THE SERIALS DIRECTORY

AN INTERNATIONAL REFERENCE BOOK

Editorial Advisory Board

Susan A. Cady
Associate Director
of Technical Services
Linderman Library
Lehigh University Libraries

Mary Elizabeth Clack
Serial Records Librarian
Harvard College Library

Genevieve Clay
Acquisitions Librarian
Eastern Kentucky University
Crabbe Library

Ludo Holans
Librarian
Campus Bibliotheekdienst
Katholiek Universiteit Leuven
Belgium

Sul H. Lee
Dean University Libraries
University of Oklahoma
Norman, Oklahoma

Joyce McDonough
Director of Technical Support &
Acquisitions
Columbia University Libraries
Butler Library

Peter Szanto
Hungarian Central Library
Budapest Hungary

Lois N. Upham
Uncle Remus Regional Library
Madison, Georgia

The 10th Edition of *The Serials Directory: An International Reference Book* was compiled and published by EBSCO Publishing, a part of the EBSCO Information Services Group.

J.T. Stephens, President-EBSCO Industries, Inc.
Tim Collins, Vice President, Division General Manager-EBSCO Publishing
Mary Beth Vanderpoorten, M.S.L.S., Vice President-EBSCO Subscription Services, General Manager-Title Information

EDITORIAL / PRODUCTION

Ann Talley, M.S.L.S., Editor
Jill Hinds, Special Projects Editor
Mona Powell, Titles Editor

Stefanie Letanosky, Production Manager
Jean Bowick, Editorial Assistant
Joe B. Crowe, Editorial Assistant
Amy Dickerson, Editorial Assistant

Kim Holder, Editorial Assistant
Tammy Lynn, Editorial Assistant

Database and publishing software
provided by Syscomp, Inc., Atlanta, Georgia, using Advanced Revelation®

Typesetting software provided by
Laser Solutions, Inc., Atlanta, Georgia using FrameMaker®

AN INTERNATIONAL
REFERENCE BOOK

AN INTERNATIONAL REFERENCE BOOK

TENTH EDITION 1996

VOLUME I

A-D

A part of the EBSCO Information Services Group

Published by EBSCO Publishing
a part of the EBSCO Information Services Group.
P.O. Box 1943, Birmingham, AL 35201-1943 USA

Copyright © 1996 by EBSCO Industries, Inc.
Printed and bound in the United States of America.

All rights reserved. Reproduction of this Directory, in whole or in part, by any method, without prior written permission of the publisher is prohibited.

Direct all editorial inquiries to EBSCO Publishing, P.O. Box 1943, Birmingham, AL 35201-1943.

Direct all other inquiries to EBSCO Publishing, 83 Pine Street, PO Box 2250, Peabody, MA 01960-7250

International Standard Book Number (5-Volume Set) 0-88751-01-0
International Standard Book Number (Volume-1) 0-88751-02-9
International Standard Book Number (Volume-2) 0-88751-03-7
International Standard Book Number (Volume-3) 0-88751-04-5
International Standard Book Number (Volume-4) 0-88751-05-3
International Standard Book Number (Volume-5) 0-88751-06-1

International Standard Serial Number 0886-4179

Every effort has been made to ensure the accuracy of information in The Serials Directory and since no payment has been made for the inclusion of any entries, the publisher cannot accept liability for errors or omissions, regardless of the cause.

CONTENTS

Preface ix
User's Guide xi
Filing Rules. xviii
Subject Headings xix
Subject Cross References xxiii
Tables xxxix
    Document Delivery xl
    Wire Services xli
    Country of Publication by Code. xlii
    Country of Publication by Country xliii
    Unit of Currency xliv
    Indexes/Abstracts. xlv

Volume 1
    Serial Listings (A–D) 3
Volume 2
    Serial Listings (E-L). 1733
Volume 3
    Serial Listings (M-Z) 4007
Volume 4
    Newspapers
      US Newspapers. 6297
      International Newspapers 6453
    Alphabetical Title Index. 6697
Volume 5
    ISSN Index. 7891
    New Title Index 8649
    Serials Online Index. 8741
    Serials on CD-ROM Index. 8809
    Peer Reviewed Index 8837
    Controlled Circulation Index 8911
    Book Review Index 9039
    Copyright Clearance Center Index. 9195
    Advertising Accepted Index. 9279

PREFACE

For EBSCO Publishing, 1995 proved to be a year of much change. In our efforts to continue providing users with valid, timely and accessible serial information, we made numerous modifications to **The Serials Directory**, including the restructuring of the format and presentation of data in the bibliographic listing and the way this information is acquired. The most significant of the various enhancements is the repositioning of the Library classification codes as presented in the Directory. While we continue to indicate new publications with a bullet (●), and place the ISSN and country code of publication at the beginning of our listings, Library of Congress and Dewey Decimal Classifications are now placed at the beginning of entries, along with CODEN designations and National Library of Medicine classification codes. These codes are now followed by Copyright Clearance Center and Peer Reviewed/ Refereed information as well as a notation for ceased titles, suspended titles or title changes for publications that are no longer active. This edition's format alterations make key elements of quality bibliographic information obtainable at a glance, increasing user's research speed and ease.

The tenth edition of **The Serials Directory** contains approximately 160,000 bibliographic entries presented in this new format. Included in Volumes I, II, and III are over 8,100 new titles, 12,151 titles known to be registered with the Copyright Clearance Center, 23,115 serials known to accept and publish book reviews, and over 25,000 serials which accept advertising.

EBSCO Publishing continues to gain timely and accurate serials information through constant contact with approximately 70,000 publishers throughout the world. This contact enables us to provide accurate title information as well as up-to-date subscription data and pricing information. Electronic data interchange will assist the editorial staff in maintaining this high level of detail.

This edition reflects our belief that customer input is the best way to achieve customer satisfaction. To this end, we consulted several professionals in the field of information science for their opinions on our Directory and for suggestions on improving it. One request which we received and expedited was for an expansion and fine tuning of our subject headings to facilitate more accurate and specific title placement. For the tenth edition that expansion was begun with the addition of approximately fifty new subject headings, as well as numerous revisions of existing subject headings and cross-references. Substantial changes include a merging of the major headings of Business and of Economics into a comprehensive subject, the addition of minor subjects in headings such as Agriculture and Education, and the alignment of all subject headings to mirror those used by the Library of Congress. For example, Medical Science and Technology is now Medical Sciences and Data Processing is now Electronic Data Processing. Other subject headings were split to provide more precise placement; these include Energy, Industry and Production and Public Health and Safety. A complete listing of our revamped Subject Headings and Cross References can be found starting on page *xix*.

The past few years have seen many exciting changes and advances occur in the serial publishing and library arenas. Most notable is the growing popularity of online access to information and people, either via the Internet or other online sources. Electronic presentation of information is quickly becoming an area of great innovation and development. This edition of **The Serials Directory** includes over 5,000 serials available in either an online or CD-ROM format. Also, notation and/or site addresses are given to titles which may be accessed via the Internet, when this information is available. This additional format availability information can be found in the text as well as in specialized indexes in Volume V.

Here at EBSCO Publishing we realize that information needs vary from organization to organization. To meet these needs, **The Serials Directory** is available in a variety of formats. This print subscription, which includes two Updates, is available along with a quarterly CD-ROM subscription. Now, for the first time, **The Serials Directory** is available online through EBSCOhost, an exciting new product from EBSCO Publishing. (For more information on the online availability of EBSCOhost in general, please call (800)653-2726).

Of interest to smaller or specialized libraries and businesses is **TSD Selects**. This product is subject specific and contains all bibliographic elements included in the tenth edition. Each **Select** can include up to 10,000 titles and is available in print or on data diskette.

EBSCO Publishing continues to offer FREE serials research. Our research line is staffed from 7:30 am to 5:30 pm Central Standard Time. Our competent and courteous research staff will be pleased to assist you in locating serial information, however obscure. You may reach us at (800)826-3024. Customers in Alabama can call collect at (205)980-2773 or (205)980-2772. Non-US customers can FAX at (205)995-1582.

Our continuous goal at EBSCO Publishing is to provide a relevant and effective serials reference authority. As the directory steadily grows and changes, we continue to hold customer satisfaction as our highest priority. Customer input is of great value to us, and we welcome all suggestions and comments to help further improve this, and all, EBSCO Publishing products.

Ann Talley
Editor

EBSCO Publishing, PO Box 1943, Birmingham, AL 35201-1943 USA
(800)826-3024 / (205)980-2773 / FAX (205)995-1582

AN INTERNATIONAL
REFERENCE BOOK

USER'S GUIDE

USER'S GUIDE

How to Use The Serials Directory.

The Serials Directory is comprised of twelve sections. Each of these sections is designed to assist the user in accessing information easily. The following is a brief explanation of each section.

- **Serial Listings (Subjects A-Z)**
  (Volumes I, II and III)
- **Newspaper Listings**
  (Volume IV)
- **Alphabetical Title Index**
  (Volume IV)
- **ISSN Index**
  (Volume V)
- **New Title Index**
  (Volume V)
- **Serials Available Online Index**
  (Volume V)
- **Serials Available on CD-ROM Index**
  (Volume V)
- **Peer Reviewed Index**
  (Volume V)
- **Controlled Circulation Index**
  (Volume V)
- **Book Review Index**
  (Volume V)
- **Copyright Clearance Center Index**
  (Volume V)
- **Advertising Accepted Index**
  (Volume V)

● Serial Listings—

The Serial Listings section is the main section of the Directory. Here, bibliographic information for serials is arranged by subject. Within each subject category, listings are arranged alphabetically (See Filing Rules—page xviii). Subject cross-references, or "see notes," are included throughout subject categories to guide users from related subject categories to the subject heading under which the full title listing appears. See pages xix-xxxviii for a complete listing of subject headings and subject cross references used in the Serials Listings section. As an additional enhancement, titles which are known to have begun publication in or after 1993 and which were active at the time data was secured for publication, are denoted with a bullet "●" in front of the listing.

● Newspaper Listings—

This section consists of listings for US and international newspapers included in our database. The US newspapers are listed alphabetically by state, while international newspapers are arranged alphabetically by country. When known, the wire service affiliations of the newspaper are included in the listings, preceded by a prefix of "**Wire Svcs**" in boldface. A chart of the abbreviations used may be found on page xli. Advertising rates for full and half-page ads are given for color and/or black and white specifications, depending on what is accepted by the publisher. Publication size and a notation for photograph inclusion will also be listed when provided.

● Alphabetical Title Index—

This index provides an alphabetical list of all titles found in the Directory, regardless of status. The country of publication code, ISSN, and MARC control number are included in each listing, when available. New titles are denoted with a bullet "●" in front of the listing. In *The Serials Directory*, a title is considered "new" if it is known to have begun publication in or after 1993 and is active at the time data was secured for publication. This edition includes over 8,100 new titles.

Titles which have ceased publication and do not have a succeeding entry (USMARC tag 785), are denoted with the word *"CEASED"* in bold italics in both the Serial Listings and the Alphabetical Title Index. Ceased titles are included in the Directory for two consecutive editions. This edition contains over 3,200 cessations.

Titles which are known to have suspended publication are denoted in both the Serial Listings and the Alphabetical Title Index with the word *"SUSPENDED"* in bold italics. These titles remain suspended until notification of a change in status is received.

Other features of the Alphabetical Title Index include additional information for Titles Changes (titles that are no longer active and have a succeeding entry) along with Main Entry-Corporate Name when applicable. For entries that have changed titles, the Directory will print "see" notes from the inactive title to the newer title for two consecutive editions. Main Entry-Corporate Names are printed in the Directory as an additional access point to the publication in question.

- **ISSN Index—**
This index lists serials found in the directory in numerical order. The ISSN will be followed by a "see" note giving the title to which the ISSN has been assigned. When the preceding ISSN is listed, it will include a "see" note to the title provided the MARC publication start date (field 008/7-10) is later than 1992. The preceding ISSN appears in italicized typeface to distinguish it from the current ISSN. The page number on which the Serial Listing may be found appears in boldface. There are over 98,542 titles included in the ISSN Index.

- **New Title Index—**
Arranged by subject then alphabetically by title, this index consists of all active titles which are known to have started publication in or after 1993. These listings include the title, country code and ISSN followed by the page number on which the main Serial Listing appears. There are over 8,100 titles included in the New Title Index.

- **Serials Available Online Index—**
Arranged alphabetically by title, this index lists all serial titles in Volumes I, II and III that are known to be available online, either as the primary format, or as an "additional" format. Included in this index are the country code, ISSN and vendor/publisher address, and telephone number(s) when available. The page number on which the Serial Listing appears prints in boldface. There are over 4,267 titles included in the Serials Available Online Index.

- **Serials Available on CD-ROM Index—**
Arranged alphabetically by title, this index lists all serial titles in Volumes I, II and III that are known to be available on CD-ROM, either as the primary format, or as an "additional" format. Included in this index are the country code, ISSN and vendor/publisher address, and telephone number(s) when available. The page number on which the Serial Listing appears prints in boldface. There are over 1,600 titles included in the Serials Available on CD-ROM Index.

- **Peer Reviewed Index—**
Arranged alphabetically by title, the Peer Reviewed Index lists all active serials found in the Directory which are known to contain refereed, or peer reviewed articles. It includes the country code, ISSN and MARC control number, when available. The boldfaced number at the end of the listing is the page on which the Serial Listing may be found. There are over 10,326 titles included in the Peer Reviewed Index.

- **Controlled Circulation Index—**
Arranged alphabetically by title, this index lists all titles in the Directory that are known to have controlled circulations. The country code, ISSN and circulation figures [printing in brackets] are provided when available. The page number on which the Serial Listing appears prints in boldface. There are over 17,980 titles included in the Controlled Circulation Index.

- **Book Review Index—**
Arranged alphabetically by title, this index lists all serial titles in Volumes I, II and III that are known to contain book reviews. Included in this index, when available, are country code, ISSN and the quantity of book reviews published "per year" (unless otherwise specified). The page number on which the Serial Listing appears prints in boldface. There are over 23,115 titles included in the Book Review Index.

- **Copyright Clearance Center Index—**
Arranged alphabetically by title, this index lists serials found in Volumes I, II and III that are known to be registered with the Copyright Clearance Center (CCC). The country code and ISSN of the publication are provided when available. The page number on which the Serial Listing appears prints in boldface. There are over 12,151 titles included in the Copyright Clearance Center Index.

- **Advertising Accepted Index—**
Arranged alphabetically by title, this index contains all serial titles found in Volumes I, II and III that are known to accept advertising. The country code, ISSN and advertising manager/telephone number(s) are also provided, when supplied. The page number on which the Serial Listing appears prints in boldface. There are over 25,000 titles included in the Advertising Accepted Index.

USER'S GUIDE/SAMPLE LISTING

SAMPLE LISTING

LC Library of Congress Classification
DD Dewey Decimal Classification
UDC Universal Decimal Classification
NLM National Library of Medicine Classification
Pr Rev. (Peer Reviewed or Refereed)
ISSN International Standard Serial Number
CODEN CODEN Designation
[CCC] Copyright Clearance Center
Country of Publication
CEASED/SUSPENDED

● **TITLE INFORMATION: KEY TITLE.** (TITLE STATEMENT). [Abbreviated Title]. **Main/Conf** Main Entry—Meeting. **Main/Corp** Main Entry—Corporate Name. **Added/Corp** Added Entry—Corporate Name. **Series/Conf** Series Statement—Meeting Name. **VFOAT** Varying Form of a Title. **VAT** Variant Access Title. Date of Publication. Type of Serial. Language(s). Frequency. Price. Publisher Name & Address. **Tel** Telephone/Telex Number/Fax/Internet Address/Email Address. (subscription address:) **ED** Editor. Index Availability. cum. index (Cumulative Index Availability). **Bk Rev** (Book reviews published), (Qty: Quantity Published). **Photos** [Photographs published]. **Ad Acc** (Advertising accepted), **Adv. Mgr**: Advertising Manager. **Tel** Telephone. Full Page (B&W) - Full page black and white ad rates. Half Page (B&W) - Half page black and white ad rates. Full Page (Color) - Full page color ad rates. Half Page (Color) - Half page color ad rates. **Pub. Size** [Publication trim size]. **Wire Svcs** [Newspaper wire services]. **Acid Free** [Acid free paper]. Circulation. (ctrl) - Controlled circulation. Document Delivery Available. Additional Physical Forms Available. *Preceding Entry-Title, Preceding Entry-ISSN. Succeeding Entry-Title, Succeeding Entry-ISSN.*

Desc: Descriptive listing.

Ind/Abst Indexes/Abstracts. Dates of Coverage. Full Text. Full/Selective Coverage

SERIAL LISTING CONTENTS

For the purpose of defining a serial, the definition as given in the USMARC Bibliographic Format is used: a bibliographic item issued in successive parts bearing numerical or chronological designations and intended to be continued indefinitely. Serials include periodicals; newspapers; annuals; the journals, memoirs, proceedings, transactions, etc., of societies; and numbered monographic series, etc.

The following data elements (when available) are shown in order of appearance within a listing. Some definitions are taken in part from USMARC Formats Bibliographic Data.

LC Classification Number. Contains the Library of Congress class/classification number, shelf number, or pseudo-call-number assigned by The Library of Congress or one of its authorized agencies. Preceded by a prefix of "**LC**" in boldface.

ISSN. International Standard Serial Number, for the main Serial Listing, appears in the top right hand corner of the listing. Not all publications have been assigned an ISSN.

Dewey Decimal Classification. Assigned according to the Dewey Decimal schedules maintained by The Library of Congress. Preceded by a prefix of "**DD**" in boldface.

CODEN Designation. Assigned by the CODEN section of Chemical Abstracts Service, this is a unique alphanumeric identifier for a specific publication. It is used primarily for scientific and technical publications. Preceded by a prefix of "**CODEN**" in boldface.

Universal Decimal Classification. Derived from the Dewey Decimal Classification, the UDC differs in arrangement and philosophy. The UDC is distinguished from the DDC by its extensive expansions. Preceded by a prefix of "**UDC**" in boldface.

Copyright Clearance Center. [CCC] indicates titles registered with the Copyright Clearance Center, a not-for-profit collective licensing organization. The Copyright Clearance Center has been authorized to grant photocopy permission and to collect any pre-set royalty fees set by the publisher.

National Library of Medicine Classification. Contains a complete NLM class/classification number. Preceded by a prefix of "**NLM**" in boldface.

Country of Publication. A two letter code indicating the place of publication, production, or execution of the Serial Listing. The Country of Publication Table may be found on Page xlii.

Peer Reviewed. If a journal is known to be peer reviewed or refereed, the abbreviation "**Pr Rev**" will appear.

Ceased. This element is present only when a title has ceased publication. This does not include titles that have a succeeding entry or have had a title change. The word "*CEASED*" appears in bold italics. Ceased titles are included in the Directory for two consecutive editions after the actual date of cessation. This edition contains over 4,700 cessations.

Suspended. Denotes temporary suspension of a serial by the publisher. The word "*SUSPENDED*" appears in bold italics. These titles remain suspended in the database until the publisher notifies *The Serials Directory* otherwise.

●Denotes titles which are known to have started publication in or after 1993, and were active at the time data was secured for publication.

Title Information. This data element may actually consist of four parts:

USER'S GUIDE/SAMPLE LISTING

Key Title. As assigned by various national centers under the auspices of the ISSN Register (formerly ISDS), is listed only if it is different from the main entry title found in the Title Statement.

Title Statement. The Title Statement consists of the title proper (including alternative title, the numerical designation of a part/section and the name of a part/section) and may also contain the medium, and other relevant title information. When both Key Title and Title Statement are present, Key Title will appear first in the listing. Title Statement will follow in uppercase and will be enclosed in parentheses. For multi-language publications, the title proper will print in all languages; each version will be separated by an equal sign (=).

Abbreviated Title. This part of the Title Statement is assigned by the ISSN Register (formerly ISDS), in accordance with ISO 4-1984, Documentation - Rules for the Abbreviation of Title Words and Titles of Publications and List of Serial Title Word Abbreviations and is based on the Key Title. It is provided for serials which might be of international interest. Within the Title Statement this information files in [brackets].

Main Entry-Meeting. A meeting or conference name may sometimes be used as a main entry for a serial publication. Main entry under a meeting name is assigned to works that contain proceedings, reports, etc. Main Entry-Meeting information is preceded by the prefix "**Main/Conf**" in boldface.

Main Entry-Corporate Name. A corporate name may also be used as a main entry for a serial publication. Main entry under corporate name is assigned to works that represent the collective thought of a body, including conference and meeting names that are entered subordinately to a corporate body. Main Entry-Corporate Name is preceded by the prefix "**Main/Corp**" in boldface.

Added Entry-Corporate Name. Contains a corporate heading used as main entry. A corporate body is identified by a name that acts or may act as an entity. Included in this definition are: associations, institutions, business firms, governments and their agencies, ships, churches and programs. The Added Entry-Corporate Name will be preceded by a prefix of "**Added/Corp**" in boldface.

Series Statement-Meeting Name. Series statement entered under a named conference or meeting. Series Statement-Meeting is preceded by "**Series/Conf**" in boldface.

Varying Form of a Title. Titles which may appear on different parts of a serial, or consisting of portions of the title proper or alternative forms of titles. Varying Form of a Title differs substantially from Key Title/Title Proper and contributes to the further identification of the serial. It is preceded by the prefix "**VFOAT**" in boldface. Multiple varying forms of the serial title are separated by commas within the Serial Listing.

Variant Access Title. A variant form of the title does not appear on the serial, and is used when the title contains an initialism, non-Roman alphabet character, etc. It provides additional access for searching purposes when access is not provided by any other title. Variant Access Title is preceded by the prefix of "**VAT**" in boldface. Multiple variant access titles are separated by commas within the Serial Listing.

Dates of Publication and Volume Information. When provided, beginning (and ending) dates of publication and volume designation will be listed. The date may consist of the year, month, or day; month or season and year; or year alone, depending upon the frequency of publication and the usage of the publisher. Dates may appear in the vernacular and/or may be abbreviated.

Type of Serial. Indicates if the serial is a periodical, monographic series, or newspaper. When available, more specific types will be used such as bibliography, catalog, bulletin, directory, government publication, newsletter, proceedings, trade publication, consumer publication, corporate report, academic scholarly publication or abstracting/indexing service.

Language(s). If the serial is published in more than one language, the predominant language will appear first and any additional languages will follow in parentheses (including languages for translations, summaries, tables of contents, etc.).

Frequency. The frequency is indicated in number of issues published per publication cycle. Exceptions are noted in parentheses following.

Price. The current annual subscription price at the time information was secured for publication. Prices are usually given in US dollars and currency of Country of Publication, if other than US. Exceptions are noted and explained.

Publisher Name and Address/Telecommunications Numbers. The complete name and address of the publisher when available. Telephone, telex and/or facsimile number as well as Internet and E-mail addresses are given for serials. Preceded by a prefix of "**Tel**" in boldface.

Subscription Address. The complete name and subscription/fulfillment address. Telecommunication numbers are listed when available.

Editor(s). Name, address and telephone number(s), when available. Preceded by a prefix of "**ED**" in boldface.

Index Availability. Shows the existence of an index, or a table of contents issued as an index, and the method of acquisition.

Cumulative Index Availability. Specifies if a cumulative index, or a table of contents issued as a cumulative index, is published. Appears in abbreviated form as "cum. index."

USER'S GUIDE/SAMPLE LISTING

Book Reviews. If book reviews are published, "**Bk Rev**" will appear in the Serial Listing.

Book Review Quantity. Quantity of book reviews published "per year," unless otherwise specified. Quantity is preceded by "Qty:" and prints in parentheses.

Photos. If photographs are included within the serial, "**Photos**" will appear in the listing.

Advertising. If advertising is accepted in a serial, the abbreviation "**Ad Acc**" will appear in boldface.

Advertising Manager/Telephone. Lists the name and telephone number of the Advertising Manager, when available. Advertising Manager name is preceded by "**Adv Mgr:**" in boldface. Telephone is preceded by the prefix "**Tel**" in boldface.

Advertising Rates. Advertising rates for full and half-page ads. (B&W) designates rates for ads in black and white. (Color) designates ads printed in color.

Publication Size. The trim size of the serial or newspaper. Preceded by the abbreviation **Pub. Size.**

Wire Services. Lists the news and photograph wire services affiliated with any given newspaper. These are preceded by a prefix of "**Wire Svcs**" in boldface. A chart of abbreviations used can be found on page xli.

Acid Free. If a publication is available on acid free paper, "**Acid Free**" will be seen in boldface.

Circulation. Annual circulation of publication, unless noted otherwise. Multiple circulation figures are separated by a comma.

Controlled Circulation. If circulation of a serial is controlled by the publisher, the abbreviation "ctrl" in parentheses follows the circulation figures. If no circulation figures are given, but the publisher has notified us that circulation is controlled, "ctrl circ" will appear.

Document Delivery. Indicates the availability of that serial for document delivery through the specified vendor(s). Refer to the chart on page xl.

Additional Physical Forms Available. Additional media in which a serial is published, other than its original or standard form.

Preceding Entry - Title/Preceding Entry - ISSN. The immediate predecessor(s) for the title, along with ISSN, appears in italics. Depending on indicators taken from the CONSER 780 field, a title's preceding entry will be preceded by one of the following: Continues, Continues in part, Supersedes, Supersedes in part, Formed by the union of... and..., Absorbed, Absorbed in part, or Separated from. If the title Continues in part, another title which is current, both titles will then be listed. Additional titles and ISSN are separated by semicolons and are preceded by one of the above, in boldface.

Succeeding Entry Title/Succeeding Entry - ISSN. The immediate successor(s) for the serial title (along with corresponding ISSN) will be listed. Multiple titles and ISSN are separated by semicolons, and preceded by one of the following: Continued by, Continued in part by, Superseded by, Superseded in part by, Absorbed by, Absorbed in part by, Split into... and..., Merged with... to form..., Merged into, or Changed back to. In cases where CONSER did not give an ending date or a title was only continued "in part" both titles will be listed.

Descriptive Listing. Description of content. Descriptions may have been edited for clarity. Description is preceded by "**Desc:**" in boldface.

Indexes/Abstracts. Specifies the publication(s) in which a serial has been indexed and/or abstracted. These are preceded by a prefix of "**Ind/Abst**" in boldface. Over 920 "active" Indexing/Abstracting services are used for the purposes of this Directory and can be found within the Serial Listings. See Indexes/Abstracts Abbreviations Table on page xlv.

Dates of Coverage. Dates of coverage are included for each index or abstract, when available. Dates are enclosed in parentheses and follow the abbreviation as used in the Serial Listing for each Indexing/Abstracting service. If no dates are provided by the Indexing/Abstracting service publisher, and we have been notified that a serial is no longer covered by a particular service, question marks will be used to notify the user that coverage of the particular serial by the service has been discontinued.

Full Text. Specifies if a journal is covered by an Indexing/Abstracting service in "Full Text." Full Text coverage indicates that all articles in the journal are indexed/abstracted completely, with any pertinent graphics, charts etc. For the purposes of this Directory, "Full Text" and "Full Image" are treated as if they were the same. These will be coded in the Serial Listing as [Full Txt.]. This notation will follow the dates of coverage in the Serial Listing.

Full/Selective Coverage — Full coverage indicates that journals are indexed/abstracted cover to cover. Selective coverage specifies serials in which the Indexing / Abstracting service selects only articles relevant to their publication. These will be coded in the Serial Listing as [Full Cov.] or [Select. Cov.]. This notation will follow the dates of coverage, when available, or will precede the Index or Abstract abbreviation when no dates of coverage are noted in the Serial Listing.

FILING RULES

A. General Rules— Filing is word for word with exceptions noted below. The order of characters applies the principle "nothing files before something," with numerals before letters, file A to Z.

1. **Spaces, hyphens, diagonal slashes, and periods** are filed as blanks:

   > AAG-AAG
   > AAG Directory / Association of American Geographers
   > AAG Newsletter
   > AAHA Directory of Membership

2. **Variant spellings** are filed as written:

   > Ageing and Society
   > Aging and Aging Disorders

B. Special Rules and Exceptions.

1. **Modified letters and diacritics—** Modified letters are written as their plain English alphabet equivalents.

2. **Punctuation—** Punctuation and non-alphabetic symbols (except those noted in A above) are ignored for filing purposes:

   > "A" Magazine
   > A Magyar Talalkozo Kronikaja
   > A.N.A. Audiologia Protesica

3. **Abbreviations—** Filed exactly as written.

   > Dr. McBirnie's Newsletter
   > St. Louis Review
   > U.N. Observer & International Report
   > U.S. Census Report

4. **Numerals—** Filed character by character according to the numeric value of each string of characters.
   Numerals precede letters:

   > 33 Metal Producing
   > 35/70; Journal of the Feature Film Industry
   > 35MM Photography London England : 1983)
   > 36 Cities : Real Estate Forecast and Review

5. **Initials, initialisms, acronyms—** Those in which each letter is separated by a space, dash, hyphen, period, or diagonal slash are regarded as a series of separate words. Those in which characters are separated by other marks or symbols, or which are not separated in any way, are regarded as single words:

   > A. C. C. L. Union List of Serials
   > A C E Q-A C G R Information
   > A/C Flyer, The
   > A.C.G.C.-Information : Bulletin d'Information de l'Association des Cadres et Gerants des Colleges du Quebec
   > A C I S
   > A. C. L. : Agence Cambodge Laos

6. **Initial Articles—** The following words are ignored when they appear at the beginning of an entry.

A	Eine	Hio	'n
al	Eit	Hin	Na
An	el-	Hinar	Nje
As	El	Hinir	Nji
Az	Els	Hinn	O
Bir	En	Ho	Os
Das	Et	Hoi	't
De	Ett	I	Ta
Dei	Gl'	Il	The
Den	Gli	Ka	To
Der	ha-	Ke	Um
Di	Hai	L'	Uma
Die	He	La	Un
Dos	he-	Las	Un'
Een	Heis	Le	Una
Eene	Hen	Les	Une
Egy	Hena	Lo	Uno
Ei	Henas	Los	Y
Ein	Het	Mia	Yr

   Exceptions— Titles composed entirely of words on the list above are filed as written, as well as place names.
   Hence:

   > A Tavola
   > A to Z of Who is Who in Australia's History, The
   > A Traverso

7. **Names and prefixes—** A prefix that is part of the name of a person or place is treated as a separate word unless it is joined to the rest of the name:

   > De Paul Law Review
   > McCall's Book for Brides
   > Van Buren Register

SUBJECT HEADINGS

The following section lists the subject headings used throughout the Directory. The list is arranged alphabetically, by subject, with the major subject (printing in boldface) followed by specific subheadings within the same category.

CROSS REFERENCES

This section combines all subject headings into one alphabetical list, regardless of whether it is a general, main subject or specific, subordinate subject. Cross references from a subject or topic not used in the Directory are made to that which is used. "See also" notes from one subject to a similar subject are included as well.

SUBJECT HEADINGS

Aeronautics, Astronautics 3
   Abstracting, Bibliographies and
      Statistics 46
   Computer Applications 47
Agriculture 47
   Abstracting, Bibliographies and
      Statistics 152
   Agricultural Economics 161
   Agricultural Equipment 169
   Computer Applications 174
   Crop Production and Soils 174
   Dairy Industry 215
   Feed Grain and Milling 225
   Livestock 230
   Poultry and Poultry Products 251
Animal Welfare 255
   Abstracting, Bibliographies and
      Statistics 257
   Pets 258
Anthropology 262
   Abstracting, Bibliographies and
      Statistics 286
Antiques 286
   Abstracting, Bibliographies and
      Statistics 290
Archaeology 291
   Abstracting, Bibliographies and
      Statistics 328
Architecture 328
   Abstracting, Bibliographies and
      Statistics 357
   Computer Applications 357
The Arts 358
   Abstracting, Bibliographies and
      Statistics 379
   Art 381
   Computer Applications 418
   Crafts and Decorative Arts 418
   Graphic Arts 427
   Performing Arts 434
Astrology 440
Astronomy 442
   Abstracting, Bibliographies and
      Statistics 456
   Computer Applications 456
Beauty and Cosmetics 456
Bicycles and Cycling 462
Biographies 464
   Abstracting, Bibliographies and
      Statistics 475
Biology 475
   Abstracting, Bibliographies and
      Statistics 507
   Bioengineering 511
   Biological Chemistry 526
   Biological Physics 547
   Botany 551
   Computer Applications 590
   Cytology 591
   Embryology 602
   Genetics 604
   Marine Biology 616
   Microbiology 623
   Microscopy 639
   Mycology 641
   Parasitology 645
   Physiology 648
Birth Control 658
   Abstracting, Bibliographies and
      Statistics 662
Boats and Boating 662
   Abstracting, Bibliographies and
      Statistics 671
Building and Construction 671
   Abstracting, Bibliographies and
      Statistics 711
   Carpentry and Woodwork 713
Business and Economics 716
   Abstracting, Bibliographies and
      Statistics 858
   Accounting 881
   Advertising and Public Relations . . . 899
   Banks and Banking 914
   Chamber of Commerce 967
   Commerce 970
   Computer Applications 1005
   Cooperatives 1009
   Economic Assistance and
      Development 1012
   Economic History, Conditions 1023
   International Economic Relations . . . 1073
   Investments 1081
   Labor 1115
   Management 1194
   Marketing and Purchasing 1233
   Office Equipment and Services 1259
   Personnel Management 1263
   Retail 1276
   Small Business 1283
Chemistry and Chemicals 1289
   Abstracting, Bibliographies and
      Statistics 1325
   Analytical Chemistry 1343
   Chemical Technology 1352
   Computer Applications 1362
   Crystallography 1363
   Electrochemistry 1366
   Inorganic Chemistry 1368
   Organic Chemistry 1372
   Physical and Theoretical
      Chemistry 1385
Children and Youth Interests 1397
   Abstracting, Bibliographies and
      Statistics 1412
Civil Defense 1412
Classical Studies 1414
   Abstracting, Bibliographies and
      Statistics 1423
Clothing Industry and Fashion 1423
   Abstracting, Bibliographies and
      Statistics 1432
College and School Publications 1432
   Abstracting, Bibliographies and
      Statistics 1441
   Alumni 1441
Communications 1448
   Abstracting, Bibliographies and
      Statistics 1471
   Computer Applications 1472
   Postal Communications 1475
   Radio 1479
   Telecommunication 1488
   Television and Cable 1514
   Video 1530
Computers 1535
   Abstracting, Bibliographies and
      Statistics 1565
   Artificial Intelligence 1568
   Automation 1576
   Computer Assisted Instruction 1581
   Computer Crimes and Security 1584
   Computer Engineering 1587
   Computer Games 1590
   Computer Graphics and Design 1591
   Computer Industry and Industry
      Directories 1595
   Computer Music 1601
   Computer Networks 1602
   Computer Sales, Service and
      Supply 1609
   Computer Systems 1610
   Cybernetics 1616
   Data Base Management 1618
   Desktop Publishing 1621
   Electronic Data Processing 1622
   Hardware 1631
   Microcomputers, Personal
      Computers 1633
   Minicomputers 1643
   Online Computing and Information . 1644
   Optical Storage, CD-ROM
      Applications 1646
   Programs and Programming 1649
   Simulation 1655
   Software 1657
   Word Processing 1669
Consumer Education and Protection . 1670
   Abstracting, Bibliographies and
      Statistics 1678
Copyright, Intellectual Property 1678
   Abstracting, Bibliographies and
      Statistics 1689
Dance 1689
   Abstracting, Bibliographies and
      Statistics 1694
Dentistry 1694
   Abstracting, Bibliographies and
      Statistics 1719
Drug Abuse and Alcoholism 1720
   Abstracting, Bibliographies and
      Statistics 1732
Earth Sciences 1733
   Abstracting, Bibliographies and
      Statistics 1743
   Computer Applications 1746
   Geology 1746
   Geophysics 1792
   Hydrology 1803
   Meteorology 1812
   Oceanography 1832
Education 1846
   Abstracting, Bibliographies and
      Statistics 1901
   Adult and Continuing Education 1909
   Computer Applications 1913
   Early Childhood and Primary
      Education 1917
   Educational Finance 1921
   Educational Research 1927
   Elementary Education 1933
   Guidance and Counseling 1935
   Higher Education 1937
   International Education 1985
   Physical Education and Training . . . 1989
   School Management and
      Organization 1995
   Tests and Measurements 2055
   Vocational Education 2058
Electronics 2066
   Abstracting, Bibliographies and
      Statistics 2093
Emigration and Immigration 2094
Encyclopedias and General Reference
   Books 2098
   Abstracting, Bibliographies and
      Statistics 2122
Energy 2127
   Abstracting, Bibliographies and
      Statistics 2155
   Atomic Energy 2159
   Computer Applications 2164
   Electric Power 2165
   Energy Conservation 2173
   Solar Energy 2174

SUBJECT HEADINGS

Engineering 2177
   Abstracting, Bibliographies and
     Statistics 2212
   Chemical Engineering 2216
   Civil Engineering 2226
   Computer Applications 2244
   Electrical Engineering 2248
   Hydraulic Engineering 2271
   Industrial Engineering 2282
   Materials Science 2288
   Mechanical Engineering and
     Machinery 2304
   Nuclear Engineering 2325
Environmental Issues 2331
   Abstracting, Bibliographies and
     Statistics 2360
   Computer Applications 2362
   Conservation and Natural
     Resources 2362
   Ecology 2391
   Pollution and Waste
     Management 2404
Ethics 2433
Ethnic Interests 2439
   Abstracting, Bibliographies and
     Statistics 2468
Fabrics and Textile Industries 2468
   Abstracting, Bibliographies and
     Statistics 2484
Family and Marriage 2485
   Abstracting, Bibliographies and
     Statistics 2498
Finance 2498
   Abstracting, Bibliographies and
     Statistics 2504
   Computer Applications 2508
   Personal Finance 2508
   Public Finance 2509
   Taxation 2536
Fire Prevention 2564
   Abstracting, Bibliographies and
     Statistics 2571
Fish and Fisheries 2571
   Abstracting, Bibliographies and
     Statistics 2597
Folklore 2599
   Abstracting, Bibliographies and
     Statistics 2607
Food and Food Industry 2607
   Abstracting, Bibliographies and
     Statistics 2646
   Beverage Industry 2647
Forests and Forestry 2659
   Abstracting, Bibliographies and
     Statistics 2687
   Lumber and Wood 2688
Funeral Service 2695
   Abstracting, Bibliographies and
     Statistics 2696
Gardening and Horticulture 2696
   Abstracting, Bibliographies and
     Statistics 2723
   Florist Trade 2723
Genealogy and Heraldry 2725
   Abstracting, Bibliographies and
     Statistics 2771
   Computer Applications 2771
General Interest 2771
   Abstracting, Bibliographies and
     Statistics 2773
   General Interest-Africa 2775
   General Interest-Asia 2777
   General Interest-Australia and
     Oceania 2785
   General Interest-Central America ... 2786
   General Interest-Europe 2788

   General Interest-Near East 2800
   General Interest-North America 2802
   General Interest-South America ... 2825
Geography 2827
   Abstracting, Bibliographies and
     Statistics 2858
   Cartography 2859
Gifts, Toys 2863
Glass and Ceramics 2865
   Abstracting, Bibliographies and
     Statistics 2876
Health 2876
   Abstracting, Bibliographies and
     Statistics 2884
   Mental Health 2885
   Physical Fitness and Hygiene 2891
Heating, Plumbing, and
   Refrigeration 2894
History 2902
   Abstracting, Bibliographies and
     Statistics 2925
   Computer Applications 2928
   History of Africa 2929
   History of Asia 2938
   History of Australia and Oceania ... 2962
   History of Europe 2965
   History of North and South America. 3018
   History of the Near East 3075
Hobbies 3085
   Abstracting, Bibliographies and
     Statistics 3095
   Numismatics 3095
   Philately 3100
Home Economics 3105
   Abstracting, Bibliographies and
     Statistics 3111
   Household Appliances 3112
   Sewing and Needlework 3114
Homosexuality 3118
Horses and Horsemanship 3122
   Abstracting, Bibliographies and
     Statistics 3130
Hotels/Motels 3130
   Abstracting, Bibliographies and
     Statistics 3137
Housing and Urban Development 3138
   Abstracting, Bibliographies and
     Statistics 3167
Humanities 3169
   Abstracting, Bibliographies and
     Statistics 3187
Industrial Health and Safety 3188
   Abstracting, Bibliographies and
     Statistics 3205
Industry and Production 3205
   Abstracting, Bibliographies and
     Statistics 3238
   Computer Applications 3240
   Manufacturing 3241
   Trade and Industrial Directories 3250
Insurance 3274
   Abstracting, Bibliographies and
     Statistics 3305
   Computer Applications 3306
Interior Design and Decoration 3306
   Home Furnishings 3314
Jewelry 3318
   Clocks and Watches 3321
Journalism 3322
   Abstracting, Bibliographies and
     Statistics 3333
Language Arts 3333
   Abstracting, Bibliographies and
     Statistics 3340
Law 3340

   Abstracting, Bibliographies and
     Statistics 3485
   Banking Law 3492
   Civil Law 3498
   Computer Applications 3507
   Constitutional Law 3509
   Corporation Law 3513
   Criminal Law 3527
   Educational Laws and Legislation .. 3533
   Entertainment Law 3537
   Environmental Law 3539
   Estate Planning 3549
   Family Law 3551
   International Law 3555
   Judicial Process 3572
   Labor Laws and Legislation 3580
   Law Enforcement and
     Criminology 3595
   Legal Aid 3619
   Maritime Law 3620
   Military Law 3623
   Taxation Law 3624
Leather and Fur Industry 3631
Leisure and Recreation 3634
   Abstracting, Bibliographies and
     Statistics 3640
   Amusements 3641
   Outdoor Recreation 3653
Library and Information Sciences 3677
   Abstracting, Bibliographies and
     Statistics 3754
   Archives and Manuscripts 3760
   Computer Applications 3766
Linguistics 3768
   Abstracting, Bibliographies and
     Statistics 3848
   Computer Applications 3850
Literary and Political Reviews 3851
   Abstracting, Bibliographies and
     Statistics 3871
Literature 3872
   Abstracting, Bibliographies and
     Statistics 3979
   Detective and Mystery 3983
   Poetry 3984
   Science Fiction, Fantasy and
     Horror 4002
Mathematics 4007
   Abstracting, Bibliographies and
     Statistics 4070
   Computer Applications 4071
Medical Sciences 4073
   Abstracting, Bibliographies and
     Statistics 4163
   Allergy and Immunologic
     Diseases 4176
   Alternative Medicine 4188
   Anatomy 4195
   Anesthesiology 4197
   Cancer and Neoplastic Syndromes. 4203
   Cardiology 4224
   Communicable Diseases 4242
   Computer Applications 4255
   Dermatology 4258
   Emergency Medicine 4265
   Endocrinology 4269
   Epidemiology 4280
   Experimental Medicine 4284
   Family Practice 4288
   Forensic Medicine, Medical
     Jurisprudence 4291
   Gastroenterology 4295
   Geriatrics 4304
   Gynecology and Obstetrics 4313
   Health Services Administration 4330

SUBJECT HEADINGS

Hematology.....................4354
Hypnosis......................4361
Internal Medicine..............4362
Medical Education..............4366
Medical Instruments and Apparatus.4371
Musculoskeletal System.........4376
Neurology.....................4383
Nursing.......................4415
Ophthalmology and Optometry....4440
Orthopedics...................4454
Otorhinolaryngology...........4462
Pathology.....................4470
Pediatrics....................4479
Physicians and Medical
  Personnel..................4493
Podiatry......................4500
Psychiatry....................4501
Radiology.....................4524
Respiratory System............4535
Sports Medicine...............4542
Surgery.......................4546
Tropical Medicine.............4568
Urology and Nephrology........4572
Men's Interests..................4581
Metals and Metallurgy............4584
  Abstracting, Bibliographies and
    Statistics..................4616
  Welding.....................4617
Metrology and Standardization....4620
  Abstracting, Bibliographies and
    Statistics..................4625
Military and Defense.............4625
  Abstracting, Bibliographies and
    Statistics..................4657
Mines and Mining.................4658
  Abstracting, Bibliographies and
    Statistics..................4681
  Computer Applications..........4683
  Mineralogy....................4683
Motion Picture....................4691
  Abstracting, Bibliographies and
    Statistics..................4710
Motorcycles......................4711
  Abstracting, Bibliographies and
    Statistics..................4714
Museums and Galleries............4715
  Abstracting, Bibliographies and
    Statistics..................4731
Music............................4731
  Abstracting, Bibliographies and
    Statistics..................4801
  Computer Applications..........4802
Natural History..................4802
  Abstracting, Bibliographies and
    Statistics..................4821
Naval Science, Navigation........4821
  Abstracting, Bibliographies and
    Statistics..................4833
New Age Publications.............4833
Nutrition and Dietetics..........4836
  Abstracting, Bibliographies and
    Statistics..................4852
Occupations and Careers..........4852
  Abstracting, Bibliographies and
    Statistics..................4863
Packaging........................4863
  Abstracting, Bibliographies and
    Statistics..................4869
Paints and Painting..............4869
  Abstracting, Bibliographies and
    Statistics..................4873
Paleontology.....................4873
  Abstracting, Bibliographies and
    Statistics..................4880
Paper and Pulp Industry..........4880

Abstracting, Bibliographies and
  Statistics....................4890
Parapsychology and Occultism......4890
  Abstracting, Bibliographies and
    Statistics..................4894
Pest Control......................4894
  Abstracting, Bibliographies and
    Statistics..................4899
Petroleum and Natural Gas.........4899
  Abstracting, Bibliographies and
    Statistics..................4939
  Computer Applications..........4941
Pharmacy and Pharmacology.........4941
  Abstracting, Bibliographies and
    Statistics..................4997
  Computer Applications..........4998
Philanthropy......................4998
  Abstracting, Bibliographies and
    Statistics..................5004
Philosophy........................5004
  Abstracting, Bibliographies and
    Statistics..................5035
Photography.......................5035
  Abstracting, Bibliographies and
    Statistics..................5048
Physical Therapy..................5048
Physically Impaired...............5053
  Abstracting, Bibliographies and
    Statistics..................5069
Physics...........................5069
  Abstracting, Bibliographies and
    Statistics..................5098
  Computer Applications..........5099
  Heat..........................5099
  Light, Optics, Radiation.......5104
  Magnetism.....................5119
  Mechanics.....................5123
  Nuclear Physics...............5129
  Sound.........................5136
Plastics..........................5139
  Abstracting, Bibliographies and
    Statistics..................5147
Political Science.................5148
  Abstracting, Bibliographies and
    Statistics..................5198
  Civil Rights..................5201
  International Relations........5215
  Socialism, Communism, Anarchism,
    Utopianism.................5243
Population Studies................5252
  Abstracting, Bibliographies and
    Statistics..................5267
Printing Industry.................5271
  Abstracting, Bibliographies and
    Statistics..................5279
Psychology........................5279
  Abstracting, Bibliographies and
    Statistics..................5337
Public Administration.............5338
  Abstracting, Bibliographies and
    Statistics..................5407
  Civil Service.................5413
  Computer Applications..........5418
  Public Utilities..............5418
Public Health and Safety..........5422
  Abstracting, Bibliographies and
    Statistics..................5462
Publishing........................5465
  Abstracting, Bibliographies and
    Statistics..................5476
  Books and Bookmaking..........5487
  Computer Applications..........5500
  Serial Publications...........5500
Real Estate.......................5504
  Abstracting, Bibliographies and
    Statistics..................5521

Religions and Theology............5521
  Abstracting, Bibliographies and
    Statistics..................5609
  Buddhism......................5611
  Catholicism...................5614
  Hinduism......................5632
  Islam.........................5633
  Judaism.......................5640
  Orthodox Eastern Churches......5650
  Other Religions, Sects and Cults..5652
  Protestantism.................5662
Restaurants.......................5681
  Abstracting, Bibliographies and
    Statistics..................5684
Rubber............................5685
  Abstracting, Bibliographies and
    Statistics..................5689
Science and Technology............5589
  Abstracting, Bibliographies and
    Statistics..................5778
  Computer Applications..........5784
Security Systems and Alarms.......5785
Senior Citizens...................5786
Sexual Life.......................5793
Social Sciences...................5795
  Abstracting, Bibliographies and
    Statistics..................5839
Societies and Clubs...............5841
Sociology.........................5851
  Abstracting, Bibliographies and
    Statistics..................5881
  Manners and Customs...........5883
  Social Services and Welfare....5885
Sound Recordings and Systems......5928
  Abstracting, Bibliographies and
    Statistics..................5933
Sports and Games..................5933
  Abstracting, Bibliographies and
    Statistics..................5991
Theater...........................5991
  Abstracting, Bibliographies and
    Statistics..................6004
Tobacco...........................6004
  Abstracting, Bibliographies and
    Statistics..................6007
Toxicology........................6007
Transportation....................6016
  Abstracting, Bibliographies and
    Statistics..................6034
  Automobiles...................6039
  Computer Applications..........6070
  Railroads.....................6070
  Recreational Vehicles..........6080
  Roads and Traffic.............6082
  Ships and Shipping............6093
  Trucking......................6107
Travel and Tourism................6110
  Abstracting, Bibliographies and
    Statistics..................6157
Veterinary Sciences...............6158
  Abstracting, Bibliographies and
    Statistics..................6187
  Computer Applications..........6166
Water Resources...................6187
  Abstracting, Bibliographies and
    Statistics..................6208
Women's Interests.................6209
  Abstracting, Bibliographies and
    Statistics..................6237
Zoology...........................6237
  Abstracting, Bibliographies and
    Statistics..................6268
  Entomology....................6270
  Ornithology...................6284

SUBJECT CROSS REFERENCES

Ability Testing —See **Education -- Tests and Measurements** pg 2055

Abortion —See **Medical Sciences -- Gynecology and Obstetrics** pg 4327

Abrasives —See **Metals and Metallurgy** pg 4584

Accessories —See **Clothing Industry and Fashion** pg 1423

Accident Prevention —See **Industrial Health and Safety** pg 3188; **Public Health and Safety** pg 5422

Accounting –pg 881; see also Law pg 3340

Acoustics —See **Physics -- Sound** pg 5136

Acquired Immune Deficiency Syndrome (AIDS) —See **Medical Sciences -- Communicable Diseases** pg 4242

Acting —See **Theater** pg 5991; see also Motion Picture pg 4691; The Arts -- Performing Arts pg 434

Actuarial Science —See **Insurance** pg 3274

Acupuncture —See **Medical Sciences -- Alternative Medicine** pg 4188

Addictions —See **Drug Abuse and Alcoholism** pg 1720; see also Psychology pg 5279

Adhesives —See **Chemistry and Chemicals -- Physical and Theoretical Chemistry** pg 1385; see also Chemistry -- Chemical Technology pg 1352; Engineering -- Chemical Engineering pg 2216; Engineering -- Materials Science pg 2288; Metals and Metallurgy -- Welding pg 4617; Paints and Painting pg 4869; Plastics pg 5139

Administrative Law —See **Law -- Constitutional Law** pg 3509

Adoption —See **Sociology -- Social Services and Welfare** pg 5885

Adult and Continuing Education –pg 1909

Adventure —See **Literature -- Detective and Mystery** pg 3983

Advertising —See **Business and Economics -- Advertising and Public Relations** pg 899

Advertising and Public Relations –pg 899

Aerobics —See **Health--Physical Fitness and Hygiene** pg 2876

Aerodynamics —See **Aeronautics, Astronautics** pg 3

Aeronautics, Astronautics –pg 3; see also Military and Defense pg 4625; Transportation pg 6016

Aerospace Medicine —See **Aeronautics, Astronautics** pg 3; **Medical Sciences** pg 4073

Aesthetics —See **The Arts -- Art** pg 381; see also Philosophy pg 5004

Africa —See **General Interest -- General Interest-Africa** pg 2775; **History -- History of Africa** pg 2929

African American History —See **History -- History of North and South America** pg 3018

African Studies —See **History -- History of Africa** pg 2929; **Literature** pg 3872

Aging —See **Medical Sciences -- Geriatrics** pg 4304; see also Senior Citizens pg 5786

Agribusiness —See **Agriculture -- Agricultural Economics** pg 161

Agricultural Aviation —See **Aeronautics, Astronautics** pg 3; see also Agriculture pg 47

Agricultural Chemistry —See **Agriculture** pg 47; see also Chemistry and Chemicals pg 1289

Agricultural Economics –pg 161

Agricultural Engineering —See **Agriculture** pg 47; see also Engineering pg 2177

Agricultural Equipment –pg 169

Agricultural Marketing —See **Agriculture** pg 47; see also Business and Economics -- Marketing and Purchasing pg 1233

Agricultural Meteorology —See **Earth Sciences -- Meteorology** pg 1812; see also Agriculture pg 47

Agriculture —See **Food and Food Industry** pg 2607; Gardening and Horticulture pg 2696, 2708

Agronomy —See **Agriculture** pg 47; see also Agriculture -- Crop Production and Soils pg 174

AIDS —See **Medical Sciences -- Communicable Diseases** pg 4242

Air Cargo —See **Transportation** pg 6016; see also Aeronautics, Astronautics pg 3

Air Conditioning —See **Heating, Plumbing, and Refrigeration** pg 2894

Air Force —See **Aeronautics, Astronautics** pg 3; **Military and Defense** pg 4625

Air Pollution —See **Environmental Issues -- Pollution and Waste Management** pg 2404

Air Travel —See **Aeronautics, Astronautics** pg 3; **Travel and Tourism** pg 6110

Airplanes —See **Aeronautics, Astronautics** pg 3

Airports —See **Aeronautics, Astronautics** pg 3

Alcoholic Beverages —See **Food and Food Industry -- Beverage Industry** pg 2647

Alcoholism —See **Drug Abuse and Alcoholism** pg 1720

Alimony —See **Law -- Family Law** pg 3551

All Terrain Vehicles —See **Transportation -- Recreational Vehicles --** pg 6080

Allergy and Immunologic Diseases –pg 4176

Almanacs —See **Encyclopedias and General Reference Books** pg 2098

Alternative Medicine –pg 4188

Alumni –pg 1441

Amateur Radio —See **Communications -- Radio** pg 1479; see also Communications pg 1448

American Studies —See **History -- History of North and South America** pg 3018

Amusements –pg 3641; see also Children and Youth Interests pg 1397

Analytical Chemistry –pg 1343

Anarchism —See **Political Science -- Socialism, Communism, Anarchism, Utopianism** pg 5243

Anatomy — pg 4195; see also Biology -- Embryology pg 602; Medical Sciences -- Pathology pg 4470

Anesthesia —See **Medical Sciences -- Anesthesiology** pg 4197; see also Medical Sciences -- Surgery pg 4546

Anesthesiology –pg 4197; see also Medical Sciences -- Surgery pg 4546

Angiology —See **Medical Sciences -- Cardiology** pg 4224

Anglo-Saxon Studies —See **History -- History of Europe** pg 2965; **Literature** pg 3872

Animal Diseases —See **Veterinary Sciences** pg 6158

Animal Husbandry —See **Agriculture -- Livestock** pg 230; see also Veterinary Sciences pg 6158

Animal Science —See **Zoology** pg 6237, 6257; see also Veterinary Sciences pg 6158

Animal Welfare –pg 255

Animals —See **Animal Welfare** pg 255; see also Animal Welfare -- Pets pg 258; Veterinary Sciences pg 6158; Zoology pg 6237

Anthropology –pg 262; see also Archaeology pg 291; Paleontology pg 4873; Sociology pg 5851

SUBJECT CROSS REFERENCES

Antibiotics —See **Pharmacy and Pharmacology** pg 4941

Antiques —pg 286; see also Hobbies pg 3085; Museums and Galleries pg 4715

Antitrust Law —See **Law -- Corporation Law** pg 3513

Anxiety —See **Medical Sciences -- Psychiatry** pg 4501; see also Psychology pg 5279

Apartments —See **Housing and Urban Development** pg 3138

Apparel —See **Clothing Industry and Fashion** pg 1423; see also Business and Economics -- Retail pg 1276; Fabrics and Textile Industries pg 2468

Appliances —See **Home Economics -- Household Appliances** pg 3112

Applied Mechanics —See **Engineering -- Materials Science** pg 2288

Apprenticeship —See **Business and Economics -- Labor** pg 1115

Aquaculture —See **Fish and Fisheries** pg 2571

Archaeology —pg 291; see also Anthropology pg 262; History pg 2902; Paleontology pg 4873

Archery —See **Sports and Games** pg 5933

Architecture —pg 328; see also Building and Construction pg 671; Engineering pg 2177; Interior Design and Decoration pg 3306

Archives and Manuscripts —pg 3760

Army —See **Military and Defense** pg 4625

Aromatherapy —See **Beauty and Cosmetics** pg 456

Art —pg 381; see also Humanities pg 3169

Art Galleries —See **Museums and Galleries** pg 4715

Art History —See **The Arts -- Art** pg 381

Art Museums —See **Museums and Galleries** pg 4715

Arthritis —See **Medical Sciences -- Musculoskeletal System** pg 4376

Artificial Intelligence —pg 1568; see also Computers -- Automation pg 1576; Science and Technology pg 5689

Arts and Sciences —See **Humanities** pg 3169; Social Sciences pg 5825

Asbestos —See **Building and Construction** pg 671; see also Public Health and Safety pg 5422

Asia —See **General Interest -- General Interest-Asia** pg 2777; **History -- History of Asia** pg 2938

Asian Studies —See **History -- History of Asia** pg 2938

Associations —See **Societies and Clubs** pg 5841

Asthma —See **Medical Sciences -- Respiratory System** pg 4535

Astrology —pg 440

Astronautics —See **Aeronautics, Astronautics** pg 3

Astronomy —pg 442

Astrophysics —See **Astronomy** pg 442

Atheism —See **Philosophy** pg 5004

Athletic Clubs —See **Health** pg 2876

Athletics —See **Sports and Games** pg 5933; see also Health pg 2876

Atlas —See **Geography** pg 2827

Atmospheric Science —See **Earth Sciences -- Meteorology** pg 1812; see also Science and Technology pg 5689

Atomic Energy —pg 2159; see also Engineering -- Nuclear Engineering pg 2325; Engineering -- Nuclear Engineering pg 2325

Attorney General —See **Law -- Judicial Process** pg 3572

Audio-Visual Education —See **Education -- Teaching and Curriculum** pg 2034

Audiocassettes —See **Sound Recordings and Systems** pg 5928

Audiology —See **Medical Sciences -- Otorhinolaryngology** pg 4462

Auditing —See **Business and Economics -- Accounting** pg 881

Audubon Society —See **Environmental Issues -- Conservation and Natural Resources** pg 2362; see also Natural History pg 4802

Australia —See **General Interest -- General Interest-Australia and Oceania** pg 2785; **History -- History of Australia and Oceania** pg 2962

Authors —See **Literature** pg 3872; see also Biographies pg 464

Automation —pg 1576

Automobile Industry and Trade —See **Transportation -- Automobiles** pg 6039

Automobile Racing —See **Sports and Games** pg 5933

Automobiles —pg 6039

Aviation —See **Aeronautics, Astronautics** pg 3

Bacteriology —See **Biology -- Microbiology** pg 623

Badminton —See **Sports and Games** pg 5933

Bahaism —See **Religions and Theology -- Other Religions, Sects and Cults** pg 5652

Bakers and Bakeries —See **Food and Food Industry** pg 2607

Balkan Studies —See **History -- History of Europe** pg 2965

Banking —See **Business and Economics -- Banks and Banking** pg 914

Banking Law —pg 3492; see also Business and Economics -- Banks and Banking pg 914; Law -- Corporation Law pg 3513

Bankruptcy —See **Law -- Banking Law** pg 3492; see also Business and Economics -- Banks and Banking pg 914

Banks and Banking —pg 914

Baptist —See **Religions and Theology -- Protestantism** pg 5662

Baseball —See **Sports and Games** pg 5933

Baseball Cards —See **Hobbies** pg 3085; see also Sports and Games pg 5933

Beauty and Cosmetics —pg 456

Beekeeping —See **Agriculture** pg 47

Behavior Therapy —See **Psychology** pg 5279

Behavioral Science —See **Psychology** pg 5279; see also Medical Sciences -- Psychiatry pg 4501

Belizean Studies —See **History -- History of North and South America** pg 3018

Beverage Industry —pg 2647

Bicycles —See **Bicycles and Cycling** pg 462

Bicycles and Cycling —pg 462

Bilingualism —See **Linguistics** pg 3768; see also Education pg 1846

Bioengineering —pg 511

Biofeedback —See **Psychology** pg 5279; see also Medical Sciences pg 4073

Biographies —pg 464

Biological Chemistry —pg 526

Biological Control Systems —See **Biology -- Physiology** pg 648

Biological Physics —pg 547

Biology —pg 475; see also Medical Sciences pg 4073; Zoology pg 6237

Biomechanics —See **Biology -- Bioengineering** pg 511

Biomedical Engineering —See **Biology -- Bioengineering** pg 511

Biomedicine —See **Biology -- Bioengineering** pg 511

Biotechnology —See **Biology -- Bioengineering** pg 511

Birds —See **Zoology -- Ornithology** pg 6284; see also Environmental Issues -- Conservation and Natural Resources pg 2362; Natural History pg 4802

Birth Control —pg 658; see also Population Studies pg 5252

SUBJECT CROSS REFERENCES

Blind —See **Physically Impaired** pg 5053; see also Education -- Special Education and Rehabilitation pg 2021; Medical Sciences -- Ophthalmology pg 4440

Blood —See **Medical Sciences -- Hematology** pg 4354

Blood Groups —See **Medical Sciences -- Hematology** pg 4354

Blood Preservation —See **Medical Sciences -- Hematology** pg 4354

Blood Transfusions —See **Medical Sciences -- Hematology** pg 4354

Boats and Boating —pg 662

Bodybuilding —See **Health** pg 2876; see also Sports and Games pg 5933

Books and Bookmaking —pg 5487

Booksellers —See **Publishing -- Books and Bookmaking** pg 5487; see also Publishing pg 5465

Botany —pg 551; see also Gardening and Horticulture pg 2696

Bowling —See **Sports and Games** pg 5933

Boxing —See **Sports and Games** pg 5933

Brahmanism —See **Hinduism** pg 5632

Braille —See **Physically Impaired** pg 5053; see also Education -- Special Education and Rehabilitation pg 2021

Breastfeeding —See **Medical Sciences -- Gynecology and Obstetrics** pg 4327

Breweries —See **Food and Food Industry -- Beverage Industry** pg 2647

Bricks —See **Building and Construction** pg 671

Bridges —See **Transportation** pg 6016; see also Engineering -- Civil Engineering pg 2226; Transportation -- Roads and Traffic pg 6082

British Studies —See **History -- History of Europe** pg 2965

Broadcasting —See **Communications -- Television and Cable** pg 1514; see also Communications -- Radio pg 1479

Buddhism —pg 5611

Budget —See **Finance -- Public Finance** pg 2536; see also Business and Economics -- Banks and Banking pg 914

Building and Construction —pg 671; see also Engineering -- Civil Engineering pg 2226; Housing and Urban Development pg 3138

Burns —See **Medical Sciences** pg 4073

Buses —See **Transportation** pg 6016

Business and Economics —pg 716

Business Education —See **Business and Economics** pg 716; see also Education pg 1846

Business Law —See **Law -- Corporation Law** pg 3513; see also Business and Economics pg 716; Law -- International Law pg 3555

Buying —See **Business and Economics -- Marketing and Purchasing** pg 1233

Cable Television —See **Communications -- Television and Cable** pg 1514

CAD/CAM —See **Computers -- Computer Graphics and Design** pg 1591; see also Computers -- Computer Engineering pg 1587

Calligraphy —See **The Arts -- Crafts and Decorative Arts** pg 418

Cameras —See **Photography** pg 5035; see also Hobbies pg 3085; Motion Picture pg 4691

Campers —See **Transportation -- Recreational Vehicles** pg 6080

Camping —See **Leisure and Recreation -- Outdoor Recreation** pg 3653

Canadian Studies —See **History -- History of North and South America** pg 3018

Cancer and Neoplastic Syndromes —pg 4203; see also Medical Sciences -- Radiology pg 4524

Canoeing —See **Boats and Boating** pg 662

Canon Law —See **Religions and Theology** pg 5521

Cardiology —pg 4224; see also Medical Sciences -- Hematology pg 4354

Careers —See **Occupations and Careers** pg 4852

Cargo —See **Transportation -- Ships and Shipping** pg 6093; see also Transportation pg 6016

Caribbean Studies —See **History -- History of North and South America** pg 3018

Carpentry and Woodwork —pg 713; see also Hobbies pg 3085; Interior Design -- Home Furnishings pg 3314

Carpet, Rugs —See **Interior Design -- Home Furnishings** pg 3314

Cars —See **Transportation -- Automobiles** pg 6039

Cartography —pg 2859

Cartooning —See **The Arts -- Graphic Arts** pg 427

Cartoons —See **Leisure and Recreation -- Amusements** pg 3641

Catalysis —See **Chemistry and Chemicals -- Physical and Theoretical Chemistry** pg 1385

Catalysts —See **Chemistry and Chemicals -- Physical and Theoretical Chemistry** pg 1385

Catering —See **Food and Food Industry** pg 2607; see also Hotels/Motels pg 3130

Catholicism —pg 5614

Cattle —See **Agriculture -- Livestock** pg 230

Caves —See **Earth Sciences -- Geophysics** pg 1792; see also Earth Sciences -- Geology pg 1746

CD-ROM —See **Computers -- Optical Storage, CD-ROM Applications** pg 1646

Celebrity Interests —See **General Interest** pg 2771; see also Motion Picture pg 4691

Cells —See **Biology -- Cytology** pg 591

Celtic Studies —See **History -- History of Europe** pg 2965

Cement —See **Building and Construction** pg 671; see also Engineering -- Civil Engineering pg 2226

Cemeteries —See **Funeral Service** pg 2695

Central America —See **General Interest -- General Interest-Central America** pg 2786; **History -- History of North and South America** pg 3018

Ceramics —See **Glass and Ceramics** pg 2865

Cereals —See **Agriculture -- Feed Grain and Milling** pg 225

Cerebral Palsy —See **Medical Sciences -- Neurology** pg 4383

Chamber of Commerce —pg 967

Charities —See **Philanthropy** pg 4998; see also Sociology -- Social Services and Welfare pg 5885

Chemical Engineering —pg 2216; see also Chemistry pg 1289; Chemistry -- Chemical Technology pg 1352

Chemical Technology —pg 1352; see also Biology -- Bioengineering pg 511; Engineering -- Chemical Engineering pg 2216

Chemistry and Chemicals —pg 1289; see also Engineering -- Chemical Engineering pg 2216

Chemotherapy —See **Medical Sciences -- Cancer and Neoplastic Syndromes** pg 4203; see also Pharmacy and Pharmacology pg 4941

Chess —See **Sports and Games** pg 5933

Child Development —See **Education -- Early Childhood and Primary Education** pg 1917

Child Psychology —See **Psychology** pg 5279

Child Welfare —See **Sociology -- Social Services and Welfare** pg 5885

Children and Youth Interests —pg 1397

SUBJECT CROSS REFERENCES

China, Tableware —See **Glass and Ceramics** pg 2865; see also Gifts, Toys pg 2863

Chinese Studies —See **History -- History of Asia** pg 2938

Chiropractic —See **Medical Sciences -- Alternative Medicine** pg 4188

Christianity —See **Religions and Theology** pg 5521

Chromatography —See **Chemistry and Chemicals -- Analytical Chemistry** pg 1343; see also Chemistry and Chemicals pg 1289

Churches —See **Religions and Theology** pg 5521; see also Religions and Theology -- Orthodox Eastern Churches pg 5650; Religions and Theology -- Protestantism pg 5662

Cinema —See **Motion Picture** pg 4691

Cinematography —See **Video** pg 1530; see also Motion Picture pg 4691

Circuits —See **Electronics** pg 2066

Citrus Industry —See **Agriculture -- Crop Production and Soils** pg 174

City Directory —See **Geography** pg 2827

City Planning —See **Housing and Urban Development** pg 3138

Civil Defense —pg 1412

Civil Engineering —pg 2226

Civil Law —pg 3498

Civil Rights —pg 5201

Civil Service —pg 5413; see also Public Administration pg 5338

Classical Studies —pg 1414; see also Archaeology pg 291; History pg 2902; Humanities pg 3169; Linguistics pg 3768; Literature pg 3872

Classroom Management —See **Education -- School Management and Organization** pg 1995

Climatology —See **Earth Sciences -- Meteorology** pg 1812

Clinical Medicine —See **Medical Sciences** pg 4073

Clocks —See **Jewelry -- Clocks and Watches** pg 3321

Clocks and Watches —pg 3321

Clothing Industry and Fashion —pg 1423; see also Leather and Fur Industry pg 3631; Textiles pg 2468

Clubs —See **Societies and Clubs** pg 5841

Coaching —See **Sports and Games** pg 5933

Coal —See **Mines and Mining** pg 4658; see also Energy pg 2127

Coast Guard —See **Naval Science, Navigation** pg 4821

Coffee —See **Food and Food Industry -- Beverage Industry** pg 2647

Coins —See **Hobbies -- Numismatics** pg 3095

Collectors and Collecting —See **Antiques** pg 286; see also Hobbies pg 3085

College and School Publications —pg 1432; see also Education -- Higher Education pg 1937

College and University Guides —See **Education -- Higher Education** pg 1937

College Costs —See **Education -- Educational Finance** pg 1921

Colleges and Universities —See **Education -- Higher Education** pg 1937; see also College and School Publications pg 1432

Combustion —See **Chemistry and Chemicals -- Physical and Theoretical Chemistry** pg 1385; **Energy** pg 2127; **Engineering** pg 2177

Comics —See **Leisure and Recreation -- Amusements** pg 3641

Commerce —pg 970

Commercial Art —See **The Arts -- Graphic Arts** pg 427

Commercial Law —See **Law -- Corporation Law** pg 3513

Commodities —See **Business and Economics -- Commerce** pg 970

Common Law —See **Law -- Civil Law** pg 3498

Communicable Diseases —pg 4242; see also Public Health and Safety pg 4242

Communication —See **Communications** pg 1448

Communications —pg 1448

Communism —See **Political Science -- Socialism, Communism, Anarchism, Utopianism** pg 5243

Community Affairs —See **Public Administration** pg 5338

Community Development —See **Housing and Urban Development** pg 3138

Compact Disc —See **Computers -- Optical Storage, CD-ROM Applications** pg 1646

Company Law —See **Law -- Corporation Law** pg 3513

Comparative Law —See **Law -- International Law** pg 3555

Composite Materials —See **Engineering -- Materials Science** pg 2288

Computer Architecture —See **Computers -- Computer Graphics and Design** pg 1591

Computer Assisted Instruction —pg 1581; see also Education -- Teaching and Curriculum pg 2034

Computer Crimes —See **Computers -- Computer Crimes and Security** pg 1584

Computer Crimes and Security —pg 1584

Computer Directories —See **Computers -- Computer Industry and Industry Directories** pg 1595

Computer Engineering —pg 1587

Computer Games —pg 1590; see also Recreation, Leisure -- Games and Amusements pg 3641

Computer Graphics and Design —pg 1591

Computer Industry —See **Computers -- Computer Industry and Industry Directories** pg 1595

Computer Industry and Industry Directories —pg 1595; see also Computers -- Computer Sales, Service and Supply pg 1609

Computer Music —pg 1601; see also Music pg 4731

Computer Networks —pg 1602

Computer Products —See **Computers -- Computer Sales, Service and Supply** pg 1609

Computer Sales, Service and Supply —pg 1609

Computer Science —See **Computers** pg 1535

Computer Simulation —See **Computers -- Simulation** pg 1655

Computer Systems —pg 1610

Computers —pg 1535

Confectioners —See **Food and Food Industry** pg 2607

Congress —See **Public Administration** pg 5338

Conservation and Natural Resources —pg 2362; see also Environmental Issues -- Ecology pg 2391; Natural History pg 4802; Water Resources pg 6187

Constitutional Law —pg 3509

Construction —See **Building and Construction** pg 671; see also Engineering -- Civil Engineering pg 2226

Consumer Education and Protection —pg 1670; see also Business and Economics pg 716

Contact Lenses —See **Medical Sciences -- Ophthalmology** pg 4440

Continuing Education —See **Education -- Adult and Continuing Education** pg 1909

Contraception —See **Birth Control** pg 658

Contractors —See **Building and Construction** pg 671; **Engineering -- Civil Engineering** pg 2226; see also Architecture pg 328

SUBJECT CROSS REFERENCES

Conventions —See **Business and Economics -- Advertising and Public Relations** pg 899; **Science and Technology** pg 5689

Cookbooks, Cooking —See **Home Economics** pg 3105

Cooperatives —pg 1009; see also Agriculture pg 47; Business and Economics -- Banking and Finance pg 914

Copyright, Intellectual Property —pg 1678

Corporate Law —See **Law -- Corporation Law** pg 3513

Corporation Law —pg 3513

Corrosion —See **Engineering -- Materials Science** pg 2288; see also Metals and Metallurgy pg 4584

Cosmetic Surgery —See **Medical Sciences -- Surgery** pg 4546

Cosmetics —See **Beauty and Cosmetics** pg 456

Cotton —See **Agriculture -- Crop Production and Soils** pg 174; see also Fabrics and Textile Industries pg 2468

Counseling —See **Psychology** pg 5279; see also Religions and Theology pg 5521

Court Rules —See **Law -- Judicial Process** pg 3572

Courts —See **Law -- Judicial Process** pg 3572

Crafts and Decorative Arts —pg 418; see also Glass and Ceramics pg 2865; Home Economics -- Sewing and Needlework pg 3114

Credit Unions —See **Business and Economics -- Banks and Banking** pg 914

Crime Prevention —See **Law -- Law Enforcement and Criminology** pg 3595

Criminal Justice —See **Law -- Law Enforcement and Criminology** pg 3595; see also Law -- Criminal Law pg 3527

Criminal Law —pg 3527; see also Law -- Law Enforcement and Criminology pg 3595

Criminal Procedure —See **Law -- Judicial Process** pg 3572; **Law -- Law Enforcement and Criminology** pg 3595; see also Law -- Criminal Law pg 3527

Criminology —See **Law -- Law Enforcement and Criminology** pg 3595

Croatian Studies —See **History -- History of Europe** pg 2965

Crop Production and Soils —pg 174

Crystallography —pg 1363

Currency —See **Business and Economics -- Banks and Banking** pg 914; see also Business and Economics -- International Economic Relations pg 1073

Curriculum —See **Education -- Teaching and Curriculum** pg 2034

Customs —See **Sociology -- Manners and Customs** pg 5883

Customs and Excise —See **Finance -- Public Finance** pg 2536; see also Law pg 3340

Cybernetics —pg 1616

Cycling —See **Bicycles and Cycling** pg 462

Cystic Fibrosis —See **Medical Sciences** pg 4073

Cytology —pg 591

Dairy Industry —pg 215

Dance —pg 1689; see also The Arts -- Performing Arts pg 434

Data Base Management —pg 1618

Data Protection —See **Computers -- Computer Crimes and Security** pg 1584

Deaf —See **Physically Impaired** pg 5053

Decorative Arts —See **The Arts -- Crafts and Decorative Arts** pg 418

Defense —See **Military and Defense** pg 4625; see also Civil Defense pg 1412

Demography —See **Population Studies** pg 5252

Dentistry —pg 1694

Department Stores —See **Business and Economics -- Retail** pg 1276; see also Business and Economics -- Marketing and Purchasing pg 1233

Dermatology —pg 4258

Desktop Publishing —pg 1621; see also Publishing pg 5465

Detective and Mystery —pg 3983

Diabetes —See **Medical Sciences -- Endocrinology** pg 4269

Diagnostic Imaging —See **Medical Sciences -- Radiology** pg 4524

Dialysis —See **Medical Sciences -- Urology and Nephrology** pg 4572

Dictionaries —See **Encyclopedias and General Reference Books** pg 2098

Diesel Trucks —See **Transportation -- Trucking** pg 6107

Dietetics —See **Nutrition and Dietetics** pg 4836

Directories —See **Encyclopedias and General Reference Books** pg 2098

Disarmament —See **Military and Defense** pg 4625; see also Law -- International Law pg 3555

Disaster Relief —See **Civil Defense** pg 1412

Disease Control —See **Public Health and Safety** pg 5422

Divorce —See **Law -- Family Law** pg 3551

Doctrinal Theology —See **Religions and Theology** pg 5521

Dog Racing —See **Sports and Games** pg 5933

Domestic Relations —See **Law -- Family Law** pg 3551

Drama —See **Theater** pg 5991; see also The Arts -- Performing Arts pg 434

Drinks —See **Food and Food Industry -- Beverage Industry** pg 2647; see also Home Economics pg 3105

Drug Abuse and Alcoholism —pg 1720

Drugs —See **Pharmacy and Pharmacology** pg 4941

Drycleaning —See **Fabrics and Textile Industries** pg 2468

Dyes and Dyeing —See **Chemistry -- Chemical Technology** pg 1352; **Fabrics and Textile Industries** pg 2468

Early Childhood and Primary Education —pg 1917

Early Childhood Education —See **Education -- Early Childhood and Primary Education** pg 1917

Earth Sciences —pg 1733

Eating Disorders —See **Medical Sciences -- Psychiatry** pg 4501

Ecology —pg 2391; see also Natural History pg 4802

Economic Assistance and Development —pg 1012

Economic Assistance, Domestic —See **Business and Economics -- Economic Assistance and Development** pg 1012

Economic Assistance, International —See **Business and Economics--Economic Assistance and Development** pg 1012

Economic Conditions —See **Business and Economics -- Economic History, Conditions** pg 1023

Economic Development, Domestic —See **Business and Economics--Economic Assistance and Development** pg 1012

Economic Development, International —See **Business and Economics--Economic Assistance and Development** pg 1012

Economic Forecasting —See **Business and Economics -- Economic History, Conditions** pg 1023

Economic History —See **Business and Economics -- Economic History, Conditions** pg 1023

Economic History, Conditions —pg 1023

Economic Theory —See **Business and Economics** pg 716

SUBJECT CROSS REFERENCES

Editing —See **Publishing** pg 5465; see also Journalism pg 3322; Literature pg 3872

Education —pg 1846

Educational Exchanges —See **Education -- International Education** pg 1985

Educational Finance —pg 1921

Educational Laws and Legislation —pg 3533

Educational Psychology —See **Psychology** pg 5279; see also Education pg 1846

Educational Research —pg 1927

Elections —See **Political Science** pg 5148

Electric Power —pg 2165

Electrical Engineering —pg 2248; see also Energy pg 2127; Heating, Plumbing and Refrigeration pg 2894

Electrochemistry —pg 1366; see also Chemistry and Chemicals -- Analytical Chemistry pg 1343; Chemistry and Chemicals -- Physical and Theoretical Chemistry pg 1385

Electronic Data Processing —pg 1622

Electronic Publishing —See **Desktop Publishing** pg 1621

Electronics —pg 2066; see also Engineering -- Electrical Engineering pg 2248

Elementary Education —pg 1933

Embroidery —See **Home Economics -- Sewing and Needlework** pg 3114

Embryology —pg 602; see also Medical Sciences -- Anatomy pg 4195

Emergencies —See **Medical Sciences -- Emergency Medicine** pg 4265

Emergency Health Services —See **Medical Sciences -- Emergency Medicine** pg 4265

Emergency Medicine —pg 4265

Emigration and Immigration —pg 2094

Employment Law —See **Law -- Labor Laws and Legislation** pg 3580

Encyclopedias and General Reference Books —pg 2098

Endocrinology —pg 4269

Energy —pg 2127; see also Engineering -- Electricity, Electrical Engineering, Electronics pg 2248; Engineering -- Nuclear Engineering pg 2325; Petroleum and Natural Gas pg 4899; Physics -- Nuclear Physics pg 5129; Public Administration -- Public Utilities pg 5418

Energy Conservation —pg 2173

Engineering —pg 2177; see also Computers -- Artificial Intelligence pg 1568

Entertainment Law —pg 3537

Entomology —pg 6270

Environmental Health —See **Environmental Issues** pg 2331; see also Public Health and Safety pg 5422

Environmental Issues —pg 2331

Environmental Law —pg 3539; see also Environmental Issues pg 2331

Environmental Protection —See **Environmental Issues** pg 2331; see also Environmental Issues -- Pollution and Waste Management pg 2404

Environmental Studies —See **Environmental Issues** pg 2331; see also Environmental Issues -- Conservation and Natural Resources pg 2362; Environmental Issues -- Ecology pg 2391; Environmental Issues -- Pollution and Waste Management pg 2404

Environmental Technology —See **Environmental Issues** pg 2331; see also Science and Technology pg 5689

Environmental Toxicology —See **Toxicology** pg 6007

Environmental Waste Management —See **Environmental Issues** pg 2331

Epidemiology —pg 4280; see also Medical Sciences -- Communicable Diseases pg 4242; Public Health and Safety pg 5422

Epilepsy —See **Medical Sciences -- Neurology** pg 4383

Episcopal —See **Religions and Theology -- Protestantism** pg 5662

Ergonomics —See **Engineering -- Industrial Engineering** pg 2282; see also Computers -- Cybernetics pg 1616

Esperanto —See **Education -- Teaching and Curriculum** pg 2034

Estate Planning —pg 3549; see also Business and Economics -- Banks and Banking pg 914; Business and Economics -- Investments pg 1081

Ethics —pg 2433

Ethnic Interests —pg 2439

Ethnology —See **Anthropology** pg 262

Europe —See **General Interest-Europe** pg 2788; **History -- History of Europe** pg 2965

European Studies —See **History -- History of Europe** pg 2965

Evangelism —See **Religions and Theology** pg 5521

Examinations —See **Education -- Tests and Measurements** pg 2055

Exceptional Children —See **Education -- Special Education and Rehabilitation** pg 2021

Exercise —See **Health--Physical Fitness and Hygiene** pg 2876

Exhibits/Exhibitions —See **Business and Economics -- Advertising and Public Relations** pg 899; **Science and Technology** pg 5689

Experimental Mechanics —See **Physics -- Mechanics** pg 5123

Experimental Medicine —pg 4284

Expert Systems —See **Computers -- Artificial Intelligence** pg 1568

Expositions —See **Business and Economics -- Advertising and Public Relations** pg 899

Fabric —See **Clothing Industry and Fashion** pg 1423; see also Home Economics -- Sewing and Needlework pg 3114

Fabrics and Textile Industries —pg 2468; see also Clothing Industry and Fashion pg 1423

Fairs —See **Leisure and Recreation -- Amusements** pg 3641

Family and Marriage —pg 2485; see also Home Economics pg 3105

Family Law —pg 3551

Family Physicians —See **Medical Sciences -- Family Practice** pg 4288; see also Medical Sciences -- Physicians and Medical Personnel pg 4493

Family Planning —See **Birth Control** pg 658; see also Family and Marriage pg 2485

Family Practice —pg 4288

Family Therapy —See **Family and Marriage** pg 2485

Fantasy —See **Science Fiction, Fantasy and Horror** pg 4002

Farm Equipment —See **Agricultural Equipment** pg 169

Fashion —See **Clothing Industry and Fashion** pg 1423

Federal Aid to Education —See **Education -- Educational Finance** pg 1921

Federal Employees —See **Public Administration -- Civil Service** pg 5413

Federal Government —See **Public Administration** pg 5338; see also Political Science pg 5148

Feed Grain and Milling —pg 225

Feminism —See **Women's Interests** pg 6209

Fencing —See **Sports and Games** pg 5933

Fertility —See **Birth Control** pg 658; **Population Studies** pg 5252; see also Medical Sciences -- Gynecology and Obstetrics pg 4327

Fertilization —See **Biology -- Physiology** pg 648

xxviii

SUBJECT CROSS REFERENCES

Fertilizers —See **Agriculture -- Crop Production and Soils** pg 174; **Chemistry -- Chemical Technology** pg 1352

Fiber Optics —See **Communications -- Telecommunication** pg 1488; **Physics -- Light, Optics, Radiation** pg 5104

Fiction —See **Literature** pg 3872; see also Literary and Political Reviews pg 3851

Films and Filmmaking —See **Motion Picture** pg 4691; see also Video pg 5035

Finance —pg 2498

Finance, Personal —See **Finance--Personal Finance** pg 2508

Finance, Public —See **Finance -- Public Finance** pg 2509

Fine Arts —See **The Arts** pg 358

Fire Prevention —pg 2564; see also Public Health and Safety pg 5422

Fish and Fisheries —pg 2571

Fishing —See **Fish and Fisheries** pg 2571; see also Leisure and Recreation -- Outdoor Recreation pg 3653

Floor Coverings —See **Interior Design -- Home Furnishings** pg 3314

Florist Trade —pg 2723

Flowers —See **Gardening and Horticulture -- Florist Trade** pg 2723

Fluid Mechanics —See **Physics -- Mechanics** pg 5123; see also Engineering -- Hydraulic Engineering pg 2271

Folk Music —See **Folklore** pg 2599

Folklore —pg 2599; see also History pg 2902; Literature pg 3872; Sociology -- Manners and Customs pg 5883

Food and Food Industry —pg 2607; see also Agriculture pg 47; Home Economics pg 3105

Food Production —See **Agriculture -- Crop Production and Soils** pg 174

Football —See **Sports and Games** pg 5933

Footwear —See **Clothing Industry and Fashion** pg 1423; see also Leather and Fur Industry pg 3631

Foreign Affairs —See **International Relations** pg 5215; see also Law -- International Law pg 3555

Foreign Study —See **Education -- International Education** pg 1985

Foreign Trade —See **Business and Economics -- Commerce** pg 970; see also Business and Economics -- International Economic Relations pg 1073

Forensic Medicine, Medical Jurisprudence —pg 4291

Forests and Forestry —pg 2659; see also Environmental Issues -- Conservation and Natural Resources pg 2362; Gardening and Horticulture pg 2696; Paper and Pulp Industry pg 4880

Franchises —See **Business and Economics** pg 716

Fraternities —See **Societies and Clubs** pg 5841

Freight —See **Aeronautics, Astronautics** pg 3; Transportation -- Railroads pg 6070

Freight and Freightage —See **Transportation -- Ships and Shipping** pg 6093; see also Transportation pg 6016

French Studies —See **History -- History of Europe** pg 2965

Frozen Foods —See **Food and Food Industry** pg 2607

Fruit —See **Agriculture -- Crop Production and Soils** pg 174; see also Food and Food Industry pg 2607

Fuel —See **Petroleum and Natural Gas** pg 4899; see also Energy pg 2127

Fund Raising —See **Philanthropy** pg 4998

Funeral Service —pg 2695

Fungi —See **Biology -- Mycology** pg 641

Fur —See **Leather and Fur Industry** pg 3631

Furniture —See **Interior Design -- Home Furnishings** pg 3314; see also Antiques pg 286; Building and Construction -- Carpentry and Woodwork pg 713; Interior Design and Decoration pg 3306

Gambling —See **Sports and Games** pg 5933; see also Psychology pg 5279; Public Administration pg 5338

Gardening and Horticulture —pg 2696

Gastroenterology —pg 4295

Gay/Lesbian —See **Homosexuality** pg 3118

Genealogy and Heraldry —pg 2725; see also History pg 2902

General Interest —pg 2771

General Interest-Africa —pg 2775

General Interest-Asia —pg 2777

General Interest-Australia and Oceania —pg 2785

General Interest-Central America —pg 2786

General Interest-Europe —pg 2788

General Interest-Near East —pg 2800

General Interest-North America —pg 2802

General Interest-South America —pg 2825

General Management and Administration —See **Business and Economics -- Management** pg 1194

General Practice —See **Medical Sciences -- Family Practice** pg 4288

General Reference Books —See **Encyclopedias and General Reference Books** pg 2098

Genetic Engineering —See **Biology -- Bioengineering** pg 511; see also Biology -- Genetics pg 604

Genetics —pg 604

Geochemistry —See **Chemistry and Chemicals** pg 1289

Geodesy —See **Earth Sciences -- Geophysics** pg 1792; **Geography** pg 2827

Geography —pg 2827; see also Travel and Tourism pg 6110

Geology —pg 1746

Geophysics —pg 1792

Geriatrics —pg 4304; see also Senior Citizens pg 5786

Germanic Studies —See **History -- History of Europe** pg 2965

Gerontology —See **Senior Citizens** pg 5786; see also Medical Sciences -- Geriatrics pg 4304

Gifted Children —See **Education -- Special Education and Rehabilitation** pg 2021

Gifts, Toys —pg 2863; see also Glass and Ceramics pg 2865; Leisure and Recreation -- Amusements pg 3641

Glass and Ceramics —pg 2865; see also The Arts -- Crafts and Decorative Arts pg 418

Golf —See **Sports and Games** pg 5933

Government —See **Public Administration** pg 5338; see also Political Science pg 5148

Government Employees —See **Public Administration -- Civil Service** pg 5413

Grants in Aid —See **Finance -- Public Finance** pg 2509; see also Education -- Educational Finance pg 1921

Graphic Arts —pg 427; see also Computers -- Computer Graphics and Design pg 1591; Printing Industry pg 5271

Guidance —See **Education -- Guidance and Counseling** pg 1935

Guidance and Counseling —pg 1935

Guns —See **Sports and Games** pg 5933; see also Military and Defense pg 4625

Gymnastics —See **Sports and Games** pg 5933

Gynecology and Obstetrics —pg 4327

Handicrafts —See **The Arts -- Crafts and Decorative Arts** pg 418

Harbors —See **Transportation -- Ships and Shipping** pg 6093

Hardware —pg 1631

SUBJECT CROSS REFERENCES

Hazardous Waste —See **Environmental Issues -- Pollution and Waste Management** pg 2404; see also Environmental Issues pg 2331

Health —pg 2876

Health Services Administration —pg 4330

Hearing Disorders —See **Medical Sciences -- Otorhinolaryngology** pg 4462

Heat —pg 5099

Heating, Plumbing, and Refrigeration —pg 2894

Helicopters —See **Aeronautics, Astronautics** pg 3

Helminthology —See **Zoology** pg 6237

Hematologic Diseases —See **Medical Sciences -- Hematology** pg 4354

Hematology —pg 4354; see also Medical Sciences -- Cardiology pg 4224; Medical Sciences -- Internal Medicine pg 4362

Hemodialysis —See **Medical Sciences -- Hematology** pg 4354

Heraldry —See **Genealogy and Heraldry** pg 2725

Heredity —See **Biology -- Genetics** pg 604

High Schools —See **Education -- Secondary Education** pg 2017

Higher Education —pg 1937

Hinduism —pg 5632

Historic Sites —See **History** pg 2902

History —pg 2902

History of Africa —pg 2929

History of Asia —pg 2938

History of Australia and Oceania —pg 2962

History of Europe —pg 2965

History of North and South America —pg 3018

History of the Middle East —See **History of the Near East** pg 3075

History of the Near East —pg 3075

History, Ancient —See **History** pg 2902

History, Modern —See **History** pg 2902

Hobbies —pg 3085; see also Home Economics -- Sewing and Needlework pg 3114; Sports and Games pg 5933; The Arts -- Crafts and Decorative Arts pg 418

Hockey —See **Sports and Games** pg 5933

Home Computing —See **Computers -- Microcomputers, Personal Computers** pg 1633

Home Economics —pg 3105; see also Family and Marriage pg 2485

Home Furnishings —pg 3314; see also Building and Construction -- Carpentry and Woodwork pg 713; Interior Design pg 3306

Homeopathy —See **Medical Sciences -- Alternative Medicine** pg 4188

Homosexuality —pg 3118

Hormones —See **Medical Sciences -- Endocrinology** pg 4269

Horoscopes —See **Astrology** pg 440

Horror —See **Science Fiction, Fantasy and Horror** pg 4002

Horse Racing —See **Horses and Horsemanship** pg 3122; see also Sports and Games pg 5933

Horses and Horsemanship —pg 3122; see also Sports and Games pg 5933

Horticulture —See **Gardening and Horticulture** pg 2696; see also Agriculture -- Crop Production and Soils pg 174; Biology -- Botany pg 551; Forests and Forestry pg 2659

Hospital Administration —See **Medical Sciences -- Health Services Administration** pg 4330

Hospitals —See **Medical Sciences -- Health Services Administration** pg 4330

Hotels/Motels —pg 3130; see also Travel and Tourism pg 6110; Restaurants pg 5681

Household Appliances —pg 3112

Housing and Urban Development —pg 3138; see also Building and Construction pg 671; Real Estate pg 5504

Human Ecology —See **Sociology** pg 5851; see also Environmental Issues -- Ecology pg 2391

Human Engineering —See **Engineering -- Industrial Engineering** pg 2282

Human Sexuality —See **Sexual Life** pg 5793

Humane Society —See **Animal Welfare** pg 255

Humanism —See **Humanities** pg 3169

Humanities —pg 3169; see also Social Sciences pg 5825; The Arts pg 358

Humor and Wit —See **Leisure and Recreation -- Amusements** pg 3641

Hunting —See **Leisure and Recreation -- Outdoor Recreation** pg 3653

Hydraulic Engineering —pg 2271; see also Earth Sciences -- Hydrology pg 1803; Energy pg 2127; Water Resources pg 6187

Hydrobiology —See **Earth Sciences -- Oceanography** pg 1832

Hydroelectric Power —See **Energy -- Electric Power** pg 2165

Hydrology —pg 1803; see also Engineering -- Hydraulic Engineering pg 2271; Water Resources pg 6187

Hygiene —See **Health -- Physical Fitness and Hygiene** pg 2891

Hypertension —See **Medical Sciences -- Cardiology** pg 4224

Hypnosis —pg 4361

Illiteracy —See **Education** pg 1846

Illustration —See **The Arts -- Graphic Arts** pg 427

Immigration —See **Emigration and Immigration** pg 2094

Immunology —See **Medical Sciences -- Allergy and Immunologic Diseases** pg 4176

Imports/Exports —See **Business and Economics -- Commerce** pg 970

Income Tax —See **Finance -- Finance--Taxation** pg 2536; see also Business and Economics -- Accounting pg 881

Industrial Arts —See **Education -- Vocational Education** pg 2058; see also Science and Technology pg 5689

Industrial Design —See **Engineering -- Industrial Engineering** pg 2282; see also Industry and Production -- Manufacturing pg 3241

Industrial Development —See **Industry and Production** pg 3205

Industrial Engineering —pg 2282

Industrial Health and Safety —pg 3188; see also Public Health and Safety pg 5422

Industrial Medicine —See **Industrial Health and Safety** pg 3188

Industry and Production —pg 3205; see also Business and Economics pg 716

Infectious Diseases —See **Medical Sciences -- Communicable Diseases** pg 4242; see also Medical Sciences -- Epidemiology pg 4280; Public Health and Safety pg 5422

Information Retrieval —See **Library and Information Sciences** pg 3677

Information Science —See **Library and Information Sciences** pg 3677

Inheritance —See **Law -- Estate Planning** pg 3549

Inorganic Chemistry —pg 1368

Insecticide —See **Pest Control** pg 4894

Insects —See **Zoology -- Entomology** pg 6270; see also Pest Control pg 4894

Insulation —See **Building and Construction** pg 671; see also Engineering -- Electrical Engineering pg 2248

Insurance —pg 3274

Insurance Law —See **Insurance** pg 3274

Integrated Circuits —See **Electronics** pg 2066; see also Engineering -- Electrical Engineering pg 2248

SUBJECT CROSS REFERENCES

Intellectual Property —See **Copyright, Intellectual Property** pg 1678

Intensive Care —See **Medical Sciences** pg 4073; see also Medical Sciences -- Nursing pg 4415

Interdisciplinary Studies —See **Humanities** pg 3169

Interior Design and Decoration —pg 3306; see also Architecture pg 328

Internal Medicine —pg 4362

Internal Revenue Service —See **Finance -- Taxation** pg 2536

International Economic Relations —pg 1073

International Education —pg 1985

International Law —pg 3555; see also Political Science -- International Relations pg 5215

International Relations —pg 5215; see also History pg 2902; Law -- International Law pg 3555; Military and Defense pg 4625

Interpersonal Communication —See **Communications** pg 1448

Invertebrates/Vertebrates —See **Zoology** pg 6237

Investing —See **Business and Economics -- Investments** pg 1081

Investments —pg 1081; see also Business and Economics -- Banking and Finance pg 914

Irish Slavonic Studies —See **History -- History of Europe** pg 2965

Irish Studies —See **History -- History of Europe** pg 2965

Irrigation —See **Engineering -- Hydraulic Engineering** pg 2271; see also Agriculture -- Crop Production and Soils pg 174

Islam —pg 5633

Jails —See **Law -- Law Enforcement and Criminology** pg 3595

Jewelry —pg 3318

Journalism —pg 3322; see also Communication -- Broadcasting pg 1514; Publishing pg 5465

Judaism —pg 5640; see also Ethnic Interests pg 2439

Judges —See **Law -- Judicial Process** pg 3572

Judicial Ethics —See **Law -- Judicial Process** pg 3572

Judicial Process —pg 3572

Judicial Statistics —See **Law -- Judicial Process** pg 3572

Judo/Karate —See **Sports and Games** pg 5933

Junior High Schools —See **Education -- Secondary Education** pg 2017

Juvenile Delinquency —See **Law -- Law Enforcement and Criminology** pg 3595

Kidneys —See **Medical Sciences -- Urology and Nephrology** pg 4572

Kindergarten —See **Education -- Early Childhood and Primary Education** pg 1917

Knitting —See **Home Economics -- Sewing and Needlework** pg 3114; see also Fabrics and Textile Industries pg 2468

Korean Studies —See **History -- History of Asia** pg 2938

Labels/Labelling —See **Packaging** pg 4863

Labor —pg 1115; see also Business and Economics -- Personnel Management pg 1263; Industrial Health and Safety pg 3188

Labor Laws and Legislation —pg 3580

Labor Unions —See **Business and Economics -- Labor** pg 1115

Laboratory Animals —See **Medical Sciences -- Experimental Medicine** pg 4284

LAN (Local Area Networks) —See **Computers -- Computer Networks** pg 1602

Land —See **Environmental Issues -- Conservation and Natural Resources** pg 2362; see also Real Estate pg 5504; Geography pg 2827

Landscape Architecture —See **Gardening and Horticulture** pg 2696

Landscaping —See **Architecture** pg 328

Language and Languages —See **Linguistics** pg 3768

Language Arts —pg 3333

Lasers —See **Physics -- Light, Optics, Radiation** pg 5104; see also Chemistry and Chemicals pg 1289; Engineering pg 2177; Medical Sciences -- Surgery pg 4546; Physics pg 5069

Latin American Studies —See **History -- History of North and South America** pg 3018

Laundry —See **Chemistry -- Chemical Technology** pg 1352; see also Fabrics and Textile Industries pg 2468

Law —pg 3340; see also Public Administration pg 5338

Law Enforcement —See **Law -- Law Enforcement and Criminology** pg 3340

Law Enforcement and Criminology —pg 3595

Law Offices —See **Law** pg 3340; see also Business and Economics -- Management pg 1194

Learning Disabilities —See **Education -- Special Education and Rehabilitation** pg 2021

Leather and Fur Industry —pg 3631; see also Clothing Industry and Fashion pg 1423

Legal Aid —pg 3619

Legislation —See **Law** pg 3340; see also Public Administration pg 5338

Leisure —See **Leisure and Recreation** pg 3634

Leisure and Recreation —pg 3634; see also Hobbies pg 3085; Travel and Tourism pg 6110

Leukemia —See **Medical Sciences -- Cancer and Neoplastic Syndromes** pg 4203

Library and Information Sciences —pg 3677

Life/Death —See **Philosophy** pg 5004

Light, Optics, Radiation —pg 5104

Linguistics —pg 3768

Liquor —See **Food and Food Industry -- Beverage Industry** pg 2647

Literacy —See **Education** pg 1846

Literary and Political Reviews —pg 3851; see also Literature pg 3872

Literary Criticism —See **Literary and Political Reviews** pg 3851

Literary Theory —See **Literary and Political Reviews** pg 3851

Literature —pg 3872; see also Linguistics pg 3768; Literary and Political Reviews pg 3851

Livestock —pg 230

Local Area Networks —See **Computers -- Computer Networks** pg 1602

Local Government —See **Public Administration** pg 5338

Lotteries —See **Public Administration** pg 5338

Lumber and Wood —pg 2688; see also Paper and Pulp Industry pg 4880

Lutheran —See **Religions and Theology -- Protestantism** pg 5662

Machinery —See **Engineering -- Mechanical Engineering and Machinery** pg 2304

Macroeconomics —See **Business and Economics** pg 716

Magic —See **Leisure and Recreation -- Amusements** pg 3641; see also Parapsychology and Occultism pg 4890

Magnetic Resonance Imaging —See **Medical Sciences -- Radiology** pg 4524

Magnetism —pg 5119

Mainframe Computing —See **Computers -- Electronic Data Processing** pg 1622

SUBJECT CROSS REFERENCES

Management –pg 1194

Manners and Customs –pg 5883

Manufacturing –pg 3241

Manufacturing Directories –See **Industry and Production -- Trade and Industrial Directories** pg 3250

Maps and Mapmaking –See **Geography -- Cartography** pg 2859

Marine Biology –pg 616; see also **Earth Sciences -- Oceanography** pg 1832; **Zoology** pg 6237

Marine Engineering –See **Engineering** pg 2177

Marine Pollution –See **Environmental Issues -- Pollution and Waste Management** pg 2404

Marines –See **Naval Science, Navigation** pg 4821

Maritime Law –pg 3620

Marketing and Purchasing –pg 1233

Marriage –See **Family and Marriage** pg 2485

Marriage Law –See **Law -- Family Law** pg 3551

Martial Arts –See **Phyiscal Fitness and Hygiene** pg 2891

Marxism –See **Political Science -- Socialism, Communism, Anarchism, Utopianism** pg 5243

Masonry –See **Building and Construction** pg 671

Mass Media –See **Communications** pg 1448

Mass Media Law –See **Law -- Entertainment Law** pg 3537

Materials Engineering –See **Engineering -- Materials Science** pg 2288

Materials Science –pg 2288

Mathematical Geography –See **Geography** pg 2827

Mathematics –pg 4007

Matrimonial Actions –See **Law -- Family Law** pg 3551

Meat –See **Food and Food Industry** pg 2607; see also **Agriculture -- Livestock** pg 230

Mechanical Engineering and Machinery –pg 2304

Mechanics –pg 5123

Media –See **Communications** pg 1448; see also **Journalism** pg 3322

Medical Centers –See **Medical Sciences -- Health Services Administration** pg 4330

Medical Education –pg 4366

Medical Instruments and Apparatus –pg 4371

Medical Jurisprudence –See **Medical Sciences -- Forensic Medicine, Medical Jurisprudence** pg 4291

Medical Malpractice –See **Law** pg 3340; see also **Medical Sciences** pg 4073

Medical Personnel –See **Medical Sciences -- Physicians and Medical Personnel** pg 4493

Medical School Directories –See **Medical Education** pg 4366

Medical Sciences –pg 4073

Medieval Studies –See **History -- History of Europe** pg 2965; see also **Classical Studies** pg 1414

Meetings –See **Business and Economics** pg 716

Memory –See **Psychology** pg 5279

Men's Interests –pg 4581

Mental Health –pg 2885; see also **Psychology** pg 5279; **Medical Sciences -- Psychiatry** pg 4501; **Sociology -- Social Services and Welfare** pg 5885

Mental Hygiene –See **Health--Mental Health** pg 2885

Mentally Disabled –See **Education -- Special Education and Rehabilitation** pg 2021; see also **Medical Sciences -- Psychiatry** pg 4501; **Psychology** pg 5279

Mergers/Acquisitions –See **Business and Economics** pg 716

Metabolic Diseases –See **Medical Sciences -- Endocrinology** pg 4269

Metallurgy –See **Metals and Metallurgy** pg 4584

Metals and Metallurgy –pg 4584; see also **Mines and Mining** pg 4658

Meteorology –pg 1812

Methodist –See **Religions and Theology -- Protestantism** pg 5662

Metrology and Standardization –pg 4620

Mexican American Studies –See **History -- History of North and South America** pg 3018

Microbiology –pg 623

Microcomputers –See **Computers -- Microcomputers, Personal Computers** pg 1633

Microcomputers, Personal Computers –pg 1633

Microeconomics –See **Business and Economics** pg 716

Microscopy –pg 639

Microwaves –See **Electronics** pg 2066

Midwifery –See **Medical Sciences -- Gynecology and Obstetrics** pg 4327

Migration –See **Emigration and Immigration** pg 2094; see also **Population Studies** pg 5252; **Business and Economics -- Labor** pg 1115; **Zoology** pg 6237

Military Administration –See **Military and Defense** pg 4625

Military and Defense –pg 4625; see also **Political Science -- International Relations** pg 5215

Military History –See **Military and Defense** pg 4625

Military Law –pg 3623

Military Medicine –See **Medical Sciences** pg 4073; see also **Military and Defense** pg 4625

Milling –See **Agriculture -- Feed Grain and Milling** pg 225

Mineral Resources –See **Earth Sciences -- Geology** pg 1746; see also **Mines and Mining -- Mineralogy** pg 4683

Mineralogy –pg 4683

Mines and Mining –pg 4658

Minicomputers –pg 1643; see also **Computers -- Microcomputers, Personal Computers** pg 1633

Mining Engineering –See **Mines and Mining** pg 4658

Mobile Homes –See **Building and Construction** pg 671

Money –See **Business and Economics -- Banks and Banking** pg 914

Monuments –See **History** pg 2902; see also **Architecture** pg 328; **The Arts -- Art** pg 381

Mormons and Mormonism –See **Religions and Theology -- Other Religions, Sects and Cults** pg 5652

Motels –See **Hotels/Motels** pg 3130

Motion Picture –pg 4691

Motocross –See **Motorcycles** pg 4711

Motor Homes –See **Transportation -- Recreational Vehicles** pg 6080

Motor Scooters –See **Motorcycles** pg 4711

Motor Vehicles –See **Transportation -- Automobiles** pg 6039

Motorcycles –pg 4711

Mountain Climbing –See **Leisure and Recreation -- Outdoor Recreation** pg 3653; see also **Sports and Games** pg 5933

Movies –See **Motion Picture** pg 4691

Multicultural Education –See **Education -- International Education** pg 1985

Multiple Sclerosis –See **Medical Sciences -- Neurology** pg 4383

SUBJECT CROSS REFERENCES

Muscular Dystrophy —See **Medical Sciences -- Musculoskeletal System** pg 4376

Musculoskeletal System —pg 4376

Museums and Galleries —pg 4715; see also The Arts -- Art pg 381

Music —pg 4731; see also Computers -- Computer Music pg 1601; Sound Recordings and Systems pg 5928; The Arts -- Performing Arts pg 434

Music Therapy —See **Music** pg 4731; see also Psychology pg 5279

Mutual Funds —See **Business and Economics -- Investments** pg 1081; see also Business and Economics -- Banks and Banking pg 914

Mycology —pg 641

Mysticism —See **Parapsychology and Occultism** pg 4890; see also Religions and Theology pg 5521

Mythology —See **Folklore** pg 2599

Narcotics —See **Drug Abuse and Alcoholism** pg 1720; see also Law -- Law Enforcement and Criminology pg 3595; Pharmacy and Pharmacology pg 4941

Native American History —See **History -- History of North and South America** pg 3018

Natural Gas —See **Petroleum and Natural Gas** pg 4899

Natural History —pg 4802; see also Biology pg 5279; Environmental Issues -- Conservation and Natural Resources pg 2362; Environmental Issues -- Ecology pg 2362

Natural Resources —See **Environmental Issues -- Conservation and Natural Resources** pg 2362

Naturalist —See **Natural History** pg 4802; see also Environmental Issues -- Ecology pg 2391

Naval Architecture —See **Architecture** pg 328

Naval Science, Navigation —pg 4821; see also Transportation -- Ships and Shipping pg 6093

Navigation —See **Naval Science, Navigation** pg 4821

Navy —See **Naval Science, Navigation** pg 4821

Needlework —See **Home Economics -- Sewing and Needlework** pg 3114

Neoplasma —See **Medical Sciences -- Cancer and Neoplastic Syndromes** pg 4203

Nephrology —See **Medical Sciences -- Urology and Nephrology** pg 4572

Neural Networks —See **Computers -- Artificial Intelligence** pg 1568

Neurology —pg 4383; see also Medical Sciences -- Psychiatry pg 4501; Psychology pg 5279

New Age Publications —pg 4833

Noise Control —See **Environmental Issues** pg 2331

North America —See **General Interest -- General Interest-North America** pg 2802; **History -- History of North and South America** pg 3018

Nuclear Engineering —pg 2325

Nuclear Medicine —See **Medical Sciences -- Internal Medicine** pg 4362; see also Medical Sciences -- Radiology pg 4524

Nuclear Physics —pg 5129

Nuclear Waste —See **Environmental Issues -- Pollution and Waste Management** pg 2404

Numismatics —pg 3095

Nursery Industry —See **Gardening and Horticulture** pg 2696

Nursing —pg 4415; see also Medical Sciences -- Surgery pg 4415

Nursing Homes —See **Medical Sciences -- Health Services Administration** pg 4330

Nutrition and Dietetics —pg 4836; see also Food and Food Industry pg 2607

Nutritional Disorders —See **Nutrition and Dietetics** pg 4836

Obesity —See **Nutrition and Dietetics** pg 4836; see also Medical Sciences -- Endocrinology pg 4269

Obstetrics —See **Medical Sciences -- Gynecology and Obstetrics** pg 4327

Occultism —See **Parapsychology and Occultism** pg 4890

Occupational Health —See **Industrial Health and Safety** pg 3188

Occupational Therapy —See **Industrial Health and Safety** pg 3188; see also Education -- Special Education and Rehabilitation pg 2021; Medical Sciences -- Psychiatry pg 4501

Occupations and Careers —pg 4852; see also Economics -- Labor pg 1115; Education -- Special Aspects of Education pg 2021

Ocean Engineering —See **Engineering -- Hydraulic Engineering** pg 2271; see also Earth Sciences -- Oceanography pg 1832

Oceania —See **General Interest -- General Interest-Australia and Oceania** pg 2785; see also History -- History of Australia and Oceania pg 2962

Oceanography —pg 1832

Off-Road Vehicles —See **Transportation -- Recreationsl Vehicles** pg 6080

Office Equipment and Services —pg 1259

Oil —See **Petroleum and Natural Gas** pg 4899

Oncology —See **Medical Sciences -- Cancer and Neoplastic Syndromes** pg 4203

Online Computing and Information —pg 1644

Opera —See **Music** pg 4731

Ophthalmology and Optometry —pg 4440

Optical Storage, CD-ROM Applications —pg 1646

Optics —See **Physics -- Light, Optics, Radiation** pg 5104

Oral Communication —See **Communications** pg 1448

Oral Surgery —See **Dentistry** pg 1694

Organic Chemistry —pg 1372

Oriental Studies —See **History -- History of Asia** pg 2938

Ornithology —pg 6284; see also Natural History pg 4802

Orthodontics —See **Dentistry** pg 1694

Orthodox Eastern Churches —pg 5650

Orthopedics —pg 4454

Other Religions, Sects and Cults —pg 5652

Otorhinolaryngology —pg 4462

Outdoor Recreation —pg 3653; see also Environmental Issues -- Conservation and Natural Resources pg 2362; Fish and Fisheries pg 2571; Sports and Games pg 5933

Pacific Studies —See **History -- History of Australia and Oceania** pg 2962

Packaging —pg 4863

Pain —See **Medical Sciences -- Neurology** pg 4383

Paints and Painting —pg 4869

Paleontology —pg 4873

Paper and Pulp Industry —pg 4880

Parachuting —See **Sports and Games** pg 5933

Paramedics —See **Medical Sciences -- Emergency Medicine** pg 4265

Parapsychology and Occultism —pg 4890

Parasitology —pg 645

Parent Guides —See **Family and Marriage** pg 2485

Parenthood —See **Family and Marriage** pg 2485

Parks —See **Leisure and Recreation** pg 3634; see also Environmental Issues -- Conservation and Natural Resources pg 2362

Parliament/House of Commons —See **Public Administration** pg 5338; see also Political Science pg 5148

SUBJECT CROSS REFERENCES

Patents —See **Copyright, Intellectual Property** pg 1678

Pathology —pg 4470; see also Medical Sciences -- Anatomy pg 4195

Pediatric Surgery —See **Medical Sciences -- Pediatrics** pg 4479

Pediatrics —pg 4479

Penology —See **Law -- Law Enforcement and Criminology** pg 3595

Pensions —See **Business and Economics -- Investments** pg 1081; see also Business and Economics -- Labor pg 1115; Insurance pg 3274

Performing Arts —pg 434; see also Dance pg 1689; Motion Picture pg 4691; Music pg 4731; Theater pg 5991

Perfumes —See **Beauty and Cosmetics** pg 456; see also Chemistry -- Chemical Technology pg 1352

Perinatology —See **Medical Sciences -- Gynecology and Obstetrics** pg 4327; see also Medical Sciences -- Pediatrics pg 4479

Personal Computers —See **Computers -- Microcomputers, Personal Computers** pg 1633

Personal Finance —pg 2508

Personal Hygiene —See **Physical Fitness and Hygiene** pg 2891

Personnel Management —pg 1263

Personnel Service in Education —See **Education -- Guidance and Counseling** pg 1935

Pest Control —pg 4894

Petroleum and Natural Gas —pg 4899; see also Energy pg 2127

Petrology —See **Earth Sciences -- Geology** pg 1746

Pets —pg 258

Pharmaceutical Industry —See **Pharmacy and Pharmacology** pg 4941

Pharmacy and Pharmacology —pg 4941; see also Toxicology pg 6007

Philanthropy —pg 4998; see also Sociology -- Social Services and Welfare pg 5885

Philately —pg 3100

Philology —See **Linguistics** pg 3768; see also Classical Studies pg 1414

Philosophy —pg 5004

Phonetics —See **Linguistics** pg 3768

Photography —pg 5035

Physical and Theoretical Chemistry —pg 1385

Physical Education —See **Education -- Physical Education and Training** pg 1989; see also Health and Personal Fitness pg 2876

Physical Education and Training —pg 1989

Physical Fitness —See **Health -- Physical Fitness and Hygiene** pg 2891; see also Physical Education and Training pg 1989; Sports and Games pg 5933

Physical Fitness and Hygiene —pg 2891

Physical Therapy —pg 5048

Physical Training —See **Education -- Physical Education and Training** pg 1989

Physically Impaired —pg 5053; see also Education -- Special Education and Rehabilitation pg 2021; Sociology -- Social Services and Welfare pg 5885

Physician's Assistants —See **Medical Sciences -- Physicians and Medical Personnel** pg 4493

Physicians —See **Medical Sciences -- Physicians and Medical Personnel** pg 4493; see also Medical Sciences -- Family Practice pg 4288

Physicians and Medical Personnel —pg 4493

Physics —pg 5069

Physiology —pg 648

Pickup Trucks —See **Transportation -- Automobiles** pg 6039

Planned Parenthood —See **Birth Control** pg 658; see also Family and Marriage pg 2485

Plant Breeding —See **Biology -- Botany** pg 551; see also Agriculture -- Crop Production and Soils pg 174; Gardening and Horticulture pg 2696

Plant Diseases —See **Biology -- Botany** pg 551

Plastic Surgery —See **Medical Sciences -- Surgery** pg 4546

Plastics —pg 5139

Plays —See **Theater** pg 5991; see also Literature pg 3872

Plumbing —See **Heating, Plumbing, and Refrigeration** pg 2894

Podiatry —pg 4500

Poetry —pg 3984; see also Literary and Political Reviews pg 3851

Political Reviews —See **Literary and Political Reviews** pg 3851

Political Science —pg 5148; see also Military and Defense pg 4625; Public Administration pg 5338

Polling —See **Public Administration** pg 5338

Pollution and Waste Management —pg 2404; see also Earth Sciences -- Ecology pg 2391; Environmental Issues -- Ecology pg 2391

Polymers —See **Chemistry and Chemicals -- Organic Chemistry** pg 1372; see also Paints and Painting pg 4869; Plastics pg 5139

Population Studies —pg 5252; see also Birth Control pg 658

Portable Computers —See **Computers -- Microcomputers, Personal Computers** pg 1633

Ports —See **Transportation -- Ships and Shipping** pg 6093

Postage Stamps —See **Hobbies -- Philately** pg 3100

Postal Communications —pg 1475; see also Public Administration -- Civil Service pg 5413

Pottery —See **Glass and Ceramics** pg 2865

Poultry —See **Agriculture -- Poultry and Poultry Products** pg 251

Poultry and Poultry Products —pg 251

Poverty —See **Business and Economics -- Economic Assistance and Development** pg 1012

Powerlifting —See **Health--Physical Fitness and Hygiene** pg 2891

Practical Theology —See **Religions and Theology** pg 5521

Presbyterian —See **Religions and Theology -- Protestantism** pg 5662

Preschool Education —See **Education -- Early Childhood and Primary Education** pg 1917

Preventive Medicine —See **Medical Sciences** pg 4073

Primary Care —See **Medical Sciences -- Family Practice** pg 4288

Primary Education —See **Education -- Early Childhood and Primary Education** pg 1917

Printing Industry —pg 5271; see also The Arts -- Graphic Arts pg 427

Prisons —See **Law -- Law Enforcement and Criminology** pg 3595

Private Schools —See **Education** pg 1846

Probation —See **Law -- Law Enforcement and Criminology** pg 3595

Proctology —See **Medical Sciences -- Gastroenterology** pg 4295

Production —See **Industry and Production** pg 3205

Programs and Programming —pg 1649; see also Computers -- Software pg 1657

Protestantism —pg 5662

Psychiatry —pg 4501; see also Medical Sciences -- Neurology pg 4383; Psychology pg 5279

Psychoanalysis —See **Medical Sciences -- Psychiatry** pg 4501; **Psychology** pg 5279

Psychology —pg 5279; see also Medical Science and Technology -- Psychiatry pg 4501; Sociology pg 5851

SUBJECT CROSS REFERENCES

Psychopathology —See **Medical Sciences -- Psychiatry** pg 4501

Psychosomatic Medicine —See **Medical Sciences** pg 4073; see also Psychology pg 5279

Psychotherapy —See **Medical Sciences -- Psychiatry** pg 4501; see also Psychology pg 5279

PTA —See **Education -- School Management and Organization** pg 1995

Public Administration —pg 5338; see also Political Science pg 5148

Public Affairs —See **Public Administration** pg 5338

Public Finance —pg 2509

Public Health and Safety —pg 5422; see also Environmental Issues pg 2331; Medical Sciences pg 4073; Medical Sciences -- Epidemiology pg 4280

Public Opinion —See **Sociology** pg 5851

Public Relations —See **Business and Economics -- Advertising and Public Relations** pg 899

Public Speaking —See **Communications** pg 1448

Public Transportation —See **Transportation** pg 6016; see also Public Administration pg 5338

Public Utilities —pg 5418

Publishing —pg 5465; see also Journalism pg 3322

Pulp Industry —See **Paper and Pulp Industry** pg 4880

Puppetry —See **The Arts -- Performing Arts** pg 434

Puzzles —See **Leisure and Recreation -- Amusements** pg 3641

Quarries —See **Industrial Health and Safety** pg 3188

Quilting —See **Home Economics -- Sewing and Needlework** pg 3114

Race Relations —See **Sociology** pg 5851; see also Ethnic Interests pg 2439

Radiation —See **Physics -- Light, Optics, Radiation** pg 5104

Radio —pg 1479

Radiology —pg 4524; see also Medical Sciences -- Cancer and Neoplastic Syndromes pg 4203

Railroad Engineering —See **Transportation -- Railroads** pg 6070

Railroads —pg 6070

Rationalism —See **Philosophy** pg 5004

Reading —See **Language Arts** pg 3333

Real Estate —pg 5504; see also Housing and Urban Development pg 3138

Record Industry —See **Music** pg 4731; see also Sound Recordings and Systems pg 5928

Recreational Vehicles —pg 6080; see also Leisure and Recreation pg 3634

Recycling —See **Environmental Issues -- Pollution and Waste Management** pg 2404

Red Cross —See **Medical Sciences** pg 4073

Reformed Church —See **Religions and Theology -- Protestantism** pg 5662

Refrigeration —See **Heating, Plumbing, and Refrigeration** pg 2894

Regional Planning —See **Housing and Urban Development** pg 3138

Rehabilitation —See **Education -- Special Education and Rehabilitation** pg 2021; see also Drug Abuse and Alcoholism pg 1720; Physical Therapy pg 5048; Sociology -- Social Services and Welfare pg 5885

Religions and Theology —pg 5521

Religious Education —See **Religions and Theology** pg 5521

Religious Music —See **Music** pg 4731

Research —See **Science and Technology** pg 5689; see also Education -- Higher Education pg 1937

Residential Homes —See **Housing and Urban Development** pg 3138

Resorts —See **Hotels/Motels** pg 3130; **Travel and Tourism** pg 6110

Respiratory System —pg 4535

Restaurants —pg 5681; see also Food and Food Industry pg 2607; Hotels/Motels pg 3130

Retail —pg 1276

Rheumatology —See **Medical Sciences -- Musculoskeletal System** pg 4376

Roads and Traffic —pg 6082

Robotics —See **Computers -- Artificial Intelligence** pg 1568; see also Computers -- Automation pg 1576

Roman Catholic Church —See **Religions and Theology -- Catholicism** pg 5614

Romance —See **Literature** pg 3872

Rubber —pg 5685

Rugby —See **Sports and Games** pg 5933

Running —See **Health--Physical Fitness and Hygiene** pg 2891

Rural Development —See **Agriculture -- Agricultural Economics** pg 161

Safety —See **Industrial Health and Safety** pg 3188; see also Public Health and Safety pg 5422

Safety Engineering —See **Engineering -- Industrial Engineering** pg 2282

Sailing —See **Boats and Boating** pg 662

Salary/Wages —See **Business and Economics -- Labor** pg 1115

Sanitation/Municipal Engineering —See **Environmental Issues -- Pollution and Waste Management** pg 2404; see also Environmental Issues -- Conservation and Natural Resources pg 2362; Environmental Issues -- Ecology pg 2391

Scholarships —See **Education -- Educational Finance** pg 1921; see also Education -- Higher Education pg 1937

School Administrators —See **Education -- School Management and Organization** pg 1995

School Attendance —See **Education -- School Management and Organization** pg 1995

School Budgets —See **Education -- School Management and Organization** pg 1995

School Counseling —See **Education -- Special Education and Rehabilitation** pg 2021

School Discipline —See **Education -- School Management and Organization** pg 1995

School Districts —See **Education -- School Management and Organization** pg 1995

School Management and Organization —pg 1995

School Sports —See **Education -- Physical Education and Training** pg 1989; see also Sports and Games pg 5933

School Taxes —See **Education -- Educational Finance** pg 1921

Science —See **Science and Technology** pg 5689

Science and Technology —pg 5689; see also Chemistry -- Chemical Technology pg 1352; Engineering pg 2177

Science Fiction, Fantasy and Horror —pg 4002

Scuba Diving —See **Leisure and Recreation -- Outdoor Recreation** pg 3653, 3654

Sculpture —See **The Arts -- Art** pg 381; see also Architecture pg 328

Secondary Education —pg 2017

Securities Law —See **Law -- Corporation Law** pg 3513

Security —See **Computers -- Computer Crimes and Security** pg 1584

Security Systems and Alarms —pg 5785

Sedimentology —See **Earth Sciences -- Geology** pg 1746; see also Earth Sciences -- Geophysics pg 1792

SUBJECT CROSS REFERENCES

Seismology —See **Earth Sciences -- Geophysics** pg 1792

Semiconductors —See **Electronics** pg 2066

Semiotics/Semantics —See **Linguistics** pg 3768

Senior Citizens —pg 5786; see also Medical Sciences -- Geriatrics pg 4304; Sociology -- Social Services and Welfare pg 5885

Serial Publications —pg 5500

Sewage —See **Environmental Issues -- Pollution and Waste Management** pg 2404; see also Water Resources pg 6187

Sewing and Needlework —pg 3114

Sexual Life —pg 5793

Sexually Transmitted Diseases —See **Medical Sciences -- Communicable Diseases** pg 4242

Ship Design —See **Naval Science, Navigation** pg 4821; see also Transportation -- Ships and Shipping pg 6093

Shipbuilding —See **Naval Science, Navigation** pg 4821

Ships and Shipping —pg 6093; see also Naval Science, Navigation pg 4821

Shoes —See **Clothing Industry and Fashion** pg 1423

Simulation —pg 1655

Skiing —See **Sports and Games** pg 5933

Slavery —See **Civil Rights** pg 5201

Slavic Studies —See **History -- History of Europe** pg 2965

Small Business —pg 1283

Smoking —See **Public Health and Safety** pg 5422; see also Tobacco pg 6004

Soap Operas —See **General Interest** pg 2771

Soccer —See **Sports and Games** pg 5933

Social Sciences —pg 5825; see also Humanities pg 3169, 3185

Social Security —See **Business and Economics -- Labor** pg 1115; see also Insurance pg 3274

Social Services and Welfare —pg 5885

Socialism —See **Political Science -- Socialism, Communism, Anarchism, Utopianism** pg 5243

Socialism, Communism, Anarchism, Utopianism —pg 5243

Societies and Clubs —pg 5841

Sociology —pg 5851

Software —pg 1657

Soil —See **Agriculture -- Crop Production and Soils** pg 174

Solar Energy —pg 2174

Sound —pg 5136

Sound Recordings and Systems —pg 5928; see also Music pg 4731

South America —See **General Interest -- General Interest-South America** pg 2825; **History -- History of North and South America** pg 3018

Special Education —See **Education -- Special Education and Rehabilitation** pg 2021

Special Education and Rehabilitation —pg 2021

Spectroscopy —See **Physics -- Light, Optics, Radiation** pg 5104

Speech Disorders —See **Medical Sciences -- Otorhinolaryngology** pg 4462; see also Education -- Special Education and Rehabilitation pg 2021; Physically Impaired pg 5053

Speech Pathology —See **Physically Impaired** pg 5053; see also Education -- Special Education and Rehabilitation pg 2021

Speleology —See **Earth Sciences -- Geophysics** pg 1792

Sports and Games —pg 5933

Sports Cars —See **Transportation -- Automobiles** pg 6039

Sports Law —See **Law -- Entertainment Law** pg 3537

Sports Medicine —pg 4542

Stained Glass —See **Glass and Ceramics** pg 2865

Standardization —See **Metrology and Standardization** pg 4620

State Government —See **Public Administration** pg 5338

Stomatology —See **Dentistry** pg 1694

Storage and Moving Industry —See **Transportation** pg 6016

Stress —See **Psychology** pg 5279

Student Aid —See **Education -- Educational Finance** pg 1921

Student Counseling —See **Education -- Guidance and Counseling** pg 1935

Sugar —See **Agriculture -- Crop Production and Soils** pg 174; see also Food and Food Industry pg 2607

Surface Chemistry —See **Chemistry and Chemicals -- Physical and Theoretical Chemistry** pg 1385

Surgeons —See **Medical Sciences -- Physicians and Medical Personnel** pg 4493

Surgery —pg 4546

Surveying —See **Engineering -- Civil Engineering** pg 2226

Swimming —See **Sports and Games** pg 5933

Tariffs —See **Finance--Taxation** pg 2536

Tax Planning —See **Law -- Estate Planning** pg 3549

Taxation —pg 2536; see also Business and Economics -- Accounting pg 881; Law -- Estate Planning pg 3549

Taxation Law —pg 3624

Taxidermy —See **Hobbies** pg 3085

Tea —See **Agriculture -- Crop Production and Soils** pg 174; see also Food and Food Industry -- Beverage Industry pg 2647

Teacher Unions —See **Education -- School Management and Organization** pg 1995

Teachers —See **Education -- School Management and Organization** pg 1995

Teaching and Curriculum —pg 2034

Teaching Materials —See **Education -- Teaching and Curriculum** pg 2034

Technical Education —See **Education -- Vocational Education** pg 2058

Technology —See **Science and Technology** pg 5689

Telecommunication —pg 1488

Telegraph —See **Communications -- Telecommunication** pg 1488

Telephone —See **Communications -- Telecommunication** pg 1488

Telephone Directories —See **Communications -- Telecommunication** pg 1488

Television —See **Communications -- Television and Cable** pg 1514

Television and Cable —pg 1514

Tennis —See **Sports and Games** pg 5933

Test Scores —See **Education -- Tests and Measurements** pg 2055

Tests and Measurements —pg 2055; see also Psychology pg 5279

Textbooks —See **Education -- Teaching and Curriculum** pg 2034

Textiles —See **Fabrics and Textile Industries** pg 2468

The Arts —pg 358

Theater —pg 5991; see also The Arts -- Performing Arts pg 434

Theology —See **Religions and Theology** pg 5521

Theoretical Chemistry —See **Chemistry and Chemicals -- Physical and Theoretical Chemistry** pg 1385

Theosophy —See **Religions and Theology -- Other Religions, Sects and Cults** pg 5652

Thrombosis —See **Medical Sciences -- Hematology** pg 4354

Tire Industry —See **Rubber** pg 5685

SUBJECT CROSS REFERENCES

Tobacco –pg 6004

Total Quality Management –See **Business and Economics -- Management** pg 1194; **Business and Economics -- Personnel Management** pg 1263

Tourism –See **Travel and Tourism** pg 6110

Toxicology –pg 6007; see also Pharmacy and Pharmacology pg 4941

Toys –See **Gifts, Toys** pg 2863

Track and Field –See **Sports and Games** pg 5933

Trade –See **Business and Economics -- Commerce** pg 970

Trade and Industrial Directories –pg 3250

Trade Regulation –See **Law -- Corporation Law** pg 3513

Trade Schools –See **Education -- Vocational Education** pg 2058

Trade Shows –See **Business and Economics -- Advertising and Public Relations** pg 899

Trade Unions –See **Business and Economics -- Labor** pg 1115

Trademarks –See **Copyright, Intellectual Property** pg 1678

Traffic –See **Transportation -- Roads and Traffic** pg 6082

Traffic Accidents –See **Transportation -- Roads and Traffic** pg 6082; see also Public Health and Safety pg 5422

Translating and Interpreting –See **Linguistics** pg 3768

Transportation –pg 6016

Travel and Tourism –pg 6110; see also Geography pg 2827; Leisure and Recreation pg 3634

Trees –See **Gardening and Horticulture** pg 2696; see also Forests and Forestry pg 2659

Triboloby –See **Physics -- Mechanics** pg 5123

Tropical Diseases –See **Medical Sciences -- Tropical Medicine** pg 4568

Tropical Medicine –pg 4568

Truck Fleets –See **Transportation -- Trucking** pg 6107

Trucking –pg 6107

Trustees –See **Law -- Estate Planning** pg 3549

Trusts –See **Law -- Estate Planning** pg 3549

Ukrainian Studies –See **History -- History of Europe** pg 2965

Ultrafication –See **Medical Sciences -- Hematology** pg 4354

Ultrasonic Therapy –See **Medical Sciences -- Radiology** pg 4524

Ultrasound –See **Medical Sciences -- Radiology** pg 4524

Unemployment –See **Business and Economics -- Labor** pg 1115

Unions –See **Business and Economics -- Labor** pg 1115

United States History –See **History -- History of North and South America** pg 3018

Universities and Colleges –See **College and School Publications** pg 1432

Urban Development –See **Housing and Urban Development** pg 3138

Urinary Tract –See **Medical Sciences -- Urology and Nephrology** pg 4572

Urology –See **Medical Sciences -- Urology and Nephrology** pg 4572

Urology and Nephrology –pg 4572

Utopianism –See **Political Science -- Socialism, Communism, Anarchism, Utopianism** pg 5243

Vacations –See **Travel and Tourism** pg 6110; see also Leisure and Recreation pg 3634

Vans –See **Transportation -- Automobiles** pg 6039

Veterans –See **Military and Defense** pg 4625

Veterinary Sciences –pg 6158; see also Zoology pg 6237

Video –pg 1530; see also Motion Picture pg 4691

Video Games/Arcades –See **Sports and Games** pg 5933

Virology –See **Biology -- Microbiology** pg 623

Virtual Reality –See **Computers -- Artificial Intelligence** pg 1568; see also Computers -- Automation pg 1576

Visual Arts –See **The Arts -- Art** pg 381

Vitamins –See **Nutrition and Dietetics** pg 4836

Viticulture –See **Agriculture -- Crop Production and Soils** pg 174

Vocational Education –pg 2058

Vocational Guidance –See **Education -- Guidance and Counseling** pg 1935; see also Occupations and Careers pg 4852

Volcanoes –See **Earth Sciences -- Geophysics** pg 1792

Volunteer Work –See **Philanthropy** pg 4998

Voting –See **Political Science** pg 5148

WAN (Wide Area Networks) –See **Computers -- Computer Networks** pg 1602

War –See **History** pg 2902; see also Political Science pg 5148

Waste Management –See **Environmental Issues -- Pollution and Waste Management** pg 2404

Watches –See **Jewelry -- Clocks and Watches** pg 3321

Water Pollution –See **Environmental Issues -- Pollution and Waste Management** pg 2404; see also Water Resources pg 6187

Water Resources –pg 6187; see also Earth Sciences -- Hydrology pg 1803; Engineering -- Hydraulic Engineering pg 2271; Environmental Issues -- Conservation and Natural Resources pg 2362

Water Utilities –See **Public Administration -- Public Utilities** pg 5418; see also Water Resources pg 6187

Water-Supply –See **Water Resources** pg 6187

Weaponry –See **Military and Defense** pg 4625

Weather –See **Earth Sciences -- Meteorology** pg 1812

Weddings –See **Family and Marriage** pg 2485

Weightlifting –See **Health--Physical Fitness and Hygiene** pg 2891; see also Sports and Games pg 5933

Weights and Measures –See **Metrology and Standardization** pg 4620

Welding –pg 4617

Welfare –See **Sociology -- Social Services and Welfare** pg 5885

Western Australian Studies –See **History -- History of Australia and Oceania** pg 2962

Who's Who –See **Biographies** pg 464

Wide Area Networks –See **Computers -- Computer Networks** pg 1602

Wildlife –See **Environmental Issues -- Conservation and Natural Resources** pg 2362; see also Environmental Issues -- Ecology pg 2391; Leisure and Recreation -- Outdoor Recreation pg 3653

Wills –See **Law -- Estate Planning** pg 3549

Wine –See **Food and Food Industry -- Beverage Industry** pg 2647; see also Home Economics pg 3105

Women's Interests –pg 6209

Wood –See **Forestry -- Lumber and Wood** pg 2688

SUBJECT CROSS REFERENCES

Woodwork —See **Building and Construction -- Carpentry and Woodwork** pg 713

Wool —See **Fabrics and Textile Industries** pg 2468

Word Processing —pg 1669

Workmen's Compensation —See **Business and Economics -- Labor** pg 1115; see also Insurance pg 3274

World History —See **History** pg 2902

World Politics —See **Political Science** pg 5148

Wrestling —See **Sports and Games** pg 5933

Writing —See **Language Arts** pg 3333; see also Journalism pg 3322

Yachts and Yachting —See **Boats and Boating** pg 662; see also Travel and Tourism pg 6110

Yearbooks —See **Encyclopedias and General Reference Books** pg 2098

Youth —See **Children and Youth Interests** pg 1397

Zoning —See **Housing and Urban Development** pg 3138; see also Real Estate pg 5504

Zoology —pg 6237; see also Veterinary Sciences pg 6158

TABLES

Document Delivery
Wire Services
Country of Publication
Unit of Currency
Indexes/Abstracts

DOCUMENT DELIVERY

The following document supplier notations, when noted in a Serial Listing, indicate the availability of that serial for document delivery through the specified service. Permission has been granted by the copyright owner and is subject to change without notice. Only the portion in boldface will appear in the listing.

ADONIS™
ADONIS B.V.
Spuistraat 112D
1012VA Amsterdam, The Netherlands

Article Express International
Engineering Information Inc.
469 Union Avenue
Westbury, New York 11590

Ask*IEEE
(in cooperation with EBSCOdoc™)
1722 Gilbreth Road
Burlingame, CA 94010

BIOSIS Document Express™
(in cooperation with EBSCOdoc™)
1722 Gilbreth Road
Burlingame, CA 94010

BLDSC
British Library Document Supply Centre - Customer Services
Boston Spa, Wetherby
LS23 7BQ, United Kingdom

CASDDS ®
Chemical Abstracts Service Document Delivery Service
PO Box 3012
Columbus, Ohio 43210-0012

Documents on Demand
Congressional Information Service
4520 East-West Highway
Bethesda, MD 20814-3389

FAXON Xpress
FAXON Research Services, Inc.
15 Southwest Park
Westwood, MA 02090

Haworth Document Delivery Service
The Haworth Press, Inc.
10 Alice Street
Binghamton, New York 13904-1580

Magazine Collection™
Information Access Company
362 Lakeside Drive
Foster City, CA 94404

Petroleum Abstracts Document Delivery Service
University of Tulsa
600 South College
Tulsa, OK 74104-3189

Quick Copies
Williams and Wilkins Company
428 East Preston Street
Baltimore, MD 21202-3993

SWETSCAN-SWETDOC
Swets & Zeitlinger bv
Heereweg 347, PO Box 830
2160 SZ Lisse, The Netherlands

The Genuine Article®
Institute for Scientific Information
3501 Market Street
Philadelphia, PA 19104

The Uncover Company
3801 East Florida Avenue
Suite 200
Denver, CO 80210

UMI Article Clearinghouse
300 North Zeeb Road
PO Box 1346
Ann Arbor, MI 48106-1346

WIRE SERVICES

The following abbreviations represent the news and photograph wire services found in the Directory. Each code is followed by the complete name of the service.

CODE:	SERVICE:
AF	Agence France Presse
AN	Alternet
AP	Associated Press
API	Associated Press International
BU	British United Press
CA	Canadian Press
CH	Chicago Tribune - New York
CN	Capital News
CM	Christian Science Monitor
CO	Copley News Service
CP	Colorado Press
CQ	Congressional Quarterly
CS	Catholic News Service
CT	Chicago Sun Times
CP	China and Taiwan News Age
CU	Canadian United Press
DJ	Dow Jones
EI	Empire Information Service
ER	Editorial Research Service
FN	Federation News Service
GN	Gannett News Service
GP	Georgia Press Association
HH	Hearst Headline Service
HN	Harris News Service
IT	Independent Television Network
IM	Iowa Medialink
JT	Jewish Telegraphic Agency
KF	King Features
KN	Knight News Service
KR	Knight-Ridder
LA	Los Angeles Times
LO	London Daily News
LT	Times of London
MG	Manchester Guardian
ML	MediaLink
MN	Morris News Service
MP	Montana Press Association
NC	NEWSCOM
NE	Newspaper Enterprises Association
NF	Newsfinder
NM	Notimex
NN	Newhouse News Service
NP	NNAP
NU	News USA
NW	National Weather Service
NY	New York Times
ON	Ottawa News Service
PN	Pacific News Service
RN	Reuters News Service
SH	Scripps-Howard Newspaper Alliance-Scripps Howard News Service
SS	SportsStats
WN	World News
WP	Washington Post Writer's Guild
WS	Women's News Service
WW	Women's Wear Daily

COUNTRY OF PUBLICATION TABLE

The following lists of country codes have been taken directly from the USMARC Bibliographic Format, with the exception being that the United States and Canada state and province codes have been grouped under their respective countries, rather than being listed individually.

COUNTRY OF PUBLICATION BY CODE

Code	Country	Code	Country	Code	Country
AA	Albania	GS	Georgia (Republic)	PY	Paraguay
AE	Algeria	GT	Guatemala	QA	Qatar
AF	Afghanistan	GU	Guam	RE	Reunion
AG	Argentina	GV	Guinea	RH	Zimbabwe
AI	Armenia	GW	Germany	RM	Romania
AJ	Azerbaijan	GY	Guyana	RW	Rwanda
AM	Anguilla	GZ	Gaza Strip	RU	Russia (Republic)
AN	Andorra	HK	Hong Kong	SA	South Africa
AO	Angola	HM	Heard and McDonald Islands	SE	Seychelles
AQ	Antigua and Barbuda	HO	Honduras	SF	Sao Tome and Principe
AS	American Samoa	HT	Haiti	SG	Senegal
AT	Australia	HU	Hungary	SH	Spanish North Africa
AU	Austria	IC	Iceland	SI	Singapore
AW	Aruba	IE	Ireland	SJ	Sudan
AY	Antarctica	II	India	SL	Sierra Leone
BA	Bahrain	IO	Indonesia	SM	San Marino
BB	Barbados	IQ	Iraq	SO	Somalia
BD	Burundi	IR	Iran	SP	Spain
BE	Belgium	IS	Israel	SQ	Swaziland
BF	Bahamas	IT	Italy	SR	Surinam
BG	Bangladesh	IV	Ivory Coast	SS	Western Sahara
BH	Belize	IY	Iraq-Saudi Arabia Neutral Zone	SU	Saudi Arabia
BI	British Indian Ocean Territory			SW	Sweden
BL	Brazil	JA	Japan	SX	Namibia
BM	Bermuda Islands	JI	Johnson Atoll	SY	Syria
BN	Bosnia Hercegovina	JM	Jamaica	SZ	Switzerland
BO	Bolivia	JO	Jordan	TA	Tajikstan
BP	Solomon Islands	KE	Kenya	TC	Turks and Caicos Islands
BR	Burma	KG	Kyrgyzstan	TG	Togo
BS	Botswana	KN	Korea (North)	TH	Thailand
BT	Bhutan	KO	Korea (South)	TI	Tunisia
BU	Bulgaria	KU	Kuwait	TK	Turkmenistan
BV	Bouvet Island	KZ	Kazakhstan	TL	Tokelau Islands
BW	Byelarus	LB	Liberia	TO	Tonga
BX	Brunei	LE	Lebanon	TR	Trinidad and Tobago
CB	Cambodia	LH	Liechtenstein	TS	Trucial States (United Arab Emirates)
CC	China	LI	Lithuania		
CD	Chad	LO	Lesotho	TU	Turkey
CE	Sri Lanka	LS	Laos	TZ	Tanzania
CF	Congo (Brazzaville)	LU	Luxembourg	UA	Egypt
CG	Zaire	LV	Latvia	UC	United States Misc. Caribbean Islands
CH	China (Republic: 1949)	LY	Libya		
CI	Croatia	MC	Monaco	UG	Uganda
CJ	Cayman Islands	MF	Mauritius	UK	United Kingdom (Including Scotland)
CK	Colombia	MG	Madagascar		
CL	Chile	MH	Macao	UN	Ukraine
CM	Cameroon	MJ	Montserrat	UP	United States Misc. Pacific Islands
CN	Canada	MK	Oman		
CP	Canton and Enderbury Islands	ML	Mali	US	United States
CQ	Comorus	MM	Malta	UV	Burkina Faso
CR	Costa Rica	MP	Mongolia	UY	Uruguay
CS	Czechoslovakia	MQ	Martinique	UZ	Uzbekistan
CU	Cuba	MR	Morocco	VB	Virgin Islands (British V.I.)
CV	Cape Verde	MU	Mauritania	VC	Vatican City
CW	Cook Islands	MV	Moldova	VE	Venezuela
CX	Central African Republic	MW	Malawi	VI	Virgin Islands (U.S.)
CY	Cyprus	MX	Mexico	VM	Vietnam
DK	Denmark	MY	Malaysia	WF	Wallis and Futuna
DM	Benin	MZ	Mozambique	WJ	West Bank of the Jordan River
DQ	Dominica	NA	Netherlands Antilles	WK	Wake Island
DR	Dominican Republic	NE	Netherlands	WS	Western Samoa
EC	Ecuador	NG	Niger	XA	Christmas Island (Indian Ocean)
EG	Equatorial Guinea	NL	New Caledonia		
ER	Estonia	NN	Vanuatu	XB	Cocos (Keeling) Islands
ES	El Salvador	NO	Norway	XC	Maldives
ET	Ethiopia	NP	Nepal	XD	Saint Kitts-Nevis
FA	Faroe Islands	NQ	Nicaragua	XE	Marshall Islands
FG	French Guiana	NR	Nigeria	XF	Midway Island
FI	Finland	NU	Nauru	XH	Niue
FJ	Fiji	NW	Northern Mariana Islands	XJ	Saint Helena
FM	Micronesia (Federated States)	NX	Norfolk Island	XK	Saint Lucia
FP	French Polynesia	NZ	New Zealand	XL	Saint Pierre and Miquelon
FR	France	OT	Mayotte	XM	Saint Vincent and the Grenadines
FS	Terres Australes et Antarctiques Francaises	PC	Pitcairn Island		
		PE	Peru	XN	Macedonia
FT	Djibouti	PF	Paracel Islands	XO	Slovakia
GB	Kiribati	PG	Guinea-Bissau	XP	Spratly Islands
GD	Grenada	PH	Philippines	XR	Czech Republic
GH	Ghana	PK	Pakistan	XS	Falkland Islands
GI	Gibralter	PL	Poland	XV	Slovenia
GL	Greenland	PN	Panama	YE	Yemen
GM	Gambia	PO	Portugal	YU	Yugoslavia
GO	Gabon	PP	Papua New Guinea	ZA	Zambia
GP	Guadeloupe	PR	Puerto Rico		
GR	Greece	PW	Palau		

COUNTRY OF PUBLICATION TABLE

COUNTRY OF PUBLICATION BY COUNTRY

Country	Code	Country	Code	Country	Code
Afghanistan	AF	Greenland	GL	Paracel Islands	PF
Albania	AA	Grenada	GD	Paraguay	PY
Algeria	AE	Guadeloupe	GP	Peru	PE
American Samoa	AS	Guam	GU	Philippines	PH
Andorra	AN	Guatemala	GT	Pitcairn Island	PC
Angola	AO	Guinea	GV	Poland	PL
Anguilla	AM	Guinea-Bissau	PG	Portugal	PO
Antarctica	AY	Guyana	GY	Puerto Rico	PR
Antigua and Barbuda	AQ	Haiti	HT	Qatar	QA
Argentina	AG	Heard and McDonald Islands	HM	Reunion	RE
Armenia	AI	Honduras	HO	Romania	RM
Aruba	AW	Hong Kong	HK	Russia (Republic)	RU
Australia	AT	Hungary	HU	Rwanda	RW
Austria	AU	Iceland	IC	Saint Helena	XJ
Azerbaijan	AJ	India	II	Saint Kitts-Nevis	XD
Bahamas	BF	Indonesia	IO	Saint Lucia	XK
Bahrain	BA	Iran	IR	Saint Pierre and Miquelon	XL
Bangladesh	BG	Iraq	IQ	Saint Vincent and the Grenadines	XM
Barbados	BB	Iraq-Saudi Arabia Neutral Zone	IY	San Marino	SM
Belgium	BE	Ireland	IE	Sao Tome and Principe	SF
Belize	BH	Israel	IS	Saudi Arabia	SU
Benin	DM	Italy	IT	Senegal	SG
Bermuda Islands	BM	Ivory Coast	IV	Seychelles	SE
Bhutan	BT	Jamaica	JM	Sierra Leone	SL
Bolivia	BO	Japan	JA	Singapore	SI
Bosnia Hercegovina	BN	Johnson Atoll	JI	Slovakia	XO
Botswana	BS	Jordan	JO	Slovenia	XV
Bouvet Island	BV	Kazakhstan	KZ	Solomon Islands	BP
Brazil	BL	Kenya	KE	Somalia	SO
British Indian Ocean Territory	BI	Kiribati	GB	South Africa	SA
Brunei	BX	Korea (North)	KN	Spain	SP
Bulgaria	BU	Korea (South)	KO	Spanish North Africa	SH
Burkina Faso	UV	Kuwait	KU	Spratly Island	XP
Burma	BR	Kyrgyzstan	KG	Sri Lanka	CE
Burundi	BD	Laos	LS	Sudan	SJ
Byelarus	BW	Latvia	LV	Surinam	SR
Cambodia	CB	Lebanon	LE	Swaziland	SQ
Cameroon	CM	Lesotho	LO	Sweden	SW
Canada	CN	Liberia	LB	Switzerland	SZ
Canton and Enderbury Islands	CP	Libya	LY	Syria	SY
Cape Verde	CV	Liechtenstein	LH	Tajikstan	TA
Cayman Islands	CJ	Lithuania	LI	Tanzania	TZ
Central African Republic	CX	Luxembourg	LU	Terres Australes et Antarctiques Francaises	FS
Chad	CD	Macao	MH		
Chile	CL	Macedonia	XN	Thailand	TH
China	CC	Madagascar	MG	Togo	TG
China (Republic: 1949)	CH	Malawi	MW	Tokelau Islands	TL
Christmas Island (Indian Ocean)	XA	Malaysia	MY	Tonga	TO
Cocos (Keeling) Islands	XB	Maldives	XC	Trinidad and Tobago	TR
Colombia	CK	Mali	ML	Trucial States (United Arab Emirates)	TS
Comoros	CQ	Malta	MM		
Congo (Brazzaville)	CF	Marshall Islands	XE	Tunisia	TI
Cook Islands	CW	Martinique	MQ	Turkey	TU
Costa Rica	CR	Mauritania	MU	Turkmenistan	TK
Croatia	CI	Mauritius	MF	Turks and Caicos Islands	TC
Cuba	CU	Mayotte	OT	Uganda	UG
Cyprus	CY	Mexico	MX	Ukraine	UN
Czech Republic	XR	Micronesia (Federated States)	FM	United Kingdom (Including Scotland)	UK
Czechoslovakia	CS	Midway Island	XF		
Denmark	DK	Moldova	MV	United States	US
Djibouti	FT	Monaco	MC	United States (Misc. Caribbean Islands)	UC
Dominica	DQ	Mongolia	MP		
Dominican Republic	DR	Montserrat	MJ	United States (Misc. Pacific Islands)	UP
Ecuador	EC	Morocco	MR	Uruguay	UY
Egypt	UA	Mozambique	MZ	Uzbekistan	UZ
El Salvador	ES	Namibia	SX	Vanuatu	NN
Equatorial Guinea	EG	Nauru	NU	Vatican City	VC
Estonia	ER	Nepal	NP	Venezuela	VE
Ethiopia	ET	Netherlands	NE	Vietnam	VM
Falkland Islands	XS	Netherlands Antilles	NA	Virgin Islands (British V.I.)	VB
Faroe Islands	FA	New Caledonia	NL	Virgin Islands (U.S.)	VI
Fiji	FJ	New Zealand	NZ	Wake Island	WK
Finland	FI	Nicaragua	NQ	Wallis and Futuna	WF
France	FR	Niger	NG	West Bank of the Jordan River	WJ
French Guiana	FG	Nigeria	NR	Western Sahara	SS
French Polynesia	FP	Niue	XH	Western Samoa	WS
Gabon	GO	Norfolk Island	NX	Yemen	YE
Gambia	GM	Northern Mariana Islands	NW	Yugoslavia	YU
Gaza Strip	GZ	Norway	NO	Zaire	CG
Georgia (Republic)	GS	Oman	MK	Zambia	ZA
Germany	GW	Pakistan	PK	Zimbabwe	RH
Ghana	GH	Palau	PW		
Gibralter	GI	Panama	PN		
Greece	GR	Papua New Guinea	PP		

UNIT OF CURRENCY TABLE

In the Serial Listing, prices are given in country of publication currency and are one-year library subscription rates, unless designated otherwise.

Country	Currency	Country	Currency	Country	Currency
Afghanistan	afghanin	Greece	Greek drachma	Papua New Guinea	kina
Albania	lek	Guadeloupe	French franc	Paraguay	guarani
Algeria	Algerian dinar	Guatemala	quetzal	Peru	sole
Angola	kwanza	Guyana	Guyana dollar	Philippines	peso
Antigua and Barbuda	East Caribbean dollar	Haiti	gourde	Papua New Guinea	kina
Argentina	peso argentino	Honduras	lempira	Paraguay	guarani
Australia	Australian dollar	Hong Kong	Hong Kong dollar	Peru	sole
Austria	schilling	Hungary	forint	Philippines	peso
Bahamas	Bahamian dollar	Iceland	krona	Poland	zloty
Bangladesh	taka	India	rupee	Portugal	escudo
Barbados	Barbados dollar	Indonesia	rupiah	Qatar	Qatar riyal
Belgium	Belgian franc	Iran	rial	Reunion	French franc
Bermuda Islands	Bermuda dollar	Iraq	Iraqi dinar	Romania	lei
Bolivia	peso	Ireland	Irish pound	Rwanda	Rwanda franc
Botswana	pula	Israel	shekel	San Marino	Italian lira
Brazil	cruzeiro	Italy	lira	Saudi Arabia	Saudi riyal
Belize	Belize dollar	Ivory Coast	CFA franc	Senegal	CFA franc
Benin	CFA franc	Jamaica	Jamaican dollar	Sierra Leone	leone
Bulgaria	lev	Japan	yen	Singapore	Singapore dollar
Burkina Faso	CFA franc	Jordan	Jordanian dinar	Somalia	Somali shilling
Burma	kyat	Kenya	Kenya shilling	South Africa	South African rand
Cameroon	CFA franc	Korea (North)	won	Southern Yemen	dinar
Canada	Canadian dollar	Korea (South)	won	Spain	pesata
Cayman Islands	cordoba/dollar	Kuwait	Kuwaiti dinar	Sri Lanka	rupee
Central African Republic	CFA franc	Lebanon	Lebanese pound	Sudan	Sudanese pound
		Liberia	U.S. dollar	Surinam	Surinam guilder
Chad	CFA franc	Libya	Libyan dinar	Swaziland	emalangeni
Chile	peso	Liechtenstein	Swiss franc	Sweden	krona
China	renminbi yuan	Luxembourg	Luxembourg franc	Switzerland	franc
China (Republic: 1949)	New Taiwan dollar	Madagascar	Malagasy franc	Syria	Syrian pound
		Malawi	Malawi kwacha	Tanzania	Tanzanian shilling
Colombia	peso	Malaysia	ringgit	Thailand	baht
Cook Islands	New Zealand dollar	Mali	CFA franc	Togo	CFA franc
Costa Rica	colon	Malta	Maltese pound	Trinidad and Tobago	Trinidad and Tobago dollar
Cuba	peso	Martinique	French franc		
Cyprus	Cyprus pound	Mauritius	Mauritian rupee	Tunisia	Tunisian dinar
Czechoslovakia	korona	Mexico	peso	Turkey	Turkish lira
Benin	CFA franc	Monaco	French franc	Uganda	Uganda shilling
Denmark	krone	Morocco	dirham	United Kingdom	pound sterling
Djibouti	Djibouti franc	Mozambique	meticais	United States	U.S. dollar
Dominican Republic	peso	Nauru	Australian dollar	Uruguay	new peso
Ecuador	sucre	Nepal	Nepalese rupee	USSR	ruble
Egypt	Egyptian pound	Netherlands	guilder	Vatican City	lira
El Salvador	colon	New Caledonia	CFP franc	Venezuela	bolivare
Ethiopia	Ethiopian birr	New Zealand	New Zealand dollar	Vietnam	dong
Fiji	Fiji dollar	Nicaragua	cordoba	Yemen (Yemen (Sana))	riyal
Finland	fim (finnmark)	Niger	CFA franc	Yugoslavia	dinar
France	French franc	Nigeria	naira	Zaire	CFA franc
Gambia	dalasi	Norway	krone	Zambia	Zambian kwacha
Germany	mark	Oman	rial	Zimbabwe	Zimbabwean dollar
Ghana	cedi	Pakistan	rupee		
		Panama	balboa		

INDEXES/ABSTRACTS TABLE

The following is a list of all publications which may index, or contain an abstract of, titles in the Directory. The Abbreviated Title in boldface is the abbreviation of the index or abstract as used in the Serial Listing. The complete title of the index or abstract follows. Succeeding information or a Ceased/Suspended indicator will follow the complete title for those serials where it applies. For services that share the same journal source list, a reference will be made to that service which will appear in the Serial Listing. This table includes over 1,300 Indexing/Abstracting services, 921 of which are active.

A.I.D. RES. DEV. ABSTR.
[US/0096-1507]
A.I.D. RESEARCH AND DEVELOPMENT ABSTRACTS.
(***Continues*** *A.I.D. Reference Center. A.I.D. Research Abstracts.*)

ABC POL SCI
[US/0001-0456]
ABC POL SCI. ADVANCE BIBLIOGRAPHY OF CONTENTS: POLITICAL SCIENCE & GOVERNMENT.

ABI/INFORM ONDISC
[US/1062-5127]
ABI/INFORM ONDISC.

ABI/INFORM ONDISC: EXPR. ED.
[US]
ABI/INFORM ONDISC: EXPRESS EDITION [COMPUTER FILE].

ABI/INFORM GLOB. ED.
[US]
ABI/INFORM GLOBAL EDITION [COMPUTER FILE].

ABR. CATHOL. PERIOD. LIT. INDEX
[US/0737-3457]
ABRIDGED CATHOLIC PERIODICAL AND LITERATURE INDEX, THE.

ABR. INDEX MED.
[US/0001-3331]
ABRIDGED INDEX MEDICUS.
(***Continues*** *American Medical Association. Abridged Index Medicus.*)

ABR. READ. GUIDE PERIOD. LIT.
[US/0001-334X]
ABRIDGED READERS' GUIDE TO PERIODICAL LITERATURE.

ABS INT. GUIDE CLASSICAL STUD.
[US]
ABS INTERNATIONAL GUIDE TO CLASSICAL STUDIES.
(***Continued by*** *International Guide to Classical Studies (1966).*)

ABSTR. ABSTR. BOOK REV. CUR. LEG. PERIOD.
[US]
ABSTRACTS : ABSTRACTS OF BOOK REVIEWS IN CURRENT LEGAL PERIODICALS.
(***Continues*** *Abstracts of Book Reviews in Current Legal Periodicals.*)

ABSTR. AIT REP. PUBL. ENERGY
[TH/0857-6181]
ABSTRACTS OF AIT REPORTS AND PUBLICATIONS ON ENERGY.
(***Continues*** *Abstracts of AIT Reports and Publications on Renewable Energy Resources.*)

ABSTR. ANTHROPOL.
[US/0001-3455]
ABSTRACTS IN ANTHROPOLOGY.

ABSTR. BIOCOMMER.
[UK/0263-6778]
ABSTRACTS IN BIOCOMMERCE.

ABSTR. BOOK REV. CURR. LEG. PERIOD.
[US/0362-1065]
ABSTRACTS OF BOOK REVIEWS IN CURRENT LEGAL PERIODICALS.
(***Continued by*** *Abstracts : Abstracts of Book Reviews in Current Legal Periodicals.*)

ABSTR. BULL. INST. PAP. SCI. TECH.
[US/1047-2088]
ABSTRACT BULLETIN OF THE INSTITUTE OF PAPER SCIENCE AND TECHNOLOGY.
(***Continues*** *Institute of Paper Chemistry (Appleton, Wis.) Abstract Bulletin of the Institute of Paper Chemistry.*)

ABSTR. BULL. INST. PAPER CHEM.
[US]
ABSTRACT BULLETIN OF THE INSTITUTE OF PAPER CHEMISTRY.
(***Continued by*** *Abstract Bulletin of the Institute of Paper Science and Technology.*)

ABSTR. CLIN. CARE GUIDEL.
[US/1042-4423]
ABSTRACTS OF CLINICAL CARE GUIDELINES.

ABSTR. CRIMINOL. PENOL.
[NE/0001-3684]
ABSTRACTS ON CRIMINOLOGY AND PENOLOGY.
(***Continued by*** *Criminology & Penology Abstracts.*)

ABSTR. ENGL. STUD.
[US/0001-3560]
ABSTRACTS OF ENGLISH STUDIES.
(Suspended)

ABSTR. ENTOMOL.
[US/0001-3579]
ABSTRACTS OF ENTOMOLOGY.
***Refer to Biological Abstracts for complete source list.

ABSTR. FOLK. STUD.
[US/0001-3587]
ABSTRACTS OF FOLKLORE STUDIES.
(Ceased)

ABSTR. GRAPHIC ARTS TECH. FOUND.
[US]
ABSTRACTS (GRAPHIC ARTS TECHNICAL FOUNDATION).
(***Continues*** *Graphic Arts Abstracts (Pittsburgh, PA. : 1968).*)

ABSTR. HEALTH CARE MANAGE. STUD.
[US/0194-4908]
ABSTRACTS OF HEALTH CARE MANAGEMENT STUDIES.
(***Continues*** *Abstracts of Hospital Management Studies.*)

ABSTR. HEALTH ENVIRON. POLLUTANTS
[US/0044-5819]
ABSTRACTS ON HEALTH EFFECTS OF ENVIRONMENTAL POLLUTANTS.
(Ceased)

ABSTR. HOSPIT. MANAGE. STUD.
[US/0001-3595]
ABSTRACTS OF HOSPITAL MANAGEMENT STUDIES.
(***Continued by*** *Abstracts of Health Care Management Studies.*)

ABSTR. HUM. COMPUT. INTERACT.
[US/1042-0193]
ABSTRACTS IN HUMAN-COMPUTER INTERACTION.
(Suspended)

ABSTR. HYG.
[UK/0001-3692]
ABSTRACTS ON HYGIENE.
(***Continued by*** *Abstracts on Hygiene and Communicable Diseases.*)

ABSTR. HYG. COMMUN. DIS.
[UK/0260-5511]
ABSTRACTS ON HYGIENE AND COMMUNICABLE DISEASES.
(***Continues*** *Abstracts on Hygiene.*)
***Refer to Tropical Diseases Bulletin for complete source list.

ABSTR. J. EARTHQ. ENG.
[US/0363-5732]
ABSTRACT JOURNAL IN EARTHQUAKE ENGINEERING.

ABSTR. MIL. BIBLIOGR.
[AG]
ABSTRACTS OF MILITARY BIBLIOGRAPHY.
(***Continues*** *Resumenes Analíticos Sobre Defensa y Seguridad Nacional.*)

ABSTR. NEW WORLD ARCHAEOL.
[US]
ABSTRACTS OF NEW WORLD ARCHAEOLOGY.
(Ceased)

ABSTR. NORTH AM. GEOL.
[US/0001-3625]
ABSTRACTS OF NORTH AMERICAN GEOLOGY.
(Ceased)

ABSTR. OF MYCOL.
[US/0001-3617]
ABSTRACTS OF MYCOLOGY.
***Refer to Biological Abstracts for complete source list.

ABSTR. PHOTOGR. SCI. ENG. LIT.
[US/0001-3633]
ABSTRACTS OF PHOTOGRAPHIC SCIENCE & ENGINEERING LITERATURE.
(***Continues*** *Monthly Abstract Bulletin from the Kodak Research Laboratories; ANSCO Abstracts.*)

ABSTR. POP. CULT.
[US/0147-2615]
ABSTRACTS OF POPULAR CULTURE.
(Ceased)

ABSTR. RES. PASTOR. CARE COUNS.
[US/0733-2599]
ABSTRACTS OF RESEARCH IN PASTORAL CARE AND COUNSELING.
(***Continues*** *Pastoral Care and Counseling Abstracts.*)

INDEXES/ABSTRACTS TABLE

ABSTR. SOC. GERONTOL.
[US/1047-4862]
ABSTRACTS IN SOCIAL GERONTOLOGY.
(*Continues* Current Literature on Aging.)

ABSTR. SOC. WORK.
[US/0001-3412]
ABSTRACTS FOR SOCIAL WORKERS.
(*Continued by* Social Work Research & Abstracts.)

ABSTR. TROP. AGRIC.
[NE/0304-5951]
ABSTRACTS ON TROPICAL AGRICULTURE.
(*Supersedes* Tropical Abstracts.)

ABSTR. WORLD MED.
[UK]
ABSTRACTS OF WORLD MEDICINE.
(*Absorbed* Abstracts of World Surgery, Obstetrics and Gynaecology.)

ACAD. ABSTR.
[US/1056-7496]
ACADEMIC ABSTRACTS.

ACAD. ABSTR. FULL TEXT ELITE
[US/1060-6750]
ACADEMIC ABSTRACTS FULL TEXT ELITE.

ACAD. IND. [COMPUTER FILE]
[US]
ACADEMIC INDEX. [COMPUTER FILE].

ACAD. SEARCH
[US/1071-2720]
ACADEMIC SEARCH.

ACCESS
[US/0095-5698]
ACCESS (SYRACUSE).
(*Absorbed* Monthly Periodical Index.)

ACCESS INDEX LITTLE MAG.
[US/0363-065X]
ACCESS INDEX TO LITTLE MAGAZINES.
(Ceased)

ACCOUNT. ART.
[US]
ACCOUNTING ARTICLES.

ACCOUNT. DATA PROCESS. ABSTR.
[UK/0001-4796]
ACCOUNTING + DATA PROCESSING ABSTRACTS.
(*Continued by* Accounting + Finance Abstracts.)

ACCOUNT. INDEX
[US]
ACCOUNTANTS INDEX.
(*Continued by* Accounting & Tax Index.)

ACCOUNT. INDEX SUPPL.
[US/0748-7975]
ACCOUNTANTS' INDEX. SUPPLEMENT.
(*Continued by* Accounting & Tax Index.)

ACCOUNT. TAX DATAB.
[US]
ACCOUNTING AND TAX DATABASE [ONLINE DATABASE].

ACCOUNT. TAX INDEX
[US/1063-0287]
ACCOUNTING AND TAX INDEX.
(*Continues* Accountants' Index. Supplement.)
***Refer to Accounting and Tax Database for complete source list.

ACCUMU. VET. INDEX
[US/0567-7033]
ACCUMULATIVE VETERINARY INDEX.
(Ceased)

ACID RAIN ABSTR.
[US/0882-1402]
ACID RAIN ABSTRACTS.
(*Absorbed by* Environment Abstracts.)

ACM GUIDE COMPUT. LIT.
[US/0149-1199]
ACM GUIDE TO COMPUTING LITERATURE.
(*Continues* Computing Reviews. Bibliography and Subject Index of Current Computing Literature.)

ACOUST. ABSTR.
[UK/0001-4974]
ACOUSTICS ABSTRACTS.

ADOLESC. MENT. HEALTH ABSTR.
[US]
ADOLESCENT MENTAL HEALTH ABSTRACTS.
(Ceased)

ADONIS
[NE]
ADONIS CD-ROM.

AERO. DEF. MARK. TECHNOL.
[US/0885-2286]
AEROSPACE/DEFENSE MARKETS & TECHNOLOGY.
(*Continues* Defense Markets & Technology.)

AESIS Q.
[AT/0313-704x]
AESIS QUARTERLY.

AFR. ABSTR.
[UK/0568-1200]
AFRICAN ABSTRACTS.
(Ceased)

AGBIOTECH NEWS INF.
[UK/0954-9897]
AGBIOTECH NEWS AND INFORMATION.

AGRIC. ENG. ABSTR.
[UK/0308-8863]
AGRICULTURAL ENGINEERING ABSTRACTS.

AGRIC. ENVIRON. BIOTECHNOL. ABSTR.
[US/1063-1151]
AGRICULTURAL & ENVIRONMENTAL BIOTECHNOLOGY ABSTRACTS.
(*Continues in part* Biotechnology Research Abstracts.)
***Refer to Biotechnology Research Abstracts for complete source list.

AGRIC. INDEX
[US/0196-5883]
AGRICULTURAL INDEX.
(*Continued by* Biological & Agricultural Index.)

AGRICOLA
[US/1050-6810]
AGRICOLA.

AGRINDEX
[IT/0254-8801]
AGRINDEX.

AGROFOR. ABSTR.
[UK/0952-1453]
AGROFORESTRY ABSTRACTS.

AIDS ABSTR.
[US/1066-1107]
AIDS ABSTRACTS (ATLANTA, GA.).

AIR POLLUT. TITLES
[US/0002-2497]
AIR POLLUTION TITLES.
(Ceased)

AIR UNIV. LIBR. INDEX MIL. PERIOD.
[US/0002-2586]
AIR UNIVERSITY LIBRARY INDEX TO MILITARY PERIODICALS.
(*Continues* Air University Periodical Index.)

AIR UNIV. PERIOD. INDEX
[US]
AIR UNIVERSITY PERIODICAL INDEX.
(*Continued by* Air University Library Index to Military Periodicals.)

ALCOHOL CLIN. UPDATE
[US/0740-1035]
ALCOHOL CLINICAL UPDATE.
(Ceased)

ALCOHOL. DIG.
[US/0093-7010]
ALCOHOLISM DIGEST.
(Ceased)

ALTERN. PRESS INDEX
[US/0002-662X]
ALTERNATIVE PRESS INDEX.

ALUM. IND. ABSTR.
[US/1066-0623]
ALUMINIUM INDUSTRY ABSTRACTS.
(*Continues* World Aluminum Abstracts.)

AM. BIBLIOGR. SLAVIC EAST EUROP. STUD.
[US/0094-3770]
AMERICAN BIBLIOGRAPHY OF SLAVIC AND EAST EUROPEAN STUDIES.
(*Continues* American Bibliography of Russian and East European Studies.)

AM. HIST. LIFE
[US/0002-7065]
AMERICA, HISTORY AND LIFE (SANTA BARBARA, CALIF. : 1989).
(*Formed by the union of* America, History and Life. Part A, Article Abstracts and Citations *and* America, History and Life. Part B, Index to Book Reviews America, History and Life. Part C, American History Bibliography, Books, Articles and Dissertations America, History and Life. Part D, Annual Index.)

AM. HIST. LIFE PART B
[US/0002-7065]
AMERICA: HISTORY AND LIFE. PART B: INDEX TO BOOK REVIEWS.
(*Merged with* America, History and Life. Part A, Article Abstracts and Citations; America, History and Life. Part C, American History Bibliography, Books, Articles and Dissertations *and* America, History and Life. Part D, Annual Index *to form* America, History and Life.)

AM. HUMANIT. INDEX
[US/0361-0144]
AMERICAN HUMANITIES INDEX, THE.

AM. INDIAN INDEX
[US/0569-5244]
AMERICAN INDIAN INDEX.
(Ceased)

AM. STAT. INDEX
[US/0091-1658]
AMERICAN STATISTICS INDEX.

ANAL. ABSTR.
[UK/0003-2689]
ANALYTICAL ABSTRACTS.
(*Continues* British Abstracts. Section C, Analysis and Apparatus.)

INDEXES/ABSTRACTS TABLE

ANBAR ACCOUNT. FINAN. ABSTR.
[UK/0961-2742]
ANBAR ACCOUNTING & FINANCE ABSTRACTS.
(*Continues* Accounting + Data Processing Abstracts.)

ANBAR MANAG. SERV. ABSTR.
[UK]
ANBAR MANAGEMENT SERVICES ABSTRACTS.
(*Superseded in part by* Accounting + Data Processing Abstracts; Marketing + Distribution Abstracts; Personnel + Training Abstracts *and* Top Management Abstracts.)

ANBAR MARK. DISTR. ABSTR.
[UK/0305-0661]
ANBAR MARKETING & DISTRIBUTION ABSTRACTS.
(*Continues* Marketing + Distribution Abstracts.)

ANBAR TOP MANAG. ABSTR.
[UK]
ANBAR TOP MANAGEMENT ABSTRACTS.
(*Continues* Top Management Abstracts.)

ANIM. BEHAV. ABSTR.
[US/0301-8695]
ANIMAL BEHAVIOR ABSTRACTS.
(*Continues* Animal Behaviour Abstracts.)

ANIM. BREED. ABSTR.
[UK/0003-3499]
ANIMAL BREEDING ABSTRACTS.
(*Formed by the union of* Imperial Bureau of Animal Breeding and Genetics. Quarterly Bulletin *and* Imperial Bureau of Animal References to Literature Contained in Periodicals Received.)

ANIM. DISEASE OCCURR.
[UK/0144-3879]
ANIMAL DISEASE OCCURRENCE.
(Ceased)

ANNALS BEHAV. MED.
[US/0883-6612]
ANNALS OF BEHAVIORAL MEDICINE.
(*Continues* Behavioral Medicine Update; *Absorbed* Behavioral Medicine Abstracts.)

ANNOT. BIBLIOGR. ECON. GEOL.
[US/0003-5076]
ANNOTATED BIBLIOGRAPHY OF ECONOMIC GEOLOGY.
(Ceased)

ANNU. BIBLIOGR. ENGL. LANG. LIT.
[UK/0066-3786]
ANNUAL BIBLIOGRAPHY OF ENGLISH LANGUAGE AND LITERATURE.
(*Continues* Bibliography of English Language and Literature.)

ANNU. INDEX POP. MUSIC REC. REV.
[US/0092-3486]
ANNUAL INDEX TO POPULAR MUSIC RECORD REVIEWS.
(*Continues* Annual Index to Popular Music Record Reviews.)

ANNU. LEG. BIBLIOGR.
[US/0073-0793]
ANNUAL LEGAL BIBLIOGRAPHY.
(Ceased)

ANTHROPOL. INDEX
[UK/0003-5467]
ANTHROPOLOGICAL INDEX TO CURRENT PERIODICALS IN THE LIBRARY OF THE ROYAL ANTHROPOLOGICAL INSTITUTE.
(*Continues* Anthropological Index to Current Periodicals in the Museum of Mankind (Library Incorporating the Royal Anthropological Institute Library).)

ANTHROPOL. LIT.
[US/0190-3373]
ANTHROPOLOGICAL LITERATURE.
(*Continues* Anthropological Literature (Cambridge, Mass. : 1984).)

ANTHROPOL. LIT. MICRO.
[US/0190-3373]
ANTHROPOLOGICAL LITERATURE.
(*Continued by* Anthropological Literature (Cambridge, Mass. : 1989).)

APAIS, AUST. PUBLIC AFF. INF. SER.
[AT/0727-8926]
APAIS. AUSTRALIAN PUBLIC AFFAIRS INFORMATION SERVICE.

API ABSTR. HEALTH ENVIRON.
[US]
API ABSTRACTS. HEALTH & ENVIRONMENT.
(*Continued by* Literature Abstracts. Health & Environment.)

API ABSTR. OIL. CHEM.
[US]
API ABSTRACTS : OILFIELD CHEMICALS.
(*Continued by* Literature & Patent Abstracts. Oilfield Chemicals.)

APIBIZ
[US]
APIBIZ [ONLINE DATABASE].
***Refer to Petroleum/Energy Business News Index for complete source list.

APIC. ABSTR.
[UK/0003-648X]
APICULTURAL ABSTRACTS.

APILIT
[US]
APILIT [ONLINE DATABASE].
***Refer to Literature & Patent Abstracts Oilfield Chemicals for a complete source list.

APPL. ECOL. ABSTR.
[UK/0305-3040]
APPLIED ECOLOGY ABSTRACTS.
(*Continued by* Ecology Abstracts.)

APPL. MECH. REV.
[US/0003-6900]
APPLIED MECHANICS REVIEWS.

APPL. SCI. TECHNOL. INDEX
[US/0003-6986]
APPLIED SCIENCE & TECHNOLOGY INDEX.
(*Continues in part* Industrial Arts Index.)

APPL. SOC. SCI. INDEX ABSTR.
[UK/0950-2238]
ASSIA. APPLIED SOCIAL SCIENCES INDEX & ABSTRACTS.

AQUALINE ABSTR.
[UK/0263-5534]
AQUALINE ABSTRACTS.
(*Continues* Water Research Centre (Great Britain). WRC Information.)

AQUAREF
[CN]
AQUAREF.
(*Continues* Canadian Environment; Environnement.)

AQUAT. SCI. FISH. ABSTR.
[UK/0044-8516]
AQUATIC SCIENCES & FISHERIES ABSTRACTS.
(*Split into* Aquatic Sciences and Fisheries Abstracts. Part 1, Biological Sciences and Living Resources *and* Aquatic Sciences and Fisheries Abstracts. Part 2, Ocean Technology, Policy and Non-Living Resources.)

AQUAT. SCI. FISH. ABSTR. (COMPUTER FILE)
[US/1064-0460]
AQUATIC SCIENCES & FISHERIES ABSTRACTS (CD-ROM ED.).

AQUAT. SCI. FISH. ABSTR. PART 1
[US/0140-5373]
AQUATIC SCIENCES AND FISHERIES ABSTRACTS. PART 1 : BIOLOGICAL SCIENCES AND LIVING RESOURCES.
(*Continued in part by* Aquatic Sciences and Fisheries Abstracts. Part 3, Aquatic Pollution and Environmental Quality.)
***Refer to Aquatic Science & Fisheries Abstracts [Computer File]: ASFA / Cambridge Scientific Abstracts for complete source list.

AQUAT. SCI. FISH. ABSTR. 2, OCEAN TECHNOL. POLICY NON-LIVING RESOUR.
[US/0140-5381]
AQUATIC SCIENCES AND FISHERIES ABSTRACTS. PART 2 : OCEAN TECHNOLOGY, POLICY AND NON-LIVING RESOURCES.
(*Continued in part by* Aquatic Sciences and Fisheries Abstracts. Part 3, Aquatic Pollution and Environmental Quality.)
***Refer to Aquatic Sciences & Fisheries Abstracts [Computer File] : ASFA / Cambridge Scientific Abstracts for complete source list.

AQUAT. SCI. FISHER. ABSTR. 3, AQUAT. POLLUT. ENVIRO. QUAL.
[US/1045-6031]
AQUATIC SCIENCES AND FISHERIES ABSTRACTS. PART 3 : AQUATIC POLLUTION AND ENVIRONMENTAL QUALITY.
(*Continues in part* Aquatic Sciences and Fisheries Abstracts. Part 1, Biological Sciences & Living Resources *and* Aquatic Sciences and Fisheries Abstracts. Part 2, Ocean Technology, Policy and Non-Living Resources.)
***Refer to Aquatic Sciences & Fisheries Abstracts [Computer File] : ASFA / Cambridge Scientific Abstracts for complete source list.

ARCHIT. PERIOD. INDEX
[UK/0266-4380]
API. ARCHITECTURAL PERIODICALS INDEX.
(*Supersedes* Royal Institute of British Architects. RIBA Library Bulletin; Royal Institute of British Architects. RIBA Annual Review of Periodical Articles.)

ARCT. BIBLIOGR.
[CN/0066-6947]
ARCTIC BIBLIOGRAPHY.
(Ceased)

ARECO Q. INDEX PERIOD. LIT. AGING
[US/0734-5569]
ARECO'S QUARTERLY INDEX TO PERIODICAL LITERATURE ON AGING.
(*Continued by* Index to Periodical Literature on Aging.)

ART ARCHAEOL. TECH. ABSTR.
[US/0004-2994]
ART AND ARCHAEOLOGY TECHNICAL ABSTRACTS.
(*Continues* I.I.C. Abstracts.)

ART DES. PHOTO
[UK/0306-817X]
ART, DESIGN, PHOTO.
(Ceased)

ART INDEX
[US/0004-3222]
ART INDEX.

INDEXES/ABSTRACTS TABLE

ART INTELL. ABSTR.
[US/0882-1410]
ARTIFICIAL INTELLIGENCE ABSTRACTS.
(**Ceased**)

ARTBIBLIOGR. CURR. TITLES
[UK/0307-9961]
ARTBIBLIOGRAPHIES. CURRENT TITLES.

ARTBIBLIOGR. MOD.
[UK/0300-466X]
ARTBIBLIOGRAPHIES MODERN.
(**Continues** LOMA; Literature on Modern Art.)

ARTS HUMANIT. CITATION INDEX
[US/0162-8445]
ARTS & HUMANITIES CITATION INDEX (PRINT ED.).

ASCATOPICS
[US/0730-8574]
ASCATOPICS.

ASCE
[US/0730-3149]
ASCE.
(**Continued by** ASCE Annual Combined Index.)

ASCE ANNU. COMB. INDEX
[US/0742-1753]
ASCE ANNUAL COMBINED INDEX.
(**Continues** American Society of Civil Engineers. ASCE.)

ASCE PUBL. INF.
[US/0734-1962]
ASCE PUBLICATIONS INFORMATION.
(**Continues** ASCE Publications Abstracts.)

ASIA.-PAC. ECON. LIT.
[UK/0818-9935]
ASIAN-PACIFIC ECONOMIC LITERATURE.

ASSIA PLUS
[UK]
ASSIA PLUS [COMPUTER FILE].
***Refer to Applied Social Sciences Index & Abstracts for complete source list.

ASTIS BIBLIOGR.
[CN/0226-1685]
ASTIS BIBLIOGRAPHY.

ASTIS CURR. AWARE. BULL.
[CN/0705-8454]
A S T I S CURRENT AWARENESS BULLETIN.
(**Continues** Arctic Institute of North America. Library Accessions.)

ASTRON. ASTROPHYS. ABSTR.
[GW/0067-0022]
ASTRONOMY AND ASTROPHYSICS ABSTRACTS.
(**Continues** Astronomischer Jahresbericht.)

AUST. EDUC. INDEX
[AT/0004-9026]
AUSTRALIAN EDUCATION INDEX.

AUST. LEG. MON. DIG.
[AT/0004-9646]
AUSTRALIAN LEGAL MONTHLY DIGEST.

AUST. LIBR. INF. SCI. ABSTR.
[AT/0810-9265]
ALISA. AUSTRALIAN LIBRARY AND INFORMATION SCIENCE ABSTRACTS.

AUST. SCI. INDEX
[AT/0005-0229]
AUSTRALIAN SCIENCE INDEX.
(**Continues** C.S.I.R.O. Science Abstracts.)

AUTOM. SUBJ. CITATION ALERT
[US]
AUTOMATIC SUBJECT CITATION ALERT.
(**Continued by** Research Alert.)

AVERY INDEX ARCHIT. PERIOD. SUPPL.
[US/0588-540X]
AVERY INDEX TO ARCHITECTURAL PERIODICALS. SUPPLEMENT.
(**Continued by** Avery Index to Architectural Periodicals. Supplement.)

AVERY INDEX ARCHIT. PERIOD. SUPPL. COLUM. UNIV.
[US/0196-0008]
AVERY INDEX TO ARCHITECTURAL PERIODICALS. SECOND EDITION. REVISED AND ENLARGED. SUPPLEMENT.
(**Continues** Avery Library. Avery Index to Architectural Periodicals. Supplement.)

AVIAT. TRADESCAN
[US/0899-1928]
AVIATION TRADESCAN.

BEHAV. ABSTR.
[UK/0262-236X]
BEHAVIOURAL ABSTRACTS.
(**Ceased**)

BEHAV. MED. ABSTR.
[US/0197-7717]
BEHAVIORAL MEDICINE ABSTRACTS.
(**Absorbed by** Annals of Behavioral Medicine.)

BER. BIOCHEM. BIOL.
[GW/0005-9013]
BERICHTE BIOCHEMIE UND BIOLOGIE.
(**Continues** Berichte uber die Wissenschaftliche Biologie.)

BHA : BIBLIO. HIST. ART
[FR/1150-1588]
BIBLIOGRAPHY OF THE HISTORY OF ART : BHA.
(**Formed by the union of** Repertoire International de la Litterature de l'Art **and** Repertoire d'Art et d'Archeologie.)

BHI PLUS
[UK/0966-8772]
BHI PLUS [COMPUTER FILE].
***Refer to British Humanities Index for complete source list.

BIBLIOGR. AGRIC.
[US/0006-1530]
BIBLIOGRAPHY OF AGRICULTURE.
(**Continues** Bibliography of Agriculture with Subject Index.)
***Refer to AGRICOLA for complete source list.

BIBLIOGR. BRAS. CIEN. INF.
[BL/0102-2865]
BIBLIOGRAFIA BRASILEIRA DE CIENCIA DA INFORMACAO.
(**Ceased**)

BIBLIOGR. BRAS. MED.
[BL/0067-6675]
BIBLIOGRAFIA BRASILEIRA DE MEDICINA.
(**Continues** Indice-Catalogo Medico Brasileiro.)

BIBLIOGR. CARTO.
[GW/0340-0409]
BIBLIOGRAPHIA CARTOGRAPHICA.
(**Supersedes** Bibliotheca Cartographica.)

BIBLIOGR. ENGL. LIT.
[UK]
BIBLIOGRAPHY OF ENGLISH LANGUAGE AND LITERATURE.
(**Continued by** Annual Bibliography of English Language and Literature.)

BIBLIOGR. HIST. MED.
[US/0067-7280]
BIBLIOGRAPHY OF THE HISTORY OF MEDICINE.
***Refer to Index Medicus for complete source list.

BIBLIOGR. INDEX GEOL.
[US/0098-2784]
BIBLIOGRAPHY AND INDEX OF GEOLOGY.
(**Continues** Bibliography and Index of Geology Exclusive of North America; **Absorbed** Bibliography of North American Geology.)
***Refer to GeoRef [Computer File] for complete source list.

BIBLIOGR. INDEX GEOL. EXCLUS. NORTH AM.
[US/0376-1673]
BIBLIOGRAPHY AND INDEX OF GEOLOGY EXCLUSIVE OF NORTH AMERICA.
(**Continued by** Bibliography and Index of Geology.)

BIBLIOGR. INDEX HEALTH EDUC. PERIOD.
[US/0278-2340]
BIBLIOGRAPHIC INDEX OF HEALTH EDUCATION PERIODICALS : BIHEP.
(**Ceased**)

BIBLIOGR. INDEX MICROPALEONTOLOGY
[US/0300-7227]
BIBLIOGRAPHY AND INDEX OF MICROPALEONTOLOGY.
***Refer to GeoRef [Computer File] for complete source list.

BIBLIOGR. MISSION.
[IT]
BIBLIOGRAFIA MISSIONARIA.
(**Continued by** Bibliographia Missionaria.)

BIBLIOGR. MISSION.
[VC/0394-9869]
BIBLIOGRAPHIA MISSIONARIA / PONTIFICAL MISSIONARY LIBRARY OF THE CONGREGATION FOR THE EVANGELIZATION OF PEOPLES.
(**Continues** Bibliografia Missionaria.)

BIBLIOGR. NORTH AM. GEOL.
[US/0740-6347]
BIBLIOGRAPHY OF NORTH AMERICAN GEOLOGY.
(**Absorbed by** Bibliography and Index of Geology.)

BIOBUSINESS
[US]
BIOBUSINESS.

BIOCONT. NEWS INF.
[UK/0143-1404]
BIOCONTROL NEWS AND INFORMATION.

BIODETER. ABSTR.
[UK/0951-0621]
BIODETERIORATION ABSTRACTS.
(**Separated from** International Biodeterioration.)

BIOENG. ABSTR.
[US/0093-8378]
BIOENGINEERING ABSTRACTS.
(**Continued by** Engineering Index Bioengineering Abstracts.)

INDEXES/ABSTRACTS TABLE

BIOENG. ABSTR.
[US/1068-5693]
BIOENGINEERING ABSTRACTS (1993).
(*Continues* Engineering Index Bioengineering and Biotechnology Abstracts.)

BIOGR. INDEX
[US/0006-3053]
BIOGRAPHY INDEX.

BIOL. ABSTR. RRM
[US/0192-6985]
BIOLOGICAL ABSTRACTS / RRM.
(*Continues* Bioresearch Index.)
***Refer to Biological Abstracts for complete source list.

BIOL. ABSTR.
[US/0006-3169]
BIOLOGICAL ABSTRACTS.
(*Formed by the union of* Abstracts of Bacteriology *and* Botanical Abstracts.)

BIOL. ABSTR. ON COMPACT DISC
[US/1058-4129]
BIOLOGICAL ABSTRACTS ON COMPACT DISC.
***Refer to Biological Abstracts for complete source list.

BIOL. AGRIC. INDEX
[US/0006-3177]
BIOLOGICAL & AGRICULTURAL INDEX.
(*Continues* Agricultural Index.)

BIOL. DIG.
[US/0095-2958]
BIOLOGY DIGEST.

BIOSTATISTICA
[US/1041-7648]
BIOSTATISTICA (DAVENPORT, IOWA).

BIOTECHNOL. ABSTR.
[UK/0262-5318]
DERWENT BIOTECHNOLOGY ABSTRACTS.
(*Continued by* Biotechnology Abstracts.)

BIOTECHNOL. ABSTR.
[UK]
BIOTECHNOLOGY ABSTRACTS.
(*Continues* Derwent Biotechnology Abstracts.)
***Refer to PESTDOC for complete source list.

BIOTECHNOL. RES. ABSTR.
[US/0733-5709]
BIOTECHNOLOGY RESEARCH ABSTRACTS.
(*Continued in part by* Medical & Pharmaceutical Biotechnology Abstracts *and* Agricultural & Environmental Biotechnology Abstracts.)

BLACK INF. INDEX
[US/0045-2173]
BLACK INFORMATION INDEX.
(Ceased)

BMT ABSTR.
[UK/0268-9650]
BMT ABSTRACTS : BRITISH MARITIME TECHNOLOGY ABSTRACTS.
(*Continues* Journal of Abstracts of the British Ship Research Association.)

BOOK REV. DIGEST
[US/0006-7326]
BOOK REVIEW DIGEST.
(*Continues* Cumulative Book Review Digest.)

BOOK REV. INDEX
[US/0524-0581]
BOOK REVIEW INDEX.

BOOK REV. MON.
[US/0006-7342]
BOOK REVIEWS OF THE MONTH.
(Ceased)

BOSTON GLOBE INDEX
[US/0893-2727]
BOSTON GLOBE INDEX (1987), THE.
(*Continues* Bell & Howell Newspaper Index to the Boston Globe.)

BOWNE DIG. CORP. SEC. LAWYERS
[US/0896-906X]
BOWNE DIGEST FOR CORPORATE & SECURITIES LAWYERS.
(*Continues* Abstracts of Legal Periodicals (Corporate & Securities Ed.).)

BR. ARCHAEOL. ABSTR.
[UK/0007-0270]
BRITISH ARCHAEOLOGICAL ABSTRACTS.
(*Continued by* British Archaeological Bibliography.)

BR. ARCHAEOL. BIBLIOGR.
[UK/0964-7104]
BRITISH ARCHAEOLOGICAL BIBLIOGRAPHY.
(*Continues* British Archaeological Abstracts.)

BR. CERAM. ABSTR.
[UK/0300-4570]
BRITISH CERAMIC ABSTRACTS.
(*Continued by* World Ceramics Abstracts.)

BR. EDUC. INDEX
[UK/0007-0637]
BRITISH EDUCATION INDEX.

BR. HUMANIT. INDEX
[UK/0007-0815]
BRITISH HUMANITIES INDEX.
(*Supersedes in part* Subject Index to Periodicals.)

BR. TECHNOL. INDEX
[UK/0007-1889]
BRITISH TECHNOLOGY INDEX.
(*Continued by* Current Technology Index.)

BULL. ANAL. ENTOMOL. MED. VET.
[FR/0007-4098]
BULLETIN ANALYTIQUE D'ENTOMOLOGIE MEDICALE ET VETERINAIRE.
(Ceased)

BULL. SIGNAL.
[FR]
BULLETIN SIGNALETIQUE.
(Ceased)

BUS. ASAP
[US]
BUSINESS ASAP [COMPUTER FILE].

BUS. DATELINE
[US]
BUSINESS DATELINE.

BUS. EDUC. INDEX
[US/0068-4414]
BUSINESS EDUCATION INDEX.

BUS. INDEX
[US/0273-3684]
BUSINESS INDEX.

BUS. PERIOD. INDEX
[US/0007-6961]
BUSINESS PERIODICALS INDEX.
(*Continues in part* Industrial Arts Index.)

BUS. SOURCE
[US]
BUSINESS SOURCE. [COMPUTER FILE].

BUS. SOURCE PLUS
[US/1083-4508]]
BUSINESS SOURCE PLUS. [COMPUTER FILE].

CA QUICK SEARCH
[US]
CA QUICK SEARCH [COMPUTER FILE].
***Refer to Concrete Abstracts for complete source list.

CA SEL., ACID RAIN ACID AIR
[US/0885-0097]
CA SELECTS: ACID RAIN & ACID AIR.
***Refer to Chemical Abstracts for complete source list.

CA SEL., ADHESIVES
[US/0162-7686]
CA SELECTS: ADHESIVES.
***Refer to Chemical Abstracts for complete source list.

CA SEL., AIDS RELAT. IMMUNODEFIC.
[US/1040-7111]
CA SELECTS: AIDS & RELATED IMMUNODEFICIENCIES.
***Refer to Chemical Abstracts for complete source list.

CA SEL., AIR POLLUT. BOOKS REV.
[US/0895-5980]
CA SELECTS: AIR POLLUTION (BOOKS & REVIEWS).
***Refer to Chemical Abstracts for complete source list.

CA SEL., ALKYL. CATAL.
[US/0895-5964]
CA SELECTS: ALKYLATION & CATALYSTS.
***Refer to Chemical Abstracts for complete source list.

CA SEL., ALUMIN. LITH. ALUMIN. CER. ALLOYS
[US/1066-1166]
CA SELECTS: ALUMINUM-LITHIUM & ALUMINUM-CERIUM ALLOYS.
***Refer to Chemical Abstracts for complete source list.

CA SEL., ALZHEIMER'S DIS. RELAT. MEM. DYSFUNC.
[US/1047-8183]
CA SELECTS: ALZHEIMER'S DISEASE & RELATED MEMORY DYSFUNCTIONS.
***Refer to Chemical Abstracts for complete source list.

CA SEL., AMINO ACIDS PEP. PROT.
[US/0275-701X]
CA SELECTS: AMINO ACIDS, PEPTIDES & PROTEINS.
***Refer to Chemical Abstracts for complete source list.

CA SEL., ANALYT. ELECTROCHEM.
[US/0160-8959]
CA SELECTS: ANALYTICAL ELECTROCHEMISTRY.
***Refer to Chemical Abstracts for complete source list.

CA SEL., ANIMAL LONG. AGING
[US/0162-7694]
CA SELECTS: ANIMAL LONGEVITY & AGING.
***Refer to Chemical Abstracts for complete source list.

CA SEL., ANTI INFLAM. AGENTS ARTHRIT.
[US/0148-2394]
CA SELECTS: ANTI-INFLAMMATORY AGENTS & ARTHRITIS.
***Refer to Chemical Abstracts for complete source list.

CA SEL., ANTIBAC. AGENTS
[US/1045-8522]
CA SELECTS: ANTIBACTERIAL AGENTS.
(*Continues* CA Selects. Bactericides, Disinfectants & Antiseptics.)
***Refer to Chemical Abstracts for complete source list.

INDEXES/ABSTRACTS TABLE

CA SEL., ANTIOXID.
[US/0275-7028]
CA SELECTS: ANTIOXIDANTS.
***Refer to Chemical Abstracts for complete source list.

CA SEL., ANTITUMOR AGENTS
[US/0148-2386]
CA SELECTS: ANTITUMOR AGENTS.
***Refer to Chemical Abstracts for complete source list.

CA SEL., ARTIF. SWEETEN.
[US/0890-1813]
CA SELECTS: ARTIFICIAL SWEETENERS.
***Refer to Chemical Abstracts for complete source list.

CA SEL., ASYMMET. SYNTH. INDUC.
[US/0890-183X]
CA SELECTS: ASYMMETRIC SYNTHESIS & INDUCTION.
***Refer to Chemical Abstracts for complete source list.

CA SEL., AT. SPECTROSC.
[US/0195-4911]
CA SELECTS: ATOMIC SPECTROSCOPY.
***Refer to Chemical Abstracts for complete source list.

CA SEL., ATHEROSCL. HEART DIS.
[US/0148-2378]
CA SELECTS: ATHEROSCLEROSIS & HEART DISEASE.
***Refer to Chemical Abstracts for complete source list.

CA SEL., AUTOM. CHEM. ANAL.
[US/0740-0683]
CA SELECTS: AUTOMATED CHEMICAL ANALYSIS.
***Refer to Chemical Abstracts for complete source list.

CA SEL., B-LACTAM ANTIB.
[US/0148-2459]
CA SELECTS: B-LACTAM ANTIBIOTICS.
***Refer to Chemical Abstracts for complete source list.

CA SEL., BACTER. DISINFECT. ANTISEP.
[US/0890-1848]
CA SELECTS: BACTERICIDES, DISINFECTANTS & ANTISEPTICS.
(*Continued by* CA Selects: Antibacterial Agents.)

CA SEL., BATTER. FUEL CELLS
[US/0162-7708]
CA SELECTS: BATTERIES & FUEL CELLS.
***Refer to Chemical Abstracts for complete source list.

CA SEL., BIOGEN. AMINES NERV. SYST.
[US/0162-7716]
CA SELECTS: BIOGENIC AMINES & THE NERVOUS SYSTEM.
***Refer to Chemical Abstracts for complete source list.

CA SEL., BIOL. INFO. TRANSF.
[US/0162-7724]
CA SELECTS: BIOLOGICAL INFORMATION TRANSFER.
(Ceased)

CA SEL., BISMUTH CHEM.
[US/1061-5342]
CA SELECTS: BISMUTH CHEMISTRY.
***Refer to Chemical Abstracts for complete source list.

CA SEL., BLOCK GRAFT POLYM.
[US/0734-8851]
CA SELECTS: BLOCK & GRAFT POLYMERS.
***Refer to Chemical Abstracts for complete source list.

CA SEL., BLOOD COAG.
[US/0162-7732]
CA SELECTS: BLOOD COAGULATION.
***Refer to Chemical Abstracts for complete source list.

CA SEL., CARBOHYDR. (CHEM. ASP.)
[US/0740-0756]
CA SELECTS: CARBOHYDRATES (CHEMICAL ASPECTS).
***Refer to Chemical Abstracts for complete source list.

CA SEL., CARBON FIBER COMPOS.
[US/0895-5956]
CA SELECTS: CARBON FIBER COMPOSITES.
***Refer to Chemical Abstracts for complete source list.

CA SEL., CARBON GRAPH. FIB.
[US/0890-1856]
CA SELECTS: CARBON & GRAPHITE FIBERS.
***Refer to Chemical Abstracts for complete source list.

CA SEL., CARBON HETERO. NMR
[US/0190-9401]
CA SELECTS: CARBON & HETEROATOM NMR.
(*Continues in part* CA Selects. Nuclear Magnetic Resonance, Chemical Aspects.)
***Refer to Chemical Abstracts for complete source list.

CA SEL., CARCIN. MUT. TERATO.
[US/0148-2408]
CA SELECTS: CARCINOGENS, MUTAGENS & TERATOGENS.
***Refer to Chemical Abstracts for complete source list.

CA SEL., CATAL. (APPL. PHYS. ASP.)
[US/0146-440X]
CA SELECTS: CATALYSIS (APPLIED AND PHYSICAL ASPECTS).
***Refer to Chemical Abstracts for complete source list.

CA SEL., CATAL. (ORG. REACT.)
[US/0146-4396]
CA SELECTS: CATALYSIS (ORGANIC REACTIONS).
***Refer to Chemical Abstracts for complete source list.

CA SEL., CATAL. KINET. ANAL.
[US/0890-1864]
CA SELECTS: CATALYTIC & KINETIC ANALYSIS.
***Refer to Chemical Abstracts for complete source list.

CA SEL., CATAL. REGEN.
[US/0734-8800]
CA SELECTS: CATALYST REGENERATION.
***Refer to Chemical Abstracts for complete source list.

CA SEL., CERAM. MATER. J.
[US/0895-5948]
CA SELECTS: CERAMIC MATERIALS (JOURNALS).
***Refer to Chemical Abstracts for complete source list.

CA SEL., CERAM. METER. PAT.
[US/0885-0100]
CA SELECTS: CERAMIC MATERIALS (PATENTS).
***Refer to Chemical Abstracts for complete source list.

CA SEL., CHELATING AGENTS
[US/0734-8797]
CA SELECTS: CHELATING AGENTS.
***Refer to Chemical Abstracts for complete source list.

CA SEL., CHEM. ENG. OPER.
[US/1040-712X]
CA SELECTS: CHEMICAL ENGINEERING OPERATIONS.
***Refer to Chemical Abstracts for complete source list.

CA SEL., CHEM. HAZ. HEALTH SAFETY
[US/0190-9398]
CA SELECTS: CHEMICAL HAZARDS, HEALTH, & SAFETY.
(*Continues* CA Selects. Chemical Hazards.)
***Refer to Chemical Abstracts for complete source list.

CA SEL., CHEM. INSTRUM.
[US/0195-4938]
CA SELECTS: CHEMICAL INSTRUMENTATION.
***Refer to Chemical Abstracts for complete source list.

CA SEL., CHEM. IR OS RH RU
[US/1040-7146]
CA SELECTS: CHEMISTRY OF IR, OS, RH, & RU.
***Refer to Chemical Abstracts for complete source list.

CA SEL., CHEM. PROCESS. APPAR.
[US/0195-4946]
CA SELECTS: CHEMICAL PROCESSING APPARATUS.
***Refer to Chemical Abstracts for complete source list.

CA SEL., CHEM. VAPOR DEPOS.
[US/0885-0119]
CA SELECTS. CHEMICAL VAPOR DEPOSITION.
***Refer to Chemical Abstracts for complete source list.

CA SEL., CHEMILUMIN.
[US/1040-7138]
CA SELECTS: CHEMILUMINESCENCE.
***Refer to Chemical Abstracts for complete source list.

CA SEL., COAL SCI. PROC. CHEM.
[US/0146-4426]
CA SELECTS: COAL SCIENCE & PROCESS CHEMISTRY.
***Refer to Chemical Abstracts for complete source list.

CA SEL., COAT. INKS REALT. PROD.
[US/0275-7036]
CA SELECTS: COATINGS, INKS, & RELATED PRODUCTS.
***Refer to Chemical Abstracts for complete source list.

CA SEL., COLLOIDS (APPL. ASP.)
[US/0160-8967]
CA SELECTS: COLLOIDS (APPLIED ASPECTS).
(*Continued by* CA Selects. Colloids (Macromolecular Aspects).)

CA SEL., COLLOIDS (MACROMOL. ASP.)
[US/0190-9444]
CA SELECTS: COLLOIDS (MACROMOLECULAR ASPECTS).
(*Supersedes in part* CA Selects. Colloids (Applied Aspects).)
***Refer to Chemical Abstracts for complete source list.

CA SEL., COLLOIDS (PHYSICO. ASP.)
[US/0160-8975]
CA SELECTS: COLLOIDS (PHYSICOCHEMICAL ASPECTS).
***Refer to Chemical Abstracts for complete source list.

CA SEL., COLOR SCI.
[US/0885-0127]
CA SELECTS: COLOR SCIENCE.
***Refer to Chemical Abstracts for complete source list.

CA SEL., COLOR. DYES
[US/0734-8789]
CA SELECTS: COLORANTS & DYES.
***Refer to Chemical Abstracts for complete source list.

CA SEL., COMPOS. MATER. (CERAM.)
[US/1066-1158]
CA SELECTS: COMPOSITE MATERIALS (CERAMIC).
***Refer to Chemical Abstracts for complete source list.

CA SEL., COMPOS. MATER. (MET.)
[US/1066-114X]
CA SELECTS: COMPOSITE MATERIALS (METALLIC).
***Refer to Chemical Abstracts for complete source list.

CA SEL., COMPOS. MATER. (POLYM.)
[US/1040-7154]
CA SELECTS: COMPOSITE MATERIALS (POLYMERIC).
***Refer to Chemical Abstracts for complete source list.

INDEXES/ABSTRACTS TABLE

CA SEL., COMPUT. CHEM.
[US/0160-9025]
CA SELECTS: COMPUTERS IN CHEMISTRY.
***Refer to Chemical Abstracts for complete source list.

CA SEL., CONDUCT. POLYM.
[US/0885-0135]
CA SELECTS: CONDUCTIVE POLYMERS.
***Refer to Chemical Abstracts for complete source list.

CA SEL., CONTROL. RELEASE TECHNOL.
[US/0740-0748]
CA SELECTS: CONTROLLED RELEASE TECHNOLOGY.
***Refer to Chemical Abstracts for complete source list.

CA SEL., CORROS.
[US/0146-4434]
CA SELECTS: CORROSION.
***Refer to Chemical Abstracts for complete source list.

CA SEL., CORROS.-INHIB. COAT.
[US/0749-7296]
CA SELECTS: CORROSION-INHIBITING COATINGS.
***Refer to Chemical Abstracts for complete source list.

CA SEL., COSMET. CHEM.
[US/0275-7044]
CA SELECTS: COSMETIC CHEMICALS.
***Refer to Chemical Abstracts for complete source list.

CA SEL., COSMOCHEM.
[US/0195-4954]
CA SELECTS: COSMOCHEMISTRY.
(Ceased)

CA SEL., CROSSLINK. REACT.
[US/0740-0721]
CA SELECTS: CROSSLINKING REACTIONS.
***Refer to Chemical Abstracts for complete source list.

CA SEL., CRYS. GROWTH
[US/0162-7740]
CA SELECTS: CRYSTAL GROWTH.
***Refer to Chemical Abstracts for complete source list.

CA SEL., DETER. SOAPS, SURFAC.
[US/0162-7767]
CA SELECTS: DETERGENTS, SOAPS, & SURFACTANTS.
***Refer to Chemical Abstracts for complete source list.

CA SEL., DISTILL. TECHNOL.
[US/0275-7052]
CA SELECTS: DISTILLATION TECHNOLOGY.
***Refer to Chemical Abstracts for complete source list.

CA SEL., DRILL. MUDS
[US/0749-730X]
CA SELECTS: DRILLING MUDS.
***Refer to Chemical Abstracts for complete source list.

CA SEL., DRUG COSMET. TOXIC.
[US/0162-7775]
CA SELECTS: DRUG & COSMETIC TOXICITY.
***Refer to Chemical Abstracts for complete source list.

CA SEL., DRUG DELIV. SYST. DOS. FORMS
[US/1040-7162]
CA SELECTS: DRUG DELIVERY SYSTEMS & DOSAGE FORMS.
***Refer to Chemical Abstracts for complete source list.

CA SEL., ELECT. AUG. SPECTRO.
[US/0146-4450]
CA SELECTS: ELECTRON & AUGER SPECTROSCOPY.
***Refer to Chemical Abstracts for complete source list.

CA SEL., ELECT. SPIN RESON. (CHEM. ASP.)
[US/0146-4469]
CA SELECTS: ELECTRON SPIN RESONANCE (CHEMICAL ASPECTS).
***Refer to Chemical Abstracts for complete source list.

CA SEL., ELECTR. CONDUCT. ORG.
[US/0885-0143]
CA SELECTS: ELECTRICALLY CONDUCTIVE ORGANICS.
***Refer to Chemical Abstracts for complete source list.

CA SEL., ELECTROCHEM. ORG. SYNTH.
[US/0734-8770]
CA SELECTS: ELECTROCHEMICAL ORGANIC SYNTHESIS.
***Refer to Chemical Abstracts for complete source list.

CA SEL., ELECTROCHEM. REAC.
[US/0146-4442]
CA SELECTS: ELECTROCHEMICAL REACTIONS.
***Refer to Chemical Abstracts for complete source list.

CA SEL., ELECTRODEPOSIT.
[US/0162-7783]
CA SELECTS: ELECTRODEPOSITION.
***Refer to Chemical Abstracts for complete source list.

CA SEL., ELECTRON. CHEM. MATER.
[US/0885-0151]
CA SELECTS: ELECTRONIC CHEMICALS & MATERIALS.
***Refer to Chemical Abstracts for complete source list.

CA SEL., ELECTROPHOR.
[US/0195-4962]
CA SELECTS: ELECTROPHORESIS.
***Refer to Chemical Abstracts for complete source list.

CA SEL., EMULS. POLYM.
[US/0195-4970]
CA SELECTS: EMULSION POLYMERIZATION.
***Refer to Chemical Abstracts for complete source list.

CA SEL., EMULSIF. & DEMULSIF.
[US/0734-8754]
CA SELECTS: EMULSIFIERS & DEMULSIFIERS.
***Refer to Chemical Abstracts for complete source list.

CA SEL., ENERGY REV. BOOKS
[US/0162-7791]
CA SELECTS: ENERGY REVIEWS & BOOKS.
***Refer to Chemical Abstracts for complete source list.

CA SEL., ENGINE EXH.
[US/0160-9033]
CA SELECTS: ENGINE EXHAUST.
(Ceased)

CA SEL., ENHANC. PETRO. RECOV.
[US/0734-8746]
CA SELECTS: ENHANCED PETROLEUM RECOVERY.
***Refer to Chemical Abstracts for complete source list.

CA SEL., ENVIRON. POLLUT.
[US/0160-9041]
CA SELECTS: ENVIRONMENTAL POLLUTION.
***Refer to Chemical Abstracts for complete source list.

CA SEL., ENZYM. APPL.
[US/0895-593X]
CA SELECTS: ENZYME APPLICATIONS.
***Refer to Chemical Abstracts for complete source list.

CA SEL., ENZYM. ASSAYS
[US/0895-5808]
CA SELECTS: ENZYME ASSAYS.
***Refer to Chemical Abstracts for complete source list.

CA SEL., EPOXY RESINS
[US/0275-7060]
CA SELECTS: EPOXY RESINS.
***Refer to Chemical Abstracts for complete source list.

CA SEL., FATS OILS
[US/0275-7079]
CA SELECTS: FATS & OILS.
***Refer to Chemical Abstracts for complete source list.

CA SEL., FERMENT. CHEM.
[US/0740-0713]
CA SELECTS: FERMENTATION CHEMICALS.
***Refer to Chemical Abstracts for complete source list.

CA SEL., FIBER OPT. OPT. COMMUN.
[US/0890-1872]
CA SELECTS: FIBER OPTICS & OPTICAL COMMUNICATION.
***Refer to Chemical Abstracts for complete source list.

CA SEL., FIBER-REINFOR. PLAST.
[US/0734-869X]
CA SELECTS: FIBER-REINFORCED PLASTICS.
***Refer to Chemical Abstracts for complete source list.

CA SEL., FLAMMABIL.
[US/0162-7805]
CA SELECTS: FLAMMABILITY.
***Refer to Chemical Abstracts for complete source list.

CA SEL., FLAV. FRAGR.
[US/0148-2327]
CA SELECTS: FLAVORS & FRAGRANCES.
***Refer to Chemical Abstracts for complete source list.

CA SEL., FLUID. SOLIDS TECHNOL.
[US/0195-4989]
CA SELECTS: FLUIDIZED SOLIDS TECHNOLOGY.
***Refer to Chemical Abstracts for complete source list.

CA SEL., FLUOROPOLY.
[US/0895-5921]
CA SELECTS: FLUOROPOLYMERS.
***Refer to Chemical Abstracts for complete source list.

CA SEL., FOOD DRUGS COSMET.
[US/1051-3914]
CA SELECTS: FOOD, DRUGS, & COSMETICS.
***Refer to Chemical Abstracts for complete source list.

CA SEL., FOOD FEED ANAL.
[US/0895-5913]
CA SELECTS: FOOD & FEED ANALYSIS.
***Refer to Chemical Abstracts for complete source list.

CA SEL., FOOD TOXIC.
[US/0162-7813]
CA SELECTS: FOOD TOXICITY.
***Refer to Chemical Abstracts for complete source list.

CA SEL., FORENS. CHEM.
[US/0362-9880]
CA SELECTS: FORENSIC CHEMISTRY.
***Refer to Chemical Abstracts for complete source list.

CA SEL., FORMUL. CHEM.
[US/0890-1880]
CA SELECTS: FORMULATION CHEMISTRY.
***Refer to Chemical Abstracts for complete source list.

CA SEL., FREE RADIC.
[US/0885-016X]
CA SELECTS: FREE RADICALS.
(Continued by CA Selects: Free Radicals (Organic Aspects).)

CA SEL., FREE RADIC. (BIOCHEM. ASP.)
[US/0895-5905]
CA SELECTS: FREE RADICALS (BIOCHEMICAL ASPECTS).
***Refer to Chemical Abstracts for complete source list.

INDEXES/ABSTRACTS TABLE

CA SEL., FREE RADIC. (ORG. ASP.)
[US/0895-5972]
CA SELECTS: FREE RADICALS (ORGANIC ASPECTS).
(*Continues* CA Selects. Free Radicals.)
***Refer to Chemical Abstracts for complete source list.

CA SEL., FUEL LUBR. ADDIT.
[US/0195-4997]
CA SELECTS: FUEL & LUBRICANT ADDITIVES.
***Refer to Chemical Abstracts for complete source list.

CA SEL., FUNGICID.
[US/0160-9068]
CA SELECTS: FUNGICIDES.
***Refer to Chemical Abstracts for complete source list.

CA SEL., GAS CHROMAT.
[US/0146-4477]
CA SELECTS: GAS CHROMATOGRAPHY.
***Refer to Chemical Abstracts for complete source list.

CA SEL., GAS. WASTE TREAT.
[US/0160-9076]
CA SELECTS: GASEOUS WASTE TREATMENT.
***Refer to Chemical Abstracts for complete source list.

CA SEL., GEL PERM. CHROMAT.
[US/0146-4485]
CA SELECTS: GEL PERMEATION CHROMATOGRAPHY.
***Refer to Chemical Abstracts for complete source list.

CA SEL., GEOCHEM.
[US/1066-5730]
CA SELECTS: GEOCHEMISTRY.
***Refer to Chemical Abstracts for complete source list.

CA SEL., HEAT-RESIST. ABLAT. POLYM.
[US/0162-7821]
CA SELECTS: HEAT-RESISTANT & ABLATIVE POLYMERS.
***Refer to Chemical Abstracts for complete source list.

CA SEL., HERBIC.
[US/0160-9084]
CA SELECTS: HERBICIDES.
***Refer to Chemical Abstracts for complete source list.

CA SEL., HIGH PERFORM. LIQ. CHROMATOGR.
[US/0195-5217]
CA SELECTS: HIGH PERFORMANCE LIQUID CHROMATOGRAPHY.
(*Continues* CA Selects. High Speed Liquid Chromatography.)
***Refer to Chemical Abstracts for complete source list.

CA SEL., HOT-MELT ADHES.
[US/0895-5891]
CA SELECTS: HOT-MELT ADHESIVES.
***Refer to Chemical Abstracts for complete source list.

CA SEL., HYPERTENS. ANTIHYPERTENS.
[US/1051-3922]
CA SELECTS: HYPERTENSION & ANTIHYPERTENSIVES.
***Refer to Chemical Abstracts for complete source list.

CA SEL., INFR. SPECTRO. (ORG. ASP.)
[US/0190-9428]
CA SELECTS: INFRARED SPECTROSCOPY (ORGANIC ASPECTS).
(*Continues in part* CA Selects. Infrared Spectroscopy.)
***Refer to Chemical Abstracts for complete source list.

CA SEL., INFR. SPECTRO. (PHYSICOCHEM. ASP.)
[US/0190-9436]
CA SELECTS: INFRARED SPECTROSCOPY (PHYSICOCHEMICAL ASPECTS).
(*Continues in part* CA Selects. Infrared Spectroscopy.)
***Refer to Chemical Abstracts for complete source list.

CA SEL., INIT. POLYMER.
[US/0734-8843]
CA SELECTS: INITIATION OF POLYMERIZATION.
***Refer to Chemical Abstracts for complete source list.

CA SEL., INORG. ANAL. CHEM.
[US/0275-7087]
CA SELECTS: INORGANIC ANALYTICAL CHEMISTRY.
***Refer to Chemical Abstracts for complete source list.

CA SEL., INORG. CHEM. REACT.
[US/0275-7095]
CA SELECTS: INORGANIC CHEMICALS & REACTIONS.
***Refer to Chemical Abstracts for complete source list.

CA SEL., INORG. FLOUR. CHEM.
[US/0195-5004]
CA SELECTS: INORGANIC FLOURINE CHEMISTRY.
(Ceased)

CA SEL., INORG. ORGANOMET. REACT. MECHAN.
[US/0195-5012]
CA SELECTS: INORGANIC & ORGANOMETALLIC REACTION MECHANISMS.
***Refer to Chemical Abstracts for complete source list.

CA SEL., INSECTIC.
[US/0160-9092]
CA SELECTS: INSECTICIDES.
***Refer to Chemical Abstracts for complete source list.

CA SEL., ION CHROMATOGR.
[US/0890-1899]
CA SELECTS: ION CHROMATOGRAPHY.
***Refer to Chemical Abstracts for complete source list.

CA SEL., ION EXCHANGE
[US/0146-4493]
CA SELECTS: ION EXCHANGE.
***Refer to Chemical Abstracts for complete source list.

CA SEL., ION-CONTAIN. POLYM.
[US/0195-5020]
CA SELECTS: ION-CONTAINING POLYMERS.
***Refer to Chemical Abstracts for complete source list.

CA SEL., ISOMERI. CATAL.
[US/0895-5883]
CA SELECTS: ISOMERIZATION & CATALYSTS.
***Refer to Chemical Abstracts for complete source list.

CA SEL., LASER APPL.
[US/0195-5039]
CA SELECTS: LASER APPLICATIONS.
***Refer to Chemical Abstracts for complete source list.

CA SEL., LASER-INDUC. CHEM REACT.
[US/0885-0178]
CA SELECTS: LASER-INDUCED CHEMICAL REACTIONS.
***Refer to Chemical Abstracts for complete source list.

CA SEL., LASERS MASERS
[US/0195-5047]
CA SELECTS: LASERS & MASERS.
(Ceased)

CA SEL., LIQ. CRYST.
[US/0148-2351]
CA SELECTS: LIQUID CRYSTALS.
***Refer to Chemical Abstracts for complete source list.

CA SEL., LIQ. WASTE TREAT.
[US/0160-9106]
CA SELECTS: LIQUID WASTE TREATMENT.
***Refer to Chemical Abstracts for complete source list.

CA SEL., LUBR. GREAS. LUBRICAT.
[US/0734-8738]
CA SELECTS: LUBRICANTS, GREASES & LUBRICATION.
***Refer to Chemical Abstracts for complete source list.

CA SEL., MACROCYCL. ANTIBIOT.
[US/0195-5055]
CA SELECTS: MACROCYCLIC ANTIBIOTICS.
(Ceased)

CA SEL., MASS SPECTRO.
[US/0362-9872]
CA SELECTS: MASS SPECTROMETRY.
***Refer to Chemical Abstracts for complete source list.

CA SEL., MEM. REC. DEVICES MATER.
[US/0890-1821]
CA SELECTS: MEMORY & RECORDING DEVICES & MATERIALS.
***Refer to Chemical Abstracts for complete source list.

CA SEL., MEMBR. SEP.
[US/1040-7197]
CA SELECTS: MEMBRANE SEPARATION.
***Refer to Chemical Abstracts for complete source list.

CA SEL., METAL. GLASS.
[US/1062-8681]
CA SELECTS: METALLIC GLASSES.
***Refer to Chemical Abstracts for complete source list.

CA SEL., METALLO ENZ. METALLO COENZ.
[US/0160-9114]
CA SELECTS: METALLO ENZYMES & METALLO COENZYMES.
***Refer to Chemical Abstracts for complete source list.

CA SEL., MOLEC. MODEL. (BIOCHEM. ASP.)
[US/1059-2784]
CA SELECTS: MOLECULAR MODELING (BIOCHEMICAL ASPECTS).
***Refer to Chemical Abstracts for complete source list.

CA SEL., NAT. PROD. SYNTH.
[US/0740-0691]
CA SELECTS: NATURAL PRODUCT SYNTHESIS.
***Refer to Chemical Abstracts for complete source list.

CA SEL., NEW ANTIBIOT.
[US/0895-5875]
CA SELECTS: NEW ANTIBIOTICS.
***Refer to Chemical Abstracts for complete source list.

CA SEL., NEW BOOKS CHEM.
[US/0148-2416]
CA SELECTS: NEW BOOKS IN CHEMISTRY.
***Refer to Chemical Abstracts for complete source list.

CA SEL., NEW PLAST.
[US/0734-8673]
CA SELECTS: NEW PLASTICS.
***Refer to Chemical Abstracts for complete source list.

CA SEL., NITROGEN FIXAT.
[US/1047-8108]
CA SELECTS: NITROGEN FIXATION.
***Refer to Chemical Abstracts for complete source list.

CA SEL., NONLINEAR OPT. MATER.
[US/0895-5867]
CA SELECTS: NONLINEAR OPTICAL MATERIALS.
***Refer to Chemical Abstracts for complete source list.

INDEXES/ABSTRACTS TABLE

CA SEL., NOV. PESTIC. HERBIC.
[US/0749-7318]
CA SELECTS: NOVEL PESTICIDES & HERBICIDES.
***Refer to Chemical Abstracts for complete source list.

CA SEL., NOVEL NAT. PROD.
[US/0734-872X]
CA SELECTS: NOVEL NATURAL PRODUCTS.
***Refer to Chemical Abstracts for complete source list.

CA SEL., NOVEL POLYM. PAT.
[US/0734-8819]
CA SELECTS: NOVEL POLYMERS FROM PATENTS.
***Refer to Chemical Abstracts for complete source list.

CA SEL., NOVEL SULFUR HETEROCYCL.
[US/0275-7109]
CA SELECTS: NOVEL SULFUR HETEROCYCLES.
***Refer to Chemical Abstracts for complete source list.

CA SEL., OMEGA THREE FAT. ACID. FISH OIL
[US/1052-1984]
CA SELECTS: OMEGA THREE FATTY ACIDS & FISH OIL.
***Refer to Chemical Abstracts for complete source list.

CA SEL., OPT. PHOTOSENSIT. MATER.
[US/0195-5063]
CA SELECTS: OPTICAL & PHOTOSENSITIVE MATERIALS.
***Refer to Chemical Abstracts for complete source list.

CA SEL., OPTIMIZ. ORG. REACT.
[US/0195-5071]
CA SELECTS: OPTIMIZATION OF ORGANIC REACTIONS.
***Refer to Chemical Abstracts for complete source list.

CA SEL., ORAGNOPHOS. CHEM.
[US/0162-783X]
CA SELECTS: ORGANOPHOSPHORUS CHEMISTRY.
***Refer to Chemical Abstracts for complete source list.

CA SEL., ORG. ANAL. CHEM.
[US/0275-7117]
CA SELECTS: ORGANIC ANALYTICAL CHEMISTRY.
***Refer to Chemical Abstracts for complete source list.

CA SEL., ORG. OPT. MATER.
[US/0885-0186]
CA SELECTS: ORGANIC OPTICAL MATERIALS.
***Refer to Chemical Abstracts for complete source list.

CA SEL., ORG. REACT. MECHAN.
[US/0162-7848]
CA SELECTS: ORGANIC REACTION MECHANISMS.
***Refer to Chemical Abstracts for complete source list.

CA SEL., ORG. STEREOCHEM.
[US/0195-508X]
CA SELECTS: ORGANIC STEREOCHEMISTRY.
***Refer to Chemical Abstracts for complete source list.

CA SEL., ORG.-TRANS. MET. COMPL.
[US/0160-9130]
CA SELECTS: ORGANO-TRANSITION METAL COMPLEXES.
***Refer to Chemical Abstracts for complete source list.

CA SEL., ORGANOBOR. CHEM. BORAN.
[US/0195-5098]
CA SELECTS: ORGANOBORON CHEMISTRY & BORANES.
(Ceased)

CA SEL., ORGANOFLOUR. CHEM.
[US/0160-905X]
CA SELECTS: ORGANOFLUORINE CHEMISTRY.
***Refer to Chemical Abstracts for complete source list.

CA SEL., ORGANOMET. ORG. SYNTH.
[US/0895-5859]
CA SELECTS: ORGANOMETALLICS IN ORGANIC SYNTHESIS.
***Refer to Chemical Abstracts for complete source list.

CA SEL., ORGANOSIL. CHEM.
[US/0362-9899]
CA SELECTS: ORGANOSILICON CHEMISTRY.
***Refer to Chemical Abstracts for complete source list.

CA SEL., ORGANOSUL. CHEM. J.
[US/1040-7189]
CA SELECTS: ORGANOSULFUR CHEMISTRY (JOURNALS).
***Refer to Chemical Abstracts for complete source list.

CA SEL., ORGANOTIN CHEM.
[US/0195-5101]
CA SELECTS: ORGANOTIN CHEMISTRY.
***Refer to Chemical Abstracts for complete source list.

CA SEL., OXID. CATAL.
[US/1040-7170]
CA SELECTS: OXIDATION CATALYSTS.
***Refer to Chemical Abstracts for complete source list.

CA SEL., OXIDE SUPERCOND.
[US/1040-7219]
CA SELECTS: OXIDE SUPERCONDUCTORS.
***Refer to Chemical Abstracts for complete source list.

CA SEL., PAINT ADDIT.
[US/0734-8762]
CA SELECTS: PAINT ADDITIVES.
***Refer to Chemical Abstracts for complete source list.

CA SEL., PAP. CHEM.
[US/1040-7200]
CA SELECTS: PAPER CHEMISTRY.
***Refer to Chemical Abstracts for complete source list.

CA SEL., PAP. THIN-LAY. CHROMATOGR.
[US/0146-4515]
CA SELECTS: PAPER & THIN-LAYER CHROMATOGRAPHY.
***Refer to Chemical Abstracts for complete source list.

CA SEL., PAPER ADDIT.
[US/0734-8711]
CA SELECTS: PAPER ADDITIVES.
***Refer to Chemical Abstracts for complete source list.

CA SEL., PHARM. ANAL.
[US/0890-1902]
CA SELECTS: PHARMACEUTICAL ANALYSIS.
***Refer to Chemical Abstracts for complete source list.

CA SEL., PHARM. CHEM. (PAT.)
[US/0890-1929]
CA SELECTS: PHARMACEUTICAL CHEMISTRY (PATENTS).
***Refer to Chemical Abstracts for complete source list.

CA SEL., PHARM. CHEM. J.
[US/0890-1910]
CA SELECTS: PHARMACEUTICAL CHEMISTRY (JOURNALS).
***Refer to Chemical Abstracts for complete source list.

CA SEL., PHASE TRANSF. CATAL.
[US/0885-0194]
CA SELECTS: PHASE TRANSFER CATALYSIS.
***Refer to Chemical Abstracts for complete source list.

CA SEL., PHOTOBIOCHEM.
[US/0148-2335]
CA SELECTS: PHOTOBIOCHEMISTRY.
***Refer to Chemical Abstracts for complete source list.

CA SEL., PHOTOCHEM.
[US/0362-9856]
CA SELECTS: PHOTOCHEMISTRY.
***Refer to Chemical Abstracts for complete source list.

CA SEL., PHOTOCHEM. ORG. SYNTH.
[US/0885-0208]
CA SELECTS: PHOTOCHEMICAL ORGANIC SYNTHESIS.
***Refer to Chemical Abstracts for complete source list.

CA SEL., PHOTORESIS.
[US/0885-0216]
CA SELECTS: PHOTORESISTS.
***Refer to Chemical Abstracts for complete source list.

CA SEL., PHOTOSENSIT. POLYM.
[US/0749-7326]
CA SELECTS: PHOTOSENSITIVE POLYMERS.
***Refer to Chemical Abstracts for complete source list.

CA SEL., PLAS. REACT. ION ETCHING
[US/0749-7334]
CA SELECTS: PLASMA & REACTIVE ION ETCHING.
***Refer to Chemical Abstracts for complete source list.

CA SEL., PLAST. ADDIT.
[US/0734-8681]
CA SELECTS: PLASTICS ADDITIVES.
***Refer to Chemical Abstracts for complete source list.

CA SEL., PLAST. FABR. USES
[US/0275-7125]
CA SELECTS: PLASTICS FABRICATION & USES.
***Refer to Chemical Abstracts for complete source list.

CA SEL., PLAST. FILMS
[US/0195-511X]
CA SELECTS: PLASTIC FILMS.
***Refer to Chemical Abstracts for complete source list.

CA SEL., PLAST. MANUF. PROCESS.
[US/0275-7133]
CA SELECTS: PLASTICS MANUFACTURING & PROCESSING.
***Refer to Chemical Abstracts for complete source list.

CA SEL., PLAT. PALLAD. CHEM.
[US/0890-1937]
CA SELECTS: PLATINUM & PALLADIUM CHEMISTRY.
***Refer to Chemical Abstracts for complete source list.

CA SEL., POLLUT. MONIT.
[US/0160-9149]
CA SELECTS: POLLUTION MONITORING.
***Refer to Chemical Abstracts for complete source list.

CA SEL., POLYACRYL. J.
[US/0890-1945]
CA SELECTS: POLYACRYLATES (JOURNALS).
***Refer to Chemical Abstracts for complete source list.

CA SEL., POLYEST.
[US/0734-8703]
CA SELECTS: POLYESTERS.
***Refer to Chemical Abstracts for complete source list.

CA SEL., POLYIMIDES
[US/0895-5840]
CA SELECTS: POLYIMIDES.
***Refer to Chemical Abstracts for complete source list.

CA SEL., POLYM. BLENDS
[US/0734-8827]
CA SELECTS: POLYMER BLENDS.
***Refer to Chemical Abstracts for complete source list.

CA SEL., POLYM. DEGRAD.
[US/0734-8835]
CA SELECTS: POLYMER DEGRADATION.
***Refer to Chemical Abstracts for complete source list.

INDEXES/ABSTRACTS TABLE

CA SEL., POLYM. KINET. PROCESS CONTROL
[US/0885-0224]
CA SELECTS: POLYMERIZATION KINETICS & PROCESS CONTROL.
***Refer to Chemical Abstracts for complete source list.

CA SEL., POLYM. MORPHOL.
[US/0195-5128]
CA SELECTS: POLYMER MORPHOLOGY.
***Refer to Chemical Abstracts for complete source list.

CA SEL., POLYURETH.
[US/0740-0705]
CA SELECTS: POLYURETHANES.
***Refer to Chemical Abstracts for complete source list.

CA SEL., PORPHYR.
[US/0195-5136]
CA SELECTS: PORPHYRINS.
***Refer to Chemical Abstracts for complete source list.

CA SEL., PROSTAGLAND.
[US/0148-2343]
CA SELECTS: PROSTAGLANDINS.
***Refer to Chemical Abstracts for complete source list.

CA SEL., PROT. MAG. RESON.
[US/0190-941X]
CA SELECTS: PROTON MAGNETIC RESONANCE.
(*Continues in part CA Selects. Nuclear Magnetic Resonance, Chemical Aspects.*)
***Refer to Chemical Abstracts for complete source list.

CA SEL., PSYCHOBIOCHEM.
[US/0362-9848]
CA SELECTS: PSYCHOBIOCHEMISTRY.
***Refer to Chemical Abstracts for complete source list.

CA SEL., QUAT. AMMON. COMP.
[US/0890-1953]
CA SELECTS: QUATERNARY AMMONIUM COMPOUNDS.
***Refer to Chemical Abstracts for complete source list.

CA SEL., RADIAT. CHEM.
[US/0146-4523]
CA SELECTS: RADIATION CHEMISTRY.
***Refer to Chemical Abstracts for complete source list.

CA SEL., RADIAT. CURING
[US/0749-7342]
CA SELECTS: RADIATION CURING.
***Refer to Chemical Abstracts for complete source list.

CA SEL., RAMAN SPECTROS.
[US/0148-2432]
CA SELECTS: RAMAN SPECTROSCOPY.
***Refer to Chemical Abstracts for complete source list.

CA SEL., RECOV. RECYCL. WASTES
[US/0160-9157]
CA SELECTS: RECOVERY & RECYCLING OF WASTES.
***Refer to Chemical Abstracts for complete source list.

CA SEL., SELEN. TELLUR. CHEM.
[US/0749-7350]
CA SELECTS: SELENIUM & TELLURIUM CHEMISTRY.
***Refer to Chemical Abstracts for complete source list.

CA SEL., SHAPE MEM. ALLOYS
[US/1062-869X]
CA SELECTS: SHAPE MEMORY ALLOYS.
***Refer to Chemical Abstracts for complete source list.

CA SEL., SILICAS SILICAT.
[US/0890-1961]
CA SELECTS: SILICAS & SILICATES.
***Refer to Chemical Abstracts for complete source list.

CA SEL., SILOX. SILIC.
[US/0895-5832]
CA SELECTS: SILOXANES & SILICONES.
***Refer to Chemical Abstracts for complete source list.

CA SEL., SILVER CHEM.
[US/0148-2440]
CA SELECTS: SILVER CHEMISTRY.
***Refer to Chemical Abstracts for complete source list.

CA SEL., SOL. ENERGY
[US/0148-236X]
CA SELECTS: SOLAR ENERGY.
***Refer to Chemical Abstracts for complete source list.

CA SEL., SOLID RADIOACT. WASTE TREAT.
[US/0160-9165]
CA SELECTS: SOLID & RADIOACTIVE WASTE TREATMENT.
***Refer to Chemical Abstracts for complete source list.

CA SEL., SOLID STATE NMR
[US/0895-5824]
CA SELECTS: SOLID STATE NMR.
***Refer to Chemical Abstracts for complete source list.

CA SEL., SOLV. EXTRACT.
[US/0146-4531]
CA SELECTS: SOLVENT EXTRACTION.
***Refer to Chemical Abstracts for complete source list.

CA SEL., SPECTROCHEM. ANAL.
[US/0885-0232]
CA SELECTS: SPECTROCHEMICAL ANALYSIS.
***Refer to Chemical Abstracts for complete source list.

CA SEL., STEROIDS (BIOCHEM. ASP.)
[US/0160-9173]
CA SELECTS: STEROIDS (BIOCHEMICAL ASPECTS).
***Refer to Chemical Abstracts for complete source list.

CA SEL., STEROIDS (CHEM. ASP.)
[US/0160-9181]
CA SELECTS: STEROIDS (CHEMICAL ASPECTS).
***Refer to Chemical Abstracts for complete source list.

CA SEL., STRESS CORROS.-MET.
[US/1066-1174]
CA SELECTS: STRESS CORROSION - METALS.
***Refer to Chemical Abstracts for complete source list.

CA SEL., STRUCT.-ACT. RELAT.
[US/0895-5816]
CA SELECTS: STRUCTURE-ACTIVITY RELATIONSHIPS.
***Refer to Chemical Abstracts for complete source list.

CA SEL., SUBSTIT. EFFECTS LIN. FREE ENERGY RELAT.
[US/0162-7856]
CA SELECTS: SUBSTITUENT EFFECTS & LINEAR FREE ENERGY RELATIONSHIPS.
(Ceased)

CA SEL., SURF. ANAL.
[US/0195-5152]
CA SELECTS: SURFACE ANALYSIS.
***Refer to Chemical Abstracts for complete source list.

CA SEL., SURF. CHEM. (PHYSICOCHEM. ASP.)
[US/0146-454X]
CA SELECTS: SURFACE CHEMISTRY (PHYSICOCHEMICAL ASPECTS).
***Refer to Chemical Abstracts for complete source list.

CA SEL., SYNFUELS
[US/0195-5160]
CA SELECTS: SYNFUELS.
***Refer to Chemical Abstracts for complete source list.

CA SEL., SYNTH. HIGH POLYM.
[US/0275-7168]
CA SELECTS: SYNTHETIC HIGH POLYMERS.
***Refer to Chemical Abstracts for complete source list.

CA SEL., SYNTH. MACROCY. COMP.
[US/0195-5179]
CA SELECTS: SYNTHETIC MACROCYCLIC COMPOUNDS.
***Refer to Chemical Abstracts for complete source list.

CA SEL., TECH. CERAM.
[US/1062-8703]
CA SELECTS: TECHNICAL CERAMICS.
***Refer to Chemical Abstracts for complete source list.

CA SEL., THERM. ANAL.
[US/0195-5187]
CA SELECTS: THERMAL ANALYSIS.
***Refer to Chemical Abstracts for complete source list.

CA SEL., THERMOCHEM.
[US/0162-7864]
CA SELECTS: THERMOCHEMISTRY.
***Refer to Chemical Abstracts for complete source list.

CA SEL., TRACE ELEM. ANAL.
[US/0160-919X]
CA SELECTS: TRACE ELEMENT ANALYSIS.
***Refer to Chemical Abstracts for complete source list.

CA SEL., ULTRAFILTR.
[US/0195-5195]
CA SELECTS: ULTRAFILTRATION.
***Refer to Chemical Abstracts for complete source list.

CA SEL., ULTRAVIOL. VISI. SPECTRO.
[US/0195-5209]
CA SELECTS: ULTRAVIOLET & VISIBLE SPECTROSCOPY.
***Refer to Chemical Abstracts for complete source list.

CA SEL., WATER TREAT.
[US/0740-073X]
CA SELECTS: WATER TREATMENT.
***Refer to Chemical Abstracts for complete source list.

CA SEL., WATER-BASED COAT.
[US/0749-7369]
CA SELECTS: WATER-BASED COATINGS.
***Refer to Chemical Abstracts for complete source list.

CA SEL., X-RAY ANAL. SPECTRO.
[US/0162-7872]
CA SELECTS: X-RAY ANALYSIS & SPECTROSCOPY.
***Refer to Chemical Abstracts for complete source list.

CA SEL., ZEOLITES
[US/0190-4949]
CA SELECTS: ZEOLITES.
***Refer to Chemical Abstracts for complete source list.

CALCIUM CALCIF. TISSUE ABSTR.
[US/1069-5540]
CALCIUM AND CALCIFIED TISSUE ABSTRACTS.
(*Continues Calcified Tissue Abstracts.*)

CALIF. PERIOD. INDEX
[US/0730-1367]
CALIFORNIA PERIODICALS INDEX.
(Ceased)

CALIF. PERIOD. MICROFI.
[US]
CALIFORNIA PERIODICALS ON MICROFILM.
(Ceased)

INDEXES/ABSTRACTS TABLE

CAN. BUS. INDEX
[CN/0227-8669]
CANADIAN BUSINESS INDEX.
(*Merged with* Canadian News Index *and* Canadian Magazine Index (Toronto, Ont.) *to form* Canadian Index (Toronto, Ont.).)

CAN. BUS. PERIOD. INDEX
[CN/0318-6717]
CANADIAN BUSINESS PERIODICALS INDEX.
(*Continued by* Canadian Business Index.)

CAN. CURR. LAW
[CN/0835-9768]
CANADIAN CURRENT LAW.
(*Split into* Jurisprudence (Scarborough, Ont.); Legislation (Scarborough, Ont.) *and* Canadian Legal Literature.)

CAN. EDUC. INDEX
[CN/0008-3453]
CANADIAN EDUCATION INDEX.
(*Absorbed* Directory of Education Studies in Canada.)

CAN. ENVIRON.
[CN]
CANADIAN ENVIRONMENT.
(*Continued by* AQUAREF.)

CAN. ESSAY LIT. INDEX
[CN/0316-0696]
CANADIAN ESSAY AND LITERATURE INDEX.
(Ceased)

CAN. INDEX
[CN/1192-4160]
CANADIAN INDEX (TORONTO).
(*Formed by the union of* Canadian Business Index *and* Canadian News Index Canadian Magazine Index (Toronto, Ont.).)

CAN. LEGAL LIT.
[CN/0832-9257]
CANADIAN LEGAL LITERATURE.
(*Continues in part* Canadian Current Law (1988).)

CAN. LIT. INDEX
[CN/0838-6021]
CANADIAN LITERATURE INDEX.
(Ceased)

CAN. MAG. INDEX
[CN/0829-8777]
CANADIAN MAGAZINE INDEX.
(*Merged with* Canadian Business Index *and* Canadian News Index *to form* Canadian Index (Toronto, Ont.).)

CAN. NEWS INDEX
[CN/0225-7459]
CANADIAN NEWS INDEX TORONTO.
(*Merged with* Canadian Business Index *and* Canadian Magazine Index (Toronto, Ont.) *to form* Canadian Index (Toronto, Ont.).)

CAN. PERIOD. INDEX
[CN/0008-4719]
CANADIAN PERIODICAL INDEX (1964).
(*Continues* Canadian Index to Periodicals and Documentary Films.)

CAN., MICROFICHE
[CN/0225-3216]
CANADIANA. MICROFICHE.
(Ceased)

CANON LAW ABSTR.
[UK/0008-5650]
CANON LAW ABSTRACTS.

CATCH. TRADE NAME INDEX : CATNI
[UK]
CATCHWORD AND TRADE NAME INDEX : CATNI.
***Refer to Current Technology Index for complete source list.

CATHOL. PERIOD. INDEX
[US/0363-6895]
CATHOLIC PERIODICAL INDEX.
(*Continued by* Catholic Periodical and Literature Index.)

CATHOL. PERIOD. LIT. INDEX
[US/0008-8285]
CATHOLIC PERIODICAL AND LITERATURE INDEX, THE.
(*Continues* Catholic Periodical Index; *Absorbed* Guide to Catholic Literature.)

CCLP CONTENTS CURR. LEG. PERIOD.
[US/0300-7391]
CCLP. CONTENTS OF CURRENT LEGAL PERIODICALS.
(*Continued by* Legal Contents.)

CERAM. ABSTR.
[US/0095-9960]
CERAMIC ABSTRACTS.
(*Continues in part* American Ceramic Society. Journal of the American Ceramic Society.)

CHEM INFORM
[GW/0931-7597]
CHEM INFORM.
(*Continues* Chemischer Informationsdienst.)

CHEM. ABSTR.
[US/0009-2258]
CHEMICAL ABSTRACTS.
(*Supersedes* Review of American Chemical Research.)

CHEM. BUS. BULL.
[UK]
CHEMICAL BUSINESS BULLETINS.

CHEM. BUS. NEWSBASE
[UK]
CHEMICAL BUSINESS NEWSBASE [ONLINE DATABASE].

CHEM. BUS. UPDATE
[UK/0950-6144]
CHEMICAL BUSINESS UPDATE.

CHEM. ENG. ABSTR.
[UK/0262-6438]
CHEMICAL ENGINEERING ABSTRACTS.
(*Continued by* Process & Chemical Engineering.)

CHEM. HAZARDS IND.
[UK/0265-5721]
CHEMICAL HAZARDS IN INDUSTRY.

CHEM. IND. NOTES
[US/0045-639X]
CHEMICAL INDUSTRY NOTES.
(*Supersedes* Plastics Industry Notes.)

CHEM. INF. DIENST.
[GW/0009-2975]
CHEMISCHER INFORMATIONSDIENST.
(*Continued by* Chem Inform.)

CHEM. TITLES
[US/0009-2711]
CHEMICAL TITLES.

CHEMORECEPT. ABSTR.
[US/0300-1261]
CHEMORECEPTION ABSTRACTS.

CHICAGO PSYCHOANAL. LIT. INDEX.
[US/0009-3661]
CHICAGO PSYCHOANALYTIC LITERATURE INDEX.
(Ceased)

CHICANO INDEX
[US/1044-3487]
CHICANO INDEX, THE.
(*Continues* Chicano Periodical Index.)

CHICOREL INDEX MENT. HEALTH BOOK REV.
[US/0149-4090]
CHICOREL INDEX TO MENTAL HEALTH BOOK REVIEWS.
(*Continues* Mental Health Book Review Index.)

CHILD DEV. ABSTR. BIBLIOGR.
[US/0009-3939]
CHILD DEVELOPMENT ABSTRACTS AND BIBLIOGRAPHY.
(*Continues* Selected Child Development Abstracts Currently Published in the Journal of Nervous and Mental Disease, the Wistar Institute Bibliographic Service, American Journal of Diseases of Children, Archives of Neurology and Psychiatry, Psychological Abstracts, Physiological Abstracts, Biological Abstracts, Chemical Abstracts, Endocrinology.)

CHILD. LIT. ABSTR.
[UK/0306-2015]
CHILDREN'S LITERATURE ABSTRACTS.

CHILD. MAG. GUIDE
[US/0743-9873]
CHILDREN'S MAGAZINE GUIDE.
(*Continues* Subject Index to Children's Magazines.)

CHRIST. PERIOD. INDEX
[US/0069-3871]
CHRISTIAN PERIODICAL INDEX.

CIS ABSTR.
[US/0302-7651]
CIS ABSTRACTS.
(*Continued by* Safety and Health at Work.)

CIS INDEX PUBL. U.S. CONGR.
[US/0007-8514]
CIS INDEX TO PUBLICATIONS OF THE UNITED STATES CONGRESS.

CIV. STRUCT. ENG. ABSTR.
[US/1063-7338]
CIVIL AND STRUCTURAL ENGINEERING ABSTRACTS.
(Ceased)

CLARK'S DIG.-ANNOT.
[US]
CLARK'S DIGEST-ANNOTATOR.
(*Continued by* New York Law Journal Digest-Annotator.)

CLASSIFIED ABSTR. ARCH. ALCOHOL LIT.
[US]
CLASSIFIED ABSTRACT ARCHIVE OF THE ALCOHOL LITERATURE.
(Ceased)

CLIN. BEHAV. THERAPY REV.
[US/0162-2269]
CLINICAL BEHAVIOR THERAPY REVIEW.
(Ceased)

COAL ABSTR.
[UK/0309-4979]
COAL ABSTRACTS.
(Ceased)

INDEXES/ABSTRACTS TABLE

COLL. STUD. PERS. ABSTR.
[US/0010-1168]
COLLEGE STUDENT PERSONNEL ABSTRACTS.
(*Continued by* Higher Education Abstracts.)

COMB. CUMUL. INDEX CARDIOL.
[US/0747-5330]
COMBINED CUMULATIVE INDEX TO CARDIOLOGY.
(**Ceased**)

COMB. CUMUL. INDEX OB. GYN.
[US/0884-8092]
COMBINED CUMULATIVE INDEX TO OBSTETRICS AND GYNECOLOGY.

COMB. CUMUL. INDEX PEDIATR.
[US/0190-4981]
COMBINED CUMULATIVE INDEX TO PEDIATRICS.

COMM. FISH. ABSTR.
[US/0010-2970]
COMMERCIAL FISHERIES ABSTRACTS.
(*Continued by* Marine Fisheries Abstracts.)

COMMUN. ABSTR.
[US/0162-2811]
COMMUNICATION ABSTRACTS.

COMMUNITY DEV. ABSTR.
[US]
COMMUNITY DEVELOPMENT ABSTRACTS.
(**Ceased**)

COMMUNITY MENT. HEALTH REV.
[US/0363-1605]
COMMUNITY MENTAL HEALTH REVIEW.
(*Continued by* Prevention in Human Services.)

COMPEND. PLUS
[US/1063-8709]
COMPENDEX PLUS.
***Refer to Engineering Index for complete source list.

COMPUMATH CIT. INDEX
[US/0730-6199]
COMPUMATH CITATION INDEX : CMCI.

COMPUT-A-CAL
[US/0742-5686]
COMPUT-A-CAL.
(**Ceased**)

COMPUT. ABSTR.
[UK/0010-4469]
COMPUTER ABSTRACTS.
(*Continues* Computer Bibliography.)

COMPUT. ASAP
[US]
COMPUTER ASAP [ONLINE DATABASE].

COMPUT. BUS.
[US/0732-8346]
COMPUTER BUSINESS (LOS ANGELES, CALIF.).

COMPUT. CONTENTS
[US/0747-0193]
COMPUTER CONTENTS.
(**Ceased**)

COMPUT. CONTROL ABSTR.
[UK/0036-8113]
COMPUTER & CONTROL ABSTRACTS.
(*Continues* Control Abstracts.)
***Refer to INSPEC [Online Database] for a complete source list.

COMPUT. DATABASE
[US]
COMPUTER DATABASE [ONLINE DATABASE].

COMPUT. IND. UPDATE
[US/0744-0081]
COMPUTER INDUSTRY UPDATE.

COMPUT. INF. SYST.
[US/0010-4507]
COMPUTER & INFORMATION SYSTEMS.
(*Continued by* Computer and Information Systems Abstracts Journal.)

COMPUT. INF. SYST. ABSTR. J.
[US/0191-9776]
COMPUTER AND INFORMATION SYSTEMS ABSTRACTS JOURNAL.
(*Continued by* Computer and Information Systems Abstracts.)

COMPUT. LIT. INDEX
[US/0270-4846]
COMPUTER LITERATURE INDEX.
(*Continues* Quarterly Bibliography of Computers and Data Processing.)

COMPUT. REV.
[US/0010-4884]
COMPUTING REVIEWS.

COMPUT. REV. INDEX
[US/1040-5003]
COMPUTER REVIEW INDEX.

COMPUT. REV., BIBLIOGR. SUBJ. INDEX CURR. COMPUT. LIT.
[US/0149-1202]
COMPUTING REVIEWS. BIBLIOGRAPHY AND SUBJECT INDEX OF CURRENT COMPUTING LITERATURE.
(*Continued by* ACM Guide to Computing Literature.)

CONCR. ABSTR.
[US/0045-8007]
CONCRETE ABSTRACTS.

CONSTR. INDEX
[US/0892-2047]
CONSTRUCTION INDEX.

CONSUM. HEALTH NUTR. INDEX
[US/0883-1963]
CONSUMER HEALTH & NUTRITION INDEX.

CONSUM. INDEX PROD. EVAL. INF. SOURCE
[US/0094-0534]
CONSUMERS INDEX TO PRODUCT EVALUATIONS AND INFORMATION SOURCES.

CONTENTS CONTEMP. MATH. J.
[US/0010-759X]
CONTENTS OF CONTEMPORARY MATHEMATICAL JOURNALS.
(*Merged with* New Publications - American Mathematical Society *to form* Contents of Contemporary Mathematical Journals and New Publications.)

CONTENTS CONTEMP. MATH. J. NEW PUBL.
[US]
CONTENTS OF CONTEMPORARY MATHEMATICAL JOURNALS AND NEW PUBLICATIONS.
(*Continued by* Current Mathematical Publications.)

CONTENTS CURR. LEG. PERIOD.
[US/0300-7391]
CONTENTS OF CURRENT LEGAL PERIODICALS.
(*Continued by* CCLP. Contents of Current Legal Periodicals.)

CONTENTS PAGES EDUC.
[UK/0265-9220]
CONTENTS PAGES IN EDUCATION.

CONTENTS RECENT ECON. J.
[UK]
CONTENTS OF RECENT ECONOMICS JOURNALS.
(**Ceased**)

CORROS. ABSTR.
[US/0010-9339]
CORROSION ABSTRACTS.
(*Supersedes in part* Corrosion.)

COT. TROP. FIBR. ABSTR. BIBLIOGR.
[UK]
COTTON AND TROPICAL FIBRES ABSTRACTS BIBLIOGRAPHY.
(*Continues* Cotton and Tropical Fibres Abstracts.)

CRIM. JUSTICE ABSTR.
[US/0146-9177]
CRIMINAL JUSTICE ABSTRACTS.
(*Continues* Crime and Delinquency Literature.)

CRIM. JUSTICE PERIOD. INDEX
[US/0145-5818]
CRIMINAL JUSTICE PERIODICAL INDEX.

CRIM. PENOL. POLICE SCI. ABSTR.
[NE/0928-8759]
CRIMINOLOGY, PENOLOGY AND POLICE SCIENCE ABSTRACTS.
(*Formed by the union of* Criminology & Penology Abstracts *and* Police Science Abstracts.)

CRIME DELINQ. ABSTR.
[US/0045-902X]
CRIME AND DELINQUENCY ABSTRACTS.
(*Continues* International Bibliography on Crime and Delinquency.)

CRIME DELINQ. LIT.
[US/0037-1327]
CRIME AND DELINQUENCY LITERATURE.
(*Continued by* Criminal Justice Abstracts.)

CRIMINOL. PENOL. ABSTR.
[NE/0166-6231]
CRIMINOLOGY & PENOLOGY ABSTRACTS.
(*Merged with* Police Science Abstracts *to form* Criminology, Penology, and Police Science Abstracts.)

CROP PHYSIOL. ABSTR.
[UK/0306-7556]
CROP PHYSIOLOGY ABSTRACTS.

CSA NEURO. ABSTR.
[US/0141-7711]
CSA NEUROSCIENCES ABSTRACTS.

CTI PLUS
[UK]
CTI PLUS [COMPUTER FILE].
***Refer to Current Technology Index for complete source list.

CUMUL. INDEX MED.
[US/0090-1423]
CUMULATED INDEX MEDICUS.
(*Continues* Quarterly Cumulative Index Medicus.)
***Refer to Index Medicus for complete source list.

CUMUL. INDEX NURS. ALLIED HEALTH LIT.
[US/0146-5554]
CUMULATIVE INDEX TO NURSING & ALLIED HEALTH LITERATURE.
(*Continued in part by* Nursing and Allied Health Index.)

CUMUL. INDEX NURS. LIT.
[US/0011-3018]
CUMULATIVE INDEX TO NURSING LITERATURE.
(*Continued by* Cumulative Index to Nursing & Allied Health Literature.)

INDEXES/ABSTRACTS TABLE

CURR. ABSTR. CHEM. INDEX CHEM.
[US/0161-455X]
CURRENT ABSTRACTS OF CHEMISTRY AND INDEX CHEMICUS.
(*Continued by* Index Chemicus : IC.)

CURR. ADV. APPL. MICROBIOL. BIOTECHNOL.
[UK/0964-8712]
CURRENT ADVANCES IN APPLIED MICROBIOLOGY & BIOTECHNOLOGY.
(*Continues* Current Advances in Microbiology.)
***Refer to Current Awareness in Biological Sciences : CABS for complete source list.

CURR. ADV. BIOCHEM.
[UK/0741-1618]
CURRENT ADVANCES IN BIOCHEMISTRY.
(*Continued by* Current Advances in Protein Biochemistry.)

CURR. ADV. CANCER RES.
[UK/0895-9803]
CURRENT ADVANCES IN CANCER RESEARCH.
***Refer to Current Awareness in Biological Sciences : CABS for complete source list.

CURR. ADV. CELL DEV. BIOL.
[UK/0741-1626]
CURRENT ADVANCES IN CELL AND DEVELOPMENTAL BIOLOGY.
(*Continues in part* Current Awareness in Biological Sciences.)
***Refer to Current Awareness in Biological Sciences : CABS for complete source list.

CURR. ADV. CLIN. CHEM.
[UK/0885-1980]
CURRENT ADVANCES IN CLINICAL CHEMISTRY.
(*Continues* Current Clinical Chemistry.)
***Refer to Current Awareness in Biological Sciences : CABS for complete source list.

CURR. ADV. ECOL. ENVIRON. SCI.
[UK/0955-6648]
CURRENT ADVANCES IN ECOLOGICAL & ENVIRONMENTAL SCIENCES.
(*Continues* Current Advances in Ecological Sciences.)
***Refer to Current Awareness in Biological Sciences : CABS for complete source list.

CURR. ADV. ECOL. SCI.
[UK/0306-3291]
CURRENT ADVANCES IN ECOLOGICAL SCIENCES.
(*Continued by* Current Advances in Ecological & Environmental Sciences.)

CURR. ADV. ENDOCRIN.
[UK/0741-1634]
CURRENT ADVANCES IN ENDOCRINOLOGY.
(*Continues in part* Current Awareness in Biological Sciences.)

CURR. ADV. ENDOCRIN. METAB.
[UK/0964-8720]
CURRENT ADVANCES IN ENDOCRINOLOGY AND METABOLISM.
(*Continues* Current Advances in Physiology.)
***Refer to Current Awareness in Biological Sciences : CABS for complete source list.

CURR. ADV. GENET. MOL. BIOL.
[UK/0741-1642]
CURRENT ADVANCES IN GENETICS & MOLECULAR BIOLOGY.
(*Continues* Current Advances in Genetics.)
***Refer to Current Awareness in Biological Sciences : CABS for complete source list.

CURR. ADV. IMMUNOL.
[UK/0741-1650]
CURRENT ADVANCES IN IMMUNOLOGY.
(*Continued by* Current Advances in Immunology & Infectious Diseases.)

CURR. ADV. IMMUNOL. INFECT. DISEAS.
[UK/0964-8747]
CURRENT ADVANCES IN IMMUNOLOGY & INFECTIOUS DISEASES.
(*Continues* Current Advances in Immunology.)
***Refer to Current Awareness in Biological Sciences : CABS for complete source list.

CURR. ADV. MICROBIOL.
[UK/0741-1669]
CURRENT ADVANCES IN MICROBIOLOGY.
(*Continued by* Current Advances in Applied Microbiology & Biotechnology.)

CURR. ADV. NEUROSCI.
[UK/0741-1677]
CURRENT ADVANCES IN NEUROSCIENCE.
(*Continues in part* Current Awareness in Biological Sciences.)
***Refer to Current Awareness in Biological Sciences : CABS for complete source list.

CURR. ADV. PHARMACOL. TOXICOL.
[UK/0741-1685]
CURRENT ADVANCES IN PHARMACOLOGY & TOXICOLOGY.
(*Continued by* Current Advances in Toxicology.)

CURR. ADV. PHYSIOL.
[UK/0741-1693]
CURRENT ADVANCES IN PHYSIOLOGY.
(*Continued by* Current Advances in Endocrinology & Metabolism.)

CURR. ADV. PLANT SCI.
[UK/0306-4484]
CURRENT ADVANCES IN PLANT SCIENCE.
***Refer to Current Awareness in Biological Sciences : CABS for complete source list.

CURR. ADV. PROT. BIOCHEM.
[UK/0965-0504]
CURRENT ADVANCES IN PROTEIN BIOCHEMISTRY.
(*Continues* Current Advances in Biochemistry.)
***Refer to Current Awareness in Biological Sciences : CABS for complete source list.

CURR. ADV. PROT. CHEM.
[UK/0965-0504]
CURRENT ADVANCES IN PROTEIN CHEMISTRY.
(*Continues* Current Advances in Biochemistry.)
***Refer to Current Awareness in Biological Sciences : CABS for complete source list.

CURR. ADV. TOXICOL.
[UK/0965-0512]
CURRENT ADVANCES IN TOXICOLOGY.
(*Continues* Current Advances in Pharmacology & Toxicology.)
***Refer to Current Awareness in Biological Sciences : CABS for complete source list.

CURR. AUST. NEW Z. LEG. LIT. INDEX
[AT]
CURRENT AUSTRALIAN AND NEW ZEALAND LEGAL LITERATURE INDEX.
(Ceased)

CURR. AWARE. BIOL. SCI., CABS
[UK/0733-4443]
CURRENT AWARENESS IN BIOLOGICAL SCIENCES.
(*Continued in part by* Current Advances in Neuroscience; Current Advances in Cell & Developmental Biology.)

CURR. AWARENESS LIBR. LIT., CALL
[US/0091-5270]
CURRENT AWARENESS-LIBRARY LITERATURE : CALL.
(Ceased)

CURR. BIOTECHNOL.
[UK/0960-5037]
CURRENT BIOTECHNOLOGY.
(*Continues* Current Biotechnology Abstracts.)

CURR. BIOTECHNOL. ABSTR.
[UK/0264-3391]
CURRENT BIOTECHNOLOGY ABSTRACTS.
(*Continued by* Current Biotechnology.)

CURR. BOOK REV. CITATIONS
[US/0360-1250]
CURRENT BOOK REVIEW CITATIONS.
(Ceased)

CURR. CHEM. REACT.
[US/0163-6278]
CURRENT CHEMICAL REACTIONS.

CURR. CIT.
[US/1074-9837]
CURRENT CITATIONS [COMPUTER FILE].

CURR. CONTENTS
[US/0272-1430]
CURRENT CONTENTS.
(*Continued by* Current Contents of Pharmaceutical Publications.)

CURR. CONTENTS AFR.
[UK/0721-5207]
CURRENT CONTENTS AFRICA.
(*Continues* CCA, Current Contents Afrika.)

CURR. CONTENTS AGRIC. BIOL. ENVIRON. SCI.
[US/0090-0508]
CURRENT CONTENTS. AGRICULTURE, BIOLOGY, & ENVIRONMENTAL SCIENCES.
(*Continues* Current Contents. Agricultural, Food & Veterinary Sciences.)

CURR. CONTENTS AGRIC. FOOD VET. SCI.
[US/0011-3379]
CURRENT CONTENTS : AGRICULTURAL, FOOD AND VETERINARY SCIENCES.
(*Continued by* Current Contents. Agriculture, Biology & Environmental Sciences.)

CURR. CONTENTS ARTS HUMANIT.
[US/0163-3155]
CURRENT CONTENTS. ARTS & HUMANITIES.

CURR. CONTENTS BEHAV. SOC. EDUC. SCI.
[US/0011-3387]
CURRENT CONTENTS: BEHAVIORAL, SOCIAL & EDUCATIONAL SCIENCES.
(*Continued by* Current Contents. Social & Behavioral Sciences.)

CURR. CONTENTS BEHAV. SOC. MANAGE. SCI.
[US/0590-384X]
CURRENT CONTENTS: BEHAVIORAL, SOCIAL & MANAGEMENT SCIENCES.
(*Continued by* Current Contents. Behavioral, Social & Educational Sciences.)

CURR. CONTENTS CLIN. MED.
[US/0891-3358]
CURRENT CONTENTS. CLINICAL MEDICINE.
(*Continues* Current Contents. Clinical Practice.)

INDEXES/ABSTRACTS TABLE

CURR. CONTENTS CLIN. PRACT.
[US/0091-1704]
CURRENT CONTENTS. CLINICAL PRACTICE.
(*Continued by* Current Contents. Clinical Medicine.)

CURR. CONTENTS EDUC.
[US/0590-3866]
CURRENT CONTENTS. EDUCATION.
(*Absorbed by* Current Contents: Behavioral, Social & Management Sciences.)

CURR. CONTENTS ENG. TECH. APPL. SCI.
[US/0095-7917]
CURRENT CONTENTS. ENGINEERING, TECHNOLOGY & APPLIED SCIENCES.
(*Continues* Current Contents: Engineering & Technology.)

CURR. CONTENTS ENG. TECH.
[US/0011-3395]
CURRENT CONTENTS: ENGINEERING & TECHNOLOGY.
(*Continued by* Current Contents. Engineering, Technology & Applied Sciences.)

CURR. CONTENTS LIFE SCI.
[US/0011-3409]
CURRENT CONTENTS. LIFE SCIENCES.
(*Continues* Current Contents. Your Weekly Guide to the Chemical, Pharmaco-Medical & Life Sciences.)

CURR. CONTENTS PHARM. PUBL.
[US/0272-1422]
CURRENT CONTENTS OF PHARMACEUTICAL PUBLICATIONS.
(*Superseded by* Current Contents of Pharmaco-Medical Publications.)

CURR. CONTENTS PHARM.-MED. PUBL.
[US/0272-1414]
CURRENT CONTENTS OF PHARMACO-MEDICAL PUBLICATIONS.
(*Continued by* Current Contents: Your Weekly Survey of Chemical, Pharmacological & Clinical Publications.)

CURR. CONTENTS PHYS. CHEM. EARTH SCI.
[US/0163-2574]
CURRENT CONTENTS. PHYSICAL, CHEMICAL & EARTH SCIENCES.
(*Continues* Current Contents. Physical and Chemical Sciences.)

CURR. CONTENTS PHYS. CHEM. SCI.
[US/0011-3417]
CURRENT CONTENTS. PHYSICAL & CHEMICAL SCIENCES.
(*Continued by* Current Contents. Physical, Chemical & Earth Sciences.)

CURR. CONTENTS SOC. BEHAV. SCI.
[US/0092-6361]
CURRENT CONTENTS. SOCIAL & BEHAVIORAL SCIENCES.
(*Continues* Current Contents. Behavioral, Social & Educational Sciences.)

CURR. CONTENTS YOUR WKLY. GUIDE CHEM. PHARM.-MED. LIFE SCI.
[US/0272-1503]
CURRENT CONTENTS: YOUR WEEKLY GUIDE OF THE CHEMICAL, PHARMACO-MEDICAL & LIFE SCIENCES.
(*Continued by* Current Contents. Life Sciences.)

CURR. CONTENTS YOUR WKLY. SURV. CHEM. PHARMACOL. CLIN. PUBL.
[US/0272-1449]
CURRENT CONTENTS: YOUR WEEKLY SURVEY OF CHEMICAL, PHARMACOLOGICAL & CLINICAL PUBLICATIONS.
(*Continued by* Current Contents. Your Weekly Guide to the Chemical, Pharmaco-Medical & Life Sciences.)

CURR. DIG. POST SOV. PRESS
[US/1067-7542]
CURRENT DIGEST OF THE POST-SOVIET PRESS, THE.
(*Continues* Current Digest of the Soviet Press.)

CURR. GEOGR. PUBL.
[US/0011-3514]
CURRENT GEOGRAPHICAL PUBLICATIONS.

CURR. INDEX J. EDUC.
[US/0011-3565]
CURRENT INDEX TO JOURNALS IN EDUCATION.

CURR. INDEX STAT.
[US/0364-1228]
CURRENT INDEX TO STATISTICS.

CURR. LAW INDEX
[US/0196-1780]
CURRENT LAW INDEX.

CURR. LIT. AGING
[US/0011-3662]
CURRENT LITERATURE ON AGING.
(*Continued by* Abstracts in Social Gerontology.)

CURR. LIT. BLOOD
[US/0001-7108]
CURRENT LITERATURE OF BLOOD.
(**Ceased**)

CURR. LIT. FAM. PLAN.
[US/0092-6000]
CURRENT LITERATURE IN FAMILY PLANNING.
(*Continues* Acquisitions List - Katharine Dexter McCormick Library.)

CURR. LIT. SCI. SCI.
[II]
CURRENT LITERATURE ON SCIENCE OF SCIENCE.
(*Supersedes* Index to Literature on Science of Science.)

CURR. MATH. PUBL.
[US/0361-4794]
CURRENT MATHEMATICAL PUBLICATIONS.
(*Continues* Contents of Contemporary Mathematical Journals and New Publications.)
***Refer to Mathematical Reviews for complete source list.

CURR. MIL. POL. LIT.
[UK/0954-3589]
CURRENT MILITARY & POLITICAL LITERATURE.
(*Continues* Current Military Literature.)

CURR. PAP. COMPUT. CONTROL
[UK/0011-3794]
CURRENT PAPERS ON COMPUTERS & CONTROL.
(*Continues* Current Papers on Control.)
***Refer to INSPEC [Online Database] for complete source list.

CURR. PAP. ELECTR. ELECTRON. ENG.
[UK/0011-3778]
CURRENT PAPERS IN ELECTRICAL & ELECTRONICS ENGINEERING.
(*Continues* Current Papers in Eletrotechnology.)
***Refer to INSPEC [Online Database] for complete source list.

CURR. PAP. PHYS.
[UK/0011-3786]
CURRENT PAPERS IN PHYSICS.
***Refer to INSPEC [Online Database] for complete source list.

CURR. PHYS. INDEX
[US/0098-9819]
CURRENT PHYSICS INDEX.

CURR. PRIMATE REF.
[US/0590-4102]
CURRENT PRIMATE REFERENCES.
(*Supersedes* Unverified Primate References.)

CURR. REF. FISH RES.
[US/0739-540X]
CURRENT REFERENCES IN FISH RESEARCH.

CURR. TECHNOL. INDEX
[UK/0260-6593]
CURRENT TECHNOLOGY INDEX : CTI.
(*Continues* British Technology Index.)

CURR. THOUGHTS TRENDS
[US/1054-8688]
CURRENT THOUGHTS AND TRENDS.
(*Continues* Current Christian Abstracts.)

CURR. TITL. DENT.
[DK/0903-3483]
CURRENT TITLES IN DENTISTRY.

CURR. TITLES ELECTROCHEM.
[II/0300-4376]
CURRENT TITLES IN ELECTROCHEMISTRY.
(*Absorbed* Electrochemical News.)

DAIRY SCI. ABSTR.
[UK/0011-5681]
DAIRY SCIENCE ABSTRACTS.

DATA PROCESS. DIG.
[US/0011-6858]
DATA PROCESSING DIGEST.

DEEP-SEA OCEANOGR. ABSTR.
[UK/0011-7471]
DEEP-SEA RESEARCH AND OCEANOGRAPHIC ABSTRACTS.
(*Continued by* Deep-Sea Research.)

DEEP-SEA RES.
[UK/0146-6291]
DEEP-SEA RESEARCH.
(*Continued by* Deep-Sea Research. Part A. Oceanographic Research Papers.)

DEEP-SEA RES., B, OCEANOGR. LIT. REV.
[UK/0198-0254]
DEEP-SEA RESEARCH. PART B. OCEANOGRAPHIC LITERATURE REVIEW.
(*Continued by* Oceanographic Literature Review.)

DENT. ABSTR.
[US/0011-8486]
DENTAL ABSTRACTS (CHICAGO).

DESALIN. ABSTR.
[IS/0011-9202]
DESALINATION ABSTRACTS.
(*Continued by* Desalination and Recycling Abstracts.)

DESALIN. RECYC. ABSTR.
[IS/0011-9172]
DESALINATION AND RECYCLING ABSTRACTS.
(*Continues* Desalination Abstracts.)

INDEXES/ABSTRACTS TABLE

DEV. DISABIL. ABSTR.
[US/0191-1600]
DEVELOPMENTAL DISABILITIES ABSTRACTS.
(*Continues* Mental Retardation & Developmental Disabilities Abstracts.)

DEV. MED. CHILD NEUROL.
[UK/0012-1622]
DEVELOPMENTAL MEDICINE & CHILD NEUROLOGY.
(*Continued in part by* American Academy For Cerebral Palsy & Developmental Medicine. Meeting. Abstracts.)

DIABETES LIT. INDEX
[US/0012-1819]
DIABETES LITERATURE INDEX.
(*Supersedes* Diabetes-Related Literature Index.)

DOANE INF. CENT. INDEX. SYST. SUBJ. INDEX
[US]
DICIS, DOANE INFORMATION CENTER INDEXING SYSTEM : SUBJECT INDEX.
(Ceased)

DOK. GEFAHRDUNG ALKOHOL, RAUCH., DROGEN, ARZNEIMITTEL
[GW/0341-8022]
DOKUMENTATION GEFAHRDUNG DURCH ALKOHOL, RAUCHEN, DROGEN, ARZNEIMITTEL.
(*Continues* Dokumentation Drogengefahrdung und Alkoholmissbrauch.)

DOK. RAUMENTWICKL.
[GW]
DOKUMENTATION ZUR RAUMENTWICKLUNG.
(*Continues* Documentatio Geographica.)

DSH ABSTR.
[US/0011-5150]
DSH ABSTRACTS.
(Ceased)

ECOL. ABSTR.
[UK/0305-196X]
ECOLOGICAL ABSTRACTS.

ECOLOGY ABSTR.
[US/0143-3296]
ECOLOGY ABSTRACTS.
(*Continues* Applied Ecology Abstracts.)

ECON. LIT. INDEX
[US]
ECONOMIC LITERATURE INDEX.

ECONLIT
[US]
ECONLIT [COMPUTER FILE].
***Refer to Economic Literature Index for a complete source list.

EDUC. ADM. ABSTR.
[US/0013-1601]
EDUCATIONAL ADMINISTRATION ABSTRACTS.

EDUC. INDEX
[US/0013-1385]
EDUCATION INDEX.

EDUC. TECHNOL. ABSTR.
[UK/0266-3368]
EDUCATIONAL TECHNOLOGY ABSTRACTS.

EI PAGE ONE
[US]
EI PAGE ONE [COMPUTER FILE].

ELECT. COMM. ABSTR.
[US/1069-5303]
ELECTRONICS AND COMMUNICATIONS ABSTRACTS.
(*Continues* Electronics & Communications Abstracts Journal.)

ELECTR. ELECTRON. ABSTR.
[UK/0036-8105]
ELECTRICAL & ELECTRONICS ABSTRACTS.
(*Continues* Science Abstracts. Electrical & Electronics Abstracts.)
***Refer to INSPEC [Online Database] for a complete source list.

ELECTROANAL. ABSTR.
[SZ/0013-4775]
ELECTROANALYTICAL ABSTRACTS.
(*Continues* Journal of Electroanalytical Chemistry. Abstracts Section.)

ELECTRON. COMMUN. ABSTR. J.
[US/0361-3313]
ELECTRONICS AND COMMUNICATIONS ABSTRACTS JOURNAL (RIVERDALE, MD.).
(*Continued by* Electronics and Communications Abstracts.)

ELECTRON. PUB. ABSTR.
[UK/0739-2907]
ELECTRONIC PUBLISHING ABSTRACTS.
(*Continued by* World Publishing Monitor.)

EMBASE LIST J. INDEXED
[NE]
EMBASE LIST OF JOURNALS INDEXED.
(*Continues* List of Journals Abstracted (1983).)
***Refer to EMBASE [Online Database] for complete source list.

EMBASE
[NE]
EMBASE [ONLINE DATABASE].

EMPLOY. RELAT. ABSTR.
[US]
EMPLOYMENT RELATIONS ABSTRACTS.
(*Continued by* Work Related Abstracts.)

ENERGY INDEX
[US/0094-6281]
ENERGY INDEX.
(*Absorbed by* Energy Information Abstracts Annual.)

ENERGY INF. ABSTR.
[US/0147-6521]
ENERGY INFORMATION ABSTRACTS.
(Ceased)

ENERGY INF. ABSTR. ANNU.
[US/0739-3679]
ENERGY INFORMATION ABSTRACTS ANNUAL.
(*Absorbed* Energy Index.)
***Refer to Energy Information Abstracts for complete source list.

ENERGY RES. ABSTR.
[US/0160-3604]
ENERGY RESEARCH ABSTRACTS.
(*Continues* ERDA Energy Research Abstracts.)

ENG. INDEX
[US/0739-4624]
ENGINEERING INDEX (1919), THE.
(*Continued by* Engineering Index Annual.)

ENG. INDEX ANNU.
[US/0360-8557]
ENGINEERING INDEX ANNUAL.
(*Continues* Engineering Index (New York, N.Y. : 1919).)

ENG. INDEX BIOENG. ABSTR.
[US/0736-6213]
ENGINEERING INDEX BIOENGINEERING ABSTRACTS.
(*Continued by* Engineering Index Bioengineering and Biotechnology Abstracts.)

ENG. INDEX ENERGY ABSTR.
[US/0093-8408]
ENGINEERING INDEX ENERGY ABSTRACTS.
***Refer to Engineering Index Annual for a complete source list.

ENG. INDEX MON.
[US/0742-1974]
ENGINEERING INDEX MONTHLY.
(*Continues* Engineering Index Monthly and Author Index.)
***Refer to Engineering Index Annual for a complete source list.

ENG. INDEX MON. AUTHOR INDEX
[US/0162-3036]
ENGINEERING INDEX MONTHLY AND AUTHOR INDEX.
(*Continued by* Engineering Index Monthly (1984).)

ENG. MATER. ABSTR.
[US/0951-9998]
ENGINEERED MATERIALS ABSTRACTS.

ENTOMOL. ABSTR.
[US/0013-8924]
ENTOMOLOGY ABSTRACTS.

ENVIRO ENERGYLINE PLUS
[US/1076-6464]
ENVIRO/ENERGYLINE ABSTRACTS PLUS.
(*Continued by* Environment Abstracts.)
***Refer to Environment Abstracts and Energy Infomation Abstracts for complete source list.

ENVIRON.
[CN/0709-8847]
ENVIRONNEMENT (MONTREAL).
(*Continues* Journal l'Environnement.)

ENVIRON. ABSTR.
[US/0093-3287]
ENVIRONMENT ABSTRACTS.
(*Continues* Environment Information Access; *Absorbed* Acid Rain Abstracts.)

ENVIRON. ABSTR.
[US]
ENVIRONMENT ABSTRACTS [COMPUTER FILE].
(*Continues* Enviro/Energyline Abstracts Plus.)
***Refer to Environment Abstracts and Energy Infomation Abstracts for complete source list.

ENVIRON. ABSTR. ANNU.
[US/0000-1198]
ENVIRONMENT ABSTRACTS ANNUAL.
(*Absorbed* Environment Index *and* Acid Raid Abstracts Annual.)
***Refer to Environment Abstracts for complete source list.

ENVIRON. ENG. ABSTR.
[US/1063-7346]
ENVIRONMENTAL ENGINEERING ABSTRACTS.
(Ceased)

ENVIRON. INDEX
[US/0090-791X]
ENVIRONMENT INDEX.
(*Absorbed by* Environment Abstracts Annual.)

INDEXES/ABSTRACTS TABLE

ENVIRON. PERIOD. BIBLIOGR.
[US/0145-3815]
ENVIRONMENTAL PERIODICALS BIBLIOGRAPHY.
(*Continues* Environmental Periodicals.)

EP COLLECT.
[US]
EP COLLECTION. [COMPUTER FILE].

ERGON. ABSTR.
[UK/0046-2446]
ERGONOMICS ABSTRACTS.
(*Continues* Ergonomics Abstracts (1959).)

ETHNIC STUD. BIBLIOGR.
[US/0149-1555]
ETHNIC STUDIES BIBLIOGRAPHY.
(Ceased)

ETHNOARTS INDEX
[US/0893-0120]
ETHNOARTS INDEX.
(*Continues* Tribal Arts Review.)

EUR. RES.
[NE/0304-4297]
EUROPEAN RESEARCH.
(*Continued by* Marketing and Research Today.)

EXCEPT. CHILD EDUC. RESOUR.
[US/0160-4309]
EXCEPTIONAL CHILD EDUCATION RESOURCES.
(*Continues* Exceptional Child Education Abstracts.)

EXCEPT. CHILD EDUC. ABSTR.
[US/0014-4010]
EXCEPTIONAL CHILD EDUCATION ABSTRACTS.
(*Continued by* Exceptional Child Education Resources.)

EXCEPT. HUM. EXP.
[US/1053-4768]
EXCEPTIONAL HUMAN EXPERIENCE.
(*Continues* Parapsychology Abstracts International.)

EXCERPTA MED. LIST J. ABSTR.
[US]
EXCERPTA MEDICA : LIST OF JOURNALS ABSTRACTED.
(*Continued by* List of Journals Abstracted.)

EXCERPTA MED., SECT. 06B, ARTHR. RHEUM.
[NE]
EXCERPTA MEDICA. SECTION 06B. ARTHRITIS AND RHEUMATISM.
(Ceased)

EXCERPTA MEDICA., SECT. 1, ANATOM. ANTHROPOL. EMBRYOL. HISTOL.
[NE/0014-4053]
EXCERPTA MEDICA. SECTION 1. ANATOMY, ANTHROPOLOGY, EMBRYOLOGY AND HISTOLOGY.
***Refer to EMBASE [Online Database] for complete source list.

EXCERPTA MED., SECT. 2, PHYSIOL.
[NE/0367-1089]
EXCERPTA MEDICA. SECTION 2A. PHYSIOLOGY.
(*Continues* Excerpta Medica. Section 2A. Physiology.)
***Refer to EMBASE [Online Database] for complete source list.

EXCERPTA MED., SECT. 2A, PHYSIOL.
[NE/0367-1089]
EXCERPTA MEDICA. SECTION 2A. PHYSIOLOGY.
(*Continued by* Excerpta Medica. Section 2. Physiology.)

EXCERPTA MED., SECT. 3, ENDOCRINOL.
[NE/0014-407X]
EXCERPTA MEDICA. SECTION 3. ENDOCRINOLOGY.
(*Continues* Excerpta Medica. Section 3. Endocrinology, Experimental and Clinical.)
***Refer to EMBASE [Online Database] for complete source list.

EXCERPTA MED., SECT. 4, MICROBIOL.
[NE/0167-4285]
EXCERPTA MEDICA. SECTION 4. MICROBIOLOGY.
(*Continued by* Excerpta Medica. Section 4, Microbiology, Bacteriology, Mycology, Parasitology, and Virology.)

EXCERPTA MED., SECT. 4, MICROBIOL. BACTERIOL. MYCOL. PARASITOL. VIROL.
[NE]
EXCERPTA MEDICA. SECTION 4. MICROBIOLOGY, BACTERIOLOGY, MYCOLOGY, PARASITOLOGY, AND VIROLOGY.
(*Continues* Excerpta Medica. Section 4, Microbiology; **Absorbed** Virology.)
***Refer to EMBASE [Online Database] for complete source list.

EXCERPTA MED., SECT. 5, GEN. PATHOL. PATHOLOGIC. ANAT.
[NE/0014-4096]
EXCERPTA MEDICA. SECTION 5. GENERAL PATHOLOGY AND PATHOLOGICAL ANATOMY.
***Refer to EMBASE [Online Database] for complete source list.

EXCERPTA MED., SECT. 6, INTERN. MED.
[NE/0014-410X]
EXCERPTA MEDICA. SECTION 6. INTERNAL MEDICINE.
***Refer to EMBASE [Online Database] for complete source list.

EXCERPTA MED., SECT. 7, PEDIATR. PEDIATR. SUR.
[NE/0373-6512]
EXCERPTA MEDICA. SECTION 7. PEDIATRICS AND PEDIATRIC SURGERY.
(*Continues* Excerpta Medica. Section 7. Pediatrics.)
***Refer to EMBASE [Online Database] for complete source list.

EXCERPTA MED., SECT. 8, NEUROL. NEUROSURG.
[NE/0014-4126]
EXCERPTA MEDICA. SECTION 8. NEUROLOGY AND NEUROSURGERY.
(*Continues* Excerpta Medica. Section 8A. Neurology and Neurosurgery.)
***Refer to EMBASE [Online Database] for complete source list.

EXCERPTA MED., SECT. 8A, NEUROL. NEUROSURG.
[NE/0014-4126]
EXCERPTA MEDICA. SECTION 8A. NEUROLOGY AND NEUROSURGERY.
(*Continued by* Excerpta Medica. Section 8. Neurology and Neurosurgery.)

EXCERPTA MED., SECT. 9, SURG.
[NE/0014-4134]
EXCERPTA MEDICA. SECTION 9. SURGERY.
(*Continued by* Excerpta Medica. Section 28, Urology.)

EXCERPTA MED., SECT. 9B, ORTHO. TRAUMATOL.
[NE]
EXCERPTA MEDICA. SECTION 9B. ORTHOPAEDICS AND TRAUMATOLOGY.
(*Continued by* Orthopedic Surgery.)

EXCERPTA MED., SECT. 10, OBSTETR. GYNECOL.
[NE/0014-4142]
EXCERPTA MEDICA. SECTION 10. OBSTETRICS AND GYNECOLOGY.
***Refer to EMBASE [Online Database] for complete source list.

EXCERPTA MED., SECT. 12, OPHTHALMOL.
[NE/0014-4169]
EXCERPTA MEDICA. SECTION 12. OPHTHALMOLOGY.
***Refer to EMBASE [Online Database] for complete source list.

EXCERPTA MED., SECT. 13, DERMATOL.
[NE/0014-4177]
EXCERPTA MEDICA. SECTION 13. DERMATOLOGY AND VENEREOLOGY.
***Refer to EMBASE [Online Database] for complete source list.

EXCERPTA MED., SECT. 14, RADIOL.
[NE/0014-4185]
EXCERPTA MEDICA. SECTION 14. RADIOLOGY.
***Refer to EMBASE [Online Database] for complete source list.

EXCERPTA MED., SECT. 16, CANCER
[NE/0014-4207]
EXCERPTA MEDICA. SECTION 16. CANCER.
(*Continues* Cancer, Experimental and Clinical.)
***Refer to EMBASE [Online Database] for complete source list.

EXCERPTA MED., SECT. 17, PUBL. HEALTH SOC. MED EPIDEM.
[NE]
EXCERPTA MEDICA. SECTION 17. PUBLIC HEALTH, SOCIAL MEDICINE AND EPIDEMIOLOGY.
(*Continues* Excerpta Medica. Section 17, Public Health, Social Medicine and Hygiene.)
***Refer to EMBASE [Online Database] for complete source list.

EXCERPTA MED., SECT. 17, PUBL. HEALTH SOC. MED. HYG.
[NE/0014-4215]
EXCERPTA MEDICA. SECTION 17. PUBLIC HEALTH, SOCIAL MEDICINE AND HYGIENE.
(*Continued by* Excerpta Medica. Section 17, Public Health, Social Medicine and Epidemiology.)

EXCERPTA MED., SECT. 18, CARDIOVASC. DISEAS. CARDIOVASC. SURG.
[NE/0014-4223]
EXCERPTA MEDICA. SECTION 18. CARDIOVASCULAR DISEASES AND CARDIOVASCULAR SURGERY.
(*Continues* Excerpta Medica. Section 18. Cardiovascular Diseases.)
***Refer to EMBASE [Online Database] for complete source list.

INDEXES/ABSTRACTS TABLE

EXCERPTA MED., SECT. 19, REHABIL. PHYS. MED.
[NE/0014-4231]
EXCERPTA MEDICA. SECTION 19. REHABILITATION AND PHYSICAL MEDICINE.
(***Continues*** Excerpta Medica. Section 19. Rehabilitation.)
***Refer to EMBASE [Online Database] for complete source list.

EXCERPTA MED., SECT. 20, GERONTOL. GERIATR.
[NE/0014-424X]
EXCERPTA MEDICA. SECTION 20. GERONTOLOGY AND GERIATRICS.
***Refer to EMBASE [Online Database] for complete source list.

EXCERPTA MED., SECT. 21, DEVELOP. BIOL. TERATOL.
[NE/0014-4258]
EXCERPTA MEDICA. SECTION 21. DEVELOPMENTAL BIOLOGY AND TERATOLOGY.
(***Continues*** Excerpta Medica. Section 21. Human Developmental Biology.)
***Refer to EMBASE [Online Database] for complete source list.

EXCERPTA MED., SECT. 22, HUMAN GENET.
[NE/0014-4266]
EXCERPTA MEDICA. SECTION 22. HUMAN GENETICS.
(***Continues*** Human Genetics Abstracts.)
***Refer to EMBASE [Online Database] for complete source list.

EXCERPTA MED., SECT. 23, NUCL. MED.
[NE/0014-4274]
EXCERPTA MEDICA. SECTION 23. NUCLEAR MEDICINE.
***Refer to EMBASE [Online Database] for complete source list.

EXCERPTA MED., SECT. 24, ANESTHESIOL.
[NE/0014-4282]
EXCERPTA MEDICA. SECTION 24. ANESTHESIOLOGY.
***Refer to EMBASE [Online Database] for complete source list.

EXCERPTA MED., SECT. 25, HEMATOL.
[NE/0014-4290]
EXCERPTA MEDICA. SECTION 25. HEMATOLOGY.
***Refer to EMBASE [Online Database] for complete source list.

EXCERPTA MED., SECT. 26, IMMUNOL. SEROL. TRANSPLANT.
[NE/0014-4304]
EXCERPTA MEDICA. SECTION 26. IMMUNOLOGY, SEROLOGY AND TRANSPLANTATION.
(***Supersedes in part*** Excerpta Medica. Section 4, Medical Microbiology, Immunology and Serology.)
***Refer to EMBASE [Online Database] for complete source list.

EXCERPTA MED., SECT. 27, BIOPHYS. BIOENG. MED. INSTRUMEN.
[NE/0014-4312]
EXCERPTA MEDICA. SECTION 27. BIOPHYSICS, BIOENGINEERING AND MEDICAL INSTRUMENTATION.
(***Continues*** Excerpta Medica. Section 27. Medical Instrumentation.)
***Refer to EMBASE [Online Database] for complete source list.

EXCERPTA MED., SECT. 28, UROL.
[NE]
EXCERPTA MEDICA. SECTION 28. UROLOGY.
(***Continued by*** Excerpta Medica. Section 28, Urology and Nephrology.)

EXCERPTA MED., SECT. 28, UROL. NEPHROL.
[NE/0014-4320]
EXCERPTA MEDICA. SECTION 28. UROLOGY AND NEPHROLOGY.
(***Continues*** Excerpta Medica. Section 28, Urology.)
***Refer to EMBASE [Online Database] for complete source list.

EXCERPTA MED., SECT. 29, CLIN. BIOCHEM.
[NE/0300-5372]
EXCERPTA MEDICA. SECTION 29. CLINICAL BIOCHEMISTRY.
(***Continues*** Excerpta Medica. Section 29. Biochemistry.)
***Refer to EMBASE [Online Database] for complete source list.

EXCERPTA MED., SECT. 30, CLIN. EXPER. PHARMACOL.
[NE]
EXCERPTA MEDICA. SECTION 30. CLINICAL AND EXPERIMENTAL PHARMACOLOGY.
(***Formed by the union of*** Excerpta Medica. Section 30, Pharmacology ***and*** Excerpta Medica. Section 130, Clinical Pharmacology.)
***Refer to EMBASE [Online Database] for complete source list.

EXCERPTA MED., SECT. 30, PHARMACOL.
[IE/0167-9643]
EXCERPTA MEDICA. SECTION 30. PHARMACOLOGY.
(***Continued in part by*** Excerpta Medica. Section 130, Clinical Pharmacology; ***Merged into*** Excerpta Medica. Section 30. Clinical and Experimental Pharmacology.)
***Refer to EMBASE [Online Database] for complete source list.

EXCERPTA MED., SECT. 32, PSYCH.
[NE/0014-4363]
EXCERPTA MEDICA. SECTION 32. PSYCHIATRY.
(***Continues*** Excerpta Medica. Section 8B, Psychiatry.)
***Refer to EMBASE [Online Database] for complete source list.

EXCERPTA MED., SECT. 35, OCCUPAT. HEALTH INDUSTR. MED.
[NE/0014-4398]
EXCERPTA MEDICA. SECTION 35. OCCUPATIONAL HEALTH AND INDUSTRIAL MEDICINE.
***Refer to EMBASE [Online Database] for complete source list.

EXCERPTA MED., SECT. 36, HEALTH POLICY ECON. MANAG.
[NE]
EXCERPTA MEDICA. SECTION 36. HEALTH POLICY, ECONOMICS, AND MANAGEMENT.
(***Continues*** Health Economics and Hospital Management.)
***Refer to EMBASE [Online Database] for complete source list.

EXCERPTA MED., SECT. 37, DRUG LIT. INDEX
[NE/0167-9171]
EXCERPTA MEDICA. SECTION 37. DRUG LITERATURE INDEX.
(***Continues*** Drug Literature Index.)

EXCERPTA MED., SECT. 38, ADVERSE REACT. TITLES
[NE/0167-9090]
EXCERPTA MEDICA. SECTION 38. ADVERSE REACTIONS TITLES.
(***Continues*** Adverse Reactions Titles.)
***Refer to EMBASE [Online Database] for complete source list.

EXCERPTA MED., SECT. 40, DRUG DEPEND. ALCOHOL ABUSE ALCOHOL.
[NE/0304-4041]
EXCERPTA MEDICA. SECTION 40. DRUG DEPENDENCE, ALCOHOL ABUSE, AND ALCOHOLISM.
(***Continues*** Excerpta Medica. Section 40, Drug Dependence.)
***Refer to EMBASE [Online Database] for complete source list.

EXCERPTA MED., SECT. 46, ENVIRON. HEALTH POLLUT. CONT.
[NE/0300-5194]
EXCERPTA MEDICA. SECTION 46. ENVIRONMENTAL HEALTH AND POLLUTION CONTROL.
(***Continues*** Environmental Health and Pollution Control.)
***Refer to EMBASE [Online Database] for complete source list.

EXCERPTA MED., SECT. 50, EPILEP. ABSTR.
[NE/0303-8459]
EXCERPTA MEDICA. SECTION 50. EPILEPSY ABSTRACTS.
(***Continues*** Epilepsy Abstracts.)
***Refer to EMBASE [Online Database] for complete source list.

EXCERPTA MED., SECT. 52, TOXICOL.
[NE/0167-8353]
EXCERPTA MEDICA. SECTION 52. TOXICOLOGY.
(***Continues in part*** Excerpta Medica. Section 30, Pharmacology and Toxicology.)
***Refer to EMBASE [Online Database] for complete source list.

EXCERPTA MED., SECT. 54, AIDS
[NE/0922-6532]
EXCERPTA MEDICA. SECTION 54. AIDS (ACQUIRED IMMUNE DEFICIENCY SYNDROME).
(Ceased)

EXCERPTA MED., SECT. 65, CANCER IMMUNOL. LIT. INDEX
[NE/0304-3789]
EXCERPTA MEDICA. SECTION 65. CANCER IMMUNOLOGY. LITERATURE INDEX.
***Refer to EMBASE [Online Database] for complete source list.

EXCERPTA MED., SECT. 130, CLINIC. PHARMACOL.
[NE/0921-4496]
EXCERPTA MEDICA. SECTION 130. CLINICAL PHARMACOLOGY.
(***Separated from*** Excerpta Medica. Section 30, Pharmacology.)

INDEXES/ABSTRACTS TABLE

EXCERPTA MED., SECT. 151, MYCOBACTER. DISEAS. LEPROSY TUBERCUL. RELATED SUBJ.
[NE/0168-8944]
EXCERPTA MEDICA. SECTION 151. MYCOBACTERIAL DISEASES--LEPROSY, TUBERCULOSIS, AND RELATED SUBJECTS.
(*Continues* Excerpta Medica. Section 51, Mycobacterial Diseases--Leprosy, Tuberculosis, and Related Subjects.)

EXPAND. ACAD. INDEX
[US]
EXPANDED ACADEMIC INDEX [COMPUTER FILE].

F & S INDEX CORP. IND.
[US/0014-567X]
F & S INDEX OF CORPORATIONS AND INDUSTRIES.
(*Continued by* Predicasts F & S Index United States (Annual Edition).)

F & S INDEX PLUS TEXT, INT.
[US/1065-5956]
F & S INDEX PLUS TEXT. INTERNATIONAL.

F & S INDEX PLUS TEXT, U.S.
[US/1065-5964]
F & S INDEX PLUS TEXT. UNITED STATES.
***Refer to F&S Index Plus Text International for complete source list.

FABA BEAN ABSTR.
[UK/0260-8456]
FABA BEAN ABSTRACTS.
(Ceased)

FAMLI, FAM. MED. LIT. INDEX
[CN/0227-2393]
FAMLI : FAMILY MEDICINE LITERATURE INDEX.
(Ceased)

FARM GARD. INDEX
[US/0736-9980]
FARM & GARDEN INDEX.
(Ceased)

FDA CLIN. EXP. ABSTR.
[US/0429-9442]
FDA CLINICAL EXPERIENCE ABSTRACTS.
(Ceased)

FED. PRINT
[US/0891-2769]
FED IN PRINT.
(*Continued by* Fed in Print: Economics and Banking Topics.)

FED. PRINT ECON. BANK. TOP.
[US]
FED IN PRINT: ECONOMICS AND BANKING TOPICS.
(*Continues* Fed in Print: Business and Banking Topics.)

FED. TAX ARTIC.
[US]
FEDERAL TAX ARTICLES: INCOME, ESTATE, GIFT, EXCISE, EMPLOYMENT TAXES.

FERT. ABSTR.
[US/0015-0290]
FERTILIZER ABSTRACTS.
(Ceased)

FIELD CROP ABSTR.
[UK/0015-069X]
FIELD CROP ABSTRACTS.

FILM LIT. INDEX
[US/0093-6758]
FILM LITERATURE INDEX.

FISH REV.
[US/1042-6299]
FISHERIES REVIEW (FORT COLLINS, COLO.).
(*Continues* Sport Fishery Abstracts; *Absorbed* Fish Health News.)

FLUID ABSTR. CIVIL ENG.
[UK/0962-7170]
FLUID ABSTRACTS. CIVIL ENGINEERING.
(*Formed by the union of* Civil Engineering Hydraulics Abstracts; Industrial Aerodynamics Abstracts; Offshore Engineering Abstracts *and* World Ports & Harbours Abstracts (Incorporating International Dredging Abstracts).)

FLUID ABSTR. PROC. ENG.
[UK/0962-7162]
FLUID ABSTRACTS. PROCESS ENGINEERING.
(*Formed by the union of* Fluid Flow Measurements Abstracts; Fluid Power Abstracts; Fluid Sealing Abstracts; Pipelines Abstracts; Pumps and Other Fluids Machinery Abstracts; Solid-Liquid Flow Abstracts; Computer-Aided Process Control Abstracts *and* Mixing and Separation Technology Abstracts.)

FLUIDEX
[UK]
FLUIDEX [ONLINE DATABASE].

FOOD SCI. TECHNOL. ABSTR.
[UK/0015-6574]
FOOD SCIENCE AND TECHNOLOGY ABSTRACTS.

FOODS ADLIBRA
[US/0146-9304]
FOODS ADLIBRA (1975).

FOR. ABSTR.
[UK/0015-7538]
FORESTRY ABSTRACTS.

FOR. PROD. ABSTR.
[UK/0140-4784]
FOREST PRODUCTS ABSTRACTS.

FOREIGN LANG. INDEX
[US/0048-5810]
FOREIGN LANGUAGE INDEX.
(*Continued by* PAIS Foreign Language Index.)

FRESH. AQUA. CONTENTS TABLES
[IT]
FRESHWATER AND AQUACULTURE CONTENTS TABLES. ACTUALITES DES EAUX DOUCES ET DE L'AQUACULTURE.

FUNK & SCOTT ANNU. INDEX CORP. LIB.
[US]
FUNK & SCOTT ANNUAL INDEX OF CORPORATIONS & INDUSTRIES, THE.
(*Continued by* F & S Index of Corporations and Industries.)

FUNK & SCOTT INDEX CORP. IND.
[US/0532-8705]
FUNK & SCOTT INDEX OF CORPORATIONS AND INDUSTRIES.
(*Continued by* Funk & Scott Annual Index of Corporations & Industries.)

FUT. SURV.
[US/0190-3241]
FUTURE SURVEY.
(*Continues* Public Policy Book Forecast.)

GARDEN LIT.
[US/1061-3722]
GARDEN LITERATURE.

GAS ABSTR.
[US/0016-4844]
GAS ABSTRACTS.

GASTROENTEROL. ABSTR. CITATIONS
[US/0016-5093]
GASTROENTEROLOGY: ABSTRACTS & CITATIONS.
(Ceased)

GEN. BUSINESSFILE
[US]
GENERAL BUSINESSFILE [COMPUTER FILE].

GEN. PERIOD. INDEX
[US]
GENERAL PERIODICALS INDEX [COMPUTER FILE].

GEN. PERIOD. ONDISC
[US/1064-8380]
GENERAL PERIODICALS ONDISC (RESEARCH 1 ED.).
***Refer to Newspaper and Periodical Abstracts for complete source list.

GEN. SCI. INDEX
[US/0162-1963]
GENERAL SCIENCE INDEX.

GEN. SCI. SOURCE
[US/1073-1954]
GENERAL SCIENCE SOURCE.

GENEALOGICAL PERIOD. ANNU. INDEX
[US/0072-0593]
GENEALOGICAL PERIODICAL ANNUAL INDEX.

GENET. ABSTR.
[US/0016-674X]
GENETICS ABSTRACTS.

GEO ABSTR.
[UK]
GEO ABSTRACTS.
(*Continued by* Geographical Abstracts : Physical Geography; Geographical Abstracts. Human Geography.)

GEOGR. ABSTR.
[UK]
GEOGRAPHICAL ABSTRACTS.
(*Continued by* Geo Abstracts.)

GEOGR. ABSTR. HUMAN GEOGR.
[UK/0953-9611]
GEOGRAPHICAL ABSTRACTS. HUMAN GEOGRAPHY.
(*Formed by the union of* Geographical Abstracts. C, Economic Geography (1986); Geographical Abstracts. D, Social and Historical Geography *and* Geographical Abstracts. F, Regional and Community Planning.)

GEOGR. ABSTR. PHYS. GEOGR.
[UK/0954-0504]
GEOGRAPHICAL ABSTRACTS : PHYSICAL GEOGRAPHY.
(*Formed by the union of* Geographical Abstracts. A, Landforms and the Quaternary; Geographical Abstracts. B, Climatology and Hydrology; Geographical Abstracts. E, Sedimentology *and* Geographical Abstracts. G, Remote Sensing, Photogrammetry, and Cartography.)

GEOL. ABSTR.
[UK/0954-0512]
GEOLOGICAL ABSTRACTS.
(*Formed by the union of* Geological Abstracts. Economic Geology; Geological Abstracts. Geophysics & Tectonics Abstracts; Geological Abstracts. Palaeontology & Stratigraphy *and* Geological Abstracts. Sedimentary Geology.)

INDEXES/ABSTRACTS TABLE

GEOL. ABSTR. ECON. GEOL.
[UK]
GEOLOGICAL ABSTRACTS. ECONOMIC GEOLOGY.
(*Merged with* Geological Abstracts. Geophysics & Tectonics Abstracts; Geological Abstracts. Palaeontology & Stratigraphy *and* Geological Abstracts. Sedimentary Abstracts *to form* Geological Abstracts.)

GEOL. ABSTR. GEOPHYS. TECTON.
[UK/0262-0847]
GEOLOGICAL ABSTRACTS. GEOPHYSICS & TECTONICS.
(*Merged with* Geological Abstracts. Economic Geology; Geological Abstracts. Palaeontology & Stratigraphy *and* Geological Abstracts. Sedimentary Geology *to form* Geological Abstracts.)

GEOL. ABSTR. PALAEON. STRAT.
[UK/0268-8018]
GEOLOGICAL ABSTRACTS. PALAEONTOLOGY & STRATIGRAPHY.
(*Merged with* Geological Abstracts. Economic Geology; Geological Abstracts. Geophysics & Tectonics Abstracts *and* Geological Abstracts. Sedimentary Geology *to form* Geological Abstracts.)

GEOL. ABSTR. SEDIMEN. GEOL.
[UK/0268-8026]
GEOLOGICAL ABSTRACTS. SEDIMENTARY GEOLOGY.
(*Merged with* Geological Abstracts. Economic Geology; Geological Abstracts. Geophysics & Tectonics Abstracts *and* Geological Abstracts. Palaeontology & Stratigraphy *to form* Geological Abstracts.)

GEOPHYS. ABSTR.
[UK/0309-4332]
GEOPHYSICAL ABSTRACTS.
(*Continued by* Geological Abstracts. Geophysics & Tectonics Abstracts.)

GEOREF
[US/0197-7482]
GEOREF (CD-ROM).

GEOSCI. ABSTR.
[US/0435-5628]
GEOSCIENCE ABSTRACTS.
(*Supersedes* Geological Abstracts.)

GEOSCI. DOC.
[UK/0016-8483]
GEOSCIENCE DOCUMENTATION.

GEOTECH. ABSTR.
[US/0016-8491]
GEOTECHNICAL ABSTRACTS.
(Ceased)

GERONTOL. ABSTR.
[US/0736-4342]
GERONTOLOGICAL ABSTRACTS.
(Ceased)

GLOB. VIEWS
[US/1078-3598]
GLOBAL VIEWS [COMPUTER FILE].

GRAPH. ARTS ABSTR.
[US/0017-3282]
GRAPHIC ARTS ABSTRACTS.
(*Continued by* Abstracts (Graphic Arts Technical Foundation).)

GRAPH. ARTS BULL. INST. PAP. SCI. TECHNOL.
[US/1064-9638]
GRAPHIC ARTS BULLETIN OF THE INSTITUTE OF PAPER SCIENCE AND TECHNOLOGY.
(*Continues* Graphic Arts Literature Abstracts.)

GRAPH. ARTS LIT. ABSTR.
[US/0090-8207]
GRAPHIC ARTS LITERATURE ABSTRACTS.
(*Continued by* Graphic Arts Bulletin of the Institute of Paper Science and Technology.)

GUIDE PERFORM. ARTS
[US/0072-873X]
GUIDE TO THE PERFORMING ARTS.
(*Absorbed* Guide to Dance Periodicals.)

GUIDE REV. BOOKS HISP. AM.
[US/0716-0348]
GUIDE TO REVIEWS OF BOOKS FROM AND ABOUT HISPANIC AMERICA.
(Ceased)

GUIDE SOC. SCI. RELIG.
[US/1054-0946]
GUIDE TO SOCIAL SCIENCE AND RELIGION.
(*Continues* Guide to Social Science and Religion in Periodical Literature.)

GUIDE SOC. SCI. RELIG. PERIOD. LIT.
[US/0017-5307]
GUIDE TO SOCIAL SCIENCE AND RELIGION IN PERIODICAL LITERATURE.
(*Continued by* Guide to Social Science and Religion.)

HEALTH DEVICES ALERTS
[US/0163-0458]
HEALTH DEVICES ALERTS.

HEALTH INDEX
[US]
HEALTH INDEX [COMPUTER FILE].

HEALTH PERIOD. DATABASE
[US]
HEALTH PERIODICALS DATABASE [ONLINE DATABASE].

HEALTH PLAN. ADMINIS.
[US/1065-0679]
HEALTH PLANNING AND ADMINISTRATION.

HEALTH SAF. SCI. ABSTR.
[US/0892-9351]
HEALTH AND SAFETY SCIENCE ABSTRACTS.
(*Continues* Safety Science Abstracts Journal.)

HEALTH SERV. ABSTR.
[UK/0268-0459]
HEALTH SERVICE ABSTRACTS.
(*Formed by the union of* Current Literature on Health Services; Current Literature on General Medical Practice *and* Hospital Abstracts.)

HEALTH SOURCE
[US/1063-9810]
HEALTH SOURCE (PEABODY, MASS.).

HEALTH SOURCE PLUS
[US]
HEALTH SOURCE PLUS. [COMPUTER FILE].

HELMINTHOL. ABSTR.
[UK/0957-6789]
HELMINTHOLOGICAL ABSTRACTS.
(*Continues* Helminthological Abstracts. Series A, Animal and Human Helminthology.)

HELMINTHOL. ABSTR. SER. A, ANIM. HUM. HELMINTHOL.
[UK/0300-8339]
HELMINTHOLOGICAL ABSTRACTS. SERIES A, ANIMAL AND HUMAN HELMINTHOLOGY.
(*Continued by* Helminthological Abstracts.)

HELMINTHOL. ABSTR. SER. B, PLANT NEMATOLOGY
[UK/0300-8320]
HELMINTHOLOGICAL ABSTRACTS. SERIES B, PLANT NEMATOLOGY.
(*Continued by* Nematological Abstracts.)

HERB. ABSTR.
[UK/0018-0602]
HERBAGE ABSTRACTS.
(*Continued by* Grasslands and Forage Abstracts.)

HIGH. EDUC. ABSTR.
[US/0748-4364]
HIGHER EDUCATION ABSTRACTS.
(*Continues* College Student Personnel Abstracts.)

HIGHW. RES. ABSTR.
[US/0018-1730]
HIGHWAY RESEARCH ABSTRACTS.
(*Continued by* Transportation Research Abstracts.)

HIGHW. RES. ABSTR.
[US/1050-0804]
HIGHWAY RESEARCH ABSTRACTS (1990).
(*Continues* HRIS Abstracts.)

HILITES
[US]
HILITES DATABASE [ONLINE DATABASE].

HISP. AM. PERIOD. INDEX
[US/0270-8558]
HISPANIC AMERICAN PERIODICALS INDEX (LOS ANGELES, CALIF.).

HIST. ABSTR.
[US/0018-2435]
HISTORICAL ABSTRACTS.
(*Split into* Historical Abstracts. Part A, Modern History Abstracts *and* Historical Abstracts. Part B, Twentieth Century Abstracts.)

HIST. ABSTR., PART A, MOD. HIST. ABSTR.
[US/0363-2717]
HISTORICAL ABSTRACTS. PART A, MODERN HISTORY ABSTRACTS.
(*Continues in part* Historical Abstracts.)
***Refer to America: History and Life for complete source list.

HIST. ABSTR., PART B, TWENT. CENTURY ABSTR.
[US/0363-2725]
HISTORICAL ABSTRACTS. PART B, TWENTIETH CENTURY ABSTRACTS.
(*Continues in part* Historical Abstracts.)
***Refer to America: History and Life for complete source list.

HIST. SOURCE
[US/1063-9799]
HISTORY SOURCE.
(*Merged into* Humanities Source CD-ROM.)

HOMEWORK HELP.
[US]
HOMEWORK HELPER [COMPUTER FILE].

HORTIC. ABSTR.
[UK/0018-5280]
HORTICULTURAL ABSTRACTS.

HOSPIT. ABSTR.
[UK/0018-5507]
HOSPITAL ABSTRACTS.
(*Merged with* Current Literature on Health Services *and* Current Literature on General Medical Practice *to form* Health Service Abstracts.)

INDEXES/ABSTRACTS TABLE

HOSPIT. HEALTH ADMIN. INDEX
[US/1077-1719]
HOSPITAL AND HEALTH ADMINISTRATION INDEX.
(*Continues* Hospital Literature Index.)

HOSPIT. LIT. INDEX
[US/0018-5736]
HOSPITAL LITERATURE INDEX.
(*Continued by* Hospital and Health Administration Index.)

HOSPIT. MANAGE. REV.
[US/0737-903X]
HOSPITAL MANAGEMENT REVIEW.

HRIS ABSTR.
[US/0017-6222]
HRIS ABSTRACTS.
(*Continued by* Highway Research Abstracts (Washington, D.C. : 1990).)

HTFS DIG.
[UK/0952-2654]
HTFS DIGEST (1987).
(*Continues* Heat Transfer & Fluid Flow Digest; *Absorbed* Fouling Prevention Research Digest.)

HUM. GENOME ABSTR.
[US/1045-4470]
HUMAN GENOME ABSTRACTS.

HUM. RESOUR. ABSTR.
[US/0099-2453]
HUMAN RESOURCES ABSTRACTS.
(*Continues* Poverty and Human Resources Abstracts.)

HUM. RIGHTS INTERN. REP.
[US/0275-049X]
HUMAN RIGHTS INTERNET REPORTER.
(*Continues* Human Rights Internet Newsletter.)

HUMANIT. INDEX
[US/0095-5981]
HUMANITIES INDEX.
(*Supersedes in part* Social Sciences & Humanities Index.)

HUMANIT. SOURCE
[US/1073-1962]
HUMANITIES SOURCE.
(*Absorbed* History Source CD-ROM.)

HUNGAR. LIBR. INFO. SCI. ABSTR.
[HU/0046-8304]
HUNGARIAN LIBRARY AND INFORMATION SCIENCE ABSTRACTS.

IAG, LIT. AUTO.
[NE/0376-9666]
IAG - LITERATURE ON AUTOMATION.
(*Continued by* New Literature on Automation.)

IMAGING ABSTR.
[US/0896-100X]
IMAGING ABSTRACTS.
(*Continues* Photographic Abstracts.)

IMMUNOL. ABSTR.
[US/0307-112X]
IMMUNOLOGY ABSTRACTS.

IND. ARTS INDEX
[US/0275-1682]
INDUSTRIAL ARTS INDEX.
(*Split into* Business Periodicals Index *and* Applied Science & Technology Index.)

IND. HYG. DIG.
[US/0019-8382]
INDUSTRIAL HYGIENE DIGEST.

INDEX AM. PERIOD. VERSE
[US/0090-9130]
INDEX OF AMERICAN PERIODICAL VERSE.

INDEX BLACK PERIOD.
[US/0899-6253]
INDEX TO BLACK PERIODICALS.
(*Continues* Index to Periodical Articles by and About Blacks.)

INDEX BOOK REV. HUMANIT.
[US/0073-5892]
INDEX TO BOOK REVIEWS IN THE HUMANITIES.
(Ceased)

INDEX BOOK REV. RELIG.
[US/0887-1574]
INDEX TO BOOK REVIEWS IN RELIGION.
(*Continues in part* Religion Index One. Periodicals.)

INDEX BUS. REPORTS
[UK]
INDEX TO BUSINESS REPORTS.
(*Continues* Index to Special Reports in UK Newspapers and Selected Periodicals.)

INDEX CAN. LEG. PERIOD. LIT.
[CN/0316-8891]
INDEX TO CANADIAN LEGAL PERIODICAL LITERATURE.

INDEX CHEM.
[US/0891-6055]
INDEX CHEMICUS (1987).
(*Continues* Current Abstracts of Chemistry and Index Chemicus (Philadelphia, Pa. : 1978).)

INDEX DENT. LIT.
[US/0019-3992]
INDEX TO DENTAL LITERATURE.
(*Continues* Index to Dental Literature in the English Language.)

INDEX ECON. ARTIC. J. COLLECT. VOL.
[US/0536-647X]
INDEX OF ECONOMIC ARTICLES IN JOURNALS AND COLLECTIVE VOLUMES.
(*Formed by the union of* Index of Economic Journals *and* Index of Economic Articles in Collective Volumes.)
***Refer to Journal of Economic Literature for complete source list.

INDEX ECON. J.
[US/0893-9527]
INDEX OF ECONOMIC JOURNALS.
(*Merged with* Index of Economic Articles in Collective Volumes *to form* Index of Economic Articles in Journals and Collective Volumes.)

INDEX FOREIGN LEG. PER.
[UK/0019-400X]
INDEX TO FOREIGN LEGAL PERIODICALS.

INDEX FREE PERIOD.
[US/0147-5630]
INDEX TO FREE PERIODICALS.
(*Merged into* Matter of Fact.)

INDEX IEEE PUBL.
[US/0099-1368]
INDEX TO IEEE PUBLICATIONS.
(*Supersedes* Institute of Electrical and Electronics Engineers. Index to IEEE Periodicals.)

INDEX INF.
[US/0073-5930]
INDEX TO HOW TO DO IT INFORMATION.

INDEX ISLAM.
[UK]
INDEX ISLAMICUS.
(*Continues* Index Islamicus. Supplement.)

INDEX ISLAM. LIT.
[UK]
INDEX OF ISLAMIC LITERATURE.

INDEX JEW. PERIOD.
[US/0019-4050]
INDEX TO JEWISH PERIODICALS.

INDEX LEG. PERIOD.
[US/0019-4077]
INDEX TO LEGAL PERIODICALS.

INDEX LIT. AM. INDIAN
[US/0091-7346]
INDEX TO LITERATURE ON THE AMERICAN INDIAN.
(Ceased)

INDEX MATH. PAP.
[US/0019-3917]
INDEX OF MATHEMATICAL PAPERS.
(Ceased)

INDEX MED.
[US/0019-3879]
INDEX MEDICUS (1960).
(*Continues* Current List of Medical Literature; *Absorbed* Monthly Bibliography of Medical Reviews.)

INDEX NEW Z. PERIOD.
[NZ]
INDEX TO NEW ZEALAND PERIODICALS.
(Ceased)

INDEX PERIOD. ARTIC. BLACKS
[US/0161-8245]
INDEX TO PERIODICAL ARTICLES BY AND ABOUT BLACKS.
(*Continued by* Index to Black Periodicals.)

INDEX PERIOD. ARTIC. NEGROES
[US/0073-5973]
INDEX TO PERIODICAL ARTICLES BY AND ABOUT NEGROES.
(*Continued by* Index to Periodical Articles by and About Blacks.)

INDEX PERIOD. ARTIC. RELAT. LAW
[US/0019-4093]
INDEX TO PERIODICAL ARTICLES RELATED TO LAW.

INDEX PERIOD. LIT. AGING
[US/0882-3405]
INDEX TO PERIODICAL LITERATURE ON AGING.
(*Continues* ARECO's Quarterly Index to Periodical Literature on Aging.)

INDEX PHILIP. PERIOD.
[PH/0073-599X]
INDEX TO PHILIPPINE PERIODICALS.

INDEX RELIG. PERIOD. LIT.
[US/0019-4107]
INDEX TO RELIGIOUS PERIODICAL LITERATURE.
(*Continued by* Religion Index One. Periodicals.)

INDEX SCI. REV.
[US/0360-0661]
INDEX TO SCIENTIFIC REVIEWS.

INDEX U.S. GOV. PERIOD.
[US/0098-4604]
INDEX TO U.S. GOVERNMENT PERIODICALS.
(Ceased)

INDEX VET.
[UK/0019-4123]
INDEX VETERINARIUS.

INDIAN GEOSCI. ABSTR.
[II]
INDIAN GEOSCIENCE ABSTRACTS.

INDEXES/ABSTRACTS TABLE

INDIAN LIBR. SCI. ABSTR.
[II/0019-5790]
INDIAN LIBRARY SCIENCE ABSTRACTS.

INDIAN SCI. ABSTR.
[II/0019-6339]
INDIAN SCIENCE ABSTRACTS.
(*Continues* Bibliography of Scientific Publications of South and South East Asia.)

INDICE AGRICOLA AM. LAT. CARIBE
[CR/0304-0119]
INDICE AGRICOLA DE AMERICA LATINA Y EL CARIBE.
(*Continues* Bibliografia Agricola Latinoamericana y del Caribe.)

INDICE HIST. ESP.
[SP/0537-3522]
INDICE HISTORICO ESPANOL.

INDICE MED. ESP.
[SP]
INDICE MEDICO ESPANOL.

INF. INSTRUC. TECHNOL.
[US]
INFORMATION & INSTRUCTION TECHNOLOGIES.

INF. MANAGE. TECHNOL.
[UK]
INFORMATION MANAGEMENT & TECHNOLOGY.
(*Continues* Information Media & Technology.)

INF. SCI. ABSTR.
[US/0020-0239]
INFORMATION SCIENCE ABSTRACTS.
(*Continues* Documentation Abstracts and Information Science Abstracts.)

INFO-SOUTH ABSTR.
[US/1059-5910]
INFO-SOUTH ABSTRACTS.

INFOBANK
[IO]
INFOBANK.

INFOMAT INT. BUS.
[US]
INFOMAT INTERNATIONAL BUSINESS [ONLINE DATABASE].

INIS ATOMINDEX
[AU/0004-7139]
INIS ATOMINDEX.
(*Continued by* INIS Atomindex.)

INIS ATOMINDEX [MICRO.]
[AU]
INIS ATOMINDEX [MICROFORM].
(*Continues* INIS Atomindex.)

INS. PERIOD. INDEX
[US/0074-073X]
INSURANCE PERIODICALS INDEX.

INSPEC
[UK]
INSPEC [ONLINE DATABASE].

INT. ABSTR. BIOL. SCI.
[UK/0020-5818]
INTERNATIONAL ABSTRACTS OF BIOLOGICAL SCIENCES.
(*Continued by* Current Awareness in Biological Sciences : CABS.)

INT. ABSTR. OPER. RES.
[UK/0020-580X]
INTERNATIONAL ABSTRACTS IN OPERATIONS RESEARCH.

INT. AEROSP. ABSTR.
[US/0020-5842]
INTERNATIONAL AEROSPACE ABSTRACTS.
(*Supersedes in part* Aerospace Engineering.)

INT. BIBLIOGR. BOOK REV.
[GW]
INTERNATIONAL BIBLIOGRAPHY OF BOOK REVIEWS.
(*Continued by* Internationale Bibliographie der Rezensionen Wissenschaftlicher Literatur (Osnabruck, Germany : 1984).)

INT. BIBLIOGR. HIST. RELIG.
[NE/0538-5105]
INTERNATIONAL BIBLIOGRAPHY OF THE HISTORY OF RELIGIONS.
(Ceased)

INT. BIBLIOGR. PERIOD. LIT.
[GW]
INTERNATIONAL BIBLIOGRAPHY OF PERIODICAL LITERATURE.
(*Continued by* Internationale Bibliographie der Zeitschriftenliteratur aus Allen Gebieten des Wissens (Osnabruck, Germany : 1984).)

INT. BIBLIOGR. REZEN. WISSEN. LIT.
[GW/0020-918X]
INTERNATIONALE BIBLIOGRAPHIE DER REZENSIONEN WISSENSCHAFTLICHER LITERATUR.
(*Continues* Internationale Bibliographie der Rezensionen.)

INT. BIBLIOGR. SOCIOL.
[UK/0085-2066]
INTERNATIONAL BIBLIOGRAPHY OF SOCIOLOGY.
(*Continues in part* Current Sociology (Paris, France).)

INT. BIBLIOGR. ZEITSCHRIFTENLITERATUR ALLEN GEBIETEN WISSENS
[GW]
INTERNATIONALE BIBLIOGRAPHIE DER ZEITSCHRIFTENLITERATUR AUS ALLEN GEBIETEN DES WISSENS.
(*Continues* Internationale Bibliographie der Zeitschriftenliteratur.)

INT. BUILD. SERV. ABSTR.
[UK/0140-4237]
INTERNATIONAL BUILDING SERVICES ABSTRACTS.
(*Continues* Thermal Abstracts.)

INT. CIVIL ENG. ABSTR.
[IE/0332-4095]
INTERNATIONAL CIVIL ENGINEERING ABSTRACTS.
(*Continues* Institution of Civil Engineers (Great Britain). I.C.E. Abstracts.)

INT. COPPER INF. BULL.
[UK/0309-2216]
INTERNATIONAL COPPER INFORMATION BULLETIN.
(*Formed by the union of* Selected Abstracts of Recent Literature on Copper and Copper Alloys *and* Kupfer-Mitteilungen.)

INT. DEV. ABSTR.
[UK/0262-0855]
INTERNATIONAL DEVELOPMENT ABSTRACTS.
(*Absorbed* International Development Index.)

INT. EXEC.
[US/0020-6652]
INTERNATIONAL EXECUTIVE.

INT. GUIDE CLASSICAL STUD.
[US/0020-6849]
INTERNATIONAL GUIDE TO CLASSICAL STUDIES.
(*Continues* ABS International Guide to Classical Studies.)

INT. INDEX
[US/0363-0382]
INTERNATIONAL INDEX.
(*Continued by* Social Sciences & Humanities Index.)

INT. INDEX FILM PERIOD.
[US/0000-0388]
INTERNATIONAL INDEX TO FILM PERIODICALS.

INT. INDEX MULTI MEDIA INF.
[US/0094-6818]
INTERNATIONAL INDEX TO MULTI-MEDIA INFORMATION.
(*Continues* Film Review Index.)

INT. INDEX PERIOD.
[US]
INTERNATIONAL INDEX TO PERIODICALS.
(*Continued by* International Index.)

INT. LABOUR DOC.
[SZ/0020-7756]
INTERNATIONAL LABOUR DOCUMENTATION.
(*Continues* International Labour Office. Library. International Labour Documentation.)

INT. NURS. INDEX
[US/0020-8124]
INTERNATIONAL NURSING INDEX.

INT. PACKAG. ABSTR.
[UK/0260-7409]
INTERNATIONAL PACKAGING ABSTRACTS.
(*Continues* PIRA Packaging Abstract.)

INT. PET. ABSTR.
[UK/0309-4944]
INTERNATIONAL PETROLEUM ABSTRACTS.
(*Continued by* International Petroleum Abstracts Incorporating Offshore Abstracts.)

INT. PHARM. ABSTR.
[US/0020-8264]
INTERNATIONAL PHARMACEUTICAL ABSTRACTS.

INT. POLIT. SCI. ABSTR.
[FR/0020-8345]
INTERNATIONAL POLITICAL SCIENCE ABSTRACTS.

INT. POLYM. SCI. TECH.
[UK/0307-174X]
INTERNATIONAL POLYMER SCIENCE AND TECHNOLOGY.
(*Formed by the union of* Soviet Plastics *and* Soviet Rubber Technology.)

INT. RISK CONTROL REV.
[US/0739-389X]
INTERNATIONAL RISK CONTROL REVIEW.
(*Continued by* International Loss Control Review.)

INT. ZEITSCHRIFTENSCHAU BIBELWISS. GRENZGEB.
[GW/0074-9745]
INTERNATIONALE ZEITSCHRIFTENSCHAU FUER BIBELWISSENSCHAFT UND GRENZGEBIETE.

IOWA DRUG INF. SERV.
[US]
IOWA DRUG INFORMATION SERVICE.

IRR. DRAIN. ABSTR.
[UK/0306-7327]
IRRIGATION AND DRAINAGE ABSTRACTS / COMMONWEALTH AGRICULTURAL BUREAUS.

INDEXES/ABSTRACTS TABLE

ISMEC BULL.
[US/0306-0039]
ISMEC BULLETIN.
(*Continued by* ISMEC, Mechanical Engineering Abstracts.)

ISMEC MECH. ENG. ABSTR.
[US/0896-7113]
ISMEC, MECHANICAL ENGINEERING ABSTRACTS.
(*Continued by* Mechanical Engineering Abstracts.)

J. ABSTR. ARTIC. INT. EDUC.
[US/1064-0746]
JOURNAL OF ABSTRACTS (AND ARTICLES) IN INTERNATIONAL EDUCATION.
(*Continues* Journal of Abstracts in International Education.)

J. ABSTR. BR. SHIP RES. ASSOC.
[UK/0141-903X]
JOURNAL OF ABSTRACTS OF THE BRITISH SHIP RESEARCH ASSOCIATION.
(*Continued by* BMT Abstracts.)

J. ABSTR. INT. EDUC.
[US/0094-2383]
JOURNAL OF ABSTRACTS IN INTERNATIONAL EDUCATION.
(*Continued by* Journal of Abstract (and Articles) in International Education.)

J. CONTENTS QUAN. METHODS
[UK/0142-5951]
JOURNAL CONTENTS IN QUANTITATIVE METHODS.

J. ECON. ABSTR.
[US/0364-281X]
JOURNAL OF ECONOMIC ABSTRACTS.
(*Continued by* Journal of Economic Literature.)

J. ECON. LIT.
[US/0022-0515]
JOURNAL OF ECONOMIC LITERATURE.
(*Continues* Journal of Economic Abstracts.)

J. FERROCEMENT
[TH/0125-1759]
JOURNAL OF FERROCEMENT.

J. PLAN. LIT.
[US/0885-4122]
JOURNAL OF PLANNING LITERATURE.

J. WATCH
[US/0896-7210]
JOURNAL WATCH.

JAZZ INDEX
[GW/0344-5399]
JAZZ INDEX.
(Ceased)

JMR ABSTR.
[US/1066-2375]
JMR ABSTRACTS.
(*Absorbed by* MRS Bulletin.)

JR. HIGH MAG. ABSTR.
[US/1045-5493]
JUNIOR HIGH MAGAZINE ABSTRACTS.
(Ceased)

KEY ABSTR., ADV. MATER.
[UK/0950-4753]
KEY ABSTRACTS. ADVANCED MATERIALS.
***Refer to INSPEC [Online Database] for complete source list.

KEY ABSTR., ANTENNAS PROPAG.
[UK/0950-4761]
KEY ABSTRACTS. ANTENNAS & PROPAGATION.
(*Continues in part* Key Abstracts. Communication Technology.)
***Refer to INSPEC [Online Database] for complete source list.

KEY ABSTR., ARTIF. INTELL.
[UK/0950-477X]
KEY ABSTRACTS. ARTIFICIAL INTELLIGENCE.
(*Continues* Key Abstracts. Systems Theory.)
***Refer to INSPEC [Online Database] for complete source list.

KEY ABSTR., BUS. AUTOMAT.
[UK/0954-9153]
KEY ABSTRACTS. BUSINESS AUTOMATION.
(*Continues* IT Focus.)
***Refer to INSPEC [Online Database] for complete source list.

KEY ABSTR., COMPUT. COMMUN. STOR.
[UK/0950-4788]
KEY ABSTRACTS. COMPUTER COMMUNICATIONS & STORAGE.
***Refer to INSPEC [Online Database] for complete source list.

KEY ABSTR., COMPUT. ELECTRON. POWER
[UK/0950-4796]
KEY ABSTRACTS. COMPUTING IN ELECTRONICS AND POWER.
***Refer to INSPEC [Online Database] for complete source list.

KEY ABSTR., ELECTR. MEAS. INSTRUM.
[UK/0307-7977]
KEY ABSTRACTS. ELECTRICAL MEASUREMENTS AND INSTRUMENTATION.
(*Continued by* Key Abstracts. Electronic Instrumentation.)

KEY ABSTR., ELECTRON. CIRC.
[UK/0306-557X]
KEY ABSTRACTS. ELECTRONIC CIRCUITS.
***Refer to INSPEC [Online Database] for complete source list.

KEY ABSTR., ELECTRON. INSTRUM.
[UK/0950-480X]
KEY ABSTRACTS. ELECTRONIC INSTRUMENTATION.
(*Continues* Key Abstracts. Electrical Measurements and Instrumentation.)
***Refer to INSPEC [Online Database] for complete source list.

KEY ABSTR., FACTORY AUTOMAT.
[UK]
KEY ABSTRACTS. FACTORY AUTOMATION.
***Refer to INSPEC [Online Database] for complete source list.

KEY ABSTR., HIGH-TEMP. SUPERCONDUC.
[UK/0953-1262]
KEY ABSTRACTS. HIGH-TEMPERATURE SUPERCONDUCTORS.
***Refer to INSPEC [Online Database] for complete source list.

KEY ABSTR., HUMAN-COMPUT. INTERACT.
[UK]
KEY ABSTRACTS. HUMAN-COMPUTER INTERACTION.
***Refer to INSPEC [Online Database] for complete source list.

KEY ABSTR., MACH. VISION
[UK/0952-7052]
KEY ABSTRACTS. MACHINE VISION.
***Refer to INSPEC [Online Database] for complete source list.

KEY ABSTR., MEAS. PHYS.
[UK/0950-4818]
KEY ABSTRACTS. MEASUREMENTS IN PHYSICS.
(*Continues* Key Abstracts. Physical Measurements and Instrumentation.)
***Refer to INSPEC [Online Database] for complete source list.

KEY ABSTR., MICROELECTRON. PRINT. CIRC.
[UK/0952-7060]
KEY ABSTRACTS. MICROELECTRONICS AND PRINTED CIRCUITS.
***Refer to INSPEC [Online Database] for complete source list.

KEY ABSTR., MICROWAVE TECHNOL.
[UK/0952-7079]
KEY ABSTRACTS. MICROWAVE TECHNOLOGY.
***Refer to INSPEC [Online Database] for complete source list.

KEY ABSTR., NEUR. NETWORKS
[UK]
KEY ABSTRACTS. NEURAL NETWORKS.
***Refer to INSPEC [Online Database] for complete source list.

KEY ABSTR., OPTOELECTRON.
[UK/0950-4826]
KEY ABSTRACTS. OPTOELECTRONICS.
(*Continues in part* Key Abstracts. Solid State Devices.)
***Refer to INSPEC [Online Database] for complete source list.

KEY ABSTR., PHYS. MEAS. INSTRUM.
[UK/0307-7969]
KEY ABSTRACTS. PHYSICAL MEASUREMENTS AND INSTRUMENTATION.
(*Continued by* Key Abstracts. Measurements in Physics.)

KEY ABSTR., POWER SYST. APPL.
[UK/0950-4834]
KEY ABSTRACTS. POWER SYSTEMS AND APPLICATIONS.
(*Continues* Key Abstracts. Power Transmission and Distribution.)
***Refer to INSPEC [Online Database] for complete source list.

KEY ABSTR., ROBOT. CONTROL
[UK/0950-4842]
KEY ABSTRACTS. ROBOTICS & CONTROL.
(*Continues* Key Abstracts. Industrial Power and Control Systems.)
***Refer to INSPEC [Online Database] for complete source list.

KEY ABSTR., SEMICOND. DEVICES
[UK/0950-4850]
KEY ABSTRACTS. SEMICONDUCTOR DEVICES.
(*Continues in part* Key Abstracts. Solid State Devices.)
***Refer to INSPEC [Online Database] for complete source list.

KEY ABSTR., SOFTW. ENG.
[UK/0950-4869]
KEY ABSTRACTS. SOFTWARE ENGINEERING.
***Refer to INSPEC [Online Database] for complete source list.

INDEXES/ABSTRACTS TABLE

KEY ABSTR., TELECOM.
[UK/0950-4877]
KEY ABSTRACTS. TELECOMMUNICATIONS.
(*Continues* Key Abstracts. Communication Technology.)
***Refer to INSPEC [Online Database] for complete source list.

KEY ECON. SCI.
[NE]
KEY TO ECONOMIC SCIENCE.
(*Continued by* Key to Economic Science and Managerial Sciences.)

KEY ECON. SCI. MANAGE. SCI.
[NE/0165-4748]
KEY TO ECONOMIC SCIENCE AND MANAGERIAL SCIENCES.
(*Continues* Key to Economic Science.)

KEY WORD INDEX WILDL. RES.
[SZ]
KEY-WORD-INDEX OF WILDLIFE RESEARCH.

KEY WORD INDEX MED. LIT.
[US/0145-9716]
KEY-WORD INDEX FOR THE MEDICAL LITERATURE.
(*Continues* Keyword Index in Internal Medicine.)

KEYWORD INDEX INTERN. MED.
[US/0097-0220]
KEYWORD INDEX IN INTERNAL MEDICINE.
(*Continued by* Key-Word Index for the Medical Literature.)

LAB. HAZARDS BULL.
[UK/0261-2917]
LABORATORY HAZARDS BULLETIN.

LABORDOC
[SZ]
LABORDOC [ONLINE DATABASE].

LANG. LANG. BEHAV. ABSTR.
[US/0023-8295]
LANGUAGE AND LANGUAGE BEHAVIOR ABSTRACTS : LLBA.
(*Continued by* Linguistics and Language Behavior Abstracts.)

LANG. TEACH.
[UK/0261-4448]
LANGUAGE TEACHING.
(*Continues* Language Teaching & Linguistics. Abstracts.)

LANG. TEACH. LINGUIST. ABSTR.
[UK/0306-6304]
LANGUAGE TEACHING & LINGUISTICS ABSTRACTS.
(*Continued by* Language Teaching.)

LAW OFFICE INF. SERV.
[US/0164-5390]
LAW OFFICE INFORMATION SERVICE.
(Ceased)

LEAD ABSTR.
[US/0023-9569]
LEAD ABSTRACTS.
(*Continued by* Leadscan.)

LEADSCAN
[UK/0950-1584]
LEADSCAN.
(*Continues* Lead Abstracts (London, England : 1962).)

LEFT INDEX
[US/0733-2998]
LEFT INDEX.

LEG. CONTENTS, LC
[US/0279-5787]
LEGAL CONTENTS : LC.
(*Continues* CCLP, Contents of Current Legal Periodicals.)

LEG. INF. MANAGE. INDEX
[US/0747-9298]
LEGAL INFORMATION MANAGEMENT INDEX.

LEG. RESOUR. INDEX
[US/0272-9296]
LEGAL RESOURCE INDEX.

LEGALTRAC
[US]
LEGALTRAC [COMPUTER FILE].

LEIS. RECREAT. TOUR. ABSTR.
[UK/0261-1392]
LEISURE, RECREATION, AND TOURISM ABSTRACTS.
(*Continues* Rural Recreation and Tourism Abstracts.)

LEUKEMIA ABSTR.
[US/0024-1466]
LEUKEMIA ABSTRACTS.
(Ceased)

LIBR. INF. SCI. ABSTR.
[UK/0024-2179]
LIBRARY & INFORMATION SCIENCE ABSTRACTS.
(*Supersedes* Library Science Abstracts.)

LIBR. LIT.
[US/0024-2373]
LIBRARY LITERATURE.

LIBR. SCI. ABSTR.
[UK/0459-262X]
LIBRARY SCIENCE ABSTRACTS.
(*Continued by* Library & Information Science Abstracts.)

LIFE SCI. COLLECT.
[US/0891-3889]
PERIODICALS SCANNED AND ABSTRACTED. LIFE SCIENCES COLLECTION.

LINGUIST. LANG. BEHAV. ABSTR.
[US/0888-8027]
LINGUISTICS AND LANGUAGE BEHAVIOR ABSTRACTS.
(*Continues* Language and Language Behavior Abstracts; *Absorbed* Reading Abstracts.)

LISA PLUS
[UK/0966-8799]
LISA PLUS [COMPUTER FILE].
***Refer to Library and Information Science Abstracts for complete source list.

LIST J. ABSTR.
[NE/0923-5582]
LIST OF JOURNALS ABSTRACTED.
(*Continued by* EMBASE List of Journals Indexed.)

LIT. ABSTR., CATAL. CATAL.
[US/1065-0539]
LITERATURE ABSTRACTS. CATALYSTS & CATALYSIS.
(*Continued by* Literature Abstracts. Catalysts/Zeolites.)

LIT. ABSTR., HEALTH ENVIRON.
[US/1065-0490]
LITERATURE ABSTRACTS. HEALTH & ENVIRONMENT.
(*Continues* API Abstracts. Health & Environment.)

LIT. ABSTR., PET. REFIN. PETROCHEM.
[US/1065-0512]
LITERATURE ABSTRACTS. PETROLEUM REFINING & PETROCHEMICALS.
(*Continues* Petroleum Refining and Petrochemicals.)

LIT. ABSTR., PET. SUBSTIT.
[US/1065-0504]
LITERATURE ABSTRACTS. PETROLEUM SUBSTITUTES.
(*Continues* Petroleum Substitutes.)

LIT. ABSTR., TRANSP. STORAGE
[US/1065-0520]
LITERATURE ABSTRACTS. TRANSPORTATION & STORAGE.
(*Continues* Transportation and Storage.)

LIT. ANALY. MICROCOMPUT. PUBL.
[US/0735-9721]
LITERATURE ANALYSIS OF MICROCOMPUTER PUBLICATIONS : LAMP.
(Ceased)

LIT. CRIT. REGIST.
[US/0733-2165]
LITERARY CRITICISM REGISTER.

LIT. PAT. ABSTR., OILFIELD CHEM.
[US/1065-0547]
LITERATURE & PATENT ABSTRACTS. OILFIELD CHEMICALS.
(*Continued in part by* Literature Abstracts. Oilfield Chemicals *and* Patent Abstracts. Oilfield Chemicals.)

LOMA LIT. MOD. ART
[US/0090-7235]
LOMA; LITERATURE ON MODERN ART.
(*Continued by* ARTbibliographies Modern.)

LOTUS NOTES
[US]
LOTUS NOTES [COMPUTER FILE].

MAG. ARTIC. SUMMAR.
[US/0895-3376]
MAGAZINE ARTICLE SUMMARIES (PRINT ED.).
(*Continues* Popular Magazine Review.)

MAG. ARTIC. SUMMAR. CD-ROM
[US/1041-1151]
MAGAZINE ARTICLE SUMMARIES (CD-ROM ED.).

MAG. ARTIC. SUMMAR. ELITE
[US/1060-6769]
MAGAZINE ARTICLE SUMMARIES FULL TEXT ELITE.

MAG. ARTIC. SUMMAR. SELECT
[US/1058-0255]
MAGAZINE ARTICLE SUMMARIES FULL TEXT SELECT.

MAG. ASAP PLUS
[US]
MAGAZINE ASAP PLUS [COMPUTER FILE].

MAG. ASAP SEL.
[US]
MAGAZINE ASAP SELECT [COMPUTER FILE].

MAG. EXPRESS
[US]
MAGAZINE EXPRESS [COMPUTER FILE].

MAG. INDEX
[US]
MAGAZINE INDEX, THE.

MAG. INDEX PLUS
[US]
MAGAZINE INDEX PLUS [COMPUTER FILE].

INDEXES/ABSTRACTS TABLE

MAG. INDEX SEL. MICROFICHE
[US]
MAGAZINE INDEX SELECT MICROFICHE.

MAG. INDEX. SEL.
[US]
MAGAZINE INDEX SELECT [COMPUTER FILE].

MAG. SEARCH
[US/1071-2739]
MAGAZINE SEARCH.

MAGYAR KONYV. SZAK. BIBLIO.
[HU/0133-736X]
MAGYAR KONYVTARI SZAKIRODALOM BIBLIOGRAFIAJA, A.

MAIZE ABSTR.
[UK/0267-2987]
MAIZE ABSTRACTS.
(*Continues* Maize Quality Protein Abstracts.)

MANAGE. BIBLIOGR. REV.
[UK/0309-0582]
MANAGEMENT BIBLIOGRAPHIES & REVIEWS.
(*Continues* Business Education.)

MANAGE. CONTENTS
[US/0360-2400]
MANAGEMENT CONTENTS.
(Ceased)

MANAGE. CONTENTS
[US]
MANAGEMENT CONTENTS [ONLINE DATABASE].

MANAGE. INDEX
[US]
MANAGEMENT INDEX.
(Ceased)

MANAGE. MARKET. ABSTR.
[UK/0308-2172]
MANAGEMENT AND MARKETING ABSTRACTS.

MANAGE. RES.
[US/0099-2224]
MANAGEMENT RESEARCH.
(*Continues* Bi-Monthly Review of Management Research.)

MANUF. PROCESS ENG. ABSTR.
[US/1063-7354]
MANUFACTURING AND PROCESS ENGINEERING ABSTRACTS.
(Ceased)

MAR. FISH. ABSTR.
[US/0735-3782]
MARINE FISHERIES ABSTRACTS.
(*Continues* Commercial Fisheries Abstracts.)

MAR. SCI. CONTENTS TABLES
[IT/0025-3308]
MARINE SCIENCE CONTENTS TABLES. ACTUALITES DES SCIENCES DE LA MER. INDICES DE REVISTAS SOBRE CIENCIAS MARINAS.
(*Continues* Current Contents in Marine Sciences; *Continues in part* International Marine Science.)

MARK. ADVERT. REF. SERV.
[US]
MARKETING AND ADVERTISING REFERENCE SERVICE [ONLINE DATABASE].

MARK. DISTR. ABSTR.
[UK]
MARKETING + DISTRIBUTION ABSTRACTS.
(*Continued by* Anbar Marketing & Distribution Abstracts.)

MARK. INF. GUIDE
[US/0025-374X]
MARKETING INFORMATION GUIDE.
(*Continues* Marketing Information Guide (Washington : 1961).)

MARK. RES. ABSTR.
[UK/0025-3596]
MARKET RESEARCH ABSTRACTS.

MARK. RES. TODAY
[NE/0923-5957]
MARKETING AND RESEARCH TODAY : THE JOURNAL OF THE EUROPEAN SOCIETY FOR OPINION AND MARKETING RESEARCH.
(*Continues* European Research.)

MASS SPECT. BULL.
[UK/0025-4738]
MASS SPECTROMETRY BULLETIN.

MASTERFILE.
[US/1080-7969]
MASTERFILE [COMPUTER FILE].

MASTERFILE FT 350.
[US]
MASTERFILE FULL TEXT 350 [COMPUTER FILE].

MASTERFILE FT 650.
[US]
MASTERFILE FULL TEXT 650 [COMPUTER FILE].

MASTERFILE FT 1000.
[US]
MASTERFILE FULL TEXT 1000 [COMPUTER FILE].

MATER. SCI. ENG. ABSTR.
[US/1063-732X]
MATERIALS SCIENCE AND ENGINEERING ABSTRACTS.
(Ceased)

MATH. REV.
[US/0025-5629]
MATHEMATICAL REVIEWS.

MECH. ENG. ABSTR.
[US/1063-7311]
MECHANICAL ENGINEERING ABSTRACTS.
(*Continues* ISMEC, Mechanical Engineering Abstracts.)

MED. ABSTR. NEWSL.
[US/0730-7810]
MEDICAL ABSTRACTS NEWSLETTER.

MED. ELECTRON. COMMUN. ABSTR.
[UK/0025-7222]
MEDICAL ELECTRONICS AND COMMUNICATIONS ABSTRACTS.
(Ceased)

MED. PHARM. BIOTECHNOL. ABSTR.
[US/1063-1178]
MEDICAL & PHARMACEUTICAL BIOTECHNOLOGY ABSTRACTS.
(*Continues in part* Biotechnology Research Abstracts.)
***Refer to Biotechnology Research Abstracts for complete source list.

MED. REV. DIG.
[US/0363-7778]
MEDIA REVIEW DIGEST.
(*Continues* Multi Media Reviews Index.)

MED. SOCIOECON. RES. SOURCE
[US/0025-7540]
MEDICAL SOCIOECONOMIC RESEARCH SOURCES.
(*Supersedes* Weekly Bulletin *and* Index to Medical Socioeconomic Literature.)

MEDOC
[US/0097-9732]
MEDOC.
(Ceased)

MENT. HEALTH BOOK REV. INDEX
[US/0076-6445]
MENTAL HEALTH BOOK REVIEW INDEX.
(*Continued by* Chicorel Index to Mental Health Book Reviews.)

MENT. RETARD. ABSTR.
[US/0025-9691]
MENTAL RETARDATION ABSTRACTS.
(*Continued by* Mental Retardation & Developmental Disabilities Abstracts.)

MENT. RETARD. DEV. DISABIL. ABSTR.
[US/0361-3798]
MENTAL RETARDATION & DEVELOPMENTAL DISABILITIES ABSTRACTS.
(*Continued by* Developmental Disabilities Abstracts.)

MET. ABSTR.
[UK/0026-0924]
METALS ABSTRACTS.
(*Formed by the union of* Metallurgical Abstracts *and* Review of Metal Literature.)

MET. ABSTR. INDEX
[UK/0026-0932]
METALS ABSTRACTS INDEX.
(*Formed by the union of* Metallurgical Abstracts *and* Review of Metal Literature.)
***Refer to Metals Abstracts for complete source list.

MET. FINISHING ABSTR.
[UK/0026-0584]
METAL FINISHING ABSTRACTS.
(*Continued by* Surface Treatment Technology Abstracts.)

METEOROL. GEOASTROPHYS. ABSTR.
[US/0026-1130]
METEOROLOGICAL AND GEOASTROPHYSICAL ABSTRACTS.
(*Continues* Meteorological Abstracts and Bibliography.)

METEOROL. GEOASTROPHYS. ABSTR. [CD-ROM]
[US/1066-2707]
METEOROLOGICAL & GEOASTROPHYSICAL ABSTRACTS.
***Refer to Meteorological and Geoastrophysical Abstracts for a complete source list.

METHODIST PERIOD. INDEX
[US]
METHODIST PERIODICAL INDEX.
(*Continued by* United Methodist Periodical Index.)

METHODS ORGAN. SYNTH.
[UK/0265-4245]
METHODS IN ORGANIC SYNTHESIS.

MICROBIOL. ABSTR. SECT. A
[US/0300-838X]
MICROBIOLOGY ABSTRACTS. SECTION A : INDUSTRIAL & APPLIED MICROBIOLOGY.
(*Continues* Microbiology Abstracts. Section A. Industrial Microbiology.)

MICROBIOL. ABSTR. SECT. B
[US/0300-8398]
MICROBIOLOGY ABSTRACTS. SECTION B, BACTERIOLOGY.
(*Continues* Microbiology Abstracts. Section B: General Microbiology and Bacteriology.)

INDEXES/ABSTRACTS TABLE

MICROBIOL. ABSTR. SECT. C
[US/0301-2328]
MICROBIOLOGY ABSTRACTS. SECTION C, ALGOLOGY, MYCOLOGY & PROTOZOOLOGY.

MICROCOMPUT. IND. UPDATE
[US/0741-6016]
MICROCOMPUTER INDUSTRY UPDATE.

MICROCOMPUT. INDEX
[US/8756-7040]
MICROCOMPUTER INDEX.
(*Continued by* Microcomputer Abstracts.)

MID. SEARCH
[US/1071-2755]
MIDDLE SEARCH.
(*Continues* Junior Search.)

MIDDLE EAST ABSTR. INDEX
[US/0162-766X]
MIDDLE EAST, ABSTRACTS AND INDEX.

MIDDLE EAST J.
[US/0026-3141]
MIDDLE EAST JOURNAL, THE.

MINERAL. ABSTR.
[UK/0026-4601]
MINERALOGICAL ABSTRACTS.

MINPROC
[CN/0828-8461]
MINPROC : MINERAL PROCESSING ABSTRACTS.
(**Ceased**)

MINTEC, MIN. TECHNOL. ABSTR.
[CN/0823-0773]
MINTEC : MINING TECHNOLOGY ABSTRACTS.
(**Ceased**)

MISSIONALIA
[SA/0256-9507]
MISSIONALIA.
(*Formed by the union of* Lux Mundi (Pretoria, South Africa) *and* Missionaria.)

MLA INT. BIBL. BOOKS ARTIC. MOD. LANG. LIT.
[US/0024-8215]
MLA INTERNATIONAL BIBLIOGRAPHY OF BOOKS AND ARTICLES ON THE MODERN LANGUAGES AND LITERATURES (COMPLETE ED.).
(*Continues* MLA International Bibliography of Books and Articles on the Modern Languages and Literatures.)

MOD. MED.
[US/0026-8070]
MODERN MEDICINE (MINNEAPOLIS).

MON. PERIOD. INDEX
[US/0197-6567]
MONTHLY PERIODICAL INDEX.
(*Absorbed by* Access.)

MOSHER PERIOD. INDEX
[US/0194-0716]
MOSHER PERIODICAL INDEX.
(*Continues* Subject Index to Select Periodical Literature.)

MRS BULL.
[US/0883-7694]
MRS BULLETIN.
(*Absorbed* JMR Abstracts.)

MULTI MEDIA REV. INDEX
[US/0091-5858]
MULTI MEDIA REVIEWS INDEX.
(*Continued by* Media Review Digest.)

MULTICULT. EDUC. ABSTR.
[UK/0260-9770]
MULTICULTURAL EDUCATION ABSTRACTS.

MUSCULAR DYSTROPHY ABSTR.
[US/0027-3732]
MUSCULAR DYSTROPHY ABSTRACTS.
(**Ceased**)

MUSEUM ABSTR.
[UK/0267-8594]
MUSEUM ABSTRACTS.

MUSIC ARTIC. GUIDE
[US/0027-4240]
MUSIC ARTICLE GUIDE.

MUSIC INDEX
[US/0027-4348]
MUSIC INDEX, THE.

N. Y. LAW J. DIG.-ANNOT.
[US/0745-4406]
NEW YORK LAW JOURNAL DIGEST-ANNOTATOR.
(*Continues* Clark's Digest-Annotator.)

NAPRALERT
[US]
NAPRALERT [ONLINE DATABASE].

NAT. PROD. UPDATES
[UK/0950-1711]
NATURAL PRODUCT UPDATES.

NATL. NEWSP. INDEX
[US/0273-3676]
NATIONAL NEWSPAPER INDEX.

NEMATOL. ABSTR.
[UK/0957-6797]
NEMATOLOGICAL ABSTRACTS.
(*Continues* Helminthological Abstracts. Series B, Plant Nematology.)

NEW LIT. AUTOMAT.
[NE]
NEW LITERATURE ON AUTOMATION.
(*Continues* IAG-Literature on Automation.)

NEW PERIOD. INDEX
[US/0146-5716]
NEW PERIODICALS INDEX.
(**Ceased**)

NEW TESTAM. ABSTR.
[US/0028-6877]
NEW TESTAMENT ABSTRACTS.

NEWSP. ABSTR.
[US/1064-993X]
NEWSPAPER ABSTRACTS ONDISC.

NEWSP. ABSTR.
[US]
NEWSPAPER ABSTRACTS.

NEWSP. PERIOD. ABSTR.
[US]
NEWSPAPER & PERIODICAL ABSTRACTS [ONLINE DATABASE].

NEXIS
[US]
NEXIS.

NONWOVENS ABSTR.
[UK/9036-1234]
NONWOVENS ABSTRACTS.

NUCL. ACIDS ABSTR.
[US/1070-2466]
NUCLEIC ACIDS ABSTRACTS (1994).
(*Continues* Cambridge Scientific Biochemistry Abstracts, Part 2: Nucleic Acids.)

NUCL. SCI. ABSTR.
[US/0029-5612]
NUCLEAR SCIENCE ABSTRACTS.
(*Continues* Abstracts of Declassified Documents; Guide to Published Research on Atomic Energy.)

NUMIS. LIT.
[US/0029-6031]
NUMISMATIC LITERATURE.

NURS. ABSTR.
[US/0195-3354]
NURSING ABSTRACTS.

NURS. ALLIED HEALTH INDEX
[US/0744-8732]
NURSING AND ALLIED HEALTH INDEX.
(*Absorbed by* Cumulative Index to Nursing & Allied Health Literature.)

NURS. DIG.
[US/0091-4215]
NURSING DIGEST.
(*Continued by* Nursing Dimensions.)

NURS. DIMEN.
[US/0164-0232]
NURSING DIMENSIONS.
(*Continues* Nursing Digest.)

NUTR. ABSTR. REV.
[UK/0029-6619]
NUTRITION ABSTRACTS AND REVIEWS.
(*Split into* Nutrition Abstracts and Reviews. Series A. Human and Experimental *and* Nutrition Abstracts and Reviews. Series B, Livestock Feeds and Feeding.)

NUTR. ABSTR. REV., SER. A, HUM. EXP.
[UK/0309-1295]
NUTRITION ABSTRACTS AND REVIEWS. SERIES A: HUMAN & EXPERIMENTAL.
(*Continues in part* Nutrition Abstracts and Reviews.)

NUTR. ABSTR. REV., SER. B, LIVE FEEDS AND FEED.
[UK/0309-135X]
NUTRITION ABSTRACTS AND REVIEWS. SERIES B. LIVESTOCK FEEDS AND FEEDING.
(*Continues in part* Nutrition Abstracts and Reviews.)

NUTR. RES. NEWSL.
[US/0736-0037]
NUTRITION RESEARCH NEWSLETTER.

OCCUP. MENT. HEALTH
[US/0090-1679]
OCCUPATIONAL MENTAL HEALTH.
(*Supersedes* Occupational Mental Health News.)

OCCUP. MENT. HEALTH NOTES
[US/0029-795X]
OCCUPATIONAL MENTAL HEALTH NOTES.
(*Superseded by* Occupational Mental Health.)

OCEAN. ABSTR.
[US/0748-1489]
OCEANIC ABSTRACTS (BETHESDA, MD.).
(*Continues* Oceanic Abstracts with Indexes.)

OCEAN. ABSTR. INDEXES
[US/0093-6901]
OCEANIC ABSTRACTS WITH INDEXES.
(*Continued by* Oceanic Abstracts (Bethesda, Md.).)

INDEXES/ABSTRACTS TABLE

OCEANIC CIT. J. ABSTR.
[US]
OCEANIC CITATION JOURNAL WITH ABSTRACTS / OCEANIC RESEARCH INSTITUTE.
(**Merged with** Oceanic Index **to form** Oceanic Abstracts with Indexes.)

OCEANIC INDEX CIT. J. ABSTR.
[US]
OCEANIC INDEX CITATION JOURNAL WITH ABSTRACTS.
(**Continued by** Oceanic Citation Journal with Abstracts.)

OCEANOGR. LIT. REV.
[UK/0967-0653]
OCEANOGRAPHIC LITERATURE REVIEW.
(**Continues** Deep-Sea Research. Part B, Oceanographic Literature Review.)

OCLC
[US]
OCLC [COMPUTER FILE].

OLD TESTAM. ABSTR.
[US/0364-8591]
OLD TESTAMENT ABSTRACTS.

ONCOG. GROWTH FACTORS ABSTR.
[US/1043-8963]
ONCOGENES AND GROWTH FACTORS ABSTRACTS.

OPER. PROD. MANAGE. ABSTR.
[UK]
OPERATIONS & PRODUCTION MANAGEMENT ABSTRACTS.
(**Continues** Management Services and Production Abstracts.)

OPER. RES. MANAG. SCI.
[US/0030-3658]
OPERATIONS RESEARCH/MANAGEMENT SCIENCE.

ORAL RES. ABSTR.
[US/0030-4212]
ORAL RESEARCH ABSTRACTS.
(Ceased)

ORNAMENTAL HORT.
[UK/0305-4934]
ORNAMENTAL HORTICULTURE.

ORTHO. SUR.
[NE/0014-4371]
ORTHOPEDIC SURGERY.
(**Continues** Orthopedics and Traumatology.)
***Refer to EMBASE [Online Database] for complete source list.

OZARK PERIOD. INDEX
[US/0275-9713]
OZARK PERIODICAL INDEX.

PAIS BULL.
[US/0898-2201]
PAIS BULLETIN.
(**Merged with** PAIS Foreign Language Index **to form** PAIS International in Print.)

PAIS FOREIGN LANG. INDEX
[US/0896-792X]
PAIS FOREIGN LANGUAGE INDEX.
(**Merged with** PAIS Bulletin **to form** PAIS International in Print.)

PAIS INT. PRINT
[US/1051-4015]
PAIS INTERNATIONAL IN PRINT.
(**Formed by the union of** PAIS Bulletin **and** PAIS Foreign Language Index.)

PAP. BOARD ABSTR.
[UK/0307-0778]
PAPER & BOARD ABSTRACTS.
(**Continues in part** Kenley Abstracts.)

PARAPSYCHOL. ABSTR. INT.
[US/0740-7629]
PARAPSYCHOLOGY ABSTRACTS INTERNATIONAL.
(**Continued by** Exceptional Human Experience.)

PASTOR. CARE COUNS. ABSTR.
[US]
PASTORAL CARE AND COUNSELING ABSTRACTS.
(**Continued by** Abstracts of Research in Pastoral Care and Counseling.)

PEACE RES. ABSTR. J.
[US/0031-3599]
PEACE RESEARCH ABSTRACTS JOURNAL.

PERIODEX
[CN]
PERIODEX: INDEX ANALYTIQUE DE PERIODIQUES DE LANGUE FRANCAISE.
(**Merged with** Radar **to form** Point de Repere.)

PERSON. MANAGE. ABSTR.
[US/0031-577X]
PERSONNEL MANAGEMENT ABSTRACTS.

PERSON. TRAIN. ABSTR.
[UK/0305-067X]
PERSONNEL + TRAINING ABSTRACTS.
(**Continues in part** Anbar Management Services Abstracts.)

PESTDOC
[UK]
PESTDOC.

PET. ABSTR.
[US/0031-6423]
PETROLEUM ABSTRACTS (TULSA, OKLA.).

PET. ENERGY BUS. NEWS INDEX
[US/0098-7743]
PETROLEUM/ENERGY BUSINESS NEWS INDEX.

PET. REFIN. PETROCHEM.
[US]
PETROLEUM REFINING AND PETROCHEMICALS.
(**Continued by** Literature Abstracts. Petroleum Refining & Petrochemicals.)

PET. SUBS.
[US]
PETROLEUM SUBSTITUTES.
(**Continued by** Literature Abstracts. Petroleum Substitutes.)

PHARM. NEWS INDEX
[US/0362-4439]
PHARMACEUTICAL NEWS INDEX.

PHILIP. ABSTR.
[PH/0031-7438]
PHILIPPINE ABSTRACTS.
(**Continued by** Philippine Science & Technology Abstracts.)

PHILIP. SCI. TECHNOL. ABSTR.
[PH/0115-8724]
PHILIPPINE SCIENCE & TECHNOLOGY ABSTRACTS.
(**Continues** Philippine Science and Technology Abstract Bibliography.)

PHILOS. INDEX
[US/0031-7993]
PHILOSOPHER'S INDEX.

PHOTOGR. ABSTR.
[UK/0031-8701]
PHOTOGRAPHIC ABSTRACTS.
(**Continued by** Imaging Abstracts.)

PHYS. ABSTR.
[UK/0036-8091]
PHYSICS ABSTRACTS.
(**Continues** Science Abstracts. Physics Abstracts.)
***Refer to INSPEC [Online Database] for a complete source list.

PHYS. BRIEFS
[UK/0170-7434]
PHYSICS BRIEFS.
(**Supersedes** Physikalische Berichte.)

PHYS. EDUC. INDEX
[US/0191-9202]
PHYSICAL EDUCATION INDEX (CAPE GIRARDEAU).

PHYS. MED. BIOL.
[UK/0031-9155]
PHYSICS IN MEDICINE & BIOLOGY.

PHYSIC. MEDLINE PLUS
[US/1065-6545]
PHYSICIAN'S MEDLINE PLUS.

PIG NEWS INF.
[UK/0143-9014]
PIG NEWS AND INFORMATION.

PINPOINTER
[AT/0031-9910]
PINPOINTER.
(Ceased)

PLANT BREED. ABSTR.
[UK/0032-0803]
PLANT BREEDING ABSTRACTS.

PLANT GROW. REG. ABSTR.
[UK/0305-9154]
PLANT GROWTH REGULATOR ABSTRACTS.

POINT REPERE
[CN/0822-8833]
POINT DE REPERE (MONTREAL).
(**Continued by** Repere.)

POLICE SCI. ABSTR.
[NE/0166-6282]
POLICE SCIENCE ABSTRACTS.
(**Merged with** Criminology & Penology Abstracts **to form** Criminology, Penology, and Police Science Abstracts.)

POLLUT. ABSTR. INDEXES
[US/0032-3624]
POLLUTION ABSTRACTS WITH INDEXES.

POLYMER CONTENTS
[UK/0883-153X]
POLYMER CONTENTS.
(**Continues** PRA Report: Polymer Contents.)

POP. MAG. REV.
[US/0740-3763]
POPULAR MAGAZINE REVIEW : PMR.
(**Continued by** Magazine Article Summaries.)

POP. PERIOD. INDEX
[US/0092-9727]
POPULAR PERIODICAL INDEX.
(Ceased)

POPUL. INDEX
[US/0032-4701]
POPULATION INDEX.
(**Continues** Population Literature.)

INDEXES/ABSTRACTS TABLE

POTATO ABSTR.
[UK/0308-7344]
POTATO ABSTRACTS.

POULT. ABSTR.
[UK/0306-1582]
POULTRY ABSTRACTS.

POVER. HUM. RESOUR.
[US/0032-5864]
POVERTY & HUMAN RESOURCES.
(*Continued by* Poverty and Human Resources Abstracts.)

POVER. HUM. RESOUR. ABSTR.
[US/0094-4394]
POVERTY & HUMAN RESOURCES ABSTRACTS.
(*Continued by* Human Resources Abstracts.)

PREDICASTS
[US/0032-7166]
PREDICASTS.
(*Continued by* Predicasts Forecasts.)

PREDICASTS F & S INDEX INT.
[US/0270-4528]
PREDICASTS F & S INDEX INTERNATIONAL.
(*Continued by* F&S Index International (Foster City, Calif.).)
***Refer to Predicasts Forecasts for a complete source list.

PREDICASTS F&S INDEX, U. S. ANNU. ED.
[US/0277-9676]
PREDICASTS F&S INDEX. UNITED STATES ANNUAL EDITION.
(*Continued by* F&S Index United States Annual.)

PREDICASTS FORECASTS
[US/0278-0135]
PREDICASTS FORECASTS.
(*Continues* Predicasts.)

PREV. HUM. SERV.
[US/0270-3114]
PREVENTION IN HUMAN SERVICES.
(*Continues* Community Mental Health Review.)

PRIM. SEARCH
[US/1065-2485]
PRIMARY SEARCH.

PRINT. ABSTR.
[UK/0031-109X]
PRINTING ABSTRACTS.

PROC. CHEM. ENG.
[UK/0960-5045]
PROCESS AND CHEMICAL ENGINEERING.
(*Continues* Chemical Engineering Abstracts.)

PROMT
[US/0161-8032]
PROMT / PREDICASTS OVERVIEW OF MARKETS AND TECHNOLOGY.
(*Formed by the union of* Chemical Market Abstracts *and* EMA, Equipment Market Abstracts.)

PROTOZOOLOG. ABSTR.
[UK/0309-1287]
PROTOZOOLOGICAL ABSTRACTS.

PSYCHEDELIC REV.
[US/0033-2631]
PSYCHEDELIC REVIEW.
(Ceased)

PSYCHOANAL. ABSTR.
[US/1066-9884]
PSYCHOANALYTIC ABSTRACTS.
(*Continues* Psyscan. Psychoanalysis.)

PSYCHOL. ABSTR.
[US/0033-2887]
PSYCHOLOGICAL ABSTRACTS.

PSYCHOL. READ. GUIDE
[SZ/0300-0443]
PSYCHOLOGICAL READER'S GUIDE.
(Ceased)

PSYCHOPHARMACOLOGY ABSTR.
[US/0033-3166]
PSYCHOPHARMACOLOGY ABSTRACTS.
(Ceased)

PSYCINFO
[US]
PSYCINFO.

PSYCLIT
[US]
PSYCLIT DATABASE.

PSYCSCAN PSYCHOANAL.
[US/0889-5236]
PSYCSCAN: PSYCHOANALYSIS.
(*Continued by* Psychoanalytic Abstracts.)

PSYCSCAN: APPL. EXP. ENG. PSYCH.
[US/0891-0685]
PSYCSCAN: APPLIED EXPERIMENTAL AND ENGINEERING PSYCHOLOGY.

PSYCSCAN: APPL. PSYCH.
[US/0271-7506]
PSYCSCAN. APPLIED PSYCHOLOGY.

PSYCSCAN: CLIN. PSYCH.
[US/0197-1484]
PSYCSCAN. CLINICAL PSYCHOLOGY.

PSYCSCAN: DEVELOP. PSYCH.
[US/0197-1492]
PSYCSCAN. DEVELOPMENTAL PSYCHOLOGY.

PSYCSCAN: LD/MR
[US/0730-1928]
PSYCSCAN. LD/MR.

PSYCSCAN: NEUROPSYCH.
[US/1058-6660]
PSYCSCAN. NEUROPSYCHOLOGY.

PTS NEWSL. DATABASE
[US]
PTS NEWSLETTER DATABASE [ONLINE DATABASE].

PUB. LIB. FT.
[US/1080-7977]
PUBLIC LIBRARY FULL TEXT [COMPUTER FILE].

PUBLIC ADM. ABSTR. INDEX ARTIC. INDIA
[II/0033-331X]
PUBLIC ADMINISTRATION ABSTRACTS AND INDEX OF ARTICLES (INDIA).
(Ceased)

PUBLIC AFF. INF. SERV. BULL.
[US/0033-3409]
PUBLIC AFFAIRS INFORMATION SERVICE BULLETIN.
(*Continued by* PAIS Bulletin (Annual).)

Q. BIBLIOGR. COMPUT. DATA PROCESS.
[US/0048-6132]
QUARTERLY BIBLIOGRAPHY OF COMPUTERS AND DATA PROCESSING.
(*Continued by* Computer Literature Index.)

Q. INDEX ISLAM.
[UK/0308-7395]
QUARTERLY INDEX ISLAMICUS.
***Refer to Index Islamicus for complete source list.

QUAL. CONTROL APPL. STAT.
[US/0033-5207]
QUALITY CONTROL AND APPLIED STATISTICS.

RAPRA ABSTR.
[UK/0033-6750]
RAPRA ABSTRACTS.
(*Formed by the union of* Plastics. RAPRA Abstracts *and* Rubbers. RAPRA Abstracts.)

READ. ABSTR.
[US/0361-6118]
READING ABSTRACTS.
(*Continued by* Linguistics and Language Behavior Abstracts.)

READ. GUIDE ABSTR.
[US/0899-1553]
READERS' GUIDE ABSTRACTS (PRINT EDITION).
(*Continued by* Readers' Guide Abstracts (School and Public Library Ed. : Monthly).)

READ. GUIDE ABSTR.
[US/1058-1219]
READERS' GUIDE ABSTRACTS (SCHOOL AND PUBLIC LIBRARY ED.).
(*Continued by* Readers' Guide Abstracts Select Edition.)

READ. GUIDE ABSTR. SELECT ED.
[US]
READERS' GUIDE ABSTRACTS SELECT EDITION.
(*Continues* Readers' Guide Abstracts School and Public Library Edition.)

READ. GUIDE PERIOD. LIT.
[US/0034-0464]
READERS' GUIDE TO PERIODICAL LITERATURE.
(*Continues* Monthly Cumulative Index to ... Important Periodicals; *Absorbed* Cumulative Index to a Selected List of Periodicals (Annual).)

RECENT. PUBL. ARTIC.
[US/0145-5311]
RECENTLY PUBLISHED ARTICLES - AMERICAN HISTORICAL ASSOCIATION.
(Ceased)

RECIPE PERIOD. INDEX
[US/0743-3484]
RECIPE PERIODICAL INDEX.
(Ceased)

REF. BOOK REV. INDEX
[US]
REFERENCE BOOK REVIEW INDEX.
(Ceased)

REF. SOURCES
[US/0163-3546]
REFERENCE SOURCES.
(Ceased)

REF. UPD. BASIC ED.
[US]
REFERENCE UPDATE BASIC EDITION [COMPUTER FILE].

REF. UPD. CLINICAL ED.
[US]
REFERENCE UPDATE CLINICAL EDITION [COMPUTER FILE].

REF. UPD. DELUXE ED.
[US]
REFERENCE UPDATE DELUXE EDITION [COMPUTER FILE].

INDEXES/ABSTRACTS TABLE

REFER. Z.
[RU]
REFERATIVNYI ZHURNAL: ORGANIZATSIIA I BEZOPASNOST DOROZHNOGO DVIZHENIIA.

REHABIL. LIT.
[US/0034-3579]
REHABILITATION LITERATURE.
(Ceased)

RELIG. INDEX ONE PERIOD.
[US/0149-8428]
RELIGION INDEX ONE. PERIODICALS.
(Continued in part by Index to Book Reviews in Religion.)

RELIG. PERIOD. INDEX
[US/0034-4117]
RELIGIOUS PERIODICALS INDEX.
(Ceased)

RELIG. THEOL. ABSTR.
[US/0034-4044]
RELIGIOUS AND THEOLOGICAL ABSTRACTS.

REPERT. ANAL. ARTIC. REV. QUE.
[CN/0315-2316]
RADAR: REPERTOIRE ANALYTIQUE D'ARTICLES DE REVUES DU QUEBEC.
(Merged with Periodex to form Point de Repere.)

RES. ALERT
[US]
RESEARCH ALERT.
(Continues Ascatopics.)

RES. HIGH. EDUC. ABSTR.
[UK/0034-5326]
RESEARCH INTO HIGHER EDUCATION ABSTRACTS.

RESOURCE/ONE ONDISC
[US]
RESOURCE/ONE ONDISC [COMPUTER FILE].

REV. AGRIC. ENTOMOL.
[UK/0957-6762]
REVIEW OF AGRICULTURAL ENTOMOLOGY.
(Continues Review of Applied Entomology. Series A, Agricultural.)

REV. APPL. ENTOMOL. SER. A, AGRIC.
[UK/0305-0076]
REVIEW OF APPLIED ENTOMOLOGY. SERIES A: AGRICULTURAL.
(Continued by Review of Agricultural Entomology.)

REV. APPL. ENTOMOL. SER. B, MED. VET.
[UK/0305-0084]
REVIEW OF APPLIED ENTOMOLOGY. SERIES B, MEDICAL AND VETERINARY.
(Continued by Review of Medical and Veterinary Entomology.)

REV. MED. VET. ENTOMOL.
[UK/0957-6770]
REVIEW OF MEDICAL AND VETERINARY ENTOMOLOGY.
(Continues Review of Applied Entomology. Series B, Medical and Veterinary.)

REV. MED. VET. MYCOLOGY
[UK/0034-6624]
REVIEW OF MEDICAL AND VETERINARY MYCOLOGY.
(Continues Annotated Bibliography of Medical Mycology.)

REV. PLANT PATHOL.
[UK/0034-6438]
REVIEW OF PLANT PATHOLOGY.
(Continues Review of Applied Mycology.)

RIBA LIB. BULL.
[UK]
RIBA LIBRARY BULLETIN.
(Superseded by Architectural Periodicals Index.)

RILA, INT. REP. LIT. ART
[US/0145-5982]
RILA : INTERNATIONAL REPERTORY OF THE LITERATURE OF ART.
(Merged with Repertoire d'Art et d'Archeologie to form Bibliography of the History of Art.)

RILM ABSTR.
[US/0033-6955]
RILM ABSTRACTS.

RINGDOC
[UK]
RINGDOC.
***Refer to PESTDOC for complete source list.

RISK ABSTR.
[CN/0824-3336]
RISK ABSTRACTS.

ROBOMATIX REPORT.
[US/0748-1624]
ROBOMATIX REPORTER.
(Continued by Robotics Abstracts.)

ROBOTICS ABSTR.
[US/0000-1139]
ROBOTICS ABSTRACTS.
(Continues Robomatix Reporter.)

ROMANT. MOVE.
[US/0557-2738]
ROMANTIC MOVEMENT.

ROTHS AM. POETRY ANNUAL
[US/1040-5461]
ROTH'S AMERICAN POETRY ANNUAL.
(Formed by the union of Annual Survey of American Poetry; Annual Index to Poetry in Periodicals and American Poetry Index.)

RURAL EXT. EDUC. TRAIN. ABSTR.
[UK/0140-4776]
RURAL EXTENSION, EDUCATION AND TRAINING ABSTRACTS.
(Ceased)

RURAL RECREAT. TOUR. ABSTR.
[UK/0308-0137]
RURAL RECREATION AND TOURISM ABSTRACTS.
(Continued by Leisure, Recreation and Tourism Abstracts.)

SAF. HEALTH WORK
[SZ/1010-7053]
SAFETY AND HEALTH AT WORK : ILO-CIS BULLETIN.
(Continues International Occupational Safety and Health Information Centre. CIS Abstracts.)

SAF. SCI. ABSTR.
[US/0092-542X]
SAFETY SCIENCE ABSTRACTS.
(Continued by Safety Science Abstracts Journal.)

SAF. SCI. ABSTR. J.
[US/0160-1342]
SAFETY SCIENCE ABSTRACTS JOURNAL.
(Continued by Health and Safety Science Abstracts.)

SAGE FAM. STUD. ABSTR.
[US/0164-0283]
SAGE FAMILY STUDIES ABSTRACTS.

SAGE PUBLIC ADM. ABSTR.
[US/0094-6958]
SAGE PUBLIC ADMINISTRATION ABSTRACTS.

SAGE RACE RELAT. ABSTR.
[UK/0307-9201]
SAGE RACE RELATIONS ABSTRACTS.
(Continues Race Relations Abstracts.)

SAGE URBAN STUD. ABSTR
[US/0090-5747]
SAGE URBAN STUDIES ABSTRACTS.

SCHOOL ORGAN. MANAGE. ABSTR.
[UK/0261-2755]
SCHOOL ORGANISATION & MANAGEMENT ABSTRACTS.

SCI. ABSTR. PHYS. ABSTR.
[UK]
SCIENCE ABSTRACTS. PHYSICS ABSTRACTS.
(Continued by Science Abstracts. Series A, Physics Abstracts.)

SCI. ABSTR. SECT. A. PHYS. ABSTR.
[UK]
SCIENCE ABSTRACTS. SECTION A, PHYSICS ABSTRACTS.
(Continued by Science Abstracts. Physics Abstracts.)

SCI. ABSTR. SER. A, PHYS. ABSTR.
[UK]
SCIENCE ABSTRACTS. SERIES A, PHYSICS ABSTRACTS.
(Continued by Physics Abstracts.)

SCI. CIT. INDEX
[US/0036-827X]
SCIENCE CITATION INDEX (PRINT ED.).

SCI. CIT. INDEX ABSTR.
[US/1061-1290]
SCIENCE CITATION INDEX WITH ABSTRACTS.
***Refer to Science Citation Index (US/0036-827X) for a complete source list.

SCI. CIT. INDEX [CD-ROM]
[US/1044-6052]
SCIENCE CITATION INDEX (COMPACT DISC ED.).
***Refer to Science Citation Index (US/0036-827X) for a complete source list.

SCI. CIT. INDEX, ABR. ED.
[US/0737-2108]
SCIENCE CITATION INDEX. ABRIDGED EDITION.
(Ceased)

SCI. FICT. FANTASY BOOK REV. INDEX
[US/1046-1922]
SCIENCE FICTION AND FANTASY BOOK REVIEW INDEX.
(Continues Science Fiction Book Review Index.)

SCI. RES. ABSTR. J.
[US/0731-0943]
SCIENCE RESEARCH ABSTRACTS JOURNAL.
(Absorbed by Solid State Abstracts Journal.)

SCI. RES. ABSTR. J. PART A.
[US/0194-7486]
SCIENCE RESEARCH ABSTRACTS JOURNAL. PART A: SUPERCONDUCTIVITY, MAGNETOHYDRODYNAMICS AND PLASMAS, THEORETICAL PHYSICS.
(Merged with Science Research Abstracts Journal. Part B: Laser and Electro-Opticreviews, Quantum Electronics and Unconventional Energy Sources to form Science Research Abstracts Journal.)

INDEXES/ABSTRACTS TABLE

SCISEARCH
[US]
SCISEARCH [ONLINE DATABASE].

SEA ABSTR.
[PH]
SEA ABSTRACTS.

SEED ABSTR.
[UK/0141-0180]
SEED ABSTRACTS.

SEL. PHILIP. PERIOD. INDEX
[PH/0037-1335]
SELECTED PHILIPPINE PERIODICAL INDEX.
(Ceased)

SEL. WATER RESOUR. ABSTR.
[US/0037-136X]
SELECTED WATER RESOURCES ABSTRACTS (WASHINGTON, D.C.).
(Ceased)

SELEC. COOP. INDEX MANAGE. PERIOD.
[FI/0782-2979]
SCIMP SELECTIVE CO-OPERATIVE INDEX OF MANAGEMENT PERIODICALS.
(Ceased)

SEVENTH-DAY ADVENTIST PERIOD. INDEX
[US/0270-3599]
SEVENTH-DAY ADVENTIST PERIODICAL INDEX.

SHIP ABSTR.
[NO/0346-1025]
SHIP ABSTRACTS.
(*Absorbed by* Journal of Abstracts of the British Ship Research Association.)

SHOCK VIBR. DIG.
[US/0583-1024]
SHOCK AND VIBRATION DIGEST, THE.

SMALL ANIM. ABSTR. BIBLIOGR.
[UK]
SMALL ANIMAL ABSTRACTS BIBLIOGRAPHY.
(*Continues* Small Animal Abstracts.)

SOC. PLANN. POLICY DEV. ABSTR.
[US/1042-8380]
SOCIAL PLANNING, POLICY & DEVELOPMENT ABSTRACTS.
(*Continues* Social Welfare, Social Planning/Policy & Social Development.)

SOC. RES. METHODOL. ABSTR.
[NE/0167-8477]
SOCIAL RESEARCH METHODOLOGY ABSTRACTS.
(*Continues in part* SRM Abstract Bulletin.)

SOC. SCI. CIT. INDEX
[US/0091-3707]
SOCIAL SCIENCES CITATION INDEX (PRINT ED.).

SOC. SCI. HUMANIT. INDEX
[US/0037-7899]
SOCIAL SCIENCES & HUMANITIES INDEX.
(*Split into* Social Sciences Index *and* Humanities Index.)

SOC. SCI. INDEX
[US/0094-4920]
SOCIAL SCIENCES INDEX.
(*Supersedes in part* Social Sciences & Humanities Index.)

SOC. SCI. INDEX FULLTEXT
[US]
SOCIAL SCIENCES INDEX / FULLTEXT.

SOC. SCI. SOURCE
[US/1063-9802]
SOCIAL SCIENCE SOURCE.

SOC. WELF. SOC. PLAN./POLICY SOC. DEV.
[US/0195-7988]
SOCIAL WELFARE, SOCIAL PLANNING/POLICY & SOCIAL DEVELOPMENT.
(*Continued by* Social Planning, Policy & Development Abstracts.)

SOC. WORK ABSTR.
[US/1070-5317]
SOCIAL WORK ABSTRACTS.
(*Continues in part* Social Work Research and Abstracts.)

SOC. WORK RES.
[US/1070-5309]
SOCIAL WORK RESEARCH.
(*Continues in part* Social Work Research and Abstracts.)
***Refer to Social Work Abstracts for a complete source list.

SOC. WORK RES. ABSTR.
[US/0148-0847]
SOCIAL WORK RESEARCH & ABSTRACTS.
(*Split into* Social Work Abstracts *and* Social Work Research.)

SOCIOL. ABSTR.
[US/0038-0202]
SOCIOLOGICAL ABSTRACTS.

SOCIOL. EDUC. ABSTR.
[UK/0038-0415]
SOCIOLOGY OF EDUCATION ABSTRACTS.

SOFT. ABSTR. ENG.
[IE/0790-150X]
SOFTWARE ABSTRACTS FOR ENGINEERS : SAFE.

SOILS FERT.
[UK/0038-0792]
SOILS AND FERTILIZERS.
(*Supersedes* Imperial Bureau of Soil Science. Monthly Letter.)

SOLID STATE ABSTR. J.
[US/0038-108X]
SOLID STATE ABSTRACTS JOURNAL.
(*Continued by* Solid State and Superconductivity Abstracts.)

SOLID STATE SUPERCOND. ABSTR.
[US/0896-5900]
SOLID STATE AND SUPERCONDUCTIVITY ABSTRACTS.
(*Continues* Solid State Abstracts Journal.)

SORGHUM MILL. ABSTR.
[UK/03082970]
SORGHUM AND MILLETS ABSTRACTS.
(Ceased)

SOUTH. BAPTIST PERIOD. INDEX
[US/0081-3028]
SOUTHERN BAPTIST PERIODICAL INDEX.

SOYABEAN ABSTR.
[UK/0141-0172]
SOYABEAN ABSTRACTS.

SPEC. EDUC. NEEDS ABSTR.
[UK/0954-0822]
SPECIAL EDUCATIONAL NEEDS ABSTRACTS.

SPIN
[US]
SPIN.

SPORT DISCUS
[US]
SPORT DISCUS [COMPUTER FILE].

SPORT FISH. ABSTR.
[US/0038-786X]
SPORT FISHERY ABSTRACTS.
(*Continued by* Fisheries Review.)

SPORTSEARCH
[US/0882-553X]
SPORTSEARCH.

STAT. REF. INDEX
[US/0885-6834]
STATISTICAL REFERENCE INDEX.

STAT. THEORY METHOD ABSTR.
[UK/0039-0518]
STATISTICAL THEORY AND METHOD ABSTRACTS.
(*Continues* International Journal of Abstracts: Statistical Theory and Method.)

STUD. WOMEN ABSTR.
[UK/0262-5644]
STUDIES ON WOMEN ABSTRACTS.

SUBJ. INDEX CHILD. MAG.
[US/0039-4351]
SUBJECT INDEX TO CHILDREN'S MAGAZINES.
(*Continued by* Children's Magazine Guide.)

SUBJ. INDEX PERIOD.
[UK]
SUBJECT INDEX TO PERIODICALS.
(*Split into* British Humanities Index *and* British Technology Index.)

SUBJ. INDEX SEL. PERIOD. LIT.
[US/0194-0708]
SUBJECT INDEX TO SELECT PERIODICAL LITERATURE.
(*Continued by* Mosher Periodical Index.)

SUG. INDUS. ABSTR.
[UK/0957-5022]
SUGAR INDUSTRY ABSTRACTS.

(*Continues* Tate & Lyle's Sugar Industry Abstracts.)

SURF. TREAT. TECHNOL. ABSTR.
[UK]
SURFACE TREATMENT TECHNOLOGY ABSTRACTS.
(*Continues* Metal Finishing Abstracts.)

TECH. DATA DIG.
[US]
TECHNICAL DATA DIGEST.
(Ceased)

TECH. EDUC. ABSTR.
[UK/0040-0920]
TECHNICAL EDUCATION ABSTRACTS.
(*Continued by* Technical Education & Training Abstracts.)

TECH. EDUC. TRAIN. ABSTR.
[UK]
TECHNICAL EDUCATION & TRAINING ABSTRACTS.
(*Continues* Technical Education Abstracts.)

TELEBASE.
[US]
TELEBASE [COMPUTER FILE].

TELEGEN ABSTR.
[US/0000-118X]
TELEGEN ABSTRACTS.
(*Continues* Telegen Reporter.)

INDEXES/ABSTRACTS TABLE

TELEGEN REPORT.
[US/0743-8443]
TELEGEN REPORTER.
(*Continued by* Telegen Abstracts.)

TERMITE ABSTR.
[UK/0144-5995]
TERMITE ABSTRACTS.
(**Ceased**)

TEXT. TECHNOL. DIG.
[US/0040-5191]
TEXTILE TECHNOLOGY DIGEST.

THEOL. RELIG. INDEX
[UK]
THEOLOGICAL AND RELIGIOUS INDEX.
(**Ceased**)

THEOR. CHEM. ENG.
[UK/0960-5053]
THEORETICAL CHEMICAL ENGINEERING.
(*Continues* Theoretical Chemical Engineering Abstracts.)

THEOR. CHEM. ENG. ABSTR.
[UK/0040-5787]
THEORETICAL CHEMICAL ENGINEERING ABSTRACTS.
(*Continued by* Theoretical Chemical Engineering.)

TOM GEN. INDEX
[US]
TOM GENERAL INDEX.

TOP MANAGE. ABSTR.
[UK/0049-4100]
TOP MANAGEMENT ABSTRACTS.
(*Continued by* Anbar Top Management Abstracts.)

TOPICATOR
[US/0040-9340]
TOPICATOR.

TOXICOL. ABSTR.
[US/0140-5365]
TOXICOLOGY ABSTRACTS.

TRADE IND. ASAP
[US]
TRADE & INDUSTRY ASAP [ONLINE DATABASE].

TRADE IND. INDEX
[US]
TRADE & INDUSTRY INDEX [ONLINE DATABASE].

TRANS. AM. SOC. CIV. ENG.
[US/0066-0604]
TRANSACTIONS OF THE AMERICAN SOCIETY OF CIVIL ENGINEERS.

TRANSP. RES. ABSTR.
[US/0095-2648]
TRANSPORTATION RESEARCH ABSTRACTS.
(*Absorbed in part by* HRIS Abstracts.)

TRANSP. STORAGE
[US]
TRANSPORTATION AND STORAGE.
(*Continued by* Literature Abstracts. Transportation & Storage.)

TROP. ABSTR.
[NE/0041-3208]
TROPICAL ABSTRACTS.
(*Superseded by* Abstracts on Tropical Agriculture.)

TROP. DIS. BULL.
[UK/0041-3240]
TROPICAL DISEASES BULLETIN.
(*Supersedes* Bulletin of the Sleeping Sickness Bureau and the Kala Azar Bulletin.)

U.S. POLIT. SCI. DOC.
[US/0148-6063]
UNITED STATES POLITICAL SCIENCE DOCUMENTS.
(*Absorbed* Asian Studies Indexed Journal Reference Guide.)

UMI ABI/INFORM--BUS. PERIOD. ONDISC
[US/1064-5381]
UMI ABI/INFORM--BUSINESS PERIODICALS ONDISC.

UNITED METHODIST PERIOD. INDEX
[US/0041-7319]
UNITED METHODIST PERIODICAL INDEX.
(*Continues* Methodist Periodical Index.)

URBAN AFF. ABSTR.
[US/0300-6859]
URBAN AFFAIRS ABSTRACTS.

VET. BULL.
[UK/0042-4854]
VETERINARY BULLETIN (LONDON).
(*Supersedes* Tropical Veterinary Bulletin; *Absorbed* Veterinary Reviews.)

VETDOC
[UK]
VETDOC.
***Refer to PESTDOC for complete source list.

VIROL. ABSTR.
[US/0042-6830]
VIROLOGY ABSTRACTS.
(*Continued by* Virology and AIDS Abstracts.)

VIROL. AIDS ABSTR.
[US/0896-5919]
VIROLOGY & AIDS ABSTRACTS.
(*Continues* Virology Abstracts.)

VIS. INDEX
[US/0049-6510]
VISION INDEX.
(**Ceased**)

VITIS VITIC. ENOL. ABSTR.
[GW/0175-8292]
VITIS, VITICULTURE AND ENOLOGY ABSTRACTS.
(*Separated from* Vitis.)

VOCAT. SEARCH
[US/1071-2747]
VOCATIONAL SEARCH.

WALL STREET J. INDEX
[US/0083-7075]
WALL STREET JOURNAL INDEX.
(**Ceased**)

WATER POLLUT. ABSTR.
[UK/0043-1281]
WATER POLLUTION ABSTRACTS.
(*Merged with* Water Research Association Library List *to form* WRC Information.)

WEED ABSTR.
[UK/0043-1729]
WEED ABSTRACTS.

WEST. HIST. Q.
[US/0043-3810]
WESTERN HISTORICAL QUARTERLY.

WHEAT BARLEY TRIT. ABSTR.
[UK/0265-7880]
WHEAT, BARLEY AND TRITICALE ABSTRACTS.
(*Continues* Triticale Abstracts.)

WILDL. REV.
[US/0043-5511]
WILDLIFE REVIEW (FORT COLLINS).

WILSON BUS. ABSTR.
[US/1057-6533]
WILSON BUSINESS ABSTRACTS.

WOMEN MANAG. REV. ABSTR.
[UK/0955-8357]
WOMEN IN MANAGEMENT REVIEW & ABSTRACTS.
(*Continued by* Women in Management Review.)

WOMEN MANAGE. REV.
[UK/0964-9425]
WOMEN IN MANAGEMENT REVIEW.
(*Continues* Women in Management Review & Abstracts.)

WOMEN STUD. ABSTR.
[US/0049-7835]
WOMEN STUDIES ABSTRACTS.

WORK RELAT. ABSTR.
[US/0273-3234]
WORK RELATED ABSTRACTS.
(*Continues* Employment Relations Abstracts.)

WORLD AGRIC. ECON. RURAL SOCIOL. ABSTR.
[UK/0043-8219]
WORLD AGRICULTURAL ECONOMICS AND RURAL SOCIOLOGY ABSTRACTS.

WORLD ALUM. ABSTR.
[US/0002-6697]
WORLD ALUMINUM ABSTRACTS.
(*Continued by* Aluminium Industry Abstracts.)

WORLD CERAM. ABSTR.
[UK/0957-8897]
WORLD CERAMICS ABSTRACTS.
(*Continues* British Ceramic Abstracts.)

WORLD FISH. ABSTR.
[IT/0043-8472]
WORLD FISHERIES ABSTRACTS.
(**Ceased**)

WORLD MAG. BANK
[US/1080-7950]
WORLD MAGAZINE BANK [COMPUTER FILE].

WORLD PUBL. MONIT.
[UK/0960-653X]
WORLD PUBLISHING MONITOR.
(*Continues* Electronic Publishing Abstracts.)

WORLD SURF. COAT. ABSTR.
[UK/0043-9088]
WORLD SURFACE COATINGS ABSTRACTS.
(*Continues* Review of Current Literature Relating to the Paint, Colour, Varnish and Allied Industries.)

WORLD TEXT. ABSTR.
[UK/0043-9118]
WORLD TEXTILE ABSTRACTS.
(*Supersedes* Textile Abstracts.)

WRC INF.
[UK/0306-6649]
WRC INFORMATION.
(*Continued by* Aqualine Abstracts.)

ZENTRALBL. MATH. IHRE GRENZGEB.
[GW/0044-4235]
ZENTRALBLATT FUER MATHEMATIK UND IHRE GRENZGEBIETE.
(*Superseded in part by* Zentralblatt fuer Mechanik.)

ZOOL. REC.
[UK/0144-3607]
ZOOLOGICAL RECORD (LONDON).
(*Continues* Record of Zoological Literature.)

AN INTERNATIONAL REFERENCE BOOK

AERONAUTICS, ASTRONAUTICS

LC TL **ISSN** 0273-608X
DD 629 US
99 NEWS, THE. [99 news]. **Added/Corp** Ninety-Nines (Organization). **VAT** Ninety-Nine News. (19??)-. Periodical. English. Ten times a year. $20.00. The 99 News, PO Box 59965, Oklahoma City OK 73159. **Tel** (405)682-7969.

LC HD9711.A1 A3 **ISSN** 0194-8652
DD 629.13 US
A/C FLYER, THE. **VFOAT** AC Flyer; Flyer. (19??)-. Periodical. English. Twelve times a year. $28.00. McGraw Hill Publishing Company, Inc., 1221 Avenue of the Americas, New York NY 10020. **Tel** (212)512-6410, (800)525-5003, FAX (212)512-6111. **(Subscription address:** AC Flyer, PO Box 609, Hightstown NJ 08520. **)** **Circ:** 60,000. available on an online database from University Microfilms International (UMI).
Desc: Provides lists of used aircraft for sale.

LC TL710 **ISSN** 0825-5229
DD 629.132/5471 CN
A.I.P. CANADA (ENGLISH ED.). (A.I.P. CANADA : AERONAUTICAL INFORMATION PUBLICATION.). [A.I.P. Can.]. **Added/Corp** Canadian Air Transportation Administration. **VAT** Aeronautical Information Publication Canada. (1980)-. Periodical. English. Irregular. Price varies. Canada Communication Group Publishers, Order Processing, Ottawa Ontario K1A 0S9 Canada. **Tel** (819)956-4800, (819)956-4802.

LC TL **ISSN** 0882-9365
DD 629 US
AAHS JOURNAL. [AAHS j.]. **Main/Corp** American Aviation Historical Society. **VAT** American Aviation Historical Society Journal. Vol. 25 (Spring 1980)-. Periodical. English. Four times a year (Mar., June, Sept., Dec.). $35.00 North America, $45.00 other Comes with American Aviation Historical Society membership. American Aviation Historical Society, 2333 Otis Street, Santa Ana CA 92704. **Tel** (714)549-4818. Index available (1956-1966 ($2.00) or 1966-1975 ($3.50)). cum. index. **Bk Rev. Ad Acc. Circ:** 3,000 (ctrl). ***Continues*** *American Aviation Historical Society. American Aviation Historical Society Journal, 0002-7553.*
Ind/Abst Am. Hist. Life (1980-).

LC TL501.A89 A25 **ISSN** 0300-6875
DD 629.13/009 US
AAHS NEWSLETTER. **Main/Corp** American Aviation Historical Society. **Added/Corp** American Aviation Historical Society. Newsletter. **VAT** American Aviation Historical Society Newsletter. (1967)-. Newsletter. English. Four times a year (Mar., June, Sept., Dec.). $35.00 North America, $45.00 other Comes with American Aviation Historical Society membership. American Aviation Historical Society, 2333 Otis Street, Santa Ana CA 92704. **Tel** (714)549-4818. **ED** Al Hansen and Bob Williams. Index available (1956-1966 ($2.00) or 1966-1975 ($3.50)). **Bk Rev. Ad Acc. Circ:** 3,000.

LC TL787 **ISSN** 0730-3564
DD 629.4 US
Pr Rev.
AAS HISTORY SERIES. [AAS hist. ser.]. **Main/Corp** American Astronautical Society. **VAT** American Astronautical Society History Series. Vol. 1 (1977)-. Monographic series. English. Irregular. Price varies per volume. Univelt Inc., PO Box 28130, San Diego CA 92128. **Tel** (619)746-4005. **ED** R. Cargill Hall. Index available. cum. index. **Circ:** 1,000. available on microfiche (out of print issues).
Desc: History series by historians who are specialists in aerospace history especially astronautics, including political and social aspects.
Ind/Abst Int. Aerosp. Abstr.

LC TL787 **ISSN** 0065-7417
DD 629.4 US
AAS MICROFICHE SERIES. (19??)-. Monographic series. English. Irregular. Price varies per volume. Univelt Inc, POB 28130, San Diego CA 92198. **Tel** (619)746-4005, FAX (619)746-3139. **ED** Horace and Robert Jacobs. Index available. **Bk Rev. Ad Acc. Circ:** 100. available on microfiche.
Desc: Complete series on Space and Astronautics.

LC TL720.7 .A2
DD 629 UK
ABC AIR CARGO GUIDE. **VFOAT** Air Cargo Guide. No. 141 (Oct. 1969)-. English. Twelve times a year. £215.00 Europe; £240.00 other. Reed Travel Group / England, World Timetable Center, Church Street Dunstable, Bedfordshire LU5 4HB United Kingdom. **Tel** 011 44 1582 600111, 011 44 1582 695569, FAX 011 44 1582 695230. **(Subscription address:** Reed Travel Group, 500 Plaza Drive, ABC International Division, Secaucus NJ 07096. **Tel** (201)902-2000.**)** ***Continues*** *ABC Air Cargo Guide and Directory.*
Desc: Gives you the comprehensive information you need to send anything anywhere by air.

LC G1046.P6 A2
DD 912/.138772 UK
ABC AIR TRAVEL ATLAS. **See** Travel and Tourism.

LC G
DD 912 FR
ABC AIRWAYS MAP OF THE WORLD. **See** Travel and Tourism.

LC G
DD 912 UK
TITLE CHANGE
ABC EXECUTIVE FLIGHT PLANNER EUROPE MID EAST & AFRICA. **See** Travel and Tourism.

LC G **ISSN** 0141-6278
DD 912 UK
ABC GUIDE TO INTERNATIONAL TRAVEL. **See** Travel and Tourism.

LC G **ISSN** 0001-0472
DD 912 UK
ABC RAIL GUIDE. **See** Travel and Tourism.

LC TL720.8 .A3
DD 656 UK
TITLE CHANGE
ABC WORLD AIRWAYS GUIDE, THE. **See** Travel and Tourism.

LC TL512 .A845 **ISSN** 0001-0502
DD 338.4/7/629102573 US
ABD. (ABD; AVIATION BUYER'S DIRECTORY.). **VAT** Aviation Business Directory; Aviation, Aerospace Buying Guide. Vol. 10, No. 4 (Oct. 1958)-. English. Four times a year (Mar., June, Sept., Dec.). $40.00. Aviation Buyers Directory, 105 Calvert Street, Harrison NY 06901. **Tel** (914)835-7200, FAX (914)835-2323. **ED** Jerry L. Greennard. **Ad Acc. Circ:** 16,000 (ctrl). ***Continues*** *Aviation Business Directory.*

LC TL **ISSN** 0172-3898
DD 629 GW
UDC 533.6
ABHANDLUNGEN AUS DEM AERODYNAMISCHEN INSTITUT DER RHEIN.-WESTF. TECHNISCHEN HOCHSCHULE AACHEN. (AACHEN, AERODYNAMISCHES INSTITUT ABHANDLUNGEN.). [Abh. Aerodyn. Inst. Rhein.-Westf. Tech. Hochsch. Aachen]. **VFOAT** Abhandlungen aus dem Aerodynamischen Institut an der Rheinisch-Westfalischen Technischen Hochschule in Aachen; Abhandlungen aus dem Aerodynamischen Institut der Technischen Hochschule Aachen. (1921)-. German. Irregular.
Ind/Abst Int. Aerosp. Abstr.

LC TL **ISSN** 1074-4312
DD 629 US
•**ACAR INTERNATIONAL.** (ACAR INTERNATIONAL : AIRLINE & COMMERCIAL AIRCRAFT REPORT.). [ACAR int.]. **Added/Corp** Airways International, Inc. **VFOAT** ACAR; International ACAR; Airline & Commercial Aircraft Report; Airline and Commercial Aircraft Report. (1994)-. Newsletter. English. Twelve times a year. $39.95. Airways International, Inc., PO Box 1109, Sandpoint ID 83864. **Tel** (208)263-5166, FAX (208)263-3313. **ED** John Wegg. **Ad Acc, Adv Mgr:** Seija Wegg-Itronen, **Tel** (208)263-5166. **Circ:** 5,000.

LC TL
DD 629 US
ACCEPTABLE METHODS, TECHNIQUES, AND PRACTICES. AIRCRAFT ALTERATIONS. **Main/Corp** United States. Federal Aviation Administration. **VFOAT** Aircraft Alterations. Government Publication. English. US Department of Transportation / Federal Aviation Administration, 800 Independence Avenue Southwest, Washington DC 20591. **Tel** (202)367-3484, FAX (202)367-3505.

LC TL **ISSN** 1014-4498
DD 629 CN
UDC 38
CODEN NU057
ACCIDENT/INCIDENT REPORTING ADREP. [Accid./incid. report. ADREP]. (1981)-. Periodical. English. Price varies per volume. International Civil Aviation Organization / ICAO, 1000 Sherbrooke Street West, Suite 400, Montreal Quebec H3A 2R2 Canada. **Tel** (514)285-8026, (514)285-8022, telex 05-24514.

LC HV **ISSN** 1057-5561
DD 363 US
ACCIDENT PREVENTION (ARLINGTON, VA.). (ACCIDENT PREVENTION.). [Accid. prev.]. **Added/Corp** Flight Safety Foundation. (19??)-. Periodical. English. Twelve times a year. $80.00. Flight Safety Foundation Inc., 2200 Wilson Boulevard, Suite 500, Arlington VA 22201. **Tel** (703)522-8300, FAX (703)525-6047, telex 901176 FSF INC AGTN. ***Continues*** *FSF Accident Prevention Bulletin, 0898-5774.*
Desc: Focuses on the flight deck, including reviews of accident reports. Topics have included subtle pilot incapacitation and techniques to prevent a runway overrun.

LC QB401
DD 523.98 NE
ACHIEVEMENTS OF ESA SCIENTIFIC SATELLITES, THE. (19??)-. English. Irregular. ESA Publications Division / ESTEC, 2200 AG Noordwijk The Netherlands. **Tel** FAX 011 31 1719 85433. **ED** T. D. Gliyenne. ***Continues*** *Report on the Scientific Satellites of the European Space Agency.*

LC UG1123 .U48a
DD 358.4/16212/0973 US
ACQUISITION FINANCIAL STATUS / AFSC COMPTROLLER. **Main/Corp** United States. Air Force. Systems Command. Comptroller. Vol. 1 (1991)-. English. Department of the Air Force / Headquarters Air Force Systems Command, Andrews AFB, Washington DC 20334-5000.

LC TL787 .A27 **ISSN** 0094-5765
DD 629.4/05 UK
CCC
CODEN AASTCF
Pr Rev.
ACTA ASTRONAUTICA. [Acta astronaut.]. **Added/Corp** International Academy of Astronautics. Vol. 1 (Jan./Feb. 1974)-. Academic Scholarly Publication. Multiple languages (English, French and Russian). Twenty-four times a year. $1861.00. Pergamon Press, An Imprint of Elsevier Science Ltd., The Boulevard, Langford Lane, Kidlington, Oxford OX5 1GB United Kingdom. **Tel** 011 44 1865 843000, 011 44 1865 843699, FAX 011 44 1865 843010. **(Subscription address:** Elsevier Science Ltd. / Oxford Fulfillment Centre, PO Box 800, Kidlington OX5 1DX United Kingdom. **Tel** 011 44 865 843355.**)** **ED** Jean-Pierre Marec (editor's address: International Academy of Astronautics, BP 62, F-75722, Paris Cedex 15 France). available on microfilm and microfiche from University Microfilms International (UMI); available on an online database from Elsevier Electronic Subscriptions (EES). Documents available from Article Express International, The Genuine Article, BIOSIS Document Express, Ask*IEEE, CASDDS, Documents on Demand. ***Supersedes*** *Astronautica Acta, 0004-6205.*
Desc: Publishes in all fields of engineering including life and social sciences and space technology related to the peaceful scientific exploration of space, its exploitation for human welfare and progress, and the conception, design, development and operation of space-borne and earth-based systems.
Ind/Abst Appl. Mech. Rev.; Bioeng. Abstr.; Biol. Abstr.; Chem. Abstr.; Curr. Cit.; Curr. Contents Eng. Comput. Technol.; Ei Page One; Energy Inf. Abstr.; Eng. Index Annu.; Environ. Abstr.; GeoRef; INSPEC (Jan./Feb. 1974-); Int. Aerosp. Abstr. (1991-); Math. Rev.; Res. Alert [Select. Cov.]; SCISEARCH; Soc. Sci. Cit. Index [Select. Cov.]; Zentralbl. Math. Ihre Grenzgeb.

LC TL522.O5 O48a
DD 353.97660087/77/06 US
ACTIVITY REPORT / OKLAHOMA AERONAUTICS COMMISSION. **Main/Corp** Oklahoma Aeronautics Commission. (19??)-. English. Oklahoma Aeronautics Commission, 200 NE 21st Street/Room 187, Oklahoma City OK 73105. **Tel** (405)521-2377, FAX (405)521-2379. ***Continues*** *Oklahoma Aeronautics Commission. Annual Report.*

LC TL787 .A277 **ISSN** 1041-102X
DD 629 US
CODEN ADASED
AD ASTRA (WASHINGTON, D.C.). (AD ASTRA / TO THE STARS : THE MAGAZINE OF THE NATIONAL SPACE SOCIETY.). [Ad astra]. **Added/Corp** National Space Society (U.S.). **VFOAT** To the Stars. Vol. 1, No. 1 (Jan. 1989)-. Periodical. English. Six times a year (Jan., Mar., May, Jul., Sept., Nov.). $40.00. National Space Society, 922 Pennsylvania Avenue Southeast, Washington DC 20003. **Tel** (202)543-1900, FAX (202)546-4189. **ED** Leonard David, Kate McMains. Index available. **Bk Rev. Ad Acc. Circ:** 30,000 (ctrl). available on microfilm and microfiche from University Microfilms International (UMI). Documents available from UMI Article Clearinghouse.
Desc: Features articles on space exploration and development, astronomy, satellites and technology, commercial space, educational activities and more.
Ind/Abst Acad. Abstr. Full Text Elite; Acad. Abstr.; Acad. Ind. [Computer File] (1989-); Acad. Search; EP Collect.; Expand. Acad. Index (1989-); Gen. Period. Index (1989-); Gen. Sci. Source; Homework Help.; Int. Aerosp. Abstr.; Mag. Artic. Summar. Elite; Mag. Artic. Summar. Select; Mag. Artic. Summar. CD-ROM; Mag. Index Plus (1989-); Mag. Index. Sel. (1989-); Mag. Search; MasterFile FullTEXT 1000; MasterFile FullTEXT 350; MasterFile FullTEXT 650; MasterFile FullTEXT (Jan. 1989-); Newsp. Period. Abstr. (1989-); OCLC; Pub. Lib. FullTEXT; Read. Guide Abstr. Select Ed.; Read. Guide Period. Lit.; Telebase; Mag. Index (1989-).

LC U1
DD 355 US
ADA. **See** Military and Defense.

LC TL698 .A37 **ISSN** 1055-9418
DD 629.134 US
ADVANCED MATERIALS IN AEROSPACE APPLICATIONS. [Adv. mater. aerosp. appl.]. **Added/Corp** Materials Information (Information Service). Industry Studies Division. (1989)-. Periodical. English. Irregular. £194.00. The Institute of Materials, 1 Carlton House Terrace, London SW1Y 5DB United Kingdom. **Tel** 011 44 171 8394071, FAX 011 171 8392078.

LC QB495 .A38 **ISSN** 0273-1177
DD 500.5 UK
CCC
CODEN ASRSDW
ADVANCES IN SPACE RESEARCH. (ADVANCES IN SPACE RESEARCH : THE OFFICIAL JOURNAL OF THE COMMITTEE ON SPACE RESEARCH (COSPAR).). [Adv. space res.]. **Added/Corp** COSPAR. Vol. 1, No. 1 (1981)-. Academic Scholarly Publication. English. Twenty-four times a year. $1980.00. Pergamon Press, An Imprint of Elsevier Science Ltd., The Boulevard, Langford Lane, Kidlington, Oxford OX5 1GB United Kingdom. **Tel** 011 44 1865 843000, 011 44 1865 843699, FAX 011 44 1865 843010. **(Subscription address:** Elsevier Science Ltd. / Oxford Fulfillment Centre, PO Box 800, Kidlington OX5 1DX United Kingdom. **Tel** 011 44 865 843355.) **ED** W. I. Axford. available on microfilm and microfiche from University Microfilms International (UMI); available on an online database from Elsevier Electronic Subscriptions (EES). Documents available from Ask*IEEE, CASDDS. ***Formed by the union of*** *Advances in Space Exploration, 0164-0046; Life Sciences and Space Research, 0075-9422* ***and*** *Space Research, 0081-3273.*
Desc: An interdisciplinary scientific organization concerned with the progress on an international scale of all kinds of fundamental research carried out with the use of balloons, rockets, or rocket propelled vehicles. Operating under the rules of ICSU, COSPAR ignores political considerations and considers all questions solely from the scientific viewpoint.
Ind/Abst Chem. Abstr.; Curr. Cit.; Ei Page One; Geogr. Abstr. Phys. Geogr.; Geol. Abstr.; GeoRef; INIS Atomindex [Micro.]; INSPEC (1982-); Int. Aerosp. Abstr.; Sci. Cit. Index.

LC TL787.A6 A2 **ISSN** 0065-3438
DD 629.4082 US
CODEN ADASA9
ADVANCES IN THE ASTRONAUTICAL SCIENCES. [Adv. astronaut. sci.]. **Added/Corp** American Astronautical Society. **VFOAT** Advances in the Astronautical Sciences. Vol. 4 (1958)-. Monographic series. English. Irregular. Price varies per volume. Univelt Inc., PO Box 28130, San Diego CA 92128. **Tel** (619)746-4005. **ED** H. Jacobs. Index available. cum. index. **Circ:** 600-800. available on microfiche. Documents available from Article Express International, Ask*IEEE, CASDDS. ***Continues*** *American Astronautical Society. Proceedings of the Annual Meeting.*
Desc: Technical series of the American Astronautical Society, based mainly on the proceedings of technical conferences in the field of astronautics.
Ind/Abst Bioeng. Abstr.; Chem. Abstr. (1957-1980); Curr. Cit.; Ei Page One; Eng. Index Annu.; INSPEC (1957-1980, 19??-).

LC TL504 .A2
DD 629.13 BL
AERO. (19??)-. Portuguese. Cr$150.00. J Ribeiro de Mendonca, Av Alfonso de Taunay 143, Barra de Tijuca, Rio de Janeiro Brazil.

LC TL500 **ISSN** 0279-7119
DD 629.13 US
SUSPENDED
AERO INDEX. (19??)-Suspended (19??). Periodical. English. Aero Economics, 19 Orchard Street, PO Box 4, Manhasset NY 11030. **Tel** (401)792-3820.

LC TL770.A1 A3 **ISSN** 0001-9232
DD 629.13334 UK
AERO MODELLER, THE. [Aero model.]. **Added/Corp** Skybird League. Air League of the British Empire. Junior Section. **VFOAT** Aeromodeller. Vol. 1, No. 1 (Nov. 1935)-. Periodical. English. Twelve times a year. $31.90. Argus Specialist Publications, Argus House, Boundary Way / Hemel, Hempstead Herts HP27ST United Kingdom. **Tel** 011 44 181 6671033, FAX 011 44 181 6889573, telex 948669 TOPJNL G. ***Continues*** *Skybird.*
Desc: In-depth coverage of model building and flying - encourages the beginner by "how-to-do-it" features and plans, and supplies the expert with the latest developments and reports worldwide.
Ind/Abst Index Inf. (1990-).

LC TL503 .A427 **ISSN** 0001-9186
DD 629.132/5217/09494 SZ
AERO REVUE. [Aero rev.]. **Added/Corp** Aero-Club der Schweiz. International Technical and Scientific Organization for Soaring Flight. (1956)-. Periodical. French (German and English). Twelve times a year. $68.83. Ringier Print Kommunikation, Zuerichstrasse 5, CH-6002 Luzern Switzerland. **Tel** 011 41 41 391589. **Bk Rev. Ad Acc. Circ:** 24,000 (ctrl). ***Supersedes*** *Schweizer Aero-Revue.*
Desc: Trade periodical for all branches of aviation.
Ind/Abst Int. Aerosp. Abstr.

LC TL **ISSN** 0326-1360
DD 629 AG
UDC 380.8
AEROCOMERCIAL. [Aerocomercial]. **VFOAT** AC/Aerocomercial. (1969)-. Periodical. Multiple languages. Six times a year. $80.00. Maipu 359 - P7, Buenos Aires Argentina. **Tel** 011 54 1 3251529, FAX 011 54 1 3253178. **ED** Liliana Cristina Noval. **Ad Acc. Circ:** 11,500 (ctrl).

LC HE9761
DD 387.7 CN
AERODROMES; INTERNATIONAL STANDARDS AND RECOMMENDED PRACTICES. ANNEX 14 TO THE CONVENTION ON INTERNATIONAL CIVIL AVIATION. **Main/Corp** International Civil Aviation Organization. (19??)-. English. $17.75. International Civil Aviation Organization / ICAO, 1000 Sherbrooke Street West, Suite 400, Montreal Quebec H3A 2R2 Canada. **Tel** (514)285-8026, (514)285-8022, telex 05-24514.

LC TL504 .R547
DD 629.13 AG
Pr Rev.
AEROESPACIO (BUENOS AIRES, ARGENTINA). (AEROESPACIO; REVISTA NACIONAL AERONAUTICA Y ESPACIAL.). **Added/Corp** Circulo de Aeronautica (Argentina). **VFOAT** Aero Espacio. Vol. 27, No. 300 (July 1967)-. Periodical. Spanish (English). Six times a year. $65.00. Aero Espacio / Redaccion y Administracion, Paraguay 748, 1057 Buenos Aires Argentina. **Tel** 011 54 1 3142753, 011 54 1 3143309, FAX 011 54 1 3142753, telex 39-21763. **ED** Fuerza Aerea Argentina. Index available (Publishes each year in its last edition). **Bk Rev**, (Qty: 10). **Ad Acc, Adv Mgr:** Liliana Carlos. Full Page (B&W) $2,800.00. Half Page (B&W) $1,800.00. **Acid Free. Circ:** 27,000 (ctrl). ***Continues*** *Revista Nacional Aeronautica y Espacial.*
Desc: Editorial articles, comments, and news on all aspects of aviation and space.

LC TL503 .D46 **ISSN** 0341-1281
DD 629.13 GW
CCC
AEROKURIER. [Aerokurier]. **Added/Corp** Deutscher Aero-Club. (1976)-. Academic Scholarly Publication. German. Twelve times a year. $82.91. Aerokurier, PO 5 Nordring 10, W-4650 Gelsenkirche-Buer Germany. **Tel** 011 49 511 20937431, FAX 011 49 511 209395398, telex 824727. **(Subscription address:** Deutscher Pressevertrieb Buch, POB 101602 Hansa GMBH, D-20010 Hamburg Germany. **Tel** 011 49 40 23711249.) **ED** Werner Pfaendler. Index available. cum. index. **Bk Rev. Ad Acc, Adv Mgr:** Reinhard Wittstamm, **Tel** 011 49 711 18201. Full Page (B&W) DM6000.00. Full Page (Color) DM11100.00. **Circ:** 48,000 (ctrl). available with charts; available with illustrations. Documents available from BLDSC, SWETS. ***Continues*** *Deutscher Aerokurier.*
Desc: Covers the entire civil aviation spectrum, from microlights and sailplanes to light aircraft, business jets, commercial aircraft and space projects.
Ind/Abst EMBASE.

LC TL **ISSN** 0394-820X
DD 629 IT
UDC 629.7
CODEN 355.45
Pr Rev.
AERONAUTICA & DIFESA. **VFOAT** Aeronautica e Difesa. (1986)-. Periodical. Italian. Eleven times a year. L32700. Edizioni Monografie SRL, Casella Postale 2118, 00100 Rome AD Italy. **Tel** 011 39 6 511-2406. **ED** Claudio Tatangelo. Index available. **Bk Rev. Ad Acc. Circ:** 45,000.
Desc: Magazine of aeronautics and space technologies.

LC TL500.5 .A2 Z6026.A2 TL587
DD 387.7 S 016.629132/54 CN
AERONAUTICAL CHART CATALOGUE / CATALOGUE DES CARTES AERONAUTIQUES / CATALOGO DE CARTAS AERONAUTICAS / KATALOG AERONAVIGATSIONNIKH KART.
Main/Corp International Civil Aviation Organization. **Added/Corp** International Civil Aviation Organization Catalogue des Cartes Aeronautiques. International Civil Aviation Organization Catalogo de Cartas Aeronauticas. **VFOAT** Catalogue des Cartes Aeronautiques; Catalogo de Cartas Aeronauticas. 1st Ed. (1960)-. English (French, Spanish and Russian). $44.00. International Civil Aviation Organization / ICAO, 1000 Sherbrooke Street West, Suite 400, Montreal Quebec H3A 2R2 Canada. **Tel** (514)285-8026, (514)285-8022, telex 05-24514.

LC TL
DD 629 CN
AERONAUTICAL CHARTS; INTERNATIONAL STANDARDS AND RECOMMENDED PRACTICES. ANNEX 4 TO THE CONVENTION ON INTERNATIONAL CIVIL AVIATION.
Main/Corp International Civil Aviation Organization. (19??)-. English. $5.50. International Civil Aviation Organization / ICAO, 1000 Sherbrooke Street West, Suite 400, Montreal Quebec H3A 2R2 Canada. **Tel** (514)285-8026, (514)285-8022, telex 05-24514.

LC TL
DD 629 US
●**AERONAUTICAL INFORMATION MANUAL.** (1995)-. English. $84.00. Superintendent of Documents, US Government Printing Office, Washington DC 20402. **Tel** (202)275-3328, FAX (202)786-2377. ***Continues*** *Airman's Information Manual.*

LC TL
DD 629 GW
AERONAUTICAL INFORMATION PUBLICATION. (19??)-. German. Irregular. DM663.00. R. Eisenschmidt GmbH, Postfache 110761, D-60042 Frankfurt Germany. **Tel** 011 49 69 7306040.
Desc: A comprehensive aeronautical publication containing regulations and data required for safe aircraft operations in the National Airspace System.

LC TL
DD 629 CN
AERONAUTICAL INFORMATION SERVICES; INTERNATIONAL STANDARDS AND RECOMMENDED PRACTICES. ANNEX 15 TO THE CONVENTION ON INTERNATIONAL CIVIL AVIATION. **Main/Corp** International Civil Aviation Organization. (19??)-. English. $5.25 (8th edition incorporating Amendments 1-27). International Civil Aviation Organization / ICAO, 1000 Sherbrooke Street West, Suite 400, Montreal Quebec H3A 2R2 Canada. **Tel** (514)285-8026, (514)285-8022, telex 05-24514.

LC TL500.5 .A2
DD 387.7 S 387.7/07 CN
AERONAUTICAL INFORMATION SERVICES PROVIDED BY STATES / SERVICES D'INFORMATION AERONAUTIQUE ASSURES PAR LES ETATS / SERVICIOS DE INFORMACION AERONAUTICA SUMINISTRADOS POR LOS ESTADOS. **Main/Corp** International Civil Aviation Organization. **Added/Corp** International Civil Aviation Organization. Services d'Information Aeronautique Assures par les Etats. International Civil Aviation Organization. Servicios de Informacion Aeronautica Suministrados por los Estados. **VFOAT** Services d'Information Aeronautique Assures par Les Etats; Servicios de Informacion Aeronautica Suministrados por Los Estados. (19??)-. English (French and Spanish). Irregular. $21.00. International Civil Aviation Organization / ICAO, 1000 Sherbrooke Street West, Suite 400, Montreal Quebec H3A 2R2 Canada. **Tel** (514)285-8026, (514)285-8022, telex 05-24514. **ED** J.C. Price. **Circ:** 2,300 (ctrl).
Desc: Compendium of services provided by states in aeronautical information publications. Notices to airmen and aeronautical information circulars.

LC TL501 .R7 **ISSN** 0001-9240
DD 387.7/05 UK
CODEN AENJAK
Pr Rev.
AERONAUTICAL JOURNAL, THE. [Aeronaut. j.]. **Added/Corp** Royal Aeronautical Society. Vol. 72 (1968)-. Academic Scholarly Publication. English. Ten times a year. $379.00. Royal Aeronautical Society, PO Box 139, Tonbridge Kent TN9 1EW United Kingdom. **Tel** 011 44 1454 620070, FAX 011 44 1454 620080. **ED** Bernard F Baldwin. Index available. cum. index. **Bk Rev. Ad Acc. Circ:** 2,000 (ctrl). available on microfilm and microfiche from University Microfilms International (UMI). Documents available from Article Express International, The Genuine Article, Ask*IEEE, CASDDS. ***Continues*** *Journal of the Royal Aeronautical Society, 0368-3931;* ***Absorbed*** *Aeronautical Quarterly.*
Desc: Composed of reports, analyses, informative charts, graphs, and equations which detail the latest aeronautical techniques and research. Topics include: aircraft design, construction, production and fabrication, aerodynamics, propulsion, policy, law, operations, management and history. Includes article summaries, notational explanations and references.
Ind/Abst Acoust. Abstr.; Alum. Ind. Abstr.; Appl. Sci. Technol. Index; BMT Abstr.; Chem. Abstr.; Curr. Cit.; Curr. Contents Eng. Comput. Technol.; Curr. Technol. Index; Ei Page One; EMBASE; Eng. Mater. Abstr.; Eng. Index Annu.; Fluid Abstr., Civil Eng.; Fluid Abstr. Proc. Eng.; FLUIDEX (1983-); INSPEC (1968-); Int. Aerosp. Abstr.; Math. Rev.; Met. Abstr.; Res. Alert [Select. Cov.]; Saf. Health Work; SCISEARCH; Shock Vibr. Dig.

LC TL501 .A3286
DD 629.13/05 CN

AERONAUTICAL NOTE. **Added/Corp** National Research Council Canada. National Aeronautical Establishment (Canada). NAE-AN-1 (Jan. 1983)-. Monographic series. English (summaries and/or abstracts in French). Irregular. Free on request. National Research Council / Canada, Publishing Department, Research-Building 55, Ottawa Ontario K1A 0R6 Canada. **Tel** (613)993-9084.

LC TL **ISSN** 0077-5541
DD 629.1 CN
CODEN NCCAAX

AERONAUTICAL REPORT LR. (AERONAUTICAL REPORT.). [Aeronaut. rep. LR]. **VAT** Aeronautical Report Laboratory Report. 1972-. English (summaries and/or abstracts in French). National Research Council / Canada, Publishing Department, Research- Building 55, Ottawa Ontario K1A 0R6 Canada. **Tel** (613)993-9084. Documents available from Article Express International. ***Continues*** *Aeronautical Report (National Research Council of Canada), 0077-5541.*
Ind/Abst Bioeng. Abstr.; Ei Page One; Eng. Index Annu.

LC TL
DD 629 CN

AERONAUTICAL TELECOMMUNICATIONS, INTERNATIONAL STANDARDS AND RECOMMENDED PRACTICES. ANNEX 10 TO THE CONVENTION ON INTERNATIONAL CIVIL AVIATION. **Main/Corp** International Civil Aviation Organization. (19??)-. English. Irregular. $35.50 (4th edition). International Civil Aviation Organization / ICAO, 1000 Sherbrooke Street West, Suite 400, Montreal Quebec H3A 2R2 Canada. **Tel** (514)285-8026, (514)285-8022, telex 05-24514.

LC TL789.8.U5 U57a **ISSN** 0277-6499
DD 629.4/0973 US

AERONAUTICS AND SPACE REPORT OF THE PRESIDENT. ACTIVITIES. (AERONAUTICS AND SPACE REPORT OF THE PRESIDENT ... ACTIVITIES / EXECUTIVE OFFICE OF THE PRESIDENT, NATIONAL AERONAUTICS AND SPACE COUNCIL.). [Aeronaut. space rep. Pres., Act.]. **Main/Corp** United States. President. **Added/Corp** United States. National Aeronautics and Space Council. United States. National Aeronautics and Space Administration. **VAT** Aeronaut. Space Rep. Pres., Act. (19??)-. English. One time a year. Free on request. NASA - National Aeronautics and Space Administration, LCG 9 NASA Headquarters, Washington DC 20546. ***Continues*** *Aeronautics and Space Report of the President, 0566-7186.*

LC TL502 .A3312 **ISSN** 0001-9275
FR
CCC
CODEN AENABS
TITLE CHANGE

AERONAUTIQUE ET L'ASTRONAUTIQUE, L'. [Aeronaut. astronaut.]. **Added/Corp** Association Francaise des Ingenieurs et Techniciens de l'Aeronautique et de l'Espace. Societe Francaise d'Astronautique. (Feb. 1968)-(1994). Periodical. French. Six times a year. Aeronautique & Astronautique de France / AAAF, 6 rue Galille, 75782 Paris Cedex 16 France. **Tel** 011 33 1 47230749, FAX 011 33 1 42277808, telex 290108. **ED** Jean Marie Riche. **Bk Rev. Ad Acc. Circ:** 2,500. Documents available from Ask*IEEE, CASDDS. ***Continues in part*** *Technique et Science Aeronautiques et Spatiales* ***and*** *Astronautique;* ***Absorbed in part*** *Doc-Air-Espace* ***and*** *Revue Francaise d-Astronautique.* ***Continued by*** *Nouvelle Revue Aeronautique Astronautique, 1247-5793.*
Desc: Studies on air and spacecraft technology: design and construction, aerodynamics, propulsion, materials and equipment.
Ind/Abst Alum. Ind. Abstr.; Chem. Abstr. (1968-1982); Energy Res. Abstr.; INSPEC (1971-1986); Int. Aerosp. Abstr. (1991-); Met. Abstr.

LC TL **ISSN** 0572-3159
DD 629 BE
CODEN AACADF

AERONOMICA ACTA. A. [Aeron. acta. A]. Academic Scholarly Publication. Multiple languages. Irregular. Price varies per volume. Inst d'Aeronomie Spatiale Belgique, Avenue Circulaire 3, B-1180 Brussels Belgium. **Tel** 02/374.27.28, FAX 02/374.84.23. ctrl circ. Documents available from CASDDS.
Ind/Abst Chem. Abstr.; Int. Aerosp. Abstr.

LC TL **ISSN** 0568-0581
DD 629 US
CODEN IELEBG

AERONOMY REPORT. [Aeron. rep.]. **Added/Corp** University of Illinois. Aeronomy Laboratory. No. 1 (Dec. 1, 1973)-. Periodical. English. University of Illinois / Department of Electrical Engineering, Urbana IL 61801. Documents available from Article Express International.
Ind/Abst Bioeng. Abstr.; Ei Page One; Eng. Index Annu.

LC TL **ISSN** 0148-6691
DD 629 US

AEROPHILE EXTRA. [Aerophile extra]. No. 1-. Monographic series. English. Price varies per volume. Aerophile, 4014 Belle Grove, San Antonio TX 78230. **Tel** (512)696-0447.

LC TL **ISSN** 0212-4556
DD 629 SP

AEROPLANO. (1983)-. Spanish. One time a year (Dec.). $18.18. Inst Historia Cultura Aeronaut, Romero Robledo 8 1A PTA, 28071 Madrid Spain. **Tel** 011 34 1 5444080 or 5446032.

LC TL501 .A55214 **ISSN** 0143-7240
DD 629.133/34/05 UK

AEROPLANT MONTHLY. [Aeropl. mon.]. **Added/Corp** IPC Transport Press. **VFOAT** Aeroplane. (19??)-. Periodical. English. Twelve times a year. $55.00. IPC Magazines Ltd., Perrymount Road, Haywards Heath, West Sussex RH16 3DH United Kingdom. **Tel** 011 44 1444 440421, FAX 011 44 1444 445599. available on microfiche from University Microfilms International (UMI).

LC TL **ISSN** 0336-626X
DD 629 FR
UDC 65

AEROPORTS MAGAZINE. (1975)-. Periodical. French. Ten times a year. 270.00F France; 330.00F Europe; 430.00F Africa; 550.00F US and Asia; 28.00F (single issue). Aeroports Magazine, 291 boulevard Raspail, 75675 Paris Cedex 14 France.

LC TL501.A688 A25 **ISSN** 0740-722X
DD 629.1/05 US
CCC
Pr Rev.

AEROSPACE AMERICA. [Aerosp. Am.]. **Added/Corp** American Institute of Aeronautics and Astronautics. Vol. 22, No. 1 (Jan. 1984)-. Academic Scholarly Publication. English. Twelve times a year. $95.00. American Institute of Aeronautics & Astronautics, 370 l'Enfant Promenade Southwest, Washington DC 20024-2518. **Tel** (202)646-7400, FAX (202)646-7508, telex 204792 AIAA UR. **ED** Jay Lowndes. Index available. **Ad Acc. Circ:** 65,000. available on microfiche from University Microfilms International (UMI); available on an online database from NEXIS; Mead Data Central; DATA-STAR; DIALOG; and (PROMPT) BRS. Documents available from Article Express International, The Genuine Article, UMI Article Clearinghouse. ***Continues*** *Astronautics & Aeronautics, 0004-6213.*
Desc: Articles cover surveys of emerging technologies, trends in aerospace technology and design, analysis of national aerospace issues, workplace changes that affect the aerospace professional, and international developments in aerospace.
Ind/Abst Acad. Abstr. Full Text Elite; Acad. Abstr.; Acad. Search; Acoust. Abstr.; Appl. Sci. Technol. Index (1984-); Aviat. Tradescan [Full Cov.]; Bioeng. Abstr.; Curr. Cit.; Curr. Contents Eng. Comput. Technol.; Ei Page One; EMBASE (1984-); Energy Inf. Abstr. (1984-?); Energy Res. Abstr. (1984-); Eng. Index Annu.; EP Collect.; Expand. Acad. Index (1992-); Homework Help.; INFO-SOUTH Abstr.; INIS Atomindex [Micro.]; Int. Aerosp. Abstr. (1984-); Mag. Artic. Summar. Elite; Mag. Artic. Summar. Select; Mag. Artic. Summar. CD-ROM; Mag. Search; MasterFile FullTEXT 1000; MasterFile FullTEXT 350; MasterFile FullTEXT 650; MasterFile FullTEXT (July 1990-); Newsp. Period. Abstr. (1992-); OCLC; Pollut. Abstr. Indexes; Pub. Lib. FullTEXT; Res. Alert [Select. Cov.]; SCISEARCH; Shock Vibr. Dig.; Soc. Sci. Cit. Index [Select. Cov.]; Telebase; Vocat. Search.

LC U **ISSN** 1051-9793
DD 355 US
CEASED

AEROSPACE & DEFENSE SCIENCE. [Aerosp. def. sci.]. **VFOAT** Aerospace and Defense Science; A&DS. Vol. 9, No. 4 (May 1990)-Vol. 10, No. 2. Periodical. English. Aerospace & Defense Science, PO Drawer 033619, Indialantic FL 32903. **Tel** (407)773-5711. ***Continues*** *DefenseScience (Campbell, Calif.), 1044-7547.*

LC Z5060.A2 A32
DD 016.6294 US

AEROSPACE BIBLIOGRAPHY. See Aeronautics, Astronautics-Abstracting, Bibliographies and Statistics.

LC TL289.8.C55 C5313 **ISSN** 1004-9711
DD 629.4/0951 CC
Pr Rev.

AEROSPACE CHINA. **Added/Corp** Hang Kung Hang Tien pu Hang Tien Ko Chi Ching Pao Yen Chiu So (China). (199?)-. Academic Scholarly Publication. English. Two times a year (July and Dec.). $50.00. Institute of Astronautics Information, PO Box 1408, Beijing 100013 China. **Tel** 011 86 1 8372847, FAX 011 86 1 4227606. **ED** Xue Fuxing (Editor-in-Chief). **Ad Acc, Adv Mgr:** A. Bo, **Tel** 011 86 1 8372847.
Desc: Provides updated information of China's national space policies, plans, activities, programs and projects. Contains the latest information of the development, design, test, production and use of launch vehicles, satellites and rockets.

LC TL **ISSN** 0954-5832
DD 629 UK
TITLE CHANGE

AEROSPACE COMPOSITES & MATERIALS. **VFOAT** Aerospace Composites and Materials. (1988)-(19??). Trade Publication. English. Shepard Press Ltd, 111 High Street, Burnham Buckinghamshire SL1 7JZ United Kingdom. **Tel** 011 44 1628 604311, FAX 011 44 1628 664334, telex 846575 AIRGO. Documents available from CASDDS. ***Continued by*** *Aerospace Materials.*
Ind/Abst Chem. Abstr. (?-?); F&S Index Plus Text, Int. [Select. Cov.]; Int. Aerosp. Abstr. (19??-19??); PROMT.

LC HD9711.5.U58 A33 **ISSN** 0193-4546
DD 338 US

AEROSPACE DAILY. [Aerosp. daily]. (19??)-. English. Five times a week (260 issues). $1475.00. McGraw Hill Publishing Company, Inc., 1221 Avenue of the Americas, New York NY 10020. **Tel** (212)512-6410, (800)525-5003, FAX (212)512-6111. **ED** William Hall. available on an online database from Lexis-Nexis; NEWSNET; Dow Jones News/Retrieval; Mead Data Central; European Space Agency; DATA-STAR; (file 624/Full-Text) DIALOG; and BRS.
Desc: News, insider tips and analysis for every professional in the aerospace and defense industry.
Ind/Abst F&S Index Plus Text, Int. [Select. Cov.]; PROMT; Trade Ind. Index.

LC TL **ISSN** 1057-1191
DD 629 US

AEROSPACE DAILY'S AEROGRAM. [Aerosp. daily's aerogram]. **VFOAT** Aerogram. (1991)-. Periodical. English. Seven times a week. $497.00. McGraw Hill Publishing Company, Inc., 1221 Avenue of the Americas, New York NY 10020. **Tel** (212)512-6410, (800)525-5003, FAX (212)512-6111.

LC HB **ISSN** 1057-333X
DD 338 US

AEROSPACE DAILY'S WEEKLY BRIEFING. [Aerosp. Dly. wkly. brief.]. **VFOAT** Weekly Briefing. (1991)-No Longer Available (19??). Periodical. English. One time a week. McGraw Hill Publishing Company, Inc., 1221 Avenue of the Americas, New York NY 10020. **Tel** (212)512-6410, (800)525-5003, FAX (212)512-6111. **(Subscription address:** McGraw Hill Aviation Newsletters, PO Box 489, Hightstown NJ 08520. **Tel** (609)426-5511.**)**

LC TL
DD 629 UK

AEROSPACE DESIGN & COMPONENTS. **VFOAT** Aerospace Design and Components. Periodical. English.

LC TL671.2 .S314 **ISSN** 0736-2536
DD 629.1/05 US
CCC

AEROSPACE ENGINEERING (WARRENDALE, PA.). (AEROSPACE ENGINEERING.). [Aerosp. eng.]. **Added/Corp** Society of Automotive Engineers. Vol. 3, No. 1 (March 1983)-. Periodical. English. Twelve times a year. $55.00. Society of Automotive Engineers, 400 Commonwealth Drive, Warrendale PA 15096. **Tel** (412)776-4970, FAX (412)776-0790. **ED** Daniel J. Holt. **Bk Rev. Ad Acc. Circ:** 45,000 (ctrl). available on an online database from DATA-STAR; BRS; and (file 648/Full-Text) DIALOG; available on microfilm and microfiche from University Microfilms International (UMI). Documents available from Article Express International. ***Continues*** *SAE in Aerospace Engineering, 0730-3017.*
Desc: Provides aerospace project managers and design engineers with state-of-the-art technology that can be applied to the development of new aerospace vehicle systems; editors have direct access to the vast SAE aerospace technical network.
Ind/Abst Acoust. Abstr.; Aviat. Tradescan [Full Cov.]; Curr. Cit.; Elect. Comm. Abstr.; Eng. Mater. Abstr.; Eng. Index Annu. [Select. Cov.]; Fluid Abstr., Civil Eng.; Fluid Abstr. Proc. Eng.; FLUIDEX; Int. Aerosp. Abstr.; Mech. Eng. Abstr.

LC TL512 .A848 **ISSN** 0143-1145
DD 629.13/029/4 UK

AEROSPACE EUROPE. 41st Edition (1988/89)-. English (table of contents in French and German). One time a year. $165.99. Miller Freeman Technical Ltd., Riverbank House, Angel Lane, Tonbridge Kent TN9 1SE United Kingdom. **Tel** 011 44 1732 362666, FAX 011 44 1732 770483, telex 95454 BBIS. ***Continues*** *Aviation Europe.*

LC TL501 .A818 **ISSN** 0898-4425
DD 629.13058 US

AEROSPACE FACTS AND FIGURES. See Aeronautics, Astronautics-Abstracting, Bibliographies and Statistics.

LC HD28 **ISSN** 1057-0950
DD 658 US
CCC
TITLE CHANGE

AEROSPACE FINANCIAL NEWS. [Aerosp. financ. news]. (1991)-(April 1993). Periodical. English. Phillips Business Information Inc., 1201 Seven Locks Road, PO Box 61130, Potomac MD 20854. **Tel** (301)424-3338, (301)340-1520, (800)777-5005, FAX (301)424-4297, telex 358149. available on an online database from DATA-STAR; NEWSNET; and (file 636/Full-Text) DIALOG. ***Absorbed*** *Defense / Aerospace Business Digest.* ***Merged into*** *Defense Daily.*
Ind/Abst PTS Newsl. Database [Full Txt.].

LC HB **ISSN** 1066-8985
DD 338 US

AEROSPACE INDUSTRY EMPLOYMENT SURVEY. [Aerosp. ind. employ. surv.]. **Added/Corp** Aerospace Industries Association of America. (19??)-. English. One time a year. Free on request. Aerospace Industries Association of America, 1250 Eye Street Northwest, Washington DC 20005. **Tel** (202)371-8561, FAX (202)371-8470, telex 710-822-0134 AIA DC TKU.

LC TL **ISSN** 0883-0096
DD 629 US
CODEN AINEE3

AEROSPACE INFORMATION REPORT. [Aerosp. inf. rep.]. **Added/Corp** Society of Automotive Engineers. Periodical. English. Irregular. Society of Automotive Engineers, 400 Commonwealth Drive, Warrendale PA 15096. **Tel** (412)776-4970, FAX (412)776-0790.
Ind/Abst Int. Aerosp. Abstr.

LC TL **ISSN** 0305-0831
DD 629 UK

AEROSPACE (LONDON, 1974). (AEROSPACE.). [Aerospace]. **Added/Corp** Royal Aeronautical Society. **VAT** Aerospace (Royal Aeronautical Society). (July 1974)-. Trade Publication. English. Twelve times a year. $162.57. Royal Aeronautical Society, PO Box 139, Tonbridge Kent TN9 1EW United Kingdom. **Tel** 011 44 1454 620070, FAX 011 44 1454 620080. **ED** R Bryanton. **Bk Rev. Ad Acc. Circ:** 15,000. available on microfilm and microfiche from University Microfilms International (UMI). ***Absorbed*** *Tech Air.*
Desc: Information on every sector of the aerospace industry with international news, new products and services, and a record of work in all aerospace fields by the Royal Aeronautical Society.
Ind/Abst Curr. Cit.; Int. Aerosp. Abstr.

LC TL
DD 629 US

AEROSPACE MATERIAL SPECIFICATIONS. **Main/Corp** Society of Automotive Engineers. (1941)-. Periodical. English. Four times a year. Society of Automotive Engineers, 400 Commonwealth Drive, Warrendale PA 15096. **Tel** (412)776-4970, FAX (412)776-0790. **(Subscription address:** SAE / Society of Automotive Engineers, Department L1094P, Pittsburgh PA 15264. **)** available on microfiche.
Desc: Over 2,000 documents offering comprehensive data on chemical composition, special properties, tolerances, quality controls, and processes for all materials used in aerospace vehicles.

LC TL
DD 629 UK
CEASED

AEROSPACE MATERIALS. (19??)-Vol. 5, No. 3. English. Shephard Press Ltd, 111 High Street, Burnham Buckinghamshire SL1 7JZ United Kingdom. **Tel** 011 44 1628 604311, FAX 011 44 1628 664334, telex 846575. ***Continues*** *Aerospace Composites & Materials.*

LC Z6664.3 .A36 **ISSN** 0001-9410
DD 629.13 US
NLM ZWD 700 A957

AEROSPACE MEDICINE AND BIOLOGY. **See** Medical Sciences.

LC TL
DD 629 UK

AEROSPACE NEWS. **Added/Corp** General Electric Company. (July 1992)-. Periodical. English. Twelve times a year. General Electric Company, 120 Erie Boulevard, Schenectady NY 12305. **Tel** (502)685-6200. ***Continues*** *Syracuse News, 0272-2917.*

LC TL
DD 629 US

AEROSPACE NEWS AND REVIEW. (19??)-. English. Twenty-four times a year. $39.00. Aerotech News and Review, PO Box 1332, Lancaster CA 93534. **Tel** (805)945-5634. **ED** Paul Kinison. **Ad Acc. Circ:** 10,000.

LC WMLC 93/1952 **ISSN** 1054-7045
DD 629 US
CCC
CEASED

AEROSPACE PRODUCTS. [Aerosp. prod.]. (19??)-(Oct. 1993). Periodical. English. Gordon Publications Inc., A Subsidiary of Cahners Publishing Company, 301 Gibraltar Drive, Box 650, Morris Plains NJ 07950. **Tel** (201)292-5100, (800)637-6081.
Desc: Serves the aerospace/aviation industry. The audience is made up of military, government, laboratory R&D, engineering managers and other industry professionals.

LC HE9761 **ISSN** 1050-5245
DD 387.7 US

AEROSPACE PROPULSION (WASHINGTON, D.C. 1990). (AEROSPACE PROPULSION.). [Aerosp. propuls.]. Vol. 1, No. 1 (May 30, 1990)-. Periodical. English. Twenty-six times a year. $605.00. McGraw Hill Publishing Company, Inc., 1221 Avenue of the Americas, New York NY 10020. **Tel** (212)512-6410, (800)525-5003, FAX (212)512-6111. available on an online database (file 624/Full-Text) from DIALOG.

LC HB **ISSN** 0129-1815
DD 338.476291095 SI
CEASED

AEROSPACE SINGAPORE. [Aerospace Singap.]. (1989)-(July 1995). Periodical. English. Asian Business Press Pte Ltd, PO Box 219, 9118 Singapore Singapore. **Tel** 011 65 2943366.

LC TL
DD 629 FR

AEROSPACE WORLD. (19??)-. English. Irregular. $78.00 US and Canada; $65.00 Western Europe; $84.00 other. Aerospace Media Publishing / France, 1 Bis Avenue de la Republique, 75011 Paris France. **Tel** 011 33 1 49293000. ***Continues*** *Air & Cosmos.*
Ind/Abst Infomat Int. Bus.; PROMT [Full Txt.].

LC TL504 .A2729
DD 629.13 BL

AEROSPACO. Vol. 1 (Mar. 1972)-. Periodical. Portuguese. One time a year. Editora Imagem Nova, rua da Graca 201, Conj 41, CEP 01125 Sao Paulo Brazil.

LC TL **ISSN** 0741-5974
DD 629 US

AEROSTATION (ALEXANDRIA, VA.). (AEROSTATION.). [Aerostation]. **Added/Corp** Association of Balloon and Airship Constructors. (1974)-. Periodical. English. Four times a year (Mar., June, Sept., Dec.). $25.00 (associate), $30.00 (commerical), $40.00 (benefactor), $55.00 (industrial) Comes with Association of Balloon and Airship Constructors membership. Association of Balloon & Airship Constructors, PO Box 90864, San Diego CA 92169. **Tel** (619)270-4049, FAX (619)270-4049. **ED** Donald E. Woodward. **Bk Rev**, (Qty: 4-8). **Ad Acc. Circ:** 400.
Desc: Features of a newsletter with detailed accounts of LTA technical meetings, calls for papers, analytical articles on current LTA events, and problems. Technical and historical articles, and lists of current publications of interest.

LC TL504 .A363 **ISSN** 0365-7442
DD 629.13 IT

AEROTECNICA MISSILI E SPAZIO, L'. [Aerote, Missili Spazio]. **Added/Corp** Associazione Italiana di Aeronautica e Astronautica. Vol. 50, No. 1 (Feb. 1971)-. Periodical. Italian (summaries and/or abstracts in English). Four times a year. L70000. Aerotecnica Missili e Spazio, P LE Golgi 40, 20133 Milan Italy. **Tel** 011 39 2 23994000. **ED** Luigi G. Napolitano. Index available. **Bk Rev. Ad Acc. Circ:** 1,000. available in microform from University Microfilms International (UMI). Documents available from CASDDS, The UnCover Company. ***Formed by the union of*** *Aerotecnica and Missili e Spazio.*
Ind/Abst Int. Aerosp. Abstr.; Zentralbl. Math. Ihre Grenzgeb.

LC HE9761 **ISSN** 0740-1434
DD 387.7092 US

AG PILOT INTERNATIONAL. (AG PILOT IINTERNATIONAL: API.). [AG pilot int.]. **VFOAT** AG-Pilot International; A.P.I.; API. (19??)-. Periodical. English. Twelve times a year. $29.95. AG Pilot International, 405 Main Street, PO Box 1607, Mount Vernon WA 98273. **Tel** (206)336-9737, (800)671-2428, FAX (206)336-2506.

LC TL **ISSN** 0549-7191
DD 629 UK
CODEN AGCPAV

AGARD CONFERENCE PROCEEDINGS. [AGARD conf. proc.]. **Main/Corp** North Atlantic Treaty Organization. Advisory Group for Aerospace Research and Development. No. 1 (1968)-. Academic Scholarly Publication. English. Documents available from Article Express International, Ask*IEEE, CASDDS.
Ind/Abst Bioeng. Abstr.; Chem. Abstr.; Curr. Cit.; Ei Page One; Energy Res. Abstr. (June 1971-); Eng. Index Annu.; INSPEC.

LC TL500.N64 A15 **ISSN** 0302-5020
DD 629.1/07/2 FR

AGARD HIGHLIGHTS. [AGARD highlights]. **Main/Corp** North Atlantic Treaty Organization. Advisory Group for Aerospace Research and Development. **VAT** Advisory Group for Aerospace Research and Development Highlights. (19??)-. English. Four times a year. Scientific Publications Office AGARD - NATO, 7 rue Ancelle, Neuilly-Sur-Seine France. ctrl circ.
Ind/Abst Int. Aerosp. Abstr.

LC TL **ISSN** 0549-7213
DD 629 FR
CODEN NAGLB5

AGARD LECTURE SERIES. [AGARD lect. ser.]. **Main/Corp** North Atlantic Treaty Organization. Advisory Group for Aerospace Research and Development. **Added/Corp** North Atlantic Treaty Organization. Advisory Group for Aerospace Research and Development. **VFOAT** AGARD-LS. **VAT** Advisory Group for Aerospace Research and Development Lecture Series. (19??)-. Monographic series. English (French). Irregular. Price varies per volume. North Atlantic Treaty Organization, Distribution Unit, 1110 Brussels Belgium. **Tel** 011 32 2 2414400. Documents available from Ask*IEEE, CASDDS.
Ind/Abst Chem. Abstr. (1954-1982); Curr. Cit.; INSPEC.

LC TL500 .N6 **ISSN** 0365-2467
DD 629.13 FR
CODEN AGAGAS

AGARDOGRAPH. [AGARDograph]. **Added/Corp** North Atlantic Treaty Organization. Advisory Group for Aeronautical Research and Development. North Atlantic Treaty Organization. Advisory Group for Aerospace Research and Development. (1954)-. English (French). Irregular. NASA - National Aeronautics and Space Administration / Report Distribution Storage Unit, Langley Field VA 23365.
Desc: Information on aeronautics and aerodynamics.
Ind/Abst Curr. Cit.

LC TL **ISSN** 0745-4864
DD 629 US

AGRICULTURAL AVIATION (WASHINGTON, D.C.). (AGRICULTURAL AVIATION.). [Agric. aviat.]. **Added/Corp** National Agricultural Aviation Association. Vol. 9, No. 11 (Nov. 1982)-. Periodical. English. Eight times a year (Jan., Feb., Mar., Apr., May, June, July, Aug./Sept, Oct., Nov./Dec.). $30.00. National Agricultural Aviation Association, 1005 East Street Southeast, Washington DC 20003. **Tel** (202)546-5722. **ED** Harold M. Collis. **Bk Rev. Ad Acc. Circ:** 8,500 (ctrl). ***Continues*** *WAA, 0192-6845.*
Desc: Reports on actions and events which affect agricultural aviation, new product and service needs, business tips, safety reports and profiles of the people involved.
Ind/Abst AGRICOLA (?-?) [Select. Cov.].

LC TL726.2 .D47 **ISSN** 0882-3367
DD 387.7/362 US

AIA DIRECTORY OF HELIPORTS & HELISTOPS IN THE UNITED STATES, CANADA, PUERTO RICO, AND DIRECTORY OF HOSPITAL HELIPORTS & HELISTOPS. **Added/Corp** Aerospace Industries Association of America. **VFOAT** A.I.A. Directory of Heliports and Helistops in the United States, Canada, Puerto Rico, and Directory of Hospital Heliports & Helistops; Directory of Heliports & Helistops in the United States, Canada, Puerto Rico, and Directory of Hospital Heliports & Helistops; Directory of Heliports and Helistops in the United States, Canada, Puerto Rico, and Directory of Hospital Heliports and Helistops. **VAT** Aerospace Industries Association Directory of Heliports and Helistops in the United States, Canada, Puerto Rico and Directory of Hospital Heliports and Helistops. (1984)-. Directory. English. $7.95. Aerospace Industries Association of America, 1250 Eye Street Northwest, Washington DC 20005. **Tel** (202)371-8561, FAX (202)371-8470, telex 710-822-0134 AIA DC TKU. ***Continues*** *AIA Directory of Heliports in the United States, Canada, Puerto Rico and Directory of Hospital Heliports.*

LC TL501.A688 A2 **ISSN** 0001-1452
DD 629.1/05 US
CCC
CODEN AIAJAH

Pr Rev.

AIAA JOURNAL. [AIAA j.]. **Main/Corp** American Institute of Aeronautics and Astronautics. **Added/Corp** American Institute of Aeronautics and Astronautics. Journal. **VAT** American Institute of Aeronautics and Astronautics Journal. Vol. 1 (Jan. 1963)-. Academic Scholarly Publication. English. Twelve times a year. $575.00. American Institute of Aeronautics & Astronautics, 370 l'Enfant Promenade Southwest, Washington DC 20024-2518. **Tel** (202)646-7400, FAX (202)646-7508, telex 204792 AIAA UR. **ED** George W. Sutton. Index Available, published separately, free-automatically sent. cum. index. **Circ:** 5,000. available on microfilm and microfiche from University Microfilms International (UMI). Documents available from Article Express International, The Genuine Article, Ask*IEEE, CASDDS. ***Formed by the union of*** *American Rocket*

Society. ARS Journal, 0097-4056 **and** *Journal of the Aero/Space Sciences, 0095-9820.*
Desc: Includes theoretical developments and experimental results on topics such as aerodynamics, the aerospace environment, lasers and plasmas, fluid mechanics and reacting flows, and structural mechanics and materials. Carries abstracts on research topics from Russian and Japanese aerospace literature.
Ind/Abst Appl. Sci. Technol. Index; Bioeng. Abstr.; Chem. Abstr.; Civ. Struct. Eng. Abstr.; Comput. Inf. Syst. Abstr. J. [Full Cov.]; Curr. Cit.; Curr. Contents Eng. Comput. Technol.; Elect. Comm. Abstr.; EMBASE; Energy Res. Abstr.; Eng. Index Annu.; Environ. Eng. Abstr.; Expand. Acad. Index (1992-); FLUIDEX (1973-); INIS Atomindex [Micro.]; INSPEC (1968-); Int. Aerosp. Abstr.; Math. Rev.; Mech. Eng. Abstr.; Res. Alert [Full Cov.]; Sci. Cit. Index; SCISEARCH; Shock Vibr. Dig.; Solid State Supercond. Abstr.

LC TK **ISSN** 0146-3705
DD 629.4 US
CCC
CODEN AAPRAQ

AIAA PAPER. [AIAA pap.]. **Main/Corp** American Institute of Aeronautics and Astronautics. **Added/Corp** American Institute of Aeronautics and Astronautics. Paper. **VAT** American Institute of Aeronautics and Astronautics Paper. (19??)-. Academic Scholarly Publication. English. Irregular (approximately 1,400 papers per year). $5400.00. American Institute of Aeronautics & Astronautics, 370 l'Enfant Promenade Southwest, Washington DC 20024-2518. **Tel** (202)646-7400, FAX (202)646-7508, telex 204792 AIAA UR. Documents available from Article Express International, CASDDS.
Desc: Bound volumes or individual papers presented at AIAA conference proceedings covering technical research and applications in various aerospace fields.
Ind/Abst Bioeng. Abstr.; Chem. Abstr.; Ei Page One; Eng. Index Annu.

LC TL501.A688 A23 **ISSN** 0001-1460
DD 629 US
CCC

AIAA STUDENT JOURNAL. [AIAA stud. j.]. **Main/Corp** American Institute of Aeronautics and Astronautics. **Added/Corp** American Institute of Aeronautics and Astronautics. Student Journal. **VAT** American Institute of Aeronautics and Astronautics Student Journal. (April 1963)-. Periodical. English. Four times a year. $18.00. American Institute of Aeronautics & Astronautics, 370 l'Enfant Promenade Southwest, Washington DC 20024-2518. **Tel** (202)646-7400, FAX (202)646-7508, telex 204792 AIAA UR. available on microfilm and microfiche from University Microfilms International (UMI).
Ind/Abst Int. Aerosp. Abstr.

LC TL **ISSN** 0992-065X
DD 629 FR
UDC 629.11

AIR ACTION. (1988)-. Periodical. French. Irregular (10-12 times per year). $91.86. Air Action, 23 Av de Wagram, F-75017 Paris France. **Tel** 011 33 1 47319311.

LC U **ISSN** 0002-2152
DD 358 FR
UDC 358.4

AIR ACTUALITES PARIS. **See** Military and Defense.

LC TL587 .A36 **ISSN** 0400-8456
DD 528/.05 US

AIR ALMANAC (1953), THE. (THE AIR ALMANAC.). [Air alm.]. **Added/Corp** United States Naval Observatory. United States Naval Observatory. Nautical Almanac Office. Great Britain. Her Majesty's Stationery Office. (Jan./April 1953)-. Government Publication. English. One time a year. Superintendent of Documents, US Government Printing Office, Washington DC 20402. **Tel** (202)275-3328, FAX (202)786-2377. ***Continues*** *American Air Almanac* **and** *British Air Almanac.*

LC K1 .I7
DD 343.09/7/05 NE

AIR AND SPACE LAW. **See** Law.

LC KF2400.A15 A37 **ISSN** 0747-7449
DD 343.73/097 347.30397 US

AIR AND SPACE LAWYER: FORUM COMMITTEE ON AIR AND SPACE LAW. AMERICAN BAR ASSOCIATION, THE. **See** Law.

LC TL501 .A55257 **ISSN** 0886-2257
DD 629.13/005 US

AIR & SPACE SMITHSONIAN. [Air space Smithson.]. **Added/Corp** Smithsonian Institution. **VFOAT** Air and Space Smithsonian; Air and Space. Vol. 1, No. 1 (April/May 1986)-. Periodical. English. Six times a year. $18.00. Smithsonian Institution, 900 Jefferson Drive, Washington DC 20560. **(Subscription address:** Neodata / Colorado, PO Box 2606, Boulder CO 80322. **) ED** George C. Larson. **Bk Rev. Ad Acc, Adv Mgr** Louis C. Kolenda. **Circ:** 300,000. available on microfilm and microfiche from University Microfilms International (UMI). ***Continues*** *Air & Space, 0193-8304.*
Desc: Covers aviation and aerospace for a non-technical audience. Features are slanted to a technically curious, but not necessarily technically knowledgeable audience. Emphasizes unique angles to aviation/aerospace stories, history, events, personalities, current and future technologies. All have a human-interest orientation.
Ind/Abst Acad. Abstr.; Acad. Search; Am. Hist. Life (1986-); EP Collect.; Homework Help.; INIS Atomindex [Micro.]; Int. Aerosp. Abstr.; Mag. Artic. Summar. Elite; Mag. Artic. Summar. Select; Mag. Artic. Summar. CD-ROM; MasterFile FullTEXT 1000; MasterFile FullTEXT 350; MasterFile FullTEXT 650; MasterFile FullTEXT (Jan. 1994-); OCLC; Pub. Lib. FullTEXT; Telebase; Vocat. Search.

LC TL **ISSN** 1075-1742
DD 629 US

•**AIR CARGO REPORT.** **See** Transportation.

LC HE9788 .C37 **ISSN** 0745-5100
DD 387.7/44/05 US
CCC

AIR CARGO WORLD. **See** Transportation.

LC HE9761 **ISSN** 0896-0577
DD 387.7 US

AIR CARRIER INDUSTRY SCHEDULED SERVICE TRAFFIC STATISTICS. [Air carr. ind. sched. serv. traffic stat. q.]. **Added/Corp** United States. Office of Aviation Information Management. United States. Civil Aeronautics Board. Data Systems Management Division. Financial Data Section. United States. Civil Aeronautics Board. Information Management Division. Financial Data Section. United States. Dept. of Transportation. Office of Airline Statistics. **VFOAT** Air Carrier Industry Scheduled Service Traffic Statistics Quarterly. (June 30, 1981)-. Statistical Publication. English. Four times a year. $250.00. US Department of Transportation Systems Center, Collection Officer, Kendall Square, Cambridge MA 02142. **Tel** (617)494-2000, (617)494-2852. Documents available from Documents on Demand. ***Continues*** *Commuter Air Carrier Traffic Statistics, 0270-448X.*
Ind/Abst Am. Stat. Index.

LC HE9815.A1 A25 **ISSN** 0008-2570
DD 387.7/4/0971 CN

AIR CARRIER OPERATIONS IN CANADA. [Air carr. oper. Can.]. **Main/Corp** Canada. Statistics Canada. Aviation Statistics Centre. **Added/Corp** Aviation Statistics Centre (Canada). Aviation Statistics Centre (Canada) Operations des Transporteurs Aeriens au Canada. **VFOAT** Operations des Transporteurs Aeriens au Canada. Vol. 2 (Jan./March 1971)-. Statistical Publication. English (French). Four times a year. 119.00Can$. Statistics Canada Publications Sales and Services, R.H. Coats Building 6th Floor, Ottawa Ontario K1A 0T6 Canada. **Tel** (613)951-5078, (800)267-6677, FAX (613)951-1584, telex 053-3585. **ED** Bradley Snider (editor's phone number: (819)997-6195, FAX: (819)953-8499). Index available. **Circ:** 380. ***Continues in part*** *Civil Aviation (Ottawa, Ont. : Annual), 0380-5247;* ***Absorbed*** *Transcontinental and Regional Air-Carrier Operations, 0380-5263.*
Desc: Presents statistics on the activities of approximately 500 Canadian air carriers. It contains information on passengers, goods and mail carried, kilometers and hours flown and financial data on operating revenues and expenses as well as statistics on employment and fuel consumption.

LC HE 9815.A1 S74b **ISSN** 0701-7928
DD 387.7/4/0971 CN
CCC

AIR CARRIER TRAFFIC AT CANADIAN AIRPORTS (QUARTERLY EDITION). (AIR CARRIER TRAFFIC AT CANADIAN AIRPORTS.). [Air carr. traffic Can. airpt.]. **Main/Corp** Statistics Canada. Transportation and Communications Division. **Added/Corp** Aviation Statistics Centre (Canada) Statistics Canada. Transportation and Communications Division. Trafic des Transporteurs Aeriens aux Aeroports Canadiens. **VFOAT** Trafic des Transporteurs Aeriens aux Aeroports Canadiens. Vol. 1, No. 1, (1st Quarter 1976)-. Statistical Publication. English (French). Four times a year. 104.05Can$. Statistics Canada Publications Sales and Services, R.H. Coats Building 6th Floor, Ottawa Ontario K1A 0T6 Canada. **Tel** (613)951-5078, (800)267-6677, FAX (613)951-1584, telex 053-3585. **ED** Rolfe Hakka (editor's telephone number: (819)953-3347, FAX (819)953-8499). Index available. **Circ:** 380. ***Continues in part*** *Aviation Statistics Centre (Canada). Airport Activity Statistics., 0576-0208;* ***Absorbed*** *Air Carrier Traffic at Canadian Airports (Annual), 0705-5781.*
Desc: Statistics on the volume of passengers, mail and cargo and the number of flights generated by scheduled airlines and international charter load information, for the top 50 airports in Canada.

LC HE9761 **ISSN** 0890-2925
DD 387 US

AIR CHARTER GUIDE, THE. **See** Transportation.

LC HE9815.Z7 C533 **ISSN** 0828-8208
DD 387.7/428/0971021 CN

AIR CHARTER STATISTICS. **Added/Corp** Aviation Statistics Centre (Canada). **VFOAT** Statistique des Affretements Aeriens. (1984)-. English (French). One time a year. 39.00Can$ Canada; $47.00 US; $55.00 other. Statistics Canada Publications Sales and Services, R.H. Coats Building 6th Floor, Ottawa Ontario K1A 0T6 Canada. **Tel** (613)951-5078, (800)267-6677, FAX (613)951-1584, telex 053-3585. **ED** Katerina Tieman (editor's telephone number: (819)997-6173, FAX: (819)953-8499). Index available. **Circ:** 325. ***Continues*** *International Air Charter Statistics (Annual), 0709-3667.*
Desc: Data on the international and domestic air charter operations of more than 80 Canadian and foreign carriers. Includes data on passenger, cargo and courier traffic.

LC TL **ISSN** 0002-2241
DD 629 US

AIR CLASSICS. [Air class.]. (19??)-. Periodical. English. Twelve times a year. $35.50. Challenge Publications Inc., 7950 Deering Avenue, Canoga Park CA 91304. **Tel** (818)887-0550.
Ind/Abst Am. Hist. Life.

LC U **ISSN** 0044-6955
DD 358 US

AIR COMBAT. (19??)-. Periodical. English. Six times a year. $20.25. Challenge Publications Inc., 7950 Deering Avenue, Canoga Park CA 91304. **Tel** (818)887-0550.

LC TL587 .A37
DD 387.7/2/0212 UK

AIR DISTANCES MANUAL. [Air distances man.]. **Added/Corp** International Air Transport Association. International Aeradio Ltd. International Aeradio PLC. (19??)-. English. One time a year (Apr.). $123.21. International Aeradio Ltd, Aeradio House, Hayes Road, Southall Mid UB2 5NJ United Kingdom. **Tel** 011 44 181 8432411, FAX 011 44 181 8433901. **ED** G. W. Adams. **Ad Acc. Circ:** 2,000.
Desc: Contains the great circle distances for over 35,000 sectors shown in kilometers, statute miles and nautical miles. Listing is alphabetical together with four-figure co-ordinates.

LC TL501 .A55318 **ISSN** 0143-5450
DD 629.13/005 UK

AIR ENTHUSIAST. (June 1971)-. Periodical. English. Four times a year. $51.33. Key Publishing Ltd., PO Box 100, Stamford Lincolnshire PE9 1XQ United Kingdom. **Tel** 011 44 1780 55131, FAX 011 44 1780 57261, telex 9312134113. **ED** William Green. **Ad Acc. Circ:** 15,300.
Desc: Contains in-depth and informative features on various types of aircrafts. Also contains exclusive photographs and detailed cutaway drawings. Includes full color art, accurate general arrangement drawings, and much more.

LC UG622 .A37 **ISSN** 0307-7411
DD 358.4/18/3 UK

AIR EXTRA. 1973. Periodical. English. Four times a year. $13.80. Ian Allan Ltd., Coombelands Lane, Addlestone Weybridge KT15 1HY United Kingdom. **Tel** 011 44 1932 858511, 011 44 1932 855909, FAX 011 44 1932 232366, 011 44 1932 854750. **ED** Martin Horseman. **Ad Acc. Circ:** 22,000.
Desc: Series on individual themes or subjects from past and present aviation and aerospace developments both commercial and military.

LC TL553.5.A1 A5 **ISSN** 0002-2322
DD 629.1325505 US

AIR FACTS. [Air facts]. Vol. 1 (Feb. 1938)-. Periodical. English. Twelve times a year. Air Facts, PO Box 2743, Oshkosh WI 54901.

LC U
DD 355 UK

AIR FORCES MONTHLY. (1992)-. English. Twelve times a year. $56.00 (US and Canada); £33.00 (Europe); £24.00 (UK); £30.00 (other). Key Publishing Ltd., PO Box 100, Stamford Lincolnshire PE9 1XQ United Kingdom. **Tel** 011 44 1780 55131, FAX 011 44 1780 57261, telex 9312134113. **ED** David Oliver. Index available. cum. index. **Bk Rev. Ad Acc. Circ:** 31,000.
Desc: Modern military aviation.

LC TL
DD 629 FR

AIR FRANCE EN. **Main/Corp** Air France. (1979)-. French. One time a year. Davsell Ltd, 145 Hudson Street/7th Floor, New York NY 10013. **Tel** (212)696-1223. ***Continues*** *Rapport d'Activite / Air France.*

LC HE9788.5.U5 A6 **ISSN** 0092-2870
DD 387.7/44/0973 US

AIR FREIGHT DIRECTORY. **See** Transportation.

LC TL
DD 629 US

AIR FREIGHT LOSS & DAMAGE CLAIMS. ANNUAL SUMMARIES. **Added/Corp** United States. Civil Aeronautics Board. Bureau of Accounts and Statistics. **VAT** Air Freight Loss and Damage Claims. Vol.1 (1974)-. English. One time a year. Civil Aeronautics Board, 1825 Connecticut Avenue, Washington DC 20428. **Tel** (202)673-5174.

LC TL695.5 .U45 **ISSN** 0090-1008
DD 629.132/51 US

AIR/GROUND SKY-WAVE PROPAGATION CHARTS FOR SELECTED WORLD WIDE STATIONS. [Air-ground sky-wave propag. charts sel. world wide stn.]. **Main/Corp** U.S. Army Communications-Electronics Engineering Installation Agency. **Added/Corp** U.S. Army Communications-Electronics Engineering Installation Agency. A/G Book. (Jan. 1971)-. English. Irregular. US Army Communications Electronics Engineering Installations Agency, Fort Huachuca AZ 85613. ***Continues*** *United States. Army Strategic Communications Command. Communications Engineering Dept. Air/Ground Sky-Wave Propagation Charts for Selected World Wide Stations.*

LC UG630.A1 A35 **ISSN** 0306-5634
DD 358.4/18/3 UK

AIR INTERNATIONAL. [Air int.]. (1974)-. Periodical. English. Six times a year. £27.00 UK; £35.00 Europe; £33.50. Key Publishing Ltd., PO Box 100, Stamford Lincolnshire PE9 1XQ United Kingdom. **Tel** 011 44 1780 55131, FAX 011 44 1780 57261, telex 9312134113. **ED** William Green. **Bk Rev. Ad Acc. Circ:** 41,500.
Desc: Contemporary aviation technology. In-depth coverage of the latest aircraft, current military airscene, flight test reports, exclusive cutaway, color and three view drawings and photographs.
Ind/Abst Int. Aerosp. Abstr.

LC U
DD 355 UK

AIR INTERNATIONAL (BOUND VOLUMES). (AIR INTERNATIONAL.). (19??)-. Periodical. English. Two times a year. Finescroll, PO Box 353, Whitestone NY 11357.

LC HB **ISSN** 1056-5051
DD 331 US

AIR JOBS DIGEST. [Air jobs digest]. Vol. 1, No. 1 (Jan. 1986)-. Periodical. English. Twelve times a year. $96.00. World Air Data, 7800 Airpark Road, Suite 23, Gaithersburg MD 20879. **Tel** (301)990-6800.
Desc: Presents the current job openings for occupations within aviation and aerospace, worldwide. Covers airlines, corporate aviation, US government vacancies, and the aerospace industry.

LC HE9761 **ISSN** 0002-2411
DD 387.7 US

AIR LINE EMPLOYEE, THE. **See** Business and Economics-Labor.

LC TL501 .A5537 **ISSN** 0002-242X
DD 629.1305 US

AIR LINE PILOT. [Air line pilot]. **Added/Corp** Air Line Pilots' Association, International. **VFOAT** Airline Pilot. Vol. 1 (Apr. 5, 1932)-. Trade Publication. English. Ten times a year. $24.00. Air Line Pilots Association International, 535 Herndon Parkway, PO Box 1169, Herndon VA 22070. **Tel** (703)689-4179, (800)448-5313, FAX (703)689-4370. **ED** Esperison Martinez Jr. Index available (included in Dec. issue). cum. index. **Bk Rev. Ad Acc. Circ:** 61,000. available on microfilm and microfiche from University Microfilms International (UMI).
Desc: Published for professional airline pilots and others in the commercial aviation industry. Editorial content emphasizes advances in air safety, flight technology, industry development and aviation, and labor relation.
Ind/Abst Aviat. Tradescan [Full Cov.]; Int. Aerosp. Abstr.; Work Relat. Abstr.

LC TL
DD 629 CN

AIR NAVIGATION PLAN, CARRIBBEAN AND SOUTH AMERICAN REGIONS = PLAN DE NAVIGATION AERIENNE, REGIONS CARAIBES ET AMERIQUE DU SUD = PLAN DE NAVEGACION AEREA, REGIONES DEL CARIBE Y DE SUDAMERICA. **Main/Corp** International Civil Aviation Organization. **VFOAT** Plan de Navigation Aerienne, Regions Caraibes et Amerique du Sud.; Plan de Navegacion Aerea, Regiones del Caribe y de Sudamerica. (19??)-. Multiple languages (English, French and Spanish). Irregular. $29.00. International Civil Aviation Organization / ICAO, 1000 Sherbrooke Street West, Suite 400, Montreal Quebec H3A 2R2 Canada. **Tel** (514)285-8026, (514)285-8022, telex 05-24514. **Bk Rev. Ad Acc.** ctrl circ.
Desc: Five year plan highlighting minimum requirements for aviation facilities and services in the region indicated.

LC TL500.5 .A2 TL726.6.A1 **ISSN** 0304-7652
DD 387.7/08 S 629.13/094 CN

AIR NAVIGATION PLAN, EUROPEAN REGION. **Main/Corp** International Civil Aviation Organization. **Added/Corp** International Civil Aviation Organization. Plan de Navigation Aerienne, Region Europe. **VFOAT** Plan de Navigation Aerienne Region Europe. (19??)-. Multiple languages (English, French, Spanish and Russian). Irregular. 118.25Can$. International Civil Aviation Organization / ICAO, 1000 Sherbrooke Street West, Suite 400, Montreal Quebec H3A 2R2 Canada. **Tel** (514)285-8026, (514)285-8022, telex 05-24514.

LC TL500.5 .A2
DD 387.7 S 629.132/545 CN

AIR NAVIGATION PLAN : MIDDLE EAST AND SOUTH EAST ASIA REGIONS = PLAN DE NAVIGATION AERIENNE : REGIONS MOYEN-ORIENT ET ASIE DU SUD-EST = PLAN DE NAVEGACION AEREA : REGIONES DEL ORIENTE MEDIO Y DEL ASIA SUDORIENTAL. **Main/Corp** International Civil Aviation Organization. **Added/Corp** International Civil Aviation. Plan de Navigation Aerienne : Regions Moyen-Orient et Asie du Sud-Est. International Civil Aviation Organization. Plan de Navegacion Aerea : Regiones del Oriente Medio y del Asia Sudoriental. **VFOAT** Plan de Navigation Aerienne : Regions Moyen-Orient et Asie du Sud-Est; Plan de Navegacion Aerea : Regiones del Medio y del Asia Sudoriental. Oriente Medio y del Asia Sudoriental. (19??)-. English (French and Spanish). $38.50. International Civil Aviation Organization / ICAO, 1000 Sherbrooke Street West, Suite 400, Montreal Quebec H3A 2R2 Canada. **Tel** (514)285-8026, (514)285-8022, telex 05-24514.

LC TL
DD 629 UK

AIR NAVIGATION - THE ORDER AND REGULATIONS. (19??)-. English. Irregular. £23.60 UK; £25.50 other. Civil Aviation Authority / England, Grenville House, 37 Gratton Road, Cheltenham Glo GL50 2BN United Kingdom. **Tel** 011 44 1242 235151, FAX 011 44 1242 584139.

LC HE9815.A1 A254 **ISSN** 0705-4343
DD 387.7/42 CN

AIR PASSENGER ORIGIN AND DESTINATION. CANADA-UNITED STATES. (AIR PASSENGER ORIGIN AND DESTINATION, CANADA-UNITED STATES REPORT. CANADA-UNITED STATES REPORT.). [Air passeng. orig. destin., Can.-U.S. rep.]. **Main/Corp** Canada. Statistics Canada Aviation Statistics Centre. **Added/Corp** Aviation Statistics Centre (Canada) Aviation Statistics Centre (Canada) Origine et Destination des Passagers Aeriens: Rapport sur le Trafic Canada-Etats-Unis. **VFOAT** Origine et Destination des Passagers Aeriens : Rapport sur le Trafic Canada-Etats-Unis. **VAT** Canada-United States Report (Ottawa). (1969)-. English (French). One time a year (Jan.). 54.00Can$. Statistics Canada Publications Sales and Services, R.H. Coats Building 6th Floor, Ottawa Ontario K1A 0T6 Canada. **Tel** (613)951-5078, (800)267-6677, FAX (613)951-1584, telex 053-3585. **ED** Lotfi Chahdi (phone: (819)997-1385, & FAX: (819)953-8499). Index available. **Circ:** 455. ***Continues*** *Aviation Statistics Centre (Canada). Airline Passenger Origin and Destination Statistics, Transborder Report.*
Desc: Presents an integrated set of Canada/US air passenger origin-destination statistics. The result of an agreement between Canada and the Civil Aeronautics Board in the US to exchange data from their respective surveys.

LC HE9815.A1 S74a **ISSN** 0703-2692
DD 387.7 CN

AIR PASSENGER ORIGIN AND DESTINATION, DOMESTIC REPORT. [Air passeng. orig. destin., Domest. rep.]. **Main/Corp** Canada. Statistics Canada. Aviation Statistics Centre. **Added/Corp** Aviation Statistics Centre (Canada) Aviation Statistics Centre (Canada) Domestic Report. Aviation Statistics Centre (Canada) Origine et Destination des Passagers Aeriens; Rapport sur le Trafic Interieur. **VFOAT** Domestic Report; Origine et Destination des Passagers Aeriens. (1969)-. English (French). One time a year. 54.00Can$. Statistics Canada Publications Sales and Services, R.H. Coats Building 6th Floor, Ottawa Ontario K1A 0T6 Canada. **Tel** (613)951-5078, (800)267-6677, FAX (613)951-1584, telex 053-3585. **ED** Lotfi Chahdi (editor's telephone number: (819)997-1386, FAX (819)953-8499). Index available. **Circ:** 430. ***Continues*** *Airline Passenger Origin and Destination Statistics, Domestic Report.*
Desc: Sets forth statistics on the volume of domestic air passenger traffic generated at Canadian cities and carried between pairs of Canadian points.

LC TL600 **ISSN** 0965-1896
DD 629.133 UK

AIR PICTORIAL INTERNATIONAL. [Air pict. int.]. (1992)-. Periodical. English. Twelve times a year. £23.00, one-year, £39.00 two-year, £61.00 three-year, UK; £29.00 one-year, £51.00 two-year, £78.00 three-year, Surface Mail; £44.00 Airmail. HPC Publishing, Drury Lane Hastings, East Sussex TN34 1XW United Kingdom. **Tel** 011 44 1424 720477, FAX 011 44 1424 443693. ***Continues*** *Air Pictorial (Ascot), 0002-2462;* ***Absorbed*** *Aviation News.*
Desc: For the air enthusiast, catering for those who maintain a keen and informed interest in all aspects of aviation.

LC UG633.A1 A515 **ISSN** 1044-016X
DD 358 US

AIR POWER HISTORY. [Air power hist.]. **Added/Corp** Air Force Historical Foundation. Vol. 36, No. 1 (Spring 1989)-. Periodical. English. Four times a year (Mar., June, Sept., Dec.). $45.00. Air Power History, Virginia Military Institute, Lexington VA 24450. **Tel** (703)464-7468, FAX (703)464-5229. **ED** Jack Neufeld, (editor's address: Office of Air Force History, 170 Luke Avenue, Suite 400, Rolling AFB, Washington, DC 20332-5113, phone: (202)767-5088 Ext. 229). **Bk Rev**, (Qty: 50). **Ad Acc, Adv Mgr:** Jack Neufeld. **Circ:** 4,000. available on magnetic tape, an online database, and CD-ROM; available on microfilm and microfiche from University Microfilms International (UMI). ***Continues*** *Aerospace Historian, 0001-9364.*
Desc: News and information on the history of airplanes and space travel. Includes scholarly and layman articles on aviation.
Ind/Abst Air Univ. Libr. Index Mil. Period.; Am. Hist. Life (1963-).

LC TL
DD 629 IT

AIR PRESS. (19??)-. Italian. Editorale Aeronautica, Via N Paganini 7, 00198 Rome Italy.

LC TL501 .A5539 **ISSN** 0002-2500
DD 629.13 US

AIR PROGRESS. [Air prog.]. (19??)-. Periodical. English. Twelve times a year. $31.95. Challenge Publications Inc., 7950 Deering Avenue, Canoga Park CA 91304. **Tel** (818)887-0550. **ED** Michael O'Leary. **Bk Rev. Ad Acc.** ctrl circ. Documents available from UMI Article Clearinghouse. ***Absorbed*** *Sport Flying.*
Desc: Covers the complete spectrum of general aviation and its technology.
Ind/Abst Access (1975-1988); Appl. Sci. Technol. Index; Bus. Index (1985-); EP Collect.; Gen. BusinessFile (1985-); Gen. Period. Index (1985-); Homework Help.; Mag. Artic. Summar. Elite; Mag. Artic. Summar. Select; Mag. Artic. Summar. CD-ROM; Mag. Index Plus (1989-); Mag. Search; MasterFile FullTEXT 1000; MasterFile FullTEXT 350; MasterFile FullTEXT 650; MasterFile FullTEXT (Jan. 1984-June 1989); Newsp. Period. Abstr. (1988-); OCLC; Pub. Lib. FullTEXT; Telebase; Mag. Index (1977-); Trade Ind. Index (1981-); Vocat. Search.

LC UG1240 .A39 **ISSN** 0885-2502
DD 623.7/46 US

AIR PROGRESS WARBIRDS INTERNATIONAL. [Air prog. warbirds int.]. **VFOAT** Warbirds; Warbirds International. (198?)-. Periodical. English. Nine times a year. $29.95. Challenge Publications Inc., 7950 Deering Avenue, Canoga Park CA 91304. **Tel** (818)887-0550.

LC TL
DD 629 CN

AIR REGULATIONS AND AERONAUTICS ACT. **Main/Corp** Canada. Ministry of Transport. (19??)-. English (French). Irregular. 12.95Can$. Canada Communication Group Publishers, Order Processing, Ottawa Ontario K1A 0S9 Canada. **Tel** (819)956-4800, (819)956-4802. ***Continues*** *Canada. Dept. of Transport. Air Regulations.*

LC KF2406.A15 A38 **ISSN** 1044-727X
DD 343.7309/7/05 347.3039705 US
CCC

AIR SAFETY WEEK. [Air saf. week]. Vol. 3. No. 9 (July 10, 1989)-. Periodical. English. Forty-eight times a year. $795.00. Phillips Business Information Inc., 1201 Seven Locks Road, PO Box 61130, Potomac MD 20854. **Tel** (301)424-3338, (301)340-1520, (800)777-5005, FAX (301)424-4297, telex 358149. available on an online database from NEWSNET; DATA-STAR; and (file 636/Full-Text) DIALOG. ***Continues*** *Air Safety Law & Technology, 0893-1003.*
Ind/Abst PTS Newsl. Database [Full Txt.].

LC HE9803.A2 A48 **ISSN** 0270-5079
DD 387.7/42 US

AIR TAXI CHARTER & RENTAL DIRECTORY OF NORTH AMERICA. [Air taxi chart. rent. dir. North Am.]. **VAT** Air Taxi Charter and Rental Directory of North America. (1975)-. Directory. English. $15.00. Aircraft Charter and Rental Tariff Information Service of North America, Box 1412, Springfield IL 62705.

LC HE
DD 387.74042 US

AIR TRAFFIC CONTROL. **Added/Corp** United States. Air Traffic Service. (1976)-. Government Publication. English. $72.00 US, $90.00 other. US Department of Transportation / US Coast Guard, 2100 Second Street Southwest, Washington DC 20953-0001. **Tel** (202)267-2229. **(Subscription address:** Superintendent of Documents, US Government Printing Office, Washington DC 20402. **)** ***Formed by the union of*** *Terminal Air Traffic Control* ***and*** *En Route Air Traffic*

Aeronautics, Astronautics

Control.
Desc: Prescribes air traffic control procedures and phraseology for personnel providing air traffic service.

LC TL
DD 629
CODEN ATCQER
ISSN 1064-3818

●**AIR TRAFFIC CONTROL QUARTERLY.** [Air traffic control q.]. **Added/Corp** Air Traffic Control Association Institute. Vol. 1, No. 1 (1993)-. Periodical. English. Four times a year. $196.00. John Wiley & Sons, Inc., 605 Third Avenue, New York NY 10158-0012. **Tel** (212)850-6000, (212)850-6645, **FAX** (212)850-6088, telex 12-7063. (**Subscription address:** John Wiley & Sons / UK, Baffins Lane, Chichester, West Sussex PO19 1UD United Kingdom. **Tel** 011 44 1243 779777, **FAX** 011 44 243 776128, telex 86290 WIBOOKG.) **ED** Anand Mundra.
Desc: An international journal of traffic and systems engineering and operations serving the needs of the global air transportation control community.

LC TL
DD 629
ISSN 0969-6725
UK

●**AIR TRAFFIC MANAGEMENT.** (1992)-. English. Six times a year. $126.00. Camrus Publishers, Neoter House, Clayhouse Yard, London EC4V 5EX United Kingdom. **Tel** 011 44 171 7798866, **FAX** 011 44 171 7798868. (**Subscription address:** Powerhouse. **Tel** 011 44 181 6610449.)
Desc: Dedicated to covering the latest technological, political and economic developments with the air traffic control industry.

LC HE
DD 387.74042
CN

AIR TRAFFIC SERVICES, AIR TRAFFIC CONTROL SERVICE, FLIGHT INFORMATION SERVICE, ALERTING SERVICE; INTERNATIONAL STANDARDS AND RECOMMENDED PRACTICES. ANNEX 11 TO THE CONVENTION OF INTERNATIONAL CIVIL AVIATION. **Main/Corp** International Civil Aviation Organization. (19??)-. English. $10.00. International Civil Aviation Organization / ICAO, 1000 Sherbrooke Street West, Suite 400, Montreal Quebec H3A 2R2 Canada. **Tel** (514)285-8026, (514)285-8022, telex 05-24514.

LC TL553.5.A1 A53
DD 629.130684
US

AIR TRANSPORT SAFETY. **Added/Corp** National Safety Council. Air Transport Section. (April 1945)-. Periodical. English. Twelve times a year. National Air Transportation Association, 4226 King Street, Alexandria VA 22302. **Tel** (703)845-9000.

LC HE
DD 387.74042
ISSN 0727-2774
AT

AIR TRANSPORT STATISTICS. FLIGHT CREW LICENCES. **See** Aeronautics, Astronautics-Abstracting, Bibliographies and Statistics.

LC HE9761.1 .A45
DD 387.7
ISSN 0002-2543
US
CCC

AIR TRANSPORT WORLD. [Air transp. world]. (May 1964)-. Trade Publication. English. Twelve times a year. $50.00. Penton Publishing, 1100 Superior Avenue, Cleveland OH 44114-2543. **Tel** (216)696-7000, **FAX** (216)696-0836. available on microfilm and microfiche from University Microfilms International (UMI); available on an online database (files 15,648/Full-Text) from DIALOG; available with charts; available with illustrations. Documents available from UMI Article Clearinghouse, Documents on Demand.
Ind/Abst ABI/INFORM Glob. Ed. (Jan. 1991-); ABI/INFORM [Computer File] (Jan. 1991-); Aviat. Tradescan [Full Cov.]; Bus. ASAP (1990-) [Full Txt.]; Bus. Index (1985-); Bus. Period. Index; Bus. Source Plus; Bus. Source; Curr. Cit.; Environ. Abstr.; EP Collect.; F&S Index Plus Text, Int. [Select. Cov.]; Gen. BusinessFile (1985-); Gen. Period. Index (1985-); Homework Help; Infobank (Jan. 1979-); Mag. Search; MasterFile FullTEXT 1000; MasterFile FullTEXT 350; MasterFile FullTEXT 650; MasterFile FullTEXT (July 1993-); OCLC; PAIS Int. Print; PROMT; Stat. Ref. Index; Telebase; Trade Ind. ASAP [Full Txt.]; Trade Ind. Index (1981-) [Full Txt.]; UMI ABI/Inform--Bus. Period. Ondisc (Jan. 1991-) [Full Txt.]; Vocat. Search; Wilson Bus. Abstr.

LC TL
DD 629
ISSN 0065-4868
US

AIR TRAVEL BARGAINS. (1965)-. English. Pocket Books Inc, PO Box 408 Coconut Grove, Miami FL 33133. **Tel** (305)445-0916.

LC Z6724.A3 U44
DD 016.3584/005
ISSN 0503-5368
US
CEASED

AIR UNIVERSITY ABSTRACTS OF RESEARCH REPORTS. **Main/Corp** Air University (U.S.). Vol. 1, No. 1 (1957)-(19??). English. Air University Library, Maxwell Air Force Base, Montgomery AL 36112-5564. **Tel** (334)953-2888.

LC U
DD 358
US

AIR UNIVERSITY CATALOG. **See** College and School Publications.

LC TL600
DD 629.133105
ISSN 1030-0090
AT

AIRBORNE MAGAZINE. [Airborne mag.]. (1977)-. Periodical. English. Twelve times a year. 45.22Aus$. Ropomod Pty Productions Limited, 67 75 Garden Drive Unit 11, Tullamarine Victoria 3043 Australia. **Tel** 011 61 3 3385696.

LC TL
DD 629
ISSN 0951-7782
UK

AIRCARGO NEWS INTERNATIONAL. **See** Transportation.

LC HE9784 .I55a
DD 614.8/69
CN
SUSPENDED

AIRCRAFT ACCIDENT DIGEST. **Main/Corp** International Civil Aviation Organization. (19??)-Suspended (19??). English. Irregular. International Civil Aviation Organization / ICAO, 1000 Sherbrooke Street West, Suite 400, Montreal Quebec H3A 2R2 Canada. **Tel** (514)285-8026, (514)285-8022, telex 05-24514.

LC TL
DD 629
CN

AIRCRAFT ACCIDENT INQUIRY; INTERNATIONAL STANDARDS AND PRACTICES. ANNEX 13 TO THE CONVENTION ON INTERNATIONAL CIVIL AVIATION. **Main/Corp** International Civil Aviation Organization. (19??)-. English. $6.00. International Civil Aviation Organization / ICAO, 1000 Sherbrooke Street West, Suite 400, Montreal Quebec H3A 2R2 Canada. **Tel** (514)285-8026, (514)285-8022, telex 05-24514.

LC HE9784.5.U5 A67
DD 387.7
US

AIRCRAFT ACCIDENT REPORTS. BRIEF FORMAT, U.S. CIVIL AND FOREIGN AVIATION. **Added/Corp** United States. National Transportation Safety Board. **VFOAT** Aircraft Accident Reports. Brief Format, U.S. Civil and Foreign Aviation. No. 1 (1982)-. English. Irregular (8 to 18 times a year). $160.00. National Technical Information Service - NTIS, Room 2027S, 5285 Port Royal Road, Springfield VA 22161. **Tel** (703)487-4630, (703)487-4660, (703)487-4650, **FAX** (703)321-8547, telex 89-9405. Documents available from Documents on Demand. **Continues** Aircraft Accident Reports. Brief Format, U.S. Civil Aviation, 0363-8324.
Ind/Abst Am. Stat. Index.

LC TL501
DD 629.13/005
ISSN 1032-9366
AT

AIRCRAFT & AEROSPACE. **Added/Corp** Royal Aeronautical Society. Australian Division. **VFOAT** Aircraft and Aerospace. (1988)-. Periodical. English. Eleven times a year. 37.00Aus$. Peter Isaacson Publications, 46-50 Porter Street, Prahran Victoria, 3181 Australia. **Tel** 011 61 3 2457777, **FAX** 011 61 3 2457606. **Continues** Aircraft (Melbourne, Vic.).

LC HE9761
DD 387.7
ISSN 1043-9382
US

AIRCRAFT BLUEBOOK MARKETLINE. [Aircr. bluebk. marketline]. **VFOAT** Marketline. Vol. 1, No. 1 (Summer 1989)-. Periodical. English. Four times a year. $45.00. Intertec Publishing Corporation, 9800 Metcalf, Overland Park KS 66212. **Tel** (913)341-1300. (**Subscription address:** Intertec Publishing Corporation, PO Box 2901, Overland Park KS 66282. **Tel** 800 441-0294.)

LC HD9711.A1 A36
DD 629.133/340422/029473
ISSN 1043-3767
US

AIRCRAFT BLUEBOOK-PRICE DIGEST. [Aircr. bluebk.-price dig.]. **VFOAT** Aircraft Bluebook Price Digest; Bluebook Price Digest; Bluebook-Price Digest. (19??)-. Periodical. English. Four times a year. $245.00. Intertec Publishing Corporation, 9800 Metcalf, Overland Park KS 66212. **Tel** (913)341-1300. (**Subscription address:** Intertec Publishing Corporation, PO Box 2901, Overland Park KS 66282. **Tel** 800 441-0294.) **Absorbed** General Aircraft Fixed- and Rotary-Winged Price Guide, 0738-6591.

LC TL671.1 .U65B
DD 363.1/2466/02573
ISSN 0747-5586
US

AIRCRAFT CERTIFICATION DIRECTORY. [Aircr. certif. dir.]. **Main/Corp** United States. Federal Aviation Administration. Office of Airworthiness. (1983)-. Government Publication. English. One time a year. US Department of Transportation / Federal Aviation Administration, 800 Independence Avenue Southwest, Washington DC 20591. **Tel** (202)367-3484, **FAX** (202)367-3505.

LC TL
DD 629
US

AIRCRAFT COST EVALUATOR : HELICOPTERS. (19??)-. English. Two times a year (Jan. & July). $295.00 US; $290.00 other. Conklin & de Decker Association Inc., PO Box 1142, Orleans MA 02653. **Tel** (508) 255-5975, **FAX** (508) 255-9380.

LC TL
DD 629
US

AIRCRAFT COST EVALUATOR : JETS. (19??)-. English. Two times a year (Jan. & July). $295.00. Conklin & de Decker Association Inc., PO Box 1142, Orleans MA 02653. **Tel** (508) 255-5975, **FAX** (508) 255-9380. **ED** Alan Conklin. **Circ:** 700.

LC TL
DD 629
US

AIRCRAFT COST EVALUATOR : TURBOPROPS. (19??)-. English. Two times a year (Jan. & July). $295.00 US; $290.00 other. Conklin & de Decker Association Inc., PO Box 1142, Orleans MA 02653. **Tel** (508) 255-5975, **FAX** (508) 255-9380. **ED** Alan Conklin. **Circ:** 700.

LC TL
DD 629
UK

AIRCRAFT ECONOMICS. (19??)-. English. Six times a year. £165.00 UK; $295.00 US. Euromoney Publications PLC, Nestor House, Playhouse Yard, London EC4Z 5EX United Kingdom. **Tel** 011 44 171 7798888, **FAX** 011 44 171 7798630, telex 290700 EUROMON G.
Desc: Specialist magazine dealing with the efficient use of aircraft, and in particular the valuation of aircraft, the operating costs of various aircraft types, the efficiencies of engine types and the costs which go into operating the aircraft.

LC TL
DD 629
UK

AIRCRAFT ENGINEERING AND AEROSPACE TECHNOLOGY. Vol. 58, No. 4 (April 1986)-. Periodical. English. Six times a year. $259.00. MCB University Press, 60 62 Toller Lane, Bradford, West Yorkshire BD8 9BY United Kingdom. **Tel** 011 44 1274 785280, **FAX** 011 44 1274 785200, telex 51317-MCBUNI-G. (**Subscription address:** MCB University Press / US and Canada Subscriptions, PO Box 10812, Birmingham AL 35201-0812. **Tel** (205)995-1567, (800)633-4931, **FAX** (205)995-1588.) **Continues** Aircraft Engineering, 0002-2667.
Ind/Abst Curr. Cit.

LC TL
DD 629
ISSN 0194-469X
US
CCC

AIRCRAFT FORECAST. (19??)-. Periodical. English. Twelve times a year. $1490.00. Forecast International / DMS Inc., 22 Commerce Road, Newtown CT 06470. **Tel** (203)426-0800, **FAX** (203)426-1964, telex 467615. Index available. available on diskette (5 1/4 (MS DOS)).
Desc: Forecasts, and special market analyses such as helicopters.

LC TL
DD 629.1
ISSN 0002-2675
CCC

AIRCRAFT ILLUSTRATED. Vol. 1, No. 1 (March 1968)-. Periodical. English. Twelve times a year. $72.48. Ian Allan Ltd., Coombelands Lane, Addlestone Weybridge KT15 1HY United Kingdom. **Tel** 011 44 1932 858511, 011 44 1932 855909, **FAX** 011 44 1932 232356, 011 44 1932 854750. **Absorbed** Air Display.

LC TL
DD 629.1
UK

AIRCRAFT ILLUSTRATED ANNUAL. (1979)-. English. One time a year. $10.27. Ian Allan Ltd., Coombelands Lane, Addlestone Weybridge KT15 1HY United Kingdom. **Tel** 011 44 1932 858511, 011 44 1932 855909, **FAX** 011 44 1932 232356, 011 44 1932 854750.

LC Z5064.A25 A57 TL670
DD 016.629133
ISSN 0147-1244
US

AIRCRAFT INDEX MAGAZINE. Vol. 1 (1975)-. English. One time a year. DHS Products, PO Box 111, Palmyra NJ 08065.

LC HE
DD 388
UK

●**AIRCRAFT MAINTENANCE EXPRESS.** (1995)-. English. Two times a year. $475.00. Air Transport Publications, 4 Loveday Road, London W13 9JS United Kingdom. **Tel** 011 44 181 9320780.

LC TL600
DD 629.1346
ISSN 0955-8063
UK

AIRCRAFT MAINTENANCE INTERNATIONAL. [Aircr. maint. int.]. (1989)-. Periodical. English. Ten times a year. $195.00. Camrus Publishers, Neoter House, Clayhouse Yard, London EC4V 5EX United Kingdom. **Tel** 011 44 171 7798866, **FAX** 011 44 171 7798868. (**Subscription address:** Powerhouse. **Tel** 011 44 181 6610449.) **ED** Alan Emmings. **Ad Acc. Circ:** 10,000 (ctrl).

Aeronautics, Astronautics

Desc: Covers the maintenance, overhaul, repair, inspection and modification of aircraft. Each issue contains business reports, technical analyses of state-of-the-art engineering processes, as well as news pages, a company profile and a regional focus.

LC TL **ISSN** 0961-6047
DD 629.1346 UK

AIRCRAFT MAINTENANCE INTERNATIONAL YEARBOOK. [Aircr. maint. int. yearb.]. (1991)-. Periodical. English. One time a year. $169.41. Euromoney Publications PLC, Nestor House, Playhouse Yard, London EC4Z 5EX United Kingdom. **Tel** 011 44 171 7798888, FAX 011 44 171 7798630, telex 290700 EUROMON G.

LC TL **ISSN** 1072-3145
DD 629 US

●**AIRCRAFT MAINTENANCE TECHNOLOGY.** [Aircr. maint. technol.]. Vol. 4, No. 6 (Sept./Oct. 1993)-. Trade Publication. English. Six times a year. $40.00. Johnson Hill Press Inc., (A Division of PTN Publishing Co.), 1233 Janesville Avenue, PO Box 803, Fort Atkinson WI 53538-0803. **Tel** (414)563-6388, FAX (414)563-1704. **ED** Greg Napert. **Ad Acc.** Full Page (B&W) $4745.00. Full Page (Color) $5670.00 (4-color). **Circ:** 41,097. ***Continues*** *Aircraft Technician, 1044-8012.*
Desc: Serves the maintenance side of the aviation industry. Included are management strategies, legal concerns, new product and equipment information.

LC TL
DD 629 CN

AIRCRAFT NATIONALITY AND REGISTRATION MARKS; INTERNATIONAL STANDARDS. ANNEX 7 TO THE CONVENTION ON INTERNATIONAL CIVIL AVIATION. **Main/Corp** International Civil Aviation Organization. (19??)-. English. $1.50. International Civil Aviation Organization / ICAO, 1000 Sherbrooke Street West, Suite 400, Montreal Quebec H3A 2R2 Canada. **Tel** (514)285-8026, (514)285-8022, telex 05-24514.

LC TL
DD 629 CN

AIRCRAFT NOISE; INTERNATIONAL STANDARDS AND RECOMMENDED PRACTICES. ANNEX 16 TO THE CONVENTION ON INTERNATIONAL CIVIL AVIATION. **Main/Corp** International Civil Aviation Organization. (19??)-. English. $20.00. International Civil Aviation Organization / ICAO, 1000 Sherbrooke Street West, Suite 400, Montreal Quebec H3A 2R2 Canada. **Tel** (514)285-8026, (514)285-8022, telex 05-24514.

LC HD9711.U58 A57
DD 338.4/7629133/0973 SZ

AIRCRAFT PRODUCTION USA. **VFOAT** Aircraft Production U.S.A. English. Interavia, PO Box 162, CH-1216 Geneva Switzerland. **Tel** 011 41 22 980505.

LC HD9711.2.U6 C87 **ISSN** 0275-4983
DD 380.1/4562913436/0973021 US

AIRCRAFT PROPELLERS. (CURRENT INDUSTRIAL REPORTS. MA-37E, AIRCRAFT PROPELLERS.). **Added/Corp** United States. Bureau of the Census. (19??)-. Government Publication. English. One time a year. US Department of Commerce / Bureau of the Census, Data User Services Division, Customer Services, Washington DC 20233-0800. **Tel** (301)763-4100. **(Subscription address:** Superintendent of Documents, US Government Printing Office, Washington DC 20402. **)**
Desc: Presents data on production, inventories, and orders.

LC TL **ISSN** 1044-8012
DD 629 US
TITLE CHANGE

AIRCRAFT TECHNICIAN. [Airc. tech.]. Vol. 1, No. 1 (Nov./Dec. 1989)-(19??). Periodical. English. Johnson Hill Press Inc., (A Division of PTN Publishing Co.), 1233 Janesville Avenue, PO Box 803, Fort Atkinson WI 53538-0803. **Tel** (414)563-6388, FAX (414)563-1704. ***Continued by*** *Aircraft Maintenance Technology, 1072-3145.*

LC TL670 **ISSN** 0967-439X
DD 629.13334 UK

AIRCRAFT TECHNOLOGY ENGINEERING & MAINTENANCE. [Aircr. technol. eng. maint.]. **VFOAT** Aircraft Technology Engineering and Maintenance. (1992)-. Periodical. English. Six times a year (Feb., Mar., May, July, Oct., Dec.). $111.23. Aviation Industry Press Ltd., 31 Palace Street, London SW1E 5HW United Kingdom. **Tel** 011 44 171 8284376, FAX 011 44 171 8289154. **ED** Paul Copping. **Ad Acc, Adv Mgr:** Lesley White. ctrl circ.

LC TL **ISSN** 0967-439X
DD 629.1334 UK

AIRCRAFT TECHNOLOGY ENGINEERING & MAINTENANCE. [Aircr. technol. eng. maint.]. **VFOAT** Aircraft Technology Engineering and Maintenance. (199?)-. Periodical. English. Six times a year. $111.23. Aviation Industry Press Ltd., 31 Palace Street, London SW1E 5HW United Kingdom. **Tel** 011 44 171 8284376, FAX 011 44 171 8289154.

LC TL
DD 629 US

AIRCRAFT TYPE CERTIFICATE DATA SHEETS AND SPECIFICATION. VOLUME I, SINGLE-ENGINE AIRPLANES. **VFOAT** Single-Engine Airplanes. English. One time a year (monthly supplements). $158.00 US; $197.50 other. Department of Transportation, 400 Seventh Street SW, Washington DC 20590. **Tel** (202)426-4000. available on microfiche (Vols. for (1985-) distributed to depository libraries). ***Continues*** *Type Certificate Data Sheets and Specifications. Volume 1, Single-Engine Airplanes, 0278-307X.*

LC TL **ISSN** 1014-0107
DD 629 CN
UDC 38
CODEN NU057

AIRCRAFT TYPE DESIGNATORS. [Aircr. type des.]. **VFOAT** Indicatifs de Type d'Aeronef; Designadores de Tipos de Aeronave. (1967)-. Multiple languages. Irregular. $9.00. International Civil Aviation Organization / ICAO, 1000 Sherbrooke Street West, Suite 400, Montreal Quebec H3A 2R2 Canada. **Tel** (514)285-8026, (514)285-8022, telex 05-24514.

LC TL **ISSN** 1071-0655
DD 629 US
CCC

●**AIRCRAFT VALUE NEWS.** **Added/Corp** Phillips Business Information, Inc. (1993)-. Periodical. English. Twenty-five times a year. $595.00. Phillips Business Information Inc., 1201 Seven Locks Road, PO Box 61130, Potomac MD 20854. **Tel** (301)424-3338, (301)340-1520, (800)777-5005, FAX (301)424-4297, telex 358149. ***Continues*** *Aircraft Value Newsletter, 1065-8688.*

LC TL **ISSN** 1065-8688
DD 629 US
CCC

AIRCRAFT VALUE NEWSLETTER. [Aircr. value newsl.]. **Added/Corp** Phillips Business Information, Inc. Airline Media Group. Vol. 1, No. 1 (Sept. 7, 1992)-. Newsletter. English. Twenty-five times a year. $595.00 US; $630.00 other. Phillips Business Information Inc., 1201 Seven Locks Road, PO Box 61130, Potomac MD 20854. **Tel** (301)424-3338, (301)340-1520, (800)777-5005, FAX (301)424-4297, telex 358149. available on an online database (file 636/Full-Text) from DIALOG. ***Continues*** *Slipstream (Haywards Heath, England), 0961-7388.*

LC HE9761 **ISSN** 0733-5407
DD 387.7 US

AIRFARE DISCOUNT BULLETIN. (AIRFARE DISCOUNT BULLETIN : ADB.). **VFOAT** ADB. Issue No. 1 (1982)-. Bulletin. English. Twelve times a year. $150.00. Airfare Discount Bulletin, PO Box 460, Riverside CA 06878. **Tel** (203)322-2086.

LC TL **ISSN** 0266-2132
DD 629 UK

AIRFINANCE ANNUAL. [Airfinance annu.]. **VFOAT** Air Finance Annual. (1984)-. Trade Publication. English. One time a year. $185.00. Airfinance Journal Ltd., 2 Church Street, Coggeshall Essex CO6 1 TU United Kingdom. **Tel** 011 44 1376 62262. **(Subscription address:** World Publication Services, PO Box 7717, East Rutherford NJ 07073. **) ED** Alison Taylor and Robert Hawkins. **Ad Acc. Circ:** 5,000 (ctrl).
Desc: Contains articles on all aspects of aviation and aerospace finance, plus directory listings for 1,000 companies internationally who specialize in aviation financing techniques.

LC HE9782 .A37 **ISSN** 0143-2257
DD 387.7/1 UK

AIRFINANCE JOURNAL. [Airfinance j.]. **VFOAT** Air Finance Journal. (1980)-. Trade Publication. English. Twelve times a year. $450.00. Euromoney Publications PLC, Nestor House, Playhouse Yard, London EC4Z 5EX United Kingdom. **Tel** 011 44 171 7798888, FAX 011 44 171 7798630, telex 290700 EUROMON G. **ED** Scott Hamilton Fadugba. **Bk Rev. Ad Acc. Circ:** 8,000 (ctrl). Documents available from UMI Article Clearinghouse.
Desc: Covers all aspects of commercial aircraft financing. Reviews the deals and transactions worldwide. Includes features on treasury management, leasing, legislation and financial structuring, presents essential information to all those involved in aircraft acquisition and management.
Ind/Abst ABI/INFORM Glob. Ed.

LC UG622 **ISSN** 0704-6804
DD 358.4/00971 CN
CCC

AIRFORCE. **Added/Corp** Royal Canadian Air Force Association. (Jan. 1977)-. Periodical. English. Four times a year. 16.01Can$. Airforce Productions Ltd., PO Box 2460 Station D, Ottawa Ontario K1P 5W6 Canada. **Tel** (613)992-5184, FAX (613)995-2196. **ED** Doug Stuebing. **Bk Rev**, (Qty: 20). **Ad Acc, Adv Mgr:** D. Slater, **Tel** (613)992-6096. **Circ:** 32,000. ***Supersedes*** *Wings at Home.*
Desc: Anecdotal stories of aviation and aerospace by the people who fly, and developments in aircraft industry.

LC TL **ISSN** 1075-8240
DD 629 US

●**AIRLINE AVIONICS.** [Airl. avion.]. (May 1994)-. Periodical. English. Twelve times a year. $165.00. Avionics Communications Inc., Leesburg Municipal Airport, PO Box 2628, Leesburg VA 22075. **Tel** (800)441-4224, (703)777-9559, FAX (703)777-9568.

LC HE9761 **ISSN** 0268-7615
DD 387.7 UK
CCC

AIRLINE BUSINESS. [Airl. bus.]. (1985)-. Trade Publication. English. Twelve times a year. $99.00. Reed Business Publishing / West Sussex, England, Perrymount Road, Haywards Heath, West Sussex RH16 3DH United Kingdom. **Tel** 011 44 1444 441212, FAX 011 44 1444 445447. available on an online database from Reuters, Ltd.; Information Access Company; and DATA-STAR. Documents available from BLDSC.
Ind/Abst Aviat. Tradescan [Full Cov.]; F&S Index Plus Text, Int. [Full Txt.] [Select. Cov.]; PROMT [Full Txt.]; Trade Ind. ASAP [Full Txt.]; Trade Ind. Index [Full Txt.].

LC HE9761 **ISSN** 1013-4050
DD 387.7/4042 CN

AIRLINE CODING DIRECTORY. [Airl. coding dir.]. **Added/Corp** International Air Transport Association. 16th Edition (April 1, 1988)-. Periodical. English. Fifteen times a year (3 main issues and monthly amendments). 138.00Can$. International Air Transport Association / Montreal, 2000 Peel Street, Room 3050, Montreal Quebec H3A 2R4 Canada. **Tel** (514)844-6311 ext. 232, FAX (514)844-5286, telex 05-267627. ***Separated from*** *Passenger Reservations Manual.*

LC TL
DD 629 US

AIRLINE DELAY TRENDS. **Added/Corp** United States. Federal Aviation Administration. Office of Systems Engineering Management. Transportation Systems Center. (1973)-. Trade Publication. English. One time a year. National Technical Information Service - NTIS, Room 2027S, 5285 Port Royal Road, Springfield VA 22161. **Tel** (703)487-4630, (703)487-4660, (703)487-4650, FAX (703)321-8547, telex 89-9405.

LC HE9761 **ISSN** 1040-5410
DD 387.7 US
CCC

AIRLINE FINANCIAL NEWS. [Airl. financ. news]. (1986)-. Periodical. English. Fifty times a year. $695.00. Phillips Business Information Inc., 1201 Seven Locks Road, PO Box 61130, Potomac MD 20854. **Tel** (301)424-3338, (301)340-1520, (800)777-5005, FAX (301)424-4297, telex 358149. available on an online database from DATA-STAR; and (file 636/Full-Text) DIALOG.
Ind/Abst PTS Newsl. Database [Full Txt.].

LC HE9768 .A37 **ISSN** 0194-0961
DD 387.7/025 US

AIRLINE INDUSTRY DIRECTORY. **VFOAT** AID, Airline Industry Directory. Vol. 1 (Spring/Summer 1979)-. Directory. English. Two times a year. $35.00 per copy. Airline Publishing Group, Suite 420/818 18th Street NW, Washington DC 20006.

LC HE9761 **ISSN** 1071-1325
DD 387.7 US
CCC

●**AIRLINE MARKETING NEWS.** [Airl. mark. news]. **Added/Corp** Phillips Business Information, Inc. (1993)-. Periodical. English. Twenty-five times a year. $595.00. Phillips Business Information Inc., 1201 Seven Locks Road, PO Box 61130, Potomac MD 20854. **Tel** (301)424-3338, (301)340-1520, (800)777-5005, FAX (301)424-4297, telex 358149.

LC TL
DD 629 US

AIRLINE NEWSLETTER. (1970)-. Newsletter. English. Twelve times a year. $89.50. Roadcap and Associates, 1030 South Green Bay Road, PO Box 291, Lake Forest IL 60045. **Tel** (312)234-4730.

LC TL
DD 629 SW

AIRLINE PASSENGER TARIFF. (19??)-. English. Four times a year. $480.00. Scandinavian Airlines System, Treasury Dept, Attn QT, S 161 87 Stockholm Sweden. **Tel** 011 46 8 797000.

LC TL
DD 629 US
AIRLINE QUARTERLY, THE. (19??)-. Periodical. English. Four times a year. $1135.00. Airline Economics International Inc., PO Box 16666, Crystal City, Arlington VA 22215. **Tel** (202)429-0247, FAX (202)429-8787.

LC HE9803.A2 A49 **ISSN** 0884-1624
DD 629.134/45 US
AIRLINE SEATING GUIDE (POCKET ED.). (AIRLINE SEATING GUIDE.). [Airl. seat. guide]. (1983?)-. Periodical. English. Four times a year (Feb., May, Aug., Nov.). $39.95. Carlson Publishing Company, PO Box 888, Los Alamitos CA 90720. **Tel** (310)493-4877, (800)728-4877.

LC HE9761 **ISSN** 1077-0151
DD 387.7 US
●**AIRLINE TRAFFIC MONTHLY.** [Airl. traffic mon.]. (1993)-. Periodical. English. Twelve times a year. $210.00. ROM Associates Inc, 49 Case Mountain Road, Manchester CT 06040. **Tel** (203)645-9852.

LC TL
DD 629 US
AIRLINER. **Added/Corp** Boeing Company. Commercial Airplane Group. Customer Services Division. (1992)-. Periodical. English. Four times a year. ***Continues*** *Boeing Airliner.*
Ind/Abst Aviat. Tradescan [Full Cov.].

LC TL685.4 .A38
DD 629.133/30423/029473 US
AIRLINER PRICE GUIDE OF COMMERCIAL-REGIONAL & COMMUTER AIRCRAFT, THE. **VFOAT** Airliner Price Guide; Airliner. (19??)-. English. Three times a year (Jan., May, Sept.). $575.00. Airliner Price Guide Incorporated, 1105 Sovereign Row, Oklahoma City OK 73108. **Tel** (800)872-0110, (405)942-8225, FAX (405)942-8620. **Ad Acc**, **Adv Mgr:** Judy Ellenburg.
Desc: Contains information on various airplanes. Lists the retail, wholesale and loan values. Provides other information such as overhaul costs on engines and airframes, commuter and commerical aircraft, appraisal points with values, and TBO's on engines and airframes.

LC TL720 .A46 **ISSN** 0090-8770
DD 387.7/05 US
CEASED
AIRLINERS INTERNATIONAL. [Airl. int.]. Vol. 1 (Summer 1973)-(19??). Periodical. English. Kalmbach Publishing Company, 21027 Crossroads Circle, PO Box 1612, Waukesha WI 53187. **Tel** (414)796-8776 ext. 411, FAX (414)796-0126.

LC HE9761.1 .A47 **ISSN** 0896-6575
DD 387 US
AIRLINERS (MIAMI, FLA.). **See** Travel and Tourism.

LC UG 633.A1 A528 **ISSN** 0002-2756
DD 358.405 US
AIRMAN (WASHINGTON, D.C.). **See** Military and Defense.

LC TL710 .U632
DD 629.132/5 US
AIRMAN'S INFORMATION MANUAL. **Added/Corp** United States. Federal Aviation Administration. **VFOAT** Basic Flight Manual and ATC Procedures; Airport Directory; Operational Data and Notices to Airmen; Notices to Airmen; Graphic Notices and Supplemental Data. (19??)-. Government Publication. English. Irregular (approximately every 112 days). $58.00 US; $72.50 other. US Department of Transportation / US Coast Guard, 2100 Second Street Southwest, Washington DC 20953-0001. **Tel** (202)267-2229. **(Subscription address:** Superintendent of Documents, US Government Printing Office, Washington DC 20402. **) ED** James Hardy. **Circ:** 16,000. ***Continues*** *United States. Federal Aviation Agency. Flight Information Division. Airman's Information Manual.* ***Continued in part by*** *Notices to Airmen, 1057-9621; Airman's Information Manual. Basic Flight Information and ATC Procedures, 1057-963X.*
Desc: Contains the fundamentals required to fly in the United States National Airspace System. Contains items of interest to pilots concerning health and medical facts, and factors affecting flight safety, pilot/controller glossary terms used in the air traffic control system, and information on safety, accident and hazard reporting.

LC TL **ISSN** 1057-963X
DD 629 US
TITLE CHANGE
AIRMAN'S INFORMATION MANUAL. BASIC FLIGHT INFORMATION AND ATC PROCEDURES. [Airman's Inf. Man., Basic flight Inf. ATC Proced.]. **Added/Corp** United States. Federal Aviation Administration. **VFOAT** Basic Flight Information and ATC Procedures; Official Guide to Basic Flight Information and ATC Procedures. (July 1978)-(1995). Government Publication. English. US Department of Transportation / Federal Aviation Administration, 800 Independence Avenue Southwest, Washington DC 20591. **Tel** (202)367-3484, FAX (202)367-3505. **(Subscription address:** Superintendent of Documents, US Government Printing Office, Washington DC 20402. **)** ***Separated from*** *Airman's Information Manual;* ***Absorbed in part*** *Graphic Notices and Supplemental Data.* ***Continued by*** *Aeronautical Information Manual.*
Desc: Contains the fundamentals required in order to fly in the United States National Airspace System. Contains items of interest to pilots concerning health and medical facts, factors affecting flight safety, a pilot/controller glossary of terms used in the Air Traffic Control System, and information on safety, accident and hazard reporting.

LC TL710 .A53 **ISSN** 0094-047X
DD 629.132/52/0973 US
AIRMAN'S INFORMATION MANUAL (FALLBROOK, CALIF.). (AIRMAN'S INFORMATION MANUAL.). (19??)-. English. One time a year (Nov.). $12.95. Tab Books Inc., 11 West 19th Street, New York NY 10011. **Tel** (212)337-5025.

LC TL
DD 629 US
AIRMAN'S INFORMATION MANUAL. PT. 3. OPERATIONAL DATA. Government Publication. English. Six times a year. US Department of Transportation / Federal Aviation Administration, 800 Independence Avenue Southwest, Washington DC 20591. **Tel** (202)367-3484, FAX (202)367-3505.

LC TL
DD 629 UK
AIRPORT ALERT. (19??)-. English. Twenty-four times a year. £565.00. ABI Building Data, The Chapter House, Hindeaton Hall Estate, Neston L64 7TS United Kingdom. **Tel** 051 353 1234. **ED** Denis Mclinden. Index available. cum. index. **Ad Acc.**
Desc: Covers new developments at airports.

LC HE9797.A1 A33
DD 387.7 CN
AIRPORT AND ROUTE FACILITIES : FINANCIAL DATA AND SUMMARY TRAFFIC DATA = INSTALLATIONS ET SERVICES D'AEROPORT ET DE ROUTE : DONNEES FINANCIERES ET STATISTIQUES DE TRAFIC SOMMAIRES. **Added/Corp** International Civil Aviation Organization. **VFOAT** Installations et Services d'Aeroport et de Route. (1976)-. English (French, Russian and Spanish). Price varies. International Civil Aviation Organization / ICAO, 1000 Sherbrooke Street West, Suite 400, Montreal Quebec H3A 2R2 Canada. **Tel** (514)285-8026, (514)285-8022, telex 05-24514.

LC HE9761 **ISSN** 1072-1797
DD 387 US
●**AIRPORT BUSINESS.** **See** Business and Economics.

LC TL726.3.C7 A57 **ISSN** 0145-4633
DD 387.7/36.025788 US
AIRPORT DIRECTORY OF THE STATE OF COLORADO. **VFOAT** Colorado Airport Directory. 1st- Ed.; 1976-. Directory. English. G A H Aviation Ltd, Box 2811, Littleton CO 80122.

LC TL725.A1 A515 **ISSN** 0742-7379
DD 387.7/36/068 US
AIRPORT EXECUTIVES. **Added/Corp** American Association of Airport Executives. Tele-Trip Co. **VFOAT** A.A.A.E. Directory; Airport Executives Directory; AAAE Directory. (19??)-. Trade Publication. English. Six times a year. $25.00. American Association of Airport Executives, 4212 King Street, Alexandria VA 22302. **Tel** (703)824-0504, FAX (703)820-1395. Index available. **Ad Acc. Circ:** 7,000.

LC HE9761
DD 387 US
AIRPORT FBO DIRECTORY. (19??)-. Directory. English. One time a year (January). $24.95. Acukwik Inc, PO Box 371035, Omaha NE 68137. **Tel** (402)592-1600, FAX (402)592-1603.
Desc: Data on airports / FBOs in the US and Canada.

LC HE9797.A1 A35 **ISSN** 0002-2802
DD 387 GW
CCC
CODEN APFRBE
AIRPORT FORUM. [Airpt. forum]. (1971)-. Periodical. Multiple languages (English and German). Six times a year. $109.00. Vereinigte Motor Verlag GmbH, Motor Presse, POB 106036, D-70049 Stuttgart Germany. **Tel** 011 49 711 1821506, 011 49 711 1821545. **(Subscription address:** Leserservice Airport Forum, Postfach 6740, W 8700 Wuerzburg F R Germany. **Tel** 011 49 931 4182548.**) ED** Manfred Momberger (editor's address: PO Box 1127, W-7255 Rutesheim Germany; editor's telephone number: 49-7152-51640). **Ad Acc. Circ:** 9,335 (ctrl). Documents available from Article Express International, Ask*IEEE.
Desc: Covers airport construction and operation, air transport and air traffic control.
Ind/Abst Archit. Period. Index (Dec. 1977-); Bioeng. Abstr.; Ei Page One; EMBASE; Eng. Index Annu. [Select. Cov.]; INSPEC (Oct. 1984-); Int. Aerosp. Abstr.; Int. Civil Eng. Abstr.; Soft. Abstr. Eng.

LC HE9761 **ISSN** 0256-3193
DD 387.7/36/05 CN
AIRPORT HANDLING MANUAL. [Airpt. handl. man.]. **Main/Corp** International Air Transport Association. **VAT** IATA Airport Handling Manual; International Air Transport Association Airport Handling Manual. (1973)-. English. One time a year. 139.00Can$. International Air Transport Association / Montreal, 2000 Peel Street, Room 3050, Montreal Quebec H3A 2R4 Canada. **Tel** (514)844-6311 ext. 232, FAX (514)844-5286, telex 05-267627.
Desc: Contains procedures adopted as industry standards for airport handling.

LC HE9761
DD 387.736 US
AIRPORT HIGHLIGHTS. (19??)-. English. Twenty-four times a year. $250.00 Airports; $495.00 Corporate; $125.00 Libraries. Airports Council International - North America, 1220 19th Street Northwest, Suite 200, Washington DC 20036. **Tel** (202)293-8500, telex 404732. **ED** Victoria Pannell. Index available. **Circ:** 1,600.

LC TL725.A1 A518 **ISSN** 1048-2091
DD 387.7/36/0973 US
AIRPORT MAGAZINE. [Airpt. mag.]. **Added/Corp** AAAE Service Corporation. **VFOAT** Airport. Vol. 1, No. 1 (Jan./Feb. 1989)-. Periodical. English. Six times a year. $30.00. American Association of Airport Executives, 4212 King Street, Alexandria VA 22302. **Tel** (703)824-0500, FAX (703)820-1395. Index available (Published Nov./Dec. $5.00 per issue). cum. index.
Desc: Information on issues and management strategies for Airport Executives worldwide.

LC TL **ISSN** 1061-3145
DD 629 US
CEASED
AIRPORT MANAGEMENT. (1992)-(19??). Periodical. English. Johnson Hill Press Inc., (A Division of PTN Publishing Co.), 1233 Janesville Avenue, PO Box 803, Fort Atkinson WI 53538-0803. **Tel** (414)563-6388, FAX (414)563-1704. ***Continues*** *Airport Services, 1041-4231.*

LC HE9761
DD 387.736 UK
CEASED
AIRPORT MANAGEMENT : THE ROLE OF PERFORMANCE INDICATORS. (19??)-(19??). English. Trasnport Studies Group, 35 Martlebone Road Pcl, London NW1 5LS United Kingdom. **Tel** 011 44 171 4865811, FAX 011 44 171 9115057, telex 25964.

LC HE9761 **ISSN** 1041-8318
DD 387.7 US
CCC
AIRPORT NOISE REPORT. [Airpt. noise rep.]. (1989)-. Periodical. English. Twenty-six times a year. $495.00. Airport Noise Report, 43978 Urbancrest Court, Ashburn VA 22011. **Tel** (703)729-4867, FAX (703)729-4528. **ED** Anne Kohut. Index available. cum. index.
Desc: News and information on the airport noise.

LC HD7260 **ISSN** 1057-5537
DD 363 US
AIRPORT OPERATIONS. [Airpt. oper.]. **Added/Corp** Flight Safety Foundation. (19??)-. Periodical. English. Six times a year. $60.00. Flight Safety Foundation Inc., 2200 Wilson Boulevard, Suite 500, Arlington VA 22201. **Tel** (703)522-8300, FAX (703)525-6047, telex 901176 FSF INC AGTN. ***Continues*** *FSF Airport Operations Safety Bulletin, 0898-574X.*
Desc: Focuses on ground operations that involve aircraft and other equipment, airport personnel and services, air traffic control, and passengers.

LC HE9797.5.U52 H32
DD 387.7/36/09969021 US
AIRPORT STATISTICS, STATEWIDE AIRPORT SYSTEM. **See** Aeronautics, Astronautics-Abstracting, Bibliographies and Statistics.

LC HE9761
DD 387.736 UK
AIRPORT SUPPORT. Vol. 1, No. 1 (1982)-. Trade Publication. English. Ten times a year. $195.00. Euromoney Publications PLC, Nestor House, Playhouse Yard, London EC4Z 5EX United Kingdom. **Tel** 011 44 171 7798888, FAX 011 44 171 7798630, telex 290700 EUROMON G. **(Subscription address:** Euromoney Publications PLC, Perrymount Road Haywards Heath, West Sussex RH16 3DH United Kingdom. **Tel** 011 44 1444 440421.**) Ad Acc.** ctrl circ.
Desc: Reports on airport operations, construction and air traffic control.

Aeronautics, Astronautics

LC HE9761
DD 387.736
ISSN 0952-7141
UK
AIRPORT TECHNOLOGY INTERNATIONAL. [Airpt. technol. int.]. (1987)-. Periodical. English. One time a year (Oct.) $94.11. Sterling Publications Ltd., 57 North Wharf Road, London W2 1XR United Kingdom. **Tel** 011 44 171 9159660, FAX 011 44 171 3338155, telex 295819. **(Subscription address:** Sterling Publications Ltd., PO Box 799, Brunel House, London W2 1XR United Kingdom. **Tel** 011 44 181 9159660.)

LC TL725.A1 A543
DD 387.7/36/05
ISSN 0002-2853
UK
CCC
AIRPORTS INTERNATIONAL. [Airpt. int.]. **Added/Corp** International Civil Airport Association. (June 1968)-. Periodical. English. Ten times a year (monthly with Jan./Feb. & July/Aug. issues combined). $119.79. SKC Communications Limited, Southfields South View Road, Wadhurst East Sussex TN5 6TP United Kingdom. **Tel** 011 44 1892 784099, FAX 011 44 1892 784089. **ED** Mark Pilling. **Ad Acc. Circ:** 12,000 (ctrl). **Ind/Abst** Aviat. Tradescan [Full Cov.]; Int. Aerosp. Abstr.

LC TL726.5.M4 S42
DD 387.7/36/02572
ISSN 0275-2077
US
AIRPORTS OF MEXICO AND CENTRAL AMERICA. [Airpt. Mex. Cent. Am.]. VFOAT Senterfitt's Airports of Mexico & Central America. English. A Senterfit J-V Fulfillment Center, PO Box 11950, Reno NV 89510.

LC HB
DD 338
ISSN 1044-9469
US
AIRPORTS (WASHINGTON, D.C.). (AIRPORTS.). [Airpt.]. (19??)-. Periodical. English. One time a week. $555.00. McGraw Hill Publishing Company, Inc., 1221 Avenue of the Americas, New York NY 10020. **Tel** (212)512-6410, (800)525-5003, FAX (212)512-6111. **(Subscription address:** McGraw Hill Executive Newsletters, PO Box 489, Hightstown NJ 08520. **Tel** (609)426-5511.) **ED** Robert Bunnell. available on an online database from Mead Data Central; NEWSNET; Dow Jones News/Retrieval; DIALOG; and NEXIS.
Desc: For airport managers, users and suppliers. Focuses on key airport issues such as funding, regulation, legal matters, noise, capacity problems, concessions, marketing and congressional action.

LC TL685.3 .A533
DD 629
ISSN 1067-1048
US
AIRPOWER (GRANADA HILLS, LOS ANGELES, CALIF.). (AIRPOWER.). [Airpower]. Vol. 1 (Sept. 1971)-. Periodical. English. Six times a year (Jan., Mar., May, July, Sept., Nov.). $18.00. Sentry Magazines, 10718 White Oak Avenue, Granada Hills CA 91344. **Tel** (310)368-2012.

LC UG633 .A69
DD 358.4/03/0973
ISSN 0897-0823
US
AIRPOWER JOURNAL. See Military and Defense.

LC HE9761
DD 387.7
SA
●**AIRREPORT.** (1994)-. English. One time a year. Airreport, PO Box 221, Morningside 2057 South Africa.

LC HE9761
DD 387.7
ISSN 0193-4538
US
AIRTRAN NEWS. **Added/Corp** National Air Transportation Association. (19??)-. Periodical. English. Twelve times a year. $30.00. National Air Transportation Association, 4226 King Street, Alexandria VA 22302. **Tel** (703)845-9000.

LC HE9761
DD 387.7
ISSN 1074-4320
US
●**AIRWAYS (SANDPOINT, IDAHO).** (AIRWAYS : A GLOBAL REVIEW OF COMMERCIAL FLIGHT.). **Added/Corp** Airways International, Inc. (1994)-. Trade Publication. English. Six times a year (bimonthly). $19.95. Airways International, Inc., PO Box 1109, Sandpoint ID 83864. **Tel** (208)263-5166, FAX (208)263-3313. **ED** John Wegg. **Ad Acc, Adv Mgr:** Seija Wegg-Itronen, **Tel** (208)263-5166. Full Page (B&W) $820.00. Full Page (Color) $1,300.00. **Circ.** 30,000.
Desc: For airline and air industry professionals and aficionados. Devoted to airlines and commercial aircraft as well as flying, operating, traveling in, and supporting them. Covers manufacturers, operators, people, technology, airports, and airways.

LC HE9761
DD 387.736
US
AIRWORTHINESS DIRECTIVE SUMMARY. **Added/Corp** United States. Civil Aeronautics Administration. (19??)-. Government Publication. English. Irregular. $189.00 US; $236.25 other (Book 2, small aircraft); $216.00 US; $270.00 other (Book 2, large aircraft). Superintendent of Documents, US Government Printing Office, Washington DC 20402. **Tel** (202)275-3328, FAX (202)786-2377.

LC TL
DD 629
UK
AIRWORTHINESS NOTICES. (19??)-. English. Irregular. £13.60 UK; £15.50 other. Civil Aviation Authority / England, Grenville House, 37 Gratton Road, Cheltenham Glo GL50 2BN United Kingdom. **Tel** 011 44 1242 235151, FAX 011 44 1242 584139.

LC TL
DD 629
CN
AIRWORTHINESS OF AIRCRAFT; INTERNATIONAL STANDARDS. ANNEX 8 TO THE CONVENTION ON INTERNATIONAL CIVIL AVIATION. **Main/Corp** International Civil Aviation Organization. (19??)-. English. $8.00. International Civil Aviation Organization / ICAO, 1000 Sherbrooke Street West, Suite 400, Montreal Quebec H3A 2R2 Canada. **Tel** (514)285-8026, (514)285-8022, telex 05-24514.

LC HE9868.5.A4 A37
DD 629.13
JO
AL-AJNIHAH. **Added/Corp** Alyah. (19??)-. Periodical. Arabic. Twelve times a year. Al-Ajnihah, PO Box 302, Amman Jordan.

LC TL
DD 629
UDC 629.73
Pr Rev
ISSN 0394-6185
IT
ALI ANTICHE. [Ali antiche]. (1983)-. Periodical. Italian. Four times a year (Mar., June, Sept., Dec.). L27250. Gruppo Amici Velivoli Storici, Casella Postale 7138, 00100 Rome Nomentano Italy. **Tel** 011 39 6 44291369, FAX 011 39 6 855-7628. **ED** Gregory Alegi. **Bk Rev** (Qty: 20). **Ad Acc. Circ:** 1,000 (ctrl).
Desc: Italian aviation history through the presentation of historic aircraft.

LC TL
DD 629
UDC 850
ISSN 1120-3277
IT
TITLE CHANGE
ALISEI. [Alisei]. (1982)-(1995). Monographic series. Italian. Touring Club Italiano, Corso Italia 10, Milan 20122 Italy. **Tel** 011 39 2 8526 1, FAX 011 39 2 8526299. **ED** Egidio Gavazzi. **Merged into** Dove.
Desc: Aimed at small aircraft owners and pilots.

LC TL
DD 629
US
AME JOURNAL. (19??)-. English. Twelve times a year. $89.00. Aviation Maintenance Employment, 109 Baybridge, Suite 201, Gulf Breeze FL 32561. **Tel** (800)786-5189, (904)932-6326, FAX (904)934-5000. **ED** Ted Hobson, (phone: (904)934-5908). **Ad Acc, Adv Mgr Tel** (904)934-5000. ctrl circ.

LC TL
DD 629
ISSN 0279-7968
US
AMERICAN AERONAUT. See Business and Economics-Labor.

LC HE9761
DD 387.7
ISSN 0744-091X
US
AMERICAN EXPRESS SKY GUIDE. **Added/Corp** American Express Company. VFOAT Sky Guide; Skyguide. (19??)-. Periodical. Twelve times a year. $55.00. Sky Guide, PO Box 3229, Harlan IA 51537. **Tel** (800)678-6738. ctrl circ.

LC HE9761
DD 387.7
ISSN 0003-1518
US
AMERICAN WAY (DALLAS, TEX.). (AMERICAN WAY.). [Am. way]. **Added/Corp** American Airlines/American Eagle. (19??)-. Periodical. English. Twenty-six times a year. AA Magazine Publications, Mail Drop 2G23, PO Box 619616, DFW Airport TX 75261-9616. **Tel** (817)967-1804, FAX (817)967-1571. **ED** Doug Crichton. **Ad Acc. Circ:** 270,000 (ctrl). available on microfilm from University Microfilms International (UMI).
Desc: Stories designed to appeal to passengers aboard American Airlines. Profiles, travel, business, entertainment, technology.

LC HE9882.8.S734 K485a
DD 387.7096
SJ
ANBA AL-KHUTUT AL-JAWWIYAH AL-SUDANIYAH. **Main/Corp** Khutut Al-Jawwiyah Al-Sudaniyah. (19??)-. Arabic. Twelve times a year. Al-Khutut Al-Jawwiyah Al-Sudaniyah, PO Box 253, Khartoum Sudan.

LC K1 .N5
DD 341.45/05
ISSN 0701-158X
CN
ANNALS OF AIR AND SPACE LAW. See Law-International Law.

LC TL500
DD 629.13
US
ANNALS OF BALLOON HISTORY AND MUSEOLOGY. (1991)-. English. Irregular. $21.50. Annals of Balloon History & Museology, 15155 County Road 32, Mayer MN 55360. **Tel** (612)657-2237. **ED** Paul Maravelas. **Bk Rev. Circ:** 200.

LC K1
DD 343.09/6
FR
ANNUAIRE DE DROIT MARITIME ET AERO-SPATIAL. See Law-Maritime Law.

LC U
DD 355
UDC 358.4(73)
US
ANNUAL BULLETIN - UNITED STATES AIR FORCE ACADEMY. See Military and Defense.

LC TL
DD 629
US
ANNUAL ECONOMIC REPORT OF AIRFREIGHT FORWARDERS; REPORTING MORE THEN $10,000,000 TRANSPORTATION REVENUES. **Added/Corp** United States. Civil Aeronautics Board. Bureau of Accounts and Statistics. Financial and Traffic Data Section. (1975)-. English. One time a year. Civil Aeronautics Board, 1825 Connecticut Avenue, Washington DC 20428. **Tel** (202)673-5174.

LC HE9803.A35 F3a
DD 387.7/0973
ISSN 1046-8838
US
TITLE CHANGE
ANNUAL FAA AVIATION FORECAST CONFERENCE PROCEEDINGS. [Annu. FAA Aviat. Forecast Conf. proc.]. **Added/Corp** United States. Office of Aviation Policy and Plans. VFOAT Annual F.A.A. Aviation Forecast Conference Proceedings; FAA Aviation Forecast Conference Proceedings. VAT Annual Federal Aviation Administration Aviation Forecast Conference proceedings; Federal Aviation Administration Aviation Forecast Conference Proceedings. (1986)-(1993). Government Publication. English. US Department of Transportation / Federal Aviation Administration, 800 Independence Avenue Southwest, Washington DC 20591. **Tel** (202)367-3484, FAX (202)367-3505. **Continues** FAA Forecast Conference. Annual FAA Forecast Conference Proceedings, 0277-7258. **Continued by** Annual FAA Commercial Aviation Forecast Conference Proceedings.

LC HE9803.A35 F3
DD 387.7
US
●**ANNUAL FAA COMMERCIAL AVIATION FORECAST CONFERENCE PROCEEDINGS.** **Added/Corp** United States. Office of Aviation Policy, Plans, and Management Analysis. VFOAT Annual F.A.A. Aviation Commercial Forecast Conference Proceedings; FAA Commercial Aviation Forecast Conference Proceedings. 19th (Mar. 4, 1994)-. Government Publication. English. US Department of Transportation / Federal Aviation Administration, 800 Independence Avenue Southwest, Washington DC 20591. **Tel** (202)367-3484, FAX (202)367-3505. **Continues** FAA Aviation Forecast Conference. Annual FAA Aviation Forecast Conference Proceedings, 1046-8838.

LC TL
DD 629
ISSN 0733-4249
US
CODEN PFASDL
ANNUAL FORUM PROCEEDINGS - AMERICAN HELICOPTER SOCIETY. (ANNUAL FORUM PROCEEDINGS.). [Annu. forum proc. - Am. Helicopter Soc.]. **Main/Corp** American Helicopter Society. VFOAT AHS Annual Forum Proceedings. 36th (1980)-. Proceedings. English. One time a year. $110.00. American Helicopter Society, 217 North Washington Street, Alexandria VA 22314. **Tel** (703)684-6777, FAX (703)739-6279. Index available. **Bk Rev. Ad Acc. Circ:** 400. Documents available from Article Express International. **Continues** American Helicopter Society. Preprint.
Desc: A compilation of the technical papers presented at the AHS annual forum and technology display.
Ind/Abst Bioeng. Abstr.; Curr. Cit.; Ei Page One; Eng. Index Annu.

LC TL
DD 629
US
ANNUAL PROCUREMENT REPORT. **Main/Corp** United States. National Aeronautics and Space Administration. **Added/Corp** United States. National Aeronautics and Space Administration. Procurement Management Division. (1964)-. English. One time a year. National Aeronautics and Space Administration Office of Procurement, (CODE AM-1), Washington DC 20546. available on microfiche (Vols. for (FY 1977) distributed to depository libraries). **Continues** United States. National Aeronautics and Space Administration. Semiannual Procurement Report.

LC HE9874.S56 S56b
DD 387.7/06/55957
SI
ANNUAL REPORT. Main/Corp Singapore Airlines. (1987)-. English. One time a year. SIA Building, 77 Robinson Road, Singapore 0106. **Formed by the union of** Singapore Airlines. Annual Report: Financial Report **and** Singapore Airlines. Annual Report: Operating Review.

Aeronautics, Astronautics

LC HE9815.A95 A47a **ISSN** 0568-3424
DD 387.7/06/571 CN
ANNUAL REPORT - AIR CANADA.
Main/Corp Air Canada. **VFOAT** Rapport Annuel. (1964)-. Periodical. English (French and English). One time a year. Free on request. Air Canada Shareholders Rel., PO Box 14000, St. Laurent Quebec H4Y 1C2 Canada. **Tel** (514)422-5785. **Continues** Trans-Canada Airline. Annual Report for the Year Ended ... .

LC HE9884.5.A1 A37a
DD 387.7/065/6891 RH
ANNUAL REPORT / AIR ZIMBABWE CORPORATION.
Main/Corp Air Zimbabwe Corporation. 3rd (1982)-. Corporate Report. English. One time a year. Free. Air Zimbabwe Corporation, PO Box AP 1, Harare Airport, Harare Zimbabwe. **Tel** 011 263 4 575111, FAX 011 263 4 575068. **Circ**: 2,000. **Continues** Air Zimbabwe Corporation. Air Zimbabwe ... Annual Report.

LC HE9881.J6 A57A **ISSN** 0376-5520
DD 387.7/065/5695 JO
ANNUAL REPORT - ALIA.
(ANNUAL REPORT / ALYAH.). **Main/Corp** Alyah. English. Royal Jordanian Airline, PO Box 302, Amman Jordan.

LC TL789.8.I5 I53a **ISSN** 0376-5466
DD 354/.54/00855 II
ANNUAL REPORT - DEPARTMENT OF SPACE. GOVERNMENT OF INDIA.
(ANNUAL REPORT - DEPARTMENT OF SPACE.). **Main/Corp** India (Republic). Dept. of Space. (19??)-. English. One time a year. Free. Department of Space, Antariksh Bhavan, New Bel Road, Bangalore 560094 India. **Tel** 080 3334474, FAX 080 3332253. **ED** S. Krish Namurthy. **Circ**: 5,000.

LC HE9803.A1 U55b
DD 353.0087/77 US
ANNUAL REPORT / FEDERAL AVIATION ADMINISTRATION.
Main/Corp United States. Federal Aviation Administration. (19??)-. Government Publication. English. One time a year. US Department of Transportation / Federal Aviation Administration, 800 Independence Avenue Southwest, Washington DC 20591. **Tel** (202)367-3484, FAX (202)367-3505. **Continues** United States. Federal Aviation Administration. Annual Financial Report.

LC WMLC L 83/6735
DD 629.13 NE
ANNUAL REPORT / KLM ROYAL DUTCH AIRLINES.
Main/Corp KLM (Airline). (19??)-. English. KLM Royal Dutch Airlines, PO Box 7700, 1117 SL Schiphol Airport The Netherlands. **Continues** Annual Report for the ... Financial Year ... to be Submitted at the General Meeting of Shareholders on ... .

LC HD9711.N44 K65a
DD 338.7/62913/009492 NE
ANNUAL REPORT / N.V. KONINKLIJKE NEDERLANDSE VLIEGTUIGENFABRIEK FOKKER.
See Industry and Production.

LC TL526.G7 R63A
DD 629.1/06041 UK
ANNUAL REPORT OF THE COUNCIL.
Main/Corp Royal Aeronautical Society. Council. English. One time a year.

LC HE9761 **ISSN** 1050-4486
DD 387.7 US
ANNUAL REPORT OF THE REGIONAL AIRLINE ASSOCIATION.
[Annu. rep. Reg. Airl. Assoc.]. **Added/Corp** Regional Airline Association (U.S.). **VFOAT** Annual Report, Regional Airline Association. (1988)-. English. One time a year. $50.00. Commuter Airline Association America, 1101 Connecticut Avenue Northwest, Suite 700, Washington DC 20036. **Tel** (202)857-1170. **Continues** Annual Report, Regional Airline Industry, 0898-8021.

LC TL
DD 629 PK
ANNUAL REPORT / PIA, PAKISTAN INTERNATIONAL.
Main/Corp Pakistan International Airlines. English. Pakistan International Airlines Building, Karachi International Airport, Karachi Pakistan. **Continues** Pakistan International Airlines Annual Report and Accounts.

LC TL **ISSN** 0735-4606
DD 629 US
ANNUAL REPORT / SYRACUSE (N.Y.) DEPT. OF AVIATION.
Main/Corp Syracuse (N.Y.). Dept. of Aviation. English. One time a year. City of Syracuse, Department of Aviation, Syracuse Hancock International Airport, Syracuse NY 13207.

LC HE17 .A47
DD 312/.4/4 US
ANNUAL REVIEW OF AIRCRAFT ACCIDENT DATA. U.S. GENERAL AVIATION.
Added/Corp United States. National Transportation Safety Board. **VFOAT** U.S. General Aviation; Statistical Review of General Aviation Accidents; US General Aviation. (1969)-. English. One time a year. National Technical Information Service - NTIS, Room 2027S, 5285 Port Royal Road, Springfield VA 22161. **Tel** (703)487-4630, (703)487-4660, (703)487-4650, FAX (703)321-8547, telex 89-9405. available on microfiche (Vols. for (1984-) distributed to depository libraries). **Continues** Annual Review of U.S. General Aviation Accidents.

LC TL
DD 629 US
ANNUAL SYMPOSIUM PROCEEDINGS / AGIFORS.
Main/Corp AGIFORS (Society). Symposium. **VFOAT** Annual Symposium. (Sept. 1979)-. Proceedings. English. One time a year (Feb. or Mar.). $60.00. AGIFORS, 2831 Airways Boulevard, Memphis TN 38132. **Tel** (901)395-7372. **ED** Joe Hinson, (phone: (901)395-7346). Index available. cum. index. **Continues** AGIFORS (Society). Symposium. AGIFORS Proceedings.

LC TL **ISSN** 1050-9690
DD 629 US
ANNUAL SYMPOSIUM PROCEEDINGS / SOCIETY OF FLIGHT TEST ENGINEERS.
[Annu. symp. proc. - Soc. Flight Test Eng.]. **Main/Corp** Society of Flight Test Engineers. National Symposium. (1977)-. Proceedings. English. One time a year. $55.00. Society of Flight Test Engineers Inc, PO Box 4047, Society Office, Lancaster CA 93539. **Tel** (805)538-9715. **Ind/Abst** Curr. Cit.

LC TL797 .W67a
DD 629.47/4 US
ANNUAL WORKSHOP ON SPACE OPERATIONS APPLICATIONS AND RESEARCH (SOAR ...).
Added/Corp United States. National Aeronautics and Space Administration. United States. Air Force. University of New Mexico. **VFOAT** SOAR. (1990)-. English. National Aeronautics and Space Administration, 600 Independence Avenue SW, Washington DC 20546. **Tel** (202)453-1000. **Continues** Workshop on Space Operations Automation and Robotics. Annual Workshop on Space Operations Automation and Robotics (SOAR ...).

LC TL527.I4 I53a
DD 629.13 II
ANTARIKSHA VIBHAGA KI ANUDANOM KI MANGEM.
Main/Corp India. Dept. of Space. **VFOAT** Anudanom ki Mangem, Antariksha Vibhaga; Demands for Grants of Department of Space. (19??)-. Multiple languages (English and Hindi). One time a year. Department of Space, Antariksh Bhavan, New Bel Road, Bangalore 560094 India. **Tel** 080 3334474, FAX 080 3332253.

LC TL
DD 629 US
ANTIQUE AIRPLANE DIGEST.
Added/Corp Antique Airplane Association. **VFOAT** International Antique Airplane Digest. Vol. 23, No. 4/6 3rd Quarter (1976)-. Periodical. English. Four times a year. $18.00. Antique Airplane Association, Route 2 Box 172, Ottumwa IA 52501. **Tel** (515)938-2773. **ED** Robert L. Taylor. **Bk Rev**. **Ad Acc**. **Circ**: 6,000. **Continues** Antique Airplane News.
Desc: News, photos, specifications and tips on antique and classic airplanes.

LC TJ1201.P55 A57 **ISSN** 1049-2607
DD 621.9/12 US
ANTIQUE & COLLECTABLE STANLEY PLANES PRICE GUIDE.
(ANTIQUE & COLLECTABLE STANLEY PLANES ... PRICE GUIDE.). [Antiq. collect. Stanley planes price guide]. **VFOAT** Antique and Collectable Stanley Planes ... Price Guide.; Stanley Planes ... Price Guide. (19??)-. English. Irregular. The Tool Merchant, PO Box 6471, Akron OH 44312.

LC HE9761 **ISSN** 0001-2084
DD 387.7092 US
Pr Rev.
AOPA PILOT, THE.
Main/Corp Aircraft Owners and Pilots Association. **VAT** Aircraft Owners and Pilots Association Pilot. (1958)-. Periodical. English. Twelve times a year. $21.00. Aircraft Owners and Pilots Association / Maryland, 421 Aviation Way, Frederick MD 21701. **Tel** (301)695-2044, FAX (301)695-2375. **ED** Thomas A Horne. **Bk Rev**. **Ad Acc**. **Circ**: 265,000 (ctrl). **Continues** AOPA Pilot.
Desc: For general aviation pilots who are members of AOPA. The magazine regularly reports on FAA activities, new aircraft, and equipment. Also has features designed to promote safer, more enjoyable flying.
Ind/Abst Aviat. Tradescan [Full Cov.].

LC TL
DD 629 US
AOPA'S AVIATION USA.
English. Aircraft Owners and Pilots Association / Maryland, 421 Aviation Way, Frederick MD 21701. **Tel** (301)695-2044, FAX (301)695-2375.

LC HE9787 .A4
DD 387.7/42/05 US
APACE.
Added/Corp Airline Passengers Association. (Fall 1976)-. English. Airline Passengers Association, 800 West Airport Freeway, Irving TX 75062. **Continues** Airline Passengers Association. News.

LC TL504 .A7
DD 629.13 AG
ARGENTINA AEREA.
(Feb. 1946)-. Periodical. Spanish. Twelve times a year. Direccion y Administracion Defensa, Buenos Aires Argentina.

LC U **ISSN** 0004-2463
DD 355 UK
ARMY, AIR FORCE AND NAVAL AIR STATISTICAL RECORD.
See Military and Defense.

LC UF **ISSN** 0004-248X
DD 358 US
ARMY AVIATION.
[Army aviat.]. (May 1954)-. Periodical. English. Ten times a year (Mar./Apr. & Aug./Sept. issues combined). $25.00. Army Aviation Association of America, 49 Richmondville Avenue, Westport CT 06880. **Tel** (203)226-8184, FAX (203)222-9863. **ED** William R. Harris. **Ad Acc**. **Circ**: 18,158. **Continues** Army Aviator.
Desc: Pertains to the Army aviation military and industry.
Ind/Abst Curr. Mil. Pol. Lit.

LC HE9859.A1 L83a **ISSN** 0800-4072
DD 387.7 NO
ARSRAPPORT.
Main/Corp Norway. Luftfartsverket. **VFOAT** Arsrapport Luftfartsverket. (1983)-. Norwegian (English). One time a year. Luftfartsverket, Postboks 8124 Den, 0032 Oslo 1 Norway. **Tel** (02)429280. **ED** Else Frisell. **Circ**: 4,000 (ctrl). **Continues** Norway. Luftfartsverket. Luftfartsverket.
Desc: Publication of the Civil Aviation Administration of Norway.

LC Z5064 .A7 P6 **ISSN** 0208-841X
DD 016.6291 PL
ARTIFICIAL SATELLITES. PLANETARY GEODESY.
See Earth Sciences-Geophysics.

LC QH657 .A84 **ISSN** 0898-4697
DD 574.19/19/05 US
ASGSB BULLETIN.
(ASGSB BULLETIN : PUBLICATION OF THE AMERICAN SOCIETY FOR GRAVITATIONAL AND SPACE BIOLOGY.). [ASGSB bull.]. **Added/Corp** American Society for Gravitational and Space Biology. **VAT** American Society for Gravitational and Space Biology Bulletin. Vol. 1 (1988)-. Bulletin. English. ASGSB-American Society for Gravitational and Space Biology, PO Box 9592, Rosslyn VA 22209.
Ind/Abst Int. Aerosp. Abstr.

LC TL **ISSN** 1021-3740
DD 629 CH
UDC 388.9
ASIAN AIR TRANSPORT.
See Transportation.

LC TL
DD 629 SI
ASIAN AVIATION.
(198?)-. Periodical. English. Eleven times a year (Dec./Jan. issues combined). $75.00. Asian Aviation Publs Pte Ltd, 2 Leng Kee Road, 04-01 Thye Hong, Singapore 0315 Singapore. **Tel** 011 65 4747088, FAX 011 65 4796668, telex RS 38587 AVMAG. **ED** Colin M. Gibson. **Ad Acc**, **Adv Mgr Tel** (65)4747088. **Circ**: 12,000 (ctrl).
Desc: Civil and military news coverage of Asia-Pacific and Gulf countries, including airlines, air forces, airports, flight training, safety and space.
Ind/Abst F&S Index Plus Text, Int. [Select. Cov.]; PROMT.

LC TL **ISSN** 1071-0663
DD 629 US
 CCC
● ### ASIAN AVIATION NEWS.
Added/Corp Phillips Business Information, Inc. (1993)-. Periodical. English. Twenty-five times a year. $695.00. Phillips Business Information Inc., 1201 Seven Locks Road, PO Box 61130, Potomac MD 20854. **Tel** (301)424-3338, (301)340-1520, (800)777-5005, FAX (301)424-4297, telex 358149.

LC TL787 .I44 **ISSN** 0304-8705
DD 629.4/05 NE
ASTRONAUTICAL RESEARCH.
(ASTRONAUTICAL RESEARCH; PROCEEDINGS OF THE CONGRESS OF THE INTERNATIONAL ASTRONAUTICAL FEDERATION.). **Main/Corp** International Astronautical Federation. **Added/Corp** International Astronautical Federation. Proceedings of the Congress of the International Astronautical Federation. (1970)-. English. One time a year. D. Reidel Publishing Company, PO Box 17, 3300 AA Dordrecht The Netherlands. **Tel** 011 31 78 334210, FAX (31) 78 183273, telex 29245 KAPGNL. Documents available from CASDDS. **Continues** International Astronautical Congress. Proceedings of the International Astronautical Congress, 0074-1795.
Ind/Abst Chem. Abstr.

LC TL787
DD 629.4 UK
ASTRONAUTICS. (1963)-. English.

LC HE9781 **ISSN** 0004-623X
DD 387.8 PL
ASTRONAUTYKA. [Astronautyka]. **Added/Corp** Polskie Towarzystwo Astronautyczne. Vol. 1 (June 1958)-. Periodical. Polish. Six times a year. Price on request. **(Subscription address:** Ars Polona-Ruch, PO Box 1001, Krakowskie Przedmiescie 7, 00-068 Warsaw Poland. **Tel** 011 48 22 261201.) ***Supersedes*** *Polskie Towarzystwo Astronautyczne. Biuletyn Informacyjny.*
Ind/Abst Energy Res. Abstr. (Jan. 1972-); Int. Aerosp. Abstr. (1991-).

LC QB460 .A876 **ISSN** 0004-640X
DD 500.5/05 NE
CCC
CODEN APSSBE
Pr Rev.
ASTROPHYSICS AND SPACE SCIENCE. **See** Astronomy.

LC QB
DD 520 NE
Pr Rev.
ASTRUIM. **See** Astronomy.

LC HE9761 **ISSN** 1070-5740
DD 387.7 US
ATC MARKET REPORT. [ATC mark. rep.]. **VFOAT** Air Traffic Control Market Report. (1992)-. Periodical. English. Twenty-six times a year. $485.00 colleges and universities; $655.00 other. McGraw Hill Publishing Company, Inc., 1221 Avenue of the Americas, New York NY 10020. **Tel** (212)512-6410, (800)525-5003, FAX (212)512-6111.

LC HE9761 **ISSN** 1183-5435
DD 387.7 CN
ATLANTIC REGION ... AVIATION BUSINESS DIRECTORY. **See** Industry and Production-Trade and Industrial Directories.

LC HJ **ISSN** 0279-9642
DD 336 US
ATPCO CARGO TARIFF SET. [41]. **Added/Corp** Airline Tariff Publishing Company. **VAT** Airline Tariff Publishing Company Cargo Tariff Set. (19??)-. Periodical. English. Twenty-four times a year. $152.00. Airline Tariff Publishing Company, PO Box 17415, Dulles International Airport, Washington DC 20041. **Tel** (703)471-7510. **ED** Neil Cleary. **Circ:** 3,230.
Desc: Rules and rates for air transportation of freight throughout the US, Canada, Mexico, Puerto Rico and the US Virgin Islands.

LC TL **ISSN** 0273-6284
DD 629 US
CEASED
ATPCO PASSENGER TARIFF SET. [ATPCO passeng. tariff set]. **Main/Corp** Airline Tariff Publishing Company. **VAT** Airline Tariff Publishing Company Passenger Tariff Set. (July 22 1980)-(19??). English. Airline Tariff Publishing Company, PO Box 17415, Dulles International Airport, Washington DC 20041. **Tel** (703)471-7510. **ED** Neil Cleary. **Circ:** 3,459.
Desc: Fares, rules and routings for air transportation of passengers throughout U.S., Canada, Mexico, Caribbean, Central and South America.

LC HE9761 **ISSN** 0813-0876
DD 387.70994 AT
AUSTRALIAN AVIATION. [Aust. aviat.]. (1982)-. Periodical. English. Ten times a year (monthly except Jan., & Feb.). 45.22Aus$. Australian Aviation, PO Box 3105, Weston Creek, Weston Creek Australian Capital Territories, 2611 Australia. **Tel** 11 61 6 2881677, FAX 011 61 6 2882021, telex 135042. ***Continues*** *Australian Aviation & Defence, 0159-611X.*

LC TL500 **ISSN** 0004-9123
DD 629.13 AT
AUSTRALIAN FLYING. [Aust. fly.]. (1961)-. Periodical. English. Six times a year. 25.90Aus$. Yaffa Publishing Group Pty Ltd., GPO Box 606, Sydney New South Wales 2001 Australia. **Tel** 011 61 2 2812333, FAX 011 61 2 2812750.

LC GV750 .A9
DD 797.5 AT
AUSTRALIAN GLIDING. **Added/Corp** Gliding Federation of Australia. (1950)-. Periodical. English. Twelve times a year. 23.67Aus$. Gliding Federation of Australia, GPO Box 1650, Adelaide 5001 South Australia. **Tel** 08 410 4711, FAX 08 410 4711. **ED** Allan Ash. **Bk Rev.** **Ad Acc, Adv Mgr:** F. Packerham. **Circ:** 4,000.
Ind/Abst SPORT Discus; SportSearch (May 1987-).

LC TL525.B8 A9 **ISSN** 0102-4876
DD 629.13009 BL
AVIACAO EM REVISTA. (Feb. 1938)-. Trade Publication. Portuguese. Twelve times a year. $100.00. Aviacao em Revista Editora Ltd, Rua Ibiraja 322, 04310 Sao Paulo SP Brazil. **Tel** 011 55 11 5786277, FAX 011 55 11 5786657, telex 56048 EDAV BR. **ED** Helcio Estrella. **Ad Acc, Adv Mgr:** Francisco Carlos Alves, **Tel** 011 55 115786577. Full Page (B&W) $3800.00. Full Page (Color) $4500.00. **Circ:** 25,000.

LC TL **ISSN** 0373-9821
DD 629 RU
CEASED
AVIACIJA I KOSMONAVTIKA. (AVIATSIIA I KOSMONAVTIKA.). [Aviac. kosmonavt.]. **Added/Corp** Soviet Union. Voenno-Vozdushnye Sily. No. 1 (1962)-(July 1994). Periodical. Russian. **(Subscription address:** East View Publications Inc., 3020 Harbor Lane North, Suite 110, Minneapolis MN 55447. **Tel** (800)477-1005, (612)550-0961, FAX (612)559-2931.) Index available in last issue of volume--attached. ***Continues*** *Vestnik Vozdushnogo Flota.*
Ind/Abst Int. Aerosp. Abstr.

LC TL **ISSN** 0772-876X
DD 629 BE
CEASED
AVIASTRO (1984). (AVIASTRO.). No. 2 (Feb. 1984)-(April 1993). Periodical. French (English). Panneels Caligrafic, rue Clement de Clety 25, B-1070 Brussels Belgium. **Tel** 32(0)2/7348878, FAX 32(0)2/5202833, telex 62388B. **ED** Didier Daoust. **Bk Rev,** (Qty: 15). **Ad Acc, Adv Mgr:** Johan A Francois, **Tel** 32 2 5373899. **Circ:** 32,000. ***Continues*** *Conquete de l'Air. Aviastro.*
Desc: Covers topics dealing with aerospace-international, industrial activities and trade matters, civil and military aeronautics, operational aspects, space activities, equipments and systems.

LC TL570 **ISSN** 0846-1414
DD 629.132 CN
CEASED
AVIATEUR AUJOURDHUI. (L'AVIATEUR AUJOURD'HUI.). [Aviat. aujourd'hui]. (Nov. 1990)-(199?). Periodical. French. L'Aviateur Aujourd'Hui, CP 9, Sainte-Foy Quebec G2E 5W1 Canada.

LC HD9715 **ISSN** 1191-8004
DD 338.4/7629/0971 CN
AVIATION, AEROSPACE & DEFENCE UPDATE. [Aviat. aerosp. def. update]. **VFOAT** Aviation, Aerospace and Defence Update. Vol. 1, No. 10 (Mar. 18, 1992)-. Periodical. English. One time a week. 168.25Can$. Baxter Publishing Company, 310 Dupont Street, Toronto Ontario M5R 1V9 Canada. **Tel** (416)968-7252, FAX (416)968-2377. ***Formed by the union of*** *Aviation & Aerospace News., 1191-7997* ***and*** *Canadian Defence Update., 0835-7129.*

LC TL501 .A7818 **ISSN** 0847-0588
DD 338.4/76291/0971 CN
CODEN AVAEET
AVIATION & AEROSPACE. [Aviat. aerosp.]. **VFOAT** Aviation and Aerospace. Vol. 63, No. 1 (Jan. 1990)-. Periodical. English. Six times a year. 32.00Can$ Canada; 42.00Can$ other. Baxter Publishing Company, 310 Dupont Street, Toronto Ontario M5R 1V9 Canada. **Tel** (416)968-7252, FAX (416)968-2377. **(Subscription address:** Baxter Publishing Co., PO Box 117, Richmond Hill, Ontario L4C 4X9 Canada. **Tel** (416)475-4145.) available on microfilm and microfiche from University Microfilms International (UMI). ***Formed by the union of*** *Canadian Aviation, 0008-2953* ***and*** *Aerospace & Defence Technology, 0838-4835.*
Ind/Abst Can. Index.

LC HE9803.A1 A9
DD 387.7 US
•**AVIATION & AEROSPACE ALMANAC, THE.** **VFOAT** Aviation and Aerospace Almanac. (1993)-. English. One time a year. $79.95. McGraw Hill Publishing Company, Inc., 1221 Avenue of the Americas, New York NY 10020. **Tel** (212)512-6410, (800)525-5003, FAX (212)512-6111. **(Subscription address:** McGraw Hill / Washington, 1200 G Street, Suite 200, Washington DC 20005. **Tel** (202)822-4673, (800)752-4959.)

LC TL500 **ISSN** 1352-4003
DD 629.13 UK
•**AVIATION & SPACE LAW REPORTS.** (1994)-. Academic Scholarly Publication. English. Twelve times a year (Annual cumulative issue). £295.00. Oxford University Press / UK, Walton Street, Oxford OX2 6DP United Kingdom. **Tel** 011 44 1865 56767, FAX 011 44 1865 267773, telex 851/837330 OXPRES G. **(Subscription address:** Oxford University Press / USA, Journals Marketing Department, Oxford University Press, 2001 Evans Road, Cary NC 27513. **Tel** (800)451-7556, (919)677-0977, FAX (919)677-1714.)

LC HE9761 **ISSN** 0711-8163
DD 387.7 CN
AVIATION BUSINESS REPORT. [Aviat. bus. rep.]. **VFOAT** Business Report. **VAT** Business Report (Thornhill). Vol. 1, No. 1 (Oct. 1981)-. Periodical. English. Irregular. Free. AirBorne Publishing, Suite 101 55 Doncaster Avenue, Thornhill Ontario L3T 1L7. ctrl circ.

LC HE9761 **ISSN** 1183-0204
DD 387.7/0971/05 CN
SUSPENDED
AVIATION CANADA MAGAZINE. [Aviat. Can. mag.]. **VFOAT** Aviation Canada. Vol. 1, No. 1 (Oct. 1990)-Suspended (199?). Periodical. English. Ten times a year. Duncannon Publishing, 395 Metheson Boulevard East, Mississauga Ontario L4Z 2H2 Canada. **Tel** (416)763-1675.

LC TL721.4 .A94 **ISSN** 0147-9911
DD 629.133/34/0422/0973 US
AVIATION CONSUMER, THE. [Aviat. consum.]. Vol. 1 (Nov. 1, 1971)-. Periodical. English. Twelve times a year. $84.00. Belvoir Publications Inc., 75 Holly Hill Lane, Greenwich CT 06836. **Tel** (203)661-6111, FAX (203)661-4802. **(Subscription address:** Palm Coast Data, PO Box 420163, Agency Department, Palm Coast FL 32142. **Tel** (904)445-4662 ext. 669, (800)829-5475.) **ED** Dick Weeyhman. Index available. **Circ:** 30,000. ***Absorbed*** *Avionics Review.*
Desc: Current news trends for general aviation pilots and plane owners. Also contains plane evaluations and consumer tips on maintenance and industry news.

LC TL501 .A676 **ISSN** 0193-4597
DD 387 US
AVIATION DAILY. [Aviat. dly.]. (1957)-. Periodical. English. Five times a week (260 issues). $1475.00. McGraw Hill Publishing Company, Inc., 1221 Avenue of the Americas, New York NY 10020. **Tel** (212)512-6410, (800)525-5003, FAX (212)512-6111. **ED** Joan Lowden. available on an online database from NEWSNET; Dow Jones News/Retrieval; (file 624) DIALOG; and NEXIS. ***Continues*** *American Aviation Daily.*
Desc: Primary reference for intelligence within the commercial aviation industry.
Ind/Abst Trade Ind. Index.

LC HE9803.A2 A93 **ISSN** 0092-2862
DD 387.7/4/0973 US
AVIATION DAILY'S AIRLINE STATISTICAL ANNUAL. **See** Aeronautics, Astronautics-Abstracting, Bibliographies and Statistics.

LC TL **ISSN** 0997-3753
DD 629 FR
UDC 629.13
AVIATION DESIGN THIAIS. (AVIATION DESIGN.). (1989)-. Periodical. French (English). Twelve times a year. $50.31. Breand Communication, 23 rue Guy Moquet, 94600 Choisy le Roi France. **Tel** 011 33 1 48539278, FAX 011 33 1 48922411. **ED** Andre Breand. Index available. cum. index. **Bk Rev.** **Ad Acc.** **Circ:** 35,000 (ctrl).
Desc: Articles about aircraft of the world; includes technical descriptions, color photos and drawings.

LC TL500
DD 629.13/002571 CN
AVIATION DIRECTORY OF CANADA. Directory. English. One time a year. Maclean Hunter Canada / Montreal, 1001 bvd. de Maisonneuve W., Montreal Quebec H3A 3E1 Canada. **Tel** (514)845-5141, FAX (514)845-4302, telex 055-60604.

LC TL
DD 629 US
AVIATION EDUCATION. **Added/Corp** United States. Federal Aviation Adminstration. Vol. 1, No. 1 (Spring 1992)-. Government Publication. English. Four times a year. US Department of Transportation / Federal Aviation Administration, 800 Independence Avenue Southwest, Washington DC 20591. **Tel** (202)367-3484, FAX (202)367-3505.

LC HB **ISSN** 1050-2149
DD 331 US
AVIATION EMPLOYMENT MONTHLY : AVIATION & AEROSPACE EMPLOYMENT OPPORTUNITIES. [Aviat. employ. mon.]. Vol. 1, No. 1 (Dec. 1986)-. Trade Publication. English. Twelve times a year. $99.95. Aviation Employment Monthly, PO Box 8058, Saddle Brook NJ 07662. **Tel** (201)797-3677, FAX (201)797-3677. **ED** Michael Carter.
Desc: Aviation Employment Monthly, is aviations largest listing of current job openings. It lists aviation and aerospace employment opportunities for pilots, mechanics, technicians and engineers. Both commercial and U.S. government positions are listed nationwide and worldwide.

LC TL671.9 .A88 **ISSN** 0745-0214
DD 629.134/6/05 US
CCC
AVIATION EQUIPMENT MAINTENANCE. [Aviat. equip. maint.]. **VFOAT** Worldwide Aviation Equipment Maintenance. Vol. 1, No. 1 (July/Aug. 1982)-. Trade Publication. English. Twelve times a year. $69.00. Phillips Business Information Inc., 1201 Seven Locks Road, PO Box 61130, Potomac MD 20854. **Tel** (301)424-3338, (301)340-1520, (800)777-5005, FAX (301)424-4297, telex 358149. **ED** Paul Berner. **Ad Acc.** **Circ:** 30,000 (ctrl).
Desc: Directed at the aviation service field.
Ind/Abst Aviat. Tradescan [Full Cov.].

LC HE **ISSN** 1058-7004
DD 387 US
AVIATION EUROPE (WASHINGTON, D.C.). (AVIATION EUROPE : A WEEKLY INTELLIGENCE REPORT BY THE PUBLISHER OF AVIATION DAILY.). [Aviat. Eur.]. **Added/Corp** McGraw-Hill, Inc. Aviation Week Group. (1991)-. Periodical. English. One time a week. $690.00. McGraw Hill Publishing Company, Inc., 1221 Avenue of the Americas, New York NY 10020. **Tel** (212)512-6410, (800)525-5003, FAX (212)512-6111. available on an online database from Dow Jones News/Retrieval; NEWSNET; DIALOG; and Lexis-Nexis.

LC TL515 .A94 **ISSN** 1076-8858
DD 629.13/005 US
•**AVIATION HISTORY.** [Aviat. hist.]. Vol. 4, No. 6 (July 1994)-. Periodical. English. Six times a year. $19.95. Cowles Magazines, PO Box 8200, Harrisburg PA 17105. **Tel** (717)657-9555, (800)435-9610. ***Continues*** *Aviation (Leesburg, Va.), 1067-4799.*

LC HD9711.A1 A95 **ISSN** 0887-9877
DD 338.4/762913334/05 US
AVIATION INTERNATIONAL NEWS. [Aviat. int. news]. **VFOAT** Aviation News. (19??)-. Periodical. English. Twelve times a year. $45.00. Convention News Company, PO Box 1985, Peterboro NJ 07608. **(Subscription address:** Aviation International News, 81 Kenosia Avenue, Danbury CT 06810. **Tel** (203)798-2400.**)** ***Continues*** *Aviation Convention News, 0164-9906.*
Ind/Abst Aviat. Tradescan [Full Cov.].

LC HE9761 **ISSN** 1073-5518
DD 387.7 US
AVIATION LATIN AMERICA & CARIBBEAN. [Aviat. Lat. Am. Caribb.]. (19??)-. Periodical. English. Twelve times a year. $399.00. Avnews Incorporated, 7008 Northwest 46th Street, Miami FL 33166. **Tel** (305)591-9526, FAX (305)591-1331. **ED** Robert C. Booth. cum. index. **Circ:** 600.

LC K4091 **ISSN** 0273-7310
DD 343.097 US
AVIATION LAW REPORTS. **See** Law.

LC TL515 .A94 **ISSN** 1067-4799
DD 629.13/005 US
TITLE CHANGE
AVIATION (LEESBURG, VA.). (AVIATION.). [Aviation]. Vol. 3, No. 3 (Jan. 1993)-Vol. 4, No. 5 (May 1994). Periodical. English. Cowles Magazines, PO Box 8200, Harrisburg PA 17105. **Tel** (717)657-9555, (800)435-9610. available on microfilm. ***Continues*** *Aviation Heritage (Leesburg, Va.), 1054-335X.* ***Continued by*** *Aviation History, 1076-8858.*

LC KF2454.A59 A95 **ISSN** 0737-7746
DD 346.7303/22 347.306322 US
AVIATION LITIGATION REPORTER. **See** Law.

LC TL **ISSN** 0005-2140
DD 629 US
AVIATION MECHANICS BULLETIN. [Aviat. mech. bull.]. **Added/Corp** Flight Safety Foundation. (1953/54)-. Trade Publication. English. Six times a year. $35.00. Flight Safety Foundation Inc., 2200 Wilson Boulevard, Suite 500, Arlington VA 22201. **Tel** (703)522-8300, FAX (703)525-6047, telex 901176 FSF INC AGTN. **ED** Robert B. Phillips. **Circ:** 22,000. available on microfilm from University Microfilms International (UMI).
Desc: Directed to the aviation maintenance technician with an emphasis on airline and corporate operations.

LC TL **ISSN** 0145-1014
DD 629 US
AVIATION MONTHLY. [Aviat. mon.]. **VFOAT** Monthly Aviation Safety Summary and Report; Monthly Aviation Safety Summary & report. Vol. 4, No. 3 (Mar. 1976)-. Periodical. English. Twelve times a year. $36.00. Peter Katz Productions Inc, PO Box 831, White Plains NY 10602. **Tel** (914)949-7443. **ED** Peter Katz. **Bk Rev**. ***Continues*** *M.A.S.S. Report.*
Desc: Report on aviation safety, aircraft operating tips, a summary of aircraft accidents and news of industry developments.

LC TL
DD 629 UK
TITLE CHANGE
AVIATION NEWS. (1972)-(1995). English. Twenty-six times a year. $79.00. HPC Publishing, Drury Lane Hastings, East Sussex TN34 1XW United Kingdom. **Tel** 011 44 1424 720477, FAX 011 44 1424 443693. Index available. **Bk Rev**, (Qty: 150). **Ad Acc**, **Adv Mgr:** Peter Smith. **Circ:** 20,000. ***Merged into*** *Air Pictorial International.*

LC HE9761 **ISSN** 1058-1014
DD 387.7 US
AVIATION NEWS FROM SOUTH FLORIDA. (AVIATION NEWS FROM SOUTH FLORIDA : AVIATION NEWS FOR THE AVIATION AND AIRLINE ENTHUSIAST.). [Aviat. news South Fla.]. (1990)-. Periodical. English. Six times a year. Aviation News from South Florida, 1711 North Anhinga Lane, Homestead FL 33035.

LC TL **ISSN** 0190-938X
DD 629 US
AVIATION NEWS (RENO). (AVIATION NEWS.). Periodical. English. Twelve times a year. $10.00 US; $13.00 Canada. Aviation News, 13920 Mt McClellan Avenue, Reno NV 89506.

LC HE9761 **ISSN** 0843-493X
DD 387.7/0971 CN
AVIATION (OTTAWA). (AVIATION : SERVICE BULLETIN.). [Aviation]. **Added/Corp** Aviation Statistics Centre (Canada). **VFOAT** Aviation : Bulletin de Service. Vol. 21, No. 1 (1989)-. Bulletin. English (French). Twelve times a year. 99.00Can$ Canada; $119.00 US; $139.00 other. Statistics Canada Publications Sales and Services, R.H. Coats Building 6th Floor, Ottawa Ontario K1A 0T6 Canada. **Tel** (613)951-5078, (800)267-6677, FAX (613)951-1584, telex 053-3585. **ED** Goro Baldwin (editor's phone number: (819)997-6942, FAX: (819)953-8499). **Circ:** 370. ***Continues*** *Service Bulletin (Aviation Statistics Centre (Canada), 0068-7057.*
Desc: Information on the air transport industry, airports, fare basis data, passenger and cargo traffic. Series of data released includes financial and operational advance statistics for Level I carriers.

LC TL501 .A98 **ISSN** 0360-8670
DD 387.7/05 US
AVIATION QUARTERLY. [Aviat. q.]. **VFOAT** AQ. Vol. 1 (1974)-. Periodical. English. Four times a year. $59.00 US; $80.00 other. Aviation Quarterly, PO Box 530622, Grand Prairie TX 75053-0622. **Tel** (214)647-2284. **ED** George E. Stanley, Frank B. Thornburg and Verna Bargsley. cum. index. **Bk Rev**. **Ad Acc.** ctrl circ.
Desc: Aviation history, from the early aeronautical experiments of the nineteenth century, to the aerospace industry of today.
Ind/Abst Am. Hist. Life (1979-1981).

LC K4091
DD 343.097 US
AVIATION REGULATORY DIGEST SERVICE. (July, 1967)-. English. Twelve times a year. $320.00. Hawkins Publishing Company, PO Box 480, Mayo MD 21106. **Tel** (410)798-1677. available in Loose-leaf.
Desc: Analysis of the decisions and orders of the Department of Transporation, its predecessor the Civil Aeronautics Board, the Federal and U.S. Supreme Courts relating to the economics regulation of airlines under the Federal Aviation Act.

LC HE9801 **ISSN** 1035-9079
DD 387.7099405 AT
AVIATION REPORT. SYDNEY. (AVIATION REPORT.). [Aviat. rep. Syd.]. (1990)-. Periodical. English. Irregular (48 issues). 550.86Aus$. AR Publishing, 515 Kent Street, 1st Floor, Sydney NSW 2000 Australia. **Tel** 011/61/2612123, FAX 011/61/2672261. **ED** Paul Somerville. Index available (bound in each issue). **Ad Acc.**

LC TL **ISSN** 0005-2159
DD 629 UK
AVIATION REPORTS. CIVIL AND/OR MILITARY. (19??)-. Trade Publication. English. One time a week. $1245.00. Aviation Studies, Sussex House Parkside, London SW19 5NB United Kingdom. **Tel** 011 44 81 946 5082. Index available. **Bk Rev.** available on diskette.
Desc: Contains equipment and intelligence data, and economic/technical acquisition needs.

LC WMLC 93/4771 **ISSN** 0277-1764
DD 629 US
AVIATION SAFETY (RIVERSIDE, CONN.). (AVIATION SAFETY.). [Aviat. saf.]. Vol. 1, No. 1 (Aug. 1981)-. Periodical. English. Twenty-four times a year. $84.00. Belvoir Publications Inc., 75 Holly Hill Lane, Greenwich CT 06836. **Tel** (203)661-6111, FAX (203)661-4802. **(Subscription address:** Palm Coast Data, PO Box 420163, Agency Department, Palm Coast FL 32142. **Tel** (904)445-4662 ext. 669, (800)829-5475.**)** **ED** Mark Lacagnina.

LC TL670 **ISSN** 1184-1907
DD 629.133/343 CN
AVIATION SAFETY, ULTRALIGHT AND BALLOON. [Aviat. saf. ultralight balloon]. **Added/Corp** Canada. Transport Canada. Aviation Safety Programs (Canada). **VFOAT** Ultralight and Balloon. (1990)-. Periodical. English. Two times a year. Transport Canada / Public Affairs Branch, Ottawa Ontario K1A 0N5 Canada. **Tel** (613)991-2309. ***Continues*** *Aviation Safety Ultralight., 0827-3359.*

LC RC1050 .A36 **ISSN** 0095-6562
DD 616.9/8 US
CCC
NLM W1 AV47 **CODEN** ASEMCG
Pr Rev.
AVIATION SPACE AND ENVIRONMENTAL MEDICINE. **See** Medical Sciences.

LC TL
DD 629 US
AVIATION SPACE DICTIONARY. 6th Ed. (1980)-. English. Irregular. Tab Books Inc., 11 West 19th Street, New York NY 10011. **Tel** (212)337-5025. ***Continues*** *Aviation & Space Dictionary.*

LC TL **ISSN** 1075-1378
DD 629 US
Pr Rev.
•**AVIATION TELEPHONE DIRECTORY. EASTERN & SOUTHWESTERN STATES.** **See** Industry and Production-Trade and Industrial Directories.

LC TL **ISSN** 1075-136X
DD 629 US
•**AVIATION TELEPHONE DIRECTORY. WESTERN & NORTHCENTRAL STATES.** **See** Industry and Production-Trade and Industrial Directories.

LC TL721.4 .A964 **ISSN** 0273-7191
DD 629.132/5217/05 US
AVIATION TRAVEL AND TIMES. [Aviat. travel times]. Vol. 1, No. 1 (Oct./Nov. 1980)-. Trade Publication. English. Six times a year. $15.00. Aviation Quarterly / Plana, Texas, 538 Haggard Street/Suite 408, Plana TX 75074. ***Continues*** *Aviation Travel, 0199-1558.*

LC TL501 .A8 **ISSN** 0005-2175
DD 629.1/05 US
CCC
AVIATION WEEK & SPACE TECHNOLOGY. [Aviat. week space technol.]. **VFOAT** Aviation Week and Space Technology. Vol. 72, No. 1 (Jan. 11, 1960)-. Periodical. English. One time a week. $82.00. McGraw Hill Publishing Company, Inc., 1221 Avenue of the Americas, New York NY 10020. **Tel** (212)512-6410, (800)525-5003, FAX (212)512-6111. **(Subscription address:** Aviation Week, PO Box 503, Hightstown NJ 08520.**)** **Ad Acc.** **Circ:** 632,840 (readership). available on microfilm and microfiche from University Microfilms International (UMI); available on an online database from NEWSNET; Lexis-Nexis; Dow Jones News/Retrieval; (file 624/Full-Text) DIALOG; and (file AIR) NEXIS. Documents available from UMI Article Clearinghouse. ***Continues*** *Aviation Week, Including Space Technology, 1042-1688.* ***Continued in part by*** *Aviation Week & Space Technology. Buyer's Guide.*
Desc: Features reports on all segments of global aerospace, including analyses of technical, business and engineering developments.
Ind/Abst ABI/INFORM Glob. Ed.; ABI/INFORM [Computer File] (Jan. 6, 1975-); Acad. Abstr. Full Text Elite; Acad. Abstr.; Acad. Ind. [Computer File] (1984-); Acad. Search; Am. Bibliogr. Slavic East Europ. Stud.; Appl. Sci. Technol. Index; Aviat. Tradescan [Full Cov.]; Bus. Index (1985-); Bus. Period. Index; Bus. Source Plus; Bus. Source; Curr. Cit.; Eng. Mater. Abstr.; EP Collect.; Expand. Acad. Index (1984-); F&S Index Plus Text, Int. [Select. Cov.]; Fluid Abstr., Civil Eng.; Fluid Abstr. Proc. Eng.; FLUIDEX (1973-1990); Gen. BusinessFile (1985-); Gen. Period. Index (1985-); Homework Help.; INFO-SOUTH Abstr.; Infobank (Jan. 1969-); Infomat Int. Bus.; INIS Atomindex [Micro.]; Int. Aerosp. Abstr. (1991-); Mag. Artic. Summar. Elite; Mag. Artic. Summar. Select; Mag. Artic. Summar. CD-ROM; Mag. Index Plus (1989-); Mag. Index. Sel. (1986-); Mag. Search; MasterFile FullTEXT 1000; MasterFile FullTEXT 350; MasterFile FullTEXT 650; MasterFile FullTEXT (Jan. 1984-); Middle East Abstr. Index; Newsp. Period. Abstr. (1986-); OCLC; PROMT; Pub. Lib. FullTEXT; Read. Guide Abstr. Select Ed.; Read. Guide Period. Lit.; Risk Abstr.; Stat. Ref. Index; Telebase; Mag. Index (1977-); Trade Ind. Index (1981-); UMI ABI/Inform--Bus. Period. Ondisc (Dec. 1987-) [Full Txt.]; Vocat. Search; Wilson Bus. Abstr.

LC HD9711.2.A1 A95
DD 629.1/029/473 US
AVIATION WEEK AND SPACE TECHNOLOGY. BUYERS' GUIDE. **VFOAT** Aviation Week Buyers' Guide. (1987)-. Consumer Publication. English. One time a year. $24.95. Aviation Week, 1221 Avenue of the Americas, New York NY 10020. ***Continues in part*** *Aviation Week & Space Technology, 0005-2175.*

LC HB **ISSN** 0195-0347
DD 338 US
AVIATORS HOT LINE. [Aviat. hot line]. Vol. 1 (July 10, 1979)-. Periodical. English. Twelve times a year. $21.95. Heartland Communications Group Inc., PO Box 916 1003 Central Ave, Fort Dodge IA 50501. **Tel** (800)247-2000, (515)955-1600, FAX (515)955-6636. Index available. **Ad Acc.** ctrl circ. ***Continues*** *Runway.*

LC HE9761.9.I9 A86 **ISSN** 0391-7738
DD 387.7 IT
AVIAZIONE. [Aviazione]. (1977)-. Periodical. Italian (summaries and/or abstracts in English). Ten times a year. $109.00. Publi & Consult Spa, Via Tagliamento 29 2, 00198 Rome Italy. **Tel** 011 39 6 8546754, 011 39 6 8546754, FAX 011 39 6 85350021, telex 622368 680251. **ED** Paolo Bancale. Index available. cum. index. **Bk Rev. Ad Acc. Circ:** 15,000 (ctrl). ***Continues*** *Aviazione di Linea, Difesa e Spazio.*
Desc: It is the main Italian publication on military and civil aviation, space and technology.

LC HD9711.N46 A925
DD 338.4/7/6291333409931 NZ
AVINEWS. Vol. 1 (Oct. 1977)-. Periodical. English. $3.00. Aviation Industry Association of New Zealand, PO Box 2045, Wellington New Zealand. ***Supersedes*** *Avinews.*

LC TL692 **ISSN** 0955-8055
DD 629.135 UK
SUSPENDED
AVIONICS INTERNATIONAL. [Avion. int.]. (1989)-(1991). Periodical. English. Four times a year. Camrus Publishers, Neoter House, Clayhouse Yard, London EC4V 5EX United Kingdom. **Tel** 011 44 171 7798866, FAX 011 44 171 7798868.
Ind/Abst Aviat. Tradescan [Full Cov.].

LC TL **ISSN** 0567-2899
DD 629 US
AVIONICS NEWS. [Avion. news]. **Added/Corp** Aircraft Electronics Association. (1963)-. Periodical. English. Twelve times a year. Free on request. Aircraft Electronics Association, PO Box 1981, Independence MO 64055. **Tel** (816)373-6565.
Ind/Abst Aviat. Tradescan [Full Cov.]; Int. Aerosp. Abstr.

LC TL **ISSN** 0273-7639
DD 629 US
CCC
AVIONICS (POTOMAC, MD.). (AVIONICS.). [Avionics]. **VFOAT** Avionics Magazine. (1980)-. Trade Publication. English. Twelve times a year. $69.00. Phillips Business Information Inc., 1201 Seven Locks Road, PO Box 61130, Potomac MD 20854. **Tel** (301)424-3338, (301)340-1520, (800)777-5005, FAX (301)424-4297, telex 358149. **ED** Len Buckwalter. **Bk Rev. Ad Acc. Circ:** 17,500 (ctrl).
Desc: Covers navigational and airborne systems in aerospace electronics for aircraft, air traffic control and military use.
Ind/Abst Aviat. Tradescan [Full Cov.].

LC TL **ISSN** 1048-9207
DD 629 US
TITLE CHANGE
AVIONICS REVIEW. [Avion. rev.]. (1990)-(19??). Periodical. English. Belvoir Publications Inc., 75 Holly Hill Lane, Greenwich CT 06836. **Tel** (203)661-6111, FAX (203)661-4802. **(Subscription address:** Belvoir Publishing Inc., PO Box 3000 Dept. AVR, Denville NJ 07834. **) ED** Gary Picou. ***Merged into*** *Aviation Consumer.*
Desc: Comparisons, evaluations and tests on aviation electronics.

LC HE9761 **ISSN** 0961-2513
DD 387.71 UK
AVMARK AVIATION ECONOMIST. [Avmark aviat. econ.]. (1984)-. Periodical. English. Ten times a year. $460.00. Avmark International Limited, 28-32 Shelton Street, London WC2H 9HP United Kingdom. **Tel** 011 44 171 8360838, FAX 011 44 171 8360839. **ED** Keith McMullan. Index available (free). cum. index. **Ad Acc, Adv Mgr:** Nick Moreno. **Circ:** 1,000. ***Continues*** *Lloyd's Aviation Economist, 0265-3311.*
Desc: In-depth report on the economic, financial, political and strategic factors affecting airlines and aviation-related services. Regular features are current affairs, market forces, corporate strategy and current airline statistical data. Contains assessments and forecasts of aviation markets, analyses of individual carrier performance, and reviews of airports and other aviation support services.
Ind/Abst Curr. Cit.; Infomat Int. Bus.

LC HE9761
DD 387.7 US
AVP BULLETIN. **Main/Corp** United States. Office of Aviation Policy. May 1975-. Bulletin. English. US Department of Transportation / Federal Aviation Administration, 800 Independence Avenue Southwest, Washington DC 20591. **Tel** (202)367-3484, FAX (202)367-3505.

LC HE9761
DD 387.7 UK
BAA AIRPORT TIMETABLE. **See** Travel and Tourism.

LC TL **ISSN** 1062-7413
DD 629 US
•**BARNSTORMER (FORT WAYNE, IND.), THE.** (THE BARNSTORMER.). [Barnstormer]. (1993)-. Newspaper. English. Ten times a year. $15.00 (individuals), $10.00 (libraries). T.I. Graphics and Communications, Inc., 3210 Mallard Drive, Fort Wayne IN 46804. **Tel** (219)432-6153. **ED** Robert Roskuski. **Bk Rev**, (Qty: 20 per year). **Ad Acc. Pub. Size:** Tabloid. **Circ:** 15,000 (ctrl).
Desc: Monthly directed to aviation enthusiasts in the Mid-West; 65% Mid-West content, 35% national and international content.

LC TL
DD 629 GW
BERICHTE ZUR LUFTFAHRTGERAETEROLLE. (19??)-. German. Irregular. DM28.00 (latest issue). R Eisenschmidt GmbH, Postfach 110761, D-60042 Frankfurt Germany. **Tel** 011 49 69 7306040.

LC TL858 .P87a
DD 629.13 IO
BERITA PUSAT RISET DIRGANTARA, LAPAN. **Main/Corp** Pusat Riset Dirgantara (Indonesia). (19??)-. Indonesian. Lembaga Penerbangan dan Antariksa Nasional, J1 LLRE Martadinata No 166, Bandung Indonesia.

LC TL527.I75 B58 **ISSN** 0302-8194
DD 629.1 IS
BI-YEAF. [Bi-yeaf]. **VFOAT** Biaf. Vol. 1, February (1972)-. Trade Publication. Hebrew. Four times a year. $22.00. Yehuda Borovik Ed. and Pub., Israel Society of Aeronautics and Astronautics, PO Box 3144, Rishon le-Zion 75131 Israel. **Tel** 972-3-9664034, FAX 972-3-9649599. **Bk Rev. Ad Acc. Circ:** 6,000.
Desc: Information on civil and military aviation.

LC HE9761
DD 387.7 UK
BLUE PRINT. (19??)-. English. One time a week. £296.00. Airclaims Ltd., Cardinal Point, Newall Road / Heathrow Airport, London TW6 2AS United Kingdom. **Tel** 011 44 181 8971066, FAX 011 44 181 8970300, telex 934679. **ED** Max Kingsley Jones. Index available. ***Continues*** *Airclaims Information Digest.*
Desc: Review of major issues in the airline and aviation industry.

LC QB1 .B65
DD 520/.5 CL
BOLETIN / ASOCIACION CHILENA DE ASTRONOMIA Y ASTRONAUTICA. **See** Astronomy.

LC HE17 .A47 HE9784.5.U5 **ISSN** 0362-8884
DD 380.5 S 387.7/4 US
BRIEFS OF ACCIDENTS INVOLVING AMATEUR/HOME BUILT AIRCRAFT, U. S. GENERAL AVIATION. **VAT** Briefs of Accidents Involving Amateur/Home Built Aircraft, United States General Aviation. English. One time a year. National Technical Information Service - NTIS, Room 2027S, 5285 Port Royal Road, Springfield VA 22161. **Tel** (703)487-4630, (703)487-4660, (703)487-4650, FAX (703)321-8547, telex 89-9405.

LC HE17 .A47
DD 363.1/2 S 363.1/2493 US
BRIEFS OF ACCIDENTS INVOLVING COMMUTER AIR CARRIERS AND ON-DEMAND AIR TAXI OPERATIONS, U.S. GENERAL AVIATION. **VAT** Briefs of Accidents Involving Commuter Air Carriers and On-Demand Air Taxi Operations, United States General Aviation. (1976)-. English. One time a year. National Technical Information Service - NTIS, Room 2027S, 5285 Port Royal Road, Springfield VA 22161. **Tel** (703)487-4630, (703)487-4660, (703)487-4650, FAX (703)321-8547, telex 89-9405. ***Continues*** *Briefs of Accidents Involving Air Taxi Operations, U.S. General Aviation.*

LC HE17 .A47 HE9784.5.U5 **ISSN** 0360-392X
DD 629.04208 S 387.7/4 US
BRIEFS OF ACCIDENTS INVOLVING MIDAIR COLLISIONS, U.S. GENERAL AVIATION. **VAT** Briefs of Accidents Involving Midair Collisions, United States General Aviation. English. One time a year. National Technical Information Service - NTIS, Room 2027S, 5285 Port Royal Road, Springfield VA 22161. **Tel** (703)487-4630, (703)487-4660, (703)487-4650, FAX (703)321-8547, telex 89-9405.

LC HE17 .A47 HE9784.5.U5 **ISSN** 0360-6813
DD 380.5 S 614.8/69 US
BRIEFS OF ACCIDENTS INVOLVING MISSING AND MISSING LATER RECOVERED AIRCRAFT, U.S. GENERAL AVIATION. **VAT** Briefs of Accidents Involving Missing and Missing Later Recovered Aircraft, United States General Aviation. (19??)-. English. One time a year. National Technical Information Service - NTIS, Room 2027S, 5285 Port Royal Road, Springfield VA 22161. **Tel** (703)487-4630, (703)487-4660, (703)487-4650, FAX (703)321-8547, telex 89-9405. ***Continues*** *Briefs of Accidents Involving Missing Aircraft, U.S. General Aviation, 0566-8352.*

LC HE9784.5.U5 U57A
DD 614.8/69 US
BRIEFS OF ACCIDENTS INVOLVING ROTORCRAFT, U.S. GENERAL AVIATION. English. One time a year. National Technical Information Service - NTIS, Room 2027S, 5285 Port Royal Road, Springfield VA 22161. **Tel** (703)487-4630, (703)487-4660, (703)487-4650, FAX (703)321-8547, telex 89-9405. ***Continues*** *Briefs of Aircraft Accidents Involving Rotorcraft, U.S. General Aviation.*

LC HE17 .A47 HE9784.5.U5 **ISSN** 0091-1399
DD 363.1/2 S 363.1/24/0973 US
BRIEFS OF AIRCRAFT ACCIDENTS INVOLVING TURBINE POWERED AIRCRAFT, U.S. GENERAL AVIATION. **Main/Corp** United States. National Transportation Safety Board. English. Office of General Manager, Accidents Records and Inquiry Section BGM-554, Washington DC 20591.

LC HE17 .A47 HE9784.5.U5 **ISSN** 0360-7127
DD 380.5 S 614.8/69 US
BRIEFS OF FATAL ACCIDENTS INVOLVING WEATHER AS A CAUSE/FACTOR, U.S. GENERAL AVIATION. **VAT** Briefs of Fatal Accidents Involving Weather as a Cause-Factor, U.S. General Aviation. English. One time a year. National Technical Information Service - NTIS, Room 2027S, 5285 Port Royal Road, Springfield VA 22161. **Tel** (703)487-4630, (703)487-4660, (703)487-4650, FAX (703)321-8547, telex 89-9405. ***Continues*** *Briefs of Accidents Involving Weather as a Cause/Factor, U.S. General Aviation, 0360-6678.*

LC HE9761
DD 387.7 UK
BRITISH CIVIL AIRWORTHINESS REQUIREMENTS. English. Irregular. Civil Aviation Authority / England, Grenville House, 37 Gratton Road, Cheltenham Glo GL50 2BN United Kingdom. **Tel** 011 44 1242 235151, FAX 011 44 1242 584139.

LC HE9761
DD 387.7 UK
BRITISH CIVIL AIRWORTHINESS REQUIREMENTS AMENDMENT SERVICE. English. Irregular. £22.60 UK; £24.50 other. Civil Aviation Authority / England, Grenville House, 37 Gratton Road, Cheltenham Glo GL50 2BN United Kingdom. **Tel** 011 44 1242 235151, FAX 011 44 1242 584139.

LC TL **ISSN** 0889-4388
DD 629 US
BUCKER NEWS LETTER, THE. [Bucker news lett.]. **VFOAT** Bucker Newsletter; Bucker Club Newsletter; Bucker News. Periodical. English. Six times a year. $15.00 US; $20.00 other. Bucker Club, 6438 West Millbrook, Remus MI 49340. **Tel** (517)561-2393. **ED** Chris Arvanites. **Ad Acc. Circ:** 200 (ctrl). ***Continues*** *Bucker Jungmann Newsletter.*
Desc: Devoted to technical information and flying of Bucker aircraft.

LC TL789 **ISSN** 0828-4938
DD 001.9/42/05 CN
BULLETIN D'INFORMATION UFOLOGIQUE. **Added/Corp** Corporation pour la Collection des Observations Inexpliquees. Vol. 1, No 1 (Sept. 1984)-. Bulletin. French. Four times a year. 12.00Can$ Canada; 15.00Can$ other. Corporation pour la Collection des Observations Inexpliquees, Bulletin of Information Ufologique, CP 161, St.-Bruno-de-Montarville Quebec J3V 4P9 Canada. **Circ:** 100 (ctrl).
Desc: A magazine on UFO cases, studies, news and opinions.

LC TL **ISSN** 1247-9799
DD 629 FR
UDC 629.7(44)
BULLETIN - GIFAS. (BULLETIN.). **VFOAT** Bulletin - Groupement des Industries Francaises Aeronautiques et Spatiales. (1989)-. Bulletin. French. Irregular. GIFAS / Groupement des Industries Francaises Aernautiques et Spatiales, 4 rue Galilee, F 75782 Paris 16 France. **Tel** 011 33 1 44431752. ***Continues*** *Informations Aeronautiques et Spatiales. Bulletin du GIFAS, 0399-4872.*

LC HE9761
DD 387.7 FR
BULLETIN OFFICIEL. SECTION II : AVIATION CIVILE ET METEOROLOGIE. **Main/Corp** France. Direction Generale de l'Aviation Civile. **VAT** Bulletin Officiel. Section Deux: Aviation Civile et Meteorologie. (Sept. 1976)-. Bulletin. French. Irregular. Direction des Journaux Officiels, 26 rue Desaix, 75727 Paris Cedex 15 France. **Tel** 011 33 1 40587500. ***Continues*** *France. Direction de la Meteorologie Nationale. Bulletin Officiel. Section II: Aviation Civile et Meteorologie.*

LC TL502 .F62a ISSN 0181-1517
DD 387.7/0944/021 FR
BULLETIN STATISTIQUE DE LA DGAC. **See** Aeronautics, Astronautics-Abstracting, Bibliographies and Statistics.

LC HE9848.A1 S4A ISSN 0302-8607
DD 387.7/0944 FR
BULLETIN STATISTIQUE DU SECRETARIAT GENERAL A L'AVIATION CIVILE. **See** Aeronautics, Astronautics-Abstracting, Bibliographies and Statistics.

LC TL609 .W5 ISSN 0361-5065
DD 629.133/2/05 US
BUOYANT FLIGHT. **Added/Corp** Lighter Than Air Society. (19??)-. English. Six times a year. Free to members of the Lighter Than Air Society. Lighter Than Air Society, 1436 Triplett Boulevard, Akron OH 44306. **ED** Eric Brothers. Index available. cum. index. **Bk Rev**, (Qty: 12). **Ad Acc. Circ:** 1,000. ***Continues** Wingfoot Lighter-Than-Air Society. Bulletin.*
Desc: Presents news of recent developments in lighter-than-air aviation, book reviews, historical analysis and summaries of regular meeting of this organization.
Ind/Abst SPORT Discus.

LC HE9761.1 .B8 ISSN 0191-4642
DD 387.7/05 US
CCC
BUSINESS AND COMMERCIAL AVIATION. [Bus. comm. aviat.]. Vol. 32, No. 1 (Jan. 1973)-. Periodical. English. Twelve times a year. $60.00. McGraw Hill Publishing Company, Inc., 1221 Avenue of the Americas, New York NY 10020. **Tel** (212)512-6410, (800)525-5003, FAX (212)512-6111. **(Subscription address:** Business and Commercial Aviation, PO Box 619, Hightstown NJ 08520. **) ED** John Olcott. **Ad Acc. Circ:** 52,000 (ctrl). available on microfilm from University Microfilms International (UMI); available on an online database from DIALOG; and NEXIS. ***Continues** Business & Commercial Aviation, 0191-4642.*
Desc: Operational and management information for those who own and fly aircraft for business purposes.
Ind/Abst Acad. Search; Appl. Sci. Technol. Index; Aviat. Tradescan [Full Cov.]; Bus. Index (1985-); Bus. Source Plus; Bus. Source; EP Collect.; Gen. BusinessFile (1985-); Gen. Period. Index (1985-); Homework Help.; INFO-SOUTH Abstr.; Int. Aerosp. Abstr.; Mag. Search; MasterFile FullTEXT 1000; MasterFile FullTEXT 350; MasterFile FullTEXT 650; MasterFile FullTEXT (July 1993-); OCLC; Telebase; Trade Ind. Index (1981-).

LC TL
DD 629 US
BUSINESS AVIATION. (19??)-. Periodical. English. One time a week. $520.00 North America; $600.00 other. McGraw Hill Publishing Company, Inc., 1221 Avenue of the Americas, New York NY 10020. **Tel** (212)512-6410, (800)525-5003, FAX (212)512-6111.

LC TL ISSN 0890-8664
DD 629 US
BUSINESS AVIATION SAFETY. [Bus. aviat. saf.]. **VFOAT** Business Aviation Safety Journal. (1985)-. English. One time a year. $15.00. Business Aviation Safety Journal, Box 2398, Wichita KS 67201. **Tel** (316)262-1492, telex 417384. **ED** William Donovan. **Ad Acc. Circ:** 20,000 (ctrl).
Desc: Written by professional pilots for pilots of high performance civil aircraft.
Ind/Abst Aviat. Tradescan [Full Cov.].

LC TL ISSN 0007-6570
DD 629 US
BUSINESS COMMERCIAL AVIATION. (Jan. 1958)-. Periodical. English. Business Commercial Aviation, Old Mansfield Road, Wooster OH 44691. available on microfilm and microfiche from University Microfilms International (UMI); available on an online database from DIALOG. ***Continues** Aviation Age.*
Ind/Abst Stat. Ref. Index.

LC TL501 .C3612 ISSN 0007-7771
DD 629.13/0971 CN
CAHS JOURNAL, THE. [CAHS j.]. **Main/Corp** Canadian Aviation Historical Society. **VAT** Canadian Aviation Historical Society Journal. (Jan. 1963)-. Periodical. English. Four times a year. 24.01Can$. Canadian Aviation Historical Society, PO Box 224 Station A, Willowdale Ontario M2N 5S8 Canada. **Tel** (416)294-4438, (416)488-2247, FAX (416)488-2247. **ED** Bill Wheeler. Index available. **Bk Rev**, (Qty: 12). **Circ:** 1,300 (ctrl).
Ind/Abst Am. Hist. Life (1990-).

LC HE9761 ISSN 0823-8219
DD 387.7/364/02571233 CN
CALGARY & AREA AIRPORT BUSINESS DIRECTORY. [Calg. area airpt. bus. dir.]. **VFOAT** Calgary Airport Business Directory. **VAT** Calgary and Area Airport Business Directory; Calgary Airport Business Directory (1984). (1984)-. Directory. English. One time a year. 5.60Can$. Corvus Publishing Group Ltd, 1224 Aviation Park Northeast, Suite 158, Calgary Alberta T2E 7E2 Canada. **Tel** (403)275-9457, FAX (403)275-3925. **ED** Gary Gaudreau. **Ad Acc. Circ:** 7,500 (ctrl). ***Continues** Calgary Airport Business Directory, 0227-1672.*
Desc: Descriptive listings of all activities of all companies that provide services for aviation in the Calgary area.

LC HE9761 ISSN 1183-7853
DD 387.7 CN
CALGARY & AREA AVIATION BUSINESS DIRECTORY. [Calg. area aviat. bus. dir.]. **VFOAT** Calgary and Area Aviation Business Directory. (1991/92)-. Directory. English. $7.50 per volume. Business Directories International #107, 5621-11 St. Northeast, Calgary Alta. T2E 6Z7 Canada. ***Continues** Calgary & Area Airport Business Directory., 0823-8219.*

LC TL
DD 629 CN
CANADA AIR PILOT. (19??)-. Periodical. English. Irregular. 70.15Can$ Canada; 82.25Can$ US; 99.15Can$ other. Receiver General for Canada / Canada Map Office, Canada Map Office, 615 Booth, Ottawa Ontario K1A 0E9 Canada. **Tel** (613)998-3865, FAX (613)957-8861, telex 0534328.

LC TK
DD 629 CN
CANADA AIR PILOT. WATER AERODROME SUPPLEMENT, THE. **Added/Corp** Canada. Surveys and Mapping Branch. **VFOAT** Water Aerodrome Supplement. (19??)-. English (French). One time a year (Spring). 15.00Can$ Canada; 16.85Can$ US; 24.30Can$ other. Receiver General for Canada / Canada Map Office, Canada Map Office, 615 Booth, Ottawa Ontario K1A 0E9 Canada. **Tel** (613)998-3865, FAX (613)957-8861, telex 0534328.

LC TL
DD 629 CN
CANADA FLIGHT SUPPLEMENT. (19??)-. Periodical. English (French). Irregular. 93.50Can$ Canada; 101.90Can$ US; 142.10Can$ other. Receiver General for Canada / Canada Map Office, Canada Map Office, 615 Booth, Ottawa Ontario K1A 0E9 Canada. **Tel** (613)998-3865, FAX (613)957-8861, telex 0534328.

LC HF1371 ISSN 1190-9722
DD 382 CN
•CANADA'S EXPORT STRATEGY, THE INTERNATIONAL TRADE BUSINESS PLAN. 3, AIRCRAFT AND PARTS. [Can. export strategy int. trade bus. plan, 3 Aircr. parts]. **Added/Corp** Canada. **VFOAT** Aircraft and Parts. (1996)-. Government Publication. English. ***Continues** Canada's International Trade Business Plan. 2, Aeronautics, 1200-1082.*

LC HF1371 ISSN 1200-4952
DD 382 CN
•CANADA'S EXPORT STRATEGY, THE INTERNATIONAL TRADE BUSINESS PLAN. 22, SPACE. [Can. export strategy int. trade bus. plan, 22 Space]. **Added/Corp** Canada. **VFOAT** Space. (1996)-. Government Publication. English. Irregular. ***Continues** Canada's International Trade Business Plan. 19, Space, 1200-1422.*

LC TL ISSN 0008-2821
DD 629 CN
CCC
CODEN CSPJAE
Pr Rev.
CANADIAN AERONAUTICS AND SPACE JOURNAL. [Can. aeronaut. space j.]. **Added/Corp** Canadian Aeronautics and Space Institute. Canadian Aeronautical Institute. Vol. 8 (Jan. 1962)-. Periodical. English. Twelve times a year. 52.36Can$. Canadian Aeronautic Space Institute, 818-130 Slater Street, Ottawa Ontario K1P 6E2 Canada. **Tel** (613)234-0191, FAX (613)234-9039. **ED** Pat Ryan. Index available. **Bk Rev. Circ:** 2,500. available on microfilm from Micromedia Limited; available on microfilm and microfiche from University Microfilms International (UMI). Documents available from Article Express International, Ask*IEEE. ***Continues** Canadian Aeronautical Journal, 0318-5974; **Absorbed** C.A.S.I. Transactions.*
Desc: Contains articles of a wide range of scientific and technical interest and news of the activities of the institute.
Ind/Abst Bioeng. Abstr.; Can. Index; Curr. Cit.; Ei Page One; Eng. Index Annu.; INSPEC (Sept. 1971-); Int. Aerosp. Abstr.; Pollut. Abstr. Indexes.

LC TL ISSN 0008-2848
DD 629 CN
CANADIAN AIRCRAFT OPERATOR, THE. Vol. 1 (May 16, 1964)-. Periodical. English. Twenty-four times a year. 31.62Can$. Arthurs Publications Ltd., 4141 Dixie Rd., PO Box 149, Mississauga Ontario, L4W 1V5 Canada. **Tel** (905)625-9660, FAX (905)625-7559. **ED** R. G. Halford. **Bk Rev. Ad Acc. Circ:** 8,200 (ctrl).
Desc: Tabloid newspaper providing news and comment of interest to the Canadian general aviation community.

LC TL501 .A7819 ISSN 1198-0176
DD 338.4/76291/0971 CN
CODEN CAVSEH
•CANADIAN AVIATION & AIRCRAFT FOR SALE. [Can aviat. aircr. sale]. **VFOAT** Canadian Aviation and Aircraft for Sale. (1993)-. Periodical. English. Six times a year. 25.61Can$. Canadian Aviation and Aircraft, PO Box 47555, Hamilton Ontario, L8H 7S7 Canada. **Tel** (905)544-0560. ***Formed by the union of** Aviation & Aerospace, 0847-0588 **and** Aircraft for Sale Magazine, 1189-9697.*

LC HE9761 ISSN 0829-2132
DD 387.7/0971 CN
CANADIAN AVIATION NEWS (1984). (CANADIAN AVIATION NEWS.). [Can. aviat. news]. **VFOAT** Canadian Western/Canadian Eastern Aviation News. **VAT** Canadian Western/Canadian Eastern Aviation News (1984). Vol. 9, Issue 19 (Sept. 24, 1984)-. Periodical. English. Twenty-five times a year. 16.80Can$. Canadian Aviation News Ltd, 202-1338T/36 Avenue Northeast, Calgary Alberta T2E 6T6 Canada. **Tel** (403)250-9833, FAX (403)291-9281. **ED** H R Engel. **Bk Rev**, (Qty: 2-6/yr). **Ad Acc. Circ:** 10,000 (ctrl). available on microfiche. ***Continues** Aviation News (Mynarski Park, Alta. : 1981), 0711-7396.*
Desc: Canadian aviation newspaper.

LC HE9761 ISSN 0527-6497
DD 387.7/334/0971 CN
CANADIAN CIVIL AIRCRAFT REGISTER. (CANADIAN CIVIL AIRCRAFT REGISTER [MICROFORM].). [Can. civ. aircr. regist.]. **Added/Corp** Canada. Transport Canada. **VFOAT** Registre d'Immatriculation des Aeronefs Civils Canadiens. (1984)-. Periodical. English (French). Twelve times a year. Canada Communication Group Publishers, Order Processing, Ottawa Ontario K1A 0S9 Canada. **Tel** (819)956-4800, (819)956-4802. ***Continues** Canadian Air Transportation Administration. Civil Aeronautics. Canadian Civil Aircraft Register., 0527-6497.*

LC HE9815.A1 A237 ISSN 0826-6026
DD 387.7/1/0971021 CN
CANADIAN CIVIL AVIATION. (CANADIAN CIVIL AVIATION = AVIATION CIVILE CANADIENNE.). [Can. civ. aviat.]. **Added/Corp** Aviation Statistics Centre (Canada). **VFOAT** Aviation Civile Canadienne. (1982)-. English (French). One time a year. 39.00Can$ Canada; $47.00 US; $55.00 other. Statistics Canada Publications Sales and Services, R.H. Coats Building 6th Floor, Ottawa Ontario K1A 0T6 Canada. **Tel** (613)951-5078, (800)267-6677, FAX (613)951-1584, telex 053-3585. **ED** Gord Baldwin. Index available. **Circ:** 375. ***Continues** Air Carrier Financial Statements, 0380-5174.*
Desc: Provides a summary of the activities of about 800 domestic air carriers operating in Canada. Includes operational and financial statistics relating to number of passengers carried, kilometers and hours flown, and income and balance sheets.

LC TL ISSN 0008-3577
DD 629 CN
CANADIAN FLIGHT. **Added/Corp** Canadian Owners and Pilots Association. (June 1955)-. Periodical. English. Six times a year. Comes with Canadian Owners and Pilots Association membership. Canadian Owners Pilot Association, PO Box 734, Ottawa Ontario K1P 5S4 Canada. **Tel** (613)236-4901, FAX (613)236-8646. **ED** William N. Peppler. **Bk Rev. Ad Acc. Circ:** 20,000 (ctrl).
Desc: Aimed at general aviation, government regulations, and current issues.

LC TL500 ISSN 0226-5648
DD 629.13/005 CN
CANADIAN GENERAL AVIATION NEWS. [Can. gen. aviat. news.]. **Added/Corp** Canadian Owners and Pilots Association. **VFOAT** General Aviation News. (July 1964)-. Periodical. English. Irregular. 40.00Can$ Comes with Canadian Owners and Pilots Association membership. Canadian Owners Pilot Association, PO Box 734, Ottawa Ontario K1P 5S4 Canada. **Tel** (613)236-4901, FAX (613)236-8646. **ED** William N. Peppler. **Bk Rev. Ad Acc. Circ:** 20,000 (ctrl).
Desc: News and information aim at general aviation, government regulations and other related issues.

LC G70.4 .C24 ISSN 0703-8992
DD 621.36/78/05 CN
CCC
CODEN CJRSDP
Pr Rev.
CANADIAN JOURNAL OF REMOTE SENSING. [Can. j. remote sens.]. **Added/Corp** Canadian Aeronautics and Space Institute. Vol. 1 (May 1975)-. Periodical. English (French). Four times a year. 74.80Can$. Canadian Aeronautic Space Institute, 818-130 Slater Street, Ottawa Ontario K1P 6E2 Canada. **Tel** (613)234-0191, FAX (613)234-9039. **ED** H. Lang-Runtz. **Bk Rev. Circ:** 600. available on microfilm and microfiche from University Microfilms International (UMI). Documents available from Article Express International, Ask*IEEE, CASDDS.
Desc: Disseminates information about remote sensing art, science, technologies and applications.
Ind/Abst AGRICOLA [Select. Cov.]; AQUAREF; Chem.

Abstr.; Curr. Cit.; Ecol. Abstr. (?-?); EMBASE; Eng. Index Annu.; Geogr. Abstr. Phys. Geogr.; Geol. Abstr.; GeoRef; INSPEC (Aug. 1978-); Int. Aerosp. Abstr.; Environ.

LC TL605 **ISSN** 0821-6673
DD 629.133/343 CN
CANADIAN ULTRALIGHT NEWS. [Can. ultralight news]. (1982)-. Periodical. English. Twelve times a year. 6.00Can$ Canada; 10.00Can$ other. Canadian Flight Publishing Company, PO Box 563 Station B, Ottawa Ontario K1P 5P7 Canada. **Tel** (613)236-4901, FAX (613)236-8646. **ED** William N. Peppler. **Bk Rev. Ad Acc. Circ:** 20,000 (ctrl).
Desc: News and information aimed at general aviation, government regulations and current situations.

LC TL **ISSN** 0930-0309
DD 629 GW
UDC 629.114.61
CODEN 796.54
CARAVAN (HERFORD. 1985). (1985)-. Periodical. German. Twelve times a year. $47.44. Westdeutsche Verlagsanstalt GmbH, Ahmser Strasse 190, 32052 Herford Germany. **Tel** 011 49 5221 7750, FAX 011 49 5221 775215, telex 175221855 WVD.

LC TL **ISSN** 1048-8898
DD 629 US
CAREER PILOT. [Career pilot]. **Added/Corp** Future Aviation Professionals of America. Vol. 8, No. 2 (Feb. 1990)-. Trade Publication. English. Twelve times a year. $39.00. Future Aviation Professionals of America, 4959 Massachusetts Boulevard, Atlanta GA 30337. **Tel** (404)997-8097 ext.190, (800)538-5627, FAX (404)997-8111. ***Continues*** *Piloting Careers, 0745-4996.*
Ind/Abst Aviat. Tradescan [Full Cov.].

LC TL **ISSN** 0891-0855
DD 629 US
CAREER PILOT JOB REPORT. [Career pilot job rep.]. **Added/Corp** Future Aviation Professionals of America. **VFOAT** FAPA Career Pilot Job Report. (19??)-. Periodical. English. Twelve times a year. comes with membership. Future Aviation Professionals of America, 4959 Massachusetts Boulevard, Atlanta GA 30337. **Tel** (404)997-8097 ext.190, (800)538-5627, FAX (404)997-8111. **ED** Brian Golden and Wes Powell. **Circ:** 15,000 (ctrl).

LC HE9761 **ISSN** 0834-9797
DD 387.7/44/0971 CN
CEASED
CARGO EXPRESS. [Cargo express]. Vol. 9, No. 1 (Dec. 1986/Jan. 1987)-Vol. 17, No. 7 (19??). Periodical. English. Baxter Publishing Company, 310 Dupont Street, Toronto Ontario M5R 1V9 Canada. **Tel** (416)968-7252, FAX (416)968-2377, telex 065-28085. ***Continues*** *Cargo Exchange, 0710-0485;* ***Absorbed*** *Transportation Business, 0821-5634.*

LC HE9761 **ISSN** 0278-0801
DD 387.744 US
CARGO FACTS. **See** Transportation.

LC TL726.5.C33 C37
DD 629.132/54/729 US
CARIBBEAN FLITE GUIDE. (19??)-. English. Four times a year. $24.00. Caribbean Flite Guide, 16504 Bridge End Road, Miami Lakes FL 33014. **Tel** (305)823-1093. **ED** Randal J. Agostini. **Bk Rev. Ad Acc. Circ:** 10,000.
Desc: A comprehensive visual flying manual for visitors to the Caribbean Islands.

LC HE9761
DD 387.744 CN
CATALOGUE OF ICAO PUBLICATIONS AND AUDIO VISUAL TRAINING AIDS. **See** Aeronautics, Astronautics-Abstracting, Bibliographies and Statistics.

LC HE9803.A1 A27 **ISSN** 0069-1437
DD 387.7/33/40973 US
CENSUS OF U.S. CIVIL AIRCRAFT. [Census U. S. civ. aircr.]. **VAT** Census of United States Civil Aircraft. (1964)-. English. One time a year. National Technical Information Service - NTIS, Room 2027S, 5285 Port Royal Road, Springfield VA 22161. **Tel** (703)487-4630, (703)487-4660, (703)487-4650, FAX (703)321-8547, telex 89-9405. ***Formed by the union of*** *Statistical Study of U.S. Civil Aircraft* ***and*** *United States Active Civil Aircraft by State and County.*

LC TL **ISSN** 0745-3523
DD 629 US
CESSNA OWNER MAGAZINE, THE. (THE CESSNA OWNER MAGAZINE : THE MONTHLY PUBLICATION OF THE CESSNA SKYHAWK ASSOCIATION, THE CESSNA SKYLANE SOCIETY, THE CESSNA CENTURION SOCIETY.). **Added/Corp** Cessna Skylane Society. Cessna Skyhawk Association. Cessna Centurion Society. Cessna Owner Organization. Vol. 8, No. 10 (Nov. 1982)-. Periodical. English. Twelve times a year. $42.00. Jones Publishing, N7450 Aanstad Road, Iola WI 54945. **Tel** (800)331-0038, (715)445-5000, FAX (715)445-4053, . **ED** Frank Hamilton. Index available. **Bk Rev. Ad Acc, Adv Mgr:** Wanda Zuege. **Circ:** 3,500. ***Formed by the union of*** *Cessna Skylane Society. CSS Newsletter, 0199-6932* ***and*** *Cessna Skyhawk Association. CSA Newsletter, 0199-6940.*
Desc: Full color publication whose thrust is toward the owner and the pilots of Cessna aircraft, all models.

LC TL501 .C57 **ISSN** 1000-9361
DD 629.13/005 CC
CCC
CODEN CJAEEZ
CHINESE JOURNAL OF AERONAUTICS. **Added/Corp** Chung-kuo Hang Kung Hsueh Hui. Vol. 1, No. 1 (Jan. 1988)-. Academic Scholarly Publication. English (translations available in Chinese). Four times a year. $365.00. Allerton Press Inc., 150 Fifth Avenue, New York NY 10011. **Tel** (212)924-3950, FAX (212)463-9684, telex 427441 ALPRES. **ED** He Qingzhi. Documents available from Article Express International.
Desc: Information on aeronautical research in China. Includes auto control, flight dynamics, avionics, testing and manufacturing.
Ind/Abst Eng. Index Annu.; Int. Aerosp. Abstr.

LC TL
DD 629 US
CHRONOLOGY OF AMERICAN AEROSPACE EVENTS, A. **Main/Corp** United States. Dept. of the Air Force. **Added/Corp** United States. Air University. Aerospace Studies Institute. United States. Air University. Research Studies Institute. (1959)-. English. Department of the Air Force, The Pentagon, Washington DC 20330. **Tel** (202)545-6700.

LC UG633 .A66 **ISSN** 0887-9680
DD 359.9/7/0973 US
CITIZEN AIRMAN. **See** Military and Defense.

LC TL **ISSN** 0009-7810
DD 629 US
CIVIL AIR PATROL NEWS. **Added/Corp** United States. Civil Air Patrol. (19??)-. Periodical. English. Twelve times a year. $5.00. Civil Air Patrol News, National Headquarters, Publication Affairs, Maxwell AFB AL 36112. **Tel** (334)293-7593. **ED** Daniel Sherwood. **Ad Acc. Circ:** 70,000 (ctrl).
Desc: Covers aerospace and aviation advances and education, plus cadet and senior member activities throughout the United States.

LC HD9711.U58 C87
DD 380.1/456291333/0973021 US
CIVIL AIRCRAFT AND AIRCRAFT ENGINES. **Added/Corp** United States. Bureau of the Census. (19??)-. Government Publication. English. Twelve times a year. US Department of Commerce / Bureau of the Census, Data User Services Division, Customer Services, Washington DC 20233-0800. **Tel** (301)763-4100. **(Subscription address:** Superintendent of Documents, US Government Printing Office, Washington DC 20402. **)** ***Continues*** *Current Industrial Reports. M37G, Civil Aircraft and Aircraft Engines (Except Military).*
Desc: Contains data on quantity and value of shipments of complete civilian aircraft and aircraft engines.

LC TL
DD 629 US
CIVIL AIRCRAFT FORECAST. (19??)-. English. Twelve times a year. $1390.00. Forecast International / DMS Inc., 22 Commerce Road, Newtown CT 06470. **Tel** (203)426-0800, FAX (203)426-1964, telex 467615. available on CD-ROM ($1595.00).

LC HE9762.5 .C58
DD 387.7/021/2 CN
CIVIL AVIATION STATISTICS OF THE WORLD. **See** Aeronautics, Astronautics-Abstracting, Bibliographies and Statistics.

LC TL **ISSN** 0960-9024
DD 629 UK
CIVIL AVIATION TRAINING : CAT. **VFOAT** CAT. (1990)-. Trade Publication. English. Six times a year. $68.45. Halldale Publishing and Media Limited, 84 Alexandra Road, Farnborough Hampshire GU14 6DD United Kingdom. **Tel** 011 44 1252 517974, FAX 011 44 1252 512714. **ED** Trevor Nash. **Bk Rev. Ad Acc. Circ:** 11,436 (ctrl).
Desc: Journal of civil aviation training; mailed directly to senior executives, training captains, and simulator managers at all regional and international airlines worldwide.

LC TL **ISSN** 0742-1508
DD 629 US
COCKPIT (LANCASTER, CALIF.). (COCKPIT.). **Main/Corp** Society of Experimental Test Pilots. (19??)-. English. Four times a year. Setp Publications Chairman, PO Box 986, Lancaster CA 93534-0986.
Ind/Abst Int. Aerosp. Abstr. (1983-).

LC TL **ISSN** 1071-3816
DD 629 US
CODE ONE. (CODE ONE : A PRODUCT SUPPORT PUBLICATION OF GENERAL DYNAMICS FORT WORTH DIVISION.). [Code one]. **Added/Corp** Lockheed Fort Worth Co. Vol. 1 (Apr. 1986)-. Periodical. English. Four times a year (Jan., Apr., July, Oct.). $12.00. Lockhead Fort Worth Co., Mail Zone 1793, PO Box 748, Fort Worth TX 76101. **Tel** (817)777-5542, FAX (817)777-5557. **ED** Eric Hens. **Circ:** 28,000 (ctrl).
Desc: Corporate publication for the aviation industry and military readers.

LC UG **ISSN** 1063-8970
DD 358 US
COMBAT EDGE, THE. [Combat edge]. Vol. 1, Issue 1 (June 1992)-. Government Publication. English. Twelve times a year. $31.00. US Department of Defense, The Pentagon, Washington DC 20301. **Tel** (703)545-6700. **(Subscription address:** Superintendent of Documents, US Government Printing Office, Washington DC 20402. **)** ***Formed by the union of*** *TAC Attack, 0494-3880* ***and*** *Combat Crew, 0010-213X.*
Desc: A publication of the Office of Safety, Air Combat Command that contains informative articles on mishap prevention.
Ind/Abst Air Univ. Libr. Index Mil. Period. (199?-).

LC HE9803.A2 C65 **ISSN** 0094-839X
DD 387.7/05 US
COME FLY WITH US. **Added/Corp** National Air Transportation Association (U. S.). Vol. 1 (1974)-. Periodical. English. Twelve times a year. Washington Fund for Public Policy Research, 1156 15th Street NW, Washington DC 20005.

LC HE9769.A3 A95b **ISSN** 0270-5249
DD 387.7/334/0216 US
COMMERCIAL AIRCRAFT FLEETS. [Commer. aircr. fleets]. **Main/Corp** Avmark, Inc. **Added/Corp** Avmark, Inc. Jet Equipped Airlines of the Free World. **VFOAT** Jet Equipped Airlines of the Free World. (1972)-. English. Two times a year (Jan. & Aug.). $295.00. Avmark Inc / Montana, Lewis & Clark Trail, Lolo MT 59847. **Tel** (406)273-2580, FAX (406)273-6779. **ED** James S. Beyer. **Circ:** 100. available on magnetic tape; available on diskette; available on an online database. ***Continues*** *Commercial Aircraft Fleets, 0270-5249.*
Desc: The complete directory of current jet fleets of the world's airlines, showing dates of order, delivery, sale, lease or loss by accident of all jet transports. Includes international, domestic, cargo, charter, and commuter airlines.

LC TL **ISSN** 1063-8598
DD 629 US
CCC
CEASED
COMMERCIAL AVIATION NEWS. **VFOAT** Aviation News. (1993)-(Oct. 1993). Periodical. English. Army Times Publishing Company, 6883 Commercial Drive, Springfield VA 22159. **Tel** (800)368-5718, (703)750-8099.

LC TL
DD 629 UK
COMMERCIAL AVIATION REPORT. (19??)-. English. Twenty-six times a year. $697.50. CAR-Commercial Aviation Report, 108A High Street, Uckfield, East Sussex TN22 1PX United Kingdom. **Tel** 011 44 1825 769226, FAX 011 44 1825 769229.

LC TL
DD 629 US
COMMERCIAL JET FLEETS. (19??)-. English. Four times a year. $1295.00. FedEx Aviation Services, 2005 Corporate Avenue, 1st Floor, Memphis TN 38132. **Tel** (901)395-3829.

LC HE9761 **ISSN** 1056-0254
DD 387.7 US
CCC
COMMUTER. [Commut./reg. airl. news int.]. **VFOAT** Commuter Regional Airline News International; C/R Airline News International. (1987)-. Periodical. English. One time a week (50 issues). $595.00. Phillips Business Information Inc., 1201 Seven Locks Road, PO Box 61130, Potomac MD 20854. **Tel** (301)424-3338, (301)340-1520, (800)777-5005, FAX (301)424-4297, telex 358149. available on an online database from NEWSNET.

LC HE9761 **ISSN** 1040-5402
DD 387.7 US
CCC
COMMUTER. [Commut./reg. airl. news]. **VFOAT** Commuter Regional Airline News; C/R News. (1982)-. Periodical. English. One time a week (50 issues). $695.00. Phillips Business Information Inc., 1201 Seven Locks Road, PO Box 61130, Potomac MD 20854. **Tel** (301)424-3338, (301)340-1520, (800)777-5005, FAX (301)424-4297, telex 358149. **ED** Kelly Murphy. Index available. **Ad Acc. Circ:** 300. available on an online database from NEWSNET; DIALOG; and DATA-STAR.
Ind/Abst PROMT [Full Txt.]; PTS Newsl. Database [Full Txt.]; Trade Ind. ASAP [Full Txt.]; Trade Ind. Index [Full Txt.].

LC TL726 .C64 **ISSN** 1054-7436
DD 387.7/42 US
CCC
TITLE CHANGE
COMMUTER AIR INTERNATIONAL. [Commut. air int.]. **Added/Corp** Communication Channels, Inc. **VFOAT** International Commuter Air; Commuter Air. (March 1990)-(1993). Periodical. English. Argus Business, 6151 Powers Ferry Road Northwest,

Atlanta GA 30339. **Tel** (404)995-2500, FAX (404)995-0400. available on microfilm and microfiche from University Microfilms International (UMI); available on an online database (file 648/Full-Text) from DIALOG. ***Continues*** *Commuter Air, 0199-2686.* ***Continued by*** *Regional Air International, 1070-065X.*
Ind/Abst Aviat. Tradescan [Full Cov.].

LC TL **ISSN** 0265-4504
DD 629 UK
COMMUTER WORLD.
[Commut. world]. **Added/Corp** European Regional Airlines Organization. Vol. 1, No. 1 (Jan.-April 1984)-. Trade Publication. English. Six times a year. $70.00. Shephard Press Ltd, 111 High Street, Burnham Buckinghamshire SL1 7JZ United Kingdom. **Tel** 011 44 1628 604311, FAX 011 44 1628 664334, telex 846575. **ED** Alexander Shepard and Ian Harbison. **Ad Acc. Circ:** 13,000 (ctrl). Documents available from Documents on Demand. ***Absorbed*** *Regional Air International.*
Desc: In-trade aviation magazine covering commuter and short-haul operators.
Ind/Abst Aviat. Tradescan [Full Cov.]; Environ. Abstr.

LC TL500
DD 629.13 FR
COMPTES DE L'EXERCICE .... .
Main/Corp Societe Nationale Industrielle Aerospatiale. (1969)-. French. Ten times a year. 164.54F France; 224.00F other. Revue Aerospatiale, 19 boulevard du Parc, 92200 Neuilly Seine Cedex France. **Tel** 011 33 1 47476399. ***Continues in part*** *Sud-Aviation (Firm). Comptes de l'Exercice ... .*

LC TL521 .N255 **ISSN** 0360-5175
DD 387.7/0973 US
CONFERENCE SUMMARY REPORT - AVIATION REVIEW CONFERENCE.
Main/Conf Aviation Review Conference. Government Publication. English. One time a year. US Department of Transportation / Federal Aviation Administration, 800 Independence Avenue Southwest, Washington DC 20591. **Tel** (202)367-3484, FAX (202)367-3505. ***Continues*** *National Aviation System Planning Review Conference. Summary Report.*

LC TL
DD 629 US
CONTRACTIONS.
Added/Corp United States. Federal Aviation Administration. United States. Air Traffic Rules and Procedures Service. (19??)-. Government Publication. English. Four times a year. $66.00 domestic; $82.50 other. US Department of Transportation / US Coast Guard, 2100 Second Street Southwest, Washington DC 20953-0001. **Tel** (202)267-2229. **(Subscription address:** Superintendent of Documents, US Government Printing Office, Washington DC 20402. **)**
Desc: Contains the approved word and phrase contractions used by personnel of the Federal Aviation Administration. It is also used by other agencies that provide air traffic control, communications, weather, charting and associated services.

LC TL **ISSN** 0010-8073
DD 629 SZ
CONTROLLER.
(THE CONTROLLER: JOURNAL OF THE INTERNATIONAL FEDERATION OF AIR TRAFFIC CONTROLLERS' ASSOCIATIONS.). [Controller]. **Added/Corp** International Federation of Air Traffic Controllers' Associations. **VFOAT** Journal of the International Federation of Air Traffic Controllers' Associations. (1961)-. Periodical. English. Four times a year. $29.04. International Federation of Air Traffic Controllers Association, PO Box 196, CH-1215 Geneva Airport Switzerland. **Tel** 011 41 22 822679. **ED** H. Harry Henschler (editor's address: 1998 Glenmore Avenue, Sherwood Park, Alberta T8A OX8 Canada; editor's telephone number: (403)467-6826). **Bk Rev. Ad Acc. Circ:** 5,000. Documents available from Ask*IEEE.
Desc: Treatment of professional aspects in systems and equipment development in ATC, and legal aspects in ATC. News for airspace users, IFATCA annual conference resume, and aviation book reviews.
Ind/Abst INSPEC (Dec. 1984-Dec. 1986); Int. Aerosp. Abstr.

LC TL787 .C2 **ISSN** 0045-8732
DD 629.4/05 UK
CCC
COSPAR INFORMATION BULLETIN.
[COSPAR inf. bull.]. **Main/Corp** COSPAR. **VAT** Committee on Space Research Information Bulletin. No. 1 (March 1960)-. Bulletin. English. Three times a year. $128.00. Pergamon Press, An Imprint of Elsevier Science Ltd., The Boulevard, Langford Lane, Kidlington, Oxford OX5 1GB United Kingdom. **Tel** 011 44 1865 843000, 011 44 1865 843699, FAX 011 44 1865 843010. **(Subscription address:** Elsevier Science Ltd. / Oxford Fulfillment Centre, PO Box 800, Kidlington OX5 1DX United Kingdom. **Tel** 011 44 865 843355.**)**
Desc: The Committee on Space Research (COSPAR) was established by the International Council of Scientific Unions in October 1958 to continue the cooperative programs of rocket and satellite research successfully undertaken during the International Geophysical Year of 1957-58. Addresses information on past and future meetings; news from national and international institutions and organizations.
Ind/Abst Int. Aerosp. Abstr.

LC TL787 .C68 **ISSN** 0746-8830
DD 629.4 US
Pr Rev.
COUNTDOWN (ATHENS, OHIO).
(COUNTDOWN.). [Countdown]. (198?)-. Periodical. English. Six times a year. $32.95. Cspace Press, PO Box 9331, Grand Rapids MI 49509-0331. **Tel** (616)452-5500, FAX (616)452-5538. **ED** Glen E. Swanson. **Bk Rev**, (Qty: 6-12). **Ad Acc. Circ:** 2,500.
Desc: Contemporary space flight magazine focusing on the space shuttle program and international space developments.

LC TL500 **ISSN** 1037-5759
DD 629.4 AT
CSIRO SPACE INDUSTRY NEWS.
VFOAT Commonwealth Scientific and Industrial Research Organization Space Industry News. (1990)-. Periodical. English. Six times a year. CSIRO Publications, PO Box 89, 314 Albert Street, East Melborne Victoria 3002 Australia. **Tel** 011 61 3 4187333, 4187217, FAX 011 61 3 4190459, telex AA 30236. ***Continues*** *COSSA Space Industry News, 0816-7044.*

LC TL **ISSN** 0889-437X
DD 629 US
CUB CLUES.
(CUB CLUES : THE NEWSLETTER OF THE CUB CLUB.). [Cub clues]. **Added/Corp** Cub Club. (1984)-. Newsletter. English. Six times a year. $20.00 US and Canada; $25.00 other. Cub Club, 6438 West Millbrook, Remus MI 49340-9625. **Tel** (517)561-2393. **ED** John B. Bergeson. Index available. cum. index. **Bk Rev. Ad Acc, Adv Mgr:** Alice Bergeson. **Circ:** 2,800 (ctrl).
Desc: Devoted to technical information and flying of Piper Cub aircraft.

LC TL514 .C87
DD 629.133/34/0294 SZ
CURRENT AIRCRAFT PRICES.
English. 150. Interavia, PO Box 162, CH-1216 Geneva Switzerland. **Tel** 011 41 22 980505. **ED** A Whitfield.
Desc: Current prices, sales status and recent contracts of current civil and military aircraft programmes.

LC TL
DD 629 US
DATES OF LATEST EDITIONS. AIRPORT OBSTRUCTION CHARTS.
Added/Corp United States. National Ocean Service. **VFOAT** Airport Obstruction Charts, Obstruction Data Sheets. Periodical. English. Four times a year. US Department of Commerce / National Oceanic & Atmospheric Administration NOAA, Room 808 Worldweather Building, Washington DC 20233. **Tel** (301) 763-4670, FAX (301)763-8125. ***Continues*** *Dates of Latest Editions. Airport Obstruction Charts.*

LC UG360 **ISSN** 0963-116X
DD 623 UK
DEFENCE HELICOPTER.
[Def. helicopter]. (1990)-. Trade Publication. English. Four times a year. $40.00. Shephard Press Ltd, 111 High Street, Burnham Buckinghamshire SL1 7JZ United Kingdom. **Tel** 011 44 1628 604311, FAX 011 44 1628 664334, telex 846575. ***Continues*** *Defence Helicopter World, 0263-5062.*

LC DA49 **ISSN** 1033-2898
DD 355.00994 AT
DEFENCE INDUSTRY AND AEROSPACE REPORT.
See Military and Defense.

LC DA49 **ISSN** 0211-3732
DD 355.00994 SP
UDC 355/359
Pr Rev.
DEFENSA MADRID.
See Military and Defense.

LC DA49 **ISSN** 0733-8082
DD 355.00994 US
DEFENSE/AEROSPACE COMPANY CONTRACT QUARTERLY.
VFOAT Contract Quarterly. **VAT** Defense Aerospace Company Contract Quarterly. (19??)-. Periodical. English. Four times a year. Forecast International / DMS Inc., 22 Commerce Road, Newtown CT 06470. **Tel** (203)426-0800, FAX (203)426-1964, telex 467615.

LC DA49
DD 355.00994 US
DEFENSE & AEROSPACE AGENCIES BRIEFING.
See Military and Defense.

LC DA49
DD 355.00994 US
DEFENSE & AEROSPACE COMPANIES.
See Military and Defense.

LC DA49
DD 355.00994 US
DEFENSE & AEROSPACE COMPANIES BRIEFING.
See Military and Defense.

LC DA49 **ISSN** 1056-747X
DD 355 US
CCC
TITLE CHANGE
DEFENSE & AEROSPACE ELECTRONICS.
See Military and Defense.

LC TL
DD 629 CN
DESIGNATED AIRSPACE HANDBOOK.
(19??)-. Periodical. English. Irregular. 56.10Can$ Canada; 61.70Can$ US; 90.15Can$ other. Receiver General for Canada / Canada Map Office, Canada Map Office, 615 Booth, Ottawa Ontario K1A 0E9 Canada. **Tel** (613)998-3865, FAX (613)957-8861, telex 0534328.

LC TL500.5 .A2 HE9768
DD 387.7 S 387.7/025 CN
DESIGNATORS FOR AIRCRAFT OPERATING AGENCIES, AERONAUTICAL AUTHORITIES AND SERVICES = INDICATIFS DES EXPLOITANTS D'AERONEF ET DES ADMINISTRATIONS ET SERVICES AERONAUTIQUES / DESIGNADORES DE EMPRESAS EXPLOTADORAS DE AERONAVES, DE ENTIDADES OFICIALES Y DE SERVICIOS AERONAUTICOS.
Main/Corp International Civil Aviation Organization. **Added/Corp** International Civil Aviation Organization. Indicatifs des Exploitants d'Aeronef et des Administrations et Services Aeronautiques. International Civil Aviation Organization. Designadores de Empresas Explotadoras de Aeronaves, de Entidades Oficiales y de Servicios Aeronauticos. International Civil Aviation Organization. Uslovnye Oboznacheniia Letno-Ekspluatatsionnykh Agentstv, Aviatsionnykh Polnomochnykh Organov i Sluzhb. **VFOAT** Indicatifs des Exploitants d'Aeronef et des Administrations et Services Aeronautiques; Designadores de Empresas Explotadoras de Aeronaves, de Entidades Oficiales y de Servicios Aeronauticos. (19??)-. English (French, Spanish and Russian). Four times a year. 160.00Can$. International Civil Aviation Organization / ICAO, 1000 Sherbrooke Street West, Suite 400, Montreal Quebec H3A 2R2 Canada. **Tel** (514)285-8026, (514)285-8022, telex 05-24514.

LC TL720.A1 I57
DD 387.7/4/0212 CN
DIGEST OF STATISTICS (INTERNATIONAL CIVIL AVIATION ORGANIZATION).
See Aeronautics, Astronautics-Abstracting, Bibliographies and Statistics.

LC TL **ISSN** 0074-2422
DD 629 CN
UDC 31:656.7
DIGEST OF STATISTICS - INTERNATIONAL CIVIL AVIATION ORGANIZATION. SERIES AT, AIRPORT TRAFFIC.
VFOAT Recueil de Statistiques - Organisation de l'Sviation Civile Internationale. Serie AT, Trafic d'Aeroport; Compendio Estadistico - Organizacion de Aviacion Civil Internacional. Serie AT, Trafico de Aeropuertos; Statisticeskij Sbornik - Mezdunarodnaja Organizacija Grazdanskoj Aviacii. Serija AT, Obem Perevozok Cerez Aeroporty. (1960)-. Periodical. English. Three times a month. Price varies. International Civil Aviation Organization / ICAO, 1000 Sherbrooke Street West, Suite 400, Montreal Quebec H3A 2R2 Canada. **Tel** (514)285-8026, (514)285-8022, telex 05-24514.

LC TL **ISSN** 0074-2449
DD 629 CN
UDC 31:656.7
DIGEST OF STATISTICS - INTERNATIONAL CIVIL AVIATION ORGANIZATION. SERIES FP, FLEET-PERSONNEL.
VFOAT Recueil de Statistiques - Organisation de l'Aviation Civile Internationale. Serie FP, Materiel Volant-Personnel; Compendio Estadistico - Organizacion de Aviacion Civil Internacional. Serie FP, Material Volante-Personal; Statisticeskij Sbornik - Mezdunarodnaja Organizacija Grazdanskoj Aviacii. Serija FP, Samoletnyj Park-Licnyj Sostav. (1947)-. Periodical. English. Price varies. International Civil Aviation Organization / ICAO, 1000 Sherbrooke Street West, Suite 400, Montreal Quebec H3A 2R2 Canada. **Tel** (514)285-8026, (514)285-8022, telex 05-24514.

LC TL **ISSN** 0074-2457
DD 629 CN
UDC 31:656.7
DIGEST OF STATISTICS - INTERNATIONAL CIVIL AVIATION ORGANIZATION. SERIES R, CIVIL AIRCRAFT ON REGISTER.
VFOAT Recueil de Statistiques - Organisation de l'Aviation Civile Internationale. Serie R, Immatriculation des Aeronefs Civils; Compendio Estadistico - Organizacion de Aviacion

Aeronautics, Astronautics

Civil Internacional. Serie R, Aeronaves Civiles Matriculadas; Statisticeskij Sbornik - Mezdunarodnaja Organizacija Grazdanskoj Aviacii. Serija TF, Registrovyj Park Grazdanskih Vozdusnyh Sudov. (1961)-. Periodical. English. Price varies. International Civil Aviation Organization / ICAO, 1000 Sherbrooke Street West, Suite 400, Montreal Quebec H3A 2R2 Canada. **Tel** (514)285-8026, (514)285-8022, telex 05-24514.

LC TL
DD 629 US
DIGITAL AERONAUTICAL CHART SUPPLEMENT. SECTION 7, STANDARD INSTRUMENT DEPARTURES. VFOAT Standard Instrument Departures SIDS. Periodical. English. Two times a year. US Department of Defense / Defense Mapping Agency, 8613 Lee Highway, Fairfax VA 22031. **Tel** (703)285-9290, FAX (703)285-9374. *Continues Controller Chart Supplement. Section 7, Standard Instrument Departures : SIDS.*

LC HE9793.U5 D57 **ISSN** 0741-0166
DD 387.7/3352/0257 US
DIRECTORY OF HELICOPTER OPERATORS IN THE UNITED STATES, CANADA, MEXICO, AND PUERTO RICO. VFOAT A.I.A. Directory of Helicopter Operators. (198?)-. Directory. English. $6.95. Aerospace Industries Association of America, 1250 Eye Street Northwest, Washington DC 20005. **Tel** (202)371-8561, FAX (202)371-8470, telex 710-822-0134 AIA DC TKU. *Continues AIA Directory of Helicopter Operators.*

LC UG1423 .D57 **ISSN** 1055-579X
DD 358.4/6/025 US
DIRECTORY OF NORTH AMERICAN MILITARY AVIATION COMMUNICATIONS, VHF/UHF. CENTRAL. [Dir. North Am. mil. aviat. commun. VHF/UHF, Cent.]. (1991)-. Directory. English. Hunterdon Aero Publishers, PO Box 754, Flemington NJ 08822.

LC UG1423 .D572 **ISSN** 1055-582X
DD 358.4/6/02574 US
DIRECTORY OF NORTH AMERICAN MILITARY AVIATION COMMUNICATIONS, VHF/UHF. NORTHEASTERN. [Dir. North Am. mil. aviat. commun. VHF/UHF, Northeast.]. (1991)-. Directory. English. Hunterdon Aero Publishers, PO Box 754, Flemington NJ 08822.

LC HE9761 **ISSN** 1055-5803
DD 387.7 US
DIRECTORY OF NORTH AMERICAN MILITARY AVIATION COMMUNICATIONS, VHF/UHF. SOUTHEASTERN. [Dir. North Am. mil. aviat. commun. VHF/UHF, Southeast.]. (1990/1991 Ed.)-. Directory. English. Huntedon Aero Publishers, PO Box 754, Flemington NJ 08822.

LC UG1423 .D573 **ISSN** 1055-5811
DD 358.4/6/02578 US
DIRECTORY OF NORTH AMERICAN MILITARY AVIATION COMMUNICATIONS, VHF/UHF. WESTERN. [Dir. North Am. mil. aviat. commun. VHF/UHF, West.]. (1990/1991)-. Directory. English. Hunterdon Aero Publishers, PO Box 754, Flemington NJ 08822.

LC TL788.3 .D57
DD 629.4/.025/41 UK
DIRECTORY OF UK SPACE CAPABILITIES. **Added/Corp** British National Space Centre. **VAT** Directory of United Kingdom Space Capabilities. (1987)-. Directory. English. Irregular. Free on request. British National Space Centre, Dean Bradley House Horse Ferry, London SW1 P2AG United Kingdom. **Tel** 011 44 171 276288, FAX 011 44 171 8215387.

LC K **ISSN** 0012-3390
DD 340 IT
DIRITTO AEREO. See Law.

LC TL
DD 629 IT
DIRITTO E PRATICA DELL'AVIAZIONE CIVILE. (19??)-. Periodical. Italian. Two times a year. L34030. Edizioni Scientifiche Italiane, Via Chiatamone 7, 80121 Naples Italy. **Tel** 011 39 81 7645768, 011 39 81 7645443, FAX 011 39 81 7646477.

LC TL **ISSN** 1061-1231
DD 629 US
DISPATCH (MIDLAND, TEX.), THE. (THE DISPATCH.). [Dispatch]. **Added/Corp** American Airpower Heritage Group. Confederate Air Force. (19??)-. Periodical. English. Four times a year. $38.00. Confederate Air Force, 9600 Wright Drive, Midland TX 79711. **Tel** (915)563-1000. *Continues CAF Dispatch.*

LC TL526.G3 D39a **ISSN** 0937-0420
DD 629.1 GW
CCC
DLR-NACHRICHTEN : MITTEILUNGSBLATT DER DEUTSCHEN FORSCHUNGSANSTALT FUER LUFT- UND RAUMFAHRT. **Added/Corp** Deutsche Forschungsanstalt fuer Luft- und Raumfahrt. **VFOAT** DLR Nachrichten; Mitteilungsblatt der Deutschen Forschungsanstalt fuer Luft- und Raumfahrt. (June 1989)-. German. Irregular. Free on request. Deutsche Forschungs Luft + Raumfahrt, Postfach 906058, D-51126 Cologne Germany. **Tel** 011 49 2203 6010, FAX 011 49 2203 67310. *Continues DFVLR Nachrichten.*
Ind/Abst Ei Page One; Int. Aerosp. Abstr.

LC TL587 .D38A **ISSN** 0278-1956
DD 629.132/54 US
DMA AERONAUTICAL CHART MONTHLY BULLETIN. [DMA aeronaut. chart mont. bull.]. **VFOAT** Aeronautical Chart Monthly Bulletin. **VAT** Defense Mapping Agency Chart Monthly Bulletin. Bulletin. English. Twelve times a year. US Department of Defense / Defense Mapping Agency, 8613 Lee Highway, Fairfax VA 22031. **Tel** (703)285-9290, FAX (703)285-9374. *Continues DMA Aeronautical Chart Bulletin, 0194-1887.*

LC TL587 .D38B **ISSN** 0195-3702
DD 629.132/54/05 US
DMA AERONAUTICAL CHART UPDATING MANUAL, CHUM. **Main/Corp** Aerospace Center (U.S.). **VAT** Defense Mapping Agency Aeronautical Chart Updating Manual. Chart Updating Manual. (Sept. 1977)-. English. Two times a year. Defense Mapping Agency / St Louis, Aerospace Center, St. Louis Air Force Station, St Louis MO 63118.

LC TL716.A1 W67 **ISSN** 1050-8910
DD 387.7/3352/021 US
DMS WORLD HELICOPTER INVENTORY & FORECAST. [DMS world helicopter inventory forecast]. **Added/Corp** Defense Marketing Services, Inc. Jane's Information Group. **VFOAT** DMS World Helicopter Inventory and Forecast; World Helicopter Inventory & Forecast; World Helicopter Inventory and Forecast. **VAT** Defense Marketing Services World Helicopter Inventory and Forecast. (1988)-. English. Jane's Information Group, Sentinel House, 163 Brighton Road, Coulsdon Surrey CR5 2NH United Kingdom. **Tel** 011 44 181 7631030, FAX 011 44 181 7630276, telex 916907-JANES-G. *Continues World Helicopter Forecast, 8755-0830.*

LC TL **ISSN** 0012-5563
DD 629 GW
DORNIER-POST. [Dornier-post]. (1935)-. Trade Publication. English.
Ind/Abst Coal Abstr.; Energy Res. Abstr. (Apr. 1975-); Int. Aerosp. Abstr.; Pollut. Abstr. Indexes.

LC TL685.15 .U45 **ISSN** 0894-1289
DD 629.133/343 US
TITLE CHANGE
EAA EXPERIMENTER. [EAA exp.]. **Added/Corp** Experimental Aircraft Association. **VFOAT** Experimenter. **VAT** Experimental Aircraft Association Experimenter. Vol. 7, No. 5 (May 1987)-Vol. 15, No. 1 (Jan. 1995). Periodical. English. Experimental Aircraft Association Inc., PO Box 3086, Oshkosh WI 54903-3086. **Tel** (414)426-4800, FAX (414)426-4828. **ED** Mary J. Jones. Bk Rev. Ad Acc. Circ: 6,500 (ctrl) *Continues EAA Light Plane World, 8750-7579.* *Continued by Experimenter (Oshkosh, Wis.), 1084-6441.*
Ind/Abst Index Inf. (1990-?).

LC GV750 **ISSN** 1070-566X
DD 797.5 US
●**EAA SPORT AVIATION FOR KIDS.** [EAA sport aviat. kids]. **Added/Corp** Experimental Aircraft Association. **VFOAT** Sport Aviation for Kids. Vol. 1, No. 1 (Jan./Feb. 1993)-. Periodical. English. Six times a year (Jan., Mar., May, July, Sept., Nov.). $15.00. Experimental Aircraft Association Inc., PO Box 3086, Oshkosh WI 54903-3086. **Tel** (414)426-4800, FAX (414)426-4828.
Desc: Dedicated to building interest in aviation among young people.

LC TL796.6.E2 E37 **ISSN** 1061-5067
DD 629.43/4/0216 US
EARTH SATELLITE CATALOG. [Earth satell. cat.]. **Added/Corp** Space Analysis and Research, Inc. **VAT** Catalog. (July 1991)-. Catalog. English. Two times a year. Space Analysis Research, Inc., 6957 Blackhawk Place, Colorado Springs CO 80919. **Tel** (719)260-0500, (719)599-3886.

LC UG622 .E23
DD 358 JA
EAWARUDO = AIR WORLD. See Military and Defense.

LC TL
DD 629 US
ECONOMIC REGULATIONS. PT. 214. TERMS, CHARTERS, AND LIMITATIONS OF FOREIGN AIR CARRIER PERMITS AUTHORIZING CHARTER TRANSPORTATION ONLY. **Main/Corp** United States. Civil Aeronautics Board. **VFOAT** Terms, Charters, and Limitations of Foreign Air Carrier Permits Authorizing Charter Transportation Only. Periodical. English. Civil Aeronautics Board, 1825 Connecticut Avenue, Washington DC 20428. **Tel** (202)673-5174.

LC HE9761 **ISSN** 1183-7861
DD 387.7 CN
EDMONTON & AREA AVIATION BUSINESS DIRECTORY. [Edmont. area aviat. bus. dir.]. **VFOAT** Edmonton and Area Aviation Business Directory. (1991/92)-. Directory. English. Consolidated Communications, 807 Manning Road Northeast, Suite 200, Calgary Alberta T2E 7M8 Canada. **Tel** (403)569-9520, FAX (403)569-9590. *Continues Edmonton & Area Airport Business Directory., 0823-8200.*

LC TL521.3.R4 U5a
DD 629.4/071073 US
EDUCATIONAL HORIZONS / NATIONAL AERONAUTICS AND SPACE ADMINISTRATION, EDUCATION DIVISION, EDUCATION PUBLICATIONS BRANCH. **Added/Corp** United States. National Aeronautics and Space Administration. Educational Publications Branch. **VFOAT** NASA Educational Horizons. Vol. 1, No. 1 (Feb. 1992)-. Periodical. English. Three times a year. Free on request. NASA - National Aeronautics and Space Administration, LCG 9 NASA Headquarters, Washington DC 20546. *Continues Report to Educators, 0883-0983.*

LC TK7805 .E14
DD 338.4/7/62138102573 US
EIA GUIDE. See Electronics.

LC TL **ISSN** 0170-5288
DD 629 GW
UDC 629.4
EISENBAHN-KURIER. (1966)-. Trade Publication. German. Irregular (monthly 4 issues of EK Special). $167.04. Eisenbahn-Kurier, Postfach 5560, D-78022 Freiburg, Breis Germany. **Tel** 011 49 761 703100, FAX 011 49 761 7031050.

LC TL570
DD 629.132 US
ENROUTE HIGH ALTITUDE, U.S. VFOAT United States Government Flight Information Publication. Periodical. English. Six times a year (issued every eight weeks). Defense Mapping Agency / St Louis, Aerospace Center, St. Louis Air Force Station, St Louis MO 63118.

LC TL
DD 629 CN
ENROUTE HIGH ALTITUDE CHARTS. (19??)-. English. Seven times a year. 28.10Can$ Canada; 31.80Can$ US; 58.00Can$ other. Receiver General for Canada / Canada Map Office, Canada Map Office, 615 Booth, Ottawa Ontario K1A 0E9 Canada. **Tel** (613)998-3865, FAX (613)957-8861, telex 0534328.

LC TL
DD 629 CN
ENROUTE LOW ALTITUDE CHARTS. (19??)-. English. Seven times a year. 58.14Can$. Receiver General for Canada / Canada Map Office, Canada Map Office, 615 Booth, Ottawa Ontario K1A 0E9 Canada. **Tel** (613)998-3865, FAX (613)957-8861, telex 0534328.

LC TL787 .E88a **ISSN** 0376-4265
DD 629.4/06/24 FR
CODEN ESABD8
Pr Rev.
ESA BULLETIN. [ESA bull.]. **Main/Corp** European Space Agency. **Added/Corp** European Space Agency. Bulletin ASE. **VFOAT** Bulletin ASE. **VAT** European Space Agency Bulletin. (June 1975)-. Bulletin. English (French). Free on request. ESA Estec, c/o De Zwaan, PO Box 299, 2200 AB Noordwijk Netherlands. **Tel** 011 31 1719 83405, FAX 011 31 1719 17408. **ED** B. Battrick. Ad Acc. ctrl circ. Documents available from The Genuine Article, Ask*IEEE. *Continues E.S.R.O., E.L.D.O. Bulletin.*
Ind/Abst Curr. Contents Eng. Comput. Technol.; EMBASE; Ergon. Abstr.; Geogr. Abstr. Phys. Geogr.; INSPEC (May 1977-); Int. Aerosp. Abstr.; Res. Alert [Select. Cov.].

LC TL787 .E88c **ISSN** 0379-2285
DD 500.5/05 FR
CODEN ESAJDW
Pr Rev. CEASED
ESA JOURNAL. [ESA j.]. **Added/Corp** European Space Agency. (1977)-(19??). Academic Scholarly Publication. English (French). ESA Estec, c/o De Zwaan, PO Box 299, 2200 AB Noordwijk Netherlands. **Tel** 011 31 1719 83405, FAX 011 31 1719 17408. **ED** B. Battrick. Ad

Aeronautics, Astronautics

Acc. ctrl circ. Documents available from Article Express International, The Genuine Article, Ask*IEEE. *Continues ESA Scientific and Technical Review.*
Desc: Journal of the European Space Agency.
Ind/Abst Bioeng. Abstr.; Curr. Cit.; Curr. Contents Eng. Comput. Technol.; Ecol. Abstr. (?-?); Ei Page One; EMBASE; Energy Res. Abstr. (Oct. 1979-); Eng. Index Annu.; Ergon. Abstr.; Geogr. Abstr. Phys. Geogr.; GeoRef; INSPEC (1977-); Int. Aerosp. Abstr.; Res. Alert [Full Cov.]; Sci. Cit. Index; SCISEARCH.

LC TL **ISSN** 0379-6566
DD 629 FR
 CODEN ESPUD4
ESA SP. [ESA SP]. Added/Corp European Space Agency.
VAT European Space Agency SP. (19??)-. Monographic series. English (French). European Space Agency, 8 10 rue Mario Nikis, 75738 Paris Cedex 15 France. **Tel** 011 33 1 42737291, telex 02746. Documents available from Ask*IEEE, CASDDS.
Ind/Abst Chem. Abstr.; Curr. Cit.; INSPEC.

LC HE9850.A1 H95a
DD 629.13 GR
ETESIA EKTHESIS PEPRAGMENON - HYPERESIA POLITIKES AEROPORIAS.
Main/Corp Greece. Hyperesia Politikes Aeroporias. (19??)-. Greek, Modern. Hyperesia Politikes Aeroporias 1 Hellenikon, Athens Greece.

LC TL788.3 .E94 **ISSN** 0765-0574
DD 629.4/025/4 FR
EUROPEAN SPACE DIRECTORY.
Added/Corp Eurospace. (1986)-. English. One time a year. $208.01. Sevig Press Publishing, 6 rue Bellart, F-75015 Paris France. **Tel** 011 33 1 42732837.

LC TL **ISSN** 0940-0842
DD 629 GW
UDC 62
EUROPEAN SPACE REPORT. (1990)-.
Periodical. English. Four times a year. European Space Report, PO Box 140280, D-80452 Munich Germany. **Tel** 011 49 89 8343051.

LC HE9761 **ISSN** 0746-9446
DD 387.7 US
EXECUTIVE AIR GUIDE. (19??)-. English.
Twelve times a year. $20.00. Executive Air Guide / Oakwood, Old Mundy Mill Road, Route 2 Box 127, Oakwood GA 30566.

LC TL
DD 629 US
EXPERIMENTAL AIRCRAFT ASSOCIATION. ANTIQUE CLASSIC DIVISION.
English. Irregular. $20.00. Experimental Aircraft Association Inc., PO Box 3086, Oshkosh WI 54903-3086. **Tel** (414)426-4800, **FAX** (414)426-4828.

LC TL **ISSN** 1062-8576
DD 629 US
EXPERIMENTAL ROCKET FLYER. (1992)-.
Periodical. English. Four times a year. $15.00. California Rocketry, Box 1242, Claremont CA 91711. **Tel** 800-266-6913. **ED** Jerry Irvine. Index available. cum. index. **Bk Rev. Ad Acc. Circ:** 2,000.

LC TL685.15 .U45 **ISSN** 1084-6441
DD 629.133/343 US
●EXPERIMENTER (OSHKOSH, WIS.).
(EXPERIMENTER.). [Experimenter]. **Added/Corp** Experimental Aircraft Association. **VFOAT** EAA Experimenter. Vol. 16, No. 2 (Feb. 1995)-. Periodical. English. Twelve times a year. Experimental Aircraft Association Inc., PO Box 3086, Oshkosh WI 54903-3086. **Tel** (414)426-4800, **FAX** (414)426-4828. **ED** Mary J. Jones. *Continues EAA Experimenter, 0894-1289.*
Desc: Contents include information for designing, building and flying aircraft. Features emphasis on technical, how-to aspects.

LC HE9803.A1 O36a **ISSN** 0276-9212
DD 387.7/4/0973 US
FAA AVIATION FORECASTS. [FAA aviat.
forecasts]. **Added/Corp** United States. Office of Aviation Policy. United States. Office of Aviation Policy and Plans. United States. Federal Aviation Administration. **VAT** Federal Aviation Administration Aviation Forecasts. (1989)-. Government Publication. English. Four times a year. $25.00. US Department of Transportation / Federal Aviation Administration, 800 Independence Avenue Southwest, Washington DC 20591. **Tel** (202)367-3484, **FAX** (202)367-3505. **(Subscription address:** Superintendent of Documents, US Government Printing Office, Washington DC 20402. **)** available on microfiche. *Continues Aviation Forecasts, Fiscal Years ..., 0565-4831.*
Ind/Abst F&S Index Plus Text, Int. [Select. Cov.]; Predicasts Forecasts.

LC HE9761.1 .F18 **ISSN** 1057-9648
DD 387.7/0973 US
FAA AVIATION NEWS (1987). (FAA
AVIATION NEWS : A DOT/FAA FLIGHT STANDARDS SAFETY PUBLICATION.). [FAA aviat. news]. **Added/Corp** United States. Flight Standards Service. Accident Prevention Program Branch. **VFOAT** Aviation News. **VAT** Federal Aviation Administration Aviation News. Vol. 26, No. 2, March-April (1987)-. Government Publication. English. Eight times a year. $26.00. US Department of Transportation / US Coast Guard, 2100 Second Street Southwest, Washington DC 20953-0001. **Tel** (202)267-2229. **(Subscription address:** Superintendent of Documents, US Government Printing Office, Washington DC 20402. **)** available on microfilm and microfiche from University Microfilms International (UMI). *Continues FAA General Aviation News.*
Desc: Designed to help airmen become safer pilots; also aimed at student pilots and ground personnel concerned with flight safety. Gives updates and major FAA Federal Aviation Administration rule changes and proposed changes, as well as refresher information on flight rules, maintenance airworthiness, avionics, accident analysis, and other related topics. Covers all types of aircraft, including helicopters, balloons, gliders, antique, sport and experimental.
Ind/Abst Aviat. Tradescan [Full Cov.].

LC TL553.5 .F29 TL553.5 .F33 **ISSN** 1056-2761
DD 363.12/45/0973 US
FAA AVIATION SAFETY JOURNAL. [FAA
aviat. saf. j.]. **Added/Corp** United States. Federal Aviation Administration. United States. Office of the Assistant Administrator for Aviation Safety. Safety Information Staff. **VFOAT** Aviation Safety Journal. **VAT** Federal Aviation Administration Aviation Safety Journal. Vol. 1, No. 1 (Winter 1991)-. Government Publication. English. Four times a year. US Department of Transportation / Federal Aviation Administration, 800 Independence Avenue Southwest, Washington DC 20591. **Tel** (202)367-3484, **FAX** (202)367-3505.
Ind/Abst Aviat. Tradescan [Full Cov.].

LC HE9761 **ISSN** 0427-8011
DD 387.7 US
FAA HORIZONS. Periodical. English. Twelve times
a year. US Government Printing Office / National Aeronautics and Space Administration, 600 Independence Avenue SW, Washington DC 20546. **Tel** (202)453-1000.

LC HE9803.A1 F43f
DD 353.008/77/025 US
FAA ORGANIZATIONAL DIRECTORY / U.S. DEPARTMENT OF TRANSPORTATION, FEDERAL AVIATION ADMINISTRATION. Main/Corp
United States. Federal Aviation Administration. **VFOAT** Federal Aviation Administration Organizational Directory; Organizational Directory; FAA Directory. (19??)-. Directory. English. US Department of Transportation / Federal Aviation Administration, 800 Independence Avenue Southwest, Washington DC 20591. **Tel** (202)367-3484, **FAX** (202)367-3505. *Continues United States. Federal Aviation Administration. FAA Directory, 0192-057X.*

LC TL521 .A41612 **ISSN** 0566-9618
DD 387.7/0973 US
FAA STATISTICAL HANDBOOK OF AVIATION. Added/Corp United States. Federal
Aviation Agency. United States. Federal Aviation Administration. **VAT** Federal Aviation Agency Statistical Handbook of Aviation; Federal Aviation Administration Statistical Handbook of Aviation. (1959)-. Statistical Publication. English. One time a year. Superintendent of Documents, US Government Printing Office, Washington DC 20402. **Tel** (202)275-3328, **FAX** (202)786-2377. *Continues CAA Statistical Handbook of Civil Aviation.*
Ind/Abst Predicasts Forecasts.

LC TL
DD 629 CN
FACILITATION; INTERNATIONAL STANDARDS AND RECOMMENDED PRACTICES. ANNEX 9 TO THE CONVENTION ON INTERNATIONAL CIVIL AVIATION. Main/Corp International Civil
Aviation Organization. (19??)-. English. $10.00. International Civil Aviation Organization / ICAO, 1000 Sherbrooke Street West, Suite 400, Montreal Quebec H3A 2R2 Canada. **Tel** (514)285-8026, (514)285-8022, telex 05-24514.

LC HE9761 **ISSN** 8756-579X
DD 387.7 US
FALCON DIGEST. Periodical. English. Irregular.
Free. MIALR Eastern Airlines, Miami International Airport, Corporate Communications Building 16/Room 805, Miami FL 33148.

LC TL
DD 629 FR
FANATIQUE DE L'AVIATION. (19??)-.
French. Twelve times a year. 285.00F (one-year), 520.00F (two-year) France; 340.00F (one-year), 640.00F (two-year) other. Editions Lariviere Naryse Mearn, 15 17 Quai de l Oise Sec. Abonn., 75166 Paris Cedex 19 France. **Tel** 011 33 1 40342207, **FAX** 011 33 1 40358441, telex 211678.

LC KF2400.A329 F38 **ISSN** 0092-3532
DD 343/.73/09705 US
FEDERAL AVIATION REGULATIONS & AIRMAN'S INFORMATION MANUAL: BASIC REFERENCE BOOK. Added/Corp
Aero Products Research, Inc. Aviation Education Dept. (19??)-. English. Irregular. Aero Products Research Inc, 11201 Hindry, Los Angeles CA 90045.

LC TL
DD 629 US
FEDERAL AVIATION REGULATIONS. PART 1. DEFINITIONS AND ABBREVIATIONS. Main/Corp United States.
Federal Aviation Administration. **VFOAT** Definitions and Abbreviations. (19??)-. Periodical. English. One time a year (supplements). $30.00 US; $37.50 other. US Department of Transportation / Federal Aviation Administration, 800 Independence Avenue Southwest, Washington DC 20591. **Tel** (202)367-3484, **FAX** (202)367-3505.

LC TL
DD 629 US
FEDERAL AVIATION REGULATIONS. PART 11. GENERAL RULE-MAKING PROCEDURES. Main/Corp United States. Federal
Aviation Administration. **VFOAT** General Rule-Making Procedures. Government Publication. English. One time a year (supplements). $27.00 US; $33.75 other. US Department of Transportation / Federal Aviation Administration, 800 Independence Avenue Southwest, Washington DC 20591. **Tel** (202)367-3484, **FAX** (202)367-3505.

LC TL
DD 629 US
FEDERAL AVIATION REGULATIONS. PART 13. ENFORCEMENT PROCEDURES. Main/Corp United States. Federal
Aviation Administration. **VFOAT** Enforcement Procedures. Government Publication. English. One time a year (supplements). $30.00 US; $37.50 other. US Department of Transportation / Federal Aviation Administration, 800 Independence Avenue Southwest, Washington DC 20591. **Tel** (202)367-3484, **FAX** (202)367-3505.
Desc: Investigation and enforcement procedures.

LC TL
DD 629 US
FEDERAL AVIATION REGULATIONS. PART 21. CERTIFICATION PROCEDURES FOR PRODUCTS AND PARTS. Main/Corp United States. Federal Aviation
Administration. **VFOAT** Certification Procedures for Products and Parts. Government Publication. English. One time a year (supplements). $34.00 US; $42.50 other. US Department of Transportation / Federal Aviation Administration, 800 Independence Avenue Southwest, Washington DC 20591. **Tel** (202)367-3484, **FAX** (202)367-3505.

LC TL
DD 629 US
FEDERAL AVIATION REGULATIONS. PART 23. AIRWORTHINESS STANDARDS, NORMAL, UTILITY, AND ACROBATIC CATEGORY AIRPLANES.
Main/Corp United States. Federal Aviation Administration. **VFOAT** Airworthiness Standards, Normal, Utility, and Acrobatic Category Airplanes. (19??)-. Government Publication. English. One time a year (supplements). $35.00 US; $43.75 other. US Department of Transportation / Federal Aviation Administration, 800 Independence Avenue Southwest, Washington DC 20591. **Tel** (202)367-3484, **FAX** (202)367-3505.

LC TL
DD 629 US
FEDERAL AVIATION REGULATIONS. PART 25. AIRWORTHINESS STANDARDS, TRANSPORT CATEGORY AIRPLANES. Main/Corp United
States. Federal Aviation Administration. **VFOAT** Airworthiness Standards, Transport Category Airplanes. Government Publication. English. One time a year (supplements). $39.00 US; $48.75 other. US Department of Transportation / Federal Aviation Administration, 800 Independence Avenue Southwest, Washington DC 20591. **Tel** (202)367-3484, **FAX** (202)367-3505.

LC TL
DD 629 US
FEDERAL AVIATION REGULATIONS. PART 27. AIRWORTHINESS STANDARDS, NORMAL CATEGORY ROTORCRAFT. Main/Corp United States. Federal
Aviation Administration. **VFOAT** Airworthiness Standards, Normal Category Rotorcraft. Government Publication. English. One time a year (supplements). $35.00 US; $43.75 other. US Department of Transportation / Federal

Aeronautics, Astronautics

Aviation Administration, 800 Independence Avenue Southwest, Washington DC 20591. **Tel** (202)367-3484, FAX (202)367-3505.

LC TL
DD 629 US
FEDERAL AVIATION REGULATIONS. PART 29. AIRWORTHINESS STANDARDS, TRANSPORT CATEGORY ROTORCRAFT. **Main/Corp** United States. Federal Aviation Administration. **VFOAT** Airworthiness Standards, Transport Category Rotorcraft. Government Publication. English. One time a year (supplements). $36.00 US; $45.00 other. US Department of Transportation / Federal Aviation Administration, 800 Independence Avenue Southwest, Washington DC 20591. **Tel** (202)367-3484, FAX (202)367-3505.

LC TL
DD 629 US
FEDERAL AVIATION REGULATIONS. PART 31. AIRWORTHINESS STANDARDS, MANNED FREE BALLOONS. **Main/Corp** United States. Federal Aviation Administration. **VFOAT** Airworthiness Standards, Manned Free Balloons. Government Publication. English. US Department of Transportation / Federal Aviation Administration, 800 Independence Avenue Southwest, Washington DC 20591. **Tel** (202)367-3484, FAX (202)367-3505.

LC TL
DD 629 US
FEDERAL AVIATION REGULATIONS. PART 33. AIRWORTHINESS STANDARDS, AIRCRAFT ENGINES. **Main/Corp** United States. Federal Aviation Administration. **VFOAT** Airworthiness Standards, Aircraft Engines. (19??)-. Government Publication. English. One time a year (supplements). $27.00 US; $33.75 other. US Department of Transportation / Federal Aviation Administration, 800 Independence Avenue Southwest, Washington DC 20591. **Tel** (202)367-3484, FAX (202)367-3505.

LC TL
DD 629 US
FEDERAL AVIATION REGULATIONS. PART 36. NOISE STANDARDS, AIRCRAFT TYPE AND AIRWORTHINESS CERTIFICATION. **Main/Corp** United States. Federal Aviation Administration. **VFOAT** Noise Standards, Aircraft Type and Airworthiness Certification. Government Publication. English. One time a year (supplements). $32.00 US; $40.00 other. US Department of Transportation / Federal Aviation Administration, 800 Independence Avenue Southwest, Washington DC 20591. **Tel** (202)367-3484, FAX (202)367-3505.

LC TL
DD 629 US
FEDERAL AVIATION REGULATIONS. PART 37. TECHNICAL STANDARD ORDER AUTHORIZATION. **Main/Corp** United States. Federal Aviation Administration. **VFOAT** Technical Standard Order Authorization. Government Publication. English. US Department of Transportation / Federal Aviation Administration, 800 Independence Avenue Southwest, Washington DC 20591. **Tel** (202)367-3484, FAX (202)367-3505.

LC TL671.1 .U65a **ISSN** 0276-1785
DD 629.134/3/05 US
FEDERAL AVIATION REGULATIONS. PART 39, AIRWORTHINESS DIRECTIVES. [Fed. aviat. regul., Part 39 Airworth. dir.]. **Main/Corp** United States. Federal Aviation Administration. **VFOAT** Airworthiness Directives; Summary of Airworthiness Directives for Small Aircraft; Summary of Airworthiness Directives for Large Aircraft. (19??)-. English. One time a year. FAA Aeronautical Center, Box 25461, Oklahoma City OK 73125. **Tel** (405)954-6901, FAX (405)954-4104.
 Desc: Published in two volumes. Volume I - small aircraft - 12,500 lbs or less. Volume II - large aircraft - more than 12,500 lbs. Each volume contains two books.

LC TL
DD 629 US
FEDERAL AVIATION REGULATIONS. PART 61. CERTIFICATION, PILOTS AND FLIGHT INSTRUCTORS. **Main/Corp** United States. Federal Aviation Administration. **VFOAT** Certification, Pilots and Flight Instructors. Government Publication. English. One time a year (supplements). $33.00 US; $41.25 other. US Department of Transportation / Federal Aviation Administration, 800 Independence Avenue Southwest, Washington DC 20591. **Tel** (202)367-3484, FAX (202)367-3505.

LC TL
DD 629 US
FEDERAL AVIATION REGULATIONS. PART 63. CERTIFICATION, FLIGHT CREWMEMBERS OTHER THAN PILOTS. **Main/Corp** United States. Federal Aviation Administration. **VFOAT** Certification, Flight Crewmembers other than Pilots. Periodical. English. One time a year (supplements). $25.00 US; $31.25 other. Certification Flight Crewmembers Other Than Pilots, US Department of Transportation, Federal Aviation Administration, Washington DC 20402.

LC TL
DD 629 US
FEDERAL AVIATION REGULATIONS. PART 67. MEDICAL STANDARDS AND CERTIFICATION. **Main/Corp** United States. Federal Aviation Administration. **VFOAT** Medical Standards and Certification. Government Publication. English. US Department of Transportation / Federal Aviation Administration, 800 Independence Avenue Southwest, Washington DC 20591. **Tel** (202)367-3484, FAX (202)367-3505.

LC TL
DD 629 US
FEDERAL AVIATION REGULATIONS. PART 91. GENERAL OPERATING AND FLIGHT RULES. **Main/Corp** United States. Federal Aviation Administration. **VFOAT** General Operating and Flight Rules. (19??)-. Government Publication. English. One time a year (supplements). $53.00 US; $66.25 other. US Department of Transportation / Federal Aviation Administration, 800 Independence Avenue Southwest, Washington DC 20591. **Tel** (202)367-3484, FAX (202)367-3505.

LC TL
DD 629 US
FEDERAL AVIATION REGULATIONS. PART 93. GENERAL AIR TRAFFIC RULES AND AIRPORT TRAFFIC PATTERNS. (FEDERAL AVIATION REGULATIONS. PART 93. SPECIAL AIR TRAFFIC RULES AND AIRPORT TRAFFIC PATTERNS.). **Main/Corp** United States. Federal Aviation Administration. **VFOAT** Special Air Traffic Rules and Airport Traffic Patterns. Government Publication. English. One time a year (supplements). $31.00 US; $38.75 other. US Department of Transportation / Federal Aviation Administration, 800 Independence Avenue Southwest, Washington DC 20591. **Tel** (202)367-3484, FAX (202)367-3505.

LC TL
DD 629 US
FEDERAL AVIATION REGULATIONS. PART 107. AIRPORT SECURITY. **Main/Corp** United States. Federal Aviation Administration. **VFOAT** Airport Security. Government Publication. English. US Department of Transportation / Federal Aviation Administration, 800 Independence Avenue Southwest, Washington DC 20591. **Tel** (202)367-3484, FAX (202)367-3505.

LC TL
DD 629 US
FEDERAL AVIATION REGULATIONS. PART 109. INDIRECT AIR CARRIER SECURITY. **Main/Corp** United States. Federal Aviation Administration. **VFOAT** Indirect Air Carrier Security. Government Publication. English. US Department of Transportation / Federal Aviation Administration, 800 Independence Avenue Southwest, Washington DC 20591. **Tel** (202)367-3484, FAX (202)367-3505.

LC TL
DD 629 US
FEDERAL AVIATION REGULATIONS. PART 121. CERTIFICATION AND OPERATIONS : DOMESTIC, FLAG, AND SUPPLEMENTAL AIR CARRIERS AND COMMERCIAL OPERATION UNITED STATES. FEDERAL AVIATION ADMINISTRATION. **Main/Corp** United States. Federal Aviation Administration. **VFOAT** Certification and Operations: Domestic, Flag, and Supplemental Air Carriers and Commercial Operation United States. Federal Aviation Administration. Government Publication. English. One time a year (supplements). $70.00 US; $87.50 other. US Department of Transportation / Federal Aviation Administration, 800 Independence Avenue Southwest, Washington DC 20591. **Tel** (202)367-3484, FAX (202)367-3505.

LC TL500
DD 629.13 US
FEDERAL AVIATION REGULATIONS. PART 123. CERTIFICATION AND OPERATIONS, AIR TRAVEL CLUBS USING LARGE AIRPLANES. **Main/Corp** United States. Federal Aviation Administration. **VFOAT** Certification and Operations, Air Travel Clubs Using Large Airplanes. (19??)-. Government Publication. English. Irregular (supplements). $60.00 US; $75.00 other. US Department of Transportation / Federal Aviation Administration, 800 Independence Avenue Southwest, Washington DC 20591. **Tel** (202)367-3484, FAX (202)367-3505.
 Desc: Prescribes the regulations necessary to administer the Federal civilian employee entitlements and allowances for per diem, travel, transportation, and relocation allowances.

LC TL
DD 629 US
FEDERAL AVIATION REGULATIONS. PART 127. CERTIFICATION AND OPERATIONS OF SCHEDULED AIR CARRIERS AND HELICOPTERS. **Main/Corp** United States. Federal Aviation Administration. **VFOAT** Certification and Operations of Scheduled Air Carriers and Helicopters. Government Publication. English. One time a year (supplements). $31.00 US; $38.75 other. US Department of Transportation / Federal Aviation Administration, 800 Independence Avenue Southwest, Washington DC 20591. **Tel** (202)367-3484, FAX (202)367-3505.

LC TL
DD 629 US
FEDERAL AVIATION REGULATIONS. PART 129. OPERATIONS OF FOREIGN AIR CARRIERS. **Main/Corp** United States. Federal Aviation Administration. **VFOAT** Operations of Foreign Air Carriers. (19??)-. Government Publication. English. One time a year (supplements). $29.00 US; $36.25 other. US Department of Transportation / Federal Aviation Administration, 800 Independence Avenue Southwest, Washington DC 20591. **Tel** (202)367-3484, FAX (202)367-3505.

LC TL
DD 629 US
FEDERAL AVIATION REGULATIONS. PART 133. ROTORCRAFT EXTERNAL-LOAD OPERATIONS. **Main/Corp** United States. Federal Aviation Administration. **VFOAT** Rotorcraft External-Load Operations. (19??)-. Government Publication. English. Irregular. US Department of Transportation / Federal Aviation Administration, 800 Independence Avenue Southwest, Washington DC 20591. **Tel** (202)367-3484, FAX (202)367-3505.

LC TL
DD 629 US
FEDERAL AVIATION REGULATIONS. PART 135. AIR TAXI OPERATORS AND COMMERCIAL OPERATORS OF SMALL AIRCRAFT. **Main/Corp** United States. Federal Aviation Administration. **VFOAT** Air Taxi Operators and Commercial Operators of Small Aircraft. Government Publication. English. One time a year (supplements). $43.00 US; $53.75 other. US Department of Transportation / Federal Aviation Administration, 800 Independence Avenue Southwest, Washington DC 20591. **Tel** (202)367-3484, FAX (202)367-3505.

LC TL
DD 629 US
FEDERAL AVIATION REGULATIONS. PART 137. AGRICULTURAL AIRCRAFT OPERATIONS. **Main/Corp** United States. Federal Aviation Administration. **VFOAT** Agricultural Aircraft Operations. Government Publication. English. One time a year (supplements). $32.00 US; $40.00 other. US Department of Transportation / Federal Aviation Administration, 800 Independence Avenue Southwest, Washington DC 20591. **Tel** (202)367-3484, FAX (202)367-3505.

LC TL
DD 629 US
FEDERAL AVIATION REGULATIONS. PART 139. CERTIFICATION AND OPERATIONS, LAND AIRPORTS SERVING CAB-CERTIFICATED SCHEDULED AIR CARRIERS. **Main/Corp** United States. Federal Aviation Administration. **VFOAT** Certification and Operations, Land Airports Serving Cab-Certificated Scheduled Air Carriers. Government Publication. English. One time a year (supplements). $14.00 US; $17.50 other. US Department of Transportation / Federal Aviation Administration, 800 Independence Avenue Southwest, Washington DC 20591. **Tel** (202)367-3484, FAX (202)367-3505.

LC TL
DD 629 US
FEDERAL AVIATION REGULATIONS. PART 145. REPAIR STATIONS. **Main/Corp** United States. Federal Aviation Administration. **VFOAT** Repair Stations. Government Publication. English. US

Aeronautics, Astronautics

Department of Transportation / Federal Aviation Administration, 800 Independence Avenue Southwest, Washington DC 20591. **Tel** (202)367-3484, FAX (202)367-3505.

LC TL
DD 629
US

FEDERAL AVIATION REGULATIONS. PART 147. AVIATION MAINTENANCE TECHNICIAN SCHOOLS. Main/Corp United States. Federal Aviation Administration. **VFOAT** Aviation Maintenance Technician Schools. Government Publication. English. US Department of Transportation / Federal Aviation Administration, 800 Independence Avenue Southwest, Washington DC 20591. **Tel** (202)367-3484, FAX (202)367-3505.

LC TL
DD 629
US

FEDERAL AVIATION REGULATIONS. PART 152. AIRPORT AID PROGRAM. Main/Corp United States. Federal Aviation Administration. **VFOAT** Airport Aid Program. Government Publication. English. One time a year (supplements). $31.00 US; $38.75 other. US Department of Transportation / Federal Aviation Administration, 800 Independence Avenue Southwest, Washington DC 20591. **Tel** (202)367-3484, FAX (202)367-3505.

LC TL
DD 629
US

FEDERAL AVIATION REGULATIONS. PART 159. NATIONAL CAPITAL AIRPORTS. Main/Corp United States. Federal Aviation Administration. **VFOAT** National Capital Airports. Government Publication. English. $30.00 US; $37.50 other. US Department of Transportation / Federal Aviation Administration, 800 Independence Avenue Southwest, Washington DC 20591. **Tel** (202)367-3484, FAX (202)367-3505.

LC TL
DD 629
US

FEDERAL AVIATION REGULATIONS. PART 183. REPRESENTATIVES OF THE ADMINISTRATOR. Main/Corp United States. Federal Aviation Administration. **VFOAT** Representatives of the Administrator. Government Publication. English. US Department of Transportation / Federal Aviation Administration, 800 Independence Avenue Southwest, Washington DC 20591. **Tel** (202)367-3484, FAX (202)367-3505.

LC TL
DD 629
US

FEDERAL AVIATION REGULATIONS. PART 191. WITHHOLDING SECURITY INFORMATION FROM DISCLOSURE UNDER THE AIR TRANSPORTATION SECURITY ACT OF 1974. Main/Corp United States. Federal Aviation Administration. **VFOAT** Withholding Security Information from Disclosure Under the Air Transportation Security Act of 1974. Government Publication. English. US Department of Transportation / Federal Aviation Administration, 800 Independence Avenue Southwest, Washington DC 20591. **Tel** (202)367-3484, FAX (202)367-3505.

LC TL
DD 629
ISSN 1040-5968
US

FEDERATION SPACE. (1990)-. Periodical. English. Six times a year. Pacific Rim Publishing Company, PO Box 99007, Anchorage AK 99509. **Tel** (907)272-7500, FAX (907)279-1037.

LC HE9898.5.A1 A37
DD 387.7/0996/11021
FJ

FIJI AIRCRAFT STATISTICS. Added/Corp Fiji. Bureau of Statistics. English. Government of Fiji / Bureau of Statistics, Box 2221, Suva Fiji Islands. **Tel** 011 679 315144. **Continues** Aircraft Statistics, Fiji.

LC TL
DD 629
ISSN 0899-4161
US

FINAL FRONTIER. [Final front.]. Vol. 1, No. 1 (April 1988)-. Periodical. English. Six times a year. $17.95. Final Frontier Publishing Company, 2400 Foshay Tower, Minneapolis MN 55402. **Tel** (612)331-3001, FAX (612)332-0034. **(Subscription address:** Kable Publishers Aide / Illinois, 308 East Hitt Street, Subscription Department, Mt. Morris IL 61054-1473. **Tel** (815)734-1261.) **ED** Tony Reichhardt. **Bk Rev. Ad Acc.** ctrl circ.
Desc: Covers international outer space exploration. Written for both space enthusiasts and professionals in the aerospace industry.

LC HE9782 .I61
DD 387.7068
CN

FINANCIAL DATA, COMMERCIAL AIR CARRIERS = RENSEIGNEMENTS FINANCIERS, TRANSPORTEURS AERIENS COMMERCIAUX = DATOS FINANCIEROS, TRANSPORTISTAS AEREOS COMERCIALES = FINANSOVYE DANNYE, KOMMERCHESKIE AVIAPEREVOZCHIKI. Added/Corp International Civil Aviation Organization. **VFOAT** Renseignements Financiers, Transporteurs Aeriens Commerciaux; Datos Financieros, Transportistas Aereos Comerciales; Finansovye Dannye, Kommercheskie Aviaperevozchiki. (19??)-. English (French, Russian and Spanish). Price varies. International Civil Aviation Organization / ICAO, 1000 Sherbrooke Street West, Suite 400, Montreal Quebec H3A 2R2 Canada. **Tel** (514)285-8026, (514)285-8022, telex 05-24514.

LC TL
DD 629
US

FISCAL YEAR BUDGET ESTIMATES - FEDERAL AVIATION ADMINISTRATION. See Finance-Public Finance.

LC TL504 .F38
DD 629.13
BL

FLAP INTERNACIONAL. (19??)-. Periodical. Portuguese. Twelve times a year. Pra a Franklin Roosevelt 108, S ao Paulo Brazil.

LC TL503 .A44
DD 629.13
GW

FLIEGER-REVUE. Added/Corp Gesellschaft fuer Sport und Technik. No. 203 (Jan. 1970)-. German. Twelve times a year. $24.84. Deutscher Judo Verband, Redaktion Ippon Segewaldweg 22, D-12557 Berlin Germany. **Tel** 011 49 711 210770, telex 051 678. **Continues** Aero-Sport.

LC TL
DD 629
US

FLIGHT GUIDE : EASTERN MANUAL. English. $16.50. Air Guide Publications, PO Box 1288, Long Beach CA 90713. **Tel** (213)437-3210.

LC TL
DD 629
US

FLIGHT GUIDE : WESTERN MANUAL. (19??)-. English. $15.50. Air Guide Publications, PO Box 1288, Long Beach CA 90713. **Tel** (213)437-3210.

LC TL501 .F5
DD 387.7/05
ISSN 0015-3710
UK
CCC

FLIGHT INTERNATIONAL. [Flight int.]. **Added/Corp** Royal Aero Club (Great Britain) United Service and Royal Aero Club (Great Britain). No. 2756 (Jan. 4, 1962)-. Trade Publication. English. One time a week (Thurs.). $220.00. Reed Business Publishing Group / England, Quadrant House, Quadrant Sutton Surrey, SM2 5AS United Kingdom. **Tel** 011 44 1444 445599, FAX 011 44 1444 440421. **(Subscription address:** Reed Electrical, Subscription Department, Garrard House 2 6 Homesdale Road, Bromley BR2 9WL United Kingdom. **Tel** 011 44 181 4028492, FAX 011 44 181 4028383.) available on microfilm and microfiche from University Microfilms International (UMI); available on an online database from Lexis-Nexis; (files 16,80,648/Full-Text) DIALOG; and DATA-STAR. Documents available from BLDSC, FAXON Xpress, The UnCover Company, SWETS, UMI Article Clearinghouse. **Continues** Flight (London : 1959); **Absorbed** Aeroplane.
Ind/Abst Curr. Technol. Index; F&S Index Plus Text, Int. [Full Txt.] [Select. Cov.]; Infomat Int. Bus.; Int. Aerosp. Abstr.; PROMT [Full Txt.]; Trade Ind. ASAP [Full Txt.]; Trade Ind. Index [Full Txt.]; World Text. Abstr.

LC TL
DD 629
UK

FLIGHT INTERNATIONAL DIRECTORY. PART 1, UNITED KINGDOM. (1988)-. Directory. English. Every 2 years. £44.00 UK; £56.00 US. Flight International Directory, PO Box 1315, Potters Bar, Hertfordshire EN6 1PU United Kingdom. **Tel** 011 44 1707 46952, FAX 011 44 1707 46936, telex 94019508. **ED** Malcolm Ginsberg. Index available. cum. index. **Bk Rev,** (Qty: 20). **Ad Acc, Adv Mgr:** Rowena Shelley, **Tel** 44 473 696661. **Circ:** 4,000. available on diskette.
Continues Flight International Directory of British Aviation.
Desc: A who's who of everyone and everything in the United Kingdom and Ireland flying scene; airports, airlines, air taxi operators, heliports, flying clubs, museums, organizations, trade and industry, press, training, civil and military aviation.

LC TL
DD 629
UK

FLIGHT INTERNATIONAL DIRECTORY. PART II, MAINLAND EUROPE AND IRELAND. VFOAT Flight International Directory. Part 2, Mainland Europe and Ireland. (1989)-. Directory.

English. Every 2 years. £45.00 UK; £57.00 US. Flight International Directory, PO Box 1315, Potters Bar, Hertfordshire EN6 1PU United Kingdom. **Tel** 011 44 1707 46952, FAX 011 44 1707 46936, telex 94019508. **ED** Malcolm Ginsberg. Index available. cum. index. **Bk Rev,** (Qty: 20). **Ad Acc. Circ:** 3,000. available on diskette.
Continues Flight International Directory of European Aviation.
Desc: A who's who of everyone and everything in the mainland Europe flying scene; airports, airlines, air taxi operators, flying clubs, museums, organizations, trade and industry, press, civil and military aviation.

LC TL501 .S665
DD 387.7/05
ISSN 0361-5030
US

FLIGHT OPERATIONS. Vol. 64 (Jan. 1975)-. Periodical. English. Twelve times a year. $15.00. Flight Operations, 2700 North Haskell Avenue, Dallas TX 75204. available on microfilm and microfiche from University Microfilms International (UMI). **Continues** Flight.

LC TL
DD 629
US

FLIGHT SAFETY BULLETIN. VFOAT U.S. Coast Guard Flight Safety Bulletin. Bulletin. English. US Department of Transportation / US Coast Guard, 2100 Second Street Southwest, Washington DC 20953-0001. **Tel** (202)267-2229.
Ind/Abst Health Saf. Sci. Abstr.

LC TL500
DD 629.13/0028/9
ISSN 0826-032X
CN

FLIGHT SAFETY BULLETIN. [Flight saf. bull.]. Bulletin. English. Twelve times a year. Free to members. Canadian Owners and Pilots Association, PO Box 734, Ottawa Ontario K1P 5S4 Canada. **Tel** (613)236-4901, FAX (613)236-8646. **ED** William N Peppler. **Bk Rev. Circ:** 20,000 (ctrl).
Desc: Aimed at general aviation, government regulations, and current situations (RE: general aviation), etc.

LC TL553.5 .F5564
DD 363.1/24/05
ISSN 1057-5588
US

FLIGHT SAFETY DIGEST (1988). (FLIGHT SAFETY DIGEST / FLIGHT SAFETY FOUNDATION.). [Flight saf. dig.]. **Added/Corp** Flight Safety Foundation. Vol. 7, No. 2 (Feb. 1988)-. Periodical. English. Twelve times a year. $95.00. Flight Safety Foundation Inc., 2200 Wilson Boulevard, Suite 500, Arlington VA 22201. **Tel** (703)522-8300, FAX (703)525-6047, telex 901176 FSF INC AGTN. **Continues** FSF Flight Safety Digest, 0898-5715.
Desc: Analyses of aviation statistics, accident and incident briefs and abstracts of information received by the FSF Jerry Lederer Aviation Safety Library.
Ind/Abst Aviat. Tradescan [Full Cov.].

LC TL
DD 629
ISSN 1057-557X
US
CEASED

FLIGHT SAFETY FOUNDATION NEWS. [Flight Saf. Found. news]. **Added/Corp** Flight Safety Foundation. (19??)-Vol. 35 (1995). Newsletter. English. Flight Safety Foundation Inc., 2200 Wilson Boulevard, Suite 500, Arlington VA 22201. **Tel** (703)522-8300, FAX (703)525-6047, telex 901176 FSF INC AGTN. **Continues** Newsletter / Flight Safety Foundation., 0428-5735.
Desc: Communicates the Foundation's activities - seminars, workshops, special projects, committee actions, awards, etc.

LC TL
DD 629
US

FLIGHT SERVICES. Added/Corp United States. Air Traffic Service. (19??)-. Government Publication. English. Irregular. $52.00 US; $65.00 other. US Department of Transportation / US Coast Guard, 2100 Second Street Southwest, Washington DC 20953-0001. **Tel** (202)267-2229. **(Subscription address:** Superintendent of Documents, US Government Printing Office, Washington DC 20402.)
Desc: Prescribes procedures and phraseology for use by personnel providing flight assistance and communications services.

LC TL521 .U63D
DD 629.13/00973
ISSN 0565-4866
US

FLIGHT STANDARDS INFORMATION MANUAL. Main/Corp United States. Federal Aviation Administration. English. Two times a year. Flight Standards Service, Federal Aviation Administration, Washington DC 20590.

LC WMLC L 83/9188
DD 629
ISSN 1047-6415
US

FLIGHT TRAINING. [Flight train.]. **VFOAT** Flight Training Magazine. (1989)-. Trade Publication. English. Twelve times a year. $19.95. Specialized Publications, 405 Main Street, Parkville MO 64152-3737. **Tel** (816)741-5151, FAX (816)741-6458. **ED** Scott Spangler. Index available. cum. index. **Bk Rev. Ad Acc, Adv Mgr:** Scott Spangler, **Tel** (816)741-5151. **Circ:** 80,000 (ctrl).
Desc: The "how-to" monthly for people who are interested in learning to fly for a career or for recreation. It is the official journal of the National Association of Flight Instructors.
Ind/Abst Aviat. Tradescan [Full Cov.].

LC TL ISSN 1066-078X
DD 629 US

•FLIGHT TRAINING ACADEMIC ENHANCER. BOOK 2, INSTRUMENTS. **VFOAT** Instruments. (1993)-. English. $9.95. Bagwell and Associates, Route 8, PO Box 401, Powell TN 37849.

LC HD6515.A43 F57 ISSN 0164-8691
DD 331.88/11387742 US

FLIGHTLOG. (FLIGHTLOG.). **VFOAT** Flight Log. (19??)-. Periodical. English. Six times a year. $1.00 (members), $6.00 (nonmembers) US; $10.00 other. Association of Flight Attendants, Communications Department, 1625 Massachusetts Avenue, Washington DC 20036. **ED** Emilie Stoltzfus.

LC TL ISSN 1320-5870
DD 629 AT

FLIGHTPATH CAPALABA. **VFOAT** Flightpath (Surrey Hills). (1988)-. Periodical. English. Four times a year. 21.37Aus$. Yaffa Publishing Group Pty Ltd., GPO Box 606, Sydney New South Wales 2001 Australia. **Tel** 011 61 2 2812333, FAX 011 61 2 2812750. ***Continues*** *Australasian Airpower.*

LC TL503 .C524 ISSN 0015-4547
DD 629.13 GW
CCC

FLUG REVUE. [Flug Rev. : Flugwelt Int.]. Issue 5 (May 1968)-. Consumer Publication. German. Twelve times a year. $78.30. Vereinigte Motor Verlag GmbH, Motor Presse, POB 106036, D-70049 Stuttgart Germany. **Tel** 011 49 711 1821506, 011 49 711 1821545. **(Subscription address:** Deutscher Pressevertrieb Buch, POB 101602 Hansa GMBH, D-20010 Hamburg Germany. **Tel** 011 49 40 23711249.**)** **ED** K. Vogel, P. Pietsch, Wolfdietrich Hoeveler. Index available. **Bk Rev. Ad Acc, Adv Mgr:** Reinhard Wittstamm, **Tel** 011 49 707 6684027. Full Page (B&W) DM8760.00. Full Page (Color) DM16206.00. **Circ:** 50,000 (ctrl). ***Continues*** *Flug-Revue International, 0935-0667;* ***Absorbed*** *Flugwelt International, 0935-0640.*
Desc: Leading German language aviation magazine reporting about all kinds of aviation and aerospace, civil, military, and general aviation.
Ind/Abst Energy Res. Abstr. (July 1982-); Int. Aerosp. Abstr.

LC TL500 ISSN 0428-7703
DD 629.13 SZ

FLUGTECHNISCHE REIHE. Vol. 1 (1954)-. Monographic series. German. Irregular. Price varies per volume. Birkhaeuser Verlag Ag, Klosterberg 23, PO Box 133, CH-4010 Basel Switzerland. **Tel** 011 41 61 2717400, FAX 011 41 61 2717666, telex 963475 birk ch.

LC HE9761 ISSN 0833-3424
DD 387.7/092/2 CN

FLYER (EDMONTON, ALTA.). (THE FLYER.). [Flyer]. (Oct. 14, 1983)-. Periodical. English. Four times a year. Free. Canada's Aviation Hall of Fame, Convention Centre, 9797 Jasper Avenue, Edmonton Alberta T5J 1N9 Canada.

LC TL512 .F53 ISSN 0738-3800
DD 629.133/340422/05 US

FLYING BUYERS' GUIDE. (FLYING BUYERS' GUIDE : COMPLETE DIRECTORY OF AIRCRAFT AND AVIONICS.). No. 1 (1982)-. Consumer Publication. English. Travel North America, One Park Avenue, New York NY 10016. **Tel** (212)206-8900, FAX (212)645-2459, telex 236735 GOPUB UR. **ED** Richard L. Collins. **Ad Acc. Circ:** 185,000.
Desc: Buyers guide including specifications for all current production models of general aviation, aircraft, avionics and accessories.

LC TL501 .P6 ISSN 0015-4806
DD 629 US

FLYING (LOS ANGELES, CALIF.). (FLYING.). [Flying]. Vol. 34 (1944)-. Periodical. English. Twelve times a year. $26.00. Hachette Magazines Inc., 1633 Broadway, New York NY 10019. **Tel** (212)767-6000. **(Subscription address:** Neodata / Colorado, PO Box 2606, Boulder CO 80322. **)** available on microfilm and microfiche from University Microfilms International (UMI). Documents available from UMI Article Clearinghouse. ***Continues*** *Flying Including Industrial Aviation.*
Desc: Coverage for everyone interested in airplanes. Reports on the latest planes, as well as features on navigation, weather and safety. Features include evaluation reports on aircraft, pilot proficiency, navigation, weather, safety, FAA regulations and equipment.
Ind/Abst Acad. Abstr. Full Text Elite; Acad. Abstr.; Acad. Search; Aviat. Tradescan [Full Cov.]; Book Rev. Index; EP Collect.; Gen. Period. Index (1985-); Homework Help.; INFO-SOUTH Abstr.; Mag. Artic. Summar. Elite; Mag. Artic. Summar. Select; Mag. Artic. Summar. CD-ROM; Mag. Index Plus (1989-); Mag. Index. Sel. (1986-); Mag. Search; MasterFile FullTEXT 1000; MasterFile FullTEXT 350; MasterFile FullTEXT 650; MasterFile FullTEXT (Oct. 1984-); Newsp. Period. Abstr. (1988-); OCLC; Pub. Lib. FullTEXT; Read. Guide Abstr. Select Ed.; Read. Guide Period. Lit.; Telebase; Mag. Index (1977-); Vocat. Search; World Mag. Bank.

LC TL ISSN 0274-5798
DD 629 US
Pr Rev.

FLYING REVIEW. **Added/Corp** New Mexico Aviation Association. (19??)-. Trade Publication. English. Twelve times a year. $18.00. Flying Review, 2502 Clark-Carr Loop, Albuquerque NM 87103. **Tel** (800)282-8839, (505)842-4184, FAX (505)842-4405. **ED** Rozonna Kinlen. Index available. cum. index. **Bk Rev**, (Qty: 12). **Ad Acc. Circ:** 30,000.
Desc: All aspects of aviation and political commentary.

LC UG633 .F55 ISSN 0279-9308
DD 358.4/00973 US

FLYING SAFETY (1981). (FLYING SAFETY.). [Flying saf.]. **Added/Corp** United States. Dept. of the Air Force. Office of the Inspector General. United States. Dept. of the Air Force. Vol. 37, No. 1 (Jan. 1981)-. Government Publication. English. Twelve times a year. $32.00. US Department of Defense, The Pentagon, Washington DC 20301. **Tel** (703)545-6700. **(Subscription address:** Superintendent of Documents, US Government Printing Office, Washington DC 20402. **)** available on microfilm and microfiche from University Microfilms International (UMI). ***Continues*** *Aerospace Safety, 0001-9429.*
Desc: Covers many fields of flight, aircraft engineering, training, and safety measures in the air and on the ground.
Ind/Abst Acad. Search; Air Univ. Libr. Index Mil. Period.; EP Collect.; Homework Help.; MasterFile FullTEXT 1000; MasterFile FullTEXT 350; MasterFile FullTEXT 650; MasterFile FullTEXT (July 1994-) [Full Txt.]; OCLC; Telebase; Vocat. Search.

LC TL789 ISSN 0015-4881
DD 001.9 UK

FLYING SAUCER REVIEW. Vol. 1, (1955)-. Periodical. English. Four times a year. $35.00. FSR Publications, PO Box 162, High Wycombe, Buckinghamshire HP13 5DZ United Kingdom. **ED** Gordon Creighton. **Bk Rev. Circ:** 3,000. ***Absorbed*** *Flying Saucer News.*
Desc: World-wide reports of UFOs.

LC TL789.A1 F577 ISSN 0015-489X
DD 001.9/42/05 US

FLYING SAUCERS. Periodical. English. Four times a year. $3.00. Palmer Publications Inc., PO Box 296, Amherst WI 54406. **Tel** (715)824-3214, FAX (715)824-5806. available on microfilm from University Microfilms International (UMI).

LC TL ISSN 0262-6950
DD 629 UK

FLYPAST. [Flypast]. **VFOAT** Fly Past. (198?)-. Periodical. English. Twelve times a year. $59.89. Key Publishing Ltd., PO Box 100, Stamford Lincolnshire PE9 1XQ United Kingdom. **Tel** 011 44 1780 55131, FAX 011 44 1780 57261, telex 9312134113.

LC TL
DD 629 UK

FOCUS ON COMMERICAL AVIATION SAFETY. (19??)-. English. Four times a year (Mar., June, Sept., Dec.). £24.00. Flight Safety Committee, Building C2 Fairoaks Airport, Woking Surrey GU24 8HX United Kingdom. **Tel** 011 44 1276 855193, FAX 011 44 1276 856126. **ED** Roy Humphreyson. **Ad Acc. Circ:** 17,000 (ctrl).

LC TL507 .D38 ISSN 0939-2963
DD 629.1/08 GW

FORSCHUNGSBERICHT / DEUTSCHE FORSCHUNGSANSTALT FUER LUFT- UND RAUMFAHRT. **Added/Corp** Deutsche Forschungsanstalt fur Luft- und Raumfahrt. **VFOAT** DLR-FB; DLR-Forschungsberichte. (1989)-. Monographic series. German (English). Price varies per volume. Deutsche Forschungsanstalt fuer, Luft und Raumfahrt DLR, Vorstandsbereich, Postfach 90 60 58, W-5000 Koeln 90 Germany. **Tel** (02203)601 3201, FAX (02203)6 73 10, telex 8810-0 DV D. Documents available from Article Express International. ***Continues*** *Forschungsbericht (Deutsche Forschungs- und Versuchsanstalt fur Luft- und Raumfahrt), 0171-1342.*
Ind/Abst Civ. Struct. Eng. Abstr.; Ei Page One; Eng. Index Annu.; Mater. Sci. Eng. Abstr.; Mech. Eng. Abstr.

LC GV750 ISSN 0827-2557
DD 797.5/5/05 CN

FREE FLIGHT (OTTAWA ONT.). **See** Sports and Games.

LC TL710 ISSN 0317-056X
DD 629.132/52 CN

FROM THE GROUND UP. (1941)-. Periodical. English (French). Irregular. 25.95Can$ (per copy). Aviation Publishers Company Ltd, PO Box 1361 Station B, Ottawa Ontario K1P 5R4 Canada. **Tel** (613)745-2943. **ED** I. L. Peppler. Index available. **Circ:** 340,000.
Desc: This widely known and respected aeronautical study text discusses in-depth all the subjects relating to operating an aircraft: theory of flight, aero engines, meteorology, navigation, radio and radio navigation, airmanship, air safety, aeronautical facilities. Regularly updated to always be current with changes in technology and legislation.
Ind/Abst Geogr. Abstr. Human Geogr.

LC TL ISSN 0898-5758
DD 629 US

FSF CABIN CREW SAFETY BULLETIN. [FSF cabin crew saf. bull.]. **Added/Corp** Flight Safety Foundation. **VFOAT** Cabin Crew Safety Bulletin. **VAT** Flight Safety Foundation Cabin Crew Safety Bulletin. (19??)-. Bulletin. English. Six times a year. $60.00. Flight Safety Foundation Inc., 2200 Wilson Boulevard, Suite 500, Arlington VA 22201. **Tel** (703)522-8300, FAX (703)525-6047, telex 901176 FSF INC AGTN.
Desc: Focuses on the cabin crew, especially in airline operations, but the special requirements of corporate operations are also presented.

LC TA ISSN 0898-5723
DD 620 US

FSF HUMAN FACTORS BULLETIN & AVIATION MEDICINE. [FSF hum. factors bull. aviat. med.]. **Added/Corp** Flight Safety Foundation. **VFOAT** FSF Human Factors Bulletin and Aviation Medicine; Human Factors Bulletin & Aviation Medicine; Human Factors Bulletin and Aviation Medicine. **VAT** Flight Safety Foundation Human Factors Bulletin & Aviation Medicine. (19??)-. Bulletin. English. Six times a year. $60.00. Flight Safety Foundation Inc., 2200 Wilson Boulevard, Suite 500, Arlington VA 22201. **Tel** (703)522-8300, FAX (703)525-6047, telex 901176 FSF INC AGTN. ***Continues*** *Human Factors Bulletin.*
Desc: Information from specialists, researchers and physicians on the training, performance and health of aviation professionals.

LC UG635.C5 A32
DD 358.4/00983 CL

FUERZA AEREA (SANTIAGO, CHILE). **See** Military and Defense.

LC TL589 .F86 ISSN 0094-3975
DD 629.1/028 629.1/028 US

FUNDAMENTALS OF AEROSPACE INSTRUMENTATION. [Fundam. aerosp. instrum.]. **Main/Conf** International Instrumentation Symposium. **VFOAT** Tutorial Program. English. One time a year. Instrument Society of America, 67 Alexander Drive, Research Triangle NC 27709. **Tel** (919)549-8411, FAX (919)549-8288, telex 802 540. Documents available from Article Express International, Ask*IEEE. ***Continues*** *Fundamentals of Aerospace Instrumentation, 0094-3975.*
Ind/Abst Ei Page One; Eng. Index Annu.; INSPEC.

LC TL787 .G28
DD 629.4 RU

GAGARINSKIE NAUCHNYE CHTENIIA PO KOSMONAVTIKE I AVIATSII. **Added/Corp** Institut Problem Mekhaniki (Akademiia Nauk SSSR). **VFOAT** Gagarinskie Nauchnye Chteniia. (198?)-. Russian. Izdatelstvo Nauka / Akademiia Nauk, (Publishing House of the Russian Academy of Sciences), Leninskii Porspekt 14, 117901 Moscow Russia. **Tel** 011 95 9542153, FAX 011 95 9382144, telex 411964. ***Continues*** *Nauchnye Chteniia po Aviatsii i Kosmonavtike.*

LC HE9761 ISSN 0887-7823
DD 387.7 US

GENERAL AVIATION ACCIDENT REPORT. **See** Law.

LC HE9796.U5 U53B ISSN 0272-4502
DD 387.7/0973 US

GENERAL AVIATION ACTIVITY AND AVIONICS SURVEY. [Gen. aviat. act. avion. surv.]. (197?)-. English. One time a year. US Department of Transportation / Federal Aviation Administration, 800 Independence Avenue Southwest, Washington DC 20591. **Tel** (202)367-3484, FAX (202)367-3505. available on microfiche (Vols. for 1984- distributed to depository libraries).

LC TL501 ISSN 1052-9136
DD 629.4 US

GENERAL AVIATION NEWS AND FLYER. **VFOAT** General Aviation News and Flyer. 42nd Year, No. 11 (July 2, 1990)-. Periodical. English. Twenty-six times a year. $29.00. General Aviation News and Flyer, PO Box 3909, Tacoma WA 98498. **Tel** (206)588-1743, (800)426-8538, FAX (206)588-4005. **ED** Dave Schir. **Bk Rev. Ad Acc, Adv Mgr:** Larry Price. **Circ:** 35,000. ***Continues*** *Western Flyer, 0274-9645.*
Desc: Presents news in general aviation with features, special reports and product information.

LC TL
DD 629 US

GENERAL AVIATION STATISTICAL DATABOOK. **See** Aeronautics, Astronautics-Abstracting, Bibliographies and Statistics.

LC HE9849.D4 D48a
DD 387.7/065/43 GW

GESCHAFTSBERICHT. **Main/Corp** Deutsche Lufthansa (1953-). (19??)-. German (English). One time a year. Deutsche Lufthansa AG, Von-Gablenz-Strasse

2-6, W-5000 Cologne 21 Germany. **Tel** 011 49 221 8261, telex 8873531. ctrl circ. ***Continues*** *Deutsche Lufthansa (1953-). Jahresbericht.*

LC GV750 **ISSN** 0883-7937
DD 797.5 US
GLIDER RIDER'S ULTRALIGHT FLYING. [Glid. rider's ultralight fly.]. **VFOAT** Ultralight Flying. (1985)-. Periodical. English. Twelve times a year. $29.95. Ultralight Flying, PO Box 6009, Chattanooga TN 37401. **Tel** (615)629-5375, FAX (615)629-5379. **ED** Sharon Hill. **Bk Rev. Ad Acc, Adv Mgr:** David Prestridge, **Tel** (615)629-5375. **Circ:** 12,000. ***Continues*** *Glider Rider, 0745-9564.*
Desc: Published for enthusiasts of ultralight and microlight aviation.

LC VG93 .G65 **ISSN** 0884-1128
DD 359.940973 US
GOLD BOOK OF NAVAL AVIATION, THE. (THE GOLD BOOK OF NAVAL AVIATION : NAVY, MARINE CORPS, COAST GUARD.). [Gold book nav. aviat.]. (1985)-. English. One time a year. $14.95 US; $16.45 other. Association of Naval Aviation, 5205 Leesburg Pike, Suite 200, Falls Church VA 22041. **Tel** (703)998-7733. Index available. **Ad Acc.** ctrl circ.
Desc: Historical overview of naval aviation.

LC TL
DD 629 US
GRUMMAN PLANE NEWS. Added/Corp Grumman Aerospace Corporation. (19??)-. Periodical. English. Six times a year. Grumman Aerospace Corporation, Grumman Corp Plant 5, Long Island NY 11714. **Tel** (516)575-7346, FAX (516)575-1400.

LC TL726.6.F8 D37
DD 629.132/54/44 FR
GUIDE DE L'AVIATION GENERALE. (19??)-. French. Irregular. Editions Lavauzelle, 20 rue de Leningrad, 75008 Paris France. ***Continues*** *Guide de l'Aviation Generale en France.*

LC TL504 .H342 **ISSN** 1000-0119
DD 629.13/05 CC
HANG KUNG CHIH SHIH. Added/Corp Chung-kuo Hang Kung Hsueh Hui. **VFOAT** Aerospace Knowledge Magazine; Hangkong Zhishi. (197?)-. Periodical. Chinese. Twelve times a year. $58.00. Chinese Society of Aeronautics and Astronautics, 37 Xueyuan Lu, Beijing 100083, People's Republic of China. **Tel** 2017247, telex 22036 BUAAT CN. **(Subscription address:** China International Book Trading Corporation, PO Box 399, Library Service Department, Beijing 100044 People's Republic of China. **Tel** 011 86 1 8414284, FAX 011 86 1 8412023, telex 22496 CIBTC CN.**) ED** Xie Chu. **Ad Acc. Circ:** 220,000.
Desc: A publication of CSAA with the largest circulation among all the aerospace magazines and newspapers in China.

LC TL504 .H343
DD 629.13/005 CC
HANG KUNG HSUEH PAO. VFOAT Acta Aeronautica et Astronautica Sinica. Periodical. Chinese (English; summaries and/or abstracts in English). Four times a year. RMBY37.00. Guozi Shudian, PO Box 399, Chegongzhuang Xilu 35, Beijing People's Republic of China. **Tel** 1 8414284, FAX 1 8412023, telex 22496. **ED** He Qingshi. **Bk Rev. Circ:** 2,000.
Desc: Fluid dynamics, flight dynamics and testing, structural design and analysis, propulsion system, avionics, automatics, materials technology, manufacture technology, aviation medicine and human engineering.
Ind/Abst Int. Aerosp. Abstr.

LC HD9711.5.A1 H35
DD 338.4762 KO
HANGGONG SANOP KWA KUKPANG KYONGJE YONGU. VFOAT Journal of Aerospace Industry and Defense Economics. Vol. 4 (Dec. 1981)-. Periodical. Korean. Two times a year. W6.000. Sejong Taehak Chulpanbu, San 2 Kunja-dong, Songdong-ku, Seoul South Korea. ***Continues*** *Kukpang Kyongje Yongu.*

LC TL570 **ISSN** 1000-8055
DD 629.1323 CC
HANGKONG DONGLI XUEBAO. VFOAT Journal of Aerospace Power. (1986)-. Periodical. Chinese. Four times a year. Documents available from Article Express International.
Ind/Abst Ei Page One; Eng. Index Annu.; Int. Aerosp. Abstr.

LC TL500 **ISSN** 1000-6893
DD 629.13 CC
HANGKONG XUEBAO. VFOAT Acta Aeronautica et Astronautica Sinica. (1980)-. Academic Scholarly Publication. Chinese. Twelve times a year. $4.00. Chinese Society of Aeronautics and Astronautics, 37 Xueyuan Lu, Beijing 100083, People's Republic of China. **Tel** 2017247, telex 22036 BUAAT CN. **Circ:** 1,900. Documents available from Article Express International.
Desc: Information on aeronautical research in China. Includes auto control, flight dynamics, avionics, testing and manufacturing.
Ind/Abst Ei Page One; Eng. Index Annu.; Int. Aerosp. Abstr.

LC HD9711.I5 I52a
DD 338.47629046 IO
HASIL RAPAT-KERJA DIREKTORAT JENDERAL PERINDUSTRIAN PENERBANGAN. Main/Corp Indonesia. Direktorat Jenderal Perindustrian Penerbangan. (19??)-. Indonesian. Kerja Direktorat Jenderal Perindustrian Penerbangan, Jln Sunda No 11, Jakarta Indonesia.

LC TL
DD 629 UK
HAWK : THE INDEPENDENT JOURNAL OF THE ROYAL AIR STAFF COLLEGE. VFOAT Hawk. English. One time a year. $6.84. Royal Airforce Staff College, Bracknell Berkshire, RG12 3DD United Kingdom. **Tel** 011 44 0344 54593 Ext 7331. **Bk Rev**, (Qty: approx. 6). **Ad Acc. Circ:** 3,000 (ctrl).
Desc: Information on the study of air power.
Ind/Abst Air Univ. Libr. Index Mil. Period. (19??-).

ISSN 0364-2488
US
HEADQUARTERS TELEPHONE DIRECTORY. Main/Corp United States. National Aeronautics and Space Administration. (19??)-. Directory. English. Four times a year. $6.45 US; $8.10 other. National Aeronautics and Space Administration, 600 Independence Avenue SW, Washington DC 20546. **Tel** (202)453-1000.

LC HE9761 **ISSN** 0143-1005
DD 387.73352 UK
HELICOPTER. [Helicopter]. **VFOAT** Helidata (1987). (1977)-. Periodical. English. Six times a year. $50.00. Avia Press Associates, 75 Elm Tree Road Locking, Weston-s-Mare Avon BS24 8EL United Kingdom. **Tel** 011 44 1934 822524, FAX 011 44 1934 822400. ***Continues*** *Helidata (1980).*

LC HD9711.25.A1 H44 **ISSN** 0739-5728
DD 387.7/4 US
Pr Rev.
HELICOPTER ANNUAL. [Helicopter annu.]. **Added/Corp** Helicopter Association International. 1st. Ed. (1983)-. Trade Publication. English. One time a year. $43.00. Helicopter Association International, 1619 Duke Street, Alexandria VA 22314. **Tel** (703)683-4646, FAX (703)683-4745, telex 89-615. **ED** Daniel P. Warsley. **Ad Acc, Adv Mgr:** M. Beames. **Circ:** 17,000 (ctrl).
Desc: A comprehensive reference guide for the civil helicopter industry. Listing the key civil aviation officials, FFA regional and HQ contacts, aviation periodicals, association committees, and many more.
Ind/Abst Stat. Ref. Index.

LC HF1401 **ISSN** 1056-7747
DD 381 US
HELICOPTER EQUIPMENT LISTS & PRICES. RECIPROCATING ENGINE HELICOPTERS. VFOAT Helicopter Equipment Lists and Prices. Reciprocating Engine Helicopters; Reciprocating Engine Helicopters; H.E.L.P.; HELP. Vol. 1, Ed. 1 (1st Quarter 1991)-. Periodical. English. Two times a year. $100.00. Helivalues Inc, PO Box 876, Lincolnshire IL 60069-0876. **Tel** (708)634-3877, FAX (708)634-5505.

LC HF1401 **ISSN** 1045-9464
DD 381 US
HELICOPTER EQUIPMENT LISTS & PRICES. TURBINE ENGINE HELICOPTERS : H.E.L.P. [Helicopter equip. lists prices. Turbine engine helicopters]. **VFOAT** Helicopter Equipment Lists and Prices; Turbine Engine Helicopters; H.E.L.P.; HELP. Vol. 1, Ed. 1 (1st Quarter 1991)-. Periodical. English. Two times a year. $300.00. Helivalues Inc, PO Box 876, Lincolnshire IL 60069-0876. **Tel** (708)634-3877, FAX (708)634-5505.

LC HE9761 **ISSN** 0363-8227
DD 387.73352 US
CCC
HELICOPTER NEWS. (Nov. 3, 1975)-. Periodical. English. Twenty-five times a year. $495.00. Phillips Business Information Inc., 1201 Seven Locks Road, PO Box 61130, Potomac MD 20854. **Tel** (301)424-3338, (301)340-1520, (800)777-5005, FAX (301)424-4297, telex 358149. **ED** Frank G. McGuire. **Bk Rev. Circ:** 1,000. available on an online database (file 636/Full-Text) from DIALOG.
Desc: Newsletter on helicopters, rotorcraft and vertical flight for military and civil users.
Ind/Abst PTS Newsl. Database [Full Txt.].

LC TL716.5 .H45 **ISSN** 1042-2048
DD 629.132/5252 US
HELICOPTER SAFETY (ARLINGTON, VA.). (HELICOPTER SAFETY.). [Helicopter saf.]. **Added/Corp** Flight Safety Foundation. Vol. 13, No. 6 (Nov./Dec. 1987)-. Periodical. English. Six times a year. $60.00 US, Canada and Mexico; $65.00 other. Flight Safety Foundation Inc., 2200 Wilson Boulevard, Suite 500, Arlington VA 22201. **Tel** (703)522-8300, FAX (703)525-6047, telex 901176 FSF INC AGTN. ***Continues*** *FSF Helicopter Safety Bulletin, 0898-8145.*
Desc: Covers real-world helicopter operations, including design principles and primary training as well as helicopter utilization in offshore applications and in emergency medical service.

LC HE9761 **ISSN** 0262-0448
DD 387.73352 UK
HELICOPTER WORLD (LONDON. 1982). (HELICOPTER WORLD.). [Helicopter world]. (1982)-. Trade Publication. English. Twelve times a year. $80.00. Shephard Press Ltd, 111 High Street, Burnham Buckinghamshire SL1 7JZ United Kingdom. **Tel** 011 44 1628 604311, FAX 011 44 1628 664334, telex 846575. **ED** Ian Parker. **Bk Rev. Ad Acc. Circ:** 12,672 (ctrl). ***Continues*** *Hereford's Helicopter World, 0262-6365.*
Desc: International magazine covering all aspects of civil and paramilitary helicopter activity.
Ind/Abst Aviat. Tradescan [Full Cov.]; Infomat Int. Bus.

LC HE9761 **ISSN** 0227-3160
DD 387.7/3352/0971 CN
HELICOPTERS. [Helicopters]. **VFOAT** Helicopters in Canada. **VAT** Helicopters in Canada (1983). Vol. 3, No. 3 (Winter 1983)-. Trade Publication. English. Four times a year. 20.95Can$. Corvus Publishing Group Ltd, 1224 Aviation Park Northeast, Suite 158, Calgary Alberta T2E 7E2 Canada. **Tel** (403)275-9457, FAX (403)275-3925. **ED** Tammi Shanahan. **Bk Rev. Ad Acc. Circ:** 7,000 (ctrl). ***Continues*** *Helicopters Canada, 0826-1237.*
Desc: Includes features stories on helicopter operations, operator profiles, flight reports, and domestic and international news. Regular features include an avionics update, reports on flight operations and safety, military news, etc. Directed toward the rotary wing profession.
Ind/Abst Aviat. Tradescan [Full Cov.].

LC HE9788.5.N7 H47 **ISSN** 0143-5906
DD 387.7/44/0257 UK
TITLE CHANGE
HEREFORD'S NORTH AMERICA. [Hereford's North Am.]. Vol. 1 (June/Nov. 1979)-(19??). Periodical. English. Hereford Press Ltd, 25 Elystan Place, London SW3 3JY United Kingdom. ***Merged into*** *Hereford's Airfreight Handbook Americas.*

LC UG633 **ISSN** 0708-4331
DD 358.4/00971 CN
SUSPENDED
HIGH FLIGHT. Vol. 1 (Apr. 1980)-(19??). Periodical. English. Six times a year. 11.61Can$. Canada's Wings Inc, PO Box 393, Stittsville Ontario K0A 3G0 Canada. **Tel** (613)836-4007. **ED** Carl Vincent. **Bk Rev. Circ:** 2,000.
Desc: Journal of military aviation in Canada, from WWI to the present. Articles on squadrons, individuals, and aircraft types, plus scale drawings and many photographs.

LC HE9850.A2 G73a
DD 629.13 GR
HODEGOS HYPERESIAS POLITIKES AEROPORIAS. Main/Corp Greece. Hyperesia Politikes Aeroporias. **Added/Corp** Greece. Hyperesia Politikes Aeroporias. Directory. **VFOAT** Directory - Civil Aviation Authority. (19??)-. Greek, Modern. Leophoros Vasileos Gerogiou, 1 Hellenikon, Athens Greece.

LC VG90 **ISSN** 0736-9220
DD 359.94 US
HOOK (BONITA, CALIF.), THE. **See** Naval Science, Navigation.

LC TL501 .G75 **ISSN** 0196-3120
DD 629.13 US
HORIZONS. (19??)-. Periodical. English. Four times a year. Free. Grumman Aerospace Corporation, Grumman Corp Plant 5, Long Island NY 11714. **Tel** (516)575-7346, FAX (516)575-1400. **ED** Bernard Kovit. **Circ:** 18,500 (ctrl). available with charts; available with illustrations. Documents available from UMI Article Clearinghouse. ***Continues*** *Grumman Aerospace Horizons, 0095-7615.*
Desc: Articles on aerospace technology, research, and development, energy and defense.
Ind/Abst Mat. Fact; Resource/One Ondisc (1986-1989).

LC TL694.C6 I57A
DD 629.132/54 CN
IATA LOCATION IDENTIFIERS HANDBOOK. Main/Corp International Air Transport Association. **VFOAT** Location Identifiers. English. Two times a year. $7.50 (members), $15.00 (nonmembers). Senior Traffic Publications Assistant, International Air Transportation Association, PO Box 550, Place de l'Aviation Internationale, 1000 Sherbrooke Street West, Montreal Quebec H3A 2R4 Canada.

LC TL
DD 629 SZ
IATA PASSENGER AGENCY CONFERENCE RESOLUTIONS MANUAL. English. 140.00F. International Air Transport Association / Geneva, PO Box 672, CH-1215 Geneva 15 Switzerland. **Tel** 011 41 22 7992525, 011 41 22 7992760.

LC TL500.5 .A33 ISSN 0018-8778
DD 629.13/005 CN
CODEN ICJOEP

ICAO JOURNAL. **Added/Corp** International Civil Aviation Organization. **VFOAT** Journal. **VAT** International Civil Aviation Organization Journal. Vol. 45, No. 1 (Jan. 1990)-. Periodical. English. Ten times a year. 20.00Can$. International Civil Aviation Organization / ICAO, 1000 Sherbrooke Street West, Suite 400, Montreal Quebec H3A 2R2 Canada. **Tel** (514)285-8026, (514)285-8022, telex 05-24514. Documents available from Documents on Demand. ***Continues*** *ICAO Bulletin, 0018-8778.*
Desc: Provides a concise account of the activities of the International Civil Aviation Organization and features additional information of interest to Contracting States and the international aeronautical world.
Ind/Abst Aviat. Tradescan [Full Cov.]; Environ. Abstr.; Meteorol. Geoastrophys. Abstr. (199?-).

LC TL504 ISSN 0445-1767
DD 629.13 FR

ICARE (ORLY). (ICARE; REVUE DE L'AVIATION FRANCAISE.). [Icare]. **Added/Corp** Syndicat National des Pilotes de Ligne (France). (195?)-. Periodical. French. Four times a year (Seasonally). $87.49. Icare / Tour Essor 93, 14 16 rue de Scandicci, 93508 Pantin Cedex France. **Tel** 011 33 1 43422089, FAX 011 33 1 48917289. Index available. cum. index. **Circ:** 10,000.
Ind/Abst Int. Aerosp. Abstr.

LC TL566 .I57A ISSN 0730-2010
DD 629.1/028/7 US

ICIASF RECORD. (ICIASF ... RECORD / INTERNATIONAL CONGRESS ON INSTRUMENTATION IN AEROSPACE SIMULATION FACILITIES.). [ICIASF rec.]. **Main/Conf** International Congress on Instrumentation in Aerospace Simulation Facilities. **VFOAT** I.C.I.A.S.F. ... Record. **VAT** International Congress on Instrumentation in Aerospace Simulation Facilities Record. 1969-?. English. Every 2 years. $40.00. IEEE / Institute of Electrical and Electronics Engineers Inc., 345 East 47th Street, New York NY 10017-2394. **Tel** (908)981-1393, FAX (908)981-9667. **(Subscription address:** IEEE / Institute of Electrical and Electronics Engineers, 445 Hoes Lane, PO Box 1331, Piscataway NJ 08855-1331. **Tel** (800)701-IEEE, (908)981-0060, FAX (908)981-9667, telex 833233.**)** Documents available from Article Express International. ***Continues*** *International Congress on Instrumentation in Aerospace Simulation Facilities. Proceedings, 0730-1790.*
Ind/Abst Civ. Struct. Eng. Abstr.; Comput. Inf. Syst. Abstr. J. [Full Cov.]; Ei Page One; Elect. Comm. Abstr.; Eng. Index Annu.; Environ. Eng. Abstr.; Index IEEE Publ.; Manuf. Process Eng. Abstr.; Mater. Sci. Eng. Abstr.; Mech. Eng. Abstr.; Solid State Supercond. Abstr.

LC TL693 .I117 ISSN 0885-8985
DD 629.135/5/05 US
CCC
CODEN IESMEA

IEEE AEROSPACE AND ELECTRONIC SYSTEMS MAGAZINE. [IEEE aerosp. electron. syst. mag.]. **Added/Corp** IEEE Aerospace and Electronic Systems Society. **VFOAT** Aerospace and Electronic Systems Magazine; IEEE AES Magazine. **VAT** Institute of Electrical and Electronics Engineers Aerospace and Electronic Systems Magazine. Vol. 1, No. 1 (Jan. 1986)-. Periodical. English. Twelve times a year. $95.00. IEEE / Institute of Electrical and Electronics Engineers Inc., 345 East 47th Street, New York NY 10017-2394. **Tel** (908)981-1393, FAX (908)981-9667. **(Subscription address:** IEEE / Institute of Electrical and Electronics Engineers, 445 Hoes Lane, PO Box 1331, Piscataway NJ 08855-1331. **Tel** (800)701-IEEE, (908)981-0060, FAX (908)981-9667, telex 833233.**)** available on microfiche. Documents available from Article Express International, Ask*IEEE. ***Continues*** *IEEE Aerospace and Electronic Systems Society Newsletter.*
Desc: Deals with functional systems for space, air, ocean or ground environments and systems interactions.
Ind/Abst Civ. Struct. Eng. Abstr.; Curr. Cit.; Ei Page One; Eng. Index Annu.; Environ. Eng. Abstr.; Index IEEE Publ. (1986-); INSPEC (1986-); Int. Aerosp. Abstr.; Mech. Eng. Abstr.

LC TL3000.A1 I53 ISSN 0018-9251
DD 629.1 US
CCC
CODEN IEARAX

Pr Rev.

IEEE TRANSACTIONS ON AEROSPACE AND ELECTRONIC SYSTEMS. **See** Electronics.

LC TL
DD 629 UK

IFALPA QUARTERLY REVIEW. (19??)-. English. Four times a year (Mar., June, Sept., Dec.). $51.33. IFALPA, Interpilot House, Gogmore Lane, Chertsey Surrey, KT16 9AP United Kingdom. **Tel** 011 44 1932 571711, FAX 011 44 1932 570920. **ED** T. Middleton. **Ad Acc. Circ:** 1,400 (ctrl).

LC GV ISSN 0894-6620
DD 797 US

IFR. [IFR]. (198?)-. Periodical. English. Twelve times a year. $59.00. Belvoir Publications Inc., 75 Holly Hill Lane, Greenwich CT 06836. **Tel** (203)661-6111, FAX (203)661-4802. **(Subscription address:** Palm Coast Data, PO Box 420163, Agency Department, Palm Coast FL 32142. **Tel** (904)445-4662 ext. 669, (800)829-5475.**)** **ED** Paul Betorelli. **Circ:** 20,000.
Desc: Offers information on technique, avionics, flight planning and operations.

LC TL726.2 .U48A ISSN 0092-3567
DD 387.7/4042 US

IFR AIRCRAFT HANDLED. **Main/Corp** United States. Aviation Forecast Branch. **VFOAT** I.F.R. Aircraft Handled. **VAT** Instrument Flight Rule Aircraft Handled. English. National Technical Information Service - NTIS, Room 2027S, 5285 Port Royal Road, Springfield VA 22161. **Tel** (703)487-4630, (703)487-4660, (703)487-4650, FAX (703)321-8547, telex 89-9405. ***Continues*** *IFR Aircraft Handled, 0092-3567.*

LC TL
DD 629 US

IFR OFF-AIRWAY ROUTES, NON PART 95. **VAT** Instrument Flying Rules Off-Airway Routes, Non Part Ninety-Five. (19??)-. English. US Department of Transportation / Federal Aviation Administration, 800 Independence Avenue Southwest, Washington DC 20591. **Tel** (202)367-3484, FAX (202)367-3505.

LC TL ISSN 0896-9868
DD 629 US

IFR REFRESHER. [IFR refresh.]. **Added/Corp** Professional Instrument Courses, Inc. **VFOAT** IFRR. **VAT** Instrument Flight Rule Refresher. (1987)-. Periodical. English. Twelve times a year. $72.00. Belvoir Publications Inc., 75 Holly Hill Lane, Greenwich CT 06836. **Tel** (203)661-6111, FAX (203)661-4802. **(Subscription address:** Palm Coast Data, PO Box 420163, Agency Department, Palm Coast FL 32142. **Tel** (904)445-4662 ext. 669, (800)829-5475.**)** **ED** Russ Lawton.

LC TL726.3.I3 I46
DD 387.7/36/025773 US

ILLINOIS AIRPORT DIRECTORY. 1953-. Directory. English. Every 2 years. $5.00. Illinois Division of Aeronautics, Capital Airport, Springfield IL 62707. **Tel** (217)785-8516. **ED** Richard M Ware. **Circ:** 25,000.
Desc: Aerial photographs and basic data for all open to the public airports in Illinois.

LC TL501 .I32 ISSN 0276-640X
DD 629.13/005 US

ILLINOIS AVIATION (SPRINGFIELD, ILL. : 1979). (ILLINOIS AVIATION.). (July/Aug. 1979)-. Periodical. English. Six times a year. Free (with $5.00 registration). Illinois Division of Aeronautics, Capital Airport, Springfield IL 62707. **Tel** (217)785-8516. **ED** Richard M Ware. **Bk Rev. Ad Acc. Circ:** 25,000 (ctrl). ***Continues*** *Aviation (Springfield, Ill.), 0146-0692.*
Desc: Aviation promotion and aviation safety.

LC Z
DD 016.2 UK

INDEX - ENGINEERING SCIENCES DATA UNIT. **See** Engineering-Abstracting, Bibliographies and Statistics.

LC DD99
DD 359 US

INDEX OF AIR FORCE-NAVY AERONAUTICAL (AN), AIR FORCE-NAVY AERONAUTICAL DESIGN (AND) AND MILITARY (MS) STANDARDS. **See** Military and Defense.

LC TL
DD 629 UK

INDEX OF AVIATION ARTICLES. English. Twelve times a year. £173.00. Airclaims Ltd., Cardinal Point, Newall Road / Heathrow Airport, London TW6 2AS United Kingdom. **Tel** 011 44 181 8971066, FAX 011 44 181 8970300, telex 934679. ***Continues*** *Index of Articles.*
Desc: Provides a listing of the major articles appearing in the aviation press.

LC TL521 .U63H
DD 343.73/097/02636 347. 3039702636 US

INDEX OF FAA NATIONAL AND WA ORDERS. **Main/Corp** United States. Federal Aviation Administration. English. Department of Transportation, 400 Seventh Street SW, Washington DC 20590. **Tel** (202)426-4000.

LC Z
DD 016.62 US

INDEX OF NATIONAL AEROSPACE STANDARDS. **Added/Corp** National Aerospace Standards Committee. (19??)-. English. Two times a year. $30.00. Information Handling Services, 15 Inverness Way East, Englewood CO 80150. **Tel** (800)525-7052, (303)790-0600, FAX (303)397-2599, telex 4322083. **ED** Kitty Stover.
Desc: Paper index to National Aerospace Standards.

LC TL ISSN 0074-249X
DD 629 CN

INDEX TO ICAO PUBLICATIONS. **Main/Corp** International Civil Aviation Organization. (19??)-. English. One time a year. $4.00 (1986 cumulated edition - last edition available). International Civil Aviation Organization / ICAO, 1000 Sherbrooke Street West, Suite 400, Montreal Quebec H3A 2R2 Canada. **Tel** (514)285-8026, (514)285-8022, telex 05-24514.

LC TL504 .A733 ISSN 0020-1006
DD 629.13 SP

INGENIERIA AERONAUTICA Y ASTRONAUTICA. **Added/Corp** Asociacion de Ingenieros Aeronauticos. No. 1 (1959)-. Periodical. Spanish. Four times a year. Asociacion de Ingenieros Aeronauticos, C. Claudio Coello 40, 2o Izda, 28001 Madrid Spain. **Tel** 011 34 1 4353021, FAX 011 34 1 4358283. **ED** Anibal Isidoro Carmona. Index available. **Bk Rev. Ad Acc. Circ:** 2,000. available with charts; available with illustrations. Documents available from BLDSC. ***Continues*** *Ingenieria Aeronautica, 0211-0598.*
Ind/Abst Int. Aerosp. Abstr.

LC TL
DD 629 US

INSIDE ASTROPHYSICS : THE ASTROPHYSICS DIVISION NEWSLETTER. **Added/Corp** United States. National Aeronautics and Space Administration. Astrophysics Division. Vol. 1, No. 1 (Summer 1991)-. Newsletter. English.

LC HE9761 ISSN 1061-4494
DD 387 US

INSIDE FLYER. [Inside fly.]. Vol. 1, Issue 1 (Jan. 1992)-. Periodical. English. Twelve times a year. Flightplan, 4715-C Town Center Drive, Colorado Springs CO 80916. ***Continues*** *Frequent Update, 1048-5759.*

LC U
DD 355 US

INSIDE THE PENTAGON'S INSIDE THE AIR FORCE. (19??)-. Periodical. English. One time a week. $620.60 Washington, DC residents; $580.00 other. Inside Washington Publishers, PO Box 7167, Benjamin Franklin Station, Washington DC 20044. **Tel** (703)416-8500, (800)424-9068.

LC TL
DD 629 US

INSTRUMENT FLYING. **Main/Corp** United States. Dept. of the Air Force. **VFOAT** Flying Training. (1961)-. Government Publication. English. Irregular. $27.00 domestic; $33.75 other. US Department of Defense, The Pentagon, Washington DC 20301. **Tel** (703)545-6700. **(Subscription address:** Superintendent of Documents, US Government Printing Office, Washington DC 20402. **)**
Desc: This manual establishes standard USAF instrument flying procedures and techniques. It serves as a text for various USAF training courses.

LC TL589 .I48 ISSN 0096-7238
DD 629.1 US
CCC
CODEN IASIBZ

Pr Rev.

INSTRUMENTATION IN THE AEROSPACE INDUSTRY. [Instrum. aerosp. ind.]. **Added/Corp** Instrument Society of America. Vol. 14 (1968)-. Academic Scholarly Publication. English. Irregular. Price varies per volume. Instrument Society of America, 67 Alexander Drive, Research Triangle NC 27709. **Tel** (919)549-8411, FAX (919)549-8288, telex 802 540. available in microform from University Microfilms International (UMI). Documents available from Article Express International, Ask*IEEE, CASDDS, BLDSC.
Desc: Proceedings of the annual symposium for the Aerospace Industry Division of the Instrument Society of America.
Ind/Abst Bioeng. Abstr.; Chem. Abstr. (1968-1983); Ei Page One; Eng. Index Annu.; INSPEC.

LC QB500.266.U6 U55a
DD 500.5/0973 US

INTEGRATED TECHNOLOGY PLAN FOR THE CIVIL SPACE PROGRAM. **Main/Corp** United States. National Aeronautics and Space Administration. **Added/Corp** United States. Office of Aeronautics and Space Technology. (1991)-. English. National Aeronautics and Space Administration Office of Aeronautics and Space Technology, Washington DC 20546.

LC HD9711.5.A1 I56
DD 338.4/76291/05 SZ
CODEN IAWOE8
TITLE CHANGE

INTERAVIA, AEROSPACE WORLD : BUSINESS & TECHNOLOGY. **VFOAT** Interavia; Interavia/Aerospace World. (Oct. 1992)-(Dec. 1993). Trade Publication. English. Aerospace Media Publishing SA, 29 Route de l'Aeroport, Box 437, CH-1215 Geneva 15 Switzerland. **Tel** 011 41 22 7882788, FAX 011 41 22 7882726. available on an online database (file

16/Full-Text) from DIALOG. ***Formed by the union of*** *Interavia (English Edition), 0020-5168* ***and*** *Aerospace World, 0983-1592.* ***Continued by*** *Interavia (1994).*
Ind/Abst Air Univ. Libr. Index Mil. Period. (199?-); Aviat. Tradescan [Full Cov.]; Int. Aerosp. Abstr.; PAIS Int. Print.

LC TL
DD 629 SZ
TITLE CHANGE
INTERAVIA AIR LETTER : WORLD AVIATION, SPACE AND ELECTRONICS. (19??)-(19??). English. Jane's Information Group, Sentinel House, 163 Brighton Road, Coulsdon Surrey CR5 2NH United Kingdom. **Tel** 011 44 181 7631030, FAX 011 44 181 7630276, telex 916907-JANES-G. ***Continued by*** *Air Letter.*
Ind/Abst F&S Index Plus Text, Int. [Select. Cov.]; PROMT.

LC HD9711.5.A1 I56
DD 338.4/76291/05 SZ
●**INTERAVIA : BUSINESS & TECHNOLOGY.** Vol. 49, No. 574 (Jan. 1994)-. Periodical. English. Twelve times a year. $128.00. Aerospace Media Publishing SA, 29 Route de l'Aeroport, Box 437, CH-1215 Geneva 15 Switzerland. **Tel** 011 41 22 7882788, FAX 011 41 22 7882726. ***Continues*** *Interavia, Aerospace World.*
Ind/Abst Curr. Cit.; MasterFile FullTEXT (July 1993-).

LC TL512 .I55 **ISSN** 0074-1116
DD 629.1/029/4 SZ
TITLE CHANGE
INTERNATIONAL ABC AEROSPACE DIRECTORY. **VFOAT** Interavia ABC. 39th Ed. (1990)-(199?). Directory. English. Jane's Information Group, Sentinel House, 163 Brighton Road, Coulsdon Surrey CR5 2NH United Kingdom. **Tel** 011 44 181 7631030, FAX 011 44 181 7630276, telex 916907-JANES-G. **(Subscription address:** Jane's Information Group / US Subscriptions, 1340 Braddock Place, Suite 300, Alexandria VA 22314. **Tel** (800)243-3852, (703)683-3700.**)** available on CD-ROM. ***Continues*** *Interavia ABC Aerospace Directory.* ***Continued by*** *Jane's International ABC Aerospace Directory.*

LC HD9711.5.A1 I57 **ISSN** 0882-6730
DD 338.7/6291/025 629 US
INTERNATIONAL AEROSPACE DIRECTORY. [Int. aerosp. dir.]. (1986)-. Directory. English. One time a year. $50.00. Eclipse Publishing Company, PO Box 1796, Centreville VA 22020. **Tel** (703)549-2138. **Ad Acc. Circ:** 10,000.
Desc: Contains 2,000 companies that provide space related services and products. Indexes by service. Includes government agencies and glossary.

LC TL **ISSN** 1056-5701
DD 629 **CEASED**
INTERNATIONAL AIR REVIEW. [Int. air rev.]. **VFOAT** Air Review. (19??)-(April 1993). Periodical. English. Challenge Publications Inc., 7950 Deering Avenue, Canoga Park CA 91304. **Tel** (818)887-0550.

LC TL **ISSN** 0045-1193
DD 629 US
INTERNATIONAL AVIATION MECHANICS JOURNAL. [Int. aviat. mech. j.]. **Added/Corp** Aviation Maintenance Foundation. **VFOAT** Aviation Mechanics Journal. (19??)-. Periodical. English. Twelve times a year. International Aviation Publishing Inc., PO Box 10000, 7383 6WN Road, Casper WY 82604. **Tel** (800)443-9250, (307)266-3838. **ED** Marlon Atkins. Index available. **Bk Rev. Ad Acc. Circ:** 36,000 (ctrl). available on microfiche.
Desc: Concerned with aviation maintenance technology.

LC TL
DD 629 US
INTERNATIONAL CONTRACTORS. (19??)-. English. Four times a year. $1025.00. Forecast International / DMS Inc., 22 Commerce Road, Newtown CT 06470. **Tel** (203)426-0800, FAX (203)426-1964, telex 467615.

LC TL504 **ISSN** 0364-0418
DD 629.13 US
INTERNATIONAL FLIGHT INFORMATION MANUAL. [Int. flight inf. man.]. **Added/Corp** United States. Federal Aviation Administration. United States. Civil Aeronautics Administration. United States. Federal Aviation Agency. National Flight Data Center (U.S.) United States. Air Traffic Rules and Procedures Service. United States. Air Traffic Rules and Procedures Service. Air Traffic Publications Branch. (19??)-. Government Publication. English. One time a year (3 quarterly supplements). $59.00 domestic; $73.75 other. US Department of Transportation / US Coast Guard, 2100 Second Street Southwest, Washington DC 20953-0001. **Tel** (202)267-2229. **(Subscription address:** Superintendent of Documents, US Government Printing Office, Washington DC 20402. **)** **ED** Avis Sorrell. **Circ:** 10,000. ***Absorbed in part*** *Graphic Notices and Supplemental Data.*

Desc: Primarily designed as a preflight and planning guide for use by United States non-scheduled operators, business and private aviators contemplating flights outside of the United States.

LC TL **ISSN** 0020-675X
DD 629 US
INTERNATIONAL FLYING FARMER. See Agriculture.

LC TL
DD 629 US
●**INTERNATIONAL JOURNAL OF SPACE RESEARCH.** (1995)-. English. Four times a year. $225.00. Nova Science Publishers Inc., 6080 Jericho Turnpike, Suite 207, Commack NY 11725-2808. **Tel** (516)499-3103, (516)499-3106, FAX (516)499-3146. ***Continues*** *Journal of Space Abstracts and Research.*

LC TL
DD 629 IS
INTERNATIONAL JOURNAL OF TURBO & JET-ENGINES. **VFOAT** International Journal of Turbo and Jet-Engines; Turbo & Jet-Engines; Turbo and Jet Engines. Vol. 1, No. 1 (1983)-. Periodical. English. Irregular. $260.00. Freund Publishing House Ltd., PO Box 35010, 61 Nachmani Street, Tel Aviv 61350 Israel. **Tel** 011 972 3 5628540, FAX 011 972 3 5628538. **(Subscription address:** Freund Publishing House Ltd., Suite 500, Chesham House 150 Regent Street, London W1R 5FA United Kingdom. **Tel** 011 44 178 172811, FAX 011 972 3 615335.**)** **ED** Benjamin Gal-Or. **Bk Rev. Ad Acc. Circ:** 350 (ctrl).
Desc: Aims to contribute to the advancement of the science and technology of air, land and marine applications of turbo and jet-engines; aimed at professionals and academics, with original papers and reviews on research, development and applications.
Ind/Abst Eng. Mater. Abstr.; Int. Aerosp. Abstr. (1984-).

LC TL725.A1 U52a **ISSN** 0364-6742
DD 629.132/52/05 US
TITLE CHANGE
INTERNATIONAL NOTICES TO AIRMEN. [Int. not. airmen]. **Added/Corp** United States. Federal Aviation Administration. (1975)-(1995). Government Publication. English. US Department of Transportation / US Coast Guard, 2100 Second Street Southwest, Washington DC 20953-0001. **Tel** (202)267-2229. **(Subscription address:** Superintendent of Documents, US Government Printing Office, Washington DC 20402. **)** ***Continues*** *International Notams.* ***Absorbed by*** *Notices to Airmen, 1057-9621.*
Desc: Gives worldwide coverage in each issue and offers purely a Notice-to-Airmen Service. It covers temporary hazardous conditions, changes in facility operational data, and foreign entry procedures and regulations.

LC TL512 .I68 **ISSN** 1041-4541
DD 629.1/025 US
INTERNATIONAL SATELLITE DIRECTORY. See Communications-Telecommunication.

LC TL
DD 629 SZ
TITLE CHANGE
INTERNATIONAL TRAFFIC FORECAST. SCHEDULED AND CHARTER FREIGHT. **Added/Corp** International Air Transport Association. Industry Automation and Finance Services Dept. **VFOAT** Scheduled and Charter Freight. (1997)-(19??). English. International Air Transport Association / Montreal, 2000 Peel Street, Room 3050, Montreal Quebec H3A 2R4 Canada. **Tel** (514)844-6311 ext. 232, FAX (514)844-5286, telex 05-267627. ***Changed back to*** *Scheduled and Charter Freight Traffic Forecast.*

LC TL789.A1 I592 **ISSN** 1062-3728
DD 001.9/42/05 US
INTERNATIONAL UFO LIBRARY MAGAZINE. [Int. UFO Libr. mag.]. **Added/Corp** UFO Library. **VFOAT** UFO. Vol. 1 (July 1991)-. Periodical. English. Six times a year. $19.95. UFO Library, 6444 Springs Street Suite 170, Long Beach CA 90815. **Tel** (714)826-6991.

LC TL789.A1 I593 **ISSN** 0730-174X
DD 001.9/42/05 US
INTERNATIONAL UFO REPORTER. [Int. UFO report.]. **Added/Corp** Center for UFO Studies (U.S.). **VFOAT** IUR. **VAT** International Unidentified Flying Object Reporter. (1976)-. Periodical. English. Six times a year. $25.00. Center for UFO Studies, 2457 West Peterson, Chicago IL 60659. **Tel** (312)271-3611.

LC TL **ISSN** 0738-2677
DD 629 US
INTERNATIONAL ULTRAVIOLET EXPLORER (IUE) NASA NEWSLETTER. **VFOAT** International Ultraviolet Explorer (I.U.E.) N.A.S.A. Newsletter; N.A.S.A. Newsletter for International Ultraviolet Explorer; I.U.E. N.A.S.A. Newsletter; IUE NASA Newsletter; NASA Newsletter for International Ultraviolet Explorer (IUE); IUE Ultraviolet Spectral Atlas. (1978)-. Newsletter. English. National Space Science Data Center, Goddard Space Flight Center, Greenbelt MD 20771.

LC TL
DD 629 BE
INTRA-EUROPEAN COUNTRY-TO-COUNTRY TRAFFIC. **Added/Corp** Association of European Airlines. (Jan. 1984)-. English. Twelve times a year. Association of European Airlines, Avenue Louise 350 BTE 4, B-1050 Brussels Belgium. **Tel** 32-2-640 31.75, FAX (322)648-4017, telex 22918. ***Continues*** *Scheduled Intra-European Passenger & Cargo Traffic of AEA Member Airlines.*

LC TL726.3.I8 I54A
DD 629.136/09777 US
IOWA AIRPORT SUFFICIENCY RATINGS. **Main/Corp** Iowa. Dept. of Transportation. Planning and Research Division. (1976)-. English. One time a year. Iowa Department of Transportation, 800 Lincoln Way, Ames IA 50010. **Tel** (515)239-1528.

LC TL504 .I76
DD 629.13 RU
ISSLEDOVANIIA PO ISTORII I TEORII RAZVITIIA AVIATSIONNOI I RAKETNO-KOSMICHESKOI NAUKI I TEKHNIKI. **Added/Corp** Institut Istorii Estestvoznaniia i Tekhniki (Akademiia Nauk SSSR). Vol. 1 (1981)-. Academic Scholarly Publication. Russian. One time a year. Izdatelstvo Nauka / Akademiia Nauk, (Publishing House of the Russian Academy of Sciences), Leninskii Porspekt 14, 117901 Moscow Russia. **Tel** 011 95 9542153, FAX 011 95 9382144, telex 411964.

LC HB **ISSN** 1064-4393
DD 338 US
TITLE CHANGE
ISSO NEWSLETTER, THE. [ISSO newsl.]. **Added/Corp** International Small Satellite Organization. **VAT** International Small Satellite Organization Newsletter. (July 1987)-(1995). Newsletter. English. New Space Information Service, 520 Huntmar Park Drive Suite 100, Herndon VA 22070. **Tel** (703)709-2240, FAX (703)709-0790. cum. index. **Bk Rev**, (Qty: 2/yr). **Ad Acc, Adv Mgr:** Melanie Horn. **Circ:** 600. ***Continued by*** *New Space Newsletter.*
Desc: Newsletter format, Industry activities, technical and policy developments in small and low cost space systems.

LC TL787 .I87 **ISSN** 0202-0734
DD 629.4 RU
CODEN IIKPA3
ITOGI NAUKI I TEHNIKI - VSESOJUZNYJ INSTITUT NAUCNOJ I TEHNICESKOJ INFORMACII. ISSLEDOVANIE KOSMICESKOGO PROSTRANSTVA. (ITOGI NAUKI I TEKHNIKI. ISSLEDOVANIE KOSMICHESKOGO PROSTRANSTVA.). [Itogi nauki teh. - Vses. inst. naucn. teh. inf., Issled. kosm. prostranstva]. **Added/Corp** Vsesoiuznyi Institut Nauchnoi i Tekhnicheskoi Informatsii (Soviet Union). **VFOAT** Issledovanie Kosmicheskogo Prostranstva; Seriia Issledovanie Kosmicheskogo Prostranstva; Itogi Nauki i Tekhniki. Seriia Issledovanie Kosmicheskogo Prostranstva. (1972)-. Monographic series. Russian. Irregular. Price varies per volume. VINITI - Vsesoyuznyi Institut Nauchno-Tekhnicheskoi Informatsii, All-Union Scientific and Technical Information Institute, Baltiiskaia ulitsa 14, 125219 Moscow Russia. **Tel** 011 7 95 2384600, FAX 011 7 95 9430060, telex 411160. Documents available from Ask*IEEE, CASDDS. ***Continues*** *Itogi Nauki. Issledovanie Kosmicheskogo Prostranstva.*
Ind/Abst Chem. Abstr.; INSPEC (1972-).

LC TL **ISSN** 0367-7966
DD 629 RU
CODEN IGOPA9
IZVESTIIA GLAVNOI ASTRONOMICHESKOI OBSERVATORII V PULKOVE. [Izv. Glavnoj astron. obs. Pulkove]. **Added/Corp** Glavnaia Astronomicheskaia Observatoriia (Pulkovo, R.S.F.S.R.). **VFOAT** Bulletin de l'Observatoire Central a Poulkovo. (1928)-. Bulletin. Russian (summaries and/or abstracts in English). Documents available from Ask*IEEE, CASDDS. ***Continues*** *Izvestiia Glavnoi Rossiiskoi Astronomicheskoi Observatorii.*
Ind/Abst Chem. Abstr. (?-1989); INSPEC (1968-); Int. Aerosp. Abstr.

LC TL **ISSN** 0579-2975
DD 629 RU
CODEN IVUAAV
Pr Rev.
IZVESTIIA VYSSHIKH UCHEBNYKH ZAVEDENII. AVIATSIONNAIA TEKHNIKA. [Izv. vyss. ucebn. zaved., Aviac. teh.]. **Added/Corp** Soviet Union. Ministerstvo Vysshego Obrazovaniia. Soviet Union. Ministerstvo Vysshego i Srednego spetsialnogo Obrazovaniia. Kazanskii Aviatsionnyi institut. Kazanskii Aviatsionnyi Institut Imeni N. Tupoleva. **VFOAT** Aviatsionnaia Tekhnika; Seriia

Aviatsionnaia Tekhnika; Izvestiia Vysshikh Uchebnykh Zavedenii MVO SSSR. Seriia Aviatsionnaia Tekhnika. Vol. 1 (1958)-. Academic Scholarly Publication. Russian (table of contents in English). Four times a year. $99.95. **(Subscription address:** East View Publications Inc., 3020 Harbor Lane North, Suite 110, Minneapolis MN 55447. **Tel** (800)477-1005, (612)550-0961, FAX (612)559-2931.) cum. index. Documents available from Article Express International, Ask*IEEE, CASDDS. **Ind/Abst** Chem. Abstr. (1958-1983); Ei Page One; Eng. Index Annu.; INSPEC (1973-); Int. Aerosp. Abstr.; Math. Rev.; SCISEARCH.

LC UG **ISSN** 0394-3437
DD 623 IT
UDC 623.74
J P 4. [J P 4]. **VFOAT** Jet Petrol quattro. (1972)-. Periodical. Italian. Twelve times a year. L51100. Ed Ai Srl, Via Guinicelli 4, 50133 Florence Italy. **Tel** 011 39 55 574774, FAX 011 39 55 570103, telex 580217. **Bk Rev. Ad Acc.**

LC TL **ISSN** 0447-256X
DD 629 GW
JAHRBUCH DER LUFT- UND RAUMFAHRT. Added/Corp Deutscher Aero-Club. Vol. 1 (1952)-. German. One time a year (Feb.). $48.28. Sudwestdeutsche Verlagsanstalt Pressehaus Am Markt, Postfach 121863, D-68069 Mannheim Germany. **Tel** 011 49 621 39203, FAX 011 49 621 1702376.

LC TL503 .D365A
DD 629.1/05 GW
JAHRBUCH. DEUTSCHE GESELLSCHAFT FUER LUFT- UND RAUMFAHRT. Main/Corp Deutsche Gesellschaft fur Luft- und Raumfahrt. **VFOAT** DGLR Jahrbuch. 1-1968-. German. One time a year. Goethestrasse 10, W-5 Cologne 51 Germany. ***Supersedes** Jahrbuch der Wissenschaftliche Gesellschaft.*

LC TL726.6.S92 Z874A
DD 387.7/36/094945 SZ
JAHRESBERICHT / FLUGHAFEN ZURICH. Main/Corp Flughafen Zurich. German (summaries and/or abstracts in English). One time a year. Direktion der Volkswirtschaft des Kantons Zurich Amt fur Luftverkehr Informations-und Pressedienst, 8058 Zurich-Flughafen Switzerland.

LC U **ISSN** 0954-3848
DD 355 UK
JANE'S AIR LAUNCHED WEAPONS. See Military and Defense.

LC TL725.3.E6 J36
DD 629.136/028 UK
TITLE CHANGE
JANE'S AIRPORT & ATC EQUIPMENT. Added/Corp Jane's Information Group. Jane's Air Transport Data. **VFOAT** Jane's Airport and ATC Equipment; Airport & ATC Equipment; Airport and ATC Equipment. **VAT** Jane's Airport & Air Traffic Control Equipment. (1992)-(199?)-. English. Jane's Information Group, Sentinel House, 163 Brighton Road, Coulsdon Surrey CR5 2NH United Kingdom. **Tel** 011 44 181 7631030, FAX 011 44 181 7630276, telex 916907-JANES-G. ***Continues** Jane's Airport Equipment. **Superseded by** Jane's Airports, Equipment and Services **and** Jane's Air Traffic Control.*

LC HE9797.A1 J35 **ISSN** 0954-7649
DD 387.7/36/05 UK
CCC
JANE'S AIRPORT REVIEW. [Jane's airpt. rev.]. **Added/Corp** Jane's Information Group. Jane's Air Transport Data. (198?)-. Trade Publication. English. Ten times a year. $130.00. Jane's Information Group, Sentinel House, 163 Brighton Road, Coulsdon Surrey CR5 2NH United Kingdom. **Tel** 011 44 181 7631030, FAX 011 44 181 7630276, telex 916907-JANES-G. **(Subscription address:** Jane's Information Group / US Subscriptions, 1340 Braddock Place, Suite 300, Alexandria VA 22314. **Tel** (800)243-3852, (703)683-3700.) available on an online database from DIALOG. Documents available from BLDSC. ***Continues** Aviation Ground Equipment Market, 0891-5148.*

LC TL725.3.E6 J36
DD 629.136/029/4 UK
•JANE'S AIRPORTS, EQUIPMENT, AND SERVICES. Added/Corp Jane's Information Group. **VFOAT** Airports, Equipment, and Services. 13th Ed. (1994-95)-. English. One time a year. $257.00. Jane's Information Group, Sentinel House, 163 Brighton Road, Coulsdon Surrey CR5 2NH United Kingdom. **Tel** 011 44 181 7631030, FAX 011 44 181 7630276, telex 916907-JANES-G. **(Subscription address:** Jane's Information Group / US Subscriptions, 1340 Braddock Place, Suite 300, Alexandria VA 22314. **Tel** (800)243-3852, (703)683-3700.) ***Continues in part** Jane's Airport & ATC Equipment.*

LC U **ISSN** 0075-3017
DD 355 UK
CCC
JANE'S ALL THE WORLD'S AIRCRAFT (LONDON, ENGLAND). See Military and Defense.

LC UG1420 .J36
DD 623/.043 UK
JANE'S AVIONICS. See Military and Defense.

LC TL512 .I55
DD 629.1/029/4 SZ
JANE'S INTERNATIONAL ABC AEROSPACE DIRECTORY. Added/Corp Jane's Information Group. **VFOAT** International ABC Aerospace Directory. (199?)-. English. One time a year. $372.00. Jane's Information Group, Sentinel House, 163 Brighton Road, Coulsdon Surrey CR5 2NH United Kingdom. **Tel** 011 44 181 7631030, FAX 011 44 181 7630276, telex 916907-JANES-G. ***Continues** International ABC Aerospace Directory, 0074-1116.*

LC TL787 .J28
DD 629.4 UK
•JANE'S SPACE DIRECTORY. VFOAT Space Directory. 9th Ed. (1993-94)-. English. One time a year. $272.00. Jane's Information Group, Sentinel House, 163 Brighton Road, Coulsdon Surrey CR5 2NH United Kingdom. **Tel** 011 44 181 7631030, FAX 011 44 181 7630276, telex 916907-JANES-G. ***Continues** Interavia Space Directory.*

LC TL501 .J35 **ISSN** 0286-0635
DD 387.7/025/52 JA
JAPAN AVIATION DIRECTORY. (19??)-. Directory. English. One time a year (June). $120.00. Wings Aviation Press Kanda, Kitamura Building, Kanda Higashi, Chiyoda ku Tokyo 101 Japan. **Tel** 011 81 3 3796 6647. **ED** H. Ohashi. **Ad Acc. Circ:** 5,000. ***Continues** Japanese Aerospace Directory, 0304-1654.*
Desc: Yearbook of Japan's military, aerospace and air transport world. Also it contains directory listings for government organizations and companies plus personnel listings.

LC TL501 .J35 **ISSN** 0304-1654
DD 338.4/7/62910952 JA
JAPANESE AEROSPACE DIRECTORY. (19??)-. Directory. English. $8.50. Koku Shinbun Sha, (Aviation Press), 14-5 Ginza 1 chome, Chuoku Tokyo 104 Japan.

LC TL
DD 629 UK
JAR. (19??)-. Periodical. English. Price varies. Civil Aviation Authority / England, Grenville House, 37 Gratton Road, Cheltenham Glo GL50 2BN United Kingdom. **Tel** 011 44 1242 235151, FAX 011 44 1242 584139.

LC G **ISSN** 0279-7984
DD 910 US
JAX FAX TRAVEL MARKETING MAGAZINE. See Travel and Tourism.

LC TL790.A1 B7 **ISSN** 0007-084X
DD 629.4/05 UK
CODEN JBISAW
JBIS. JOURNAL OF THE BRITISH INTERPLANETARY SOCIETY. (JOURNAL OF THE BRITISH INTERPLANETARY SOCIETY.). [JBIS, J. Br. Interplanet. Soc.]. **Added/Corp** British Interplanetary Society. **VFOAT** JBIS; J.B.I.S. Vol. 1, No. 1 (Jan. 1934)-. Periodical. English. Twelve times a year. $378.00. British Interplanetary Society Ltd, 27/29 South Lambeth Road, London SW8 1SZ United Kingdom. **Tel** 011 44 171 7353160, FAX 011 44 171 8201504. Index available in last issue of volume--attached. **Circ:** 1,500. available on microfilm and microfiche from University Microfilms International (UMI). Documents available from Article Express International, Ask*IEEE. ***Absorbed** British Interplanetary Society Bulletin of the British Interplanetary Society.*
Desc: Contributions in space research, technology and astronautics. Published with specialist subjects: communications, remote sensing, solar system exploration and space stations.
Ind/Abst Bioeng. Abstr.; Curr. Cit.; Ei Page One; EMBASE; Energy Res. Abstr. (March 1983-); Eng. Index Annu.; GeoRef; INSPEC (Dec. 1968-); Int. Aerosp. Abstr.; Meteorol. Geoastrophys. Abstr.

LC TL
DD 629 US
JENS JURGEN'S ... CHARTER FLIGHT DIRECTORY AND GUIDE TO OTHER AIR TRAVEL BARGAINS. VFOAT Charter Flight Directory and Guide to Other Air Travel Bargains; Charter Flight Directory. (1978)-. Directory. English. Travel Information Bureau, PO Box 883, Amityville NY 11701. **Tel** (516)454-0880. ***Continues** Charter Flight Directory.*

LC TL501 .J46A **ISSN** 0364-331X
DD 629.13/005 US
JEPPESEN SANDERSON AVIATION YEARBOOK. Main/Corp Jeppesen Sanderson, Inc. **VFOAT** Aviation Yearbook. English. One time a year. Jeppesen Sanderson Inc, 55 Inverness Drive East, Inglewood CO 80112.

LC HF1001 **ISSN** 0710-5932
DD 380/.097123/3 CN
JET (CALGARY). (JET.). [Jet]. (1950)-. Periodical. English. Twelve times a year. Jet, 3115 Carleton Street South West, Calgary Alberta T2T 3L5 Canada.

LC HE9761 **ISSN** 0021-6003
DD 387.7/44/05 US
JET CARGO NEWS. See Transportation.

LC TL500
DD 629.13 UK
JET PROGRAMS. (19??)-. English. Four times a year. £403.00. Airclaims Ltd., Cardinal Point, Newall Road / Heathrow Airport, London TW6 2AS United Kingdom. **Tel** 011 44 181 8971066, FAX 011 44 181 8970300, telex 934679.
Desc: Review of western and eastern built jet airliner types and their manufacturers. Includes development history, performance, market and immediate competition.

LC TL
DD 629 UK
JOINT AVIATION REQUIREMENTS AMENDMENT SERVICE. English. Irregular. £50.00 UK; £65.00 other. Civil Aviation Authority / England, Grenville House, 37 Gratton Road, Cheltenham Glo GL50 2BN United Kingdom. **Tel** 011 44 1242 235151, FAX 011 44 1242 584139.

LC TL **ISSN** 0110-5493
DD 629 NZ
CCC
JOURNAL - AVIATION HISTORICAL SOCIETY OF NEW ZEALAND. [J. - Aviat. Hist. Soc. N.Z.]. (1976)-. Periodical. English. Three times a year (Apr., Aug., Dec.). $32.95. Aviation Society of New Zealand, PO Box 12-009, Wellington New Zealand. **Tel** 011 64 4 4714704, FAX 011 64 4 4710395. **Circ:** 600. ***Continues** AHSNZ Journal, 0005-2124.*

LC TL870 **ISSN** 0893-1321
DD 629.47 US
CCC
CODEN JAEEEZ
JOURNAL OF AEROSPACE ENGINEERING. [J. aerosp. eng.]. **Added/Corp** American Society of Civil Engineers. Aerospace Division. Vol. 1, No. 1 (Jan. 1988)-. Periodical. English. Four times a year. $144.00. American Society of Civil Engineers / ASCE, 345 East 47th Street, New York NY 10017-2398. **Tel** (212)705-7179, FAX (212)705-7300, telex 422847 ASCE UI. **(Subscription address:** American Society of Civil Engineers, Publisher Fulfillment Agency, Box 828, Somerset NJ 08875. **Tel** (800)548-2723, (212)705-7539.) **ED** Robert F. Seedlock. Index available. cum. index. ctrl circ. available on microfilm and microfiche from University Microfilms International (UMI); available on CD-ROM from American Society of Civil Engineers. Documents available from Article Express International, Documents on Demand.
Ind/Abst Appl. Sci. Technol. Index; ASCE Annu. Comb. Index (1988-); ASCE Publ. Inf. (1989-); Ei Page One; Eng. Index Annu.; Environ. Abstr.; Expand. Acad. Index (1992-); Fluid Abstr., Civil Eng.; Fluid Abstr. Proc. Eng.; FLUIDEX; GeoRef; Int. Aerosp. Abstr.; Int. Civil Eng. Abstr.

LC K10 .O835 **ISSN** 0021-8642
DD 629.13 387.7 US
JOURNAL OF AIR LAW AND COMMERCE, THE. See Law.

LC TL725.3.T7 J6 **ISSN** 0021-8650
DD 629.136 US
Pr Rev.
JOURNAL OF AIR TRAFFIC CONTROL, THE. [J. air traffic control]. **Added/Corp** Air Traffic Control Association. **VFOAT** Journal of ATC; Air Traffic Control. Vol. 1 (July 1958)-. Trade Publication. English. Four times a year (Jan., Apr., July, Oct.). $35.00. Air Traffic Control Association, 2300 Clarendon Boulevard, Suite 711, Arlington VA 22201. **Tel** (703)522-5717, FAX (703)527-7251. **ED** Suzette Matthews. Index available (Jan./Mar. issue for preceding year). cum. index. **Bk Rev. Ad Acc, Adv Mgr:** Aida Gregory. **Circ:** 4,100. available in reprints; available with illustrations; available with charts.
Desc: Progress in the art and science of air traffic control.
Ind/Abst Aviat. Tradescan [Full Cov.]; Health Saf. Sci. Abstr.; Int. Aerosp. Abstr.

LC HE9781 .J68 **ISSN** 0969-6997
DD 387.7/068 UK
•JOURNAL OF AIR TRANSPORT MANAGEMENT. Vol. 1, No. 1 (March 1994)-. Periodical. English. Four times a year. $229.00. Butterworth Heinemann Publishers, Linacre House Jordan Hill, Oxford OX2 8DP United Kingdom. **Tel** 011 44

1865 310366, FAX 011 44 1865 310898. **(Subscription address:** Elsevier Science Ltd. / Oxford Fulfillment Centre, PO Box 800, Kidlington OX5 1DX United Kingdom. **Tel** 011 44 865 843355.) available on microfilm; available on an online database from Elsevier Electronic Subscriptions (EES).

LC TL501 .J63 **ISSN** 0021-8669
DD 629 US
CCC
CODEN JAIRAM

Pr Rev.
JOURNAL OF AIRCRAFT. [J. aircr.]. **Added/Corp** American Institute of Aeronautics and Astronautics. **VFOAT** J. Aircraft. Vol. 1 (Jan./Feb. 1964)-. Periodical. English. Six times a year. $315.00. American Institute of Aeronautics & Astronautics, 370 l'Enfant Promenade Southwest, Washington DC 20024-2518. **Tel** (202)646-7400, FAX (202)646-7508, telex 204792 AIAA UR. **ED** Thomas M. Weeks. **Circ:** 3,500. available on microfilm and microfiche from University Microfilms International (UMI). Documents available from Article Express International, The Genuine Article, Ask*IEEE, CASDDS.
Desc: Covers advanced design concepts and operating advances in aircraft. Papers on military and civilian aircraft, ground effect machines, V/STOL and supersonic and hypersonic aircraft are presented with emphasis on practical engineering.
Ind/Abst Acoust. Abstr.; Bioeng. Abstr.; BMT Abstr.; Chem. Abstr.; Curr. Cit.; Curr. Contents Eng. Comput. Technol.; Ei Page One; EMBASE; Eng. Mater. Abstr.; Eng. Index Annu.; Expand. Acad. Index (1992-); Fluid Abstr., Civil Eng.; Fluid Abstr. Proc. Eng.; FLUIDEX (1973-); INSPEC (Sept./Oct. 1968-); Int. Aerosp. Abstr.; Res. Alert [Select. Cov.]; SCISEARCH; Shock Vibr. Dig.; SportSearch.

LC WMLC 90/1002 **ISSN** 1065-1136
DD 629 US
JOURNAL OF AVIATION/AEROSPACE EDUCATION & RESEARCH, THE. [J. aviat./aerosp. educ. res.]. **VFOAT** Journal of Aviation Aerospace Education & Research; Journal of Aviation/Aerospace Education and Research; JAAER. Vol. 1, No. 1 (Spring 1990)-. Periodical. English. Three times a year. $50.00. Journal of Aviation/Aerospace Education and Research, JAAER, 600 South Clyde Morris Boulevard, Daytona Beach FL 32114. **Tel** (904)226-6855, FAX (904)226-6012.
Ind/Abst Aviat. Tradescan [Full Cov.].

LC TL676 .J65 **ISSN** 0731-5090
DD 629.1/1/05 US
CCC
CODEN JGCODS
JOURNAL OF GUIDANCE, CONTROL, AND DYNAMICS. (JOURNAL OF GUIDANCE, CONTROL, AND DYNAMICS : A PUBLICATION OF THE AMERICAN INSTITUTE OF AERONAUTICS AND ASTRONAUTICS DEVOTED TO THE TECHNOLOGY OF DYNAMICS AND CONTROL.). [J. guid. control dyn.]. **Added/Corp** American Institute of Aeronautics and Astronautics. **VFOAT** J. Guidance. Vol. 5, No. 1 (Jan./Feb. 1982)-. Periodical. English. Six times a year. $325.00. American Institute of Aeronautics & Astronautics, 370 l'Enfant Promenade Southwest, Washington DC 20024-2518. **Tel** (202)646-7400, FAX (202)646-7508, telex 204792 AIAA UR. **ED** Donald C. Fraser. Index available. **Circ:** 2,600. available on microfilm and microfiche from University Microfilms International (UMI). Documents available from Article Express International, The Genuine Article, Ask*IEEE. ***Continues** Journal of Guidance and Control, 0162-3192.*
Desc: Dynamics, guidance, control, navigation, optimization, electronics, information processing related to aeronautical and astronautical systems.
Ind/Abst Acoust. Abstr.; Appl. Sci. Technol. Index; Curr. Cit.; Curr. Contents Eng. Comput. Technol.; Ei Page One; Eng. Index Annu.; INSPEC (May-June 1982-); Int. Aerosp. Abstr.; Math. Rev.; Pollut. Abstr. Indexes; Res. Alert [Full Cov.]; Sci. Cit. Index; SCISEARCH; Zentralbl. Math. Ihre Grenzgeb.

LC UG622 .J68 **ISSN** 1057-8307
DD 358.4/005 US
JOURNAL OF MILITARY AVIATION. [J. mil. aviat.]. **VFOAT** Military Aviation; JMA. Vol. 1, No. 1 (Jan/Feb. 1992)-. Periodical. English. Six times a year (Jan., Mar., May., July, Sept., Nov.). $25.00 one-year; $40.00 two-year. Withers Publishing, 528 Dunkle School Road, Halifax PA 17032. **Tel** (717)896-3173, FAX (717)896-2902. **ED** Thomas J. Kaminski, (phone: (717)896-3173). **Bk Rev**, (Qty: 18). **Circ:** 5,000.

LC TL787 .J68 **ISSN** 1046-8757
DD 629.4 US
CODEN JPSPE5
Pr Rev. **TITLE CHANGE**
JOURNAL OF PRACTICAL APPLICATIONS OF SPACE. [J. pract. appl. space]. **VFOAT** JPAS. (1989)-(1995). Periodical. English. Space Transportation Association and High Frontier, 2800 Shirlington Road, Suite 405A, Arlington VA 22206. **Tel** (703)671-4111, FAX (703)931-6432. **ED** Aleta Jackson. (bound in June issue). cum. index. **Bk Rev**, (Qty: 1-10). **Circ:** 500 (ctrl). ***Absorbed** Space Power.* ***Continued by** Space Energy and Transportation.*
Desc: Covers practical matters involved with space science, technology and development, including energy, transportation, settlement and commercial development.
Ind/Abst Int. Aerosp. Abstr.

LC TL **ISSN** 0748-4658
DD 629 US
CCC
CODEN JPPOEL
Pr Rev.
JOURNAL OF PROPULSION AND POWER. [J. propuls. power]. **Added/Corp** American Institute of Aeronautics and Astronautics. Vol. 1, No. 1 (Jan.-Feb. 1985)-. Academic Scholarly Publication. English. Six times a year. $345.00. American Institute of Aeronautics & Astronautics, 370 l'Enfant Promenade Southwest, Washington DC 20024-2518. **Tel** (202)646-7400, FAX (202)646-7508, telex 204792 AIAA UR. **ED** R. H. Woodward Waesche. Index available. **Circ:** 2,000. available on microfilm and microfiche from University Microfilms International (UMI). Documents available from Article Express International, The Genuine Article, CASDDS.
Desc: Advancements in airbreathing, electric and exotic propulsion, solid and liquid rockets, fuels and propellants, power generation and conversion for aerospace vehicles.
Ind/Abst Acoust. Abstr.; Chem. Abstr. (1985-); Civ. Struct. Eng. Abstr.; Curr. Cit.; Curr. Contents Eng. Comput. Technol.; Ei Page One; Elect. Comm. Abstr.; Eng. Index Annu.; Environ. Eng. Abstr.; INIS Atomindex [Micro.]; Int. Aerosp. Abstr.; Mater. Sci. Eng. Abstr.; Mech. Eng. Abstr.; Res. Alert [Full Cov.]; Sci. Cit. Index; SCISEARCH; Solid State Supercond. Abstr.

LC TL **ISSN** 1081-1435
DD 629 US
TITLE CHANGE
JOURNAL OF SPACE ABSTRACTS AND RESEARCH. (1995)-(1995). Periodical. English. Nova Science Publishers Inc., 6080 Jericho Turnpike, Suite 207, Commack NY 11725-2808. **Tel** (516)499-3103, (516)499-3106, FAX (516)499-3146. ***Continues** Space Information Review, 0895-6596.* ***Continued by** International Journal of Space Research.*

LC JX1 .J63 **ISSN** 0095-7577
DD 341.4/7 US
JOURNAL OF SPACE LAW. See Law.

LC TL787.A62 A2 **ISSN** 0022-4650
DD 629.4 US
CCC
CODEN JSCRAG
Pr Rev.
JOURNAL OF SPACECRAFT AND ROCKETS. [J. spacecr. rockets]. **Added/Corp** American Institute of Aeronautics and Astronautics. Vol. 1 (Jan./Feb. 1964)-. Academic Scholarly Publication. English. Six times a year. $295.00. American Institute of Aeronautics & Astronautics, 370 l'Enfant Promenade Southwest, Washington DC 20024-2518. **Tel** (202)646-7400, FAX (202)646-7508, telex 204792 AIAA UR. **ED** E. Vincnet Zoby. Index available. **Circ:** 3,100. available on microfilm and microfiche from University Microfilms International (UMI); available with charts; available with illustrations. Documents available from Article Express International, The Genuine Article, Ask*IEEE, CASDDS, BLDSC, FAXON Xpress, SWETS.
Desc: Original papers on science and technology of spacecraft and missle systems, applied areas of fluid mechanics and aerothermodynamics and application to other fields.
Ind/Abst Acoust. Abstr.; Appl. Sci. Technol. Index; Bioeng. Abstr.; Chem. Abstr.; Curr. Cit.; Curr. Contents Eng. Comput. Technol.; Ei Page One; EMBASE; Energy Res. Abstr.; Eng. Mater. Abstr.; Eng. Index Annu.; INSPEC (Oct. 1968-); Int. Aerosp. Abstr.; Pollut. Abstr. Indexes; Res. Alert [Full Cov.]; Sci. Cit. Index; SCISEARCH; Shock Vibr. Dig.

LC TL504 .A3556 **ISSN** 0001-9267
DD 629.13/00954 II
CODEN JANIAK
JOURNAL OF THE AERONAUTICAL SOCIETY OF INDIA, THE. [J. Aeronaut. Soc. India]. **Main/Corp** Aeronautical Society of India. Vol. 1 (Feb. 1949)-. Periodical. English. Four times a year. $65.00. Journal of the Aeronautical Society of India, c/o Aeronautical Development Establishment, CV Raman Nagar, Bangalore 560 093 India. **Tel** 011 91 540386, telex 0845-8461 ADE-IN. **(Subscription address:** Prints India, 11 Darya Ganj, New Delhi 110002 India. **Tel** 011 91 11 3268645, FAX 011 91 11 3275542, telex 31-61087 PRIN-IN.) **ED** K Rajaiah. Index available. **Bk Rev. Ad Acc. Circ:** 2,300. Documents available from Ask*IEEE.
Desc: Covers all aspects of aeronautics and space such as aerodynamics, structures, propulsions, space sciences, etc., fracture mechanics and finite elements.
Ind/Abst Curr. Cit.; INSPEC (1983-1991); Int. Aerosp. Abstr.

LC TL716.A1 A513 **ISSN** 0002-8711
DD 629.13335 US
CODEN JHESAK
JOURNAL OF THE AMERICAN HELICOPTER SOCIETY. [J. Am. Helicopter Soc.]. **Main/Corp** American Helicopter Society. Vol. 1 (Jan. 1956)-. Periodical. English. Four times a year (Jan., April, July and Oct.). $35.00. American Helicopter Society, 217 North Washington Street, Alexandria VA 22314. **Tel** (703)684-6777, FAX (703)739-9279. **Bk Rev. Ad Acc. Circ:** 8,000 (ctrl). Documents available from Article Express International, The Genuine Article, Ask*IEEE.
Desc: Publishes original technical papers dealing with the theory and practice of vertical flight.
Ind/Abst Acoust. Abstr.; Bioeng. Abstr.; Curr. Cit.; Curr. Contents Eng. Comput. Technol.; Ei Page One; Eng. Index Annu.; INSPEC (April 1984-); Int. Aerosp. Abstr.; Pollut. Abstr. Indexes; Res. Alert [Full Cov.]; Sci. Cit. Index; SCISEARCH.

LC TL **ISSN** 0021-9142
DD 629 US
CODEN JALSA6
Pr Rev.
JOURNAL OF THE ASTRONAUTICAL SCIENCES, THE. [J. astronaut. sci.]. **Added/Corp** American Astronautical Society. Vol. 5, No. 1 (Spring 1958)-. Periodical. English. Four times a year. $140.00. American Astronautical Society, 6352 Mill Place, Suite 102, Springfield VA 22152-2354. **Tel** (703)866-0020, FAX (703)866-3526. **ED** Kyle T. Alfriend. Index available (bound in last issue). cum. index. **Bk Rev. Circ:** 1,400. available on microfiche. Documents available from Article Express International, The Genuine Article, Ask*IEEE. ***Continues** Journal of Astronautics;* ***Absorbed in part** Astronautical Sciences Review.*
Desc: Devoted to the science and technology of astronautics. Presents significant new results and surveys in all areas of astrophysics, celestial mechanics, etc.
Ind/Abst Bioeng. Abstr.; Curr. Contents Eng. Comput. Technol.; Ei Page One; Eng. Index Annu.; INSPEC (March-April 1969-); Int. Aerosp. Abstr.; Math. Rev.; Res. Alert [Full Cov.]; Sci. Cit. Index; SCISEARCH.

LC TL501 .J68 **ISSN** 0257-3423
DD 629.1 II
JOURNAL OF THE INSTITUTION ENGINEERS (INDIA). AEROSPACE ENGINEERING DIVISION. **VFOAT** Aerospace Engineering Division. Periodical. English. Two times a year. Institution of Engineers India, 8 Gokhale Road, Calcutta 700020 India. **Tel** 011 91 33 288311, 011 91 33 288334, FAX 011 91 33 288345, telex 21 7885 IEIC IN. ***Continues** Journal of the Institution of Engineers (India), 0368-2498.*
Ind/Abst Ei Page One.

LC TL **ISSN** 0021-4663
DD 629 JA
CCC
CODEN NKGAB8
JOURNAL OF THE JAPAN SOCIETY FOR AERONAUTICAL AND SPACE SCIENCES. (NIHON KOKU UCHU GAKKAISHI.). [J. Jpn. Soc. Aeronaut. Space Sci.]. **Added/Corp** Nihon Koku Uchu Gakkaishi. **VFOAT** Journal of the Japan Society for Aeronautical and Space Sciences. Vol. 16, No. 174 (July 1968)-. Periodical. Japanese. Twelve times a year. $260.00. Nihon Koku Uchu Gakkai, (Japan Society for Aeronautical & Space Sciences), 18-2 Shinbashi 1 Chome, Arakawaku Tokyo 105 Japan. Documents available from Ask*IEEE. ***Continues** Nihon Koku Gakkaishi.*
Ind/Abst INSPEC (1984-); Int. Aerosp. Abstr.

LC TL789.A1 J67 **ISSN** 0730-5478
DD 001.9/42/05 US
Pr Rev.
JOURNAL OF UFO STUDIES, THE. [J. UFO stud.]. **VFOAT** Journal of U.F.O. Studies. **VAT** Journal of Unidentified Flying Object Studies. (1989)-. Periodical. English. One time a year. $18.00. Center for UFO Studies, 2457 West Peterson, Chicago IL 60659. **Tel** (312)271-3611. **ED** Michael D Swords. **Bk Rev. Ad Acc. Circ:** 500 (ctrl).
Desc: A collection of papers on significant aspects of the UFO phenomenon, written for advanced students of the subject and scientists.
Ind/Abst Except. Hum. Exp.

LC TL **ISSN** 0449-5152
DD 629 FR
JOURNAL OFFICIEL DES COMMUNAUTES EUROPEENNES : COMMUNICATIONS ET INFORMATIONS. 11.- Vol.; 12. Jan. 1968-. French. Irregular. Communautes Europeennes, 61 rue des Delle-Feuilles, Paris 16E France. ***Supersedes in part** Journal Officiel des Communautes Europeennes, 0022-5479.*
Ind/Abst Rev. Med. Vet. Entomol.

LC HE9769.A3 J68
DD 387.7/334/0216 SZ
JP AIRLINE-FLEETS INTERNATIONAL. **VFOAT** J.P. Airline-Fleets International; JP Airline Fleets International; Airline Fleets International; Airline-Fleets International. English (German). One time a year. 45.00F Switzerland; $39.50 US. Bucher Publications, PO Box 44, CH-8058 Zurich-Airport Switzerland. **Tel** 011 41 1 8100311. **ED** U Klee and F Bucher. Index available. **Ad**

Aeronautics, Astronautics

Acc. Circ: 10,000 (ctrl). available on diskette (5 1/4 IBM MSDOS).
Desc: Airline-fleetlist reference book.

LC TL **ISSN** 0892-9661
DD 629 US
JPL PUBLICATION. [JPL publ.]. Main/Corp Jet Propulsion Laboratory (U.S.). VAT Jet Propulsion Laboratory Publication. (19??)-. Monographic series. English. Irregular. Free on request. Jet Propulsion Laboratory, 4800 Oak Grove Drive / MS264-786, Pasadena CA 91103. **Tel** (818)354-5090. Documents available from CASDDS.
Ind/Abst Chem. Abstr.

LC TL
DD 629 US
JPRS REPORT. SCIENCE & TECHNOLOGY. CENTRAL EURASIA. SPACE. Added/Corp United States. Joint Publications Research Service. United States. Foreign Broadcast Information Service. VFOAT Science & Technology. Space; Science and Technology. Space; Central Eurasia. Space. (Jan. 27, 1992)-. Periodical. English (translations available in Russian). *Continues JPRS Report. Science & Technology. USSR. Space.*

LC TL770.A1 J8 **ISSN** 0090-4937
DD 629.133/1/340 US
JR. AMERICAN MODELER. VAT Junior American Modeler. (19??)-. Periodical. English. Six times a year. $4.50. Potomac Aviation Publications, 733-15th Street NW, Washington DC 20005.

LC TL **ISSN** 0273-9895
DD 629 US
KANSAS CITY AVIATION. Vol. 1, No. 1 (Dec. 1980)-. Periodical. English. Twelve times a year. Pilot News Inc, PO Box 22373, Kansas City MO 64113.

LC HE9797.5.D42 C655c
DD 629.13 DK
KBENHAVNS LUFTHAVN, ARSRAPPORT. Main/Corp Kbenhavns Lufthavnsven (Denmark). (1970)-. Danish. One time a year. Kbenhavns Lufthavnsvsen, Havnedministrationen 2770, Kastrup Denmark. **Tel** 45 31 509333, FAX 45 31 511133. **ED** Bo Harigaard.
Desc: Annual report for the Copenhagen airport.

LC TL726.3.K4 A3
DD 629.136058 US
KENTUCKY AIRPORT DIRECTORY. Main/Corp Kentucky. Dept. of Aeronautics. Directory. English. Free. Kentucky Office of Aeronautics, Frankfort KY 40622. **Tel** (502)564-4480. **ED** Ben Prewitt. **Circ:** 3,000.
Desc: Directory of public use airports. Lists runway length and width radio frequencies, phone numbers, fuels, lighting, repairs, and navigation. Also location and layout maps.

LC WMLC L 83/6766 **ISSN** 0891-1851
DD 745 US
KITPLANES. [Kitplanes]. VFOAT Kit Planes. (198?)-. Periodical. English. Twelve times a year. $26.97. Fancy Publications, PO Box 6050, Mission Viejo CA 92690. **Tel** (714)855-8822, (800)426-2516, FAX (714)855-3045. **(Subscription address:** Palm Coast Data, PO Box 420163, Agency Department, Palm Coast FL 32142. **Tel** (904)445-4662 ext. 669, (800)829-5475.) **ED** Dave Martin. Index available. **Bk Rev. Ad Acc. Circ:** 70,000. *Continues Private Pilot's Guide to Kitplanes.*
Desc: Is edited for the aviation enthusiast interested in designing, building and flying his own airplane.

LC TL504 .K596
DD 629.13 JA
KOKU NENKAN = AVIATION ANNUAL OF JAPAN. Added/Corp Nihon Koku Kyokai. VFOAT Aviation Annual of Japan. No. 23 (1976)-. Periodical. Japanese. One time a year. ¥10000. Nihon Koku Kyokai, Kokukaikan Bunkan, 1-18-2 Shinbashi Minatoku, Tokyo 105 Japan. **Tel** 011 81 3 35021206, FAX 011 81 3 35031375. **ED** Yasunobu Sekiba. *Continues Koku Uchu Nenkan.*

LC TL568.K6 K64a
DD 629.13 JA
KOKU UCHU GIJUTSU KENKYUJO. Main/Corp Koku Uchu Gijutsu Kenkyujo. Added/Corp Koku Uchu Gijutsu Kenkyujo. NAL; National Aerospace Laboratory. VFOAT NAL National Aerospace Laboratory. (19??)-. Japanese. Irregular. Koku Uchu Gijutsu Kenkyujo, 1880 Jindaijimachi, Chofu 182 Japan. **Tel** 011 81 3 422475911, FAX 011 81 3 422421371. *Continues Koku Uchu Gijutsu Kenkyujo. Koku Gijutsu Kenkyujo Yoran.*

LC HE9877.A1 U58b
DD 629.13 JA
KOKU YUSO TOKEI NENPO. Main/Corp Japan. Unyusho. Unyusho Daijin Kambo Joho Kanribu. (1971)-. Periodical. Japanese. Unyusho Daijin Kambo Joho Kanribu, c/o Daijin Kambo Chosha, 3-Gokan 1-3 Kasumigaseki, Chiyoda-Ku Japan. *Continues Koku Yuso Tokei Nempo.*

LC QB495 .K86 **ISSN** 0254-6124
DD 500.5/05 CC
CODEN KKXUDK
KONGJIAN KEXUE XUEBAO. (KUNG CHIEN KO HSUEH PAO.). [Kongjian kexue xuebao]. Added/Corp Chung-kuo Kung Chien Ko Hsueh Hsueh Hui. VFOAT Chinese Journal of Space Science; Chinese Journal of Space Sciences. (1981)-. Periodical. Chinese (summaries and/or abstracts in English). Four times a year. $36.10. **(Subscription address:** China International Book Trading Corporation, PO Box 399, Library Service Department, Beijing 100044 People's Republic of China. **Tel** 011 86 1 8414284, FAX 011 86 1 8412023, telex 22496 CIBTC CN.) Documents available from Ask*IEEE, CASDDS.
Ind/Abst Chem. Abstr. (-1988); INSPEC (1984-); Int. Aerosp. Abstr. (1983-).

LC QB500 .K63 **ISSN** 0023-4206
DD 500.5 RU

NLM W1 KO627 **CODEN** KOISAW
KOSMICESKIE ISSLEDOVANIJA. (KOSMICHESKIE ISSLEDOVANIIA.). [Kosm. issled.]. Added/Corp Akademiia Nauk SSSR. Vol. 1 (July/Aug. 1963)-. Academic Scholarly Publication. Russian. Six times a year. $315.00. Izdatelstvo Nauka / Akademiia Nauk, (Publishing House of the Russian Academy of Sciences), Leninskii Porspekt 14, 117901 Moscow Russia. **Tel** 011 95 9542153, FAX 011 95 9382144, telex 411964. **(Subscription address:** East View Publications Inc., 3020 Harbor Lane North, Suite 110, Minneapolis MN 55447. **Tel** (800)477-1005, (612)550-0961, FAX (612)559-2931.) Documents available from Ask*IEEE, CASDDS. *Supersedes Iskusstvennye Sputniki Zemli.*
Ind/Abst Chem. Abstr.; INSPEC (1968-); Int. Aerosp. Abstr.; Math. Rev.

LC TL504 .V683 **ISSN** 0130-2701
DD 629.13 RU
KRYLIA RODINY. Added/Corp Vsesoiuznoe Dobrovolnoe Obshchestvo Sodeistviia Aviatsii (Soviet Union) DOSAAF SSSR. Vol. 1, (1950)-. Periodical. Russian. Twelve times a year. $99.95. Novo-Ryazanskaya, Moscow Russia. **(Subscription address:** East View Publications Inc., 3020 Harbor Lane North, Suite 110, Minneapolis MN 55447. **Tel** (800)477-1005, (612)550-0961, FAX (612)559-2931.) **ED** L.F. Yasnopl'skii. **Bk Rev Circ:** 80,000. available on microfilm; available with illustrations. Documents available from BLDSC.

LC QA930 .K76 **ISSN** 0258-1825
DD 533/.62/05 CC
Pr Rev.
KUNG CHI TUNG LI HSUEH HSUEH PAO. Added/Corp Chung-kuo Kung Chi Tung li Hsueh Yen Chiu Hui. VFOAT Kung Chi Tung li Hsueh; Acta Aerodynamica Sinica; Kongqidonglixue Xuebao. (19??)-. Periodical. Chinese (summaries and/or abstracts in English). Four times a year. Zhongguo Kongqi Dongli Yanjiu yu Fazhan Zhongxin, PO Box 211, Mianyang Sichuan 621000, People's Republic of China. **Tel** 0816-22490. **ED** Z. Fenggan.
Ind/Abst Int. Aerosp. Abstr.

LC TL504 .K84
DD 629.13/005 CC
KUO CHI HANG KUNG = GUOJI HANGKONG. VFOAT Guoji Hangkong; International Aviation. (1979)-. Periodical. Chinese. Twelve times a year. Science Press, 16 Donghuangchenggen North Street, Beijing 100707, People's Republic of China. **Tel** 011 86 1 4019821, 011 86 1 4010642, FAX 011 86 1 4012180, 011 86 1 4019810, telex 210147. **ED** Leng Yuan-You. **Ad Acc. Circ:** 50,000.
Desc: A comprehensive and informational magazine for aeronautical science and technology. Covering a wide range of subjects, such as aircraft, engines, avionics, equipment, airborne systems, and etc.

LC TL **ISSN** 8756-5331
DD 629 US
L5 NEWS (TUCSON, ARIZ. : 1986). (L5 NEWS.). [L5 news]. VFOAT L 5 News; L Five News. Vol. 1, No. 1 (1986)-. Periodical. English. Twelve times a year. L-5 Society, 600 Maryland Avenue SW #203W, Washington DC 20024. *Continues L5 News, 8756-5331.*

LC TL **ISSN** 0364-7587
DD 629 US
LANDSAT NON-U.S. STANDARD CATALOG. VAT Landsat Non-United States Standard Catalog. (19??)-. Catalog. English. Twelve times a year. User Services, Eros Data Center, Sioux Falls SD 57198. **Tel** (703)487-4650. *Continues Earth Resources Technology Satellite: Non-U.S. Standard Catalog.*

LC TL **ISSN** 0364-7560
DD 629 US
LANDSAT U.S. STANDARD CATALOG. VAT Landsat United States Standard Catalog. English. Twelve times a year. User Services, Eros Data Center, Sioux Falls SD 57198. **Tel** (703)487-4650. *Continues Earth Resources Technology Satellite: U.S. Standard Catalog.*

LC TL
DD 629 US
LARGE SPACE STRUCTURES & SYSTEMS IN THE SPACE STATION ERA. Added/Corp United States. National Aeronautics and Space Administration. Scientific and Technical Information Division. VFOAT Large Space Structures and Systems in the Space Station Era. (Nov. 1990)-. English. National Technical Information Service - NTIS, Room 2027S, 5285 Port Royal Road, Springfield VA 22161. **Tel** (703)487-4630, (703)487-4660, (703)487-4650, FAX (703)321-8547, telex 89-9405. *Formed by the union of Space Station Systems. Supplement and Technology for Large Space Structures. Supplement.*

LC TL **ISSN** 0364-6793
DD 629 US
LATEST EDITIONS OF U.S. AIR FORCE AERONAUTICAL CHARTS. See Military and Defense.

LC TL
DD 629 US
LEGISLATIVE HISTORY OF CAB REGULATIONS. See Law.

LC TL504 .L39
DD 629.1300 XR
LETECKY OBZOR. Added/Corp Czechoslovak Republic. Ministerstvo Dopravy a Spoju. Czechoslovak Republic. Ministerstvo Dopravy. (19??)-. Periodical. Czech. Six times a year. $27.00. Nakladatelstvi Dopravy a Spoju, Transport and Communications, Hybernska 5, 11578 Prague 1 Czech Republic. **Tel** 011 42 2 2365774, FAX 011 42 2 2356772. **(Subscription address:** Artia Pegas Press Ltd., Palac Metro Narodni Trida 25, 11210 Prague 1 Czech Republic. **Tel** 011 42 2 24196265, 011 42 2 24196266.) **ED** Miluse Kristova. **Bk Rev. Ad Acc. Circ:** 4,0001. available with charts; available with illustrations.

LC TL504 .L414 **ISSN** 0024-1156
DD 629.13 XR
LETECTVI + [I.E. A] KOSMONAUTIKA. Added/Corp Svaz pro Spolupraci s Armadou. (1952)-. Periodical. Czech. Twenty-six times a year. $164.90. **(Subscription address:** Kubon & Sagner, ABT Zeitschriftenimport, D 80328 Munich Germany. **Tel** 011 49 89 54218130.) **ED** Zdenek Formanek.

LC TL501 .L53
DD 629.133/34 UK
LIGHT AVIATION. Apr. 1968-. Periodical. English. Four times a year. £8.00. Aircraft Owners and Pilots Association / UK, 50 Cambridge Street, London SW1V 4QQ United Kingdom. **Tel** 0.834-5631. **ED** David F Ogilvy. **Bk Rev. Ad Acc. Circ:** 4,000 (ctrl). *Supersedes British Light Aviation.*

LC TL671.9 .L47 **ISSN** 0278-8950
DD 629.134/6 US
LIGHT PLANE MAINTENANCE. [Light plane maint.]. (19??)-. Periodical. English. Twelve times a year. $75.00. Belvoir Publications Inc., 75 Holly Hill Lane, Greenwich CT 06836. **Tel** (203)661-6111, FAX (203)661-4802. **(Subscription address:** Palm Coast Data, PO Box 420163, Agency Department, Palm Coast FL 32142. **Tel** (904)445-4662 ext. 669, (800)829-5475.) **ED** John Likakis. **Circ:** 15,000.
Desc: Newsletter of interest to aircraft owners and private pilots containing maintenance information, sources of discount parts, etc.
Ind/Abst Index Inf. (May 1987-).

LC TL
DD 629 US
LIST OF CERTIFICATED PILOT SCHOOLS. (1975)-. Government Publication. English. US Department of Transportation / Federal Aviation Administration, 800 Independence Avenue Southwest, Washington DC 20591. **Tel** (202)367-3484, FAX (202)367-3505. *Continues List of Certificated Pilot Flight and Ground Schools.*

LC TL
DD 629 US
LIST OF CERTIFICATED U.S. AIR CARRIERS. English. Civil Aeronautics Board, 1825 Connecticut Avenue, Washington DC 20428. **Tel** (202)673-5174. *Continues List of U.S. Air Carriers.*

LC HE17 .A47 HE9784.5.U5 **ISSN** 0360-3954
DD 387.7/0973 US
LISTING OF AIRCRAFT ACCIDENTS/INCIDENTS BY MAKE AND MODEL, U.S. CIVIL AVIATION. English. One time a year. National Technical Information Service - NTIS, Room 2027S, 5285 Port Royal Road, Springfield VA 22161. **Tel** (703)487-4630, (703)487-4660, (703)487-4650, FAX (703)321-8547, telex 89-9405.

Aeronautics, Astronautics

LC HE9761   **ISSN** 1043-4968
DD 387.7   US
Pr Rev.
LITE FLYER. [Lite flyer]. Vol. 1, No. 1 (1st Qtr. 1989)-. Periodical. English. Five times a year. $10.00 US; $15.00 other. LW Amacker, 939 South 3rd Avenue, Walla Walla WA 99362. **Tel** (509)522-0158, **FAX** (509)525-3929. **ED** LeBaron W Amacker and Heather Gatimu. Index available. cum. index. **Bk Rev. Circ:** 750.
Desc: Contains airframe, powerplant, and other information vital to flight safety.

LC HE9761   **ISSN** 1043-495X
DD 387.7   US
Pr Rev.
LITE FLYER SAFETY ALERT ACTIONGRAM. [Lite flyer saf. alert actiongram]. Vol. 1 (1989)-. Periodical. English. Irregular (three to six times per year). $10.00 US; $15.00 other. LW Amacker, 939 South 3rd Avenue, Walla Walla WA 99362. **Tel** (509)522-0158, **FAX** (509)525-3929. **ED** LeBaron W Amacker and Heather Gatimu. Index available. cum. index. **Circ:** 750.

LC HE9803.A1 C57C   **ISSN** 0146-7549
DD 387.7/42/0973   US
LOCAL SERVICE CARRIERS PASSENGER ENPLANEMENTS. **Main/Corp** United States. Civil Aeronautics Board. Bureau of Operating Rights. English. Civil Aeronautics Board, 1825 Connecticut Avenue, Washington DC 20428. **Tel** (202)673-5174.

LC TL   **ISSN** 0364-5282
DD 629   US
LOCATION IDENTIFIERS. **Added/Corp** United States. Air Traffic Service. United States. Air Traffic Operations Service. United States. Air Traffic Rules and Procedures Service. (1970)-. Government Publication. English. Six times a year. $46.00. US Department of Transportation / US Coast Guard, 2100 Second Street Southwest, Washington DC 20953-0001. **Tel** (202)267-2229. (**Subscription address:** Superintendent of Documents, US Government Printing Office, Washington DC 20402.)
Desc: Lists location identifiers authorized by the Federal Aviation Administration, Department of the Navy, and Canadian Ministry of Transport. Also lists United States airspace fixes and procedure codes and includes guidelines for requesting identifiers and procedures for making assignments.

LC TL500.5 .A2 TL694.C6
DD 387.7 S 629.132/54   CN
LOCATION INDICATORS. INDICATEURS D'EMPLACEMENT. INDICADORES DE LUGAR. **Main/Corp** International Civil Aviation Organization. **Added/Corp** International Civil Aviation Organization. Indicateurs d'Emplacement. International Civil Aviation Organization. Indicadores de Lugar. **VFOAT** Indicateurs d'Emplacement; Omdocadpres de Lugar. (19??)-. English (French, Spanish and Russian). $36.00. International Civil Aviation Organization / ICAO, 1000 Sherbrooke Street West, Suite 400, Montreal Quebec H3A 2R2 Canada. **Tel** (514)285-8026, (514)285-8022, telex 05-24514.

LC HD4973 .B85C HD4966.A45 A452U5   **ISSN** 0273-432X
DD 331.2/973 331.2/8291/09794   US
LOCKHEED AIRCRAFT CORPORATION.
See Business and Economics-Labor.

LC TL501 .L5925   **ISSN** 0459-6773
DD 629   US
    CODEN LCHZA9
LOCKHEED HORIZONS. [Lockheed horiz.]. **Added/Corp** Lockheed Aircraft Corporation. Lockheed-California Company. Issue 1 (Spring 1965)-. Periodical. English. Lockheed California Co., Procurement Division Box 551, Burbank CA 90603. Documents available from Article Express International. **Ind/Abst** Bioeng. Abstr.; Ei Page One; Eng. Index Annu.; Int. Aerosp. Abstr. (1984-).

LC TL501 .B7   **ISSN** 0024-5798
DD 629.1305   UK
LOG (HAYES), THE. (THE LOG; THE OFFICIAL ORGAN OF THE BRITISH AIR LINE PILOTS). Vol 1 (Aug. 1937)-. Periodical. English. Six times a year. $34.23. British Air Line Pilots Association, 81 New Road Harlington, Hayes UB3 5BG Middlesex United Kingdom. **Tel** 011 44 181 7599331, FAX 011 44 181 5647957. **ED** Captain I G Frow. **Bk Rev. Ad Acc. Circ:** 7,000 (ctrl).
Desc: Letters, articles (serious and humorous) connected with flying environment.
Ind/Abst Int. Aerosp. Abstr.

LC KF2400.A15 L38   **ISSN** 0274-9319
DD 343.73/097/05 347.3303705   US
LPBA JOURNAL. See Law.

LC TL504 .H3
DD 629.13   NE
LUCHT- EN RUIMTEVAART TECHNIEK LITERATUUROVERZICHT. (19??)-. Dutch. Twelve times a year. 60.00. Wetenschappelijk en Technisch Documentatie-en Informatiecentrum Voor de Krijgsmacht Frederikkazerne, Gebouw 140 Van der Burchlaan 31, 2597 PC S-Gravenhage Netherlands. **Continues** Technische Documentatie- en Informatiecentrum voor de Krijgsmacht. Luchtvaarttechniek.
Ind/Abst Fluid Abstr., Civil Eng.; Fluid Abstr. Proc. Eng.; FLUIDEX.

LC TL503 .L74   **ISSN** 0173-6264
DD 629.13/005   GW
    CCC
LUFT- UND RAUMFAHRT. [Luft- Raumfahrt]. **Added/Corp** Deutsche Gesellschaft fuer Luft- und Raumfahrt. (1980)-. Periodical. German. Four times a year. DM36.00 Germany; DM42.00 other. Aviatic Verlag P Pletschacher, Hofmarktstrasse 30, D-82152 Planegg Germany. **Tel** 011 49 89 8596711. **Bk Rev. Ad Acc. Circ:** 10,000.
Ind/Abst Int. Aerosp. Abstr.

LC TL671.1 .N67a
DD 629.1333   GW
LUFTFAHRT-NORMEN-VERZEICHNIS. **Main/Corp** Normenstelle Luftfahrt. (19??)-. German (English). One time a year. Beuth Verlag GmbH, Burggrafenstrasse 6, D-10787 Berlin Germany. **Tel** 011 49 30 260112573, FAX 011 49 30 24399926. **Ad Acc.**

LC HE9859.A1 L82   **ISSN** 0800-4072
DD 387.7/09481/021   NO
LUFTFARTSSTATISTIKK = CIVIL AVIATION STATISTICS NORWAY. See Aeronautics, Astronautics-Abstracting, Bibliographies and Statistics.

LC HE9860.A1 S93a
DD 629.13   SW
LUFTFARTSVERKET. **Main/Corp** Sweden. Luftfartsverket. **VFOAT** Board of Civil Aviation. (19??)-. English (Swedish). One time a year. Luftfartsverket / Sweden, Fack, S-601 01, Norrkoping Sweden. **Continues** Sweden. Kungl. Luftfartsstyrelsen. Luftfartsverket.

LC U
DD 355   GW
Pr Rev.   CEASED
LUFTWAFFEN-FORUM. (19??)-(Nov. 1994). German. Gruner und Jahr Ag & Co, Abonnenten Service, D-20080 Hamburg Germany. **Tel** 011 49 40 37030, FAX 011 49 40 37030763. (**Subscription address:** Deutscher Pressevertrieb Buch, POB 101602 Hansa GMBH, D-20010 Hamburg Germany. **Tel** 011 49 40 23711249.)
Index available. **Bk Rev. Ad Acc. Circ:** 24,000.
Desc: Covers military aviation worldwide.

LC TL   **ISSN** 0889-4361
DD 629   US
LUSCOMBE ASSOCIATION NEWS. [Luscombe Assoc. news]. **VFOAT** Association News; Luscombe Association Newsletter. Periodical. English. Six times a year. $15.00 US; $20.00 Canada; $25.00 other. Luscombe Association, 6438 West Millbrook, Remus MI 49340. **Tel** (517)561-2393. **ED** John B Bergeson. Index available. cum. index. **Ad Acc. Circ:** 1,200 (ctrl).
Desc: Devoted to technical information and flying of Luscombe aircraft.

LC HE9803.A1 M33   **ISSN** 8756-9019
DD 387.7/0973/021   US
MAJOR AIRLINES ANALYSIS OF FULL YEAR ... FINANCIAL AND OPERATING RESULTS. (1983)-. English. Donaldson Lufkin & Jenrette Securities Corporation, 140 Broadway, New York NY 10005. **Continues** Major Airlines ... Financial and Operating Review, 0884-1071.

LC TL
DD 629   AT
MAJOR AUSTRALIAN AIRLINES. (1995)-. English. Two times a year. 29.60Aus$. Department of Transport / Australia, PO Box 594, Canberra ACT 2601 Australia. **Tel** 011 61 6 2747642. **Continues** Domestic Airlines.

LC TL
DD 629   UK
MANDATORY AIRCRAFT MODIFICATIONS AND INSPECTIONS SUMMARY. (19??)-. English. Twelve times a year. £26.80 UK; £29.20 other. Civil Aviation Authority / England, Grenville House, 37 Gratton Road, Cheltenham Glo GL50 2BN United Kingdom. **Tel** 011 44 1242 235151, FAX 011 44 1242 584139.

LC TL
DD 629   CN
MARITIME PATROL AVIATION. (19??)-. English. Two times a year (March, Sep.). 15.00Can$ (one-year), 28.00Can$ (two-year) North America; 20.00Can$ (one-year), 38.00Can$ (two-year) other. VP International, Canadian Forces Base, Greenwood Nova Scotia B0P 1N0 Canada. **Tel** (902)765-3391, FAX (902)765-5688. **ED** Flt. Lt. Mike Price, RAAF. **Bk Rev,** (Qty: 6). **Ad Acc. Circ:** 5,000 (ctrl).
Desc: Provides a medium for the exchange of ideas of importance to the free world in the broader aspects of Maritime Air doctrine and employment of Maritime Air Forces. Will report on advancement in the application of Maritime Air Weapons Systems, and related high-technology systems that are operational or are being introduced.

LC TD883.5.M3 M36a   **ISSN** 0191-2194
DD 363.7/3922/09752   US
MARYLAND STATE YEARLY AIR QUALITY DATA REPORT. (MARYLAND STATE YEARLY AIR QUALITY DATA REPORT.). **Added/Corp** Maryland. Air Management Administration. Maryland. Division of Air Monitoring. Maryland. Bureau of Air Quality Control. Maryland. Bureau of Air Quality and Noise Control. Maryland. Air Quality Programs. **VFOAT** Maryland Air Quality Data Report. (1972)-. English. Free. Maryland Department of the Environment, Air Management Administration, 201 West Preston Street, Baltimore MD 21201. **Tel** (410)225-5275. **Circ:** 400. available on magnetic tape (nine track). **Continues** State - Local Cooperative Air Sampling Program Yearly Data Report, 0094-4629.
Desc: Sampling monitoring reports for Maryland ambient air quality.

LC TL500
DD 629.13   CN
METEOROLOGY; INTERNATIONAL STANDARDS AND RECOMMENDED PRACTICES. ANNEX 3 TO THE CONVENTION ON INTERNATIONAL CIVIL AVIATION. **Main/Corp** International Civil Aviation Organization. (19??)-. English. $20.00. International Civil Aviation Organization / ICAO, 1000 Sherbrooke Street West, Suite 400, Montreal Quebec H3A 2R2 Canada. **Tel** (514)285-8026, (514)285-8022, telex 05-24514.

LC HE9761   **ISSN** 1054-9838
DD 387   US
MIDDLE EAST CIVIL AVIATION. [Middle East civil aviat.]. (1991)-. Periodical. English. Twenty-six times a year (MECA and supplement published monthly). $375.00. Phoenix Publishing Inc., 11490 Commerce Park Drive, Suite 360, Reston VA 22091-1532. **Tel** (703)318-8108, FAX (703)318-8107. **ED** Azin Hatefi (phone: (703)264-7708). **Bk Rev,** (Qty: 12). **Ad Acc. Circ:** 5,000 (ctrl).
Desc: Review of Middle East Civil Aviation news and analysis.

LC TL   **ISSN** 0273-7515
DD 629   US
MIDWEST FLYER MAGAZINE. **VFOAT** Midwest Flyer. Vol. 2, No. 11 (Oct. 1980)-. English. Twelve times a year. $15.00. Flyer Publishing CP, PO Box 199, Oregon WI 53575-0199. **Tel** (608)835-7063. **ED** Dave Weiman. **Bk Rev,** (Qty: 6). **Ad Acc. Circ:** 25,000 (ctrl). **Continues** Wisconsin Flyer, 0194-5068.
Desc: News and information combined with feature articles specifically dear to the Midwest aviation community. Circulation includes all owners of four-place and larger aircraft.

LC U
DD 355   US
MILITARY AIRCRAFT FORECAST. See Military and Defense.

LC UG485 .M484   **ISSN** 1046-9079
DD 623/.043/05   US
    CCC
MILITARY & AEROSPACE ELECTRONICS. See Military and Defense.

LC G   **ISSN** 0743-7897
DD 355   CCC
MILITARY SPACE. See Military and Defense.

LC TL   **ISSN** 0026-4709
DD 629   IT
MINERVA AEROSPAZIALE. [Minerva aerosp.]. (1969)-. Periodical. Italian. Two times a year. L130000. Edizioni Minerva Medica, Corso Bramante 83-85, 10126 Turin Italy. **Tel** 011 39 11 678282, FAX 011 39 11 674502.

LC GV   **ISSN** 0889-4809
DD 797   US
MINNESOTA FLYER. [Minn. fly.]. **Added/Corp** Minnesota Airport Operators Association. Minnesota Airport Operations Association. Minnesota Aviation Trades Association. **VFOAT** Minnesota Flyer Magazine. Vol. 1 (Jan. 1960)-. Periodical. English. Twelve times a

year. $15.00. Minnesota Flyer Magazine, PO Box 750, Sandstone MN 55072. **Tel** (612)245-2111, FAX (612)245-2438. **ED** Richard A. Coffey. **Bk Rev**, (Qty: 3). **Ad Acc, Adv Mgr:** Mary Ellen. **Circ:** 4,000.
Desc: Covers general aviation, pilots and FBO's.

LC TL
DD 629 CN
MINUTES. Main/Corp International Air Transport Association. General Meeting. (Oct. 1981)-. English. One time a year. Free on request. International Air Transport Association / Montreal, 2000 Peel Street, Room 3050, Montreal Quebec H3A 2R4 Canada. **Tel** (514)844-6311 ext. 232, FAX (514)844-5286, telex 05-267627. ***Continues*** *International Air Transport Association. General Meeting. Reports and Proceedings.*

LC HE9761 **ISSN** 0848-791X
DD 387.7/2/097105 CN
MINUTES OF PROCEEDINGS AND EVIDENCE OF THE SPECIAL COMMITTEE ON CANADA-UNITED STATES AIR TRANSPORT SERVICES. (MINUTES OF PROCEEDINGS AND EVIDENCE OF THE SPECIAL COMMITTEE ON CANADA-UNITED STATES AIR TRANSPORT SERVICES = PROCES-VERBAUX ET TEMOIGNAGES DU COMITE SPECIAL SUR LES SERVICES DE TRANSPORT AERIEN ENTRE LE CANADA ET LES ETATS-UNIS.). [Minutes proc. evid. Spec. Comm. Can.-U.S. Air Transp. Serv.]. **Main/Corp** Canada. Parliament. House of Commons. Special Committee on Canada-United States Air Transport Services. **VFOAT** Canada-United States Air Transport Services; Proces-Verbaux et Temoignages du Comite Special sur les Services de Transport Aerien entre le Canada et les Etats-Unis. 34th Parliament, 2nd Session, Issue No. 1 (Nov. 7/Nov. 20, 1990)-. Proceedings. English (French).

LC TL726.3.M8 M47 **ISSN** 0160-4562
DD 629.132/54/778 US
MISSOURI AIRPORT DIRECTORY. Directory. English. Missouri Department of Transportation, Division of Aviation, Jefferson City MO.

LC TL
DD 629 GW
MITTEILUNGEN. Main/Corp Forschungsinstitut fur Physik der Strahlantriebe (Stuttgart, Germany). Periodical. German. R Oldenbourg Verlag, Postfach 801360, D-81613 Munich Germany. **Tel** 011 49 89 450190, FAX 011 49 89 45019305.

LC TL507 .G6 **ISSN** 0374-1257
DD 629.1332 GW
MITTEILUNGEN AUS DEM MAX-PLANCK-INSTITUT FUER STROMUNGSFORSCHUNG UND DER AERODYNAMISCHEN VERSUCHSANSTALT. (MITTEILUNGEN.). [Mitt. Max-Planck-Inst. Stroem.forsch. Aerodyn. Vers.anst.]. **Main/Corp** Max-Planck-Institut fuer Stromungsforschung. **Added/Corp** Aerodynamische Versuchsanstalt Gottingen. (1950)-. Monographic series. German (English). Irregular. Price varies per volume. Deutsche Forschungs & Versuchsanstalt, Bunsenstr 10, D-37073 Goettingen Germany. **(Subscription address:** MPI fuer Stromungsjorshcung, Postfach 2853, D 3400 Gottingen Germany. **Tel** 011 49 551 7091.**) ED** E.A. Mueller. Index available. **Bk Rev. Circ:** 300. Documents available from BLDSC.

LC UC333 .M33
DD 355 US
MOBILITY FORUM : THE JOURNAL OF THE AIR MOBILITY COMMAND, THE. **Added/Corp** United States. Air Mobility Command. Chief of Safety. Vol. 1, No. 4 (July/Aug. 1992)-. Government Publication. English. Six times a year. $22.00. US Department of Defense, The Pentagon, Washington DC 20301. **Tel** (703)545-6700. **(Subscription address:** Superintendent of Documents, US Government Printing Office, Washington DC 20402. **)** ***Continues*** *MAC Forum, 1067-8999.*
Desc: Contains articles designed to promote safety and efficiency.
Ind/Abst Air Univ. Libr. Index Mil. Period. (199?-).

LC TL770 .A1U5 **ISSN** 0026-7295
DD 629.133 US
MODEL AIRPLANE NEWS. See Hobbies.

LC TL600 **ISSN** 0317-7831
DD 629.133/1/3406271 CN
MODEL AVIATION CANADA. Added/Corp Model Aeronautics Association of Canada. Vol. 4 (Jan. 1975)-. English. Six times a year. 12.00Can$ Canada; $18.00 US. Model Aeronautics Association of Canada, 5100 South Service Road, Unit 9, Burlington Ontario L7L 6A5 Canada. **Tel** (416)632-9808, FAX (416)632-3304. **ED** Peter Perry. **Bk Rev. Ad Acc. Circ:** 12,000 (ctrl). ***Continues*** *Competition Canada, 0315-2200.*
Desc: Editorial for the hobby/sport of radio controlled model airplanes, boats, gliders, cars, etc.

LC TL501 .M62 **ISSN** 0196-1527
DD 629.13 US
MODERN AVIATION LIBRARY. Vol. 1 (1979)-. Monographic series. English. Price varies per volume. Modern Aviation Library, Blue Ridge Summit PA 17214.

LC TL **ISSN** 0942-3478
DD 629 GW
UDC 656.71
•**MOMBERGER AIRPORT INFORMATION.** [Momb. airpt. inf.]. **VFOAT** Airport Information (Rutesheim). (1992)-. Periodical. English. Twenty-four times a year. $330.00. Momberger Airport Information, PO Box 1127, D-71723 Rutesheim Germany. **Tel** 011 49 9715251640, FAX 011 49 9715255005. ***Continues*** *Airport Forum News, 0174-3279.*

LC TL
DD 629 US
MONITORING OF CONCORDE OPERATIONS AT DULLES INTERNATIONAL AIRPORT. VFOAT Concorde Monitoring Monthly Report, Dulles International Airport. Government Publication. English. Twelve times a year. US Department of Transportation / Federal Aviation Administration, 800 Independence Avenue Southwest, Washington DC 20591. **Tel** (202)367-3484, FAX (202)367-3505.

LC TL
DD 629 US
CODEN AIMODR
MONOGRAPHS. Main/Corp American Institute of Aeronautics and Astronautics. **Added/Corp** American Institute of Aeronautics and Astronautics. A.I.A.A. Monographs. American Institute of Aeronautics and Astronautics. Los Angeles Section Monographs. American Institute of Aeronautics and Astronautics. Los Angeles Section. **VFOAT** Los Angeles Section Monographs; AIAA Los Angeles Section Monographs; A.I.A.A. Monographs. (1966)-. Monographic series. English. Irregular. Price varies per volume. Western Periodicals Company, 424 East Main Street, Ventura CA 93001. **Tel** (805)641-2665, FAX (805)643-4854. **Bk Rev.** Documents available from Article Express International.
Ind/Abst Bioeng. Abstr.; Ei Page One; Eng. Index Annu.

LC HE9761 **ISSN** 1188-6676
DD 387.7 CN
MONTREAL & AREA AVIATION BUSINESS DIRECTORY. [Montr. area aviat. bus. dir.]. **VFOAT** Montreal and Area Aviation Business Directory; Montreal et Region, Annuaire Commercial des Aeroports; Montreal Aviation Directory. (1992)-. Directory. English (French). Consolidated Communications, 807 Manning Road Northeast, Suite 200, Calgary Alberta T2E 7M8 Canada. **Tel** (403)569-9520, FAX (403)569-9590. ***Continues*** *Montreal & Area Airport Business Directory., 0849-1887.*

LC HE9761 **ISSN** 1188-6676
DD 387.7 CN
MONTREAL & AREA AVIATION BUSINESS DIRECTORY (FRENCH EDITION). [Montr. area aviat. bus. dir.]. **VFOAT** Montreal and Area Aviation Business Directory; Montreal et Region, Annuaire Commercial des Aeroports; Montreal Aviation Directory. (1992)-. Directory. French (English). Consolidated Communications, 807 Manning Road Northeast, Suite 200, Calgary Alberta T2E 7M8 Canada. **Tel** (403)569-9520, FAX (403)569-9590. ***Continues*** *Montreal & Area Airport Business Directory., 0849-1887.*

LC TL **ISSN** 1381-8708
DD 629 NE
UDC 629.125+797
MOTORBOOT ROTTERDAM. See Engineering.

LC TL
DD 629 US
MOUNTAIN PILOT. (1995)-. English. Six times a year. $14.95. Wiesner Publishing, 7009 South Potomac Street, Englewood CO 80112. **Tel** (303)397-7600, (800)945-0973, FAX (303)397-7619. ***Continues*** *Wings West.*

LC TL789.A1 M8 **ISSN** 0270-6822
DD 001.9/42/05 US
MUFON UFO JOURNAL, THE. [MUFON UFO j.]. **Added/Corp** Mutual UFO Network. **VAT** Mutual Unidentified Flying Object Network Unidentified Flying Object Journal. (June 1967)-. Periodical. English. Twelve times a year. $25.00. Mutual UFO Network Inc., 103 Oldtowne Road, Seguin TX 78155-4099. **Tel** (210)379-9216, FAX (210)372-9439. **ED** Dennis W. Stacy, (editor's address: PO Box 12434, San Antonio, TX 78212, phone: (210)828-4507). **Bk Rev. Circ:** 5,000 (ctrl). ***Continues*** *Skylook.*
Desc: Devoted to the investigation, study and research of the phenomenon known as unidentified flying objects (UFO's) on an international scope.
Ind/Abst Mag. Index (1977-Feb. 1984);(1977-).

LC TL550 **ISSN** 1187-0575
DD 629.13/074/71 CN
MUSEUM NEWSLETTER - CANADIAN MUSEUM OF FLIGHT AND TRANSPORTATION (1990). (MUSEUM NEWSLETTER.). [Mus. newsl. - Can. Mus. Flight Transp.]. **Added/Corp** Canadian Museum of Flight and Transportation. **VFOAT** Mini Newsletter. (1990)-. Newsletter. English. Four times a year. Free to members. Canadian Museum of Flight and Transportation, 13527 Crescent Road, Surrey BC V4A 2W1 Canada. ***Continues*** *Newsletter (Canadian Museum of Flight and Transportation : 1990)., 1184-065X.*

LC TL **ISSN** 1077-9647
DD 629 US
MUSEUM OF FLIGHT NEWS. See Museums and Galleries.

LC TL796 .A4 **ISSN** 0130-6863
DD 629.46 RU
NABLIUDENIIA ISKUSSTVENNYKH NEBESNYKH TEL. Added/Corp Akademiia Nauk SSSR. Astronomicheskii Sovet. **VFOAT** Biulleten Stantsii Opticheskogo Nabliudeniia Iskusstvennykh Sputnikov Zemli. (1971)-. Monographic series. Russian (summaries and/or abstracts in English). Irregular. Price varies per volume. Izdatelstvo Nauka / Akademiia Nauk, (Publishing House of the Russian Academy of Sciences), Leninskii Porspekt 14, 117901 Moscow Russia. **Tel** 011 95 9542153, FAX 011 95 9382144, telex 411964. ***Continues*** *Biulleten Stantsii Opticheskogo Nabliudeniia Iskusstvennykh Sputnikov Zemli.*
Ind/Abst Astron. Astrophys. Abstr.

LC TL
DD 629 US
NADA RETAIL AIRCRAFT APPRAISAL GUIDE. (19??)-. English. Three times a year. $85.00. NADA Appraisal Guides, PO Box 7800, Costa Mesa CA 92628. **Tel** (714)556-8511, (800)966-6232, FAX (714)556-8715.

LC TL693 .N3 **ISSN** 0547-3578
DD 629.1 US
CCC
CODEN NASEA9
NAECON. (PROCEEDINGS OF THE IEEE NATIONAL AEROSPACE AND ELECTRONICS CONFERENCE, NAECON.). [NAECON]. **Main/Conf** IEEE National Aerospace and Electronics Conference. **Added/Corp** Institute of Electrical and Electronics Engineers. Dayton Section. IEEE Aerospace and Electronic Systems Society. **VFOAT** NAECON. (1974)-. Proceedings. English. One time a year. IEEE / Institute of Electrical and Electronics Engineers Inc., 345 East 47th Street, New York NY 10017-2394. **Tel** (908)981-1393, FAX (908)981-9667. **(Subscription address:** IEEE / Institute of Electrical and Electronics Engineers, 445 Hoes Lane, PO Box 1331, Piscataway NJ 08855-1331. **Tel** (800)701-IEEE, (908)981-0060, FAX (908)981-9667, telex 833233.**)** Documents available from Article Express International, Ask*IEEE. ***Continues*** *National Aerospace Electronics Conference. Proceedings of the National Aerospace Electronics Conference.*
Ind/Abst Bioeng. Abstr.; Curr. Cit.; Ei Page One; Eng. Index Annu.; Index IEEE Publ.; INSPEC.

LC TL568.K63 K64a
DD 629.13 JA
NAL; NATIONAL AEROSPACE LABORATORY, JAPAN. Main/Corp Koku Uchu Gijutsu Kenkyujo. **VAT** National Aerospace Laboratory: Koku Uchu Gijutsu Kenkyujo. (19??)-. Periodical. English. National Aerospace Laboratory / Japan, 7-44-1 Jindaijihigashi-machi, Chofu Tokyo Japan. **Tel** 0422 47 5911.

LC TL500 .B34a
DD 629.13/007/205487 II
NAL NEWS LETTER. Main/Corp Bangalore, India (City). National Aeronautical Laboratory. **VAT** National Aeronautical Laboratory News Letter. Vol. 1 (Aug. 1973)-. Periodical. English. Twelve times a year. National Aeronautical Laboratory, Box 1779 Kodihalli, Bangalore 560017 India.

LC TL500 **ISSN** 1000-1956
DD 629.13 CC
NANJING HANGKONG XUEYUAN XUEBAO. VFOAT Journal of Nanjing Aeronautical Institute. (1956)-. Academic Scholarly Publication. Chinese. Six times a year. $33.24. Nanjing Hangkong Hangtian Daxue, 29 Yudai Street, Nanjing Jiangsu 210016, People's Republic of China. **Tel** 025-4492492, FAX 025-4494880. **ED** Zhang Azhou. **Bk Rev. Ad Acc. Circ:** 1,500. available on an online database from Knight-Ridder Information, Inc. Documents available from Article Express International, CASDDS.
Ind/Abst Ei Page One; Eng. Index Annu.; Int. Aerosp. Abstr.

Aeronautics, Astronautics

LC TL
DD 629
ISSN 0191-7811
US
CODEN NACPDX
NASA CONFERENCE PUBLICATION.
[NASA conf. publ.]. **Added/Corp** United States. National Aeronautics and Space Administration. **VFOAT** NASA CP. **VAT** National Aeronautics and Space Administration Conference Publication. (1977)-. Academic Scholarly Publication. English. NASA - National Aeronautics and Space Administration, LCG 9 NASA Headquarters, Washington DC 20546. Documents available from Article Express International, CASDDS.
Ind/Abst Bioeng. Abstr.; Ceram. Abstr. (19??-); Chem. Abstr.; Curr. Cit.; Ei Page One; Eng. Index Annu.; GeoRef.

LC TL
DD 629
ISSN 0565-7059
US
CODEN NSCRAQ
NASA CONTRACTOR REPORT. [NASA contract. rep.].
VFOAT Contractor Report; NASA CR. **VAT** National Aeronautics and Space Administration Contractor Report. (1963)-. Academic Scholarly Publication. English. Irregular. Price varies per volume. National Aeronautics and Space Administration, 600 Independence Avenue SW, Washington DC 20546. **Tel** (202)453-1000. Documents available from Article Express International, BIOSIS Document Express, CASDDS.
Ind/Abst Aquat. Sci. Fish. Abstr. [CD-ROM Ed.]; Bioeng. Abstr.; Biol. Abstr.; Chem. Abstr.; Ei Page One; Eng. Mater. Abstr.; Eng. Index Annu.; GeoRef; Life Sci. Collect.

LC TL500
DD 629.13
US
NASA GEODYNAMICS PROGRAM ANNUAL REPORT FOR ... . Main/Corp United
States. Office of Space and Terrestrial Applications. Geodynamics Branch. (1979)-. English. One time a year. National Aeronautics and Space Administration Scientific and Technical Information Office, 5285 Port Royal Road, Springfield VA 22161. available on microfiche (Vols. for (fifth annual report, Oct. 1984-) distributed to depository libraries).

LC TL521.3 N16
DD 353
US
CEASED
NASA MAGAZINE. Main/Corp United States.
National Aeronautics and Space Administration. (Fall 1991)-(Winter 1994). Government Publication. English. Superintendent of Documents, US Government Printing Office, Washington DC 20402. **Tel** (202)275-3328, FAX (202)786-2377. **Continues** NASA Activities, 0190-3292.
Ind/Abst Index U.S. Gov. Period.

LC QC878.5 .N36
DD 551.5/14/0973
US
NASA/MSFC FY ... GLOBAL SCALE ATMOSPHERIC PROCESSES RESEARCH PROGRAM REVIEW.
Added/Corp George C. Marshall Space Flight Center. Global Scale Atmospheric Processes Research Program. United States. National Aeronautics and Space Administration. Scientific and Technical Information Division. **VFOAT** Global Scale Atmospheric Processes Research Program Review. **VAT** National Aeronautics and Space Administration/Marshall Space Flight Center FY ... Global Scale Atmospheric Processes Research Program Review. (19??)-. English. National Technical Information Service - NTIS, Room 2027S, 5285 Port Royal Road, Springfield VA 22161. **Tel** (703)487-4630, (703)487-4660, (703)487-4650, FAX (703)321-8547, telex 89-9405. **Continues** NASA/MSFC FY- ... Atmospheric Processes Research Review.
Desc: Information on the upper atmosphere, astronautics and aeronautics in meteorology, and mesometeorology.

LC Z
DD 016.62
US
NASA PATENT ABSTRACTS BIBLIOGRAPHY. Main/Corp United States.
National Aeronautics and Space Administration. Scientific and Technical Information Program. **VFOAT** National Aeronautics and Space Administration Patent Abstracts Bibliography. (July 1991)-. Bibliography. English. Two times a year. National Aeronautics and Space Administration, 600 Independence Avenue SW, Washington DC 20546. **Tel** (202)453-1000.
(Subscription address: National Technical Information Service, 5285 Port Royal Road, Springfield VA 22161.)
Continues United States. National Aeronautics and Space Administration. Scientific and Technical Information Division. NASA Patent Abstracts Bibliography.

LC TL521.3 .N17
DD 608
ISSN 0148-8589
US
CODEN NRPUDS
NASA REFERENCE PUBLICATION. [NASA ref. publ.].
VAT National Aeronautics and Space Administration Reference Publication. (19??)-. Periodical. English. National Aeronautics and Space Administration Scientific and Technical Information, Washington DC 20546. Documents available from Article Express International.
Ind/Abst Bioeng. Abstr.; Ei Page One; Eng. Mater. Abstr.; Eng. Index Annu.; GeoRef; Life Sci. Collect.

LC TL858 .U54a
DD 629.4/05
ISSN 0273-4362
US
NASA SPACE SYSTEMS TECHNOLOGY MODEL. [NASA space syst. technol. model].
Added/Corp United States. National Aeronautics and Space Administration. United States. Office of Aeronautics and Space Technology. **VFOAT** Space Systems Technology Model. (19??)-. English. One time a year. NASA - National Aeronautics and Space Administration, NASA Headquarters Code RS-5, Washington DC 20546.

LC Z
DD 016.62
US
NASA SPECIAL PUBLICATIONS.
Added/Corp United States. National Aeronautics and Space Administration. (19??)-. Government Publication. English. Two times a year. Superintendent of Documents, US Government Printing Office, Washington DC 20402. **Tel** (202)275-3328, FAX (202)786-2377.
Ind/Abst Alum. Ind. Abstr.; Ceram. Abstr. (19??-); Met. Abstr.

LC TL521.3.T4 A3
DD 629.13
ISSN 0499-9320
US
CODEN NATMA4
NASA TECHNICAL MEMORANDUM. [NASA tech. memo.].
Added/Corp United States. National Aeronautics and Space Administration. **VFOAT** N.A.S.A. Technical Memorandum; NASA TM; N.A.S.A. T.M. **VAT** National Aeronautics and Space Administration Technical Memorandum. (196?)-. Government Publication. English. Irregular. NASA Center for Aerospace Information, 800 Elkridge Landing Road, Linthicum Heights MD 21090. **Tel** (301)621-0153, FAX (301)621-0134. available on microfilm. Documents available from CASDDS. **Continues** United States. National Aeronautics and Space Administration. Technical Memorandum.
Ind/Abst Aquat. Sci. Fish. Abstr. [CD-ROM Ed.]; Chem. Abstr.; Soils Fert.

LC TL521.3 .N18
DD 600
ISSN 0148-8341
US
CODEN NTPADG
NASA TECHNICAL PAPER. [NASA tech. pap.].
VFOAT N.A.S.A. Technical Paper. **VAT** National Aeronautics and Space Administration Technical Paper. English. National Aeronautics and Space Administration Scientific and Technical Information, Washington DC 20546. Documents available from Article Express International.
Ind/Abst Aquat. Sci. Fish. Abstr. [CD-ROM Ed.]; Bioeng. Abstr.; Ei Page One; Eng. Mater. Abstr.; Eng. Index Annu.; GeoRef; Life Sci. Collect.

LC TL521 .A3312
DD 629.13
ISSN 0077-314X
US
CODEN NASNAZ
NASA TECHNICAL REPORT. [NASA tech. rep.].
Main/Corp United States. National Aeronautics and Space Administration. **Added/Corp** United States. National Aeronautics and Space Administration. **VFOAT** NASA TR; Technical Report; NASA Report. **VAT** National Aeronautics and Space Administration Technical Report. Vol. 1 (1959)-. Monographic series. English. Irregular. Price varies per volume. Superintendent of Documents, US Government Printing Office, Washington DC 20402. **Tel** (202)275-3328, FAX (202)786-2377. Documents available from Article Express International, CASDDS. **Continues** Report (United States. National Advisory Committee for Aeronautics), 0096-7599.
Ind/Abst Chem. Abstr.; Ei Page One; Eng. Mater. Abstr.; Eng. Index Annu.; GeoRef.

LC TL
DD 629
NLM W2 A N144NX
ISSN 0499-9355
US
CODEN NASSAH
NASA TECHNICAL TRANSLATION. [NASA tech. transl.].
Main/Corp United States. National Aeronautics and Space Administration. **Added/Corp** United States. National Aeronautics and Space Administration. **VFOAT** Technical Translation; NASA TT. (Aug. 1959)-. Monographic series. English. Irregular. Price varies per volume. NASA STI Facility, PO Box 8785, Baltimore Washington International, Baltimore MD 21240. **Tel** (202)453-2906. Documents available from Article Express International, BIOSIS Document Express, CASDDS. **Supersedes** NASA Republication.
Ind/Abst Biol. Abstr.; Chem. Abstr.; Ei Page One; Eng. Index Annu.; GeoRef.

LC HD28
DD 658
ISSN 1051-225X
US
NASA TOTAL QUALITY MANAGEMENT ... ACCOMPLISHMENT REPORT. See
Business and Economics-Management.

LC TL521.3.T4 A3 TL521.312 312
DD 629.1/08,500.5/07/2073
ISSN 0566-9847
US
NASA'S UNIVERSITY PROGRAM. VAT
National Aeronautics and Space Administrations's University Program. (July 1, 1968)-. English. One time a year. National Aeronautics and Space Administration, 600 Independence Avenue SW, Washington DC 20546. **Tel** (202)453-1000.

LC TL501 .N322
DD 629.13/005
ISSN 0005-2116
US
NATIONAL AERONAUTICS. [Natl. aeronaut.].
Added/Corp National Aeronautic Association (U.S.) Vol. 1 (Spring 1973)-. Periodical. English. Four times a year. $25.00. National Aeronautics Association, 806 15th Street Northwest, Washington DC 20005. **Tel** (202)898-1313. **ED** Don Berliner. **Circ:** 4,500 (ctrl).
Desc: Covers sport aviation: records, competition and sanctions.

LC TL
DD 629
US
NATIONAL AEROSPACE STANDARDS.
Main/Corp National Aerospace Standards Committee (U.S.). Vol. 5 (19??)-. Periodical. English. Irregular. $875.00. Global Engineering Documents Services, 15 Inverness Way East, Englewood CO 80112. **Tel** (800)624-3974, (800)854-7179, FAX (303)790-0730. **ED** Kitty Stover. **Continues** National Aircraft Standards.
Desc: Contains over 2,500 primarily procurement documents for parts and components of high technology systems.

LC TL
DD 629
ISSN 1059-6127
US
NATIONAL AIR AND SPACE MUSEUM OCCASIONAL PAPER SERIES. [Natl. Air
Space Mus. occas. pap. ser.]. **Added/Corp** National Air and Space Museum. No. 1 (1991)-. Monographic series. English. Two times a year. Free. National Air and Space Museum, 6th Avenue & Independence Street SW, Washington DC 20560.

LC TL725.3.T7 U674A
DD 387.7/4042
ISSN 0747-976X
US
NATIONAL AIRSPACE SYSTEM PLAN. ENGINEERING AND DEVELOPMENT.
Main/Corp United States. Federal Aviation Administration. Government Publication. English. One time a year. US Department of Transportation / Federal Aviation Administration, 800 Independence Avenue Southwest, Washington DC 20591. **Tel** (202)367-3484, FAX (202)367-3505.

LC TL521 .U63F
DD 384.7/362/0973
ISSN 0566-6775
US
NATIONAL AVIATION SYSTEM PLAN, THE. Main/Corp United States. Federal Aviation
Administration. 1969-. English. One time a year. $2.00. US Department of Transportation, 800 Independence Avenue SW, Washington DC 20591.

LC TL726.2 .U49a
DD 387.7/362/0973
US
●NATIONAL PLAN OF INTEGRATED AIRPORT SYSTEMS. Added/Corp United
States. Federal Aviation Administration. **VFOAT** NPIAS. (1984-1993)-. English. Superintendent of Documents, US Government Printing Office, Washington DC 20402. **Continues** National Airport System Plan, 0161-3103.

LC U
DD 355
ISSN 0028-1417
NAVAL AVIATION NEWS. [Nav. aviat. news].
Added/Corp United States. Office of the Chief of Naval Operations. Naval Historical Center (U.S.) United States. Naval Air Systems Command. (19??)-. Government Publication. English. Six times a year. $20.00. US Department of Defense, The Pentagon, Washington DC 20301. **Tel** (703)545-6700. **(Subscription address:** Superintendent of Documents, US Government Printing Office, Washington DC 20402.) available on microfilm and microfiche from University Microfilms International (UMI).
Desc: Presents articles of interest on all phases of Navy and Marine air activity.
Ind/Abst Acad. Search; EP Collect.; Homework Help.; MasterFile FullTEXT 1000; MasterFile FullTEXT 350; MasterFile FullTEXT 650; MasterFile FullTEXT (July 1994-) [Full Txt.]; OCLC; Predicasts F&S Index, U. S. Annu. Ed.; Pub. Lib. FullTEXT; Telebase; Vocat. Search.

LC VK2 .N3
DD 359
ISSN 0028-1530
FR
CODEN NVGNAL
NAVIGATION (PARIS). See Naval Science,
Navigation.

LC VK1 .N33
DD 527.05
ISSN 0028-1522
US
CCC
CODEN NAVIB3
NAVIGATION (WASHINGTON). See Naval
Science, Navigation.

LC TL522.N2 A3
DD 353.97820087/77
US
NEBRASKA DEPARTMENT OF AERONAUTICS : ANNUAL REPORT.
Main/Corp Nebraska. Dept. of Aeronautics. (1981)-.

Aeronautics, Astronautics

English. Nebraska Department of Aeronautics, Lincoln NE 68508. **Continues** Annual Report / Nebraska. Dept. of Aeronautics.

LC TL726.3.N5 N48
DD 387.7/36/025749
US
NEW JERSEY AIRPORT DIRECTORY.
Added/Corp New Jersey. Office of Aviation. (19??)-. Directory. English. New Jersey Department of Transportation, 1035 Parkway Avenue, CN 600, Trenton NJ 08625. **Tel** (609)292-1530. available with illustrations. **Continues** Airport Directory.

LC HE767.N5 N48 **ISSN** 0742-2695
DD 387.1/64/02947471
US
NEW JERSEY AND NEW YORK PORT HANDBOOK. See Transportation-Ships and Shipping.

LC HB **ISSN** 1064-4393
DD 338
US
●NEW SPACE NEWSLETTER. (1995)-.
Newsletter. English. Six times a year. $55.00. New Space Information Service, 520 Huntmar Park Drive Suite 100, Herndon VA 22070. **Tel** (703)709-2240, FAX (703)709-0790. cum. index. **Bk Rev. Ad Acc. Continues** ISSO Newsletter.
Desc: Industry activities, technical and policy developments in small and low cost space systems.

LC TL553.5 .F555 **ISSN** 0112-8949
DD 629.132/52/0289
NZ
NEW ZEALAND FLIGHT SAFETY.
Added/Corp New Zealand. Civil Aviation Division. Flight Standards Branch. **VFOAT** Flight Safety. Vol. 13, No. 1 (Feb. 1986)-. Periodical. English. Ten times a year. $26.51. Civil Aviation Authority / New Zealand, Flight Safety Sub, PO Box 31441, Lower Hut New Zealand. **Tel** 11 64 4 5600596, FAX 11 64 4 5692024, telex NZ31524. **ED** C.F.L. Jenks. **Circ:** 13,000. **Continues** Flight Safety.
Desc: Educational articles on aviation topics aimed at aircraft accident prevention in general, particularly in New Zealand.

LC TL **ISSN** 0110-1471
DD 629
NZ
NEW ZEALAND WINGS. [N.Z. Wings.] VFOAT
NZ Wings. (1973)-. Trade Publication. English. Eleven times a year (Not published in Jan.) $52.29. New Zealand Wings, PO Box 120, Otaki New Zealand. **Tel** 011 64 69 26423, 011 64 6 3646423, FAX 011 64 69 46423, 011 64 6 3647797. **ED** Ross Macpherson (editor's phone: 011 64 06 3646423). **Bk Rev**, (Qty: 25/year). **Ad Acc. Circ:** 20,000 (ctrl). **Continues** Wings, 0043-5899.
Desc: Emphasis on all aspects of New Zealand aviation--civil and military.

LC HE9761 **ISSN** 0713-536X
DD 387.7/4042
CN
NEWS UPDATE. [News update - Can. Air Traffic Control Assoc.]. VAT Update (Canadian Air Traffic Control Association). Vol. 1, Issue 1 (Jan. 22, 1982). Periodical. English. One time a year. Canadian Air Traffic Control Association - CATCA, 162 Cleopatra Drive, Nepean Ontario K2G 5X2 Canada. **Tel** (613)225-3553. **Continues** Canadian Air Traffic Control Association. Information Bulletin, 0319-1745.

LC TL500 **ISSN** 1184-065X
DD 629.13/0074/71
CN
NEWSLETTER - CANADIAN MUSEUM OF FLIGHT AND TRANSPORTATION (1990). (NEWSLETTER.). [Newsl. - Can. Mus. Flight Transp.]. **Added/Corp** Canadian Museum of Flight and Transportation. (Sept. 24, 1990)-. Newsletter. English. Canadian Museum of Flight and Transportation, 13527 Crescent Road, Surrey BC V4A 2W1 Canada. **Continues** Museum Newsletter (Canadian Museum of Flight and Transportation)., 0820-8336.

LC TL500 **ISSN** 0826-1997
DD 629.13/005
CN
NEWSLETTER / CANADIAN OWNERS & PILOTS ASSOCIATION. **Added/Corp** Canadian Owners and Pilots Association. **VFOAT** COPA Newsletter; Canadian Owners & Pilots Association Newsletter. (1953)-. Newsletter. English. Irregular. 40.00Can$. COPA / Canadian Owners & Pilots Association, PO Box 734, Ottawa Ontario K1P 5S4 Canada. **Tel** (613)236-4901. **ED** William N. Peppler. **Circ:** 20,000 (ctrl).
Desc: Concerned with government regulations, current situations on general aviation issues, etc.

LC TL **ISSN** 0428-5735
DD 629
US
TITLE CHANGE
NEWSLETTER - FLIGHT SAFETY FOUNDATION. (NEWSLETTER / FLIGHT SAFETY FOUNDATION.). [Newsl. - Flight Saf. Found.]. **Added/Corp** Flight Safety Foundation. **VFOAT** Flight Safety Foundation Newsletter. (19??-19??). Newsletter. English. Flight Safety Foundation Inc., 2200 Wilson Boulevard, Suite 500, Arlington VA 22201. **Tel** (703)522-8300, FAX (703)525-6047, telex 901176 FSF INC AGTN. **Continued by** Flight Safety Foundation News.

LC TL787 .S37 **ISSN** 0147-3417
DD 629.4
US
NEWSLETTER - SEARL NATIONAL SPACE RESEARCH CONSORTIUM, UNITED KINGDOM DIVISION. Main/Corp
Searl National Space Research Consortium, United Kingdom Division. Newsletter. English. $1.50 single issue. Rochester UFO Study Group, William T Sherwood, 220 Pinnacle Road South, Rochester NY 14623.

LC TL506.N7 N67
DD 069.62913/0025/7
US
NORTH AMERICAN AIRCRAFT & AEROSPACE MUSEUM GUIDE. VFOAT
North American Aircraft and Aerospace Museum Guide; Aircraft and Aerospace Museum Guide; N.A. Aircraft and Aerospace Museum Guide; N.A. Aircraft & Aerospace Museum Guide. (1990)-. English. Bruce/Beeson Publishers, 2428 East 56th Place, Tulsa OK 74105. **Continues** North American Aircraft Museum Guide.

LC TL **ISSN** 1057-9621
DD 629
US
NOTICES TO AIRMEN. [Not. airmen].
Added/Corp United States. Federal Aviation Administration. United States. Air Traffic Operations Service. Airspace Rules and Aeronautical Information Division. **VFOAT** Class Two NOTAMS. (April 6, 1978)-. Government Publication. English. Twenty-six times a year. $172.00. US Department of Transportation / Federal Aviation Administration, 800 Independence Avenue Southwest, Washington DC 20591. **Tel** (202)367-3484, FAX (202)367-3505. (**Subscription address:** Superintendent of Documents, US Government Printing Office, Washington DC 20402.) **Continues** Airman's Information Manual. Pt. 3A. Notices to Airmen; **Separated from** Airman's Information Manual; **Absorbed** International Notices to Airmen.
Desc: Contains current Notices to Airmen (NOTAMs) which are considered essential to the safety of flight. Includes current FDC NOTAMs, which are regulatory in nature, issued to establish restrictions to flight or amend charts or published Instrument Approach Procedures.

LC TL789 **ISSN** 0319-4345
DD 001.9/4/05
CN
NOUVEAU COSMOS-EXPRESS, LE. No.
1- July. 1975-. Periodical. French. 8.00Can$. Cosmos-Express, CP 3, Jonquiere Quebec G7X 7V8 Canada. **Supersedes** Cosmos-Express Ed. Francaise, 0319-4337.

LC TL **ISSN** 1247-5793
DD 629
FR
●NOUVELLE REVUE D'AERONAUTIQUE ET D'ASTRONAUTIQUE. (1993)-. Periodical.
French. Six times a year. 548.48F France; 750.00F others. Dunod Gauthier Villars, 15 rue Gossin, 92543 Montrouge Cedex France. **Tel** 011 33 1 46565266, 011 33 1 40926527, FAX 011 33 1 40926597. (**Subscription address:** Centrale des Revues, 11 rue Gossin, 92543 Montrouge Cedex France. **Tel** 011 33 1 46565266.) **Continues** Aeronautique et d Astronautique.

LC QB500.25
DD 500.5
US
NSSDC NEWS. **Added/Corp** National Space Science Data Center. **VFOAT** News. **VAT** National Space Science Data Center News. (1986)-. Newsletter. English. Four times a year. Free. National Space Science Data Center, Goddard Space Flight Center, Greenbelt MD 20771. available via Internet (http://nssdc.gsfc.nasa/gov/nssdc_news/toc.html). **Continues** National Space Science Data Center Newsletter.
Desc: Newsletter of the National Space Science Data Center.

LC TL
DD 629
US
NTIS ALERT. SPACE TECHNOLOGY.
(19??)-. Periodical. English. Twenty-four times a year. $160.00 US; $225.00 other. National Technical Information Service - NTIS, Room 2027S, 5285 Port Royal Road, Springfield VA 22161. **Tel** (703)487-4630, (703)487-4660, (703)487-4650, FAX (703)321-8547, telex 89-9405.

LC HE9802
DD 387.74
SA
●OAG AFRICA FLIGHT GUIDE. (1995)-.
English. Six times a year. $29.22. Houston Travel Marketing Service, PO Box 75262, Gardenview 2047 South Africa. **Tel** 011 27 11 6224600.

LC HE9761 **ISSN** 0191-152X
DD 387.7
US
OAG AIR CARGO GUIDE. See Transportation.

LC TL501
DD 629.13
UK
OAG FLIGHT PLANNER EUROPE, MIDDLE EAST & AFRICA. See Travel and Tourism.

LC TL501
DD 629.13
UK
OAG FLIGHTDISK PREMIUM WORLDWIDE EDITION. See Travel and Tourism.

LC TL501
DD 629.13
UK
OAG TRAVEL DISC [CD ROM]. See Travel and Tourism.

LC TL501
DD 629.13
UK
OAG WAG FARES SUPPLEMENT. See Travel and Tourism.

LC HE9761
DD 387.7
UK
OAG WORLD AIRWAYS GUIDE. (19??)-.
English. Twenty-four times a year. $645.00 US; $798.00 other. Reed Travel Group / England, World Timetable Center, Church Street Dunstable, Bedfordshire LU5 4HB United Kingdom. **Tel** 011 44 1582 600111, 011 44 1582 695569, FAX 011 44 1582 695230. (**Subscription address:** Reed Reference Publishing / Illinois, 2000 Clearwater Drive, Oak Brook IL 60521. **Tel** (708)574-7082.) **Continues** ABC World Airways Guide.

LC TL500
DD 629.13
UK
OBJECTIVE TESTING FOR PROFESSIONAL PILOTS LICENCES.
(19??)-. English. Irregular. £7.20 4th edition. Civil Aviation Authority / England, Grenville House, 37 Gratton Road, Cheltenham Glo GL50 2BN United Kingdom. **Tel** 011 44 1242 235151, FAX 011 44 1242 584139.

LC TL **ISSN** 1056-7755
DD 629
US
OFFICIAL HELICOPTER BLUE BOOK. RECIPROCATING ENGINE HELICOPTERS. VFOAT Reciprocating Engine Helicopters. Vol. 8, Ed. 1 (1st quarter 1991)-. Periodical. English. Four times a year. $150.00. International Helicopter Financial Services Inc, 4256 North Arlington Heights Road #205, Arlington Heights IL 60004-1372. **Tel** (312)259-7711, FAX (312)259-2202, telex 720 493 HELIBLUEBOOK. **Continues in part** Official Helicopter Blue Book, 0890-7498.

LC TL **ISSN** 1056-7763
DD 629
US
OFFICIAL HELICOPTER BLUE BOOK. TURBINE ENGINE HELICOPTERS. VFOAT
Turbine Engine Helicopters. Vol. 8, Ed. 1 (1st quarter 1991)-. Periodical. English. Four times a year. $250.00. International Helicopter Financial Services Inc, 4256 North Arlington Heights Road #205, Arlington Heights IL 60004-1372. **Tel** (312)259-7711, FAX (312)259-2202, telex 720 493 HELIBLUEBOOK. **Continues in part** Official Helicopter Blue Book, 0890-7498.

LC TL720.A1 I57 HE9778
DD 387.7 S 387.7/4042
CN
ON-FLIGHT ORIGIN AND DESTINATION = ORIGINE ET DESTINATION PAR VOL.
Main/Corp International Civil Aviation Organization. **Added/Corp** International Civil Aviation Organization. Origine et Destination par Vol. **VFOAT** Origine et Destination par Vol. (Mar. 1977)-. Periodical. English (summaries and/or abstracts in French, Spanish and Russian). Price varies per volume. International Civil Aviation Organization / ICAO, 1000 Sherbrooke Street West, Suite 400, Montreal Quebec H3A 2R2 Canada. **Tel** (514)285-8026, (514)285-8022, telex 05-24514.

LC S **ISSN** 0030-235X
DD 630
US
ON THE DECK. See Agriculture.

LC TL500 **ISSN** 0708-6008
DD 629.132/54/71
CN
ON TRACK. 1978-. English. Irregular. $34.78.
Skylark Aviation, 807-72 Avenue NW, Calgary Alberta T2K 0P5 Canada. **Tel** (403)274-8710.

LC TL600 **ISSN** 0951-9904
DD 629.133
UK
ONLINE HELIDATA. [Online helidata]. VFOAT
Helidata (1987). (1987)-. Periodical. English. Twenty-four times a year (25 issues per year). $450.00. Avia Press Associates, 75 Elm Tree Road Locking, Weston-s-Mare Avon BS24 8EL United Kingdom. **Tel** 011 44 1934 822524, FAX 011 44 1934 822400. **Ad Acc. Circ:** 10,000 (ctrl). **Continues** Helidata (1980).
Desc: Provides world-wide coverage of civil and military helicopter operations and manufacturers.

LC TL504 .O6
DD 629.13
NE
ONZE LUCHTMACHT. **Added/Corp** Vereniging Onze Luchtmacht. (1949)-. Six times a year. Fl40.00. WYT Uitgevers, Postbus 268, 3000 AG Rotterdam The Netherlands. **Tel** 011 31 10 4762566. Index available. **Bk Rev. Ad Acc. Circ:** 11,500. available with illustrations.

LC TL500
DD 629.13 CN
OPERATION OF AIRCRAFT; INTERNATIONAL STANDARDS AND RECOMMENDED PRACTICES. ANNEX 6 TO THE CONVENTION ON INTERNATIONAL CIVIL AVIATION.
Main/Corp International Civil Aviation Organization. (19??)-. English. Irregular. $9.50 (Part I), $6.00 (Part II), $14.00 (Part III). International Civil Aviation Organization / ICAO, 1000 Sherbrooke Street West, Suite 400, Montreal Quebec H3A 2R2 Canada. **Tel** (514)285-8026, (514)285-8022, telex 05-24514.

LC TL522.V8 V56A ISSN 0147-7730
DD 353.9/755/008777 US
OPERATIONS REPORT - STATE CORPORATION COMMISSION, DIVISION OF AERONAUTICS. **Main/Corp** Virginia. Division of Aeronautics. English. One time a year. State Corporation Commission, 4508 South Laburnum Avenue, Richmond VA 23231.

LC TL522.V8 V56A
DD 353.97550087/77 US
OPERATIONS REPORT / VIRGINIA DEPARTMENT OF AVIATION. **Main/Corp** Virginia. Dept. of Aviation. July 1, 1979-June 30, 1980-. English. One time a year. Virginia Department of Aviation, PO Box 7716, Richmond VA 23231. ***Continues*** *Virginia. Division of Aeronautics. Operations Report.*

LC TL503
DD 629.13 US
ORIGIN-DESTINATION SURVEY OF AIRLINE PASSENGER TRAFFIC - DOMESTIC. **Main/Corp** United States. Civil Aeronautics Board. **Added/Corp** Air Transport Association of America. (1968)-. Periodical. English. Irregular. Civil Aeronautics Board, 1825 Connecticut Avenue, Washington DC 20428. **Tel** (202)673-5174. ***Continues*** *Domestic Origin-Destination Survey of Airline Passenger Traffic.*

LC TL789.8.R9 O79
DD 629.409 RU
OSVOENIE KOSMICHESKOGO PROSTRANSTVA V SSSR. **Added/Corp** Institut Kosmicheskikh Issledovanii (Akademiia Nauk SSSR). (1967)-. Academic Scholarly Publication. Russian. Irregular. Izdatelstvo Nauka / Akademiia Nauk, (Publishing House of the Russian Academy of Sciences), Leninskii Porspekt 14, 117901 Moscow Russia. **Tel** 011 95 9542153, FAX 011 95 9382144, telex 411964.

LC TL500 ISSN 0843-1566
DD 629.13/006/071 CN
OUTBOUND (WILLOWDALE). (OUTBOUND : CANADIAN AVIATION HISTORICAL SOCIETY NEWSLETTER.). [Outbound]. **Added/Corp** Canadian Aviation Historical Society. No. 59 (Fall 1988)-. Newsletter. English. Four times a year. 25.00Can$ Canada; 26.00Can$ US and Pan America; 28.00Can$ Europe; 29.00Can$ other. Canadian Aviation Historical Society, PO Box 224 Station A, Willowdale Ontario M2N 5S8 Canada. **Tel** (416)294-4438, (416)488-2247, FAX (416)488-2247. **ED** W. J. Wheeler. **Bk Rev. Circ:** 1,000. ***Continues*** *Canadian Aviation Historical Society. C A H S Newsletter., 0382-4489.*

LC D600 .O85 ISSN 0888-272X
DD 940.4/4/05 US
OVER THE FRONT. **See** History.

LC TL501
DD 629.13 US
PACIFIC FLYER AVIATION NEWS. (19??)-. English. Twelve times a year. $18.50 (one-year), $30.25 (two-year). Pacific Flyer, 3355 Mission Avenue, Number 213, Oceanside CA 92054. **Tel** (619)439-4466.

LC TX907 .P24 ISSN 0742-4981
DD 917.4/0443 US
PAGES (NORTHEAST ED.). **See** Travel and Tourism.

LC TL501 .S6378 ISSN 0737-657X
DD 387.7/09757 US
PALMETTO AVIATION. **Added/Corp** South Carolina. Aeronautics Commission. (Oct. 1979)-. Periodical. English. Twelve times a year. South Carolina Aeronautics Commission, PO Drawer 1987, Columbia SC 29202. ***Continues*** *South Carolina Aviation News Letter.*

LC TL720.9.P313 A34 ISSN 0278-1263
DD 910/.5 US
CEASED
PAN AM CLIPPER. [Pan Am clipp.]. **Added/Corp** Pan American World Airways, Inc. **VFOAT** Clipper Magazine. (19??)-(19??). Periodical. English. Ziff-Davis, One Park Avenue, 5th Floor, New York NY 10016. **Tel** (212)503-3500. ***Continues*** *Clipper (Los Angeles, Calif.).*

LC HE9761 ISSN 0256-3282
DD 387.7/42/05 CN
PASSENGER SERVICES CONFERENCE RESOLUTIONS MANUAL. [Passeng. serv. conf. resolut. man.]. **Main/Corp** International Air Transport Association. (Jan. 1981)-. English. One time a year. $163.00. International Air Transport Association / Montreal, 2000 Peel Street, Room 3050, Montreal Quebec H3A 2R4 Canada. **Tel** (514)844-6311 ext. 232, FAX (514)844-5286, telex 05-267627.
Desc: Text of all resolutions and recommended practices adopted by the Passenger Services Conference.

LC TL501
DD 629.13 CN
PERSONNEL LICENSING; INTERNATIONAL STANDARDS AND RECOMMENDED PRACTICES. ANNEX TO THE CONVENTION ON INTERNATIONAL CIVIL AVIATION.
Main/Corp International Civil Aviation Organization. (19??)-. English. $13.00. International Civil Aviation Organization / ICAO, 1000 Sherbrooke Street West, Suite 400, Montreal Quebec H3A 2R2 Canada. **Tel** (514)285-8026, (514)285-8022, telex 05-24514.

LC TL500 ISSN 0898-6371
DD 629.13 US
PFEIFFER'S OFFICIAL FREQUENT FLYER GUIDE. **VFOAT** Official Frequent Flyer Guide. (1989)-. Periodical. English. Six times a year. Pegasus Press, 8535 Production Avenue, San Diego CA 92121.

LC GV750 ISSN 1381-1827
DD 797.55 NE
UDC 797.55
●**PILOOT & VLIEGTUIG.** [Piloot vliegtuig]. **VFOAT** Piloot en Vliegtuig. (1994)-. Consumer Publication. Dutch. Twelve times a year. S & F Publications, PO Box 1005, 6040 KA Roermond Netherlands. **Tel** 011 31 4750 24702, FAX 011 31 4750 22234. **Bk Rev. Ad Acc.**

LC TL721.4 .P52 ISSN 0300-1695
DD 629.132/5217/05 UK
PILOT (CLAYGATE). (PILOT.). (19??)-. Periodical. English. Twelve times a year. $63.31. Pilot Publishing Company Ltd., Clock House, 28 Oldtown Clapham, London SW4 0L8 United Kingdom. **Tel** 011 44 171 4982506, FAX 011 44 171 4986920.

LC TL ISSN 0380-6618
DD 629 CN
PILOT (MONTREAL). (PILOT.). **Added/Corp** Canadian Air Line Pilots Association. Vol. 27, No. 3 (Autumn 1970)-. Periodical. English. Four times a year. Canadian Airline Pilots Association, 1300 Steeles Avenue East, Brampton Ontario L6T 1A2 Canada. **Tel** (905)453-8210, FAX (905)453-8757. **ED** Roger Burgess-Webb. **Bk Rev. Ad Acc. Circ:** 5,000. ***Continues*** *Canadian Air Line Pilot, 0380-660X.*

LC TL503 .P54
DD 629.13/005 GW
PILOT UND FLUGZEUG. (19??)-. Periodical. German (German). Twelve times a year. $118.83. Heiko Teegen, Wiesbadener Strasse 59B, D-61462 Koenigstein Germany. **Tel** 011 49 6174 5302, telex 934801. Index available. **Ad Acc. Circ:** 15,000. ***Absorbed*** *Luftfahrt International.*
Desc: Concentrates on practical subjects, serves the interests of pilots of powered aircraft in aviation generally and assists in their basic and further training.

LC TL ISSN 0897-7666
DD 629 US
PILOT'S AUDIO UPDATE [SOUND RECORDING]. [Pilot's audio update]. Vol. 1, No. 1 (Jan. 1979)-. Periodical. English. Twelve times a year. $96.00. Belvoir Publications Inc., 75 Holly Hill Lane, Greenwich CT 06836. **Tel** (203)661-6111, FAX (203)661-4802. **(Subscription address:** Belvoir Publishing Inc., PO Box 3000 Dept. AVR, Denville NJ 07834. **)**

LC TL501
DD 629.13 US
PILOTS GUIDE TO CALIFORNIA AIRPORTS. (19??)-. English (French). Three times a year (Published Feb., June, Oct.). $34.95. Optima Publications, 180 Second Street, Los Altos CA 94022. **Tel** (415)941-4333. **ED** Dana Maresh.
Desc: Pilots guide for general aviation pilots in California.

LC TL721.4 .P57 ISSN 0032-0617
DD 629.132/52/05 US
PLANE & PILOT. [Plane pilot]. **VAT** Plane and Pilot. (Dec. 1965)-. Periodical. English. Twelve times a year. $16.95. Werner Publishing Corporation, 12121 Wilshire Boulevard, Suite 1220, Los Angeles CA 90025. **Tel** (310)820-1500, FAX (310)826-5008. **(Subscription address:** Neodata / Colorado, PO Box 2606, Boulder CO 80322. **) ED** Steve Werner. **Bk Rev. Ad Acc. Circ:** 112,000 (ctrl). available on microfilm and microfiche from University Microfilms International (UMI).
Desc: Edited for THS and single- and twin-engine pilots. Includes flight test reports, buyer's guides, updates and features on training, schools, safety and more.

LC QB600 .P54 ISSN 0736-3680
DD 523.4/05 US
PLANETARY REPORT, THE. **See** Astronomy.

LC TL726.6.G7 P66
DD 629.132/5441 UK
POOLEY'S FLIGHT GUIDE, UNITED KINGDOM AND IRELAND. **Added/Corp** Great Britain. Civil Aviation Authority. (19??)-. English. One time a year. $33.37. Airtour International Ltd., Elstree Aerodome, Elstree Hertfordshire WD6 DAW United Kingdom. **Tel** 011 44 1953 4870, FAX 011 44 1953 5219.

LC TL500 ISSN 0032-4493
DD 629.13 UK
POPULAR FLYING. (19??)-. Newsletter. English. Six times a year (Jan., May, May, July, Sept., Nov.). £32.00 Comes with Popular Flying Association membership. Popular Flying Association, Terminal Building, Shoreham Airport, Shoreham-by-Sea West Sussex BN4 5FF United Kingdom. **Tel** 011 44 1273 461616, FAX 011 44 1273 463390. **ED** Roger Jones (editor's address: 76 Kempe Road, Enfield Middlesex, UK EN1 4QS England, phone: 011 44 81 807 3383). **Bk Rev**, (Qty: 12). **Ad Acc, Adv Mgr:** J. Willeit. Full Page (B&W) £535.00. Full Page (Color) £700.00. **Circ:** 8,000 (ctrl). available with charts; available with illustrations.

LC TL787.P67 A3 ISSN 0373-5982
DD 629.4 PL
CODEN POASBE
POSTEPY ASTRONAUTYKI. [Post. astronaut.]. **Added/Corp** Polskie Towarzystwo Astronautyczne. (1967)-. Polish (summaries and/or abstracts in English and Russian). Four times a year. $24.00. Polskie Towarzystwo Astronautczyne / Polish Astronautical Society, Ul. Z. Krasinskiego 54, 01 755 Warsaw Poland. **Tel** 011 48 22 302703. **(Subscription address:** Ars Polona-Ruch, PO Box 1001, Krakowskie Przedmiescie 7, 00-068 Warsaw Poland. **Tel** 011 48 22 261201.**) ED** Pawel Elsztein. Index available. **Bk Rev. Circ:** 500. available with charts; available with illustrations. Documents available from CASDDS.
Desc: Contains original papers on astronautics.
Ind/Abst Chem. Abstr. (1967-1983); Int. Aerosp. Abstr.

LC TL ISSN 1066-7431
DD 629 US
●**PRECISNEWS. CAMEA.** (PRECISNEWS. CAMEA : A MID-MONTH REVIEW OF CIVIL AVIATION IN THE MIDDLE EAST & AFRICA.). [PrecisNews, CAMEA]. **VFOAT** Precis News. CAMEA; Civil Aviation, Middle East and Africa; A.Civil aviation, Middle East & Africa; A.CAMEA. Vol. 1, No. 1 (Jan. 15, 1993)-. Periodical. English. Twelve times a year. $80.00 US and Canada. Phoenix Publishing Inc., 11490 Commerce Park Drive, Suite 360, Reston VA 22091-1532. **Tel** (703)318-8108, FAX (703)318-8107.

LC TL790 .P67 ISSN 1018-8657
DD 629.4/07204 NE
CODEN PRFUEZ
PREPARING FOR THE FUTURE : ESA'S TECHNOLOGY PROGRAMME QUARTERLY. **Added/Corp** European Space Agency. **VFOAT** ESA's Technology Programme Quarterly; Technology Programme Quarterly. **VAT** European Space Agency's Technology Programme Quarterly. Vol. 1 No. 1 (Sept. 1991)-. Periodical. English. Four times a year. European Space Agency, 8 10 rue Mario Nikis, 75738 Paris Cedex 15 France. **Tel** 011 33 1 42737291, telex 02746. **(Subscription address:** European Space Agency / Publishing Division, Estec PO Box 299, 2200 AG Noordwijk Netherlands. **Tel** 011 31 1719 83405.**) ED** M. Perry. **Circ:** 20,000 (ctrl).
Desc: State of the art of space related projects and programs.

LC TL721.4 .P7 ISSN 0032-8901
DD 797 US
PRIVATE PILOT (NEW YORK, N.Y.). (PRIVATE PILOT.). [Priv. pilot]. Vol. 1, (Oct./Nov. 1965)-. Periodical. English. Twelve times a year. $23.97. Fancy Publications, PO Box 6050, Mission Viejo CA 92690. **Tel** (714)855-8822, (800)426-2516, FAX (714)855-3045. **(Subscription address:** Neodata / Colorado, PO Box 2606, Boulder CO 80322. **) ED** Dennis Shattuck. **Circ:** 86,377.

LC G ISSN 0713-7060
DD 910 CN
CCC
CODEN CSRSDK
PROCEEDINGS - CANADIAN SYMPOSIUM ON REMOTE SENSING. (PROCEEDINGS.). [Proc. - Can. Symp. Remote Sens.]. **VAT** Proceedings of the Canadian Symposium on Remote Sensing; Compte Rendu du Symposium Canadien Sur la Teledetection. (1972)-. Proceedings. English. Irregular. 48.02Can$. Canadian Aeronautic Space Institute, 818-130 Slater Street, Ottawa Ontario K1P 6E2 Canada. **Tel** (613)234-0191, FAX (613)234-9039.
Ind/Abst GeoRef.

LC K **ISSN** 0069-5831
DD 341.520631 US
PROCEEDINGS / COLLOQUIUM ON THE LAW OF OUTER SPACE. **See** Law.

LC TL722 .C67a **ISSN** 0736-4709
DD 363.1/24/05 US
PROCEEDINGS - CORPORATE AVIATION SAFETY SEMINAR. (PROCEEDINGS / FLIGHT SAFETY FOUNDATION, INC., CORPORATE AVIATION SAFETY SEMINAR.). [Proc. - Corp. Aviat. Saf. Semin.]. **Main/Conf** Corporate Aviation Safety Seminar. **Added/Corp** Flight Safety Foundation. **VFOAT** Proceedings of the ... Corporate Aviation Safety Seminar. 24th (1979)-. Proceedings. English. One time a year. $65.00 nonmembers; $45.00 members. Flight Safety Foundation Inc., 2200 Wilson Boulevard, Suite 500, Arlington VA 22201. **Tel** (703)522-8300, FAX (703)525-6047, telex 901176 FSF INC AGTN. **ED** Roger Rozelle. ctrl circ. ***Continues*** *Corporate Aircraft Safety Seminar. Proceedings.*

LC Z5063.A2 P7 TL545 **ISSN** 0032-9568
DD 016.6291 US
NLM W 3.5 P963 **CODEN** PPRNA
PROCEEDINGS IN PRINT. **See** Aeronautics, Astronautics-Abstracting, Bibliographies and Statistics.

LC TL553.5 .F565a **ISSN** 0270-5176
DD 629.132/5/0289 US
PROCEEDINGS - INTERNATIONAL AIR SAFETY SEMINAR. (INTERNATIONAL AIR SAFETY SEMINAR PROCEEDINGS.). [Int. air saf. semin. proc.]. **Main/Corp** Flight Safety Foundation. **Added/Corp** Flight Safety Foundation. **VFOAT** Proceedings of the Annual International Air Safety Seminar. (19??)-. Proceedings. English. One time a year. $65.00. Flight Safety Foundation Inc, 2200 Wilson Boulevard, Suite 500, Arlington VA 22201. **Tel** (703)522-8300, FAX (703)525-6047, telex 901176 FSF INC AGTN. Documents available from Article Express International.
Ind/Abst Bioeng. Abstr.; Ei Page One; Eng. Index Annu.

LC TK399 .I63a **ISSN** 0884-5123
DD 621.37/9 US
CODEN ITCOD6
PROCEEDINGS - INTERNATIONAL TELEMETERING CONFERENCE (U.S.). **See** Engineering-Electrical Engineering.

LC TL500
DD 629.13 JA
PROCEEDINGS OF INTERNATIONAL SYMPOSIUM OF SPACE TECHNOLOGY & SCIENCE. (19??)-. Proceedings. English. One time a year. $90.00. **(Subscription address:** Maruzen Company Ltd., PO Box 5050, Import & Export Department, Tokyo 100 31 Japan. **Tel** 011 81 3 32789224.)

LC TL725.3.T7 A38a **ISSN** 0192-8740
DD 629.136/6/05 US
PROCEEDINGS OF THE ANNUAL AIR TRAFFIC CONTROL ASSOCIATION FALL CONFERENCE. (PROCEEDINGS OF THE ANNUAL AIR TRAFFIC CONTROL ASSOCIATION FALL CONFERENCE. ASSOCIATION FALL CONFERENCE.). **Main/Corp** Air Traffic Control Association. (1977)-. Proceedings. English. One time a year (Fall). $30.00. Air Traffic Control Association, 2300 Clarendon Boulevard, Suite 711, Arlington VA 22201. **Tel** (703)522-5717, FAX (703)527-7251. **Circ:** 2,000. ***Continues*** *Air Traffic Control Association. Technical Papers Presented at the Annual Meeting.*
Desc: Technical papers pertaining to the subject matter of the meeting.

LC TL693 .R25a **ISSN** 0145-9589
DD 629.135/5 US
PROCEEDINGS OF THE ANNUAL ASSEMBLY MEETING. **Main/Corp** Radio Technical Commission for Aeronautics (U.S.). (19??)-. Proceedings. English. One time a year (Nov.). $29.00. R. T. C. A. Inc., 1140 CT Avenue New, Suite 1020, Washington DC 20036. **Tel** (202)833-9339. **ED** Joann C. Alcorn.
Desc: Technical papers presented at the annual assembly meeting and technical symposium of RTCA.

LC VK560 .I59A **ISSN** 0278-9396
DD 623.89/32/05 US
PROCEEDINGS OF THE ... ANNUAL MEETING. **See** Naval Science, Navigation.

LC TL697.S3 N3 **ISSN** 0743-846X
DD 629.134/43/05 US
PROCEEDINGS OF THE ... ANNUAL SYMPOSIUM, SAFE ASSOCIATION. [Proc. annu. Symposium SAFE Assoc.]. **Main/Corp** SAFE Association (U.S.). Symposium. **VFOAT** S.A.F.E. Symposium Proceedings; SAFE Symposium Proceedings. **VAT** Proceedings of the Annual Symposium, Survival and Flight Equipment Association. (Sept. 13-16, 1976)-. Proceedings. English. One time a year. $27.50. SAFE Association, 34834 Shoreview Drive, Suite 23, Cottage Grove OR 97424. **Tel** (503)942-3538, FAX (503)942-0387. **ED** Russ Burton (editor's address: PO Box 38 Cottage Grove OR 97424). Index available. **Circ:** 1,000. Documents available from Article Express International. ***Continues*** *SAFE Association (U.S.). Conference and Trade Exhibit. Proceedings of the ... Annual Conference and Trade Exhibit, SAFE Association, 0743-8451.*
Desc: Covers Annual Symposium.
Ind/Abst Eng. Index Annu.

LC TJ1 .P867 **ISSN** 0954-4100
DD 629.1 UK
CCC
CODEN PMGEEP
PROCEEDINGS OF THE INSTITUTION OF MECHANICAL ENGINEERS. PART G, JOURNAL OF AEROSPACE ENGINEERING. [Proc. Inst. Mech. Eng., G J. aerosp. eng.]. **Added/Corp** Institution of Mechanical Engineers (Great Britain). **VFOAT** Journal of Aerospace Engineering; Proceedings IMechE. Part G, Journal of Aerospace Engineering. Vol. 203, No. G1 (1989)-. Proceedings. English. Four times a year. $309.00. Mechanical Engineering Publications, PO Box 24, Northgate Avenue, Bury St. Edmunds, Suffolk IP32 6BW United Kingdom. **Tel** 011 44 1284 763277, FAX 011 44 1284 704006, telex 817376. **(Subscription address:** Mechanical Engineering Publications / Western Hemisphere Subscriptions, Subscription Office, PO Box 361, Birmingham AL 35201-0361. **Tel** (800)633-4931 (US and Canada), (205)991-1177, FAX (205)995-1588.) **ED** F.K.E. Behennah. available on microfilm and microfiche from University Microfilms International (UMI). Documents available from Ask*IEEE. ***Continues in part*** *Proceedings of the Institution of Mechanical Engineers. Part D, Transport Engineering, 0265-1904.*
Desc: Contains papers of a high standard on aeronautical and space subjects relevant to mechanical engineers and covers both academic and practical aspects.
Ind/Abst Appl. Sci. Technol. Index (1991-); Curr. Cit.; INSPEC (1989-); Int. Aerosp. Abstr.

LC HE9788 .I5 **ISSN** 1043-4712
DD 387.7/44/05 US
PROCEEDINGS OF THE INTERNATIONAL AIR CARGO FORUM. **See** Transportation.

LC TL589 .I48 **ISSN** 0277-7576
DD 629.1 S 629.1 US
CCC
PROCEEDINGS OF THE INTERNATIONAL INSTRUMENTATION SYMPOSIUM. [Proc. Int. Instrum. Symp.]. **Main/Conf** International Instrumentation Symposium. Vol. 20 (1974)-. Proceedings. English. One time a year. $95.00 plus shipping. Instrument Society of America, 67 Alexander Drive, Research Triangle NC 27709. **Tel** (919)549-8411, FAX (919)549-8288, telex 802 540. Documents available from Article Express International. ***Continues*** *ISA Aerospace Instrumentation Symposium. Proceedings of the International ISA Aerospace Instrumentation Symposium.*
Desc: Proceedings of the Annual Symposium for the Aerospace and Test Measurement Industries Division of the Instrument Society of America.
Ind/Abst Curr. Cit.; Eng. Index Annu.

LC U
DD 355 UK
TITLE CHANGE
PROCEEDINGS OF THE ROYAL AIR FORCE HISTORICAL SOCIETY, THE. **Added/Corp** Royal Air Force Historical Society. (Jan. 1987)-(1993). Proceedings. English. Royal Air Force Historical Society, Silverhill House, Coombe Wotton, Edge Gloucestershire, GL12 7ND United Kingdom. **Tel** 011 44 1903 263732. ***Continued by*** *Royal Air Force Historical Society Journal.*
Desc: Transactions of meetings of the Royal Air Force Historical Society.

LC TL799 **ISSN** 0288-433X
DD 629.455 JA
PROCEEDINGS OF THE SYMPOSIUM ON MECHANICS FOR SPACE FLIGHT. **Main/Corp** Symposium on Mechanics for Space Flight. **Added/Corp** Uchu Kagaku Kenkyujo (Japan). (1982)-. Proceedings. English. One time a year. Uchu Kagaku Kenkyujo, (Institute of Space and Astronautical Science), 1-1 Yoshinodai 3 chome, Sagamiharashi Kanagawaken 229 Japan. Documents available from BLDSC.

LC TL **ISSN** 0584-6099
DD 629 US
CODEN SPCPBL
PROCEEDINGS / SPACE CONGRESS. [Proc. - Space Cong.]. **Main/Conf** Space Congress. **Added/Corp** Canaveral Council of Technical Societies. (1964)-. English. One time a year (Apr.). $70.00. Canaveral Council of Technical Societies, PO Box 245, Cape Canaveral FL 32930. **Tel** (407)868-1623. **(Subscription address:** Space Congress Proceedings, 1255 Leslie Drive, Merrett Island FL 32952. **Tel** (407)453-4162.) **Circ:** 1,000 (ctrl). available on microfiche (from Western Periodicals, North Hollywood, California.). Documents available from Article Express International.
Desc: Proceedings and presentations from guest speakers, latest technologies in the USA space program and research and development.
Ind/Abst Bioeng. Abstr.; Ei Page One; Eng. Index Annu.

LC TL502
DD 629.13 US
PRODUCTIVITY AND COST OF EMPLOYMENT. LOCAL SERVICE CARRIERS. **See** Business and Economics-Labor.

LC TL501 .P75 **ISSN** 0191-6238
DD 629 US
PROFESSIONAL PILOT. [Prof. pilot]. (1967)-. Trade Publication. English. Twelve times a year. $36.00. Professional Pilot, 3014 Colvin Street, Alexandria VA 22314. **Tel** (800)222-3212, (703)370-0606, FAX (703)370-8072, telex 517267 PRO PILOT. **ED** Mary Silitch. Index available (bound in first issue, December, Price $5.00 is sold separately , included in subscription.). cum. index (Only in December issue). **Ad Acc, Adv Mgr:** Earlene Chandler. **Circ:** 3,520 (ctrl).
Desc: For the career professional pilots by aviation professionals. Editorial covers current and future issues, trends, techniques, safety, salaries, equipment checks and commentary.
Ind/Abst Aviat. Tradescan [Full Cov.].

LC HE9803.A1 A93b
DD 387.7/0973 US
PROFILES OF SCHEDULED AIR CARRIER OPERATIONS BY STAGE LENGTH. **Main/Corp** United States. Aviation Forecast Branch. (19??)-. Government Publication. English. Irregular. US Department of Transportation / Federal Aviation Administration, 800 Independence Avenue Southwest, Washington DC 20591. **Tel** (202)367-3484, FAX (202)367-3505.

LC HE9803.A1 A93A **ISSN** 0360-0041
DD 387.7/364/0973 US
PROFILES OF SCHEDULED AIR CARRIER PASSENGER TRAFFIC, TOP 100 U.S. AIRPORTS. **Main/Corp** United States. Aviation Forecast Branch. **VAT** Profiles of Scheduled Air Carrier Passenger Traffic, Top One Hundred United States Airports. Government Publication. English. US Department of Transportation / Federal Aviation Administration, 800 Independence Avenue Southwest, Washington DC 20591. **Tel** (202)367-3484, FAX (202)367-3505.

LC HE9850.A1 H95b
DD 629.13 GR
PROGRAMMA DRASEOS HYPERESIAS POLITIKES AEROPORIAS. (19??)-. Greek, Modern. Hyperesia Politikes Aeroporias 1 Hellenikon, Athens Greece.

LC TL500 .P7 **ISSN** 0376-0421
DD 629.1/05 UK
CCC
CODEN PAESD6
PROGRESS IN AEROSPACE SCIENCES. [Prog. aerosp. sci.]. Vol. 11 (1970)-. Periodical. English (French and German). Six times a year. $557.00. Pergamon Press, An Imprint of Elsevier Science Ltd., The Boulevard, Langford Lane, Kidlington, Oxford OX5 1GB United Kingdom. **Tel** 011 44 1865 843000, 011 44 1865 843699, FAX 011 44 1865 843010. **(Subscription address:** Elsevier Science Ltd. / Oxford Fulfillment Centre, PO Box 800, Kidlington OX5 1DX United Kingdom. **Tel** 011 44 865 843355.) **ED** Alec Young. available on microfilm from Microfilms International Marketing Corp.; available on microfilm and microfiche from University Microfilms International (UMI); available on an online database from Elsevier Electronic Subscriptions (EES). Documents available from Article Express International, Ask*IEEE. ***Continues*** *Progress in Aeronautical Sciences, 0079-6026.*
Ind/Abst Acoust. Abstr.; Bioeng. Abstr.; Ei Page One; Eng. Index Annu.; Expand. Acad. Index (1992-); INSPEC (March 1975-); Int. Aerosp. Abstr.; Met. Abstr.; Zentralbl. Math. Ihre Grenzgeb.

LC TL507 .P75 **ISSN** 0079-6050
DD 629 US
CODEN PAAEA9
PROGRESS IN ASTRONAUTICS AND AERONAUTICS. [Prog. astronaut. aeronaut.]. **Added/Corp** American Institute of Aeronautics and Astronautics. (1963)-. Academic Scholarly Publication. English. Irregular. Price varies per volume. American Institute of Aeronautics & Astronautics, 370 l'Enfant Promenade Southwest, Washington DC 20024-2518. **Tel** (202)646-7400, FAX (202)646-7508, telex 204792 AIAA UR. **ED** Martin Summerfield. Documents available from Article Express International, Ask*IEEE, CASDDS. ***Continues*** *Progress in Astronautics and Rocketry, 0096-4824.*
Desc: Hard cover books of papers and monographs covering topics in astronautical and aeronautical

technology and science.
Ind/Abst Bioeng. Abstr.; Chem. Abstr.; Ei Page One; Energy Res. Abstr.; Eng. Index Annu.; GeoRef; INSPEC.

LC TL787 **ISSN** 0555-4306
DD 629.4082 NE
PROGRESS IN THE ASTRONAUTICAL SCIENCES. Vol. 1-. English. North Holland Publishing Company, PO Box 211, Amsterdam The Netherlands. **Tel** 31-20-5803579. **ED** S F Singer.

LC TL501 **ISSN** 0269-4018
DD 629.13 UK
PROPLINER. [Propliner]. **VFOAT** Propliner Aviation Magazine. (1979)-. Consumer Publication. English. Four times a year. £14.00 Europe; £17.00 other. Propliner Magazine Ltd, 6 Millside, Bourne End, Buckinghamshire SL8 5 UN United Kingdom. **Tel** 011 44 1628 520349, FAX 011 44 1628 532488. **ED** Tony Merton Jones. available with charts; available with illustrations.

LC TL **ISSN** 1065-7738
DD 629 US
Pr Rev.
QUEST (GRAND RAPIDS, MICH.). (QUEST : THE HISTORY OF SPACEFLIGHT MAGAZINE.). [Quest]. **VFOAT** Quest Magazine. Vol. 1, No. 2 (Summer 1992)-. Periodical. English. Four times a year. $19.95. Cspace Press, PO Box 9331, Grand Rapids MI 49509-0331. **Tel** (616)452-5500, FAX (616)452-5538. **ED** Glen E. Swanson. **Bk Rev**, (Qty: 4-12). **Circ:** 1,000. ***Continues** Liftoff (Grand Rapids, Mich.), 1060-7692.*
Desc: Covers the past international achievements in manned and unmanned space flight.
Ind/Abst Mag. Search.

LC HD3860 .R15 **ISSN** 0033-6793
DD 650 US
CEASED
R&D CONTRACTS MONTHLY. **See** Science and Technology.

LC TL789.8.F8 A3
DD 629.4/072044 FR
RAPPORT ANNUEL / CENTRE NATIONAL D'ETUDES SPATIALES.
Main/Corp Centre National d'Etudes Spatiales (France). **VFOAT** Annual Report. (1989)-. English (French). One time a year. Free. Centre National d'Etudes Spatiales, 18 Avenue Edouard-Berlin, 31055 Toulouse Cedex France. **Tel** 33 (61)27 31 31, telex 531081. ctrl circ. ***Continues** Rapport d'Activite (Centre National d'Etudes Spatiales. France).*

LC JS **ISSN** 0034-0111
DD 352 GW
RAUMFORSCHUNG UND RAUMORDNUNG. [Raumforsch. Raumordn.]. **Added/Corp** Institut fuer Raumforschung. Reichsarbeitsgemeinschaft fuer Raumforschung. Akademie fuer Raumforschung und Landesplanung (Germany). Vol. 1 (1936)-. Periodical. German. Six times a year. $99.03. Carl Heymanns Verlag KG, Luxemburger Strasse 449, D-50939 Cologne Germany. **Tel** 011 49 221 460100, telex 8 881 888. Index available. **Bk Rev**. **Ad Acc. Circ:** 2,000 (ctrl).
Desc: Scientific treatises on space regulations and space research.
Ind/Abst Bibliogr. Carto.; EMBASE; Int. Labour Doc.; PAIS Int. Print.

LC TL770.A1 R14 **ISSN** 0033-6866
DD 629.133/1 US
RC MODELER (1969). **See** Hobbies.

LC TL5010 **ISSN** 1013-9044
DD 629.13 NE
CODEN RESKEZ
REACHING FOR THE SKIES. [Reach. skies]. **Added/Corp** European Space Agency Publications Division. Vol. 1, No. 1 (June 1989)-. Periodical. English (French). Four times a year. free on request. ESA Publications Division / ESTEC, 2200 AG Noordwijk The Netherlands. **Tel** FAX 011 31 1719 85433. **ED** D. Guyenne and N. Longdon. **Circ:** 20,000. available with illustrations.

LC TL502 .R32 **ISSN** 0034-1223
DD 629.1/05 FR
CODEN REARAU
Pr Rev.
RECHERCHE AEROSPATIALE. (LA RECHERCHE AEROSPATIALE : BULLETIN BIMESTRIEL DE L'OFFICE NATIONAL D'ETUDES ET DE RECHERCHES AEROSPATIALES.). [Rech. aerosp.]. **Added/Corp** France. Office National d'Etudes et de Recherches Aerospatiales. No. 94 (May/June 1963)-. Bulletin. French. Six times a year. $183.72. Dunod Gauthier Villars, 15 rue Gossin, 92543 Montrouge Cedex France. **Tel** 011 33 1 46565266, 011 33 1 40926527, FAX 011 33 1 40926597. **(Subscription address:** Centrale des Revues, 11 rue Gossin, 92543 Montrouge Cedex France. **Tel** 011 33 1 46565266.) Documents available from Article Express International, The Genuine Article, Ask*IEEE, CASDDS. ***Continues** Recherche Aeronautique, 0370-3533.*
Ind/Abst Alum. Ind. Abstr.; Chem. Abstr.; Civ. Struct. Eng. Abstr.; Comput. Inf. Syst. Abstr. J.; Curr. Cit.; Curr. Contents Eng. Comput. Technol.; EMBASE; Energy Res. Abstr.; Eng. Index Annu.; Fluid Abstr., Civil Eng.; Fluid Abstr. Proc. Eng.; FLUIDEX (1973-); INSPEC (Nov./Dec. 1969-); Int. Aerosp. Abstr.; Leadscan; Math. Rev.; Mech. Eng. Abstr.; Met. Abstr.; Res. Alert; Sci. Cit. Index; SCISEARCH; Zentralbl. Math. Ihre Grenzgeb.

LC TL502 .R33 **ISSN** 0244-9056
DD 629.1/05 FR
CODEN RAEEDK
RECHERCHE AEROSPATIALE (ENGLISH ED.), LA. (LA RECHERCHE AEROSPATIALE : BULLETIN BIMESTRIEL DE L'OFFICE NATIONAL D'ETUDES ET DE RECHERCHES AEROSPATIALES.). [Rech. aerosp.]. **Added/Corp** France. Office National d'Etudes et de Recherches Aerospatiales. **VFOAT** Bulletin Bimestriel de l'Office National d'Etudes et de Recherches Aerospatiales; Bimonthly Bulletin of Office National d'Etudes et de Recherches Aerospatiales. (1974)-. Bulletin. English. Six times a year. $192.48. Office National d'Etudes et de Recherches Aerospatiales, BP 72, 92322 Chatillon Cedex France. **Tel** 011 33 1 46734040. Documents available from Article Express International, Ask*IEEE.
Ind/Abst Bioeng. Abstr.; Ei Page One; EMBASE; Eng. Index Annu.; INSPEC (1969-); Int. Aerosp. Abstr.; Math. Rev.

LC TL500
DD 629.13 US
RECIPIENTS OF LOCAL SERVICE AIR CARRIERS' UNIT COSTS. **Added/Corp** United States. Civil Aeronautics Board. (1970)-. English. US Civil Aeronautics Board, 1825 Connecticut Avenue NW, Washington DC 20428. **Tel** (202)673-5174.

LC TL500 **ISSN** 0845-8391
DD 629.133/343 CN
RECREATIONAL FLYER, THE. [Recreat. fly.]. **Added/Corp** Experimental Aircraft Association of Canada. Recreational Aircraft Association Canada. (Summer 1986)-. Periodical. English (French; summaries and/or abstracts in French). Six times a year (Jan., March, May, July, Sept., Nov.). comes with Recreational Aircraft Association of Canada membership. Recreational Aircraft Association Canada, 152 Harwood Avenue South, Ajax Ontario L1S 2H6 Canada. **Tel** (902)683-3517, FAX (902)428-2415. **Ad Acc. Circ:** 2,000 (ctrl).

LC K **ISSN** 0883-5837
DD 341 US
REFLECTIONS ON SPACE. [Reflect. space]. Vol. 1, No. 1 (Sept. 1983)-. Periodical. English. Twelve times a year. $18.00. Reflections on Space, MIT Branch, PO Box 49, Cambridge MA 02139. **Tel** (617)969-2495. **ED** Michael M. Bernard.
Desc: An independent, experimental publication now in it's 9th year, founded at M.I.T. for the purpose of exploring the various concepts of space in science, technology, and the arts.

LC TL726 .C64 **ISSN** 1070-065X
DD 387.7/42 US
TITLE CHANGE
REGIONAL AIR INTERNATIONAL. [Reg. air int.]. Vol. 15, No. 6 (June 1993)-(1995). Trade Publication. English. Argus Business, 6151 Powers Ferry Road Northwest, Atlanta GA 30339. **Tel** (404)995-2500, FAX (404)995-0400. ***Continues** Commuter Air International, 1054-7436. **Merged into** Commuter World.*

LC HE9785 .R44
DD 387.7/42/025 US
REGIONAL AIRLINE DIRECTORY, THE. **Added/Corp** Phillips Publishing, Inc. (19??)-. Directory. English. One time a year. $235.00. Phillips Business Information Inc., 1201 Seven Locks Road, PO Box 61130, Potomac MD 20854. **Tel** (301)424-3338, (301)340-1520, (800)777-5005, FAX (301)424-4297, telex 358149.
Desc: Provides information on individual carrier fleets and route data, traffic and aircraft forecasts, aircraft maintenance and modification, and manufacturers of engine systems.

LC HB **ISSN** 1044-9450
DD 338 US
REGIONAL AVIATION WEEKLY. [Reg. aviat. wkly.]. (1986)-. Periodical. English. One time a week. $425.00 (one-year), $280.00 (six month). McGraw Hill Publishing Company, Inc., 1221 Avenue of the Americas, New York NY 10020. **Tel** (212)512-6410, (800)525-5003, FAX (212)512-6111. available on an online database (file 624/Full-Text) from DIALOG; and NEXIS.
Desc: Complete and continual statistics, facts, field reports, business analysis and more for the regional aviation industry. Top-quality reporting you can't afford to be without.

LC TL500
DD 629.13 US
REGULATIONS OF THE CIVIL AERONAUTICS BOARD. **Main/Corp** United States. Civil Aeronautics Board. (19??)-. Periodical. English. Irregular. US Department of Commerce / Civil Aeronautics Board, Washington DC 20402.
Desc: Contains regulations of the CAB, pts. 200-399, except pt. 241 which is issued separately.

LC TL1 .R36 **ISSN** 0163-643X
DD 623.74/69/05 US
REMOTELY PILOTED MAGAZINE. **Added/Corp** National Association for Remotely Piloted Vehicles. (19??)-. Periodical. English. Six times a year. $10.00. National Association for RPVS, 4130 Linden Avenue, Suite 256, Dayton OH 45432.

LC TL **ISSN** 0484-3916
DD 629 US
RENDEZVOUS (BUFFALO, N.Y.). (RENDEZVOUS.). [Rendezvous]. **Added/Corp** Bell Aerosystems Company. Bell Aerospace Textron. Vol. 1 (Apr./May 1962)-. Periodical. English. Six times a year. (ia93).
Ind/Abst Am. Hist. Life (1967-).

LC TL500.5 .A22 HE9797.4.F F4
DD 387.7 S 387.7/1 CN
REPERTOIRE DE TARIFS D'AEROPORTS ET DE TARIFS D'INSTALLATIONS ET DE SERVICES DE NAVIGATION AERIENNE. **Main/Corp** International Civil Aviation Organization. French. $22.50. Organisation de l'Aviation Civile Internationale, Service de Distribution, CP 400, Succursale Place de l'Aviation Internationale, 1000 Ouest rue Sherbrooks, Montreal Quebec H3A 2R2 Canada.

LC TL500.5 .I56A **ISSN** 0828-2536
DD 387.7/1/05 CN
REPORT AND MINUTES - ECONOMIC COMMISSION. INTERNATIONAL CIVIL AVIATION ORGANIZATION. (REPORT AND MINUTES / ECONOMIC COMMISSION.). [Rep. minutes - Econ. Comm., Int. Civ. Aviat. Organ.]. **Main/Corp** International Civil Aviation Organization. Economic Commission. 23rd Session (Sept. 16-Oct. 7, 1980)-. English (French, Spanish, Russian and Arabic). Every 3 years. $5.75. Document Sales Unit of the International Civil Aviation Organization, 1000 Sherbrooke Street West/Suite 400, Montreal Quebec H3A 2R2 Canada. ***Formed by the union of** International Civil Aviation Organization. Economic Commission. Report of the Economic Commission **and** International Civil Aviation Organization. Economic Commission. Minutes of the Economic Commission.*

LC TL **ISSN** 0285-6808
DD 629.1/05 JA
CODEN IASRDU
REPORT - INSTITUTE OF SPACE AND ASTRONAUTICAL SCIENCE, TOKYO. (THE INSTITUTE OF SPACE AND ASTRONAUTICAL SCIENCE REPORT.). [Rep. - Inst. Space Astronaut. Sci., Tokyo]. **Added/Corp** Uchu Kagaku Kenkyujo (Japan). **VFOAT** ISAS Report; I.S.A.S. Report; Report. (Nov. 1981)-. Academic Scholarly Publication. English. Irregular. Free on request. Institute of Space and Astronautical Science, 6-1-4 Chome Komaba Meguro-ku, Tokyo 153 Japan. Documents available from CASDDS. ***Continues** Report (Tokyo Daigaku. Uchu Koku Kenkyujo), 0372-1418.*
Ind/Abst Chem. Abstr.; Int. Aerosp. Abstr.

LC TL796
DD 629.4 US
REPORT ON ACTIVE AND PLANNED SPACECRAFT AND EXPERIMENTS. (1974)-. English. Irregular. Free. National Space Science Data Center (NSSDC), World Data Center A for Rockets and Satellites (WDC-A-R & S), National Aeronautics and Space Administration, Greenbelt MD 20771. **Tel** (301)286-6695. **ED** N J Scholfield and L Blasso. **Circ:** 2,000.
Desc: This report provides information on current and planned spacecraft activity for a broad range of scientific disciplines.

LC TL720.9.S34 A3
DD 387.7065 387.74 SW
REPORT - SCANDINAVIAN AIRLINES SYSTEM. **Main/Corp** Scandinavian Airlines System. English. Scandinavian Airlines System, Treasury Dept, Attn QT, S 161 87 Stockholm Sweden. **Tel** 011 46 8 797000.

LC TL789.8.U6 S574A **ISSN** 0090-5453
DD 629.44/5 US
REPORT TO THE ADMINISTRATOR ON THE SKYLAB PROGRAM. [Rep. adm. skylab prog.]. **Main/Corp** United States. National Aeronautics and Space Administration. Aerospace Safety Advisory Panel. Periodical. English. One time a year. US National Aeronautics and Space Administration, Aerospace Safety Advisory Board, Washington DC 20546.

LC TL501 **ISSN** 0231-3928
DD 629.13 HU
UDC 016
REPULESI SZAKIRODALMI TAJEKOZTATO. (1983)-. Abstracting/Indexing Service. Hungarian. Six times a year. 3000ft. Orszagos Muszaki Informacios Kozpont es Konyvtar (O.M.I.K.K.), National Technical Information Centre and Library Museum, Muzeum u. 17, PO Box 12, 1428 Budapest

Hungary. **Tel** 011 36 1 1181994, FAX 011 36 1 1382414, telex 22-4944 OMIKK H. **ED** Ferenc Bardosi. Index available. cum. index. **Bk Rev**. **Ad Acc**. **Circ:** 200 (ctrl).
Desc: Information on aircrafts and airports.

LC HE9761.1 .I18
DD 387.7/06/01 SZ
REVIEW (INTERNATIONAL AIR TRANSPORT ASSOCIATION). (IATA REVIEW.). **VFOAT** IATA Review. (Jan.-March 1985)-. Periodical. English. Four times a year. International Air Transport Association / Montreal, 2000 Peel Street, Room 3050, Montreal Quebec H3A 2R4 Canada. **Tel** (514)844-6311 ext. 232, FAX (514)844-5286, telex 05-267627. cum. index. ***Continues*** *World Airline Cooperation Review, 0376-642X.*
Ind/Abst Leis., Rec., Tour. Abstr.

LC TL501
DD 629.13 US
REVISION SERVICE FOR FEDERAL REGULATORY LIBRARY WITH I ADS. INSPECTIONS AIRWOTHINESS & DIRECTIVES. (19??)-. English. Twenty-six times a year. $625.00. Aircraft Technical Publishers, 101 South Hill Drive, Brisbane CA 94005. **Tel** (800)227-4610, FAX (415)468-1596, telex 171048.

LC TL526 **ISSN** 0279-4519
DD 629.13 US
REVISTA AEREA. (19??)-. Trade Publication. Spanish. Ten times a year (monthly with combined Dec./Jan. and June/July). $50.00. Strato Publishing Company Inc., 310 East 44th Street/Suite 1601, New York NY 10017. **Tel** (212)370-1740, FAX (212)949-6756, telex 130412. **ED** Elaine Asch. **Bk Rev**. **Ad Acc, Adv Mgr:** D. Dicker, **Tel** (212)370-1740. Full Page (B&W) $6060.00. Full Page (Color) $9845.00. **Circ:** 10,000 (ctrl). available with illustrations. ***Continues*** *Revista Aerea Latinoamericana, 0034-6934.*
Desc: Publishes news in Spanish of the aviation and aerospace world to readers in Latin America, Spain, and the Philippines.

LC UG635.B5 R48
DD 358.4009 BO
REVISTA AERONAUTICA. **See** Military and Defense.

LC TL
DD 629 SP
REVISTA DE AERONAUTICA Y ASTRONAUTICA. (April 1932/July 1936)-. Periodical. Spanish. Twelve times a year. $56.82. Institute Historia Cultura Aeronautica, Princesa 88 Bajo, 28008 Madrid Spain. **Tel** 011 34 1 5444080.
Ind/Abst Int. Aerosp. Abstr.

LC WMLC 93/4367
DD 629.13 FR
REVUE AEROSPATIALE. **VFOAT** Aerospatiale. (198?)-. Periodical. French (English). Ten times a year. $61.24. Revue Aerospatiale, 19 boulevard du Parc, 92200 Neuilly Seine Cedex France. **Tel** 011 33 1 47476399.

LC JX5760 .R48
DD 340 FR
REVUE FRANCAISE DE DROIT AERIEN ET SPATIAL. **Added/Corp** Societe Francaise de Droit Aerien et Spatial. Vol. 169, No. 1 (Jan./March 1989)-. Periodical. French. Four times a year. $100.00. Editions Pedone, 13 rue Soufflot, 75005 Paris France. **Tel** 011 33 1 43540597. ***Continues*** *Revue Francaise de Droit Aerien, 0035-287X.*

LC HE9761 **ISSN** 0035-3191
DD 387.73 FR
REVUE GENERALE DES ROUTES ET DES AERODROMES. [Rev. gen. routes aerodr.]. No. 1 (1926)-. Academic Scholarly Publication. French (English, German and Spanish; summaries and/or abstracts in English, French, German and Spanish). Thirteen times a year (publishes 11 issues with July/Aug. issues combined and Hors Serie two issues per year). $288.71. Revue Generale des Routes et des Aerodromes, 9 rue Magellan, 75008 Paris France. **Tel** 011 33 1 40738000, FAX 011 33 1 49520180, telex CCP 887-03 X Paris. **ED** Bernard Dollon (phone: 011 33 1 40738002). Index Available, published separately, free-automatically sent.
Ind/Abst EMBASE; Int. Aerosp. Abstr. (1984-); Int. Civil Eng. Abstr.; Soft. Abstr. Eng.

LC TL504 .R54
DD 629.1305 IT
RIVISTA AERONAUTICA. (19??)-. Periodical. Italian. Six times a year (Feb., Apr., June, Aug., Oct., Dec.). L54500. Stato Maggiore Aeronautica, Viale Dell Universita 4, 00185 Rome Italy. **Tel** 011 39 6 49861. **ED** Antonio Duma. Index available. **Bk Rev**. **Ad Acc**. **Circ:** 20,000.
Desc: Covers military policy and strategy. Economic and industrial fallout; civil and military aviation; the Italian air force; space; and history.

LC TL780 .R625 **ISSN** 0035-7499
DD 629.1333805 US
ROCKET-JET FLYING. Vol. 101 (Fall 1945)-. Periodical. English. Four times a year. Auerbach Publishers Inc., Park Square Building, 31 St. James Avenue, Boston MA 02116. **Tel** (800)950-1207.

LC HB **ISSN** 0897-831X
DD 338 US
Pr Rev.
ROTOR (ALEXANDRIA, VA.). (ROTOR.). [Rotor]. **Added/Corp** Helicoptor Association International. Vol. 1, No. 1 (Spring 1988)-. Trade Publication. English. Four times a year (Spring, Summer, Fall, Winter). $15.00. Helicopter Association International, 1619 Duke Street, Alexandria VA 22314. **Tel** (703)683-4646, FAX (703)683-4745, telex 89-615. **ED** Daniel P. Warsley. **Ad Acc, Adv Mgr:** M. Beames. **Circ:** 17,000 (ctrl). ***Continues*** *Rotor News, 0889-4272.*
Desc: Comprehensive reports and a guide to the civil helicopters industry.

LC TL **ISSN** 1066-8098
DD 629 US
ROTOR & WING (1992). (ROTOR & WING.). [Rotor wing]. **VFOAT** Rotor and Wing. (199?)-. Periodical. English. Twelve times a year. $49.00 US; $80.00 other. Phillips Business Information Inc., 1201 Seven Locks Road, PO Box 61130, Potomac MD 20854. **Tel** (301)424-3338, (301)340-1520, (800)777-5005, FAX (301)424-4297, telex 358149. ***Continues*** *Rotor & Wing International, 0191-6408.*

LC TL716.A1 R63 **ISSN** 0191-6408
DD 629.133/352/05 US
CCC
CODEN RWINEI
TITLE CHANGE
ROTOR & WING INTERNATIONAL. [Rotor wing int.]. **VFOAT** Rotor and Wing International. **VAT** Rotor and Wing International. Vol. 10, No. 4 (July/Aug. 1976)-(199?). Trade Publication. English. Phillips Business Information Inc., 1201 Seven Locks Road, PO Box 61130, Potomac MD 20854. **Tel** (301)424-3338, (301)340-1520, (800)777-5005, FAX (301)424-4297, telex 358149. **ED** Don Toler. **Ad Acc**. **Circ:** 40,000 (ctrl). ***Continues*** *Rotor & Wing.* ***Continued by*** *Rotor & Wing (Potomac, Md.), 1066-8098.*
Desc: Coverage of worldwide rotorcraft industry, military and commercial activity.
Ind/Abst Aviat. Tradescan [Full Cov.]; Infomat Int. Bus.; Int. Aerosp. Abstr. (19??-19??).

LC HE9769.A3 R68
DD 387.7/3352/05 US
ROTOR ROSTER. (19??)-. English. One time a year. $25.00. Air Track, PO Box 610, Hilliard FL 32046. **Tel** (912)496-3504, (800)288-7024, FAX (912)496-7513. **ED** Glenn Wonnacott. **Ad Acc**. **Circ:** 7,000. available on diskette.
Desc: Listing of civil helipoter owners worldwide.

LC GV **ISSN** 1041-2735
DD 797 US
ROTORCRAFT (CLINTON, LA.). **See** Sports and Games.

LC U
DD 355 UK
ROYAL AIR FORCE HISTORICAL SOCIETY JOURNAL. (19??)-. Proceedings. English. Two times a year. £15.00 Comes with membership. Royal Air Force Historical Society, Silverhill House, Coombe Wotton, Edge Gloucestershire, GL12 7ND United Kingdom. **Tel** 011 44 1903 263732. ***Continues*** *Proceedings of the Royal Air Force Historical Society.*
Desc: Transactions of meetings of the Royal Air Force Historical Society.

LC TL500 **ISSN** 0954-092X
DD 629.13 UK
ROYAL AIR FORCE YEARBOOK. (19??)-. Periodical. English. One time a year. Royal Air Force Benevolent Fund, Building 15, RAF Fairford Gloucestershire GL7 4DL United Kingdom. **Tel** 011 44 1285 713300, FAX 011 44 1285 285 713268, telex 43511 IATFFDG. **ED** Peter R March. **Ad Acc**. **Circ:** 96,500 (ctrl).
Desc: Provides a medium to promote the service to as wide an audience as possible.

LC TL
DD 629 CN
RULES OF THE AIR; INTERNATIONAL STANDARDS. ANNEX 2 TO THE CONVENTION ON INTERNATIONAL CIVIL AVIATION. **Main/Corp** International Civil Aviation Organization. (19??)-. English (French, Spanish and Russian). Irregular. $5.75 (9th edition incorporating Amendments 1-29). International Civil Aviation Organization / ICAO, 1000 Sherbrooke Street West, Suite 400, Montreal Quebec H3A 2R2 Canada. **Tel** (514)285-8026, (514)285-8022, telex 05-24514.

LC TL504 .R76144 **ISSN** 1068-7998
DD 629.13/00947 US
CCC
RUSSIAN AERONAUTICS. [Russ. aeronaut.]. Vol. 35, 1 (1992)-. Academic Scholarly Publication. English (translations available in Russian). Four times a year. $915.00. Allerton Press Inc., 150 Fifth Avenue, New York NY 10011. **Tel** (212)924-3950, FAX (212)463-9684, telex 427441 ALPRES. Documents available from CASDDS. ***Continues*** *Soviet Aeronautics, 0364-8117.*
Ind/Abst Chem. Abstr.; Int. Aerosp. Abstr.; Math. Rev.

LC TL789.8.R9 N6813 **ISSN** 1078-1188
DD 629.4/0947 US
CEASED
RUSSIAN SPACE NEWS. (RUSSIAN SPACE NEWS = NOVOSTI KOSMONAVTIKI.). [Russ. space news]. **VFOAT** Novosti Kosmonavtiki. (199?)-(199?). Periodical. English (translations available in Russian). Tranquest Corporation, PO Box 30208, Cleveland OH 44130. **Tel** (216)888-3991.

LC T174.3 .R88
DD 605 US
•**RUSSIAN TECH BRIEFS : THE OFFICIAL TECHNOLOGY TRANSFER PUBLICATION OF THE RUSSIAN SPACE AGENCY.** **Added/Corp** Russian Space Agency. Moscow Space Club. Vol. 1, No. 1 (Mar. 1994)-. Periodical. English. Six times a year. $195.00. Associated Business Publishing Inc., 41 East 42nd Street, Suite 921, New York NY 10017. **Tel** (212)490-3999.

LC TL500 **ISSN** 0382-1153
DD 629.13 CN
S R F B NEWSLETTER. **Main/Corp** National Research Council of Canada. Space Research Facilities Branch. No. 1 (Mar. 1969)-. Newsletter. English. National Research Council of Canada, Receiver General for Canada, Ottawa Ontario K1A 0R6 Canada. **Tel** (613)993-0362, FAX (613)952-7656.

LC TL671.1 .S24 **ISSN** 1056-1897
DD 016.62913/00218/73 US
SAE AEROSPACE STANDARDS INDEX. [SAE aerosp. standards index]. **Added/Corp** Society of Automotive Engineers. Cooperative Engineering Program. **VAT** Society of Automotive Engineers Standards Index. English. Twelve times a year. $36.00. Society of Automotive Engineers, 400 Commonwealth Drive, Warrendale PA 15096. **Tel** (412)776-4970, FAX (412)776-0790. ***Continues*** *SAE Aerospace Index, 0741-7551.*

LC TL553.5 .S27 **ISSN** 0191-6319
DD 363.1/247/05 US
CODEN SAFJDH
Pr Rev.
SAFE JOURNAL. [Safe j.]. **Added/Corp** SAFE Association (U.S.). **VFOAT** S.A.F.E. Journal; SAFE Journal. (19??)-. Academic Scholarly Publication. English. Four times a year (Jan., Apr., July, Oct.). $25.00. SAFE Association, 34834 Shoreview Drive, Suite 23, Cottage Grove OR 97424. **Tel** (503)942-3538, FAX (503)942-0387. **ED** Russ Burton. Index available. **Bk Rev**, (Qty: varies). **Ad Acc**. **Circ:** 1,000.
Desc: Safety and survival in all areas where man ventures. Flight equipment applications.
Ind/Abst EMBASE; Int. Aerosp. Abstr.

LC TL **ISSN** 0882-858X
DD 629 US
SAFETY MANUAL. [Saf. man. - Helicopter Assoc. Int.]. **Added/Corp** Helicopter Association International. **VFOAT** HAI Safety Manual. (1984)-. Trade Publication. English. One time a year. $95.00-$115.00. Helicopter Association International, 1619 Duke Street, Alexandria VA 22314. **Tel** (703)683-4646, FAX (703)683-4745, telex 89-615. **ED** Glenn A. Leister. Index available. **Circ:** 15,000 (ctrl).
Desc: A manual for safe helicopter operations, including a helicopter safety reference guide.

LC TL **ISSN** 1065-951X
DD 629 US
•**SAGA DIRECTORY OF INTERNATIONAL AVIATION PRODUCTS AND SERVICES.** **Added/Corp** Sport and General Aviation, Inc. **VFOAT** Directory of International Aviation Products and Services. **VAT** Sport and General Aviation Directory of International Aviation Products and Services. (1993)-. Directory. English. $14.95. Evergreen Professional and Technical Center, 6851 Highway 73, Evergreen CO 80439. **Tel** (303)674-5086, FAX (303)674-8289.

LC TL **ISSN** 1065-9501
DD 629 US
•**SAGA INTERNATIONAL AVIATOR.** **Added/Corp** Sport and General Aviation, Inc. **VFOAT** Directory of International Aviation Products and Services. **VAT** Sport and General Aviation International Aviator. (1993)-. Periodical. English. Four times a year. $40.00. Evergreen Professional and Technical Center, 6851 Highway 73, Evergreen CO 80439. **Tel** (303)674-5086, FAX (303)674-8289.

Aeronautics, Astronautics

LC TL760.A1 B734   ISSN 0036-2735
DD 629.1333   UK
SAILPLANE & GLIDING. [Sailplane glid.]. **VAT** Sailplane and Gliding. (1955)-. Periodical. English. Six times a year. $29.78. British Gliding Association, Kimberly House, Vaughn Way, Leicester LE1 4SE United Kingdom. **Tel** 011 44 533 531051. Index Available, published separately, free-automatically sent. available on microfilm from University Microfilms International (UMI). **Continues** Gliding; **Absorbed** Sailplane and Glider.
Ind/Abst SPORT Discus; SportSearch.

LC PN   ISSN 1060-3581
DD 071   US
    CEASED
SAT-VIEW. VFOAT Sat View; Satview. (1992)-(199?). Periodical. English. Terr Publishing Company, PO Box 460, Salamanca NY 14779-0460. **ED** Tim Jackson Sr. **Circ:** 23,000.
Desc: Information on satellite programs.

LC TL
DD 629   UK
SATELLITE NEWS. [Satell. news]. (1963)-. English. Twelve times a year. $92.00. Geoffrey Falworth, 15 Whitefield Road, Penwortham, Preston PR1 0XJ United Kingdom. **ED** Geoffrey Falworth. **Ad Acc.**
Desc: Complete record of space activity, satellite launches and spacecraft data. Contains orbital data for all new space objects, technical reviews of new spacecraft, future military space plans and developments in Europe and elsewhere.

LC TL796.A1 S33   ISSN 0267-6389
DD 629.44   UK
SATELLITE TECHNOLOGY. Periodical. English. Twelve times a year. $80.00. Satellite Technology, 12-13 Little Newport Street, London WC2H 7PP United Kingdom.

LC GV
DD 797   UK
SCALE AIRCRAFT MODELLING. See Sports and Games.

LC TL770.A1 S27   ISSN 0036-5424
DD 629.133/134/05   US
SCALE MODELER. (19??)-. Periodical. English. Twelve times a year. $35.50. Challenge Publications Inc., 7950 Deering Avenue, Canoga Park CA 91304. **Tel** (818)887-0550. **Absorbed** Military Modeler, 0195-1467.

LC TL501
DD 629.13   SZ
●**SCHEDULED AND CHARTER FREIGHT TRAFFIC FORECAST. Added/Corp** International Air Transport Association. Management Information Division. **VFOAT** International Traffic Forecast. Scheduled and Charter Freight; International Traffic Forecast; Traffic Forecast. (199?)-. English. International Air Transport Association / Montreal, 2000 Peel Street, Room 3050, Montreal Quebec H3A 2R4 Canada. **Tel** (514)844-6311 ext. 232, FAX (514)844-5286, telex 05-267627. **Continues** International Traffic Forecast. Scheduled and Charter Freight.
Ind/Abst Predicasts Forecasts.

LC TL500
DD 629.13   SZ
    TITLE CHANGE
SCHEDULED AND CHARTER FREIGHT TRAFFIC FORECAST. Added/Corp International Air Transport Association. Management Information Division. **VFOAT** International Traffic Forecast. Scheduled and Charter Freight; International Traffic Forecast; Traffic Forecast. (1995)-(1996). English. International Air Transport Association / Montreal, 2000 Peel Street, Room 3050, Montreal Quebec H3A 2R4 Canada. **Tel** (514)844-6311 ext. 232, FAX (514)844-5286, telex 05-267627. **Continues** Freight Traffic Forecast. **Continued by** International Traffic Forecast. Scheduled and Charter Freight.
Ind/Abst Predicasts Forecasts (?-?).

LC TL500
DD 629.13   US
SCHEDULED CARGO TRAFFIC & REVENUE. Added/Corp United States. Civil Aeronautics Baord. Bureau of Accounts and Statistics. (1977)-. Periodical. English. Four times a year. Civil Aeronautics Board, 1825 Connecticut Avenue, Washington DC 20428. **Tel** (202)673-5174. **Continues** Quarterly Cargo Review.

LC TL500
DD 629.13   SZ
SCHEDULED PASSENGER TRAFFIC FORECAST. Added/Corp International Air Transport Association. Industry Automation and Finance Services Dept. International Air Transport Association. Management Information Division. **VFOAT** Passenger Traffic Forecast ... Region Air and Country-Region Forecasts. (1991)-. English. One time a year. International Air Transport Association / Montreal, 2000 Peel Street, Room 3050, Montreal Quebec H3A 2R4 Canada. **Tel** (514)844-6311 ext. 232, FAX (514)844-5286, telex 05-267627. **Continues** Total Market Scheduled Passenger Traffic Forecasts.
Ind/Abst F&S Index Plus Text, Int. [Select. Cov.]; Predicasts Forecasts.

    NE
SCHIPHOLLAND. Dutch. Irregular. Free. Facility Management Schiphol, Abon Schiphol, Postbus 7501, 1118 ZG Schiph Cnt Netherlands. **Tel** 011 31 20 6012409, FAX 011 31 20 6041475.

LC TL500   ISSN 1381-8481
DD 629.13   NE
UDC 656.7
SCHIPHOLLAND SCHIPHOL. (SCHIPHOLLAND.). [Schipholland Schiphol]. (1977)-. Periodical. Dutch. Irregular. Free. Facility Management Schiphol, Abon Schiphol, Postbus 7501, 1118 ZG Schiph Cnt Netherlands. **Tel** 011 31 20 6012409, FAX 011 31 20 6041475.

LC TA   ISSN 0278-4017
DD 620   US
    CODEN AASTBE
SCIENCE AND TECHNOLOGY SERIES. (SCIENCE AND TECHNOLOGY SERIES : AN AMERICAN ASTRONAUTICAL SOCIETY PUBLICATION.). [Sci. technol. ser.]. **Added/Corp** American Astronautical Society. (1977)-. Monographic series. English (French and German). Irregular (four or five issues per year). Price varies per volume. Univelt Inc., PO Box 28130, San Diego CA 92128. **Tel** (619)746-4005. **ED** H. Jacobs and Carol Stoker. Index available. cum. index. **Circ:** 2,000. available on microfiche. Documents available from Article Express International, BIOSIS Document Express, Ask*IEEE. **Continues** AAS Science and Technology Series, 0080-7451.
Desc: Series of monographs and proceedings of technical conferences dealing with space technology and related fields.
Ind/Abst Bioeng. Abstr.; Biol. Abstr.; Ei Page One; Eng. Index Annu.; GeoRef; INSPEC.

LC TL500 .S35   ISSN 0036-8741
DD 629.1/05   US
    CODEN STAEA5
    CEASED
SCIENTIFIC AND TECHNICAL AEROSPACE REPORTS. Added/Corp United States. National Aeronautics and Space Administration. Office of Scientific and Technical Information. United States. National Aeronautics and Space Administration. Scientific and Technical Information Division. United States. National Aeronautics and Space Administration. Scientific and Technical Information Office. United States. National Aeronautics and Space Administration. Scientific and Technical Information Branch. United States. National Aeronautics and Space Administration. Scientific and Technical Information Program. NASA Scientific and Technical Information Facility. **VFOAT** STAR, An Abstract Journal; STAR; S.T.A.R. Vol. 1, No. 1 (Jan. 8, 1963)-(Dec. 1995). Periodical. English. Twelve times a year. $108.00. NASA Center for Aerospace Information, 800 Elkridge Landing Road, Linthicum Heights MD 21090. **Tel** (301)621-0153, FAX (301)621-0134. available on microfilm and microfiche from University Microfilms International (UMI). Documents available from CASDDS. **Continues** Technical Publications Announcements / United States. National Aeronautics and Space Administration; **Absorbed** Scientific and Technical Aerospace Reports. Index.
Desc: Announces abstracts and indexes reports issued by the National Aeronautics and Space Administration, as well as by other government agencies, universities, industry, and research organizations, in the United States and abroad.
Ind/Abst Chem. Abstr.; Corros. Abstr.; Ergon. Abstr.; Fluid Abstr.; Civil Eng.; Fluid Abstr. Proc. Eng.; FLUIDEX (1973-); GeoRef; Int. Aerosp. Abstr.; Mass Spect. Bull.

LC Z5064.P62 S34 TL943   ISSN 0160-581X
DD 016.6297/044   US
SCIENTIFIC PUBLICATIONS AND PRESENTATIONS RELATING TO PLANETARY QUARANTINE. See Aeronautics, Astronautics-Abstracting, Bibliographies and Statistics.

LC TL501   ISSN 1023-7151
DD 629.13   UK
UDC 384
SDL NEWSLETTER LUTTERWORTH. [SDL newsl. Lutterworth]. (1981)-. Periodical. English. One time a year. Free on request. TSE Ltd., 13 Weston House, 18-22 Church Street, Leicestershire, LE17 4AW United Kingdom. **Tel** 011 44 1455 559655, FAX 011 44 1455 550396. **ED** Rick Reed.

LC TL501
DD 629.13   CN
SEARCH AND RESCUE; INTERNATIONAL STANDARDS AND RECOMMENDED PRACTICES. ANNEX 12 TO THE CONVENTION ON INTERNATIONAL CIVIL AVIATION. Main/Corp International Civil Aviation Organization. (19??)-. English. $4.00. International Civil Aviation Organization / ICAO, 1000 Sherbrooke Street West, Suite 400, Montreal Quebec H3A 2R2 Canada. **Tel** (514)285-8026, (514)285-8022, telex 05-24514.

LC TL500   ISSN 0362-8647
DD 629.13   US
SELECCIONES DE AIR UNIVERSITY REVIEW. Added/Corp Air University (U.S.). Vol. 1 (1973)-. Periodical. Spanish. Four times a year. Air University / Alabama, Building 1211, Montgomery AL 36112.

LC TL500
DD 629.13   US
SEMIANNUAL REPORT TO CONGRESS ON THE EFFECTIVENESS OF THE CIVIL AVIATION SECURITY PROGRAM. Main/Corp United States. Federal Aviation Administration. (1981)-. Government Publication. English. Two times a year. US Department of Transportation / Federal Aviation Administration, 800 Independence Avenue Southwest, Washington DC 20591. **Tel** (202)367-3484, FAX (202)367-3505. available on microfiche (Vols. for(July/Dec. 1981- July/Dec. 1982) distributed to depository libraries). **Continues** Semiannual Report to Congress on the Effectiveness of the Civil Aviation Security Program.

LC TL504 .S29
DD 629.13   CH
SHI CHI HANG KUNG. VFOAT Century Aviation. (1978)-. Chinese (Chinese). $15.00. Tien Kung Shu Chu, 77 Wu Chang Chieh Lst Sect, Taipei Taiwan.

LC TL725.3.M2 C32A   ISSN 0402-1681
DD 387.7/36   US
SHORT COURSE IN AIRPORT MANAGEMENT. Main/Corp California. University. Institute of Transportation and Traffic Engineering. English. One time a year. University of California / Berkeley, Berkeley CA 94720.

LC HE884.6.S52 S5
DD 387.5/44/0255952   SI
SINGAPORE SHIPPING & AIR TRANSPORTATION INDUSTRIES DIRECTORY. See Transportation-Ships and Shipping.

LC TL724.5.N57 N6   ISSN 0037-6639
DD 338   US
SKYLINE (PITTSBURGH, PA.). (SKYLINE.). [Skyline]. Vol. 1 (1951)-. Periodical. English. Four times a year. North American Aviation Inc, 600 Grant Street, Pittsburgh PA 15219.
Ind/Abst Int. Aerosp. Abstr.

LC TL501 .S6344
DD 387.7/05   II
SKYWAYS. Vol. 30 (Jan. 1976)-. English. Twelve times a year (monthly). Aeronautical Publications of India Pvt Ltd, Santacruz Airport, Bombay 400029 India. **Tel** 612 4448/6128221, telex 11-71086 AWIB IN. **(Subscription address:** Prints India, 11 Darya Ganj, New Delhi 110002 India. **Tel** 011 91 11 3268645, FAX 011 91 11 3275542, telex 31-61087 PRIN-IN.) **ED** D.M. Heble. **Bk Rev. Ad Acc. Circ:** 10,000 (ctrl). **Continues** Asia and Indian Skyways.
Desc: Focuses on policy and developments in civil and military aerospace, with particular reference to India, Asia, Africa, Australia and the Pacific.

LC TL   ISSN 1051-6956
DD 629   US
SKYWAYS (POUGHKEEPSIE, N.Y.). (SKYWAYS : JOURNAL OF THE AIRPLANE 1920-1940.). **Added/Corp** World War I Aeroplanes (Association). No. 1 (Jan. 1987)-. Periodical. English. Four times a year. $25.00. World War I Aeroplanes Inc, 15 Crescent Road, Poughkeepsie NY 12601. **Tel** (914)473-3679. **ED** Ken Rust (editor's address: PO Box 3366 Glendale CA 91221; editor's phone: (818)243-6820). **Bk Rev**, (Qty: Varies). **Ad Acc. Circ:** 1,500.

LC TL760.A1 S6   ISSN 0037-7503
DD 629.1333305   US
SOARING. [Soaring]. **Added/Corp** Soaring Society of America. **VFOAT** Soaring and Motorgliding; Soaring & Motorgliding. Vol. 1 (Jan. 1937)-. Periodical. English. Twelve times a year. $30.00. Soaring Society of America Inc, PO Box E, Hobbs NM 88241. **Tel** (505)392-1177, FAX (505)392-8154. cum. index. **Bk Rev. Ad Acc. Circ:** 18,000 (ctrl). **Supersedes** Gliding and Soaring Bulletin.
Desc: All aspects of gliding including sailplanes, pilot techniques, weather, safety, and personal experiences.
Ind/Abst Gen. Period. Index (Jan. 1985-Dec. 1985); SPORT Discus; Mag. Index (1977-Dec. 1985).

LC HE9761   ISSN 1073-8304
DD 387.7   US
SOUTHERN AVIATOR, THE. [South. aviat.]. (19??)-. Periodical. English. Twelve times a year. $18.00. Solo Publications, PO Box 1089, Clayton NC 27520. **Tel** (919)550-1600.

LC TL504 **ISSN** 0275-7281
DD 629.13 US
SOVIET SCIENTIFIC REVIEWS SUPPLEMENT SERIES. ASTROPHYSICS AND SPACE PHYSICS REVIEWS. **VFOAT** Astrophysics and Space Physics Reviews. (1990)-. Monographic series. English. Irregular. Price varies per volume. Harwood Academic Publishers / New York, PO Box 786, Cooper Station, New York NY 10276. **Tel** (212)206-8900, (201)643-7500. **ED** R A Syunyaev. Index available. available in microform. Documents available from BLDSC, The UnCover Company.

LC TL787 .S626 **ISSN** 0267-954X
DD 629.4/05 UK
SPACE. [Space]. Vol. 1, No. 1 (June 1985)-. Trade Publication. English. Six times a year (Jan., March, May, July, Sept., Nov.). $84.00. Parker Publications Ltd., 42 Keephatch Road, Wokingham Berks RG11 1QD United Kingdom. **Tel** 011 44 1734 774000, FAX 011 44 1734 774001. **ED** Mark Williamson (editor's phone number: 011 44 1768 361040). **Ad Acc**, **Adv Mgr:** J. Alexander. **Circ:** 12,000 (ctrl).
Desc: International coverage of industry, commerce, technology, business, and military aspects of space. Focus on spacecraft and missions.
Ind/Abst Trade Ind. Index.

LC TL500 **ISSN** 1064-2064
DD 629.13 US
SPACE 2000. (SPACE 2000 [COMPUTER FILE].). [Space 2000]. **Added/Corp** Space Analysis and Research, Inc. **VFOAT** Space Two Thousand. (1992)-. Periodical. English. Four times a year. $200.00. Space Analysis Research, Inc., 6957 Blackhawk Place, Colorado Springs CO 80919. **Tel** (719)260-0500, (719)599-3886. **(Subscription address:** Space Analysis and Research Inc., PO Box 49446, Colorado Springs CO 80949. **)** ***Continues*** *Space - 90.*
Desc: An historical work of space-related activity. Searchable data includes names of launch sites, launch times, initial orbit data, and geostationary position for missions completed before 1957, as well as information on future missions.

LC TL787
DD 629.4 US
TITLE CHANGE
SPACE ABSTRACTS ON DISKETTE. **See** Aeronautics, Astronautics-Abstracting, Bibliographies and Statistics.

LC TK7800 .S65 **ISSN** 0091-0554
DD 621.381/05 US
SPACE AGE NEWS. [Space age news]. (19??)-. Periodical. English. Six times a year. $15.00. Brentwood Publishing, 1640 5th Street, Santa Monica CA 90401. **Tel** (310)826-8388, telex 71-371-7714.

LC TL787 .S627 **ISSN** 0738-0968
DD 629.4/05 US
SPACE AGE TIMES. [Space age times]. **Added/Corp** United States Space Education Association. News Operations Division. United States Space Education Association. International Public Relations Committee. (19??)-. Periodical. English. Six times a year. Comes with United States Space Education Association membership. United States Space Education Association Operations Division, International Headquarters, PO Box 249, Rheems PA 17570. **Tel** (717)367-3265. **ED** Stephen M. Cobaugh. **Bk Rev**. **Ad Acc**. **Circ:** 1,000 (ctrl). ***Continues*** *USSEA Takes Up Space.*
Desc: Devoted to worldwide space news. Designed to provide a variety of articles on space exploration.

LC TL **ISSN** 1071-2569
DD 629 US
SPACE AND SECURITY NEWS. [Space secur. news]. **Added/Corp** Institute for Space and Security Studies. **VFOAT** S&SN. **VAT** Space & Security News. (19??)-. Periodical. English. Four times a year. $25.00. Institute for Space and Security Studies, 5115 S AIA, Melbourne FL 32951. **Tel** (407)952-0600. **ED** Robert Bowman. Index available (every five years). **Bk Rev**. **Ad Acc**. **Circ:** 8,500 (ctrl).

LC HB **ISSN** 1068-0233
DD 332 US
CEASED
SPACE AVAILABLE. (SPACE AVAILABLE : THE SPACE BUSINESS NEWSLETTER.). [Space available]. (1993)-(Dec. 1994). Newsletter. English. Space Available, PO Box 1346, Anacortes WA 98221. **Tel** (206)293-1339, (800)455-7722. ***Continues*** *Space Times, 1062-8762.*

LC TL **ISSN** 0738-9884
DD 629 US
CCC
SPACE BUSINESS NEWS. [Space bus. news]. **VFOAT** Space. (July 18, 1983)-. Periodical. English. Twenty-five times a year. $595.00. Phillips Business Information Inc., 1201 Seven Locks Road, PO Box 61130, Potomac MD 20854. **Tel** (301)424-3338, (301)340-1520, (800)777-5005, FAX (301)424-4297, telex 358149. available on an online database (files 16,636,648/Full-Text) from DIALOG. ***Continues*** *Space Commerce Week;* ***Absorbed*** *Russian Aerospace & Technology; Space Exploration Technology* ***and*** *Space Station News, 0895-8947.*
Desc: Provides the latest developments on business and political trends in the commercial space industry, covering space stations, launch vehicles, financing, Congress and the international scene.
Ind/Abst F&S Index Plus Text, Int. [Select. Cov.]; PTS Newsl. Database [Full Txt.].

LC TL **ISSN** 0741-1731
DD 629 US
SPACE CALENDAR. (SPACE CALENDAR.). [Space cal.]. Vol. 1, No. 1 (May 1, 1982)-. Periodical. English. One time a week. $139.00. Space Age Publishing Company, 10020 North De Anza Boulevard, Cupertino CA 95014. **Tel** (408)996-9210, FAX (408)996-2125. **(Subscription address:** Space Age Publishing Co., 75 5751 Kuakini Highway, Suite 209, Kailua Kona HI 96740. **Tel** (808)326-2014, FAX (808)36-1825.**)** **ED** Steve Durst, Brian McMahon, Bill Fennie. Index available. **Ad Acc**. **Circ:** 625. ***Absorbed*** *Space Newsletter.*
Desc: Departments include space entrepreneurs, international activities, American space movement, space stations, space transportation systems and American space education.

LC HD9711.75.A1 S67 **ISSN** 1043-934X
DD 338.0919/05 SZ
CCC
CODEN SCOMEI
SPACE COMMERCE. [Space commer.]. Vol. 1, No. 1 (1990)-. Periodical. English. Four times a year. Price varies. Gordon & Breach Science Publishers, PO Box 90, Reading, Berkshire RG1 8JL United Kingdom. **Tel** 011 44 1734 560080, FAX 011 44 1734 568211. **(Subscription address:** Gordon & Breach Science Publishers / US, 820 Town Center Drive, Langhorne PA 19047. **Tel** (215)750-2642.**)**

LC TL787 .J68
DD 629.4 US
•SPACE ENERGY AND TRANSPORTATION. (1995)-. English. Four times a year. $200.00. High Frontier Space Transportation, 2800 Shirlington Road, Suite 405A, Arlington VA 22206. **Tel** (703)671-4116.

LC TL787 .S645 **ISSN** 1052-3383
DD 338.4/76294 US
CCC
TITLE CHANGE
SPACE EXPLORATION TECHNOLOGY. [Space explor. technol.]. Vol. 1, No. 1 (1990)-(Sept. 1993). Periodical. English. Phillips Business Information Inc., 1201 Seven Locks Road, PO Box 61130, Potomac MD 20854. **Tel** (301)424-3338, (301)340-1520, (800)777-5005, FAX (301)424-4297, telex 358149. available on an online database (file 636/Full-Text) from DIALOG. ***Merged into*** *Space Business News.*
Ind/Abst PTS Newsl. Database [Full Txt.].

LC TL **ISSN** 1048-2652
DD 629 US
TITLE CHANGE
SPACE FAX DAILY. [Space fax dly.]. (1990)-(199?). Periodical. English. Space Age Publishing Company, 10020 North De Anza Boulevard, Cupertino CA 95014. **Tel** (408)996-9210, FAX (408)996-2125. ***Continues*** *Space Daily, 1048-3616.* ***Split into*** *Space Fax Daily (Global Ed.), 1074-8881* ***and*** *Space Fax Daily (Asia Ed.).*

LC TL787
DD 629.4 US
•SPACE FAX DAILY (ASIA ED.). (SPACE FAX DAILY.). (1994)-. Periodical. English. Seven times a week. $295.00 (institutions), $195.00 (individuals). Space Age Publishing Company, 10020 North De Anza Boulevard, Cupertino CA 95014. **Tel** (408)996-9210, FAX (408)996-2125. ***Continues in part*** *Space Fax Daily, 1048-2652.*

LC TL **ISSN** 1074-8881
DD 629 US
•SPACE FAX DAILY (GLOBAL ED.). (SPACE FAX DAILY.). (1994)-. Periodical. English. Seven times a week. $295.00. Space Age Publishing Company, 10020 North De Anza Boulevard, Cupertino CA 95014. **Tel** (408)996-9210, FAX (408)996-2125. ***Continues in part*** *Space Fax Daily, 1048-2652.*

LC TL787 .S665 **ISSN** 0191-4480
DD 300/.919 US
SPACE HUMANIZATION SERIES, THE. 1979-. Periodical. English. Institute for the Social Science Study of Space, 2135 Wisconsin Avenue NW, Suite 401, Washington DC 20007.

LC TL789.8.J3 J35a
DD 629.4/07/2052 JA
SPACE IN JAPAN. **Main/Corp** Japan. Kagaku Gijutsucho. (19??)-. Periodical. English. Every 2 years. ¥1500. Science and Technology Agency / Japan, 2-1 Kasumigaseki, 2-chome, Chiyoda-ku Tokyo 100 Japan. **Tel** 03 3581 5271.
Ind/Abst F&S Index Plus Text, Int. [Select. Cov.]; Predicasts Forecasts.

LC TL501
DD 629.13 US
SPACE LETTER. (19??)-. English. Twenty-four times a year. $190.00 US; $200.00 other. Callahan Publications, PO Box 1173, McLean VA 22101. **Tel** (703)356-1925, FAX (703)356-9614. **ED** Vincent F. Callahan. **Bk Rev**, (Qty: 6).
Desc: Contracting opportunities, marketing data, and research and development with NASA; also Army, Navy, Air Force, NOAA, and commercial space ventures.

LC TL787 .S6724 **ISSN** 1046-6940
DD 629.4 US
CCC
Pr Rev.
SPACE NEWS (SPRINGFIELD, VA.). (SPACE NEWS.). [Space news]. Vol. 1, No. 1 (Jan. 15-21, 1990)-. Periodical. English. Forty-eight times a year. $99.00. Army Times Publishing Company, 6883 Commercial Drive, Springfield VA 22159. **Tel** (800)368-5718, (703)750-8099. **ED** Theresa Foley. Index available. cum. index. **Bk Rev**. **Ad Acc**. **Circ:** 20,000 (ctrl). available on microfilm.
Desc: Covers the international politics and business of the space industry. Includes administration officials and foreign leaders, the National Space Council, members of Congress and other decision makers in space related industries. Covers competition, corporate strategies, new markets and the latest developments in space technologies and applications.
Ind/Abst F&S Index Plus Text, Int. [Select. Cov.]; PROMT.

LC TL1102.N8 S95a **ISSN** 1041-2824
DD 629.47/53/05 US
CODEN SNPSEG
SPACE NUCLEAR POWER SYSTEMS. (SPACE NUCLEAR POWER SYSTEMS : PROCEEDINGS OF THE ... SYMPOSIUM ON SPACE NUCLEAR POWER SYSTEMS.). [Space nucl. power syst.]. 1st (1984)-. Academic Scholarly Publication. English. Orbit Book Co., 2005 Township Road, Malabar FL 32950. Documents available from CASDDS.
Ind/Abst Chem. Abstr. (1986-).

LC TL787 .S673 **ISSN** 0265-9646
DD 338.4/76294 UK
CCC
CODEN SPCPEO
Pr Rev.
SPACE POLICY. [Space policy]. Vol. 1, No. 1 (Feb. 1985)-. Periodical. English. Four times a year. $668.00. Butterworth Heinemann Publishers, Linacre House Jordan Hill, Oxford OX2 8DP United Kingdom. **Tel** 011 44 1865 310366, FAX 011 44 1865 310898. **(Subscription address:** Elsevier Science Ltd. / Oxford Fulfillment Centre, PO Box 800, Kidlington OX5 1DX United Kingdom. **Tel** 011 44 865 843355.**)** Index available. **Ad Acc**. available on microfilm and microfiche from University Microfilms International (UMI); available on an online database from Elsevier Electronic Subscriptions (EES). Documents available from The Genuine Article.
Desc: Provides a forum for the consideration of space activities and developments in their industrial, economic, political, legal and social contexts. The journal is explicitly interdisciplinary and the readership is international. Publishes articles on space use, activities and developments, providing information, analysis and a means for the exchange of ideas and opinion.
Ind/Abst Commun. Abstr. (?-?); Curr. Contents Soc. Behav. Sci.; Curr. Lit. Sci. Sci.; Curr. Mil. Pol. Lit.; Expand. Acad. Index (1992-); Int. Aerosp. Abstr.; PAIS Int. Print (?-?); Res. Alert [Full Cov.]; Soc. Sci. Cit. Index [Full Cov.].

LC TL **ISSN** 0733-8678
DD 629 US
SPACE PRESS. [Space press]. Vol. 1, No. 1 (Nov. 1981)-. Periodical. English. Twelve times a year. Vernuccio Publications, 645 West End Avenue, New York NY 10025. **Tel** (201)368-4553.

LC HE9761 **ISSN** 0743-8982
DD 387.7 US
SPACE R & D ALERT. [Space RD alert]. **VFOAT** Space R&D Alert; Space R and D Alert. (1984)-. Periodical. English. Twenty-six times a year. $195.00. Aerospace Communications, 5902 Mount Eagle Drive/Suite 417, Alexandria VA 22303-3516. **Tel** (212)927-8919. **ED** Jeffrey K Mawber. **Ad Acc**. **Circ:** 500.
Desc: Concise summations of ongoing commercial space research. Impacting on the pharmaceutical, computer and semiconductor industries. Coverage of venture capital and legislation also included.

LC TL796
DD 629.46 UK
SPACE REVIEW. (19??)-. English. Twelve times a year. £477.00. Airclaims Ltd., Cardinal Point, Newall Road / Heathrow Airport, London TW6 2AS United Kingdom. **Tel** 011 44 181 8971066, FAX 011 44 181 8970300, telex 934679. ***Continues*** *Space Statistics Review.*
Desc: Data and statistics on the success and failures in the launching and positioning of satellites with particular emphasis on communication satellites.

Aeronautics, Astronautics

LC TL796.6.E2 S67
DD 384.5/1
US
SPACE SATELLITE HANDBOOK. (1986)-.
English. One time a year. $39.95. Gulf Publishing Company / Texas, PO Box 2608, Houston TX 77252. **Tel** (800)231-6275, (713)529-4301, FAX (713)520-4433.

LC TL500 **ISSN** 1061-8686
DD 629 US
SPACE SHUTTLE DATABASE REPORT.
Added/Corp Progressive Management. **VFOAT** Report. (1992)-. Periodical. English. Six times a year. $75.00. Progressive Management, PO Box 98, Sewell NJ 08080.

LC TL500 **ISSN** 1061-5350
DD 629 US
SPACE STATION FREEDOM NEWS.
[Space stn. freedom news]. (1992)-. Periodical. English. Twenty-six times a year. $90.00. Randall M. Schuller, PO Box 98, Sewell NJ 08080-0098. **Tel** (609)478-6396.

LC TL **ISSN** 0895-8947
DD 629 US
CCC
TITLE CHANGE
SPACE STATION NEWS. [Space stn. news].
VFOAT Space Station News and Advanced Space Technology. (1987)-(Feb. 1995). Periodical. English. Phillips Business Information Inc., 1201 Seven Locks Road, PO Box 61130, Potomac MD 20854. **Tel** (301)424-3338, (301)340-1520, (800)777-5005, FAX (301)424-4297, telex 358149. available on an online database (file 636/Full-Text) from DIALOG. **Merged into** Space Business News, 0738-9884.
Ind/Abst PTS Newsl. Database [Full Txt.].

LC TL500
DD 629.13 UK
TITLE CHANGE
SPACE STATISTICS REVIEW. (19??)-(1993).
English. Airclaims Ltd., Cardinal Point, Newall Road / Heathrow Airport, London TW6 2AS United Kingdom. **Tel** 011 44 181 8971066, FAX 011 44 181 8970300, telex 934679. **Continued by** Space Review.

LC TL787
DD 629.4 US
●SPACE TECHNOLOGY INNOVATION.
Added/Corp United States. National Aeronautics and Space Administration. Office of Advanced Concepts and Technology. **VFOAT** Innovation. Vol. 1, No. 1 (Jan./Feb. 1993)-. Periodical. English. Six times a year. Free. National Aeronautics Space Administration, Code 300, E Street Southwest, Washington DC 20456. **Tel** (202)358-4562, FAX (202)358-3878. **ED** Sandra Dressel. **Circ**: 10,000 (ctrl). available on an online database. **Continues** Commercial Space Opportunities.
 Desc: Provides information to the people in industry, academia and the public about the relevance and status of OSAT supported R&D activities and the resources and opportunities available to them from OSAT.

LC TL787 .A29 **ISSN** 0892-9270
DD 629.4 UK
CCC
CODEN SPTEE8
SPACE TECHNOLOGY (OXFORD).
(SPACE TECHNOLOGY.). [Space technol.]. Vol. 7, No. 1/2 (1987)-. Periodical. English. Six times a year. $692.00. Pergamon Press, An Imprint of Elsevier Science Ltd., The Boulevard, Langford Lane, Kidlington, Oxford OX5 1GB United Kingdom. **Tel** 011 44 1865 843000, 011 44 1865 843699, FAX 011 44 1865 843010. (**Subscription address**: Elsevier Science Ltd. / Oxford Fulfillment Centre, PO Box 800, Kidlington OX5 1DX United Kingdom. **Tel** 011 44 865 843355.) **ED** Roldofo Monti. available on microfilm and microfiche from University Microfilms International (UMI); available on an online database from Elsevier Electronic Subscriptions (EES). Documents available from Article Express International, The Genuine Article, Ask*IEEE. **Continues** Earth-Oriented Applications of Space Technology, 0277-4488.
 Ind/Abst Curr. Cit.; Curr. Contents Eng. Comput. Technol.; Ei Page One; Eng. Index Annu. (1987-); Environ. Period. Bibliogr. (1987-?); Geogr. Abstr. Phys. Geogr. (1987-); GeoRef (1987-); INSPEC (1987-); Int. Aerosp. Abstr. (1987-); Int. Civil Eng. Abstr. (1987-); Leadscan; Life Sci. Collect. (1987-); Pollut. Abstr. Indexes (1987-); Res. Alert [Select. Cov.]; Soft. Abstr. Eng. (1987-).

LC TL
DD 629 US
SPACE TIMES. **Added/Corp** American
Astronautical Society. **VFOAT** Newsletter of the American Astronautical Society. Vol. 25, No. 1 (Jan./Feb. 1986)-. Periodical. English. Six times a year (Jan., Mar., May, July, Sept., Nov.). $65.00. American Astronautical Society, 6352 Mill Place, Suite 102, Springfield VA 22152-2354. **Tel** (703)866-0020, FAX (703)866-3526. **Continues** American Astronautical Society. Newsletter - American Astronautical Society.

LC HB **ISSN** 1062-8762
DD 332 US
TITLE CHANGE
SPACE TIMES (SEATTLE, WASH.).
(SPACE TIMES: THE SPACE BUSINESS NEWSLETTER.). [Space times]. Vol. 1, No. 1 (Apr. 1992)-(199?). Newsletter. English. Space Available, PO Box 1346, Anacortes WA 98221. **Tel** (206)293-1339, (800)455-7722. **Continued by** Space Available, 1068-0233.

LC TL780
DD 621.4356 US
SPACE TRANSPORTATION SYSTEM USER HANDBOOK. **Added/Corp** United States.
National Aeronautics and Space Administration. (1977)-. Trade Publication. English. National Aeronautics and Space Administration, 600 Independence Avenue SW, Washington DC 20546. **Tel** (202)453-1000. Full Page (B&W) $3800.00. Full Page (Color) $4500.00.

LC TL4050 **ISSN** 0709-7999
DD 629.4/05 CN
SPACE TRAVEL MAGAZINE. [Space travel mag.]. Vol. 2, No. 2 (Summer 1979)-. Periodical. English. Four times a year. Free to members. North American Interplanetary Society, 150 Montreal Street, Victoria B.C. V8V 1Y8. **Continues** North American Interplanetary Society. Newsmagazine, 0709-7980.

LC TL787 **ISSN** 0561-3078
DD 629/.4058 US
SPACE VOLUME. 1960-. Periodical. English. One
time a year. Government Data Publications / New York, GDP Building, 1661 McDonald Avenue, Brooklyn NY 11230. **Tel** (718)627-0819.

LC TL **ISSN** 1058-2576
DD 629 US
SPACE YEAR. [Space year]. (1991)-. English.
Motorbooks International Publishers & Wholesalers, PO Box 2, 729 Prospect Avenue, Osceola WI 54020. **Tel** (800)826-6600, (715)294-3345.

LC HD28 **ISSN** 8756-517X
DD 338 US
SPACEBUSINESS CONFERENCE DIGEST, THE. See Industry and Production.

LC TL787 .B725 **ISSN** 0038-6340
DD 629.4/05 UK
CODEN SPFLAN
SPACEFLIGHT. [Spaceflight]. **Added/Corp** British
Interplanetary Society. Vol. 1 (Oct. 1956)-. Periodical. English. Twelve times a year. $81.00. British Interplanetary Society Ltd, 27/29 South Lambeth Road, London SW8 1SZ United Kingdom. **Tel** 011 44 171 7353160, FAX 011 44 171 8201504. **ED** G. V. Groves. Index available. **Bk Rev**, (Qty: 100). **Ad Acc, Adv Mgr**: S.A. Parry. **Circ**: 12,000. available on microfilm and microfiche from University Microfilms International (UMI). Documents available from Article Express International, CASDDS.
 Desc: The international magazine of space and aeronautics; includes news, features and correspondence.
 Ind/Abst Appl. Sci. Technol. Index; Bioeng. Abstr.; Chem. Abstr.; Curr. Technol. Index; Ei Page One; Eng. Index Annu.; Int. Aerosp. Abstr.

LC HE9761 **ISSN** 0271-2598
DD 387.7 US
SPEEDNEWS. [Speednews]. **VAT** Speed News.
(1979)-. Trade Publication. English. One time a week. $547.00. SPEEDNEWS, 1801 Avenue of the Stars/Suite 210, Los Angeles CA 90067-5902. **Tel** (310)203-9603, FAX (310)203-9352, telex 292674. **ED** Ann M. Speed. **Bk Rev**, (Qty: 2 per week). **Ad Acc, Adv Mgr**: Scott Daniels. **Circ**: 3,000 (ctrl). available on an online database.
 Desc: An aviation equipment marketing intelligence newsletter providing updates on aircraft and equipment ordered by the world's airlines.

LC U **ISSN** 1060-1368
DD 355 US
SPEEDNEWS DEFENSE BIWEEKLY.
[Speednews def. biwkly.]. **VFOAT** Defense Biweekly. 1st Issue (Sept. 13, 1991)-. Periodical. English. Twenty-six times a year. $200.00. SPEEDNEWS, 1801 Avenue of the Stars/Suite 210, Los Angeles CA 90067-5902. **Tel** (310)203-9603, FAX (310)203-9352, telex 292674. **ED** Ann More.

LC TL711.S8 S66 **ISSN** 0161-5351
DD 797.5/4/05 US
SPORT AEROBATICS. See Sports and Games.

LC GV758 **ISSN** 0038-7835
DD 629 US
SPORT AVIATION. See Sports and Games.

LC GV **ISSN** 8750-8117
DD 797 US
SPORT FLYER. See Sports and Games.

LC GV **ISSN** 1040-5798
DD 797 US
SPORT PILOT HOT KITS & HOMEBUILTS. See Sports and Games.

LC TL844 .M62 **ISSN** 1076-2701
DD 629.47/5/0228 US
SPORT ROCKETRY. See Hobbies.

LC TL721.4 .S66 **ISSN** 0279-1749
DD 629.132/5217/05 US
SPORTSMAN PILOT (HALES CORNERS, WIS.). (SPORTSMAN PILOT.). Vol. 1, No. 1 (Spring
1981)-. Periodical. English. Four times a year. $8.00. Sportsman Pilot, Box 2768, Oshkosh WI 54903. **Tel** (414)231-6657. **ED** J.B. Jack Cox. **Circ**: 3,000.

LC TL686.S7 S73A **ISSN** 0149-1458
DD 629.133/343 US
SRA "OUTFIT" NEWSLETTER. **Main/Corp**
Stearman Restorers Association. **VAT** Stearman Restorers Association Outfit Newsletter. Newsletter. English. Twelve times a year. Stearman Restorer Association, 823 Kingston Lane, Crystal Lake IL 60014.

LC TL **ISSN** 0898-8242
DD 629 US
SSI UPDATE. **Added/Corp** Space Studies Institute.
VAT Space Studies Institute Update. (19??)-. Periodical. English. Six times a year (Jan., Mar., May, July, Sept, Nov.). $25.00 (individuals); $50.00 (institutions). Space Studies Institute, PO Box 82, Princeton NJ 08542. **Tel** (609)921-0377, FAX (609)921-0389. **ED** Bettle Greber. **Bk Rev**, (Qty: 2). **Circ**: 5,000 (ctrl).
 Desc: Each issue presents a brief summary of current topics in space research.

LC TL500
DD 629.13 US
STANDARD INSTRUMENT APPROACH PROCEDURES, TAKEOFF MINIMUMS/DEPARTURES, AND FIX ACTIONS. **Main/Corp** United States. Federal
Aviation Administration. (19??)-. Periodical. English. Twenty-six times a year. Department of Transportation, 400 Seventh Street SW, Washington DC 20590. **Tel** (202)426-4000.

LC KF2422.5 .F43
DD 343/.73/0978 US
STATISTICAL SUMMARY : AIR CARRIER ENFORCEMENT CASES. See
Aeronautics, Astronautics-Abstracting, Bibliographies and Statistics.

LC HE9788.5.I4 S73
DD 382/.0954/005 II
STATISTICS OF THE AIR BORNE FOREIGN TRADE OF INDIA. See Aeronautics,
Astronautics-Abstracting, Bibliographies and Statistics.

LC HE9778 .W46A
DD 387.7/4/0212 FR
STATISTIQUES DE TRAFIC. See Aeronautics,
Astronautics-Abstracting, Bibliographies and Statistics.

LC HE9842.A4 **ISSN** 0078-947X
DD 387.7 FR
STATISTIQUES DE TRAFIC : GRANDS AEROPORTS DE L'OUEST DE L'EUROPE. See Aeronautics,
Astronautics-Abstracting, Bibliographies and Statistics.

LC TL787 .C415
DD 001.9/4 SP
STENDEK; SERVICIO INFORMATIVO.
Main/Corp Centro de Estudios Interplanetarios. Periodical. Spanish. Balmes 86, Entresuelo 2A Apartado 282, Barcelona Spain.

LC TL501
DD 629.13 US
STI BULLETIN. **Added/Corp** United States.
National Aeronautics and Space Administration. Scientific and Technical Information Branch. United States. National Aeronautics and Space Administration. Scientific and Technical Information Division. United States. National Aeronautics and Space Administration. Scientific and Technical Information Program. **VAT** Scientific and Technical Information Bulletin. (19??)-. Bulletin. English. NASA STI Facility, PO Box 8785, Baltimore Washington International, Baltimore MD 21240. **Tel** (202)453-2906. **Continues** STI-RECON Bulletin & Technical Information News.
 Ind/Abst Int. Aerosp. Abstr.

LC TL795.5 .S77 **ISSN** 1066-1263
DD 629.44/1/05 US
STS MISSION PROFILES : COMPLETE SPACE SHUTTLE MISSION COVERAGE.
[STS mission profiles]. Vol. 1, Issue 1 (Jan. 1992)-. Periodical. English. Ten times a year. $35.00. STS Mission Profiles, PO Box 751387, Memphis TN 38175.

Desc: Preflight publication dedicated to NASA Space Mission coverage. Includes crew interviews, experiments, test and medical objectives, and previous missions.

LC TL570 **ISSN** 0364-6416
DD 629.1323 US
CEASED

SUMMARY OF SUPPLEMENTAL TYPE CERTIFICATES.
Main/Corp United States. Federal Aviation Administration. **Added/Corp** United States. Federal Aviation Administration. **VFOAT** Summary of Federal Aviation Administration Supplemental Type Certificates. (19??)-(1993). English. Department of Transportation, 400 Seventh Street SW, Washington DC 20590. **Tel** (202)426-4000.
Desc: Lists all FAA supplemental type certificates, which the holders have indicated will be made available to others.

LC HE9875.A1 S87
DD 387.7 IO

SURVEY ANGKUTAN UDARA.
VFOAT Air Transport Survey. (1980)-. Indonesian. One time a year. Rp2000 Indonesia; $2.00 US. Biro Pusat Statistik / Central Bureau of Statistics, 8 Jalan Dr. Sutomo No. 8, Box 3, Jakarta Pusat 10710 Indonesia. **Tel** 011 62 21 372808, 011 62 21 374908 ext.342. ctrl circ.

LC TL789 **ISSN** 0707-7106
DD 001.9/42/05 CN

SWAMP GAS JOURNAL, THE.
No. 1- Sept. 1978-. Periodical. English. Irregular. Free. C Rutkowski, Box 1918 Winnipeg General Post Office, Winnipeg Manitoba R3C 3R2 Canada. **ED** C Rutkowski. **Bk Rev. Circ:** 150 (ctrl).
Desc: An open forum for discussions relating to unidentified flying objects.

LC TL671.7 .S55a **ISSN** 0742-3705
DD 629.134/53 US

SYMPOSIUM PROCEEDINGS / THE SOCIETY OF EXPERIMENTAL TEST PILOTS.
[Symp. proc. - Soc. Exp. Test Pilots, Symp.]. **Main/Corp** Society of Experimental Test Pilots. Symposium. **VFOAT** Report to the Aerospace Profession; SETP Technical Review. (1967)-. Proceedings. English. Five times a year (Jan., Apr., July, Oct., Nov.). $45.00. Society of Experimental Test Pilots, PO Box 986, Lancaster CA 93534. **Tel** (805)942-9574. **Circ:** 2,000. ***Continues in part** Society of Experimental Test Pilots. Technical Review - The Society of Experimental Test Pilots, 0096-8781.*

LC HE9778 .T33
DD 387.7/021 FR

TABLEAU DE BORD DU TRANSPORT AERIEN DANS LE MONDE / WORLD AIR TRANSPORT DATA GUIDE.
Added/Corp Institut du Transport Aerien. **VFOAT** World Air Transport Data Guide. (19??)-. English (French). One time a year. $218.73. Institut Du Transport Aerien, 103 rue de la Boetie, 75008 Paris France. **Tel** 011 33 1 43593868.

LC TL
DD 629 NE
Pr Rev.

TACT : THE AIR CARGO TARIFF.
(19??)-. Periodical. English (Spanish, Italian and French). Six times a year. Fl450.00. Tact The Air Cargo Tariff, PO Box 903, 2130 EA Hoofddorp Netherlands. **Tel** 011 31 0 250373520, FAX 011 31 0 250373515. Index available. **Bk Rev. Ad Acc.** ctrl circ. available on diskette; available on magnetic tape.
Desc: Provides information on the subject of air cargo rates and the rules to apply these rates. The rates published are either IATA rates or carriers own rates. Domestic and international are published.

LC HE9764.76.K6 T3317
DD 387.7 KO

TAEHAN HANGGONG HYOPHOE HOEBO = K.A.A. BULLETIN.
Added/Corp Taehan Hanggong Hyophoe. **VFOAT** K.A.A. Bulletin; KAA Bulletin. (19??)-. Bulletin. Korean. Korea Aeronautic Association, 132-5 1-ka Bongnae-dong Choong-ku, Seoul Korea.

LC QB539.T4 T34
DD 500.5 JA

TAIYO CHIKYU KEIHO EISEI CHOSA HOKOKU = SOLAR-TERRESTRIAL ALERT SATELLITES : SOTAS.
Added/Corp Yuseisho Denpa Kenkyujo (Japan). Uchu Kukan Kenkyushitsu. **VFOAT** Solar-Terrestrial Alert Satellites : SOTAS; SOTAS; S.O.T.A.S.; Solar-Terrestrial Alert Satellites. No. 1 (1980)-. Japanese. Free. Yuseisho Tsushin Sogo Kenkyujo Kenkyushitsu, 2-1 Nukui, Kita-Machi 4-chome, Koganei-shi Tokyo-to 184 Japan. **Tel** 0423-27-7578, telex 2832611 DEMPA J. **ED** T. Ondoh. **Bk Rev. Ad Acc. Circ:** 150 (ctrl).
Desc: Used for predicting solar-terrestrial electromagnetic disturbances. The system includes a geostationary satellite and an elliptical orbit satellite for observing the plasma pause, magnetic field, plasma waves, particles and solar radiations.

LC TL501
DD 629.13 US

TAKE OFF MAGAZINE.
(19??)-. English. Four times a year. Intermedia Publishing, PO Box 73, Blaine WA 98230. **Tel** (206)380-1000.

LC Z **ISSN** 0565-6141
DD 016 500 US

TECHNICAL ABSTRACTS - U. S. GODDARD SPACE FLIGHT CENTER.
Main/Corp United States. Goddard Space Flight Center, Greenbelt, Maryland. Vol. 1 (Oct./Dec. 1962)-. Periodical. English. Four times a year. Goddard Space Flight Center NASA, Code 513, Greenbelt MD 20771. **Tel** (301)286-8956.

LC TL760.A1 **ISSN** 0744-8996
DD 629.132 US

TECHNICAL SOARING.
[Tech. Soar.]. **Added/Corp** Soaring Society of America. Organisation Scientifique et Technique Internationale du Vol a Voile. (19??)-. Periodical. English. Four times a year. $30.00. Soaring Society of America Inc, PO Box E, Hobbs NM 88241. **Tel** (505)392-1177, FAX (505)392-8154. **ED** Rob Sjostedt. **Bk Rev. Circ:** 500 (ctrl).
Desc: Technical and scientific aspects of soaring flight including design, aerodynamics, structures, materials, meteorology instruments and pilot technique.
Ind/Abst SPORT Discus; SportSearch (May 1987-).

LC TL504 .T38 **ISSN** 0040-1145
DD 629.13 PL
CODEN TLASB3

TECHNIKA LOTNICZA I ASTRONAUTYCZNA.
[Tech. lot. astronaut.]. (1966)-. Academic Scholarly Publication. Polish (summaries and/or abstracts in English and Russian). Twelve times a year. $93.00. Oficyna Wydawnicza SIMP Press Ltd., Swietokrzyska 14A, 00-050 Warsaw Poland. **Tel** 011 48 22 272542. **(Subscription address:** Ars Polona-Ruch, PO Box 1001, Krakowskie Przedmiescie 7, 00-068 Warsaw Poland. **Tel** 011 48 22 261201.**)** **ED** W.J. Gawrych. **Bk Rev. Ad Acc. Circ:** 3,500. Documents available from CASDDS, BLDSC.
Desc: History of airplane and air technics.
Ind/Abst Chem. Abstr. (-1983).

LC TL501
DD 629.13 GW

TELE SATELLIT.
(19??)-. German. Twelve times a year. DM96.00 Germany; DM144.00 other. Tele Audiovision Mediengesells, Postfach 801965, D-8000 Munich 80 Germany. **Tel** 011 49 89 41860809. **(Subscription address:** Computer Service, Postfach 801965, D 8000 Munich 5 Germay. **)**

LC TL726.3.T4 D5
DD 629.136/025/764 US
Pr Rev.

TEXAS AIRPORT DIRECTORY.
Directory. English. One time a year. $5.00. Texas Department of Aviation, PO Box 12607, Austin TX 78711. **Tel** (512)476-9262, FAX (512)479-0294. **ED** Yolanda Alvarez, Nona Gold and Jim Cummins. Index available. cum. index. **Ad Acc. Circ:** 3,600. ***Continues** Directory of Texas Airports.*
Desc: This directory is distributed by the Texas Department of Aviation to help promote safer flying by providing detailed information about the public-use airports in Texas.

LC HE9761 **ISSN** 0256-4459
DD 387.7/364 CN

TICKETING HANDBOOK.
[Ticketing handb.]. **Main/Corp** International Air Transport Association. **VFOAT** IATA Ticketing Handbook. **VAT** International Air Transport Association Ticketing Handbook. (1968)-. English (French and Spanish). One time a year. 34.50Can$. International Air Transport Association / Montreal, 2000 Peel Street, Room 3050, Montreal Quebec H3A 2R4 Canada. **Tel** (514)844-6311 ext. 232, FAX (514)844-5286, telex 05-267627.
Desc: Detailed procedures for the issuance and reissuance of airline tickets.

LC TL862.T T63a
DD 629.4 JA

TOKYO DAIGAKU UCHU KOKU KENKYUJO TEIKI HOKOKU.
Main/Corp Tokyo Daigaku. Uchu Koku Kenkyujo. (1970/74)-. Japanese. Irregular. 6-4 Komaba 4-chome Meguro-ku, 153 Tokyo Japan.

LC HE9761 **ISSN** 0822-7748
DD 387.7/364/025713541 CN

TORONTO & AREA AIRPORT BUSINESS DIRECTORY.
[Tor. area airpt. bus. dir.]. **VFOAT** Toronto Airport Directory. **VAT** Airport Business Directory (1984). 1983/84-. Directory. English. One time a year. $5.00 US. Toronto & Area Airport Business Directory, 5621 11th Street NE/Suite 107, Calgary Alberta T2E 6Z7 Canada. **Tel** (403)295-9200, FAX (403)275-3925. **ED** Gary Gaudreau. **Ad Acc. Circ:** 10,000 (ctrl). ***Continues** Toronto Airport Business Directory, 0714-8593.*
Desc: Directory listing all companies connected with aviation in the area of Toronto. Listings show company, personnel, operations, who's where at the airports, directory of services provided by the companies listed.

LC TL
DD 629 BE

TRAFFIC AND OPERATING DATA OF AEA AIRLINES.
Main/Corp Association of European Airlines. (1973)-. English. One time a year (Sept.). 35.00F. Association of European Airlines, Avenue Louise 350 BTE 4, B-1050 Brussels Belgium. **Tel** 32-2-640 31.75, FAX (322)648-4017, telex 22918.

LC TL720.A1 I57 subser.
DD 387.7/4/0212 CN

TRAFFIC BY FLIGHT STAGE = TRAFIC PAR ETAPES.
Main/Corp International Civil Aviation Organization. **Added/Corp** International Civil Aviation Organization. **VFOAT** Trafic par Etapes. (March 1976)-. Periodical. English (French, Russian and Spanish). One time a year. 49.50Can$. International Civil Aviation Organization / ICAO, 1000 Sherbrooke Street West, Suite 400, Montreal Quebec H3A 2R2 Canada. **Tel** (514)285-8026, (514)285-8022, telex 05-24514. available on magnetic tape. ***Continues** Traffic Flow.*
Desc: Digest of statistics on traffic.

LC TL500
DD 629.13 CN

TRAFFIC FLOW.
(TRAFFIC FLOW = TRAFIC PAR ETAPES = MOVIMIENTO DEL TRAFICO.). **Main/Corp** International Civil Aviation Organization. Secretariat. **VFOAT** Trafic par Etapes; Movimiento del Trafico. (1947)-. Multiple languages (English, French, Russian and Spanish). Two times a year. International Civil Aviation Organization / ICAO, 1000 Sherbrooke Street West, Suite 400, Montreal Quebec H3A 2R2 Canada. **Tel** (514)285-8026, (514)285-8022, telex 05-24514.
Desc: Addendum accompany some numbers.

LC HE9788.5.F8 A35A
DD 387.7/44/0944 FR

TRAFIC INTERNATIONAL DU FRET.
Main/Corp Aeroport de Paris. Section Etudes Statistiques. French. Aeroports de Paris, Orly Sud 103, 94396 Orly, Aerogare Cedex France.

LC TL501 .T73 **ISSN** 0549-3811
DD 629.13/005 JA
CCC
CODEN TJASAM

TRANSACTIONS OF THE JAPAN SOCIETY FOR AERONAUTICAL AND SPACE SCIENCES.
[Trans. Jpn. Soc. Aeronaut. Space Sci.]. **Main/Corp** Nihon Koku Gakkai. **Added/Corp** Nihon Koku Uchu Gakkai. Vol. 2 (1958)-. Academic Scholarly Publication. English. Four times a year. $120.00. Nihon Koku Uchu Gakkai, (Japan Society for Aeronautical & Space Sciences), 18-2 Shinbashi 1 Chome, Arakawaku Tokyo 105 Japan. **(Subscription address:** Maruzen Company Ltd., PO Box 5050, Import & Export Department, Tokyo 100 31 Japan. **Tel** 011 81 3 32789224.**)** **ED** Kanichiro Kato. **Circ:** 3,500 (ctrl). Documents available from Article Express International, The Genuine Article, Ask*IEEE, CASDDS. ***Continues** Transactions of the Japan Society of Aeronautical Engineering.*
Desc: Technical documents and theses of aeronautical and space sciences.
Ind/Abst Acoust. Abstr.; Alum. Ind. Abstr.; Bioeng. Abstr.; Chem. Abstr.; Curr. Contents Eng. Comput. Technol.; Ei Page One; Eng. Mater. Abstr.; Eng. Index Annu.; INSPEC (Nov. 1983-); Int. Aerosp. Abstr.; Met. Abstr.; Res. Alert [Select. Cov.].

LC HE9803.A1 C57D **ISSN** 0148-9356
DD 387.7/42/0973 US

TRUNKLINE CARRIER DOMESTIC PASSENGER ENPLANEMENTS.
Main/Corp United States. Civil Aeronautics Board. Bureau of Operating Rights. Standards Division. English. US Civil Aeronautics Board / Bureau of Operating Rights, Standards Division, 1825 Connecticut Avenue NW, Washington DC 20428. **Tel** (202)673-5174.

LC TJ **ISSN** 1073-8703
DD 621 US
CCC
CODEN TSJOEK

•TSAGI JOURNAL, THE.
(THE TSAGI JOURNAL : JOURNAL OF THE CENTRAL AERO-HYDRODYNAMIC INSTITUTE (TSAGI).). [TsAGI j.]. **Added/Corp** TSentralnyi Aerogidrodinamicheskii Institut Imeni Prof. N.E. Zhukovskogo. Vol. 1, No. 1 (Jan./Mar. 1994)-. Academic Scholarly Publication. English. Four times a year. $250.00. Begell House Inc., 79 Madison Avenue, New York NY 10016-7892. **Tel** (212)725-1999, FAX (212)213-8368.
Desc: Devoted to the science and technology of aviation. Publishes articles on fundamental and applied aspects of aero-hydrodynamics of flying vehicles, stability, strength, and aeroacoustics, experimental and computational research and other areas related to the development of aerospace engineering.

Aeronautics, Astronautics

LC TL501
DD 629.13
US
TURBOJET/TURBOFAN AIRCRAFT OPERATING COST AND PERFORMANCE TRENDS. DOMESTIC OPERATIONS OF TRUNK AND LOCAL SERVICE CARRIERS. Added/Corp United States. Civil Aeronautics Board. Financial and Cost Analysis Division. United States. Civil Aeronautics Board. Financial Analysis and Cost Division. **VFOAT** Domestic Operations of Trunk and Local Service Carriers; Domestic Jet Trends. (19??)-. English. Every 2 years. Financial and Cost Analysis Division, Office of Economic Analysis, Civil Aeronautics Board, Washington DC 20428.

LC U
DD 355
TU
TURKISH DEFENCE & AEROSPACE UPDATE. See Military and Defense.

LC TL500
DD 629.13
ISSN 0278-3037
US
TYPE CERTIFICATE DATA SHEETS AND SPECIFICATIONS. VOLUME VI, AIRCRAFT LISTING & AIRCRAFT ENGINE & PROPELLER LISTING. Added/Corp United States. Federal Aviation Administration. **VFOAT** Aircraft Listing & Aircraft Engine & Propeller Listing; Aircraft Listing and Aircraft Engine and Propeller Listing. **VAT** Type Certificate Data Sheets and Specifications. Volume Six, Aircraft Listing and Aircraft Engine and Propeller Listing. (1977)-. Government Publication. English. Irregular. Price varies per volume. Superintendent of Documents, US Government Printing Office, Washington DC 20402. **Tel** (202)275-3328, FAX (202)786-2377.

LC TL789
DD 001.9/42/05
ISSN 0227-1559
CN
U F O UPDATE. [UFO update]. Vol. 1 (Sept. 1977)-. Periodical. English. $9.00. Northeastern UFO Organization, Suite 402 573 North Service Road, Mississauga Ontario L5A 1B6 Canada.

LC TL521 .U617
DD 331.1/1
ISSN 0364-927X
US
U.S. CIVIL AIRMEN STATISTICS. See Aeronautics, Astronautics-Abstracting, Bibliographies and Statistics.

LC TL500
DD 629.13
US
U.S. INTERNATIONAL AIR TRAVEL STATISTICS (CALENDAR YEAR). See Aeronautics, Astronautics-Abstracting, Bibliographies and Statistics.

LC UG1243 .U55
DD 358.4/18/3
ISSN 1064-1459
US
U.S. MILITARY AIRCRAFT DATA BOOK. See Military and Defense.

LC TL500
DD 629.13
US
U.S. TERMINAL PROCEDURES. ALASKA. Added/Corp United States. National Ocean Service. **VFOAT** US Terminal Procedures. Alaska; Alaska Terminal. (Dec. 1990/Feb. 1991)-. Periodical. English. Six times a year. US Department of Commerce / National Oceanic & Atmospheric Administration NOAA, Room 808 Worldweather Building, Washington DC 20233. **Tel** (301) 763-4670, FAX (301)763-8125.

LC TL500
DD 629.13
US
U.S. TERMINAL PROCEDURES. CHANGE NOTICE (CN). Added/Corp United States. National Ocean Service. **VFOAT** US Terminal Procedures. Change Notice (CN). (Jan 1991 to Feb 1991)-. Periodical. English. Six times a year. US Department of Commerce / National Oceanic & Atmospheric Administration NOAA, Room 808 Worldweather Building, Washington DC 20233. **Tel** (301) 763-4670, FAX (301)763-8125. **Continues** Instrument Approach Procedures. Change Notice (CN).
Desc: Focuses on instrument flying.

LC TL500
DD 629.13
US
U.S. TERMINAL PROCEDURES. EAST CENTRAL (EC). Added/Corp United States. National Ocean Service. **VFOAT** US Terminal Procedures. East Central (EC). (Dec. 1990/Feb. 1991)-. Periodical. English. Six times a year. US Department of Commerce / National Oceanic & Atmospheric Administration NOAA, Room 808 Worldweather Building, Washington DC 20233. **Tel** (301) 763-4670, FAX (301)763-8125. **Continues in part** Standard Terminal Arrival (STAR), United States; Standard Instrument Departures (Civil). Eastern United States including Puerto Rico and the Virgin Islands.

LC TL500
DD 629.13
US
U.S. TERMINAL PROCEDURES. NORTH CENTRAL (NC). Added/Corp United States. National Ocean Service. **VFOAT** US Terminal Procedures. North Central (NC). (Dec. 1990/Feb. 1991)-. Periodical. English. Six times a year. US Department of Commerce / National Oceanic & Atmospheric Administration NOAA, Room 808 Worldweather Building, Washington DC 20233. **Tel** (301) 763-4670, FAX (301)763-8125. **Continues** Instrument Approach Procedures. U.S. North Central; **Continues in part** Standard Terminal Arrival (STAR), United States; Standard Instrument Departures (Civil). Western United States.

LC TL500
DD 629.13
US
U.S. TERMINAL PROCEDURES. NORTHEAST (NE). Added/Corp United States. National Ocean Service. **VFOAT** US Terminal Procedures. Northeast (NE). (Dec. 1990/Feb. 1991)-. Periodical. English. Six times a year. US Department of Commerce / National Oceanic & Atmospheric Administration NOAA, Room 808 Worldweather Building, Washington DC 20233. **Tel** (301) 763-4670, FAX (301)763-8125. **Continues** Instrument Approach Procedures. U.S. Northeast; **Continues in part** Standard Terminal Arrival (STAR), United States; Standard Instrument Departures (Civil). Eastern United States including Puerto Rico and the Virgin Islands.

LC TL500
DD 629.13
US
U.S. TERMINAL PROCEDURES. SOUTH CENTRAL (SC). Added/Corp United States. National Ocean Service. **VFOAT** US Terminal Procedures. South Central (SC). (Dec. 1990/Feb. 1991)-. Periodical. English. Six times a year. US Department of Commerce / National Oceanic & Atmospheric Administration NOAA, Room 808 Worldweather Building, Washington DC 20233. **Tel** (301) 763-4670, FAX (301)763-8125. **Continues in part** Instrument Approach Procedures. U.S. South Central; Standard Terminal Arrival (STAR), United States; Standard Instrument Departures (Civil). Western United States.

LC TL500
DD 629.13
US
U.S. TERMINAL PROCEDURES. SOUTHWEST (SW). Added/Corp United States. National Ocean Service. **VFOAT** US Terminal Procedures. Southwest (SW). (Dec. 1990/Feb. 1991)-. Periodical. English. Six times a year. US Department of Commerce / National Oceanic & Atmospheric Administration NOAA, Room 808 Worldweather Building, Washington DC 20233. **Tel** (301) 763-4670, FAX (301)763-8125. **Continues in part** Instrument Approach Procedures. U.S. Southwest; Instrument Approach Procedures. U.S. South Central; Standard Terminal Arrival (STAR), United States; Standard Instrument Departures (civil). Western United States.

LC TL570 .M62a
DD 629.1323
ISSN 0321-3439
RU
CODEN UZTAAG
UCENYE ZAPISKI CAGI. (UCHENYE ZAPISKI TSAGI.). [Uc. zap. CAGI]. **Main/Corp** TSentralnyi Aerogidrodinamicheskii Institut Imeni Prof. N.E. Zhukovskogo. **VAT** Uchenye Zapiskie Tsentralnogo Aero-Gidrodinamicheskogo Instituta. (1970)-. Academic Scholarly Publication. Russian. Four times a year. $545.00 US and Canada; $555.00 Europe; $570.00 other. Nauchno-Memorialnyi Muzei N E Zhukovskogo, B-S Ulitsa Radio, 17 Moscow Russia. (**Subscription address:** East View Publications Inc., 3020 Harbor Lane North, Suite 110, Minneapolis MN 55447. **Tel** (800)477-1005, (612)550-0961, FAX (612)559-2931.) Documents available from CASDDS.
Ind/Abst Chem. Abstr.; Int. Aerosp. Abstr.; Math. Rev.

LC TL794 .U27a
DD 629.13
JA
UCHU KAIHATSU HANDOBUKKU.
Main/Corp Uchu Kaihatsu Suishin Kaigi. **Added/Corp** Japan. Kagaku Gijutsucho. KenkyAu Choseikyoku. (1969)-. Japanese. ¥2000. Uchu Kaihatsu Suishin Kaigi, c/o Keidanren Kaikan, 9-4 Otemachi-1 Chi Yoda-ku, Tokyo Japan.

LC TL504
DD 629.13
JA
CODEN UKJHDL
UCHU KAIHATSU JIGYODAN GIJUTSU HOKOKU. [Uchu Kaihatsu Jigyodan gijutsu hokoku]. **VFOAT** Technical Report of National Space Development Agency of Japan. (1973)-. Academic Scholarly Publication. Japanese. Irregular. Uchu Kaihatsu Jigyodan 4-1 Hamamatsu-cho 2 chome, Minato-ku Tokyo 105 Japan. Documents available from CASDDS.
Ind/Abst Chem. Abstr. (1973-1979).

LC TL789.A1 U15
DD 001.9/42/05
US
UFO ANNUAL (BROOKLYN). (UFO ANNUAL.). **VFOAT** Saga's Special UFO Annual. **VAT** Unidentified Flying Objects Annual. English. One time a year. $1.50. Executive & Editorial Offices, 333 Johnson Avenue, Brooklyn NY 11206.

LC TL789.A1 U19
DD 001.9/4
DK
UFO CONTACT. (Feb. 1973)-. Periodical. English. Six times a year. $2.00. Igap Information Service, Tvaerborre 6, Mlholm 7100 Vejle Denmark.

LC TL789.A1 U195
DD 001.9/42/05
ISSN 0148-6438
US
UFO REPORT (BROOKLYN). (UFO REPORT.). **VFOAT** Unidentified Flying Objects Report. Periodical. English. Irregular. $12.50. Gambi Publications, 333 Johnson Avenue, Brooklyn NY 11206. **Continues** Saga's UFO Report, 0148-3412.

LC TL789
DD 001.942
ISSN 0958-4846
UK
UFO TIMES. [UFO times]. **VFOAT** Unidentified Flying Object Times. (1989)-. Periodical. English. Six times a year. £14.00 UK; £16.00 other. British Unindentified Flying Objects Research Association, 16 Southway, Burgess Hill RH15 9ST United Kingdom. **Tel** 011 44 46 6738. **ED** Mike Wooten. **Bk Rev. Ad Acc. Circ:** 500 (ctrl). Documents available from BLDSC.
Continues BUFORA Bulletin, 0265-1947; Journal of Transient Aerial Phenomena, 0143-8840.
Desc: Anonymous phenomena, UFO events, and space science.

LC TL789
DD 001.942
BL
UFONTAS, AS. Added/Corp Centro de Estudos Ufologicos. (19??)-. Portuguese. Two times a year. Cr$10.00 Brazil; $10.00 North America; $12.00 other. Centro de Estudos Ufologicos, Jean Alencar, Caixa Postal 689 Brazil. **Tel** 55-085-239.24.29. **ED** Jean Alencar. **Bk Rev. Ad Acc. Circ:** 300 (ctrl).
Desc: Presents original articles and reprints from the world-wide press, in translation, on the occurrence, history and analysis of unidentified flying objects.

LC TL501 .U46
DD 629.133/343
ISSN 0736-2447
US
ULTRALIGHT PILOT. (ULTRALIGHT PILOT : AN OFFICIAL PUBLICATION OF THE AIRCRAFT OWNERS AND PILOTS ASSOCIATION.). [Ultralight pilot]. **VFOAT** Pilot. Periodical. English. Six times a year. $15.00. Ultralight Pilot, PO Box 5800, Bethesda MD 20814.

LC UG633 .A377164
DD 358.4/00973
US
CEASED
UNITED STATES ARMY AVIATION DIGEST. Added/Corp U.S. Army Aviation Center. U.S. Army Aviation School. (Feb. 1955)-(Mar./Apr. 1995). Government Publication. English. Superintendent of Documents, US Government Printing Office, Washington DC 20402. **Tel** (202)275-3328, FAX (202)786-2377.
Desc: Provides information of an operational or functional nature concerning safety and aircraft accident prevention, training, maintenance, operations, research and development, aviation medicine and other related data.
Ind/Abst Air Univ. Libr. Index Mil. Period.

LC TL
DD 629
US
●**UNITED STATES LOW ALTITUDE IFR - AFR PLANNING REPORT.** (1995)-. English. One time a year. $9.00. National Ocean Service, NOAA Distribution Branch NCG33, Riverdale MD 20737. **Tel** (301)436-6993.

LC TL
DD 629
US
UNITED STATES OF AMERICA AIP, AERONAUTICAL INFORMATION PUBLICATION. Added/Corp National Flight Data Center (U.S.) United States. Air Traffic Service. Flight Services Division. United States. Air Traffic Service. Flight Information Division. United States. Air Traffic Operations Service. Flight Information and Obstructions Branch. United States. Air Traffic Rules and Procedures Service. Air Traffic Publications Program. **VFOAT** AIP, Aeronautical Information Publication; Aeronautical Information Publication; AIP. (19??)-. Government Publication. English. Irregular. $87.00 US; $108.75 other. US Department of Transportation / US Coast Guard, 2100 Second Street Southwest, Washington DC 20953-0001. **Tel** (202)267-2229. (**Subscription address:** Superintendent of Documents, US Government Printing Office, Washington DC 20402.)
Desc: Comprehensive aeronautical publication containing regulations and data required for safe aircraft operations in the National Airspace System.

Aeronautics, Astronautics

LC TL500
DD 629.13 US
UNITED STATES SPACE FOUNDATION PROCEEDINGS. (19??)-. Proceedings. English. One time a year. $50.00, ($3.00 postage) $50.00, (5.00 postage) other (twenty percent discount for standing orders). Univelt Inc, POB 28130, San Diego CA 92198. **Tel** (619)746-4005, FAX (619)746-3139. **ED** US Space Foundation. **Bk Rev. Ad Acc. Circ:** 2,000.
Desc: Journal containing information on space planning, programs, government, and management.

LC TL500 **ISSN** 0741-4587
DD 629.1 US
UPDATE (ELIZABETHTOWN, PA.). (UPDATE / UNITED STATES SPACE EDUCATION ASSOCIATION.). [Updat.]. **Added/Corp** United States Space Education Association. (19??)-. Periodical. English. Twelve times a year. $26.00 US and Canada; $32.00 other. USSEA / US Space Education Association, International Headquarters, PO Box 249, Rheems PA 17570. **Tel** (717)367-3265. **ED** Stephen M. Cobaugh. **Circ:** 1,000 (ctrl).
Desc: Important timely space-related news, legislative and political space news, listings of upcoming conferences, seminars and workshops of aerospace interest.

LC UG622
DD 358.4 US
USAF WEAPONS REVIEW. Added/Corp USAF Weapons School. **VFOAT** Weapons Review. Vol. 40, Issue 3 (Fall 1992)-. Periodical. English. Four times a year. Free. USAF Weapons Review, Department of the Air Force, 57th Tactical Training, Nellis Air Force Base NV 89191. ***Continues*** *USAF Fighter Weapons Review, 0274-6824.*
Ind/Abst Air Univ. Libr. Index Mil. Period. (199?-).

LC TL **ISSN** 0082-5255
DD 629.1 CN
CODEN TIRPBO
UTIAS REPORT. [UTIAS rep.]. **VFOAT** U.T.I.A.S. Report. **VAT** University of Toronto Institute for Aerospace Studies Report. (196?)-. Academic Scholarly Publication. English. Irregular. Price varies per volume. University of Toronto Institute for Aerospace Studies, 4925 Dufferin Street, Downsview Ontario M3H 5T6 Canada. **Tel** 667-7723. available on microfiche (from Updata). Documents available from Article Express International, CASDDS. ***Continues*** *UTIA Report.*
Desc: Research results in aerospace disciplines, including aeroacoustics, gas dynamics, subsonic aerodynamics, materials science, fusion energy, air cushion technology, space dynamics and laser and photonic sensor technology.
Ind/Abst Bioeng. Abstr.; Chem. Abstr.; Ei Page One; Eng. Index Annu.

LC TL507 .T6 **ISSN** 0082-5263
DD 629.1 CN
CODEN TIATAI
UTIAS TECHNICAL NOTE. [UTIAS tech. note]. **Main/Corp** University of Toronto. Institute of Aerospace Studies. **VAT** University of Toronto Institute of Aerospace Studies. No. 68-. Academic Scholarly Publication. English. Irregular. Price varies per volume. University of Toronto Institute for Aerospace Studies, 4925 Dufferin Street, Downsview Ontario M3H 5T6 Canada. **Tel** 667-7723. **Circ:** 325. available on microfiche (by Updata). Documents available from Article Express International, CASDDS. ***Continues*** *UTIA Technical Note.*
Desc: Research results in aerospace disciplines, including aeroacoustics, gas dynamics, subsonic aerodynamics, materials, science, fusion energy, air cushion technology, space dynamics and laser resonance interaction.
Ind/Abst Acoust. Abstr.; Bioeng. Abstr.; Chem. Abstr.; Ei Page One; Eng. Index Annu.

LC HE9761 **ISSN** 0828-4504
DD 387.7/364/025711 CN
VANCOUVER & AREA AIRPORT BUSINESS DIRECTORY. [Vanc. area airpt. bus. dir.]. **VAT** Vancouver Airport Business Directory (1984); Vancouver and Area Airport Business Directory. 1984-. Directory. English. One time a year. $5.00. Vancouver & Area Airport Business Directory, 5621 11th Street NE/Suite 107, Calgary Alberta T2E 6Z7 Canada. **Tel** (403)295-9200, FAX (403)275-3925. **ED** Gary Gaudreau. **Ad Acc. Circ:** 8,000 (ctrl). ***Continues*** *Vancouver Airport Business Directory, 0227-1680.*
Desc: Descriptive listing of all aviation related companies and services in the Vancouver area.

LC HE9761 **ISSN** 1188-2778
DD 387.7 CN
VANCOUVER & AREA ... AVIATION BUSINESS DIRECTORY. [Vanc. area aviat. bus. dir.]. **VFOAT** Vancouver and Area ... Aviation Business Directory; Vancouver Aviation Directory. (1992)-. Directory. English. $7.50 per volume. Consolidated Communications, 807 Manning Road Northeast, Suite 200, Calgary Alberta T2E 7M8 Canada. **Tel** (403)569-9520, FAX (403)569-9590. ***Continues*** *Vancouver & Area Airport Business Directory., 0828-4504.*

LC HE9848.A1 A36b
DD 387.7/0944/363 FR
VENTILATION DU TRAFIC COMMERCIAL. Main/Corp Aeroport de Paris. Departement Informatique. Statistiques. (19??)-. French. Twelve times a year. 440.00F. Aeroports de Paris, Orly Sud 103, 94396 Orly, Aerogare Cedex France.

LC HE9849.A1 A33
DD 629.13 GW
VERKEHR. REIHE 6 : LUFTVERKEHR. Main/Corp Germany (West). Statistisches Bundesamt. **Added/Corp** Germany (West). Statistisches Bundesamt. Luftverkehr. **VAT** Verkehr. Reihe Sechs: Luftverkehr. (1976)-. German. One time a year. DM11.80. Metzler Poeschel Verlag Veroeffen, Statist Bundesamt Kernerstr 43, D-70182 Stuttgart Germany. **Tel** 011 49 7071 935350. ***Continues*** *Verkehr. Reihe 3: Luftverkehr.*

LC TL716.A1 A514 **ISSN** 0042-4455
DD 629 US
CODEN VEFLAD
VERTIFLITE. [Vertiflite]. **Added/Corp** American Helicopter Society. **VFOAT** Vertiflite. (1963)-. Periodical. English. Five times a year. $35.00. American Helicopter Society, 217 North Washington Street, Alexandria VA 22314. **Tel** (703)684-6777, FAX (703)739-9279. **ED** Christopher R. Colligan. **Bk Rev. Ad Acc. Circ:** 9,000 (ctrl). Documents available from Article Express International. ***Continues*** *Verti-Flite Newsletter;* ***Absorbed*** *American Helicopter Society. Directory of Members, 0090-4627.*
Desc: An official publication of the American Helicopter Society, publishes articles for the advancement of vertical flight technology and its useful application throughout the world.
Ind/Abst Aviat. Tradescan [Full Cov.]; Bioeng. Abstr.; Curr. Cit.; Ei Page One; Eng. Index Annu. [Select. Cov.]; Int. Aerosp. Abstr.; Pollut. Abstr. Indexes.

LC TL500
DD 629 US
VFR TERMINAL AREA CHART. BALTIMORE--WASHINGTON. Main/Corp United States. National Ocean Service. **VFOAT** Baltimore--Washington; Washington Tri-Area Terminal Control Area; Tri-Area Flyway, Chartered VFR Flyway Planning Chart. 42nd Ed. (Aug. 23, 1990)-. Periodical. English. Two times a year. US Department of Commerce / National Marine Fisheries Service, 1335 East-West Highway, Silver Spring MD 20910. **Tel** (301)713-2239, FAX (301)713-2258. ***Continues*** *VFR Terminal Area Chart. Washington.*

LC TL506.G7 R55
DD 629.133/34/075 UK
VINTAGE AIRCRAFT DIRECTORY. Directory. English. One time a year. £0.85. G Riley Esq, 16 Church End, Weston Colville, Chambridgeshire CB1 5PE United Kingdom.

LC TL506.A1 V55 **ISSN** 0091-6943
DD 629.133/34/05 US
VINTAGE AIRPLANE, THE. Added/Corp Experimental Aircraft Association. Antique and Classic Division. Vol. 1 (Dec. 1972)-. Periodical. English. Twelve times a year. Comes with membership. Experimental Aircraft Association Inc., PO Box 3086, Oshkosh WI 54903-3086. **Tel** (414)426-4800, FAX (414)426-4828. **ED** Gene R. Chase. **Bk Rev. Ad Acc. Circ:** 4,000 (ctrl).
Desc: Contents include information on antique and classic aircrafts. and stories on events and people associated with such aircrafts. Also some technical data.
Ind/Abst Index Inf.

LC TL796.6.E2 V57
DD 629.43/7 FI
VISUAL OBSERVATIONS OF ARTIFICIAL EARTH SATELLITES IN FINLAND. English. One time a year. University of Helsinki, Siltavuoren Penger 20C, SF 00170 Helsinki 17 Finland.

LC TL500 **ISSN** 0042-7705
DD 629.13 NE
UDC 355
VLIEGENDE HOLLANDER. [Vliegende Holl.]. (1945)-. Government Publication. Dutch. Twelve times a year. Fl42.50. Ministserie van Defensie, Directie Voorlichting, Postbus 20701, 2500 ES The Hague Netherlands. **Tel** 011 31 70 3188335, FAX 011 31 70 3188426. **ED** Martin Zijlstra. **Bk Rev. Ad Acc. Circ:** 40,000. available with charts; available with illustrations. ***Continues*** *Bericht, Beschouwing, Raad, 0167-0700.*

LC GV **ISSN** 1121-5607
DD 797 IT
UDC 629.73
VOLARE. ROZZANO. See Sports and Games.

LC TL789.A1 V83
DD 001.9/05 FR
VUES NOUVELLES. Vol. 1 (1974)-. Periodical. French. 46.00F. Vues Nouvelles, C C P 27 24 26 Lyon, 43400 Le Chambon-sur-Lignon.

LC TL506.A1 W67 **ISSN** 0736-198X
DD 629.133/343/09041 US
W.W. 1 AERO. [W.W.1 aero]. **Added/Corp** World War I Aeroplanes (Association). **VFOAT** Aero; WW1 Aero; World War 1 Aeroplanes. (19??)-. Periodical. English. Four times a year. $25.00. World War I Aeroplanes Inc, 15 Crescent Road, Poughkeepsie NY 12601. **Tel** (914)473-3679. **ED** Leonard E Opdycke. **Bk Rev,** (Qty: Varies). **Ad Acc. Circ:** 2,000. ***Continues*** *World War I Aeroplanes, 0160-6816.*
Desc: Plans, projects, lists of materials, collections of parts, engines, aircraft books, and models to assist builders and restorers of early aeroplanes.

LC UG1243 .W35 **ISSN** 0744-6624
DD 358.4/183/0973 US
WARBIRDS. (WARBIRDS / WARBIRDS OF AMERICA.). [Warbirds]. **Added/Corp** Warbirds of America. Vol. 5, No. 5 (May 1982)-. Periodical. English. Eight times a year. $30.00. Experimental Aircraft Association Inc., PO Box 3086, Oshkosh WI 54903-3086. **Tel** (414)426-4800, FAX (414)426-4828. **ED** Gene R. Chase. **Bk Rev. Ad Acc. Circ:** 4,000 (ctrl). ***Continues*** *Warbirds Newsletter, 0744-1312.*
Desc: Focus on vintage military aircraft and the people who fly them. Includes technical tips on restoration and maintenance of these special airplanes.

LC TL500 **ISSN** 0739-6538
DD 629.13 US
WASHINGTON REMOTE SENSING LETTER. [Washington remote sens. lett.]. **VFOAT** RSL; R.S.L. Vol. 1, No. 1 (July 1981)-. Periodical. English. Twenty-two times a year (bimonthly except monthly in Jan. and Aug.). $410.00. Washington Remote Sensing Letter, PO Box 2075, Washington DC 20013. **Tel** (202)393-3640. **ED** Dr. Murray Felsher. **Bk Rev,** (Qty: 50). **Photos.** available on an online database from NEWSNET.
Desc: Reporting and analysis of U.S. and international news dealing with satellite remote sensing of Earth. Including photography, imagery, surveillance, reconnaissance, and monitoring of the earth from space.

LC TL684 .W38 **ISSN** 0733-1754
DD 629.133/347/05 US
WATER FLYING. [Water fly.]. **Added/Corp** Seaplane Pilots Association (U.S.). (1981)-. Periodical. English. Four times a year. Free to members, $2.00 nonmembers. Seaplane Pilots Association, 421 Aviation Way, Frederick MD 21701. **Tel** (301)695-2083. ***Continues*** *Water Flying News, 0736-6485.*

LC TL684 .W37 **ISSN** 0193-4198
DD 629.132/5247/05 US
WATER FLYING ANNUAL. [Water fly. annu.]. **Added/Corp** U.S. Seaplane Pilots Association. Seaplane Pilots Association. (19??)-. English. One time a year. $11.00. US Seaplane Pilots Association, 421 Aviation Way, Frederick MD 21701. **Tel** (301)695-2083.

LC HB **ISSN** 0509-9528
DD 338 US
WEEKLY OF BUSINESS AVIATION, THE. [Wkly. bus. aviat.]. **VFOAT** Business Aviation. Vol. 1 No. 1 (Sept. 1965)-. Periodical. English. One time a week. $520.00. McGraw Hill Publishing Company, Inc., 1221 Avenue of the Americas, New York NY 10020. **Tel** (212)512-6410, (800)525-5003, FAX (212)512-6111. available on an online database from NEWSNET; Lexis-Nexis; Dow Jones News/Retrieval; and (file 624/Full-Text) DIALOG.
Desc: A source of general aviation news, government trends, business facts, figures and analysis.
Ind/Abst Trade Ind. Index.

LC TL
DD 629 CN
Pr Rev.
•**WEST COAST AVIATOR.** (1995)-. English. Six times a year (Feb., April, June, Aug., Oct., Dec.). 19.20Can$. Pilot Press Ltd., Box 2065, Sydney BC V8L 3S3 Canada. **Tel** (604)656-7598, FAX (604)655-4090. **ED** Jack Schofield (editor's phone number: (604)658-1267). Index available. cum. index. **Bk Rev,** (Qty: 2). **Ad Acc. Circ:** 5,000. ***Continues*** *BC Aviator.*
Desc: An historical aviation event is paralleled with a current profile of individual/airline'aircraft/event. Circulation and editorial content applies to "Canada" (west coast) only.

LC TL **ISSN** 0388-1032
DD 629.13 JA
WING NEWSLETTER. [Wing newsl.]. **VFOAT** Japan's Aerospace and Aviation Weekly. (1978)-. Periodical. English. Fifty times a year (Wed.). $1160.00. **(Subscription address:** Maruzen Company Ltd., PO Box 5050, Import & Export Department, Tokyo 100 31 Japan. **Tel** 011 81 3 32789224.) ***Continues*** *Wing (Tokyo. 1973), 0388-1024.*
Ind/Abst PROMT [Full Txt.].

Aeronautics, Astronautics

LC TL501
DD 629.13
AT
WINGS. (19??)-. English. Four times a year (Feb., May, Aug., Nov.). 8.00Aus$ Australia; 15.00Aus$ other. Air Forces Association, PO Box E147, St. James Sydney, New South Wales, 2000 Australia. **Tel** 011 61 2 267 2722.

LC HE9761
DD 387.7/0971
ISSN 0701-1369
CN
TITLE CHANGE
WINGS (CALGARY). (WINGS.). Vol. 18, No. 8 (Aug./Sept. 1976)-(19??). Periodical. English. Corvus Publishing Group Ltd, 1224 Aviation Park Northeast, Suite 158, Calgary Alberta T2E 7E2 Canada. **Tel** (403)275-9457, FAX (403)275-3925. **ED** Tammi Shanahan. **Bk Rev. Ad Acc. Circ:** 11,500 (ctrl). **Continues** Canadian Wings, 0008-5367. **Continued by** Wings Magazine.
Desc: Covers commercial, corporate and military aviation. Nonfiction, historical, technical, informational, new products, profile (Canadian), photo features, and a news magazine.

LC TL501
DD 629.13
CN
WINGS MAGAZINE. (19??)-. English. Six times a year. £26.17 Canada; £41.00 US; £59.00 other. Corvus Publishing Group Ltd, 1224 Aviation Park Northeast, Suite 158, Calgary Alberta T2E 7E2 Canada. **Tel** (403)275-9457, FAX (403)275-3925. **Continues** Wings, 0701-1369.

LC TL
DD 629
ISSN 0161-6331
US
WINGS (NEVADA CITY). (WINGS.). **Added/Corp** Institute for the Development of the Harmonious Human Being. (1978)-. Periodical. English. Six times a year (Feb., Apr., May, July, Sept., Dec.). $18.00. Sentry Magazines, 10718 White Oak Avenue, Granada Hills CA 91344. **Tel** (310)368-2012. **Continues** Sufi Times, 0149-5135.

LC G149
DD 910.4
US
WINGS OF ALOHA. See Travel and Tourism.

LC VG93 .W496
DD 359
ISSN 0274-7405
US
WINGS OF GOLD (PENSACOLA, FLA.). (WINGS OF GOLD.). **Added/Corp** Association of Naval Aviation (U.S.). Vol. 1, No. 1 (April 1976)-. Periodical. English. Four times a year (Mar., June, Sept., Dec.). $25.00. Association of Naval Aviation, 5205 Leesburg Pike, Suite 200, Falls Church VA 22041. **Tel** (703)998-7733. **ED** Rosario M. Rausa. Index available. cum. index. **Bk Rev**, (Qty: 4). **Ad Acc, Adv Mgr:** Nancy Fullen. **Circ:** 15,000.
Desc: Strategic considerations for USA, naval and aeronautical developments, tactical operations, training, manpower and logistic support, military pay and compensation.
Ind/Abst Predicasts.

LC GV
DD 797
ISSN 1049-7781
US
TITLE CHANGE
WINGS WEST. See Sports and Games.

LC TL500
DD 629.1309
ISSN 0955-9000
UK
WINGSPAN HIGH WYCOMBE. (WINGSPAN.). [Wingspan High Wycombe]. (1985)-. Periodical. English. Twelve times a year. $53.05. Wingspan, 5 Riverside Woodburn Moor Nr, Wycombe Buckinghamshire HP10 0NU United Kingdom. **Tel** 011 44 16285 2358. **Continues** Planes (High Wycombe).
Ind/Abst F&S Index Plus Text, Int. [Select. Cov.].

LC QB461
DD 523.01
ISSN 0363-3675
US
CODEN WIASDH
WISCONSIN ASTROPHYSICS. [Wis. astrophys.]. **Added/Corp** Washburn Observatory. No. 1 (1974)-. Academic Scholarly Publication. English. Twelve times a year. University of Wisconsin / Washburn Observatory, Madison WI. Documents available from CASDDS.
Ind/Abst Chem. Abstr. (?-1992).

LC TL500
DD 629.13
GW
WISSENSCHAFTLICH-TECHNISCHER BERICHT. Main/Corp Deutsche Forschungs- und Versuchsanstalt fur Luft- und Raumfahrt. Bereich Wissenschaftlich-Technische Betriebseinrichtungen. **VFOAT** Wissenschaftlich Technischer Bericht. (1983)-. German. Deutsche Forschungs Luft + Raumfahrt, Postfach 906058, D-51126 Cologne Germany. **Tel** 011 49 2203 6010, FAX 011 49 2203 67310.

LC TL501
DD 629.13
US
WORLD AEROSPACE & DEFENSE INTELLIGENCE. (19??)-. Bulletin. English. Fifty times a year. $565.00. Forecast International / DMS Inc., 22 Commerce Road, Newtown CT 06470. **Tel** (203)426-0800, FAX (203)426-1964, telex 467615.

LC TL500 .W67
DD 629.4/05
ISSN 0268-8670
UK
WORLD AEROSPACE PROFILE : THE INTERNATIONAL REVIEW OF AEROSPACE DESIGN AND DEVELOPMENT. (1986)-. Periodical. English. One time a year. Free (senior design engineers and key personnel of major aerospace and allied manufacturing corporations and to civil defence aircraft operators worldwide). Sterling Publications Ltd., 57 North Wharf Road, London W2 1XR United Kingdom. **Tel** 011 44 171 9159660, FAX 011 44 171 3338155, telex 295819. **ED** Arthur Reed.

LC UG622 .W67
DD 358.4/005
ISSN 0959-7050
UK
WORLD AIR POWER JOURNAL. [World air power j.]. (Spring 1990)-. Periodical. English. Four times a year. $58.00. Air Time Publ Inc, 10 Bay Street, Westport CT 06880.

LC TL500
DD 629.13
UK
WORLD AIRLINE ACCIDENT SUMMARY. (19??)-. English. Irregular. £36.80 UK; £39.20 other. Civil Aviation Authority / England, Grenville House, 37 Gratton Road, Cheltenham Glo GL50 2BN United Kingdom. **Tel** 011 44 1242 235151, FAX 011 44 1242 584139. **Continues** World Helicopter Accident Summary & Binders.

LC HE9769.A3 E55
DD 387.7/334/0216
UK
WORLD AIRLINE FLEETS. (1977)-. English. One time a year. £5.50.

LC TL
DD 629
ISSN 0951-8673
UK
WORLD AIRLINE FLEETS NEWS. See Transportation.

LC TL501
DD 629.13
US
● **WORLD AIRLINE MAINTENANCE FORECAST.** (1994)-. English. Four times a year. $3490.00. Forecast International / DMS Inc., 22 Commerce Road, Newtown CT 06470. **Tel** (203)426-0800, FAX (203)426-1964, telex 467615.

LC HE9761
DD 387.7
ISSN 1059-4183
US
CCC
WORLD AIRLINE NEWS. [World airl. news]. (1991)-. Periodical. English. One time a week (50 issues). $595.00. Phillips Business Information Inc., 1201 Seven Locks Road, PO Box 61130, Potomac MD 20854. **Tel** (301)424-3338, (301)340-1520, (800)777-5005, FAX (301)424-4297, telex 358149.
Ind/Abst PROMT [Full Txt.]; PTS Newsl. Database [Full Txt.].

LC TL500
DD 629.13
ISSN 0261-2399
SA
WORLD AIRNEWS. [World airnews]. (1973)-. Periodical. English. Twelve times a year. $25.35. Tom Chalmers Enterprises Ltd., PO Box 35082, Northway 4065, Durban Natal South Africa. **Tel** 011 27 31 841319, FAX 011 27 31 837115. **ED** M. T. Chalmers. **Ad Acc. Circ:** 13,200.
Desc: Contains aviation information.

LC TL
DD 629
ISSN 1078-1420
US
● **WORLD AIRPORT WEEK.** (1994)-. Newsletter. English. One time a week. $495.00. Phillips Business Information Inc., 1201 Seven Locks Road, PO Box 61130, Potomac MD 20854. **Tel** (301)424-3338, (301)340-1520, (800)777-5005, FAX (301)424-4297, telex 358149. **ED** Jim Brown. available on an online database from INFO ACCESS.
Desc: Information on airport finance and technology.

LC HB
DD 338
ISSN 0888-5265
US
WORLD AIRSHOW NEWS. Vol. 1, No. 1 (First Quarter 1986)-. Trade Publication. English. Six times a year (Jan., Mar., May, July, Sept., Nov.). $20.00. World Airshow News, PO Box 199, Oregon WI 53575. **Tel** (608)835-7063. **ED** Dave Weiman. **Bk Rev**, (Qty: 6). **Ad Acc. Circ:** 3,300 (ctrl).
Desc: Trade magazine for the airshow entertainment industry. Covers airshow promoters, performers, and vendors.

LC TL537 .W66
DD 629.13
ISSN 0890-510X
US
WORLD AND UNITED STATES AVIATION AND SPACE RECORDS AS OF ... . [World U.S. aviat. space rec.]. **Added/Corp** National Aeronautic Association. **VFOAT** World and U.S. Aviation-space Records; World and U.S. Aviation Space Records; World and Space Records, World and United States; World and United States Aviation & Space Records. (19??)-. Irregular (Book plus 4 annual updates). $39.00. National Aeronautic Association, 1815 North Fort Meyer Drive, Suite 700, Arlington VA 22209-1805. **Tel** (703)527-0226, FAX (703)527-0229. **ED** Arthur W. Greenfield. Index available. **Ad Acc. Circ:** 7,500.

LC TL512 .A63
DD 629
ISSN 0043-826X
US
WORLD AVIATION DIRECTORY. [World aviat. dir.]. (1958)-. Periodical. English. Two times a year. $250.00. McGraw Hill Publishing Company, Inc., 1221 Avenue of the Americas, New York NY 10020. **Tel** (212)512-6410, (800)525-5003, FAX (212)512-6111. **(Subscription address:** World Aviation Directory, Box 416, Hightstown NJ 08520. **) ED** Donna Kaulkin. available on CD-ROM. **Continues** American Aviation World Wide Directory.; **Absorbed** World Space Directory, 0043-9045. Continued in part by World Aviation Buyer's Guide, 1064-0495.
Desc: Global communications reference source for all market sectors of the aviation/aerospace industry (civil, military, government) worldwide. Volume one features industry trends, company profiles and capabilities with key personnel. Volume two features products and services included in a world buyer's guide.
Ind/Abst Int. Aerosp. Abstr.

LC TL512 .W67
DD 629
ISSN 1064-0509
US
WORLD AVIATION DIRECTORY. BUYER'S GUIDE. [World aviat. dir., Buy. guide]. **VFOAT** Buyer's Guide. No. 13 (Summer 1992)-. Directory. English. Two times a year. $160.00 US; $185.00 other. McGraw Hill Publishing Company, Inc., 1221 Avenue of the Americas, New York NY 10020. **Tel** (212)512-6410, (800)525-5003, FAX (212)512-6111. **Continues** World Aviation Buyer's Guide, 1064-0495.

LC TL501
DD 629.13
US
WORLD COMMERCIAL AIRCRAFT : ENGINES ORDERS & OPTIONS. (19??)-. English. Four times a year. $1025.00. Forecast International / DMS Inc., 22 Commerce Road, Newtown CT 06470. **Tel** (203)426-0800, FAX (203)426-1964, telex 467615.

LC TL770.A1 W67
DD 796.1/5
ISSN 0191-3247
US
WORLD FREE FLIGHT REVIEW. Vol. 1 (1975/77)-. English. World Free Flight Press, 7513 Sausalito Avenue, Canoga Park CA 91307.

LC UG1230 .W67
DD 358.4/183
SZ
CEASED
WORLD HELICOPTER SYSTEMS. **Added/Corp** Interavia Data (Firm). (19??)-(19??). English. Jane's Information Group, Sentinel House, 163 Brighton Road, Coulsdon Surrey CR5 2NH United Kingdom. **Tel** 011 44 181 7631030, FAX 011 44 181 7630276, telex 916907-JANES-G. **(Subscription address:** Jane's Information Group / US Subscriptions, 1340 Braddock Place, Suite 300, Alexandria VA 22314. **Tel** (800)243-3852, (703)683-3700.**)**

LC TL501
DD 629.13
US
WORLD MILITARY & CIVIL AIRCRAFT BRIEFING. (19??)-. English. Twelve times a year. $995.00 US and Canada; $1,150.00 other. Teal Group Corporation, 3900 University Drive, Suite 220, Fairfax VA 22030. **Tel** (703)385-1992, FAX (703)691-9591.

LC HE9762.5 .W67
DD 387.7
CN
WORLD OF CIVIL AVIATION, THE. **Added/Corp** International Civil Aviation Organization. (1992)-. English. One time a year. 20.00Can$. International Civil Aviation Organization / ICAO, 1000 Sherbrooke Street West, Suite 400, Montreal Quebec H3A 2R2 Canada. **Tel** (514)285-8026, (514)285-8022, telex 05-24514.

LC TL500
DD 629.13
FR
WORLD SPACE INDUSTRY SURVEY. TEN YEAR OUTLOOK. (19??)-. English (French). One time a year. $2450.00. Euroconsult, 71 boulevard Richard Lenoir, 75011 Paris France. **Tel** 011 33 1 43380600. **ED** Rachel Villain. ctrl circ.
Desc: This report is an indispensable analytical tool geared toward financial and economic decision - makers involved in the development of space programs and applications. It presents worldwide trends in space activity and analyzes them in terms of their economic, financial and industrial aspects.

LC TL501
DD 629.13
US
WORLD SPACE SYSTEMS BRIEFING. (19??)-. English. Irregular. $995.00 US and Canada; $1,150.00 other. Teal Group Corporation, 3900 University Drive, Suite 220, Fairfax VA 22030. **Tel** (703)385-1992, FAX (703)691-9591.

LC TL500 **ISSN** 0737-8548
DD 629.1 US
WORLD SPACEFLIGHT NEWS. VFOAT
World Space Flight News. Vol. 1, No. 1 (Aug. 1983)-. Periodical. English. Twelve times a year. £16.20 (one-year), £31.50 (two-year). Randall M. Schuller, PO Box 98, Sewell NJ 08080-0098. **Tel** (609)478-6396.
Ind/Abst Int. Aerosp. Abstr.

LC HE9761 **ISSN** 1056-7925
DD 387 US
WSN EXPRESS. [WSN express]. VAT World
Spaceflight News Express. (1991)-. Periodical. English. One time a week. $180.00. Progressive Management, PO Box 98, Sewell NJ 08080.

LC TL501 .S63518
DD 629.13/006/273 US
YEAR BOOK & DIRECTORY - SOCIETY OF AIRWAY PIONEERS. Main/Corp Society of
Airway Pioneers. **VFOAT** Airway Pioneer. Directory. English. Society of Airway Pioneers, PO Box 530, Santa Rosa CA 95402.

LC TL500
DD 629.13 BE
YEARBOOK (ASSOCIATION OF EUROPEAN AIRLINES). (YEARBOOK.).
Added/Corp Association of European Airlines. (1984)-. English. One time a year. Association of European Airlines, Avenue Louise 350 BTE 4, B-1050 Brussels Belgium. **Tel** 32-2-640 31.75, FAX (322)648-4017, telex 22918. ***Formed by the union of** Annual Traffic and Operating Data **and** Association of European Airlines. Facts and Figures.*

LC TL787 .Y83 **ISSN** 1000-1328
DD 629.4/05 CC
YU HANG HSUEH PAO. Added/Corp
Chung-kuo yu Hang Hsueh hui. **VFOAT** Yuhang Xuebao; Journal of Chinese Society of Astronautics. (19??)-. Periodical. Chinese (summaries and/or abstracts in English). Four times a year. $15.70. **(Subscription address:** China International Book Trading Corporation, PO Box 399, Library Service Department, Beijing 100044 People's Republic of China. **Tel** 011 86 1 8414284, FAX 011 86 1 8412023, telex 22496 CIBTC CN.)
Ind/Abst Int. Aerosp. Abstr.

LC HE9885.5.A2 G47a
DD 629.13 GW
ZAIRE : LUFTVERKEHR. Main/Corp
Bundesstelle fur Aussenhandelsinformation (Germany). (19??)-. German. Bundesstelle fuer Aussenhandelsinformation, Agrippastrasse 87 93, D-50676 Cologne Germany. **Tel** 011 49 221 2057316, FAX 011 49 221 2057212.

LC TL503 .Z43 **ISSN** 0342-068X
DD 629.13 GW
CCC
CODEN ZFWEDT
ZEITSCHRIFT FUER FLUGWISSENSCHAFTEN UND WELTRAUMFORSCHUNG. [Z. Flugwiss.
Weltraumforsch.]. **Added/Corp** Deutsche Gesellschaft fur Luft- und Raumfahrt. Deutsche Forschungs- und Versuchsanstalt fur Luft- und Raumfahrt. Vol. 1 (Jan./Feb. 1977)-. Academic Scholarly Publication. German. Six times a year. $223.00. Springer-Verlag GmbH & Company KG, Heidelberger Platz 3, D-14197 Berlin Germany. **Tel** 011 49 30 8207223, FAX 011 49 30 8214091, telex 183 319 SPBLN D. **(Subscription address:** Springer-Verlag New York Inc. / North America, PO Box 2485, Journal Fulfillment, Secaucus NJ 07096. **Tel** (201)348-4033, (800)777-4643, FAX (201)348-4505.) **ED** G Madelung, H Tolle, W Krolly, H Sax, U Renner. **Bk Rev. Ad Acc. Circ:** 3,400 (ctrl). available on microfilm and microfiche from University Microfilms International (UMI). Documents available from Article Express International, The Genuine Article, Ask*IEEE, CASDDS. ***Formed by the union of** Zeitschrift fur Flugwissenschaften, 0044-2739 **and** Raumfahrtforschung, 0034-0103.*
Desc: Publishes original papers and review articles from all areas of aerospace research and technology, as well as from associated fields of interest.
Ind/Abst Acoust. Abstr.; Alum. Ind. Abstr.; Bioeng. Abstr.; Chem. Abstr.; Curr. Contents Eng. Comput. Technol.; Ei Page One; EMBASE; Energy Res. Abstr. (April 1978-); Eng. Mater. Abstr.; Eng. Index Annu.; Fluid Abstr., Civil Eng.; Fluid Abstr. Proc. Eng.; FLUIDEX (1977-); INSPEC (1977-); Int. Aerosp. Abstr.; Met. Abstr.; Res. Alert [Select. Cov.]; Sci. Cit. Index (19??-19??); SCISEARCH; World Alum. Abstr.; Zentralbl. Math. Ihre Grenzgeb.

LC K30 .E6 **ISSN** 0340-8329
DD 343.09/7/05 GW
CCC
ZEITSCHRIFT FUER LUFT- UND WELTRAUMRECHT. See Law.

LC TL **ISSN** 0889-4353
DD 629 US
ZENAIR NEWS. [Zenair news]. Added/Corp Zenair
(Firm). **VFOAT** Zenair. (19??)-. Periodical. English. Six times a year (Jan., Mar., May, July, Sept., Nov.). $15.00. Zenair News, 6438 West Millbrook Road, Remus MI 49340. **Tel** (517)561-2393. **ED** John B. Bergeson. **Bk Rev. Ad Acc. Circ:** 250 (ctrl).
Desc: Devoted to technical information related to building Zenair aircraft and also flying them.

LC TL **ISSN** 1002-7742
DD 629.1 CC
Pr Rev.
ZHONGGUO HANGTIAN. VFOAT Aerospace
China. (1991)-. Periodical. Chinese. Twelve times a year (Aug.). $130.00. Aerospace China Press, PO Box 1408, Beijing 100013 People's Republic of China. **Tel** 8373440, FAX 4227606. **ED** L. Jiyuan. ***Continues** Shijie Daodan yu Hangtian, 1001-4144.*
Desc: Discusses aspects of space science and technology.
Ind/Abst Int. Aerosp. Abstr.

LC TL787 **ISSN** 1000-758X
DD 629.4 CC
ZHONGGUO KONGJIAN KEXUE JISHU.
VFOAT Chinese Space Science and Technology. (1980)-. Periodical. Chinese. Six times a year. $19.70. Chinese Academy of Space Technology, PO Box 2417, No. 48, Beijing 100081 People's Republic of China. **Tel** 011 86 1 8378204. **(Subscription address:** China National Publishers / Industry & Trade, PO Box 782, Beijing, China. **Tel** 011 86 1 4215031.) **ED** H. Shenyuan.
Ind/Abst Int. Aerosp. Abstr.

LC TL501 **ISSN** 0044-5355
DD 629.13 XR
UDC 629.13
ZPRAVODAJ VZLU. [Zpr. VZLU]. VFOAT
Zpravodaj Vyzkumneho a Zkhusebniho Leteckeho Ustavu. (1962)-. Academic Scholarly Publication. Multiple languages. Five times a year (Exchange basis only). SNTL - Nakladatelstvi Technicke Literatury, Technical Literature, Spalena 51, 113 02 Prague 1 Czech Republic. **Tel** (2)297670. **ED** Ladislav Vymetal. available with charts; available with illustrations; available in microform.
Ind/Abst Int. Aerosp. Abstr.

ABSTRACTING, BIBLIOGRAPHIES AND STATISTICS

LC Z5063.A2 A28 **ISSN** 0163-4941
DD 016.62913 US
AERONAUTICAL ENGINEERING (WASHINGTON, DC.). (AERONAUTICAL
ENGINEERING.). **Added/Corp** United States. National Aeronautics and Space Administration. Scientific and Technical Information Branch. United States. National Aeronautics and Space Administration. Scientific and Technical Information Office. United States. National Aeronautics and Space Administration. Scientific and Technical Information Division. United States. National Aeronautics and Space Administration. Scientific and Technical Information Program. NASA Scientific and Technical Information Facility. (1970)-. Periodical. English. Twelve times a year. $355.00 US, Canada and Mexico; $705.00 other. National Aeronautics and Space Administration, 600 Independence Avenue SW, Washington DC 20546. **Tel** (202)453-1000. **(Subscription address:** National Technical Information Service, 5285 Port Royal Road, Springfield VA 22161.)
Desc: A selection of annotated references to unclassified reports and journal articles that were introduced into the NASA scientific and technical information system.
Ind/Abst Corros. Abstr.

LC Z5060.A2 A32
DD 016.6294 US
AEROSPACE BIBLIOGRAPHY. Added/Corp
National Aerospace Education Council (U.S.) United States. National Aeronautics and Space Administration. Educational Programs Division. United States. National Aeronautics and Space Administration. (1966)-. Bibliography. English. Irregular. Superintendent of Documents, US Government Printing Office, Washington DC 20402. **Tel** (202)275-3328, FAX (202)786-2377.

LC TL501 .A818 **ISSN** 0898-4425
DD 629.13058 US
AEROSPACE FACTS AND FIGURES.
Added/Corp Aerospace Industries Association of America. 1st Ed. (1945)-. Trade Publication. English. One time a year (Dec.). $37.01. Aerospace Industries Association of America, 1250 Eye Street Northwest, Washington DC 20005. **Tel** (202)371-8561, FAX (202)371-8470, telex 710-822-0134 AIA DC TKU. **ED** Virginia C. Lopez. Index available. **Circ:** 3,000. available on diskette.
Desc: Comprehensive statistical summary of the US aerospace industry.
Ind/Abst Predicasts Forecasts; Stat. Ref. Index.

LC HE **ISSN** 0727-2774
DD 387.74042 AT
AIR TRANSPORT STATISTICS. FLIGHT CREW LICENCES. [Air transp. stat., Flight crew
licences]. (1980)-. English. One time a year. Department of Transport and Communications, GPO Box 594, Canberra Australian Capital Territory 2601 Australia. **Tel** (062)687111, FAX (062)572505, telex 62018. **Circ:** 285 (ctrl).
Desc: Presents data compiled from statistical returns submitted regularly by the department's regional offices.

LC HE9788.5.U5 A63 **ISSN** 0190-552X
DD 387.7/0973 US
AIR TRANSPORT (WASHINGTON). (AIR
TRANSPORT.). **Main/Corp** Air Transport Association of America. (1971)-. Statistical Publication. English. One time a year (June). $10.00. Air Transport Association, 1301 Pennsylvania Avenue Northwest, Suite 1100, Washington DC 20006-5206. **Tel** (202)626-4000. ***Continues** Air Transport Facts & Figures.*
Desc: Statistical report of the US airlines.
Ind/Abst Predicasts Forecasts.

LC HE9797.5.U52 H32
DD 387.7/36/09969021 US
AIRPORT STATISTICS, STATEWIDE AIRPORT SYSTEM. (1981)-. English. One time a
year. Airports Division, Department of Transportation, Honolulu International Airport, Honolulu HI 96819. ***Continues** State of Hawaii Airport Statistics.*

LC HE9803.A2 A93 **ISSN** 0092-2862
DD 387.7/4/0973 US
AVIATION DAILY'S AIRLINE STATISTICAL ANNUAL. VFOAT Airline
Statistical Annual. Statistical Publication. English. One time a year. $12.00. Murdoch Magazines, 200 Madison Avenue, 8th Floor, New York NY 10016. **Tel** (212)447-4700, (212)447-4732.

LC HE9761 **ISSN** 0899-1928
DD 387 US
AVIATION TRADESCAN. (AVIATION
TRADESCAN : THE AVIATION INFORMATION MANAGEMENT SYSTEM.). [Aviat. tradescan]. **VFOAT** Tradescan. Vol. 1, No. 1 (Jan. 1984)-. Abstracting/Indexing Service. English. Twelve times a year. $175.00. Aerospace Research Group, 2812 Summit Ridge, Grapevine TX 76051. **Tel** (817)488-9161, FAX (817)421-5418. **ED** Catherine Heinzer. Index available. cum. index. **Circ:** 200. available on an online database.
Desc: A guide to industry journals and reports. Indexes and abstracts articles and reports from principal industry periodicals and aviation-related items from general news and business journals.

LC TL502 .F62a **ISSN** 0181-1517
DD 387.7/0944/021 FR
BULLETIN STATISTIQUE DE LA DGAC.
Added/Corp France. Direction Generale de l'Aviation Civile. **VFOAT** Bulletin Statistique de la D.G.A.C. (1960)-. Statistical Publication. French. One time a year. Direction Generale de l'Aviation Civile, Service de Coordination Economique, Bureau Statistiques, 48 rue Camille Desmoulins, 92452 Issy les Moulineaux Cedex France. ***Continues** France. Direction Generale de l'Aviation Civile. Bulletin Statistique de la Direction Generale a l'Aviation Civile.*

LC HE9848.A1 S4A **ISSN** 0302-8607
DD 387.7/0944 FR
BULLETIN STATISTIQUE DU SECRETARIAT GENERAL A L'AVIATION CIVILE. (BULLETIN STATISTIQUE
DU SECRETARIAT GENERAL A L'AVIATION CIVILE (FRANCE).). **Main/Corp** France. Secretariat General a l'Aviation Civile. Bulletin. French. Secretariat General a l'Aviation Civile, 246 rue Lecourbe, Paris France.

LC HE9761
DD 387.744 CN
CATALOGUE OF ICAO PUBLICATIONS AND AUDIO VISUAL TRAINING AIDS.
Main/Corp International Civil Aviation Organization. **VFOAT** Catalogue of ICAO Publications and Audio Visual Aids. (199?)-. Catalog. English (French, Russian and Spanish). One time a year. Free on request. International Civil Aviation Organization / ICAO, 1000 Sherbrooke Street West, Suite 400, Montreal Quebec H3A 2R2 Canada. **Tel** (514)285-8026, (514)285-8022, telex 05-24514. ***Formed by the union of** International Civil Aviation Organization. Catalogue of ICAO Publications **and** International Civil Aviation Organization. Catalogue of ICAO Audio Visual Aids.*
Desc: Contains the titles and prices of all current salable publications, audio visual training aids and details of some of the publications offered free on request.

LC TK **ISSN** 1005-7870
DD 629 CC
•CHINA ASTRONAUTICS AND MISSILERY ABSTRACTS. (1994)-.
Abstracting/Indexing Service. English (Chinese). Six times a year (Jan., Mar., May, Jul., Sept., Nov.). $250.00. Institute of Astronautics Information, PO Box 1408,

Beijing 100013 China. **Tel** 011 86 1 8372847, FAX 011 86 1 4227606. **ED** An Bo. Index available ($60.00). cum. index. **Ad Acc, Adv Mgr:** An Bo, **Tel** 011 86 1 8372847.
Desc: A bilingual reference journal exhaustively citing the latest aerospace-related books, technical reports, standards, conference papers and journal articles recently produced in China.

LC HE9762.5 .C58
DD 387.7/021/2   CN
CIVIL AVIATION STATISTICS OF THE WORLD. **Added/Corp** International Civil Aviation Organization. 1st Ed. (1975)-. English. One time a year. 27.00Can$. International Civil Aviation Organization / ICAO, 1000 Sherbrooke Street West, Suite 400, Montreal Quebec H3A 2R2 Canada. **Tel** (514)285-8026, (514)285-8022, telex 05-24514.

LC TL720.A1 I57
DD 387.7/4/0212   CN
DIGEST OF STATISTICS (INTERNATIONAL CIVIL AVIATION ORGANIZATION). (DIGEST OF STATISTICS - INTERNATIONAL CIVIL AVIATION ORGANIZATION.). **Added/Corp** International Civil Aviation Organization. International Civil Aviation Organization. Recueil de Statistiques. **VFOAT** Recueil de Statistiques - Organisation de l'Aviation Civile Internationale. (19??)-. Monographic series. English (French, Russian and Spanish). Irregular. Price varies per volume. International Civil Aviation Organization / ICAO, 1000 Sherbrooke Street West, Suite 400, Montreal Quebec H3A 2R2 Canada. **Tel** (514)285-8026, (514)285-8022, telex 05-24514. **Continues** International Civil Aviation Organization. Secretariat. Digest of Statistics.

LC TL
DD 629   US
GENERAL AVIATION STATISTICAL DATABOOK. **Added/Corp** General Aviation Manufacturers' Association. (1982)-. Statistical Publication. English. One time a year (Fall). $10.00. General Aviation Manufacturing Association, 1400 K Street Northwest, Suite 801, Washington DC 20005. **Tel** (202)393-1500, FAX (202)842-4063. **Circ:** 2,000. **Continues** General Aviation Statistical Data.

LC TL500 .I57   **ISSN** 0020-5842
DD 629.1/08   US
                         CCC
NLM Z 5064.S7 I61   **CODEN** IAEAA8
INTERNATIONAL AEROSPACE ABSTRACTS. [Int. aerosp. abstr.]. **Added/Corp** American Institute of Aeronautics and Astronautics. Technical Information Service. United States. National Aeronautics and Space Administration. Institute of the Aerospace Sciences. Technical Information Service. Vol. 1 (Jan. 1961)-. Abstracting/Indexing Service. English. Twelve times a year (plus annual index). $1,625.00 North America; $2,240 other. American Institute of Aeronautics & Astronautics / New York, 85 John Street, 4th Floor, New York NY 10038. **Tel** (212)349-1120, FAX (212)582-4861. (**Subscription address:** American Institute of Aeronautics and Astronautics, 370 I'Enfant Promenade Southwest, Washington DC 20024. **Tel** (202)646-7400.) Index available. **Circ:** 1,000. available on CD-ROM (as OnDisc Aerospace Database) from DIALOG.
Supersedes in part Aerospace Engineering, 0096-669X.
Desc: Professionally prepared summaries and bibliographic data for recently published monographs, technical preprints, conference proceedings, and journal articles in 75 technical areas from over 40 countries and international organizations.

LC TL   **ISSN** 1081-1435
DD 629   US
                     TITLE CHANGE
JOURNAL OF SPACE ABSTRACTS AND RESEARCH. See Aeronautics, Astronautics.

LC HE9859.A1 L82   **ISSN** 0800-4072
DD 387.7/09481/021   NO
LUFTFARTSSTATISTIKK = CIVIL AVIATION STATISTICS NORWAY. **Added/Corp** Norway. Luftfartsverket. **VFOAT** Civil Aviation Statistics Norway. (19??)-. English (Norwegian). One time a year. Luftfartsverket, Postboks 8124 Den, 0032 Oslo 1 Norway. **Tel** (02)429280. **ED** Else Frisell. Index available. **Circ:** 5,000 (ctrl)

LC Z5063.A2 P7 TL545   **ISSN** 0032-9568
DD 016.6291
NLM W 3.5 P963   **CODEN** PPRNA
PROCEEDINGS IN PRINT. **Added/Corp** Special Libraries Association. Aerospace Section. Special Libraries Association. Aerospace Division. Vol. 1, Oct. (1964)-. Proceedings. English. Six times a year. $610.00 US and Canada; $640.50 Massachusetts; $675.00 other. Proceedings in Print Inc., PO Box 369, Halifax MA 02338. **Tel** (617)294-8011, FAX (617)294-8012.

                                          US
QUARTERLY AIRCRAFT OPERATING COSTS AND STATISTICS. Statistical Publication. English. Four times a year (published Mar., June, Sept., Dec.). $250.00. Avmark Inc / Virginia, 1911 North Fort Myer Drive, Arlington VA 22209. **Tel** (703)528-5610, FAX (703)528-3689. **ED** Larry C. Benton. ctrl circ.
Desc: A statistical publication detailing direct operating costs (by aircraft) from airline (U.S. carriers only) financial reports to the U.S. Department of Transportation.

LC Z5064.P62 S34 TL943   **ISSN** 0160-581X
DD 016.6297/044   US
SCIENTIFIC PUBLICATIONS AND PRESENTATIONS RELATING TO PLANETARY QUARANTINE. **Added/Corp** George Washington University. Medical Center. Science Communication Division. (19??)-. English. One time a year. George Washington University / Department of Medical and Public Affairs, Science Communications Division, 1343 H Street Northwest, Washington DC 20005.

LC TL787
DD 629.4   US
                     TITLE CHANGE
SPACE ABSTRACTS ON DISKETTE. (19??)-(19??). Abstracting/Indexing Service. English. Nova Science Publishers Inc., 6080 Jericho Turnpike, Suite 207, Commack NY 11725-2808. **Tel** (516)499-3103, (516)499-3106, FAX (516)499-3146. **Continues** Space Abstracts on Microfiche, 0895-6596. **Continued by** Journal of Space Abstracts and Research.

LC TL787
DD 629.4   US
                     TITLE CHANGE
SPACE ABSTRACTS ON MICROFICHE. (19??)-(19??). Abstracting/Indexing Service. English. Nova Science Publishers Inc., 6080 Jericho Turnpike, Suite 207, Commack NY 11725-2808. **Tel** (516)499-3103, (516)499-3106, FAX (516)499-3146. **Continues** Space Information Review, 0895-6596. **Continued by** Space Abstracts on Diskette.

LC TL   **ISSN** 0898-8242
DD 629   US
SSI UPDATE. See Aeronautics, Astronautics.

LC KF2422.5 .F43
DD 343/.73/0978   US
STATISTICAL SUMMARY : AIR CARRIER ENFORCEMENT CASES. **Main/Corp** United States. Federal Aviation Administration. Office of the General Counsel. **VFOAT** Air Carrier Enforcement Cases. Government Publication. English. One time a year. US Department of Transportation / Federal Aviation Administration, 800 Independence Avenue Southwest, Washington DC 20591. **Tel** (202)367-3484, FAX (202)367-3505.

LC HE9788.5.I4 S73
DD 382/.0954/005   II
STATISTICS OF THE AIR BORNE FOREIGN TRADE OF INDIA. English. Government of India, 214 Archaryа Jagadish Bose Road, Calcutta 70017 India.

LC HE9778 .W46A
DD 387.7/4/0212   FR
STATISTIQUES DE TRAFIC. **Main/Corp** Western European Airport Association. Multiple languages (English and French). Aeroports de Paris, Orly Sud 103, 94396 Orly, Aerogare Cedex France.

LC HE9842.A4   **ISSN** 0078-947X
DD 387.7   FR
STATISTIQUES DE TRAFIC : GRANDS AEROPORTS DE L'OUEST DE L'EUROPE. **Main/Corp** Aeroport de Paris. Service Statistique. 1951-. French. Western European Airport Association, 291 B D Raspazl, 75014 Paris France.

LC TL521 .U617   **ISSN** 0364-927X
DD 331.1/1   US
U.S. CIVIL AIRMEN STATISTICS. **VAT** United States Civil Airmen Statistics. (19??)-. English. One time a year. US Department of Transportation / Federal Aviation Administration, 800 Independence Avenue Southwest, Washington DC 20591. **Tel** (202)367-3484, FAX (202)367-3505. available on microfiche (Vols. for (1983-) distributed to depository libraries).

LC TL500
DD 629.13   US
U.S. INTERNATIONAL AIR TRAVEL STATISTICS (CALENDAR YEAR). (U.S. INTERNATIONAL AIR TRAVEL STATISTICS.). **VFOAT** US International Air Travel Statistics. **VAT** United States International Air Travel Statistics. (1979)-. English. Irregular. $275.00. DOT, Transportation Systems Center, Collection Officer, Kendall Square, Cambridge MA 02142. **Tel** (617)494-2450.
Desc: Number of U.S. citizens and aliens arriving and departing U.S. gateways on all international flights by world area and country.

LC HA37.Y8 A37
                                         YU
UTICAJ POPISIVACA NA REZULTATE PROBNOG ISTRAZIVANJA U SAP VOJVODINI ... GODINE = ENUMERATORS INFLUENCE ON PILOT INQUIRY RESULTS IN SAP VOJVODINA / SAVEZNI ZAVOD ZA STATISTIKU. **Added/Corp** Savezni Zavod za Statistiku (Yugoslavia). **VFOAT** Enumerators Influence on Pilot Inquiry Results in SAP Vojvodina. (19??)-. Serbo-Croatian (Roman). Irregular. 80.00Din. Savenzi Zavod za Statistiku, Kneza Milosa 20, Belgrad Yugoslavia.

COMPUTER APPLICATIONS

LC QA76.6 .D57   **ISSN** 1043-9935
DD 005.3/029/473   US
COSMIC SOFTWARE CATALOG. [COSMIC softw. cat.]. (19??)-. Catalog. English. One time a year. $25.00 US; $60.00 Canada and Mexico. COSMIC/The University of Georgia, 112 Barrow Hall, Athens GA 30602. **Tel** (706)542-3265, FAX (706)542-4807. **ED** Richard Saunders. Index available. **Circ:** 8,000. available on microfiche; available on an online database. **Continues** Directory of Computer Programs Available from Cosmic, 0090-9793.
Desc: Catalog describing 1,200 computer programs developed by the National Aeronautics and Space Administration, (NASA).

AGRICULTURE

LC S   **ISSN** 1182-9796
DD 630/.6/071271   CN
4-H NORTHERN NEWS. [4-H north. news]. **Added/Corp** Manitoba. 4-H Office. **VAT** Four-H Northern News. No. 1 (1990)-. English.

LC S   **ISSN** 0511-0726
DD 630   NE
A.A.G. BIJDRAGEN. [A.A.G. bydr.]. **Added/Corp** Landbouwhogeschool Wageningen. Afdeling Agrarische Geschiedenis. **VFOAT** AAG Bijdragen. **VAT** Afdeling Agrarische Geschiedenis Bijdragen. (1959)-. Monographic series. Dutch (English). Price varies per volume.
Ind/Abst Am. Hist. Life (1978-).

LC S   **ISSN** 0095-2486
DD 630   US
A.G.R. [AGR]. **Main/Corp** University of Kentucky. Agronomy Dept. **Added/Corp** University of Kentucky. Cooperative Extension Service. No. 1 (Feb. 1972)-. Monographic series. English. Irregular. Price varies per volume. University of Kentucky Department of Agricultural Economics, College of Agriculture, Lexington KY 40546. **Tel** (606)757-7273.
Ind/Abst AGRICOLA [Full Cov.].

LC S   **ISSN** 0183-7656
DD 630   FR
UDC 63
A.G.R.A. FRANCE. [A.G.R.A. Fr.]. **VFOAT** Agence Generale de Renseignements Agricoles et Alimentaires France. (1964)-. Periodical. French. One time a week. 5406.46F France; 5460.00F French overseas departments; 5800.00F other. Agra Presse, 29 rue du General Foy, 75008 Paris France. **Tel** 011 33 1 43871586. **Continues** AGRA Quotidien. Edition France, 0339-4425.

LC S21.R44 A18   **ISSN** 0092-1939
DD 630/.8   US
                     CODEN XAGSBY
A.R.S. S. AGRICULTURAL RESEARCH SERVICE. SOUTHERN REGION. (ARS-S.). [A.R.S. S. Agric. Res. Serv. South. Reg.]. **Main/Corp** United States. Agricultural Research Service. **VAT** Agricultural Research Service. Southern Region. Academic Scholarly Publication. English. Price varies per volume. US Department of Agriculture / Agricultural Research Service, 14th and Independence Avenue SW, Washington DC 20250. Documents available from CASDDS.
Ind/Abst Chem. Abstr.

LC S
DD 630   ET
AAASA NEWSLETTER. **Main/Corp** Association for the Advancement of Agricultural Sciences in Africa. (19??)-. Newsletter. English (French). Four times a year. $5.00 Africa; $6.00 other. AAASA, PO 30087-MA, Addis Ababa Ethiopia.

LC S **ISSN** 1037-8286
DD 630 AT
ABARE RESEARCH REPORT. Added/Corp Australian Bureau of Agricultural and Resource Economics. **VAT** Australian Bureau of Agricultural and Resource Economics Research Report. (1992)-. Monographic series. English. Irregular (15 to 20 per year). 180.06Aus$. ABARE / Australian Bureau of Agriculture and Resource Economics, GPO Box 1563, Canberra ACT 2601 Australia. **Tel** 011 61 6 2722000, FAX 011 61 6 2722001. ***Formed by the union of*** *Discussion Paper (Australian Bureau of Agricultural and Resource Economics), 1030-9527; Technical Paper (Australian Bureau of Agriculture and Resource Economics), 1035-767X; Submission to the ..., 1035-803X* ***and*** *Occasional Paper (Australian Bureau of Agricultural and Resource Economics).*

LC S **ISSN** 0373-4625
DD 630 FR
ABEILLE DE FRANCE ET L'APICULTEUR, L'. [Abeille Fr. apic.]. No. 528 (May 1970)-. Periodical. French. Eleven times a year (July/Aug. issues combined). 132.00F France; 190.00F other. Abeille de France, 5 rue Copenhague, F 75008 Paris France. **Tel** 011 33 1 45224842, FAX 011 33 1 42937785. **ED** Vedrenne Yves. **Bk Rev. Ad Acc, Adv Mgr:** Chong Wing. ***Formed by the union of*** *Apiculteur (Societe Centrale d'Apiculture)* ***and*** *Abeille de France,.*
Ind/Abst AGRICOLA; Sug. Indus. Abstr.

LC HD9502.A64 A25
DD 338.1 QA
ABRAJUNA. See Industry and Production.

LC SB192.G3 G46a
DD 633.1 GW
ABSCHLUSSBERICHT UEBER DIE BESONDERE ERNTEERMITTLUNG BEI GETREIDE UND KARTOFFELN. Main/Corp Germany (Federal Republic, 1949-). Bundesministerium fur Ernahrung, Landwirtschaft und Forsten. Abteilung 2, Planungskoordination und Wirtschaftsbeobachtung. Referat 221. **Added/Corp** Germany (West). Bundesministerium fur Ernahrung, Landwirtschaft und Forsten. Abteilung VI. Wirtschatsbeobachtung, Verbraucherangelegenheiten. Referat VI A 2. Germany (West). Bundesministerium fur Ernahrung, Landwirtschaft und Forsten. Abteilung 2, Planungskoordination und Wirtschaftsbeobachtung. Referat 221. Germany (West). Bundesministerium fur Ernahrung, Landwirtschaft und Forsten. Abteilung 2. Allgemeine Angelegenheiten der Agrarpolitik. Referat 212. **VFOAT** Besondere Ernteermittlung, Getreide, Kartoffeln; Besondere Ernteermittlung. (19??)-. English. One time a year.

LC S **ISSN** 0325-3902
DD 630 AG
ACAECER. Added/Corp Asociacion de Cooperativos Argentinas. (19??)-. Periodical. Spanish. Twelve times a year. Asociacion de Cooperativos Argentinos, Editorial Interior, 2000 Rosario Argentina.

LC SB203 **ISSN** 0814-4133
DD 633.3072094 AT
ACIAR FOOD LEGUME NEWSLETTER. [ACIAR food legume newsl.]. **Added/Corp** Australian Centre for International Agricultural Research. Food Legume Program. **VFOAT** Australian Centre for International Agricultural Research Food Legume Newsletter. (1984)-. Periodical. English. Two times a year. Australian Centre for International Agricultural Research, GPO Box 1571, Canberra ACT 2601 Australia. **Tel** 011 61 6 2488588.
Ind/Abst Field Crop Abstr.; Soils Fert.

LC S
DD 630 AT
ACIAR MONOGRAPH SERIES. [ACIAR monogr. ser.]. **Added/Corp** Australian Centre for International Agricultural Research. **VFOAT** Australian Centre for International Agricultural Research Monograph Series. (1986)-. Monographic series. English. Irregular. Price varies per volume. Australian Centre for International Agricultural Research, GPO Box 1571, Canberra ACT 2601 Australia. **Tel** 011 61 6 2488588.
Ind/Abst Agrofor. Abstr. (1991-); For. Prod. Abstr. (1991-); For. Abstr.; Grass. Forage Abstr.; Rev. Agric. Entomol.; Seed Abstr.

LC S **ISSN** 1038-6920
DD 630 AT
ACIAR PROCEEDINGS. [ACIAR proc.]. **VFOAT** Australian Center for International Agriculture Research Proceedings. (1985)-. English. Irregular. Australian Centre for International Agricultural Research, GPO Box 1571, Canberra ACT 2601 Australia. **Tel** 011 61 6 2488588. ***Continues*** *ACIAR Proceedings Series, 0816-4266.*
Ind/Abst Curr. Cit.; Rev. Agric. Entomol.

LC S
DD 630 AT
ACIAR TECHNICAL REPORTS. Added/Corp Australian Centre for International Agricultural Research. **VFOAT** A.C.I.A.R. Technical Reports. **VAT** Australian Centre for International Agricultural Research Technical Reports. (198?)-. Monographic series. English. Irregular. Price varies per volume. Australian Centre for International Agricultural Research, GPO Box 1571, Canberra ACT 2601 Australia. **Tel** 011 61 6 2488588.
Ind/Abst Agric. Eng. Abstr. (1991-); Rice Abstr.

LC SB51 **ISSN** 0816-7923
DD 630.72094 AT
ACIAR TECHNICAL REPORTS SERIES. [aACIAR tech. rep. ser.]. **Added/Corp** Australian Centre for International Agricultural Research. **VFOAT** Australian Centre for International Agricultural Research Technical Reports Series. (1985)-. Monographic series. English. Irregular. Australian Centre for International Agricultural Research, GPO Box 1571, Canberra ACT 2601 Australia. **Tel** 011 61 6 2488588.
Ind/Abst Hortic. Abstr.; Postharvest News Inf.; Potato Abstr.; Rice Abstr.; Weed Abstr.; World Agric. Econ. Rural Sociol. Abstr.

LC S **ISSN** 0819-7857
DD 630 AT
ACIAR WORKING PAPER. [ACIAR work. pap.]. **Added/Corp** Australian Centre for International Agricultural Research. **VFOAT** Australian Centre for International Agricultural Research Working Paper. (1987)-. English. Irregular. Australian Centre for International Agricultural Research, GPO Box 1571, Canberra ACT 2601 Australia. **Tel** 011 61 6 2488588.
Ind/Abst Hortic. Abstr.; Index Vet.; Plant Breed. Abstr.; Postharvest News Inf.; Rev. Agric. Entomol.; Rev. Plant Pathol.; World Agric. Econ. Rural Sociol. Abstr.

LC S
DD 630 CL
ACONEX. Added/Corp Exportadora Aconcagua Ltda. **VFOAT** ACONEX International. No. 1 (July/Aug./Sept. 1982)-. Periodical. Spanish (English). Four times a year (Mar., June, Sept., Dec.). $16.00. Aconex, N 16 Las Condes, Santiago Chile. **Tel** 011 56 2 2314627.

LC S451.5 **ISSN** 0712-2535
DD 630/.9714 CN
ACQ INFORME. [ACQ inf.]. **Added/Corp** Association des Cultivateurs du Quebec. **VAT** Association des Cultivateurs du Quebec Informe. Vol. 1, No. 1 (Feb. 1980)-. Periodical. French. Four times a year. Association des Cultivateurs du Quebec, 155 St. Thomas St. Elzear, Beauce Quebec G0S 2J0 Canada.

LC S
DD 630 US
ACRES, U.S.A. (1971)-. Periodical. English. Twelve times a year. $20.00. Acres U.S.A., PO Box 8800, Metairie LA 70011-8800. **Tel** (504)889-2100, FAX (504)889-2777. **ED** Charles Walters Jr. (phone: (816)737-0064). **Ad Acc. Circ:** 10,000. ***Continues*** *Fuel Alcohol U.S.A.*
Desc: A voice for eco-agriculture. Presents information needed to make agriculture ecological and more economical.

LC HD1491.U5 A654 **ISSN** 0277-8025
DD 334/.683/0973 US
ACS SERVICE REPORT. See Business and Economics-Cooperatives.

LC S **ISSN** 0860-2832
DD 630 PL
CODEN ATOAE5
ACTA ACADEMIAE AGRICULTURAE AC TECHNICAE OLSTENENSIS. AGRICULTURA. (AGRICULTURA.). [Acta Acad. Agricult. Techn. Olst., Agricult.]. **Added/Corp** Akademia Rolniczo-Techniczna w Olsztynie. (1985)-. Monographic series. Polish (English; summaries and/or abstracts in English and Russian). Irregular. Price varies per volume. Wydawnictwo Akademia Rolniczo-Techniczna w Olsztynie / Agricultural and Technical Academy in Olsztyn, Blok 21, 10-957 Olsztyn-Kortowo Poland. **Tel** 011 48 89 273310. **(Subscription address:** Ars Polona-Ruch, PO Box 1001, Krakowskie Przedmiescie 7, 00-068 Warsaw Poland. **Tel** 011 48 22 261201.) Documents available from CASDDS. ***Continues*** *Zeszyty Naukowe Akademii Rolniczo-Technicznej w Olsztynie. Rolnictwo.*
Ind/Abst Biocont. News Inf.; Chem. Abstr.; Hortic. Abstr.; Nutr. Abstr. Rev., Ser. B, Live Feeds and Feed.; Plant Breed. Abstr.; Plant Genet. Resour. Abstr.; Postharvest News Inf.; Potato Abstr.; Rev. Agric. Entomol.; Seed Abstr.; Soils Fert.; Weed Abstr.

LC S **ISSN** 0065-0919
DD 630 PL
ACTA AGRARIA ET SILVESTRIA. SERIES AGRARIA. [Acta agrar. silv., ser. agrar.]. (1966)-. Academic Scholarly Publication. Polish (summaries and/or abstracts in English and Russian; table of contents in English and Russian). Two times a year. **(Subscription address:** Ars Polona-Ruch, PO Box 1001, Krakowskie Przedmiescie 7, 00-068 Warsaw Poland. **Tel** 011 48 22 261201.) Documents available from BIOSIS Document Express. ***Continues*** *Acta Agraria et Silvestria. Seria Rolnicza.*
Ind/Abst Biol. Abstr.; EMBASE; Plant Breed. Abstr.; Plant Grow. Reg. Abstr.; Potato Abstr.

LC S11 .A183 **ISSN** 0065-0943
DD 630 SW
CODEN AASNAT
ACTA AGRICULTURAE SCANDINAVICA. SUPPLEMENTUM. [Acta agric. scand. Suppl.]. Vol. 1 (1957)-. Monographic series. English (Swedish). Price varies per volume. Munksgaard International Publishers Ltd, PO Box 2148, DK-1016 Copenhagen K Denmark. **Tel** 011 45 33 127030, FAX 011 45 33 129387, telex 19431 MUNKS DK. Documents available from BIOSIS Document Express, CASDDS.
Ind/Abst Biodeter. Abstr.; Biol. Abstr.; Chem. Abstr.; Life Sci. Collect.; Rev. Agric. Entomol.

LC S **ISSN** 0238-0161
DD 630 HU
CCC
CODEN AAHUEX
ACTA AGRONOMICA HUNGARICA. [Acta agron. Hung.]. **Added/Corp** Magyar Tudomanyos Akademia. Vol. 35, No. 1/2 (1986)-. Academic Scholarly Publication. English. Four times a year. $96.00. Akademiai Kiado, Publishing House of the Hungarian Academy of Sciences, Prielle Kornelia u. 19-35, H-1117 Budapest Hungary. **Tel** 011 36 1 1811991, FAX 011 36 1 1811991, telex 22-6228 AKNYO H. **ED** Istvan Tamassy and Akos Mathe (editorial address: Acta Agronomica, Menesi ut 44, H-1118 Budapest Hungary). Documents available from BIOSIS Document Express, CASDDS. ***Continues*** *Acta Agronomica Academiae Scientiarum Hungaricae, 0001-513X.*
Ind/Abst AgBiotech News Inf.; Anim. Breed. Abstr.; Biol. Abstr.; Chem. Abstr.; Cot. Trop. Fibr. Abstr. Bibliogr.; Crop Physiol. Abstr.; Dairy Sci. Abstr.; Field Crop Abstr.; Food Sci. Technol. Abstr.; Grass. Forage Abstr.; Hortic. Abstr.; Index Vet.; Irr. Drain. Abstr.; Maize Abstr.; Nutr. Abstr. Rev., Ser. B, Live Feeds and Feed.; Nutr. Abstr. Rev., Ser. A, Hum. Exp.; Pig News Inf.; Plant Breed. Abstr.; Plant Grow. Reg. Abstr.; Postharvest News Inf.; Potato Abstr.; Rev. Plant Pathol.; Rice Abstr.; Seed Abstr.; Soils Fert.; Sorghum Mill. Abstr.; Soyabean Abstr.; Vet. Bull.; Vitis Vitic. Enol. Abstr.; Weed Abstr.; Wheat Barley Trit. Abstr.

LC S **ISSN** 0044-5959
DD 630 CK
CODEN ACAGAY
ACTA AGRONOMICA (PALMIRA). (ACTA AGRONOMICA.). [Acta agron.]. **Added/Corp** Universidad Nacional de Colombia. Facultad de Ciencias Agropecuarias. Universidad Nacional de Colombia. Facultad de Agronomia. Vol. 1 (Dec. 1950)-. Periodical. Spanish (English). Four times a year. Facultad de Ciencias Agropecuarias / Palmira, Apdo 237, Palmira Colombia. **Tel** FAX 931-32477. Documents available from BIOSIS Document Express, CASDDS.
Ind/Abst Biol. Abstr.; Chem. Abstr.; Hortic. Abstr.; Maize Abstr.; Nutr. Abstr. Rev., Ser. B, Live Feeds and Feed.; Poult. Abstr.; Rev. Agric. Entomol.; Rice Abstr.; Seed Abstr.; Soils Fert.

LC S **ISSN** 0120-2812
DD 630 CK
ACTA AGRONOMICA (UNIVERSIDAD NACIONAL DE COLOMBIA. FACULTAD DE CIENCIAS AGROPECUARIAS). (ACTA AGRONOMICA.). **Added/Corp** Universidad Nacional de Colombia. Facultad de Ciencias Agropecuarias. (1971)-. Periodical. Spanish. Four times a year. Facultad de Ciencias Agropecuarias / Palmira, Apdo 237, Palmira Colombia. **Tel** FAX 931-32477. ***Continues*** *Acta Agronomica (Universidad Nacional de Colombia. Facultad de Agronomia), 0044-5959.*
Ind/Abst Biocont. News Inf.; Field Crop Abstr.; For. Abstr.; Nematol. Abstr.; Life Sci. Collect.; Pig News Inf.; Plant Breed. Abstr.; Poult. Abstr.

LC S **ISSN** 0567-7432
DD 630 XO
CODEN ACFYAB
ACTA FYTOTECHNICA. See Gardening and Horticulture.

LC S
DD 630 CS
ACTA PRUHONICIANA. Added/Corp Ceskoslovenska Akademie Zemedelskych Ved. Vyzkumny Ustav Okrasneho Zahradnictvi v Pruhonicich. Vol. 1 (1960)-. Monographic series. Czech (summaries and/or abstracts in English, German and Russian). Irregular. Price varies per volume. Research and Breeding Institute of Ornamental Gardening, Pruhonice 252 43.
Ind/Abst Agrofor. Abstr.; Biocont. News Inf.; For. Abstr.; Hortic. Abstr.; Ornamental Hort. (1991-); Plant Breed. Abstr.; Rev. Agric. Entomol.; Weed Abstr.

LC S
DD 630 XR
ACTA UNIVERSITATIS AGRICULTURAE FACULTAS AGROECONOMICA. Main/Corp Brunn. Vysoka Skola Zemedelska. Fakulta Provozne Ekonomicka. Vol. 3 (1967)-. Academic Scholarly Publication. Czech (English, German and Russian; summaries and/or abstracts in English, German and Russian; table of contents in English, German and Russian). Four times a year.

$20.00. Vysoka Skola Zemedelska, Zemedelska 1, 61300 Brno Czech Republic. **Tel** FAX 42 05 452 11128. **ED** Jan Hradilik. Index available. **Circ:** 400. available with charts. ***Continues*** *Brunn. Vysoka Skola Zemedelska. Fakulta Provozne Ekonomicka. Sborník Vysoke Skoly Zemedelske v Brne. Rada D. Spisy Fakulty Provozne Ekonomicke, 0524-7446.*
Ind/Abst Agric. Eng. Abstr. (1991-); Curr. Contents Agric. Biol. Environ. Sci.; Dairy Sci. Abstr.; Grass. Forage Abstr.; Hortic. Abstr.; Maize Abstr.; Nutr. Abstr. Rev., Ser. B, Live Feeds and Feed.; Postharvest News Inf.; Poult. Abstr.; Seed Abstr.; Soils Fert.; Sug. Indus. Abstr.

LC S17 **ISSN** 0524-7403
DD 630 XR
CODEN AUAAB7

ACTA UNIVERSITATIS AGRICULTURAE. FACULTAS AGRONOMICA. [Acta Univ. Agric., Fac. agron.]. **Main/Corp** Vysoka Skola Zemedelska v Brne. Fakulta Agronomicka. **VFOAT** Sbornik Vysoka Skoly Zemedelske v Brne; Facultas Agronomica; Spisy Fakulty Agronomicke; Sbornik Selskokhoziaistvennogo Instituta G. Brno; Publications of the University of Agriculture in Brno; Mitteilungen der Hochschule fur Landwirtschaft Brno; Travaux de l'Universite d'Agriculture Brno. Vol. 15 (1967)-. Academic Scholarly Publication. Czech (English, German and Russian; summaries and/or abstracts in English, German and Russian; table of contents in English). Four times a year. Vysoka Skola Zemedelska, Zemedelska 1, 61300 Brno Czech Republic. **Tel** FAX 42 05 452 11128. Documents available from CASDDS. ***Continues*** *Vysoka Skola Zemedelska v Brne. Fakulta Agronomicka. Sbornik Vysoke Skoly Zemedelske v Brne. Rada A. Spisy Fakulty Agronomicke, 0524-7403.*
Desc: Covers agriculture and agricultural research.
Ind/Abst Chem. Abstr.; Crop Physiol. Abstr.; EMBASE; Field Crop Abstr.; For. Prod. Abstr.; For. Abstr.; Helminthol. Abstr.; Hortic. Abstr.; Index Vet.; Irr. Drain. Abstr.; Maize Abstr.; Nutr. Abstr. Rev., Ser. B, Live Feeds and Feed.; Ornamental Hort. (1991-); Plant Breed. Abstr.; Plant Grow. Reg. Abstr.; Postharvest News Inf.; Potato Abstr.; Soils Fert.; Weed Abstr.; Wheat Barley Trit. Abstr.

LC SF **ISSN** 0851-0466
DD 636 MR
CODEN AIAHEF

ACTES DE L'INSTITUT AGRONOMIQUE ET VETERINAIRE HASSAN II. [Actes Inst. agron. vet. Hassan II]. **Added/Corp** Institut Agronomique et Veterinaire Hassan II. **VFOAT** Abhat Mahad Al-Hassan Al-Thani Li-Al-Ziraah Wa-Al-Baytarah. (1980)-. Periodical. French (English; summaries and/or abstracts in French and English). Four times a year. $40.00 (individuals); $200.00 (institutions). Institute Agron Veterinaire Hassan, BP 6202 Rabat Instituts, Rabat Morocco. **Tel** 011 212 7 74351.
Ind/Abst Anim. Breed. Abstr.; Biodeter. Abstr. (1991-); For. Prod. Abstr. (1991-); Hortic. Abstr.; Nutr. Abstr. Rev., Ser. B, Live Feeds and Feed.; Nutr. Abstr. Rev., Ser. A, Hum. Exp.; Plant Breed. Abstr.; Rev. Agric. Entomol.; Soils Fert.; Wheat Barley Trit. Abstr.

LC S
DD 630 FR

ACTES ET COMMUNICATIONS. **Added/Corp** Institut National de la Recherche Agronomique (France). Departement d'Economie et de Sociologie Rurales. (198?)-. Monographic series. French.
Ind/Abst Maize Abstr.; Plant Breed. Abstr.; Rev. Plant Pathol.; Weed Abstr.; Wheat Barley Trit. Abstr.

LC S540.8.C44 A28 **ISSN** 0304-2529
DD 630/.9728 CR
CEASED

ACTIVIDADES EN TURRIALBA. **Added/Corp** Centro Agronomico Tropical de Investigacion y Ensenanza. **VFOAT** CATIE, Actividades en Turrialba. (19??-19??). Periodical. Spanish. CATIE, Turrialba 7170, Costa Rica.
Ind/Abst Agrofor. Abstr. (19??-19??); For. Abstr.

LC S
DD 630 SP

ACTUALIDAD TABAQUERA. (19??)-. Spanish. Twelve times a year. $30.00. Tabapress Sa Banco de Urquijo, CC 01 8623199 01 2 Alcala 47, Madrid 14 Spain.

LC S **ISSN** 0181-0979
DD 630 FR

ACTUALITES SCIENTIFIQUES ET AGRONOMIQUES DE L'I.N.R.A. [Actual. sci. agron. I.N.R.A.]. 1-. Monographic series. French. Irregular. Price varies per volume. CCLS, BP 22, 41353 Vineuil France. **Tel** 011 33 54 787741.

LC S **ISSN** 0764-8650
DD 630 FR
UDC 664

ACTUALITES SCIENTIFIQUES ET TECHNIQUES DANS LES INDUSTRIES AGRO-ALIMENTAIRES. **VFOAT** Actualites Scientifiques des Industries Utilisatrices de Produits Agricoles. (1981)-. Monographic series. French.
Ind/Abst Dairy Sci. Abstr.; Sug. Indus. Abstr.

LC S **ISSN** 0980-0611
DD 630 FR
UDC 634

ADALIA. [Adalia]. (1986)-. Periodical. French. Four times a year. 120.00F France; 150.00F other. Rhodiagri Littorale, 13 Parc Club Mill, 34036 Montpellier Cedex 1 France. **Tel** 011 33 67 697600.

LC J2 **ISSN** 0835-2305
DD 354.71240082/33042 CN
CODEN ADFNEN

ADF NEWS. (ADF NEWS : AGRICULTURE DEVELOPMENT FUND NEWSLETTER.). [ADF news]. **Added/Corp** Agriculture Development Fund (Sask.). **VAT** Agriculture Development Fund News. (Dec. 1986)-. Newsletter. English. Twelve times a year. ***Continues*** *Research & Development Newsletter, 0844-9759.*
Ind/Abst Foods Adlibra.

LC S **ISSN** 0172-4207
DD 630 US

ADVANCED SERIES IN AGRICULTURAL SCIENCES. (1975)-. Monographic series. English. Irregular. Price varies per volume. Springer-Verlag New York Inc., 175 Fifth Avenue, New York NY 10010. **Tel** (212)460-1500 ext 256, FAX (212)533-3503, telex 232 235 SPB UR. **(Subscription address:** Springer-Verlag New York Inc. / North America, PO Box 2485, Journal Fulfillment, Secaucus NJ 07096. **Tel** (201)348-4033, (800)777-4643, FAX (201)348-4505.**)** **ED** B. Yaron, H. Van Keulen, G.W. Thomas, L.D. Van Vleck.
Ind/Abst Math. Rev.

LC S405 .A24 **ISSN** 0065-2113
DD 630.72 US
CCC
CODEN ADAGA7

ADVANCES IN AGRONOMY. [Adv. agron.]. **Added/Corp** American Society of Agronomy. Vol. 1 (1949)-. Monographic series. English. Irregular. Price varies per volume. Academic Press Inc., 6277 Sea Harbor Drive, Orlando FL 32887. **Tel** (800)543-9534, (407)345-4100, FAX (407)352-3445. Documents available from The Genuine Article, BIOSIS Document Express, CASDDS.
Ind/Abst AgBiotech News Inf.; AGRICOLA [Full Cov.]; Agrofor. Abstr. (1991-); Biol. Agric. Index; Biol. Abstr.; Chem. Abstr.; Field Crop Abstr.; For. Abstr.; GeoRef; Grass. Forage Abstr.; Hortic. Abstr.; Index Sci. Rev. [Full Cov.]; Life Sci. Collect.; Plant Breed. Abstr.; Res. Alert [Full Cov.]; Rev. Agric. Entomol.; Rev. Plant Pathol.; Rice Abstr.; Sci. Cit. Index; SCISEARCH; Seed Abstr.; Soils Fert.; Sorghum Mill. Abstr.; Weed Abstr.; Wheat Barley Trit. Abstr.; World Agric. Econ. Rural Sociol. Abstr.

LC HB **ISSN** 1068-4883
DD 338 US

ADVANCES IN STRAWBERRY RESEARCH. [Adv. strawb. res.]. **Added/Corp** North American Strawberry Growers Association. Vol. 11 (1992)-. English. One time a year (July). $45.00. North America Strawberry Growers Association, PO Box 160, West Paducah KY 42086. **Tel** (502)488-2116. ***Continues*** *Advances in Strawberry Production, 0732-3506.*
Desc: Provides growers with information in the area of strawberry research.

LC S **ISSN** 1036-0867
DD 630 AT

ADVISORY BULLETIN. **Added/Corp** NSW Agriculture & Fisheries. No. 1 (1991)-. Bulletin. English. New South Wales Agriculture & Fisheries / Division of Rural and Resource Economics, PO Box K220, Haymarket New South Wales 20000 Australia. **Tel** 011 61 2 2175166, FAX 011 61 2 2175156. ***Formed by the union of*** *Advisory Note* ***and*** *Advisory Bulletin.*

LC SF **ISSN** 0561-0095
DD 636 US

AE (SOUTH CAROLINA CROP AND LIVESTOCK REPORTING SERVICE). (AE.). [AE]. **Added/Corp** South Carolina Crop and Livestock Reporting Service. South Carolina Agricultural Experiment Station. Dept. of Agricultural Economics and Rural Sociology. **VFOAT** A.E. **VAT** Agricultural Economics. (1951)-. Monographic series. English.
Ind/Abst AGRICOLA [Full Cov.].

LC S **ISSN** 0832-8773
DD 630 CN

AEB, AGRICULTURAL ECONOMICS AND BUSINESS. (AEB.). [AEB, Agric. Econ. Bus.]. **Added/Corp** Ontario Agricultural College. Dept. of Agricultural Economics and Business. **VFOAT** Ontario Farm Management Analysis Project. **VAT** Agricultural Economics and Business. Vol. 1, Sept. (1985)-. Monographic series. English. Price varies per volume. University of Guelph / Agricultural College, Ontario Agricultural College, Guelph Ontario N7G 2W1 Canada. ***Continues*** *AEEE.*
Ind/Abst Poult. Abstr.

LC S451.5 **ISSN** 0845-5007
DD 630/.97123 CN

AF&R, ALBERTA FARM & RANCH MAGAZINE. [AF&R, Alta. farm ranch mag.]. **VFOAT** Alberta Farm & Ranch. **VAT** Alberta Farm & Ranch Magazine. Vol. 7, No. 2 (Feb. 1989)-. Periodical. English. Twelve times a year. 16.01Can$. North Hill News Inc., 4000-19 Street Northeast, Calgary Alberta T2E 6P8, Canada. **Tel** (403)520-6633, FAX (403)291-0502. ***Continues*** *Alberta FARMagazine., 0833-4463.*

LC S
DD 630 US

AFPC POLICY RESEARCH REPORT. **Added/Corp** Agricultural and Food Policy Center (Tex.). **VFOAT** Policy Research Report. **VAT** Agricultural and Food Policy Center Policy Research Report. (1989)-. Monographic series. English. Price varies per volume. Prentice-Hall General Reference and Travel, 200 Old Tappan Road, Old Tappan NJ 07675. **Tel** (800)922-0579. ***Continues in part*** *AFPC Staff Report.*
Ind/Abst World Agric. Econ. Rural Sociol. Abstr.

LC HB **ISSN** 1053-1653
DD 338 US

AFPC POLICY WORKING PAPER. [AFPC policy work. pap.]. **Added/Corp** Agricultural and Food Policy Center (Tex.). **VFOAT** AFPC Working Paper; AFPC Policy Center Working Paper; Policy Working Paper. **VAT** Agricultural and Food Policy Center Policy Working Paper; Agricultural and Food Policy Center Working Paper; Agricultural and Food Policy Center Policy Center Working Paper. 89-1 (April 1989)-. Monographic series. English. Agricultural and Food Policy Center, Department of Agricultural Economics, Texas Agricultural Experiment Station, Texas Agricultural Extension Service, Texas A&M University, College Station TX 77843. ***Continues in part*** *AFPC Staff Report.*
Ind/Abst AGRICOLA [Full Cov.]; Dairy Sci. Abstr.; Maize Abstr.; Soyabean Abstr.; World Agric. Econ. Rural Sociol. Abstr.

LC S **ISSN** 0267-8489
DD 630 UK

AFRC NEWS. **Added/Corp** Agricultural and Food Research Council (Great Britain). **VAT** Agricultural and Food Research Council News. (1983)-. Periodical. English. Three times a year. Agricultural and Food Research Council / Swindon, England, Wiltshire Court, Farnsby Street, Swindon SN1 5AT United Kingdom. **Tel** 011 44 1628 823631, FAX 011 44 1628 823630. Documents available from Documents on Demand. ***Continues*** *ARC News (Agricultural Research Council (Great Britain)), 0140-539X.*
Desc: Information on agricultural biotechnology.
Ind/Abst AgBiotech News Inf.; Anim. Breed. Abstr.; Dairy Sci. Abstr.; Environ. Abstr.; Index Vet.; Nematol. Abstr.; Nutr. Abstr. Rev., Ser. B, Live Feeds and Feed.; Pig News Inf.; Poult. Abstr.

LC HF46 .A25 SUPPL.
DD 338.1/096 UK

AFRICA AGRICULTURE. Issue No. 1-. Periodical. English. One time a year. £1.00. Africa Journal Ltd, Kirkman House, 54A Tottenham Court Road, London W1P 0BT United Kingdom. **Tel** 011 44 171 6379341, telex 8952670.

LC S **ISSN** 1053-8623
DD 630 US

AFRICAN FARMER (ENGLISH ED.). (AFRICAN FARMER : THE KEY TO AFRICA'S FUTURE.). [Afr. farmer]. **Added/Corp** Hunger Project. No. 1 (1988)-. Periodical. English. Four times a year. Free in Africa; $5.00 other. The Hunger Project, One Madison Avenue, New York NY 10010. **Tel** (212)532-4255.
Ind/Abst Geogr. Abstr. Human Geogr.; Int. Dev. Abstr.

LC TP368
DD 664 UK

AFRICAN FARMING AND FOOD PROCESSING. (Jan./Feb. 1984)-. Periodical. English. Six times a year. $75.00. Alain Charles Publishing Ltd., 27 Wilfred Street, London SW1E 6PR United Kingdom. **Tel** 011 44 171 8347676, FAX 011 44 171 9730076, telex 297165. **ED** Jonquil Phelan. **Ad Acc. Circ:** 8,000 (ctrl). ***Continues*** *West African Farming and Food Processing.*
Desc: Covers agriculture and food processing related to Africa.
Ind/Abst Dairy Sci. Abstr.; Food Sci. Technol. Abstr.; Helminthol. Abstr.; Index Vet.; Maize Abstr.; Nutr. Abstr. Rev., Ser. B, Live Feeds and Feed.; Poult. Abstr.; Rice Abstr.; Wheat Barley Trit. Abstr.

LC S401 .A84a **ISSN** 0253-5955
DD 630/.96 ET
CODEN AFJADH

AFRICAN JOURNAL OF AGRICULTURAL SCIENCES. [Afr. j. agric. sci.]. **Added/Corp** Association for the Advancement of Agricultural Sciences in Africa. Vol. 5, No. 1 (Jan. 1978)-. Academic Scholarly Publication. English (French). Two times a year (Jan., July). AAASA, PO 30087-MA, Addis Ababa Ethiopia. Documents available from CASDDS. ***Continues*** *Journal of the Association for the Advancement of Agricultural Sciences in Africa.*
Ind/Abst Anim. Breed. Abstr.; Chem. Abstr.; Dairy Sci. Abstr.; Field Crop Abstr.; Grass. Forage Abstr.; Hortic. Abstr.; Maize Abstr.; Nutr. Abstr. Rev., Ser. B, Live Feeds and Feed.; Nutr. Abstr. Rev., Ser. A, Hum. Exp.; Pig News

Inf.; Rev. Agric. Entomol.; Rev. Plant Pathol.; Rice Abstr.; Rural Dev. Abstr.; Seed Abstr.; Soils Fert.; World Agric. Econ. Rural Sociol. Abstr.

LC SD411 **ISSN** 1022-0119
DD 333.76 SA

●**AFRICAN JOURNAL OF RANGE & FORAGE SCIENCE.** **Added/Corp** Grassland Society of Southern Africa. **VFOAT** African Journal of Range and Forage Science; Afr j Range for Sci. Vol. 10, No. 1 (Apr. 1993)-. Periodical. English. Three times a year. $75.00. Science Africa, PO Box 40221, Arcadia 0007 South Africa. **Tel** 011 27 12 3486660. **(Subscription address:** Grasslands Society of Southern Africa, PO Box 100327, Scottsville 3209 Rep South Africa. **)** **Circ:** 800 (ctrl). Documents available from BIOSIS Document Express. ***Continues*** *Journal of the Grassland Society of Southern Africa, 0256-6702.*
Ind/Abst Agrofor. Abstr. (19??-19??); Biol. Abstr.; Crop Physiol. Abstr.; For. Abstr.; Grass. Forage Abstr.; Irr. Drain. Abstr.; Nutr. Abstr. Rev., Ser. B, Live Feeds and Feed.; Plant Breed. Abstr.; Plant Genet. Resour. Abstr.; Plant Grow. Reg. Abstr.; Soils Fert.

LC S **ISSN** 0337-9515
DD 630 FR

AFRIQUE AGRICULTURE. [Afr. agric.]. No. 1 (Sept. 1975)-. Periodical. French. Eleven times a year. $108.27. Globaledit, 6 rue du Docteur Solomon, 60119 Henonville France. **Tel** 011 33 44 498387. **ED** B. Catrisse. Index available. **Bk Rev**. **Ad Acc**. **Circ:** 8,950. available on audiocassette; available on videocassette.
Desc: Magazine concerned with the development of agriculture in Africa.
Ind/Abst Leis., Rec., Tour. Abstr.; Rural Dev. Abstr.; Soils Fert.; World Agric. Econ. Rural Sociol. Abstr.

LC S
DD 630 US

AFSIC NOTES. **Added/Corp** Alternative Farming Systems Information Center (U.S.). **VAT** Alternative Farming Systems Information Center Notes. No. 1 (1991)-. Monographic series. English. Free. National Agricultural Library, 10301 Baltimore Boulevard, Beltsville MD 20705.

LC S **ISSN** 0161-5408
DD 630 US

AG ALERT. **Added/Corp** California Farm Bureau Federation. (1974)-. Periodical. English. Forty-eight times a year (weekly except 2 issues in July and Dec.). California Farm Bureau Federation, 1601 Exposition Boulevard, Sacramento CA 95815. **Tel** (916)924-4140. **ED** Steve Adler. **Bk Rev**. **Ad Acc**. **Circ:** 51,316 (ctrl).
Desc: Agriculture newsletter concerned with the business of farming. Edited for commercial farmers.

LC S
DD 630 CN

AG-ALERT (LONDON, ONT.). (AG-ALERT.). **VFOAT** Agriculture Alert. (1982)-. English. Twelve times a year. 184.07Can$. Deputter Publishing Ltd, 190 Wortley Road, Suite 200, London Ontario N6C 4Y7 Canada. **Tel** (519)663-2224, FAX (519)663-9124. **ED** John DePutter. **Circ:** 500 (ctrl).
Desc: Provides agricultural commodity market information for farmers and agricultural companies.

LC HD9660.P3 A37 **ISSN** 1072-7361
DD 632 US

AG CHEM NEW COMPOUND REVIEW. [Ag chem new compd. rev.]. Vol. 10 (1992)-. English. One time a year (Apr.). $350.00. Agricultural Chemical Information Service, 6705 East 71st Street, Indianapolis IN 46220. **Tel** (317)842-1959, FAX (317)841-1210. ***Continues*** *Ag Chem New Product Review.*

LC S583 **ISSN** 0894-7155
DD 631 US
CCC

AG CONSULTANT. [Ag consult.]. **VFOAT** Ag Consultant and Fieldman. (1986)-. Trade Publication. English. Eight times a year. $24.00. Meister Publishing Company, 37733 Euclid Avenue, Willoughby OH 44094-5992. **Tel** (216)942-2000, (800)572-7740, FAX (216)942-0662. available on microfilm and microfiche from University Microfilms International (UMI). ***Continues*** *AG Consultant and Fieldman, 0199-6460.*
Desc: Focuses on providing crop consultants with information on environmental stewardship, new products and production approaches, and developments in precision application.
Ind/Abst Bibliogr. Agric. (1986-).

LC S **ISSN** 0196-0857
DD 630 US
UDC 338.43

AG IMPACT. [Ag impact]. Vol. 1 (1974)-. Periodical. English. Twelve times a year. Agricultural Division of Co-Op NY 14411. **Tel** (716)589-5561. **Ad Acc**. ctrl circ.
Ind/Abst AGRICOLA [Full Cov.].

LC S583 **ISSN** 1074-1186
DD 631 US

●**AG/INNOVATOR (LINN GROVE, IOWA).** (AG/INNOVATOR.). [Ag/innovator]. **Added/Corp** Agricultural Information Management Network. **VFOAT** Ag Innovator. (1993)-. Periodical. English. Twelve times a year. $48.00. Agri-Info Management Network, 7014 Highway C-13, Linn Grove IA 51033. **Tel** (712)296-3615, (800)564-4005.

LC S **ISSN** 0744-1452
DD 630 US

AG. MARKET CHARTS. [Ag. mark. charts]. **Added/Corp** Ag. Marketing Services, Inc. **VFOAT** Agricultural Market Charts. (19??)-. Periodical. English. One time a week. $220.00. Phi Marketing Services Inc., PO Box 1176, Mankato MN 56001. **Tel** (507)625-1241. ***Continues*** *Farm Market Charts, 0195-220X.*

LC HD9483.U5 F48 **ISSN** 1072-9267
DD 338.4/766862/0973 US

●**AG RETAILER.** [Ag retail.]. **Added/Corp** Agricultural Retailers Association. **VFOAT** Ag Retailer Magazine. Vol. 37, No. 6 (Oct. 1993)-. Periodical. English. Six times a year. $35.00. Ag Retailer, 11701 Borman Dr., St Louis MO 63146. ***Continues*** *Solutions, 0199-9869.*
Ind/Abst Bibliogr. Agric.

LC S **ISSN** 0194-6625
DD 630 US

AG. REVIEW (PUTNAM, CONN.). (AG. REVIEW.). [Ag. rev.]. **Added/Corp** Farm Resource Center (Putnam, Conn.). **VFOAT** AgReview. **VAT** Agricultural Review. (19??)-. Periodical. English. Twelve times a year. Farm Resource Center, 16 Grove Street, Putnam CT 06260. **Tel** (203)928-7778. **ED** Lucien Laliberty Jr. **Ad Acc**. **Circ:** 45,000 (ctrl).
Desc: New information, technology, practices and products for commercial farms. Serves dairy, beef, field and cash crop operations.

LC S **ISSN** 8756-7733
DD 630 US
TITLE CHANGE

AGACCESS. [AgAccess]. **VFOAT** AG Access. Vol. 5 No. 1 (Jan/Feb 1985)-(Aug. 1993). Periodical. English. Agaccess, PO Box 2008, Davis CA 95617. **Tel** (916)756-7177, FAX (916)756-7177. **ED** David Katz and Karen Van Epen. **Bk Rev**. **Circ:** 150,000. ***Continues*** *Agricultural Books Magazine.* ***Continued by*** *Agricultural Books & Information.*

LC S **ISSN** 1066-0569
DD 630 US

AGBIOTECH STOCK LETTER. **See** Biology-Bioengineering.

LC HB **ISSN** 8756-243X
DD 338 US

AGCHEMPRICE. [Agchemprice]. **Added/Corp** AgMarket Research, Inc. **VFOAT** AG Chem Price. (1984)-. Periodical. English. Three times a year. $395.00. DPRA Incorporated, PO Box 727, Manhattan KS 66502. **Tel** (913)539-3565, FAX (913)539-5353. **ED** Ben Y. Mason. available on diskette (from IBM PC compatible).

LC HD9001 .A86 **ISSN** 1047-4781
DD 382/.41/097305 US
CODEN AGEXEZ

AGEXPORTER (WASHINGTON, D.C.). (AGEXPORTER.). [AgExporter]. **Added/Corp** United States. Foreign Agricultural Service. **VFOAT** Ag Exporter. Vol. 1, No. 1 (Jan. 1989)-. Government Publication. English. Twelve times a year. $28.00. US Department of Agriculture, 14th Street and Independence Avenue SW, Washington DC 20250. **Tel** (202)720-5457. **(Subscription address:** Superintendent of Documents, US Government Printing Office, Washington DC 20402 **)** Index available in last issue of volume--attached. available on an online database (file 648/Full-Text) from DIALOG. ***Continues*** *Foreign Agriculture (Washington, D.C. : 1963), 0015-7163.*
Desc: Targeted at business firms selling United States farm products overseas. Provides timely information on overseas trade opportunities, including reports on marketing activities and how-to's of agricultural exporting.
Ind/Abst AGRICOLA [Full Cov.]; BioBusiness; Biol. Agric. Index; Dairy Sci. Abstr.; Foods Adlibra; Geogr. Abstr. Human Geogr.; Pig News Inf.; Soyabean Abstr.; Trade Ind. ASAP [Full Txt.]; Trade Ind. Index [Full Txt.]; Wheat Barley Trit. Abstr.; World Agric. Econ. Rural Sociol. Abstr.

LC S **ISSN** 0725-7759
DD 630 AT

AGFACTS. **Added/Corp** New South Wales. Dept. of Agriculture. (19??)-. Periodical. English. Twelve times a year. 41.11Aus$. New South Wales Department of Agriculture & Fisheries, Division of Agriculture Services, PMB 21, Orange S NSW 2800 Australia. **Tel** 011 61 63 913100, FAX 011 61 63 629059.
Desc: A guide to farming in a small way. Covers many topics and issues in the business of farming, rural environment, farming basics, pastures and crops, fruit and nuts, larger and smaller farm animals and pests and diseases.
Ind/Abst Cot. Trop. Fibr. Abstr. Bibliogr.; Maize Abstr.

LC S **ISSN** 0899-7535
DD 630 US

AGFOCUS (MIDDLETOWN, N.Y.). (AGROFUCUS : A PUBLICATION OF CORNELL COOPERATIVE EXTENSION-ORANGE COUNTY.). [Agfocus]. **Added/Corp** Cornell University. Cooperative Extension. Orange County Agriculture Program. **VFOAT** Ag Focus. (June 1988)-. Periodical. English. Twelve times a year. $10.00 Comes with Orange County Cooperative Extension Agricultural Division membership. Cornell Cooperative Extension Orange County Agriculture, Program Education Center, 239 Wisner Avenue, Middleton NY 10940. **Tel** (914)343-1105. ***Continues*** *Orange County Extension News, 0891-6233.*

LC S **ISSN** 0339-4409
DD 630 FR
UDC 63

AGRA ALIMENTATION. [AGRA aliment.]. **VFOAT** Agence Generale d'Informations Agricoles et Alimentaires. (1964)-. Periodical. French. Forty-Five times a year. $1718.66. Agra Alimentation, 29 rue du General Foy, 75008 Paris France. **Tel** 011 33 1 43871593.
Ind/Abst Infomat Int. Bus.

LC HD1428 **ISSN** 0266-3570
DD 338.181 UK

AGRA-BRIEFING. [Agra-brief.]. (1984)-. English. Irregular. Price varies per volume. Agra Europe London Limited, 25 Frant Road, Tunbridge Wells, Kent TN2 5JT United Kingdom. **Tel** 011 44 1892 533813, FAX 011 44 1892 544895, telex 95114 AGRATW G.
Ind/Abst World Agric. Econ. Rural Sociol. Abstr.

LC S **ISSN** 0141-2221
DD 630 UK

AGRA EUROPE. POTATO MARKETS. [Agra Eur. Potato mark.]. **VFOAT** Potato Markets. (1976)-. Trade Publication. English. One time a week. £675.00 UK; £750.00 other. Agra Europe London Limited, 25 Frant Road, Tunbridge Wells, Kent TN2 5JT United Kingdom. **Tel** 011 44 1892 533813, FAX 011 44 1892 544895, telex 95114 AGRATW G. available on an online database from DIALOG.
Desc: Written for traders on the futures market. Production, price, and marked information from Europe, North America and other significant potato countries.
Ind/Abst F&S Index Plus Text, Int. [Full Txt.] [Select. Cov.]; PTS Newsl. Database.

LC HD9275.E86 **ISSN** 0142-422X
DD 338 UK

AGRA EUROPE SPECIAL REPORT. [Agra Eur. spec. rep.]. (1978)-. Monographic series. English. Irregular. Price varies per volume. Agra Europe London Limited, 25 Frant Road, Tunbridge Wells, Kent TN2 5JT United Kingdom. **Tel** 011 44 1892 533813, FAX 011 44 1892 544895, telex 95114 AGRATW G.
Ind/Abst Curr. Cit.; World Agric. Econ. Rural Sociol. Abstr.

LC S
DD 630 IT

AGRA PRESS. (19??)-. Italian. Coop Outsider, Via IN Lucina 15, 00186 Rome Italy. **Tel** 011 39 6 6871185, 011 39 6 6893000.

LC S **ISSN** 0568-2339
DD 630 II

AGRA UNIVERSITY JOURNAL OF RESEARCH. LETTERS. **Main/Corp** Agra University. **Added/Corp** Agra University. Journal of Research. Letters. **VFOAT** Journal of Research. Letters. Vol. 1 (Nov. 1952)-. Periodical. English. Two times a year. Agra University / Journal of Research Science, Agra 282004 Uttar Pradesh India.
Ind/Abst Ceram. Abstr. (19??-).

LC S **ISSN** 0167-3246
DD 630 NE
UDC 631.1 :666.97

AGRABETON HERTOGENBOSCH. (AGRABETON.). [Agrabeton-Hertogenbosch]. (1972)-. Periodical. Dutch. Three times a year (Apr., Sept., Dec.). Free on request. Vereniging Nederlandse Cemntin, Postbus 3011, 5203 Da Den Bosch Netherlands. **Tel** 011 31 73 401150.
Ind/Abst Agric. Eng. Abstr.

LC S
DD 630 UK

AGRAFILE. (19??)-. English. Twelve times a year. £110.00 UK; £116.00 Europe; £119.00 other. Agra Europe London Limited, 25 Frant Road, Tunbridge Wells, Kent TN2 5JT United Kingdom. **Tel** 011 44 1892 533813, FAX 011 44 1892 544895, telex 95114 AGRATW G. **ED** Guy Faulkner.
Desc: Monthly overview of the current market situation with selected information.

LC SF101 **ISSN** 0950-4958
DD 636.0883 UK

AGRAFILE. LIVESTOCK & MEAT. [Agrafile, Livest. meat]. **VFOAT** Livestock & Meat. (1986)-. English. Irregular. £220.00 UK; £250.00 other. Agra Europe London Limited, 25 Frant Road, Tunbridge Wells, Kent TN2 5JT United Kingdom. **Tel** 011 44 1892 533813, FAX 011 44 1892 544895, telex 95114 AGRATW G.

LC HD **ISSN** 1354-4128
DD 338.195 UK

●**AGRAFOOD ASIA.** [AgraFood Asia]. **Added/Corp** Agra Europe. (1994)-. English. Twelve times a year. $718.71. Agra Europe London Limited, 25 Frant Road,

Agriculture

Tunbridge Wells, Kent TN2 5JT United Kingdom. **Tel** 011 44 1892 533813, **FAX** 011 44 1892 544895, telex 95114 AGRATW G.

LC S
DD 630 GW
AGRAR- UND UMWELTFORSCHUNG IN BADEN-WURTTEMBERG. Added/Corp Baden-Wurttemberg (Germany). Ministerium fur Ernahrung, Landwirtschaft, Umwelt und Forsten. (1982)-. Monographic series. German. Price varies per volume. Verlag Eugen Ulmer, Postfach 700561, D-70574 Stuttgart Germany. **Tel** 011 49 711 4507108, **FAX** 011 49 711 4507120, telex 7-23634. Documents available from CASDDS.
Ind/Abst Chem. Abstr.

LC HA1320.N6 A32 HD1960.N67
DD 314.3 GW
AGRARBERICHTERSTATTUNG NORDRHEIN-WESTFALEN. VIEHHALTUNG UND BODENNUTZUNG DER LANDWIRTSCHAFTLICHEN BETRIEBE. VFOAT Viehhaltung und Bodennutzung der Landwirtschaftlichen Betriebe. (1981)-. German. DM21.00. Landesamt fuer Datenverarbeitung und Statistik Nordrhein-Westfalen, Postfach 101105, 40002 Duesseldorf Germany. **Tel** (0211)944901, **FAX** (0211)442006, telex 8586654 LDST D.

LC S ISSN 1022-663X
DD 630 SZ
AGRARFORSCHUNG BERN. (19??)-. German. Eleven times a year. $54.69. Eidgen Forschungsanst Viehwirt Produktion, Monika Boltshauser, CH-1725 Posieux Switzerland. **Tel** 011 44 37 877221. **Continues** Landwirtschaft Schweiz.

LC K16 .A25 ISSN 0167-4242
DD 343 NE
AGRARISCH RECHT. See Law.

LC S ISSN 0002-1075
DD 630 NE
AGRARISCH WEEKOVERZICHT. Main/Corp Landbouw-Economisch Instituut. Afdeling Statistiek. **Added/Corp** Landbouw-Economisch Instituut (Netherlands). Afdeling Statistiek. Landbouw-Economisch Instituut (Netherlands). Afdeling Algemeen Economisch Onderzoek en Statistiek. Sectie Prijzenstatistiek. (19??)-. Periodical. Dutch. One time a week. Fl.87.50. Landbouw-Economisch Instituut, Postbus 29703, 2502 LS Hague Netherlands. **Tel** 011 31 70 3308330, **FAX** 011 31 70 615624.

LC HD9015.P7 N47a
DD 382/.41/509438 NE
AGRARISCHE BUITENLANDSE HANDEL VAN POLEN, DE. Main/Corp Netherlands (Kingdom, 1815-). Ministerie Van Landbouw en Visserij. Directie Algemene Zaken. Afdeling Statistiek en Documentatie. (19??)-. Dutch. Ministerie van Landbouw en Visserij, Directie Algemene Zaken Afdeling Statistiek en Documentatie, Koningin Julianaplein 3, S-Gravenhage Netherlands.

LC S ISSN 0002-0710
DD 630 AU
AGRARISCHE RUNDSCHAU. [Agrar. Rundsch.]. (1947)-. Trade Publication. German. Six times a year. $56.19. Oesterreichischer Agrarverlag, Inkustr 1 7 Bueropark Donau, A 3400 Klosterneuberg Austria. **Tel** 011 43 2243 33300. **ED** Ernst Scheiber. **Bk Rev. Ad Acc. Circ:** 3,000.
Ind/Abst Leis., Rec., Tour. Abstr.; Rural Dev. Abstr.; World Agric. Econ. Rural Sociol. Abstr.

LC S13 .V38
DD 630 RU
●**AGRARNAIA NAUKA = AGRARIAN SCIENCE. VFOAT** Agrarian Science. (1993)-. Periodical. Russian (summaries and/or abstracts in English). Six times a year. **(Subscription address:** East View Publications Inc., 3020 Harbor Lane North, Suite 110, Minneapolis MN 55447. **Tel** (800)477-1005, (612)550-0961, **FAX** (612)559-2931.**) Continues** Vestnik Selskokhoziaistvennoi Nauki, 0206-6335.

LC S
DD 630 GW
AGRAROKOLOGIE. (1991)-. Periodical. German. Verlag Paul Haupt, Falkenplatz 11, CH-3001 Bern Switzerland. **Tel** 011 41 31 3012435, **FAX** 011 41 31 243023, telex 912 906 HAUP CH.

LC K1 .G7 ISSN 0340-840X
DD 343/.43/076 GW
CCC
AGRARRECHT. See Law.

LC S ISSN 0515-6866
DD 630 GW
AGRARWIRTSCHAFT. SONDERHEFT. Vol. 1 (1954)-. Monographic series. German. Price varies per volume. Deutscher Fachverlag GmbH, Verlagsgruppe, D-60264 Frankfurt Germany. **Tel** 011 49 69 75951001, telex 411 862.

Ind/Abst Dairy Sci. Abstr.; Maize Abstr.; Nutr. Abstr. Rev., Ser. A, Hum. Exp.; Pig News Inf.; Potato Abstr.; Poult. Abstr.; World Agric. Econ. Rural Sociol. Abstr.

LC HD1401 .A32
DD 338.1/05 SZ
AGRARWIRTSCHAFT UND AGRARSOZIOLOGIE. Added/Corp Schweiz. Gesellschaft fur Agrarwirtschaft und Agrarsoziologie. **VFOAT** Economie et Sociologie Rurales. (19??)-. Periodical. German (French). Two times a year.
Ind/Abst World Agric. Econ. Rural Sociol. Abstr.

LC HD1401 .A33 ISSN 0303-1853
DD 338.1 SA
AGREKON. [Agrekon]. **Added/Corp** South Africa. Dept. of Agricultural Economics and Marketing. Vol. 1 (Jan. 1962)-. Periodical. English. Four times a year. $50.00. Agrekon, PO Box 25549 Monument Park, Pretoria 0105 South Africa. **Tel** 011 27 11 313 3029, **FAX** 011 27 313 3086. **ED** G. Van Zyl, N. Vinh, and G. K. Loetzel. Index available. **Bk Rev. Circ:** 700.
Ind/Abst AGRICOLA [Full Cov.]; Agric. Eng. Abstr. (1991-); Field Crop Abstr.; Hortic. Abstr.; Leis., Rec., Tour. Abstr.; Maize Abstr.; Ornamental Hort. (1991-); Protozoolog. Abstr.; Rural Dev. Abstr.; Soils Fert.; Soyabean Abstr.; World Agric. Econ. Rural Sociol. Abstr.

LC S ISSN 0998-4186
DD 630 FR
UDC 31(44)
AGRESTE. ANALYSES & ETUDES. VFOAT Agreste. Analyses et Etudes. (1989)-. Monographic series. French. Irregular. Price varies per volume. SCEES, 4 Avenue de Saint-Mande, 75570 Paris Cedex 12 France. **Tel** 011 33 1 49558576. **Continues** Collection de Statistiques Agricoles, 0336-5638.

LC S ISSN 0998-4178
DD 630 FR
UDC 31(44)
AGRESTE. ANALYSES & ETUDES, CAHIERS. VFOAT Agreste. Cahiers; Agreste. Analyses et Etudes, Cahiers. (1990)-. Periodical. French. Four times a year. 250.00F France; 280.00F other. Ministere de l'Agriculture et de la Peche, Service Central des Enquetes et Etudes Statistiques, 4 avenue de Saint Mande, 75570 Paris Cedex 12 France. **Tel** 011 33 1 49558585, **FAX** 011 33 1 49558503.
Ind/Abst World Agric. Econ. Rural Sociol. Abstr.

LC S ISSN 1150-1987
DD 630 FR
UDC 31(449.8/.9)
AGRESTE. ANALYSES & ETUDES, COUP D'OEIL SUR RHONE-ALPES. (1990)-. Periodical. French. Four times a year. 165.00F. Ministere de l'Agriculture et de la Peche, Direction des Affaires Financieres et Economiques, Service Central des Enquetes et Etudes Statistiques, 4 Avenue de Saint-Mande, 75570 Paris Cedex 12 France. **Tel** 011 33 1 43444633, 16 61288305.

LC S ISSN 1167-4563
DD 630 FR
UDC 31(441.1/.5)
AGRESTE. ANALYSES & ETUDES, TRAJECTOIRES BRETAGNE. VFOAT Agreste. Analyses et Etudes, Trajectoires Bretagne; Trajectoires Bretagne. (1991)-. Periodical. French. Four times a year. 120.00F France; 140.00F other. Ministere de l'Agriculture et de la Peche, Direction des Affaires Financieres et Economiques, Service Central des Enquetes et Etudes Statistiques, 4 Avenue de Saint-Mande, 75570 Paris Cedex 12 France. **Tel** 011 33 1 43444633, 16 61288305.

LC S ISSN 1148-5604
DD 630 FR
UDC 31(44) CODEN 663/664(44)
AGRESTE. CONJONCTURE, COMMERCE EXTERIEUR AGRO-ALIMENTAIRE. (1990)-. Periodical. French. Twelve times a year. 160.00F France; 180.00F other. Ministere de l'Agriculture et de la Peche, Direction des Affaires Financieres et Economiques, Service Central des Enquetes et Etudes Statistiques, 4 Avenue de Saint-Mande, 75570 Paris Cedex 12 France. **Tel** 011 33 1 43444633, 16 61288305.

LC S ISSN 0998-416X
DD 630 FR
AGRESTE. CONJONCTURE, CONJONCTURE GENERALE. [Agreste, Conjonct. Conjonct. gen.]. **Added/Corp** France. Service Central des Enquete et Etudes Statistiques. **VFOAT** Conjoncture Generale; Statistique Agricole; Agreste - Conjoncture Generale. (1990)-. Periodical. French. Twelve times a year. 420.00F France; 490.00F other. Ministere de l'Agriculture et de la Peche, Direction des Affaires Financieres et Economiques, Service Central des Enquetes et Etudes Statistiques, 4 Avenue de Saint-Mande, 75570 Paris Cedex 12 France. **Tel** 011 33 1 43444633, 16 61288305. **Continues** France. Service Central des Enquetes et Etudes Statistiques. Situation Agricole en France. Conjoncture Generale, 0222-5220.

LC S ISSN 1148-5620
DD 630 FR
UDC 31(44)
AGRESTE. CONJONCTURE, GRANDES CULTURES. (1990)-. Periodical. French. Twelve times a year. 160.00F France; 180.00F other. Ministere de l'Agriculture et de la Peche, Direction des Affaires Financieres et Economiques, Service Central des Enquetes et Etudes Statistiques, 4 Avenue de Saint-Mande, 75570 Paris Cedex 12 France. **Tel** 011 33 1 43444633, 16 61288305.

LC S
DD 630 FR
AGRESTE. CONJONCTURE. INFOS RAPIDES HAUTE ET BASSE-NORMANDIE. (199?)-. Periodical. French. Twelve times a year. 100.00F. Ministere de l'Agriculture et de la Peche, Direction des Affaires Financieres et Economiques, Service Central des Enquetes et Etudes Statistiques, 4 Avenue de Saint-Mande, 75570 Paris Cedex 12 France. **Tel** 011 33 1 43444633, 16 61288305.

LC S ISSN 1167-1416
DD 630 FR
UDC 31(442.7/.8)
AGRESTE CONJONCTURE NORD-PAS-DE-CALAIS. (1992)-. Periodical. French. Eight times a year. 170.00F. Ministere de l'Agriculture et de la Peche, Direction des Affaires Financieres et Economiques, Service Central des Enquetes et Etudes Statistiques, 4 Avenue de Saint-Mande, 75570 Paris Cedex 12 France. **Tel** 011 33 1 43444633, 16 61288305.

LC S ISSN 1150-1707
DD 630 FR
UDC 31(447.7/.8)
AGRESTE. CONJONCTURE, NOTE DE CONJONCTURE AGRICOLE MIDI-PYRENEES. VFOAT Note de Conjoncture Agricole Midi-Pyrenees. (1990)-. Periodical. French. Twelve times a year. 170.00F. Ministere de l'Agriculture et de la Peche, Direction des Affaires Financieres et Economiques, Service Central des Enquetes et Etudes Statistiques, 4 Avenue de Saint-Mande, 75570 Paris Cedex 12 France. **Tel** 011 33 1 43444633, 16 61288305.

LC S ISSN 1167-3931
DD 630 FR
UDC 31(443.4/.5)
AGRESTE CONJONCTURE, PICARDIE. (199?)-. Periodical. French. Eight times a year. 170.00F. Ministere de l'Agriculture et de la Peche, Direction des Affaires Financieres et Economiques, Service Central des Enquetes et Etudes Statistiques, 4 Avenue de Saint-Mande, 75570 Paris Cedex 12 France. **Tel** 011 33 1 43444633, 16 61288305.

LC S ISSN 1150-1693
DD 630 FR
UDC 31(446.1/.5)
AGRESTE. CONJONCTURE, POITOU-CHARENTES. (1990)-. Periodical. French. Four times a year. 42.00F. Ministere de l'Agriculture et de la Peche, Direction des Affaires Financieres et Economiques, Service Central des Enquetes et Etudes Statistiques, 4 Avenue de Saint-Mande, 75570 Paris Cedex 12 France. **Tel** 011 33 1 43444633, 16 61288305.

LC S ISSN 1148-5167
DD 630 FR
UDC 31(449)
AGRESTE. CONJONCTURE, PROVENCE ALPES COTE D'AZUR. VFOAT Agreste. Conjoncture, L'Agriculture en Provence Alpes Cote d'Azur. (1990)-. Periodical. French. Twelve times a year. 180.00F. Ministere de l'Agriculture et de la Peche, Direction des Affaires Financieres et Economiques, Service Central des Enquetes et Etudes Statistiques, 4 Avenue de Saint-Mande, 75570 Paris Cedex 12 France. **Tel** 011 33 1 43444633, 16 61288305.

LC S ISSN 1157-3554
DD 630 FR
UDC 31(443.6)
AGRESTE. CONJONCTURE, REGION ILE-DE-FRANCE. VFOAT Agreste. Conjoncture, Note Bleue Ile-de-France. (1991)-. Periodical. French. Twelve times a year. 80.00F. Ministere de l'Agriculture et de la Peche, Direction des Affaires Financieres et Economiques, Service Central des Enquetes et Etudes Statistiques, 4 Avenue de Saint-Mande, 75570 Paris Cedex 12 France. **Tel** 011 33 1 43444633, 16 61288305.

LC S ISSN 1148-5671
DD 630 FR
UDC 31(449.8/.9)
AGRESTE. CONJONCTURE, RHONE-ALPES. VFOAT Agreste. La Conjoncture du Mois Rhone-Alpes. (1990)-. Periodical. French. Twelve times a year. 165.00F. Ministere de l'Agriculture et de la Peche, Direction des Affaires Financieres et

Economiques, Service Central des Enquetes et Etudes Statistiques, 4 Avenue de Saint-Mande, 75570 Paris Cedex 12 France. **Tel** 011 33 1 43444633, 16 61288305.

LC S **ISSN** 1255-6726
DD 630 FR
UDC 31(446.6/.7)

●**AGRESTE CONJONCTURE TENDANCES LIMOUSIN. VFOAT** Agreste Limousin. Tendances. (1994)-. Periodical. French. Four times a year. Ministere de l'Agriculture et de la Peche, Direction des Affaires Financieres et Economiques, Service Central des Enquetes et Etudes Statistiques, 4 Avenue de Saint-Mande, 75570 Paris Cedex 12 France. **Tel** 011 33 1 43444633, 16 61288305.

LC S **ISSN** 1142-3218
DD 630 FR

AGRESTE, SER. BULL. (AGRESTE. SERIES, LE BULLETIN.). [Agreste. Series, Le Bulletin]. **Added/Corp** France. Service Central des Enquetes et Etudes Statistiques. **VFOAT** Agreste, Le Bulletin; Bulletin; Statistique Agricole. (19??)-. Bulletin. French. Twelve times a year. 530.00F France; 590.00F other. Ministere de l'Agriculture et de la Peche, Direction des Affaires Financieres et Economiques, Service Central des Enquetes et Etudes Statistiques, 4 Avenue de Saint-Mande, 75570 Paris Cedex 12 France. **Tel** 011 33 1 43444633, 16 61288305. ***Continues** Bulletin Mensuel de Statistique Agricole, 0997-1122.*

LC S **ISSN** 1150-2037
DD 630 FR
UDC 31(443.83)

AGRESTE. SERIES, BULLETIN ALSACE. (1990)-. Periodical. French. Four times a year. 180.00F. Ministere de l'Agriculture et de la Peche, Direction des Affaires Financieres et Economiques, Service Central des Enquetes et Etudes Statistiques, 4 Avenue de Saint-Mande, 75570 Paris Cedex 12 France. **Tel** 011 33 1 43444633, 16 61288305.

LC S **ISSN** 1148-5558
DD 630 FR
UDC 31(448)

AGRESTE. SERIES, BULLETIN MENSUEL LANGUEDOC-ROUSSILLON. (1990)-. Periodical. French. Twelve times a year. 300.00F. Ministere de l'Agriculture et de la Peche, Direction des Affaires Financieres et Economiques, Service Central des Enquetes et Etudes Statistiques, 4 Avenue de Saint-Mande, 75570 Paris Cedex 12 France. **Tel** 011 33 1 43444633, 16 61288305.

LC S **ISSN** 1148-5361
DD 630 FR
UDC 31(444.5/.7)

AGRESTE. SERIES, LE BULLETIN DE FRANCHE-COMTE. (1990)-. Periodical. French. Four times a year. 190.00F. Ministere de l'Agriculture et de la Peche, Direction des Affaires Financieres et Economiques, Service Central des Enquetes et Etudes Statistiques, 4 Avenue de Saint-Mande, 75570 Paris Cedex 12 France. **Tel** 011 33 1 43444633, 16 61288305.

LC S **ISSN** 1155-4088
DD 630 FR
UDC 31(446.1/.5)

AGRESTE. SERIES, LE BULLETIN POITOU-CHARENTES. (1990)-. Periodical. French. Three times a year. 120.00F. Ministere de l'Agriculture et de la Peche, Direction des Affaires Financieres et Economiques, Service Central des Enquetes et Etudes Statistiques, 4 Avenue de Saint-Mande, 75570 Paris Cedex 12 France. **Tel** 011 33 1 43444633, 16 61288305.

LC S **ISSN** 1150-1537
DD 630 FR
UDC 31(446.6/.7)
TITLE CHANGE

AGRESTE SERIES, LE BULLETIN TRIMESTRIEL LIMOUSIN. VFOAT Bulletin Trimestriel Limousin. (1990)-(1993). Periodical. French. Ministere de l'Agriculture et de la Peche, Direction des Affaires Financieres et Economiques, Service Central des Enquetes et Etudes Statistiques, 4 Avenue de Saint-Mande, 75570 Paris Cedex 12 France. **Tel** 011 33 1 43444633, 16 61288305. ***Continued by** Agreste. Conjoncture. Tendances Limousin, 1255-6726.*

LC S451.5 **ISSN** 0705-3878
DD 630/.971 CN

AGRI-BOOK MAGAZINE. Vol. 1 (Oct. 1975)-. Periodical. English (French). Six times a year. 30.67Can$. AIS Communications Limited, 145 Thames Road West, Exeter Ontario N0M 1S3 Canada. **Tel** (519)235-2400, FAX (519)235-0798. **ED** Peter Darbishire. **Ad Acc.** ctrl circ. available in microform from Micromedia Limited.
Desc: Each Agri-Book is the market leader in its particular segment of agriculture.

LC S
DD 630 CN

AGRI-BOOK MAGAZINE. TOP CROP MANAGER. (19??)-. English. Three times a year (Mar., Apr., Aug.). $18.00 US and Canada; $36.00 other. AIS Communications Limited, 145 Thames Road West, Exeter Ontario N0M 1S3 Canada. **Tel** (519)235-2400, FAX (519)235-0798. **Bk Rev. Ad Acc. Circ:** 23,000 (ctrl). available on microfiche.
Desc: Articles on crop production and technology to assist the producer in achieving maximum economic yield.

LC HG2051.U5 A5968 **ISSN** 0002-1164
DD 332.7/1/097305 US

AGRI FINANCE. See Business and Economics-Banks and Banking.

LC HD **ISSN** 0849-2360
DD 338.1/09714 CN

●**AGRI-FOOD AND FISHERIES PROJECT, THE.** [Agri-food fish. proj.]. **Added/Corp** Quebec (Province).Ministere de l'Agriculture, des Pecheries et de l'Alimentation. **VFOAT** Projet Bio-Alimentaire. (1993)-. English.

LC HD9014.C2 M37 **ISSN** 1193-8277
DD 338.1 CN

AGRI-FOOD PERSPECTIVES. [Agri-food perspect.]. **Added/Corp** Canada. Agriculture Canada. Economic Analysis Division. **VFOAT** Agri Food Perspectives. (May 1992)-. Government Publication. English. Three times a year. Free on request. Agriculture Canada, Communications Branch, Ottawa Ontario K1A 0C7 Canada. ***Continues** Market Commentary, 0823-4760.*
Ind/Abst Food Sci. Technol. Abstr.

LC S **ISSN** 1192-7704
DD 630 CN

AGRI-FOOD RESEARCH IN ONTARIO. [Agri-food res. Ont.]. **Added/Corp** Agricultural Research Institute of Ontario. Ontario. Ministry of Agriculture and Food. **VFOAT** Recherche Agro-Alimentaire en Ontario. (1992)-. Periodical. English (summaries and/or abstracts in French). Four times a year (Mar., Jun., Sep., Dec.). Free on request. Ministry of Agriculture and Food Education Research Division, Box 1030 Guelph Agriculture Ct., Guelph Ontario N1H 6N1 Canada. **Tel** (519)823-5700 ext. 229, FAX (519)824-6941. **ED** Robyn Meerveld (Editor's Address: 95 Stone Rd. West Guelph, Ontario N1H837; Editor's Telephone: (519)767-6287). Index available (In March). **Circ:** 8,000. ***Continues** Highlights of Agricultural and Food Research in Ontario, 1183-5796.*

LC S239 .A64
DD 630/.9492 NE

AGRI-HOLLAND. Added/Corp Netherlands (Kingdom, 1815-). Ministerie van Landbouw en Visserij. Foreign Marketing Service. (1977)-. Periodical. English. Six times a year. ***Continues** Agricultural Newsletter from the Netherlands.*
Ind/Abst Hortic. Abstr.; Soils Fert.

LC S **ISSN** 1383-6455
DD 630 NE

●**AGRI MONITOR.** (Oct. 1995)-. Dutch. Six times a year. Fl.60.00. Landbouw-Economisch Instituut, Postbus 29703, 2502 LS Hague Netherlands. **Tel** 011 31 70 3308330, FAX 011 31 70 615624.

LC S **ISSN** 0882-9292
DD 630 US
UDC 63

AGRI-NATURALIST. [Agri-nat.]. **VFOAT** Agri Naturalist. Issue 1 (Autumn 1984)-. Periodical. English. Three times a year. $2.00. Ohio State University / College of Agriculture, Room 204 / Ag Administration, 2120 Fyffe Road, Columbus OH 43210. **Tel** (614)292-6671. **ED** Thad Welch, Lynn Hamilton, and Michelle Stevens. **Circ:** 2,000. ***Continues** Buckeye Tribune, 0274-9785.*

LC S **ISSN** 1073-1776
DD 631 US

AGRI-PLASTICS REPORT, THE. See Plastics.

LC SF **ISSN** 0745-452X
DD 636 US

AGRI-PRACTICE. [Agri-Pract.]. **VFOAT** Agripractice; Agriculture Practice. Vol. 4, No. 1 (Jan. 1983)-. Periodical. English. Ten times a year. $38.00. Veterinary Practice Publishing Company, PO Box 4457, Santa Barbara CA 93140-4457. **Tel** (805)965-1028, FAX (805)965-0722. **ED** G. Rupp, J. Reneau, B. Bennett, and K. McKean. available on microfilm from University Microfilms International (UMI). Documents available from The Genuine Article. ***Continues** Bovine Practice, 0199-5456.*
Desc: Journal of medicine and surgery for the food animal practitioner.
Ind/Abst AgBiotech News Inf.; AGRICOLA [Full Cov.]; Agric. Eng. Abstr. (1991-); Anim. Breed. Abstr.; BioBusiness; Curr. Cit.; Curr. Contents Agric. Biol. Environ. Sci.; Dairy Sci. Abstr.; Grass. Forage Abstr.; Helminthol. Abstr. (19??-19??); Index Vet.; Nutr. Abstr. Rev., Ser. B, Live Feeds and Feed.; Pig News Inf.; Postharvest News Inf.; Protozoolog. Abstr.; Res. Alert [Select. Cov.]; Rev. Med. Vet. Entomol.; Rev. Med. Vet. Mycology; SCISEARCH; Small Anim. Abstr. Bibliogr.; Vet. Bull.; Wheat Barley Trit. Abstr.; World Agric. Econ. Rural Sociol. Abstr.

LC SB **ISSN** 0884-7606
DD 634 US

AGRI-PULSE. VFOAT Agri Pulse. (198?)-. Periodical. English. Twenty-six times a year. $49.00. Agri-Pulse Commission Inc., 63 Harbor Bend, Lake St. Louis MO 63367. **Tel** (314)625-3013, FAX (314)625-3015.

LC HD **ISSN** 1021-4240
DD 338 BE
UDC 338(4):63

AGRI-SERVICE INTERNATIONAL. [Agri-serv. int.]. (1979)-. Periodical. English (French). Twenty-four times a year. $861.95. Europe Information Service, rue de Geneve 6, 1140 Brussels Belgium. **Tel** 011 32 2 242 6020, FAX 011 32 2 242 9549. **Bk Rev. Circ:** 1,000.

LC S **ISSN** 0887-2910
DD 630 US

AGRI-TIMES NORTHWEST. [Agri-times northwest]. **VFOAT** Agritimes Northwest. (198?)-. Periodical. English. One time a week. $20.00. Agri Times Northwest, PO Box 189, Pendleton OR 97801. **Tel** (503)276-7845. **ED** Virgil Rupp and James Eardley. **Bk Rev. Ad Acc. Circ:** 5,500.

LC S **ISSN** 1052-2255
DD 630 US

AGRI-TOPICS (BELTSVILLE, MD.). (AGRI-TOPICS.). **Added/Corp** National Agricultural Library (U.S.). **VFOAT** Agri Topics. (1990)-. Monographic series. English.
Ind/Abst AGRICOLA [Full Cov.].

LC S
DD 630 US

AGRI-VIEW. VFOAT Agri View. Vol. 9, No. 43 (Oct. 28, 1983)-. Newspaper. English. One time a week. $18.00. Krause Publications, 700 East State Street, Iola WI 54990-0001. **Tel** (715)445-2214, FAX (715)445-4087, telex 55 6461. ***Continues in part** Agri-View (Marshfield, Wis. : Northwest Ed.).*

LC S
DD 630 US

AGRI VIEW. (19??)-. Newsletter. English. Twenty-six times a year. $7.00. Vermont Department of Agriculture, Food & Markets, 116 State Street / Drawer 20, Montpelier VT 05620-2901. **Tel** (802)828-2500, FAX (802)828-2361. **ED** Jennifer Grahovac (editor's phone: (802)828-2416). **Ad Acc, Adv Mgr:** Jeffrey Cook. **Circ:** 4,000.
Desc: News relating to the agricultural community of the state of Vermont.

LC S **ISSN** 0115-2440
DD 630 PH

AGRIASIA. Added/Corp Agricultural Information Bank for Asia. Southeast Asian Regional Centre for Graduate Study and Research in Agriculture. Vol. 1 (1977)-. Periodical. English. Two times a year (July, & Dec.). $150.00. Agricultural Information Bank of Asia, Southeast Asian College, Laguana 3720 Philippines. **Tel** 011 63 2 2317, FAX 011 63 2 813 5697, telex 40904. Index available. **Circ:** 60.

LC S **ISSN** 0938-0337
DD 630 GW
CCC
CODEN AGRREE

AGRIBIOLOGICAL RESEARCH. [Agribiol. res.]. **Added/Corp** Verband Deutscher Landwirtschaftlicher Untersuchungs- und Forschungsanstalten. Vol. 43, No. 1 (1990)-. Periodical. German (English; summaries and/or abstracts in French). Four times a year. $168.12. J. D. Sauerlaender Verlag, Finkenhofstrasse 21, D-60322 Frankfurt Germany. **Tel** 011 49 69 555217, FAX 011 49 69 5964344. **ED** M. Kircheessner. Index available. **Bk Rev.** Documents available from The Genuine Article, CASDDS. ***Continues** Landwirtschaftliche Forschung, 0023-8147.*
Desc: Covers agricultural chemistry and biology, investigation of soil and fertilizer, food and feedstuff analysis, soil fertility, pesticide residue and heavymetal, feedstuff evaluation.
Ind/Abst Biodeter. Abstr. (1991-); Chem. Abstr.; Curr. Cit.; Dairy Sci. Abstr.; Field Crop Abstr.; Grass. Forage Abstr.; Nutr. Abstr. Rev., Ser. B, Live Feeds and Feed.; Nutr. Abstr. Rev., Ser. A, Hum. Exp.; Pig News Inf.; Postharvest News Inf.; Potato Abstr.; Res. Alert [Full Cov.]; Rev. Med. Vet. Mycology; Sci. Cit. Index; SCISEARCH; Seed Abstr.; Soils Fert.; Sorghum Mill. Abstr.; Wheat Barley Trit. Abstr.

LC S **ISSN** 1079-9060
DD 630 US

●**AGRIBIOSCAN (PHOENIX, ARIZ.).** (AGRIBIOSCAN : THE AGRICULTURAL BIOTECHNOLOGY DIRECTORY.). **VFOAT** Agri Bio Scan; Agricultural Biotechnology Directory. (1995)-. Periodical. English. Three times a year. $395.00. Oryx

Press, 4041 North Central Avenue #700, Phoenix AZ 85012-3397. **Tel** (800)279-6799, (602)265-2651, FAX (602)265-6250, (800)279-4663, (800)279-6799.

LC HD1401 .A333 **ISSN** 0742-4477
DD 338.1/05 US
CCC
CODEN AGRBEY

AGRIBUSINESS (NEW YORK, N.Y.).
(AGRIBUSINESS.). [Agribusiness]. Vol. 1, No. 1 (Spring 1985)-. Periodical. English. Six times a year. $396.00. John Wiley & Sons, Inc., 605 Third Avenue, New York NY 10158-0012. **Tel** (212)850-6000, (212)850-6645, FAX (212)850-6088, telex 12-7063. **(Subscription address:** John Wiley & Sons / UK, Baffins Lane, Chichester, West Sussex PO19 1UD United Kingdom. **Tel** 011 44 1243 779777, FAX 011 44 243 776128, telex 86290 WIBOOKG.**)** **ED** Michael Woolverton, Gail Cramer, and Timothy Hammonds. **Ad Acc. Circ:** 700. available on microfilm and microfiche from University Microfilms International (UMI). Documents available from UMI Article Clearinghouse, Documents on Demand.
Desc: Research journal encompassing all sectors of agribusiness. Primarily serves the large and growing non-farm sectors of the food and fiber system. Contains articles that deal with all the business aspects of agricultural production. Contributors include practitioners, researchers and academicians.
Ind/Abst ABI/INFORM Glob. Ed.; ABI/INFORM [Computer File] (Jan. 1988-); AGRICOLA [Full Cov.]; BioBusiness; Biol. Agric. Index; Bus. Index (1992-); Curr. Cit.; Dairy Sci. Abstr.; Energy Inf. Abstr.; Environ. Abstr.; Gen. BusinessFile (1992-); Grass. Forage Abstr.; Hortic. Abstr.; Maize Abstr.; Pig News Inf.; Postharvest News Inf.; Poult. Abstr.; Rev. Agric. Entomol.; Soyabean Abstr.; World Agric. Econ. Rural Sociol. Abstr.

LC HD **ISSN** 0899-1294
DD 338 US
Pr Rev.

AGRIBUSINESS NEWS FOR KENTUCKY.
[Agribus. news Ky.]. **Added/Corp** University of Kentucky. Cooperative Extension Service. (Feb./March 1988)-. Periodical. English. Six times a year. University of Kentucky Department of Agricultural Economics, College of Agriculture, Lexington KY 40546. **Tel** (606)757-7273. Index available. **Circ:** 3,500 (ctrl). ***Continues** Kentucky Agri-Business News.*
Desc: Peer-reviewed submissions on topics of interest to Kentucky agribusiness managers and marketers.
Ind/Abst AGRICOLA [Full Cov.].

LC S **ISSN** 0897-3237
DD 630 US
CEASED

AGRICOLA ; CRIS.
(AGRICOLA ; CRIS [COMPUTER FILE].). [AGRICOLA CRIS]. **Added/Corp** OCLC. National Agricultural Library (U.S.) United States. Cooperative State Research Service. Current Research Information System. **VFOAT** CRIS. (Sept. 1987)-(19??). Periodical. English. OCLC Asia Pacific Services, 6565 Frantz Road, Dublin OH 43017. **Tel** (800)848-5878, (614)764-6394 or 6000, FAX (614)764-6096.
Desc: AGRICOLA is a compilation of materials by the National Agricultural Library and cooperating institutions. CRIS is produced by the Cooperative State Research Service of the U.S. Department of Agriculture.

LC S **ISSN** 0211-2728
DD 631 SP

AGRICOLA VERGEL.
(1980)-. Periodical. Spanish. Twelve times a year. $78.90. Ediciones y Promociones Lav S.L., Apartado 473, 46080 Valencia Spain. **Tel** 011 34 6 963720261, FAX 011 34 6 963710516. **ED** Francisco Salvador Planes. **Ad Acc. Circ:** 4,300.
Desc: Articles on the growth of of plants, flowers and fruit.

LC S
DD 630 IT
SUSPENDED

AGRICOLTURA 2000.
(19??)-Suspended (May 1990)-. Periodical. Italian. Twelve times a year. Valentini Editore, Via F Filzi 19, 20100 Milan Italy. **Tel** 011 39 2 6080343.

LC S **ISSN** 0400-776X
DD 630 IT

AGRICOLTURA DELL VENEZIE.
(1947)-. Italian.
Ind/Abst Fish Rev. (Jan. 1989-July 1992); Wildl. Rev. (Jan. 1989-July 1992).

LC S **ISSN** 0002-127X
DD 631 IT
UDC 621.039 : 63

AGRICOLTURA D'ITALIA.
[Agric. Ital.]. (1955)-. Periodical. Italian. Twelve times a year. L34060. Istituto Studi Nucleari Agricoltura, Via 4 Novembre 152, 00187 Rome Italy. **Tel** 011 39 6 6784991, FAX 011 39 6 6782904. **Bk Rev.**
Desc: Covers atomic energy as applied to agriculture.

LC S **ISSN** 0394-2805
DD 630 IT
UDC 63
SUSPENDED

AGRICOLTURA E INNOVAZIONE.
[Agric. innov.]. (1987)-Suspended (1995). Periodical. Multiple languages. Four times a year. L27250. ENEA, V le Regina Margherita 125, 00198 Rome Italy. **Tel** 011 39 6 85281.

LC S **ISSN** 0394-0438
DD 630 IT

AGRICOLTURA MEDITERRANEA (OSPEDALETTO).
(AGRICOLTURA MEDITERRANEA.). [Agric. mediterr.]. Vol. 117, No. 1 (1987)-. Periodical. English (French, Italian and Spanish). Four times a year. L200000. Pacini Editore Srl, via A Gherardesca 1, 56121 Ospedaletto Pisa Italy. **Tel** 011 39 50 982439. ***Continues** Agricoltura Italiana, 0375-8389.*
Ind/Abst Agric. Eng. Abstr. (1991-); Anim. Breed. Abstr.; Crop Physiol. Abstr.; Curr. Cit.; Field Crop Abstr.; For. Abstr.; Grass. Forage Abstr.; Hortic. Abstr.; Irr. Drain. Abstr.; Maize Abstr.; Nutr. Abstr. Rev., Ser. B, Live Feeds and Feed.; Nutr. Abstr. Rev., Ser. A, Hum. Exp.; Ornamental Hort. (1991-); Plant Breed. Abstr.; Plant Genet. Resour. Abstr.; Plant Grow. Reg. Abstr.; Seed Abstr.; Soils Fert.; Sorghum Mill. Abstr.; Soyabean Abstr.; Weed Abstr.; Wheat Barley Trit. Abstr.

LC S **ISSN** 0392-5609
DD 630 IT
UDC 63
SUSPENDED

AGRICOLTURA RICERCA.
[Agric. ric.]. (1978)-Suspended with 150 (1993). Periodical. Italian. Twelve times a year. Free on request (in Italy only). ISMEA Inst Mercato Agricolo, Via Nomentana 183, 00183 Rome Italy. **Tel** 39 6 6657680.
Ind/Abst Field Crop Abstr.; Irr. Drain. Abstr.; Postharvest News Inf.; Potato Abstr.; Rev. Agric. Entomol.; Seed Abstr.; Soils Fert.; Weed Abstr.

LC S
DD 630 IT

AGRICOLTURE DELLE VENEZIE : ORGANO MENSILE DELLA CONSULTA REGIONALE PER L'AGRICOLTURA E LE FORESTE DELLE VENEZIE... .
Added/Corp Consulta per l'Agricoltura e le Foreste delle Venezie. Consulta Regionale per l'Agricoltura e le Foreste delle Venezie. Vol. 1, No. 1-2 (Jan./Feb) 1947)-. Periodical. Italian. Ten times a year. L27250. Consulta Agric Foreste Venezie, San Marco 2746, 30124 Venice Italy. **Tel** 011 39 41 5220760.

LC S **ISSN** 0770-285X
DD 630 BE
UDC 263

AGRICONTACT ED. FRANCAISE.
[Agricontact Ed. fr.]. **VFOAT** Courier du Ministere de l'Agriculture. (1971)-. Government Publication. French (Dutch). Eleven times a year (monthly except July). 360F Belgium; 480F other. Ministere de l'Agriculture / Belgium, Manhattan Centre Office Tower, Avenue du Boulevard 21-13e Etage, 1210 Brussels Belgium. **Tel** 011 32 2 2117211, FAX 011 32 2 2117209, telex AGRILA 22033. **ED** M De Baeremaeker. Index available. **Bk Rev,** (Qty: 150). **Circ:** 2,300.
Desc: Contains European Union News, market news, presentation of one agricultural sector each month, brief news of the Department of Agriculture, extension papers on various subjects, and more.

LC S
DD 630 IT

AGRICOTURA BIOLOGICA.
(19??)-. Italian. Federico Ceratti Editore, C Postale 1, Via XXV Aprile 11, 20060 Vignate Milan Italy. **Tel** 011 39 2 9560530.

LC S15 .A37
DD 630.987 VE

AGRICULTOR VENEZOLANO, EL.
Added/Corp Venezuela. Ministerio de Agricultura y Cria. Vol. 1 (May 1936)-. Spanish. Twelve times a year. Ministerio de Agricultura Cria, Caracas Venezuela.

LC S
DD 630 BL

AGRICULTURA & COOPERATIVISMO.
Added/Corp Federacao das Cooperativas Brasileiras de Trigo e Soja. Vol. 1. No. 1 (May 1976)-. Periodical. Portuguese. Twelve times a year. $35.00. Fecotrico, Caixa Postal 2679, 90000 Porto Agegre RS Brazil.

LC S **ISSN** 0002-1350
DD 630 US
CCC

AGRICULTURA DE LAS AMERICAS (OVERLAND PARK, KANS.).
(AGRICULTURA DE LAS AMERICAS.). [Agric. Am.]. **Added/Corp** Intertec Publishing Corporation. Vol. 5, No. 5 (May 1956)-. Periodical. Spanish. Six times a year. $65.00. Keller International Publishing, 150 Great Neck Road, Great Neck NY 11021. **Tel** (516)829-9210 ext. 302, FAX (516)829-5414, telex 221574 KELLE. **ED** Victor Prieto (editor's address: 16645 West 147th Street, Olathe KS 66026; telephone: (913)829-5753). cum. index. **Ad Acc. Circ:** 40,000 (ctrl). ***Continues** Implementos y Tractores.*
Desc: Suggestions for better animal health and more productive crops, new agri-products available, where to purchase any given farm equipment, and association news.
Ind/Abst Dairy Sci. Abstr.; Field Crop Abstr.; Grass. Forage Abstr.; Life Sci. Collect.; Protozoolog. Abstr.

LC S **ISSN** 0044-6793
DD 630 BL
UDC 338.43(81)

AGRICULTURA EM SAO PAULO.
[Agric. Sao Paulo]. 1951-. Portuguese. One time a year. $2.50. Instituto de Economia Agricola, Caixa Postal 8114, Sao Paulo 01000 Brazil. **Tel** (011)34067 SAGR-SAO PAULO-BRASIL, telex (011) 34067 SAGR. cum. index. **Circ:** 2,000 (ctrl).
Ind/Abst Int. Dev. Abstr. (?-?); Maize Abstr.; Rice Abstr.; Soyabean Abstr.

LC S **ISSN** 0002-1334
DD 630 SP
UDC 338.43(460) **CCC**
Pr Rev.

AGRICULTURA (MADRID, SPAIN).
(AGRICULTURA : REVISTA AGROPECUARIA.). Vol. 1, No. 1 (Jan. 1929)-. Periodical. Spanish (Castilian). Twelve times a year. $79.90. Editorial Agricola Espanola SA, Caballero de Gracia 24 #3 IZ, 28013 Madrid Spain. **Tel** 34 (1) 5211633, FAX 34 (1) 5224872. **ED** Cristobal de la Puerta Costello. Index available. cum. index. **Bk Rev. Ad Acc. Circ:** 8,000 (ctrl). available on microfilm from University Microfilms International (UMI).
Ind/Abst For. Abstr.; Seed Abstr.; Soyabean Abstr.

LC HD9014.B8 B68E
DD 338.17 BL
UDC 338.43(81)

AGRICULTURA : PERSPECTIVAS - BRAZIL. COMISSAO DE FINANCIAMENTO DA PRODUCAO.
Main/Corp Brazil. Comissao de Financiamento da Producao. Portuguese. Setor de Edificios Publicos, Comissao de Financiamento da Producao, W 3 Norte - Q 514 Bl B 70.000, Brasilia Brazil.

LC S
DD 630 RM
UDC 338.43(498)
CEASED

AGRICULTURA SOCIALISTA.
(19??)-(19??). Periodical. Romanian. **(Subscription address:** Rompresfilatelia, PO Box 12 201, Bucharest Romania. **Tel** 011 40 0 10376.**)**
Desc: Socio-political and economic review. Publishes articles on agricultural problems.

LC S15 .A384 **ISSN** 0365-2807
DD 630.5 CL
CODEN AGTCA9
Pr Rev.

AGRICULTURA TECNICA.
[Agric. tec.]. **Added/Corp** Chile. Direccion General de Agricultura. Instituto de Investigaciones Agropecuarias. Chile. Ministerio de Agricultura. Vol. 4 (July 1944)-. Academic Scholarly Publication. Spanish. Four times a year. $35.00. Instituto de Investigaciones / Chile, Agropecuarias Casilla 439 CR 3, Santiago Chile. **Tel** 011 56 2 5417223, FAX 2258773, telex 242207 INIA-CL. **ED** Nora Aedo Marchant. Index available. cum. index. **Bk Rev. Circ:** 1,000. Documents available from BIOSIS Document Express, CASDDS. ***Continues** Boletin de Sanidad Vegetal.*
Desc: Agriculture production research results: crops, horticulture (fruit trees, vegetable crops), livestock (meat, dairy and wool production), pastures, soil and fertilizers, irrigation, crops and animals management, etc.
Ind/Abst AgBiotech News Inf.; Agrindex; Anim. Breed. Abstr.; Biocont. News Inf.; Biol. Abstr.; Chem. Abstr.; Dairy Sci. Abstr.; Field Crop Abstr.; Food Sci. Technol. Abstr.; Grass. Forage Abstr.; Hortic. Abstr.; Irr. Drain. Abstr.; Maize Abstr.; Nematol. Abstr.; Nutr. Abstr. Rev., Ser. B, Live Feeds and Feed.; Nutr. Abstr. Rev., Ser. A, Hum. Exp.; Plant Breed. Abstr.; Plant Grow. Reg. Abstr.; Postharvest News Inf.; Protozoolog. Abstr.; Rev. Agric. Entomol.; Rev. Med. Vet. Mycology; Rev. Plant Pathol.; Seed Abstr.; Soils Fert.; Sorghum Mill. Abstr.; Sug. Indus. Abstr.; Weed Abstr.; Wheat Barley Trit. Abstr.

LC S **ISSN** 0568-2517
DD 630 MX

AGRICULTURA TECNICA EN MEXICO.
Added/Corp Mexico. Instituto Nacional de Investigaciones Agricolas. Mexico. Direccion General de Agricultura. Mexico. Secretaria de Agricultura Ganaderia. No. 1 (July 1955)-. Periodical. Spanish (summaries and/or abstracts in English, French and German). Instituto Nacional de Investigaciones Agricolas, Apartado Postal 6 882, Mexico 6 DF Mexico.
Ind/Abst Potato Abstr.; Rice Abstr.

LC S
DD 630 XR
CODEN ATSUEH

AGRICULTURA TROPICA ET SUBTROPICA.
Added/Corp Vysoka Skola Zemedelska v Praze. Institut Tropickeho a Subtropickeho

Zemedelstvi. Vysoka Skola Zemedelska v Praze. Provozne Ekonomicka Fakulta. Vol. 8 (1975)-. English (French and Spanish; summaries and/or abstracts in Czech and Russian). One time a year. ***Continues** Vysoka Skola Zemedelska v Praze. Institut Tropickeho a Subtropickeho Zemedelskvi. Sbornik Provozne Ekonomicke Fakulty, Vysoke Skoly Zemedelske v Praze.*
Ind/Abst Anim. Breed. Abstr.; Cot. Trop. Fibr. Abstr. Bibliogr.; Dairy Sci. Abstr.; Field Crop Abstr.; Hortic. Abstr.; Index Vet.; Irr. Drain. Abstr.; Plant Breed. Abstr.; Plant Grow. Reg. Abstr.; Potato Abstr.; Poult. Abstr.; Protozoolog. Abstr.; Rural Dev. Abstr.; Soils Fert.; Soyabean Abstr.; World Agric. Econ. Rural Sociol. Abstr.

LC S
DD 630.5 CK
AGRICULTURA Y GANADERIA. No. 1-. Periodical. Spanish. Ministerio Agricultura, Centro de Publicaciones, Calle Alfonso XII 56, 28071 Madrid Spain. **Tel** 011 34 1 3475551, FAX 011 34 1 3475722.

LC S
DD 630 SP
Pr Rev.
AGRICULTURA Y SOCIEDAD. Added/Corp Spain. Ministerio de Agricultura. Vol. 1 (Oct./Dec. 1976)-. Periodical. Spanish (summaries and/or abstracts in English and French). Four times a year (Jan., Apr., Aug., Dec.). $75.50. Ministerio Agricultura, Centro de Publicaciones, Calle Alfonso XII 56, 28071 Madrid Spain. **Tel** 011 34 1 3475551, FAX 011 34 1 3475722. **ED** Cristobal Gomez Benito. Index available. cum. index. **Bk Rev. Circ:** 1,500 (ctrl).
Desc: Social sciences on agriculture, fishing, and nourishment.
Ind/Abst AgBiotech News Inf.; Int. Bibliogr. Sociol.; Leis., Rec., Tour. Abstr.; Maize Abstr.; Rice Abstr.; Rural Dev. Abstr.; Wheat Barley Trit. Abstr.; World Agric. Econ. Rural Sociol. Abstr.

LC HD1417 .B74a **ISSN** 0713-0465
DD 338.1/81/091724 CN
AGRICULTURAL AID TO DEVELOPING COUNTRIES. See Business and Economics-Economic Assistance and Development.

LC SF **ISSN** 0567-431X
DD 636 UK
AGRICULTURAL AND VETERINARY CHEMICALS. VFOAT AVC; AVC and Agricultural Engineering; Journal of AVC. Vol. 1 (May/June 1960)-. Periodical. English. Six times a year (Feb., Apr., June, Aug., Oct., Dec.). $70.00. Chandler Publications Ltd, 10 South Street, Totnes Devon TQ9 5DZ United Kingdom. **Tel** 011 44 1803 864668, FAX 011 44 1803 805049, telex 42928. **ED** J R D Heming. **Bk Rev. Ad Acc. Circ:** 2,000.
Desc: A news sheet for research chemists, research stations, converters and formulators of agricultural and veterinary chemicals.

LC TL **ISSN** 0745-4864
DD 629 US
AGRICULTURAL AVIATION (WASHINGTON, D.C.). See Aeronautics, Astronautics.

LC S
DD 630 US
AGRICULTURAL BOOKS AND INFORMATION. (19??)-. English. Two times a year (Feb., & Sept.). Free on request. Agaccess, PO Box 2008, Davis CA 95617. **Tel** (916)756-7177, FAX (916)756-7177.

LC HD2056 .F37 **ISSN** 0568-2606
DD 338.1/095 US
AGRICULTURAL DATA BOOK FOR THE FAR EAST AND OCEANIA, THE. Added/Corp United States. Dept. of Agriculture. Economic Research Service. (1968)-. English. One time a year. US Department of Agriculture, 14th Street and Independence Avenue SW, Washington DC 20250. **Tel** (202)720-5457. ***Continues** Far East and Oceania Agricultural Data Book, 0162-4997.*

LC HD2131 .A13
DD 338.1/096891 RH
UDC 338.43(689.1)
AGRICULTURAL ECONOMICS AND MARKETS REPORT. (July/Dec. 1971)-. English. Two times a year. Economics and Research Branch, Ministry of Agriculture, Zimbabwe Rhodesia. ***Continues** Biannual Economics & Markets Report.*

LC S530 .A3 **ISSN** 0732-4677
DD 630/.7/1 US
AGRICULTURAL EDUCATION MAGAZINE (1980), THE. (THE AGRICULTURAL EDUCATION MAGAZINE.). [Agric. educ. mag.]. Vol. 52, No. 7 (Jan. 1980)-. Periodical. English. Twelve times a year. $10.00. Agricultural Education, 10171 Suzanne Drive, Mechanicville VA 23111. **Tel** (804)746-3538. **ED** Phillip Zurbrick. Index available. cum. index. **Bk Rev. Circ:** 5,500 (ctrl). available on microfilm from Xerox; available on microfilm and microfiche from University Microfilms International (UMI). ***Continues** Agricultural Education (Danville, Ill. : 1962), 0002-144X.*
Desc: Professional articles on instruction leadership, supervision, and curriculum development in agricultural education in the United States and other countries.
Ind/Abst AGRICOLA [Select. Cov.]; Curr. Index J. Educ.; Educ. Index; Life Sci. Collect.

LC S
DD 630 US
AGRICULTURAL EDUCATORS DIRECTORY. (19??)-. Directory. English. One time a year. Free. Charles M. Henry Printing Co., PO Box 68, Greensburg PA 15601. **Tel** (412)834-7600, FAX (412)836-7759. **ED** Sarah L. Henry. **Circ:** 12,000 (ctrl). ***Continues** Agriculture Teachers Directory.*

LC S **ISSN** 0308-5732
DD 630 UK
AGRICULTURAL ENGINEER, THE. [Agric. eng.]. **Added/Corp** Institution of Agricultural Engineers. Vol. 27 (Spring 1972)-. Periodical. English. Four times a year. $75.29. Institution of Agricultural Engineers, West End Road Silsoe, Bedford MK45 4DU United Kingdom. **Tel** 011 45 1525 861096, FAX 011 45 1525 861660. **ED** B.W. Sheppard. Index available. cum. index. **Bk Rev. Ad Acc. Circ:** 4,000 (ctrl). available on microfilm from University Microfilms International (UMI). ***Continues** Journal and Proceedings of the Institution of Agricultural Engineers.*
Desc: Technical articles and papers on the subject of agricultural engineering. Proceedings of conferences of the Institution of Agricultural Engineers. Reviews of agricultural engineering literature.
Ind/Abst AGRICOLA [Full Cov.]; Agric. Eng. Abstr.; Dairy Sci. Abstr.; Field Crop Abstr.; Grass. Forage Abstr.; Hortic. Abstr.; Int. Abstr. Oper. Res. [Select. Cov.]; Irr. Drain. Abstr.; Maize Abstr.; Pig News Inf.; Postharvest News Inf.; Potato Abstr.; Seed Abstr.; Soils Fert.; Stat. Theory Method Abstr. (1959-1963); World Agric. Econ. Rural Sociol. Abstr.

LC S671 .A3 **ISSN** 0002-1458
DD 630 US
CCC
CODEN AGENAZ
Pr Rev. **TITLE CHANGE**
AGRICULTURAL ENGINEERING. [Agric. eng.]. **Added/Corp** American Society of Agricultural Engineers. Vol. 1 (Sept. 1920)-(Mar. 1994). Periodical. English. American Society of Agricultural Engineers, Department 2510, 2950 Niles Road, St. Joseph MI 49085-9659. **Tel** (616)429-0300, FAX (616)429-3852. **ED** Mark Zimmerman. Index available. cum. index. **Bk Rev. Ad Acc.** available on microfilm and microfiche from University Microfilms International (UMI). Documents available from Article Express International, The Genuine Article, Ask*IEEE, UMI Article Clearinghouse, Documents on Demand. ***Merged with** Within ASAE, 0741-0387 **to form** Resource (Saint Joseph, Mich.), 1076-3333.*
Desc: Broad interest articles and continuing departments spotlight agricultural process with emphasis on mechanization, plus trends influencing contemporary events.
Ind/Abst AgBiotech News Inf.; Agric. Eng. Abstr. (19??-19??); BioBusiness; Bioeng. Abstr.; Biogr. Index; Biol. Agric. Index; Curr. Aware. Biol. Sci., CABS; Curr. Cit.; Curr. Contents Agric. Biol. Environ. Sci.; Dairy Sci. Abstr.; Educ. Index; Ei Page One; EMBASE; Eng. Index Annu. [Select. Cov.]; Environ. Abstr.; Environ. Period. Bibliogr.; Expand. Acad. Index (1992-); Field Crop Abstr.; Grass. Forage Abstr.; Hortic. Abstr.; INIS Atomindex [Micro.]; INSPEC (Aug. 1971-Feb. 1973); Int. Aerosp. Abstr.; Irr. Drain. Abstr.; Newsp. Period. Abstr. (1992-); Life Sci. Collect.; Protozoolog. Abstr.; Res. Alert [Select. Cov.]; SCISEARCH; Soc. Sci. Cit. Index [Select. Cov.]; Soils Fert.

LC S **ISSN** 0044-6807
DD 630 AT
Pr Rev.
AGRICULTURAL ENGINEERING AUSTRALIA. [Agric. eng. Aust.]. **Added/Corp** Agricultural Engineering Society (Australia). (19??)-. Periodical. English. Two times a year (June & Dec.). 41.11Aus$. Society Engineering in Agriculture National Office, 11 National Circuit, Barton ACT 2600 Australia. **Tel** 011 61 6 2706555, FAX 011 61 6 7420202. **ED** M. P. Foster. **Bk Rev. Circ:** 600. ***Continues** Agricultural Engineering Society (Australia). Newsletter.*
Desc: Scientific papers and technical reports on Australian agricultural engineering research.
Ind/Abst AGRICOLA [Full Cov.]; Agric. Eng. Abstr.; Soils Fert.

LC S
DD 630 II
AGRICULTURAL ENGINEERING TODAY. Added/Corp Indian Society of Agricultural Engineers. (19??)-. Periodical. English. Six times a year. $70.00. Indian Society of Agricultural Engineers, Satya Mansion, Flats No 305-306, Community Centre, Ranjit Nagar New Delhi 100 008 India. **(Subscription address:** Prints India, 11 Darya Ganj, New Delhi 110002 India. **Tel** 011 91 11 3268645, FAX 011 91 11 3275542, telex 31-61087 PRIN-IN.)

LC S
DD 630 AT
AGRICULTURAL GAZETTE OF TASMANIA. (19??)-. Periodical. English.

LC S1 .A16 **ISSN** 0002-1482
DD 630.5 US
CCC
Pr Rev.
AGRICULTURAL HISTORY. [Agric. hist.]. **Added/Corp** Agricultural History Society. Vol. 1 (Jan. 1927)-. Periodical. English. Four times a year (Jan., Apr., July, Oct.). $63.00. University of California Press, 2120 Berkeley Way, Berkeley CA 94720. **Tel** (510)642-4191, (510)642-3907, FAX (510)642-9917. **ED** R. Douglas Hurt. **Bk Rev. Ad Acc. Circ:** 1,250 (ctrl). available on microfilm and microfiche from University Microfilms International (UMI). Documents available from The Genuine Article, UMI Article Clearinghouse. ***Supersedes** Agricultural History Society. Papers.*
Desc: Study of agriculture, in all countries and historical periods, from social, technological and scientific viewpoints.
Ind/Abst AGRICOLA [Full Cov.]; Am. Hist. Life (1954-); Am. Bibliogr. Slavic East Europ. Stud.; Arts Humanit. Citation Index [Full Cov.]; Biocont. News Inf.; Br. Archaeol. Bibliogr. (?-19??); Curr. Cit.; Curr. Contents Agric. Biol. Environ. Sci.; Curr. Contents Arts Humanit.; Curr. Geogr. Publ. (199?-); Dairy Sci. Abstr.; EP Collect.; Expand. Acad. Index (1989-); Geogr. Abstr. Human Geogr.; Homework Help.; Humanit. Index; Humanit. Source; Mag. Search; MasterFile FullTEXT 1000; MasterFile FullTEXT 350; MasterFile FullTEXT 650; MasterFile FullTEXT (Jan. 1993-); Middle East Abstr. Index; Newsp. Period. Abstr. (1991-); Nutr. Abstr. Rev., Ser. A, Hum. Exp.; OCLC; Life Sci. Collect.; Plant Breed. Abstr.; Res. Alert [Full Cov.]; Rev. Agric. Entomol.; Rev. Med. Vet. Entomol.; SCISEARCH; Soc. Sci. Cit. Index [Select. Cov.]; Soils Fert.; Telebase; Vocat. Search; West. Hist. Q.

LC S **ISSN** 0002-1490
DD 630 UK
UDC 63(09)
AGRICULTURAL HISTORY REVIEW, THE. [Agric. hist. rev.]. Vol. 1 (1953)-. Periodical. English. Two times a year. $47.92. British Agricultural History Society, Institute of Agricultural History, The University of Reading, Whiteknights, PO Box 229, Reading Berkshire RG6 2AG United Kingdom. **Tel** 011 44 1734 318660. **ED** J Chartres. Index available. cum. index. **Bk Rev. Ad Acc. Circ:** 1,000 (ctrl). available on microfilm and microfiche from University Microfilms International (UMI). Documents available from The Genuine Article.
Desc: The object of the journal is to encourage the study of the history of agriculture and rural economy.
Ind/Abst AGRICOLA [Full Cov.]; Am. Hist. Life (1955-); Anim. Breed. Abstr.; Arts Humanit. Citation Index [Full Cov.]; Br. Archaeol. Bibliogr.; Br. Humanit. Index; Curr. Contents Arts Humanit.; Dairy Sci. Abstr.; Geogr. Abstr. Human Geogr.; Middle East Abstr. Index; Life Sci. Collect.; Res. Alert [Full Cov.]; Soc. Sci. Cit. Index [Select. Cov.]; Soils Fert.; West. Hist. Q.

LC HD9014.A57 A37
DD 338.1/7/0972774 AQ
AGRICULTURAL INFORMATION BULLETIN / PRODUCTION AND MARKETING INTELLIGENCE SERVICE, ANTIGUA & BARBUDA. Added/Corp Antigua and Barbuda. Production and Marketing Intelligence Service. (198?)-. Bulletin. English. Twelve times a year. Production & Marketing Intelligence Service, St. John's Antigua & Barbuda.

LC S562.C2 A4a
DD 630.68 CN
AGRICULTURAL INPUT PRICES, PRICE INDICES AND AVAILABILITY IN ALBERTA. Main/Corp Alberta. Engineering and Home Design Branch. (1974/75)-. English. Alberta Agriculture, Engineering and Home Design Branch, Family Farm Division, Edmonton Alberta Canada.

LC S
DD 630 US
AGRICULTURAL ISSUES OVERVIEW. Added/Corp National Agricultural Library (U.S.). No. 1 (1981)-. English.

LC HD2196.5 .A34
DD 338.1/0995/3021 PP
AGRICULTURAL LARGEHOLDINGS (PRELIMINARY). Added/Corp Papua New Guinea. National Statistical Office. (Dec. 31, 1979)-. English. One time a year. k7.00. National Statistical Office / New Guinea, PO Wards Strip NCO, Papua New Guinea. **Tel** 011 675 27182 271172, FAX 011 657 255057, telex FINANCE NE 22312. ***Continues** Rural Industries (Port Moresby, Papua New Guinea). Largeholdings Covered. Preliminary Statement.*

LC KF1681.A15 A38 **ISSN** 1051-2780
DD 349.73/02463 347.3002463 US
AGRICULTURAL LAW DIGEST. See Law.

LC Z675.A8 A29 ISSN 0095-2699
DD 026/.63/0973 US
AGRICULTURAL LIBRARIES INFORMATION NOTES. See Library and Information Sciences.

LC S
DD 630 US
AGRICULTURAL LIBRARIES INFORMATION NOTES. SUPPLEMENT. See Library and Information Sciences.

LC S583 ISSN 1075-3354
DD 631 US
•**AGRICULTURAL NEWS (HAMDEN, N.Y.).** (AGRICULTURAL NEWS : A PUBLICATION OF CORNELL COOPERATIVE EXTENSION IN DELAWARE COUNTY.). [Agric. news]. **Added/Corp** Cornell Cooperative Extension. Delaware County. Agricultural Program. Vol. 1, No. 1 (Feb. 1994)-. Periodical. English. Twelve times a year. Cooperative Extension Association of Delaware County Center, Route 10, PO Box 184, Hamden NY 13782. ***Continues*** *Extension Connection, 0747-1769.*

LC S
DD 630 II
UDC 338.43(540)
AGRICULTURAL NEWS LETTER (SRINAGAR, INDIA). (AGRICULTURAL NEWS LETTER.). **Added/Corp** Jammu and Kashmir (India). Agriculture Information Service. Periodical. English. Irregular. ***Continues*** *Agriculture News Letter.*

LC S451.5 ISSN 0228-2038
DD 630/.9713/133 CN
UDC 63(713)
AGRICULTURAL NEWSLETTER (SUDBURY). (AGRICULTURAL NEWSLETTER.). [Agric. newsl.]. **Added/Corp** Ontario. Ministry of Agriculture and Food. **VFOAT** Lettre de Nouvelles Agricoles. Newsletter. English (French). Free. Ministry of Agriculture & Food Ontario, Extension Branch, 1414 Lasalle Blvd., Sudbury Ontario P3A 1Z6. ctrl circ. ***Continues*** *Ontario. Ministry of Agriculture and Food. Newsletter, 0228-202X.*

LC HD9000.1 .A473 ISSN 1015-1540
DD 338.1/8/05 FR
TITLE CHANGE
AGRICULTURAL POLICIES, MARKETS, AND TRADE. [Agric. policies mark. trade]. **Added/Corp** Organisation for Economic Co-Operation and Development. (1988)-(1994). English. OECD Publications and Information Center, 2 rue Andre-Pascal, 75775 Paris Cedex 16 France. **Tel** 011 33 1 49104262, US:(202)785-6323, FAX 011 33 1 45248500, 011 33 1 45248176, telex 620 160 OCDE. **(Subscription address:** OECD Publications Center, 2001 L Street, Suite 700, Washington DC 20036. **Tel** (202)822-3873, (202)785-6323.**)** ***Continued in part by*** *Agricultural Policies, Markets, and Trade. In the Central and Eastern European Countries, the New Independent States, and China;* ***Continued by*** *Agricultural Policies, Markets and Trade in OECD Countries.*
Desc: Reviews developments in the agricultural economy of OECD countries. Examines the outlook for cereals and feeds, sugar and other sweeteners, dairy products, meat, and fruit and vegetables. Examines developments in agricultural trade, presents data on levels of subsidies to agriculture by commodity and by country, and presents brief summaries of agricultural policy changes taken in selected countries.

LC HD9000.1 .A473
DD 338.1/8/05 FR
•**AGRICULTURAL POLICIES, MARKETS AND TRADE IN OECD COUNTRIES.** **Added/Corp** Organisation for Economic Co-Operation and Development. **VFOAT** Agricultural Policies, Markets and Trade. In OECD Countries; In OECD Countries. (1995)-. English. OECD Publications and Information Center, 2 rue Andre-Pascal, 75775 Paris Cedex 16 France. **Tel** 011 33 1 49104262, US:(202)785-6323, FAX 011 33 1 45248500, 011 33 1 45248176, telex 620 160 OCDE. **(Subscription address:** OECD Publications Center, 2001 L Street, Suite 700, Washington DC 20036. **Tel** (202)822-3873, (202)785-6323.**)** ***Continues*** *Agricultural Policies, Markets, and Trade, 1015-1540.*

LC HD9000.1 .A474
DD 338.1/8/05 FR
•**AGRICULTURAL POLICIES, MARKETS, AND TRADE. IN THE CENTRAL AND EASTERN EUROPEAN COUNTRIES, THE NEW INDEPENDENT STATES, AND CHINA.** **Added/Corp** Organisation for Economic Co-Operation and Development. Centre for Co-Operation with Economies in Transition. **VFOAT** In the Central and Eastern European Countries, the New Independent States, and China; Agricultural Policies, Markets, and Trade. In the Central and Eastern European Countries (CEECs), the New Independent States (NIS), Mongolia and, China; In the Central and Eastern European countries (CEECs), the New Independent States (NIS), Mongolia, and China. (1993)-. English. One time a year. 150.00F France; 195.00F other. OECD Publications and Information Center, 2 rue Andre-Pascal, 75775 Paris Cedex 16 France. **Tel** 011 33 1 49104262, US:(202)785-6323, FAX 011 33 1 45248500, 011 33 1 45248176, telex 620 160 OCDE. **(Subscription address:** OECD Publications Center, 2001 L Street, Suite 700, Washington DC 20036. **Tel** (202)822-3873, (202)785-6323.**)** ***Continues in part*** *Agricultural Policies, Markets and Trade, 1015-1540.*

LC HD ISSN 0895-9781
DD 338 US
AGRICULTURAL POLICY AND ECONOMIC ISSUES. [Agric. policy econ. issues]. **Added/Corp** United States. Dept. of Agriculture. Oklahoma State University. Cooperative Extension Service. Oklahoma State University. Dept. of Agricultural Economics. Oklahoma State University. Dept. of Agricultural Economics. Division of Agriculture. (1978)-. Periodical. English. Ten times a year. Free on request. Oklahoma State University / Agriculture, Department of Agricultural Economics, 313 AG Hall, Stillwater OK 74078. **Tel** (405)744-5398.

LC HD ISSN 0112-0603
DD 338.1 NZ
AGRICULTURAL POLICY DISCUSSION PAPER. [Agric. policy discuss. pap.]. **VFOAT** Discussion Paper - Centre for Agricultural Policy Studies, Massey University. (1982)-. Monographic series. English. Irregular.
Ind/Abst World Agric. Econ. Rural Sociol. Abstr.

LC S ISSN 0111-6339
DD 630 NZ
AGRICULTURAL POLICY PROCEEDINGS. [Agric. policy proc.]. (1981)-. Periodical. English. Three times a week.
Ind/Abst Nutr. Abstr. Rev., Ser. B, Live Feeds and Feed.; Pig News Inf.; Postharvest News Inf.; Poult. Abstr.; Rice Abstr.; Sorghum Mill. Abstr.; World Agric. Econ. Rural Sociol. Abstr.

LC S
DD 630 FR
AGRICULTURAL POLICY REPORTS (SERIES). **Main/Corp** Organization for Economic Cooperation and Development. (19??)-. Monographic series. English. Irregular. Price varies per volume. OECD Publications and Information Center, 2 rue Andre-Pascal, 75775 Paris Cedex 16 France. **Tel** 011 33 1 49104262, US:(202)785-6323, FAX 011 33 1 45248500, 011 33 1 45248176, telex 620 160 OCDE.

LC S ISSN 0065-4493
DD 630 UK
AGRICULTURAL PROGRESS. **Added/Corp** Agricultural Education Association. Vol. 1 (1924)-. English. One time a year (Aug.). $27.37. Agricultural Education Association, 5 Capel Close, Oxford OX2 7LA United Kingdom. **Tel** 011 44 1865 58654. **ED** A. R. Staniforth. **Bk Rev**. **Ad Acc**. **Circ:** 800.
Desc: Agricultural development and education.
Ind/Abst AGRICOLA [Full Cov.]; Agric. Eng. Abstr. (1991-); Anim. Breed. Abstr.; Dairy Sci. Abstr.; Field Crop Abstr.; Grass. Forage Abstr.; Index Vet.; Leis., Rec., Tour. Abstr.; Maize Abstr.; Nutr. Abstr. Rev., Ser. B, Live Feeds and Feed.; Nutr. Abstr. Rev., Ser. A, Hum. Exp.; Plant Breed. Abstr.; Postharvest News Inf.; Rural Dev. Abstr.; Soils Fert.; Vet. Bull.; World Agric. Econ. Rural Sociol. Abstr.

LC HD319.A4 A29b ISSN 0701-7502
DD 333.3/35/097123 CN
AGRICULTURAL REAL ESTATE VALUES IN ALBERTA. See Real Estate.

LC S530.5 .F37
DD 630/.72 UK
AGRICULTURAL RESEARCH CENTRES. 7th Ed. (1983)-. Trade Publication. English. Every 3 years. $508.00. Longman Group Ltd., Fourth Avenue, Longman House, Harlow Essex CM19 5SR United Kingdom. **Tel** 011 44 1279 429655, FAX 011 44 1279 431067, telex 81259. **(Subscription address:** Gale Research Co., 835 Penobscot Building, Detroit MI 48226. **Tel** (800)347-4253.**)** ***Continues*** *Agricultural Research Index.*
Desc: Covers more than 130 countries with more than 8,000 detailed profiles of agricultural research and technology laboratories.

LC S ISSN 0749-2197
DD 630 US
UDC 63(047.31)(781)
AGRICULTURAL RESEARCH IN KANSAS. [Agric. res. Kans.]. **Main/Corp** Kansas Agricultural Experiment Station. **VFOAT** Biennial Report of the Agricultural Experiment Station; Report of the Director for the Biennium Ending .... 29th (1978)-. English. Every 2 years. Agricultural Experiment Station / Kansas, Kansas State University, Manhattan KS 66506. **Tel** (913)532-6147. **ED** E K Schofield and S C Morgan. **Circ:** 3,000 (ctrl). ***Continues*** *Biennial Report of the Director. Kansas Agricultural Experiment Station, 0361-1558.*
Desc: Contains highlights of agricultural research at Kansas State University, plus lists of all publications related to that research and of grants received during the Biennium.
Ind/Abst AGRICOLA [Full Cov.].

LC S ISSN 0002-1628
DD 630 II
CODEN ARJKAQ
AGRICULTURAL RESEARCH JOURNAL OF KERALA. [Agric. res. j. Kerala]. **Added/Corp** Kerala Agricultural University. Trivandrum, India (City). Agricultural College and Research Institute. (1962)-. Periodical. English. Two times a year. $50.00. Agricultural Research Journal, Vellanikkara 680654 Triehor, Kerala India. **Tel** 21822. **(Subscription address:** Prints India, 11 Darya Ganj, New Delhi 110002 India. **Tel** 011 91 11 3268645, FAX 011 91 11 3275542, telex 31-61087 PRIN-IN.**)** Documents available from BIOSIS Document Express, CASDDS.
Ind/Abst Agrofor. Abstr. (19??-19??); Biocont. News Inf.; Biol. Abstr.; Chem. Abstr.; Hortic. Abstr.; Life Sci. Collect.; Plant Grow. Reg. Abstr.; Rev. Plant Pathol.; Rice Abstr.; Soils Fert.

LC S
DD 630 II
AGRICULTURAL RESEARCH NEWS LETTER. Vol. 1 (Aug. 1973)-. Periodical. English. Four times a year. $25.00 one-year; $45.00 two-year; $60.00 three-year. Agricultural Research Communication Centre, Sadar Karnal 132001, Haryana India. **Tel** 011 91 3036. **ED** R.D. Goel. **Circ:** 2,000.
Desc: Reports original research with new theories on all aspects of plant and soil sciences, animal husbandry, and veterinary and dairy sciences.

LC S ISSN 0193-2853
DD 630 US
AGRICULTURAL RESEARCH RESULTS. (SOUTHERN SERIES). (AGRICULTURAL RESEARCH RESULTS. SOUTHERN SERIES - MICROFORM.). **Added/Corp** United States. Science and Education Administration. Agricultural Research. Southern Region. United States. Agricultural Research Service. Southern Region. **VFOAT** Agricultural Research Results. ARR-S. (1979)-. English. Agricultural Research Southern Region, US Department of Agriculture, PO Box 53326, New Orleans LA 70153.

LC S ISSN 0374-5252
DD 630 UA
CODEN AGRRAA
AGRICULTURAL RESEARCH REVIEW. [Agric. res. rev.]. Vol. 1 (1922)-. Academic Scholarly Publication. English. Editing Publication and Library Sub-Dept, Agrarian Culture Department, Ministry of Agriculture, Cairo Arab Republic of Egypt. Documents available from BIOSIS Document Express, CASDDS.
Ind/Abst Biocont. News Inf. (19??-19??); Biodeter. Abstr. (1991-); Biol. Abstr.; Chem. Abstr.; Cot. Trop. Fibr. Abstr. Bibliogr.; Dairy Sci. Abstr.; Hortic. Abstr.; Index Vet.; Nutr. Abstr. Rev., Ser. A, Hum. Exp.; Plant Breed. Abstr.; Postharvest News Inf.; Potato Abstr.; Poult. Abstr.; Rev. Agric. Entomol.; Rev. Med. Vet. Entomol.; Rev. Plant Pathol.; Rice Abstr.; Seed Abstr.; Small Anim. Abstr. Bibliogr.; Soils Fert.; Sorghum Mill. Abstr.; Weed Abstr.; Wheat Barley Trit. Abstr.

LC S1 .A1815 ISSN 0002-161X
DD 630.72 US
CODEN AGREA5
Pr Rev.
AGRICULTURAL RESEARCH (WASHINGTON). (AGRICULTURAL RESEARCH / U.S. DEPARTMENT OF AGRICULTURE.). [Agric. res.]. **Added/Corp** United States. Science and Education Administration. United States. Agricultural Research Administration. United States. Agricultural Research Service. Vol. 1, No. 1 (Jan. 1953)-. Government Publication. English. Twelve times a year. $38.00. US Department of Agriculture, 14th Street and Independence Avenue SW, Washington DC 20250. **Tel** (202)720-5457. **(Subscription address:** Superintendent of Documents, US Government Printing Office, Washington DC 20402.**)** cum. index. available on microfilm and microfiche from University Microfilms International (UMI). Documents available from The Genuine Article, UMI Article Clearinghouse, Documents on Demand.
Desc: Presents results of United States Department of Agriculture research projects in livestock management, crops, soils, fruits and vegetables, poultry, and related agricultural fields.
Ind/Abst AGRICOLA [Full Cov.]; BioBusiness; Biol. Dig.; Coal Abstr.; Curr. Cit.; Curr. Contents Agric. Biol. Environ. Sci.; Energy Res. Abstr.; Environ. Abstr.; EP Collect.; Expand. Acad. Index (1992-); F&S Index Plus Text, Int. [Select. Cov.]; Foods Adlibra; Garden Lit. (1992-); Homework Help.; Index Vet.; INIS Atomindex [Micro.]; Mag. Search; MasterFile FullTEXT 1000; MasterFile FullTEXT 350; MasterFile FullTEXT 650; MasterFile FullTEXT (July 1993-) [Full Txt.]; Newsp. Period. Abstr. (1988-); OCLC; PESTDOC; Pollut. Abstr. Indexes; Potato Abstr.; Poult. Abstr.; PROMT; Res. Alert [Select. Cov.]; Rev. Med. Vet. Entomol.; SCISEARCH; Telebase; Trade Ind. ASAP [Full Txt.]; Trade Ind. Index [Full Txt.]; Vitis Vitic. Enol. Abstr.; Vocat. Search.

LC HD1917 .U5
DD 338.1/094 US
AGRICULTURAL REVIEW FOR EUROPE.
Added/Corp United Nations. FAO/ECE Agriculture and Timber Division. No. 27 (1983-1984)-. Government Publication. English. One time a year. United Nations Publications, 2 United Nations Plaza, Room DC2 0853, Department 007C, New York NY 10017. **Tel** (212)963-8303, (800)253-9646. ***Continues*** *Review of the Agricultural Situation in Europe at the End of ..., 0085-5618;* ***Absorbed*** *Agricultural Trade in Europe.*
Ind/Abst Dairy Sci. Abstr.; Maize Abstr.; Potato Abstr.; Rice Abstr.; Sorghum Mill. Abstr.; Wheat Barley Trit. Abstr.; World Agric. Econ. Rural Sociol. Abstr.

LC S **ISSN** 0253-1496
DD 630 II
AGRICULTURAL REVIEWS.
Vol. 1, No. 1 (June 1980)-. Periodical. English. Four times a year. $55.00. Agricultural Research Communication Centre, Sadar Karnal 132001, Haryana India. **Tel** 011 91 3036. **(Subscription address:** Prints India, 11 Darya Ganj, New Delhi 110002 India. **Tel** 011 91 11 3268645, FAX 011 91 11 3275542, telex 31-61087 PRIN-IN.)
Desc: Review articles reporting original research with a new theory on all aspects of plant and soil sciences, animal husbandry, veterinary & dairy sciences.
Ind/Abst Anim. Breed. Abstr.; Biocont. News Inf.; Curr. Cit.; Dairy Sci. Abstr.; Field Crop Abstr.; Irr. Drain. Abstr.; Nutr. Abstr. Rev., Ser. B, Live Feeds and Feed.; Plant Breed. Abstr.; Postharvest News Inf.; Potato Abstr.; Rev. Agric. Entomol.; Rev. Plant Pathol.; Soils Fert.; Sorghum Mill. Abstr.; Weed Abstr.; Wheat Barley Trit. Abstr.

LC S269.F5 A335 **ISSN** 0789-600X
DD 630/.5 FI
CODEN ASFIEB
AGRICULTURAL SCIENCE IN FINLAND.
Added/Corp Maatalouden Tutkimuskeskus (Finland) Suomen Maataloustieteellinen Seura. Meijeritieteellinen Seura. Vol. 1, No. 1 (1992)-. Periodical. English (summaries and/or abstracts in Finnish). Six times a year. Fmk500. Agricultural Research Centre of Finland, Data & Information Services, SF 31600 Jokionen Finland. **Tel** 011 358 16 1881, FAX 011 358 16 188339, telex 6741 MTTK SF. **ED** Professor Dr. Aarne Kurppa. Index available (indexed in databases). **Ad Acc, Adv Mgr:** Sari Torkko, **Tel** 358-16-1881. **Circ:** 1,500 (ctrl). Documents available from The Genuine Article. ***Formed by the union of*** *Annales Agriculture Fenniae, 0570-1538; Journal of Agricultural Science in Finland, 0782-4386* ***and*** *Finnish Journal of Dairy Science.* ***Continued in part by*** *Finnish Journal of Dairy Science (Helsinki, Finland : 1994).*
Desc: An international journal publishing original reports on agricultural research advancing Finnish agriculture. It is also open for foreign authors. Reports on basic as well as applied research are published.
Ind/Abst Curr. Contents Agric. Biol. Environ. Sci.; Food Sci. Technol. Abstr.; Poult. Abstr.; Res. Alert [Select. Cov.].

LC S530.52.N4 A35
DD 607/.0492 NE
UDC 63(492)
AGRICULTURAL SCIENCE IN THE NETHERLANDS.
English. Fl1,500.00. International Agricultural Centre, PO Box 88, 6700 AB Wageningen The Netherlands. **Tel** 08370-90111, telex 45888 INTAS NL.

LC S **ISSN** 1030-4614
DD 630 II
AGRICULTURAL SCIENCE. MELBOURNE.
(AGRICULTURAL SCIENCE : THE JOURNAL OF THE AUSTRALIAN INSTITUTE OF AGRICULTURAL SCIENCE.). [Agric. sci. Melb.]. **Added/Corp** Australian Institute of Agricultural Science. **VFOAT** Journal of the Institute of Agricultural Science; Journal of the Australian Institute of Agricultural Science and the New Zealand Institute of Agricultural Science. Vol. 1, No. 1 (Dec. 1987)-. Periodical. English. Six times a year. 150.00Aus$. Australian Institute of Agricultural Science, 1st Floor, 91 Rathdowne Street, Carlton Victoria 3053 Australia. **Tel** 011 61 3 6621077, FAX 011 61 3 6622727. **ED** Simon Field. **Ad Acc, Adv Mgr:** Amanda Davis. Full Page (B&W) 530.00Aus$. Half Page (B&W) 350.00Aus$. **Circ:** 4,000. ***Continues*** *Journal of the Australian Institute of Agricultural Science, 0045-0545.*
Desc: Presents topics which cover research and commerical innovation in agriculture throughout Australia.

LC S **ISSN** 0970-0722
DD 630 II
UDC 63
CODEN ASPREK
AGRICULTURAL SCIENCE PROGRESS.
[Agric. sci. prog.]. **Added/Corp** Academy for the Advancement of Agricultural Sciences. Indian Society for Plant Physiology. Vol. 1 (1983)-. Academic Scholarly Publication. English. $20.00. Academy for the Advancement of Agricultural Sciences, Indian Society for Plant Physiology, New Delhi India. Documents available from CASDDS.
Ind/Abst Chem. Abstr. (1983-).

LC HD1775.N9 N58a
DD 338.1/09784 US
AGRICULTURAL SITUATION AND OUTLOOK.
Main/Corp North Dakota State University. Cooperative Extension Service. (19??)-. English. North Dakota State University / CES, Cooperative Extension Service, Fargo ND 58105.

LC HD2071 .A75 **ISSN** 0002-1679
DD 338.1 II
AGRICULTURAL SITUATION IN INDIA.
Added/Corp India (Republic). Ministry of Agriculture . Directorate of Economics and Statistics. (19??)-. Periodical. English. Twelve times a year. $36.00. Directorate of Economics and Statistics / Agriculture, Ministry of Agriculture, A-Block 2E/3, Curzoor Old Barracks, Kasturba Ganothi Marg 110001 New Delhi. **Tel** 381523. **(Subscription address:** Prints India, 11 Darya Ganj, New Delhi 110002 India. **Tel** 011 91 11 3268645, FAX 011 91 11 3275542, telex 31-61087 PRIN-IN.) **ED** Shri Brajesh Kumar Gantam. Index available. **Bk Rev. Ad Acc. Circ:** 1,100 (ctrl).
Desc: Covers agricultural economics and allied subjects.
Ind/Abst Agric. Eng. Abstr. (1991-); Agrofor. Abstr. (19??-19??); Anim. Breed. Abstr.; Cot. Trop. Fibr. Abstr. Bibliogr.; Dairy Sci. Abstr.; Field Crop Abstr.; For. Prod. Abstr. (1991-); For. Abstr.; Int. Dev. Abstr. (?-?); Int. Labour Doc.; Irr. Drain. Abstr.; Leis., Rec., Tour. Abstr.; Maize Abstr.; Pig News Inf.; Postharvest News Inf.; Potato Abstr.; Poult. Abstr.; Rice Abstr.; Rural Dev. Abstr.; Seed Abstr.; Soils Fert.; Sorghum Mill. Abstr.; Soyabean Abstr.; Weed Abstr.; Wheat Barley Trit. Abstr.; World Agric. Econ. Rural Sociol. Abstr.

LC HD1920.5 .A18a
DD 338.1/094 BE
TITLE CHANGE
AGRICULTURAL SITUATION IN THE COMMUNITY; REPORT, THE.
Main/Corp Commission of the European Communities. (1975)-(1993). English. Commission of the European Communities, Directorate of General Information, Avenue D Auderghem, 45 Breydel boulevard, B 1049 Brussels Belgium. **Tel** 011 32 2 2357639, telex 21877 COMEU B. ***Continued by*** *Agricultural Situation in the European Union.*

LC HD1920.5 .A18a
DD 338.1/094 BE
•AGRICULTURAL SITUATION IN THE EUROPEAN UNION, THE.
Added/Corp European Commission. (1994)-. English. Commission of the European Communities, Directorate of General Information, Avenue D Auderghem, 45 Breydel boulevard, B 1049 Brussels Belgium. **Tel** 011 32 2 2357639, telex 21877 COMEU B. ***Continues*** *Commission of the European Communities. Agricultural Situation in the Community.*

LC HD2067 .U54A **ISSN** 0360-3393
DD 338.1/0951 US
UDC 338.43(51)
AGRICULTURAL SITUATION IN THE PEOPLE'S REPUBLIC OF CHINA AND OTHER COMMUNIST ASIAN COUNTRIES, THE.
Main/Corp United States. Dept. of Agriculture. Economic Research Service. 1973/74-. Government Publication. English. US Department of Agriculture / Economic Research Service, 1301 New York Avenue, Room 208, Washington DC 20250. **Tel** (202)447-4111.

LC HD1992 .U56 **ISSN** 0360-4098
DD 338.1/0947 US
UDC 338.43(47)
AGRICULTURAL SITUATION IN THE SOVIET UNION, THE.
Main/Corp United States. Dept. of Agriculture. Economic Research Service. Government Publication. English. US Department of Agriculture / Economic Research Service, 1301 New York Avenue, Room 208, Washington DC 20250. **Tel** (202)447-4111.

LC S530 **ISSN** 0228-1090
DD 630/.607123 CN
AGRICULTURAL SOCIETIES NEWSLETTER.
[Agric. soc. newsl.]. **Added/Corp** Alberta. Farm Development Division. Alberta. Engineering and Rural Services Division. Alberta. Rural Services Division. (1???)-. Newsletter. English. Six times a year. Free on request. Alberta Agriculture / Market Analysis, 7000 113th Street, Edmonton Alberta T5K 2C8 Canada. **Tel** (403)427-2121, FAX (403)435-4725.

LC S
DD 630 TZ
AGRICULTURAL STATISTICAL BULLETIN.
(1991)-. Bulletin. English.

LC S3 .A57 **ISSN** 0308-521X
DD 630 UK
CCC
CODEN AGSYD5
Pr Rev.
AGRICULTURAL SYSTEMS.
[Agric. syst.]. Vol. 1 (Jan. 1976)-. Academic Scholarly Publication. English. Twelve times a year. $1090.00. Elsevier Applied Science, An Imprint of Elsevier Science Ltd., The Boulevard, Langford Lane, Kidlington, Oxford OX5 1GB United Kingdom. **Tel** 011 44 1865 843000, 011 44 1865 843699, FAX 011 44 1865 843010. **(Subscription address:** Elsevier Science Ltd. / Oxford Fulfillment Centre, PO Box 800, Kidlington OX5 1DX United Kingdom. **Tel** 011 44 865 843355.) **ED** C. R. W. Spedding. **Bk Rev. Ad Acc.** available on microfilm and microfiche from University Microfilms International (UMI); available on an online database from Elsevier Electronic Subscriptions (EES). Documents available from The Genuine Article, BIOSIS Document Express, Documents on Demand. ***Absorbed*** *Agricultural Administration and Extension, 0269-7475.*
Desc: Publishes the results of studies of whole agricultural systems or relevant parts of them whether at the level of a production process, enterprise, farm, regional agriculture or on a world basis.
Ind/Abst AGRICOLA [Full Cov.]; Agric. Eng. Abstr. (19??-19??); Agrofor. Abstr. (19??-19??); Anim. Breed. Abstr.; BioBusiness (1989-); Biol. Abstr.; Cot. Trop. Fibr. Abstr. Bibliogr.; Curr. Aware. Biol. Sci., CABS; Curr. Cit.; Curr. Contents Agric. Biol. Environ. Sci.; Dairy Sci. Abstr.; Ecol. Abstr.; Energy Inf. Abstr.; Environ. Abstr.; Environ. Period. Bibliogr.; Field Crop Abstr.; For. Prod. Abstr. (19??-19??); For. Abstr.; Geogr. Abstr. Phys. Geogr. (?-?); Geogr. Abstr. Human Geogr.; Grass. Forage Abstr.; Hortic. Abstr.; Index Vet.; Int. Abstr. Oper. Res. [Select. Cov.]; Int. Dev. Abstr.; Int. Labour Doc.; Irr. Drain. Abstr.; Maize Abstr.; Nutr. Abstr. Rev., Ser. B, Live Feeds and Feed.; Plant Breed. Abstr.; Postharvest News Inf.; Potato Abstr.; Res. Alert [Full Cov.]; Rev. Agric. Entomol.; Rice Abstr. (1989-); Rural Dev. Abstr.; Sci. Cit. Index; SCISEARCH; Seed Abstr.; Soc. Sci. Cit. Index [Select. Cov.]; Soils Fert.; Sorghum Mill. Abstr.; Soyabean Abstr.; Vet. Bull.; Weed Abstr.; Wheat Barley Trit. Abstr.; Wildl. Rev.; World Agric. Econ. Rural Sociol. Abstr.

LC S
DD 630 US
AGRICULTURAL TRADE HIGHLIGHTS.
See Business and Economics-Commerce.

LC S **ISSN** 0705-8101
DD 630 AT
AGRICULTURAL TRENDS (BRISBANE, QLD.).
(AGRICULTURAL TRENDS.). **Added/Corp** Queensland. Dept. of Primary Industries. Marketing Services Branch. Vol. 1, No. 1 (March 1981)-. Periodical. English. Irregular. Department of Primary Industries / Queensland Australia, GPO Box 46, Brisbane Queensland 4001 Australia. **Tel** 011 61 7 2393111, FAX 011 61 7 2212490, telex AA41620.

LC S494.5.W3 A37 **ISSN** 0378-3774
DD 631.6 NE
CCC
CODEN AWMADF
Pr Rev.
AGRICULTURAL WATER MANAGEMENT.
[Agric. water manage.]. Vol. 1 (Dec. 1976)-. Academic Scholarly Publication. English. Nine times a year. $713.00. Elsevier Science Publishers BV, PO Box 211, 1000 AE Amsterdam Netherlands. **Tel** 011 31 20 4853641, 011 31 20 4853642, FAX 011 31 20 4853598. **ED** J Wesseling and N A de Ridder. available on microfilm and microfiche from University Microfilms International (UMI); available on an online database from Elsevier Electronic Subscriptions (EES). Documents available from The Genuine Article, BIOSIS Document Express, Documents on Demand.
Desc: Concerned with the publication of scientific papers of international significance to the management of agricultural water.
Ind/Abst AGRICOLA; Agric. Eng. Abstr. (1991-); AQUAREF; BioBusiness; Biol. Agric. Index; Biol. Abstr.; Crop Physiol. Abstr.; Curr. Aware. Biol. Sci., CABS; Curr. Cit.; Curr. Contents Agric. Biol. Environ. Sci.; Ecol. Abstr.; Energy Inf. Abstr.; Environ. Abstr.; Environ. Period. Bibliogr.; Field Crop Abstr.; Geogr. Abstr. Phys. Geogr.; Geogr. Abstr. Human Geogr.; GeoRef; Grass. Forage Abstr.; Hortic. Abstr.; Int. Abstr. Oper. Res. [Select. Cov.]; Int. Dev. Abstr.; Irr. Drain. Abstr.; Maize Abstr.; Meteorol. Geoastrophys. Abstr.; Life Sci. Collect.; Plant Breed. Abstr.; Pollut. Abstr. Indexes; Potato Abstr.; Res. Alert [Full Cov.]; Rice Abstr.; Rural Dev. Abstr.; Sci. Cit. Index; SCISEARCH; Soils Fert.; Sorghum Mill. Abstr.; Soyabean Abstr.; Weed Abstr.; Wheat Barley Trit. Abstr.; World Agric. Econ. Rural Sociol. Abstr.

LC HD1501
DD 305.555 US
AGRICULTURAL WORK FORCE OF ... .
Added/Corp United States. Dept. of Agriculture. Economic Research Service. (1985)-. Government Publication. English. Every 2 years. US Department of Agriculture, 14th Street and Independence Avenue SW, Washington DC 20250. **Tel** (202)720-5457. ***Continues*** *Hired Farm Working Force.*

LC QL ISSN 0269-0543
DD 591 UK
CCC
CODEN AZREE6

AGRICULTURAL ZOOLOGY REVIEWS.
See Zoology.

LC S ISSN 0194-4452
DD 630 US

AGRICULTURE ACROSS MICHIGAN.
Added/Corp Michigan Agricultural Reporting Service. Michigan Agricultural Statistics Service. Issue No. 79-01 (Jan. 15, 1979)-. Government Publication. English. Twelve times a year. $10.00. US Department of Agriculture / National Agricultural Statistics Service (NASS), Room 5829 South Building, Washington DC 20250. **Tel** (202)720-4020, FAX (314)875-5231.
Ind/Abst Field Crop Abstr.; Grass. Forage Abstr.

LC S323 .A35
DD 338.1/096 FR
UDC 338.43(6)

AGRICULTURE AFRICAINE, L'. 1st Ed.;
1970-. French. One time a year. Ediafric la Documentation Africaine, 10 rue Vineuse, 75116 Paris France. **Tel** 011 33 1 44308100, FAX 011 33 1 45208174.

LC S
DD 630 FR

AGRICULTURE ALGERIENNE. A64.
(19??)-. French. Irregular. 990.00F. IC Publications Ediafric, 10 rue Vineuse, 75116 Paris France. **Tel** 011 33 1 44308100.

LC HD1401 ISSN 0002-1725
DD 338.1/0954 II

AGRICULTURE AND AGRO-INDUSTRIES JOURNAL. [Agric. agro-ind. j.].
Vol. 1 (Feb. 1968)-. Periodical. English. Twelve times a year. $1.24. Chary Publications, 14 Sidh Prasad Ghatkopar Mahul Road, Tilak Nagar PO 89, Bombay India. **Tel** 011 91 22 5518254.
Ind/Abst EMBASE.

LC Z ISSN 0364-7994
DD 016.63 US
TITLE CHANGE

AGRICULTURE & FOOD.
Added/Corp United States. National Technical Information Service. **VAT** Agriculture and Food. (19??)-(1991). English. National Technical Information Service - NTIS, Room 2027S, 5285 Port Royal Road, Springfield VA 22161. **Tel** (703)487-4630, (703)487-4660, (703)487-4650, FAX (703)321-8547, telex 89-9405. Index Available in last issue of each volume--loose separately paged. ***Continued by** NTIS Alert. Agriculture & Food.*
Desc: Provides information on agricultural chemistry, equipment and resource surveys, agronomy, plant pathology, animal husbandry, etc.

LC S451.5 ISSN 0705-3983
DD 630/.97123 CN
CCC
CODEN AFBUD3
SUSPENDED

AGRICULTURE AND FORESTRY BULLETIN.
Added/Corp University of Alberta. Faculty of Agriculture and Forestry. No. 33 (Spring 1977)-(19??). Bulletin. English. Four times a year. Free. Agricultural and Forestry Bulletin, University of Alberta, Faculty of Extension, Edmonton Alberta T6G 2G4 Canada. **Tel** (403)492-3029, FAX (403)493-9009. **ED** P. Jerome Martin. **Ad Acc. Circ:** 11,500. available on microfilm and microfiche from University Microfilms International (UMI). Documents available from CASDDS. ***Continues** Agriculture Bulletin, 0568-9074.*
Ind/Abst AGRICOLA [Full Cov.]; Anim. Breed. Abstr. (-1988); Chem. Abstr. (Vol. 14, No. 1-4, 1991); Dairy Sci. Abstr.; Field Crop Abstr.; For. Prod. Abstr.; For. Abstr.; Grass. Forage Abstr.; Index Vet.; Leis., Rec., Tour. Abstr.; Nutr. Abstr. Rev., Ser. B, Live Feeds and Feed.; Pig News Inf.; Poult. Abstr.; Rev. Med. Vet. Entomol.; Rural Dev. Abstr.; Soils Fert.; Soyabean Abstr.; World Agric. Econ. Rural Sociol. Abstr.

LC S
DD 630 US

AGRICULTURE & HUMAN RESOURCE SERIES AGRICULTURE. CD-ROM. (19??)-.
English. $145.60 Minnesota residents; $137.80 other. Alde Publishing, PO Box 39326, Minneapolis MN 55396. **Tel** (612)474-3755.

LC HD1401 .A344 ISSN 0889-048X
DD 307.7/2 US
CODEN AHVAEO
Pr Rev.

AGRICULTURE AND HUMAN VALUES.
[Agric. human values]. **Added/Corp** University of Florida. Humanities and Agriculture Program. Vol. 1, No. 1 (Winter 1984)-. Periodical. English. Four times a year (Feb., May, Aug., Nov.). $40.00. Agriculture & Human Values Inc, PO Box 14938, Gainesville FL 32604. **Tel** (904)392-2080, FAX (904)392-3584. **ED** Richard P. Haynes (Philosophy Department, University of Florida, Gainesville, FL 32611). Index available. **Bk Rev**, (Qty: 10/yr). **Ad Acc, Adv Mgr:** Richard Haynes. **Circ:** 650.
Desc: Covers a wide range of topics related in raising some important questions about the direction that agricultural development has taken in the modern world.
Ind/Abst AgBiotech News Inf.; AGRICOLA [Full Cov.]; Curr. Cit.; Dairy Sci. Abstr.; For. Abstr.; Index Vet.; Nematol. Abstr.; Nutr. Abstr. Rev., Ser. B, Live Feeds and Feed.; Philos. Index; Plant Genet. Resour. Abstr.; Rev. Agric. Entomol.; Rural Dev. Abstr.; Soils Fert.; West. Hist. Q.; World Agric. Econ. Rural Sociol. Abstr.

LC HD2151 .A64 ISSN 1032-9722
DD 338.1/0994/05 AT
CODEN ARQUER
TITLE CHANGE

AGRICULTURE & RESOURCES QUARTERLY. [Agric. resour. q.].
Added/Corp Australian Bureau of Agricultural and Resource Economics. **VFOAT** Agriculture and Resources Quarterly. Vol. 1 (Mar. 1989)-(1994). Periodical. English. ABARE / Australian Bureau of Agriculture and Resource Economics, GPO Box 1563, Canberra ACT 2601 Australia. **Tel** 011 61 6 2722000, FAX 011 61 6 2722001. Index available. cum. index. ctrl circ. available on diskette. ***Formed by the union of** Quarterly Review of the Rural Economy, 0156-7446 **and** Resource Trends. **Continued by** Australian Commodities.*
Desc: Commodity forecasts and brief articles on commodities and macroeconomic issues.
Ind/Abst AESIS Q.; AGRICOLA [Select. Cov.]; APAIS, Aust. Public Aff. Inf. Ser.; Dairy Sci. Abstr.; For. Prod. Abstr. (1991-); Leis., Rec., Tour. Abstr.; Maize Abstr.; Sug. Indus. Abstr.; Wheat Barley Trit. Abstr.; World Agric. Econ. Rural Sociol. Abstr.

LC S133 .A37 ISSN 1200-1627
CN

AGRICULTURE CANADA ANNUAL REPORT.
(THE AGRICULTURE CANADA ANNUAL REPORT.). [Agric. can. annu. rep.]. **Main/Corp** Canada. Agriculture Canada. **VFOAT** Rapport Annuel d'Agriculture Canada. (1988/1989)-. Government Publication. English (French). One time a year. Free on request. Agriculture Canada, Communications Branch, Ottawa Ontario K1A 0C7 Canada. ***Continues** Canada. Agriculture Canada. Annual Report for the Year Ended 31 March ..., 1187-8363.*

LC S ISSN 0821-2732
DD 630/.2/74505 CN
UDC 63

AGRICULTURE DE L'AVENIR, L'. [Agric. avenir].
VAT Agriculture de l'Avenir. Vol. 2, No. 1 (Spring 1982)-. French. One time a year. $1.00 per number. Services Agricules Eaton Valley, CP 25, Sawyerville Quebec J0B 3A0 Canada. ***Continues** Agriculture pour l'Avenir, 0821-2732.*

LC KF5900 ISSN 0002-1741
DD 343/.73/07602636 US
UDC 338.23:63(73)

AGRICULTURE DECISIONS.
(AGRICULTURE DECISIONS : DECISIONS OF THE SECRETARY OF AGRICULTURE UNDER THE REGULATORY LAWS ADMINISTERED IN THE UNITED STATES DEPARTMENT OF AGRICULTURE.). **Main/Corp** United States. Dept. of Agriculture. Vol. 1, No. 1 (Jan. 1942)-. Government Publication. English. Twelve times a year. US Department of Agriculture, 14th Street and Independence Avenue SW, Washington DC 20250. **Tel** (202)720-5457. available on microfilm and microfiche from University Microfilms International (UMI).
Desc: Up to 1988, the December issue contains a cumulative list of decisions reported for the year, by act, docket numbers arranged in consecutive order, and cumulative subject-index, by act.

LC S560 ISSN 0833-6210
DD 338.1/3/0971/021 CN

AGRICULTURE ECONOMIC STATISTICS. [Agric. econ. stat.].
Added/Corp Statistics Canada. Farm Income and Prices Section. (Sept. 1986)-. English (French). Irregular. 40.01Can$. Statistics Canada Publications Sales and Services, R.H. Coats Building 6th Floor, Ottawa Ontario K1A 0T6 Canada. **Tel** (613)951-5078, (800)267-6677, FAX (613)951-1584, telex 053-3585.
Desc: Presents estimates of eight agricultural economic indicators: farm income, farm cash receipts, farm operating expenses and depreciation charges, the index of farm production, current values of farm capital, farm debt outstanding, the farm product price index and direct program payments.

LC S601 .A364 ISSN 0167-8809
DD 630/.2/74505 NE
CCC
CODEN AEENDO
Pr Rev.

AGRICULTURE, ECOSYSTEMS & ENVIRONMENT. [Agric. ecosyst. environ.].
VFOAT Agriculture, Ecosystems, and Environment. Vol. 9, No. 1 (Feb. 1983)-. Academic Scholarly Publication. English. Fifteen times a year (5 volumes). $1210.00. Elsevier Science Publishers BV, PO Box 211, 1000 AE Amsterdam Netherlands. **Tel** 011 31 20 4853641, 011 31 20 4853642, FAX 011 31 20 4853598. **ED** J W Sturrock and T L V Ulbricht. available on microfilm and microfiche from University Microfilms International (UMI); available on an online database from Elsevier Electronic Subscriptions (EES). Documents available from The Genuine Article, BIOSIS Document Express, CASDDS, Documents on Demand. ***Formed by the union of** Agriculture and Environment, 0304-1131 **and** Agro-Ecosystems, 0304-3746; **Absorbed** Protection Ecology, 0378-4339.*
Desc: Concerned with the interaction of methods of agricultural production, agro-ecosystems, and the environment.
Ind/Abst AGRICOLA [Full Cov.]; Agric. Eng. Abstr. (1991-); Agrofor. Abstr. (19??-19??); BioBusiness; Biocont. News Inf. (19??-19??); Biodeter. Abstr. (19??-19??); Biol. Agric. Index; Biol. Abstr.; Chem. Abstr. (1983-); Chemorecept. Abstr.; Coal Abstr.; Cot. Trop. Fibr. Abstr. Bibliogr.; Crop Physiol. Abstr.; Curr. Aware. Biol. Sci., CABS; Curr. Cit.; Curr. Contents Agric. Biol. Environ. Sci.; Dairy Sci. Abstr.; Ecol. Abstr.; Ecology Abstr.; EMBASE; Energy Inf. Abstr.; Entomol. Abstr.; Environ. Abstr.; Environ. Period. Bibliogr.; Field Crop Abstr.; Fish Rev.; Food Sci. Technol. Abstr.; For. Abstr.; Genet. Abstr.; Geogr. Abstr. Phys. Geogr.; Geogr. Abstr. Human Geogr.; GeoRef; Grass. Forage Abstr.; Health Saf. Sci. Abstr.; Hortic. Abstr.; Int. Dev. Abstr.; Irr. Drain. Abstr.; Maize Abstr.; Microbiol. Abstr. Sect. A; Microbiol. Abstr. Sect. C; Nematol. Abstr.; Ornamental Hort. (1991-); Life Sci. Collect.; Plant Breed. Abstr.; Pollut. Abstr. Indexes; Postharvest News Inf.; Potato Abstr.; Res. Alert [Full Cov.]; Rev. Agric. Entomol.; Rev. Med. Vet. Entomol.; Rev. Plant Pathol.; Rice Abstr.; Rural Dev. Abstr.; Sci. Cit. Index; SCISEARCH; Seed Abstr.; Soc. Sci. Cit. Index [Select. Cov.]; Soils Fert.; Sorghum Mill. Abstr.; Soyabean Abstr.; Vitis Vitic. Enol. Abstr.; Weed Abstr.; Wheat Barley Trit. Abstr.; Wildl. Rev.; World Agric. Econ. Rural Sociol. Abstr.

LC S ISSN 1181-955X
DD 630 FR
CEASED

AGRICULTURE ET COOPERATION.
(19??)-(19??). French. Sodiap, 18 rue des Pyramides, 75001 Paris France. **Tel** 011 33 1 426031264, FAX 011 31 1 42610692. **ED** Michel Anore.
Ind/Abst LABORDOC.

LC S ISSN 1249-9951
DD 630 FR
Pr Rev.

•AGRICULTURE ET DEVELOPPEMENT (MONTPELLIER).
(AGRICULTURE ET DEVELOPPEMENT.). **Added/Corp** CIRAD (Organization). Departement des Cultures Annuelles. (1994)-. Academic Scholarly Publication. French (summaries and/or abstracts in English, French and Spanish). Four times a year. $109.36. CIRAD CA, Service Editions BP 5035, 34032 Montpellier Cedex France. **Tel** 011 33 67 615918, FAX 011 33 67 615921. **ED** Herve St. Macery. **Bk Rev. Circ:** 2,000. available with illustrations. Documents available from BLDSC. ***Continues** Agronomie Tropicale, 0002-1946.*
Desc: Includes articles on tropical crops; covers natural resources management, food crops, cash crops, etc.

LC Z5075.G8 G83a
DD 016.63/0941 UK

AGRICULTURE, FISHERIES, FOOD.
Main/Corp Great Britain. Ministry of Agriculture, Fisheries and Food. (19??)-. English. Ministry of Agriculture Fisheries and Food, Tolcarne Drive, Pinner HA5 2DT United Kingdom.

LC HD1440.J3 N67a
DD 354.520082/33045 JA

AGRICULTURE, FORESTRY, AND FISHERIES FINANCE CORPORATION : REPORT.
Main/Corp Norin Gyogyo Kinyu Koko. (19??)-. English. Agriculture Forestry and Fisheries Finance Corporation, Head Office 9-3 Otemachi 1-chome, Chiyoda-ku Tokyo Japan.

LC S21 .A37 ISSN 0065-4612
DD 630 US
UDC 63
CODEN XAAHA4

AGRICULTURE HANDBOOK (UNITED STATES. DEPT. OF AGRICULTURE).
(AGRICULTURE HANDBOOK.). [Agric. handb.]. No. 1 (1950)-. Monographic series. English. Price varies per volume. US Department of Agriculture / Forest Service, 201 14th Street SW, Washington DC 20250. **Tel** (202)205-1661, FAX (202)205-1181. Documents available from BIOSIS Document Express, CASDDS.
Ind/Abst Abstr. Bull. Inst. Pap. Sci. Tech.; AGRICOLA [Full Cov.]; Biol. Abstr.; Chem. Abstr.; For. Prod. Abstr.; For. Abstr.; GeoRef; Grass. Forage Abstr.; Hortic. Abstr.; Leis., Rec., Tour. Abstr.; Nutr. Abstr. Rev., Ser. B, Live Feeds and Feed.; Nutr. Abstr. Rev., Ser. A, Hum. Exp.; Ornamental Hort. (1991-); Plant Breed. Abstr.; Postharvest News Inf.; Rev. Agric. Entomol.; Rev. Med. Vet. Mycology; Rev. Plant Pathol.; Rural Dev. Abstr.; Soils Fert.; World Agric. Econ. Rural Sociol. Abstr.

Agriculture

LC S **ISSN** 0279-1412
DD 630 US
AGRICULTURE IN IDAHO. [Agric. Idaho].
Added/Corp Idaho Crop and Livestock Reporting Service. (19??)-. Periodical. English. Twenty-six times a year. $10.00. Idaho Agricultural Statistics Service, Box 1699, Boise ID 83701. **Tel** (208)334-1507.

LC S
DD 630 IE
AGRICULTURE IN NORTHERN IRELAND (1986). (AGRICULTURE IN NORTHERN IRELAND.). Vol. 1, No. 1 (Oct. 1986)-. Periodical. English. Twelve times a year. Northern Ireland Department of Agriculture, Dundonald House, Upper Newtownard, Belfast BT4 3SB 5RU United Kingdom. **Tel** 011 44 1232 650111. **Continues** Agriculture in Northern Ireland, 0002-175X.

LC S21 .A74 **ISSN** 0065-4639
DD 630.82 US
UDC 63
CODEN XAAIA7
AGRICULTURE INFORMATION BULLETIN. [Agric. inf. bull.]. **VFOAT** AIB. No. 1-. Bulletin. English. Price varies per volume. US Department of Agriculture, 14th Street and Independence Avenue SW, Washington DC 20250. **Tel** (202)720-5457.
Ind/Abst Agric. Eng. Abstr. (1991-); Dairy Sci. Abstr.; For. Prod. Abstr.; For. Abstr.; GeoRef; Irr. Drain. Abstr.; Maize Abstr.; Pig News Inf.; Poult. Abstr.; Rev. Agric. Entomol.; Rev. Med. Vet. Mycology; Rev. Plant Pathol.; Rice Abstr.; Soils Fert.; Soyabean Abstr.; Wheat Barley Trit. Abstr.; World Agric. Econ. Rural Sociol. Abstr.

LC S **ISSN** 0895-5506
DD 630 US
AGRICULTURE MATERIALS IN LIBRARIES. See Library and Information Sciences.

LC S **ISSN** 0002-1687
DD 630 CN
CEASED
AGRICULTURE (MONTREAL). (AGRICULTURE.). [Agriculture]. **Added/Corp** Ordre des Agronomes du Quebec. Corporation des Agronomes de la Province de Quebec. (1944)-(Feb. 1995). Periodical. French. Ordre des Agronomes du Quebec, 1259 Berri Street, Suite 710, Montreal Quebec H2L 4C7 Canada. **Tel** (514)844-3833, FAX (514)844-7462. **ED** Rhonda Beauregard. Index available. **Bk Rev**. **Ad Acc**. **Circ:** 4,000 (ctrl).
Desc: Covers agricultural science and food processing, with research reports on education, farm economy, communication and extension.
Ind/Abst Pig News Inf.; Plant Breed. Abstr.; Repere (1983-); Soils Fert.; Weed Abstr.; World Agric. Econ. Rural Sociol. Abstr.

LC S451.5 **ISSN** 0712-7375
DD 630/.9719 CN
UDC 63(798)
AGRICULTURE NORTH. [Agric. north]. Vol. 1, No. 1 (Jan. 20, 1982)-. Periodical. English. Twelve times a year. $25.00. Agriculture North/Monarch Mountain Press, PO Box 104, Atlin British Columbia V0W 1A0 Canada. **ED** Mac Mackay.
Desc: A newsletter of helpful information aimed at farmers, growers and stock owners in Alaska, Yukon, Northwest Territory and other northern areas.

LC S
DD 630 US
AGRICULTURE RESEARCH DIGEST.
Added/Corp United States. Cooperative State Research Service. Vol. 1, No. 1 (Spring 1991)-. Periodical. English. Four times a year.

LC HD1769 .D36a **ISSN** 0733-1517
DD 338.1/0973 US
AGRICULTURE REVIEW (LEXINGTON, MASS.). (AGRICULTURE REVIEW / DATA RESOURCES, INC.). [Agric. rev.]. **Added/Corp** Data Resources, Inc. **VFOAT** Data Resources Agriculture Review. Vol. 6, No. 4 (Winter 1981)-. Periodical. English. Four times a year. DRI McGraw Hill, 24 Hartwell Avenue, Lexington MA 02173. **Tel** (617)863-5100, FAX (617)860-6464, (617)860-6416. (Subscription address: Data Resources, PO Box 5 0210, Woburn MA 01815.) **Continues** DRI Agriculture Service Quarterly Review, 0145-8523.

LC S
DD 630 US
AGRICULTURE (SAINT LOUIS, MO.).
(AGRICULTURE.). **Added/Corp** Federal Reserve Bank of St. Louis, Mo. (19??)-. Periodical. English. Four times a year. Free. Federal Reserve Bank of St. Louis, PO Box 66953, St Louis MO 63166. **Tel** (314)444-8444, (314)444-8660.

LC S **ISSN** 0895-2442
DD 630 US
AGRICULTURE TODAY. (AGRICULTURE TODAY : OFFICIAL PUBLICATION OF FRESNO COUNTY FARM BUREAU.). [Agri. today]. **Added/Corp** Fresno County Farm Bureau (Fresno, Calif. **VFOAT** Fresno County Farm Bureau News. Vol. 40, No. 11 (July 24, 1987)-. Periodical. English. Twenty-four times a year. $4.00. Fresno County Farm Bureau, 1274 Hedges Avenue, Fresno CA 93728. **Tel** (209)237-0263.
Continues Fresno County Farm Bureau News, 0893-8318.

LC HD2155.W4 A37
DD 338.1/09941 AT
AGRICULTURE, WESTERN AUSTRALIA. **Added/Corp** Australian Bureau of Statistics. Western Australian Office. (1979/1980)-. English. One time a year. 14.60Aus$. Australian Bureau of Statistics, PO Box 2796Y, Melbourne 3001 Australia. **Tel** 011 61 3 6157843. **Continues in part** Agriculture, Forestry, Fishing, and Hunting, Western Australia.
Desc: Six-year summaries of agricultural land utilization, crop production, fruit production, livestock and livestock products; agricultural land use and selected inputs, structural and financial statistics, gross value of agricultural commodities produced.
Ind/Abst Biocont. News Inf. (1991-); Helminthol. Abstr. (1991-); Rev. Plant Pathol.

LC S **ISSN** 0888-1804
DD 630 US
AGRIDATA NETWORK REVIEW. [AgriData netw. rev.]. (1986)-. English. AgriData Resources Inc, 330 East Kilbourn Avenue, Milwaukee WI 53202. **Tel** (414)278-7676.

LC S361 .A44
SX
AGRIFORUM. **Added/Corp** Namibia Agricultural Union. (199?)-. Periodical. Afrikaans (English). Twelve times a year. $12.53. Namibia Agricultural Union, Private Bag X13255, Windhoek 9000 Namibia. **Tel** 011 264 61 37838.

LC S **ISSN** 0394-5537
DD 630 IT
UDC 63
AGRIGIORNALE DEL COMMERCIO.
(1987)-. Periodical. Italian. Eleven times a year. L80000. Edagricole, PO Box 2157, 40100 Bologna Italy. **Tel** 011 39 51 492211 Ext. 22, FAX 011 39 51 493660, telex 510336 EDAGRI.

LC S **ISSN** 0925-2762
DD 630 NE
UDC 631
CEASED
AGRILOPER WAGENINGEN. (AGRILOPER.). [Agriloper Wageningen]. (1990)-(1993). Periodical. Dutch. PUDOC, PO Box 4, 6700 AA Wageningen Netherlands. **Tel** 011 31 8370 84541, FAX 31 8370 84761, telex 45015 BLUWG NL. **Continues** Landbouwdocumentatie ('s-Gravenhage), 0023-7760.

LC S
DD 630 US
AGRIS [CD-ROM]. (19??)-. English. Four times a year. $825.00 (1991-present) single user, $1238.00 (1991-present) multi-user. Silverplatter Information Inc., 100 River Ridge Drive, Norwood MA 02062. **Tel** (800)343-0064, (617)769-2599, FAX (617)769-8763.
Desc: Covers all aspects of agriculture, including forestry, animal husbandry, aquatic sciences and fisheries, and human nutrition from over 110 participating countries. Literature covered includes unique material such as unpublished scientific and technical reports, these, conference papers, government publications and more.

LC SB **ISSN** 0840-8289
DD 630/.971 CN
Pr Rev. **SUSPENDED**
AGRISCIENCE (OTTAWA). (AGRISCIENCE.). [Agriscience]. **Added/Corp** Agricultural Institute of Canada. (Jan. 1989)-Suspended (Dec. 1995). Trade Publication. English. Eleven times a year (monthly with July/Aug. issues combined). 9.61Can$. Agrican Publishers Inc, 151 Slater Street/Suite 907, Ottawa Ontario K1P 5H4 Canada. **Tel** (613)232-9459, FAX (613)594-5190. **ED** John Watts. **Bk Rev**. **Ad Acc**. **Circ:** 5,800. available in microform from Micromedia Limited. **Formed by the union of** Agrologist, 0044-684X **and** Agrinews, 0318-658X.
Desc: Articles on agricultural research, economics, mechanization, and policy. Written for and by agricultural professionals.
Ind/Abst Dairy Sci. Abstr.; Rev. Agric. Entomol.; World Agric. Econ. Rural Sociol. Abstr.

LC S
DD 630 AG
Pr Rev.
AGRISCIENTIA. **Added/Corp** Universidad Nacional de Cordoba. Facultad de Ciencias Agropecuarias. Vol. 8 (1991)-. Academic Scholarly Publication. Spanish (summaries and/or abstracts in English). One time a year. $12.00. Facultad de Ciencias Agropecuarias / Cordoba, Casilla de Correo 509, 5000 Cordoba Argentina. **Tel** 54 51 681763, 54 51 681764, FAX 54 51 681765. **Ad Acc**. **Circ:** 500. **Continues** Revista de Ciencias Agropecuarias.
Desc: Publishes original scientific papers concerned with agricultural sciences and related issues (veterinary, biology, and biotechnology).

LC S **ISSN** 0751-7378
DD 630 FR
SUSPENDED
AGRISCOPE : REGARDS SUR L'AGRICULTURE. **Added/Corp** Ecole Superieure d'Agriculture (Angers, France) Syndicat d'Enseignement Agronomique et de Recherches Agricoles (Angers, France). Vol. 1, No. 1 (1983)-Suspended with Iss. 11 (1988). Periodical. French. Two times a year. Agriscope, 33 rue Rabelais, BP 748, 49007 Angers Cedex 01 France. **Tel** 011 33 41 885812.

LC S
DD 630 US
UDC 63
AGRISEARCH (CARBONDALE, ILL.).
(AGRISEARCH.). June 1983-. Periodical. English. Free. Southern Illinois University / Carbondale - Agriculture, School of Agriculture, Carbondale IL 62901. **Tel** (618)536-7733. **Circ:** 7,000 (ctrl).
Desc: Publication of semi-technical articles of selected research projects of the SIU agriculture faculty, written by the researchers.

LC S
DD 630 US
AGRISEARCH [COMPUTER FILE] : CRIS, SIS-SPAAR, ICAR, ARRIP, AGREP. **Added/Corp** United States. Dept. of Agriculture. Special Program for African Agricultural Research (International Bank for Reconstruction and Development) Canadian Agricultural Research Council. Australia. Dept. of Primary Industries and Energy. European Economic Community. SilverPlatter Information, Inc. **VFOAT** CRIS; SIS-SPAAR; ICAR; ARRIP; AGREP. **VAT** Current Research Information System; SPAAR Information System; Special Program for African Agricultural Information System; Inventory of Canadian Agri-Food Research; Australian Rural Research in Progress; Agricultural Research Projects. (Aug. 1992)-. English. Two times a year. $795.00. Silverplatter Information Inc., 100 River Ridge Drive, Norwood MA 02062. **Tel** (800)343-0064, (617)769-2599, FAX (617)769-8763. **Continues** CRIS / ICAR.

LC S
DD 630 AT
AGRITALK. (19??)-. English. One time a year (Dec). 5.00Aus$. Victorian Agricultural Teacher, Drovin High School, PO Box 196, Drovin Victoria 3818 Australia.
Ind/Abst Aust. Educ. Index (1981-19??).

LC HD9560.3
DD 338.1 UK
AGRITRADE. (March 1978)-. Periodical. English. Twelve times a year. **Continues** Agricultural Merchant.
Ind/Abst Dairy Sci. Abstr.

LC S297 .A55 **ISSN** 0126-0537
DD 338.1/09598 IO
CODEN AGRIDK
AGRIVITA. [Agrivita]. Vol. 1 (1978)-. Academic Scholarly Publication. Indonesian. Six times a year. Bagian Penerbitan Universitas Brawijaya, JL Laks Martadinata 80, Malang Indonesia. Documents available from CASDDS.
Ind/Abst Chem. Abstr.

LC S
DD 630 TH
AGRO-CHEMICALS NEWS IN BRIEF.
Added/Corp Fertilizer Advisory, Development, and Information Network for Asia and the Pacific. Economic and Social Commission for Asia and the Pacific. Food and Agriculture Organization of the United Nations. United Nations Industrial Development Organization. **VFOAT** Agro Chemicals News in Brief News in Brief. Vol. 6, No. 1 (Jan. 1983)-. Periodical. English. Six times a year (quarterly with 2 special issues). $60.00. ESCAP, Rajadamnern Avenue, UN Building, Bangkok 10200 Thailand. **Tel** 011 66 2 2829161, 2829200, FAX 011 66 2 2812403, 2829602, telex 82392, 82315. **ED** Ivy M. Rodricks (editor's phone: 011 66 2 2829161 Ext. 1348). **Circ:** 1,000. **Continues** News in Brief (Bangkok, Thailand).
Ind/Abst Agric. Eng. Abstr. (1991-); Field Crop Abstr.; Rice Abstr.; Soils Fert.; World Agric. Econ. Rural Sociol. Abstr.

LC S **ISSN** 0716-1689
DD 630 CL
AGRO-CIENCIA. **Added/Corp** Universidad de Concepcion. Facultad de Ciencias Agropecuarias y Forestales. (198?)-. Periodical. Spanish (summaries and/or abstracts in English). Two times a year.
Ind/Abst Agric. Eng. Abstr.; Biocont. News Inf.; Hortic. Abstr.; Postharvest News Inf.; Rev. Agric. Entomol.; Seed Abstr.; Soils Fert.; Weed Abstr.; Wheat Barley Trit. Abstr.

LC S **ISSN** 1000-0267
DD 630 CH

AGRO-ENVIRONMENTAL PROTECTION. (????)-. Periodical. Chinese. The Chinese Society of Agro-Environmental Protection, Tianjin China.
Ind/Abst Rev. Plant Pathol.

LC TP368 **ISSN** 1120-6012
DD 664 IT
CODEN AIHTEI

AGRO-INDUSTRY HI-TECH. (AGROFOODINDUSTRY HI-TECH.). [Agro-Ind. Hi-Tech]. **VFOAT** Agrofoodindustry Hi Tech; Agro Food Industry Hi-Tech; Agro Food Industry Hi Tech; Agro-Industry Hi-Tech; Agro Industry Hi Tech. (1990)-. Periodical. English. Six times a year. L88470. Tekno Scienze, Via Vincenzo Gioberti 1, 20123 Milan Italy. **Tel** 011 39 2 4818118. Index available (free). Documents available from The Genuine Article.
Ind/Abst Abstr. BioCommer.; Res. Alert [Full Cov.].

LC S **ISSN** 1166-7729
DD 630 FR
UDC 631/635(44)

AGRO MAGAZINE (PARIS). (AGRO MAGAZINE.). [Agro mag.]. **VFOAT** Agro Magazine Agriculture. No 1 (March 1992)-. Periodical. French. Four times a year. $39.37. EditAgro, 64 rue de la Boetie, 75008 Paris France. **Tel** 011 33 1 45610406. ***Continues*** *Agriculture (Paris, France), 0002-1709.*

LC S
DD 630 MX

AGRO-SINTESIS. Vol. 1 No. 1 (Feb. 1971)-. Periodical. Spanish. Twelve times a year. $42.00. Editorial Ano Dos Mil SA, Indianapolis 70, 03810 Mexico DF Mexico. **Tel** 5 23 99 12, 5 23 30 07.

LC QH **ISSN** 0304-8802
DD 574 CL
CODEN AGSUDR

AGRO SUR. [Agro sur]. **Added/Corp** Universidad Austral de Chile. Facultad de Ciencias Agrarias. (1973)-. Academic Scholarly Publication. Spanish (English). Two times a year (Aug. and Dec.). $40.00. Universidad Austral Chile, Casilla 567, Ciencias Agrarias, Valdivia Chile. **Tel** 011 56 213911, FAX 011 56 212598, telex 271035. **ED** Fernando Mujicz. cum. index. **Bk Rev**. **Ad Acc. Circ:** 500 (ctrl). Documents available from BIOSIS Document Express, CASDDS.
Desc: Covers crop and horticulture production, soil science, dairy science, livestock and poultry, etc.
Ind/Abst AGRICOLA; Agric. Eng. Abstr. (1991-); Agrindex; Anim. Breed. Abstr.; Biol. Abstr. (1974-1988); Chem. Abstr. (1973-1982); Curr. Aware. Biol. Sci., CABS; Dairy Sci. Abstr.; Field Crop Abstr.; Food Sci. Technol. Abstr.; Grass. Forage Abstr.; Hortic. Abstr.; Irr. Drain. Abstr.; Maize Abstr.; Nutr. Abstr. Rev., Ser. B, Live Feeds and Feed.; Nutr. Abstr. Rev., Ser. A, Hum. Exp.; Life Sci. Collect.; Plant Breed. Abstr.; Potato Abstr.; Rev. Med. Vet. Mycology; Rev. Plant Pathol.; Seed Abstr.; Soils Fert.; Vitis Vitic. Enol. Abstr.; Wheat Barley Trit. Abstr.

LC HD1491 **ISSN** 0100-4298
DD 338.1 BL

AGROANALYSIS. (19??)-. Periodical. Portuguese. Twelve times a year. $150.00. Fundacao Getulio Vargas, Praia de Botafogo, 190 6 Andar, 22253-900 Rio de Janeiro RJ Brazil. **Tel** 011 5521 551 0698, FAX 011 5521 551 1596, 011 5521 551 5755.
Desc: Each issue provides a comprehensive survey of Brazilian agrobusiness and shows how it is affected by both the national and international economic policies.

LC S33 .E26 **ISSN** 0002-1822
DD 630 US
CODEN AGBOBO
Pr Rev.

AGROBOREALIS. [Agroborealis]. **Added/Corp** University of Alaska, Fairbanks. Agricultural Experiment Station. University of Alaska, Fairbanks. Institute of Agricultural Sciences. Vol. 1 (April 1969)-. Periodical. English. One time a year (Jan.). Free on request. Agricultural and Forestry Experiment Station, School of Agriculture and Land Resources Management, University of Alaska, 309 O'Neill Resources Building, 905 Koyukuk Avenue North, Fairbanks AK 99775-0080. **Tel** (907)474-6923. **ED** J. Stephen Lay. Index available. cum. index. **Circ:** 7,000. Documents available from BIOSIS Document Express, Documents on Demand.
Desc: Journal written by agriculture and forestry experiment station.
Ind/Abst ASTIS Curr. Aware. Bull. (1978-); ASTIS Bibliogr. (1978-); Biol. Abstr.; Crop Physiol. Abstr.; Dairy Sci. Abstr.; EMBASE; Environ. Abstr.; Fish Rev. (Jan. 1989-July 1992); Food Sci. Technol. Abstr.; Grass. Forage Abstr.; Nutr. Abstr. Rev., Ser. B, Live Feeds and Feed.; Nutr. Abstr. Rev., Ser. A, Hum. Exp.; Ornamental Hort.; Life Sci. Collect.; Plant Grow. Reg. Abstr.; Postharvest News Inf.; Soils Fert.; Soyabean Abstr.; Wheat Barley Trit. Abstr.; Wildl. Rev. (Jan. 1989-July 1992); World Agric. Econ. Rural Sociol. Abstr.

LC S **ISSN** 0002-1849
DD 630 PL
CODEN AGROD4

AGROCHEMIA. [Agrochemia]. **Added/Corp** Poland Ministerstwo Przemyslu Chemicznego. Poland. Ministerstwo Rolnictwa. Panstwowe Wydawnictwo Rolnicze i Lesne. (1961)-. Academic Scholarly Publication. Polish. Twelve times a year. $33.00. **(Subscription address:** Ars Polona-Ruch, PO Box 1001, Krakowskie Przedmiescie 7, 00-068 Warsaw Poland. **Tel** 011 48 22 261201.) Documents available from CASDDS.
Ind/Abst Chem. Abstr.

LC S **ISSN** 0002-1830
DD 630 XO
CODEN AGROB2

AGROCHEMIA (BRATISLAVA). (AGROCHEMIA.). [Agrochemia]. (1961)-. Academic Scholarly Publication. Slovak (summaries and/or abstracts in English, German and Russian). Twelve times a year. $120.94. **(Subscription address:** Slovart GTG Ltd., Krupinska 4, 852 99 Bratislava Slovakia. **Tel** 011 42 7 839471 2.) Documents available from BIOSIS Document Express, CASDDS.
Ind/Abst Biocont. News Inf.; Biol. Abstr.; Chem. Abstr.; EMBASE; Field Crop Abstr.; Grass. Forage Abstr.; Irr. Drain. Abstr.; Plant Grow. Reg. Abstr.; Postharvest News Inf.; Protozoolog. Abstr.; Rev. Agric. Entomol.; Rev. Plant Pathol.; Soils Fert.; Weed Abstr.

LC S
DD 630 UK

AGROCHEMICAL SERVICE. (19??)-. English. Irregular. £2,950.00. Wood Mackenzie Consultants Ltd., Kintore House, 74 77 Queen Street, Edinburgh EH2 4NS United Kingdom. **Tel** 011 44 131 2258525, FAX 011 44 131 2434435, telex 72555.

LC S
DD 630 UK
TITLE CHANGE

AGROCHEMICALS HANDBOOK. (19??)-(19??). English. Royal Society of Chemistry, Thomas Graham House, Science Park, Cambridge CB4 4WF United Kingdom. **Tel** 011 44 1223 420066, FAX 011 44 1223 423623, telex 818293 ROYAL. **(Subscription address:** Royal Society of Chemistry, Turpin Distribution Services Ltd., Blackhorse Road, Letchworth, Hertfordshire SG6 1HN United Kingdom. **Tel** 011 44 1462 672555, FAX 011 44 1462 480947.) **ED** H. Kidd and D. Hartley. available on an online database (file 306/Full-Text) from DIALOG. ***Merged into*** *The Pesticide Manual.*
Desc: Contains information on a wide variety of active components of agricultural chemical products used in crop protection and pest control. Includes herbicides, fungicides, insecticides, nematicides, aracnicides and rodenticides.

LC S583 .A42 **ISSN** 0002-1857
DD 631.4/1/05 IT
CODEN AGRCAX
Pr Rev.

AGROCHIMICA. [Agrochimica]. **Added/Corp** Universita di Pisa. Istituto di Chimica Agraria. Vol. 1 (Dec. 1956)-. Periodical. English (French, German, Italian and Spanish). Six times a year. L170310. Ind Grafiche V Lischi & Figli, Via XXIV Maggio 28, 56123 Pisa Italy. **Tel** 011 39 50 563371, FAX 011 39 50 562726. **ED** Prof. L. Carloni. Index available. **Bk Rev**. **Circ:** 700. Documents available from The Genuine Article, CASDDS.
Desc: Information on agricultural chemistry.
Ind/Abst AGRICOLA; Chem. Abstr.; Crop Physiol. Abstr.; Curr. Aware. Biol. Sci., CABS; Curr. Cit.; Curr. Contents Agric. Biol. Environ. Sci.; Dairy Sci. Abstr.; EMBASE; Field Crop Abstr.; For. Abstr.; GeoRef; Grass. Forage Abstr.; Hortic. Abstr.; Irr. Drain. Abstr.; Leadscan; Maize Abstr.; Nucl. Sci. Abstr.; Ornamental Hort.; Life Sci. Collect.; Plant Breed. Abstr.; Plant Grow. Reg. Abstr.; Postharvest News Inf.; Potato Abstr.; Protozoolog. Abstr.; Res. Alert [Select. Cov.]; Rev. Agric. Entomol.; Rice Abstr.; SCISEARCH; Seed Abstr.; Soils Fert.; Soyabean Abstr.; Weed Abstr.; Wheat Barley Trit. Abstr.

LC S **ISSN** 0188-3038
DD 630 MX
Pr Rev.

AGROCIENCIA. SERIE CIENCIA ANIMAL. [Agrocienc., Ser. cienc. anim.]. (1990)-. Periodical. Spanish. Three times a year. $25.00. Colegio de Postgraduados, Gen Lazardo Cardenas 24 La Paz, 56170 Texcoco Mexico. **Tel** 011 52 595 47011. ***Continues*** *Agrociencia (Montecillo, Edo. Mex.), 0185-0288.*

LC S **ISSN** 0188-302X
DD 630 MX
Pr Rev.

AGROCIENCIA. SERIE FITOCIENCIA. [Agrocienc., Ser. fitocienc.]. (1990)-. Monographic series. Multiple languages. Four times a year. $25.00. Colegio de Postgraduados, Gen Lazardo Cardenas 24 La Paz, 56170 Texcoco Mexico. **Tel** 011 52 595 47011. ***Continues*** *Agrociencia, 0185-0288.*

LC S **ISSN** 0188-3046
DD 630 MX
Pr Rev.

AGROCIENCIA. SERIE PROTECCION VEGETAL. [Agrocien., Ser. prot. veg.]. (1990)-. Periodical. Spanish. Three times a year. $25.00. Colegio de Postgraduados, Gen Lazardo Cardenas 24 La Paz, 56170 Texcoco Mexico. **Tel** 011 52 595 47011. ***Continues*** *Agrociencia (Montecillo, Edo. Mex.), 0185-0288.*

LC S **ISSN** 0188-3062
DD 630 MX
Pr Rev.

AGROCIENCIA. SERIE RECURSOS NATURALES RENOVABLES. [Agrocien., Ser. recur. nat. renov.]. (1990)-. Periodical. Spanish. Three times a year. $25.00. Colegio de Postgraduados, Gen Lazardo Cardenas 24 La Paz, 56170 Texcoco Mexico. **Tel** 011 52 595 47011. ***Continues*** *Agrociencia (Montecillo, Edo. Mex.), 0185-0288.*

LC S **ISSN** 0188-3089
DD 630 MX
Pr Rev.

AGROCIENCIA. SERIE SUELO, AGUA Y CLIMA. [Agrocienc., Ser. suelo agua clima]. (1990)-. Periodical. Spanish. Four times a year. $25.00. Colegio de Postgraduados, Gen Lazardo Cardenas 24 La Paz, 56170 Texcoco Mexico. **Tel** 011 52 595 47011. ***Continues*** *Agrociencia (Montecillo, Edo. Mex.), 0185-0288.*

LC S185 .A43
DD 630/.98 CL

AGROECOLOGIA Y DESARROLLO. **Added/Corp** Consorcio Latinoamericano de Agroecologia y Desarrollo. Vol. 1, No. 1 (March 1991)-. Periodical. Spanish. Two times a year. $15.00. CET, Casilla 97 Correo 9, Santiago Chile.
Desc: Provides information on agricultural ecology, traditional farming, sustainable agriculture, and other agricultural topics.

LC HD1940.C9 A38
DD 630 XO

AGROEKONOMIKA. (1992)-. Periodical. Slovak (table of contents in English, German and Russian). Twelve times a year. DM189.00. **(Subscription address:** Kubon & Sagner, ABT Zeitschriftenimport, D 80328 Munich Germany. **Tel** 011 49 89 54218130.) ***Continues*** *Ekonomika Pol'Nohospodarstva.*

LC S
DD 630 SP

AGROEUROPA. (19??)-. Spanish. One time a week. 63300.00ptas. AgroEuropa, C Ayala 20 5 A, 28001 Madrid Spain. **Tel** 011 34 1 5762700.

LC S **ISSN** 1019-1984
DD 630 CR

AGROFORESTERIA (TURRIALBA). (AGROFORESTERIA.). [Agroforesteria]. (19??)-. Periodical. Spanish.
Ind/Abst Agrofor. Abstr.

LC SB **ISSN** 0952-1453
DD 634 UK

AGROFORESTRY ABSTRACTS. **See** Forests and Forestry-Abstracting, Bibliographies and Statistics.

LC SB **ISSN** 0167-4366
DD 634 NE
CCC
CODEN AGSYE6
Pr Rev.

AGROFORESTRY SYSTEMS. [Agrofor. syst.]. **Added/Corp** International Council for Research in Agroforestry. Vol. 1, No. 1 (1982)-. Periodical. English. Twelve times a year. $754.00. Kluwer Academic Publishers, Postbus 322, 3300 AH Dordrecht The Netherlands. **Tel** 011 31 78 524400, FAX 011 31 78 183273, telex 20083. **ED** H J von Maydell. **Bk Rev**. **Ad Acc**. **Acid Free. Circ:** 500. available on microfilm and microfiche from University Microfilms International (UMI). Documents available from The Genuine Article, BIOSIS Document Express, Documents on Demand.
Desc: An international, multidisciplinary journal which provides a rapid publication outlet for all types of research concerned with the various aspects of agroforestry systems and for critical reviews on all sustainable land management systems which combine agriculture, animal husbandry, and trees on the same unit of land.
Ind/Abst Agrofor. Abstr. (19??-19??); Biol. Abstr.; Curr. Aware. Biol. Sci., CABS; Curr. Cit.; Curr. Contents Agric. Biol. Environ. Sci.; Ecol. Abstr.; Environ. Abstr.; Environ. Period. Bibliogr.; Field Crop Abstr.; Fish Rev. (Jan. 1989-July 1992); For. Prod. Abstr. (1991-); For. Abstr.; Geogr. Abstr. Phys. Geogr.; Geogr. Abstr. Human Geogr.; Grass. Forage Abstr.; Hortic. Abstr.; Int. Dev. Abstr.; Int. Labour Doc.; Irr. Drain. Abstr.; Maize Abstr. (1990-); Plant Breed. Abstr.; Plant Genet. Resour. Abstr.; Potato Abstr.; Res. Alert [Select. Cov.]; Rice Abstr.; Rural Dev. Abstr.; SCISEARCH; Seed Abstr.; Soc. Sci. Cit. Index [Select. Cov.]; Soils Fert.; Soyabean Abstr.; Weed Abstr.; Wheat Barley Trit. Abstr.; Wildl. Rev. (Jan. 1989-July 1992); World Agric. Econ. Rural Sociol. Abstr.

LC SB ISSN 0255-8173
DD 634 KE
AGROFORESTRY TODAY. [Agro. today]. **Added/Corp** International Council for Research in Agroforestry. Vol. 1, No. 1 (Jan./Mar. 1989)-. Periodical. English. Four times a year. Free on request. ICRAF, PO Box 30677, Nairobi Kenya. **Tel** 011 254 2 521450. ***Continues*** *Newsletter & Agroforestry Review, 1013-9575.*
Ind/Abst Agrofor. Abstr.; Field Crop Abstr.; For. Abstr.; Grass. Forage Abstr.; Hortic. Abstr.; Rev. Agric. Entomol.; Soils Fert.

LC S ISSN 0002-1865
DD 630 YU
CODEN AGHJA4
AGROHEMIJA. [Agrohemija]. Academic Scholarly Publication. Serbo-Croatian (Roman). Six times a year. Documents available from BIOSIS Document Express, CASDDS.
Ind/Abst Biol. Abstr.; Chem. Abstr.; EMBASE; Plant Grow. Reg. Abstr.; Potato Abstr.

LC S583 .A43 ISSN 0002-1881
DD 630 RU
CCC
CODEN AGKYAU
AGROHIMIJA. (AGROKHIMIIA.). [Agrohimija]. **Added/Corp** Akademiia Nauk SSSR. Soviet Union. Ministerstvo Selskogo Khoziaistva. (1964)-. Academic Scholarly Publication. Russian (table of contents in English). Twelve times a year. $287.50. Izdatelstvo Nauka / Akademiia Nauk, (Publishing House of the Russian Academy of Sciences), Leninskii Porspekt 14, 117901 Moscow Russia. **Tel** 011 95 9542153, FAX 011 95 9382144, telex 411964. **(Subscription address:** East View Publications Inc., 3020 Harbor Lane North, Suite 110, Minneapolis MN 55447. **Tel** (800)477-1005, (612)550-0961, FAX (612)559-2931.**)** Documents available from BIOSIS Document Express, CASDDS.
Desc: Information on agricultural chemistry.
Ind/Abst Biocont. News Inf.; Biol. Abstr.; Chem. Abstr.; Cot. Trop. Fibr. Abstr. Bibliogr.; Curr. Biotechnol.; Field Crop Abstr.; Food Sci. Technol. Abstr.; For. Abstr.; Hortic. Abstr.; PESTDOC; Plant Grow. Reg. Abstr.; Potato Abstr.; Rev. Agric. Entomol.; Rev. Med. Vet. Entomol.; Rev. Plant Pathol.; Rice Abstr.; Soils Fert.; Sorghum Mill. Abstr.; Soyabean Abstr.; Vitis Vitic. Enol. Abstr.; Weed Abstr.

LC S ISSN 0377-9424
DD 630 CR
CODEN AGCODV
AGRONOMIA COSTARRICENSE. [Agron. costarric.]. **Added/Corp** Costa Rica. Ministerio de Agricultura y Granderia. Universidad de Costa Rica. Colegio de Ingenieros Agronomos. Vol. 1, No. 1 (Mar. 1977)-. Academic Scholarly Publication. Spanish (summaries and/or abstracts in English). Two times a year. $20.00. University de Costa Rica, Apartado 75 2060, Ciudad Universite, San Jose Costa Rica. **Tel** 011 506 2247051, 011 506 2253133, telex 2544. **ED** Floria Bertsch Hernandez. **Circ:** 1,400 (ctrl). available with charts. Documents available from CASDDS.
Desc: Covers all aspects of agriculture, including planting, crop production, insects and feed grains.
Ind/Abst Agrofor. Abstr. (19??-19??); Biodeter. Abstr. (1991-); Chem. Abstr.; Crop Physiol. Abstr.; Dairy Sci. Abstr.; Field Crop Abstr.; For. Prod. Abstr. (1991-); For. Abstr.; Grass. Forage Abstr.; Hortic. Abstr.; Nematol. Abstr.; Nutr. Abstr. Rev., Ser. B, Live Feeds and Feed.; Ornamental Hort. (1991-); Life Sci. Collect.; Pig News Inf.; Postharvest News Inf.; Potato Abstr.; Rev. Med. Vet. Mycology; Rice Abstr.; Seed Abstr.; Soils Fert.; Sorghum Mill. Abstr.; Soyabean Abstr.; Sug. Indus. Abstr.; Weed Abstr.

LC S15 .A4 ISSN 0002-1911
DD 633/.09469 PO
CCC
CODEN AGLUAN
AGRONOMIA LUSITANA. [Agron. lusit.]. **Added/Corp** Estacao Agronomica Nacional (Portugal). Vol. 1 (1939)-. Academic Scholarly Publication. Portuguese (English, French, German, Latin and Portuguese). Irregular. $10.00. Estacao Agronomica Nacional, Oeiras Portugal. cum. index. Documents available from BIOSIS Document Express, CASDDS.
Ind/Abst Biol. Abstr.; Chem. Abstr.; Field Crop Abstr.; For. Prod. Abstr.; For. Abstr.; GeoRef; Grass. Forage Abstr.; Hortic. Abstr.; Leis., Rec., Tour. Abstr.; Plant Breed. Abstr.; Protozoolog. Abstr.; Rev. Med. Vet. Mycology; Rev. Plant Pathol.; Rural Dev. Abstr.; Soils Fert.; Vitis Vitic. Enol. Abstr.; World Agric. Econ. Rural Sociol. Abstr.

LC S ISSN 0400-8111
DD 630 BL
UDC 338.43:633
CODEN AGSLAV
AGRONOMIA SULRIOGRANDENSE. (AGRONOMIA SULRIOGRANDENSE : BOLETIM TECNICO DA DIRECTORIA DA PRODUCAO VEGETAL.). [Agron. sulriogrand.]. Vol. 1, No. 1 A 4 (Jan./Dec. 1954)-. Academic Scholarly Publication. Portuguese. Two times a year. Instituto de Pesquisas Agronomicas, Departmento de Pesquisa, Diretoria Greal Secretaria da Agricultura, Porto Alegre Brazil. Documents available from BIOSIS Document Express, CASDDS.
Ind/Abst Biocont. News Inf.; Biol. Abstr.; Chem. Abstr.; Field Crop Abstr.; Grass. Forage Abstr.; Maize Abstr.; Plant Breed. Abstr.; Protozoolog. Abstr.; Rev. Med. Vet. Mycology; Rev. Plant Pathol.; Soils Fert.; Sorghum Mill. Abstr.; Soyabean Abstr.; Vitis Vitic. Enol. Abstr.

LC S ISSN 0002-192X
DD 630 VE
CODEN ATMVAK
AGRONOMIA TROPICAL. (AGRONOMIA TROPICAL : REVISTA DEL INSTITUTO NACIONAL DE AGRICULTURA.). **Added/Corp** Fondo Nacional de Investigaciones Agropecuarias (Venezuela) Instituto Nacional de Agricultura (Venezuela) Centro de Investigaciones Agronomicas (Venezuela) Centro Nacional de Investigaciones Agropecuarias (Venezuela). Vol. 1 (Apr./June 1951)-. Periodical. Spanish (summaries and/or abstracts in English). Six times a year. Agronomia Tropical / FONAIAP, Apdo 4653 A, Maracay 2101 Venezuela. **ED** Aydee Cabrera de Green. cum. index. **Bk Rev. Circ:** 1,500. Documents available from BIOSIS Document Express, CASDDS.
Ind/Abst Agric. Eng. Abstr. (1991-); Agrofor. Abstr.; Anim. Breed. Abstr.; Biodeter. Abstr.; Biol. Abstr.; Chem. Abstr.; Field Crop Abstr.; Hortic. Abstr.; Index Vet.; Irr. Drain. Abstr.; Maize Abstr.; Nutr. Abstr. Rev., Ser. B, Live Feeds and Feed.; Nutr. Abstr. Rev., Ser. A, Hum. Exp.; Plant Breed. Abstr.; Plant Grow. Reg. Abstr.; Postharvest News Inf.; Potato Abstr.; Protozoolog. Abstr.; Rev. Med. Vet. Mycology; Rev. Plant Pathol.; Rice Abstr.; Seed Abstr.; Soils Fert.; Sorghum Mill. Abstr.; Soyabean Abstr.; Vet. Bull.; Weed Abstr.

LC S
DD 630 BL
UDC 631.4; 632
AGRONOMICO, O. Vol. 1 (19??)-. Academic Scholarly Publication. Portuguese. Irregular. Instituto Agronomico, Caiza Postal 28, 13.100 Campinas Brazil. **Tel** 011 55 192 315422. **ED** Rubens R. A. Lordello. **Bk Rev. Circ:** 2,200. Documents available from BIOSIS Document Express, CASDDS.
Desc: Covers fertilizers, plant breeding, plant diseases and insects, pedology, crop physiology and nutrition, crop management, agricultural technology, seeds, mycology, bacteriology and virology, and soil fertility.
Ind/Abst AGRICOLA; Biol. Abstr.; Chem. Abstr.; Field Crop Abstr.; Hortic. Abstr.; Maize Abstr.; Plant Breed. Abstr.; Plant Genet. Resour. Abstr.; Soyabean Abstr.

LC S ISSN 0065-4663
DD 630 US
CODEN AGRYAV
AGRONOMY. [Agronomy]. **Added/Corp** American Society of Agronomy. Crop Science Society of America. Soil Science Society of America. Vol. 1 (1949)-. Monographic series. English. Irregular. Price varies per volume. American Society of Agronomy, 677 South Segoe Road, Madison WI 53711. **Tel** (608)273-8080, FAX (608)273-2021. Documents available from BIOSIS Document Express, CASDDS.
Ind/Abst AGRICOLA [Full Cov.]; Agric. Eng. Abstr. (1991-); BioBusiness; Biol. Abstr.; Chem. Abstr.; Ei Page One; Field Crop Abstr.; GeoRef; Grass. Forage Abstr.; Irr. Drain. Abstr.; Maize Abstr.; Life Sci. Collect.; Potato Abstr.; Soils Fert.; Sorghum Mill. Abstr.; Wheat Barley Trit. Abstr.

LC S583 ISSN 0375-5495
DD 631 US
CODEN AGABBE
AGRONOMY ABSTRACTS (MADISON, WIS.). (AGRONOMY ABSTRACTS.). [Agron. abstr.]. **Added/Corp** American Society of Agronomy. Crop Science Society of America. Crop Science Society of America. Agronomic Education Division. Soil Science Society of America. (19??)-. English. One time a year. $13.00. American Society of Agronomy, 677 South Segoe Road, Madison WI 53711. **Tel** (608)273-8080, FAX (608)273-2021. ***Continues*** *Abstracts (American Society of Agronomy).*
Desc: Includes abstracts of the annual meetings of the American Society of Agronomy; Soil Science Society of America; Crop Science Society of America ... .
Ind/Abst GeoRef; Plant Breed. Abstr.

LC S ISSN 0886-4381
DD 630 US
AGRONOMY DEPARTMENT SERIES. [Agron. Dept. ser.]. **Added/Corp** Ohio Agricultural Research and Development Center. Dept. of Agronomy. **VFOAT** Agronomy Department Mimeograph Series.; Agronomy Mimeo. (19??)-. Monographic series. English.
Ind/Abst AGRICOLA [Full Cov.].

LC S
DD 630 II
UDC 63
AGRONOMY NEWS LETTER. **VFOAT** Agronomy Newsletter. English. One time a year.

LC S583 ISSN 0886-4403
DD 631 US
AGRONOMY RESEARCH REPORT. [Agron. res. rep.]. **Main/Corp** Louisiana Agricultural Experiment Station. Dept. of Agronomy. No. 1 (Aug. 1968)-. Periodical. English.
Ind/Abst AGRICOLA [Full Cov.].

LC S583 ISSN 0886-4373
DD 631 US
UDC 63(047.31)
AGRONOMY RESEARCH REPORT AG. [Agron. res. rep. AG]. **Main/Corp** Florida. University. Dept. of Agronomy. (No. 73-1- Nov. 1972)-. Periodical. English. University of Florida Department of Agronomy, Agricultural Experiment Station, IFAS, Gainesville FL. ***Continues*** *Florida. Agricultural Experiment Station, Gainesville. Agronomy Mimeo Report AG.*
Ind/Abst AGRICOLA [Full Cov.].

LC S ISSN 0103-0779
DD 630 BL
AGROPECUARIA CATARINENSE. **Added/Corp** Empresa Catarinense de Pesquisa Agropecuaria. Vol. 1, No. 1 (March/May 1988)-. Periodical. Portuguese. Four times a year (Mar., June, Sept., Dec.). $30.00. EMPASC, Caixa Postal 1460, 88001 Florianopolis SC Brazil. **Tel** 011 55 842 340066, FAX 011 55 842 341024. **ED** Dr. Voltaire Mesquita Cesar. **Bk Rev**, (Qty: 4/yr). **Ad Acc.**
Desc: Scientific and technical magazine concerning agricultural production.
Ind/Abst Agrofor. Abstr. (1991-); Field Crop Abstr.; For. Abstr.; Grass. Forage Abstr.; Helminthol. Abstr. (1991-); Hortic. Abstr.; Index Vet.; Rice Abstr.; Soils Fert.

LC S
DD 630 BL
AGROPECUARIA : PRECOS, MEDIOS E INDICES DE ARRENDAMENTOS, VENDAS DE TERRAS, SALARIOS, SERVICOS. **Main/Corp** Centro de Estudos Agricolas (Instituto Brasileiro de Economia). Portuguese. Irregular. Free. Caixa Postal 9052 20.000, Rio de Janeiro Brazil. **Tel** 233-6040, telex 212-3840 FGUE BR. **Circ:** 2,800 (ctrl).

LC S17 .A74
DD 630.5 SA
UDC 63(680)
AGROPLANTAE. Afrikaans (English; summaries and/or abstracts in English and French). ***Supersedes in part*** *Suid-Afrikaanse Tydskrif Vir Landbouwetenskap.*
Ind/Abst Field Crop Abstr.; Grass. Forage Abstr.; Hortic. Abstr.; Plant Breed. Abstr.; Soils Fert.; Weed Abstr.

LC S13 .S432 ISSN 0235-2958
KZ
AGROPROMYSHLENNYI KOMPLEKS KAZAKHSTANA. **Added/Corp** Qazaqstan KP Ortalyq Komiteti. (1987)-. Periodical. Russian. Twelve times a year. Izdatelstvo TSK Kompartii Kazakhstana, Ulitsa M. Gorkogo 50, Alma-Ata 480044 Kazakhstan. ***Continues*** *Selskoe Khoziaistvo Kazakhstana (Alma-Ata, Kazakh S.S.R. : 1953).*

LC S ISSN 0568-3114
DD 630 CU
UDC 63(8)
CODEN AGCUDF
AGROTECNIA DE CUBA. [Agrotec. Cuba]. Vol. 1 (Oct./Dec. 1963)-. Periodical. Spanish (summaries and/or abstracts in English; table of contents in English). Two times a year. $12.00. Ediciones Cubanas, Obispo 527 Altos ESQ Bernaza, CP 10100 Havana Cuba. **Circ:** 400,000 (ctrl). Documents available from CASDDS.
Desc: Extensive information on the most important events that have taken place during the week, especially in Latin America. Articles and commentaries on the most burning issues of the day; includes features and interviews.
Ind/Abst Agrindex; Biodeter. Abstr.; Chem. Abstr. (1963-1981); Crop Physiol. Abstr.; Field Crop Abstr.; Hortic. Abstr.; Nematol. Abstr.; Plant Breed. Abstr.; Potato Abstr.; Rev. Agric. Entomol.; Seed Abstr.; Soils Fert.

LC HD2055.5 .A14
DD 630 GR
AGROTIKE (ATHENS, GREECE, : 1983). (AGROTIKE.). **Added/Corp** Agrotike Trapeza tes Hellados. Tmema Demosion Scheseon. (19??)-. Periodical. Greek, Modern. Twelve times a year. Free. Agrotike Trapeza Tes Hellados, Tmema Demosion Scheseon Hodos Edouardou Lo 19, Athens Greece. **Tel** 01-32.33.442, telex 021-5810. **Circ:** 30,000 (ctrl). ***Continues*** *Agrotike Trapeza.*

Agriculture

LC S ISSN 0103-3816
DD 630 BL
CODEN AGROE5
AGROTROPICA. [Agrotropica]. **Added/Corp** Centro de Pesquisas do Cacau. Vol. 1 No. 1 (Jan./Arril 1989)-. Periodical. Portuguese (English and Spanish). Three times a year. **Continues** Revista Theobroma, 0370-7962.
 Ind/Abst For. Prod. Abstr. (1991)-; For. Abstr.

LC TP ISSN 0268-313X
DD 660 UK
CCC
AGROW. (AGROW WORLD CROP PROTECTION NEWS.). [AGROW]. **VFOAT** AGROW. (198?)-. Trade Publication. English. Two times a week. £325.00 UK and Europe; $640.00 US and Canada; ¥95,000 Japan; £325.00 N. Africa/Mid East; £350.00 other. PJB Publications, 18-20 Hill Rise, Richmond Surrey TW10 6UA United Kingdom. **Tel** 011 44 181 9483262, FAX 011 44 181 3328998. **ED** Jane Sackett. **Bk Rev**. **Ad Acc**. **Circ**: 12,000. available on an online database (file 129,130/Full-Text) from DIALOG; DATA-STAR; and BRS. Documents available from BLDSC, SWETS.
 Desc: Commercial, financial, political and technical news on the world crop protection market and industry.
 Ind/Abst Trade Ind. Index.

LC S ISSN 0279-666X
DD 630 US
AGSCENE. **Added/Corp** Illinois. Dept. of Agriculture. **VFOAT** Ag Scene; Illinois Ag Scene. Vol. 1, No. 8 (Jan. 1974)-. Periodical. English. Twelve times a year. Free on request. Agscene, Emmerson Building, State Fairground, Springfield IL 62706. **Tel** (217)782-6675. **ED** Mia Jazo. **Circ**: 9,000 (ctrl). **Continues** Illinois Agricultural Scene.
 Desc: Newsletter highlighting current events, programs and projects of the Illinois Department of Agriculture.

LC HD ISSN 0887-9133
DD 333 US
TITLE CHANGE
AGVENTURE. [AgVenture]. **Added/Corp** Wisconsin Farm Bureau Federation. Vol. 1, No. 1 (Jan./Feb. 1986)-(Jan. 1995). Periodical. English. Wisconsin Farm Bureau Federation, PO Box 5550, Madison WI 53705. **Tel** (608)833-8070. **Continues** Badger Farm Bureau News, 0005-3740. **Continued by** Farm Bureau's Rural Route, 1082-1368.

LC S ISSN 0884-6162
DD 630 US
UDC 63
AGWEEK. Vol. 1, No. 1 (August 5, 1985)-. Periodical. English. One time a week. $32.00. Agweek, PO Box 6008, Grand Forks ND 58206. **Tel** (701)780-1230. **ED** Jim Durkin. **Ad Acc**. **Continues** Farm and Home (Grand Forks, N.D.), 8750-1783.

LC S478 ISSN 0728-859X
DD 630.994 AT
AIAS OCCASIONAL PUBLICATION. [AIAS occas. publ.]. **VFOAT** Australian Institute of Agricultural Science Occasional Publication. (1982)-. Monographic series. English. Irregular. Australian Institute of Agricultural Science, 1st Floor, 91 Rathdowne Street, Carlton Victoria 3053 Australia. **Tel** 011 61 3 6621077, FAX 011 61 3 6622727. **Continues** A.I.A.S Symposium Series, 0813-9245.
 Ind/Abst Hortic. Abstr. (?-?).

LC S
DD 630 CR
AIBDA ACTUALIDADES. See Library and Information Sciences.

LC S ISSN 0388-7995
DD 630 JA
CODEN ANKHDV
AICHI-KEN NOGYO SOGO SHIKENJO KEKNYU HOKOKU. [Aichi-ken Nogyo Sogo Shikenjo kenkyu hokoku]. **VFOAT** Research Bulletin of the Aichi-Ken Agricultural Research Center. No. 11 (Oct. 1979)-. Academic Scholarly Publication. Japanese. One time a year. Aichiken Nogyo Sogo Shikenjo, (Aichiken Agricultural Research Center), Nagakutecho, Aichigun Aichiken 480-11 Japan. Documents available from BIOSIS Document Express, CASDDS. **Formed by the union of** Aichi-Ken Nogyo Sogo Shikenjo Kenkyu Hokoku. A, Sakumotsu, 0388-7944; Aichi-Ken Nogyo Sogo Shikenjo Kenkyu Hokoku. B, Engei, 0388-7952; Aichi-Ken Nogyo Sogo Shikenjo Kenkyu Hokoku. C, Yokei, 0388-7960; Aichi-Ken Nogyo Sogo Shikenjo Kenkyu Hokoku. D, Sangyo, 0388-7979 **and** Aichi-Ken Nogyo Sogo Shikenjo Kenkyu Hokoku. E, Chikusan, 0388-7987.
 Ind/Abst Agric. Eng. Abstr.; Biodeter. Abstr.; Biol. Abstr. (1986-); Chem. Abstr.; Crop Physiol. Abstr.; Field Crop Abstr.; Index Vet.; Ornamental Hort. (1991-); Plant Grow. Reg. Abstr.; Postharvest News Inf.; Rev. Plant Pathol.; Rice Abstr.; Seed Abstr.; Weed Abstr.; World Agric. Econ. Rural Sociol. Abstr.

LC S
DD 630 NE
AKKERBOUW. Added/Corp Landbouw-Economisch Instituut (Netherlands). Afdeling Landbouw. (19??)-. Dutch. Irregular. Fl.23.75. Landbouw-Economisch Instituut, Postbus 29703, 2502 LS Hague Netherlands. **Tel** 011 31 70 3308330, FAX 011 31 70 615624. **ED** M. N. de Groot. **Circ**: 400.
 Desc: Outline of the development of prices, costs and profitability of Dutch arable farming over a period of five years.

LC S ISSN 0347-9293
DD 630 SW
AKTUELLT FRAN LANTBRUKSUNIVERSITETET. **Added/Corp** Sveriges Lantbruksuniversitet. (19??)-. Periodical. Swedish. Sveriges Lantbruksuniversitet Institutionen foer Virkeslaera, Swedish University of Agricultural Sciences, Box 7008, S-750 07 Uppsala Sweden. **Continues** Uppsala. Lantbrukshogskolan. Aktuellt Fran Lantbrukshogskolan.
 Ind/Abst Agric. Eng. Abstr.; Dairy Sci. Abstr.

LC S
DD 630 US
ALABAMA FARMER. (1986)-. Periodical. English. Twelve times a year. $12.00. Rural Press USA, 7701 Six Forks Road, Suite 132, Raleigh NC 27615. **Tel** (800)934-2472, (919)676-3276, FAX (919)676-9803. **ED** Eva Ann Davis (editor's telephone: (601)489-1777). **Ad Acc**. **Circ**: 12,134 (ctrl).
 Desc: General farm magazine serving Alabama agriculture.

LC S ISSN 1015-8499
DD 630 WS
ALAFUA AGRICULTURAL BULLETIN. [Alafua agric. bull.]. (1976)-. Periodical. English. Three times a year.
 Ind/Abst World Agric. Econ. Rural Sociol. Abstr.

LC S451.5 ISSN 0823-6720
DD 630/.97123 CN
UDC 63(712)
ALBERTA FARM & RANCH. [Alta. farm ranch]. **VAT** Alberta Farm and Ranch. Apr. 1983-. Periodical. English. Four times a year. North Hill Publications, 4000 19th Street NE, Calgary Alberta P2E 6P8 Canada. **Tel** (403)250-6633.

LC HD1401 ISSN 0832-4867
DD 338.1/025/7123 CN
ALBERTA FARM & RANCH, FARM DIRECTORY. [Alta. farm ranch farm dir.]. **Added/Corp** Rural Education and Development Association. **VFOAT** Alberta Farm and Ranch, Farm Directory; Greenbook; Farm Directory. (1986)-. Directory. English. Rural Education and Development Association, 14815 119 Avenue, Edmonton Alberta T5L 2N9 Canada. **Tel** 451-5959. **Continues** Alberta Co-Operative and Farm Organization Directory., 0822-7209.

LC S451.5 ISSN 0707-9818
DD 630/.97123 CN
UDC 63(712)
ALBERTA RURAL DEVELOPMENT STUDIES. **Main/Corp** Rural Education and Development Association. (1971/1972)-. English. One time a year. $1.00 per issue. Rural Education and Development Association, 14815 119 Avenue, Edmonton Alberta T5L 2N9 Canada. **Tel** 451-5959. **ED** Richard Stringham. **Circ**: 880.
 Desc: Series of information papers on current trends and problems in rural Alberta and on ways to improve one's lifestyle.

LC S451.5 ISSN 0823-0218
DD 630/.97123 CN
UDC 63(712)
ALBERTA RURAL MONTH. [Alta. rural mon.]. **VFOAT** Rural Month. Mar. 1983-. Periodical. English. Twelve times a year. $15.00. Alberta Rural Month, 4000-19 Street NE, Calgary Alberta T2E 6P8 Canada. **Continues** Calgary Rural Week, 0714-8399.

LC KF6369.8.F3 A14 ISSN 0190-9657
DD 343/.73/053 US
ALI-ABA COURSE OF STUDY. SELECTED PROBLEMS IN TAX PLANNING FOR AGRICULTURE : MATERIALS. See Law-Taxation Law.

LC KF6369.8.F3 A16 ISSN 0272-8133
DD 343.7305/581 347.3035581 US
ALI-ABA COURSE OF STUDY. TAX PLANNING FOR AGRICULTURE : MATERIALS. See Law-Taxation Law.

LC S
DD 630 SP
ALIMARKET MONTHLY. (19??)-. Spanish. Eleven times a year. 29000ptas Spain; 39000ptas other. Alimarket, O'Donnel 18 Plt 2 G, 28009 Madrid Spain. **Tel** 011 34 1 5778225.

LC S ISSN 1082-1570
DD 630 US
●**ALL AROUND KENTUCKY. Added/Corp** Kentucky Farm Bureau Federation. Vol. 1, No. 1 (Jan. 1995)-. Periodical. English. Six times a year. Kentucky Farm Bureau News, Box 20700, Louisville KY 40220. **Tel** (502)495-5112, FAX (502)495-5114. **Continues** Kentucky Farm Bureau Federation Kentucky Farm Bureau News, 0023-0200.

LC S ISSN 0587-4815
DD 630 HU
ALLAMI GAZDASAG. [All. gazd.]. Vol. 9, No. 1 (1968)-. Periodical. Hungarian. Twelve times a year. $22.00 US. Allami Gazdasag, Akademia u. 1-3, 1054 Budapest Hungary. **Tel** 1 112 4617, FAX 1 111 4877. (**Subscription address**: Kultura, PO Box 143, H-1300 Budapest 3 Hungary. **Tel** 011 36 1 2500194.) **ED** P. Gorgenyi. **Bk Rev**
 Desc: Information on state farming.
 Ind/Abst Agric. Eng. Abstr. (1991-); Leis., Rec., Tour. Abstr.; Pig News Inf.; Rural Dev. Abstr.; Sug. Indus. Abstr.; World Agric. Econ. Rural Sociol. Abstr.

LC HD1401 ISSN 1052-7540
DD 338 US
ALLEGANY AGRICULTURE. Added/Corp Cornell University. Cooperative Extension. Cooperative Extension Association of Allegany County. State University of New York. United States. Dept. of Agriculture. (197?)-. Periodical. English. Twelve times a year.
 Ind/Abst AGRICOLA [Select. Cov.].

LC S ISSN 0569-0803
DD 630 IO
ALMAMATER. Indonesian. Bagain Penerangan/Publikasi, Dewan Mahasiswa IPB, Campus IPB Baranangsiang, Bogar Indonesia.
 Ind/Abst Bibliogr. Mission.

LC S
DD 630 GW
ALMBAUER, DER. Added/Corp Almwirtschaftlicher Verein Oberbayern. (19??)-. Periodical. German. Twelve times a year. $32.24. BLV Verlagsgesellschaft MBH, Lothstrasse 29, D80797 Munich Germany. **Tel** 011 49 89 12705214.

LC S ISSN 1100-116X
DD 630 SW
ALTERNATIV ODLING. [Altern. odl.]. **Added/Corp** Sveriges Lantbruksuniversitet. Forsknings- och Forsoksnamnden for Alternativ Odling. **VFOAT** Alternative Agriculture. (1988)-. Monographic series. Swedish (English).
 Ind/Abst World Agric. Econ. Rural Sociol. Abstr.

LC S583 ISSN 8755-4941
DD 631 US
CODEN AAGNE7
ALTERNATIVE AGRICULTURE NEWS. [Altern. agric. news]. **Added/Corp** Institute for Alternative Agriculture (U.S.). Vol. 1, No. 1 (Mar. 1983)-. Periodical. English. Twelve times a year. $16.00. H. A. Wallace / Institute for Alternative Agriculture Inc., 9200 Edmonston Road, Suite 117, Greenbelt MD 20770. **Tel** (301)441-8777.
 Ind/Abst BioBusiness (1991-).

LC S539.I5 M434
DD 630.72 IO
ALUMNI FAKULTAS PERTANIAN UNIVERSITAS SUMATERA UTARA. See College and School Publications-Alumni.

LC S ISSN 0745-001X
DD 630 US
AMERICAN AGRICULTURE NEWS. (197?)-. Periodical. English. Twenty-six times a year. American Agriculture News, PO Box 100, Iredell TX 76649.

LC S ISSN 0161-8237
DD 630 US
AMERICAN AGRICULTURIST (1976). (AMERICAN AGRICULTURIST.). [Am. agric.]. Vol. 173, No. 4, April (1976)-. Periodical. English. Twelve times a year. $19.95. Farm Progress Publishing, 191 South Gary Avenue, Carol Stream IL 60188-2089. **Tel** (708)462-2890 or 2891. (**Subscription address**: CDS / SIFD Agency Control, 1901 Bell Avenue, Des Moines IA 50315. **Tel** (515)246-6812.) **ED** Gordon L. Conklin. **Ad Acc**. **Circ**: 74,000. available on microfilm and microfiche from University Microfilms International (UMI). **Continues** American Agriculturist, Rural New Yorker, 0002-7219.
 Desc: Regional magazine for Northeast agriculture and agribusiness covering wide spectrum of daily, other livestock, field crops and horticultural production.

LC SF521 .A5 ISSN 0002-7626
DD 638.1405 US
CODEN ABJOAS
Pr Rev.
AMERICAN BEE JOURNAL. [Am. bee j.]. Vol. 1 (Jan. 1861)-. Trade Publication. English. Twelve times a year. $17.50. Dadant and Sons, 51 South 2nd Street,

Hamilton IL 62341. **Tel** (217)847-3324. **ED** Joe M. Graham. Index available. **Bk Rev. Ad Acc. Circ:** 16,000. available on microfilm and microfiche from University Microfilms International (UMI). Documents available from The Genuine Article, BIOSIS Document Express, CASDDS. ***Absorbed** National Bee Journal.*
Desc: Covers all aspects of beekeeping information for both hobbyist and professional. Practical, scientific and industry news of honey handling, colony management and the latest in scientific research.
Ind/Abst AGRICOLA [Full Cov.]; BioBusiness; Biol. Abstr.; Chem. Abstr. (1861-1988); Curr. Aware. Biol. Sci., CABS; Curr. Cit.; Curr. Contents Agric. Biol. Environ. Sci.; Entomol. Abstr.; Index Vet.; Nutr. Abstr. Rev., Ser. A, Hum. Exp.; Life Sci. Collect.; Protozoolog. Abstr.; Res. Alert [Select. Cov.]; Rev. Agric. Entomol.; Rev. Med. Vet. Entomol.; Rev. Plant Pathol.; SCISEARCH; Soc. Sci. Cit. Index [Select. Cov.]; Soils Fert.; Sug. Indus. Abstr.

LC HD3443 .A7 **ISSN** 0065-793X
DD 334 US
AMERICAN COOPERATION. **See** Business and Economics-Cooperatives.

LC S605.5 .A48 **ISSN** 0889-1893
DD 630 US
CODEN AJAAEZ
AMERICAN JOURNAL OF ALTERNATIVE AGRICULTURE. [Am. j. altern. agric.]. **Added/Corp** Institute for Alternative Agriculture (U.S.). **VFOAT** Alternative Agriculture. Vol. 1, No. 1 (Winter 1986)-. Trade Publication. English. Four times a year. $44.00. H. A. Wallace / Institute for Alternative Agriculture Inc., 9200 Edmonston Road, Suite 117, Greenbelt MD 20770. **Tel** (301)441-8777. Documents available from The Genuine Article, UMI Article Clearinghouse, Documents on Demand.
Desc: Covers organic farming and agricultural conservation systems.
Ind/Abst AgBiotech News Inf.; AGRICOLA [Full Cov.]; Agric. Eng. Abstr. (1991-); Agrofor. Abstr. (1991-); BioBusiness; Biocont. News Inf.; Biol. Agric. Index; Curr. Cit.; Environ. Abstr.; Environ. Period. Bibliogr.; Expand. Acad. Index (1992-); Field Crop Abstr.; For. Abstr.; Geogr. Abstr. Human Geogr.; Irr. Drain. Abstr.; Maize Abstr.; Newsp. Period. Abstr. (1992-); Res. Alert [Select. Cov.]; Rev. Agric. Entomol.; Soc. Sci. Cit. Index [Select. Cov.]; Soils Fert.; Sorghum Mill. Abstr.; Weed Abstr.; Wheat Barley Trit. Abstr.; World Agric. Econ. Rural Sociol. Abstr.

LC S
DD 630 US
•**AMERICAN OSTRICH : OFFICIAL PUBLICATION OF THE AMERICAN OSTRICH ASSOCIATION.** **Added/Corp** American Ostrich Association. **VFOAT** Ostrich Report. (Jan. 1994)-. Trade Publication. English. Twelve times a year. American Ostrich Association, 3480 Hulen, Suite 210, Fort Worth TX 76107. **Tel** (817)731-8597, FAX (817)731-8446. ***Continues** Ostrich Report.*

LC S583 **ISSN** 1064-7473
DD 631 US
AMERICAN SMALL FARM MAGAZINE. [Am. small farm mag.]. **VFOAT** American Small Farm; Small Farm. Vol. 1, No. 1 (Nov./Dec. 1992)-. Periodical. English. Ten times a year. $15.00. Magnet Communications, 9420 Topanga Canyon Boulevard, Suite 202, Chatsworth CA 91311-5759. **Tel** (818)727-2236.

LC S **ISSN** 0871-0635
DD 630 PO
UDC 63(05)
ANAIS DA UTAD. [An. UTAD]. (1988)-. Periodical. Multiple languages. Irregular.
Ind/Abst Field Crop Abstr.; Potato Abstr.; Soils Fert.

LC S15 .S373 **ISSN** 0365-1800
DD 630/.94655 SP
Pr Rev.
ANALES DE LA ESTACION EXPERIMENTAL DE AULA DEI. [An. estac. exp. Aula Dei]. **Main/Corp** Estacion Experimental de Aula Dei. Vol. 1 (1948)-. Periodical. Spanish (English). One time a year. 3300ptas Spain; 4950ptas other. Estacion Experimental de Aula, Dei Apartado de Correos 202, 50080 Zaragoza Spain. **Tel** 011 34 76 575611, 011 34 76 576414. **ED** Angel Sanchez Gomez. Index available. **Circ:** 1,000 (ctrl).
Desc: Publishes articles of high scientific value, exposing the research results of the authors on the areas of agriculture, horticulture, vegetal genetics and pedology.
Ind/Abst Field Crop Abstr.; Grass. Forage Abstr.; Hortic. Abstr.; Maize Abstr.; Plant Breed. Abstr.; Potato Abstr.; Seed Abstr.; Soils Fert.; Vitis Vitic. Enol. Abstr.; Wheat Barley Trit. Abstr.

LC S
DD 630 BL
ANALISE DO SETOR AGROPECUARIO DE SERGIPE. **Main/Corp** Comissao Estadual de Planejamento Agricola de Sergipe. Portuguese. Comissao Estadual de Planejamento Agricole de Sergipe, rua Riachuelo 1200 49.000, Aracaju Brazil.

LC S15 .A76
DD 630/.97291 CU
UDC 63(729.1)
ANAP. **Main/Corp** ANAP (Organization). Spanish. Twelve times a year. $20.00 US. Ediciones Cubanas, Obispo 527 Altos ESQ Bernaza, CP 10100 Havana Cuba. **Bk Rev. Ad Acc. Circ:** 20,000.
Desc: Reflects the economic, cultural and social developments of this farmer's association.

LC [S279] **ISSN** 0003-2956
DD 630 II
ANDHRA AGRICULTURAL JOURNAL, THE. **Added/Corp** Andhra Agricultural Union. (Jan. 1954)-. Periodical. English. Four times a year. $20.00. Andhra Agricultural Journal, Agricultural College Campus, Bapatla 522101 India. **Tel** 26 86 45. **(Subscription address:** Prints India, 11 Darya Ganj, New Delhi 110002 India. **Tel** 011 91 11 3268645, FAX 011 91 11 3275542, telex 31-61087 PRIN-IN.) **ED** G. V. Hanumantha Rao. **Bk Rev. Ad Acc. Circ:** 1,200 (ctrl).
Desc: Published to disseminate knowledge pertaining to the latest development in agriculture research among the scientists and moderate farmers.
Ind/Abst Food Sci. Technol. Abstr.; Plant Breed. Abstr.; Rev. Med. Vet. Mycology; Rev. Plant Pathol.; Rice Abstr.

LC SF **ISSN** 1057-2120
DD 636 US
ANIMAL AGRICULTURE UPDATE NEWSLETTER. **Added/Corp** University of Maryland Cooperative Extension Service. University of Maryland, College Park. Dept. of Animal Sciences. (19??)-. Newsletter. English. Six times a year.
Ind/Abst AGRICOLA [Select. Cov.].

LC SB599 **ISSN** 1057-2457
DD 632 US
ANIMAL DAMAGE CONTROL. [Anim. damage control]. **Added/Corp** Purdue University. Cooperative Extension Service. U.S. Fish and Wildlife Service. (1985)-. Monographic series. English.
Ind/Abst AGRICOLA [Full Cov.].

LC S
DD 630 PH
ANIMAL HUSBANDRY AND AGRICULTURAL JOURNAL. Vol. 1 (Jan. 1966)-. Periodical. English. Twelve times a year.
Ind/Abst Philip. Sci. Technol. Abstr.

LC S
DD 630 US
ANIMAL NUTRITION RESEARCH HIGHLIGHTS. (19??)-. English. Four times a year. Free. American Soybean Association, 540 Maryville Ctr. Dr., Suite 390, St. Louis MO 63141. **Tel** (314)576-1770, FAX (314)576-2786. **ED** Ron Kohlmeier. **Circ:** 6,000 (ctrl).
Desc: Summaries of recent research on animal nutrition.

LC S **ISSN** 0303-9099
DD 630 BE
CODEN AGEMAW
ANNALES DE GEMBLOUX. [Ann. Gembloux]. **Added/Corp** Gembloux, Belgium. Institut Agronimique de l'Etat. Vol. 15 (1905)-. Academic Scholarly Publication. French. Four times a year. 1415.09F Belgium; 1698.11F other European Union; 1792.45F other. Faculte des Sciences Agronomiques de Gembloux, Passage des Deportes 2, Com Ed, B 5030 Gembloux Belgium. **Tel** 011 32 81 622103, FAX 011 32 81 614544. **ED** R. Paul. **Bk Rev. Ad Acc. Circ:** 1,500. ***Continues** Ingenieur Agricole de Gembloux.*
Desc: Synthesis in agronomic sciences including any related field such as forestry, fish culture, biotechnology.
Ind/Abst AgBiotech News Inf.; Agric. Eng. Abstr.; Anim. Breed. Abstr.; Biocont. News Inf.; EMBASE; Field Crop Abstr.; For. Prod. Abstr.; For. Abstr.; GeoRef; Grass. Forage Abstr.; Hortic. Abstr.; Leis., Rec., Tour. Abstr.; Maize Abstr.; Nutr. Abstr. Rev., Ser. B, Live Feeds and Feed.; Nutr. Abstr. Rev., Ser. A, Hum. Exp.; Ornamental Hort. (1991-); Life Sci. Collect.; Plant Breed. Abstr.; Protozoolog. Abstr.; Rev. Agric. Entomol.; Rural Dev. Abstr.; Soils Fert.; Sug. Indus. Abstr.; World Agric. Econ. Rural Sociol. Abstr.

LC S **ISSN** 0373-0816
DD 630 FR
ANNALES DE L'INSTITUT NATIONAL AGRONOMIQUE. [Ann. inst. nat. agron.]. **Main/Corp** Institut National Agronomique. (Algeria). Vol. 1, No. 1 (1972)-. Periodical. French (Arabic).
Ind/Abst Biocont. News Inf.; Potato Abstr.

LC SB29.T8 A3 **ISSN** 0365-4761
DD 630 TI
ANNALES DE L'INSTITUT NATIONAL DE LA RECHERCHE AGRONOMIQUE DE TUNISIE. **Added/Corp** Mahad al-Qawmi lil-Buhuth al-Ziraiyah al-Tunisiyah. Vol. 32 (1959)-. Academic Scholarly Publication. French. One time a year. price varies. Institut National de la Recherche Agronomique de Tunisie, Service de Documentation, Rue Hedi Karray, 2080 Ariana Tunis Tunisia. **Circ:** 800. Documents available from BLDSC. ***Continues** Annales du Service Botanique et Agronomique.*
Desc: Scientific publication detailing the results of Tunisian agricultural research.
Ind/Abst Anim. Breed. Abstr.

LC SB599 .K5 **ISSN** 0365-5814
DD 632.05 GR
CODEN APYBAQ
Pr Rev.
ANNALES DE L'INSTITUT PHYTOPATHOLOGIQUE BENAKI. [Ann. Inst. phytopathol. Benaki]. **Main/Corp** Mpenakeion Phytopathologikon Institouton. **Added/Corp** Benakeio Phytopathologiko Institouto. **VFOAT** Chronika tou Benakeiou Phytopathologikou Institoutou. (1935)-. Academic Scholarly Publication. French (English and Greek, Modern). Irregular. Dr3000 (libraries and institutions), Dr1600 (individuals), Dr1000 (students) Greece; $40.00 (libraries, institutions, and individuals) other. Institut Phytopathologique Benaki, rue Delta 8, 14561 Kiphissia Athens Greece. **Tel** 01 8077506, FAX 01 8077506. Index available (published separately). cum. index. **Circ:** 1,000 (ctrl). Documents available from CASDDS.
Desc: Research and experimental work covering the plant protection field.
Ind/Abst Chem. Abstr.; Hortic. Abstr.; Ornamental Hort.; PESTDOC; Plant Breed. Abstr.; Plant Grow. Reg. Abstr.; Potato Abstr.; Protozoolog. Abstr.; Rev. Med. Vet. Mycology; Rev. Plant Pathol.; Soils Fert.; Weed Abstr.

LC S **ISSN** 0298-7929
DD 630 FR
ANNALES D'HISTOIRE DES ENSEIGNEMENTS AGRICOLES. **Added/Corp** INRAP (Organization) Service d'Histoire de l'Education de l'I.N.R.P. (Dec. 1986)-. French. INRAP, 2 rue des Champs Prevois, 21000 Dijon France.
Ind/Abst Am. Hist. Life (1986-).

LC S13 .L8 **ISSN** 0365-1118
DD 630 PL
CODEN ACEAA2
ANNALES UNIVERSITATIS MARIAE CURIE-SKLODOWSKA. SECTIO E. AGRICULTURA. [Ann. univ. Mariae Curie-Sklodowska., sect. E.]. **Main/Corp** Uniwersytet Marii Curie-Sklodowskiej. **VFOAT** Roczniki Uniwersytetu Marii Curie-Skodowskiej w Lublinie. Dzial E. Nauki Rolnicze. Vol. 1 (1946)-. Academic Scholarly Publication. Polish (English; summaries and/or abstracts in English and Russian; table of contents in Russian and English). One time a year. Price varies per volume. Uniwersytet Marii Curie-Sklodowskiej, Biuro Wydawnictwo, Pl. Marii Curie-Sklodowskiej 5, 20-031 Lublin Poland. **Tel** 011 48 81 375304, FAX 011 48 81 336699, telex 0643223. **Circ:** 650. Documents available from CASDDS.
Ind/Abst Chem. Abstr. (-1983); EMBASE; Plant Grow. Reg. Abstr.

LC S **ISSN** 0304-0534
DD 630 IT
UDC 634.63
ANNALI DELL' ISTITUTO SPERIMENTALE PER L'OLIVICOLTURA. [Ann. Ist. sper. olivic.]. (1973)-. Periodical. Italian. One time a year. Istituto Sperimentale per l'Olivicoltura, Via Silvio Pellico 50, 87036 Commenda di Rende, Cosenza Italy.
Ind/Abst Crop Physiol. Abstr.; Hortic. Abstr.; Plant Grow. Reg. Abstr.

LC S **ISSN** 0540-049X
DD 630 IT
CODEN AFAGAL
ANNALI DELLA FACOLTA DI AGRARIA UNIVERSITA CATTOLICA DEL SACRO CUORE MILANO. (ANNALI DELLA FACOLTA DI AGRARIA.). [Ann. Fac. Agrar. Univ. cattol. Sacro Cuore Milano]. **Main/Corp** Universita Cattolica del Sacro Cuore. Facolta di Agraria. **Added/Corp** Societa Editrice Vita e Pensiero. (1955)-. Academic Scholarly Publication. Italian. Two times a year. L93000. Vita e Pensiero Pubblic University, Largo Gemelli 1, 20123 Milan Italy. **Tel** 011 39 2 72342310, 011 39 2 72342370. Documents available from BIOSIS Document Express, CASDDS.
Ind/Abst Biol. Abstr.; Chem. Abstr.; Crop Physiol. Abstr.; Dairy Sci. Abstr.; EMBASE; Field Crop Abstr.; Food Sci. Technol. Abstr.; Grass. Forage Abstr.; Hortic. Abstr.; Maize Abstr.; Nutr. Abstr. Rev., Ser. B, Live Feeds and Feed.; Plant Breed. Abstr.; Plant Grow. Reg. Abstr.; Rev. Agric. Entomol.; Vitis Vitic. Enol. Abstr.; World Agric. Econ. Rural Sociol. Abstr.

LC SF **ISSN** 0373-2673
DD 630 IT
ANNALI DELLA FACOLTA DI AGRARIA. UNIVERSITA DEGLI STUDI DI PERUGIA. [Ann. Fac. Agrar., Univ. Studi Perugia]. (1???)-. Periodical. Italian. Annali Della Facolta di Agraria, Universita Degli Studi di Perugia, 06100 Perugia Italy.
Ind/Abst Field Crop Abstr.; Plant Breed. Abstr.

Agriculture

LC S
DD 630
ISSN 0374-4981
IT
CODEN AASPAZ

ANNALI DELLA FACOLTA DI AGRARIA UNIVERSITA PERUGIA. (ANNALI DELLA FACOLTA DI AGRARIA.). [Ann. Fac. Agrar. Univ. Perugia]. **Main/Corp** Perugia. Universita. Facolta di Agraria. Vol. 1 (1942)-. Academic Scholarly Publication. Italian. Documents available from CASDDS.
Ind/Abst Chem. Abstr.; EMBASE; For. Abstr.; Hortic. Abstr.; Plant Grow. Reg. Abstr.; Seed Abstr.; Soyabean Abstr.

LC S
DD 630
ISSN 0365-799X
IT
CODEN AUNPAE

ANNALI DELLA FACOLTA DI SCIENZE AGRARIE DELLA UNIVERSITA DEGLI STUDI DI NAPOLI, PORTICI. [Ann. fac. sci. agrar. Univ. stud. Napoli, Portici]. **Added/Corp** Universita di Napoli. Facolta di Scienze Agrarie, Portici. (1951-1953)-Vol. 30 (1964-1965)-. Periodical. Italian (summaries and/or abstracts in English). One time a year. L10000. Universita Degli Studi Napoli Federico II, Facolta di Agraria Biblioteca Centrale, 80055 Portici Naples Italy. **Tel** 081 273739. Documents available from CASDDS.
Continues Annali del Facolta di Agrari di Portici Della Universita di Napoli.
Ind/Abst Chem. Abstr.; Crop Physiol. Abstr.; Ecology Abstr.; Fish Rev. (Jan. 1989-July 1992); Grass. Forage Abstr.; Index Vet.; Nutr. Abstr. Rev., Ser. B, Live Feeds and Feed; Life Sci. Collect.; Plant Breed. Abstr.; Plant Grow. Reg. Abstr.; Rev. Plant Pathol.; Sorghum Mill. Abstr.; Wildl. Rev. (Jan. 1989-July 1992).

LC QH301
DD 574
ISSN 0082-6871
IT

ANNALI DELLA FACOLTA DI SCIENZE AGRARIE DELLA UNIVERSITA DEGLI STUDI DI TORINO. [Ann. Fac. Sci. Agrar. Univ. Studi Torino]. **Main/Corp** Universita di Torino. Facolta di Scienze Agrarie. Vol. 1 (1961-62)-. Italian. Universita di Torino, Facolta di Scienze Agrarie, Turin Italy. Documents available from BIOSIS Document Express.
Ind/Abst Biol. Abstr.; Life Sci. Collect.; Rev. Agric. Entomol.; Rev. Plant Pathol.; Soils Fert.

LC S
DD 630
IT

ANNALI DELL'INSTITUTO SPERIMENTALE PER LA MECCANIZZAZIONE AGRICOLA.
Main/Corp Istituto Sperimentale per la Meccanizzazione Agricola. Vol. 1 (1970)-. Italian (summaries and/or abstracts in English; table of contents in English). One time a year.
Ind/Abst Agric. Eng. Abstr.

LC S539.5
DD 630.72
ISSN 0304-0615
IT

ANNALI DELL'ISTITUTO SPERIMENTALE AGRONOMICO. [Ann. ist. sper. agron.]. **Main/Corp** Istituto Sperimentale Agronomico. Vol. 1 (1970)-. Periodical. Italian (English, French, German and Italian; summaries and/or abstracts in English and Italian). Two times a year.
Ind/Abst Field Crop Abstr.; Irr. Drain. Abstr.; Seed Abstr.; Soils Fert.; Sorghum Mill. Abstr.; Wheat Barley Trit. Abstr.

LC S
DD 630
ISSN 0304-0569
IT
CODEN AIFCBM

ANNALI DELL'ISTITUTO SPERIMENTALE PER LA FRUTTICOLTURA. [Ann. Ist. sper. fruttic.]. **Main/Corp** Istituto Sperimentale per la Frutticoltura (Rome, Italy). Vol. 1 (1970)-. Italian (summaries and/or abstracts in English). One time a year. Documents available from BIOSIS Document Express. **Supersedes** Istituto Sperimentale per la Frutticoltura (Rome, Italy). Pubblicazioni dell'Istituto Sperimentale per la Frutticoltura.
Ind/Abst Agric. Eng. Abstr.; Biol. Abstr.

LC S
DD 630
ISSN 0970-3179
II
CODEN AAGREJ

ANNALS OF AGRICULTURAL RESEARCH. [Ann. agric. res.]. **Added/Corp** Indian Society of Agricultural Science. (19??)-. Periodical. English. Four times a year. $125.00. Indian Society of Agricultural Science, New Delhi India. (**Subscription address:** Prints India, 11 Darya Ganj, New Delhi 110002 India. **Tel** 011 91 11 3268645, FAX 011 91 11 3275542, telex 31-61087 PRIN-IN.) **Bk Rev. Ad Acc. Circ:** 500. Documents available from BIOSIS Document Express.
Desc: Provides opportunities to scientists to address themselves with problems of Indian agriculture and express their views on a scientific basis.
Ind/Abst Agrofor. Abstr. (1991-); Anim. Breed. Abstr.; Biol. Abstr.; Cot. Trop. Fibr. Abstr. Bibliogr.; Crop Physiol. Abstr.; Field Crop Abstr.; For. Prod. Abstr. (1991-); For. Abstr.; Grass. Forage Abstr.; Hortic. Abstr.; Irr. Drain. Abstr.; Maize Abstr.; Nematol. Abstr.; Ornamental Hort.; Plant Breed. Abstr.; Plant Grow. Reg. Abstr.; Rev. Agric. Entomol.; Rev. Plant Pathol.; Rice Abstr.; Seed Abstr.; Soils Fert.; Sorghum Mill. Abstr.; Soyabean Abstr.; Weed Abstr.; Wheat Barley Trit. Abstr.

LC S19. C3
DD 630
UA

ANNALS OF AGRICULTURAL SCIENCE. **VFOAT** Hawliyat Al-Ulum Al-Ziraiyah. (June 1956)-. Periodical. English (summaries and/or abstracts in Arabic; table of contents in Arabic). Two times a year. Faculty of Agriculture, University of Ain Shams, Cairo Egypt.
Ind/Abst Biocont. News Inf. (19??-19??); Biodeter. Abstr. (1991-); Cot. Trop. Fibr. Abstr. Bibliogr.; Crop Physiol. Abstr.; Dairy Sci. Abstr.; Field Crop Abstr.; Grass. Forage Abstr.; Hortic. Abstr.; Irr. Drain. Abstr.; Maize Abstr.; Nematol. Abstr.; Nutr. Abstr. Rev., Ser. B, Live Feeds and Feed; Plant Breed. Abstr.; Plant Grow. Reg. Abstr.; Postharvest News Inf.; Potato Abstr.; Rev. Agric. Entomol.; Rev. Med. Vet. Entomol.; Rev. Med. Vet. Mycology; Rev. Plant Pathol.; Rice Abstr.; Seed Abstr.; Soils Fert.; Sorghum Mill. Abstr.; Soyabean Abstr.; Sug. Indus. Abstr.; Weed Abstr.; Wheat Barley Trit. Abstr.

LC S
DD 630
ISSN 0570-1783
UA
CODEN AAGSAI

ANNALS OF AGRICULTURAL SCIENCE. [Ann. Agric. Sci.]. (1956)-. English. Two times a year. Ain-Shams University, Abbasseyah, Cairo Egypt.
Ind/Abst Curr. Cit.; Postharvest News Inf.

LC S341 .A6
DD 630.962
UA
Pr Rev.

ANNALS OF AGRICULTURAL SCIENCE, MOSHTOHOR. (1974)-. Periodical. English (summaries and/or abstracts in Arabic). Four times a year. Zagazig University, Faculty of Agricultural Science, Moshtohor-Tukh Arab Republic of Egypt.
Ind/Abst Biocont. News Inf.; Biodeter. Abstr.; Cot. Trop. Fibr. Abstr. Bibliogr.; Nematol. Abstr.; Plant Breed. Abstr.; Poult. Abstr.; Rev. Med. Vet. Entomol.; Soyabean Abstr.

LC S
DD 630
PL

ANNALS OF WARSAW AGRICULTURAL UNIVERSITY, SGGW. AGRICULTURE. **Added/Corp** Szkola Glowna Gospodarstwa Wiejskiego--Akademia Rolnicza w Warszawie. (19??)-. Academic Scholarly Publication. English (French, German and Russian; summaries and/or abstracts in Polish). Irregular. SGGW - Szkola Glowna Gospodarstwa Wiejskiego / Akademia Rolnicza w Warszawie, Ul. Nowoursynowska 166, 02-766 Warsaw Poland. **Continues** Annals of Warsaw Agricultural University, SGGW--AR. Agriculture, 0208-5712.

LC S
DD 630
ISSN 0208-5712
PL
TITLE CHANGE

ANNALS OF WARSAW AGRICULTURAL UNIVERSITY, SGGW--AR. AGRICULTURE. **Added/Corp** Szkola Glowna Gospodarstwa Wiejskiego--Akademia Rolnicza w Warszawie. **VFOAT** No. 19 (1986)-(19??). Academic Scholarly Publication. English (French, German and Russian; summaries and/or abstracts in Polish). SGGW - Szkola Glowna Gospodarstwa Wiejskiego / Akademia Rolnicza w Warszawie, Ul. Nowoursynowska 166, 02-766 Warsaw Poland. **Continues** Zeszyty Naukowe Szkoly Glownej Gospodarstwa Wiejskiego--Akademii Rolniczej w Warszawie. Rolnictwo, 0511-1692. **Continued by** Annals of Warsaw Agricultural University, SGGW. Agriculture.
Ind/Abst For. Abstr.; Maize Abstr.

LC S
DD 630
UDC 63
ISSN 0208-5771
PL
CODEN AWARD6

ANNALS OF WARSAW AGRICULTURAL UNIVERSITY SGGW-AR. LAND RECLAMATION. (ANNALS OF WARSAW AGRICULTURAL UNIVERSITY.). [Ann. Wars. Agric. Univ. SGGW-AR, Land reclam.]. **VFOAT** Land Reclamation. No. 19-. Academic Scholarly Publication. Polish. Irregular. Warsaw Agricultural University Press, Ul Nowoursynowska 166, 02-766 Warsaw Poland. Documents available from CASDDS. **Continues** Melioracje Rolne.
Ind/Abst Chem. Abstr.

LC HD1491.F72 R493a
DD 334/.683/0944582
FR

ANNUAIRE DES ORGANISMES COOPERATIFS, REGION RHONE-ALPES. See Business and Economics-Cooperatives.

LC S230.L38 A6
DD 338.1/0944/8
FR

ANNUAIRE REGIONAL: STATISTIQUE AGRICOLE. **Added/Corp** France. Service Regional de Statistique Agricole, Region Languedoc. **VFOAT** Statistique Agricole, Languedoc; Annuaire Regional. (1970)-. Statistical Publication. French. One time a year. 60.00F. Service Regional de Statistique Agricole/Region Languedoc-Rousillon, BP 3054, 34034 Montpellier Cedex 01 France. **Tel** 011 33 67 101850, FAX 011 33 67 100102.

LC S280.M3 A36
DD 354.54/82008233
UDC 338.43(540)
II

ANNUAL ADMINISTRATION REPORT FOR THE YEAR ... / GOVERNMENT OF TAMIL NADU, AGRICULTURE DEPARTMENT. **Main/Corp** Tamil Nadu (India). Agriculture Dept. English. One time a year. **Continues** Tamil Nadu (India). Agriculture Dept. Administration Report of the Agriculture Department for the Year ... .

LC HD9198.I4 A23
DD 354.540082/333
II

ANNUAL ADMINISTRATION REPORT FOR THE YEAR ... / TEA BOARD (INDIA). See Public Administration.

LC S
DD 630
US

ANNUAL FERTILIZER REPORT. **Added/Corp** New Mexico. Division of Producer Services. New Mexico State University. 47th (1976)-. English. New Mexico Department of Agriculture, Department 3189, Las Cruces NM 88003. **Tel** (505)646-3007, FAX (505)827-4824.

LC S117 .D42A
DD 363.97640082/33
US

ANNUAL FINANCIAL REPORT. **Main/Corp** Texas. Dept. of Agriculture. (1987)-. English. One time a year. Texas Department of Agriculture, 18th & Congress Street, PO Box 12847, Austin TX 78711. **Tel** (512)463-7435, FAX (512)463-7643. **Continues** Annual Report. Texas Dept. of Agriculture.

LC HD1491
DD 338.1
CN

ANNUAL MEETING PROCEEDINGS / CANADIAN AGRICULTURAL ECONOMICS AND FARM MANAGEMENT SOCIETY. **Main/Corp** Canadian Agricultural Economics and Farm Management Society. Meeting. Vol. 31 (1983)-. English. One time a year. Comes with The Canadian Journal of Agricultural Economics. Canadian Agricultural Economics and Farm Management Society, 151 Slater Street / Suite 907, Ottawa Ontario K1P 5H4 Canada. **Tel** (613)232-9459, FAX (613)594-5190. **Continues** Canadian Agricultural Economics Society. Meeting. Proceedings of the Annual Meeting of the Canadian Agricultural Economics Society, 0707-4816.

LC S541.5.L82 L685A
DD 630/.9763
UDC 63(047.31)
ISSN 0742-3764
US

ANNUAL PROGRESS REPORT - LOUISIANA. NORTHEAST RESEARCH STATION. (ANNUAL PROGRESS REPORT ... NORTHEAST RESEARCH STATION, ST. JOSEPH, LA., AND MACON RIDGE RESEARCH STATION, WINNSBORO, LA.). **Main/Corp** Louisiana. Northeast Research Station. English. One time a year. Louisiana State University, Baton Rouge LA 70803. **Tel** (504)388-2855.

LC HD1401
DD 338.10941
ISSN 0267-999X
UK

ANNUAL REGISTER OF MERCHANTS' PREMISES. [Annu. regist. merch. premises]. (1985)-. English. Thirteen times a year. $80.42. Pharmaceutical Press, 1 Lambeth High Street, London SE1 7JN United Kingdom. **Tel** 011 44 171 7359141, FAX 011 44 171 7357629, telex 265871. **Acid Free. Circ:** 200.
Desc: A comprehensive list of the names and addresses of all agricultural merchants.

LC S
DD 630
UK
CEASED

ANNUAL REPORT. **Added/Corp** Northern Ireland. Dept. of Agriculture. (1989/90)-(1993). English. Northern Ireland Department of Agriculture, Dundonald House, Upper Newtownard, Belfast BT4 3SB 5RU United Kingdom. **Tel** 011 44 1232 650111. **Continues** Northern Ireland Agriculture.

LC S
DD 630
II

ANNUAL REPORT. **Main/Corp** India. Dept. of Agricultural Research and Education. (1980/1981)-. English. One time a year. Government of India / Department of Agriculture, International Archives of India, Janpath New Delhi India. **Continues** India. Dept. of

Agriculture

Agricultural Research and Education. Report - Government of India, Department of Agricultural Research and Education, Ministry of Agriculture.
LC HN682.5 .A25
DD 354.540081/8 II

●ANNUAL REPORT. See Business and Economics-Economic History, Conditions.

LC HD1483 .A37A ISSN 0741-2568
DD 334/.05 US
ANNUAL REPORT / AGRICULTURAL COOPERATIVE DEVELOPMENT INTERNATIONAL. [Annu. rep. - Agric. Coop. Dev. Int.]. **Main/Corp** Agricultural Cooperative Development International. English. One time a year. Agricultural Cooperative Service, US Department of Agriculture, 14th Street and Independence Avenue SW, Washington DC 20250. Tel (202)653-6973, FAX (202)653-7033.

LC SB401.C6 P48a
DD 354/.599/008233 PH
ANNUAL REPORT - AGRICULTURAL RESEARCH DEPARTMENT, PHILIPPINE COCONUT AUTHORITY. **Main/Corp** Philippine Coconut Authority. Agricultural Research Dept. (1974)-. English. One time a year. Philippine Coconut Authority, Dilliman Quezon City Philippines. cum. index. **Ad Acc**.
Ind/Abst Hortic. Abstr.

LC HD2131.5 .A23A
DD 354.68940081/8/06 ZA
UDC 338.43(689.4)
ANNUAL REPORT AND ACCOUNTS FOR THE YEAR ENDED 31ST MARCH ... - RURAL DEVELOPMENT CORPORATION OF ZAMBIA. Main/Corp Rural Development Corporation of Zambia. English. One time a year. Rural Development Corporation of Zambia, PO Box 31957, Lusaka Zambia. **Continues** *Rural Development and Corporation of Zambia. Annual Report.*

LC S
DD 630 KE
ANNUAL REPORT & ACCOUNTS / THE TEA BOARD OF KENYA. Main/Corp Tea Board of Kenya. **VFOAT** Annual Report and Accounts; Report On the Operations of the Tea Board of Kenya for the Year ended 30th June ... . English. Tea Board of Kenya, PO Box 820, Kericho Kenya.

LC S219 .A22
DD 354.4150082/33 IE
●**ANNUAL REPORT : ANNUAL REPORT OF THE MINISTER FOR AGRICULTURE, FOOD AND FORESTRY. Main/Corp** Ireland. Dept. of Agriculture, Food, and Forestry. **VFOAT** Annual Report of the Minister for Agriculture, Food and Forestry. (1993)-. English. One time a year. Government Publications, 4 5 Harcourt Road, Dublin 2 Ireland. Tel 011 353 1 6613111 ext.4005. **Continues** *Ireland. Dept. of Agriculture and Food. Annual Report of the Minister for Agriculture and Food, 0791-0177.*

LC HC415.I52 A74a ISSN 0066-846X
DD 341.7/59 JA
ANNUAL REPORT - ASIAN PRODUCTIVITY ORGANIZATION. See Industry and Production.

LC S
DD 630 US
ANNUAL REPORT / COLLEGE OF AGRICULTURAL & ENVIRONMENTAL SCIENCES. Added/Corp University of Georgia. College of Agricultural & Environmental Sciences. (1991)-. English. University of Georgia College of Agriculture Extension Service, Athens GA 30602. **Continues** *Annual Report (University of Georgia. College of Agriculture).*

LC S399 .D46a ISSN 1062-4929
DD 353.99690082/33/06 US
ANNUAL REPORT / DEPARTMENT OF AGRICULTURE. Main/Corp Hawaii. Dept. of Agriculture. (19??)-. English. Department of Agriculture / Hawaii, PO Box 22159, Honolulu HI 96823. Tel (808)973-9599, FAX (808)973-9613. **Continues** *Biennial Report (Hawaii. Dept. of Agriculture), 0162-8089.*

LC S544.5.E8 E87A
DD 354/.63/0082330715 ET
ANNUAL REPORT - ETHIOPIA. YAERSA MINISTER. EXTENSION AND PROJECT IMPLEMENTATION DEPT. Main/Corp Ethiopia. Yaersa Minister. Extension and Project Implementation Dept. (1972)-. English. One time a year. EPID, PO Box 3824, Addis Ababa Ethiopia.

LC HD1491 ISSN 0382-1501
DD 338.1 CN
ANNUAL REPORT - FARM CREDIT CORPORATION. See Business and Economics-Banks and Banking.

LC S ISSN 0890-2038
DD 630 US
UDC 63(047.31)
ANNUAL REPORT - FLORIDA COOPERATIVE EXTENSION SERVICE. [Annu. rep. - Fla. Coop. Ext. Serv.]. **Main/Corp** Florida. University. Cooperative Extension Service. (1970)-. Periodical. English. One time a year. Institute of Food and Agricultural Sciences, University of Florida, Building 664, Gainesville FL 32611. Tel (904)392-1773. **Continues** *Annual Report - Florida Agricultural Experiment Station, 0090-4740.*
Ind/Abst AGRICOLA [Full Cov.].

LC J961 .H835 HD9118.F529 F529
DD 300/.996/11 354.96/11008233 FJ
UDC 338.439.4:633.61(961.1)
ANNUAL REPORT FOR ... SEASON (FIJI. SUGAR BOARD). Main/Corp Fiji. Sugar Board. **VFOAT** Annual Report ... Cane Harvesting and Crushing Season. English. One time a year.

LC SB113
DD 631.531 SY
ANNUAL REPORT FOR ... / SEED UNIT. Main/Corp International Center for Agricultural Research in the Dry Areas. Seed Unit. (1990)-. English. One time a year. International Center for Agricultural Research in the Dry Areas, PO Box 5466, Aleppo Syria. Tel 213433, telex 331206. **Continues** *International Center for Agricultural Research in the Dry Areas. Seed Production Unit.*

LC S605 .I5 ISSN 0165-1803
DD 631.6/05 NE
CODEN AILRAS
ANNUAL REPORT - INTERNATIONAL INSTITUTE FOR LAND RECLAMATION AND IMPROVEMENT. (ANNUAL REPORT.). [Annu. rep. - Int. Inst. Land Reclam. Improv.]. **Main/Corp** International Institute for Land Reclamation and Improvement. (1958)-. English. Irregular. Free on request. International Institute for Land Reclamation and Improvement, PO Box 45, 6700 AA Wageningen Netherlands. Tel 011 31 837019100, FAX 11524, telex 75230 NL.

LC SF756.37.K42 K44a
DD 354.676/20082/336 KE
ANNUAL REPORT / KENYA AGRICULTURAL RESEARCH INSTITUTE, VETERINARY RESEARCH DEPARTMENT. See Veterinary Sciences.

LC S69 .E2
DD 630 US
●**ANNUAL REPORT / MAINE AGRICULTURAL AND FOREST EXPERIMENT STATION, UNIVERSITY OF MAINE. Main/Corp** Maine Agricultural and Forest Experiment Station. **VFOAT** MAFES Annual Report. 108th (1992-1993)-. English. One time a year. Maine Agricultural Experiment Station, 103 Winslow Hall, University of Maine, Orono ME 04469. **Continues** *Maine Agricultural Experiment Station. MAES Annual Report.*
Ind/Abst Biol. Abstr.

LC HD6820.6.Z7 A294a ISSN 0580-5120
DD 338.1/09595/1 MY
ANNUAL REPORT - MALAYAN AGRICULTURAL PRODUCERS ASSOCIATION. Main/Corp Malayan Agricultural Producers Association. (19??)-. English. One time a year. Malayan Agricultural Products Association, Bangunan Getah Asli/First Floor, Jalan Ampang, PO Box 1063, Kuala Lumpur Malaysia. available in microform.

LC HG9968.C75 ISSN 0542-5395
DD 368.1 CN
ANNUAL REPORT - MANITOBA CROP INSURANCE CORPORATION. See Insurance.

LC S71 .E2 ISSN 0096-8676
DD 630 US
ANNUAL REPORT - MARYLAND AGRICULTURAL EXPERIMENT STATION. Main/Corp Maryland Agricultural Experiment Station. (1888)-. English.
Ind/Abst AGRICOLA [Full Cov.].

LC HD9014.C2 N37
DD 331.7 CN
TITLE CHANGE
ANNUAL REPORT / NATIONAL FARM PRODUCTS COUNCIL. Main/Corp Canada. National Farm Products Council. **Added/Corp** Canada. National Farm Products Council. **VFOAT** Rapport Annuel. (1993)-(1993). English. Agriculture Canada, Communications Branch, Ottawa Ontario K1A 0C7 Canada. **Continues** *Canada. National Farm Products Marketing Council. Annual Report, 0383-414X.* **Continued by** *Canada. National Farm Products Council. Annual Review.*

LC JL198 ISSN 1185-0418
DD 354.7180082/33/05 CN
ANNUAL REPORT / NEWFOUNDLAND FARM PRODUCTS CORPORATION. [Annu. rep. - Nfld. Farm Prod. Corp.]. **Main/Corp** Newfoundland Farm Products Corporation. (1989/1990)-. English.

LC S542.N5 N53A
DD 354/.669/008233 NR
UDC 338.43(669)
ANNUAL REPORT OF AGRICULTURAL RESEARCH COUNCIL OF NIGERIA. Main/Corp Agricultural Research Council of Nigeria. No. 1 (1971/72)-. English. Agricultural Research Council of Nigeria, Dr T I Ashaye PMB, 5029 Ibadan Nigeria.

LC JL198 ISSN 0842-6430
DD 354.710082/33044 CN
ANNUAL REPORT OF THE AGRICULTURAL PRODUCTS BOARD. (ANNUAL REPORT OF THE AGRICULTURAL PRODUCTS BOARD FOR THE YEAR ENDED MARCH 31.). [Annu. rep. Agric. Prod. Board]. **Main/Corp** Canada. Agricultural Products Board. **VFOAT** Rapport Annuel de l'Office des Produits Agricoles pour l'Annee se Terminant le 31 Mars. (1988)-. Government Publication. English (French). One time a year. Free on request. Agriculture Canada, Communications Branch, Ottawa Ontario K1A 0C7 Canada. **Continues** *Canada. Agricultural Products Board. Annual Report to the Minister of Agriculture., 0383-2325.*

LC S153 .A22 ISSN 0703-5977
DD 354.7160082/33/06 CN
ANNUAL REPORT OF THE DEPARTMENT OF AGRICULTURE AND MARKETING (HALIFAX). (ANNUAL REPORT - DEPARTMENT OF AGRICULTURE AND MARKETING.). **Main/Corp** Nova Scotia. Dept. of Agriculture and Marketing. **VAT** Annual Report - Department of Agriculture and Marketing (Halifax). (1959)-. Periodical. English. One time a year. Department of Agriculture and Marketing, Hollis Building, Halifax Nova Scotia B3J 2M4 Canada. Tel (902)895-1571. **Continues** *Report of the Department of Agriculture and Marketing, Province of Nova Scotia, 0703-5969.*

LC S83 .D46A ISSN 0092-9786
DD 353.9/786/00823305 US
UDC 338.43(786)
ANNUAL REPORT OF THE DEPARTMENT OF AGRICULTURE (MONTANA). (ANNUAL REPORT.). [Annu. rep. Dept. Agric.]. **Main/Corp** Montana. Dept. of Agriculture. English. One time a year. George Lackman, Capitol Annex Building, Helena MT 59601.

LC S328 .D45A
DD 354.968/0082/3306 SA
UDC 338.43(680)
ANNUAL REPORT OF THE DIRECTOR GENERAL, AGRICULTURE AND FISHERIES FOR THE PERIOD 1 APRIL ... TO 31 MARCH / REPUBLIC OF SOUTH AFRICA. Main/Corp South Africa. Dept. of Agriculture and Fisheries. **VFOAT** Report of the Director General, Agriculture and Fisheries for Period 1 April ... to 31 March ...; Annual Report. 1980/1982-. English. One time a year.

LC S328 .D47A
DD 338.1/0968 SA
UDC 338.43(680)
ANNUAL REPORT OF THE DIRECTOR GENERAL, AGRICULTURE FOR THE PERIOD ... . **Main/Corp** South Africa. Dept. of Agriculture. **VFOAT** Department of Agriculture Annual Report. 1 Apr. 1981 to 31 Mar. 1982-. English. One time a year. R2.90 South Africa; R3.50 other. **Continues** *South Africa. Dept. of Agriculture and Fisheries. Annual Report of the Director General, Agriculture and Fisheries.*

LC S219 .A22 ISSN 0791-0177
DD 354.4150082/33 IE
TITLE CHANGE
ANNUAL REPORT OF THE MINISTER FOR AGRICULTURE AND FOOD (DUBLIN). (ANNUAL REPORT OF THE MINISTER FOR AGRICULTURE AND FOOD.). [Annu. rep. Minist. Agric. Food]. **Main/Corp** Ireland. Dept. of Agriculture and Food. (1987)-(1992). English. Government Publications, 4 5 Harcourt Road, Dublin 2 Ireland. Tel 011 353 1 6613111 ext.4005. **Continues** *Ireland. Dept. of Agriculture. Annual Report of the Minister for Agriculture.* **Continued by** *Ireland. Dept. of Agriculture, Food, and Forestry. Annual Report.*

LC HG9969.C2 C36a ISSN 0711-8198
DD 354.710082/33045 CN
ANNUAL REPORT OF THE MINISTER UNDER THE CROP INSURANCE ACT. [Annu. rep. Minist. crop Insur. Act]. **Main/Corp** Canada. Agriculture Canada. **VFOAT** Rapport Annuel du Ministre, Loi sur l'Assurance-Recolte; Rapport Annuel du Ministre pour l'Annee Financiere ... en Marge de la Loi sur l'Assurance-Recolte. **VAT** Rapport Annuel du Ministre. Loi sur l'Assurance-Recolte; Rapport Annuel du Ministre en Marge de l Loi sur l'Assurance-Recolte. (19??)-. Government Publication. English (French). Free on request. Agriculture Canada, Communications Branch, Ottawa Ontario K1A 0C7 Canada.

LC SB354 ISSN 0099-7838
DD 634 US
ANNUAL REPORT OF THE NORTHERN NUT GROWERS ASSOCIATION. (ANNUAL REPORT / NORTHERN NUT GROWERS ASSOCIATION.). [Annu. rep. North. Nut Grow. Assoc.]. **Main/Corp** Northern Nut Growers Association. **VFOAT** Annual Report of the Northern Nut Growers Association. (1942)-. English. One time a year. $12.00. Northern Nut Growers Association - Connecticut, 13 Broken Arrow Road, Hamden CT 06518. **Tel** (203)288-1026. **ED** William Reid. Index available (Additional $5.00). cum. index. ***Continues*** *Northern Nut Growers Association. Report of the Proceedings at the Annual Meeting.*
Ind/Abst Plant Breed. Abstr.

LC K ISSN 0318-5044
DD 343/.7123/0760269 CN
ANNUAL REPORT - OFFICE OF THE FARMERS' ADVOCATE (ALBERTA). See Law.

LC S21 .A26A ISSN 0882-2026
DD 353.0082/33/072 US
ANNUAL REPORT ON THE FOOD AND AGRICULTURAL SCIENCES, FROM THE SECRETARY OF AGRICULTURE TO THE PRESIDENT AND THE CONGRESS OF THE UNITED STATES. (ANNUAL REPORT ON THE FOOD AND AGRICULTURAL SCIENCES, FROM THE SECRETARY OF AGRICULTURE TO THE PRESIDENT AND THE CONGRESS OF THE UNITED STATES / UNITED STATES DEPARTMENT OF AGRICULTURE, RESEARCH AND EDUCATION COMMITTEE.). [Annu. rep. food agric. sci. Secr. Agric. Pres. Congr. U.S.]. **Main/Corp** United States. Dept. of Agriculture. Research and Education Committee. (1982)-. Government Publication. English. One time a year. US Department of Agriculture, 14th Street and Independence Avenue SW, Washington DC 20250. **Tel** (202)720-5457.

LC HD1775.V5 V464A ISSN 0735-3243
DD 353.97550082/33/06 US
ANNUAL REPORT. PLANNING AND DEVELOPMENT. (ANNUAL REPORT. PLANNING AND DEVELOPMENT (VIRGINIA).). [Annu. rep., Plan. dev.]. **Main/Corp** Virginia. Dept. of Agriculture and Consumer Services. (1978)-. English. One time a year. Virginia Department of Agriculture & Consumer Services, 1100 Bank Street, Washington Building, Suite 210, Richmond VA 23219. **Tel** (804)786-2373, FAX (804)371-7679. ***Continues*** *Virginia. Dept. of Agriculture and Commerce. Annual Report.*

LC S605.2.C2 C363a ISSN 0829-1772
DD 354/.71/008233 CN
ANNUAL REPORT - PRAIRIE FARM REHABILITATION ADMINISTRATION. [Annu. rep. - Prairie Farm Rehabil. Adm.]. **Main/Corp** Canada. Prairie Farm Rehabilitation Administration. **Added/Corp** Canada. Prairie Farm Rehabilitation Administration. Rapport Annuel. **VFOAT** Rapport Annuel - Administration du Retablissement Agricole des Prairies. (19??)-. English (French).
Ind/Abst Rev. Agric. Entomol.; Rev. Plant Pathol.

LC KEB503.A72 A35 ISSN 0708-4048
DD 354.7110082/326 CN
ANNUAL REPORT - PROVINCIAL AGRICULTURAL LAND COMMISSION (BRITISH COLUMBIA). **Main/Corp** British Columbia. Provincial Agricultural Land Commission. (1978)-. English. One time a year. Provincial Agricultural Land Commission, 4333 Ledger Avenue, Burnaby BC. ***Continues*** *British Columbia. Provincial Land Commission. Annual Report, 0703-2374.*

LC HD9435.C23 S277 ISSN 0715-2965
DD 354.71240082/336 CN
ANNUAL REPORT ... SASKATCHEWAN AGRICULTURAL RETURNS STABILIZATION FUND. [Annu. rep., Sask. Agric. Returns Stab. Fund]. **Main/Corp** Saskatchewan. **VFOAT** Saskatchewan Agricultural Returns Stabilization Fund. (1979)-. English. One time a year. Saskatchewan Government Services, Regina Saskatchewan Canada. ***Continues*** *Annual Report of the Saskatchewan Agricultural Returns Stabilization Fund.*

LC JL198 ISSN 0842-4632
DD 354.71270082/326 CN
ANNUAL REPORT / THE MANITOBA FARM LANDS OWNERSHIP BOARD. [Annu. rep. - Manit. Farm Lands Ownersh. Board]. **Main/Corp** Manitoba Farm Lands Ownership Board. **Added/Corp** Manitoba. Manitoba Agriculture. (1984/85)-. English. Manitoba Department of Agriculture, 903 Norquay Building, Winnipeg Manitoba R3C 0P8 Canada. ***Continues*** *Annual Report / Manitoba Agricultural Lands Protection Board, 0711-4796.*

LC S ISSN 0527-4664
DD 630 CN
ANNUAL REPORT TO THE MINISTER OF AGRICULTURE (AGRICULTURAL STABILIZATION BOARD). (ANNUAL REPORT TO THE MINISTER OF AGRICULTURE.). **Main/Corp** Canada. Agricultural Stabilization Board. **VAT** Annual Report - Agricultural Stabilization Board; Annual Report of the Agricultural Stabilization Board; Rapport Annuel - Office de Stabilisation des Prix Agricoles (1976); Rapport Annuel de l'Office de Stabilisation des Prix Agricoles (1976); Rapport Annuel Presente au Ministre de l'Agriculture (Office de Stabilisation des Prix Agricoles. 1976). (1957)-. Government Publication. English. One time a year. Free on request. Agriculture Canada, Communications Branch, Ottawa Ontario K1A 0C7 Canada. ***Supersedes*** *Canada. Agricultural Prices Support Board. Annual Report to the Minister of Agriculture.*

LC JK404 .U54A
DD 353.0081/8 US
UDC 338.43(73)
ANNUAL REPORT - UNITED STATES. DEPT. OF AGRICULTURE. **Main/Corp** United States. Dept. of Agriculture. Government Publication. English. One time a year. US Department of Agriculture, 14th Street and Independence Avenue SW, Washington DC 20250. **Tel** (202)720-5457.

LC HD1775.V5 V475a ISSN 0883-0967
DD 353.97550082/33045 US
ANNUAL REPORT / VIRGINIA AGRICULTURAL DEVELOPMENT AUTHORITY. [Annu. rep. - Va. Agric. Dev. Auth.]. **Main/Corp** Virginia Agricultural Development Authority. 1st (1981-82)-. Periodical. English. One time a year. Virginia Agricultural Development Authority, PO Box 1163, Richmond VA 23209. **Tel** (804)786-3538. **ED** James R. Kee. **Circ:** 20.
Desc: Provides long-term low-interest farm loans through the use of Industrial Development Bonds.

LC HD1775.V5 V476A ISSN 0883-1017
DD 372.951/132 US
ANNUAL REPORT / VIRGINIA AGRICULTURAL FOUNDATION. [Annu. rep. - Va. Agric. Found.]. **Main/Corp** Virginia Agricultural Foundation. English. One time a year. Virginia Agricultural Foundation, Department of Agriculture and Consumer Services, PO Box 1163, Richmond VA 23209.

LC HD9014.C2 N37
DD 331.7 CN
•**ANNUAL REVIEW / NATIONAL FARM PRODUCTS COUNCIL.** **Main/Corp** Canada. National Farm Products Council. **Added/Corp** Canada. National Farm Products Council. **VFOAT** Revue Annuelle. (1994)-. English. Agriculture Canada, Communications Branch, Ottawa Ontario K1A 0C7 Canada. ***Continues*** *Canada. National Farm Products Council. Annual Report.*

LC S ISSN 0953-6884
DD 630 UK
CODEN AESAEM
ANNUAL REVIEW / THE EDINBURGH SCHOOL OF AGRICULTURE. [Annu. rev. - Edinb. Sch. Agric.]. **Main/Corp** Edinburgh School of Agriculture. (1987)-. English. One time a year. Edinburgh School of Agriculture, West Mains Road, Edinburgh EH9 3JG United Kingdom. Documents available from BIOSIS Document Express. ***Continues*** *Annual Report - Edinburgh School of Agriculture, 0307-2355.*
Ind/Abst Biol. Abstr. (1988-).

LC HD1970 .I73 ISSN 0304-0666
DD 630 IT
ANNUARIO DELL'AGRICOLTURA ITALIANA. Vol. 2 (1948)-. Italian (summaries and/or abstracts in English and French). One time a year. Societa Editrice il Mulino, Strada Maggiore 37, 40125 Bologna Italy. **Tel** 011 39 51 256011, FAX 011 39 51 256034. ***Continues*** *Annuario dell'Economia Agraria Italiana.*

LC HD9015.I6 A67
DD 338.1 IT
ANNUARIO SEAT. VOL. H, AGRICOLTURA ED ALIMENTAZIONE. **VFOAT** Agricoltura Ed Alimentazione; Annuario S.E.A.T. Vol. H, Agricoltura Ed Alimentazione. Italian. One time a year. L35000. Casella Postale N 512, 10100 Torino Centro Italy. **Tel** 011-33301, FAX 4472953, telex 212248 I. **Bk Rev.** **Circ:** 21,500.
Desc: Yearbook of Italian companies operating in agriculture, animals, food and drinks classified by categories. Additional information on specific market situations in Italy is available.

LC S471.J32 A544
DD 630.95 JA
AOMORI-KEN NOGYO SHIKENJO KENKYU HOKOKU. **VFOAT** Aomori Ken Nogyo Shikenjo Kenkyu Hokoku; Bulletin of the Aomori Agricultural Experiment Station. Bulletin. Japanese (summaries and/or abstracts in English). Aomoriken Nogyo Shikenjo, (Aomori Agricultural Experiment Station), 1-1 Sakaimatsu, Kurioshishi Aomoriken 036-03 Japan.
Ind/Abst Postharvest News Inf.; Rice Abstr.

LC SF521 ISSN 1010-3619
DD 638.1 SZ
APE, L'. [Ape]. **Added/Corp** Societa Ticinese di Apicoltura. **VFOAT** Rivista Svizzera di Apicoltura. Vol. 1 (1917)-. Periodical. Italian. Twelve times a year.
Ind/Abst AGRICOLA; Sug. Indus. Abstr.

LC S21 .A85735 ISSN 0094-3797
DD 353.81 US
APHIS 91. **Main/Corp** United States. Animal and Plant Health Inspection Service. **VAT** Animal and Plant Health Inspection Service Ninety One. Monographic series. English. Price varies per volume. US Department of Agriculture / Animal & Plant Health Inspection Service, 741 Federal Building 1, 6505 Belcres Road, Hyattsville MD 20782. **Tel** (301)436-7817.

LC SF521 ISSN 0003-6455
DD 638.1 RM
APIACTA. [Apiacta]. **Added/Corp** Apimondia. (196?)-. Periodical. English (French, German, Spanish, Russian and Romanian). Four times a year. L28000. **(Subscription address:** Kubon & Sagner, ABT Zeitschriftenimport, D 80328 Munich Germany. **Tel** 011 49 89 54218130.) **ED** Dumitrascu Erika. **Ad Acc. Circ:** 6,000 (ctrl). available on microfilm and microfiche from University Microfilms International (UMI).
Desc: A magazine for apicultural technical and scientifical information.
Ind/Abst Rev. Agric. Entomol.

LC SF521 ISSN 0393-4241
DD 638.1 IT
APICOLTURA : RIVISTA SCIENTIFICA DI APIDOLOGIA. **Added/Corp** Istituto Sperimentale per la Zoologia Agraria (Italy) Istituto Sperimentale per la Zoologia Agraria (Italy). Sezione Operativa di Apicoltura. Vol. 1 (1985)-. Periodical. Italian (English). One time a year. L54500. Institute Sperim Zoologia Agraria, via Lanciola 12A Cascine Riccio, 50125 Florence Italy. **Tel** 011 39 55 209182.
Ind/Abst Sug. Indus. Abstr.

LC SF521 ISSN 1081-843X
DD 638 US
APICULTURAL INFORMATION AND ISSUES (ONLINE). (APICULTURAL INFORMATION AND ISSUES [COMPUTER FILE] : APIS : FLORIDA EXTENSION BEEKEEPING NEWSLETTER.). [Apic. inf. issues]. **Added/Corp** Florida Cooperative Extension Service. University of Florida. Institute of Food and Agricultural Sciences. University of Florida. Dept. of Entomology and Nematology. **VFOAT** APIS. (198?)-. Newsletter. English. Twelve times a year. Free. APIS, Building 970, Box 110620, Gainesville FL 32611-0620. **Tel** (904)392-1801, FAX (904)392-0190. available via Internet (http://gnv.ifas.ufl.edu:7999/~entweb/apis/apis.htm); available in print.
Desc: Covers bee culture and beekeeping.

LC S13 .S874 ISSN 0235-2443
DD 630.5 RU
APK-EKONOMIKA, UPRAVLENIE. **Added/Corp** Gosudarstvennyi Agropromyshlennyi Komitet SSSR. **VFOAT** APK, Ekonomika, Upravlenie; APK; Ekonomike, Upravlenie. Vol. 1 (1988)-. Periodical. Russian. Twelve times a year. $119.95. Izdatelstvo Kolos, Sadovaia-Spasskaia 18, 107807 Moscow Russia. **(Subscription address:** East View Publications Inc., 3020 Harbor Lane North, Suite 110, Minneapolis MN 55447. **Tel** (800)477-1005, (612)550-0961, FAX (612)559-2931.) ***Continues*** *Ekonomika Selskogo Khoziaistva, 0013-3094.*
Ind/Abst Hortic. Abstr.; Maize Abstr.; Potato Abstr.; Poult. Abstr.; Soils Fert.; Wheat Barley Trit. Abstr.; World Agric. Econ. Rural Sociol. Abstr.

LC HC415.I52 A66 ISSN 0919-0589
DD 338/.06/09500 JA
•**APO PRODUCTIVITY JOURNAL.** **Added/Corp** Asian Productivity Organization. (Spring 1993)-. English. Two times a year. $40.00. Asian Productivity Organization, 4-14 Akasaka 8 Chome, Minato-ku Tokyo 107 Japan. **Tel** 011 81 3 4087221, FAX 011 81 3 34087220, telex APOFFICE J26477. **(Subscription address:** UNIPUB, 4611 F Assembly Drive, Lanham MD 20706. **Tel** (800)274-4888, (301)459-7666.) **ED** Raymond S. L. Wan. **Bk Rev**, (Qty: 10). **Circ:** 1,000.

LC S
DD 630 US
APPLICATION TECHNOLOGY. (19??)-. Periodical. English. Six times a year. $10.50 (one-year), $18.00 (two-year). Meister Publishing Company, 37733 Euclid Avenue, Willoughby OH 44094-5992. **Tel** (216)942-2000, (800)572-7740, FAX (216)942-0662.
Desc: Information on successful agricultural application.

LC S **ISSN** 0883-8542
DD 630 US
CCC
Pr Rev.
APPLIED ENGINEERING IN AGRICULTURE. [Appl. eng. agric.]. **Added/Corp** American Society of Agricultural Engineers. Vol. 1, No. 1 (June 1985)-. Periodical. English. Six times a year. $74.50. American Society of Agricultural Engineers, Department 2510, 2950 Niles Road, St. Joseph MI 49085-9659. **Tel** (616)429-0300, FAX (616)429-3852. Index available (free). Documents available from Article Express International.
Desc: Contributors representing industry, education, agricultural extension, and government research share studies of unique installations and applications, successful methods of technology transfer, and critical reviews of new technology.
Ind/Abst AgBiotech News Inf.; AGRICOLA [Full Cov.]; Agric. Eng. Abstr. (1991-); Biodeter. Abstr. (19??-19??); Cot. Trop. Fibr. Abstr. Bibliogr.; Curr. Cit.; Dairy Sci. Abstr.; Eng. Index Annu.; Field Crop Abstr.; Food Sci. Technol. Abstr.; Grass. Forage Abstr.; Hortic. Abstr.; Index Vet.; Irr. Drain. Abstr.; Maize Abstr.; Nematol. Abstr.; Ornamental Hort. (19??-19??); Pig News Inf.; Plant Genet. Resour. Abstr.; Postharvest News Inf.; Rev. Agric. Entomol.; Rice Abstr.; Seed Abstr.; Soils Fert.; Sorghum Mill. Abstr.; Soyabean Abstr.; Vet. Bull.; Weed Abstr.; Wheat Barley Trit. Abstr.; World Agric. Econ. Rural Sociol. Abstr.

LC S17
DD 630 NR
APPROVED RESEARCH PROGRAMME - FEDERAL DEPARTMENT OF AGRICULTURAL RESEARCH. Main/Corp Nigeria. Dept. of Agricultural Research. (1974)-. Periodical. English. ***Continues*** *An Index of Agricultural Research and Related Subjects in Nigeria.*
Ind/Abst Hortic. Abstr.; Rev. Med. Vet. Mycology; Rev. Plant Pathol.

LC HD1511.G72 A3
DD 354.4110082/33 UK
Pr Rev.
APUA NEWSLETTER. Main/Corp Scotland. Crofters Commission. (1958)-. Newsletter. English. One time a year. $35.00 (individuals), $75.00 (institutions). Alliance For the Prudent Use of Antibiotics, PO Box 1372, Boston MA 02117. **Tel** (617)956-6765, FAX (617)956-0458. **ED** Stuart B Levy. Index available. cum. index. **Bk Rev. Circ:** 625 (ctrl). ***Continues*** *Report / Scotland. Crofters Commission.*
Desc: International forum on antibiotic usage and resistance worldwide. Tailored for mass readability on medical subjects.

LC S **ISSN** 0267-0216
DD 630 BA
ARAB WORLD AGRIBUSINESS. VFOAT Ziraah Fial-Alam Al-Arabi. Vol. 1, No. 1 (1985)-. Trade Publication. English (Arabic). Nine times a year. $60.00. Fanar Publishing, PO Box 10131, 8th Bahrain Towers, Manama Bahrain. **Tel** 011 973 213900, FAX 011 973 211765.
Desc: Contains a variety of articles and special features on the latest technical processes and developments, farming systems, husbandry practices, mechanization improvements and scientific advances in agriculture and horticulture.
Ind/Abst Index Vet.; Rev. Med. Vet. Entomol.; Soils Fert.

LC S **ISSN** 0269-6797
DD 630 UK
ARABLE FARMING. [Arable farming]. Vol. 1, No. 1 (Jan. 1974)-. Periodical. English. Twelve times a year. $63.00. Farming Press, Royal Sovereign House, 40 Beresford Street, Woolwich London SE18 6BO United Kingdom. **Tel** 011 44 181 8557777, FAX 011 44 181 3173938. **(Subscription address:** Morgan Grampian, 40 Beresford Street, London SE18 6BQ United Kingdom. **Tel** 011 44 171 8557777, FAX 011 44 181 8555548.**) ED** G R Rumsey. **Ad Acc. Circ:** 32,000 (ctrl). ***Continues*** *Arable Farmer and Vegetable Grower, 0300-2829.*
Desc: Informs farmers of developments in growing, harvesting and marketing their crops, with emphasis on practical experience.
Ind/Abst Agric. Eng. Abstr.; Field Crop Abstr.; Grass. Forage Abstr.; Hortic. Abstr.; Nematol. Abstr.; Soils Fert.; Weed Abstr.

LC SD411
DD 634.9 PH
ARANETA RESEARCH JOURNAL. Added/Corp Araneta University Foundation. Vol. 19, (Jan./Mar. 1972)-. Periodical. English. Four times a year. $20.00 Philippines; $100.00 other. Gregorio Araneta University, Victoneta Park Malabon Metro, Manila 3104 Philippines. **Tel** 34-64-21. ***Continues*** *Araneta Journal of Agriculture, 0003-7575.*
Ind/Abst Field Crop Abstr.; Grass. Forage Abstr.; Hortic. Abstr.; Plant Breed. Abstr.; Rev. Med. Vet. Mycology; Rev. Plant Pathol.; Soils Fert.

LC S **ISSN** 0233-0652
DD 630 GW
UDC 63
ARBEITEN ZUR MECHANISIERUNG DER PFLANZEN- UND TIERPRODUKTION. [Arb. Mech. Pflanzen-Tierprod.]. (1984)-. Monographic series. German. Irregular.
Ind/Abst Agric. Eng. Abstr.; Field Crop Abstr.; Hortic. Abstr.; Nutr. Abstr. Rev., Ser. B, Live Feeds and Feed.; Postharvest News Inf.; Potato Abstr.

LC HA1248.L69 S73
DD 331.11/8/094359 GW
UDC 331.5:63(430-317)
ARBEITSKRAEFTE IN DEN LANDWIRTSCHAFTLICHEN BETRIEBEN. German. One time a year. DM5.40. Niedersaechsisches Landesamt fuer Statistik, Postfach 4460, D-30044 Hannover Germany. **Tel** 011 49 511 9898321, FAX 011 49 511 9898400. **Bk Rev. Circ:** 150.
Desc: Manpower in the agricultural sector.

LC HD1536.G3 S23A
DD 331.7/63/094359 GW
ARBEITSKRAFTEERHEBUNG IN DER LANDWIRTSCHAFT. See Business and Economics-Labor.

LC S
DD 630 FR
ARDENNE AGRICOLE. (1944)-. French. One time a week. 115.00F. Ardenne Agricole, 1 Ave du Petit Bois, PO Box 416, 08107 Charleville France. **Tel** 24 33 53 00.

LC HD1862 .G47A
DD 338.1/0982 GW
UDC 338.43(82)
ARGENTINIEN, LANDWIRTSCHAFT / BUNDESSTELLE FUR AUSSENHANDELSINFORMATION. German. DM5.00. Bundesstelle fuer Aussenhandelsinformation, Agrippastrasse 87 93, D-50676 Cologne Germany. **Tel** 011 49 221 2057316, FAX 011 49 221 2057212. ***Continues*** *Argentinien, Landwirtschaft und Agrarpolitik.*

LC S **ISSN** 0004-1262
DD 630 YU
CODEN APNAA2
ARHIV ZA POLJOPRIVREDNE NAUKE. [Arh. poljopr. nauke]. **VFOAT** Journal for Scientific Agricultural Research. (1948)-. Periodical. Serbo-Croatian (Roman). Documents available from CASDDS. ***Continues*** *Arhiv za Poljoprivredne Nauke i Tehniku, 0365-5601.*
Ind/Abst Chem. Abstr.; Food Sci. Technol. Abstr.; Life Sci. Collect.; Plant Breed. Abstr.; Poult. Abstr.

LC S **ISSN** 0274-7014
DD 630 US
ARIZONA FARM BUREAU NEWS. Main/Corp Arizona Farm Bureau Federation. **VFOAT** AFB News. (19??)-. Periodical. English. Twenty-four times a year. Arizona Farm Bureau Federation, 2618 South 21st Street, Phoenix AZ 85034. **Tel** (602)257-8655. **ED** Deb Flowers. **Circ:** 4,300.

LC S **ISSN** 1071-6521
DD 630 US
•**ARIZONA FARMER (1993).** (ARIZONA FARMER.). Vol. 72, No. 6 (July 1993)-. Trade Publication. English. Twelve times a year. Western Farmer Stockman, Box 2160, Spokane WA 99210. **Tel** (509)459-5361, FAX (509)459-5102. ***Continues*** *Arizona Farmer-Stockman, 8750-6432.*

LC S **ISSN** 0744-5474
DD 630 US
ARIZONA LAND & PEOPLE. (ARIZONA LAND & PEOPLE; MAGAZINE OF THE COLLEGE OF AGRICULTURE, UNIVERSITY OF ARIZONA.). [Ariz. land people]. **Added/Corp** University of Arizona. College of Agriculture. **VFOAT** Arizona Land and People. Vol. 33, No. 1 (March 1982)-. Periodical. English. Four times a year. Free on request. University of Arizona / Agriculture, College of Agriculture, Tucson AZ 85721. **Tel** (602)626-4885. **(Subscription address:** Agricultural Sciences Communications, 715 North Park Avenue, Tucson AZ 85721. **) ED** Jan McCoy. **Circ:** 5,000. ***Continues*** *Progressive Agriculture in Arizona, 0033-0744.*
Desc: Concerns agriculture, natural resources and home economics in Arizona.
Ind/Abst Field Crop Abstr.; Grass. Forage Abstr.; Life Sci. Collect.

LC S **ISSN** 0004-1785
DD 630 US
CODEN AKFRAC
Pr Rev. **CEASED**
ARKANSAS FARM RESEARCH. [Ark. farm res.]. **Added/Corp** University of Arkansas (Fayetteville Campus). Agricultural Experiment Station. University of Arkansas, Fayetteville. Agricultural Experiment Station. Vol. 1 (Spring 1952)-Vol. 43 (Nov./Dec. 1994). Periodical. English. Irregular. Arkansas Agricultural Experiment Station, University of Arkansas, Fayetteville AR 72701. **Tel** (501)575-5647, FAX (501)575-7273. **ED** Raymond Barclay Jr., Howell Medders. Index available. cum. index. **Circ:** 9,800. Documents available from CASDDS.
Desc: Reports findings of research in agriculture, forestry and home economics in Arkansas.
Ind/Abst AGRICOLA [Full Cov.]; Biocont. News Inf. (19??-19??); Biodeter. Abstr.; Chem. Abstr. (1952-1983); Cot. Trop. Fibr. Abstr. Bibliogr.; Crop Physiol. Abstr.; Dairy Sci. Abstr.; EMBASE; Field Crop Abstr.; Food Sci. Technol. Abstr.; Grass. Forage Abstr.; Hortic. Abstr.; Index Vet.; Irr. Drain. Abstr.; Maize Abstr.; Nematol. Abstr.; Nutr. Abstr. Rev., Ser. B, Live Feeds and Feed.; Nutr. Abstr. Rev., Ser. A, Hum. Exp.; Ornamental Hort. (1991-); Life Sci. Collect.; Plant Breed. Abstr.; Postharvest News Inf.; Poult. Abstr.; Protozoolog. Abstr.; Rev. Agric. Entomol.; Rev. Med. Vet. Entomol.; Rev. Med. Vet. Mycology; Rev. Plant Pathol.; Rice Abstr.; Seed Abstr.; Soils Fert.; Sorghum Mill. Abstr.; Soyabean Abstr.; Vitis Vitic. Enol. Abstr.; Weed Abstr.; Wheat Barley Trit. Abstr.

LC S **ISSN** 0004-1890
DD 630 US
CEASED
ARKANSAS VALLEY JOURNAL. (19??)-(19??). Trade Publication. English. Arkansas Valley Journal, PO Box 500, La Junta CO 81050-0500. **Tel** (303)384-8121. **ED** Daniel R. Hyatt. **Ad Acc. Circ:** 5,893 (ctrl). available on microfilm (Woodcraft Memorial Library).
Desc: Covers agriculture in Colorado and northern New Mexico, including all livestock, equestrian activities and crops. Includes lifestyle-type stories that relate to rural living.

LC S **ISSN** 0100-2481
DD 630 BL
ARQUIVOS DA UNIVERSIDADE FEDERAL RURAL DO RIO DE JANEIRO. Added/Corp Universidade Federal Rural do Rio de Janeiro. Vol. 1 (1971)-. Periodical. Portuguese (summaries and/or abstracts in English). Four times a year.
Ind/Abst Biocont. News Inf.; Biodeter. Abstr.; Index Vet.; Rev. Agric. Entomol.; Small Anim. Abstr. Bibliogr.

LC NOT IN LC **ISSN** 0020-3653
DD 630 BL
NLM W1 AR921KI **CODEN** AIBOA3
ARQUIVOS DO INSTITUTO BIOLOGICO (SAO PAULO). See Biology.

LC SB188 **ISSN** 0120-2634
DD 633.18 CK
Pr Rev.
ARROZ EN LAS AMERICAS. Added/Corp Programa de Arroz (Centro Internacional de Agricultura Tropical). (198?)-. Newsletter. Spanish. Two times a year. Free on request. Centro Internacional de Agricultura Tropical, Apartado Aereo 67-13, Cali Colombia. **Tel** 57 23 4450000, FAX 57 23 4450273, telex 05769 CIAT CO. **ED** Francisco Motta. **Circ:** 1,200. ***Continues*** *Arroz del CIAT America Latina, 0120-2634.*
Desc: Information on irrigated and upland rice research done mainly in Latin America and the Caribbean. Information on rice research and events from IRRI and other Asian institutes.
Ind/Abst Field Crop Abstr.; Irr. Drain. Abstr.; Rice Abstr.

LC S **ISSN** 1052-5386
DD 630 US
ARS. (ARS / UNITED STATES DEPARTMENT OF AGRICULTURE, AGRICULTURAL RESEARCH SERVICE.). [ARS]. **VFOAT** A.R.S. **VAT** Agricultural Research Service. (1984)-. Monographic series. English. Price varies per volume. US Department of Agriculture / Agricultural Research Service / Maryland, Hyattsville MD 20782. ***Formed by the union of*** *Advances in Agricultural Technology. AAT-NE, 0193-371X; Agricultural Research Results. ARR-NE, 0193-3809; Agricultural Reviews and Manuals. ARM-NE, 0193-3752; Advances in Agricultural Technology. AAT-NC, 0193-3701; Agricultural Reviews and Manuals. ARM-NC; Agricultural Research Results. North Central Series, 0193-3825; Advances in Agricultural Technology. AAT-S, 0193-3728; Agricultural Reviews and Manuals. ARM-S, 0193-3779; Agricultural Research Results. Southern Series, 0193-2853; Advances in Agricultural Technology. AAT-W, 0193-3736; Agricultural Reviews and Manuals. Western Series, 0193-3760* **and** *Agricultural Research Results. ARR-W, 0193-3817.*
Ind/Abst AGRICOLA [Full Cov.].

Agriculture

LC S441 .A13 ISSN 0498-224X
DD 338.1 US
ARS 43. Main/Corp United States. Agricultural Research Service. **Added/Corp** United States. Agricultural Research Service. **VFOAT** ARS Forty Three. **VAT** Agricultural Research Service 43; Agricultural Research Service. No. 1, (Aug. 1954)-. Monographic series. English. Irregular. Price varies per volume. US Department of Agriculture / Agricultural Research Service, 14th and Independence Avenue SW, Washington DC 20250. **Continues** PERB. United States. Agricultural Research Service. Production Economics Research Branch.

LC S
DD 630 US
ARS DIRECTORY. Main/Corp United States. Agricultural Research Service. **VFOAT** Directory of the Agricultural Research Service. **VAT** Agricultural Research Service Directory. (19??)-. Directory. English. Two times a year. US Department of Agriculture / Agricultural Research Service, National Center for Agricultural Utilization Research, 1815 North University, Peoria IL 61604. **Tel** (309)685-4011. **Continues** United States. Agricultural Research Service Directory of the Agricultural Research Service, 0196-3511.

LC S ISSN 0098-2946
DD 630 US
  CODEN XARHDO
ARS-H. Main/Corp United States. Agricultural Research Service. **VAT** Agricultural Research Service-Hyattsville. (1972)-. Academic Scholarly Publication. English. Price varies per volume. US Department of Agriculture / Agricultural Research Service / Maryland, Hyattsville MD 20782. Documents available from CASDDS.
Ind/Abst Chem. Abstr.

LC S ISSN 0102-4418
DD 630 BL
ARTICULACAO PESQUISA-EXTENSAO. [Articul. pesqui.-ext.]. **Added/Corp** Empresa Capixaba de Pesquisa Agropecuaria. Empresa de Assistencia Tecnica e Extensao Rural do Estado do Espirito Santo. **VFOAT** Articulacao Pesquisa Extensao. No. 1 (1984)-. Monographic series. Portuguese. Embrapa, Dept. Dif. Tecnologiaogi, Caixa Postal 040315, 07770 901 Brasilia DF Brazil. **Tel** 011 55 61 2724241.
Ind/Abst Hortic. Abstr.

LC S1 .A453 ISSN 0066-0566
DD 630/.5 US
  CODEN AASPC3
ASA SPECIAL PUBLICATION. [ASA spec. publ.]. **Added/Corp** American Society of Agronomy. Crop Science Society of America. **VAT** American Society of Agronomy Special Publication. No. 1 (1963)-. Monographic series. English. Irregular. Price varies per volume. American Society of Agronomy, 677 South Segoe Road, Madison WI 53711. **Tel** (608)273-8080, FAX (608)273-2021. Documents available from BIOSIS Document Express, CASDDS.
Ind/Abst AGRICOLA [Full Cov.]; Biol. Abstr.; Chem. Abstr.; GeoRef; Maize Abstr.; Rice Abstr.; Soils Fert.; Soyabean Abstr.

LC S ISSN 0197-1662
DD 630 US
  CODEN ASPUDS
ASAE PUBLICATION. [ASAE publ.]. **Main/Corp** American Society of Agricultural Engineers. **VAT** American Society of Agricultural Engineers Publication. (19??)-. Academic Scholarly Publication. English. American Society of Agricultural Engineers, Department 2510, 2950 Niles Road, St. Joseph MI 49085-9659. **Tel** (616)429-0300, FAX (616)429-3852. Documents available from Article Express International, CASDDS.
Ind/Abst Biodeter. Abstr.; Bioeng. Abstr.; Chem. Abstr.; Ei Page One; Eng. Index Annu.; Maize Abstr.; Soyabean Abstr.

LC S671 .A32 ISSN 8755-1187
DD 631/.0218 US
  CODEN ASEPER
ASAE STANDARDS. (ASAE STANDARDS : STANDARDS, ENGINEERING PRACTICES AND DATA ADOPTED BY THE AMERICAN SCCIETY OF AGRICULTURAL ENGINEERS). [ASAE stand.]. **Main/Corp** American Society of Agricultural Engineers. **VAT** American Society of Agricultural Engineers Standards. (1984)-. English. One time a year (June). $135.00. American Society of Agricultural Engineers, Department 2510, 2950 Niles Road, St. Joseph MI 49085-9659. **Tel** (616)429-0300, FAX (616)429-3852. **ED** Russel Hahn. Index available (free) cum. index. **Continues** Agricultural Engineers Yearbook of Standards, 0882-1224.
Desc: Presents performance criteria for products, materials, and systems; readily available design data; safety information; and a basis for codes and regulations.
Ind/Abst AgBiotech News Inf.; Agric. Eng. Abstr. (1991-); Dairy Sci. Abstr.; Ei Page One; Irr. Drain. Abstr.; Maize Abstr.; Nutr. Abstr. Rev., Ser. B, Live Feeds and Feed.; Pig News Inf.; Postharvest News Inf.; Soils Fert.

LC S
DD 630 US
  TITLE CHANGE
ASCS COMMODITY FACT SHEET. HONEY. Added/Corp United States. Agricultural Stabilization and Conservation Service. **VFOAT** Honey; A.S.C.S. Commodity Fact Sheet. Honey. **VAT** Agricultural Stabilization and Conservation Commodity Fact Sheet. (19??)-(1993). Government Publication. English. US Department of Agriculture / Agricultural Stabilization and Conservation, 14th and Independence Avenue SW, Washington DC 20250. **Continued by** FSA Commodity Fact Sheet. Honey.

LC S ISSN 0344-5712
DD 630 GW
ASG - MATERIALSAMMLUNG. Added/Corp Agrarsoziale Gesellschaft. (197?)-. Periodical. German. **Continues** Agrarsoziale Gesellschaft, Gottingen. Materialsammlung, 0065-4388.
Ind/Abst Leis., Rec., Tour. Abstr.; World Agric. Econ. Rural Sociol. Abstr.

LC S
DD 630 US
ASIA-PACIFIC AGRIBUSINESS REPORT. (19??)-. English. Twelve times a year. $240.00. Asia-Pacific AgriBusiness Report, PO Box 88189, Los Angeles CA 90009. **Tel** (852)262950, FAX (852)267131, telex HX 61166 HKNW. **ED** Charles Smith, Josephine Chang, Neal Donnelly and Cesar Dalagan. **Bk Rev**.
Desc: Provides a wide range of analytical coverage on significant trends and developments in Asia's biggest business, agribusiness.

LC S
DD 630 II
ASSAM REVIEW AND TEA NEWS, THE. (19??)-. Periodical. English. Twelve times a year. $50.00. Assam Review Publishing Company, 29 Waterloo Street, 700 069 Calcutta India. **Tel** 011 91 33 282251.
(Subscription address: Prints India, 11 Darya Ganj, New Delhi 110002 India. **Tel** 011 91 11 3268645, FAX 011 91 11 3275542, telex 31-61087 PRIN-IN.)

LC S
DD 630 BS
ATIP WORKING PAPER. Added/Corp Agricultural Technology Improvement Project (Botswana) Botswana. Dept. of Agricultural Research. MidAmerica International Agricultural Consortium. **VAT** Agricultural Technology Improvement Project Working Paper. (1989)-. Monographic series. English. **Continues** Working Paper (Agricultural Technology Improvement Project (Botswana)).
Ind/Abst Agric. Eng. Abstr.; Anim. Breed. Abstr.; Dairy Sci. Abstr.; Index Vet.; Nutr. Abstr. Rev., Ser. B, Live Feeds and Feed.; Protozoolog. Abstr.; Rev. Med. Vet. Entomol.; World Agric. Econ. Rural Sociol. Abstr.

LC HD ISSN 0703-5357
DD 334/.09715 CN
ATLANTIC CO-OPERATOR, THE. See Business and Economics-Cooperatives.

LC S ISSN 0067-0286
DD 630 FR
ATLAS DES STRUCTURES AGRAIRES AU SUD DU SAHARA. Added/Corp O.R.S.T.O.M. Paris. Ecole Pratique des Hautes Etudes. Section des Sciences Economiques et Sociales. Maison des Sciences de l'Homme (Paris, France). (1967)-. Monographic series. French. Irregular. Price varies per volume. Editions EHESS, 131 boulevard Saint Michel, 75005 Paris France. **Tel** 011 33 1 43544715, FAX 011 33 1 43548073.
Ind/Abst Int. Dev. Abstr. (?-?).

LC S
DD 630 IT
ATTI DELL'ISTITUTO SPERIMENTALE PER LA VALORIZZAZIONE TECNOLOGICA DEI PRODOTTI AGRICOLI, MILANO. Added/Corp Istituto Sperimentale per la Valorizzazione Tecnologica dei Prodotti Agricoli. Vol. 1 (1978)-. Periodical. Italian. One time a year.
Ind/Abst Agric. Eng. Abstr.; Hortic. Abstr.; Postharvest News Inf.

LC S ISSN 0365-0014
DD 630 IT
ATTI E MEMORIE DELLA ACCADEMIA DI AGRICOLTURA, SCIENZE E LETTERE DI VERONA. [Atti mem. Accad. agric., sci. lett. Verona]. **Added/Corp** Accademia di Agricoltura, Scienze e Lettere di Verona. (1913)-. Italian. One time a year. **Continues** Atti e Memorie dell' Accademia d'Agricoltura, Scienze, Lettere, Arti e Commercio di Verona.
Ind/Abst BHA : Biblio. Hist. Art.

LC S537.A43 T46A ISSN 0148-2777
DD 630/.7/1976969 US
AUDIT REPORT, DEPARTMENT OF EDUCATION, ALVIN C. YORK AGRICULTURAL INSTITUTE. [Audit rep., Dep. Educ. Alvin C. York Agric. Inst.]. **Main/Corp** Tennessee. Division of State Audit. English. Tennessee Comptroller of the Treasury, Nashville TN 37219.

LC S534.T2 T64a ISSN 0148-043X
DD 630/.71/7 US
AUDIT REPORT, DEPARTMENT OF EDUCATION, TENNESSEE ASSOCIATION OF THE FUTURE FARMERS OF AMERICA. Main/Corp Tennessee. Division of State Audit. (19??)-. English. Tennessee Comptroller of the Treasury, Nashville TN 37219.

LC S ISSN 0045-0049
DD 630 GW
AUSBILDUNG UND BERATUNG IN LAND- UND HAUSWIRTSCHAFT / LAND- UND HAUSWIRTSCHAFTLICHER AUSWERTUNGS- UND INFORMATIONSDIENST. Added/Corp Land- und Hauswirtschaftlicher Auswertungs- und Informationsdienst e.V. Vol. 8, No. 10 (Oct. 1955)-. Trade Publication. German. Eleven times a year. DM64.80. Landwirtschaftsverlag GmbH, Postfach 480249, D-48079 Muenster Hiltrup Germany. **Tel** 011 49 2501 8010, FAX 011 49 2501 801204, telex 892665 LANDV D. **Continues** Nutzen Und Ordnung **and** Ausbildung Und Beratung in der Landwirtschaft.

LC S ISSN 0004-8313
DD 630 AT
AUSTRALASIAN BEEKEEPER, THE. Vol.1 (1899)-. Periodical. English. Twelve times a year (Published on the 15th of each month). $31.00 Australia; $36.00 other. Pender Beekeeping Supplies, P M B 19, Maitland New South Wales, 2320 Australia. **Tel** 011 61 49 327244, FAX 011 61 49 327621. **ED** Robert Rutherford. Index available. **Bk Rev. Ad Acc**; **Adv Mgr:** J. Gardner. **Circ:** 2,350. **Absorbed** Commonwealth Beekeeper **and** Australian Beekeeper.
Desc: Concentrating on the beekeeping industry of Australia and the honeybee.

LC S ISSN 0045-0294
DD 630 AT
AUSTRALIAN BEE JOURNAL. Added/Corp Victorian Apiarists' Association. (19??)-. Periodical. English. Twelve times a year. 35.00Au$. Victorian Apiarists Association, PO Box 40, % Kerrin Williams, California Gull, 3556 Australia. **Tel** 11 61 54 461455. **ED** J Peterson. Index available. **Bk Rev. Ad Acc. Circ:** 1,000 (ctrl). **Continues** Victorian Bee Journal.
Desc: All aspects of beekeeping and related issues including: practical beekeeping equipment, techniques and management, original research, case histories, public image and education studies and experiences, legal aspects and developments; economic, social and political assessment and commentaries; reviews of beekeeping literature.

LC S ISSN 0157-3039
DD 630 AT
AUSTRALIAN CANEGROWER.
Added/Corp Queensland Cane Growers' Association. New South Wales Cane Growers' Association. Australian Cane Growers' Association. Vol. 1, No. 1, (March 1979)-. Trade Publication. English. Twenty-five times a year. Canegrowers, GPO Box 1032, 190 194 Edward Street, Brisbane Queensland 4001 Australia. **Tel** 011 61 7 8646444, FAX 011 61 7 8646429, telex 41263. **ED** Carmel Tremble. **Ad Acc. Circ:** 7,924 (ctrl).
Desc: Special features of interest to the canegrowing industry.

LC HD2151 .A64 ISSN 1321-7844
DD 630 AT
●**AUSTRALIAN COMMODITIES. Added/Corp** Australian Bureau of Agricultural and Resource Economics. Vol. 1, No. 1 (Mar. 1994)-. Periodical. English. Four times a year. 102.77Au$. ABARE / Australian Bureau of Agriculture and Resource Economics, GPO Box 1563, Canberra ACT 2601 Australia. **Tel** 011 61 6 2722000, FAX 011 61 6 2722001. **Continues** Agriculture & Resource Quarterly, 1032-9722.

LC S ISSN 1036-6474
DD 630 AT
AUSTRALIAN FARM JOURNAL. VFOAT Farm Journal. (Mar. 1991)-. Periodical. English. Twelve times a year. 53.44Au$. Rural Press / Victoria, PO Box 160, Port Melbourne Victoria 3207 Australia. **Tel** 11 61 3 2870900, telex 35668. **Formed by the union of** Farm (Sydney, N.S.W.), 0725-3338 **and** Australian Rural Times (Richmond, N.S.W.), 1034-5809.
Ind/Abst EP Collect.; Homework Help.; MasterFile FullTEXT 1000; MasterFile FullTEXT 350; MasterFile FullTEXT 650; MasterFile FullTEXT (Sept. 1994-); Telebase; World Mag. Bank.

LC S ISSN 1035-1914
DD 630.68 AT
AUSTRALIAN FARM MANAGER, THE. [Aust. farm manager]. **Added/Corp** Australian Farm Management Society. (1990)-. Periodical. English. Six times a year. 20.00Aus$. South Australia Department of Agriculture / Adelaide, 25 Grenfell Street, Adelaide SA 5000 Australia. **Tel** 011 61 8 226-0348. **Bk Rev. Ad Acc.** ***Continues*** *Farming Forum, 0311-1431* ***and*** *Newsletter - Australian Farm Management Society, 0311-8665.*
Desc: Articles on farm management, especially farm business management.

LC S17 .A94 ISSN 0004-9409
DD 630/.994 AT
CCC
CODEN AJAEA9
Pr Rev.
AUSTRALIAN JOURNAL OF AGRICULTURAL RESEARCH. [Aust. j. agric. res.]. **Added/Corp** Commonwealth Scientific and Industrial Research Organization (Australia) Australian Institute of Agricultural Science. Australian Veterinary Association. Australian Academy of Science. Vol. 1 (Jan. 1950)-. Periodical. English. Eight times a year. 280.00Aus$. CSIRO Publications, PO Box 89, 314 Albert Street, East Melborne Victoria 3002 Australia. **Tel** 011 61 3 4187333, 4187217, FAX 011 61 3 4190459, telex AA 30236. **ED** M. J. Sharkey. **Ad Acc. Acid Free. Circ:** 1,000 (ctrl). available on microfilm and microfiche from University Microfilms International (UMI). Documents available from The Genuine Article, BIOSIS Document Express, CASDDS, Documents on Demand.
Desc: Publishes papers that make an original contribution towards the understanding of some part of the physical, chemical, or biological aspects of an agricultural system having relevance to the Australasian region. Either primary research papers or review articles may be submitted.
Ind/Abst AgBiotech News Inf.; AGRICOLA [Full Cov.]; Agric. Eng. Abstr.; Agrofor. Abstr. (1991-); Anim. Breed. Abstr.; BioBusiness; Biol. Abstr.; Ceram. Abstr.; Chem. Abstr.; Crop Physiol. Abstr.; Curr. Aware. Biol. Sci., CABS; Curr. Biotechnol.; Curr. Cit.; Curr. Contents Agric. Biol. Environ. Sci.; Dairy Sci. Abstr.; Ecol. Abstr.; Environ. Abstr.; Environ. Period. Bibliogr.; Field Crop Abstr.; Food Sci. Technol. Abstr.; For. Abstr.; Geogr. Abstr. Phys. Geogr.; Geogr. Abstr. Human Geogr.; Grass. Forage Abstr.; Helminthol. Abstr. (1991-); Hortic. Abstr.; Index Vet.; Irr. Drain. Abstr.; Leadscan; Meteorol. Geoastrophys. Abstr.; Nematol. Abstr.; Nutr. Abstr. Rev., Ser. B, Live Feeds and Feed.; Life Sci. Collect.; PESTDOC; Plant Breed. Abstr.; Plant Genet. Resour. Abstr.; Plant Grow. Reg. Abstr.; Potato Abstr.; Poult. Abstr.; Protozoolog. Abstr.; Res. Alert [Full Cov.]; Rev. Agric. Entomol.; Rev. Med. Vet. Entomol.; Rev. Med. Vet. Mycology; Rev. Plant Pathol.; Rice Abstr.; Sci. Cit. Index; SCISEARCH; Seed Abstr.; Soils Fert.; Sorghum Mill. Abstr.; Soyabean Abstr.; Stat. Theory Method Abstr. (1959-1963); Vet. Bull.; Vitis Vitic. Enol. Abstr.; Weed Abstr.; Wheat Barley Trit. Abstr.; World Agric. Econ. Rural Sociol. Abstr.

LC S ISSN 0816-1089
DD 630 AT
CCC
CODEN AJEAEL
Pr Rev.
AUSTRALIAN JOURNAL OF EXPERIMENTAL AGRICULTURE. [Aust. j. exp. agric.]. **Added/Corp** Commonwealth Scientific and Industrial Research Organization (Australia). Vol. 25, No. 1 (1985)-. Academic Scholarly Publication. English. Eight times a year. 250.00Aus$. CSIRO Publications, PO Box 89, 314 Albert Street, East Melborne Victoria 3002 Australia. **Tel** 011 61 3 4187333, 4187217, FAX 011 61 3 4190459, telex AA 30236. **ED** C. A. Anderson. Index available. **Ad Acc. Acid Free. Circ:** 1,400. available on microfilm and microfiche from University Microfilms International (UMI). Documents available from The Genuine Article, BIOSIS Document Express, CASDDS. ***Continues*** *Australian Journal of Experimental Agriculture and Animal Husbandry, 0045-060X.*
Desc: Publishes original research into applied agriculture. Articles are of interest to agricultural scientists in many parts of the world. Publishes research papers in animal husbandry, animal-plant interactions, pasture and fodder crops, field crops and horticulture. Also publishes reviews, negative evidence, short notes, records, descriptions of new cultivars, comments and replies, and papers about techniques and equipment. Work from other countries may be accepted if clearly relevant to Australian conditions.
Ind/Abst AgBiotech News Inf.; AGRICOLA [Full Cov.]; Agric. Eng. Abstr. (1991-); Agrofor. Abstr. (19??-19??); Anim. Breed. Abstr.; BioBusiness; Biocont. News Inf.; Biodeter. Abstr. (19??-19??); Biol. Abstr. (1985-); Chem. Abstr. (1985-); Cot. Trop. Fibr. Abstr. Bibliogr.; Crop Physiol. Abstr.; Curr. Aware. Biol. Sci., CABS; Curr. Cit.; Curr. Contents Agric. Biol. Environ. Sci.; Dairy Sci. Abstr.; Ecol. Abstr.; EMBASE; Field Crop Abstr.; Food Sci. Technol. Abstr.; For. Abstr.; Geogr. Abstr. Phys. Geogr.; Grass. Forage Abstr.; Helminthol. Abstr. (19??-19??); Hortic. Abstr.; Index Vet.; Irr. Drain. Abstr.; Leadscan; Maize Abstr.; Nematol. Abstr.; Nutr. Abstr. Rev., Ser. B, Live Feeds and Feed.; Ornamental Hort.; Life Sci. Collect.; PESTDOC; Pig News Inf.; Plant Breed. Abstr.; Plant Grow. Reg. Abstr.; Postharvest News Inf.; Potato Abstr.; Poult. Abstr.; Res. Alert [Full Cov.]; Rev. Agric. Entomol.; Rev. Med. Vet. Entomol.; Rev. Plant Pathol.; Rice Abstr.; Sci. Cit. Index; SCISEARCH; Seed Abstr.; Soils Fert.; Sorghum Mill. Abstr.; Soyabean Abstr.; Sug. Indus. Abstr.; Vet. Bull.; Vitis Vitic. Enol. Abstr.; Weed Abstr.; Wheat Barley Trit. Abstr.

LC S ISSN 0158-3999
DD 630 AT
CCC
AUSTRALIAN STANDARD. (1980)-. Periodical. English. Eleven times a year. 50.00Aus$. Standards Australia, 132 Arthur Street, Level 7, North Sydney 2060 Australia. **Tel** 011 61 2 7464600, FAX 011 61 2 7463333, telex 26514.
Ind/Abst AESIS Q.; Agric. Eng. Abstr.

LC S ISSN 0326-1131
DD 630 AG
AVANCE AGROINDUSTRIAL. (19??)-. Spanish.
Ind/Abst Field Crop Abstr.; Grass. Forage Abstr.; Hortic. Abstr.; Plant Breed. Abstr.; Postharvest News Inf.; Rev. Agric. Entomol.; Seed Abstr.; Soils Fert.; Wheat Barley Trit. Abstr.

LC S
DD 630 MX
UDC 338.1:63(72)
AVANCES DE INVESTIGACION AGRICOLA EN ZONAS DE RIEGO Y TEMPORAL / CIAN. Spanish. One time a year. Apartado Postal No 247, Torreon Coah Mexico.

LC S ISSN 0188-7890
DD 630 MX
Pr Rev.
AVANCES EN INVESTIGACION AGROPECUARIA. (1992)-. Academic Scholarly Publication. Spanish (English and French). Three times a year. $40.00. AgroSystems Editing, Universidad de Colima, Justo Sierra 592, Colima 28010 Colima Mexico. **Tel** 331 4 11 33, FAX 331 2 75 81. **(Subscription address:** Avances en Investigacion Agropecuaria, AP 22, Colima 28045, Colima Mexico. **) ED** Janet Hummel Oliver. Each issue contains an index to its own contents (no volume index)--loose. **Bk Rev. Circ:** 250. available on an online database from Internet.
Desc: Dedicated to publishing original and applied research in tropical agriculture, including animal production, biotechnology and the biological sciences.

LC HD1491 ISSN 1192-8077
DD 338.1 CN
•**AVERAGE PRICES OF SELECTED FARM INPUTS.** (AVERAGE PRICES OF SELECTED FARM INPUTS = LE PRIX MOYEN DE CERTAINES ENTREES AGRICOLES.). [Aver. prices sel. farm inputs]. **Added/Corp** Statistics Canada. Prices Division. **VFOAT** Prix Moyen de Certaines Entrees Agricoles. Vol. 1, No. 1 (Apr. 1993)-. Periodical. English (French). Twelve times a year. 38.42Can$. Statistics Canada Publications Sales and Services, R.H. Coats Building 6th Floor, Ottawa Ontario K1A 0T6 Canada. **Tel** (613)951-5078, (800)267-6677, FAX (613)951-1584, telex 053-3585.

LC TP ISSN 0816-1623
DD 668.6029494 AT
AVPI. AGRICULTURAL AND VETERINARY PRODUCT INDEX. [AVPI, Agric. vet. prod. index]. **VFOAT** Agricultural and Veterinary Product Index. (1984)-. Periodical. English. Two times a year. 25.00Aus$ Australia; 30.70Aus$ New Zealand and Papua New Guinea; 35.20Aus$ other. Mims Australia, 48 Albany Street, Crows Nest New South Wales 2065 Australia. **Tel** 011 61 2 9067966, FAX 011 61 2 9063955. **ED** Linda Badewitz-Dodd. **Ad Acc, Adv Mgr:** G Hand.
Desc: Condensed information of agricultural and animal health products.

LC S ISSN 0005-2361
DD 630 IT
UDC 338.1:63(45)
AVVENIRE AGRICOLE, L'. (1892)-. Periodical. Italian. Twelve times a year. Conf Coltivatori di Novara, Corso Mazzini 31, 28100 Novara Italy.

LC S367 .A94 ISSN 0572-2721
DD 631/.0964 MR
AWAMIA, AL. [Awamia]. **Added/Corp** Morocco. Idarat al-Bahth al-Zirai. Morocco. Direction de la Recherche Agronomique et de l'Enseignement Agricole. **VFOAT** Awwamiyah. Vol. 1 (1961)-. Periodical. French (summaries and/or abstracts in Arabic, English and Spanish). Irregular. $50.00. Institut National Recherche Agronomique, BP 415, Avenue de la Victoire, Rabat Morocco. **Tel** 212/74003.
Ind/Abst Hortic. Abstr.; Plant Breed. Abstr.; Soils Fert.; Weed Abstr.

LC S
DD 630 US
B / AGRICULTURAL EXTENSION SERVICE, UNIVERSITY OF WYOMING. **Added/Corp** University of Wyoming. Agricultural Extension Service. Wyoming Agricultural Experiment Station. University of Wyoming. Cooperative Extension Service. **VFOAT** Bulletin. **VAT** Bulletin. (1973)-. Bulletin. English. ***Continues*** *Bulletin (Wyoming Agricultural Experiment Station), 0084-313X.*
Ind/Abst AGRICOLA [Full Cov.].

LC S
DD 630 GW
UDC 63(434.6)
BADISCHE BAUERN-ZEITUNG. Vol. 10, No. 1, (1957)-. Periodical. German. One time a week. Badischer Landwirtschaftsvg, Postfach 209, 78 Frieburg Germany. ***Continues*** *Bauern-Zeitung.*

LC S
DD 630 PH
BAECON BI-MONTHLY REPORTER. **Main/Corp** Philippines. Bureau of Agricultural Economics. Vol. 3, No. 19 (June 1972)-. Periodical. English. Six times a year. ***Continues*** *Baecon Bi-Monthly.*

LC Z5075.B795 B35 S475.B7 ISSN 0101-0697
DD 016.63/0981 BL
BANCO DE BIBLIOGRAFIAS / EMBRAPA, EMPRESA BRASILEIRA DE PESQUISA AGROPECUARIA, DEPARTAMENTO DE INFORMACAO E DOCUMENTACAO. Periodical. Portuguese. Three times a year.

LC S
DD 630 BG
BANGLADESH AGRICULTURAL SCIENCES ABSTRACTS. **Added/Corp** Bangladesh Agricultural University Old Boys' Association. Vol. 1 (1974)-. English. One time a year. Bangladesh Agricultural University, Bureau of Socioeconomic Research, Mymensingh Bangladesh. **Tel** 011 880 569597 09.

LC S17 ISSN 0258-7122
DD 630 BG
BANGLADESH JOURNAL OF AGRICULTURAL RESEARCH. **Added/Corp** Bangladesh Agricultural Research Institute. Vol. 1 (Dec. 1974)-. Periodical. English. Two times a year.
Ind/Abst Irr. Drain. Abstr.; Rev. Plant Pathol.; Rice Abstr.; Soils Fert.; Wheat Barley Trit. Abstr.

LC S ISSN 0379-4296
DD 630 BG
CODEN BJAGAQ
BANGLADESH JOURNAL OF AGRICULTURAL SCIENCES. Vol. 1 (Jan. 1974)-. Academic Scholarly Publication. English. Two times a year. Bangladesh Agricultural University, Bureau of Socioeconomic Research, Mymensingh Bangladesh. **Tel** 011 880 569597 09. Documents available from CASDDS. ***Continues in part*** *Bangladesh Journal of Biological and Agricultural Sciences, 0045-1428.*
Ind/Abst Chem. Abstr.; Food Sci. Technol. Abstr.

LC S ISSN 0253-5408
DD 630 BG
CODEN BJOADD
BANGLADESH JOURNAL OF AGRICULTURE. [Bangladesh j. agric.]. **Added/Corp** Bamladesa Krshi Gabeshana Kaunsila. (July 1976)-. Academic Scholarly Publication. English. Two times a year. Bangladesh Agricultural Research Council, Airport Road Farm Gate, Dacca 15 Bangladesh. Documents available from BIOSIS Document Express, CASDDS.
Ind/Abst Biodeter. Abstr.; Biol. Abstr. (1985-); Chem. Abstr. (1976-1980); Cot. Trop. Fibr. Abstr. Bibliogr.; Field Crop Abstr.; Hortic. Abstr.; Plant Grow. Reg. Abstr.; Rev. Agric. Entomol.; Rice Abstr.; Soyabean Abstr.; Weed Abstr.

LC S ISSN 1013-0306
DD 630 BG
BANGLADESH JOURNAL OF TRAINING AND DEVELOPMENT. [Bangladesh j. train. dev.]. (1988)-. Periodical. English. Two times a year. Bangladesh Agricultural University, Mymensingh Graduate Training Institute, Mymensingh Bangladesh.
Ind/Abst Field Crop Abstr.; Nutr. Abstr. Rev., Ser. B, Live Feeds and Feed.; Poult. Abstr.; Rice Abstr.; World Agric. Econ. Rural Sociol. Abstr.

LC HD1491 ISSN 1188-8911
DD 338.1 CN
BARLEY COUNTRY. [Barley ctry.]. **Added/Corp** Alberta Barley Commission. Vol. 1, No. 1 (Spring 1992)-. Periodical. English. Four times a year.

LC Z5074.E3 B37 HD1941 ISSN 0242-2921
DD 016.3381/0944 FR
BASE DE DONNEES ECONOMIQUES, FINANCIERES ET SOCIALES RESEDA. **Added/Corp** Reseau de Documentation Socio-Economique en Agriculture (Association : France). **VFOAT** RESEDA. (19??)-. French. Twelve times a year.

Documentation Francaise, 29 quai Voltaire, 75344 Paris Cedex 7 France. **Tel** 011 33 1 40157000, FAX 011 33 1 40157230, telex 204 826 DOCFRAN.

LC S
DD 630 GW
BAUBRIEFE LANDWIRTSCHAFT. (19??)-. German. Irregular. Price varies per volume. Landwirtschaftsverlag GmbH, Postfach 480249, D-48079 Muenster Hiltrup Germany. **Tel** 011 49 2501 8010, FAX 011 49 2501 801204, telex 892665 LANDV D.

LC TH **ISSN** 0171-7952
DD 690 GW
BAUEN FUER DIE LANDWIRTSCHAFT (ZEITSCHRIFT). **See** Building and Construction.

LC S
DD 630 SZ
UDC 63(494)
BAUERN-ECHO. Periodical. German. Seven times a week. Deutscher Judo Verband, Redaktion Ippon Segewaldweg 40, D-12557 Berlin Germany. **Tel** 011 49 711 210770, telex 051 678.

LC HD2330 **ISSN** 0847-1444
DD 338.1/09711 CN
BC AGRICULTURE. [B.C. agric.]. **Added/Corp** British Columbia Federation of Agriculture. **VFOAT** BC Agriculture Magazine. **VAT** British Columbia Agriculture. Vol. 1, No. 1 (Dec. 1989)-. Periodical. English. Eleven times a year (monthly except July). 29.95Can$. BC Fed Agricultural Publications Ltd, 846 Broughton Street, Victoria BC V8W 1E4 Canada. **Tel** (604)383-7171, FAX (604)383-5031. **ED** Lloyd Mackey and Barb Schmidt. **Ad Acc. Circ:** 9,000 (ctrl).
Desc: Farming and agriculture in Bristish Columbia.

LC SB175 **ISSN** 1066-0607
DD 635 US
BEAN MARKET NEWS. [Bean mark. news]. (19??)-. Periodical. English. One time a week. $55.00. US Department of Agriculture / Colorado, Agricultural Marketing Service, 711 O Street, Greely CO 80631. **Tel** (303)353-9750, FAX (303)353-9790.

LC S
DD 630 NE
BEDRIJFSUITKOMSTEN IN DE LANDBOUW. **Main/Corp** Landbouw-Economisch Instituut (Netherlands). Afdeling Landbouw. (19??)-. Dutch. One time a year. Fl.30.25 Netherlands; $17.00 US. Landbouw-Economisch Instituut, Postbus 29703, 2502 LS Hague Netherlands. **Tel** 011 31 70 3308330, FAX 011 31 70 615624. **ED** M. N. de Groot. **Circ:** 800. ***Continues*** *Hague. Landbouw-Economisch Instituut. Afdeling Bedrijfseconomisch Onderzoek Landbouw. Bedrijfsuitkomsten in de Landbouw.*
Desc: Outline of income and profitability of arable and stock farms in the Netherlands on the basis of the Landbouw-Economisch Instituut bookkeeping network.

LC SF521 .G5 **ISSN** 1071-3190
DD 638 US
Pr Rev.
●**BEE CULTURE.** [Bee cult.]. (Jan. 1993)-. Trade Publication. English. Twelve times a year. $17.00. A I Root Company, 623 West Liberty Street, PO Box 706, Medina OH 44258. **Tel** (216)725-6677, FAX (216)725-5624, telex 753856. **ED** Kim Flottum. Index available ($2.00). cum. index. **Bk Rev**, (Qty: 12-15). **Ad Acc, Adv Mgr:** D. Feagan, **Tel** (216)725-6677 Ext.3220. **Circ:** 12,000 (ctrl). available on microfilm from University Microfilms International (UMI). ***Continues*** *Gleanings in Bee Culture, 0017-114X.*
Desc: For all size beekeepers. This magazine covers issues ranging from honey plants and honey markets to how-to beekeep.

LC S
DD 630 UK
BEEKEEPING. **Added/Corp** Devon Beekeepers' Association. Vol. 1, (May 1935)-. Periodical. English. Three times a year (Feb., June, Oct.). $15.83. Devon Beekeepers Association, 9 Darwin Crescent Plymouth, Devon PL3 6DT United Kingdom. **ED** P. P. Rosenfeld. **Bk Rev. Ad Acc. Circ:** 1,200.
Desc: Presents a wealth of information on the British Beekeepers Association and its functions. Details most aspects of the group's founding, its history, and charter, etc. Not to be confused with information on CONBA-The Council of National Beekeeping Associations of the UK.

LC SF522 .A87
DD 338.1/7/810994 AT
UDC 338.43:638.1(94)
BEEKEEPING, AUSTRALIA. **Main/Corp** Australian Bureau of Statistics. (1974/75)-. English. One time a year. ***Continues*** *Bee Farming, Australia, 0587-5781.*

LC S19 .H77 **ISSN** 0479-8007
DD 630/.5 CC
BEIJING NONGYE DAXUE XUEBAO. (HSUEH PAO.). [Beijing nongye daxue xuebao]. **Added/Corp** Pei-ching Nung Yeh ta Hsueh. **VFOAT** Acta Agriculturae Universitatis Pekinensis; Pei-Ching Nung Yeh Ta Hsueh Hsueh Pao. (1955)-. Periodical. Chinese (summaries and/or abstracts in English). Four times a year. Beijing Nongye Daxue, Xuebao Bianjibu, Haidian-qu Beijing 100094 People's Republic of China. **Tel** 2582244. **ED** Z. Shimai. Documents available from BLDSC. ***Continues*** *Pei-ching Nung Yeh ta Hsueh Hsueh Pao.*
Ind/Abst AGRICOLA; Crop Physiol. Abstr.; Field Crop Abstr.; Helminthol. Abstr. (1991-); Index Vet.; Plant Breed. Abstr.; Plant Grow. Reg. Abstr.; Postharvest News Inf.; Potato Abstr.; Poult. Abstr.; Rev. Agric. Entomol.; Rev. Med. Vet. Entomol.; Rev. Plant Pathol.; Rice Abstr.; Seed Abstr.; Soils Fert.; Wheat Barley Trit. Abstr.

LC S671 **ISSN** 1000-1514
DD 631.3 CC
BEIJING NONGYE GONGCHENG DAXUE XUEBAO. (PEI-CHING NUNG YEH KUNG CHENG TA HSUEH HSUEH PAO.). **Added/Corp** "Pei-ching Nung yeh Kung Cheng ta Hsueh Hsueh pao" Pien chi pu. Pei-Ching Nung yeh Kung Cheng ta Hsueh. **VFOAT** Journal of Beijing Agricultural Engineering University; Beijing Nongye Gongcheng Daxue Xuebao. (1981)-. Academic Scholarly Publication. Chinese (summaries and/or abstracts in English). Four times a year. Beijing Nongye Gongcheng Daxue, Zuebao Bianjibu Qinghua Donglu, Beijing 100083, People's Republic of China. **ED** Li Xingchang.
Ind/Abst Agric. Eng. Abstr.; Poult. Abstr.; Seed Abstr.; World Agric. Econ. Rural Sociol. Abstr.

LC S **ISSN** 0301-567X
DD 630 GW
NLM W1 BE461L **CODEN** BTLVBR
TITLE CHANGE
BEITRAEGE ZUR TROPISCHEN LANDWIRTSCHAFT UND VETERINARMEDIZIN. **See** Veterinary Sciences.

LC S **ISSN** 0892-8606
DD 630 US
BELLE GLADE EREC RESEARCH REPORT. [Belle Glade EREC res. rep.]. **VAT** Belle Glade Everglades Research and Education Center Research Report. (1984)-. Monographic series. English. Price varies per volume. ***Continues*** *AREC-Belle Glade Research Report, 0892-8592.*
Ind/Abst AGRICOLA [Select. Cov.]; Rice Abstr.

LC S **ISSN** 0160-3612
DD 630 US
CODEN BSARDN
BELTSVILLE SYMPOSIA IN AGRICULTURAL RESEARCH. (BELTSVILLE SYMPOSIA IN AGRICULTURAL RESEARCH; INVITED PAPERS PRESENTED AT A SYMPOSIUM.). [Beltsville symp. agric. res.]. **Main/Corp** Beltsville Symposium in Agricultural Research. **Added/Corp** Beltsville Agricultural Research Center. **VFOAT** BARC Symposia. (1976)-. English. Documents available from BIOSIS Document Express, CASDDS.
Ind/Abst Biol. Abstr.; Chem. Abstr.; Index Vet.

LC S **ISSN** 0256-4270
DD 630 AU
UDC 63
BERATER-INFORMATION - LBL. [Berat.-Inf. - LBL]. **VFOAT** Berater-Information - Landwirtschaftliche Beratungszentrale Lindau; LBL Berater-Information. (1???)-. Periodical. German. Irregular.
Ind/Abst Soyabean Abstr.

LC S **ISSN** 0105-6883
DD 630 DK
BERETNING FRA STATENS HUSDYRBRUGSFORSG. [Beret. statens husdyrbrugsfors.]. **Main/Corp** Denmark. Statens Husdyrbrugsforsg. No. 424 (1975)-. Danish (English). Documents available from BIOSIS Document Express. ***Continues*** *Beretning fra Forsgslaboratoriet.*
Ind/Abst Anim. Breed. Abstr.; Biol. Abstr.; Food Sci. Technol. Abstr.; Grass. Forage Abstr.; Index Vet.; Nutr. Abstr. Rev., Ser. B, Live Feeds and Feed.; Poult. Abstr.; Vet. Bull.; Wheat Barley Trit. Abstr.

LC S **ISSN** 0906-2181
DD 630 DK
BERETNING - FRA STATENS PLANTEAVLSFORSOEG OG STATENS HUSDYRBRUGSFORSOEG. **VFOAT** Fllesberetning - Landbrugsministeriet, Statens Planteavlsforsg, Statens Husdyrbrugsforsoeg (Koebenhavn. 1990). (1990)-. English. Statens Planteavlsforsoeg Statens Husdyrbrugsforsoeg, Copenhagen Denmark.
Ind/Abst Agric. Eng. Abstr.; Field Crop Abstr.

LC S7 .K36
DD 630/.9436/3 AU
UDC 63(436.8)
BERICHT - KAMMER FUR LAND- UND FORSTWIRTSCHAFT IN SALZBURG. **Main/Corp** Kammer fur Land- Und Forstwirtschaft in Salzburg. **VFOAT** Salzburger Land- Und Forstwirtschaft. 1970-. German. ***Continues*** *Tatigkeitsbericht / Kammer fur Land- und Forstwirtschaft in Salzburg.*

LC TS2120 .A74A TS2149
DD 664.7 GW
BERICHT UEBER DIE ... TAGUNG FUER GETREIDECHEMIE. German. Granum-Verlag, Postfach 23, Detmold Germany.

LC HD1951 .A3 **ISSN** 0005-9080
DD 338.1/0943 GW
CCC
CODEN BERLAN
Pr Rev.
BERICHTE UEBER LANDWIRTSCHAFT. [Ber. Landwirtsch.]. **Added/Corp** Germany (West). Bundesministerium fuer Ernahrung, Landwirtshaft und Forsten. Vol. 1 (1907)-. Periodical. German. Four times a year. $374.61. Landwirtschaftsverlag GmbH, Postfach 480249, D-48079 Muenster Hiltrup Germany. **Tel** 011 49 2501 8010, FAX 011 49 2501 801204, telex 892665 LANDV D. Index available. cum. index. **Bk Rev. Ad Acc. Circ:** 2,500. Documents available from The Genuine Article, BIOSIS Document Express, CASDDS.
Ind/Abst AgBiotech News Inf.; Anim. Breed. Abstr.; Biol. Abstr.; Chem. Abstr.; Curr. Aware. Biol. Sci., CABS; Curr. Contents Agric. Biol. Environ. Sci.; Dairy Sci. Abstr.; EMBASE; Energy Res. Abstr. (Mar. 1973-); Field Crop Abstr.; Food Sci. Technol. Abstr.; GeoRef; Grass. Forage Abstr.; Hortic. Abstr.; Int. Labour Doc.; Irr. Drain. Abstr.; Leis., Rec., Tour. Abstr.; Maize Abstr.; PAIS Int. Print (1991-); Life Sci. Collect.; Pig News Inf.; Plant Breed. Abstr.; Potato Abstr.; Poult. Abstr.; Res. Alert [Select. Cov.]; Rural Dev. Abstr.; SCISEARCH; Soc. Sci. Cit. Index [Select. Cov.]; Soils Fert.; Vitis Vitic. Enol. Abstr.; Weed Abstr.; Wheat Barley Trit. Abstr.; World Agric. Econ. Rural Sociol. Abstr.

LC S **ISSN** 0301-2689
DD 630 GW
CODEN BELWAQ
BERICHTE UEBER LANDWIRTSCHAFT. SONDERHEFT. [Ber. Landwirtsch. Sonderh.]. **Added/Corp** Germany (West). Bundesministerium fuer Ernahrung, Landwirtschaft und Forsten. (1924)-. Monographic series. German. Irregular. Price varies per volume. Blackwell Wissenschafts-Verlag, Kurfuerstendamm 57, D-10707 Berlin Germany. **Tel** 011 49 30 32790623, 011 49 30 32790624, FAX 011 49 30 327 90610. Documents available from BIOSIS Document Express.
Ind/Abst AGRICOLA; Bibliogr. Agric.; Biol. Abstr.; GeoRef.

LC SB298 **ISSN** 0127-6581
DD 633.85 MY
BERITA ISOPB. (NEWSLETTER / ISOPB, INTERNATIONAL SOCIETY FOR OIL PALM BREEDERS = BERITA / PERSATUAN AHLI-AHLI PEMBIAK BAIK KELAPA SAWIT ANTARA BANGSA.). [Ber. ISOPB]. **Added/Corp** International Society for Oil Palm Breeders. **VFOAT** Berita. (1984)-. Periodical. English. Four times a year. Palm Oil Research Institute of Malaysia, PO Box 10620, 50720 Kuala Lumpur Malaysia. **Tel** 011 60 3 8259155.
Ind/Abst Plant Breed. Abstr.

LC S
DD 630 MY
BERITA PENYELIDIKAN INSTITUT PENYELIDIKAN DAN KEMAJUAN PERTANIAN MALAYSIA. **Added/Corp** Malaysian Agricultural Research and Development Institute. **VFOAT** Berita Penyelidikan; Berita Penyelidikan MARDI. (Sept. 1979)-. Periodical. Malay (English). Four times a year.
Ind/Abst Nematol. Abstr.

LC SB354 **ISSN** 1189-4172
DD 634/.7/09713505 CN
TITLE CHANGE
BERRY & VEGETABLE INFORMER. [Berry veg. inf.]. **Added/Corp** Ontario. Ministry of Agriculture and Food. **VAT** Berry and Vegetable Informer. (Feb. 1992)-(Jan. 1994). Periodical. English. ***Continues*** *Berry News and Views., 0848-7243.* ***Continued by*** *Berry & Vegetable Informer & Pomiculture, Combination Newsletter, 1189-2285.*

LC SB354 **ISSN** 1189-2285
DD 634/.7/09713505 CN
●**BERRY & VEGETABLE INFORMER & POMICULTURE, COMBINATION NEWSLETTER.** [Berry veg. inf. pomic. comb. newsl.]. **VFOAT** Berry and Vegetable Informer and Pomiculture, Combination Newsletter. (1994)-. Periodical. English. Twelve times a year. Ontario Ministry of Agriculture and Food, 801 Bay Street, Toronto Ontario M7A 2B2 Canada. **Tel** (416)965-1064, (416)326-3400. ***Continues*** *Berry & Vegetable Informer, 1189-4172.*

LC S
DD 630 AU
BESSERES OBST. (19??)-. German. Twelve times a year. S540.00 Austria; S638.00 other. Oesterreichischer Agrarverlag, Inkustr 1 7 Bueropark Donau, A 3400 Klosterneuberg Austria. **Tel** 011 43 2243 33300.
Ind/Abst Agric. Eng. Abstr. (1991-); Hortic. Abstr.;

Agriculture

Nematol. Abstr.; Plant Breed. Abstr.; Plant Grow. Reg. Abstr.; Rev. Plant Pathol.; Weed Abstr.; World Agric. Econ. Rural Sociol. Abstr.

LC HD1960.S6 L35A
DD 338.1/0943/512
UDC 338.3:63(430-317)
GW
BETRIEBSERGEBNISSE : DURCHSCHNITTSERGEBNISSE.
Main/Corp Landwirtschaftskammer Schleswig-Holstein. German. Landwirtschafts-Kammer Schleswig-Holstein, Holstenstrasse 106-108, Kiel 23 Germany.

LC S **ISSN** 0179-5066
DD 630 GW
BETRIEBSWIRTSCHAFTLICHE NACHRICHTEN FUER DIE LANDWIRTSCHAFT. Added/Corp Hauptverband
der Landwirtschaftlichen Buchstellen und Sachverstandigen (Germany). (19??)-. Periodical. German. Twelve times a year. DM35.00. Verlag Pflug und Feder GmbH, Koelnstrasse 202, D-53757 St. Augustin 2 Germany. **Tel** 011 49 2241 204084.

LC S **ISSN** 0303-3821
DD 630 II
BHARTIYA KRISHI ANUSANDHAN PATRIKA. Added/Corp Agricultural Research
Communication Centre (India). **VFOAT** Research Journal of Agriculture & Animal Science. Vol. 1 (June 1973)-. Periodical. Multiple languages (English and Hindi). Four times a year. $50.00 one-year; $90.00 two-year; $125.00 three-year. Agricultural Research Communication Centre, Sadar Karnal 132001, Haryana India. **Tel** 011 91 3036.
Desc: The research papers of agriculture, animal, dairy, food & home sciences.
Ind/Abst Agrofor. Abstr. (1991-); Field Crop Abstr.; Ornamental Hort.; Plant Breed. Abstr.; Plant Grow. Reg. Abstr.; Postharvest News Inf.; Rice Abstr.; Sorghum Mill. Abstr.

LC Z5073 .B618 S493 **ISSN** 0364-829X
DD 016.63 US
BIBLIOGRAPHY OF AGRICULTURE : ANNUAL CUMULATION. Added/Corp
National Agricultural Library (U.S.). (19??)-. Bibliography. English. One time a year (Jan.). $645.00. Oryx Press, 4041 North Central Avenue #700, Phoenix AZ 85012-3397. **Tel** (800)279-6799, (602)265-2651, FAX (602)265-6250, (800)279-4663, (800)279-6799. cum. index. **Bk Rev**. **Ad Acc**. **Acid Free**. **Circ**: 550 (ctrl).
Desc: Each issue contains about 8,000 main entry citations and about 30,000 subject references to journal literature in agriculture and allied sciences.

LC SF521 **ISSN** 0006-212X
DD 638.1 GW
BIENE, DIE. [Biene]. (1955)-. Periodical. German.
Twelve times a year. $41.22. Deutscher Landwirtschaftsverlag, Grabbaallee 41, D-13156 Berlin Germany. **Tel** 011 49 30 48320311. **Ad Acc** *Continues Hessische Biene; Absorbed Rheinische Bienenzeitung.*
Ind/Abst AGRICOLA.

LC SF521 **ISSN** 0006-2146
DD 638.1 AU
BIENENVATER. [Bienen-vater]. Added/Corp
Osterreichischer Imkerbund. Osterreichischer Reichsverein fuer Bienenzucht. (1869)-. Periodical. German. Eleven times a year. $32.73. Oesterreichischer Imkerbund, Georg Koch Platz 3 11A, A 1010 Vienna Austria. **Tel** 011 43 1 5125429.
Desc: Bee culture.
Ind/Abst AGRICOLA; Rev. Agric. Entomol.; Sug. Indus. Abstr.

LC S **ISSN** 0818-8726
DD 630 AT
BIENNIAL REPORT / AGRICULTURAL RESEARCH AND ADVISORY STATION, CONDOBOLIN. [Bienn. rep. - Agric. Res. Advis.
Stn. Condobolin]. **Main/Corp** Agricultural Research and Advisory Station, Condobolin. (1985/87)-. English. Every 2 years. Agricultural Research and Advisory Station, Condobolin NSW Australia.

LC S **ISSN** 0814-3595
DD 630 AT
BIENNIAL REPORT / GLEN INNES AGRICULTURAL RESEARCH AND ADVISORY STATION. Main/Corp Glen Innes
Agricultural Research and Advisory Station. **Added/Corp** New South Wales. Dept. of Agriculture. New England, Hunter, and Metropolitan Region. (19??)-. English. Every 2 years. New South Wales Department of Agriculture / Hunter and Metropolitan Region, New England, Sydney NSW Australia.

LC S **ISSN** 0144-6584
DD 630 UK
UDC 63(047.1)(411)
BIENNIAL REPORT / SCOTTISH INSTITUTE OF AGRICULTURAL ENGINEERING. English. Every 2 years.
Ind/Abst Hortic. Abstr.

LC HD1775.W6 W55a **ISSN** 0277-0660
DD 353.97750082/33 US
BIENNIAL REPORT / WISCONSIN DEPARTMENT OF AGRICULTURE, TRADE, AND CONSUMER PROTECTION. Main/Corp Wisconsin. Dept. of
Agriculture, Trade, and Consumer Protection. (1977)-. English. Every 2 years. Free on request. Wisconsin Agriculture, Trade & Consumer Protection Department, PO Box 8911, Madison WI 53708. **Tel** (608)224-5012, FAX (608)266-1300. *Continues Wisconsin. Dept. of Agriculture. Biennial Report.*

LC S
DD 630 AT
BIENNIAL RESEARCH REPORT.
Main/Corp Agricultural Research and Advisory Station, Grafton. **VFOAT** Research Report. (July 1987/June 1989)-. English. Every 2 years. *Continues Agricultural Research and Advisory Station, Grafton. Biennial Report, 1032-4291.*

LC SB111 **ISSN** 1195-0358
DD 631.5/84/0971405 CN
BIO-BULLE. [Bio-bulle]. Added/Corp Institut de
Technologie Agro-Alimentaire de La Pocatiere. Institut de Technologie Agro-Alimentaire de La Pocatiere. Centre d'Agriculture Biologique. Vol. 1, No 1 (Nov. 1989)-. Periodical. French. Six times a year. 14.05Can$. Centre for Agriculture Biologique Pocatiere, 401 rue Poire, LaPocatiere Quebec G0R 1Z0 Canada. **Tel** (418)856-1110.

LC SB **ISSN** 0143-1404
DD 574/630 UK
BIOCONTROL NEWS AND INFORMATION. See Biology.

LC S **ISSN** 0144-8765
DD 630 UK
UDC 632.9 CCC
CODEN BIAHDP
Pr Rev.
BIOLOGICAL AGRICULTURE & HORTICULTURE. (BIOLOGICAL AGRICULTURE
& HORTICULTURE : AN INTERNATIONAL JOURNAL.). [Biol. agric. hortic.]. **VFOAT** Biological Agriculture and Horticulture. Vol. 1, No. 1 (1982)-. Academic Scholarly Publication. English. Four times a year. £69.00 UK; $129.00 US. AB Academic Publishers, PO Box 42 Bicester, Oxfordshire OX6 7NW United Kingdom. **Tel** 011 44 1869 320949, FAX 011 44 1869 320949. **ED** R D Hodges. **Bk Rev**. **Ad Acc**. Documents available from The Genuine Article, CASDDS.
Desc: Publishes research and reviews related to biological, integrated agriculture and comparative studies.
Ind/Abst AgBiotech News Inf.; AGRICOLA [Full Cov.]; Agrofor. Abstr. (19??-19??); Biocont. News Inf. (1991-); Chem. Abstr.; Coal Abstr.; Crop Physiol. Abstr.; Curr. Aware. Biol. Sci.; CABS; Curr. Cit.; Curr. Contents Agric. Biol. Environ. Sci.; Ecol. Abstr.; Entomol. Abstr.; Environ. Period. Bibliogr.; Field Crop Abstr.; Geogr. Abstr. Human Geogr.; Grass. Forage Abstr.; Helminthol. Abstr. (1991-); Hortic. Abstr.; Int. Dev. Abstr.; Maize Abstr.; Ornamental Hort. (1991-); Life Sci. Collect.; Plant Breed. Abstr.; Res. Alert [Select. Cov.]; Rev. Agric. Entomol.; Rev. Plant Pathol.; Rice Abstr.; Soils Fert.; Soyabean Abstr.; Weed Abstr.; Wheat Barley Trit. Abstr.; World Agric. Econ. Rural Sociol. Abstr.

LC SB732.6 .B58 **ISSN** 0887-2236
DD 632 US
BIOLOGICAL AND CULTURAL TESTS FOR CONTROL OF PLANT DISEASES.
(BIOLOGICAL AND CULTURAL TESTS FOR CONTROL OF PLANT DISEASES : B & C TESTS.). [Biol. cult. tests control plant dis.]. **VFOAT** B & C Tests. Vol. 1 (1986)-. English. One time a year. $28.00. American Phytopathological Society, 3340 Pilot Knob Road, St. Paul MN 55121. **Tel** (612)454-7250, (800)328-7560, FAX (612)454-0766, telex 6502439657 (MCI UW).
Ind/Abst Nematol. Abstr.; Plant Breed. Abstr.; Soyabean Abstr.

LC Z695.1.B5 B56 **ISSN** 0154-0262
DD 025.4/9574 FR
BIOLOGIE VEGETALE, SCIENCES AGRICOLES. LEXIQUE. (19??)-. French.
Informascience, Centre de Documentation Scientifique et Technique Service des Abonnements, 26 rue Boyer, 75971 Paris Cedex 20 France.

LC TP360 .B5957 **ISSN** 0960-8524
DD 662/.88/05 UK
CCC
CODEN BIRTEB
Pr Rev.
BIORESOURCE TECHOLOGY. See
Environmental Issues-Pollution and Waste Management.

LC TP248 **ISSN** 0934-943X
DD 660 US
CCC
BIOTECHNOLOGY IN AGRICULTURE AND FORESTRY. See Biology-Bioengineering.

LC S **ISSN** 0960-202X
DD 630 UK
CODEN BIAGEN
BIOTECHNOLOGY IN AGRICULTURE SERIES. [Biotechnol. agric. ser.]. Added/Corp C.A.B.
International. **VFOAT** Biotechnology in Agriculture. (1990)-. Monographic series. English. CAB International Centre, Wallingford, Oxfordshire OX10 8DE United Kingdom. **Tel** 011 44 1491 832111, FAX 011 44 1491 833508, telex 847964 COMAGG G.
Ind/Abst AGRICOLA; Biol. Abstr. (1992-); Curr. Cit.

LC S
DD 630 YU
BIOTEHNIKA. (1973)-. Periodical. Multiple
languages (Albanian and Serbo-Croatian (Roman); summaries and/or abstracts in English and Russian). Four times a year. 20.00 Din.

LC S **ISSN** 0373-7837
DD 630 PL
UDC 631.52
BIULETYN INSTYTUTU HODOWLI I AKLIMATYZACJI ROSLIN. [Biul. Inst. Hod.
Aklim. Rosl.]. (1951)-. Periodical. Polish. Four times a year. $33.00. (**Subscription address:** Ars Polona-Ruch, PO Box 1001, Krakowskie Przedmiescie 7, 00-068 Warsaw Poland. **Tel** 011 48 22 261201.)
Ind/Abst Hortic. Abstr.; Plant Breed. Abstr.; Potato Abstr.; Rev. Agric. Entomol.; Rev. Plant Pathol.; Seed Abstr.; Wheat Barley Trit. Abstr.

LC SB211.P8 I56b **ISSN** 0137-1576
DD 635.1 PL
CODEN BIZIDH
BIULETYN INSTYTUTU ZIEMNIAKA. See
Food and Food Industry.

LC S **ISSN** 0137-155X
DD 630 PL
UDC 631.52
BIULETYN OCENY ODMIAN - CENTRALNY OSRODEK BADANIA ODMIAN ROSLIN UPRAWNYCH W SLUPI WIELKIEJ POW. SRODA WLKP.
Added/Corp Warszawa Panstwowe Wydawnictwo Naukowe, Oddzial Poznan. **VFOAT** Cultivar Testing Bulletin. (1972)-. Multiple languages. Three times a week.
Ind/Abst Plant Breed. Abstr.; Potato Abstr.; Wheat Barley Trit. Abstr.

LC S **ISSN** 0006-5471
DD 630 AU
UDC 631.4
CODEN BODEA2
Pr Rev.
BODENKULTUR (1964). (DIE
BODENKULTUR.). [Bodenkultur]. Vol. 15, No. 1 (March 1964)-. Academic Scholarly Publication. German (summaries and/or abstracts in English). Four times a year. $311.15. Oesterreichischer Agrarverlag, Inkustr 1 7 Bueropark Donau, A 3400 Klosterneuburg Austria. **Tel** 011 43 2243 33300. **ED** Otto Steineck. **Bk Rev**. **Ad Acc**. **Circ**: 2,100. Documents available from The Genuine Article, CASDDS. *Formed by the union of Bodenkultur. Ausgabe A, Biologischtechnischer Teil and Bodenkultur. Ausgabe B, Agrarwirtschaftlicher Teil.*
Ind/Abst AGRICOLA; Agric. Eng. Abstr. (1991-); Anim. Breed. Abstr.; Biodeter. Abstr.; Chem. Abstr.; Curr. Aware. Biol. Sci.; CABS; Curr. Cit.; Curr. Contents Agric. Biol. Environ. Sci.; Dairy Sci. Abstr.; EMBASE; Field Crop Abstr.; GeoRef; Grass. Forage Abstr.; Hortic. Abstr.; Irr. Drain. Abstr.; Leis., Rec., Tour. Abstr.; Maize Abstr.; Nutr. Abstr. Rev., Ser. B, Live Feeds and Feed.; Nutr. Abstr. Rev., Ser. A, Hum. Exp.; Ornamental Hort.; Life Sci. Collect.; PESTDOC; Pig News Inf.; Plant Breed. Abstr.; Potato Abstr.; Poult. Abstr.; Protozoolog. Abstr.; Res. Alert [Select. Cov.]; Rev. Agric. Entomol.; Rev. Med. Vet. Entomol.; Rev. Med. Vet. Mycology; Rev. Plant Pathol.; Rural Dev. Abstr.; SCISEARCH; Soils Fert.; Soyabean Abstr.; Weed Abstr.; Wheat Barley Trit. Abstr.; World Agric. Econ. Rural Sociol. Abstr.

LC S
DD 630 BE
BOER EN DE TUINDER, DE. Added/Corp
Belgische Boerenbond. (18??)-. Periodical. Flemish. One time a week (Publish on Friday). $104.48. Belgische Boerenbond, Minderbroederstraat 8, B3000 Leuven Belgium. **Tel** 011 32 16 242111. **ED** Belgian Farmer's Union. **Bk Rev**. **Ad Acc**, **Adv Mgr**: Van Eylen, **Tel** 016 242246. **Circ**: 40,000 (ctrl).
Desc: News and articles pertaining to the farmers and the horticulturist.
Ind/Abst Plant Breed. Abstr.

LC S
DD 630 NE
BOERDERIJ, DE. (19??)-. Periodical. Dutch. One
time a week. $208.13. Misset Uitgeverij BV / Doetinchem, Postbus 4, 7000 BA Doetinchem Netherlands. **Tel** 011 31 8340 49911, 011 31 8340 49562, FAX 011 31 8340 43839, 011 31 8340 40515.

Agriculture

LC S
DD 630 — BL
BOLETIM DE PESQUISA. Added/Corp Centro de Pesquisa Agroflorestal da Amazonia Oriental (Brazil). (199?)-. Monographic series. Portuguese (summaries and/or abstracts in English). Price varies per volume. Boletim de Pesquisa, Caixa Postal 48, 66000 Belem Pa Brazil. *Continues* Boletim de Pesquisa (Centro de Pesquisa Agropecuaria do Tropico Umido (Empresa Brasileira de Pesquisa Agropecuaria), 0100-8102.

LC S — **ISSN** 0100-8102
DD 630 — BL
TITLE CHANGE
BOLETIM DE PESQUISA. Added/Corp Centro de Pesquisa Agropecuaria do Tropico Umido (Empresa Brasileira de Pesquisa Agropecuaria). No. 1 (Jan. 1980)-(199?). Monographic series. Portuguese (summaries and/or abstracts in English). Boletim de Pesquisa, Caixa Postal 48, 66000 Belem Pa Brazil. *Continued by* Boletim de Pesquisa (Centro de Pesquisa Agroflorestal da Amazonia Oriental (Brazil)).
Ind/Abst Abstr. Trop. Agric.; Agrindex; Agrofor. Abstr.; For. Abstr.; Maize Abstr.; Nutr. Abstr. Rev., Ser. B, Live Feeds and Feed.; Nutr. Abstr. Rev., Ser. A, Hum. Exp.; Rev. Agric. Entomol.

LC S — **ISSN** 0101-966X
DD 630 — BL
BOLETIM DE PESQUISA - EMPAER.
(BOLETIM DE PESQUISA.). [Bol. pesqui. - EMPAER]. Added/Corp EMPAER (Organizacion : Mato Grosso do Sul, Brazil). (1982)-. Monographic series. Portuguese (summaries and/or abstracts in English).
Ind/Abst Field Crop Abstr.; Rice Abstr.; Soyabean Abstr.

LC HD9200.B7 B73a
DD 630 — BL
BOLETIM ESTATISTICO DO CACAU.
Main/Corp Brazil. Comissao Executiva do Plano de Recuperacao Economico-Rural da Lavoura Cacaueira. (19??)-. Trade Publication. Portuguese. Assessoria de Programacao e Avaliacao - Assessoria Estatistica - Secretaria General, Avenue Nilo Pecanha 50-Grupo, 710 GB Rio de Janeiro Brazil.

LC S — **ISSN** 0377-2152
DD 630 — PO
UDC 311:63(469)
BOLETIM MENSAL DAS ESTATISTICAS DA AGRICULTURA E DA PESCA.
(BOLETIM MENSAL DAS ESTATISTICAS DA AGRICULTURA E DA PESCA : CONTINENTE E ILHAS ADJACENTES.). [Bol. mens. estat. agric. pesca]. Main/Corp Portugal. Instituto Nacional de Estatistica. Servicos Centrais. VFOAT Bulletin Mensuel des Statistiques de l'Agriculture et de la Peche : Continent et Iles Adjacentes. Vol. 1, (1976)-. Bulletin. French (Portuguese). Twelve times a year. Instituto Nacional de Estatistica, Avenida Antonio Jose de Almeida, 1078 Lisbon Codex Portugal. **Tel** 011 351 1 8470050.

LC S
DD 630 — BL
BOLETIM TECNICO. Added/Corp Empresa de Pesquisa Agropecuaria e Difusao de Tecnologia de Santa Catarina. (19??)-. Monographic series. Portuguese. Price varies per volume. EMPASC, Caixa Postal 1460, 88001 Florianopolis SC Brazil. **Tel** 011 55 842 340066, FAX 011 55 842 341024. *Continues* Boletim Tenico (Empresa Catarinense de Pesquisa Agropecuaria), 0100-7416.

LC S — **ISSN** 0102-5511
DD 630 — BL
UDC 63
BOLETIM TECNICO - COMISSAO EXECUTIVA DO PLANO DA LAVOURA CACAUEIRA, DEPARTAMENTO ESPECIAL DA AMAZONIA. (BOLETIM TECNICO.). [Bol. tec. - Com. Exec. Plano Lavoura Cacau. Dep. Espec. Amazonia]. **VFOAT** Boletim Tecnico CEPLAC. (1985)-. Monographic series. Multiple languages. Irregular. Price varies per volume. Organizacao das Cooperativas Estado do Parana - OCEPAR, Programa de Pesquisa, BR 467 - KM 19-, Rodovia Cascavel-Toledo, Caixa Postal 1203 85 800, Cascavel Parana Brazil. *Continues* Comunicado Tecnico - Departamento Especial da Amazonia. Comissfao Executiva do Plano da Lavoura Cacaueira, 0100-9907.
Ind/Abst Hortic. Abstr.; Postharvest News Inf.

LC S — **ISSN** 0100-4417
DD 630 — BL
BOLETIM TECNICO - COORDENDORIA DE ASSISTENCIA TECNICA INTEGRAL.
(BOLETIM TECNICO - GOVERNO DO ESTADO DE SAO PAULO, SECRETARIA DA AGRICULTURA, COORDENDORIA DE ASSISTENCIA TECNICA INTEGRAL.). [Bol. tec. - Coord. Assist. Tec. Integral]. Main/Corp Sao Paulo, Brazil (State). Secretaria da Agricultura. Coordenadoria de Assistencia Tecnica Integral. No. 81 (Nov. 1974)-. Monographic series. Portuguese. Price varies per volume. Secretaria da Agricultura Supervisao de Apoio Tecnico, Unidade de Economia Agricola, 585 - 70. Andar 90.000, Porto Alegre Brazil.

LC S
DD 630 — BL
BOLETIM TECNICO DA ESCOLA SUPERIOR DE AGRICULTURA DE LAVRAS. Added/Corp Escola Superior de Agricultura de Lavras. (19??)-. Monographic series. Portuguese. Irregular. Price varies per volume.
Ind/Abst Biodeter. Abstr.

LC S
DD 630 — PE
BOLETIN AGROPECUARIO ANDINO.
Added/Corp Junta del Acuerdo de Cartagena. Sistema de Informacion Comercial. Departamento de Desarrollo Agropecuario. (19??)-. Periodical. Spanish. Sistema de Informacion Comercial, Departamento de Desarrollo Agropecuario, Junta del Acuerdo de Cartagena, Casilla 3237, Lima Peru.

LC S
DD 630 — VE
BOLETIN AGROPECUARIO (INDUSTRIA LACTEA VENEZOLANA. DEPARTAMENTO DE ASISTENCIA TECNICA AGROPECUARIA). (BOLETIN AGROPECUARIO / INDULAC, ASISTENCIA TECNICA AGROPECUARIA.). Periodical. Spanish. Four times a year. Apartado No 1548, Caracas Venezuela. *Continues* Boletin Agropecuario Indulac.

LC S — **ISSN** 0325-2167
DD 630 — AG
BOLETIN DE DIVULGACION TECNICA.
Added/Corp Estacion Experimental Regional Agropecuaria Anguil. (19??)-. Periodical. Spanish.
Ind/Abst Soyabean Abstr.; Wheat Barley Trit. Abstr.

LC HD9014.M6 B63
DD 331.7 — MX
BOLETIN DE INFORMACION OPORTUNA DEL SECTOR ALIMENTARIO. Added/Corp Instituto Nacional de Estadistica, Geografia e Informatica (Mexico) PRONAL. (19??)-. Spanish. Twelve times a year. Free on request. INEGI / Instituto Nacional de Estadistica, Geografia e Informatica, Avenida Patriotismo 711 Segundo Piso, 03750 Mexico DF Mexico. **Tel** 011 52 5 5639935, 011 52 5 5988935, FAX 011 52 55987941. (**Subscription address:** INEGI / Instituto Nacional de Estadistica, Geografia e Informatica, Avenida Heroe de Nacozari 2301 Sur, Fracc. Jardines del Parque, CP 20270, Aguascalientes Mexico. **Tel** 011 52 49 182998.)

LC S — **ISSN** 0797-0315
DD 630 — UY
BOLETIN DE INVESTIGACION - FACULTAD DE AGRONOMIA (MONTEVIDEO). (BOLETIN DE INVESTIGACION.). [Bol. investig. - Fac. Agron. (Montev.)]. Added/Corp Universidad de la Republica (Uruguay). Facultad de Agronomia. No. 1 (1987)-. Monographic series. Spanish (summaries and/or abstracts in English). *Continues* Boletin (Universidad de la Republica(Uruguay). Facultad de Agronomia), 0077-1260.
Ind/Abst For. Prod. Abstr. (1991-); For. Abstr.; Hortic. Abstr.

LC S — **ISSN** 0213-3407
DD 630 — SP
UDC 338.43
CEASED
BOLETIN DE PRECIOS AGRARIOS ED. SEMANAL. (1980)-(19??). Periodical. Spanish. Ministerio Agricultura, Centro de Publicaciones, Calle Alfonso XII 56, 28071 Madrid Spain. **Tel** 011 34 1 3475551, FAX 011 34 1 3475722.

LC S
DD 630 — CU
BOLETIN DE RESENAS (CENTRO DE INFORMACION Y DOCUMENTACION AGROPECUARIO). (BOLETIN DE RESENAS. ARROZ.). **VFOAT** Arroz. (May 1980)-. Spanish. Centro de Informacion y Documentacion Agropecuario, Calle 11 No 1057, Vedado Habana Cuba.
Ind/Abst Field Crop Abstr.; Postharvest News Inf.; Rice Abstr.; Soils Fert.; Weed Abstr.

LC S
DD 630 — CU
BOLETIN DE RESENAS. TABACO.
Added/Corp Centro de Informacion y Documentacion Agropecuario (Cuba) Estacion Central de Tabaco. Cuba. Ministerio de Agricultura. Estacion Central de Tabaco. **VFOAT** Tabaco. (19??)-. Monographic series. Spanish.
Ind/Abst Crop Physiol. Abstr.; Field Crop Abstr.; Soils Fert.

LC SB226 .B65
DD 633.6/1/05 — CU
BOLETIN INICA. Added/Corp Instituto Nacional de Investigaciones de la Cana de Azucar (Cuba). (19??)-. Spanish. Four times a year.
Ind/Abst Field Crop Abstr.; Hortic. Abstr.; Rev. Agric. Entomol.; Weed Abstr.

LC S — **ISSN** 0188-4360
DD 630 — MX
BOLETIN MENSUAL DE INFORMACION BASICA DEL SECTOR AGROPECUARIO Y FORESTAL. Added/Corp Mexico. Secretaria de Agricultura y Recursos Hidraulicos. Direccion General de Estadistica. Statistical Publication. Spanish. Twelve times a year.

LC S — **ISSN** 0574-203X
DD 630 — CR
UDC 63
BOLETIN TECNICO. Main/Corp Inter-American Institute of Agricultural Sciences. (1949)-. Periodical. Spanish. Inter-American Institute of Science, Oficina de Dist de Publ, Turrialba Costa Rica.

LC S — **ISSN** 0577-7925
DD 630 — CL
BOLETIN TECNICO. Main/Corp Chile. Direccion de Agricultura y Pesca. (19??)-. Periodical. Spanish. Twenty-four times a year. Coordinador de Experimentacion, Casilla 16065, Santiago 9 Chile.

LC S
DD 630 — AG
BOLETIN TECNICO - ESTACION EXPERIMENTAL REGIONAL AGROPECUARIA BALCARCE. Main/Corp Estacion Experimental Regional Agropecuaria Balcarce. (1971)-. Monographic series. Spanish (summaries and/or abstracts in English). *Continues* Estacion Experimental Agropecuaria Balcarce. Boletin Tecnico - Estacion Experimental Agropecuaria Balcarce.
Ind/Abst Weed Abstr.

LC S — **ISSN** 0304-5552
DD 630 — CL
UDC 630(83)
BOLETIN TECNICO - UNIVERSIDAD DE CHILE, FACULTAD DE AGRONOMIA.
[Bol. tec. - Fac. Agron. Univ. Chile]. Main/Corp Universidad de Chile. Facultad de Agronomia. No. 36- Dec. 1972-. Monographic series. Spanish (summaries and/or abstracts in English). Price varies per volume. Universidad de Chile / Agronomia, Facultad de Agronomia, Casilla 1004, Santiago Chile. *Continues* Maipu, Chile. Estacion Experimental Agronomia. Boletin Tecnio.

LC S — **ISSN** 0506-533X
DD 630 — VE
BOLETIN - VENEZUELA. INSTITUTO AGRARIO NACIONAL. Main/Corp Instituto Agrario Nacional (Venezuela). No. 1 (Jan. 31, 1964)-. Bulletin. Spanish. Twenty-four times a year. Instituto Agrario Nacional, Caracas 1071 Venezuela.

LC HD1401 — **ISSN** 0006-7741
DD 338.1 634 — HU
CODEN BORGBB
BORGAZDASAG. [Borgazdasag]. (19??)-. Periodical. Multiple languages (French and German). Documents available from CASDDS.
Ind/Abst Chem. Abstr.

LC S530
DD 630.717 — US
BR. Added/Corp University of Vermont. Extension Service. University of Vermont. Extension System. **VFOAT** Brieflet. (19??)-. Monographic series. English. University of Vermont Agricultural Extension Service, Burlington VT 05405. *Continues* Brieflet (University of Vermont. Extension Service).

LC HD1401 — **ISSN** 0709-0102
DD 338.1/7/409711 — CN
BRITISH COLUMBIA GROWER.
Added/Corp Association of British Columbia Grape Growers. British Columbia Fruit Growers Association. **VFOAT** British Columbia Grower Magazine. **VAT** British Columbia Grower Magazine. Vol. 1 (Jan. 1979)-. Periodical. English. Twelve times a year. $7.50 Canada; $9.00 other. The British Columbia Grower Magazine, PO Box 1527, Kelowna BC V1Y 7V8.

LC S — **ISSN** 0267-6338
DD 630.941 — UK
BRITISH FARMER (1985). [Br. farmer 1985]. (1985)-. Trade Publication. English. Ten times a year. £23.00 UK; £28.00 Europe; £48.50 other. TG Scott Subscriber Services, 6 Bourne Enterprise Center, Sevenoaks Kent TN15 8DG United Kingdom. **Tel** 011 44 1732 884023, FAX 011 44 1732 884034. *Continues* British Farmer and Stockbreeder, 0007-0688.
Desc: Represents about 100,000 farmers and growers in England and Wales. Reports to them on the work the NFU is doing on their behalf and provides information and analysis on issues affecting their businesses.

Agriculture

LC S
DD 630 US
● **BROADCASTERS LETTER.** **Added/Corp** United States. Dept. of Agriculture. Office of Communications. (July 15, 1994)-. Periodical. English. One time a week. US Department of Agriculture / Office of Communication, Room 1618-S, Washington DC 20250. **Tel** (202)720-2791. *Continues Farm Broadcasters Letter.*

LC S
DD 630 FR
BTI : BULLETIN TECHNIQUE D'INFORMATION. **Added/Corp** France. Ministere de l'Agriculture et de la Foret. **VFOAT** Bulletin Technique d'Information; BTI. (Jan/Feb 1991)-. Bulletin. French. Six times a year. *Continues Bulletin Technique d'Information (France. Ministere de l'Agriculture).*
Ind/Abst Agric. Eng. Abstr.

ISSN 0007-2834
DD 630 US
BUCKEYE FARM NEWS. **Added/Corp** Ohio Farm Bureau Federation. (19??)-. Periodical. English. Eleven times a year. $5.00. Ohio Farm Bureau Federation, Box 479, Columbus OH 43216. **Tel** (614)249-2483, FAX (614)249-2200. **ED** C Dunham. Index available. **Bk Rev. Ad Acc. Circ:** 130,000. available with illustrations.

LC S ISSN 0744-3447
DD 630 US
BUFFALO FRUIT AND VEGETABLE REPORT. **Added/Corp** New York (State). Dept. of Agriculture and Markets. Division of Market Development. United States. Agricultural Marketing Service. Fruit and Vegetable Division. Federal-State Market News Service. (19??)-. Trade Publication. English. Two times a week. Federal-State Market News Service, 1220 N Street, Suite 216, Box 942871, Sacramento CA 94271-0001. **Tel** (916)654-0298, FAX (916)654-1046.

LC S539.M4 U547
DD 338.1 MY
BUKU PANDUAN - UNIVERSITI PERTANIAN MALAYSIA. **Main/Corp** Universiti Pertanian Malaysia. Malay. Universiti Pertanian Malaysia, Peti Surat 203 Sungai Besi, Serdang Malaysia.

LC QA ISSN 0127-2799
DD 515.5 MY
BULETIN KAJICUACA-PERTANIAN. See Earth Sciences-Meteorology.

LC S297 .B82 ISSN 0216-3500
DD 638.09598 IO
BULETIN PENELITIAN INSTITUT PERTANIAN BOGOR. Periodical. English (Indonesian). Irregular. Lembaga Penelitian, Institut Pertanian Bogor, JL Raya Pajaranjan, Bogor Indonesia. **Tel** (0251) 28105. **ED** Tonny Ungerer, Amris Makmur, Sitanala Arsyad, Sudirman Yahya, Edi Guhardja, I G B Teken, and Soewondo Djojosoebagyo. **Circ:** 500 (ctrl). **Desc:** Published the papers presented in the Seminars on the research results conducted by IPB.
Ind/Abst Biocont. News Inf.; Biodeter. Abstr.

LC S
DD 630 IO
BULETIN PERKEBUNAN. Vol. 16, No. 1 (April 1985)-. Periodical. Indonesian (summaries and/or abstracts in English). *Continues Bulletin Balai Penelitian Perkebunan Medan.*
Ind/Abst Agrofor. Abstr. (19??-19??); Biocont. News Inf.; For. Abstr.; Hortic. Abstr.; Plant Breed. Abstr.; Plant Grow. Reg. Abstr.; Rural Dev. Abstr.; Weed Abstr.; World Agric. Econ. Rural Sociol. Abstr.

LC WMLC L 83/5184 ISSN 0563-573X
DD 630 AA
CODEN BSBUAY
BULETINI I SHKENCAVE BUJQESORE. **Added/Corp** Instituti Larte Shteteror te Bujqesise (Tirana, Albania) Institucione Kerkimore Shkencore te Bujqesise. Institucione Kerkimore Shkencore dhe Mesimore te Bujqesise. (1962)-. Periodical. Albanian (summaries and/or abstracts in French). Four times a year. Institutions de Recherches Scientifiques Agricoles, Tirane, Albania. **ED** L. Veshi. Documents available from CASDDS.
Ind/Abst Chem. Abstr. (19??-1987); Field Crop Abstr.; Hortic. Abstr.; Irr. Drain. Abstr.; Maize Abstr.; Plant Breed. Abstr.; Seed Abstr.; Sug. Indus. Abstr.; Wheat Barley Trit. Abstr.

LC S ISSN 0557-465X
DD 630 RM
CODEN BIAAD4
BULETINUL INSTITUTULUI AGRONOMIC CLUJ-NAPOCA. SERIA AGRICULTURA. [Bul. Inst. Agron. Cluj-Napoca. Ser. agric.]. **Main/Corp** Institutul Agronomic "Dr. Petru Groza.". **VFOAT** Seria Agricultura; Buletin IACN-A. Vol. 32 (1978)-(19??). Academic Scholarly Publication. Romanian (English). One time a year. Universitatea de Stiinte Agricole, Str. Manastur Nr. 3, Cluj-Napoca Romania. **Tel** 011 40 951 193792. **ED** Alexandru Salontai. **Circ:** 500 (ctrl). Documents available from BIOSIS Document Express, CASDDS. *Supersedes in part Institutul Agronomic "Dr. Petru Groza." Buletinul Institutului Agronomic Cluj-Napoca, 0378-0554. Continued by Buletinul Universitatii de Stiinte Agricole Cluj-Napoca Seria Agricultura si Horticultura.*
Ind/Abst Biodeter. Abstr.; Biol. Abstr.; Chem. Abstr. (1978-1981); Field Crop Abstr.; Grass. Forage Abstr.; Hortic. Abstr.; Maize Abstr.; Nutr. Abstr. Rev., Ser. B, Live Feeds and Feed.; Ornamental Hort. (1991-); Plant Breed. Abstr.; Plant Genet. Resour. Abstr.; Potato Abstr.; Refer. Z.; Rev. Med. Vet. Mycology; Rev. Plant Pathol.; Soils Fert.; Soyabean Abstr.

LC S ISSN 1220-8450
DD 630 RM
BULETINUL UNIVERSITATII DE STIINTE AGRICOLE CLUJ-NAPOCA. SERIA AGRICULTURA SI HORTICULTURA. **Added/Corp** Universitatea de Stiinte Agricole Cluja-Napoca. **VFOAT** Seria Agricultura si Horticultura; Buletin USACN A-H. Vol. 46, Nr. 1 (1992)-. Bulletin. Romanian (English). Two times a year. Universitatea de Stiinte Agricole, Str. Manastur Nr. 3, Cluj-Napoca Romania. **Tel** 011 40 951 193792. **ED** Leon Muntean. **Circ:** 200 (ctrl). *Continues Buletinul Institutului Agronomic Cluj-Napoca. Seria Agricultura si Horticultura.*

LC S469.B8 B78
DD 334./68/3094977 BU
BULGARIAN CO-OPERATIVE REVIEW. See Business and Economics-Cooperatives.

LC S ISSN 0156-2452
DD 630 AT
UDC 338.439.4:633.1(944)
BULK WHEAT. English. One time a year. Grain Handling Authority of New South Wales, PO Box A268, Sydney New South Wales 2000 Australia.

LC S
DD 630 US
BULLETIN. **Added/Corp** Illinois Agricultural Experiment Station. (June 1977)-. Bulletin. English. *Continues Bulletin.*
Ind/Abst GeoRef; Rev. Plant Pathol.

LC S ISSN 0708-5702
DD 630 CN
BULLETIN AGRICOLE, DISTRICT DE TIMISKAMING. **Added/Corp** Ontario. Ministere de l'Agriculture et de l'Alimentation. (1???)-. Bulletin. French. Ministere de l'Agriculture et de l'Alimentation, CP G, New Liskeard Ontario P0J 1P0 Canada.

LC S
DD 630 RW
BULLETIN AGRICOLE DU RWANDA. **Added/Corp** Rwanda. Office des Cafes. (1968)-. Bulletin. French. Four times a year.
Ind/Abst Helminthol. Abstr. (1991-); Index Vet.; Maize Abstr.; Soyabean Abstr.

LC S181 ISSN 0097-5486
DD 630 PR
UDC 63(63(761))
CODEN PRABAH
BULLETIN - AGRICULTURAL EXPERIMENT STATION, RIO PIEDRAS. **Main/Corp** University of Puerto Rico. Agricultural Experiment Station, Rio Piedras. **VFOAT** Boletin - Estacion Experimental Agricola, Rio Piedras. No. 3 - 19 -. Bulletin. Multiple languages. Price varies per volume. Agricultural Experiment Station / Puerto Rico, Rio Piedras, Mayaguez Puerto Rico 00708. Documents available from CASDDS. *Continues Bulletin - Experiment Station, Rio Piedras.*
Ind/Abst Chem. Abstr. (19??-1981).

LC S ISSN 0765-0787
DD 630 GP
CODEN 631(882)
BULLETIN AGRONOMIQUE PETIT-BOURG. (1983)-. Periodical. French. Two times a year.
Ind/Abst Plant Breed. Abstr.

LC S
DD 630 US
BULLETIN (ALABAMA AGRICULTURAL EXPERIMENT STATION). (BULLETIN.). **Added/Corp** Alabama Agricultural Experimental Station. (1981)-. Bulletin. English. Irregular. Price varies per volume. Alabama Agricultural Experiment Station, Auburn University, 110 Comer Hall, Auburn University AL 36849. **Tel** (334)844-4877, FAX (334)844-5892. *Continues Bulletin (Auburn University. Agricultural Experiment Station), 0271-0544.*
Ind/Abst Fish Rev. (Jan. 1989-July 1992); For. Abstr.; Potato Abstr.; Wildl. Rev. (Jan. 1989-July 1992).

LC SB992 ISSN 1084-3051
DD 632.6 US
BULLETIN - ASSOCIATION OF APPLIED INSECT ECOLOGISTS. (BULLETIN.). **Added/Corp** Association of Applied Insect Ecologists. **VFOAT** Quarterly Bulletin; AAIE Bulletin. (19??)-. Bulletin. English. Four times a year. $15.00. Association of Applied Insect Ecologists, 1008 10 Street, Suite 549, Sacramento CA 95814. **Tel** (916)441-5224. **ED** John F. Plain. **Photos. Ad Acc.** Full Page (B&W) $100.00. Half Page (B&W) $75.00. **Pub. Size:** Standard. *Continues Newsletter of the Association of Applied Insect Ecologists.*
Desc: Articles and information of interest to professional entomologists, researchers, pest control advisors, and others dedicated to controlling agricultural, ornamental and landscape pests through integrated pest management and biological control measures.

LC S17 ISSN 0886-473X
DD 630 US
BULLETIN B - OKLAHOMA STATE UNIVERSITY. AGRICULTURAL EXPERIMENT STATION. (BULLETIN B.). [Bull. B - Okla. State Univ., Agric. Exp. Stn.]. **Main/Corp** Oklahoma Agricultural Experiment Station. (19??)-. Bulletin. English.
Ind/Abst Wheat Barley Trit. Abstr.

LC S43 .E22 ISSN 0097-0905
DD 630 US
BULLETIN / CONNECTICUT AGRICULTURE EXPERIMENT STATION. [Bull. - Conn. Agric. Exp. Stn.]. **Added/Corp** Connecticut Agricultural Experiment Station. (198?)-. Bulletin. English. Irregular. Connecticut Agricultural Experiment Station, 123 Huntington Street, Box 1106, New Haven CT 06504-1106. **Tel** (203)789-7272, FAX (203)789-7232. Documents available from Documents on Demand.
Ind/Abst AGRICOLA [Select. Cov.]; EMBASE; Environ. Abstr.; For. Abstr.; GeoRef; Nematol. Abstr.; Ornamental Hort.; Plant Breed. Abstr.; Rev. Agric. Entomol.

LC S ISSN 0092-9077
DD 630 US
BULLETIN - COOPERATIVE EXTENSION SERVICE (ATHENS). See Business and Economics-Cooperatives.

LC S451.5 ISSN 1187-4392
DD 630/.9715/1 CN
BULLETIN DE LA F.A.A.F., N.-B, LE. [Bull. F.A.A.F. N.-B.]. **Added/Corp** Federation des Agriculteurs et Agricultrices Francophones du N.-B. **VFOAT** Bulletin de la Federation des Agriculteurs et Agricultrices Francophones du Nouveau-Brunswick. Vol. 6, No 1/2 (Sept./Oct. 1991)-. Bulletin. French. Twelve times a year. Federation des Agriculteurs et Agricultrices Francophones, Du N. B. 500 Boulevard Mgr. Pichette, Edmundston New Brunswick E3V 2S8 Canada. *Continues Le Bulletin de la Federation., 0834-1451.*

LC S ISSN 0378-8997
DD 630 RM
CODEN BAAFBT
BULLETIN DE L'ACADEMIE DES SCIENCES AGRICOLES ET FORESTIERES. [Bull. Acad. sci. agric. for.]. **Main/Corp** Academia de Stiinte Agricole Si Silvice. **VFOAT** Bulletin of the Academy of Agricultural and Forestry Sciences. No. 1 (1972)-. Bulletin. French (English). One time a year. **(Subscription address:** Ilexim Press Department, PO Box 1, 136-1-137, Bucharest, Romania. **Tel** 011 40 1 173836.) Documents available from BIOSIS Document Express, CASDDS.
Ind/Abst Anim. Breed. Abstr.; Biol. Abstr.; Chem. Abstr. (1972-1980); For. Abstr.; Maize Abstr.; Potato Abstr.; Poult. Abstr.; Vitis Vitic. Enol. Abstr.

LC S ISSN 0029-7127
DD 630 FR
CODEN BLOVAJ
BULLETIN DE L'OIV. (BULLETIN.). [Bull. OIV]. **Main/Corp** Office International de la Vigne et du Vin. (1928)-. Bulletin. French. Six times a year. $150.92. Office Internationale la Vigne et du Vin, 11 rue Roquepine, 75008 Paris France. **Tel** 011 33 1 44948080, FAX 011 33 1 42669063, telex 281196. **ED** Robert Tinlot. Index available. cum. index. **Bk Rev,** (Qty: 6): **Circ:** 1,200 (ctrl). Documents available from CASDDS.
Desc: Scientific review concerning wine and vineyards.
Ind/Abst Chem. Abstr.; Curr. Cit.; Food Sci. Technol. Abstr.; Hortic. Abstr.; Plant Breed. Abstr.; Soils Fert.; Vitis Vitic. Enol. Abstr.; Weed Abstr.

LC S
DD 630 AT
UDC 63(941)
BULLETIN - DEPT. OF AGRICULTURE. **Main/Corp** Western Australia. Department of Agriculture. Bulletin. English. Price varies per volume. Western Australia Department of Agriculture / South Perth, Information Branch / Baron-Hay Court, South Perth Western Australia 6151 Australia. **Tel** 011 61 9 3683231, FAX 011 61 9 4742018, telex AA 93304.

LC S ISSN 0007-4446
DD 630 CN
BULLETIN DES AGRICULTEURS. [Bull. agric.]. Vol. 1 (1915)-. Trade Publication. French. Twelve times a year (2 issues in Mar. with July/Aug. issue combined). 19.96Can$. Le Bulletin des Agriculteurs, 75

Agriculture

rue de Port Royal Bur 200, Montreal Quebec H3L 3T1 Canada. **Tel** (514)382-4350, FAX (514)382-4356. **ED** Marc-Alain Soucy. **Ad Acc**. **Circ:** 35,000 (ctrl). available on an online database.
 Desc: French farm magazine covering Quebec, and the French areas of Ontario and New Brunswick. Dairy farming, field crops, machinery and equipment, and farm management are included.
 Ind/Abst Repere (1983-).

LC SF521
DD 638.1
ISSN 0435-2033
BE
CODEN BRAGBF
Pr Rev.

BULLETIN DES RECHERCHES AGRONOMIQUES DE GEMBLOUX.
(BULLETIN DES RECHERCHES AGRONOMIQUES DE GEMBLOUX.). [Bull. rech. agron. Gembloux]. **Added/Corp** Gembloux, Belgium. Faculte des Sciences Agronomiques de l'Etat. Centre de Recherches Agronomiques de l'Etat, Gembloux. Vol. 1 (1966)-. Bulletin. French (summaries and/or abstracts in Dutch, English and German). Four times a year. $59.70. Faculte des Sciences Agronomiques de Gembloux, Passage des Deportes 2, Com Ed, B 5030 Gembloux Belgium. **Tel** 011 32 81 622103, FAX 011 32 81 614544. **ED** B. Cuvelier, G. Hanotiaux, R. Paul, M. Populer, G. Sommereyns. Index available (published every 5 years). cum. index. **Bk Rev**. **Circ:** 1,000 (ctrl). Documents available from BIOSIS Document Express, CASDDS. **Supersedes** Gembloux, Belgium. Institut Agronomique de l'Etat. Bulletin de l'Institut Agronomique et des Stations de Recherches de Gembloux.
 Desc: Covers the areas of general agriculture, use and conservation, integrated development, satellite and aircraft remote sensing, animal husbandry, forestry, and allied subjects in temperate and tropical areas.
 Ind/Abst Agric. Eng. Abstr.; Agrindex; Biol. Abstr.; Chem. Abstr.; Cot. Trop. Fibr. Abstr.; Bibliogr.; Dairy Sci. Abstr.; EMBASE; Field Crop Abstr.; Food Sci. Technol. Abstr.; For. Prod. Abstr. (19??-19??); For. Abstr.; GeoRef; Grass. Forage Abstr.; Hortic. Abstr.; Index Vet.; Nematol. Abstr.; Nutr. Abstr. Rev., Ser. B, Live Feeds and Feed.; Nutr. Abstr. Rev., Ser. A, Hum. Exp.; Pig News Inf.; Plant Breed. Abstr.; Plant Genet. Resour. Abstr.; Potato Abstr.; Rev. Med. Vet. Mycology; Rev. Plant Pathol.; Rice Abstr.; Seed Abstr.; Soils Fert.; Sorghum Mill. Abstr.; Vitis Vitic. Enol. Abstr.; Wheat Barley Trit. Abstr.

LC S
DD 630
UDC 63(44)
FR

BULLETIN D'INFORMATION DU MINISTERE DE L'AGRICULTURE (FRANCE). **Main/Corp** France. Ministere de l'Agriculture. Bulletin. French. Sous-Direction de l'Information, des Relations Republiques et de la Documentation, 78 rue de Varenne 7E, Paris France. **Continues** France. Ministere de l'Agriculture et du Developpement Rural. Bulletin d'Information.

LC S
DD 630
BD

BULLETIN D'INFORMATION IRAZ.
 Added/Corp Institut de Recherche Agronomique et Zootechnique. (1989)-. Bulletin. French.
 Ind/Abst Hortic. Abstr.; Seed Abstr.; Wheat Barley Trit. Abstr.

LC HD1916 .E75a
DD 338.1/094
SZ

BULLETIN D'INFORMATIONS CEA.
 Main/Corp European Confederation of Agriculture. Secretariat General. **VFOAT** Bulletin d'Informations C.E.A. (19??)-. Bulletin. French. Four times a year. Confederation Europeenne de l'Agriculture, Secretariat General, Brougg Switzerland. **Continues** European Confederation of Agriculture. Secretariat General. Bulletin d'Information.

LC S
DD 630
UDC 632
ISSN 1015-8219
TG

BULLETIN DU SERVICE DE LA PROTECTION DES VEGETAUX. [Bull. Serv. prot. veg.]. (198?)-. Periodical. French.
 Ind/Abst Postharvest News Inf.; Rev. Agric. Entomol.

LC S537
DD 630.9758
UDC 63(758)
US

BULLETIN - GEORGIA. UNIVERSITY. COLLEGE OF AGRICULTURE. EXTENSION SERVICE. **Main/Corp** Georgia. University. College of Agriculture. Extension Service. Vol. 1 (1912)-. Bulletin. English. Price varies per volume. University of Georgia College of Agriculture Extension Service, Athens GA 30602.
 Desc: Each Bulletin includes Annual Report of the Extension Service for previous year.

LC SB16
DD 630/.6/0715
UDC 63(71)
ISSN 0712-8835
CN
CEASED

BULLETIN - INSTITUT DES AGRONOMES DU N.-B. INSTITUT AGRICOLE DU CANADA. (BULLETIN / N.B. INSTITUTE OF AGROLOGISTS.). [Bull. - Inst. agron. N.-B.]. **VFOAT** Newsletter; Bulletin - Institut Agricole du Canada. (May 1981)-(199?). Bulletin. English. Bulletin / Fredericton, c/o I A N B, CP 20280, Research Station, Fredericton New Brunswick E3B 4X7 Canada. **Continues** Lettre Circulaire de l'I.A.N.-B, 0712-8827.

LC S
DD 630
ISSN 0097-0484
US

BULLETIN - KANSAS AGRICULTURAL EXPERIMENT STATION. (BULLETIN / KANSAS AGRICULTURAL EXPERIMENT STATION, KANSAS STATE UNIVERSITY.). [Bull. - Kans. Agric. Exp. Stn.]. **Added/Corp** Kansas Agricultural Experiment Station. (1888)-. Bulletin. English. Irregular. Price varies per volume. Agricultural Experiment Station / Kansas, Kansas State University, Manhattan KS 66506. **Tel** (913)532-6147. **ED** Eileen Schofield, Steve Morgan. cum. index. **Circ:** 3,000 (ctrl).
 Ind/Abst AGRICOLA [Select. Cov.]; Field Crop Abstr.; Grass. Forage Abstr.; Maize Plant Breed. Abstr.; Soils Fert.; Soyabean Abstr.

LC S69 .E92
DD 338.1/09741
ISSN 1070-1494
US

●BULLETIN - MAINE AGRICULTURAL AND FOREST EXPERIMENT STATION. (BULLETIN.). [Bull. - Maine Agric. Forest Exp. Stn.]. **Added/Corp** Maine Agricultural and Forest Experiment Station. (Jan. 1994)-. Monographic series. English. University of Maine at Orono, College Life Sciences and Agriculture Experience, Orono ME 04473. **Tel** (207)581-2723. **Continues** Experiment Station Bulletin (Maine Agricultural Experiment Station), 0734-9548.

LC S
DD 630
FR

BULLETIN MENSUEL D'INFORMATION ET DE LIAISON DES CHAMBRES D'AGRICULTURE. Bulletin. English. Twelve times a year. $35.10. APPCA Service de l'Enseignement Etdela, 9 Avenue Geor, 75008 Paris France.

LC SB354
DD 634
UDC 63
ISSN 0898-0497
US
Pr Rev.

BULLETIN (MISSISSIPPI AGRICULTURAL AND FORESTRY EXPERIMENT STATION). (BULLETIN.). [Bull. - Miss. Agric. For. Exp. Stn.]. No. 781 (Sept. 1970)-. Bulletin. English. Irregular. Price varies per volume. Mississippi State University / Information Services, PO Box 5446, Mississippi State MS 39762. **Tel** (601)325-7774. **ED** Keith H Remy. Index available. cum. index. **Circ:** 850. **Continues** Bulletin - Mississippi State College, Agricultural Experiment Station, 0096-7696.
 Desc: Includes technical data and discussion of experiment station research.
 Ind/Abst AGRICOLA [Select. Cov.]; Agric. Eng. Abstr.; Field Crop Abstr.; Sorghum Mill. Abstr.; Soyabean Abstr.

LC S91 .E23
DD 630
ISSN 0096-6398
US

BULLETIN - NEW JERSEY AGRICULTURAL EXPERIMENT STATION, RUTGERS UNIVERSITY. (BULLETIN / NEW JERSEY AGRICULTURAL EXPERIMENT STATION.). **Added/Corp** New Jersey Agricultural Experiment Station. No. 1 (1880)-. Bulletin. English. Irregular. Price varies per volume. Department of Agriculture Economics and Marketing / New Jersey, New Jersey Agricultural Experiment Station, Cook College, New Brunswick NJ 08903.
 Ind/Abst Protozoolog. Abstr.; Soils Fert.

LC S
DD 630
ISSN 0149-9866
US
CODEN NEXAAG
Pr Rev.

BULLETIN / NEW MEXICO STATE UNIVERSITY, AGRICULTURAL EXPERIMENT STATION. [Bull. - N.M. State Univ., Agric. Exp. Stn.]. **Added/Corp** New Mexico State University. Agricultural Experiment Station. (1973)-. Bulletin. English. Irregular (occasional). Price varies per volume. New Mexico State University, Agricultural Experiment Station, Las Cruces NM 88003. **Tel** (505)646-2701, FAX (505)646-2702. **ED** Susan Pieper (editor's address: Box 30003, Department 3AI, Las Cruces NM 88003; telephone): (505)646-1163). Documents available from BIOSIS Document Express, CASDDS. **Continues** Agricultural Experiment Station Bulletin.
 Desc: Reports of research completed by the Agricultural Experiment Station at New Mexico State University.
 Ind/Abst Biol. Abstr.; Chem. Abstr. (?-1986); GeoRef (?-1986).

LC S
DD 630
ISSN 0096-7874
US

BULLETIN OF THE AGRICULTURAL EXPERIMENT STATION OF THE LOUISIANA STATE UNIVERSITY AND A & M COLLEGE. **Main/Corp** Louisiana Agricultural Experiment Station. **VAT** Bulletin of the Agricultural Experiment Station of the Louisiana State University and Agricultural and Mechanical College. Bulletin. English. Louisiana Agricultural Experiment Station, PO Box 25055, Baton Rouge LA 70894-5055. **Tel** (504)388-5649.
 Ind/Abst AGRICOLA [Full Cov.]; Grass. Forage Abstr.; Nematol. Abstr.; Rev. Plant Pathol.; Rice Abstr.; Soyabean Abstr.

LC S
DD 630
ISSN 0440-8772
JA

BULLETIN OF THE HIROSHIMA AGRICULTURAL COLLEGE. **Main/Corp** Hiroshima Nogyo Tanki Daigaku, Saijo, Japan. Vol. 1 (May 1958)-. Bulletin. Multiple languages (Japanese and English). Price varies per volume. Hiroshima Nogyo Tanki Daigaku, (Hiroshima Agricultural College), Saijocho, Higashihiroshimashi Hiroshimaken 724 Japan.
 Ind/Abst For. Prod. Abstr.; For. Abstr.; Plant Breed. Abstr.; Vitis Vitic. Enol. Abstr.; World Agric. Econ. Rural Sociol. Abstr.

LC S
DD 630
ISSN 0915-499X
JA

BULLETIN OF THE INSTITUTE OF TROPICAL AGRICULTURE, KYUSHU UNIVERSITY. [Bull. Inst. Trop. Agric., Kyushu Univ.]. **VFOAT** Nettai Nogaku Kenkyu. (1975)-. Bulletin. Multiple languages. One time a year. Kyushu Daigaku Nettai Nogaku Kenkyu Senta, (Inst. of Tropical Agriculture Kyushu University), 10-1 Hakozaki 6 Chome Higashiku, Fukuokashi Fukuokaken 812 Japan.
 Ind/Abst Field Crop Abstr.; For. Abstr.; Rice Abstr.; Seed Abstr.

LC S227 .B84
DD 630/.5
ISSN 0237-8930
HU

BULLETIN OF THE UNIVERSITY OF AGRICULTURAL SCIENCES, GODOLLO. **Added/Corp** Godolloi Agrartudomanyi Egyetem. (19??)-. Bulletin. English (summaries and/or abstracts in Russian and Hungarian). One time a year. Central Library of the University of Agricultural Sciences, 2103 Godollo Hungary.
 Ind/Abst Agric. Eng. Abstr. (1991-); Field Crop Abstr.; For. Prod. Abstr. (1991-); Maize Abstr.; Plant Grow. Reg. Abstr.; Postharvest News Inf.; Poult. Abstr.; Rev. Agric. Entomol.; Rice Abstr.; Seed Abstr.

LC S19
DD 630
NLM W1 BU893
ISSN 0366-3353
JA
CODEN BSKBAM

BULLETIN OF THE UNIVERSITY OF OSAKA PREFECTURE. SERIES B: AGRICULTURE AND BIOLOGY. [Bull. univ. Osaka Prefect. Ser. B.]. **Main/Corp** Osaka Furitsu Daigaku. **VFOAT** Osaka Furitsu Daigaku Kiyo: Nogaku, Seibutsugaku. Vol. 1 (1950)-. Bulletin. English (Japanese). One time a year. University of Osaka Prefecture, Sakai Japan. Documents available from CASDDS.
 Ind/Abst AGRICOLA [Select. Cov.]; Chem. Abstr.; GeoRef; Plant Grow. Reg. Abstr.; Rev. Plant Pathol.; SEA Abstr.

LC QH301
DD 574
ISSN 0952-8245
UK
Pr Rev.

BULLETIN - OVERSEAS DEVELOPMENT NATURAL RESOURCES INSTITUTE. (NATURAL RESOURCES INSTITUTE BULLETIN.). [Bull. - Overseas Dev. Nat. Resour. Inst.]. **Added/Corp** Overseas Development Natural Resources Institute. (1987)-. Bulletin. English. Irregular. Natural Resources Institute, Central Avenue, Chatham Maritime, Chatham Kent ME4 4TB United Kingdom. **Tel** 011 44 1634 880088, FAX 011 44 1634 880066, telex 203907 8 LONG. **Circ:** 500-1,000. **Formed by the union of** Tropical Development and Research Institute (Report Series G), 0264-763X and Tropical Development and Research Institute (Report Series. L), 0264-7648.
 Desc: Covers different aspects of agriculture relevant to the developing countries of the world.
 Ind/Abst Agric. Eng. Abstr. (1991-); For. Prod. Abstr. (1991-); For. Abstr.; Hortic. Abstr.; Postharvest News Inf.; Rev. Agric. Entomol.; Rice Abstr.; Sorghum Mill. Abstr.; Wheat Barley Trit. Abstr.; World Agric. Econ. Rural Sociol. Abstr.

LC S107
DD 630
UDC 63
ISSN 0362-4013
US
CODEN PAABAY

BULLETIN - PENNSYLVANIA STATE UNIVERSITY, COLLEGE OF AGRICULTURE, AGRICULTURAL EXPERIMENT STATION. [Bull. - Pa. State Univ.

Agriculture

Coll. Agric. Agric. Exp. Stn.]. **Main/Corp** Pennsylvania State University. Agricultural Experiment Station. 573-Dec. 1953-. Bulletin. English. Price varies per volume. Pennsylvania State University, 211 Weaver Building, University Park PA 16802. Documents available from BIOSIS Document Express, CASDDS. *Continues Bulletin - Pennsylvania State College, School of Agriculture, Agricultural Experiment Station, 0096-0969.*
Ind/Abst Anim. Breed. Abstr.; Biol. Abstr.; Chem. Abstr.; Field Crop Abstr.; Grass. Forage Abstr.; Leis., Rec., Tour. Abstr.; Soils Fert.

LC S **ISSN** 0216-7867
DD 630 IO
BULLETIN PERKARETAN. (1983)-. Bulletin. Indonesian. One time a year.
Ind/Abst Hortic. Abstr.; Plant Grow. Reg. Abstr.; Rev. Plant Pathol.; Rice Abstr.

LC S **ISSN** 1011-999X
DD 630 AE
BULLETIN SIGNALETIQUE - INSTITUT NATIONAL AGRONOMIQUE EL HARRACH. [Bull. signal. - Inst. natl. agron. El Harrach]. (1???)-. Periodical. French. Irregular.
Ind/Abst Agrofor. Abstr.

LC S229 .A365 **ISSN** 0303-1721
DD 630/.944 FR
BULLETIN TECHNIQUE D'INFORMATION (FRANCE. MINISTERE DE L'AGRICULTURE ET DU DEVELOPPEMENT RURAL). (BULLETIN TECHNIQUE D'INFORMATION.). [Bull. tech. inf., Minist. agric. dev. rural]. **Added/Corp** France. Ministere de l'Agriculture et du Developpement Rural. (19??)-. Bulletin. French. Irregular. $98.43. Ministere de l'Agriculture, 78 rue de Varenne, 75007 Paris France. **Tel** 011 33 1 49554955 ext. 2718. *Continues Bulletin Technique d'Information des Ingenieurs des Services Agricole, Directions Departementales et Etablissements d'Enseignement.*
Ind/Abst Agric. Eng. Abstr. (1991-); EMBASE.

LC S117 **ISSN** 0096-6061
DD 630 US
CODEN TAEBAU
BULLETIN - TEXAS AGRICULTURAL EXPERIMENT STATION. (BULLETIN.). [Bull. Tex. Agric. Exp. Stn.]. **Main/Corp** Texas. Agricultural Experiment Station, College Station. **Added/Corp** Texas Agricultural Experiment Station. Texas A & M University System. (1888)-. Bulletin. English. Price varies per volume. Texas A & M University / Agriculture, Texas Agricultural Experiment Station, College Station TX 77843. Documents available from BIOSIS Document Express, CASDDS.
Ind/Abst Agrofor. Abstr.; Biol. Abstr.; Chem. Abstr.; Field Crop Abstr.; For. Abstr.; Sorghum Mill. Abstr.; Wheat Barley Trit. Abstr.; World Agric. Econ. Rural Sociol. Abstr.

LC S37 .E2 **ISSN** 0097-3491
DD 630 US
BULLETIN - UNIVERSITY OF ARKANSAS, FAYETTEVILLE. AGRICULTURAL EXPERIMENT STATION. (BULLETIN. / ARKANSAS AGRICULTURAL EXPERIMENT STATION AT ARKANSAS INDUSTRIAL UNIVERSITY.). [Bull. - Univ. Ark. Fayettev. Agric. Exp. Stn.]. **Added/Corp** University of Arkansas, Fayetteville. Agricultural Experiment Station. No. 1 (1886)-. Bulletin. English. Price varies per volume. Arkansas Agricultural Experiment Station, University of Arkansas, Fayetteville AR 72701. **Tel** (501)575-5647, FAX (501)575-7273.
Ind/Abst Anim. Breed. Abstr.; Field Crop Abstr.; For. Prod. Abstr. (1991-); For. Abstr.; Index Vet.; World Agric. Econ. Rural Sociol. Abstr.

LC S **ISSN** 1044-4823
DD 630 US
BULLETIN - UNIVERSITY OF CALIFORNIA (SYSTEM). DIVISION OF AGRICULTURE AND NATURAL RESOURCES. (BULLETIN / UNIVERSITY OF CALIFORNIA, DIVISION OF AGRICULTURE AND NATURAL RESOURCES.). [Bull. - Univ. Calif. (Syst.), Div. Agric. Nat. Resour.]. **Added/Corp** University of California (System). Division of Agriculture and Natural Resources. (Jan. 1984)-. Bulletin. English. *Continues Bulletin (University of California (System). Division of Agricultural Sciences), 0363-8707.*
Ind/Abst For. Abstr.

LC S45 .E22 **ISSN** 0097-1367
DD 630/.9751 US
BULLETIN - UNIVERSITY OF DELAWARE, AGRICULTURAL EXPERIMENT STATION. (BULLETIN.). [Bull. - Univ. Del. Agric. Exp. Stn.]. **Added/Corp** University of Delaware. Agricultural Experiment Station. **VFOAT** Agricultural Experiment Station Bulletin; Delaware Agricultural Experiment Station Bulletin. No. 1 (1888)-. Bulletin. English. Price varies per volume. University of Delaware Agricultural Experiment Station, Newark DE 19716.
Ind/Abst Biocont. News Inf.; Fish Rev. (Jan. 1989-July 1992); Wildl. Rev. (Jan. 1989-July 1992).

LC S49 .E2 **ISSN** 0096-607X
DD 630/.9759 US
CODEN FASBAE
BULLETIN - UNIVERSITY OF FLORIDA, AGRICULTURAL EXPERIMENT STATIONS. (BULLETIN.). [Bull. - Univ. Fla., Agric. Exp. Stn.]. **Main/Corp** University of Florida. Agricultural Experiment Station. No. 1 (1888)-. Bulletin. English. Price varies per volume. University of Florida Agricultural Experiment Station, Gainesville FL 32601. Documents available from BIOSIS Document Express.
Ind/Abst Biol. Abstr.; For. Abstr.; Hortic. Abstr.; Protozool. Abstr.; Rev. Agric. Entomol.; Rev. Plant Pathol.; Soils Fert.

LC S
DD 630 UK
BULLETIN / UNIVERSITY OF READING, AGRICULTURAL EXTENSION AND RURAL DEVELOPMENT CENTRE. **Main/Corp** University of Reading. Agricultural Extension and Rural Development Centre. **VFOAT** Reading and Rural Development Communications. Bulletin. English. University of Reading / London Road, London Road, Reading RG1 5AQ United Kingdom.

LC S **ISSN** 0096-6088
DD 630 US
Pr Rev.
BULLETIN / VIRGINIA AGRICULTURAL EXPERIMENT STATION. [Bull. - Va. Agric. Exp Stn.]. **Added/Corp** Virginia Polytechnic Institute and State University. Virginia Agricultural Experiment Station. Vol. 1 (1981)-. Bulletin. English. Price varies per volume. Virginia Agricultural Experiment Station, Virginia Polytechnic Institute and State University, Blacksburg VA 24061-0402. **Tel** (703)231-3766. **ED** Mary C Holliman. *Continues Bulletin - Virginia Agricultural Experiment Station, 0096-6088.*
Desc: Reports of research too long for journals.
Ind/Abst For. Abstr.; Maize Abstr.; World Agric. Econ. Rural Sociol. Abstr.

LC S **ISSN** 0748-1268
DD 630 US
CODEN WVABAK
BULLETIN / WEST VIRGINIA UNIVERSITY AGRICULTURAL AND FORESTRY EXPERIMENT STATION. [Bull. - W. Va. Univ., Agric. For. Exp. Stn.]. No. 648 (Oct. 1976)-. Bulletin. English. Irregular. Price varies per volume. West Virginia University / Foundation Department for Languages, Chitwood Hall, Morgantown WV 26506. **Tel** (304)293-5121. Documents available from BIOSIS Document Express. *Continues Bulletin (West Virginia University. Agricultural Experiment Station), 0096-6096.*
Ind/Abst Biocont. News Inf.; Biol. Abstr.; Hortic. Abstr.; Postharvest News Inf.; Rev. Plant Pathol.

LC HD1694 .A1565A **ISSN** 0565-0674
DD 353.008/232 US
UDC 631.61(73)
BUREAU OF RECLAMATION PROGRESS. **Main/Corp** United States. Bureau of Reclamation. **VFOAT** Progress - Bureau of Reclamation. 1949-. Periodical. English. Two times a year. Bureau of Reclamation, PO Box 25007, Denver CO 80225. **Tel** (303)234-3000. *Continues Progress Report - Bureau of Reclamation.*

LC S
DD 630 AU
BURGENLANDISCHER AGRAR KURIER. **Added/Corp** Burgenlandischer Bauernbund. **VFOAT** Buregnlandischer Agrarkurier. Vol. 23, No.1 (1970)-. Periodical. German. Twelve times a year. DM160.00. Oesterreichischer Agrarverlag, Inkustr 1 7 Bueropark Donau, A 3400 Klosterneuberg Austria. **Tel** 011 43 2243 33300. *Continues Burgenlandische Bauernbundler.*

LC S **ISSN** 1012-6910
DD 630 IC
CODEN BUVIEE
BUVISINDI (REYKJAVIK). (BUVISINDI.). [Buvisindi]. **Added/Corp** Rannsoknastofnun Landbunaarins. **VFOAT** Icelandic Agricultural Sciences. (1988)-. Icelandic (Danish, English and Swedish). Documents available from BIOSIS Document Express. *Continues Islenzkar Landbunaar Rannsoknir.*
Ind/Abst Biol. Abstr.; Index Vet.

LC S
DD 630 UK
C.A.P. MONITOR. English. Agra Europe London Limited, 25 Frant Road, Tunbridge Wells, Kent TN2 5JT United Kingdom. **Tel** 011 44 1892 533813, FAX 011 44 1892 544895, telex 95114 AGRATW G.

LC S20 **ISSN** 0706-9782
DD 630/.6/21 CN
C A S A S NEWS. **Main/Corp** Commonwealth Association of Scientific Agricultural Societies. **VAT** Commonwealth Association of Scientific Agricultural Societies News. No. 1 (Oct. 1978)-. Periodical. English. Commonwealth Association of Scientific Agricultural Societies, 151 Slater Street/Suite 907, Ottawa Ontario K1P 5H4 Canada.

LC SB950.9 **ISSN** 0160-9068
DD 632.952 US
CODEN CSFNDD
CA SELECTS: FUNGICIDES. See Chemistry and Chemicals-Abstracting, Bibliographies and Statistics.

LC SB950.9 **ISSN** 0160-9084
DD 632.954 US
CODEN CSHEDU
CA SELECTS: HERBICIDES. See Chemistry and Chemicals-Abstracting, Bibliographies and Statistics.

LC SB951.145 **ISSN** 0160-9092
DD 632.951 US
CODEN CSEIDR
CA SELECTS: INSECTICIDES. See Chemistry and Chemicals-Abstracting, Bibliographies and Statistics.

LC QD241 **ISSN** 0749-7318
DD 547 US
CODEN CASHE3
CA SELECTS: NOVEL PESTICIDES & HERBICIDES. See Chemistry and Chemicals-Abstracting, Bibliographies and Statistics.

LC S
DD 630 CN
CAAR COMMUNICATOR. (19??)-. English. Four times a year. 12.01Can$. CAAR Communicator, 1090 Waverly Street, Suite 107, Winnepeg Manitoba R3T 0P4 Canada. **Tel** (204)989-9300. *Continues WFCD Communicator, 0822-8183.*
Desc: Magazine for independent fertilizer and chemical dealers and their suppliers.

LC S
DD 630 US
CAB ABSTRACTS ON CD-ROM [COMPUTER FILE]. **Added/Corp** SilverPlatter Information, Inc. Commonwealth Agricultural Bureaux. **VFOAT** C.A.B. Abstracts; CAB Abstracts on Silverplatter. **VAT** Commonwealth Agricultural Bureaux Abstracts on CD-ROM. Vol. 1 (1984)-. Periodical. English. One time a year. $8000.00 nonmember countries; $6000.00 member countries. CAB International Centre, Wallingford, Oxfordshire OX10 8DE United Kingdom. **Tel** 011 44 1491 832111, FAX 011 44 1491 833508, telex 847964 COMAGG G.

LC S3 .C7
DD 630/.6/01 UK
CAB ANNUAL REPORT. **Main/Corp** Commonwealth Agricultural Bureaux. **VFOAT** C.A.B. Annual Report. (1980/81)-. English. One time a year. CAB International Centre, Wallingford, Oxfordshire OX10 8DE United Kingdom. **Tel** 011 44 1491 832111, FAX 011 44 1491 833508, telex 847964 COMAGG G. *Continues Commonwealth Agricultural Bureaux. Executive Council. Annual Report of the Executive Council.*

LC S **ISSN** 0308-8480
DD 630 UK
CAB INTERNATIONAL NEWS. **Added/Corp** C.A.B. International. **VAT** Commonwealth Agricultural Bureaux International News. (Oct. 1986)-. Periodical. English. Two times a year. Free on request. CAB International Centre, Wallingford, Oxfordshire OX10 8DE United Kingdom. **Tel** 011 44 1491 832111, FAX 011 44 1491 833508, telex 847964 COMAGG G. *Continues CAB News.*

LC S
DD 630 NE
CABO-VERSLAG. **Added/Corp** Centrum voor Agrobiologisch Onderzoek (Netherlands). **VFOAT** Verslagen. **VAT** Centrum voor Agrobiologisch Onderzoek-Verslag. (1977?)-. Monographic series. Dutch (English). *Continues Verslagen (Centrum voor Agrobiologisch Onderzoek (Netherlands)).*
Ind/Abst Crop Physiol. Abstr.; Plant Grow. Reg. Abstr.; Rev. Plant Pathol.; Soyabean Abstr.

LC HD9199.A35 C33
DD 338.1/7373/096 IV
CAFE D'AFRIQUE. See Food and Food Industry-Beverage Industry.

LC S **ISSN** 0525-7951
DD 630 MR
CAHIERS DE LA RECHERCHE AGRONOMIQUE, LES. **Added/Corp** Institut National de la Recherche Agronomique, Rabat. Morocco. Service de la Recherche Agronomique et de l'Experimentation Agricole. Morocco. Service de la Recherche Agronomique et de l'Enseignement Agricole. Morocco. Sous-Direction de la Recherche Agronomique et de l'Enseignement Agricole. Morocco. Direction de la

Recherche Agronomique et de l'Enseignement Agricole. Rabat, Moracco. Centre de Recherches Agronomiques. No. 1 (1948)-. Periodical. French (summaries and/or abstracts in Spanish and English; table of contents in Arabic). Irregular. $40.00. Institut National Recherche Agronomique, BP 415, Avenue de la Victoire, Rabat Morocco. **Tel** 212/74003.
Ind/Abst Field Crop Abstr.; Grass. Forage Abstr.; Hortic. Abstr.; Plant Breed. Abstr.

LC S **ISSN** 0760-579X
DD 630 FR
CAHIERS DE LA RECHERCHE DEVELOPPEMENT, LES. (198?)-. Periodical. French (summaries and/or abstracts in English and Spanish; table of contents in English and Spanish). Four times a year. $65.61. CIRAC CA, Services Editiones, BP 5035, 34032 Montpellier Cedex France. **Tel** 33 1 67615800.
Ind/Abst AGRICOLA; Agrofor. Abstr. (1991-); Anim. Breed. Abstr.; For. Abstr.; Maize Abstr.; Rice Abstr.; Rural Dev. Abstr.; Soils Fert.; Wheat Barley Trit. Abstr.; World Agric. Econ. Rural Sociol. Abstr.

LC S
DD 630 FR
CAHIERS DE STATISTIQUES AGRICOLES. **Main/Corp** France. Service Central des Enquetes et Etudes Statistiques. French. 85.00. Monsieur le Regisseur des Recettes de l'Administration, Centrale du Ministere de l'Agriculture, CCP No 9062, 44 Paris France. ***Continues** Statistique Agricole: Cahiers.*

LC S **ISSN** 0575-0865
DD 630 FR
CODEN CIAGAU
CAHIERS DES INGENIEURS AGRONOMES. (CAHIERS DES INGENIEURS AGROMONES PARIS GRIGNON.). [Cah. ing. agron.]. (1945)-. Periodical. French. Ten times a year. $43.74. Association Anciens Eleves de l'Ina, 5 Quai Voltaire, 75007 Paris France. **Tel** 011 33 1 426002500.
Ind/Abst GeoRef.

LC S **ISSN** 0575-5298
DD 338 US
CALIFORNIA AGRICULTURAL DIRECTORY (BERKELEY, CALIF.). (CALIFORNIA AGRICULTURAL DIRECTORY.). [Calif. agric. dir.]. (1965)-. Directory. English. Every 2 years. $33.00. California Service Agency, 1601 Exposition Boulevard, FB 10, Sacramento CA 95815. **Tel** (916)924-4060, FAX (916)929-1680. **ED** Clark Biggs. **Circ:** 1,000 (ctrl). ***Supersedes** California Agriculture Cooperative Directory.*
Desc: Lists agencies, associations, cooperatives, and organizations concerned with California agriculture.

LC S
DD 630 US
CALIFORNIA AGRICULTURAL EXPORTER. **VFOAT** California Agricultural Export Directory. Vol. 1, No. 1 (Winter 1989)-. Periodical. English. Eight times a year. $16.00; $20.00 other. California Agricultural Statistics Service, California Department of, Food and Agriculture, PO Box 1258, Sacramento CA 95812. **Tel** (916)551-1533. **ED** Richard Van Brackle. **Ad Acc. Circ:** 12,000 (ctrl). ***Continues in part** California Agricultural Export Directory.*
Desc: Provides information for growers, processors, shippers, traders and brokers of agricultural products.

LC HF1371 **ISSN** 1064-9670
DD 382 US
CALIFORNIA AGRICULTURAL EXPORTS ANNUAL BULLETIN AND STATISTICAL APPENDIX. [Calif. agric. exports annu. bull. stat. append.]. **Added/Corp** California. Dept. of Food and Agriculture. **VFOAT** Annual Bulletin and Statistical Appendix. (1992)-. Bulletin. English. One time a year (August). $39.00. Worldtariff, 220 Montgomery Street, Suite 432, San Francisco CA 94104-3410. **Tel** (415)391-7501, FAX (415)391-7537. **ED** Scott D. Morse. ***Formed by the union of** California Agricultural Exports **and** California Agricultural Exports Appendix.*
Desc: Tables and analysis of California State agricultural export totals, products, and foreign markets. Published in cooperation with the California Department of Food & Agriculture.

LC S1 .C15 **ISSN** 0008-0845
DD 630.72 US
CODEN CAGRA3
Pr Rev.
CALIFORNIA AGRICULTURE (BERKELEY, CALIF.). (CALIFORNIA AGRICULTURE.). [Calif. agric.]. **Added/Corp** University of California (System). Division of Agricultural Sciences. California Agricultural Experiment Station. Vol. 1 (Dec. 1946)-. Periodical. English. Six times a year (Jan., Mar., May, July, Sept., Nov.). Free on request. California Agriculture, 300 Lakeside Drive, Subs Department, Oakland CA 94612. Index available (Bound in next issue, in Nov/Dec.). **Circ:** 20,000. Documents available from BIOSIS Document Express, CASDDS, Documents on Demand.
Desc: Reports of progress in research by the Division of Agriculture and Natural Resources, University of California.
Ind/Abst AGRICOLA [Full Cov.]; Agric. Eng. Abstr.; Agrofor. Abstr.; BioBusiness; Biocont. News Inf.; Biodeter. Abstr. (1946-1983); Biol. Abstr.; Calif. Period. Index; Calif. Period. Microfi.; Chem. Abstr. (1946-1983); Cot. Trop. Fibr. Abstr. Bibliogr.; Curr. Cit.; Dairy Sci. Abstr.; EMBASE; Entomol. Abstr.; Environ. Abstr.; Field Crop Abstr.; Food Sci. Technol. Abstr.; For. Prod. Abstr.; For. Abstr.; Health Saf. Sci. Abstr.; INIS Atomindex [Micro.]; Irr. Drain. Abstr.; Nematol. Abstr.; Nutr. Abstr. Rev., Ser. B, Live Feeds and Feed.; Ornamental Hort.; Life Sci. Collect.; PESTDOC; Plant Breed. Abstr.; Plant Grow. Reg. Abstr.; Pollut. Abstr. Indexes (-1990); Rev. Plant Pathol.; Rice Abstr.; Risk Abstr.; Soils Fert.; Sorghum Mill. Abstr.; Vitis Vitic. Enol. Abstr.; Weed Abstr.

LC S **ISSN** 0164-5331
DD 630 US
CALIFORNIA-ARIZONA FARM PRESS. **VAT** California Arizona Farm Press. Vol. 1 (Jan. 9, 1979)-. Trade Publication. English. Forty-two times a year. $30.00. California-Arizona Farm Press, 6151 Powers Ferry Road Northwest, Atlanta GA 30339. **Tel** (800)253-3160, FAX (404)618-0345.

LC S
DD 630 US
CALIFORNIA CERTIFIED ORGANIC FARMERS CERTIFICATION HANDBOOK. (1991)-. Periodical. English.

LC SB354 **ISSN** 1041-7028
DD 634 US
CALIFORNIA EUCALYPTUS GROWER. (CALIFORNIA EUCALYPTUS GROWER : NEWSLETTER OF THE EUCALYPTUS IMPROVEMENT ASSOCIATION.). **Added/Corp** Eucalyptus Improvement Association. Vol. 4, No. 1 (Jan. 1989)-. Periodical. English. Four times a year. $10.00. California Eucalyptus Improvement Association, PO Box 4460, Davis CA 95617. **Tel** (913)753-4535. ***Continues** Newsletter (Eucalyptus Improvement Association), 0892-7405.*

LC S **ISSN** 0008-1051
DD 630 US
CALIFORNIA FARMER. (Jan. 16, 1960)-. Periodical. English. Nineteen times a year (publishes twice a month except May, June, July, Aug. and Dec.). $30.00. Farm Progress Publishing, 191 South Gary Avenue, Carol Stream IL 60188-2089. **Tel** (708)462-2890 or 2891. **(Subscription address:** CDS / SIFD Agency Control, 1901 Bell Avenue, Des Moines IA 50315. **Tel** (515)246-6812.**)** **ED** Len Richardson. **Ad Acc. Circ:** 56,633. Documents available from Documents on Demand. ***Continues** Arizona Farmer Stockman.*
Desc: Edited to serve the interests of agriculture in matters affecting the state's agriculture economy. Coverage of major crops is provided on growing, harvesting, distribution and marketing.
Ind/Abst Calif. Period. Index (19??-); Environ. Abstr.

LC S **ISSN** 0279-263X
DD 630 US
CALIFORNIA FRUIT & NUT REVIEW. **VAT** California Fruit and Nut Review. Vol. 1, No. 1 (July 15, 1981)-. English. Twelve times a year. $10.00 US; $20.00 other. California Agricultural Statistics Service, California Department of, Food and Agriculture, PO Box 1258, Sacramento CA 95812. **Tel** (916)551-1533.
Desc: Grape, citrus, deciduous, and nut acreage, production, price and utilization.

LC S **ISSN** 0008-1108
DD 630 US
UDC 338.1:63(794)
CALIFORNIA FUTURE FARMER. [Calif. future farmer]. Vol. 1 (March 1932)-. Periodical. English. Four times a year. Bureau of Agricultural Education, California Polytechnic State University, San Luis Obispo CA 93401.

LC S **ISSN** 0008-1124
DD 630 US
CALIFORNIA GRANGE NEWS. **See** Newspapers.

LC S **ISSN** 0279-4551
DD 630 US
UDC 638.14.06; 339.13:638.16(794)
CALIFORNIA HONEY REPORT. (CALIFORNIA HONEY REPORT / FEDERAL-STATE MARKET NEWS SERVICE.). [Calif. honey rep.]. Periodical. English. Twelve times a year. $15.00 US; $30.00 other. Federal-State Market News Service, 1220 N Street, Suite 216, Box 942871, Sacramento CA 94271-0001. **Tel** (916)654-0298, FAX (916)654-1046.
Desc: Covers prices and market situation, exports and imports.

LC S **ISSN** 0279-2613
DD 630 US
CALIFORNIA VEGETABLE REVIEW. English. Twelve times a year. $10.00 US; $20.00 other. California Agricultural Statistics Service, California Department of, Food and Agriculture, PO Box 1258, Sacramento CA 95812. **Tel** (916)551-1533.
Desc: Processing and fresh market vegetable, potato, berry acreage, production, and value.

LC S19 .C33 **ISSN** 0527-4257
DD 630/.967/11 CM
UDC 63(671.1)
CAMEROUN AGRICOLE, PASTORAL ET FORESTIER, LE. [Cameroun agric. pastor. for.]. (19??)-. Periodical. French (English). Twelve times a year.
Ind/Abst AGRICOLA.

LC S
DD 630 CL
UDC 63(83)
CAMPESINO, EL. Vol. 1 (Oct. 16, 1869)-. Periodical. Spanish. Irregular. $25.00 US. Sociedad Nacional Agricultura Tenderini, 187 Casilla 40-D, Santiago Chile. **Tel** 396710, telex 240760 SNA CL. **Bk Rev. Ad Acc. Circ:** 10,000 (ctrl).
Desc: Covers plant production, animal production, plant physiology, agriculture news and flower production.

LC S **ISSN** 0212-2146
DD 630 SP
CAMPO, EL. [Campo]. No. 13 (Feb. 1969)-. Periodical. Spanish. Six times a year.

LC S **ISSN** 0008-2473
DD 630 MX
CAMPO; REVISTA MENSUAL AGRICOLA Y GANADERA. (1924)-. Periodical. Spanish. Twelve times a year. $20.00. EL Campo, Mar Negro 147, Apartado Postal 17 506, Mexico 17 DF Mexico. **Tel** 011 52 7 4554.

LC HF1371 **ISSN** 1190-9706
DD 382 CN
•**CANADA'S EXPORT STRATEGY, THE INTERNATIONAL TRADE BUSINESS PLAN. 2, AGRICULTURE AND FOOD PRODUCTS.** [Can. export strategy int. trade bus. plan, 2 Agric. food prod.]. **Added/Corp** Canada. **VFOAT** Agriculture and Food Products. (1996)-. Government Publication. English. ***Continues** Canada's International Trade Business Plan. 3, Agri-Food Products, 1200-1104.*

LC S **ISSN** 0045-432X
DD 630 CN
CCC
CODEN CAEOAI
Pr Rev.
CANADIAN AGRICULTURAL ENGINEERING. [Can. agric. eng.]. **Added/Corp** Canadian Society of Agricultural Engineering. (Jan. 1959)-. Periodical. English (French). Four times a year. 45.00Can$. Canadian Society of Agricultural Engineering, PO Box 306, RPO University, Saskatoon Saskatoon S7N 4J8 Canada. **Tel** (306)966-5335, FAX (306)966-5334. **(Subscription address:** American Society of Agricultural Engineering, 2950 Niles Road, St. Joseph MI 49085. **Tel** (616)429-0300.**)** **ED** E. McKyes. **Circ:** 1,000. Documents available from Article Express International, The Genuine Article, BIOSIS Document Express, CASDDS.
Desc: Scientific research on agricultural engineering machinery, equipment, structures and processes.
Ind/Abst AgBiotech News Inf.; AGRICOLA [Full Cov.]; Agric. Eng. Abstr. (1991-); BioBusiness; Biodeter. Abstr. (1991-); Bioeng. Abstr.; Biol. Abstr.; Chem. Abstr. (1959-1982); Curr. Cit.; Curr. Contents Agric. Biol. Environ. Sci.; Curr. Contents Eng. Comput. Technol.; Dairy Sci. Abstr.; Ei Page One; EMBASE; Eng. Index Annu. [Select. Cov.]; Field Crop Abstr.; Food Sci. Technol. Abstr.; Grass. Forage Abstr.; Hortic. Abstr.; Index Vet.; Irr. Drain. Abstr.; Maize Abstr.; Ornamental Hort. (19??-19??); Pig News Inf.; Plant Breed. Abstr.; Postharvest News Inf.; Potato Abstr.; Res. Alert [Full Cov.]; Rev. Agric. Entomol.; Rev. Med. Vet. Mycology; Rev. Plant Pathol.; Rice Abstr.; Sci. Cit. Index; SCISEARCH; Seed Abstr.; Weed Abstr.; Wheat Barley Trit. Abstr.

LC S **ISSN** 0068-8185
DD 630 CN
UDC 632.7
CODEN CAIPA7
CANADIAN AGRICULTURAL INSECT PEST REVIEW, THE. [Can. agric. insect pest rev.]. **VFOAT** La Revue Canadienne des Insectes Nuisibles aux Cultures. Vol. 46 (1968)-. English (French). One time a year. Free on request. Research Program Service, Canadian Department of Agriculture, Ottawa Ontario K1A 0C6 Canada. Documents available from BIOSIS Document Express. ***Continues** Canadian Insect Pest Review, 0374-7018.*
Ind/Abst Biol. Abstr.; Maize Abstr.

LC S **ISSN** 0008-2961
DD 630 CN
CANADIAN AYRSHIRE REVIEW. **Added/Corp** Ayrshire Breeders' Association of Canada. Canadian Ayrshire Breeders' Association. (May 1920)-. Periodical. English (French). Ten times a year. 25.00Can$. Ayrshire Breeders Association of Canada, PO Box 188, St. Ann-de-Bellevue Quebec H9X 3V9 Canada. **Tel** (514)398-7970, FAX (514)398-7972. **ED**

Agriculture

Patrice Prevost, (editor's address: 21 111 Lakeshore Road, Ste-Anne-de-Bellevue, Quebec, CN H9X 3V9). **Ad Acc. Circ:** 1,800 (ctrl).
 Desc: Intended to keep members informed of breed programs, cattle sales, exhibitions and news related to the Ayrshire breed and dairy cattle farming.

LC SF191   **ISSN** 0576-4688
DD 636.2   CN
CANADIAN BEEKEEPING. [Can. beekeep.].
(July 1968)-. Periodical. English. Twelve times a year. $18.69 US; 20.00Can$ Canada; $37.38 other. Canadian Beekeeping, Box 676, Tottenham Ontario L0G 1W0 Canada. **Tel** (416)983-9372, FAX (416)623-6161. **ED** William Arnott. **Bk Rev. Ad Acc, Adv Mgr:** WJR Arnott.
 Desc: Contains information on the beekeeping industry in Canada.

LC SF191   **ISSN** 1198-5135
DD 636.2   CN
●CANADIAN ELK & DEER FARMER, THE.
[Can. elk deer farmer]. **Added/Corp** Canadian Venison Council. **VFOAT** Canadian Elk and Deer Farmer. Vol. 1, No. 1 (Spring 1994)-. Periodical. English. Four times a year. 37.40Can$. Canadian Elk and Deer Farmer, 3016 19th Street Northeast, Suite 205, Calgary Alberta T2E 6Y9 Canada.

LC KE5270.F37 N37   **ISSN** 0700-1320
DD 343.71/078690892 347.10378690892   CN
CANADIAN FARM BUILDING CODE. See
Building and Construction.

LC KE5600   **ISSN** 0823-6089
DD 343.7105/2   CN
CANADIAN FARMTAX. See Finance-Taxation.

LC S
DD 630   CN
CANADIAN PAPERS IN RURAL HISTORY.
Vol. 1 (1978)-. Monographic series. English. Every 2 years. 36.02Can$. Langdale Press, Rural Route 1, Gananoque Ontario K7G 2V3 Canada. **ED** DH Akenson. **Circ:** 1,000.
 Ind/Abst Am. Hist. Life (1978-).

LC S   **ISSN** 0317-6401
DD 630   CN
CANADIAN PLAINS PROCEEDINGS. See
History-History of North and South America.

LC HF5410   **ISSN** 0715-3651
DD 380.1/4/3853/0971   CN
CANOLA DIGEST. [Canola dig.]. Added/Corp
Canola Council of Canada. Vol. 14, No. 6 (June 1980)-. Periodical. English. Six times a year. 24.01Can$. Canola Council of Canada, 400 167 Lombard Avenue, Winnipeg Manitoba R3B OT6 Canada. **Tel** (204)982-2100. **ED** Dawn Harris. **Circ:** 1,000. **Continues** Canola-Rapeseed Digest, 0715-3643.
 Desc: Topics of interest to canola producers, growers and anyone in the canola industry.

LC S   **ISSN** 0953-5586
DD 630   UK
CAP LEGISLATION. See Law.

LC S   **ISSN** 0142-5633
DD 630   UK
CAP MONITOR. [CAP monit.]. VFOAT Common
Agricultural Policy Monitor. (1979)-. Trade Publication. English. Irregular. $1232.07. Agra Europe London Limited, 25 Front Road, Tunbridge Wells, Kent TN2 5JT United Kingdom. **Tel** 011 44 1892 533813, FAX 011 44 1892 544895, telex 95114 AGRATW G.

LC S
DD 630   UK
CAP MONITOR UPDATES. (19??)-. Periodical.
English. £460.00 UK; £480.00 Europe; £525.00 other. Agra Europe London Limited, 25 Front Road, Tunbridge Wells, Kent TN2 5JT United Kingdom. **Tel** 011 44 1892 533813, FAX 011 44 1892 544895, telex 95114 AGRATW G.

LC HD   **ISSN** 0953-5594
DD 338.181   UK
TITLE CHANGE
CAP WEEKLY. [CAP wkly]. (1987)-(19??). Trade
Publication. English. Agra Europe London Limited, 25 Front Road, Tunbridge Wells, Kent TN2 5JT United Kingdom. **Tel** 011 44 1892 533813, FAX 011 44 1892 544895, telex 95114 AGRATW G. available on an online database (file 636/Full-Text) from DIALOG. **Continues** Agra Europe. Express Monitor, 0951-2063. **Absorbed by** CAP Legislation.
 Ind/Abst PTS Newsl. Database [Full Txt.].

LC S
DD 630   US
●CARBON FORMS FUNCTIONS IN FOREST SOIL.
(1995)-. English. Soil Science Society of America, 677 South Segoe Road, Madison WI 53711. **Tel** (608)273-8080, FAX (608)273-2021.

LC HD1401   **ISSN** 0886-3970
DD 338   US
CARD REPORT (AMES, IOWA. 1986).
(CARD REPORT.). [CARD rep.]. **Added/Corp** Iowa State University. Center for Agricultural and Rural Development. **VAT** Center for Agricultural and Rural Development Report. Vol. 1, No. 1 (Oct. 1986)-. Periodical. English. Four times a year. Iowa State University Center for Agricultural & Rural Development, 578 Heady Hall, Ames IA 50011. **Tel** (515)294-7519. **Continues** CARD Report.
 Desc: Periodical of policy research from the Center for Agricultural and Rural Development.

LC S
DD 630   US
CARD WORKING PAPER SERIES. VFOAT
CARD Working Paper; Working Paper. No. 86-WP1 (1986)-. Monographic series. English. Price varies per volume. Iowa State University Center for Agricultural & Rural Development, 578 Heady Hall, Ames IA 50011. **Tel** (515)294-7519.
 Ind/Abst Field Crop Abstr.; Maize Abstr.; Potato Abstr.; Poult. Abstr.; Soils Fert.; Soyabean Abstr.

LC S
DD 630   US
CARGILL BULLETIN. (June 1982)-. Bulletin.
English. Twelve times a year. $12.00, one-year; $22.00, two-year; Cargill Bulletin, PO Box 5625, Minneapolis MN 55440. **Tel** (612)742-6218, FAX (612)742-6208, telex 290625. **ED** Linda Thrane. **Circ:** 8,000. **Continues** Cargill Crop Bulletin.
 Desc: Reviewing current domestic and international market conditions and public policy questions involving agriculture and world trade.

LC S   **ISSN** 0744-2033
DD 630   US
UDC 631/635(756)
CAROLINA FARMER (NORTH CAROLINA ED.). (CAROLINA FARMER.).
Periodical. English. Twelve times a year. Carolina Farmer, PO Box 13269, Greensboro NC 27415. **Tel** (919)621-1446. **ED** Bob Garsson.

LC S583   **ISSN** 0890-7528
DD 631   US
   CODEN CBAGEJ
CAS BIOTECH UPDATES. AGRICULTURE. [CAS bioTech updates, Agric.].
Added/Corp American Chemical Society. Chemical Abstracts Service. **VAT** Agriculture. CAS Chemical Abstracts Service BioTech Updates. Agriculture. Issue 1 (Jan. 12, 1987)-. Periodical. English. Twenty-six times a year. $220.00. Chemical Abstracts Service, (Subsidiary of The American Chemical Society), 2540 Olentangy River Road, PO Box 3012, Columbus OH 43210-0012. **Tel** (614)447-3731, (800)753-4227, FAX (614)447-3751. **(Subscription address:** Chemical Abstracts Service, Customer Service Department, PO Box 3012, Columbus OH 43210. **Tel** (800)848-6538, (614)447-3600.)

LC S
DD 630   UK
CAS PAPER. Added/Corp University of Reading.
Centre for Agricultural Strategy. **VAT** Centre for Agricultural Strategy Paper. (1977)-. Monographic series. English.
 Ind/Abst Index Vet.; Nematol. Abstr.; Nutr. Abstr. Rev., Ser. A, Hum. Exp.; Pig News Inf.; Rev. Agric. Entomol.; Soils Fert.; Vet. Bull.

LC S
DD 630   UK
CAS REPORT. Added/Corp University of Reading.
Centre for Agricultural Strategy. (1976)-. Monographic series. English.
 Ind/Abst World Agric. Econ. Rural Sociol. Abstr.

LC S   **ISSN** 0970-2423
DD 630   II
UDC 634.573
CASHEW COCHIN. (THE CASHEW.). [Cashew Cochin].
VFOAT Di Kaissyu. (1987)-. Periodical. English. Four times a year. $25.00. Directorate of Cashew Development, Karimpatta Cross Road, Cochin 682016 India. **Tel** 011 91 484 682011. **(Subscription address:** UBS Publishers Distributors, 5 Ansari Road, PO Box 7015, New Delhi 110 002 India. **Tel** 011 91 11 3273601, 011 91 11 3266645.) **Circ:** 500. **Continues** Cashew Causerie, 0970-1818.
 Desc: Contains scientific articles on different aspects of cashews.

LC NOT IN LC   **ISSN** 0970-2423
   II
CASHEW = DI KAISYU, THE. Added/Corp
India. Directorate of Cashewnut Development. **VFOAT** Kaisyu. (19??)-. Periodical. English (Hindi). Four times a year. $25.00. Directorate of Cashew Development, Karimpatta Cross Road, Cochin 682016 India. **Tel** 011 91 484 682011.

LC S
DD 630   CK
Pr Rev.
●CASSAVA BIBLIOGRAPHIC BULLETIN.
(1994)-. Bulletin. Spanish. Four times a year. $20.00. Centro Internacional de Agricultura Tropical, Apartado Aereo 67-13, Cali Colombia. **Tel** 57 23 4450000, FAX 57 23 4450273, telex 05769 CIAT CO. **Acid Free. Circ:** 3,000 (ctrl).
 Desc: Markets current bibliographic information on Cassava available to researchers, extensionists, and producers.

LC HC59.69 .C37   **ISSN** 0904-4698
DD 330.9172/4   DK
CDR PROJECT PAPER. Added/Corp Centret
for Udviklingsforskning (Denmark). **VFOAT** CDR Project Papers. **VAT** Centre for Development Research Project Paper. (19??)-. Monographic series. English. Centre for Development Research, Gammel Kongeuej 5, DK-1610 Copenhagen Denmark. **Tel** 011 45 33 251200, FAX 011 45 33 258110. **Continues** CDR Project Papers. A, 0106-0805.
 Ind/Abst Wheat Barley Trit. Abstr.; World Agric. Econ. Rural Sociol. Abstr.

LC S   **ISSN** 0008-8692
DD 630   HO
   CODEN CEIBAR
CEIBA. [CEIBA]. Added/Corp Escuela Agricola
Panamericana. (Jan. 23, 1950)-. English. Two times a year. $20.00. Escuela Agricola Panamericana, Apartado 93, Tegucigalpa Honduras. **Tel** 011 504 322660. Documents available from BIOSIS Document Express, CASDDS.
 Ind/Abst Anim. Breed. Abstr.; Biocont. News Inf.; Biol. Abstr.; Chem. Abstr.; Field Crop Abstr.; For. Abstr.; Helminthol. Abstr. (1991-); Nutr. Abstr. Rev., Ser. B, Live Feeds and Feed.; Pig News Inf.; Rev. Agric. Entomol.; Seed Abstr.; Sorghum Mill. Abstr.; Weed Abstr.

LC S
DD 630   CY
CENSUS OF AGRICULTURE (1985).
English. One time a year. £8.00 Cyprus; £10.00 other. Department of Statistics and Research / Cyprus, 13 Lord Byron Avenue, Nicosia 162 Cyprus. **Tel** 011 357 2 303286. Index available. **Circ:** 400.
 Desc: Results of the census refer to the structure of farms, areas planted, livestock numbers, employment on farms, machinery used, etc.

LC S
DD 630   US
CENSUS OF AGRICULTURE. V. 3. AGRICULTURAL SERVICES. Added/Corp
United States. Bureau of the Census. (1969)-. Government Publication. English. Irregular. US Department of Commerce / Bureau of the Census, Data User Services Division, Customer Services, Washington DC 20233-0800. **Tel** (301)763-4100. **(Subscription address:** Superintendent of Documents, US Government Printing Office, Washington DC 20402.)

LC S
DD 630   US
CENTER FOR RURAL AFFAIRS NEWSLETTER.
Newsletter. English. Twelve times a year. Free (donations accepted annually). Center for Rural Affairs, 101 South Taliman, PO Box 405, Walthill NE 68067. **Tel** (402)846-5428. **ED** Marty Strange. **Circ:** 7,000.
 Desc: Information for small family farms, farm legislation, rural development opportunity and world agricultural issues.

LC S   **ISSN** 0253-5785
DD 630   CU
   CODEN CEAGD5
CENTRO AGRICOLA. [Cent. agric.]. Vol. 1
(1974)-. Academic Scholarly Publication. Spanish (summaries and/or abstracts in English; table of contents in English). Four times a year. Ediciones Cubanas, Obispo 527 Altos ESQ Bernaza, CP 10100 Havana Cuba. Documents available from BIOSIS Document Express, CASDDS.
 Ind/Abst Agrofor. Abstr.; Biocont. News Inf.; Biodeter. Abstr.; Biol. Abstr.; Chem. Abstr.; Field Crop Abstr.; Hortic. Abstr.; Maize Abstr.; Nematol. Abstr.; Plant Breed. Abstr.; Plant Grow. Reg. Abstr.; Potato Abstr.; Rev. Agric. Entomol.; Rev. Plant Pathol.; Rice Abstr.; Seed Abstr.; Soils Fert.; Soyabean Abstr.; Sug. Indus. Abstr.; Weed Abstr.

LC HN980 .F66a   **ISSN** 0009-0379
DD 909/.09724   IT
NLM W1 CE585   **CODEN** CERSBM
CERES (ROME, ENGLISH EDITION).
(CERES.). [Ceres]. **Added/Corp** Food and Agriculture Organization of the United Nations. Vol. 1, No. 2 (March/April 1968)-. Periodical. English (French, Arabic and Spanish). Six times a year. L30000. Food Agriculture Organization (FAO) / Italy, GIPCI66 via Terme di Caracalla, 00100 Rome Italy. **Tel** 011 39 6 52252925, FAX 011 39 6 52253152. available on microfilm and microfiche from University Microfilms International (UMI). Documents available from UMI Article Clearinghouse, Documents on Demand. **Continues** FAO Review.

Desc: A general review of FAO policies and activities presented in an attractive, accessible format with illustrations.
Ind/Abst Agric. Eng. Abstr.; Agrofor. Abstr.; BioBusiness (1991-); Environ. Abstr.; Expand. Acad. Index (1992-); Field Crop Abstr.; For. Prod. Abstr.; For. Abstr.; Grass. Forage Abstr.; Hum. Rights Intern. Rep.; Index Vet.; Int. Dev. Abstr.; Int. Labour Doc.; Leis., Rec., Tour. Abstr.; Newsp. Period. Abstr. (1989-); Nutr. Abstr. Rev., Ser. B, Live Feeds and Feed.; Nutr. Abstr. Rev., Ser. A, Hum. Exp.; PAIS Int. Print (1991-); Life Sci. Collect.; Plant Breed. Abstr.; Rev. Med. Vet. Entomol.; Rice Abstr.; Rural Dev. Abstr.; Soils Fert.; World Agric. Econ. Rural Sociol. Abstr.

LC S **ISSN** 0379-5837
DD 630 RM
CERETARI AGRONOMICE IN MOLDOVA. (CERCETARI AGRONOMICE IN MOLDOVA / ACADEMIA DE STIINTE AGRICOLE SI SILVICE.). [Ceret. agron. Mold.]. **Added/Corp** Academia de Stiinte Agricole si Silvice. Vol. 1 (1978)-. Romanian (summaries and/or abstracts in French; table of contents in English, French and Russian). Editura Academia Republicii Socialiste Romania, Calea Victoriei Nr 125, R-79717 Bucuresti Romania. **Tel** telex 10376 PRSFI R.
Ind/Abst Agric. Eng. Abstr. (1991-); Biocont. News Inf.; Dairy Sci. Abstr.; Field Crop Abstr.; Grass. Forage Abstr.; Hortic. Abstr.; Maize Abstr.; Nematol. Abstr.; Ornamental Hort. (1991-); Plant Breed. Abstr.; Plant Grow. Reg. Abstr.; Potato Abstr.; Seed Abstr.; Soils Fert.; Vitis Vitic. Enol. Abstr.; Weed Abstr.; Wheat Barley Trit. Abstr.; World Agric. Econ. Rural Sociol. Abstr.

LC S
DD 630 XR
CESKE A MORAVSKOSLEZSKE ZEMEDELSKE NOVINY. VFOAT Zemedelske Noviny; ZN. Vol. 1 No. 1 (1991)-. Periodical. Czech. Seven times a week. DM350.00. **(Subscription address:** Kubon & Sagner, ABT Zeitschriftenimport, D 80328 Munich Germany. **Tel** 011 49 89 54218130.) ***Continues*** *Zemedelske Noviny.*
Ind/Abst PROMT.

LC S
DD 630 US
•**CFSA COMMODITY FACT SHEET. HONEY. Added/Corp** United States. Consolidated Farm Service Agency. **VFOAT** Consolidated Farm Service Agency Commodity Fact Sheet. Honey; Honey. (1995)-. English. US Department of Agriculture / Agricultural Stabilization and Conservation, 14th and Independence Avenue SW, Washington DC 20250. ***Continues*** *FSA Commodity Fact Sheet. Honey.*

LC SB272.J25 J37A
DD 633.7 JA
CHA TOKEI NEMPO. Main/Corp Japan. Norinsho. Norin Keizaikyoku. Tokei Johobu. (19??)-. Japanese. Norin Keizaikyoku, 1 Kasumigaseki 2 Chiyoda-ku, Tokyo Japan. ***Continues*** *Cha Chosa Hokokusho.*
Desc: Information on the tea industry.

LC S
DD 630 AG
CHACRA & CAMPO MODERNO. Vol. 524 (July 1974)-. Periodical. Spanish. Twelve times a year. Editorial Atlantida SA, Azopado 579, 1307 Buenos Aires Argentina. **Tel** 33 4591. ***Continues*** *Chacra.*

LC S **ISSN** 0396-7883
DD 630 FR
CHAMBRES D'AGRICULTURE. [Chamb. agric.]. (1938)-. Periodical. French. Irregular. APPCA Service de l'Enseignement Etdela, 9 Avenue Geor, 75008 Paris France. ***Continues*** *Travaux des Chambres d'Agriculture.*
Ind/Abst Agric. Eng. Abstr.; Dairy Sci. Abstr.; Index Vet.; Int. Labour Doc.; Maize Abstr.; Poult. Abstr.; Wheat Barley Trit. Abstr.; World Agric. Econ. Rural Sociol. Abstr.

LC TA501 .R6 Suppl
DD 338.1/0941 UK
CHARTERED SURVEYOR: RURAL QUARTERLY. See Engineering-Civil Engineering.

LC S
DD 630 US
CHAUTAUQUA COUNTY AGRICULTURAL NEWS. Vol. 51, No. 1 (Jan. 1967)-. Periodical. English. Twelve times a year. Cooperative Extension Association of Chautauqua County, Road 2 Turner Road, Jamestown NY 14701. ***Continues*** *Chautauqua Farm and Home News.*

LC S **ISSN** 0528-9017
DD 630 CC
CHEJIANG NONGYE KEXUE. (CHE-CHIANG NUNG YEH KO HSUEH.). **Added/Corp** Che-Chiang Sheng Nung Yeh ko Hsueh Yuan. Che-Chiang Nung Yeh ta Hsueh. **VFOAT** Zhejiang Nongye Kexue. (1961)-. Academic Scholarly Publication. Chinese. Six times a year. Zhejiang Nongye Kexueyuan, Zhejiang Academy of Agricultural Science, 48 Shiqiao Lu Hangzhou, Zhejiang 310021 People's Republic of China. **Tel** 42701. **ED** Z. Jiefang.
Ind/Abst Hortic. Abstr.; Postharvest News Inf.

LC S583-587.5
DD 631 GW
CHEMIE UND TECHNIK IN DER LANDWIRTSCHAFT : DER RARGEBER FUER DIE GENOSSENCHAFTLICHE WARENVERMITTLUNG. Added/Corp Deutsche Raiffeisen-Warenzentrale. (19??)-. Academic Scholarly Publication. German. Twelve times a year.
Ind/Abst EMBASE.

LC S19 .C4857
DD 630/.5 CC
CHIANG-SU NUNG HSUEH YUAN HSUEH PAO. Added/Corp Chiang-su Nung Hsueh Yuan. **VFOAT** Jiangsu Nongxueyuan Xuebao; Journal of Jiangsu Agricultural College. (19??)-. Periodical. Chinese (summaries and/or abstracts in English). Four times a year. Jiangsu Academy of Agricultural Sciences, Nanjing 210014, People's Republic of China.
Ind/Abst Crop Physiol. Abstr.; Field Crop Abstr.; Helminthol. Abstr. (1991-); Maize Abstr.; Plant Breed. Abstr.; Rice Abstr.; Seed Abstr.

LC S471.J32 C463 **ISSN** 0577-6880
DD 630.95 JA
CHIBA-KEN NOGYO SHIKENJO KENKYU HOKOKU. Added/Corp Chiba-Ken Nogyo Shikenjo. **VFOAT** Chiba Ken Nogyo Shikenjo Kenkyu Hokoku; Bulletin of the Chiba-Ken Agricultural Experiment Station; Bulletin of the Chiba Ken Agricultural Experiment Station. (1953)-. Bulletin. Japanese. Do Shinkenjo, Chiba-Ken Nogyo Shinkenjo, 808-Banchi, Daizenno-Machi, Chiba-Shi 280-02 Japan.
Ind/Abst Agrofor. Abstr.; Hortic. Abstr.; Rev. Plant Pathol.; Rice Abstr.; Seed Abstr.; Soils Fert.; Weed Abstr.; Wheat Barley Trit. Abstr.

LC S
DD 630 HK
CHINA AGRIBUSINESS REPORT. English. Twenty-six times a year. $595.00. China Agribusiness Report, PO Box 92619, Worldway Post Center, Los Angeles CA 90009. **Tel** (852)5262950, FAX (852)5267131, telex 4X61166 HKNW. **ED** Charles Smith. **Bk Rev.**
Desc: Comprehensive coverage of the agribusiness sector of China's biggest and most important economic sector.

LC S277 .C48
DD 338.1/0951 CC
CHINA AGRICULTURE YEARBOOK. VFOAT Chung-kuo Nung Yeh Nien Chien. (1985)-. Trade Publication. English (Chinese). One time a year. $29.50. **(Subscription address:** China International Book Trading Corporation, PO Box 399, Library Service Department, Beijing 100044 People's Republic of China. **Tel** 011 86 1 8414284, FAX 011 86 1 8412023, telex 22496 CIBTC CN.)

LC S
DD 630 US
UDC 63(51)
CHINA REPORT. AGRICULTURE. VFOAT Agriculture. No. 46 (July 3, 1979)-. Trade Publication. English (translations available in Chinese). available on microfiche (Vols. for (Dec. 10, 1986-) distributed to depository libraries). ***Continues*** *People's Republic of China. Agriculture.*

LC S **ISSN** 0009-4919
DD 630 PL
UDC 621.56/.59
CHODNICTWO. [Chodnictwo]. (1966)-. Periodical. Polish. Twelve times a year. Price on request. **(Subscription address:** Ars Polona-Ruch, PO Box 1001, Krakowskie Przedmiescie 7, 00-068 Warsaw Poland. **Tel** 011 48 22 261201.)
Ind/Abst Postharvest News Inf.

LC HD1401 **ISSN** 0886-5558
DD 338 US
CHOICES (AMES, IOWA). (CHOICES.). [Choices]. **Added/Corp** American Agricultural Economics Association. 1st Quarter (1986)-. Periodical. English. Four times a year. $20.00. American Agricultural Economics Association, 1110 Buckeye Avenue, Ames IA 50011. **Tel** (515)233-3202, FAX (515)233-3101. **ED** Lyle P. Schertz. **Ad Acc. Circ:** 14,000.
Desc: Magazine of food, farm and resource issues.
Ind/Abst Acad. Search; AGRICOLA [Full Cov.]; EP Collect.; Homework Help.; MasterFile FullTEXT 1000; MasterFile FullTEXT 350; MasterFile FullTEXT 650; MasterFile FullTEXT (Jan. 1993-); OCLC; Telebase; Vocat. Search.

LC S19 .C49
DD 630 KO
CHON'GUK TAEHAKSAENG HAKSUL YON'GU PALPYO NONMUNJIP: NONGSUSAN, HAEYANGHAK PUNYA. Added/Corp Chonbuk Taehakkyo Hakto Hoguktan. Vol. 1, Series (1977)-. Periodical. Korean (summaries and/or abstracts in English). Chonbuk Taehakkyo Hakto Hoguktan, 53 3-ka Myongyun-dong, Chongno-U Seoul South Korea.

LC S **ISSN** 0137-9070
DD 630 PL
UDC 631(438)
CODEN 338(438)
CHOPSKA DROGA. (1945)-. Periodical. Polish. One time a week. $52.00. **(Subscription address:** Ars Polona-Ruch, PO Box 1001, Krakowskie Przedmiescie 7, 00-068 Warsaw Poland. **Tel** 011 48 22 261201.)

LC S **ISSN** 0913-4239
DD 630 JA
CHUGOKU NOGYO SHIKENJO KENKYU HOKOKU. [Chugoku Nogyo Shikenjo Kenkyu Hokoku]. **VFOAT** Bulletin of the Chugoku National Agricultural Experiment Station. (1987)-. Bulletin. Multiple languages. One time a year. Noein Suisansho Chugoku Nogyo Shikenjo, (Chugoku National Agricultural Experiment Station Ministry of Agriculture Forestry & Fisheries), 12-1 Nishifukatsucho 6 Chome, Fukuyamashi Hiroshimaken 721 Japan. ***Formed by the union of*** *Chugoku Nogyo Shikenjo Hokoku. A, Sakumotsubu, 0366-7227; Chugoku Nogyo Shikenjo Hokoku. B, Chikusanbu, 0366-7464; Chugoku Nogyo Shikenjo Hokoku. C, Nogyo Keieibu, 0385-6550; Chugoku Nogyo Shikenjo Hokoku. D, Kikaku Renrakushitsu, Kaku-bu, 0385-6569* ***and*** *Chugoku Nogyo Shikenjo Hokoku. E, Kankyobu, 0366-726X.*
Ind/Abst Agric. Eng. Abstr.; Crop Physiol. Abstr.; Rice Abstr.; Seed Abstr.; Soils Fert.; World Agric. Econ. Rural Sociol. Abstr.

LC S562.J3 J32a
DD 338.1 JA
CHUGOKU SHIKOKU NOGYO JOSEI HOKOKU. Main/Corp Japan. Chugoku Shikoku Noseikyoku. (1964)-. Periodical. Japanese. One time a year. Norinsho Suisansho Chugoku Shikoku Noseikyoku, (Chugoku Shikoku Agricultural Administration Bureau, Ministry of Agriculture Forestry and Fisheries), 9-24 Tenjincho, Okayamashi Okayamaken 700 Japan.

LC S **ISSN** 0376-477X
DD 630 CH
CODEN CHNCDB
CHUNG-HUA NUNG YEH YEN CHIU. [Chung-hua nung yeh yen chiu]. **Added/Corp** T'ai-wan Sheng Nung yeh Shih yen so, T'ai-pei. **VFOAT** Journal of Agricultural Research of China. Vol. 24, No. 1/2 (Sept. 1975)-. Academic Scholarly Publication. Chinese (English; summaries and/or abstracts in English; table of contents in English). Four times a year. Free on request. Taiwan Agricultural Research Institute, 189 Chungcheng Rd, Wanfeng Wufe, Taichung Taiwan. **Tel** 886 4 330 2301. Documents available from CASDDS. ***Continues*** *Nung Yeh Yen Chiu, 0022-4847.*
Ind/Abst Biocont. News Inf.; Chem. Abstr.; Crop Physiol. Abstr.; For. Abstr.; Hortic. Abstr.; Ornamental Hort. (1991-); Plant Grow. Reg. Abstr.; Postharvest News Inf.; Potato Abstr.; Rev. Agric. Entomol.; Rev. Plant Pathol.; Rice Abstr.; Seed Abstr.; Soils Fert.; Soyabean Abstr.; World Agric. Econ. Rural Sociol. Abstr.

LC S **ISSN** 0578-1736
DD 631.9 CH
CODEN CKNHAA
CHUNG-KUO NUNG YEH HUA HSUEH. HUI CHIH. [Chung-kuo nung yeh hua hsueh hui chih]. **Main/Corp** Chung-Kuo Nung Yeh Hua Hsueh Hui. **VFOAT** Journal of the Chinese Agricultural Chemical Society. Vol. 1 (Oct. 1963)-. Academic Scholarly Publication. Chinese (summaries and/or abstracts in English; table of contents in English). Four times a year. $10.00 per issue. Chinese Agricultural Chemical Society, 1 Roosevelt Road, Taipei Taiwan. **Tel** 011 886 2 3630231. Documents available from BIOSIS Document Express, CASDDS.
Ind/Abst Biol. Abstr. (1988-); Chem. Abstr.; Curr. Biotechnol.; Curr. Cit.; Maize Abstr.; Postharvest News Inf.; Rev. Agric. Entomol.; Rice Abstr.; Soyabean Abstr.

LC S539.5 **ISSN** 0578-1752
DD 630.72 CC
CODEN CKNYAR
CHUNG-KUO NUNG YEH KO HSUEH. [Chung-kuo Nung yeh ko Hsueh]. **Added/Corp** Chung-kuo Nung yeh ko Hsueh Yuan. **VFOAT** Zhongguo Nongye Kexue; Chinese Agricultural Science; Selskokhoziaistvennaia Nauk Kitaia. (1960)-. Academic Scholarly Publication. Chinese. Six times a year. $136.50. Chinese Academy of Agricultural Sciences, (Zhonguo Nongye Kexueyuan), Zhonguo Nongye Kexue Zazhishe, 30 Baishiqiao Lu, Beijing 100081, People's Republic of China. **Tel** 011 86 1 8314433, FAX 011 86 1 8315465. **(Subscription address:** China Books & Periodicals Inc., 2929 24th Street, San Francisco CA 94110. **Tel** (415)282-2994.) **ED** Liu Gengling. **Circ:** 15,000. Documents available from BIOSIS Document Express, CASDDS. ***Continues*** *Chung Kuo Nung Yeh Ko Hsueh Tung Hsun, 0369-6480.*
Ind/Abst AGRICOLA; Biol. Abstr.; Chem. Abstr.; Food Sci. Technol. Abstr.; NAPRALERT.

Agriculture

LC S
DD 630   CK
CIAT INTERNATIONAL. **Added/Corp** Centro Internacional de Agricultura Tropical. **VFOAT** C.I.A.T International. **VAT** Centro Internacional de Agricultura Tropical International. Vol. 1, No. 1 (Sept. 1982)-. Newsletter. English (Spanish). Two times a year. Free. Centro Internacional de Agricultura Tropical, Apartado Aereo 67-13, Cali Colombia. **Tel** 57 23 4450000, FAX 57 23 4450273, telex 05769 CIAT CO. **ED** Thomas R. Hargrove. **Bk Rev**, (Qty: 10). **Acid Free. Circ:** 8,000 (ctrl).
Desc: Highlights research and international collaborative activities of CIAT. Dedicated to the alleviation of hunger and poverty in developing countries of the tropics by applying science to agriculture, increasing food production while sustaining the natural resource base.

LC SF521   **ISSN** 0045-6888
DD 638.1
     CODEN CIAGDX
CIENCIA AGRONOMICA. [Cienc. agron.]. Vol 1, No. 1 (July 1971)-. Academic Scholarly Publication. Portuguese. Irregular. Escola de Agronomica, Universidade Federal do Ceara, Fortaleza Ceara Brazil. **Tel** 223-4931. Documents available from CASDDS.
Ind/Abst Chem. Abstr. (1971-1982).

LC S
DD 630   MX
CIENCIA AGROPECUARIA. **Added/Corp** Universidad Autonoma de Nuevo Leon. Facultad de Agronomia. Vol. 1, No. 1 (Jan. 1988)-. Periodical. Spanish. Two times a year.
Ind/Abst Hortic. Abstr.; Postharvest News Inf.

LC S   **ISSN** 0304-5609
DD 630   CL
     CODEN CINADC
CIENCIA E INVESTIGACION AGRARIA. [Cienc. invest. agrar.]. **Added/Corp** Santiago de Chile. Universidad Catolica. Escuela de Agronomia. Vol. 1 (1974)-. Academic Scholarly Publication. Spanish (summaries and/or abstracts in English). Three times a year. $30.00 (two-year). Ciencia e Investigacion, Facultad de Agronomia, Casilla 6177, Santiago Chile. **ED** Horacio Urzua. **Ad Acc. Circ:** 500 (ctrl). Documents available from BIOSIS Document Express, CASDDS.
Desc: Applied research on soil science, horticulture, animal science and agriculture economics and crops.
Ind/Abst Anim. Breed. Abstr.; Biol. Abstr. (1983-1988); Chem. Abstr.; Crop Physiol. Abstr.; Dairy Sci. Abstr.; Field Crop Abstr.; Food Sci. Technol. Abstr.; Grass. Forage Abstr.; Hortic. Abstr.; Maize Abstr.; Nutr. Abstr. Rev., Ser. B, Live Feeds and Feed.; Nutr. Abstr. Rev., Ser. A, Hum. Exp.; Postharvest News Inf.; Poult. Abstr.; Rev. Agric. Entomol.; Rev. Plant Pathol.; Rice Abstr.; Seed Abstr.; Soils Fert.; Soyabean Abstr.; Weed Abstr.; Wheat Barley Trit. Abstr.; World Agric. Econ. Rural Sociol. Abstr.

LC S   **ISSN** 0100-3267
DD 630   BL
     CODEN CPRADD
CIENCIA E PRATICA. [Cienc. prat.]. **Added/Corp** Escola Superior de Agricultura de Lavras. Vol. 1 (Jan./June 1977)-. Periodical. Portuguese (summaries and/or abstracts in English). Two times a year. Documents available from BIOSIS Document Express, CASDDS.
Ind/Abst Biol. Abstr.; Chem. Abstr.

LC S   **ISSN** 0103-8478
DD 630   BL
     CODEN CIRUEP
CIENCIA RURAL : REVISTA CIENTIFICA DO CENTRO DE CIENCIAS RURAIS DA UNIVERSIDADE FEDERAL DE SANTA MARIA. **Added/Corp** Universidade Federal de Santa Maria. Centro de Ciencias Rurais. Vol. 21, No. 1 (1991)-. Periodical. Portuguese (summaries and/or abstracts in English). Three times a year. Universidade Federal de Santa Maria, Centro de Ciencias Rurais, Campus Universitario, 97119-900 Santa Maria, Rio Grande do Sul Brazil. **Tel** 011 55 55 2262347. **Continues** *Universidade Federal de Santa Maria. Centro de Ciencias Rurais. Revista do Centro de Ciencias Rurais*, 0085-5901.

LC S
DD 630   CU
     CODEN CAGPDY
CIENCIA Y TECNICA EN LA AGRICULTURA. Vol. 1, No. 1-2 (Aug. 1978)-. Academic Scholarly Publication. Spanish. Ediciones Cubanas, Obispo 527 Altos ESQ Bernaza, CP 10100 Havana Cuba. Documents available from BIOSIS Document Express, CASDDS.
Ind/Abst Biol. Abstr. (1985-); Chem. Abstr. (1978-1982).

LC S
DD 630   CU
UDC 63
CIENCIA Y TECNICA EN LA AGRICULTURA (CENTRO DE INFORMACION Y DOCUMENTACION AGROPECUARIO). (CIENCIA Y TECNICA EN LA AGRICULTURA. RUMIANTES.). **VFOAT** Ruminates : Ciencia y Tecnica en la Agricultura. (197?)-. Spanish (summaries and/or abstracts in English; table of contents in English). Two times a year. $11.38. Ediciones Cubanas, Obispo 527 Altos ESQ Bernaza, CP 10100 Havana Cuba.
Ind/Abst Biodeter. Abstr.; Nutr. Abstr. Rev., Ser. B, Live Feeds and Feed.; Nutr. Abstr. Rev., Ser. A, Hum. Exp.

LC SF521   **ISSN** 0100-0039
DD 638.1
     CODEN CNTFBM
CIENTIFICA (JABOTICABAL). See Veterinary Sciences.

LC S
DD 630   US
CIRCULAR (ALABAMA AGRICULTURAL EXPERIMENT STATION). (CIRCULAR.). **Added/Corp** Alabama. Agricultural Experiment Station. No. 252 (May 1981)-. English. Alabama Agricultural Experiment Station, Auburn University, 110 Comer Hall, Auburn University AL 36849. **Tel** (334)844-4877, FAX (334)844-5892. **Continues** *Circular (Auburn University. Agricultural Experiment Station)*.

LC S   **ISSN** 0099-7676
DD 334   US
CIRCULAR (FLORIDA COOPERATIVE EXTENSION SERVICE). See Business and Economics-Cooperatives.

LC S   **ISSN** 0100-3356
DD 630   BL
CIRCULAR - FUNDACAO INSTITUTO AGRONOMICO DO PARANA. **Main/Corp** Instituto Agronomica do Parana. **VFOAT** Circular IAPAR. No. 1 (Feb. 1977)-. Monographic series. Portuguese.
Ind/Abst Field Crop Abstr.; Rev. Plant Pathol.

LC S67 .E42   **ISSN** 0889-7506
DD 630   US
CIRCULAR - LOUISIANA AGRICULTURAL EXPERIMENT STATION. (CIRCULAR.). [Circ. - La. Agric. Exp. Stn.]. **Main/Corp** Louisiana Agricultural Experiment Station. **Added/Corp** Louisiana Agricultural Experiment Station. **VFOAT** Cir. (1955)-. Monographic series. English. Irregular. Price varies per volume. Louisiana Agricultural Experiment Station, PO Box 25055, Baton Rouge LA 70894-5055. **Tel** (504)388-5649. **Continues** *Louisiana Circular*.

LC S91 .A325   **ISSN** 0275-0600
DD 630.9749   US
UDC 63(749)
CIRCULAR - NEW JERSEY DEPARTMENT OF AGRICULTURE. **Main/Corp** New Jersey. Dept. of Agriculture. Monographic series. English. Price varies per volume. New Jersey Department of Agriculture, John Fitch Plaza, CN-330, Trenton NJ 08625. **Tel** (609)292-3976, FAX (609)292-3978.

LC S   **ISSN** 0102-3691
DD 630   BL
UDC 63
CIRCULAR TECNICA - EMPA-MT. (CIRCULAR TECNICA.). [Circ. tec. - EMPA-MT]. **VFOAT** Circular Tecnica - Empresa de Pesquisa Agropecuaria do Estado de MatoGrosso. (1985)-. Monographic series. Portuguese. Irregular.
Ind/Abst Potato Abstr.

LC S   **ISSN** 0101-9678
DD 630   BL
UDC 633
CIRCULAR TECNICA - EMPAER. [Circ. tec. - EMPAER]. **VFOAT** Circular Tecnica - Empresa de Pesquisa Assistencia Tecnica e Extensão Rural de Mato Grosso do Sul. (1982)-. Monographic series. Portuguese. Irregular.
Ind/Abst Plant Grow. Reg. Abstr.

LC S   **ISSN** 0100-3003
DD 630   BL
CIRCULAR TECNICA / EMPRESA GOIANA DE PESQUISA AGROPECUARIA. No. 1 (March 1981)-. Monographic series. Portuguese. Price varies per volume.
Ind/Abst Soyabean Abstr.

LC S   **ISSN** 0734-8452
DD 630   US
CIRCULAR - UNIVERSITY OF FLORIDA. AGRICULTURAL EXPERIMENT STATIONS. (CIRCULAR.). [Circ. - Univ. Fla., Agric. Exp. Stn.]. **Added/Corp** University of Florida. Agricultural Experiment Station. (May 1949)-. Monographic series. English. Price varies per volume. University of Florida Agricultural Experiment Station, Gainesville FL 32601.
Ind/Abst AGRICOLA [Select. Cov.]; Hortic. Abstr.; Nutr. Abstr. Rev., Ser. B, Live Feeds and Feed.; Ornamental Hort. (1991-); Plant Breed. Abstr.; Potato Abstr.; Sug. Indus. Abstr.

LC S537 .G3526
DD 630.9758   US
CIRCULAR - UNIVERSITY OF GEORGIA. COLLEGE OF AGRICULTURE. **Main/Corp** Georgia. University. College of Agriculture. Cooperative Extension Service. **Added/Corp** United States Department of Agriculture. No. 1 (1913)-. English. University of Georgia Cooperative Extension Service, Athens GA 30602.

LC S   **ISSN** 0889-8065
DD 630   US
CIRCULAR / WEST VIRGINIA UNIVERSITY AGRICULTURAL AND FORESTRY EXPERIMENT STATION. [Circ. - W.V. Univ., Agric. For. Exp. Stn.]. **Added/Corp** West Virginia University. Agricultural and Forestry Experiment Station. (197?)-. Monographic series. English. Price varies per volume. **Continues** *West Virginia University. Agricultural Experiment Station. Circular*, 0096-7734.
Ind/Abst AGRICOLA [Select. Cov.]; For. Prod. Abstr. (1991-).

LC S   **ISSN** 0746-4533
DD 630   US
CLARK COUNTY FARM BUREAU NEWS (MARTINSVILLE, ILL.). (CLARK COUNTY FARM BUREAU NEWS.). Periodical. English. Six times a year. $2.00. Clark County Farm Bureau, PO Box W, Martinsville IL 62442.

LC S   **ISSN** 0250-7692
DD 630   BE
UDC 33
CLEO-SCHRIFTEN. [CLEO-Schr.]. **VFOAT** Centrum voor Landbouw-Economisch Onderzoek-Schriften. (19??)-. Periodical. Dutch. Six times a year.
Ind/Abst Sug. Indus. Abstr.

LC S   **ISSN** 0115-0405
DD 630   PH
     CODEN CSCJDK
CLSU SCIENTIFIC JOURNAL. [CLSU sci. j.]. **Main/Corp** Central Luzon State University. **Added/Corp** Central Luzon State University. Scientific Journal. **VFOAT** Scientific Journal. **VAT** Central Luzon State University Scientific Journal. Vol. 1 (1965)-. Academic Scholarly Publication. English. Two times a year. $10.00. CLSU Publications House, Central Luzon State University, Munoz Nueva Ecija Philippines. Documents available from CASDDS.
Ind/Abst Chem. Abstr.; Philip. Sci. Technol. Abstr.

LC S   **ISSN** 0116-7847
DD 630   PH
     CCC
     TITLE CHANGE
CMU JOURNAL OF SCIENCE. See Science and Technology.

LC S   **ISSN** 0315-1204
DD 630   CN
CO-OPERATEUR AGRICOLE, LE. [Coop. agric.]. **Added/Corp** Cooperative Federee de Quebec. Vol. 1 (Jan. 1972)-. Periodical. French. Twelve times a year. 8.00Can$. Cooperative Federee de Quebec, CP 500 Station Youville, Montreal Quebec H2P 2W2 Canada. **Tel** (514)384-6450, FAX (514)384-8772. **ED** Andre Piette. **Ad Acc**, **Adv Mgr:** Andre Leger. **Circ:** 26,000.
Ind/Abst AGRICOLA.

LC S   **ISSN** 0737-1756
DD 630   US
UDC 63(761)
COASTAL PLAINS FARMER. ALABAMA, FLORIDA ED. (COASTAL PLAINS FARMER.). [Coast. plains farmer, Ala., Fla. ed.]. Periodical. English. Twelve times a year. $10.00. Specialized Agricultural Publications, 3000 Highwoods Boulevard, Suite 300, Raleigh NC 27625. **Tel** (919)872-5040. **ED** Sid Reynolds. **Ad Acc. Circ:** 100,000 (ctrl).
Desc: Farming information geared to the economic development of farms in the Southeastern United States.

LC S   **ISSN** 0737-1748
DD 630   US
UDC 63(756)
COASTAL PLAINS FARMER NORTH CAROLINA, VIRGINIA ED. (COASTAL PLAINS FARMER.). [Coast. plains farmer]. (1983)-. Periodical. English. Twelve times a year. Specialized Agricultural Publications, 3000 Highwoods Boulevard, Suite 300, Raleigh NC 27625. **Tel** (919)872-5040.

LC S
DD 630   US
COCOA. (19??)-. Periodical. English. Two times a year. comes with Tropical Products. US Department of Agriculture / Foreign Agricultural Service, 14th Street & Independence Avenue Southwest, Washington DC 20250. **Tel** (202)720-9445, FAX (202)720-7729. **Continues** *World Cocoa Situation*.

Agriculture

LC SB281 **ISSN** 0215-1502
DD 633.58 IO
COCOMUNITY NEWSLETTER. (THE COCOMUNITY : NEWSLETTER.). [Cocomunity newsl.].
Added/Corp Asian and Pacific Coconut Community. (1971)-. Newsletter. English. Twenty-four times a year. $100.00. Asian & Pacific Coconut Community, PO Box 1343, Jakarta 10013 Indonesia. **Tel** 011 62 21 5250073, FAX 011 62 21 5205160, telex 62863. **ED** Jo Suharto, (editor's address: APCC, 3rd Floor, Wisma Bakrie, JL. H. R. Rasuna Said, PO Box 1343, Jakarta 10013 Indonesia). **Circ:** 200 (ctrl).
Desc: All the news about the world of coconut. It brings the latest facts and figures regarding coconut agriculture, processing of coconut products and their marketing, domestically and internationally.

LC S
DD 630 US
CODE OF FEDERAL REGULATIONS. 7, AGRICULTURE. See Law.

LC S
DD 630 FR
COLLECTIONS DE STATISTIQUE AGRICOLE. ETUDE.
Main/Corp France. Service Central des Enquetes et Etudes Statistiques. No. 124 (May 1974)-. Periodical. French. SCEES - Service Central des Enquetes et Etudes Statistiques, 4 Avenue de Saint-Mande, 75570 Paris Cedex 12 France. **Tel** 011 33 1 49558576. **Continues** Statistique Agricole. Supplement Serie Etudes.
Ind/Abst Dairy Sci. Abstr.; Poult. Abstr.; World Agric. Econ. Rural Sociol. Abstr.

LC TX560.C63 I57a
DD 641.3/373 SZ
Pr Rev.
COLLOQUE SCIENTIFIQUE INTERNATIONAL SUR LE CAFE : [PROCEEDINGS].
Added/Corp International Scientific Association of Coffee. **VFOAT** International Conference on Coffee Science. (Nov./ Dec. 1977)-. Proceedings. French (English, German and Spanish). Every 2 years. 700.00F. Association Scientifique Internationale du Cafe, Avenue Nestle 55, 1800 Vevey Switzerland. **Circ:** 300. Documents available from CASDDS. **Continues** International Colloquium on the Chemistry of Coffee. Colloque International sur la Chimie des Cafes Verts, Torrefies et leurs Derives.
Desc: Articles on physiology, chemistry, technology, agronomy of coffee.
Ind/Abst Chem. Abstr.; Curr. Cit.

LC S **ISSN** 0293-1915
DD 630 FR
CODEN COLIEZ
COLLOQUES DE L'INRA, LES. [Colloq. INRA].
Added/Corp Institut National de la Recherche Agronomique (France). **VFOAT** Colloques de l'I.N.R.A. **VAT** Colloques de l'Institut National de la Recherche Agronomique. (1981)-. Academic Scholarly Publication. French (English). Five times a year. 90.00F. INRA Editions / Institut National de la Recherche Agronomique, Route de Saint-Cyr, 78026 Versailles Cedex France. **Tel** 011 33 1 30833406, FAX 011 33 1 30833449, telex INRAPUB 699 368 F. **Circ:** 600. Documents available from BIOSIS Document Express, CASDDS.
Desc: Created in 1981, this collection is designed for the rapid publication of proceedings of national or international conferences organized by INRA. Includes 54 titles some of which are out of print.
Ind/Abst Anim. Breed. Abstr.; Biocont. News Inf.; Biodeter. Abstr.; Biol. Abstr.; Chem. Abstr.; Cot. Trop. Fibr. Abstr. Bibliogr.; Crop Physiol. Abstr.; Curr. Cit.; Ecology Abstr.; Maize Abstr.; Nutr. Abstr. Rev., Ser. B, Live Feeds and Feed; Plant Breed. Abstr.; Poult. Abstr.; Rice Abstr.; Seed Abstr.; Soils Fert.; Soyabean Abstr.; Wheat Barley Trit. Abstr.

LC S1 **ISSN** 0710-572X
DD 630/.5 CN
COLLOQUES SCIENTIFIQUES. No. 1-.
Periodical. French (English). Gouvernement du Quebec, 875 2nd Floor Grande Allee Est. Ed., Quebec G1R 4Y8 Canada.

LC HD1775.C6 C617 **ISSN** 0732-7226
DD 338.1/09788 US
UDC 338.43(788)
COLORADO AGRIBUSINESS ROUNDUP. [Colo. agribus. roundup].
Periodical. English. Two times a year. Colorado State University Cooperative Extension Service, County Courth, BX543, Fort Collins CO 80522.

LC S **ISSN** 0010-1729
DD 630 US
COLORADO RANCHER AND FARMER.
[Colo. rancher farmer]. **Added/Corp** Nebraska Farmer Co. **VFOAT** Colorado Rancher & Farmer. (19??)-. Periodical. English. Fifteen times a year. $19.95. Farm Progress Publishing, 191 South Gary Avenue, Carol Stream IL 60188-2089. **Tel** (708)462-2890 or 2891. **(Subscription address:** CDS / SIFD Agency Control, 1901 Bell Avenue, Des Moines IA 50315. **Tel** (515)246-6812.)
Ind/Abst AGRICOLA.

LC S
DD 630 IT
COLTIVATORE : SETTIMANALE DELLA CONFEDERAZIONE NAZIONALE DEI COLTIVATORI DIRETTI, IL. **Added/Corp**
Confederazione Nazionale dei Coltivatori Diretti. Vol. 1, No. 1 (Jan. 1, 1945)-. Periodical. Italian. One time a week. L5450. Coldiretti Il Colivatore Amm, Via 24 Maggio 43, 00187 Rome Italy. **Tel** 011 39 6 4682252.

LC S
DD 630 SP
COMERCIALIZACION HORTOFRUTICOLA.
(19??)-. Spanish. Twelve times a year. 6000.00ptas Spain; 7000.00ptas other. Ediciones CH SL, Plaza del Punto, Edif Anton 8 K, 21003 Huelva Spain. **Tel** 011 34 955 262730.

LC HD1401 **ISSN** 0010-3101
DD 338 US
UDC 63
COMMERCIAL REVIEW (PORTLAND, OR.). (COMMERCIAL REVIEW.). [Commer. rev.].
Periodical. English. Four times a year. $20.00. Commercial Review, 1725 NW 24th, Portland OR 97210-2507. **Tel** (503)226-2758. **ED** Dennis Hays. **Ad Acc. Circ:** 1,000 (ctrl).
Desc: General agriculture and news about various agricultural associations in the Pacific northwest.

LC HD9000.1 .F55
DD 338.14 IT
COMMODITY BULLETIN SERIES.
Main/Corp Food and Agriculture Organization of the United Nations. No. 30 (1958)-. Monographic series. English. Price varies per volume. Food Agriculture Organization (FAO) / Italy, GIPCI66 via Terme di Caracalla, 00100 Rome Italy. **Tel** 011 39 6 52252925, FAX 011 39 6 52253152. **Continues** Food and Agriculture Organization of the United Nations. FAO Commodity Series. Bulletin.

LC S
DD 630 IT
COMMODITY POLICY STUDIES.
Added/Corp Food and Agriculture Organization of the United Nations. **VFOAT** FAO Commodity Policy Studies. No. 1 (Sept. 1952)-. Monographic series. English.

LC HD1401 .F63A
DD 338.1/05 IT
UDC 338.1
COMMODITY REVIEW AND OUTLOOK.
1982-83-. English. One time a year. UNIPUB, 4611-F Assembly Drive, Lanham MD 20706-4391. **Tel** (800)274-4888, FAX (301)459-0056, telex 28787 GATT CH. **Continues** FAO Commodity Review and Outlook, 0071-7002.

LC S **ISSN** 0817-685X
DD 630 AT
COMMODITY STATISTICAL BULLETIN.
Added/Corp Australia. Bureau of Agricultural Economics. Australian Bureau of Agricultural and Resource Economics. (1985)-. Bulletin. English. One time a year. 50.00Aus$ Australia; 62.00Aus$ US and Europe; 58.50Aus$ other. ABARE / Australian Bureau of Agriculture and Resource Economics, GPO Box 1563, Canberra ACT 2601 Australia. **Tel** 011 61 6 2722000, FAX 011 61 6 2722001.
Ind/Abst AESIS Q.

LC SB188 **ISSN** 0228-2232
DD 633.1/09717 CN
COMPETITIONS, SUMMARIES, PROJECTS, TRIALS. [Compet., summ., proj., trials].
Main/Corp Prince Edward Island Soil & Crop Improvement Association. (1976)-. English. One time a year. Free. Prince Edward Island Soil & Crop Improvement Association, PO Box 1600, Charlottetown Prince Edward Island, C1A 7N3 Canada. **Tel** (902)368-5633, FAX (902)368-5661. **ED** Blair Van Omme and Winston Cousins. **Circ:** 500. **Continues** Prince Edward Island Soil & Crop Improvement Association. Demonstrations, Summaries, Projects, Trials, 0228-2224.

LC S **ISSN** 0314-0164
DD 630 AT
SUSPENDED
COMPLAN HANDBOOK. **Added/Corp** New
South Wales. Dept. of Agriculture. Agricultural Business Research Instiue (N.S.W.). (19??)-(1988/1989). Monographic series. English. One time a year. Agricultural Business Research Institute, University of New England, Armidale New South Wales 2351 Australia. **Tel** 067 73 3555.

LC S
DD 630 FR
COMPTE RENDU DE LA CONFERENCE DU COLUMA. **Main/Corp** Comite Francais de Lutte
Contre les Mauvaises Herbes. **Added/Corp** Federation Nationale des Groupements de Protection des Cultures. **VFOAT** Compte Rendu des Journees d'Etudes sur les Herbicides, PNGPC-COLUMA; COLUMA Conference; Journees d'Etudes sur les Herbicides. Compte Rendu. (1961)-. Periodical. French. Comite Francais de Lutte Contre les Mauvaises Herbes, 8 Avenue du President Wilson, 75116 Paris France.
Ind/Abst PESTDOC.

LC S
DD 630 FR
COMPTE RENDU DES ESSAIS. **Added/Corp**
Union Nationale Interprofessionnelle des Legumes Transformes. **VAT** Union Nationale Interprofessionnelle des Legumes Transformes. (19??)-. Periodical. French.
Ind/Abst Agric. Eng. Abstr.; Plant Grow. Reg. Abstr.; Rev. Plant Pathol.

LC S **ISSN** 0379-184X
DD 630 BE
COMPTE RENDU DES RECHERCHES (STATION DAMELIORATION DES PLANTES, GEMBLOUX). (COMPTE RENDU
DES RECHERCHES.). [C.-r. rech. - Stn. amelior. plantes Gembloux]. **Added/Corp** Station d'Amelioration des Plantes (Gembloux, Belgium). (1971)-. French. Every 2 years. **Continues** Station d'Amelioration des Plantes (Gembloux, Belgium) Rapport d'Activite, 0774-949X.

LC HD1941 .S47A
DD 338.1/0944 FR
UDC 311:63(44)
COMPTES DE L'AGRICULTURE, LES.
Main/Corp France. Service Central des Enquetes et Etudes Statistiques. (19??)-. French. 7 rue Scribe, 75436 Paris Cedex 09 France.

LC S5 .A32 **ISSN** 0989-6988
DD 630 FR
CODEN CRAFEQ
COMPTES RENDUS DE L'ACADEMIE D'AGRICULTURE DE FRANCE. [C. r. Acad.
agric. Fr.]. **Added/Corp** Academie d'Agriculture de France. Vol. 73, No. 1 (1987)-. Periodical. French. Eight times a year. $157.47. Academie d'Agriculture France, 18 rue de Bellechasse, 75007 Paris France. **Tel** 011 33 1 47051037, FAX 011 33 1 45550978. **ED** Andie Cauderon. Index available. cum. index. **Bk Rev** (Qty: 1). **Circ:** 1,400 (ctrl). Documents available from BIOSIS Document Express, CASDDS. **Continues** Comptes Rendus des Seances (Academie d'Agriculture de France), 0151-1335.
Ind/Abst AgBiotech News Inf.; Agric. Eng. Abstr. (1991-); Anim. Breed. Abstr.; Biol. Abstr. (1987-); Chem. Abstr.; Crop Physiol. Abstr.; Curr. Cit.; Dairy Sci. Abstr.; Field Crop Abstr.; Food Sci. Technol. Abstr.; Hortic. Abstr.; Nutr. Abstr. Rev., Ser. A, Hum. Exp.; PESTDOC; Pig News Inf.; Plant Breed. Abstr.; Potato Abstr.; Rev. Agric. Entomol.; Rev. Plant Pathol.; Vitis Vitic. Enol. Abstr.; Wheat Barley Trit. Abstr.; World Agric. Econ. Rural Sociol. Abstr.

LC HD2021 .C66 **ISSN** 0214-0322
DD 338.1 /2 20 SP
COMUNICACIONES I.N.I.A. SERIE ECONOMIA. **Added/Corp** Instituto Nacional de
Investigaciones Agrarias. Instituto Nacional de Investigacion y Tecnologia Agraria y Alimentaria (Spain). **VFOAT** Comunicaciones INIA. Serie Economia; Serie Economia. **VAT** Comunicaciones Instituto Nacional de Investigaciones Agrarias. Serie Economia. (1986)-. Monographic series. Spanish (summaries and/or abstracts in English). **Continues** Comunicaciones I.N.I.A. Serie Economia y Sociologia Agrarias, 0210-332X.
Ind/Abst Wheat Barley Trit. Abstr.

LC S **ISSN** 0210-3311
DD 630 SP
COMUNICACIONES I.N.I.A. SERIE GENERAL. **VFOAT** Serie General. No. 1 (1976)-.
Monographic series. Spanish. Price varies per volume. Instituto Nacional de Investigaciones Agrarias / Madrid, Avda de Puerta de Hierro S/N, Madrid Spain.

LC SD206 .C56 **ISSN** 0210-3338
DD 634.9/046 SP
COMUNICACIONES I.N.I.A. SERIE RECURSOS NATURALES. **Added/Corp**
Instituto Nacional de Investigaciones Agrarias. **VFOAT** Serie Recursos Naturales; Recursos Naturales. (197?)-. Monographic series. Spanish.
Ind/Abst For. Abstr.; GeoRef.

LC S **ISSN** 0210-2560
DD 630 SP
CODEN CISTDQ
COMUNICACIONES I.N.I.A. SERIE TECNOLOGIA AGRARIA. [Comun. I.N.I.A. ser.
tecnol. agrar.]. **Added/Corp** Instituto Nacional de Investigaciones Agrarias. **VFOAT** Serie Tecnologia Agraria. (19??)-. Monographic series. Spanish. Documents available from CASDDS. **Continues** Comunicaciones I.N.I.A. Serie Tecnologia.
Ind/Abst Chem. Abstr. (1974-1982); For. Prod. Abstr. (1991-).

Agriculture

LC S
DD 630
ISSN 0871-1763
PO

COMUNICACOES - INSTITUTO DE INVESTIGACAO CIENTIFICA TROPICAL. SERIE DE CIENCIAS AGRARIAS. (COMUNICACOES. SERIE DE CIENCIAS AGRARIAS.). [Comun. - Inst. Investig. Cient. Trop., Ser. cienc. agrar.]. **Added/Corp** Instituto de Investigacao Cientifica Tropical (Portugal) Portugal. Secretaria de Estado da Ciencia e Tecnologia. **VFOAT** Serie de Ciencias Agrarias; Comunicacoes do Instituto de Investigacao Cientifica Tropical Serie de Ciencias Agrarias. No. 1 (1989)-. Monographic series. Portuguese (summaries and/or abstracts in English). Irregular. Price varies per volume. Instituto de Investigacao Cientifica Tropical, Centro de Documentacao e Informacao, rua Jau 47, 1 300 Lisbon Portugal. **Tel** 645321. **Circ:** 1,000 (ctrl).
Ind/Abst Agrofor. Abstr. (1991-); Field Crop Abstr.; For. Abstr.; Grass. Forage Abstr.; Soyabean Abstr.

LC S
DD 630
ISSN 0100-6061
BL

COMUNICADO TECNICO (CENTRO DE PESQUISA AGROPECUARIA DO TROPICO SEMI-ARIDO). (COMUNICADO TECNICO / CENTRO DE PESQUISA AGROPECUARIO DO TROPICO SEMI-ARIDO.). Monographic series. Portuguese. Price varies per volume.
Ind/Abst Agric. Eng. Abstr. (1991-); Field Crop Abstr.; Nutr. Abstr. Rev., Ser. B, Live Feeds and Feed.; Soils Fert.

LC S
DD 630
UDC 664
ISSN 0101-5508
BL

COMUNICADO TECNICO - CENTRO DE TECNOLOGIA AGRICOLA E ALIMENTAR. [Comun. Tec. - Cent. Tecnol. Agric. Aliment.]. **VFOAT** Comunicado Tecnico. CTAA. (1982)-. Monographic series. Portuguese. Three times a week.
Ind/Abst Soyabean Abstr.

LC S
DD 630
UDC 633/636
ISSN 0101-7683
BL

COMUNICADO TECNICO - EMCAPA. [Comun. tec. - EMCAPA]. **VFOAT** Comunicado Tecnico - Empresa Capixaba de Pesquisa Agropecuaria. (1982)-. Monographic series. Portuguese. Irregular. **Continues** Comunicado EMCAPA, 0100-8609.
Ind/Abst Hortic. Abstr.; Nematol. Abstr.; Plant Grow. Reg. Abstr.

LC S17
DD 630
BL

COMUNICADO TECNICO - EMPRESA BRASILEIRA DE PESQUISA AGROPECUARIA, UNIDADE DE EXECUCAO DE PESQUISA DE AMBITO ESTADUAL, MANAUS. **Main/Corp** Empresa Brasileira de Pesquisa Agropecuaria. Unidade de Execucao de Pesquisa de Ambito Estadual de Manaus. No. 1- March 1976-. Periodical. Portuguese.
Ind/Abst Maize Abstr.; Plant Breed. Abstr.

LC S17
DD 630
ISSN 0100-896X
BL

COMUNICADO TECNICO - EMPRESA DE PESQUISA AGROPECUARIA DO ESTADO DO RIO DE JANEIRO. [Comun. tec. - Empresa pesqui. agropecu. Estado Rio J.]. **Main/Corp** Empresa de Pesquisa Agropecuaria do Estado de Rio de Janeiro. No. 1 (1978)-. Monographic series. Portuguese. Twelve times a year. Price varies per volume.
Ind/Abst AGRICOLA; Field Crop Abstr.; Hortic. Abstr.; Maize Abstr.; Plant Genet. Resour. Abstr.; Soils Fert.

LC S17
DD 630
BL

COMUNICADO TECNICO - EMPRESA GOIANA DE PESQUISA AGROPECUARIA. **Main/Corp** Empresa Goiana de Pesquisa Agropecuaria. (19??)-. Periodical. Portuguese.
Ind/Abst Soyabean Abstr.

LC S
DD 630
UDC 338.12:63(81)
BL

CONJUNTURA AGRICOLA. **Main/Corp** Rio Grande do Sul, Brazil (State). Unidade de Economia Agricola. Portuguese. Secretaria da Agricultura Supervisao de Apoio Tecnico, Unidade de Economia Agricola, 585 - 70. Andar 90.000, Porto Alegre Brazil.

LC S
DD 630
ISSN 1059-8723
US

CONNECTICUT WEEKLY AGRICULTURAL REPORT. **Added/Corp** Connecticut. Dept. of Agriculture. **VFOAT** Agricultural Report. (199?)-. Periodical. English. One time a week. $10.00. Connecticut Weekly Agriculture Report, Connecticut Department of Agriculture, State Office Building, Hartford CT 06106. **Tel** (203)566-4845. **ED** Patricia V. Bussa. **Ad Acc. Circ:** 2,400. **Continues** Connecticut Market Bulletin, 0161-5858.
Desc: Agriculture information.

LC S451.5
DD 630/.7/1171374
ISSN 0228-1759
CN

CONTACT (KEMPTVILLE COLLEGE OF AGRICULTURAL TECHNOLOGY). (CONTACT.). [Contact - Kemptv. Coll. Agric. Technol.]. **Added/Corp** Kemptville College of Agricultural Technology. Vol. 1 (April 1975)-. Periodical. English. Two times a year. 16.01Can$. KCAT Alumni, RRI 4903 Farmers Way, Carlsbad Springs Ontario K0A 1K0 Canada. **Tel** (613)822-1340.

LC S410.N45 H34
DD 630/.2/05931
UDC 63(058.7)(931)
NZ

CONTACTS IN AGRICULTURE. English. Every 2 years. $25.00 per issue. Contacts in Agriculture Primedia, Ministry of Agriculture and Fisheries, PO Box 2526, Wellington New Zealand. **Tel** (04)720367, FAX (04)727-161, telex MAFWN NZ 31532. Index available. **Ad Acc. Circ:** 10,000. **Continues** Handbook of New Zealand Agriculture.
Desc: Directory of key contacts in agriculture and related organizations in New Zealand.

LC S
DD 630
UDC 334.4:63(75); 631.115.8(75)
ISSN 0010-8448
US

COOPERATIVE FARMER. **VFOAT** SS Cooperative Farmer. Vol. 29, No. 9- (Nov./Dec. 1973)-. Periodical. English. Twelve times a year. Southern States Cooperative, PO Box 26234, Richmond VA 23260. **Continues** Southern States Cooperative Farmer.

LC HD1491.U5 C619
DD 334/.683/0973
ISSN 0742-9487
US

COOPERATIVE INFORMATION REPORT. [Coop. inf. rep.]. **Added/Corp** United States. Agricultural Cooperative Service. United States. Dept. of Agriculture. Economics, Statistics, and Cooperatives Service. (197?)-. English. Irregular. Agricultural Cooperative Service, US Department of Agriculture, 14th Street and Independence Avenue SW, Washington DC 20250. **Tel** (202)653-6973, FAX (202)653-7033.
Ind/Abst AGRICOLA; Leis., Rec., Tour. Abstr.; Rural Dev. Abstr.; World Agric. Econ. Rural Sociol. Abstr.

LC S
DD 630
IT

COOPERAZIONE IN AGROCOLTURA. Italian. Ed Cooperativa, Via Guattani 13, 00161 Rome Italy. **Tel** 011 39 6 8440507, 011 39 6 8844942, FAX 011 39 6 84439216.

LC S
DD 630
UDC 58.006(754); 63027(754)
US

CORE ARBORETUM BULLETIN. Vol. 1, No. 1 (Fall/Winter 1975/76)-. Bulletin. English. Two times a year. **Continues** Arboretum Newsletter (Morgantown, W. Va.).

LC S
DD 630
ISSN 1049-7021
US

CORNELL COOPERATIVE EXTENSION AGRICULTURAL NEWS. **Added/Corp** Cooperative Extension Association of Saratoga County. Cornell University. Cooperative Extension. **VFOAT** Extension News; Agricultural News. Periodical. English. Twelve times a year. Canadian Pulp & Paper Association, 1155 Metcalfe Street, 19th Floor, Montreal Quebec H3B 4T6 Canada. **Tel** (514)866-6621, FAX (514)866-3035, telex 055-60690. **Continues** Extension News, 0199-7564.

LC S1 .C77
DD 630
ISSN 0010-8782
US

CORNELL COUNTRYMAN. **Added/Corp** Cornell University. College of Agriculture. New York State College of Agriculture. New York State College of Agriculture and Life Sciences. Vol. 1, No. 1 (Dec. 1903)-. Periodical. English. Six times a year. $12.00. Cornell University / Joan Payton, 324 Kennedy Hall, Ithaca NY 14853. **Tel** (607)255-2111, FAX (607)255-7905. **ED** Jane E Hardy (editor's phone: (607)255-2171). **Circ:** 2,400. available on microfilm from University Microfilms International (UMI).
Desc: Activities, research, profiles and history related to the New York State College of Agriculture and Life Sciences at Cornell University.

LC S
DD 630
ISSN 1067-585X
US

CORNELL FOCUS. (CORNELL FOCUS : A PUBLICATION OF CORNELL UNIVERSITY'S COLLEGE OF AGRICULTURE AND LIFE SCIENCES.). [Cornell focus]. **Added/Corp** New York State Agricultural Experiment Station. Cornell University. Agricultural Experiment Station. New York State College of Agriculture and Life Sciences. Vol. 1, No. 1 (1992)-. Periodical. English. Three times a year. Free on request. Cornell Focus, Cornell University Media Service, 1150 Comstock Hall, Ithaca NY 14853. **Tel** (607)255-1876. Documents available from BIOSIS Document Express. **Continues** New York's Food & Life Sciences Quarterly, 0361-5367.
Ind/Abst AGRICOLA; Biol. Abstr.; Coal Abstr.; Foods Adlibra.

LC S
DD 630
UDC 63
ISSN 0363-8693
US

CODEN CIABDI

CORNELL INTERNATIONAL AGRICULTURE BULLETIN. [Cornell int. agric. bull.]. Vol. 24 (1973)-. Bulletin. English. Price varies per volume. Cornell University Distribution Center, 7 Research Park, Ithaca NY 14850. **Tel** (607)255-7660. Documents available from CASDDS. **Continues** Cornell International Agricultural Development Bulletin, 0589-7084.
Ind/Abst Chem. Abstr. (1963-1979).

LC S
DD 630
UDC 630
ISSN 0391-6774
IT

CORRIERE DI ROMA. [Corr. Roma]. (1950)-. Periodical. Italian. Twenty-four times a year. L34060. Corriere di Roma, Via IV Novembre 152, 00187 Rome Italy. **Tel** 011 39 6 6784964.

LC S
DD 630
ISSN 1043-5557
US

CORTLAND COUNTY CONNECTION. **VFOAT** Cortland. Vol. 1, No. 1 (March 10, 1989). Periodical. English. Twelve times a year. Cornell Cooperative Extension of Cortland County, 60 Central Avenue, PO Box 5590, Cortland NY 13045. **Continues** Cortland County Farm and Home News, 0194-6501.

LC HD9075 .U54A
DD 338.1/3
ISSN 0092-9530
US

COST OF STORING AND HANDLING COTTON AT PUBLIC STORAGE FACILITIES. **Main/Corp** United States. Dept. of Agriculture. Economic Research Service. Government Publication. English. US Department of Agriculture / Economic Research Service, 1301 New York Avenue, Room 208, Washington DC 20250. **Tel** (202)447-4111.

LC HF
DD 380.1
US

CODEN CWMTER

●COTTON, WORLD MARKETS & TRADE. **Added/Corp** United States. Foreign Agricultural Service. United States. World Agricultural Outlook Board. **VFOAT** Cotton, World Markets and Trade. (Jan. 1994)-. Trade Publication. English. Twelve times a year. $69.00. US Department of Agriculture / Foreign Agricultural Service, 14th Street & Independence Avenue Southwest, Washington DC 20250. **Tel** (202)720-9445, FAX (202)720-7729. (**Subscription address:** NTIS, 5285 Port Royal Road, Springfield VA 22161. **Tel** (703)487-4630.) **Circ:** 750. available on microfiche; available on an online database (file 648/Full-Text). **Continues** World Cotton Situation.
Desc: Information on world cotton production, consumption, and trade, market development, export opportunities and prices.

LC S
DD 630
US

COUNCIL FOR AGRICULTURAL SCIENCE AND TECHNOLOGY PUBLICATIONS SUBSCRIPTION. English. Irregular. $35.00 US; $50.00 other. Council for Agricultural Science and Technology, 4420 West Lincoln Way, Ames IA 50010. **Tel** (515)292-2125, FAX (515)292-4512. **ED** Kayleen A Niyo. **Circ:** 5,000.
Desc: Subscription includes task force reports, comments from CAST, special publications, NewsCAST, and Science of Food and Agriculture.

LC HB241
DD 338
ISSN 1065-1756
US

COUNTRY FOLKS GROWER. [Ctry. folks grow.]. (1992)-. Periodical. English. Twelve times a year. $9.00. Country Folks Grows, PO Box 97, Subscription Department, Canajohari NY 13317-0097.

LC S
DD 630
UK

COUNTRY GENTLEMEN'S MAGAZINE, THE. Vol. 67, No. 1 (Jan. 1967)-. Periodical. English. Twelve times a year. Country Gentlemens Association Letchworth, Hertfordshire SG6 4AP United Kingdom. **Continues** Country Gentlemen's Estate Magazine.

LC S
DD 630
ISSN 0011-0140
CN

COUNTRY GUIDE. (1908)-. Periodical. English. Eleven times a year. 23.00Can$. Public Press Ltd., 1760 Ellice Avenue, Winnipeg Manitoba R3H 0B6 Canada. **Tel** (204)774-1861. **Ad Acc. Circ:** 226,759.
Desc: Edited for farmers across Canada, especially those with medium or large farms, who are interested in increasing the efficiency and profitability of their operations.
Ind/Abst Can. Index (?-?).

LC S
DD 630 UK
UDC 332.21
COUNTRY LANDOWNER : JOURNAL OF THE COUNTRY LANDOWNERS' ASSOCIATION. Vol. 1, Pt. 1 (Feb. 1950)-. Periodical. English. Six times a year.

LC S **ISSN** 0011-0183
DD 630 CN
COUNTRY LIFE IN BRITISH COLUMBIA. [Ctry. life B.C.]. **Added/Corp** British Columbia Federation of Agriculture. **VFOAT** Country Life. Vol. 1 (1915)-. Periodical. English. Twelve times a year. 9.61Can$. Country Life Ltd, 3308 King George Highway, Surrey British Columbia V4P 1A8 Canada. **Tel** (604)536-7622, FAX (604)536-5677. **ED** D.M. Young. **Bk Rev. Ad Acc. Circ:** 8,200.
Desc: Presents news and articles on all phases of agriculture in British Columbia. Directed to the working farmer, with an emphasis on farm organizations.

LC S1 **ISSN** 0095-5558
DD 630/.5 US
UDC 63
COUNTRY PLACE. Periodical. English. Six times a year. $5.00. Farm Wife Inc, 1726 First Street, Milwaukee WI 53212.

LC S **ISSN** 1185-3387
DD 630 CN
COUNTRY ROADS (VANCOUVER). (COUNTRY ROADS.). [Ctry. roads]. Vol. 1, No. 1 (Dec. 1990)-. Periodical. English. Six times a year. Limited free distribution. DoMac Publications Ltd., 207 West Hastings Street, Suite 810, Vancouver BC V68 1J8, Canada. **Tel** (604)684-8255.

LC S544 .C64 **ISSN** 0164-3932
DD 630/.7/15 US
COUNTY AGENT, THE. [Cty. agent]. Vol. 1, (Feb. 1941)-. Periodical. English. Four times a year. $10.00. Aiken County Cooperative Extension Service Office, PO Drawer 2007, Aiken SC 29802. **Tel** (803)646-6297. **ED** Allen Bayles. **Circ:** 7,500 (ctrl).
Desc: Professional improvement and association business. Official publication of the National Association of County Agricultural Agents.

LC S **ISSN** 0739-4330
DD 630 US
COUNTY AGENTS. (COUNTY AGENTS : THE ANNUAL REFERENCE DIRECTORY FOR AGRICULTURAL EXTENSION WORKERS.). **VFOAT** County Agents Directory. 67th Ed. (1982-83)-. Directory. English. Every 2 years. $22.95. Century Communications Inc., 6201 Howard Street, Niles IL 60714-3435. **Tel** (708)647-1200, FAX (708)647-7055. ***Continues*** *County Agent Directory.*

LC S
DD 630 US
COUNTY ESTIMATES OF FEED GRAIN. English. One time a year (Mar.). Free. Agricultural Statistics Division, PO Box 27767, Raleigh NC 27611. **Tel** (919)856-4394.

LC S
DD 630 US
COUNTY ESTIMATES OF SOYBEAN AND WHEAT. English. One time a year. Free. Agricultural Statistics Division, PO Box 27767, Raleigh NC 27611. **Tel** (919)856-4394.

LC HD1401 **ISSN** 0823-6887
DD 338.1/09713/31 CN
COUNTY GROWER. [Cty. grow.]. Periodical. English. Twelve times a year. Free to members of Essex County Associated Growers. County Grower, 139 Oak Street West, Leamington Ontario N8H 3E4 Canada.

LC S **ISSN** 0011-0450
DD 630 FR
TITLE CHANGE
COURRIER AVICOLE, LE. [Courr. avic.]. **Added/Corp** Centre de Recherches Scientifiques d'Auxances. Association des Elevages Francais Garantis Agglutines. No. 1 (Jan. 1946)-(19??). Periodical. French. SPI, 35 rue de Chaillot, 75116 Paris France. **Tel** (1)40 70 19 49. ***Merged into*** *Cultivar.*
Ind/Abst PESTDOC (?-?).

LC HD1775.S6 S6
DD 338.1/08 US
CROP AND LIVESTOCK SERIES. English. ***Continues*** *Crops and Livestock Series / South Carolina Crops Reporting Service.*

LC S
DD 630 AT
CROP REPORT. (19??)-. English. Five times a year. 94.00Aus$ Australia; 119.00Aus$ other. ABARE / Australian Bureau of Agriculture and Resource Economics, GPO Box 1563, Canberra ACT 2601 Australia. **Tel** 011 61 6 2722000, FAX 011 61 6 2722001.

LC S **ISSN** 0327-4950
DD 630 AG
UDC 631(82)
CUADERNO DE ACTUALIZACION TECNICA - ESTACION EXPERIMENTAL AGROPECUARIA MANFREDI. (CUADERNO DE ACTUALIZACION TECNICA.). [Cuad. actual. tec. - Estac. exp. agropecu. Manfredi]. (1984)-. Monographic series. Spanish. Irregular.
Ind/Abst Seed Abstr.

LC S **ISSN** 0253-5815
DD 630 CU
CODEN CJASB6
Pr Rev.
CUBAN JOURNAL OF AGRICULTURAL SCIENCE. [Cuban j. agric. sci.]. **Added/Corp** Instituto de Ciencia Animal. Universidad de La Habana Estacion Experimental de Pastos y Forrajes. Vol. 7 (Mar. 1973)-. Academic Scholarly Publication. English (summaries and/or abstracts in Russian). Three times a year. $30.00. Revista Cubana de Ciencia Agricola, Apartado 24, San Jose de las Lajas, La Habana, Cuba. **ED** M. Valdivic. Index available. cum. index. **Bk Rev**, (Qty: varies). **Ad Acc, Adv Mgr:** Renan Alvarez. Full Page (B&W) $200.00. Half Page (B&W) $125.00. **Circ:** 400 (ctrl). Documents available from The Genuine Article, BIOSIS Document Express, CASDDS, UMI Article Clearinghouse. ***Continues*** *Revista Cubana de Ciencia Agricola.*
Desc: Brings together the different and diverse aspects of animal nutrition, genetics and pasture and forage production in one publication. Deals with the study of these sciences which could be regarded as being useful for animal feeding purposes.
Ind/Abst Abstr. Trop. Agric.; AgBiotech News Inf.; AGRICOLA; Agrofor. Abstr. (1991-); Anim. Breed. Abstr.; Biodeter. Abstr. (1991-); Biol. Abstr.; Chem. Abstr.; Curr. Contents Agric. Biol. Environ. Sci.; Dairy Sci. Abstr.; EMBASE; Food Sci. Technol. Abstr.; For. Abstr.; Grass. Forage Abstr.; Nutr. Abstr. Rev., Ser. B, Live Feeds and Feed.; Life Sci. Collect.; Pig News Inf.; Plant Breed. Abstr.; Pollut. Abstr. Indexes; Res. Alert [Select. Cov.]; Rev. Agric. Entomol.; SCISEARCH; Soils Fert.; Soyabean Abstr.; Sug. Indus. Abstr.; Weed Abstr.; Wheat Barley Trit. Abstr.; World Agric. Econ. Rural Sociol. Abstr.

LC S
DD 630 SP
CULTIVADOR MODERNO, EL. (19??)-. Periodical. Spanish. Eleven times a year. 6784ptas Spain; 8900ptas other. Raul Maria Mir Rague, Escoles Pies 45, 08017 Barcelona Spain. **Tel** 93 212 43 67, FAX 93 418 92 79. **ED** Raul Maria Mir Rague. **Bk Rev. Ad Acc. Circ:** 11,000.
Desc: Covers the news in the field of agriculture such as, livestock, machinery, equipment and companies.

LC S **ISSN** 1143-7405
DD 630 FR
UDC 631
CULTIVAR (1989). (CULTIVAR.). (1989)-. Periodical. French. Twenty-two times a year. $87.93. Documentation Agricole, 228 rue du Faubourg St. Martin, 75010 Paris France. **Tel** 011 33 1 40051818, 011 33 1 40380880. **(Subscription address:** Cultivar Service Abonnements, BP 210, 60732 S Genevieve Cdx 9 France. **Tel** 011 33 44 034000.) ***Continues*** *Cultivar 2000 (Lille), 1143-7391.*

LC HT401 .C85 **ISSN** 1048-4876
DD 307.72/05 US
CULTURE & AGRICULTURE. (CULTURE & AGRICULTURE : BULLETIN OF THE ANTHROPOLOGICAL STUDY GROUP ON AGRARIAN SYSTEMS.). [Cult. agric.]. **Added/Corp** Anthropological Study Group on Agrarian Systems (U.S.) Culture and Agriculture Group (U.S.). **VFOAT** Bulletin of the Anthropological Study Group on Agrarian Systems; Bulletin of the Culture and Agriculture Group; C and A; C & A; Culture and Agriculture. No. 1 (Jan. 77)-. Bulletin. English. Irregular. $25.00. American Anthropological Association, 4350 North Fairfax Dr, Suite 640, Arlington VA 22203. **Tel** (703)528-1902 ext. 3031, FAX (703)528-3546. **(Subscription address:** Culture and Agriculture, 1703 New Hampshire Avenue NW AAA, Washington DC 20009. **)**
Ind/Abst Postharvest News Inf.; Potato Abstr.; World Agric. Econ. Rural Sociol. Abstr.

LC S **ISSN** 0256-6885
DD 630 II
CODEN CREREE
CURRENT RESEARCH REPORTER. [Curr. res. report.]. Vol. 1, No. 1 (Jan. 1985)-. Academic Scholarly Publication. English. Two times a year. Mahatma Phule Agricultural University, Rahuri-413722, Dist Ahmednagar, Maharashtra India. Documents available from BIOSIS Document Express, CASDDS.
Ind/Abst Biocont. News Inf.; Biol. Abstr. (1986-); Chem. Abstr. (1985-); Nematol. Abstr.; Plant Grow. Reg. Abstr.; Soils Fert.

LC SF521 **ISSN** 0253-7133
DD 638.1 II
CODEN UACRBC
CURRENT RESEARCH - UNIVERSITY OF AGRICULTURAL SCIENCES. [Curr. res. - Univ. Agric. Sci.]. **Main/Corp** University of Agricultural Sciences. (197?)-. Academic Scholarly Publication. English. Twelve times a year. $30.00. University of Agricultural Sciences, Post Bag No 2477, Hebbal Bangalore 560 024 India. **Tel** 35383. **(Subscription address:** Prints India, 11 Darya Ganj, New Delhi 110002 India. **Tel** 011 91 11 3268645, FAX 011 91 11 3275542, telex 31-61087 PRIN-IN.) Documents available from CASDDS.
Ind/Abst Agric. Eng. Abstr. (1991-); Agrofor. Abstr.; Anim. Breed. Abstr.; Biocont. News Inf. (19??-19??); Chem. Abstr. (1972-1981); Dairy Sci. Abstr.; Field Crop Abstr.; Food Sci. Technol. Abstr.; For. Abstr.; Hortic. Abstr.; Index Vet.; Irr. Drain. Abstr.; Maize Abstr.; Nematol. Abstr.; Ornamental Hort.; Plant Breed. Abstr.; Plant Genet. Resour. Abstr.; Plant Grow. Reg. Abstr.; Potato Abstr.; Protozoolog. Abstr.; Rev. Agric. Entomol.; Rev. Plant Pathol.; Rice Abstr.; Seed Abstr.; Soils Fert.; Sorghum Mill. Abstr.; Soyabean Abstr.; Vet. Bull.; Weed Abstr.; Wheat Barley Trit. Abstr.

LC HD1775.L8 L7 **ISSN** 0886-4861
DD 338 US
D.A.E. RESEARCH REPORT. [D.A.E. res. rep.]. **VFOAT** DAE Research Report. No. 321 (June 1963)-. Monographic series. English. Irregular. Price varies per volume. Louisiana State University Agriculture & Mechanics, Department of Agricultural Economics & Agribusiness, Baton Rouge LA 70821. **Tel** (504)388-3282, FAX (504)388-2716. ***Continues*** *D.A.E. Circular.*
Ind/Abst AGRICOLA.

LC S **ISSN** 0199-7122
DD 630 US
DAKOTA FAMILY. (March 1980)-. Periodical. English. Twelve times a year. North Dakota Farm Bureau, Box 2064, Fargo ND 58107. **ED** Dawn Hvinden (editor's address: P.O. Box 2793, Bismarck, ND 58502). **Ad Acc. Circ:** 25,500 (ctrl). ***Continues in part*** *North Dakota Farm Bureau News.*

LC S **ISSN** 0198-6171
DD 630 US
UDC 631/635(783/784)
DAKOTA FARMER, THE. [Dak. farmer]. **VFOAT** The Farmer/The Dakota Farmer. Vol. 98 (Jan. 5, 1980)-. Periodical. English. Twenty-four times a year. $6.00 (Minnesota, North Dakota, South Dakota), $15.00 all other. Webb Publishing Company, 1999 Shepard Road, St Paul MN 55116. **Tel** (612)690-7203. ***Formed by the union of*** *Farmer (North & South Dakota Ed.)* ***and*** *Dakota Farmer, 0011-5789.*

LC S **ISSN** 0548-2739
DD 630 GW
DBZ, NEUE DEUTSCHE BAUERNZEITUNG. **Added/Corp** Sozialistische Einheitspartei Deutschlands. Zentral Komitee. **VFOAT** Neue Deutsche Bauernzeitung. Vol. 17, No. 23 (June 4, 1976)-. Periodical. German. Twenty-four times a year. Deutscher Judo Verband, Redaktion Ippon Segewaldweg 40, D-12557 Berlin Germany. **Tel** 011 49 711 210770, telex 051 678.
Ind/Abst Dairy Sci. Abstr.

LC HD9483.U5 F47 **ISSN** 1043-3104
DD 338.4/766862/097305 US
CODEN DEPREN
DEALER PROGRESS. [Deal. prog.]. **Added/Corp** Fertilizer Institute. Vol. 19, No. 6 (Nov./Dec. 1988)-. Trade Publication. English. Six times a year. $40.00. Fertilizer Institute, 501 2nd Street Northeast, Washington DC 20002. **Tel** (202)675-8250. ***Continues*** *Progress (Washington, D.C.), 0895-1616.*
Ind/Abst BioBusiness; Soils Fert.

LC HD1901 .D4
DD 630 PE
DEBATE AGRARIO. **Added/Corp** Centro Peruano de Estudios Sociales. (1987)-. Periodical. Spanish. Four times a year. Centro Peruano de Estudios Sociales, Cespes Avenue Slavery 818, Lima 11 Peru.
Ind/Abst Nutr. Abstr. Rev., Ser. A, Hum. Exp.; Seed Abstr.; Wheat Barley Trit. Abstr.; World Agric. Econ. Rural Sociol. Abstr.

LC S17
DD 630 HU
DEBRECENI AGRARTUDOMANYI EGYETEM TUDOMANYOS KOZLEMENYEI, A. **Added/Corp** Debreceni Agrartudomanyi Egyetem. **VFOAT** Studia Universitatis Scientiarum Agriculturae Debreceniensis. Vol. 20 (1978)-. Hungarian (summaries and/or abstracts in English, German and Russian; table of contents in English, German and Russian). One time a year. ***Formed by the union of*** *Debreceni Agrartudomany Egyetem Tudomanyos Kozlemenyei. Agrobiologiai Sorozat; Debreceni Agrartudomanyi Egyetem Tudomanyos Kozlemenyei. Allattenyesztesi Sorozat; Debreceni Agrartudomanyi Egyetem Tudomanyos Kozlemenyei.*

Agriculture

Fizikai es Muszaki Sorozat; Debreceni Agrartudomanyi Egyetem Tudomanyos Kozlemenyei. Mezogazdasagi-Okonomiai Sorozat and *Debreceni Agrartudomanyi Egyetem Tudomanyos Kozlemenyei. Novenytermesztesi Sorozat.*
Ind/Abst Agric. Eng. Abstr.; Dairy Sci. Abstr.; Field Crop Abstr.; Grass. Forage Abstr.; Maize Abstr.; Plant Breed. Abstr.; Postharvest News Inf.; Rev. Agric. Entomol.; Soils Fert.

LC QC989.S57 D45   **ISSN** 0352-180X
DD 551.6   XV
DEKADNI AGROMETEOROLOSKI BILTEN. **Added/Corp** Hidrometeoroloski Zavod Republike Slovenije. Agrometeoroloski Oddelek. (199?)-. Slovenian. Three times a month. Hidrometeoroloski Zavod SR Slovenije, Oddelek za Agrometeorologiju, Vojkova ul. 1-b, 61000 Ljubljana Slovenia. **Tel** 011 38 61327461, FAX 011 38 61320466, telex 31620. **Continues** Dekadno Agrometeorolosko Porocilo.

LC S
DD 630   US
DEL-MAR-VA HEARTLAND. VFOAT Heartland. **VAT** Delaware, Maryland, Virginia Heartland. (19??)-. Periodical. English. Heartland Publications, PO Box 249, Denton MD 21629.

LC S   **ISSN** 0194-2964
DD 630   US
DELMARVA FARMER, THE. Periodical. English. One time a week. Chesapeake Publishing Corporation / Maryland, 1 Airpark Drive, Box 600, Easton MD 21601. **Tel** (410)479-3174. **Continues** Central Shore Farmer.

LC S   **ISSN** 1051-7936
DD 630   US
DELTA COUNCIL NEWS, THE. Added/Corp Delta Council (Miss.). Vol. 1, No. 1 (Nov. 1938)-. Periodical. English. Twelve times a year. Comes with Delta Council membership. Delta Council News, PO Box 257, Stonwville MS 38776. **Tel** (601)686-4041.

LC S   **ISSN** 0011-8036
DD 630   US
DELTA FARM PRESS. [Delta farm press]. (19??)-. Newspaper. English. One time a week. $30.00. Farm Press Publishers Inc, PO Box 1420, Clarksdale MS 38614. **Tel** (601)624-8503.

LC S530 .N44A   **ISSN** 0090-7391
DD 630/.7/10782   US
UDC 63(782)
DEPARTMENT OF AGRICULTURAL EDUCATION REPORT. (REPORT.). **Main/Corp** Nebraska. University. Dept. of Agricultural Education. English. University of Nebraska / Department of Agricultural Education, Lincoln NE 68588.

LC S
DD 630   US
DEPARTMENTAL INFORMATION REPORT. Added/Corp Texas Agricultural Experiment Station. Dept. of Agricultural Economics. Texas A. & M. University. Dept. of Rural Sociology. (1974)-. Monographic series. English. Four times a year. available on microfilm. **Continues** Departmental Information Report (Texas A & M University. Dept. of Agricultural Economics and Rural Sociology).
Ind/Abst Potato Abstr.

LC K4 .E7   **ISSN** 0304-2820
DD 340.05   VE
DERECHO Y REFORMA AGRARIA; REVISTA. See Law.

LC S   **ISSN** 0302-8038
DD 630   UA
     CODEN DIBLAR
     TITLE CHANGE
DESERT INSTITUTE BULLETIN, A.R.E. [Desert Inst. bull. A.R.E.]. **Main/Corp** Mahad al-Sahara al-Misriyah. **VFOAT** Bulletin of the Desert Institute, A.R.E. **VAT** Desert Institute Bulletin, Arab Republic of Egypt. (19??)-(19??). Periodical. English. National Information & Documentation Center, A1-Tahrir St Dokki Awqaf PO, Cairo Egypt. **Tel** 011 20 2 701696, telex 93069. **Continues** Mahad al-Sahara al-Misriyah. Bulletin de l'Institut du Desert d'Egypte. **Continued by** Deser Institute Bulletin, 1110-0605.
Ind/Abst Chem. Abstr. (-1977).

LC S280.T3 T34a
DD 354/.54/82008233   II
DETAILED AGRICULTURE BUDGET. **Main/Corp** Tamil Nadu (India). (19??)-. English. One time a year. Rs5.00. Tamil Nadu India, Madras India.

LC S   **ISSN** 0343-3846
DD 630   GW
UDC 63(430.1)
DEUTSCH BAUERN-KORRESPOONDENZ. (DEUTSCHE BAUERN-KORRESPOONDENZ : MITTEILUNGSBLATT DES DEUTSCHEN BAUERNVERBANDES.). [Dtsch. Bauern-Korresp.]. (1948)-. Trade Publication. German. Twelve times a year.
Ind/Abst EMBASE.

LC SF521   **ISSN** 0943-2914
DD 638.1   GW
●**DEUTSCHES BIENEN JOURNAL.** **Added/Corp** Imkerverband Berlin. (1993)-. Periodical. German. Twelve times a year. DM34.50. Deutscher Bauernverlag GmbH, PO Box 130, D-10108 Berlin Germany. **Tel** 011 49 37 228930. **Formed by the union of** Neue BienenZeitung (Berlin, Germany) **and** Deutsches Imker Journal, 0863-3592.
Desc: Provides information on bees and bee culture.

LC S
DD 630   NE
DEVELOPMENT ORIENTED RESEARCH IN AGRICULTURE. (19??)-. English. Koninklijk Instituut voor de Tropen, Mauritskade 63, 1092 AD Amsterdam Netherlands. **Tel** 011 31 20 5688272, FAX 011 31 20 5688286.

LC HD1407 .R4   **ISSN** 0486-0837
DD 338.1   UK
DEVELOPMENT STUDIES. Added/Corp University of Reading. Dept. of Agricultural Economics. University of Reading. Dept. of Agricultural Economics and Management. **VFOAT** Development Study. No. 1 (1966)-. Monographic series. English. Price varies per volume. University of Reading Department of Agricultural Economics, 4 Earley / Whiteknights, PO Box 237, Reading RG6 2AR United Kingdom.

LC S   **ISSN** 0167-4137
DD 630   NE
     CODEN DAENDT
Pr Rev.
DEVELOPMENTS IN AGRICULTURAL ENGINEERING. [Dev. agric. eng.]. (1980)-. Academic Scholarly Publication. English. Irregular. Price varies per volume. Elsevier Science Publishers BV, PO Box 211, 1000 AE Amsterdam Netherlands. **Tel** 011 31 20 4853641, 011 31 20 4853642, FAX 011 31 20 4853598. Documents available from BIOSIS Document Express, CASDDS.
Ind/Abst AGRICOLA [Full Cov.]; Biol. Abstr. (1985-); Chem. Abstr.; GeoRef.

LC HD1501
DD 305.555   US
DIGNIDAD. Added/Corp Farm Labor Research Project, Inc. Vol. 1 (June 1991)-. Periodical. English. **Continues** Update (Farm Labor Organizing Committee (Ohio) : 1986).

LC SF98.A2 D57
     US
●**DIRECT-FED MICROBIAL, ENZYME & FORAGE ADDITIVE COMPENDIUM.** **Added/Corp** Miller Publishing Company. **VFOAT** Direct-fed Microbial, Enzyme and Forage Additive Compendium. (1993)-. Periodical. English. One time a year. $75.00. Miller Publishing Company, 12400 Whitewater Drive, Suite 160, Minnetonka MN 55343. **Tel** (612)931-0211. (**Subscription address:** CDS / SIFD Agency Control, 1901 Bell Avenue, Des Moines IA 50315. **Tel** (515)246-6812.)

LC S494.5.C6 A38A   **ISSN** 8755-5972
DD 630/.7/15   US
Pr Rev.
DIRECTORY - AGRICULTURAL COMMUNICATORS IN EDUCATION (U.S.). (DIRECTORY / AGRICULTURAL COMMUNICATORS IN EDUCATION, ACE.). [Dir. - Agric. Commun. Educ. (U.S.)]. **Main/Corp** Agricultural Communicators in Education (U.S.). Directory. English. One time a year. $75.00. ACE Headquarters, PO Box 35, Evinston FL 32633-0035. **Tel** telex (904)392-8583. Index available. ctrl circ.
Desc: Name, address, position, agency, telephone and mailing address of all ACE members.

LC HD1775.M4 M35a   **ISSN** 0145-661X
DD 338.1/025/744   US
DIRECTORY - MASSACHUSETTS DEPARTMENT OF FOOD AND AGRICULTURE. Main/Corp Massachusetts. Dept. of Food and Agriculture. (19??)-. Directory. English. Massachusetts Department of Food and Agriculture, 100 Cambridge Street, Room 2103, Boston MA 02202. **Tel** (617)727-3003, FAX (617)727-7235.

LC S409.5.N5 D57   **ISSN** 0095-5205
DD 630/.6/2749   US
UDC 061:63(749); 63(058)(749)
DIRECTORY : NEW JERSEY AGRICULTURAL ORGANIZATIONS. **VFOAT** New Jersey Agricultural Organizations. Directory. English. New Jersey Department of Agriculture, John Fitch Plaza, CN-330, Trenton NJ 08625. **Tel** (609)292-3976, FAX (609)292-3978.

LC S
     UK
DIRECTORY OF AGRICULTURAL CO-OPERATIVES IN THE UNITED KINGDOM. Added/Corp Horace Plunkett Foundation. Food from Britain (Organization) Federation of Agricultural Co-Operatives (U.K.). (1990)-. Directory. English. One time a year. £27.50. Plunkett Foundation, 23 Hanborough Business Park, Long Hanborough, Oxfordshire OX8 8LH United Kingdom. **Tel** 011 44 1993 883636, FAX 011 44 1993 883576. **Ad Acc**. **Circ**: 1,000. **Continues** Directory of Agricultural, Horticultural and Fishery Co-Operatives in the United Kingdom.

LC S494.5.C6 D57
DD 630/.1/41   US
DIRECTORY OF COMMUNICATORS IN AGRICULTURE. (19??)-. Directory. English. $5.00. Agricultural Relations Council, Chicago IL 60603.

LC TD169.6 .D5693   **ISSN** 0882-6048
DD 363.7/0025/7   US
DIRECTORY OF CONSULTANTS IN ENVIRONMENTAL SCIENCE, THE. See Environmental Issues.

LC HD1759 .D57   **ISSN** 0148-5091
DD 362.5   US
DIRECTORY OF FEDERAL DROUGHT ASSISTANCE. (19??)-. Directory. English. Institute For Policy Research, Western Governors, 2480 West 26th Avenue, Denver CO 80211.

LC S
DD 630   US
DIRECTORY OF MAJOR U.S. CORPORATIONS INVOLVED IN AGRIBUSINESS. Added/Corp Agribusiness Accountability Project. **VFOAT** Agbiz Directory. (1976)-. Directory. English. Irregular. Agribusiness ACCT Project, 3410 19th Street, PO Box 5646, San Francisco CA 94101. **Tel** (415)626-1266.

LC S21 .A37 S530.52.U6   **ISSN** 0732-8524
DD 630 630/.2/0573   US
DIRECTORY OF PROFESSIONAL WORKERS IN STATE AGRICULTURAL EXPERIMENT STATIONS AND OTHER COOPERATING STATE INSTITUTIONS. **VFOAT** Professional Workers in State Agricultural Experiment Stations and Other Cooperating State Institutions. (1981)-. Directory. English. One time a year. US Department of Agriculture, 14th Street and Independence Avenue SW, Washington DC 20250. **Tel** (202)720-5457. **Continues** Directory, Professional Workers in State Agricultural Experiment Stations and Other Cooperating State Institutions, 0732-8524.

LC S133 .A34835
DD 354.710082/33 354.710082/33042   CN
DIRECTORY OF RESEARCH / RESEARCH BRANCH = ANNUAIRE DE LA RECHERCHE / DIRECTION GENERALE DE LA RECHERCHE. Main/Corp Canada. Agriculture Canada. Research Branch. **VFOAT** Annuaire de la Recherche. (1992)-. English (French). Research Program Service, Canadian Department of Agriculture, Ottawa Ontario K1A 0C6 Canada. **Continues** Research Branch Report (Canada. Agriculture Canada. Research Branch), 0025-7580.

LC S571.5 .D57
DD 338.13   US
DIRECTORY TO ROADSIDE MARKETS AND U-PICK FARMS. Added/Corp Indiana. Office of the Commissioner of Agriculture. **VFOAT** Grown in Indiana.; Grown in Indiana Guide to Roadside Markets and U-Pick Farms. (1991)-. Directory. English. Every 2 years. Office of the Commissioner of Agriculture, One N. Capitol / Suite 700, Indianapolis IN 46204-2288. **Continues** Guide to Direct Sources of Indiana Agricultural Products.

LC S
DD 630   UK
DISCUSSION PAPER. Added/Corp University of Newcastle Upon Tyne. Dept. of Agricultural Economics. University of Newcastle Upon Tyne. Dept. of Agricultural Marketing. **VFOAT** DP; D.P. Vol. 1 (March 1982)-. Monographic series. English. Irregular. Price varies per volume. University of Newcastle Upon Tyne, Department of Agricultural Economics & Food Marketing, Newcastle Upon Tyne NE1 7RU United Kingdom.
Desc: Agricultural research.

LC S
DD 630   NZ
DISCUSSION PAPER. Added/Corp Lincoln College (University of Canterbury). Dept. of Horticulture, Landscape, and Parks. No. 1 (1981)-. English. Royal New Zealand Institute of Horticulture, PO Box 12, Lincoln College, Canterbury New Zealand. **Tel** 011 03 252811 ext 788. **ED** R.L. Sheppard. **Circ**: 300.

Agriculture

Desc: Economic and marketing papers on agricultural subjects including policy, management, transport, business, resources and education.

LC HD1483   **ISSN** 0113-4507
DD 338.109931   NZ

DISCUSSION PAPER - AGRIBUSINESS & ECONOMICS RESEARCH UNIT, LINCOLN COLLEGE. (DISCUSSION PAPER.).
[Discuss. pap. - Agribus. Econ. Res. Unit. Linc. Coll.]. (1987)-. Monographic series. English. Irregular. Price varies per volume. **Continues** *Discussion Paper - Agricultural Economics Research Unit. Lincoln College, 0110-7720.*
Ind/Abst Irr. Drain. Abstr.

LC S   **ISSN** 0951-1873
DD 630   UK

DISCUSSION PAPER - AGRICULTURAL ADMINISTRATION, RESEARCH AND EXTENSION, NETWORK.
[Discuss. pap. - Agric. Adm. Res. Ext. Netw.]. (1986)-. Monographic series. English. Two times a year. **Continues** *Network Paper - Agricultural Administration Network, 0952-2468.*
Ind/Abst World Agric. Econ. Rural Sociol. Abstr.

LC S   **ISSN** 0956-1110
DD 630   UK

DISCUSSION PAPER SERIES - UNIVERSITY OF LEEDS. SCHOOL OF BUSINESS AND ECONOMIC STUDIES.
(DISCUSSION PAPER SERIES). [Discuss. pap. ser. - Univ. Leeds, Sch. Bus. Econ. Stud.]. (1989)-. English. **Continues** *Discussion Paper Series - University of Leeds. School of Economic Studies. Series A, 0951-7030.*
Ind/Abst World Agric. Econ. Rural Sociol. Abstr.

LC S   **ISSN** 0178-3335
DD 630   GW
UDC 338.432

DISKUSSIONSBEITRAGE - UNIVERSITAET KIEL, INSTITUT FUER AGRARPOLITIK UND MARKTLEHRE.
[Diskuss.beitr. - Univ. Kiel Inst. Agrarpolit. Marktlehre]. (1980)-. Monographic series. Multiple languages. Irregular. Price varies per volume. **Continues** *Diskussionsbeitrage - Universitat Kiel, Lehrstuhl fur Agrarpolitik, 0178-3327.*
Ind/Abst World Agric. Econ. Rural Sociol. Abstr.

LC S   **ISSN** 0256-4246
DD 630   AU
UDC 63

DISSERTATIONEN DER UNIVERSITAET FUER BODENKULTUR IN WIEN.
[Diss. Univ. Bodenkult. Wien]. (1976)-. Periodical. German. Irregular. Verband der Wissenschaftlichen Gesellschaften Osterreichs, Lindengasse 37, A-1070 Vienna Austria. **Tel** 011 43 1 932166, 011 43 1 934756, telex 847/134981. **Continues** *Dissertationen der Hochschule fuer Bodenkultur in Wien.*
Ind/Abst Agrofor. Abstr.; For. Abstr.; Grass. Forage Abstr.

LC S   **ISSN** 0588-778X
DD 630   UK

DISTRIBUTION MAPS OF PESTS. SERIES A (AGRICULTURAL). Main/Corp
Commonwealth Institute of Entomology, London. Map No. 109 (June 1960)-. English. Two times a year (Jul. and Dec.). $115.00. CAB International Centre, Wallingford, Oxfordshire OX10 8DE United Kingdom. **Tel** 011 44 1491 832111, FAX 011 44 1491 833508, telex 847964 COMAGG G. **ED** J. R. Metcalfe. **Ad Acc. Continues** *Commonwealth Institute of Entomology, London. Distribution Maps of Insect Pests. Series A.*
Desc: Gives the world distribution, together with supporting references, of a particular arthropod pest. Presently dealing with pests of importance in relation to agriculture or forestry or their products.
Ind/Abst For. Prod. Abstr. (1991-); For. Abstr.; Wheat Barley Trit. Abstr.

LC S
DD 630   UK

DIVISIONAL NOTE. See Engineering.

LC S   **ISSN** 0267-5471
DD 630   UK

DIVISIONAL NOTE - NATIONAL INSTITUTE OF AGRICULTURAL ENGINEERING.
[Div. note - Natl. Inst. Agric. Eng.]. (1981)-. Monographic series. English. Irregular.
Ind/Abst World Agric. Econ. Rural Sociol. Abstr.

LC S
DD 630   GW

DLG MITTEILUNGEN AGRAR-INFORM.
Added/Corp Deutsche Landwirtschafts-Gesellschaft. **VFOAT** DLG Mitteilungen Agrarinform; DLG-Mitteilungen; DLG-Mitteilungen/Agrar-Inform. (Oct. 1990)-. Periodical. German. Twelve times a year. DM103.00 Germany; DM117.30 other. Deutsche Landwirtschafts Gesellschaft, Verlags GmbH, Eschborner Landstr 122, D-60489 Frankfurt Germany. **Tel** 011 49 69 247880, FAX 011 49 69 24788580. **Formed by the union of** *DLG-Mitteilungen, 0341-0412* **and** *Agrar-Inform, 0863-4491.*
Ind/Abst Agric. Eng. Abstr.

LC S   **ISSN** 0417-8254
DD 630   BL

DOCUMENTARIO DA VIDA RURAL.
(1952)-. Monographic series. Portuguese. Price varies per volume. Ministerio Agricultura, Centro de Publicaciones, Calle Alfonso XII 56, 28071 Madrid Spain. **Tel** 011 34 1 3475551, FAX 011 34 1 3475722.

LC S
DD 630   BL

DOCUMENTOS. Added/Corp
Empresa de Pesquisa Agropecuaria e Difusao de Tecnologia de Santa Catarina. (19??)-. Monographic series. Portuguese. Price varies per volume. EMPASC, Caixa Postal 1460, 88001 Florianopolis SC Brazil. **Tel** 011 55 842 340066, FAX 011 55 842 341024. **Continues** *Documentos (Empresa Catarinense de Pesquisa Agropecuaria), 0100-8986.*

LC S   **ISSN** 0100-9729
DD 630   BL

DOCUMENTOS (CENTRO DE PESQUISA AGROPECUARIA DO TROPICO SEMI-ARIDO).
(DOCUMENTOS / EMBRAPA, CENTRO DE PESQUISA AGROPECUARIA DO TROPICO SEMI-ARIDO.). [Doc. - Cent. Pesqui. Agropecu. Trop. Semi-Arido]. Monographic series. Portuguese. Price varies per volume.
Ind/Abst Agric. Eng. Abstr. (1991-); Field Crop Abstr.; Grass. Forage Abstr.; Helminthol. Abstr.; Index Vet.; Nutr. Abstr. Rev., Ser. B, Live Feeds and Feed.; Soils Fert.; Sorghum Mill. Abstr.

LC S   **ISSN** 0102-9185
DD 630   BL
UDC 63

DOCUMENTOS - CENTRO NACIONAL DE PESQUISA DE COCO. (DOCUMENTOS.).
[Doc. - Cent. Nac. Pesqui. Coco]. **VFOAT** Documentos - CNPCo. (1985)-. Monographic series. Portuguese. Irregular. **Continues** *Documentos - UEPAE Aracaju, 0102-3101.*
Ind/Abst Rev. Plant Pathol.

LC S
DD 630   BL

DOCUMENTOS DDT / EMBRAPA, DEPARTAMENTO DE DIFUSAO DE TECNOLOGIA AND CENTRONACIONAL DE PESQUISA DE SOJA.
No. 1 (April 1980)-. Portuguese.
Ind/Abst Biocont. News Inf.; Field Crop Abstr.

LC S   **ISSN** 0101-8949
DD 630   BL

DOCUMENTOS - EMCAPA.
(DOCUMENTOS.). [Doc. - EMCAPA]. **Added/Corp** Empresa Capixaba de Pesquisa Agropecuaria. No. 1 (April 1983)-. Monographic series. Portuguese.
Ind/Abst Plant Breed. Abstr.

LC S   **ISSN** 0102-2423
DD 630   BL

DOCUMENTOS / EMPA-MT. Added/Corp
Empresa de Pesquisa Agropecuaria do Estado de Mato Grosso. **VFOAT** Documentos; Documento. (1984)-. Periodical. Portuguese. Empresa de Pesquisa Agropecuaria de Mato Grosso, Cuiaba Brazil.
Ind/Abst Weed Abstr.

LC S   **ISSN** 0102-5651
DD 630   BL

DOCUMENTOS / UEPAE DOURADOS.
Added/Corp Empresa Brasileira de Pesquisa Agropecuaria-EMBRAPA. Unidade de Execucao de Pesquisa de Ambito Estadual de Dourados. **VFOAT** Documentos. (1983)-. Periodical. Portuguese. EMBRAPA, Unidade de Execucao de Pesquisa de Ambito Estadual de Dourados, Dourados Brazil.
Ind/Abst Irr. Drain. Abstr.; Seed Abstr.; Soils Fert.; Soyabean Abstr.

LC S   **ISSN** 1010-7649
DD 630   TU

DOGA. TURK TARIM VE ORMANCLK DERGISI.
(DOGA. TURK TARIM VE ORMANCLK DERGISI = DOGA. TURKISH JOURNAL OF AGRICULTURE AND FORESTRY.). [Doga. Turk tarim orman. derg.]. **Added/Corp** Turkiye Bilimsel be Teknik Arastrma Kurumu. **VFOAT** Doga. Turkish Journal of Agriculture and Forestry; Turk Tarim ve Ormanclk Dergisi; Turkish Journal of Agriculture and Forestry. (1986)-. Academic Scholarly Publication. Turkish (summaries and/or abstracts in German). Six times a year. $150.00. Tubitak, Ataturk Bulvari, No: 221, 06100 Kavaklidere Ankara Turkey. **(Subscription address:** Tubitak, Bilimsel Dergiler, Yazi Isleri Mudurlugu, PO Box 5, Kizilay 06420 Ankara Turkey. **Tel** 011 90 312 4685300 ext. 1122, 011 90 312 4270493, FAX 011 90 312 4271336.) **ED** Ferhan Hatipoglu. **Circ:** 700. Documents available from CASDDS. **Continues** *Doga Bilim Dergisi. Seri D2, Tarim ve Ormanclk, 1011-0917.*
Desc: Covers all fields of agriculture, research in soil and harvest, agricultural technology and mechanization, and forestry (technology and environment).
Ind/Abst Agric. Eng. Abstr.; Chem. Abstr.; Crop Physiol. Abstr.; Ecol. Abstr.; Field Crop Abstr.; For. Prod. Abstr.; Geogr. Abstr. Human Geogr.; Grass. Forage Abstr.; Nutr. Abstr. Rev., Ser. B, Live Feeds and Feed.; Postharvest News Inf.; Potato Abstr.; Rev. Plant Pathol.; Rice Abstr.; Seed Abstr.; Soils Fert.; Weed Abstr.

LC S   **ISSN** 0587-2650
DD 630   BU

DOKLADY. Main/Corp
Akademiia Na Selskostopanskite Nauki. (1968)-. Multiple languages (English, French, German and Russian). Four times a year. **(Subscription address:** Hemus Foreign Trade Organization, 1B Raiko Daskalov Sq Books, 1000 Sofia Bulgaria. **Tel** 011 359 2 882544, 011 359 2 801575.)

LC S
DD 630   RU

CODEN DRASE8

DOKLADY ROSSIISKOI AKADEMII SELSKOKHOZIAISTVENNYKH NAUK.
Added/Corp Rossiiskaia Akademiia Selskokhoziaistvennykh Nauk. **VFOAT** Doklady Rosselkhozakademii. (1992)-. Periodical. Russian. Six times a year. $79.95. Izdatelstvo Kolos, Sadovaia-Spasskaia 18, 107807 Moscow Russia. **(Subscription address:** East View Publications Inc., 3020 Harbor Lane North, Suite 110, Minneapolis MN 55447. **Tel** (800)477-1005, (612)550-0961, FAX (612)559-2931.) **Continues** *Doklady Vsesoiuznoi Akademii Selskokhoziaistvennykh Nauk Imeni V.I. Lenina, 0042-9244.*

LC S
DD 630   RU

CODEN DVASAW

DOKLADY VSESOIUZNOI ORDENA LENINA I ORDENA TRUDOVOGO KRASNOGO ZNAMENI AKADEMII SELSKOKHOZIAISTVENNYKH NAUK IMENI V. I LENINA.
Added/Corp Vsesoiuznaia Akademiia Selskokhoziaistvennykh Nauk Imeni V.I. Lenina. No. 9 (Sept. 1979)-. Periodical. Russian (table of contents in English). Twelve times a year. Izdatelstvo Kolos, Sadovaia-Spasskaia 18, 107807 Moscow Russia. Documents available from BIOSIS Document Express. **Continues** *Doklady Vsesoiuznoi Ordena Lenina Akademii Selskokhoziaistvennykh Nauk Imeni V.I. Lenina.*
Ind/Abst AgBiotech News Inf.; Agric. Eng. Abstr.; Anim. Breed. Abstr.; Biol. Abstr.; Dairy Sci. Abstr.; Field Crop Abstr.; For. Abstr.; Hortic. Abstr.; Index Vet.; Maize Abstr.; Nematol. Abstr.; Plant Breed. Abstr.; Plant Genet. Resour. Abstr.; Plant Grow. Reg. Abstr.; Postharvest News Inf.; Potato Abstr.; Poult. Abstr.; Rev. Med. Vet. Mycology.

LC S   **ISSN** 0253-228X
DD 630   CC

CODEN DNXUDW

DONGBEI NONGXUEYUAN XUEBAO.
(TUNG-PEI NUNG HSUEH YUAN HSUEH PAO.). [Dongbei nongxueyuan xuebao]. **Added/Corp** Tung-pei Nung Hsueh Yuan. **VFOAT** Journal of Northeast Agricultural College. (19??)-. Academic Scholarly Publication. Chinese (English). Four times a year. $60.00. Dongbei Nongye Daxue, Xuebao Bianjibu Xiangfang-qu, Harbin Heilongjiang 150030, People's Republic of China. **Tel** 5665886, FAX 5663336. **ED** Li Wenxiong. **Circ:** 6,000. Documents available from CASDDS.
Desc: Contains information from scientific experiments in agricultural science.
Ind/Abst Agrofor. Abstr.; Chem. Abstr. (?-1983); NAPRALERT.

LC SB951 .D58   **ISSN** 0012-5792
DD 630.2405   US
UDC 63

CODEN DOEAAH

DOWN TO EARTH.
[Down earth]. Vol. 1. (May 1945)-. Periodical. English. Three times a year. Free. Dow Chemical Company, 2020 Dow Center, Barstow Building, Midland MI 48640. **Tel** (517)636-1000. Index available. **Bk Rev. Circ:** 6,000 (ctrl). Documents available from BIOSIS Document Express, CASDDS.
Desc: A journal of agricultural research and product developments, directed primarily at agricultural researchers in university and government laboratories, extension services, and corporations.
Ind/Abst Biol. Abstr.; Chem. Abstr.; Hortic. Abstr.; Maize Abstr.; Protozoolog. Abstr.; Rev. Med. Vet. Entomol.; Rev. Plant Pathol.; Soils Fert.; Weed Abstr.; Wildl. Rev.

LC HA1631 .A33 HD2045.5
DD 314.971   YU

DRUSTVENA POLJOPRIVREDNA GAZDINSTVA. Main/Corp
Savezni Zavod za Statistiku (Yugoslavia). (19??)-. Serbo-Croatian (Roman). Savezni Zavod za Statistiku / Federal Statistical Office, Kneza Milosa 20, Belgrade 11000 Yugoslavia.

Agriculture

LC S13 .P45a
PL

DZIENNIK URZEDOWY MINISTERSTWA ROLNICTWA, LESNICTWA I GOSPODARKI ZYWNOSCIOWEJ.
Main/Corp Poland. Ministerstwo Rolnictwa, Lesnictwa i Gospodarki Zywnosciowej. (198?)-. Periodical. Polish. Irregular. Price on request. **(Subscription address:** Ars Polona-Ruch, PO Box 1001, Krakowskie Przedmiescie 7, 00-068 Warsaw Poland. **Tel** 011 48 22 261201.)
Continues Dziennik Urzedowy Ministerstwa Rolnictwa i Gospodarki Zywnosciowej.

LC HD2330 **ISSN** 1183-630X
DD 338.1
CN

EARTHKEEPING ONTARIO. [Earthkeep. Ont.].
Added/Corp Jubilee Centre for Agricultural Research. (1991)-. Newsletter. English. Six times a year. 12.01Can$. Christian Farmers Federation of Ontario, 115 Woolwich Street, Guelph Ontario N1H 3V1 Canada. **Tel** (519)837-1620, FAX (519)310-1835. **Circ:** 3,500 (ctrl). **Continues** Earthkeeping (Guelph, Ont.), 0833-823X.
Ind/Abst Christ. Period. Index (19??-).

LC S **ISSN** 0012-8325
DD 630
UDC 63(676)
KE

EAST AFRICAN AGRICULTURAL AND FORESTRY JOURNAL. Vol. 1, (July 1935)-.
Periodical. English. Four times a year. Sh300.00. Kenya Agricultural Research Institute Library, PO Box 30148, Nairobi Kenya. **Tel** 0154-32880-1-6, telex KARI NAIROBI. **ED** Joseph Oloo Mugah. Index available. cum. index. **Bk Rev. Ad Acc. Circ:** 3,000 (ctrl). Documents available from CASDDS.
Desc: Original research findings in agriculture, forestry, and animal sciences.
Ind/Abst AgBiotech News Inf.; Agrofor. Abstr. (1991-); Anim. Breed. Abstr.; Biodeter. Abstr.; Chem. Abstr.; Cot. Trop. Fibr. Abstr. Bibliogr.; Dairy Sci. Abstr.; Field Crop Abstr.; Food Sci. Technol. Abstr.; For. Prod. Abstr.; For. Abstr.; Grass. Forage Abstr.; Hortic. Abstr.; Index Vet.; Maize Abstr.; Nutr. Abstr. Rev., Ser. B, Live Feeds and Feed.; Nutr. Abstr. Rev., Ser. A, Hum. Exp.; Pig News Inf.; Plant Breed. Abstr.; Poult. Abstr.; Protozoolog. Abstr.; Rev. Agric. Entomol.; Rev. Med. Vet. Mycology; Rev. Plant Pathol.; Rice Abstr.; Seed Abstr.; Soils Fert.; Sorghum Mill. Abstr.; Vet. Bull.; Weed Abstr.

LC HD1920.7 .A2
DD 630
UK

EAST EUROPE. AGRICULTURE AND FOOD.
Added/Corp Agra Europe (London) Limited. **VFOAT** Agriculture and Food. No. 114 (March 1992)-. Periodical. English. Twelve times a year. $727.26. Agra Europe London Limited, 25 Frant Road, Tunbridge Wells, Kent TN2 5JT United Kingdom. **Tel** 011 44 1892 533813, FAX 011 44 1892 544895, telex 95114 AGRATW G.
Continues East Europe & USSR. Agriculture and Food.

LC HD1401 .E27 **ISSN** 0377-7103
DD 338.1/0967
UG

EASTERN AFRICA JOURNAL OF RURAL DEVELOPMENT. [East. Afr. j. rural dev.]. Vol. 6 (1973)-.
English. Two times a year. Eastern Africa Agricultural Economics Society, Department of Rural Economy and Extension, PO Box 7062, Kampala Uganda. available on microfilm and microfiche from University Microfilms International (UMI). **Continues** East African Journal of Rural Development.
Ind/Abst Int. Labour Doc.

LC S **ISSN** 0967-7852
DD 630
UK

EC PACKAGING REPORT.
English. Twelve times a year. £285.00 Europe; £300.00 other. Agra Europe London Limited, 25 Frant Road, Tunbridge Wells, Kent TN2 5JT United Kingdom. **Tel** 011 44 1892 533813, FAX 011 44 1892 544895, telex 95114 AGRATW G.

LC S583 **ISSN** 1057-1949
DD 631
US

EC - UNIVERSITY OF ARKANSAS, FAYETTEVILLE. COOPERATIVE EXTENSION SERVICE. (EC.). [EC - Univ. Ark. Fayettev., Coop. Ext. Serv.].
Added/Corp University of Arkansas (System). Cooperative Extension Service. United States. Dept. of Agriculture. **VFOAT** E.C. VAT Extension Circular. (197?)-. Monographic series. English. **Continues** Circular (University of Arkansas (System). Cooperative Extension Service).
Ind/Abst AGRICOLA [Full Cov.].

LC S
DD 630
GW

ECOLOGY AND FARMING : INTERNATIONAL IFOAM MAGAZINE.
Added/Corp International Federation of Organic Agriculture Movements. **VFOAT** Ecology + Farming. No. 1 (1990)-. Periodical. English (French and Spanish). Three times a year. DM30.00 Europe; DM48.00 other. IFOAM - International Federation of Organic Agriculture, Oekozentrum Imsbach, D-66636 Tholey Theley Germany. **Tel** 011 49 6853 5190, FAX 011 49 6853 30110. **ED** Franz Frey. **Bk Rev. Ad Acc. Continues** IFOAM Bulletin.
Desc: Reports on the development of organic agriculture worldwide. It covers practice, research, agropolitics, news items as well as conference reports and book reviews.

LC S **ISSN** 0886-5345
DD 630
UDC 338.43; 63
US

ECONOMIC AND SOCIAL ISSUES. [Econ. soc. issues].
Main/Corp University of California, Davis. Cooperative Extension. (Feb./March 1975)-. Periodical. English. Six times a year. Free. University of California Department of Agriculture, Economic Extension, Davis CA 95616.
Ind/Abst AGRICOLA [Full Cov.].

LC S **ISSN** 1191-3576
DD 630
CN

ECONOMIC PLANNING IN FREE SOCIETIES. [Econ. plann. free soc.]. Vol. 27, No. 6 (Nov./Dec. 1991)-.
Periodical. English. Six times a year. 24.00Can$ US and Canada; 28.00Can$ other. Academic Publishing Company, PO Box 145, Mount Royal Quebec, H3P 3B9 Canada. **Tel** (514)738-5255. **ED** Dr. Peter Harsany. Index Bound in First Issue. **Bk Rev. Circ:** 1,200. **Continues** Economic Planning, 0013-0222.
Desc: News and information in agricultural economics, planning in general, world food supply and privatization.

LC S
DD 630
US

ECONOMIC SUMMARY OF EXTENSION TECHNICAL BULLETIN NO. ..., AN.
Added/Corp University of Arkansas (System). Cooperative Extension Service. (1988)-. Bulletin. English. Price varies per volume.

LC S **ISSN** 0100-4107
DD 630
BL
CODEN ECSSE4

ECOSSISTEMA / FACULDADE DE AGRONOMIA E ZOOTECNIA "MANOEL CARLOS GONCALVES.". Added/Corp
Faculdade de Agronomia e Zootecnia Manoel Carlos Goncalves. Vol. 1, No. 1 (1976)-. Periodical. Portuguese (summaries and/or abstracts in English and Portuguese). One time a year. Faculdade de Agronomia e Zootecnia Manoel Carlos Goncalves, Av. Helio Vergueiro Leiti, S/N Caixa Postal 5 Espirito Santo, de Pinhal Sao Paulo Brazil. **Bk Rev. Ad Acc. Circ:** 1,000 (ctrl).
Desc: Publishes mainly agricultural and veterinary research.
Ind/Abst AgBiotech News Inf.; Biocont. News Inf.; Biodeter. Abstr.; Field Crop Abstr.; Hortic. Abstr.; Maize Abstr.; Plant Breed. Abstr.; Postharvest News Inf.; Rev. Agric. Entomol.; Rev. Med. Vet. Entomol.; Rev. Plant Pathol.; Rice Abstr.; Seed Abstr.; Soils Fert.; Soyabean Abstr.; Wheat Barley Trit. Abstr.

LC S **ISSN** 0422-7212
DD 630
ER
CODEN EPSNA8

EESTI POLLUMAJANDUSE AKADEEMIA TEADUSLIKE TOODE KOGUMIK. VFOAT Sbornik Nauchnykh Trudov. 1 (1955)-.
Periodical. Russian (Estonian, English and German; summaries and/or abstracts in Russian, English and German). $20.00.
Ind/Abst AGRICOLA; Anim. Breed. Abstr.

LC HD1920.5.Z775 E44
DD 338.1/3/09401
LU

EG-AGRARPREISINDIZES. VORSCHATZUNG DER EG-AGRARPREISINDIZES (OUTPUT AND INPUT) FUR ... . VFOAT
Vorschatzung der EG-Agrarpreisindizes (Output und Input) fur ...; Forecast of the EC Agricultural Price Indices (Output and Input) for ...; EC Agricultural Price Indices. Forecast of the EC Agricultural Price Indices (Output and Input) for ... . English (French, German and Italian).

LC S **ISSN** 1018-8851
DD 630
TU

EGE UNIVERSITESI ZIRAAT FAKULTESI DERGISI. [Ege Üniv. Ziraat fak. derg.]. VFOAT
Journal of Agricultural Faculty of Ege University; Ziraat Fakultesi Dergisi (Bornova). (1975)-. Periodical. Turkish. Three times a year. Documents available from CASDDS. **Continues** Ege Universitesi, Ziraat Fakultesi, Dergisi, Seri A, 0367-1550.
Ind/Abst Biodeter. Abstr.; Chem. Abstr.; Field Crop Abstr.; Irr. Drain. Abstr.; Rev. Med. Vet. Mycology; Rev. Plant Pathol.; Seed Abstr.; Wheat Barley Trit. Abstr.

LC S **ISSN** 0424-6829
DD 630
JA
CODEN ECPMAZ

EHIME DAIGAKU NOGAKUBU KIYO.
(EHIME DAIGAKU NOGAKUBU KIYO. MEMOIRS OF THE COLLEGE OF AGRICULTURE, EHIME UNIVERSITY.). [Ehime Daigaku Nogakubu kiyo]. **Main/Corp** Ehime Daigaku. Nogakubu. **Added/Corp** Ehime Daigaku. Nogakubu. Ehime Daigaku Nogakubu Kiyo. **VFOAT** Memoirs of the College of Agriculture, Ehime University. Vol. 13 (1968)-. Academic Scholarly Publication. Japanese (English). Price varies per volume. Ehime University, College of Agriculture, 3-ban Bunkyo-cho, Matsuyama-shi 790 Japan. Documents available from CASDDS. **Continues** Ehime Daigaku. Memoirs of the Ehime University. Sect. VI (Agriculture).
Ind/Abst AGRICOLA; Chem. Abstr.; For. Abstr.; Plant Breed. Abstr.; Plant Grow. Reg. Abstr.; Rev. Plant Pathol.; Seed Abstr.; World Agric. Econ. Rural Sociol. Abstr.

LC S **ISSN** 0389-2859
DD 630
JA
CODEN ECSHD4

EHIME-KEN CHIKUSAN SHIKENJO KENKYU HOKOKU. [Ehime-ken Chikusan Shikenjo kenkyu hokoku]. VFOAT
Bulletin of the Ehime Prefectural Animal Husbandry Experiment Station. (1975)-. Academic Scholarly Publication. Japanese. Ehimeken Chikusan Shikenjo, (Ehime Prefectural Animal Husbandry Experiment Station), Age Nomuracho, Higashiuwagun Ehimeken 797-12 Japan. Documents available from CASDDS.
Ind/Abst Chem. Abstr. (1975-1982).

LC S
DD 630
UDC 338.43(476)
BW

EKONOMICHESKIE VOPROSY RAZVITIIA SELSKOGO KHOZIAISTVA BSSR.
Russian. Uradzhai / Harvest Publishing House, Masherova 11, 220600 Minsk Byelarus. **Tel** 0172 23-64-94.

LC S
DD 630
YU

EKONOMIKA PROIZVODNJE HRANE.
Vol. 24 (Jan./Feb. 1977)-. Periodical. Serbo-Croatian (Roman) (summaries and/or abstracts in Russian). 750.00. U1 Kneza Milosa Br 9/1, Postanski FAH 577, Belgrad Yugoslavia. **Continues** Ekonomika Poljoprivrede.
Ind/Abst Leis., Rec., Tour. Abstr.; Rural Dev. Abstr.; World Agric. Econ. Rural Sociol. Abstr.

LC HD1491.R9 U35 **ISSN** 0235-2494
DD 338.1
RU

EKONOMIKA SELSKOKHOZIAISTVENNYKH I PERERABATYVAIUSHCHIKH PREOPRIIATII.
Added/Corp Gosudarstvennyi Agropromyshlennyi Komitet SSSR. (1988)-. Periodical. Russian. Twelve times a year. Izdatelstvo Kolos, Sadovaia-Spasskaia 18, 107807 Moscow Russia. **(Subscription address:** East View Publications Inc., 3020 Harbor Lane North, Suite 110, Minneapolis MN 55447. **Tel** (800)477-1005, (612)550-0961, FAX (612)559-2931.) **Continues** Planirovanie i Uchet v Selskokhoziaistvennykh Predpriiatiiakh, 0206-5703.
Desc: Information on collective farms, state farms and agricultural industries.
Ind/Abst Agric. Eng. Abstr.; Sug. Indus. Abstr.

LC S
DD 630
AT

ELDERS WEEKLY. (19??)-.
Periodical. English. Irregular (every Thurs.). 92.50Aus$ (includes Farm Weekly). Western Farmer & Grazier, PO Box 1268, Victoria Park East, 6101 Australia. **Tel** 011 61 9 3560356. **Continues** Western Farmer & Grazier, 0311-7804.

LC S **ISSN** 0886-9693
DD 630
US

EMPIRE STATE FARMER. (198?)-.
Periodical. English. Twenty-four times a year. Jefferson County Journal / NY, PO Box 68, 7 Main Street, Adams NY 13605. **Tel** (315)232-2141, (315)232-4586, FAX (315)232-4586. **Continues** North Country Farmer, 0194-7516.

LC SF **ISSN** 1077-355X
DD 636
US
TITLE CHANGE

EMU MARKETPLACE. [Emu marketpl.]. VFOAT
Marketplace. (199?)-(19??). Periodical. English. Ratite Marketplace, 114 North Mason, PO Box 1613, Bowie TX 76230. **Tel** (817)872-6189, (800)972-7730, FAX (817)872-3559. **Continued by** Ratite Marketplace.

LC S
DD 630
CK

ENCUESTA AGROPECUARIA NACIONAL.
Main/Corp Colombia. Departamento Administrativo Nacional de Estadistica. Periodical. Spanish. **Continues** Encuesta Agricola Nacional.

LC S **ISSN** 0100-3593
DD 630
BL
CODEN ENAGDM

ENERGIA NUCLEAR E AGRICULTURA.
See Energy-Atomic Energy.

LC S **ISSN** 0921-9757
DD 630
NE
CODEN EWAGEI

ENERGY IN WORLD AGRICULTURE.
[Energy world agric.]. Vol. 1 (1986)-. Monographic series. English. Irregular. Price varies per volume. Elsevier Science Publishers BV, PO Box 211, 1000 AE

Agriculture

Amsterdam Netherlands. **Tel** 011 31 20 4853641, 011 31 20 4853642, FAX 011 31 20 4853598. **(Subscription address:** Elsevier Science Inc. / New York Books, 655 Avenue of the Americas, New York NY 10010. **Tel** (212)633-3650.) Documents available from BIOSIS Document Express.
 Ind/Abst AGRICOLA [Full Cov.]; Biocont. News Inf.; Biol. Abstr. (1987-).

LC S   ISSN 0100-6916
DD 630
     BL
     CODEN EARIDM
ENGENHARIA AGRICOLA. [Eng. agric.].
(1972)-. Academic Scholarly Publication. Portuguese. Documents available from BIOSIS Document Express, CASDDS.
 Ind/Abst Biol. Abstr.; Chem. Abstr.

LC S
DD 630   UK
     CEASED
ENTERPRISE FARMING. (19??)-(Apr. 19, 1994).
English. Cooperative Development Division Food Britain, New Covent Garden Market, 301-344 Market Towers, London SW8 5NQ United Kingdom. **Tel** 011 44 181 7202144, FAX 011 44 181 6270616, telex 267901. **ED** Mary Curnock Cook. **Circ:** 160,000 (ctrl). **Continues** Farming Business.
 Desc: Highlights successful agricultural enterprises.

LC S   ISSN 0343-6462
DD 630   GW
UDC 63.341.232   CCC
     CODEN 63.339.96
ENTWICKLUNG + LANDLICHER RAUM.
VFOAT Entwicklung und Landlicher Raum. (1974)-. Trade Publication. German. Six times a year. $50.67. Deutsche Landwirtschafts Gesellschaft, Verlags GmbH, Eschborner Landstr 122, D-60489 Frankfurt Germany. **Tel** 011 49 69 247880, FAX 011 49 69 24788580.
 Ind/Abst Field Crop Abstr.; Hortic. Abstr.; Index Vet.; Irr. Drain. Abstr.; Nutr. Abstr. Rev., Ser. B, Live Feeds and Feed.; Nutr. Abstr. Rev., Ser. A, Hum. Exp.; Postharvest News Inf.; Potato Abstr.; Protozoolog. Abstr.; World Agric. Econ. Rural Sociol. Abstr.

LC QH301 .E58   ISSN 0970-0420
DD 574/.05   II
UDC 614.7
     CODEN ENECEV
ENVIRONMENT & ECOLOGY. See Biology.

LC S   ISSN 1121-2896
DD 630   IT
UDC 633.8
ERBORISTA MILANO, L'. (L'ERBORISTA.).
[Erborista Milano]. (1992)-. Periodical. Italian. Six times a year. L45000 Italy; L70000 Europe; L80000 other. Tecniche Nuove SPA, Via Ciro Menotti 14, 20129 Milan Italy. **Tel** 011 39 2 75701, FAX 011 39 2 7570205, telex 334647 TECHS I.

LC S   ISSN 0521-3851
DD 630   HU
UDC 634.0
ERDESZETI KUTATASOK. [Erdesz. Kut.].
(1954)-. Periodical. Multiple languages. Two times a year. **Continues** Erdeszeti Kiserletek, 0367-1291.
 Ind/Abst Plant Grow. Reg. Abstr.; Rev. Agric. Entomol.

LC S21.R44 E18A   ISSN 0361-9524
DD 664/.008   US
ERRL PUBLICATION. Main/Corp United States.
Agricultural Research Service. Eastern Regional Research Laboratory. English. Eastern Utilization Research & Development Division, Agricultural Research Service, U.S. Dept of Agriculture, 600 East Mermaid Lane, Philadelphia PA 19118. **Continues** United States. Agricultural Research Service. Eastern Marketing and Nutrition Research Division. EMN Publication.

LC S   ISSN 0082-9730
DD 630   US
UDC 338.43(73)
ERS. [ERS]. Main/Corp United States. Dept. of Agriculture. Economics, Statistics, and Cooperatives Service. VAT Economic Research Service.
Monographic series. English. Price varies per volume. Department of Agriculture / Economics Statistics and Cooperative, Economics Statistics and Cooperatives Service, 14th Street and Independence Avenue SW, Washington DC 20250. **Tel** (202)720-2791. **Continues** ERS, 0082-9730.
 Ind/Abst AGRICOLA.

LC HD9014.M6 E84
DD 338.1/0972   MX
UDC 338.439.4(72)
ESTIMACION DE LA PRODUCCION AGRICOLA EN LOS DISTRITOS DE RIEGO.
Spanish. One time a year. Secretaria de Agricultura y Recursos Hidraulicos, Direccion General de Economia, Agricola Carolina No 132 - 120, Piso Delegacion Benito, Juarez Codigo Postal 03720 Mexico DF.

LC HC111 .A15a
DD 354.710082   CN
●ESTIMATES. PART III, AGRICULTURE AND AGRIFOOD CANADA EXPENDITURE PLAN. Main/Corp Canada.
VFOAT Agriculture and Agrifood Canada Expenditure Plan; Budget des Depenses. Partie III, Agriculture et Agro-Alimentaire Canada Plan de Depenses. (1994)-. English (French). Canada Communication Group Publishers, Order Processing, Ottawa Ontario K1A 0S9 Canada. **Tel** (819)956-4800, (819)956-4802. **Formed by the union of** Canada. Estimates. Part III, Agriculture Canada; Canada. Estimates. Part III, Consumer and Corporate Affairs Expenditure Plan **and** Canada. Estimates. Part III, Industry, Science and Technology Canada. Expenditure Plan.

LC HD1781 .C36a
DD 354.710082/33   CN
     TITLE CHANGE
ESTIMATES. PART III, AGRICULTURE CANADA. Main/Corp Canada. VFOAT Budget des Depenses. Partie III, Agriculture Canada.
(19??)-(199?). English (French). Canada Communication Group Publishers, Order Processing, Ottawa Ontario K1A 0S9 Canada. **Tel** (819)956-4800, (819)956-4802. **Absorbed by** Canada. Estimates. Part III, Consumer and Corporate Affairs Expenditure Plan; Canada. Estimates. Part III, Industry, Science and Technology Canada. Expenditure Plan **and** Canada. Estimates. Part III, Agriculture and Agrifood Canada Expenditure Plan.

LC S401.U6 A22
DD 630.82   US
ESTUDIOS AGROPECUARIOS DE LA FAO. Main/Corp Food and Agriculture Organization of the United Nations.
No. 1-. Spanish (English). UNIPUB, 4611-F Assembly Drive, Lanham MD 20706-4391. **Tel** (800)274-4888, FAX (301)459-0056, telex 28787 GATT CH.

LC HD1790.5 .A27   ISSN 0120-0747
DD 338.1   CK
ESTUDIOS RURALES LATINOAMERICANOS. Added/Corp Consejo Latinoamericano de Ciencias Sociales. Secretaria Ejecutiva. Consejo Latinoamericano de Ciencias Sociales. Comision de Estudios Rurales.
Vol. 1 (Jan./April 1978)-. Periodical. Spanish. One time a year. $50.00. Estudios Rurales Latinoamericanos, Apartado Aereo 11386, Bogota Colombia. **Tel** 011 57 1 2837771. cum. index.
 Ind/Abst Hisp. Am. Period. Index, HAPI; Int. Labour Doc.; LABORDOC.

LC S469.S7 E78   ISSN 0210-4830
DD 630.94   SP
ESTUDIS D'HISTORIA AGRARIA. [Estud. hist. agrar.]. Added/Corp Centro de Estudios Historicos Internacionales (Barcelona, Spain).
(1978)-. Periodical. Catalan (Spanish). One time a year. 2010ptas. Curial Ediciones Catalanes S A, Bruc 144 Baixos, 08037 Barcelona Spain. **Tel** 011 34 3 2588101, FAX 207 74 27. **ED** Rafael Aracil, Llorenc Ferrer, Emili Giralt, Antoni Riera, Antoni Segura, Jaume Suau. cum. index.
 Desc: Review devoted to the agrarian history of the Iberian peninsula, from neolithic from today.
 Ind/Abst AGRICOLA; Am. Hist. Life.

LC S   ISSN 0257-2605
DD 630   ET
UDC 63
ETHIOPIAN JOURNAL OF AGRICULTURAL SCIENCES. [Ethiop. j. agric. sci.]. VFOAT EJAS.
(1979)-. Periodical. English. Irregular. $75.00. Ethiopian Journal of Agricultural Sciences, PO Box 5509, Addis Ababa Ethiopia. **Tel** 011 251 1 2572.
 Ind/Abst Agric. Eng. Abstr.; Field Crop Abstr.; Rev. Agric. Entomol.; Rev. Med. Vet. Mycology; Rev. Plant Pathol.; Seed Abstr.; Sorghum Mill.; Soyabean Abstr.; Weed Abstr.; Wheat Barley Trit. Abstr.

LC S   ISSN 0967-7844
DD 630   UK
EUROCHEM MONITOR. (19??)-. Trade
Publication. English. Two times a year. $2053.45. Agra Europe London Limited, 25 Frant Road, Tunbridge Wells, Kent TN2 5JT United Kingdom. **Tel** 011 44 1892 533813, FAX 011 44 1892 544895, telex 95114 AGRATW G.

LC S
DD 630   UK
EUROCHEM MONITOR UPDATES. (19??)-.
Periodical. English. £220.00 UK and Europe; £245.00 other. Agra Europe London Limited, 25 Frant Road, Tunbridge Wells, Kent TN2 5JT United Kingdom. **Tel** 011 44 1892 533813, FAX 011 44 1892 544895, telex 95114 AGRATW G.

LC S
DD 630   UK
EUROFOOD MONITOR UPDATES. (19??)-.
Periodical. English. £165.00 UK and Europe; £175.00 other. Agra Europe London Limited, 25 Frant Road, Tunbridge Wells, Kent TN2 5JT United Kingdom. **Tel** 011 44 1892 533813, FAX 011 44 1892 544895, telex 95114 AGRATW G.

LC S
DD 630   FR
EUROLETTRE PARIS. (EUROLETTRE.).
(198?)-. Periodical. French. Twenty-four times a year. $407.03. Eurolettre / de M. F. Guillaume, 13 Square Gabriel Faure, F-75017 Paris France. **Tel** 011 33 1 42671375. **Circ:** 500.
 Desc: Covers European and world political problems in agriculture and the food industry.

LC S
DD 630   UK
EUROPEAN FERTILIZER REVIEW. (19??)-.
English. Twenty-four times a year. £490.00 UK; $980.00 North America; 1125.00Can$ Canada. Ferteeon Limited, 25 Copperfield Street, Suite B, London SE1 0EN United Kingdom. **Tel** 011 44 171 2619998, FAX 011 44 171 9287911.
 Desc: Market report on European industry.

LC S583   ISSN 1381-2335
DD 631   NE
UDC 631/632:371
Pr Rev.
●EUROPEAN JOURNAL OF AGRICULTURAL EDUCATION AND EXTENSION. [Eur. j. agric. educ. ext.]. (1994)-.
Academic Scholarly Publication. English. Four times a year. European Journal of Agricultural Education and Extension, PO Box 194, 6700 AD Wageningen Netherlands. **Tel** 011 31 837084018.

LC S   ISSN 0755-1134
DD 630   FR
UDC 63
     TITLE CHANGE
EVOLUTION AGRICOLE. (1961)-(1993).
Periodical. French. AFIP Editions Diffusion, 2 rue Paul Escudier, 75009 Paris France. **Tel** 011 33 1 48745288. **Merged with** Trans Rural Express, 0766-8007; **Changed back to** Trans Rural Initiatives, 1165-6166.

LC S
DD 630   IT
EVOLUZIONE AGRICOLA; MENSILE DI ATTUALITA E TECNICA ZOOAGRICOLA. (1???)-. Periodical. Italian.
Twelve times a year. L30000 Italy; L80000 other. Sigma 2, Via Pietro da Cemmo 3, 20155 Milan Italy. **Tel** 011 39 2 33002856.

LC S3 .E9   ISSN 0014-4797
DD 630   UK
     CCC
     CODEN EXAGAL
Pr Rev.
EXPERIMENTAL AGRICULTURE. [Exp. agric.].
Vol. 1, No. 1 (Jan. 1965)-. Academic Scholarly Publication. English. Four times a year (January, April, July and October). $192.00. Cambridge University Press, The Edinburgh Building, Shaftesbury Road, Cambridge CB2 2RU United Kingdom. **Tel** 011 44 1223 312393, FAX 011 44 1223 315052, telex 851-817256. **(Subscription address:** Cambridge University Press / North America, 110 Midland Avenue, Port Chester NY 10573. **Tel** (800)431-1580, (914)937-9600.) **ED** F. G. H. Lupton. **Bk Rev.** Documents available from The Genuine Article, BIOSIS Document Express, CASDDS, Documents on Demand. **Continues** Empire Journal of Experimental Agriculture.
 Desc: Publishes the results of analytical research into the agronomy of crops, particularly the food, forage, and industrial crops of the warmer regions of the earth. Especially concerned with experimental work conducted in the field and designed to explain agronomic results in biological and environmental terms. Publishes accounts of new methods of experimental crop production and discussions of problems arising from the rapid expansion of agricultural production. Particular emphasis is placed on papers covering farming systems and sustainability in tropical regions.
 Ind/Abst AgBiotech News Inf.; AGRICOLA [Select. Cov.]; Agrofor. Abstr. (19??-19??); BioBusiness; Biol. Agric. Index; Biol. Abstr.; Chem. Abstr.; Cot. Trop. Fibr. Abstr. Bibliogr.; Crop Physiol. Abstr.; Curr. Aware. Biol. Sci., CABS; Curr. Cit.; Curr. Contents Agric. Biol. Environ. Sci.; Dairy Sci. Abstr.; Ecol. Abstr.; Energy Inf. Abstr.; Environ. Abstr.; Field Crop Abstr.; Food Sci. Technol. Abstr.; Geogr. Abstr. Human Geogr.; Grass. Forage Abstr.; Hortic. Abstr.; Index Vet.; Int. Dev. Abstr.; Irr. Drain. Abstr.; Leadscan; Leis., Rec., Tour. Abstr.; Maize Abstr.; Nutr. Abstr. Rev., Ser. B, Live Feeds and Feed.; Nutr. Abstr. Rev., Ser. A, Hum. Exp.; Rev. Stat. Collect.; Plant Breed. Abstr.; Plant Genet. Resour. Abstr.; Plant Grow. Reg. Abstr.; Potato Abstr.; Protozoolog. Abstr.; Res. Alert [Full Cov.]; Rev. Agric. Entomol.; Rev. Med. Vet. Mycology; Rev. Plant Pathol.; Rice Abstr.; Rural Dev. Abstr.; Sci. Cit. Index; SCISEARCH; Seed Abstr.; Soils Fert.; Sorghum Mill. Abstr.; Soyabean Abstr.; Stat. Theory Method Abstr. (1967-1969, 1971, 1977-1978, 1980-1981, 1983); Vet. Bull.; Weed Abstr.; Wheat Barley Trit. Abstr.; World Agric. Econ. Rural Sociol. Abstr.

LC S270 .E9
DD 630/.95 CH
EXTENSION BULLETIN (ASIAN AND PACIFIC COUNCIL. FOOD & FERTILIZER TECHNOLOGY CENTER). (EXTENSION BULLETIN.). **Added/Corp** Asian and Pacific Council. Food & Fertilizer Technology Center. No. 1 (1970)-. Bulletin. English. Price varies per volume. ASPAC Food & Fertilizer Technology Center, Agriculture Building, 14 Wen Chow Street, Taipei Taiwan.
Ind/Abst Agrofor. Abstr.; Biocont. News Inf.; Crop Physiol. Abstr.; Hortic. Abstr.; Index Vet.; Nematol. Abstr.; Nutr. Abstr. Rev., Ser. B, Live Feeds and Feed.; Philip. Sci. Technol. Abstr.; Poult. Abstr.; Rev. Agric. Entomol.; Rev. Plant Pathol.; Rice Abstr.; Rural Dev. Abstr.; Seed Abstr.

LC HD1401 **ISSN** 0316-8808
DD 338.1 CN
EXTENSION BULLETIN - DEPARTMENT OF AGRICULTURAL ECONOMICS AND FARM MANAGEMENT FACULTY OF AGRICULTURE. UNIVERSITY OF MANITOBA. (EXTENSION BULLETIN.). **Added/Corp** University of Manitoba. Dept. of Agricultural Economic and Farm Management. (1970)-. Bulletin. English. Irregular. Price varies per volume. University of Manitoba Department of Agricultural Economics, Winnipeg Manitoba R3T 2N2 Canada. **Tel** (204)474-9436, FAX (204)269-6629, telex 07587721.
Circ: 100.
Desc: Publications which communicate information and research results in the field of agricultural economics of a general or specific nature to the general public.

LC S
DD 630 US
EXTENSION BULLETIN - MICHIGAN. STATE UNIVERSITY, EAST LANSING. COOPERATIVE EXTENSION SERVICE. **Main/Corp** Michigan. State University, East Lansing. Cooperative Extension Service. **Added/Corp** Michigan. State University, East Lansing. Cooperative Extension Service. Bulletin, Extension Series. No. 1 (Jan. 1916)-. Bulletin. English. Two times a year. Michigan State University Extension Service, East Lansing MI 48824.
Ind/Abst AGRICOLA.

LC S **ISSN** 0748-125X
DD 630 US
EXTENSION BULLETIN - WASHINGTON STATE UNIVERSITY. COOPERATIVE EXTENSION. (EXTENSION BULLETIN.). [Ext. bull. - Wash. State Univ., Coop. Ext.]. **Added/Corp** Washington State University. Cooperative Extension. (Nov. 1978)-. Bulletin. English. Price varies per volume. Washington State University / Enginerrig Extension Service, Engineering Extension Service, Pullman WA 99164. **Tel** (509)335-3530. ***Continues*** *Washington State University. Extension Service. Extension Bulletin.*
Ind/Abst AGRICOLA [Select. Cov.]; Biodeter. Abstr.; Field Crop Abstr.; Index Vet.; Leis., Rec., Tour. Abstr.; Maize Abstr.; Ornamental Hort. (19??-19??); Plant Breed. Abstr.; Rev. Med. Vet. Entomol.; Rev. Plant Pathol.; Rural Dev. Abstr.; Soils Fert.; World Agric. Econ. Rural Sociol. Abstr.

LC S530 **ISSN** 0703-9166
DD 630/.715/0971 CN
EXTENSION INFORMATION BULLETIN. **Added/Corp** Canadian Society of Extension. Issue No. 1, (Apr. 1977)-. Bulletin. English. Free to members. Agricultural Institute of Canada, 151 Slater Street, Suite 907, Ottawa Ontario K1P 5H4 Canada. **Tel** (613)232-9459, (613)238-2271, FAX (613)594-5190.
Circ: 400 (ctrl). ***Continues*** *Stop-Gap, 0318-1308.*
Desc: News bulletin distributed to the members of the Canadian Society of Extension.

LC S **ISSN** 1061-4613
DD 630 US
EXTENSION NEWS & ADVISOR. [Ext. news advis.]. **Added/Corp** North Carolina Agricultural Extension Service. North Carolina Cooperative Extension Service. **VFOAT** Extension News and Advisor. Vol. 76, No. 2 (Jan. 1991)-. Periodical. English. Six times a year. North Carolina Cooperative Extension Service, North Carolina State University, Raleigh NC 27695-7603.
Formed by the union of *Extension News (Raleigh, N.C.)* ***and*** *North Carolina Agricultural Extension Advisor, 0274-8231.*

LC S **ISSN** 0940-8541
DD 630 GW
UDC 66/68
F. O. LICHT'S INTERNATIONAL SUGAR AND SWEETENER REPORT. [F. O. Licht's int. sugar sweeten. rep.]. **VFOAT** International Sugar and Sweetener Report. (1990)-. English. Three times a month. ***Continues*** *F. O. Licht's International Sugar Report, 0940-8533.*
Ind/Abst Sug. Indus. Abstr.

LC S
DD 630 US
FACT BOOK OF AGRICULTURE.
Added/Corp United States. Dept. of Agriculture. Office of Public Affairs (1989-). (1990)-. Government Publication. English. US Department of Agriculture, 14th Street and Independence Avenue SW, Washington DC 20250. **Tel** (202)720-5457. ***Continues*** *Fact Book of U.S. Agriculture, 0501-9273.*

LC HD2195.5 .A26A
DD 338.1/09931 NZ
FACTS & FIGURES ON NEW ZEALAND AGRICULTURE. **Main/Corp** New Zealand. Ministry of Agriculture and Fisheries. Information Services. English. One time a year. 4.50NZ$ per issue. Ministry of Agriculture and Fisheries, PO Box 2526, Wellington New Zealand. **Tel** (64)(04)720-367, telex MAFWN N231532.
Circ: 2,500.
Desc: Pocket-size, illustrated guide to key statistical details of New Zealand agriculture.

LC S
DD 630 US
FACULTY PAPER SERIES. **Added/Corp** Texas A & M University. Dept. of Agricultural Economics. (19??)-. Monographic series. English.
Ind/Abst Soyabean Abstr.

LC S **ISSN** 0352-3020
DD 630 YU
FAGOPYRUM (LJUBLJANA).
(FAGOPYRUM : NOVOSTI O AJDI.). [Fagopyrum]. **Added/Corp** International Buckwheat Research Association. Univerza Edvarda Kardelja v Ljubljana. VTOZD za Agronomijo. **VFOAT** Novosti o Ajdi; Buckwheat Newsletter. (1982)-. English (Russian; summaries and/or abstracts in Polish and Serbo-Croatian (Roman)). One time a year. ***Continues*** *Buckwheat Newsletter, 0351-7942.*
Ind/Abst Plant Breed. Abstr.; Rev. Plant Pathol.; Seed Abstr.; Weed Abstr.

LC S **ISSN** 1010-1365
DD 630 IT
FAO AGRICULTURAL SERVICES BULLETIN. [FAO agric. serv. bull.]. **Added/Corp** Food and Agriculture Organization of the United Nations. **VFOAT** F.A.O. Agricultural Services Bulletin. **VAT** Food and Agriculture Organization of the United Nations Agricultural Services Bulletin. (1977)-. Bulletin. English. Irregular. Price varies per volume. Food Agriculture Organization (FAO) / Italy, GIPCI66 via Terme di Caracalla, 00100 Rome Italy. **Tel** 011 39 6 52252925, FAX 011 39 6 52253152. **(Subscription address:** UNIPUB, 4611 F Assembly Drive, Lanham MD 20706. **Tel** (800)274-4888, (301)459-7666.) ***Continues*** *Agricultural Services Bulletin, 0378-2182.*
Ind/Abst Agric. Eng. Abstr. (1991-); Leis., Rec., Tour. Abstr.; Nutr. Abstr. Rev., Ser. B, Live Feeds and Feed.; Nutr. Abstr. Rev., Ser. A, Hum. Exp.; Life Sci. Collect.; Postharvest News Inf.; Rural Dev. Abstr.; Soils Fert.; World Agric. Econ. Rural Sociol. Abstr.

LC HD1411 .F57
DD 338.1 IT
FAO COMMODITY POLICY STUDIES.
Main/Corp Food and Agriculture Organization of the United Nations. No. 1-. English. Food Agriculture Organization (FAO) / Italy, GIPCI66 via Terme di Caracalla, 00100 Rome Italy. **Tel** 011 39 6 52252925, FAX 011 39 6 52253152.

LC S **ISSN** 0071-7002
DD 630 IT
FAO COMMODITY REVIEW AND OUTLOOK. **Main/Corp** Food and Agriculture Organization of the United Nations. Commodities and Trade Division. **Added/Corp** Food and Agriculture Organization of the United Nations. Commodities Division. (1961)-. Monographic series. Multiple languages (English, French and Spanish). One time a year. $50.00. Food Agriculture Organization (FAO) / Italy, GIPCI66 via Terme di Caracalla, 00100 Rome Italy. **Tel** 011 39 6 52252925, FAX 011 39 6 52253152. **(Subscription address:** UNIPUB, 4611 F Assembly Drive, Lanham MD 20706. **Tel** (800)274-4888, (301)459-7666.)
Desc: Provides analysis of the worldwide market and trade groups for more than 20 commodity groups.
Ind/Abst Nutr. Abstr. Rev., Ser. B, Live Feeds and Feed.; Nutr. Abstr. Rev., Ser. A, Hum. Exp.

LC S
DD 630 IT
FAO ECONOMIC AND SOCIAL DEVELOPMENT PAPER. **Added/Corp** Food and Agriculture Organization of the United Nations. **VFOAT** Economic and Social Development Paper. (1978)-. Monographic series. English. Irregular. Price varies per volume. Food Agriculture Organization (FAO) / Italy, GIPCI66 via Terme di Caracalla, 00100 Rome Italy. **Tel** 011 39 6 52252925, FAX 011 39 6 52253152.
Ind/Abst Postharvest News Inf.; World Agric. Econ. Rural Sociol. Abstr.

LC S
DD 630 IT
FAO ECONOMIC AND SOCIAL DEVELOPMENT SERIES. **Added/Corp** Food and Agriculture Organization of the United Nations. **VFOAT** Economic and Social Development Series. (1976)-. Monographic series. English. Irregular. Price varies per volume. Food Agriculture Organization (FAO) / Italy, GIPCI66 via Terme di Caracalla, 00100 Rome Italy. **Tel** 011 39 6 52252925, FAX 011 39 6 52253152.
Ind/Abst AGRICOLA; For. Prod. Abstr.

LC S
DD 630 IT
FAO ENVIRONMENT AND ENERGY PAPER. **Added/Corp** Food and Agriculture Organization of the United Nations. **VAT** Food and Agriculture Organization Environment and Energy Paper. (1985)-. Monographic series. English. Food Agriculture Organization (FAO) / Italy, GIPCI66 via Terme di Caracalla, 00100 Rome Italy. **Tel** 011 39 6 52252925, FAX 011 39 6 52253152. ***Continues*** *FAO Environment Paper.*
Ind/Abst Rice Abstr.; World Agric. Econ. Rural Sociol. Abstr.

LC S401 .F64D
DD 354.1/8233 IT
FAO IN ... . **Main/Corp** Food and Agriculture Organization of the United Nations. **VFOAT** F.A.O. in ... . English.

LC S **ISSN** 0071-7045
DD 630 IT
FAO LEGISLATIVE SERIES. **Main/Corp** Food and Agriculture Organization of the United Nations. No. 1, (1957)-. Monographic series. English. Price varies per volume. Food Agriculture Organization (FAO) / Italy, GIPCI66 via Terme di Caracalla, 00100 Rome Italy. **Tel** 011 39 6 52252925, FAX 011 39 6 52253152.

LC S
DD 630 IT
FAO RESEARCH AND TECHNOLOGY PAPER. **Added/Corp** Food and Agriculture Organization of the United Nations. **VAT** Food and Agriculture Organization of the United Nations Research and Technology Paper. (1986)-. Monographic series. English. Irregular. Price varies per volume. Food Agriculture Organization (FAO) / Italy, GIPCI66 via Terme di Caracalla, 00100 Rome Italy. **Tel** 011 39 6 52252925, FAX 011 39 6 52253152.

LC S
DD 630 IT
FAO STATISTICAL DEVELOPMENT SERIES. Vol. 1 (1986)-. Statistical Publication. English. Price varies per volume. Food Agriculture Organization (FAO) / Italy, GIPCI66 via Terme di Caracalla, 00100 Rome Italy. **Tel** 011 39 6 52252925, FAX 011 39 6 52253152.

IT
FAO TRAINING SERIES. **Added/Corp** Food and Agriculture Organization of the United Nations. (1980)-. Monographic series. English. Irregular. Price varies per volume. Food Agriculture Organization (FAO) / Italy, GIPCI66 via Terme di Caracalla, 00100 Rome Italy. **Tel** 011 39 6 52252925, FAX 011 39 6 52253152. **(Subscription address:** UNIPUB, 4611 F Assembly Drive, Lanham MD 20706. **Tel** (800)274-4888, (301)459-7666.)
Ind/Abst Aquat. Sci. Fish. Abstr. [CD-ROM Ed.]; For. Prod. Abstr. (1991-); Hortic. Abstr.; Postharvest News Inf.

LC HD9483.A1 F65
DD 338.4/766862/04 IT
FAO YEARBOOK. FERTILIZER = FAO ANNUAIRE. ENGRAIS. **Added/Corp** Food and Agriculture Organization of the United Nations. **VFOAT** Fertilizer; Engrais; FAO Annuaire. Engrais. **VAT** Food and Agriculture Organization of the United Nations Yearbook. Fertilizer. Vol. 37 (1987)-. English (French and Spanish). One time a year. $40.00. Food Agriculture Organization (FAO) / Italy, GIPCI66 via Terme di Caracalla, 00100 Rome Italy. **Tel** 011 39 6 52252925, FAX 011 39 6 52253152. **(Subscription address:** UNIPUB, 4611 F Assembly Drive, Lanham MD 20706. **Tel** (800)274-4888, (301)459-7666.) ***Continues*** *Food and Agriculture Organization of the United Nations. FAO Fertilizer Yearbook, 0251-1525.*
Desc: Provides information on the world production, consumption, and trade of fertilizers.

LC S
DD 630 US
FAPRI STAFF REPORT. **VFOAT** FAPRI; Card Staff Report. Monographic series. English. Price varies per volume.
Ind/Abst Cot. Trop. Fibr. Abstr. Bibliogr.; Poult. Abstr.; Soyabean Abstr.

LC S **ISSN** 0266-8025
DD 630 UK
FAR EASTERN AGRICULTURE. [Far East. agric.]. (Jan. 1983)-. Trade Publication. English. Six times a year. $75.00. Alain Charles Publishing Ltd., 27 Wilfred Street, London SW1E 6PR United Kingdom. **Tel** 011 44 171 8347676, FAX 011 44 171 9730076, telex 297165.
Ind/Abst Dairy Sci. Abstr.; Helminthol. Abstr.; Index Vet.; Maize Abstr.; Poult. Abstr.; Sorghum Mill. Abstr.

LC S ISSN 0046-3299
DD 630 CN
FARM AND COUNTRY (TORONTO).
(FARM AND COUNTRY.). [Farm ctry.]. Vol. 31, No. 12, (Mar. 14, 1967)-. Trade Publication. English. Irregular. 12.71Can$. Agricultural Publishing Company Ltd, 100 Broadview Avenue, Suite 402, Toronto Ontario M4M 3H3 Canada. **Tel** (416)463-8306. **ED** John Phillips. **Ad Acc. Circ:** 71,000. ***Continues*** *Rural Co-Operator, 0315-9361.*
Desc: A comprehensive paper for the Ontario farmer.

LC S
DD 630 IE
CODEN FFOOE4
FARM & FOOD. Added/Corp Teagasc (Organization). **VFOAT** Farm and Food. Vol. 1, No. 1 (Jan./Mar. 1991)-. Periodical. English. Six times a year. 12.00p. Teagasc, 19 Sandymount Avenue, Dublin 4 Ireland. **Tel** 011 353 1 688188, FAX 011 353 1 688023, telex 30459. ***Continues*** *Farm and Food Research, 0046-3302.*
Ind/Abst World Agric. Econ. Rural Sociol. Abstr.

LC S521.5.A2 F37 ISSN 0276-170X
DD 630/.973 US
FARM & RANCH LIVING. VAT Farm and Ranch Living. Vol. 1 (March 1978)-. Periodical. English. Six times a year. $16.98. Reiman Publications, 5400 South 60th Street, Greendale WI 53129. **Tel** (414)423-0100 Ext. 421, FAX (414)423-1143. **ED** Bob Ottum. **Circ:** 325,000. available on microfilm from University Microfilms International (UMI).
Desc: A unique look at the lifestyle of farmers and ranchers. It captures the charm and character of the country.

LC S ISSN 0364-5444
DD 630 US
TITLE CHANGE
FARM BROADCASTERS LETTER. Added/Corp United States. Dept. of Agriculture. Radio and Television Division. United States. Dept. of Agriculture. Radio and Television Service. United States. Dept. of Agriculture. Broadcasting and Film. United States. Dept. of Agriculture. Office of Communications. (19??)-(July 1, 1994). Government Publication. English. US Department of Agriculture / Office of Information, Radio and Television Division/Room 410-A, Washington DC 20250. **Tel** (202)447-4330, FAX (202)447-5340. **ED** Marci Hilt. **Circ:** 1,200. ***Continued by*** *Broadcasters Letter.*
Desc: For and about farm broadcasters. Included recent developments at USDA and in agriculture. Includes news tips and news services available.

LC HD1401 ISSN 0826-2985
DD 338.1/097127 CN
FARM BULLETIN (ST. PIERRE, MAN.).
(FARM BULLETIN.). [Farm bull.]. **VFOAT** Farm Bulletin Supplement. Vol. 1, No. 1 (Mar. 22, 1983)-. Bulletin. English. Twelve times a year. Free. Compass Publishing, PO Box 269, St. Pierre Manitoba R0A 1V0 Canada. ctrl circ.

LC S ISSN 1077-1859
DD 630 US
FARM BUREAU JOURNAL. Added/Corp Oklahoma Farm Bureau. (199?)-. Newspaper. English. Eleven times a year (Jan./Feb. issues combined). $1.00 (members) Farm Bureau; $5.00 (nonmembers). Oklahoma Farm Bureau, 2501 North Stiles, Oklahoma City OK 73105-3196. **Tel** (405)523-2300, FAX (405)523-2439. **ED** Mike Nichols. **Ad Acc. Circ:** 105,000 (ctrl). available on microfiche. ***Continues*** *Oklahoma Farm Bureau. Oklahoma Farm Bureau Farmer, 0048-1599.*
Desc: Articles and information concerning legislative issues about agriculture.

LC S ISSN 0197-5617
DD 630 US
FARM BUREAU NEWS (WASHINGTON).
(FARM BUREAU NEWS.). [Farm Bur. news]. **Main/Corp** American Farm Bureau Federation. Vol. 51, (1972)-. Periodical. English. Fifty-one times per year. $10.00. American Farm Bureau Federation, 600 Maryland Avenue Southwest, Suite 800, Washington DC 20024. **Tel** (202)484-3600, FAX (202)484-3604. **ED** Joan Waldoch, (phone: (202)484-3625). **Circ:** 50,000 (ctrl). ***Continues*** *American Farm Bureau Federation. Official Newsletter.*
Desc: National legislative and regulatory news of significance to agriculture.

LC S ISSN 0744-4990
DD 630 US
FARM BUREAU PERSPECTIVE. [Farm bur. perspect.]. Vol. 1, No. 1 (Apr. 9, 1982)-. Periodical. English. Twenty-six times a year. $5.00. Farm Bureau Perspective, Route 9-W, Glenmont NY 12077. ***Continues*** *This Week in Farm Bureau (Glenmont, N.Y.).*

LC HD ISSN 1082-1368
DD 333 US
•**FARM BUREAU'S RURAL ROUTE.** [Farm Bur. rural route]. **Added/Corp** Wisconsin Farm Bureau Federation. **VFOAT** Rural Route. Vol. 1, No. 1 (Winter 1995)-. Periodical. English. Four times a year. $5.00. Wisconsin Farm Bureau Federation, PO Box 5550, Madison WI 53705. **Tel** (608)833-8070. ***Continues*** *AgVenture, 0887-9133.*

LC HD9483.U5 F35 ISSN 0092-0053
DD 338.4/7/66860973 US
CCC
CODEN FARCAC
FARM CHEMICALS (1973). (FARM CHEMICALS.). [Farm chem.]. Vol. 136, No. 5 (May 1973)-. Trade Publication. English. Twelve times a year. $34.50. Meister Publishing Company, 37733 Euclid Avenue, Willoughby OH 44094-5992. **Tel** (216)942-2000, (800)572-7740, FAX (216)942-0662. available on microfilm and microfiche from University Microfilms International (UMI). Documents available from CASDDS, Documents on Demand. ***Formed by the union of*** *Farm Chemicals and Crop Life, 0014-7885* ***and*** *Ag Chem & Commercial Fertilizer, 0092-0037.*
Desc: Serving dealers, distributors, formulators, applicators, manufacturers, and others involved in the agricultural chemical and fertilizer market. Focus is on new equipment, dealer stewardship, conservation tillage, and ongoing monitoring of the agrichemical industry.
Ind/Abst AGRICOLA; Agric. Eng. Abstr. (1991-); BioBusiness (1984-); Chem. Abstr.; Chem. Bus. Bull.; Chem. Bus. NewsBase (1987-); Chem. Bus. Update; Chem. Ind. Notes; Energy Inf. Abstr.; Environ. Abstr.; F&S Index Plus Text, Int. [Select. Cov.]; Field Crop Abstr.; Index Vet.; Maize Abstr.; PESTDOC; PROMT; Rev. Agric. Entomol.; Soils Fert.; Soyabean Abstr.; Vet. Bull.; Weed Abstr.

LC HB241 ISSN 1043-8858
DD 338 US
FARM CHEMICALS INTERNATIONAL.
[Farm chem. int.]. (1987)-. Trade Publication. English. Four times a year. $34.50. Meister Publishing Company, 37733 Euclid Avenue, Willoughby OH 44094-5992. **Tel** (216)942-2000, (800)572-7740, FAX (216)942-0662.
Desc: Global perspective on the agrichemical industry.
Ind/Abst Chem. Bus. Bull.; Chem. Bus. NewsBase (1987-); Chem. Bus. Update; PESTDOC; Rev. Agric. Entomol.; Rev. Plant Pathol.; Rice Abstr.; Weed Abstr.

LC S
DD 630 UK
FARM DEVELOPMENT REVIEW. (19??)-. English. Thirteen times a year. $299.00. MCB University Press, 60 62 Toller Lane, Bradford, West Yorkshire BD8 9BY United Kingdom. **Tel** 011 44 1274 785280, FAX 011 44 1274 785200, telex 51317-MCBUNI-G. **(Subscription address:** MCB University Press / US and Canada Subscriptions, PO Box 10812, Birmingham AL 35201-0812. **Tel** (205)995-1567, (800)633-4931, FAX (205)995-1588.**) ED** John Williams. Index available. cum. index. **Bk Rev. Circ:** 1,200.
Desc: Provides down-to-earth advice on the likely success of ventures that co-exist with the main farm business. It aims to provide an illuminating digest of everything that is relevant to the farmer or landowner with an interest in diversification.

LC S451.5 ISSN 1185-2119
DD 630/.97123/05 CN
FARM FAMILY WEST. [Farm fam. west]. Vol. 10, No. 4 (Oct. 1990)-. Periodical. English. Four times a year. $4.00 per issue. Alberta Publications, 10234 24th Street/Suite 105, Edmonton Alberta T5N 1P9 Canada. **Tel** (403)488-7484, FAX (403)488-7523. ***Continues*** *Alberta Junior Farm Quarterly., 0836-1010.*

LC S451.5 ISSN 0705-8748
DD 630/.971 CN
FARM GATE, THE. (1977)-. Periodical. English. Twelve times a year. 12.00Can$ Canada; 20.00Can$ other. North Waterloo Publishing Ltd., 15 King Street, Elmira Ontario N3B 2R1 Canada. **Tel** (519)669-5155, FAX (519)669-5928. **ED** Bob Verdun. **Ad Acc. Circ:** 24,500 (ctrl).
Desc: Innovative analysis of crucial issues facing agriculture. Official organ of Waterloo federation of agriculture. Exclusive locally written cooking column.

LC S
DD 630 UK
FARM INCOME SERIES / MINISTRY OF AGRICULTURE AND FISHERIES. No. 1-. Monographic series. English. Irregular. Price varies per volume.

LC S ISSN 0744-7787
DD 630 US
FARM INDUSTRY NEWS SUNBELT. VFOAT Farm Industry News. Periodical. English. Twelve times a year. Farm Industry News, 1999 Shepard Road, St Paul MN 55116. ***Continues*** *Farm Industry News South, 0161-4347.*

LC HD1781 .S85d ISSN 0383-4875
DD 338.1/3/0971 CN
FARM INPUT PRICE INDEX. (FARM INPUT PRICE INDEXES.). [Farm input price index]. **Added/Corp** Statistics Canada. Prices Division. Indice des Prix des Entrees dans l'Agriculture. Statistics Canada. Prices Division. Statistics Canada. Statistics Canada. Industrial Prices Section. **VFOAT** Farm Input Price Index; Indice de Prix des Entrees dans l'Agriculture; Indices des Prix des Entrees dans l'Agriculture. 3rd Quarter (1973)-. Periodical. English (French). Four times a year. 64.02Can$. Statistics Canada Publications Sales and Services, R.H. Coats Building 6th Floor, Ottawa Ontario K1A 0T6 Canada. **Tel** (613)951-5078, (800)267-6677, FAX (613)951-1584, telex 053-3585. ***Continues*** *Price Index Numbers of Commodities and Services Used by Farmers, 0383-4867.*
Desc: Indexes of prices of farming commodities and services used in Canadian farming operations for eastern, western and all of Canada.

LC S1 .F25 ISSN 0014-8008
DD 630/.5 US
FARM JOURNAL (PHILADELPHIA. 1956). (FARM JOURNAL.). [Farm j.]. Vol. 80, No. 12 (Dec. 1956)-. Trade Publication. English. Thirteen times a year. $14.00. Farm Journal Inc, 230 West Washington Square, Philadelphia PA 19106. **Tel** (215)829-4700, (800)331-9310. **ED** Earl Ainsworth. **Bk Rev. Ad Acc. Circ:** 890,000. available on microfilm and microfiche from University Microfilms International (UMI). Documents available from UMI Article Clearinghouse. ***Continues*** *Farm Journal and Country Gentlemen.*
Desc: A business magazine published for families who own or operate farms and/or ranches.
Ind/Abst Acad. Abstr. Full Text Elite; Acad. Abstr.; Bus. Index (1979-March 1984); EP Collect.; Homework Help.; Mag. Artic. Summar. Elite; Mag. Artic. Summar. Select; Mag. Artic. Summar. CD-ROM; Mag. Search; MasterFile FullTEXT 1000; MasterFile FullTEXT 350; MasterFile FullTEXT 650; MasterFile FullTEXT (July 1989-); Newsp. Period. Abstr. (1988-1992); OCLC; Pub. Lib. FullTEXT; Telebase; Mag. Index (1977-March 1984); Trade Ind. Index; Vocat. Search.

LC S
DD 630 US
FARM LABOR AND WAGE RATES / IOWA CROP AND LIVESTOCK REPORTING SERVICE. **See** Business and Economics-Labor.

LC HD1527.W9 W94A ISSN 0095-389X
DD 331.7/63/09787 US
FARM LABOR REPORT (CASPER). **See** Business and Economics-Labor.

LC S451.5 ISSN 0229-2106
DD 630/.97123 CN
CEASED
FARM LIGHT & POWER (ALBERTA EDITION). (FARM LIGHT & POWER.). [Farm light power]. **VFOAT** Alberta Seed Guide. (1958)-(1995). Trade Publication. English. Farm Light & Power, 2330 15th Avenue, Regina Saskatchewan S4P 1A2 Canada. **Tel** (306)525-3305.

LC S451.5 ISSN 0229-2092
DD 630/.97127 CN
CEASED
FARM LIGHT & POWER (MANITOBA EDITION). (FARM LIGHT & POWER.). [Farm light power]. (1958)-(1995). Trade Publication. English. Farm Light & Power, 2330 15th Avenue, Regina Saskatchewan S4P 1A2 Canada. **Tel** (306)525-3305.

LC S
DD 630 US
FARM MANAGEMENT NEWS AND VIEWS. VFOAT News and Views. English.

LC S ISSN 0430-084X
DD 630 TH
FARM MANAGEMENT NOTES FOR ASIA AND THE FAR EAST. Added/Corp Food and Agriculture Organization of the United Nations. Regional Commission on Farm Management for Asia and the Far East. Food and Agriculture Organization of the United Nations. Regional Working Party on Farm Management for Asia and the Far East. Vol. 1 (Jan. 1965)-. Periodical. English. Four times a year. Free on request. Food and Agriculture Organization of the United Nations, Regional Office for Asia and the Pacific, Maliwan Mansion, Phra Atit Road, Bangkok 10200 Thailand. **Circ:** 300.
Ind/Abst Agrofor. Abstr.; For. Abstr.; Rice Abstr.; World Agric. Econ. Rural Sociol. Abstr.

LC S
DD 630 US
FARM NEWS AND VIEWS. Added/Corp Oklahoma Farmers Union. Vol. 67, No. 9 (Sept. 1986)-. Periodical. English. Twelve times a year. Oklahoma Union Farmer, PO Box 24000, Oklahoma City OK 73124. ***Continues*** *Oklahoma Union Farmer, 0030-1620.*

LC S
DD 630 US
FARM NEWS OF ERIE AND WYOMING COUNTIES. Vol. 72, No. 11 (Nov. 1986)-. Periodical. English. Twelve times a year. $12.00. Farm News of Erie and Wyoming Counties, 21 South Grove Street, East Aurora NY 14052. **Tel** (716)652-5401. **ED** David E Weaver. **Bk Rev. Ad Acc. Circ:** 1,600 (ctrl). ***Formed by the union of*** *Erie County Farm News* ***and*** *Wyoming County Farm, Home and 4-H News.*
Desc: Contains information of interest to agriculture producers within the circulation area.

Agriculture

LC S451.5
DD 630/.97123
ISSN 0846-0442
CN
FARM OUTLOOK (LLOYDMINSTER). (FARM OUTLOOK.). [Farm outlook]. (Feb. 25, 1990)-. Periodical. English. Irregular. Farm Outlook, 4828 44th Street, Lloydminister Saskatchewan, S9V 0G8 Canada.

LC HD2330
DD 338.1/097127
ISSN 0715-5042
CN
FARM PAPER, THE. [Farm pap.]. **Added/Corp** Stouffers of Souris (Association). Vol. 1 No. 1 (Oct. 5, 1977)-. Periodical. English. Twenty-six times a year. Farm Paper, PO Box 488, Souris Manitoba R0K 2C0 Canada.

LC S561 .U5115A
DD 338.1/3
ISSN 0191-0531
US
FARM PRODUCTION EXPENDITURES. 1983. Statistical Publication. English. One time a year. Agricultural Statistics Board, Inependence Avenue, Room 5829, South Building, Washington DC 20250. available on microfiche (Vols. for 1983 distributed to depository libraries). *Continues* Farm Production Expenditures for ..., 0191-0531.

LC S
DD 630
ISSN 0192-9437
US
FARM, RANCH & SUBURBAN ACREAGE. **VFOAT** Acreage. **VAT** Farm, Ranch and Suburban Acreage. Periodical. English. Twelve times a year. Malheur Publishing Company, 1160 SW 4th Street Box 130, Ontario OR 97914-0130.

LC HD1295.U5 F37
DD 338.1
ISSN 0071-4003
US
FARM REAL ESTATE TAXES. **Added/Corp** United States. Dept. of Agriculture. Economic Research Service. United States. Dept. of Agriculture. Economics and Statistics Service. United States. Agricultural Research Service. (19??)-. Government Publication. English. One time a year. Free on request. US Department of Agriculture / Livestock and Seed Division, AMS/LMGS S Agr Building/Room 2623, PO Box 96456, Washington DC 20090. **Tel** (202)720-1050, (202)720-6231. available on microfiche.

LC S
DD 630
US
FARM REVIEW (JOLIET, ILL.). (FARM REVIEW.). **VFOAT** Chicago Farmers Farm Review. Periodical. English. One time a week. $12.00. Farmers Weekly Review, 100 Manhattan Road, Joliet IL 60433. **Tel** (815)727-4811. **ED** P J Cleary. **Bk Rev**. **Ad Acc**. **Circ:** 10,240. **Desc:** General news, farm news, family history, and legal articles.

LC S
DD 630
US
FARM SMART. (19??)-. Periodical. English. Four times a year. $18.00. FBS Systems Inc, Drawer 248, Aledo IL 61231. **Tel** (309)582-5628.

LC HD2151 .F37
DD 338.1/0994
ISSN 0818-027X
AT
FARM SURVEYS REPORT. [Farm surv. rep.]. **Added/Corp** Australia. Bureau of Agricultural Economics. (Apr. 1986)-. English. One time a year. 25.00Aus$ Australia; 28.50Aus$ Asia and Pacific; 30.00Aus$ other. ABARE / Australian Bureau of Agriculture and Resource Economics, GPO Box 1563, Canberra ACT 2601 Australia. **Tel** 011 61 6 2722000, FAX 011 61 6 2722001. *Separated from* Quarterly Review of the Rural Economy, 0156-7446. **Ind/Abst** AGRICOLA [Select. Cov.].

LC S
DD 630
AT
FARM TAXATION. *See* Finance-Taxation.

LC WMLC 93/348
ISSN 1011-0488
RH
FARMER, THE. Vol. 59, No. 32 (Aug. 10, 1989)-. Periodical. English. One time a week. $153.96. Modern Farming International Harare, Ground Floor Agriculture House, Moffat Street, PO Box 1622, Harare Zimbabwe. **Tel** 011 263 4 753278. *Continues* Farmer Including Tobacco News.

LC S
DD 630
ISSN 0014-8369
II
FARMER AND PARLIAMENT. **Added/Corp** Farmers' Parliamentary Forum. Vol. 1 (1966)-. Periodical. Multiple languages (English and Hindi). Twelve times a year. $15.00. S. N. Bhalla for Farmers Parliamentary Forum, New Delhi India. (**Subscription address:** Prints India, 11 Darya Ganj, New Delhi 110002 India. **Tel** 011 91 11 3268645, FAX 011 91 11 3275542, telex 31-61087 PRIN-IN.)

LC HD1491.U5 C619
DD 334/subser.683/0973 S 334/.683/0973
ISSN 0742-9495
FARMER COOPERATIVE STATISTICS. *See* Business and Economics-Abstracting, Bibliographies and Statistics.

LC S451.5
DD 630
ISSN 0896-5579
US
FARMER (MINNESOTA ED.). (THE FARMER.). [Farmer]. Vol. 53, No. 1 (Jan. 5, 1935)-. Periodical. English. Twenty-four times a year. Webb Publishing Company, 1999 Shepard Road, St Paul MN 55116. **Tel** (612)690-7203. *Continues in part* Farmer and Farm, Stock and Home.

LC S451.5
DD 630/.97124/2
ISSN 1185-2178
CN
FARMER-RANCHER. [Farmer-rancher]. Vol. 1, No. 3 (Oct. 7, 1990)-. Trade Publication. English. Irregular. Limited free distribution. McIntosh Publications Co Ltd, Box 430, North Battleford, 291 2Y5 Canada. **Tel** (306)445-7477, FAX (306)445-1977. *Continues* North West Farmer, Rancher., 0822-5737.

LC S
DD 630
ISSN 0739-9235
US
FARMER STOCKMAN OF THE MIDWEST. **VFOAT** Farmer Stockman; Farmer-Stockman of the Midwest. (19??)-. Periodical. English. One time a week. $22.00. Farmer Stockman of the Midwest, PO Box 349, Belleville KS 66935. **Tel** (913) 527-2224, FAX (913)527-2225. **ED** Merele M. Miller. **Ad Acc**, **Adv Mgr:** Robert Deterding. ctrl circ.

LC S
DD 630
ISSN 1074-0163
US
●**FARMER TO FARMER.** (FARMER TO FARMER : CALIFORNIA FARMING AT ITS BEST.). [Farmer farmer]. **Added/Corp** Community Alliance with Family Farmers Foundation. (1993)-. Periodical. English. Four times a year. $15.00. Community Alliance Family Farm Fund, PO Box 73674, Davis CA 95617. **Tel** (916)756-8518.

LC S21 .A6
DD 630/.08
ISSN 0193-4392
US
FARMERS' BULLETIN (UNITED STATES. DEPT. OF AGRICULTURE). (FARMERS' BULLETIN.). [Farmers' bull.]. (1889)-. Bulletin. English. Price varies per volume. US Department of Agriculture, 14th Street and Independence Avenue SW, Washington DC 20250. **Tel** (202)720-5457. cum. index.
Ind/Abst AGRICOLA.

LC S
DD 630
ISSN 0430-0998
UK
FARMERS BULLETIN (WEST CUMBERLAND). (FARMERS BULLETIN.). [Farmers bull.]. No. 43 (Autumn 1963)-. Bulletin. English. Four times a year. *Continues* Bulletin (West Cumberland Farmers' Trading Society).
Ind/Abst AGRICOLA.

LC S451.5
DD 630/.97123/05
ISSN 1182-1248
CN
FARMERS' CHOICE. (FARMERS CHOICE.). [Farmers' choice]. Vol. 1, No. 1 (March 2, 1993)-. Periodical. English. Twelve times a year. 14.40Can$. Red Deer Advocate, 2950 Bremner Avenue, Red Deer Alberta T4N JG3 Canada. **Tel** (403)343-2400.
Desc: Farm and agriculture related articles.

LC S
DD 630
UK
FARMERS' CLUB JOURNAL (LONDON, ENGLAND). (THE FARMERS' CLUB JOURNAL.). Periodical. English. Six times a year. *Continues* Journal of the Farmers' Club.

LC S
DD 630
ISSN 0046-3337
US
FARMER'S DIGEST. [Farmer's dig.]. Vol. 1 (May 1937)-. Trade Publication. English. Ten times a year (monthly except June/July and Aug./Sept. combined) $20.95. Farmers Digest, PO Box 624, Brookfield WI 53008-0624. **Tel** (414)782-4480. **ED** Frank Lessiter. Index available. **Bk Rev**. **Ad Acc**. **Circ:** 25,000. available on microfilm and microfiche from University Microfilms International (UMI).
Desc: Selects information in more than 300 farm and technical publications, USDA and University sources. It presents 1,000 pages of farm information each year.

LC S
DD 630
US
FARMER'S EXCHANGE, THE. Vol. 1, (Nov. 5, 1926)-. Periodical. English. One time a week. $17.00. Farmers Exchange, PO Box 45, New Paris IN 46553. **Tel** (219)831-2138, FAX (219)831-2131. **ED** Paul Hershberger. **Ad Acc**. **Circ:** 14,500.

LC S
DD 630
US
FARMERS EXCHANGE. English. Twelve times a year. Exchange Inc, Box 490, Fayetteville TN 37334. **Tel** (615)433-7010. **ED** William F Thomas. **Ad Acc**. **Circ:** 20,000 (ctrl).
Desc: Buying and selling of equipment and stock.

LC S
US
FARMERS FASTLINE - ILLINOIS EDITION. English. Fastline Publications, 4900 Fox Run Road, Buckner KY 40010. **Tel** (502)222-0146.

LC S
DD 630
US
FARMERS FASTLINE (INDIANA EDITION). (FARMERS FASTLINE.). (19??)-. English. Twelve times a year. $8.00 US; $36.00 Canada and Mexico. Fastline Publications, 4900 Fox Run Road, Buckner KY 40010. **Tel** (502)222-0146.

LC S
DD 630
US
FARMERS FASTLINE - IOWA EDITION. English. Fastline Publications, 4900 Fox Run Road, Buckner KY 40010. **Tel** (502)222-0146.

LC S
DD 630
US
FARMERS FASTLINE - KENTUCKY EDITION. English. Fastline Publications, 4900 Fox Run Road, Buckner KY 40010. **Tel** (502)222-0146.

LC HD28
DD 338
ISSN 0192-6322
US
FARMERS HOT LINE. [Farmers hot line]. (1975)-. English. One time a week. $29.00. Heartland Communications Group Inc, PO Box 916 1003 Central Ave, Fort Dodge IA 50501. **Tel** (800)247-2000, (515)955-1600, FAX (515)955-6636. Index available. **Ad Acc**. ctrl circ.

LC S
DD 630
ISSN 0014-844X
AT
FARMERS' NEWSLETTER. **Added/Corp** Australia. Commonwealth Scientific and Industrial Research Organization. Irrigation Research and Extension Committee. Griffith, Australia. Irrigation Research Laboratory. No. 1 (1944)-. Newsletter. English. Irregular (4 issues). 8.23Aus$. Irrigation Res & Extension Com, CSIRO PMB, Griffith New South Wales 2680 Australia. **Tel** 011 61 69 62 0550. Documents available from Documents on Demand.
Ind/Abst Am. Stat. Index; Hortic. Abstr.; Leis., Rec., Tour. Abstr.; Rural Dev. Abstr.; World Agric. Econ. Rural Sociol. Abstr.

LC S
DD 630
ISSN 0467-5282
AT
FARMERS' NEWSLETTER, LARGE AREA. No. 1 (1951)-. Newsletter. English. Four times a year. 10.00Aus$. Irrigation Res & Extension Com, CSIRO PMB, Griffith New South Wales 2680 Australia. **Tel** 011 61 69 62 0550. **Ad Acc**. **Circ:** 2,600 (ctrl).
Ind/Abst Irr. Drain. Abstr.; Rice Abstr.; Soils Fert.; Weed Abstr.

LC S
DD 630
ISSN 0014-8474
UK
CCC
FARMER'S WEEKLY. Vol. 1 (1934)-. Trade Publication. English. One time a week. $155.00. Reed Business Publishing / West Sussex, England, Perrymount Road, Haywards Heath, West Sussex RH16 3DH United Kingdom. **Tel** 011 44 1444 441212, FAX 011 44 1444 445447. *Continues* Big Farm Weekly; *Absorbed* Power Farming.
Ind/Abst Anim. Breed. Abstr.; Dairy Sci. Abstr.; Field Crop Abstr.; Grass. Forage Abstr.; Hortic. Abstr.; Leis., Rec., Tour. Abstr.; Rural Dev. Abstr.; World Agric. Econ. Rural Sociol. Abstr.

LC WMLC 93/1280
DD 338
ISSN 0091-1305
US
FARMFUTURES. [Farm futures]. **VFOAT** Farm Futures. Vol. 1 (1973)-. Periodical. English. Thirteen times a year. $36.00. Miller Publishing Company, 12400 Whitewater Drive, Suite 160, Minnetonka MN 55343. **Tel** (612)931-0211. (**Subscription address:** CDS / SIFD Agency Control, 1901 Bell Avenue, Des Moines IA 50315. **Tel** (515)246-6812.) **ED** Claudia Waterloo, Bryce Knorr, Andy Jacobitz, Jennifer Lieffers. **Ad Acc**. **Circ:** 200,000 (ctrl).
Desc: Published for the operator of a large, full-time farming business. Focuses on the objective of helping a farming business make and keep profit.

LC S
DD 630
US
FARMING ALTERNATIVES FOR SUSTAINABLE AGRICULTURE IN NEW YORK STATE. **Added/Corp** Cornell Farming Alternatives Program. **VFOAT** Farming Alternatives. Vol. 1, No. 1 (Fall 1992)-. Periodical. English. Four times a year. $10.00. Cornell University, Rural Society Department, Ithaca NY 14853. **Tel** (607)225-1400.

LC HD2330
DD 338.1/0971
ISSN 0835-6246
FARMING FACTS. [Farming facts]. **Added/Corp** Statistics Canada. Statistics Canada. Agriculture Statistic Division. Statistics Canada. Agriculture/Natural Resources Division. (1980)-. English (French). One time a year. Free on request. Statistics Canada Publications

Agriculture

Sales and Services, R.H. Coats Building 6th Floor, Ottawa Ontario K1A 0T6 Canada. **Tel** (613)951-5078, (800)267-6677, FAX (613)951-1584, telex 053-3585. cum. index.
Desc: Reference report covering highlights on virtually every kind of Canadian agricultural activity- from oilseed production to honey and wax production.

LC S **ISSN** 0821-2724
DD 630/.2/74505 **CN**
FARMING FOR THE FUTURE. [Farming future]. Vol. 1, No. 1 (Spring 1981)-. English. One time a year. $1.00 per no. Eaton Valley Agricultural Services, PO Box 25, Sawyerville Quebec J0B 3A0 Canada.

LC S
DD 630 **JA**
FARMING JAPAN. Added/Corp Kaigai Gijutsu Kyoryoku Jigyodan. (196?)-. Periodical. English. Six times a year. $123.00. **(Subscription address:** Maruzen Company Ltd., PO Box 5050, Import & Export Department, Tokyo 100 31 Japan. **Tel** 011 81 3 32789224.) **Ad Acc. Circ:** 18,000 (ctrl).
Desc: Covers agriculture, forestry, and fishery; purpose is to promote mutual comprehension with the people on their way to expansion through soil making.
Ind/Abst Irr. Drain. Abstr.; Plant Breed. Abstr.

LC S
DD 630 **UK**
FARMING NEWS. English. One time a week. £60.00 UK and Northern Ireland; $130.00 other. Morgan Grampian, 40 Beresford Street Woolwich, London SE18 6BQ United Kingdom. **Tel** 011 44 181 8557777, FAX 011 44 181 8555548, telex 896238. **Bk Rev. Ad Acc Circ:** 102,000 (ctrl). available on microfilm and microfiche from University Microfilms International (UMI).
Desc: Topical farming newspaper.
Ind/Abst Nutr. Abstr. Rev., Ser. B, Live Feeds and Feed.; Postharvest News Inf.; Sug. Indus. Abstr.

LC HD1483 **ISSN** 0265-1645
DD 338.10941 **UK**
FARMING NEWS (LONDON. 1982). [Farming news Lond. 1982]. (1982)-. Trade Publication. English. One time a week.
Ind/Abst Index Vet.

LC S338.K38 F37
DD 338.1/09676/2 **KE**
FARMING REVIEW (NAIROBI, KENYA). (Feb. 1985)-. Periodical. English. Twelve times a year. Nation Newspapers Limited, PO Box 49010, Nairobi Kenya. **Tel** 011 254 2 228831.

LC SF **ISSN** 0925-6563
DD 636 **NE**
UDC 63
FARMING SYSTEMS ANALYSIS PAPER. [Farming syst. anal. pap.]. (1989)-. Monographic series. English. Irregular. Price varies per volume.
Ind/Abst Field Crop Abstr.; Rice Abstr.; World Agric. Econ. Rural Sociol. Abstr.

LC S **ISSN** 0932-6154
DD 630 **GW**
UDC 631.1(213.5)
FARMING SYSTEMS AND RESOURCE ECONOMICS IN THE TROPICS. [Farming syst. resour. econ. trop.]. (1988)-. Monographic series. English. Irregular.
Ind/Abst Irr. Drain. Abstr.; Soils Fert.

LC S **ISSN** 0893-424X
DD 630 **US**
FARMING SYSTEMS RESEARCH PAPER SERIES. [Farming syst. res. pap. ser.]. **VFOAT** FSR Paper Series. (1982)-. Monographic series. English. Irregular. Price varies per volume. International Agricultural Programs, Waters Hall, Kansas State University, Manhattan KS 66506.
Ind/Abst Potato Abstr.

LC S
DD 630 **US**
FARMING SYSTEMS SUPPORT PROJECT NEWSLETTER. Added/Corp Farming Systems Support Project. University of Florida. Institute of Food and Agricultural Sciences. **VFOAT** FSSP Newsletter. Vol. 1, No. 1 (Spring 1983)-. Newsletter. English. Four times a year. Institute of Food and Agricultural Sciences, University of Florida, Building 664, Gainesville FL 32611. **Tel** (904)392-1773.

LC HD2330 **ISSN** 0838-8512
DD 338.1/09713/4 **CN**
FARMING TODAY (WELLINGTON-WATERLOO-PERTH ED.). (FARMING TODAY.). [Farming today]. (November 11, 1981)-. Periodical. English. Twenty-four times a year. Alliston Press, 28 Main Street North, Milverton Ontario N0K 1M0 Canada. **Formed by the union of** Farming Today (Wellington Edition), 0838-8520 **and** Farming Today (Perth Edition), 0711-6160.

LC S **ISSN** 0093-5832
DD 630 **US**
FARMLAND NEWS. Added/Corp Farmland Industries. Vol. 38, No. 18, (Sept. 30, 1971)-. Periodical. English. Twenty-three times a year. Farmland Industries, Department 38, PO Box 7305, Kansas City MO 64116. **Continues** Farmland, 0014-8539.

LC R **ISSN** 0382-781X
DD 614.8/52/09713 **CN**
FARMSAFE. Vol. 1, (Jan. 1976)-. Periodical. English. Six times a year. Farm Safety Association, Suite 22-23/340 Woodlawn Road West, Guelph Ontario N1H 7K9 Canada. **Tel** (519)823-5600.

LC S **ISSN** 0197-6680
DD 630 **US**
FARMWEEK (BLOOMINGTON). (FARMWEEK.). **VAT** Farm Week. (197?)-. Periodical. English. One time a week. $2.00, included in membership fee. Farmweek, PO Box 2901, Bloomington IL 61701.

LC S **ISSN** 0164-8640
DD 630 **US**
FARMWEEK (EASTERN ED.). (FARMWEEK.). **VFOAT** Farm Week. (197?)-. Periodical. English. One time a week. $18.95. Mayhill Publications Inc, PO Box 90, Knightstown IN 46148. **Tel** (800)876-5133, FAX (317)345-5133. **ED** Rod Everhart and Nancy Searfoss. **Ad Acc. Circ:** 28,000. **Continues in part** Eastern Indiana Farmer, 0420-3690.
Desc: Covers general agriculture news, markets, sales, and other information pertaining to farmers and agribusiness in Indiana, Western Ohio, and Kentucky.

LC S **ISSN** 1018-502X
DD 630 **SZ**
UDC 63
FAT-BERICHTE. [FAT-Ber.]. **VFOAT** Forschungsanstalt fur Betriebswirtschaft und Landtechnik-Berichte. (19??)-. Periodical. German. Irregular. Eidgenossische Forschungsanstalt fuer Betriebswirtschaft und Landtechnik (FAT), 8356 Tanikon, TG Switzerland.
Ind/Abst Index Vet.; Postharvest News Inf.; Soyabean Abstr.

LC S
DD 630 **US**
FCS SPECIAL REPORT. Main/Corp United States. Farmer Cooperative Service. No. 13 (June 1975)-. Periodical. English.

LC S **ISSN** 0195-3346
DD 630 **US**
FCX CAROLINA COOPERATOR. [FCX Carol. coop.]. **Main/Corp** FCX. (1976)-. Periodical. English. Ten times a year (with combined July-Aug. and Nov.-Dec.) $1.00. FCX Inc, 125 East Davie Street, Raleigh NC 27602. **Tel** (919)828-4411. **ED** Dean A. Deter. **Bk Rev. Ad Acc. Circ:** 60,000 (ctrl) **Continues** Carolina Cooperator.
Desc: Farming and cooperation, especially in the Southeast.

LC S **ISSN** 0866-482X
DD 630 **HU**
UDC 612.398
FEHERJE ES BIOTERMEK. (1990)-. Periodical. Multiple languages. Four times a year. Agroinform, Kitaibel Pal 4, 1024 Budapest Hungary. **Tel** 135-1927, FAX 135-0344, telex 224439.
Ind/Abst Soyabean Abstr.

LC S
DD 630 **FR**
FEL ACTUALITES HEBDO : MARCHES EUROPEENS DES FRUITS ET LEGUMES. VAT Fruits et Legumes Actualites Hebdo. (1984)-. Periodical. French. Twelve times a year. **Continues in part** MFL.

LC S **ISSN** 0014-9799
DD 630 **GW**
FELDWIRTSCHAFT. [Feldwirtschaft]. **Main/Corp** Deutsche Akademie der Landwirtschaftswissenschaften zu Berlin. Vol. 7, No. 1 (Jan. 1966)-. Periodical. German. Twelve times a year. Deutscher Judo Verband, Redaktion Ippon Segewaldweg 40, D-12557 Berlin Germany. **Tel** 011 49 711 210770, telex 051 678. **Continues** Deutsche Landwirtschaft (Berlin, Germany : 1950).
Ind/Abst AGRICOLA; Hortic. Abstr.; Irr. Drain. Abstr.; Leis., Rec., Tour. Abstr.; Maize Abstr.; Nematol. Abstr.; Nutr. Abstr. Rev., Ser. B, Live Feeds and Feed.; Nutr. Abstr. Rev., Ser. A, Hum. Exp.; Plant Grow. Reg. Abstr.; Postharvest News Inf.; Potato Abstr.; Rev. Plant Pathol.; Rural Dev. Abstr.; Soils Fert.; Wheat Barley Trit. Abstr.; World Agric. Econ. Rural Sociol. Abstr.

LC S
DD 630 **II**
FERTILISER MARKETING NEWS. [Fertil. market. news.]. **Added/Corp** Fertiliser Association of India. Vol. 6, No. 1 (1978)-. Periodical. English. Twelve times a year. $10.00 (one-year); $25.00 (three-year). Fertiliser Association of India, 10 Shaheed Jit Singh Marg, New Delhi 110067 India. **Tel** 011 91 11 667144, telex 031-73056. Index available. **Ad Acc.** available on diskette.
Desc: Fertiliser production and marketing analysis.
Ind/Abst AGRICOLA; Field Crop Abstr.; Soils Fert.; World Agric. Econ. Rural Sociol. Abstr.

LC S631 .F36 **ISSN** 0015-0266
DD 631.8 **II**
CODEN FENEAQ
FERTILISER NEWS. [Fertil. news]. **Added/Corp** Fertiliser Association of India. (1957)-. Academic Scholarly Publication. English. Twelve times a year. $60.00. Fertiliser Association of India, 10 Shaheed Jit Singh Marg, New Delhi 110067 India. **Tel** 011 91 11 667144, telex 031-73056. **ED** K. P. Sundaram. **Bk Rev. Ad Acc.** ctrl circ. available on diskette. Documents available from CASDDS.
Desc: New developments and requirements in the fertiliser industry.
Ind/Abst AgBiotech News Inf.; AGRICOLA; Agric. Eng. Abstr. (1991-); Agrofor. Abstr. (1991-); Biodeter. Abstr.; Chem. Abstr.; Curr. Cit.; EMBASE; Field Crop Abstr.; For. Prod. Abstr. (1991-); Hortic. Abstr.; Irr. Drain. Abstr.; Leis., Rec., Tour. Abstr.; Plant Breed. Abstr.; Potato Abstr.; Rice Abstr.; Rural Dev. Abstr.; Seed Abstr.; Soils Fert.; Sorghum Mill. Abstr.; Soyabean Abstr.; Wheat Barley Trit. Abstr.; World Agric. Econ. Rural Sociol. Abstr.

LC S **ISSN** 0015-0304
DD 630 **UK**
CODEN FRZIAJ
FERTILIZER INTERNATIONAL. [Fert. int.]. No. 1 (July 1969)-. Trade Publication. English. Twelve times a year. $290.00. British Sulphur Corporation Ltd, 31 Mount Pleasant, London WC1X 0AD United Kingdom. **Tel** 011 44 171 8375600, FAX 011 44 171 8370292, telex 918918 SULFEX G. **(Subscription address:** CRU International Ltd., 31 Mount Pleasant, London WC1X 0AD United Kingdom. **Tel** 011 44 171 8375600, FAX 011 44 171 8370292.) **ED** Mark Evans. **Ad Acc.** available on an online database (file 648/Full-Text) from DIALOG. Documents available from CASDDS.
Desc: Reporting on commerical and technical developments in the world fertilizer industry.
Ind/Abst Chem. Abstr.; Chem. Bus. Bull.; Chem. Bus. NewsBase (1985-); Chem. Bus. Update; Chem. Ind. Notes; Curr. Cit.; F&S Index Plus Text, Int. [Select. Cov.]; Infomat Int. Bus.; PROMT; Soils Fert.; Trade Ind. ASAP [Full Txt.]; Trade Ind. Index [Full Txt.].

LC S
DD 630 **UK**
FERTILIZER MARKET BULLETIN. Vol. 1, No. 1 (Feb. 22, 1982)-. Bulletin. English. One time a week. $1711.21. FMB Publications Ltd., FMB House 6, Windmill Road Hampton Hill, Middlesex TW12 1RH United Kingdom. **Tel** 011 44 181 9797866.

LC HD9483.A1 F43 **ISSN** 1051-9130
DD 380.1/4566862/05 **US**
FERTILIZER MARKETS. [Fertil. mark.]. **Added/Corp** British Sulphur North America, Inc. (1990)-. Periodical. English. One time a week. $849.00. British Sulphur North America, 7500 Greenway Center Drive, Suite 1045, Greenbelt MD 20770. **Tel** (301)441-4724, FAX (301)441-4726. **ED** Karen Chesez.
Desc: News and information that represents domestic prices market levels as determined by surveys of buyers and sellers and are not representations of actual transactions.

LC S **ISSN** 0071-4623
DD 630 **US**
CCC
CODEN FZSTA5
FERTILIZER SCIENCE AND TECHNOLOGY SERIES. [Fertil. sci. technol. ser.]. Vol. 1 (1968)-. Monographic series. English. Irregular. Price varies per volume. Marcel Dekker Inc., 270 Madison Avenue, New York NY 10016. **Tel** (212)696-9000, (800)228-1160, FAX (212)685-4540, telex 421419. **(Subscription address:** Marcel Dekker Inc., PO Box 5017, Monticello NY 12701. **Tel** (800)228-1160.) **ED** A. V. Slack. Documents available from CASDDS.
Desc: Each title covers a different topic in fertilizer science and technology. Topics include fertilizer processing and fertilizer nitrates.
Ind/Abst AGRICOLA [Full Cov.]; Chem. Abstr. (1968-1983).

LC S **ISSN** 0367-3073
DD 630 **SA**
CODEN FSAJA6
FERTILIZER SOCIETY OF SOUTH AFRICA JOURNAL. (FSSA JOURNAL.). [Fertil. Soc. S. Afr. j.]. **Added/Corp** Fertilizer Society of South Africa. **VFOAT** MVSA Joernaal; Fertilizer Society of South Africa Journal. **VAT** Fertilizer Society of South Africa Journal; Misstofvereniging van Suid-Afrika Joernaal. (19??)-. Periodical. English (Afrikaans and English). Two times a year.
Ind/Abst Soils Fert.; Wheat Barley Trit. Abstr.

LC S631 .U5 S631 .U48 ISSN 0146-1850
DD 338.1/62 US
FERTILIZER SUMMARY DATA. **Added/Corp** National Fertilizer Development Center (U.S.). (1968)-. English. Every 2 years. $10.00. Tennessee Valley Authority, Technical Library, National Fertilizer Development Center, Muscle Shoals AL 35660. **Tel** (205)386-2601. **Circ:** 3,500. available on microfiche (Vols. for (1980-) distributed to depository libraries). ***Continues*** *National Fertilizer Development Center (U.S.). Fertilizer Summary Data, by States and Geographic Areas.*
Desc: Fertilizer consumption data by state, region, and nation. Includes consumption of nutrients, fertilizer by class, popular grades. Gives average application rates, expenditures and incomes.
Ind/Abst Predicasts Forecasts.

LC S ISSN 1069-806X
DD 630 US
FFA NEW HORIZONS. [FFA new horiz.]. **Added/Corp** Future Farmers of America. National FFA Organization. **VFOAT** New Horizons. **VAT** Future Farmers of America New Horizons. Vol. 38, No. 2 (Dec./Jan. 1989/90)-. Periodical. English. Six times a year (Jan., Mar., May, July, Sept., Nov.). $5.00. National FFA Organization, PO Box 15160, Alexandria VA 22309. **Tel** (703)360-3600, FAX (703)360-5524, telex 899121. **ED** Andrew Markwart, (editor's address: 5632 Mount Vernon Memorial Highway, Alexandria, VA 22309). ***Continues*** *National Future Farmer, 0027-9315.*
Desc: News and events of the FFA organizations.

LC S400.F5 A63 ISSN 0015-0886
DD 630/.996/11 FJ
CODEN FJAJAB
FIJI AGRICULTURAL JOURNAL. [Fiji agric. j.]. **Added/Corp** Fiji. Ministry of Agriculture, Fisheries & Forests. Fiji. Dept. of Agriculture. New Series, Vol. 32, (Jan./June 1970)-. Academic Scholarly Publication. English. Two times a year (Jan. & July). Ministry of Agriculture & Fisheries, Information Section, PO Box 358, Suva Fiji. **Tel** 311233. **Circ:** 350 (ctrl). Documents available from CASDDS. ***Continues*** *Fiji Farmer.*
Desc: Presents scientific research, agricultural data and evaluation.
Ind/Abst AGRICOLA; Agrofor. Abstr.; Anim. Breed. Abstr.; Chem. Abstr.; Dairy Sci. Abstr.; Field Crop Abstr.; Grass. Forage Abstr.; Helminthol. Abstr.; Hortic. Abstr.; Index Vet.; Maize Abstr.; Life Sci. Collect.; Plant Breed. Abstr.; Protozoolog. Abstr.; Rev. Med. Vet. Mycology; Rev. Plant Pathol.; Rice Abstr.; Soils Fert.; Vet. Bull.; Weed Abstr.

LC TP557 .C27A ISSN 0271-6127
DD 338.4/766322041/09794 US
FINAL GRAPE CRUSH REPORT. **Main/Corp** California. Dept. of Food and Agriculture. **VFOAT** Grape Crush Report. English. One time a year. $20.00. California Agricultural Statistics Service, California Department of, Food and Agriculture, PO Box 1258, Sacramento CA 95812. **Tel** (916)551-1533.

LC HD1995.5 .A275
DD 338.1/094897 GW
FINNLAND, LAND-, FORST- UND HOLZWIRTSCHAFT. German. DM5.00. Bundesstelle fuer Aussenhandelsinformation, Agrippastrasse 87 93, D-50676 Cologne Germany. **Tel** 011 49 221 2057316, FAX 011 49 221 2057212.

LC HD1995.5 .A28
DD 338.1/094897 GW
FINNLAND, LANDWIRTSCHAFT. German. 5.00. Bundesstelle fuer Aussenhandelsinformation, Agrippastrasse 87 93, D-50676 Cologne Germany. **Tel** 011 49 221 2057316, FAX 011 49 221 2057212.

LC S
DD 630 US
•**FISCAL YEAR ... PRIORITIES AND FISCAL YEAR ... ACCOMPLISHMENTS FOR RESEARCH, EXTENSION, AND HIGHER EDUCATION.** **Main/Corp** Joint Council on Food and Agricultural Sciences (U.S.). **Added/Corp** United States. Dept. of Agriculture. (1996)-. English. Joint Council on Food and Agricultural Sciences, Administration Building / Room 321A, 14th and Independence Avenue SW, Washington DC 20250-2200. **Tel** (202)447-8662. ***Formed by the union of*** *Accomplishments for Research, Extension, and Higher Education* ***and*** *Joint Council on Food and Agricultural Sciences (U.S.). Priorities for Research, Extension, and Higher Education.*

LC SB369.2.F6 F65B ISSN 0092-3656
DD 338.1/74304/09759021 US
FLORIDA AGRICULTURAL STATISTICS. COMMERCIAL CITRUS INVENTORY. [Fla. agric. stat., Commer. citrus invent.]. **VFOAT** Commercial Citrus Inventory. English. Florida Agricultural Statistics Service, 1222 Woodward Street, Orlando FL 32803. ***Continues*** *Florida Agricultural Statistics: Inventory of Commercial Citrus Acreage, 0092-3656.*

LC HD9220.U53 F64 ISSN 0428-6456
DD 338.17 US
FLORIDA AGRICULTURAL STATISTICS: VEGETABLE SUMMARY. **Added/Corp** Florida. Marketing Bureau Section. Florida Crop and Livestock Reporting Service. (1961/1962)-. English. One time a year. $3.00. USDA NASS Florida Agricultural Statistics Service, 1222 Woodward Street, Orlando FL 32803. **Tel** (407)648-6013. ***Continues*** *Florida Vegetable Crops. Annual Statistical Summary.*

LC S ISSN 0015-4091
DD 630 US
CODEN FGRAAE
FLORIDA GROWER & RANCHER. [Fla. grow. rancher]. **VFOAT** Florida Grower and Rancher. (1953)-. Trade Publication. English. Twelve times a year. $48.00. FGR Incorporated, 1331 North Mills Avenue, Orlando FL 32803-7194. **Tel** (407)894-6522, FAX (407)894-6511. **ED** Frank Garner. **Ad Acc, Adv Mgr:** Sondra Abrahamson. **Circ:** 18,000 (ctrl). available on microfilm and microfiche from University Microfilms International (UMI). Documents available from CASDDS. ***Continues*** *Florida Grower.*
Desc: Serves all interests of Florida crop and livestock farmers: production, marketing, etc.
Ind/Abst AGRICOLA; Chem. Abstr.

LC S ISSN 0046-4120
DD 630 US
FLORIDA MARKET BULLETIN. **Added/Corp** Florida. Dept. of Agriculture and Consumer Services. Vol. 18, No. 9 (Oct. 15, 1976)-. Periodical. English. Twenty-four times a year. $10.00. Florida Department of Agriculture and Consumer Relations, 545 East Tennessee Street, Tallahassee FL 32308. **Tel** (904)487-8000. ***Continues*** *Florida. Dept. of Agriculture and Consumer Services. Division of Marketing. Market Bulletin - Florida Department of Agriculture and Consumer Services.*

LC HD9007.F6 F58A
DD 381/.41/09759 US
FLORIDA STATE FARMERS' MARKETS ... ANNUAL SUMMARY. **Main/Corp** Florida. Dept. of Agriculture and Consumer Services. Decision of Marketing. (19??)-. English. One time a year. ***Continues*** *Florida State Farmers' Markets.*

LC S ISSN 0430-7887
DD 630 US
FLORIDA TURF GROWER. **Added/Corp** University of Florida. Agricultural Experiment Stations. Vol. 1 (Oct. 1966)-. Periodical. English. University of Florida Agricultural Experiment Station, Gainesville FL 32601.

LC S ISSN 0015-3869
DD 338 US
FLORIDAGRICULTURE (GAINESVILLE, FLA.). (FLORIDAGRICULTURE : A FARM BUREAU PUBLICATION.). [FloridAgriculture]. **Added/Corp** Florida Farm Bureau Federation. **VAT** Florida Agriculture. (19??)-. Trade Publication. English. Twelve times a year. $176.55. Florida Farm Bureau Federation, PO Box 147030, Gainesville FL 32614-7030. **Tel** (904)374-1523. **ED** Rick Bush; Telephone: (904)374-1517. **Bk Rev**, (Qty: 2-3). **Ad Acc. Circ:** 84,000. ***Continues*** *Florida Agriculture.*
Desc: Reports on agriculture for associate members interested in agriculture in Florida.

LC S ISSN 0745-8355
DD 630 US
FOCUS ON FARMING. [Focus farming]. (19??)-. Periodical. English. Two times a week (104 per year). $18.00. Moravia Republican Register, 6 Central Street, PO Box 591, Moravia NY 13118. **Tel** (315)497-1551. **ED** B. F. McGuerty, III. **Ad Acc. Circ:** 15,000.
Desc: General agricultural information and advertising.

LC S ISSN 0015-525X
DD 630 AU
FOERDERUNGSDIENST, DER. [Foerderungsdienst]. **Added/Corp** Austria. Bundesministerium fuer Land- und Forstwirtschaft. Vol. 1 No. 1 (Jan. 1953)-. Periodical. German. Twelve times a year. Bundesministerium fuer Land- und Forstwirtschaft, Stubenring 1, 1010 Vienna Austria.
Ind/Abst AGRICOLA; Agric. Eng. Abstr.; EMBASE; Leis., Rec., Tour. Abstr.; Nutr. Abstr. Rev., Ser. B, Live Feeds and Feed.; Pig News Inf.; Potato Abstr.; Seed Abstr.; Soils Fert.; Soyabean Abstr.; Wheat Barley Trit. Abstr.; World Agric. Econ. Rural Sociol. Abstr.

LC LC5256.D4 F63
DK
FOLKEHJSKOLER OG LANDBRUGSSKOLER SAMT HUSHOLDNINGKOLER. **VFOAT** Folk High Schools, Agricultural and Domestic Science Schools. Danish (Danish).

LC S
DD 630 VE
FONAIAP DIVULGA / FONDO NACIONAL DE INVESTIGACIONES AGROPECURAIAS. **VAT** Fondo Nacional de Investigaciones Agropecuarias Divulga. Vol. 1, No. 1 (Nov./Dec. 1981)-. Periodical. Spanish. Six times a year.
Ind/Abst Index Vet.; Maize Abstr.; Pig News Inf.; Rice Abstr.; Sorghum Mill. Abstr.

LC RB37 ISSN 0954-0105
DD 616.075/6 UK
CCC
NLM W1; FO402L CODEN FAIMEZ
FOOD AND AGRICULTURAL IMMUNOLOGY. **See** Biology-Microbiology.

LC S ISSN 0015-6221
DD 630 IT
FOOD AND AGRICULTURAL LEGISLATION. **Added/Corp** Food and Agriculture Organization of the United Nations. Vol. 1, No. 1 (1952)-. Periodical. English (French and Spanish). One time a year. L26000. Food Agriculture Organization (FAO) / Italy, GIPCI66 via Terme di Caracalla, 00100 Rome Italy. **Tel** 011 39 6 52252925, FAX 011 39 6 52253152. cum. index. ***Continues*** *Annuaire International de Legislation Agricole.*
Desc: Presents information on laws and regulations currently in force and governing food and agriculture in FAO member states. Provides coverage of legislation and legislative activities within those nations.
Ind/Abst For. Abstr.

LC S
DD 630 US
NLM ZWA 695; U58f
FOOD AND AGRICULTURE : BIBLIOGRAPHY OF GAO DOCUMENTS. (Dec. 1988)-. Bibliography. English. US General Accounting Office / District of Columbia, 441 G Street Northwest, Room 4528, Washington DC 20548. **Tel** (202)275-2812. ***Continues*** *Food Bibliography, 0738-6737.*

LC HD1491
DD 338.19 ET
FOOD AND AGRICULTURE IN AFRICA. **See** Business and Economics-Economic Assistance and Development.

LC S ISSN 0090-9688
DD 630 US
FOOD AND HOME NOTES. [Food home notes]. **Added/Corp** United States. Dept. of Agriculture. Office of Communication. United States. Dept. of Agriculture. Office of Information. (1???)-. Government Publication. English. One time a week. US Department of Agriculture / Office of Communication, Room 1618-S, Washington DC 20250. **Tel** (202)720-2791.
Ind/Abst AGRICOLA.

LC S530 ISSN 0712-2934
DD 630/.7/1171133 CN
FOOD FOR THOUGHT (VANCOUVER). (FOOD FOR THOUGHT.). [Food thought]. Vol. 1, No. 1 (Oct. 1981)-. Periodical. English. Six times a year. Free. Agricultural Sciences, University of British Columbia Vancouver British Columbia V6T 2A2 Canada. **Tel** (604)228-5072. **ED** Maureen R Garland. **Circ:** 750 (ctrl). ***Continues*** *AG Sciences News, 0712-2926.*
Desc: Newsletter on current teaching, research and public service activities.

LC RA601 .F63 ISSN 1014-806X
DD 363.8/05 IT
NLM W1; FO428H
FOOD, NUTRITION AND AGRICULTURE. (FOOD, NUTRITION, AND AGRICULTURE / ALIMENTATION, NUTRITION ET AGRICULTURE.). [Food nutr. agric.]. **Added/Corp** Food and Agriculture Organization of the United Naitons. **VFOAT** Alimentacion Nutricion y Agricultura; Alimentation Nutrition et Agriculture. Vol. 1 (1991)-. Periodical. English. Three times a year. Free on request. Food Agriculture Organization (FAO) / Italy, GIPCI66 via Terme di Caracalla, 00100 Rome Italy. **Tel** 011 39 6 52252925, FAX 011 39 6 52253152. ***Continues*** *Food and Nutrition, 0304-8942.*
Ind/Abst Food Sci. Technol. Abstr.

LC S ISSN 0778-7065
DD 630 BE
UDC 641/642
FOOD POLICY INTERNATIONAL. [Food policy int.]. (1991)-. Trade Publication. English. Twelve times a year. $453.47. Agra Europe London Limited, 25 Frant Road, Tunbridge Wells, Kent TN2 5JT United Kingdom. **Tel** 011 44 1892 533813, FAX 011 44 1892 544895, telex 95114 AGRATW G.

LC S ISSN 0045-4168
DD 633 CN
FORAGE NOTES. (FORAGE NOTES. NOTES SUR LES FOURRAGES.). **Added/Corp** Canada. Dept. of Agriculture. Research Branch. Canada. Forage Crops Division. Canada. Agriculture Canada. Research Branch. **VFOAT** Notes sur les Fourrages. Vol. 1 (June 1955)-.

Agriculture

Periodical. English. Four times a year.
Ind/Abst Grass. Forage Abstr.; Irr. Drain. Abstr.; Nematol. Abstr.; Seed Abstr.; Soils Fert.

LC S ISSN 0379-0444
DD 630 II
CODEN FOREDH
FORAGE RESEARCH. [Forage res.].
Added/Corp Indian Society of Forage Research. Vol. 1 July (1975)-. Periodical. English. Two times a year. $30.00. Indian Society of Forage Research, Hissar India. **(Subscription address:** Prints India, 11 Darya Ganj, New Delhi 110002 India. **Tel** 011 91 11 3268645, FAX 011 91 11 3275542, telex 31-61087 PRIN-IN.)

LC SB193 ISSN 1186-7175
DD 633.2 CN
FORAGE SEED UPDATE. [Forage seed update]. **Added/Corp** Manitoba. Manitoba Agriculture. (Apr. 1991)-. Periodical. English. Four times a year. **Continues** The Leafcutter., 0825-5687.

LC S ISSN 0272-5290
DD 630 US
FORD FERGIE FARMER. Periodical. English. Six times a year. $5.00. J Todd Miles, Greystones Farm, Millbury MA 01527. **Continues** Small Farmer.

LC S US
DD 630
FOREIGN AGRICULTURAL TRADE OF THE UNITED AND STATES FISCAL YEAR ... SUPPLEMENT. Added/Corp United States. Dept. of Agriculture. Economic Research Service. **VFOAT** FATUS. Fiscal Year ... Supplement. (1984)-. Government Publication. English. One time a year. $21.00. Superintendent of Documents, US Government Printing Office, Washington DC 20402. **Tel** (202)275-3328, FAX (202)786-2317. **Continues in part** U.S. Foreign Agricultural Trade Statistical Report.
Desc: Consists of tables and statistics of exports and imports of agricultural commodities in the United States.
Ind/Abst Predicasts Forecasts.

LC HD9001 .F654 ISSN 0046-4546
DD 382/.41/0973 US
FOREIGN AGRICULTURAL TRADE OF THE UNITED STATES. [Foreign agric. trade U.S.]. **VFOAT** F.A.T.U.S.; FATUS; Foreign Agricultural Trade. Aug. 1962-. Government Publication. English. Six times a year (2 supplements). $40.00. US Department of Agriculture, 14th Street and Independence Avenue SW, Washington DC 20250. **Tel** (202)720-5457. **(Subscription address:** Superintendent of Documents, US Government Printing Office, Washington DC 20402.)
Formed by the union of Foreign Agricultural Trade of the United States Digest **and** Foreign Agricultural Trade of the United States, Statistical Report.
Desc: Consisting chiefly of tables and statistics, contains information on exports and imports of agricultural commodities in the United States.
Ind/Abst Middle East Abstr. Index; Predicasts Forecasts; Soyabean Abstr.; World Agric. Econ. Rural Sociol. Abstr.

LC S ISSN 1157-3201
DD 630 FR
UDC 630 449.1/.5
CODEN 372.86
FORET PROFESSIONNELLE LA BASTIDE-DES-JOURDANS, LA. (LA FORET PROFESSIONNELLE.). (1990)-. Periodical. French. Six times a year. $13.12. Foret Professionnelle, 84240 Bastide Jourdans France. **Tel** 011 33 90778001.

LC S GW
DD 630
FORSCHUNGSBERICHT AGRARTECHNIK DES ARBEITSKREISES FORSCHUNG UND LEHRE DER MAX-EYTH-GESELLSCHAFT (MEG).
Added/Corp Arbeitskreis Forschung und Lehre der Max-Eyth-Gesellschaft. (19??)-. Monographic series. German. **Continues** Forschungsbericht Agrartechnik des Arbeitskreises Forschung und Lehre der MEG.
Ind/Abst Agric. Eng. Abstr.; Dairy Sci. Abstr.; Field Crop Abstr.; Hortic. Abstr.; Index Vet.; Maize Abstr.; Nutr. Abstr. Rev., Ser. B, Live Feeds and Feed.; Postharvest News Inf.; Rev. Agric. Entomol.; Wheat Barley Trit. Abstr.

LC S AU
DD 630
FORSCHUNGSBERICHTE DER BUNDESANSTALT FUER LANDTECHNIK, WIESELBURG.
Added/Corp Bundesanstalt fuer Landtechnik, Wieselburg. (1983)-. Monographic series. German. Irregular. Price varies per volume. Bundesanstalt fur Wassergute des Bundesministeriums fur Land und Forstwirtschaft, Schiffmuhlenstrasse 120, Postfach 52, A-1223 Vienna Austria. **Continues** Forschungsberichte der Bundesversuchs- und Prufungsanstalt fur Landwirtschaftliche Maschinen und Gerate, Wieselburg.
Ind/Abst Agric. Eng. Abstr.

LC S542.G3 F65 ISSN 0931-2277
DD 630/.72043 GW
FORSCHUNGSREPORT, ERNAHRUNG, LANDWIRTSCHAFT, FORSTEN.
[Forsch.-Rep., ErnEähr., Landwirtsch., Forsten].
Added/Corp Germany (West). Bundesministerium fuer Ernahrung, Landwirtschaft und Forsten. Senat der Forschungsanstalten. Germany. Bundesministerium fuer Ernahrung, Landwirtschaft und Forsten. Senat der Forschungsanstalten. **VFOAT** Forschungs Report, Ernahrung, Landwirtschaft, Forsten. Vol. 1 (1986)-. Periodical. German.

LC S ISSN 0939-7701
DD 630 GW
FORSCHUNGSVORHABEN. (1990)-.
Bibliography. German. One time a year. DM15.00. Zentralstelle fuer Agrardokumentation und Information, Villichgasse 17, PO Box 201415, D-53144 Bonn Germany. **Tel** 0228 95480, FAX 0228 9548 149. Index available. cum. index. Circ: 1,200 (ctrl).
Desc: Provides information on current German research in the fields of nutrition, agriculture, forestry and veterinary medicine.

LC S AU
DD 630
FORTSCHRITTLICHE LANDWIRT, DER.
(19??)-. German (English). Twenty-six times a year. S651.00 Italy; S638.00 Austria; $765.00 other. Leopold Stocker Verlag, Hofgasse 11 a, A 8011 Graz Austria. **Tel** 011 43 316 821636, FAX 011 43 316 835612. **Bk Rev**, (Qty: 50); **Ad Acc**. Circ: 35,000 (ctrl).
Desc: Contains articles on agriculture.

LC S GW
DD 630
FORTSCHRITTSBERICHTE FUER ERNAHRUNG UND HANDWIRTSCHAFT. Added/Corp Institut fur Landwirtschaftliche Information und Dokumentation (Akademie der Landwirtschaftswissenschaften der DDR). (1990)-. Monographic series. German. **Continues** Fortschrittsberichte fur Ernahrung und Landwirtschaft.
Ind/Abst Nutr. Abstr. Rev., Ser. B, Live Feeds and Feed.; Pig News Inf.; Potato Abstr.

LC S ISSN 0721-474X
DD 630 GW
FORUM - KIELER WISSENSCHAFTSVERLAG VAUK.
(FORUM.). [Forum - Kiel. Wiss.verl. Vauk.]. (1981)-. Monographic series. German.
Ind/Abst World Agric. Econ. Rural Sociol. Abstr.

LC S IO
DD 630
FORUM PASCASARJANA. Periodical. Indonesian (English; summaries and/or abstracts in Indonesian). Institut Pertanian, Fakultas Pascasarjana, Bogor Indonesia. **Continues** Forum Sekolah Pasca Sarjana, 0126-1886.
Ind/Abst Potato Abstr.

LC S FR
DD 630
FRANCE AGRICOLE, LA. Vol. 24, No. 1175 (Jan. 5, 1968)-. Periodical. French. Fifty times a year. $135.17. Nouvelles Editions Publs Agricoles, 8 Cite Paradis, F 75010 Paris Cedex 10 France. **Tel** 011 33 1 40227900, 011 33 1 40227974.

LC SB317.5 ISSN 1072-2831
DD 635 US
●**FRESH CUT.** [Fresh cut]. Vol. 1, No. 1 (1993)-. Periodical. English. Nine times a year. $15.00. Columbia Publishing Company / Washington, 2809 A Fruitvale, Yakima WA 98907. **Tel** (509)248-2452, (800)788-2452, FAX (509)575-3080. **(Subscription address:** Columbia Publishing Company, PO Box 1467, Yakima WA 98907.)

LC S US
DD 630
FRESH FRUIT AND VEGETABLES, ORNAMENTAL CROPS. WEEKLY SUMMARY--SHIPMENTS AND UNLOADS. VFOAT Weekly Summary--Shipments and Unloads. No. WS-03-81 (Jan. 21, 1981)-. Government Publication. English. One time a week. US Department of Agriculture, 14th Street and Independence Avenue SW, Washington DC 20250. **Tel** (202)720-5457. Documents available from Documents on Demand. **Continues** Fresh Fruit and Vegetable Market News. Weekly Summary, Shipments--Unloads, 0094-4858.
Ind/Abst Am. Stat. Index.

LC S ISSN 0890-8176
DD 630 US
FRIEND OF THE FAMILY FARM, THE. Vol. 1, No. 1 (Nov. 1984)-. Periodical. English. Six times a year. Free. The Friend of the Family Farm, PO Box 504, Wisconsin Rural Development Center, Black Earth WI 53515. **Tel** (608)767-2539.

LC HD9000 ISSN 0961-0464
DD 338.175 UK
FRUIT AND VEGETABLE MARKETS.
[Fruit Veg. Mark.]. (1990)-. English. Twelve times a year. $530.48. Agra Europe London Limited, 25 Frant Road, Tunbridge Wells, Kent TN2 5JT United Kingdom. **Tel** 011 44 1892 533813, FAX 011 44 1892 544855, telex 95114 AGRATW G. **Continues** Fruits and Vegetables, 0950-4931.

LC S ISSN 0744-0197
DD 630 US
FRUIT AND VEGETABLE TRUCK RATE REPORT (SAN FRANCISCO, CALIF.).
(FRUIT AND VEGETABLE TRUCK RATE REPORT.).
Added/Corp California. Bureau of Market News. (1???)-. Periodical. English. One time a week. US Department of Agriculture / Agricultural Marketing Service / New York, Fruit and Vegetable Market News Branch, 4A New York City Terminal Market, New York NY 10474. **Tel** (212)542-2225.

LC S US
DD 630
FRUIT COUNTRY. English. Twelve times a year. $12.00 US; $18.00 Canada and Mexico; $56.00 other. Columbia Publishing and Design, 2809-A Fruitvale Boulevard, Box 1467, Yakima WA 98907-1467. **Tel** (509)248-2452, FAX (509)248-4056. **ED** Ken Hodge. **Bk Rev**. **Ad Acc**. Circ: 11,500.
Desc: For progressive fruit growers in the Pacific Northwest. Editorial emphasis is on human interest. Features may be on successful growers who are facing and overcoming current industry challenges or on agribusinesses serving the industry. Focus is on production techniques and services which can help growers' profitability.

LC SB354 ISSN 0427-6906
DD 634 US
FRUIT NOTES. [Fruit notes]. **Added/Corp**
University of Massachusetts (Amherst Campus). Dept. of Plant and Soil Sciences. University of Massachusetts (Amherst Campus). Cooperative Extension Service. (Jan./Feb., 1968)- . Periodical. English. Six times a year. $8.00. University of Massachusetts Department of Plant and Soil Science, Bowditch Hall, Amherst MA 01003. **Tel** (413)545-2963, FAX (413)545-0260. **ED** Wesley R Autio.
Circ: 700.
Ind/Abst AGRICOLA [Full Cov.].

LC S17 US
DD 630
FS. Main/Corp Oregon State University. Extension Service. No. 1 (Feb. 1962)-. Periodical. English.
Ind/Abst AGRICOLA; World Agric. Econ. Rural Sociol. Abstr.

LC S US
DD 630 TITLE CHANGE
FSA COMMODITY FACT SHEET. HONEY. (1993)-(1995). English. US Department of Agriculture / Agricultural Stabilization and Conservation, 14th and Independence Avenue SW, Washington DC 20250. **Continued by** CFSA Commodity Fact Sheet. Honey.

LC S471.C62 F844 ISSN 0253-2301
DD 630/.951245 CC
FU-CHIEN NUNG YEH KO CHI. Added/Corp
Fu-chien Sheng Nung Yeh ko Hsueh Yuan. **VFOAT**
Fujian Agricultural Science and Technology. (19??)-. Periodical. Chinese. Six times a year. $48.00. Fujian Nongye Kexueyuan / Fujian Academy of Agricultural Science, 41 Hualin lu, Fuzhou Fujian 350003, People's Republic of China. **Tel** 841771. **ED** Yang Hui. Documents available from CASDDS.
Ind/Abst Biocont. News Inf.; Biodeter. Abstr.; Field Crop Abstr.; Hortic. Abstr.; Nematol. Abstr.; Plant Breed. Abstr.; Plant Grow. Reg. Abstr.; Postharvest News Inf.; Rev. Agric. Entomol.; Rice Abstr.; Seed Abstr.; Soyabean Abstr.

LC S ISSN 0253-2301
DD 630 CC
CODEN FNKED9
FUJIAN NONGYE KEJI. (FU-CHIEN NUNG YEH KO CHI.). [Fujian nongye keji]. **Added/Corp**
Fu-Chien Sheng Nung Yeh ko Hsueh Yuan. (19??)-. Academic Scholarly Publication. Chinese. Six times a year. $48.00. Fujian Nongye Kexueyuan / Fujian Academy of Agricultural Science, 41 Hualin lu, Fuzhou Fujian 350003, People's Republic of China. **Tel** 841771. **ED** Y. Hui. **Ad Acc**. Documents available from CASDDS.
Ind/Abst NAPRALERT.

LC S ISSN 0388-7790
DD 630 JA
CODEN FNSHDO
FUKUI-KEN NOGYO SHIKENJO HOKOKU. [Fukui-ken Nogyo Shikenjo hokoku]. **Added/Corp** Fukui-Ken Nogyo Shikenjo. **VFOAT** Fukui Noshi Ho; Bulletin of the Fukui Agricultural Experiment Station. (1964)-. Bulletin. Japanese. One time a year. Do Shinkenjo, Chiba-Ken Nogyo Shinkenjo, 808-Banchi, Daizenno-Machi, Chiba-Shi 280-02 Japan. Documents available from CASDDS.

Agriculture

Ind/Abst Agric. Eng. Abstr.; Chem. Abstr. (1964-1976); Field Crop Abstr.; Rev. Plant Pathol.; Rice Abstr.; Seed Abstr.

LC S
DD 631   ISSN 0388-7723
JA
FUKUSHIMA-KEN NOGYO SHIKENJO KENKYU HOKOKU. [Fukushima-ken Nogyo Shikenjo kenkyu hokoku]. **VFOAT** Bulletin of the Fukushima Prefecture Agricultural Experiment Station. (1965)-. Periodical. Multiple languages. One time a year. **(Subscription address:** Japan Publications Trading Company Ltd., PO Box 5030, Tokyo International, Tokyo 100-31 Japan. **Tel** 011 81 3 3292 3753.)
Ind/Abst Rev. Plant Pathol.

LC S
DD 631   ISSN 0387-3714
JA
FUKUSHIMA-KEN NOGYO SHIKENJO TOKUBETSU KENKYU HOKOKU. [Fukushima-ken Nogyo Shikenjo tokubetsu kenkyu hokoku]. **VFOAT** Special Bulletin of the Fukushima Prefecture Agricultural Experiment Station. (1978)-. Periodical. Multiple languages. **(Subscription address:** Japan Publications Trading Company Ltd., PO Box 5030, Tokyo International, Tokyo 100-31 Japan. **Tel** 011 81 3 3292 3753.)
Ind/Abst Rice Abstr.

LC S
DD 630   US
FURROW. CORNBELT EDITION, THE. (THE FURROW.). **Added/Corp** Deere & Company. (Jan. 1981)-. Periodical. English. Seven times a year. Free to qualified subscribers. Deere & Company, John Deere Road, Moline IL 61265. **Tel** (309)765-8000. **Continues in part** Furrow, 0016-3112.

LC S
DD 630   US
FURROW. SOUTHEAST EDITION, THE. (THE FURROW.). **Added/Corp** Deere & Company. Vol. 86, Issue 1 (Jan. 1981)-. Periodical. English. Seven times a year. Free to qualified subscribers. Deere & Company, John Deere Road, Moline IL 61265. **Tel** (309)765-8000. **ED** George Sollenberger. **Continues in part** Furrow, 0016-3112.
Ind/Abst Mat. Fact.

LC S
DD 630   UK
FUTURE EUROPEAN AGRICULTURE. (19??)-. English. One time a year. £140.00 UK; £143.00 other. The Economist Intelligence Unit, 40 Duke Street, London W1A 1DW United Kingdom. **Tel** 011 44 171 8301000. **(Subscription address:** Economist Intelligence Unit / North America Subscriptions, 111 West 57th Street, New York NY 10019. **Tel** 800 938-4685, (212)554-0600, **FAX** (212)586-1181, (212)586-1182.)

LC S
DD 630   US
FUTURES CHART SERVICE. AGRICULTURAL. **VFOAT** Commodity Research Bureau Futures Chart Service; CRB Futures Chart Service. Vol. 35, No. 31 (Aug. 3, 1990)-. Periodical. English. One time a week. $230.00. Knight Ridder Financial Publishing, 30 South Wackler Drive, Suite 1820, Chicago IL 60606. **Tel** (312)454-1801, (800)621-5271, **FAX** (312)454-0239. **Continues in part** CRB Futures Chart Service.

LC S
DD 630   ISSN 0748-1578
US
FUTURES (EAST LANSING, MICH.). (FUTURES.). [Futures]. No. 1 (Winter 1982)-. Periodical. English. Four times a year. Agricultural Experiment Station, Michigan State University, East Lansing MI 48824-1039. **Tel** (517)355-0123. **Continues** Michigan Science in Action, 0076-809X.
Ind/Abst AGRICOLA [Select. Cov.].

LC HD9001 .U53a   ISSN 0090-3078
DD 380.1/41/4097   US
FVUS. **Main/Corp** United States. Agricultural Marketing Service. Fruit and Vegetable Division. **Added/Corp** United States. Agricultural Marketing Service. Fruit and Vegetable Division. Market News Branch. (1971)-. English. US Department of Agriculture / Agricultural Marketing Service / Washington, DC, Market News Branch, Fruit and Vegetable Division, Washington DC 20250. **Tel** (202)720-2745, (202)720-3343, **FAX** (202)720-7502. **Continues in part** C & MS (Series).

LC S
DD 630   ISSN 0374-7859
SI
CODEN GABUAV
GARDENS' BULLETIN, SINGAPORE, THE. [Gard. bull., Singapore]. **Added/Corp** Botanic Gardens (Singapore). **VFOAT** Gardens' Bulletin. (1942)-. Bulletin. English. Two times a year (June & Dec.). 40.00Sing$. National Parks Board Singapore, Botanic Gardens Cluny Road, Singapore 1025 Singapore. **Tel** 011 65 4709917, telex RS22603 PRD. **ED** S. Y. Geh. Index available. **Bk Rev. Ad Circ:** 300 (ctrl). Documents available from BIOSIS Document Express. **Continues** Gardens' Bulletin, Straits Settlements.
Ind/Abst AGRICOLA [Full Cov.]; Biol. Abstr.; Field Crop Abstr.; For. Prod. Abstr.; For. Abstr.; Grass. Forage Abstr.; Hortic. Abstr.; Ornamental Hort. (19??-19??); Plant Breed. Abstr.; Plant Grow. Reg. Abstr.; Rev. Med. Vet. Mycology; Rev. Plant Pathol.; Soils Fert.

LC S
DD 630   ISSN 0046-5437
NO
CODEN GARTA6
GARTNERYRKET. [Gartneryrket]. **VFOAT** Gartner Yrket. Vol. 37 (Dec. 15, 1947)-. Academic Scholarly Publication. Norwegian. One time a week. Documents available from CASDDS. **Continues** Norsk Gartnerforenings Tidsskrift.
Ind/Abst AGRICOLA; Agric. Eng. Abstr. (1991-); Biocont. News Inf.; Biodeter. Abstr.; Chem. Abstr.; Field Crop Abstr.; For. Abstr.; Hortic. Abstr.; Nematol. Abstr.; Ornamental Hort. (1991-); Plant Breed. Abstr.; Plant Grow. Reg. Abstr.; Postharvest News Inf.; Rev. Agric. Entomol.; Rev. Plant Pathol.; Soils Fert.

LC S
DD 630   ISSN 1018-7235
UK
GATEKEEPER SERIES. [Gatekeep. ser.]. **Added/Corp** International Institute for Environment and Development. Sustainable Agriculture Programme. No. SA1 (1987)-. Monographic series. English.
Ind/Abst World Agric. Econ. Rural Sociol. Abstr.

LC HD2129.5 .A33a
DD 338.1/869/1   MG
GAZATIM-BAOVAO - MINISTERAN'NY FAMPANDROSOANA NY AMBANIVOHITRA SY NY FANAVAOZANA NY FIZAKAN-TANY. **Main/Corp** Malagasy Republic. Ministere du Developpement Rural et de la Reforme Agraire. **Added/Corp** Malagasy Republic. Ministere du Developpement Rural et de la Reforme Agraire. Bulletin d'information. **VFOAT** Bulletin d'Information - Ministere du Developpement Rural et de la Reforme Agraire. (1975)-. Bulletin. French (Malagasy). Repoblika Malagasy, Ministeranny Fampandrosoana Ny Ambanivohitra Sy Ny Fanavaozana Ny Fizakan-tany, Tananarive Malagasy. **Continues** Gazetim-Baovao - Ministeran'ny Fampandrosoana Ny Ambanivohitra.

LC S
DD 630   AO
GAZETA AGRI'COLA DE ANGOLA. **Added/Corp** Associacao dos Agricultores de Angola. Vol. 1, No. 1 (July 1956)-. Periodical. Portuguese. Twelve times a year. Associacao dos Agricultores de Angola, Luanda Angola.

LC S
DD 630   JA
GENDAI NOGYO. Vol. 39, No. 11 (Nov. 1960)-. Periodical. Japanese. Twelve times a year. Nosangyoson Bunka Kyokai, 6-1 Akasaka 7 Chome, Minatoku Tokyo 107 Japan. **Continues** Noson Bunka.

LC S
DD 630   ISSN 0016-6863
IT
GENIO RURALE. [Genio rurale]. Vol. 11, No. 1 (Jan/Feb. 1948)-. Periodical. Italian. Eleven times a year. L51780. Edagricole, PO Box 2157, 40100 Bologna Italy. **Tel** 011 39 51 492211 Ext. 22, **FAX** 011 39 51 493660, telex 510336 EDAGRI. Index available in last issue of volume--attached.
Ind/Abst AgBiotech News Inf.; AGRICOLA; Agric. Eng. Abstr. (19??-19??); Dairy Sci. Abstr.; Maize Abstr.; PAIS Int. Print (1991-); Pig News Inf.; Rev. Agric. Entomol.; Soils Fert.; Soyabean Abstr.

LC S
DD 630   ISSN 0735-696X
US
GEORGIA FARM BUREAU NEWS. [Ga. Farm Bur. news]. **Added/Corp** Georgia Farm Bureau Federation. Georgia Farm Bureau. **VFOAT** Farm Bureau News. (19??)-. Periodical. English. Twelve times a year. $9.00. Georgia Farm Bureau Federation, 2960 Riverside Drive, Box 7068, Macon GA 31298. **Tel** (912)474-8411. **Continues** News Letter of the State Association of County Chapters of the United Georgia Farmers.
Ind/Abst AGRICOLA [Select. Cov.].

LC S
DD 630   ISSN 0741-1251
US
GEORGIA FARMER (BALTIMORE, MD.). (GEORGIA FARMER.). [Ga. farmer]. Vol. 1, No. 1 (Oct. 1983)-. Periodical. English. Twelve times a year. $6.00. Wittman Publications, Box 3689, Baltimore MD 21214. **Tel** (301)377-0202.

LC S
DD 630   US
GEORGIA FUTURE FARMER, THE. **Added/Corp** Future Farmers of America. Georgia Association. Vol. 26, No. 1 (Oct. 1957)-. Periodical. English. Four times a year. **Continues** G.A.F.F.A.
Ind/Abst AGRICOLA.

LC S
DD 630   ISSN 0239-1260
HU
GEORGICON FOR AGRICULTURE. [Georgicon agric.]. **Added/Corp** Keszthelyi Mezogazdasagtudomanyi Kar. Pannon Agrartudomanyi Egyetem. Georgicon Faculty. (1988)-. Periodical. English. Two times a year.
Ind/Abst Field Crop Abstr.; Grass. Forage Abstr.; Nutr. Abstr. Rev., Ser. B, Live Feeds and Feed.; Pig News Inf.; Seed Abstr.; Soils Fert.; Wheat Barley Trit. Abstr.

LC S17
DD 630   GR
GEORGIKE EREUNA - HYPERESIA GEORGIKON EREUNON, GREECE. **Main/Corp** Greece. Hyperesia Georgikon Ereunon. Periodical. Greek, Modern (summaries and/or abstracts in English and French).
Ind/Abst Biocont. News Inf.; Dairy Sci. Abstr.; Maize Abstr.; Plant Breed. Abstr.; Soils Fert.

LC S9 .A16   ISSN 0367-4134
DD 630.6245   IT
GEORGOFILI; ATTI DELLA ACCADEMIA DEI GEORGOFILI, I. **Added/Corp** Accademia Economico-Agraria dei Georgofili, Florence. (1792)-. Periodical. Italian. Four times a year. cum. index.
Ind/Abst Agric. Eng. Abstr.

LC S
DD 630   ISSN 0046-5917
GH
GHANA FARMER, THE. [Ghana farmer]. Vol. 1, No. 4 (May 1957)-. Periodical. English. Two times a year. **Continues** New Gold Coast Farmer.
Ind/Abst AGRICOLA; Field Crop Abstr.; Grass. Forage Abstr.; Hortic. Abstr.; Plant Breed. Abstr.

LC S
DD 630   NE
GIDS VOOR ZIEKTEN EN ONKRUIDBESTRIJDING IN DE LAND EN TUINBOUW. (19??)-. Dutch. One time a year. Plantenziektenkundige Dienst, Postbus 9102, 6700 HC Wageningen Netherlands. **Tel** 011 31 8340-96799, **FAX** 011 31 8340-21701.

LC S
DD 630   ISSN 0435-9763
GW
GIESSENER BEITRAEGE ZUR ENTWICKLUNGSFORSCHUNG. REIHE 2 : MONOGRAPHIEN. (GIESSENER BEITRAEGE ZUR ENTWICKLUNGSFORSCHUNG. REIHE II MONOGRAPHIEN.). [Giess. Beitr. Entwicklungsforsch., 2]. **Added/Corp** Justus-Liebig Universitat. Tropeninstitut. (1967)-. Monographic series. German (English). Price varies per volume.
Ind/Abst Ecol. Abstr.; Int. Dev. Abstr.

LC HD9482.A1 I57a
DD 338.7/6686/025   BE
GIFAP DIRECTORY. See Industry and Production-Trade and Industrial Directories.

LC S
DD 630   ISSN 0072-4513
JA
CODEN GNKEAH
GIFU DAIGAKU NOGAKUBU KENKYU HOKOKU. [Gifu Daigaku Nogakubu kenkyu hokoku]. **Main/Corp** Gifu Daigaku. Nogakubu. **Added/Corp** Gifu Daigaku. Nogakubu. Kenkyu Hokoku. Gifu Daigaku. Nogakubu. Research Bulletin of the Faculty of Agriculture, Gifu University. **VFOAT** Kenkyu Hokoku; Research Bulletin of the Faculty of Agriculture, Gifu University. No 1 (Dec 1951)-. Academic Scholarly Publication. Japanese (English; summaries and/or abstracts in English). Documents available from BIOSIS Document Express, CASDDS.
Ind/Abst Agric. Eng. Abstr. (1991-); Biol. Abstr. (-1983); Chem. Abstr.; EMBASE; Food Sci. Technol. Abstr.; For. Prod. Abstr. (1991-); Hortic. Abstr.; Index Vet.

LC S
DD 630   ISSN 0304-064X
UDC 630   IT
CODEN GIAGA
SUSPENDED
GIORNALE DI AGRICOLTURA. [G. agric.]. (1890)-(Dec. 1991). Newspaper. Italian. One time a week. Reda Ramo Edit Agricoltori, Via di Tor Sapienza 172, 00155 Rome Italy. **Tel** 011 39 6 2280077.

LC S
DD 630   ISSN 1064-9972
US
●**GLOBAL ALABAMA.** (1993)-. Periodical. English. Twelve times a year. $24.00. Agro-Eco Global Ltd., PO Box 2674, Savannah GA 31402.

LC S
DD 630   ISSN 1064-9956
US
●**GLOBAL NORTH CAROLINA.** (1993)-. Periodical. English. Twelve times a year. $24.00. Agro-Eco Global Ltd., PO Box 2674, Savannah GA 31402.

LC S
DD 630   ISSN 1064-9964
US
●**GLOBAL SOUTH CAROLINA.** (1993)-. Periodical. English. Twelve times a year. $24.00. Agro-Eco Global Ltd., PO Box 2674, Savannah GA 31402.

LC S ISSN 1064-9980
DD 630 US
•GLOBAL TEXAS. (1993)-. Periodical. English. Twelve times a year. $24.00. Agro-Eco Global Ltd., PO Box 2674, Savannah GA 31402.

LC S ISSN 0351-9112
DD 630 XN
CODEN GZFSDJ
GODISEN ZBORNIK NA ZEMJODELSKIOT FAKULTET NA UNIVERZITETOT VO SKOPJE. [God. zb. zemjod. fak. univ. Skopje]. **Added/Corp** Univerzitet "Kiril i Metodij"--Skopje. Zemjodelski Fakultet. **VFOAT** Annuaire de la Faculte d'Agriculture de l'Universite de Skopje. (1977)-. Macedonian (summaries and/or abstracts in English and French). One time a year. Documents available from CASDDS. ***Continues*** *Godisen Zbornik na Zemjodelsko-Sumarskiot Fakultet na Univerzitetot--Skopje. Zemjodelstvo, 0367-5580.*
Ind/Abst Chem. Abstr.

LC SB320 ISSN 0888-5672
DD 635 US
Pr Rev.
GOURD, THE. [Gourd]. **Added/Corp** American Gourd Society. Vol. 1, No. 1 (Feb. 1971)-. Periodical. English. Four times a year (Jan., Apr., July, Sept.). $10.00 (one-year), $19.00 (two-year), $28.00 (three-year) US; $16.00 (one-year), $30.00 (two-year), $44.00 (three-year) other, Comes with American Gourd Society membership. American Gourd Society, PO Box 274, Mt Gilead OH 43338. **Tel** (419)362-6446, FAX (419)362-6446. **ED** Ted Medvowski. Index available ((published annually)). cum. index. **Bk Rev. Circ:** 4,000 (ctrl). Documents available from the publisher.

LC S
DD 630 UK
GRAIN AND OILSEEDS. (19??)-. Periodical. English. Twelve times a year. £220.00 Europe; £250.00 other. Agra Europe London Limited, 25 Frant Road, Tunbridge Wells, Kent TN2 5JT United Kingdom. **Tel** 011 44 1892 533813, FAX 011 44 1892 544895, telex 95114 AGRATW G.

LC S ISSN 0744-1533
DD 630 US
GRAIN MARKET NEWS (BELL, CALIF.). (GRAIN MARKET NEWS.). **VFOAT** Weekly Grain Market News. Periodical. English. One time a week. $42.00. Federal-State Market News Service, 1220 N Street, Suite 216, Box 942871, Sacramento CA 94271-0001. **Tel** (916)654-0298, FAX (916)654-1046.

LC HD9049.W3 M37
DD 331.7 UK
GRAIN MARKET REPORT. Added/Corp International Wheat Council. (Nov. 1990)-. English (French, Spanish and Russian). Eleven times a year. $400.00. International Wheat Council, One Canada Square, Canary Wharf, London E14 5AE United Kingdom. **Tel** 011 44 171 5131122, FAX 011 44 171 7120071, telex 8813241. ***Continues*** *Market Report (International Wheat Council).*

LC S ISSN 0043-0587
DD 630 US
GRANGE NEWS, THE. (THE GRANGE NEWS : VOICE OF WASHINGTON AGRICULTURE.). [Grange news]. **Added/Corp** Washington State Grange. **VFOAT** Washington Grange News. (19??)-. Periodical. English. Twelve times a year. $4.75. Grange News, PO Box 1186, Olympia WA 98507. **Tel** (206)943-9911. **ED** Bill Thorness. **Bk Rev. Ad Acc. Circ:** 43,250 (ctrl).
Desc: Official publication of the Washington State Grange devoted to informing the agri-business community.

LC S
DD 630 BL
GRANJA : UMA REVISTA RURAL AO SERVICO DO RIO GRANDE DO SUL, A. (1944)-. Periodical. English. Twelve times a year. Editora Centaurus Ltda, Caixa Postal 2890, 90000 Porto Alegre-RS Brazil.

LC HD1941 .G7 ISSN 0242-2085
DD 338.1/0944 FR
GRAPH-AGRI : ANNUAIRE DE GRAPHIQUES AGRICOLES. VFOAT Graph Agri; Annuaire de Graphiques Agricoles. French. One time a year. 125.00F France; 135.00F other. SCEES, 4 Avenue de Saint-Mande, 75570 Paris Cedex 12 France. **Tel** 011 33 1 49558576.
Desc: Gives recent data in the form of charts, maps and graphs, with concise comments, on the agricultural sector and its evolution through the last decade.

LC HD1941 .G73 ISSN 0755-1908
DD 630 FR
GRAPH AGRI REGIONS. Added/Corp France. Service Central des Enquetes et Etudes Statistiques. (1984)-. French. Every 3 years. SCEES - Service Central des Enquetes et Etudes Statistiques, 4 Avenue de Saint-Mande, 75570 Paris Cedex 12 France. **Tel** 011 33 1 49558576.

LC HD1492 ISSN 0310-2890
DD 335.994 AT
GRASS ROOTS SHEPPARTON. [Grass roots Sheppart.]. (1973)-. Periodical. English. Six times a year (Feb., April, June, Aug., Oct., Dec.). 24.25Aus$. Night Owl Publishers Pty Ltd., PO Box 242, Euroa Victoria 3666 Australia. **Tel** 011 61 3 57947256, FAX 011 61 3 57947285. Index available (Back iss. avail.). **Bk Rev**, (Qty: 18). **Ad Acc, Adv Mgr:** C. Ballard, **Tel** 057-947-256. **Circ:** 32,000.
Desc: Covers crafts and self-sufficiency for down to earth people.

LC SB354 ISSN 1057-2430
DD 634 US
GRAZIER (CORVALLIS, OR.), THE. (THE GRAZIER.). [Grazier]. **Added/Corp** Oregon State College. Extension Service. Oregon State University. Extension Service. United States. Dept. of Agriculture. No. 1 (May 4, 1939)-. Periodical. English.
Ind/Abst AGRICOLA [Full Cov.].

LC S
DD 630 US
GREAT BLAFIGRIA IS, THE. No. 1 (1975)-. Academic Scholarly Publication. English. The Great Blafigria Is, Box 1054, Santa Fe MN 87501. Documents available from BIOSIS Document Express, CASDDS.
Ind/Abst Biol. Abstr.; Chem. Abstr.; GeoRef.

LC S ISSN 0705-7210
DD 630/.2/02 CN
GREAT CANADIAN HOMESTEADER, THE. Vol. 1- April 1977-. Periodical. English. Irregular. .50 cents per no. The Great Canadian Homesteader, 5320 198 A Street, Langley British Columbia, V3A 7B6 Canada. **Tel** (604)530-1328.

LC HD1920.5.Z8 G73 ISSN 0250-5886
DD 338.1/81/094 UK
GREEN EUROPE (BRUSSELS, BELGIUM). (GREEN EUROPE.). 1967. Periodical. English. Twelve times a year. £132.00 UK; £138.00 Europe; £143.00 other. Agra Europe London Limited, 25 Frant Road, Tunbridge Wells, Kent TN2 5JT United Kingdom. **Tel** 011 44 1892 533813, FAX 011 44 1892 544895, telex 95114 AGRATW G. **ED** Edgar Phillips. **Circ:** 400. ***Continues*** *Newsletter on the Common Agricultural Policy.*
Desc: Digest, written mainly for British Isles readers; gives background information on CAP and other matters affecting agriculture and allied industries.
Ind/Abst Geogr. Abstr. Human Geogr.; Leis., Rec., Tour. Abstr.; Potato Abstr.; Rural Dev. Abstr.; World Agric. Econ. Rural Sociol. Abstr.

LC S ISSN 0149-5569
DD 630 US
GREEN MARKETS. (197?)-. Periodical. English. Fifty times a year. $1320.00. Pike & Fischer Inc., 4600 East-West Highway, Suite 200, Bethesda MD 20814-1438. **Tel** (301)654-6262, FAX (301)654-6297. **ED** Thomas Woodall, Sara Hansard, Philip Finnegan and Karen Chasez. **Circ:** 1,200. available via fax; available on an online database from NEXIS; and DIALOG.
Desc: Covers world fertilizer industry including company news, market developments, and wholesale fertilizer prices.

LC S
DD 630 PH
GREENFIELDS : THE TOTAL AGRICULTURAL MAGAZINE. (19??)-. Periodical. English. Twelve times a year. P130.00. Planters Products Inc, Esteban St Legaspi Village, Makati Manila Philippines. **Tel** 011 63 8182154, 011 63 8182110.
Ind/Abst Philip. Sci. Technol. Abstr.

LC S ISSN 0017-4092
DD 630 UK
GREENSWARD. Added/Corp South West Scotland Grassland Society. Central Scotland Grassland Society. South West Scotland Grassland Society. Journal of the South West Scotland Grassland Society. No. 1 (Nov. 1962)-. English. One time a year. £5.00. Southwest Scotland Grassland Society, Auchincruive Ayr United Kingdom. **Tel** 011 44 1292 520331, telex 777400. **ED** D. Reid. **Bk Rev. Ad Acc. Circ:** 800 (ctrl).
Ind/Abst Field Crop Abstr.; Grass. Forage Abstr.

LC S ISSN 0137-9208
DD 630 PL
GROMADA ROLNIK POLSKI. [Grom. Rol. Pol.]. **VFOAT** Gromada-Rolnik Polski. (1952)-. Newspaper. Polish. Irregular (104 issues). $52.00. **(Subscription address:** Ars Polona-Ruch, PO Box 1001, Krakowskie Przedmiescie 7, 00-068 Warsaw Poland. **Tel** 011 48 22 261201.) ***Formed by the union of*** *Gromada, 0867-5058* ***and*** *Rolnik Polski, 0867-5066.*

LC S
DD 630 SZ
GRUNE, DIE. Added/Corp Schweizerischer Landwirtschaftlicher Verein. Vol. 1 (1873)-. Periodical. German. One time a week. $92.41. Verlag die Grune, Klausstr NR 10, CH-8008 Zurich Switzerland. **Tel** 011 44 1 478086.
Ind/Abst Grass. Forage Abstr.; Plant Breed. Abstr.; Rev. Plant Pathol.; Saf. Health Work; Seed Abstr.; Soils Fert.

LC S ISSN 1000-2553
DD 630 CC
GUANGXI NONGXUEYUAN XUEBAO. VFOAT Journal of Guangxi Agricultural College. (1982)-. Periodical. Chinese. Two times a year.
Ind/Abst Seed Abstr.

LC S ISSN 0101-4684
DD 630 BL
GUIA BRASILEIRO DE INSTITUCOES DE PESQUISA EM AGRICULTURA / MINISTERIO DA AGRICULTURA, BINAGRI. 1979/1981-. Portuguese. CENAGRI, Centro Nacional de Informacao Documental Agricola Brasilia DF Brazil. **Tel** (061)218 2613. **Circ:** 1,000.
Desc: Agriculture research institutions.

LC S338.M28 G84 ISSN 0542-3007
DD 338.1/09689/7 MW
GUIDE TO AGRICULTURAL PRODUCTION IN MALAWI. English. Ministry of Agriculture, Zomba Malawi. ***Continues*** *Guide to Agricultural Production in Malawi, 0542-3007.*

LC SF521
DD 638.1 UK
GUIDE TO THE DEPARTMENT, UNIVERSITY FARMS AND EXPERIMENTAL STATIONS WITH A SUMMARY OF RESEARCH. Main/Corp Reading, Eng. University. Dept. of Agriculture and Horticulture. (1975-). Periodical. English. One time a year. ***Continues*** *Guide to the University Farms and Agricultural Experimental Stations.*

LC SF521 ISSN 0250-5193
DD 638.1 II
CODEN GAUJDS
GUJARAT AGRICULTURAL UNIVERSITY RESEARCH JOURNAL. [Gujarat Agric. Univ. res. j.]. **Main/Corp** Gujarat Agricultural University. Vol. 1 (July 1975)-. Academic Scholarly Publication. English. Two times a year. $10.00. Gujarat Agricultural University, Shahibag, Ahmedabad 380004 India. **Tel** 66431. **(Subscription address:** Prints India, 11 Darya Ganj, New Delhi 110002 India. **Tel** 011 91 11 3268645, FAX 011 91 11 3275542, telex 31-61087 PRIN-IN.) **ED** K. Janakiraman. **Ad Acc. Circ:** 450 (ctrl). Documents available from CASDDS.
Ind/Abst AGRICOLA; Anim. Breed. Abstr.; Biocont. News Inf. (19??-19??); Chem. Abstr.; Cot. Trop. Fibr. Abstr. Bibliogr.; Dairy Sci. Abstr.; Field Crop Abstr.; Food Sci. Technol. Abstr.; Grass. Forage Abstr.; Hortic. Abstr.; Index Vet.; Irr. Drain. Abstr.; Leis., Rec., Tour. Abstr.; Maize Abstr.; Nematol. Abstr.; Nutr. Abstr. Rev., Ser. B, Live Feeds and Feed.; Nutr. Abstr. Rev., Ser. A, Hum. Exp.; Plant Breed. Abstr.; Plant Grow. Reg. Abstr.; Postharvest News Inf.; Rev. Agric. Entomol.; Rev. Med. Vet. Mycology; Rev. Plant Pathol.; Rice Abstr.; Rural Dev. Abstr.; Seed Abstr.; Soils Fert.; Sorghum Mill. Abstr.; Vet. Bull.; Weed Abstr.; Wheat Barley Trit. Abstr.; World Agric. Econ. Rural Sociol. Abstr.

LC S ISSN 0289-4610
DD 631 JA
GUNMA NOGYO KENKYU. A, SOGO. [Gunma nogyo kenkyu. A, Sogo]. **VFOAT** Gunma Journal of Agricultural Research. Series A, General. (1984)-. Periodical. Multiple languages. One time a year. Gunmaken Nogyo Sogo Shikenjo, (Gunma Agricultural Research Center), 1251 Egimachi Maebashishi, Gunmaken 371 Japan. ***Continues*** *Gunma-ken Nogyo Shikenjo Hokoku, 0533-6651.*
Ind/Abst Agric. Eng. Abstr.; Rice Abstr.; Seed Abstr.; Soils Fert.

LC HD1741.J3 H324a
DD 333.7153 JA
GYOMU NEMPO - HACHIROGATA SHINNOSON KENSETSU JIGYODAN. Main/Corp Hachirogata Shinnoson Kensetsu Jigyodan. (1966)-. Periodical. Japanese. Akita Kenritsu Chikusan, Kaikan Building, 7-9 Nakadori 6-chome, Akita 010 Japan. ***Continues*** *Hachirogata Shinnoson Kensetsu Jigyodan Nempo.*

LC S15 .H2 ISSN 0017-6486
DD 630 US
HACIENDA, LA. Vol. 1, No. 1 (Oct. 1905)-. Periodical. Spanish. Six times a year. La Hacienda Inc, 639 NE 125th Street/Box 61-1197, North Miami FL 33161.

LC S
DD 630 IS
HAKLAUT BE-YISRAEL. VFOAT Haklauth Beisrael; Agriculture in Israel. Year 3- September 1957-. Periodical. Hebrew (English; summaries and/or abstracts in English). Irregular. TA Publications Department, Hakirya, Tel Aviv Israel. ***Continues*** *Alon La-Madrikh Ha-Haklai.*

LC SL **ISSN** 1192-0785
DD 630 CN
HALTON-PEEL FARM NEWS. [Halton-Peel farm news]. **Added/Corp** Georgetown Field Office (Ont.). Vol. 1 (May/June 1992)-. Periodical. English. Six times a year. Ontario Ministry of Agriculture and Food, 801 Bay Street, Toronto Ontario M7A 2B2 Canada. **Tel** (416)965-1064, (416)326-3400. ***Formed by the union of*** *Halton Farm News., 0704-9226* ***and*** *Peel Farm News., 0226-6520.*

LC S671 .H36a **ISSN** 0253-3146
DD 630.208 KO
CODEN HNHAD4
HANGUG NONGON HAGHOI JI. (HAN'GUK NONGGONG HAKHOE CHI. JOURNAL OF THE KOREAN SOCIETY OF AGRICULTURAL ENGINEERS.). [Hangug nongon haghoi ji]. **Main/Corp** Han'guk Nonggong Hakhoe. **Added/Corp** Han'guk Hanggong Uju Hakhoe. Journal. **VFOAT** Journal of the Korean Society of Agricultural Engineers. (19??)-. Academic Scholarly Publication. Korean (summaries and/or abstracts in English). Four times a year. Documents available from CASDDS.
Ind/Abst Chem. Abstr.

LC S583 .H36 **ISSN** 0368-2897
DD 631 KO
CODEN JKACA7
HAN'GUK NONGHWA HAKHOE CHI. [Han'guk Nonghwa Hakhoe chi.]. **Added/Corp** Han'guk Nonghwa Hakhoe. **VFOAT** Journal of the Korean Agricultural Chemical Society. (19??)-. Academic Scholarly Publication. Korean (English). Four times a year. $60.00. Han'Guk Nonghwa Hakhoe, 103 Sodun-dong, Department of Agricultural Chemistry, Seoul National University, Suwon 441 744 Korea. **Tel** 82 331 290 2415, FAX 82 331 293 8608. **ED** Jaf-Koo Lee. Index available. **Bk Rev. Ad Acc. Circ:** 1,000. Documents available from BIOSIS Document Express, CASDDS.
Ind/Abst Biol. Abstr. (1986-); Chem. Abstr.; Curr. Biotechnol.; Curr. Cit.; Soyabean Abstr.

LC S
DD 630 UK
HARAMATA. Added/Corp International Institute for Environment and Development. No. 1 (July 1988)-. Periodical. English (French). Four times a year. $30.00. International Institute for Environment and Development, #13 Endsleigh Street, London WC1 H 0DD United Kingdom. **Tel** 011 44 171 3882117. **ED** Robin Sharp and Camilla Toulnin.
Desc: Bulletin of the Drylands: people, policies, programs.

LC SB129 **ISSN** 0378-8865
DD 631.55 PP
CODEN HARVDQ
HARVEST (PORT MORESBY). (HARVEST.). [Harvest]. (19??)-. Academic Scholarly Publication. English. Two times a year. $13.17. Department of Agriculture and Livestock / Papua New Guinea, PO Box 417, Konedobu Papua New Guinea. **Tel** 011 675 230268, 011 675 258191, 011 675 214699, FAX 011 675 214526, telex 23280. **ED** Ray Kumar. **Bk Rev. Ad Acc. Circ:** 3,100. available on diskette. Documents available from CASDDS.
Desc: Developments, projects, experiments and practical agriculture in Papua New Guinea.
Ind/Abst Chem. Abstr.; Rev. Plant Pathol.

LC S
DD 630 US
HARVEST TODAY. Periodical. English. Four times a year. Worldteam, 1607 Ponce de Leon Boulevard, Box 343038, Coral Gables FL 33134.

LC S **ISSN** 0367-5610
DD 630 II
CODEN HAJRA5
HARYANA AGRICULTURAL UNIVERSITY JOURNAL OF RESEARCH. [Haryana agric. univ. j. res.]. **Main/Corp** Haryana Agricultural University. Vol. 1 (1971)-. Academic Scholarly Publication. English. Four times a year. $20.00. Haryana Agricultural University, Directorate of Research, Hissar India. **(Subscription address:** Prints India, 11 Darya Ganj, New Delhi 110002 India. **Tel** 011 91 11 3268645, FAX 011 91 11 3275542, telex 31-61087 PRIN-IN.**)** Documents available from CASDDS.
Ind/Abst AGRICOLA; Anim. Breed. Abstr.; Biocont. News Inf. (1991-); Biodeter. Abstr.; Chem. Abstr.; Cot. Trop. Fibr. Abstr. Bibliogr.; Crop Physiol. Abstr.; Field Crop Abstr.; Hortic. Abstr.; Nematol. Abstr.; Plant Breed. Abstr.; Plant Grow. Reg. Abstr.; Postharvest News Inf.; Potato Abstr.; Poult. Abstr.; Rev. Agric. Entomol.; Rev. Plant Pathol.; Seed Abstr.; Soils Fert.; Weed Abstr.; Wheat Barley Trit. Abstr.

LC S
DD 630 II
CODEN HJAGES
HARYANA JOURNAL OF AGRONOMY. Added/Corp Haryana Agronomists Association. Vol. 1, No. 1 (Jan./June 1985)-. Periodical. English. Two times a year. Documents available from CASDDS.
Ind/Abst Chem. Abstr. (1985-); Field Crop Abstr.; Grass. Forage Abstr.; Hortic. Abstr.; Maize Abstr.; Plant Breed. Abstr.; Potato Abstr.; Rice Abstr.; Seed Abstr.; Soils Fert.; Sorghum Mill. Abstr.; Weed Abstr.; Wheat Barley Trit. Abstr.; World Agric. Econ. Rural Sociol. Abstr.

LC S19 .S27 **ISSN** 0017-8314
DD 630 IS
HASSADEH. Added/Corp Histadrut ha-Poalim ha-ha Klaim be-E. Y. Histadrut ha-Poalim ha-Haklaim be-Yisrael. Minhal ha-Mehkar ha-Haklai (Israel) Israel. Misrad ha-ha klaut. Sherut hadrakhah u-Miktsoa. Histadrut ha-Poalim ha-ha Klaim be-Yisrael. Merkaz ha-ha Klai. **VFOAT** Hassadeh. (1920)-. Periodical. Hebrew. Twelve times a year. $80.00. Hassadeh, PO Box 40044, Tel Aviv 61400 Israel. **Tel** 011 927 3 6929978. **ED** J.M. Margalit. **Bk Rev. Ad Acc. Circ:** 8,000. Documents available from BIOSIS Document Express.
Desc: Techniques and economics of crop production and protection of field, vegetable, flower and plantation crops, livestock management, soil conservation, fertilization and irrigation.
Ind/Abst AGRICOLA; Biocont. News Inf. (1991-); Biol. Abstr.; Cot. Trop. Fibr. Abstr. Bibliogr.; Crop Physiol. Abstr.; Field Crop Abstr.; For. Abstr.; Grass. Forage Abstr.; Hortic. Abstr.; Index Vet.; Irr. Drain. Abstr.; Maize Abstr.; Nematol. Abstr.; Nutr. Abstr. Rev., Ser. B, Live Feeds and Feed.; Ornamental Hort. (19??-19??); Plant Breed. Abstr.; Plant Grow. Reg. Abstr.; Postharvest News Inf.; Potato Abstr.; Poult. Abstr.; Rev. Agric. Entomol.; Rev. Plant Pathol.; Seed Abstr.; Soils Fert.; Weed Abstr.

LC S
DD 630 IS
HASSADEH QUARTERLY : ISRAELI REVIEW OF AGRICULTURE. Added/Corp Histadrut ha-Poalim ha-Haklaim be-Yisrael. Vol. 1, No. 1 (19??)-. Periodical. English. Four times a year.
Ind/Abst Irr. Drain. Abstr.; Postharvest News Inf.

LC HD9107.H3 H76 **ISSN** 1048-9428
DD 338.1/7361/0996905 US
HAWAIIAN SUGAR MANUAL. [Hawaii. sugar man.]. **Added/Corp** Hawaiian Sugar Planters' Association. **VFOAT** H.S.P.A. Sugar Manual; HSPA Sugar Manual. (1983)-. English. Royal Assn Disability & Rehabilitation, 25 Mortimer Street, London W1N 8AB United Kingdom. **Tel** 071 637 5700, FAX 071 637 1827. ***Continues*** *HSPA Sugar Manual, 0735-441X.*

LC S
DD 630 US
HAZELNUT PRODUCTION. Added/Corp United States. Agricultural Statistics Board. United States. National Agricultural Statistics Service. Hazelnut (Filbert) Production. (1991)-. Government Publication. English. US Department of Agriculture / Statistical Reporting Service, 14th Street & Independence Avenue SW, Washington DC 20250.

LC HD2001 .H45 **ISSN** 0108-6561
DD 630 DK
HELTIDSLANDBRUGETS KONOMI. [Heltidslandbr. ekon.]. Danish. 15.-. Jordbrugskonomisk Institut, Valby Langgade 19, 2500 Valby, Copenhagen. **ED** T Due Pedersen and Svend Sorensen. **Circ:** 1,200.
Desc: Covers economic results on full-time farms and income disparity.

LC S338.M28 A23
DD 630/.9689/7 MW
HIGHLIGHTS. Main/Corp Malawi. Ministry of Agriculture and Natural Resources. English. Ministry of Agriculture and Natural Resources, Zomba Malawi.

LC S **ISSN** 1183-5796
DD 630 CN
HIGHLIGHTS OF AGRICULTURAL AND FOOD RESEARCH IN ONTARIO. [Highlights agric. food res. Ont.]. **Added/Corp** Ontario. Ministry of Agriculture and Food. Technology and Field Services. Ontario. Ministry of Agriculture and Food. Agricultural Research Institute of Ontario. **VFOAT** Agricultural and Food Research in Ontario. Vol. 13, No. 3 (Sept. 1990)-. Periodical. English (French). Four times a year. ***Continues*** *Highlights of Agricultural Research in Ontario, 0706-5213.*
Ind/Abst Agric. Eng. Abstr.

LC S **ISSN** 0018-1668
DD 630 US
CODEN HARAAS
Pr Rev.
HIGHLIGHTS OF AGRICULTURAL RESEARCH. [Highlights agr. res.]. **Added/Corp** Auburn University. Agricultural Experiment Station. Vol. 1 (Summer 1954)-. Periodical. English. Four times a year (Mar., June, Sept., Dec.). Free on request. Alabama Agricultural Experiment Station, Auburn University, 110 Comer Hall, Auburn University AL 36849. **Tel** (334)844-4877, FAX (334)844-5892. **ED** J. R. Roberson, R. A. Hearn, and C. L. Smith. **Circ:** 11,000 (ctrl). Documents available from CASDDS, Documents on Demand.
Desc: Timely summaries of research findings by scientists at Auburn University.
Ind/Abst AGRICOLA [Full Cov.]; Chem. Abstr. (1954-1983); Environ. Abstr.; Hortic. Abstr.; Nematol. Abstr.; Ornamental Hort. (1991-); Soyabean Abstr.

LC S1 .H5 **ISSN** 0073-2230
DD 630 US
CODEN HILGA4
Pr Rev.
HILGARDIA. (HILGARDIA : A JOURNAL OF AGRICULTURAL SCIENCE.). [Hilgardia]. Vol. 1, No. 1; 1925-. Monographic series. English. Irregular. Price varies per volume. University of California / Division of Agriculture and Natural Resources, 300 Lakeside Drive, 6th Floor, Oakland CA 94612-3560. available on microfilm and microfiche from University Microfilms International (UMI). Documents available from The Genuine Article, BIOSIS Document Express, CASDDS. ***Continues*** *Technical Paper - Agricultural Experiment Station, Berkeley, California.*
Ind/Abst AGRICOLA [Full Cov.]; Biocont. News Inf.; Biol. Agric. Index; Biol. Abstr.; Chem. Abstr.; Cot. Trop. Fibr. Abstr. Bibliogr.; Curr. Contents Agric. Biol. Environ. Sci.; Ecol. Abstr.; For. Abstr.; Geogr. Abstr. Phys. Geogr. (?-?); GeoRef; Key Word Index Wildl. Res.; Life Sci. Collect.; Res. Alert [Full Cov.]; Rev. Med. Vet. Entomol.; Sci. Cit. Index (19??-19??); SCISEARCH; Vitis Vitic. Enol. Abstr.

LC S583 **ISSN** 0235-2516
DD 631 RU
HIMIZACI A SELSKOGO HOZAJSTVA. (KHIMIZATSIIA SELSKOGO KHOZIAISTVA.). [Him. selskogo hoz.]. **Added/Corp** Gosudarstvennyi Agrompromyshlennyi Komitet SSSR. Soviet Union. Ministerstvo po Proizvodstvu Mineralnykh Udobrenii. Soviet Union. Ministerstvo Khimicheskoi Promyshlennosti. Vol. 1 (1988)-. Periodical. Russian. Twelve times a year. Agropromizdat, Sadovo-Spasskaia 18, 107807 Moscow Russia. Documents available from CASDDS. ***Continues*** *Khimiia v Selskom Khoziaistve, 0023-1185.*
Ind/Abst Agric. Eng. Abstr.; Chem. Abstr.; Plant Grow. Reg. Abstr.; Potato Abstr.; Soils Fert.

LC S **ISSN** 0073-229X
DD 630 JA
CODEN HIROAO
HIROSAKI DAIGAKU NOGAKUBU GAKUJUTSU HOKOKU. (BULLETIN OF THE FACULTY OF AGRICULTURE, HIROSAKI UNIVERSITY.). [Hirosaki Daigaku Nogakubu Gakujutsu hokoku]. **Main/Corp** Hirosaki Daigaku. Nogakubu. No. 1 (1955)-. Bulletin. Japanese (summaries and/or abstracts in English). Hirodaki University, Faculty of Agriculture, Hirosaki Japan. Documents available from BIOSIS Document Express, CASDDS.
Ind/Abst Biol. Abstr.; Chem. Abstr.

LC S **ISSN** 0439-1799
DD 630 JA
CODEN HNSKBJ
HIROSHIMA KENRITSU NOGYO SHIKENJO HOKOKU. [Hiroshima Kenritsu Nogyo Shikenjo hokoku]. **VFOAT** Bulletin of the Hiroshima Prefectural Agricultural Experiment Station. **VAT** Hiroshima-Kenritsu Nogyo Shikenjo Hokoku. (1978)-. Academic Scholarly Publication. Japanese. Irregular. Documents available from CASDDS.
Ind/Abst AGRICOLA; Chem. Abstr.; Rev. Plant Pathol.; Rice Abstr.

LC S **ISSN** 0439-2027
DD 630 NE
HISTORIA AGRICULTURAE. [Hist. agric.]. **Added/Corp** Nederlands Agronomisch-Historisch Instituut. Vol. 1-12, (1953-1978)-. Dutch. Nederlands Agronomisch Historisch Instituut, NL 5826 Groiningen Netherlands.
Ind/Abst Am. Hist. Life (1956-1965).

LC S **ISSN** 0378-7524
DD 630 II
HISTORY OF AGRICULTURE. [Hist. agric.]. **Added/Corp** International Association for the History of Agriculture. Vol. 1 No. 1 (Feb. 1973)-. Periodical. English. Four times a year. $67.00. K.K. Roy Private Ltd., PO Box 10210, 55 Gariahat Road, Calcutta 700019 India. **Tel** 011 91 33 4754872, 011 91 33 4755069.
Ind/Abst Am. Hist. Life (1974-).

LC S589.5 .H63 **ISSN** 1000-8551
DD 630/.2/13975205 CC
CODEN HEXUEE
HO NUNG HSUEH PAO. Added/Corp Chung-kuo Yuan Tzu Neng Nung Hsueh Hui. Chung-kuo Nung Yeh ko Hsueh Yuan. Yuan Tzu Neng li Yung Yen Chiu so. **VFOAT** Acta Agriculturae Nucleatae Sinica. (1987)-. Academic Scholarly Publication. Chinese (summaries and/or abstracts in English). Four times a year. Zhongguo Nongye Kexueyuan / Yuanzineng Liyong Yanjiusuo, Chinese Academy of Agricultural Sciences, Institute of Nuclear Energy Utilization, PO Box 5109, Beijing 100094 People's Republic of China. **Tel** 2581177. **ED** Xu Guanren. Documents available from CASDDS.
Ind/Abst Biocont. News Inf.; Biodeter. Abstr.; Chem. Abstr. (1990-); Crop Physiol. Abstr.; Field Crop Abstr.; Hortic. Abstr.; Plant Breed. Abstr.; Plant Grow. Reg. Abstr.; Postharvest News Inf.; Rev. Agric. Entomol.; Rev. Plant Pathol.; Rice Abstr.; Seed Abstr.; Soils Fert.; Soyabean Abstr.; Weed Abstr.

Agriculture

LC S
DD 630   PL
HODOWCA DROBNEGO INWENTARZA.
(19??)-. Periodical. Polish. Twelve times a year. $39.00. **(Subscription address:** Ars Polona-Ruch, PO Box 1001, Krakowskie Przedmiescie 7, 00-068 Warsaw Poland. **Tel** 011 48 22 261201.)

LC S   **ISSN** 0340-9783
DD 630   GW
   CODEN HOARDR
HOHENHEIMER ARBEITEN.
(HOHENHEIMER ARBEITEN : SCHRIFTENREIHE DER UNIVERSITAET HOHENHEIM (LH.).). [Hohenheimer Arb.]. No. 53 (1971)-. Academic Scholarly Publication. German (summaries and/or abstracts in English). Price varies per volume. Verlag Eugen Ulmer, Postfach 700561, D-70574 Stuttgart Germany. **Tel** 011 49 711 4507108, FAX 011 49 711 4507120, telex 7-23634. Documents available from CASDDS. **Continues** Arbeiten der Universitat Hohenheim (Landwirtschaftliche Hochschule).
Ind/Abst Chem. Abstr.; GeoRef.

LC S253 .A47
DD 630.946   SP
HOJAS DIVULGADORAS. Added/Corp Spain.
Ministerio de Agricultura. Spain. Ministerio de Agricultura. Seccion de Publicaciones, Prensa y Propaganda. Spain. Ministerio de Agricultura, Pesca y Alimentacion. (1907)-. Monographic series. Spanish. Irregular. Price varies per volume. INT Reforma Desarrollo Agrario, Corazon de Maria 8, 28002 Madrid Spain. **(Subscription address:** Centro Publicaciones del Mapa, Paseo de Infanta Isabel No. 1, 28014 Madrid Spain.**)**
Ind/Abst Agric. Eng. Abstr. (1991-); Seed Abstr.; World Agric. Econ. Rural Sociol. Abstr.

LC S   **ISSN** 0213-2613
DD 630   SP
HOJAS DIVULGADORAS - MINISTERIO DE AGRICULTURA, PESCA Y ALIMENTACION. [Hojas divulg. - Minist. Agric. Pesca Aliment.]. **VFOAT** Hojas Divulgadoras del Ministerio de Agricultura, Pesca y Alimentacion. (1981)-. Monographic series. Spanish. Twenty-four times a year. **Continues** Hojas Divulgadoras - Ministerio de Agricultura y Pesca, 0213-2605.
Ind/Abst Poult. Abstr.

LC S   **ISSN** 0367-5726
DD 630   JA
   CODEN HDNHAG
HOKKAIDO DAIGAKU NOGAKUBU HOBUN KIYO. (HOKKAIDO DAIGAKU NOGAKUBU HOBUN KIYO. MEMOIRS OF THE FACULTY OF AGRICULTURE, HOKKAIDO UNIVERSITY.). [Hokkaido Daigaku Nogakubu hobun kiyo]. **Main/Corp** Hokkaido Daigaku. Nogakubu. **Added/Corp** Hokkaido Daigaku, Sapporo, Japan. Nogakubu. Memoirs of the Faculty of Agriculture, Hokkaido University. **VFOAT** Memoirs of the Faculty of Agriculture, Hokkaido University. Vol. 1 (Dec. 1951)-. Periodical. Japanese (summaries and/or abstracts in English; table of contents in English). Four times a year. Hokkaido University / Agriculture, Faculty of Agriculture, Sapporo Japan. Documents available from BIOSIS Document Express, CASDDS.
Ind/Abst Biol. Abstr.; Chem. Abstr. (-1987); For. Prod. Abstr. (1991-); For. Abstr.; Plant Breed. Abstr.; Plant Grow. Reg. Abstr.; Postharvest News Inf.; Rice Abstr.; Soils Fert.; Soyabean Abstr.

LC S   **ISSN** 0385-6445
DD 630   JA
   CODEN HDNHDJ
HOKKAIDO DAIGAKU NOGAKUBU NOJO KENKYU HOKOKU. [Hokkaido Daigaku Nogakubu Nojo kenkyu hokoku]. **VFOAT** Research Bulletin of the University Farm Hokkaido University. Academic Scholarly Publication. Japanese. Irregular. Hokkaido Daigaku Nogakubu Fuzoku Nojo Chuo-ku, Nishi 3-chome Kita 4-Jo, Sapporo-Shi 060 Japan. Documents available from CASDDS.
Ind/Abst Chem. Abstr. (1929-1985); Field Crop Abstr.; Potato Abstr.

LC S
DD 630   JA
HOKKAIDO NOGYO SHIKENJO. Main/Corp
Hokkaido Nogyo Shikenjo (Japan). (1964)-. Japanese. Norinsho Hokkaido Nogyo Shikenjo, Hitsujigaoka, Sapporo 061-01 Japan.

LC S   **ISSN** 0367-5955
DD 630   JA
   CODEN HKNSBV
HOKKAIDO NOGYO SHIKENJO KENKYU HOKOKU. (HOKKAIDO NOGYO SHIKENJO KENKYU HOKOKU. RESEARCH BULLETIN OF THE HOKKAIDO NATIONAL AGRICULTURAL EXPERIMENT STATION.). [Hokkaido Nogyo Shikenjo kenkyu hokoku]. **Added/Corp** Hokkaido Nogyo Shikenjo (Japan). Research Bulletin of the Hokkaido National Agricultural Experiment Station. Hokkaido Nogyo Shikenjo (Japan). Kenkyu Hokoku. **VFOAT** Research Bulletin of the Hokkaido National Agricultural Experiment Station. No. 101 (March 1972)-. Bulletin. Japanese (summaries and/or abstracts in English). Two times a year. Hokkaido National Agricultural Experiment Station, 1 Hitsujigaoka Toyohira-ku, Sapporo-shi Hokkaido 062 Japan. **Tel** 011-851-9141, FAX 011-853-2178. **ED** Toshiaki Hirashima. Documents available from CASDDS. **Continues** HokkaidÃo Nogyo Shikenjo. Hokkaido Nogyo Shikenjo Iho.
Ind/Abst AGRICOLA; Chem. Abstr.; Field Crop Abstr.; Index Vet.; Nematol. Abstr.; Plant Breed. Abstr.; Protozoolog. Abstr.; Soils Fert.; Soyabean Abstr.; Wheat Barley Trit. Abstr.

LC S   **ISSN** 0441-0807
DD 630   JA
   CODEN HOSSAF
HOKKAIDO NOGYO SHIKENJO SHUHO. [Hokkaido Nogyo Shikenjo shuho]. **Added/Corp** Hokkaido Nogyo Shikenjo. **VFOAT** Bulletin of Hokkaido Agricultural Experiment Stations. (19??)-. Bulletin. Japanese. Documents available from BIOSIS Document Express, CASDDS.
Ind/Abst Biol. Abstr.; Chem. Abstr.

LC S   **ISSN** 0367-6048
DD 630   JA
   CODEN HNSKAI
HOKKAIDORITSU NOGYO SHIKENJO HOKOKU. [Hokkaidoritsu Nogyo Shikenjo hokoku]. **Main/Corp** Hokkaidoritsu Nogyo Shikenjo. **VFOAT** Report of Hokkaido Prefectural Agricultural Experiment Station. (1951)-. Academic Scholarly Publication. Japanese (summaries and/or abstracts in English). Price varies per volume. Hokkaidoritsu Chuo Nogyo Shikenjo, (Hokkaido Central Agricultural Experiment Station), Higashi Rokusen Kita 15, Naganumamachi Yubarigun, Hokkaido 069-13 Japan. Documents available from BIOSIS Document Express, CASDDS.
Ind/Abst Biol. Abstr.; Chem. Abstr.; Nutr. Abstr. Rev., Ser. B, Live Feeds and Feed.; Potato Abstr.

LC S   **ISSN** 0040-8697
DD 630   JA
   CODEN TNKHBY
HOKOKU (TOHOKU DAIGAKU. NOGAKU KENKYUJO). (HOKOKU.). **VFOAT** Bulletin of the Institute for Agricultural Research, Tohoku University. Bulletin. Japanese (summaries and/or abstracts in English; table of contents in English). Two times a year. Tohoku University, Sendai 980 Japan. **Tel** 0222-27-6200. Documents available from BIOSIS Document Express. **Continues** IHO.
Ind/Abst Biol. Abstr. (-1988); Rice Abstr.

LC S   **ISSN** 0439-3600
DD 630   JA
   CODEN HNGSAG
HOKURIKU NOGYO SHIKENJO HOKOKU. **Main/Corp** Norin Suisansho Hokuriku Nogyo Shikenjo. **VFOAT** Bulletin of the Hokuriku Agricultural Experiment Station. (March 1960)-. Academic Scholarly Publication. Japanese (summaries and/or abstracts in English). Price varies per volume. Norin Suisansho Hokuriku Nogyo Shikenjo, (Hokuriku National Agricultural Experiment Station Ministry of Agriculture Forestry & Fisheries), Inada Joetsushi, Niigataken 943-01 Japan. Documents available from BIOSIS Document Express, CASDDS. **Supersedes** Hokuriku Nogyo Shikenjo Kenkyu.
Ind/Abst AGRICOLA; Biol. Abstr.; Chem. Abstr. (1960-1985); EMBASE; Rice Abstr.; Soils Fert.; Soyabean Abstr.

LC HD   **ISSN** 1069-2789
DD 333   US
●HOLISTIC RESOURCE MANAGEMENT QUARTERLY. [Holist. resour. manage. q.]. **Added/Corp** Center for Holistic Resource Management. **VFOAT** HRM quarterly. No. 39 (Spring 1993)-. Periodical. English. Four times a year. $20.00. Center for Holistic Resource Management, PO Box 7128, Albuquerque NM 87194. **Tel** (505)842-5252, FAX (505)843-7900. **Continues** Holistic Resource Management Newsletter, 1048-8472.

LC S367 .H64
DD 630/.964   MR
HOMMES, TERRE & I.E. ET EAUX. VAT
Hommes, Terre et Eaux. (19??)-. Periodical. French. Four times a year. Anafid-Anpa-Anappav-Institut Agronomique et Veterinaire, Hassan II BP 704, Rabat-Maroc Morocco. **Continues** Hommes, la Terre, l'Eau.
Ind/Abst AGRICOLA; Field Crop Abstr.; Fish Rev. (Jan. 1989-July 1992); Grass. Forage Abstr.; Soils Fert.; Wildl. Rev. (Jan. 1989-July 1992).

LC S
DD 630   HK
HONG KONG CHENG FU YU NUNG CHU KAN WU. **VFOAT** Agriculture and Fisheries Department Bulletin. (19??)-. Monographic series. English (Chinese). Irregular. Price varies per volume.

LC HD1775.H3 H38A   **ISSN** 0148-3358
DD 338.1/3   US
HONOLULU WHOLESALE PRICES EGGS, POULTRY, PORK, BEEF AND RICE. Main/Corp Hawaii. Market News Service Branch. **VFOAT** Honolulu Prices: Wholesale Eggs, Poultry, Pork, Beef and Rice. (19??)-. Periodical. English. One time a year. Market News Service, Hawaii State Department of Agriculture, PO Box 5425, Honolulu HI 96814.

LC S   **ISSN** 0018-4748
DD 630   US
HOOSIER FARMER. Periodical. English. Twelve times a year. $12.00 (members), $5.00 (nonmembers). Indiana Farm Bureau Inc, 130 East Washington Street, Indianapolis IN 46206.

LC S
DD 630   ZA
"HOW TO GROW" SERIES. Main/Corp
Zambia. Dept. of Agriculture. No. 1, (1974)-. Monographic series. English. Irregular. Price varies per volume.

LC S471.C62 S5974
DD 630/.9516   CH
HSIN-CHIANG NUNG YEH KO HSUEH / HSIN-CHIANG NUNG YEH KO HSUEH YUAN, HSIN-CHIANG PA I NUNG HSUEH YUAN. VFOAT Agriculture Science of Xinjiang. Periodical. Chinese (Chinese). Six times a year. Wu-Lu-Mu-Chi Shih Yu Cheng, Chu Hsin-Chiang, People's Republic of China.

LC S19 .H78
DD 630/.5   CH
HSUEH SHU YEN TAO HUI PAO KAO.
VFOAT Scientific Meeting Report; Tai-Wan Sheng Tai-Nan Chu Nung Yeh Kai Liang Chang ... Hsueh Shu Yen Tao Hui Pao Kao; Scientific Meeting Report of Tainan District Agricultural Improvement Station. Periodical. Chinese (summaries and/or abstracts in English). One time a year. Tainan District Agricultural Improvement, Station 350/First Section Lin Sen Road, Tainan Taiwan.
Ind/Abst Plant Breed. Abstr.

LC S19 .H8
DD 630/.5   CH
HUA-KANG NUNG KO HSUEH PAO / CHUNG-KUO WEN HUA HSUEH YUAN NUNG HSUEH PU. VFOAT Hua Kang Journal of Agriculture. Vol. 1 (March 1980)-. Periodical. Chinese (summaries and/or abstracts in English; table of contents in English). One time a year. $500.00. Chung-Kuo Wen Hua Ta Hsueh Chu Pan Pu, Hua-Kang Yu Cheng Road, Yan-Ming-Shan Taipei Taiwan.

LC S19 .H82 u   **ISSN** 1000-7091
   CC
HUA PEI NUNG HSUEH PAO. Added/Corp
Tien-Chin Shih Nung Yeh Ko Hsueh Yuan. **VFOAT** Acta Agriculturae Boreali-Sinica. (19??)-. Periodical. Chinese (summaries and/or abstracts in English). Four times a year.
Ind/Abst Sorghum Mill. Abstr.

LC S   **ISSN** 0864-7410
DD 630   HU
HUNGARIAN AGRICULTURAL ENGINEERING. [Hung. agric. eng.]. (1988)-. English. One time a year.
Ind/Abst Agric. Eng. Abstr.; Postharvest News Inf.; Soils Fert.; Soyabean Abstr.; Weed Abstr.; Wheat Barley Trit. Abstr.

LC S   **ISSN** 1216-4526
DD 630   HU
HUNGARIAN AGRICULTURAL RESEARCH. Added/Corp Hungary.
Foldmuvelesugyi Miniszterium. Vol. 1, No. 1 (Sept. 1992)-. Periodical. English. Four times a year. $37.00. Agrinform Kiado es Nyomda Kft., Kitaibel u. 4, 1024 Budapest Hungary. **Tel** 011 36 4 135 1927, FAX 011 36 1 135 0344.

LC S760.K6 H85
DD 631.3   KO
HUNGNONGGYE. Periodical. Korean. Twelve times a year. Nongop Chinhung Kongsa, Anyang Ucheguk Sasoham 12-ho, Sihung-gun Kyonggi-do Korea.

LC S21 .A46 GB705   **ISSN** 0503-5139
DD 630   US
HYDROLOGIC DATA FOR EXPERIMENTAL AGRICULTURAL WATERSHEDS IN THE UNITED STATES.
See Earth Sciences-Hydrology.

LC S279   **ISSN** 0537-1309
DD 630   II
I.C.A.R. TECHNICAL BULLETIN (AGRIC). Main/Corp Indian Council of Agricultural Research. No. 1- 1965-. Bulletin. English. Price varies per

volume. Indian Council of Agricultural Research, Mgr Krishi Anusandham Bhavan, New Delhi 110 012 India. **Tel** 011 91 11 5713657, telex 031-62249 ICAR IN.

LC S
DD 630 SZ

I.S.T.A. NEWS BULLETIN. **Added/Corp** International Seed Testing Association. (19??)-. Periodical. English (French and Spanish). Four times a year. Free upon request. ISTA / International Seed Testing Association, PO Box 412, CH-8046 Zurich Switzerland. **Tel** 011 41 1 3713133, FAX 011 41 1 3713427. **Bk Rev**, (Qty: 20-30). **Ad Acc. Circ:** 1,400.

LC S **ISSN** 1015-9762
DD 630 ET

IAR NEWSLETTER OF AGRICULTURAL RESEARCH. [IAR newsl. agri. res.]. **Added/Corp** YaErsa Meremer Instityut. **VFOAT** Newsletter of Agricultural Research. **VAT** Institute of Agricultural Research Newsletter of Agricultural Research. (1986)-. Newsletter. English. Four times a year.
Ind/Abst Field Crop Abstr.; Plant Breed. Abstr.; Rev. Plant Pathol.; Soils Fert.; Sorghum Mill. Abstr.; Weed Abstr.; Wheat Barley Trit. Abstr.

LC S **ISSN** 0445-1694
DD 630 JA
CODEN IDNGAO

IBARAKI DAIGAKU NOGAKUBU GAKUJUTSU HOKOKU. [Ibaraki Daigaku Nogakubu gakujutsu hokoku]. **Main/Corp** Ibaraki Daigaku. Nogakubu. **VFOAT** Scientific Reports of the Faculty of Agriculture, Ibaraki Uiversity. No. 1 (Oct. 1953)-. Academic Scholarly Publication. Japanese. Ibaraki Daigaku Nogakubu, (Faculty of Agriculture Ibaraki University), 3998 Amimachi, Inashikigun, Ibarakiken 300-03 Japan. Documents available from CASDDS.
Ind/Abst Chem. Abstr.; EMBASE; Hortic. Abstr.; Ornamental Hort. (1991-); Rice Abstr.; Seed Abstr.; Soils Fert.

LC SB **ISSN** 1076-3112
DD 630 US
TITLE CHANGE

IBSNAT VIEWS. [IBSNAT views]. **Added/Corp** International Benchmark Sites Network for Agrotechnology Transfer. No. 1 (Sept. 1993)-(1995). Periodical. English. University of Hawaii / IBSNAT Project, 2500 Dole Street, Honolulu HI 96822. **Tel** (808)948-8858, telex 9423 UHBSP HR. ***Continues*** *Agrotechnology Transfer, 0883-8631.* ***Continued by*** *ICASA News, 1084-3736.*

LC S
DD 630 NO

IBT-RAPPORT. **Added/Corp** Norges Landbrukshgskole. Institutt for Bygningsteknikk. **VFOAT** IBT Rapport. **VAT** Instituut for Byginingsteknikk-Rapport. (198?)-. Monographic series. Norwegian (summaries and/or abstracts in English). ***Continues*** *Stensiltrykk (Norges Landbrukshgskole. Institutt for bygningsteknikk).*
Ind/Abst AgBiotech News Inf.; For. Prod. Abstr. (1991-); Hortic. Abstr.; Ornamental Hort. (1991-).

LC S **ISSN** 0046-9920
DD 630 CK

ICA INFORMA. **Added/Corp** Instituto Colombiano Agropecuario. (1966)-. Periodical. Spanish. Four times a year. Instituto Colombiano Agropecuario Division de Comunicacion Tecnica, Apdo. Aereo 151123, Bogota Colombia. ***Absorbed*** *Temas Didacticos.*
Ind/Abst Bibliogr. Agric.

LC S
DD 630 SY

ICARDA. **Added/Corp** International Center for Agricultural Research in the Dry Areas. **VAT** International Center for Agricultural Research in the Dry Areas. (19??)-. Monographic series. English (French and Arabic). Price varies per volume. International Center for Agricultural Research in the Dry Areas, PO Box 5466, Aleppo Syria. **Tel** 213433, telex 331206.
Ind/Abst Nematol. Abstr.; Seed Abstr.

LC S612.5 .I57A
DD 631.5/86/05 SY

ICARDA ANNUAL REPORT / INTERNATIONAL CENTER FOR AGRICULTURAL RESEARCH IN THE DRY AREAS. **Main/Corp** International Center for Agricultural Research in the Dry Areas. **VAT** International Center for Agricultural Research in the Dry Areas Annual Report. (1980/81)-. English. One time a year. Free. International Center for Agricultural Research in the Dry Areas, PO Box 5466, Aleppo Syria. **Tel** 213433, telex 331206. **ED** S Varma. **Circ:** 3,000. ***Continues*** *International Center for Agricultural Research in the Dry Areas. Report on Research Program at ICARDA.*
Desc: Reports research concerning improvement of barley, wheat, lentil, faba bean, and chickpea production and farming systems in dry areas of West Asia and North Africa and other parts of the world.
Ind/Abst Plant Breed. Abstr.

LC SB **ISSN** 1084-3736
DD 630 US

●**ICASA NEWS.** [ICASA news]. **Added/Corp** International Consortium for Agricultural Systems Applications. **VFOAT** International Consortium for Agricultural Systems Applications News. (1995)-. Periodical. English. Every 2 years. University of Hawaii / IBSNAT Project, 2500 Dole Street, Honolulu HI 96822. **Tel** (808)948-8858, telex 9423 UHBSP HR. ***Continues*** *IBSNAT Views, 1079-3112.*

LC GB841 .I5 **ISSN** 0538-5318
DD 333.7/3 US
CODEN ICPUD4

ICASALS PUBLICATION. **See** Geography.

LC S
DD 630 JA

IDACA NEWS: THE INSTITUTE FOR THE DEVELOPMENT OF AGRICULTURAL COOPERATION IN ASIA. (19??)-. English. Two times a year. Free. Institute for the Development of Agricultural Cooperatives in Asia, 4771 Aihara-Cho Machida-Shi, Tokyo 194-02 Japan. **Tel** 427 82 4331.

LC S **ISSN** 0073-4675
DD 630 CL
CODEN IDESBG
Pr Rev.

IDESIA. [Idesia]. **Added/Corp** Universidad del Norte. Departamento de Agricultura. Universidad de Tarapaca. Instituto de Agronomia. No. 1 (August 1970)-. Academic Scholarly Publication. Spanish (summaries and/or abstracts in English). One time a year. $6.00. Universidad de Tarapaca / Instituto de Agronomia, Casilla 6-D, Arica Chile. **Tel** FAX 011 56 58 226737. **ED** Mauricio Jimenez and R. Luis Tapia I. Index available. cum. index. **Bk Rev. Circ:** 1,000 (ctrl). Documents available from CASDDS.
Desc: Covers arid land agriculture, crop production, conservation and natural resources, entomology, nematology, and plant disease.
Ind/Abst Agric. Eng. Abstr. (1991-); Chem. Abstr.; Hortic. Abstr.; Index Vet.; Irr. Drain. Abstr.; Nematol. Abstr.; Ornamental Hort. (1991-); Plant Breed. Abstr.; Soils Fert.

LC S **ISSN** 0018-9081
DD 630 AG

IDIA, INFORMATIVO DE INVESTIGACIONES AGRICOLAS. **VFOAT** Informativo de Investigaciones Agricolas. No. 1 (1948)-. Periodical. Spanish. Instituto Nacional de Tecnologia Agropecuaria, Centro de Investigaciones de Recursos Naturales, Cervino 3101, Buenos Aires Argentina.
Ind/Abst Maize Abstr.; Vitis Vitic. Enol. Abstr.

LC QC878.5 **ISSN** 0367-7443
DD 551.5 HU

IDOJARAS (BUDAPEST 1897). **See** Earth Sciences-Meteorology.

LC S
DD 630 US

IED STAFF REPORT. **See** Business and Economics-International Economic Relations.

LC S
DD 630 IT

IFAD UPDATE. (19??)-. Newsletter. English (French, Spanish and Arabic). International Fund for Agricultural Development / IFAD, Via del Serafico 107, 00142 Rome Italy. **Tel** 011 39 396 54591, FAX 011 39 396 5043463, telex 620330. **Circ:** 14,000.

LC S583 **ISSN** 0149-5852
DD 631 US

IFCD REPORT (SPANISH EDITION). (IFDC REPORT.). [IFDC rep.]. **Main/Corp** International Fertilizer Development Center. **VAT** International Fertilizer Development Center Report. Vol. 1, No. 3 (Aug. 1976)-. Periodical. Spanish (Spanish and French). Four times a year. Free. IFDC, PO Box 2040, Muscle Shoals AL 35662. **Tel** (205)381-6600, FAX (205)381-7408, telex TWX 810 731 3970. **ED** Marie K. Thompson. **Circ:** 5,000 (ctrl).
Desc: An update on the work and progress at IFDC.

LC S583 **ISSN** 0149-3434
DD 631 US

IFDC REPORT. [IFDC rep.]. **Main/Corp** International Fertilizer Development Center. **Added/Corp** International Fertilizer Development Center. Report. **VAT** International Fertilizer Development Center Report. (1976)-. Periodical. English (Spanish and French). Four times a year. Free on request. IFDC, PO Box 2040, Muscle Shoals AL 35662. **Tel** (205)381-6600, FAX (205)381-7408, telex TWX 810 731 3970. **ED** Marie K. Thompson. **Circ:** 5,000 (ctrl).
Desc: Contains updated information on the work and progress at IFDC.

LC S **ISSN** 0205-3845
DD 630 BU

IKONOMIKA I UPRAVLENIE NA SELSKOTO STOPANSTVO. **Added/Corp** Selskostopanska Akademiia (Bulgaria) Asotsiatsiia "Natsionalen Agrarno-Promishlen Suiuz" (Bulgaria). **VFOAT** Rural Economics and Management. (1988)-. Periodical. Bulgarian (summaries and/or abstracts in English and Russian; table of contents in English and Russian). Eight times a year. $92.00. **(Subscription address:** Hemus Foreign Trade Organization, 1B Raiko Daskalov Sq Books, 1000 Sofia Bulgaria. **Tel** 011 359 2 882544, 011 359 2 801575.) ***Formed by the union of*** *Ikonomika na Selskoto Stopanstvo, 0019-1760* ***and*** *Upravlenie na Selskoto Stopanstvo i Khranitelnata Promishlenost, 0204-9279.*
Ind/Abst Agric. Eng. Abstr. (1991-); Dairy Sci. Abstr.; Grass. Forage Abstr.; Hortic. Abstr.; Maize Abstr.; Pig News Inf.; Plant Breed. Abstr.; Postharvest News Inf.; Poult. Abstr.; Rev. Agric. Entomol.; Seed Abstr.; Soils Fert.; Weed Abstr.; Wheat Barley Trit. Abstr.; World Agric. Econ. Rural Sociol. Abstr.

LC S **ISSN** 0194-7443
DD 630 US

ILLINOIS AGRI-NEWS. (19??)-. Periodical. English. One time a week. $17.00. Agri-News Publications, 420 Second Street, La Salle IL 61301. **Tel** (815)223-2558, FAX (815)223-5997. **ED** Kevin Conerton and Warren Pufhal. **Bk Rev. Ad Acc. Circ:** 43,000 (ctrl). ***Continues*** *AG-News.*
Desc: News of agriculture: local, state and national.

LC S **ISSN** 0019-2201
DD 630 US

ILLINOIS RESEARCH. [Ill. res.]. **Added/Corp** University of Illinois at Urbana-Champaign. Agricultural Experiment Station. University of Illinois (Urbana-Champaign Campus). Agricultural Experiment Station. Vol. 1 (1959)-. Academic Scholarly Publication. English. Four times a year. Free on request. Illinois Agricultural Experiment Station, 211 Mumford Hall, 1301 West Gregory Drive, Urbana IL 61801. **Tel** (217)333-2548. **ED** Mary Overmier. **Ad Acc. Circ:** 9,000 (ctrl).
Desc: Designed for the nonspecialist with an interest in agriculture, human resources, and family studies. Written by research scientists and faculty at the University of Illinois and Urbana-Champaign.
Ind/Abst AGRICOLA [Select. Cov.]; Biol. Dig.; EMBASE; Field Crop Abstr.; Grass. Forage Abstr.; Hortic. Abstr.; Nematol. Abstr.; Life Sci. Collect.; Plant Breed. Abstr.; Pollut. Abstr. Indexes; Protozoolog. Abstr.; Soils Fert.; Soyabean Abstr.

LC SB950 **ISSN** 0964-069X
DD 632.9 UK
CEASED

IMPACT AGBIOINDUSTRY. **See** Biology-Bioengineering.

LC S **ISSN** 0748-2353
DD 630 US
CODEN IMPCEL

IMPACT (GAINESVILLE, FLA.). (IMPACT / IFAS, INSTITUTE OF FOOD AND AGRICULTURAL SCIENCES, UNIVERSITY OF FLORIDA.). [Impact]. Spring 1984-. Periodical. English. Three times a year. IFAS, Gozz McCarty Hall, Gainesville FL 32611. Documents available from BIOSIS Document Express.
Ind/Abst Anim. Breed. Abstr.; Biol. Abstr.; Hortic. Abstr.

LC S **ISSN** 8750-5355
DD 630 US

IMPERIAL COUNTY FARM BUREAU MONTHLY. **Added/Corp** Imperial County Farm Bureau (Calif.). **VFOAT** Farm Bureau Monthly. (19??)-. Periodical. English. Twelve times a year. Imperial County Farm Bureau, 1000 Broadway, El Centro CA 92243.

LC S **ISSN** 1065-1527
DD 630 US

IN GOOD TILTH. [In good tilth]. **Added/Corp** Oregon Tilth, Inc. Vol. 1, No. 1 (Aug. 1990)-. Periodical. English. Twelve times a year. $15.00. Oregon Tilth, Subscription Department, 31615 Fern Road, Philomath OR 97370. ***Continues*** *Oregon Tilth.*

LC HD1761 .I53 **ISSN** 0430-0785
DD 338.1/873 US

INCREASING UNDERSTANDING OF PUBLIC PROBLEMS AND POLICIES. [Increasing underst. public probl. policies]. 1951-. English. One time a year. Farm Foundation, 1211 West 22nd Street, Oak Brook IL 60521.
Ind/Abst AGRICOLA [Full Cov.].

LC S **ISSN** 0872-315X
DD 630 PO
UDC 582

INDEX SEMINUM QUAE HORTUS ET MUSAEUM AGRICOLUM TROPICUM SEMINA ET PROPAGALUM PRO MUTUA COMMUTATIONE OFFERT. [Index semin. Hortus Mus. Agric. Trop. semina propagalum mutua commut. offert]. **VFOAT** Index Seminum quae Hortus et Musaeum Agricolum Ultramarinum pro Mutua Commutatione Offert. (19??)-. Periodical. Latin. Every 2 years. 400$00. Instituto de Investigacao Cientifica Tropical, Centro de Documentacao e Informacao, rua Jau 47, 1 300 Lisbon Portugal. **Tel** 645321. **Circ:** 500 (ctrl). ***Continues*** *Index Seminum quae Hortus Colonialis Olisiponensis pro Mutua Commutatione Offert, 0872-3141.*

LC S **ISSN** 0536-8510
DD 630 II
INDIAN AGRICULTURE IN BRIEF. 1st- Ed.; 1955-. English. Irregular. $13.36. Government of India / Ministry of Works and Housing, Department of Publications, Civil Lines, New Delhi 111054 India.

LC S539.5 **ISSN** 0019-4336
DD 630.72 II
CODEN INAGAT
INDIAN AGRICULTURIST. [Indian agric.]. **Added/Corp** Agricultural Society of India. Vol. 1 Jan. (1957)-. Periodical. English. Four times a year. $50.00. Agricultural Society of India, 35 Ballygunge Circular Road, Calcutta 19 India. **(Subscription address:** Prints India, 11 Darya Ganj, New Delhi 110002 India. **Tel** 011 91 11 3268645, FAX 011 91 11 3275542, telex 31-61087 PRIN-IN.**)** Documents available from CASDDS.
Ind/Abst AGRICOLA; Biodeter. Abstr. (1991-); Chem. Abstr.; Cot. Trop. Fibr. Abstr. Bibliogr.; Crop Physiol. Abstr.; Field Crop Abstr.; Food Sci. Technol. Abstr.; For. Abstr.; Grass. Forage Abstr.; Hortic. Abstr.; Irr. Drain. Abstr.; Nematol. Abstr.; Ornamental Hort. (1991-); Life Sci. Collect.; Plant Breed. Abstr.; Plant Genet. Resour. Abstr.; Plant Grow. Reg. Abstr.; Postharvest News Inf.; Potato Abstr.; Rev. Agric. Entomol.; Rev. Plant Pathol.; Rice Abstr.; Seed Abstr.; Soils Fert.; Sorghum Mill. Abstr.; Sug. Indus. Abstr.; Vitis Vitic. Enol. Abstr.; Weed Abstr.; Wheat Barley Trit. Abstr.; World Agric. Econ. Rural Sociol. Abstr.

LC SF521 **ISSN** 0019-4425
DD 638.1 II
INDIAN BEE JOURNAL. [Indian bee j.]. **Added/Corp** All India Beekeepers' Association. Vol. 1 (1939)-. Periodical. English. Four times a year. $110.00. All India Beekeepers' Association, Poona India. **(Subscription address:** Prints India, 11 Darya Ganj, New Delhi 110002 India. **Tel** 011 91 11 3268645, FAX 011 91 11 3275542, telex 31-61087 PRIN-IN.**) ED** S G Shende. **Bk Rev. Ad Acc. Circ:** 800 (ctrl).
Desc: Journal to beekeepers and bee scientists. Gives information on beekeeping and bee research in India and abroad.
Ind/Abst AGRICOLA; Rev. Agric. Entomol.

LC S
DD 630 II
INDIAN FARMERS' DIGEST. (1968)-. Periodical. English. Twelve times a year. $20.00. Pant University of Agriculture and Technology, Pantnagar Directorate of Communication and Publication, Pantnagar India. **(Subscription address:** Prints India, 11 Darya Ganj, New Delhi 110002 India. **Tel** 011 91 11 3268645, FAX 011 91 11 3275542, telex 31-61087 PRIN-IN.**)**

LC S17 .I5 **ISSN** 0019-4786
DD 630.5 II
INDIAN FARMING. [Indian farming]. **Added/Corp** Indian Council of Agricultural Research. Indian Council of Agricultural Research. Vol. 1 Jan. (1940)-. Periodical. English. Twelve times a year. $20.00. Indian Council of Agricultural Research, Mgr Krishi Anusandham Bhavan, New Delhi 110 012 India. **Tel** 011 91 11 5713657, telex 031-62249 ICAR IN. **(Subscription address:** Prints India, 11 Darya Ganj, New Delhi 110002 India. **Tel** 011 91 11 3268645, FAX 011 91 11 3275542, telex 31-61087 PRIN-IN.**) ED** P. L. Jaiswal. **Bk Rev. Ad Acc. Circ:** 10,000. available on microfilm from University Microfilms International (UMI). ***Supersedes*** *Agriculture and Livestock in India;* ***Absorbed*** *Indian Livestock.*
Desc: Journal on agriculture, animal husbandry and allied subjects. Conveys results of proven research in a popular language which are of practical benefit to the farmers.
Ind/Abst AGRICOLA; Agric. Eng. Abstr. (1991-); Agrofor. Abstr. (19??-19??); Anim. Breed. Abstr.; Dairy Sci. Abstr.; EMBASE; Field Crop Abstr.; For. Prod. Abstr. (19??-19??); For. Abstr.; Grass. Forage Abstr.; Hortic. Abstr.; Index Vet.; Irr. Drain. Abstr.; Maize Abstr.; Nematol. Abstr.; Nutr. Abstr. Rev., Ser. B, Live Feeds and Feed.; Life Sci. Collect.; Plant Breed. Abstr.; Potato Abstr.; Poult. Abstr.; Rev. Agric. Entomol.; Rev. Plant Pathol.; Rice Abstr.; Rural Dev. Abstr.; Seed Abstr.; Soils Fert.; Sorghum Mill. Abstr.; Soyabean Abstr.; Sug. Indus. Abstr.; Vet. Bull.; Wheat Barley Trit. Abstr.; World Agric. Econ. Rural Sociol. Abstr.

LC S **ISSN** 0970-6399
DD 630 II
UDC 63 :577.1
INDIAN JOURNAL OF AGRICULTURAL BIOCHEMISTRY. [Indian J. Agric. Biochem.]. (1988)-. Periodical. English. Two times a year. Indian Society of Agricultural Biochemists, Kanpur India. Documents available from CASDDS.
Ind/Abst Chem. Abstr.

LC S **ISSN** 0367-8229
DD 630 II
CODEN IJACBO
INDIAN JOURNAL OF AGRICULTURAL CHEMISTRY. [Indian j. agric. chem.]. **Added/Corp** Indian Society of Agricultural Chemists. (19??)-. Periodical. English. Three times a year. Price varies. Indian Society of Agricultural Chemists, Allahabad India. **(Subscription address:** Prints India, 11 Darya Ganj, New Delhi 110002 India. **Tel** 011 91 11 3268645, FAX 011 91 11 3275542, telex 31-61087 PRIN-IN.**)** Documents available from CASDDS.
Ind/Abst Chem. Abstr.; Crop Physiol. Abstr.; Field Crop Abstr.; Grass. Forage Abstr.; Maize Abstr.; Nematol. Abstr.; Nutr. Abstr. Rev., Ser. B, Live Feeds and Feed.; Plant Breed. Abstr.; Rice Abstr.; Soils Fert.; Sorghum Mill. Abstr.; Weed Abstr.

LC S **ISSN** 0971-2356
DD 630 II
INDIAN JOURNAL OF AGRICULTURAL ENGINEERING, THE. [Indian J. Agric. Eng.]. **Added/Corp** Indian Council of Agricultural Research. Vol. 1, No. 1 (Sept. 1991)-. Periodical. English. Four times a year. $20.00. Indian Council of Agricultural Research, Mgr Krishi Anusandham Bhavan, New Delhi 110 012 India. **Tel** 011 91 11 5713657, telex 031-62249 ICAR IN. **(Subscription address:** Prints India, 11 Darya Ganj, New Delhi 110002 India. **Tel** 011 91 11 3268645, FAX 011 91 11 3275542, telex 31-61087 PRIN-IN.**)** ***Continues*** *Journal of Agricultural Engineering, 0256-6524.*
Ind/Abst Field Crop Abstr.

LC S19 .I59 **ISSN** 0367-8245
DD 630 II
CODEN IJARC2
INDIAN JOURNAL OF AGRICULTURAL RESEARCH. [Indian j. agric. res.]. **Added/Corp** Agricultural Research Communication Centre (India). Vol. 5, No. 1 (March 1971)-. Academic Scholarly Publication. English. Four times a year. $60.00. Agricultural Research Communication Centre, Sadar Karnal 132001, Haryana India. **Tel** 011 91 3036. **ED** Kirti Singh. cum. index. **Bk Rev. Ad Acc. Circ:** 5,000. Documents available from BIOSIS Document Express, CASDDS. ***Continues*** *Indian Journal of Science & Industry. Section A, Agricultural Sciences, 0367-8296.*
Desc: Publishes original research articles by scientists and book reviews on all aspects of plant and soil sciences.
Ind/Abst AGRICOLA; Agric. Eng. Abstr. (1991-); Biol. Abstr.; Chem. Abstr.; Cot. Trop. Fibr. Abstr. Bibliogr.; Curr. Contents; Dairy Sci. Abstr.; EMBASE; Field Crop Abstr.; Grass. Forage Abstr.; Hortic. Abstr.; Indian Sci. Abstr.; Irr. Drain. Abstr.; Leis., Rec., Tour. Abstr.; Maize Abstr.; Nucl. Sci. Abstr.; Life Sci. Collect.; Plant Breed. Abstr.; Plant Grow. Reg. Abstr.; Potato Abstr.; Protozoolog. Abstr.; Rev. Med. Vet. Mycology; Rev. Plant Pathol.; Rice Abstr.; Rural Dev. Abstr.; Sci. Cit. Index (19??-19??); Seed Abstr.; Soils Fert.; Sorghum Mill. Abstr.; Soyabean Abstr.; Trop. Abstr.; Weed Abstr.; World Agric. Econ. Rural Sociol. Abstr.

LC S19 .I6 **ISSN** 0019-5022
DD 630 II
CODEN IJASA3
Pr Rev.
INDIAN JOURNAL OF AGRICULTURAL SCIENCES, THE. [Indian j. agric. sci.]. Vol. 1 (Feb. 1931)-. Academic Scholarly Publication. English. Twelve times a year. $50.00. Indian Council of Agricultural Research, Mgr Krishi Anusandham Bhavan, New Delhi 110 012 India. **Tel** 011 91 11 5713657, telex 031-62249 ICAR IN. **(Subscription address:** Prints India, 11 Darya Ganj, New Delhi 110002 India. **Tel** 011 91 11 3268645, FAX 011 91 11 3275542, telex 31-61087 PRIN-IN.**) ED** S. N. Tata, R. S. Gupta, R. P. Sharma. Index available. cum. index. **Bk Rev. Ad Acc. Circ:** 3,000. available on microfilm and microfiche from University Microfilms International (UMI). Documents available from The Genuine Article, BIOSIS Document Express, CASDDS. ***Continues*** *Agricultural Journal of India, 0365-3641;* ***Absorbed*** *Indian Potato Journal, 0537-2437; Agricultural Research (New Delhi, India), 0374-5287.*
Ind/Abst AgBiotech News Inf.; AGRICOLA; Agric. Eng. Abstr. (1991-); Agrindex; Agrofor. Abstr. (1991-); BioBusiness; Biocont. News Inf.; Biodeter. Abstr. (19??-19??); Biol. Abstr.; Chem. Abstr.; Cot. Trop. Fibr. Abstr. Bibliogr.; Crop Physiol. Abstr.; Curr. Cit.; Curr. Contents Agric. Biol. Environ. Sci.; Dairy Sci. Abstr.; EMBASE; Field Crop Abstr.; Food Sci. Technol. Abstr.; For. Prod. Abstr. (19??-19??); For. Abstr.; Grass. Forage Abstr.; Hortic. Abstr.; Irr. Drain. Abstr.; Leadscan; Leis., Rec., Tour. Abstr.; Maize Abstr.; Microbiol. Abstr. Sect. A; Nematol. Abstr.; Nutr. Abstr. Rev., Ser. B, Live Feeds and Feed.; Nutr. Abstr. Rev., Ser. A, Hum. Exp.; Ornamental Hort. (1991-); Life Sci. Collect.; Plant Breed. Abstr.; Plant Genet. Resour. Abstr.; Plant Grow. Reg. Abstr.; Postharvest News Inf.; Potato Abstr.; Protozoolog. Abstr.; Res. Alert [Select. Cov.]; Rev. Agric. Entomol.; Rev. Med. Vet. Mycology; Rev. Plant Pathol.; Rice Abstr.; Rural Dev. Abstr.; SCISEARCH; SEA Abstr.; Seed Abstr.; Soils Fert.; Sorghum Mill. Abstr.; Soyabean Abstr.; Sug. Indus. Abstr.; Vitis Vitic. Enol. Abstr.; Weed Abstr.; Wildl. Rev.; World Agric. Econ. Rural Sociol. Abstr.

LC SB4 **ISSN** 0537-197X
DD 631/.0954 II
CODEN IJAGAZ
INDIAN JOURNAL OF AGRONOMY. [Indian j. agron.]. **Added/Corp** Indian Society of Agronomy. Vol. 1 (Aug. 1956)-. Periodical. English. Four times a year (March, June, Sep., Dec.). $150.00. Indian Society of Agronomy, Secretary, Indian Agricultural Research Institute, New Delhi 110012 India. **(Subscription address:** Prints India, 11 Darya Ganj, New Delhi 110002 India. **Tel** 011 91 11 3268645, FAX 011 91 11 3275542, telex 31-61087 PRIN-IN.**) ED** Dr. S.P. Singh. **Ad Acc. Circ:** 1,800 (ctrl). available on microfiche; available on microfilm; available in microform. Documents available from The Genuine Article, CASDDS.
Desc: Disseminates knowledge of agronomy, research in the field of soil, water, and crop management and provides a suitable forum for exchange of ideas to research workers.
Ind/Abst AGRICOLA; Agric. Eng. Abstr. (1991-); Agrofor. Abstr. (1991-); Chem. Abstr.; Cot. Trop. Fibr. Abstr. Bibliogr.; Curr. Aware. Biol. Sci., CABS; Curr. Cit.; Curr. Contents Agric. Biol. Environ. Sci.; Field Crop Abstr.; For. Prod. Abstr. (19??-19??); For. Abstr.; Grass. Forage Abstr.; Hortic. Abstr.; Irr. Drain. Abstr.; Maize Abstr.; Nutr. Abstr. Rev., Ser. B, Live Feeds and Feed.; Nutr. Abstr. Rev., Ser. A, Hum. Exp.; Plant Breed. Abstr.; Plant Grow. Reg. Abstr.; Potato Abstr.; Poult. Abstr.; Protozoolog. Abstr.; Res. Alert [Select. Cov.]; Rev. Agric. Entomol.; Rev. Med. Vet. Mycology; Rev. Plant Pathol.; Rice Abstr.; Rural Dev. Abstr.; SCISEARCH; Seed Abstr.; Soils Fert.; Sorghum Mill. Abstr.; Soyabean Abstr.; Sug. Indus. Abstr.; Weed Abstr.; Wheat Barley Trit. Abstr.; World Agric. Econ. Rural Sociol. Abstr.

LC S612 .I53
II
INDIAN JOURNAL OF DRYLAND AGRICULTURAL RESEARCH AND DEVELOPMENT. **Added/Corp** Indian Society of Dryland Agriculture. (19??)-. Periodical. English. Two times a year. $40.00. Central Research Institute of Dryland Agriculture, Hyderabad India. **(Subscription address:** Prints India, 11 Darya Ganj, New Delhi 110002 India. **Tel** 011 91 11 3268645, FAX 011 91 11 3275542, telex 31-61087 PRIN-IN.**)**

LC S544.5.I5 I5 **ISSN** 0537-1996
DD 630 II
INDIAN JOURNAL OF EXTENSION EDUCATION. See Education.

LC S **ISSN** 0253-8040
DD 630 II
CODEN IJWSAB
INDIAN JOURNAL OF WEED SCIENCE. [Indian j. weed sci.]. **Added/Corp** Indian Society of Weed Science. (1969)-. Academic Scholarly Publication. English. Four times a year. $20.00. Taru Books & Journals, G-159 Pashchim Vihar, New Delhi 110063 India. **Tel** 384851. **(Subscription address:** Prints India, 11 Darya Ganj, New Delhi 110002 India. **Tel** 011 91 11 3268645, FAX 011 91 11 3275542, telex 31-61087 PRIN-IN.**)** Documents available from CASDDS.
Ind/Abst Chem. Abstr.; Field Crop Abstr.; Grass. Forage Abstr.; Maize Abstr.; Potato Abstr.; Rice Abstr.; Seed Abstr.; Soils Fert.; Sorghum Mill. Abstr.; Weed Abstr.; Wheat Barley Trit. Abstr.

LC S **ISSN** 0745-7103
DD 630 US
INDIANA AGRI-NEWS. **VFOAT** Indiana Agrinews. (198?)-. Periodical. English. One time a week. $13.00. Agri-News Publications, 420 Second Street, La Salle IL 61301. **Tel** (815)223-2558, FAX (815)223-5997.

LC S
DD 630 US
INDIANA AGRICULTURAL STATISTICS. (1986)-. English. One time a year. $5.00. Indiana Agricultural Statistics, Agricultural Administration Building, West Lafayette IN 47907. **ED** Ralph Q Gann. **Circ:** 2,000 (ctrl). ***Continues*** *Annual Crop and Livestock Summary.*

LC S **ISSN** 0162-7104
DD 630 US
INDIANA PRAIRIE FARMER. [Indiana prairie farmer]. (19??)-. Trade Publication. English. Twenty-four times a year. $19.95. Farm Progress Publishing, 191 South Gary Avenue, Carol Stream IL 60188-2089. **Tel** (708)462-2890 or 2891. **(Subscription address:** CDS / SIFD Agency Control, 1901 Bell Avenue, Des Moines IA 50315. **Tel** (515)246-6812.**)**

LC HD1527.I6 I57a **ISSN** 0092-3222
DD 331.7/63/09772 US
INDIANA RURAL MANPOWER REPORT. See Business and Economics-Labor.

LC HD9014.B8 I5
DD 338.1/3/0981 BL
CEASED
INDICES AGROPECUARIOS. **Added/Corp** Centro de Estudos Agricolas (Instituto Brasileiro de Economia). (1974)-(19??). Portuguese. Fundacao Getulio Vargas, Praia de Botafogo, 190 6 Andar, 22253-900 Rio de Janeiro RJ Brazil. **Tel** 011 5521 551 0698, FAX 011 5521 551 1596, 011 5521 551 5755. **ED** Sylvio Wanick Ribeiro.

LC S
DD 630 LU
INDICES CE DE PRECIOS AGRICOLAS. GLOSSARIUM. **VFOAT** Glossarium, Indices de de Precios Agricolas; Glossarium, Ec Agricultural Price Indexes; Ec Agricultural Price Indices. Glossarium.

Agriculture

LC HD2081 .I48
DD 630   IO

INDIKATOR PEMBANGUNAN INDUSTRI PERTANIAN. **Added/Corp** Indonesia. Bagian Statistik Agro Industri. **VFOAT** Indikator Pertanian Industri. (1981)-. Indonesian. Biro Pusat Statistik / Central Bureau of Statistics, 8 Jalan Dr. Sutomo No. 8, Box 3, Jakarta Pusat 10710 Indonesia. **Tel** 011 62 21 372808, 011 62 21 374909 ext.342. Index available. **Bk Rev**. **Ad Acc**. ctrl circ.

LC S17
DD 630   IO

INDONESIAN AGRICULTURAL RESEARCH & DEVELOPMENT JOURNAL. **Added/Corp** Indonesia. Badan Penelitian dan Pengembangan Pertanian. **VAT** Indonesian Agricultural Research and Development Journal. Vol. 1 (1979)-. Periodical. English.
Ind/Abst Agrofor. Abstr.; Biocont. News Inf.; Cot. Trop. Fibr. Abstr. Bibliogr.; Fish Rev. (Jan. 1989-July 1992); Maize Abstr.; Wildl. Rev. (Jan. 1989-July 1992).

LC S   **ISSN** 0325-0326
DD 630   AG

INDUSTRIA AZUCARERA, LA. [Ind. azucar.]. (18??)-. Periodical. English. Twelve times a year. $45.00. Centro Azucarero, Argentino Reconquista 336, 1335 Buenos Aires Argentina. **Tel** 394-0257. **Bk Rev**. **Ad Acc**. **Circ:** 3,000. **Continues** Revista Azucarera.
Ind/Abst AGRICOLA; Agric. Eng. Abstr. (1991-); Food Sci. Technol. Abstr.; Hortic. Abstr.; Sug. Indus. Abstr.

LC S   **ISSN** 0215-8981
DD 630   IO
    CODEN ICRJEG

INDUSTRIAL CROPS RESEARCH JOURNAL. [Ind. crops res. j.]. **Added/Corp** Pusat Penelitian dan Pengembangan Tanaman Industri (Indonesia). Vol. 1, No. 1 (Nov. 1988)-. Periodical. English. Two times a year.
Ind/Abst Agrofor. Abstr. (1991-); Biocont. News Inf. (1991-); Field Crop Abstr.; Food Sci. Technol. Abstr.; For. Abstr.; Hortic. Abstr.; Plant Breed. Abstr.; Plant Grow. Reg. Abstr.; Rev. Agric. Entomol.; Rev. Plant Pathol.; Seed Abstr.; Soils Fert.

LC S   **ISSN** 0749-145X
DD 630   US

INDUSTRIAL VEGETATION MANAGEMENT (1982). (INDUSTRIAL VEGETATION MANAGEMENT.). [Ind. veg. manage.]. Periodical. English. Industrial Vegetation Management, PO Box 54, Jefferson WI 53549. **Tel** (414)694-4026. **Continues** Industrial Vegetation and Pest Management.
Ind/Abst Weed Abstr.

LC S   **ISSN** 0019-9311
DD 630   FR
    CODEN IALAA9

INDUSTRIES ALIMENTAIRES ET AGRICOLES. [Ind. aliment. agr.]. **Added/Corp** Association des Chimistes, Ingenieurs et Cadres des Industries Agricoles et Alimentaires. Association des Anciens Eleves de l'Ecole Nationale Superieure des Industries Agricoles et Alimentaires. Commission Internationale des Industries Agricoles. (1955)-. Academic Scholarly Publication. French. Twelve times a year. $166.22. Assoc. des Chimistes Ingenieurs, 2 rue de l'Oratoire, 75001 Paris France. **Tel** 33 1 42974138, FAX 33 1 42601198, telex 212555. **ED** G Dardenne (editor's phone: 33 1 44081838). Documents available from CASDDS. **Continues** Industries Agricoles et Alimentaires.
Ind/Abst AGRICOLA; Biodeter. Abstr.; Chem. Abstr.; Curr. Cit.; Dairy Sci. Abstr.; EMBASE; Energy Res. Abstr.; Food Sci. Technol. Abstr.; Hortic. Abstr.; Nutr. Abstr. Rev., Ser. A, Hum. Exp.; Plant Breed. Abstr.; Poult. Abstr.; Rev. Agric. Entomol.; Rice Abstr.; Seed Abstr.; Soyabean Abstr.; Sug. Indus. Abstr.; World Agric. Econ. Rural Sociol. Abstr.

LC LB2335.86
DD 331.88113711   SZ

INFO / FITPAS = IFPAAW / FITPASC. See Business and Economics-Labor.

LC S20   **ISSN** 0822-7314
DD 630/.6/0714   CN

INFO-RURAL. (INFO-RURAL : BULLETIN D'INFORMATION DE L'ASSOCIATION DE LA JEUNESSE RURALE DU QUEBEC.). [Info-rural]. Vol. 2, No. 2, (April/May 1983)-. Bulletin. French. Six times a year. Free. Association de la Jeunesse Rurale du Quebec, Local 4326 Pavillon Comtois Universite Laval, Quebec G1K 7P4 Canada. ctrl circ. **Continues** AJRQ, 0826-2497.

LC S
DD 630   PO

INFORMACAO BIBLIOGRAFICA. **Added/Corp** Empresa Publica de Abastecimento de Cereais. Centro de Documentacao e Biblioteca. (19??)-. Periodical. Portuguese. Irregular. CIDAC, R Pinheiro Chagas 77 2 E, 1000 Libson Portugal.

LC AS171   **ISSN** 0939-9534
DD 63   GW
UDC 63

INFORMATIK IN DER LAND-, FORST- UND ERNAHRUNGSWIRTSCHAFT. (1987)-. Periodical. German. One time a week. Gesellschaft fuer Informatik in der Land-, Forst- und Ernahrungswirtschaft, Stuttgart Germany.
Ind/Abst Agric. Eng. Abstr.

LC S   **ISSN** 0019-994X
DD 630   FR

INFORMATION AGRICOLE, L'. [Inf. agric.]. **Added/Corp** Federation Nationale des Syndicats d'Exploitants Agricoles. (1952)-. Periodical. French. Eleven times a year (monthly with combined July/Aug.). $54.68. FNSEA, 11 rue de la Baume, 75008 Paris France. **Tel** 011 33 1 45631177, FAX 011 33 1 45639125.
Ind/Abst AGRICOLA; Leis., Rec., Tour. Abstr.; Rural Dev. Abstr.; World Agric. Econ. Rural Sociol. Abstr.

LC S
DD 630   US

INFORMATION BULLETIN - MISSISSIPPI. AGRICULTURAL AND FORESTRY EXPERIMENT STATION, MISSISSIPPI STATE. **Main/Corp** Mississippi. Agricultural and Forestry Experiment Station Mississippi State. 1-. Bulletin. English. Price varies per volume.

LC S   **ISSN** 1013-9915
DD 630   NL

INFORMATION CIRCULAR / SOUTH PACIFIC COMMISSION. [Inf. circ. - S. Pac. Comm.]. **Main/Corp** South Pacific Commission. (1978)-. Periodical. English. South Pacific Commission, PO Box D5, Noumea Cedex New Caledonia. **Tel** 011 687 262000, FAX 011 687 263818.
Ind/Abst AGRICOLA.

LC S   **ISSN** 0742-7425
DD 630   US
    CODEN ISVSE5
Pr Rev.

INFORMATION SERIES - VIRGINIA POLYTECHNIC INSTITUTE AND STATE UNIVERSITY. COLLEGE OF AGRICULTURE AND LIFE SCIENCES. (INFORMATION SERIES.). **Added/Corp** Virginia Polytechnic Institute and State University. College of Agriculture and Life Sciences. (1982)-. Monographic series. English. Irregular (30 per year). $150.00. National Institute for Public Policy, 8408 Arlington Virginia, Fairfax VA 22031. **Tel** (703)698-0563. **ED** Mary C. Holliman. **Circ:** 800 (ctrl). Documents available from BIOSIS Document Express.
Desc: Reviews, proceedings, historical progress reports, scientific data.
Ind/Abst AGRICOLA; Biol. Abstr. (1986-).

LC S   **ISSN** 0090-256X
DD 630   US

INFORMATION SHEET - MISSISSIPPI STATE UNIVERSITY. AGRICULTURAL AND FORESTRY EXPERIMENT STATION. (INFORMATION SHEET.). **Main/Corp** Mississippi. Agricultural and Forestry Experiment Station. No. 1122-. Monographic series. English. Price varies per volume. Assoc of British Theatre Tech, 4 7 Great Pulteney Street, London W1R 3DF United Kingdom. **Tel** 011 44 171 4343901. **Continues** Mississippi. Agricultural Experiment Station, State College. Information Sheet.

LC S   **ISSN** 0886-5787
DD 630   US

INFORMATION SHEET - MISSISSIPPI STATE UNIVERSITY. COOPERATIVE EXTENSION SERVICE. See Business and Economics-Cooperatives.

LC S   **ISSN** 0271-9908
DD 630   US

INFORMATION TEXT SERIES - HAWAII INSTITUTE OF TROPICAL AGRICULTURE AND HUMAN RESOURCES. (INFORMATION TEXT SERIES.). [Inf. text ser. - Hawaii Inst. Trop. Agric. Hum. Resour.]. **Added/Corp** Hawaii Institute of Tropical Agriculture and Human Resources. (1980)-. Monographic series. English. Price varies per volume. University of Hawaii College of Tropical Agriculture and Human Resources, Office of Publications and Information, 2500 Dole Street / Room 107, Honolulu HI 96822.
Ind/Abst AGRICOLA [Select. Cov.].

LC S   **ISSN** 0300-3981
DD 630   SZ

INFORMATIONEN ZUR ORTS-, REGIONAL- UND LANDESPLANUNG. Periodical. Multiple languages (English, French, German and Italian). Four times a year. Verlag der Fachvereine Austieferung, Postfach 566, CH-6314 Unteraegeri Switzerland.

LC S   **ISSN** 0755-2181
DD 630   FR
UDC 63
    TITLE CHANGE

INFORMATIONS TECHNIQUES - CEMAGREF. [Inf. tech. - CEMAGREF]. **VFOAT** Informations Techniques - Centre National du Machinisme Agricole, du Genie Rural, des Eaux et des Forets. (1981)-(19??). Periodical. French. Centre National du Machinisme Agricole du Genie Rural des Eaux et des Forets / CEMAGREF, BP 22, 92162 Antony Cedex France. **Tel** 011 33 1 40966121. (**Subscription address:** Lavoisier Abonnements, 14 rue de Provigny, 94236 Cachan Cedex France. **Tel** 011 33 1 47406700.) **Continues** Informations Techniques - C.T.G.R.E.F., 0755-2173. **Continued by** Ingenieries.
Ind/Abst Agric. Eng. Abstr.; Geogr. Abstr. Phys. Geogr.; Geogr. Abstr. Human Geogr.; GeoRef; Irr. Drain. Abstr.; Pig News Inf.; Soils Fert.

LC S
DD 630   CL

INFORMATIVO DEL MINISTERIO / MINISTERIO DE AGRICULTURA, CHILE. **Added/Corp** Chile. Ministerio de Agricultura. (1990)-. Periodical. Spanish.

LC HD9014.B83 G62A
DD 630   BL

INFORMATIVO ESTATISTICO DE MERCADO AGRICOLA DE GOIAS. **Main/Corp** Brazil. Divisao de Informacao de Mercado Agricola. Vol. 3, No. 26 (Feb. 1972)-. Periodical. Portuguese. Divisao de Informacao de Mercado Agricola, Setor Universitario - S/N Caixa Postal - 77, Goiania Brazil. **Continues** Informativo Estatistico Agropecuario de Goias.

LC S
DD 630   PE

INFORMATIVO LEGAL AGRARIO : UNA PUBLICACION MENSUAL DEL CEPES. **Added/Corp** Centro Peruano de Estudios Sociales. No. 1 (Oct. 1980)-. Periodical. Spanish. Twelve times a year.
Ind/Abst Hum. Rights Intern. Rep.

LC S   **ISSN** 0020-0689
DD 630   IT
UDC 63

INFORMATORE AGRARIO, L'. [Inf. agrar.]. (1945)-. Periodical. Italian. Fifty times a year. L122630. Informatore Agrario SRL, Largo Caldera 11, PO Box 520, 37122 Verona Italy. **Tel** 011 39 45 597855, FAX 011 39 45 597510, telex 481117 INFAGR I. Index available (free, published in Dec.).
Ind/Abst Curr. Cit.

LC S
DD 630   IT

INFORMATORE AGRARIO, L'. (1945)-. Periodical. Italian. Fifty times a year. L102000 Italy; L180000 other. Informatore Agrario SRL, Largo Caldera 11, PO Box 520, 37122 Verona Italy. **Tel** 011 39 45 597855, FAX 011 39 45 597510, telex 481117 INFAGR I. **ED** M. Mistruzzi. Index available. **Bk Rev**. **Ad Acc**. **Circ:** 55,000.
Desc: Deals with all aspects of agriculture, technics, experimentation, politics and economics.
Ind/Abst Agric. Eng. Abstr.; Agrofor. Abstr.; Anim. Breed. Abstr.; Biocont. News Inf.; Biodeter. Abstr.; Cot. Trop. Fibr. Abstr. Bibliogr.; Crop Physiol. Abstr.; Field Crop Abstr.; For. Abstr.; Grass. Forage Abstr.; Hortic. Abstr.; Index Vet.; Irr. Drain. Abstr.; Leis., Rec., Tour. Abstr.; Maize Abstr.; Nematol. Abstr.; Nutr. Abstr. Rev., Ser. B, Live Feeds and Feed.; Ornamental Hort.; Pig News Inf.; Plant Breed. Abstr.; Plant Grow. Reg. Abstr.; Postharvest News Inf.; Potato Abstr.; Protozoolog. Abstr.; Rev. Agric. Entomol.; Rev. Med. Vet. Entomol.; Rev. Plant Pathol.; Rice Abstr.; Seed Abstr.; Soils Fert.; Sorghum Mill. Abstr.; Soyabean Abstr.; Vitis Vitic. Enol. Abstr.; Weed Abstr.; Wheat Barley Trit. Abstr.

LC HD1875.M5 I54   **ISSN** 0100-3364
DD 338.1/0981/5   BL

INFORME AGROPECUARIO (BELO HORIZONTE). (INFORME AGROPECUARIO.). [Inf. agropecu.]. **Added/Corp** Empresa de Pesquisa Agropecuaria de Minas Gerais. (1977)-. Periodical. Portuguese. Six times a year. $50.00. EPAMIG / Empresa de Pesquisa Agropecuaria de Minas Gerais, Avenida Amazonas 115 s/614, CEP 30180-902 Belo Horizonte MG Brazil. **Tel** 011 55 31 2733544 ext. 137 or 149, FAX 011 55 31 2733884, telex 313906. **ED** Geraldo Magel Carozzi de Miranda. Index available. **Ad Acc**. **Circ:** 15,000 (ctrl). available with charts. **Continues** Informe Agropecuario. Conjuntura e Estatistica, 0100-445X.
Desc: Information on agriculture, livestock, research

results, applied technology, crop diseases, climate, soil, seed, dairy, poultry, economic analysis, survey, and fodder.
Ind/Abst AGRICOLA; Agrindex; Agrofor. Abstr.; Cot. Trop. Fibr. Abstr. Bibliogr.; Crop Physiol. Abstr.; Dairy Sci. Abstr.; Field Crop Abstr.; Grass. Forage Abstr.; Hortic. Abstr.; Index Vet.; Irr. Drain. Abstr.; Maize Abstr.; Nematol. Abstr.; Nutr. Abstr. Rev., Ser. B, Live Feeds and Feed.; Ornamental Hort.; Pig News Inf.; Plant Grow. Reg. Abstr.; Postharvest News Inf.; Rev. Agric. Entomol.; Rice Abstr.; Soils Fert.; Soyabean Abstr.; Weed Abstr.; World Agric. Econ. Rural Sociol. Abstr.

LC S
DD 630 CK
INFORME ANUAL - CENTRO INTERNACIONAL DE AGRICULTURA TROPICAL. **Main/Corp** Centro Internacional de Agricultura Tropical. English. One time a year. Free. Centro Internacional de Agricultura Tropical, Apartado Aereo 67-13, Cali Colombia. **Tel** 57 23 4450000, FAX 57 23 4450273, telex 05769 CIAT CO. **ED** Jack Reeves, Susana Amaya, and Elizabeth de Paez. ctrl circ.
Ind/Abst Anim. Breed. Abstr.

LC S
DD 630 VE
INFORME ANUAL / UNIVERSIDAD CENTRAL DE VENEZUELA, FACULTAD DE AGRONOMIA, INSTITUTO DE PRODUCCION ANIMAL. **Main/Corp** Universidad Central de Venezuela. Instituto de Produccion Animal. Spanish. One time a year. $5.00. UDPPA Facultad de Agronomia, UCV Apartado 4579, Maracay Venezuela.

LC S192.P27 I54 **ISSN** 0100-9508
BL
INFORME DA PESQUISA. [Inf. Pesqui.]. **Added/Corp** Fundacao Instituto Agronomico do Parana. **VFOAT** Informe da Pesquisa Iapar. (1977)-. Monographic series. Portuguese. Fundacao Instituto Agronomico do Parana, Caixa Postal 1331, Londrina 86.100 Brazil.
Ind/Abst Agrofor. Abstr.; Anim. Breed. Abstr.; Field Crop Abstr.; For. Abstr.; Maize Abstr.; Rev. Agric. Entomol.; Seed Abstr.; Weed Abstr.

LC S
DD 630 MX
INFORME DE INVESTIGACION - DIVISION DE CIENCIAS AGROPECUARIAS Y MARITIMAS, INSTITUTO TECNOLOGICO DE MONTEREY. **Main/Corp** Monterey, Mexico. Instituto Tecnologico y de Estudios Superiores. Division de Ciencias Agropecuarias y Maritimas. **VFOAT** Informe de Investigacion - Escuela de Agricultura y Ganaderia, Itesm. Periodical. Spanish. One time a year. Division de Ciencias, Estudios Superiores de Monterey, Monterey Mexico.
Ind/Abst Biocont. News Inf.; Biodeter. Abstr.; Nematol. Abstr.; Plant Grow. Reg. Abstr.; Potato Abstr.; Soils Fert.

LC S **ISSN** 0325-1799
DD 630 AG
INFORME TECNICO - ESTACION EXPERIMENTAL REGIONAL AGROPECUARIA PERGAMINO. (INFORME TECNICO.). [Inf. tec. - Estac. exp. reg. agropecu. Pergamino]. (1971)-. Monographic series. Spanish (summaries and/or abstracts in English). Price varies per volume. ***Continues*** *Informe Tecnico.*
Ind/Abst AGRICOLA; Nutr. Abstr. Rev., Ser. B, Live Feeds and Feed.; Pig News Inf.; Rev. Plant Pathol.; World Agric. Econ. Rural Sociol. Abstr.

LC S
DD 630 EC
INFORME TECNICO - INSTITUTO NACIONAL DE INVESTIGACIONES AGROPECUARIAS. **Main/Corp** Instituto Nacional de Investigaciones Agropecuarias. Spanish. Instituto Nacional de Investigaciones, Casilla 2600, Quito Ecuador. ***Continues*** *Informe Anual - Instituto Nacional de Investigaciones Agropecuarias.*

LC S **ISSN** 0758-5373
DD 630 FR
UDC 63 : 331.88
INFOS PARIS. **VFOAT** Info C.T.I.F.L. (1984)-. Periodical. French. Ten times a year (monthly with Jan./Feb. & July/Aug. issues combined). 300.00F France; 450.00F other. CTIFL, 22 rue Bergere, F-75009 Paris France. **Tel** 33 1 47701693, FAX 33 1 42462113. **ED** Anne-Jeanne Aesmazeaud. cum. index. **Bk Rev**, (Qty: 10). **Circ:** 1,500.
Ind/Abst For. Abstr.

LC S
DD 630 FR
INGENIERIES. (19??)-. French. Six times a year (publishes four regular issues and two special issues). $94.05. Centre National du Machinisme Agricole du Genie Rural des Eaux et des Forets / CEMAGREF, BP 22, 92162 Antony Cedex France. **Tel** 011 33 1 40966121. ***Continues*** *Informations Techniques du Cemagref, 0755-2181.*
Ind/Abst Agric. Eng. Abstr.; Geogr. Abstr. Phys. Geogr.; Geogr. Abstr. Human Geogr.; GeoRef; Irr. Drain. Abstr.; Pig News Inf.; Soils Fert.

LC S
DD 630 US
INNOVATIONS. **Added/Corp** West Central Experiment Station, Morris. Vol. 1, Issue 1 (Spring 1991)-. Periodical. English. Three times a year. ***Continues*** *West Central Experiment Station News.*
Ind/Abst AGRICOLA.

LC S **ISSN** 0020-4919
DD 630 II
INTENSIVE AGRICULTURE. (THE INTENSIVE AGRICULTURE.). [Intensive agric.]. **Added/Corp** India. Farm Information Unit. Vol. 1, No. 1 (Mar. 1963)-. Periodical. English. Twelve times a year. $20.00. **(Subscription address:** Prints India, 11 Darya Ganj, New Delhi 110002 India. **Tel** 011 91 11 3268645, FAX 011 91 11 3275542, telex 31-61087 PRIN-IN.**)** ***Continues*** *Extension.*

LC S **ISSN** 1048-2962
DD 631 US
INTERNATIONAL AG-SIEVE. [Int. ag-sieve]. **Added/Corp** Rodale Institute. Rodale International. Vol. 1, No. 1 (May/June 1988)-. Periodical. English. Six times a year (Jan., Mar., May, July, Sept., Nov.). $18.00. Rodale International, 222 Main Street, Emmaus PA 18098. **Tel** (610)683-6383, FAX (215)683-8548. **ED** Katie Carruth (editor's address: 611 Siegfriedale, Kutztown, PA 19530). **Bk Rev**, (Qty: 10). **Circ:** 1,000. available on an online database.
Desc: A collection of the latest information in the field of sustainable agriculture in the Tropics. Contains the technical information that the scientific community needs, and the practical information the field worker can use but does not require. Covers the latest in tropical forest products, training opportunities, seeds and biodiversity, women in agriculture and agroforestry.

LC S **ISSN** 0261-4413
DD 630 UK
INTERNATIONAL AGRICULTURAL DEVELOPMENT (CROWBOROUGH, EAST SUSSEX). (INTERNATIONAL AGRICULTURAL DEVELOPMENT.). [Int. agric. dev.]. Vol. 1, No. 1 (Nov./Dec. 1980)-. Trade Publication. English. Six times a year (Jan., Mar., May, July, Sept., Nov.). $51.33. International Agricultural Development, 19 Woodford Close Caversham, Reading Berkshire RG4 7HN United Kingdom. **Tel** 011 44 1734 476063, FAX 011 44 1734 470367, telex 95596. **ED** John Madeley. **Bk Rev**, (Qty: 15-20). **Ad Acc. Circ:** 1,500 (ctrl). Documents available from Documents on Demand.
Ind/Abst Dairy Sci. Abstr.; Environ. Abstr.; Environ. Period. Bibliogr.; Int. Labour Doc.; Plant Breed. Abstr.; Plant Genet. Resour. Abstr.; Seed Abstr.; Soils Fert.

LC TL **ISSN** 0020-675X
DD 629 US
INTERNATIONAL FLYING FARMER. [Int. fly. farmer]. **Added/Corp** International Flying Farmers. (19??)-. Periodical. English. Nine times a year. $15.00. International Flying Farmer, PO Box 9124, Mid Continent Airport, Wichita KS 67277. **Tel** (316)943-4234. **ED** Angie Blakley-Reid. **Ad Acc. Circ:** 2,000 (ctrl). ***Continues*** *National Flying Farmer.*
Desc: Articles on members, and aviation and agriculture as it relates to our members. Chapter activities.

LC SB950.A1 P18 **ISSN** 0967-0874
UK
NLM W1; IN771RW
•**INTERNATIONAL JOURNAL OF PEST MANAGEMENT.** **VFOAT** IJPM; Pest Management. Vol. 39, No. 1 (Jan.-Mar. 1993)-. Academic Scholarly Publication. English (summaries and/or abstracts in French and Spanish). Four times a year. $275.00. Taylor & Francis Ltd. / UK, Rankine Road, Basingstoke, Hampshire RG24 8PR United Kingdom. **Tel** 011 44 1256 840366, FAX 011 44 1256 479438, telex 858540. **(Subscription address:** Taylor & Francis Inc., 1900 Frost Road, Suite 101, Bristol PA 19007-1598. **Tel** (215)785-5800, (800)821-8312, FAX (215)785-5515.**)** **ED** Neil Kidd and Mark Jarvis. Documents available from BIOSIS Document Express, CASDDS. ***Continues*** *Tropical Pest Management, 0143-6147.*
Desc: Publishes original research papers concerning the control of pests and diseases of plants of economic, conservation, medicinal and amenity value within the areas of agriculture, horticulture, forestry, conservation, and stored products research. The journal also contains a "Forum" section aimed at facilitating discussion and debate between readers and authors on important issues in pest management.
Ind/Abst Abstr. Trop. Agric.; AGRICOLA; Apic. Abstr.; Biol. Abstr.; Chem. Abstr.; Curr. Aware. Biol. Sci., CABS; Curr. Cit.; Life Sci. Collect.; PESTDOC; Sci. Cit. Index (19??-19??).

LC S **ISSN** 0254-8755
DD 630 II
CODEN IJTADD
Pr Rev.
INTERNATIONAL JOURNAL OF TROPICAL AGRICULTURE. [Int. j. trop. agric.]. **VFOAT** Antarrashtriya Ushnakatibandhiya Krshi-Sodha Patrika. Vol. 1, No. 1 (March 1983)-. Academic Scholarly Publication. English. Four times a year. $130.00. **(Subscription address:** Prints India, 11 Darya Ganj, New Delhi 110002 India. **Tel** 011 91 11 3268645, FAX 011 91 11 3275542, telex 31-61087 PRIN-IN.**)** **ED** R. D. Laura. **Bk Rev. Circ:** 400 (ctrl). Documents available from BIOSIS Document Express, CASDDS.
Ind/Abst Anim. Breed. Abstr.; Biol. Abstr.; Chem. Abstr. (1983-); Cot. Trop. Fibr. Abstr. Bibliogr.; Curr. Cit.; Dairy Sci. Abstr.; Field Crop Abstr.; Food Sci. Technol. Abstr.; Hortic. Abstr.; Irr. Drain. Abstr.; Plant Breed. Abstr.; Potato Abstr.; Rev. Agric. Entomol.; Rice Abstr.; SCISEARCH; Seed Abstr.; Soils Fert.; Soyabean Abstr.; Weed Abstr.; Wheat Barley Trit. Abstr.

LC S **ISSN** 0782-7784
DD 630 FI
CODEN IPEJE8
INTERNATIONAL PEAT JOURNAL. [Int. peat j.]. **Added/Corp** International Peat Society. No. 1 (1986)-. Academic Scholarly Publication. English (German and Russian). One time a year. $20.00. International Peat Society, Kuokkalantie 4, SF 40420, Jyska Finland. **Tel** 358 41 674042. **ED** R.A. Robertson. **Bk Rev. Circ:** 1,500 (ctrl). Documents available from CASDDS.
Desc: All aspects of peat and peatlands study and utilizations, environment, energy.
Ind/Abst Chem. Abstr. (1986-); Coal Abstr.

LC SB599 **ISSN** 1046-8366
DD 632 US
INTERNATIONAL PERMACULTURE SOLUTIONS JOURNAL. [Int. permac. solut. j.]. **VFOAT** TIPS Journal. Vol. 1, No. 1 (1990)-. Periodical. English. $27.50 (U.S. and Mexico), $30.00 (elsewhere). Yankee Permaculture, PO Box 264, Maloy IA 50852. ***Continues*** *International Permaculture Species Yearbook, 0896-5781.*

LC S **ISSN** 0863-1840
DD 630 RU
CEASED
INTERNATIONALE AGRAR-INDUSTRIE-ZEITSCHRIFT. (INTERNATIONALE AGRARINDUSTRIE ZEITSCHRIFT.). [Int. agrar-ind.-z.]. **Added/Corp** Council for Mutual Economic Assistance. Komitet po Sotrudnichestvu v Oblasti Agropromyshlennogo Kompleksa. **VFOAT** Internationale Agrar Industrie Zeitschrift; International Agroindustrial Journal; Revista Internacional Agroindustrial. (1989)-(19??). Periodical. German (table of contents in English and Spanish). Deutscher Landwirtschaftsverlag, Grabbaallee 41, D-13156 Berlin Germany. **Tel** 011 49 30 48320311. ***Continues*** *Internationale Zeitschrift der Landwirtschaft, 0535-420X.*
Ind/Abst AgBiotech News Inf.; Agric. Eng. Abstr.; Anim. Breed. Abstr.; Dairy Sci. Abstr.; Grass. Forage Abstr.; Index Vet.; Irr. Drain. Abstr.; Maize Abstr.; Nutr. Abstr. Rev., Ser. B, Live Feeds and Feed.; Nutr. Abstr. Rev., Ser. A, Hum. Exp.; PESTDOC; Pig News Inf.; Plant Breed. Abstr.; Potato Abstr.; Rev. Plant Pathol.; Rice Abstr.; Soils Fert.; Sug. Indus. Abstr.; Vet. Bull.; Wheat Barley Trit. Abstr.; World Agric. Econ. Rural Sociol. Abstr.

LC WMLC L 83/3096
AU
CODEN IGGKEQ
INTERNATIONALE GESELLSCHAFT FUER GETREIDEWISSENSCHAFT UND -TECHNOLOGIE. **Main/Corp** International Association for Cereal Science and Technology. Congress. **VFOAT** International Association for Cereal Science and Technology : B.[Papers]. (19??)-. English (German, French and Russian). Documents available from BIOSIS Document Express. ***Continues*** *International Association for Cereal Chemistry. Congress. Berichte der Internationalen Gesellschaft fur Getreidechemie, 0534-6665.*
Ind/Abst Biol. Abstr. (1987-).

LC S230.B7 I53
DD 338.1/0944/1 FR
INVENTAIRE AGRICOLE REGIONAL. **VFOAT** Annuaire Statistique Agricole de Bretagne. French. Service Regional de Statistique Agricole Region Bretagne, 21 Bd du Colombier, 35000 Remmes France.

LC S541 .U6524A **ISSN** 0360-5841
DD 338.1/072073 US
INVENTORY OF AGRICULTURAL RESEARCH. (INVENTORY OF AGRICULTURAL RESEARCH / ISSUED BY TECHNICAL INFORMATION SYSTEMS, SCIENCE AND EDUCATION ADMINISTRATION, U.S. DEPARTMENT OF AGRICULTURE.). [Inventory agric. res.]. English. One time a year. Cooperative State Research Service,

Agriculture

Science and Education, US Department of Agriculture, Washington DC 20250. available on microfiche (Vols. for 1979- distributed to depository libraries).

LC S **ISSN** 0113-051X
DD 630.993 NZ
INVERMAY TECHNICAL REPORT.
[Invermay tech. rep.]. (1987)-. Monographic series. English. Irregular. *Continues Technical Report - Invermay Research Centre, 0110-649X.*
Ind/Abst Agric. Eng. Abstr.

LC HD2021 .I58 **ISSN** 0213-635X
DD 630 SP
INVESTIGACION AGRARIA. ECONOMIA.
Added/Corp Instituto Nacional de Investigaciones Agrarias. Spain. Ministerio de Agricultura, Pesca y Alimentacion. **VFOAT** Economia. (June/Dec. 1986)-. Periodical. Spanish (English; summaries and/or abstracts in English). Three times a year. $84.38. Instituto Nacional de Investigaciones Agrarias, C. Jose Abascal 56, 28003 Madrid Spain. **Tel** 011 34 1 3473906, FAX (91)4423587, telex 48989 INIA E. **Bk Rev. Circ:** 1,500 (ctrl). *Continues Serie : Economia y Sociologia Agrarias.*
Ind/Abst Hortic. Abstr.; Pig News Inf.; World Agric. Econ. Rural Sociol. Abstr.

LC S
DD 630 UY
INVESTIGACIONES AGRONOMICAS.
Added/Corp Centro de Investigaciones Agricolas "Alberto Boerger.". Vol. 1, No. 1 (1980)-. Periodical. Spanish. Centro de Investigaciones Agricolas Alberto Berger, La Estanzuela, Colonia Uruguay.
Ind/Abst Field Crop Abstr.; Rev. Plant Pathol.; Rice Abstr.; Wheat Barley Trit. Abstr.

LC S **ISSN** 0021-051X
DD 630 US
IOWA FARM BUREAU SPOKESMAN.
Added/Corp Iowa Farm Bureau Federation. **VFOAT** Spokesman. (19??)-. Periodical. English. One time a week. Comes with Iowa Farm Bureau membership. Iowa Farm Bureau Spokesman, 608 Eighth Street, Grundy Center IA 50638.

LC S **ISSN** 0092-5209
DD 630 US
IOWA FARM OUTLOOK. [Iowa farm outlook].
Main/Corp Iowa. Cooperative Extension Service. (Apr. 30, 1964)-. English. Twenty-four times a year. $10.00. Iowa State University Publications Distribution Center, Ames IA 50011. **Tel** (515) 294-5247. *Continues Iowa Farm Outlook Letter, 0092-5195.*
Ind/Abst AGRICOLA [Full Cov.].

LC S **ISSN** 1013-9885
DD 630 IR
  CODEN IAGRE5
IRAN AGRICULTURAL RESEARCH.
[Iran agric. res.]. **Added/Corp** Danishgah-i Shiraz. Danishkadah-i Kishavarzi. **VFOAT** Tahqiqat-i Kishavarzi-i Iran. (19??)-. Periodical. English (Persian). Two times a year. Documents available from BIOSIS Document Express, CASDDS.
Ind/Abst Biol. Abstr. (1986-1988); Chem. Abstr.; Crop Physiol. Abstr.; Field Crop Abstr.; Hortic. Abstr.; Rice Abstr.; Weed Abstr.; Wheat Barley Trit. Abstr.

LC S17 **ISSN** 1017-5652
DD 630 IR
  CODEN IRJADJ
IRANIAN JOURNAL OF AGRICULTURAL SCIENCE.
[Iran j. agric. sci.]. **VFOAT** Majallah-i Ulum-i Kishavarzi Kishavarzi Iran. Vol. 1 (Dec. 1977)-. Academic Scholarly Publication. Persian (summaries and/or abstracts in English). Four times a year. Documents available from CASDDS.
Ind/Abst Chem. Abstr.; Crop Physiol. Abstr.; Seed Abstr.; Soyabean Abstr.; Sug. Indus. Abstr.

LC S
DD 630 IQ
IRAQI JOURNAL OF AGRICULTURAL SCIENCES ZANCO.
VFOAT Iraqi Journal of Agricultural Sciences. (1983)-. Periodical. English (Arabic). Four times a year. University of Salahaddin, College of Agriculture, Arbil Iraq.
Ind/Abst AGRICOLA; Biocont. News Inf.; For. Prod. Abstr.; For. Abstr.; Nematol. Abstr.; Plant Grow. Reg. Abstr.; Poult. Abstr.; Protozoolog. Abstr.; Rev. Med. Vet. Entomol.

LC S **ISSN** 1015-8502
DD 630 WS
IRETA'S SOUTH PACIFIC AGRICULTURAL NEWS.
[IRETA S. Pac. agric. news]. **VFOAT** Institute for Research, Extension & Training in Agriculture's South Pacific Agricultural News. (1983)-. Periodical. English. Twelve times a year.
Ind/Abst Agrofor. Abstr.

LC S
DD 630 IE
IRISH FARMER'S JOURNAL. Periodical.
English. One time a week. $292.62. Agricultural Trust, Irish Farm Center Bluebell, Dublin 12 Ireland. **Tel** 01-501166, FAX 520876, telex 33338. **ED** P O'Keeffe.

Bk Rev. Ad Acc. Circ: 72,000.
Desc: Includes news and notes of the agriculture industry in Europe.

LC S **ISSN** 0791-6833
DD 630 IE
  CODEN IAFREY
IRISH JOURNAL OF AGRICULTURAL AND FOOD RESEARCH.
Added/Corp Teagasc (Organization). Vol. 31, No. 1 (May 1992)-. Periodical. English. Two times a year. $85.56. Teagasc, 19 Sandymount Avenue, Dublin 4 Ireland. **Tel** 011 353 1 688188, FAX 011 353 1 688023, telex 30459. Documents available from The Genuine Article, CASDDS. *Formed by the union of Irish Journal of Agricultural Research, 0578-7483 and Irish Journal of Agricultural Economics and Rural Sociology, 0021-1249 Irish Journal of Food Science and Technology, 0332-0375.*
Ind/Abst AGRICOLA; Chem. Abstr.; Curr. Aware. Biol. Sci., CABS; Curr. Cit.; Curr. Contents Agric. Biol. Environ. Sci.; Res. Alert [Select. Cov.].

LC S **ISSN** 0115-2467
DD 630 PH
IRRI REPORTER, THE. Main/Corp International
Rice Research Institute. Vol. 1 (Jan. 1965)-. Periodical. English. Four times a year. Free on request. International Rice Research Institute, PO Box 933, 1099 Manila Philippines. **Tel** (011)63 2 8181926, FAX (011)63 2 8182087, telex 45365, 7425365.
Ind/Abst Philip. Sci. Technol. Abstr.

LC S **ISSN** 0021-1680
DD 630 IT
IRRIGAZIONE, L'. [Irrigazione]. Added/Corp
Centro Internazionale per Gli Studi Sulla Irrigazione. Vol. 5, No. 2 (1958)-. Periodical. Italian. Four times a year. L44000. Edagricole, PO Box 2157, 40100 Bologna Italy. **Tel** 011 39 51 492211 Ext. 22, FAX 011 39 51 493660, telex 510336 EDAGRI.
Ind/Abst AGRICOLA; Agric. Eng. Abstr.; Leis., Rec., Tour. Abstr.; Rural Dev. Abstr.; World Agric. Econ. Rural Sociol. Abstr.

LC S
DD 630 JA
ISHIKAWA NOGYO NO KENKYU. (1971)-.
Japanese. Ishikawaken Nogyo Tanki Daigaku, (Ishikawa Agricultural College), 1-308 Uematsu Nonoichimachi, Ishikawagun Ishikawaken 921 Japan.

LC HD1401 **ISSN** 0823-7735
DD 338.1/09717 CN
ISLAND FARMER. [Isl. farmer]. Vol. 1, No. 1 (Mar. 19, 1974)-. Periodical. English. Twenty-six times a year (every 2nd Monday). 10.00Can$ Prince Edward Island; 4.00Can$ other Provinces. Island Farmer, PO Box 88, Montague Prince Edward Island C0A 1R0 Canada. **ED** Jim MacNeill.

LC S **ISSN** 0926-3225
DD 630 NE
ISNAR SMALL-COUNTRIES STUDY PAPER. (STUDY PAPER.). [ISNAR small-ctries. study pap.]. Added/Corp
International Service for National Agricultural Research. **VFOAT** Small-Countries Study Paper; Small Countries Study Paper; ISNAR Small-Countries Study Paper. **VAT** International Service for National Agricultural Research Small-Countries Study Paper. (1991-). Monographic series. English.
Ind/Abst World Agric. Econ. Rural Sociol. Abstr.

LC S
DD 630 IS
ISRAEL AGRICULTURE. (19??)-. Periodical.
English. Four times a year. Embassy of Israel, 3514 International Drive, Washington DC 20008.
Ind/Abst Leis., Rec., Tour. Abstr.; Rural Dev. Abstr.; World Agric. Econ. Rural Sociol. Abstr.

LC JF201 **ISSN** 0886-635X
DD 351 US
ISSUE BRIEFING PAPER. See Public Administration.

LC S **ISSN** 0021-275X
DD 630 IT
  CODEN IAGRAZ
  SUSPENDED
ITALIA AGRICOLA, L'. [Ital. agric.].
(1???)-Suspended (Dec. 1991). Academic Scholarly Publication. Italian. Twelve times a year. Ramo Editoriale Degli Agricoltori (REDA), Via Nazionale No 89A, 00184 Rome Italy. Documents available from BIOSIS Document Express, CASDDS. *Absorbed Giornale di Agricoltura.*
Ind/Abst AGRICOLA; Biodeter. Abstr.; Biol. Abstr.; Chem. Abstr.; Index Vet. (-1987); For. Prod. Abstr. (1991-); For. Abstr.; Index Vet. (?-?); Nematol. Abstr.; Postharvest News Inf.; Rev. Agric. Entomol.; World Agric. Econ. Rural Sociol. Abstr.

LC S671 **ISSN** 0802-8532
DD 631.3 NO
ITF RAPPORT. Added/Corp Norges
Landbrukshgskole. Institutt for Tekniske Fag. **VAT** Institutt for Tekniske Fag Rapport. (19??)-. Monographic series. Norwegian.

Ind/Abst Agric. Eng. Abstr.; Nutr. Abstr. Rev., Ser. B, Live Feeds and Feed.; Postharvest News Inf.; Potato Abstr.

LC SF521 **ISSN** 0579-2746
DD 638.1 JA
  CODEN IDNHAR
IWATE DAIGAKU NOGAKUBU HOKOKU.
(HOKOKU. JOURNAL OF THE FACULTY OF AGRICULTURE, IWATE UNIVERSITY.). [Iwate Daigaku Nogakubu Hokoku]. **Added/Corp** Iwate Daigaku, Morioka, Japan. Nogakubu. **Added/Corp** Iwate Daigaku, Morioka, Japan. Nogakubu. Journal of the Faculty of Agriculture, Iwate University. **VFOAT** Journal of the Faculty of Agriculture, Iwate University. Vol. 1 (1953)-. Academic Scholarly Publication. Japanese (summaries and/or abstracts in English; table of contents in English). Iwate University, Faculty of Agriculture, Morioka Japan. Documents available from BIOSIS Document Express, CASDDS. *Supersedes Morioka Koto Norin Gakko. Gakujutsu Hokoku.*
Ind/Abst AGRICOLA; Biol. Abstr.; Chem. Abstr.; Index Vet.; Nutr. Abstr. Rev., Ser. B, Live Feeds and Feed.; Rice Abstr.; Vet. Bull.

LC QH301 **ISSN** 0321-1746
DD 574 TK
NLM W1 IZ652V **CODEN** ITUBAK
  TITLE CHANGE
IZVESTIIA AKADEMIIA NAUK TURKMENSKOI SSR. SERIIA BIOLOGICHESKIKH NAUK. See Biology.

LC S **ISSN** 0021-342X
DD 630 RU
IZVESTIIA TIMIRIAZEVSKOI SELSKOKHOZIAISTVENNOI AKADEMII.
[Izv. Timirjazevsk. selskohoz. akad.]. **Added/Corp** Moskvskaia Selskokhoziaistvennaia Akademiia Imeni K.A. Timiriazeva. **VFOAT** Izvestiia Tskha. (1952)-. Academic Scholarly Publication. Russian (summaries and/or abstracts in English). Four times a year. $79.95. **(Subscription address:** East View Publications Inc.; 3020 Harbor Lane North, Suite 110, Minneapolis MN 55447. **Tel** (800)477-1005, (612)550-0961, FAX (612)559-2931.) Index available in last issue of volume--attached. Documents available from BIOSIS Document Express, CASDDS. *Continues Izvestiia Selskokhoziaistvennoi Akademii Imeni K.A. Timiriazeva.*
Ind/Abst AGRICOLA; Biol. Abstr.; Chem. Abstr.; Index Vet.; Maize Abstr.; Nutr. Abstr. Rev., Ser. B, Live Feeds and Feed.; Plant Breed. Abstr.; Plant Grow. Reg. Abstr.; Potato Abstr.

LC S **ISSN** 0406-8386
DD 630 NE
JAARBOEK - PROEFSTATION VOOR DE BOOMKWEKERIJ. Main/Corp Boskoop,
Netherlands. Proefstation voor de Boomkwekerij. (1???)-. Dutch (English). One time a year. $13.71. Proefstation voor Boomkwekerij, Postbus 118, 2770 AC, Boskoop Netherlands. **Tel** 011 31 1727 19797.

LC HD1335.N4 N47a
DD 333.33 NE
JAARVERSLAG. See Real Estate.

LC HD1987 .P76A
DD 338.1 NE
JAARVERSLAG - PRODUKTSCHAP VOOR LANDBOUWZAAIZADEN.
Main/Corp Produktschap Voor Landbouwzaaizaden. Dutch. One time a year. Produktschap Voor Landbouwzaaizaden, Stadhoudersplantsoen 12, S-Gravenhage Netherlands. **Tel** 070-708708, FAX 070-461400, telex 32579 HOVA NL. ctrl circ.

LC SF **ISSN** 0417-1489
DD 636 GE
JAHRESBERICHT. Main/Corp Deutsche
Akademie der Landwirtschaftswissenschaften, Berlin Stitut for Tierzuchtforschung Dummerstorf. (1953)-. Periodical. German. Deutsche Akademie der Landwirtschaftswissenschaften, Berlin Germany.

LC S
DD 630 SZ
JAHRESBERICHT ... DES ZURCHER LANDWIRTSCHAFTLICHER KANTONALVEREINS UND DES ZURCHER BAUERNSEKRETARIATES.
1974-. Periodical. German.

LC S
DD 630 JA
JAPAN AGRINFO NEWSLETTER : JAPAN'S FOOD AND AGRICULTURE-NEWS AND VIEWS.
Added/Corp Japan International Agricultural Council. (1983)-. Newsletter. English. Twelve times a year. $35.00. Japan International Agriculture Council, Zenkokunogyokyosai Kaikan 19 Ichibancyo, Chiyoda KY Tokyo Japan. **Tel** 81 3 262-5046. **ED** Yutaka Yoshioka.
Desc: Provide news on current developments in food

and agricultural situations and policies in Japan and offers views of various indigenous circles on relevant issues.

LC S **ISSN** 0021-3551
DD 630 JA
CODEN JARJA9

Pr Rev.
JARQ. JAPAN AGRICULTURAL RESEARCH QUARTERLY. (JARQ.). [JARQ. Jpn. agric. res. q.]. **Added/Corp** Nettai Nogyo Kenkyu Senta. **VFOAT** Japan Agricultural Research Quarterly. (19??)-. Academic Scholarly Publication. English. Four times a year. Free on request. Tropical Agriculture Research Center, 1 2 Owashi Tsukubashi, Ibarakiken 305 Japan. Index available. cum. index. **Circ:** 2,000 (ctrl). Documents available from The Genuine Article, CASDDS.
Ind/Abst AgBiotech News Inf.; AGRICOLA; Agric. Eng. Abstr. (1991-); Agrofor. Abstr. (19??-19??); Anim. Breed. Abstr.; Biocont. News Inf. (19??-19??); Chem. Abstr.; Crop Physiol. Abstr.; Curr. Aware. Biol. Sci., CABS; Curr. Cit.; Curr. Contents Agric. Biol. Environ. Sci.; Dairy Sci. Abstr.; EMBASE; Field Crop Abstr.; Food Sci. Technol. Abstr.; For. Prod. Abstr. (1991-); For. Abstr.; Hortic. Abstr.; Index Vet.; Irr. Drain. Abstr.; Microbiol. Abstr. Sect. A; Nematol. Abstr.; Nutr. Abstr. Rev., Ser. B, Live Feeds and Feed.; Life Sci. Collect.; Plant Breed. Abstr.; Plant Genet. Resour. Abstr.; Plant Grow. Reg. Abstr.; Potato Abstr.; Poult. Abstr.; Protozoolog. Abstr.; Res. Alert [Select. Cov.]; Rev. Agric. Entomol.; Rev. Plant Pathol.; Rice Abstr.; Rural Dev. Abstr.; SCISEARCH; Seed Abstr.; Sorghum Mill. Abstr.; Soyabean Abstr.; Sug. Indus. Abstr.; Vet. Bull.; Wheat Barley Trit. Abstr.; World Agric. Econ. Rural Sociol. Abstr.

LC HD1940.5 .A26
DD 333 HU
JELENTES A MEZOGAZDASAG ... EVI FEJLODESEROL. (19??)-. Hungarian. One time a year.

LC S **ISSN** 1002-1302
DD 630 CH
JIANGSU NONGYE KEXUE. VFOAT Jiangsu Agricultural Sciences. (1979)-. Periodical. Chinese. Six times a year. Jiangsu Academy of Agricultural Sciences, Nanjing 210014, People's Republic of China.
Ind/Abst Cot. Trop. Fibr. Abstr. Bibliogr.; Crop Physiol. Abstr.; Hortic. Abstr.; Maize Abstr.; Seed Abstr.

LC S **ISSN** 1000-4440
DD 630 CC
JIANGSU NONGYE XUEBAO. VFOAT Journal of Agricultural Sciences. (1985)-. Academic Scholarly Publication. Chinese. Four times a year. Jiangsu Academy of Agricultural Sciences, Nanjing 210014, People's Republic of China.
Ind/Abst Crop Physiol. Abstr.; Index Vet.; Nutr. Abstr. Rev., Ser. B, Live Feeds and Feed.; Plant Breed. Abstr.; Rev. Plant Pathol.; Rice Abstr.; Seed Abstr.; Soils Fert.; Soyabean Abstr.

LC SF **ISSN** 0289-5277
DD 636.085 JA
JIKYU SHIRYO. [Jikyu shiryo]. **VFOAT** Nippon Sochi Gakkaishi. Jitsuyo-hen. (1984)-. Periodical. Japanese. Two times a year. Nihon Sochi Gakkai, (Japanese Soc. of Grassland Science), c/o Norin Suisansho Sochi Shikenjo, 768 Senbonmatsu Nishinasunomachi, Nasugun Tochigiken 329-27 Japan.

LC S19 .C485 **ISSN** 1000-5684
DD 630/.5 CC
JILIN NONGYE DAXUE XUEBAO. (CHI-LIN NUNG YEH TA HSUEH HSUEH PAO.). **Added/Corp** Chi-lin Nung yeh ta Hsueh. **VFOAT** Acta Agriculturae Universitatis Jilinensis; Jilin Nongye Daxue Xuebao. (Sept. 1979)-. Periodical. Chinese (summaries and/or abstracts in English). Four times a year. Jilin Nongye Daxue, Jilin University of Agriculture, Donghuan Lunan Changchun, Jilin 130118, People's Republic of China. **Tel** 42112. **ED** X. Zhendou. Documents available from BLDSC.
Ind/Abst Agrofor. Abstr.; For. Prod. Abstr. (1991-); For. Abstr.; Plant Breed. Abstr.; Plant Grow. Reg. Abstr.; Rice Abstr.; Soyabean Abstr.; Wheat Barley Trit. Abstr.

LC S17 .J36 **ISSN** 0021-3721
DD 630 II
CODEN JNRJAW
JNKVV RESEARCH JOURNAL. Main/Corp Jawaharlal Nehru. Agricultural University. **Added/Corp** Jawaharlal Nehru Agricultural University. Research Journal. **VFOAT** Research Journal. Vol. 1 (1967)-. Academic Scholarly Publication. English. Four times a year (Jan., Apr., July, Oct.). $12.00. Jawaharlal Neh Kris Vish Vidyl Officer, Information & Publ. Relations Officer, Jabalpur Madhya Pradesh India. Documents available from CASDDS.
Ind/Abst Chem. Abstr.

LC S **ISSN** 0746-3766
DD 630 US
CODEN JOHAEY
CEASED
JOJOBA HAPPENINGS. [Jojoba happen.]. **Added/Corp** University of Arizona. Office of Arid Lands Studies International Committee on Jojoba Research and Development. International Council on Jojoba. (July 1972)-(1993). Periodical. English. Jojoba Happenings, 6641 West Frye Road, Chandler AZ 85226. **Tel** (602)276-2626. **ED** Ken Lucas. **Bk Rev. Ad Acc. Circ:** 2,000 (ctrl).
Desc: Covers jojoba, an arid land commercial crop, producing an oil chemically the same as that of the endangered sperm whale.
Ind/Abst AGRICOLA [Select. Cov.]; Agric. Eng. Abstr. (1991-); Agrofor. Abstr.; BioBusiness; Hortic. Abstr.; Irr. Drain. Abstr.; Plant Breed. Abstr.; Seed Abstr.; Soils Fert.

LC S **ISSN** 0906-7043
DD 630 DK
JORD OG VIDEN. Added/Corp Danmarks Jordbrugsvidenskabelige Kandidatforbund. (1992)-. Trade Publication. Danish. Twenty-six times a year. kr900.00. Danmarks Jordbrugsvidenskabelige Kandidatforbund, Strandvejen 863, 2930 Klampenborg Denmark. **Tel** 31 63 11 66, FAX 31 63 88 11. **ED** Marianne Tinggaard. **Bk Rev. Ad Acc.** ***Continues*** *Ugeskrift for Jordbrug.*

LC HD4801
DD 331 SW
JORDBRUKETS ARBETSKRAFT. See Business and Economics-Labor.

LC S **ISSN** 0021-7441
DD 630 SW
JORDBRUKSEKONOMISKA MEDDELANDEN: JEM. [Jordbruksekon. medd.]. **VFOAT** Journal of Agricultural Economics; JEM. (1939)-. Periodical. Swedish (summaries and/or abstracts in English; table of contents in English). Twelve times a year.
Ind/Abst AGRICOLA; Dairy Sci. Abstr.; Nutr. Abstr. Rev., Ser. A, Hum. Exp.; Pig News Inf.; Postharvest News Inf.; Potato Abstr.; Poult. Abstr.; Wheat Barley Trit. Abstr.

LC S
DD 630 SW
JORDBRUKSSTATISTISK ARSBOK. VFOAT Statistical Yearbook of Agriculture. 1965-. Swedish (summaries and/or abstracts in English). One time a year. Liber Distribution, Prenumerationsorder, Forlagsorder 162 89, Stockholm Sweden. ***Continues*** *Jordbruk Och Boskapsskotsel.*

LC HC190.P6 J67
DD 331.5 BL
JORNAL DOS TRABALHADORES RURAIS SEM TERRA. Added/Corp Movimento dos Trabalhadores Rurais sem Terra (Brazil) Associacao Nacional de Cooperacao Agricola (Brazil). **VFOAT** Sem Terra. (1988)-. Periodical. Portuguese. Twelve times a year. $25.00. Movimento dos Trabalhadores Rurais sem Terra - JST, rua Ministro Godoy 1484, 05015 900 Sao Paulo SP Brazil. ***Continues*** *Jornal dos Trabalhadores sem Terra.*
Ind/Abst Hum. Rights Intern. Rep.

LC S19 .C52 **ISSN** 0300-550X
DD 630/.5 CH
CODEN CHNHAN
JOURNAL - AGRICULTURAL ASSOCIATION OF CHINA. (CHUNG-HUA NUNG HSUEH HUI PAO.). [J. - Agric. Assoc. China]. **Added/Corp** Chung-hua Nung Hsueh Hui. **VFOAT** Chung-Hua Nung Hsueh Hui Tsung Kan; Journal of the Agricultural Association of China. (1918)-. Periodical. Chinese (English). Four times a year. Chung-Hua Nung Hseuh Hui, 14 Wen-Chow Street, Taipei 106 Taiwan. Documents available from The Genuine Article, BIOSIS Document Express, CASDDS.
Ind/Abst Biol. Abstr.; Chem. Abstr.; CSA Neuro. Abstr. (?-?); Leadscan; Life Sci. Collect.; Plant Breed. Abstr.; Plant Grow. Reg. Abstr.; Poult. Abstr.; Res. Alert [Select. Cov.].

LC S583 .A7
DD 630/.24 US
JOURNAL - ASSOCIATION OF OFFICIAL ANALYTICAL CHEMISTS. Main/Corp Association of Official Analytical Chemists. Vol. 1 (1915/16)-. Periodical. English. Six times a year. Association of Official Analytical Chemists, Box 540, Benjamin Franklin Station, Washington DC 20044.
Ind/Abst Agric. Eng. Abstr.; Dairy Sci. Abstr.; Grass. Forage Abstr.; Hortic. Abstr.; Index Vet.; Maize Abstr.; NAPRALERT; Nutr. Abstr. Rev., Ser. B, Live Feeds and Feed.; Nutr. Abstr. Rev., Ser. A, Hum. Exp.; Pig News Inf.; Protozoolog. Abstr.; Rev. Med. Vet. Entomol.; Soils Fert.; Soyabean Abstr.; Vet. Bull.

LC QK **ISSN** 0183-5173
DD 581 FR
CODEN JATADT
SUSPENDED
JOURNAL D'AGRICULTURE TRADITIONNELLE ET DE BOTANIQUE APPLIQUEE. [J. agric. tradit. bot. appl.]. **VFOAT** JATBA. Vol. 24 (1977)-Suspended with Vol. 35 (1988). Periodical. French (English). Four times a year. Laboratoire d'Ethnobotanique, 57 rue Cuvier, 75 Paris 5EME France. **Bk Rev.** Documents available from BIOSIS Document Express. ***Continues*** *Journal d'Agriculture Tropicale et de Botanique Appliquee, 0021-7662.*
Ind/Abst Agrofor. Abstr.; Biol. Abstr. (-1982); For. Prod. Abstr.; Hortic. Abstr.; Leis., Rec., Tour. Abstr.; Plant Breed. Abstr.; Rice Abstr.; Rural Dev. Abstr.; Soils Fert.; World Agric. Econ. Rural Sociol. Abstr.

LC S **ISSN** 1052-5394
DD 630 US
JOURNAL FOR HAWAIIAN AND PACIFIC AGRICULTURE. [J. Hawaii. Pac. agric.]. **Added/Corp** University of Hawaii at Hilo. College of Agriculture. Vol. 1, No. 1 (1988)-. Periodical. English. Journal for Hawaiian and Pacific Agriculture, College of Agriculture, University of Hawaii at Hilo, Hilo HI 67620-4091.
Ind/Abst AGRICOLA [Full Cov.].

LC S
DD 630 AT
JOURNAL / HACOBU. Added/Corp Hawkesbury Agricultural College. **VFOAT** Hawkesbury Journal. (19??)-. Periodical. English. Six times a year. University of Western Sydney / Hawkesbury, Bourke Street, Richmond NSW 2753 Australia. **Tel** 011 61 45 784647, FAX 011 61 45 885612. ***Continues*** *Hawkesbury Agricultural College Journal.*

LC HD1401 .J677 **ISSN** 0738-8950
DD 338.1/0973 US
JOURNAL OF AGRIBUSINESS. [J. agribusiness]. **Added/Corp** Agricultural Economics Association of Georgia. University of Georgia. Division of Agricultural Economics. **VFOAT** JAB. Vol. 1, No. 1 (Feb. 1983)-. Periodical. English. Two times a year. $35.00. Agricultural Economics Association, University of Georgia, 301 Conner Hall, Athens GA 30602. **Tel** (706)542-0847. **ED** Joseph M Broder and Chung L Huang (editor's phone: (706)542-0751). **Circ:** 1,400 (ctrl).
Ind/Abst AGRICOLA [Full Cov.]; Dairy Sci. Abstr.; For. Prod. Abstr. (1991-); Leis., Rec., Tour. Abstr.; World Agric. Econ. Rural Sociol. Abstr.

LC BJ **ISSN** 1187-7863
DD 174/.963/05 CN
CCC
CODEN JAETEC
Pr Rev.
JOURNAL OF AGRICULTURAL & ENVIRONMENTAL ETHICS. See Ethics.

LC S494.5.I47 J68 **ISSN** 1049-6505
DD 026/.63 US
CODEN JFOIEU
Pr Rev.
•**JOURNAL OF AGRICULTURAL & FOOD INFORMATION.** [J. agric. food inf.]. **VFOAT** Journal of Agricultural and Food Information. Vol. 1, No. 1 (1993)-. Periodical. English. Four times a year. $50.00. The Haworth Press Inc., 10 Alice Street, Binghamton NY 13904-1580. **Tel** (607)722-5857, (800)3-HAWORTH, FAX (607)722-1424. **ED** Robyn Frank. **Bk Rev. Ad Acc. Acid Free.** available on microfiche. Documents available from Haworth Document Delivery Service.
Desc: Forum for the communication of research, practice and opinion on all aspects of agricultural and food information. The journal includes not only the traditional subjects of plant and animal husbandry, but also food and nutrition science and technology, aquaculture and fisheries, marine science involving food products, veterinary medicine, agricultural engineering, agricultural economics, applied entomology, natural products, and rural sociology.

LC S **ISSN** 1042-0541
DD 630 US
Pr Rev.
JOURNAL OF AGRICULTURAL EDUCATION. [J. agric. educ.]. **Added/Corp** American Association of Teacher Educators in Agriculture. Vol. 30, No. 1 (Spring 1989)-. Periodical. English. Four times a year (Mar., June, Sept., Dec.). $95.00. Texas A & M University / Agricultural Education, Department of Agricultural Education and Mechanization, FE Box 2588, College Station TX 77843. **Tel** (409)845-6601, FAX (409)845-6608. **ED** Jamie Cand (editor's address: 208 Agriculture Administration Building, 2120 Fyffe Road, Columbus, OH 43210). Index available. **Circ:** 500. available on microfilm and microfiche from University Microfilms International (UMI). ***Continues*** *American Association of Teacher Educators in Agriculture. Journal of the American Association of Teacher Educators in Agriculture, 0002-7480.*
Ind/Abst AGRICOLA [Full Cov.]; Curr. Index J. Educ. (March 1990).

LC S671 .J6 **ISSN** 0021-8634
DD 631.305 UK
CCC
CODEN JAERA2
Pr Rev.
JOURNAL OF AGRICULTURAL ENGINEERING RESEARCH. [J. agric. eng. res.]. Vol. 1 (1956)-. Academic Scholarly Publication. English. Twelve times a year. $533.89. Academic Press Ltd., A Division of Harcourt Brace & Company Ltd., 24-28 Oval Road, London NW1 7DX United Kingdom. **Tel** 011 44 171 2674466, FAX 011 44 171 4822293, 011 44 171

4854752, telex 25775 ACPRES G. **(Subscription address:** Harcourt Brace & Company, Ltd., Foots Cray High Street, Sidcup Kent DA14 5HP United Kingdom. **Tel** 011 44 181 3003322, FAX 011 44 181 3090807, telex 896 377 ACADEM.) **ED** D. J. White. Index available (bound in last issue). Documents available from The Genuine Article, BIOSIS Document Express, CASDDS.
Desc: Reflects the broad spectrum of interdisciplinary interests inherent in this field. Publishes mainly original research papers but also includes in-depth review articles and short research notes.
Ind/Abst AgBiotech News Inf.; AGRICOLA [Full Cov.]; Agric. Eng. Abstr. (19??-19??); Anim. Breed. Abstr.; Biodeter. Abstr. (19??-19??); Biol. Agric. Index; Biol. Abstr.; Chem. Abstr.; Curr. Cit.; Curr. Contents Agric. Biol. Environ. Sci.; Curr. Contents Eng. Comput. Technol.; Dairy Sci. Abstr.; EMBASE; Field Crop Abstr.; Fluid Abstr., Civil Eng.; Fluid Abstr. Proc. Eng.; FLUIDEX (1973-); Food Sci. Technol. Abstr.; For. Abstr.; Grass. Forage Abstr.; Hortic. Abstr.; Int. Abstr. Oper. Res. [Select. Cov.]; Irr. Drain. Abstr.; Maize Abstr.; Nutr. Abstr. Rev., Ser. B, Live Feeds and Feed.; Ornamental Hort. (19??-19??); Life Sci. Collect.; Pig News Inf.; Plant Genet. Resour. Abstr.; Postharvest News Inf.; Potato Abstr.; Res. Alert [Full Cov.]; Rev. Agric. Entomol.; Rice Abstr.; Sci. Cit. Index; SCISEARCH; Seed Abstr.; Soils Fert.; Soyabean Abstr.; Weed Abstr.

LC SB818 .J68 **ISSN** 0735-939X
DD 630/.2/957 US
CODEN JAENES
Pr Rev.

JOURNAL OF AGRICULTURAL ENTOMOLOGY. See Zoology-Entomology.

LC HV **ISSN** 1074-7583
DD 363 US

●**JOURNAL OF AGRICULTURAL SAFETY AND HEALTH.** [J. agric. saf. health]. **Added/Corp** American Society of Agricultural Engineers. Vol. 1, No. 1 (Feb. 1995)-. Periodical. English. Four times a year. $68.00. American Society of Agricultural Engineers, Department 2510, 2950 Niles Road, St. Joseph MI 49085-9659. **Tel** (616)429-0300, FAX (616)429-3852.

LC S3 .J84 **ISSN** 0021-8596
DD 630.5 UK
CCC
CODEN JASIAB
Pr Rev.

JOURNAL OF AGRICULTURAL SCIENCE, THE. [J. agric. sci.]. Vol. 1 (1905/1906)-. Academic Scholarly Publication. English. Eight times a year. $495.00. Cambridge University Press, The Edinburgh Building, Shaftesbury Road, Cambridge CB2 2RU United Kingdom. **Tel** 011 44 1223 312393, FAX 011 44 1223 315052, telex 851-817256. **(Subscription address:** Cambridge University Press / North America, 110 Midland Avenue, Port Chester NY 10573. **Tel** (800)431-1580, (914)937-9600.) **ED** WJ Whittington. **Bk Rev**. available on microfilm and microfiche from University Microfilms International (UMI). Documents available from BIOSIS Document Express, CASDDS, Documents on Demand.
Desc: Publishes papers concerned with the advance of agriculture and the use of land resources throughout the world. Publishes original scientific work related to strategic and applied studies in agronomy and crop physiology, breeding, genetics and pathology, soil science, animal nutrition, physiology and genetics, and the mathematical and statistical methods used in experimentation and data analysis.
Ind/Abst AgBiotech News Inf.; AGRICOLA [Full Cov.]; Agric. Eng. Abstr. (19??-19??); Agrofor. Abstr.; Anim. Breed. Abstr.; Biol. Agric. Index; Biol. Abstr.; Chem. Abstr.; Crop Physiol. Abstr.; Curr. Aware. Biol. Sci., CABS; Curr. Cit.; Dairy Sci. Abstr.; EMBASE; Environ. Abstr.; Field Crop Abstr.; Food Sci. Technol. Abstr.; For. Abstr.; Geogr. Abstr. Phys. Geogr.; Geogr. Abstr. Human Geogr.; Grass. Forage Abstr.; Hortic. Abstr.; Irr. Drain. Abstr.; Maize Abstr.; Nematol. Abstr.; Nutr. Abstr. Rev., Ser. B, Live Feeds and Feed.; Life Sci. Collect.; PESTDOC; Pig News Inf.; Plant Breed. Abstr.; Plant Grow. Reg. Abstr.; Postharvest News Inf.; Potato Abstr.; Poult. Abstr.; Protozoolog. Abstr.; Rev. Agric. Entomol.; Rev. Med. Vet. Mycology; Rev. Plant Pathol.; Rice Abstr.; Seed Abstr.; Soils Fert.; Sorghum Mill. Abstr.; Soyabean Abstr.; Stat. Theory Method Abstr. (1959-1963, 1967, 1969-1971, 1976, 1978, 1980-1983); Weed Abstr.

LC S **ISSN** 0041-994X
DD 630 PR
CODEN JAUPA8
Pr Rev.

JOURNAL OF AGRICULTURE OF THE UNIVERSITY OF PUERTO RICO, THE. [J. agric. Univ. P. R.]. **Main/Corp** University of Puerto Rico (Rio Piedras Campus). **Added/Corp** University of Puerto Rico (Rio Piedras Campus). Agricultural Experiment Station. Vol. 18, No. 1/2 (Jan./April 1934)-. Academic Scholarly Publication. English (Spanish). Four times a year (Jan., Apr., July, Oct.). $25.00. University of Puerto Rico Agricultural Experiment Station, Mayaguez Puerto Rico 00708. **Tel** (809)832-4040. **ED** Samuel O. Velez Delgado. available on microfilm and microfiche from University Microfilms International (UMI). Documents available from The Genuine Article, BIOSIS Document Express, CASDDS. ***Continues*** *Journal of the Department of Agriculture of Puerto Rico.*
Ind/Abst AGRICOLA [Full Cov.]; Biocont. News Inf. (19??-19??); Biodeter. Abstr. (1991-); Biol. Abstr.; Chem. Abstr.; Crop Physiol. Abstr.; Curr. Cit.; Field Crop Abstr.; Fish Rev. (Jan. 1989-July 1992); Food Sci. Technol. Abstr.; For. Prod. Abstr. (1991-); For. Abstr.; Grass. Forage Abstr.; Hortic. Abstr.; Irr. Drain. Abstr.; Maize Abstr.; Nematol. Abstr.; Life Sci. Collect.; PESTDOC; Plant Breed. Abstr.; Postharvest News Inf.; Poult. Abstr.; Res. Alert [Select. Cov.]; Rev. Agric. Entomol.; Rev. Med. Vet. Entomol.; Rev. Plant Pathol.; SCISEARCH; Seed Abstr.; Soils Fert.; Sorghum Mill. Abstr.; Soyabean Abstr.; Weed Abstr.; Wildl. Rev. (Jan. 1989-July 1992).

LC S397 .D46a **ISSN** 0021-8618
DD 630/.5 AT
Pr Rev.

JOURNAL OF AGRICULTURE (SOUTH PERTH). (JOURNAL OF AGRICULTURE.). [J. agric.]. **Added/Corp** Western Australia. Dept. of Agriculture. Vol. 13, No. 1 (Mar. 1972)-. Periodical. English. Four times a year. 23.84Aus$. Western Australia Department of Agriculture / South Perth, Information Branch / Baron-Hay Court, South Perth Western Australia 6151 Australia. **Tel** 011 61 9 3683231, FAX 011 61 9 4742018, telex AA 93304. **ED** G.P. Ayling. Index available. **Circ:** 5,000. ***Continues*** *Journal of Agriculture, Western Australia, 1032-3023.*
Desc: Articles relating to agricultural research by the Western Australian Department of Agriculture.
Ind/Abst AGRICOLA [Full Cov.]; Anim. Breed. Abstr.; Dairy Sci. Abstr.; Field Crop Abstr.; Grass. Forage Abstr.; Hortic. Abstr.; Index Vet.; Nutr. Abstr. Rev., Ser. B, Live Feeds and Feed.; Life Sci. Collect.; Plant Breed. Abstr.; Rev. Med. Vet. Mycology; Rev. Plant Pathol.; Soils Fert.; Vet. Bull.; Weed Abstr.

LC RC965.A5 **ISSN** 1059-924X
DD 616.9/803 US
NLM W1; JO534JD

●**JOURNAL OF AGROMEDICINE.** See Industrial Health and Safety.

LC S583 .A7 **ISSN** 1060-3271
DD 630.24 US
CCC
CODEN JAINEE

JOURNAL OF AOAC INTERNATIONAL. See Chemistry and Chemicals-Analytical Chemistry.

LC S1 .J78 **ISSN** 0047-2425
DD 631 US
CCC
NLM W1 JO644BG **CODEN** JEVQAA
Pr Rev.

JOURNAL OF ENVIRONMENTAL QUALITY. See Environmental Issues-Ecology.

LC S544.5.I5 J68
DD 630/.7/15054 II
Pr Rev.

JOURNAL OF EXTENSION SYSTEMS. **Added/Corp** National Dairy Research Institute (India). Vol. 1 (Dec. 1985)-. Periodical. English. Two times a year. $30.00. Journal of Extension Systems, CGS Col Sec 2 47 507 Koliwada, Bombay 400037 India. **Tel** 11 91 22 484355. **(Subscription address:** Prints India, 11 Darya Ganj, New Delhi 110002 India. **Tel** 011 91 11 3268645, FAX 011 91 11 3275542, telex 31-61087 PRIN-IN.) **ED** O.S. Verma.
Ind/Abst Irr. Drain. Abstr.; Rev. Agric. Entomol.; Rural Dev. Abstr.; World Agric. Econ. Rural Sociol. Abstr.

LC S **ISSN** 1051-6786
DD 631 US
Pr Rev.

JOURNAL OF FARMING SYSTEMS RESEARCH-EXTENSION. [J. farming syst. res.-ext.]. **Added/Corp** Association of Farming Systems Research-Extension. **VFOAT** Journal for Farming Systems Research-Extension. Vol. 1, No. 1 (1990)-. Periodical. English. Irregular (2 or 3 per year). $20.00 (students); $125.00 (institutions), $20.00 (individuals) developing countries; $125.00 (institutions), $65.00 (individuals) other. University of Arizona / Office of Arid Land Studies, AFSRE / Association for Farming Systems Research-Extension, 845 North Park Avenue, Tucson AZ 85719-4896. **Tel** (602)621-8582, (602)621-2796, (602)621-1955, FAX (602)621-3816, telex 1561507 ARID UT. **ED** Tim Frankenberger (editor's address: 151 Ellis Street NE, Atlanta, GA 30303; phone: (404)681-2552). **Circ:** 500.
Ind/Abst AGRICOLA [Full Cov.]; Agrofor. Abstr.; Cot. Trop. Fibr. Abstr. Bibliogr.; Field Crop Abstr.; For. Abstr.; Rice Abstr.; Soils Fert.; World Agric. Econ. Rural Sociol. Abstr.

LC S **ISSN** 0794-7194
DD 630 NR
CODEN JFAGEM

JOURNAL OF FOOD & AGRICULTURE. See Food and Food Industry.

LC S **ISSN** 1001-7364
DD 630 CC

JOURNAL OF FRUIT SCIENCE. (1992)-. Periodical. Chinese.
Ind/Abst AgBiotech News Inf.; Hortic. Abstr.; Plant Breed. Abstr.; Plant Genet. Resour. Abstr.; Rev. Plant Pathol.; Seed Abstr.; Vitis Vitic. Enol. Abstr.

LC HD9000.1 .J68 **ISSN** 0897-4438
DD 382 US
CODEN JIFMEI
Pr Rev.

JOURNAL OF INTERNATIONAL FOOD & AGRIBUSINESS MARKETING. See Food and Food Industry.

LC S530 .J68 **ISSN** 1059-9053
DD 570/.5 US
CCC
CODEN JRLEEJ

JOURNAL OF NATURAL RESOURCES AND LIFE SCIENCES EDUCATION. [J. nat. resour. life sci. educ.]. **Added/Corp** American Society of Agronomy. Vol. 21, No. 1 (Spring 1992)-. Academic Scholarly Publication. English. Two times a year. $18.00. American Society of Agronomy, 677 South Segoe Road, Madison WI 53711. **Tel** (608)273-8080, FAX (608)273-2021. Documents available from BIOSIS Document Express, CASDDS. ***Continues*** *Journal of Agronomic Education, 0094-2391.*
Ind/Abst AGRICOLA; Biol. Abstr.; Chem. Abstr.; Curr. Index J. Educ.

LC S589.5 .J68 **ISSN** 0379-5489
DD 630/.24/138805 II
CODEN JNABDS

JOURNAL OF NUCLEAR AGRICULTURE AND BIOLOGY. [J. nucl. agric. biol.]. **Added/Corp** Indian Society for Nuclear Techniques in Agriculture and Biology. Vol. 4, No. 1 (March 1975)-. Academic Scholarly Publication. English. Four times a year. $65.00. Indian Society of Nuclear Technology Agriculture and Biology, Nuclear Research Laboratory, Indian Agriculture Research Institute, New Delhi 110012 India. **Tel** 584454. **(Subscription address:** Prints India, 11 Darya Ganj, New Delhi 110002 India. **Tel** 011 91 11 3268645, FAX 011 91 11 3275542, telex 31-61087 PRIN-IN.) **ED** G. R. Sethi. **Bk Rev. Ad Acc. Circ:** 300 (ctrl). Documents available from BIOSIS Document Express, CASDDS. ***Supersedes*** *Indian Society for Nuclear Techniques in Agriculture and Biology. Newsletter.*
Desc: Includes original research and invited review articles involving the use of nuclear tools in agriculture, biology, and animal sciences.
Ind/Abst AGRICOLA; Biol. Abstr.; Chem. Abstr.; Cot. Trop. Fibr. Abstr. Bibliogr.; Crop Physiol. Abstr.; EMBASE; Energy Res. Abstr. (March 1975-); Field Crop Abstr.; Grass. Forage Abstr.; Hortic. Abstr.; Index Vet.; Irr. Drain. Abstr.; Nematol. Abstr.; Nutr. Abstr. Rev., Ser. B, Live Feeds and Feed.; Nutr. Abstr. Rev., Ser. A, Hum. Exp.; Ornamental Hort. (19??-19??); Life Sci. Collect.; Plant Breed. Abstr.; Postharvest News Inf.; Potato Abstr.; Protozoolog. Abstr.; Rev. Agric. Entomol.; Rev. Med. Vet. Entomol.; Rev. Med. Vet. Mycology; Rev. Plant Pathol.; Rice Abstr.; Seed Abstr.; Soils Fert.; Sorghum Mill. Abstr.; Soyabean Abstr.; Wheat Barley Trit. Abstr.

LC S **ISSN** 0931-1785
DD 630 GW
CCC

JOURNAL OF PHYTOPATHOLOGY (1986). **VFOAT** Phytopathologische Zeitschrift (1986). (1986)-. Periodical. Multiple languages. Twelve times a year. $1268.17. Blackwell Wissenschafts-Verlag, Kurfuerstendamm 57, D-10707 Berlin Germany. **Tel** 011 49 30 32790623, 011 49 30 32790624, FAX 011 49 30 327 90610. **ED** Alfred Bronnimann, Alan Brunk, Rudolf Heitefuss.
Desc: Publishes original scientific articles and short communications on all aspects of phytopathology, and on relevant related subjects.
Ind/Abst Agrofor. Abstr.; Curr. Cit.; Postharvest News Inf.; Rev. Agric. Entomol.; Seed Abstr.

LC SF85 .J67 **ISSN** 0022-409X
DD 636.08423 636.081* US
CODEN JRMGAQ
Pr Rev.

JOURNAL OF RANGE MANAGEMENT. [J. range manage.]. **Added/Corp** Society for Range Management. American Society of Range Management. Vol. 1 (Oct. 1948)-. Academic Scholarly Publication. English. Six times a year. $95.00. Society for Range Management, 1839 York Street, Denver CO 80206. **Tel** (303)355-7070, (303)571-0174. **ED** Gary Frasier. Index available. cum. index. **Bk Rev. Ad Acc. Circ:** 6,800 (ctrl). available on microfilm and microfiche from University Microfilms International (UMI). Documents available from The Genuine Article, BIOSIS Document Express, CASDDS, Documents on Demand.
Desc: Technical articles on range management including range plant physiology, grazing effects, wildlife, watershed and economics.
Ind/Abst AGRICOLA [Full Cov.]; Agrofor. Abstr. (19??-19??); Anim. Breed. Abstr.; AQUAREF; Biocont. News Inf.; Biol. Agric. Index; Biol. Abstr.; Biol. Dig.; Can. Environ.; Chem. Abstr.; Coal Abstr.; Crop Physiol. Abstr.;

Curr. Aware. Biol. Sci., CABS; Curr. Cit.; Curr. Contents Agric. Biol. Environ. Sci.; Ecol. Abstr.; Ecology Abstr.; EMBASE; Environ. Abstr.; Environ. Period. Bibliogr.; Fish Rev.; For. Abstr.; Geogr. Abstr. Phys. Geogr.; Geogr. Abstr. Human Geogr.; GeoRef; Grass. Forage Abstr.; INIS Atomindex [Micro.]; Int. Abstr. Oper. Res. [Select. Cov.]; Irr. Drain. Abstr.; Key Word Index Wildl. Res.; Nematol. Abstr.; Nucl. Sci. Abstr.; Nutr. Abstr. Rev., Ser. B, Live Feeds and Feed.; Life Sci. Collect.; PESTDOC; Plant Breed. Abstr.; Plant Genet. Resour. Abstr.; Plant Grow. Reg. Abstr.; Res. Alert [Full Cov.]; Rev. Agric. Entomol.; Sci. Cit. Index; SCISEARCH; Seed Abstr.; Sel. Water Resour. Abstr.; Soc. Sci. Cit. Index [Select. Cov.]; Soils Fert.; Weed Abstr.; Wildl. Rev.; World Agric. Econ. Rural Sociol. Abstr.

LC S
DD 630 II

JOURNAL OF RESEARCH APAU, THE.
VFOAT J. Res. APAU. **VAT** Journal of Research Andhra Pradesh Agricultural University. Periodical. English. Four times a year.
Ind/Abst Biocont. News Inf. (1991-); Crop Physiol. Abstr.; Field Crop Abstr.; Irr. Drain. Abstr.; Plant Breed. Abstr.; Plant Grow. Reg. Abstr.; Rev. Agric. Entomol.; Rev. Plant Pathol.; Rice Abstr.; Soils Fert.; Sorghum Mill. Abstr.; Wheat Barley Trit. Abstr.

LC S **ISSN** 0258-1728
DD 630 II
CODEN JRAUDB

JOURNAL OF RESEARCH / ASSAM AGRICULTURAL UNIVERSITY. [J. Res. - Assam Agric. Univ.]. (1980)-. Academic Scholarly Publication. English. Two times a year. Documents available from BIOSIS Document Express, CASDDS.
Ind/Abst Biocont. News Inf. (1991-); Biol. Abstr.; Chem. Abstr.; Cot. Trop. Fibr. Abstr. Bibliogr.; Field Crop Abstr.; Food Sci. Technol. Abstr.; Index Vet.; Life Sci. Collect.; Rev. Agric. Entomol.; Rice Abstr.

LC S
DD 630 II

JOURNAL OF RESEARCH (ORISSA UNIVERSITY OF AGRICULTURE AND TECHNOLOGY). (JOURNAL OF RESEARCH.). **Added/Corp** Orissa University of Agriculture and Technology. (19??)-. Periodical. English. Two times a year. Orissa University of Agriculture & Technology, Dean of Research, Bhubaneswar Orissa India. **(Subscription address:** Prints India, 11 Darya Ganj, New Delhi 110002 India. **Tel** 011 91 11 3268645, FAX 011 91 11 3275542, telex 31-61087 PRIN-IN.)

LC S17 .P823 **ISSN** 0048-6019
DD 630.5 II
CODEN JRPUAF

JOURNAL OF RESEARCH, PUNJAB AGRICULTURAL UNIVERSITY. (JOURNAL OF RESEARCH.). [J. Res., Punjab Agr. Univ.]. **Main/Corp** Punjab Agricultural University. **Added/Corp** Punjab Agricultural University. Vol. 1 (June 1964)-. Periodical. English. Four times a year. $20.00. Punjab Agricultural University, Ludhiana India. **(Subscription address:** Prints India, 11 Darya Ganj, New Delhi 110002 India. **Tel** 011 91 11 3268645, FAX 011 91 11 3275542, telex 31-61087 PRIN-IN.) Documents available from BIOSIS Document Express, CASDDS.
Ind/Abst AGRICOLA; Biodeter. Abstr.; Biol. Abstr.; Chem. Abstr.; Cot. Trop. Fibr. Abstr. Bibliogr.; Crop Physiol. Abstr.; Field Crop Abstr.; Food Sci. Technol. Abstr.; Helminthol. Abstr. (1991-); Hortic. Abstr.; Index Vet.; Leis., Rec., Tour. Abstr.; Maize Abstr.; Nematol. Abstr.; Nutr. Abstr. Rev., Ser. B, Live Feeds and Feed.; Ornamental Hort. (1991-); Plant Breed. Abstr.; Plant Grow. Reg. Abstr.; Potato Abstr.; Poult. Abstr.; Protozoolog. Abstr.; Rev. Plant Pathol.; Rice Abstr.; Rural Dev. Abstr.; Soils Fert.; Vitis Vitic. Enol. Abstr.; Wheat Barley Trit. Abstr.

LC S **ISSN** 0971-1724
DD 630 II
UDC 63

JOURNAL OF RESEARCH RANCHI. [J. Res.Ranchi]. (1990)-. Periodical. English. Two times a year. ***Continues*** *BAU Journal of Research, 0971-1201.*
Ind/Abst Index Vet.; Potato Abstr.; Protozoolog. Abstr.; Rev. Plant Pathol.

LC HD1491.A1 J68 **ISSN** 0377-7480
DD 334/.683/05 IS
CODEN JRCOE4

JOURNAL OF RURAL COOPERATION.
See Business and Economics-Cooperatives.

LC HD2095.5 .A25 **ISSN** 1013-0764
DD 630 KO

JOURNAL OF RURAL DEVELOPMENT.
[J. rural dev.]. Nov. 1978-. Periodical. English. Two times a year. W4000 South Korea; $5.00 US. Korea Rural Economics, Institute Hoegi-dong, Dongdaemoon-ku, Seoul 131 Korea. **ED** Kim Young-Jin. **Circ:** 800 (ctrl). Documents available from The Genuine Article.
Ind/Abst AGRICOLA [Full Cov.]; Appl. Soc. Sci. Index Abstr.; Curr. Contents Soc. Behav. Sci.; Dairy Sci. Abstr.; Int. Dev. Abstr.; J. Plan. Lit.; Middle East Abstr. Index; Res. Alert [Full Cov.]; Rice Abstr.; Soc. Sci. Cit. Index [Full Cov.]; World Agric. Econ. Rural Sociol. Abstr.

LC S494.5.S86 J68 **ISSN** 1044-0046
DD 630/.5 US
CODEN JSAGEB
Pr Rev.

JOURNAL OF SUSTAINABLE AGRICULTURE. [J. sustain. agric.]. Vol. 1, No. 1 (1990)-. Periodical. English. Four times a year. $90.00. The Haworth Press Inc., 10 Alice Street, Binghamton NY 13904-1580. **Tel** (607)722-5857, (800)3-HAWORTH, FAX (607)722-1424. **ED** Raymond Poincelot (editor's address: Biology Department, Fairfield University, Fairfield, CT 06430). **Bk Rev. Ad Acc. Acid Free. Circ:** 339. available on microfilm and microfiche from University Microfilms International (UMI). Documents available from The Genuine Article, Haworth Document Delivery Service, Documents on Demand.
Desc: Specifically devoted to the rapidly growing field of sustainable agriculture. Aimed at increasing professional and public awareness and gaining support for necessary changes in our agricultural industry. The goal is to promote the study and application of sustainable agriculture for solutions to the problems of resource depletion and environmental misuse.
Ind/Abst AGRICOLA [Full Cov.]; Biocont. News Inf. (1991-); Biol. Dig.; Curr. Aware. Biol. Sci., CABS; Ecol. Abstr.; Energy Inf. Abstr.; Environ. Abstr.; Environ. Period. Bibliogr.; Food Sci. Technol. Abstr.; Foods Adlibra (1990-); Geogr. Abstr. Phys. Geogr.; Geogr. Abstr. Human Geogr.; Grass. Forage Abstr.; Hortic. Abstr.; Ornamental Hort. (1991-); PAIS Int. Print (1991-); Res. Alert [Select. Cov.]; Rice Abstr.; Soc. Plann. Policy Dev. Abstr.; Soc. Sci. Cit. Index [Select. Cov.]; Soils Fert.; World Agric. Econ. Rural Sociol. Abstr.

LC S **ISSN** 0368-1327
DD 630 TR
SUSPENDED

JOURNAL OF THE AGRICULTURAL SOCIETY OF TRINIDAD & TOBAGO. [J. agric. soc. Trinidad Tobago]. **Main/Corp** Agricultural Society of Trinidad & Tobago. Vol. 1 (1894)-?. Periodical. English. Four times a year. $10.00. Agricultural Society of Trinidad and Tobago, PO Box 256, Port of Spain Trinidad.
Ind/Abst Anim. Breed. Abstr.; Biocont. News Inf.; Dairy Sci. Abstr.; Field Crop Abstr.; Grass. Forage Abstr.; Hortic. Abstr.; Leis., Rec., Tour. Abstr.; Life Sci. Collect.; Plant Breed. Abstr.; Protozoolog. Abstr.; Rev. Med. Vet. Mycology; Rev. Plant Pathol.; Rural Dev. Abstr.; Soils Fert.; World Agric. Econ. Rural Sociol. Abstr.

LC S **ISSN** 0003-116X
DD 630 US

JOURNAL OF THE AMERICAN SOCIETY OF FARM MANAGERS AND RURAL APPRAISERS. [J. Am. Soc. Farm Manage. Rural Appraisers]. **Main/Corp** American Society of Farm Managers and Rural Appraisers. **Added/Corp** American Society of Farm Managers and Rural Appraisers. Journal. **VFOAT** Journal of the ASFMRA. Vol. 1 (1937)-. Trade Publication. English. One time a year (June). $24.00. American Society of Farm Managers & Rural Appraisers, 950 South Cherry Street, Suite 508, Denver CO 80222. **Tel** (303)758-3513, FAX (303)758-0190. **ED** Deborah Long Hunt. cum. index. **Circ:** 4,700.
Desc: For persons who manage and appraise rural properties and those in the agribusiness complex who need insight into modern farm and ranch management, rural property valuations, real estate investment, agricultural finance and related areas.
Ind/Abst AGRICOLA.

LC S **ISSN** 0018-344X
DD 630 JA
CODEN JFAGAI

JOURNAL OF THE FACULTY OF AGRICULTURE. HOKKAIDO UNIVERSITY. (JOURNAL OF THE FACULTY OF AGRICULTURE.). [J. Fac. Agric., Hokkaido Univ.]. **Main/Corp** Sapporo, Japan. Hokkaido University. Faculty of Agriculture. (1952)-. Academic Scholarly Publication. English. Dean of the Faculty, Faculty of Agriculture, Hokkaido University, Sapporo Japan. Documents available from BIOSIS Document Express, CASDDS. ***Continues*** *Hokkaido Imperial University. College of Agriculture. Journal.*
Ind/Abst Abstr. Bull. Inst. Pap. Sci. Tech.; Biol. Abstr.; Chem. Abstr. (-1982); Field Crop Abstr.; Fish Rev. (Jan. 1989-July 1992); Grass. Forage Abstr.; Maize Abstr.; Plant Breed. Abstr.; Rev. Agric. Entomol.; Rev. Med. Vet. Mycology; Rev. Plant Pathol.; Rice Abstr.; Seed Abstr.; Soils Fert.; Wildl. Rev. (Jan. 1989-July 1992).

LC S **ISSN** 0023-6152
DD 630 JA
CODEN JFAKAU

JOURNAL OF THE FACULTY OF AGRICULTURE, KYUSHU UNIVERSITY.
[J. Fac. Agric., Kyushu Univ.]. **VFOAT** Kyushu Daigaku Nogokubu Kiyo. (194?)-. English. Irregular. Kyushu University / Department of Agriculture, Department of Agriculture, 33 Fukuoka 812 Japan. Documents available from The Genuine Article, BIOSIS Document Express, CASDDS. ***Continues*** *Journal of the Department of Agriculture, Kyushu Imperial University, 0368-1831.*
Ind/Abst Biol. Abstr.; Chem. Abstr.; Crop Physiol. Abstr.; Curr. Aware. Biol. Sci., CABS; Curr. Cit.; Curr. Contents Agric. Biol. Environ. Sci.; Field Crop Abstr.; Fish Rev. (Jan. 1989-July 1992); Nematol. Abstr.; Ornamental Hort. (1991-); PESTDOC; Plant Breed. Abstr.; Res. Alert [Full Cov.]; Rev. Agric. Entomol.; Rev. Med. Vet. Entomol.; Rev. Plant Pathol.; Rice Abstr.; Sci. Cit. Index; SCISEARCH; Seed Abstr.; Soyabean Abstr.; Wildl. Rev. (Jan. 1989-July 1992).

LC S539.5 **ISSN** 0082-5360
DD 630.72 JA
CODEN JFALAX

JOURNAL OF THE FACULTY OF AGRICULTURE, TOTTORI UNIVERSITY.
[J. Fac. Agric., Tottori Univ.]. **Main/Corp** Tottori Daigaku. Nogakubu. **VFOAT** Tottori Daigaku Nogakubu Kiyo. Vol. 1 (Feb 1951)-. English. One time a year. Tottori Daigaku Nogakubu, (Faculty of Agriculture Tottori University), Minami 4-101 Koyamacho, Tottorishi Tottoriken 680 Japan. Documents available from BIOSIS Document Express, CASDDS.
Ind/Abst AGRICOLA; Anim. Breed. Abstr.; Biol. Abstr.; Chem. Abstr.; Dairy Sci. Abstr.; For. Prod. Abstr. (1991-); Grass. Forage Abstr.; Index Vet.; Irr. Drain. Abstr.; Nutr. Abstr. Rev., Ser. B, Live Feeds and Feed.; Rice Abstr.; Soils Fert.; Vet. Bull.

LC S **ISSN** 0256-6702
DD 630 SA
CODEN JGSAEX
Pr Rev. **TITLE CHANGE**

JOURNAL OF THE GRASSLAND SOCIETY OF SOUTHERN AFRICA, THE.
[J. Grassl. Soc. South. Afr.]. **VFOAT** Tydskrif Van die Weidingsvereniging Van Suidelike Afrika. Vol. 1, No. 1 (1984)-(1993). Periodical. English (Afrikaans). Grassland Society of Southern Africa, PO Box 10327, Scottsville 3209 South Africa. **Tel** FAX 0331 63497, telex 643719. **ED** Maureen M Wolfson and Greg Stuart Hill. Index available. **Circ:** 800 (ctrl). Documents available from BIOSIS Document Express. ***Continues*** *Proceedings / Grassland Society of Southern African.* ***Continued by*** *African Journal of Range and Forage Science.*
Ind/Abst Agrofor. Abstr. (19??-19??); Biol. Abstr.; Crop Physiol. Abstr.; For. Abstr.; Grass. Forage Abstr.; Irr. Drain. Abstr.; Nutr. Abstr. Rev., Ser. B, Live Feeds and Feed.; Plant Breed. Abstr.; Plant Genet. Resour. Abstr.; Plant Grow. Reg. Abstr.; Soils Fert.

LC S
DD 630 NP

JOURNAL OF THE INSTITUTE OF AGRICULTURE AND ANIMAL SCIENCE.
Added/Corp Institute of Agriculture and Animal Science (Nepal). (198?)-. Periodical. English. Institute of Agriculture and Animal Science, PO Box 984 GPO, Kathmandu Nepal.
Ind/Abst Field Crop Abstr.; Fish Rev. (Jan. 1989-July 1992); For. Abstr.; Hortic. Abstr.; Maize Abstr.; Plant Grow. Reg. Abstr.; Poult. Abstr.; Rev. Agric. Entomol.; Rev. Plant Pathol.; Seed Abstr.; Soils Fert.; Soyabean Abstr.; Weed Abstr.; Wheat Barley Trit. Abstr.; Wildl. Rev. (Jan. 1989-July 1992).

LC S671 .J63 **ISSN** 0257-3431
DD 631 II

JOURNAL OF THE INSTITUTION OF ENGINEERS (INDIA). AGRICULTURAL ENGINEERING DIVISION. [J. Inst. Eng., India, Agric. eng. div.]. **Added/Corp** Institution of Engineers (India). Agricultural Engineering Division. **VFOAT** Agricultural Engineering Division; IE (I) Journal-AG. (1982)-. Periodical. English. Two times a year. $5.00. Institution of Engineers India, 8 Gokhale Road, Calcutta 700020 India. **Tel** 011 91 33 288311, 011 91 33 288334, FAX 011 91 33 288345, telex 21 7885 IEIC IN. ***Continues in part*** *Journal of the Institution of Engineers (India), 0368-2498.*
Ind/Abst Agric. Eng. Abstr.; Maize Abstr.; Postharvest News Inf.; Rice Abstr.; Seed Abstr.

LC S17 **ISSN** 0547-3616
DD 630/.095493 CE
CODEN NASJAO

JOURNAL OF THE NATIONAL AGRICULTURAL SOCIETY OF CEYLON. **Main/Corp** National Agricultural Society of Ceylon. Vol. 1 (Mar. 1964)-. English. One time a year. $10.00. University of Sri Lanka Faculty of Agriculture, Peradeneya Sri Lanka. **Tel** (08)88041. **ED** H P M Gunasena. **Bk Rev. Ad Acc. Circ:** 200 (ctrl). Documents available from CASDDS.
Desc: Includes articles on tropical agriculture, horticulture and livestock production; also education and agricultural research management.
Ind/Abst Chem. Abstr. (1964-1980); Dairy Sci. Abstr.; Field Crop Abstr.; Grass. Forage Abstr.; Hortic. Abstr.; Leis., Rec., Tour. Abstr.; Plant Breed. Abstr.; Rev. Med. Vet. Mycology; Rev. Plant Pathol.; Rural Dev. Abstr.; World Agric. Econ. Rural Sociol. Abstr.

LC S3 .R8 **ISSN** 0080-4134
DD 630 UK
CODEN JRAGAY

JOURNAL OF THE ROYAL AGRICULTURAL SOCIETY OF ENGLAND. [J. R. Agric. Soc. Engl.]. **Main/Corp** Royal Agricultural Society of England. Vol. 1 (1840)-.

Agriculture

English. One time a year (December). $60.00. Royal Agricultural Society of England, Stoneleigh Kenilworth, Warwickshire CV8 2LZ United Kingdom. **Tel** 011 44 1203 696577, FAX 011 44 1203 696900, telex 31697. cum. index. **Ad Acc**. **Circ**: 16,000. available on microfilm and microfiche from University Microfilms International (UMI). Documents available from BIOSIS Document Express, CASDDS.
Desc: Includes articles dealing with recent scientific advances in agriculture, developments in farm and estate management and changes in rural land use and management. Also covers aspects of farming in other countries and some material of general historic interest.
Ind/Abst AGRICOLA; Agric. Eng. Abstr. (1991-); Anim. Breed. Abstr.; Biol. Abstr.; Chem. Abstr.; Curr. Aware. Biol. Sci., CABS; Curr. Cit.; Dairy Sci. Abstr.; Food Sci. Technol. Abstr.; Geogr. Abstr. Human Geogr.; Index Vet.; Maize Abstr.; Nutr. Abstr. Rev., Ser. B, Live Feeds and Feed.; Pig News Inf.; Poult. Abstr.; Rev. Agric. Entomol.; Rev. Plant Pathol.; Soils Fert.; Wheat Barley Trit. Abstr.

LC S
DD 630 ISSN 0022-5142
UK
CCC
NLM W1 JO954 CODEN JSFAAE
Pr Rev.

JOURNAL OF THE SCIENCE OF FOOD AND AGRICULTURE. See Food and Food Industry.

LC S
DD 630 ISSN 1055-1387
US
Pr Rev.

JOURNAL OF TREE FRUIT PRODUCTION. See Agriculture-Crop Production and Soils.

LC Z5076 .C75a S493
DD 016.63/05 UK

JOURNAL SUBSCRIPTION PRICE LIST.
Added/Corp Commonwealth Agricultural Bureaux. (19??)-. English. CAB International Centre, Wallingford, Oxfordshire OX10 8DE United Kingdom. **Tel** 011 44 1491 832111, FAX 011 44 1491 833508, telex 847964 COMAGG G. **Continues** Publications List (Commonwealth Agricultural Bureaux).

LC S
DD 630 CC

JUA NAN NUNG YEH TA HSUEH HSUEH PAO. Added/Corp Hua Nan Nung Yeh Ta Hsueh.
Hsueh Pao Pien Wei Hui. **VFOAT** Journal of South China Agricultural University. Vol. 5, No. 3 (Sept. 1984)-. Periodical. Chinese (summaries and/or abstracts in English). Four times a year. **Continues** Hua-Nan Nung Hsueh Yuan Hsueh Pao.
Ind/Abst AGRICOLA; Biocont. News Inf.; Crop Physiol. Abstr.; Field Crop Abstr.; For. Abstr.; Hortic. Abstr.; Index Vet.; Maize Abstr.; Nematol. Abstr.; Ornamental Hort. (1991-); Pig News Inf.; Plant Breed. Abstr.; Plant Grow. Reg. Abstr.; Rev. Agric. Entomol.; Rev. Plant Pathol.; Seed Abstr.; Soils Fert.; Wheat Barley Trit. Abstr.

LC S3 .M35a ISSN 0128-0686
MY
CODEN MRJOE4

JURNAL PENYELIDIKAN MARDI.
Added/Corp Institut Penyelidikan dan Kemajuan Pertanian Malaysia. **VFOAT** MARDI Research Journal. **VAT** Malaysian Agricultural Research and Development Institute Research Journal. Vol. 16, No. 1 (June 1988)-. Periodical. English (Malay). Two times a year (June & Dec.). $50.00. Malaysian Agriculture Research Development Institute, PO Box 12301, 50774 Kuala Lumpur Malaysia. **Tel** 011 60 3 9486601, telex 37115. Documents available from BIOSIS Document Express. **Continues** Penyelidikan dan Kemajuan Pertanian Malaysia. MARDI Buletin Penyelidikan, 0126-5709.
Ind/Abst Biol. Abstr. (1991-); Crop Physiol. Abstr.; Irr. Drain. Abstr.; Plant Breed. Abstr.; Plant Grow. Reg. Abstr.; Postharvest News Inf.

LC S
DD 630 II

JUTE DEVELOPMENT JOURNAL. Vol. 1,
No. 1 (Jan./March 1981)-. Periodical. English. Four times a year. Government of India / Directorate of Jute Development, Ministry of Agriculture, Calcutta India. **Continues** Jute Bulletin.
Ind/Abst Cot. Trop. Fibr. Abstr. Bibliogr.; Field Crop Abstr.; Hortic. Abstr.; Plant Breed. Abstr.; Potato Abstr.; Rev. Agric. Entomol.; Rev. Plant Pathol.; Rice Abstr.; Seed Abstr.; Soils Fert.; Wheat Barley Trit. Abstr.; World Agric. Econ. Rural Sociol. Abstr.

LC SB183 ISSN 0125-0485
DD 633.05 TH

KAEN KASET. [Kaen Kaset]. (1973)-. Periodical.
Thai. Six times a year.
Ind/Abst Agrofor. Abstr.; Anim. Breed. Abstr.; Biocont. News Inf.; Crop Physiol. Abstr.; Field Crop Abstr.; For. Abstr.; Index Vet.; Irr. Drain. Abstr.; Nutr. Abstr. Rev., Ser. B, Live Feeds and Feed. (1991-); Plant Grow. Reg. Abstr.; Postharvest News Inf.; Poult. Abstr.; Rev. Agric. Entomol.; Rev. Plant Pathol.; Soils Fert.

LC QD415.A1 K35 ISSN 0453-073X
DD 574 JA
NLM W1 KA367E CODEN KASEAA

KAGAKU TO SEIBUTSU. See Biology-Biological Chemistry.

LC S
DD 630 ISSN 0368-5128
JA
CODEN KDNGAC

KAGAWA DAIGAKU NOGAKUBU GAKUJUTSU HOKOKU. [Kagawa Daigaku
Nogakubu gakujutsu hokoku]. **Added/Corp** Kagawa Daigaku. Nogakubu. **VFOAT** Technical Bulletin of Faculty of Agriculture, Kagawa University. (1956)-. Bulletin. Japanese (summaries and/or abstracts in English). One time a year. Kagawa Daigaku Nogakubu, (Faculty of Agriculture Kagawa University), Mikicho Kidagun Kagawaken 761-07, Japan. Documents available from BIOSIS Document Express, CASDDS. **Continues** Kagawa-Kenritsu Noka Daigaku Gakujutsu Hokoku.
Ind/Abst Biol. Abstr.; Chem. Abstr.; Plant Breed. Abstr.

LC S17 ISSN 0453-0764
DD 630 JA
CODEN KDNKAO

KAGAWA DAIGAKU NOGAKUBU KIYO.
[Kagawa Daigaku Nogakubu kiyo]. **Main/Corp** Kagawa Daigaku. Nogakubu. **VFOAT** Memoirs of Faculty of Agriculture, Kagawa University; Memoirs of Kagawa Agricultural College. (March 1955)-. Academic Scholarly Publication. Japanese. Price varies per volume. Kagawa University, Faculty of Agriculture, Mikityo Kagawa-ken Japan. Documents available from BIOSIS Document Express, CASDDS.
Ind/Abst AGRICOLA; Biol. Abstr.; Chem. Abstr. (1957-1984); For. Abstr.; Plant Grow. Reg. Abstr.; Soils Fert.

LC S
DD 630 ISSN 0453-0845
JA
CODEN KADNAU

KAGOSHIMA DAIGAKU NOGAKUBU GAKUJUTSU HOKOKU. (KAGOSHIMA
DAIGAKU NOGAKUBU GAKUJUTSU HOKOKU. BULLETIN OF THE FACULTY OF AGRICULTURE, KAGOSHIMA UNIVERSITY.). **Added/Corp** Kagoshima Daigaku. Nogakubu. **VFOAT** Bulletin of the Faculty of Agriculture, Kagoshima University. No. 1 (1952)-. Bulletin. Japanese (summaries and/or abstracts in English). Kagoshima University Faculty of Agriculture, 21-24 Koorimoto 1 chome, Kagoshimashi Kagoshimaken 890 Japan. Documents available from CASDDS. **Continues** Kagoshima Koto Norin Gakko Gakujutsu Hokoku.
Ind/Abst AGRICOLA; Biodeter. Abstr.; Chem. Abstr.; For. Abstr.; For. Prod. Abstr.; Hortic. Abstr.; Index Vet.; Nutr. Abstr. Rev., Ser. B, Live Feeds and Feed.; Nutr. Abstr. Rev., Ser. A, Hum. Exp.; Ornamental Hort. (1991-); Poult. Abstr.; Rev. Plant Pathol.; Rice Abstr.; SEA Abstr.; Small Anim. Abstr. Bibliogr.; Soyabean Abstr.; Vet. Bull.

LC SB267 ISSN 0911-4785
DD 633.72 JA

KAGOSHIMA-KEN CHAGYO SHIKENJO KENKYU HOKOKU. [Kagoshima-ken Chagyo
Shikenjo kenkyu hokoku]. **VFOAT** Bulletin of the Kagoshima Tea Experiment Station. (1985)-. Bulletin. Multiple languages. One time a year. Kagoshimaken Chagyo Shikenjo, (Kagoshima Prefecture Tea Experiment Station), 3964 Nagasato Chirancho, Kawanabegun Kagoshimaken 897-03, Japan. Documents available from CASDDS.
Ind/Abst Chem. Abstr.

LC SF521 ISSN 0388-8215
DD 638.1 JA
CODEN KNHODB

KAGOSHIMA-KEN NOGYO SHIKENJO KENKYU HOKOKU. [Kagoshima-ken Nogyo
Shikenjo kenkyu hokoku]. **Main/Corp** Kagoshima-Ken Nogyo Shikenjo. **VFOAT** Bulletin of the Kagoshima Agricultural Experiment Station. No. 1 (March 1973)-. Academic Scholarly Publication. Japanese. Kagoshimaken Nogyo Shikenjo, (Kagoshima Agricultural Experiment Station), 5500 Kamifukumotocho, Kagoshimashi Kagoshimaken 891-01, Japan. Documents available from CASDDS.
Ind/Abst AGRICOLA; Chem. Abstr. (1973-1983).

LC S
DD 630 ISSN 0372-7785
JA

KAIHO. Main/Corp Yamagata Norin Gakkai.
Added/Corp Yamagata Norin Gakkai. Journal of the Yamagata Agriculture and Forestry Society. **VFOAT** Journal of the Yamagata Agriculture and Forestry Society. No. 1 (1951)-. Japanese (summaries and/or abstracts in English; table of contents in English). One time a year.
Ind/Abst Postharvest News Inf.; Rev. Plant Pathol.; Soils Fert.

LC S
DD 630 ISSN 0388-8231
JA
CODEN KNSGB6

KANAGAWA-KEN NOGYO SOGO KENKYUJO KENKYU HOKOKU.
[Kanagawa-ken Nogyo Sogo Kenkyujo kenkyu hokoku]. **VFOAT** Bulletin of the Agricultural Research Institute of Kanagawa Prefecture. (1962)-. Academic Scholarly Publication. Japanese. Irregular. Agricultural Research Institute of Kanagawa, Prefecture Teradanawa Hiratsuka-shi, Kanagawa-ken Japan. Documents available from CASDDS.
Ind/Abst Agric. Eng. Abstr.; Chem. Abstr.; Field Crop Abstr.; Hortic. Abstr.; Plant Breed. Abstr.; Potato Abstr.; Rev. Plant Pathol.; Rice Abstr.; Soils Fert.; World Agric. Econ. Rural Sociol. Abstr.

LC SF541 .K36a
DD 638.2 JA

KANAGAWA-KEN SANGYO SENTA SHIKEN KENKYU KOKOKU. Main/Corp
Kanagawa-Ken Sangyo Senta. Vol. 1, Issue 47 (1972)-. Japanese. Kanagawa-Ken Sangyo Senta, 2010 Nakashinden, Ebina Japan. **Supersedes** Kanagawa-Ken Sangyo Senta. Shiken Chosa Seiseki Gaiyo.

LC S63 .S72a
DD 338.1/09781 US

KANSAS AGRICULTURE. Main/Corp Kansas
State Board of Agriculture. **VFOAT** Annual Report of Kansas State Board of Agriculture. (1988)-. English. Kansas State Board of Agriculture, 109 SW 9th Street, Topeka KS 66612-1280.

LC S
DD 630 ISSN 0022-8583
US

KANSAS FARMER. [Kans. farmer]. (19??)-.
Periodical. English. Fifteen times a year. $19.95 Kansas; $30.00 US; $35.00 Canada and Mexico; $45.00 other. Farm Progress Publishing, 191 South Gary Avenue, Carol Stream IL 60188-2089. **Tel** (708)462-2890 or 2891. **(Subscription address:** CDS / SIFD Agency Control, 1901 Bell Avenue, Des Moines IA 50315. **Tel** (515)246-6812.)

LC S
GW

KARTOFFELFORSCHUNG AKTUELL.
(19??)-. German. Institut fuer Kartoffelforschung, Akademie der Landwirtschaftswissenschaften der Deutschen Demokratischen Republik, 2551 Gross Lusewitz 2551 Germany.
Ind/Abst Field Crop Abstr.; Grass. Forage Abstr.; Postharvest News Inf.

LC S
DD 630 US

KCSA NEWSLETTER. Added/Corp Kerr Center
for Sustainable Agriculture. **VAT** Kerr Center for Sustainable Agriculture Newsletter. Vol. 17, No. 1 (Jan. 1991)-. Newsletter. English. Six times a year. Free on request. Kerr Center for Sustainable Agriculture, PO Box 588, Poteau OK 74953. **Tel** (918)647-9123. **ED** Heidi Carter. **Circ**: 1,500. **Continues** Newsletter (Kerr Center for Sustainable Agriculture).

LC S
DD 630 ISSN 0388-3116
JA
CODEN HCHOD3

KENKYU HOKOKU. [Hyogo Kenritsu Chikusan
Shikenjo kenkyu hokoku]. **VFOAT** Bulletin of Hyogo Prefectural Experiment Station of Animal Husbandry. Academic Scholarly Publication. Japanese. One time a year. Documents available from CASDDS.
Ind/Abst Chem. Abstr. (1969-1980).

LC SF521 ISSN 0495-7318
DD 638.1 JA
CODEN TNSKAE

KENKYU HOKOKU TOHOKU NOGYO SHIKENJO. (KENKYU HOKOKU.). [Kenkyu hokoku
Tohoku Nogyo Shikenjo]. **Main/Corp** Tohoku Nogyo Shikenjo, Morioka, Japan. **Added/Corp** Thoku Nogyo Shikenjo, Morioka, Japan. Bulletin. **VFOAT** Bulletin of the Tohoku National Agricultural Experiment Station. No. 1 (Apr. 1950)-. Academic Scholarly Publication. Japanese (summaries and/or abstracts in English; table of contents in English). Two times a year. Norin Suisansho Tohoku Nogyo Shikenjo, (Tohoku National Agricultural Experiment Station Ministry of Agriculture Forestry & Fisheries), 4 Akahira Shimokuriyagawa, Moriokashi Iwateken 020-01, Japan. Documents available from CASDDS.
Ind/Abst AGRICOLA; Chem. Abstr. (1950-1986); EMBASE; GeoRef; Plant Breed. Abstr.; Rev. Plant Pathol.; Rice Abstr.; Soyabean Abstr.; World Agric. Econ. Rural Sociol. Abstr.

LC HD1401 ISSN 8750-9792
DD 338 US

KENTUCKY AGRI-NEWS. [Ky. agri-news].
English. Twenty-four times a year. Kentucky Crop & Livestock Reporting Service, PO Box 1120, 645 Post Office Building, Louisville KY 40201. **Continues** Agri-News (Louisville, KY.), 0744-1878.

LC S
DD 630 US

KENTUCKY BEEKEEPERS' QUARTERLY. Vol. 1 (19??)-. Periodical. English.
Four times a year. Kentucky Department of Agriculture, 500 Mero Street, 7th Floor, Frankfort KY 40601. **Tel** (502)564-4696, FAX (502)564-6527.

LC S ISSN 0023-0219
DD 630 US
KENTUCKY FARMER, THE. (19??)-. Periodical. English. Twelve times a year. $12.00. Rural Press USA, 7701 Six Forks Road, Suite 132, Raleigh NC 27615. **Tel** (800)934-2472, (919)676-3276, FAX (919)676-9803. **ED** Wayne Harr (editor's telephone: (615)831-9673). **Ad Acc. Circ:** 20,700 (ctrl).
Desc: General farm magazine serving Kentucky agriculture.

LC S
DD 630 KE
KENYA AGRICULTURAL ABSTRACTS. CURRENT SERIES. Added/Corp Kenya Agricultural Documentation Centre. **VFOAT** Current Series. No. 1 (1979)-. English.

LC S ISSN 0023-1088
DD 630 II
KHETI. Added/Corp Indian Council of Agricultural Research. (1948)-. Periodical. Hindi. Twelve times a year. Rs84.00. Indian Council of Agricultural Research, Mgr Krishi Anusandham Bhavan, New Delhi 110 012 India. **Tel** 011 91 11 5713657, telex 031-62249 ICAR IN.

LC S13 .S4315 ISSN 0869-1479
BW
KHOZIAIN. Added/Corp Soiuz Agrarnikov BSSR. Gosudarstvennyi Komitet Belorusskoi SSR po Selskomu Khoziaistvu I Prodovolstviiu. Byelorussian S.S.R. Ministerstvo Slskogo Khoziaistva I Prodovolstviia. Soiuz Agrarnikov (Byelorussian S.S.R.). (1991)-. Periodical. Russian. Twelve times a year. ***Continues*** *Selskoe Khoziaistvo Belorussii, 0131-6311.*

LC S13 .S4344 ISSN 0868-7188
RU
KHOZIAIN. Added/Corp Russian S.F.S.R. Ministerstvo Selskogo Khoziaistva. Russian S.F.S.R. Ministerstvo Selskogo Khoziaistva i Prodovolstviia. (1990)-. Periodical. Russian. Six times a year. $79.95. **(Subscription address:** East View Publications Inc., 3020 Harbor Lane North, Suite 110, Minneapolis MN 55447. **Tel** (800)477-1005, (612)550-0961, FAX (612)559-2931.) ***Continues*** *Agropromyshlennyi Kompleks Rossii, 0235-2613.*

LC S338.K4 K54
DD 338.1/09676/2 KE
KILIMO NEWS : NEWSLETTER OF THE MINISTRY OF AGRICULTURE. Added/Corp Kenya. Ministry of Agriculture. Agricultural Information Centre (Kenya). (Apr. 1979)-. Newsletter. English. Four times a year. Sh30.00. Agricultural Information Centre, PO Box 14733, Nairobi Kenya. **ED** James Wahome. **Ad Acc. Circ:** 8,000. available on diskette.
Desc: Covers technological developments that can be used to increase crop production in Kenya.

LC S ISSN 0453-8889
DD 630 JA
CODEN KDNOA2
KINKI DAIGAKU NOGAKUBU KIYO. [Kinki Daigaku Nogakubu kiyo]. **Added/Corp** Kinki Daigaku. Nogakubu. **VFOAT** Memoirs of the Faculty of Agriculture of Kinki University. (1960)-. Japanese (English). Kinki Daigaku Nogakubu, (Faculty of Agriculture Kinki University), 4-1 Kowakae 3 Chome, Higashiosakashi Osakafu 577, Japan. Documents available from CASDDS.
Ind/Abst Chem. Abstr.; Crop Physiol. Abstr.

LC S
DD 630 JA
KINKI NORIN SUISAN TOKEI. Added/Corp Japan. Kinki Noseikyoku. (19??)-. Periodical. Japanese. Kinki Noseikyoku, Nishi Doindori Shimochojamachi Sagaru Kamikyo-ku, Kyoto Japan.

LC HD1751 .K56 ISSN 0023-1746
DD 338.1/0973 US
KIPLINGER AGRICULTURE LETTER, THE. [Kiplinger agric. lett.]. **Added/Corp** Kiplinger Washington Editors, Inc. Vol. 57, No. 3 (Jan. 31, 1986)-. Periodical. English. Twenty-six times a year. $54.00. Kiplinger Washington Editors, 1729 H Street Northwest, Washington DC 20006. **Tel** (202)887-6400, (800)544-0155, FAX (202)331-1206. **(Subscription address:** Kiplinger Washington Editors, 3401 East West Highway, c/o Rick Topolski, Editors Park MD 20782. **Tel** (800)544-0155, (301)853-6600.) **ED** M. Bristow. **Circ:** 18,000. ***Continues*** *Kiplinger Agricultural Letter, 0023-1746.*
Desc: News and summary forecasts for agriculturists or people who deal in the business of agriculture.

LC SB599 ISSN 0368-623X
DD 632 JA
CODEN KNBKAY
KITA NIHON BYOGAICHU KENKYUKAIHO. VFOAT Annual Report of the Society of Plant Protection of North Japan; Kita Nihon Byogaichu Kenkyukai Nenpo. (1950)-. Academic Scholarly Publication. Japanese. One time a year. ¥3000.00. Kita Nihon Byogaichu Kenkyukai, c/o Tohoku National Agricultural Experiment Station, 3 Shimofurumichi Yotsuya, Omagari-shi Akita-ken 014-01 Japan. **ED** H Miura. Index available. cum. index. **Ad Acc.** Documents available from CASDDS.
Ind/Abst Chem. Abstr.

LC SF521 ISSN 0452-2370
DD 638.1 JA
CODEN KNGKAP
KOBE DAIGAKU NOGAKU-BU KENKYU HOKOKU. SCIENCE REPORTS OF FACULTY OF AGRICULTURE, KOBE UNIVERSITY. Main/Corp Kobe Daigaku. Nogaku-bu. **VFOAT** Science Reports of Faculty of Agriculture, Kobe University. Vol. 9 (1971)-. Periodical. Japanese (English; table of contents in English). Two times a year. Kobe Daigaku Nogakubu, (Faculty of Agriculture Kobe University), 1 Rokkodaimachi Nadaku, Kobeshi Hyogoken 657, Japan. **Tel** FAX 011 81 78 8718450. Documents available from BIOSIS Document Express, CASDDS. ***Continues*** *Hyogo Noka Daigaku, Sasayama, Japan. Kenkyu Hokoku.*
Ind/Abst AGRICOLA; Biol. Abstr.; Chem. Abstr.; Food Sci. Technol. Abstr.; Helminthol. Abstr. (1991-); Nutr. Abstr. Rev., Ser. B, Live Feeds and Feed.; Pig News Inf.; Plant Breed. Abstr.; World Agric. Econ. Rural Sociol. Abstr.

LC S ISSN 0389-0473
DD 630 JA
CODEN KDGHBF
KOCHI DAIGAKU GAKUJUTSU KENKYU HOKOKU. NOGAKU. [Kochi Daigaku gakujutsu kenkyu hokoku, Nogaku]. **VFOAT** Research Reports of the Kochi University; Nogaku. (1970)-. Academic Scholarly Publication. Japanese. One time a year. Kochi Daigaku, (Kochi University), 5-1 Akebonocho 2 Chome, Kochishi Kochiken 780, Japan. Documents available from CASDDS. ***Continues*** *Kochi Daigaku Gakujutsu Kenkyu Hokoku. 2, Shizen Kagaku.*
Ind/Abst AGRICOLA; Chem. Abstr.; Crop Physiol. Abstr.; GeoRef; Hortic. Abstr.; Ornamental Hort. (1991-); Plant Grow. Reg. Abstr.; Rev. Plant Pathol.; Rice Abstr.; Soils Fert.

LC S ISSN 0428-4372
DD 630 FI
KOETUSSELOSTUS - VAKOLA. (KOETUSSELOSTUS.). [Koetusselos. - Vakola]. **Added/Corp** Valtion Maatalouskoneiden Tutkimuslaitos. Valtion Maatalousteknologian Tutkimuslaitos. **VFOAT** Test Report. (1949)-. Periodical. Finnish (summaries and/or abstracts in English).
Ind/Abst Agric. Eng. Abstr.; For. Prod. Abstr. (1991-).

LC S583 ISSN 0023-334X
DD 631 JA
UDC 632.95
CODEN KONODE
KONGETSU NO NOYAKU. See Chemistry and Chemicals.

LC S328 .K67
DD 630.096 SA
KORTBEGRIP VAN LANDBOUSTATISTIEK. See Agriculture-Abstracting, Bibliographies and Statistics.

LC S
DD 630 II
KRISHAK SAMACHAR. Added/Corp Bharat Krishak Samaj. (1956)-. Periodical. English (Hindi). Twelve times a year. Rs10.00. Bharat Krishak Samaj, Farmer's Forum India, A-1 Nizamuddin West, New Delhi 110013 India. **Tel** 011 91 11 619508. **ED** K. Prabhakar Reddy. **Bk Rev. Ad Acc. Circ:** 12,000 English, 30,000 Hindi. available with charts; available with illustrations.

LC S ISSN 0023-4850
DD 630 CI
CODEN KRMIA9
KRMIVA. [Krmiva]. **Added/Corp** Mjesecnik za Pitanja Ishrane Stoke i Proizvodnje Stocne Hrane. Casopis Poslovnog Udruzenja Proizvodaca Krmnih Smjesa. Vol. 1 (Jan. 1959)-. Academic Scholarly Publication. Serbo-Croatian (Roman). Twelve times a year. Feed Manufacturers Association, Gunduliceva 45, 41000 Zagreb Croatia. **ED** Hrvoje Zlatic. **Bk Rev. Ad Acc. Circ:** 1,000. Documents available from CASDDS.
Ind/Abst AGRICOLA; Biodeter. Abstr. (1991-); Chem. Abstr.; Dairy Sci. Abstr.; Field Crop Abstr.; Grass. Forage Abstr.; Index Vet.; Maize Abstr.; Nutr. Abstr. Rev., Ser. B, Live Feeds and Feed.; Pig News Inf.; Postharvest News Inf.; Poult. Abstr.; Protozoolog. Abstr.; Rev. Med. Vet. Mycology; Seed Abstr.; Soyabean Abstr.; Wheat Barley Trit. Abstr.

LC S
DD 630 GW
KTBL-ARBEITSPAPIER. Added/Corp Kuratorium fuer Technik und Bauwesen in der Landwirtschaft. **VFOAT** K.T.B.L.-Arbeitspapier. **VAT** Kuratorium fuer Technik und Bauwesen in der Landwirtschaft Arbeitspapier. (19??)-. Monographic series. German. Irregular. Price varies per volume. Kuratorium fuer Technik und Bauwesen in der Landwirtschaft, Bartningstr 49, 64289 Darmstadt Germany.
Ind/Abst Agric. Eng. Abstr. (1991-); Maize Abstr.; Rev. Plant Pathol.; Weed Abstr.; World Agric. Econ. Rural Sociol. Abstr.

LC S ISSN 0173-2811
DD 630 GW
KTBL-SCHRIFT. VFOAT KTBL-Schriften. (1972)-. Monographic series. German. Irregular. KTBL EV, Bartningstr 49, D-64289 Darmstadt Germany.
Ind/Abst Agric. Eng. Abstr.; Index Vet.; Vet. Bull.

LC S11 .S86 ISSN 0023-5350
DD 630.5 SW
KUNGL. SKOGS- OCH LANTBRUKSAKADEMIENS TIDSKRIFT. (KUNGL. SKOGS- OCH LANTBRUKSAKADEMIENS TIDSKRIFT = ZEITSCHRIFT DER KGL. SCHWEDISCHEN AKADEMIE DER LAND- UND FORSTWIRTSCHAFT = JOURNAL OF THE ROYAL SWEDISH ACADEMY OF AGRICULTURE AND FORESTRY = ANNALES DE L'ACADEMIE ROYALE D'AGRICULTURE ET DE SYLVICULTURE DE SUEDE.). [K. Skogs- lantbruksakad. tidskr.]. **Added/Corp** Kungl. Skogs- och Lantbruksakademien (Sweden). **VFOAT** Journal of the Royal Swedish Academy of Agriculture and Forestry; Zeitschrift der KGL. Schwedischen Akademie der Land- und Stwirtschaft; Annales de l'Academie Royale d'Agriculture et de Sylviculture Suede. (1956)-. Academic Scholarly Publication. Swedish (summaries and/or abstracts in English). Irregular. $40.07. Royal Swedish Academy of Sciences, Publications Department, Box 50005, S-104 05 Stockholm Sweden. **Tel** 011 46 8 6739500, FAX 011 46 8 1550670, 011 46 8 6739590, telex 17073 ROYACOD S. Documents available from CASDDS. ***Continues*** *Kungl. Lantbruksakademiens Tidskrift.*
Ind/Abst AGRICOLA; Agrofor. Abstr.; Chem. Abstr.; Dairy Sci. Abstr.; Field Crop Abstr.; Fish Rev. (Jan. 1989-July 1992); For. Prod. Abstr.; Grass. Forage Abstr.; Index Vet.; Leis., Rec., Tour. Abstr.; Potato Abstr.; Wildl. Rev. (Jan. 1989-July 1992); World Agric. Econ. Rural Sociol. Abstr.

LC S
DD 630 JA
KYOTO FURITSU DAIGAKU NOGAKUBU GAKUJUTSU HOKOKU: NOGAKU. SCIENTIFIC REPORTS OF THE KYOTO PREFECTURAL UNIVERSITY: AGRICULTURE. Main/Corp Kyoto Furitsu Daigaku. Nogakubu. **Added/Corp** SaikyÂo Daigaku. Nogakubu. Kyoto Furitsu Daigaku. Scientific Reports of Kyoto Prefectural University: Agriculture. **VFOAT** Gakujutsu Hokoku: Nogaku; Scientific Reports of the Saikyo University: Agriculture; Scientific Reports of the Kyoto Prefectural University: Agriculture. No. 1 (Apr. 1951)-. Japanese (English and German; table of contents in English). One time a year. Kyoto Prefectural University / Faculty of Agriculture, Library, Shimogamo Kyoto 606 Japan.
Ind/Abst Crop Physiol. Abstr.; For. Abstr.; Irr. Drain. Abstr.; Plant Breed. Abstr.; Plant Grow. Reg. Abstr.; Poult. Abstr.; Seed Abstr.

LC S ISSN 0368-6264
DD 630 JA
CODEN KNGZA2
KYUSHU DAIGAKU NOGAKUBU GAKUGEI ZASSHI. (GAKUGEI ZASSHI.). [Kyushu Daigaku Nogakubu gakugei zasshi]. **VFOAT** Science Bulletin of the Faculty of Agriculture, Kyushu University; Kyushu Daigaku Nogakubu Gakugei Zasshi. (19??)-. Academic Scholarly Publication. Japanese (summaries and/or abstracts in English). Kyushu University / Department of Agriculture, Department of Agriculture, 33 Fukuoka 812 Japan. Documents available from BIOSIS Document Express, CASDDS. ***Continues*** *Kyushu Teikoku Daigaku Nogakubu Gakugei Zasshi.*
Ind/Abst AGRICOLA; Biol. Abstr.; Chem. Abstr.; Food Sci. Technol. Abstr.; For. Abstr.; Hortic. Abstr.; Irr. Drain. Abstr.; Leis., Rec., Tour. Abstr.; Plant Grow. Reg. Abstr.; Potato Abstr.; Soyabean Abstr.

LC S562.J3 J35a
DD 338.1 JA
KYUSHU NOGYO JOSEI HOKOKU. Main/Corp Japan. Kyushu Noseikyoku. (1964)-. Periodical. Japanese. One time a year. Norin Suisansho Kyushu Noseikyoku, (Kyushu Agricultural Administration Bureau, Ministry of Agriculture Forestry and Fisheries), 1-2 Ninomaru Kumamotoshi, Kumamotoken 860 Japan.

LC S17 ISSN 0376-0685
DD 630 JA
CODEN KSHKBW
KYUSHU NOGYO SHIKENJO HOKOKU. [Kyushu Nogyo Shikenjo hokoku]. **Main/Corp** Kyushu Nogyo Shikenjo Nogyo Shikenjo. **VFOAT** Bulletin of the Kyushu National Agricultural Experiment Station. Vol. 20, No. 1/2 (1978)-. Academic Scholarly Publication. Japanese (summaries and/or abstracts in English). Norin Suisansho Kyushu Nogyo Shikenjo, (Kyushu National Agricultural Experiment Station Ministry of Agriculture Forestry & Fisheries), Izumi Chikugoshi Fukuokaken 833, Japan. Documents available from CASDDS. ***Continues*** *Norinsho Kyushu Nogyo Shikenjo. Bulletin.*

Agriculture

LC SF521
DD 638.1   JA
KYUSHU NOSHI NEMPO. **Main/Corp** Japan. Nogyo Shikenjo, Kyushu. **VFOAT** Annual Report of the Kyushu Agricultural Experiment Station. 1974-. Periodical. Japanese. Norin Suisansho Kyushu Nogyo Shikenjo, (Kyushu National Agricultural Experiment Station Ministry of Agriculture Forestry & Fisheries), Izumi Chikugoshi Fukuokaken 833, Japan.
Ind/Abst AGRICOLA; Agric. Eng. Abstr.; Chem. Abstr.; Nutr. Abstr. Rev., Ser. B, Live Feeds and Feed.; Rev. Plant Pathol.

LC S471.J3 K9
DD 630.95   JA
CODEN KDNKDR
KYUSHU TOKAI DAIGAKU NOGAKUBU KIYO. [Kyushu Tokai Daigaku Nogakubu kiyo]. **VFOAT** Proceedings of Faculty of Agriculture, Kyushu Tokai University. Vol. 1 (1982)-. Academic Scholarly Publication. English (Japanese). Kyushu Tokai Daigaku, Nogakubu Nawayo, Choyo-mura, Aso-Gun, Kumamoto-ken 869-14 Japan. Documents available from CASDDS.
Ind/Abst Chem. Abstr.; Plant Breed. Abstr.; Plant Grow. Reg. Abstr.; Poult. Abstr.

LC S
DD 630   ISSN 0440-4904   US
L.S.B. BULLETIN. See Earth Sciences-Geology.

LC HD1940.A96 N5a
DD 338.1/09436/12   AU
LAGEBERICHT DER NIEDEROSTERREICHISCHEN LAND- UND FORSTWIRTSCHAFT. **Main/Corp** Niederosterreichische Landes-Landwirtschaftskammer. (19??)-. German. Irregular. Niederosterreichischen Landwirtschaft, Lowelstr 16, 1014 Vienna Austria.

LC S
DD 630   ISSN 0023-7485   US
LANCASTER FARMING. (1955)-. Trade Publication. English. One time a week. $25.00. Lancaster Farming, PO Box 609, Ephrata PA 17522. **Tel** (717)733-6397, (717)394-3047, FAX (717)733-6058. **ED** Everett Nearwanger. **Ad Acc, Adv Mgr:** Gary Myer. **Circ:** 52,000 (ctrl). available on microfilm from University Microfilms International (UMI).
Desc: General agricultural publication.

LC S
DD 630   ISSN 0176-2389   GW
LAND AGRARWIRTSCHAFT UND GESELLSCHAFT. Vol. 1, No. 1 (July 1984)-. Periodical. German. Three times a year. $34.54. Landwirtschaftsverl Hessen GmbH, Taunusstrasse 151, D-34369 Friedrichsdorf Germany. **Tel** 011 49 6172 714060.
Ind/Abst Leis., Rec., Tour. Abstr.; Rural Dev. Abstr.; World Agric. Econ. Rural Sociol. Abstr.

LC S
DD 630   AU
LAND JUGEND. **Added/Corp** Austria. Bundesministerium fuer Land- und Forstwirtschaft. Landjugend Osterreich. **VFOAT** Landjugend. (19??)-. Periodical. German. Twelve times a year. S290.00 Austria; S384.00 other. Oesterreichischer Agrarverlag, Inkustr 1 7 Bueropark Donau, A 3400 Klosterneuburg Austria. **Tel** 011 43 2243 33300. **ED** Renate Gailer and Franz Kammleitner. **Bk Rev. Ad Acc. Circ:** 40,000.

LC S
DD 630   ISSN 0279-1633   US
LAND (MANKATO, MINN.), THE. (THE LAND : SOUTHERN MINNESOTA'S FARM PUBLICATION.). [Land]. (19??)-. Newspaper. English. Twenty-six times a year. $12.00. Free Press Company Inc, PO Box 3169, Mankato MN 56001. **Tel** (507)345-4523, FAX (507)388-4353. **Ad Acc. Circ:** 40,000 (ctrl). available on microfilm.

LC HD101 .L35
DD 333.3/23/05   ISSN 0251-1894   IT
LAND REFORM, LAND SETTLEMENT AND COOPERATIVES. See Business and Economics-Cooperatives.

LC S
DD 630   US
LAND REPORT, THE. **Added/Corp** Land Institute. (197?)-. Periodical. English. Three times a year. $5.00. The Land Institute, 2440 East Water Well Road, Salina KS 67401.
Ind/Abst Environ. Period. Bibliogr.

LC HA1320.B2 A32 HD1960.B2 B27
DD 314.3/46 S 338.1/0943/46   GW
LAND- UND FORSTWIRTSCHAFT, DIE. See Agriculture-Abstracting, Bibliographies and Statistics.

LC S
DD 630   GW
LAND- UND FORSTWIRTSCHAFT, FISCHEREI. REIHE 2.1.1 : BETREIBSGROSSENSTRUKTUR. **Main/Corp** Germany (West). Statistisches Bundesamt. **VFOAT** Fachserie 3. **VAT** Land- und Forstwirtschaft, Fischerei. Reihe Zwei.Eins. Eins: Betreibsgrossenstruktur. 1976-. Periodical. German. One time a year. W. Kohlhammer Verlag GmbH, Postfach 800430, D-70549 Stuttgart Germany. **Tel** 011 49 711 78630, FAX 011 49 711 7863430, telex 7-255820. **Continues** Land- und Forstwirtschaft, Fischerei. Reihe 5: Betriebe, Arbeitskrafte und Einkommensverhaltnisse. I. Betriebsgrossenstruktur.

LC S231 .S78a
DD 630   GW
LAND- UND FORSTWIRTSCHAFT, FISCHEREI. REIHE 3, LANDWIRTSCHAFTLICHE BODENNUTZUNG UND PFLANZLICHE ERZEUGUNG. **Added/Corp** Germany (West). Statistisches Bundesamt. **VFOAT** Landwirtschaftliche Bodennutzung und Pflanzliche Erzeugung; Fachserie 3. (1990)-. German. Hermann Leins GmbH & Co., Verlags-KG, Holzwiesenstrasse 2, Postfach 11 52, D-7408 Kusterdingen Germany. **Continues** Land- und Forstwirtschaft, Fischerei. Reihe 3, Bodennutzung und Pflanzliche Erzeugung.

LC S
DD 630   GW
LAND- UND FORSTWIRTSCHAFT, FISCHEREI. REIHE 3.2, HEUERNTE / HERAUSGEBER STATISTISCHES BUNDESAMT. **VFOAT** Heuernte; Fachserie 3. German.

LC S
DD 630   GW
LAND- UND FORSTWIRTSCHAFT, FISCHEREI. REIHE 3.2, WACHSTUMSTAND FUR WINTERGETREIDE UND WINTEROLFRUCHTE. **VFOAT** Wachstumstand fur Wintergetreide und Winterolfruchte; Fachserie 3. Periodical. German.

LC S17
DD 630   ISSN 0458-6859   GW
CODEN LVOEAC
LANDBAUFORSCHUNG VOELKENRODE. [Landbauforsch. voelkenrode]. **Added/Corp** Forschungsanstalt fuer Landwirtschaft Braunschweig-Voelkenrode. Bundesforschungsanstalt fuer Landwirtschaft (Germany). (1951)-. Government Publication. German (summaries and/or abstracts in English). Four times a year (quarterly). DM60.00. Bundesforschungsanstalt fuer Landwirtschaft Braunschweig-Voelkenrode, Infod Bundesalle 50, D-38116 Braunschweig Germany. **Tel** 011 49 531 5961, FAX 011 49 531 596814. **Circ:** 800. Documents available from The Genuine Article, CASDDS.
Ind/Abst AGRICOLA; Agric. Eng. Abstr. (1991-); Anim. Breed. Abstr.; Biodeter. Abstr.; Chem. Abstr.; Cot. Trop. Fibr. Abstr.; Publics. Bibliogr.; Curr. Cit.; Curr. Contents Agric. Biol. Environ. Sci.; Dairy Sci. Abstr.; EMBASE; Hortic. Abstr.; Index Vet.; Irr. Drain. Abstr.; Nature Abstr.; Nematol. Abstr.; Life Sci. Collect.; Pig News Inf.; Plant Breed. Abstr.; Plant Genet. Resour. Abstr.; Plant Grow. Reg. Abstr.; Postharvest News Inf.; Potato Abstr.; Poult. Abstr.; Res. Alert [Select. Cov.]; Rev. Med. Vet. Entomol. [Select. Cov.]; SCISEARCH; Seed Abstr.; Soc. Sci. Cit. Index [Select. Cov.]; Sug. Indus. Abstr.; Vet. Bull.; Vitis Vitic. Enol. Abstr.; Weed Abstr.; Wheat Barley Trit. Abstr.; World Agric. Econ. Rural Sociol. Abstr.

LC S
DD 630   ISSN 0376-0723   GW
CODEN LVSWAI
LANDBAUFORSCHUNG VOELKENRODE, SONDERHEFT. (LANDBAUFORSCHUNG VOELKENRODE. SONDERHEFT : WISSENSCHAFTLICHE MITTEILUNGEN DER FORSCHUNGSANSTALT FUER LANDWIRTSCHAFT.). [Landbauforsch. Voelkenrode, Sonderh.]. **Added/Corp** Forschungsanstalt fuer Landwirtschaft Braunschweig-Voelkenrode. Bundesforschungsanstalt fuer Landwirtschaft (Germany). (1969)-. Monographic series. German (summaries and/or abstracts in English). Irregular. Price varies per volume. Bundesforschungsanstalt fuer Landwirtschaft Braunschweig-Voelkenrode, Infod Bundesalle 50, D-38116 Braunschweig Germany. **Tel** 011 49 531 5961, FAX 011 49 531 596814.
Ind/Abst Pig News Inf.

LC S
DD 630   GW
LANDBOTE, DER. Periodical. German. One time a week. Zeitschriften Verlag/Germany, Abeggstrafe 2, 62 Wiesbaden 1 Germany. **Tel** 06121/52 40 28-29. **ED** Fraund. **Ad Acc. Circ:** 5,700 (ctrl).
Desc: Corn growing, agricultural economy, plant protection, fertilization, advice, feeding, marketing (crops, beans, vegetables and fruit cultural question of environment); science of agriculture.

LC S
DD 630   NE
LANDBOUW-ECONOMISCH INSTITUUT, AFDELING LANDBOUW: PUBLIKATIE. **Added/Corp** Landbouw-Economisch Instituut (Netherlands). Afdeling Landbouw. **VFOAT** Publikatie. No. 3.49 (1974)-. Monographic series. Dutch. Price varies per volume. Landbouw-Economisch Instituut, Postbus 29703, 2502 LS Hague Netherlands. **Tel** 011 31 70 3308330, FAX 011 31 70 615624. **Continues** Landbouw-Economisch Instituut. Afdeling Bedrijfseconomisch Onderzoek Landbouw. [Publikatie] 3.
Ind/Abst Poult. Abstr.

LC S
DD 630   NE
LANDBOUWBLAD, HET. (1992)-. Periodical. Dutch. One time a week. $157.59. Fries-Flevolandse Land en Tuinbouw Organisatie, Postbus 613, 8901 BK Leeuwarden, Netherlands. **Tel** 011 31 58 133441, FAX 011 38 58 126040. **Continues** Fries Landbouwblade.

LC S
DD 630   ISSN 0436-5569   NE
LANDBOUWCIJFERS. See Agriculture-Abstracting, Bibliographies and Statistics.

LC S
DD 630   ISSN 0772-7240   BE
UDC 631
LANDBOUWLEVEN. [Landbouwleven]. (1951)-. Periodical. Dutch. One time a week. Landelijke Uitgeveryen, 92 Leon Grosjeanlaan, B-1140 Brussels Belgium. **Tel** 02 730 3317, FAX 02 730 3324. **ED** De Mol Andre. **Ad Acc, Adv Mgr:** Eyben Sylvie, **Tel** 02 730 3316.

LC S
DD 630   BE
LANDBOUWSTATISTIEKEN. See Agriculture-Abstracting, Bibliographies and Statistics.

LC S
DD 630   ISSN 0776-2143   BE
UDC 63
LANDBOUWTIJDSCHRIFT (1988). [Landbouwtijdschr. 1988]. **VFOAT** Revue de l'Agriculture (1988). (1988)-. Periodical. Multiple languages (Dutch, English and German). Six times a year. 600F Belgium; 800F other. Manhattan Center-Office Tower, Avenue du Boulevard 21, 13 eme Etage, 1210 Brussels Belgium. **Tel** 011 32 2 2117211, FAX 011 32 2 2117214, telex AGRILA 22033. Index available. cum. index. **Bk Rev. Circ:** 2,000. Documents available from The Genuine Article. **Formed by the union of** Revue de l'Agriculture, 0035-1296 **and** Landbouwtijdschrift, 0774-6385.
Desc: Publishes results of scientific research and articles on technical, economic, social matters and agriculture.
Ind/Abst Leadscan; PAIS Int. Print (1991-); Res. Alert [Select. Cov.]; SCISEARCH.

LC HD9015.E8 L36
DD 338.1/3/094   BE
LANDBRUGSMARKEDER. FORKLARINGER, PRISER. **Added/Corp** Commission of the European Communities. Directorate-General for Agriculture. Directorate General Matters. **VFOAT** Agrarmarkte. Erlauterungen, Preise; Agricultural Markets. Explanatory Note, Prices. (19??)-. Danish (Dutch, English, French, German and Italian). One time a year. £100.00. Office for Official Publications of the European Communities, 2 rue Mercier, 2985 Luxembourg Luxembourg. **Tel** 011 352 499281, FAX 011 352 292942763.

LC HD2001 .L354
DD 630   ISSN 0107-5675   DK
LANDBRUGSREGNSKABSSTATISTIK. **Added/Corp** Jordbrugskonomisk Institut (Denmark). **VFOAT** Economic Results in Danish Agriculture. (1981)-. Danish (summaries and/or abstracts in English). One time a year. kr40.00. **Continues in part** Beretning (Jordbrugskonomisk Institut (Denmark)).
Ind/Abst World Agric. Econ. Rural Sociol. Abstr.

LC S245 .L19
DD 338.1/09489   DK
LANDBRUGSSTATISTIK. See Agriculture-Abstracting, Bibliographies and Statistics.

LC S
DD 630   NO
LANDBRUKSDIREKTRENS ARSMELDING. **Main/Corp** Norway. Landbruksdepartementet. Norwegian. 4 Landburgskontor Akersgt, 42 Oslo-Dep Norway.

Agriculture

LC S
DD 630
SA
LANDOUNUUS = AGRICULTURAL NEWS. Added/Corp South Africa. Dept. of Agricultural Technical Services. South Africa. Dept. of Agriculture and Fisheries. South Africa. Dept. of Agriculture and Water Supply. South Africa. Dept. of Agricultural Economics and Marketing South Africa. Dept. of Agriculture. **VFOAT** Agricultural News. No. 9 (Sept. 27, 1957)-. Periodical. English (Afrikaans). One time a week. Free. South Africa Department of Agricultural Technical Services, Privantsak Private Bag X144, Pretoria 0001 South Africa. **Tel** 21-3111 X 150. **Continues** Nuusbrief (South Africa. Dept. of Agriculture).

LC S
DD 630
ISSN 0011-5010
GW
CCC
LANDTECHNISCHE ZEITSCHRIFT. (DLZ.). [Landtech. Z.]. **VFOAT** Deutsche Landtechnische Zeitschrift; Landtechnische Zeitschrift; Landwirtschaftliche Zeitschrift fur Produktion--Technik--Management. Vol. 5, No. 1 (Jan. 1954)-. Trade Publication. German. Twelve times a year. $78.30. BLV Verlagsgesellschaft MBH, Lothstrasse 29, D80797 Munich Germany. **Tel** 011 49 89 12705214. **Continues** Traktor; **Absorbed** Agrar Praxis, 0014-9748.
Ind/Abst AGRICOLA; Agric. Eng. Abstr. (1991-); Maize Abstr.; Wheat Barley Trit. Abstr.

LC S
DD 630
GW
LANDWIRTSCHAFT IN NORDRHEIN-WESTFALEN, DIE. Main/Corp North Rhine-Westphalia (Germany). Landesamt fur Datenverarbeitung und Statistik. German. One time a year. DM25.50. Landesamt fuer Datenverarbeitung und Statistik Nordrhein-Westfalen, Postfach 101105, 40002 Duesseldorf Germany. **Tel** (0211)944901, FAX (0211)442006, telex 8586654 LDST D. Circ: 260.
Desc: Statistical survey on agriculture in North Rhine-Westphalia.

LC S
DD 630
SZ
TITLE CHANGE
LANDWIRTSCHAFT SCHWEIZ. (June 1988)-(19??). Periodical. German (summaries and/or abstracts in English and French). Landwirtschaft Schweiz Teko Consultants, Postfach 507, CH-1290 Versoix Switzerland. **Tel** 011 41 22 7555241, FAX 011 41 22 7555967. Index available in last issue of volume--attached. **Formed by the union of** Mitteilungen fuer die Schweizerische Landwirtschaft **and** Schweizerische Landwirtschaftliche Monatshefte, 0036-7648. **Continued by** Agrarforschung Bern, 1022-663X.
Ind/Abst Agric. Eng. Abstr. (1991-); Anim. Breed. Abstr.; Biocont. News Inf.; Biodeter. Abstr. (1991-); Dairy Sci. Abstr.; Field Crop Abstr.; Grass. Forage Abstr.; Index Vet.; Irr. Drain. Abstr.; Maize Abstr.; Nematol. Abstr.; Nutr. Abstr. Rev., Ser. B, Live Feeds and Feed.; Pig News Inf.; Plant Breed. Abstr.; Plant Grow. Reg. Abstr.; Postharvest News Inf.; Potato Abstr.; Poult. Abstr.; Rev. Agric. Entomol.; Seed Abstr.; Soils Fert.; Soyabean Abstr.; Vet. Bull.; Wheat Barley Trit. Abstr.; World Agric. Econ. Rural Sociol. Abstr.

LC S257 .A34
DD 630
ISSN 0023-8171
SZ
CEASED
LANDWIRTSCHAFTLICHES JAHRBUCH DER SCHWEIZ. ANNUAIRE AGRICOLE DE LA SUISSE. [Landwirtsch. Jahrb. Schweiz]. Added/Corp Switzerland. Volkswirtschafts Departement. Switzerland Paul Sunday Pioneer Press, Apr. 7, 1918-Dec. 30, 1984. **VFOAT** Annuaire Agricole de la Suisse. (1887)-(1993). Periodical. German (French). Bundesamt fuer Landwirtschaft, Mattenhofstrasse 5, CH-3003 Bern Switzerland. **Tel** 011 41 31 612111. cum. index.
Ind/Abst AGRICOLA; Nematol. Abstr.

LC S
DD 630
GW
LANDWIRTSCHAFTLICHES WOCHENBLATT FUR WESTFALEN UND LIPPE. Periodical. German. One time a week. DM180.20. Landwirtschaftsverlag GmbH, Postfach 480249, D-48079 Muenster Hiltrup Germany. **Tel** 011 49 2501 8010, FAX 011 49 2501 801204, telex 892665 LANDV D. Index available. **Bk Rev. Ad Acc. Circ:** 61,000 (ctrl).
Desc: Contains information about crop and animal production, agricultural technology and market, especially for farmers in Westphalia.

LC HD6668.A3 L3
DD 331.8813
UK
LANDWORKER, THE. See Business and Economics-Labor.

LC S
DD 630
SW
LANTMANNEN. Added/Corp Sveriges Allmanna Lantbrukssallskap. Vol. 75, No. 1 (Jan. 4, 1964)-. Periodical. Swedish. Twelve times a year. $72.13. LRF Media AB, Lantmannen, S-105 33 Stockholm Sweden. **Tel** 011 46 8 7875710. **ED** Jan-Olov Johansson. Index available. **Bk Rev. Ad Acc.** Circ: 20,000 (ctrl).
Desc: Magazine for progressive agriculture, plants, soil, machinery, animal/husbandry, economics, pesticides and field crops.
Ind/Abst Field Crop Abstr.; Plant Breed. Abstr.; Wheat Barley Trit. Abstr.

LC S
DD 630
IO
LAPORAN - SURVEY AGRO EKONOMI INDONESIA. Main/Corp Survey Agro Ekonomi Indonesia. No. 4 (July 4, 1970)-. Periodical. Indonesian.

LC S
DD 630
MY
LAPURAN TAHUNAN - JABATAN PERTANIAN NEGERI PAHANG. Main/Corp Pahang. Jabatan Pertanian Negeri. (19??)-. Malay.

LC S
DD 630
ISSN 0023-9143
BL
CODEN LARRAL
LAVOURA ARROZEIRA. [Lavoura arrozeira]. Added/Corp Instituto Rio Grandense do Arroz. (1947)-. Academic Scholarly Publication. Portuguese. Six times a year. $50.00. Instituto Rio Grandense do Arrozeira Missoe, 342 Navegantes, 90230 Porto Alegre RS Brazil. **Tel** 011 55 51 2265144. **ED** Jacques Alkalai Wainberg. **Ad Acc.** Circ: 19,000. Documents available from CASDDS.
Desc: Rice culture, agronomy, soil sciences, and irrigation.
Ind/Abst Abstr. Trop. Agric.; AGRICOLA; Biocont. News Inf.; Biodeter. Abstr.; Chem. Abstr.; Field Crop Abstr.; Grass. Forage Abstr.; Irr. Drain. Abstr.; Maize Abstr.; Plant Breed. Abstr.; Plant Genet. Resour. Abstr.; Postharvest News Inf.; Rev. Agric. Entomol.; Rev. Med. Vet. Entomol.; Rice Abstr.; Seed Abstr.; Soils Fert.; Sorghum Mill. Abstr.; Soyabean Abstr.; Weed Abstr.; World Agric. Econ. Rural Sociol. Abstr.

LC S
DD 630
ISSN 0268-8727
UK
LEAFLET - ADAS. MINISTRY OF AGRICULTURE, FISHERIES AND FOOD. [Leafl. - ADAS, Minist. Agric. Fish. Food]. **VFOAT** Leaflet - Agricultural Development and Advisory Service. Ministry of Agriculture, Fisheries and Food. (19??)-. Monographic series. English. Irregular. Price varies per volume. Agricultural Development and Advisory Service, Whitehall Place, London SW1 United Kingdom.
Ind/Abst Irr. Drain. Abstr.

LC S
DD 630
UK
LEAFLET (GREAT BRITAIN. AGRICULTURAL DEVELOPMENT AND ADVISORY SERVICE). (LEAFLET / MINISTRY OF AGRICULTURE, FISHERIES AND FOOD, AGRICULTURAL DEVELOPMENT AND ADVISORY SERVICE.). Added/Corp Great Britain. Agricultural Development and Advisory Service. (19??)-. Trade Publication. English. Ministry of Agriculture, Fisheries and Food, Agricultural and Advisory Service, London SW1A 2HH United Kingdom.
Ind/Abst Poult. Abstr.

LC SB203
DD 633.3
ISSN 0250-5371
II
CODEN LRESDD
LEGUME RESEARCH. [Legume res.]. Added/Corp Agricultural Research Communication Centre (India). Vol. 1, No. 1 (July 1977)-. Academic Scholarly Publication. English. Four times a year. $60.00. Agricultural Research Communication Centre, Sadar Karnal 132001, Haryana India. **Tel** 011 91 3036. **ED** S. Chandra. Index available. cum. index. Circ: 1,000. Documents available from BIOSIS Document Express, CASDDS.
Desc: The journal is designed to highlight the fundamental and applied aspects of legume physiology, genetics, breeding, bacterial activity, product quality and technological aspects of cultivation, processing and evaluation.
Ind/Abst Agrofor. Abstr. (1991-); Biodeter. Abstr.; Biol. Abstr.; Chem. Abstr.; Crop Physiol. Abstr.; Field Crop Abstr.; Food Sci. Technol. Abstr.; Grass. Forage Abstr.; Index Vet.; Irr. Drain. Abstr.; Maize Abstr.; Nutr. Abstr. Rev., Ser. B, Live Feeds and Feed.; Plant Breed. Abstr.; Rev. Agric. Entomol.; Rev. Plant Pathol.; Rice Abstr.; Seed Abstr.; Soils Fert.; Soyabean Abstr.; Weed Abstr.

LC S
DD 630
FR
LETTRE DE L'OIV. (19??)-. French. Irregular (approximately every 5 week). 190.00F EEC countries; 250.00F other. Office Internationale la Vigne et du Vin, 11 rue Roquepine, 75008 Paris France. **Tel** 011 33 1 44948080, FAX 011 33 1 42669063, telex 281196. **ED**

Robert Tinlot. Index Bound in First Issue. **Bk Rev.** ctrl circ.
Desc: Newsletter covering wine and vineyards.

LC S
DD 630
ISSN 0254-8364
CH
LEUCAENA RESEARCH REPORTS. [Leucaena res. rep.]. Added/Corp Nitrogen Fixing Tree Association. University of Hawaii at Manoa. Dept. of Horticulture. Hsing Cheng Yuan Nung Yeh Fa Chan Wei Yuan Hui (China). Vol. 2 (July 1981)-. English (Spanish and French). One time a year. $7.00. Council for Agricultural Planning and Development, 37 Nanhai Road, Taipei Taiwan. **Continues** Leucaena Newsletter.
Ind/Abst Agrofor. Abstr.; Crop Physiol. Abstr.; Field Crop Abstr.; Grass. Forage Abstr.; Rev. Agric. Entomol.; Rice Abstr.

LC S
DD 630
ISSN 0883-685X
US
LEWIS LIVING. (LEWIS LIVING.). June 1985-. Periodical. English. Twelve times a year. Lewis Living, Box 72, Outer Stowe Street, Lowville NY 13367. **Continues** Lewis County Farm, Home and 4-H News.

LC Z881.U4 L5
DD 016.63
US
LIBRARY LIST. See Library and Information Sciences.

LC SF521
DD 638.1
ISSN 1010-3740
LY
CODEN LJAGD3
LIBYAN JOURNAL OF AGRICULTURE, THE. [Libyan j. agric.]. Vol. 1 (June 1971)-. Academic Scholarly Publication. English. One time a year. Documents available from BIOSIS Document Express, CASDDS.
Ind/Abst AGRICOLA; Biol. Abstr.; Chem. Abstr.; GeoRef.

LC S
DD 630
LI
LIETUVOS ZEMDIRBYSTES MOKSLINIO TYRIMO INSTITUTO DARBAI. [Liet. zemdirb. moksl. tyrimo inst. darb.]. **VFOAT** Trudy Litovskogo Naucno-Issledovatelskogo Instituta Zemledelija. (19??)-. Lithuanian. Lietuvos TSR Valstybinis Agropramoninis Komitetas, Lenino pr 19 232025, Vilnius Lithuania.
Ind/Abst Maize Abstr.; Plant Grow. Reg. Abstr.; Soils Fert.

LC S530.5 .L56
DD 630/.7/20171241
UK
LIST OF RESEARCH WORKERS IN THE AGRICULTURAL SCIENCES IN THE COMMONWEALTH. Added/Corp Commonwealth Agricultural Bureaux. Executive Council. (1978)-. English. CAB International Centre, Wallingford, Oxfordshire OX10 8DE United Kingdom. **Tel** 011 44 1491 832111, FAX 011 44 1491 833508, telex 847964 COMAGG G.

LC Z5076 .V45
DD 016.63
VE
LISTA DE LIBROS Y FOLLETOS RECIBIDOS. Main/Corp Venezuela. Ministerio de Agricultura y Cria. Biblioteca. **VFOAT** Boletin Informativo. Periodical. Spanish. Three times a year.

LC HD
DD 338
ISSN 1076-2183
US
●**LIVESTOCK, DAIRY, AND POULTRY SITUATION AND OUTLOOK.** [Livest. dairy poult. situat. outlook]. Added/Corp United States. Dept. of Agriculture. Economic Research Service. United States. World Agricultural Outlook Board. LDP-M-1 (Jan. 25, 1994)-. English. Five times a year. $22.00. U.S. Department of Agriculture, ERS-NASS, 341 Victory Drive, Herndon VA 22070. **Tel** (800)999-6779, (703)834-0125.
Formed by the union of Livestock and Poultry Update, 1048-1605; Situation and Outlook Report. Dairy, 1050-9151 **and** Situation and Outlook Report. Livestock and Poultry, 1054-0849.

LC S
DD 630
ISSN 0024-5313
US
LIVINGSTON COUNTY AGRICULTURAL NEWS. **VFOAT** Agricultural News. Vol. 29, No. 1 (Jan. 1956)-. Periodical. English. Twelve times a year. Livingston County Extension Service Association, Agricultural Department, Mt Morris NY 14510. **Continues** Livingston County Farm Bureau News.

LC SF
DD 636
ISSN 0899-6202
US
LLAMA BANNER. [Llama banner]. Vol. 1, No. 1 (July/Aug. 1988)-. Periodical. English. Six times a year. $24.00. Llama Banner, PO Box 1968, Manhattan KS 66502. **Tel** (913)537-0320. **ED** Doug Able. **Ad Acc.**

LC S ISSN 0024-6735
DD 630 US
CODEN LOAGAZ
LOUISIANA AGRICULTURE. [La. agric.]. Vol. 1 (Fall 1957)-. English. Four times a year. Free on request. Louisiana Agricultural Experiment Station, PO Box 25055, Baton Rouge LA 70894-5055. **Tel** (504)388-5649. Documents available from BIOSIS Document Express, CASDDS, Documents on Demand.
Ind/Abst AGRICOLA [Full Cov.]; Agric. Eng. Abstr. (1991-); Agrofor. Abstr.; Anim. Breed. Abstr.; Biol. Abstr.; Chem. Abstr. (1957-1983); Dairy Sci. Abstr.; EMBASE; Environ. Abstr.; Field Crop Abstr.; Food Sci. Technol. Abstr.; For. Abstr.; Grass. Forage Abstr.; Helminthol. Abstr. (1991-); Index Vet.; Irr. Drain. Abstr.; Maize Abstr.; Nutr. Abstr. Rev., Ser. B, Live Feeds and Feed.; Life Sci. Collect.; Plant Breed. Abstr.; Pollut. Abstr. Indexes; Postharvest News Inf.; Rev. Agric. Entomol.; Rev. Med. Vet. Entomol.; Rev. Plant Pathol.; Rice Abstr.; Seed Abstr.; Soils Fert.; Sorghum Mill. Abstr.; Soyabean Abstr.; Vet. Bull.; Weed Abstr.; Wheat Barley Trit. Abstr.; World Agric. Econ. Rural Sociol. Abstr.

LC S
DD 630 US
LOUISIANA COUNTRY. Periodical. English. Twelve times a year. Associations of Louisiana Electric Cooperatives Inc, 10725 Airline Highway, Baton Rouge LA 70816. ***Continues*** *Rural Louisiana.*

LC S ISSN 0273-883X
DD 630 US
LOUISIANA FARM REPORTER. **Added/Corp** Louisiana Crop and Livestock Reporting Service. (19??)-. Government Publication. English. Twenty-four times a year. $10.00. US Department of Agriculture / National Agricultural Statistics Service (NASS), Room 5829 South Building, Washington DC 20250. **Tel** (202)720-4020, FAX (314)875-5231. **ED** Bergen A. Nelson. **Circ:** 1,000 (ctrl).
Desc: Contains information on crops, livestock, poultry, prices, stocks, farm-labor, economic analysis, and other items of special interest.

LC SD144.L8 L17 ISSN 0458-5682
DD 634 US
LSU FORESTRY NOTES. [LSU for. notes]. **Main/Corp** Louisiana Agricultural Experiment Station. **Added/Corp** Louisiana Agricultural Experiment Station. Forestry Notes. **VAT** Louisiana State University Forestry Notes. No. 1 (1953)-. English. Louisiana State University / School of Forestry, Wildlife, and Fish, 227 Forestry Wildlife and Fish Building, Baton Rouge LA 70803. **Tel** (504)388-4131.
Ind/Abst Abstr. Bull. Inst. Pap. Sci. Tech.; AGRICOLA [Full Cov.].

LC S298.J36 L8
DD 638.095 IO
LUAS TANAH MENURUT PENGGUNAANNYA DI JAWA & MADURA. (19??)-. Indonesian (English). One time a year. Rp4,500 Indonesian; $1.35 US. Biro Pusat Statistik / Central Bureau of Statistics, 8 Jalan Dr. Sutomo No. 8, Box 3, Jakarta Pusat 10710 Indonesia. **Tel** 011 62 21 372808, 011 62 21 374908 ext.342. ctrl circ.

LC S
DD 630 RM
LUCRARI STIINTIFICE - INSTITUTUL AGRONOMIC ION IONESCU DE LA BRAD. SERIA ZOOTEHNIE - MEDICINA VETERINARA. **Main/Corp** Jassy. Institutul Agronomic Profesor Ion Ionescu de la Brad. (1968)-. Romanian (English, French, German and Russian). One time a year. ***Supersedes in part*** *Lucrari Stiintifice - Institutul Agronomic Ion Ionescu de la Brad.*
Ind/Abst Poult. Abstr.

LC S ISSN 0563-5578
DD 630 RM
LUCRARI STIINTIFICE, INSTITUTUL AGRONOMIC TIMISOARA, SERIA AGRONOMIE. (LUCRARI STIINTIFICE. SERIA AGRONOMIE.). [Lucr. stiint. Inst. Agron. Timisoara Ser. agron.]. **Added/Corp** Institutul Agronomic Timisoara. **VFOAT** Lucrari Stiintifice. Agronomie; Seria Agronomie; Agronomie. Vol. 8 (1965)-. Romanian. One time a year. DM164.00. **(Subscription address:** Kubon & Sagner, ABT Zeitschriftenimport, D 80328 Munich Germany. **Tel** 011 49 89 54218130.) ***Continues in part*** *Lucrari Stiintifice Ale Institutului Agronomic Timisoara.*
Ind/Abst Maize Abstr.; Life Sci. Collect.; Sorghum Mill. Abstr.; Soyabean Abstr.; Vitis Vitic. Enol. Abstr.

LC S ISSN 1010-1349
DD 630 RM
LUCRARI STIINTIFICE - INSTITUTUL DE CERCETARI SI PROIECTARI PENTRU VALORIFICAREA SI INDUSTRIALIZAREA LEGUMELOR SI FRUCTELOR. [Lucr. stiint. - Inst. cercet. proiect. pentru valorif. ind. legum. fruct.]. (1???)-. Periodical. Romanian.
Ind/Abst Plant Grow. Reg. Abstr.; Postharvest News Inf.; Potato Abstr.

LC HA1448 .F4 HD1995.5 ISSN 0357-5527
DD 314.7 FI
MAA- JA METSATALOUS. **VFOAT** Jord- Och Skogsbruk; Agriculture and Forestry. (1978)-. Finnish (Swedish). Irregular. Tilastokeskus, PL 504, Annankatu 44, 00101 Helsinki Finland. **Tel** 011 358 0 17341, FAX 011 358 0 17342474, telex 1002111 TILASTO SF.

LC S ISSN 0784-8404
DD 630 FI
UDC 311.3
CODEN 630
MAA- JA METSATALOUS (HELSINKI. 1988). **See** Agriculture-Abstracting, Bibliographies and Statistics.

LC S242.F5 A3
DD 630 FI
MAATALOUSTILASTOLLINEN KUUKAUSIKATSAUAS. MONTHLY REVIEW OF AGRICULTURAL STATISTICS. **See** Agriculture-Abstracting, Bibliographies and Statistics.

LC HA1448 .F4 ISSN 0785-7500
DD 314.7 FI
MAATILAREKISTERI. [Maatilarekisteri]. **Added/Corp** Finland. Maatilahallitus. **VFOAT** Lantbruksregister; Farm Register. (19??)-. Finnish (Swedish and English). One time a year (Oct). Fmk150.00. Information Centre of the Ministry of Argriculture and Forestry Statistics, PO Box 250, Liisankatu 8, SF-00171 Helsinki Finland. **Tel** 358 0 134 211, FAX 358 0 1342 1573.
Desc: Provides information about the number of farms, use of arable land and farm ownership.

LC HC340.2.Z9 I5175 HD199
DD 330 FI
MAATILATALOUDEN YRITYS- JA TULOTILASTO ... TULO- JA VEROTUSTIEDOT. **VFOAT** Gardsbrukets Foretags- Och Inkomststatistik ... Inkomst- Och Beskattningsuppgifter. Finnish (Swedish). One time a year. Government Printing Centre, PO Box 516, SF-00101 Helsinki 10 Finland.

LC S17 .M25 ISSN 0024-9602
DD 630.954 II
CODEN MAAJAP
MADRAS AGRICULTURAL JOURNAL, THE. [Madras agric. j.]. **Added/Corp** Madras Agricultural Students' Union (Coimbatore, India). (1929)-. Academic Scholarly Publication. English. Twelve times a year. $100.00. Madras Agricultural Students Union, Agricultural College and, Research Institute, Coimbatore 641003 India. **Tel** 011 91 41222. **(Subscription address:** Prints India, 11 Darya Ganj, New Delhi 110002 India. **Tel** 011 91 11 3268645, FAX 011 91 11 3275542, telex 31-61087 PRIN-IN.) **ED** K. Sivaprakasam. **Ad Acc. Circ:** 2,200 (ctrl). Documents available from BIOSIS Document Express, CASDDS. ***Continues*** *Madras Agricultural Students' Union. Journal.*
Desc: A scientific publication on agricultural sciences.
Ind/Abst Agric. Eng. Abstr. (1991-); Agrofor. Abstr. (19??-19??); Biocont. News Inf. (19??-19??); Biodeter. Abstr.; Biol. Abstr.; Chem. Abstr.; Cot. Trop. Fibr. Abstr. Bibliogr.; Crop Physiol. Abstr.; EMBASE; Field Crop Abstr.; Food Sci. Technol. Abstr.; For. Prod. Abstr. (1991-); Grass. Forage Abstr.; Hortic. Abstr.; Irr. Drain. Abstr.; Maize Abstr.; Nematol. Abstr.; Nutr. Abstr. Rev., Ser. B, Live Feeds and Feed.; Ornamental Hort. (19??-19??); PESTDOC; Plant Breed. Abstr.; Plant Grow. Reg. Abstr.; Postharvest News Inf.; Potato Abstr.; Protozoolog. Abstr.; Rev. Agric. Entomol.; Rev. Med. Vet. Entomol.; Rev. Plant Pathol.; Rice Abstr.; Seed Abstr.; Soils Fert.; Sorghum Mill. Abstr.; Soyabean Abstr.; Weed Abstr.; Wheat Barley Trit. Abstr.

LC S ISSN 0024-9645
DD 630 DK
MAELKERITIDENDE. [Maelkeritidende]. (1888)-. Periodical. Danish.
Ind/Abst AgBiotech News Inf.; AGRICOLA; Agric. Eng. Abstr. (1991-); Dairy Sci. Abstr.; Food Sci. Technol. Abstr.; Index Vet.; Nutr. Abstr. Rev., Ser. B, Live Feeds and Feed.; Nutr. Abstr. Rev., Ser. A, Hum. Exp.; Soyabean Abstr.; Vet. Bull.

LC S ISSN 0091-4460
DD 630 US
MAFES RESEARCH HIGHLIGHTS. [MAFES res. highlights]. **Main/Corp** Mississippi Agricultural and Forestry Experiment Station. **Added/Corp** Mississippi Agricultural and Forestry Experiment Station. Research Highlights. **VFOAT** Research Highlights. **VAT** Mississippi Agricultural and Forestry Experiment Station Research Highlights. Vol. 36 (Jan. 1973)-. Periodical. English. Six times a year. Free on request. Mississippi State University / Information Services, PO Box 5446, Mississippi State MS 39762. **Tel** (601)325-7774. **ED** Troy Kight. Index available. cum. index. **Circ:** 13,000. ***Continues*** *Mississippi Farm Research, 0026-6221.*
Desc: A tabloid of popular interpretation and discussion of experimental station research.
Ind/Abst AGRICOLA [Select. Cov.].

LC S590 ISSN 0258-3275
DD 638.1 UA
CODEN AJASDK
MAGALLA ASYUT AL-ULUM AZ-ZIRAIYYA. (ASSIUT JOURNAL OF AGRICULTURAL SCIENCES.). [Magalla Asyut al-ulum az-ziraiyya]. **Added/Corp** Jamiat Asyut. Kulliyat al-Ziraah. **VFOAT** Majallat Asyut Lil-ulum Al-ziraiyah. Vol. 1 (1970)-. Academic Scholarly Publication. English (summaries and/or abstracts in Arabic). Irregular. Assiut University, Faculty of Agriculture, Assiut Egypt. Documents available from CASDDS.
Ind/Abst Biocont. News Inf. (19??-19??); Chem. Abstr.; Cot. Trop. Fibr. Abstr. Bibliogr.; Dairy Sci. Abstr.; Field Crop Abstr.; Food Sci. Technol. Abstr.; For. Prod. Abstr. (1991-); Grass. Forage Abstr.; Hortic. Abstr.; Index Vet.; Maize Abstr.; Nutr. Abstr. Rev., Ser. B, Live Feeds and Feed.; Plant Breed. Abstr.; Plant Grow. Reg. Abstr.; Poult. Abstr.; Rev. Agric. Entomol.; Rev. Med. Vet. Entomol.; Rev. Plant Pathol.; Rice Abstr.; Seed Abstr.; Soyabean Abstr.; Weed Abstr.; Wheat Barley Trit. Abstr.; World Agric. Econ. Rural Sociol. Abstr.

LC S322.I7 M34
DD 630 IQ
CODEN JAWRES
MAGALLAT AL-BUHUT AL-ZIRAIYYAT WA-AL-MAWARID AL-MAIYYAT. (MAJALLAT AL-BUHUTH AL-ZIRAIYAH WA-AL-MAWARID AL-MAIYAH.). [Magallat al-Buhut al-Ziraiyyat wa-al-Mawarid al-Maiyyat]. **Added/Corp** Markaz Al-Buhuth Al-Ziraiyah Wa-al-Mawarid Al-Maiyah (Majlis Al-Bahth Al-Ilmi). **VFOAT** Journal of Agriculture and Water Resources Research; Intaj al-Hayawani; Intaj al-Nabati; Turbah wa-Masadir al-Miyah; JAWRR. (19??)-. Periodical. Arabic (English). Two times a year. $50.00 (institutions), $20.00 (individuals). Sikirtir al-Tahrir, Majallet al-Buhuth al-Ziraiyan, Wa-al-Mawarid al-Maiyah Markaz al-Buhuth, al-Ziraiyah Wa-al-Mawarid al-Maiyah, S B 2416 Baghdad Al-Iraq. Documents available from BIOSIS Document Express, CASDDS.
Ind/Abst Biodeter. Abstr.; Biol. Abstr. (?-1989); Chem. Abstr. (1985).

LC S ISSN 1012-3466
DD 630 IQ
MAGALLAT AL-BUHUT AL-ZIRA'IYYAT WA-AL-MAWARID AL-MA'IYYAT. AL-INTAG AL-HAYAWANI. **VFOAT** Journal of Agriculture and Water Resources Research. Animal Production. (1986)-. Periodical. Multiple languages. Two times a year. Agriculture and Water Resources Research Center, PO Box 2416, Baghdad Iraq. Documents available from CASDDS.
Ind/Abst Agrindex; Chem. Abstr.

LC S ISSN 1012-3474
DD 630 IQ
MAGALLAT AL-BUHUT AL-ZIRA'IYYAT WA-AL-MAWARID AL-MA'IYYAT. AL-INTAG AL-NABATI. **VFOAT** Journal of Agriculture and Water Resources Research. Plant Production. (1986)-. Periodical. Multiple languages. Two times a year. Agriculture and Water Resources Research Center, PO Box 2416, Baghdad Iraq. Documents available from CASDDS.
Ind/Abst Agrindex; Chem. Abstr.; Irr. Drain. Abstr.; Plant Grow. Reg. Abstr.; Soyabean Abstr.

LC S ISSN 1018-3590
DD 630 SU
UDC 63
MAGALLAT GAMIAT AL-MALIK SAUD. AL-ULUM AL-ZIRAIYYAT. **VFOAT** Journal of King Saud University. Agricultural Sciences. (1989)-. Periodical. Multiple languages. Two times a year. King Saud University, University Libraries, PO Box 22480, 11495 Riyadh Saudi Arabia.
Ind/Abst Rev. Med. Vet. Mycology; Rev. Plant Pathol.; Seed Abstr.

LC S ISSN 0763-8922
DD 630 FR
UDC 63 : 331.88
MAGASIN AGRICOLE (PARIS). (MAGASIN AGRICOLE.). (1984)-. Periodical. French. Irregular. 120.00F France; 180.00F other. Promapress, 28 rue Bayard, 75008 Paris France. **Tel** 1 47 23 72 98.
Ind/Abst Chem. Bus. Bull.; Chem. Bus. NewsBase (1985-); Chem. Bus. Update.

LC S
DD 630 II
MAGAZINE - COLLEGE OF AGRICULTURE, NAGPUR. **Main/Corp** College of Agriculture, Nagpur. (19??)-. English (Hindi).
Ind/Abst Nematol. Abstr.

LC S
DD 630 HU
MAGYAR MEZOGAZDASAG. (19??)-. Periodical. Hungarian. One time a week.

Agriculture

LC S227 .M27   **ISSN** 0521-4238
HU
MAGYAR MEZOGAZDASAGI MUZEUM KOZLEMENYEI, A. **Added/Corp** Magyar Mezogazdasagi Muzeum. **VFOAT** Kozlemenyek; Mitteilungen des Ungarischen Handwirtschaftlichen Muzeums. (19??)-. Hungarian (summaries and/or abstracts in English and German; table of contents in English and German).
Ind/Abst Am. Hist. Life (1981-).

LC S544.5.I5 M29
DD 630/.7/15054792
II
MAHARASHTRA JOURNAL OF EXTENSION EDUCATION. Vol. 1, No. 1 (Oct. 1982)-. English. One time a year. Rs100.00 India; $10.00 US. Maharashtra Society of Extension Education, Directorate of Extension, PO Krishi Nagar, Akola 444104 India. **Tel** 6849/6841, telex 0725-215 PKV. **ED** R R Sinha. **Circ:** 750 (ctrl).
Desc: Publishes contents on research articles of agricultural extension, sociology, communication, education and home science.
Ind/Abst Maize Abstr.

LC S   **ISSN** 1062-2691
DD 630   US
MAINE AGRICULTURAL REPORT. [Maine agric. rep.]. **Added/Corp** Maine. Dept. of Agriculture. Division of Production and Market Development. (1992)-. Periodical. English. One time a week. $15.00. Maine Department of Agriculture, Food & Rural Resources, Blossom Lane, State House, Station 28, Augusta ME 04333. **Tel** (207)289-3871, FAX (207)289-7548. **Continues** Maine-ly Agriculture.

LC S   **ISSN** 0891-9194
DD 630   US
MAINE ORGANIC FARMER & GARDENER, THE. [Me. org. farmer gard.]. **Added/Corp** Maine Organic Farmers and Gardeners Association. **VAT** Maine Organic Farmer and Gardener. Vol. 5, No. 1 (Jan./Feb. 1978)-. Periodical. English. Six times a year (Jan., Mar., May, July, Sept., Nov.). $12.00. Maine Organic Farmers & Gardeners Association, 283 Water Street/Box 2176, Augusta ME 04330. **Tel** (207)622-3118. **ED** Jean English (editor's address: RR 2 Box 594, Lincolnville ME 04849) (phone: (207)763-3043). Index available (bound in Jan./Feb. issue; $1.50). cum. index. **Bk Rev**. **Ad Acc**, **Adv Mgr** Janice Clark. **Circ:** 5,000.
Desc: Dedicated to healthy soil, pollution free environment, renewable resources, humane practices in livestock, husbandry, and a strong agricultural economy.

LC SB317.5   **ISSN** 1193-3046
DD 635   CN
MAIS-GRAIN, RESULTATS D'ESSAIS ..., HYBRIDES RECOMMANDES EN ... / CONSEIL DES PRODUCTIONS VEGETALES DU QUEBEC. [Mais-grain result. essais hybrides recomm.]. **Added/Corp** Conseil des Productions Vegetales du Quebec. (1992)-. French.

LC S   **ISSN** 0541-7406
DD 630   IO
CODEN MJPGAI
MAJALAH PERUSAHAAN GULA. **Added/Corp** Pasuruan, Indonesia (City). Balai Penyelidikan Perusahaan Perkebunan Gula. (1973)-. Periodical. Indonesian (English). Four times a year. **Continues** Madjalah Perusahaan Gula.
Ind/Abst Field Crop Abstr.; Hortic. Abstr.; Soils Fert.

LC S410.M3 A37
DD 630/.2/05595
MY
MALAYSIA AGRICULTURAL DIRECTORY & INDEX. **VFOAT** Malaysia Agricultural Directory and Index. (1984/85)-. Directory. English. Two times a year. 80.00Mal$. Pantai Maju Sdn Bhd, 78B Jalan SS22, 21 Damansara Jaya Petaling, Jaya Selangor Malaysia. **Tel** 7195272, FAX 603-7181050. **ED** Ch'ng Guan Choo, Kho Boon Lian, Lee Loy Fatt, Lim Tong Kwee, Tan Swee Lian, Tay Tian Hock. Index available. cum. index. **Ad Acc**. **Circ:** 4,000. **Continues** Agricultural Directory of Malaysia, 0376-5644.
Desc: Complete guide to Malaysian agriculture. Includes about 4,000 key personnel, both government and commercial agriculture organizations.

LC S17 .M3   **ISSN** 0025-1321
DD 630   MY
CODEN MAGJAL
MALAYSIAN AGRICULTURAL JOURNAL, THE. [Malays. agric. j.]. **Added/Corp** Malaya. Ministry of Agriculture and Cooperatives. Malaysia. Kementerian Pertanian dan Pembangunan Luar Bandar. Vol. 45, No. 1 (Jan. 1985)-. Periodical. English. Two times a year (July & Dec.). $12.05. Ministry of Agricultural, Jalan Swettonham, Kuala Lampur Malaysia. **Tel** 982011. Documents available from BIOSIS Document Express, CASDDS. **Continues** Malayan Agricultural Journal.
Ind/Abst AGRICOLA; Biol. Abstr.; Chem. Abstr. (1965-1981); Nutr. Abstr. Rev., Ser. B, Live Feeds and Feed.; Nutr. Abstr. Rev., Ser. A, Hum. Exp.; Rev. Med. Vet. Entomol.; SEA Abstr.; Soils Fert.; Soyabean Abstr.; Wheat Barley Trit. Abstr.

LC S   **ISSN** 0126-8643
DD 630   MY
CODEN MABIDU
Pr Rev.
MALAYSIAN APPLIED BIOLOGY. (MALAYSIAN APPLIED BIOLOGY = BIOLOGI GUNAAN MALAYSIA.). [Malays. appl. biol.]. **Added/Corp** Persatuan Biologi Gunaan Malaysia. **VFOAT** Biologi Gunaan Malaysia. Vol. 6 (June 1977)-. Academic Scholarly Publication. English (summaries and/or abstracts in Malay). Two times a year. $50.00. Malaysian Society of Applied Biology, c/o Faculty of Fisheries & Marine Science, Universiti Pertanian, Serdang 43400, Selangor Malaysia. **Tel** 011 63 3 8292861, FAX 011 63 3 8252698. **ED** Ismail Sahid. **Ad Acc**. **Circ:** 300. Documents available from BIOSIS Document Express, CASDDS. **Continues** Malaysian Agricultural Research, 0126-5458.
Ind/Abst AGRICOLA [Full Cov.]; Biol. Abstr.; Chem. Abstr.; EMBASE; Fish Rev.; Food Sci. Technol. Abstr.; Wildl. Rev.

LC S   **ISSN** 1016-0469
DD 630   CR
Pr Rev.
MANEJO INTEGRADO DE PLAGAS. [Manejo integr. plagas]. (1986)-. Academic Scholarly Publication. Spanish. Four times a year. $25.00. Centro Agronomico Tropical de Investigacion y Ensenanza, CATIE 7170 Turrialba Costa Rica. **Tel** 011 506 556 6431, 556 0169, 556 1632, FAX 011 506 556 1533, 556 0606, telex 8005 CATIE C.R. **ED** Laura Rodriguez Amador. Index available. cum. index. **Ad Acc**. Full Page (B&W) $345.00. Half Page (B&W) $245.00. Full Page (Color) $480.00. Half Page (Color) $365.00. **Circ:** 1,000.
Ind/Abst Biocont. News Inf.; For. Abstr.; Hortic. Abstr.; Maize Abstr.; Potato Abstr.; Rev. Agric. Entomol.; Rev. Plant Pathol.; Seed Abstr.; Weed Abstr.

LC SB950   **ISSN** 0228-7927
DD 632/.951   CN
MANITOBA INSECT CONTROL GUIDE. Trade Publication. English. One time a year. Manitoba Department of Agriculture Entomology Division, 910 Norquay Building, Manitoba R3C 0V8 Canada.

LC HD2022 .M33
DD 630   SP
MANUAL DE ESTADISTICA AGRARIA. See Agriculture-Abstracting, Bibliographies and Statistics.

LC HD72   **ISSN** 0826-6433
DD 338.9171   CN
MANUSCRIPT REPORTS - INTERNATIONAL DEVELOPMENT RESEARCH CENTRE. See Business and Economics-Economic Assistance and Development.

LC S   **ISSN** 0279-4543
DD 630   US
MARKET NEWS. LIVESTOCK, MEAT, GRAIN AND SEED DIVISION. **Added/Corp** Nebraska. Division of Agriculture Development and Marketing. United States. Dept. of Agriculture. **VFOAT** Livestock Market News, Nebraska Edition. (198?)-. Periodical. English. One time a week. Nebraska Department of Agriculture, PO Box 94947, Lincoln NE 68509. **Tel** (402)471-2341, FAX (402)471-3252. **Continues** Market News. Livestock, Poultry, Grain and Seed Divisions, 0199-7718.

LC HD9007.V8 V56a   **ISSN** 0507-066X
DD 381/.41/09755   US
MARKET NEWS (RICHMOND). (MARKET NEWS.). **Main/Corp** Virginia. Division of Markets. (1967)-. English. One time a year. Virginia Department of Agriculture & Consumer Services, 1100 Bank Street, Washington Building, Suite 210, Richmond VA 23219. **Tel** (804)786-2373, FAX (804)371-7679.

LC S
DD 630   US
MARKETING CALIFORNIA, COLORADO, IDAHO, NEW MEXICO, OREGON, AND WASHINGTON ONIONS. English. One time a year. $10.00. US Department of Agriculture / Washington State, 2015 South First Street, Room 4, Yakima WA 98903. **Tel** (509)575-2494, FAX (509)457-7132.

LC S
DD 630   US
●MARKETING GREAT LAKES VEGETABLES. (1995)-. English. One time a year. $20.00. Michigan Department of Agriculture, PO Box 30017, Lansing MI 48909. **Tel** (517)373-1050, FAX (517)335-0628. **Continues** Marketing Michigan Vegetables.

LC S
DD 630   US
MARKETING NORTHWEST APPLES. **Added/Corp** United States. Agricultural Marketing Service. Fruit and Vegetable Division. Market News Branch. Idaho. Dept. of Agriculture. Washington (State). Dept. of Agriculture. Federal-State Market News Service. (1975)-. Periodical. English. One time a year. $10.00. US Department of Agriculture / Washington State, 2015 South First Street, Room 4, Yakima WA 98903. **Tel** (509)575-2494, FAX (509)457-7132.

LC S
DD 630   US
MARKETING WESTERN POTATOES. English. One time a year. $10.00 North America; $20.00 other. US Department of Agriculture / Washington State, 2015 South First Street, Room 4, Yakima WA 98903. **Tel** (509)575-2494, FAX (509)457-7132.

LC AP   **ISSN** 1052-5785
DD 051   US
MARTHA'S VINEYARD. [Martha's Vineyard]. **VFOAT** Martha's Vineyard Magazine. (1985)-. Periodical. English. Four times a year (May, July, Aug., Sept.). $15.00. Vineyard Gazette, PO Box 66, Edgartown MA 02539. **Tel** (508)627-4311, FAX (508)627-7444. **ED** Lawrence Michie. **Ad Acc**. ctrl circ.

LC S   **ISSN** 0745-4317
DD 630   US
MARYLAND AGRI-VIEWS. [Md. agri-views]. **Added/Corp** Maryland. Dept. of Agriculture. **VAT** Maryland Agri Views. Vol. 1, No. 1 (May 1974)-. Periodical. English. Four times a year. Agriculture Views, Crop Reporting Service, Room 3124/Symons Hall, College Park MD 20742. **Continues** Agricultural Review.

LC S
DD 630   US
MARYLAND AGRICULTURAL STATISTICS SUMMARY FOR... . See Agriculture-Abstracting, Bibliographies and Statistics.

LC S   **ISSN** 0279-7895
DD 630   US
MARYLAND FARMER (BALTIMORE, MD. : 1979). (MARYLAND FARMER.). Vol. 1, No. 1 (May 1979)-. Newspaper. English. Twelve times a year. $12.00. Rural Press USA, 7701 Six Forks Road, Suite 132, Raleigh NC 27615. **Tel** (800)934-2472, (919)676-3276, FAX (919)676-9803. **ED** Julie Gochenour (editor's telephone: (703)459-3209). **Ad Acc**. **Circ:** 10,353 (ctrl).
Desc: A locally-edited newspaper which serves the agricultural interests of the state and its neighboring counties.

LC S73 .N48A   **ISSN** 0092-9794
DD 338.1/09774   US
MASSACHUSETTS AGRICULTURAL STATISTICS. See Agriculture-Abstracting, Bibliographies and Statistics.

LC S73 .D46A   **ISSN** 0739-8867
DD 338.1/09744   US
MASSACHUSETTS AGRICULTURE. [Mass. agric.]. **Main/Corp** Massachusetts. Dept. of Food and Agriculture. English. One time a year. Massachusetts Department of Food and Agriculture, 100 Cambridge Street, Room 2103, Boston MA 02202. **Tel** (617)727-3003, FAX (617)727-7235. **Continues** Massachusetts. Dept. of Food and Agriculture. Annual Report.

LC S   **ISSN** 0025-6153
DD 630   IT
CODEN MYDCAH
Pr Rev.
MAYDICA. [Maydica]. Vol. 1- 1956-. Periodical. English. Four times a year. L160000 Italy; $115.00 US. Istituto Sperimentale Per La Cerealicoltura, Sezione di Bergamo, Via Stezzano 24, 24100 Bergamo Italy. **Tel** 35/313132, FAX 35/316054. **ED** A Bianchi and P A Peterson. Index available. cum. index. **Bk Rev**. **Circ:** 320 (ctrl). Documents available from The Genuine Article, CASDDS.
Desc: A journal devoted to maize and allied species.
Ind/Abst AgBiotech News Inf.; AGRICOLA; Chem. Abstr.; Crop Physiol. Abstr.; Curr. Aware. Biol. Sci.; CABS; Curr. Cit.; Curr. Contents Agric. Biol. Environ. Sci.; Field Crop Abstr.; Genet. Abstr.; Irr. Drain. Abstr.; Maize Abstr.; Life Sci. Collect.; Plant Breed.; Plant Grow. Reg. Abstr.; Res. Alert [Full Cov.]; Rev. Agric. Entomol.; Rev. Plant Pathol.; Rice Abstr.; Sci. Cit. Index; SCISEARCH; Seed Abstr.

LC S   **ISSN** 0368-3419
DD 630   SW
MEDDELANDE - JORDBRUKSTEKNISKA INSTITUTET. [Medd. - Jordbruksek. inst.]. **Main/Corp** Jordbruksekniska Institutet (Sweden). (1945)-. Monograph series. Swedish (summaries and/or abstracts in English). Price varies per volume. **Continues**

Agriculture

in part Jordbrukstekniska Foreningen. Meddelande - Jordbrukstekniska Foreningen.
Ind/Abst Agric. Eng. Abstr.; Potato Abstr.; Soils Fert.

LC S
DD 630 BE
MEDEDELING. Added/Corp Proinciaal Onderzoeken Voorlichtingscentrum voor Land- en Tuinbouw (Beitem-Roeselare). (19??)-. Dutch.
Ind/Abst Hortic. Abstr.; Plant Breed. Abstr.

LC S
DD 630 BE
MEDEDELINGEN / FACULTEIT LANDBOUWKUNDIGE EN TOEGEPASTE BIOLOGISCHE WETENSCHAPPEN. (1993)-. Periodical. German. Four times a year. 4000.00F. Faculteit Landbouwwetenschappen, Coupure 653, B-9000 Ghent Belgium. **Tel** 011 32 91 236961. *Continues* Rijksuniversiteit te Gent. Faculteit van de Landbouwwetenschappen Mededelingen, 0368-9697.
Ind/Abst Curr. Cit.

LC S **ISSN** 0303-9056
DD 630 BE
MEDEDELINGEN VAN HET RIJKSSTATION VOOR LANDBOUWTECHNICK. [Meded. rijksstn. landbouwtech.]. (1964)-. Monographic series. Dutch (summaries and/or abstracts in English, French and German). Irregular. Price varies per volume. Rijksstation voor Landbouwtechniek, van Gansberghelaan 115, B-9820 Merelbeke Belgium. **Tel** 011 32 9 252 521821, **FAX** 011 32 9 252 5244234. **ED** J. Daelemans. ctrl circ.
Ind/Abst Agric. Eng. Abstr.; Postharvest News Inf.

LC S **ISSN** 0368-9697
DD 630 BE
MEDELDELINGEN VAN DE FACULTEIT LANDBOUWWETENSCHAPPEN, RIJKSUNIVERSITEIT, GENT. [Meded. fac. landbouwwet., Rijksuniv., Gent]. **Main/Corp** Rijksuniversiteit te Gent. Faculteit van de Landbouwwetenschappen, Ghent. Mededelingen - Rijksfaculteit Landbouwwetenschapen te Gent. French. Four times a year. 4000.00F. Faculteit Landbouwwetenschappen, Coupure 653, B-9000 Ghent Belgium. **Tel** 011 32 91 236961. *Continues* Rijksfaculteit der Landbouwwetenschappen, Ghent. Mededelingen - Rijksfaculteit Landbouwwetenschapen te Gent.
Ind/Abst AGRICOLA; Field Crop Abstr.; Index Vet.; Nematol. Abstr.; Rev. Agric. Entomol.; Vitis Vitic. Enol. Abstr.; Weed Abstr.

LC S **ISSN** 0166-8129
DD 630 NE
MEDELINGEN - LANDBOUW-ECONOMISCH INSTITUUT. [Meded. - Landbouw-Econ. Inst.]. **Main/Corp** Landbouw-Economisch Instituut (Netherlands). No. 138 (March 1976)-. Monographic series. Dutch. Price varies per volume. Landbouw-Economisch Instituut, Postbus 29703, 2502 LS Hague Netherlands. **Tel** 011 31 70 3308330, **FAX** 011 31 70 615624. *Continues* Mededelingen & Overdrukken.
Ind/Abst AGRICOLA; Poult. Abstr.

LC S **ISSN** 1120-6403
DD 630 IT
UDC 33
CODEN 504
MEDIT. (1990)-. Periodical. Italian. Four times a year. L64720. Edagricole, PO Box 2157, 40100 Bologna Italy. **Tel** 011 39 51 492211 Ext. 22, **FAX** 011 39 51 493660, telex 510336 EDAGRI.

LC S
DD 630 GW
MEINUNGEN ZUR AGRAR- UND UMWELTPOLITIK. Added/Corp Deutsche Gesellschaft fur Agrar- und Umweltpolitik. (1978)-. German.
Ind/Abst World Agric. Econ. Rural Sociol. Abstr.

LC S
DD 630 AT
CEASED
MELBOURNE NOTES ON AGRICULTURAL EXTENSION. Added/Corp Melbourne. University. Faculty of Agriculture and Forestry. Victoria, Australia. Dept. of Agriculture. Melbourne. University. Faculty of Agriculture. No.4 (Apr. 1970)-(19??). Periodical. English.
Ind/Abst Aust. Educ. Index (?-?).

LC S
DD 630 NO
MELDING. Added/Corp Norges Landbrukshgskole. Institutt for Landbruksokonomi. **VFOAT** Report. (19??)-. Monographic series. Norwegian (summaries and/or abstracts in English). Price varies per volume. *Continues* Norges Landbrukshgskole. Institutt for Driftslaere og Landbruksokonomi. Melding.
Ind/Abst World Agric. Econ. Rural Sociol. Abstr.

LC S560 **ISSN** 0225-0985
DD 630/.68 CN
CEASED
MEMBERS' DIGEST - ONTARIO FEDERATION OF AGRICULTURE. [Memb. dig. - Ont. Fed. Agric.]. **Main/Corp** Ontario Federation of Agriculture. Vol. 1 (July 1979)-(1993). Periodical. English. Ontario Federation Agriculture, Suite 502, 387 Bloor Street East, Toronto Ontario M4W 1H9. *Supersedes* Management Digest, 0380-4380.

LC S230.D67 M45
DD 638.0944 FR
MEMENTO DE STATISTIQUE AGRICOLE : DORDOGNE. See Agriculture-Abstracting, Bibliographies and Statistics.

LC LAW **ISSN** 0766-6160
DD 343.44/076/05 344.4037605 FR
MEMENTO PRATIQUE FRANCIS LEFEBVRE: AGRICULTURE. See Law.

LC S
DD 630 FR
MEMOIRES DE LA SOCIETE D'AGRICULTURE, COMMERCE, SCIENCES ET ARTS DU DEPARTEMENT DE LA MARNE. Main/Corp Societe d'Agriculture, Commerce, Sciences et Arts du Departement de la Marne, Chalons-Sur-Marne. (1855)-. French. One time a year. $13.40. Societe d'Agriculture Commerce Sciences et Arts de la Marne, 13 rue Pasteur, Chalons-Sur Marne 51000 France. **Tel** 26 68 06 69. Index available. cum. index. **Circ**: 900. *Supersedes* Societe d'Agriculture, Commerce, Sciences et Arts du Departement de la Marne, Chalons-sur-Marne. Seance Publique.
Ind/Abst Avery Index Archit. Period. Suppl. Colum. Univ. (?-199?); BHA : Biblio. Hist. Art.

LC S19 .K34 **ISSN** 0453-0853
DD 630/.5 JA
CODEN MAKUA6
MEMOIRS OF THE FACULTY OF AGRICULTURE, KAGOSHIMA UNIVERSITY. [Mem. Fac. Agric., Kagoshima Univ.]. **Added/Corp** Kagoshima Daigaku. Nogakubu. **VFOAT** Kagoshima Daigaku Nogakubu Kiyo. (March 1952)-. Academic Scholarly Publication. English. One time a year. Kagoshima University Faculty of Agriculture, 21-24 Koorimoto 1 chome, Kagoshimashi Kagoshimaken 890 Japan. Documents available from CASDDS.
Ind/Abst Biocont. News Inf.; Chem. Abstr.; Dairy Sci. Abstr.; EMBASE; Field Crop Abstr.; Plant Grow. Reg. Abstr.; Rice Abstr.; SEA Abstr.; Seed Abstr.; Trop. Dis. Bull.

LC S539.5 **ISSN** 0372-0322
DD 630.72 JA
CODEN TOAMB6
MEMOIRS OF THE TOKYO UNIVERSITY OF AGRICULTURE. [Mem. Tokyo univ. agric.]. **Main/Corp** Tokyo Nogyo Daigaku. Vol. 7 (1963)-. Multiple languages (English and German). Tokyo Nogyo Daigaku, (Tokyo University of Agriculture). 1-1 Sakuragaoka 1 Chome, Setagayaku Tokyo 156 Japan. Documents available from BIOSIS Document Express, CASDDS. *Continues* Tokyo Nogyo Daigaku. Journal.
Ind/Abst Biol. Abstr.; Chem. Abstr.

LC S
DD 630 SP
MEMORIA DEL ICONA. (19??)-. Spanish. One time a year. 600ptas. Ministerio Agricultura, Centro de Publicaciones, Calle Alfonso XII 56, 28071 Madrid Spain. **Tel** 011 34 1 3475551, **FAX** 011 34 1 3475722.

LC S
DD 630 AG
MEMORIA Y BALANCE GENERAL. Main/Corp Cooperativa Agricola General Pueyrredon. (1???)-. Portuguese.

LC HD9014.B8 M47
DD 630 BL
MERCADO EM ANALISE. Periodical. Portuguese. Ministerio Agricultura, Centro de Publicaciones, Calle Alfonso XII 56, 28071 Madrid Spain. **Tel** 011 34 1 3475551, **FAX** 011 34 1 3475722.

LC HD9015.A1 L36 **ISSN** 1014-8159
DD 338.1/3/094021 LU
MERCADOS AGRARIOS. PRECIOS / COMISION DE LAS COMUNIDADES EUROPEAS / LANDSBRUGSMARKEDER. PRISER / KOMMISSIONEN FOR DE EUROPAEISKE FAELLESSKABER / AGRICULTURAL MARKETS. PRICES / COMMISSION OF THE EUROPEAN COMMUNITIES. See Agriculture-Abstracting, Bibliographies and Statistics.

LC HD9014.B8 B35A
DD 338.1 BL
MERCADOS AGRICOLAS : INFORMACOES. Main/Corp Banco do Nordeste do Brasil. Departamento Rural. Divisao de Estudos e Projetos Especiais. Portuguese. Banco do Nordeste do Brasil / SEBIB, Avenue Paranjana 5700, 60715 Fortaleza CE Brazil. **Tel** 011 55 2993175, telex (085)2259. *Continues* Mercados Agricolas: Informacoes.

LC S
DD 630 IT
MERCATI AGRICOLI : PREZZI. (19??)-. Multiple languages. Four times a year. L206000.00. Office for Official Publications of the European Communities, 2 rue Mercier, 2985 Luxembourg Luxembourg. **Tel** 011 352 499281, **FAX** 011 352 292942763. **(Subscription address:** Licosa s.p.a., PO Box 552, 50125 Florence Italy. **Tel** 011 39 55 645415.)

LC S159 .D46B
DD 630/.7/9 CN
MERITE AGRICOLE ET MERITE DU DEFRICHEUR. Main/Corp Quebec (Province). Dept. of Agriculture and Colonization. French. Ministere de l'Agriculture et de la Colonisation, Quebec Quebec.

LC S **ISSN** 0177-865X
DD 630 GW
UDC 63
MERKBLATT- DEUTSCHE LANDWIRTSCHAFTS-GESELLSCHAFT V. [Merkbl. - Dtsch. Landwirtsch.-Ges. e.V.]. **VFOAT** Merkblatt - DLG. (1978)-. Monographic series. German. Irregular. Deutsche Landwirtschafts Gesellschaft, Verlags GmbH, Eschborner Landstr 122, D-60489 Frankfurt Germany. **Tel** 011 49 69 247880, **FAX** 011 49 69 24788580. *Continues* DLG-Merkblatt, 0177-8641.

LC S17 **ISSN** 0379-7791
DD 630 IQ
CODEN MJAGDE
MESOPOTAMIA JOURNAL OF AGRICULTURE. [Mesop. j. agric.]. **VFOAT** Majallah Ziraah Al-rafidayn. Vol. 5-6, (1970-71)-. Academic Scholarly Publication. English (English). Irregular. University of Mosul, College of Agriculture and Forestry, Hammam Al-Alil Iraq. Documents available from BIOSIS Document Express, CASDDS. *Continues* Mesopotamia Agriculture.
Ind/Abst Agrofor. Abstr. (1991-); Anim. Breed. Abstr.; Biodeter. Abstr.; Biol. Abstr.; Chem. Abstr.; Cot. Trop. Fibr. Abstr. Bibliogr.; Crop Physiol. Abstr.; Dairy Sci. Abstr.; Field Crop Abstr.; Food Sci. Technol. Abstr.; For. Prod. Abstr. (19??-19??); For. Abstr.; Hortic. Abstr.; Index Vet.; Irr. Drain. Abstr.; Maize Abstr.; Nematol. Abstr.; Plant Breed. Abstr.; Postharvest News Inf.; Rev. Agric. Entomol.; Rev. Med. Vet. Entomol.; Soils Fert.; Wheat Barley Trit. Abstr.

LC S **ISSN** 0230-2810
DD 630 HU
MEZOGAZDASAGI GEPUZEMELTETES. [Mezogazd. gepuzemelt.]. (1981)-. Monographic series. Hungarian. Irregular.
Ind/Abst World Agric. Econ. Rural Sociol. Abstr.

LC HD1492.H8 H87a
DD 335 HU
MEZOGAZDASAGI SZOVETKEZETEK GAZDALKODASA A SZAMOK TUKREBEN. Main/Corp Hungary. Termeloszovetkezetek Orszagos Tanacsa. (19??)-. Hungarian.

LC S409.5.M5 M53 **ISSN** 0092-2250
DD 631/.025/774 US
MICHIGAN CENTENNIAL FARMS DIRECTORY. Directory. English. Irregular. Michigan Bureau of History, Department of State, Lansing MI 48918. **Tel** (517)335-2740.
Desc: A listing of farm addresses organized by county.

LC S **ISSN** 1063-598X
DD 630 US
MICHIGAN FARM NEWS (1990). (MICHIGAN FARM NEWS : PUBLICATION OF MICHIGAN FARM BUREAU.). **Added/Corp** Michigan Farm Bureau. (Oct.15, 1990)-. Periodical. English. Twenty-four times a year. Michigan Farm Bureau, PO Box 30690, Lansing MI 48909. **Tel** (517)323-7000, **FAX** (517)323-6793. *Separated from* Rural Living (Lansing, Mich. : 1981), 0743-9962.

LC S **ISSN** 0026-2153
DD 630 US
MICHIGAN FARMER. [Mich. farmer]. (19??)-. Periodical. English. Fifteen times a year. $19.95. Farm Progress Publishing, 191 South Gary Avenue, Carol Stream IL 60188-2089. **Tel** (708)462-2890 or 2891. **(Subscription address:** CDS / SIFD Agency Control, 1901 Bell Avenue, Des Moines IA 50315. **Tel** (515)246-6812.) available on microfilm from University Microfilms International (UMI). Documents available from

Agriculture

Documents on Demand. **Continues** Michigan Farmer and Livestock Journal.
Ind/Abst Energy Inf. Abstr.; Environ. Abstr.

LC S ISSN 0759-0644
DD 630 FR
MICROBIOLOGIE, ALIMENTS, NUTRITION = MICROBIOLOGY, FOODS AND FEEDS, NUTRITION. See Biology-Microbiology.

LC HD2330 ISSN 1040-1423
DD 338 US
MID AMERICA FARMER GROWER, THE. Vol. 5 No. 29 (July 21, 1988)-. Newspaper. English. One time a week. $51.57. SJS Publishing Company, PO Box 323, Perryville MO 63775. **Tel** (314)547-2244, FAX (314)547-5663. **ED** Lisa K. LaRose, Sales Manager, (phone: (314)547-2244). **Ad Acc, Adv Mgr:** Lisa LaRose, **Tel** (314)547-2244. **Circ:** 27,000 (ctrl). available on an online database (modem). **Continues** MidAmerica Farmer, 0896-6788.
Desc: Information relevant to agriculture nationwide. It is of importance to our large acre readers in Missouri, Southern Illinois, Southwest Indiana, Kentucky, Tennessee, and Arkansas.

LC KF1681.A15 M53 ISSN 0738-6753
DD 343.77/076/05 347.7037605 US
MIDWEST AGRICULTURAL LAW JOURNAL. See Law.

LC S
DD 630 US
MINNESOTA REPORT (UNIVERSITY OF MINNESOTA. AGRICULTURAL EXPERIMENT STATION). (MINNESOTA REPORT.). **Added/Corp** University of Minnesota. Agricultural Experiment Station. (19??)-. Monographic series. English. Price varies per volume. **Continues** Miscellaneous Report (University of Minnesota. Agricultural Experiment Station).
Ind/Abst AGRICOLA [Select. Cov.].

LC S ISSN 0026-5675
DD 630 US
MINNESOTA SCIENCE. Added/Corp University of Minnesota. Agricultural Experiment Station. Vol. 23 (Sept. 1966)-. Periodical. English. Three times a year. Free on request. University of Minnesota / Minnesota Science, 405 Coffey Hall, St Paul MN 55108. **Tel** (612)373-0751. **ED** David L. Hansen. **Circ:** 23,000 (ctrl). **Continues** Minnesota Farm and Home Science, 0096-655x.
Desc: Results of research in agriculture, natural resources, human ecology, biology, the environment, and rural life from the University of Minnesota.
Ind/Abst AGRICOLA [Select. Cov.].

LC S ISSN 0815-7162
DD 630 AT
MISCELLANEOUS BULLETIN (NEW SOUTH WALES. DIVISION OF AGRICULTURAL SERVICES). (MISCELLANEOUS BULLETIN - DIVISION OF AGRICULTURAL SERVICES.). [Misc. bull. - Div. Agric. Serv.]. **Added/Corp** New South Wales. Division of Agricultural Services. (1988)-. Bulletin. English. Irregular. Price varies per volume. New South Wales Department of Agriculture, Locked Bag 21, Orange NSW 2800 Australia. **Tel** 011 61 63 913197.

LC S ISSN 0083-6990
DD 630 NE
CODEN LBMPAV
MISCELLANEOUS PAPERS - LANDBOUWHOGESCHOOL WAGENINGEN. (MISCELLANEOUS PAPERS.). [Misc. pap., Landbouwhogesch. Wageningen]. (1968)-. Monographic series. Dutch. Irregular. Price varies per volume. Drukkerij Veenman BV, Postbus 7, 6700 AA Wageningen Netherlands. **Tel** 011/31/8370/19045, telex 45626. Documents available from BIOSIS Document Express, CASDDS.
Ind/Abst Biol. Abstr.; Chem. Abstr.

LC S471.J3 T626A
DD 630.9 JA
MISCELLANEOUS PUBLICATION OF THE TOHOKU NATIONAL AGRICULTURAL EXPERIMENT STATION. Main/Corp Tohoku Nogyo Shikenjo. **VFOAT** Tohoku Nogyo Shikenjo Kenkyu Shiryo. No. 1-Mar. 1978-. Multiple languages (English and Japanese). Norin Suisansho Tohoku Nogyo Shikenjo, (Tohoku National Agricultural Experiment Station Ministry of Agriculture Forestry & Fisheries), 4 Akahira Shimokuriyagawa, Moriokashi Iwateken 020-01, Japan.
Ind/Abst Plant Breed. Abstr.; Rev. Agric. Entomol.; Seed Abstr.; Soyabean Abstr.

LC S ISSN 0097-6334
DD 630 US
CODEN TAEMAT
MISCELLANEOUS PUBLICATION - TEXAS AGRICULTURAL EXPERIMENT STATION. [Misc. publ., Tex. Agric. Exp. Stn.]. **Main/Corp** Texas Agricultural Experiment Station. No. 1 (Nov. 1946)-. Academic Scholarly Publication. English. Price varies per volume. Texas A & M University / Agriculture, Texas Agricultural Experiment Station, College Station TX 77843. Documents available from BIOSIS Document Express, CASDDS.
Ind/Abst AGRICOLA [Select. Cov.]; Biol. Abstr.; Chem. Abstr. (1946-1983); Field Crop Abstr.; Hortic. Abstr.; Irr. Drain. Abstr.; Plant Genet. Resour. Abstr.; Potato Abstr.; Seed Abstr.; Soyabean Abstr.; World Agric. Econ. Rural Sociol. Abstr.

LC S21 .A46 ISSN 0097-0212
DD 630 US
CODEN XAMPAK
MISCELLANEOUS PUBLICATION - UNITED STATES DEPARTMENT OF AGRICULTURE. (MISCELLANEOUS PUBLICATION / UNITED STATES DEPARTMENT OF AGRICULTURE.). [Misc. publ. - U. S. Dep. Agric.]. **VFOAT** U.S. Department of Agriculture Miscellaneous Publication. No. 1 (1927)-. Monographic series. English. Irregular. Price varies per volume. US Department of Agriculture, 14th Street and Independence Avenue SW, Washington DC 20250. **Tel** (202)720-5457. Documents available from BIOSIS Document Express, CASDDS. **Continues** Miscellaneous Circular - Dept. of Agriculture, 0889-8766.
Ind/Abst AGRICOLA [Full Cov.]; Biol. Abstr.; Chem. Abstr.; Geogr. Abstr. Human Geogr. (?-?); GeoRef; Irr. Drain. Abstr.; Life Sci. Collect.; World Agric. Econ. Rural Sociol. Abstr.

LC S ISSN 0725-847X
DD 630 AT
MISCELLANEOUS PUBLICATION - WESTERN AUSTRALIA DEPARTMENT OF AGRICULTURE. (MISCELLANEOUS PUBLICATION.). [Misc. pub. - West. Aust. Dep. Agric.]. **Added/Corp** Western Australian Dept. of Agriculture. (1982)-. Monographic series. English.
Ind/Abst Nutr. Abstr. Rev., Ser. B, Live Feeds and Feed.; Plant Breed. Abstr.; Postharvest News Inf.; Rev. Agric. Entomol.; Sorghum Mill. Abstr.

LC S ISSN 0428-6103
DD 630 US
MISCELLANEOUS PUBLICATIONS - FLORIDA. AGRICULTURAL EXPERIMENT, GAINESVILLE. LIBRARY. Main/Corp Florida. Agricultural Experiment Station, Gainesville. Library. No. 1 (1961)-. Monographic series. English. Price varies per volume. Institute of Food and Agricultural Sciences, University of Florida, Building 664, Gainesville FL 32611. **Tel** (904)392-1773. **ED** Ida Keeling Cresap, Janie Lee Tyson and Albert C Strickland.

LC S ISSN 0253-6749
DD 630 CY
CODEN MRCIEJ
MISCELLANEOUS REPORTS - MINISTRY OF AGRICULTURE AND NATURAL RESOURCES. AGRICULTURAL RESEARCH INSTITUTE. (MISCELLANEOUS REPORTS.). [Misc. rep. - Minist. Agric. Nat. Resour., Agric. Res. Inst.]. **Added/Corp** Institouton Georgikon Ereunon (Cyprus). (19??)-. Monographic series. English (Greek, Modern). Institouton Georgikon Ereunon / Agricultural Research Institute, Ministry of Agriculture and Natural Resources, Nicosia Cyprus. Documents available from BIOSIS Document Express.
Ind/Abst Biol. Abstr.; Postharvest News Inf.; Potato Abstr.; Rev. Plant Pathol.

LC S ISSN 0026-6205
DD 630 US
MISSISSIPPI FARM BUREAU NEWS. [Miss. Farm Bur. news]. **Added/Corp** Mississippi Farm Bureau Federation. Mississippi Farm Bureau Federation. News. (19??)-. Periodical. English. Ten times a year. Mississippi Farm Bureau News, 429 Mississippi Street, Box 1570, Jackson MS 39205. **ED** Glynda Phillips. **Ad Acc. Circ:** 160,000 (ctrl).
Desc: Covers agricultural news and organizational news.

LC S81 .M57 ISSN 0544-5507
DD 338.1/09778 US
MISSOURI FARM FACTS. Added/Corp Missouri Crop and Livestock Reporting Service. (1966)-. English. One time a year. $5.00. Missouri Agricultural Statistics Office, PO Box L, Columbia MO 65201. **Tel** (314)875-5233. **Circ:** 5,500 (ctrl). **Supersedes** Missouri Farm Census by Counties.
Desc: Publication providing latest county and state agricultural statistics for Missouri.

LC S ISSN 0026-6574
DD 630 US
MISSOURI FB NEWS. (MISSOURI FARM BUREAU NEWS.). **Added/Corp** Missouri Farm Bureau Federation. **VAT** Missouri Farm Bureau News. (19??)-. Periodical. English. Nine times a year. Missouri Farm Bureau, PO Box 658, Jefferson City MO 65102. **Tel** (314)893-1469, FAX (314)893-1540. **ED** Chris Fennewald. **Ad Acc. Circ:** 75,000 (ctrl).
Desc: Covers activities of Missouri Farm Bureau Federation and its members; it is primarily agricultural in nature.

LC S ISSN 0026-668X
DD 630 US
MISSOURI RURALIST. (19??)-. Periodical. English. Irregular. $19.95. Farm Progress Publishing, 191 South Gary Avenue, Carol Stream IL 60188-2089. **Tel** (708)462-2890 or 2891. **Absorbed** Breeder's Special **and** Journal of Agriculture (Saint Louis, Mo. : 1916).
Ind/Abst Ozark Period. Index.

LC SF521 ISSN 0388-2217
DD 638.1 JA
CODEN MIKAE6
MITSUBACHI KAGAKU = HONEYBEE SCIENCE. Added/Corp Tamagawa Daigaku. Mitsubachi Kagaku Kenkyujo. **VFOAT** Honeybee Science. Vol. 1 No. 1 (Jan. 1980)-. Academic Scholarly Publication. Japanese (summaries and/or abstracts in English). Four times a year. Institute of Honeybee Science, Tamagawa University, Machida Shi, Tokyo 194 Japan. **Tel** 011 81 3 427283395, FAX 011 81 3 427283099. **ED** Tetsuo Sakai. Index available. cum. index. **Circ:** 1,000 (ctrl). Documents available from CASDDS.
Desc: Information on agriculture and honey production. Study on mutagenicity of royal jelly, honey vernoms, artificial honey comb and its usage.
Ind/Abst Chem. Abstr.; Sug. Indus. Abstr.

LC S ISSN 0540-4894
DD 630 JA
CODEN MNDGAK
MIYAGI-KEN NOGYO TANKI DAIGAKU GAKUJUTSU HOKOKU. [Miyagi-Ken Nogyo Tanki Daigaku Gakujutsu Hokoku]. **VFOAT** Scientific Reports of the Miyagi Agricultural College. (1954)-. Japanese. One time a year. Miyagiken Nogyo Tanki Daigaku, (Miyagi Agricultural College), 2-1 Hatatate 2 Chome, Sendaishi Miyagiken 982-02, Japan.
Ind/Abst Index Vet.

LC S ISSN 0386-8370
DD 630 JA
CODEN MNTDBO
MIYAGI-KEN NOGYO TANKI DAIGAKU KIYO. [Miyagi-ken Nogyo Tanki Daigaku kiyo]. **VFOAT** Bulletin of the Miyagi Agricultural College. (1966)-. Academic Scholarly Publication. Japanese. Irregular. Documents available from CASDDS.
Ind/Abst Chem. Abstr. (1966-1980).

LC S ISSN 0544-6066
DD 630 JA
CODEN MDNKAC
MIYAZAKI DAIGAKU NOGAKUBU KENKYU JIHO. Main/Corp Miyazaki Daigaku. Nogakubu. **VFOAT** Bulletin of the Faculty of Agriculture, Miyazaki University. Vol. 1 (Feb. 1955)-. Bulletin. Japanese (summaries and/or abstracts in English; table of contents in English). Two times a year. Miyazaki University, Faculty of Agriculture, Miyazaki Japan. Documents available from BIOSIS Document Express, CASDDS.
Ind/Abst Agric. Eng. Abstr.; Agrofor. Abstr.; Biodeter. Abstr.; Biol. Abstr. (-1988); Chem. Abstr.; EMBASE; Field Crop Abstr.; Food Sci. Technol. Abstr.; For. Abstr.; Index Vet.; Nutr. Abstr. Rev., Ser. B, Live Feeds and Feed.; Plant Grow. Reg. Abstr.; Postharvest News Inf.; Poult. Abstr.; Rice Abstr.; Soils Fert.; Sorghum Mill. Abstr.; Vet. Bull.; World Agric. Econ. Rural Sociol. Abstr.

LC S301 .M6
DD 630/.5 PH
MODERN AGRICULTURE AND INDUSTRY. English. $12.00. Multiples Publamark Inc, Femil Building/Suite 334, Aduana Street, PO Box 3332, Manila Philippines.
Ind/Abst Philip. Sci. Technol. Abstr.

LC S
DD 630 AT
MODERN MANAGEMENT (COLLINGWOOD, VIC.). (MODERN MANAGEMENT.). **Added/Corp** McColl Partners (Aust.) Pty. Ltd. ACIL Australia Pty. Ltd. (19??)-. Periodical. English. Twelve times a year. 40.00Aus$. McColl Partners Pty. Ltd., ACIL Australia Pty. Ltd., 30 Cambridge Street, Collingwood Victoria 3066 Australia.
Ind/Abst Manage. Market. Abstr.

LC SB175 ISSN 0145-0662
DD 635 US
MOLASSES MARKET NEWS. (MOLASSES MARKET NEWS. UNITED STATES DEPARTMENT OF AGRICULTURE, AGRICULTURAL MARKETING

SERVICE, GRAIN DIVISION.). [Molasses mark. news]. **Added/Corp** United States. Agricultural Marketing Service. Grain Division. United States. Agricultural Marketing Service. Livestock Division. (19??)-. Periodical. English. One time a week. $40.00. US Department of Agriculture / Colorado, Agricultural Marketing Service, 711 O Street, Greely CO 80631. **Tel** (303)353-9750, FAX (303)353-9790. **ED** Keith L. Padgett.

LC S **ISSN** 0567-1248
DD 630 AU
MONATSBERICHTE UEBER DIE OESTERREICHISCHE LANDWIRTSCHAFT. [Mon.ber. Eosterr. Landwirtsch.]. **Added/Corp** Agrarwirtschaftliches Institut des Bundesministeriums fuer Land- und Forstwirtschaft (Austria) Bundesanstalt fuer Agrarwirtschaft (Austria). (19??)-. Periodical. German. Twelve times a year. S1031.25. Bundesanstalt Agrarwirtschaft, Schweizertalstrasse 36, A 1133 Vienna Austria. **Tel** 011 43 1 8773651. **ED** Werner Pevetz. **Circ:** 680.
Desc: Covers agricultural situations, statistics, and forecasts.
Ind/Abst For. Prod. Abstr. (1991-); For. Abstr.; Maize Abstr.; Pig News Inf.; Soyabean Abstr.; Sug. Indus. Abstr.; Wheat Barley Trit. Abstr.; World Agric. Econ. Rural Sociol. Abstr.

LC S
DD 630 IT
MONDO AGRICOLO. (June 25, 1950)-. Periodical. Italian. One time a week. L34060. Sepe Mondo Agricolo, C So Vitt Emanuele 101, 00186 Rome Italy. **Tel** 011 39 6 6852374.

LC S
DD 630 SP
MONOGRAFIAS I.N.I.A. **Added/Corp** Instituto Nacional de Investigaciones Agrarias. No. 2 (1973)-. Periodical. Spanish.
Ind/Abst Agrofor. Abstr.

LC S
DD 630 UK
MONOGRAPH. BRITISH SOCIETY FOR PLANT GROWTH REGULATION. (19??)-. Monographic series. English. Irregular. Price varies per volume. University of Bristol / Department of Agriculture Science, Long Ashton Research Station, Bristol BS18 9AF United Kingdom.
Ind/Abst Field Crop Abstr.; Grass. Forage Abstr.; Ornamental Hort. (1991-); Plant Genet. Resour. Abstr.; Plant Grow. Reg. Abstr.; Rev. Agric. Entomol.

LC S **ISSN** 0899-3874
DD 630 US
CODEN MUFSEH
MONOGRAPH - UNIVERSITY OF FLORIDA. AGRICULTURAL EXPERIMENT STATION. (MONOGRAPH.). [Monograph - Univ. Fla., Agric. Exp. Stn.]. **Added/Corp** University of Florida. Agricultural Experiment Station. No. 12 (Jan. 1984)-. Monographic series. English. Irregular. Price varies per volume. Institute of Food and Agricultural Sciences, University of Florida, Building 664, Gainesville FL 32611. **Tel** (904)392-1773. Documents available from BIOSIS Document Express. ***Continues*** *Florida Agricultural Experiment Stations Monograph Series, 0735-0465.*
Ind/Abst Biol. Abstr.; Soyabean Abstr.

LC S
DD 630 ET
MONOGRAPHS IN ETHIOPIAN LAND TENURE. **Added/Corp** Haile Selassie I University. Institute of Ethiopian Studies. (1965)-. Monographic series. English. Irregular. Price varies per volume. Oxford University Press / UK, Walton Street, Oxford OX2 6DP United Kingdom. **Tel** 011 44 1865 56767, FAX 011 44 1865 267773, telex 851/837330 OXPRES G.

LC S **ISSN** 0895-1489
DD 630 US
MONTANA AGRESEARCH. [Mont. agresearch]. **Added/Corp** Montana Agricultural Experiment Station. **VFOAT** Montana ag Research. Vol. 1 (Spring 1984)-. Periodical. English. Four times a year. ***Continues*** *Focus on Montana Agriculture.*
Ind/Abst Field Crop Abstr.; Soils Fert.; Weed Abstr.; Wheat Barley Trit. Abstr.

LC HD1775.M9 M6
DD 338.1 US
MONTANA AGRICULTURAL STATISTICS. **See** Agriculture-Abstracting, Bibliographies and Statistics.

LC HD1483 **ISSN** 1182-8919
DD 338.1/097123/05 CN
MONTHLY COMMENTARY AND OUTLOOK. [Mon. comment. outl.]. **Added/Corp** Alberta. Alberta Agriculture. **VAT** Alberta Agriculture Monthly Commentary and Outlook. (Nov. 1990)-. Periodical. English. Twelve times a year. 24.01Can$. Alberta Agriculture Food and Rural Development, Market Analysis and Statistics Branch, #302 7000 - 113 Street, Edmonton Alberta T6H 5T6 Canada. **Tel** (403)427-5387. ***Formed by the union of*** *Alberta. Alberta Agriculture. Market Analysis Branch. The Weekly Grains and Oilseeds Review., 0381-3940* ***and*** *Alberta. Alberta Agriculture. Market Analysis Branch. The Weekly Livestock Market Review., 0381-3959.*

LC S
DD 630 UK
MONTHLY ECONOMIC SURVEY. English. Twelve times a year. £24.00. Scottish Agricultural College, Kings Building / West Mains Road, Edinburgh EH93JG United Kingdom. **Tel** 011 44 131 6671041, FAX 011 44 131 6672601.

LC S
DD 630 US
MONTHLY SUMMARY OF EXPORT CREDIT GUARANTEE PROGRAM ACTIVITY. (19??)-. Government Publication. English. Twelve times a year. $50.00. US Department of Agriculture / Foreign Agricultural Service, 14th Street & Independence Avenue Southwest, Washington DC 20250. **Tel** (202)720-9445, FAX (202)720-7729. **(Subscription address:** NTIS, 5285 Port Royal Road, Springfield VA 22161. **Tel** (703)487-4630.**)**

LC HD **ISSN** 0891-8309
DD 338 US
MONTHLY SUMMARY - UNITED STATES. AGRICULTURAL MARKETING SERVICE. POULTRY DIVISION. MARKET NEWS BRANCH. (MONTHLY SUMMARY / U.S. DEPARTMENT OF AGRICULTURE, AGRICULTURAL MARKETING SERVICE, POULTRY DIVISION, MARKET NEWS BRANCH.). [Mon. summ. - U.S., Agric. Mark. Serv., Poult. Div., Mark. News Branch]. **Added/Corp** United States. Agricultural Marketing Service. Poultry Division. Market News Branch. (19??)-. Periodical. English. Twelve times a year. $75.00. USDA AMS Poultry Market, 800 Roosevelt Road, Building A Suite 310, Glen Ellyn IL 60137. **Tel** (708)790-6910, FAX (708)790-6948.

LC S **ISSN** 0324-5705
DD 630 HU
CODEN MMKZA3
MOSONMAGYAROVARI MEZOGAZDASAGTUDOMANYI KAR KOZLEMENYEI, A. [Mosonmagyarovari Mezogazdasagtud. Kar Kozl.]. **Main/Corp** Agrartudomanyi Egyetem, Keszthely. Mosonmagyarovari Mezogazdasagtudomanyi Kar. (19??)-. Periodical. Hungarian (summaries and/or abstracts in English). ***Continues*** *Mosonmagyarovari Agrartudomanyi Foiskola Kozlemenyei.*
Ind/Abst Dairy Sci. Abstr.; Maize Abstr.; Poult. Abstr.

LC HD9220.P43 L56 **ISSN** 0302-9409
DD 338.17 PE
MOVIMIENTO DE PRODUCTOS AGRICOLAS ALIMENTICIOS INGRESADOS A LIMA METROPOLITANA. **Main/Corp** Peru. Servicio de Informacion de Mercadeo Agropecuario. Spanish. Servico de Informacion de Mercadeo Agropecuario, Edicicio Ministerio de Tracajo 9 Piso, Lima Peru. ***Continues*** *Movimiento de Hortalizas, Tuberculos Y Frutas Ingresados a Lima por el Mercado Mayorista.*

LC S
DD 630 US
MSU INTERNATIONAL DEVELOPMENT PAPERS : REPRINT. (1986)-. Monographic series. English. Price varies per volume. Agriculture Hall, Michigan State University, Department of Agricultural Economics, East Lansing MI 48824-1039.
Ind/Abst World Agric. Econ. Rural Sociol. Abstr.

LC HD1265.J3 A25
DD 387.7/36/095123 JA
MUSHIRO-BATA. **VFOAT** The Strawmat Banner; Strawmat Banner. No. 1- July 1981-. Periodical. English (English). Mushiro-Bata, c/o Parc, PO Box 5250, Tokyo International Japan.

LC S
DD 630 FR
MUTUALITE SOCIALE AGRICOLE EN ... / MSA, MUTUALITE SOCIALE AGRICOLE, LA. **See** Agriculture-Abstracting, Bibliographies and Statistics.

LC S **ISSN** 0047-8539
DD 630 II
CODEN MJASAD
MYSORE JOURNAL OF AGRICULTURAL SCIENCES. [Mysore j. agric. sci.]. **Added/Corp** University of Agricultural Sciences. Vol. 1 (1967)-. Periodical. English. Four times a year. $20.00. University of Agricultural Sciences, Post Bag No 2477, Hebbal Bangalore 560 024 India. **Tel** 35383. **(Subscription address:** Prints India, 11 Darya Ganj, New Delhi 110002 India. **Tel** 011 91 11 3268645, FAX 011 91 11 3275542, telex 31-61087 PRIN-IN.**)** available on microfilm from University Microfilms International (UMI). Documents available from BIOSIS Document Express, CASDDS.
Ind/Abst AGRICOLA; Agrofor. Abstr.; Anim. Breed. Abstr.; Biocont. News Inf.; Biodeter. Abstr. (19??-19??); Biol. Abstr.; Chem. Abstr.; Cot. Trop. Fibr. Abstr. Bibliogr.; Dairy Sci. Abstr.; Field Crop Abstr.; Fish Rev. (Jan. 1989-July 1992); Food Sci. Technol. Abstr.; Grass. Forage Abstr.; Helminthol. Abstr. (19??-19??); Maize Abstr.; Nematol. Abstr.; Nutr. Abstr. Rev., Ser. B, Live Feeds and Feed.; Life Sci. Collect.; Plant Breed. Abstr.; Plant Grow. Reg. Abstr.; Postharvest News Inf.; Potato Abstr.; Poult. Abstr.; Protozoolog. Abstr.; Rev. Agric. Entomol.; Rev. Med. Vet. Entomol.; Rev. Plant Pathol.; Rice Abstr.; Seed Abstr.; Small Anim. Abstr. Bibliogr.; Sorghum Mill. Abstr.; Soyabean Abstr.; Weed Abstr.; Wildl. Rev. (Jan. 1989-July 1992).

LC S20 **ISSN** 0848-8851
DD 630/.6/07151 CN
N.B.I.A. NEWSLETTER (1989). (N.B.I.A. NEWSLETTER.). [N.B.I.A. newsl.]. **Added/Corp** New Brunswick Institute of Agrologists. **VAT** New Brunswick Institute of Agrologists Newsletter (1989). Vol. 1, No. 1 (Winter 1989)-. Newsletter. English (French). Four times a year. Free to members. New Brunswick Institute of Agrologists, PO Box 3479, Postal Station B, Fredericton New Brunswick E3A 5H2 Canada. ***Continues*** *NBIA News, 0832-5235.*

LC S **ISSN** 0149-4910
DD 630 US
NACTA JOURNAL. [NACTA j.]. **Main/Corp** National Association of Colleges and Teachers of Agriculture. **Added/Corp** National Association of Colleges and Teachers of Agriculture. Journal. **VAT** National Association of Colleges and Teachers of Agriculture Journal. Vol. 19, (March 1975)-. Periodical. English. Four times a year (Mar., June, Sept., Dec.). $20.00. National Association of Colleges and Teachers of Agriculture, PO Box 2088, South Houston State University, Huntsville TX 77341. **Tel** (409)294-1226. **ED** Jack Everly. Index available. **Bk Rev**. **Ad Acc. Circ:** 1,800 (ctrl). available on microfilm and microfiche from University Microfilms International (UMI). ***Continues*** *Journal of the National Association of Colleges and Teachers of Agriculture.*
Desc: To improve the teaching in post-secondary agriculture.
Ind/Abst AGRICOLA [Full Cov.].

LC S19 .N28 **ISSN** 1000-2030
DD 630/.5 CC
CODEN NNDXEI
NANJING NONGYE DAXUE XUEBAO. (NAN-CHING NUNG YEH TA HSUEH HSUEH PAO.). [Nanjing nongye daxue xuebao]. **Added/Corp** Nan-Ching Nung yeh ta Hsueh. **VFOAT** Journal of Nanjing Agricultural University; Nanjing Nongye Daxue Xuebao. Vol. 1 (1986)-. Academic Scholarly Publication. English (Chinese). Four times a year. $13.14. Nanjing Agricultural University, Nan-Ching, People's Republic of China. **(Subscription address:** China National Publishers / Industry & Trade, PO Box 782, Beijing, China. **Tel** 011 86 1 4215031.**)** Documents available from CASDDS. ***Continues*** *Nan-Ching Nung Hsueh Yuan Hsueh Pao, 0465-7918.*
Ind/Abst Chem. Abstr.; Cot. Trop. Fibr. Abstr. Bibliogr.; For. Abstr.; Plant Breed. Abstr.; Plant Grow. Reg. Abstr.; Poult. Abstr.; Protozoolog. Abstr.; Rev. Plant Pathol.; Soyabean Abstr.

LC DU1 .N35 **ISSN** 0389-5351
DD 993 JA
NANKAIKEN KIYO = MEMOIRS OF THE KAGOSHIMA UNIVERSITY RESEARCH CENTER FOR THE SOUTH PACIFIC. **Added/Corp** Kagoshima Daigaku. Nanpo Kaiiki Kenkyu Senta. **VFOAT** Memoirs of the Kagoshima University Research Center for the South Pacific. Vol. 2, No. 1 (1981)-. Periodical. English (Japanese). Two times a year. Kagoshima Daigaku Nanpo Kaiiki Kenkyu Senta, (Research Center for the South Pacific), 1-21-24 Korimoto, Kagoshima 890 Japan. ***Continues*** *Nansoken Kiyo.*

LC S **ISSN** 0388-8371
DD 630 JA
CODEN NNSHDA
NARA-KEN NOGYO SHIKENJO KENKYU HOKOKU. [Nara-ken Nogyo Shikenjo kenkyu hokoku]. **VFOAT** Bulletin of the Nara Agricultural Experiment Station. (1969)-. Academic Scholarly Publication. Japanese. One time a year. Naraken Nogyo Shikenjo, (Nara Prefectural Agricultural Experiment Station), Shijocho Kashiharashi, Naraken 634 Japan. Documents available from CASDDS.
Ind/Abst Chem. Abstr. (1969-1983); Hortic. Abstr.; Ornamental Hort. (1991-); Rice Abstr.

LC S **ISSN** 0970-230X
DD 630 II
CODEN NDJRES
NARENDRA DEVA JOURNAL OF AGRICULTURAL RESEARCH. [Narendra Deva j. agric. res.]. **Added/Corp** Narendra Deva University of Agriculture and Technology. Directorate of Research. (19??)-. Periodical. English. Documents available from BIOSIS Document Express.

Ind/Abst Agrofor. Abstr.; Biol. Abstr.; Crop Physiol. Abstr.; Hortic. Abstr.; Maize Abstr.; Rev. Plant Pathol.; Seed Abstr.; Soils Fert.; World Agric. Econ. Rural Sociol. Abstr.

LC S542.T35 T36A
DD 630/.7/20678 TZ
NATIONAL AGRICULTURAL RESEARCH PROGRAMME. **Main/Corp** Tanzania. Crop Development Division. English. PO Box 9071, Dar es Salaam Tanzania.

LC HG3288.N37 N37
DD 332.2 II
NATIONAL BANK NEWS REVIEW. **See** Business and Economics-Economic History, Conditions.

LC HD1401 **ISSN** 0822-7969
DD 338.1/8711 CN
NATIONAL FARMERS UNION REGION 8 SUBMISSION TO THE GOVERNMENT OF BRITISH COLUMBIA ... . [Natl. Farmers Union Reg. 8 submiss. Gov. B.C.]. **Main/Corp** National Farmers Union (Canada). Region 8. 1981-. English. One time a year. Free. National Farmers Union / Canada, 250C 2nd Avenue South, Saskatoon Saskatchewan S7K 1K9 Canada. ctrl circ. ***Continues*** *National Farmers Union Region 8 Submission to the Government of British Columbia ..., 0822-7950.*

LC S **ISSN** 0027-9226
DD 630 US
NATIONAL FARMERS UNION WASHINGTON NEWSLETTER. **Added/Corp** National Farmers' Union (U.S.). **VFOAT** Washington Newsletter. (19??)-. Newsletter. English. Eighteen times a year. $10.00. National Farmers Union / Denver, 10065 East Harvard Avenue, Denver CO 80251. **Tel** (303)337-5500, FAX (303)368-1390. **ED** Marilyn Wentz (editor's address: 11900 East Cornell Avenue Aurora CO 80014-3194). **Circ:** 30,000.

LC SF521
DD 638.1 US
NATIONAL HONEY MARKET NEWS. **Added/Corp** United States. Agricultural Marketing Service. Fruit and Vegetable Division. (198?)-. Periodical. English. Twelve times a year. $36.00. US Department of Agriculture / Washington State, 2015 South First Street, Room 4, Yakima WA 98903. **Tel** (509)575-2494, FAX (509)457-7132. **ED** Linda Verstrate. Documents available from Documents on Demand. ***Continues*** *Honey Market News, 0364-2054.*
Ind/Abst Am. Stat. Index.

LC S
DD 630 US
NATURAL FARMER : PUBLICATION OF THE NATURAL ORGANIC FARMERS ASSOCIATION, THE. **Added/Corp** Natural Organic Farmers Association. **VFOAT** TNF. (1???)-. Periodical. English. Four times a year. $10.00. Natural Organic Farmers Association, RFD 2, Barreker MA 01005. **Tel** (508)355-2853.

LC S **ISSN** 0470-3715
DD 630 US
SUSPENDED
NATURAL FOOD & FARMING. [Nat. food farming]. **Added/Corp** Natural Food Associates. **VAT** Natural Food and Farming. Vol. 1 (Apr. 1954)-Suspended (July-Aug. 1994). Periodical. English. Six times a year. $15.00. Natural Food Associates, PO Box 210, Atlanta TX 75551. **Tel** (903)796-4136.

LC S **ISSN** 0182-7146
DD 630 FR
UDC 57
CODEN 57
NATURE ET PROGRES PARIS. (1964)-. Periodical. French. Six times a year. $39.37. Revue Nature et Progres, BP 6, 69921 Oullins Cedex France. **Tel** 33 72 390436, FAX 33 78 505437.
Ind/Abst Dairy Sci. Abstr.

LC S **ISSN** 0204-6385
DD 630 BU
CODEN NTVVA4
NAUCHNI TRUDOVE - VISSH SELSKOSTOPANSKI INSTITUT "VASIL KOLAROV" PLOVDIV. (NAUCHNI TRUDOVE - VISSH SELSKOSTOPANSKI INSTITUT.). [Nauchni tr. - Vissh Selskostop. Inst. "Vasil Kolarov" Plovdiv]. **Main/Corp** Plovdiv, Bulgaria. Vissh Selskostopanski Institut. (1952)-. Academic Scholarly Publication. Bulgarian (summaries and/or abstracts in English; table of contents in English). Documents available from CASDDS.
Ind/Abst Chem. Abstr.

LC S589 .L54
DD 338.1 RU
CODEN NTBFEU
NAUCHNO-TEKHNICHESKII BIULLETEN PO AGRONOMICHESKOI FIZIKE. **Added/Corp** Agrofizicheskii Nauchno-Issledovatelskii Institut (Vsesoiuznaia Akademiia Selskokhoziaistvennykh Nauk Imeni V.I. Lenina). (19??)-. Academic Scholarly Publication. Russian. Izdatelstvo Nauka / Akademiia Nauk, (Publishing House of the Russian Academy of Sciences), Leninskii Porspekt 14, 117901 Moscow Russia. **Tel** 011 95 9542153, FAX 011 95 9382144, telex 411964. Documents available from CASDDS. ***Continues*** *Biulleten Nauchno-Tekhnicheskoi Informatsii Po Agronomicheskoi Fizike, 0457-4362.*
Ind/Abst Chem. Abstr. (1983-);(1983); Field Crop Abstr.; Seed Abstr.

LC S
DD 630 US
NC STATE ECONOMIST. **Added/Corp** North Carolina Agricultural Extension Service. North Carolina State University. Dept. of Economics and Business. **VAT** North Carolina State Economist. (Jan. 1989)-. Periodical. English. Twelve times a year. North Carolina State University / Economics, Department of Economics, Raleigh NC 27695. **Tel** (919)737-2258. ***Continues*** *Tar Heel Economist.*

LC S
DD 630 US
NCALRI NEWSLETTER. **Main/Corp** National Center for Agricultural Law Research and Information (U.S.). **Added/Corp** National Center for Agricultural Law Research and Information (U.S.). **VFOAT** Newsletter / National Center for Agricultural Law Research and Information. (1991)-. Newsletter. English.

LC Z5071
DD 016.63 US
NEBRASKA AGRICULTURAL STATISTICS. **See** Agriculture-Abstracting, Bibliographies and Statistics.

LC S1 .N454 **ISSN** 1049-1880
DD 630.5 US
NEBRASKA FARMER, THE. [Nebr. farmer]. (1877)-. Periodical. English. Fifteen times a year. $19.95. Farm Progress Publishing, 191 South Gary Avenue, Carol Stream IL 60188-2089. **Tel** (708)462-2890 or 2891. **(Subscription address:** CDS / SIFD Agency Control, 1901 Bell Avenue, Des Moines IA 50315. **Tel** (515)246-6812.) **ED** Dave Howe. **Ad Acc. Circ:** 50,000.
Desc: Farm magazine for farmers and ranchers of Nebraska.

LC S471.C62 I565
DD 630/.951/77 CC
NEI MENG-KU NUNG MU CHANG. **VFOAT** Neimenggu Nongmuchang; Nei Meng Gu Nong Mu Chang. Periodical. Chinese. Twelve times a year. RMBY0.15. Post Office / Hu Ho Hao Shih, Hu Ho Hao Shih, People's Republic of China.

LC S **ISSN** 0391-9749
DD 630 IT
NEMATOLOGIA MEDITERRANEA. [Nematol. mediter.]. **Added/Corp** Laboratorio di Nematologia Agraria (Italy) Istituto di Nematologia Agraria (Italy). Vol. 1, No. 1 (June 1973)-. Periodical. English (Italian, Portuguese and French). Two times a year. L68130. Instituto di Nematologia Agraria del C N R, Agraria App. Veg/V. Amendola 165, 70126 Bari Italy. **Tel** 011 39 80 5484186/7, FAX 011 39 80 5484165. **ED** Franco Lamberti, C E Taylor. Each issue contains an index to its own contents (no volume index)--loose.
Desc: Specialized journal intended to expand knowledge in nematology, stimulate contacts and exchange of information among those nematologists concerned with problems arising in the Mediterranean region.
Ind/Abst AGRICOLA; Agrofor. Abstr.; Biocont. News Inf.; Cot. Trop. Fibr. Abstr. Bibliogr.; Crop Physiol. Abstr.; Field Crop Abstr.; For. Prod. Abstr. (19??-19??); Hortic. Abstr.; Maize Abstr.; Nematol. Abstr.; Plant Breed. Abstr.; Potato Abstr.; Protozoolog. Abstr.; Rev. Med. Vet. Entomol.; Rev. Plant Pathol.; Rice Abstr.; Seed Abstr.; Soils Fert.; Sorghum Mill. Abstr.; Soyabean Abstr.; Vitis Vitic. Enol. Abstr.; Weed Abstr.; Wheat Barley Trit. Abstr.

LC S
DD 630 NP
NEPAL THESIS ABSTRACTS. **Added/Corp** Agricultural Projects Services Centre (Kathmandu, Nepal) National Agricultural Documentation Centre (Kathmandu, Nepal). (Oct. 1984)-. Periodical. English. ***Continues*** *Nepal Agricultural Abstracts.*

LC S11 .N53 **ISSN** 0028-2928
DD 630 NE
CODEN NETMAW
Pr Rev.
NETHERLANDS JOURNAL OF AGRICULTURAL SCIENCE. [Neth. j. agric. sci.]. **Added/Corp** Koninklijk Genootschap voor Landbouwwetenschap (Netherlands). Vol. 1 (Feb. 1953)-. Periodical. English (French and German). Four times a year. $116.48. Royal Netherlands Society for Agricultural Science, PO Box 79, 6700 AB Wageningen The Netherlands. **Tel** 011 31 8370-83537. **ED** M.L.van Beusichem. Index available. cum. index. **Ad Acc.** ctrl circ. available on microfilm and microfiche from University Microfilms International (UMI). Documents available from The Genuine Article, BIOSIS Document Express, CASDDS.
Desc: 30 papers and circa 100 synopses per volume on research related to agriculture and biology.
Ind/Abst AgBiotech News Inf.; AGRICOLA; Agric. Eng. Abstr. (1991-); Anim. Breed. Abstr.; Biol. Abstr.; Chem. Abstr.; Crop Physiol. Abstr.; Curr. Aware. Biol. Sci., CABS; Curr. Cit.; Curr. Contents Agric. Biol. Environ. Sci.; Dairy Sci. Abstr.; Ecol. Abstr.; EMBASE; Field Crop Abstr.; Fish Rev. (Jan. 1989-July 1992); For. Abstr.; Geogr. Abstr. Phys. Geogr.; Grass. Forage Abstr.; Hortic. Abstr.; Index Vet.; Int. Dev. Abstr.; Irr. Drain. Abstr.; Leadscan; Maize Abstr.; Nematol. Abstr.; Nutr. Abstr. Rev., Ser. B, Live Feeds and Feed.; Ornamental Hort. (19??-19??); Life Sci. Collect.; Pig News Inf.; Plant Breed. Abstr.; Plant Grow. Reg. Abstr.; Postharvest News Inf.; Potato Abstr.; Res. Alert [Full Cov.]; Rice Abstr.; Sci. Cit. Index; SCISEARCH; Soils Fert.; Vet. Bull.; Weed Abstr.; Wheat Barley Trit. Abstr.; Wildl. Rev. (Jan. 1989-July 1992); World Agric. Econ. Rural Sociol. Abstr.

LC S **ISSN** 0021-5260
DD 630 JA
CODEN NENOA8
NETTAI NOGYO. [Nettai nogyo]. **Added/Corp** Nihon Nettai Nogyo Gakkai. **VFOAT** Japanese Journal of Tropical Agriculture. (1957)-. Periodical. Japanese (summaries and/or abstracts in English). Four times a year. $170.00. Nihon Nettai Nogyo Gakkai, (Tropical Agriculture Research Assoc. of Japan), Tsukuba Daigaku Noringakkei, Tennodai Tsukubashi, Ibarakiken 305 Japan. **(Subscription address:** Maruzen Company Ltd., PO Box 5050, Import & Export Department, Tokyo 100 31 Japan. **Tel** 011 81 3 32789224.) Documents available from CASDDS.
Ind/Abst Agrofor. Abstr.; Chem. Abstr.; Cot. Trop. Fibr. Abstr. Bibliogr.; Crop Physiol. Abstr.; For. Abstr.; Nutr. Abstr. Rev., Ser. B, Live Feeds and Feed.; Plant Breed. Abstr.; Plant Grow. Reg. Abstr.; Rice Abstr.; Seed Abstr.; Soils Fert.

LC S481 .N47
DD 630.9 JA
NETTAI NOKEN SHUHO. **Added/Corp** Nettai Nogyo Kenkyu Senta. (1980)-. Japanese. Norin Suisansho Nettai Nogyo Kenkyu Senta Yatabemachi, Tsukuba-gun, Ibaraki-ken 305 Japan.

LC S **ISSN** 0951-1873
DD 630 UK
NETWORK PAPER / ODI, AGRICULTURAL ADMINISTRATION (RESEARCH AND EXTENSION) NETWORK. **Added/Corp** Agricultural Administration (Research and Extension) Network. Overseas Development Institute (London, England). Agricultural Administration Unit. (1988)-. Monographic series. English.
Ind/Abst Agrofor. Abstr.; Anim. Breed. Abstr.; Dairy Sci. Abstr.; Plant Breed. Abstr.; Potato Abstr.; Seed Abstr.; Wheat Barley Trit. Abstr.

LC S
DD 630 GW
NEUE BIENENZUCHT, DIE. **Added/Corp** Landesverband Schleswig-Holsteinischer und Hamburger Imker. Vol. 1 (1974)-. Periodical. German. Twelve times a year. $23.03. Landesverband Schleswig Holst Imker, Hamburger Strasse 109, D-23795 Bad Segeberg Germany. **Tel** 011 49 4551 2436, FAX 011 49 4551 93194. **Circ:** 4,000. ***Supersedes*** *Bienenzucht.*

LC S
DD 630 GW
NEUE LANDWIRTSCHAFT. (19??)-. Periodical. German. Twelve times a year. DM90.00. Deutscher Landwirtschaftsverlag, Grabbaallee 41, D-13156 Berlin Germany. **Tel** 011 49 30 48320311. ***Continues*** *Tierzucht.*

LC S **ISSN** 0196-0636
DD 630 US
NEVADA AGRICULTURAL STATISTICS. **See** Agriculture-Abstracting, Bibliographies and Statistics.

LC S **ISSN** 0971-0647
DD 630 II
NEW AGRICULTURIST. [New Agric.]. **Added/Corp** Bioved Research Society. (1990)-. Periodical. English. Two times a year. $75.00. Bioved Research Society, Allahabad India. **(Subscription address:** Prints India, 11 Darya Ganj, New Delhi 110002 India. **Tel** 011 91 11 3268645, FAX 011 91 11 3275542, telex 31-61087 PRIN-IN.)
Ind/Abst Rev. Plant Pathol.; Weed Abstr.

LC S **ISSN** 1056-2133
DD 630 US
NEW AMERICAN FARMER. (1992)-. Periodical. English. Six times a year. $35.00. DeVault Publ, 3502 Main Road East, Emmaus PA 18049.

LC SF **ISSN** 1064-8763
DD 636 US
NEW CHIHUAHUA, THE. (Nov./Dec. 1992)-. Periodical. English. Six times a year. $38.00. The New Chihuahua, PO Box 126, Corte Madera CA 94976.

LC S ISSN 0193-0923
DD 630 US
NEW ENGLAND FARMER (ST. JOHNSBURY). (NEW ENGLAND FARMER.). **VFOAT** New England Farm. (197?)-. Periodical. English. Twelve times a year. $12.00. Rural Press USA, 7701 Six Forks Road, Suite 132, Raleigh NC 27615. **Tel** (800)934-2472, (919)676-3276, FAX (919)676-9803. **ED** Gus Howe (editor's telephone: (603)526-2602). **Ad Acc. Circ:** 18,074 (ctrl). available on microfilm from University Microfilms International (UMI). ***Continues*** *New England Farmer and Vermont Farm.*
Desc: New England agriculture, including dairy, beef, sheep, maple sugar and fruit and vegetable producers.

LC S ISSN 0099-426X
DD 630 US
CODEN NEMFAA
NEW ENGLAND FRUIT MEETINGS. [N. Engl. fruit meet.]. **Main/Corp** Massachusetts Fruit Growers' Association. Vol.72 (1966)-. Academic Scholarly Publication. English. One time a year. $25.00. Massachusetts Fruit Growers Association Inc, PO Box 632, North Amherst MA 01059. **Tel** (413)549-1876. **ED** James F. Anderson. **Ad Acc. Circ:** 800 (ctrl). Documents available from CASDDS. ***Continues*** *Report of the ... Annual Meeting. Ed. States. Geological Survey.*
Desc: Contains the proceedings of the annual meeting of the Massachusetts Fruit Growers' Association.
Ind/Abst AGRICOLA [Select. Cov.]; Chem. Abstr.

LC S1 .N48 ISSN 0163-0369
DD 631 US
CODEN NEFAEW
CEASED
NEW FARM, THE. [New farm]. **Added/Corp** Rodale Institute. Vol. 1 (Jan. 1979)-Vol. 17 (May/June 1995). Periodical. English. Rodale Press Inc., 400 South 10th Street, Emmaus PA 18098. **Tel** (610)967-5171, (800)666-2503, FAX (610)967-8964, telex 847338. **(Subscription address:** CDS Agency Hard Copy, PO Box 4966, Des Moines IA 50340. **Tel** (515)247-7569.**)** available on microfilm and microfiche from University Microfilms International (UMI).
Ind/Abst AGRICOLA [Select. Cov.]; BioBusiness; Environ. Period. Bibliogr.

LC SB126 ISSN 0952-1402
DD 631.584 UK
NEW FARMER AND GROWER. [New farmer grow.]. (1983)-. Trade Publication. English. Four times a year (Apr., July, Oct., Dec.). $34.23. British Organic Farmers, 86-88 Colston Street, Bristol BS1 5BB United Kingdom. **Tel** 011 44 117 929988, FAX 011 44 117 9252504. **ED** Mark Redman. Index available (free). **Bk Rev. Ad Acc. Circ:** 2,000.
Desc: Keep in touch with organic development, techniques, events, research, news, and views.
Ind/Abst Agric. Eng. Abstr. (1991-); Environ. Period. Bibliogr.; Weed Abstr.

LC S
DD 630 US
NEW HOLLAND NEWS (NEW HOLLAND, PA. : 1986). (NEW HOLLAND NEWS.). **VFOAT** News. (April/May 1986)-. Periodical. English (French). Eight times a year. New Holland News, New Holland PA 17557. **Tel** (717)355-1276, FAX (717)355-3600. **ED** Gary Martin. **Circ:** 350,000 (ctrl). ***Continues*** *Sperry New Holland News.*

LC HD1775.N6 N4 ISSN 0077-8540
DD 630 US
NEW MEXICO AGRICULTURAL STATISTICS. **See** Agriculture-Abstracting, Bibliographies and Statistics.

LC S ISSN 0028-6192
DD 630 US
NEW MEXICO FARM AND RANCH. (1945)-. Trade Publication. English. Eleven times a year (1 double issue included). $9.00. New Mexico Fram Ranch, 421 North Water Street, Las Cruces NM 88001. **Tel** (505)526-5521, FAX (505)525-0858. **ED** Erik L. Ness. **Bk Rev**, (Qty: 2). **Ad Acc, Adv Mgr:** Erik Ness, **Tel** (505)526-5521. **Circ:** 10,000 (ctrl).
Desc: Supplies farmers and ranchers in New Mexico with newest information on equipment and techniques. Also contains items pertaining to agriculture.

LC HD1751 .A9322G ISSN 0148-0820
DD 338.1/8/747 US
NEW YORK ANNUAL PROGRAM SUMMARY. **Main/Corp** United States. Agricultural Stabilization and Conservation Service. English. One time a year. US Department of Agriculture / New York, Federal Building/Room 811, 100 South Clinton Street, Syracuse NY 13210.

LC S ISSN 0744-317X
DD 630 US
NEW YORK CITY FRUIT AND VEGETABLE REPORT. Trade Publication. English. Two times a week. Federal-State Market News Service, 1220 N Street, Suite 216, Box 942871, Sacramento CA 94271-0001. **Tel** (916)654-0298, FAX (916)654-1046.

LC S
DD 630 US
NEW YORK CITY WHOLESALE FRUIT AND VEGETABLE REPORT. **See** Food and Food Industry-Abstracting, Bibliographies and Statistics.

LC S
DD 630 US
NEW YORK STATE GUIDE TO FARM FRESH FOOD. **Added/Corp** New York (State). Dept. of Agriculture and Markets. **VFOAT** Guide to Farm Fresh Food. (19??)-. English. Irregular. New York Department of Agriculture & Markets, 1 Winners Circle, Capitol Plaza, Albany NY 12235. **Tel** (518)457-4188, FAX (518)457-3087.

LC S ISSN 0099-5223
DD 630 US
CODEN NYFSBJ
NEW YORK'S FOOD AND LIFE SCIENCES BULLETIN. [N. Y. food life sci. bull.]. **Added/Corp** New York State Agricultural Experiment Station. No. 1 (Aug. 1970)-. Bulletin. English. Irregular. Price varies per volume. New York State Agricultural Experiment Station, Publications Department, Jordan Hall, Geneva NY 14456. Documents available from BIOSIS Document Express, BIOSIS Document Express, CASDDS. ***Formed by the union of*** *New York State Agricultural Experiment Station. Research Circular - New York State Agricultural Experiment Station, 0548-7498; Bulletin (Cornell University. Agricultural Experiment Station)* ***and*** *Bulletin (New York State Agricultural Experiment Station).*
Ind/Abst AGRICOLA [Full Cov.]; Biol. Abstr.; Chem. Abstr.

LC SB950 ISSN 0114-4022
DD 632.90993 NZ
NEW ZEALAND AGRICHEMICAL AND PLANT PROTECTION MANUAL. [N.Z. agrichem. plant prot. man.]. **VFOAT** Agrichemical and Plant Protection Manual; NZ Agrichemical Manual. (1990)-. English. Every 3 years. $60.89. Wham Group Ltd., PO Box 11092, Wellington New Zealand. **Tel** 011 64 4 4739243, FAX 011 64 4 4734530. **Ad Acc. Circ:** 7,000. ***Continues*** *New Zealand Agrichemical Manual, 0112-2290.*
Desc: Contains information for safe and effective use of agrichemicals; at its heart are Agrichemical Product Listings, which provide detailed information on the recommended uses of individual products.

LC S ISSN 0549-0146
DD 630 NZ
TITLE CHANGE
NEW ZEALAND AGRICULTURAL SCIENCE. [N. Z. agric. sci.]. **Added/Corp** New Zealand Institute of Agricultural Science. **VFOAT** Agricultural Science. Vol. 1 (July 1965)-(1993). Periodical. English. New Zealand Institute of Agricultural Science, PO Box 19-560, Christchurch 8002 New Zealand. **Tel** 011 64 3 3842432, FAX 011 64 3 842432. cum. index. **Circ:** 1,400 (ctrl). ***Continued by*** *Proceedings of the New Zealand Institute of Agricultural Science and the New Zealand Society for the Horticultural Science Annual Convention.*
Ind/Abst AGRICOLA [Full Cov.]; Agric. Eng. Abstr. (1991-); Ecol. Abstr. (?-?); Geogr. Abstr. Human Geogr.; Hortic. Abstr.; Int. Dev. Abstr. (?-?); Irr. Drain. Abstr.; Postharvest News Inf.

LC S
DD 630 NZ
NEW ZEALAND BEEKEEPER, THE. **Added/Corp** National Beekeepers Association of New Zealand. Vol. 1 (1939)-. Periodical. English. Four times a year. $16.00. National Beekeepers of New Zealand, Circulation Department, PO Box 4048, Wellington New Zealand. **Tel** 011 64 4 728102, FAX 011 64 4 712882. **ED** M Burgess. **Bk Rev. Ad Acc. Circ:** 1,550.
Desc: General beekeeping, disorders in New Zealand honey bees, hive maintenance; reports from regions, and general matters pertaining to beekeepers.
Ind/Abst Rev. Agric. Entomol.

LC S
DD 630 NZ
NEW ZEALAND FARMER, THE. (19??)-. Periodical. English. Fifty times a year. $157.56. New Zealand Rural Press LTD, PO Box 4233, Auckland New Zealand. **Tel** 011 64 9 5209451. **ED** John Cornwell. Index available. **Bk Rev. Ad Acc. Circ:** 30,000.
Desc: General farming magazine covering all aspects of agriculture in New Zealand plus information on world markets.

LC S ISSN 0028-8233
DD 630 NZ
CCC
CODEN NEZFA7
Pr Rev.
NEW ZEALAND JOURNAL OF AGRICULTURAL RESEARCH. [N.Z. j. agric. res.]. **Added/Corp** New Zealand. Dept. of Scientific and Industrial Research. Vol. 1 (Feb. 1958)-. Periodical. English. Four times a year (Mar., June, Sep., Dec.). $200.00. SIR Publishing, PO Box 399, Wellington New Zealand. **Tel** 011 64 4 472 7421, FAX 011 64 4 473 1841. **ED** Anne Greenwood. **Bk Rev. Ad Acc. Circ:** 1,300 (ctrl). Documents available from The Genuine Article, BIOSIS Document Express, CASDDS, Documents on Demand. ***Continues*** *New Zealand Journal of Science and Technology. A. Agricultural Research Section, 0369-6952.*
Desc: Covers animal husbandry, horticulture, agronomy, soil science, fertilizer trials, weed research, plant pathology. Publishes New Zealand-based research papers.
Ind/Abst AgBiotech News Inf.; AGRICOLA; Agrofor. Abstr. (1991-); Anim. Breed. Abstr.; Biocont. News Inf. (1991-); Biol. Agric. Index; Biol. Abstr.; Chem. Abstr.; CSA Neuro. Abstr. (?-?); Curr. Aware. Biol. Sci., CABS; Curr. Cit.; Curr. Contents Agric. Biol. Environ. Sci.; Ecol. Abstr.; EMBASE; Energy Inf. Abstr.; Environ. Abstr.; Field Crop Abstr.; Food Sci. Technol. Abstr.; For. Abstr.; Geogr. Abstr. Phys. Geogr.; Geogr. Abstr. Human Geogr.; Grass. Forage Abstr.; Helminthol. Abstr. (1991-); Index Vet.; Irr. Drain. Abstr.; Maize Abstr.; Microbiol. Abstr. Sect. A; Microbiol. Abstr. Sect. C; Nematol. Abstr.; Nutr. Abstr. Rev., Ser. B, Live Feeds and Feed.; Life Sci. Collect.; PESTDOC; Pig News Inf.; Plant Breed. Abstr.; Plant Grow. Reg. Abstr.; Pollut. Abstr. Indexes; Protozoolog. Abstr.; Res. Alert [Full Cov.]; Rev. Agric. Entomol.; Rev. Med. Vet. Entomol.; Rev. Med. Vet. Mycology; Rev. Plant Pathol.; Sci. Cit. Index; SCISEARCH; SEA Abstr.; Seed Abstr.; Small Anim. Abstr. Bibliogr.; Soils Fert.; Vet. Bull.; Vitis Vitic. Enol. Abstr.; Weed Abstr.; Wheat Barley Trit. Abstr.; Wildl. Rev. (19??-199?).

LC S ISSN 0048-0215
DD 630 US
NEWS & FARMER. [News farmer]. **VAT** News and Farmer. Periodical. English. One time a week. Caroline Publishing Company, PO Box 459, Preston MD 21655-0459.

LC S ISSN 1194-823X
DD 630 CN
•NEWS FROM THE OC CORRAL. **VFOAT** News from the Ottaw-Carleton Corral. (1993)-. Periodical. English. Ottawa-Carleton Junior Farmers, c/o Junior Farmer's Association of Ontario, PO Box 1030, Guelph Ontario N1H 6N1 Canada. ***Continues*** *Ottawa-Carleton Headliner, 1183-4374.*

LC S20 ISSN 0229-7728
DD 630/.6/0714 CN
NEWS SPREADER, THE. [News spreader]. Vol. 1, No. 1 (July 1980)-. Periodical. English. Irregular. Free. The News Spreader, c/o Extension Department, Box 24, MacDonald College, Ste-Anne-de-Bellevue Quebec H9X 1C0 Canada. ctrl circ. ***Continues*** *Quebec Young Farmers' News Spreader, 0229-771X.*

LC S
DD 630 BE
NEWSFLASH GREEN EUROPE. **Added/Corp** Commission of the European Communities. Agricultural Information Service. **VFOAT** Newsflash. (1984)-. Periodical. English. Agricultural Information Service of the Directorate-General for Information, European Community Commission. ***Continues*** *Green Europe Newsletter in Brief.*
Ind/Abst Rice Abstr.

LC HD1334 ISSN 0823-8561
DD 333.33/5 CN
NEWSLETTER - ALBERTA SURFACE RIGHTS FEDERATION. (NEWSLETTER : A PUBLICATION OF THE ALBERTA SURFACE RIGHTS FEDERATION.). [Newsl. - Alta. Surf. Rights Fed.]. Aug. 1982-. Newsletter. English. Four times a year. Alberta Surface Rights Federation, PO Box 720, Elk Point Alberta T0A 1A0 Canada. **Tel** (403)724-2296. **ED** Alban Bugej.

LC SF521
DD 638.1 UK
NEWSLETTER FOR BEEKEEPERS IN TROPICAL & SUBTROPICAL COUNTRIES. No. 6 (March 1985)-. Newsletter. English. Two times a year. International Bee Research Association, 18 North Road, Cardiff CF1 3DY United Kingdom. **Tel** 011 44 1222 372409, FAX 011 44 1222 665522, telex 23152. ***Continues*** *Newsletter for Tropical Apiculture.*
Ind/Abst Agrofor. Abstr. (1991-); For. Abstr.

LC S ISSN 0919-8822
DD 630 JA
•NEWSLETTER FOR INTERNATIONAL COLLABORATION. **Added/Corp** Japan International Research Center for Agricultural Sciences. **VFOAT** Newsletter; JIRCAS Newsletter. **VAT** Japan International Research Center for Agricultural Sciences Newsletter. Vol. 1, 1 (Oct. 1993)-. Newsletter. English. Two times a year. Japan International Research Center, Tsukuba Ibaraki Japan. ***Continues*** *Newsletter (Nettai Nogyo Kenkyu Senta), 0915-7476.*

Agriculture

LC S **ISSN** 0316-3369
DD 630 CN
NEWSLETTER - NATIONAL FARMERS UNION. Main/Corp National Farmers Union (Canada). Vol. 2, No. 18 (May 14, 1971)-. Newsletter. English. Twenty-six times a year. National Farmers Union / Canada, 250C 2nd Avenue South, Saskatoon Saskatchewan S7K 1K9 Canada. **Continues** National Newsletter, 0316-3377.

LC S583 **ISSN** 0004-5764
DD 631 US
NEWSLETTER OF THE ASSOCIATION OF OFFICIAL SEED ANALYSTS, THE. [Newsl. Assoc. Off. Seed Anal.]. **VFOAT** News Letter of the Association of Official Seed Analysts. (19??)-. Newsletter. English. Three times a year. $20.00. Association of Official Seed Analysts, 268 Plant Science Building, Lincoln NE 68583. **Tel** (402)472-1444. **ED** Larry Prentice. **Bk Rev. Circ:** 600.
Ind/Abst AGRICOLA; Cot. Trop. Fibr. Abstr. Bibliogr.

LC HQ1871 **ISSN** 1186-2041
DD 305.43/63/097105 CN
NEWSLETTER / ONTARIO FARM WOMEN'S NETWORK. See Women's Interests.

LC SB111 **ISSN** 0317-0527
DD 631.5/8 CN
NEWSLETTER - ORGANIC GROWERS CO-OPERATIVE. Main/Corp Organic Growers Co-Operative. No. 1- Aug. 1974-. Newsletter. English. Twelve times a year. Free to members, membership $6.00. Organic Growers Co-Operative, PO Box 493, Middleton NS B0S 1P0, Canada.

LC S **ISSN** 1055-2634
DD 630 US
NFO REPORTER, THE. [NFO report.]. Main/Corp National Farmers Organization (U.S.). **VAT** National Farmers Organization Reporter. (19??)-. Trade Publication. English. Twelve times a year. $5.00. National Farmers Association, 2505 Elwood Drive, Ames IA 50010-8288. **Tel** (515)292-2000.

LC HD1986 .N53
DD 338.1/09492 GW
NIEDERLANDE, LANDWIRTSCHAFT / BUNDESSTELLE FUR AUSSENHANDELSINFORMATION. German. One time a year. 3.00. Bundesstelle fuer Aussenhandelsinformation, Agrippastrasse 87 93, D-50676 Cologne Germany. **Tel** 011 49 221 2057316, FAX 011 49 221 2057212.

LC SB298 **ISSN** 0795-8692
DD 633.85 NR
NIGERIAN JOURNAL OF PALMS AND OIL SEEDS. [Niger. j. palms oil seeds]. Added/Corp Nigerian Institute for Oil Palm Research. Vol. 8, No. 1 (May 1987)-. Periodical. English. Irregular. $30.00 (per copy). Nigerian Institute for Oil Palm Research, PMB 1030, Benin City Nigeria. **Continues** Journal of the Nigerian Institute for Oil Palm Research, 0078-0715.

LC S **ISSN** 0078-0839
DD 630 JA
CODEN NIPDAD
NIHON DAIGAKU NOJUIGAKUBU GAKUJUTSU KENKYU HOKOKU. (GAKUJUTSU KENKYU HOKOKU.). [Nihon Daigaku Nojuigakubu Gakujutsu kenkyu hokoku]. Main/Corp Nihon Daigaku, Tokyo. Nojuigakubu. **VFOAT** Bulletin of the College of Agriculture and Veterinary Medicine, Nihon University. (1953)-. Monographic series. English (Japanese). Price varies per volume. Nihon Daigaku Nojuikubu, 34 1 Shiouma 3 Chome Setagayak, Tokyo 154 Japan. Documents available from BIOSIS Document Express.
Ind/Abst Biol. Abstr.; Index Vet.; Vet. Bull.

LC S
DD 630 JA
NIHON NOGAKU TOSHOKAN KYOGIKAI KAIHO. Main/Corp Nihon Nogaku Toshokan Kyogikai. Added/Corp Nihon Nogaku Toshokan Kyogikai. **VFOAT** Bulletin of the Japan Association of Agricultural Librarians and Documentalists. (19??)-. Bulletin. Japanese. Nihon Nogaku Toshokan Kyogikai, Seio Building, 29-31 Sakuragaoka Shibuya-ku, Tokyo Japan.
Ind/Abst World Agric. Econ. Rural Sociol. Abstr.

LC SF521 **ISSN** 0385-8634
DD 638.1 JA
CODEN NDNHDH
NIIGATA DAIGAKU NOGAKUBU KENKYU HOKOKU. [Niigata Daigaku Nogakubu kenkyu hokoku]. Main/Corp Niigata Daigaku. Nogakubu. **VFOAT** Bulletin of the Faculty of Agriculture, Niigata University. No. 29 (Mar. 1977)-. Academic Scholarly Publication. Japanese (summaries and/or abstracts in English; table of contents in English). One time a year. Niigata University / Agriculture, Faculty of Agriculture, 8050 Igarashi 2, Niigata-shi 950-21 Japan. Documents available from BIOSIS Document Express, CASDDS. **Continues** Niigata Norin Kenkyu.
Ind/Abst AGRICOLA; Biodeter. Abstr.; Biol. Abstr. (1986-); Chem. Abstr.; Crop Physiol. Abstr.; EMBASE; Field Crop Abstr.; Hortic. Abstr.; Pig News Inf.; Potato Abstr.; Rev. Plant Pathol.; Rice Abstr.; Wheat Barley Trit. Abstr.; World Agric. Econ. Rural Sociol. Abstr.

LC S **ISSN** 0549-4826
DD 630 JA
NIIGATA DAIGAKU NOGAKUBU KIYO. MEMOIRS OF THE FACULTY OF AGRICULTURE, NIIGATA UNIVERSITY. **VFOAT** Memoirs of the Faculty of Agriculture, Niigata University. No. 1 (Mar. 1961)-. Japanese (English; summaries and/or abstracts in English). One time a year. Niigata Daigaku Nogakubu, (Faculty of Agriculture Niigata University), 8050 Igarashi Ninocho, Niigatashi Niigataken 950-21, Japan.
Ind/Abst Agric. Eng. Abstr.

LC S **ISSN** 0549-4869
DD 630 JA
CODEN NNSHA7
NIIGATA-KEN NOGYO SHIKENJO KENKYU HOKOKU. (NIIGATA-KEN NOGYO SHIKENJO KENKYU HOKOKU. JOURNAL OF THE NIIGATA AGRICULTURAL EXPERIMENT STATION.). [Niigata-ken Nogyo Shikenjo kenkyu hokoku]. **Main/Corp** Niigata-Ken Nogyo Shikenjo. Added/Corp Niigata-Ken Nogyo Shikenjo. Journal. Niigata-Ken Nogyo Shikenjo. Kenkyu Hokoku. **VFOAT** Journal of the Niigata Agricultural Experiment Station. No. 1 (1951)-. Periodical. Japanese (summaries and/or abstracts in English; table of contents in English).
Ind/Abst Soyabean Abstr.

LC S **ISSN** 1002-204X
DD 630 CH
NINGXIA NONG-LIN KE-JI. **VFOAT** Ningxia Journal of Agro-Forestry Science and Technology. (1987)-. Periodical. Chinese. Six times a year.
Ind/Abst For. Abstr.; Hortic. Abstr.; Plant Grow. Reg. Abstr.

LC QD415 **ISSN** 0002-1407
DD 631 JA
CODEN NNKKAA
Pr Rev.
NIPPON NOGEI KAGAKU KAISHI. [Nippon nogei kagakukaishi]. Added/Corp Nippon Nogei-Kagakukai. **VFOAT** Journal of the Agricultural Chemical Society of Japan. Vol. 1, No. 1 (Oct. 1924)-. Academic Scholarly Publication. Japanese (summaries and/or abstracts in English). Twelve times a year. $200.00. Nippon Nogei Kagakkai, (Agricultural Chemical Soc. of Japan), Gakkai Senta Biru, 4-16 Yayoi 2 Chome, Bunkyoku Tokyo 113 Japan. **(Subscription address:** Maruzen Company Ltd., PO Box 5050, Import & Export Department, Tokyo 100 31 Japan. **Tel** 011 81 3 32789224.) Documents available from The Genuine Article, BIOSIS Document Express, CASDDS.
Ind/Abst AgBiotech News Inf.; Biocont. News Inf.; Biodeter. Abstr.; Biol. Abstr.; Chem. Abstr.; Chem. Titles; Curr. Biotechnol.; Curr. Chem. React.; Curr. Cit.; Dairy Sci. Abstr.; EMBASE; Food Sci. Technol. Abstr.; Grass. Forage Abstr.; Index Chem.; Index Vet.; Maize Abstr.; Mass Spect. Bull.; Methods Organ. Synth.; NAPRALERT; Plant Breed. Abstr.; Plant Grow. Reg. Abstr.; Potato Abstr.; Res. Alert [Select. Cov.]; Rev. Med. Vet. Entomol.; Rice Abstr.; SCISEARCH; Soyabean Abstr.; Vet. Bull.

LC S
DD 630 TH
NITROGEN FIXING TREE RESEARCH REPORTS : A PUBLICATION OF THE NITROGEN FIXING TREE ASSOCIATION (NFTA). See Forests and Forestry.

LC S671 .N62 **ISSN** 0287-0029
DD 631.3 JA
NOGYO DOBOKU SHIKENJO GIHO. HE, SUIKO. **VFOAT** Technical Report of the National Research Institute of Agricultural Engineering. HE. No. 1 (March 1983)-. Japanese. Norin Suisansho Nogyo Doboku Shikenjo, (National Reserach Institute of Agricultural Engineering Ministry of Agriculture Forestry & Fisheries), 1-2 Kannondai 2 Chome, Tsukubashi Ibarakiken 305, Japan. **Continues in part** Nogyo Doboku Shikenjo Giho. B: Suiri.

LC S605.2.J3 N64 **ISSN** 0287-0029
DD 631.45 JA
NOGYO DOBOKU SHIKENJO GIHO. LI, NOCHI SEIBI. **VFOAT** Technical Report of the National Research Institute of Agricultural Engineering. LI. Japanese. Norin Suisansho Nogyo Doboku Shikenjo, (National Reserach Institute of Agricultural Engineering Ministry of Agriculture Forestry & Fisheries), 1-2 Kannondai 2 Chome, Tsukubashi Ibarakiken 305, Japan. **Continues in part** Nogyo Doboku Shikenjo Giho. A: Tochi Kairyo.

LC S562.J3 N577A **ISSN** 0077-4863
DD 338.1 JA
NOGYO GIJUTSU KENKYUJO HOKOKU. H : KEIEI TOCHI RIYO. Main/Corp Norinsho Nogyo Gijutsu Kenkyujo (Japan). **VFOAT** Bulletin of the National Institute of Agricultural Sciences. Farm Management and Land Utilization. No. 1- ; 1951-. Bulletin. Multiple languages (Japanese and English). Morinsho Nogyo Gijutsu Kenkyujo, 1-7 Nishigahara 2 Chome, Chuo-Ku (114).
Ind/Abst AGRICOLA.

LC S
DD 630 JA
NOGYO HAKUSHO. Main/Corp Japan. Norinsho. (1973)-. Periodical. Japanese. ¥950. Norin Tokei Kyokai, (Association of Agriculture & Forestry Statistics), 11-14 Meguro 2 Chome, Meguroku Tokyo 153 Japan.

LC S **ISSN** 0911-9450
DD 630 JA
CODEN NKGHEW
NOGYO KANKYO GIJUTSU KENKYUJO HOKOKU. [Nogyo Kankyo Gijutsu Kenkyujo hokoku]. **VFOAT** Bulletin of the National Institute of Agro-Environmental Sciences. (1986)-. Academic Scholarly Publication. Japanese. Documents available from BIOSIS Document Express, CASDDS.
Ind/Abst Biol. Abstr. (1986-); Chem. Abstr.; Nematol. Abstr.; Rice Abstr.; Soyabean Abstr.

LC S494.5.I5 N635a **ISSN** 0910-2000
DD 630 JA
NOGYO KANKYO GIJUTSU KENKYUJO NENPO. Main/Corp Norin Suisansho Nogyo Kankyo Gijutsu Kenkyujo (Japan). Added/Corp Norin Suisansho Nogyo Kankyo Gijutsu Kenkyujo (Japan) Periodicals. No. 1 (1983)-. Japanese. One time a year. Norin Suisansho Nogyo Kankyo Gijutsu Kenkyujo, 1-1 Kannondai 3 chome, Tsukubashi Ibarakiken 305 Japan. **Continues** Nogyo Gijutsu Kenkujo Nenpo.

LC HD2091 .N62
DD 338.1 JA
NOGYO KEIEI KENKYU SEIKA SHUHO. Added/Corp Norin Suisansho Nogyo Gijutsu Kenkyujo (Japan). No. 1 (1980)-. Japanese. Norin Suisansho Nogyo Kenkyu Center, 3-1-1 Kannondai, Tsukuba-shi, Ibaraki-ken 305 Japan. **Circ:** 900 (ctrl).

LC S303 .N58 **ISSN** 0289-3207
DD 630 JA
NOGYO KENKYU SENTA KENKYU HOKOKU. Added/Corp Norin Suisansho Nogyo Kenkyu Senta (Japan). **VFOAT** Bulletin of the National Agriculture Research Center. (1983)-. Bulletin. Japanese (English). Norin Suisansho Nogyo, (National Agriculture Research Center Ministry of Agriculture Forestry & Fisheries), 1-1 Kannondai 3 Chome, Tsukubashi Ibarakiken 305, Japan. **Continues** Norin Suisansho Noji Shikenjo (Japan) Noji Shikenjo Kenkyu Hokoku, 0549-5873.
Ind/Abst Plant Breed. Abstr.; Rev. Agric. Entomol.; Rev. Plant Pathol.; Rice Abstr.

LC S **ISSN** 0369-5247
DD 630 JA
CODEN NOOEAJ
NOGYO OYOBI ENGEI. [Nogyo oyobi engei]. **VFOAT** Agriculture and Horticulture. Vol. 1 (1926)-. Periodical. Japanese. Twelve times a year. $269.00. Yokendo, 5-30-15 Hongo, Bunkyo-ku Tokyo Japan. **Tel** 814-0911. **(Subscription address:** Japan Publications Trading Company Ltd., PO Box 5030, Tokyo International, Tokyo 100-31 Japan. **Tel** 011 81 3 3292 3753.) Documents available from CASDDS.
Ind/Abst AGRICOLA; Agric. Eng. Abstr.; Chem. Abstr.; Crop Physiol. Abstr.; Field Crop Abstr.; Hortic. Abstr.; Irr. Drain. Abstr.; Plant Breed. Abstr.; Plant Grow. Reg. Abstr.; Postharvest News Inf.; Potato Abstr.; Rev. Agric. Entomol.; Rice Abstr.; Soils Fert.; Soyabean Abstr.; Weed Abstr.; World Agric. Econ. Rural Sociol. Abstr.

LC S
DD 630 JA
NOGYO ROPPO. See Law.

LC S770 **ISSN** 0388-8517
DD 631.2 JA
NOGYO SHISETSU. [Nogyo shisetsu]. **VFOAT** Journal of the Society of Agricultural Structures, Japan. (1971)-. Periodical. Japanese. Two times a year. Nogyo Shisetsu Gakkai, (Soc. of Agricultural Structures Japan), Tsukuba Daigaku Nokogakukei, 1-1 Tennodai 1 Chome, Tsukubashi Ibarakiken 305, Japan.
Ind/Abst Agric. Eng. Abstr.; Index Vet.; Seed Abstr.; World Agric. Econ. Rural Sociol. Abstr.

LC S **ISSN** 0387-3242
DD 630 JA
NOGYO SOGO KENKYU. (NOGYO SOGO KENKYU. QUARTERLY JOURNAL OF AGRICULTURAL ECONOMY.). [Nogyo Sogo Kenkyu]. Added/Corp Nogyo Sogo Kenkyujo (Japan). **VFOAT** Quarterly Journal of Agricultural Economy. Vol. 1 (Nov. 1947)-. Periodical. Japanese (table of contents in English). Four times a year. Free on request. National

Agriculture

Research Institute Agricultural Economics, 2 2 1 Nishigahara, Tokyo 114 Japan. **Ind/Abst** Rice Abstr.; World Agric. Econ. Rural Sociol. Abstr.

LC HD2092 .N525
DD 338.1
JA
NOGYO TO KEIZAI. Added/Corp Fumin Kyokai. (April 1934)-. Periodical. Japanese. Twelve times a year. ¥5000. Fumin Shuppanbu, (Better Farming Association), Mainichi Shimbunsha, 1-1 Hitotsubashi, 1-chome Chiyodaku, Tokyo 100 Japan.

LC HD2091 .N65g
DD 630
JA
NOKA KEIZAI CHOSA HOKOKU.
Main/Corp Japan. Norin Suisansho. Keizaikyoku. Tokei Johobu. (1977)-. Periodical. Japanese. ¥4300. Norin Tokei Kyokai, (Association of Agriculture & Forestry Statistics), 11-14 Meguro 2 Chome, Meguroku Tokyo 153 Japan. **Continues** Norinsho Noka Keizai Chosa Hokoku.

LC HD1513.J3 J36a
DD 305.555
JA
NOKA SHUGYO DOKO CHOSA HOKOKUSHO. Main/Corp Japan. Norin Suisansho. Keizaikyoku. Tokei Johobu. (1977)-. Japanese. Norin Tokei Kyokai, (Association of Agriculture & Forestry Statistics), 11-14 Meguro 2 Chome, Meguroku Tokyo 153 Japan. **Continues** Noka Shugyo Doko Chosa Hokokusho.

LC S
DD 630
JA
NOKO TO ENGEI. VFOAT Agriculturist and Horticulturist; Agriculturist. (1946)-. Periodical. Japanese. Twelve times a year. $200.00. Seibundo Shinkosha, (Seibundo Sinkosha Publishing Co. Ltd.), 5-5 Kanda Nishikicho 1 Chome, Chiyodaku Tokyo 101 Japan.

LC S
DD 630
ISSN 0331-6742
NR
NOMA. Added/Corp Ahmadu Bello University. Institute for Agricultural Research and Special Services. Vol. 1 (Aug. 1978)-. Periodical. English. Four times a year. Free on request. Ahmadu Bello University / Institute of Agricultural Research, Samaru/PMB 1044, Zaria Nigeria. **Tel** 011 234 50571, 011 234 44052. **ED** B.O. Uchegbu. **Bk Rev**. **Ad Acc**. **Circ**: 500. **Continues** Samaru Agricultural Newsletter.
Desc: Deals with an agricultural issue relating to Nigeria and the Savanna ecological zone.
Ind/Abst Field Crop Abstr.; Soils Fert.; Sorghum Mill. Abstr.; Wheat Barley Trit. Abstr.

LC HD28
DD 338
ISSN 1057-7912
US
NONCITRUS FRUITS & NUTS. MID-YEAR SUPPLEMENT. [Noncitrus fruits nuts, Mid-year suppl.]. **Added/Corp** United States. Agricultural Statistics Board. United States. Crop Reporting Board. **VFOAT** Noncitrus Fruits and Nuts. Mid-Year Supplement; Mid-Year Supplement. (19??)-. Government Publication. English. Two times a year. $7.50 US; $9.40 other. Superintendent of Documents, US Government Printing Office, Washington DC 20402. **Tel** (202)275-3328, FAX (202)786-2377.
Ind/Abst Foods Adlibra.

LC HD9244 .U55A
DD 338.1/74/0973021
ISSN 1060-2666
US
NONCITRUS FRUITS AND NUTS. SUMMARY. VFOAT Noncitrus Fruits and Nuts. Annual Summary; Noncitrus Fruits and Nuts Annual; Noncitrus Fruits & Nuts Annual. (1983)-. Government Publication. English. Two times a year. $7.50 US; $9.40 other. US Department of Agriculture, 14th Street and Independence Avenue SW, Washington DC 20250. **Tel** (202)720-5457. (**Subscription address**: Superintendent of Documents, US Government Printing Office, Washington DC 20402.) available on microfiche (Vols. for 1986- distributed to depository libraries). **Continues** Noncitrus Fruits & Nuts. Annual Summary, 0093-4569.
Ind/Abst Foods Adlibra (1983-).

LC S19 .N794
DD 630/.5
ISSN 0550-3744
CH
CODEN NLHPAU
NONG-LIN XUE BAO. (NUNG LIN HSUEH PAO.). [Nong-lin xue bao]. **VFOAT** Journal of Agriculture and Forestry; Journal of Agriculture & Forestry. (Jan. 1952)-. Academic Scholarly Publication. Chinese (summaries and/or abstracts in English). One time a year. Japan Hymenopterist Association, Taipei Taiwan. Documents available from BIOSIS Document Express, CASDDS.
Ind/Abst Biol. Abstr. (1986-); Chem. Abstr.; For. Prod. Abstr.; For. Abstr.; Index Vet.; Protozoolog. Abstr.; Rev. Plant Pathol.; Soils Fert.; Soyabean Abstr.

LC HD9016.K6 N6
DD 338.17
KO
NONGCHON MULKA CHONGNAM. See Agriculture-Abstracting, Bibliographies and Statistics.

LC S19 .N63
DD 630.5
KO
CODEN NONODD
NONGNIM NONJIP. Added/Corp Koryo Taehakkyo. Nongkwa Taehak. **VFOAT** Theses Collection of Agriculture & Forestry. (19??)-. Academic Scholarly Publication. English (Korean). Documents available from CASDDS.
Ind/Abst Chem. Abstr. (1983-).

LC HD2095.5 .A489
DD 630
KO
NONGOP KIBAN CHOSONG SAOP TONGGYE YONBO. See Agriculture-Abstracting, Bibliographies and Statistics.

LC S542.K8 N66
DD 630.72
ISSN 1225-5440
KO
CODEN RASAEB
●**NONGOP KWAHAK NONMUNJIP.**
Added/Corp Korea (South). Nongchon Chinhungchong. **VFOAT** Journal of Agricultural Science; Nongop Nonmunjip; RDA Journal of Agricultural Science. (1993)-. Periodical. Korean (summaries and/or abstracts in English). Four times a year. **Continues** Nongsa Sihom Yongu Nonmunjip.

LC S19 .N644
KO
NONGOP KWAHAK YONGU. Added/Corp Chungnam Taehakkyo. Nongop Kwahak Yonguso. **VFOAT** Journal of Agricultural Science; Chungnam Taehakkyo Nongop Kwahak Yongu. (1989)-. Academic Scholarly Publication. Korean (summaries and/or abstracts in English). Two times a year. Documents available from CASDDS. **Continues** Nongop Kisul Yongu Pogo.
Ind/Abst Chem. Abstr.

LC S
DD 630
KO
NONGSA SIHOM Y'ONGU POGO. NOGKI, NOGKA, NOGKY'UNG. VFOAT Research Reports of the Office of Rural Development. VOol 22 (Dec. 1980)-. Korean (summaries and/or abstracts in English). One time a year. Office of Rural Development, Ministry of Agriculture and Fisheries, Suweon Korea. **Continues in part** Nongsa Sihom Yongu Pogo. Wonye, Nongkong Pyon.

LC S
DD 630
KO
NONGSA SIHOM YONGU POGO. NONGKONG, NONGCHON KYUNGYON, JAMUP. See Agriculture-Agricultural Equipment.

LC S
DD 630
ISSN 0802-0957
NO
NORAGRIC OCCASIONAL PAPERS. SERIES C : DEVELOPMENT AND ENVIRONMENT. [NorAgric occas. pap., C : Dev. environ.]. (1988)-. Monographic series. English. Irregular.
Ind/Abst Agrofor. Abstr.; For. Abstr.; Plant Genet. Resour. Abstr.; Rev. Agric. Entomol.; Rev. Plant Pathol.

LC S
DD 630
NO
NORDEN; NORD-NORGES LANDBRUKSTIDSSKRIFT. No. 1 (Jan. 6, 1956)-. Periodical. Norwegian. Sixteen times a year. $74.13. Norden, Vagones Forkingsstasjon, N 8001 Bodo Norway. **Tel** 011 47 77 584840, FAX 011 47 77 584175. **ED** Hakon Renolen. **Bk Rev**. **Ad Acc**. **Circ**: 3,500.

LC S
DD 630
ISSN 0048-0495
NO
NORDISK JORDBRUGSFORSKNING.
Added/Corp Nordiske Jordbrugsforskeres Forening. (1919)-. Trade Publication. Norwegian. Four times a year. Fmk90.00. Nordiska Jordbruksforskares Foerening, T T S - Instituett, PO Box 28, FIN-00211 Helsinki Finland. **Tel** 358 0 6922445, FAX 358 0 9922084. **ED** Erkki Oksanen. cum. index. **Bk Rev**.
Ind/Abst AgBiotech News Inf.; Anim. Breed. Abstr.; Hortic. Abstr.; Index Vet.; Nutr. Abstr. Rev., Ser. B, Live Feeds and Feed.; Plant Breed.; Potato Abstr.; Rev. Plant Pathol.; Vet. Bull.

LC HD1401 .N67
DD 338.1
SW
NORDISKT LANTBRUK. Periodical. Swedish. Irregular. Lantbrukarnas Riksforbund, Trycksaksbestallningen, 105 33 Stockholm Sweden. **Tel** 08-787 50 00. **Continues** Nordisk Lantbrunsekonomisk Tidskrift.

LC S542.J3 N67
DD 630
JA
NORIN SUISAN KANKEI SHIKEN KENKYU YORAN. Added/Corp Norin Suisan Gijutsu Kaigi. (19??)-. Japanese. Norin Tokei Kyokai, (Association of Agriculture & Forestry Statistics), 11-14 Meguro 2 Chome, Meguroku Tokyo 153 Japan.

LC S303 .N63
DD 638.0952
ISSN 0388-8436
JA
NORIN SUISAN KENKYU KEISAN SENTA HOKOKU. A = BULLETIN OF THE COMPUTING CENTER FOR RESEARCH IN AGRICULTURE, FORESTRY, AND FISHERY. SERIES A.
Added/Corp Norin Suisan Kenkyu Senta (Japan). **VFOAT** Bulletin of the Computing Center for Research in Agriculture, Forestry, and Fishery. Series A. (19??)-. Bulletin. Japanese. Norin Suisansho Norin Suisan Gijutsu Kaigi Jimukyoku, (Agriculture Forestry & Fisheries Research Council Ministry of Agriculture Forestry & Fisheries), 2-1 Kasumigaseki 1 Chome, Chiyodaku Tokyo 100 Japan. **Continues** Norin Kenkyu Keisan Senta (Japan). Norin Kenkyu Keisan Senta Hokoku. A.

LC S494.5.D3 N67
DD 630
ISSN 0389-3103
JA
NORIN SUISAN KENKYU KEISAN SENTA HOKOKU. B. Added/Corp Norin Suisan Kenkyu Keisan Senta (Japan). **VFOAT** Bulletin of the Computing Centre for Research in Agriculture, Forestry, and Fishery. Series B. (19??)-. Bulletin. Japanese (summaries and/or abstracts in English). Norin Suisansho Norin Suisan Gijutsu Kaigi Jimukyoku, (Agriculture Forestry & Fisheries Research Council Ministry of Agriculture Forestry & Fisheries), 2-1 Kasumigaseki 1 Chome, Chiyodaku Tokyo 100 Japan.

LC S
DD 630
JA
NORIN SUISAN TOKEI SHIHYO.
Added/Corp Japan. Norinsho. Norin Keizaikyoku. Tokei Chosabu. Japan. Norinsho. Norin Keizaikyoku. Tokei Johobu. (1956)-. Periodical. Japanese. Norin Tokei Kyokai, (Association of Agriculture & Forestry Statistics), 11-14 Meguro 2 Chome, Meguroku Tokyo 153 Japan.

LC S19 .A23
DD 630
JA
NORIN SUISANSHO KOHO. VFOAT Agriculture Forestry Fishery : AFF. Periodical. English (Japanese). Twelve times a year. ¥5400. Norin Tokei Kyokai, (Association of Agriculture & Forestry Statistics), 11-14 Meguro 2 Chome, Meguroku Tokyo 153 Japan. **Continues** AFF (Tokyo, Japan).

LC HD2091 .N65B
DD 630
JA
NORIN SUISANSHO TOKEIHYO.
Main/Corp Japan. Norin Suisansho. Keizaikyoku. Tokei Johobu. **VFOAT** Statistical Yearbook of Ministry of Agriculture, Forestry and Fisheries; Japan Agricultural Statistics. 1977/78-. Japanese (English). One time a year. ¥5000. Norin Tokei Kyokai, (Association of Agriculture & Forestry Statistics), 11-14 Meguro 2 Chome, Meguroku Tokyo 153 Japan. **Ad Acc**. **Continues** Norinsho Tokeihyo.

LC S
DD 630
JA
NORINSHO NEMPO. Main/Corp Japan. Norinsho. (1953)-. Japanese. ¥3000. Norin Kosaikai, 1-2-1 Kasumigaseki Chiyoda-ku, Tokyo 100 Japan. **Continues** Norin Suisan Nenkan.

LC S
DD 630
CU
NORMA CUBANA. See Agriculture-Abstracting, Bibliographies and Statistics.

LC S
DD 630
NO
NORSK LANDBRUK. Vol. 1 (July 5, 1935)-. Periodical. Norwegian. Twenty-four times a year. Kr410.00 Scandinavia; Kr625.00 other. Landbruksforlaget, PO Box 9303, Gronland 0135 Oslo Norway. **Tel** 011 47 2 173340. **ED** Stein Hoset. **Bk Rev**. **Ad Acc**. **Circ**: 25,500 (ctrl).
Desc: Concerned with plant production, machinery, meat and milk production, economics, farm structures, rural conditions, forestry, etc.
Ind/Abst Plant Breed. Abstr.

LC S
DD 630
ISSN 0801-5333
NO
CODEN NOLAEU
NORSK LANDBRUKSFORSKING. [Nor. landbr. forsk.]. **Added/Corp** Statens Fagtjeneste for Landbruket (Norway). **VFOAT** Norwegian Agricultural Research. (1987)-. Periodical. Norwegian (summaries and/or abstracts in English). Four times a year. Kr400.00. Norwegian Agricultural Advisory Centre, Moerveien 12, N 1430 AS Norway. **Tel** 011 47 2 941365. Documents available from BIOSIS Document Express. **Continues in part** Forskning og Forski Landbruket, 0429-1913; Meldinger Fra Norges Landbrukshgskole, 0025-8946.
Ind/Abst AgBiotech News Inf.; Agric. Eng. Abstr. (1991-); Biodeter. Abstr. (1991-); Biol. Abstr. (1987-); Field Crop Abstr.; Fish Rev. (Jan. 1989-July 1992); Grass. Forage Abstr.; Hortic. Abstr.; Index Vet.; Irr. Drain. Abstr.; Maize Abstr.; Nutr. Abstr. Rev., Ser. B, Live Feeds and Feed.; Ornamental Hort. (1991-); Plant Breed. Abstr.; Plant Grow. Reg. Abstr.; Postharvest News Inf.; Potato Abstr.; Poult. Abstr.; Rev. Agric. Entomol.; Rev. Plant

Agriculture

Pathol.; Soils Fert.; Weed Abstr.; Wheat Barley Trit. Abstr.; Wildl. Rev. (Jan. 1989-July 1992); World Agric. Econ. Rural Sociol. Abstr.

LC S ISSN 0802-0914
DD 630 NO
NORSK LANDBRUKSFORSKING. SUPPLEMENT. [Nor. landbr. forsk. Suppl.]. VFOAT Norwegian Agricultural Research. No. 1 (1987)-. Monographic series. Norwegian (summaries and/or abstracts in English). Price varies per volume. Norwegian Agricultural Advisory Centre, Moerveien 12, N 1430 AS Norway. **Tel** 011 47 2 941365.

LC S ISSN 0091-7508
DD 630 US
NORTH CAROLINA AGRICULTURAL CHEMICALS MANUAL. [N.C. agric. chem. man.]. **Added/Corp** North Carolina State University at Raleigh. Division of Continuing Education. North Carolina State University at Raleigh. Pesticide Fertilizer School. (1970)-. Periodical. English. One time a year. $10.00. North Carolina State University / Raleigh, PO Box 7603, Raleigh NC 27695. **Tel** (919)737-2808. **Continues** North Carolina Pesticide-Fertilizer Manual.

LC S97 .Z24 ISSN 0091-3693
DD 638.0974 US
NORTH CAROLINA AGRICULTURAL STATISTICS. [N.C. agric. stat.]. **Added/Corp** North Carolina. Crop Reporting Service. United States. Agricultural Marketing Service. North Carolina. Division of Agricultural Statistics. United States. Bureau of Agricultural Economics. North Carolina. Crop & Livestock Reporting Service. United States. Dept. of Agriculture. North Carolina. Dept. of Agriculture. VFOAT Agricultural Statistics; Agricultural Statistics, North Carolina; North Carolina Agricultural Statistics, Crop and Livestock Report. (1937/1938/1939/1940)-. English. Free on request. Agricultural Statistics Division, PO Box 27767, Raleigh NC 27611. **Tel** (919)856-4394. **Continues** North Carolina Farm Forecaster Agricultural Statistics.

LC S ISSN 0744-9593
DD 630 US
NORTH CAROLINA FARM BUREAU NEWS. [N.C. Farm Bur. news]. VFOAT Farm Bureau News. Periodical. English. Twelve times a year. $0.25 (members), $0.50 (nonmembers). North Carolina Farm Bureau News, 5301 Glenwood Avenue/Box 27766, Raleigh NC 27612. **ED** Bill Critcher. **Ad Acc. Circ:** 285,000.

LC S
DD 630 US
NORTH CAROLINA FARM INCOME. English. North Carolina Crop and Livestock Reporting Service, PO Box 27767, 1 West Edenton Street, Raleigh NC 27611.

LC S
DD 630 US
NORTH COUNTRY FARM NEWS. Vol. 1 (Jan. 1979)-. Periodical. English. Twelve times a year. Clinton County Cooperative Extension News, Clinton County Court House, Plattsburgh NY 12901.

LC S99 .Z28 ISSN 0737-1624
DD 338.1/09784 US
Pr Rev.
NORTH DAKOTA AGRICULTURAL STATISTICS (FARGO, N.D.). See Agriculture-Abstracting, Bibliographies and Statistics.

LC S ISSN 0196-9897
DD 630 US
NORTH DAKOTA FARM REPORTER. **Added/Corp** North Dakota Crop and Livestock Reporting Service. VFOAT Farm Reporter. (1955)-. Government Publication. English. Irregular. $10.00. US Department of Agriculture / National Agricultural Statistics Service (NASS), Room 5829 South Building, Washington DC 20250. **Tel** (202)720-4020, FAX (314)875-5231. **ED** Janice C. Kjesbo. **Circ:** 1,900.
Desc: Provides basic state and national estimates.

LC S ISSN 0097-5338
DD 630 US
NORTH DAKOTA FARM RESEARCH. [N. D. farm res.]. **Added/Corp** North Dakota Agricultural Experiment Station (Fargo). Vol. 20, No. 4 (March/April 1958)-. Periodical. English. Six times a year. Free on request. North Dakota University, Bulletin Room #10, PO Box 5655, Fargo ND 58105. **Tel** (701)237-8011. **ED** Gary Moran. **Circ:** 9,000. **Continues** North Dakota Agricultural Experiment Station, Fargo. Bimonthly Bulletin.
Desc: Reports of agricultural research conducted at North Dakota State University experiment stations.
Ind/Abst AGRICOLA [Full Cov.]; Anim. Breed. Abstr.; Coal Abstr.; Dairy Sci. Abstr.; Energy Res. Abstr. (March 1977-); Field Crop Abstr.; Hortic. Abstr.; Irr. Drain.; Maize Abstr.; Nutr. Abstr. Rev., Ser. B, Live Feeds and Feed; Life Sci. Collect.; Plant Breed. Abstr.; Potato Abstr.; Risk Abstr.; Seed Abstr.; Soils Fert.; Soyabean Abstr.; Weed Abstr.; World Agric. Econ. Rural Sociol. Abstr.

LC S451.5 ISSN 0715-4674
DD 630/.97123 CN
NORTHERN ALBERTA FARMER (FORT SASKATCHEWAN). (NORTHERN ALBERTA FARMER.). [North. Alta. farmer]. VAT Farmer (Fort Saskatchewan). (Nov. 12, 1980)-. Periodical. English. One time a week. $15.00 Canada, $40.00 other. Ootes Press Ltd, 10308 100th Avenue, Suite 100, Fort Saskatchewan T8L 1Z1 Canada. **Tel** (403)998-1419, FAX (403)992-1646.

LC S
DD 630 US
NORTHWEST BERRY PROCESSING REPORT. (19??)-. English. Four times a year. $32.00 North America; $64.00 other. US Department of Agriculture / Washington State, 2015 South First Street, Room 4, Yakima WA 98903. **Tel** (509)575-2494, FAX (509)457-7132.

LC S ISSN 0801-5341
DD 630 NO
NORWEGIAN JOURNAL OF AGRICULTURAL SCIENCES. [Nor. j. agric. sci.]. **Added/Corp** Statens Fagtjeneste for Landbruket (Norway). Vol. 1, No. 1 (1987)-. Periodical. English. Four times a year (Feb., May, Aug., Nov.). $87.21. Norwegian Agricultural Advisory Centre, Moerveien 12, N 1430 AS Norway. **Tel** 011 47 2 941365. **Continues in part** Forskning og Forsk i Landbruket, 0429-1913 **and** Meldinger fra Norges Landbrukshgskole, 0025-8946.
Ind/Abst Curr. Cit.; Field Crop Abstr.; Grass. Forage Abstr.; Hortic. Abstr.; Maize Abstr.; Nutr. Abstr. Rev., Ser. A, Hum. Exp.; Postharvest News Inf.; Wheat Barley Trit. Abstr.

LC S
DD 630 NO
NORWEGIAN JOURNAL OF AGRICULTURAL SCIENCES. SUPPLEMENT. (1987)-. Monographic series. English. Irregular. Price varies per volume.
Ind/Abst Agric. Eng. Abstr. (1991-); Anim. Breed. Abstr.; Crop Physiol. Abstr.; Dairy Sci. Abstr.; For. Abstr.; Irr. Drain.; Nutr. Abstr.; Nutr. Abstr. Rev., Ser. B, Live Feeds and Feed.; Ornamental Hort. (1991-); Pig News Inf.; Plant Breed. Abstr.; Plant Grow. Reg. Abstr.; Potato Abstr.; Poult. Abstr.; Rev. Plant Pathol.; Soils Fert.

LC S ISSN 0389-1763
DD 631 JA
NOSAGYO KENKYU. [Nosagyo Kenkyu]. VFOAT Japanese Journal of Farm Work Research; Farm Work Research; Journal of Farm Work Society of Japan. (1966)-. Periodical. Multiple languages. Three times a year. Nihon Nosagyo Gakkai, (Japanese Soc. of Farm Work Research), Norin Suisansho Nogyo Kenkyu Senta, 1-1 Kannondai 3 Chome, Tsukubashi Ibarakiken 305, Japan.
Ind/Abst Agric. Eng. Abstr.

LC S ISSN 0797-0323
DD 630 UY
NOTAS TECNICAS - FACULTAD DE AGRONOMIA (MONTEVIDEO). (NOTAS TECNICAS : NT.). [Notas tec. - Fac. Agron.]. **Added/Corp** Universidad de la Republica (Uruguay). Facultad de Agronomia. VFOAT NT. No 1 (1987)-. Monographic series. Spanish. Departamento de Documentacion, Facultad de Agronomia, Garzon 780, Montevideo Uruguay.
Ind/Abst For. Abstr.

LC S ISSN 0771-0607
DD 630 BE
CODEN NTCGD3
NOTE TECHNIQUE DU CENTRE DE RECHERCHES AGRONOMIQUE DE LETAT. (NOTE TECHNIQUE.). [Note tech. Cent. Rech. Agron. Etat.]. **Added/Corp** Belgium. Centre de Rrecherches Aagronomiques de Letat. VFOAT Note Technique du Centre de Recherches Agronomiques de Letat. (19??)-. Academic Scholarly Publication. French. Price varies per volume. Royaume De Belgique, Centre De Recherches Agronomiques, Administration De La Recherche, Agronomique Ministere, De L'Agriculture Gembloux Belgium. Documents available from CASDDS. **Continues** Station de Phytopharmacie de Letat. Note Technique.
Ind/Abst Chem. Abstr.; Dairy Sci. Abstr.; Plant Grow. Reg. Abstr.

LC HD2150.6 .A4 ISSN 0335-4024
DD 338.1/0969/81 FR
NOTES DE CONJONCTURE (FRANCE. DIRECTION DEPARTEMENTALE DE L'AGRICULTURE DE LA REUNION. SERVICE DE STATISTIQUE AGRICOLE). (NOTES DE CONJONCTURE / DIRECTORY DEPARTEMENTALE DE L'AGRICULTURE, SERVICE DE STATISTIQUE AGRICOLE.). (19??)-. Directory. French. Twelve times a year. Boulevard de la Providence, 97489 Saint Denis Reunion.

LC HD2021 .N68 ISSN 1132-1261
DD 630 SP
CODEN NHAGEC
Pr Rev.
NOTICIARIO DE HISTORIA AGRARIA. **Added/Corp** Seminario de Historia Agraria (Association) Grupo de Historia Agraria de la Universidad de Murcia. No. 1 (Jan./June 1991)-. Academic Scholarly Publication. Spanish (Italian). Two times a year. 3500ptas (individuals); 4000ptas (institutions). Seminario de Historia Agraria, University de Zaragoza, Facultdad de Ciencias Economia y Empresariales, C. Dr. Cerrada 1 50005, Zaragoza Spain. **ED** Jose Miguel Martinez. Index available. cum. index. **Bk Rev. Ad Acc. Circ:** 600.
Ind/Abst Am. Hist. Life (1992-); Hist. Abstr. (1992-).

LC S
DD 630 FR
NOUVEL AGRICULTEUR, LE. (July 18, 1986)-. French. One time a week. 408.00F France; 683.00F US and Canada; 421.20F other. Le Nouvel Agriculteur, 21 rue du Faubourg St Antoine, 75550 Paris Cedex 11 France. **Formed by the union of** Agri Sept **and** Producteur Agricole Francais.

LC S583 ISSN 0369-4658
DD 631 JA
CODEN NKHOAK
NOYAKU KENSAJO HOKOKU. [Noyaku Kensajo hokoku]. **Main/Corp** Norinsho Noyaku Kensajo. VFOAT Bulletin of the Agricultural Chemicals Inspection Station, Ministry of Agriculture and Forestry. Academic Scholarly Publication. Japanese (summaries and/or abstracts in English). Norin Suisansho Noyaku Kensajo, (Agricultural Chemicals Inspection Station Ministry of Agriculture Forestry & Fisheries), 2-772 Suzukicho Kodairashi, Tokyo 187 Japan. Documents available from BIOSIS Document Express, CASDDS.
Ind/Abst AGRICOLA; Biol. Abstr.; Chem. Abstr.; EMBASE; Index Vet.; Rice Abstr.

LC S ISSN 0226-8124
DD 630/.5 CN
NOYAU, LE. [Noyau]. No. 1 (Jan./Feb. 1980)-. Periodical. French. Six times a year. $6.97. Le Noyau, CP 37, Causapscal Quebec G0J 1J0 Canada. **Tel** (418)756-5651.

LC HD2091 .N646A
DD 630 JA
NPGUO CHOSA HOKOKUSHO. **Main/Corp** Japan. Norin Suisansho. Keizaikyoku. Tokei Johobu. (19??)-. Japanese. Norin Tokei Kyokai, (Association of Agriculture & Forestry Statistics), 11-14 Meguro 2 Chome, Meguroku Tokyo 153 Japan.

LC S
DD 630 AT
NSW AGRICULTURE TODAY. English. Eleven times a year (monthly except Jan.). 25.00Aus$. Rural Press Ltd. / New South Wales, PO Box 999, North Richmond NSW 2754 Australia. **Tel** 011 61 45 704444, FAX 011 61 45 704649. **Continues** NSW Farmer and Grazier.

LC S
DD 630 US
NTIS ALERT. AGRICULTURE & FOOD. **Added/Corp** United States. National Technical Information Service. (1992)-. English. Twenty-four times a year. $135.00 US; $195.00 other. National Technical Information Service - NTIS, Room 2027S, 5285 Port Royal Road, Springfield VA 22161. **Tel** (703)487-4630, (703)487-4660, (703)487-4650, FAX (703)321-8547, telex 89-9405. Index Available in last issue of each volume--loose separately paged. **Continues** Agriculture & Food / NTIS, 0364-7994.
Desc: Provides information on agricultural chemistry, equipment and resource surveys, agronomy, plant pathology, animal husbandry, etc.

LC S
DD 630 US
NUMBER OF FARMS AND LAND IN FARMS / IOWA CROP AND LIVESTOCK REPORTING SERVICE. (19??)-. English. One time a year. The Service, Full Depository, 707 Savings and Loan Building, Des Moines IA 50309.
Desc: Statistical report on number of farms, average size, and land in farms.

LC HD2181 .B85A ISSN 0157-065X
DD 338.1/09946 AT
NUMBER OF RURAL ESTABLISHMENTS, IRRIGATION AND FERTILISER USAGE, TASMANIA / AUSTRALIAN BUREAU OF STATISTICS. (19??)-. English. One time a year. Australian Bureau Statistics / Tasmanian Office, Commonwealth Government Centre, 188 Collins Street, Hobart GPO Box 66A, Hobart Tasmania 7001 Australia. **Tel** 011 61 2 205889. **Continues** Number of Farms, Employment, Machinery, Irrigation and Fertiliser Usage, Tasmania.

Agriculture

LC S
DD 630   **ISSN** 1002-8889
   CC
NUNG TSUN CHING CHI YU SHE HUI = RURAL ECONOMY AND SOCIETY.
Added/Corp Chung-kuo she hui ko Hsueh Yuan. Nung Tsun fa Chan yen Chiu so. **VFOAT** Rural Economy and Society. (1988)-. Periodical. Chinese (table of contents in English). Six times a year. Zhongguo Shehui Kexueyuan, Nongcun Fazhan Yanjiusuo, (Chinese Academy of Social Sciences), Institute of Rural Development, 2 Yuetan Beixiaojie, Beijing 100836, People's Republic of China. **Tel** 8312466.
Ind/Abst World Agric. Econ. Rural Sociol. Abstr.

LC S471.C6 N836
DD 354.510082/33   CC
NUNG TSUN KUNG TSO TUNG HSUN.
VFOAT Nongcun Gongzuo Tongxun. (19??)-. Periodical. Chinese. Twelve times a year. RMBY0.22. Nung Tsun Kung Tso Tung Hsun, Post Office, Beijing, People's Republic of China.

LC HD1401 .N755
DD 338.1   **ISSN** 0546-9600
   CH
NUNG YEH CHING CHI. [Nongye jingji]. **VFOAT** Journal of Agricultural Economics. (1963)-. Periodical. Chinese (summaries and/or abstracts in English). Two times a year.
Ind/Abst AGRICOLA.

LC HD2100.L5 N86
DD 338.1/0951/82   CH
NUNG YEH CHING CHI (SHEN-YANG SHIH, CHINA). (NUNG YEH CHING CHI.). **VFOAT** Nong Ye Jing Ji. (19??)-. Periodical. Chinese. Six times a year. NT$0.34. Post Office Shen-Yang Shih, Shen-Yang Shih, People's Republic of China.

LC S471.C62 K9766
DD 630/.95134   CC
NUNG YEH CHING YING KUAN LI. **VFOAT** Nongyejingyingguanli. (19??)-. Periodical. Chinese. Twelve times a year. Chinese Academy of Sciences, Fujian Institute of Research, Box 143, Fuzhou Fujian 350002 China. **Tel** 011 86 591 37113682151, FAX 011 86 591 714946.

LC S589.75 .N86
DD 363.7/31   **ISSN** 1000-0267
   CC
Pr Rev.
NUNG YEH HUAN CHING PAO HU. See Environmental Issues-Pollution and Waste Management.

LC S
DD 630   US
OARDC RESEARCH BULLETIN. Bulletin. English. Ohio Agricultural Research and Development Center, Ohio State University, 1680 Madison Avenue, Wooster OH 44691. **Tel** (216)263-3775.
Ind/Abst For. Abstr.

LC S
DD 630   US
OARDC RESEARCH CIRCULAR.
Main/Corp Ohio Agricultural Research and Development Center. **Added/Corp** Ohio Agricultural Research and Development Center. **VFOAT** Ohio Agricultural Research and Development Center Research Circular. (1991)-. Periodical. English. Ohio Agricultural Research and Development Center, Ohio State University, 1680 Madison Avenue, Wooster OH 44691. **Tel** (216)263-3775. **Continues** Research Circular.

LC S590
DD 638.1   **ISSN** 0470-925X
   JA
   CODEN OBIHAK
OBIHIRO CHIKUSAN DAIGAKU GAKUJUTSU KENKYU HOKOKU DAI-1-BU. (GAKUJUTSU KENKYU HOKOKU. DAIICHIBU. RESEARCH BULLETIN OF OBIHIRO UNIVERSITY. SERIES I.). [Obihiro Chikusan Daigaku Gakujutsu kenkyu hokoku. Dai-1-bu]. **Main/Corp** Obihiro Chikusan Daigaku. **VFOAT** Research Bulletin of Obihiro University. Series I. Vol. 9, No. 1 (Dec. 1974)-. Bulletin. Japanese (summaries and/or abstracts in English). Obihiro University, Department of Agriculture and Veterinary Medicine, Obihiro Japan. Documents available from BIOSIS Document Express, CASDDS. **Continues** Obihiro, Japan. Zootechnical University. Research Bulletin.
Ind/Abst AGRICOLA; Agric. Eng. Abstr.; Biol. Abstr.; Chem. Abstr.; EMBASE; For. Abstr.; Hortic. Abstr.; Nutr. Abstr. Rev., Ser. A, Hum. Exp.; Life Sci. Collect.; Potato Abstr.; Soils Fert.

LC HD1401
DD 338.17   GW
OBSTBAU. **Added/Corp** Bundesausschuss Obst und Gemuse. Fachgruppe Obstbau. Vol. 1, No. 3 (Mar. 1976)-. Periodical. German. Twelve times a year. $115.15. Alfred Grossgebour, Grossgebauer, Bodesberger Allee 142-148, 5300 Bonn 2 Germany. **Tel** 011 49 228 373499.
Ind/Abst AGRICOLA; Hortic. Abstr.; Plant Breed. Abstr.; Rev. Agric. Entomol.; Rev. Plant Pathol.; World Agric. Econ. Rural Sociol. Abstr.

LC S
DD 630   GW
OBSTERNTE. REIHE 3.4 / HERAUSGEBER, STATISTISCHES BUNDEMAST, WIESBADEN. (197?)-. German. **Continues** Gartenbau und Weinwirtschaft. II. Obst.

LC S
DD 630   AT
OCCASIONAL PAPER (SOUTH PACIFIC SMALLHOLDER PROJECT). (SOUTH PACIFIC SMALLHOLDER PROJECT.). (1986)-. English. Irregular. South Pacific Smallholders Project, University of New England, Department of Agricultural and Resource Economics, Armidale New South Wales 2351 Australia. **Tel** 011 61 67 732232, FAX 011 61 67 711531. **ED** J.B. Hardaker. **Circ:** 200.

LC SD411
DD 333.76   **ISSN** 0957-0985
   UK
OCCASIONAL PAPER / WYE COLLEGE, UNIVERSITY OF LONDON, DEPARTMENT OF AGRICULTURE, HORTICULTURE AND THE ENVIRONMENT. **Added/Corp** Wye College. Dept. of Agriculture, Horticulture and the Environment. **VFOAT** Occasional Papers. (198?)-. Monographic series. English. **Continues** Occasional Paper (Wye College. Dept. of Environmental Studies and Countryside Planning).
Ind/Abst Agrofor. Abstr.; For. Abstr.

LC S
DD 630   **ISSN** 0029-8239
   PL
OCHRONO ROSLIN. [Ochr. rosl.]. **Added/Corp** Poland. Ministerstwo Rolnictwa. Vol. 4, No. 1 (Jan./March 1960)-. Periodical. Polish. Twelve times a year. Price on request. **(Subscription address:** Ars Polona-Ruch, PO Box 1001, Krakowskie Przedmiescie 7, 00-068 Warsaw Poland. **Tel** 011 48 22 261201.) **Continues** Biuletyn Kwarantanny i Ochrony Roalin.
Ind/Abst AGRICOLA; Nematol. Abstr.; PESTDOC; Plant Grow. Reg. Abstr.; Potato Abstr.; Seed Abstr.

LC SB298
DD 633.85   FR
●**OCL : OLEAGINEUX CORPS GRAS LIPIDES.** **VFOAT** Oleagineux Corps Gras Lipides; OCL. Vol. 1, No. 1 (Aug./Sept. 1994)-. Periodical. French (English). Six times a year. $273.40. John Libbey Eurotext Ltd., 127 avenue de la Republique, 92120 Montrouge France. **Tel** 011 33 1 46730660, FAX 011 33 1 40840999. **(Subscription address:** ATEI John Libbey Eurotext, 3 avenue Pierre Kerautret, 93230 Romainville France. **Tel** 011 33 1 48408686.) **Formed by the union of** Informations Techniques, 0374-1451; Revue Francaise des Corps Gras, 0035-3000 and Oleagineux, 0030-2082.

LC S19 .O33
DD 630.5   KO
OEGUK KWAHAK KISUL TONGBO. NONGOP. **VFOAT** Nongop. (19??)-. Periodical. Korean. Twelve times a year.

LC S
DD 630   **ISSN** 0923-4195
   NE
OFCOR, COMPARATIVE STUDY. **VFOAT** OFCORA Comparative Study Paper. (1988)-. Monographic series. English. Price varies per volume.
Ind/Abst World Agric. Econ. Rural Sociol. Abstr.

LC SF
DD 636
UDC 63   **ISSN** 1019-6544
   NE
OFCOR DISCUSSION PAPER. [OFCOR discuss. pap.]. **VFOAT** On-Farm Client-Oriented Research Discussion Paper. (1989)-. Monographic series. English. Irregular. Price varies per volume.
Ind/Abst World Agric. Econ. Rural Sociol. Abstr.

LC HD1751 .U54b
DD 353.81/05   US
OFFICE OF INSPECTOR GENERAL SEMIANNUAL REPORT TO CONGRESS / UNITED STATES DEPARTMENT OF AGRICULTURE, OFFICE OF INSPECTOR GENERAL. **Main/Corp** United States. Dept. of Agriculture. Office of the Inspector General. (1989)-. English. Two times a year. US Department of Agriculture, 14th Street and Independence Avenue SW, Washington DC 20250. **Tel** (202)720-5457. **Continues** United States. Dept. of Agriculture. Office of the Inspector General.; Semiannual Report to Congress.

LC S409.5.P4 O36
DD 630/.6/2748   **ISSN** 0160-2594
   US
OFFICERS OF PENNSYLVANIA AGRICULTURAL ORGANIZATIONS. **Added/Corp** Pennsylvania. Dept. of Agriculture. (19??)-. Periodical. English. One time a year. Free. Pennsylvania Department of Agriculture, 2301 North Cameron Street, Harrisburg PA 17110-9408. **Tel** (717)787-5085. **ED** Sandi Duncan. Index available. **Circ:** 3,000.
Desc: A listing of agricultural organizations, officers, addresses and phone numbers.

LC S641 .A77a
DD 363.1/79   **ISSN** 0094-8764
   US
   CODEN OPAAAN
OFFICIAL PUBLICATION - ASSOCIATION OF AMERICAN PLANT FOOD CONTROL OFFICIALS. [Off. publ. - Ass. Amer. Plant Food Control Off.]. **Main/Corp** Association of American Plant Food Control Officials. No. 23 (1970)-. English. One time a year (Apr.). $20.00. Virginia Department of Agriculture & Consumer Services, 1100 Bank Street, Washington Building, Suite 210, Richmond VA 23219. **Tel** (804)786-2373, FAX (804)371-7679. **Continues** Official Publication - Association of American Fertilizer Control Officials.
Ind/Abst AGRICOLA.

LC S
DD 630   **ISSN** 0030-0896
   US
OHIO FARMER, THE. [Ohio farmer]. (19??)-. Periodical. English. Irregular (15 issues). $17.95 Ohio; $25.00 US; $35.00 Canada and Mexico; $45.00 other. Farm Progress Publishing, 191 South Gary Avenue, Carol Stream IL 60188-2089. **Tel** (708)462-2890 or 2891.

LC S
DD 630   **ISSN** 0749-4009
   US
OHIO GRANGER. **Added/Corp** Ohio State Grange. (Jan./Feb. 1984)-. Periodical. English. Six times a year. $2.00. Ohio State Grange, 1031 East Broad Street, Columbus OH 43205. **Tel** (614)258-9569. **ED** Bernard Shoemaker. **Ad Acc. Circ:** 14,500. **Continues** Ohio Grange, 0030-0926.

LC S
DD 630   **ISSN** 0030-1442
   US
   CODEN OMGAAW
OIL MILL GAZETTEER. [Oil mill gazet.]. **Added/Corp** International Oil Mill Superintendents. Tri-States Oil Mill Superintendents Association. (19??)-. Trade Publication. English. Twelve times a year. $13.00. Oil Mill Gazetteer, PO Box 590483, Houston TX 77259. **Tel** (713)480-7889, FAX (713)334-4619. **ED** Paula Kolmar. cum. index. **Ad Acc. Circ:** 1,300.
Desc: Contains information on oilseed processing.
Ind/Abst BioBusiness (1988-); Food Sci. Technol. Abstr.; Rice Abstr.

LC SB298
DD 633.85   GW
OIL WORLD ANNUAL. **Added/Corp** International Seed Testing Association. (1987)-. English. One time a year. DM152.00. Ista Mielke GmbH, Langenberg 25, 21077 Hamburg Germany. **Tel** 011 49 40 7610500. **Continues** Oil World Semi-Annual.
Desc: Study on the global situation and prospects of oilseeds, oils, fats and meals with breakdown by commodities and countries.

LC HD9490.I38 .O3
DD 338.17   **ISSN** 0369-769X
   II
OILS AND OILSEEDS JOURNAL. [Oils oilseeds j.]. **Added/Corp** Oil Merchant's Chamber Ltd. (Bombay, India) Bombay Oilseeds Exchange. Bombay Oilseeds & Oils Exchange. **VFOAT** Oils and Oilseeds Journal. (July 1948)-. Periodical. English (Gujarati). Four times a year. $15.00. Bombay Oils & Oilseed Exchange Meherali Road, Jenabai Building Yusuf Meherali, PO Box 13009, Bombay 400 003 India. **Tel** 324361/321510. **Ad Acc. Circ:** 1,000 (ctrl).
Ind/Abst AGRICOLA; Food Sci. Technol. Abstr.

LC S
DD 630   **ISSN** 0265-0002
   UK
   TITLE CHANGE
OILSEEDS. (198?)-Vol. 11, No. 4 (Feb. 1994). Periodical. English. Satsouth Limited, 34 Cavendish Road, London NW6 7XP United Kingdom. **Tel** 011 44 171 4595330. **ED** Herbert Daybell. Index available. cum. index. **Continued by** Oilseeds & Industrial Crops.

LC SB298
DD 633.85   UK
●**OILSEEDS & INDUSTRIAL CROPS.** **VFOAT** Oilseeds and Industrial Crops; Oilseeds. Vol. 11, No. 5 (May 1994)-. Periodical. English. Four times a year. $22.25. Satsouth Limited, 34 Cavendish Road, London NW6 7XP United Kingdom. **Tel** 011 44 171 4595330. **ED** Herbert Daybell. Index available. cum. index. **Continues** Oilseeds, 0265-0002.

LC S
DD 630   **ISSN** 0474-0254
   JA
   CODEN ODNGAMODNG-A
OKAYAMA DAIGAKA NOGAKUBU GAKUJUTSU HOKUKU. (OKAYAMA DAIGAKA NOGAKUBU GAKUJUTSU HOKUKU. SCIENTIFIC REPORTS OF THE FACULTY OF AGRICULTURE, OKAYAMA UNIVERSITY.). [Okayama Daigaka Nogakubu gakujutsu hokuku]. **Main/Corp** Okayama Daigaku. Nogakubu. **VFOAT** Scientific Reports of the Faculty of Agriculture, Okayama University. No. 1 (1952)-. Academic Scholarly Publication. Japanese (English). Okayama Daigaku Nogakubu, (Faculty of Agriculture

Agriculture

Okayama University), 1-1 Tsushima Naka 1 Chome, Okayamashi Okayamaken 700, Japan. Documents available from CASDDS.
Ind/Abst AGRICOLA; AGRICOLA; Chem. Abst.; EMBASE; Hortic. Abstr.; Irr. Drain. Abstr.; Plant Grow. Reg. Abstr.; Rice Abstr.

LC S
DD 630 JA
OKINAWA-KEN TOKEISHO. Main/Corp
Japan. Norinsho. Norin Keizaikyoku. Tokei Johobu. **VFOAT** Okinawa Nogyo Sensasu. (1971)-. Japanese. Norin Tokei Kyokai, (Association of Agriculture & Forestry Statistics), 11-14 Meguro 2 Chome, Meguroku Tokyo 153 Japan.

LC S304.O57 O55A
DD 638.09599 JA
OKINAWA NOGYO SENSASU HOKOKUSHO. Main/Corp Okinawa (Prefecture).
Tokeika. (1971)-. Japanese. Tokeika, 1-2-32 Kamiizumicho Naha, Okinawa Japan.

LC S
DD 630 JA
OKINAWA NORIN SUISAN TOKEI NEMPO. (19??)-. Japanese. Okinawa Kaihatsucho
Okinawa Sogo Jimukyoku Norin Suisanbu, 21-5 Maejima 2, Naha 900 Japan.

LC S103 .O38
DD 338.1/09766 US
OKLAHOMA AGRICULTURAL STATISTICS. See Agriculture-Abstracting, Bibliographies and Statistics.

LC S **ISSN** 0145-9392
DD 630 US
OKLAHOMA FARMER-STOCKMAN, THE. VAT Oklahoma Farmer Stockman. (19??)-.
Periodical. English. Twelve times a year. $25.00 US; $45.00 other. HBJ Farm Publications, PO Box 5467, Lincoln NE 68505. **Tel** (402)489-8845. **(Subscription address:** Farm Progress Companies, PO Box 10972, Des Moines IA 50345. **Tel** (800)888-7580.) **ED** Ernest Shiner. **Ad Acc. Circ:** 227,000.
Desc: General farming, livestock, farm, home and country life.

LC HD1527.O3 O43a **ISSN** 0090-8037
DD 331.7/63/09766 US
OKLAHOMA RURAL MANPOWER REPORT. See Business and Economics-Labor.

LC TP680 .O4 **ISSN** 0472-8602
DD 665.3 HU
CODEN OSZKAT
OLAJ, SZAPPAN, KOZMETIKA. (19??)-.
Periodical. Hungarian. Four times a year. $29.00. **(Subscription address:** Kultura, PO Box 143, H-1300 Budapest 3 Hungary. **Tel** 011 36 1 2500194.)
Ind/Abst Field Crop Abstr.; Nutr. Abstr. Rev., Ser. A, Hum. Exp.; Seed Abstr.

LC TP670 .O4 **ISSN** 0030-2082
DD 630 FR
CODEN OLEAAF
Pr Rev. **TITLE CHANGE**
OLEAGINEUX (PARIS). (OLEAGINEUX.).
[Oleagineux]. **Added/Corp** Institut de Recherches pour les Huiles de Palme et Oleagineux. Institut de Recherches pour les Huiles et Oleagineux. Institut des Corps Gras (Paris, France) Institut Colonial de Marseille. Institut Francais d'Outre-mer, Marseille. Vol. 1 (Sept. 1946)-(1994). Periodical. French (English and Spanish; summaries and/or abstracts in English and Spanish; table of contents in English and Spanish). Revue Internationale des Corps Gras, IRHO/CIRAD, Avenue du Val-de-Montferrand, Boite Postale 5035, 34032 Montpellier France. **Tel** 011 33 67 615800, FAX 011 33 67 615986, telex 480762F. **ED** Irho Cirad. (Bound in last issue). cum. index. **Bk Rev.** **Ad Acc.** Documents available from The Genuine Article, CASDDS. **Continues** *Institut Colonial de Marseille. Bulletin des Matieres Grasses, 0366-1202;* **Absorbed** *Industries des Corps Gras.* **Merged with** *Informations Techniques (Paris, France), 0374-1451* **and** *Revue Francais des Corps Gras, 0035-3000 OCL Cafe, Cacao, The, 0007-9510* **to form** *Plantations, Recherche, Developpement, 1254-7670.*
Desc: Agronomy, chemistry technology uses, economy of tropical oil plants, oil palm coconut, groundnut, soybean, sesame castor.
Ind/Abst AgBiotech News Inf.; AGRICOLA; Agrofor. Abstr. (19??-19??); Biocont. News Inf. (19??-19??); Chem. Abstr.; Crop Physiol. Abstr.; Curr. Aware. Biol. Sci.; CABS; Curr. Cit.; Curr. Contents Agric. Biol. Environ. Sci.; Field Crop Abstr.; Food Sci. Technol. Abstr.; Hortic. Abstr.; Irr. Drain. Abstr.; Nematol. Abstr.; Life Sci. Collect.; PESTDOC; Plant Breed. Abstr.; Plant Grow. Reg. Abstr.; Postharvest News Inf.; Res. Alert [Select. Cov.]; Rev. Agric. Entomol.; Rev. Plant Pathol.; SCISEARCH; Seed Abstr.; Soils Fert.; Soyabean Abstr.; World Agric. Econ. Rural Sociol. Abstr.

LC S **ISSN** 1153-4664
DD 630 FR
UDC 663/664
OLEOSCOPE PARIS. (OLEOSCOPE.). (1991)-.
Periodical. French. Six times a year. $85.30. CETIOM, 174 Avenue Victor Hugo, 75116 Paris France. **Tel** 011 33 1 44347200, 011 33 1 44347239. **Continues** *Bulletin CETIOM, 0374-1443.*

LC S **ISSN** 0748-2345
DD 630 US
ON LINE (GAINESVILLE, FLA.). (ON LINE / IFAS, INSTITUTE OF FOOD AND AGRICULTURAL SCIENCES.). [On line]. VFOAT Online; I.F.A.S. Online;
IFAS Online. Vol. 1, No. 1 (Jan. 1984)-. Periodical. English. Twelve times a year. IFAS, Gozz McCarty Hall, Gainesville FL 32611.

LC S **ISSN** 0030-235X
DD 630 US
ON THE DECK. [On deck]. Added/Corp California
Agricultural Aircraft Association. (19??)-. Periodical. English. Twelve times a year. $10.00. On the Deck, 5999 Freeport Boulevard, Sacramento CA 95822. **Tel** (916)427-1171.

LC S451.5 **ISSN** 0831-3865
DD 630/.9713/4 CN
TITLE CHANGE
ONTARIO FARMER (WESTERN ED.).
(ONTARIO FARMER.). [Ont. farmer]. **VFOAT** Ontario Pork Congress. Vol. 18, No. 23 (Aug. 7, 1985)-(1993). Periodical. English. Bowes Publishers, PO Box 7400 Station E, London Ontario N5Y 4X3 Canada. **Tel** (519)472-7601, FAX (519)473-2256. **Continues** *Western Ontario Farmer, 0049-7460.* **Merged with** *Ontario Farmer (Eastern ed.), 0831-3873* **to form** *Ontario Farmer (London, Ont. : 1994), 1199-3529.*

LC J2 **ISSN** 1189-7627
DD 354.710082 CN
OPERATIONAL REVIEW ... FARM DEBT REVIEW BOARDS. [Oper. rev. Farm Debt Rev.
Boards]. **Main/Corp** Canada. Farm Debt Review Board. **VFOAT** Examen Operationnel ... Bureaux d'Examen de l'Endettement Agricole. (1992)-. Government Publication. English (French). Free on request. Agriculture Canada, Communications Branch, Ottawa Ontario K1A 0C7 Canada. **Separated from** *Canada. Farm Debt Review Board. Annual Report ... Farm Debt Review Boards., 1196-0140.*

LC S
DD 630 UK
OPPORTUNITIES IN AGRICULTURE, DEVELOPMENT & BIOLOGICALLY RELATED ARTS & SCIENCES. English.
Twelve times a year. $20.00. Agraria Press, Yew Tree House, Horne Horley, Surrey RH6 9JP United Kingdom. **Tel** 011 44 134 2843173, FAX 011 44 134 2843173. **Ad Acc. Circ:** 14,000.
Desc: Situations in worldwide agriculture, development, and biologically-related arts and sciences.

LC S **ISSN** 1016-121X
DD 630 FR
OPTIONS MEDITERRANEENNES. SERIE A : SEMINAIRES MEDITERRANEENS.
[Options mediterr., Ser. A : semin. mediterr.]. **Added/Corp** Centre International de Hautes Etudes Agronomiques Mediterraneenne. (1989)-. Monographic series. French (English and French).
Ind/Abst AgBiotech News Inf.; Field Crop Abstr.; Grass. Forage Abstr.; Irr. Drain. Abstr.; Nutr. Abstr. Rev., Ser. B, Live Feeds and Feed.; Plant Breed. Abstr.; Rev. Agric. Entomol.; Rev. Plant Pathol.; Seed Abstr.; Weed Abstr.; World Agric. Econ. Rural Sociol. Abstr.

LC S **ISSN** 1016-1228
DD 630 FR
OPTIONS MEDITERRANEENNES. SERIE B : ETUDES ET RECHERCHES. [Options
mediterr., Ser. B : etud. rech.]. **Added/Corp** Centre International de Hautes Etudes Agronomiques Mediterraneenne. No 1 (1989)-. Monographic series. French.
Ind/Abst Grass. Forage Abstr.; Nutr. Abstr. Rev., Ser. B, Live Feeds and Feed.

LC HD1428 **ISSN** 0127-8436
DD 338.18 MY
OPTIONS SERDANG. [OptionsSerdang]. VFOAT
Newsletter of the Centre for Agricultural Policy Studies, Universiti Pertanian Malaysia. (1986)-. Periodical. English. Two times a year. Centre for Agricultural Policy Studies, Universiti Pertanian Malaysia, 43400 Serdan Selangor Malaysia.
Ind/Abst For. Prod. Abstr. (1991-); For. Abstr.

LC SB354 **ISSN** 1180-2251
DD 634/.074/711 CN
ORCHARD (KELOWNA). See Food and Food Industry.

LC S **ISSN** 0279-0874
DD 630 US
OREGON AGRI-FACTS. (OREGON
AGRI-FACTS : ISSUED SEMI-MONTHLY BY OREGON CROP AND LIVESTOCK REPORTING SERVICE.). **Added/Corp** Oregon Crop and Livestock Reporting Service. Vol. 1-81 (May 19, 1981)-. Government Publication. English. Twenty-four times a year. $12.00. US Department of Agriculture / National Agricultural Statistics Service (NASS), Room 5829 South Building, Washington DC 20250. **Tel** (202)720-4020, FAX (314)875-5231.

LC HD1775.O7 O75
DD 338.1/09795/021 US
OREGON AGRICULTURE & FISHERIES STATISTICS. Added/Corp Oregon Agricultural
Statistics Service. United States. National Agricultural Statistics Service. Oregon. State Dept. of Agriculture. **VFOAT** Oregon Agriculture and Fisheries Statistics. (1986/987)-. English. Oregon Agricultural Statistics Service, 1735 Federal Building, 1220 SW Third Avenue, Portland OR 97204. **Tel** (503)221-2131. **Continues** *Oregon Agricultural Statistics, 0748-2647.*

LC S **ISSN** 0162-5179
DD 630 US
OREGON FARM BUREAU NEWS. VFOAT
Farm Bureau News. Periodical. English. Twenty-four times a year. Oregon Farm Bureau Federation, Box 2209, Salem OR 97308-2209. **Circ:** 10,500 (ctrl). **Continues** *Oregon Agriculture, 0030-4611.*

LC S **ISSN** 0030-4697
DD 630 US
OREGON GRANGE BULLETIN. (19??)-.
Bulletin. English. Twenty-four times a year. Oregon Grange Bulletin, 1313 SE 12th Avenue, Portland OR 97214.

LC S **ISSN** 0474-4721
DD 630 US
OREGON'S AGRICULTURAL PROGRESS. [Or. agric. prog.]. Added/Corp Oregon
State University. Agricultural Experiment Station. Vol. 1, No. 1 (Fall 1953)-. Periodical. English. Three times a year. Free on request. Oregon State University Extension Service, Administrative Services A422, Corvallis OR 97331. **Tel** (503)737-3379. **ED** Andy Duncan. **Circ:** 11,000.
Ind/Abst AGRICOLA [Full Cov.].

LC S **ISSN** 1063-6803
DD 630 US
CEASED
ORGANIC FARMER (MONTPELIER, VT.).
(ORGANIC FARMER.). [Org. farmer]. **Added/Corp** Rural Vermont (Organization) Rural Education Action Project. (Winter 1990)-Vol. 5, No. 1 (Winter 1994). Trade Publication. English. Rural Education Action Project Inc., 15 Barre Street, Montpelier VT 05602. **Tel** (802)223-7222, FAX (802)223-0269. **ED** Grace Gershuny. **Bk Rev.** (Qty: 8-10). **Ad Acc. Circ:** 5,000.
Desc: Committed to building communication and encouraging dialogue among people involved in organic and sustainable agriculture. Strives to educate and mobilize support for progressive farm & food policies and to build a healthy, life-affirming agriculture.

LC S
DD 630 US
CEASED
ORGANIC FOOD MATTERS; THE JOURNAL OF SUSTAINABLE AGRICULTURE. (1988)-(19??). Periodical.
English. Committee Sustainable Agriculture, PO Box 1300, Colfax CA 95713. **Tel** (916)346-2777, FAX (916)346-6884.

LC S
DD 630 US
SUSPENDED
ORGANIC WHOLESALE MARKET REPORT. Added/Corp Organic Market News and
Information Service (California) California Certified Organic Farmers. Steering Committee for Sustainable Agriculture. (1985)- Suspended (19??). Periodical. English. Twenty-five times a year. $45.00. Committee Sustainable Agriculture, PO Box 1300, Colfax CA 95713. **Tel** (916)346-2777, FAX (916)346-6884.

LC HD1401 **ISSN** 0382-7852
DD 338.1/09714 CN
ORIENTATIONS ET POLITIQUES DE L'U P A. [Orientat. polit. UPA]. Main/Corp Union de
Producteurs Agricoles. **VFOAT** Orientation et Politiques de l'UPA; Orientation et Politiques de l'Union des Producteurs Agricoles; Orientation et Politiques - Union des Producteurs Agricoles. (1974)-. French. One time a year. Union des Producteurs Agricoles, 555 boulevard Roland Therrien, Longueuil Quebec J4H 3Y9 Canada. **Tel** (514)679-0535. **Supersedes** *Union des Producteurs Agricoles. Congres General, 1er, Sainte-Adele, Quebec, 1972. Politiques de l'U P A*

LC S
DD 630 VE
ORIENTE AGROPECUARIO. Vol. 1 (July/Dec. 1968)-. Periodical. Spanish. Two times a year. Bs60.00 Venezuela; $4.00 US. Universidad de Oriente, Jusepin Venezuela. **Tel** 092-21024, telex UDONM 91180 VC. **ED** Clemente Larez. **Circ:** 500.
Desc: Publication of the Institute of Agricultural Research of the Universidad de Oriente, Venezuela. Publishes original articles on agricultural and animal sciences.
Ind/Abst Nutr. Abstr. Rev., Ser. B, Live Feeds and Feed.

LC S ISSN 0970-728X
DD 630 II
ORISSA JOURNAL OF AGRICULTURAL RESEARCH. (THE ORISSA JOURNAL OF AGRICULTURAL RESEARCH.). [Orissa J. Agric. Res.]. (1988)-. Periodical. English. Four times a year. Orissa University of Agriculture & Technology, Dean of Research, Bhubaneswar Orissa India.
Ind/Abst Agric. Eng. Abstr.; Biodeter. Abstr.; Field Crop Abstr.; Hortic. Abstr.; Irr. Drain. Abstr.; Maize Abstr.; Plant Breed. Abstr.; Plant Grow. Reg. Abstr.; Postharvest News Inf.; Rev. Agric. Entomol.; Rev. Plant Pathol.; Rice Abstr.; Seed Abstr.; Soils Fert.; Sorghum Mill. Abstr.; Soyabean Abstr.; Weed Abstr.; Wheat Barley Trit. Abstr.

LC S ISSN 0078-6888
DD 630 GW
OSTEUROPASTUDIEN DER HOCHSCHULEN DES LANDES HESSEN. REIHE I, GIESSENER ABHANDLUNGEN ZUR AGRAR- UND WIRTSCHAFTSFORSCHUNG DES EUROPAISCHEN OSTENS. **VFOAT** Giessener Abhandlungen zur Agrar- und Wirtschaftsfouschung des Europaischen Ostens. Vol. 1 (1957)-. Monographic series. German. Price varies per volume. Wilhalm Schmitz Verlag, Postfach 21108, Pestalvzstr 1-3, W-6300 Giessen Germany.
Ind/Abst GeoRef; Plant Grow. Reg. Abstr.; Rev. Med. Vet. Entomol.; World Agric. Econ. Rural Sociol. Abstr.

LC SF511 .N384 ISSN 1068-5774
DD 636.6 US
OSTRICH NEWS RATITE DIRECTORY, THE. See Veterinary Sciences.

LC S
DD 630 US
●**OUTLOOK FOR FARM COMMODITY PROGRAM SPENDING, THE.** **Added/Corp** United States. Congressional Budget Office. (1993)-. Newspaper. English. The Congressional Budget Office, 2nd and D Streets Southwest, Washington DC 20515. **Tel** (202)226-2115.

LC HD9001 .O9 ISSN 0739-8891
DD 382/.41/0973 US
OUTLOOK FOR U.S. AGRICULTURAL EXPORTS (1982). (OUTLOOK FOR U.S. AGRICULTURAL EXPORTS.). [Outlook U.S. agric. exports.]. **Added/Corp** United States. World Agricultural Outlook Board. United States. Dept. of Agriculture. Economic Research Service. United States. Foreign Agricultural Service. **VFOAT** Outlook for US Agricultural Exports. **VAT** Outlook for United States Agricultural Exports. (Nov. 1982)-. Government Publication. English. Four times a year. $18.00. US Department of Agriculture, 14th Street and Independence Avenue SW, Washington DC 20250. **Tel** (202)720-5457. **(Subscription address:** Superintendent of Documents, US Government Printing Office, Washington DC 20402. **)** available on microfiche (Vols. for 1986- distributed to depository libraries). ***Continues** Agricultural Exports (Washington, D.C.), 0740-5758.*
Desc: Analyzes prospects for U.S. agricultural trade, including total exports and imports, volume and value of major commodities, and regional breakdowns.
Ind/Abst F&S Index Plus Text, Int. [Select. Cov.]; Predicasts Forecasts.

LC S539.5 ISSN 0030-7270
DD 630.72 UK
CODEN OUAGA8
Pr Rev.
OUTLOOK ON AGRICULTURE. [Outlook agric.]. **Added/Corp** Imperial Chemical Industries, Ltd. Plant Protection Division. Vol. 1 (Spring 1956)-. Periodical. English. Four times a year. $226.00. CAB International Centre, Wallingford, Oxfordshire OX10 8DE United Kingdom. **Tel** 011 44 1491 832111, FAX 011 44 1491 833508, telex 847964 COMAGG G. available on microfilm and microfiche from University Microfilms International (UMI). Documents available from The Genuine Article, BIOSIS Document Express, CASDDS, Documents on Demand. ***Continues** Imperial Chemical Industries, Ltd. Agricultural Research Station, Jealott's Hill, England. Bulletin.*
Ind/Abst AgBiotech News Inf.; AGRICOLA [Select. Cov.]; Agric. Eng. Abstr. (1991-); Agrofor. Abstr. (19??-19??); Anim. Breed. Abstr.; Biocont. News Inf. (1991-); Biodeter. Abstr.; Biol. Abstr.; Chem. Abstr.; Crop Physiol. Abstr.; CSA Neuro. Abstr. (?-?); Curr. Aware. Biol. Sci., CABS; Curr. Cit.; Curr. Contents Agric. Biol. Environ. Sci.; Dairy Sci. Abstr.; Ecol. Abstr. (?-?); Energy Inf. Abstr.; Environ. Abstr.; Field Crop Abstr.; Food Sci. Technol. Abstr.; For. Prod. Abstr. (1991-); For. Abstr.; Geogr. Abstr. Human Geogr. (?-?); Grass. Forage Abstr.; Hortic. Abstr.; Int. Dev. Abstr. (?-?); Maize Abstr.; Nematol. Abstr.; Nutr. Abstr. Rev., Ser. B, Live Feeds and Feed.; Life Sci. Collect.; PESTDOC; Pig News Inf.; Plant Breed. Abstr.; Plant Grow. Reg. Abstr.; Postharvest News Inf.; Potato Abstr.; Protozoolog. Abstr.; Res. Alert [Full Cov.]; Rev. Agric. Entomol.; Rev. Med. Vet. Entomol.; Rice Abstr.; Sci. Cit. Index; SCISEARCH; Sel. Water Resour. Abstr.; Soc. Sci. Cit. Index [Select. Cov.]; Soils Fert.; Soyabean Abstr.; Weed Abstr.; World Agric. Econ. Rural Sociol. Abstr.

LC HG2051.U5 A168A ISSN 0271-7654
DD 353.0082/33045 US
OVERVIEW - FARMERS HOME ADMINISTRATION. **Main/Corp** United States. Farmers Home Administration. Government Publication. English. One time a year. US Department of Agriculture, 14th Street and Independence Avenue SW, Washington DC 20250. **Tel** (202)720-5457.

LC HD1401 .O95
DD 338.1/05 UK
TITLE CHANGE
OXFORD AGRARIAN STUDIES.
Added/Corp University of Oxford. Institute of Agricultural Economics. Queen Elizabeth House. Agricultural Economics Unit. Vol. 1 (1972)-(1995). Periodical. English. Carfax Publishing Company, PO Box 25, Abingdon, Oxfordshire OX14 3UE United Kingdom. **Tel** 011 44 1235 555335, FAX 011 44 1235 553559, telex 817484. **ED** G.T. Jones. cum. index. **Circ:** 600. available on microfiche. ***Supersedes** Farm Economist. **Continued by** Oxford Development Studies.*
Ind/Abst Contents Recent Econ. J.; Cot. Trop. Fibr. Abstr. Bibliogr.; Dairy Sci. Abstr.; For. Prod. Abstr. (1991-); Geogr. Abstr. Human Geogr.; Int. Abstr. Oper. Res. [Select. Cov.]; Int. Bibliogr. Sociol.; Int. Dev. Abstr.; Int. Labour Doc.; Irr. Drain. Abstr.; Maize Abstr.; Poult. Abstr.; Rice Abstr.; World Agric. Econ. Rural Sociol. Abstr.

LC S
DD 630 UK
●**OXFORD DEVELOPMENT STUDIES.**
(1995)-. English. Three times a year. $388.00. Carfax Publishing Company, PO Box 25, Abingdon, Oxfordshire OX14 3UE United Kingdom. **Tel** 011 44 1235 555335, FAX 011 44 1235 553559, telex 817484. ***Continues** Oxford Agrarian Studies.*

LC S ISSN 1071-6548
DD 630 US
●**PACIFIC FARMER.** Vol. 118, No. 6 (July 1993)-. Periodical. English. Twelve times a year. Western Farmer Stockman, Box 2160, Spokane WA 99210. **Tel** (509)459-5361, FAX (509)459-5102. ***Continues** Pacific Farmer-Stockman, 1062-256X.*

LC S449 .P32 ISSN 1062-256X
DD 630 US
TITLE CHANGE
PACIFIC FARMER - STOCKMAN. [Pac. farmer-stockm.]. **VFOAT** Pacific Farmer Stockman. Vol. 1, No. 1 (Jan. 1992)-(19??). Trade Publication. English. Western Farmer Stockman, Box 2160, Spokane WA 99210. **Tel** (509)459-5361, FAX (509)459-5102. ***Continues in part** Oregon Farmer-Stockman, 1041-2719; Washington Farmer-Stockman, 1041-2727. **Continued by** Pacific Farmer, 1071-6548.*

LC HD9003 .P32 ISSN 0147-6378
DD 380.1/41/02573 US
PACKER'S PRODUCE AVAILABILITY AND MERCHANDISING GUIDE, THE. **VFOAT** Produce Availability and Merchandising Guide. (1971)-. Periodical. English. One time a year. $20.00. Vance Publishing Corporation, 400 Knightsbridge Parkway, Lincolnshire IL 60069. **Tel** (800)255-5113, (708)634-2600.

LC S ISSN 0253-2883
DD 630 PK
PAKISTAN AGRICULTURE. [Pak. agric.]. (1979)-. Periodical. English. Twelve times a year. $65.00. International Book Fair, PO Box 7469, Saddar Karachi 74400 Pakistan. **Tel** 011 92 21 522781.
Ind/Abst AGRICOLA; Cot. Trop. Fibr. Abstr. Bibliogr.; Poult. Abstr.

LC S ISSN 0251-0480
DD 630 PK
CODEN PJARDC
PAKISTAN JOURNAL OF AGRICULTURAL RESEARCH. [Pak. j. agric. res.]. **Added/Corp** Agricultural Research Council (Pakistan). Vol. 1, No. 1 (Jan./March 1980)-. Academic Scholarly Publication. English. Four times a year (Jan., Apr., July, Oct.). $30.00. NGM Communication, 3-D-1 Gulberg III, Near TP Exchange, Lahore 54660 Pakistan. **Tel** 011 92 21 428625, FAX 011 92 21 613854. **ED** CM Anwar Khan. Documents available from BIOSIS Document Express, CASDDS. ***Continues** Agriculture Pakistan, 0002-1776.*
Ind/Abst Biodeter. Abstr.; Biol. Abstr. (-1988); Chem. Abstr.; Crop Physiol. Abstr.; Dairy Sci. Abstr.; Field Crop Abstr.; Food Sci. Technol. Abstr.; For. Prod. Abstr. (1991-); Index Vet.; Irr. Drain. Abstr.; Maize Abstr.; Nutr. Abstr. Rev., Ser. B, Live Feeds and Feed.; Plant Grow. Reg. Abstr.; Potato Abstr.; Seed Abstr.; Soyabean Abstr.; Wheat Barley Trit. Abstr.

LC HD2075.5 .A43
DD 338.1/09549/1 PK
PAKISTAN JOURNAL OF AGRICULTURAL SOCIAL SCIENCES : BI-ANNUAL JOURNAL OF PAKISTAN AGRICULTURAL RESEARCH COUNCIL, ISLAMABAD. Vol. 1, No. 1 (July/Dec. 1986)-. Periodical. English. Two times a year. Rs50.00 Pakistan; $20.00 US. Pakistan Agricultural Research Council, PO Box 1031, Islamabad Pakistan.
Ind/Abst AGRICOLA; Rice Abstr.; Rural Dev. Abstr.; Weed Abstr.; World Agric. Econ. Rural Sociol. Abstr.

LC S ISSN 1015-3055
DD 630 PK
PAKISTAN JOURNAL OF AGRICULTURE, AGRICULTURAL ENGINEERING & VETERINARY SCIENCES. **Added/Corp** Sind Agriculture University. Vol. 1, No. 1 (Jan. 1985)-. English. Two times a year (Jan., July). $40.00. Secretary Editorial Board / Pakistan, Sindh Agriculture University, Tando Jam Pakistan. **Tel** 011 92 22 33625. **ED** Dr. Abdul Jabbar Malik. **Ad Acc. Circ:** 10,000.

LC S ISSN 0215-2711
DD 630 IO
PALAWIJI NEWS. (PALAWIJA NEWS : THE CGPRT CENTRE NEWSLETTER.). [Palawiji News]. (1983)-. Newsletter. English. Four times a year.
Ind/Abst Maize Abstr.; Postharvest News Inf.; Potato Abstr.; Rice Abstr.

LC HD9490.5.P343 M46
DD 338.1/73851/09595 MY
PALMOIL STATISTICAL HANDBOOK.
See Agriculture-Abstracting, Bibliographies and Statistics.

LC S13 ISSN 0552-9778
DD 630/.5 PL
CODEN PMPLAJ
PAMIETNIK PUAWSKI. [Pam. pu.]. No. 1 (1961)-. Academic Scholarly Publication. Polish (summaries and/or abstracts in English and Russian; table of contents in English and Russian). Irregular (two or three issues per year). Price varies per volume. Panstwowe Wydawnictwo Rolnicze i Lesne, Al. Jerozolimskie 28, PO Box 374, 00 024 Warsaw Poland. **Tel** 011 48 22 266451, telex 642410 IUNG PL. **(Subscription address:** Instytut Uprawy Nawozenia i Gleboznawstwa, Zaklad Wdrazania i Upowszechniania Wynikow Badan, 24-100 Pulawy Poland. **)** Index available. ctrl circ. Documents available from CASDDS.
Ind/Abst AGRICOLA; Chem. Abstr.; Crop Physiol. Abstr.; EMBASE; Field Crop Abstr.; Hortic. Abstr.; Maize Abstr.; Nematol. Abstr.; Nutr. Abstr. Rev., Ser. B, Live Feeds and Feed.; PESTDOC; Plant Breed. Abstr.; Plant Grow. Reg. Abstr.; Potato Abstr.; Seed Abstr.; Soils Fert.

LC S583 ISSN 0149-9890
DD 631 US
CODEN AAEPCZ
PAPER - AMERICAN SOCIETY OF AGRICULTURAL ENGINEERS. [Pap. - Am. Soc. Agric. Eng.]. **Main/Corp** American Society of Agricultural Engineers. **VFOAT** Transcript; ASAE Paper; ASAE Technical Paper. (196?)-. Academic Scholarly Publication. English. Two times a year. Price varies per volume. American Society of Agricultural Engineers, Department 2510, 2950 Niles Road, St. Joseph MI 49085-9659. **Tel** (616)429-0300, FAX (616)429-3852. **ED** James Basselman. Index available. cum. index. available on microfiche. Documents available from Article Express International, CASDDS.
Desc: Papers presented at Summer and Winter meetings of the Society.
Ind/Abst AgBiotech News Inf.; AGRICOLA; Agric. Eng. Abstr.; Anim. Breed. Abstr.; Biodeter. Abstr. (19??-19??); Bioeng. Abstr.; Chem. Abstr.; Cot. Trop. Fibr. Abstr. Bibliogr.; Dairy Sci. Abstr.; Ei Page One; Energy Res. Abstr. (Sept. 1978-); Eng. Index Annu.; Field Crop Abstr.; For. Prod. Abstr. (19??-19??); For. Abstr.; GeoRef; Grass. Forage Abstr.; Hortic. Abstr.; Index Vet.; Irr. Drain. Abstr.; Maize Abstr.; Nematol. Abstr.; Nutr. Abstr. Rev., Ser. B, Live Feeds and Feed.; Nutr. Abstr. Rev., Ser. A, Hum. Exp.; Ornamental Hort. (1991-); Pig News Inf.; Plant Genet. Resour. Abstr.; Postharvest News Inf.; Potato Abstr.; Poult. Abstr.; Rice Abstr.; Seed Abstr.; Sorghum Mill. Abstr.; Soyabean Abstr.; Vet. Bull.; Weed Abstr.; Wheat Barley Trit. Abstr.; World Agric. Econ. Rural Sociol. Abstr.

LC HD1483 ISSN 0956-5280
DD 338.109416 UK
PAPERS IN AGRICULTURAL AND FOOD ECONOMICS NORTHERN IRELAND. [Pap. agric. food econ. North. Irel.]. (1988)-. English. One time a year.
Ind/Abst Hortic. Abstr.; Pig News Inf.; World Agric. Econ. Rural Sociol. Abstr.

Agriculture

LC S **ISSN** 1031-1009
DD 630 AT
PARTNERS IN RESEARCH FOR DEVELOPMENT. [Partn. res. dev.]. **Added/Corp** Australian Centre for International Agricultural Research. No. 1 (April 1988)-. Periodical. English. Partners in Research for Development ACIAR, GPO Box 1571, Canberra A C T, 2601 Australia.
Ind/Abst Index Vet.; World Agric. Econ. Rural Sociol. Abstr.

LC S **ISSN** 0258-5987
DD 630 CU
UDC 631
PASTOS Y FORRAJES. [Pastos forrajes].
(1978)-. Periodical. Spanish. Three times a year. $18.00 North and South America; $20.00 Europe. Ediciones Cubanas, Obispo 527 Altos ESQ Bernaza, CP 10100 Havana Cuba.
Ind/Abst Biocont. News Inf.; Postharvest News Inf.

LC S
DD 630 CK
PASTOS Y FORRAJES; BOLETIN DE LA CAMPANA NACIONAL DE PASTOS.
Added/Corp Colombia. Ministerio de Agricultura. (Mar. 1962)-. Periodical. Spanish.
Ind/Abst Field Crop Abstr.; Nutr. Abstr. Rev., Ser. B, Live Feeds and Feed.

LC SB193 **ISSN** 1012-7410
DD 633.202 CK
Pr Rev.
PASTURAS TROPICALES. [Pasturas trop.].
Added/Corp Centro Internacional de Agricultura Tropical. Vol. 10, No. 1 (1988)-. Academic Scholarly Publication. Spanish (summaries and/or abstracts in English). Three times a year. Free. Centro Internacional de Agricultura Tropical, Apartado Aereo 67-13, Cali Colombia. **Tel** 57 23 4450000, **FAX** 57 23 4450273, telex 05769 CIAT CO. **ED** Alberto Ramirez. **Bk Rev.** (Qty: 10). **Acid Free.** ctrl circ.
Continues Pasturas Tropicales Boletin, 0120-6915.
Desc: A means of communication among researchers belonging to the international tropical pastures evaluation network and others involved in the introduction, evaluation, and use of tropical forage grasses and legumes.
Ind/Abst Agrofor. Abstr.; Seed Abstr.; Soils Fert.

LC TP **ISSN** 1065-0482
DD 665 US
PATENT ABSTRACTS. AGRICULTURALS. See Copyright, Intellectual Property.

LC S **ISSN** 0479-7353
DD 630 FR
PAYSANS. [Paysans]. (1956)-. Periodical. French. Six times a year. $54.68. Paysans, 6 Bis Av Henri Barbus, 919210 Draveil France. **Tel** 011 33 16 9427474.
Ind/Abst Irr. Drain. Abstr.; Soils Fert.; World Agric. Econ. Rural Sociol. Abstr.

LC S **ISSN** 0116-3140
DD 630 PH
PCARRD MONITOR, THE. [PCARRD monit.].
Added/Corp Philippine Council for Agriculture and Resources Research and Development. **VFOAT** P.C.A.R.R.D. Monitor. **VAT** Philippine Council for Agriculture and Resources Research and Development Monitor. Vol. 10, No. 8 (Oct. 1982)-. Periodical. English. Twelve times a year. Philippine Council for Agriculture and Resources Research and Development, Los Banos, Laguna 3270 Philippines. **Continues** Monitor, 0115-0529.
Ind/Abst AGRICOLA; Agrofor. Abstr. (1991-); Cot. Trop. Fibr. Abstr. Bibliogr.; Dairy Sci. Abstr.; Helminthol. Abstr. (1991-); Index Vet.; Maize Abstr.; Nutr. Abstr. Rev., Ser. B, Live Feeds and Feed.; Philip. Sci. Technol. Abstr.; Rev. Agric. Entomol.; Rev. Med. Vet. Entomol.; Rice Abstr.

LC SF521 **ISSN** 0369-8629
DD 638.1 RU
CODEN PCLVAR
PCHELOVODSTVO. (Oct. 1921)-. Periodical. Russian. Six times a year. $99.95. Izdatelstvo Kolos, Sadovaia-Spasskaia 18, 107807 Moscow Russia. **(Subscription address:** East View Publications Inc., 3020 Harbor Lane North, Suite 110, Minneapolis MN 55447. **Tel** (800)477-1005, (612)550-0961, **FAX** (612)559-2931.)
Desc: Articles deal with bee-keeping.

LC S451.5 **ISSN** 0848-6786
DD 630/.971187 CN
PEACE RIVER NEWSLETTER. [Peace River newsl.]. **Added/Corp** British Columbia. Ministry of Agriculture and Fisheries. (Autumn 1990)-. Newsletter. English. **Continues** Peace River Farm News., 0827-0260.

LC HD1711 **ISSN** 0706-1307
DD 333.7 CN
PEAT NEWS. **Added/Corp** Newfoundland and Labrador Peat Association. (April 1979)-. Periodical. English. Four times a year. 10.00Can$. Newfoundland & Labrador Peat Association, PO Box 8335 Postal Station A, St. John's Newfoundland A1B 3N7 Canada. **ED** A.F. Rayment. **Bk Rev. Ad Acc. Circ:** 100.
Desc: Peat resource inventory, classification, conservation and utilization - forestry, agriculture, horticulture, fuel and industrial uses.

LC S
DD 630 US
PECAN SOUTH. **Added/Corp** Texas Pecan Growers Association. Vol. 25, No. 5 (1992)-. Periodical. English. **Continues** Pecan South Including Pecan Quarterly.

LC S **ISSN** 0889-5929
DD 630 US
PENNSTATE AGRICULTURE. [PennState agric.]. **Added/Corp** Pennsylvania State University. College of Agriculture. **VFOAT** Penn State Agriculture. (Spring 1984)-. Periodical. English. Two times a year. Free on request. Penn State Agriculture, 106 Agricultural Administration Building, University Park PA 16802. **Tel** (814)863-2708. **ED** Evelyn Buckalew. **Continues** Science in Agriculture, 0048-9670.
Desc: For alumni, friends, and students of the college.
Ind/Abst AGRICOLA [Select. Cov.]; Biol. Dig.

LC S451.P4 P4 S494.5.E5
DD 630/.9748 S 333.79 US
PENNSYLVANIA FARM FUEL SURVEY.
Main/Corp Pennsylvania Crop Reporting Service. English. Pennsylvania Department of Agriculture, 2301 North Cameron Street, Harrisburg PA 17110. **Tel** (717)772-2853, **FAX** (717)787-2387.

LC S1 .P43 **ISSN** 0031-4471
DD 630 US
PENNSYLVANIA FARMER. [Pa. farmer]. (1877)-. Periodical. English. Twelve times a year. $19.95. Farm Progress Publishing, 191 South Gary Avenue, Carol Stream IL 60188-2089. **Tel** (708)462-2890 or 2891. **(Subscription address:** CDS / SIFD Agency Control, 1901 Bell Avenue, Des Moines IA 50315. **Tel** (515)246-6812.) **ED** John Vogel. **Absorbed** Pennsylvania Stockman and Farmer.

LC HD891.A1 P46
DD 333.7309598 IO
PENYULUH LANDREFORM & AGRARIA.
Added/Corp Yayasan Dana Landreform. No. 8/9 (Feb./March. 1973)-. Periodical. Indonesian. Twelve times a year. Yayasan Dana Landreform, Jl Singamangaraja No 2, Kebayoran Baru Indonesia. **Continues** Penjuluh Landreform & Agraria.

LC S **ISSN** 0031-6792
DD 630 YU
UDC 636.5
PERADARSTVO. [Peradarstvo]. (1966)-. Periodical. Multiple languages. Twelve times a year. Savez Zinivara SR Srbije, Bulevar JNA 18, Belgrade Yugoslavia. **ED** M Gancic. **Bk Rev. Ad Acc.**
Ind/Abst Index Vet.; Maize Abstr.; Soyabean Abstr.; Vet. Bull.

LC HD2080.6.Z9 S2742
DD 338.1/.09595/4 MY
PERANGKAAN PERTANIAN SARAWAK. See Agriculture-Abstracting, Bibliographies and Statistics.

LC S280.M43 D46a
DD 354.54/1640072/2368233 II
PERFORMANCE BUDGET. **Main/Corp** Meghalaya (India). Dept. of Agriculture. (1979)-. English. One time a year. The Government Press, Vadodara India.

LC HJ66.M5 C12A
DD 354/.54/792008232 II
PERFORMANCE BUDGET: IRRIGATION AND POWER DEPARTMENT. See Finance-Public Finance.

LC S280.G8 A55A
DD 354.54/750072 II
PERFORMANCE BUDGET OF AGRICULTURE, FORESTS, AND CO-OPERATION DEPARTMENT. AGRICULTURE. **Main/Corp** Gujarat (India). Agriculture, Forests, and Cooperation Dept. 1978/79-. Periodical. English. Agriculture Forests and Co-Operation Department, Gujarat India.

LC HD3540.A3 G816A
DD 354.54/7500722253 II
PERFORMANCE BUDGET OF AGRICULTURE, FORESTS, AND CO-OPERATION DEPARTMENT. CO-OPERATION. See Business and Economics-Cooperatives.

LC SD88.G8 A35A
DD 354.54/750082338 II
PERFORMANCE BUDGET OF AGRICULTURE, FORESTS, AND CO-OPERATION DEPARTMENT. FOREST. **Main/Corp** Gujarat (India). Agriculture, Forests, and Co-Operation Department. 1978/79-. English. Agriculture Forests and Co-Operation Department, Gujarat India.

LC S **ISSN** 0897-7348
DD 630 US
PERMACULTURE ACTIVIST, THE.
[Permac. act.]. **Added/Corp** Permaculture Institute of North America. (198?)-. Trade Publication. English. Four times a year. $16.00. Permaculture Activist, PO Box 1209, Black Mountain NC 28711.
Ind/Abst Environ. Period. Bibliogr.

LC S **ISSN** 1037-8480
DD 630 AT
PERMACULTURE INTERNATIONAL JOURNAL. (1989)-. Periodical. English. Four times a year (Mar., June, Sep., Dec). 15.00Aus$ Australia; $20.00 other. Permaculture International, Ltd., PO Box 6039, South Lismore NSW 2480 Australia. **Tel** 011 61 66 22020, **FAX** 011 61 66 220579. **ED** Steve Payne. Index available. cum. index. **Bk Rev**, (Qty: 12). **Ad Acc. Circ:** 16,000. **Continues** International Permaculture Journal, 1033-4947.
Ind/Abst Environ. Period. Bibliogr.

LC S
DD 630 IO
PERTANIAN. **VFOAT** Agriculture. (19??)-. Indonesian (English).

LC S3 .P46
MY
Pr Rev.
●PERTANIKA JOURNAL OF TROPICAL AGRICULTURAL SCIENCE. **VFOAT** Tropical Agricultural Science. Vol. 16, No. 1 (Apr. 1993)-. Periodical. English (Malay). Three times a year. $70.00. Universiti Pertanian Malaysia Agriculture, University of Agriculture Malaysia, 43400 Serdng Selangor Malaysia. **Tel** 011 60 3 9486101, **FAX** 011 60 3 9482507, telex UNIPER MA 37454. **ED** Chin Hoong Fong. Index available in last issue of volume--attached. **Circ:** 300. **Continues** Pertanika, 0126-6128.

LC S **ISSN** 0100-204X
DD 630 BL
CODEN PEABBT
Pr Rev.
PESQUISA AGROPECUARIA BRASILEIRA. [Pesqui. agropecu. bras.]. Vol. 12 (1977)-. Academic Scholarly Publication. Portuguese (English; summaries and/or abstracts in English). Twelve times a year. $180.00. Embrapa, Dept. Dif. Tecnologiaogi, Caixa Postal 040315, 07770 901 Brasilia DF Brazil. **Tel** 011 55 61 2724241. **ED** Luis Carlos Cruz-Riascos. Index available. **Circ:** 1,600 (ctrl). Documents available from The Genuine Article, BIOSIS Document Express, CASDDS. **Formed by the union of** Pesquisa Agropecuaria Brasileira. Serie Agronomia; Pesquisa Agropecuaria Brasileira. Serie Veterinaria, 0369-8122 **and** Pesquisa Agropecuaria Brasileira. Serie Zootecnia, 0304-372X.
Desc: Articles in the areas of agropecuary, rural sociology, rural economy, genetics, and others.
Ind/Abst AgBiotech News Inf.; AGRICOLA; Agric. Eng. Abstr. (1991-); Agrindex; Agrofor. Abstr. (19??-19??); Anim. Breed. Abstr.; BioBusiness; Biocont. News Inf. (19??-19??); Biodeter. Abstr.; Biol. Abstr.; Chem. Abstr.; Crop Physiol. Abstr.; Curr. Contents Agric. Biol. Environ. Sci.; Field Crop Abstr.; Food Sci. Technol. Abstr.; For. Prod. Abstr.; For. Abstr.; Grass. Forage Abstr.; Helminthol. Abstr.; Hortic. Abstr.; Index Vet.; Irr. Drain. Abstr.; Leadscan; Maize Abstr.; Nematol. Abstr.; Nutr. Abstr. Rev., Ser. B, Live Feeds and Feed.; Pig News Inf.; Plant Breed. Abstr.; Plant Genet. Resour. Abstr.; Plant Grow. Reg. Abstr.; Postharvest News Inf.; Potato Abstr.; Poult. Abstr.; Protozoolog. Abstr.; Res. Alert [Select. Cov.]; Rev. Agric. Entomol.; Rev. Med. Vet. Entomol.; Rev. Med. Vet. Mycology; Rice Abstr.; SCISEARCH; Seed Abstr.; Soils Fert.; Sorghum Mill. Abstr.; Soyabean Abstr.; Sug. Indus. Abstr.; Vet. Bull.; Weed Abstr.; Wheat Barley Trit. Abstr.; World Agric. Econ. Rural Sociol. Abstr.

LC S **ISSN** 0101-9651
DD 630 BL
UDC 633
PESQUISA EM ANDAMENTO - EMPAER.
[Pesqui. andam. - EMPAER]. **VFOAT** Pesquisa em Andamento - Empresa de Pesquisa Assistencia Tecnica e Extensfao Rural de Mato Grosso do Sul. (1982)-. Monographic series. Portuguese. Irregular.
Ind/Abst Soyabean Abstr.

LC S
DD 630 US
PEST-BANK [COMPUTER FILE]. See Pest Control.

LC S
DD 630 UK
PESTICIDE MANUAL, THE. (19??)-. Academic Scholarly Publication. English. £110.00 UK; $190.00 US. Royal Society of Chemistry, Thomas Graham House, Science Park, Cambridge CB4 4WF United Kingdom. **Tel** 011 44 1223 420066, **FAX** 011 44 1223 423623, telex

Agriculture

818293 ROYAL. **(Subscription address:** Royal Society of Chemistry, Turpin Distribution Services Ltd., Blackhorse Road, Letchworth, Hertfordshire SG6 1HN United Kingdom. **Tel** 011 44 1462 672555, FAX 011 44 1462 480947.) **ED** Dr. Clive Tomlin. available on an online database; available on magnetic tape. *Absorbed The Agrochemicals Handbook.*
Desc: Geared to the diversity of interests in pesticides and their impact on the environment. Details over seven hundred pesticide active ingredients as well as over five hundred superceded ones. Herbicides, fungicides, insecticides, acaricides, nematicides, plant growth regulators and rodenticides.

LC S ISSN 0031-7454
DD 630 PH
 CODEN PHAGAU
Pr Rev.
PHILIPPINE AGRICULTURIST, THE. [Philipp. agric.]. **Added/Corp** University of the Philippines. College of Agriculture. **VFOAT** University of the Philippines Publications: Series A. Vol. 7 (Aug. 1918)-. Academic Scholarly Publication. English. Four times a year. $65.00. University of Philippines at Los Banos College of Agriculture, Laguna Philippines 4031. **Tel** 011 63 94 2379, 011 63 94 3274. **ED** Teresita L. Rosario. **Circ:** 500. Documents available from BIOSIS Document Express, CASDDS. *Continues Philippine Agriculturalist and Forester.*
Desc: Original research papers and reviews on plant, animal, soil, and food sciences, agricultural processing and technology, agricultural biotechnology, agricultural education and rural sociology, devt. communication, agribusiness, and agricultural economics and management.
Ind/Abst AGRICOLA; Agric. Eng. Abstr. (1991-); Agrofor. Abstr. (1991-); Anim. Breed. Abstr.; Biocont. News Inf. (1991-); Biodeter. Abstr. (1991-); Biol. Abstr.; Chem. Abstr.; Crop Physiol. Abstr.; Dairy Sci. Abstr.; EMBASE; Field Crop Abstr.; Food Sci. Technol. Abstr.; For. Abstr.; GeoRef; Hortic. Abstr.; Irr. Drain. Abstr.; Maize Abstr.; Nematol. Abstr.; Nutr. Abstr. Rev., Ser. B, Live Feeds and Feed.; Life Sci. Collect.; Philip. Sci. Technol. Abstr.; Pig News Inf.; Plant Breed. Abstr.; Postharvest News Inf.; Potato Abstr.; Rev. Agric. Entomol.; Rev. Med. Vet. Entomol.; Rev. Plant Pathol.; Rice Abstr.; Rural Dev. Abstr.; Seed Abstr.; Soils Fert.; Sorghum Mill. Abstr.; Soyabean Abstr.; Wheat Barley Trit. Abstr.

LC S17 .P53 ISSN 0115-0928
DD 630.5 PH
PHILIPPINE FARMERS' JOURNAL. Vol. 1 (Jan. 1959)-. Periodical. English. Twelve times a year.
Ind/Abst Philip. Sci. Technol. Abstr.

LC SB ISSN 1164-6993
DD 630 FR
UDC 631/635
PHYTOMA, LA DEFENSE DES VEGETAUX. (1991)-. French. Twelve times a year. Editions le Carousel, 26 rue Daniel Casanova, 75002 Paris France. **Tel** 011 33 1 40209474. **(Subscription address:** Phytoma SVC Abonnement, 4 rue Andre Boulle, 94942 Creteil Cedex 09 France. **Tel** 011 33 1 49819117.)
Ind/Abst Curr. Cit.; PESTDOC.

LC S
DD 630 UK
●**PLA NOTES.** (1995)-. English. Three times a year. $25.67. Sustainable Agri Programme, IIED 3 Endsleigh Street, London WC1H ODD United Kingdom. **Tel** 011 44 171 3882117. *Continues RRA Notes.*

LC HD601.A1 P55 ISSN 0260-8642
DD 352.94/18/0942 UK
PLANNING AND DEVELOPMENT STATISTICS ... ACTUALS / CIPFA, STATISTICAL INFORMATION SERVICE. See Finance-Abstracting, Bibliographies and Statistics.

LC S295 .P58 ISSN 0126-575X
DD 630/.9595 MY
 CODEN PLTRBH
PLANTER, THE. [Planter]. **Added/Corp** Incorporated Society of Planters. (1920)-. Academic Scholarly Publication. English. Twelve times a year. $73.18. Incorp Society of Planters, Box 10262, 50708 Kuala Lumpur Malaysia. **Tel** 011 60 3 2425561, FAX 011 60 3 2426898. **ED** M. Rajadurai. **Bk Rev**, (Qty: 3800 x 12). **Ad Acc. Circ:** 3,600. available on microfilm. Documents available from CASDDS.
Desc: Original technical articles in tropical agriculture. Papers relating to the Society's technical education scheme and other contributions of more general interest.
Ind/Abst Agric. Trop. Agric.; AgBiotech News Inf.; Agric. Eng. Abstr. (1991-); Agrofor. Abstr.; Biocont. News Inf.; Chem. Abstr. (1920-1983); Curr. Cit.; EMBASE; For. Prod. Abstr.; Hortic. Abstr.; Index Vet.; Irr. Drain. Abstr.; Nematol. Abstr.; Nutr. Abstr. Rev., Ser. A, Hum. Exp.; Plant Breed. Abstr.; Postharvest News Inf.; Rev. Agric. Entomol.; Rev. Med. Vet. Entomol.; Rev. Plant Pathol.; Soils Fert.; Weed Abstr.; World Agric. Econ. Rural Sociol. Abstr.

LC S ISSN 0032-0986
DD 630 II
PLANTERS JOURNAL AND AGRICULTURIST, THE. (1???)-. Periodical. English. Twelve times a year. Planters Journal and Agriculturist, 13 Ezra Mansions, Box 2361, Calcutta 1 India.

LC S
DD 630 FR
PLASTICULTURE. See Plastics.

LC S ISSN 0920-0959
DD 631 NE
UDC 63
 CODEN 639-2
PLATFORM. (1985)-. Periodical. Dutch. Eleven times a year. Free on request. Min Van Landvouw en Visserij, Direct Veb Kamer 6192, PB 20401, 2500 EK Hague Netherlands. **Tel** 011 33 70 3793604.

LC S ISSN 0922-2197
DD 630 NE
UDC 631
PLATTELANDS POST. (1988)-. Periodical. Dutch. Ten times a year (monthly except July and Aug.). $19.53. Plattelands Post Magazine, Postbus 3, 46001 AA Bergen OP Netherlands. **Tel** 011 31 1640 37564, FAX 011 31 1640 47605. **ED** Van Wezel. **Bk Rev. Ad Acc.**

LC S
DD 630 FR
POINT DE VUE IMAGES DU MONDE. (19??)-. French. Union Agricole, 31 Cours des Juliottes, 94704 Maison Alfort Cedex France.

LC S
DD 630 JA
POKETTO NORIN SUISAN TOKEI. **Added/Corp** Norin Tokei Kyokai. (19??)-. Statistical Publication. English. One time a year. Norin Suisansho Kyushu Noseikyoku, (Kyushu Agricultural Administration Bureau, Ministry of Agriculture Forestry and Fisheries), 1-2 Ninomaru Kumamotoshi, Kumamotoken 860 Japan. *Continues Kyushu Norin Suisan Tokei.*

LC S ISSN 0967-7836
DD 630 UK
POLICY IMPACT ANALYSIS. (19??)-. Trade Publication. English. Irregular. $1420.30. Agra Europe London Limited, 25 Frant Road, Tunbridge Wells, Kent TN2 5JT United Kingdom. **Tel** 011 44 1892 533813, FAX 011 44 1892 544895, telex 95114 AGRATW G.

LC S ISSN 0992-4426
DD 630 FR
POLISH AGRICULTURE. No. 1 (Jan. 1986)-. Periodical. English. Four times a year. Kontakt / Vanves, France, 42 rue Raymond Marcheron, 92170 Vanves France. **Tel** 011 33 1 46458716.
Desc: Provides some useful information on a very important aspect of Polish economic situation, i.e. the agriculture.

LC S
DD 630 IT
POLITICA AGRARIA. Periodical. Spanish. Four times a year. Edagricole, PO Box 2157, 40100 Bologna Italy. **Tel** 011 39 51 492211 Ext. 22, FAX 011 39 51 493660, telex 510336 EDAGRI.

LC S ISSN 0554-5579
DD 630 YU
 CODEN PPVSAN
POLJOPRIVREDA I SUMARSTVO. [Poljopr. sumar.]. Academic Scholarly Publication. Serbo-Croatian (Roman). Four times a year. Poljoprivredni Instityt, 81000 Titograd Yugoslavia. Documents available from CASDDS. *Continues NASA Poljoprivreda I Sumerstvo.*
Ind/Abst AGRICOLA; Chem. Abstr.; Ecol. Abstr. (?-?).

LC S13 .P48 ISSN 0370-0291
DD 630 YU
 CODEN PJZSAZ
POLJOPRIVREDNA ZNANSTVENA SMOTRA. [Poljopr. znan. smotra]. **VFOAT** Revisio Scientifica Agriculturae; Agriculturae Conspectus Scientificus. (1939)-. Academic Scholarly Publication. Serbo-Croatian (Roman) (table of contents in English and German). Poljoprivredni Instityt, 81000 Titograd Yugoslavia. Documents available from BIOSIS Document Express, CASDDS.
Ind/Abst AGRICOLA; Biol. Abstr.; Chem. Abstr.; Ecol. Abstr.; Life Sci. Collect.; Plant Grow. Reg. Abstr.; Seed Abstr.; Soyabean Abstr.; Vitis Vitic. Enol. Abstr.; Wheat Barley Trit. Abstr.

LC S
DD 630 XO
POLNOHOSPODARSKA VEDA. SERIA A, POLNOHOSPODARSTVO. **Added/Corp** Slovenska Akademia Vied. **VFOAT** Polnohospodarstvo; Selskokhoziaistvennaia Nauka; Agricultural Science. (19??)-. Monographic series. Czech. Irregular. Price varies per volume. Slovenska Akademia Vied / Slovak Academy of Sciences, PO Box 57, 81005 Bratislava Slovakia. **Tel** 011 42 7 3782715, 011 42 7 3782925, FAX 011 42 7 3782910, telex 93261.

LC S ISSN 0551-3677
DD 630 XO
 CODEN POLNAJ
POLNOHOSPODARSTVO. (POLNOHOSPODARSTVO. SELSKOE KHOZIAISTVO. AGRICULTURE.). [Polnohospodarstvo]. **Added/Corp** Slovenska Akademia Vied. **VFOAT** Selskoe Khoziaistvo; Agriculture. (1955)-. Academic Scholarly Publication. Slovak (summaries and/or abstracts in English and Russian). Twelve times a year. $159.95. Veda, Publishing House of the Slovak Academy of Sciences, Klemensova 19, 814 30 Bratislava Slovakia. **Tel** (7)583-15. **ED** Jan Plesnik. Documents available from CASDDS. *Continues Podohospodarstvo.*
Ind/Abst AGRICOLA; Agric. Eng. Abstr.; Biodeter. Abstr.; Chem. Abstr.; Curr. Cit.; EMBASE; Field Crop Abstr.; Food Sci. Technol. Abstr.; Index Vet.; Maize Abstr.; Nutr. Abstr. Rev., Ser. B, Live Feeds and Feed.; Life Sci. Collect.; Pig News Inf.; Plant Breed. Abstr.; Plant Genet. Resour. Abstr.; Plant Grow. Reg. Abstr.; Postharvest News Inf.; Potato Abstr.; Poult. Abstr.; Rev. Agric. Entomol.; Rev. Med. Vet. Entomol.; Rev. Med. Vet. Mycology; Rev. Plant Pathol.; Seed Abstr.; Soils Fert.; Soyabean Abstr.; Vet. Bull.; Vitis Vitic. Enol. Abstr.; Wheat Barley Trit. Abstr.; World Agric. Econ. Rural Sociol. Abstr.

LC S
DD 630 PL
PORADNIK GOSPODARSKI. Vol. 31 (Jan. 4, 1920)-. Periodical. Polish. Twelve times a year. $36.00. **(Subscription address:** Ars Polona-Ruch, PO Box 1001, Krakowskie Przedmiescie 7, 00-068 Warsaw Poland. **Tel** 011 48 22 261201.)

LC S ISSN 0127-0257
DD 630 MY
PORIM TECHNOLOGY. [PORIM technol.]. **Added/Corp** Institut Penyelidikan Minyak Kelapa Sawit Malaysia. **VFOAT** Palm Oil Research Institute of Malaysia Technology. **VAT** Palm Oil Research Institute of Malaysia Technology. (Apr. 1981)-. Monographic series. English.
Ind/Abst Nutr. Abstr. Rev., Ser. B, Live Feeds and Feed.

LC HE560.L44 P67
DD 387.1/096981 RE
PORT DE LA POINTE DES GALETS, STATISTIQUES PORTUAIRES. French. One time a year. Ministere de l'Agriculture, Direction Departementale de l'Agriculture Service Statistique, 7 Place Francheville, 24016 Perigueux France.

LC S571 .P67 ISSN 0739-4284
DD 664 US
POST HARVEST SCIENCE AND TECHNOLOGY RESEARCH. (POST HARVEST SCIENCE AND TECHNOLOGY RESEARCH / UNITED STATES DEPARTMENT OF AGRICULTURE, AGRICULTURAL RESEARCH SERVICE.). [Post harvest sci. technol. res.]. Government Publication. English. One time a year. US Department of Agriculture / Agricultural Research Service, 14th and Independence Avenue SW, Washington DC 20250. available on microfiche (Vols. for (1982-) distributed to depository libraries).

LC S ISSN 0032-5457
DD 630 PL
 CODEN PNROAB
POSTEPY NAUK ROLNICZYCH. [Post. nauk roln.]. **Added/Corp** Polska Akademia Nauk. Wydzia Nauk Rolniczych i Lesnych. (1954)-. Academic Scholarly Publication. Polish. Six times a year. Price on request. **(Subscription address:** Ars Polona-Ruch, PO Box 1001, Krakowskie Przedmiescie 7, 00-068 Warsaw Poland. **Tel** 011 48 22 261201.) Documents available from CASDDS.
Ind/Abst AGRICOLA; Chem. Abstr.

LC S ISSN 0968-7661
DD 630 UK
●**POTATO BUSINESS WORLD.** See Food and Food Industry.

LC S
DD 630 US
●**POTATO GROWER : POTATO GROWER OF IDAHO MAGAZINE.** See Agriculture-Crop Production and Soils.

LC S
DD 630 UK
POTATOES. **VFOAT** Results of Agriculture Service Experiments: Potatoes. English. Seven times a year. $9.00 US; $11.25 (3 issues and 1 special report) other.

LC S ISSN 1058-1138
DD 630 US
PR - TEXAS AGRICULTURAL EXPERIMENT STATION. (PR.). [PR - Tex. Agric. Exp. Sta.]. **Added/Corp** Texas Agricultural Experiment Station. **VFOAT** P.R.; CPR; Consolidated Progress Report. (Nov. 1976)-. Monographic series. English. *Continues Progress Report (Texas Agricultural Experiment Station),* 0099-5142.
Ind/Abst Weed Abstr.

Agriculture

LC S
DD 630
ISSN 0079-4708
PL
CODEN PTPWAX

PRACE KOMISJI NAUK ROLNICZYCH I KOMISJI NAUK LESNYCH. [Pr. Kom. Nauk Roln. Kom. Nauk Les.]. **Main/Corp** Poznanskie Towarzystwo Przyjacio Nauk. Komisja Nauk Rolniczych. **Added/Corp** Poznanskie Towarzystwo Przyjacio Nauk. Komisja Nauk Lesnych. Prace. Vol. 7 (1960)-. Academic Scholarly Publication. Polish (summaries and/or abstracts in English and German). Irregular. **(Subscription address:** Ars Polona-Ruch, PO Box 1001, Krakowskie Przedmiescie 7, 00-068 Warsaw Poland. **Tel** 011 48 22 261201.) Documents available from CASDDS. **Continues** Poznanskie Towarzystwo Przyjacio Nauk. Komisja Nauk Rolniczych i Lesnych. Prace Komisji Nauk Rolniczych i Lesnych, 0079-4708.
Ind/Abst AGRICOLA; Chem. Abstr.; Hortic. Abstr.; Ornamental Hort. (1991-); Plant Breed. Abstr.

LC S
DD 630
ISSN 0968-0136
UK

PRACTICAL FARM IDEAS QUARTERLY. **VFOAT** Farm Ideas. (1992)-. Periodical. English. Four times a year. $32.42. Mido Publications Ltd., PO Box 1 Whitland Dyfed, SA34 OHZ United Kingdom. **Tel** 011 44 1994 448315, **FAX** 011 44 1994 448315.

LC S
DD 630
ISSN 0032-6615
US

PRAIRIE FARMER. [Prairie farmer]. Periodical. English. Twenty-four times a year (21 issues a year). $10.00 in Illinois; $20.00 other. Prairie Farmer Publishing Company, 191 S Gary Avenue, Carol Stream IL 60188. available on microfilm and microfiche from University Microfilms International (UMI).

LC S
DD 630
AU

PRAKTISCHE LANDTECHNIK. Trade Publication. German. Twelve times a year. S595.00 Austria; S696.00 other. Oesterreichischer Agrarverlag, Inkustr 1 7 Bueroparke Donau, A 3400 Klosterneuberg Austria. **Tel** 011 43 2243 33300.

LC HD1481.G3 B38A
DD 338.17
GW

PRAMIERUNG VON FLURBEREINIGUNGEN. **Main/Corp** Bavario. Staatsministerium fur Ernahrung, Landwirtschaft und Forsten. Abteilung Landliche Neuordnung Durch Flurbereinigung. German. 22 Ludwigstrasse 2, W-8 Munich 22 Germany.

LC S
DD 630
ISSN 0326-1565
AG

PRECIO$ AGROPECUARIOS. **VFOAT** Precios Agropecuarios. (Nov. 1981)-. Periodical. Spanish. Twelve times a year.

LC HD9014.U8 U78A
DD 338.1
UY

PRECIOS DE PRODUCTOS E INSUMOS AGROPECUARIOS. **Main/Corp** Uruguay. Direccion de Investigaciones Economicas Agropecuarias. Spanish. Twelve times a year. Free. Direccion de Investigaciones Economicas Agropecuarias, Division de Comercializacion, Rincon 422-Piso 2, Montevideo Uruguay. **Tel** 955172. Index available. cum. index. **Ad Acc. Circ:** 3,000.
Desc: Monthly review of prices of inputs and products referred to the previous month.

LC HD1872.75 .P74
DD 630
BL

PRECOS MINIMOS: REGIOES CENTRO-OESTE, SUDESTE E SUL. **Added/Corp** Companhia de Financiamento da Producao (Brazil). Portuguese. Ministerio Agricultura, Centro de Publicaciones, Calle Alfonso XII 56, 28071 Madrid Spain. **Tel** 011 34 1 3475551, **FAX** 011 34 1 3475722. **Formed by the union of** Precos Minimos: Norte-Nordeste **and** Precos Minimos: Regioes Centro-Oeste, Sudeste e sul.

LC S
DD 630
UDC 37
ISSN 0339-0055
FR

PRESENCE DE L'ENSEIGNEMENT AGRICOLE PRIVE. [Presence enseign. agric. prive]. (1975)-. Periodical. French. Six times a year. 59.00F. CNEAP Presence, 277 rue St. Jacques, 75005 Paris France. **Tel** 011 33 1 43548675, **FAX** 011 33 1 43254325.

LC S
DD 630
US

PRESS HANDBOOK. **Main/Corp** Tennessee Valley Authority. **VFOAT** TVA News; TVA Press Handbook. **VAT** Tennessee Valley Authority News. 1972-. English. One time a year. US Tennessee Valley Authority, W12D140 C K, 400 Commerce Avenue, Knoxville TN 37902. **Continues** Tennessee Valley Authority Press Handbook.

LC S
DD 630
IT

PREZZI AGRICOLI. (19??)-. French (English). Four times a year. Office for Official Publications of the European Communities, 2 rue Mercier, 2985 Luxembourg Luxembourg. **Tel** 011 352 499281, **FAX** 011 352 292942763. **(Subscription address:** Licosa s.p.a., PO Box 552, 50125 Florence Italy. **Tel** 011 39 55 645415.)

LC HD9015.A3 U452a
DD 300/.8 S 388.1/3/094
US

PRICES OF AGRICULTURAL PRODUCTS AND SELECTED INPUTS IN EUROPE AND NORTH AMERICA. **Main/Corp** United Nations. Economic Commission for Europe. **Added/Corp** Food and Agriculture Organization of the United Nations. (1974)-. Government Publication. English. One time a year. Price varies per volume. United Nations Publications, 2 United Nations Plaza, Room DC2 0853, Department 007C, New York NY 10017. **Tel** (212)963-8303, (800)253-9646. **Continues** Prices of Agricultural Products and Selected Inputs in Europe.

LC HD9018.A8 T32
DD 338.1/09946
ISSN 0157-0641
AT

PRINCIPAL AGRICULTURAL COMMODITIES, TASMANIA. **Added/Corp** Australian Bureau of Statistics. (19??)-. English. One time a year. Australian Bureau Statistics / Tasmanian Office, Commonwealth Government Centre, 188 Collins Street, Hobart GPO Box 66A, Hobart Tasmania 7001 Australia. **Tel** 011 61 2 205889.
Desc: Information on the produce trade in Australia.

LC S612 .P76
DD 631.6
ISSN 0032-9428
TK
CODEN POSPBR

PROBLEMY OSVOENIIA PUSTYN. [Probl. osvo. pustyn]. **Added/Corp** Nauchnyi Sovet po Probleme Pustyn (Turkmenistan SSR Ylymlar Akademiiasy) Coller Institutly (Turkmenistan SSR Ylymlar Akademiiasy). **VFOAT** Cholleri Oeleshdirmeging Problemalary; Problems of Desert Development. Vol. 1 (1967)-. Periodical. Russian (summaries and/or abstracts in English). Twelve times a year. $149.95. Izdatelstvo Ylym, Ulitsa Engelsa 6, 744000 Ashkhabad Turkmenistan. **Tel** 3632 9 04 84. **(Subscription address:** East View Publications Inc., 3020 Harbor Lane North, Suite 110, Minneapolis MN 55447. **Tel** (800)477-1005, (612)550-0961, **FAX** (612)559-2931.) Documents available from BIOSIS Document Express.
Desc: Information on desert resource development and desert ecology.
Ind/Abst AGRICOLA; Biol. Abstr.; Ecol. Abstr.; Fish Rev. (19??-199?); Geogr. Abstr. Phys. Geogr.; Geogr. Abstr. Human Geogr.; Geol. Abstr.; GeoRef; Grass. Forage Abstr.; Hortic. Abstr.; Int. Dev. Abstr.; Irr. Drain. Abstr.; Life Sci. Collect.; Wildl. Rev. (19??-199?).

LC SB193 .A45
US

PROCEEDINGS. AMERICAN FORAGE AND GRASSLAND COUNCIL. **Main/Corp** American Forage and Grassland Council. **VFOAT** American Forage and Grassland Council Proceedings. Vol. 1 (Apr. 5-9, 1992)-. English. One time a year. $30.00. American Forage & Grassland Council Management, PO Box 94, Georgetown TX 78627. **Tel** (512)863-2444. **ED** John R. Rodgers. **Circ:** 1,000 (ctrl). **Continues** Forage and Grassland Conference Proceedings of the ... Forage and Grassland Conference.
Ind/Abst AGRICOLA.

LC S539.5 .A37A
DD 338.1/05
ISSN 0148-2572
US

PROCEEDINGS AND MINUTES, ANNUAL MEETING OF THE AGRICULTURAL RESEARCH INSTITUTE. [Proc. minutes, Annu. meet. Agric. Res. Inst.]. **Main/Corp** Agricultural Research Institute (U.S.). No. 22- 1973-. Proceedings. English. One time a year. $5.00. US Department of Agriculture, 14th Street and Independence Avenue SW, Washington DC 20250. **Tel** (202)720-5457. **Continues** Proceedings, Annual Meeting of the Agricultural Research Institute.
Ind/Abst AGRICOLA [Full Cov.].

LC S
DD 630
Pr Rev.
ISSN 0110-6589
NZ

PROCEEDINGS ... ANNUAL CONFERENCE / AGRONOMY SOCIETY OF NEW ZEALAND. [Proc. annu. conf. - Agron. Soc. N.Z.]. **Main/Corp** Agronomy Society of New Zealand. **VFOAT** Agronomy. (1971)-. Proceedings. English. One time a year. $20.00. Agronomy Society of New Zealand, Private Bag 4704, Christchurch New Zealand. **Tel** 011 64 3 3256400, **FAX** 011 64 3 3252074. **ED** G Hill. **Circ:** 200. Documents available from BIOSIS Document Express.
Desc: Covers all agronomic aspects of research conducted in New Zealand on arable crop species.
Ind/Abst Biol. Abstr.; Crop Physiol. Abstr.; Grass. Forage Abstr.; Hortic. Abstr.; Irr. Drain. Abstr.; Maize Abstr.; Ornamental Hort.; Plant Breed. Abstr.; Plant Grow. Reg. Abstr.; Postharvest News Inf.; Seed Abstr.

LC S
DD 630
US

PROCEEDINGS - DISTILLERS FEED RESEARCH COUNCIL CONFERENCE. **Main/Corp** Distillers Feed Research Council. (194?)-. Proceedings. English.

LC S
DD 630
ISSN 0370-2057
II
CODEN PSUTA8

PROCEEDINGS OF THE ANNUAL CONVENTION OF THE SUGAR TECHNOLOGISTS' ASSOCIATION OF INDIA. [Proc. annu. conv. Sugar Technol. Assoc. India]. **Main/Corp** Sugar Technologists' Association of India. (1927)-. Proceedings. English. One time a year. $30.00. Sugar Technologists' Association of India, Kalyanpur Kanpur India. **(Subscription address:** Prints India, 11 Darya Ganj, New Delhi 110002 India. **Tel** 011 91 11 3268645, **FAX** 011 91 11 3275542, telex 31-61087 PRIN-IN.)

LC SB317.5
DD 635
ISSN 0749-4327
US

PROCEEDINGS OF THE ANNUAL MEETING / ARKANSAS STATE HORTICULTURAL SOCIETY. See Gardening and Horticulture.

LC SF521
DD 638.1
US

PROCEEDINGS OF THE ANNUAL MEETING - FLORIDA STATE BEEKEEPERS ASSOCIATION. **Main/Corp** Florida. State Beekeepers Association. Proceedings. English.

LC S535.T35 N37A
DD 630/.7/10678
TZ

PROCEEDINGS OF THE ANNUAL MEETING - NATIONAL COUNCIL FOR AGRICULTURAL EDUCATION. **Main/Corp** National Council for Agricultural Education. Proceedings. English. One time a year. Manpower Development Division, Ministry of Agriculture, PO Box 2066, Dar es Salaam Tanzania.

LC HD9014 .C2 C29a
DD 338.1/0971
ISSN 0704-2426
CN

PROCEEDINGS OF THE CANADIAN AGRICULTURAL OUTLOOK CONFERENCE. (PROCEEDINGS OF THE CANADIAN AGRICULTURAL OUTLOOK CONFERENCE / EDITED AND PUBLISHED BY INFORMATION DIVISION, AGRICULTURE CANADA.). **Added/Corp** Canada. Agriculture Canada. Information Division. Canada. Dept. of Agriculture. Canada. Agriculture Canada. Economics Branch. Canada. Agriculture Canada. Policy, Planning and Economics Branch. Canada. Agriculture Canada. Marketing and Economics Branch. **VFOAT** Market Commentary; Canadian Agricultural Outlook Conference Report. **VAT** Canadian Agricultural Outlook Conference Report. (19??)-. Government Publication. English. One time a year. Agriculture Canada, Communications Branch, Ottawa Ontario K1A 0C7 Canada.
Ind/Abst AGRICOLA.

LC S
DD 630
ISSN 0078-2092
UK
CODEN PEANAU

PROCEEDINGS OF THE EASTER SCHOOL IN AGRICULTURAL SCIENCE, UNIVERSITY OF NOTTINGHAM. (PROCEEDINGS.). [Proc. Easter Sch. Agric. Sci., Univ. Notting.]. **Main/Corp** Easter School in Agricultural Science. (1963)-. Proceedings. English. Butterworth & Co. Ltd. / UK, Halsbury House, 35 Chancery Lane, London WC2A 1EL United Kingdom. **Tel** 011 44 171 4002500. Documents available from CASDDS. **Continues** Proceedings of the University of Nottingham Easter School in Agricultural Science, 0308-2393.
Ind/Abst Chem. Abstr.

LC S27
DD 630
ISSN 0434-5835
US

PROCEEDINGS OF THE GREAT PLAINS AGRICULTURAL COUNCIL. **Main/Corp** Great Plains Agricultural Council. Proceedings. English.
Ind/Abst AGRICOLA [Full Cov.].

LC S
DD 630
JA

PROCEEDINGS OF THE INTERNATIONAL GRASSLAND CONGRESS. (19??)-. Proceedings. English. Irregular (Published every 4 years by the host country). $112.00. International Grassland Congress, Sir Publishing, PO Box 399, Wellington New Zealand. **Tel** 011 64 4 4727421, **FAX** 011 64 4 4731841.

Agriculture

LC S
DD 630
Pr Rev.
ISSN 1073-1768
US

PROCEEDINGS OF THE ... NATIONAL AGRICULTURAL PLASTICS CONGRESS. See Plastics.

LC S
DD 630
ISSN 0369-3902
NZ

PROCEEDINGS OF THE NEW ZEALAND GRASSLAND ASSOCIATION. [Proc. N. Z. Grassl. Assoc.]. Main/Corp New Zealand Grassland Association. Vol. 1 (1931)-. Proceedings. English. One time a year. $25.07. New Zealand Grassland Association, Agres Grassland, Private Bag, 11008 Palmerston New Zealand. ED M Baker. cum. index. Ad Acc. Circ: 1,700 (ctrl).
Ind/Abst AgBiotech News Inf.; AGRICOLA; Agrofor. Abstr.; Anim. Breed. Abstr.; Dairy Sci. Abstr.; Grass. Forage Abstr.; Index Vet.; Nematol. Abstr.; Nutr. Abstr. Rev., Ser. B, Live Feeds and Feed.; Plant Breed. Abstr.; Rev. Agric. Entomol.; Seed Abstr.; Soils Fert.; Weed Abstr.; World Agric. Econ. Rural Sociol. Abstr.

LC S
DD 630
ISSN 1172-2827
NZ

PROCEEDINGS OF THE NEW ZEALAND INSTITUTE OF ARGRICULTURAL SCIENCE & THE NEW ZEALAND SOCIETY HORTICULTURAL SCIENCE ANNUAL CONVENTION. (19??)-. English. One time a year (Oct.). 24.00Aus$. New Zealand Institute of Agricultural Science, PO Box 19-560, Christchurch 8002 New Zealand. Tel 011 64 3 3842432, FAX 011 64 3 842432. Continues New Zealand Institute of Argricultural Science, 0549-0146.

LC S
DD 630
ISSN 0110-5272
NZ
CODEN PRFCDE

PROCEEDINGS OF THE RUAKURA FARMERS' CONFERENCE. [Proc. Ruakura Farmers' Conf.]. (1971)-. Proceedings. English. One time a year (June). $17.91. Ruakura Agricultural Research Center, Private Bag, Hamilton New Zealand. Tel 011 64 71 62839, FAX 011 64 71 62839. ED John Lomas (Editor's telephone: 011 64 71 8385092). Continues Proceedings of the Ruakura Farmers' Conference Week, 0485-5752.

LC HD1781 .C37B
DD 338.1/0971
ISSN 0842-3008
CN

PROCEEDINGS OF THE STANDING SENATE COMMITTEE ON AGRICULTURE AND FORESTRY. [Proc. Standing Senate Comm. Agric. For.]. Main/Corp Canada. Parliament. Senate. Standing Committee on Agriculture and Forestry. VFOAT Deliberations du Comite Senatorial Permanent de l'Agriculture et des Forets; Agriculture and Forestry. Proceedings. English (French). Irregular. Canadian Government Publishing Center, Supply and Services Canada, Hull Quebec K1A 0S9 Canada. Tel (613)990-8116, telex 053-4296. Continues in part Proceedings of the Standing Senate Committee on Agriculture, Fisheries and Forestry, 0826-7820.

LC TP375 .T4A
DD 664/.122/05
UDC 664.11
ISSN 0730-6490
US

PROCEEDINGS OF THE ... SUGAR PROCESSING RESEARCH CONFERENCE. [Proc. Sugar Process. Res. Conf.]. Main/Conf Sugar Processing Research Conference. 1982-. Academic Scholarly Publication. English. Every 2 years. Free. Agricultural Research Southern Region, US Department of Agriculture, PO Box 53326, New Orleans LA 70153. Documents available from CASDDS. Continues Proceedings of the ... Technical Session on Cane Sugar Refining Research, 0197-7288.
Ind/Abst AGRICOLA [Full Cov.]; Chem. Abstr.

LC HD1401
DD 338.1/0971
ISSN 0707-4808
CN

PROCEEDINGS OF THE WORKSHOP OF THE CANADIAN AGRICULTURAL ECONOMICS SOCIETY. Main/Corp Canadian Agricultural Economics Society. Workshop. VFOAT C. A. E. S. Workshop Proceedings. VAT Proceedings. Annual Workshop - Canadian Agricultural Economics Society; Canadian Agricultural Economics Society. Workshop Proceedings. 1968-. Proceedings. English. One time a year. Canadian Agricultural Economics and Farm Management Society, 151 Slater Street / Suite 907, Ottawa Ontario K1P 5H4 Canada. Tel (613)232-9459, FAX (613)594-5190. Supersedes Report of the Annual Workshop, Canadian Agricultural Economics Society, 0068-8177.

LC HD1875.P4 P45a
DD 330.9
BL

PRODUCAO AGRICOLA. Main/Corp
Superintendencia dos Servicos de Estatistica. Servicos de Estatistica. (1973)-. Portuguese. Secretaria de Coordenacao Geral, Superintendica dos Servios de Estatistica de Peenambuco, Av Marques de Olinda 55, Recife Brazil.

LC S
DD 630
ISSN 1183-9929
CN

PRODUCTEUR PLUS, LE. [Prod. plus]. VFOAT
Producteur +. Vol. 1, No. 1 (Summer 1991)-. Periodical. French. Ten times a year (monthly with combined July/Aug. and Nov./Dec.). 19.96Can$. Les Editions Imago Inc., PO Box 147, Farnham Quebec J2N 2R4 Canada. Tel (514)293-8282, FAX (514)293-8554. ED Leonard Pigeon. Ad Acc. Circ: 23,955 (ctrl). Absorbed Le Producteur Horticole; Le Producteur Laitier and Le Producteur de Porc Quebecoise.

LC S631
DD 631.8
ISSN 0430-3288
II

PRODUCTION AND CONSUMPTION OF FERTILISERS; ANNUAL REVIEW.
Main/Corp Fertiliser Association of India. 1959-. English. One time a year. Fertiliser Association of India, 10 Shaheed Jit Singh Marg, New Delhi 110067 India. Tel 011 91 11 667144, telex 031-73056.

LC S21 .Z2382
DD 630/.8
ISSN 0082-979X
US
CODEN XAPRA7

PRODUCTION RESEARCH REPORT - UNITED STATES DEPARTMENT OF AGRICULTURE. (PRODUCTION RESEARCH REPORT.). [Prod. res. rep. - U. S. Dep. Agric.]. Main/Corp United States. Dept. of Agriculture. No. 1-. Monographic series. English. Price varies per volume. US Department of Agriculture, 14th Street and Independence Avenue SW, Washington DC 20250. Tel (202)720-5457. Documents available from BIOSIS Document Express.
Ind/Abst AGRICOLA [Full Cov.]; Biol. Abstr. (-1982).

LC S
DD 630
US

PRODUCTORES DE HORTALIZAS.
(19??)-. Trade Publication. Spanish. Twelve times a year. $45.00. Meister Publishing Company, 37733 Euclid Avenue, Willoughby OH 44094-5992. Tel (216)942-2000, (800)572-7740, FAX (216)942-0662.
Desc: For the Mexican vegetable grower. Focuses on technification of Mexican agriculture, bringing new production technology from the US to Mexico.

LC S
DD 630
UDC 63
SP

PRODUCTOS DEL MAR. (19??)-. Periodical. Spanish. Twelve times a year. 12000ptas Spain. Pub Tecnicas Alimentarias S A, Triana 52 Bajo IZQ, 28016 Madrid Spain. Tel 011 34 1 3505319, 011 34 1 3595798.

LC SB354.6.I5 P76
IO

PRODUKSI BUAH-BUAHAN DI JAWA.
Added/Corp Indonesia. Biro Pusat Statistik. VFOAT Production of Fruits in Java. VAT Produksi Buah Buahan di Jawa. Indonesian. Biro Pusat Statistik / Central Bureau of Statistics, 8 Jalan Dr. Sutomo No. 8, Box 3, Jakarta Pusat 10710 Indonesia. Tel 011 62 21 372808, 011 62 21 374908 ext.342. Continues in part Produksi Buah-buahan di Jawa & [i.e. dan] Madura.

LC HD9015.I6 I85A
DD 338.17
IT

PRODUZIONE E COMMERCIO : PRODOTTI AGRICOLO-ALIMENTARI E FLORICOLI. Main/Corp Italy. Istituto Nazionale per il Commercio Estero. Servizio Economico Agrario. (19??)-. Italian. Istituto Nazionale Per Il Commercio Estero, 21 Via Liszt, 00100 Rome Italy.
Desc: Information about agricultural and food product markets in the world.

LC S
DD 630
UDC 63
ISSN 0937-1583
GW

PROFI MUNSTER. (PROFI.). [Profi Munst.].
(1989)-. Trade Publication. German. Twelve times a year. $108.93. Landwirtschaftsverlag GmbH, Postfach 480249, D-48079 Muenster Hiltrup Germany. Tel 011 49 2501 8010, FAX 011 49 2501 801204, telex 892665 LANDV D.

LC S
DD 630
BL

PROGNOSTICO AGRICOLA. Added/Corp
Sao Paulo (Brazil : State). Instituto de Economia Agricola. Vol. 1 (1988-1989)-. Portuguese. Instituto de Economia Agricola, Caixa Postal 8114, Sao Paulo 01000 Brazil. Tel (011)34067 SAGR-SAO PAULO-BRASIL, telex (011) 34067 SAGR. Continues Prognostico (Sao Paulo, Brazil), 0100-5316.

LC S542.B6 P77
DD 630/.72/081
BL

PROGRAMA NACIONAL DE PESQUISA AGROPECUARIA : PRONAPA. VFOAT
PRONAPA; P.R.O.N.A.P.A. Portuguese. One time a year. Ministerio Agricultura, Centro de Publicaciones, Calle Alfonso XII 56, 28071 Madrid Spain. Tel 011 34 1 3475551, FAX 011 34 1 3475722.

LC HD9235.G362 M66
DD 338.1/7526
MX

PROGRAMA SIEMBRA-EXPORTACION DE AJO / DGEA. VFOAT Programa Siembra Exportacion de Ajo. Spanish. Secretaria de Agricultura y Recursos Hidraulicos, Direccion General de Economia, Agricola Carolina No 132 - 120, Piso Delegacion Benito, Juarez Codigo Postal 03720 Mexico DF.

LC HD9235.S782 .M66
DD 338.1/7562/0972
MX

PROGRAMA SIEMBRA-EXPORTACION DE CALABACITA / DGEA. VFOAT Programa Siembra Exportacion de Calabactia. Spanish. Secretaria de Agricultura y Recursos Hidraulicos, Direccion General de Economia, Agricola Carolina No 132 - 120, Piso Delegacion Benito, Juarez Codigo Postal 03720 Mexico DF.

LC HD9235.O62 M66
DD 338.1/7525/0972
MX

PROGRAMA SIEMBRA-EXPORTACION DE CEBOLLA. VFOAT Programa Siembra-Exportacion de Cebolla. Spanish. Secretaria de Agricultura y Recursos Hidraulicos, Direccion General de Economia, Agricola Carolina No 132 - 120, Piso Delegacion Benito, Juarez Codigo Postal 03720 Mexico DF.

LC HD1491
DD 338.1
ISSN 1194-8493
CN

●PROGRAMME AIDE AUX EXPLOITATIONS AGRICOLES. P.REGION DU SUD-OUEST DE MONTREAL. [Programme Aide exploit. agric., Reg. Sud-ouest Montr.]. Main/Corp Quebec (Province). Ministere de l'Agriculture, des Pecheries et de l'Alimentation. (1996)-. Government Publication. French. Every 3 years.

LC HD1491
DD 338.1
ISSN 1194-854X
CN

●PROGRAMME AIDE AUX EXPLOITATIONS AGRICOLES. REGION DE BEAUCE-APPALACHES. (PROGRAMME AIDE AUX EXPLOITATIONS AGRICOLES. REGION DE BEAUCE-APPALACHES.). [Programme Aide exploit. agric., Reg. Beauce-Appalaches]. Main/Corp Quebec (Province). Ministere de l'Agriculture, des Pecheries et de l'Alimentation. (1996)-. Government Publication. French. Every 3 years.

LC HD1491
DD 338.1
ISSN 1194-8558
CN

●PROGRAMME AIDE AUX EXPLOITATIONS AGRICOLES. REGION DE LA MAURICIE. (PROGRAMME AIDE AUX EXPLOITATIONS AGRICOLES. REGION DE LA MAURICIE.). [Programme Aide exploit. agric., Reg. Mauricie]. Main/Corp Quebec (Province). Ministere de l'Agriculture, des Pecheries et de l'Alimentation. (1996)-. French. Every 3 years.

LC HD1491
DD 338.1
ISSN 1194-8574
CN

●PROGRAMME AIDE AUX EXPLOITATIONS AGRICOLES. REGION DE L'ABITIBI-TEMISCAMINGUE. [Programme Aide exploit. agric., Reg. Abitibi-Temiscamingue]. Main/Corp Quebec (Province). Ministere de l'Agriculture, des Pecheries et de l'Alimentation. (1996)-. Government Publication. French. Every 3 years.

LC HD1491
DD 338.1
ISSN 1194-8582
CN

●PROGRAMME AIDE AUX EXPLOITATIONS AGRICOLES. REGION DE L'ESTRIE. [Programme Aide exploit. agric., R,eg. Estrie]. Main/Corp Quebec (Province). Ministere de l'Agriculture, des Pecheries et de l'Alimentation. (1996)-. Government Publication. French. Every 3 years.

LC HD1491
DD 338.1
ISSN 1194-8507
CN

●PROGRAMME AIDE AUX EXPLOITATIONS AGRICOLES. REGION DE L'OUTAOUAIS-LAURENTIDES. [Programme Aide exploit. agric., Reg. Outaouais-Laurent.]. Main/Corp Quebec (Province). Ministere de l'Agriculture, des Pecheries et de l'Alimentation. (1996)-. Government Publication. French. Every 3 years.

LC HD1491
DD 338.1
ISSN 1194-8531
CN

●PROGRAMME AIDE AUX EXPLOITATIONS AGRICOLES. REGION DE QUEBEC. [Programme Aide exploit. agric., Reg.

Agriculture

Que.]. **Main/Corp** Quebec (Province). Ministere de l'Agriculture, des Pecheries et de l'Alimentation. (1996)-. Government Publication. French. Every 3 years.

LC HD1491   **ISSN** 1194-8523
DD 338.1   CN
●**PROGRAMME AIDE AUX EXPLOITATIONS AGRICOLES. REGION DES BOIS-FRANCS.** (PROGRAMME AIDE AUX EXPLOITATIONS AGRICOLES. REGION DES BOIS-FRANCS.). [Programme Aide exploit. agric., Reg. Bois-Francs]. **Main/Corp** Quebec (Province). Ministere de l'Agriculture, des p„echeries et de l'alimentation. (1996)-. Government Publication. French. Every 3 years.

LC HD1491   **ISSN** 1194-8515
DD 338.1   CN
●**PROGRAMME AIDE AUX EXPLOITATIONS AGRICOLES. REGION DU BAS-SAINT-LAURENT--GASPESIE--ILES-DE-LA-MADELEINE.** [Programme Aide exploit. agric., Reg. Bas-St.-Laurent-Gaspesie-Iles-de-Madeleine]. **Main/Corp** Quebec (Province). Ministere de l'Agriculture, des Pecheries et de l'Alimentation. (1996)-. Government Publication. French. Every 3 years.

LC HD1491   **ISSN** 1194-8566
DD 338.1   CN
●**PROGRAMME AIDE AUX EXPLOITATIONS AGRICOLES. REGION DU NORD DE MONTREAL.** [Programme Aide exploit. agric., Reg. nord Montr.]. **Main/Corp** Quebec (Province). Ministere de l'Agriculture, des Pecheries et de l'Alimentation. (1996)-. French. Every 3 years.

LC HD1491   **ISSN** 1194-8477
DD 338.1   CN
●**PROGRAMME AIDE AUX EXPLOITATIONS AGRICOLES. REGION DU RICHELIEU--SAINT-HYACINTHE.** [Programme Aide exploit. agric., R,eg. Richelieu St.-Hyacinthe]. **Main/Corp** Quebec (Province). Ministere de l'Agriculture, des Pecheries et de l'Alimentation. (1996)-. Government Publication. French. Every 3 years.

LC HD1491   **ISSN** 1194-8485
DD 338.1   CN
●**PROGRAMME AIDE AUX EXPLOITATIONS AGRICOLES. REGION DU SAGUENAY--LAC-SAINT-JEAN--COTE-NORD.** [Programme Aide exploit. agric., R,eg. Saguenay-Lac-St.-Jean C„ote-Nord]. **Main/Corp** Quebec (Province). Ministere de l'Agriculture, des Pecheries et de l'Alimentation. (1996)-. Government Publication. French. Every 3 years.

LC S   **ISSN** 0369-8173
DD 630   FR
PROGRES AGRICOLE ET VITICOLE, LE. [Prog. agric. vitic.]. Vol. 8 (1887)-. Periodical. French. Twenty-two times a year. $161.85. Progres Agricole et Viticole, 1 Bis rue de Verdun, 34000 Montpellier France. **Tel** 011 33 67585976. Index available. cum. index. **Bk Rev**. **Ad Acc. Circ:** 11,000.
Ind/Abst AGRICOLA; Agric. Eng. Abstr. (1991-); Energy Res. Abstr. (Feb. 1982-); Hortic. Abstr.; Plant Breed. Abstr.; Rev. Plant Pathol.; Seed Abstr.; Soils Fert.; Weed Abstr.; World Agric. Econ. Rural Sociol. Abstr.

LC S631 .U47   **ISSN** 0730-7322
DD 631.8/1/060761915   US
PROGRESS (MUSCLE SHOALS, ALA.). (PROGRESS ... / NATIONAL FERTILIZER DEVELOPMENT CENTER, TENNESSEE VALLEY AUTHORITY.). [Progress]. **Main/Corp** National Fertilizer Development Center (U.S.). (1980)-. English. One time a year. Free. National Fertilizer Development Center, Tennessee Valley Authority, Muscle Shoals AL 35660. **Tel** (205)386-2871. **ED** Harold Parker. **Circ:** 5,500.
Continues National Fertilizer Development Center (U.S.). Annual Report, 0077-4510.

LC S17   **ISSN** 0886-7038
DD 630   US
PROGRESS REPORT - IDAHO. AGRICULTURAL EXPERIMENT STATION. (PROGRESS REPORT - AGRICULTURAL EXPERIMENT STATION, UNIVERSITY OF IDAHO.). [Prog. rep. - Ida., Agric. Exp. Stn.]. **Main/Corp** Idaho. Agricultural Experiment Station. (1976)-. Monographic series. English. Price varies per volume. ***Continues*** Idaho Agricultural Research Progress Report.
Ind/Abst AGRICOLA.

LC S113 .S68A
DD 630/.720783272   US
PROGRESS REPORT - SOUTHEAST SOUTH DAKOTA EXPERIMENT FARM. **Main/Corp** Southeast South Dakota Experiment Farm. English. One time a year. South Dakota State University / Agricultural Experiment Station, Box 2231, Brookings SD 57007. **Tel** (605)688-4187, FAX (605)688-4018.

LC S   **ISSN** 0033-0760
DD 630   US
PROGRESSIVE FARMER. **VFOAT** Progressive Farmer/Southwest. (1???)-. Periodical. English. Twelve times a year. $18.00. Progressive Farmer, 820 Shades Creek Parkway, PO Box 2581, Birmingham AL 35202. **Tel** (205)877-6000, FAX (205)877-6450. **(Subscription address:** Media Services Inc., 500 Office Park, Birmingham AL 35223. **Tel** (205)877-6505.) **ED** Tom Curl and Jack Odle. **Bk Rev**. **Ad Acc. Circ:** 536,071 (ctrl). available on microfilm and microfiche from University Microfilms International (UMI).
Desc: Editorial content is geared to farm production and management of crops and livestock produced in the southern United States, plus the family interests of recipients.

LC S
DD 630   US
PROGRESSIVE FARMER FOR FLORIDA, THE. Vol. 90, No. 2 (Feb. 1975)-. Periodical. English. Twelve times a year.

LC S
DD 630   PK
    CODEN PFIPDI
PROGRESSIVE FARMING (ISLAMABAD, PAKISTAN). (PROGRESSIVE FARMING.). (Jan./Feb. 1981)-. Periodical. English. Six times a year. Rs15.00. Pakistan Agricultural Research Council, PO Box 1031, Islamabad Pakistan. Documents available from BIOSIS Document Express.
Ind/Abst Agrofor. Abstr. (1991-); Biol. Abstr. (-1988); Dairy Sci. Abstr.; For. Prod. Abstr. (1991-); For. Abstr.; Hortic. Abstr.; Index Vet.; Irr. Drain. Abstr.; Maize Abstr.; Nematol. Abstr.; Nutr. Abstr. Rev., Ser. A, Hum. Exp.; Rev. Agric. Entomol.; Rev. Plant Pathol.; Rice Abstr.; Rural Dev. Abstr.; Soils Fert.; Weed Abstr.; Wheat Barley Trit. Abstr.; World Agric. Econ. Rural Sociol. Abstr.

LC S
DD 630   CN
PROJECT REPORT (UNIVERSITY OF ALBERTA. DEPT. OF RURAL ECONOMY). (PROJECT REPORT.). **VFOAT** Rural Economy Project Report. Monographic series. English. Irregular. Price varies per volume. University of Alberta / Rural Economy, Department of Rural Economy, Edmonton Alberta T6G 2H1 Canada. **Tel** (403)492-4225.

LC HD1483   **ISSN** 0849-2352
DD 338.1/09714   CN
PROJET BIO-ALIMENTAIRE. [Proj. bio-aliment.]. **Added/Corp** Quebec (Province). Ministere de l'Agriculture, des Pecheries et de l'Alimentation. **VFOAT** Strategie d'Action. (1991)-. French.

LC S   **ISSN** 0921-5506
DD 630   NE
UDC 582.4
PROPHYTA. See Gardening and Horticulture.

LC HD1883 .P76
DD 338.1/8861   CK
PROYECCIONES AGROPECUARIAS / MINISTERIO DE AGRICULTURA. Spanish. One time a year. Ministerio Agricultura, Centro de Publicaciones, Calle Alfonso XII 56, 28071 Madrid Spain. **Tel** 011 34 1 3475551, FAX 011 34 1 3475722.

LC S
DD 630   AG
PUBLICACION ESR. **Main/Corp** Argentine Republic. Direccion Nacional de Economia y Sociologia Rural. (19??)-. Spanish. Paseo Colon No 974, 3er Piso, Buenos Aires Argentina.

LC S
DD 630   AG
    CODEN PMECE9
PUBLICACION MISCELANEA / ESTACION EXPERIMENTAL AGRO-INDUSTRIAL OBISPO COLOMBRES. **Added/Corp** Estacion Experimental Agro-Industrial "Obispo Colombres.". No. 64 (1979)-. Monographic series. Spanish. Irregular. Price varies per volume. San Miguel de Tucuman, Estacion Experimental Agro-Industrial Obispo Colombres, Buenos Aires Argentina. Documents available from BIOSIS Document Express. ***Continues*** Publicacion Miscelanea (Estacion Experimental Agricola de Tucuman), 0367-0163.
Ind/Abst Biol. Abstr. (1988-); Maize Abstr.; Potato Abstr.; Soyabean Abstr.

LC S   **ISSN** 0325-2132
DD 630   AG
PUBLICACION TECNICA (ESTACION EXPERIMENTAL REGIONAL AGROPECUARIAANGUIL). (PUBLICACION TECNICA.). **Added/Corp** Estacion Experimental Regional Agropecuaria Anguil. (19??)-. Monographic series. Spanish. Irregular. Price varies per volume.

LC S   **ISSN** 0577-8425
DD 630   SP
PUBLICACIONES EN CIENCIAS AGRICOLAS. **Main/Corp** Chile. Universidad, Santiago. Facultad de Agronomia. No. 1- 1967-. Periodical. Spanish. Universidad de Santiago / Publicaciones, Servicio de Publicaciones e Intercambio Cientifico, Campus Universitario, Santiago de Compostela, E-15706 Santiago Spain. **Tel** 011 34 59-35-00.

LC S133 .A346   **ISSN** 0828-2870
DD 638.09071   CN
PUBLICATION - AGRICULTURE CANADA (ENGLISH ED.). (PUBLICATION.). [Publ. - Agric. Can.]. **Added/Corp** Canada. Agriculture Canada. **VFOAT** Publication; Agriculture Canada Publication. (1972)-. Government Publication. English. Agriculture Canada, Communications Branch, Ottawa Ontario K1A 0C7 Canada. ***Continues*** Publication (Canada. Dept. of Agriculture), 0068-7340.
Ind/Abst Biocont. News Inf.; Nutr. Abstr. Rev., Ser. B, Live Feeds and Feed.; Postharvest News Inf.; Rev. Plant Pathol.; Vet. Bull.

LC S   **ISSN** 0379-3494
DD 630   II
UDC 626.81/85:621.3
    CODEN IBPBD
PUBLICATION - CENTRAL BOARD OF IRRIGATION AND POWER. [Publ. - Cent. Board Irrig. Power]. (19??)-. Periodical. English. Irregular. Price varies. Central Board of Irrigation Power, Maalcha Marg Chanakyapuri, New Delhi 110021 India. **(Subscription address:** Prints India, 11 Darya Ganj, New Delhi 110002 India. **Tel** 011 91 11 3268645, FAX 011 91 11 3275542, telex 31-61087 PRIN-IN.)

LC S
DD 630   US
    CODEN PUCREW
PUBLICATION / DIVISION OF AGRICULTURE AND NATURAL RESOURCES, UNIVERSITY OF CALIFORNIA. **Added/Corp** University of California (System). Division of Agriculture and Natural Resources. (198?)-. Monographic series. English. Division of Agriculture and Natural Resources, University of California, 300 Lakeside Drive/6th Floor, Oakland CA 94612-3560. **Tel** (510)987-0044. ***Continues*** Publication (University of California (System). Division of Agricultural Sciences).
Ind/Abst Rev. Agric. Entomol.; Rev. Med. Vet. Entomol.; Rev. Plant Pathol.; Weed Abstr.

LC S17   **ISSN** 0308-5708
DD 630   UK
PUBLICATION - THE SCOTTISH AGRICULTURAL COLLEGES. [Publ. - Scott. Agric. Coll.]. **Main/Corp** East of Scotland College of Agriculture. **Added/Corp** North of Scotland College of Agriculture. West of Scotland Agricultural College. No. 1 (June 1974)-. Monographic series. English. Twelve times a year. $30.80. Scottish Agricultural College, Kings Building / West Mains Road, Edinburgh EH93JG United Kingdom. **Tel** 011 44 131 6671041, FAX 011 44 131 6672601.
Ind/Abst AGRICOLA.

LC S
DD 630   US
PUBLICATION (UNIVERSITY OF ALASKA (SYSTEM). COOPERATIVE EXTENSION SERVICE). See Business and Economics-Cooperatives.

LC Z5073 .U53a S21.R44   **ISSN** 0098-566X
DD 016.63/0208   US
PUBLICATIONS AND PATENTS OF THE EASTERN UTILIZATION RESEARCH AND DEVELOPMENT DIVISION. (PUBLICATIONS AND PATENTS - EASTERN UTILIZATION RESEARCH AND DEVELOPMENT DIVISION, AGRICULTURAL RESEARCH SERVICE.). **Main/Corp** United States. Agricultural Research Service. Eastern Utilization Research and Development Division. July/Dec. 1956-. Catalog. English. Two times a year. Eastern Utilization Research & Development Division, Agricultural Research Service, U.S. Dept of Agriculture, 600 East Mermaid Lane, Philadelphia PA 19118. ***Continues*** Publications and Patents of the Eastern Utilization Research Branch.

LC Z5074.E3 F55A HD1775.F6   **ISSN** 0149-4481
DD 016.3381/09759   US
PUBLICATIONS OF THE FOOD AND RESOURCE ECONOMICS DEPARTMENT, UNIVERSITY OF FLORIDA. **Main/Corp** University of Florida. Food and Resource Economics Dept. (19??)-. English. Institute of

Agriculture

Food and Agricultural Sciences, University of Florida, Building 664, Gainesville FL 32611. **Tel** (904)392-1773. **ED** C N Smith and M A Petty.

LC S
DD 630 NE
PUBLIKATIE 1 / LANDBOUW-ECONOMISCH INSTITUUT, STAFAFDELING. Added/Corp Landbouw-Economisch Instituut. Stafafdeling. (197?)-. Monographic series. Dutch. Price varies per volume. Landbouw-Economisch Instituut, Postbus 29703, 2502 LS Hague Netherlands. **Tel** 011 31 70 3308330, FAX 011 31 70 615624. **ED** M. N. de Groof. *Continues Landbouw-Economisch Instituut. Afdeling Algemeen Economisch Onderzoek. [Publikatie] 1.*
Ind/Abst Agric. Eng. Abstr.; Potato Abstr.; World Agric. Econ. Rural Sociol. Abstr.

LC S
DD 630 NE
PUBLIKATIE 2 - LANDBOUW-ECONOMISCH INSTITUUT, AFDELING STRUCTUURONDERZOEK. Main/Corp Landbouw-Economisch Instituut. Afdeling Structuuronderzoek. No. 60 (March 1974)-. Monographic series. Dutch. Price varies per volume. Landbouw-Economisch Instituut, Postbus 29703, 2502 LS Hague Netherlands. **Tel** 011 31 70 3308330, FAX 011 31 70 615624. *Continues Landbouw-Economisch Instituut. Afdeling Streekonderzoek. [Publikatie] 2.*
Ind/Abst Dairy Sci. Abstr.

LC S ISSN 0169-2143
DD 630 NE
PUBLIKATIE - INSTITUUT VOOR MECHANISATIE, ARBEID EN GEBOUWEN. [Publ. - Inst. Mech., Arb. Gebouwen]. Main/Corp Instituut voor Mechanisatie, Arbeid en Gebouwen (Wagenngen, Netherlands). No. 1 (Sept. 1974)-. Monographic series. Dutch (summaries and/or abstracts in English). Price varies per volume. *Supersedes in part Publikatie - Instituut voor Landbouwbedrifsgebowen; Publikatie - Instituut voor Landbouwtechniek en Rationalisatie; Continues Publikatie - Instituut voor Tuinbouwtechniek, 0511-0718.*
Ind/Abst AGRICOLA.

LC S17
DD 630 NE
PUBLIKATIE - PROEFSTATION VOOR DE AKKERBOUW EN DE GROENTETEELT IN DER VOLLEGROND. Main/Corp Proefstation voor de Akkerbouw en de Groenteteelt in de Vollegrond. No. 1-4-Oct. 1977-. Periodical. Dutch. *Supersedes in part Proefstation voor de Akker- en Weidebouw. Publicatie (12 W12).*
Ind/Abst Agric. Eng. Abstr. (1991-).

LC S
DD 630 US
PUBLISHED SEARCH BIBLIOGRAPHIES FROM THE NTIS BIBLIOGRAPHIC DATA BASE. AGRICULTURE AND FOOD. *See Agriculture-Abstracting, Bibliographies and Statistics.*

LC S ISSN 0395-8655
DD 630 FR
UDC 631
PURPAN. [Purpan]. (1957)-. Periodical. French. Four times a year. $65.61. Revue Purpan, 75 Voie du Toec, 31076 Toulouse Cedex France. **Tel** 33 61 492311, FAX 33 61 319148. Index available. cum. index. **Bk Rev**. **Circ:** 2,000.
Desc: Scientific, technical, and legal studies about agriculture and countryside.

LC S ISSN 0274-8339
DD 630 US
PURPLE CIRCLE. (Sept. 1980)-. Periodical. English. Nine times a year (monthly with Dec./Jan., May/June, July/Aug. issues combined). $20.00. Purple Circle Magazine, 303 North Center, Brownwood TX 76801. **Tel** (915)643-5426. **ED** Wade Stephens. Index available. cum. index. **Ad Acc**, **Adv Mgr:** Gary Cramblet. **Circ:** 3,500.

LC SB952.P9 P94 ISSN 0048-6043
DD 633.8/98 KE
CODEN PYRPAN
PYRETHRUM POST. [Pyrethrum post]. **Added/Corp** Pyrethrum Bureau. Pyrethrum Board of Kenya. African Pyrethrum Research Council. African Pyrethrum Technical Information Centre. Vol. 1 (July 1948)-. Academic Scholarly Publication. English. Two times a year. $30.00. Pyrethrum Technology Information Center, PO Box 420, Nakuru Kenya. **Tel** 011 254 37 40311, FAX 011 254 37 45274, telex 22087. Index available. cum. index. **Circ:** 1,000. Documents available from CASDDS.
Desc: Publishes technical information on Pyrethrum and related chemicals.

Ind/Abst AGRICOLA [Full Cov.]; Chem. Abstr.; Dairy Sci. Abstr.; EMBASE; Hortic. Abstr.; Irr. Drain. Abstr.; Maize Abstr.; PESTDOC; Plant Breed. Abstr.; Plant Grow. Reg. Abstr.; Postharvest News Inf.; Rev. Agric. Entomol.; Rev. Med. Vet. Entomol.

LC S
DD 630 IT
QUADERNI DELLA RIVISTA DI POLITICA AGRARIA. Monographic series. Italian. Irregular. Price varies per volume. Edagricole, PO Box 2157, 40100 Bologna Italy. **Tel** 011 39 51 492211 Ext. 22, FAX 011 39 51 493660, telex 510336 EDAGRI.

LC S
DD 630 IT
UDC 63
QUADERNI DI AGRONOMIA. Main/Corp Palermo. Universita. Instituto di Agronomia Generale e Coltivazioni Erbacee. (1965)-. Periodical. Italian.
Ind/Abst For. Abstr.

LC HD2130.Z15 A3
DD 338.1/09689/4 ZA
QUARTERLY AGRICULTURAL STATISTICAL BULLETIN. *See Agriculture-Abstracting, Bibliographies and Statistics.*

LC Z672 .I5
DD 026.63 NE
QUARTERLY BULLETIN OF THE INTERNATIONAL ASSOCIATION OF AGRICULTURAL INFORMATION SPECIALISTS. Added/Corp International Association of Agricultural Information Specialists. **VFOAT** Quarterly Bulletin; Bulletin Trimestriel de l'Association Internationale des Specialistes de l'Information Agricole; Quarterly Bulletin of the IAALD; IAALD Quarterly Bulletin. Vol. 35, No. 3 (1990)-. Bulletin. English (French, German and Spanish). Four times a year. 40.00F. International Association of Agricultural Librarians & Documentalists, PO Box 4, PUDOC, 6700 AA Wageningen Netherlands. available on microfilm. *Continues International Association of Agricultural Librarians and Documentalists. Quarterly Bulletin of the International Association of Agricultural Librarians & Documentalists, 0020-5966.*

LC S ISSN 0895-5158
DD 630 US
QUARTERLY LIST OF PUBLICATIONS / UNITED STATES DEPARTMENT OF AGRICULTURE, OFFICE OF GOVERNMENTAL AND PUBLIC AFFAIRS. [Q. list publ. - United States. Dep. Agric. Off. Gov. Public Aff.]. **Added/Corp** United States. Dept. of Agriculture. Office of Governmental and Public Affairs. (Jan. 1986)-. Catalog. English. Six times a year (Jan., Mar., May, July, Sept., Nov.). Free on request. US Department of Arigreculture, Room 504A, Washington DC 20250. **Tel** (202)720-4585. *Continues Publications and Visuals, 0737-3570.*
Ind/Abst Abstr. Bull. Inst. Pap. Sci. Tech.

LC S
DD 630 US
QUARTERLY REPORT OF SELECTED RESEARCH PROJECTS. Added/Corp United States. Agricultural Research Service. **VFOAT** Quarterly Report. (19??)-. Periodical. English. Four times a year.
Ind/Abst Foods Adlibra.

LC S ISSN 0033-6084
DD 630 AT
UDC 63(943)
QUEENSLAND COUNTRY LIFE. Periodical. English. One time a week. 115.44Aus$. Queensland Country Life Ltd, 432 Queens Street, UGA Building, Brisbane Queensland 4001 Australia. **Tel** 011 61 832 2171. **ED** Peter Owen. **Bk Rev**. **Ad Acc**. **Circ:** 35,000 (ctrl). *Continues Graziers' Review.*
Desc: Newspaper relating to farming, agriculture, machinery, stock.

LC S ISSN 0481-3553
DD 630 GW
QUELLEN UND FORSCHUNGEN ZUR AGRARGESCHICHTE. Vol. 1 (1955)-. Monographic series. German. Irregular. Price varies per volume. Gustav Fischer Verlag Stuttgart, Postfach 720143, D-70577 Stuttgart Germany. **Tel** 011 49 711 458030, FAX 011 49 711 4580334, telex 2627-7111488. **ED** G. Franz, P. Blickle. **Circ:** 600.

LC S
DD 630 IT
QUESTIONE AGRARIA : QA, LA. **VFOAT** QA. (1981)-. Periodical. Italian. Four times a year. L65330. Franco Angeli Riviste SRL, Viale Monza 106, 20127 Milan Italy. **Tel** 011 39 2 2827651, 011 39 2 289562, FAX 011 39 2 258004, telex 051-511650.
Ind/Abst AgBiotech News Inf.; Dairy Sci. Abstr.; For. Prod. Abstr. (1991-); For. Abstr.; Rural Dev. Abstr.; World Agric. Econ. Rural Sociol. Abstr.

LC S ISSN 1052-5378
DD 630 US
QUICK BIBLIOGRAPHY SERIES. (QUICK BIBLIOGRAPHY SERIES - NATIONAL AGRICULTURAL LIBRARY.). [Quick bibliogr. ser.]. Main/Corp National Agricultural Library (US). **Added/Corp** National Agricultural Library (U.S.). (Oct. 1976)-. Bibliography. English. Price varies per volume. National Agricultural Library, 10301 Baltimore Boulevard, Beltsville MD 20705.
Ind/Abst AGRICOLA [Full Cov.]; Index Vet.; Vet. Bull.

LC S
DD 630 US
●**R.B.** Added/Corp New York State College of Agriculture and Life Sciences. Dept. of Agricultural, Resource, and Managerial Economics. **VFOAT** RB. **VAT** Research bulletin. (1994)-. Monographic series. English. Irregular. New York State College, Department of Agricultural Economics, Ithaca NY. *Continues A.E. Res., 0554-4441.*

LC S ISSN 0997-7503
DD 630 FR
UDC 616-091
RACHIS CLICHY. (RACHIS : REVUE DE PATHOLOGIE VERTEBRALE.). (1989)-. Periodical. French. Six times a year. $218.73. Edimedica, 146 boulevard Voltaire, 92600 Asnieres France. **Tel** 011 33 1 47935603.
Ind/Abst Field Crop Abstr.; Food Sci. Technol. Abstr.; Irr. Drain. Abstr.; Maize Abstr.; Plant Breed. Abstr.; Rev. Agric. Entomol.; Rice Abstr.; Wheat Barley Trit. Abstr.

LC SD383 ISSN 1171-1124
DD 634.97512099305 A338.17498099305 NZ
RADIATA BULLETIN. [Radiata bull.]. (1991)-. Periodical. English. Twenty-four times a year. 135.65Aus$. Bulletin Publishing, PO Box 106 063, Auckland 1 New Zealand. **Tel** 011 64 9 3020289.

LC S
DD 630 BN
RADOVI POLJOPRIVREDNOG FAKULTETA UNIVERZITETA U SARAJEVU. Added/Corp Univerzitet u Sarajevu. Poljoprivredni Fakultet. **VFOAT** Works of the Agricultural Faculty of the University of Sarajevo. (1959)-. Serbo-Croatian (Roman). *Continues Radovi Poljoprivredno-Sumarskog Fakulteta Univerziteta u Sarajevu. A, Poljoprivreda.*
Ind/Abst Dairy Sci. Abstr.; Food Sci. Technol. Abstr.; Hortic. Abstr.; Plant Genet. Resour. Abstr.; Rev. Agric. Entomol.; Weed Abstr.

LC TP248
DD 660.6 US
RAFI COMMUNIQUE. *See Biology-Bioengineering.*

LC S ISSN 0090-0281
DD 630 US
RANCHER. SOUTHERN SAN JOAQUIN VALLEY EDITION. (THE RANCHER.). **VFOAT** California Rancher. Vol. 24, No. 8 (Aug. 1970)-. Periodical. English. Twelve times a year. Rancher Publications, Box 1060 V0X 1A0 Canada. **Tel** (604)8565418. *Supersedes in part Rancher. San Joaquin County Edition.*

LC S
DD 630 US
RANGE AND PASTURE. Added/Corp Oklahoma. Crop and Livestock Reporting Service. United States. Dept. of Agriculture. Statistical Reporting Service. (Dec. 1973)-. Periodical. English. Twelve times a year.

LC S ISSN 0812-4930
DD 630 AT
RANGE MANAGEMENT NEWSLETTER. (1976)-. English. Three times a year. 32.88Aus$. Australian Rangeland Society, PO Box 718, Victoria Park WA 6100 Australia. **Tel** 011 9 2227084, FAX 011 61 9 3221598. **ED** Gary Bastin. **Circ:** 400.

LC S ISSN 0277-9404
DD 630 US
RANGE SCIENCE SERIES (FORT COLLINS, COLO.). (RANGE SCIENCE SERIES.). [Range sci. ser.]. Main/Corp Colorado State University. Range Science Dept. **VFOAT** Science Series. (1976)-. Academic Scholarly Publication. English. Irregular. Price varies per volume. Range Science Department, Colorado State University, Fort Collins CO 80523. **Tel** (303)491-6677. Documents available from CASDDS. *Continues Science Series, 0190-1478.*
Ind/Abst Chem. Abstr.; GeoRef.

LC SD411 ISSN 1036-9872
DD 333.76 AT
RANGELAND JOURNAL, THE. *See Forests and Forestry.*

Agriculture

LC S
DD 636
ISSN 0190-0528
US
CODEN RNGLE7

RANGELANDS. [Rangelands]. **Added/Corp** Society for Range Management. Vol. 1 (Feb. 1979)-. Periodical. English. Six times a year. $50.00. Society for Range Management, 1839 York Street, Denver CO 80206. **Tel** (303)355-7070, (303)571-0174. **ED** Gary Frasier. Index available. cum. index. **Bk Rev. Ad Acc. Circ:** 7,000 (ctrl). available on microfilm and microfiche from University Microfilms International (UMI). *Continues Rangeman's Journal, 0095-6236.*
Desc: Society news, practical experiences in range management, range history, political events affecting rangelands.
Ind/Abst AGRICOLA [Select. Cov.]; Biocont. News Inf.; Field Crop Abstr.; For. Abstr.; Grass. Forage Abstr.; Index Vet.; Nutr. Abstr. Rev., Ser. B, Live Feeds and Feed.; Plant Genet. Resour. Abstr.; Rev. Agric. Entomol.; Seed Abstr.; Vet. Bull.; Weed Abstr.; Wildl. Rev.

LC HD1920.5 .A22
DD 630
ISSN 1017-5776
LU
TITLE CHANGE

RAPID REPORTS. AGRICULTURE, FORESTRY, AND FISHERIES. **Added/Corp** Statistical Office of the European Communities. **VFOAT** Agriculture, Forestry, and Fisheries. (1991)-(1994). Periodical. English. Office for Official Publications of the European Communities, 2 rue Mercier, 2985 Luxembourg Luxembourg. **Tel** 011 352 499281, FAX 011 352 292942763. **(Subscription address):** Unipub, 4611 F Assembly Drive, Lanham MD 20706. **Tel** (800)274-4888, (301)459-7666.) *Continues Rapid Reports. Agriculture. Continued by Statistics in Focus. Agriculture, Forestry and Fisheries.*
Ind/Abst Anim. Breed. Abstr.

LC S339 .I58A
DD 630/.9675/1
CG

RAPPORT ANNUEL - INSTITUT NATIONAL POUR L'ETUDE ET LA RECHERCHE AGRONOMIQUE. **Main/Corp** Institut National pour l'Etude et la Recherche Agronomique. **VFOAT** Rapport pour l'Exercice. French. Institut National pour l'Etude et la Recherche Agronomique, Box 257, Kinshasa 11 Zaire.

LC S159 .Q436A
DD 630/.9714
ISSN 0701-6557
CN

RAPPORT ANNUEL. MERITE AGRICOLE. (MERITE AGRICOLE, RAPPORT ANNUEL.). [Rapp. annu., Merite agric.]. **Main/Corp** Quebec (Province). Ministere de l'Agriculture, des Pecheries et de l'Alimentation. **VFOAT** Rapport Annuel du Merite Agricole. 1979-. French. One time a year. *Continues Quebec (Province). Ministere de l'Agriculture. Rapport Annuel, Merite Agricole, 0701-6557.*

LC HD1790.Q4 Q45A
DD 354.7140682/33/06
ISSN 0715-6219
CN

RAPPORT ANNUEL / MINISTERE DE L'AGRICULTURE, DES PECHERIES ET DE LA'ALIMENTATION. **See** Public Administration.

LC S159 .S65A
DD 630/.6/0714
ISSN 0708-6059
CN

RAPPORT ANNUEL - SOCIETE QUEBECOISE D'INITIATIVES AGRO-ALIMENTAIRES. **Main/Corp** Societe du Quebecoise d'Initiatives Agro-Alimentaires. 1977/78-. French. One time a year. Societe Quebecoise d'Initiatives Argro-Alimentaire, 4 Parc Samuel-Holland/Bureau 1802, Quebec Quebec G1S 3R3 Canada. *Absorbed Societe Quebecoise d'Initiatives Agro-Alimentaire. Etats Financiers, 0708-6040.*

LC HD2144.5.Z9 S466
DD 338.1/0966/3
SG

RAPPORT D'ACTIVITES - SOCIETE D'AMENAGEMENT ET D'EXPLOITATION DES TERRES DU DELTA. **Main/Corp** Societe d'Amenagement et d'Exploitation des Terres du Delta. French. Republique du Senegal, Ministere du Developpement Industriel et de l'Artisanat, Direction de l'Industrie, Route de Ouakam B P 3179, Dakar Senegal.

LC HD9000.9.F7 A14A
DD 354.440077/82
FR

RAPPORT GENERAL D'ACTIVITE / MINISTERE DE L'AGRICULTURE, DIRECTION DE LA QUALITE. **See** Public Administration.

LC S
DD 630
ISSN 0922-3282
NE

RAPPORT - INSTITUUT VOOR VEEVOEDINGSONDERZOEK. **See** Agriculture-Livestock.

LC S
DD 630
ISSN 0108-7401
DK

RAPPORT / STATENS JORDBRUGSKONOMISK INSTITUT. [Rapp. - Statens Jordbrugskon. Inst.]. **Added/Corp** Statens Jordbrugskonomisk Institut (Denmark). (1983)-. Monographic series. Danish (English). Irregular. Price varies per volume. Statens Jordbrugsokonomiske Institut, Rolighedsvej 25, 1958 Frederiksberg C Denmark. **Tel** 39 70 00. *Continues Rapport (Jordbrugskonomisk Institut (Denmark)), 0107-5357.*
Ind/Abst Postharvest News Inf.; Potato Abstr.

LC SB191.R5 S44A
DD 338.1/7/31809663
SG

RAPPORT SUR LA CULTURE DU RIZ PLUVIAL AU SENEGAL ORIENTAL. **Main/Corp** Senegal. Direction Generale de la Production Agricole. (19??)-. French. C F D T - Senegal, BP 3216, Dakar Senegal.

LC S
DD 630
ISSN 0348-0259
SW
CODEN RLIBD6

RAPPORT - SVERIGES LANTBRUKSUNIVERSITET INSTITUTIONEN FOR BYGGNADSTEKNIK. (RAPPORT / INSTITUTIONEN FOR LANTBRUKETS BYGGNADSTEKNIK = REPORT / SWEDISH UNIVERSITY OF AGRICULTURAL SCIENCES, DEPARTMENT OF FARM BUILDINGS.). [Rapp. - Sver. lantbruksuniv. inst. byggnadstek.]. **Added/Corp** Sveriges Lantbruksuniversitet. Institutionen for Lantbrukets Byggnadsteknik. **VFOAT** Report. (1978)-. Monographic series. English. Documents available from BIOSIS Document Express.
Ind/Abst AGRICOLA; Agric. Eng. Abstr.; Biol. Abstr.; Hortic. Abstr.; Index Vet.; Nutr. Abstr. Rev., Ser. B, Live Feeds and Feed.; Ornamental Hort. (1991-).

LC S
DD 630
ISSN 0284-3153
SW

RAPPORT (SVERIGES LANTBRUKSUNIVERSITET. INSTITUTIONEN FOR EKONOMI). (RAPPORT / INSTITUTIONEN FOR EKONOMI.). **VFOAT** Report. Monographic series. Swedish (English). Irregular. Price varies per volume. *Continues Rapport Fran Institutionen for Ekonomi och Statisti, 0346-5241.*
Ind/Abst AgBiotech News Inf.; Dairy Sci. Abstr.; Rice Abstr.

LC QR
DD 576
ISSN 0348-4041
SW

RAPPORT / SVERIGES LANTBRUKSUNIVERSITET. INSTITUTIONEN FOR MIKROBIOLOGI. **Added/Corp** Sveriges Lantbruksuniversitet. Institutionen for Mikrobiologi. **VFOAT** Report. (19??)-. Monographic series. English.
Ind/Abst Biodeter. Abstr.; For. Abstr.; Nutr. Abstr. Rev., Ser. B, Live Feeds and Feed.

LC S
DD 338.17
YU

RATARSTVO, VOCARSTVO I VINOGRADARSTVO. **Main/Corp** Savenzi Zavod za Statistiku (Yugoslavia). Serbo-Croatian (Roman). 10.00. Savezni Zavod za Statistiku, Kneza Milosa 20, Belgrad Yugoslavia.

LC S
DD 630
ISSN 0352-5686
XV

RAZISKAVE IN STUDIJE - KMETIJSKI INSTITUT SLOVENIJE. [Razisk. stud. - Kmet. inst. Slov.]. **Main/Corp** Kmetijski Institut Slovenije. 44-. Monographic series. Slovenian (summaries and/or abstracts in German and English). Price varies per volume. *Continues Kmetijski Institut Slovenije Publikacije.*
Ind/Abst AGRICOLA.

LC Z5074.R27 R39 SF84.86
DD 016.6332/02
US

RECENT PUBLICATION OF RANGE RESEARCH. English. US Department of Agriculture / California, Agriculture Research Service, Western Region, 800 Buchann, Albany CA 94701-1105.

LC K3870.A12 N38
DD 016.343/076 016.342376
ISSN 0899-0662
US

RECENT TITLES IN LAW FOR THE SUBJECT SPECIALIST. AGRICULTURE, ANIMAL, AND FOOD LAW. **See** Law.

LC S604.8 .R4
DD 631.6
ISSN 0160-788X
UK
CODEN REREDB
SUSPENDED

RECLAMATION REVIEW. [Reclam. rev.]. **Added/Corp** Canadian Land Reclamation Association. Vol. 1 (Mar. 1978)-(19??). Academic Scholarly Publication. English. Four times a year. $90.00. Canadian Land Reclamation Association, Box 682, Guelph Ontario N1H 6L3 Canada. **Tel** (914)592-9141. available on microfilm and microfiche from University Microfilms International (UMI). Documents available from CASDDS.
Ind/Abst AGRICOLA; Chem. Abstr.; Coal Abstr.; Energy Res. Abstr. (June 1980-); GeoRef; Life Sci. Collect.

LC S338.E3 A33
DD 630/.9676/2
KE

RECORD OF RESEARCH. **Main/Corp** Kenya Agricultural Research Institute. Agricultural Research Dept. **VFOAT** Record of Research, Annual Report; Annual Report. (1981)-. Periodical. English. One time a year. Free. Kenya Agricultural Research Institute Library, PO Box 30148, Nairobi Kenya. **Tel** 0154-32880-1-6, telex KARI NAIROBI. ctrl circ. *Continues Record of Research for the Period ... Annual Report.*

LC S560
DD 630/.68
ISSN 0225-0977
CN
CEASED

RECUEIL DES MEMBRES - LA FEDERATION DE L'AGRICULTURE DE L'ONTARIO. [Recl. memb. - Fed. agric. Ont.]. **Main/Corp** Federation de l'Agriculture de l'Ontario. Vol. 1 (July 1979)-(1993). Periodical. French. Federation De L'Agriculture De L'Ontario, 387 Est rue Bloor, Toronto Ontario M4W 1H9 Canada. *Supersedes Management Digest, 0701-1628.*

LC S253 .R43
DD 338.1/0945
SP

RED CONTABLE AGRARIA NACIONAL / MINISTERIO DE AGRICULTURA, SECRETARIA GENERAL TECNICA. **Added/Corp** Spain. Ministerio de Agricultura. Secretaria General Tecnica. (19??)-. Spanish. Irregular. 1800ptas. Ministerio de Agricultura, Pesca y Alimentacion, Secretaria General Tecnica, Centro de Publicaciones, Paseo de la Infanta Isabel 1, 28071 Madrid Spain. **Tel** 011 91 347 55 51. available with charts.

LC SF521
DD 638.1
ISSN 0132-358X
RU

REFERATIVNYI ZHURNAL: PCHELOVODSTVO, SHELKOVODSTVO. **Added/Corp** Vsesoiuznyi Nauchno-Issledovatelskii Institut Informatsii i Tekhniko-Ekonomicheskikh Issledovanii po Selskomu Khoziaistvu. **VFOAT** Pchelovodstvo, Shelkovodstvo. No. 1 (Jan. 1978)-. Periodical. Russian. Twelve times a year. VINITI - Vsesoyuzny Institut Nauchno-Tekhnicheskoi Informatsii, All-Union Scientific and Technical Information Institute, Baltiiskaia ulitsa 14, 125219 Moscow Russia. **Tel** 011 7 95 2384600, FAX 011 7 95 9430060, telex 411160. *Continues in part Referativnyi Zhurnal: Pchelovodstvo, Shelkovodstvo, Rybovodstvo.*

LC S
DD 630
ISSN 0134-2878
RU

REFERATIVNYI ZHURNAL. SERIIA 2, ZEMLEDELIE. **Added/Corp** Vsesoiuznyi Nauchno-Issledovatelskii Institut Informatsii i Tekhniko-Ekonomicheskikh Issledovanii po Selskomu Khoziaistvu. **VFOAT** Zemledelie. No. 1 (Jan., 1978)-. Abstracting/Indexing Service. Russian. Twelve times a year. $61.00. VINITI - Vsesoyuzny Institut Nauchno-Tekhnicheskoi Informatsii, All-Union Scientific and Technical Information Institute, Baltiiskaia ulitsa 14, 125219 Moscow Russia. **Tel** 011 7 95 2384600, FAX 011 7 95 9430060, telex 411160. **(Subscription address):** Victor Kamkin, 4956 Boiling Brook Parkway, Rockville MD 20852. **Tel** (301)881-5973.) *Continues in part Referativnyi Zhurnal: Zemledelie, Agrokhimiia, Pochvovedenie.*

LC HD491.A1 R4
DD 630
ISSN 0102-1184
BL

REFORMA AGRARIA. [Reforma agrar.]. **Added/Corp** Associacao Brasileira de Reforma Agraria. Associacao Brasileira de Reforma Agraria. Boletim da Associacao Brasileira de Reforma Agraria. **VFOAT** Boletim da Associacao Brasileira de Reforma Agraria. (19??)-. Periodical. Portuguese. Three times a year (Apr., Aug., Dec). $50.00. Associacao Brasileiro de Reforma Agraria, Caixa Postal 1396, 13001 Campinas Sao Paulo Brazil. **Tel** 011 55 192426590.

LC HD1428
DD 338.1/8717/05
ISSN 0822-4250
CN

REGION 1 SUBMISSION TO THE GOVERNMENT OF PRINCE EDWARD ISLAND. (SUBMISSION TO THE GOVERNMENT OF PRINCE EDWARD ISLAND ... / REGION 1.). [Reg. 1 submiss. Gov. P.E.I.]. **Main/Corp** National Farmers Union (Canada). Region 1. **VAT** Region One Submission to the Government of Prince Edward Island. English. Every 2 years. National Farmers Union / Canada, 250C 2nd Avenue South, Saskatoon Saskatchewan S7K 1K9 Canada.

LC S17
DD 630
US

REGIONAL RESEARCH REPORT - OHIO AGRICULTURAL RESEARCH AND DEVELOPMENT CENTER. **Main/Corp** Ohio.

Agriculture

Agricultural Research and Development Center. No. 1- Apr. 1973-. Monographic series. English. Price varies per volume.
Ind/Abst Plant Grow. Reg. Abstr.

LC S
DD 630 BL
RELATORIO TECNICO ANUAL DO CENTRO DE TECHNOLOGIA AGRICOLA E ALIMENTAR. Portuguese. One time a year.

LC SB16 **ISSN** 0822-9430
DD 630/.6/0714 CN
REPERTOIRE DES MEMBRES. [Repert. memb. - Ordre agron. Que.]. **Main/Corp** Order of Agrologists of Quebec. (1983)-. English (French). Every 2 years. Ordre des Agronomes du Quebec, 1259 Berri Street, Suite 710, Montreal Quebec H2L 4C7 Canada. **Tel** (514)844-3833, **FAX** (514)844-7462. **Bk Rev. Ad Acc. Circ:** 3,500. **Continues** Order of Agrologist of Quebec. Tableau des Membres, 0705-7512.
Desc: Includes research reports, agri-business, agriculture extension, and food progressing.

LC S **ISSN** 0531-5344
DD 630 UK
REPORT - AGRICULTURAL ECONOMICS UNIT. UNIVERSITY OF EXETER. [Rep. - Agric. Econ. Unit., Univ. Exeter]. (1932)-. Monographic series. English. Irregular.
Ind/Abst World Agric. Econ. Rural Sociol. Abstr.

LC HD9017.Z55 S68A
DD 354.68910082/61/06 RH
REPORT AND ACCOUNTS FOR THE YEAR ENDED 30TH JUNE ... / AGRICULTURAL MARKETING AUTHORITY. **Main/Corp** Southern Rhodesia. Agricultural Marketing Authority. English. One time a year. Agricultural Marketing Authority, PO Box 8094, Causeway, Harare Zimbabwe.

LC HD9118.M45 M38A
DD 354.69/820082333 MF
REPORT AND STATEMENT OF ACCOUNT. See Public Administration.

LC S542.V632 C643a
DD 630/.7207297/22 VI
REPORT / COLLEGE OF THE VIRGIN ISLANDS. AGRICULTURAL EXPERIMENT STATION. (REPORT.). **Main/Corp** College of the Virgin Islands. Agricultural Experiment Station. **Added/Corp** College of the Virgin Islands. Cooperative Extension Service. (1981/82)-. English. Every 2 years. **Continues** Annual Report (College of the Virgin Islands, Agricultural Experiment Station).

LC QK
DD 581 AT
REPORT / CSIRO DIVISION OF PLANT INDUSTRY. See Biology-Botany.

LC J905 .L3 HD9258.A8
DD 300/.994 354.940082/42 AT
REPORT FOR THE ... PERIOD OF THE AUSTRALIAN DRIED FRUITS CORPORATION FOR THE PERIOD ... . **Main/Corp** Australian Dried Fruits Corporation. 1st (Jan. 1979 to 30th June 1980)-. English. One time a year. 2.75Aus$. Australian Dried Fruits Association, 9 Queens Road, Melbourne Victoria 3004 Australia. **Tel** 011 61 3 2678322, telex AA39479. **Continues** Annual Report of the Australian Dried Fruits Control Board for the Year Ended 30th June ... .
Desc: Annual report of the Australian Dried Fruits Corporation.

LC S542.G72 A377 **ISSN** 0961-6071
DD 630/.72041 UK
REPORT / IGER. **Added/Corp** AFRC Institute of Grassland and Environmental Research. **VFOAT** IGER Report. (1990)-. English. One time a year. £10.00. Institute of Grassland and Environmental Research, Plas Goggerdan, Aberystwyth, Dyted Wales SY23 3EB United Kingdom. **Continues** AFRC Institute for Grassland and Animal Production. Report, 0953-7295.
Desc: Covers agricultural ecology, biotechnology, and the livestock of the grasslands.

LC HD1775.R4 .U54A **ISSN** 0147-3263
DD 338.1/8745 US
REPORT OF ACCOMPLISHMENTS, RHODE ISLAND. (REPORT OF ACCOMPLISHMENTS - AGRICULTURAL STABILIZATION AND CONSERVATION SERVICE.). **Main/Corp** United States. Agricultural Stabilization and Conservation Service. Government Publication. English. US Department of Agriculture / Agricultural Stabilization and Conservation, 14th and Independence Avenue SW, Washington DC 20250.

LC HD1775.M2 M34A **ISSN** 0738-8438
DD 338.1/8741 US
REPORT OF ... COMMISSIONER OF AGRICULTURE, FOOD AND RURAL RESOURCES TO THE ... REGULAR SESSION OF THE ... MAINE STATE LEGISLATURE. [Rep. Comm. Agric., Food Rural Resour. regul. sess. Me. State Legis.]. **Main/Corp** Maine. Dept. of Agriculture, Food, and Rural Resources. English. One time a year. **Continues** Maine. Dept. of Agriculture. Report of the Commissioner of Agriculture, 0148-7590.

LC S217
DD 630.6342 UK
REPORT OF PROCEEDINGS - COMMONWEALTH AGRICULTURAL BUREAUX REVIEW CONFERENCE. **Main/Conf** Commonwealth Agricultural Bureaux Review Conference. 1946-. Proceedings. English. Irregular.

LC HD1491 **ISSN** 0915-5457
DD 338.1 JA
REPORT OF STUDY GROUP ON INTERNATIONAL ISSUES, FAPRC. [Rep. Stud. Group Int. Issues, FAPRC]. **VFOAT** Report of Study Group on International Issues, Food and Agriculture Policy Research Center; Bulletin of the Food and Agriculture Policy Research Center, Japan. (1989)-. Bulletin. English. Irregular.
Ind/Abst Rice Abstr.; World Agric. Econ. Rural Sociol. Abstr.

LC S **ISSN** 0706-425X
DD 630 CN
REPORT OF THE AGRICULTURAL RESEARCH INSTITUTE OF ONTARIO. **Main/Corp** Agricultural Research Institute of Ontario. 1973/74-. English (French). One time a year. Ontario Ministry of Agriculture and Food, 801 Bay Street, Toronto Ontario M7A 1B3 Canada. **Tel** (416)965-1064, (416)326-3400. **Circ:** 2,000. **Continues** Research Report of the Agricultural Research Institute of Ontario, 0706-4241.
Ind/Abst Anim. Breed. Abstr.

LC HD9887.S7 S66A
DD 331.7 SA
REPORT OF THE AUDITOR-GENERAL ON THE ACCOUNTS OF THE COTTON BOARD FOR THE FINANCIAL YEAR ... . **VFOAT** Verslag van die Ouditeur-Generaal oor die Rekeninge van die Katoenraad vir die Boekjaar ... . Afrikaans (English). One time a year. R1.00. Staatsdrukker, Bosmanstraat, Privaatsak X85, Pretoria 0001 South Africa. **Continues** Report of the Controller and Auditor-General on the Accounts of the Cotton Board.

LC S
DD 630 IT
REPORT OF THE CONFERENCE OF FAO. See Food and Food Industry.

LC S401.U6 A29
DD 338.10611 IT
REPORT OF THE COUNCIL OF FAO (ENGLISH EDITION). See Food and Food Industry.

LC S441 .A12
DD 338.106173 US
REPORT OF THE GOVERNMENT OF THE UNITED STATES OF AMERICA TO THE FOOD AND AGRICULTURE ORGANIZATION OF THE UNITED NATIONS. **Main/Corp** United States. FAO Interagency Committee. **VFOAT** U.S. Report to FAO. 1st (1947)-. Periodical. English. UNIPUB, 4611-F Assembly Drive, Lanham MD 20706-4391. **Tel** (800)274-4888, **FAX** (301)459-0056, telex 28787 GATT CH.

LC S
DD 630 AT
SUSPENDED
REPORT OF THE RURAL ASSISTANCE BOARD. **Main/Corp** New South Wales. Rural Assistance Board. (1971/72)-?. Periodical. English. Irregular. $0.29. NSW Government Printing Office, PO Box 256, Regents Park 2143 Australia. **Tel** 011 61 02 7438777, **FAX** 011 61 02 954455.

LC HD1393 .N49 **ISSN** 0545-2376
DD 333.33/5/09749 US
REPORT OF THE STATE FARMLAND EVALUATION ADVISORY COMMITTEE. **Main/Corp** New Jersey. State Farmland Evaluation Advisory Committee. 1964-. English. One time a year. Local Property and Public Utility Branch, Division of Taxation Building, West State and Willow Streets, Trenton NJ 08625.

LC HD1751 .A9322F **ISSN** 0361-2260
DD 338.1/873 US
REPORT ON PARTICIPATION IN ASCS COUNTY PROGRAMS AND OPERATIONS BY RACIAL GROUPS. **VFOAT** Report on Participation in A.S.C.S. County Programs and Operations by Racial Groups. **VAT** Report on Participation in Agricultural Stabilization and Conservation Service County Programs and Operations by Racial Groups. Government Publication. English. US Department of Agriculture / Agricultural Stabilization and Conservation, 14th and Independence Avenue SW, Washington DC 20250.

LC S **ISSN** 0097-5370
DD 630 US
REPORT SERIES - AGRICULTURAL EXPERIMENT STATION, DIVISION OF AGRICULTURE, UNIVERSITY OF ARKANSAS. **Added/Corp** University of Arkansas. Agricultural Experiment Station. (1945)-. Monographic series. English. Price varies per volume. Arkansas Agricultural Experiment Station, University of Arkansas, Fayetteville AR 72701. **Tel** (501)575-5647, **FAX** (501)575-7273.
Ind/Abst AGRICOLA; Anim. Breed. Abstr.; Cot. Trop. Fibr. Abstr. Bibliogr.; Field Crop Abstr.; Sorghum Mill. Abstr.; Soyabean Abstr.

LC S
DD 630 US
REPORT SERIES - UNIVERSITY OF ARKANSAS AGRICULTURAL EXPERIMENT STATION. **Main/Corp** University of Arkansas Agricultural Experiment Station. No. 1- April 1945-. Academic Scholarly Publication. English.
Ind/Abst EMBASE; Plant Breed. Abstr.; Plant Grow. Reg. Abstr.; Rice Abstr.

LC S541 .U656a **ISSN** 1045-1579
DD 630/.72073 US
REPORT TO THE PRESIDENT AND CONGRESS / NATIONAL AGRICULTURAL RESEARCH AND EXTENSION USERS ADVISORY BOARD. [Rep. Pres. Congr. - U. S., Natl. Agric. Res. Ext. Users Advis. Board]. **Main/Corp** United States. National Agricultural Research and Extension Users Advisory Board. **VFOAT** Appraisal of the Proposed ... Budget for Food and Agricultural Sciences. (19??)-. Periodical. English. One time a year. National Agricultural Research and Extension User Advisory Board, Room 432-A, Administration Building / USDA, 14th Street and Independence Avenue SW, Washington DC 20250.

LC S
DD 630 US
REPORT TO THE SENATE ON THE JURISDICTION AND A SUMMARY OF ACTIVITIES OF THE COMMITTEE ON AGRICULTURE, NUTRITION, AND FORESTRY FOR THE ... CONGRESS. **Main/Corp** United States. Congress. Senate. Committee on Agriculture, Nutrition, and Forestry. English. Every 2 years.

LC S **ISSN** 0963-6536
DD 630 UK
REPORT - UNIVERSITY OF NEWCASTLE UPON TYNE. DEPARTMENT OF AGRICULTURAL ECONOMICS AND FOOD MARKETING. (REPORT.). [Rep. - Univ. Newctle upon Tyne, Dept. Agric. Econ. Food Mark.]. (1989)-. English. **Continues** Report - University of Newcastle upon Tyne. Department of Agricultural and Food Marketing, 0956-6740.
Ind/Abst World Agric. Econ. Rural Sociol. Abstr.

LC S
DD 630 CU
REPORTE DE INVESTIGACION DEL INSTITUTO DE INVESTIGACIONES FUNDAMENTALES EN AGRICULTURA TROPICAL. **Added/Corp** Instituto de Investigaciones Fundamentales en Agricultura Tropical Alejandro de Humboldt. Academia de Ciencias de Cuba. No. 1 (1982)-. Monographic series. Spanish. Academia de Ciencias de Cuba, Industria No 452, La Habana 2 Cuba.
Ind/Abst Rev. Plant Pathol.; Soyabean Abstr.

LC S **ISSN** 0414-0494
DD 630 UK
REPORTS. A - INTER-AFRICAN CONFERENCE. AGRICULTURE. (REPORTS: A.). **Main/Conf** Inter-African Conference. Agriculture. **Added/Corp** Commission for Technical Co-operation in Africa South of the Sahara. **VFOAT** Reports: Agriculture. (19??)-. Periodical. English. Europa Publications Ltd., 18 Bedford Square, London WC1B 3JN United Kingdom. **Tel** 011 44 171 5808236, telex 21540 EUROPA G.

LC S
DD 630 PH
RESEARCH AT LOS BANOS. Added/Corp University of the Philippines at Los Banos. Dept. of Development Communication. Vol. 1, No. 1 (March 1982)-. Periodical. English. Four times a year. $20.00. Research at Los Banos / University of Philippines, Director of Research, Laguna Philippines. ***Continues*** *Agriculture at Los Banos.*
Ind/Abst Biodeter. Abstr.; Poult. Abstr.

LC S51 .R4
US
RESEARCH BULLETIN. Added/Corp University of Georgia. Georgia Agricultural Experiment Stations. (1991)-. Bulletin. English. University of Georgia Agricultural Experiment Station, Athens GA 30602. **Tel** (404)542-3621. ***Continues*** *Research Bulletin (University of Georgia. College of Agriculture. Experiment Stations), 0435-4680.*

LC S
DD 630 II
RESEARCH BULLETIN. (1991)-. Bulletin. English.

LC SF521
DD 638.1 US
RESEARCH BULLETIN - ALABAMA AGRICULTURAL AND MECHANICAL UNIVERSITY, SCHOOL OF AGRICULTURE AND ENVIRONMENTAL SCIENCE. Main/Corp Alabama. Agricultural and Mechanical University. School of Agriculture and Environmental Science. **Added/Corp** United States. Cooperative State Research Service. No. 1 (July 1975)-. Bulletin. English.

LC S73 .R47 **ISSN** 0271-7212
DD 630 US
RESEARCH BULLETIN / MASSACHUSETTS AGRICULTURAL EXPERIMENT STATION. (RESEARCH BULLETIN.). [Res. bull. - Mass. Agric. Exp. Stn.]. **Added/Corp** Massachusetts Agricultural Experiment Station (1906-). **VFOAT** Bulletin. No. 602 (June 1973)-. Bulletin. English. Irregular. Price varies per volume. University of Massachusetts Bulletin Center, Cottage A-Thatcher Way, Amherst MA 01003. **Tel** (413)545-1044. ***Continues*** *Bulletin (Massachusetts Agricultural Experiment Station, 0097-6776.*
Ind/Abst AGRICOLA; Biocont. News Inf.; Potato Abstr.

LC S **ISSN** 0435-9844
DD 630 JA
RESEARCH BULLETIN OF THE FACULTY OF AGRICULTURE, GIFU UNIVERSITY. Main/Corp Gifu University. Faculty of Agriculture. (1951)-. Bulletin. Multiple languages (English and Japanese; summaries and/or abstracts in English; table of contents in English). One time a year. Gifu University / Faculty of Agriculture, 1-1 Yanagido, Gifushi Gifuken 501-11 Japan. ***Supersedes*** *Gifu Daigaku. Nogakubu. Research Bulletin of the Gifu College of Agriculture.*
Ind/Abst Agric. Eng. Abstr.; Dairy Sci. Abstr.; Field Crop Abstr.; Food Sci. Technol. Abstr.; For. Abstr.; Grass. Forage Abstr.; Maize Abstr.; Ornamental Hort. (1991-); Pig News Inf.; Plant Breed. Abstr.; Plant Grow. Reg. Abstr.; Postharvest News Inf.; Poult. Abstr.; Rev. Agric. Entomol.; Rice Abstr.; Seed Abstr.; Small Anim. Abstr. Bibliogr.; Vet. Bull.; Weed Abstr.; World Agric. Econ. Rural Sociol. Abstr.

LC UNC **ISSN** 0078-3951
DD 30/.9771 US
CODEN OARBB7
RESEARCH BULLETIN - OHIO AGRICULTURAL RESEARCH AND DEVELOPMENT CENTER. (RESEARCH BULLETIN.). [Res. bull. - Ohio Agr. Res. Develop. Cent.]. **Added/Corp** Ohio Agricultural Research and Development Center. **VFOAT** OARDC Research Bulletin. **VAT** Ohio Agricultural Research and Development Center Research Bulletin. (1965)-. Monographic series. English. Price varies per volume. Ohio Agricultural Research and Development Center, Ohio State University, 1680 Madison Avenue, Wooster OH 44691. **Tel** (216)263-3775. Documents available from BIOSIS Document Express. ***Continues*** *Research Bulletin (Ohio Agricultural Experiment Station), 0741-7500.*
Ind/Abst Biol. Abstr.; Rev. Plant Pathol.; Soyabean Abstr.; World Agric. Econ. Rural Sociol. Abstr.

LC S
DD 630 PP
RESEARCH BULLETIN / PAPUA NEW GUINEA DEPT. OF AGRICULTURE AND LIVESTOCK. (RESEARCH BULLETIN.). **Added/Corp** Papua New Guinea. Dept. of Agriculture and Livestock. (198?)-. Bulletin. English. Irregular. Price varies per volume. Department of Agriculture and Livestock / Papua New Guinea, PO Box 417, Konedobu Papua New Guinea. **Tel** 011 675 230268, 011 675 258191, 011 675 214699, FAX 011 675 214526, telex 23280. ***Continues*** *Research Bulletin (Papua New Guinea. Dept. of Primary Industry).*

LC S81
DD 630 US
RESEARCH BULLETIN - UNIVERSITY OF MISSOURI-COLUMBIA. AGRICULTURAL EXPERIMENT STATION. Main/Corp University of Missouri-Columbia. Agricultural Experiment Station. No. 1- 1910-. Bulletin. English.
Ind/Abst AGRICOLA; Field Crop Abstr.

LC S123 .V56A **ISSN** 0097-1510
DD 630/.8 US
CODEN VPSRA3
RESEARCH DIVISION REPORT - VIRGINIA POLYTECHNIC INSTITUTE AND STATE UNIVERSITY. (REPORT.). [Res. Div. rep. - Va. Polytech. Inst. State Univ.]. (197?)-. Monographic series. English. Price varies per volume. Research Division Report, Virginia Polytechnic Institute and State Report Research Division, Blacksburg VA 24061. Documents available from CASDDS. ***Continues*** *Report - Research Division, Virginia Polytechnic Institute, 0145-9260.*
Ind/Abst Chem. Abstr. (1970-1980).

LC S52.5 .R47 **ISSN** 0271-9916
DD 630/.5 US
CODEN REHRDY
RESEARCH EXTENSION SERIES. [Res. ext. ser. - Hawaii Inst. Trop. Agric. Hum. Resour.]. (1980)-. Academic Scholarly Publication. English. Irregular. Price varies per volume. University of Hawaii College of Tropical Agriculture and Human Resources, Office of Publications and Information, 2500 Dole Street / Room 107, Honolulu HI 96822. Documents available from CASDDS.
Ind/Abst AgBiotech News Inf.; AGRICOLA [Select. Cov.]; Agrofor. Abstr. (1991-); Anim. Breed. Abstr.; Chem. Abstr. (1980-1981); Field Crop Abstr.; For. Prod. Abstr.; Hortic. Abstr.; Irr. Drain. Abstr.; Nematol. Abstr.; Ornamental Hort.; Plant Breed. Abstr.; Plant Grow. Reg. Abstr.; Rev. Agric. Entomol.; Rev. Plant Pathol.; Rice Abstr.; Seed Abstr.; Soils Fert.; Sug. Indus. Abstr.

LC HD9000.1 .R49 **ISSN** 0276-1653
DD 338.1/072 US
RESEARCH IN DOMESTIC AND INTERNATIONAL AGRIBUSINESS MANAGEMENT. **See** Business and Economics.

LC S
DD 630 JA
RESEARCH PAPER. Added/Corp Nogyo Sogo Kenyujo (Japan). (1987)-. Monographic series. English.
Ind/Abst World Agric. Econ. Rural Sociol. Abstr.

LC S97 .R47 **ISSN** 0732-4766
DD 630/.720756 US
RESEARCH PERSPECTIVES (RALEIGH, N.C.). (RESEARCH PERSPECTIVES.). [Res. perspec.]. **Added/Corp** North Carolina Agricultural Research Service. Vol. 1, No. 1 (Fall 1981)-. Periodical. English. Four times a year. Free on request, US; $4.00 other. Research Perspectives, Campus Box 7603, NC State University, Raleigh NC 27695. **Tel** (919)737-3173. **ED** L.B. Padgett. **Circ:** 5,000. ***Continues*** *Research and Farming, 0034-5121.*
Desc: Reports on developments in agricultural and biological sciences at North Carolina State University.
Ind/Abst AGRICOLA [Select. Cov.].

LC HD2195.5 .A45 **ISSN** 0113-4485
DD 338.1 NZ
RESEARCH REPORT. Added/Corp Lincoln University (Canterbury, N.Z.). Agribusiness and Economics Research Unit. No. 203 (Mar. 1990)-. Monographic series. English. ***Continues*** *Research Report (Lincoln College (University of Canterbury). Agribusiness and Economics Research Unit), 0113-4485.*
Ind/Abst Leis., Rec., Tour. Abstr.

LC S537 .E34
US
RESEARCH REPORT. [Res. rep. - Univ. Ga., Coll. Agric., Exp. Stn.]. **Added/Corp** University of Georgia. Georgia Agricultural Experiment Stations. No. 600 (1992)-. Monographic series. English. Irregular. Free on request. University of Georgia Agricultural Experiment Station, Athens GA 30602. **Tel** (404)542-3621. Documents available from CASDDS. ***Continues*** *Research Report (University of Georgia. College of Agriculture. Experiment Stations), 0435-4699.*
Ind/Abst AgBiotech News Inf. (?-?); AGRICOLA (?-?) [Select. Cov.]; Chem. Abstr. (1967-1983); Dairy Sci. Abstr. (?-?); For. Prod. Abstr. (?-?); Maize Abstr. (?-?); Ornamental Hort. (1991-?); Pig News Inf. (?-?); Plant Breed. Abstr. (?-?); Potato Abstr. (?-?); Poult. Abstr. (?-?); Rev. Plant Pathol. (?-?); Sorghum Mill. Abstr. (?-?); Soyabean Abstr. (?-?).

LC S **ISSN** 0094-3878
DD 630 US
RESEARCH REPORT - AGRICULTURAL EXPERIMENT STATION. UTAH STATE UNIVERSITY. (RESEARCH REPORT.). **Main/Corp** Utah. Agricultural Experiment Station. No. 1 (Nov. 1972)-. Monographic series. English. Four times a year. Free on request. Agriculture Bulletin Room, PO Box 3313, Laramie WY 82071. **Tel** (307)766-3667, (301)766-2115.
Desc: Contains educational materials from the Cooperative Extension Service and Agricultural Experiment Station of the College of Agriculture at University of Wyoming in Laramie, Wyoming.
Ind/Abst Field Crop Abstr.; Grass. Forage Abstr.; Irr. Drain. Abstr.

LC SB610 **ISSN** 0829-6200
DD 632.58 CN
RESEARCH REPORT - EXPERT COMMITTEE ON WEEDS. EASTERN CANADA SECTION. (RESEARCH REPORT - EXPERT COMMITTEE ON WEEDS, EASTERN SECTION = RAPPORT DE RECHERCHES - COMITE CONSULTATIF MALHERBOLOGIE, SECTION DE L'EST.). [Res. rep. - Expert Comm. Weeds, East. Can. Sect.]. **Main/Corp** Expert Committee on Weeds. Eastern Section. **VFOAT** Rapport de Recherches - Comite Consultatif Malherbologie, Section de l'Est. (1978)-. English (French). Expert Committee on Weeds / Ontario, Eastern Canada Section, Ontario Canada. ***Continues*** *Canada Weed Committee. Eastern Section. Research Report - Canada Weed Committee, Eastern Section.*
Desc: Publication concerned with weeds and weed control.
Ind/Abst PESTDOC.

LC SB610 **ISSN** 0829-7584
DD 632.58 CN
RESEARCH REPORT - EXPERT COMMITTEE ON WEEDS. WESTERN CANADA SECTION. (RESEARCH REPORT - EXPERT COMMITTEE ON WEEDS, WESTERN CANADA = RAPPORT DE RECHERCHES - COMITE CONSULTATIF MALHERBOLOGIE, CANADA DE L'OUEST.). [Res. rep. - Expert Comm. Weeds, West. Can. Sect.]. **Main/Corp** Expert Committee on Weeds. Western Canada. **VFOAT** Rapport de Recherches - Comite Consultatif Malherbologie, Canada de l'Ouest. (1978)-. English (French). Expert Committee on Weeds, Western Canada Section, Saskatchewan Canada. ***Continues*** *Canada Weed Committee. Western Section. Research Report - Canada Weed Committee, Western Section.*
Desc: Publication concerned with weeds and weed control.
Ind/Abst PESTDOC.

LC S **ISSN** 0543-8233
DD 630 US
RESEARCH REPORT FROM THE MICHIGAN STATE UNIVERSITY AGRICULTURAL EXPERIMENT STATION, EAST LANSING. [Res. rep. Mich. State Univ. Agric. Exp. Stn. East Lansing]. **Main/Corp** Michigan State University. Agricultural Experiment Station. **Added/Corp** Michigan State University. Agricultural Experiment Station. **VFOAT** Research Report. No. 1 (1963)-. Monographic series. English. Agricultural Experiment Station, Michigan State Univeristy, East Lansing MI 48824-1039. **Tel** (517)355-0123.
Ind/Abst AGRICOLA [Select. Cov.].

LC S **ISSN** 0147-2186
DD 630 US
CODEN RRMSDH
Pr Rev.
RESEARCH REPORT - MISSISSIPPI AGRICULTURAL & FORESTRY EXPERIMENT STATION. (RESEARCH REPORT.). [Res. rep., Miss. Agric. For. Exp. Stn.]. **Added/Corp** Mississippi Agricultural and Forestry Experiment Station. Vol. 1, No. 1 (Feb. 1975)-. Academic Scholarly Publication. English. Free. Mississippi State University / Information Services, PO Box 5446, Mississippi State MS 39762. **Tel** (601)325-7774. **ED** Keith H Remy. Index available. cum. index. **Circ:** 800. Documents available from CASDDS.
Desc: Includes technical data and discussion of experiment station research.
Ind/Abst AGRICOLA [Select. Cov.]; Chem. Abstr.; Cot. Trop. Fibr. Abstr. Bibliogr.; Hortic. Abstr.; Irr. Drain. Abstr.; Nematol. Abstr.; Ornamental Hort. (1991-); Plant Breed. Abstr.; Plant Grow. Reg. Abstr.; Poult. Abstr.; Rev. Agric. Entomol.; Rev. Plant Pathol.; Rice Abstr.

LC S89 .R47 **ISSN** 0077-832X
DD 630/.5 US
RESEARCH REPORT / NEW HAMPSHIRE AGRICULTURAL EXPERIMENTAL STATION. (RESEARCH REPORT.). [Res. rep. - N.H. Agric. Exp. Stn.]. Monographic series. English. Irregular. Price varies per volume. New Hampshire Agricultural Experiment Station, University of New Hampshire, Durham NH 03824. ctrl

Agriculture

circ.
Ind/Abst AGRICOLA [Select. Cov.]; Hortic. Abstr.; World Agric. Econ. Rural Sociol. Abstr.

LC SB610 .R47   **ISSN** 1062-421X
DD 632   US

RESEARCH REPORT - NORTH CENTRAL WEED SCIENCE SOCIETY (U.S.).
(RESEARCH REPORT / NORTH CENTRAL WEED SCIENCE SOCIETY.). [Res. rep. - North Cent. Weed Sci. Soc. (U.S.)]. **Added/Corp** North Central Weed Science Society (U.S.). **VFOAT** NCWSS Research Report. Vol. 46 (1989)-. English. One time a year. $25.00. North Central Weed Control, 309 West Clark Street, Champaign IL 61820. **Tel** (217)356-3182, FAX (217)398-4119. *Continues* Research Report (North Central Weed Control Conference : 1979), 0099-9547.
Ind/Abst AGRICOLA; PESTDOC.

LC S   **ISSN** 0361-5804
DD 630   US
    CODEN OAERBO

RESEARCH REPORT P.
[Res. rep. P]. (1972)-. Monographic series. English. Irregular. Price varies per volume. Oklahoma State University / Research Report P, Classroom Building, Stillwater OK 74078. Documents available from BIOSIS Document Express.
Ind/Abst AGRICOLA [Select. Cov.]; Biol. Abstr.; For. Abstr.; GeoRef; Hortic. Abstr.; Rev. Agric. Entomol.; Rev. Plant Pathol.; World Agric. Econ. Rural Sociol. Abstr.

LC S
DD 630   US

RESEARCH REPORT SERIES. Added/Corp
Alabama Agricultural Experiment Station. No. 1 (May 1983)-. Monographic series. English. Alabama Agricultural Experiment Station, Auburn University, 110 Comer Hall, Auburn University AL 36849. **Tel** (334)844-4877, FAX (334)844-5892.
Ind/Abst For. Abstr.; Irr. Drain. Abstr.; Plant Grow. Reg. Abstr.; Rev. Agric. Entomol.; Rev. Plant Pathol.

LC S
DD 630   AT

RESEARCH REPORT (UNIVERSITY OF SYDNEY. DEPT. OF AGRICULTURAL ECONOMICS).
(RESEARCH REPORT.). No. 7 (1978)-. Monographic series. English. Irregular. Price varies per volume. *Continues* Mimeographed Report (University of Sydney. Dept. of Agricultural Economics).

LC S   **ISSN** 1051-3140
DD 630   US
    CODEN RSUSEV

RESEARCH SERIES / UNIVERSITY OF ARKANSAS, FAYETTVILLE. AGRICULTURAL EXPERIMENT STATION.
(RESEARCH SERIES.). [Res. ser. - Univ. Ark. Fayettev., Agric. Exp. Stn.]. **Added/Corp** University of Arkansas, Fayetteville. Agricultural Experiment Station. **VFOAT** Arkansas Experiment Station Research Series. No. 326 (Oct. 1985)-. Monographic series. English. Price varies per volume. Arkansas Agricultural Experiment Station, University of Arkansas, Fayetteville AR 72701. **Tel** (501)575-5647, FAX (501)575-7273. Documents available from BIOSIS Document Express. *Continues* Mimeograph Series (University of Arkansas, Fayetteville. Agricultural Experiment Station).
Ind/Abst AGRICOLA; Biol. Abstr.; Cot. Trop. Fibr. Abstr. Bibliogr.; Hortic. Abstr.; Irr. Drain. Abstr.; Plant Grow. Reg. Abstr.; Rev. Plant Pathol.; Seed Abstr.; Sorghum Mill. Abstr.

LC S
DD 630   CE

RESEARCH STUDY / AGRARIAN RESEARCH AND TRAINING INSTITUTE.
(RESEARCH STUDY.). **Added/Corp** Agrarian Research and Training Institute. Monographic series. English. Price varies per volume. *Continues* Research Study Series (Agrarian Research and Training Institute).

LC HD1950.B7 R47
DD 338.1/0944/1   FR

RESEAU D'INFORMATION COMPTABLE AGRICOLE. REGION BRETAGNE. VFOAT
Region Bretagne. French. 15 Avenue de Cucille, 35047 Rennes Cedex France.

LC S229 .R47   **ISSN** 0243-8941
DD 338.1/09445/021   FR

RESEAU D'INFORMATION COMPTABLE AGRICOLE. REGION CENTRE.
1979 A 1982-. French. Circonscription d'Action Regionale Centre, Cite Administrative Coligny, 131 rue du Faubourg Bannier, 45042 Orleans Cedex France. *Continues in part* Reseau d'Information Comptable Agricole. Circonscription Centre, Ile de France.

LC S229 .M56A HD1491.F7
DD 338.1/0944 334/.683/0944   FR

RESULTATS DE L'ENQUETE ANNUELLE SUR LA COOPERATION AGRICOLE. Main/Corp
France. Service Central des Enquetes et Etudes Statistiques. French. Ministry of Agriculture, 78 rue de Varenne, 75007 Paris France.

LC SB191.O2 R44   **ISSN** 0733-9283
DD 633.1/33/0973   US

RESULTS FROM THE COOPERATIVE COORDINATED OAT BREEDING NURSERIES, AND THE UNIFORM WINTER-HARDINESS NURSERIES. See
Agriculture-Feed Grain and Milling.

LC S   **ISSN** 0827-4339
DD 630   CN

RESUME DES RECHERCHES - STATION DE RECHERCHES. SAINT-JEAN, QUEBEC.
(RESUME DES RECHERCHES / AGRICULTURE CANADA, DIRECTION DE LA RECHERCHE.). [Resume rech. - Stn rech., St.-Jean, Que.]. **VFOAT** Research Summary. Vol. 7 (1978)-. French (summaries and/or abstracts in English). One time a year. *Continues* Resume des Recherches en Cultures Fruitieres et Maraicheres.
Ind/Abst Nematol. Abstr.; Ornamental Hort.; Soyabean Abstr.

LC S   **ISSN** 0120-2944
DD 630   CK

RESUMENES ANALITICOS SOBRE PASTOS TROPICALES.
Vol. 1 (Dec. 1979)-. Periodical. Spanish. Three times a year. $40.00. CIAT Publication Distribution, Apartado Aereo 6713, Cali Colombia. Index available in last issue of volume--attached.
Ind/Abst Grass. Forage Abstr.; Nematol. Abstr.; Rev. Agric. Entomol.

LC HD9000
DD 338.173/18   LB

RETROSPECTIVE INDEX - WEST AFRICA RICE DEVELOPMENT ASSOCIATION. Main/Corp
West Africa Rice Development Association. **VFOAT** Index Retrospectif - Association pour le Developpement de la Riziculture en Afrique de l'Ouest. No. 1- ; Dec. 1975-. English (French). Documentation Centre Warda/Adrao, PO Box 1019, Monrovia Liberia.

LC S   **ISSN** 0070-2307
DD 630   CY

REVIEW FOR ... / AGRICULTURAL RESEARCH INSTITUTE.
(1991)-. Periodical. English.

LC S
DD 630   CY

REVIEW FOR ... / AGRICULTURAL RESEARCH INSTITUTE, REPUBLIC OF CYPRUS. Main/Corp
Institouton Georgikon Ereunon (Cyprus). **Added/Corp** Cyprus. Grapheio Typou kai PlerophoriAon. Cyprus. Hypourgeio Georgias kai Physikon Poron. (1991)-. English. *Continues* Annual Report - Cyprus Agricultural Research Institute, 0070-2307.
Ind/Abst Ornamental Hort. (1991-).

LC S540.8.K66 K66A
DD 630/.913   NE

REVIEW OF AGRICULTURAL PROGRAMMES AND ADVISORY ACTIVITIES. Main/Corp
Koninklijk Instituut voor de Tropen. 1982-. English. One time a year. Royal Tropical Institute, Information & Documentation, Mauritskade 63, 1092 AD Amsterdam Netherlands. **Tel** 11 31 20 5688330, FAX 11 31 20 6654423, telex 15080 KIT NL. *Continues* Koninklijk Instituut Voor de Tropen. Afdeling Agrarisch Onderzoek. Report.

LC S401.F64B
DD 338.1   IT

REVIEW OF THE REGULAR PROGRAMME. Main/Corp
Food and Agriculture Organization of the United Nations. English. Every 2 years. Food Agriculture Organization (FAO) / Italy, GIPCI66 via Terme di Caracalla, 00100 Rome Italy. **Tel** 011 39 6 52252925, FAX 011 39 6 52253152.

LC HD1861 .R48
DD 630   AG

REVISTA ARGENTINA DE ECONOMIA AGRARIA. Added/Corp
Asociacion Argentina de Economia Agraria. (1987)-. Spanish. One time a year. Asociacion Argentina de Economia Agraria, Buenos Aires Argentina.
Ind/Abst Dairy Sci. Abstr.; Int. Dev. Abstr.; Postharvest News Inf.; Potato Abstr.; World Agric. Econ. Rural Sociol. Abstr.

LC S   **ISSN** 0101-563X
DD 630   BL
    CODEN REBMDN
Pr Rev.

REVISTA BRASILEIRA DE MANDIOCA.
[RBM, Rev. Bras. Mandioca]. **Added/Corp** Sociedade Brasileira de Mandioca. **VFOAT** RBM; R.B.M.; R.B.M., Revista Brasileira de Mandioca; Cassava Brasilian Journal. Vol. 1, No. 1 (1982)-. Periodical. Portuguese (summaries and/or abstracts in English). Two times a year. $12.00. Sociedad Brasileira de Mandioca, Centro Nacional de Pesquisa de Mandioca e Fruticultura, Caixa Postal 007, CEP 44 380, Cruz das Almas Bahia Brazil. **Tel** 075 721-2120, FAX 075 721-1118, telex 075 2074. **ED** Laercio Duarte Souza. Index available. **Circ:** 500 (ctrl). available on diskette. Documents available from BLDSC, CASDDS.
Desc: Original articles on cassava agronomy matters.
Ind/Abst Chem. Abstr.

LC S   **ISSN** 0101-3122
DD 630   BL

REVISTA BRASILEIRA DE SEMENTES.
VFOAT Brazilian Seed Journal. Vol. 1, No. 1-. Periodical. Portuguese. Three times a year. $30.00. Secretario Executivo Abrates, Palacio do Desenvolvimento, 9O Andar 70.057, Brasilia DF Brazil.
Ind/Abst Field Crop Abstr.; Grass. Forage Abstr.; Maize Abstr.; Postharvest News Inf.; Rice Abstr.; Seed Abstr.

LC S15 .C46   **ISSN** 0034-737X
DD 630/.5   BL
    CODEN RCERA2

REVISTA CERES. Added/Corp
Universidade Federal de Vicosa. Universidade Rural do Estado de Minas Gerais. Escola Superior de Agricultura. Universidade Rural do Estado de Minas Gerais. (Sept./Oct. 1944)-. Periodical. English (Portuguese). Six times a year (Feb., Apr., June, Aug., Oct., Dec.). $40.00. Universidade Federal de Vicosa, Commisao Editorial 36 570, Vocosa Minas Gerais Brazil. **Tel** 011 55 31 8992136, FAX 011 55 31 8992108. **Circ:** 1,100 (ctrl). Documents available from BIOSIS Document Express, CASDDS. *Continues* Ceres.
Ind/Abst Agric. Eng. Abstr. (1991-); Agrofor. Abstr.; Biol. Abstr.; Chem. Abstr.; Crop Physiol. Abstr.; Field Crop Abstr.; Fish Rev. (Jan. 1989-July 1992); Food Sci. Technol. Abstr.; For. Prod. Abstr. (1991-); For. Abstr.; Grass. Forage Abstr.; Hortic. Abstr.; Int. Dev. Abstr. (?-?); Irr. Drain. Abstr.; Maize Abstr.; Nematol. Abstr.; Plant Breed. Abstr.; Plant Genet. Resour. Abstr.; Potato Abstr.; Rev. Plant Pathol.; Rice Abstr.; Seed Abstr.; Soils Fert.; Sorghum Mill. Abstr.; Soyabean Abstr.; Weed Abstr.; Wildl. Rev. (Jan. 1989-July 1992); World Agric. Econ. Rural Sociol. Abstr.

LC S   **ISSN** 0186-3231
DD 630   MX
    CODEN REVCEQ

REVISTA CHAPINGO. [Rev. Chapingo].
Added/Corp Universidad Autonoma Chapingo. Vol. 7, No. 33/34 (Jan./Apr. 1982)-. Periodical. Spanish. Six times a year. Documents available from BIOSIS Document Express. *Continues* Chapingo, 0186-7075.
Ind/Abst Anim. Breed. Abstr.; Biol. Abstr.; Dairy Sci. Abstr.; Field Crop Abstr.; Grass. Forage Abstr.; Hortic. Abstr.; Index Vet.; Irr. Drain. Abstr.; Maize Abstr.; Plant Breed. Abstr.; Rev. Agric. Entomol.; Rev. Plant Pathol.; Seed Abstr.; Soils Fert.; Weed Abstr.

LC S671
DD 631.3   CU

REVISTA CIENCIAS TECNICAS AGROPECUARIAS. Added/Corp
Centro de Mecanizacion Agropecuaria (Cuba) Instituto Superior de Ciencias Agropecuarias de la Habana. **VFOAT** Ciencias Tecnicas Agropecuarias; CTA. Vol. 1, No. 1 (1988)-. Periodical. Spanish. Three times a year. Comerical Mercadu S.A., Calle 30 #768-1 E/C 39 Y 41, Nuevo Vedado COD 10 600, Ciudad de la Habana Cuba.
Ind/Abst Agric. Eng. Abstr.; Grass. Forage Abstr.; Hortic. Abstr.; Irr. Drain. Abstr.; Postharvest News Inf.; World Agric. Econ. Rural Sociol. Abstr.

LC S   **ISSN** 0034-7655
DD 630   BL
    CODEN RAPCAW

REVISTA DE AGRICULTURA. [Rev. agric.].
Vol. 1 (1925)-. Periodical. Portuguese. Four times a year. Revista de Agricultura, Rua Moraes e Barros 829, POB 60, Sao Paul Brazil. Documents available from BIOSIS Document Express, CASDDS.
Ind/Abst Biocont. News Inf. (1991-); Biol. Abstr.; Chem. Abstr.; Cot. Trop. Fibr. Abstr. Bibliogr.; Crop Physiol. Abstr.; Grass. Forage Abstr.; Hortic. Abstr.; Maize Abstr.; Nematol. Abstr.; Plant Grow. Reg. Abstr.; Potato Abstr.; Rev. Agric. Entomol.; Rev. Med. Vet. Entomol.; Rice Abstr.; Seed Abstr.; Soils Fert.; Sorghum Mill. Abstr.; Weed Abstr.

LC K19 .D573
DD 340.05   BL

REVISTA DE DIREITO AGRARIO. See Law.

LC HD1872 .R45
DD 630 BL
REVISTA DE ECONOMIA E SOCIOLOGIA RURAL. **Added/Corp** Sociedade Brasileira de Economia e Sociologia Rural. Vol. 26, No. 1 (Jan./March 1988)-. Periodical. Portuguese (summaries and/or abstracts in English). Irregular. $65.00. Soc Brasileira Econ Rural, Srtn Av W/3N.Quadra702/1049-50, 70-710 Brasilia DF Brazil. **Tel** 011 55 61 225-6144. ***Continues*** *Revista de Economia Rural, 0100-4905.*

LC HD101 .R38 **ISSN** 0034-8155
DD 333.73 SP
Pr Rev. **TITLE CHANGE**
REVISTA DE ESTUDIOS AGRO-SOCIALES. [Rev. estud. agro-soc.]. **Added/Corp** Spain. Ministerio de Agricultura, Pesca y Alimentacion. Secretaria General Tecnica. Instituto e Relaciones Agrarias (Spain) Instituto de Estudios Agro-Sociales (Spain). (Oct.-Dec. 1952)-(1995). Spanish. Ministerio Agricultura, Centro de Publicaciones, Calle Alfonso XII 56, 28071 Madrid Spain. **Tel** 011 34 1 3475551, FAX 011 34 1 3475722. **ED** Carlos San Juan Mesonada. Index available. cum. index. **Bk Rev. Ad Acc. Circ:** 2,500 (ctrl). Documents available from BLDSC. ***Continued by*** *Revista Espanola de Economia Agraria.*
Ind/Abst Dairy Sci. Abstr.; For. Abstr.; Int. Labour Doc.; Maize Abstr.; PAIS Int. Print; Rice Abstr.; Soyabean Abstr.; World Agric. Econ. Rural Sociol. Abstr.

LC S **ISSN** 0210-1742
DD 630 SP
REVISTA DE EXTENSION AGRARIA. [Rev. ext. agrar.]. **Added/Corp** Spain. Servicio de Extension Agraria. Spain. Direccion General de Capacitacion y Extension Agrarias. Spain. Direccion General de Investigacion y Capacitacion Agrarias. Vol. 1, No. 1 (Oct. 1961)-. Periodical. Spanish. Four times a year. 1000.00ptas Spain and Latin America; 1500.00ptas other. Ministerio Agricultura, Centro de Publicaciones, Calle Alfonso XII 56, 28071 Madrid Spain. **Tel** 011 34 1 3475551, FAX 011 34 1 3475722. ***Continues*** *Boletin Informativo (Spain. Servicio de Extension Agraria), 0210-1734.*

LC S
DD 630 EC
REVISTA DE LA CAMARA DE AGRICULTORA DE LA PRIMERA ZONA. ANO. (19??)-. Periodical. Spanish.

LC S **ISSN** 0041-8285
DD 630 VE
SUSPENDED
REVISTA DE LA FACULTAD DE AGRONOMIA. **Main/Corp** Universidad Central de Venezuela. Facultad de Agronomia. Vol. 1 (June 1952)-?. Spanish (summaries and/or abstracts in English and French). Three times a year. $20.00 Venezuela; $25.00 US. Universidad Central de Venezuela / Facultad de Agronomia Revista de la Facultad de Agronomia, Maracay Venezuela. **Tel** 011 58 43 28996, FAX 011 58 43 25204. **ED** Alex Moreno. Index available. cum. index. **Circ:** 1,000.
Desc: Research work in agronomy field.
Ind/Abst Abstr. Trop. Agric.; Agrindex; Plant Breed. Abstr.; Rev. Agric. Entomol.; Rice Abstr.; Soils Fert.; Sorghum Mill. Abstr.; Soyabean Abstr.

LC S **ISSN** 0376-0030
DD 630 VE
Pr Rev.
REVISTA DE LA FACULTAD DE AGRONOMIA DE LA UNIVERSIDAD CENTRAL DE VENEZUELA. ALCANCE. [Rev. Fac. Agron. Univ. Cent. Venez., Alcance]. Monographic series. Spanish (summaries and/or abstracts in English and French). Irregular. Price varies per volume. Universidad Central de Venezuela / Facultad de Agronomia Revista de la Facultad de Agronomia, Maracay Venezuela. **Tel** 011 58 43 28996, FAX 011 58 43 25204. **ED** Alex Moreno. **Circ:** 1,000. ***Continues*** *Revista de la Facultad de Agronomia. Alcance.*
Desc: Agriculture and similar subjects.
Ind/Abst Field Crop Abstr.; Grass. Forage Abstr.; Hortic. Abstr.; Irr. Drain. Abstr.; Maize Abstr.; Life Sci. Collect.; Plant Breed. Abstr.; Seed Abstr.; Weed Abstr.

LC S **ISSN** 0370-4661
DD 630 AG
UDC 63
CODEN RFACAQ
REVISTA DE LA FACULTAD DE CIENCIAS AGRARIAS, UNIVERSIDAD NACIONAL DE CUYO. [Rev. Fac. Cienc. Agrar. Univ. Nac. Cuyo]. (1949)-. Spanish. Irregular.
Ind/Abst Hortic. Abstr.; Postharvest News Inf.; Rev. Agric. Entomol.; Rev. Plant Pathol.; Soils Fert.

LC S **ISSN** 0325-9846
DD 630 AG
REVISTA DE LOS CREA. (REVISTA DE LOS CREA - CONSORCIOS REGIONALES DE EXPERIMENTACION AGRICOLA.). [Rev. CREA]. **Main/Corp** Asociacion Argentina de Consorcios Regionales de Experimentacion Agricola. Vol. 5, No. 26 (Dec. 1970)-. Periodical. Spanish. Six times a year. CREA / Consorcios Regionales de Experimentacion Agricola, Buenos Aires Argentina.
Ind/Abst AGRICOLA; Field Crop Abstr.; Grass. Forage Abstr.; Index Vet.; Maize Abstr.; Nutr. Abstr. Rev., Ser. B, Live Feeds and Feed.; Weed Abstr.

LC HD1792 .R46 **ISSN** 0034-9097
DD 338.1/0972 MX
REVISTA DEL MEXICO AGRARIO. [Rev. Mex. agrar.]. **Added/Corp** Confederacion Nacional Campesina (Mexico). 1 (Nov./Dec. 1967)-. Periodical. Spanish. Six times a year. $12.00. Libreria Mexico Agraria, Apartado Postal 59-007, Mexico 1 DF Mexico.
Ind/Abst Foreign Lang. Index (-1984); PAIS Foreign Lang. Index (1985-).

LC S **ISSN** 0085-5901
DD 630 BL
CODEN RCCRDT
TITLE CHANGE
REVISTA DO CENTRO DE CIENCIAS RURAIS. [Rev. Cent. Cienc. Rurais]. **Main/Corp** Santa Maria, Brazil (Rio Grande do Sul). Universidade Federal. Centro de Ciencias Rurais. Vol. 1 (1971)-(199?). Academic Scholarly Publication. Portuguese (Spanish; summaries and/or abstracts in English). Universidade Federal de Santa Maria, Centro de Ciencias Rurais, Campus Universitario, 97119-900 Santa Maria, Rio Grande do Sul Brazil. **Tel** 011 55 55 2262347. **ED** Dionisio Link. Index available. cum. index. **Circ:** 470 (ctrl). Documents available from CASDDS. ***Continued by*** *Ciencia Rural, 0103-8478.*
Desc: Plant breeding, economic entomology, weed control, plant pathology, veterinary surgical methods, livestock, poultry, microbiology, forestry.
Ind/Abst AGRICOLA; Anim. Breed. Abstr.; Biocont. News Inf.; Biodeter. Abstr.; Chem. Abstr.; Field Crop Abstr.; For. Abstr.; Grass. Forage Abstr.; Helminthol. Abstr. (1991-); Index Vet.; Irr. Drain. Abstr.; Maize Abstr.; Nutr. Abstr. Rev., Ser. B, Live Feeds and Feed.; Pig News Inf.; Plant Breed. Abstr.; Postharvest News Inf.; Rev. Agric. Entomol.; Seed Abstr.; Small Anim. Abstr. Bibliogr.; Soils Fert.; Soyabean Abstr.

LC S **ISSN** 0100-607X
DD 630 BL
REVISTA DO SECTOR DE CIENCIAS AGRARIAS. Vol. 1, No. 1 (Aug./Dec. 1979)-. Periodical. Portuguese. Two times a year.
Ind/Abst For. Prod. Abstr. (1991-); For. Abstr.; Poult. Abstr.

LC S
DD 630 SP
Pr Rev.
•**REVISTA ESPANOLA DE ECONOMIA AGRARIA.** (1995)-. Spanish. Four times a year. $75.50. Ministerio Agricultura, Centro de Publicaciones, Calle Alfonso XII 56, 28071 Madrid Spain. **Tel** 011 34 1 3475551, FAX 011 34 1 3475722. ***Continues*** *Revista de Estudios Agro-Sociales.*

LC S15 .C65 **ISSN** 0304-2847
DD 630 CK
REVISTA FACULTAD NACIONAL DE AGRONOMIA, MEDELLIN. (REVISTA, FACULTAD NACIONAL DE AGRONOMIA.). [Rev fac. nac. agron., Medellin]. **Added/Corp** Universidad Nacional de Colombia. Facultad Nacional de Agronomia. **VFOAT** Revista, Facultad Nacional de Agronomia, Medellin. Vol. 1, No. 1 (Aug. 1939)-. Periodical. Spanish (summaries and/or abstracts in English and Spanish). 4000Col$. Facultad Nacional de Agronomia Medellin, Biblioteca Facultad de Agronomia, Universidad Nacional de Colombia, Apartado 568, Medellin Colombia. **Tel** 011 57 4 2303802, FAX 011 57 4300420. cum. index. **Circ:** 1,000 (ctrl). Documents available from BLDSC.
Ind/Abst Nutr. Abstr. Rev., Ser. B, Live Feeds and Feed.

LC SB354 **ISSN** 0716-534X
DD 634 CL
REVISTA FRUTICOLA. [Rev. frutic.]. **Added/Corp** Cooperativa Agricola y Fruticola de Curico. (19??)-. Periodical. Spanish. Three times a year (May, Sept., Dec.). $25.00. Copefrut, Castilla 23-A, Curico Chile. **Tel** 011 56 75 310531. Index available ($25.00 extra.).
Ind/Abst Hortic. Abstr.; Rev. Agric. Entomol.

LC HD2025.G3 R45
DD 338.1/0946/105 SP
REVISTA GALEGA DE ESTUDIOS AGRARIOS. Spanish.

LC S195 .I513
DD 630/.720861 CK
CODEN RICAEL
REVISTA ICA : PUBLICACION CIENTIFICA DEL INSTITUTO COLOMBIANO AGROPECUARIO. **VFOAT** Revista. Periodical. Spanish. Four times a year. Ministerio Agricultura, Centro de Publicaciones, Calle Alfonso XII 56, 28071 Madrid Spain. **Tel** 011 34 1 3475551, FAX 011 34 1 3475722. ***Continues*** *Revista - Instituto Colombiano Agropecuario.*

LC S **ISSN** 0250-5479
DD 630 VE
CODEN RLCAD7
REVISTA LATINOAMERICANA DE CIENCIAS AGRICOLAS. [Rev. latinoam. cienc. agric.]. Vol. 12 (1976)-. Academic Scholarly Publication. Multiple languages (Spanish and Portuguese; summaries and/or abstracts in Spanish, Portuguese and English). Asociacion Latinoamericana De Ciencias Agricolas, Apartado Postal 29-280, Caracas 06720 Mexico. Documents available from CASDDS. ***Continues*** *Fitotecnia Latinoamericana.*
Ind/Abst Chem. Abstr.

LC S **ISSN** 0035-0222
DD 630 CK
REVISTA NACIONAL DE AGRICULTURA (BOGOTA). (REVISTA NACIONAL DE AGRICULTURA.). [Rev. nac. agric.]. Vol. 1, No. 1 (1906)-. Periodical. Spanish. Four times a year. $150.00. Sociedad Agricultores Colombia, Aptd 3638 Carr 724 89 Piso 44, Bogota de Columbia. **Tel** 011 57 1 2418013. ***Supersedes*** *Agricultor.*
Ind/Abst AgBiotech News Inf.; AGRICOLA; Dairy Sci. Abstr.; Maize Abstr.; Rice Abstr.; Soyabean Abstr.; Sug. Indus. Abstr.; World Agric. Econ. Rural Sociol. Abstr.

LC SB193 **ISSN** 0210-1270
DD 633.202 SP
REVISTA PASTOS. (PASTOS : REVISTA DE LA SOCIEDAD ESPANOLA PARA EL ESTUDIO DE LOS PASTOS.). [Rev. pastos]. **Added/Corp** Sociedad Espanola para el Estudio de los Pastos. **VFOAT** Revista de la Sociedad Espanola para el Estudio de los Pastos; Revista Pastos. (1971)-. Periodical. Spanish (summaries and/or abstracts in English). Two times a year (June and Dec.). $28.42. Revista Pathos, Apartado 212, 39080 Santander Spain. **Tel** 011 34 42 221106. Index available (free).
Ind/Abst Irr. Drain. Abstr.; Nutr. Abstr. Rev., Ser. B, Live Feeds and Feed.; Pig News Inf.

LC S **ISSN** 0370-3576
DD 630 MF
CODEN RASMA9
REVUE AGRICOLE ET SUCRIERE DE L'ILE MAURICE. (REVUE AGRICOLE ET SUCRIERE DE L'ILE MAURICE : ORGANE OFFICIEL DE LA SOCIETE DE TECHNOLOGIE AGRICOLE ET SUCRIERE DE L'ILE MAURICE.). [Rev. agric. sucr. Ile Maurice]. **Added/Corp** Societe de Technologie Agricole et Sucriere de l'Ile Maurice. Vol. 34, No. 1 (Jan./Feb. 1955)-. Academic Scholarly Publication. French (English). Four times a year. $17.00. Revue Agricole & Sucriere, C O M S I R I, Reduit Mauritius. Documents available from BIOSIS Document Express, CASDDS. ***Continues*** *Revue Agricole de l'Ile Maurice.*
Ind/Abst AGRICOLA; Agric. Eng. Abstr. (1991-); Biol. Abstr.; Chem. Abstr.; EMBASE; Food Sci. Technol. Abstr.; Hortic. Abstr.; Maize Abstr.; Ornamental Hort. (1991-); Plant Breed. Abstr.; Potato Abstr.; Rev. Agric. Entomol.; Rev. Plant Pathol.; Soils Fert.; Sug. Indus. Abstr.; Weed Abstr.

LC S5 .B362 **ISSN** 0035-1296
DD 630/.5 BE
CODEN RVAGAE
TITLE CHANGE
REVUE DE L'AGRICULTURE. [Rev. Agric.]. Vol. 1 (Jan. 1948)-(19??). Periodical. French (Dutch). Manhattan Center-Office Tower, Avenue du Boulevard 21, 13 eme Etage, 1210 Brussels Belgium. **Tel** 011 32 2 2117211, FAX 011 32 2 2117216, telex AGRILA 22033. Index available. cum. index. **Bk Rev. Circ:** 1,100. Documents available from CASDDS. ***Continued by*** *Revue de l'Agriculture - Landbouwtijdschrift, 0776-2143.*
Desc: Publishes results of scientific research and articles on technical, economic and social matters. Each year, a special issue is devoted to one specific subject.
Ind/Abst AgBiotech News Inf.; Agric. Eng. Abstr.; Anim. Breed. Abstr.; Biocont. News Inf. (19??-19??); Biodeter. Abstr. (1991-); Chem. Abstr.; Crop Physiol. Abstr. (?-?); Dairy Sci. Abstr.; Field Crop Abstr.; Food Sci. Technol. Abstr.; Grass. Forage Abstr.; Helminthol. Abstr. (1991-); Hortic. Abstr.; Index Vet.; Nematol. Abstr.; Nutr. Abstr. Rev., Ser. B, Live Feeds and Feed.; Nutr. Abstr. Rev., Ser. A, Hum. Exp.; Ornamental Hort. (1991-); Life Sci. Collect.; Pig News Inf.; Plant Grow. Reg. Abstr.; Postharvest News Inf.; Poult. Abstr.; Protozoolog. Abstr.; Seed Abstr.; Soils Fert.; Soyabean Abstr.; Vet. Bull.; Weed Abstr.; World Agric. Econ. Rural Sociol. Abstr.

LC S
DD 630 FR
REVUE DES AGRICULTEURS DE FRANCE. French. Six times a year. 250.00F France; 244.85F other. Soc Agriculteurs de France, 8 rue d Athenes, 75009 Paris France. **Tel** 011 33 1 42857227, FAX 011 33 1 42806334.

LC S **ISSN** 0035-2853
DD 630 FR
REVUE FRANCAISE D'APICULTURE. **Added/Corp** Union Nationale de l'Apiculture Francaise. Syndicat des Producteurs de Miel de France. No. 1 (1946)-. Periodical. French. Eleven times a year (July and

August issues are combined). $48.12. Revue Francaise d'Apiculture, 26 rue des Tournelles, 75004 Paris France. Index available. cum. index. **Bk Rev. Ad Acc.** ctrl circ.

LC S **ISSN** 0375-1325
DD 630 SZ
REVUE SUISSE D'AGRICULTURE. [Rev. suisse agric.]. **Added/Corp** Station Federale de Recherches Agronomiques de Lausanne. Switzerland. Service Romand de Vulgarisation Agricole. Vol. 1, (Jan./Feb. 1969)-. Periodical. French (summaries and/or abstracts in English, German and Italian). Six times a year. $41.47. Revue Suisse d'Agriculture, M Magnenat, Case Postale 190, CH-1260 Nyon Switzerland. **Tel** 011 41 22 615454, FAX 011 41 22 621325. **ED** Michel Magnenat. Index available. cum. index. **Ad Acc, Adv Mgr:** E. Grandgirard. **Circ:** 7,500 (ctrl).
Ind/Abst AgBiotech News Inf.; Dairy Sci. Abstr.; EMBASE; Field Crop Abstr.; Food Sci. Technol. Abstr.; Grass. Forage Abstr.; Index Vet.; Irr. Drain. Abstr.; Nutr. Abstr. Rev., Ser. B, Live Feeds and Feed.; PESTDOC; Potato Abstr.; Soils Fert.; Soyabean Abstr.

LC S109 .R47 **ISSN** 0035-4635
DD 333.7/2/09745 US
RHODE ISLAND RESOURCES. Added/Corp University of Rhode Island. Agricultural Experiment Station. University of Rhode Island. Cooperative Extension Service. Vol. 16, (Mar. 1970)-. Periodical. English. Rhode Island Resources, University of Rhode Island, 10 Woodward Hall, Kingston RI 02881. **Tel** (401)792-2465. **ED** Jacqueline McGrath. **Ad Acc. Circ:** 16,000. ***Continues** Rhode Island Agriculture.*
Desc: It provides Rhode Islanders and others with general information on gardening, food and nutrition, research of our natural resources, household problems, energy and family life.

LC S **ISSN** 0364-8087
DD 630 US
RICE MARKET NEWS. (RICE MARKET NEWS.). **Added/Corp** Federal-State Market News Service. California. Bureau of Market News. United States. Agricultural Marketing Service. Livestock, Meat, Grain & Seed Division. United States. Agricultural Marketing Service. Livestock & Seed Division. (19??)-. Periodical. English. Fifty-one times per year. $70.00. USDA NFC / US Department of Agriculture, Market News Office, PO Box 391, Little Rock AR 72203. **ED** Steve Cheney. **Circ:** 500.
Desc: Rice marketing information.

LC S **ISSN** 0035-6026
DD 630 IT
CODEN RSTTAP
RIVISTA DI AGRICOLTURA SUBTROPICALE E TROPICALE. [Riv. agric. subtrop. trop.]. **Added/Corp** Florence. Instituto Agronomico per lltremare. (194?)-. Academic Scholarly Publication. Italian (English, French and Spanish). Four times a year. L100000. Istituto Agronomico per l'Oltremare, Via A Cocchi 4, 50131 Florence Italy. **Tel** 011 39 55 573201, FAX 011 39 55 580314, telex 574549 IAO I. **(Subscription address:** Rivista de Agricoltura Subtropicale, C SO Brescia 75, 10152 Turin Italy. **Tel** 011 39 11 2480870.**) ED** A. Bramdolimi. **Bk Rev. Circ:** 1,000. Documents available from CASDDS. ***Continues** Agricoltura Coloniale.*
Desc: A review dealing with several aspects of tropical and subtropical agriculture: cultures, soil, livestock, development economics, crop protection, forestry, etc.
Ind/Abst AGRICOLA; Agric. Eng. Abstr. (1991-); Anim. Breed. Abstr.; Chem. Abstr.; Crop Physiol. Abstr.; EMBASE; Field Crop Abstr.; Grass. Forage Abstr.; Hortic. Abstr.; Int. Dev. Abstr. (?-?); Irr. Drain. Abstr.; Nutr. Abstr. Rev., Ser. B, Live Feeds and Feed.; Nutr. Abstr. Rev., Ser. A, Hum. Exp.; Life Sci. Collect.; Plant Breed. Abstr.; Plant Genet. Resour. Abstr.; Plant Grow. Reg. Abstr.; Postharvest News Inf.; Potato Abstr.; Rev. Agric. Entomol.; Rev. Plant Pathol.; Rural Dev. Abstr.; Seed Abstr.; Soils Fert.; Sorghum Mill. Abstr.; World Agric. Econ. Rural Sociol. Abstr.

LC S **ISSN** 0035-6034
DD 630 IT
RIVISTA DI AGRONOMIA. Added/Corp Societa Italiana di Agronomia. (Mar. 1967)-. Academic Scholarly Publication. Italian. Four times a year. L47010. Edagricole, PO Box 2157, 40100 Bologna Italy. **Tel** 011 39 51 492211 Ext. 22, FAX 011 39 51 493660, telex 510336 EDAGRI. Index available in last issue of volume--attached. Documents available from CASDDS.
Ind/Abst Chem. Abstr.; Crop Physiol. Abstr.; Field Crop Abstr.; Grass. Forage Abstr.; Hortic. Abstr.; Irr. Drain. Abstr.; Maize Abstr.; Plant Breed. Abstr.; Plant Grow. Reg. Abstr.; Seed Abstr.; Soils Fert.; Sorghum Mill. Abstr.; Soyabean Abstr.; Weed Abstr.; Wheat Barley Trit. Abstr.

LC S **ISSN** 0035-6190
DD 630 IT
RIVISTA DI ECONOMIA AGRARIA. [Riv. econ. agrar.]. **Added/Corp** Istituto Nazionale di Economia Agraria. Vol. 1 (May 1946)-. Periodical. Italian. Four times a year. L81750. Societa Editrice il Mulino, Strada Maggiore 37, 40125 Bologna Italy. **Tel** 011 39 51 256011, FAX 011 39 51 256034. cum. index.
Ind/Abst Dairy Sci. Abstr.; For. Prod. Abstr. (1991-); Int. Labour Doc.; PAIS Int. Print; Life Sci. Collect.; Pig News Inf.; Poult. Abstr.; Wheat Barley Trit. Abstr.; World Agric. Econ. Rural Sociol. Abstr.

LC S **ISSN** 0034-916X
DD 630 IT
RIVISTA DI INGEGNERIA AGRARIA.
Added/Corp Associazione Italiana de Genio Rurale. Utenti Motori Agricoli. Vol. 1 (Mar 1970)-. Periodical. Italian (summaries and/or abstracts in English, French and German). Four times a year. L51100. Edagricole, PO Box 2157, 40100 Bologna Italy. **Tel** 011 39 51 492211 Ext. 22, FAX 011 39 51 493660, telex 510336 EDAGRI.
Ind/Abst AgBiotech News Inf.; Agric. Eng. Abstr. (1991-); Dairy Sci. Abstr.; Food Sci. Technol. Abstr.; For. Prod. Abstr. (1991-); For. Abstr.; Hortic. Abstr.; Irr. Drain. Abstr.; Maize Abstr.; Nutr. Abstr. Rev., Ser. A, Hum. Exp.; Plant Breed. Abstr.; Postharvest News Inf.; Rev. Agric. Entomol.; Rice Abstr.; Seed Abstr.; Soils Fert.; Soyabean Abstr.; World Agric. Econ. Rural Sociol. Abstr.

LC S **ISSN** 0035-645X
DD 630 IT
RIVISTA DI POLITICA AGRARIA. [Riv. polit. agrar.]. (1954)-. Periodical. Italian. Six times a year. L51100. Edagricole, PO Box 2157, 40100 Bologna Italy. **Tel** 011 39 51 492211 Ext. 22, FAX 011 39 51 493660, telex 510336 EDAGRI.
Ind/Abst AGRICOLA.

LC S **ISSN** 0393-4810
DD 630 IT
UDC 63
RIVISTA DI POLITICA AGRARIA. RASSEGNA DELLA AGRICOLTURA ITALIANA. [Riv. polit. agrar., Rass. agric. ital.]. (1983)-. Periodical. Italian. Four times a year. L80000. Edagricole, PO Box 2157, 40100 Bologna Italy. **Tel** 011 39 51 492211 Ext. 22, FAX 011 39 51 493660, telex 510336 EDAGRI. ***Formed by the union of** Rivista di Politica Agraria, 0035-645X **and** Rassegna dell'Agricoltura Italiana, 0393-4829.*
Ind/Abst Pig News Inf.; World Agric. Econ. Rural Sociol. Abstr.

LC S **ISSN** 0557-1359
DD 630 IT
RIVISTA DI STORIA DELL'AGRICOLTURA. (RIVISTA DI STORIA DELL'AGRICOLTURA.). [Riv. stor. agric.]. **Added/Corp** Accademia Economico-Agraria dei Georgofili (Florence, Italy) Istituto di Tecnica e Propaganda Agraria (Rome, Italy) Centro Studi e Ricerche per la Museologia Agraria (Sant'Angelo Lodigiano, Italy). Vol. 1 (Oct./Dec. 1961)-. Periodical. Italian (summaries and/or abstracts in English, French and German). Four times a year. L20440. Rivista Storia Agricoltura, Accademia Economico-Agraria dei Georgofili, Loggia Uffizzi, 50122 Firenze Italy. **Tel** 011 39 55 213360.
Ind/Abst AGRICOLA.

LC S
DD 630 PL
ROBOTNIK ROLNY. (19??)-. Periodical. Polish. One time a week. **(Subscription address:** Ars Polona-Ruch, PO Box 1001, Krakowskie Przedmiescie 7, 00-068 Warsaw Poland. **Tel** 011 48 22 261201.**)**

LC S **ISSN** 0035-7650
DD 630 US
ROCKY MOUNTAIN UNION FARMER.
Added/Corp Farmers Educational and Cooperative Union of America. Rocky Mountain Division. (1912)-. Trade Publication. English. Six times a year. $7.00. Rocky Mountain Farmers Union, 10800 East Bethany Drive, Aurora CO 80014-2632. **Tel** (303)752-5800, FAX (303)752-5810. **ED** Melissa Elliott. **Bk Rev. Circ:** 8,600 (ctrl).
Desc: Co-operative, political and educational information for family farmers and ranchers in in Colorado, Wyoming and New Mexico.

LC HD1995.7 .A53
DD 338.1 PL
•ROCZNIK STATYSTYCZNY ROLNICTWA.
Added/Corp Poland. Gowny Urzad Statystyczny. (1993)-. Polish (table of contents in English). Zaklad Wydawnictw Statystycznych, Al. Niepodleglosci 208, 00-925 Warsaw Poland. **Tel** 011 48 22 250345, telex 814581 A GUS PL. ***Continues** Rolnictwo i Gospodarka Zywnosciowa.*

LC S **ISSN** 0080-3650
DD 630 PL
CODEN RNRAAP
ROCZNIKI NAUK ROLNICZYCH. SERIA A. PRODUKCJA ROSLINNA. Added/Corp Polska Akademia Nauk. Komitet Uprawy i Hodowli Roslin. **VFOAT** Annaly Selskokhoziaistvennykh Nauk; Polish Agricultural Annual. (1953)-. Monographic series. Polish. Irregular. Price varies per volume. Panstwowe Wydawnictwo Naukowe / PWN, (Polish Scientific Publishers PWN Ltd.), Ul. Miodowa 10, PO Box 391, 00-251 Warsaw Poland. **Tel** 011 48 22 312738, FAX 011 48 22 267163. **Circ:** 750. ***Supersedes in part** Roczniki Nauk Rolniczych.*
Ind/Abst Field Crop Abstr.; Hortic. Abstr.; Soils Fert.; Wheat Barley Trit. Abstr.

LC S13 .R76
DD 630.5 PL
ROLNICTWO. (1972)-. Periodical. Polish (summaries and/or abstracts in English, German and Russian). ***Continues** Wyzsza Szkoa Rolnicza W Szczecinie. Rolnictwo.*
Ind/Abst Field Crop Abstr.

LC SF521
DD 638.1 RM
ROMANIA APICOLA. Added/Corp Asociatia Crescatorilor de Albine din Romania. (19??)-. Periodical. Romanian (table of contents in English, French, German and Russian). Twelve times a year. DM169.00. Beekeepers' Association / Romania, Str. I, Fucik 17, 70231 Bucharest Romania. **Tel** 137877. **(Subscription address:** Kubon & Sagner, ABT Zeitschriftenimport, D 80328 Munich Germany. **Tel** 011 49 89 54218130.**) ED** Elisei Tarta. **Circ:** 25,000. ***Continues** Apicultura in Romania, 0378-2425.*
Desc: Provides information on bees and bee culture.

LC HD1401
DD 338.1 AT
RONALD ANDERSON'S PRIMARY INDUSTRY NEWSLETTER. Main/Corp Ronald Anderson and Associates. **VFOAT** Primary Industry Newsletter. No. 563 (June 15, 1977)-. Newsletter. English. Forty-eight times a year. 242.54Aus$. Australian Press Services, PO Box E160, Queen Victoria Terrace, ACT 2600 Australia. **Tel** 011 61 6 2731600. **ED** Kenneth Randall.
Desc: Comprehensive coverage of relevant information concerning all primary industry happenings.

LC S **ISSN** 0234-1727
DD 630 RU
ROSSIIA MOLODAIA. Added/Corp Gosagroprom Nechernozemnoi Zony RSFSR. (1990)-. Periodical. Russian. Twelve times a year. $79.95. **(Subscription address:** East View Publications Inc., 3020 Harbor Lane North, Suite 110, Minneapolis MN 55447. **Tel** (800)477-1005, (612)550-0961, FAX (612)559-2931.**) *Continues** Nechernozeme, 0207-639X.*

LC S **ISSN** 0138-3299
DD 630 GW
ROSTOCKER AGRARWISSENSCHAFTLICHE BEITRAEGE. Monographic series. German. Price varies per volume. Ministerium fur Verkehrswesen, Redaktion Tizl, 1189 Berlin Schonefeld Germany. **Tel** 6722263.

LC S **ISSN** 0298-119X
DD 630 FR
ROUSSILLON AGRICOLE. [Roussillon agric.]. **Added/Corp** Chambre d'Agriculture du Roussillon. (1985)-. Bulletin. French. Four times a year. 400.00F France; 450.00F other. Chambre Agriculture Pyrenees, 19 Avenue de Grande Bretagne, 66025 Perpignan Cedex France. **Tel** 011 33 68 348021. **Circ:** 400 (ctrl). ***Continues** Bulletin Technique (Chambre d'Agriculture du Rousillon).*

LC S **ISSN** 0239-6467
DD 630 PL
CODEN RZARB8
ROZPRAWY - AKADEMIA ROLNICZA W SZCZECINIE. Main/Corp Akademia Rolnicza w Szczecinie. No. 32 (1973)-. Monographic series. Polish (summaries and/or abstracts in English and Russian). Irregular. Price varies per volume. Akademia Rolnicza w Szczecinie / Agricultural University in Szczecin, Dzial Wydawnictwo, Ul. Doktora Judyma 22, 71-460 Szczecin Poland. **Tel** 011 48 91 541639, FAX 011 48 91 541642. ***Continues** Rozprawy - Wyzsza Szkola Rolnicza w Szczecinie, 0585-265X.*
Ind/Abst Agric. Eng. Abstr.; Soils Fert.; Wheat Barley Trit. Abstr.

LC S
DD 630 UK
TITLE CHANGE
RRA NOTES. Added/Corp International Institute for Environment and Development. Sustainable Agriculture Programme. **VAT** Rapid Rural Appraisal Notes. (1988)-(1995). Periodical. English. Human Settlements Programme, IIED, 3 Endsleigh Street, London WC1H 0DD United Kingdom. **Tel** 011 44 171 3882117, FAX 011 44 171 3882826, telex 261681. ***Continued by** PLA Notes.*

LC S **ISSN** 0927-0655
DD 630 NE
UDC 636
RSP-BULLETIN LELYSTAD. (RSP-BULLETIN.). [RSP-bull. Lelystad]. **VFOAT** Rundvee-, Schapen- en Paardenhouderij-Bulletin (Lelystad). (1991)-. Bulletin. Dutch. Six times a year. $40.73. IKC-Afdeling RSP, Runderweg 2, 8219 PK Lelystad Netherlands. **Tel** 011 31 3200 93311, FAX 011 31 3200 26733.

LC S
DD 630 EC
RUMIPAMBA. Vol. 1, No. 1-. Periodical. Spanish. Two times a year. Universidad Central Facultad de Ciencias Agricolas Biblioteca, Apartado A 25-20, Quito Ecuador.

LC HC501 .R8 **ISSN** 0085-5839
DD 301.3/5/0967 US
TITLE CHANGE
RURAL AFRICANA. **See** Business and Economics-Economic History, Conditions.

LC S **ISSN** 1031-3079
DD 630.994 AT
RURAL BUSINESS MAGAZINE. [Rural bus. mag.]. (1988)-. Periodical. English. Twelve times a year. 39.46Aus$. Richard Milne Pty Ltd., PO Box 113, Pyrmont NSW 2009 Australia. **Tel** 011 61 2 8197322, FAX 011 61 2 8197650. **ED** Rex Holyoake. **Bk Rev**. **Ad Acc**. **Circ:** 4,000 (ctrl). ***Continues*** *Rural Merchant Magazine, 0729-5588.*
Desc: Trade publication for rural resellers.

LC HN90.C6 R87 **ISSN** 1063-5866
DD 630 US
RURAL CONDITIONS AND TRENDS. [Rural cond. trends]. **Added/Corp** United States. Dept. of Agriculture. Economic Research Service. Vol. 1, No. 1 (Spring 1990)-. Periodical. English. Four times a year. $13.00. U.S. Department of Agriculture, ERS-NASS, 341 Victory Drive, Herndon VA 22070. **Tel** (800)999-6779, (703)834-0125. Documents available from Documents on Demand.
Ind/Abst Am. Stat. Index.

LC JS1721.S3 R85 **ISSN** 0036-0007
DD 352.071 CN
RURAL COUNCILLOR, THE. **Added/Corp** Saskatchewan Association of Rural Municipalities. Rural Municipal Secretary-Treasurers' Association of Saskatchewan. Vol. 1 (Mar. 1966)-. Periodical. English. Ten times a year. 12.81Can$. Saskatchewan Association of Rural Municipalities, 2075 Hamilton Street, Regina Saskatchewan S4P 2E1 Canada. **ED** Patricia Smith; Telephone: (306)757-3577. **Ad Acc**. **Circ:** 3,250 (ctrl).
Desc: Monthly account of rural Saskatchewan issues, concerns, legislative and member information.

LC HN90.C6 R767 **ISSN** 0271-2172
DD 307.7/2/0973 US
RURAL DEVELOPMENT PERSPECTIVES. (RURAL DEVELOPMENT PERSPECTIVES : RDP.). [Rural dev. perspect.]. **Added/Corp** United States. Dept. of Agriculture. Economic Research Service. **VFOAT** RDP. Vol. 1, Issue 1 (Oct. 1984)-. Government Publication. English. Every 3 years. $14.00. Superintendent of Documents, US Government Printing Office, Washington DC 20402. **Tel** (202)275-3328, FAX (202)786-2377. Documents available from Documents on Demand. ***Continues*** *Rural Development Perspectives, 0271-2172.*
Desc: Covers factors influencing rural development, and persistent and emerging problems.
Ind/Abst AGRICOLA [Full Cov.]; Am. Stat. Index; Curr. Index J. Educ.; PAIS Int. Print.

LC HB **ISSN** 0886-7585
DD 330 US
RURAL DEVELOPMENT RESEARCH REPORT. (RURAL DEVELOPMENT RESEARCH REPORT.). [Rural dev. res. rep.]. No. 1-. Monographic series. English. Price varies per volume. US Department of Agriculture, 14th Street and Independence Avenue SW, Washington DC 20250. **Tel** (202)720-5457.
Ind/Abst AGRICOLA; World Agric. Econ. Rural Sociol. Abstr.

LC HD2196.5 .A45
DD 338.1/0995/3 PP
RURAL INDUSTRIES (KONEDOBU, PAPUA NEW GUINEA). (RURAL INDUSTRIES.). English. One time a year. k3.00 Papua New Guinea; k3.50 (surface mail), k5.00 (airmail) other. National Statistical Office / New Guinea, PO Wards Strip NCO, Papua New Guinea. **Tel** 011 675 27182 271172, FAX 011 657 255057, telex FINANCE NE 22312. ***Continues in part*** *Production Bulletin (Konedobu, Papua New Guinea).*

LC SB **ISSN** 0743-9962
DD 630 US
RURAL LIVING (LANSING, MICH.). (RURAL LIVING / MICHIGAN FARM BUREAU.). **Added/Corp** Michigan Farm Bureau. Vol. 11, No. 1 (Winter 1992)-. Newspaper. English. Four times a year. Michigan Farm Bureau, PO Box 30690, Lansing MI 48909. **Tel** (517)323-7000, FAX (517)323-6793. **ED** Dennis Rudat. **Circ:** 46,640. ***Continues*** *Rural Living (Lansing, Mich. : 1981), 0743-9962.*

LC S **ISSN** 0199-6401
DD 630 US
RURAL MONTANA. **Added/Corp** Montana Associated Utilities, Inc. Montana Electric Cooperative Association. Vol. 27, No. 6 (Feb. 1980)-. Periodical. English. Twelve times a year. Free. Rural Montana, PO Box 1641, Great Falls MT 59403. **Tel** (406)761-8333. **ED** Mack McConnell. **Ad Acc**. **Circ:** 68,000 (ctrl). ***Continues*** *Montana Rural Electric News, 0047-7974.*
Desc: Statewide publication for consumers, farmers, and ranchers, served by rural electric and rural telephone cooperatives and systems.

LC S
DD 630 US
RURAL NEW ENGLAND MAGAZINE. (19??)-. English. Twelve times a year. $18.00. Rural New England Magazine, Upper Street, Buckland MA 01338. **Tel** (413)586-6475. **ED** Robert Kalderbach. **Bk Rev**, (Qty: 20). **Ad Acc**, **Adv Mgr:** Robert Kalderbach. **Circ:** 4,000.
Desc: Covers New England small town life. Reviews country real estate for sale and small farming.

LC S381 .R87 **ISSN** 1034-6074
DD 630/.5 AT
CODEN RUREEM
RURAL RESEARCH. (RURAL RESEARCH : A CSIRO QUARTERLY.). [Rural res.]. **Added/Corp** Commonwealth Scientific and Industrial Research Organization (Australia). (Dec. 1972)-. Periodical. English. Four times a year. 18.09Aus$. CSIRO Publications, PO Box 89, 314 Albert Street, East Melborne Victoria 3002 Australia. **Tel** 011 61 3 4187333, 4187217, FAX 011 61 3 4190459, telex AA 30236. ***Continues*** *Rural Research in C.S.I.R.O., 0036-0090.*
Ind/Abst AESIS Q.; AgBiotech News Inf.; AGRICOLA [Full Cov.]; Anim. Breed. Abstr.; BioBusiness (1989-); Biocont. News Inf. (19??-19??); EP Collect.; Field Crop Abstr.; Helminthol. Abstr.; Homework Help.; Hortic. Abstr.; Index Vet.; MasterFile FullTEXT 1000; MasterFile FullTEXT 350; MasterFile FullTEXT 650; MasterFile FullTEXT (Jan. 1994-); Nematol. Abstr.; Pig News Inf.; Plant Breed. Abstr.; Rev. Agric. Entomol.; Rev. Med. Vet. Entomol.; Rev. Med. Vet. Mycology; Rev. Plant Pathol.; Soils Fert.; Telebase; Weed Abstr.; Wheat Barley Trit. Abstr.; World Mag. Bank.

LC HD **ISSN** 0818-1713
DD 338.4763609941 AT
RURAL UPDATE. [Rural update]. (1986)-. Periodical. English. Twenty-six times a year. Pastoralist and Graziers Association, 789 Wellington Street, Perth Western Australia 6000 Australia.

LC S **ISSN** 0700-5385
DD 630/.9713/2 CN
RURAL VOICE (BLYTH). (THE RURAL VOICE.). [Rural voice]. Vol. 1 (June 1975)-. Periodical. English. Twelve times a year. 12.01Can$. The Rural Voice, PO Box 429, 136 Queen Street, Blyth Ontario N0M 1H0 Canada. **Tel** (519)523-4311, FAX (519)523-9140. **ED** Keith Roulston. **Bk Rev**, (Qty: 5-6). **Ad Acc**, **Adv Mgr:** Gerry Fortune. **Circ:** 15,000.
Desc: Provides coverage of the agricultural scene with in-depth articles, personality profiles and farm issues. Regular sections feature rural heritage, news, product reports, management ideas and marketing information. Lively columns are presented by writers who either live on a farm or have an agricultural background.

LC S **ISSN** 1068-3674
DD 630 US
CCC
•**RUSSIAN AGRICULTURAL SCIENCES.** (1993)-. Periodical. English (translations available in Russian). Twelve times a year. $975.00. Allerton Press Inc., 150 Fifth Avenue, New York NY 10011. **Tel** (212)924-3950, FAX (212)463-9684, telex 427441 ALPRES. ***Continues*** *Soviet Agricultural Sciences, 0735-2700.*

LC S **ISSN** 0370-4246
DD 630 JA
CODEN RDNGBM
RYUKYU DAIGAKU NOGAKUBU GAKUJUTSU HOKOKU. [Ryukyu Daigaku Nogakubu gakujutsu hokoku]. **Main/Corp** Ryukyu Daigaku. Nogakubu. **Added/Corp** Ryukyu Daigaku. Nogakubu. Science Bulletin. **VFOAT** Science Bulletin of the College of Agriculture, University of the Ryukyus. (1967)-. Academic Scholarly Publication. Japanese (English). One time a year. Ryukyu Daigaku Rigakubu, 59-banchi Aza Senbaru, Nishihara-cho, Okinawa-ken Japan. Documents available from CASDDS. ***Continues*** *Ryukyu Daigaku. Nokasei Kogakubu. Ryukyu Daigaku Nokasei Kogakubu Gakujutsu Hokoku.*
Ind/Abst AGRICOLA; Agrofor. Abstr.; Chem. Abstr.; Crop Physiol. Abstr.; For. Prod. Abstr. (1991-); For. Abstr.; Index Vet.; Rev. Plant Pathol.; Soils Fert.

LC S **ISSN** 1052-6781
DD 630 US
NLM W1; SA104K
SAAS BULLETIN, BIOCHEMISTRY AND BIOTECHNOLOGY. **See** Biology-Bioengineering.

LC S **ISSN** 0953-4148
DD 630 UK
SAC ECONOMIC REPORT. [SAC econ. rep.]. **VFOAT** Scottish Agricultural Colleges Economic Report. (1988)-. Monographic series. English. Irregular.
Ind/Abst Potato Abstr.; World Agric. Econ. Rural Sociol. Abstr.

LC S305 .S23
DD 638.09519 KO
SAE MAUL YONGU. **VFOAT** Sae Maul Research. Periodical. Korean (summaries and/or abstracts in English). Choson Taehakkyo Sae Maul Yonguso, 17 Pullo-dong, Tong-ku Kwangju-si Korea.

LC S **ISSN** 0581-2801
DD 630 JA
CODEN SDNID7
SAGA DAIGAKU NOGAKUBU IHO. [Saga Daigaku Nogakubu iho]. **Added/Corp** Saga Daigaku. Nogakubu. **VFOAT** Bulletin of the Faculty of Agriculture, Saga University. No. 51, Nov. (1981)-. Academic Scholarly Publication. Japanese (summaries and/or abstracts in English). Two times a year. Saga Daigaku Nogakubu, (Faculty of Agriculture Saga University), 1 Honjomachi, Sagashi Sagaken 840, Japan. Documents available from CASDDS. ***Continues*** *Saga Daigaku Nogaku Iho, 0581-2801.*
Ind/Abst Agric. Eng. Abstr.; Biocont. News Inf.; Chem. Abstr.; Plant Breed. Abstr.; Postharvest News Inf.; Rev. Plant Pathol.; Soils Fert.

LC S **ISSN** 0331-7285
DD 630 NR
SAMARU: JOURNAL OF AGRICULTURE RESEARCH. **Added/Corp** Ahmadu Bello University. Institute for Agricultural Research. Ahmadu Bello University. Faculty of Agriculture. Vol. 1, No. 1 (Apr. 1981)-. Periodical. English.
Ind/Abst Cot. Trop. Fibr. Abstr. Bibliogr.; Hortic. Abstr.; Irr. Drain. Abstr.; Soils Fert.; Sorghum Mill. Abstr.; Weed Abstr.

LC K23 .A517 **ISSN** 1055-422X
DD 343.73/076 347.30376 US
SAN JOAQUIN AGRICULTURAL LAW REVIEW. **See** Law.

LC AP95.J2 S26
JA
SANDE MAINICHI. **VFOAT** Sunday Mainichi. (1922)-. Periodical. Japanese. One time a week. $412.20. **(Subscription address:** Kinokuniya Company Ltd., 38-1 Sakuragaoka 5, chome Setagaya-ku, Tokyo 156 Japan. **Tel** FAX 011 03 3439 0136.**)**

LC HD2092 .S28
DD 630 JA
SANSON SHINKO KONSARUTANTO IKENSHO SORAN. **Added/Corp** Sanson Shinko Chosakai. (19??)-. Periodical. Japanese. Sanson Shinko Chosakai, c/o Zenkoku Chosen Kaikan, 4-kai 11-35 Nagatacho 1 Chiyoda-ku, Tokyo Japan.

LC S13 .S35
DD 630 RU
CODEN SNRIDT
SARATOVSKII SELSKOKHOZIAISTVENNYI INSTITUT. TRUDY. (SBORNIK NAUCHNYKH RABOT - SARATOVSKII SELSKOKHOZIAISTVENNYI INSTITUT.). [Sb. nauchn. rab. - Sarat. s-h. inst.]. **Main/Corp** Saratovskii Selskokhoziaistvennyi Institut. (1971)-. Academic Scholarly Publication. Russian. Price varies per volume. Pl Revoliutsii 1, Saratov Russia. Documents available from CASDDS. ***Continues*** *Trudy / Saratovskii Selskokhoziaistvennyi Institut.*
Ind/Abst Chem. Abstr.

LC S322.P27 S27 **ISSN** 1010-6103
DD 630/.9549/14 PK
CODEN SJAGED
SARHAD JOURNAL OF AGRICULTURE. [Sarhad j. agric.]. **Added/Corp** N.W.F.P. Agricultural University. Vol. 1, No. 1 (July 1985)-. Periodical. English. Two times a year. Rs40.00 per issue. Documents available from BIOSIS Document Express.
Ind/Abst Agrofor. Abstr. (1991-); Anim. Breed. Abstr.; Biodeter. Abstr. (1991-); Biol. Abstr. (1987-); Curr. Cit.; Dairy Sci. Abstr.; Field Crop Abstr.; Food Sci. Technol. Abstr.; For. Prod. Abstr. (1991-); Grass. Forage Abstr.; Hortic. Abstr.; Index Vet.; Irr. Drain. Abstr.; Maize Abstr.; Nutr. Abstr. Rev., Ser. B, Live Feeds and Feed.; Nutr. Abstr. Rev., Ser. A, Hum. Exp.; Plant Breed. Abstr.; Plant Genet. Resour. Abstr.; Postharvest News Inf.; Potato Abstr.; Poult. Abstr.; Protozoolog. Abstr.; Rev. Agric. Entomol.; Rev. Plant Pathol.; Rice Abstr.; Seed Abstr.; Soils Fert.; Sorghum Mill. Abstr.; Soyabean Abstr.; Sug. Indus. Abstr.; Vet. Bull.; Weed Abstr.; Wheat Barley Trit. Abstr.; World Agric. Econ. Rural Sociol. Abstr.

LC S
DD 630 CN
SASKATCHEWAN PULSE CROP DEVELOPMENT BOARD NEWSLETTER. Newsletter. English. Six times a year (Jan., Mar., May, July, Sept., Nov.). $10.00. Saskatchewan Pulse Crop Development Board, PO Box 516, Regina SASK S4P 3A2 Canada. **Tel** (306)781-7475, FAX (306)525-4173. **ED** Donald R. Jaques. **Circ:** 6,500 (ctrl).

Agriculture

LC S
DD 630
UDC 631
ISSN 0350-2953
YU

SAVREMENA POLJOPRIVREDNA TEHNIKA. [Savrem. poljopr. teh.]. **VFOAT** Advanced Agricultural Engineering. (1975)-. Periodical. Serbo-Croatian (Roman) (summaries and/or abstracts in English). Four times a year. Vojvodjansko Drustvo za Poljoprivrednu Tehniku, Trg Dositeja Obradovica 8, 21000 Novi Sad Yugoslavia. **ED** Radovan Popov.
Ind/Abst Agric. Eng. Abstr.; Hortic. Abstr.; Postharvest News Inf.

LC AP95.A6 S257
DD 016.63
KU

SAWT AL-KHALIJ. (1962)-. Periodical. Arabic. One time a week. Sawt al-Khalij, SP 659, Al-Safat Kuwait.

LC S
DD 630
XR
CODEN SVSSEJ

SBORNIK VYSOKE SKOLY ZEMEDELSKE V PRAZE, FAKULTA AGRONOMICKA. RADA A-C, ROSTLINNA VYROBA-ZEMEDELSKE MELIORACE A STAVBY. Added/Corp Vysoka Skola Zemedelska v Praze. Agronomicka Fakulta v Ceskych Budejovicich. **VFOAT** Rostlinna Vyroba-Zemedelske Meliorace a Stavby; Zemedelske Meliorace a Stavby; Crop Production - Agricultural Buildings and Constructions; Agricultural Buildings and Constructions; Journal, University of Agriculture Prague, Agronomy. Series A-C, P.Crop Production - Agricultural Buildings and Constructions. (1990)-. Academic Scholarly Publication. Czech (summaries and/or abstracts in English and Russian). Vysoka Skola Zemedelska, Zemedelska 1, 61300 Brno Czech Republic. **Tel** FAX 42 05 452 11128. Documents available from CASDDS. **Formed by the union of** Sbornik Vysoke Skoly Zemedelske v Praze, Fakulta Agronomicka. Rada A, Rostlinnna Vyroba **and** Sbornik Vysoke Skoly Zemedelske v Praze, Fakulta Agronomicka. Rada C, Zemedelske Meliorace, Zemedelske Stavby.
Ind/Abst Biodeter. Abstr.; Chem. Abstr.; Potato Abstr.; Seed Abstr.

LC S
DD 630
XR

SBORNIK VYSOKE SKOLY ZEMEDELSKE V PRAZE, FAKULTA AGRONOMICKA. RADA C: ZEMEDELSKE MELIORACE, ZEMEDELSKE STAVBY. Main/Corp Prague. Vysoka Skola Zemedelska. Fakulta Agronomicka. **VFOAT** Jahrbuch der Hochschule fur Landwirtschaft Prag, Agronomische Fakultat. Reihe C: Landwirtschaftliche Meliorationen, Landwirtschaftliche Bauten. (1972)-. Periodical. Czech (summaries and/or abstracts in English, German and Russian). Vysoka Skola Zemedelska, Zemedelska 1, 61300 Brno Czech Republic. **Tel** FAX 42 05 452 11128. **Continues** Prague. Vysoka Skola Zemedelska. Sbornik ... Acta.
Ind/Abst Irr. Drain. Abstr.

LC S
DD 630
AT

SCA TECHNICAL REPORT SERIES. Added/Corp Australian Agricultural Council. Standing Committee on Agriculture. **VAT** Standing Committee on Agriculture Technical Report Series. (19??)-. Monographic series. English. Price varies per volume. CSIRO Publications, PO Box 89, 314 Albert Street, East Melbourne Victoria 3002 Australia. **Tel** 011 61 3 4187333, 4187217, FAX 011 61 3 4190459, telex AA 30236.

LC SD411
DD 333.76
ISSN 0925-1413
NE

SCAN (WAGENINGEN). See Environmental Issues-Conservation and Natural Resources.

LC S
DD 630
GW

SCHRIFTENREIHE DER AGRARWISSENSCHAFTLICHEN FAKULTAT DER UNIVERSITAET KIEL. Added/Corp Universitat Kiel. Agrarwissenschaftliche Fakultat. No. 61 (1980)-. Monographic series. German. Irregular. Price varies per volume. Dekan Agrarwissenschaftlichen Fakultat, Olshausenstr. 40-60, D-24118 Kiel Germany. **Continues** Universitat Kiel. Agrarwissenschaftlicher Fachbereich Schriftenreihe des Agrarwissenschaftlichen Fachbereichs der Universitat Kiel.
Desc: Publishes papers from the faculty of the Universitat Kiel.

LC S
DD 630
AU

SCHRIFTENREIHE DER BUNDESANSTALT FUER AGRARWIRTSCHAFT. Added/Corp Bundesanstalt fur Agrarwirtschaft. **VFOAT** Schriftenreihe. (1983)-. Monographic series. German (summaries and/or abstracts in English). **Continues** Schriftenreihe des Agrarwirtschaftlichen Institutes des Bundesministeriums fur Land- und Forstwirtschaft.
Ind/Abst Agrofor. Abstr.; For. Abstr.; World Agric. Econ. Rural Sociol. Abstr.

LC S
DD 630
ISSN 0723-7847
GW

SCHRIFTENREIHE DES BUNDESMINISTERS FOR ERNAHRUNG, LANDWIRTSCHAFT UND FORSTEN. REIHE A, ANGEWANDTE WISSENSCHAFT. [Schriftenr. Bundesminist. Ernahr., Landwirtsch. Forsten, Reihe A, Angew. Wiss.]. **Added/Corp** Germany (West). Bundesministerium fur Ernahrung, Landwirtschaft und Forsten. **VFOAT** Angewandte Wissenschaft. Heft 246 (1981)-. Academic Scholarly Publication. German. Price varies per volume. Landwirtschaftsverlag GmbH, Postfach 480249, D-48079 Muenster Hiltrup Germany. **Tel** 011 49 2501 8010, FAX 011 49 2501 801204, telex 892665 LANDV D. Documents available from CASDDS. **Continues** Schriftenreihe des Bundesministers fur Ernahrung, Landwirtschaft und Forsten. Reihe A, Landwirtschaft-Angewandte Wissenschaft.
Ind/Abst Chem. Abstr.; EMBASE; Field Crop Abstr.; For. Abstr.; GeoRef; Hortic. Abstr.; Maize Abstr.; Rev. Plant Pathol.; Seed Abstr.; Vitis Vitic. Enol. Abstr.; World Agric. Econ. Rural Sociol. Abstr.

LC S
DD 630
GW

SCHRIFTENREIHE DES BUNDESMINISTERS FUER ERNAHRUNG, LANDWIRTSCHAFT UND FORSTEN. REIHE B, FLURBEREINIGUNG. Added/Corp Germany (West). Bundesministerium fuer Ernahrung, Landwirtschaft und Forsten. **VFOAT** Flurbereinigung. (1979)-. Monographic series. German. Irregular. Price varies per volume. Landwirtschaftsverlag GmbH, Postfach 480249, D-48079 Muenster Hiltrup Germany. **Tel** 011 49 2501 8010, FAX 011 49 2501 801204, telex 892665 LANDV D. **Continues** Schriftenreihe fuer Flurbereinigung, 0487-7322.
Ind/Abst World Agric. Econ. Rural Sociol. Abstr.

LC S
DD 630
ISSN 0177-6673
GW

SCHRIFTENREIHE DES FACHBEREICHS INTERNATIONALE AGRARENTWICKLUNG. (SCHRIFTENREIHE DES FACHBEREICHS.). [Schr.reihe Fachbereichs Int. Agrarentwickl.]. **Added/Corp** Technische Universitat Berlin. Fachbereich Internationale Agrarentwicklung. **VFOAT** Serial Publications on the Faculty; Schriftenreihe des Fachbereiches. No 81 (1984)-. Monographic series. English (German, English and Spanish). Price varies per volume. **Formed by the union of** Reihe: Forschung, 0177-6452 **and** Schriftenreihe des Fachbereichs Internationale Agrarentwicklung. Reihe: Organisation, 0177-6436 Reihe: Studien, 0177-6460 Schriftenreihe des Fachbereichs Internationale Agrarentwicklung. Reihe: Lehre, 0177-6444.

LC S
DD 630
ISSN 0036-6986
AU

SCHRIFTTUM DER AGRARWIRTSCHAFT, DAS. Added/Corp Austria. Bundesministerium fuer Land- und Forstwirtschaft. (1961)-. Periodical. German. Six times a year. $98.19. Bundesanstalt Agrarwirtschaft, Schweizerstrasse 36, A 1133 Vienna Austria. **Tel** 011 43 1 8773651. **ED** Hans Alfons. **Bk Rev. Circ:** 380. **Supersedes** Schrifttum der Bodenkultur.
Desc: Covers agriculture, agricultural economics, rural sociology, rural spatial planning, agricultural development, rural conservation.

LC S
DD 630
GW

SCHWEINE-ZUCHT. (19??)-. German. Twelve times a year. DM77.00 Germany; DM92.00 other. Verlag M & H Schaper GmbH & Co, Postfach 1642, D-31046 Alfeld Leine Germany. **Tel** 011 49 5181 80090, FAX 011 49 5181 800933.

LC S
DD 630
SZ

SCHWEIZER LANDTECHNIK. Vol. 34, No. 1 (1972)-. Trade Publication. German. Twelve times a year. Technique Agricole, Postfach 53, Aussersdorfstrasse 31, CH-5223 Riniken Switzerland. **Tel** 011 41 56 412022. **Continues** Traktor und die Landmaschine.

LC S
DD 630
ISSN 0036-763X
SZ
CODEN SLWFAS

SCHWEIZERISCHE LANDWIRTSCHAFTLICHE FORSCHUNG. [Schweiz. landwirtsch. forsch.]. **Added/Corp** Switzerland. Eidgenossisches Volkswirtschaftsdepartement. Abteilung fuer Landwirtschaft. **VFOAT** Recherche Agronomique en Suisse. (1962)-. Periodical. French (German and Italian; summaries and/or abstracts in English). Four times a year. $13.55. Banteli Verlag, Bern Switzerland, CH-3018 Bern Switzerland. Documents available from CASDDS.
Ind/Abst AGRICOLA; Chem. Abstr. (1962-1983); EMBASE; Nematol. Abstr.; Nutr. Abstr. Rev., Ser. A, Hum. Exp.; Soils Fert.; Weed Abstr.; Wheat Barley Trit. Abstr.

LC SB170
DD 634.99
KE

SCIENCE AND PRACTICE OF AGROFORESTRY. (1984)-. Monographic series. English. Irregular. Price varies per volume.
Ind/Abst Agrofor. Abstr.

LC S
DD 630
ISSN 0084-3156
US

SCIENCE MONOGRAPH. [Sci. monogr.]. **Main/Corp** Wyoming Agricultural Experiment Station. **Added/Corp** Wyoming Agricultural Experiment Station. (1966)-. Monographic series. English. Price varies per volume. University of Wyoming Agricultural Experiment Station, Laramie WY 82071.
Ind/Abst AGRICOLA [Select. Cov.].

LC S1 .S342
DD 630
ISSN 0738-9310
US
CEASED

SCIENCE OF FOOD AND AGRICULTURE. See Food and Food Industry.

LC S
DD 630
ISSN 0103-9016
BL

SCIENTIA AGRICOLA. (1992)-. Periodical. Portuguese (summaries and/or abstracts in English). Two times a year. $45.00. Universidade de Sao Paulo / Piracicaba, Caixa Postal 9, CEP 13400, Piracicaba SP Brazil. **Tel** 011 55 11 194 330011. **Continues** Anais da Escola Superior de Agricultura "Luiz de Queiroz".

LC S
DD 630
IT

SCIENZA E TECNICA AGRARIA. Italian. Six times a year. Assn Prov Dottori Scien Agrari, Viale Unita D Italia 24, 70125 Bari Italy. **Tel** 011 39 80 363655.

LC S
DD 630
UK

SCOTTISH BEE JOURNAL. English. Robert Skilling Frsa, 34 Rennie Street, Kilmavmock Scotland United Kingdom.

LC SF521
DD 638.1
ISSN 0370-8918
UK

SCOTTISH BEEKEEPER. [Scott. beekeep.]. **Added/Corp** Scottish Beekeepers' Association. Vol. 1 (July 1924)-. Periodical. English. Twelve times a year. £10.00. Scottish Beekeepers Association, 27 Moss Road, Ross Shire IV19 1HH United Kingdom. **Tel** 011 44 1862 892351. **ED** J Stoakley. **Bk Rev. Ad Acc. Circ:** 1,500 (ctrl).
Desc: All about beekeeping.
Ind/Abst AGRICOLA.

LC SB29.C2 O65
DD 634/.09713
ISSN 0474-1560
CN

SEASONAL FRUIT AND VEGETABLE REPORT. Main/Corp Ontario. Ministry of Agriculture and Food. Economics Branch. **VAT** Fruit and Vegetable Production in Ontario. No. 184 (May 1972)-. Periodical. English. Six times a year. Free on request. Ontario Ministry of Agriculture and Food, 801 Bay Street, Toronto Ontario M7A 2B2 Canada. **Tel** (416)326-3400. **ED** John King and Bill McGee. **Circ:** 3,000. **Continues** Ontario. Farm Economics, Co-Operatives and Statistics Branch. Seasonal Fruit and Vegetable Report, 0474-1560.

LC HD2111.P32 M47C
DD 630
IS

SEDAROT STATISTIYOT. See Agriculture-Abstracting, Bibliographies and Statistics.

LC SB113
DD 631.531
UK

SEED PATHOLOGY AND MICROBIOLOGY. Added/Corp C.A.B. International. Bureau of Crop Protection. Frpatologisk Institut for Udviklingslandene. Vol. 1 (1990)-. English. One time a year. $53.00 US. CAB International Centre, Wallingford, Oxfordshire OX10 8DE United Kingdom. **Tel** 011 44 1491 832111, FAX 011 44 1491 833508, telex 847964 COMAGG G.

LC SB114.U7 P47
DD 353.97482/333
ISSN 0740-2996
US

SEED REPORT (PENNSYLVANIA. DEPT. OF AGRICULTURE : 1980). (SEED REPORT.). 1980-. English. One time a year. Pennsylvania Department of Agriculture, 2301 North Cameron Street, Harrisburg PA 17110. **Tel** (717)772-2853, FAX (717)787-2387. **Continues** Seed Report, 0740-2996.

Agriculture

LC SB114.A1 S4   ISSN 0251-0952
DD 631.5/21/05   SZ
CODEN SSTCBK

SEED SCIENCE AND TECHNOLOGY.
[Seed sci. tech.]. **Added/Corp** International Seed Testing Association. Vol. 1 (1973)-. Periodical. English (French and German; summaries and/or abstracts in English). Three times a year. 250.00F. ISTA / International Seed Testing Association, PO Box 412, CH-8046 Zurich Switzerland. **Tel** 011 41 1 3713133, FAX 011 41 1 3713427. **Circ:** 1,200 (ctrl). available on microfilm from University Microfilms International (UMI). Documents available from The Genuine Article, BIOSIS Document Express, CASDDS.
 Desc: Original papers in all areas of science technology applied to production, sampling, testing, storing, processing and distribution of seed and international rules for testing seed.
 Ind/Abst AgBiotech News Inf.; Agric. Eng. Abstr. (1991-); Agrofor. Abstr.; BioBusiness; Biol. Abstr.; Chem. Abstr.; Cot. Trop. Fibr. Abstr. Bibliogr.; Crop Physiol. Abstr.; Curr. Aware. Biol. Sci., CABS; Curr. Cit.; Curr. Contents Agric. Biol. Environ. Sci.; Field Crop Abstr.; Maize Abstr.; Ornamental Hort.; Life Sci. Collect.; PESTDOC; Plant Breed. Abstr.; Plant Genet. Resour. Abstr.; Plant Grow. Reg. Abstr.; Postharvest News Inf.; Res. Alert [Select. Cov.]; Rice Abstr.; Seed Abstr.; Sorghum Mill. Abstr.; Soyabean Abstr.

LC SB113   ISSN 0960-2585
DD 631.531   UK
CODEN SESREX

SEED SCIENCE RESEARCH. [Seed sci. res.].
Added/Corp C.A.B. International. Vol. 1, No. 1 (Mar. 1991)-. Periodical. English. Four times a year. $270.00. CAB International Centre, Wallingford, Oxfordshire OX10 8DE United Kingdom. **Tel** 011 44 1491 832111, FAX 011 44 1491 833508, telex 847964 COMAGG G.
 Ind/Abst AgBiotech News Inf.; AGRICOLA; Crop Physiol. Abstr.; Curr. Aware. Biol. Sci., CABS; Curr. Cit.; Field Crop Abstr.; Grass. Forage Abstr.; Hortic. Abstr.; Ornamental Hort. (1991-); Plant Breed. Abstr.; Plant Genet. Resour. Abstr.; Seed Abstr.; Weed Abstr.

LC S   ISSN 0037-0789
DD 630   US

SEED TRADE NEWS. (19??)-. Trade Publication. English. Fourteen times a year (2 issues in June and Nov.). $25.00. Dean Enterprises Inc., 9995 West 69th Street, Eden Prairie MN 55344. **Tel** (612)941-5820. **ED** Frank Zaworski. **Ad Acc, Adv Mgr** James R. Laird. **Circ:** 2,923.

LC HD9225.J3 J36i
DD 338.17   JA

SEIKABUTSU NISUGATA CHOSA KEKKA. See Industry and Production.

LC HD2092 .J38b
DD 330.9   JA

SEISAN NOGYO SHOTOKU TOKEI.
Main/Corp Japan. Norinsho. Norin Keizaikyoku. Tokei Johoku. (19??)-. Japanese. In Norin Tokei Kyokai, (Association of Agriculture & Forestry Statistics), 11-14 Meguro 2 Chome, Meguroku Tokyo 153 Japan.

LC S   ISSN 0370-9841
DD 630   JA
CODEN SGIKA6

SEITO GIJUTSU KENKYUKAI SHI. (SEITO GIJUTSU KENKYUKAI SHI. PROCEEDINGS OF THE RESEARCH SOCIETY OF JAPAN SUGAR REFINERIES' TECHNOLOGISTS.). [Seito Gijutsu Kenkyukai shi]. **Main/Corp** Seito Gijutsu Kenkyukai. **Added/Corp** Seito Gijutsu Kenkyukai. Proceedings of the Research Society of Japan Sugar Refineries' Technologists. **VFOAT** Proceedings of the Research Society of Japan Sugar Refineries' Technologists. (1952)-. Academic Scholarly Publication. Japanese (summaries and/or abstracts in English). Two times a year. Seito Kogyokai Gijutsu Kenkyukai, (Research Soc. of Japan Sugar Refineries' Technologists), 5-7 Sanbancho Chiyodaku, Tokyo 102 Japan. Documents available from CASDDS.
 Ind/Abst AGRICOLA; Chem. Abstr.; Curr. Biotechnol.; Field Crop Abstr.; Food Sci. Technol. Abstr.; SEA Abstr.; Sug. Indus. Abstr.

LC S   ISSN 0037-1122
DD 630   BL
CODEN SEVAAR
SUSPENDED

SEIVA. [Seiva]. **Added/Corp** Universidade Federal de Vicosa. Universidade Rural do Estado de Minas Gerais. (1944)-Suspended. Periodical. Portuguese (summaries and/or abstracts in English). Universidade Federal de Vicosa, Academico Editoral 36 570, Vocosa Minas Gerais Brazil. **Tel** 011 55 31 8992156, FAX 011 55 31 8992108. Documents available from BIOSIS Document Express.
 Ind/Abst Biol. Abstr. (-1987); For. Prod. Abstr. (1991-); For. Abstr.; Soils Fert.

LC S   ISSN 0131-6273
DD 630   RU

SELSKIE ZORI. **Added/Corp** Soviet Union. Ministerstvo Selskogo Khoziaistva. (19??)-. Periodical. Russian. Six times a year. $99.95. **Continues** Selskokhoziaistvennoe Proizvodstvo Severnogo Kavkaza i Tscho.

LC S
DD 630   RU

SELSKII KALENDAR. **Added/Corp** Gosudarstvennoe Izdatelstvo Selskokhoziaistvennoi Literatury (Soviet Union). (19??)-. Russian. Two times a year. $49.95.

LC S   ISSN 0131-6370
DD 630   UZ

SELSKOE KHOZIAISTVO UZBEKISTANA. **Added/Corp** Uzbek S.S.R. Ministerstvo Proizvodstva i Zagotovok Selskokhoziaistvennykh Produktov. Uzbek S.S.R. Ministerstvo Selskogo Khoziaistva. Uzbekistan Kommunistik Partiiasi. Markazii Komiteti. (Jan. 1965)-. Periodical. Russian. Twelve times a year. 0.30rub single issue. Izdatelstvo Tsk Kompartii Uzbekistana, Ulitsa Pravdy Vostoka 26, Tashkent Uzbekistan. **Supersedes** Kolkhozno-Sovkhoznoe Proizvodstvo Uzbekistana.
 Ind/Abst Seed Abstr.

LC S   ISSN 0037-1688
DD 630   RU

SELSKOKHOZIAISTVENNAIA LITERATURA SSSR. **Added/Corp** Moscow. Tsentralnaia Nauchnaia Selskokhoziaistvennaia Biblioteka. (1???)-. Periodical. Russian. Twelve times a year. $79.95. **(Subscription address:** East View Publications Inc., 3020 Harbor Lane North, Suite 110, Minneapolis MN 55447. **Tel** (800)477-1005, (612)550-0961, FAX (612)559-2931.) Index available.

LC S
DD 630   BU

•**SELSKOSTOPANSKA NAUKA I PROIZVODSTVO = AGRICULTURAL SCIENCE AND PRODUCTION.** **Added/Corp** Selskostopanska Akademiia (Bulgaria) Bulgaria. Ministerstvo na Zemedelieto. **VFOAT** Agricultural Science and Production. (1994)-. Periodical. Bulgarian (summaries and/or abstracts in English and Russian; table of contents in English and Russian). Six times a year. **(Subscription address:** Kubon & Sagner, ABT Zeitschriftenimport, D 80328 Munich Germany. **Tel** 011 49 89 54218130.) **Continues** Selskostopanska Nauka, 0002-1636.

LC S   ISSN 0002-1636
DD 630   BU
CODEN SENAAL
TITLE CHANGE

SELSKOSTOPANSKA NAUKA : ORGAN NA PREZIDIUMA NA ASN. **Added/Corp** Akademiia Selskostopanskite Nauki. Selskostopanska Akademiia Georgi Dimitrov. Bulgaria. Ministerstvo na Zemedelieto i Khranitelnata Promishlenost. Natsionalen Agrarno-Promishlen Suiuz (Bulgaria) Selskostopanska Akademiia (Bulgaria). **VFOAT** Agricultural Science. (1962)-(1993). Academic Scholarly Publication. Bulgarian (summaries and/or abstracts in English and Russian; table of contents in English and Russian). **(Subscription address:** Kubon & Sagner, ABT Zeitschriftenimport, D 80328 Munich Germany. **Tel** 011 49 89 54218130.) Documents available from CASDDS. **Continued by** Selskostopanska Nauka i Proizvodstvo.
 Ind/Abst Agric. Eng. Abstr. (1991-); Anim. Breed. Abstr.; Biocont. News Inf.; Chem. Abstr. (1962-1983); Cot. Trop. Fibr. Abstr. Bibliogr.; Dairy Sci. Abstr.; Hortic. Abstr.; Index Vet.; Irr. Drain. Abstr.; Maize Abstr.; Plant Breed. Abstr.; Potato Abstr.; Poult. Abstr.; Rev. Agric. Entomol.; Rev. Plant Pathol.; Seed Abstr.; Soils Fert.; Vet. Bull.; Wheat Barley Trit. Abstr.; World Agric. Econ. Rural Sociol. Abstr.

LC S   ISSN 0395-8930
DD 630   FR
UDC 631.52

SEMENCES ET PROGRES. [Semences prog.]. (1974)-. Periodical. French. Four times a year. $72.18. Semences et Progres, 44 rue du Louvre, 75001 Paris France. **Tel** 011 33 1 42363960. Index available. **Bk Rev. Ad Acc.** **Circ:** 11,500.

LC S
DD 630   US

SENECA COUNTY FARM & HOME NEWS. **Added/Corp** Seneca County Extension Service. Agricultural Dept. **VFOAT** Seneca County Farm and Home News. (195?)-. Periodical. English. Twelve times a year. Seneca County Extension Service, East William and Mill Streets, Waterloo NY 13165. **Continues** Seneca County Farm Bureau News (1954).

LC QH301 .S772A   ISSN 0377-5232
DD 547/.05   KO
CODEN SNBAAO

SEOUL NATIONAL UNIVERSITY FACULTY PAPERS : BIOLOGY AND AGRICULTURE SERIES. See Biology.

LC S
DD 630   PL

SERIA HISTORYCZNA. **Main/Corp** Akademia Rolnicza w Warszawie. (1973)-. Polish (summaries and/or abstracts in Russian and French). Irregular. Akademia Rolnicza w Warszawie, Ul. Rakowiecka 41, Warsaw Poland. **Tel** telex 81 47 90 SGGW-AR PL. **Continues** Seria Historyczna.

LC S
DD 630   CR

SERIE BIBLIOTECOLOGIA Y DOCUMENTACION. **Added/Corp** Biblioteca Conmemorativa Orton. No. 2 (1980)-. Monographic series. Spanish. **Continues** Serie Bibliotecologica (Biblioteca Conmemorativa Orton).
 Ind/Abst For. Abstr.

LC S
DD 630   CL

SERIE DESARROLLO RURAL. BOLETIN. **Added/Corp** Universidad de Chile. Facultad de Agronomia. Departameto de Desarrollo Rural. (19??)-. Periodical. Spanish. Universidad de Chile / Agronomia, Facultad de Agronomia, Casilla 1004, Santiago Chile.
 Ind/Abst Soc. Plann. Policy Dev. Abstr.

LC S   ISSN 0325-2493
DD 630   AG

SERIE DIDACTICA - FACULTAD DE AGRONOMIA Y ZOOTECNIA. UNIVERSIDAD NACIONAL TUCUMAN. (SERIE DIDACTICA / UNIVERSIDAD NACIONAL DE TUCUMAN, FACULTAD DE AGRONOMIA Y ZOOTECNIA.). [Ser. didact. - Fac. agron. zootec., Univ. Nac. Tucuman]. **Added/Corp** Universidad Nacional de Tucuman. Facultad de Agronomia y Zootecnia. (1967)-. Monographic series. Spanish. Irregular. Price varies per volume. Universidad Nacional de Tucuman / Facultad de Agronomia y Zootecnia, Buenos Aires Argentina.
 Ind/Abst AGRICOLA; Life Sci. Collect.

LC S
DD 630   AG

SERIE ESTADISTICA (MENDOZA) (ARGENTINA : PROVINCE). (DIRECCION AGROPECUARIA). See Agriculture-Abstracting, Bibliographies and Statistics.

LC S
DD 630   FR

SERIE ETUDES ET RECHERCHES / MINISTERE DE L'AGRICULTURE, INSTITUT NATIONAL DE LA RECHERCHE AGRONOMIQUE.
Added/Corp Institut National de la Recherche Agronomique (France). Station d'Economie et Sociologie Rurales (Montpellier). (19??)-. Monographic series. French. Irregular. Price varies per volume.
 Ind/Abst AGRICOLA.

LC S   ISSN 0588-3970
DD 630   CK

SERIE INSTRUMENTOS DE POLITICA AGRARIA. **Main/Corp** Colombia. Ministerio de Agricultura. No. 1- 1968-. Periodical. Spanish. PO Box 2157, 40100 Bologna Italy.

LC S
DD 630   FR

SERIE NOTES ET DOCUMENTS.
Added/Corp Institut National de la Recherche Agronomique (France) Institut National de la Recherche Agronomique (France). Station d'Economie et Sociologie Rurales (Montpellier). (19??)-. Monographic series. French. Price varies per volume.
 Ind/Abst Sug. Indus. Abstr.

LC S
DD 630   SP

SERIE : RECURSOS NATURALES. **VFOAT** Recursos Naturales. Spanish. Instituto Nacional de Investigaciones Agrarias / Madrid, Avda de Puerta de Hierro S/N, Madrid Spain.

LC S
DD 630   FR

SESAME BULLETIN. (199?)-. Periodical. English (French). Five times a year (published four times per year plus annual index). $120.30. CIRAD/UCIST, Service Editions BP 5035, 34032 Montpellier, Cedex France. **Tel** 011 33 1 67615565. Index available (annual). **Continues** Agritrop, 0399-1539.

LC S ISSN 0239-9342
DD 630 PL
SESJA NAUKOWA. Added/Corp Akademia Rolnicza im. H. Kollataja w Krakowie. **VFOAT** Nauchnaia Sessiia. (1980)-. Polish (English, German and Russian). Adademia Rolnicza im. Hugona Kollataja w Krakowie, Al. 29 Listopada 46, 31-425 Krakow Poland. **Tel** 011 48 12 119144, FAX 011 48 12 336245. ***Continues*** *Sesja Naukowa (Akademia Rolnicza w Krakowie).*
Ind/Abst For. Abstr.; Seed Abstr.

LC S ISSN 0192-4184
DD 630 US
SEVEN COUNTY FARM AND HOME NEWS. VFOAT C. (19??)-. Periodical. English. Twelve times a year. Farm and Home Publications, 10 Lourdes Road, Binghamton NY 13905. ***Continues*** *Columbia, Luzerne, Wyoming Farm and Home News.*

LC S469.R92 N587 ISSN 0582-8902
DD 630.94 RU
SEVERO-ZAPAD EVROPEISKOI CHASTI SSSR. Added/Corp Leningradskii Gosudarstvennyi Universitet Imeni A.A. Zhdanova. No. 1 (1963)-. Russian. One time a year. St. Petersburg State University / Izdatelstvo Leningradskogo Universiteta, Universitetskaia Nab 7/9, 199034 St. Petersburg Russia. **Tel** 011 7 812 2189788, FAX 011 7 812 2185152, telex 121481.

LC S ISSN 1000-193X
DD 630 CC
SHANGHAI NONGXUEYUAN XUEBAO. VFOAT Journal of Shanghai Agricultural College. (1983)-. Periodical. Chinese. Four times a year. RMBY2.50. Shanghai Nongxueyuan, Shanghai Agricultural College, No. 31 Qishen Lu, Shanghai 201101 People's Republic of China. **Tel** 923010. **ED** Wu Jinkang. **Ad Acc. Circ:** 1,000. Documents available from BLDSC.
Ind/Abst Index Vet.

LC S ISSN 1000-3924
DD 630 CC
SHANGHAI NONYE XUEBAO. (SHANG-HAI NUNG YEH HSUEH PAO SHANG-HAI SHIH NUNG HSUEH HUI, SHANG-HAI NUNG YEH KO HSUEH YUAN CHU PAN.). **Added/Corp** Shang-hai Shih Nung Hsueh hui. Shang-hai Shih Nung yeh ko Hsueh Yuan. **VFOAT** Acta Agriculturae Shanghai. (1985)-. Periodical. Chinese (summaries and/or abstracts in English; table of contents in English). Four times a year. Shanghai Academy of Agricultural Sciences, 2901 Bei Di Road, Shanghai, People's Republic of China.
Ind/Abst Biocont. News Inf.; Crop Physiol. Abstr.; Field Crop Abstr.; For. Abstr.; Nematol. Abstr.; Plant Breed. Abstr.; Plant Genet. Resour. Abstr.; Plant Grow. Reg. Abstr.; Potato Abstr.; Rev. Agric. Entomol.; Rev. Med. Vet. Mycology; Rev. Plant Pathol.; Rice Abstr.; Soils Fert.; Weed Abstr.; Wheat Barley Trit. Abstr.

LC S ISSN 0953-9026
DD 630.5 UK
SHELL AGRICULTURE (1988). [Shell agric. 1988]. (1988)-. Periodical. English. Three times a year. ***Continues*** *Span (Derby), 0584-8024.*
Ind/Abst Biocont. News Inf.; Food Sci. Technol. Abstr.; Geogr. Abstr. Phys. Geogr.; Geogr. Abstr. Human Geogr.; Hortic. Abstr.; Rev. Plant Pathol.; Weed Abstr.

LC S
DD 630 CC
SHEN-YANG NUNG YEH TA HSUEH HSUEH PAO. Added/Corp Shen-Yang Nung Yeh Ta Hsueh. **VFOAT** Journal of Shenyang Agricultural University. (1986)-. Periodical. Chinese (summaries and/or abstracts in English; table of contents in English). Four times a year. ***Continues*** *Shen-Yang Nung Hsueh Yuan Hsueh Pao.*
Ind/Abst Agrofor. Abstr.; Crop Physiol. Abstr.; Maize Abstr.; Pig News Inf.; Plant Breed. Abstr.; Postharvest News Inf.; Rev. Plant Pathol.; Rice Abstr.; Seed Abstr.; Sorghum Mill. Abstr.; Wheat Barley Trit. Abstr.

LC S ISSN 0285-8800
DD 630 JA
CODEN SHIKDG
SHIBAKUSA KENKYU. [Shibakusa kenkyu]. **VFOAT** Journal of Japan Turfgrass Research Association. (1972)-. Academic Scholarly Publication. Japanese (summaries and/or abstracts in English). Two times a year. Nihon Shibakusa kenkyukai, (Japanese Soc. of Turfgrass Science), Tokyo Nogyo Daigaku Zoen, Gakka Zeon Chihi Shokusaigaku, Kenkyushitsu 1-1 Sakuragaoka, 1 Chome Setagayaku, Tokyoto 156 Japan. Documents available from CASDDS.
Ind/Abst AGRICOLA; Chem. Abstr. (1972-1983).

LC S471.J32 S557a ISSN 0037-3702
DD 630.95 JA
CODEN SNSKA3
SHIKOKU NOGYO SHIKENJO HOKOKU. [Shikoku Nogyo Shikenjo Hokoku]. **Main/Corp** Shikoku Nogyo Shikenjo. **Added/Corp** Shikoku Nogyo Shikenjo. Bulletin of the Shikoku Agricultural Experiment Station. **VFOAT** Bulletin of the Shikoku Agricultural Experiment Station. Vol. 1 (1953)-. Bulletin. Multiple languages (Japanese and English). Norin Suisansho Shikoku Nogyo Shikenjo, (Shikoku National Agricultural Experiment Station Ministry of Agriculture Forestry & Fisheries), 3-1 Sen'yucho 1 Chome, Zentsujishi Kagawaken 765, Japan. Documents available from BIOSIS Document Express, CASDDS. ***Supersedes in part*** *Chugoku Shikoku Nogyo Shikenjo. Chugoku Shikoku Nogyo Shikenjo Hokoku.*
Ind/Abst AGRICOLA; Agric. Eng. Abstr.; Agrofor. Abstr.; Biol. Abstr.; Chem. Abstr. (?-1987); EMBASE; For. Abstr.; Nutr. Abstr. Rev., Ser. B, Live Feeds and Feed.; Plant Grow. Reg. Abstr.

LC S ISSN 0370-940X
DD 630 JA
CODEN SDNKBB
SHIMANE DAIGAKU NOGAKUBU KENKYU HOKOKU. [Shimane Daigaku Nogakubu kenkyu hokoku]. **Main/Corp** Shimane Daigaku, Matsue, Japan. Nogakubu. **VFOAT** Bulletin of the Faculty of Agriculture, Shimane University. (1967)-. Academic Scholarly Publication. Japanese (summaries and/or abstracts in English). One time a year. Shimane University, Faculty of Agriculture, Matsue Japan. Documents available from BIOSIS Document Express, CASDDS. ***Continues*** *Shimane Noka Daigaku Kenkyu Hokoku, 0559-8311.*
Ind/Abst AGRICOLA; Biol. Abstr.; Chem. Abstr.; EMBASE; For. Abstr.; Hortic. Abstr.; Nutr. Abstr. Rev., Ser. B, Live Feeds and Feed.; Life Sci. Collect.; Rice Abstr.

LC S ISSN 0388-905X
DD 630 JA
CODEN SNSHDV
SHIMANE-KEN NOGYO SHIKENJO KENKYU HOKOKU. [Shimane-ken Nogyo Shikenjo kenkyu hokoku]. **VFOAT** Bulletin of the Shimane Agricultural Experiment Station. (1956)-. Academic Scholarly Publication. Japanese. One time a year. Shimaneken Nogyo Shikenjo, (Shimane Agricultural Experiment Station), 2440 Ashiwatarimachi, Izumoshi Shimaneken 693, Japan. Documents available from CASDDS.
Ind/Abst Biocont. News Inf.; Chem. Abstr. (1956-1981); Plant Grow. Reg. Abstr.

LC S19 .S574a ISSN 0583-0621
DD 630 JA
CODEN SDNOAM
SHINSHU DAIGAKU NOGAKUBU KIYO. [Shinshu Daigaku Nogakubu kiyo]. **Main/Corp** Shinshu Daigaku. Nogakubu. **VFOAT** Journal of the Faculty of Agriculture, Shinshu University. Vol. 1 (1951)-. Academic Scholarly Publication. Japanese (English; summaries and/or abstracts in German). Shinshu Daigaku Nogakubu, (Faculty of Agriculture Shinshu University), 8304 Minamiminowamura, Kamiinagun Naganoken 399-45, Japan. Documents available from BIOSIS Document Express, CASDDS. ***Continues*** *Shinshu Daigaku. Shinshu Daigaku Kiyo.*
Ind/Abst AGRICOLA; Biol. Abstr.; Chem. Abstr.; EMBASE; Plant Grow. Reg. Abstr.

LC S
DD 630 JA
CODEN SKKHD4
SHINSHU MISO KENKYUJO KENKYU HOKOKU. [Shinshu Miso Kenkyujo kenkyu hokoku]. **Added/Corp** Shinshu Miso Kenkyujo. **VFOAT** Reports of the Shinshu-Miso Research Institute. (1959)-. Academic Scholarly Publication. Japanese. Shinshu Miso Kenkyujo, (Shinshu Miso Research Inst.), 496-6 Nakagosho Naganoshi, Naganoken 380 Japan. Documents available from CASDDS.
Ind/Abst Chem. Abstr.; Soyabean Abstr.

LC S ISSN 0559-8850
DD 630 JA
CODEN SDNKAA
SHIZUOKA DAIGAKU NOGAKUBU KENKYU HOKOKU. [Shizuoka Daigaku Nogakubu kenkyu hokoku]. **Added/Corp** Shizuoka Daigaku. Nogakubu. **VFOAT** Bulletin of the Faculty of Agriculture, Shizuoka University. (1949)-. Academic Scholarly Publication. Japanese (English). Shizuoka Daigaku Nogakubu, (Faculty of Agriculture Shizuoka University), 836 Oya Shizuokashi, Shizuokaken 420 Japan. Documents available from CASDDS.
Ind/Abst AGRICOLA; Chem. Abstr.; Crop Physiol. Abstr.; For. Prod. Abstr. (1991-); Hortic. Abstr.; Postharvest News Inf.; Rev. Agric. Entomol.; Rev. Plant Pathol.; Rice Abstr.

LC S ISSN 0583-094X
DD 630 JA
CODEN SNSKC5
SHIZUOKA-KEN NOGYO SHIKENJO KENKYU HOKOKU. [Shizuoka-ken Nogyo Shikenjo kenkyu hokoku]. **VFOAT** Bulletin of the Shizuoka Agricultural Experiment Station. (1956)-. Academic Scholarly Publication. Japanese. One time a year. Shizuokaken Nogyo Shikenjo, (Shizuoka Agricultural Experiment Station), 678-1 Tomigaoka Toyodamachi, Iwatagun Shizuokaken 438, Japan. Documents available from CASDDS.
Ind/Abst Chem. Abstr. (1956-1979).

LC S ISSN 0037-4091
DD 630 JA
CODEN SHBOAO
SHOKUBUTSU BOEKI. [Shokubutsu boeki]. **Added/Corp** Nihon Shokubutsu Boeki Kyokai. (1946)-. Academic Scholarly Publication. Japanese. Twelve times a year. $114.00. Nihon Shokubutsu Boeki Kyokai, (Japan Plant Protection Assoc.), 43-11 Komagome 1 Chome, Toshimaku Tokyo 170 Japan. Index available in last issue of volume--attached. Documents available from CASDDS.
Ind/Abst AGRICOLA; Chem. Abstr.

LC S ISSN 0441-0807
DD 630 JA
SHUHO. BULLETIN OF THE HOKKAIDO PREFECTURAL AGRICULTURAL EXPERIMENT STATIONS. Main/Corp Hokkaidoritsu Nogyo Shikenjo. **VFOAT** Bulletin of the Hokkaido Prefectural Agricultural Experimental Stations. (March 1957)-. Bulletin. Japanese (summaries and/or abstracts in English; table of contents in English). Two times a year.
Ind/Abst AgBiotech News Inf.; Dairy Sci. Abstr.; Nematol. Abstr.; Plant Breed. Abstr.; Potato Abstr.; Rev. Plant Pathol.; Rice Abstr.

LC AP95.J2 S546
JA
SHUKAN YOMIURI. VFOAT Weekly Yomiuri. (1952)-. Periodical. Japanese. One time a week. $304.00. **(Subscription address:** Japan Publications Trading Company Ltd., PO Box 5030, Tokyo International, Tokyo 100-31 Japan. **Tel** 011 81 3 3292 3753.) ***Continues*** *Junkan Yomiuri.*

LC S ISSN 0370-8799
DD 630 RU
CODEN SBVSAQ
SIBIRSKII VESTNIK SELSKOKHOZIAISTVENNOI NAUKI. [Sib. vestn. s-h. nauki]. **Added/Corp** Vsesoiuznaia Akademiia Selskokhoziaistvennykh Nauk Imeni V.I. Lenina. Sibirskoe Otdelenie. (1971)-. Academic Scholarly Publication. Russian (summaries and/or abstracts in English; table of contents in English). Four times a year. $99.95. **(Subscription address:** East View Publications Inc., 3020 Harbor Lane North, Suite 110, Minneapolis MN 55447. **Tel** (800)477-1005, (612)550-0961, FAX (612)559-2931.) Documents available from CASDDS.
Ind/Abst AgBiotech News Inf.; Agric. Eng. Abstr. (1991-); Agrofor. Abstr. (19??-19??); Anim. Breed. Abstr.; Biocont. News Inf.; Chem. Abstr.; Crop Physiol. Abstr.; Dairy Sci. Abstr.; Field Crop Abstr.; For. Abstr.; Helminthol. Abstr.; Hortic. Abstr.; Index Vet.; Maize Abstr.; Nematol. Abstr.; Nutr. Abstr. Rev., Ser. B, Live Feeds and Feed.; Plant Breed. Abstr.; Plant Genet. Resour. Abstr.; Plant Grow. Reg. Abstr.; Postharvest News Inf.; Potato Abstr.; Poult. Abstr.; Rev. Med. Vet. Entomol.; Rev. Plant Pathol.; Soils Fert.; Soyabean Abstr.

LC S ISSN 1000-2650
DD 630 CC
SICHUAN NONGYE DAXUE XUEBAO. VFOAT Journal of Sichuan Agricultural University. (1985)-. Periodical. Chinese. Four times a year.
Ind/Abst For. Abstr.

LC S
DD 630 US
SIGNALS. Added/Corp Agricultural Communicators in Education (U.S.). Vol. 1, No. 1 (Jan./Feb. 1990)-. Periodical. English. Six times a year. ***Continues*** *Agricultural Communicators in Education.*

LC S
DD 630 UN
SILSKI VISTI. Added/Corp Komunistychna Partiia Ukrainy. Tsentralnyi Komitet. **VFOAT** Selskie Vesti. (19??)-. Newspaper. Ukrainian. Five times a week (260 issues per year). $264.95. **(Subscription address:** East View Publications Inc., 3020 Harbor Lane North, Suite 110, Minneapolis MN 55447. **Tel** (800)477-1005, (612)550-0961, FAX (612)559-2931.)

LC S ISSN 0965-8106
DD 630.72041 UK
SILSOE LINK. [Silsoe link]. (1991)-. English. Three times a year. $59.89. Silsoe Link, Silsoe Research Institute, Wrest Park Silso, Bedford MK45 4HS United Kingdom. **Tel** 011 44 525 860000, FAX 011 44 525 860156.
Desc: Liaison between organizations in Silsoe Village which are involved with agricultural and horticultural engineering.

LC S
DD 630 CR
SILVOENERGIA. Added/Corp Centro Agronomico Tropical de Investigacion. (19??)-. Periodical. Spanish.
Ind/Abst Irr. Drain. Abstr.

LC S **ISSN** 0037-5403
DD 630 CL
CODEN SMNTAW

SIMIENTE. [Simiente]. **Added/Corp** Sociedad Agronomica de Chile. (1931)-. Academic Scholarly Publication. Spanish. Four times a year. Sociedad de Agronomica de Chile, Alonso Ovalle 1638, 2 Piso, Casilla 4109 Santiago Chile. Documents available from CASDDS.
Ind/Abst AGRICOLA; Biodeter. Abstr. (1991-); Chem. Abstr. (1931-1983); Crop Physiol. Abstr.; Field Crop Abstr.; Grass. Forage Abstr.; Hortic. Abstr.; Irr. Drain. Abstr.; Maize Abstr.; Plant Breed. Abstr.; Plant Grow. Reg. Abstr.; Postharvest News Inf.; Potato Abstr.; Rev. Agric. Entomol.; Seed Abstr.; Soils Fert.; Vitis Vitic. Enol. Abstr.; Weed Abstr.; Wheat Barley Trit. Abstr.

LC S322.S55 S55 **ISSN** 0129-6485
DD 630/.5 SI
CODEN SJPIDP

SINGAPORE JOURNAL OF PRIMARY INDUSTRIES. [Singapore j. primary ind.]. **Added/Corp** Singapore. Primary Production Dept. Vol. 1 (Jan. 1973)-. English. Two times a year (June & Dec.). $12.00. Director of Primary Production, 3TH National Dev. Building, Maxwell Road, Singapore 0106 Singapore. **Tel** 011 65 3226634, FAX 011 65 2206068, telex PPD RS 28851. **ED** Ngiam Tong Tau. **Ad Acc. Circ:** 500. Documents available from CASDDS.
Desc: Agricultural research, horticulture research, animal husbandry, veterinary science, fish diseases, fish biology and aquaculture.
Ind/Abst AGRICOLA; Chem. Abstr. (1973-1982); Hortic. Abstr.; Index Vet.; Nematol. Abstr.; Nutr. Abstr. Rev., Ser. B, Live Feeds and Feed.; Pig News Inf.; Plant Grow. Reg. Abstr.; Poult. Abstr.; Protozoolog. Abstr.

LC HD1751 .U54a
DD 338.1/3/0973 US

SITUATION AND OUTLOOK REPORT. AGRICULTURAL INCOME AND FINANCE / UNITED STATES DEPARTMENT OF AGRICULTURE, ECONOMIC RESEARCH SERVICE. **Added/Corp** United States. Dept. of Agriculture. Economic Research Service. United States. World Agricultural Outlook Board. **VFOAT** Agricultural Income and Finance; Agricultural Income and Finance Situation and Outlook. (May 1988)-. Periodical. English. Four times a year. $18.00. Economic Research Service USDA, 341 Victory Drive, Herndon VA 22070. **Tel** (800) 999-6779. ***Continues** Situation and Ooutlook Report. Agricultural Finance.*
Ind/Abst World Agric. Econ. Rural Sociol. Abstr.

LC HD9241 .A3 **ISSN** 1051-7901
DD 338.1/745/0973 US

SITUATION AND OUTLOOK REPORT. FRUIT AND TREE NUTS. [Situat. outlook rep., Fruit tree nuts]. **Added/Corp** United States. Dept. of Agriculture. Economic Research Service. United States. World Agricultural Outlook Board. **VFOAT** Fruit and Tree Nuts; Situation and Outlook Yearbook. Fruit and Tree Nuts; Fruit and Tree Nuts. Situation and Outlook Report Yearbook. TFS-245 (Mar. 1988)-. Periodical. English. Four times a year. $21.00. Economic Research Service USDA, 341 Victory Drive, Herndon VA 22070. **Tel** (800) 999-6779. **(Subscription address:** Superintendent of Documents, US Government Printing Office, Washington DC 20402. **)** available on an online database (file 648/Full-Text) from DIALOG. ***Continues** Situation and Outlook Report. Fruit, 1051-8916.*
Desc: Reports, consisting chiefly of tables and statistics, contain information on supply, demand and price research.
Ind/Abst Trade Ind. ASAP [Full Txt.]; Trade Ind. Index [Full Txt.]; World Agric. Econ. Rural Sociol. Abstr.

LC HD9066.A1 U45 **ISSN** 1051-9149
DD 338.1/7318/05 US
CEASED

SITUATION AND OUTLOOK REPORT. RICE. (SITUATION AND OUTLOOK REPORT. RICE.). [Situat. outlook rep., Rice]. **Added/Corp** United States. Dept. of Agriculture. Economic Research Service. United States. World Agricultural Outlook Board. **VFOAT** Rice; Situation and Outlook Yearbook. Rice; Rice Situation and Outlook. (May 1986)-(1994). Government Publication. English. Superintendent of Documents, US Government Printing Office, Washington DC 20402. **Tel** (202)275-3328, FAX (202)786-2377. ***Continues** Outlook and Situation Report. Rice, 0882-7834.*
Ind/Abst AGRICOLA; F&S Index Plus Text, Int. [Select. Cov.]; Foods Adlibra; Rice Abstr.; Trade Ind. ASAP [Full Txt.]; Trade Ind. Index [Full Txt.]; World Agric. Econ. Rural Sociol. Abstr.

LC HD9101 .S888 **ISSN** 0896-0240
DD 338.1/736/0973 US

SITUATION AND OUTLOOK REPORT. SUGAR AND SWEETENER. [Situat. outlook rep., Sugar sweeten.]. **Added/Corp** United States. Dept. of Agriculture. Economic Research Service. United States. World Agricultural Outlook Board. **VFOAT** Sugar and Sweetener; Situation and Outlook Yearbook. Sugar and Sweetener; Sugar and Sweetener Situation and Outlook. SSRV11N3 (Sept. 1986)-. Government Publication. English. Four times a year. $22.00. Superintendent of Documents, US Government Printing Office, Washington DC 20402. **Tel** (202)275-3328, FAX (202)786-2377. ***Continues** Outlook and Situation Report. Sugar and Sweetener, 8755-8548.*
Ind/Abst F&S Index Plus Text, Int. [Select. Cov.]; Foods Adlibra; Sug. Indus. Abstr.; Trade Ind. ASAP [Full Txt.]; Trade Ind. Index [Full Txt.].

LC HD9049.W5 U658 **ISSN** 0895-1454
DD 338.1/7311/0973 US
CEASED

SITUATION AND OUTLOOK REPORT. WHEAT. [Situat. outlook rep., Wheat]. **Added/Corp** United States. Dept. of Agriculture. Economic Research Service. United States. World Agricultural Outlook Board. **VFOAT** Situation and Outlook Yearbook. Wheat; Wheat Situation and Outlook. (May 1986)-(Nov. 1994). Government Publication. English. Superintendent of Documents, US Government Printing Office, Washington DC 20402. **Tel** (202)275-3328, FAX (202)786-2377. available on microfiche (Vols. for 1986- distributed to depository libraries). ***Continues** Outlook and Situation Report. Wheat, 0884-6391.*
Desc: Reports, consisting chiefly of tables and statistics, containing information on supply, demand and price research.
Ind/Abst F&S Index Plus Text, Int. [Select. Cov.]; Foods Adlibra; Predicasts Forecasts; Wheat Barley Trit. Abstr.

LC HD9018.P16 S57
DD 338.1/09182/3021 US

•SITUATION AND OUTLOOK SERIES. ASIA AND PACIFIC RIM INTERNATIONAL AGRICULTURE AND TRADE REPORTS / UNITED STATES DEPARTMENT OF AGRICULTURE, ECONOMIC RESEARCH SERVICE. See Business and Economics-Commerce.

LC HD2096 .C483
DD 338.1/0951/05 US

•SITUATION AND OUTLOOK SERIES. CHINA INTERNATIONAL AGRICULTURE AND TRADE REPORTS. **Added/Corp** United States. Dept. of Agriculture. Economic Research Service. United States. World Agricultural Outlook Board. **VFOAT** China; China International Agriculture and Trade Report; International Agriculture and Trade Report. (July 1993)-. Government Publication. English. US Department of Agriculture / Economic Research Service, 1301 New York Avenue, Room 208, Washington DC 20250. **Tel** (202)447-4111. ***Continues** Situation and Outlook Series. China Agriculture and Trade Report, 1051-8703.*
Ind/Abst F&S Index Plus Text, Int.; Predicasts Forecasts; Wheat Barley Trit. Abstr.; World Agric. Econ. Rural Sociol. Abstr.

LC HD9018.D44 S57
DD 338.1/09172/4021 US

SITUATION AND OUTLOOK SERIES. DEVELOPING ECONOMIES AGRICULTURE AND TRADE REPORT / UNITED STATES DEPARTMENT OF AGRICULTURE, ECONOMIC RESEARCH SERVICE. **Added/Corp** United States. Dept. of Agriculture. Economic Research Service. United States. World Agricultural Outlook Board. **VFOAT** Developing Economies; Developing Economies Agriculture and Trade Report; Agriculture and Trade Report. (19??)-. English. U.S. Department of Agriculture, ERS-NASS, 341 Victory Drive, Herndon VA 22070. **Tel** (800)999-6779, (703)834-0125.
Ind/Abst F&S Index Plus Text, Int. [Select. Cov.]; Predicasts Forecasts.

LC HD1751 .I56
DD 338.1/3/0973 UK
CEASED

SITUATION AND OUTLOOK SUMMARY. AGRICULTURAL RESOURCES, AGRICULTURAL LAND VALUES. **Added/Corp** United States. Dept. of Agriculture. Economic Research Service. United States. World Agricultural Outlook Board. **VFOAT** Agricultural Resources, Agricultural Land Values. (19??)-(Oct. 1993). Government Publication. English. Superintendent of Documents, US Government Printing Office, Washington DC 20402. **Tel** (202)275-3328, FAX (202)786-2377. ***Continues** Situation and Ooutlook Report. Agricultural Resources, 1057-8447.*

LC S **ISSN** 0251-1460
DD 630 IT
UDC 613.2:63

SITUATION MONDIALE DE L'ALIMENTATION ET DE L'AGRICULTURE, LA. (1947)-. Periodical. French. One time a year. Food Agriculture Organization (FAO) / Italy, GIPCI66 via Terme di Caracalla, 00100 Rome Italy. **Tel** 011 39 6 52252925, FAX 011 39 6 52253152.
Ind/Abst LABORDOC.

LC S **ISSN** 1330-0121
DD 630 CI
UDC 631
CODEN SJVOE6

SJEMENARSTVO ZAGREB. (SJEMENARSTVO.). [Sjemenarstvo Zagreb]. (1991)-. Periodical. Serbo-Croatian (Roman). Six times a year. Zagreb Poljoprivredni Vjesnik, 41000 Zagreb Croatia. ***Continues** Semenarstvo (Zagreb), 0352-3047.*

LC S **ISSN** 0137-4796
DD 630 PL

SLUZBA ROLNA. [Suz. rolna]. No. 1 (Jan. 1976)-. Periodical. Polish.
Ind/Abst AGRICOLA.

LC S **ISSN** 0253-5211
DD 630 SZ
CODEN SSLADA

SLZ. SCHWEIZERISCHE LABORATORIUMS-ZEITSCHRIFT. (SCHWEIZERISCHE LABORATORIUMS-ZEITSCHRIFT : SLZ.). [SLZ, Schweiz. Lab.-Z.]. **Added/Corp** Schweizerischer Laborpersonal-Verband. **VFOAT** Revue Suisse de Laboratoire; SLZ; S.L.Z. (1978)-. Academic Scholarly Publication. French (German). Twelve times a year. SLV, Postfach 428, 4005 Basel Postcheck 40-16388 Switzerland. Documents available from CASDDS.
Ind/Abst Chem. Abstr.; Curr. Biotechnol.; Curr. Cit.; Rev. Agric. Entomol.; Rev. Plant Pathol.; Saf. Health Work.

LC HD1476.U5 S58 **ISSN** 0273-5237
DD 338.1/873 US

SMALL FARM PROGRAMS AND ACTIVITIES, STATE REPORTS. [Small farm programs act. State rep.]. 1979-. English. Science and Education Administration, Washington DC 20250.

LC S **ISSN** 0892-6301
DD 630 US

SMALL FARM TODAY. Vol. 9, No. 2 (Apr. 1992)-. Periodical. English. Six times a year. $21.00 (one-year), $39.00 (two-year), $54.00 (three-year). Missouri Farm Publishing Inc., 3903 W. Ridge Trail Rd., Clark MO 65243. **Tel** (314)687-3525. **ED** Ron Macher (Editor's telephone: (314)687-3333). Index available (Published separately). **Bk Rev**, (Qty: 12). **Ad Acc**, **Adv Mgr Tel** 800 633-2535. **Circ:** 12,000 (ctrl). ***Continues** Missouri Farm, 0892-6301.*
Desc: A how-to magazine of alternative and traditional crops, livestock, and direct marketing.
Ind/Abst Bibliogr. Agric.

LC S **ISSN** 0743-9989
DD 630 US

SMALL FARMER'S JOURNAL. [Small farmer's j.]. (1976)-. Periodical. English. Four times a year. $22.00. Small Farmers Journal, PO Box 2805, Eugene OR 97402. **Tel** (503)683-6486. **ED** Lynn R Miller. **Bk Rev**. **Ad Acc. Circ:** 23,000 (ctrl).
Desc: A magazine devoted to the betterment of the independent family farm. Each issue features practical horse farming and covers all facets of small-scale diversified agriculture.
Ind/Abst AGRICOLA.

LC SB354
DD 634 US

SMALL FRUIT CROPS, DISEASE IDENTIFICATION SHEET. **Added/Corp** Cornell Cooperative Extension. New York State Integrated Pest Management Program. New York (State). Dept. of Agriculture and Markets. **VFOAT** Disease Identification Sheet. No. 2 (1991)-. English. Cornell Focus, Cornell University Media Service, 1150 Comstock Hall, Ithaca NY 14853. **Tel** (607)255-1876. ***Continues** Small Fruit IPM, Disease Identification Sheet.*

LC SB354 **ISSN** 0227-8863
DD 634/.7/05 CN

SMALL FRUIT INFORMATION LETTER. [Small fruit inf. lett.]. No. 1/80 (April 16, 1980)-. Periodical. English. Ministry of Agriculture & Food Ontario, Extension Branch, 1414 Lasalle Blvd., Sudbury Ontario P3A 1Z6. ***Continues** Small Fruit Newsletter, 0708-5664.*

LC S **ISSN** 0383-6312
DD 630/.9711 CN

SMALLHOLDER, THE. No. 1- March 1974-. Periodical. English. Irregular. $3.50 Canada; $4.00 other. The Smallholder, Argentina British Columbia V0G 1B0 Canada.

LC HD **ISSN** 0265-7473
DD 338.642 UK

SMALLHOLDER STOWMARKET. [Smallholder Stowmarket]. (1983)-. Periodical. English. Twelve times a year. $49.20. Smallholder Publications Ltd, High Street Stoke, Ferry Kings Lynn, Norfolk PE33 9SF United Kingdom. **Tel** 011 44 1366 501035. ***Continues** Goatkeeper & Smallholder, 0265-4598.*

Agriculture

LC TP375 .S67
DD 664/.122
ISSN 0049-0849
CU
CODEN SDCAAR
TITLE CHANGE

SOBRE LOS DERIVADOS DE LA CANA DE AZUCAR. [Sobre deriv. ca‰na de az,ucar].
Added/Corp ICIDCA. **VFOAT** Boletin Sobre los Derivados. (1967)-(19??). Academic Scholarly Publication. Spanish (summaries and/or abstracts in English). Documents available from CASDDS. *Continued by* Revista Sobre los Derivados de la Cana de Azucar.
Desc: Contains information on sugar.
Ind/Abst Abstr. Bull. Inst. Pap. Sci. Tech. (?-?); Chem. Abstr.

LC S
DD 630
ISSN 0385-0196
JA
CODEN SSKHBO

SOCHI SHIKENJO KENKYU HOKOKU.
[Sochi Shikenjo kenkyu hokoku]. **Main/Corp** Sochi Shikenjo, Tochigi, Japan. **Added/Corp** Sochi Shikenjo, Tochigi, Japan. Bulletin. **VFOAT** Bulletin of the National Grassland Research Institute. No. 1 (March 1972)-. Academic Scholarly Publication. Japanese (summaries and/or abstracts in English). National Grassland Research Institute, Cong Secretariat Nishinasuno, Tochigi 329 27 Japan. **Tel** 011 606 278 0177. Documents available from BIOSIS Document Express, CASDDS.
Ind/Abst AGRICOLA; Agrofor. Abstr.; Biol. Abstr.; Chem. Abstr.; EMBASE; Field Crop Abstr.; Grass. Forage Abstr.; Index Vet.; Nutr. Abstr. Rev., Ser. B, Live Feeds and Feed.; Rev. Plant Pathol.; Seed Abstr.

LC S21. A46 TJ811
DD 630 016.621042
ISSN 0741-5419
US

SOLAR ENERGY AND NONFOSSIL FUEL RESEARCH. (SOLAR ENERGY AND NONFOSSIL FUEL RESEARCH : A DIRECTORY OF PROJECTS RELATED TO AGRICULTURE.). [Solar energy nonfoss. fuel res.].
(1976/79)-. Directory. English. One time a year. US Department of Agriculture, 14th Street and Independence Avenue SW, Washington DC 20250. **Tel** (202)720-5457. available on microfiche (Vols. for 1981- distributed to depository libraries).

LC HD9483.U5 F48
DD 338.4/766862/0973
ISSN 0199-9869
TITLE CHANGE

SOLUTIONS (1980). (SOLUTIONS.). [Solut.].
Added/Corp National Fertilizer Solutions Association. Vol. 24, No. 1 (Jan./Feb. 1980)-(1993). Periodical. English. Ag Retailer, 11701 Borman Dr., St Louis MO 63146. available on microfilm from University Microfilms International (UMI). *Continues* Fertilizer Solutions, 0015-0312. *Continued by* AG Retailer, 1072-9267.
Ind/Abst AGRICOLA (?-?) [Select. Cov.].

LC S
DD 630
ISSN 03082970
UK
CEASED

SORGHUM AND MILLETS ABSTRACTS.
See Agriculture-Abstracting, Bibliographies and Statistics.

LC HV
DD 363
ISSN 1062-581X
US

SOUND SAFETY. (SOUND SAFETY [SOUND RECORDING]: AUDIO SERVICE TO THE AGRI-CHEMICAL & FERTILIZER INDUSTRIES.). [Sound saf.].
Prog. No. 1 (1992)-. Periodical. English. Six times a year. $175.00. Simpson Bayne Communications, PO Box 20087, Spokane WA 99204.

LC HD9117.S7 S2
DD 338.17361
SA

SOUTH AFRICAN SUGAR YEAR BOOK, THE.
(19??)-. English. One time a year. R25.00. South African Sugar Yearbook, PO Box 507, Durban 4000 South Africa. **Tel** (031) 318952. **ED** Glen Dewey. **Bk Rev. Ad Acc. Circ:** 3,000 (ctrl).
Desc: General news and technical material relating to the South African sugar industry.

LC S
DD 630
ISSN 0889-1834
US

SOUTH CAROLINA FARMER : THE SOUTH CAROLINA FARM BUREAU FEDERATION NEWS. [S.C. farmer].
Added/Corp South Carolina Farm Bureau Federation. **VFOAT** Farmer; South Carolina Farm Bureau Federation News. (19??)-. Periodical. English. Six times a year. $2.00. South Carolina Farm Bureau Federation, PO Box 754, Columbia SC 29202. **Tel** (803)796-6700.

LC S
DD 630
ISSN 1079-8889
US

SOUTH CAROLINA'S YOUNG FARMER & FFA MAGAZINE. [S.C. young farmer futur. FFA mag.].
Added/Corp South Carolina Future Farmers Associations. South Carolina Young Farmer Association. **VFOAT** Young Farmer & FFA; Young Farmer & FFA Magazine; South Carolina's Young Farmer & FFA Magazine; South Carolina's Young Farmer & Future Farmers of America Magazine. (199?)-. Periodical. English. Four times a year. South Carolina Young Farmer Association, South Carolina Future Farmers Association, 922 Rutledge Building, Columbia SC 29201.

LC S583
DD 631
ISSN 1045-8999
US

SOUTH DAKOTA CROP & LIVESTOCK REPORTER. [S.D. crop livest. report.]. VFOAT
South Dakota Crop and Livestock Reporter. (19??)-. Periodical. English. National Agriculture Statistics Service, South Building USDA/Room 5829, Washington DC 20250.

LC S113 .E48
DD 630.72
ISSN 0038-3295
US
CODEN SDFHAT

SOUTH DAKOTA FARM & HOME RESEARCH. [S. D. farm home res.]. Added/Corp
South Dakota Agricultural Experiment Station. **VAT** South Dakota Farm and Home Research. (1949)-. Periodical. English. Four times a year. Free. South Dakota State University / Agricultural Experiment Station, Box 2231, Brookings SD 57007. **Tel** (605)688-4187, FAX (605)688-4018. **ED** Mary Brashier (Editor's address: SDSU, ACC Box 2231 Brookings, South Dakota 57007; Editor's telephone: (605)688-4648). **Circ:** 5,000 (ctrl). Documents available from BIOSIS Document Express, CASDDS.
Desc: Summarizes current agricultural and home economics research projects underway by the Agricultural Experiment Station at South Dakota State University. Other articles on topics of current interest to South Dakota residents also appear.
Ind/Abst AGRICOLA [Select. Cov.]; Biol. Abstr.; Chem. Abstr.; Dairy Sci. Abstr.; Index Vet.; Irr. Drain. Abstr.; Maize Abstr.; Life Sci. Collect.; Pig News Inf.

LC S
DD 630
ISSN 0279-2486
US

SOUTH TEXAS AGRINEWS.
(1981)-. Trade Publication. English. Twenty-six times a year. Big River Press, 1217 North Conway, Mission TX 78572.

LC S
DD 630
ISSN 0194-0937
US

SOUTHEAST FARM PRESS.
(197?)-. Trade Publication. English. Twenty times a year. $30.00. Farm Press Publications Ltd, PO Box 1420, Clarksdale MS 38614. **Tel** (601)624-8503.

LC S445 .S67
DD 338.1/0975
ISSN 0096-8498
US

SOUTHERN COOPERATIVE SERIES BULLETIN. (SOUTHERN COOPERATIVE SERIES.). [South. coop. ser. bull.]. VFOAT
Southern Cooperative Series Bulletin. No. 1 (Nov. 1943)-. Monographic series. English. Price varies per volume.
Ind/Abst Soyabean Abstr.; World Agric. Econ. Rural Sociol. Abstr.

LC S
DD 630
ISSN 0194-0945
US

SOUTHWEST FARM PRESS.
(19??)-. Trade Publication. English. Fifty times a year (Thurs.). $25.00 North America; $100.00 other. Farm Press Publications Ltd, PO Box 1420, Clarksdale MS 38614. **Tel** (601)624-8503.

LC S
DD 630
ISSN 1055-0607
US

SOVIET AGRICULTURAL SCIENCES.
Added/Corp Akademiia sel'Skokhoziaistvennykh nauk Imeni V. I. Lenina. Doklady 0042-9244. No. 1 (1977)-. Periodical. English (Russian). Twelve times a year. $55.00. Stagnito Publishing Company, 1935 Sherner Road, Suite 100, Northbrook IL 60062. **Tel** (708)205-5660, FAX (708)205-5680. Documents available from CASDDS. *Continues* Soviet Agriculture Sciences.
Ind/Abst Biodeter. Abstr.; Chem. Abstr.; Nutr. Abstr. Rev., Ser. A, Hum. Exp.; Potato Abstr.; Seed Abstr.

LC S
DD 630
ISSN 0735-2700
US
CCC
CODEN SAGSDF
TITLE CHANGE

SOVIET AGRICULTURAL SCIENCES.
[Sov. agric. sci.]. (1977)-(1993). Academic Scholarly Publication. English (Russian). Allerton Press Inc., 150 Fifth Avenue, New York NY 10011. **Tel** (212)924-3950, FAX (212)463-9684, telex 427441 ALPRES. Documents available from BIOSIS Document Express. *Continues* Vsesoiuznaia Akademiia Selskokhozia Istvennykh Nauk. Soviet Agriculture Sciences, 0735-2700. *Continued by* Russian Agricultural Sciences.
Ind/Abst AgBiotech News Inf.; AGRICOLA [Full Cov.]; Agric. Eng. Abstr. (1991-); Agrofor. Abstr. (19??-19??); Anim. Breed. Abstr.; Biocont. News Inf. (19??-19??); Biol. Abstr. (-1983); Cot. Trop. Fibr. Abstr. Bibliogr.; Crop Physiol. Abstr.; Dairy Sci. Abstr.; EMBASE; Field Crop Abstr.; For. Prod. Abstr. (1991-); For. Abstr.; Hortic. Abstr.; Index Vet.; Irr. Drain. Abstr.; Maize Abstr.; Nematol. Abstr.; Nutr. Abstr. Rev., Ser. B, Live Feeds and Feed.; Nutr. Abstr. Rev., Ser. A, Hum. Exp.; Pig News Inf.; Plant Breed. Abstr.; Plant Grow. Reg. Abstr.; Postharvest News Inf.; Potato Abstr.; Poult. Abstr.; Rev. Agric. Entomol.; Rev. Plant Pathol.; Rice Abstr.; Soils Fert.; Sorghum Mill. Abstr.; Soyabean Abstr.; Sug. Indus. Abstr.; Vet. Bull.

LC S
DD 630
ISSN 1041-0120
US

SOYA WORLD. Added/Corp Soyfoods Center.
(1991)-. English. One time a year. $75.00. Soyfoods Center, PO Box 234, Lafayette CA 94549. **Tel** (510)283-2991.

LC Z5071
DD 016.63
ISSN 0141-0172
UK

SOYABEAN ABSTRACTS. See
Agriculture-Abstracting, Bibliographies and Statistics.

LC HD2021 .S66
DD 338.1/0946/021
GW

SPANIEN, LAND- UND FORSTWIRTSCHAFT, FISCHEREI.
Added/Corp Bundesstelle fuer Aussenhandelsinformation (Germany). (19??)-. German. DM5.00. Bundesstelle fuer Aussenhandelsinformation, Agrippastrasse 87 93, D-50676 Cologne Germany. **Tel** 011 49 221 2057316, FAX 011 49 221 2057212.

LC HD2021
DD 338.1/0946
GW

SPANIEN, LANDWIRTSCHAFT. German.
DM5.00. Bundesstelle fuer Aussenhandelsinformation, Agrippastrasse 87 93, D-50676 Cologne Germany. **Tel** 011 49 221 2057316, FAX 011 49 221 2057212.

LC S
DD 630
ISSN 1057-1663
US

SPECIAL BULLETIN / MISSISSIPPI AGRICULTURAL AND FORESTRY EXPERIMENT STATION. (SPECIAL BULLETIN.).
Added/Corp Mississippi Agricultural and Forestry Experiment Station. (1985)-. Bulletin. English. Irregular. Price varies per volume. Mississippi State University / Information Services, PO Box 5446, Mississippi State MS 39762. **Tel** (601)325-7774.
Ind/Abst Cot. Trop. Fibr. Abstr. Bibliogr.; Poult. Abstr.

LC S539.J3 U8
DD 630
ISSN 0566-4683
JA

SPECIAL BULLETIN OF THE COLLEGE OF AGRICULTURE, UTSUNOMIYA UNIVERSITY. Added/Corp Utsunomiya Daigaku.
Nogakubu. **VFOAT** Gakujutsu Hokoku Tokushu. (1954)-. Bulletin. Japanese (summaries and/or abstracts in English). Utsunomiya University / Agriculture, College of Agriculture, Utsunomiya Japan.
Ind/Abst For. Abstr.

LC S
DD 630
ISSN 0736-8003
US

SPECIAL CIRCULAR - OHIO AGRICULTURAL RESEARCH AND DEVELOPMENT CENTER. [Spec. circ. - Ohio Agric. Res. Dev. Cent.]. Main/Corp Ohio Agricultural Research and Development Center. VFOAT OARDC
Special Circular. (19??)-. Monographic series. English. Irregular. Free on request. Ohio Agricultural Research and Development Center, Ohio State University, 1680 Madison Avenue, Wooster OH 44691. **Tel** (216)263-3775. *Continues* Special Circular - Ohio Agricultural Experiment Station, 0097-062X.
Ind/Abst AGRICOLA [Select. Cov.]; Hortic. Abstr.; Ornamental Hort. (1991-); Plant Grow. Reg. Abstr.; Rev. Plant Pathol.; World Agric. Econ. Rural Sociol. Abstr.

LC S
DD 630
ISSN 0334-2484
IS

SPECIAL PUBLICATION - AGRICULTURAL RESEARCH ORGANIZATION. (SPECIAL PUBLICATION.). [Spec. pub. - Agric. Res. Organ.]. Added/Corp Minhal Ha-Mehkar Ha-Hakla'i (Israel). VFOAT Pirsum Meyuhad.
No. 6 (1972)-. Monographic series. English (Hebrew). Agricultural Research Organization, Division of Scientific Publishing, Volcani Center, PO Box 6, Bet Dagan Israel. **Tel** 03-9683215. *Continues* Special Publication (Mekhon Volkani Le-Heker Ha-Haklaut).
Ind/Abst Hortic. Abstr.; Rev. Plant Pathol.

LC SF521
DD 638.1
ISSN 0334-2484
IS

SPECIAL PUBLICATION - AGRICULTURAL RESEARCH ORGANIZATION, THE VOLCANI CENTER. [Spec. pub. - Agric. Res. Organ.].
Main/Corp Agricultural Research Organization. Volcani Center. Division of Scientific Publications. No. 3 (1971)-. Monographic series. Multiple languages. Irregular. Price varies per volume. Agricultural Research Organization, Division of Scientific Publishing, Volcani Center, PO Box 6, Bet Dagan Israel. **Tel** 03-9683215. ctrl circ.

Agriculture

LC S   **ISSN** 0194-407X
DD 630   US
Pr Rev
SPECIAL PUBLICATION - COUNCIL FOR AGRICULTURAL SCIENCE AND TECHNOLOGY. [Spec. publ. - Counc. Agric. Sci. Technol.]. **Main/Corp** Council for Agricultural Science and Technology. **Added/Corp** Council for Agricultural Science and Technology. No. 1 (1972)-. Monographic series. English. Irregular. Price varies per volume. Council for Agricultural Science and Technology, 4420 West Lincoln Way, Ames IA 50010. **Tel** (515)292-2125, FAX (515)292-4512. **ED** Kayleen A. Niyo.
Ind/Abst AGRICOLA [Full Cov.].

LC S   **ISSN** 0748-0032
DD 630   US
SPECIAL PUBLICATION / THE UNIVERSITY OF GEORGIA, COLLEGE OF AGRICULTURE, EXPERIMENT STATION. [Spec. pub. - Univ. Ga., Coll. Agric., Exp. Stn.]. English. Irregular. Free. Agricultural Experiment Station / Georgia, University of Georgia, Athens GA 30602. **Tel** (706)542-3621. **ED** Katheleen Sheridan. **Circ:** 2,000.
Desc: All fields of agricultural research.
Ind/Abst Cot. Trop. Fibr. Abstr. Bibliogr.; Hortic. Abstr.; Maize Abstr.; Nutr. Abstr. Rev., Ser. B, Live Feeds and Feed.; Ornamental Hort. (1991-); Sorghum Mill. Abstr.; Soyabean Abstr.; World Agric. Econ. Rural Sociol. Abstr.

LC S   **ISSN** 1052-536X
DD 630   US
SPECIAL REFERENCE BRIEFS. [Spec. ref. briefs]. **Added/Corp** National Agricultural Library (U.S.). Reference Section. NAL SRB (Feb. 1982)-. Monographic series. English. **Continues** Special Publication Series (National Agricultural Library (U.S.)).
Ind/Abst AGRICOLA [Full Cov.].

LC S   **ISSN** 0258-2708
DD 630   CH
TITLE CHANGE
SPECIAL REPORT. **Added/Corp** Tai-Chung chu Nung yeh kai Liang Chang. (19??)-(19??). Monographic series. English. **Continued by** Special Publication (Tai-Chung chu Nung yeh kai Liang Chang), 0258-2708.
Ind/Abst World Agric. Econ. Rural Sociol. Abstr. (?-?).

LC S   **ISSN** 0571-0189
DD 630   US
     CODEN AUARAN
SPECIAL REPORT - AGRICULTURAL EXPERIMENT STATION, DIVISION OF AGRICULTURE, UNIVERSITY OF ARKANSAS, FAYETTEVILLE. (SPECIAL REPORT.). [Spec. rep. - Agric. Exp. Stn. Div. Agric. Univ. Ark. Fayettev.]. **Added/Corp** University of Arkansas. Agricultural Experiment Station. Vol. 17 (1969)-. Monographic series. English. Price varies per volume. Arkansas Agricultural Experiment Station, University of Arkansas, Fayetteville AR 72701. **Tel** (501)575-5647, FAX (501)575-7273. **Continues** Special Report (University of Arkansas (Fayetteville Campus). Agricultural Experiment Station).
Ind/Abst Index Vet.; Nutr. Abstr. Rev., Ser. B, Live Feeds and Feed.; Plant Breed. Abstr.; Rev. Med. Vet. Mycology; Soils Fert.; Weed Abstr.

LC S   **ISSN** 0886-7623
DD 630   US
SPECIAL REPORT - NEW YORK STATE AGRICULTURAL EXPERIMENT STATION. (SPECIAL REPORT - NEW YORK STATE AGRICULTURAL EXPERIMENT STATION, GENEVA.). [Spec. rep. - N. Y. State Agric. Exp. Stn.]. **Main/Corp** New York State Agricultural Experiment Station. No. 1-. Monographic series. English. Price varies per volume.
Ind/Abst AGRICOLA [Select. Cov.].

LC S81 .A53a
DD 630.5   US
SPECIAL REPORT / UNIVERSITY OF MISSOURI--COLUMBIA, AGRICULTURAL EXPERIMENT STATION. **Added/Corp** University of Missouri--Columbia. Agricultural Experiment Station. **VFOAT** Missouri Special Report; SR. (1968)-. Monographic series. English. **Continues** Special Report (University of Missouri. Agricultural Experiment Station), 0544-4977.
Ind/Abst Plant Breed. Abstr.

LC HD1401   **ISSN** 0190-6798
DD 338   US
SPEEDY BEE, THE. Vol. 1 (Feb. 1972)-. Trade Publication. English. Twelve times a year. $15.75. The Speedy Bee, PO Box 998, Jesup GA 31545. **Tel** (912)427-4018. **ED** Troy Fore. **Bk Rev**. **Ad Acc**. **Circ:** 4,000.
Desc: Tabloid newspaper for beekeepers and honey industry. News, how-to's, features, advertising.

LC S   **ISSN** 1011-0054
DD 630   NE
SPORE (ENGLISH ED.). (SPORE : BIMONTHLY BULLETIN OF THE TECHNICAL CENTRE FOR AGRICULTURAL AND RURAL COOPERATION FOR DISSEMINATION OF SCIENTIFIC AND TECHNICAL INFORMATION.). [Spore (Engl. ed.)]. **Added/Corp** Centre Technique de Cooperation Agricole et Rurale. (1986)-. Bulletin. English. Six times a year. CTA, BP 380, 6700 A J, Wageningen The Netherlands.
Ind/Abst Geogr. Abstr. Human Geogr.; Int. Dev. Abstr.

LC S   **ISSN** 0038-8661
DD 630   US
SPUDMAN. (SPUDMAN; VOICE OF THE POTATO INDUSTRY.). (19??)-. Trade Publication. English. Eight times a year. $1.00. Spudman Magazine, PO Box 1752, Monterey VA 93942. **Tel** (408)373-7991, FAX (408)373-2923. **ED** Donald S. Miller. **Bk Rev**, (Qty: 1-2/yr). **Ad Acc**. **Circ:** 17,600.
Desc: Information for growers, packers and processors of potatoes nationally. Articles range from scientific research reports to grower profiles and industry news.

LC S
DD 630   RU
SPUTNIK SELSKOI MOLODEZHI. (19??)-. Russian. One time a year. 0.35rub. Izdatelstvo Molodaia Gvardiia, Novodmitrovskaya Ulitsa 5A, 125015 Moscow Russia. **Tel** 011 95 285 1935.

LC S
DD 630   CE
SRI LANKAN JOURNAL OF AGRICULTURAL SCIENCES. **Added/Corp** National Agricultural Society of Sri Lanka. Vol. 20 (1983)-. Periodical. English. $5.00. National Agricultural Society of Sri Lanka, Faculty of Agriculture, Dr. HPM Gunasena, Peradeniya Sri Lanka. **Tel** 08 88375. **Continues** National Agricultural Society of Ceylon. Journal of the National Agricultural Society of Ceylon.
Ind/Abst Field Crop Abstr.; Postharvest News Inf.

LC S   **ISSN** 0090-1334
DD 630   US
STAFF PAPER P. [Staff pap. P]. **Added/Corp** University of Minnesota. Dept. of Agricultural and Applied Economics. **VFOAT** Staff Papers Series. (19??)-. Monographic series. English.
Ind/Abst For. Abstr.; Soyabean Abstr.

LC S
DD 630   US
STAFF PAPERS SERIES / MISSISSIPPI AGRICULTURAL AND FORESTRY EXPERIMENT STATION. DEPT. OF AGRICULTURAL ECONOMICS. (STAFF PAPERS SERIES.). **Added/Corp** Mississippi Agricultural and Forestry Experiment Station. Dept. of Agricultural Economics. No. 1 (1970)-. Monographic series. English. Price varies per volume.

LC S
DD 630   CN
STAFF PAPERS : UNIVERSITY OF ALBERTA. DEPARTMENT OF RURAL ECONOMY. English. Irregular. Free. University of Alberta / Rural Economy, Department of Rural Economy, Edmonton Alberta T6G 2H1 Canada. **Tel** (403)492-4225. ctrl circ.

LC JC345
DD 929.82
STALSBY WILSON'S WHO'S WHO IN FERTILIZER AND AG-CHEMICAL SUPPLY. See Biographies.

LC S   **ISSN** 8750-4960
DD 630   US
STANISLAUS FARM NEWS. (19??)-. Periodical. English. One time a week. $5.00. Stanilaus Farm News, PO Box 3070, Modesto CA 95353. **Tel** (209)522-7278. **ED** Jan Ennenga. Each issue contains an index to its own contents (no volume index)--loose. **Ad Acc**. **Circ:** 6,000 (ctrl).

LC HD1751 .A9322A   **ISSN** 0277-9307
DD 338.1/0973   US
STATE DATA PROFILES, CALENDAR YEAR. [State data profiles, cal. year.]. Government Publication. English. One time a year. US Department of Agriculture / Agricultural Stabilization and Conservation, 14th and Independence Avenue SW, Washington DC 20250. **Continues** State Data Profiles, 0095-8204.

LC S401.U6 A317   **ISSN** 0081-4539
DD 338.1/05   IT
NLM W1 ST314X   **CODEN** FAONEY
STATE OF FOOD AND AGRICULTURE, THE. (THE STATE OF FOOD AND AGRICULTURE : REVIEW AND OUTLOOK.). [State food agric.]. **Added/Corp** Food and Agriculture Organization of the United Nations. (1951)-. English (Spanish). One time a year. $50.00. Food Agriculture Organization (FAO) / Italy, GIPCI66 via Terme di Caracalla, 00100 Rome Italy. **Tel** 011 39 6 52252925, FAX 011 39 6 52253152.
(Subscription address: UNIPUB, 4611 F Assembly Drive, Lanham MD 20706. **Tel** (800)274-4888, (301)459-7666.) Documents available from BIOSIS Document Express. **Continues** World Outlook and State of Food and Agriculture.
Desc: Includes facts and figures on the global agricultural situation, an analysis of the economic environment surrounding agriculture, an appraisal of the sector's future prospects, and a report on regional trends and policy developments as well as selected country performances.
Ind/Abst Biol. Abstr.; F&S Index Plus Text, Int. [Select. Cov.]; Int. Labour Doc.; LABORDOC; Predicasts Forecasts.

LC S401 .S74a
DD 630   KO
STATE OF FOOD AND AGRICULTURE. (SEGYE SINGNYANG NONGOP PAEKSO.). **Added/Corp** Food and Agriculture Organization of the United Nations. FAO Hanguk Hyophoe. (19??)-. Korean (English; translations available in English). One time a year. Fao Hanguk Hyophoe, 731 Socho-dong Kangnam-ku, Seoul Seoul Korea.

LC HD1401   **ISSN** 0318-4838
DD 338.1/8/71   CN
STATEMENT ON FARM POLICY ISSUES PRESENTED TO MEMBERS OF PARLIAMENT AND THE SENATE. **Main/Corp** National Farmers Union (Canada). (1974)-. Periodical. English. One time a year. National Farmers Union / Canada, 250C 2nd Avenue South, Saskatoon Saskatchewan S7K 1K9 Canada. **Supersedes** National Farmers Union (Canada). Submission to the Government of Canada, 0470-0198.

LC S   **ISSN** 0362-8167
DD 630   US
     CODEN MXSBAE
STATION BULLETIN - AGRICULTURAL EXPERIMENT STATION. (STATION BULLETIN.). [Stn. bull. - Agric. Exp. Stn.]. **Added/Corp** University of Minnesota. Agricultural Experiment Station. United States. Bureau of Agricultural Economics. No. 416 (1953)-. Bulletin. English. Irregular. Price varies per volume. University of Minnesota Agricultural Experiment Station, 220 Coffee Hall, 1420 Eckles Avenue, St. Paul MN 55108. **Tel** (612)625-4211. Documents available from BIOSIS Document Express, CASDDS. **Continues** University of Minnesota. Agricultural Experiment Station. Bulletin - Agricultural Experiment Station, University of Minnesota, 0196-8742.
Ind/Abst AGRICOLA; Biol. Abstr.; Chem. Abstr.

LC S   **ISSN** 0077-8338
DD 630   US
STATION BULLETIN - NEW HAMPSHIRE AGRICULTURAL EXPERIMENT STATION. (STATION BULLETIN.). [Stn. bull. - N.H. Agric. Exp. Stn.]. **Added/Corp** New Hampshire Agricultural Experiment Station. **VFOAT** Bulletin. (1888)-. Bulletin. English.
Ind/Abst AGRICOLA; Leis., Rec., Tour. Abstr.

LC S   **ISSN** 0096-1078
DD 630   US
STATION BULLETIN - OREGON STATE UNIVERSITY, AGRICULTURAL EXPERIMENT STATION. (STATION BULLETIN.). [Stn. bull. - Or. State Univ., Agric. Exp. Stn.]. **Added/Corp** Oregon State University. Agricultural Experiment Station. (1961)-. Bulletin. English. Oregon State University / Agricultural Experiment Station, Corvallis OR 97331. **Continues** Station Bulletin (Oregon State College. Agricultural Experiment Station).
Ind/Abst Field Crop Abstr.; Soils Fert.; Weed Abstr.

LC HD1751 .A5
DD 338.1/0973   US
STATISTICAL BULLETIN / UNITED STATES DEPARTMENT OF AGRICULTURE. See Agriculture-Abstracting, Bibliographies and Statistics.

LC S557.T752 S247
DD 630/.74/0972983   SP
STATISTICAL REPORT ON THE NATIONAL AGRICULTURAL EXHIBITION / REPUBLIC OF TRINIDAD & TOBAGO, CENTRAL STATISTICAL OFFICE. See Agriculture-Abstracting, Bibliographies and Statistics.

LC HD1930.N65 S83
DD 338.1/09416   IE
STATISTICAL REVIEW OF NORTHERN IRELAND AGRICULTURE See Agriculture-Abstracting, Bibliographies and Statistics.

Agriculture

LC S
DD 630 LU
● **STATISTICS IN FOCUS. AGRICULTURE, FORESTRY AND FISHERIES.** See Agriculture-Abstracting, Bibliographies and Statistics.

LC Z5071
DD 016.63 AT
STATISTICS OF WESTERN AUSTRALIA: RURAL INDUSTRIES. See Agriculture-Abstracting, Bibliographies and Statistics.

LC S239 .A3854
DD 338.1/09492 NE
STATISTIEK VAN DE LAND- EN TUINBOUW / CENTRAAL BUREAU VOOR DE STATISTIEK, HOOFDAFDELING LANDBOUWSTATISTIEKEN. See Agriculture-Abstracting, Bibliographies and Statistics.

LC HD1950.P35 S8
DD 630 FR
STATISTIQUE AGRICOLE : REGION PARISIENNE. See Agriculture-Abstracting, Bibliographies and Statistics.

LC HD9014.C4 Q482 **ISSN** 0828-2501
DD 338.1/09713/021 CN
STATISTIQUES DE L'AGRICULTURE, DES PECHES ET DE L'ALIMENTATION. See Agriculture-Abstracting, Bibliographies and Statistics.

LC HD2001 .S72 **ISSN** 0108-5522
DD 630 DK
STATISTISKE EFTERRETNINGER. LANDBRUG. See Agriculture-Abstracting, Bibliographies and Statistics.

LC HD1751 .A91854 HD1476.U U5 **ISSN** 0270-1154
DD 338.1 338.1/6 US
STATUS OF THE FAMILY FARM, ANNUAL REPORT TO THE CONGRESS. **Main/Corp** United States. Dept. of Agriculture. Economics, Statistics, and Cooperatives Service. National Economics Division. Government Publication. English. One time a year. Department of Agriculture / Economics Statistics and Cooperative, Economics Statistics and Cooperative Service, 14th Street and Independence Avenue SW, Washington DC 20250. **Tel** (202)720-2791.

LC S13 .S4373 **ISSN** 0131-9140
DD 630.5 RU
STEPNYE PROSTORY. [Stepnye prostory]. **Added/Corp** Russian S.F.S.R. Ministerstvo Selskogo Khoziaistva. Vol. 1 (Jan. 1968)-. Periodical. Russian. Twelve times a year. $119.95. Saratov N.G. Chernyshevskii State University, Astrakhanskaya Ulitsa 83, 410071 Saratov Russia. **Tel** 011 7 241696, **FAX** 011 7 240146, telex 241125. **(Subscription address:** East View Publications Inc., 3020 Harbor Lane North, Suite 110, Minneapolis MN 55447. **Tel** (800)477-1005, (612)550-0961, **FAX** (612)559-2931.) **Continues** Selskokhoziaistvennoe Proizvodstvo Povolzhia.

LC S
DD 630 CI
STOCARSTVO. Vol. 1 (1947)-. Periodical. Serbo-Croatian (Roman). Six times a year.
Ind/Abst Grass. Forage Abstr.; Index Vet.; Nutr. Abstr. Rev., Ser. B, Live Feeds and Feed.; Pig News Inf.; Poult. Abstr.; Sorghum Mill. Abstr.; Soyabean Abstr.

LC S **ISSN** 0039-1565
DD 630 AT
STOCK & LAND. (1993)-. English. One time a week. 71.53Aus$. Rural Press / Victoria, PO Box 160, Port Melbourne Victoria 3207 Australia. **Tel** 11 61 3 2870900, telex 35668.

LC S
DD 630 US
STOCKS OF GRAINS, OILSEEDS, AND HAY, FINAL ESTIMATES BY STATES. Statistical Publication. English. US Department of Agriculture / Statistical Reporting Service, 14th Street & Independence Avenue SW, Washington DC 20250. available on microfiche (Vols. for (1978-83)- distributed to depository libraries).

LC HF1371 **ISSN** 1190-9714
DD 382 CN
● **STRATEGIE D'EXPORTATION DU CANADA, PLAN DE PROMOTION DU COMMERCE EXTERIEUR. 2, AGRICULTURE ET PRODUITS ALIMENTAIRES.** [Strateg. export. Can. plan promot. commer. exter., 2 Agric. prod. aliment.]. **Added/Corp** Canada. **VFOAT** Agriculture et Produits Alimentaires. (1996)-. Government Publication. French. **Continues** Plan de Promotion du Commerce Exterieur du Canada. 3, Produits Agro-Alimentaires, 1200-1112.

LC HF1371 **ISSN** 1190-9730
DD 382 CN
● **STRATEGIE D'EXPORTATION DU CANADA, PLAN DE PROMOTION DU COMMERCE EXTERIEUR. 3, AERONAUTIQUE ET PIECES D'AERONEFS.** [Strateg. export. Can. plan promot. commer. exter., 3 Aeronaut. pieces aeronefs]. **Added/Corp** Canada. **VFOAT** Aeronautique et Pieces d'Aeronefs. (1996)-. Government Publication. French. **Continues** Plan de Promotion du Commerce Exterieur du Canada. 2, Aeronautique, 1200-1090.

LC S
DD 630 FR
STRATEGIES ALIMENTAIRES. (19??)-. French. Solidarite Agro-Alimentaire, 13 boulevard Saint-Martin, 75003 Paris France.

LC S348.B45 B45a
DD 338.1/0966/83 DM
STRUCTURE DES EXPLOITATIONS AGRICOLES TRADITIONNELLES DE LA REPUBLIQUE POPULAIRE DU BENIN. **Main/Corp** Benin. Ministere du Developpement Rural et de l'Action Cooperative. Service des Etudes et de la Statistique. (19??)-. French. Ministere du Developpement Rural et de l'Action Cooperative, Service des Etudes et de la Statistique, Porto-Novo Dahomey.

LC TH4911 .M52A **ISSN** 0149-1245
DD 690/.8/9 US
Pr Rev.
STRUCTURES AND ENVIRONMENT HANDBOOK. See Building and Construction.

LC S **ISSN** 0177-2503
DD 630 GW
STUDIEN ZUR INTEGRIERTEN LANDLICHEN ENTWICKLUNG. (19??)-. Monographic series. German. Irregular. Price varies per volume. Verlag Weltarchiv GmBH, Neuer Jungfernstieg 21, D-20354 Hamburg Germany. **Tel** 011 49 40 3562500.
Ind/Abst Agric. Eng. Abstr.; Nutr. Abstr. Rev., Ser. A, Hum. Exp.; Potato Abstr.; Rural Dev. Abstr.; World Agric. Econ. Rural Sociol. Abstr.

LC S **ISSN** 0139-5084
DD 630 XR
UDC 631.17
STUDIJNI INFORMACE. ZEMEDELSKA TECHNIKA. (1970)-. Periodical. Multiple languages. Irregular.
Ind/Abst Agric. Eng. Abstr.

LC S **ISSN** 0257-3148
DD 630 US
STUDY PAPER - CGIAR. (STUDY PAPER / CONSULTATIVE GROUP ON INTERNATIONAL AGRICULTURAL RESEARCH.). [Study pap. - CGIAR]. **Added/Corp** Consultative Group on International Agricultural Research. **VFOAT** CGIAR Study Paper. No. 1 (1985)-. Monographic series. English. Price varies per volume. CGIAR, Pub H-2007, 1818 H Street NW, Washington DC 20433.
Ind/Abst Geogr. Abstr. Human Geogr.; Int. Dev. Abstr.

LC HD2330 **ISSN** 0714-4644
DD 338.1/09715 CN
SUBMISSION TO THE GOVERNMENT OF NEW BRUNSWICK / NATIONAL FARMERS UNION, REGION 1. [Submiss. Gov. N.B. - Natl. Farmers Union, Reg. 1]. **Main/Corp** National Farmers Union (Canada). Region 1. 1977-. English. Every 2 years. National Farmers Union / Canada, 250C 2nd Avenue South, Saskatoon Saskatchewan S7K 1K9 Canada. **Continues** Submission to the Province of New Brunswick on the Subjects of Collective Bargaining Legislation and In-Storage Crop Loss.

LC HD1871 .S72
DD 338.1/881 BL
SUBSIDIOS PARA A FIXACAO DOS PRECOS MINIMOS. Portuguese. Ministerio da Agricultura Comissao de Financiamento da Producao CFP Setor De Edificios Publicos W, 3 Norte Q514 BL B Brasilia DF CEP 70760 Brazil.

LC S1 .S93 **ISSN** 0039-4432
DD 631 US
SUCCESSFUL FARMING. [Success. farming]. **VFOAT** SF. Vol. 1, (1902)-. Periodical. English. Twelve times a year. $14.00. Meredith Corporation, Locust at 17th, Des Moines IA 50309. **Tel** (515)284-3000, **FAX** (515)284-2568. **(Subscription address:** Neodata / Colorado, PO Box 2606, Boulder CO 80322.) **ED** Loren Kruse. **Ad Acc**. **Circ:** 576,000 (ctrl). available on microfilm and microfiche from University Microfilms International (UMI); available on an online database (files 647,648/Full-Text) from DIALOG. Documents available from UMI Article Clearinghouse, Magazine Collection. **Absorbed** Dairy Farmer **and** Successful Farming in the South.
Desc: The magazine for families that make farming their business.

Ind/Abst Abr. Read. Guide Period. Lit.; Acad. Abstr. Full Text Elite; Acad. Abstr. Full Text (1992-) [Full Txt.]; Bus. Index (1985-); EP Collect.; Gen. BusinessFile (1985-); Gen. Period. Index (1985-); Homework Help.; Mag. Artic. Summar. Elite; Mag. Artic. Summar. Select; Mag. Artic. Summar. CD-ROM; Mag. Index Plus (1989-); Mag. Search; MasterFile FullTEXT 1000; MasterFile FullTEXT 350; MasterFile FullTEXT 650; MasterFile FullTEXT (Dec. 1988-); Newsp. Period. Abstr. (1988-); OCLC; Pub. Lib. FullTEXT; Read. Guide Abstr. Select Ed.; Read. Guide Period. Lit.; Telebase; Mag. Index (1977-); TOM Gen. Index (1985-) [Full Txt.]; Trade Ind. ASAP [Full Txt.]; Trade Ind. Index [Full Txt.]; Vocat. Search.

LC S **ISSN** 0039-467X
DD 630 US
SUFFOLK COUNTY AGRICULTURAL NEWS. **Added/Corp** Cooperative Extension Association of Suffolk County. Suffolk County Extension Service Association. Vol. 1 (May 1917)-. Periodical. English. Twelve times a year. $15.00. Cooperative Extension of Suffolk County, 246 Griffing Avenue, Riverhead NY 11901. **Tel** (516)727-7850, **FAX** (516)727-7130. Index available. **Ad Acc, Adv Mgr:** Caryn Popowitch. **Circ:** 1,000.
Desc: Information on potato, vegetable, greenhouse, nursery, fruit, and etc. for growers.

LC S
DD 630 US
SUFFOLK COUNTY AGRICULTURAL NEWS. Vol. 55, No. 1 (Jan. 1971)-. Periodical. English. Twelve times a year. $15.00 US; $20.00 other. Cooperative Extension of Suffolk County, 246 Griffing Avenue, Riverhead NY 11901. **Tel** (516)727-7850, **FAX** (516)727-7130. **ED** Patricia Edwards. **Ad Acc. Circ:** 1,450 (ctrl). **Continues** Suffolk County Farm Bureau News (1932).
Desc: Commercial agricultural news articles.

LC HD1401 **ISSN** 0039-4742
DD 338
CODEN SUAZA7
SUGAR Y AZUCAR. [Sugar azucar]. **Added/Corp** International Society of Sugar Cane Technologists. Vol. 51, No. 10 (Oct. 1956)-. Trade Publication. English (Spanish). Twelve times a year. $75.00. Ruspam Communications, 452 Hudson Terrace, Englewood Cliffs NJ 07632. **Tel** (201)871-9200, **FAX** (201)871-9639. **ED** Richard B. Miles. **Ad Acc, Adv Mgr:** Alan Berg. **Circ:** 5,000. available on microfilm and microfiche from University Microfilms International (UMI). Documents available from CASDDS. **Formed by the union of** Sugar, 0361-0063 **and** Mundo Azucarero.
Ind/Abst AGRICOLA; BioBusiness (1989--); Chem. Abstr.; Field Crop Abstr.; Food Sci. Technol. Abstr.; Hortic. Abstr.; Nutr. Abstr. Rev., Ser. B, Live Feeds and Feed.; Nutr. Abstr. Rev., Ser. A, Hum. Exp.; Life Sci. Collect.; Sug. Indus. Abstr.; World Agric. Econ. Rural Sociol. Abstr.

LC S **ISSN** 0301-603X
DD 630.71505 SA
SUID.-AFRIKAANSE TYDSKRIF VIR LANDBOUVOORLIGTING. [S. Afr. tydskr. l. ndbouvoorligt.]. **VFOAT** South African Journal of Agricultural Extension. (1972)-. Periodical. Afrikaans (English; summaries and/or abstracts in Afrikaans and English). One time a year. R30.00. South African Society for Agricultural Extension, University of Pretoria, Department of Agriculture, Pretoria 0002 South Africa. **Tel** 011 27 12 4203244, **FAX** 011 27 12 3422713. **ED** J.J. van der Wateren. Index available (author). **Bk Rev. Ad Acc**. ctrl circ.
Ind/Abst World Agric. Econ. Rural Sociol. Abstr.

LC S **ISSN** 0373-1332
DD 630 CI
SUMARSKI LIST. [Sumar. list]. (1???)-. Periodical. Serbo-Croatian (Roman). Twelve times a year. $176.00. **(Subscription address:** Jugoslovenska Knjiga, PO Box 36, YU 11001 Belgrade Yugoslovia. **Tel** 011 38 11 621055, **FAX** 011 38 11 325970.)
Ind/Abst AGRICOLA; Rev. Agric. Entomol.

LC S **ISSN** 1033-8772
DD 630 AT
CEASED
SUMMARY OF CROPS AUSTRALIA. See Agriculture-Abstracting, Bibliographies and Statistics.

LC S **ISSN** 0039-5471
DD 630 FI
CODEN SUOOAA
SUO. [Suo]. **Added/Corp** Suoseura. (1950)-. Academic Scholarly Publication. Finnish. Four times a year. Fmk100.00. Suo Seura / Finnish Peatland Society, Unioninkatu 40, SF-00170 Helsinki Finland. **Tel FAX** 011 358 0 1917605. **(Subscription address:** Academic Bookstore Akateeminen, Postilokero 23, FIN 00371 Helsinki Finland. **Tel** 011 358 0 12141.) Documents available from BIOSIS Document Express, CASDDS.
Ind/Abst Biol. Abstr.; Chem. Abstr.; Coal Abstr.; EMBASE; Energy Res. Abstr. (Jan. 1982)-; For. Prod. Abstr.; For. Abstr.; GeoRef.; Life Sci. Collect.; Soils Fert.

Agriculture

LC S **ISSN** 0358-9153
DD 630 FI
UDC 08
SUOMEN AKATEMIAN JULKAISUJA.
[Suom. akat. julk.]. **VFOAT** Publications of the Academy of Finland. (1977)-. Monographic series. Multiple languages. Three times a week.
Ind/Abst For. Abstr.; Irr. Drain. Abstr.

LC S
DD 630 US
SURCO LATINOAMERICANA, EL.
Added/Corp Deere and Company. **VFOAT** Surco. (1???)-. Periodical. Spanish. Four times a year. Free on request to qualified subscribers. Deere & Company, John Deere Road, Moline IL 61265. **Tel** (309)765-8000.

LC S **ISSN** 0228-2305
DD 312/.43/09713 CN
SURVEY OF AGRICULTURAL LOST TIME INJURIES. (SURVEY OF AGRICULTURAL LOST TIME INJURIES FOR THE YEAR ...). [Surv. agric. lost time inj.]. 1976-. English. One time a year. Farm Safety Association, Suite 22-23/340 Woodlawn Road West, Guelph Ontario N1H 7K9 Canada. **Tel** (519)823-5600.

LC S
DD 630 IO
SURVEY PERTANIAN. Main/Corp Indonesia.
Biro Pusat Statistik. (19??)-. Multiple languages (English and Indonesian). Biro Pusat Statistik / Central Bureau of Statistics, 8 Jalan Dr. Sutomo No. 8, Box 3, Jakarta Pusat 10710 Indonesia. **Tel** 011 62 21 372808, 011 62 21 374908 ext.342.

LC SF **ISSN** 0944-307X
DD 636 GW
UDC 63
SUS. SCHWEINEZUCHT UND SCHWEINEMAST. [SUS, Schweinezucht und Schweinemast]. **VFOAT** Schweinezucht und Schweinemast. (1992)-. Periodical. German. Six times a year. DM48.60 Germany; DM57.60 other. Landwirtschaftsverlag GmbH, Postfach 480249, D-48079 Muenster Hiltrup Germany. **Tel** 011 49 2501 8010, FAX 011 49 2501 801204, telex 892665 LANDV D. **Continues** Schweinezucht und Schweinemast, 0036-7176.

LC S602.5 **ISSN** 1180-1506
DD 631.5/84/0971 CN
SUSTAINABLE FARMING. (SUSTAINABLE FARMING : THE QUARTERLY MAGAZINE OF RESOURCE EFFICIENT AGRICULTURAL PRODUCTION.). [Sustain. farming]. **Added/Corp** REAP-Canada. **VFOAT** Magazine of Resource Efficient Agricultural Production. Vol. 1, No. 1 (Spring 1990)-. Periodical. English. Four times a year (During the seasons). 12.81Can$. Reap-Canada, Glenaladale House, Box 125, St. Anne Bellevue H9X1CO Canada. **Tel** (514)298-7743, FAX (514)398-7972. **ED** Roger Samson. **Bk Rev**, (Qty: 4). **Ad Acc**, **Ad Adv Mgr**: R. Samson. **Circ**: 1,200 (ctrl). **Continues** R.E.A.P. (Newsletter)., 0847-477X.
Desc: The magazine of Resource Efficient Agricultural Production.

LC S **ISSN** 0049-2701
DD 630 SW
 CCC
 CODEN SJARB9
Pr Rev.
SWEDISH JOURNAL OF AGRICULTURAL RESEARCH. [Swed. j. agric. res.]. (1971)-. Academic Scholarly Publication. English. Four times a year. $112.00. Scandinavian University Press, PO Box 2959 Toeyen, N 0608 Oslo 6 Norway. **Tel** 011 47 2 2575400, FAX 011 47 2 2575353, telex 71896 UROR N. (**Subscription address**: Scandinavian University Press, 200 Meacham Ave., Elmont NY 11003. **Tel** (516)352-7300, FAX (516)352-7377.) **ED** Goran Grant. ctrl circ. Documents available from The Genuine Article, BIOSIS Document Express, CASDDS. **Supersedes** Uppsala. Lantbrukshogskolan Och Statens Lantbruksforsok. Annaler.
Desc: Presents to international readership essential contributions of research originating from the faculty of Agriculture at the Swedish University of Agricultural Sciences.
Ind/Abst AGRICOLA; Agric. Eng. Abstr. (1991-); Anal. Abstr.; Anim. Breed. Abstr.; Biol. Abstr.; Chem. Abstr.; Crop Physiol. Abstr.; Curr. Aware. Biol. Sci., CABS; Curr. Cit.; Curr. Contents Agric. Biol. Environ. Sci.; Dairy Sci. Abstr.; Ecol. Abstr. (?-?); Ecology Abstr.; EMBASE; Energy Res. Abstr. (April 1972-); Field Crop Abstr.; Food Sci. Technol. Abstr.; Grass. Forage Abstr.; Helminthol. Abstr.; Hortic. Abstr.; Maize Abstr.; Nutr. Abstr. Rev., Ser. B, Live Feeds and Feed.; Life Sci. Collect.; Pig News Inf.; Plant Breed. Abstr.; Postharvest News Inf.; Potato Abstr.; Poult. Abstr.; Res. Alert [Full Cov.]; Rev. Agric. Entomol.; Rev. Plant Pathol.; Sci. Cit. Index; SCISEARCH; Seed Abstr.; Soils Fert.; Soyabean Abstr.; Weed Abstr.; Wildl. Rev.

LC HD1393 .N497a
DD 333.14 JA
TAHATA KAKAKU OYOBI KOSAKURYO SHIRABE. Main/Corp Nihon Fudosan Kenkyujo. (19??)-. Japanese (English). One time a year. ¥310. Nihon Fudosan Kenkyujo, (Japan Real Estate Institute), Kangin-Fujiya Building, 1-3-2 Toranomon Minato-ku, Tokyo Japan. **Tel** 011 81 3 5035335, FAX 011 81 3 5978063. Index available. cum. index. **Circ**: 5,200.
Desc: Agricultural land prices and rents in Japan compiled by the Japan Real Estate Institute.

LC S19 **ISSN** 0253-276X
DD 630/.951249 CH
 CODEN TNYKDD
TAI-WAN NUNG YEH = TAIWAN AGRICULTURE BIMONTHLY. (TAIWAN NONGYE SHUANG-YUEKAN). [Taiwan nongye shuang-yuekan]. **VFOAT** Taiwan Agriculture Bimonthly. (1979)-. Academic Scholarly Publication. Chinese (summaries and/or abstracts in English; table of contents in English). Six times a year. Free. Taiwan Department of Agriculture and Forestry, Taiwan Provincial Government, Taiwan 543. **ED** Ren-der Yan. **Circ**: 3,000. Documents available from CASDDS. **Continues** Tai-Wan Nung Yeh Chi Kan.
Desc: Purposes are to report agricultural policies, science, achievements, news, and regulations, etc.
Ind/Abst AGRICOLA; Agric. Eng. Abstr.; Chem. Abstr. (1979-1983); Field Crop Abstr.; Hortic. Abstr.; Plant Grow. Reg. Abstr.; Postharvest News Inf.; Rev. Agric. Entomol.; Rev. Plant Pathol.; Seed Abstr.; Soyabean Abstr.; World Agric. Econ. Rural Sociol. Abstr.

LC S304.F6 T3 **ISSN** 0429-1255
DD 630 CH
TAI-WAN NUNG YEH NIEN PAO.
Added/Corp Taiwan. Nung Lin Ting. **VFOAT** Taiwan Agricultural Yearbook. (1920)-. Chinese (English). One time a year. Free on request. Taiwan Department of Agriculture & Forestry, Chung Hsing New Villa, Nantou Taiwan.

LC S542.T332 T347
DD 630.72 CH
 TITLE CHANGE
TAI-WAN SHENG TAI-NAN CHU NUNG YEH KAI LIANG CHANG YEN CHIU HUI PAO. **Added/Corp** Tai-wan Sheng Tai-nan chu Nung yeh kai Liang Chang. **VFOAT** Yen Chiu hui pao; Research Bulletin of the Tainan District Agricultural Improvement Station. (19??)-(19??). Bulletin. Chinese (English). **Continued by** Yen Chiu hui pao (Tai-wan Sheng Tai-nan chu Nung yeh kai Liang Chang).
Ind/Abst Maize Abstr. (?-?); Rev. Agric. Entomol.

LC S **ISSN** 0255-6103
DD 630 CH
TAIWAN NONGYE. [Taiwan nongye]. **VFOAT** Taiwan Agriculture Bimonthly. (1965)-. Periodical. Multiple languages. Four times a year.
Ind/Abst Biocont. News Inf.; Ornamental Hort. (1991-); Rice Abstr.

LC S **ISSN** 0258-2708
DD 630 CH
 CODEN STPSEO
TAIWAN-SHENG TAIZHONG-QU NONGYE GAILIANG CHANG TEKAN ... HAO. (SPECIAL PUBLICATION.). [Taiwan-sheng Taizhong-qu nongye gailiang chang tekan ... hao]. **Added/Corp** Tai-Chung Chu Nung yeh kai Liang Chang. (1985)-. Monographic series. English. Documents available from BIOSIS Document Express. **Continues** Special Report (Tai-Chung chu Nung yeh kai Liang Chang).
Ind/Abst Agric. Eng. Abstr.; Biol. Abstr. (1987-); Field Crop Abstr.; Hortic. Abstr.; Leis., Rec., Tour. Abstr.; Maize Abstr.; Ornamental Hort. (1991-); Postharvest News Inf.; Soils Fert.; World Agric. Econ. Rural Sociol. Abstr.

LC S539.5 **ISSN** 0082-156X
DD 630.72 JA
 CODEN TDNHAC
TAMAGAWA DAIGAKU NOGAKUBU KENKYU HOKOKU. (KENKYU HOKOKU.).
[Tamagawa daigaku nogakubu kenkyu hokoku]. **Main/Corp** Tamagawa Daigaku, Tokyo. Nogakubu. **VFOAT** Bulletin of the Faculty of Agriculture, Tamagawa University. No. 1 (1960)-. Academic Scholarly Publication. Multiple languages (English and Japanese). Kenkyu Hokulu / Tamagawa University, Faculty of Agriculture, Machida Shi, Tokyo 194 Japan. Documents available from BIOSIS Document Express, CASDDS.
Ind/Abst Biol. Abstr.; Chem. Abstr.; EMBASE.

LC S
DD 630 TU
 TITLE CHANGE
TARM, ORMAN, VE KOYISLERI BAKANLG DERGISI. **Added/Corp** Turkey. Tarm, Orman, ve Koyisleri Bakanlg. **VFOAT** Tarm, Orman, Koy; Tarm, Orman, Koyisleri Bakanlg Dergisi. (Mar. 1986)-(19??). Periodical. Turkish. **Continued by** Tarm ve Koyisleri Bakanlg Dergisi.
Ind/Abst Index Vet.

LC S **ISSN** 1057-7017
DD 630 US
TASK FORCE REPORT. [Task force rep. - Counc. Agric. Sci. Technol.]. **Added/Corp** Council for Agricultural Science and Technology. **VFOAT** Report. No. 115, June (1989)-. Monographic series. English. Price varies per volume. Council for Agricultural Science and Technology, 4420 West Lincoln Way, Ames IA 50010. **Tel** (515)292-2125, FAX (515)292-4512. **Circ**: 4,000. **Continues** Report (Council for Agricultural Science and Technology), 0194-4088.
Desc: Reports on topics in food and agricultural science written by multidisciplinary groups of scientists.
Ind/Abst AGRICOLA [Full Cov.].

LC S562.I5 T37
DD 630.68 II
TATAM. Periodical. Tamil (Tamil). Twelve times a year. 8.00.

LC HD1536.A9 L35A
DD 305.555 GW
TATIGKEITSBERICHT DER LANDARBEITERKAMMER FUR TIROL.
Main/Corp Landarbeiterkammer fur Tirol. German. Landarbeiterkammer fur Tirol, Brixner Strasse 1, A-6020 Innsbruck Austria.

LC S **ISSN** 0191-1716
DD 630 US
TB (SOUTH DAKOTA AGRICULTURAL EXPERIMENT STATION). (TB.). **VFOAT** T.B. **VAT** Technical Bulletin. Monographic series. English. Irregular. Price varies per volume. South Dakota Agricultural Experiment Station, Agricultural Information Bulletin Room, Old Extension Building, South Dakota University, Brookings SD 57007. **Continues** Technical Bulletin (South Dakota Agricultural Experiment Station).
Ind/Abst AGRICOLA [Select. Cov.].

LC S **ISSN** 0747-0746
DD 630 US
TCM GROWER, THE. **Added/Corp** Texas Citrus Mutual. **VFOAT** T.C.M. Grower; Grower. **VAT** Texas Citrus Mutual Growe. (19??)-. Periodical. English. Texas Citrus Mutual, PO Box 2648, McAllen TX 78502.

LC L
DD 371 US
TEACHER EDUCATION RESEARCH SERIES (PENNSYLVANIA STATE UNIVERSITY. DEPT. OF AGRICULTURAL AND EXTENSION EDUCATION). See Education-Teaching and Curriculum.

LC S
DD 630 PK
TECHNICAL BULLETIN. **Added/Corp** National Fertilizer Development Centre (Pakistan). Planning and Development Division. (19??)-. Bulletin. English.
Ind/Abst Field Crop Abstr.; Irr. Drain. Abstr.; Maize Abstr.; Potato Abstr.; Soils Fert.

LC S
DD 630 AT
TECHNICAL BULLETIN. **Added/Corp** NSW Agriculture. (1991)-. Bulletin. English. **Continues** Technical Bulletin (NSW Agriculture & Fisheries), 1032-9129.

LC S
DD 630 MF
TECHNICAL BULLETIN. **Added/Corp** Mauritius. Ministry of Agriculture, Fisheries, and Natural Resources. (198?)-. Bulletin. English. **Continues** Technical Bulletin (Mauritius. Ministry of Agriculture and Natural Resources and the Environment).
Ind/Abst Index Vet.

LC S **ISSN** 0362-8159
DD 630 US
 CODEN OATBAG
TECHNICAL BULLETIN - AGRICULTURAL EXPERIMENT STATION, OKLAHOMA STATE UNIVERSITY. (TECHNICAL BULLETIN / OKLAHOMA AGRICULTURAL AND MECHANICAL COLLEGE, AGRICULTURAL EXPERIMENT STATION.).
[Tech. bull. - Agri. Exp. Stn. Okla. State Univ.]. **Added/Corp** Oklahoma Agricultural Experiment Station. No. 1 (1938)-. Bulletin. English. Documents available from BIOSIS Document Express, CASDDS.
Ind/Abst Biol. Abstr.; Chem. Abstr.; GeoRef; Poult. Abstr.

Agriculture

LC S
DD 630   CN
TECHNICAL BULLETIN / AGRICULTURE CANADA.
Added/Corp Agriculture Canada. Research ;Branch. **VFOAT** Technical Bulletin. (19??)-. Bulletin. English.
Ind/Abst Soils Fert.

LC S   **ISSN** 0070-2315
DD 630   CY
CODEN CYABAP
TECHNICAL BULLETIN - CYPRUS AGRICULTURAL RESEARCH INSTITUTE. (TECHNICAL BULLETIN.). [Tech. bull. - Cyprus Agric. Res. Inst.]. **Added/Corp** Institouton Georgikon Ereunon (Cyprus). (1966)-. Bulletin. English. Institouton Georgikon Ereunon / Agricultural Research Institute, Ministry of Agriculture and Natural Resources, Nicosia Cyprus. Documents available from BIOSIS Document Express.
Ind/Abst Biol. Abstr.; Hortic. Abstr.; Rev. Plant Pathol.; Seed Abstr.

LC S
DD 630   MY
TECHNICAL BULLETIN - DEPARTMENT OF AGRICULTURE, SABAH, MALAYSIA.
Main/Corp Sabah. Dept. of Agriculture. No.1 (1975)-. Bulletin. English.
Ind/Abst Hortic. Abstr.; Plant Breed. Abstr.; Rev. Agric. Entomol.; Rev. Plant Pathol.

LC S   **ISSN** 1070-1524
DD 630   US
●TECHNICAL BULLETIN - MAINE AGRICULTURAL AND FOREST EXPERIMENT STATION. (TECHNICAL BULLETIN.). **Added/Corp** Maine Agricultural and Forest Experiment Station. **VFOAT** Experiment Station Technical Bulletin; Maine Agricultural and Forest Experiment Station Technical Bulletin. (1994)-. Monographic series. English. Irregular. Free. Maine Agricultural Experiment Station, 103 Winslow Hall, University of Maine, Orono ME 04469. **Continues** Technical Bulletin (Maine Agricultural Experiment Station : 1982), 0734-9556.
Ind/Abst EMBASE.

LC S   **ISSN** 0734-9556
DD 630   US
CODEN TBMSEU
TITLE CHANGE
TECHNICAL BULLETIN - MAINE AGRICULTURAL EXPERIMENT STATION (1982). (TECHNICAL BULLETIN / MAINE AGRICULTURAL EXPERIMENT STATION, UNIVERSITY OF MAINE AT ORONO.). [Tech. bull. - Me. Agric. Exp. Stn.]. **Added/Corp** Maine Agricultural Experiment Station. Maine. Division of Entomology. **VFOAT** Experiment Station Technical Bulletin; Maine Agricultural Experiment Station Technical Bulletin; MAES Technical Bulletin. (Oct. 1982)-(Apr. 1993). Bulletin. English. Maine Agricultural Experiment Station, 103 Winslow Hall, University of Maine, Orono ME 04469. Documents available from BIOSIS Document Express. **Continues** Technical Bulletin - Life Sciences and Agriculture Experiment Station, 0097-5087. **Continued by** Technical Bulletin (Maine Agricultural and Forest Experiment Station), 1070-1524.
Ind/Abst Biocont. News Inf. (?-?); Biol. Abstr. (1987-?); EMBASE (?-?); Fish Rev. (?-?); For. Prod. Abstr. (1991-?); For. Abstr. (?-?); Wildl. Rev. (?-?).

LC S   **ISSN** 0277-5506
DD 630   US
TECHNICAL BULLETIN - MISSISSIPPI AGRICULTURAL AND FORESTRY EXPERIMENT STATION. [Tech. bull. - Miss. Agric. For. Exp. Stn.]. **Main/Corp** Mississippi Agricultural and Forestry Experiment Station. No. 57- July 1970-. Bulletin. English. Irregular. Price varies per volume. Mississippi State University / Information Services, PO Box 5446, Mississippi State MS 39762. **Tel** (601)325-7774. **ED** Keith H Remy. Index available. cum. index. **Circ**: 950. **Continues** Technical Bulletin - Mississippi State University Agricultural Experiment Station.
Desc: Series includes technical data and discussion of experiment station research.
Ind/Abst AgBiotech News Inf.; AGRICOLA [Select. Cov.]; Agric. Eng. Abstr. (1991-); Cot. Trop. Fibr. Abstr. Bibliogr.; For. Prod. Abstr. (1991-); For. Abstr.; Irr. Drain. Abstr.; Nematol. Abstr.; Nutr. Abstr. Rev., Ser. A, Hum. Exp.; Plant Breed. Abstr.; Rev. Agric. Entomol.; Rev. Plant Pathol.; Rice Abstr.; Soils Fert.; Soyabean Abstr.; World Agric. Econ. Rural Sociol. Abstr.

LC S   **ISSN** 0158-2763
DD 630   AT
TECHNICAL BULLETIN / NORTHERN TERRITORY, DEPARTMENT OF PRIMARY PRODUCTION. Bulletin. English.
Price varies per volume. Department of Primary Production, GPO Box 4160, Darwin Northern Territory 5794 Australia. **Continues** Technical Bulletin (Northern Territory. Animal Industry and Agriculture Branch).

LC S21 .A72   **ISSN** 0082-9811
DD 630   US
CODEN XATBAD
TECHNICAL BULLETIN / UNITED STATES DEPARTMENT OF AGRICULTURE. [Tech. bull. - U. S. Dep. Agric.]. **Added/Corp** United States. Dept. of Agriculture. No. 1 (1927)-. Bulletin. English. Price varies per volume. US Department of Agriculture, 14th Street and Independence Avenue SW, Washington DC 20250. **Tel** (202)720-5457. cum. index. Documents available from BIOSIS Document Express, CASDDS. **Absorbed** United States Dept. of Agriculture. Department Bulletin, 0097-0824.
Ind/Abst AGRICOLA; Biol. Abstr.; Chem. Abstr.; Dairy Sci. Abstr.; EMBASE; Field Crop Abstr.; For. Abstr.; GeoRef; Maize Abstr.; Life Sci. Collect.; Potato Abstr.; Poult. Abstr.; Rev. Agric. Entomol.; Rev. Med. Vet. Entomol.; Soils Fert.; Soyabean Abstr.; World Agric. Econ. Rural Sociol. Abstr.

LC S   **ISSN** 0083-8675
DD 630   AT
TECHNICAL BULLETIN - WESTERN AUSTRALIAN DEPARTMENT OF AGRICULTURE. (TECHNICAL BULLETIN.). [Techn. bull. - West. Aust. Dept. Agric.]. **Added/Corp** Western Australia. Dept. of Agriculture. No. 1 (1969)-. Bulletin. English.
Ind/Abst Soils Fert.

LC S   **ISSN** 1012-7100
DD 630   SA
TECHNICAL COMMUNICATION (SOUTH AFRICA. DEPT. OF AGRICULTURE AND WATER SUPPLY). (TECHNICAL COMMUNICATION / DEPARTMENT OF AGRICULTURE AND WATER SUPPLY, REPUBLIC OF SOUTH AFRICA.). **VFOAT** Tegniese Mededeling. (1984)-. Monographic series. English. Irregular. Price varies per volume. South Africa Department of Agriculture and Water Supply, Pretoria South Africa. Documents available from BIOSIS Document Express. **Continues** Technical Communication (South Africa. Dept. of Agriculture).
Ind/Abst Biol. Abstr.; Cot. Trop. Fibr. Abstr. Bibliogr.; Irr. Drain. Abstr.; Protozoolog. Abstr.; Rev. Plant Pathol.; Wheat Barley Trit. Abstr.

LC S   **ISSN** 0142-7695
DD 630   UK
TECHNICAL NOTE - SCOTTISH AGRICULTURAL COLLEGES. [Tech. note - Scott. Agric. Coll.]. (1974)-. English. Irregular. Scottish Agricultural College, Kings Building / West Mains Road, Edinburgh EH93JG United Kingdom. **Tel** 011 44 131 6671041, **FAX** 011 44 131 6672601. **Absorbed** Technical Note - East of Scotland College of Agriculture, 0142-7709; Technical Note - West of Scotland Agricultural College **and** Technical Note - North of Scotland College of Agriculture.
Ind/Abst Index Vet.; Poult. Abstr.; Protozoolog. Abstr.

LC S
DD 630   TZ
TECHNICAL PAPER (UNIVERSITY OF DAR ES SALAAM. DEPT. OF RURAL ECONOMY). (TECHNICAL PAPER.). **Added/Corp** Chu Kikuu cha Dar es Salaam. Dept. of Rural Economy. (19??)-. Monographic series. English. Price varies per volume. University of Dar es Salaam, PO Box 35189, Dar es Salaam Tanzania. **Tel** 011 255 51 48235.

LC TS1600   **ISSN** 0111-0950
DD 677.31   NZ
TECHNICAL PAPERS - WOOL RESEARCH ORGANISATION OF NEW ZEALAND. [Tech. pap. - Wool Res. Organ. N.Z.]. (1980)-. Monographic series. English. Irregular. price varies. Wool Research Organisation of New Zealand inc, Private Bag 4749, Christchurch New Zealand. **Tel** 011 64 3 3252421, **FAX** 011 64 3 3252717. **ED** B.H. Vaile.
Continues Technical Papers on New Zealand Wools.
Desc: Reviews and bibliograhies.

LC S542.R5 R48B
DD 630/.7/206891   RH
TECHNICAL REPORT - AGRICULTURAL RESEARCH COUNCIL OF RHODESIA.
Main/Corp Rhodesia, Southern. Agricultural Research Council. 1976-. English. One time a year. Agricultural Research Council, PO Box 8108, Causeway Salisbury Zimbabwe.

LC S542.R5 R48b
DD 630/.7206891   RH
TECHNICAL REPORT / AGRICULTURAL RESEARCH COUNCIL OF ZIMBABWE RHODESIA. **Main/Corp** Zimbabwe. Agricultural Research Council. English. Agricultural Research Council, PO Box 8108, Causeway Salisbury Zimbabwe. **Continues** Technical Report - Agricultural Research Council of Rhodesia.

LC S   **ISSN** 0727-601X
DD 630   AT
TECHNICAL REPORT / DEPARTMENT OF AGRICULTURE, SOUTH AUSTRALIA. [Tech. rep. - Dep. Agric. S. Aust.]. **Added/Corp** South Australia. Dept. of Agriculture. No. 1, (1982)-. Monographic series. English. Irregular. Price varies per volume.
Ind/Abst Agric. Eng. Abstr. (1991-); Field Crop Abstr.; Grass. Forage Abstr.; Hortic. Abstr.; Irr. Drain. Abstr.; Maize Abstr.; Potato Abstr.; Soils Fert.; Wheat Barley Trit. Abstr.; World Agric. Econ. Rural Sociol. Abstr.

LC S583   **ISSN** 0715-8629
DD 631   CN
TECHNICAL REPORT - SCHOOL OF ENGINEERING, UNIVERSITY OF GUELPH. [Tech. rep. - Univ. Guelph, Sch. Eng.]. **Main/Corp** Ontario Agricultural College. School of Engineering. **Added/Corp** Ontario Agricultural College. School of Engineering. (1???)-. Monographic series. English. Price varies per volume. University of Guelph School of Engineering, Guelph Ontario N1G 2W1 Canada. **Continues** Engineering Technical Publications.
Ind/Abst Maize Abstr.

LC S   **ISSN** 0815-2357
DD 630   AT
TECHNICAL REPORT SERIES (VICTORIA. DEPT. OF AGRICULTURE AND RURAL AFFAIRS). (TECHNICAL REPORT SERIES / DEPARTMENT OF AGRICULTURE AND RURAL AFFAIRS.). **Added/Corp** Victoria. Dept. of Agriculture and Rural Affairs. (1985)-. Monographic series. English. Irregular. Price varies per volume. **Continues** Technical Report Series (Victoria. Dept. of Agriculture), 0314-8912.
Ind/Abst Agric. Eng. Abstr. (1991-); Anim. Breed. Abstr.

LC S   **ISSN** 0111-932X
DD 631   NZ
TECHNICAL REPORT SOUTHERN SOUTH ISLAND REGION, AGRICULTURAL RESEARCH DIVISION, MINISTRY OF AGRICULTURE & FISHERIES. [Tech. rep. - South. South Isl. Reg. Agric. Res. Div. Minist. Agric. Fish.]. (1982)-. Monographic series. English. Irregular. **Continues** Technical Report - Invermay Research Centre, 0110-649X.
Ind/Abst Ornamental Hort. (1991-).

LC S
DD 630   FR
TECHNICIEN D'AGRICULTURE TROPICALE, LE. **Added/Corp** Agence de Cooperation Culturelle et Technique. Centre Technique de Cooperation Agricole et Rurale. (1983)-. Monographic series. French.
Ind/Abst Weed Abstr.

LC S
DD 630   SZ
TECHNIQUE AGRICOLE. (19??)-. French. Twelve times a year. 50.00F Switzerland; 68.00F other. Technique Agricole, Postfach 53, Ausserdorfstrasse 31, CH-5223 Riniken Switzerland. **Tel** 011 41 56 412022.
Ind/Abst Field Crop Abstr.; Grass. Forage Abstr.; Postharvest News Inf.; Potato Abstr.

LC S
DD 630   IT
TECNICA AGRICOLA / EDITA A CURA DELL'ASSOCIAZIONE DEI DOTTORI IN SCIENZE AGRARIE DELLA PROVINCIA DI CATANIA. **Added/Corp** Associazione dei Dottori in Scienze Agrarie della Provincia di Catania. (1949)-. Periodical. Italian. Six times a year.
Ind/Abst Grass. Forage Abstr.; Nutr. Abstr. Rev., Ser. B, Live Feeds and Feed.; Rev. Agric. Entomol.; Wheat Barley Trit. Abstr.

LC S   **ISSN** 0355-0567
DD 630   FI
Pr Rev.
TEHO. **Added/Corp** Tyotehoseura (Finland). Vol. 1 (1950)-. Academic Scholarly Publication. Finnish (summaries and/or abstracts in English). Six times a year. Fmk155.00 Finland; Fmk195.00 other. Tyotehoseura PY, PO Box 28, Melkonkatu 16 A, SF-00211 Helsinki Finland. **Tel** 011 358 0 6922445, **FAX** 011 358 0 6922084. **ED** Tarmo Luoma. **Ad Acc**, **Adv Mgr**: Atte Kaksonen, **Tel** 011 358 90 6922445. **Circ**: 5,500 (ctrl). **Continues** Tyotehotietoa.
Desc: A professional journal with results of research in technical, economical, ergonomical, energetical and environmental topics, also experiences of practice and computer use.
Ind/Abst Agrofor. Abstr. (1991-); Dairy Sci. Abstr.; For. Abstr.

Agriculture

LC S ISSN 0282-6674
DD 630 SW
TEKNIK FOR LANTBRUKET. [Tek. lantbr.].
Added/Corp Jordbrukstekniska institutet. (1985)-.
Monographic series. Swedish. Irregular.
Jordbrukstekniska Institutet (Swedish Institute of Agricultural Engineering), Box 7033 750 07, Uppsala Sweden. **Continues** Cirkular - Jordbrukstekniska Institutet, 0368-3427.
Ind/Abst For. Prod. Abstr. (1991-); For. Abstr.

LC S ISSN 0127-7979
DD 630 MY
TEKNOLOGI KOKO-KELAPA. (1989)-.
Periodical. Malay.
Ind/Abst Irr. Drain. Abstr.; Soils Fert.; Sug. Indus. Abstr.

LC S
DD 630 FR
TENDANCES DES MARCHES : BULLETIN DE L'INSTITUT TECHNIQUE DE L'AVICOLE, TDM. (19??)-. Bulletin. French. Seventy-eight times a year. 1077.38F France; 1250.00F other. ITAVI, 28 rue du Rocher, F 75008 Paris France. **Tel** 011 33 1 45226240.

LC S115 T46
DD 630 US
CODEN TASCF6
●**TENNESSEE AGRI SCIENCE : CONTRIBUTING TO THE DEVELOPMENT OF TENNESSEE AGRICULTURE. Added/Corp** University of Tennessee, Knoxville. Agricultural Experiment Station. **VFOAT** Tennessee Agriscience. No. 173 (Winter 1995)-. Academic Scholarly Publication. English. Four times a year. Free. University of Tennessee Agricultural Ext. Ser., PO Box 1071, Knoxville TN 37901-1071. **Tel** (615)974-7145, FAX (615)974-7448. **Circ:** 4,000. Documents available from The UnCover Company. **Continues** Tennessee Farm and Home Science, 0040-3229.

LC S115 .T46 ISSN 0497-2317
DD 338.1/09768 US
TENNESSEE AGRICULTURAL STATISTICS. See Agriculture-Abstracting, Bibliographies and Statistics.

LC S ISSN 0040-3229
DD 630 US
CODEN TFHSAT
TITLE CHANGE
TENNESSEE FARM AND HOME SCIENCE. (TENNESSEE FARM AND HOME SCIENCE : PROGRESS REPORT.). [Tenn. farm home sci.]. **Added/Corp** University of Tennessee, Knoxville. Agricultural Experiment Station. University of Tennessee (Knoxville Campus). Agricultural Experiment Station. **VFOAT** Farm and Home Science. (1952)-(1994). Academic Scholarly Publication. English. Free. University of Tennessee Agricultural Ext. Ser., PO Box 1071, Knoxville TN 37901-1071. **Tel** (615)974-7145, FAX (615)974-7448. **ED** P.A. Clark. Index available. cum. index. **Circ:** 4,000. Documents available from BIOSIS Document Express, CASDDS. **Continued by** Tennessee Agri Science.
Desc: Publishes results of research performed in conjunction with the Tennessee Agricultural Experiment Station.
Ind/Abst AGRICOLA [Full Cov.]; Agric. Eng. Abstr.; Biol. Abstr.; Chem. Abstr.; Field Crop Abstr.; Food Sci. Technol. Abstr.; For. Prod. Abstr. (1991-); For. Abstr.; Hortic. Abstr.; Maize Abstr.; Ornamental Hort.; Life Sci. Collect.; Plant Breed. Abstr.; Plant Grow. Reg. Abstr.; Rev. Med. Vet. Mycology; Rev. Plant Pathol.; Soils Fert.; Soyabean Abstr.; Weed Abstr.

LC S ISSN 0744-7388
DD 630 US
TENNESSEE FARM FACTS. Added/Corp Tennessee Crop Reporting Service. (19??)-. Government Publication. English. Twelve times a year. $10.00. US Department of Agriculture / National Agricultural Statistics Service (NASS), Room 5829 South Building, Washington DC 20250. **Tel** (202)720-4020, FAX (314)875-5231. **(Subscription address:** Agricultural Statistics Board, Room 5829, South Building / USDA NASS, Washington DC 20250.)

LC S ISSN 0040-3245
DD 630 US
TENNESSEE FARMER (NASHVILLE, TENN.). (TENNESSEE FARMER.). [Tenn. farmer]. (1954)-. Periodical. English. Twelve times a year. $12.00. Rural Press USA, 7701 Six Forks Road, Suite 132, Raleigh NC 27615. **Tel** (800)934-2047, (919)676-3276, FAX (919)676-9803. **ED** Wayne Harr (editor's telephone: (615)831-9673). **Ad Acc. Circ:** 20,136 (ctrl).
Desc: General farm magazine serving Tennessee agriculture.

LC S ISSN 0731-6240
DD 630 US
TENNESSEE NURSERY DIGEST. [Tenn. nurs. digest]. **Added/Corp** University of Tennessee, Knoxville. Agricultural Extension Service. (19??)-. Periodical. English. Twelve times a year. Free on request. University of Tennessee Agricultural Extension Service, PO Box 1071, Knoxville TN 37901. **Tel** (615)974-7145.

LC S
DD 630 NE
TER HERKENNING. Vol. 1 (Feb. 1973)-. Periodical. Dutch. Six times a year. $9.59. SDU Uitgeverij, Postbus 20014, Christoffel Plantijnstraat, 2500 EA Den Haag Netherlands. **Tel** 011 31 70 3789911. Index available. **Bk Rev. Ad Acc. Formed by the union of** Christus en Israel **and** Kerk en Israel.

LC S
DD 630 IT
TERMINOLOGY BULLETIN (FOOD AND AGRICULTURE ORGANIZATION OF THE UNITED NATIONS. TERMINOLOGY AND REFERENCE SECTION). (TERMINOLOGY BULLETIN.). **Added/Corp** Food and Agriculture Organization of the United Nations. Terminology and Reference Section. **VFOAT** Bulletin de Terminologie. (19??)-. Bulletin. English (French and Spanish). Irregular. United Nations Publications, 2 United Nations Plaza, Room DC2 0853, Department 007C, New York NY 10017. **Tel** (212)963-8303, (800)253-9646.

LC S ISSN 0040-3776
DD 630 IT
TERRA E VITA. (1960)-. Periodical. Italian. Forty-nine times a year. L74940. Edagricole, PO Box 2157, 40100 Bologna Italy. **Tel** 011 39 51 492211 Ext. 22, FAX 011 39 51 493660, telex 510336 EDAGRI. Index available in last issue of volume--attached. **Absorbed** Raccolto.
Ind/Abst Chem. Bus. Bull.; Chem. Bus. NewsBase (1989-); Chem. Bus. Update; Nematol. Abstr.

LC S451.5 ISSN 0823-2784
DD 630/.9714 CN
TERRE DE CHEZ NOUS. DOSSIER D'INFORMATION TECHNIQUE ET PROFESSIONNELLE, LA. Vol. 1, No 1 (24 Feb. 1983)-. Periodical. French. Twelve times a year. 16.00Can$. Union des Producteurs Agricoles, 555 boulevard Roland Therrien, Longueuil Quebec J4H 3Y9 Canada. **Tel** (514)679-0535. **Bk Rev. Ad Acc. Circ:** 50,000 (ctrl).
Desc: All subjects concerning agriculture and forestry.

LC S ISSN 0040-3830
DD 630 CN
TERRE DE CHEZ NOUS (MONTREAL). (LA TERRE DE CHEZ NOUS.). [Terre chez nous]. **Added/Corp** Union Catholique des Cultivateurs. Union Catholique des Cultivateurs de la Province de Quebec. Union des Producteurs Agricoles. Vol. 1 (Mar. 6 1929)-. Periodical. French. Fifty times a year (publishes on Thurs.). 20.81Can$. L'Union Producteurs Agricoles, 555 boulevard Roland-Therrien, Longueuil Quebec J4H 9Z9 Canada. **Tel** (514)679-0530. **Bk Rev. Ad Acc. Circ:** 50,000 (ctrl).
Desc: Information to farmers on markets, union activities, agricultural policies and all social and economic issues in agriculture.

LC S ISSN 0099-7730
DD 630 US
CODEN TAELA
TEXAS AGRICULTURAL EXPERIMENT STATION LEAFLET. [Tex. Agric. Exp. Stn. Leafl.]. (19??)-. English.
Ind/Abst World Agric. Econ. Rural Sociol. Abstr.

LC S
DD 630 US
TEXAS AGRICULTURAL FACTS. See Agriculture-Abstracting, Bibliographies and Statistics.

LC S
DD 630 US
●**TEXAS AGRICULTURAL STATISTICS.** (1995)-. Statistical Publication. English. One time a year. $30.00. Texas Agricultural Statistics Service, PO Box 70, Austin TX 78767. **Tel** (512)482-5581. **Absorbed** Texas Livestock Statistics **and** Texas Crop Statistics.

LC S
DD 630 US
TEXAS AGRICULTURE (NORTH TEXAS EDITION : 1987). (TEXAS AGRICULTURE.). Periodical. English. Twenty-four times a year. Texas Farm Bureau, Box 2689, Waco TX 76702-2689. **Continues** Texas Agriculture Weekly (North Texas Edition).

LC F386 .T334A ISSN 0272-8400
DD 976.4 US
TEXAS FAMILY LAND HERITAGE REGISTRY. Main/Corp Texas. Dept. of Agriculture. English. One time a year. Texas Department of Agriculture, 18th & Congress Street, PO Box 12847, Austin TX 78711. **Tel** (512)463-7435, FAX (512)463-7643.

LC S ISSN 8750-9873
DD 630 US
TEXAS FARMER. (TEXAS FARMER = TEXASKY ROLNIK.). **Added/Corp** Farmers Mutual Protective Association of Texas. **VFOAT** Texasky Rolnik. (19??)-. Periodical. English. Four times a year. $0.50. Texas Farmer, 2301 South 37th Street, Temple TX 76501.

LC S ISSN 0279-165X
DD 630 US
TEXAS FARMER STOCKMAN. VFOAT Texas Farmer Stockman. (19??)-. Periodical. English. Twelve times a year. $19.95. HBJ Farm Publications, PO Box 5467, Lincoln NE 68505. **Tel** (402)489-8845. **ED** Charles Taylor. **Ad Acc. Circ:** 227,000.
Desc: General farming livestock, farm home and country life.

LC S ISSN 0893-8997
DD 630 US
TEXAS FFA MAGAZINE. Added/Corp Texas Association of Future Farmers of America. **VAT** Texas Future Farmers of America Magazine. (198?)-. Periodical. English. Six times a year. Texas Association of Future Farmers of America, 1701 North Congress Avenue, Austin TX 78701. **Tel** (512)280-7239, (512)463-9687. **Continues** Texas Future Farmer, 0040-4330.
Desc: Information for agricultural students and societies.

LC S ISSN 0891-5466
DD 351 US
Pr Rev.
TEXAS JOURNAL OF AGRICULTURE AND NATURAL RESOURCES. (TEXAS JOURNAL OF AGRICULTURE AND NATURAL RESOURCES : A PUBLICATION OF THE AGRICULTURAL CONSORTIUM OF TEXAS.). [Tex. j. agric. nat. resour.]. **Added/Corp** Agricultural Consortium of Texas. Vol. 1 (1987)-. English. One time a year. $5.00. Texas Journal of Agricultural Natural Resources, Campus Box 156, Texas A & M University, Kingsville TX 78363. **Tel** (512)595-3719.
Ind/Abst AGRICOLA [Select. Cov.].

LC S
DD 630 US
TEXAS NEIGHBORS. Vol. 50, No. 9 (July/August 1985)-. Periodical. English. Six times a year. Texas Farm Bureau, Box 2689, Waco TX 76702-2689. **Continues** Texas Agriculture (Waco, Tex. : 1979).

LC S ISSN 0049-3589
DD 630 TH
CODEN TJASBN
THAI JOURNAL OF AGRICULTURAL SCIENCE. [Thai j. agric. sci.]. **Added/Corp** Samakhom Witthayasat Kankaset Hng Prathet Thai. **VFOAT** Witthayasat Kaset; Journal of Agricultural Science. Vol.1 (1968)-. Periodical. English. Four times a year. $38.00. Agricultural Science Society of Thailand, 196 Phahonyothin Road, Bangkok 10900 Thailand. **ED** Prapandh Boonklinkajorn (editor's address: Po Box 1070, Kasetsart University, Bangkok 10903 Thailand). Index available (bound in fourth issue). **Ad Acc. Circ:** 1,000. available on CD-ROM; available on diskette; available on audiocassette; available on videocassette; available on microfilm from University Microfilms International (UMI). Documents available from CASDDS.
Desc: Agriculture, biology, soil, entomology, forestry, genetics, fisheries, animal science, cropping, system, agricultural development, breeding, and food technology.
Ind/Abst Abstr. AIT Rep. Publ. Energy; Agrofor. Abstr.; Biocont. News Inf. (1991-); Chem. Abstr.; Cot. Trop. Fibr. Abstr. Bibliogr.; Dairy Sci. Abstr.; Food Sci. Technol. Abstr.; Irr. Drain. Abstr.; Maize Abstr.; Nutr. Abstr. Rev., Ser. B, Live Feeds and Feed.; Life Sci. Collect.; Plant Breed. Abstr.; Plant Grow. Reg. Abstr.; Poult. Abstr.; Rice Abstr.; Soyabean Abstr.

LC S
DD 630 DK
TIDSSKRIFT FOR JORDEMODRE. Danish. Twelve times a year. kr320.00. Almindelige Danske Jordemoder, Norre Voldgade 90, 1358 Copenhagen K Denmark. **Tel** 011 45 1 33138211.

LC S ISSN 0788-5199
DD 630 FI
TIEDONANTOJA - MAATALOUDEN TALOUDELLINEN TUTKIMUSLAITOS. (TIEDONANTOJA.). [Tied. - Maatal. tal. tutk.l.]. **VFOAT** Research Reports - Agricultural Economics Research Institute, Finland; Research Reports - Agricultural Economics Research Institute, Finland. (1989)-. Monographic series. Multiple languages. Irregular. **Continues** Maatalouden Taloudellinen Tutkimuslaitoksen Tiedonantoja, 0355-0877.
Ind/Abst Pig News Inf.; Soils Fert.; Wheat Barley Trit. Abstr.

LC S **ISSN** 0921-481X
DD 630 NE
UDC 631 :303
Pr Rev.
TIJDSCHRIFT VOOR SOCIAAL WETENSCHAPPELIJK ONDERZOEK VAN DE LANDBOUW. (1986)-. Periodical. Dutch (English). Four times a year. $51.39. Stichting TSL, P/A LEI Postbus 29703, 2502 LS Den Haag Netherlands. **Tel** 011 599 070 3614161. **ED** G. van Huylenbroeck. **Bk Rev**, (Qty: 20). **Ad Acc**, **Adv Mgr:** J.H.M. Wijnands. **Circ:** 350 (ctrl).
Desc: Information on agriculture, economics, sociology, physical planning and research.
Ind/Abst Rural Dev. Abstr.; World Agric. Econ. Rural Sociol. Abstr.

LC S
DD 630 GT
TIKALIA. 1982-. Spanish. Two times a year. Q.4.00 Guatemala; $3.00 US; $4.00 other. Universidad de San Carlos de Guatemala / Agronomia, Facultad de Agronomia, Ciudad Universitaria Zona 12, Apartado Postal No 1545, Guatemala Central America. **ED** Dennis Orlando Escobar Galicia. Index available. cum. index. **Bk Rev. Circ:** 1,000 (ctrl).
Desc: Journal specializing in agriculture and natural resources.

LC S **ISSN** 0739-0092
DD 630 US
TODAY'S FARMER. Added/Corp Midcontinent Farmers Association. (19??)-. English. Ten times a year. MFA Inc, 615 Locust Street, Columbia MO 65201. **Tel** (314)876-5205. ***Continues** Missouri Farmer.*
Ind/Abst Ozark Period. Index.

LC S19 .T59 **ISSN** 0040-8719
DD 630 JA
CODEN TJARAJ
TOHOKU JOURNAL OF AGRICULTURAL RESEARCH. [Tohoku j. agric. res.]. **Added/Corp** Tohoku Daigaku. Nogakubu. Vol. 1 (March 1950)-. Periodical. English. Two times a year. Tohoku Daigaku Nogakubu, (Faculty of Agriculture Tohoku University), 1-1 Amamiyacho Tsutsumi Doori, Sendaishi Miyagiken 980, Japan. Documents available from BIOSIS Document Express, CASDDS.
Ind/Abst AgBiotech News Inf.; Anim. Breed. Abstr.; Biol. Abstr.; Chem. Abstr.; Fish Rev.; Life Sci. Collect.; SEA Abstr.; Soyabean Abstr.; Wildl. Rev.

LC S
DD 630 JA
TOKAI NORIN SUISAN TOKEI. Added/Corp Japan. Tokai Noseikyoku. Tokei Johobu. (19??)-. Periodical. Japanese. Tokai Nosei Kyoku Tokei Johobu, 2-2 Sannomaru 1-chome Naka-ku 460, Nagaya Japan.

LC S **ISSN** 0375-9202
DD 630 JA
TOKYO NOGYO DAIGAKU NOGAKU SHUHO. [Tokyo Nogyo Daigaku nogaku shuho]. **VFOAT** Nogaku Shuho; Journal of Agricultural Science, Tokyo Nogyo Daigaku. (1937)-. Academic Scholarly Publication. Japanese. Four times a year. Tokyo Nogyo Daigaku, (Tokyo University of Agriculture), 1-1 Sakuragaoka 1 Chome, Setagayaku Tokyo 156 Japan. Documents available from CASDDS.
Ind/Abst Chem. Abstr.; Hortic. Abstr.; Potato Abstr.; Rev. Plant Pathol.; Soyabean Abstr.; World Agric. Econ. Rural Sociol. Abstr.

LC S **ISSN** 0447-8959
DD 630 JA
CODEN TNDNAG
TOKYO NOGYO DAIGAKU NOGAKU SHUHO. (JOURNAL OF AGRICULTURAL SCIENCE.). [Tokyo Nogyo Daigaku nogaku shuho]. **Added/Corp** Tokyo Nogyo Daigaku. **VFOAT** Tokyo Nogyo Daigaku Nogaku Shuho. Vol. 1 (July 1937)-. Periodical. Multiple languages (English and Japanese; summaries and/or abstracts in English). Four times a year. Academia Scientific Book Inc., 39 6 Hongo 2 Chome Bunkyo ku, Tokyo 113 Japan. **Tel** 011 81 3 38139805, 011 81 3 38128509. Documents available from The Genuine Article, CASDDS.
Ind/Abst AgBiotech News Inf.; AGRICOLA; Agric. Eng. Abstr.; Anim. Breed. Abstr.; BioBusiness; Biodeter. Abstr.; Chem. Abstr.; Curr. Contents Agric. Biol. Environ. Sci.; Dairy Sci. Abstr.; Ecol. Abstr.; Environ. Period. Bibliogr.; Fish Rev. (Jan. 1989-July 1992); Geogr. Abstr. Phys. Geogr.; Helminthol. Abstr. (1991-); Index Vet.; Int. Dev. Abstr.; Irr. Drain. Abstr.; Nutr. Abstr. Rev., Ser. B, Live Feeds and Feed.; Ornamental Hort.; PESTDOC; Pig News Inf.; Plant Breed. Abstr.; Plant Grow. Reg. Abstr.; Postharvest News Inf.; Poult. Abstr.; Res. Alert [Full Cov.]; Rev. Agric. Entomol.; Rev. Med. Vet. Entomol.; Rice Abstr.; Sci. Cit. Index; SCISEARCH; Soils Fert.; Wheat Barley Trit. Abstr.; Wildl. Rev. (Jan. 1989-July 1992).

LC S
DD 630 JA
TOKYO NORIN SUISAN TOKEI NEMPO. Added/Corp Japan. Norinsho. Tokyo Tokei Chosa Jimusho. Japan. Kanto Noseikyoku. Tokei Chosabu. Japan. Kanto Noseikyoku. Tokei Johobu. **VFOAT** Tokyo Norin Suisan Tokei Nempo. (19??)-. Periodical. Japanese. One time a year. Otemachi Godo Chosha, 3-2 Otemachi 1 Chiyoda-ku 100, Tokyo Japan.

LC HD1537.S72 T65
DD 305.555 CE
TOLILALAR PATAI. See Business and Economics-Labor.

LC HD9483.U53 M575
DD 381/.45/6696209762 US
TONNAGE OF FERTILIZER SOLD IN MISSISSIPPI. Main/Corp Mississippi. Feed and Fertilizer Control Division. (19??)-. English. One time a year. Mississippi Department of Agriculture and Commerce, PO Box 1609, Jackson MS 39205.

LC HD9483.U53 M578
DD 381/.45/6686209762 US
TONNAGE OF FERTILIZER SOLD IN MISSISSIPPI BY GRADES. English. One time a year. Mississippi Department of Agriculture and Commerce, PO Box 1609, Jackson MS 39205.

LC S
DD 630 GW
TOP AGRAR : DAS MAGAZIN FUR MODERNE LANDWIRTSCHAFT. German. Twelve times a year. DM89.40. Landwirtschaftsverlag GmbH, Postfach 480249, D-48079 Muenster Hiltrup Germany. **Tel** 011 49 2501 8010, FAX 011 49 2501 801204, telex 892665 LANDV D. Index available. **Bk Rev. Ad Acc. Circ:** 110,000 (ctrl).
Desc: Magazine for modern agriculture containing high level information about agricultural management, crop production, agricultural technology, animal production and market.

LC S **ISSN** 0372-0349
DD 630 JA
UDC 63
CODEN TODNAN
TOTTORI DAIGAKU NOGAKUBU KENKYU HOKOKU. [Tottori Daigaku Nogakubu Kenkyu Hokoku]. **VFOAT** Bulletin of the Faculty of Agriculture, Tottori University. (1970)-. Bulletin. Japanese (summaries and/or abstracts in English). One time a year. Tottori Daigaku Nogakubu, (Faculty of Agriculture Tottori University), Minami 4-101 Koyamacho, Tottorishi Tottoriken 680 Japan. ***Continues** Tottori Nogakkaiho, 0372-0438.*
Ind/Abst Agric. Eng. Abstr.; Soils Fert.

LC S
DD 630 JA
TOTTORI DAIGAKU NOGAKUBU KENKYU HOKOKU. BULLETIN OF THE FACULTY OF AGRICULTURE, TOTTORI UNIVERSITY. Main/Corp Tottori Daigaku. Nogaku-bu. **VFOAT** Bulletin of the Faculty of Agriculture, Tottori University. Vol. 22 (March 1970)-. Bulletin. Japanese. Tottori University, Faculty of Agriculture, Tottori Japan. Documents available from CASDDS. ***Continues** Tottori Society of Agricultural Science. Transactions.*
Ind/Abst Chem. Abstr.; Crop Physiol. Abstr.; Plant Breed. Abstr.; Rev. Plant Pathol.; Rice Abstr.; World Agric. Econ. Rural Sociol. Abstr.

LC S **ISSN** 0814-4540
DD 630.'5 AT
TOWN AND COUNTRY FARMER. [Town ctry. farmer]. (1984)-. Periodical. English. Four times a year. 21.05Aus$. Town & Country Farmer, PO Box 798, Benalla VIC 3672 Australia. **Tel** 011 61 57 641348. **ED** Shirley Hurley, Glenn Hurley. **Ad Acc.**
Desc: News and information on livestock, farming and other agricultural topics.

LC HF
DD 380.1 US
CEASED
TRADE LEADS. Added/Corp AgExport Connections (U.S.). **VFOAT** AgExport Trade Leads. (October 9, 1990)-(199?). Government Publication. English. US Department of Agriculture / Foreign Agricultural Service, 14th Street & Independence Avenue Southwest, Washington DC 20250. **Tel** (202)720-9445, FAX (202)720-7729. ***Continues** Export Briefs.*

LC S
DD 630 US
TRADE REPORT SERVICE: WEEKLY TRADE REPORT. Added/Corp New York Cotton Exchange. **VFOAT** Weekly Trade Report. Report No. 534 (April 12, 1937)-. Periodical. English. One time a week. $100.00. New York Cotton Exchange, 4 World Trade Center, 8th Floor, New York NY 10048. **Tel** (212)938-2664. ***Continues** Weekly Trade Report.*

LC S530 .T7 **ISSN** 0251-1495
DD 630/.7/1 IT
TRAINING FOR AGRICULTURE AND RURAL DEVELOPMENT. [Train. agric. rural dev.]. **Added/Corp** Food and Agricultural Organization of the United Nations. Unesco International Labour Organisation. (1975)-. English (French). Irregular. Price varies per volume. Food Agriculture Organization (FAO) / Italy, GIPCI66 via Terme di Caracalla, 00100 Rome Italy. **Tel** 011 39 6 52252925, FAX 011 39 6 52253152. **(Subscription address:** UNIPUB, 4611 F Assembly Drive, Lanham MD 20706. **Tel** (800)274-4888, (301)459-7666.) ***Continues** Training for Agriculture.*
Ind/Abst AGRICOLA.

LC S **ISSN** 0766-8007
DD 630 FR
UDC 63 : 070.431
TITLE CHANGE
TRANS RURAL EXPRESS. (1984)-(1993). Periodical. French. AFIP Editions Diffusion, 2 rue Paul Escudier, 75009 Paris France. **Tel** 011 33 1 48745288. ***Merged with** Evolution Agricole, 0755-1134; **Changed back to** Trans Rural Initiatives, 1165-6166.*

LC S **ISSN** 1165-6166
DD 630 FR
UDC 63-051(44)
•**TRANS RURAL INITIATIVES. Added/Corp** Association pour la Formation et l'Information Paysannes (France). (1993)-. Periodical. French. Twenty-four times a year. AFIP Editions Diffusion, 2 rue Paul Escudier, 75009 Paris France. **Tel** 011 33 1 48745288. ***Formed by the union of** Trans Rural Express, 0766-8007 **and** Evolution Agricole, 0755-1134.*

LC SB110 **ISSN** 0970-3918
DD 631.586 II
CCC
CODEN TISTEA
TRANSACTIONS OF INDIAN SOCIETY OF DESERT TECHNOLOGY. (TRANSACTIONS OF INDIAN SOCIETY OF DESERT TECHNOLOGY.). [Trans. Indian Soc. Desert Technol.]. **Added/Corp** Indian Society of Desert Technology. Vol. 12, No. 1 (Jan. 1987)-. English. One time a year. $25.00. Indian Society of Desert Technology, Jodhpur India. **(Subscription address:** Prints India, 11 Darya Ganj, New Delhi 110002 India. **Tel** 011 91 11 3268645, FAX 011 91 11 3275542, telex 31-61087 PRIN-IN.) ***Continues** Indian Society of Desert Technology. Transactions of Indian Society of Desert Technology and University Centre of Desert Studies, 0379-0568.*

LC S671 .A452 **ISSN** 0001-2351
DD 631.3/05 US
CCC
CODEN TAAEAJ
Pr Rev.
TRANSACTIONS OF THE ASAE. [Trans. ASAE]. **Main/Corp** American Society of Agricultural Engineers. **VAT** Transactions of the American Society of Agricultural Engineers. Vol. 1 (1958)-. Academic Scholarly Publication. English. Six times a year. $212.00. American Society of Agricultural Engineers, Department 2510, 2950 Niles Road, St. Joseph MI 49085-9659. **Tel** (616)429-0300, FAX (616)429-3852. **ED** James Basselman. Index available ($6.25). cum. index. **Circ:** 2,200 (ctrl). Documents available from Article Express International, The Genuine Article, BIOSIS Document Express, CASDDS, Documents on Demand. ***Supersedes** Transactions of the American Society of Agricultural Engineers.*
Desc: Full length technical articles describe the application of engineering principles to the solution of agricultural problems.
Ind/Abst AgBiotech News Inf.; AGRICOLA [Full Cov.]; Agric. Eng. Abstr.; Biodeter. Abstr. (1991-); Bioeng. Abstr.; Biol. Agric. Index; Biol. Abstr.; Chem. Abstr.; Civ. Struct. Eng. Abstr.; Coal Abstr.; Comput. Inf. Syst. Abstr. J. [Full Cov.]; Cot. Trop. Fibr. Abstr. Bibliogr.; Curr. Aware. Biol. Sci., CABS; Curr. Cit.; Curr. Contents Agric. Biol. Environ. Sci.; Curr. Contents Eng. Comput. Technol.; Dairy Sci. Abstr.; Ei Page One; Elect. Comm. Abstr.; EMBASE; Energy Inf. Abstr.; Eng. Index Annu.; Environ. Abstr.; Environ. Eng. Abstr.; Field Crop Abstr.; Fluid Abstr., Civil Eng.; Fluid Abstr. Proc. Eng.; FLUIDEX (1973-); Food Sci. Technol. Abstr.; For. Prod. Abstr. (19??-19??); For. Abstr.; Grass. Forage Abstr.; Hortic. Abstr.; Int. Abstr. Oper. Res. [Select. Cov.]; Irr. Drain. Abstr.; Maize Abstr.; Manuf. Process Eng. Abstr.; Mater. Sci. Eng. Abstr.; Mech. Eng. Abstr.; Nutr. Abstr. Rev., Ser. B, Live Feeds and Feed.; Ocean. Abstr.; Ornamental Hort. (19??-19??); Life Sci. Collect.; Pig News Inf.; Plant Genet. Resour. Abstr.; Postharvest News Inf.; Potato Abstr.; Poult. Abstr.; Res. Alert [Full Cov.]; Rev. Agric. Entomol.; Rev. Med. Vet. Entomol.; Rev. Med. Vet. Mycology; Rev. Plant Pathol.; Rice Abstr.; Sci. Cit. Index; SCISEARCH; Seed Abstr.; Soils Fert.; Solid State Supercond. Abstr.; Sorghum Mill. Abstr.; Soyabean Abstr.; Sug. Indus. Abstr.; Weed Abstr.

LC S
DD 630 US
TRANSLATIONS ON USSR AGRICULTURE. Added/Corp United States. Joint Publications Research Service. (196?)-. Periodical. English (Russian). National Technical Information Service - NTIS, Room 2027S, 5285 Port Royal Road, Springfield VA 22161. **Tel** (703)487-4630, (703)487-4660, (703)487-4650, FAX (703)321-8547, telex 89-9405. ***Continues** Translations on Soviet Agriculture.*

LC S **ISSN** 0399-9688
DD 630 FR
UDC 63
TRAVAUX ET INNOVATIONS. [Trav. innov.]. (1977)-. Periodical. French. Eight times a year. $126.85. Sarec, 9 11 rue de la Baume, 75008 Paris France. **Tel** 011 33 1 44950800. ***Continues*** *Techni C.E.T.A., 0399-9696.*

LC S **ISSN** 0041-2481
DD 630 US
CODEN TTCRAV
TRI-OLOGY TECHNICAL REPORT. (TRI-OLOGY TECHNICAL REPORT : ENTOMOLOGY, NEMATOLOGY, PATHOLOGY.). [Tri-ology tech. rep.]. **Added/Corp** Florida. Division of Plant Industry. **VFOAT** Tri-Ology; Triology Technical Report; Triology. Vol. 1 No. 1 (May 1962)-. Periodical. English. Twelve times a year. Florida Department of Agriculture & Consumer Services, State Capitol, 10th Floor, Tallahassee FL 32399. **Tel** (904)488-6971, FAX (904)488-8087.
Ind/Abst Nematol. Abstr.; Weed Abstr.

LC S
DD 630 US
TROPAG & RURAL [COMPUTER FILE]. **Added/Corp** SilverPlatter Information, Inc. **VFOAT** Tropag and Rural. (19??)-. English. Two times a year. $750.00. Silverplatter Information Inc., 100 River Ridge Drive, Norwood MA 02062. **Tel** (800)343-0064, (617)769-2599, FAX (617)769-8763. available in print (as: Abstracts on Tropical Agriculture; and, Abstracts on Rural Development in the Tropics).

LC S
DD 630 GW
CODEN BTLVBR
•**TROPENLANDWIRT BEITRAEGE ZUR TROPISCHEN LANDWIRTSCHAFT UND VETERINAERMEDIZIN.** **See** Veterinary Sciences.

LC S **ISSN** 0041-3186
DD 630 GW
TITLE CHANGE
TROPENLANDWIRT : ZEITSCHRIFT FUER DIE LANDWIRTSCHAFT IN DEN TROPEN UND SUBTROPEN, DER. **Added/Corp** Deutsches Institut fuer Tropische und Subtropische Landwirtschaft (Witzenhausen, Germany) Verband der Tropenlandwirte aus Witzenhausen (Germany) Gesellschaft zur Foerderung des Deuschen Instituts fuer Tropische und Subtropische Landwirtschaft (Witzenhausen, Germany). (1966)-(1994). Trade Publication. German (table of contents in English). Verband der Tropenlandwirte, Steinstr 19, Postfach 68, D-37213 Witzenhausen Germany. **Tel** 011 49 5542 9801216. Documents available from The Genuine Article. ***Continues*** *Deutsche Tropenlandwirt (Not in NAL).* ***Merged into*** *Tropenlandwirt Beitraege zur Tropischen Landwirtschaft und Veterinaermedizin.*
Ind/Abst Agrofor. Abstr.; Anim. Breed. Abstr.; Curr. Aware. Biol. Sci., CABS; Curr. Contents Agric. Biol. Environ. Sci.; Dairy Sci. Abstr.; GeoRef; Hortic. Abstr.; Index Vet.; Irr. Drain. Abstr.; Maize Abstr.; Nutr. Abstr. Rev., Ser. B, Live Feeds and Feed.; Ornamental Hort. (1991-); Poult. Abstr.; Res. Alert [Select. Cov.]; Rev. Med. Vet. Entomol.; Soils Fert.; Weed Abstr.; World Agric. Econ. Rural Sociol. Abstr.

LC S **ISSN** 0041-3224
DD 630 CE
TROPICAL AGRICULTURIST. **Added/Corp** Sri Lanka. Krasikarma Departmentuva. Ceylon Agricultural Society. (June 1881)-. Trade Publication. English. Irregular. Central Library Director of Agriculture, Department of Agriculture, PO Box 47, Peradeniya Sri Lanka.
Ind/Abst Field Crop Abstr.; Grass. Forage Abstr.; Hortic. Abstr.; Maize Abstr.; Nematol. Abstr.; Postharvest News Inf.; Rev. Agric. Entomol.; Rice Abstr.; Seed Abstr.; Soils Fert.; Sorghum Mill. Abstr.; Soyabean Abstr.; Weed Abstr.

LC S **ISSN** 0926-9495
DD 630 NE
UDC 502(213.5)
TROPICAL RESOURCE MANAGEMENT PAPERS. [Trop. resour. manag. pap.]. (1991)-. Monographic series. Multiple languages. Irregular. Price varies per volume.
Ind/Abst Agrofor. Abstr.; For. Abstr.

LC S3 .T7 **ISSN** 0041-3291
DD 630.5 UK
NLM W1 TR887 **CODEN** TROSAC
TROPICAL SCIENCE. [Trop. sci.]. **Added/Corp** Tropical Products Institute (Great Britain). Vol. 1 (1959)-. Academic Scholarly Publication. English. Four times a year. $162.00. Whurr Publishers Ltd., 19B Compton Terrace, London N1 2UN United Kingdom. **Tel** 011 44 171 3595979, FAX 011 44 171 2265290. **(Subscription address:** Turpin Distribution Services Limited, Blackhorse Road, Letchworth, Hertfordshire SH6 1HN United Kingdom. **Tel** 011 44 1462 672555, FAX 011 44 1462 480947.) **ED** Geoffrey R. Ames. Index available. **Ad Acc.** Full Page (B&W) £250.00. Half Page (B&W) £150.00. **Acid Free.** available on microfilm from University Microfilms International (UMI). Documents available from CASDDS. ***Supersedes*** *Colonial Plant and Animal Products, 0143-7442;* ***Formed by the union of*** *Tropical Stored Products Information, 0564-3325.*
Desc: Makes better use of natural resources, particularly plant and animal products, in hotter climates.
Ind/Abst AGRICOLA [Full Cov.]; Agric. Eng. Abstr. (1991-); Agrofor. Abstr. (19??-19??); Biodeter. Abstr. (1991-); Chem. Abstr.; Crop Physiol. Abstr.; Curr. Aware. Biol. Sci., CABS; Curr. Cit.; Dairy Sci. Abstr.; EMBASE (-1988); Field Crop Abstr.; Food Sci. Technol. Abstr.; For. Prod. Abstr. (19??-19??); For. Abstr.; Hortic. Abstr.; Int. Packag. Abstr.; Maize Abstr.; Nutr. Abstr. Rev., Ser. A, Hum. Exp.; Plant Breed. Abstr.; Plant Genet. Resour. Abstr.; Plant Grow. Reg. Abstr.; Postharvest News Inf.; Potato Abstr.; Rev. Agric. Entomol.; Rev. Med. Vet. Mycology; Rev. Plant Pathol.; Rice Abstr.; Rural Dev. Abstr.; Seed Abstr.; Soils Fert.; Soyabean Abstr.; Wheat Barley Trit. Abstr.; World Agric. Econ. Rural Sociol. Abstr.

LC Z5074.A83 T76 S616.B6
DD 016.63/0915/4 BL
TROPICO SEMI-ARIDO : RESUMOS INFORMATIVOS. Vol. 1 (1977)-. Portuguese. Irregular. $80.00. Empresa Brasileira de Pesquisa Agropecuaria, Centro de Pesquisa Agropecuria do Tropico Semi-Arido, Caixa Postal No 23, 56.300 Petrolina - PE Brazil. **Tel** (081)961-4411, telex (081)1878.
Desc: Contains abstracts of the published papers about the Brazilian semi-arid regions (agriculture and animal production).

LC S **ISSN** 0771-3312
DD 630 BE
Pr Rev.
TROPICULTURA. (1983)-. Periodical. French (English, Dutch and Spanish). Four times a year. Free on request. Agri Overseas Bruxelles Agcd, 4 rue du Trone, Bureau 405, B-1050 Brussels Belgium. **Tel** 011 32 2 5190377. **ED** J. Hardouin. Index available. **Bk Rev**, (Qty: 10). **Circ:** 2,000. Documents available from BIOSIS Document Express.
Ind/Abst Biol. Abstr.; Index Vet.; Nutr. Abstr. Rev., Ser. B, Live Feeds and Feed.; Pig News Inf.; Postharvest News Inf.; Poult. Abstr.; Protozoolog. Abstr.; Rev. Med. Vet. Entomol.

LC S
DD 630 FR
TROTTEUR DE FRANCE. (19??)-. Periodical. French. Eight times a year. 231.87F France; 415.00F other. Province Courses, BP 3, 50290 Brehal France. **Tel** 011 33 33 616264.

LC S **ISSN** 0126-0057
DD 630 IO
TRUBUS. Vol. 1- (No. 1-); Dec. 1969-. Periodical. Indonesian. Twelve times a year. Rp30,000. Yayasan Sosial Tani Membangun, Jl Gunung Sahari 111/7 Tromol Pos 456, Jakarta Indonesia. **Tel** 354700. **ED** F Rahardi. Index available. **Bk Rev. Ad Acc. Circ:** 50,000 (ctrl).
Desc: Covers livestock, poultry, horticulture and plants, fish culture and fisheries, hobbies, home economics, dairy and related technologies, water resources, zoology, veterinary medicine, animal culture, etc.

LC S13 .K55 **ISSN** 0371-8794
DD 630/.5 MV
CODEN TKSFAC
TRUDY (INSTITUTUL AGRIKOL M.V. FRUNZE). (TRUDY / KISHINEVSKII SELSKOKHOZIAISTVENNYI INSTITUT IM. M.V. FRUNZE.). **Added/Corp** Institutul Agrikol "M.V. Frunze.". (1949)-. Academic Scholarly Publication. Russian. Price varies per volume. Documents available from CASDDS.
Ind/Abst Chem. Abstr. (?-1977).

LC S16.L3 L3
LV
CODEN LLRADG
TRUDY LSKHA. **Added/Corp** Latvijas Lauksaimniecibas Akademija. **VFOAT** LLA Raksti. **VAT** Trudy Latviiskoi Selskokhoziaistvennoi Akademii; Latvijas Lauksaimniecibas Akademijas Raksti. (19??)-. Monographic series. Latvian (Russian; summaries and/or abstracts in English). Documents available from CASDDS. ***Continues*** *Ar Darba SarkanÂa Karoga Ordeni Apbalvotas Latvijas Lauksaimniecibas Akademijas Raksti.*
Ind/Abst Agric. Eng. Abstr.; Chem. Abstr.

LC S **ISSN** 0372-3283
DD 630 RU
CODEN TVZKA3
TRUDY VSESOUZNOGO NAUCNO-ISSLEDOVATELSKOGO INSTITUTA ZERNOVOGO HOZAJSTVA. (TRUDY.). [Tr. Vses. naucno-issled. inst. zern. hoz.]. **Main/Corp** Vsesoiuznyi Nauchno-Issledovatelskii Institut Zernovogo Khoziaistva. **Added/Corp** Vsesoiuznaia Akademiia Selskokhoziaistvennykh Nauk Imeni V.I. Lenina. (1964)-. Academic Scholarly Publication. Russian. Irregular. Izdatelstvo Kolos, Sadovaia-Spasskaia 18, 107807 Moscow Russia. Documents available from CASDDS.
Ind/Abst Chem. Abstr. (1961-1980).

LC S **ISSN** 0744-7086
DD 630 US
TULARE COUNTY FARM BUREAU NEWS. **VFOAT** FB News. Periodical. English. Twelve times a year. Tulare Company, Farm Bureau News, POB 748, Visalia CA 93279.

LC HD1401 .T84
DD 338.1/09595 MY
TUMBUH. Periodical. English. University of Malaya Agricultural Graduates Alumni, No 21 Jalan 11/6, Petaling Jaya Malaysia.

LC S346.5 .T86
DD 638.0965 TI
TUNIS AL-KHADRA. **VFOAT** Tounes el Khadra. Periodical. Arabic. 10. Al-Ittihad Al-Qawmi Lil-Fallahin, 6 Al-Habeeb Thamir Street, Tunis Tunisia.

LC S **ISSN** 0254-5454
DD 630 TU
CODEN TBKDD8
TURKIYE BITKI KORUMA DERGISI. [Turk. bitki koruma derg.]. **VFOAT** Turkish Journal of Plant Protection. Academic Scholarly Publication. English (German). Documents available from CASDDS.
Ind/Abst Chem. Abstr.; Life Sci. Collect.; Rev. Med. Vet. Entomol.

LC S13 .A573
DD 630.5 TK
TURKMENISTAN YLYMLAR AKADEMIIASYNYNG KHABARLARY. BIOLOGIK YLYMLARYNG SERIIASY. **See** Biology.

LC S **ISSN** 0041-4360
DD 630 CR
CODEN TURRAB
Pr Rev. **CEASED**
TURRIALBA : REVISTA INTERAMERICANO DE CIENCIAS AGRICOLAS. [Turrialba]. **Added/Corp** Inter-American Institute of Agricultural Sciences. (July 1950)-(1995). Periodical. Spanish (French, Portuguese and English). Instituto Interamericano de Cooperacion Para la Agricultura, Apartado Postal, 552200 Coronado, San Jose Costa Rica. **Tel** 011 506 290222, FAX 011 506 294741, 011 506 292659. **Bk Rev. Circ:** 800 (ctrl). available on microfilm and microfiche from University Microfilms International (UMI). Documents available from The Genuine Article, CASDDS.
Desc: The object of the journal is to serve as a tool for technical, scientific and general interest for professionals in the field to express their findings and experiences.
Ind/Abst AgBiotech News Inf.; Agrofor. Abstr. (19??-19??); Anim. Breed. Abstr.; Biocont. News Inf. (19??-19??); Chem. Abstr.; Crop Physiol. Abstr.; Curr. Cit.; Curr. Contents Agric. Biol. Environ. Sci.; Dairy Sci. Abstr.; Ecol. Abstr. (?-?); Field Crop Abstr.; Food Sci. Technol. Abstr.; For. Prod. Abstr.; For. Abstr.; Geogr. Abstr. Phys. Geogr. (?-?); GeoRef; Helminthol. Abstr.; Hortic. Abstr.; Int. Dev. Abstr. (?-?); Irr. Drain. Abstr.; Maize Abstr.; Nematol. Abstr.; Nutr. Abstr. Rev., Ser. B, Live Feeds and Feed.; Life Sci. Collect.; PESTDOC; Plant Breed. Abstr.; Plant Grow. Reg. Abstr.; Postharvest News Inf.; Potato Abstr.; Res. Alert [Select. Cov.]; Rev. Agric. Entomol.; Rev. Plant Pathol.; Rice Abstr.; Seed Abstr.; Soils Fert.; Sorghum Mill. Abstr.; Soyabean Abstr.; Weed Abstr.; Wildl. Rev. (19??-199?).

LC S **ISSN** 0496-5201
DD 630 II
TWO AND A BUD. **Added/Corp** Tea Research Association. Indian Tea Association. Vol. 1 (Apr. 1954)-. Periodical. English. Two times a year. $30.00. Tea Research Association, Tocklai Experimental Station, Jorhat 785008 Assam India. **(Subscription address:** UBS Publishers Distributors, 5 Ansari Road, PO Box 7015, New Delhi 110002 India. **Tel** 011 91 11 3273601, 011 91 11 3266645.)
Ind/Abst Agrofor. Abstr. (1991-); Biocont. News Inf. (1991-); Crop Physiol. Abstr.; Food Sci. Technol. Abstr.; Hortic. Abstr.; Plant Breed. Abstr.; Plant Grow. Reg. Abstr.; Rev. Agric. Entomol.; Rev. Plant Pathol.; Seed Abstr.; Soils Fert.; Weed Abstr.

LC S **ISSN** 0355-0710
DD 630 FI
TYOTEHOSEURAN JULKAISUJA. [Tyotehoseuran julk.]. **VFOAT** Tyotehoseuranjulkaisu. Monographic series. Finnish (summaries and/or abstracts in Swedish and English). Irregular. Price varies per volume. ***Continues*** *Maatalouden Tyotehoseuran Julkaisuja.*
Ind/Abst Agric. Eng. Abstr. (1991-); Agrofor. Abstr. (1991-); For. Prod. Abstr. (1991-); For. Abstr.; Wheat Barley Trit. Abstr.

LC S
DD 630 CN
TYPE ANALYSIS FOR TOP 50 LPI SERIES. (19??)-. English. Two times a year (Mar., Sept.). 28.01Can$. Holstein Association of Canada, PO Box 610, Brantford Ontario, N3T 5R4 Canada. **Tel** (519)756-8300, FAX (519)756-5878, (519)756-3502, telex 06181139.

Agriculture

LC HD1751 .U18   **ISSN** 0895-545X
DD 338.1/873   US
U.S. AGRICULTURAL POLICY GUIDE.
See Public Administration.

LC S   **ISSN** 0041-7637
DD 630   US
U.S. FARM NEWS. Added/Corp U.S. Farmers Association. **VAT** United States Farm News. (19??)-. Periodical. English. Eleven times a year (monthly except April). $5.00. US Farmers Association, 909-5th Avenue Southeast, Hampton IA 50441. **Tel** (515)456-4470. **ED** Fred W. Stover. **Bk Rev. Circ:** 4,000 (ctrl). available on microfilm.
 Desc: Farm legislation, foreign affairs, peace and civil rights.

LC HD1751 .A5 HD9490.U5   **ISSN** 0146-8782
DD 338.1/0973 S 338.4/7/66430973   US
U.S. FATS AND OILS STATISTICS. See Agriculture-Abstracting, Bibliographies and Statistics.

LC S   **ISSN** 0856-0838
DD 630   TZ
UKULIMA WA KISASA. (1955)-. Afrikaans.

LC HD1491.R95 U58
DD 334/.683/0967571   RW
UMUNYAMUYANGO. See Business and Economics-Cooperatives.

LC S   **ISSN** 0317-2279
DD 630/.6/2714   CN
UNION DES PRODUCTEURS AGRICOLES. See Business and Economics-Labor.

LC S21 .A
DD 630   US
UNITED STATES. DEPT. OF AGRICULTURE. ANNUAL REPORT OF THE SECRETARY OF AGRICULTURE. (19??)-. Government Publication. English. One time a year. Free. US Department of Agriculture, 14th Street and Independence Avenue SW, Washington DC 20250. **Tel** (202)720-5457. **Continues** Report of the Secretary of Agriculture.

LC S   **ISSN** 0273-5016
DD 630   US
URNER BARRY'S PRICE-CURRENT. WEST COAST EDITION. (URNER BARRY'S PRICE-CURRENT.). (198?)-. Periodical. English. Two times a week. $121.00. Urner Barry Publications Inc., PO Box 389, Toms River NJ 08754. **Tel** (908)240-5330, (800)932-0617, FAX (908)341-0891. **ED** Bud O'Shaughnessy and John Carter. **Ad Acc. Circ:** 100. **Continues** Producers' Price Current. West Coast Edition, 0270-420X.
 Desc: Regional prices and conditions for poultry, dairy and eggs.

LC HD9014.U8 U79
DD 338.1/09895   GW
URUGUAY, ENTWICKLUNG DER LANDWIRTSCHAFT / BUNDESSTELLE FUR AUSSENHANDELSINFORMATION. German. DM3.00. Bundesstelle fuer Aussenhandelsinformation, Agrippastrasse 87 93, D-50676 Cologne Germany. **Tel** 011 49 221 2057316, FAX 011 49 221 2057212.

LC S
DD 630   PH
USM CA RESEARCH JOURNAL, THE. Added/Corp University of Southern Mindanao. College of Agriculture. **VFOAT** Journal of the College of Agriculture, University of Southern Mindanao; USMCARJ; University of Southern Mindanao College of Agriculture Research Journal; Research Journal; USM Coll. Agric. Res. J.; USM CARJ. Vol. 1, No. 1 (Apr. 1990)-. English.
 Ind/Abst Field Crop Abstr.; Hortic. Abstr.; Rev. Plant Pathol.; Rice Abstr.; Soils Fert.; Sorghum Mill. Abstr.; Weed Abstr.

LC S119 .U8
DD 338.1/09792/021   US
UTAH AGRICULTURAL STATISTICS AND UTAH DEPARTMENT OF AGRICULTURE ANNUAL REPORT. **VFOAT** Utah Department of Agriculture Agricultural Statistics, Utah Department of Agriculture; UAL Report; Annual Report. 1988-. English. One time a year. Utah Agriculture Statistic Service, POB 25007, Salt Lake City UT 84125. **Formed by the union of** Biennial Report - Utah State Dept. of Agriculture **and** Utah Agricultural Statistics, 0276-0193.

LC S   **ISSN** 1071-653X
DD 630
●**UTAH FARMER (1993).** (UTAH FARMER.). Vol. 113, No. 7 (July 1993)-. Trade Publication. English. Twelve times a year. $18.00 US / $32.00 Canada and Mexico; $52.00 other. Western Farmer Stockman, Box 2160, Spokane WA 99210. **Tel** (509)459-5361, FAX (509)459-5102. **Continues** Utah Farmer-Stockman, 1041-1666.

LC S   **ISSN** 1041-1666
DD 630   US
      TITLE CHANGE
UTAH FARMER-STOCKMAN. [Utah farmer-stockm.]. **VFOAT** Utah Farmer Stockman. (19??)-(19??). Periodical. English. Utah Farmer Stockman, PO Box 2160, Spokane WA 99210. **Tel** (509)459-5361, FAX (509)459-5234. **Continues** Utah Farmer. **Continued by** Utah Farmer (Spokane, Wash. : 1993), 1071-653X.

LC S   **ISSN** 0042-1502
DD 630   S
      CODEN UTSCBA
UTAH SCIENCE. [Utah sci.]. **Added/Corp** Utah Agricultural Experiment Station. Vol. 28 (March 1967)-. Periodical. English. Irregular. Free. Utah Agricultural Experiment Station, Utah State University, UMC 48, Logan UT 84322. **Tel** (801)750-2206, FAX (801)750-3321. **ED** Kurt Gutknecht. Index available. **Circ:** 2,600 (ctrl). Documents available from BIOSIS Document Express. **Continues** Utah Farm and Home Science, 0097-1588.
 Desc: Articles written by UAES staff covering the variety of research done through the Utah Agricultural Experiment Station.
 Ind/Abst AgBiotech News Inf. (19??-); AGRICOLA (19??-) [Select. Cov.]; Anim. Breed. Abstr. (19??-); Biol. Abstr. (19??-); Crop Physiol. Abstr. (19??-); Curr. Ref. Fish Res. (19??-); Dairy Sci. Abstr. (19??-); Environ. Period. Bibliogr. (?-?); For. Abstr. (19??-); GeoRef (19??-); Grass. Forage Abstr. (19??-); Index Vet. (19??-); Mat. Fact (19??-); Nematol. Abstr. (19??-); Nutr. Abstr. Rev., Ser. B, Live Feeds and Feed. (19??-); Life Sci. Collect. (19??-); Plant Breed. Abstr. (19??-); Pollut. Abstr. Indexes (19??-); Soyabean Abstr. (19??-); Wildl. Rev. (19??-); World Agric. Econ. Rural Sociol. Abstr. (19??-).

LC S539.J3 U82   **ISSN** 0566-4691
DD 630/.952   JA
      CODEN UDNGAK
UTSUNOMIYA DAIGAKU NOGAKUBU GAKUJUTSU HOKOKU. (GAKUJUTSU HOKOKU.). [Utsunomiya Daigaku Nogakubu Gakujutsu hokoku]. **VFOAT** Bulletin of the College of Agriculture, Utsunomiya University. (Feb. 1950)-. Bulletin. Japanese (summaries and/or abstracts in English). Utsunomiya University / Agriculture, College of Agriculture, Utsunomiya Japan. Documents available from BIOSIS Document Express, CASDDS. **Continues** Gakujutsu Hokoku. Dai 1-Shu, Nogaku, Ringaku, Juigaku, Nogyo Dobokugaku, Nogei Nagaku; Gakujutsu Hokoku. Dai 2-Shu, Norin Keizai.
 Ind/Abst AGRICOLA; Agric. Eng. Abstr.; Biol. Abstr.; Chem. Abstr. (1950-1986); Rice Abstr.

LC S280.T3 V34
DD 630   II
VALARUM VELANMAI. Added/Corp Tamil Nadu Agricultural University. (19??)-. Periodical. Tamil (Tamil). Four times a year. 1.00 single issue. Tamil Nadu Agricultural University, Coimbatore India.

LC S
DD 630   SP
VALENCIA FRUITS. (19??)-. Periodical. Spanish. One time a week. 10500ptas Spain; 14000ptas Europe; 20000ptas other. Edita Sucro SA, Hernan Cortes 5, Valencia 4 Spain. **Tel** 011 34 6 3525301. **ED** Fidel Pascual Teules. **Bk Rev. Ad Acc. Circ:** 13,000 (ctrl).
 Desc: Covers agricultural economics.

LC SB175   **ISSN** 0889-4787
DD 635   US
VALLEY POTATO GROWER. [Val. potato grow.]. **Added/Corp** Red River Valley Potato Growers Association (East Grand Forks, Minn.). (1946)-. Trade Publication. English. Twelve times a year. Free on request. Valley Potato Grower, PO Box 301, East Grand Forks MN 56721. **Tel** (218)773-3633, FAX (218)773-6227. **ED** Christle Johnson. **Ad Acc. Circ:** 11,500. **Continues** Red River Valley Potato Grower.
 Desc: Deals with all facets of the potato industry: advertising and promotion, marketing, transportation, legislation, research and extension work.

LC HD2151 .V34
DD 338.1/0994   AT
VALUE OF AGRICULTURAL COMMODITIES PRODUCED, AUSTRALIA. See Agriculture-Abstracting, Bibliographies and Statistics.

LC S209   **ISSN** 1184-8170
DD 635/.217/0971   CN
VARIETES DE POMMES DE TERRE AU CANADA. [Var. pommes terre Can.]. **Added/Corp** Nouveau-Brunswick. Ministere de l'Agriculture. Entente de Cooperation Canada/Nouveau-Brunswick sur le Developpement du Secteur Agro-Alimentaire 1989-1994. Association des Producteurs de Pommes de Terre de Semence du Nouveau-Brunswick. Agence de la Pomme de Terre du N.-B. (1991)-. French. **Continues** Liste de Varietes de Pommes de Terre au Canada., 0845-9258.

LC S   **ISSN** 0340-7810
DD 630   GW
VDL NACHRICHTEN. [VDL Nachr.]. **Main/Corp** Verband Deutscher Akademiker fur Landwirtschaft, Ernahrung und Landespflege. Vol. 24, No. 1 (Jan. 1974)-. Periodical. German. Twelve times a year. BLV Verlagsgesellschaft MBH, Lothstrasse 29, D80797 Munich Germany. **Tel** 011 49 89 12705214. **Continues** Der Diplomlandwirt.
 Ind/Abst AGRICOLA.

LC S
DD 630   GW
VDLUFA KONGRESSBAND. (19??)-. German. DM292.00. J. D. Sauerlaender Verlag, Finkenhofstrasse 21, D-60322 Frankfurt Germany. **Tel** 011 49 69 555217, FAX 011 49 69 5964344.
 Desc: Annual reports of congresses held by the Organization of German Agricultural Research Stations.

LC S   **ISSN** 0173-8712
DD 630   GW
VDLUFA-SCHRIFTENREIHE. [VDLUFA-Schr. reihe]. **Added/Corp** Verband Deutscher Landwirtschaftlicher Untersuchungs- und Forschungsanstalten. **VAT** Verband Deutscher Landwirtschaftlicher Untersuchungs- und Forschungsanstalten Schriftenreihe. (1980)-. Academic Scholarly Publication. German. Documents available from CASDDS.
 Ind/Abst Chem. Abstr.

LC S13 .M66   **ISSN** 0130-0911
DD 630.5   RU
      CODEN VSPRED
VDNKH SSSR. Added/Corp Vystavka Dostizhenii Narodnogo Khoziaistva SSSR (Moscow, R.S.F.S.R.). **VFOAT** V.D.N.K.H. S.S.S.R. (19??)-. Periodical. Russian. Twelve times a year. $11.50. VDNKh SSSR, Redaktsionno-Izdatelskii Otdel 129223, Moscow I-223 Russia. **Continues** Vystavka Dostizhenii Narodnogo Khoziiaistva SSSR (Moscow, R.S.F.S.R.). Informatsionnyi Biulleten.

LC S
DD 630   XO
VEDECKE PRACE VYSKUMNEHO USTAVU RASTLINNEJ VYROBYV PIESTANOCH. OBILNINY. Added/Corp Vyskumny Ustav Rastlinnej Vyroby. **VFOAT** Scientific Papers of the Research Institute for Plant Production at Piestany. Cereals. Vol. 18 (1981)-. Slovak (summaries and/or abstracts in English and Russian). One time a year. Documents available from BIOSIS Document Express. **Continues** Vedecke Prace Vyskumneho Ustavu Rastlinnej Vyroby v Piestanoch. Obilniny-Strakoviny.
 Ind/Abst Biol. Abstr.

LC S
DD 630   US
VERMONT SCIENCE : RESEARCH OF THE AGRICULTURAL EXPERIMENT STATION, UNIVERSITY OF VERMONT. Vol. 1, No. 1 (Winter 1977)-. Periodical. English. Two times a year. Free. University of Vermont Agricultural Experiment Station, Burlington VT 05405-0106. **Tel** (802)656-3024. **ED** LaRae Donnellan. **Circ:** 9,000 (ctrl). **Formed by the union of** Vermont Farm and Home Science **and** Science Serves Vermont.
 Desc: Popularized articles on Vermont Agricultural Experiment Station research. Topics include acid rain, maple syrup production, embryo transplants, nutrition of the elderly, and winter hardiness.

LC S   **ISSN** 1010-6146
DD 630   AU
VEROFFENTLICHUNGEN DER BUNDESANSTALT FUER ALPENLANDISCHE LANDWIRTSCHAFT GUMPENSTEIN. [Veroff. Bundesanst. alpenland. Landwirtsch. Gumpenstein]. **Added/Corp** Bundesanstalt fur Alpenlandische Landwirtschaft Gumpenstein. **VFOAT** Veroffentlichungen. (1987)-. Monographic series. German.
 Ind/Abst Agric. Eng. Abstr.; Anim. Breed. Abstr.; Weed Abstr.; World Agric. Econ. Rural Sociol. Abstr.

LC S
DD 630   NE
VERSLAGEN EN MEDEDELING - PLANTENZIEKTENKUNDIGE DIENST. **Main/Corp** Netherlands (Kingdom, 1815-). Plantenziektenkundige Dienst. (1916)-. Dutch. Plantenziektenkundige Dienst, Postbus 9102, 6700 HC

Wageningen Netherlands. **Tel** 011 31 8340-96799, FAX 011 31 8340-21701.
Ind/Abst Nematol. Abstr.

LC S900 **ISSN** 0174-1993
DD 634.45 GW
VERZEICHNIS DER WISSENSCHAFTLICHEN FILME. TEILVERZEICHNIS B.
(WISSENSCHAFTLICHE FILME : TEILVERZEICHNIS B. ZOOLOGIE, MIKROBIOLOGIE, BOTANIK, BIOCHEMIE, UMWELTSCHUTZ, HUMANETHOLOGIE, LAND- UND FORSTWIRTSCHAFT, JAGD/FISCHEREI.). (1976)-. German. ***Continues*** *Verzeichnis der Wissenschaftliche Filme. Teilverzeichnis B, 0174-1993.*

LC S **ISSN** 0042-4684
DD 630 KZ
CODEN VSNKBD
VESTNIK SELSKOHOZJAJSTVENNOJ NAUKI KAZAHSTANA.
(VESTNIK SELSKOKHOZIAISTVENNOI NAUKI KAZAKHATANA : EZHEMESIACHNYI ZHURNAL.). [Vestn. s-h. nauki Kazahstana]. **Added/Corp** Kazak S.S.R. Ministerstvo Selskogo Khoziaistva. Vsesoiuznaia Akademiia Selskokhoziastvennykh Nauki Imeni V.I. Lenina. Vostochnoe Otdelenie. (Jan. 1973)-. Academic Scholarly Publication. Russian. Twelve times a year. $61.00 domestic airmail; $71.00 international airmail. **(Subscription address:** Victor Kamkin, 4956 Boiling Brook Parkway, Rockville MD 20852. **Tel** (301)881-5973.**)** Documents available from CASDDS. ***Continues*** *Vestnik Selskokhoziaistvennoi Nauki.*
Ind/Abst AGRICOLA; Chem. Abstr.; Nematol. Abstr.; Plant Breed. Abstr.; Plant Grow. Reg. Abstr.; Protozoolog. Abstr.

LC S13 .V38 **ISSN** 0206-6335
DD 630 RU
CODEN VSNLAF
TITLE CHANGE
VESTNIK SELSKOKHOZIAISTVENNOI NAUKI.
[Vestn. s.-h. nauki]. **Added/Corp** Soviet Union. Ministerstvo Selskogokhoziaistva. Vsesoiuznaia Akademiia Selskokhoziaistvennykh M Nauk Imeni V.I. Lenina. (1956)-(19??). Periodical. Russian (German; summaries and/or abstracts in English, French and German; table of contents in Chinese, English, French and German). **Circ:** 8,310. available on microfilm. Documents available from CASDDS. ***Absorbed*** *Vsesoiuznaia Akademiia Selskokhoziaistvennykh naukk Imeni V.I. Lenina. Doklad.* ***Continued by*** *Agrarnaia Nauka.*
Ind/Abst AgBiotech News Inf.; AGRICOLA; Agric. Eng. Abstr.; Agrofor. Abstr.; Anim. Breed. Abstr.; Chem. Abstr.; Cot. Trop. Fibr. Abstr. Bibliogr.; Crop Physiol. Abstr.; Dairy Sci. Abstr.; Field Crop Abstr.; Grass. Forage Abstr.; Helminthol. Abstr.; Hortic. Abstr.; Index Vet.; Maize Abstr.; Nutr. Abstr. Rev., Ser. B, Live Feeds and Feed.; Ornamental Hort.; Plant Breed. Abstr.; Plant Genet. Resour. Abstr.; Plant Grow. Reg. Abstr.; Postharvest News Inf.; Potato Abstr.; Poult. Abstr.; Rev. Med. Vet. Entomol.; Rev. Plant Pathol.; Seed Abstr.; Soils Fert.; Vet. Bull.

LC S
DD 630 BW
VESTSI AKADEMII NAVUK BELARUSKAI SSR. SERYIA SELSKAHASPADARCHYKH NAVUK.
[Vestsi Akad Navuk BSSR, Ser. selskahaspad. Navuk]. **Added/Corp** Akademiia Navuk Belaruskai SSR. **VFOAT** Seryia Selskagaspadarchykh Navuk; Agricultural Series; Seriia Selskokhoziaistvennykh Nauk; Izvestiia Akademii Nauk Belorusskoi SSR. Seriia Selskokhoziaistvennykh Nauk. (19??)-. Periodical. Byelorussian (Russian; summaries and/or abstracts in Russian). Four times a year. $55.00. **(Subscription address:** East View Publications Inc., 3020 Harbor Lane North, Suite 110, Minneapolis MN 55447. **Tel** (800)477-1005, (612)550-0961, FAX (612)559-2931.**)** Documents available from BIOSIS Document Express, CASDDS. ***Continues*** *Vestsi Akademii Navuk Belaruskai SSR. Seryia Selskahaspadarchykh Navuk, 0321-1657.*
Desc: Provides information on the transactions of the Belorussian Academy of Sciences Agricultural Series.
Ind/Abst AGRICOLA (19??-); Biol. Abstr. (19??-); Chem. Abstr. (19??-); Dairy Sci. Abstr. (19??-); Index Vet. (19??-); Nutr. Abstr. Rev., Ser. B, Live Feeds and Feed. (19??-); Pig News Inf. (19??-); Poult. Abstr. (19??-).

LC S
DD 630 SP
VIDA RURAL.
(19??)-. Periodical. Spanish. Eleven times a year. 11000ptas. Edagricole Espana SA, Castello 32, 28001 Madrid Spain. **Tel** 011 34 1 5780534, 011 34 1 5780820. ***Absorbed*** *MT Maquinas y Tractores Agricolas.*

LC HD1995.7 .A57
DD 338.1/09438 PL
VILLAGE AND AGRICULTURE.
Added/Corp Instytut Rozwoju Wsi i Rolnictwa (Polska Akademia Nauk). Vol. 1 (1973-1974)-. English (Polish). Every 2 years. **(Subscription address:** Ars Polona-Ruch, PO Box 1001, Krakowskie Przedmiescie 7, 00-068 Warsaw Poland. **Tel** 011 48 22 261201.**)**

LC HD1775.V5 V478 HD1775.V5 A3 **ISSN** 0360-3830
DD 338.1/09755 S 338.1/09755/021 US
VIRGINIA AGRICULTURAL STATISTICS.
See Agriculture-Abstracting, Bibliographies and Statistics.

LC S **ISSN** 0744-513X
DD 630 US
VIRGINIA CROPS AND LIVESTOCK.
(VIRGINIA CROPS AND LIVESTOCK / CROP REPORTING SERVICE.). [Va. crops livest.]. **Added/Corp** United States. Bureau of Agricultural Economics. Virginia. Division of Agricultural Statistics. United States. Division of Agricultural Statistics. United States. Division of Crop and Livestock Estimates. Virginia Crop Reporting Service. United States. Dept. of Agriculture. Virginia. Dept. of Agriculture and Consumer Services. Virginia Agricultural Statistics Service. **VFOAT** Virginia Farm Production. Vol. 1, No. 1 (Aug. 14, 1929)-. Government Publication. English. Twenty-four times a year. $10.00. US Department of Agriculture / National Agricultural Statistics Service (NASS), Room 5829 South Building, Washington DC 20250. **Tel** (202)720-4020, FAX (314)875-5231.

LC S **ISSN** 0746-1186
DD 630 US
VIRGINIA FARMER (BALTIMORE, MD.).
(VIRGINIA FARMER.). (19??)-. Periodical. English. Twelve times a year. $12.00. Rural Press USA, 7701 Six Forks Road, Suite 132, Raleigh NC 27615. **Tel** (800)934-2472, (919)676-3276, FAX (919)676-9803. **ED** Julie Gochenour (editor's telephone: (703)459-3209). **Ad Acc. Circ:** 17,554 (ctrl).

LC HB241 **ISSN** 1064-4083
DD 338 US
VIRGINIA FRUIT AND VEGETABLE MARKET INFORMATION.
See Food and Food Industry.

LC SD **ISSN** 0848-3809
DD 634.9/09714/77 CN
VISION, TERRE ET FORET.
See Forests and Forestry.

LC S **ISSN** 1120-3005
DD 630 IT
VITA IN CAMPAGNA.
[Vita camp.]. (1983)-. Periodical. Italian. Eleven times a year. L34060. L'Informatore Agrario Srl, Largo Caldera 11, PO Box 520, 37122 Verona Italy. **Tel** 011 39 45 597855.
Ind/Abst Agrofor. Abstr.; Biocont. News Inf. (1991-); For. Prod. Abstr. (1991-); For. Abstr.; Index Vet.; Pig News Inf.; Plant Breed. Abstr.; Rev. Agric. Entomol.; Rev. Med. Vet. Entomol.; Small Anim. Abstr. Bibliogr.

LC S **ISSN** 1131-5679
DD 630 SP
UDC 634.8
Pr Rev.
VITICULTURA ENOLOGIA PROFESIONAL.
(1989)-. Periodical. Spanish. Five times a year. $51.52. Agro Latino, Apartado Correos 20 151, 08080 Barcelona Spain. **Tel** (93) 456 85 63, FAX (93)235 91 04. **ED** Daniel Aradas Llorens. Index available. cum. index. **Ad Acc.**

LC S **ISSN** 0703-8852
DD 630/.5 CN
VOICE OF THE ESSEX FARMER, THE.
VFOAT Essex Farmer. (Mar. 8, 1977)-. Periodical. English. Six times a year. Leader Publications / Canada, Box 490, Dresden Ontario N0P 1M0 Canada. **Tel** (519)882-1270, (519)683-4485.

LC S451.5 **ISSN** 0715-4372
DD 630/.9713/22 CN
VOICE OF THE HURON FARMER, THE.
[Voice Huron farmer]. Vol. 1, Issue 1 (Sept. 16, 1981)-. Periodical. English. Twenty-four times a year. $10.00. Leader Publications / Canada, Box 490, Dresden Ontario N0P 1M0 Canada. **Tel** (519)882-1270, (519)683-4485.

LC S451.5 **ISSN** 0709-1915
DD 630/.9713/25 CN
VOICE OF THE MIDDLESEX FARMER, THE.
VFOAT Middlesex Farmer; Rural Reflections. Vol. 1 (Sept. 6, 1977)-. Periodical. English. Twenty-four times a year. 15.21Can$. Leader Publications / Canada, Box 490, Dresden Ontario N0P 1M0 Canada. **Tel** (519)882-1270, (519)683-4485. ctrl circ.

LC S **ISSN** 0742-4302
DD 630 US
VOICE (ORLAND PARK, ILL), THE.
(THE VOICE : PUBLICATION OF UNITED FARMERS AGENTS ASSOCIATION.). Periodical. English. Four times a year. United Farmers Agents Association Inc, PO Box 182, Orland Park IL 60462.

LC QH301 **ISSN** 0166-6053
DD 630 NE
UDC 631
VRUCHTBARE AARDE.
See Biology.

LC S **ISSN** 0139-7265
DD 630 CS
UDC 636.2
VYZKUM V CHOVU SKOTU.
[Vyzk. Chovu Skotu]. **VFOAT** Acta Taurologica. (1959)-. Periodical. Multiple languages. Four times a year. Vyzkumny Ustav pro Chov Skotv, Rapotin Nr., Sumperk.
Ind/Abst Index Vet.; Wheat Barley Trit. Abstr.

LC S **ISSN** 0889-3233
DD 630 US
WACO FARM AND LABOR JOURNAL (1986).
(WACO FARM AND LABOR JOURNAL.). (1986)-. Periodical. English. One time a week. $6.50. Waco Farm and Labor Journal, PO Box 402, Waco TX 76703-0402. **Tel** (817)753-3863. **ED** Roger Jones, (phone: (817)753-3871). Index available. **Ad Acc. Circ:** 120 (ctrl). ***Continues*** *Waco Labor Journal, 0737-4941.*
Desc: General news to interest to farm and organized labor.

LC S
DD 630 NE
Pr Rev.
WAGENINGEN AGRICULTURAL UNIVERSITY PAPERS.
Added/Corp Landbouwhogeschool Wageningen. **VFOAT** Agricultural University Wageningen Papers. (1989)-. Monographic series. English. Irregular. Price varies per volume. PUDOC, PO Box 4, 6700 AA Wageningen Netherlands. **Tel** 011 31 8370 84541, FAX 31 8370 84761, telex 45015 BLUWG NL. **ED** L. J. G. Van der Maesen. ***Continues*** *Agricultural University Wageningen Papers, 0169-345X.*
Desc: This series reports on research done at the Agricultural University, Wageningen.
Ind/Abst Ecol. Abstr. (19??-); Int. Dev. Abstr. (19??-).

LC HM7.W34 **ISSN** 0923-4365
DD 301.05 NE
WAGENINGSE SOCIOLOGISCHE STUDIES : WSS.
See Sociology.

LC HD1401 **ISSN** 0043-0129
DD 338 US
WALLACES FARMER (1959).
(WALLACES FARMER.). [Wallaces farmer]. **Added/Corp** Wallace-Homestead Co. **VFOAT** Wallaces Farmer and Iowa Homestead. Vol. 84, No. 1 (Jan. 1959)-. Periodical. English. Twenty-one times a year. $19.95. Farm Progress Publishing, 191 South Gary Avenue, Carol Stream IL 60188-2089. **Tel** (708)462-2890 or 2891. **(Subscription address:** CDS / SIFD Agency Control, 1901 Bell Avenue, Des Moines IA 50315. **Tel** (515)246-6812.**)** available on microfilm and microfiche from University Microfilms International (UMI). ***Continues*** *Wallace's Farmer and Iowa Homestead.*

LC S **ISSN** 0195-0673
DD 630 US
WASHINGTON AGRICULTURAL RECORD, THE.
Added/Corp Agro/Info. (1971)-. Periodical. English. Forty-eight times a year. $65.00. Washington Agricultural Record, PO Box 25001, Georgetown Station, Washington DC 20007. **Tel** (202)463-4455. **ED** Mark C. Pyle. **Circ:** 2,300.
Desc: Concise weekly update of the Washington and international agricultural news. Primary news sources, USDA, foreign governments, congress, administration and national farm trade associations.

LC S125 .W37A **ISSN** 0095-4330
DD 338.1/09797 US
WASHINGTON AGRICULTURAL STATISTICS.
See Agriculture-Abstracting, Bibliographies and Statistics.

LC HB3525.W2 W35 **ISSN** 1063-0155
US
WASHINGTON COUNTS.
Added/Corp Washington State University. Cooperative Extension. No. 1 (Apr. 29, 1991)-. Monographic series. English. ***Continues*** *Census Notes.*
Ind/Abst AGRICOLA.

LC T1 **ISSN** 0891-6373
DD 605 US
WASHINGTON'S LAND & PEOPLE.
[Wash. land people]. **Added/Corp** Washington State University. College of Agriculture and Home Economics. **VFOAT** Washington's Land and People. Vol. 1, No. 1 (Spring 1987)-. Periodical. English. Two times a year.
Ind/Abst AGRICOLA [Full Cov.].

LC S605 .W3 **ISSN** 0043-0951
DD 630 GW
CCC
CODEN WUBOAN
WASSER UND BODEN.
[Wasser & Boden]. **Added/Corp** Germany (West). Bundesministerium fuer Ernahrung, Landwirtschaft und Forsten. (1949)-. Academic Scholarly Publication. German. Twelve times a year. DM202.00. Paul Parey Verlag, PO Box 106304, D 20043 Hamburg Germany. **Tel** 011 49 40 33969134. **ED** H. Zoelsmann and D. Ruchay. Index available. cum. index. **Bk Rev. Ad Acc. Circ:** 2,500.
Desc: Covers water management and supply, soil and environmental protection.

Agriculture

Ind/Abst AGRICOLA; Aquat. Sci. Fish. Abstr. [CD-ROM Ed.]; Coal Abstr.; EMBASE; Energy Res. Abstr. (Jan. 1972-); GeoRef; Int. Civil Eng. Abstr.; Soft. Abstr. Eng.

LC S
DD 630 US
WATER SPOUTS. No. 1- 1973-. Periodical. English. North Dakota State University of Agriculture Cooperative Extension Service, US Department of Agriculture, Fargo ND 58102.

LC S
DD 630 US
WATI/TS-VIEW [COMPUTER FILE].
Added/Corp United States. Dept. of Agriculture. Economic Research Service. (19??-)-. Government Publication. English. Irregular. Superintendent of Documents, US Government Printing Office, Washington DC 20402. **Tel** (202)275-3328, FAX (202)786-2377. available in print (World Agricultural Trends and Indicators).
Desc: System requirements: IBM or compatible; 330K RAM; MS-DOS or PC-DOS; hard disk with at least 650K storage; VGA, EGSA, MCGA, CGA, and Hercules monochrome hardware for graphics support.

LC HD
DD 333 **ISSN** 1073-4813 US
●**WEBSTER AGRICULTURAL LETTER, THE.** [Webster agric. lett.]. **Added/Corp** Webster Communications Corporation. Vol. 1, No. 1 (Jan. 1, 1994)-. Periodical. English. Twenty-four times a year. $295.00. Webster Communications Corporation, 1530 North Key Boulevard PH2, Arlington VA 22209. **Tel** (703)525-4512, FAX (703)525-4917. **ED** James Webster. *Formed by the union of Agricultural Credit Letter, 0887-7521 and Washington Farmletter, 0739-6783.*

LC SB183
DD 633.089954 **ISSN** 1033-3061 AT
WEED CONTROL IN SUMMER CROPS.
[Weed control summer crops]. (1989)-. English. One time a year. **Continues** Weed Control in Sorghum, Maize, Soybeans and Sunflower, 0812-5651.

LC SB611
DD 632/.52/05 **ISSN** 0043-1745 US
CODEN WEESA6
Pr Rev.
WEED SCIENCE. [Weed sci.]. (Jan. 1968). Academic Scholarly Publication. English. Four times a year. $125.00. Weed Science Society of America, 1508 West University Avenue, Champaign IL 61821. **Tel** (217)352-4212, FAX (217)398-4114. Index available (Bound in Oct. issue). **Circ:** 3,700. available on microfilm and microfiche from University Microfilms International (UMI). Documents available from The Genuine Article, BIOSIS Document Express, CASDDS. **Continues** Weeds.
Ind/Abst AGRICOLA (19??-) [Full Cov.]; Agrofor. Abstr. (1991-); BioBusiness (19??-); Biocont. News Inf. (19??-19??); Biol. Agric. Index (19??-); Biol. Abstr. (19??-); Chem. Abstr. (19??-); Cot. Trop. Fibr. Abstr. Bibliogr. (19??-); Crop Physiol. Abstr. (19??-); Curr. Cit.; Curr. Contents Agric. Biol. Environ. Sci. (19??-); Ecology Abstr. (19??-); EMBASE (19??-); Environ. Period. Bibliogr. (19??-); Field Crop Abstr. (19??-); For. Abstr. (19??-); Grass. Forage Abstr. (19??-); Hortic. Abstr. (19??-); Index Vet. (19??-); Nematol. Abstr. (19??-); Ornamental Hort. (19??-19??); Plant Breed. Abstr. (19??-); Plant Genet. Resour. Abstr. (19??-); Plant Grow. Reg. Abstr. (19??-); Potato Abstr. (19??-); Res. Alert (19??-) [Full Cov.]; Rev. Agric. Entomol. (19??-); Rev. Plant Pathol. (19??-); Rice Abstr. (19??-); Sci. Cit. Index (19??-); SCISEARCH (19??-); Seed Abstr. (19??-); Soils Fert. (19??-); Sorghum Mill. Abstr. (19??-); Soybean Abstr. (19??-); Weed Abstr. (19??-); Wheat Barley Trit. Abstr. (19??-).

LC SB599
DD 632 **ISSN** 0890-037X US
CODEN WETEE9WEEST4
WEED TECHNOLOGY. (WEED TECHNOLOGY: A JOURNAL OF THE WEED SCIENCE SOCIETY OF AMERICA.). [Weed technol.]. **Added/Corp** Weed Science Society of America. Vol. 1, No. 1 (Jan. 1987)-. Academic Scholarly Publication. English. Four times a year. $75.00. Weed Science Society of America, 1508 West University Avenue, Champaign IL 61821. **Tel** (217)352-4212, FAX (217)398-4114. available on microfilm and microfiche from University Microfilms International (UMI). Documents available from The Genuine Article, BIOSIS Document Express, CASDDS.
Ind/Abst AgBiotech News Inf. (19??-); AGRICOLA (19??-) [Full Cov.]; Agrofor. Abstr. (1991-); Biocont. News Inf. (1991-); Biol. Abstr. (19??-); Chem. Abstr. (19??-); Cot. Trop. Fibr. Abstr. Bibliogr. (19??-); Curr. Aware. Biol. Sci., CABS (19??-); Curr. Cit.; Curr. Contents Agric. Biol. Environ. Sci. (19??-); Ecology Abstr. (19??-); Environ. Period. Bibliogr. (19??-); Field Crop Abstr. (19??-); For. Abstr. (19??-); Grass. Forage Abstr. (19??-); Hortic. Abstr. (19??-); Index Vet. (19??-); Maize Abstr. (19??-); Ornamental Hort. (1991-); PESTDOC (19??-); Plant Breed. Abstr. (19??-); Plant Grow. Reg. Abstr. (19??-); Potato Abstr. (19??-); Res. Alert (19??-) [Select. Cov.]; Rev. Agric. Entomol. (19??-); Rev. Plant Pathol. (19??-); Rice Abstr. (19??-); Seed Abstr. (19??-); Soils Fert.

(19??-); Sorghum Mill. Abstr. (19??-); Soyabean Abstr. (19??-); Weed Abstr. (19??-); Wheat Barley Trit. Abstr. (19??-); World Agric. Econ. Rural Sociol. Abstr. (19??-).

LC S
DD 630 UK
WEEKLY RAW COTTON REPORT. No. 32/69 (Aug. 11, 1969)-. English. One time a week. **Continues** Weekly Cotton Report.

LC S
DD 630 US
WEEKLY REPORT OF CERTIFICATED STOCK IN LICENSED WAREHOUSES.
Added/Corp United States. Agricultural Marketing Service. Cotton Division. (19??-). Periodical. English. One time a week. $27.00. New York Cotton Exchange, 4 World Trade Center, 8th Floor, New York NY 10048. **Tel** (212)938-2664.

LC HD1930.W3 W4 **ISSN** 0262-8325
DD 338.1/09429 UK
WELSH AGRICULTURAL STATISTICS / WELSH OFFICE = YSTADEGAU AMAETHYDDOL CYMRU / Y SWYDDFA GYMREIG. **Added/Corp** Great Britain. Welsh Office. **VFOAT** Ystadegau Amaethyddol Cymru. No. 1 (1979)-. Statistical Publication. English. One time a year. Welsh Office Publications Unit, Crown Building, Cathay's Park, Cardiff CF1 3NQ United Kingdom. **Tel** 011 44 1222 825111, FAX 011 44 1222 823036. **Continues in part** Agricultural Statistics, England and Ws.

LC S127 .A12 HD1775.W4
DD 630/.9754 338.1/09754 US
WEST VIRGINIA AGRICULTURAL STATISTICS. See Agriculture-Abstracting, Bibliographies and Statistics.

LC S
DD 631 **ISSN** 0164-6001 US
WESTERN FRUIT GROWER. [West. fruit grow.]. Vol. 94 No. 7 (July 1974)-. Trade Publication. English. Twelve times a year. $27.00. Meister Publishing Company, 37733 Euclid Avenue, Willoughby OH 44094-5992. **Tel** (216)942-2000, (800)572-7740, FAX (216)942-0662. *Absorbed American Fruit Grower: Western Edition.*
Desc: Information on growing, from planning to harvesting and marketing.
Ind/Abst AGRICOLA.

LC S
DD 630 **ISSN** 0043-4094 CN
WESTERN PRODUCER. (1923)-. Newspaper. English. One time a week. 28.81Can$. Western Producer, PO Box 2500, Saskatoon Saskatchewan S7K 2C4 Canada. **Tel** (306)665-3521, FAX (306)653-1255. **ED** R.K. Dryden. **Bk Rev**. **Ad Acc**. **Circ:** 133,000.
Desc: A weekly newspaper serving Western Canadian farmers.

LC HD9680 **ISSN** 0822-8183
DD 338.4/766862/09712 CN
TITLE CHANGE
WFCD COMMUNICATOR. (WFCD COMMUNICATOR.). [WFCD commun.]. **Added/Corp** Western Fertilizer and Chemical Dealers Association. **VAT** Western Fertilizer and Chemical Dealers Association Communicator; Communicator = Western Fertilizer and Chemical Dealers Association. - (1980)-(19??). Trade Publication. English. CAAR Communicator, 1090 Waverly Street, Suite 107, Winnepeg Manitoba R3T 0P4 Canada. **Tel** (204)989-9300. **ED** Jacqueline Ryrie. **Ad Acc**. **Circ:** 2,700. (ctrl). *Continued by CAAR Communicator.*
Desc: Magazine for independent fertilizer and chemical dealers and their suppliers.

LC HD1751 .W45 **ISSN** 0749-5854
DD 338.1/0973 US
WHARTON AGRICULTURE SERVICE.
[Wharton agric. serv.]. English. WEFA / Philadelphia, PO Box 8500, Suite 1995, Philadelphia PA 19178. **Tel** (215)667-6000, telex 710 6700575.

LC HD1401 .W53 **ISSN** 0749-579X
DD 338.1/05 US
WHARTON INTERNATIONAL AGRICULTURE SERVICE. LONG-TERM FORECAST. [Wharton int. agric. serv., Long-term forecast]. English. Two times a year. WEFA / Philadelphia, PO Box 8500, Suite 1995, Philadelphia PA 19178. **Tel** (215)667-6000, telex 710 6700575.

LC HD1401 .W54 **ISSN** 0749-5803
DD 338.1/05 US
WHARTON INTERNATIONAL AGRICULTURE SERVICE. MEDIUM TERM FORECAST. [Wharton int. agric. serv., Medium term forecast]. English. Four times a year. WEFA / Philadelphia, PO Box 8500, Suite 1995, Philadelphia PA 19178. **Tel** (215)667-6000, telex 710 6700575.

LC S
DD 630 UK
WHAT'S NEW IN FARMING. No. 9 (June 1978)-. Trade Publication. English. Eight times a year. $150.00. Morgan Grampian, 40 Beresford Street Woolwich, London SE18 6BQ United Kingdom. **Tel** 011 44 181 8557777, FAX 011 44 181 8555548, telex 896258. **ED** Stephen Mitchell. Index available. **Bk Rev**. **Ad Acc**. **Circ:** 76,000. (ctrl). available on microfilm and microfiche from University Microfilms International (UMI).
Desc: Comprehensive guide to all new products for the ARABLE and livestock farmer, backed by an express inquiry card system.
Ind/Abst AgBiotech News Inf.; Helminthol. Abstr.; Pig News Inf.

LC Z5071 **ISSN** 0706-8662
DD 016.63 CN
WHAT'S NEW IN PUBLICATIONS (EDMONTON). See Agriculture-Abstracting, Bibliographies and Statistics.

LC S **ISSN** 0510-3517
DD 630 JA
CODEN WINSAB
WHEAT INFORMATION SERVICE.
Added/Corp Kihara Institute for Biological Research. Wheat Information Service. Kyoto Daigaku. Biological Institute. Laboratory of Genetics. Kyoto Daigaku. Kyoyobu. Seibutsugaka Kyoshitsu. No. 1 (Oct. 1954)-. Monographic series. English. Irregular. Price varies per volume. Kihara Seibutsugaku Kenkyusho, 122-23 3-chome Mutsugawa, Yokohama-shi 233 Japan. Documents available from BIOSIS Document Express.
Ind/Abst Biol. Abstr. (?-1987); Field Crop Abstr.; Plant Breed. Abstr.; Plant Genet. Resour. Abstr.; Plant Grow. Reg. Abstr.; Rev. Plant Pathol.; Seed Abstr.; Wheat Barley Trit. Abstr.

LC S **ISSN** 0043-4701
DD 630 US
●**WHEAT LIFE.** **Added/Corp** Washington Association of Wheat Growers. Washington Wheat Commission. (19??)-. Periodical. English. Eleven times a year. $12.00. Washington Association Wheat Growers, 109 East 1st Street, Ritzville WA 99169. **Tel** (509)659-0610. **Bk Rev**. **Ad Acc**. **Circ:** 13,000 (ctrl).
Desc: Research, market developments, policy, laws affecting Pacific Northwest wheat industry. Activities of the Washington Association of Wheat Growers, Washington Wheat Commission, and Washington Barley Commissions.

LC S **ISSN** 0137-3838
DD 630 PL
WIADOMOSCI ZIELARSKIE.
[Wiad.zielarskie]. (1972)-. Periodical. Polish. Twelve times a year. $51.00. **(Subscription address:** Ars Polona-Ruch, PO Box 1001, Krakowskie Przedmiescie 7, 00-068 Warsaw Poland. **Tel** 011 48 22 261201.)
Ind/Abst AGRICOLA.

LC S **ISSN** 1230-0659
DD 630 PL
UDC 338.43
CODEN 438
WIES I PANSTWO. (1938)-. Periodical. Polish. Four times a year. Price on request. **(Subscription address:** Ars Polona-Ruch, PO Box 1001, Krakowskie Przedmiescie 7, 00-068 Warsaw Poland. **Tel** 011 48 22 261201.)

LC TP500 **ISSN** 0043-583X
DD 663 US
WINES AND VINES. See Food and Food Industry-Beverage Industry.

LC S129 .W48 **ISSN** 0512-1329
DD 338.1/09775 US
WISCONSIN AGRICULTURAL STATISTICS. See Agriculture-Abstracting, Bibliographies and Statistics.

LC S **ISSN** 0043-6356
DD 630 US
WISCONSIN AGRICULTURIST (1958).
(WISCONSIN AGRICULTURIST.). [Wis. agric.]. **VFOAT** Wisconsin Agriculturist, The Wisconsin Farmer. Vol. 85, No. 20 (Oct. 1958)-. Trade Publication. English. Twenty-four times a year. $17.95. Farm Progress Publishing, 191 South Gary Avenue, Carol Stream IL 60188-2089. **Tel** (708)462-2890 or 2891. **(Subscription address:** CDS / SIFD Agency Control, 1901 Bell Avenue, Des Moines IA 50315. **Tel** (515)246-6812.) **ED** Al Morrow. **Ad Acc**. **Circ:** 50,000. **Continues** Wisconsin Agriculturist and Farmer.

LC S
DD 630 US
WISCONSIN CROP WEATHER. English.
Irregular (weekly during growing season). $12.00. Wisconsin Agricultural Statistics Service, PO Box 9160, Madison WI 53713. **Tel** (608)264-5317.
Desc: Focusing on crop condition and development, temperature and rainfall, growing degree days and weather summaries.

LC S129 .Z8 **ISSN** 0043-6461
DD 338.1/09775 US
WISCONSIN FARM REPORTER.
Added/Corp Wisconsin Statistical Reporting Service. Wisconsin Agriculture Reporting Service. Wisconsin Agricultural Statistics Service. **VFOAT** Farm Reporter. Vol. 1 (April 1969)-. Periodical. English. Twenty-four times a year (semimonthly). $12.00. Wisconsin Agricultural Statistics Service, PO Box 9160, Madison WI 53713. **Tel** (608)264-5317. **(Subscription address:** US Department of Agriculture Publications Unit, 14th Independence Avenue Southwest, Room 5829, Washington DC 20250. **)** ***Continues*** *Wisconsin Dairying;* ***Absorbed*** *Livestock Review.*

LC S129
DD 338.1/09775 US
WISCONSIN FARM REPORTER : DAIRY, CROPS, LIVESTOCK. Main/Corp Wisconsin
Agriculture Reporting Service. Vol. 10, No. 3 (1978)-. Periodical. English. Twenty-four times a year. $10.00. Wisconsin Agricultural Statistics Service, PO Box 9160, Madison WI 53713. **Tel** (608)264-5317. **ED** Carrol D Spencer. **Circ:** 2,624. ***Continues*** *Wisconsin Farm Reporter.*
Desc: Contains narrative and statistical information describing agricultural conditions primarily in Wisconsin in order to provide facts for decision making.

LC S **ISSN** 0417-1411
DD 630 GW
WISSENSCHAFTLICHE ABHANDLUNGEN. Main/Corp Deutsche
Akademie der Landwirtschaftswissenschaften. (1953)-. Periodical. German. Deutsche Akademie der Landwirtschaftswissenschaften, Berlin Germany.

LC S **ISSN** 0863-0658
DD 630 GW
UDC 63
WISSENSCHAFTLICHE ZEITSCHRIFT DER HUMBOLDT-UNIVERSITAT ZU BERLIN REIHE AGRARWISSENSCHAFTEN. [Wiss. Z.
Humboldt-Univ. Berl., Agrarwiss.]. (1988)-. Academic Scholarly Publication. German. Four times a year. Humboldt Universitaet Berlin, Mittelstrasse 7-8 Wissenschaftl, D-12167 Berlin Germany. Documents available from CASDDS. ***Continues in part*** *Wissenschaftliche Zeitschrift der Humboldt-Universitat zu Berlin. Mathematisch-Naturwissenschaftliche Reihe, 0522-9863.*
Ind/Abst Agric. Eng. Abstr.; Biocont. News Inf.; Chem. Abstr.; For. Abstr.; World Agric. Econ. Rural Sociol. Abstr.

LC S **ISSN** 0741-0387
DD 630 US
TITLE CHANGE
WITHIN ASAE. [Within ASAE]. Added/Corp
American Society of Agricultural Engineers. **VFOAT** Within A.S.A.E. **VAT** Within American Society of Agricultural Engineers. Vol. 1, No. 1 (Nov. 1983)-(Apr. 1994). Periodical. English. American Society of Agricultural Engineers, Department 2510, 2950 Niles Road, St. Joseph MI 49085-9659. **Tel** (616)429-0300, FAX (616)429-3852. ***Merged with*** *Agricultural Engineering, 0002-1458* ***to form*** *Resource (Saint Joseph, Mich.), 1076-3333.*
Desc: Broad interest articles and continuing departments spotlight agricultural process with emphasis on mechanization, plus trends influencing contemporary events.

LC S
DD 630 TH
WITTHAYASAN KASETSART. SAKHA THAMMACHT = KASETSART JOURNAL. NATURAL SCIENCES. Added/Corp
Mahawitthayalai Kasetsat. **VFOAT** Kasetsart Journal. Natural Sciences; Sakha Thammacht; Natural Sciences. Vol. 13, No. 1-2 (Jan./Dec. 1979)-. Periodical. Thai (English; summaries and/or abstracts in Thai). Four times a year. Kasetsart University Main Library, Bangkok 9 Thailand. ***Continues in part*** *Witthayasan Kasetsart.*
Ind/Abst Agric. Eng. Abstr. (1991-); Biocont. News Inf. (19??-19??); Biodeter. Abstr. (1991-); For. Abstr.; Hortic. Abstr.; Ornamental Hort. (1991-); Plant Genet. Resour. Abstr.; Plant Grow. Reg. Abstr.; Postharvest News Inf.; Rev. Plant Pathol.; Rice Abstr.; Seed Abstr.; Soils Fert.; Soyabean Abstr.

LC SF **ISSN** 1079-9052
DD 636 US
•WOLF CLAN. [Wolf clan]. Vol. 1, No. 1 (Dec. 1994)-.
Periodical. English. Six times a year. $18.00. Wolf Clan Publications, 3952 North Southport Avenue / Suite 122, Chicago IL 60613.

LC S **ISSN** 0043-7875
DD 630 AT
Pr Rev.
WOOL TECHNOLOGY AND SHEEP BREEDING. [Wool technol. sheep breed.].
Added/Corp University of New South Wales. Vol. 5 (1958)-. English. Four times a year. 61.66Aus$. Wool Technology and Sheep Breeding, Robert Webster Building University, Room 265, Sydney 2052 Australia. **Tel** 011 61 2 3854493, FAX 011 61 2 313-6404. **ED** Dr D. Cottle. **Bk Rev**. **Ad Acc**. **Circ:** 4,000 (ctrl). Documents available from The Genuine Article. ***Continues*** *Wool Technology.*
Desc: A modern review of developments in science and commerce of the sheep and wool industry of Australia.
Ind/Abst Anim. Breed. Abstr.; Curr. Contents Agric. Biol. Environ. Sci.; Index Vet.; Nutr. Abstr. Rev., Ser. B, Live Feeds and Feed.; Life Sci. Collect.; Res. Alert [Select. Cov.]; Soc. Sci. Cit. Index [Select. Cov.]; Text. Technol. Dig.; Vet. Bull.; World Agric. Econ. Rural Sociol. Abstr.; World Text. Abstr.

LC TS
DD 677 AT
•WOOLTEL. (1994)-. English. Twelve times a year.
100Aus$. Wool Information Services, L2 275 Wattletree Road, Malvern Vic 32144 Australia. **Tel** FAX 011 61 3 5091055. **ED** Dr Lionel Ward.
Desc: Provides information on Australian and international wool industries.

LC S539.5 .W67
DD 338.1 NE
WORKING PAPER. Added/Corp International
Service for National Agricultural Research. **VFOAT** Documents de Travail; ISNAR Working Papers. No. 1 (Jan. 1985)-. Monographic series. English (French).
Ind/Abst World Agric. Econ. Rural Sociol. Abstr.

LC S **ISSN** 0815-7596
DD 630 AT
WORKING PAPER / NATIONAL CENTRE FOR DEVELOPMENT STUDIES, AUSTRALIAN NATIONAL UNIVERSITY.
Added/Corp Australian National University. National Centre for Development Studies. (1985)-. Monographic series. English. ***Continues*** *Working Paper (Australian National University. Development Studies Centre : 1984), 0814-1266.*
Ind/Abst World Agric. Econ. Rural Sociol. Abstr.

LC S
DD 630 CN
WORKING PAPER. POLICY BRANCH, AGRICULTURE CANADA. (WORKING
PAPER.). **VFOAT** Document de Travai. (198?)-. English.
Ind/Abst World Agric. Econ. Rural Sociol. Abstr.

LC S
DD 630 US
WORKING PAPER SERIES. Added/Corp
University of California (System). Center for Cooperatives. No. 1 (July 1989)-. Monographic series. English. Irregular. UC Regents Center Cooperatives, University of California at Davis, Davis CA 95616. **Tel** (916)752-2408.

LC S **ISSN** 1100-8679
DD 630 SW
WORKING PAPER / SWEDISH UNIVERSITY OF AGRICULTURAL SCIENCES, INTERNATIONAL RURAL DEVELOPMENT CENTRE. [Work. pap. - Swed.
Univ. Agric. Sci., Int. Rural Dev. Cent.]. **Added/Corp** Sveriges Lantbruksuniversitet. International Rural Development Centre. **VFOAT** Arbetsrapport. (1989)-. Monographic series. English (French and Spanish). ***Continues*** *Arbetsrapport (Sveriges Lantbruksuniversitet. U-Landsavdelningen), 0280-4301.*
Ind/Abst Agric. Eng. Abstr. (1991-); Agrofor. Abstr. (1991-); Anim. Breed. Abstr.; For. Abstr.; Hortic. Abstr.; Leis., Rec., Tour. Abstr.; Plant Breed. Abstr.; Rev. Med. Vet. Entomol.; Rural Dev. Abstr.

LC S
DD 630 CN
WORKING PAPER / THE GEORGE MORRIS CENTRE. Added/Corp George Morris
Centre. **VFOAT** Working Paper Series. (1990)-. Monographic series. English. Price varies per volume.
Ind/Abst Postharvest News Inf.; World Agric. Econ. Rural Sociol. Abstr.

LC S21.F6 W67 **ISSN** 1052-0279
DD 338.1/021 US
WORLD AGRICULTURAL PRODUCTION. [World agric. prod.]. Added/Corp
United States. Foreign Agricultural Service. United States. Foreign Agricultural Service. Foreign Production Estimates Division. United States. World Agricultural Outlook Board. (Jan. 1988)-. Government Publication. English. Twelve times a year. $75.00. Department of Agriculture / Foreign Agricultural Service, 14th Street and Independence Avenue SW, Washington DC 20250-1000. **Tel** (202)720-3935, FAX (202)720-7729. available on microfiche (Vols. for (1988) distributed to depository libraries). ***Continues*** *World Crop Production, 1046-3224.*

LC HD1401 .W65 **ISSN** 1060-9741
DD 338 US
WORLD AGRICULTURE (WASHINGTON, D.C. 1991). (WORLD AGRICULTURE.). [World
agric.]. **Added/Corp** United States. Dept. of Agriculture. Economic Research Service. Issue 62 (Apr. 1991)-. Government Publication. English. Four times a year. US Department of Agriculture / Economics and Statistics Service, Washington DC 20250. Documents available from Documents on Demand. ***Continues*** *Situation and Outlook Report. World Agriculture, 1057-8242.*
Ind/Abst Am. Stat. Index.

LC S **ISSN** 0253-7494
DD 630 US
WORLD BANK TECHNICAL PAPER.
[World Bank tech. pap.]. (1982)-. Monographic series. English. Irregular. Price varies per volume. World Bank Publications, 1818 H Street Northwest, Washington DC 20043. **Tel** (202)473-1155, (202)473-1155, FAX (202)522-3224, telex WUI 64145 WORLDBANK. Documents available from BIOSIS Document Express.
Ind/Abst AgBiotech News Inf.; Agrofor. Abstr. (1991-); Biol. Abstr.; Curr. Cit.; Dairy Sci. Abstr.; Ecol. Abstr.; For. Prod. Abstr.; For. Abstr.; Geogr. Abstr. Phys. Geogr.; Geogr. Abstr. Human Geogr.; GeoRef; Int. Dev. Abstr.; Leis., Rec., Tour. Abstr.; Plant Genet. Resour. Abstr.; Rural Dev. Abstr.; Soils Fert.; Wheat Barley Trit. Abstr.; World Agric. Econ. Rural Sociol. Abstr.

LC HD9199.A1 F67
DD 382/.41373/0973021 US
TITLE CHANGE
WORLD COFFEE SITUATION. Added/Corp
United States. Foreign Agricultural Service. United States. World Agricultural Outlook Board. (Feb. 1987)-(1993). Statistical Publication. English. Department of Agriculture / Foreign Agricultural Service, 14th Street and Independence Avenue SW, Washington DC 20250-1000. **Tel** (202)720-3935, FAX (202)720-7729. **Circ:** 796. available on microfiche (Vols. for 1987- distributed to depository libraries). ***Continues*** *Foreign Agriculture Circular. Coffee, 0145-0913.* ***Continued by*** *Tropical Products, World Markets and Trade.*
Desc: Contains the latest statistical data on world coffee production, consumption, trade and prices.
Ind/Abst F&S Index Plus Text, Int. [Select. Cov.]; Predicasts Forecasts.

LC S
DD 630 US
TITLE CHANGE
WORLD COTTON SITUATION. Added/Corp
United States. Foreign Agricultural Service. (Jan. 1987)-(1993). Trade Publication. English. Department of Agriculture / Foreign Agricultural Service, 14th Street and Independence Avenue SW, Washington DC 20250-1000. **Tel** (202)720-3935, FAX (202)720-7729. **Circ:** 750. available on microfiche; available on an online database (file 648/Full-Text) from DIALOG. ***Continues*** *Foreign Agriculture Circular. Cotton, World Cotton Situation.* ***Continued by*** *Cotton, World Markets & Trade.*
Desc: Information on world cotton production, consumption, and trade, market development, export opportunities and prices.
Ind/Abst F&S Index Plus Text, Int. (?-?) [Select. Cov.]; Predicasts Forecasts (?-?); Text. Technol. Dig. (?-?); Trade Ind. ASAP (?-?) [Full Txt.]; Trade Ind. Index (?-?) [Full Txt.].

LC S
DD 630 UK
•WORLD DIRECTORY OF FERTILIZER MANUFACTURERS. 8th Edition (Oct. 1993)-.
Directory. English. Irregular. £250.00. British Sulphur Corporation Ltd, 31 Mount Pleasant, London WC1X 0AD United Kingdom. **Tel** 011 44 171 8375600, FAX 011 44 171 8370292, telex 918918 SULFEX G.
Desc: Lists the main fertilizer producers throughout the world, giving extensive information on each. Also listed are the major national and international fertilizer associations.

LC S
DD 630 UK
WORLD DIRECTORY OF FERTILIZER PRODUCTS. Added/Corp British Sulphur
Corporation, Ltd. 1st Ed. (1967)-. Directory. English. Irregular. Price varies per volume. British Sulphur Corporation Ltd, 31 Mount Pleasant, London WC1X 0AD United Kingdom. **Tel** 011 44 171 8375600, FAX 011 44 171 8370292, telex 918918 SULFEX G. **(Subscription address:** CRU International Ltd., 31 Mount Pleasant, London WC1X 0AD United Kingdom. **Tel** 011 44 171 8375600, FAX 011 44 171 8370292.**)** **Ad Acc**. **Circ:** 1,200.
Desc: A useful reference book not just for those in the fertilizer industry, but also for government agencies,

international organizations, banks, research bodies, libraries, educational establishments, and all concerned with world food supply and problems.

LC HG3881 .U6228 **ISSN** 0364-7234
DD 338.1/05 US

WORLD ECONOMIC CONDITIONS IN RELATION TO AGRICULTURAL TRADE. **See** Business and Economics-Commerce.

LC S
DD 630 SZ

WORLD FARMERS' TIMES : A WORLD FARMERS' TIMES FOUNDATION PUBLICATION. **Added/Corp** World Farmers' Times Foundation. (19??)-. Periodical. English. Twelve times a year. $20.00. World Farmers Times, Talstrasse 39, CH Zuerich Switzerland. **Tel** 011 41 1 2119912.
Ind/Abst Agric. Eng. Abstr.; Dairy Sci. Abstr.; Geogr. Abstr. Phys. Geogr. (?-?); Geogr. Abstr. Human Geogr.; Int. Dev. Abstr.; Soils Fert.

LC S
DD 630 UK

WORLD FERTILIZER PLANT LIST AND ATLAS. English. Irregular. £250.00. British Sulphur Corporation Ltd, 31 Mount Pleasant, London WC1X 0AD United Kingdom. **Tel** 011 44 171 8375600, FAX 011 44 171 8370292, telex 918918 SULFEX G. **(Subscription address:** CRU International Ltd., 31 Mount Pleasant, London WC1X 0AD United Kingdom. **Tel** 011 44 171 8375600, FAX 011 44 171 8370292.**)**
Desc: The plant list and atlas details of over 1,000 fertilizer plant sites throughout the world. Maps shows the exact location of each listed plant.

LC TX353 .F58
DD 613.2 IT

WORLD FOOD SURVEY. **Main/Corp** Food and Agriculture Organization of the United Nations. (July 1946)-. English. UNIPUB, 4611-F Assembly Drive, Lanham MD 20706-4391. **Tel** (800)274-4888, FAX (301)459-0056, telex 28787 GATT CH.

LC SB442 **ISSN** 0846-3212
DD 380.1/413/025 CN

WORLD GRAIN LIST. [World grain list]. (1991)-. English. $90.00 per year. Stat Publishing, PO Box 8110-361, Blaine WA 98230. **Tel** (604)535-8505, FAX (604)531-8818.

LC S
DD 630 US

WORLD HARVEST. Vol. 1 (1962)-. Periodical. English. Six times a year. World Harvest, PO Box 12, South Bend IN 46624. **Tel** (219)291-3292. **ED** Lorraine Nagle. **Circ:** 75,000.
Desc: Activities of LeSea Ministries and LeSea Broadcasting (TV stations, shortwave - religious programming). World hunger program.

LC S **ISSN** 0043-8979
DD 630 IT
CODEN WRAPAY

WORLD REVIEW OF ANIMAL PRODUCTION. [World rev. anim. prod.]. Periodical. English. Four times a year. L160000. International Publishing Entr, Via di Tor Vergata 85-87, 00133 Rome Italy. **Tel** 6140653. Documents available from CASDDS.
Ind/Abst AGRICOLA [Full Cov.]; Anim. Breed. Abstr.; Chem. Abstr.; Dairy Sci. Abstr.; Food Sci. Technol. Abstr.; Index Vet.; Maize Abstr.; Nutr. Abstr. Rev., Ser. B, Live Feeds and Feed.; Life Sci. Collect.; PESTDOC; Pig News Inf.; Poult. Abstr.; Soyabean Abstr.

LC S
DD 630 US

WRAES QUARTERLY. **Main/Corp** Western Regional Agricultural Engineering Service. (Fall 1975)-. Periodical. English. Four times a year.

LC S **ISSN** 1057-2465
DD 630 US

WREP. [WREP]. **VAT** Western Regional Extension Publication. (1977)-. Monographic series. English. Irregular. Price varies per volume. Cooperative Extension, Washington State Unviersity, Pullman WA 91163.
Ind/Abst AGRICOLA [Select. Cov.].

LC S7 .W82
DD 630.5 GW

WURTTEMBERGISCHES WOCHENBLATT FUR LANDWIRTSCHAFT. 1.- Yearly volume; Jan. 1878-. Periodical. German. One time a week. DM115.80 Germany; $62.00 US. Verlag Eugen Ulmer, Postfach 700561, D-70574 Stuttgart Germany. **Tel** 011 49 711 4507108, FAX 011 49 711 4507120, telex 7-23634. Index available. **Bk Rev. Ad Acc. Circ:** 45,000 (ctrl). ***Supersedes** Wochenblatt fur Land- und Forstwirtschaft.*
Desc: Specialized periodical for the farmer, his wife and inhabitants of agrarian localities.

LC S269.P6 G56a
DD 630 PL

WYNIKI SPISU ROLNICZEGO. **Main/Corp** Poland. Gowny Urzad Statystyczny. (19??)-. Polish. One time a year. $14.00 Poland; $17.00 North America; $16.00 other. Zaklad Wydawnictw Statystycznych, Al. Niepodleglosci 208, 00-925 Warsaw Poland. **Tel** 011 48 22 250345, telex 814581 A GUS PL. **Circ:** 800 (ctrl).
Desc: Result of the agricultural registration.

LC S131 .W94 **ISSN** 0363-9339
DD 630/.9787 US

WYOMING AGRICULTURAL STATISTICS. **See** Agriculture-Abstracting, Bibliographies and Statistics.

LC HD28 **ISSN** 0043-9800
DD 338 US

WYOMING STOCKMAN FARMER. [Wyo. stockm. farmer]. **VFOAT** Stockman Farmer; Wyoming Stockman-Farmer; Wyoming Industrial Journal. (19??)-. Trade Publication. English. Twelve times a year. $12.00. Wyoming Stockman-Farmer, 702 West Lincolnway, Cheyenne WY 82001. **Tel** (307)634-7964. **ED** Frank W. McCrea. **Bk Rev. Ad Acc. Circ:** 5,600.
Desc: Informs farm families in the area of agriculture practices that are successful under Wyoming conditions.

LC S **ISSN** 0513-4676
DD 630 JA
CODEN YDKNA2

YAMAGATA DAIGAKU KIYO : NOGAKU. [Yamagata Daigaku kiyo: nogaku]. **Main/Corp** Yamagata Daigaku. **VFOAT** Bulletin of the Yamagata University: Agricultural Science. (1950)-. Academic Scholarly Publication. Japanese (English). Yamagata Daigaku, (Yamagata University), Kojirakawamachi Yamagatashi, Yamagataken 990 Japan. Documents available from CASDDS.
Ind/Abst AGRICOLA; Chem. Abstr.; Rice Abstr.

LC S **ISSN** 0513-1715
DD 630 JA
CODEN YDNGAU

YAMAGUCHI DAIGAKU NOGAKUBU GAKUJUTSU HOKOKU. **Main/Corp** Yamaguchi Daigaku. Nogakubu Shimonoseki. **VFOAT** Bulletin of the Faculty of Agriculture, Yamaguti University. (1950)-. Academic Scholarly Publication. Japanese (summaries and/or abstracts in English; table of contents in English). Price varies per volume. Yamaguti University, Faculty of Agriculture, Yamaguti Japan. Documents available from BIOSIS Document Express, CASDDS.
Ind/Abst Biol. Abstr.; Chem. Abstr. (1950-1982); Rev. Agric. Entomol.; Rice Abstr.

LC S
DD 630 UK

YEAR BOOK - NATIONAL AURICULA & PRIMULA SOCIETY (NORTHERN SECTION). **Added/Corp** National Auricula and Primula Society. Northern Section. **VFOAT** Auriculas. Vol. 1 (1950)-. English. One time a year. $5.14. National Auricula & Primula Society, 146 Queens Road, Cheadle Chestershire SK8 5HY United Kingdom. **Tel** 011 44 161 4856371. **ED** J. J. Wemmys-Cooke. **Bk Rev. Ad Acc. Circ:** 400 (ctrl).
Ind/Abst AGRICOLA.

LC HD1775.V5 V465A **ISSN** 0748-0423
DD 353.97550082/33043 US

YEAR IN REVIEW (RICHMOND, VA.), THE. (THE YEAR IN REVIEW.). **Main/Corp** Virginia. Dept. of Agriculture and Consumer Services. 1980-81-. English. One time a year. Virginia Department of Agriculture & Consumer Services, 1100 Bank Street, Washington Building, Suite 210, Richmond VA 23219. **Tel** (804)786-2373, FAX (804)371-7679. ***Continues in part** Bulletin - The Virginia Department of Agriculture and Consumer Services, 0198-8298.*

LC S19 **ISSN** 0255-5905
DD 630/.72 CH
CODEN TCNPEX

YEN CHIU HUI PAO. [Taizhong qu nongye gailiang chang yanjiu huibao]. **VFOAT** Bulletin of Taichung District Agricultural Improvement Station; Tai-Chung Chu Nung Yeh Kai Lian Chang Yen Chiu Hui Pao. (19??)-. Bulletin. Chinese. Two times a year. Documents available from BIOSIS Document Express.
Ind/Abst Agric. Eng. Abstr.; Biol. Abstr. (1985-); Field Crop Abstr.; Hortic. Abstr.; Plant Breed. Abstr.; Rev. Plant Pathol.; Rice Abstr.; Soils Fert.; Sorghum Mill. Abstr.; Weed Abstr.

LC S542.T332 T347
DD 630/.724 CH

YEN CHIU HUI PAO (TAI-WAN SHENG TAI-NAN CHU NUNG YEH KAI LIANG CHANG). (YEN CHIU HUI PAO.). **Added/Corp** Tai-wan Sheng Tai-nan chu Nung yeh kai Liang Chang. **VFOAT** Tai-Nan Chu Nung Yeh Kai Liang Chang Yen Chiu Hui Pao; Research Bulletin; Research Bulletin of Tainan District Agricultural Improvement Station. (19??)-. Bulletin. Chinese (English). One time a year. Tainan District Agricultural Improvement, Station 350/First Section Lin Sen Road, Tainan Taiwan. ***Continues** Tai-Wan Sheng Tai-Nan Chu Nung Yeh Kai Liang Chang Yen Chiu Hui Pao.*
Ind/Abst AGRICOLA; Agric. Eng. Abstr.; Rice Abstr.

LC S **ISSN** 0077-5819
DD 630 CH
CODEN KTNYA8

YEN CHIU PAO KAO. [Yen chiu pao kao]. **Main/Corp** Taiwan Ta Hsueh, Tai-Pei. Nung Hsueh Yuan. **Added/Corp** Kuo li Taiwan ta Hsueh. Nung Hsueh Yuan. **VFOAT** Memoirs of the College of Agriculture, National Taiwan University; Memoires de la Faculte d'Agriculture de l'Universite Nationale Taiwan. Vol. 1 (Dec. 1946)-. Academic Scholarly Publication. Chinese (English). Four times a year. National Taiwan University - Agriculture, College of Agriculture, Taipei Taiwan. Documents available from BIOSIS Document Express, CASDDS.
Ind/Abst AGRICOLA; Agric. Eng. Abstr. (1991-); Biocont. News Inf.; Biodeter. Abstr.; Biol. Abstr.; Chem. Abstr.; Crop Physiol. Abstr.; EMBASE; Field Crop Abstr.; For. Prod. Abstr. (1991-); For. Abstr.; Hortic. Abstr.; Index Vet.; Nutr. Abstr. Rev., Ser. B, Live Feeds and Feed.; Plant Breed. Abstr.; Postharvest News Inf.; Rev. Plant Pathol.; Rice Abstr.; Seed Abstr.; Soils Fert.; Sorghum Mill. Abstr.; Vet. Bull.

LC HD2126.5 .A47
DD 338.1/3/096762 KE

YIELDS, COSTS, PRICES. (19??)-. English. One time a year. Ministry of Agriculture, Central Development & Marketing Unit, PO Box 30028, Nairobi Kenya.

LC S **ISSN** 0253-3596
DD 630 CC
CODEN YTNYDT

YUANZINENG NONGYE YINGYONG. **See** Energy.

LC S **ISSN** 0044-1600
DD 630 PL

ZAGADNIENIA EKONOMIKI ROLNEJ. [Zag. ekon. rol.]. **Added/Corp** Polskie Towarzystwo Ekonomiczne. Sekcja Ekonomiki Rolnictwa. Polska Akademia Nauk. Komitet Organizacji Produkcji Rolnej i WyŻywienia Kraju. Instytut Ekonomiki Rolnej (Warsaw, Poland) Polskie Towarzystwo Ekonomiczne, Warsaw. Sekcja Ekonomiki Rolnictwa. Polska Akademia Nauk. Komitet Ekonomiki Rolnictwa. **VFOAT** Voprosy Ekonomiki Selskigo Khoziaistva; Problems of Agricultural Economics. (Aug. 1952)-. Periodical. Polish (summaries and/or abstracts in English and Russian; table of contents in English and Russian). Six times a year. $99.00. **(Subscription address:** Ars Polona-Ruch, PO Box 1001, Krakowskie Przedmiescie 7, 00-068 Warsaw Poland. **Tel** 011 48 22 261201.**)** cum. index.
Ind/Abst AGRICOLA; Agric. Eng. Abstr. (1991-); Dairy Sci. Abstr.; Wheat Barley Trit. Abstr.

LC S
DD 630 XV

ZBORNIK BIOTEHNISKE FAKULTETE UNIVERZE V LJUBLJANI. KMETIJSTVO = RESEARCH REPORTS, BIOTECHNICAL FACULTY, UNIVERSITY OF LJUBLJANA. AGRICULTURAL ISSUE. **Added/Corp** Univerza v Ljubljani. Biotehniska Fakulteta. Univerza v Ljubljani. VTOZD za Agronomijo. Kmetijski Institut Slovenije. Zveza Drustev Kmetijskih Inzenirjev in Teknikov Slovenije. Univerza v Ljubljani. VTOZD za Zivinorejo. **VFOAT** Research Reports, Biotechnical Faculty, University of Ljubljana. Agricultural Issue; Kmetijstvo; Agricultural Issue. (1990)-. Periodical. Slovenian (summaries and/or abstracts in English and German). Twenty-four times a year. Centralna Knjiznica Biotehniske Fakultete Univerze v Ljubljani, Krekov Trg 1, PP 486, 61001 Ljubljana Slovenia. ***Continues** Zbornik Biotehniske Fakultete Univerze Edvarda Kardelja v Ljubljani. Kmetijstvo, 0352-0994.*

LC HD1401 .Z4 **ISSN** 0044-2194
DD 338.1/05 GW
CCC

ZEITSCHRIFT FUER AGRARGESCHICHTE UND AGRARSOZIOLOGIE. [Z. agrarges. agrarsoziol.]. **Added/Corp** Deutsche Landwirtschafts-Gesellschaft (Germany : West). Landvolksabteilung. Deutsche Landwirtschafts-Gesellschaft (Germany : West). Landvolksabteilung. Gesellschaft fuer Agrargeschichte. Deutsche Landwirtschafts-Gesellschaft (Germany : West). Vol. 1 (Apr. 1953)-. Trade Publication. German. Two times a year. DM111.00. Deutsche Landwirtschafts Gesellschaft, Verlags GmbH, Eschborner Landstr 122, D-60489 Frankfurt Germany. **Tel** 011 49 69 247880, FAX 011 49 69 24788580. **ED** H. Winkel and U. Planck. Index available.
Desc: Articles on history of farming to development of modern industrial agriculture. Of interest to the farmer, historian, sociologist and folklorist.
Ind/Abst AGRICOLA; Am. Hist. Life (1987-); Bibliogr. Carto.

LC SB599 .Z37 **ISSN** 0044-2240
DD 632.705 GW
NLM W1 ZE231N **CODEN** ZANEAE

ZEITSCHRIFT FUER ANGEWANDTE ENTOMOLOGIE. **See** Zoology-Entomology.

LC S **ISSN** 0049-8599
DD 630 GW
CCC

ZEITSCHRIFT FUER AUSLANDISCHE LANDWIRTSCHAFT. (QUARTERLY JOURNAL OF INTERNATIONAL AGRICULTURE.). [Z. ausl. Landwirtsch.]. Vol. 19, No. 1 (Jan./Mar. l980)-. Trade Publication. English (German; summaries and/or abstracts in German). Four times a year. $143.55. Deutsche Landwirtschafts Gesellschaft, Verlags GmbH, Eschborner Landstr 122, D-60489 Frankfurt Germany. **Tel** 011 49 69 247880, FAX 011 49 69 24788580. **ED** Sachs, Caesar, and Horst. **Bk Rev. Ad Acc. Circ:** 400 (ctrl). ***Continues*** *Zeitschrift fur Auslandische Landwirtschaft, 0049-8599.*
Desc: Agricultural development policy, crop and animal production economics, extension education, marketing economics, world nutrition, irrigation and soil economics, cooperative movement.
Ind/Abst AgBiotech News Inf.; AGRICOLA; Agrofor. Abstr. (1991-); Curr. Cit.; For. Abstr.; Geogr. Abstr. Human Geogr.; Grass. Forage Abstr.; Int. Dev. Abstr.; Int. Labour Doc.; Maize Abstr.; Postharvest News Inf.; Rev. Agric. Entomol.; Rice Abstr.; Rural Dev. Abstr.; Soils Fert.; Soyabean Abstr.; Wheat Barley Trit. Abstr.; World Agric. Econ. Rural Sociol. Abstr.

LC HD101 .C87 **ISSN** 0139-570X
DD 333.73 XR

ZEMEDELSKA EKONOMIKA. (VEDECKY CASOPIS ZEMEDELSKA EKONOMIKA.). [Zemed. ekon.]. **Added/Corp** Czechoslovakia. Ministerstvo Zemedelstvi, Lesniho a Vodniho Hospodarstvi. Ustav Vedeckotechnickych Informaci. Ustredi Zemedelskeho a Potravinarskeho Vyzkumu (Czechoslovakia). Ustav Vedeckotechnickych Informaci. Ceskoslovenska Akademie Zemedelska. Ustav Vedeckotechnickych Informaci. Ceskoslovenska Akademie Zemedelska. Ustav Vedeckotechnickych Informaci pro Zemedelstvi. **VFOAT** Zemedelska Ekonomika. Vol. 11, 1 (Jan. 1965)-. Periodical. Czech (summaries and/or abstracts in English, German and Russian). Twelve times a year. $112.00. PNS Expedice Tisku, Oddeleni Vyvozu Tisku Jindrisska Ulice 14, Prague 1 Czech Republic. ***Continues*** *Zemedelska Ekonomika.*
Ind/Abst AGRICOLA; Nematol. Abstr.; Poult. Abstr.; Sug. Indus. Abstr.

LC S13 .Z48 **ISSN** 0044-3913
DD 630 RU
CODEN ZMLDAH

ZEMLEDELIE. [Zemledelie]. **Added/Corp** Soviet Union. Ministerstvo Selskogo Khoziaistva i Zagotovok. Soviet Union. Ministerstvo Selskogo Khoziaistva. Soviet Union. Ministerstvo Sovkhozov. Vsesoiuznaia Akademiia Selßkokhoziaistvennykh Nauk Imeni V.I. Lenina. Nauchno-Tekhnicheskoe Obshchestvo Selskogokhoziaistva. Tsentralnoe Pravlenie. Gosudarstvennyi Agropromyshlennyi Komitet SSSR. Vol. 1 (June 1953)-. Periodical. Russian. Six times a year. $69.95. **(Subscription address:** East View Publications Inc., 3020 Harbor Lane North, Suite 110, Minneapolis MN 55447. **Tel** (800)477-1005, (612)550-0961, FAX (612)559-2931.**)** Index available. **Bk Rev. Ad Acc.** Documents available from CASDDS. ***Formed by the union of*** *Selektsiia i Semenovodstvo, 0582-5075; Sovetskaia Agronomiia; Udobrenie i Urozhai; Obmen Opytom v Selskom Khoziaistve. Zernovye i Kormovye Kultury* ***and*** *Obmen Opytom v Selskom Khoziaistve. Tekhnicheskie i Maslichnye Kultury.*
Ind/Abst AGRICOLA; Chem. Abstr.

LC S **ISSN** 0869-1487
DD 630 UN

ZEMLIA I LIUDY UKRAINY. **Added/Corp** Derzhavnyi Ahropromyslovyi Komitet Ukrainskoi RSR. (19??)-. Periodical. Ukrainian. Six times a year. $89.95. **(Subscription address:** East View Publications Inc., 3020 Harbor Lane North, Suite 110, Minneapolis MN 55447. **Tel** (800)477-1005, (612)550-0961, FAX (612)559-2931.**)** ***Continues*** *Khliborob Ukrainy, 0131-7482.*

LC S
DD 630 RU

ZEMLIA SIBIRSKAIA, DAL'NEVOSTOCHNAIA. **Added/Corp** Russia. Ministerstvo Sel'skogo Khoziaistva. No. 2 (1970)-. Periodical. Russian. Twelve times a year. ***Continues*** *Sel'Skokhoziaistvennoe Proizvodstvo Sibiri I Dal'Nego Vostoka.*

LC S590 .Z4 **ISSN** 0514-6658
DD 630 YU
CODEN ZMBLAP

ZEMLJISTE I BILJKA. (ZEMLJISTE I BILJKA; CASOPIS ZA PEDOLOGIJU ISHRANU BILJA ZEMLJISNU MIKROBIOLOGIJU I DUBRIVA.). [Zemlj. biljka]. **VFOAT** Acta Biologica Iugoslavica Serija A: Zemlijiste i Bilka. Vol. 1 (1952)-. Periodical. Bikol (Serbo-Croatian (Roman)).
Ind/Abst AGRICOLA; For. Abstr.; Maize Abstr.; Plant Grow. Reg. Abstr.; Soyabean Abstr.

LC S **ISSN** 0235-2532
DD 630 RU

ZERNOVYE KULTURY. **Added/Corp** Soviet Union. Gosudarstvennyi Agropromyshlennyi Komitet. No. 1 (Jan./Feb. 1988)-. Periodical. Russian. Four times a year. $99.95. Agropromizdat, Sadovo-Spasskaia 18, 107807 Moscow Russia. **(Subscription address:** East View Publications Inc., 3020 Harbor Lane North, Suite 110, Minneapolis MN 55447. **Tel** (800)477-1005, (612)550-0961, FAX (612)559-2931.**)** ***Continues*** *Zernovoe Khoziaistvo.*

LC S **ISSN** 0867-7379
DD 630 PL
CODEN ZARSA8

ZESZYTY NAUKOWE - AKADEMIA ROLNICZA W SZCZECINIE. **Main/Corp** Akademia Rolnicza w Szczecinie. 38 (1972)-. Academic Scholarly Publication. Polish (summaries and/or abstracts in English, German and Russian). Irregular. Price varies per volume. Akademia Rolnicza w Szczecinie / Agricultural University in Szczecin, Dzial Wydawnictwo, Ul. Doktora Judyma 22, 71-460 Szczecin Poland. **Tel** 011 48 91 541639, FAX 011 48 91 541642. Documents available from CASDDS. ***Continues*** *Wyzsza Szkola Rolnicza. Zeszyty Naukowe - Wyzsza Szkola Rolnicza, 0082-1233.*
Ind/Abst Chem. Abstr.; EMBASE.

LC S **ISSN** 0137-1886
DD 630 PL

ZESZYTY NAUKOWE AKADEMII ROLNICZEJ W KRAKOWIE. ROLNICTWO. (ROLNICTWO.). [Zesz. nauk. Akad. Roln. Krak., Roln.]. (1956)-. Polish (summaries and/or abstracts in English, French and Russian; table of contents in English and French). Irregular. Akademia Rolnicza w Warszawie, Ul. Rakowiecka 41, Warsaw Poland. **Tel** telex 81 47 90 SGGW-AR PL.

LC S **ISSN** 0137-1959
DD 630 PL
UDC 631

ZESZYTY NAUKOWE AKADEMII ROLNICZEJ WE WROCLAWIU. ROLNICTWO. [Zesz. Nauk. Akad. Rol. Wroc., Rol.]. **Added/Corp** Akademia Rolnicza we Wroclawiu. (1972)-. Monographic series. Multiple languages. Irregular. Price varies per volume. Akademia Rolnicza we Wroclawiu, Ul. Norwida 25, 50-375 Wroclaw Poland. **Tel** 011 48 71 229576. Documents available from CASDDS. ***Continues*** *Zeszyty Naukowe Wyzszej Szkoly Rolniczej we Wroclawiu. Rolnictwo, 0520-9307.*
Ind/Abst Agric. Eng. Abstr.; Chem. Abstr.; Dairy Sci. Abstr.; For. Prod. Abstr. (1991-); Maize Abstr.; Postharvest News Inf.; Potato Abstr.; Soils Fert.

LC S **ISSN** 0867-1427
DD 630 PL
TITLE CHANGE

ZESZYTY NAUKOWE AKADEMII ROLNICZEJ WE WROCLAWIU. ROZPRAWA HABILITACYJNA.
Added/Corp Akademia Rolnicza we Wroclawiu. **VFOAT** Rozprawa Habilitacyjna. (1990)-(1994). Monographic series. Polish (summaries and/or abstracts in English). Akademia Rolnicza we Wroclawiu, Ul. Norwida 25, 50-375 Wroclaw Poland. **Tel** 011 48 71 229576. ***Continues*** *Zeszyty Naukowe Akademii Rolniczej we Wroclawiu. Rozprawy, 0209-1321.* ***Continued by*** *Zeszyty Naukowe Akademii Rolniczy we Wroclawiu. Rozprawy.*
Ind/Abst Helminthol. Abstr. (1991-).

LC S
DD 630 PL

•**ZESZYTY NAUKOWE AKADEMII ROLNICZEJ WE WROCLAWIU. ROZPRAWY.** (1994)-. Monographic series. Polish (summaries and/or abstracts in English). Irregular. Price varies per volume. Akademia Rolnicza we Wroclawiu, Ul. Norwida 25, 50-375 Wroclaw Poland. **Tel** 011 48 71 229576. **Circ:** 300. ***Continues*** *Zeszyty Naukowe Akademii Rolniczej we Wroclawiu. Rozprawa Habilitacyjna, 0867-1427.*

LC S **ISSN** 0137-2017
DD 630 PL

ZESZYTY NAUKOWE AKADEMII ROLNICZEJ WE WROCLAWIU. ZOOTECHNIKA. **Added/Corp** Akademia Rolnicza we Wroclawiu. **VFOAT** Zootechnika. (1956)-. Academic Scholarly Publication. Polish (summaries and/or abstracts in English and Russian; table of contents in English and Russian). Irregular. Price varies per volume. Akademia Rolnicza we Wroclawiu, Ul. Norwida 25, 50-375 Wroclaw Poland. **Tel** 011 48 71 229576. Documents available from CASDDS. ***Continues*** *Zeszyty Naukowe Wyzszej Szkoly Rolniczej we Wroclawiu.*
Ind/Abst Chem. Abstr.; Index Vet.; Vet. Bull.

LC TA501 .G39 **ISSN** 0324-9174
DD 624.1517 PL

ZESZYTY NAUKOWE AKADEMII ROLNICZO-TECHNICZNEJ W OLSZTYNIE. GEODEZJA I URZADZENIA ROLNE. (GEODEZJA I URZADZENIA ROLNE.). [Zesz. nauk. akad. roln. - tech. Olszt. geod. urzadz. rolne]. Monographic series. Polish (summaries and/or abstracts in English, French and Russian). Price varies per volume. Akademia Rolniczo-Technicznej W Olsztynie, Ksiegarnia Akademicka, Olsztyn Poland. ***Supersedes*** *Zeszyty Naukowe Wyzszej Szkoly Rolniczej w Olsztynie. Seria F. Inzynieria; Zeszyty Naukowe Wyzszej Szkoty Rolniczej w Olsztynie. Seria F. Inzynieria. Suplement.*
Ind/Abst AGRICOLA.

LC S **ISSN** 0084-5477
DD 630 PL
CODEN ZPPRAW

ZESZYTY PROBLEMOWE POSTEPOW NAUK ROLNICZYCH. [Zesz. probl. post. nauk roln.]. **Added/Corp** Polska Akademia Nauk. Wydzial Nauk Rolniczych i Lesnych. Polska Akademia Nauk. Komitet Ekonomiki Rolnictwa. (1956)-. Monographic series. Polish (summaries and/or abstracts in English, German and Russian). Irregular. Price varies per volume. Panstwowe Wydawnictwo Naukowe / PWN, (Polish Scientific Publishers PWN Ltd.), Ul. Miodowa 10, PO Box 391, 00-251 Warsaw Poland. **Tel** 011 48 22 312738, FAX 011 48 22 267163. **(Subscription address:** Ars Polona-Ruch, PO Box 1001, Krakowskie Przedmiescie 7, 00-068 Warsaw Poland. **Tel** 011 48 22 261201.**)** Documents available from CASDDS. ***Continued in part by*** *Phytopathologia Polonica, 1230-0462.*
Ind/Abst AGRICOLA; Biocont. News Inf.; Chem. Abstr.; EMBASE; Food Sci. Technol. Abstr.; Hortic. Abstr.; Ornamental Hort. (1991-); Plant Breed. Abstr.; Potato Abstr.; Rev. Agric. Entomol.; Wheat Barley Trit. Abstr.

LC S **ISSN** 0044-4464
DD 630 RU

ZHILISHCHNOE I KOMMUNALNOE KHOZIAISTVO. **Added/Corp** Russian S.F.S.R. Ministerstvo Kommunalnogo Khoziaistva. Profsoiuz Rabochikh Kommunalno-Bytovykh Predpriiatii (Soviet Union). TSK. Russian S.F.S.R. Ministerstvo Zhilishchno-Kommunalnogo Khoziaistva. Profsoiuz Rabochikh Mestnoi Promyshlennosti i Kommunalno-Bytovykh Predpriiatii. TSK. (1965)-. Periodical. Russian. Twelve times a year. $79.95. Stroiizdat, Ulitsa Shchousseva rm. 60, 103001 Moscow Russia. **(Subscription address:** East View Publications Inc., 3020 Harbor Lane North, Suite 110, Minneapolis MN 55447. **Tel** (800)477-1005, (612)550-0961, FAX (612)559-2931.**)** ***Continues*** *Zhilishchno-Kommunalnoe Khoziaistvo.*

LC SF521 **ISSN** 0253-8938
DD 638 CH
UDC 638.121

ZHONGHUA YANGFENG. [Zhonghua yangfeng]. (1977)-. Academic Scholarly Publication. Chinese. Six times a year. $12.00. Chinese Academy of Agricultural Sciences, (Zhonguo Nongye Kexueyuan), Zhonguo Nongye Kexue Zazhishe, 30 Baishiqiao Lu, Beijing 100081, People's Republic of China. **Tel** 011 86 1 8314433, FAX 011 86 1 8315465. **ED** Li Jiyong. **Ad Acc, Adv Mgr:** Ye Zhensheng. **Circ:** 20,000. available on an online database from Knight-Ridder Information, Inc. Documents available from BLDSC.

LC S **ISSN** 1017-5156
DD 630 RH
CODEN ZIAJEO

ZIMBABWE AGRICULTURAL JOURNAL. [Zimb. agric. j.]. **Added/Corp** Zimbabwe. Ministry of Agriculture. Vol. 77, No. 3 (May/June 1980)-. Periodical. English. Six times a year. R & S S Information Services, PO Box 8108, Causeway Harare Zimbabwe. **Tel** 011 263 0 704531, telex 2455 AGRC ZW. **ED** R.J. Fenner. Index available. cum. index. **Bk Rev. Ad Acc. Circ:** 1,250 (ctrl). Documents available from BIOSIS Document Express. ***Continues*** *Zimbabwe Rhodesia Agricultural Journal, 0256-7164.*
Desc: Agriculture, research, soil, agronomy, chemistry, and horticulture.
Ind/Abst AGRICOLA; BioBusiness; Biol. Abstr. (1985-); Int. Dev. Abstr. (?-?); Life Sci. Collect.

LC S338.Z55 Z56 **ISSN** 0251-1045
DD 630 RH
CODEN ZJARDK

ZIMBABWE JOURNAL OF AGRICULTURAL RESEARCH, THE. [Zimb. j. agric. res.]. **Added/Corp** Zimbabwe. Dept. of Research and Specialist Services. Southern African Centre for Co-operation in Agricultural Research. Vol. 18 (1980)-. Academic Scholarly Publication. English. Two times a year. 10.00Zin$ Zimbabwe; $16.00 other. R & S S Information Services, PO Box 8108, Causeway Harare Zimbabwe. **Tel** 011 263 0 704531, telex 2455 AGRC ZW. **ED** C.L. Keswani. cum. index. **Bk Rev. Ad Acc. Circ:** 1,000. Documents available from BIOSIS Document Express. ***Continues*** *Rhodesian Journal of Agricultural Research.*
Desc: Covers soil, crops, livestock, forestry, irrigation,

Agriculture

hydrology, wildlife, fisheries, and research notes. **Ind/Abst** Biodeter. Abstr.; Biol. Abstr.; EMBASE; Food Sci. Technol. Abstr.; Maize Abstr.; Nutr. Abstr. Rev., Ser. B, Live Feeds and Feed.; Nutr. Abstr. Rev., Ser. A, Hum. Exp.; Life Sci. Collect.; Rev. Med. Vet. Mycology; Rev. Plant Pathol.; Weed Abstr.

LC SF521
DD 638.1 TU
ZIRRAT FAKULTESI DERGISI. SERI: A.
Main/Corp Ege Universitesi. Ziraat Fakultesi. **VFOAT** Review of the Faculty of Agriculture Ege University. Periodical. Turkish (English, French and German; summaries and/or abstracts in Turkish, English, French and German). Three times a year. Ege Universitesi / Ziraat, Ziraat Fakultesi, Bornova Turkey.
Ind/Abst AGRICOLA; Life Sci. Collect.; Potato Abstr.

LC S ISSN 0133-3682
DD 630 HU
CODEN ZKIBDJ
ZOLDSEGTERMESZTESI KUTATO INTEZET BULLETINJE. See Gardening and Horticulture.

LC S
DD 630 HU
ZOLDSEGTERMESZTESI KUTATO INTEZET BULLETINJE. See Gardening and Horticulture.

ABSTRACTING, BIBLIOGRAPHIES AND STATISTICS

JA
ABSTRACT OF STATISTICS ON AGRICULTURE, FORESTRY AND FISHERIES, JAPAN. Added/Corp Japan. Norinsho. (1960)-. Statistical Publication. English. One time a year. $43.00. **(Subscription address:** Japan Publications Trading Company Ltd., PO Box 5030, Tokyo International, Tokyo 100-31 Japan. **Tel** 011 81 3 3292 3753.**) Continues** Japan. Norinsho. Statistical Abstracts of Ministry of Agriculture and Forestry, Japan.

LC Z5071
DD 016.63 CK
CEASED
ABSTRACTS OF FIELD BEANS (PHASEOLUS VULGARIS L.). (1976)-(Jan. 1993). English. CIAT Publication Distribution, Apartado Aereo 6713, Cali Colombia.
Ind/Abst Nematol. Abstr.

LC S295 .A55
DD 016.63 MY
ABSTRACTS OF MARDI PUBLICATIONS. Added/Corp Malaysian Agricultural Research and Development Institute. Vol. 1 (1975)-. English. Every 2 years. $22.00 (surface mail), $29.00 (airmail). Mardi Director General, PO Box 202 Unipertama, Serdang Selangor Malaysia. **Tel** 011 60 3 58660112. **ED** Jariah Jais.
Ind/Abst Soils Fert.

ISSN 0749-3193
DD 338 US
ABSTRACTS OF STAFF REPORTS. [Abstr. staff rep.]. **Added/Corp** United States. Dept. of Agriculture. Economic Research Service. United States. Dept. of Agriculture. Statistical Reporting Service. (June-July 1981)-. Government Publication. English. US Department of Agriculture / Economic Research Service, 1301 New York Avenue, Room 208, Washington DC 20250. **Tel** (202)447-4111. **Continues** Abstracts of ESS Staff Reports.
Ind/Abst Sug. Indus. Abstr.

LC S
DD 630 NE
ABSTRACTS ON SUSTAINABLE AGRICULTURE : ABSTRECO. Added/Corp Landbouwhogeschool Wageningen. Dept. of Ecological Agriculture. **VFOAT** ABSTRECO. Vol. 3, No. 2 (July 1989)-. Periodical. English. Four times a year (March, Juns, Sept., Dec.). $61.66. Department of Ecological Agriculture, Haarweg 333, 6709 RZ Wageningen Netherlands. **Tel** 011 31 837083522, FAX 011 31 837084575, telex 45015. **Continues** Abstract Bulletin on Sustainable Agriculture : ABSTRECO.

LC SB111.A2 A26 ISSN 0304-5951
DD 630/.913 NE
ABSTRACTS ON TROPICAL AGRICULTURE. Added/Corp Koninklijk Instituut voor de Tropen. Afdeling Agrarisch Onderzoek. Vol. 1, (Jan. 1975)-. Abstracting/Indexing Service. English. Twelve times a year. $342.59. Royal Tropical Institute, Information & Documentation, Mauritskade 63, 1092 AD Amsterdam Netherlands. **Tel** 11 31 20 5688330, FAX 11 31 20 6654423, telex 15080 KIT NL. **ED** CJ Pesch. Index available. cum. index (provided at the end of the volume).
Bk Rev. Ad Acc. Circ: 1,000 (ctrl). available on CD-ROM (as: TROPAG and RURAL [Computer File]) from SilverPlatter (US); and (KIT Abstracts) KIT Institute; available on an online database from ORBIT.
Supersedes Tropical Abstracts.
Desc: Abstracts on practical aspects of crop production in tropical and subtropical regions, also paying attention to farming systems, environmental relationships and post-harvest operations.

LC S494.5.B563 A36 ISSN 0954-9897
DD 630 UK
AGBIOTECH NEWS AND INFORMATION. [AgBiotech news inf.]. Vol. 1, No. 1 (Feb. 1989)-. Abstracting/Indexing Service. English. Twelve times a year. $675.00. CAB International Centre, Wallingford, Oxfordshire OX10 8DE United Kingdom. **Tel** 011 44 1491 832111, FAX 011 44 1491 833508, telex 847964 COMAGG G. **Bk Rev.** available on magnetic tape and CD-ROM; available on an online database from Tsukuba Daigaku; CAN/OLE; STN International; JICST; DATA-STAR; DIMDI; ESA-IRS; BRS; and DIALOG.
Desc: Focuses on the impact of biotechnology in agriculture; the policy issues as well as the purely scientific ones. Covers molecular genetics, genetic engineering, in vitro culture and diagnostics for animals and plants. Includes news and a reviews section.
Ind/Abst Abstr. BioCommer.; AgBiotech News Inf.; Anim. Breed. Abstr.; Curr. Cit.; Food Sci. Technol. Abstr.; Hortic. Abstr.; Index Vet.; Nematol. Abstr.; Plant Breed. Abstr.; Postharvest News Inf.; Rev. Agric. Entomol.; Vet. Bull.

LC HA1248.L69 S73
DD 338.1/76/0094359 GW
UDC 338.43:637.5(430-317)
AGRARBERICHTERSTATTUNG. HEFT 4, VIEHHALTUNG. VFOAT Viehhaltung. German. Every 2 years. DM17.70. Niedersaechsisches Landesamt fuer Statistik, Postfach 4460, D-30044 Hannover Germany. **Tel** 011 49 511 9898321, FAX 011 49 511 9898400. **Bk Rev. Circ:** 210.
Desc: Important statistical results about livestock and poultry in Niedersaechsen (Lower-Saxony).

ISSN 1150-224X
FR
UDC 31(443.83)
AGRESTE. CONJONCTURE, BULLETIN REGIONAL CHAMPAGNE-ARDENNE. (1990)-. Periodical. French. Six times a year. 180.00F. Ministere de l'Agriculture et de la Peche, Direction des Affaires Financieres et Economiques, Service Central des Enquetes et Etudes Statistiques, 4 Avenue de Saint-Mande, 75570 Paris Cedex 12 France. **Tel** 011 33 1 43444633, 16 61288305.

ISSN 1150-1898
FR
UDC 31(444.1/.4)
AGRESTE. DONNEES, BULLETIN BOURGOGNE. VFOAT Bulletin Bourgogne. (1990)-. Bulletin. French. Four times a year. 180.00F. Ministere de l'Agriculture et de la Peche, Direction des Affaires Financieres et Economiques, Service Central des Enquetes et Etudes Statistiques, 4 Avenue de Saint-Mande, 75570 Paris Cedex 12 France. **Tel** 011 33 1 43444633, 16 61288305.

ISSN 1150-1901
FR
UDC 31(447.1/.6)
AGRESTE. DONNEES, BULLETIN DE STATISTIQUE AGRICOLE D'AQUITAINE. VFOAT Bulletin de Statistique Agricole d'Aquitaine. (1990)-. Bulletin. French. Four times a year. 165.00F. Ministere de l'Agriculture et de la Peche, Direction des Affaires Financieres et Economiques, Service Central des Enquetes et Etudes Statistiques, 4 Avenue de Saint-Mande, 75570 Paris Cedex 12 France. **Tel** 011 33 1 43444633, 16 61288305.

ISSN 1155-4037
GP
UDC 31(729.74)
AGRESTE. DONNEES, BULLETIN DE STATISTIQUE AGRICOLE GUADELOUPE. VFOAT Bulletin de Statistique Agricole Guadeloupe; Statistiques Agricoles - Direction de l'Agriculture et de la Foret de la Guadeloupe. (1990)-. Bulletin. French. Four times a year. 120.00F. Ministere de l'Agriculture et de la Peche, Direction des Affaires Financieres et Economiques, Service Central des Enquetes et Etudes Statistiques, 4 Avenue de Saint-Mande, 75570 Paris Cedex 12 France. **Tel** 011 33 1 43444633, 16 61288305.

ISSN 1150-1723
FR
UDC 631(442.1/.5-14)
AGRESTE. DONNEES, BULLETIN DE STATISTIQUE AGRICOLE HAUTE ET BASSE-NORMANDIE. VFOAT Bulletin de Statistique Agricole Haute et Basse-Normandie. (1990)-. Bulletin. French. Four times a year. 160.00F. Ministere de l'Agriculture et de la Peche, Direction des Affaires
Financieres et Economiques, Service Central des Enquetes et Etudes Statistiques, 4 Avenue de Saint-Mande, 75570 Paris Cedex 12 France. **Tel** 011 33 1 43444633, 16 61288305.

ISSN 1155-4479
MQ
AGRESTE. DONNEES, BULLETIN DE STATISTIQUE AGRICOLE MARTINIQUE. VFOAT Bulletin de Statistique Agricole Martinique. (1990)-. Bulletin. French. Four times a year. 120.00F. Ministere de l'Agriculture et de la Peche, Direction des Affaires Financieres et Economiques, Service Central des Enquetes et Etudes Statistiques, 4 Avenue de Saint-Mande, 75570 Paris Cedex 12 France. **Tel** 011 33 1 43444633, 16 61288305.

ISSN 1150-1448
RE
UDC 31(698.1)
AGRESTE. DONNEES, BULLETIN DE STATISTIQUE AGRICOLE REUNION. VFOAT Bulletin de Statistique Agricole Reunion. (1990)-. Bulletin. French. Twelve times a year. 280.00F. Ministere de l'Agriculture et de la Peche, Direction des Affaires Financieres et Economiques, Service Central des Enquetes et Etudes Statistiques, 4 Avenue de Saint-Mande, 75570 Paris Cedex 12 France. **Tel** 011 33 1 43444633, 16 61288305.

ISSN 1146-5751
FR
UDC 31(441)
AGRESTE. SERIES, BULLETIN BIMESTRIEL DE STATISTIQUE AGRICOLE DES PAYS DE LA LOIRE. VFOAT Bulletin Bimestriel de Statistique Agricole des Pays de la Loire. (1990)-. Bulletin. French. Six times a year. 150.00F. Ministere de l'Agriculture et de la Peche, Direction des Affaires Financieres et Economiques, Service Central des Enquetes et Etudes Statistiques, 4 Avenue de Saint-Mande, 75570 Paris Cedex 12 France. **Tel** 011 33 1 43444633, 16 61288305.

ISSN 1157-3546
FR
UDC 31(443.6)
AGRESTE. SERIES, BULLETIN DE STATISTIQUE AGRICOLE ILE DE FRANCE. (1991)-. Periodical. French. Four times a year. 170.00F. Ministere de l'Agriculture et de la Peche, Direction des Affaires Financieres et Economiques, Service Central des Enquetes et Etudes Statistiques, 4 Avenue de Saint-Mande, 75570 Paris Cedex 12 France. **Tel** 011 33 1 43444633, 16 61288305.

ISSN 1150-1731
FR
UDC 31(447.7/.8)
AGRESTE. SERIES, BULLETIN DE STATISTIQUE AGRICOLE REGION MIDI-PYRENEES. VFOAT Bulletin Trimestriel de Statistique Agricole de Midi-Pyrenees; Bulletin de Statistique Agricole Region Midi-Pyrenees. (1990)-. Bulletin. French. Four times a year. 160.00F. Ministere de l'Agriculture et de la Peche, Direction des Affaires Financieres et Economiques, Service Central des Enquetes et Etudes Statistiques, 4 Avenue de Saint-Mande, 75570 Paris Cedex 12 France. **Tel** 011 33 1 43444633, 16 61288305.

US
AGRI/STATS I. CD-ROM. (19??)-. English. $69.00 Minnesota residents; $65.00 US and Canada; $150.00 Africa, Russia, and Eastern Europe; $130.00 India; $115.00 other. Hopkins Technology, 421 Hazel Lane, Suite 120, Hopkins MN 55343. **Tel** (612)931-9376, FAX (612)931-9377.
Desc: Eight agricultural databases of US statistics including: Crop Estimates, Grain Stocks, Count Estimates - Crops and Livestock, Hog and Pig Estimates, Cattle Inventory and Cattle on Feed. Bonus: Corn Production in 42 African countries since 1966.

ISSN 1053-9603
US
DD 630
AGRI-VIEW. [Agri-view]. Periodical. English. Twenty-four times a year. $10.00. USDA SRS, Crop and Livestock Reporting Service, Room 5829/S Building, Washington DC 20250. **Tel** (612)296-2230.

ISSN 1050-6810
US
DD 630
AGRICOLA [COMPUTER FILE].
Added/Corp National Agricultural Library (U.S.) Silverplatter Information, Inc. (19??)-. Abstracting/Indexing Service. English. Four times a year. $825.00 (single user networked). Silverplatter Information Inc., 100 River Ridge Drive, Norwood MA 02062. **Tel** (800)343-0064, (617)769-2599, FAX (617)769-8763.
Desc: The Indexing Branch of the National Agricultural Library's bibliographic database.

LC S494.5.B563 A363 **ISSN** 1063-1151
DD 660 US

•AGRICULTURAL & ENVIRONMENTAL BIOTECHNOLOGY ABSTRACTS.

[Agric. environ. biotechnol. abstr.]. **Added/Corp** Cambridge Scientific Abstracts, Inc. **VFOAT** Agricultural and Environmental Biotechnology Abstracts. Vol. 1, No. 1 (1993)-. Abstracting/Indexing Service. English. Six times a year. $325.00. Cambridge Scientific Abstracts, 7200 Wisconsin Avenue, #601, Bethesda MD 20814-4823. **Tel** (301)961-6750, (800)843-7751, FAX (301)961-6720. available on magnetic tape, an online database, and CD-ROM; available via Internet (to the current year's abstracts and five-year backfiles) from Cambridge Scientific Abstracts; available on an online database from STN International; and (File no.76) DIALOG; available on CD-ROM from National Information Service Corporation (NISC). ***Continues in part*** *Biotechnology Research Abstracts, 0733-5709.*
Desc: Biotechnology research in plant genome studies, the food industry, agricultural products, and environmental protection are covered in this volume. Specific areas of coverage include: legislation and regulation - new product approval - soil microorganisms - transgenic plants and animals - food safety tests - biopesticides, and more.

LC SB
DD 630 II

AGRICULTURAL CENSUS.

Main/Corp Gujarat. (19??)-. Periodical. English.

LC Z5074.C7 A36 HD1439
DD 016.3327/1 IT
UDC 336.77:338.43(01)

AGRICULTURAL CREDIT BIBLIOGRAPHY.

VFOAT Bibliographie du Credit Agricole. No. 1 (1978)-. Bibliography. English (French and Spanish).

LC HD1407 .A33 **ISSN** 0148-2920
DD 338.1/0212 US

AGRICULTURAL ECONOMICS STATISTICAL SERIES.

[Agric. econ. stat. ser.]. **Added/Corp** North Dakota State University. Dept. of Agricultural Economics. United States. Dept. of Agriculture. Economic Research Service. Farm Production Economics Division. **VFOAT** Ag. Economics Statistics Series. **VAT** Agricultural Economics Statistical Series. (196?)-. Statistical Publication. English. Price varies per volume. Extension Communications, PO Box 3166, North Dakota State University, Fargo ND 58105. **Tel** (701)239-5306, FAX (701)239-5613. ***Continues*** *Agricultural Economics Statistical Series.*

LC Z5074.E6 A36 S675 **ISSN** 0308-8863
DD 016.63 UK

AGRICULTURAL ENGINEERING ABSTRACTS.

Added/Corp Commonwealth Agricultural Bureaux. National Institute of Agricultural Engineering (Great Britain). Scientific Information Dept. (March 1976)-. Abstracting/Indexing Service. English. Twelve times a year. $560.00. CAB International Centre, Wallingford, Oxfordshire OX10 8DE United Kingdom. **Tel** 011 44 1491 832111, FAX 011 44 1491 833508, telex 847964 COMAGG G. **ED** J. R. Metcalfe. **Bk Rev. Ad Acc. Circ:** 450. available on magnetic tape and CD-ROM; available on an online database from Tsukuba Daigaku; CAN/OLE; STN International; JICST; DATA-STAR; DIMDI; ESA-IRS; BRS; and DIALOG. Documents available from BLDSC.
Desc: Produced in collaboration with the Silsoe Research Institute, keeps readers informed about significant research developments in agricultural engineering and instrumentation. Aspects include: mechanical power; crop production; crop harvesting and threshing; crop processing and storage; aquaculture; land improvement; protected cultivation; handling and transport; farm buildings and equipment.
Ind/Abst Dairy Sci. Abstr.; Field Crop Abstr.; Grass. Forage Abstr.; Weed Abstr.

ISSN 0733-1770
US
CCC

AGRICULTURAL ENGINEERING INDEX.

[Agric. eng. index]. **Added/Corp** American Society of Agricultural Engineers. (1961)-. English. Irregular. Price varies per volume. American Society of Agricultural Engineers, Department 2510, 2950 Niles Road, St. Joseph MI 49085-9659. **Tel** (616)429-0300, FAX (616)429-3852. **ED** James Basselman. Index available. cum. index. **Circ:** 4,000.
Desc: Lists over 8,000 books, articles, and technical papers published by U.S. and international agricultural engineering technical societies.

ISSN 0791-3346
DD 630.2012 630.9417 IE

AGRICULTURAL INPUT PRICE INDEX DUBLIN.

(AGRICULTURAL INPUT PRICE INDEX.). [Agric. input price index Dublin]. (1987)-. Government Publication. English. Twelve times a year. 24.00p. Central Statistics Office / Ireland, Ardee Road, Dublin 6 Ireland. **Tel** 011 353 1 4977144. ***Continues*** *Agricultural Input Price Index Numbers.*
Desc: Monitors the prices of agricultural inputs.

LC HD319.B8 A65 **ISSN** 0713-1631
DD 333.76/16/09711 CN
UDC 332(711)

AGRICULTURAL LAND RESERVE STATISTICS.

[Agric. land reserve stat.]. English. One time a year. Provincial Agricultural Land Commission, 4333 Ledger Avenue, Burnaby BC.

ISSN 0791-3354
DD 630.2012 630.9417 IE

AGRICULTURAL OUTPUT PRICE INDEX DUBLIN.

(AGRICULTURAL OUTPUT PRICE INDEX.). [Agric. output price index Dublin]. (1987)-. Government Publication. English. Twelve times a year. 24.00p. Central Statistics Office / Ireland, Ardee Road, Dublin 6 Ireland. **Tel** 011 353 1 4977144. ***Continues*** *Agricultural Output Price Index Numbers.*
Desc: Monitors changes in the prices of agricultural outputs.

LU

AGRICULTURAL STATISTICS.

Added/Corp Statistical Office of the European Community. **VFOAT** Statistique Agricole; Agrarstatistik; Statistica Agraria; Landbouwstatistiek; Landbrugsstatistik. (19??)-. Statistical Publication. Multiple languages (French, German, English, Italian, Dutch and Danish; summaries and/or abstracts in Dutch and Danish). Eight times a year. 300.00F. Office for Official Publications of the European Communities, 2 rue Mercier, 2985 Luxembourg Luxembourg. **Tel** 011 352 499281, FAX 011 352 292942763. **(Subscription address:** UNIPUB, 4611 F Assembly Drive, Lanham MD 20706. **Tel** (800)274-4888, (301)459-7666.**)**
Desc: World market prices and official support prices for products under the EC common agricultural policy and current statistics on plant products: land use, areas and products harvested, selection of yield, and agro-meteorological conditions.

LC HD1790.P74 A38 **ISSN** 0715-1438
DD 338.1/3/09717 CN

AGRICULTURAL STATISTICS AND REVIEW OF AGRICULTURE.

[Agric. stat. rev. agric.]. **Added/Corp** Prince Edward Island. Dept. of Agriculture and Forestry. Economics, Marketing and Statistics Branch. Statistics Canada. Maritime Office. Prince Edward Island. Dept. of Agriculture and Forestry. Economics, Planning and Marketing Branch. Prince Edward Island. Dept. of Agriculture and Forestry. Office of Policy Development and Planning. Prince Edward Island. Dept. of Agriculture and Forestry. Marketing Branch. Statistics Canada. Atlantic Office. Prince Edward Island. Dept. of Agriculture. Marketing Branch. **VFOAT** Agricultural Statistics. Vol. 9 (1973)-. Statistical Publication. English. One time a year. Free on request. PEI Department of Agriculture & Forestry, PO Box 2000, Marketing Branch, Charlottetown PEI C1A 7N8 Canada. **Tel** (902)892-4101. **Circ:** 1,000. ***Absorbed*** *Agricultural Statistics (Charlottetown, P.E.I.), 0715-142X.*

US

AGRICULTURAL STATISTICS FOR ARKANSAS.

Added/Corp Arkansas Crop Reporting Service. (19??)-. Government Publication. English. One time a year (July). free on request, $2.00 postage. US Department of Agriculture / National Agricultural Statistics Service (NASS), Room 5829 South Building, Washington DC 20250. **Tel** (202)720-4020, FAX (314)875-5231.

LC HD1790.O6 A63 **ISSN** 0568-2894
DD 338.1/09713/021 CN

AGRICULTURAL STATISTICS FOR ONTARIO.

[Agric. stat. Ont.]. **Main/Corp** Ontario. Ministry of Agriculture and Food Statistics Section. **Added/Corp** Ontario. Ministry of Agriculture and Food. Statistics Section. Ontario. Dept. of Agriculture. Statistics Section. Ontario. Dept. of Agriculture. Ontario. Dept. of Agriculture and Food. Ontario. Ministry of Agriculture and Food. (1924)-. Statistical Publication. English. Irregular. $21.60. Statistics Canada Publications Sales and Services, R.H. Coats Building 6th Floor, Ottawa Ontario K1A 0T6 Canada. **Tel** (613)951-5078, (800)267-6677, FAX (613)951-1584, telex 053-3585. ***Continues*** *Ontario. Dept. of Agriculture. Statistics Branch. Annual Report of the Statistics Branch.*

LC SB23 **ISSN** 0791-3524
DD 630.9417 630.20112 IE

AGRICULTURAL STATISTICS, JUNE ..., LAND UTILISATION AND NUMBERS OF LIVESTOCK, REGIONAL ANALYSIS.

[Agric. stat. June land util. numbers livest. reg. anal.]. (1986)-. Government Publication. English. One time a year. 2.00p. Central Statistics Office / Ireland, Ardee Road, Dublin 6 Ireland. **Tel** 011 353 1 4977144. ***Continues*** *Agricultural Statistics, June ..., Final Results.*
Desc: Crops and livestock numbers.

LC S296.S3 D45A
DD 338.1/09595/3 MY
UDC 338.43(595)

AGRICULTURAL STATISTICS OF SABAH.

Main/Corp Sabah. Dept. of Agriculture. Statistical Publication. English (Malayalam). One time a year. Free. Agricultural Information Division, Department of Agriculture, Sabah Malaysia. **Tel** 088-55155. **ED** Fung Pui Ken. **Circ:** 300.
Desc: Contains agricultural crops planted area, inport and export of agricultural commodities of Sabah state.

LC HD1751 .A43 **ISSN** 0082-9714
DD 338.10973 US

AGRICULTURAL STATISTICS (WASHINGTON, D.C.).

(AGRICULTURAL STATISTICS.). [Agric. Stat.]. **Added/Corp** United States. Dept. of Agriculture. United States. National Agricultural Statistics Service. (1936)-. Government Publication. English. One time a year. Superintendent of Documents, US Government Printing Office, Washington DC 20402. **Tel** (202)275-3328, FAX (202)786-2377. available on microfilm and microfiche from University Microfilms International (UMI). ***Continues in part*** *Yearbook of Agriculture (Washington, D.C. : 1926), 0084-3628.*
Ind/Abst Anim. Breed. Abstr.; Predicasts Forecasts.

US

AGRICULTURE STATISTICS. CD-ROM.

(19??)-. Statistical Publication. English. One time a year. $670.00 (nonprofit institutions), $745.00 other. Slater Hall Information Products, 1301 Pennsylvania Avenue Northwest, Washington DC 20004. **Tel** (202)393-2666.

LC Z5073 .A485 S18 **ISSN** 0254-8801
DD 630/.1/6 IT

AGRINDEX.

Added/Corp AGRIS Coordinating Centre. Food and Agriculture Organization of the United Nations. Vol. 1 (1975)-. Abstracting/Indexing Service. English (French and Spanish). Twelve times a year. $500.00 North America. Food Agriculture Organization (FAO) / Italy, GIPCI66 via Terme di Caracalla, 00100 Rome Italy. **Tel** 011 39 6 52252925, FAX 011 39 6 52253152. **(Subscription address:** Her Majesty's Stationery Office, PO Box 276, Public Centre, London SW8 5DT United Kingdom. **Tel** 011 44 171 8738499, 011 44 171 8738456.**)** available on an online database from Orbit Search Service; DIALOG; and DIMDI.
Desc: Bibliography compiled from information submitted by centers worldwide participating in AGRIS, the International Information System for Agricultural Sciences and Technology. Provides complete bibliographic information on all items listed, with availability information and reference number for each entry.
Ind/Abst Dairy Sci. Abstr.; Leis., Rec., Tour. Abstr.; Protozoolog. Abstr.; Rural Dev. Abstr.; Weed Abstr.; World Agric. Econ. Rural Sociol. Abstr.

LC S31 .A37 **ISSN** 0270-2436
DD 338.1/09761 US

ALABAMA AGRICULTURAL STATISTICS.

(ALABAMA AGRICULTURAL STATISTICS. BULLETIN.). [Ala. agric. stat.]. **Added/Corp** Alabama. Division of Agricultural Statistics. United States. Bureau of Agricultural Economics. United States. Agricultural Marketing Service. United States. Dept. of Agriculture. Statistical Reporting Service. Alabama. Dept. of Agriculture and Industries. Alabama Crop Reporting Service. Alabama Crop and Livestock Reporting Service. (1948)-. Bulletin. English. One time a year. Free on request. Alabama Agriculture Industries, PO Box 1071, 1445 Federal Drive, Montgomery AL 36193. **Tel** (334)832-7263.

LC S33 .D45a
DD 338.1/09798 US

ALASKA AGRICULTURAL STATISTICS.

Added/Corp Alaska Crop and Livestock Reporting Service. United States. Dept. of Agriculture. Statistical Reporting Service. United States. Dept. of Agriculture. Economics, Statistics, and Cooperatives Service. **VFOAT** Alaska Farm Production. (1963)-. Statistical Publication. English. One time a year (June). $5.00. Alaska Agricultural Statistics Service, PO Box 799, Palmer AK 99645. **Tel** (907)745-4272. ***Continues*** *Alaska Farm Production, 0516-4850.*
Desc: Contains Alaska agricultural statistics.

LC SF1 .A63 **ISSN** 0003-3499
DD 636.05 UK
NLM ZW 1 A573

ANIMAL BREEDING ABSTRACTS.

[Anim. breed. abstr.]. **Added/Corp** Imperial Bureau of Animal Breeding. Imperial Bureau of Animal Breeding and Genetics. Commonwealth Bureau of Animal Breeding and Genetics. Vol. 1 (April 1933)-. Abstracting/Indexing Service. English. Twelve times a year. $735.00. CAB International Centre, Wallingford, Oxfordshire OX10 8DE United Kingdom. **Tel** 011 44 1491 832111, FAX 011 44 1491 833508, telex 847964 COMAGG G. **ED** J. R. Metcalfe. Index Available, published separately, free-automatically sent. cum. index. **Ad Acc. Circ:** 1,400. available on magnetic tape and CD-ROM; available on an online database from Tsukuba Daigaku; CAN/OLE; STN International; JICST; DATA-STAR; DIMDI; ESA-IRS; BRS; DIALOG; and CISTI. Documents available from BLDSC. ***Formed by the union of*** *Imperial Bureau of Animal Breeding and Genetics. Quarterly Bulletin* ***and*** *Imperial Bureau of Animal References to Literature Contained in Periodicals Received.*
Desc: A source of information on the reproduction, genetics, breeding and management of farm livestock, poultry, fur-bearing animals and laboratory mammals, and the reproduction and genetics of species used in aquaculture. Covers the application of biotechnology to

Agriculture — Abstracting, Bibliographies and Statistics

animal breeding (e.g. genetic engineering and new reproductive techniques).
 Ind/Abst Anim. Breed. Abstr.; Dairy Sci. Abstr.; Field Crop Abstr.; Grass. Forage Abstr.; Index Vet.; Leis., Rec., Tour. Abstr.; Pig News Inf.; Rural Dev. Abstr.; Vet. Bull.; World Agric. Econ. Rural Sociol. Abstr.
UK

UDC 338.43(01)
ANNOTATED BIBLIOGRAPHY. SERIES B - COMMONWEALTH BUREAU OF AGRICULTURAL ECONOMICS. Main/Corp
Commonwealth Bureau of Agricultural Economics. No. 1-. Bibliography. English. Price varies per volume. Her Majesty's Stationery Office, 51 Nine Elms Lane, London SW8 5DR United Kingdom. **Tel** 011 44 171 8738459, 011 44 171 8738499, FAX 011 44 171 8738499, 011 44 171 8738456, telex 297138. **(Subscription address:** Her Majesty's Stationery Office, PO Box 276, Public Centre, London SW8 5DT United Kingdom. **Tel** 011 44 171 87384998456.)
 Ind/Abst Leis., Rec., Tour. Abstr.; Rural Dev. Abstr.; World Agric. Econ. Rural Sociol. Abstr.

LC S230.R49 A55
DD 338.1/0944
FR
ANNUAIRE ABREGE DE STATISTIQUES AGRICOLES, REGION RHONE-ALPES.
Added/Corp France. Service Regional de Statistique Agricole, Rhone-Alpes. (1966/1967)-. French. One time a year. 40.00F France. DRAF, Service Regional de Statistique Agricole-Rhone-Alpes, 165 rue Garibaldi, BP 3202, 69401 Lyon Cedex 03 France. **Tel** 78.63.13.13. Index available. **Ad Acc. Circ:** 300. available on microfiche.
 Desc: Topics covered are surfaces and plant production, animal numbers and production, material inventories, accounts, etc.

LC HD1950.P65 A55a
DD 338.1/0944/6   **ISSN** 0243-6507
FR
ANNUAIRE DE STATISTIQUE AGRICOLE (FRANCE. SERVICE REGIONAL DE STATISTIQUE AGRICOLE, POITOU-CHARENTES).
(ANNUAIRE DE STATISTIQUE AGRICOLE.). **Added/Corp** France. Service Regional de Statistique Agricole, Poitou-Chaentes. **VFOAT** Annuaire Poitou-Charentes. (19??)-. French. 47 rue de la Cathedrale, 86020 Poitiers Cedex France.

LC S230.F7 A55
DD 338.1/0944/45
FR
ANNUAIRE REGIONAL DE STATISTIQUE AGRICOLE.
French. Ministere de l'Agriculture, 78 rue de Varenne, 75007 Paris France. **Tel** 011 33 1 49554955 ext. 2718.

LC S230.B87 F68a
DD 338.1/0944/4
FR
ANNUAIRE REGIONAL - SERVICE CENTRAL DES ENQUETES ET ETUDES STATISTIQUES, REGION DE PROGRAMME BOURGOGNE. Main/Corp
France. Service Central des Enquetes et Etudes Statistiques. Region de Programme Bourgogne. (19??)-. French. SCEES - Service Central des Enquetes et Etudes Statistiques, 4 Avenue de Saint-Mande, 75570 Paris Cedex 12 France. **Tel** 011 33 1 49558576.

LC S253 .A6
DD 630
UDC 338.43(460)
SP
ANUARIO DE ESTADISTICA AGRARIA.
VFOAT Anuario Estadistica Agraria. 1972-. Statistical Publication. Spanish. One time a year. Secretaria General Tecnica Ser Publ Agrar, Paseo de Infanta Isabel 1, Madrid 7 Spain.

LC HD9014.B8 B68A
DD 338.1/881
BL
ANUARIO ESTATISTICO - COMISSAO DE FOMAMCIAMENTO DA PRODUCAO, DEPARTAMENTO DE PESQUISAS ECONOMICAS. Main/Corp
Brazil. Comissao de Financiamento da Producao. Departamento de Pesquisas Economicas. (19??)-. Portuguese. Ministerio Agricultura, Centro de Publicaciones, Calle Alfonso XII 56, 28071 Madrid Spain. **Tel** 011 34 1 3475551, FAX 011 34 1 3475722.

LC SF531 .A87a
DD 638/.1/09946
AT
BEE FARMING STATISTICS, TASMANIA. Main/Corp
Australian Bureau of Statistics. Tasmanian Office. (19??)-. Statistical Publication. English. One time a year. Australian Bureau Statistics / Tasmanian Office, Commonwealth Government Centre, 188 Collins Street, Hobart GPO Box 66A, Hobart Tasmania 7001 Australia. **Tel** 011 61 2 205889. **Continues** Bee Farming Statistics, Tasmania.

LC Z3277.A26 B52 DS6 S646.15.A8
IO
BIBLIOGRAFI DAERAH ISTIMEWA ACEH : BDIA.
VFOAT BDIA; B.D.I.A. No. 1 Pelita 3 (July 1980)-. Bibliography. Indonesian. Proyek Pengembangan Perpustakaan Daerah Istimewa Aceh, Perpustakaan Wilayah Banda Aceh, Jln Jenderal Sudirman No 5, Banda Aceh Indonesia.

LC Z5074.C6 B5 SB191.M2
DD 015
BL
BIBLIOGRAFIA DO MILHO. Added/Corp
Cenafor. Secao de Biblioteca e Documentacao Cientifica. Vol. 1 (Sept. 1975)-. Bibliography. Portuguese. Cenafor, rua Rodolfo Miranda 636, 01121 Sao Paulo Brazil.

LC Z5074.E3 B56 HD1941   **ISSN** 0982-3417
DD 016.63
FR
BIBLIOGRAPHIE - INSTITUT NATIONAL DE LA RECHERCHE AGRONOMIQUE, DEPARTEMENT D'ECONOMIE ET DE LA SOCIOLOGIE RURALES.
(BIBLIOGRAPHIE / DEPARTEMENT D'ECONOMIE ET DE SOCIOLOGIE RURALES.). [Bibliog. - inst. natl. rech. agron. Dep. econ. sociol. rurales]. **Main/Corp** Institut National de la Recherche Agronomique (France). **Added/Corp** Institut National de la Recherche Agronomique (France). Departement d'Economie et de Sociologie Rurales. **VFOAT** INRA Economie et Sociologie Rurales, Bibliographie. **VAT** Institut National de la Recherche Agronomique Economie et Sociologie Rurales, Bibliographie. No. 1 (1985)-. Bibliography. French. One time a year. INRA Editions / Institut National de la Recherche Agronomique, Route de Saint-Cyr, 78026 Versailles Cedex France. **Tel** 011 33 1 30833406, FAX 011 33 1 30833449, telex INRAPUB 699 368 F. **Continues** Bulletin d'Information du Departement d'Economie et de Sociologie Rurales, 0339-2945.

ISSN 0163-0873
US
UDC 63(01); 63(048.3)
BIBLIOGRAPHIES AND LITERATURE OF AGRICULTURE.
[Bibliogr. lit. agric.]. 1/1977-. Bibliography. English. Price varies per volume. US Department of Agriculture / Science and Education Administration / Maryland, Belcrest Road, Beltsville MD 20705. Index available. cum. index. available on microfiche.
 Desc: Contains in-depth subject bibliographies on various agriculture topics.
 Ind/Abst For. Prod. Abstr. (1991-); For. Abstr.; Hortic. Abstr.; Index Vet.; Nematol. Abstr.; Potato Abstr.; Rev. Agric. Entomol.; Rev. Plant Pathol.; Soils Fert.; Soyabean Abstr.; Weed Abstr.; World Agric. Econ. Rural Sociol. Abstr.

LC Z5071   **ISSN** 0074-6436
DD 016.63
NE
CODEN BIIIDY
BIBLIOGRAPHY - INTERNATIONAL INSTITUTE FOR LAND RECLAMATION AND IMPROVEMENT.
[Bibliogr. - Int. Inst. land reclam. improv.]. **Main/Corp** International Institute for Land Reclamation and Improvement. No. 1 (1960)-. Bibliography. English. Irregular. Price varies per volume. International Institute for Land Reclamation and Improvement, PO Box 45, 6700 AA Wageningen Netherlands. **Tel** 011 31 837019100, FAX 11524, telex 75230 NL. ctrl circ.
 Desc: Bibliography dealing with hydrology, soil science, water management, irrigation, drainage, and geoscience.
 Ind/Abst Field Crop Abstr.; GeoRef; Grass. Forage Abstr.; Int. Dev. Abstr. (?-?); Leis., Rec., Tour. Abstr.; Rural Dev. Abstr.; Soils Fert.; World Agric. Econ. Rural Sociol. Abstr.

LC Z5073 .U572 S493   **ISSN** 0006-1530
DD 0163.63
US
BIBLIOGRAPHY OF AGRICULTURE.
[Bibliogr. agric.]. **Added/Corp** National Agricultural Library (U.S.). Vol. 44, No. 1-2 (Jan./Feb. 1980)-. Abstracting/Indexing Service. English. Twelve times a year. $1295.00. Oryx Press, 4041 North Central Avenue #700, Phoenix AZ 85012-3397. **Tel** (800)279-6799, (602)265-2651, FAX (602)265-6250, (800)279-4663, (800)279-6799. cum. index. available on microfilm and microfiche from University Microfilms International (UMI); available on CD-ROM from SilverPlatter (US); available on an online database from CISTI. **Continues** Bibliography of Agriculture with Subject Index, 0006-1530.
 Desc: Each issue contains main entry citations and about 20,000 subject index references to journal articles, pamphlets, government documents, special reports, and proceedings in agriculture.

LC HD9012.4 .F75d
DD 338.1/0944
FR
BILANS ALIMENTAIRES ET AUTRES BILANS. Main/Corp
France. Service Central des Enquetes et Etudes Statistiques. (1967)-. French. SCEES - Service Central des Enquetes et Etudes Statistiques, 4 Avenue de Saint-Mande, 75570 Paris Cedex 12 France. **Tel** 011 33 1 49558576.

LC Z5073 .A46   **ISSN** 0006-3177
DD 016.63/05
US
NLM ZS 419 A278
Pr Rev.
BIOLOGICAL & AGRICULTURAL INDEX.
See Biology-Abstracting, Bibliographies and Statistics.

LC Z5073
DD 574 630
US
BIOLOGICAL & AGRICULTURAL INDEX [COMPUTER FILE]. See Biology-Abstracting,
Bibliographies and Statistics.

LC HD2026 .I56b
DD 338/.09469
PO
BOLETIM TRIMESTRAL DAS ESTATISTICAS DA AGRICULTURA E DA PESCA: CONTINENTE E ILHAS ADJACENTES. BULLETIN TRIMESTRIEL DES STATISTIQUES DE L'AGRICULTURE ET DE LA PECHE: CONTINENT ET ILES ADJACENTES.
Main/Corp Instituto Nacional de Estatistica (Portugal). Servicos Centrais. **Added/Corp** Instituto Nacional de Estatistica (Portugal). Servicos Centrais. Bulletin Trimestriel des Statistiques de l'Agriculture et de la Peche: Continent et Iles Adjacentes. **VFOAT** Bulletin Trimestriel des Statistiques de l'Agriculture et de la Peche : Continent et Iles Adjacentes. (19??)-. Bulletin. Multiple languages (French and Portuguese). Instituto Nacional de Estatistica, Avenida Antonio Jose de Almeida, 1078 Lisbon Codex Portugal. **Tel** 011 351 1 8470050.

ISSN 0007-4160
FR
BULLETIN BIBLIOGRAPHIQUE INTERNATIONAL DU MACHINISME AGRICOLE.
VFOAT International Farm Machinery Abstracts. 1- 1966-. Bulletin. French (English, Spanish and German). Twelve times a year. 330.00F. Centre National du Machinisme, Agricole du Genie Rural des Eaux et des Forets, Parc de Tourvoie, Antony 91160 France. **Tel** 46-66-21-09, telex 204565. Index available. **Circ:** 550. **Absorbed** Antony, France. Centre National d'Etudes et d'Experimentation de Machinisme Agricole. Bulletin Bibliographique.
 Desc: Abstracts from agricultural machinery journals received at the Cemagref Library.
 Ind/Abst Agric. Eng. Abstr.

ISSN 0997-1122
FR
TITLE CHANGE
BULLETIN MENSUEL DE STATISTIQUE AGRICOLE (PARIS).
(BULLETIN MENSUEL DE STATISTIQUE AGRICOLE.). [Bull. mens. stat. agric.]. **Added/Corp** France. Service Central des Enquetes et Etudes Statistiques. (Feb. 1988)-(19??)-. Bulletin. French. SCEES - Service Central des Enquetes et Etudes Statistiques, 4 Avenue de Saint-Mande, 75570 Paris Cedex 12 France. **Tel** 011 33 1 49558576. **Continues** France. Service Central des Enquetes et Etudes Statistiques. Bulletin de Statistique Agricole, 0336-9919. **Continued by** Agreste. Series, le Bulletin, 1142-3218.

LC HD9017.T3 B84
DD 338.1/09678
TZ
BULLETIN OF CROP AND LIVESTOCK STATISTICS.
1976-. Bulletin. English. One time a year. Statistics Section, Planning Division, Ministry of Agriculture, PO Box 9192, Dar es Salaam Tanzania. **Continues** Bulletin of Crop Statistics.

LC S39 .C42
DD 338.1/09794/021
US
UDC 311:63(794)
CALIFORNIA AGRICULTURE STATISTICAL REVIEW.
(1985)-. Statistical Publication. English. One time a year. Media Office, California Department of Food and Agriculture, 1220 North Street, Sacramento CA 96814. **Continues** California Agriculture (California. Dept. of Food and Agriculture).

LC SB193
DD 633
US
CEASED
CALIFORNIA FIELD CROPS STATISTICS (1987).
(CALIFORNIA FIELD CROPS STATISTICS.). **VFOAT** Field Crops Statistics. (1987)-(1993). Statistical Publication. English. California Agricultural Statistics Service, California Department of, Food and Agriculture, PO Box 1258, Sacramento CA 95812. **Tel** (916)551-1533. **Continues** Field Crops Statistics, California.

LC TP368
DD 664
US
CALIFORNIA FRUIT & NUT STATISTICS.
VFOAT California Fruit and Nut Statistics. (1967)-. Statistical Publication. English. One time a year. $4.00. California Agricultural Statistics Service, California Department of, Food and Agriculture, PO Box 1258, Sacramento CA 95812. **Tel** (916)551-1533. **Continues**

California Fruit and Nut Crops.
Desc: Acreage, production, value, and utilization of fruit and nut crops with historical data.

CN
CANADIAN GRAINS INDUSTRY; STATISTICAL HANDBOOK. **Main/Corp** Canada Grains Council. **Added/Corp** Canadian Grain Commission. Winnipeg Commodity Exchange. (1974)-. Statistical Publication. English. One time a year (Feb.). 33.62Can$. Canada Grains Council, 760 360 Main Street, Winnipeg Manitoba R3C 3Z3 Canada. **Tel** (204)942-2254, FAX (204)947-0992. **Ad Acc. Circ:** 1,200.

LC Z5071
DD 016.63 BL
CENSO AGROPECUARIO : VIII RECENSEAMENTO GERAL, 1970.
Main/Corp Instituto Brasileiro de Geografia e Estatistica. Vol.1 (1974)-. Government Publication. Portuguese. Irregular. $110.00. Fundacao Instituto Brasileiro de Geografia e Estatistica, Centro de Documentacao e Disseminacao de Informacoes, Rua General Canabarro 666, 10 andar Maracana 20271-201, Rio de Janeiro, Brazil. **Tel** 011 55 21 2645424, FAX 011 55 21 2289575.

LC Z5071
DD 016.63 PH
COCONUT STATISTICS. **Added/Corp** United Coconut Association of the Philippines. Research Dept. (19??)-. Statistical Publication. English. One time a year. $70.00. United Coconut Association of the Philippines, 4th Floor, G&A 2303 Pasong Tamo Ex, Manila Philippines. **Tel** 011 63 2 8167495. **ED** Yvonne T.V. Agustin. **Bk Rev. Ad Acc. Circ:** 500 (ctrl).
Desc: Statistics pertinent to the coconut industry in the Philippines and elsewhere. World oils/fats production, imports, exports, prices, Philippine coco trade directory, current policies related to industry.

LC HD9199.I4 A32 **ISSN** 0536-7093
DD 331.7 II
COFFEE STATISTICS. (COFFEE STATISTICS - (INDIA).). **Main/Corp** India (Republic). Coffee Board. **VFOAT** Coffee in India. 1954/55-. Statistical Publication. English. Coffee Board, Box 5366, Bangalore 560001 India. **Tel** 24920.

LC Z5074.E6 C65 S675 **ISSN** 1061-1827
DD 632 US
COMPREHENSIVE INDEX OF PUBLICATIONS - AMERICAN SOCIETY OF AGRICULTURAL ENGINEERS.
(COMPREHENSIVE INDEX OF PUBLICATIONS.). [Compr. index publ. - Am. Soc. Agric. Eng.]. **Added/Corp** American Society of Agricultural Engineers. (1985)-. English. One time a year. $5.00. American Society of Agricultural Engineers, Department 2510, 2950 Niles Road, St. Joseph MI 49085-9659. **Tel** (616)429-0300, FAX (616)429-3852. ***Continues*** *American Society of Agricultural Engineers. Comprehensive Index of ASAE Publications (1979), 0889-6798.*

LC Z5071
DD 016.63 UK
COTTON AND TROPICAL FIBRES ABSTRACTS BIBLIOGRAPHY. (19??)-. Abstracting/Indexing Service. English. One time a year (published in Dec.). $57.00. CAB International Centre, Wallingford, Oxfordshire OX10 8DE United Kingdom. **Tel** 011 44 1491 832111, FAX 011 44 1491 833508, telex 847964 COMAGG G. available on magnetic tape and CD-ROM; available on an online database from Tsukuba Daigaku; CAN/OLE; STN International; JICST; DATA-STAR; DIMDI; ESA-IRS; BRS; and DIALOG. ***Continues*** *Cotton and Tropical Fibres Abstracts., 0308-6577.*
Desc: Cover studies in the tropics and other zones on cotton, sisal, ramie, kapol, coir, juts, kenaf, and minor fibres. Includes breeding, ecology, planting, crop protection, harvesting, handling, processing, and uses.

LC HD9093.U4 A32 **ISSN** 0010-9827
DD 338.1/3 US
COTTON PRICE STATISTICS. **Added/Corp** United States. Agricultural Marketing Service. Cotton Division. United States. Agricultural Marketing Service. Cotton Division. Market News Branch. Vol. 53, No. 8 (Mar. 1972)-. Statistical Publication. English. Twelve times a year (also annual edition). $31.00 monthly edition; $6.00 annual edition. US Department of Agriculture / Tennessee, Agricultural Marketing Service, 4841 Summer Avenue, Memphis TN 38122. **Tel** (901)766-2934, 766-2931. Documents available from Documents on Demand. ***Continues*** *United States. Consumer and Marketing Service. Cotton Division. Cotton Price Statistics, 0010-9827.*
Desc: A summary of various cotton prices and transactions.
Ind/Abst Am. Stat. Index.

LC TS1565.U6 C65 **ISSN** 0098-7026
DD 677/.21/30973 US
COTTON QUALITY CROP. (COTTON QUALITY CROP OF ...). **Added/Corp** United States. Agricultural Marketing Service. Cotton Division. United States. Consumer and Marketing Service. Cotton Division. (1960)-. English. One time a year. $11.00. US Department of Agriculture / Tennessee, Agricultural Marketing Service, 4841 Summer Avenue, Memphis TN 38122. **Tel** (901)766-2934, 766-2931.
Desc: A report of quality statistics for the crop, by states and the United States.

LC Z6662 **ISSN** 0306-7556
DD 016.61 UK
CROP PHYSIOLOGY ABSTRACTS.
Added/Corp Commonwealth Agricultural Bureaux. Vol. 1 (Jan. 1975)-. Abstracting/Indexing Service. English. Six times a year. $575.00. CAB International Centre, Wallingford, Oxfordshire OX10 8DE United Kingdom. **Tel** 011 44 1491 832111, FAX 011 44 1491 833508, telex 847964 COMAGG G. **ED** R. E. Hill BSc. Each issue contains an index to its own contents (no volume index)--loose. **Ad Acc. Circ:** 250. available on magnetic tape and CD-ROM; available on an online database from Tsukuba Daigaku; CAN/OLE; STN International; JICST; DATA-STAR; DIMDI; ESA-IRS; CISTI; BRS; and DIALOG.
Desc: Covers world scientific literature on the physiology of crop plants. All higher plants of economic importance are dealt with.

LC Z5071 .C86 **ISSN** 0090-0508
DD 016.63 US
NLM Z 5071 C976 **CODEN** CABEA
CURRENT CONTENTS. AGRICULTURE, BIOLOGY, & ENVIRONMENTAL SCIENCES. [Curr. contents, Agric. biol. environ. sci.]. **Added/Corp** Institute for Scientific Information. **VFOAT** Agriculture, Biology, & Environmental Sciences. **VAT** Current Contents. Agriculture, Biology and Environmental Sciences. Vol. 4 (1973)-. Abstracting/Indexing Service. English. One time a week. $530.00. Institute for Scientific Information, 3501 Market Street, Philadelphia PA 19104. **Tel** (215)386-0100, (800)523-1850, FAX (215)386-6362, telex 84-5305. **(Subscription address:** Institute for Scientific Information, PO Box 71416, Chicago IL 60694. **)** available on diskette; available on magnetic tape and an online database (as Current Contents Search); available on CD-ROM; available on an online database from BRS. Documents available from The Genuine Article. ***Continues*** *Current Contents. Agricultural, Food & Veterinary Sciences, 0011-3379.*
Desc: Provides electronic access to full bibliographic data on the articles contained in agricultural, biology and environmental sciences journals.
Ind/Abst Abstr. Bull. Inst. Pap. Sci. Tech.; Curr. Contents Agric. Biol. Environ. Sci.; Res. Alert [Full Cov.]; Rev. Med. Vet. Entomol.; Sci. Cit. Index; SCISEARCH; Soc. Sci. Cit. Index [Full Cov.].

LC Z5071 **ISSN** 1073-1245
DD 016 US
●**CURRENT CONTENTS. AGRICULTURE, BIOLOGY & ENVIRONMENTAL SCIENCES (CD-ROM VERSION).**
(CURRENT CONTENTS. AGRICULTURE, BIOLOGY & ENVIRONMENTAL SCIENCES [COMPUTER FILE].). **Added/Corp** Institute for Scientific Information. **VFOAT** Current Contents. Agriculture, Biology and Environmental Sciences; Agriculture, Biology & Environmental Sciences; Agriculture, Biology and Environmental Sciences. (1994)-. English. One time a week. $2125.00. Institute for Scientific Information, 3501 Market Street, Philadelphia PA 19104. **Tel** (215)386-0100, (800)523-1850, FAX (215)386-6362, telex 84-5305. **(Subscription address:** Institute for Scientific Information, PO Box 71416, Chicago IL 60694. **)** available on diskette; available on magnetic tape and an online database; available in print.
Desc: Provides access to bibliographic data on articles contained in agricultural, biological and environmental sciences journals.

LC Z5071 **ISSN** 1062-3167
DD 016 US
CURRENT CONTENTS ON DISKETTE. AGRICULTURE, BIOLOGY & ENVIRONMENTAL SCIENCES. (CURRENT CONTENTS ON DISKETTE. AGRICULTURE, BIOLOGY & ENVIRONMENTAL SCIENCES [COMPUTER FILE].). [Curr. contents diskette, Agric. biol. environ. sci.]. **Added/Corp** Institute for Scientific Information. **VFOAT** Agriculture, Biology & Environmental Sciences.; Agriculture, Biology and Environmental Sciences; Current Contents. Agriculture, Biology & Environmental Sciences. Vol. 20, Issue 32 (Aug. 7, 1989)-. Periodical. English. One time a week. $530.00. Institute for Scientific Information, 3501 Market Street, Philadelphia PA 19104. **Tel** (215)386-0100, (800)523-1850, FAX (215)386-6362, telex 84-5305. **(Subscription address:** Institute for Scientific Information, PO Box 71416, Chicago IL 60694. **)** available in print; available on magnetic tape and an online database; available on CD-ROM.
Desc: Provides access to full bibliographic data on the articles contained in agricultural, biology and environmental sciences journals.

LC Z5071 **ISSN** 1062-3124
DD 016 US
CURRENT CONTENTS ON DISKETTE WITH ABSTRACTS. AGRICULTURE, BIOLOGY & ENVIRONMENTAL SCIENCES. (CURRENT CONTENTS ON DISKETTE WITH ABSTRACTS. AGRICULTURE, BIOLOGY & ENVIRONMENTAL SCIENCES [COMPUTER FILE].). [Curr. contents diskette abstr., Agric. biol. environ. sci.]. **Added/Corp** Institute for Scientific Information. **VFOAT** Agriculture, Biology & Environmental Sciences; Agriculture, Biology and Environmental Sciences. Vol. 22, Issue 18, (May 6, 1991)-. Periodical. English. One time a week. $840.00. Institute for Scientific Information, 3501 Market Street, Philadelphia PA 19104. **Tel** (215)386-0100, (800)523-1850, FAX (215)386-6362, telex 84-5305. **(Subscription address:** Institute for Scientific Information, PO Box 71416, Chicago IL 60694. **)** available in print; available on magnetic tape and an online database; available on CD-ROM.
Desc: Provides access to bibliographic data on articles contained in agricultural, biology and environmental sciences journals.

LC HD9014.B83 M373A
DD 331.7 BL
UDC 311:63(817.2)
DADOS ESTATISTICOS : PRODUTOS AGRO PECUARIOS SAIDOS DE MATO GROSSO. **Main/Corp** Acordo de Classificacao no Estado de Mato Grosso. (19??)-. Periodical. Portuguese. Presidente Marques, Departamento de Estatistica, 559 Brazil.

LC SF233.I4 D326
DD 338.1/771/0954 II
DAIRY INDIA. (1983)-. English. One time a year. $90.00. Dairy India Yearbook, A-25 Priyadarshini Vihar, Delhi 110092 India. **Tel** 243039. **(Subscription address:** Prints India, 11 Darya Ganj, New Delhi 110002 India. **Tel** 011 91 11 3268645, FAX 011 91 11 3275542, telex 31-61087 PRIN-IN.) **ED** P. R. Gupta. **Ad Acc. Circ:** 1,500.
Desc: Sourcebook of reference data, directory and trends in dairy management and marketing. Also serves as handbook, buyer's guide and who's who. Over 7,000 organizations and personalities are listed by their business and location.

LC HD9275.U3 D315 **ISSN** 0098-6690
DD 338.1/77/0973 US
DAIRY MARKET STATISTICS, ANNUAL SUMMARY. **Added/Corp** United States. Agricultural Marketing Service. United States. Agricultural Marketing Service. Dairy Division. United States. Agricultural Marketing Service. Dairy Division. Market Information Branch. (1974)-. Statistical Publication. English. One time a year. $4.00. US Department of Agriculture / Wisconsin, PO Box 8911, Madison WI 53708. **Tel** (608)264-5254, FAX (608)264-5011. **Circ:** 2500. ***Continues*** *Dairy Market Statistics, 0091-2123.*

ISSN 0300-0753
DD 338.1/77/0971 CN
DAIRY REVIEW, THE. [Dairy rev.]. **Added/Corp** Canada. Dominion Bureau of Statistics. Agriculture Division. Canada. Dominion Bureau of Statistics. Statistics Canada. Livestock and Animal Products Section. **VFOAT** Revue Laitiere. Vol. 11, No. 1 (Jan. 1950)-. Periodical. English (French). Twelve times a year. 166.00Can$. Statistics Canada Publications Sales and Services, R.H. Coats Building 6th Floor, Ottawa Ontario K1A 0T6 Canada. **Tel** (613)951-5078, (800)267-6677, FAX (613)951-1584, telex 053-3585. ***Absorbed in part*** *Statistics Canada. Livestock and Animal Products Section. Stocks of Dairy and Frozen Poultry Products.;* ***Continues*** *Monthly Dairy Review of Canada.*
Desc: Statistical summary of the dairy situation in Canada and the provinces, including farm sales of milk for fluid and manufacturing purposes and cash receipts from farm sales.

LC HD1401 **ISSN** 0011-5681
DD 338.47637 UK
DAIRY SCIENCE ABSTRACTS. **Added/Corp** Commonwealth Bureau of Dairy Science and Technology, Shinfield, Eng. Commonwealth Agricultural Bureau. Imperial Bureau of Dairy Science, Shinfield, Eng. Vol. 1 (May 1939)-. Abstracting/Indexing Service. English. Twelve times a year. $710.00. CAB International Centre, Wallingford, Oxfordshire OX10 8DE United Kingdom. **Tel** 011 44 1491 832111, FAX 011 44 1491 833508, telex 847964 COMAGG G. **ED** E.J. Mann. **Ad Acc. Circ:** 1,500. available on diskette; available on magnetic tape and CD-ROM; available on an online database from Tsukuba Daigaku; (File Nos.16 & 124/CAB) European Space Agency; CAN/OLE; STN International; JICST; DATA-STAR; DIMDI; ESA-IRS; BRS; DIALOG; CISTI; and Ovid Technologies, Inc.; available with illustrations; available with charts. Documents available from BLDSC.
Desc: Provides information on all aspects of milk production, secretion and processing and milk products. A guide for research workers, farmers, extension workers, dairy industrialists, teachers and students.
Ind/Abst Anim. Breed. Abstr.; Dairy Sci. Abstr.; Field Crop Abstr.; Grass. Forage Abstr.; Index Vet.; Leis., Rec., Tour. Abstr.; Nutr. Abstr. Rev., Ser. B, Live Feeds and

Feed.; Nutr. Abstr. Rev., Ser. A, Hum. Exp.; Rural Dev. Abstr.; Vet. Bull.; Trop. Dis. Bull.; World Agric. Econ. Rural Sociol. Abstr.

LC HD1775.D3 D45
DD 338.1/09751/02 US

DELAWARE AGRICULTURAL STATISTICS / PREPARED BY DELAWARE CROP REPORTING SERVICE. **Added/Corp** Delaware Crop Reporting Service. Delaware. Dept. of Agriculture. United States. Dept. of Agriculture. Statistical Reporting Service. United States. National Agricultural Statistics Service. Delaware Agricultural Statistical Service. **VFOAT** Delaware Agricultural Statistics Summary. (1983)-. Statistical Publication. English. One time a year. free. Delaware Agricultural Statistics Service, Delaware Department of Agriculture, 2320 South DuPont Highway, Dover DE 19901. **Tel** (302)739-4811, (800)282-8685 (Delaware only).

LC HF1921 .A365
DD 630 UK

DIGEST OF AGRICULTURAL CENSUS STATISTICS, UNITED KINGDOM, THE. **Added/Corp** Great Britain. Ministry of Agriculture, Fisheries and Food. (1991)-. Statistical Publication. English. Her Majesty's Stationery Office, 51 Nine Elms Lane, London SW8 5DR United Kingdom. **Tel** 011 44 171 8738459, 011 44 171 8738499, FAX 011 44 171 8738499, 011 44 171 8738456, telex 297138. ***Continues*** *Agricultural Statistics, United Kingdom, 0065-4590.*

ISSN 0962-0036
DD 630.72 UK

DIRECTORY OF RESEARCH WORKERS IN AGRICULTURE AND ALLIED SCIENCES. [Dir. res. work. agric. allied sci.]. (1989)-. Directory. English. Irregular. £85.00. CAB International Centre, Wallingford, Oxfordshire OX10 8DE United Kingdom. **Tel** 011 44 1491 832111, FAX 011 44 1491 833508, telex 847964 COMAGG G. **ED** R. Vernon. Documents available from BLDSC. ***Continues*** *List of Research Workers in the Agricultural Sciences in the Commonwealth and in the Republic of Ireland, 0069-6897.*
Desc: Contains research information on over 29,000 agriculturalists indexed by name, institution and subject.

LC Z5074.E3 C29 **ISSN** 0527-0936
DD 015 US
UDC 63

ECONOMIC RESEARCH OF INTEREST TO AGRICULTURE. **Main/Corp** California Agricultural Experiment Station. English. Irregular.

LC S631 **ISSN** 0252-354X
DD 631.8 TH

ESCAP AGRICULTURE DIVISION, ARSAP/FADINAP, REGIONAL INFORMATION SUPPORT SERVICE (RISS). (RISS : REGIONAL INFORMATION SUPPORT SERVICE : AN ABSTRACT JOURNAL ON FERTILIZER-RELATED SUBJECTS.). [ESCAP Agric. Div., ARSAP/FADINAP, Reg. Inf. Support Serv. (RISS)]. **Added/Corp** Fertilizer Advisory, Development, and Information Network for Asia and the Pacific. **VFOAT** Regional Information Support Service; R.I.S.S. (197?)-. Periodical. English. Twelve times a year. $40.00 Thailand; $50.00 other. United Nations Economic Society Comm., United Nations Building, Rajadamnern Avenue, Bangkok 2 Thailand. **Tel** 011 66 2 2829161, FAX 011 66 2 2812403, telex 82392 ESCAP TH. **ED** Marianne Vespry. Index available. cum. index. **Bk Rev. Circ:** 500. available on diskette.
Desc: Contains bibliogrpahic citations and abstracts of documents relating to fertilizers and pesticides.

LC HD1901 .M55A
PE
UDC 311:63(85)

ESTADISTICA - MINISTERIO DE ALIMENTACION DIRECCION GENERAL DE INFORMATICA Y ESTADISTICA. **Main/Corp** Peru. Ministerio de Alimentacion. Direccion General de Informatica y Estadistica. **VFOAT** Estadistica Agropecuaria. Statistical Publication. Spanish. Cahuide 852 - Jesus Maria, Lima Peru.

LC S562.P33 P35a
DD 630 PN

ESTADISTICA PANAMENA. SERIE H.2 : INFORMACION AGROPECUARIA, PRECIOS PAGADOS POR EL PRODUCTOR AGROPECUARIO. **Main/Corp** Panama. Direccion de Estadistica y Censo. **VFOAT** Informacion Agropecuaria, Precios Pagados por el Productor Agropecio. (19??)-. Statistical Publication. Spanish. Direccion de Estadistica y Censo, Contraloria General, Apartado 5213, Panama 5 Panama. **Tel** 011 507 640777 Ext. 269 or 203.

UY

ESTADISTICAS AGROPECUARIAS. (19??)-. Statistical Publication. Spanish. Comcorde Secretaria Tecnica, Avda Rondeau 1908, Montevideo Uruguay.

ISSN 1015-9924
LU
UDC 63

EUROSTAT. AGRICULTURAL PRICES. PRICE INDICES AND ABSOLUTE PRICES. QUARTERLY STATISTICS. [EUROSTAT, Agric. prices, Price indices absol. prices, Q. stat.]. **VFOAT** EUROSTAT. Prix Agricoles. Indices de Prix et Prix Absolus. Statistiques Trimestrielles; Agricultural Prices. Price Indices and Absolute Prices. Quarterly Statistics; Prix Agricoles. Indices de Prix et Prix Absolus. Statistiques Trimestrielles. (1990)-. Periodical. Multiple languages. Four times a year. £50.50 UK; 54.70p Ireland. Office for Official Publications of the European Communities, 2 rue Mercier, 2985 Luxembourg Luxembourg. **Tel** 011 352 499281, FAX 011 352 292942763.

LC Z5073 .F2
DD 016.63 IT

FAO DOCUMENTATION. CURRENT BIBLIOGRAPHY / DOCUMENTATION DE LA FAO. BIBLIOGRAPHIE COURANTE / DOCUMENTACION DE LA FAO. BIBLIOGRAFIA CORRIENTE. **Added/Corp** Food and Agriculture Organization of the United Nations. Documentation Center. Food and Agriculture Organization of the United Nations. Food and Agriculture Organization of the United Nations. Library and Documentation Systems Division. David Lubin Memorial Library. **VFOAT** Documentation de la FAO. Bibliographie Courante; Documentacion de la FAO. Bibliografia Corriente. **VAT** Food and Agricultural Organization Documentation. Current Bibliography; Food and Agricultural Organization Documentation. Bibliographie Courante; Food and Agricultural Organization Documentacion. Bibliografia Courriente. (Jan. 1972)-. Bibliography. English (French and Spanish). Twelve times a year. Free on request. Food Agriculture Organization (FAO) / Italy, GIPCI66 via Terme di Caracalla, 00100 Rome Italy. **Tel** 011 39 6 52252925, FAX 011 39 6 52253152. **(Subscription address:** Food Agriculture Organization, D Lubin Memorial Library, 100100 Rome Italy. **)** ***Continues*** *FAO Documentation. Current Index.*
Ind/Abst Aquat. Sci. Fish. Abstr. [CD-ROM Ed.]; Field Crop Abstr.; Grass. Forage Abstr.; Nutr. Abstr. Rev., Ser. B, Live Feeds and Feed.; Nutr. Abstr. Rev., Ser. A, Hum. Exp.

LC HD9000.4 .F65a **ISSN** 1011-8780
DD 338.1/021 IT

FAO QUARTERLY BULLETIN OF STATISTICS. **Added/Corp** Food and Agriculture Organization of the United Nations. **VFOAT** Bulletin Trimestriel FAO de Statistiques; Boletin Trimestral FAO de Estadisticas. Vol. 1 (1988)-. Bulletin. English (French and Spanish). Four times a year. L15000. Food Agriculture Organization (FAO) / Italy, GIPCI66 via Terme di Caracalla, 00100 Rome Italy. **Tel** 011 39 6 52252925, FAX 011 39 6 52253152. Documents available from UMI Article Clearinghouse. ***Continues*** *FAO Monthly Bulletin of Statistics, 0379-0010.*
Ind/Abst Dairy Sci. Abstr.; Expand. Acad. Index (1992-); Newsp. Period. Abstr. (1992-); Nutr. Abstr. Rev., Ser. B, Live Feeds and Feed.; Nutr. Abstr. Rev., Ser. A, Hum. Exp.; World Agric. Econ. Rural Sociol. Abstr.

LC HD1421 .P76
DD 338.1/021 IT

FAO YEARBOOK. PRODUCTION. **VFOAT** Production; FAO Annuaire. Production; FAO Anuario. Produccion. **VAT** Food and Agriculture Organization of the United Nations Yearbook. Production. Vol. 41 (1987)-. Statistical Publication. English (French and Spanish). One time a year (Jan.). $52.50. Food Agriculture Organization (FAO) / Italy, GIPCI66 via Terme di Caracalla, 00100 Rome Italy. **Tel** 011 39 6 52252925, FAX 011 39 6 52253152. **(Subscription address:** UNIPUB, 4611 F Assembly Drive, Lanham MD 20706. **Tel** (800)274-4888, (301)459-7666.**)** ***Continues*** *Food and Agriculture Organization of the United Nations. FAO Production Yearbook, 0071-7118.*
Desc: Strives to give a global picture of world agricultural output. Contains statistics for land use and irrigation, population, production indices for crops and livestock, yield by country for every type of food crop, and more.

LC HD1751 .A5 HD9282.U3A28 **ISSN** 0501-4670
DD 338.1/0973 S 381/.41/710973 US

FEDERAL MILK ORDER MARKET STATISTICS. (FEDERAL MILK ORDER MARKET STATISTICS. ANNUAL SUMMARY / UNITED STATES DEPARTMENT OF AGRICULTURE, AGRICULTURAL MARKETING SERVICE.). **Added/Corp** United States. Agricultural Marketing Service. United States. Consumer and Marketing Service. (1962)-. English. Thirteen times a year (monthly plus 1 annual end of the year report). Free on request. US Department of Agriculture / Federal Milk Order Market Statistics, Agricultural Marketing Service, 14th Street & Independence Avenue SW, #2768, Washington DC 20250. **Tel** (202)720-7461, FAX (202)720-4844. **ED** John P. Rourke (editor's address: PO Box 96456, Washington, DC 20090-6456). **Circ:** 600. available on microfiche (Vols. for (1982-) distributed to depository libraries). ***Continues*** *Federal Milk Order Market Statistics. Supplement.*
Desc: Data on the amount of milk marketed by dairy farmers, prices paid for milk, and production and consumption of milk and dairy products.

LC HD9483.I4 F47
DD 338.4/766862/09541 II

FERTILISER & ALLIED AGRICULTURAL STATISTICS, NORTHERN REGION. **VFOAT** Fertiliser and Allied Agricultural Statistics, Northern Region. English. One time a year. Rs15.00. Fertiliser Association of India, 10 Shaheed Jit Singh Marg, New Delhi 110067 India. **Tel** 011 91 11 667144, telex 031-73056.

LC Z5071 **ISSN** 0430-327X
DD 016.63 II

FERTILISER STATISTICS. **Main/Corp** Fertiliser Association of India. (1955)-. Statistical Publication. English. One time a year. $10.00. Fertiliser Association of India, 10 Shaheed Jit Singh Marg, New Delhi 110067 India. **Tel** 011 91 11 667144, telex 031-73056.

LC SB183 .F5 **ISSN** 0015-069X
DD 633/.05 UK

FIELD CROP ABSTRACTS. **Added/Corp** Commonwealth Agricultural Bureaux. Commonwealth Bureau of Pastures and Field Crops. Vol. 1 (Jan. 1948)-. Abstracting/Indexing Service. English. Twelve times a year. $940.00. CAB International Centre, Wallingford, Oxfordshire OX10 8DE United Kingdom. **Tel** 011 44 1491 832111, FAX 011 44 1491 833508, telex 847964 COMAGG G. **ED** J. R. Metcalfe. Index Available, published separately, free-automatically sent. **Ad Acc. Circ:** 1,300. available on magnetic tape and CD-ROM; available on an online database from Tsukuba Daigaku; CAN/OLE; STN International; JICST; DATA-STAR; DIMDI; ESA-IRS; BRS; DIALOG; and CISTI. Documents available from BLDSC.
Desc: Covers literature on agronomy, filed production, crop botany and physiology of all annual field crops, both temperate and tropical.
Ind/Abst Anim. Breed. Abstr.; Dairy Sci. Abstr.; For. Prod. Abstr.; For. Abstr.; Leis., Rec., Tour. Abstr.; Plant Breed. Abstr.; Protozoolog. Abstr.; Rural Dev. Abstr.; Weed Abstr.; World Agric. Econ. Rural Sociol. Abstr.

LC HD9259.C54 U569
DD 338.1/7/4309759 US

FLORIDA AGRICULTURAL STATISTICS. **Main/Corp** Florida Crop and Livestock Reporting Service. **Added/Corp** Florida. Division of Plant Industry. **VFOAT** Commercial Citrus Inventory. (1966?)-. Statistical Publication. English. USDA NASS Florida Agricultural Statistics Service, 1222 Woodward Street, Orlando FL 32803. **Tel** (407)648-6013.

LC HD9259.C54 F637A **ISSN** 0428-6413
DD 338.1/7/4309759 US

FLORIDA AGRICULTURAL STATISTICS. CITRUS SUMMARY. **Main/Corp** Florida Crop and Livestock Reporting Service. (1961/62)-. Statistical Publication. English. One time a year. $2.50. USDA NASS Florida Agricultural Statistics Service, 1222 Woodward Street, Orlando FL 32803. **Tel** (407)648-6013. ctrl circ. ***Continues in part*** *Florida Agricultural Statistics : Citrus Summary.*

LC HD9282.U5 F55
DD 331.7 US

FLORIDA AGRICULTURAL STATISTICS. DAIRY SUMMARY. **Added/Corp** Florida Agricultural Statistics Service. Florida Crop and Livestock Reporting Service. (19??)-. Statistical Publication. English. One time a year (July). USDA NASS Florida Agricultural Statistics Service, 1222 Woodward Street, Orlando FL 32803. **Tel** (407)648-6013. ctrl circ. ***Continues in part*** *Florida. Marketing Bureau. Agricultural Statistical Summary; Acreage, Production, Value, Disposition and Transportation Analysis, with Seasonal Comparisons.*

LC HD9433.U5 F55
DD 331.7 US

FLORIDA AGRICULTURAL STATISTICS. LIVESTOCK SUMMARY. **Added/Corp** Florida Crop and Livestock Reporting Service. Florida Agricultural Statistics Service. Florida. Marketing Bureau Section. Florida. Dept. of Agriculture. Division of Marketing. Florida. Dept. of Agriculture and Consumer Services. Division of Marketing. United States. Dept. of Agriculture. **VFOAT** Livestock Summary. (1963)-. Statistical Publication. English. One time a year (June). USDA NASS Florida Agricultural Statistics Service, 1222 Woodward Street, Orlando FL 32803. **Tel** (407)648-6013. ***Continues in part*** *Florida. Marketing Bureau. Agricultural Statistical Summary.*

ISSN 0381-3010
CN

GRAIN STATISTICS WEEKLY. Main/Corp Canadian Grain Commission. Economics and Statistics Division. Aug. 11, 1971-. Statistical Publication. English. One time a week. 26.00Can$ (non-delivered), 55.00Can$ (delivered) Licensee subscribers; 52.00Can$ (non-delivered), 105.00Can$ (delivered) other. Receiver General of Canada CDN Grain Commission, 600 303 Main Street, Winnipeg Manitoba R3C 3G8 Canada. **Tel** (204)983-1570, FAX (204)983-0248. ***Supersedes*** *Canadian Grain Position, 0410-5125.*

LC SB183 .H47 **ISSN** 1350-9837
DD 633.005/6 UK

●**GRASSLANDS AND FORAGE ABSTRACTS. Added/Corp** C.A.B. International. Division of Crop Production. (1993)-. Abstracting/Indexing Service. English. Twelve times a year. $560.00. CAB International Centre, Wallingford, Oxfordshire OX10 8DE United Kingdom. **Tel** 011 44 1491 832111, FAX 011 44 1491 833508, telex 847964 COMAGG G. **ED** J R Metcalfe. Index Available, published separately, free-automatically sent. **Ad Acc**. available on magnetic tape and CD-ROM; available on an online database from Tsukuba Daigaku; CAN/OLE; STN International; JICST; DATA-STAR; DIMDI; ESA-IRS; BRS; DIALOG; and CISTI. Documents available from BLDSC. ***Continues*** *Herbage Abstracts, 0018-0602.*
Desc: Concentrates on current research literature on the management and evaluation of sown grasslands, natural grasslands and fodder crops.
Ind/Abst Anim. Breed. Abstr.; Dairy Sci. Abstr.; For. Prod. Abstr.; For. Abstr.; Leis., Rec., Tour. Abstr.; Plant Breed. Abstr.; Rural Dev. Abstr.; Weed Abstr.; World Agric. Econ. Rural Sociol. Abstr.

LC Z5071 **ISSN** 0018-0602
DD 016.63 UK
TITLE CHANGE

HERBAGE ABSTRACTS. Added/Corp Commonwealth Bureau of Pastures and Field Crops, Hurley, Eng. (Berkshire). Vol. 1 (June 1931)-(19??). Abstracting/Indexing Service. English. CAB International Centre, Wallingford, Oxfordshire OX10 8DE United Kingdom. **Tel** 011 44 1491 832111, FAX 011 44 1491 833508, telex 847964 COMAGG G. **ED** J R Metcalfe. Index Available, published separately, free-automatically sent. **Ad Acc**. available on magnetic tape and CD-ROM; available on an online database from Tsukuba Daigaku; CAN/OLE; STN International; JICST; DATA-STAR; DIMDI; ESA-IRS; BRS; and DIALOG. ***Continued by*** *Grasslands and Forage Abstracts.*
Desc: Concentrates on current research literature on the management and evaluation of sown grasslands, natural grasslands and fodder crops.
Ind/Abst Anim. Breed. Abstr.; Dairy Sci. Abstr.; For. Prod. Abstr.; For. Abstr.; Leis., Rec., Tour. Abstr.; Plant Breed. Abstr.; Rural Dev. Abstr.; Weed Abstr.; World Agric. Econ. Rural Sociol. Abstr.

LC S53 .I3a **ISSN** 0094-1271
DD 338.1/09796 US

IDAHO AGRICULTURAL STATISTICS. Main/Corp Idaho Crop and Livestock Reporting Service. (1972)-. Statistical Publication. English. One time a year. $5.00. Idaho Agricultural Statistics Service, Box 1699, Boise ID 83701. **Tel** (208)334-1507.
Ind/Abst Stat. Ref. Index.

LC S55 .Z5 **ISSN** 0442-2562
DD 338.1 US

ILLINOIS AGRICULTURAL STATISTICS. (ILLINOIS AGRICULTURAL STATISTICS ANNUAL SUMMARY.). [Ill. agric. stat.]. **Added/Corp** Illinois Cooperative Crop Reporting Service. United States. Dept. of Agriculture. Statistical Reporting Service. United States. Dept. of Agriculture. Economics, Statistics, and Cooperative Service. Illinois. Bureau of Agricultural Statistics. Illinois. Agricultural Statistics Section. Illinois. Bureau of Agricultural Statistics. Division of Marketing. United States. National Agricultural Statistics Service. Illinois Agricultural Statistics Service. (1951)-. Government Publication. English. One time a year. $5.00. US Department of Agriculture / National Agricultural Statistics Service (NASS), Room 5829 South Building, Washington DC 20250. **Tel** (202)720-4020, FAX (314)875-5231. ctrl circ.

FR

IMAGES ECONOMIQUES DES ENTREPRISES. INDUSTRIES AGRICOLES ET ALIMENTAIRES AU ... . Added/Corp Institut National de la Statistique et des Etudes Economiques (France). **VFOAT** Industries Agricoles et Alimentaires au ... . (19??)-. French. One time a year. Institut National de la Statistique et des Etudes Economiques, 18 Bd Adolphe Pinard, 75675 Paris 14 France.

LC Z
DD 016.63 US

IOWA AGRICULTURAL STATISTICS. Added/Corp Iowa Agricultural Statistics. United States. National Agricultural Statistics Service. Iowa State University. Extension to Agriculture. (199?)-. Statistical Publication. English. One time a year. $7.50. Iowa Department of Agriculture, 833 Federal Building, 210 Walnut Street, Des Moines IA 50309. **Tel** (515)284-4340. ***Continues*** *Agricultural Statistics (Des Moines, IA).*

LC HD9086.J3 J45 **ISSN** 0447-5321
DD 331.7 JA

JAPAN COTTON STATISTICS AND RELATED DATA, THE. Added/Corp Nippon Menka Kyokai. Menka Keizai Kenkyujo. (19??)-. English. One time a year. $35.00. Japan Cotton Traders Association, 2 9 Awajimachi 3 Chome Chuo Ku, Osaka 541 Japan. **Tel** 011 81 6 201 2215, FAX 011 81 6 231 5122, telex 0524-2177-JCTA-J.
Desc: Covers the cotton trade.

LC Z5071 **ISSN** 0019-6363
DD 016.63 II

JOURNAL OF THE INDIAN SOCIETY OF AGRICULTURAL STATISTICS. [J. Indian soc. agric. stat.]. **Main/Corp** Indian Society of Agricultural Statistics. (March 1948)-. Statistical Publication. English (Hindi). Three times a year. $45.00. Institute of Agricultural Research Statistics, Post Box 310, New Delhi 12 India. **Tel** 581861. **(Subscription address:** Prints India, 11 Darya Ganj, New Delhi 110002 India. **Tel** 011 91 11 3268645, FAX 011 91 11 3275542, telex 31-61087 PRIN-IN.) **ED** Prem Narain. **Bk Rev**. **Circ:** 600 (ctrl).
Desc: The journal publishes original articles in statistics and its application to agriculture and allied fields; also reviews books and periodicals recently brought out.
Ind/Abst AGRICOLA; Math. Rev.; Plant Breed. Abstr.; Stat. Theory Method Abstr. (1959-1963, 1969-1971, 1973-1975, 1977-1978, 1986-1987).

LC S328 .K67
DD 630.096 SA

KORTBEGRIP VAN LANDBOUSTATISTIEK. Added/Corp South Africa. Division of Agricultural Marketing Research. South Africa. Dept. of Agriculture. Division of Economic Services. South Africa. Agricultural Economic Trends Division. South Africa. Directorate Agricultural Economic Trends. **VFOAT** Abstract of Agricultural Statistics. (19??)-. Afrikaans (English). One time a year. $4.47. Directorate Divisio Agricultural Information, Private Bag X246, Pretoria 0001 South Africa. **Tel** 011 27 12 2062183.

LC HA1320.B2 A32 HD1960.B2 B27
DD 314.3/46 S 338.1/0943/46 GW

LAND- UND FORSTWIRTSCHAFT, DIE. Main/Corp Statistisches Landesamt Baden-Wurttemberg. German.

LC S **ISSN** 0436-5569
DD 630 NE

LANDBOUWCIJFERS. Added/Corp Landbouw-Economisch Instituut. Netherlands. Centraal Bureau voor de Statistiek. **VFOAT** Agricultural Data. (1954)-. Dutch. One time a year. $41.80. Landbouw-Economisch Instituut, Postbus 29703, 2502 LS Hague Netherlands. **Tel** 011 31 70 3308330, FAX 011 31 70 615624. **ED** W. van Veen. Index available. **Circ:** 2,200. ***Continues*** *Zakboekje - Landbouw-Economisch Instituut.*
Desc: Statistical data on number and size of agricultural holdings, income, production, means of production, and areas in Dutch agriculture.

LC S
DD 630 BE

LANDBOUWSTATISTIEKEN. Main/Corp Institut National de Statistique (Belgium). (1967)-. Periodical. Dutch (French). Five times a year. $44.77. Institut National de Statistique / Belgium, rue de Louvain 44, 1000 Brussels Belgium. **Tel** 011 32 2 5486211, FAX 011 32 2 5486367. **Circ:** 400 (ctrl).
Desc: Agricultural statistics.

LC S245 .L19
DD 338.1/09489 DK

LANDBRUGSSTATISTIK. Added/Corp Danmarks Statistik. **VFOAT** Agricultural Statistics. (19??)-. Danish (English). One time a year. kr60.66. Danmarks Statistik, Sejrgade 11, DK-2100 Copenhagen Denmark. **Tel** 011 45 3 9173917, FAX 011 45 31 18 48 01, telex 1 62 36. ***Continues*** *Landbrugsstatistik Herunder Gartneri Og Skovbrug.*

LC Z5071 **ISSN** 0812-2598
DD 016.63 AT

LIVESTOCK AND LIVESTOCK PRODUCTS, AUSTRALIA. [Livest. livest. prod. Aust.]. **Added/Corp** Australian Bureau of Statistics. (1982)-. English. One time a year. 21.40Aus$. Australian Bureau of Statistics, PO Box 2796Y, Melbourne 3001 Australia. **Tel** 011 61 3 6157843. ***Continues*** *Livestock Australia.*
Desc: Numbers of cattle and sheep classified by age, sex and purpose; numbers of pigs and poultry; lambing; exports of livestock and livestock products; and more.

AT

LIVESTOCK AND LIVESTOCK PRODUCTS, SOUTH AUSTRALIA. Added/Corp Australian Bureau of Statistics. (19??)-. English. One time a year. 16.00Aus$. Australian Bureau of Statistics, PO Box 2796Y, Melbourne 3001 Australia. **Tel** 011 61 3 6157843.
Desc: Number of cattle and sheep classified by age, sex and purpose, number of pigs and poultry, lambing, exports of livestock and livestock products, consumption of selected livestock products, livestock slaughtering, etc.

LC HD9428.A83 W465
DD 338.1/76/009941 AT

LIVESTOCK AND LIVESTOCK PRODUCTS, WESTERN AUSTRALIA. Added/Corp Australian Bureau of Statistics. Western Australian Office. (19??)-. English. One time a year. 16.30Aus$. Australian Bureau of Statistics, PO Box 2796Y, Melbourne 3001 Australia. **Tel** 011 61 3 6157843.
Desc: Number of cattle and sheep classified by age, sex and purpose; number of pigs and poultry; lambing; exports of livestock and livestock products, consumption of selected livestock products, livestock slaughtering, etc.

LC SF
DD 636 AT

LIVESTOCK PRODUCTS, AUSTRALIA. Added/Corp Australian Bureau of Statistics. (19??)-. Periodical. English. Twelve times a year. 98.66Aus$. Australian Bureau of Statistics, PO Box 2796Y, Melbourne 3001 Australia. **Tel** 011 61 3 6157843.
Desc: Provides statistics on livestock slaughterings, meat production, milk intake by factories, market milk sales by factories, receivals of wool by brokers and dealers, exports of meat and stocks of frozen meat.

CN

●**LIVESTOCK STATISTICS.** (Apr. 1993)-. English. Four times a year. 144.00Can$ Canada; $173.00 US; $202.00 other. Statistics Canada Publications Sales and Services, R.H. Coats Building 6th Floor, Ottawa Ontario K1A 0T6 Canada. **Tel** (613)951-5078, (800)267-6677, FAX (613)951-1584, telex 053-3585. ***Formed by the union of*** *Livestock Report (1985), 0828-3095; Live Stock and Animal Products Statistics, 0068-7154; Fur Production, 0318-787X* ***and*** *Report on Fur Farms, 0318-7888.*

LC S **ISSN** 0784-8404
DD 630 FI
UDC 311.3
CODEN 630

MAA- JA METSATALOUS (HELSINKI. 1988). (1988)-. Finnish (Swedish and English). One time a year (Oct.). Fmk190.00. Information Centre of the Ministry of Argriculture and Forestry Statistics, PO Box 250, Liisankatu 8, SF-00171 Helsinki Finland. **Tel** 358 0 134 211, FAX 358 0 1342 1573.
Desc: A national compendium of agricultural statistics which serves as a source of and a guide to statistical informations.

LC S242.F5 A3
DD 630 FI

MAATALOUSTILASTOLLINEN KUUKAUSIKATSAUAS. MONTHLY REVIEW OF AGRICULTURAL STATISTICS. Main/Corp Finland. Maatilahallitus. Tilastotoimisto. **Added/Corp** Finland. Maatilahallitus. Tilastotoimisto. Monthly Review of Agricultural Statistics. **VFOAT** Monthly Review of Agricultural Statistics. (1950)-. Finnish (English and Swedish). Twelve times a year. Fmk240.00. Information Centre of the Ministry of Argriculture and Forestry Statistics, PO Box 250, Liisankatu 8, SF-00171 Helsinki Finland. **Tel** 358 0 134 211, FAX 358 0 1342 1573. Index available. **Circ:** 1,500. ***Continues*** *Finland. Maataloushallitus. Tilastotoimisto. Maataloustilastollinen Kuukausikatsaus.*
Desc: News and information on agriculture. Statistics on dairies and slaughterhouses yields and used of arable land and numbers of livestocks.

LC Z5071 **ISSN** 0267-2987
DD 016.63 UK

MAIZE ABSTRACTS. Added/Corp Commonwealth Agricultural Bureaux. International Maize and Wheat Improvement Center. Vol. 1, No. 1 (Jan. 1985)-. Abstracting/Indexing Service. English. Six times a year. $480.00. CAB International Centre, Wallingford, Oxfordshire OX10 8DE United Kingdom. **Tel** 011 44 1491 832111, FAX 011 44 1491 833508, telex 847964 COMAGG G. **Circ:** 850. available on magnetic tape and CD-ROM; available on an online database from Tsukuba Daigaku; CAN/OLE; STN International; JICST; DATA-STAR; DIMDI; ESA-IRS; CISTI; BRS; and DIALOG. ***Continues*** *Maize Quality Protein Abstracts, 0305-9162.*
Desc: Covers plant breeding and genetics, plant physiology, soil science, pests and diseases, agricultural engineering, crop science, seeds and grains, weeds and weed control, agricultural economics, nutrition and quality.

ISSN 0713-3359
DD 338.1/097127 CN

MANITOBA AGRICULTURE STATISTICS. [Manit. agric. stat.]. **Added/Corp** Manitoba. Dept. of Agriculture. Statistics Canada.

Manitoba. Dept. of Agriculture. Statistics Section. July 1979-. Periodical. English. Free. Manitoba Department of Agriculture Statistics Section, 903-401 York Avenue, Winnipeg Manitoba R3C 0P8 Canada. **Tel** (204)945-3503, FAX (204)945-8692. **ED** Errol T Lewis. **Circ:** 300-600 (ctrl).
Desc: Major responsibility is to acquire and provide selected data on Manitoba agriculture for use by government, farm organizations and farmers, researchers and the general public.

LC HD2022 .M33
DD 630 SP
MANUAL DE ESTADISTICA AGRARIA. **Added/Corp** Spain. Ministerio de Agricultura. Secretaria General Tecnica. (19??)-. Statistical Publication. Spanish. One time a year. 200ptas. Ministerio Agricultura, Centro de Publicaciones, Calle Alfonso XII 56, 28071 Madrid Spain. **Tel** 011 34 1 3475551, FAX 011 34 1 3475722.

LC S
DD 630 US
MARYLAND AGRICULTURAL STATISTICS SUMMARY FOR... . **Added/Corp** Maryland. Dept. of Agriculture. Maryland Agricultural Statistics Service. **VFOAT** Maryland Agricultural Statistics. (19??)-. Periodical. English. One time a year. free. Maryland Department of Agriculture / Annapolis, Agricultural Statistics Service, 50 Harry S Truman Parkway, Annapolis MD 21401.
Desc: Summary of the major series of agricultural statistics compiled by the Maryland Agricultural Statistics Service. Includes crop production data, livestock and poultry numbers, production, prices, and income. Provides two years of county data for selected data series.

LC S73 .N48A **ISSN** 0092-9794
DD 338.1/09774 US
MASSACHUSETTS AGRICULTURAL STATISTICS. **Main/Corp** New England Crop and Livestock Reporting Service. **VFOAT** Agricultural Statistics, Massachusetts. (1972)-. English. One time a year. Massachusetts Department of Food and Agriculture, 100 Cambridge Street, Room 2103, Boston MA 02202. **Tel** (617)727-3003, FAX (617)727-7235.

LC S230.D67 M45
DD 638.0944 FR
MEMENTO DE STATISTIQUE AGRICOLE : DORDOGNE. French. Ministere de l'Agriculture, Direction Departementale de l'Agriculture Service Statistique, 7 Place Francheville, 24016 Perigueux France.

LC HD9015.A1 L36 **ISSN** 1014-8159
DD 338.1/3/094021 LU
MERCADOS AGRARIOS. PRECIOS / COMISION DE LAS COMUNIDADES EUROPEAS / LANDSBRUGSMARKEDER. PRISER / KOMMISSIONEN FOR DE EUROPAEISKE FAELLESSKABER / AGRICULTURAL MARKETS. PRICES / COMMISSION OF THE EUROPEAN COMMUNITIES. **Added/Corp** Commission of the European Communities. Office for Official Publications of the European Communities. **VFOAT** Landbrugsmarkeder. Priser; Agricultural Markets. Prices. (1990)-. Periodical. Spanish (Multiple languages). Four times a year. Office for Official Publications of the European Communities, 2 rue Mercier, 2985 Luxembourg Luxembourg. **Tel** 011 352 499281, FAX 011 352 292942763. ***Continues*** *Landbrugsmarkeder. Priser (Monthly), 0250-9601.*
Desc: World market prices and official support prices for products under the EC common agricultural policy.

LC HD1940.5 .A28 **ISSN** 0238-7891
HU
MEZOGAZDASAGI ELELMISZERIPARI STATISZTIKAI ZSEBKONYU. **VFOAT** Mezogazdasagi Zsebkonyv. Hungarian. One time a year. 71.00ft. Statisztikai Kiado Vallalat, PO Box 99, H-1033 Budapest 3 Hungary. **Tel** 803-311, telex 22-6699-SKV-H. **Ad Acc. Circ:** 3,500.
Desc: Statistical data on farming results such as the value, sale and price of agricultural products. It also includes information on the cultivation of plants, livestock farming, forestry, food industry and weather conditions.

ISSN 0026-900X
SP
MOLINERIA Y PANADERIA. [Molin. panad.]. (1906)-. Abstracting/Indexing Service. Spanish. Twelve times a year. $220.00. Montagu Editores, Ausias Marc 25, 1RO, 08010 Barcelona Spain. **Tel** 011 34 3 3182082, FAX 011 34 3 3025083.
Ind/Abst AGRICOLA.

LC HD1775.M9 M6
DD 338.1 US
MONTANA AGRICULTURAL STATISTICS. **Added/Corp** Montana Crop and Livestock Reporting Service. Montana. Dept. of Agriculture, Labor, and Industry. United States. Bureau of Agricultural Economics. Montana. Dept. of Agriculture. United States. Agricultural Marketing Service. United States. Dept. of Agriculture. Statistical Reporting Service. United States. Dept. of Agriculture. Economics, Statistics, and Cooperatives Service. Vol. 1 (1946)-. English. One time a year. $5.00. Montana Department of Agricultural Statistics, PO Box 4369, Helena MT 59604. **Tel** (406)449-5303, FAX (406)449-5330.

US
MONTANA AGRICULTURAL STATISTICS BULLETIN. (19??)-. Bulletin. English. One time a year (November). $5.00. Montana Department of Agricultural Statistics, PO Box 4369, Helena MT 59604. **Tel** (406)449-5303, FAX (406)449-5330.

LC S
DD 630 FR
MUTUALITE SOCIALE AGRICOLE EN ... / MSA, MUTUALITE SOCIALE AGRICOLE, LA. **Main/Corp** Mutualite Sociale Agricole (France). **VFOAT** Statistiques; Resultats d'Ensemble. (1984)-. French. One time a year. C.C.M.S.A., Direction du Financement et des Statistique Etudes Financieres, 8-10 rue d'Astorg, 75380 Paris Cedex 08 France. ***Continues*** *Statistiques (Caisses Centrales de Mutualite Sociale Agricole (France)).*

LC Z5071
DD 016.63 US
NEBRASKA AGRICULTURAL STATISTICS. **Added/Corp** Nebraska Crop and Livestock Reporting Service. Nebraska. Dept. of Agriculture. Nebraska. Dept. of Agriculture and Inspection. (19??)-. Statistical Publication. English. One time a year. $5.00. USDA Statistical Reporting Service, PO Box 81069, Lincoln NE 68501. **Tel** (402)471-5541.

LC S **ISSN** 0196-0636
DD 630 US
NEVADA AGRICULTURAL STATISTICS. **Main/Corp** Nevada Crop and Livestock Reporting Service. Abstracting/Indexing Service. English. One time a year. Free. Agricultural Statistician, PO Box 8888, Reno NV 89507.

LC HD1775.N6 N4 **ISSN** 0077-8540
DD 630 US
NEW MEXICO AGRICULTURAL STATISTICS. [N.M. agric. stat.]. **Added/Corp** New Mexico Crop and Livestock Reporting Service. New Mexico. Dept. of Agriculture. United States. Dept. of Agriculture. Statistical Reporting Service. Field Operations Division. United States. National Agricultural Statistics Service. Vol. 1 (1962)-. Statistical Publication. English. One time a year. Free on request. USDA / New Mexico, PO Box 1809, Las Cruces NM 88004. **Tel** (505)525-6023. **ED** Don Gerhardt. **Circ:** 1,500 (ctrl).
Desc: New Mexico agricultural statistics.
Ind/Abst Stat. Ref. Index.

LC Z5074.S7 N45A **ISSN** 0110-165X
DD 016.6314/9931 NZ
NEW ZEALAND SOIL BUREAU BIBLIOGRAPHIC REPORT. [N.Z. Soil Bur. bibl. rep.]. No. 1- 1971-. English. Irregular. New Zealand Soil Bureau, Department of Scientific and Industrial Research, Private Bag, Lower Hutt New Zealand. **Tel** 673 119.
Desc: Bibliographic details of subjects of interest in soil science.
Ind/Abst AGRICOLA [Select. Cov.]; GeoRef.

LC HD9016.K6 N6
DD 338.17 KO
NONGCHON MULKA CHONGNAM. **VFOAT** Statistics on Prices in Rural Areas. English (Korean). Nongop Hyoptong Chohap Chunganghoe, 75 Chungjongno 1-ka Chung-ku, Seoul Korea.

LC HD2095.5 .A489
DD 630 KO
NONGOP KIBAN CHOSONG SAOP TONGGYE YONBO. **VFOAT** Yearbook of Land and Water Development Statistics. English (Korean). One time a year. Agricultural Development Corporation, 487 Poli-ri, Euiwangeub Siheung-gun, Kyonggi-do South Korea.

LC Z5075.J3 J36A
DD 016.63 JA
NORIN-SUISANGYO NI KANSURU CHIIKI BUNSEKISHO SORAN. **Main/Corp** Japan. Norin Suisansho. Keizaikyoku. Tokei Johobu. Kikaku Johoka. (1977)-. Japanese. Norin Tokei Kyokai, (Association of Agriculture & Forestry Statistics), 11-14 Meguro 2 Chome, Meguroku Tokyo 153 Japan. ***Continues*** *Norin-Suisangyo Ni Kansuru Bhiiki Bunsekisho Soran.*

LC S
DD 630 CU
NORMA CUBANA. **Main/Corp** Cuba. Direccion General de Normas. (1960)-. Spanish.
Ind/Abst Agric. Eng. Abstr.; For. Prod. Abstr. (1991-).

LC S99 .Z28 **ISSN** 0737-1624
DD 338.1/09784 US
Pr Rev.
NORTH DAKOTA AGRICULTURAL STATISTICS (FARGO, N.D.). (NORTH DAKOTA AGRICULTURAL STATISTICS.). [N.D. agric. stat.]. **Added/Corp** North Dakota Crop and Livestock Reporting Service. North Dakota Agricultural Experiment Station (Fargo) United States. Dept. of Agriculture. Economics, Statistics, and Cooperatives Service. North Dakota State University. United States. Dept. of Agriculture. Statistical Reporting Service. **VFOAT** Agricultural Statistics. (19??)-. Statistical Publication. English. One time a year. $10.00. Extension Communications, PO Box 3166, North Dakota State University, Fargo ND 58105. **Tel** (701)239-5306, FAX (701)239-5613. Index available. cum. index. **Circ:** 2,000. ***Continues*** *North Dakota Crop & Livestock Statistics.*

LC SF95 .N867 **ISSN** 0309-135X
DD 636.08/5/05 UK
NUTRITION ABSTRACTS AND REVIEWS. SERIES B. LIVESTOCK FEEDS AND FEEDING. (NUTRITION ABSTRACTS AND REVIEWS, B: LIVESTOCK FEEDS AND FEEDING.). [Nutr. abstr. rev., Ser. B, Livest. feeds feed.]. **Added/Corp** Commonwealth Bureau of Nutrition. **VFOAT** Nutrition Abstracts & Reviews, Series B, Livestock Feeds and Feeding. Vol. 47 (Jan. 1977)-. Abstracting/Indexing Service. English. Twelve times a year. $625.00. CAB International Centre, Wallingford, Oxfordshire OX10 8DE United Kingdom. **Tel** 011 44 1491 832111, FAX 011 44 1491 833508, telex 847964 COMAGG G. **ED** D. J. Fleming. **Ad Acc. Circ:** 1,500. available on magnetic tape and CD-ROM; available on an online database from Tsukuba Daigaku; CAN/OLE; STN International; JICST; DATA-STAR; DIMDI; ESA-IRS; CISTI; BRS; and DIALOG. ***Continues in part*** *Nutrition Abstracts and Reviews, 0029-6619.*
Desc: Reviews highlights aspects of particular importance to animal nutrition research centres, agricultural colleges, feed suppliers and manufacturers, school of veterinary science, animal health specialists and aquaculturalists.
Ind/Abst AgBiotech News Inf.; Dairy Sci. Abstr.; Fish Rev. (Jan. 1989-July 1992); Index Vet.; Nutr. Abstr. Rev., Ser. B, Live Feeds and Feed.; Pig News Inf.; Soyabean Abstr.; Wildl. Rev. (Jan. 1989-July 1992).

LC SF191
DD 636.2 AT
OFFICIAL HERD RECORDING STATISTICS. **Main/Corp** New South Wales. Dept. of Agriculture. Division of Dairying. (1975/76)-. Statistical Publication. English. New South Wales Department of Agriculture / Division of Dairying, Sydney NSW Australia.

LC S103 .O38
DD 338.1/09766 US
OKLAHOMA AGRICULTURAL STATISTICS. **Added/Corp** Oklahoma. State Dept. of Agriculture Oklahoma Crop and Livestock Reporting Service. (1976)-. English. One time a year. $5.00. Oklahoma State Department of Agriculture, 2800 North Lincoln Boulevard, Oklahoma City OK 73105. **Tel** (405)521-3864, FAX (405)521-4912. **ED** Barry Bloyd. **Circ:** 2,000 (ctrl). ***Continues*** *Oklahoma Agriculture.*
Desc: Crop and livestock production estimates at state, district, and county level for the state of Oklahoma.

ISSN 0279-7712
US
OKLAHOMA FARM STATISTICS. (OKLAHOMA FARM STATISTICS / OKLAHOMA CROP & LIVESTOCK REPORTING SERVICE.). Vol. 1, No. 1 (Jan. 20, 1981)-. Government Publication. English. Twenty-four times a year. $10.00. US Department of Agriculture / National Agricultural Statistics Service (NASS), Room 5829 South Building, Washington DC 20250. **Tel** (202)720-4020, FAX (314)875-5231.

LC HD9490.5.P343 M46
DD 338.1/73851/09595 MY
PALMOIL STATISTICAL HANDBOOK. (1980)-. Statistical Publication. English. $5.00. Porla, PO Box 2184, Kuala Lumpur 01-02 Malaysia.

LC Z6915 .P43
DD 016.6314 IE
PEAT ABSTRACTS. **Added/Corp** Bord na Mona. (1946-). Oifig Ealadhanta. (19??)-. Abstracting/Indexing Service. English. Three times a year. $22.50. Peat Abstracts, Bord na Mona, Research & Development Department, Newbridge Co Kildare Ireland. **Tel** 011 353 45 33106. **ED** Tony McKenna. **Circ:** 400 (ctrl).
Desc: Abstracts world literature on all aspects of peat production and utilization for fuel, horticulture and general peatland development.
Ind/Abst Coal Abstr.; Hortic. Abstr.

LC HD2080.6.Z9 S2742
DD 338.1/09595/4 MY
PERANGKAAN PERTANIAN SARAWAK. (1976)-. English (English). One time a year. ***Continues*** *Agricultural Statistics of Sarawak.*

LC S **ISSN** 0921-7169
DD 630 NE
UDC 339.562
PERIODIEKE RAPPORTAGE - LANDBOUW-ECONOMISCH INSTITUUT. (PERIODIEKE RAPPORTAGE.). (1982)-. Government Publication. Dutch. Irregular. Price varies per volume. Landbouw-Economisch Instituut, Postbus 29703, 2502 LS Hague Netherlands. **Tel** 011 31 70 3308330, FAX 011 31 70 615624.
Ind/Abst For. Abstr.; Potato Abstr.; World Agric. Econ. Rural Sociol. Abstr.

LC Z5074 **ISSN** 0143-9014
DD 016.63 UK
CODEN PNINEZ
PIG NEWS AND INFORMATION. [Pig news inf.]. **Added/Corp** Commonwealth Agricultural Bureaux. Vol. 1 (Mar. 1980)-. Abstracting/Indexing Service. English. Four times a year. $150.59. CAB International Centre, Wallingford, Oxfordshire OX10 8DE United Kingdom. **Tel** 011 44 1491 832111, FAX 011 44 1491 833508, telex 847964 COMAGG G. **ED** J. R. Metcalfe. **Ad Acc.** available on magnetic tape and CD-ROM; available on an online database from Tsukuba Daigaku; CAN/OLE; STN International; JICST; DATA-STAR; DIMDI; ESA-IRS; CISTI; BRS; and DIALOG. Documents available from The UnCover Company, SWETS.
Desc: Contains abstracts, reviews, news and views, short review articles, conference reports and an international diary of pig events. Acting as a single source for all those involved in the pig industry.
Ind/Abst AGRICOLA [Full Cov.]; Anim. Breed. Abstr.; Food Sci. Technol. Abstr.; Index Vet.; Nutr. Abstr. Rev., Ser. B, Live Feeds and Feed.; Life Sci. Collect. (1985-); Pig News Inf.; Postharvest News Inf.; Poult. Abstr.; Soyabean Abstr.; World Agric. Econ. Rural Sociol. Abstr.

ISSN 0791-3044
DD 636.4 IE
PIG STATISTICS, NUMBER AND WEIGHT OF PIGS SLAUGHTERED AT BACON FACTORIES. [Pig stat. number weight pigs slaught. bacon fact.]. (1984)-. Government Publication. English. Twelve times a year. 24.00p. Central Statistics Office / Ireland, Ardee Road, Dublin 6 Ireland. **Tel** 011 353 1 4977144.
Desc: Information on the slaughtering of pigs in bacon factories.

ISSN 0791-3095
DD 636.4 IE
PIG SURVEY AUGUST DUBLIN. [Pig surv. August Dublin]. (1987)-. Government Publication. English. One time a year. 2.00p. Central Statistics Office / Ireland, Ardee Road, Dublin 6 Ireland. **Tel** 011 353 1 4977144. ***Continues*** *Pig Enumeration, August (Dublin), 0791-3087.*

LC Z5071 **ISSN** 0032-0803
DD 016.63 UK
PLANT BREEDING ABSTRACTS. **Added/Corp** Commonwealth Bureau of Plant Breeding and Genetics, Cambridge, Eng. Imperial Bureau of Plant Breeding and Genetics, Cambridge, Eng. Vol. 1 (Jan./June 1930)-. Abstracting/Indexing Service. English. Twelve times a year. $835.07. CAB International Centre, Wallingford, Oxfordshire OX10 8DE United Kingdom. **Tel** 011 44 1491 832111, FAX 011 44 1491 833508, telex 847964 COMAGG G. **ED** J. R. Metcalfe. **Ad Acc. Circ:** 1,600. available on magnetic tape and CD-ROM; available on an online database from Tsukuba Daigaku; CAN/OLE; STN International; JICST; DATA-STAR; DIMDI; ESA-IRS; CISTI; BRS; and DIALOG. Documents available from BLDSC.
Desc: Covers the breeding, genetics, cytology, taxonomy and resistance to stresses, diseases and pests of individual crops.
Ind/Abst AgBiotech News Inf.; Plant Breed. Abstr.; Plant Genet. Resour. Abstr.; Seed Abstr.; Weed Abstr.; Wheat Barley Trit. Abstr.; World Agric. Econ. Rural Sociol. Abstr.

LC Z5071 **ISSN** 0305-9154
DD 016.63 UK
PLANT GROWTH REGULATOR ABSTRACTS. **Added/Corp** Commonwealth Agricultural Bureaux. Vol. 1 (Jan. 1975)-. Abstracting/Indexing Service. English. Four times a year. $253.25. CAB International Centre, Wallingford, Oxfordshire OX10 8DE United Kingdom. **Tel** 011 44 1491 832111, FAX 011 44 1491 833508, telex 847964 COMAGG G. **ED** J. L. Mayall. **Ad Acc. Circ:** 550. available on magnetic tape and CD-ROM; available on an online database from Tsukuba Daigaku; CAN/OLE; STN International; JICST; DATA-STAR; DIMDI; ESA-IRS; CISTI; BRS; and DIALOG.
Desc: Deals with the role of chemicals in plant growth regulation and in modifying beneficially the growth processes of plants.

LC SB129 .P59 **ISSN** 0957-7505
DD 631.55 UK
Pr Rev.
POSTHARVEST NEWS AND INFORMATION. **Added/Corp** C.A.B. International. Information Services. Vol. 1, No. 1 (Feb. 1990)-. Abstracting/Indexing Service. English. Six times a year. $430.00. CAB International Centre, Wallingford, Oxfordshire OX10 8DE United Kingdom. **Tel** 011 44 1491 832111, FAX 011 44 1491 833508, telex 847964 COMAGG G. **ED** AJ Rendell-Dunn. Index available. cum. index. **Bk Rev. Ad Acc. Circ:** 300. available on magnetic tape and CD-ROM; available on an online database from Tsukuba Daigaku; CAN/OLE; STN International; JICST; DATA-STAR; DIMDI; ESA-IRS; BRS; and DIALOG.
Desc: Covers the research into drying, cleaning, grading, sorting, handling, packing, storage, transport, postharvest physiology, storage pests, diseases and postharvest losses of food and non-food products of plant origin.
Ind/Abst Agric. Eng. Abstr. (1991-); Biocont. News Inf. (1991-); Biodeter. Abstr. (1991-); Curr. Aware. Biol. Sci., CABS; Food Sci. Technol. Abstr.; Grass. Forage Abstr.; Hortic. Abstr.; Ornamental Hort. (1991-); Plant Breed. Abstr.; Plant Grow. Reg. Abstr.; Postharvest News Inf.; Rev. Agric. Entomol.; Rev. Plant Pathol.; Seed Abstr.

LC Z5071 **ISSN** 0308-7344
DD 016.63 UK
POTATO ABSTRACTS. **Added/Corp** Commonwealth Agricultural Bureaux. Vol. 1 (Mar. 1976)-. Abstracting/Indexing Service. English. Four times a year. $290.00. CAB International Centre, Wallingford, Oxfordshire OX10 8DE United Kingdom. **Tel** 011 44 1491 832111, FAX 011 44 1491 833508, telex 847964 COMAGG G. **ED** M. S. Mahal PhD. Index available. **Ad Acc. Circ:** 350. available on magnetic tape and CD-ROM; available on an online database from Tsukuba Daigaku; CAN/OLE; STN International; JICST; DATA-STAR; DIMDI; ESA-IRS; CISTI; BRS; and DIALOG.
Desc: Covers all aspects of the potato (solanum tubersum), including breeding, agronomy, fertilizers, weeds, pests and diseases, botany and physiology, harvesting, storage and quality, processing, and utilization.

LC HD9235.P82 U67 **ISSN** 0739-0238
DD 338.1/7421/0973 US
POTATO STATISTICAL YEARBOOK. [Potato stat. yearb.]. (19??)-. Statistical Publication. English. One time a year. $20.00. National Potato Council, 9085 East Mineral Circle #155, Englewood CO 80112-3418. **Tel** (303)790-1141. **ED** Ron Walker. **Ad Acc. Circ:** 11,800.
Desc: Contains all statistics on potatoes--from production to varieties to costs to per consumption. Combines historical and current data on the potato industry.

ISSN 0306-1582
UK
POULTRY ABSTRACTS. **Added/Corp** Commonwealth Agricultural Bureaux. Vol. 1 (Jan. 1975)-. Abstracting/Indexing Service. English. Twelve times a year. $405.00. CAB International Centre, Wallingford, Oxfordshire OX10 8DE United Kingdom. **Tel** 011 44 1491 832111, FAX 011 44 1491 833508, telex 847964 COMAGG G. **ED** A. Rostron BSc. **Circ:** 500. available on magnetic tape and CD-ROM; available on an online database from Tsukuba Daigaku; CAN/OLE; STN International; JICST; DATA-STAR; DIMDI; ESA-IRS; CISTI; BRS; and DIALOG.
Desc: Covers the world periodical literature on all aspects of poultry production.

LC HD1751 .A5 HD9437.U6 **ISSN** 0565-1980
DD 338.1/0973 S 338.1/7/6500973 US
UDC 338.3:636.5(73)
POULTRY MARKET STATISTICS. **Main/Corp** United States. Agricultural Marketing Service. 1972-. Government Publication. English. One time a year. US Department of Agriculture / Agricultural Marketing Service / Washington, DC, Market News Branch, Fruit and Vegetable Division, Washington DC 20250. **Tel** (202)720-2745, (202)720-3343, FAX (202)720-7502. ***Continues*** *Poultry Market Statistics, 0565-1980.*

US
POULTRY MARKET STATISTICS ... ANNUAL SUMMARY / UNITED STATES DEPARTMENT OF AGRICULTURE, AGRICULTURAL MARKETING SERVICE. **Added/Corp** United States. Agricultural Marketing Service. United States. Poultry Market News Branch. (19??)-. Statistical Publication. English. One time a year. $15.00. USDS AMS / Poultry Division, 210 Walnut Street, Room 769, Des Moines IA 50309. **Tel** (515)284-4471.

ISSN 0791-3036
DD 637.09417 637.0212 IE
PRODUCTION OF MILK AND MILK PRODUCTS. [Prod. milk milk prod.]. (1987)-. Government Publication. English. One time a week. 40.00p. Central Statistics Office / Ireland, Ardee Road, Dublin 6 Ireland. **Tel** 011 353 1 4977144. **Bk Rev. Ad Acc.** ctrl circ. ***Continues*** *Production of Butter and Separated Milk.*
Desc: Production of butter and separated milk powder.

LC S
DD 630 US
PUBLISHED SEARCH BIBLIOGRAPHIES FROM THE NTIS BIBLIOGRAPHIC DATA BASE. AGRICULTURE AND FOOD. **Added/Corp** United States. National Technical Information Service. **VFOAT** Published Search Bibliographies from the N.T.I.S. Bibliographic Data Base. Agriculture and Food; Agriculture and Food. (19??)-. Trade Publication. English. Irregular. Free on request. National Technical Information Service - NTIS, Room 2027S, 5285 Port Royal Road, Springfield VA 22161. **Tel** (703)487-4630, (703)487-4660, (703)487-4650, FAX (703)321-8547, telex 89-9405.

LC HD2130.Z15 A3
DD 338.1/09689/4 ZA
QUARTERLY AGRICULTURAL STATISTICAL BULLETIN. **Main/Corp** Zambia. Ministry of Rural Development. Statistics Section. Bulletin. English. K50.00. Ministry of Rural Development, Statistics Section, Lusaka Zambia. ***Continues*** *Zambia. Ministry of Rural Development. Statistics Section. Statistical Bulletin.*

LC Z5075.T8 I63A SB111
DD 016.63/0913 NR
RECORD OF PUBLICATIONS. **Main/Corp** International Institute of Tropical Agriculture. (1980)-. English. International Institute of Tropical Agriculture, Oyo Road, PMB 5320, Ibadan Nigeria. **Tel** 022 400 300.

LC HA1173 .A27 SF196.A8
DD 314.36 AU
UDC 338.3:636.2(436)
RINDERRASSENERHEBUNG. **Main/Corp** Osterreichisches Statistisches Zentralamt. German. Kommissionsverlag Osterreichische Staatsdruckerei, Rennweg 12A, 1037 Vienna Austria.

LC HD2111.P32 M47C
DD 630 IS
SEDAROT STATISTIYOT. **Main/Corp** Ha-Merkaz Le-Tikhnun U-Fituah Haklai Ve-Hityashvuti. **VFOAT** Statistical Series. Hebrew (summaries and/or abstracts in English). Hakiria, POB 7011, Tel Aviv Israel.

LC Z **ISSN** 0141-0180
DD 016.631 UK
SEED ABSTRACTS. **Added/Corp** Commonwealth Agricultural Bureaux. International Food Information Service. Vol. 1 (1978)-. Abstracting/Indexing Service. English. Twelve times a year. $355.00. CAB International Centre, Wallingford, Oxfordshire OX10 8DE United Kingdom. **Tel** 011 44 1491 832111, FAX 011 44 1491 833508, telex 847964 COMAGG G. **ED** J. Armstrong. **Ad Acc. Circ:** 450. available on magnetic tape and CD-ROM; available on an online database from Tsukuba Daigaku; CAN/OLE; STN International; JICST; DATA-STAR; DIMDI; ESA-IRS; CISTI; BRS; and DIALOG.
Desc: Covers seed morphology and anatomy, physiology and development, chemistry, germination, production, storage and longevity, pests, diseases, breeding, selection, processing, assessment, testing, techniques, legislation.

LC S
DD 630 AG
SERIE ESTADISTICA (MENDOZA) (ARGENTINA : PROVINCE). (DIRECCION AGROPECUARIA). (SERIE ESTADISTICA.). **Added/Corp** Mendoza (Argentina : Province). Direccion Agropecuaria. No. 1 (1979)-. Statistical Publication. Spanish.

AG
SINTESIS ESTADISTICA - MINISTERIO DI ECONOMIA, JUNTA NACIONAL DE CARNES DE LA REPUBLICA ARGENTINA. **Main/Corp** Argentine Republic. Junta Nacional de Carnes. **Added/Corp** Argentine Republic. Junta Nacional de Carnes. Resena. (19??)-. Statistical Publication. Spanish.

LC S590 .S67 **ISSN** 0038-0792
DD 631.405 UK
CODEN SOFEAT
SOILS AND FERTILIZERS. [Soils fert.]. **Added/Corp** C.A.B. International. Information Services. Imperial Bureau of Soil Science. Commonwealth Bureau of Soil Science. Commonwealth Bureau of Soils. Vol. 1 (1938)-. Abstracting/Indexing Service. English. Twelve times a year. $1065.00. CAB International Centre, Wallingford, Oxfordshire OX10 8DE United Kingdom. **Tel** 011 44 1491 832111, FAX 011 44 1491 833508, telex 847964 COMAGG G. **Ad Acc. Circ:** 1,900. available on magnetic tape and CD-ROM; available on an online database from Tsukuba Daigaku; CAN/OLE; STN International; JICST; DATA-STAR; DIMDI; ESA-IRS; CISTI; BRS; and DIALOG. Documents available from CASDDS, BLDSC. ***Supersedes*** *Imperial Bureau of Soil Science. Monthly Letter.*
Desc: The major source of reference for specialists in the soil and fertilizer sciences.
Ind/Abst Chem. Abstr. (?-1984); Life Sci. Collect.

Agriculture —Abstracting, Bibliographies and Statistics

LC Z8825.76 .S65 PG3488.O4
DD 891.73/44
ISSN 0731-2261
US
SUSPENDED
SOLZHENITSYN STUDIES. [Solzhenitsyn stud.]. Vol. 1, No. 1 (Spring 1980)-Suspended with Vol. 2, No. 1 (1981). Periodical. English. Four times a year. $10.50. University Lancaster, Russian Soviet, Studies Department, Lancaster LA1 4YN United Kingdom.

LC S
DD 630
ISSN 03082970
UK
CEASED
SORGHUM AND MILLETS ABSTRACTS. Added/Corp Commonwealth Agricultural Bureaux. Vol. 1, No. 1 (Jan. 1976)-(19??). Abstracting/Indexing Service. English. CAB International Centre, Wallingford, Oxfordshire OX10 8DE United Kingdom. **Tel** 011 44 1491 832111, FAX 011 44 1491 833508, telex 847964 COMAGG G. **ED** A. M. Doroszenko BSc, PhD. **Ad Acc. Circ:** 250.
Desc: Produced by CABI in collaboration with the International Crops Research Institute for the Semi-Arid Tropics (ICRISAT), it attempts to disseminate useful scientific and technical information on sorghum and millets for the benefit of workers in the semi-arid tropics (SAT).

LC Z5071
DD 016.63
ISSN 0141-0172
UK
SOYABEAN ABSTRACTS. Added/Corp Commonwealth Agricultural Bureaux. International Food Information Service. (Oct. 1977)-. Abstracting/Indexing Service. English. Four times a year. $260.00. CAB International Centre, Wallingford, Oxfordshire OX10 8DE United Kingdom. **Tel** 011 44 1491 832111, FAX 011 44 1491 833508, telex 847964 COMAGG G. **ED** Susan E. Hill. **Ad Acc. Circ:** 250. available on magnetic tape and CD-ROM; available on an online database from Tsukuba Daigaku; CAN/OLE; STN International; JICST; DATA-STAR; DIMDI; ESA-IRS; CISTI; BRS; and DIALOG.
Desc: Covers breeding, agronomy, weeds, pests and diseases, botany and physiology, harvesting, storage and quality, economics, processing and utilization.

LC Z
DD 016.63
CN
SPECIAL BIBLIOGRAPHY. Added/Corp Ontario. Ministry of Agriculture and Food Library. No. 1-. Bibliography. English. Price varies per volume.

LC HG6047.C57 S7
DD 332.64/4
ISSN 0731-9576
US
STATISTICAL ANNUAL / COFFEE, SUGAR & COCOA EXCHANGE INC. [Stat. annu. - Coffee, Sugar Cocoa Exch.]. **Added/Corp** Coffee, Sugar & Cocoa Exchange, Inc. (1980)-. Statistical Publication. English. Four time a year. Coffee Sugar & Cocoa Exchange Inc, Four World Trade Center, New York NY 10048.

ISSN 0736-1092
US
STATISTICAL ANNUAL - MINNEAPOLIS GRAIN EXCHANGE. (STATISTICAL ANNUAL.). **Main/Corp** Minneapolis Grain Exchange. 99th (Year Ending Dec. 31, 1981)-. Statistical Publication. English. One time a year (August). $30.00. Minneapolis Grain Exchange, 400 South 4th Street, Suite 130, Minneapolis MN 55415. **Tel** (612)338-6212, FAX (612)339-1155. **ED** Jenny Hendrix. **Continues** Minneapolis Grain Exchange. Annual Report.

CN
STATISTICAL ANNUAL / THE WINNIPEG COMMODITY EXCHANGE. Added/Corp Winnipeg Commodity Exchange. (19??)-. Statistical Publication. English. One time a year. 13.60Can$. Winnipeg Commodity Exchange, 500-360 Main Street, Winnipeg Manitoba R3C 3Z4 Canada. **Tel** (204)925-5000, FAX (204)943-5448. **Circ:** 200-300. available on diskette.
Desc: Statistical publication concerning agricultural futures.

LC HD1751 .A5
DD 338.1/0973
US
STATISTICAL BULLETIN / UNITED STATES DEPARTMENT OF AGRICULTURE. VFOAT USDA Statistical Bulletin; U.S.D.A. Statistical Bulletin. No. 1 (Aug. 1923)-. Bulletin. English. Price varies per volume.
Ind/Abst Cot. Trop. Fibr. Abstr. Bibliogr.; Irr. Drain. Abstr.; Maize Abstr.; Nutr. Abstr. Rev., Ser. B, Live Feeds and Feed.; Nutr. Abstr. Rev., Ser. A, Hum. Exp.; Poult. Abstr.; Soils Fert.; Soyabean Abstr.; World Agric. Econ. Rural Sociol. Abstr.

LC S557.T752 S247
DD 630/.74/0972983
SP
STATISTICAL REPORT ON THE NATIONAL AGRICULTURAL EXHIBITION / REPUBLIC OF TRINIDAD & TOBAGO, CENTRAL STATISTICAL OFFICE. Statistical Publication. English. Government Printery / Trinidad, Central Statistical Office, 35 41 Queen Street, Port of Spain Trinidad. **Tel** (809)625-4970, FAX (809)625-3802.

LC HD1930.N65 S83
DD 338.1/09416
IE
STATISTICAL REVIEW OF NORTHERN IRELAND AGRICULTURE / DEPARTMENT OF AGRICULTURE FOR NORTHERN IRELAND. (1974/75)-. Statistical Publication. English. One time a year. £10.00. Northern Ireland Department of Agriculture, Dundonald House, Upper Newtownard, Belfast BT4 3SB 5RU United Kingdom. **Tel** 011 44 1232 650111.

LC HD3537 .R4
DD 334.058
II
STATISTICAL STATEMENTS RELATING TO THE COOPERATIVE MOVEMENT IN INDIA. Main/Corp Reserve Bank of India. **Added/Corp** India. Dept. of Statistics. India. Commercial Intelligence Dept. Reserve Bank of India. Statements Showing Progress of the Co-operative Movement in India. (19??)-. Statistical Publication. English. Reserve Bank of India, Economic Department, PO Box 1036, Bombay 400001 India.

LC S
DD 630
LU
●**STATISTICS IN FOCUS. AGRICULTURE, FORESTRY AND FISHERIES. Added/Corp** Statistical Office of the European Communities. **VFOAT** Agriculture, Forestry and Fisheries. (1995)-. Periodical. English (French and German). Fifty times a year. $320.00. Office for Official Publications of the European Communities, 2 rue Mercier, 2985 Luxembourg Luxembourg. **Tel** 011 352 499281, FAX 011 352 292942763. **(Subscription address:** Unipub, 4611 F Assembly Drive, Lanham MD 20706. **Tel** (800)274-4888, (301)459-7666.) **Continues** Rapid Reports. Agriculture, Forestry and Fisheries.
Ind/Abst Anim. Breed. Abstr.

LC Z5071
DD 016.63
AT
STATISTICS OF WESTERN AUSTRALIA: RURAL INDUSTRIES. Main/Corp Australia. Bureau of Statistics. Western Australian Office. (1972/73)-. Periodical. English. Irregular. **Continues** Statistics of Western Australia, Rural Industries.

LC S239 .A3854
DD 338.1/09492
NE
STATISTIEK VAN DE LAND- EN TUINBOUW / CENTRAAL BUREAU VOOR DE STATISTIEK, HOOFDAFDELING LANDBOUWSTATISTIEKEN. VFOAT Statistics on Agriculture. Dutch (summaries and/or abstracts in English). one time a year. Centraal Bureau voor de Statistiek, AFD ALG Zaken, Postbus 959, 2270 AZ Voorburg Netherlands. **Tel** 011 31 70 3373800, FAX 011 31 70 0387429, telex 32692 CBS NL.

LC SB176.I5 S8
DD 630
IO
STATISTIK TANAMAN BAHAN MAKANAN. Indonesian. Kantor Statistik Propinsi Bali, JL Raya Puputan, Denpasar Indonesia.

LC S230.N673 S7
DD 338.1/0944/27
ISSN 0243-7155
FR
STATISTIQUE AGRICOLE. PRINCIPAUX RENSEIGNEMENTS, REGIONS NORD-PAS DE CALAIS ET PICARDIE / MINISTERE DE L'AGRICULTURE, SERVICE REGIONAL DE STATISTIQUE AGRICOLE. Added/Corp France. Service Regional de Statistique Agricole Nord-Pas de Calais et Picardie. **VFOAT** Principaux Renseignements, Regions Nord-Pas de Calais et Picardie. (19??)-. French. One time a year. 49.00F. International Thomson Retail, 9889 Willow Creek Rd., San Diego CA 92131. **Continues** Statistique Agricole. Regions Nord-Picardie.
Desc: Significant data on agricultural statistics as of Dec. 31 of each year for the French departments Nord, Pas de Calais and Picardie.

LC HD1950.P35 S8
DD 630
FR
STATISTIQUE AGRICOLE : REGION PARISIENNE. French. Ministere de l'Agriculture, 78 rue de Varenne, 75007 Paris France. **Tel** 011 33 1 49554955 ext. 2718.

LC HD9014.C4 Q482
DD 338.1/09713/021
ISSN 0828-2501
CN
STATISTIQUES DE L'AGRICULTURE, DES PECHES ET DE L'ALIMENTATION. [Stat. agric. pech. aliment.]. (19??)-. French. Statistique Quebec, 117 rue St Andre, Quebec Quebec G1K 3Y3 Canada. **Tel** (514)283-2642.

LC HD2001 .S72
DD 630
ISSN 0108-5522
DK
STATISTISKE EFTERRETNINGER. LANDBRUG. VFOAT Landbrug. 1983 1-. Monographic series. Danish. Price varies per volume. Danmarks Statistik, Sejrgade 11, DK-2100 Copenhagen Denmark. **Tel** 011 45 3 9173917, FAX 011 45 31 18 48 01, telex 1 62 36. **Continues in part** Danmarks Statistik. Statistiske Efterretninger.
Desc: Statistics on production and prices, crops, cereal stocks, feeding stuff consumption, stocks of pigs and cattle, factor incomes, capital formation and forest fellings; includes volume and price indexes.

LC TP375 .T37
DD 016.664/12
ISSN 0957-5022
UK
SUGAR INDUSTRY ABSTRACTS. Added/Corp C.A.B. International. Information Services. C.A.B. International. Bureau of Horticulture and Plantation Crops. Tate & Lyle, Ltd. Vol. 52, No. 1 (January 1990)-. Abstracting/Indexing Service. English. Six times a year. $485.00. CAB International Centre, Wallingford, Oxfordshire OX10 8DE United Kingdom. **Tel** 011 44 1491 832111, FAX 011 44 1491 833508, telex 847964 COMAGG G. **ED** M. E. Cope BSc, MIInfSc. available on magnetic tape and CD-ROM; available on an online database from Tsukuba Daigaku; CAN/OLE; STN International; JICST; DATA-STAR; DIMDI; ESA-IRS; BRS; and DIALOG. **Continues** Tate & Lyle's Sugar Industry Abstracts.
Desc: Covers such topics as sugar processing, sugar factory equipment manufacture, sugar technology research and more.

LC S
DD 630
ISSN 1033-8772
AT
CEASED
SUMMARY OF CROPS AUSTRALIA. Added/Corp Australian Bureau of Statistics. (1987/1988)–(1993). Government Publication. English. Australian Bureau of Statistics, PO Box 2796Y, Melbourne 3001 Australia. **Tel** 011 61 3 6157843. **Formed by the union of** Crops and Pastures, Australia, 0813-3336; Fruit Australia and Agricultural Land Use and Selected Inputs, Australia.
Desc: Contains summary tables of data on agricultural land use, area and production of crops and pastures, tree numbers and production of orchard fruit, production of other fruit and grapes, and fertilizer usage.

LC S478
DD 630.9941
ISSN 1037-5678
AT
SUMMARY OF CROPS, WESTERN AUSTRALIA. [Summ. crops West. Aust]. **Added/Corp** Australian Bureau of Statistics. Western Australian Office. (1991)-. English. One time a year. 27.50Aus$. Australian Bureau of Statistics, PO Box 2796Y, Melbourne 3001 Australia. **Tel** 011 61 3 6157843. **Formed by the union of** Crops and Pastures, Western Australia, 0812-6801; Fruit, Western Australia, 1031-2250 **and** Agricultural Land Use and Selected Inputs, Western Australia, 0812-5627.
Desc: Area and land utilization of agricultural establishments, numbers of agricultural establishments by size of establishment, area artificially fertilized, area of irrigation, and more.

LC S115 .T46
DD 338.1/09768
ISSN 0497-2317
US
TENNESSEE AGRICULTURAL STATISTICS. Added/Corp Tennessee Crop Reporting Service. United States. Dept. of Agriculture. Statistical Reporting Service. United States. Dept. of Agriculture. Economics, Statistics, and Cooperatives Service. Tennessee. Dept. of Agriculture. (1963)-. Government Publication. English. one time a year (Aug.). Free on request. US Department of Agriculture / National Agricultural Statistics Service (NASS), Room 5829 South Building, Washington DC 20250. **Tel** (202)720-4020, FAX (314)875-5231.

LC HD9275.U7 T28
DD 338.1/77/09768
ISSN 0748-4119
US
TENNESSEE DAIRY STATISTICS. (TENNESSEE DAIRY STATISTICS.). [Tenn. dairy stat.]. **Added/Corp** Tennessee. Dairy Division. Tennessee. Food and Dairy Division. Tennessee Crop Reporting Service. **VFOAT** Tennessee Dairy Statistics and Summary. (1979)-. English.

LC S
DD 630
US
TEXAS AGRICULTURAL FACTS. Main/Corp Texas Crop and Livestock Reporting Service. (19??)-. Periodical. English. Twenty-four times a year. $10.00. Texas Crop and Livestock Reporting Service, PO Box 70, Austin TX 78767. **Tel** (512)482-5581.
Desc: Provides a summary of crop, livestock and other agricultural reports.

LC HD9417.T4 T49a
DD 338.1/7/6009764
ISSN 0091-1550
US
TITLE CHANGE
TEXAS LIVESTOCK STATISTICS. Main/Corp Texas Crop and Livestock Reporting Service. (19??)–(19??). English. Texas Agricultural Statistics

Service, PO Box 70, Austin TX 78767. **Tel** (512)482-5581. ***Merged into*** *Texas Agricultural Statistics.*

LC HD1751 .A5 HD9490.U5 **ISSN** 0146-8782
DD 338.1/0973 S 338.4/7/66430973 US

U.S. FATS AND OILS STATISTICS. **Main/Corp** United States. Dept. of Agriculture. Economic Research Service. **VAT** United States Fats and Oils Statistics. Government Publication. English. One time a year. US Department of Agriculture / Economic Research Service, 1301 New York Avenue, Room 208, Washington DC 20250. **Tel** (202)447-4111.

LC HD2151 .V34
DD 338.1/0994 AT

VALUE OF AGRICULTURAL COMMODITIES PRODUCED, AUSTRALIA. **Added/Corp** Australian Bureau of Statistics. (19??)-. English. One time a year. 22.40Aus$. Australian Bureau of Statistics, PO Box 2796Y, Melbourne 3001 Australia. **Tel** 011 61 3 6157843. **Circ:** 1,000.
Desc: Detailed statistics of the gross and local value of crops and pastures and grasses, fruits and nuts, vegetables, livestock products, livestock slaughterings by type, etc.

LC HD1775.V5 V478 HD1775.V5 A3 **ISSN** 0360-3830
DD 338.1/09755 S 338.1/09755/021 US

VIRGINIA AGRICULTURAL STATISTICS. [Va. agric. stat.]. **Main/Corp** Virginia Cooperative Crop Reporting Service. **Added/Corp** Virginia Agricultural Statistics Service. United States. National Agricultural Statistics Service. Virginia. Dept. of Agriculture and Consumer Services. Virginia Cooperative Crop Reporting Service. Virginia. Dept. of Agriculture and Commerce. United States. Dept. of Agriculture. Statistical Reporting Service. (19??)-. English. One time a year. US Department of Agriculture / National Agricultural Statistics Service (NASS), Room 5829 South Building, Washington DC 20250. **Tel** (202)720-4020, FAX (314)875-5231.

LC Z7951 **ISSN** 0175-8292
DD 016.64122 GW

VITIS, VITICULTURE AND ENOLOGY ABSTRACTS. [Vitis vitic. enol. abstr.]. **Added/Corp** Bundesforschungsanstalt fuer Rebenzuechtung Geilweilerhof. International Food Information Service. **VFOAT** Viticulture and Enology Abstracts. Vol. 23, No. 1 (March 1984)-. Abstracting/Indexing Service. English (French, German, Italian and Spanish). Four times a year. Comes with Vitis Berichte Ueber Rebenforschung. Vitis / Bundesanstalt fuer Zuechtungsforschung, Forschung Wein Geilweilerhof, D-76833 Siebeldingen Germany. **Tel** 011 49 6345 410. Index available. **Bk Rev. Circ:** 700 (ctrl). available on an online database from STN International; and IFIS. ***Separated from*** *Vitis, 0042-7500.*
Desc: Abstracts of scientific papers on viticulture, enology and grapevine breeding.

LC S125 .W37A **ISSN** 0095-4330
DD 338.1/09797 US

WASHINGTON AGRICULTURAL STATISTICS. **Main/Corp** Washington Crop and Livestock Reporting Service. English. Washington Agricultural Statistics Service, 417 West 4th Avenue, Olympia WA 98501. ***Continues*** *Annual Crop Report.*
Ind/Abst Stat. Ref. Index.

LC SB611 .W35 **ISSN** 0043-1729
DD 632/.58 UK

WEED ABSTRACTS. **Added/Corp** Weed Research Organization. British Weed Control Council. Commonwealth Agricultural Bureaux. (1952)-. Abstracting/Indexing Service. English. Twelve times a year. $450.00. CAB International Centre, Wallingford, Oxfordshire OX10 8DE United Kingdom. **Tel** 011 44 1491 832111, FAX 011 44 1491 833508, telex 847964 COMAGG G. **ED** J. R. Metcalfe. **Ad Acc. Circ:** 2,250. available on magnetic tape and CD-ROM; available on an online database from Tsukuba Daigaku; CAN/OLE; STN International; JICST; DATA-STAR; DIMDI; ESA-IRS; CISTI; BRS; and DIALOG.
Desc: Covers the literature on the control of weeds in annual and herbage crops, in vegetables, fruit, ornamental and plantation crops and in forestry; control of individual weed species, woody weeds and aquatic weeds, including weeds in non-agricultural situations.

ISSN 0160-4872
US

WEEKLY INSIDERS POULTRY REPORT. (Nov. 22, 1972)-. Periodical. English. One time a week. $292.00. Urner Barry Publications Inc., PO Box 389, Toms River NJ 08754. **Tel** (908)240-5330, (800)932-0617, FAX (908)341-0891. **ED** Bud O'Shaughnessy. **Circ:** 120. ***Continues in part*** *Weekly Insiders Poultry Letter, 0276-0274.*
Desc: Data for trucklot whole chickens, whole legs, slaughter, storage holdings, broiler production, chicken availability, U.S.D.A and industry news.

ISSN 0160-4910
US

WEEKLY INSIDERS TURKEY LETTER. (Nov. 22, 1972)-. Periodical. English. One time a week. $149.00. Urner Barry Publications Inc., PO Box 389, Toms River NJ 08754. **Tel** (908)240-5330, (800)932-0617, FAX (908)341-0891. **ED** Paul B. Brown. **Bk Rev. Ad Acc. Circ:** 260 (ctrl). ***Continues in part*** *Weekly Insiders Poultry Letter, 0276-0274.*
Desc: Turkey parts, storage stocks, slaughter, school lunch, poverty program purchases and meat production.

LC S127 .A12 HD1775.W4
DD 630/.9754 338.1/09754 US

WEST VIRGINIA AGRICULTURAL STATISTICS / WEST VIRGINIA CROP REPORTING SERVICE. English. One time a year. $5.00. West Virginia Agricultural Statistics, c/o State Department of Agriculture, Charleston WV 25305.

LC Z5071 **ISSN** 0706-8662
DD 016.63 CN

WHAT'S NEW IN PUBLICATIONS (EDMONTON). (WHAT'S NEW IN PUBLICATIONS.). **Added/Corp** Alberta. Dept. of Agriculture. Communications Branch. Vol. 1 (Jan. 1976)-. Periodical. English. Twelve times a year. Free on request. Alberta Agriculture / Market Analysis, 7000 113th Street, Edmonton Alberta T5K 2C8 Canada. **Tel** (403)427-2121, FAX (403)435-4725.
Desc: Brief listing of the available publications, brochures, factsheets, etc. from Alberta Agriculture. Also supplements annual publications list.

LC Z5071 **ISSN** 0265-7880
DD 016.63 UK

WHEAT, BARLEY AND TRITICALE ABSTRACTS. **Added/Corp** Commonwealth Agricultural Bureaux. International Maize and Wheat Improvement Center. Vol. 1, No. 1 (Feb. 1984)-. Abstracting/Indexing Service. English. Six times a year. $570.00. CAB International Centre, Wallingford, Oxfordshire OX10 8DE United Kingdom. **Tel** 011 44 1491 832111, FAX 011 44 1491 833508, telex 847964 COMAGG G. **Ad Acc. Circ:** 150. available on magnetic tape and CD-ROM; available on an online database from Tsukuba Daigaku; CAN/OLE; STN International; JICST; DATA-STAR; DIMDI; ESA-IRS; CISTI; BRS; and DIALOG. Documents available from BLDSC. ***Continues*** *Triticale Abstracts.*
Desc: Provides research findings and developments in these three cereals, and also rye.

LC S129 .W48 **ISSN** 0512-1329
DD 338.1/09775 US

WISCONSIN AGRICULTURAL STATISTICS. 1965-. English. One time a year. $5.00. Wisconsin Agricultural Statistics Service, PO Box 9160, Madison WI 53713. **Tel** (608)264-5317. **ED** Carrol Spencer. **Circ:** 3,000. ***Supersedes in part*** *Special Bulletin - Wisconsin Department of Agriculture.*
Desc: Contains crop and livestock statistical data.

LC HD1491 **ISSN** 0043-8219
DD 016.338 UK

WORLD AGRICULTURAL ECONOMICS AND RURAL SOCIOLOGY ABSTRACTS. [World Agric. Econ. Rural Sociol. Abstr.]. **Added/Corp** C.A.B. International. Information Services. Commonwealth Bureau of Agricultural Economics. International Association of Agricultural Librarians and Documentalists. International Association of Agricultural Economists. **VFOAT** World Agricultural Economics Abstracts. Vol. 1 (April 1959)-. Abstracting/Indexing Service. English. Twelve times a year. $725.00. CAB International Centre, Wallingford, Oxfordshire OX10 8DE United Kingdom. **Tel** 011 44 1491 832111, FAX 011 44 1491 833508, telex 847964 COMAGG G. **ED** J. R. Metcalfe. **Ad Acc. Circ:** 1,250. available on magnetic tape and CD-ROM; available on an online database from Tsukuba Daigaku; CAN/OLE; STN International; JICST; DATA-STAR; DIMDI; ESA-IRS; CISTI; BRS; and DIALOG. Documents available from BLDSC.
Desc: Provides a review of literature on a broad range of agricultural economics and rural sociology. Users include farm business managers, bankers, economists, investments analysts, planners and sociologists.
Ind/Abst Int. Dev. Abstr. (?-?).

LC S131 .W94 **ISSN** 0363-9339
DD 630/.9787 US

WYOMING AGRICULTURAL STATISTICS. **Added/Corp** Wyoming. Crop and Livestock Reporting Service. United States. Dept. of Agriculture. Statistical Reporting Service. University of Wyoming. Wyoming. Dept. of Agriculture. (1973)-. Government Publication. English. One time a year (Nov.). Free. US Department of Agriculture / National Agricultural Statistics Service (NASS), Room 5829 South Building, Washington DC 20250. **Tel** (202)720-4020, FAX (314)875-5231. **ED** Samuel J Hundley.
Desc: Statistics about agriculture in Wyoming at the state and county level on crops, livestock and prices.

NE

YEARBOOK OF AGRICULTURAL STATISTICS. (19??)-. English. One time a year. Fl63.60. SDU Uitgeverij, Postbus 20014, Christoffel Plantijnstraat, 2500 EA Den Haag Netherlands. **Tel** 011 31 70 3789911.

AGRICULTURAL ECONOMICS

LC HD1407 .C67 **ISSN** 0545-4441
DD 630 US
TITLE CHANGE

A.E. RES. [A.E. res.]. **Added/Corp** New York State College of Agriculture. Dept. of Agricultural Economics. New York State College of Agriculture and Life Sciences. Dept. of Agricultural Economics. **VFOAT** AE Res.; A.E. Research; AE Research. **VAT** Agricultural Economics Research. (July 1958)-(1993). Monographic series. English. New York State College, Department of Agricultural Economics, Ithaca NY. ***Continues in part*** *AE (New York State College of Agriculture. Dept. of Agricultural Economics).* ***Continued by*** *R.B. (New York State College of Agriculture and Life Sciences. Dept. of Agricultural, Resource, and Managerial Economics).*
Ind/Abst Bibliogr. Agric.

ISSN 0888-9651
DD 338 US

AAEA NEWSLETTER (AMES, IOWA). (AAEA NEWSLETTER.). [AAEA newsl.]. **Main/Corp** American Agricultural Economics Association. **Added/Corp** American Agricultural Economics Association. **VAT** American Agricultural Economics Association Newsletter. Vol. 1, No. 1 (Jan. 1979)-. Newsletter. English. Six times a year. $12.00. American Agricultural Economics Association, 1110 Buckeye Avenue, Ames IA 50011. **Tel** (515)233-3202, FAX (515)233-3101. **ED** Bruce Greenshields. **Ad Acc. Circ:** 5,000.

LC S469.P72 0654 **ISSN** 0324-9166
PL

ACTA ACADEMIAE AGRICULTURAE AC TECHNICAE OLSTENENSIS. OECONOMICA. (OECONOMICA.). [Acta Acad. Agric. Tech. Olst., Oecon.]. **Added/Corp** Akademia Rolniczo-Techniczna w Olsztynie. **VFOAT** Sel'Skohozajstvenno-Tehniceskaa Akademia v Ol'Styne - Ekonomika; Agricultural and Technical Academy in Olsztyn - Economics. (1986)-. Academic Scholarly Publication. Polish (summaries and/or abstracts in English and Russian; table of contents in English and Russian). Irregular. Price varies per volume. Wydawnictwo Akademia Rolniczo-Techniczna w Olsztynie / Agricultural and Technical Academy in Olsztyn, Blok 21, 10-957 Olsztyn-Kortowo Poland. **Tel** 011 48 89 273310. **(Subscription address:** Ars Polona-Ruch, PO Box 1001, Krakowskie Przedmiescie 7, 00-068 Warsaw Poland. **Tel** 011 48 22 261201.) ***Continues*** *Zeszyty Naukowe Akademii Rolniczo-Technicznej w Olsztynie. Ekonomika.*
Ind/Abst Agric. Eng. Abstr.; Dairy Sci. Abstr.; Field Crop Abstr.; Nutr. Abstr. Rev., Ser. B, Live Feeds and Feed.; Pig News Inf.; Potato Abstr.

ISSN 0549-544X
XO

ACTA OPERATIVO-OECONOMICA. ZBORNIK VYSOKEJ SKOLA POLNOHOSPODARSKEJ V NITRE. **Added/Corp** Vysoka Skola Polnohospodarska v Nitre. Vysoka Skola Pol'Nohospodarska v Nitre. Prevadzkovo-Ekonomicka Fakulta. Vysoka Skola Polnohospodarska v Nitre. Prevadzkovo-Ekonomicka Fakulta. Sbornik. **VFOAT** Zbornik Vysokej Skoly Polnohospodarskej v Nitre. (1960)-. Monographic series. Czech (summaries and/or abstracts in English and Russian; table of contents in Russian and English). Irregular. Price varies per volume. Vysoka Skola Polnohospodarska, Nitra Slovakia.
Ind/Abst Irr. Drain. Abstr.; Potato Abstr.; Poult. Abstr.

LC HJ **ISSN** 0988-9183
DD 336 FR
UDC 336.71

ADMINISTRATEUR DU CREDIT AGRICOLE, L'. **VFOAT** Administrateur du Credit Agricole Mutuel. (1968)-. Periodical. French. Six times a year. Administrateur du Credit, 48 de la Boetie, 75008 Paris France. **Tel** 011 33 1 45630300.

US

AFPC POLICY ISSUES . **Added/Corp** Agricultural and Food Policy Center (Tex.). **VFOAT** Policy Issues Paper. **VAT** Agricultural and Food Policy Center Staff Report. (1989)-. Monographic series. English. Irregular. Price varies per volume. Prentice-Hall General Reference and Travel, 200 Old Tappan Road, Old

Tappan NJ 07675. **Tel** (800)922-0579. ***Continues in part*** *AFPC Staff Report.*
Ind/Abst Cot. Trop. Fibr. Abstr. Bibliogr.

LC S **ISSN** 0279-9014
DD 630 US
UDC 63

AG UPDATE. [Ag update]. **Added/Corp** United States. Dept. of Agriculture. Colorado Crop & Livestock Reporting Service. Vol. 1, No. 1 (Apr. 7, 1981)-. English. Twenty-four times a year. $12.00. Colorado Department of Agriculture, Agricultural Statistics Service, PO Box 150969, Lakewood CO 80215. **Tel** (303)236-2300.
Desc: Containing the most recently issued agricultural estimates and forecasts for Colorado and the United States.

ISSN 0002-1024
UK

AGRA EUROPE (BRITISH EDITION). (AGRA EUROPE.). [Agra Eur.]. (1963)-. Trade Publication. English. One time a week (51 issues). $2113.34. Agra Europe London Limited, 25 Frant Road, Tunbridge Wells, Kent TN2 5JT United Kingdom. **Tel** 011 44 1892 533813, FAX 011 44 1892 544895, telex 95114 AGRATW G. **ED** Edgar Phillips. Index available. cum. index. **Circ:** 900. available on an online database (file 16,648/Full-Text) from DIALOG.
Desc: European and world developments affecting the production and marketing of food and agricultural commodities, and the common agricultural policy.
Ind/Abst Dairy Sci. Abstr.; F&S Index Plus Text, Int. [Full Txt.] [Select. Cov.]; Leis., Rec., Tour. Abstr.; Maize Abstr.; Nutr. Abstr. Rev., Ser. B, Live Feeds and Feed.; Potato Abstr.; Poult. Abstr.; PROMT [Full Txt.]; Rural Dev. Abstr.; Soyabean Abstr.; Sug. Indus. Abstr.; Trade Ind. ASAP [Full Txt.]; Trade Ind. Index [Full Txt.]; Wheat Barley Trit. Abstr.; World Agric. Econ. Rural Sociol. Abstr.

LC HD101 .A416 **ISSN** 0002-1121
GW
CCC

AGRARWIRTSCHAFT. [Agrarwirtschaft]. Vol. 1 (Feb. 1952)-. Trade Publication. German. Twelve times a year. Price varies. Deutscher Fachverlag GmbH, Verlagsgruppe, D-60264 Frankfurt Germany. **Tel** 011 49 69 75951001, telex 411 862. **ED** H. E. Buchholz. **Bk Rev. Ad Acc. Circ:** 3,000.
Desc: Science of business administration, market research, and book reviews.
Ind/Abst Agric. Eng. Abstr. (1991-); Anim. Breed. Abstr.; Dairy Sci. Abstr.; Int. Labour Doc.; Irr. Drain. Abstr.; Leis., Rec., Tour. Abstr.; Maize Abstr.; Nutr. Abstr. Rev., Ser. B, Live Feeds and Feed.; Nutr. Abstr. Rev., Ser. A, Hum. Exp.; Pig News Inf.; Potato Abstr.; Poult. Abstr.; Rural Dev. Abstr.; Soils Fert.; Soyabean Abstr.; Sug. Indus. Abstr.; World Agric. Econ. Rural Sociol. Abstr.

ISSN 1182-9133
DD 338.1/75/09717 CN

AGRI-FOOD BUSINESS IN P.E.I. [Agri-food bus. P.E.I.]. **Added/Corp** Canada. Agriculture Canada. Prince Edward Island. Dept. of Agriculture. **VAT** Agri-Food Business in Prince Edward Island. Vol. 1, Issue 1 (Oct. 1990)-. Periodical. English. Twelve times a year.

ISSN 0002-1180
US
UDC 338.43

AGRI MARKETING. Vol. 1, No. 1 (Spring 1963)-. Trade Publication. English. Twelve times a year. $30.00 US; $60.00 other. Century Communications Inc., 6201 Howard Street, Niles IL 60714-3435. **Tel** (708)647-1200, FAX (708)647-7055. **ED** Carroll Merry. **Bk Rev. Ad Acc. Circ:** 10,000 (ctrl). available on microfilm and microfiche from University Microfilms International (UMI); available on an online database (file 15/Full-Text) from DIALOG. Documents available from UMI Article Clearinghouse.
Desc: Written for marketers and advertising agencies of items that farmers purchase.
Ind/Abst ABI/INFORM Glob. Ed. (Jan. 1991-); ABI/INFORM [Computer File] (Jan. 1991-); Bus. Period. Index; Bus. Source Plus; Bus. Source; Curr. Cit.; EP Collect.; Homework Help.; Mag. Search; Mark. Advert. Ref. Serv.; MasterFile FullTEXT 1000; MasterFile FullTEXT 350; MasterFile FullTEXT 650; MasterFile FullTEXT (July 1993-); OCLC; Telebase; Wilson Bus. Abstr.

ISSN 0311-0370
AT

AGRIBUSINESS DECISION. [Agribus. decis.]. **Added/Corp** Agribusiness Counsellors. (Oct. 1976)-. Periodical. English. Eleven times a year. 61.66Aus$. Agriplan Pty Ltd, Lawton House, 105 Broadway, Suite 6, Nedlands Western 6009 Australia. **Tel** 011 61 9 3867115, FAX 011 61 9 3863206. **ED** R. S. Watt. **Circ:** 500 (ctrl).
Desc: Articles by agricultural consultants on farming topics, especially relevant to the sheep and wheat areas of Western Australia. Plus technical information, price and cost outlook, management and business decisions.

LC HB241 **ISSN** 0199-1671
DD 338 US
CODEN AWORD8
SUSPENDED

AGRIBUSINESS WORLDWIDE. [Agribus. worldw.]. Vol. 1 (Sept./Oct. 1979)-Suspended (1995). Periodical. English. Six times a year. $57.00. Sosland Publishing Company / Missouri, 4800 Main Street, Suite 100, Kansas City MO 64112. **Tel** (816)756-1000, FAX (816)756-0494, telex 820182. available on an online database from BRS; and (file 648/Full-Text) DIALOG.
Ind/Abst Agric. Eng. Abstr.; BioBusiness (1990-); Dairy Sci. Abstr.; F&S Index Plus Text, Int. [Select. Cov.]; Helminthol. Abstr.; Index Vet.; Irr. Drain. Abstr.; PESTDOC; Postharvest News Inf.; Potato Abstr.; Poult. Abstr.; PROMT; Protozoolog. Abstr.; Soils Fert.; Trade Ind. ASAP [Full Txt.]; Trade Ind. Index [Full Txt.]; World Agric. Econ. Rural Sociol. Abstr.

LC HD1773.A2 N67a **ISSN** 1068-2805
DD 338.1/0974 USUS

●**AGRICULTURAL AND RESOURCE ECONOMICS REVIEW.** [Agric. resour. econ. rev.]. **Added/Corp** Northeastern Agricultural and Resource Economics Association (U.S.). Vol. 21, No. 1 (Apr. 1993)-. Periodical. English. Two times a year (Apr. & Oct.). $15.00. NE Agriculture Resource Economics, 203 Armsby Building, University Park PA 16802. **Tel** (302)831-5211. ***Continues*** *Northeastern Journal of Agricultural and Resource Economics, 0899-367X.*

LC HG1501 **ISSN** 0737-948X
DD 332.1 US

AGRICULTURAL CREDIT CONDITIONS SURVEY. [Agric. credit cond. surv.]. **Added/Corp** Federal Reserve Bank of Minneapolis. Research Dept. **VFOAT** Agricultural Credit Conditions. (19??)-. Periodical. English. Free on request. Federal Reserve Bank of Minneapolis, 250 Marquette Avenue, Publ Affairs, Minneapolis MN 55480. **Tel** (612)340-2356. **ED** Stanley L. Graham. **Circ:** 4,000 (ctrl).
Desc: Analysis of farm credit conditions in the 9th Federal Reserve District. Based on a survey of rural bankers in Minnesota, Montana, North and South Dakota, and Northwestern Wisconsin.

LC HG1501
DD 332.1 PK

AGRICULTURAL CREDIT INDICATORS. (1991)-. Periodical. English. State Bank of Pakistan - Public Relation Department, PO Box 4456, Central Directorate, Karachi Pakistan. **Tel** 011 92 21 2414141310, telex 2754 SBP.

ISSN 0887-7521
DD 332 US
TITLE CHANGE

AGRICULTURAL CREDIT LETTER, THE. [Agric. cred. lett.]. **Added/Corp** Webster Communications Corporation. (1985)-(199?). Periodical. English. Webster Communications Corporation, 1530 North Key Boulevard PH2, Arlington VA 22209. **Tel** (703)525-4512, FAX (703)525-4917. **ED** James C. Webster. **Bk Rev.** ***Merged with*** *Washington Farmletter, 0739-6783* ***to form*** *Webster Agricultural Letter, 1073-4813.*

LC HD1751 .A91854 **ISSN** 0083-0445
DD 338.1/08 US
UDC 338.43(73)

AGRICULTURAL ECONOMIC REPORT (WASHINGTON, D.C.). (AGRICULTURAL ECONOMIC REPORT / UNITED STATES DEPARTMENT OF AGRICULTURE, ECONOMICS, STATISTICS, AND COOPERATIVES SERVICE.). [Agric. econ. rep.]. **VFOAT** Agricultural Economic Research Report. No. 1 (1961)-. Monographic series. English. Irregular. Price varies per volume. US Department of Agriculture / Economic Research Service, 1301 New York Avenue, Room 208, Washington DC 20250. **Tel** (202)447-4111. available in microform.
Ind/Abst AgBiotech News Inf.; Dairy Sci. Abstr.; Leis., Rec., Tour. Abstr.; Maize Abstr.; Nutr. Abstr. Rev., Ser. B, Live Feeds and Feed.; Poult. Abstr.; Rice Abstr.; Rural Dev. Abstr.; Sorghum Mill. Abstr.; World Agric. Econ. Rural Sociol. Abstr.

ISSN 0169-5150
NE
CCC
CODEN AGECE6
Pr Rev.

AGRICULTURAL ECONOMICS. (AGRICULTURAL ECONOMICS : THE JOURNAL OF THE INTERNATIONAL ASSOCIATION OF AGRICULTURAL ECONOMISTS.). [Agric. econ.]. **Added/Corp** International Association of Agricultural Economists. Vol. 1, No. 1 (Dec. 1986)-. Academic Scholarly Publication. English. Six times a year (two volumes). $485.00. Elsevier Science Publishers BV, PO Box 211, 1000 AE Amsterdam Netherlands. **Tel** 011 31 20 4853641, 011 31 20 4853642, FAX 011 31 20 4853598. **ED** Douglas Hedley. available on microfilm and microfiche from University Microfilms International (UMI); available on an online database from Elsevier Electronic Subscriptions (EES). Documents available from The Genuine Article.
Desc: Publishes articles covering the range of work done on agricultural economics.
Ind/Abst AGRICOLA [Full Cov.]; BioBusiness (1987-); Biol. Agric. Index; Cot. Trop. Fibr. Abstr. Bibliogr.; Curr. Aware. Biol. Sci., CABS; Curr. Cit.; Dairy Sci. Abstr.; Geogr. Abstr. Human Geogr.; Int. Dev. Abstr.; Irr. Drain. Abstr.; Maize Abstr.; Nutr. Abstr. Rev., Ser. B, Live Feeds and Feed.; Pig News Inf.; Postharvest News Inf.; Potato Abstr.; Res. Alert [Select. Cov.]; Rev. Agric. Entomol.; Rice Abstr.; Rural Dev. Abstr.; SCISEARCH; Soc. Sci. Cit. Index [Select. Cov.]; Soils Fert.; Sorghum Mill. Abstr.; Soyabean Abstr.; Sug. Indus. Abstr.; World Agric. Econ. Rural Sociol. Abstr.

ISSN 0313-377X
AT

AGRICULTURAL ECONOMICS BULLETIN (ARMIDALE, N.S.W.). (AGRICULTURAL ECONOMICS BULLETIN.). **Added/Corp** University of New England. Dept. of Agricultural Economics and Business Management. (19??)-. Bulletin. English. Price varies per volume. Department of Agricultural Economics and Business Management, University of New England, Armidale NSW 2350 Australia. **Tel** 02 228-5333.
Ind/Abst World Agric. Econ. Rural Sociol. Abstr.

ISSN 0811-4447
AT

AGRICULTURAL ECONOMICS BULLETIN (SYDNEY). (AGRICULTURAL ECONOMICS BULLETIN.). [Agric. econ. bull.]. **Added/Corp** New South Wales. Dept. of Agriculture. Division of Marketing and Economic Services. NSW Agriculture & Fisheries. Division of Rural and Resource Economics. No. 1 (1982)-. Bulletin. English.
Ind/Abst AGRICOLA [Full Cov.].

AT

AGRICULTURAL ECONOMICS DISCUSSION PAPER. **Added/Corp** University of Queensland. Dept. of Agriculture. **VFOAT** Agricultural Economics Discussion Papers Series. (19??)-. Monographic series. English. Price varies per volume. University of Queensland Department of Agriculture, St. Lucia Queensland 4067 Australia.

AT

AGRICULTURAL ECONOMICS REPORT. **Main/Corp** Melbourne. University. School of Agriculture and Forestry. (197?)-. Periodical. English. University of Melbourne / School of Agriculture and Forestry, Parkville Victoria 3052 Australia. ***Continues*** *Melbourne. University. Faculty of Agriculture. Agricultural Economics Report.*

LC HD2057 .A15 **ISSN** 0379-0827
DD 338.1/095693/05 CY

AGRICULTURAL ECONOMICS REPORT. AGRICULTURAL RESEARCH INSTITUTE (NICOSIA). (AGRICULTURAL ECONOMICS REPORT.). [Agr. Econ. Rep., Agric. Res. Insst. (Nicos.)]. **Added/Corp** Institouton Georgikon Ereunon (Cyprus). No. 1 (1973)-. Monographic series. English. Price varies per volume. Institouton Georgikon Ereunon / Agricultural Research Institute, Ministry of Agriculture and Natural Resources, Nicosia Cyprus.
Ind/Abst Agrofor. Abstr.; World Agric. Econ. Rural Sociol. Abstr.

LC HD1407 .M5 **ISSN** 0065-4442
DD 630 US

AGRICULTURAL ECONOMICS REPORT (MICHIGAN STATE UNIVERSITY. DEPT. OF AGRICULTURAL ECONOMICS). (AGRICULTURAL ECONOMICS REPORT.). [Agric. econ. rep.]. (1965)-. Monographic series. English. Price varies per volume. Agriculture Hall, Michigan State University, Department of Agricultural Economics, East Lansing MI 48824-1039.
Ind/Abst AGRICOLA [Full Cov.]; Poult. Abstr.

LC SB205.S7 N64 **ISSN** 0549-8295
DD 630 US

AGRICULTURAL ECONOMICS REPORT (NORTH DAKOTA AGRICULTURAL EXPERIMENT STATIONS (FARGO)). (AGRICULTURAL ECONOMICS REPORT.). **Added/Corp** North Dakota Agricultural Experiment Station (Fargo) United States. Bureau of Reclamation. (1951)-. Monographic series. English. Irregular. Price varies per volume. US Department of Interior / Agriculture Experiment Station, North Dakota Agricultural College and Bureau of Reclamation, Fargo ND.

US
Pr Rev.

AGRICULTURAL ECONOMICS RESEARCH REPORT (MISSISSIPPI AGRICULTURAL AND FORESTRY EXPERIMENT STATION). (AGRICULTURAL ECONOMICS RESEARCH REPORT.). **Added/Corp** Mississippi Agricultural and Forestry Experiment Station. No. 149, (1984)-. Monographic series. English. Irregular. Price varies per volume. Mississippi State University / Information Services, PO Box 5446, Mississippi State MS

39762. **Tel** (601)325-7774. **ED** Earl Stennis. ***Continues*** *AEC Research Report, 0886-7593.*
Desc: Photocopy production - departmental series produced and distributed by department.

LC HD1407 .A33 **ISSN** 0148-2920
DD 338.1/0212 US

AGRICULTURAL ECONOMICS STATISTICAL SERIES. See
Agriculture-Abstracting, Bibliographies and Statistics.

ISSN 0883-0088
DD 338 US
Pr Rev.

AGRICULTURAL ECONOMICS TECHNICAL PUBLICATION.
[Agric. econ. tech. publ.]. **Added/Corp** Mississippi Agricultural and Forestry Experiment Station. **VFOAT** Technical Publication. (1982)-. Monographic series. English. Irregular. Price varies per volume. Mississippi State University / Information Services, PO Box 5446, Mississippi State MS 39762. **Tel** (601)325-7774. **ED** Earl Stennis. ***Continues*** *AEC Tech. Pub.*
Desc: Departmental publication of ag economics research.
Ind/Abst Bibliogr. Agric.

ISSN 1070-6755
DD 338 US

AGRICULTURAL FINANCE DATABOOK (WASHINGTON, D.C. 1989).
(AGRICULTURAL FINANCE DATABOOK.). [Agric. finance datab.]. **Added/Corp** Board of Governors of the Federal Reserve System (U.S.). Division of Research and Statistics. (Jan. 1989)-. Periodical. English. Four times a year. $5.00. Board of Governors of the Federal Reserve System, Mail Stop 127, Washington DC 20551. **Tel** (202)452-3244, (202)452-3245. ***Continues*** *Agricultural Finance Databook. Quarterly Series, 0735-942X.*

LC HG2051.U5 A59 **ISSN** 0002-1466
DD 332.71 332.31* US
Pr Rev.

AGRICULTURAL FINANCE REVIEW.
(AGRICULTURAL FINANCE REVIEW / UNITED STATES DEPARTMENT OF AGRICULTURE, ECONOMIC RESEARCH SERVICE.). [Agric. financ. rev.]. **Added/Corp** United States. Dept. of Agriculture. Economic Research Service. United States. Bureau of Agricultural Economics. United States. Dept. of Agriculture. Economics and Statistics, and Cooperatives Service. New York State College of Agriculture. Dept. of Agricultural Economics. Vol. 1 (May 1938)-. Trade Publication. English. One time a year (fall). Free on request. Cornell University / S Allen, 155 Warren Hall, Ithaca NY 14853-7801. **Tel** (607)255-1587, FAX (607)255-9984. **ED** Eddy L LaDue. **Circ:** 1,800 (ctrl). available on microfilm and microfiche from University Microfilms International (UMI). ***Continued in part by*** *Agricultural Finance Statistics.*
Desc: Provides a forum for presentation of research and discussion of issues in agricultural finance. Contains articles contributed by scholars in the field.
Ind/Abst AGRICOLA [Full Cov.]; Dairy Sci. Abstr.; Stat. Ref. Index; World Agric. Econ. Rural Sociol. Abstr.

US

AGRICULTURAL MANAGEMENT AND ECONOMICS.
(1991)-. Monographic series. English. Two times a year. Price varies per volume. Springer-Verlag New York Inc., 175 Fifth Avenue, New York NY 10010. **Tel** (212)460-1500 ext 256, FAX (212)533-3503, telex 232 235 SPB UR. **(Subscription address:** Springer-Verlag New York Inc. / North America, PO Box 2485, Journal Fulfillment, Secaucus NJ 07096. **Tel** (201)348-4033, (800)777-4643, FAX (201)348-4505.**)** **ED** G.C. Rausser.
Desc: Presents topics of research interest in the management and economics of agricultural systems. The series focuses on future developments that are likely to make significant changes in farming, commodity markets, food processing and manufacturing, nutrition and diets, and the consumption of food throughout the developing and developed world.

LC HD1751 .D46a **ISSN** 0099-1066
DD 338.1/0973 US
CODEN AGOUD7

AGRICULTURAL OUTLOOK (WASHINGTON, D.C. : 1975).
(AGRICULTURAL OUTLOOK / UNITED STATES DEPARTMENT OF AGRICULTURE, ECONOMIC RESEARCH SERVICE.). [Agric. Outlook]. **Added/Corp** United States. Dept. of Agriculture. Economic Research Service. United States. Dept. of Agriculture. Economics, Statistics, and Cooperatives Service. United States. Dept. of Agriculture. Economics and Statistics Service. Vol. 1 (June 1975)-. Periodical. English. Eleven times a year. $42.00. US Department of Agriculture, 14th Street and Independence Avenue SW, Washington DC 20250. **Tel** (202)720-5457. **(Subscription address:** Superintendent of Documents, US Government Printing Office, Washington DC 20402. **)** available on microfilm and microfiche from University Microfilms International (UMI). Documents available from Documents on Demand. ***Continues in part*** *Farm Income Situation;* ***Continues*** *Marketing and Transportation Situation.*
Desc: An update and analysis of the developments affecting the outlook for the United States food and fiber economy; highlights the major interrelated developments in farming, input industries and produce marketing. Discusses potential impact on US agriculture and the consumer.
Ind/Abst AGRICOLA [Select. Cov.]; Am. Stat. Index; BioBusiness (1986-); F&S Index Plus Text, Int. [Select. Cov.]; Foods Adlibra; PAIS Int. Print; Poult. Abstr.; Predicasts Forecasts; Trade Ind. ASAP [Full Txt.]; Trade Ind. Index [Full Txt.]; World Agric. Econ. Rural Sociol. Abstr.

LC HB233.A3 U5125
DD 338.1/3/0973021 US

AGRICULTURAL PRICES ... SUMMARY.
Added/Corp United States. Crop Reporting Board. United States. Agricultural Statistics Board. **VFOAT** Agricultural Prices Annual Summary; Annual Price Summary. (1983)-. Statistical Publication. English. One time a year (July). $15.00. US Department of Agriculture / National Agricultural Statistics Service (NASS), Room 5829 South Building, Washington DC 20250. **Tel** (202)720-4020, FAX (314)875-5231. ***Continues*** *Agricultural Prices, Annual Summary.*

LC HD9004 .U523a **ISSN** 0002-1601
DD 338.1/3/0973 US

AGRICULTURAL PRICES (WASHINGTON, D.C.).
(AGRICULTURAL PRICES.). [Agric. prices]. **Added/Corp** United States. Crop Reporting Board. United States. Bureau of Agricultural Economics. United States. Agricultural Marketing Service. United States. Agricultural Statistics Board. (1942)-. Government Publication. English. Twelve times a year. $50.00. US Department of Agriculture, 14th Street and Independence Avenue SW, Washington DC 20250. **Tel** (202)720-5457. **(Subscription address:** Superintendent of Documents, US Government Printing Office, Washington DC 20402. **)** available on microfiche (Vols. for (1986-) distributed to depository libraries); available on an online database from DIALOG. Documents available from Documents on Demand. ***Continues*** *United States. Bureau of Agricultural Economics. Farm Product Prices.*
Desc: Provides comparative information on prices received by farmers for various commodities, and prices paid by farmers for commodities and services, interest, taxes and farm wages.
Ind/Abst Am. Stat. Index.

LC S **ISSN** 0188-3054
DD 630 MX
Pr Rev.

AGROCIENCIA. SERIE MATEMATICAS APLICADAS, ESTADISTICA Y COMPUTACION.
[Agrocienc., Ser. mat. apl. estad. comput.]. (1990)-. Periodical. Spanish. Three times a year. $25.00. Colegio de Postgraduados, Gen Lazardo Cardenas 24 La Paz, 56170 Texcoco Mexico. **Tel** 011 52 595 47011. ***Continues*** *Agrociencia (Montecillo, Edo. Mex.), 0185-0288.*

US

AGRONOMIST, THE.
Added/Corp University of Maryland, College Park. Agronomy Dept. University of Maryland Cooperative Extension Service. United States. Dept. of Agriculture. **VFOAT** UM Newsletter. **VAT** University of Maryland newsletter. (1964)-. Periodical. English. Four times a year. University of Maryland Agronomy Department, College Park MD 20742.

ISSN 0516-3854
US

ALABAMA AGRIBUSINESS.
[Ala. agribus.]. Periodical. English. Four times a year. Auburn University Cooperative Extension Service, Auburn AL 36830.
Ind/Abst AGRICOLA [Full Cov.].

LC S560 .J6 **ISSN** 0002-9092
DD 338.1/05 US
CODEN AJAEBA
Pr Rev.

AMERICAN JOURNAL OF AGRICULTURAL ECONOMICS.
[Am. j. agric. econ.]. **Added/Corp** American Agricultural Economics Association. American Agricultural Economics Association. Proceedings. American Agricultural Economics Association. Directory. Vol. 50 (Feb. 1968)-. Periodical. English. Five times a year. $90.00. American Agricultural Economics Association, 1110 Buckeye Avenue, Ames IA 50011. **Tel** (515)233-3202, FAX (515)233-3101. **ED** Peter Barry. **Bk Rev. Ad Acc.** available on microfilm and microfiche from University Microfilms International (UMI). Documents available from The Genuine Article, UMI Article Clearinghouse, Documents on Demand. ***Continues*** *Journal of Farm Economics, 1071-1031.*
Ind/Abst ABI/INFORM Glob. Ed.; ABI/INFORM [Computer File] (Nov. 1972-Dec. 1974); Acad. Search; AgBiotech News Inf.; AGRICOLA [Full Cov.]; Agric. Eng. Abstr. (1991-); BioBusiness; Biol. Agric. Index; Biostatistica (19??-19??); Bus. Index (1985-); Bus. Period. Index; Bus. Source Plus; Bus. Source; Coal Abstr.; Contents Recent Econ. J.; Cot. Trop. Fibr. Abstr. Bibliogr.; Curr. Cit.; Curr. Contents Agric. Biol. Environ. Sci.; Curr. Contents Soc. Behav. Sci.; Dairy Sci. Abstr.; Ecol. Abstr. (?-?); Econ. Lit. Index; Energy Inf. Abstr.; Energy Res. Abstr. (May 1977-); Environ. Abstr.; EP Collect.; Expand. Acad. Index (1992-); Field Crop Abstr.; For. Abstr.; Gen. BusinessFile (1985-); Gen. Period. Index (1985-); Geogr. Abstr. Phys. Geogr.; Geogr. Abstr. Human Geogr.; GeoRef; Grass. Forage Abstr.; Homework Help.; INFO-SOUTH Abstr.; INIS Atomindex [Micro.]; Int. Abstr. Oper. Res. [Select. Cov.]; Int. Bibliogr. Sociol.; Int. Dev. Abstr.; Int. Labour Doc.; Irr. Drain. Abstr.; J. Econ. Lit.; Leis., Rec., Tour. Abstr.; Mag. Search; Maize Abstr.; MasterFile FullTEXT 1000; MasterFile FullTEXT 350; MasterFile FullTEXT 650; MasterFile FullTEXT (Jan. 1993-); Middle East Abstr. Index; Nematol. Abstr.; Newsp. Period. Abstr. (1992-1992); Nutr. Abstr. Rev., Ser. B, Live Feeds and Feed.; Nutr. Abstr. Rev., Ser. A, Hum. Exp.; OCLC; Oper. Res./Manage. Sci.; PAIS Int. Print (1991-); Pig News Inf.; Postharvest News Inf.; Potato Abstr.; Poult. Abstr.; Qual. Control Appl. Stat.; Res. Alert [Full Cov.]; Rev. Agric. Entomol.; Rice Abstr.; Risk Abstr.; Rural Dev. Abstr.; Sci. Cit. Index; SCISEARCH; Soc. Sci. Cit. Index [Full Cov.]; Soils Fert.; Soyabean Abstr.; Sug. Indus. Abstr.; Telebase; Vocat. Search; Wheat Barley Trit. Abstr.; Wilson Bus. Abstr.; World Agric. Econ. Rural Sociol. Abstr.

LC HG1501
DD 332.1 US

ANALYSIS AND SUMMARY OF CONDITION AND PERFORMANCE OF THE FARM CREDIT BANKS AND ASSOCIATIONS.
Added/Corp United States. Farm Credit Administration. Policy and Risk Analysis Division. (Sept. 30, 1991)-. Periodical. English. Four times a year. Farm Credit Administration / McLean, 1501 Farm Credit Drive, McLean VA 22102. **Tel** (703)883-4056.

TI

ANNALES.
Main/Corp Institut National de la Recherche Agronomique de Tunisie. Vol. 32 (1959)-. French (English and Arabic). Irregular. 7,200TD. Institut National de la, Recherche Agronomique de Tunisie, Ave de l'Independence, 2080-Ariana Tunisia. **Tel** 011 216 1 230024. **Ad Acc.** ctrl circ. ***Continues*** *Annales du Service Botanique et Agronomique.*
Ind/Abst Crop Physiol. Abstr.; Dairy Sci. Abstr.; Field Crop Abstr.; For. Abstr.; Grass. Forage Abstr.; Hortic. Abstr.; Nutr. Abstr. Rev., Ser. B, Live Feeds and Feed.; Plant Breed. Abstr.; Soils Fert.; Weed Abstr.

ISSN 0270-4188
US

ANNUAL PRICE REVIEW.
(19??)-. English. $389.00 (with Monthly Price Review). Urner Barry Publications Inc., PO Box 389, Toms River NJ 08754. **Tel** (908)240-5330, (800)932-0617, FAX (908)341-0891. **ED** Paul B Brown and Richard A Brown. **Ad Acc, Adv Mgr:** Lisa Sharkus, **Tel** (800)932-0617. **Circ:** 500.
Desc: Lists prices for the month of eggs, turkeys, chickens, fowl, butter, margarine, cheese and concentrated milk products. Includes an annual summary.

US

ANNUAL REPORT FOR FISCAL YEAR ... / COMMODITY CREDIT CORPORATION.
Main/Corp Commodity Credit Corporation. (1988)-. Government Publication. English. US Department of Agriculture / Commodity Credit Corporation, 14th Street & Independence Avenue SW, Room 200-A, Washington DC 20250. **Tel** (202)720-3631, FAX (202)205-2883. ***Formed by the union of*** *Report of the President of the Commodity Credit Corporation / United States Department of Agriculture, Production and Marketing Administration, Commodity Credit Corporation* ***and*** *Report of the Financial Condition and Operations as of ... / U.S. Department of Agriculture, Production and Marketing Administration, Commodity Credit Corporation, 0414-0818.*

LC HG2051.U5 A57 **ISSN** 0883-329X
DD 353.0082/33045 US
UDC 336.77:338.43(73)

ANNUAL REPORT OF THE FARM CREDIT ADMINISTRATION.
[Annu. rep. Farm Credit Adm. Coop. Farm Credit Syst.]. **Main/Corp** United States. Farm Credit Administration. **VFOAT** Annual Report; Annual Report of the Farm Credit Administration on the Work of the Cooperative Farm Credit System. 1st (1934)-. Periodical. English. One time a year. Farm Credit Administration, Public Affairs Division, Washington DC 20578. **Tel** (202)755-2195. available on microfiche (Vols. for (1980-) distributed to depository libraries).

US

ANNUAL REPORT OF THE FARM CREDIT ADMINISTRATION AND THE COOPERATIVE FARM CREDIT SYSTEM.
Main/Corp United States. Farm Credit Administration. 1st. (1933)-. Periodical. English. Farm Credit Administration, Public Affairs Division, Washington DC 20578. **Tel** (202)755-2195. ***Absorbed*** *Characteristics of Federal Land Bank Loans, 0147-4979.*

LC HD9014.B8 B68A
DD 338.1/881 BL
ANUARIO ESTATISTICO - COMISSAO DE FOMAMCIAMENTO DA PRODUCAO, DEPARTAMENTO DE PESQUISAS ECONOMICAS. **See** Agriculture-Abstracting, Bibliographies and Statistics.

ISSN 0257-7992
II
UDC 336.77:338.43
ARDC NEWS. [ARDC news]. **Main/Corp** Agricultural Refinance and Development Corporation. Vol. 4, No. 4, (Jan./Mar. 1976)-. Periodical. English. Agricultural Refinance and Development Corporation, Worli, Bombay 400 018 India. ***Continues** ARC News.*
Ind/Abst Leis., Rec., Tour. Abstr.; Rural Dev. Abstr.; World Agric. Econ. Rural Sociol. Abstr.

AT
•AUSTRALIAN FARMING PRICE INDEXES. (1995)-. English. Four times a year. 61.66Aus$. ABARE / Australian Bureau of Agriculture and Resource Economics, GPO Box 1563, Canberra ACT 2601 Australia. **Tel** 011 61 6 2722000, FAX 011 61 6 2722001. ***Continues** Index of Prices Received and Paid by Farmers.*

LC HD1401 .A9 **ISSN** 0004-9395
DD 338.1/0994 AT
Pr Rev.
AUSTRALIAN JOURNAL OF AGRICULTURAL ECONOMICS, THE. [Aust. j. agric. econ.]. **Added/Corp** Australian Agricultural Economics Society. Australian Agricultural Economics Society. Proceedings of the Conference. Vol. 1 (1957)-. Academic Scholarly Publication. English. Three times a year (Apr., Aug., Dec.). 67.42Aus$. Australian Agricultural Economics Society Inc, PO Box 319, East Melbourne 3002 Australia. **Tel** 011 61 3 345035, FAX 011 61 3 3445570. **ED** J.O.S. Kennedy, Bill Malcolm. Index available. cum. index. **Bk Rev. Ad Acc.** Documents available from The Genuine Article.
Desc: Publishes material with relevance to the economics of agriculture, natural resources or issues which have a direct impact on agriculture.
Ind/Abst AGRICOLA [Full Cov.]; APAIS, Aust. Public Aff. Inf. Ser. (1963-); Contents Recent Econ. J.; Curr. Contents Agric. Biol. Environ. Sci.; Curr. Contents Soc. Behav. Sci.; Dairy Sci. Abstr.; Econ. Lit. Index; For. Prod. Abstr.; Geogr. Abstr. Human Geogr.; Grass. Forage Abstr.; Int. Dev. Abstr.; J. Econ. Lit.; Leis., Rec., Tour. Abstr.; Postharvest News Inf.; Poult. Abstr.; Res. Alert [Full Cov.]; Rice Abstr.; Rural Dev. Abstr.; SCISEARCH; Soc. Sci. Cit. Index [Full Cov.]; Wheat Barley Trit. Abstr.; World Agric. Econ. Rural Sociol. Abstr.

LC HD2075.6 .B37
DD 338.1/09549/2 BG
BANGLADESH JOURNAL OF AGRICULTURAL ECONOMICS, THE. **Added/Corp** Bangladesh Agricultural University. Bureau of Socio-Economic Research and Training. Vol. 1, No. 1 (June 1978)-. Periodical. English. Two times a year (June and Dec.). $40.00. Bangladesh Agricultural University, Bureau of Socioeconomic Research, Mymensingh Bangladesh. **Tel** 011 880 569597 09. Index available (free).
Ind/Abst Int. Labour Doc.; Nutr. Abstr. Rev., Ser. A, Hum. Exp.; Rice Abstr.; World Agric. Econ. Rural Sociol. Abstr.

ISSN 0274-6050
US
UDC 338.43(698.1)
BIG FARMER ENTREPRENEUR. [Big farmer entrep.]. Vol. 52, No. 6 (June 1980)-. Periodical. English. Twelve times a year. Big Farmer Entrepreneur, 131 Lincoln Highway, Frankfort IL 60423. available on microfilm and microfiche from University Microfilms International (UMI). ***Continues** Big Farmer, 0006-2189.*

LC HB **ISSN** 0886-4489
DD 330 US
BIG SKY ECONOMICS. [Big sky econ.]. **Added/Corp** Montana State University. Cooperative Extension Service. (19??)-. Monographic series. English. Irregular. Montana State University, Bozeman MT 59715.
Ind/Abst AGRICOLA [Full Cov.].

DR
UDC 338.43(729.3)
BOLETIN INFORMATIVO DE PRECIOS Y MERCADOS. **Main/Corp** Dominican Republic. Departamento de Economia Agropecuaria. (197?)-. Periodical. Spanish. ***Continues** Boletin Informativo - Departamento de Economia Agropecuaria, Division de Mercadeo.*

ISSN 0366-2403
IT
CODEN BOZAAW
BOLLETTINO DI ZOOLOGIA AGRARIA E DI BACHICOLTURA. [Boll. zool. agrar. bachic.]. **Added/Corp** Milan. R. Istituto Superiore Agrario. Laboratorio di Zoologia Agraria e Bachicoltura. Bollettino. Universita di Milano. Istituto di Entomologia Agraria. Vol. 1, (1929)-. Periodical. Italian (summaries and/or abstracts in English). Two times a year. L60000. Istituto Entomologia Agraria dell'Universita, Via Celoria 2, 20133 Milan Italy. **Tel** 011 39 2 236 3439. cum. index. **Circ:** 250 (ctrl). Documents available from BIOSIS Document Express.
Ind/Abst Biocont. News Inf.; Biol. Abstr.; For. Abstr.; Rev. Agric. Entomol.; Seed Abstr.; Weed Abstr.; Wheat Barley Trit. Abstr.

LC HF5410 **ISSN** 0711-7590
DD 380.1/41/05 CN
BROADWATER MARKET LETTER. [Broadwater mark. lett.]. **Added/Corp** Broadwater Farm News Services. Vol. 7, No. 26 , (Aug. 10 1981)-. Periodical. English. Fifty times a year (weekly except Christmas & New Years). 149.00Can$ Canada; 159.00Can$ other. Deputter Publishing Ltd, 190 Wortley Road, Suite 200, London Ontario N6C 4Y7 Canada. **Tel** (519)663-2224, FAX (519)663-9124. **ED** Ruth Belcher. ctrl circ. ***Formed by the union of** Broadwater Farm News Services. Broadwater Grain Lletter., 0383-0128 **and** Broadwater Livestock Letter., 0705-7350.*
Desc: A summary of farm commodity prices, trends and policies edited for Canadian farmers, and agri-business from coast to coast.

UK
BULLETIN - DEPARTMENT OF AGRICULTURAL ECONOMICS. **Main/Corp** Victoria University of Manchester. Agricultural Economics Dept. (1???)-. Bulletin. English. Price varies per volume. Victoria University of Manchester, Department of Agricultural Economics, Manchester M13 9PL United Kingdom.
Ind/Abst Potato Abstr.; Poult. Abstr.; Wheat Barley Trit. Abstr.; World Agric. Econ. Rural Sociol. Abstr.

LC HB235.I4 **ISSN** 0445-5983
II
UDC 338.5:63(540)
BULLETIN OF AGRICULTURAL PRICES (INDIA). **Main/Corp** India (Republic). Directorate of Economics and Statistics. Vol. 1 (June 2, 1951)-. Bulletin. English. Rs100.00. Government of India / Ministry of Urban Development, Department of Publication, Civil Lines, Delhi 110054 India.

LC HC **ISSN** 0008-3976
DD 338.1/0971 CN
CCC
Pr Rev.
CANADIAN JOURNAL OF AGRICULTURAL ECONOMICS. [Can. j. agric. econ.]. **Added/Corp** Canadian Agricultural Economics and Farm Management Society. Canadian Agricultural Economics Society. **VFOAT** Revue Canadienne d'Economie Rurale. Vol. 1 (Fall 1952)-. Periodical. English (French; summaries and/or abstracts in French). Four times a year (quarterly with Dec. issue divided into two parts). 71.06Can$. Canadian Agricultural Economics and Farm Management Society, 151 Slater Street / Suite 907, Ottawa Ontario K1P 5H4 Canada. **Tel** (613)232-9459, FAX (613)594-5190. **ED** Z.A. Hassan and H.B. Huff. **Bk Rev. Circ:** 1,050. available on microfilm and microfiche from University Microfilms International (UMI). Documents available from The Genuine Article.
Desc: Research level texts in agricultural economics with particular reference to the Canadian economy.
Ind/Abst AgBiotech News Inf.; AGRICOLA [Full Cov.]; Biol. Agric. Index; Can. Period. Index; Curr. Cit.; Curr. Contents Agric. Biol. Environ. Sci.; Curr. Contents Soc. Behav. Sci.; Dairy Sci. Abstr.; Econ. Lit. Index; Field Crop Abstr.; Food Sci. Technol. Abstr.; For. Prod. Abstr. (1991-); For. Abstr.; Geogr. Abstr. Human Geogr.; Index Vet.; J. Econ. Lit.; Leis., Rec., Tour. Abstr.; Maize Abstr.; Nutr. Abstr. Rev., Ser. B, Live Feeds and Feed.; Nutr. Abstr. Rev., Ser. A, Hum. Exp.; PAIS Int. Print (1991-); Pig News Inf.; Plant Breed. Abstr.; Potato Abstr.; Poult. Abstr.; Res. Alert [Full Cov.]; Rev. Agric. Entomol.; Rev. Med. Vet. Entomol.; Risk Abstr. (19??-19??); Rural Dev. Abstr.; Sci. Cit. Index; SCISEARCH; Soc. Sci. Cit. Index [Full Cov.]; Soils Fert.; Soyabean Abstr.; Wheat Barley Trit. Abstr.; World Agric. Econ. Rural Sociol. Abstr.

US
CASH RECEIPTS FROM FARMING / IOWA CROP AND LIVESTOCK REPORTING SERVICE. Periodical. English. Two times a year. The Service, Full Depository, 707 Savings and Loan Building, Des Moines IA 50309.
Desc: Cash receipts from farm marketings, and by commodities and commodity groups.

LC HG2051.I4 A145a
DD 354.540082/33045 II
CIRCULARS OF THE AGRICULTURAL REFINANCE AND DEVELOPMENT CORPORATION FROM ... . **Main/Corp** Agricultural Refinance and Development Corporation. **Added/Corp** Agricultural Refinance and Development Corporation. **VFOAT** Agricultural Refinance and Development Corporation, Circulars ... . (19??)-. English. Irregular. Rs14.75. Agricultural Refinance and Development Corporation, Worli, Bombay 400 018 India.

ISSN 0318-6334
DD 338.1/09714 CN
COLLECTION DU DEPARTEMENT D'ECONOMIQUE. **Main/Corp** Universite de Sherbrooke. Departement d'Economique. (1???)-. Monographic series. French (English; summaries and/or abstracts in English). Irregular. Price varies per volume. Sherbrooke University, Department de Economie, Sherbrooke Quebec J1K 2R1 Canada.

LC HG2051.U5 C563
US
COMMODITY CREDIT CORPORATION CHARTS / UNITED STATES DEPARTMENT OF AGRICULTURE, PRODUCTION AND MARKETING ADMINISTRATION. **VFOAT** Charts, Commodity Credit Corporation; Charts Providing a Graphic Summary of Operations. Government Publication. English. One time a year. US Department of Agriculture / Commodity Credit Corporation, 14th Street & Independence Avenue SW, Room 200-A, Washington DC 20250. **Tel** (202)720-3631, FAX (202)205-2883. available on microfiche (Vols. for (1984-) distributed to depository libraries).

LC HD1401 **ISSN** 0822-7144
DD 338.1/3/0973 CN
COURRIER AGRIROYAL. (LE COURRIER AGRIROYAL.). [Courr. agriRoyal]. **Added/Corp** Banque Royale du Canada. Services Agricoles. **VAT** Courrier Agricole (1983). (April 1983)-. Periodical. English (French). Twelve times a year. Free. Royal Bank of Canada Agricultural Department, 13th Floor 220 Portage Avenue, Box 923, Winnipeg Manitoba R3C 2T5 Canada. **Tel** (204)988-6027, 988-4209, FAX (204)942-2822. **Circ:** 1,800 (ctrl). ***Continues** Courrier Agricole, 0821-6444.*
Desc: Provides information related to the financial side of farming.

LC HD2021 .C83
DD 338.1/0946 SP
UDC 338.43(460)
CUENTAS DEL SECTOR AGRARIO. No. 1 (Nov. 1975)-. Spanish. One time a year. Ministerio Agricultura, Centro de Publicaciones, Calle Alfonso XII 56, 28071 Madrid Spain. **Tel** 011 34 1 3475551, FAX 011 34 1 3475722.

LC HD9014.B83 M373A
DD 331.7 BL
UDC 311:63(817.2)
DADOS ESTATISTICOS : PRODUTOS AGRO PECUARIOS SAIDOS DE MATO GROSSO. **See** Agriculture-Abstracting, Bibliographies and Statistics.

ISSN 0926-5589
NE
DEVELOPMENTS IN AGRICULTURAL ECONOMICS. [Dev. agric. econ.]. (1983)-. Monographic series. English. Irregular. Price varies per volume. Elsevier Science Publishers BV, PO Box 211, 1000 AE Amsterdam Netherlands. **Tel** 011 31 20 4853641, 011 31 20 4853642, FAX 011 31 20 4853598.
Desc: Series containing information on agricultural economics. Volumes have included topics such as wine economy and marketing sugar.

ISSN 0110-2044
NZ
DISCUSSION PAPER IN NATURAL RESOURCE ECONOMICS / DEPARTMENT OF AGRICULTURAL ECONOMICS AND FARM MANAGEMENT, MASSEY UNIVERSITY. **Added/Corp** Massey University. Dept. of Agricultural Economics and Farm Management. (19??)-. Monographic series. English. Irregular. Price varies per volume. Massey University / New Zealand, Department of Agriculture & Economics, Palmerston North New Zealand. **Tel** 69099. **ED** R. L. Sheppard. **Circ:** 300.
Desc: Economic and marketing papers on agricultural subjects including policy, management, transport, business, resources, and education.
Ind/Abst Leis., Rec., Tour. Abstr.

LC HA1634.C7 D78
CI
DRUSTVENI PROIZVOD I NARODNI DOHODAK ... POLJOPRIVREDE INDIVIDUALNOG SEKTORA. (1979)-. Periodical. Serbo-Croatian (Roman). One time a year. 70.00 Din. Republicki Zavod za Statistiku, Central Bureau of Statistics of the Republic of Croatia, Ilica 3, Zagreb Croatia. **Tel** 011 385 41 45 44 22, FAX 011 385 41 42 94 13, 011 385 41 42 37 11, telex 21130 DZSTAT RH.

LC HD1769 .E294 **ISSN** 0895-2051
DD 338 US
ECONOMIC INDICATORS OF THE FARM SECTOR. NATIONAL FINANCIAL SUMMARY. (ECONOMIC INDICATORS OF THE FARM SECTOR. NATIONAL FINANCIAL SUMMARY.).

[Econ. indic. farm sect., Natl. financ. summ.]. **Added/Corp** United States. Dept. of Agriculture. Economic Research Service. **VFOAT** National Financial Summary. (1984)-. English. One time a year. US Department of Agriculture, 14th Street and Independence Avenue SW, Washington DC 20250. **Tel** (202)720-5457. **(Subscription address:** Superintendent of Documents, US Government Printing Office, Washington DC 20402. **)** ***Continues*** *Economic Indicators of the Farm Sector. Income and Balance Sheet Statistics, 0747-8585.*
Ind/Abst World Agric. Econ. Rural Sociol. Abstr.

LC HD1751 .E296
DD 338.1/3/0973021 US
CEASED

ECONOMIC INDICATORS OF THE FARM SECTOR. STATE FINANCIAL SUMMARY. **Added/Corp** United States. Dept. of Agriculture. Economic Research Service. **VFOAT** State Financial Summary. (1984)-Vol. 13, No. 3 (1995). Government Publication. English. Superintendent of Documents, US Government Printing Office, Washington DC 20402. **Tel** (202)275-3328, FAX (202)786-2377. ***Continues*** *Economic Indicators of the Farm Sector. State Income and Balance Sheet Statistics, 0747-8569.*
Ind/Abst Soyabean Abstr.; World Agric. Econ. Rural Sociol. Abstr.

LC UNC **ISSN** 0886-4845
DD 330 US

ECONOMIC INFORMATION REPORT (GAINESVILLE, FLA.). (ECONOMIC INFORMATION REPORT.). [Econ. inf. rep.]. **Added/Corp** University of Florida. Food and Resource Economics Dept. University of Florida. Agricultural Experiment Station. Florida Cooperative Extension Service. University of Florida. Institute of Food and Agricultural Sciences. (Mar. 1975)-. Monographic series. English. Price varies per volume. University of Florida / Institute of Food and Agricultural Sciences / Food and Resources Economics Department, PO Box 110240, Gainesville FL 32611-6015. **Tel** (904)392-1733.
Ind/Abst Soyabean Abstr.

ISSN 1048-7573
DD 338 US

ECONOMIC PERSPECTIVES. AGRICULTURAL CREDIT OUTLOOK. [Econ. perspect., Agric. credit outlook]. **Added/Corp** United States. Farm Credit Administration. **VFOAT** Agricultural Credit Outlook. (1988)-. English. One time a year. Free. Farm Credit Administration, Public Affairs Division, Washington DC 20578. **Tel** (202)755-2195. **Circ:** 1,000. ***Continues*** *Agricultural and Credit Outlook, 0732-6009.*

LC HD1407 .C5 HD9049.W5N53
DD 338.1 S 338.1/3311/09931 NZ
UDC 338.439.4:633.1(931)

ECONOMIC SURVEY OF NEW ZEALAND WHEATGROWERS : FINANCIAL ANALYSIS, AN. **Main/Corp** Lincoln College, Lincoln, N.Z. Agricultural Economics Research Unit. 1977/78-. English. $4.50. Bookshop, Lincoln College, Canterbury New Zealand.

LC HD2075.P8 A26
DD 338.1/0954/552 II

ECONOMICS OF AGRICULTURAL PRODUCTION AND FARM MANAGEMENT IN PUNJAB. **Main/Corp** Punjab, India (State). Economic and Statistical Organisation. (1968)-. English. Government Press / Economical and Statistical Organization, Chandigarh India.

LC S49 .E4 **ISSN** 0428-6782
DD 338.1 US

ECONOMICS SERIES- FLORIDA. UNIVERSITY, GAINESVILLE. AGRICULTURAL EXTENSION SERVICE. **Main/Corp** Florida. University, Gainesville. Agricultural Extension Service. 55-1 (Feb. 1955)-. English. Irregular. Florida University, Agricultural Extension Service, Gainesville FL 32611.

ISSN 0981-8715
FR
UDC 664

ECONOMIE AND GESTION AGRO-ALIMENTAIRE. (198?)-. Periodical. French. Four times a year. $74.36. Econ Gestion Agro Aliment IGIA, 13 boulevard de l'Hautil, 95092 Cergy Pntoise CDX France. **Tel** 011 33 1 30756085, FAX 011 33 1 30756081. **ED** Frederic Oble. Index available. **Bk Rev**. **Ad Acc. Circ:** 700 (ctrl).
Ind/Abst World Agric. Econ. Rural Sociol. Abstr.

ISSN 0070-8798
FR

ECONOMIE ET FINANCES AGRICOLES. (ECONOMIE & FINANCES AGRICOLES : REVUE DE LA CAISSE NATIONALE DE CREDIT AGRICOLE.). [Econ. financ. agric.]. **Added/Corp** Caisse Nationale de Credit Agricole (France). **VFOAT** Economie et Finances Agricoles. (1971)-. Periodical. English. Five times a year. $65.61. Caisse National Credit of Agricole, 91 93 BD Pasteur, 75015 Paris France.
Ind/Abst Leis., Rec., Tour. Abstr.; PAIS Int. Print; Pig News Inf.; Potato Abstr.; Soyabean Abstr.; Wheat Barley Trit. Abstr.; World Agric. Econ. Rural Sociol. Abstr.

LC HC **ISSN** 0013-0559
FR

ECONOMIE RURALE. [Econ. rurale]. **Added/Corp** Societe Francaise d'Economie Rurale. No. 15 (April 1953)-. Periodical. French (summaries and/or abstracts in English). Six times a year. $157.47. Societe Francaise Economie Rurale, 16 rue Claude Bernard, 75231 Paris Cedex 05 France. **Tel** 011 33 1 47074786. **ED** Philippe Lacombe. **Bk Rev. Circ:** 1,000 (ctrl). ***Continues*** *Bulletin de la Societe Francaise d'Economie Rurale.*
Ind/Abst AGRICOLA; Dairy Sci. Abstr.; Int. Labour Doc.; Leis., Rec., Tour. Abstr.; Maize Abstr.; PAIS Int. Print (1991-); Rice Abstr.; Rural Dev. Abstr.; Sorghum Mill. Abstr.; Wheat Barley Trit. Abstr.; World Agric. Econ. Rural Sociol. Abstr.

LC S562.E95 S73a
DD 338.1/3/094 LU

EG-INDIZES DER EINKAUFSPREISE LANDWIRTSCHAFTLICHER BETRIEBSMITTEL. **Main/Corp** Statistical Office of the European Communities. **Added/Corp** Statistical Office of the European Communities. EC-Indices of Purchase Prices of the Means of Agricultural Production. **VFOAT** EC-Indices of Purchase Prices of the Means of Agricultural Production. (1978)-. English (French, German and Italian).

ISSN 1350-4460
DD 338.1094 UK

EUROPEAN AGRIBUSINESS. [Eur. agribus.]. **Added/Corp** Agra Europe. (1992)-. Newspaper. English. Twelve times a year. $444.92. Agra Europe London Limited, 25 Frant Road, Tunbridge Wells, Kent TN2 5JT United Kingdom. **Tel** 011 44 1892 533813, FAX 011 44 1892 544895, telex 95114 AGRATW G. ***Continues*** *Green Europe, 0141-2213.*

LC HD1401 **ISSN** 0165-1587
DD 338.1 NE
CCC
CODEN ERAEDA

EUROPEAN REVIEW OF AGRICULTURAL ECONOMICS. [Eur. rev. agric. econ.]. Vol. 1 (1973)-. Trade Publication. English. Four times a year. $252.00. Walter de Gruyter Inc., PO Box 303421, D-10728 Berlin Germany. **Tel** 011 49 30 260050, FAX 011 49 30 26005251, telex 184027. **ED** Arie Oskam. **Bk Rev. Ad Acc. Circ:** 600. Documents available from BLDSC, FAXON Xpress, The UnCover Company, SWETS.
Desc: Serves as a forum for discussions about the development of theoretical and applied agricultural economics research in Europe.
Ind/Abst AGRICOLA; Agrindex; Contents Recent Econ. J.; Curr. Cit.; Dairy Sci. Abstr.; Econ. Lit. Index; Geogr. Abstr. Human Geogr.; Int. Dev. Abstr.; Int. Labour Doc.; Irr. Drain. Abstr.; J. Econ. Lit.; LABORDOC; Leis., Rec., Tour. Abstr.; Maize Abstr.; Nutr. Abstr. Rev., Ser. B, Live Feeds and Feed.; Rice Abstr.; Rural Dev. Abstr.; Soc. Plann. Policy Dev. Abstr.; Soc. Sci. Cit. Index [Full Cov.]; Sociol. Abstr.; Soils Fert.; Sug. Indus. Abstr.; Wheat Barley Trit. Abstr.; World Agric. Econ. Rural Sociol. Abstr.

US

FARM BUREAU NEWS (KANSAS FARM BUREAU). (FARM BUREAU NEWS.). Periodical. English. Twelve times a year. Kansas Farm Bureau, 2321 Anderson Avenue, Manhattan KS 66502.

ISSN 0703-7945
DD 338.1/3/0971 CN

FARM CASH RECEIPTS (QUARTERLY ED.). (FARM CASH RECEIPTS.). [Farm cash receipts]. **Added/Corp** Statistics Canada. Farm Income and Prices Section. Statistics Canada. Agriculture Division. **VFOAT** Recettes Monetaires Agricoles. (1971)-. Periodical. English (French). Four times a year. 49.62Can$. Statistics Canada Publications Sales and Services, R.H. Coats Building 6th Floor, Ottawa Ontario K1A 0T6 Canada. **Tel** (613)951-5078, (800)267-6677, FAX (613)951-1584, telex 053-3585. ***Continues*** *Farm Cash Receipts (Canada. Dominion Bureau of Statistics : Quarterly), 0703-7945.*
Desc: Estimates income received by farmers from the sale of farm products by provinces and main commodities, cumulative from January to reference month.

LC HG3691 **ISSN** 0825-7019
DD 332.7/1/0971 CN

FARM CREDIT STATISTICS. [Farm credit stat.]. **VFOAT** Statistiques du Credit Agricole. 1983-. English (French). One time a year. Farm Credit Corporation, 1800 Hamilton Street, Suite 900, Regina Saskatchewan S4P 4K7 Canada. **Tel** (306)780-8100. ***Continues*** *Federal Farm Credit Statistics (1981), 0823-4264.*

ISSN 0886-5906
DD 338 US

FARM ECONOMICS : FACTS AND OPINIONS. [Farm econ. facts opin.]. **Added/Corp** University of Illinois (Urbana-Champaign Campus). Dept. of Agricultural Economics Illinois. University. Cooperative Extension Service. (Mar. 1976)-. Periodical. English. Irregular (18 issues per year). $15.00. Agricultural Newsletter Service, University of Illinois, 116 Mumford Hall, Urbana IL 61801. **Tel** (217)333-2666. ***Continues*** *Farm Management.*
Desc: Covers agricultural extension work.
Ind/Abst AGRICOLA [Full Cov.].

ISSN 0555-9456
DD 338 US

FARM ECONOMICS (UNIVERSITY PARK, PA.). (FARM ECONOMICS.). [Farm econ.]. **Added/Corp** Pennsylvania State University. Agricultural Economics Extension. Pennsylvania State University. Agricultural Extension Service. Pennsylvania State University. Cooperative Extension Service. **VFOAT** Farm and Family Economics. (Aug. 1, 1957)-. Periodical. English. Six times a year. Free on request. Pennsylvania State University, 211 Weaver Building, University Park PA 16802. available on microfilm. ***Continues*** *Pennsylvania Farm Economics.*
Ind/Abst AGRICOLA [Full Cov.]; Field Crop Abstr.; Grass. Forage Abstr.

LC HD2075.6 .A28
DD 338.1/09549/2 BG

FARM ECONOMY. Vol. 1, (1979)-. Periodical. English (Bengali).

LC HG1501
DD 332.1 US

FARM FINANCE REVIEW. (Dec. 1975)-. Periodical. English. Twelve times a year. $28.50. Farm Finance Review, 416 Wren Drive, Mt. Vernon IL 62864. **Tel** (618)242-2736. **ED** G. Mitchell Kane.
Desc: A review of economic situations in agri-business.

ISSN 0883-2188
DD 338 US

FARM FINANCIAL CONDITIONS REVIEW. (FARM FINANCIAL CONDITIONS REVIEW (FFCR).). [Farm financ. cond. rev.]. **Added/Corp** Farm Sector Economics Associates. **VFOAT** FFCR. (1985)-. Periodical. English. Twelve times a year. $595.00. Farm Sector Economics Inc, PO Box 10017, Colorado Springs CO 80932. **Tel** (800)835-9100, FAX (719)78-0800. **ED** Paul T. Prentice. **Circ:** 150 (ctrl).
Desc: Analysis of financial conditions in the U.S. agricultural economy. Forecasts of key farm sector financial indicators are made. Developments in the economy are related to U.S. agriculture.

LC HD1525 .F293 **ISSN** 0363-8545
DD 331.12/53/0973 US

FARM LABOR (WASHINGTON). (FARM LABOR.). [Farm labor]. (Nov. 13, 1943)-. Government Publication. English. Four times a year. $17.00. US Department of Agriculture / National Agricultural Statistics Service (NASS), Room 5829 South Building, Washington DC 20250. **Tel** (202)720-4020, FAX (314)875-5231. available on microfiche (Vols. for (1986-) distributed to depository libraries). Documents available from Documents on Demand. ***Continues*** *Farm Labor Report (United States. Bureau of Agricultural Economics).*
Ind/Abst Am. Stat. Index.

ISSN 0014-8059
UK

FARM MANAGEMENT (KENILWORTH). (FARM MANAGEMENT.). [Farm manage.]. **Added/Corp** Canadian Farm Management Association. Vol. 1, (Feb. 1967)-. Periodical. English. Four times a year (Jan., Apr., July, Oct.). $37.64. Centre of Management in Agriculture, Farm Management Unit, University of Reading, PO Box 236, Reading RG6 2AT United Kingdom. **Tel** 011 44 1734 351458, FAX 011 44 1734 352421. **ED** D. Brown. Index available. cum. index. **Bk Rev**, (Qty: 4). **Circ:** 1,800 (ctrl).
Desc: Business management journal for agriculture.
Ind/Abst AGRICOLA; Agric. Eng. Abstr. (1991-); Agrofor. Abstr.; Dairy Sci. Abstr.; Grass. Forage Abstr.; Int. Abstr. Oper. Res. [Select. Cov.]; Leis., Rec., Tour. Abstr.; Manage. Market. Abstr.; Potato Abstr.; Rural Dev. Abstr.; World Agric. Econ. Rural Sociol. Abstr.

LC HD1491.U5 N4 **ISSN** 0364-0736
DD 334/.683/0973 US

FARMER COOPERATIVES. (FARMER COOPERATIVES / ECONOMICS, STATISTICS, AND COOPERATIVES SERVICE, U.S. DEPARTMENT OF AGRICULTURE.). [Farmer coop.]. **Added/Corp** United States. Dept. of Agriculture. Economics, Statistics, and Cooperatives Service. United States. Farmer Cooperative Service. United States. Agricultural Cooperative Service. Vol. 42, No. 11 (Feb. 1976)-. Government Publication. English. Twelve times a year. $31.00. US Department of Agriculture, 14th Street and Independence Avenue SW, Washington DC 20250. **Tel** (202)720-5457. **(Subscription address:** Superintendent of Documents, US Government Printing Office, Washington DC 20402. **)** **ED** Patrick Duffey. **Circ:** 18,000. ***Continues*** *News for Farmer Cooperatives.*
Desc: Reports actions of cooperatives and views of

cooperative leaders in industry, government and education; reports the activities of the publishing agency.
Ind/Abst Acad. Search; AGRICOLA [Full Cov.]; EP Collect.; Homework Help.; MasterFile FullTEXT 1000; MasterFile FullTEXT 350; MasterFile FullTEXT 650; MasterFile FullTEXT (July 1994-) [Full Txt.]; OCLC; PAIS Int. Print (1991-); Telebase; Vocat. Search.

ISSN 0889-5619
DD 630 US

FARMERS & CONSUMERS MARKET BULLETIN. [Farmers and consumers market bulletin]. **Added/Corp** Georgia. Dept. of Agriculture. **VFOAT** Farmers and Consumers Market Bulletin; Market Bulletin. Vol. 55, No. 10 (Mar. 5, 1969)-. Trade Publication. English. One time a week. Free on request. Georgia Department of Agriculture, 19 Martin Luther King Drive, Room 226, Capitol Square, Atlanta GA 30334-4250. **Tel** (404)656-3600, (404)656-3722, FAX (404)656-9380, (404)651-7957. **ED** Lisa Ray and Carlton Moore. ***Continues** Georgia. Dept. of Agriculture. Georgia Farmers' Market Bulletin.*
Desc: A publication for Georgia farmers to market their goods and services.
Ind/Abst AGRICOLA.

LC KF6289.8.F3 F36 **ISSN** 0731-4612
DD 343.7304/024631 347.3034024631 US

FARMERS FEDERAL TAX ALERT. **Added/Corp** Research Institute of America, inc. (19??)-. Periodical. English. Twelve times a year. $90.00. Research Institute of America, 117 East Stevens Avenue, Valhalla NY 10595. **Tel** (800)431-9025, FAX (800)820-3135 (914)749-5300. **ED** James E Cheeks.
Desc: Highlights developments in the field of agribusiness.

LC HD1751 .F34 **ISSN** 0270-5672
DD 338.1/0973 US
CODEN FRMLEZ
CEASED

FARMLINE. [Farmline]. **Added/Corp** United States. Dept. of Agriculture. Economics, Statistics, and Cooperatives Service. United States. Dept. of Agriculture. Economics and Statistics Service. United States. Dept. of Agriculture. Economic Research Service. United States. Dept. of Agriculture. Statistical Reporting Service. **VAT** Farm line. Vol. 1, No. 1 (Apr. 1980)-(1993). Government Publication. English. Superintendent of Documents, US Government Printing Office, Washington DC 20402. **Tel** (202)275-3328, FAX (202)786-2377. ***Formed by the union of** Agricultural Situation (Washington, D.C.), 0002-1660 **and** Farm Index, 0014-7982.*
Desc: Written for a general agricultural audience, including farm analysts, agribusinesses, and farmers who want to keep up with major economic developments in the farm sector through the research and analysis of USDA's Economic Research Service. Wide-ranging articles report and analyze trends in farm production, foreign trade, commodity prices, land use and land values, farm finances, rural populations and employment, productivity, policy, and other subjects.
Ind/Abst AGRICOLA [Full Cov.]; BioBusiness; Biol. Dig.; Field Crop Abstr.; Foods Adlibra; Maize Abstr.; Potato Abstr.; Rice Abstr.; Sug. Indus. Abstr.; Wheat Barley Trit. Abstr.; World Agric. Econ. Rural Sociol. Abstr.

LC HD9003 .F43 HD1751. A91845 **ISSN** 0363-2288
DD 016.3801/41/072073 US

FEDERAL-STATE MARKET NEWS REPORTS; A DIRECTORY OF SERVICES AVAILABLE. **Added/Corp** United States. Agricultural Marketing Service. United States. Consumer and Marketing Service. (19??)-. Government Publication. English. US Department of Agriculture / Agricultural Marketing Service / Washington, DC, Market News Branch, Fruit and Vegetable Division, Washington DC 20250. **Tel** (202)720-2745, (202)720-3343, FAX (202)720-7502.

LC HG2051.I4 A24 **ISSN** 0015-2110
II

FINANCING AGRICULTURE. [Financ. agric.]. **Added/Corp** Agricultural Finance Corporation. Vol. 1 No. 1 & 2 (Apr.-July 1969)-. Periodical. English. Four times a year. $35.00. UBS Publishers Distributors, 5 Ansari Road, PO Box 7015, New Delhi 110002 India. **Tel** 011 91 11 3273601.
Ind/Abst Agrofor. Abstr.; Dairy Sci. Abstr.; World Agric. Econ. Rural Sociol. Abstr.

US

FOREIGN AGRICULTURAL ECONOMIC REPORT. **Main/Corp** United States. Dept. of Agriculture. Economics, Statistics, and Cooperatives Service. No. 143- Jan. 1978-. Government Publication. English. Department of Agriculture / Economics Statistics and Cooperative, Economics Statistics and Cooperatives Service, 14th Street and Independence Avenue SW, Washington DC 20250. **Tel** (202)720-2791. ***Continues** Foreign Agricultural Economic Report, 0429-0577.*
Ind/Abst Maize Abstr.; Rural Dev. Abstr.; World Agric. Econ. Rural Sociol. Abstr.

LC HD9015.E8 S73a
DD 338.1/094 LU

FORSYNINGSBALANCER. VERSORGUNGSBILANZEN. SUPPLY BALANCE SHEETS. See Agriculture-Crop Production and Soils.

US

FYI/FMHA : FOR YOUR INFORMATION / INFORMATION STAFF, FARMERS HOME ADMINISTRATION, U.S. DEPARTMENT OF AGRICULTURE. **VFOAT** For Your Information. **VAT** For Your Information/Farmers Home Administration. Government Publication. English. One time a week. US Department of Agriculture / Farmers Home Administration, 14th Street & Independence Avenue SW, Room 5014, Washington DC 20250. **Tel** (202)690-1533, FAX (202)690-0311.

ISSN 0710-8915
DD 336.2/7863/0971 CN

GUIDE D'IMPOT SUR LE REVENU DES AGRICULTEURS. [Guide impot revenu agric.]. French. One time a year. Revenue Canada Impot, 875 Heron Road, Ottawa Ontario K1A 0L8 Canada. ***Continues in part** Impot (Canada). Guide d'Impot des Agriculteurs et Pecheurs, 0700-1649.*

LC S562.D4 H3
DD 338.1/09489 DK

HAANDBOG FOR DRIFTSPLANLGNING. **Added/Corp** Denmark. Landbrugsministeriet. Driftskonomiudvalget. (19??)-. Academic Scholarly Publication. Danish. One time a year. kr40.00 Denmark; $16.00 US. Landbrugets Informationskontor, Udkaersvej 15 Skejby, 8200 Arhus N Denmark. **Tel** 011 45 86 10 90 11, FAX 011 45 86 10 90 22. **Circ:** 8,000.
Desc: Farm management data: crop husbandry, animal husbandry, farm buildings, labour, financing, investments and prices.

LC HD1431 I57a
DD 341.7/592/05 IT

IFAD ANNUAL REPORT. **Main/Corp** International Fund for Agricultural Development. **VAT** International Fund for Agricultural Development Annual Report. (198?)-. English. One time a year. International Fund for Agricultural Development / IFAD, Via del Serafico 107, 00142 Rome Italy. **Tel** 011 39 396 54591, FAX 011 39 396 5043463, telex 620330. ***Continues** Annual Report / International Fund for Agricultural Development.*

LC HD9000.1 .I49A **ISSN** 0272-3700
DD 338.1/9/05 US

IFPRI REPORT. [IFPRI rep.]. **Main/Corp** International Food Policy Research Institute. **VAT** International Food Policy Research Institute Report. (1976/78)-. English (French and Spanish). Four times a year. Free. IFPRI, 1776 Massachusetts Avenue NW, Washington DC 20036. **Tel** (202)862-5600, FAX (202)467-4439, telex 440054. **ED** Barbara Alison Rose. **Circ:** 7,500 (ctrl).
Desc: A newsletter detailing research perspectives, and upcoming publications. Includes a commentary; intended audiences are agricultural economists interested in food policy.

FR

IMAGES ECONOMIQUES DES ENTREPRISES. INDUSTRIES AGRICOLES ET ALIMENTAIRES AU ... . See Agriculture-Abstracting, Bibliographies and Statistics.

ISSN 0961-4745
UK

IMPACT AGBIOBUSINESS. (1990)-. Periodical. English. Four times a year. CAB International Centre, Wallingford, Oxfordshire OX10 8DE United Kingdom. **Tel** 011 44 1491 832111, FAX 011 44 1491 833508, telex 847964 COMAGG G.
Ind/Abst Biocont. News Inf.; Rev. Agric. Entomol.; Rev. Med. Vet. Entomol.; Rev. Plant Pathol.; Weed Abstr.

AT
TITLE CHANGE

INDEXES OF PRICES RECEIVED AND PAID BY FARMERS. **Added/Corp** Australian Bureau of Agricultural and Resource Economics. **VFOAT** Prices Received and Paid by Farmers. (19??)-(1995). Periodical. English. ABARE / Australian Bureau of Agriculture and Resource Economics, GPO Box 1563, Canberra ACT 2601 Australia. **Tel** 011 61 6 2722000, FAX 011 61 6 2722001. ***Continued by** Australian Farming Price Indexes.*

LC HD101 .I533 **ISSN** 0019-5014
II

INDIAN JOURNAL OF AGRICULTURAL ECONOMICS, THE. [Indian j. agric. econ.]. **Added/Corp** Indian Society of Agricultural Economics. Vol. 1, No. 1 (July 1946)-. Periodical. English. Four times a year. $80.00. Indian Society Agricultural Economics, 46/48 Esplanade Mansions, Mahatma Gandhi Road, Bombay 400001 India. **Tel** 242542. **(Subscription address:** Prints India, 11 Darya Ganj, New Delhi 110002 India. **Tel** 011 91 11 3268645, FAX 011 91 11 3275542, telex 31-61087 PRIN-IN.) **ED** N. A. Mujumdar. Index available. **Bk Rev. Ad Acc. Circ:** 1,800 (ctrl).
Desc: Provides a forum for dissemination and exchange of findings of research on agricultural economics. Contents cover studies on production economics, agrarian structure, agrarian relations and much more.
Ind/Abst Agric. Eng. Abstr. (1991-); Agrofor. Abstr.; Cot. Trop. Fibr. Abstr. Bibliogr.; Dairy Sci. Abstr.; Field Crop Abstr.; Food Sci. Technol. Abstr.; For. Prod. Abstr. (19??-19??); Geogr. Abstr. Human Geogr.; Int. Bibliogr. Sociol.; Int. Dev. Abstr.; Int. Labour Doc.; Irr. Drain. Abstr.; J. Plan. Lit.; Leis., Rec., Tour. Abstr.; Maize Abstr.; Rice Abstr.; Rural Dev. Abstr.; Soils Fert.; Stat. Theory Method Abstr. (1959-1963); Wheat Barley Trit. Abstr.; World Agric. Econ. Rural Sociol. Abstr.

LC HD1875.S3 I58A **ISSN** 0100-4409
DD 338.18 BL

INFORMACOES ECONOMICAS - INSTITUTO DE ECONOMIA AGRICOLA. (INFORMACOES ECONOMICAS.). [Inf. econ. - Inst. econ. agric.]. **VFOAT** Agricultura en Sao Paulo. (1971)-. Portuguese. Twelve times a year. $7.00. Instituto de Economia Agricola, Caixa Postal 8114, Sao Paulo 01000 Brazil. **Tel** (011)34067 SAGR-SAO PAULO-BRASIL, telex (011) 34067 SAGR. ctrl circ. available with charts.
Ind/Abst AGRICOLA; Postharvest News Inf.; Potato Abstr.; Rural Dev. Abstr.; World Agric. Econ. Rural Sociol. Abstr.

LC HF1371 **ISSN** 1199-1429
DD 382 CN
CEASED

INTERNATIONAL TRADE BUSINESS PLAN. [Int. trade bus. plan]. **Added/Corp** Canada. External Affairs and International Trade Canada. **VFOAT** Integrated Plan for Trade, Investment and Technology Promotion and Development. (1992/1993)-(1993/1994). Government Publication. English. Agriculture Canada, Communications Branch, Ottawa Ontario K1A 0C7 Canada.

LC HD9086.J3 J45 **ISSN** 0447-5321
DD 331.7 JA

JAPAN COTTON STATISTICS AND RELATED DATA, THE. See Agriculture-Abstracting, Bibliographies and Statistics.

LC HD1401 .S67 **ISSN** 1074-0708
DD 338.1/0975 US
CODEN JAIAE9
Pr Rev.

•**JOURNAL OF AGRICULTURAL AND APPLIED ECONOMICS.** [J. agric. appl. econ.]. **Added/Corp** Southern Agricultural Economics Association. **VFOAT** Journal of the Southern Agricultural Economics Association. Vol. 25, No. 1 (July 1993)-. Academic Scholarly Publication. English. Two times a year. $20.00. Department of Agriculture Economics / Auburn, 202 Comer Hall, Auburn University / SAEA, Auburn AL 36849. **Tel** (334)844-5611, (334)844-6520, FAX (334)844-5639. ***Continues** Southern Journal of Agricultural Economics, 0081-3052.*
Desc: Creative and scholarly work in agricultural economics including theory, methodology, and applications in teaching, research, extension, agribusiness, and microcomputer software.
Ind/Abst Bibliogr. Agric.; BioBusiness; Curr. Cit.; Energy Inf. Abstr.; Environ. Abstr.; Index Econ. Artic. J. Collect. Vol.

LC HD1401 .W47 **ISSN** 1068-5502
DD 338.1/0973/05 US

JOURNAL OF AGRICULTURAL AND RESOURCE ECONOMICS. [J. agric. resour. econ.]. **Added/Corp** Western Agricultural Economics Association. **VFOAT** JARE. Vol. 17, No. 1 (July 1992)-. Periodical. English. Two times a year (July and Dec.). $40.00. Western Agricultural Economics Association, 513 AG Hall, Oklahoma State University, Lincoln NE 68583. **Tel** (405)744-9821. Documents available from The Genuine Article. ***Continues** Western Journal of Agricultural Economics, 0162-1912.*
Ind/Abst Curr. Contents Agric. Biol. Environ. Sci.; Curr. Contents Soc. Behav. Sci.; Econ. Lit. Index; Res. Alert [Full Cov.]; Soc. Sci. Cit. Index [Full Cov.].

LC HD1401 .J68 **ISSN** 0021-857X
DD 338.1/05 UK
CODEN JAGEA7
Pr Rev.

JOURNAL OF AGRICULTURAL ECONOMICS. [J. agric. econ.]. **Added/Corp** Agricultural Economics Society (Great Britain). Vol. 11 (June 1954)-. Periodical. English. Three times a year (Jan., May, Sept.). $61.60. Agricultural Economics Society, Wye College, Ashford TN25 5AH Kent United Kingdom. **Tel** 011 44 1233 812401, telex 73458 UNIABN G. **ED** D.I. Buteman. **Bk Rev. Ad Acc. Circ:** 1,800. Documents available from Documents on Demand. ***Continues** Agricultural Economics Society (Great Britain). Journal of Proceedings of the Agricultural Economic Society.*
Desc: Economics of agriculture world wide.
Ind/Abst AGRICOLA; Agrofor. Abstr. (19??-19??);

BioBusiness; Contents Recent Econ. J.; Curr. Cit.; Dairy Sci. Abstr.; Econ. Lit. Index (19??-); Environ. Abstr.; Food Sci. Technol. Abstr.; Geogr. Abstr. Human Geogr.; Int. Abstr. Oper. Res. (1986-) [Select. Cov.]; Int. Dev. Abstr.; Irr. Drain. Abstr.; J. Econ. Lit.; J. Plan. Lit.; Leis., Rec., Tour. Abstr.; Maize Abstr.; Nutr. Abstr. Rev., Ser. B, Live Feeds and Feed.; Nutr. Abstr. Rev., Ser. A, Hum. Exp.; PAIS Int. Print (1991-); Pig News Inf.; Potato Abstr.; Poult. Abstr.; Rice Abstr.; Rural Dev. Abstr.; Sci. Cit. Index; Soc. Sci. Cit. Index [Full Cov.]; Soils Fert.; Sorghum Mill. Abstr.; Sug. Indus. Abstr.; Wheat Barley Trit. Abstr.; World Agric. Econ. Rural Sociol. Abstr.

LC HC **ISSN** 0300-1717 PH

JOURNAL OF AGRICULTURAL ECONOMICS AND DEVELOPMENT. [J. agric. econ. dev.]. **Added/Corp** Philippine Agricultural Economics Association. Farm Economics Association of the Philippines. Philippine Council for Agriculture and Resources Research. Philippine Council for Agricultural Research. National Research Council of the Philippines. (1971)-. Periodical. English. Two times a year. Philippines Agricultural Economics Association, CDEM U P at Los Banos College, Laguna Philippines.
Ind/Abst AGRICOLA.

LC HD101 .A425 **ISSN** 1043-3309
DD 338.1/05 US
CODEN JAERE6
CEASED

JOURNAL OF AGRICULTURAL ECONOMICS RESEARCH, THE. [J. agric. econ. res.]. **Added/Corp** United States. Dept. of Agriculture. Economic Research Service. **VFOAT** Agricultural Economics Research. Vol. 39 No. 2 (Spring 1987)-Vol. 45 No. 4 (19??). Periodical. English. **(Subscription address:** Superintendent of Documents, US Government Printing Office, Washington DC 20402. **)** available on microfilm and microfiche from University Microfilms International (UMI). Documents available from The Genuine Article, Documents on Demand. ***Continues*** *Agricultural Economics Research, 0002-1423.*
Desc: Contains papers relating to economic and statistical research in agriculture by Government bureaus and other cooperating agencies.
Ind/Abst AGRICOLA [Full Cov.]; Am. Stat. Index; BioBusiness; Biol. Agric. Index; Econ. Lit. Index; Geogr. Abstr. Human Geogr.; Irr. Drain. Abstr.; J. Econ. Lit.; J. Plan. Lit.; Maize Abstr.; PAIS Int. Print; Pig News Inf.; Postharvest News Inf.; Poult. Abstr.; Res. Alert [Full Cov.]; Rev. Agric. Entomol.; Sci. Cit. Index (19??-19??); SCISEARCH; Soyabean Abstr.; Wheat Barley Trit. Abstr.; World Agric. Econ. Rural Sociol. Abstr.

LC HG1501
DD 332.1 US

JOURNAL OF AGRICULTURAL LENDING. **Added/Corp** American Bankers Association. Agricultural Bankers Division. Vol. 1, No. 1 (Winter 1987)-. Periodical. English. Four times a year (Feb., May, Aug., Nov.). $90.00. American Bankers Association, 1120 Connecticut Avenue Northwest, Washington DC 20036. **Tel** (202)663-5221, (202)663-5000, FAX (202)828-4544. **ED** Kris Myszka (editor's address: Century Communications, 6201 West Howard Street, Niles, IL 60714; phone: (708)647-1200 ext. 330). **Ad Acc, Adv Mgr:** K Gotsick, **Tel** (202)663-5111. **Circ:** 1,000.

ISSN 0967-0785
DD 338.1068 UK

JOURNAL OF INTERNATIONAL FARM MANAGEMENT. [J. int. farm manag.]. (1992)-. Periodical. English. Four times a year. $37.64. Centre of Management in Agriculture, Farm Management Unit, University of Reading, PO Box 236, Reading RG6 2AT United Kingdom. **Tel** 011 44 1734 351458, FAX 011 44 1734 352421. ***Continues*** *Farm Management International, 0967-0777.*

ISSN 0738-7296
US
CEASED

KANSAS CITY GRAIN MARKET REVIEW. **See** Agriculture-Feed Grain and Milling.

LC HB1 .J65 **ISSN** 0023-7639
DD 333.05 US
CCC
CODEN LAECAD

LAND ECONOMICS. [Land econ.]. **Added/Corp** University of Wisconsin. University of Wisconsin--Madison. Vol. 24, No. 1 (Feb. 1948)-. Periodical. English. Four times a year (Feb., May, Aug., Nov.). $75.00. University of Wisconsin Press, Journal Division, 114 North Murray Street, Madison WI 53715. **Tel** (608)262-4952, FAX (608)262-8909. Index available (bound in last issue). available on microfilm and microfiche from University Microfilms International (UMI); available on an online database (file 648/Full-Text) from DIALOG. Documents available from The Genuine Article, UMI Article Clearinghouse, Documents on Demand. ***Continues*** *Journal of Land & Public Utility Economics.*
Ind/Abst ABI/INFORM Glob. Ed.; ABI/INFORM [Computer File] (Nov. 1971-); Acad. Abstr.; Acad. Search; AGRICOLA [Select. Cov.]; Am. Hist. Life (1964-); AQUAREF; Avery Index Archit. Period. Suppl. Colum. Univ. (1990-); BioBusiness; Bus. ASAP (1990-) [Full Txt.]; Bus. Index (1985-); Bus. Period. Index; Coal Abstr.; Curr. Cit.; Curr. Contents Soc. Behav. Sci.; Econ. Lit. Index; EMBASE; Energy Inf. Abstr.; Energy Res. Abstr.; Environ. Abstr.; EP Collect.; Expand. Acad. Index (1984-); For. Prod. Abstr.; Gen. BusinessFile (1985-); Gen. Period. Index (1985-); Geogr. Abstr. Human Geogr.; GeoRef; Homework Help.; Index Period. Artic. Relat. Law; INFO-SOUTH Abstr.; Int. Dev. Abstr.; Int. Labour Doc.; Irr. Drain. Abstr.; J. Econ. Lit. (199?-); Leis., Rec., Tour. Abstr.; Mag. Search; Manage. Contents; MasterFile FullTEXT 1000; MasterFile FullTEXT 350; MasterFile FullTEXT 650; MasterFile FullTEXT (Jan. 1992-); Middle East Abstr. Index; Newsp. Period. Abstr. (1991-); OCLC; PAIS Int. Print; Res. Alert [Full Cov.]; Rural Dev. Abstr.; Sage Urban Stud. Abstr; Soc. Sci. Source; Soc. Sci. Cit. Index [Full Cov.]; Soc. Sci. Index; Soc. Sci. Index Fulltext (Nov. 1988-) [Full Txt.]; Soils Fert.; SportSearch; Telebase; Trade Ind. Index (1981-) [Full Txt.]; UMI ABI/Inform--Bus. Period. Ondisc (Nov. 1987-) [Full Txt.]; West. Hist. Q.; Wilson Bus. Abstr.; World Agric. Econ. Rural Sociol. Abstr.

ISSN 0800-5974
DD 338.1 NO

LANDBRUKS KONOMISK FORUM. (LANDBRUKSOKONOMISK FORUM.). [Landbr. kon. forum]. (1984)-. Periodical. Norwegian. Four times a year. $57.56. Scandinavian University Press, PO Box 2959 Toeyen, N 0608 Oslo 6 Norway. **Tel** 011 47 2 2575400, FAX 011 47 2 2575353, telex 71896 UROR N. **(Subscription address:** Scandinavian University Press, 200 Meacham Ave., Elmont NY 11003. **Tel** (516)352-7300, FAX (516)352-7377.**)**
Desc: A Norwegian journal on agricultural economics. Covers agriculture in a wide sense, with economic, environmental and social issues.
Ind/Abst Agric. Eng. Abstr. (1991-); Rural Dev. Abstr.; Wheat Barley Trit. Abstr.; World Agric. Econ. Rural Sociol. Abstr.

LC HD2016 .L36
SW

LANTBRUKSARET / LRF. **Added/Corp** Lantbrukarnas Riksforbund. (19??)-. Swedish. One time a year. Lantbrukarnas Riksforbund, Trycksaksbestallningen, 105 33 Stockholm Sweden. **Tel** 08-787 50 00.
Desc: Description of the Swedish agricultural year mainly in economic terms related to the agricultural co-op sector.

LC HD1775.L8 L75 **ISSN** 8756-6273
DD 338 US

LOUISIANA RURAL ECONOMIST. [La. rural econ.]. **Added/Corp** Louisiana Agricultural Experiment Station. Dept. of Agricultural Economics and Agribusiness. Louisiana Agricultural Experiment Station. Dept. of Agricultural Economics. Louisiana State University and Agricultural and Mechanical College. Agricultural Extension Service. Vol. 1 (Jan. 1939)-. Periodical. English. Four times a year. Free on request. Louisiana State University Agriculture & Mechanics, Department of Agricultural Economics & Agribusiness, Baton Rouge LA 70821. **Tel** (504)388-3282, FAX (504)388-2716. **ED** Alvin Schupp. **Circ:** 1,500 (ctrl).
Desc: Publishes short articles giving results of experiment station research and independent scientific reasoning of agricultural economists in Louisiana.
Ind/Abst AGRICOLA.

ISSN 0084-0793
US

LTC PAPER. **Added/Corp** University of Wisconsin--Madison. Land Tenure Center. **VFOAT** LTC. **VAT** Land Tenure Center Paper. No. 124 (1985)-. Monographic series. English. Irregular. Price varies per volume. Land Tenure Center, 1300 University Avenue, University of Wisconsin, Madison WI 53706. **Tel** (608)262-3657. ***Continues*** *LTC (Series), 0193-5674.*
Desc: Deals with land tenure.
Ind/Abst World Agric. Econ. Rural Sociol. Abstr.

LC HD2080.6 .M35
DD 338.1/09595 MY

MALAYSIAN JOURNAL OF AGRICULTURAL ECONOMICS, THE. **VFOAT** Jurnal Ekonomi Pertanian Malaysia. Vol. 1, No. 1 (Dec. 1984)-. Periodical. English (English). Two times a year. $25.00. Malaysian Agricultural Economics Association, c/o Faculty of Resource Economics and Agribusiness, Universiti Pertanian Malaysia, Serdang, Selangor Malaysia.
Ind/Abst World Agric. Econ. Rural Sociol. Abstr.

UK

MANCHESTER WORKING PAPERS IN AGRICULTURAL ECONOMICS. **Added/Corp** University of Manchester. Dept. of Agricultural Economics. (1986)-. Monographic series. English.
Ind/Abst Wheat Barley Trit. Abstr.

ISSN 0713-3359
DD 338.1/097127 CN

MANITOBA AGRICULTURE STATISTICS. **See** Agriculture-Abstracting, Bibliographies and Statistics.

ISSN 0542-8297
US

MARYLAND AGRI-ECONOMICS. [Md. agriecon.]. **Main/Corp** Maryland. Cooperative Extension Service. (19??)-. English. University of Maryland Cooperative Extension Service, College Park MD 20742. ***Continues*** *Maryland Farm Economics, 0093-5867.*

LC S560 **ISSN** 0802-9210
DD 338.1 NO

MELDING / NORGES LANDBRUKSHGSKOLE, INSTITUTT FOR KONOMI OG SAMFUNNSFAG = REPORT / AGRICULTURAL UNIVERSITY OF NORWAY, DEPARTMENT OF ECONOMICS AND SOCIAL SCIENCES. **Added/Corp** Norges Landbrukshgskole. Institutt for Konomi og Samfunns- fag. **VFOAT** Report. (1990)-. Monographic series. Norwegian (summaries and/or abstracts in English). ***Continues*** *Melding (Norges Landbrukshgskole. Institutt for Landbrukskonomi).*
Ind/Abst Agric. Eng. Abstr.

LC HG1501
DD 332.1 SP

MEMORIA / BANCO DE CREDITO AGRICOLA (MICROFORM). **See** Business and Economics-Banks and Banking.

LC HD101 .F3 **ISSN** 0885-4874
DD 338 US

MINNESOTA AGRICULTURAL ECONOMIST. [Minn. agric. econ.]. **Added/Corp** University of Minnesota. Agricultural Extension Service. University of Minnesota. Dept. of Agricultural Economics. University of Minnesota. Dept. of Agricultural and Applied Economics. No. 510 (Sept. 1968)-. Periodical. English. Four times a year. Free on request. Waite Library / University of Minnesota, 1994 Burford Avenue, Department of Applied Economics, St. Paul MN 55108. **Tel** (612)625-1705. ***Continues*** *Minnesota Farm Business Notes (1951).*
Ind/Abst PAIS Int. Print; World Agric. Econ. Rural Sociol. Abstr.

LC KE1700.A23 A372 **ISSN** 0825-0146
DD 343.71/076/0262 347.103760262 CN

MINUTES OF PROCEEDINGS AND EVIDENCE OF THE SUB-COMMITTEE OF THE STANDING COMMITTEE ON AGRICULTURE ON FARM CREDIT ARRANGEMENTS. [Minutes proc. evid. Sub-Comm. Standing Comm. Agric. Farm Credit Arrange.]. **Main/Corp** Canada. Parliament. House of Commons. Sub-Committee of the Standing Committee on Agriculture on Farm Credit Arrangements. **VFOAT** Proces-Verbaux et Temoignages du Sous-Comite du Comite Permanent de l'Agriculture Charge d'Etudier Arrangements; Accords Relatifs au Credit Agricole. 32nd Parliament, 1st Session, Issue No. 1 (Mar. 24/29, 1983)-. English (French). Canada Communication Group Publishers, Order Processing, Ottawa Ontario K1A 0S9 Canada. **Tel** (819)956-4800, (819)956-4802.

II

MONOGRAPH - CENTRE FOR MANAGEMENT IN AGRICULTURE, INDIAN INSTITUTE OF MANAGEMENT. **Main/Corp** Indian Institute of Management. Centre for Management in Agriculture. (1977)-. Monographic series. English. Irregular. Price varies per volume. Centre Management Agriculture, Indian Institute of Management, Vastrapur Ahmedabad India. ***Continues*** *CMA Monograph.*

LC WMLC 93/1781 **ISSN** 0251-6438
SZ

MONTHLY COMMODITY PRICE BULLETIN. **Added/Corp** United Nations Conference on Trade and Development. Commodities Division. **VFOAT** Boletin Mensual de Precios de Productos Basicos; Bulletin Mensuel des Prix Produits de Base. (1969)-. Bulletin. English (French and Spanish). Twelve times a year. $125.00. United Nations Publications, 2 United Nations Plaza, Room DC2 0853, Department 007C, New York NY 10017. **Tel** (212)963-8303, (800)253-9646. **(Subscription address:** United Nations Publications, Subscription Office, PO Box 361, Birmingham AL 35201-0361. **Tel** (800)633-4931, (205)995-1567 (outside US and Canada), FAX (205)995-1588.**)**

LC HD9890.1 .N3 **ISSN** 0028-0410
DD 338.1/763145 US
TITLE CHANGE

NATIONAL WOOL GROWER. [Natl. wool grower]. **Added/Corp** National Wool Growers Association (U.S.) National Lamb Feeders Association (U.S.). Vol. 1 (1911)- Vol. 83, No. 10 (1993). Periodical. English. American Sheep Industry Association, 6911 South Yosemite Street, Englewood CO 80112. **Tel** (303)771-3500, FAX (303)771-8200. **ED** Janic Grauberger. Index available. **Ad Acc. Circ:** 20,000.

Agriculture —Agricultural Economics

available on microfilm and microfiche from University Microfilms International (UMI). **Continued by** *National Lamb & Wool Grower, 1075-0231*.
Desc: For the producers of sheep, lambs, and wool. Editorial coverage includes activities of the American Sheep Industry Association on lamb and wool promotion and legislative issues in addition to practical management features and agriculture technology.
Ind/Abst AGRICOLA; Life Sci. Collect.

LC HD2091 .N65h

JA
NOGYO KANSOKU. Main/Corp
Japan. Norin Suisansho. Daijin Kambo. Chosaka. 45 (1978)-. Periodical. Japanese. One time a year. ¥1,800. Norin Suisansho Daijin Kanbo, (Minister's Secretariat, Ministry of Agriculture Forestry, and Fisheries), 2-1 Kasumigaseki 1-chome, Chiyodaku Tokyo 100 Japan. **Tel** 03-492-2942. **Continues** *Nogyo Kansoku.*

LC HD2091 .N64

JA
NOGYO SHOTOKU TOKEI. Added/Corp
Japan. Norinsho. Norin Keizaikyoku. Tokei Chosabu. (19??)-. Periodical. Japanese. Norin Tokei Kyokai, (Association of Agriculture & Forestry Statistics), 11-14 Meguro 2 Chome, Meguroku Tokyo 153 Japan.

LC HD2091 .N65d

JA
NOKA SHIKIN DOTAI TOKEI. Main/Corp
Japan. Norinsho. Norin Keizaikyoku. Tokei Johobu. (19??)-. Periodical. Japanese. Norin Tokei Kyokai, (Association of Agriculture & Forestry Statistics), 11-14 Meguro 2 Chome, Meguroku Tokyo 153 Japan.
Continues *Noka Shikin Dotai Tokei.*

LC S561 .N73A **ISSN** 0097-7853
DD 658/.93/071 US
NORTH DAKOTA VOCATIONAL AGRICULTURE FARM BUSINESS MANAGEMENT EDUCATION.
(NORTH DAKOTA VOCATIONAL AGRICULTURE FARM BUSINESS MANAGEMENT EDUCATION : ANNUAL REPORT.). **Main/Corp** North Dakota. State University of Agriculture and Applied Science, Fargo. Dept. of Agricultural Economics. (19??)-. English. One time a year. Extension Communications, PO Box 3166, North Dakota State University, Fargo ND 58105. **Tel** (701)239-5306, FAX (701)239-5613.

AT
OCCASIONAL PAPER / BUREAU OF AGRICULTURAL ECONOMICS, CANBERRA. Added/Corp
Australia. Bureau of Agricultural Economics. (1977)-. Monographic series. English. Irregular. Price varies per volume. Australian Government Publishing Service, GPO Box 84, Canberra ACT 2601 Australia. **Tel** 011 61 6 2954411, FAX 011 61 6 2954455.
Ind/Abst AESIS Q.

II
OCCASIONAL PAPER - ECONOMICS PROGRAM. Main/Corp
International Crops Research Institute for the Semi-Arid Tropics. Economics Program. No. 13 (Mar. 1977)-. Monographic series. English. Price varies per volume.

ISSN 0197-9361
US
CEASED
OLSEN'S AGRIBUSINESS REPORT.
Main/Corp G. V. Olsen Associates. **Added/Corp** G. V. Olsen Associates. Agribusiness Report. **VFOAT** Agribusiness Report. (1979)-(19??)-. Periodical. English. G V Olsen Associates, 123 Picketts Ridge Road, West Redding CT 06896. **Tel** (203)938-4188, FAX (203)938-4186. **ED** Gus Olsen. **Bk Rev**, (Qty: 12). **Circ:** 150.
Desc: News and trends in agriculture and agribusiness; articles on companies involved in food.

LC HD9014.B8 I55a
DD 338.1/3 BL
PRECOS RECEBIDOS PELOS AGRICULTORES. Main/Corp
Instituto Brasileiro de Economia. Centro de Estudos Agricolas. (19??)-. Portuguese. Instituto Brasileiro de Economia, Fundacao Getulio Vargas, Caixa Postal 9052, ZC-02, Rio de Janeiro 20.000 Brazil.

LC HD9016.P5 P5b
DD 338.1/3 PH
PRICES RECEIVED BY FARMERS.
Main/Corp Philippines. Bureau of Agricultural Economics. Economics. (19??)-. English. Bureau of Agricultural Economics / Philippines, De los Santos Building 582, Quezon City 3008 Philippines.

LC HD9282.U5 M66
DD 338.1/371/0973021 US
PRICES RECEIVED. MINNESOTA-WISCONSIN MANUFACTURING GRADE MILK.
Added/Corp United States. Crop Reporting Board.

United States. Agricultural Statistics Board. **VFOAT** Minnesota Wisconsin Manufacturing Grade Milk; Minnesota Wisconsin Manufacturing Grade Milk. (19??)-. Statistical Publication. English. One time a year (June). $7.50. U.S. Department of Agriculture, ERS-NASS, 341 Victory Drive, Herndon VA 22070. **Tel** (800)999-6779, (703)834-0125. **Continues** *Prices Received by Farmers. Minnesota-Wisconsin Manufacturing Grade Milk Price Series and Final Two-state estimates for ...* .

LC HD1831 .W4
DD 338.1/09729/05 TR
PROCEEDINGS OF THE ... WEST INDIES AGRICULTURAL ECONOMICS CONFERENCE. Main/Cont
West Indies Agricultural Economics Conference. **Added/Corp** University of the West Indies (St. Augustine, Trinidad and Tobago). Dept. of Agricultural Economics and Farm Management. Caribbean Agro-Economic Society. **VFOAT** Proceedings of the West Indian Agricultural Economics Conference. 8th (1973)-. Proceedings. English. One time a year. $25.00. Department of Agricultural & Economical Farm Management, University of West Indies, St. Augustine Trinidad. **Tel** (809)663-1334 ext. 3275. **Continues** *Proceedings of the West Indian Agricultural Economics Conference, 0511-5701.*
Ind/Abst Field Crop Abstr.

LC HG3691
DD 332.71 US
REPORT TO STOCKHOLDERS. Main/Corp
Sacramento Bank for Cooperatives. (1977)-. Periodical. English. One time a year.

ISSN 1059-8022
DD 630 AT
CODEN RBWCEA
RESEARCH BULLETIN - WASHINGTON STATE UNIVERSITY. COLLEGE OF AGRICULTURE AND HOME ECONOMICS. RESEARCH CENTER.
(RESEARCH BULLETIN.). [Res. bull. - Wash. State Univ., Coll. Agric. Home Econ., Res. Center].
Added/Corp Washington State University. College of Agriculture and Home Economics. Research Center. **VFOAT** Research Bulletin XB. (1988)-. Bulletin. English. Washington State University College of Agriculture and Home Economics. Documents available from BIOSIS Document Express. **Continues** *Research Bulletin (Washington State University. Agricultural Research Center), 0889-7212.*
Ind/Abst Biol. Abstr.; Hortic. Abstr.; Postharvest News Inf.

LC HD107 .W52 **ISSN** 0090-7170
DD 333/.008 US
RESEARCH PAPER (UNIVERSITY OF WISCONSIN--MADISON. TENURE CENTER).
(A RESEARCH PAPER / LAND TENURE CENTER, UNIVERSITY OF WISCONSIN-MADISON.).
Added/Corp University of Wisconsin--Madison. Land Tenure Center. No. 46 (1968)-. Monographic series. English (Portuguese and Spanish). Irregular. Price varies per volume. Land Tenure Center, 1300 University Avenue, University of Wisconsin, Madison WI 53706. **Tel** (608)262-3657. **Ad Acc. Continues** *University of Wisconsin. Land Tenure Center. Research Paper - Land Tenure Center, 0084-0815.*

ISSN 0812-1664
AT
RESEARCH REPORT OR OCCASIONAL PAPER / THE UNIVERSITY OF NEWCASTLE, DEPARTMENT OF ECONOMICS. Added/Corp
University of Newcastle. Dept. of Economics. (1976)-. Monographic series. English. Irregular. 18.09Aus$. University of Newcastle / Department of Economics, Newcastle New South Wales, 2308 Australia. **Tel** 011 61 49 685551, FAX 011 61 49 676845. **ED** John Stanton & Duncan McDonald. **Circ:** 200 (ctrl).
Desc: Papers on various economic topics.
Ind/Abst Leis., Rec., Tour. Abstr.; Pig News Inf.; Potato Abstr.; Rice Abstr.

LC HD1930.I6 F67a **ISSN** 0791-7376
DD 338.1/09415 IE
RESEARCH REPORT / TEAGASC.
[Res. rep. - Teagasc]. **Added/Corp** Teagasc (Organization). **VFOAT** Teagasc Research Report. (1990)-. English. Teagasc, 19 Sandymount Avenue, Dublin 4 Ireland. **Tel** 011 353 1 688188, FAX 011 353 1 688023, telex 30459. *Formed by the union of Research Report. Animal Production, 0332-1207; Foras Taluntais. Economics and Rural Welfare Research Report, 0332-0251; Research Report. Horticulture, 0790-2964; Research Report. Plant Sciences and Crop Husbandry, 0790-2956; Research Report. Soils and Grassland Production, 0790-2980 and Research Report. Food Science and Technology, 0790-2999.*

ISSN 1058-7195
DD 338 US
Pr Rev
REVIEW OF AGRICULTURAL ECONOMICS.
[Rev. agric. econ.]. **VFOAT** RAE. Vol. 13, No. 1 (Jan. 1991)-. Periodical. English. Two times a year. $20.00. Department of Agricultural Economics, 324B Waters Hall, Kansas State Univeristy, Manhattan KS 66506. **Tel** (913)532-4488. **ED** Ted C. Schroeder. **Circ:** 600. **Continues** *North Central Journal of Agricultural Economics, 0191-9016.*
Desc: Serves as a medium for communicating applied and empirical findings to agricultural economists in research, teaching, extension, business and government.
Ind/Abst AGRICOLA [Full Cov.].

ISSN 0034-6403
MY
REVIEW OF AGRICULTURAL ECONOMICS MALAYSIA. Added/Corp
Federal Agricultural Marketing Authority. Vol. 1 (June 1967)-. Periodical. English. Two times a year (June & Dec.). Federal Agricultural Marketing Authority, 17 & 19 Jalan Selangor, Petaling Jaya Selangor Malaysia.

LC HD9018.A7 R4 **ISSN** 0034-6616
AT
REVIEW OF MARKETING AND AGRICULTURAL ECONOMICS.
[Rev. mark. agric. econ.]. **Added/Corp** New South Wales. Division of Marketing and Agricultural Economics. New South Wales. Dept. of Agriculture. Division of Marketing and Economics. New South Wales. Dept. of Agriculture. Division of Marketing and Economic Services. NSW Agriculture & Fisheries. Division of Marketing and Economic Services. NSW Agriculture & Fisheries. Division of Rural and Resource Economics. Australian Agricultural Economics Society. (1945)-. Periodical. English. Three times a year (Apr., Aug., Dec.). 59.20Aus$. Australian Agricultural Economics Society Inc, PO Box 319, East Melbourne 3002 Australia. **Tel** 011 61 3 345035, FAX 011 61 3 3445570. **ED** R.W.M. Johnson. Index available. cum. index. **Bk Rev**. **Circ:** 700. **Continues** *Monthly Marketing Review.*
Desc: Covers economics analysis of farming, fisheries and forestry including forward and backward linkages. Primary emphasis is the Australian rural sector.
Ind/Abst AGRICOLA [Full Cov.]; APAIS, Austr. Public Aff. Inf. Ser. (1963-); Dairy Sci. Abstr.; Econ. Lit. Index; J. Econ. Lit.; Maize Abstr.; Wheat Barley Trit. Abstr.; World Agric. Econ. Rural Sociol. Abstr.

ISSN 0886-8611
DD 333 US
RURAL DEVELOPMENT NEWS. [Rural dev. news]. Added/Corp
North Central Regional Center for Rural Development. (19??)-. Periodical. English. Five times a year. Free on request. North Central Regional Center for Rural Development, 317-D East Hall, Iowa State University, Ames IA 50011. **Tel** (515)294-8321. Documents available from Documents on Demand.
Ind/Abst AGRICOLA [Full Cov.]; Environ. Abstr.

ISSN 0969-6350
DD 338.1091724 UK
RURAL EXTENSION BULLETIN. [Rural ext. bull.]. Added/Corp
Agricultural Extension and Rural Development Centre. (1993)-. Periodical. English. University of Reading / London Road, London Road, Reading RG1 5AQ United Kingdom. **Continues** *Bulletin - Reading Rural Development Communications, 0261-0914.*

LC HD9225.J3 J36D **ISSN** 0303-5859
JA
SEIKABUTSU SEISAN SHUKKA TOKEI.
(SEIKABUTSU SEISAN SHUKKA TOKEI; SHICHOSONBETSU HEN.). [Seikabutsu seisan shukka tokei]. **Main/Corp** Japan. Norinsho. Norin Keizaikyoku. Tokei Johobu. Japanese. Norin Tokei Kyokai, (Association of Agriculture & Forestry Statistics), 11-14 Meguro 2 Chome, Meguroku Tokyo 153 Japan.

LC HC307.M5 C23a
IT
SITUAZIONE ECONOMICA PROVINCIALE / A CURA DEL SERVIZIO STUDI. Main/Corp
Camera di Commercio, Industria, Artigianato E Agricoltura, Milan. **Added/Corp** Camera di Commercio, Industria, Artigianato e Agricoltura di Milano. Servizio Studi. (19??)-. Periodical. Italian. Four times a year. Camera di Commercio Industria Artigianato E Agricoltura di Milano, via Meravigli 9 B, 20123 Milan Italy. **Tel** 011 39 2 85154516. **Continues** *Situazione Economica in Provincia di Milano nel Mese di ...* .

LC S542.E78 Y38a
DD 630/.72063 ET
SOCIO-ECONOMICS DEPARTMENT RESEARCH PROGRAMME. Main/Corp
Yaersa Meremer Enestiyut. Socio-Economics Dept. **Added/Corp** Yaersa Meremer Derejet. Socio-Economics Dept. Research Programme. (19??)-. English. One time a year. $5.00. Institute of Agricultural Research, PO Box 2003, Addis Ababa Ethiopia. **Tel** telex 21548 IAR ET. **ED** Helen Van Houten, Abebe Kineb and Haiw G Mariam.

Agriculture —Agricultural Equipment

ISSN 0958-9732
UK

SPECIAL STUDIES IN AGRICULTURAL ECONOMICS - UNIVERSITY OF READING, DEPARTMENT OF AGRICULTURAL ECONOMICS & MANAGEMENT. (SPECIAL STUDIES IN AGRICULTURAL ECONOMICS.). **Added/Corp** University of Reading. Dept. of Agricultural Economics and Management. (1988)-. Monographic series. English. **Continues** *Agricultural Enterprise Studies in England and Wales Economic Report, 0306-8900.*
 Ind/Abst Pig News Inf.; World Agric. Econ. Rural Sociol. Abstr.

CN

STATISTICAL ANNUAL / THE WINNIPEG COMMODITY EXCHANGE. See Agriculture-Abstracting, Bibliographies and Statistics.

LC S560
DD 338.1
UK

STUDY/ UNIVERSITY OF READING, DEPARTMENT OF AGRICULTURAL ECONOMICS & MANAGEMEMT. (19??)-. Monographic series. English. Irregular. price varies.
 Ind/Abst World Agric. Econ. Rural Sociol. Abstr.

ISSN 0043-1850
US

WEEKLY MARKET BULLETIN (CONCORD). (WEEKLY MARKET BULLETIN.). **Main/Corp** New Hampshire. Bureau of Markets. (1918)-. Bulletin. English. One time a week. $20.00. New Hampshire Department of Agriculture, PO Box 2042, Concord NH 03302-2042. **Tel** (603)271-2505. **ED** Stephen H. Taylor. **Ad Acc. Circ:** 10,000 (ctrl).
 Desc: Listings confined to items such as farm products, standard farm animals, tools and equipment, farm land, farm labor and articles of agricultural nature only. Advertising by subscribers only.

CN

WORKING PAPER / DEPARTMENT OF AGRICULTURAL ECONOMICS AND BUSINESS, UNIVERSITY OF GUELPH. **Added/Corp** Ontario Agricultural College. Dept. of Agricultural Economics and Business. **VFOAT** Working Paper Series; Working Papers Series. (1987)-. Monographic series. English. **Continues** *Ontario Agricultural College. School of Agricultural Economics and Extension Education. Working Paper - Ontario Agricultural College, School of Agricultural Economics and Extension Education, 0318-1790.*
 Ind/Abst World Agric. Econ. Rural Sociol. Abstr.

LC HD2131 .A46
DD 338.1/096891/05
RH

WORKING PAPER (UNIVERSITY OF ZIMBABWE. DEPT. OF AGRICULTURAL ECONOMICS & EXTENSION). (WORKING PAPER / DEPARTMENT OF AGRICULTURAL ECONOMICS & EXTENSION, UNIVERSITY OF ZIMBABWE.). Monographic series. English. Price varies per volume. University of Zimbabwe / Department of Agricultural Economics, PO Box MP167, Mount Pleasant Harare Zimbabwe.
 Ind/Abst Agrofor. Abstr. (1991-); Cot. Trop. Fibr. Abstr. Bibliogr.; For. Abstr.; Maize Abstr.; Rural Dev. Abstr.; World Agric. Econ. Rural Sociol. Abstr.

LC HD1491
DD 016.338
ISSN 0043-8219
UK

WORLD AGRICULTURAL ECONOMICS AND RURAL SOCIOLOGY ABSTRACTS. See Agriculture-Abstracting, Bibliographies and Statistics.

LC HD9001 .U55b
DD 338.1/05
ISSN 0277-3139
US

WORLD AGRICULTURAL SUPPLY AND DEMAND ESTIMATES. [World agric. supply demand estim.]. **Added/Corp** United States. Dept. of Agriculture. Economics and Statistics Service. United States. Foreign Agricultural Service. United States. World Food and Agricultural Outlook and Situation Board. United States. Dept. of Agriculture. Economic Research Service. United States. World Agricultural Outlook Board. (Oct. 14, 1980)-. Government Publication. English. Twelve times a year. $37.00. Superintendent of Documents, US Government Printing Office, Washington DC 20402. **Tel** (202)275-3328, **FAX** (202)786-2377. **Continues** *Agricultural Supply & Demand Estimates, 0162-5586.*
 Desc: Consisting chiefly of tables and statistics, this publication also contains news items projecting the supply and demand of agricultural commodities.
 Ind/Abst Text. Technol. Dig.

AGRICULTURAL EQUIPMENT

LC TJ1480
DD 631.3
UK

A.E.A. DIRECTORY OF TRACTORS AND AGRICULTURAL MACHINERY. Main/Corp Agricultural Engineers Association. **VFOAT** Directory of Tractors and Agricultural Machinery. 1972-. Directory. English. One time a year.

LC TJ1480
DD 631.3
UDC 631.17
ISSN 0860-2956
PL

ACTA ACADEMIAE AGRICULTURAE AC TECHNICAE OLSTENENSIS. AEDIFICATIO ET MECHANICA. **VFOAT** Selskohozajstvenno-Tehniceskaa Akademia v Olstyne - Mehanika i Stroitelstvo; Agricultural and Technical Academy in Olsztyn - Mechanics and Buildings. (1986)-. Academic Scholarly Publication. Multiple languages. Irregular. Price varies per volume. Wydawnictwo Akademia Rolniczo-Techniczna w Olsztynie / Agricultural and Technical Academy in Olsztyn, Blok 21, 10-957 Olsztyn-Kortowo Poland. **Tel** 011 48 89 273310. (**Subscription address:** Ars Polona-Ruch, PO Box 1001, Krakowskie Przedmiescie 7, 00-068 Warsaw Poland. **Tel** 011 48 22 261201.)

LC TJ1480
DD 631.3
US

AERIAL APPLICATOR, FARM, FOREST AND FIRE. (19??)-. Periodical. English. Nine times a year. $4.50. Aerial Applicator, 8420 Aviation Avenue, Santa Fe Springs CA 90670. **Tel** (310)948-3713. **ED** Robert G. Rosenblatt. **Bk Rev. Ad Acc. Circ:** 8,214 (ctrl).
 Desc: Interest of agriculture, forestry, fire control and new methods and technology for aerial applicators. Includes government regulations, new chemical research, coverage of pest control and regulations for AG pilots and farmers.

LC TJ1480
DD 631.3
US

AG-EQUIPMENT POWER. (19??)-. Periodical. English. Twelve times a year. $12.00. Clintron Publishers, Inc., PO Box 6, Spokane WA 99210. **Tel** (509)575-6774, (800)869-7923, **FAX** (509)457-3885. **ED** Ken Hodge. **Ad Acc. Circ:** 11,203. **Continues** *Agri-Equipment & Chemical, 0192-9526.*
 Desc: Features new and used equipment, successful farmers and dealers, chemical and cultural practices, new products and marketing strategies in Washington, Oregon and Idaho.

LC TJ1480
DD 631.3
GW

AGRARTECHNIK INTERNATIONAL. Vol. 53, No. 1 (Jan. 1974)-. Periodical. German. Vogel Verlag, Postfach 6740, D-97064 Wuerzburg Germany. **Tel** 011 49 931 4182145, 011 49 931 4182483, **FAX** 011 49 931 4182670, telex 841 680131. **Bk Rev. Ad Acc. Circ:** 15,450 (ctrl). **Continues** *Landmaschinen-Markt.; Landmaschinen-Markt. Europa-Ausgabe.).*
 Ind/Abst Agric. Eng. Abstr.; Leis., Rec., Tour. Abstr.; Rural Dev. Abstr.; World Agric. Econ. Rural Sociol. Abstr.

LC TJ1480
DD 631.3
ISSN 0192-9526
US
TITLE CHANGE

AGRI-EQUIPMENT & CHEMICAL. **VFOAT** Agri Equipment & Chemical; Agri-Equipment and Chemical. (1986)-(19??). Periodical. English. Clintron Publishers, Inc., PO Box 6, Spokane WA 99210. **Tel** (509)575-6774, (800)869-7923, **FAX** (509)457-3885. **ED** Ken Hodge. **Ad Acc. Circ:** 11,203. **Continues** *Agri-Equipment Today.* **Continued by** *Ag-Equipment Power.*
 Desc: Features new and used equipment, successful farmers and dealers, chemical and cultural practices, new products and marketing strategies in Washington, Oregon and Idaho.

LC TJ1480
DD 631.3
ISSN 0140-4822
UK

AGRICULTURAL SUPPLY INDUSTRY. [Agric. supply ind.]. Vol. 1, No. 1 (April 2, 1971)-. Trade Publication. English. One time a week. $315.00. PJB Publications, 18-20 Hill Rise, Richmond Surrey TW10 6UA United Kingdom. **Tel** 011 44 181 9483262, **FAX** 011 44 181 3328998. available on an online database from BRS; and (file 648/Full-Text) DIALOG.
 Ind/Abst Abstr. BioCommer.; Chem. Bus. Bull.; Chem. Bus. NewsBase (1985-); Chem. Bus. Update; F&S Index Plus Text, Int. [Select. Cov.]; Infomat Int. Bus.; PROMT.

LC TJ1480
DD 631.3
UK

AGRICULTURE & EQUIPMENT INTERNATIONAL. **VFOAT** Agriculture and Equipment International; Agric & E Intl. **VAT** Agriculture and equipment international. Vol. 44, No. 9 & 10 (1992)-. Periodical. English. Six times a year. $81.00. Research Information Ltd., 222 Mayland Avenue Hemel Hempstead, Hertfordshire HP2 7TD United Kingdom. **Tel** 011 44 1442 259884. **Formed by the union of** *Agriculture International, 0269-2457* **and** *Farm Equipment International.*
 Ind/Abst Curr. Cit.

LC TJ1480
DD 631.3
JA

AMA, AGRICULTURAL MECHANIZATION IN ASIA. Added/Corp Farm Machinery Industrial Research Corporation. Shin-Norinsha Company. International Farm Mechanization Research Service. Vol. 1 (Spring 1971)-. Periodical. English. Four times a year. $121.50. Farm Machinery Industrial Research Corporation Ltd., 7 2-chome Kanda Nishike Cho, Chiyoda-ku Tokyo 101 Japan. **Tel** 011 81 3 3291 3674, **FAX** 011 81 3 3291 5717. (**Subscription address:** Japan Publications Trading Company Ltd., PO Box 5030, Tokyo International, Tokyo 100-31 Japan. **Tel** 011 81 3 3292 3753.)
 Ind/Abst Abstr. AIT Rep. Publ. Energy; Wheat Barley Trit. Abstr.

LC TJ1480
DD 631.3
ISSN 0084-5841
JA
CODEN AMAADL

AMA. AGRICULTURAL MECHANIZATION IN ASIA, AFRICA AND LATIN AMERICA. (AGRICULTURAL MECHANIZATION IN ASIA, AFRICA AND LATIN AMERICA.). [AMA, Agric. mech. Asia, Afr. Lat. Am.]. **Added/Corp** Farm Machinery Industrial Research Corporation. Shin-Norin Sha. International Farm Mechanization Research Service. **VFOAT** AMA, Agricultural Mechanization in Asia, Africa and Latin America; A.M.A. Agricultural Mechanization in Asia, Africa and Latin America. Vol. 12, No. 1 (Winter 1981)-. Periodical. English. Four times a year. $86.48. Farm Machinery Industrial Research Corporation Ltd., 7 2-chome Kanda Nishike Cho, Chiyoda-ku Tokyo 101 Japan. **Tel** 011 81 3 3291 3674, **FAX** 011 81 3 3291 5717. **ED** Yoshisuke Kishida. Index available. **Bk Rev. Ad Acc. Circ:** 15,000. Documents available from Article Express International. **Continues** *AMA, Agricultural Mechanization in Asia, 0084-5841.*
 Desc: Specializes in agricultural mechanization in developing countries.
 Ind/Abst AGRICOLA; Agric. Eng. Abstr. (1991-); Agrofor. Abstr.; Bioeng. Abstr.; Cot. Trop. Fibr. Abstr. Bibliogr.; Curr. Cit.; Dairy Sci. Abstr.; Ei Page One; Eng. Index Annu. [Select. Cov.]; Field Crop Abstr.; Food Sci. Technol. Abstr.; For. Prod. Abstr. (1991-); For. Abstr.; Grass. Forage Abstr.; Hortic. Abstr.; Int. Abstr. Oper. Res. [Select. Cov.]; Irr. Drain. Abstr.; Maize Abstr.; Pig News Inf.; Postharvest News Inf.; Potato Abstr.; Rice Abstr.; Seed Abstr.; Soils Fert.; Sorghum Mill. Abstr.; Soyabean Abstr.; Weed Abstr.; World Agric. Econ. Rural Sociol. Abstr.

LC TJ1480
DD 631.3
ISSN 0730-8701
US
CODEN ADLDDM

ASAE DISTINGUISHED LECTURE SERIES; TRACTOR DESIGN. [ASAE disting. lect. ser., Tract. des.]. **Main/Corp** American Society of Agricultural Engineers. **VAT** American Society of Agricultural Engineers Distinguished Lecture Series. Tractor Design. No. 1 (Dec. 1975)-. Monographic series. English. Irregular. Price varies per volume. American Society of Agricultural Engineers, Department 2510, 2950 Niles Road, St. Joseph MI 49085-9659. **Tel** (616)429-0300, **FAX** (616)429-3852.
 Ind/Abst Agric. Eng. Abstr.

LC TJ1480
DD 338.47681763
ISSN 1036-4242
AT
Pr Rev.

AUSTRALIAN FARMERS' AND DEALERS' JOURNAL. [Aust. farmers' deal. j.]. **VFOAT** AFDJ. (1990)-. Periodical. English. Four times a year. 24.67Aus$. Norley Pty Ltd., 3 Lygon Street, South Caulfield Victoria 3162 Australia. **Tel** 011 61 3 95789122, **FAX** 011 61 3 95782784. **ED** Peter Levy. **Bk Rev**, (Qty: 4). **Ad Acc, Adv Mgr:** Garry Kennedy, **Tel** 11 61 3 6576130. **Circ:** 17,500 (ctrl). **Continues** *Australian Farm Dealers Journal, 0818-2183.*
 Desc: A record of industry news and new products for the agricultural industry within Australia.

LC TJ1480
DD 631.3
ISSN 0249-4779
FR

BULLETIN D'INFORMATION (CENTRE NATIONAL DU MACHINISME AGRICOLE, DU GENIE RURAL, DES EAUX ET DES FORETS (FRANCE). (BULLETIN D'INFORMATION / CEMAGREF.). No. 324 (Jan. 1985)-. Bulletin. French. Twelve times a year. Centre National du Machinisme Agricole, rue du Genie Rural des Eaux et des Forets, Parc de Tourvoie, Antony 92160 France. **Continues** *Bulletin d'Information du CEMAGREF.*

Agriculture —Agricultural Equipment

LC TJ1480
DD 631.3 FR
BULLETIN TECHNIQUE DU MACHINISME ET DE L'EQUIPMENT AGRICOLES.
(1986)-. Bulletin. French. Twelve times a year. 360.00F. Index available. cum. index. **Bk Rev. Circ:** 2,750.
Desc: Includes articles about agricultural equipment.
Ind/Abst Agric. Eng. Abstr. (1991-); Dairy Sci. Abstr.; Irr. Drain. Abstr.; Maize Abstr.; Ornamental Hort. (19??-19??); Pig News Inf.; Postharvest News Inf.; Rice Abstr.; Soyabean Abstr.

LC TJ1480 **ISSN** 1041-9640
DD 338 US
CATALOG (FORT ATKINSON, WIS.).
(CATALOG.). (1989)-. English. One time a year (Jan.). $15.00 US; $20.00 Canada and Mexico; $25.00 other. Johnson Hill Press Inc., (A Division of PTN Publishing Co.), 1233 Janesville Avenue, PO Box 803, Fort Atkinson WI 53538-0803. **Tel** (414)563-6388, FAX (414)563-1704.
Desc: Provides farm operators with a comprehensive guide of farm machinery, grain handling, and livestock products.

LC S760.S6 S7a
DD 631.3 SP
CENSO DE MAQUINARIA AGRICOLA.
Main/Corp Spain. Direccion General de Agricultura, Seccion 7a. (19??)-. Spanish. One time a year. Ministerio Agricultura, Centro de Publicaciones, Calle Alfonso XII 56, 28071 Madrid Spain. **Tel** 011 34 1 3475551, FAX 011 34 1 3475722.

LC TJ1480 **ISSN** 1010-2000
DD 631.3 CU
CODEN CAMAEK
CIENCIA Y TECNICA EN LA AGRICULTURA. MECANIZACION DE LA AGRICULTURA.
[Cienc. tec. agric., Mec. agric.]. **VFOAT** Mecanizacion de la Agricultura. Vol. 1, No. 1 (June 1978)-. Spanish (summaries and/or abstracts in English; table of contents in English). Ediciones Cubanas, Obispo 527 Altos ESQ Bernaza, CP 10100 Havana Cuba. Documents available from BIOSIS Document Express.
Ind/Abst Agric. Eng. Abstr. (1991-); Biol. Abstr. (1986-); For. Abstr.; Postharvest News Inf.; Potato Abstr.

LC S699 .C65 **ISSN** 0148-6470
DD 631.3/5 US
CEASED
COMBINE FACTS.
(1978)-(19??). Periodical. English. Intertec Publishing Corporation, 9800 Metcalf, Overland Park KS 66212. **Tel** (913)341-1300.

LC HD9710.P8 C66
DD 338.4/76292/09469 PO
COMERCIO E A INDUSTRIA AUTOMOVEL EM PORTUGAL, O. See
Industry and Production.

LC TJ1480
DD 631.3 IT
CONTOTERZISTA, IL.
Italian. Eleven times a year. L48000.00. Edagricole, PO Box 2157, 40100 Bologna Italy. **Tel** 011 39 51 492211 Ext. 22, FAX 011 39 51 493660, telex 510336 EDAGRI.

LC S562.E95 S73a
DD 338.1/3/094 LU
EG-INDIZES DER EINKAUFSPREISE LANDWIRTSCHAFTLICHER BETRIEBSMITTEL. See Agriculture-Agricultural Economics.

LC TJ1480 **ISSN** 0013-8142
DD 631.3 US
ENGINEERS AND ENGINES MAGAZINE.
(19??)-. Periodical. English. Six times a year. $18.00. Engineers & Engines Magazine, 1118 North Raymor Avenue, Joliet IL 60435. **Tel** (815)727-1830. **ED** Donald D. Knowles. **Bk Rev. Ad Acc. Circ:** 9,500 (ctrl).
Desc: A magazine for all steam, gas, tractor, railroad, locomotive and farm machinery enthusiasts.

LC TJ1480 **ISSN** 0383-3445
DD 631.3 CN
EVALUATION REPORT - PRAIRIE AGRICULTURAL MACHINERY INSTITUTE.
(EVALUATION REPORT.). [Eval. rep. - Prairie Agric. Mach. Inst.]. **Added/Corp** Prairie Agricultural Machinery Institute (Canada). **VFOAT** Prairie Agricultural Machinery Institute Evaluation Report. (1981)-. Periodical. English. Thirty times a year. 10.00Can$ Alberta, Manitoba and Saskatchewan; 20.00Can$ other Canada; 25.00Can$ other. Prairie Agricultural Machinery Institute, PO Box 1900, Humboldt Saskatchewan S0K 2A0 Canada. **Tel** (306)682-2555, FAX (306)682-5080. **Continues** PAMI Evaluation Report., 0383-3445.

LC TJ1480 **ISSN** 0892-6085
DD 631 US
Pr Rev. **TITLE CHANGE**
FARM & POWER EQUIPMENT DEALER.
(FARM & POWER EQUIPMENT DEALER : OFFICIAL PUBLICATION OF THE NATIONAL FARM & POWER EQUIPMENT DEALERS ASSOCIATION.). [Farm power equip. deal.]. **Added/Corp** National Farm & Power Equipment Dealers Association (U.S.). **VFOAT** Farm and Power Equipment Dealer. Vol. 83, No. 1 (Jan. 1987)-(199?). Trade Publication. English. Admore Publishing Inc, 9701 Gravois Avenue, St Louis MO 63123. **Tel** (314)638-4050, FAX (314)638-3880. **ED** Rick Null. **Ad Acc. Circ:** 11,500 (ctrl). **Continues** Farm & Power Equipment, 0014-7834. **Continued by** NAEDA Equipment Dealer, 1074-5017.
Desc: Serves the retailer, wholesaler, manufacturer, jobber and distributor of farm and industrial and out-door power equipment, accessories, repair parts and others allied to the field served.

LC TJ1480 **ISSN** 0309-4111
DD 631.3 UK
FARM BUILDING PROGRESS.
[Farm build. prog.]. **Added/Corp** Scottish Farm Buildings Investigation Unit. (19??)-. Periodical. English. Four times a year (Jan., April, July, Oct.). $63.31. Centre for Rural Building, Craibstone Bucksburn, Aberdeen AB2 9TR United Kingdom. **Tel** 011 44 1224 713622, FAX 011 44 1224 716433. **ED** Martin Sommer. Index available. **Bk Rev**, (Qty: varies). **Ad Acc, Adv Mgr:** Martin Sommer. **Circ:** 600. Documents available from The Genuine Article.
Desc: Includes research and development news and reviews on current practice in design and construction, and the use of agricultural buildings for livestock and crop production, storage and processing.
Ind/Abst AgBiotech News Inf.; Agric. Eng. Abstr. (19??-19??); Archit. Period. Index (1965-); Curr. Contents Agric. Biol. Environ. Sci.; Dairy Sci. Abstr.; Index Vet.; Nutr. Abstr. Rev., Ser. B, Live Feeds and Feed.; Pig News Inf.; Postharvest News Inf.; Potato Abstr.; Poult. Abstr.; Res. Alert [Select. Cov.]; SCISEARCH; Vet. Bull.

LC S
DD 630 UK
FARM BUILDINGS TOPICS. Added/Corp
East of Scotland College of Agriculture. Farm Buildings Advisory and Development Dept. (19??)-. Periodical. English.
Ind/Abst Archit. Period. Index (Nov. 1972-Apr. 1977).

LC TJ1480 **ISSN** 0014-7958
DD 631 US
FARM EQUIPMENT.
[Farm equip.]. (1962)-. Trade Publication. English. Seven times a year. $28.00. Johnson Hill Press Inc., (A Division of PTN Publishing Co.), 1233 Janesville Avenue, PO Box 803, Fort Atkinson WI 53538-0803. **Tel** (414)563-6388, FAX (414)563-1704. **ED** Jim Wedde. **Ad Acc.** Full Page (B&W) $3610.00. Full Page (Color) $4505.00 (4-color). **Circ:** 13,598 (ctrl).
Desc: Serves owners and managers of farm equipment dealerships in North America. Provides business management, product news, and industry information.

LC TJ1480 **ISSN** 0892-8312
DD 633 US
CCC
FARM INDUSTRY NEWS (1984). (FARM INDUSTRY NEWS.).
[Farm ind. news]. Vol. 17, No. 1 (Jan. 1984)-. Periodical. English (Chinese). Eleven times a year. $12.94. Intertec Publishing Corporation, 9800 Metcalf, Overland Park KS 66212. **Tel** (913)341-1300. (Subscription address: Intertec Publishing Corporation, PO Box 2901, Overland Park KS 66282. **Tel** 800 441-0294.) **ED** Joe Degnan. **Ad Acc. Circ:** 270,000 (ctrl). available on microfilm and microfiche from University Microfilms International (UMI). **Continues** Farm Industry News Midwest, 0199-6924.
Desc: For high-income farmers in 12 midwestern states.

LC HD9486.U3 C87 **ISSN** 0278-9035
DD 380.1/45681763/0973 US
FARM MACHINERY AND LAWN AND GARDEN EQUIPMENT.
(CURRENT INDUSTRIAL REPORTS. MA-35A, FARM MACHINERY AND LAWN AND GARDEN EQUIPMENT.). **Added/Corp** United States. Bureau of the Census. **VFOAT** Farm Machinery and Lawn and Garden Equipment. (1941)-. Government Publication. English. One time a year. $1.25. US Department of Commerce / Bureau of the Census, Data User Services Division, Customer Services, Washington DC 20233-0800. **Tel** (301)763-4100. (Subscription address: Superintendent of Documents, US Government Printing Office, Washington DC 20402.) **Continues** Current Industrial Reports. MA-35A, Farm Machinery and Equipment.
Desc: Shows statistics on the quantity and value of manufacturers' shipments of farm machinery and lawn and garden equipment.

LC S671 .F33 **ISSN** 0192-8317
DD 629.22/5 US
CEASED
FARM MACHINERY & TRACTOR FACTS. VAT
Farm Machinery and Tractor Facts. (19??)-(19??). English. Intertec Publishing Corporation, 9800 Metcalf, Overland Park KS 66212. **Tel** (913)341-1300.

LC TJ1480 **ISSN** 0709-6216
DD 631.3 CN
FARM MACHINERY COSTS AS A GUIDE TO CUSTOM RATES. Added/Corp
Alberta. Farm Business Management Branch. (1???)-. English. Free. Alberta Agriculture / Farm Business Management Branch, Box 2000, Olds Alberta T0M 1P0 Canada. **Tel** (403)427-2442, FAX (403)556-7545.

LC TJ1480 **ISSN** 0225-9346
DD 338.1/3 CN
FARM MACHINERY CUSTOM AND RENTAL RATES, DETAILED SUPPLEMENT.
[Farm mach. cust. rent. rates, Detailed suppl.]. 1979-. English. One time a year. Saskatchewan Agriculture, Crop Production Section, Regina Saskatchewan Canada.

LC TJ1480 **ISSN** 0163-4518
DD 631.3 US
FARM SHOW.
[Farm show]. Vol. 1, (1977)-. Trade Publication. English. Six times a year (Jan., Mar., May, July, Sept., Nov.). $15.95. Farm Show, 20088 Kenwood Trail, PO Box 1029, Lakeville MN 55044. **Tel** (612)469-5572, FAX (612)469-5575. **ED** Mark Newhail. Index available. cum. index. **Circ:** 150,000. **Absorbed** Ag World, 0190-4515.
Desc: Focuses on latest new products and ideas including made-it- myself ideas from farm workshops.

LC S677 **ISSN** 1072-9038
DD 381 US
FARM SUPPLY RETAILING.
[Farm supply retail.]. (19??)-. Periodical. English. Six times a year. $40.00. Farm Supply Retailing, PO Box 23536, Minneapolis MN 55423. **Tel** (612)854-5101, FAX (612)854-8191.

LC TJ1480
DD 631.3 US
FURROW. DAIRYLAND EDITION, THE.
(THE FURROW.). **Added/Corp** Deere & Company. (19??)-. Periodical. English. Seven times a year. Free to qualified subscribers. Deere & Company, John Deere Road, Moline IL 61265. **Tel** (309)765-8000. **Continues in part** Furrow, 0016-3112.

LC TJ1480
DD 631.3 US
FURROW. GREAT PLAINS EDITION, THE.
(THE FURROW.). **Added/Corp** Deere & Company. (198?)-. Periodical. English. Seven times a year. Free to qualified subscribers. Deere & Company, John Deere Road, Moline IL 61265. **Tel** (309)765-8000. **Continues in part** Furrow, 0016-3112.

LC TJ1480
DD 631.3 US
FURROW. NORTH PLAINS EDITION, THE.
(THE FURROW.). **Added/Corp** Deere & Company. (19??)-. Periodical. English. Seven times a year. Free to qualified subscribers. Deere & Company, John Deere Road, Moline IL 61265. **Tel** (309)765-8000. **Continues in part** Furrow, 0016-3112.

LC TJ1480
DD 631.3 US
FURROW. NORTHERN EDITION, THE.
(THE FURROW.). **Added/Corp** Deere & Company. (198?)-. Periodical. English. Seven times a year. Free to qualified subscribers. Deere & Company, John Deere Road, Moline IL 61265. **Tel** (309)765-8000. **Continues in part** Furrow, 0016-3112.

LC TJ1480
DD 631.3 US
FURROW. NORTHWEST EDITION, THE.
(THE FURROW.). **Added/Corp** Deere & Company. (19??)-. Periodical. English. Seven times a year. Free to qualified subscribers. Deere & Company, John Deere Road, Moline IL 61265. **Tel** (309)765-8000. **Continues in part** Furrow, 0016-3112.

LC TJ1480
DD 631.3 US
FURROW. PLAINS EDITION, THE.
(THE FURROW.). **Added/Corp** Deere & Company. (19??)-. Periodical. English. Seven times a year. Free to qualified subscribers. Deere & Company, John Deere Road, Moline IL 61265. **Tel** (309)765-8000. **Continues in part** Furrow, 0016-3112.

LC TJ1480
DD 631.3 US
FURROW. SOUTHLAND EDITION, THE.
(THE FURROW.). **Added/Corp** Deere & Company. (19??)-. Periodical. English. Seven times a year. Free to qualified subscribers. Deere & Company, John Deere Road, Moline IL 61265. **Tel** (309)765-8000. **Continues in part** Furrow, 0016-3112.

LC TJ1480
DD 631.3 US
FURROW. STRIPPER/COTTON EDITION, THE.
(THE FURROW.). **Added/Corp** Deere & Company. (19??)-. Periodical. English. Seven

times a year. Free to qualified subscribers. Deere & Company, John Deere Road, Moline IL 61265. **Tel** (309)765-8000. ***Continues in part*** *Furrow, 0016-3112.*

LC TJ1480
DD 631.3 US
FURROW. SUN BELT EDITION, THE. (THE FURROW.). **Added/Corp** Deere & Company. (19??)-. Periodical. English. Seven times a year. Free to qualified subscribers. Deere & Company, John Deere Road, Moline IL 61265. **Tel** (309)765-8000. ***Continues in part*** *Furrow, 0016-3112.*

LC TJ1480
DD 631.3 US
FURROW. TRANS-WEST EDITION, THE. (THE FURROW.). **Added/Corp** Deere & Company. (19??)-. Periodical. English. Seven times a year. Free to qualified subscribers. Deere & Company, John Deere Road, Moline IL 61265. **Tel** (309)765-8000. ***Continues in part*** *Furrow, 0016-3112.*

LC TJ1480
DD 631.3 US
FURROW. VALLEY EDITION, THE. (THE FURROW.). **Added/Corp** Deere & Company. (198?)-. Periodical. English. Seven times a year. Free to qualified subscribers. Deere & Company, John Deere Road, Moline IL 61265. **Tel** (309)765-8000. ***Continues in part*** *Furrow, 0016-3112.*

LC TJ1480
DD 631.3 US
FURROW. WESTERN EDITION, THE. (THE FURROW.). **Added/Corp** Deere & Company. (19??)-. Periodical. English. Seven times a year. Free to qualified subscribers. Deere & Company, John Deere Road, Moline IL 61265. **Tel** (309)765-8000. ***Continues in part*** *Furrow, 0016-3112.*

LC TK **ISSN** 0435-1304
DD 621 US
GAS ENGINE MAGAZINE. **See** Engineering.

LC Z7164.G8 G7 TH9445.G7
DD 016.6331/0468/0289 US
GRAIN DUST ABSTRACTS / COMPILED BY FANG S. LAI. **See** Agriculture-Feed Grain and Milling.

LC TJ1480 **ISSN** 0017-3932
DD 631.3 UK
TITLE CHANGE
GREEN BOOK (LONDON). (THE GREEN BOOK.). [Green book]. Vol. 20, No. 42 (1971)-(198?). Trade Publication. English. Industrial Newspapers Ltd, Queensway House, 2 Queensway, Redhill Surrey RH1 1QS United Kingdom. **Tel** 011 44 1737 68611. **ED** H Catling. **Ad Acc. Circ:** 4,000. ***Continues*** *Tractors and Farm Machinery.* ***Continued by*** *Institution of Agricultural Engineers. Members' Handbook and Buyers' Guide, 0965-867X.*
Desc: The authority on tractors, agricultural and forestry equipment, and supplies.

LC HD9486.D4 D35A **ISSN** 0302-5349
DD 338.1 DK
HANDBOG - DANSK MASKINHANDLERFORENING. (HANDBOG.). [Handb. - Dan. maskinhandlerforen.]. **Main/Corp** Dansk Maskinhandlerforening. Danish.

LC TJ1480 **ISSN** 1060-6718
DD 629 US
HEAVY EQUIPMENT & FARM MACHINERY MAGAZINE. [Heavy equip. farm mach. mag.]. **VFOAT** Heavy Equipment and Farm Machinery Magazine. (Dec. 1991)-. Periodical. English. Six times a year. $6.00. G S M Publishing, 113 West Chestnut Ct., Wauseon OH 43567.

LC HD9486.U3 F28 **ISSN** 0743-7730
DD 629.2/25 US
HOT LINE FARM EQUIPMENT GUIDE'S QUICK REFERENCE GUIDE FOR FARM TRACTORS AND COMBINES. [Hot line farm equip. guide's quick ref. guide farm tract. comb.]. **VFOAT** Farm Equipment Guide's Quick Reference Guide for Farm Tractors and Combines; Hot Line Farm Equipment Guide's Quick Reference Guide. Vol. 2 (1983)-. English. One time a year. $35.95. Heartland Communications Group Inc., PO Box 916 1003 Central Ave, Fort Dodge IA 50501. **Tel** (800)247-2000, (515)955-1600, FAX (515)955-6636. Index available. **Ad Acc.** ctrl circ. ***Continues*** *Farm Blue Book's Quick Reference Guide for Farm Tractors and Combines, 0743-7722.*
Desc: Information on used farm tractors and combines.

LC TJ1480 **ISSN** 0019-2953
DD 631.3 US
IMPLEMENT & TRACTOR. [Implement tract.]. **VFOAT** Implement and Tractor. (19??)-. Trade Publication. English. Six times a year. $25.00. Farm Press Publishers Inc, PO Box 1420, Clarksdale MS 38614. **Tel** (601)624-8503. **ED** Bill Fogarty. **Ad Acc. Circ:** 27,000. available on an online database (file 648/Full-Text) from DIALOG. ***Continues*** *Implement & Tractor Trade Journal (Kansas City, Mo. :1929).;* ***Absorbed*** *Farm Implement News.*
Desc: Covers worldwide farm and industrial equipment industry.
Ind/Abst Agric. Eng. Abstr.; Bus. ASAP (1990-) [Full Txt.]; Bus. Index (1985-); EP Collect.; F&S Index Plus Text, Int. [Select. Cov.]; Gen. BusinessFile (1985-); Gen. Period. Index (1985-); Homework Help.; Mag. Search; MasterFile FullTEXT 1000; MasterFile FullTEXT 350; MasterFile FullTEXT 650; MasterFile FullTEXT (July 1993-); OCLC; PROMT; Stat. Ref. Index; Telebase; Trade Ind. ASAP [Full Txt.]; Trade Ind. Index (1981-) [Full Txt.]; Vocat. Search.

LC TJ1480 **ISSN** 0047-0597
DD 631.3 US
INTERNATIONAL BARBED WIRE GAZETTE, THE. **Added/Corp** Barbed Wire Collectors. (197?)-. Periodical. English. Twelve times a year. $10.00. Cow Puddle Press, Sunset Trading Post, Sunset TX 76270. **Tel** (817)872-2027.

LC TJ1480 **ISSN** 0952-5513
DD 631.3 UK
JOURNAL OF THE HISTORIC FARM BUILDINGS GROUP. **See** Building and Construction.

LC S677 **ISSN** 1199-1836
DD 381.4563151/0971 CN
KEEPING TRACK (BURLINGTON). (KEEPING TRACK.). [Keep. track]. **Added/Corp** Canadian Farm and Industrial Equipment Institute. **VFOAT** CFIEI Keeping Track; Canadian Farm and Industrial Equipment Institute Keeping Track. (1992)-. Trade Publication. English. Irregular. Limited free distribution. Canadian Farm and Industrial Equipment Institute, 1243 Islington Avenue, Toronto Ontario M8X 1Y9 Canada. ***Continues*** *Bulletin (Canadian Farm and Industrial Equipment Institute)., 0821-7513.*

LC TJ1480
DD 631.3 JA
KIKAIKA NOGYO. **Added/Corp** Shin Norin Sha. **VFOAT** Farming Mechanization. No. 2500 (September 1960)-. Periodical. Japanese. Twelve times a year. ¥8500. Shin-Norinsha Company Limited, 7 2-chome Kanda Nishikicho, Chiyoda-ku Tokyo Japan. **Tel** 011 81 3 2913674, FAX 011 81 3 2915717. **ED** Yoshisuke Kishida. **Bk Rev. Ad Acc. Circ:** 100,000 (ctrl).
Desc: Publishes articles on agricultural equipment.
Ind/Abst AGRICOLA; Agric. Eng. Abstr.; Hortic. Abstr.; Soyabean Abstr.

LC TJ1480 **ISSN** 0023-1371
DD 631.3 JA
KIKAIKA NOGYO. **VFOAT** Farming Mechanization. (1940)-. Periodical. Japanese. Twelve times a year. $91.88. Shin-Norinsha Company Limited, 7 2-chome Kanda Nishikicho, Chiyoda-ku Tokyo Japan. **Tel** 011 81 3 2913674, FAX 011 81 3 2915717.
Ind/Abst Postharvest News Inf.

LC TJ1480.A1 K65
DD 631.3 UN
KONSTRUIROVANIE I TEKHNOLOGIIA PROIZVODSTVA SELSKOKHOZIAISTVENNYKH MASHIN. Vol. 3 (1973)-. Russian. 0.79rub. Izdatelstvo Tekhnika, Pushkinskaia 28, Kiev Ukraine. **Tel** 011 7 44 282243. ***Continues*** *Konstruirovanie I Proizvodstvo Selskokhoziaistvennykh Mashin.*

LC HD9486.N4 N47a
DD 338.1 NE
LANDBOUWMACHINE-INDUSTRIE. **Added/Corp** Netherlands. Centraal Bureau voor de Statistiek. Hoofdafdeling Statistieken van Industrie en Bouwnijverheid. **VFOAT** Manufacture of Agricultural Machinery and Equipment. (19??)-. Dutch (summaries and/or abstracts in English). One time a year. Fl7.00. Centraal Bureau voor de Statistiek, AFD ALG Zaken, Postbus 959, 2270 AZ Voorburg Netherlands. **Tel** 011 31 70 3373800, FAX 011 31 70 0387429, telex 32692 CBS NL. ***Continues*** *Netherlands. Centraal Bureau Voor de Statistiek. Produktiestatistieken: Landbouwmachine-Industrie.*

LC TJ1480 **ISSN** 0023-7795
DD 631.3 NE
LANDBOUWMECHANISATIE. **Added/Corp** Stichting Mechanisatie-Centrum. Instituut voor Landbouwtechniek en Rationalisatie. (1950)-. Academic Scholarly Publication. Dutch. Twelve times a year. $103.28. Wageningen Pers, Postbus 42, 6700 AA Wageningen Netherlands. **Tel** 011 31 8370 76511, FAX 011 31 8370 26044. **ED** J Heeres. **Bk Rev. Ad Acc. Circ:** 23,000 (ctrl).
Desc: Specializes in agricultural equipment. Publishes research reports in the field of agricultural machinery, buildings, automation and news on new equipment and trade.
Ind/Abst AgBiotech News Inf.; AGRICOLA; Agric. Eng. Abstr. (1991-); Biodeter. Abstr.; Dairy Sci. Abstr.; EMBASE; Field Crop Abstr.; For. Prod. Abstr.; Hortic. Abstr.; Index Vet.; Maize Abstr.; Nematol. Abstr.; Ornamental Hort.; Pig News Inf.; Postharvest News Inf.; Potato Abstr.; Saf. Health Work; Soils Fert.; Weed Abstr.; World Agric. Econ. Rural Sociol. Abstr.

LC TJ1480 .L3 **ISSN** 0023-8082
DD 631 GW
Pr Rev.
LANDTECHNIK, DIE. [Landtechnik]. (Jan. 1946)-. Trade Publication. German. Ten times a year. $138.33. Landwirtschaftsverlag GmbH, Postfach 480249, D-48079 Muenster Hiltrup Germany. **Tel** 011 49 2501 8010, FAX 011 49 2501 801204, telex 892665 LANDV D. Index available. cum. index. **Bk Rev. Ad Acc. Circ:** 4,000 (ctrl). ***Absorbed*** *Landarbeit, 0023-771X.*
Desc: Deals with agricultural work and the economy of agriculture.
Ind/Abst AgBiotech News Inf.; AGRICOLA; Agric. Eng. Abstr.; Biodeter. Abstr.; Coal Abstr.; Curr. Cit.; Dairy Sci. Abstr.; EMBASE; Energy Res. Abstr. (April 1977-); Field Crop Abstr.; For. Prod. Abstr. (1991-); Grass. Forage Abstr.; Hortic. Abstr.; Index Vet.; Irr. Drain. Abstr.; Life Sci. Collect.; Pig News Inf.; Postharvest News Inf.; Potato Abstr.; Seed Abstr.; Soils Fert.; Soyabean Abstr.; Weed Abstr.; Wheat Barley Trit. Abstr.

LC HD9710.4.U6 L4 **ISSN** 1043-089X
DD 629.225 US
CEASED
LAWN, GARDEN, AND FARM TRACTOR TRADE-IN GUIDE. [Lawn gard. farm tract. trade-in guide]. **Added/Corp** Intertec Publishing Corporation. Technical Publications Division. **VFOAT** Lawn, Garden & Farm Tractor Trade-in Guide. (198?)-(19??). Consumer Publication. English. Intertec Publishing Corporation, 9800 Metcalf, Overland Park KS 66212. **Tel** (913)341-1300. ***Formed by the union of*** *Lawn & Garden Tractor Trade-In Guide, 8756-5110* ***and*** *Farm Tractor Trade-In Guide.*

LC TJ1480 **ISSN** 0024-8967
DD 631.3 IT
MACCHINE E MOTORI AGRICOLI. [Macch. mot. agric.]. (1941)-. Periodical. Italian. Twelve times a year. L54500. Edagricole, PO Box 2157, 40100 Bologna Italy. **Tel** 011 39 51 492211 Ext. 22, FAX 011 39 51 493660, telex 510336 EDAGRI.
Ind/Abst AgBiotech News Inf.; Agric. Eng. Abstr.; Field Crop Abstr.; Postharvest News Inf.; Saf. Health Work; Sorghum Mill. Abstr.

LC TJ1480 **ISSN** 0242-2565
DD 631.3 FR
CODEN MAATBM
SUSPENDED
MACHINISME AGRICOLE TROPICAL. No. 1- Jan./Mar. 1963-Suspended with Issue 18, 1989. Periodical. French (summaries and/or abstracts in English and Spanish). Four times a year. 130.00F France; 150.00F US. CEEMAT, Parc de Tourvoie, 92160 Antony France. **Tel** 46 68 61 02, 201296 F. Index available. cum. index. **Bk Rev. Ad Acc.** Documents available from BIOSIS Document Express.
Desc: Contains agricultural equipment for tropical areas.
Ind/Abst Biol. Abstr.; Cot. Trop. Fibr. Abstr. Bibliogr.; Irr. Drain. Abstr.; Maize Abstr.; Rice Abstr.

LC S671 .M39 **ISSN** 0206-572X
DD 630.208/ 631.3 RU
ME, MEHANIZACIA I ELEKTRIFIKACIA SELSKOGO HOZAISTVA (MOSKVA). (MEKHANIZATSIIA I ELEKTRIFIKATSIIA SELSKOGO KHOZIAISTVA.). [ME, Meh. elektr. selskogo hoz. (Mosk.)]. **Added/Corp** Vsesoiuznaia Akademiia Selskokhoziaistvennykh nauk Imeni V. I. Lenina. **VFOAT** ME. (1930)-. Periodical. Russian. Twelve times a year. $89.95. Izdatelstvo Kolos, Sadovaia-Spasskaia 18, 107807 Moscow Russia. **(Subscription address:** East View Publications Inc., 3020 Harbor Lane North, Suite 110, Minneapolis MN 55447. **Tel** (800)477-1005, (612)550-0961, FAX (612)559-2931.**)**
Ind/Abst Biodeter. Abstr.; Hortic. Abstr.; Index Vet.; Nutr. Abstr. Rev., Ser. B, Live Feeds and Feed.; Ornamental Hort. (1991-); Plant Breed. Abstr.; Potato Abstr.; Rev. Med. Vet. Entomol.; Rice Abstr.; Seed Abstr.; Soils Fert.; Soyabean Abstr.; Vet. Bull.

LC S671 .P75
DD 631.3/05 RM
MECANIZAREA AGRICULTURII. **Added/Corp** Romania. Ministerul Agriculturii. Vol. 31, Nr. 1 (Jan. 1987)-. Periodical. Romanian (table of contents in English, French and Russian). Twelve times a year. lei96.00. **(Subscription address:** Rompresfilatelia, PO Box 12 201, Bucharest Romania. **Tel** 011 40 0 10376.**)** ***Continues*** *Productia Vegetala. Mecanizarea Agriculturii.*
Ind/Abst Irr. Drain. Abstr.; Maize Abstr.; Rev. Agric. Entomol.; Soyabean Abstr.

LC TJ1480 **ISSN** 0373-6776
DD 631.3 XR
MECHANIZACE ZEMEDELSTVI. [Mech. zemed.]. (1951)-. Periodical. Czech. Six times a year. $43.10. **(Subscription address:** Artia Pegas Press Ltd., Palac Metro Narodni Trida 25, 11210 Prague 1 Czech Republic. **Tel** 011 42 2 24196265, 011 42 2 24196266.**)**
Ind/Abst Agric. Eng. Abstr. (1991-); Biodeter. Abstr.; Dairy Sci. Abstr.; Field Crop Abstr.; Hortic. Abstr.; Irr.

Drain. Abstr.; Maize Abstr.; Pig News Inf.; Postharvest News Inf.; Potato Abstr.; Rev. Agric. Entomol.; Saf. Health Work; Seed Abstr.; Soils Fert.; Soyabean Abstr.

LC TJ1480 **ISSN** 0461-5220
DD 631.3 PL
MECHANIZACJA ROLNICTWA.
[Mech. roln.]. (1954)-. Periodical. Polish. Twelve times a year. $48.00. **(Subscription address:** Ars Polona-Ruch, PO Box 1001, Krakowskie Przedmiescie 7, 00-068 Warsaw Poland. **Tel** 011 48 22 261201.)
Ind/Abst AGRICOLA.

LC TJ1480 **ISSN** 0965-867X
DD 631.3 UK
MEMBERS' HANDBOOK & BUYERS' GUIDE : THE GREEN BOOK / THE INSTITUTION OF AGRICULTURAL ENGINEERS.
Main/Corp Institution of Agricultural Engineers. **VFOAT** Official Membership Register; Members' Handbook and Buyers' Guide; Institution of Agricultural Engineers Members' Handbook & Buyers' Guide; Green Book. (1992)-. Consumer Publication. English. Industrial Newspapers Ltd, Queensway House, 2 Queensway, Redhill Surrey RH1 1QS United Kingdom. **Tel** 011 44 1737 68611. ***Absorbed** Green Book (London, England), 0017-3932.*

LC S760.H8 M49
DD 631.3 HU
MEZOGAZDASAGI ERO- ES MUNKAGEPEK.
Added/Corp Hungary. Kozponti Statisztikai Hivatal. Hungary. Kozponti Statisztikai Hivatal. Mezogazdasagi Statisztikai Fosztaly. (19??)-. Hungarian. One time a year. 67.00ft. Statisztikai Kiado Vallalat, PO Box 99, H-1033 Budapest 3 Hungary. **Tel** 803-311, telex 22-6699-SKV-H. **Circ:** 800.
Desc: Presents a survey on all power engines and machineries used in agriculture in Hungary. Reports stocks on Dec. 31 of each year, detailed by categories and territories.

LC S **ISSN** 0521-422X
DD 630 HU
MEZOGAZDASAGI GEPESITESI TANULMANYOK.
Main/Corp Budapest. Mezogazdasasgi Gepkiserleti Intezet. Vol. 1, (1957)-. Periodical. Hungarian (summaries and/or abstracts in English). Mezogazdasagi Gepesitesi Tanulmanyok, PO Box 149, Budapest 62 Hungary.

LC TJ1480
DD 631.3 PK
MILLAT TRACTORS LIMITED.
(ANNUAL REPORT.). **Main/Corp** Millat Tractors Limited. (19??)-. English. One time a year.

LC HD9007.M6 M49 **ISSN** 0883-4385
DD 338.7/63/025776 US
MINNESOTA AG MANUAL, THE.
[Minn. ag man.]. English. $49.50. Minnesota Agri-Growth Council, 8030 Cedar Avenue South/Suite 213, Minneapolis MN 55420.

LC TJ1480
DD 631.3 US
MOBIL FARM FUTURE.
Main/Corp Mobil Oil Corporation. Wholesale Programs Dept. (Aug. 1974)-. Periodical. English. Mobil Oil Corporation / Technical Publications, Technical Publications, 3225 Gallows Road, Fairfax VA 22037.

LC TJ1480 **ISSN** 1156-1556
DD 631.3 FR
MOTORISATION (PARIS).
(MOTORISATION.). No. 1 (Nov. 1990)-. Periodical. French. Six times a year. Nouvelles Editions Publications Agricoles, 8 Cite Paradis, F 75010 Paris France. **Tel** 011 33 1 40227900.

LC TJ1480 **ISSN** 0214-9206
DD 631.3 SP
UDC 631.3
TITLE CHANGE
MT. MAQUINAS Y TRACTORES AGRICOLAS.
[MT, Maquinas tract. agric.]. **VFOAT** Maquinas y Tractores Agricolas; M.T. Maquinas y Tractores. (1990)-(Jan. 1994). Periodical. Spanish. Edagricole Espana SA, Castello 32, 28001 Madrid Spain. **Tel** 011 34 1 5780534, 011 34 1 5780820. ***Merged into** Vida Rural.*
Ind/Abst Agric. Eng. Abstr. (1991-); Dairy Sci. Abstr.; Field Crop Abstr.; Hortic. Abstr.; Maize Abstr.; Postharvest News Inf.; Seed Abstr.; Soils Fert.; Wheat Barley Trit. Abstr.; World Agric. Econ. Rural Sociol. Abstr.

LC SL **ISSN** 1074-5017
DD 631 US
NAEDA EQUIPMENT DEALER.
[NAEDA equip. dealer]. **Added/Corp** North American Equipment Dealers Association. **VFOAT** Equipment Dealer. (199?)-. Periodical. English. Twelve times a year. $40.00. North American Equipment Dealers Association, 10877 Watson Road, St Louis MO 63127. **Tel** (314)821-7220, FAX (314)821-0674. **ED** Mike Kraemer. **Bk Rev**, (Qty: 1). **Ad Acc, Adv Mgr:** Larry Krueger. ctrl circ. ***Continues** Farm & Power Equipment Dealer, 0892-6085.*
Desc: For NAEDA members; for those involved in the management of or suppliers to farm and outdoor power equipment dealerships.

LC TJ1480 **ISSN** 0713-0236
DD 338.4/76218/05 CN
NATIONAL FACTORY & EQUIPMENT NEWS.
[Natl. fact. equip. news]. **VFOAT** Factory & Equipment; Factory & Equipment News. **VAT** Factory and Equipment News; National Factory and Equipment News; Factory and Equipment. Periodical. English. Twelve times a year. $12.00 Canada; $16.00 other. Bobcat Communications Inc, Unit 9/150 Milner Avenue, Scarborough Ontario M1S 3R3 Canada.

LC HD9486.U3 N3 **ISSN** 0193-7642
DD 338.4/7/629225 US
CEASED
NATIONAL FARM TRACTOR AND IMPLEMENT BLUE BOOK.
VFOAT Tractor Blue Book. (1939)-(19??). English. Intertec Publishing Corp, 29 North Wacker Drive, Chicago IL 60606-3298. **Tel** (312)726-2802, FAX (312)726-3091. **(Subscription address:** Maclean Hunter Market Reports, 29 North Wacker Drive, Chicago IL 60606.)

LC TJ1480 **ISSN** 0093-1489
DD 631.3 US
NEBRASKA TRACTOR TEST.
[Nebr. tractor test]. **Added/Corp** University of Nebraska--Lincoln. Dept. of Agricultural Engineering. University of Nebraska (Lincoln Campus). Dept. of Agricultural Engineering. University of Nebraska--Lincoln. Agricultural Experiment Station. (19??)-. English. One time a year (Feb.). $14.00. Nebraska Tractor Testing Lab, University of Nebraska-Lincoln, East Campus, Lincoln NE 68583-0832. **Tel** (402)472-2242, FAX (402)472-8367. **ED** Brent Sampson. Index available. cum. index. **Circ:** 300.
Desc: Reports performance of tractors from US and overseas. Includes power, pull, fuel conservation, hydraulic lift cap, lugging ability, sound levels and other descriptive data.
Ind/Abst AGRICOLA [Full Cov.].

LC TJ1480 **ISSN** 0824-3972
DD 631.3/09713 CN
NEW FARMER'S FINDER.
[New farmer's finder]. **VFOAT** Farmer's Finder. **VAT** Farmer's Finder (1983). Feb. 1983-. Periodical. English. Free. New Farmer's Finder, 31 Armstrong Avenue, Georgetown Ontario L7G 4S1 Canada. ***Continues** Farmer's Finder Pocket Shopper (1983), 0821-4239.*

LC TJ1480 **ISSN** 0714-3044
DD 631.3 CN
NEWSLETTER / CANADIAN SOCIETY OF AGRICULTURAL ENGINEERING.
[Newsl. - Can. Soc. Agric. Eng.]. **Added/Corp** Canadian Society of Agricultural Engineering. (197?)-. Newsletter. English. Canadian Society of Agricultural Engineering, PO Box 306, RPO University, Saskatoon Saskatoon S7N 4J8 Canada. **Tel** (306)966-5335, FAX (306)966-5334.

LC TJ1480 **ISSN** 0917-9720
DD 631.3 JA
NOGYO KIKAI GAKKAI KYUSHU SHIBUSHI.
VFOAT Journal of Kyushu Branch of the Japanese Society of Agricultural Machinery. (1950)-. Periodical. Japanese. One time a year.
Ind/Abst Agric. Eng. Abstr.; Hortic. Abstr.; Soyabean Abstr.

LC TJ1480 **ISSN** 0285-2543
DD 631.3 JA
NOGYO KIKAI GAKKAISHI.
(JOURNAL OF THE SOCIETY OF AGRICULTURAL MACHINERY, JAPAN.). [Nogyo Kikai Gakkai]. **Main/Corp** Nogyo Kikai Gakkai. **Added/Corp** Nogyo Kikai Gakkai. **VFOAT** Journal of the Society of Agricultural Machinery, Japan; Journal of the Japanese Society of Agricultural Machinery. Vol. 1 (1937)-. Periodical. Japanese (summaries and/or abstracts in English; table of contents in English). Six times a year (Jan., Mar., May, July, Sept., Nov.). $180.00. Japan Society of Agricultural Machinery, Iam Brain Nissin, Cho 1 40 Z, Omiya City Saitama 331 Japan. **Tel** 011 81 48 652 4119. **(Subscription address:** Maruzen Company Ltd., PO Box 5050, Import & Export Department, Tokyo 100 31 Japan. **Tel** 011 81 3 32789224.)
Ind/Abst AGRICOLA; For. Prod. Abstr.; Maize Abstr.; Postharvest News Inf.; Potato Abstr.; Rice Abstr.; Seed Abstr.; Soils Fert.

LC TJ1480 **ISSN** 0387-8139
DD 631.3 JA
NOGYO KIKAIKA KENKYUSHO HOKOKU.
VFOAT Technical Report of the Institute of Agricultural Machinery. No. 15 (Mar. 1981)-. Japanese (summaries and/or abstracts in English). Nogyo Kikaika Kenkyujo, (Inst. of Agricultural Machinery), 40-2 Nisshincho 1 Chome, Omiyashi Saitamaken 331, Japan. ***Continues** Kenkyujo Hokoku. Technical Report.*

LC S760.K6 N64
DD 631.3 KO
NONGOP KIGYE YONGAM.
VFOAT Agricultural Machinery Yearbook, Republic of Korea. (19??)-. English (Korean). One time a year. Hanguk Nonggigu Kongop Hyoptong Chohap, 19-6 1-ka To-dong Yongsan-ku, Seoul Korea.

LC S
DD 630 KO
NONGSA SIHOM YONGU POGO. NONGKONG, NONGCHON KYUNGYON, JAMUP.
Added/Corp Korea (South). Nongchon Chinhungchong. **VFOAT** Research Reports of the Office of Rural Development. Agri-Eng., Farm Management & Sericulture. Vol. 24 (Dec. 1982)-. Periodical. Korean (summaries and/or abstracts in English). Two times a year. Rural Development Administration, Plant Environment Mycology and Farm Products Utilization, Suweon 170 Korea. ***Continues** Nongsa Sihom Yongu Pogo. Nongkong, Nongsanmul Hwalyong, Nongchon Kyungyong.*
Ind/Abst Rev. Plant Pathol.

LC TS500 **ISSN** 1000-1298
DD 681.763 CC
NONGYE JIXIE XUEBAO.
VFOAT Transactions of The Chinese Society of Agricultural Machinery. (1957)-. Academic Scholarly Publication. Chinese. Four times a year. Zhongguo Nongye Jixie Xuehui, (Chinese Society of Agricultural Machinery), 1 Bei Shatan, Dewai, Beijing 100083 People's Republic of China. **(Subscription address:** China International Book Trading Corporation, PO Box 399, Library Service Department, Beijing 100044 People's Republic of China. **Tel** 011 86 1 8414284, FAX 011 86 1 8412023, telex 22496 CIBTC CN.) **ED** H Zhong.
Ind/Abst Irr. Drain. Abstr.

LC TJ1480
DD 631.3 US
CEASED
NORTH AMERICAN FARM EQUIPMENT JOURNAL.
(April/May 1994)-(March 1995). Periodical. English. Northwest Farm Equipment Journal, PO Box 1210, Marshfield WI 54449. **Tel** (715)389-2234, FAX (715)389-2380. **ED** Gerald Petcher. **Ad Acc. Circ:** 2,800. ***Continues** Northwest Farm Equipment Journal, 0029-3350.*
Desc: Industry news of the interest to retailers, manufacturers, wholesalers and manufacture agents.

LC TJ1480 **ISSN** 0029-3350
DD 631 US
TITLE CHANGE
NORTHWEST FARM EQUIPMENT JOURNAL.
[Northwest farm equip. j.]. **VFOAT** Farm Equipment Journal. (19??)-Vol. 108, Nos. 1-2-3 (Jan./Feb./Mar. 1994). Trade Publication. English. Northwest Farm Equipment Journal, PO Box 1210, Marshfield WI 54449. **Tel** (715)389-2234, FAX (715)389-2380. **ED** Gerald Petcher. **Ad Acc. Circ:** 2,800 (ctrl). ***Continues** Farm Implements and Tractors.* ***Continued by** North American Farm Equipment Journal.*
Desc: Industry news of interest to retailers, manufacturers, wholesalers and manufacture agents.

LC S671 .85
DD 681/.763/05 CH
NUNG YEH CHI HSIEH.
VFOAT Nongye Jixie; Farm Machinery. Periodical. Chinese. Twelve times a year. NT$0.20. Science Press, 16 Donghuangchenggen North Street, Beijing 100707, People's Republic of China. **Tel** 011 86 1 4019821, 011 86 1 4010642, FAX 011 86 1 4012180, 011 86 1 4019810, telex 210147.

LC S671 .N86
DD 681/.763/05 CC
NUNG YEH CHI HSIEH HSUEH PAO.
Added/Corp Chung-kuo Nung yeh chi Hsieh Hsueh hui. **VFOAT** Transactions of the Chinese Society of Agricultural Machinery; Acta Agromechanica Sinica. (19??)-. Periodical. Chinese (summaries and/or abstracts in English). Four times a year. 0.80. Science Press, 16 Donghuangchenggen North Street, Beijing 100707, People's Republic of China. **Tel** 011 86 1 4019821, 011 86 1 4010642, FAX 011 86 1 4012180, 011 86 1 4019810, telex 210147. ***Continues** Nung yeh chi Hsieh i pao.*
Ind/Abst AGRICOLA; Agric. Eng. Abstr.; Field Crop Abstr.; Maize Abstr.; Nutr. Abstr. Rev., Ser. B, Live Feeds and Feed.; Pig News Inf.; Postharvest News Inf.; Potato Abstr.; Rev. Agric. Entomol.; Rice Abstr.; Seed Abstr.; Soils Fert.; Wheat Barley Trit. Abstr.; World Agric. Econ. Rural Sociol. Abstr.

LC S713 .O33 **ISSN** 0735-6676
DD 629.2/25 US
OFFICIAL GUIDE, OUTDOOR POWER EQUIPMENT.
[Off. guide, outdoor power equip.]. **Added/Corp** National Farm & Power Equipment Dealers Association (U.S.). **VFOAT** Outdoor Power Equipment; Outdoor Power Equipment Official Guide. (1982)-. Trade Publication. English. One time a year. $15.00. National Farm and Power Services Inc, 10877 Watson Road, St

Louis MO 63127. **Circ:** 3,200 (ctrl).
Desc: Deals solely with lawn and compact tractors up to 50 HP.

LC S677 .O34 **ISSN** 0162-6809
DD 381/.45/681763102573 US
OFFICIAL GUIDE, TRACTORS AND FARM EQUIPMENT. **Added/Corp** National Farm & Power Equipment Dealers Association (U.S.). (Spring 1969)-. Trade Publication. English. Two times a year. $217.58. Alabama Farm and Power Equipment Dealers Association, 369 South College Street, PO Box 2580, Auburn AL 36831-2580. **Tel** (334)335-5627. **Ad Acc.** ***Supersedes*** *Official Tractor and Farm Equipment Guide.*

LC TJ1480
DD 631.3 GW
PFLANZENSCHUTZMITTEL-VERZEICHNIS. TEIL 6: ANERKANNTE PFLANZENSCHUTZ- UND VORRATSSCHUTZGERATE. **Main/Corp** Biologische Bundesanstalt fur Land- und Forstwirtschaft. Abteilung fur Pflanzenschutzmittel und -Gerate. (19??)-. Periodical. German. ***Supersedes in part*** *Biologische Bundesanstalt fur Land- und Forstwirtschaft. Abteilung fuer Pflanzenschutzmittel und -Gerate. Pflanzenschutzmittel-Verzeichnis (SB950.A1B5).*
Ind/Abst Rev. Plant Pathol.

LC TJ1480 **ISSN** 0311-1911
DD 631.3 AT
POWER FARMING MAGAZINE. [Power farming mag.]. **VFOAT** Power Farming. Vol. 82 No. 10 (Oct. 1973)-. Periodical. English. Six times a year. 34.53Aus$. Diverse Publishing Company Pty Limited, PO Box 370, North Melbourne Victoria 3051 Australia. **Tel** 011 61 3 3296040. **ED** Jeremy Bayard. **Bk Rev. Ad Acc.** ***Continues*** *Power Farming in Australia and New Zealand, Better Farming Digest.*
Desc: Latest in farm buildings, farming techniques and tractors.
Ind/Abst AGRICOLA; Agric. Eng. Abstr.

LC TJ1480 **ISSN** 0968-0136
DD 338.160941 UK
PRACTICAL FARM IDEAS QUARTERLY. [Pract. farm ideas q.]. (19??)-. English. Four times a year (Apr., July, Oct., Jan.). $32.42. Mido Publications Ltd., PO Box 1 Whitland Dyfed, SA34 OHZ United Kingdom. **Tel** 011 44 1994 448315, FAX 011 44 1994 448315. **ED** Michael Donovan. Index available. **Bk Rev**, (Qty: 8). **Circ:** 3,000.

LC TJ1480 **ISSN** 0867-8243
DD 631.3 PL
PREZEGLAD TECHNIKI ROLNICZEJ I LESNEJ. (1992)-. Periodical. Polish. Twelve times a year. $90.00. **(Subscription address:** Ars Polona-Ruch, PO Box 1001, Krakowskie Przedmiescie 7, 00-068 Warsaw Poland. **Tel** 011 48 22 261201.) ***Continues*** *Maszyny i Ciagniki Rolnicze.*

LC TJ1480 **ISSN** 0033-1481
DD 631.3 SA
PROSPECT (AFRICAN EXPLOSIVES AND CHEMICAL INDUSTRIES). (PROSPECT / AECI.). **Added/Corp** African Explosives and Chemical Industries. (19??)-. Periodical. English. Four times a year. AECI Ltd, Carlton Centre, PO Box 1122, JHB Johannesburg South Africa. **Tel** (01127-11)223-9111, FAX 223-1929, telex 48-7048 SA. **ED** F. Putero. Index available. **Circ:** 15,000 (ctrl).
Desc: Articles in non-technical style describing interesting uses of AECI products by customers. Covers plastics, chemicals, fertilizers, paints and explosives.

LC TJ1480
DD 631.3 FR
RAPPORTS D'ESSAI DE TRACTEUR. French. 2260.00F France; 2660.00F other. Centre National du Machinisme Agricole du Genie Rural des Eaux et des Forets / CEMAGREF, BP 22, 92162 Antony Cedex France. **Tel** 011 33 1 40966121.

LC HD9680.I8 A78a
DD 338.1 IT
REPERTORIO ASSOCIATE ANIMA = DIRECTORY OF ANIMA MEMBER-FIRMS. **Main/Corp** Associazione Nazionale Industria Meccanica Varia Ed Affine. **VFOAT** Directory of ANIMA Member-Firms; A.N.I.M.A. (19??)-. Directory. English (French, German, Italian and Spanish). Two times a year. L50.000 Italy; L60.000 other. ANIMA / Associazione Nazionale Industria Meccanica Varia ed Affine, Casella Postale 18265, Florence Italy. **Tel** 011 39 55 698185. **ED** Francesco Donfrancesco. Index available. cum. index. **Circ:** 500 (ctrl).

LC S760.G7 R47
DD 631.3/09416 IE
RESULTS OF AGRICULTURAL MACHINERY AND EQUIPMENT CENSUS / DEPARTMENT OF AGRICULTURE, NORTHERN IRELAND. **Added/Corp** Northern Ireland. Dept. of Agriculture. (19??)-. English. One time a year. £12.50. Economics and Statistics, Division Dundonald House, Upper Newtownards Road, Belfast BT4 3SB United Kingdom. **Tel** 0232 524655, FAX 0232 524676. **ED** W. Hunter.

LC TJ1480 **ISSN** 0223-0135
DD 631.3 FR
UDC 631 CCC
REVUE TECHNIQUE MACHINISME AGRICOLE. (1979)-. Periodical. French. Six times a year. $178.26. Editions Techniques pour l'Automobile et l'Industrie (ETAI), 94 96 rue de Paris, 92100 Boulogne Billancourt France. **Tel** 011 33 1 46992411. **Bk Rev. Ad Acc. Circ:** 15,000.
Ind/Abst Agric. Eng. Abstr. (1991-).

LC TJ1480 **ISSN** 0252-3582
DD 631.3 TH
RNAM NEWSLETTER. [RNAM newsl.]. **VFOAT** Regional Network for Agricultural Machinery Newsletter; Newsletter - Regional Network for Agricultural Machinery. (1978)-. Periodical. English. Three times a year.
Ind/Abst Agric. Eng. Abstr.; Cot. Trop. Fibr. Abstr. Bibliogr.; Field Crop Abstr.; Hortic. Abstr.; Irr. Drain. Abstr.; Postharvest News Inf.; Rice Abstr.; Seed Abstr.

LC TJ1480 **ISSN** 0080-3677
DD 631.3 PL
CODEN RNTRAI
ROCZNIKI NAUK ROLNICZYCH. SERIA C. TECHNIKA ROLNICZA. [Rocz. nauk roln., Ser. C]. **Added/Corp** Polska Akademia Nauk. Komitet Techniki Rolniczej. **VFOAT** Annaly Sel'skokhoziaistvennykh Nauk. Seriia C : Sel'skokhoziaistvennaia Tekhnika; Polish Agricultural Annual. Series C : Agricultural Engineering. Vol. 69 (1972)-. Polish (summaries and/or abstracts in English, Polish and Russian). Irregular. Panstwowe Wydawnictwo Naukowe / PWN, (Polish Scientific Publishers PWN Ltd.), Ul. Miodowa 10, PO Box 391, 00-251 Warsaw Poland. **Tel** 011 48 22 312738, FAX 011 48 22 267163. **(Subscription address:** Ars Polona-Ruch, PO Box 1001, Krakowskie Przedmiescie 7, 00-068 Warsaw Poland. **Tel** 011 48 22 261201.) Documents available from BIOSIS Document Express. ***Continues*** *Roczniki Nauk Rolniczych. Seria C : Mechanizacja Rolnictwa.*
Ind/Abst Agric. Eng. Abstr.; Biol. Abstr.; Field Crop Abstr.; Hortic. Abstr.; Postharvest News Inf.; Potato Abstr.; Seed Abstr.; Soils Fert.; Wheat Barley Trit. Abstr.; World Agric. Econ. Rural Sociol. Abstr.

LC S671 .S337
DD 631.3 XR
SBORNIK MECHANIZACNI FAKULTY VYSOKE SKOLY ZEMEDELSKE V PRAZE. **Added/Corp** Vysoka Skola Zemedelska v Praze. Mechanizacni Fakulta. **VFOAT** Sbornik Fakulteta Mekhanizatsii Selskokhoziastvennogo Instituta v Prage; Collection of Papers. (19??)-. Periodical. Czech (summaries and/or abstracts in English, German and Russian). One time a year. College of Agriculture in Prague, Faculty of Mechanization, Prague Czech Republic.
Ind/Abst Agric. Eng. Abstr. (1991-); Dairy Sci. Abstr.; Field Crop Abstr.; Hortic. Abstr.; Irr. Drain. Abstr.; Postharvest News Inf.; Potato Abstr.; Wheat Barley Trit. Abstr.

LC TJ1480 **ISSN** 0037-1718
DD 631.3 BU
CODEN STFMBL
SELSKOSTOPANSKA TEKHNIKA. [Selskostop. teh.]. **Added/Corp** Akademiia na Selskostopansjute Nauki. (1964)-. Academic Scholarly Publication. Bulgarian. Eight times a year. DM217.00. **(Subscription address:** Kubon & Sagner, ABT Zeitschriftenimport, D 80328 Munich Germany. **Tel** 011 49 89 54218130.) Documents available from CASDDS.
Ind/Abst AGRICOLA; Agric. Eng. Abstr. (1991-); Chem. Abstr. (1968-1983); Dairy Sci. Abstr.; EMBASE; Field Crop Abstr.; For. Prod. Abstr.; Hortic. Abstr.; Irr. Drain. Abstr.; Maize Abstr.; Nutr. Abstr. Rev., Ser. B, Live Feeds and Feed.; Pig News Inf.; Postharvest News Inf.; Potato Abstr.; Rev. Agric. Entomol.; Rice Abstr.; Seed Abstr.; Soils Fert.; Soyabean Abstr.; Vitis Vitic. Enol. Abstr.; Weed Abstr.; Wheat Barley Trit. Abstr.

LC TJ1480
DD 631.3 US
STARKS OFF HIGHWAY LEDGER. (19??)-. Periodical. English. Twenty-four times a year. $770.00. JC Communications Co Inc, 176 West Adams Street, Chicago IL 60603. **Tel** (312)236-5122, FAX (312)236-3297. **ED** Jeanne Hoch.
Desc: Covers the production, sales, and inventories of trucks, farm & construction machinery.

LC TJ1480
DD 631.3 UK
SUGAR INDUSTRY BUYERS GUIDE. **See** Industry and Production.

LC TJ1480 **ISSN** 0040-2265
DD 631.3 RU
TEKHNIKA V SELSKOM KHOZIAISTE. [Teh. selsk. hoz.]. **Added/Corp** Soviet Union. Ministerstvo Selskogo Khoziaistva. Vol. 18, No. 9 (Sept. 1958)-. Russian (French, German and Chinese; table of contents in English, French, German and Chinese). Six times a year. $77.00. ***Continues*** *Mashino-Traktornaia Stantsiia.*
Ind/Abst Agric. Eng. Abstr.; Biodeter. Abstr.; Cot. Trop. Fibr. Abstr. Bibliogr.; Field Crop Abstr.; Hortic. Abstr.; Index Vet.; Postharvest News Inf.; Potato Abstr.; Seed Abstr.

LC TJ1480 **ISSN** 0040-3768
DD 631.3 IT
UDC 630
TERRA E SOLE. [Terra sole]. (1945)-. Periodical. Italian. Eleven times a year. L30660. Iacico Srl, Via A Poliziano 80, 00184 Rome Italy. **Tel** 011 39 6 4873183.
Ind/Abst Agric. Eng. Abstr. (1991-); Agrofor. Abstr. (1991-); Biocont. News Inf. (1991-); Cot. Trop. Fibr. Abstr. Bibliogr.; Field Crop Abstr.; For. Abstr.; Grass. Forage Abstr.; Hortic. Abstr.; Plant Breed. Abstr.; Rev. Plant Pathol.; Rice Abstr.; Seed Abstr.; Soils Fert.; Wheat Barley Trit. Abstr.

LC S419 .T64 **ISSN** 0563-8887
DD 630.94 DK
TOOLS & TILLAGE. [Tools tillage]. **VFOAT** Tools and Tillage. **VAT** Tools and Tillage. Vol. 1 (1968)-. English (German; summaries and/or abstracts in German). Every 3 years (published every 3 years). kr85.00. Poul Kristensens Forlag, Akirkebyvej 2, DK 7400 Herning Denmark. **Tel** 011 45 97121022.
Ind/Abst Agric. Eng. Abstr. (1991-); Am. Hist. Life (1980-); Br. Archaeol. Bibliogr.; MLA Int. Bibl. Books Artic. Mod. Lang. Lit.

LC TJ1480 **ISSN** 0754-121X
DD 631.3 FR
UDC 631.3
TRACTEURS & MACHINES AGRICOLES PARIS. [Tract. Mach. Agric. Paris]. **VFOAT** Tracteurs Machines Agricoles (Paris); TMA (Paris); TMA Hebdo; _aTMA Tracteurs machines agricoles; _aTracteurs et machines agricoles (Paris). (1982)-. Periodical. French. Ten times a year. 410.00F France; $125.00. SEPA, BP 107, 95170 Deuil la Barre France. **Tel** 011 33 1 40280567, FAX 011 33 1 40280565, or 39842787. **Bk Rev. Ad Acc. Circ:** 8,000. ***Continues*** *Tracteurs & Machines Agricoles. Edition Marchands Reparateurs, 0395-9422; Tracteurs & Machines Agricoles. Fermes Modernes, 0241-287X.*
Desc: Deals with all the equipment and the companies in the agricultural sector.
Ind/Abst Agric. Eng. Abstr. (1991-); Postharvest News Inf.; Soyabean Abstr.

LC TJ1480 **ISSN** 0162-3427
DD 631.3 US
TRACTOR AND FARM IMPLEMENT LUBRICATION GUIDE. (19??)-. English. One time a year. $41.35. H.M Gousha & Company, PO Box 49006, 2001 The Alameda, San Jose CA 95161. **Tel** (800)662-6277, FAX (404)296-1300. **ED** Daniel Doornbos. **Circ:** 10,000.
Desc: Covers specifications of lubricants in SAE, API, and industry terms plus refill capacities and service intervals for farm tractors and implements up to 15 years old.

LC Discard **ISSN** 0731-4698
DD 631.3 US
TRACTOR DIGEST. [Tract. dig.]. **Added/Corp** H.M. Gousha Company. Vol. 1. No. 1 (Jan. 1982)-. Periodical. English. Four times a year. $9.15. H.M Gousha & Company, PO Box 49006, 2001 The Alameda, San Jose CA 95161. **Tel** (800)662-6277, FAX (404)296-1300. **ED** Jo Phelps. **Circ:** 6,000.
Desc: Covers new models of farm tractors and self-propelled implements with lubrication and service data.

LC TJ1480 **ISSN** 1057-0306
DD 629 US
TRACTOR MAGAZINE, THE. (THE TRACTOR MAGAZINE : TM.). [Tractor mag.]. **VFOAT** TM. No. 1 (1991)-. Periodical. English. Six times a year. $18.80. Tractor Magazine, PO Box 174, Spencer NB 68777.

LC TL233.A1 V75a
DD 629.22/5/0947 RU
TRACTOROEXPORT. **Main/Corp** Vsesoiuznoe Obedinenie Traktoroeksport. (19??)-. Periodical. English (English). Four times a year. V/O Tractorexport, 21/5 Kuznetsky Most, 103031 Moscow Russia.

LC HD9710.4.U6 C87 **ISSN** 0145-5249
DD 338.4/76817631 US
TRACTORS, EXCEPT GARDEN TRACTORS. (CURRENT INDUSTRIAL REPORTS. M35S, TRACTORS (EXCEPT GARDEN TRACTORS).). [Tract. except gard. tract.]. **Added/Corp** United States. Bureau of the Census. (19??)-. Government Publication. English. Twelve times a year. US Department of Commerce / Bureau of the Census, Data User Services Division, Customer Services, Washington DC 20233-0800. **Tel** (301)763-4100. **(Subscription address:** Superintendent of Documents, US Government Printing Office, Washington DC 20402.) Documents available from Documents on Demand.
Desc: Presents data on production, inventories, and orders.
Ind/Abst Am. Stat. Index.

Agriculture —Agricultural Equipment

LC S671 .T7 **ISSN** 0235-8573
DD 631.3 RU
TRAKTORY I SELSKOKHOZIAISTVENNYE MASHINY. **Added/Corp** Soviet Union. Ministerstvo Avtomobilnogo i Selskokhoziaistvennogo Mashinostroeniia. (1988)-. Periodical. Russian. Twelve times a year. $159.95. Agropromizdat, Sadovo-Spasskaia 18, 107807 Moscow Russia. **(Subscription address:** East View Publications Inc., 3020 Harbor Lane North, Suite 110, Minneapolis MN 55447. **Tel** (800)477-1005, (612)550-0961, FAX (612)559-2931.**) Continues** *Traktory i Selkhozmashiny.*
Ind/Abst Agric. Eng. Abstr.; Hortic. Abstr.; Postharvest News Inf.; Potato Abstr.; Seed Abstr.

LC TJ1480 **ISSN** 1031-4695
DD 631.3 AT
SUSPENDED
WEEKLY TIMES TECHNICAL ANNUAL. **VFOAT** Technical Annual. (198?)-. English. One time a year. M & S Media Services, 2 Railway Place, Preston VIC Australia. **Tel** 011 61 3 4803074. **Continues** *Power Farming Technical Annual.*

LC HD28 **ISSN** 0896-6834
DD 658 US
YARD & GARDEN. See Gardening and Horticulture.

LC TJ1480 **ISSN** 0044-3883
DD 631.3 XR
ZEMEDELSKA TECHNIKA. Added/Corp Ceskoslovenska Akademie Zemedelska, Prague. Ustav Vedeckotechnickych Informaci. (1955)-. Periodical. Czech (summaries and/or abstracts in English, German and Russian; table of contents in French). Quarterly. DM76.00. **(Subscription address:** Kubon & Sagner, ABT Zeitschriftenimport, D 80328 Munich Germany. **Tel** 011 49 89 54218130.**) Supersedes in part** *Ceskoslovenska Akademie Zemedelskych Ved. Sbornik Ceskoslovenske Akademie Zemedelskych ved. Rada A* **and** *Ceskoslovenska Akademie Zemedelskych Ved. Sbornik Ceskoslovenske Akademie Zemedelskych ved. Rada B.*
Ind/Abst AgBiotech News Inf.; AGRICOLA; Agric. Eng. Abstr.; Dairy Sci. Abstr.; Field Crop Abstr.; Grass. Forage Abstr.; Hortic. Abstr.; Maize Abstr.; Nutr. Abstr. Rev., Ser. B, Live Feeds and Feed.; Pig News Inf.; Plant Genet. Resour. Abstr.; Postharvest News Inf.; Potato Abstr.; Rev. Agric. Entomol.; Seed Abstr.; Soils Fert.; Soyabean Abstr.; Wheat Barley Trit. Abstr.

COMPUTER APPLICATIONS

  ISSN 0738-5978
  US
  CODEN AGRCE3
AGRICOMP. [AgriComp]. (198?)-. Periodical. English. Six times a year. $24.00. Agricomp, 103 Outdoors Building, Columbia MO 65201. **Tel** (314)443-4316. **ED** Mark Wilsdorf. **Bk Rev. Ad Acc. Circ:** 5,000. Documents available from Ask*IEEE.
  Desc: Information for using a computer in a farm business. Management oriented, focusing on applications, tutorials, reviews, etc.
  Ind/Abst INSPEC (Sep./Oct. 1984-).

LC S **ISSN** 0188-3054
DD 630 MX
Pr Rev.
AGROCIENCIA. SERIE MATEMATICAS APLICADAS, ESTADISTICA Y COMPUTACION. See Agriculture-Agricultural Economics.

  ISSN 0899-3025
DD 004 US
COMPUTER RAMBLINGS. [Comput. rambl.]. **Added/Corp** United States. Dept. of Agriculture. South Dakota State University. Extension Computer Services. South Dakota State University. Cooperative Extension Service. Vol. 1, No. 1 (July 1985)-. Periodical. English. Twelve times a year.
  Ind/Abst AGRICOLA [Full Cov.].

  ISSN 0168-1699
  NE
  CCC
  CODEN CEAGE6
Pr Rev.
COMPUTERS AND ELECTRONICS IN AGRICULTURE. [Comput. electron. agric.]. Vol. 1, No. 1 (Oct. 1985)-. Academic Scholarly Publication. English. Eight times a year (2 volumes). $500.00. Elsevier Science Publishers BV, PO Box 211, 1000 AE Amsterdam Netherlands. **Tel** 011 31 20 4853641, 011 31 20 4853642, FAX 011 31 20 4853598. **ED** S W R Cox (editor's address: Manor Close, Hitchin, Herts, SG4 9ES United Kingdom). available on microfilm and microfiche from University Microfilms International (UMI); available on an online database from Elsevier Electronic Subscriptions (EES). Documents available from Article Express International, BIOSIS Document Express, Ask*IEEE.

Desc: Aim is to provide international coverage of advances in the application of computers and electronic instrumentation and control systems to agriculture and related industries.
Ind/Abst AgBiotech News Inf.; AGRICOLA [Full Cov.]; Agric. Eng. Abstr. (19??-19??); Anim. Breed. Abstr.; Biol. Abstr. (1985-); Cot. Trop. Fibr. Abstr. Bibliogr.; Curr. Cit.; Dairy Sci. Abstr.; Ecol. Abstr.; Ei Page One; Eng. Index Annu.; Field Crop Abstr.; Food Sci. Technol. Abstr.; Geogr. Abstr. Phys. Geogr.; Geogr. Abstr. Human Geogr.; Grass. Forage Abstr.; Hortic. Abstr.; Index Vet.; Inf. Sci. Abstr.; INSPEC (1985-); Int. Abstr. Oper. Res. [Select. Cov.]; Int. Dev. Abstr.; Irr. Drain. Abstr.; Maize Abstr.; Nutr. Abstr. Rev., Ser. B, Live Feeds and Feed.; Ornamental Hort. (19??-19??); Pig News Inf.; Plant Breed. Abstr.; Plant Genet. Resour. Abstr.; Rev. Agric. Entomol.; Rice Abstr.; Soils Fert.; Vet. Bull.; Wheat Barley Trit. Abstr.; World Agric. Econ. Rural Sociol. Abstr.

  ISSN 0748-9897
DD 631 US
EASTERN COMPUTING FARMER. (EASTERN COMPUTING FARMER : THE PUBLICATION OF EASTERN COMPUTING FARMERS ASSOCIATION.). [East. comput. farmer]. **Added/Corp** Eastern Computing Farmers Association (United States). Vol. 1, No. 1 (Aug. 1984)-. Periodical. English. Twelve times a year. $35.00. Eastern Computing Farmer's Association, PO Box 336, State College PA 16804. **Tel** (814)466-7645.

  AT
FARM COMPUTING. English. Four times a year (Feb., May, Aug., Nov.). 20.00 Aus$ (one-year), 36.00 Aus$ (two-year). Agram Computer Services, PO Box 122, Canterbury VICT 3126 Australia. **Tel** 11 61 3 8425311.

  ISSN 1182-8986
DD 630/.285 CN
NOVA SCOTIA FARM COMPUTING NEWS, THE. [N.S. farm comput. news]. **Added/Corp** Nova Scotia. Farm Business Management Section. Vol. 1, Issue 1 (Fall 1990)-. Periodical. English. Four times a year. **Continues** *RAM-Blings, Farm Computer News., 1182-8978.*

LC HD9000.1 .S64 **ISSN** 8756-1050
DD 630/.68 US
SOFTWHERE. AGRI-BUSINESS. [Softwhere, Agri-bus.]. **VFOAT** Agri-Business Softwhere. Summer 1984-. English. Two times a year. $49.95. Moore Data Management Services, Minneapolis MN 55416. **Tel** (612)588-7205. **ED** Richaro Winther. **Circ:** 10,000.

CROP PRODUCTION AND SOILS

LC SB608 **ISSN** 0165-6031
DD 635.21 NE
AARDAPPELWERELD. Added/Corp Federatie voor de Handel in Pootaardappelen. No. 4 (Oct. 1985)-. Periodical. Dutch. Twelve times a year. F29.00. Aardappelwereld, PO Box 80537, 2508 GM Den Haag Netherlands. **Continues** *Pootaardappelen, 0165-6031.*
Ind/Abst Biocont. News Inf.; Potato Abstr.

LC S
DD 630 US
  TITLE CHANGE
ABSTRACTS, MEETING OF THE WEED SCIENCE SOCIETY OF AMERICA. **Main/Corp** Weed Science Society of America. (1956)-(19??). English. Weed Science Society of America, 1508 West University Avenue, Champaign IL 61821. **Tel** (217)352-4212, FAX (217)398-4114. **Continued by** *WSSA Abstracts. Meeting of the Weed Science Society of America.*
Ind/Abst PESTDOC.

LC Z5071
DD 016.63 CK
  CEASED
ABSTRACTS OF FIELD BEANS (PHASEOLUS VULGARIS L.). See Agriculture-Abstracting, Bibliographies and Statistics.

LC SB211.C3 A15 **ISSN** 0120-288X
DD 633.6/82/05 CK
  CEASED
ABSTRACTS ON CASSAVA (MANIHOT ESCULENTA CRANTZ). [Abstr. cassava]. Vol. 2 (1976)- (Jan. 1993). English. CIAT International, Apartado Aereo 6713, Cali Colombia. **Tel** 675050, telex 05769 CIAT CO ITT. **Continues** *2,000 Abstracts on Cassava (Manihot Esculenta Crantz).*
Ind/Abst Nematol. Abstr.; Plant Breed. Abstr.; Rev. Agric. Entomol.; Weed Abstr.

LC SB111.A2 A26 **ISSN** 0304-5951
DD 630/.913 NE
ABSTRACTS ON TROPICAL AGRICULTURE. See Agriculture-Abstracting, Bibliographies and Statistics.

LC SB320.6 .A25 **ISSN** 0565-1905
DD 338.1/8 US
ACREAGE MARKETING GUIDES. SPRING VEGETABLES AND MELONS. (SPRING VEGETABLES AND MELONS.). Government Publication. English. One time a year. Department of Agriculture / Foreign Agricultural Service, 14th Street and Independence Avenue SW, Washington DC 20250-1000. **Tel** (202)720-3935, FAX (202)720-7729. **Continues** *Spring Vegetables, Spring Melons.*

LC S900 **ISSN** 1030-8857
DD 630.2745 AT
ACRES AUSTRALIA. [Acres Aust.]. (1988)-. Periodical. English. Six times a year. 14.79Aus$. Independent Rural Publishers, PO Box 27, Eumundi Queensland 4562 Australia. **Tel** 011 61 74 491881. **ED** Lindsay E. Bock. **Bk Rev**, (Qty: 24). **Ad Acc, Adv Mgr:** Pam Feldman. **Circ:** 7,500 (ctrl).
  Desc: Covers topics such as organic and bio-dynamic farming, landcare, agro forestry, marketing, property, ecology, eco tourism, and health and wellbeing.

LC SB13 .A27 **ISSN** 0906-4710
DD 630 DK
  CCC
  CODEN AASBEV
ACTA AGRICULTUR SCANDINAVICA. SECTION B, SOIL AND PLANT SCIENCE. **Added/Corp** Kungl. Skogs- och Lantbruksakademien (Sweden) Scandinavian Agricultural Research Workers' Association. **VFOAT** Soil and Plant Science. Vol. 42, No. 1 (Mar. 1992)-. Periodical. English. Four times a year. $150.00. Scandinavian University Press, PO Box 2959 Toeyen, N 0608 Oslo 6 Norway. **Tel** 011 47 2 2575400, FAX 011 47 2 2575353, telex 71896 UROR N. **(Subscription address:** Scandinavian University Press, 200 Meacham Ave., Elmont NY 11003. **Tel** (516)352-7300, FAX (516)352-7377.**) ED** Ake Barklund. Documents available from The Genuine Article. **Continues in part** *Acta Agricultur Scandinavica, 0001-5121.*
  Desc: Articles concerning agricultural research of relevance to Scandinavian conditions. Discusses results of research in soils and plant science related to fertilizers; land preparation; drainage and water management; environmental considerations; general agronomy; crop production science, including horticulture; plant protection, including plant pathology and entomology; plant breeding and genetics, and harvesting and processing.
  Ind/Abst Curr. Aware. Biol. Sci.; CABS; Res. Alert [Full Cov.]; Sci. Cit. Index; SCISEARCH.

LC SB363.2.U6 V52 **ISSN** 0092-8348
DD 353.9/755/008233 US
ACTIVITY REPORT OF THE VIRGINIA STATE APPLE COMMISSION. (ACTIVITY REPORT.). **Main/Corp** Virginia State Apple Commission. (19??)-. English. State Apple Commission, PO Box 718, Staunton VA 22401.

LC S590 **ISSN** 0715-4844
DD 631.5/21/05 CN
ACTUALITE-SEMENCE. [Acual.-semen.]. Vol. 31, No. 1 (March 1982)-. Periodical. French. Actualite-Semence, a/s Association Canadienne des Producteurs de Semences, CP 8455, Ottawa Ontario K1G 3T1 Canada. **Tel** (613)236-0497, FAX (613)563-7855. **Continues** *Seed Scoop. Ed. Francaise, 0384-7314.*

LC S **ISSN** 0169-0566
DD 630 NE
ADVANCES IN AGRICULTURAL BIOTECHNOLOGY. [Adv. agric. biotechnol.]. (1984)-. Monographic series. English. Irregular. Price varies per volume. Kluwer Academic Publishers, Postbus 322, 3300 AH Dordrecht The Netherlands. **Tel** 011 31 78 524400, FAX 011 31 78 183273, telex 20083. **(Subscription address:** Kluwer Academic Publishers / US Subscriptions, PO Box 253, Accord Station, Hingham MA 02018. **Tel** (617)871-6600.**)**
  Ind/Abst AGRICOLA [Full Cov.]; Hortic. Abstr.; Ornamental Hort. (1991-); Postharvest News Inf.

LC S583
DD 631 UK
●**ADVISOR, THE.** (1994)-. Trade Publication. English. Four times a year. £20.00. Carter Spencer Publishing Ltd., Chancery Court, Lincoln Road, High Wycombe, Buckinghamshire HP12 3RE United Kingdom. **Tel** 011 44 1494 442424, FAX 011 44 1494 472790. **ED** Hans Luers. **Ad Acc, Adv Mgr:** David Spencer. **Circ:** 3,500. available with charts; available with illustrations.

LC SB188 **ISSN** 0950-494X
DD 633.1 UK
AGRAFILE. GRAIN & OILSEEDS. [Agrafile, Grain oilseeds]. **VFOAT** Grain & Oilseeds. (1986)-. Trade Publication. English. Twelve times a year. £135.00 (institutions) UK. Agra Europe London Limited, 25 Frant Road, Tunbridge Wells, Kent TN2 5JT United Kingdom. **Tel** 011 44 1892 533813, FAX 011 44 1892 544595, telex

95114 AGRATW G. **ED** Guy Faulkner.
Desc: Overview of the current market situation with selected information.

LC S **ISSN** 1148-5639
DD 630 FR
UDC 31(44)
AGRESTE. CONJONCTURE, FRUITS.
(1990)-. Periodical. French. Twelve times a year. 160.00F France; 180.00F other. Ministere de l'Agriculture et de la Peche, Direction des Affaires Financieres et Economiques, Service Central des Enquetes et Etudes Statistiques, 4 Avenue de Saint-Mande, 75570 Paris Cedex 12 France. **Tel** 011 33 1 43444633, 16 61288305.

LC S **ISSN** 1148-5655
DD 630 FR
UDC 31(44)
AGRESTE. CONJONCTURE, LEGUMES.
(1990)-. Periodical. French. Twelve times a year. 160.00F France; 180.00F other. Ministere de l'Agriculture et de la Peche, Direction des Affaires Financieres et Economiques, Service Central des Enquetes et Etudes Statistiques, 4 Avenue de Saint-Mande, 75570 Paris Cedex 12 France. **Tel** 011 33 1 43444633, 16 61288305.
Desc: Vegetable production in France.

LC S **ISSN** 1148-5663
DD 630 FR
UDC 31(44)
AGRESTE. CONJONCTURE, VITICULTURE. **VFOAT** Agreste. Conjoncture, Vin. (1990)-. Periodical. French. Twelve times a year. 65.00F France; 75.00F other. Ministere de l'Agriculture et de la Peche, Direction des Affaires Financieres et Economiques, Service Central des Enquetes et Etudes Statistiques, 4 Avenue de Saint-Mande, 75570 Paris Cedex 12 France. **Tel** 011 33 1 43444633, 16 61288305. ***Continues** Informations Rapides - Ministere de l'Agriculture. Viticulture, 0243-6116.*

LC QK725 .A37 **ISSN** 0738-145X
DD 630 US
CCC
AGRICELL REPORT. **Added/Corp** Agritech Consultants, Inc. Vol. 1, No. 1 (July 1983)-. Periodical. English. Twelve times a year. $298.00. Agritech Consultants Inc, PO Box 255, Shrub Oak NY 10588. **Tel** (914)528-3469.
Ind/Abst Abstr. Bull. Inst. Pap. Sci. Tech.; Abstr. BioCommer.; AgBiotech News Inf.; Potato Abstr.

LC S **ISSN** 0168-1923
DD 630 NE
CCC
Pr Rev.
AGRICULTURAL AND FOREST METEOROLOGY. [Agric. for. meteorol.]. Vol. 31, No. 1 (Feb. 1984)-. Academic Scholarly Publication. English (French and German; summaries and/or abstracts in French and German). Twenty times a year (5 volumes). $1464.00. Elsevier Science Publishers BV, PO Box 211, 1000 AE Amsterdam Netherlands. **Tel** 011 31 20 4853641, 011 31 20 4853642, FAX 011 31 20 4853598. **ED** W E Reifsnyder, M N Hough and K G McNaughton. available on microfilm and microfiche from University Microfilms International (UMI); available on an online database from Elsevier Electronic Subscriptions (EES). Documents available from The Genuine Article, Documents on Demand. ***Continues** Agricultural Meteorology, 0002-1571.*
Desc: Specialized channel of communication in the interdisciplinary field of meteorology and climatology applied to agriculture and forestry.
Ind/Abst Agric. Eng. Abstr. (1991-); Agrofor. Abstr. (19??-19??); Coal Abstr.; Crop Physiol. Abstr.; Curr. Aware. Biol. Sci., CABS; Curr. Cit.; Curr. Contents Agric. Biol. Environ. Sci.; Ecol. Abstr.; Ecology Abstr.; Environ. Abstr.; Environ. Period. Bibliogr.; Field Crop Abstr.; For. Abstr.; Geogr. Abstr. Phys. Geogr.; Geogr. Abstr. Human Geogr.; GeoRef; Hortic. Abstr.; Index Vet.; Int. Dev. Abstr.; Irr. Drain. Abstr.; Maize Abstr.; Meteorol. Geoastrophys. Abstr. (199?-); Nutr. Abstr. Rev., Ser. B, Live Feeds and Feed.; Ornamental Hort. (1991-); Life Sci. Collect.; Plant Breed. Abstr.; Potato Abstr.; Res. Alert [Full Cov.]; Rev. Agric. Entomol.; Rev. Plant Pathol.; Rice Abstr.; Sci. Cit. Index; SCISEARCH; Soils Fert.; Sorghum Mill. Abstr.; Soyabean Abstr.; Vet. Bull.; Vitis Vitic. Enol. Abstr.; Wheat Barley Trit. Abstr.

LC HD9016.I4 A34 **ISSN** 0002-1555
DD 338.17 II
AGRICULTURAL MARKETING. **Added/Corp** India (Republic). Directorate of Marketing and Inspection. (1958)-. Periodical. English. Four times a year. $20.00. Controller of Publications / Marketing, Directorate of Marketing and Inspection, New Delhi India. **(Subscription address:** Prints India, 11 Darya Ganj, New Delhi 110002 India. **Tel** 011 91 11 3268645, FAX 011 91 11 3275542, telex 31-61087 PRIN-IN.)
Ind/Abst Postharvest News Inf.; Potato Abstr.; Rice Abstr.; Rural Dev. Abstr.; Sug. Indus. Abstr.; World Agric. Econ. Rural Sociol. Abstr.

LC S **ISSN** 0253-150X
DD 630 II
CODEN ASDIDY
AGRICULTURAL SCIENCE DIGEST (AGRICULTURAL RESEARCH COMMUNICATION CENTER.).
(AGRICULTURAL SCIENCE DIGEST.). [Agric. sci. dig.]. **Added/Corp** Agricultural Research Communication Centre (India). Vol. 1, No. 1 (Mar. 1981)-. Academic Scholarly Publication. English. Four times a year. $55.00. Agricultural Research Communication Centre, Sadar Karnal 132001, Haryana India. **Tel** 011 91 3036. **ED** S. Srivastava and J. Chaudharg. cum. index. **Circ:** 1,500. Documents available from CASDDS.
Desc: Original research notes/short communications on plant and soil sciences.
Ind/Abst AgBiotech News Inf.; Agrofor. Abstr. (19??-19??); Biocont. News Inf. (1991-); Biodeter. Abstr. (19??-19??); Chem. Abstr.; Cot. Trop. Fibr. Abstr. Bibliogr.; Crop Physiol. Abstr.; EMBASE; Field Crop Abstr.; For. Abstr.; Hortic. Abstr.; Index Vet.; Irr. Drain. Abstr.; Maize Abstr.; Nematol. Abstr.; Plant Breed. Abstr.; Plant Grow. Reg. Abstr.; Postharvest News Inf.; Potato Abstr.; Rev. Agric. Entomol.; Rev. Plant Pathol.; Rice Abstr.; Seed Abstr.; Soils Fert.; Sorghum Mill. Abstr.; Soyabean Abstr.; Vet. Bull.; Weed Abstr.; Wheat Barley Trit. Abstr.

LC SB23 **ISSN** 0791-3524
DD 630.9417 630.20112 IE
AGRICULTURAL STATISTICS, JUNE ..., LAND UTILISATION AND NUMBERS OF LIVESTOCK, REGIONAL ANALYSIS. **See** Agriculture-Abstracting, Bibliographies and Statistics.

LC S **ISSN** 0995-5178
DD 630 FR
AGRICULTURES ACTUALITE. [Agric. actual.]. (1988)-. Periodical. French. Four times a year. 100.00F (individuals) France; 180.00F (individuals) other. Geyser, rue Grande 04870 St Michael, L Observatoire France. **Tel** 011 33 92 766244. ***Formed by the union of** Alternatives Agricoles **and** Bioactuel, 0982-5762.*

LC S
DD 630 JA
AGROCHEMICALS JAPAN. (19??)-. Japanese. Two times a year. $115.00. Sun Publications Service Ltd, Ishii Building, 3 37 Sakumacho Kanda, Chiyoda-ku Tokyo 101 Japan. **Tel** 011 81 3 38669897, FAX 011 81 3 38617715. ***Continues** Japan Pesticide Information, 0368-265X.*

LC S590 **ISSN** 0002-1873
DD 631.4 HU
CODEN AKTLAUAKTLUA
AGROKEMIA ES TALAJTAN. (AGROKEMIA ES TALAJTAN. AGROKHIMIIA I POCHVOVEDENIE. AGROCHEMISTRY AND SOIL SCIENCE.). [Agrokem. talajt.]. **Added/Corp** Magyar Tudomanyos Akademia, Budapest. Talajtani es Agrokemiai Kutato Intezet. **VFOAT** Agrokhimiia I Pochvovedenie; Agrochemistry and Soil Science. Vol. 1 (1951)-. Academic Scholarly Publication. Hungarian (summaries and/or abstracts in English, French, German, Russian and Spanish). Four times a year. $38.00. Akademiai Kiado, Publishing House of the Hungarian Academy of Sciences, Prielle Kornelia u. 19-35, H-1117 Budapest Hungary. **Tel** 011 36 1 1811991, FAX 011 36 1 1811991, telex 22-6228 AKNYO H. **ED** I. Szabolcs, A. Muranyi. cum. index. **Bk Rev. Ad Acc. Circ:** 1,200. Documents available from CASDDS. ***Supersedes** Agrokemia, 0365-2734.*
Ind/Abst Chem. Abstr.; Crop Physiol. Abstr.; Field Crop Abstr.; Grass. Forage Abstr.; Hortic. Abstr.; Irr. Drain. Abstr.; Maize Abstr.; Life Sci. Collect.; Plant Breed. Abstr.; Potato Abstr.; Soils Fert.; Soyabean Abstr.; Weed Abstr.

LC SB761 **ISSN** 0120-9965
DD 635.97 CK
AGRONOMIA COLOMBIANA. **Added/Corp** Universidad Nacional de Colombia. Facultad de Agronomia. Vol. 1, No. 1 (Aug./Dec. 1983)-. Periodical. Spanish. Two times a year. Universidad Nacional de Colombia Facultad de Agronomia, Bogota Colombia.
Desc: Publication providing information on plants, agronomy and agriculture.
Ind/Abst Field Crop Abstr.; Hortic. Abstr.; Maize Abstr.; Ornamental Hort. (1991-); Rice Abstr.; Soils Fert.; Wheat Barley Trit. Abstr.

LC SB7 .A36 **ISSN** 0249-5627
DD 631.5 FR
CCC
CODEN AGRNDZ
Pr Rev.
AGRONOMIE. [Agronomie]. **Added/Corp** Institut National de la Recherche Agronomique (France). Vol. 1, No. 1 (1981)-. Academic Scholarly Publication. English (French). Ten times a year. $471.00. Editions Scientifique Elsevier, 141 rue de Javel, 75747 Paris Cedex 15 France. **Tel** 011 33 1 45589067, FAX 011 33 1 45589424. **(Subscription address:** Editions Scientifiques Elsevier / for North America, PO Box 7247-7576, Philadelphia PA 19170-7576. **) ED** M. Rives. Index available. **Bk Rev. Circ:** 1,600. available on microfilm and microfiche from University Microfilms International (UMI); available on an online database from Elsevier Electronic Subscriptions (EES). Documents available from The Genuine Article, BIOSIS Document Express, CASDDS. ***Formed by the union of** Annales Agronomiques (Institut National de la Recherche Agronomique (France)); Annales de L'Amelioration des Plantes, 0003-4053 **and** Annales de Phytopathologie.*
Desc: Articles concerning fundamental or applied problems of plant growing and agrarian systems considered by their different biological, physiological, ecological and economical aspects.
Ind/Abst BioBusiness; Biocont. News Inf. (19??-19??); Biol. Abstr.; Chem. Abstr. (?-1981); Cot. Trop. Fibr. Abstr. Bibliogr.; Crop Physiol. Abstr.; Curr. Aware. Biol. Sci., CABS; Curr. Cit.; Curr. Contents Agric. Biol. Environ. Sci.; Ecol. Abstr.; Ecology Abstr.; EMBASE; Energy Res. Abstr. (Dec. 1982-); Entomol. Abstr.; Field Crop Abstr.; For. Abstr.; Geogr. Abstr. Phys. Geogr.; Geogr. Abstr. Human Geogr.; Grass. Forage Abstr.; Hortic. Abstr.; Int. Dev. Abstr.; Irr. Drain. Abstr.; Leadscan; Maize Abstr.; Nematol. Abstr.; Nutr. Abstr. Rev., Ser. B, Live Feeds and Feed.; Ornamental Hort. (19??-19??); Life Sci. Collect.; PESTDOC; Plant Breed. Abstr.; Plant Genet. Resour. Abstr.; Plant Grow. Reg. Abstr.; Potato Abstr.; Res. Alert [Select. Cov.]; Rev. Agric. Entomol.; Rev. Plant Pathol.; SCISEARCH; Seed Abstr.; Soc. Sci. Cit. Index [Select. Cov.]; Soils Fert.; Soyabean Abstr.; Weed Abstr.; Wheat Barley Trit. Abstr.; World Agric. Econ. Rural Sociol. Abstr.

LC S590
DD 631.4 US
AGRONOMY AND SOILS DEPARTMENTAL SERIES. **Added/Corp** Alabama Agricultural Experiment Station. (19??)-. Monographic series. English. Alabama Agricultural Experiment Station, Auburn University, 110 Comer Hall, Auburn University AL 36849. **Tel** (334)844-4877, FAX (334)844-5892.
Ind/Abst Field Crop Abstr.; GeoRef; Maize Abstr.; Plant Breed. Abstr.; Rev. Plant Pathol.; Sorghum Mill. Abstr.; Wheat Barley Trit. Abstr.

LC S **ISSN** 0002-1962
DD 630 US
CCC
CODEN AGJOAT
AGRONOMY JOURNAL. [Agron. j.]. **Added/Corp** American Society of Agronomy. Vol. 41 Jan. (1949)-. Academic Scholarly Publication. English. Six times a year. $117.00. American Society of Agronomy, 677 South Segoe Road, Madison WI 53711. **Tel** (608)273-8080, FAX (608)273-2021. cum. index. Documents available from BIOSIS Document Express, CASDDS. ***Continues** Journal - American Society of Agronomy, 0095-9650.*
Desc: Papers on all aspects of crop and soil sciences including crop physiology, production and management along with their relationship to soil fertility and climatic conditions.
Ind/Abst AgBiotech News Inf.; AGRICOLA; Agric. Eng. Abstr.; Agrofor. Abstr.; BioBusiness; Biogr. Index; Biol. Agric. Index; Biol. Abstr.; Chem. Abstr.; Crop Physiol. Abstr.; Curr. Aware. Biol. Sci., CABS; Curr. Cit.; Curr. Contents Agric. Biol. Environ. Sci.; Dairy Sci. Abstr.; EMBASE; Environ. Period. Bibliogr.; Field Crop Abstr.; Food Sci. Technol. Abstr.; For. Abstr.; Grass. Forage Abstr.; Hortic. Abstr.; Index Vet.; INIS Atomindex [Micro.]; Int. Aerosp. Abstr.; Irr. Drain. Abstr.; Leadscan; Leis., Rec., Tour. Abstr.; Maize Abstr.; Meteorol. Geoastrophys. Abstr.; Nematol. Abstr.; Nutr. Abstr. Rev., Ser. B, Live Feeds and Feed.; Nutr. Abstr. Rev., Ser. A, Hum. Exp.; Ornamental Hort.; Life Sci. Collect.; PESTDOC; Plant Breed. Abstr.; Plant Genet. Resour. Abstr.; Plant Grow. Reg. Abstr.; Postharvest News Inf.; Potato Abstr.; Res. Alert; Rev. Agric. Entomol.; Rev. Med. Vet. Mycology; Rev. Plant Pathol.; Rice Abstr.; Rural Dev. Abstr.; Sci. Cit. Index; SCISEARCH; Seed Abstr.; Soc. Sci. Cit. Index; Soils Fert.; Sorghum Mill. Abstr.; Soyabean Abstr.; Stat. Theory Method Abstr.; Vet. Bull.; Weed Abstr.; World Agric. Econ. Rural Sociol. Abstr.

LC S **ISSN** 0568-3106
DD 630 US
CCC
AGRONOMY NEWS. **Added/Corp** American Society of Agronomy. Crop Science Society of America. Soil Society of America. (March/April 1956)-. Periodical. English. Twelve times a year. $12.00. American Society of Agronomy, 677 South Segoe Road, Madison WI 53711. **Tel** (608)273-8080, FAX (608)273-2021. **ED** Keith R. Schlesinger. **Bk Rev. Circ:** 12,500.
Desc: Contains information about Society members and activities. It also includes news of recent developments in other agronomy related fields and countries.

LC S590 **ISSN** 1057-1698
DD 631.4 US
AGRONOMY NOTES. **Added/Corp** United States. Dept. of Agriculture. University of Kentucky. Agronomy Dept. University of Kentucky. Cooperative

Extension Service. (19??)-. Monographic series. English. University of Kentucky Department of Agricultural Economics, College of Agriculture, Lexington KY 40546. **Tel** (606)757-7273.
Ind/Abst AGRICOLA [Full Cov.].

LC S594 .A36 **ISSN** 0743-5479
DD 631.4/32/028 US
AIRCRAFT REMOTE SENSING OF SOIL MOISTURE AND HYDROLOGIC PARAMETERS, CHICKASHA, OKLA., ... DATA REPORT. English. Hydrology Laboratory, Beltsville Agricultural Research Center-West, Beltsville MD 20705.

LC S **ISSN** 0385-3152
DD 630 JA
AKITA-KEN KAJU SHIKENJUO KENKYUU HUOKOKU. (BULLETIN OF THE AKITA FRUIT-TREE EXPERIMENT STATION.). [Akita-ken Kaju Shikenjuo kenkyuu huokoku]. **Main/Corp** Akita, Japan, Akita Fruit-Tree Experiment Station. (1969)-. Bulletin. Japanese. Akita Fruit-Tree Experiment Station, Daigo, Hiraka Akita, Japan.
Ind/Abst Crop Physiol. Abstr.; Hortic. Abstr.; Plant Breed. Abstr.

LC SB183 **ISSN** 0379-3575
DD 633 UA
CODEN EJAGDS
AL-MAGALLA AL-MISRIYYA LI-L-MAHASIL. (EGYPTIAN JOURNAL OF AGRONOMY.). [Magalla al-misriyya li-l-mahasil]. **Added/Corp** Egyptian Society of Crop Science. Markaz al-Qawmi Lil-Ila Wa-al-Tawthiq. **VFOAT** Majallah Al-Misriyah Lil-Mahasil. Vol. 1 (1976)-. Periodical. English (summaries and/or abstracts in Arabic; table of contents in Arabic). Irregular. $57.00 (latest volume). National Information & Documentation Center, A1-Tahrir St Dokki Awqaf PO, Cairo Egypt. **Tel** 011 20 2 701696, telex 93069. Documents available from CASDDS.
Ind/Abst Chem. Abstr.; Field Crop Abstr.; Irr. Drain. Abstr.; Maize Abstr.; Nutr. Abstr. Rev., Ser. B, Live Feeds and Feed.; Nutr. Abstr. Rev., Ser. A, Hum. Exp.; Plant Breed. Abstr.; Plant Grow. Reg. Abstr.; Seed Abstr.; Soils Fert.; Sorghum Mill. Abstr.; Soyabean Abstr.; Weed Abstr.; Wheat Barley Trit. Abstr.

LC S605.2.C2 A42 **ISSN** 0713-1224
DD 631.6/07207123 CN
ALBERTA'S RECLAMATION RESEARCH PROGRAM. [Alta. reclam. res. pro.]. English. Dr P F Ziemkiewicz Chairman, Reclamation Research, Technical Advisory Committee, Alberta Energy & Natural Resources, 9915 - 108 Street, Edmonton Alberta Canada.

LC SB354 **ISSN** 0886-4365
DD 634 US
ALMOND FACTS. **Main/Corp** California Almond Growers Exchange, Sacramento, Calif. Vol. 1 (1937)-. Periodical. English. Six times a year. $25.00. Blue Diamond Growers, PO Box 1768, Sacramento CA 95812. **Tel** (916)442-0771. **ED** Dan Campbell. **Ad Acc. Circ:** 9,000 (ctrl).
Desc: Published for the 5,800 grower/members of the California Almond Growers Exchange, with information on cultural practices, and on the cooperative which markets under the Blue Diamond label.
Ind/Abst Bibliogr. Agric.

LC SB354.6.I75 A45 **ISSN** 0333-8886
DD 634 IS
ALON HA-NOTEA. **Added/Corp** Irgun Megadle Perot (Israel). (1945)-. Periodical. Hebrew. Twelve times a year. $60.00. Israel Fruit Growers Association, 8 Shaul Hamelekh, PO Box 40007, Tel-Aviv 61400 Israel. **Tel** 972-3-6966267, FAX 972-3-6917625. **ED** J. Kovetz. **Circ:** 5,000. Documents available from BLDSC.
Ind/Abst Biocont. News Inf. (19??-19??); Crop Physiol. Abstr.; Plant Breed. Abstr.; Plant Grow. Reg. Abstr.; Postharvest News Inf.

LC SB188 **ISSN** 0883-0142
DD 633 US
AMARANTH TODAY. Vol. 1, No. 1 (1985)-. Periodical. English. Four times a year. $15.00 US; $21.00 Canada. Amaranth Toady, 33 East Minor Street, Emmaus PA 18049.

LC SB428 .A6 **ISSN** 0569-3845
DD 338.1/7/4975 US
CODEN ACTJB3
AMERICAN CHRISTMAS TREE JOURNAL. [Am. Christmas tree j.]. **Added/Corp** National Christmas Tree Association. (19??)-. Academic Scholarly Publication. English. Four times a year (Jan., April, July, Oct.). $125.00. National Christmas Tree Association Inc, 611 East Wells Street, Milwaukee WI 53202. **Tel** (414)276-6410, FAX (414)276-3349. **ED** Dennis Tompkins. Index available. cum. index. **Ad Acc. Circ:** 2,000 (ctrl). Documents available from CASDDS. ***Continues*** *American Christmas Tree Growers' Journal.*
Desc: Covers Christmas tree production and marketing.
Ind/Abst Chem. Abstr.

LC SB354 **ISSN** 0002-8568
DD 634 US
CCC
CODEN AMFGAR
AMERICAN FRUIT GROWER (WILLOUGHBY, OHIO : 1931). (AMERICAN FRUIT GROWER.). [Am. fruit grow.]. Vol. 51 (Jan. 1931)-. Trade Publication. English. Twelve times a year. $27.00. Meister Publishing Company, 37733 Euclid Avenue, Willoughby OH 44094-5992. **Tel** (216)942-2000, (800)572-7740, FAX (216)942-0662. available on microfilm and microfiche from University Microfilms International (UMI). Documents available from Documents on Demand. ***Continues*** *American Fruit Grower Magazine.*
Ind/Abst Biocont. News Inf. (1991-); Biol. Agric. Index; Curr. Cit.; Energy Inf. Abstr.; Environ. Abstr.; Hortic. Abstr.; Postharvest News Inf.; Rev. Agric. Entomol.; Rev. Plant Pathol.; Weed Abstr.

LC S **ISSN** 0003-0589
DD 630 US
CODEN APOJAY
Pr Rev.
AMERICAN POTATO JOURNAL. [Am. potato j.]. **Added/Corp** Potato Association of America. (1926)-. Academic Scholarly Publication. English (summaries and/or abstracts in Spanish). Twelve times a year. $65.00. Potato Association of America, 157 park st, STE 23, Bangor ME 04401. **Tel** (207)942-9732, FAX (207)942-9733. **ED** Hugh Murphy. cum. index. **Bk Rev. Circ:** 1,500 (ctrl). available on microfilm and microfiche from University Microfilms International (UMI); available on CD-ROM. Documents available from The Genuine Article, BIOSIS Document Express, CASDDS, Documents on Demand. ***Continues*** *Potato News Bulletin.*
Desc: Research in disease and insect control, crop fertilization, storage, marketing, physiology, and processings; principally in research, extension, industry: worldwide circulation 60 countries.
Ind/Abst AgBiotech News Inf.; AGRICOLA [Full Cov.]; Agric. Eng. Abstr. (1991-); Biodeter. Abstr. (19??-19??); Biol. Abstr.; Chem. Abstr.; Crop Physiol. Abstr.; Curr. Aware. Biol. Sci., CABS; Curr. Cit.; Curr. Contents Agric. Biol. Environ. Sci.; EMBASE; Energy Inf. Abstr.; Environ. Abstr.; Field Crop Abstr.; Food Sci. Technol. Abstr.; Grass. Forage Abstr.; Irr. Drain. Abstr.; Nematol. Abstr.; Nutr. Abstr. Rev., Ser. B, Live Feeds and Feed.; Nutr. Abstr. Rev., Ser. A, Hum. Exp.; Life Sci. Collect.; Plant Breed. Abstr.; Plant Genet. Resour. Abstr.; Plant Grow. Reg. Abstr.; Postharvest News Inf.; Potato Abstr.; Protozoolog. Abstr.; Res. Alert [Full Cov.]; Rev. Agric. Entomol.; Rev. Med. Vet. Mycology; Rev. Plant Pathol.; Sci. Cit. Index; SCISEARCH; Seed Abstr.; Soils Fert.; Weed Abstr.; World Agric. Econ. Rural Sociol. Abstr.

LC SB320 **ISSN** 0741-9848
DD 635 US
CCC
CODEN AMVGA5
AMERICAN VEGETABLE GROWER (1983). (AMERICAN VEGETABLE GROWER.). [Am. veg. grow.]. Vol. 31, No. 1 (Jan. 1983)-. Trade Publication. English. Twelve times a year. $27.00. Meister Publishing Company, 37733 Euclid Avenue, Willoughby OH 44094-5992. **Tel** (216)942-2000, (800)572-7740, FAX (216)942-0662. available on microfilm and microfiche from University Microfilms International (UMI). ***Continues*** *American Vegetable Grower and Greenhouse Grower, 0161-8946.*
Desc: Coverage of the vegetable market.
Ind/Abst BioBusiness (1988-); Biol. Agric. Index; Food Sci. Technol. Abstr.; Ornamental Hort.

LC SB761 **ISSN** 0253-1682
DD 635.97 RM
CODEN ACPCBU
ANALELE INSTITUTULUI DE CERCETARI PENTRU CEREALE SI PLANTE TEHNICE, FUNDULEA. [An. Inst. Cercet. Cereale Plante Teh., Fundulea]. **Main/Corp** Institutul de Cercetari Pentru Cereale si Plante Tehnice Fundulea. **Added/Corp** Academia de Stiinte Agricole si Silvice. Vol. 41 (1973)-. Academic Scholarly Publication. Romanian (summaries and/or abstracts in English and Russian). One time a year. Documents available from CASDDS. ***Formed by the union of*** *Institutul de Cercetari Pentru Cereale si Plante Tehnice Analele Institutului de Cercetari Pentru Cereale si Plante Tehnice. Seria B: Agrofitotehnie si Agrochimie Rumania.* ***and*** *Institutul de Cercetari Pentru Cereale si Plante Tehnice. Analele ... Seria C, Ameliorare, Genetica, Fiziologie, Biochimie si Protectia Plantelor.*
Ind/Abst Chem. Abstr.; Field Crop Abstr.; Irr. Drain. Abstr.; Maize Abstr.; Plant Grow. Reg. Abstr.; Potato Abstr.; Rev. Agric. Entomol.; Rev. Plant Pathol.; Rice Abstr.; Seed Abstr.; Sorghum Mill. Abstr.; Soyabean Abstr.; Wheat Barley Trit. Abstr.

LC S590 **ISSN** 0258-6959
DD 631.4 RM
CODEN AICAD3
ANALELE INSTITUTULUI DE CERCETARI PENTRU PEDOLOGIE SI AGROCHIMIE. [An. Inst. Cercet. pentru Pedol. Agrochim.]. **Main/Corp** Institutul de Cercetari Pentru Pedologie Si Agrochimie (Romania). **Added/Corp** Academia de Stiinte si Silvice. **VFOAT** Analele I.C.P.A. Vol. 41 (1975)-. Academic Scholarly Publication. Romanian (summaries and/or abstracts in English and Russian; table of contents in English and Russian). One time a year. **(Subscription address:** Ilexim Press Department, PO Box 1, 136-1-137, Bucharest, Romania. **Tel** 011 40 1 173836.) Documents available from CASDDS. ***Continues*** *Institutul de Studii si Cercetari Pedologice (Romania). Analele - Institutul de Studii si Cercetari Pedologice, 0365-3099.*
Ind/Abst Chem. Abstr.

LC S
DD 630 NE
ANALYTICAL METHODS FOR RESIDUES OF PESTICIDES IN FOODSTUFFS. See Pest Control.

LC S9 .I56a **ISSN** 0365-7043
DD 630 IT
CODEN ASNPBZ
ANNALI DELL'ISTITUTO SPERIMENTALE PER LA NUTRIZIONE DELLE PIANTE. [Ann. Ist. sper. nutr. piante]. **Added/Corp** Istituto Sperimentale per la Nutrizione delle Piante. (1968)-. Italian (summaries and/or abstracts in English). Documents available from BIOSIS Document Express.
Ind/Abst Biol. Abstr.; Soyabean Abstr.

LC S539.2
DD 630.72 IT
ANNALI DELL'ISTITUTO SPERIMENTALE PER L'AGRUMICOLTURA. **Main/Corp** Istituto Sperimentale per l'Agrumicoltura. Vol. 1/2 (1970)-. Periodical. Italian (summaries and/or abstracts in English and French). One time a year.
Ind/Abst Hortic. Abstr.; Plant Grow. Reg. Abstr.

LC SB110 .A6 **ISSN** 0570-1791
DD 630/.9154 II
CODEN ANAZBX
Pr Rev.
ANNALS OF ARID ZONE. [Ann. Arid Zone]. **Added/Corp** Arid Zone Research Association of India. Vol. 1 (Dec. 1962)-. Periodical. English. Four times a year (Mar., June, Sept., Dec.). $55.00. Arid Zone Research Association India, Jodhpur 342 003, Rajasthan India. **Tel** telex 218 CAZRI_IN_JU. **(Subscription address:** Prints India, 11 Darya Ganj, New Delhi 110002 India. **Tel** 011 91 11 3268645, FAX 011 91 11 3275542, telex 31-61087 PRIN-IN.) **ED** Dr. S. Kathju. Index available (Bound in 4th issue, Publish in December). cum. index. **Bk Rev**, (Qty: 1000). **Ad Acc. Circ:** 1000. Documents available from The Genuine Article, BIOSIS Document Express, CASDDS, Documents on Demand.
Desc: Multidisciplinary of arid land research.
Ind/Abst AGRICOLA (-1986); Agrofor. Abstr. (1991-); Anim. Breed. Abstr.; Biol. Abstr.; Chem. Abstr.; Crop Physiol. Abstr.; Curr. Cit.; Curr. Contents Agric. Biol. Environ. Sci.; Energy Inf. Abstr.; Environ. Abstr.; Field Crop Abstr.; For. Prod. Abstr. (19??-19??); For. Abstr.; Grass. Forage Abstr.; Hortic. Abstr.; Indian Geosci. Abstr.; Irr. Drain. Abstr.; Leis., Rec., Tour. Abstr.; Life Sci. Collect.; Plant Breed. Abstr.; Plant Grow. Reg. Abstr.; Res. Alert [Select. Cov.]; Rev. Plant Pathol.; Rural Dev. Abstr.; SCISEARCH; Seed Abstr.; Soc. Plann. Policy Dev. Abstr.; Soc. Sci. Cit. Index [Select. Cov.]; Sociol. Abstr. (?-?); Soils Fert.; Sorghum Mill. Abstr.; Weed Abstr.; Wheat Barley Trit. Abstr.; Wildl. Rev.; World Agric. Econ. Rural Sociol. Abstr.

LC SB183
DD 633 US
ANNUAL CROP SUMMARY. **VFOAT** Crop Production : Annual Crop Summary; Crops : Annual Crop Summary. (19??)-. English. One time a year. The Service, Full Depository, 707 Savings and Loan Building, Des Moines IA 50309.
Desc: Contains Iowa and United States acreage, crop yield, and production.

LC TC401 .C64a **ISSN** 0198-1994
DD 333.91/009172/4 US
ANNUAL PROGRESS REPORT - WATER MANAGEMENT RESEARCH PROJECT. See Water Resources.

LC SB320
DD 635 US
ANNUAL REPORT. **Main/Corp** Vegetable Growers Association of America, Inc. (19??)-. English.

LC HD9235.P82 W49A
DD 338.17 AT
ANNUAL REPORT AND ACCOUNTS / WESTERN AUSTRALIAN POTATO MARKETING BOARD. **Main/Corp** Western Australian Potato Marketing Board. 32nd (1979/80)-. English. One time a year. Western Australian Potato Marketing Board, 103 Outram Street, Perth Western Australia 6005 Australia. ***Continues*** *Annual Report and Accounts Covering ... Season / Western Australian Potato Marketing Board.*

LC S **ISSN** 0700-6691
DD 630 CN
ANNUAL REPORT AND MINUTES OF THE ANNUAL MEETING - CANADIAN SEED GROWERS' ASSOCIATION.
Main/Corp Canadian Seed Growers' Association. (194?)-. English (French). One time a year. Canadian Seed Growers' Association, PO Box 8455, Ottawa Ontario K1G 3T1 Canada. **Tel** (613)236-0497, FAX (613)563-7855. **Circ:** 10,000. ***Continues*** *Canadian Seed Growers' Association. Annual Report, 0068-9610.*

LC SB354
DD 634 US
ANNUAL REPORT, ARIZONA FRUITS AND VEGETABLES. **Main/Corp** Arizona Fruit and Vegetable Standardization Service. (1975)-. Periodical. English. One time a year.

LC S
DD 630 US
ANNUAL REPORT / BLUE DIAMOND.
Main/Corp Blue Diamond Growers. (1987/88)-. English. ***Continues*** *Annual Report.*

LC JL1 **ISSN** 1184-2075
DD 354.71230082/326 CN
ANNUAL REPORT - CANADA-ALBERTA SOIL CONSERVATION INITIATIVE. (CASCI ANNUAL REPORT.). [Annu. rep. - Can.-Alta. Soil Conserv. Initiat.]. **Main/Corp** Canada--Alberta Soil Conservation Initiative. (1989/1990)-. English.

LC S599.7.A1 A9a **ISSN** 1032-5441
DD 631.4/072094 AT
ANNUAL REPORT - CSIRO DIVISION OF SOILS (1987). (ANNUAL REPORT / CSIRO AUSTRALIA, DIVISION OF SOILS.). [Annu. rep. - CSIRO Div. Soils]. **Main/Corp** Commonwealth Scientific and Industrial Research Organization (Australia). Division of Soils. **VFOAT** CSIRO Division of Soils Annual Report. (1987)-. English. One time a year. CSIRO Publications, PO Box 89, 314 Albert Street, East Melborne Victoria 3002 Australia. **Tel** 011 61 3 4187333, 4187217, FAX 011 61 3 4190459, telex AA 30236. ***Continues*** *Research Report (Commonwealth Scientific and Industrial Research Organization (Australia). Division of Soils), 0729-4336.*

LC SB271 .T37A **ISSN** 0258-4476
DD 633.7/2/005 KE
ANNUAL REPORT FOR THE YEAR ... / TEA RESEARCH FOUNDATION OF KENYA. **Main/Corp** Tea Research Foundation of Kenya. 1980-. English. One time a year. $50.00 (add postage). Timbilil Estate, PO Box 820, Kericho Kenya. ***Continues*** *Tea Research Institute of East Africa. Report.*

LC HD9259.F53 U56a
DD 353.97950082/333 US
ANNUAL REPORT / HAZELNUT MARKETING BOARD. **Main/Corp** Oregon. Hazelnut Marketing Board. (1986)-. English. Filbert/Hazelnut Marketing Board, PO Box 23126, Tigard OR 97223. **Tel** (503)639-3118. ***Continues*** *Oregon. Filbert/Hazelnut Marketing Board. Annual Report, 0735-1739.*

LC S590 **ISSN** 0748-5875
DD 631 US
ANNUAL REPORT / INTERNATIONAL FERTILIZER DEVELOPMENT CENTER. [Annu. rep. - Int. Fertil. Dev. Cent.]. **Main/Corp** International Fertilizer Development Center. (1982)-. English. One time a year. Free. IFDC, PO Box 2040, Muscle Shoals AL 35662. **Tel** (205)381-6600, FAX (205)381-7408, telex TWX 810 731 3970. **ED** Marie K Thompson. **Circ:** 4,000 (ctrl). ***Continues*** *International Fertilizer Development Center. IFDC Annual Report, 0734-4376.*
Desc: An account of the progress of the International Fertilizer Development Center in its four program areas, research, training, technical assistance, and national programs.

LC HD9117.T34 K544
DD 338.7/66/412209678 TZ
ANNUAL REPORT - KILOMBERO SUGAR COMPANY. **Main/Corp** Kilombero Sugar Company. (19??)-. English. Kilombero Sugar Company, PO Box 4355, Dar es Salaam Tanzania.

LC S590 **ISSN** 0820-3997
DD 631.4 CN
Pr Rev.
ANNUAL REPORT - LAND RESOURCE SCIENCE. UNIVERSITY OF GUELPH. (ANNUAL REPORT / LAND RESOURCE SCIENCE.). [Annu. rep. - Land Resour. Sci., Univ. Guelph]. **Main/Corp** Ontario Agricultural College. Dept. of Land Resource Science. **VFOAT** Land Resource Science Annual Report. (1985)-. English. One time a year. Department of Land Resource Science, University of Guelph, Guelph Ontario N1G 2W1 Canada. **Tel** (519)824-4120 Ext 6365, FAX (519)824-5730. ctrl circ. ***Continues*** *Ontario Agricultural College. Dept. of Land Resource Science. Progress Report (1983).*
Desc: Provides information on developments in teaching, research and extension which have occurred in the Department of Land Resource Science in the past year.
Ind/Abst GeoRef.

LC S590 **ISSN** 0954-7010
DD 631.4 UK
ANNUAL REPORT / MACAULAY LAND USE RESEARCH INSTITUTE. **Main/Corp** Macaulay Land Use Research Institute. 1987-. English. One time a year. MacAulay Land Use Research Institute, Craigiebuckler, Aberdeen AB9 2YJ United Kingdom. **Tel** 011 44 1226 318611, telex 738847 MISR G. **Circ:** 850 (ctrl). ***Formed by the union of*** *Annual Report / Macaulay Institute for Soil Research* ***and*** *Biennial Report / Hill Farming Research Organisation.*
Desc: Account of work of this scientific institute during year of reprint.

LC S **ISSN** 0510-002X
DD 630 UK
ANNUAL REPORT - NATIONAL VEGETABLE RESEARCH STATION.
Main/Corp Wellesbourne, Eng. National Vegetable Research Station. **Added/Corp** British Society for the Promotion of Vegetable Research. (1950)-. English. One time a year. National Vegetable Research Station, Wellesbourne United Kingdom.
Ind/Abst Vitis Vitic. Enol. Abstr.

LC SB327 .B36 **ISSN** 0084-7747
DD 635 US
ANNUAL REPORT OF THE BEAN IMPROVEMENT COOPERATIVE. [Annu. rep. Bean Improv. Coop.]. **Main/Corp** Bean Improvement Cooperative. (19??)-. English. One time a year (Apr. or May). $10.00 Comes with Bean Improvement Cooperative membership. Bean Improvement Cooperative, Colorado State University, Department of Plant Pathology, Fort Collins CO 80523. **Tel** (303)491-6987, FAX (303)491-0564. Index available. cum. index. **Ad Acc.**
Ind/Abst AGRICOLA [Full Cov.].

LC SB113
DD 631.521 SA
ANNUAL REPORT OF THE OILSEED CONTROL BOARD FOR THE PERIOD ...
See Public Administration.

LC SB267 .U54A **ISSN** 0374-5759
DD 633/.74/09729 TR
CODEN ARCRBD
ANNUAL REPORT ON CACAO RESEARCH. [Annu. Rep. Cacao Res. Reg. Res. Cent. Imp. Coll. Trop. Agric. Univ.West Indies]. **Main/Corp** University of the West Indies (Saint Augustine, Trinidad and Tobago). English. University of the West Indies / Main Library, St. Augustine, Trinidad and Tobago. **Tel** FAX 011 809 6629238, telex 24 520 UWI-WG. Documents available from BIOSIS Document Express.
Ind/Abst Biol. Abstr.; Hortic. Abstr.; Rev. Med. Vet. Mycology; Rev. Plant Pathol.

LC HD1775.N9 N56A **ISSN** 0270-8892
DD 338.1/09784 US
ANNUAL REPORT ON MARKETING, IRRIGATION, PRODUCTION. (ANNUAL REPORT ON MARKETING, IRRIGATION, PRODUCTION (NORTH DAKOTA).). **Main/Corp** North Dakota. Agricultural Experiment Station, Fargo. MIP Interdisciplinary Research Team. **VFOAT** MIP Report. (1974)-. English. One time a year. Extension Communications, PO Box 3166, North Dakota State University, Fargo ND 58105. **Tel** (701)239-5306, FAX (701)239-5613.

LC HD9049.W5 C295a **ISSN** 0316-4128
DD 382/.41/311097124 CN
ANNUAL REPORT - SASKATCHEWAN WHEAT POOL. **Main/Corp** Saskatchewan Wheat Pool. (1954)-. English. One time a year. Free on request. Saskatchewan Wheat Pool, 2625 Victoria Avenue, Regina Saskatchewan S4T 7T9 Canada. **Tel** (306)569-4411, FAX (306)569-4885, telex 0712284. **Circ:** 75,000. ***Continues*** *Saskatchewan Co-operative Producers. Annual Report, 1182-6045.*
Desc: Provides an overview of Saskatchewan Wheat Pool's current operations, policy and financial status. Includes all operating divisions and associated companies.

LC S **ISSN** 0263-7200
DD 630 UK
ANNUAL REPORT / SCOTTISH CROP RESEARCH INSTITUTE. **Main/Corp** Scottish Crop Research Institute. (1981)-. English. One time a year. £7.00. Scottish Crop Research Institute, Mylnefield Invergowrie, Dundee DD2 5DA United Kingdom. **Tel** 011 44 1382 826731. **ED** R. Exley. **Circ:** 1,200. ***Continues*** *Scottish Horticultural Research Institute. Annual Report.*

LC S622 **ISSN** 0817-4245
DD 631.45 AT
ANNUAL REPORT / SOIL CONSERVATION SERVICE OF NSW.
Main/Corp New South Wales. Soil Conservation Service. (19??)-. English. One time a year. Soil & Water Conservation Australia, 9 The Crest, Killara New South Wales 2071 Australia. **Tel** 011 61 2 4843703, FAX 011 61 2 9806728. ***Continues*** *Report of the Soil Conservation Service of New South Wales.*

LC S599.4.G72 E57a **ISSN** 0141-1675
DD 631.4/7/072041 UK
CODEN ARSWD8
ANNUAL REPORT - SOIL SURVEY. ENGLAND AND WALES. (THE SOIL SURVEY, ENGLAND AND WALES : ANNUAL REPORT.). [Annu. rep. - Soil Surv., Engl. Wales]. **Main/Corp** Soil Survey of England and Wales. (19??)-. English. One time a year. £2.50. Lawes Agricultural Research, Rothamsted Experimental Statistics, Harpenden Hertfordshire United Kingdom. **Tel** 011 44 1525 60428. **ED** M. Hodgson. Index available. **Circ:** 200 (ctrl). ***Continues*** *Report - Soil Survey of Great Britain.*
Desc: Report of the work carried out by the soil survey of England and Wales including soil mapping and research with lists of publications.
Ind/Abst GeoRef.

LC SB231 **ISSN** 0530-0371
DD 633.6 II
ANNUAL REPORT - SUGARCANE BREEDING INSTITUTE. **Main/Corp** Coimbatore, India (City). Sugarcane Breeding Institute. 1950/51-. English. Free. Sugarcane Breeding Institute, Indian Council Agric Research, Coimbatore 641 007 India. **Tel** 41621. ***Supersedes in part*** *Scientific Reports - Indian Agricultural Research Institute.*
Ind/Abst Plant Breed. Abstr.; Rev. Med. Vet. Mycology; Rev. Plant Pathol.

LC HD1471.M34 U54A **ISSN** 0304-8349
DD 338.1/06/2595 MY
ANNUAL REPORT - UNITED PLANTING ASSOCIATION OF MALAYSIA. [Annu. rep. - United Plant. Assoc. Malaysia]. **Main/Corp** United Planting Association of Malaysia. **VFOAT** Laporan Tahunan. (1968)-. English. One time a year. United Planting Association of Malaysia, PO Box 10272, 50708 Kuala Lumpur Malaysia. **Bk Rev. Circ:** 1,100 (ctrl). ***Continues*** *Annual Report - United Planting Association of Malaya, 0304-8330.*

LC SB191.R5 W44A
DD 341.7/59 LB
ANNUAL REPORT - WEST AFRICA RICE DEVELOPMENT ASSOCIATION.
Main/Corp West Africa Rice Development Association. (1971/74)-. English. West Africa Rice Development Association, PO Box 1019, Monrovia Liberia.

LC S67 .E7
DD 630 US
ANNUAL RESEARCH REPORT / RED RIVER RESEARCH STATION. **Added/Corp** Red River Research Station (La.). (1983)-. English. One time a year. Red River Research Station, Bossier City LA. ***Continues*** *Red River Valley Agricultural Experiment Station (La.). Annual Research Report - Red River Valley Agricultural Experiment Station.*

LC SB191.R5 L6 **ISSN** 1054-8300
DD 633.1/8/05 US
ANNUAL RESEARCH REPORT / RICE RESEARCH STATION. [Annu. res. rep. - La. State Univ. (Baton Rouge La.), Rice Res. Stn.]. **Main/Corp** Louisiana State University (Baton Rouge, La.). Rice Research Station. English. One time a year. Louisiana State University / Rice Research Station, Baton Rouge LA 70803. ***Continues*** *Annual Progress Report.*

LC HF
DD 380.1 SP
ANUARIO HORTOFRUTICOLA ESPANOL. (1975)-. Periodical. Spanish. One time a year. 8500ptas. Sucro SA, Hernan Cortes 5-1, 46004 Valencia Spain. **Tel** 011 34 6 3510295, FAX 011 34 6 3525752. **ED** Fidel Pascual Tecles. **Circ:** 5,000.
Desc: International annual on horticulture and fruit growing.

LC SB981 .A334
DD 353/.008/233 US
APHIS 82. See Agriculture-Livestock.

LC S590 **ISSN** 0259-5605
DD 631.4 SA
Pr Rev.
APPLIED PLANT SCIENCE. **Added/Corp** Southern African Weed Science Society. South African Society of Crop Production. Soil Science Society of South Africa. **VFOAT** Toegepaste Plantwetenskap. Vol. 1, No. 1 (1987)-. Periodical. English (Afrikaans; summaries and/or abstracts in English and Afrikaans). Two times a year (Jan., & July). $30.00. University of Pretoria / Department of Plant Production, Pretoria 0001 South Africa. **Tel** 011

27 12 4209111, 011 27 12 4203224, FAX 011 27 12 3422713. **ED** Dr. C. F. Reinhardt. Index available. **Circ:** 800 (ctrl).
Desc: Original research papers, short communications, and reviews on topics in agriculture.
Ind/Abst AGRICOLA [Full Cov.]; Agric. Eng. Abstr. (1991-); Hortic. Abstr.; Maize Abstr.; Nematol. Abstr.; Plant Grow. Reg. Abstr.; Postharvest News Inf.; Soils Fert.; Wheat Barley Trit. Abstr.

LC QH541.5.S6 A6 **ISSN** 0929-1393
DD 631.45 NE
CCC
Pr Rev.
•APPLIED SOIL ECOLOGY : A SECTION OF AGRICULTURE, ECOSYSTEMS & ENVIRONMENT. Vol. 1, No. 1 (Apr. 1994)-. Academic Scholarly Publication. English. Six times a year. $540.00. Elsevier Science Publishers BV, PO Box 211, 1000 AE Amsterdam Netherlands. **Tel** 011 31 20 4853641, 011 31 20 4853642, FAX 011 31 20 4853598. available on an online database from Elsevier Electronic Subscriptions (EES).

LC S **ISSN** 1033-9280
DD 630 AT
AQIS BULLETIN. [AQIS bull.]. **Added/Corp** Australian Quarantine and Inspection Service. **VFOAT** Bulletin. **VAT** Australian Quarantine and Inspection Service Bulletin. Vol. 1, No. 1 (Sept. 1989)-. Bulletin. English. Eleven times a year. Free on request. AQUIS, GPO Box 858, Canberra 2601 Australia. **Tel** 011 61 06 272-4730.
Ind/Abst Potato Abstr.

LC S **ISSN** 0003-794X
DD 630 FR
CODEN AFRUAC
ARBORICULTURE FRUITIERE, L'. [Arboric. fruit.]. No. 1 (Feb. 1954)-. Periodical. French. Twelve times a year. $96.46. Arboriculture Fruitiere, 4 Bis rue de Clery, 75002 Paris France. **Tel** 1 44 82 30 40, FAX 1 44 82 30 01. **Bk Rev. Ad Acc. Circ:** 5,000 (ctrl). Documents available from BIOSIS Document Express.
Desc: Professional and specialized review on all subjects referring fruits and table grapes, from orchard production to commercialization.
Ind/Abst AGRICOLA; Agric. Eng. Abstr.; Biol. Abstr.; Hortic. Abstr.; Leis., Rec., Tour. Abstr.; Plant Breed. Abstr.; Postharvest News Inf.; Rev. Agric. Entomol.; Rural Dev. Abstr.; Soils Fert.; Vitis Vitic. Enol. Abstr.; World Agric. Econ. Rural Sociol. Abstr.

LC S590 **ISSN** 0365-0340
DD 631 SW
CCC
CODEN AAPBCE
Pr Rev. **TITLE CHANGE**
ARCHIV FUER ACKER- UND PFLANZENBAU UND BODENKUNDE. [Arch. Acker- Pflanzenbau Bodenkd.]. **Added/Corp** Deutsche Akademie der Landwirtschaftswissenschaften zu Berlin. Akademie der Landwirtschaftswissenschaften der DDR. **VFOAT** Archives of Agronomy and Soil Science. Vol. 15, Issue 7 (1971)-(199?). Academic Scholarly Publication. German (summaries and/or abstracts in English and Russian; table of contents in English and Russian). Harwood Academic Publishers, PO Box 90, Reading RG1 8JL United Kingdom. **Tel** 011 44 1734 560080, FAX 011 44 1734 568211. Documents available from The Genuine Article, BIOSIS Document Express, CASDDS. ***Formed by the union of*** *Kuhn-Archiv* ***and*** *Archiv fur Bodenfruchtbarkeit und Pflanzenproduktion.* ***Continued by*** *Kuhn-Archiv (1992), 0940-3507.*
Ind/Abst Agric. Eng. Abstr. (1991-); Biodeter. Abstr.; Biol. Abstr.; Chem. Abstr.; Coal Abstr.; Crop Physiol. Abstr.; Curr. Cit.; Curr. Contents Agric. Biol. Environ. Sci.; EMBASE; Field Crop Abstr.; For. Prod. Abstr.; For. Abstr.; GeoRef; Grass. Forage Abstr.; Hortic. Abstr.; INIS Atomindex [Micro.]; Irr. Drain. Abstr.; Leis., Rec., Tour. Abstr.; Maize Abstr.; Life Sci. Collect.; Plant Breed. Abstr.; Plant Grow. Reg. Abstr.; Potato Abstr.; Protozoolog. Abstr.; Res. Alert [Full Cov.]; Rural Dev. Abstr.; Sci. Cit. Index (19??-19??); SCISEARCH; Soils Fert.; Vitis Vitic. Enol. Abstr.; Weed Abstr.; World Agric. Econ. Rural Sociol. Abstr.

LC S592.17.A73 A74 **ISSN** 0890-3069
DD 631 US
CCC
CODEN ASRREU
ARID SOIL RESEARCH & REHABILITATION. [Arid soil res. rehabil.]. Vol. 1, No. 1 (1987)-. Periodical. English. Four times a year. $150.00. Taylor & Francis Ltd. / UK, Rankine Road, Basingstoke, Hampshire RG24 8PR United Kingdom. **Tel** 011 44 1256 840366, FAX 011 44 1256 479438, telex 858540. **(Subscription address:** Taylor & Francis Inc., 1900 Frost Road, Suite 101, Bristol PA 19007-1598. **Tel** (215)785-5800, (800)821-8312, FAX (215)785-5515.**)** **ED** J. Skujins (editor's address: Utah State University, Department of Biology, Logan UT 84322-5500). available on microfilm and microfiche from University Microfilms International (UMI). Documents available from The Genuine Article, BIOSIS Document Express, CASDDS.
Desc: Provides a useful source for articles on fundamental basic and applied aspects of arid and semiarid soils. Subjects covered in the journal include: soil biology in nonirrigated soils, arid land rehabilitation, and arid soil biotechnology.
Ind/Abst AgBiotech News Inf.; AGRICOLA [Full Cov.]; Agric. Eng. Abstr. (1991-); Agrofor. Abstr. (1991-); Biol. Abstr.; Chem. Abstr.; Crop Physiol. Abstr.; Curr. Aware. Biol. Sci., CABS; Curr. Cit.; Curr. Contents Agric. Biol. Environ. Sci.; Ecol. Abstr.; Ecology Abstr.; Environ. Period. Bibliogr.; Field Crop Abstr.; For. Abstr.; Geogr. Abstr. Phys. Geogr.; Grass. Forage Abstr.; Hortic. Abstr.; Int. Dev. Abstr.; Irr. Drain. Abstr.; Maize Abstr.; Ornamental Hort.; Plant Breed. Abstr.; Res. Alert [Select. Cov.]; Rev. Agric. Entomol.; Rev. Plant Pathol.; Rice Abstr.; SCISEARCH; Seed Abstr.; Soils Fert.; Sorghum Mill. Abstr.; Soyabean Abstr.; Wheat Barley Trit. Abstr.

LC S
DD 630 SP
ARROZ / FEDERACION SINDICAL DE AGRICULTORES ARROCEROS DE ESPANA, DEPARTMENTO DE INFORMATION, PRENSA Y PROGAGANDE. Periodical. Spanish. Ediciones Cubanas, Obispo 527 Altos ESQ Bernaza, CP 10100 Havana Cuba.
Ind/Abst Biocont. News Inf.; Plant Breed. Abstr.; Plant Genet. Resour. Abstr.; Rice Abstr.; Seed Abstr.; Soils Fert.; Weed Abstr.; World Agric. Econ. Rural Sociol. Abstr.

LC S900 **ISSN** 0498-2231
DD 631.45 US
UDC 338.43(73)
ARS 41. **Main/Corp** United States. Agricultural Research Service. **VAT** Agricultural Research Service 41. 1- Dec. 1954-. Monographic series. English. Price varies per volume. Department of Agriculture / Foreign Agricultural Service, 14th Street and Independence Avenue SW, Washington DC 20250-1000. **Tel** (202)720-3935, FAX (202)720-7729.

LC S631
DD 631.8 UK
ASIAFAB : ASIA FERTILIZER AND AGROCHEMICALS BULLETIN. **VFOAT** Asia Fertilizer and Agrochemicals Bulletin. (Sept. 1992)-. Bulletin. English. Two times a year. $120.00. British Sulphur Corporation Ltd, 31 Mount Pleasant, London WC1X 0AD United Kingdom. **Tel** 011 44 171 8375600, FAX 011 44 171 8370292, telex 918918 SULFEX G. **(Subscription address:** CRU International Ltd., 31 Mount Pleasant, London WC1X 0AD United Kingdom. **Tel** 011 44 171 8375600, FAX 011 44 171 8370292.**)** **ED** Mark Evans. **Ad Acc, Adv Mgr:** Helen Kelly.
Desc: Contains information on the Asian fertilizer and agrochemical markets.

LC S
DD 630 NZ
ASPARAGUS RESEARCH NEWSLETTER. **Added/Corp** Massey University. Dept. of Horticulture & Plant Health. Vol. 1, No. 1 (June 1983)-. Newsletter. English. Two times a year. Massey University / Department of Plant Science, Palmerston North New Zealand. **Tel** 011 64 63 69099.
Ind/Abst Agric. Eng. Abstr. (1991-); Hortic. Abstr.; Ornamental Hort.; Plant Breed. Abstr.; Plant Genet. Resour. Abstr.; Plant Grow. Reg. Abstr.; Rev. Agric. Entomol.; Rev. Plant Pathol.; Seed Abstr.; Weed Abstr.

LC SB354.6.I8 A84
DD 338.1/74/0945021 IT
ASPETTI STRUTTURALI DELLE PRINCIPALI COLTIVAZIONI LEGNOSE AGRARIE. **Added/Corp** Istituto Centrale di Statistica (Italy). (19??)-. Italian. Istituto Nazionale Statistica, GBP SEZ4 Via Cesare Balbo 16, 00184 Rome Italy. **Tel** 011 39 6 46735118.

LC S **ISSN** 0159-1290
DD 630 AT
AUSTRALIAN COTTON GROWER. (THE AUSTRALIAN COTTONGROWER.). **VFOAT** Australian Cotton Grower. (1980)-. English. Six times a year. 20.55Aus$. Australian Grain, PO Box 766, Toowoomba Queensland 4350 Australia. **Tel** 011 61 76 971199, FAX 011 61 76 971184. **ED** Lloyd O'Connell. **Bk Rev. Ad Acc, Adv Mgr:** Brian O'Connell. **Circ:** 18,500.
Desc: Technical and marketing information on the cotton industry.

LC SB183
DD 633 AT
AUSTRALIAN GRAIN. (199?)-. Periodical. English. Six times a year. 22.20Aus$. Australian Grain, PO Box 766, Toowoomba Queensland 4350 Australia. **Tel** 011 61 76 971199, FAX 011 61 76 971184. **ED** Lloyd O'Connell. **Bk Rev. Ad Acc, Adv Mgr:** Brian O'Connell. **Circ:** 18,500.
Desc: Technical and marketing information on the grain industry.

LC S590 .A83 **ISSN** 0004-9573
DD 631.4 AT
CCC
CODEN ASORAB
Pr Rev.
AUSTRALIAN JOURNAL OF SOIL RESEARCH. [Aust. j. soil res.]. **Added/Corp** Commonwealth Scientific and Industrial Research Organization (Australia). Vol. 1 (Feb. 1963)-. Periodical. English. Six times a year. 270.00Aus$. CSIRO Publications, PO Box 89, 314 Albert Street, East Melborne Victoria 3002 Australia. **Tel** 011 61 3 4187333, 4187217, FAX 011 61 3 4190459, telex AA 30236. **ED** M. J. Sharkey. Index available. **Ad Acc. Acid Free. Circ:** 1,000. available on microfilm from University Microfilms International (UMI). Documents available from The Genuine Article, BIOSIS Document Express, CASDDS, Documents on Demand.
Desc: Journal of soil science, covering soil genesis, soil morphology, and classification; soil physics and hydrology; soil chemistry and mineralogy; soil fertility and plant nutrition; soil biology and biochemistry; soil and water management and conservation.
Ind/Abst AESIS Q.; AGRICOLA [Select. Cov.]; Agric. Eng. Abstr. (1991-); Biol. Abstr.; Ceram. Abstr.; Chem. Abstr.; Curr. Aware. Biol. Sci., CABS; Curr. Cit.; Curr. Contents Agric. Biol. Environ. Sci.; Ecol. Abstr.; EMBASE; Energy Inf. Abstr.; Environ. Abstr.; Environ. Period. Bibliogr.; Field Crop Abstr.; For. Prod. Abstr.; For. Abstr.; Geogr. Abstr. Phys. Geogr.; Geol. Abstr.; GeoRef; Grass. Forage Abstr.; Hortic. Abstr.; Irr. Drain. Abstr.; Maize Abstr.; Nucl. Sci. Abstr.; Life Sci. Collect.; Pollut. Abstr. Indexes; Res. Alert [Full Cov.]; Rev. Agric. Entomol.; Rice Abstr.; Sci. Cit. Index; SCISEARCH; Sel. Water Resour. Abstr.; Soils Fert.; Sorghum Mill. Abstr.; Soyabean Abstr.; Weed Abstr.; Wheat Barley Trit. Abstr.

LC SB354 **ISSN** 0819-7849
DD 634.505 AT
AUSTRALIAN NUTGROWER. [Aust. nutgrow.]. (1987)-. Periodical. English. Four times a year. 23.02Aus$. Australian Nut Industry Council, PO Box 394, Yarra Glen Victoria 3775 Australia. **Tel** 011 61 08 2332063, FAX 011 61 03 97235955. **ED** Jane Bean. **Ad Acc. Circ:** 600 (ctrl). ***Continues*** *Victorian Nutgrower, 0819-7830.*

LC S
DD 630 AT
AUSTRALIAN WEEDS RESEARCH NEWSLETTER. **Added/Corp** Commonwealth Scientific and Industrial Research Organization (Australia). (1962)-. Newsletter. English. CSIRO Publications, PO Box 89, 314 Albert Street, East Melborne Victoria 3002 Australia. **Tel** 011 61 3 4187333, 4187217, FAX 011 61 3 4190459, telex AA 30236.

LC S **ISSN** 0271-5864
DD 630 US
BADGER COMMON TATER, THE. **Added/Corp** Wisconsin Potato & Vegetable Grower's Association. Wisconsin Potato Growers Association. **VFOAT** Badger Common 'Tater. **VAT** Badger common 'tater. (19??)-. Trade Publication. English. Twelve times a year. $12.00. Wisconsin Potato & Vegetable Growers Association, 700 5th Avenue Box 327, Antigo WI 54409. **Tel** (715)623-7683, FAX (715)623-3176. **ED** Tamas Houlihan. **Bk Rev. Ad Acc. Circ:** 3,850.
Desc: News related to the potato and vegetable industry in Wisconsin and throughout the U.S.

LC QK **ISSN** 0289-2111
DD 584.93 JA
BAMBOO JOURNAL. [Bamboo j.]. (1983)-. Periodical. Japanese. One time a year. Documents available from CASDDS. ***Continues*** *Take, 0389-5513.*
Ind/Abst Chem. Abstr.

LC S
DD 630 CC
BAMBOO RESEARCH. **Added/Corp** Nan-Ching Lin Chan Kung Yeh Hsueh Yuan. **VFOAT** Chu Lei Yen Chiu. Vol. 1 (1981)-. Periodical. English. Nanjing Technological College of Forest Products, Nanjing, People's Republic of China.
Ind/Abst Hortic. Abstr.; Rev. Plant Pathol.

LC S **ISSN** 1018-0818
DD 630 BG
BANGLADESH JOURNAL OF CROP SCIENCE. [Bangladesh j. crop sci.]. (1990)-. Periodical. English. Two times a year.
Ind/Abst Field Crop Abstr.; Rice Abstr.

LC S590 .P3 **ISSN** 0253-5440
DD 631.4/05 BG
CODEN BJSSDJ
BANGLADESH JOURNAL OF SOIL SCIENCE. [Bangladesh j. soil sci.]. Vol. 7 (Jan. 1971)-. Academic Scholarly Publication. English. Dacca University / Department of Soil Science, Dacca 2 Bangladesh. Documents available from CASDDS. ***Continues*** *Pakistan Journal of Soil Science.*
Ind/Abst Chem. Abstr. (1971-1981); Field Crop Abstr.; Grass. Forage Abstr.

Agriculture —Crop Production and Soils

LC Z5074.P75 E48a SB211.P8
DD 016.63
BL
BATATINHA : RESUMOS INFORMATIVOS. Main/Corp Empresa Brasileira de Perquisa Agropecuaria. Unidade de Execucao de Perquisa de Ambito Estadual de Brasilia. (19??)-. Portuguese. Unidade de Execucao de Pesquisa de Ambito Estadual de Brasilia, Caixa Postal 1316, 70.000 Brasilia Brazil.

LC SB761
DD 635.67
UK
BCPC MONOGRAPH. Added/Corp British Crop Protection Council. **VAT** British Crop Protection Council Monograph. No. 34 (1986)-. Monographic series. English. Irregular. Price varies per volume. British Crop Protection Council, Bear Farm Binfield, Bracknell Berkshire RG12 5QE United Kingdom. **Tel** 011 44 1734 341998. Index available. cum. index. **Bk Rev**, (Qty: 10). Documents available from CASDDS. *Continues British Crop Protection Council. Monograph, 0306-3941.*
Ind/Abst Agric. Eng. Abstr.; Chem. Abstr.; Hortic. Abstr.; Plant Breed. Abstr.; Potato Abstr.; Rev. Agric. Entomol.; Soils Fert.; Weed Abstr.

LC S
DD 630
ISSN 0274-5054
US
BEAN COMMISSION JOURNAL, THE. Main/Corp Michigan Bean Commission. **Added/Corp** Michigan Bean Commission. Journal. (197?)-. Periodical. English. Four times a year. Free on request. Michigan Bean Commission, PO Box 22037, Lansing MI 48909. **Tel** (517)694-1171.

LC S
DD 630
ISSN 0744-9909
US
BENTON HARBOR FRUIT MARKET (1982). (BENTON HARBOR FRUIT MARKET.). **Added/Corp** Michigan. Dept. of Agriculture. (1982)-. Periodical. English. Three times a year. $20.00. Michigan Department of Agriculture, PO Box 30017, Lansing MI 48909. **Tel** (517)373-1050, FAX (517)335-0628. *Continues Michigan Fruit & Vegetable Report, 0279-6937.*

LC S
DD 630
ISSN 0345-1410
SW
BETODLAREN. (BETODLAREN : ORGAN FOR SVERIGES BETODLARES CENTRALFORENING.). [Betodlaren]. **Added/Corp** Sveriges Betodlares Centralforening. (1964)-. Periodical. Swedish. Four times a year. *Continues Sveriges Betodlares Centralforenings Tidskrift.*
Ind/Abst Field Crop Abstr.; Seed Abstr.

LC S631
DD 631.8
ISSN 0006-0089
US
BETTER CROPS WITH PLANT FOOD.
[Better crops plant food]. **Added/Corp** Potash & Phosphate Institute (Atlanta, Ga.). Vol. 9, No. 1 (June 1927)-. Trade Publication. English. Four times a year (Jan., April, July, Oct.). Free on request. Potash & Phosphate Institute, 655 Engineering Drive, Suite 110, Norcross GA 30092. **Tel** (404)447-0335, FAX (404)448-0439. **ED** Donald L Armstrong. Index available. cum. index. **Bk Rev**. Circ: 20,000 (ctrl). available on microfilm and microfiche from University Microfilms International (UMI). *Formed by the union of Better Crops and Pland Food.*
Desc: Primarily features short articles from university and private research organizations highlighting recent results of studies.
Ind/Abst Field Crop Abstr.; Grass. Forage Abstr.; Hortic. Abstr.; Maize Abstr.; Nutr. Abstr. Rev., Ser. B, Live Feeds and Feed.; Plant Breed. Abstr.; Protozoolog. Abstr.; Rev. Plant Pathol.; Soils Fert.; Soyabean Abstr.; Wheat Barley Trit. Abstr.

LC S590
DD 631.4
II
BETTER FARMING IN SALTED AFFECTED SOILS. Added/Corp Central Soil Salinity Research Institute (Karnal, India) Indian Council of Agricultural Research. (1985)-. Periodical. English.
Ind/Abst Irr. Drain. Abstr.

LC S
DD 630
ISSN 0405-6701
FR
BETTERAVIER FRANCAIS, LE. [Better. fr.]. (1952)-. Periodical. French. Twenty-six times a year. $52.49. S E D A, 25 rue de Madrid, 75008 Paris France. **Tel** 44 70 74 94, FAX 44 70 74 99. *Continues Planteurs de Betteraves.*
Ind/Abst Energy Res. Abstr. (Dec. 1982-).

LC HD1401
DD 338.174772
ISSN 1322-0055
AT
BGF BULLETIN. [BGF bull.]. **VFOAT** Banana Growers Federation Bulletin. (1989)-. Periodical. English. Twelve times a year. 30.00Aus$ Australia; 35.00Aus$ other. Banana Growers Federation Cooperative, PO Box 31, Murwillumbah New South Wales 2484 Australia. **Tel** 011 066 72 2488. Index available.
Ind/Abst Hortic. Abstr.

LC S590
DD 631.4
UK
BGRG RESEARCH MONOGRAPH. VFOAT Research Monograph. **VAT** British Geomorphological Research Group Research Monograph. Vol. 1- 1980-. Monographic series. English. Price varies per volume. Institute British Geographers, 1 Kensington Gore, London SW7 2AR United Kingdom. **Tel** 011 44 171 5846371, FAX 011 44 171 5819918.

LC S
DD 630
UDC 633.61
ISSN 0970-6240
II
BHARATIYA SUGAR. [Bharatiya Sugar]. (1986)-. Periodical. English. Twelve times a year. *Continues Maharashtra Sugar, 0970-6496.*
Ind/Abst Crop Physiol. Abstr.; Hortic. Abstr.; Postharvest News Inf.; Rev. Agric. Entomol.; Rev. Plant Pathol.; Sug. Indus. Abstr.

LC Z5071
DD 016.63
ISSN 0074-6436
NE
CODEN BIIIDY
BIBLIOGRAPHY - INTERNATIONAL INSTITUTE FOR LAND RECLAMATION AND IMPROVEMENT. See Agriculture-Abstracting, Bibliographies and Statistics.

LC S1 .B5
DD 630.5
ISSN 0006-2863
US
BIO-DYNAMICS. Added/Corp Bio-Dynamic Farming and Gardening Association. **VFOAT** Biodynamics. Vol. 1, No. 1/2 (Summer 1941)-Vol. 12, No. 4 (Fall 1954); No. 36 (Winter-Spring 1955)-. Periodical. English. Six times a year (Jan., Mar., May, July, Sept., Nov.). $30.00 (regular members); $50.00 (contributing members); $75.00 (supporting members); $250.00 (sustaining members). Bio-Dynamic Literature, PO Box 550, Kimberton PA 19442. **Tel** (610)935-7797, FAX (610)983-3196. **ED** Jean W. Yeager. Index available. cum. index. **Bk Rev**. **Ad Acc**. **Circ:** 1,200. available on microfilm from University Microfilms International (UMI).
Desc: The US journal for Bio dynamic agriculture. Also the largest source of information about community supported agriculture.
Ind/Abst Environ. Period. Bibliogr.

LC SB975 .B562
DD 632.96
ISSN 0958-3157
UK
CCC
BIOCONTROL SCIENCE & TECHNOLOGY. Vol. 1, No. 1 (1991)-. Periodical. English. Four times a year (Mar., Jun, Sep., Dec.). $476.00. Carfax Publishing Company, PO Box 25, Abingdon, Oxfordshire OX14 3UE United Kingdom. **Tel** 011 44 1235 555335, FAX 011 44 1235 553559, telex 817484. available on microfiche. Documents available from The Genuine Article.
Ind/Abst Curr. Aware. Biol. Sci.; CABS; Curr. Cit.; Curr. Contents Agric. Biol. Environ. Sci.; Res. Alert [Full Cov.]; Rev. Plant Pathol.

LC S590
DD 631.4
ISSN 0178-2762
GW
CCC
CODEN BFSOEE
Pr Rev.
BIOLOGY AND FERTILITY OF SOILS.
[Biol. fertil. soils]. Vol. 1, No. 1 (1985)-. Academic Scholarly Publication. English. Eight times a year. $1158.00. Springer-Verlag GmbH & Company KG, Heidelberger Platz 3, D-14197 Berlin Germany. **Tel** 011 49 30 8207223, FAX 011 49 30 8214091, telex 183 319 SPBLN D. **(Subscription address:** Springer-Verlag New York Inc. / North America, PO Box 2485, Journal Fulfillment, Secaucus NJ 07096. **Tel** (201)348-4033, (800)777-4643, FAX (201)348-4505.**) ED** J C G Ottow, K Vlassak, and W G Whitford. available on microfilm and microfiche from University Microfilms International (UMI). Documents available from The Genuine Article, BIOSIS Document Express, CASDDS.
Desc: Reports on new developments in fundamental and applied aspects of biology and productivity of soils.
Ind/Abst AgBiotech News Inf.; AGRICOLA [Full Cov.]; Agrofor. Abstr. (19??-19??); Biol. Abstr. (1987-); Chem. Abstr. (1985-); Crop Physiol. Abstr.; Curr. Aware. Biol. Sci., CABS; Curr. Cit.; Curr. Contents Agric. Biol. Environ. Sci.; Ecol. Abstr. (?-?); Field Crop Abstr.; For. Prod. Abstr. (1991-); For. Abstr.; Geogr. Abstr. Phys. Geogr.; Grass. Forage Abstr.; Hortic. Abstr.; Int. Dev. Abstr.; Irr. Drain. Abstr.; Maize Abstr.; Nematol. Abstr.; Ornamental Hort. (1991-); Plant Breed. Abstr.; Plant Grow. Reg. Abstr.; Potato Abstr.; Res. Alert [Full Cov.]; Rev. Agric. Entomol.; Rev. Plant Pathol.; Rice Abstr.; Sci. Cit. Index; SCISEARCH; Soils Fert.; Sorghum Mill. Abstr.; Soyabean Abstr.; Weed Abstr.; Wheat Barley Trit. Abstr.

LC SB599 .B53
DD 632.05/6
ISSN 0406-3597
TU
BITKI KORUMA BULTENI. (BITKI KORUMA BULTENI. PLANT PROTECTION BULLETIN.). [Bitki koruma bul.]. **Added/Corp** Zirai Mucadele Ilac ve Aletleri Enstitusu. Turkey. Zirai Mucadele ve Zirai Karantina Genel Mudurlugu. **VFOAT** Plant Protection Bulletin. Vol. 1 (August 1959)-. Bulletin. Turkish (summaries or abstracts in English and German). Four times a year.
Ind/Abst Seed Abstr.

LC S583
DD 631
PL
BIULETYN / INSTYTUT HODOWLI I AKLIMATYZACJI ROSLIN = BULLETIN / INSTITUTE OF PLANT BREEDING AND ACCLIMATIZATION. Main/Corp Instytut Hodowli i Aklimatyzacji Roslin. (1951)-. Bulletin. Polish. Irregular. Instytut Hodowli i Aklimatyzacji Roslin, Radzikow, 05-870 Blonie Poland. **Tel** 011 48 22 552611, FAX 011 48 22 554714. **(Subscription address:** Ars Polona-Ruch, PO Box 1001, Krakowskie Przedmiescie 7, 00-068 Warsaw Poland. **Tel** 011 48 22 261201.**) Bk Rev**. **Ad Acc**. available in reprints.
Desc: Information on plant breeding and genetics, phytopathology, seed production, genotype creation, etc.
Ind/Abst Crop Physiol. Abstr.; Soyabean Abstr.; Weed Abstr.

LC SB320
DD 635
ISSN 0509-6839
PL
CODEN BIWAA9
BIULETYN WARZYWNICZY. BULLETIN OF VEGETABLE CROPS RESEARCH WORK. BIULLETEN PO OVOSHCHEVODSTVU. Added/Corp Instytut Warzywnictwa. Warsaw. Instytut Uprawy, Nawozenia i Gleboznawstwa. Zaklad Warzywnictwa. **VFOAT** Bulletin of Vegetable Crops Research Work; Biulleten po Ovoshchevodstvu. (19??)-. Monographic series. Polish (summaries and/or abstracts in English and Russian). Irregular. $19.20. Instytut Warzywnictwa / Research Institute of Vegetable Crops, Ul. Konstutucji 3, Maja 1-3, 96-100 Skierniewice Poland. Index available. cum. index.
Circ: 400. available on Cards. Documents available from CASDDS.
Desc: Research and developments in vegetable crop research.
Ind/Abst Agric. Eng. Abstr. (1991-); Chem. Abstr. (1953-1979); Field Crop Abstr.; Hortic. Abstr.; Plant Breed. Abstr.; Plant Grow. Reg. Abstr.; Rev. Plant Pathol.; Seed Abstr.; Weed Abstr.

LC S
DD 630
ISSN 0202-5531
RU
BIULLETEN NAUCNO-TEHNICESKOJ INFORMACII VSESOUZNOGO NAUCNO-ISSLEDOVATELSKOGO INSTITUTA RISA. (BIULLETEN NAUCHNO-TEKHNICHESKOI INFORMATSII VSESIUZNOGO NAUCHNO-ISSLEDOVATELSKOGO INSTITUTA RISA.). [Bull. nauco-teh. inf. Vses. naucno-issled. inst. risa]. **Main/Corp** Vsesoiuznyi Nauchno-Issledovatelskii Institut Risa. **Added/Corp** Vsesoiuznyi Nauchno-Issledovatelskii Institut Risa. Vsesoiuznaia Akademiia Selskokhoziaistvennykh Nauk. (1968)-. Periodical. Russian (summaries and/or abstracts in English).
Ind/Abst AGRICOLA.

LC S590
DD 631.4
RU
BIULLETEN POCHVENNOGO INSTITUTA IMENI V. V. DOKUCHAEVA. Main/Corp Pochvennyi Institut Imeni V. V. Dokuchaeva. **Added/Corp** Vsesoiuznaia Akademiia Sel'skokhoziaistvennykh Nauk. (19??)-. Periodical. Russian. **ED** V. V. Egorov. Documents available from CASDDS.
Ind/Abst Chem. Abstr.

LC S583
DD 631
ISSN 1081-5228
US
●**BLUEBOOK UPDATE.** (1994)-. Newsletter. English. Four times a year. $48.00 US and Canada. Soyatech Inc., 318 Main Street, Bar Harbor ME 04609. **Tel** (207)288-4969, (800)424-SOYA, FAX (207)288-5264. **Circ:** 3,000.

LC HD9014.B8 B35a
DD 338.1/3/09813
BL
BOLETIM DE MERCADOS AGRICOLAS, INFORMACOES. See Industry and Production.

LC S
DD 630
ISSN 0102-292X
BL
BOLETIM DE PESQUISA. Added/Corp Empresa de Pesquisa Agropecuaria do Ceara. No. 1 (Feb. 1984)-. Monographic series. Portuguese.
Ind/Abst For. Abstr.; Hortic. Abstr.

LC S590
DD 631.4
ISSN 0101-6431
BL
BOLETIM DE PESQUISA - UNIDADE DE EXECUCAO DE PESQUISA DE AMBITO ESTADUAL DE PORTO VELHO. (BOLETIM DE PESQUISA.). [Bol. pesqui. - Unid. Exec. Pesqui. Ambito Estadual Porto Velho]. **Added/Corp** Empresa Brasileira de Pesquisa Agropecuaria. Unidade de Execucao de Pesquisa de Ambito Estadual de Porto Velho. No 1 (1982)-. Monographic series. Portuguese (summaries and/or abstracts in English).
Ind/Abst Field Crop Abstr.; Hortic. Abstr.; Rev. Agric. Entomol.; Rice Abstr.

Agriculture —Crop Production and Soils

LC SB215
DD 633.6
BL
BOLETIM TECNICO COPERSUCAR.
Main/Corp Coopertiva Central dos Produtores de Acucar e Alcool do Estado de Sao Paulo. Departamento Tecnico. No. 3 (Dez. 1976)-. Bulletin. Portuguese.
Ind/Abst Field Crop Abstr.; Hortic. Abstr.; Irr. Drain. Abstr.; Rev. Agric. Entomol.; Sug. Indus. Abstr.; World Agric. Econ. Rural Sociol. Abstr.

LC TC841 .A32
DD 631.5/87/0981
ISSN 0374-6658
BL
BOLETIM TECNICO - DEPARTAMENTO NACIONAL DE OBRAS CONTRA AS SECAS. (BOLETIM TECNICO.). [Bol. tec. dep. nac. obras contra secas]. Vol. 28, No. 1 (Jan./June 1970)-. Bulletin. Portuguese. Two times a year. Banco do Brazil SA, Carteira de Cambio Agencia de Itabuna, 45600 Itabuna Bahia Brazil. **Continues** Boletim (Brazil). Departamento Nacional de Obras Contra As Secas).

LC S
DD 630
BL
BOLETIM TECNICO / ORGANIZACAO DAS COOPERATIVAS DO ESTADO DO PARANA, PROGRAMA DE PESQUISA. Monographic series. Portuguese. Price varies per volume.
Ind/Abst Nematol. Abstr.; Soyabean Abstr.

LC S
DD 630
CU
BOLETIN DE CULTIVOS TROPICALES : REVISTA DEL MINISTERIO DE EDUCACION SUPERIOR DE LA REPUBLICA DE CUBA. Added/Corp Instituto de Ciencia Agricola (Cuba) Cuba. Ministerio de Educacion Superior. (19??)-. Monographic series. Spanish.
Ind/Abst Field Crop Abstr.; Hortic. Abstr.; Plant Grow. Reg. Abstr.; Sug. Indus. Abstr.

LC S
DD 630
ISSN 0213-6910
SP
BOLETIN DE SANIDAD VEGETAL. PLAGAS. See Pest Control.

LC S
DD 630
CU
BOLETIN / INSTITUTO NACIONAL DE CIENCIAS AGRICOLAS. Added/Corp Instituto de Ciencia Agricola (Cuba). (198?)-. Monographic series. Spanish.
Ind/Abst Field Crop Abstr.; Postharvest News Inf.; Potato Abstr.; Soils Fert.

LC SB183
DD 633
ISSN 0100-3054
BL
BOLETIN TECNICO - IAPAR. (BOLETIM TECNICO - INSTITUTO AGRONOMICO DO PARANA.). [Boletin tec. - IAPAR]. **Main/Corp** Instituto Agronomico do Parana. **Added/Corp** Fundacao Instituto Agronomico do Parana. No. 2, (1976)-. Monographic series. Portuguese. Price varies per volume.
Ind/Abst Anim. Breed. Abstr.; Field Crop Abstr.; Grass. Forage Abstr.; Seed Abstr.; Soils Fert.; World Agric. Econ. Rural Sociol. Abstr.

LC S
DD 630
US
BOOKS IN SOILS, PLANTS, AND THE ENVIRONMENT. Monographic series. English. Irregular. Price varies per volume. Marcel Dekker Inc., 270 Madison Avenue, New York NY 10016. **Tel** (212)696-9000, (800)228-1160, FAX (212)685-4540, telex 421419. **(Subscription address:** Marcel Dekker Inc., PO Box 5017, Monticello NY 12701. **Tel** (800)228-1160.)
Desc: Covers topics such as soil biochemistry, transgenic plants, soil analysis, and soil reclamation processes.

LC SB13
DD 630.5
ISSN 0006-8705
BL
CODEN BRGTAF
BRAGANTIA : BOLETIM TECNICO DO INSTITUTO AGRONOMICO DO ESTADO DE SAO PAULO. [Bragantia]. Vol. 1 (Jan. 1941)-. Bulletin. Portuguese (summaries and/or abstracts in English). One time a year. $70.00. Institute Agronomico, Caiza Postal 28, 13 100 Campinas Brazil. **Tel** (0192)315422. **ED** Angela Maria Cangiani Furlani. Index available. cum. index. **Circ:** 1,100. Documents available from BIOSIS Document Express, CASDDS. **Supersedes** Sao Paulo (Brazil : State). Instituto Agronomico. Boletim; Sao Paulo (Brazil : State). Instituto Agronomico. Boletim Tecnico; San Paulo (Brazil : State). Instituto Agronomico. Circular.
Desc: Covers fertilizers, plant breeding, plant diseases and insects, pedology, crop physiology and nutrition, crop management, agricultural technology, seeds, mycology, bacteriology and virology, soil fertility and nematology.
Ind/Abst Abstr. Trop. Agric.; Agric. Eng. Abstr. (1991-); Agrofor. Abstr. (1991-); Biol. Abstr.; Chem. Abstr.; Cot. Trop. Fibr. Abstr. Bibliogr.; Crop Physiol. Abstr.; Field Crop Abstr.; Food Sci. Technol. Abstr.; For. Prod. Abstr.; For. Abstr.; Grass. Forage Abstr.; Irr. Drain. Abstr.; Maize Abstr.; Plant Breed. Abstr.; Plant Grow. Reg. Abstr.; Potato Abstr.; Rev. Agric. Entomol.; Rev. Plant Pathol.; Seed Abstr.; Soils Fert.; Sorghum Mill. Abstr.; Soyabean Abstr.; Weed Abstr.; Wheat Barley Trit. Abstr.

LC S
DD 630
ISSN 0955-1514
UK
CODEN BCPWE2
BRIGHTON CROP PROTECTION CONFERENCE--WEEDS. [Brighton Crop Prot. Conf. . Weeds]. **Added/Corp** British Crop Protection Council. **VFOAT** Proceedings. (1989)-. Academic Scholarly Publication. English. Every 2 years. £112.00. BCPC Publications Sales, Bear Farm, Binfield Bracknell, Berkshire RG12 5QE United Kingdom. **Tel** 011 44 1734 342727, FAX 011 44 1734 341998. Index available. **Circ:** 2,250. Documents available from CASDDS. **Continues** British Crop Protection Conference--Weeds. British Crop Protection Conference--Weeds, 0144-1604.
Ind/Abst AGRICOLA [Full Cov.]; Chem. Abstr.; Curr. Cit.

LC S590
DD 631.4/7/711
ISSN 0375-5886
CN
CODEN BCSRBX
BRITISH COLUMBIA SOIL SURVEY, REPORT. [Rep., B.C. Soil Surv.]. **Added/Corp** Canada. Experimental Farms Service. Canada. Dept. of Agriculture. Research Branch. Canada. Agriculture Canada. Research Branch. University of British Columbia. British Columbia. Dept. of Agriculture. **VAT** Report of British Columbia Soil Survey. (1969)-. Monographic series. English. Free on request.
Ind/Abst GeoRef.

LC S
DD 630
ISSN 0007-1854
UK
BRITISH SUGAR BEET REVIEW. [Br. sugar beet rev.]. (1927)-. Periodical. English. Four times a year (Mar., June, Sept., Dec.). Free on request. British Sugar Beet Review, PO Box 26, Peterborough PE2 9QU United Kingdom. **Tel** 011 44 1733 63171, FAX 011 44 1733 63068, telex 32149-32273. **ED** Bill Hollowell. Index available. cum. index. **Bk Rev. Ad Acc. Circ:** 15,500 (ctrl). **Continues** Sugar Beet Review and British Beet Grower.
Ind/Abst Field Crop Abstr.; Grass. Forage Abstr.; Leis., Rec., Tour. Abstr.; Nutr. Abstr. Rev., Ser. B, Live Feeds and Feed.; Life Sci. Collect.; Plant Breed.; Plant Genet. Resour. Abstr.; Postharvest News Inf.; Protozoolog. Abstr.; Rev. Plant Pathol.; Soils Fert.; Sug. Indus. Abstr.; Weed Abstr.; Wheat Barley Trit. Abstr.; World Agric. Econ. Rural Sociol. Abstr.

LC S
DD 630
ISSN 0141-1969
UK
BRITISH SUGAR NEWS. (1974)-. English.
Ind/Abst Fluid Abstr., Civil Eng.; Fluid Abstr. Proc. Eng.; FLUIDEX (19??-).

LC SB215
DD 633.6
ISSN 0810-3240
AT
BSES BULLETIN. Added/Corp Queensland. Bureau of Sugar Experiment Stations. **VAT** Bureau of Sugar Experiment Stations Bulletin. No. 1 (Jan. 1983)-. Bulletin. English. Four times a year. 26.31Aus$. Bureau of Sugar Experiment Stations, PO Box 86, Indooroopilly Queensland 4068 Australia. **Tel** 011 61 7 371 6100, FAX 011 61 7 871 0383, telex 42227. **Continues** Cane Growers' Quarterly Bulletin, 0008-5553.
Ind/Abst Agric. Eng. Abstr. (1991-); Biocont. News Inf.; Field Crop Abstr.; Hortic. Abstr.; Plant Breed. Abstr.; Sug. Indus. Abstr.; Weed Abstr.

LC HD1401
DD 338.1/731/0971
ISSN 0843-2309
CN
CEASED
BUDGET - ALBERTA WHEAT POOL. (BUDGET.). [Budg. - Alta. Wheat Pool]. **Added/Corp** Alberta Wheat Pool. **VFOAT** Wheat Pool Budget. **VAT** Alberta Pool Budget. (Jan. 22, 1988)-(Aug. 1995). Periodical. English. Alberta Wheat Pool, Box 2700, 505 2nd Street Southwest, Calgary Alberta T2P 2P5 Canada. **Tel** (403)290-4648. **Continues** Wheat Pool "Budget", 0382-0807; **Absorbed** Crop Report / Alberta Wheat Pool.

LC SB187.Q4 A3
DD 630
AT
BULLETIN. Main/Corp Queensland. Division of Plant Industry. (1924)-. Bulletin. English. CSIRO / Division of Plant Industry, GPO Box 1600, Canberra ACT 2601 Australia. **Tel** 011 61 62 465483.
Ind/Abst Plant Breed. Abstr.

LC S590
DD 631.4
SZ
BULLETIN / BODENKUNDLICHE GESELLSCHAFT DER SCHWEIZ.
Added/Corp Bodenkundliche Gesellschaft der Schweiz. (19??)-. Bulletin. German (French).
Ind/Abst For. Abstr.; Irr. Drain. Abstr.; Maize Abstr.; Wheat Barley Trit. Abstr.

LC S590
DD 631.4
ISSN 0366-0672
II
CODEN BISOAV
BULLETIN - INDIAN SOCIETY OF SOIL SCIENCE. [Bull. - Indian Soc. Soil Sci.]. **Main/Corp** Indian Society of Soil Science. No. 1 (1938)-. Bulletin. English. One time a year. Price varies per volume. Indian Society of Soil Science Institute, New Delhi 110012 India. **Tel** 5720991. **(Subscription address:** Prints India, 11 Darya Ganj, New Delhi 110002 India. **Tel** 011 91 11 3268645, FAX 011 91 11 3275542, telex 31-61087 PRIN-IN.)

LC S
DD 630
NZ
BULLETIN - NEW ZEALAND. SOIL BUREAU. Main/Corp New Zealand. Soil Bureau. Vol. 1; 1947-. Bulletin. English. Irregular. New Zealand Soil Bureau, Department of Scientific and Industrial Research, Private Bag, Lower Hutt New Zealand. **Tel** 673 119.

LC S599.N56 A3
DD 631.49931
UDC 631.4(931)
ISSN 0077-9644
NZ
CODEN NZSBB6
BULLETIN - NEW ZEALAND. SOIL BUREAU. [Soil Bur. bull.]. **Main/Corp** New Zealand. Soil Bureau. **VFOAT** New Zealand Soil Bureau Bulletin. **Main/Corp** English. New Zealand. Soil Bureau, Department of Scientific and Industrial Research, Private Bag, Lower Hutt New Zealand. **Tel** 673 119.
Ind/Abst GeoRef.

LC S
DD 630
ISSN 0250-8052
FR
CCC
CODEN OEPBAO
BULLETIN OEPP. [Bull. OEPP]. **Main/Corp** European and Mediterranean Plant Protection Organisation. **Added/Corp** European and Mediterranean Plant Protection Organisation. EPPO Bulletin. **VFOAT** EPPO Bulletin. No. 1 (May 1971)-. Bulletin. English (French; summaries and/or abstracts in French). Four times a year. $266.00. European and Mediterranean Plant Protection Organization, 1 rue le Notre, 75016 Paris France. **Tel** 011 33 1 45207794. **(Subscription address:** Blackwell Publishers / UK, 108 Cowley Road, Oxford OX4 1JF United Kingdom. **Tel** 011 44 1865 791100, FAX 011 44 1865 791347.) **ED** I. M. Smith. **Bk Rev. Circ:** 700. available on microfilm and microfiche from University Microfilms International (UMI). Documents available from BIOSIS Document Express, CASDDS. **Absorbed** European and Mediterranean Plant Protection Organization. Rapport Annuel - European and Mediterranean Plant Protection Organization, 0300-1490; **Supersedes** European and Mediterranean Plant Protection Organization. Publications de l'OEPP. Serie A.
Desc: Scientific papers, guidelines, data sheets, etc. on all aspects of crop and forest protection.
Ind/Abst AgBiotech News Inf.; Agrofor. Abstr. (1991-); Biocont. News Inf. (1991-); Biodeter. Abstr.; Biol. Abstr. (1991-); Biol. Abstr.; Chem. Abstr. (1971-1983); Cot. Trop. Fibr. Abstr. Bibliogr.; Curr. Cit.; Field Crop Abstr.; For. Abstr.; Hortic. Abstr.; Maize Abstr.; Nematol. Abstr.; Ornamental Hort. (1991-); PESTDOC; Plant Genet. Resour. Abstr.; Potato Abstr.; Protozoolog. Abstr.; Rev. Agric. Entomol.; Rev. Plant Pathol.; Rice Abstr.; Seed Abstr.; Soils Fert.; Soyabean Abstr.; Weed Abstr.; Wheat Barley Trit. Abstr.

LC HD9017.T3 B84
DD 338.1/09678
TZ
BULLETIN OF CROP AND LIVESTOCK STATISTICS. See Agriculture-Abstracting, Bibliographies and Statistics.

LC S539.2
DD 630.72
JA
BULLETIN OF THE FRUIT TREE RESEARCH STATION. SERIES B. (OKITSU). Main/Corp Kaju Shikenjo, Hiratsuka, Japan. (1974)-. Bulletin. Japanese (summaries and/or abstracts in English). Norin Suisansho Kaju Shikenjo Okitsu Shijo, (Okitsu Branch Fruit Tree Research Station Ministry of Agriculture Forestry & Fisheries), Okitsunakamachi, Shimizushi Shizuokaken 424-02 Japan.
Ind/Abst AgBiotech News Inf.; Biocont. News Inf. (1991-); Plant Grow. Reg. Abstr.; Postharvest News Inf.; Rev. Agric. Entomol.; Seed Abstr.

LC S
DD 630
ISSN 0020-8760
IT
BULLETIN OF THE INTERNATIONAL SOCIETY OF SOIL SCIENCE = BULLETIN DE L'ASSOCIATION INTERNATIONALE DE LA SCIENCE DU SOL = MITTEILUNGEN DER INTERNATIONALEN BODENKUNDLICHEN GESELLSCHAFT.
Main/Corp International Society of Soil Science. **VFOAT** Bulletin de l'Association Internationale de la Science du Sol; Mitteilungen der Internationalen Bodenkundlichen Gesellschaft. (1952)-. Bulletin. English (French and German). Two times a year. $50.00. International Soil Science Society, Zuercherstr 111, CH-8903 Birmensdorf

Switzerland. **Tel** 011 41 1 7392299, FAX 011 41 1 7392215. **ED** Professor Dr. Winfried E. H. Blum and Drs. J. Hans V. van Baren. cum. index.

LC S **ISSN** 0498-1308
DD 630 II
CODEN BUPDD2

BULLETIN - UNITED PLANTERS' ASSOCIATION OF SOUTHERN INDIA, SCIENTIFIC DEPARTMENT. [Bull., United Plant. Assoc. South. India, Sci. Dep.]. **Main/Corp** United Planters' Association of Southern India. Scientific Dept. (19??)-. Bulletin. English. Documents available from CASDDS.
Ind/Abst Chem. Abstr.; Hortic. Abstr.; Rev. Agric. Entomol.; Rev. Plant Pathol.

LC HD1401 **ISSN** 0826-2942
DD 338.1/06/071 CN

C.S.A. NEWSLETTER - CANADIAN SOCIETY OF AGRONOMY (1983). (C.S.A. NEWSLETTER.). [C.S.A. newsl. - Can. Soc. Agron.]. **Main/Corp** Canadian Society of Agronomy. **VAT** Canadian Society of Agronomy Newsletter (1983). March 1983-. Newsletter. English. Free. Canadian Society of Agronomy, Suite 907/151 Slater Street, Ottawa Ontario K1P 5H4 Canada. ***Continues** Canadian Society of Agronomy. Newsletter, 0712-6948.*

LC S **ISSN** 0102-7344
DD 630 BL

CABRA & BODES. [Cabra bodes]. **VFOAT** Cabra e Bodes. (1985)-. Periodical. Portuguese. Six times a year.
Ind/Abst Index Vet.; Nutr. Abstr. Rev., Ser. B, Live Feeds and Feed.; Sug. Indus. Abstr.

LC S **ISSN** 1010-3503
DD 630 PE

CAFE PERU - CENTRAL DE COOPERATIVAS AGRARIAS CAFE PERU. [Cafe Peru]. Vol. 1, No. 1; 1977-. Periodical. Spanish. One time a year.

LC HN49.C6 C34 **ISSN** 0755-9208
DD 307.1/412/05 FR

CAHIERS D'ECONOMIE ET SOCIOLOGIE RURALES. **Added/Corp** Institut National de la Recherche Agronomique (France). No. 1 (June 1984)-. Periodical. French. Four times a year (quarterly). 390.00F France and EEC; 480.00 other. INRA Editions / Institut National de la Recherche Agronomique, Route de Saint-Cyr, 78026 Versailles Cedex France. **Tel** 011 33 1 30833406, FAX 011 33 1 30833449, telex INRAPUB 699 368 F. **ED** Y. Leon.
Desc: Deals with agriculture and related activities (the agro-food industries in particular) in terms of their economics, their social characteristics and their relations with the national and international economy or with society as a whole. Intended for readers interested in research trends, methods and results - specialist civil servants, decision makers and specialists in the food and agriculture sectors of the economy, as well as teachers and instructors.
Ind/Abst Dairy Sci. Abstr.; Maize Abstr.; PAIS Int. Print; Pig News Inf.; Poult. Abstr.; Soyabean Abstr.; World Agric. Econ. Rural Sociol. Abstr.

LC S **ISSN** 0029-7259
DD 630 FR

CAHIERS O.R.S.T.O.M. PEDOLOGIE. (CAHIERS O.R.S.T.O.M. SERIE PEDOLOGIE.). [Cah. O.R.S.T.O.M., Pedol.]. **Main/Corp** O.R.S.T.O.M. (Agency : France). (1964)-. Periodical. French (summaries and/or abstracts in English, French and Spanish). Two times a year. 180.00F France; 225.00F other. Orstom Editions, 72 route d'Aulnay, F-93143 Bondy Cedex France. **Tel** 011 33 1 48025500. **ED** G. Pedro. cum. index. available with charts; available with illustrations. Documents available from CASDDS. ***Continues** Cahiers O.R.S.T.O.M. Pedologie.*
Desc: Review devoted to tropical and arid soils: morphology, mineralogical and physico-chemical features classification, problems in relation with geomorphology, salts, water, erosion, fertility.
Ind/Abst Agric. Eng. Abstr. (1991-); Agrofor. Abstr. (1991-); Chem. Abstr.; Energy Res. Abstr. (July 1975-); Geogr. Abstr. Phys. Geogr.; Geol. Abstr.; GeoRef; Int. Dev. Abstr.; Rev. Plant Pathol.; Soils Fert.

LC S **ISSN** 0008-0578
DD 630 US

CALAVO NEWSLETTER. [Calavo news.]. 1959-. Newsletter. English. Twelve times a year. Free. Calavo Growers of California, PO Box 26081, Santa Ana CA 92799-6081. **Tel** (714)259-1166, FAX (714)259-1973. **ED** Dean E Borton. **Circ:** 4,200.
Desc: Current news of interest to the commercial avocado grower and related industry.

LC SB354 **ISSN** 0092-2145
DD 634 US
TITLE CHANGE

CALIFORNIA AND WESTERN STATES GRAPE GROWER. [Calif. west. states grape grow.]. Vol. 1, No. 5 (Jan. 1971)-(19??). Periodical. English. Western Agricultural Publishing Company, 1755 North Fine Avenue, Fresno CA 93727. **Tel** (209)252-7000, FAX (209)252-7387. **ED** Harry Cline. **Ad Acc. Circ:** 14,714. ***Continues** California Grape Grower (Fresno, Calif.). **Continued by** Grape Grower (Fresno, Calif.), 1049-670X.*

LC S **ISSN** 0008-090X
DD 630 US

CALIFORNIA-ARIZONA COTTON. **VFOAT** California Arizona Cotton; Cotton: California-Arizona. **VAT** California Arizona Cotton. Vol. 1 (1965)-. Trade Publication. English. Twelve times a year. $19.95. Western Agricultural Publishing Company, 1755 North Fine Avenue, Fresno CA 93727. **Tel** (209)252-7000, FAX (209)252-7387. **ED** Harry Cline. **Ad Acc. Circ:** 15,000.

LC SB183 **ISSN** 0279-2648
DD 633 US

CALIFORNIA FIELD CROP REVIEW. **Main/Corp** California. Crop and Livestock Reporting Service. **Added/Corp** California. Dept. of Food and Agriculture. United States. Dept. of Agriculture. (1980)-. English. Twelve times a year. $15.00. California Agricultural Statistics Service, California Department of, Food and Agriculture, PO Box 1258, Sacramento CA 95812. **Tel** (916)551-1533.
Desc: Grain, cotton, hay, sugar beet, etc. acreage, production, value, price, warehouse, and farm labor data.

LC SB193
DD 633 US
CEASED

CALIFORNIA FIELD CROPS STATISTICS (1987). **See** Agriculture-Abstracting, Bibliographies and Statistics.

LC S **ISSN** 0527-2181
DD 630 US

CALIFORNIA FRUIT & NUT ACREAGE. **Main/Corp** California Crop and Livestock Reporting Service. **VFOAT** California Fruit and Nut Crop Acreage Estimates; Fruit & Nut Acreage Bulletin. **VAT** California Fruit and Nut Acreage (1959). 1959-. Bulletin. English. One time a year. $4.00 US; $8.00 other. California Agricultural Statistics Service, California Department of, Food and Agriculture, PO Box 1258, Sacramento CA 95812. **Tel** (916)551-1533. ***Continues** Acreage Estimates, California Fruit and Nut Crops.*
Desc: Acreages of fruit and nut crops by year planted, variety and county.

LC TP368
DD 664 US

CALIFORNIA FRUIT & NUT STATISTICS. **See** Agriculture-Abstracting, Bibliographies and Statistics.

LC HD9259.G7 U514 **ISSN** 0146-7344
DD 338.1/7/4809794 US

CALIFORNIA GRAPES, RAISINS, AND WINE. (CALIFORNIA GRAPES, RAISINS, AND WINE : PRODUCTION AND MARKETING.). **Main/Corp** California Crop and Livestock Reporting Service. 1975-. English. One time a year. $4.00. California Agricultural Statistics Service, California Department of, Food and Agriculture, PO Box 1258, Sacramento CA 95812. **Tel** (916)551-1533. ***Continues** Production and Marketing California Grapes, Raisins and Wine.*

LC SB354 **ISSN** 0888-1715
DD 634 US

CALIFORNIA GROWER (VISTA, CALIF.). (CALIFORNIA GROWER.). [Calif. grow.]. Vol. 9, No. 9 (Sept. 1985)-. Trade Publication. English. Twelve times a year. $22.00. Rincon Information Management Corporation, PO Box 370, Carpinteria CA 93104. **Tel** (805)684-6581, FAX (805)684-1535. **ED** Willard Thompson. Index Bound in First Issue (Part of Subscription.). **Ad Acc, Adv Mgr:** R. Belieff, **Tel** (805)684-0916. **Circ:** 5,000 (ctrl). ***Continues** Avocado Grower, 0193-399X.*
Desc: For citrus, avocado and specialty crop growers. Provides easy to understand information on yield maximization, marketing, finances and other agri-business topics.
Ind/Abst AGRICOLA [Select. Cov.].

LC S **ISSN** 0744-2653
DD 631 US

CALIFORNIA ORNAMENTAL CROPS REPORT. [Calif. ornam. crops rep.]. **Added/Corp** California. Bureau of Market News. United States. Agricultural Marketing Service. Fruit and Vegetable Division. (19??)-. Periodical. English. Two times a week (104 per year). $180.00. US Department of Agriculture / Federal-State Market News, 630 Sansome Street, Room 727, San Francisco CA 94111. **Tel** (415)705-1300, FAX (415)705-1301. **ED** F. Teensma. **Circ:** 200 (ctrl).
Desc: Shipping point information on cut flowers for California and other areas.

LC S **ISSN** 0194-8504
DD 631 US

CALIFORNIA STRAWBERRY REPORT. **Added/Corp** California. Bureau of Market News. United States. Agricultural Marketing Service. Fruit and Vegetable Division. (19??)-. English. Irregular (Feb-Oct.). $135.00. US Department of Agriculture / Federal-State Market News, 630 Sansome Street, Room 727, San Francisco CA 94111. **Tel** (415)705-1300, FAX (415)705-1301. **ED** F. Teensma. **Circ:** 100 (ctrl).
Desc: Shipping point information on strawberries and raspberries.

LC S **ISSN** 0527-3277
DD 630 US

CALIFORNIA TOMATO GROWER, THE. **Added/Corp** California Tomatoe Growers Association. (19??)-. Periodical. English. Nine times a year (May/June and July/Aug. issues combined). $30.00. California Tomato Growers Association Inc, PO Box 7398, Stockton CA 95207. **Tel** (209)478-1761. **ED** David L. Zollinger. **Bk Rev. Ad Acc. Circ:** 2,200.
Desc: Deals with various issues; advertising, seed companies, equipment, chemicals, fieldmen's report, classifieds, news releases and articles on pesticides. Also articles dealing with California Tomato Growers Association.

LC S **ISSN** 0045-4885
DD 630 CN
CODEN CAFRAW

CANADIAN FRUITGROWER. [Can. fruitgrow.]. Vol. 12 (1956)-. Periodical. English. Nine times a year (Jan., Feb., Mar., Apr., May, June, July, Sept., Nov.). 12.81Can$. NCC Publishing, 222 Argyle Avenue, Delhi Ontario N4B 2Y2 Canada. **Tel** (519)582-2513, FAX (519)582-4040. **ED** Ben Steidman. **Ad Acc, Adv Mgr:** Jim Countryman. **Circ:** 4,000 (ctrl). ***Continues** Canadian Fruitgrower and Gardener.*

LC S **ISSN** 0008-4271
DD 630 CN
CCC
CODEN CJSSAR
Pr Rev.

CANADIAN JOURNAL OF SOIL SCIENCE. [Can. j. soil sci.]. **Added/Corp** Agricultural Institute of Canada. Canadian Society of Soil Science. National Committee on Agricultural Services. **VFOAT** Revue Canadienne de la Science du Sol. Vol. 37 (Feb. 1957)-. Periodical. English (French). Four times a year. 72.02Can$. Agricultural Institute of Canada, 151 Slater Street, Suite 907, Ottawa Ontario K1P 5H4 Canada. **Tel** (613)232-9459, (613)238-2271, FAX (613)594-5190. **ED** U. C. Gupta. **Ad Acc. Circ:** 1,600. available in microform from Micromedia Limited; available on microfilm and microfiche from University Microfilms International (UMI). Documents available from The Genuine Article, BIOSIS Document Express, CASDDS. ***Continues in part** Canadian Journal of Agricultural Science, 0366-6557.*
Desc: Presents research in various fields of soil science including agriculture, engineering, forestry, geology and geography, agronomy (grains, forages and weeds), and horticulture (fruits, vegetables and ornamentals).
Ind/Abst AgBiotech News Inf.; AGRICOLA [Full Cov.]; AQUAREF; Biol. Agric. Index; Biol. Abstr.; Ceram. Abstr.; Chem. Abstr.; Crop Physiol. Abstr.; Curr. Aware. Biol. Sci., CABS; Curr. Cit.; Curr. Contents Agric. Biol. Environ. Sci.; Ecol. Abstr.; Ecology Abstr.; EMBASE; Environ. Period. Bibliogr.; Field Crop Abstr.; For. Prod. Abstr.; For. Abstr.; Geogr. Abstr. Phys. Geogr.; Geogr. Abstr. Human Geogr. (?-?); Geol. Abstr.; GeoRef; Grass. Forage Abstr.; Health Saf. Sci. Abstr.; Hortic. Abstr.; Irr. Drain. Abstr.; Maize Abstr.; Microbiol. Abstr. Sect. A; Nematol. Abstr.; Life Sci. Collect.; Plant Breed. Abstr.; Plant Grow. Reg. Abstr.; Pollut. Abstr. Indexes; Potato Abstr.; Protozoolog. Abstr.; Res. Alert [Full Cov.]; Rev. Agric. Entomol.; Sci. Cit. Index; SCISEARCH; Soils Fert.; Sorghum Mill. Abstr.; Soyabean Abstr.; Weed Abstr.; Wheat Barley Trit. Abstr.

LC SB215
DD 633.6 PH

CANEFARM NEWS. (1977)-. Periodical. English. Six times a year. ***Continues** Farm News.*
Ind/Abst Philip. Sci. Technol. Abstr.

LC SB320 **ISSN** 1071-6653
DD 635 US

•**CARROT COUNTRY.** [Carrot ctry.]. (1993)-. Periodical. English. Four times a year. Columbia Publishing and Design, 2809-A Fruitvale Boulevard, Box 1467, Yakima WA 98907-1467. **Tel** (509)248-2452, FAX (509)248-4056. **ED** Ken Hodge. **Ad Acc. Circ:** 3,800.
Desc: Features are designed for all segments of the carrot growing industry.

LC S **ISSN** 0120-1824
DD 630 CK
Pr Rev.

CASSAVA NEWSLETTER. **Added/Corp** Centro de Informacion sobre Yuca (Centro Internacional de Agricultura Tropical). No. 1 (Jan./June 1977)-. Newsletter. English (Spanish and French). Two times a year. Free. Cassava Biotechnology Network, CIAT, Apartado Aereo 67-13, Cali Colombia. **Tel** 57 23 445 00 00, FAX 57 26 445 0273, telex 05769 CIAT CO. **ED** Dr. Rupert Best. Index available. cum. index. **Bk Rev**, (Qty: 6-12 per year). **Acid Free. Circ:** 2,200 (ctrl).
Desc: Provides progress reports from Cassava researchers and developers in tropical countries, interchange of technical notes, and other news.
Ind/Abst Agrofor. Abstr. (1991-); Biocont. News Inf.; Food Sci. Technol. Abstr.; For. Abstr.; Nematol. Abstr.; Life Sci. Collect. (1985-); Plant Breed. Abstr.

Agriculture — Crop Production and Soil

LC S590
DD 631.4
ISSN 0341-8162
GW
CCC
CODEN CIJPD3
Pr Rev.
CATENA (GIESSEN). (CATENA.). [Catena]. **Added/Corp** Justus Liebig-Universitat Giessen. Geographisches Institut. International Society of Soil Science. Vol. 1 (Dec. 1973)-. Academic Scholarly Publication. English (French and German). Twelve times a year (3 volumes). $704.00. Elsevier Science Publishers BV, PO Box 211, 1000 AE Amsterdam Netherlands. **Tel** 011 31 20 4853641, 011 31 20 4853642, **FAX** 011 31 20 4853598. **ED** R.B. Bryan, R. Herrmann, P. Jungerius, J. Poesen, R. Webster, and D. Yaalon. cum. index. **Bk Rev**. **Ad Acc**. **Acid Free**. **Circ:** 500. available on an online database from Elsevier Electronic Subscriptions (EES). Documents available from The Genuine Article, BIOSIS Document Express, CASDDS.
Desc: Publishes original contributions in the fields of geoecology and landscape evolution.
Ind/Abst AESIS Q.; AGRICOLA; AQUAREF; Biol. Abstr. (1991-); Chem. Abstr.; Curr. Cit.; Curr. Contents Agric. Biol. Environ. Sci.; Curr. Geogr. Publ. (19??-); Ecol. Abstr.; EMBASE; For. Abstr.; Geogr. Abstr. Phys. Geogr.; GeoRef; Int. Dev. Abstr.; Irr. Drain. Abstr.; Meteorol. Geoastrophys. Abstr. (199?-); Res. Alert [Full Cov.]; Rev. Agric. Entomol.; Sci. Cit. Index; SCISEARCH; Soils Fert.; Wheat Barley Trit. Abstr.

LC S
DD 630
ISSN 1022-1492
CK
●**CBN NEWSLETTER.** (1992)-. Newsletter. English. Two times a year. Free. Cassava Biotechnology Network, CIAT, Apartado Aereo 67-13, Cali Colombia. **Tel** 57 23 445 00 00, **FAX** 57 26 445 0273, telex 05769 CIAT CO. **ED** Ann Marie Thro. **Circ:** 900 (ctrl).
Desc: News of Cassava Biotechnology Network activities; short feature articles on research priorities and objectives, methods, results, or other issues of current concern.

LC S
DD 630
ISSN 0120-0275
CK
CODEN CENIA5
CENICAFE. See Food and Food Industry-Beverage Industry.

LC SB320
DD 635
CH
CENTERPOINT (ASIAN VEGETABLE RESEARCH AND DEVELOPMENT CENTER). (CENTERPOINT.). **Added/Corp** Asian Vegetable Research and Development Center. (Spring 1980)-. Periodical. English. One time a year. Office of Information Services, The Asian Vegetable Research and Development Center, PO Box 42, Shanhua Tainan 741 Taiwan. **Tel** (06)5837801, telex 73560 AVRDC. **ED** B. T. Mclean. **Circ:** 7,000. **Continues** About AVRDC.
Desc: Provides information on AVRDC's research, training, publishing and development activities.
Ind/Abst Hortic. Abstr.; Nematol. Abstr.; Plant Breed. Abstr.; Soyabean Abstr.

LC HD9056.A1 C47
DD 338.17
IT
CEREAL POLICIES REVIEW. **Added/Corp** Food and Agriculture Organization of the United Nations. Commodities and Trade Division.a40. (1990/1991)-. English. Food Agriculture Organization (FAO) / Italy, GIPC166 via Terme di Caracalla, 00100 Rome Italy. **Tel** 011 39 6 52252925, **FAX** 011 39 6 52253152.

LC S
DD 630
ISSN 1013-8609
NE
CEREAL RUSTS AND POWDERY MILDEWS BULLETIN. **Added/Corp** European and Mediterranean Cereal Rusts Foundation. Vol. 16, No. 1 (1988)-. Bulletin. English. Two times a year. $50.00. European & Mediterranean Cereal Rusts Foundation, Postbus 271, 6700 AG Wageningen, Netherlands. **Continues** Cereal Rusts Bulletin.
Ind/Abst Plant Breed. Abstr.; Rev. Plant Pathol.; Wheat Barley Trit. Abstr.

LC S
DD 630
ISSN 0399-0001
FR
UDC 66/68
CETIM INFORMATIONS. [CETIM inf.]. **VFOAT** Informations - CETIM; Centre Technique des Industries Mecaniques Informations. (1967)-. Periodical. French (English). Six times a year. $102.36. CETIM, Service Diffusion BP 67, F-60304 Senlis France. **Tel** 011 33 44 583266.
Desc: Market reports on world fertilizer industry.

LC S
DD 630
ISSN 0009-1308
GW
CODEN CHMPDB
CHAMPIGNON. [Champignon]. (1961)-. Academic Scholarly Publication. German. Twelve times a year. $169.65. Bund Deutscher ChampignonZuechter, Godesberger Allee 142-148, D-53175 Bonn Germany. **Tel** 011 49 30 3235251. Documents available from CASDDS.
Ind/Abst Agric. Eng. Abstr. (1991-); Chem. Abstr.; Food Sci. Technol. Abstr.; Hortic. Abstr.; Maize Abstr.; Nutr. Abstr. Rev., Ser. A, Hum. Exp.; Life Sci. Collect. (1985-); Postharvest News Inf.; Rev. Plant Pathol.; Rice Abstr.; Soils Fert.; World Agric. Econ. Rural Sociol. Abstr.

LC SB320
DD 635
ISSN 0009-1316
NE
CHAMPIGNONCULTUUR, DE. [Champignoncult.]. Vol. 1 (May 1957)-. Periodical. Dutch. Ten times a year. $99.35. Champignoncultuur, PO Box 6042, 5960 AA Horst Netherlands. **Tel** 011 31 47641944, **FAX** 04764-1567. **Ad Acc**. **Acc. Circ:** 1,725 (ctrl).
Desc: Publishes technical information on all aspects of mushroom cultivation including cultivation techniques, breeding, pests and diseases, substrates, and climate.
Ind/Abst AGRICOLA; Hortic. Abstr.; Soyabean Abstr.

LC S
DD 630
ISSN 0193-8835
US
CHERRIES (ALBANY, N.Y.). (CHERRIES.). **Main/Corp** New York Crop Reporting Service. (1971)-. English. One time a year. New York Crop Reporting Service, c/o Department of Agriculture & Markets Building, 8 State Campus, Albany NY 12235. **Continues** Tart Cherry Report, 0193-8843.
Desc: Includes data for New York, Pennsylvania, Ohio, Michigan, and Wisconsin.

LC S
DD 630
ISSN 0735-7389
US
CHERRY UTILIZATION. **Added/Corp** United States. Crop Reporting Board. **VFOAT** Cherries. (Oct. 6, 1976)-. Government Publication. English. One time a year (Oct.). $5.00. US Department of Agriculture / National Agricultural Statistics Service (NASS), Room 5829 South Building, Washington DC 20250. **Tel** (202)720-4020, **FAX** (314)875-5231.
Desc: Production, utilization, price and value of crops.

LC S542.C4 C44
DD 631/.05
CC
CHIANG-SU NUNG YEH KO HSUEH. **Added/Corp** Chiang-Su Sheng Nung Yeh Ko Hsueh Yuan. **VFOAT** Jiangsu Nongye Kexue. (19??)-. Periodical. Chinese. Six times a year. RMBY0.25.
Ind/Abst Maize Abstr.; Plant Breed. Abstr.; Plant Grow. Reg. Abstr.; Rev. Agric. Entomol.; Rice Abstr.; Soyabean Abstr.

LC SB354
DD 634
US
CHICAGO FRUIT & VEGETABLE REPORTER. **Added/Corp** Chicago Fruit & Vegatable Reporter (Firm). **VFOAT** Chicago Fruit and Vegetable Reporter. (19??)-. Periodical. English. Seven times a week. Chicago Produce Publishing Company, 1656 West 35th Street, Chicago IL 60609.

LC SB188
DD 633
ISSN 0577-943X
XR
CHMELARSTVI. (19??)-. Periodical. Czech. Twelve times a year. DM114.00. (Subscription address: Kubon & Sagner, ABT Zeitschriftenimport, D 80328 Munich Germany. **Tel** 011 49 89 54218130.)
Ind/Abst Agric. Eng. Abstr. (1991-); Biocont. News Inf.; Hortic. Abstr.; Irr. Drain. Abstr.; Rev. Agric. Entomol.; Soils Fert.

LC SB271 .C58
DD 633.7/2/05
CC
CHUNG-KUO CHA YEH. **VFOAT** China Tea. (May 1979)-. Periodical. Chinese. Six times a year. RMBY0.25. Post Office Hang-Chou Shih, Hang-Chou Shih, People's Republic of China.

LC SB354 .C48
DD 634/.05
CC
CHUNG-KUO KUO SHU = ZHONG GUO GUOSHU. **Added/Corp** Chung-Kuo Nung Yeh Ko Hsueh Yuan. Kuo Shu Yen Chiu So. **VFOAT** Zhong Guo Guoshu. (19??)-. Periodical. Chinese.

LC SB242.C6 C57
DD 633.5/0951
CC
CHUNG-KUO MA TSO. **Added/Corp** Chung-kuo Nung yeh ko Hsueh Yuan. Ma lei yen Chiu so. **VFOAT** China's Fiber Crops. (19??)-. Periodical. Chinese. Four times a year. RMBY0.30. Science Press, 16 Donghuangchenggen North Street, Beijing 100707, People's Republic of China. **Tel** 011 86 1 4019821, 011 86 1 4010642, **FAX** 011 86 1 4012180, 011 86 1 4019810, telex 210147.
Ind/Abst Biocont. News Inf.; Hortic. Abstr.; Plant Genet. Resour. Abstr.; Seed Abstr.

LC SB245 .C483
DD 633.5/1/0951
CC
CHUNG-KUO MIEN HUA. **Added/Corp** Chung-kuo Nung yeh ko Hsueh Yuan. Mien hua yen Chiu so.41. **VFOAT** Zhongguo Mianhua; China Cottons. (19??)-. Periodical. Chinese. Six times a year. RMBY0.25. Post Office An-Yang Shih, An-Yang Shih, People's Republic of China.
Ind/Abst Biocont. News Inf.; Cot. Trop. Fibr. Abstr. Bibliogr.; Seed Abstr.

LC S625.C555 C52
DD 631.4/05
CC
CHUNG-KUO SHUI TU PAO CHIH. **VFOAT** Zhongguo Shuitubaochi; Soil and Water Conservation in China. Periodical. Chinese. Six times a year. RMBY0.20. Post Office Cheng-chou Shih, Cheng-chou Shih, People's Republic of China.

LC SB298.5.C6 C485
DD 633.8/5/05
CC
CHUNG-KUO YU LIAO. **Added/Corp** Chung-Kuo Nung yeh ko Hsueh Yuan. Yu Liao tso wu yen Chiu so. **VFOAT** Oil Crops of China. (19??)-. Periodical. Chinese (summaries and/or abstracts in English). Four times a year.
Ind/Abst Biocont. News Inf.; Crop Physiol. Abstr.; Field Crop Abstr.; Hortic. Abstr.; Nematol. Abstr.; Plant Breed. Abstr.; Plant Genet. Resour. Abstr.; Plant Grow. Reg. Abstr.; Rev. Plant Pathol.; Seed Abstr.; Soyabean Abstr.

LC SB320
DD 635
CU
CIENCIA Y TECNICA EN LA AGRICULTURA (CENTRO DE INFORMACION Y DOCUMENTACION AGROPECUARIO). (CIENCIA Y TECNICA EN LA AGRICULTURA. VIANDAS, HORTALIZAS Y GRANOS.). **Added/Corp** Centro de Informacion y Documentacion Agropecuario. Estacion de Investigaciones en Raices y Tuberculos Tropicales "Fructuoso Rodriquez". **VFOAT** Viandas, Hortalizas y Granos: Ciencia y Tecnica en la Agricultura. Vol. 1, No. 1 (May 1978)-. Periodical. Spanish (summaries and/or abstracts in English; table of contents in English). Ediciones Cubanas, Obispo 527 Altos ESQ Bernaza, CP 10100 Havana Cuba.
Ind/Abst Hortic. Abstr.

LC SB354
DD 634
CU
CIENCIA Y TECNICA EN LA AGRICULTURA. CITRICOS Y OTROS FRUTALES. **Added/Corp** Centro de Informacion y Documentacion Agropecuario. Estacion Central de Citricos y Otros Frutales. **VFOAT** Citricos y Otros Frutales : Ciencia y Tecnica en la Agricultura. Vol. 1, No. 1 (Mar. 1978)-. Spanish (summaries and/or abstracts in English; table of contents in English). Ediciones Cubanas, Obispo 527 Altos ESQ Bernaza, CP 10100 Havana Cuba.
Ind/Abst Crop Physiol. Abstr.; Hortic. Abstr.; Postharvest News Inf.; Soils Fert.

LC SB761
DD 635.97
CU
CODEN CTHFE7
CIENCIA Y TECNICA EN LA AGRICULTURA. HORTALIZAS, PAPAS, GRANOS Y FIBRAS. **VFOAT** Hortalizas, Papas, Granos y Fibras. Vol. 1, No. 1 (May 1982)-. Spanish. Two times a year. Ediciones Cubanas, Obispo 527 Altos ESQ Bernaza, CP 10100 Havana Cuba. Documents available from BIOSIS Document Express. **Continues** Boletin de Resenas. Viandas, Hortalizas y Granos.
Ind/Abst Biol. Abstr. (1986-); Cot. Trop. Fibr. Abstr. Bibliogr.; Plant Grow. Reg. Abstr.

LC SB761
DD 635.97
ISSN 0259-2924
CU
CODEN CAPFEG
CIENCIA Y TECNICA EN LA AGRICULTURA. PASTOS Y FORRAJES. [Cienc. tec. agric., Pastos y forrajes]. **VFOAT** Pastos y Forrajes. Spanish (summaries and/or abstracts in English; table of contents in English). Ediciones Cubanas, Obispo 527 Altos ESQ Bernaza, CP 10100 Havana Cuba. Documents available from BIOSIS Document Express.
Ind/Abst Agrofor. Abstr. (19??-19??); Biol. Abstr. (1986-); For. Abstr.; Grass. Forage Abstr.; Plant Genet. Resour. Abstr.; Rev. Agric. Entomol.; Seed Abstr.; Soyabean Abstr.; Sug. Indus. Abstr.; Weed Abstr.

LC S
DD 630
ISSN 1013-9850
CU
CODEN CARDEK
CIENCIA Y TECNICA EN LA AGRICULTURA. RIEGO Y DRENAJE. See Engineering-Hydraulic Engineering.

LC SB761
DD 635.97
ISSN 1010-1578
CU
CODEN CAPPDB
CIENCIAS Y TECNICA EN LA AGRICULTURA. PROTECCION DE PLANTAS. [Cienc. tec. agric., Prot. plantas]. **VFOAT** Proteccion de Plantas. Academic Scholarly Publication. Spanish (English; summaries and/or abstracts in English; table of contents in English). Centro de Informacion y Documentacion Agropecuario, Calle 11 No 1057, Vedado Habana Cuba. Documents available from BIOSIS Document Express, CASDDS.
Ind/Abst Biocont. News Inf.; Biol. Abstr. (1985-); Chem. Abstr. (1978-1981).

LC HA1911 .A3 HD9016.T8
DD 338.17 TU
CIFTCININ ELINE GECEN FIYATLAR = PRICES RECEIVED BY FARMERS.
Added/Corp Devlet Istatistik Enstitusu (Turkey). **VFOAT** Prices Received by Farmers. (1976)-. English (Turkish). One time a year. $30.00. Turkish State Institute of Statistics, Necatibey Cadessi 114, Ankara 016100 Turkey. **Tel** 011 90 4 1188719, FAX 011 90 4 1253387, telex 46347 DIETR. Index available. cum. index. **Circ:** 700.

LC S **ISSN** 0304-548X
DD 630 MX
UDC 633.1
CIMMYT REPORT ON MAIZE IMPROVEMENT. VFOAT CIMMYT ... Maize. (1975)-. Periodical. English. One time a year. Centrl Internacional de Mejoramiento de Maiz y Trigo, Apartado 6/641 Londres 40, 06600 Mexico City DF Mexico. ***Continues*** *CIMMYT Maize Improvement.*

LC SB189 .I59A **ISSN** 0304-5463
DD 633/.11/072072 MX
CIMMYT REVIEW. Main/Corp International Maize and Wheat Improvement Center. **VAT** Centro Internacional de Mejoramiento de Maiz y Trigo Review. English. Centro Internacional de Mejoramiento de Maiz y Trigo, Apartado 6, 641 Londres 40, 06600 Mexico City DF Mexico.
Ind/Abst Field Crop Abstr.; Grass. Forage Abstr.

LC S **ISSN** 0744-4095
DD 630 US
CINCINNATI FRESH FRUIT AND VEGETABLE REPORT. (19??)-. Trade Publication. English. Seven times a week. $144.00. USDA Fruit & Vegetable, Market News Service/Room 9522, Federal Office Building, 550 Main Street, Cincinnati OH 45202. **Tel** (513)684-3194. **Circ:** 105.
Desc: Collects and disseminates information from fruit and vegetable wholesalers on prices, demands, market trends, quality, condition, and supplies of fresh fruit and vegetables.

LC SB608 **ISSN** 0256-8632
DD 635.21 PE
CIP CIRCULAR (ENGLISH ED.). (CIP CIRCULAR.). [CIP circ.]. **Main/Corp** International Potato Center. (19??)-. Periodical. English (Spanish and French). Four times a year. Free on request. Centro Internacional de Papa, Apartado 5969, Lima Peru. **Tel** 51 14 366920, FAX 51 14 351570, telex 25672 PE. **ED** Linda Peterson. Index available. ctrl circ.
Ind/Abst AgBiotech News Inf.; Biocont. News Inf.; Field Crop Abstr.; Grass. Forage Abstr.; Plant Breed. Abstr.; Potato Abstr.

LC S **ISSN** 0751-6037
DD 630 FR
UDC 63
CIRCUITS CULTURE PARIS. [Circuits cult. Paris]. (1973)-. Periodical. French. Twenty-one times a year. $110.02. Documentation Agricole, 228 rue du Faubourg St. Martin, 75010 Paris France. **Tel** 011 33 1 40051818, 011 33 1 40380880.
Ind/Abst Chem. Bus. Bull.; Chem. Bus. NewsBase (1988-); Chem. Bus. Update.

LC S
DD 630 UK
CIRCULAR / LONDON RICE BROKERS' ASSOCIATION. English. London Rice Brokers Assn, 48 Upper Thames Street, London EC4V 3EP United Kingdom. ***Continues*** *Weekly Circular (London Rice Brokers' Association).*

LC SB183
DD 633 BL
CIRCULAR TECNICA (CENTRO NACIONAL DE PESQUISA DE ARROZ E FEIJAO). (CIRCULAR TECNICA.). **Added/Corp** Centro Nacional de Pesquisa de Arroz e Feijao. (19??)-. Periodical. Portuguese. Embrapa, Dept. Dif. Tecnologiaogi, Caixa Postal 040315, 07770 901 Brasilia DF Brazil. **Tel** 011 55 61 2724241.

LC S **ISSN** 0100-6886
DD 630 BL
CIRCULAR TECNICA - UNIDADE DE EXECUCAO DE PESQUISA DE AMBITO ESTADUAL DE DOURADOS. [Circ. tec. - Unidade Exec. Pesqui. Ambito Estadual Dourados]. (1980)-. Monographic series. Portuguese. Irregular. Price varies per volume. MS Unidade de Execucao de Pesquisa de Ambito Estadual, Dourados Brazil.
Ind/Abst Plant Breed. Abstr.; Rice Abstr.; Weed Abstr.

LC SB354 **ISSN** 0009-7578
DD 634 US
CITROGRAPH (FRESNO, CALIF.). (CITROGRAPH.). Vol. 54, No. 5 (Mar. 1969)-. Trade Publication. English. Twelve times a year (May/June, Jul./Aug., & Nov./Dec. issues combined). $19.95. Western Agricultural Publishing Company, 1755 North Fine Avenue, Fresno CA 93727. **Tel** (209)252-7000, FAX (209)252-7387. **ED** Lewis Robinson. Index available (bound in Oct. issue). ***Continues*** *California Citrograph.*
Ind/Abst BioBusiness; Biocont. News Inf.; Food Sci. Technol. Abstr.; Hortic. Abstr.; Nematol. Abstr.; Plant Genet. Resour. Abstr.; Plant Grow. Reg. Abstr.; Postharvest News Inf.; Rev. Agric. Entomol.; Rev. Med. Vet. Mycology; Rev. Plant Pathol.

LC SB354 **ISSN** 0257-2095
DD 634 SA
CODEN CSFJAW
CEASED
CITRUS AND SUB-TROPICAL FRUIT JOURNAL, THE. (CITRUS & SUBTROPICAL FRUIT JOURNAL.). [Citrus sub-trop. fruit j.]. **VFOAT** Citrus and Subtropical Fruit Journal. (1973)-(19??). Academic Scholarly Publication. English (Afrikaans). Citrus and Subtropical Fruit Journal, PO Box 1410, Krugersdorp, 1740 Transvaal South Africa. **Tel** 662-1233. **ED** N G Hulley. **Bk Rev. Ad Acc. Circ:** 3,750 (ctrl). Documents available from CASDDS. ***Continues*** *Citrus Grower and Subtropical Fruit Journal.*
Desc: Serves the citrus and subtropical fruit industries. Includes first publication of original research. Supported by the South African citrus exchange.
Ind/Abst Agrofor. Abstr.; Biocont. News Inf.; Chem. Abstr.; Food Sci. Technol. Abstr.; Hortic. Abstr.; Nematol. Abstr.; Plant Breed. Abstr.; Soyabean Abstr.; Weed Abstr.

LC SB354 **ISSN** 0009-7586
DD 634 US
CODEN CVGMAX
CITRUS AND VEGETABLE MAGAZINE. [Citrus veg. mag.]. Vol. 23 (1960)-. Periodical. English. Twelve times a year. $25.00. Vance Publishing Corporation, 400 Knightsbridge Parkway, Lincolnshire IL 60069. **Tel** (800)255-5113, (708)634-2600. **ED** Gordon Smith. **Ad Acc, Adv Mgr:** Alicia Fremont, **Tel** (913)451-6694. **Circ:** 12,500 (ctrl). ***Continues*** *Citrus Magazine, 1065-9005.*
Desc: Information of interest to commercial citrus and vegetable growers, packers and processors in Florida.
Ind/Abst BioBusiness (1986-); Energy Inf. Abstr.; Food Sci. Technol. Abstr.; Hortic. Abstr.; Nematol. Abstr.; Life Sci. Collect. (1985-); Plant Breed. Abstr.; Postharvest News Inf.; Rev. Agric. Entomol.

LC HD **ISSN** 0749-4475
DD 338 US
CITRUS DIGEST. See Industry and Production.

LC HD9259.C54 U5 **ISSN** 0883-2870
DD 338.1/7435/0973021 US
CITRUS FRUITS (1976). (CITRUS FRUITS.). [Citrus fruits]. **Added/Corp** United States. Crop Reporting Board. United States. Agricultural Statistics Board. (1976)-Crop Year. Government Publication. English. One time a year (Sept.). $10.00. US Department of Agriculture / National Agricultural Statistics Service (NASS), Room 5829 South Building, Washington DC 20250. **Tel** (202)720-4020, FAX (314)875-5231. ***Continues*** *Citrus Fruits by States ..., 0732-3476.*

LC S **ISSN** 0045-7256
DD 630 UK
Pr Rev.
COCOA GROWERS' BULLETIN.
Added/Corp Cadbury Brothers, Ltd., Bournville, Eng. No. 1 (Aug. 1963)-. Bulletin. English. Two times a year. Free on request. Cadbury Ltd., Bourneville, Birmingham B30 2LU United Kingdom. **Tel** 011 44 121 4582000.
Ind/Abst Biocont. News Inf.; Plant Breed. Abstr.; Plant Genet. Resour. Abstr.; Rev. Plant Pathol.; World Agric. Econ. Rural Sociol. Abstr.

LC S **ISSN** 0255-4119
DD 630 CE
COCONUT BULLETIN (LUNUWILA, SRI LANKA). (COCONUT BULLETIN.). Vol. 1, No. 1 (June 1984)-. Bulletin. English. Two times a year. Rs10.00 Sri Lanka; $2.50 US. Coconut Research Institute, Publications Officer, Lunuwila Sri Lanka. **Tel** 011 94 030 3795. **ED** R Mahindapala, P A Henry Nimal. **Ad Acc. Circ:** 2,000. ***Continues*** *Ceylon Coconut Planters' Review.*
Desc: Extension publication for coconut growers in Sri Lanka.
Ind/Abst Agrofor. Abstr.; Plant Breed. Abstr.

LC S **ISSN** 0115-1541
DD 630 PH
COCONUT FARMERS BULLETIN, THE. Bulletin. English. Irregular. Philippine Coconut Authority, PO Box 295, Davao Philippines.
Ind/Abst Philip. Sci. Technol. Abstr.

LC Z5071
DD 016.63 PH
COCONUT STATISTICS. See Agriculture-Abstracting, Bibliographies and Statistics.

LC S **ISSN** 0116-2837
DD 630 PH
COCONUTS TODAY. [Coconuts today]. **Added/Corp** United Coconut Association of the Philippines. (1983)-. Periodical. English. Two times a year. $40.00. United Coconut Association of the Philippines, 4th Floor, G&A 2303 Pasong Tamo Ex, Manila Philippines. **Tel** 011 63 2 8167495.

LC S **ISSN** 0255-4100
DD 630 CE
CODEN COCSEK
COCOS : JOURNAL OF THE COCONUT RESEARCH INSTITUTE OF SRI LANKA.
Added/Corp Coconut Research Institute of Sri Lanka. Vol. 1 (1983)-. Periodical. English. Two times a year. $5.00. Coconut Research Institute, Publications Officer, Lunuwila Sri Lanka. **Tel** 011 94 030 3795. **ED** R. Mahindapala. **Bk Rev. Circ:** 800. ***Continues*** *Ceylon Coconut Quarterly, 0009-5844.*
Ind/Abst Agrofor. Abstr. (19??-19??); Biocont. News Inf.; Hortic. Abstr.; Irr. Drain. Abstr.; Nematol. Abstr.; Plant Breed. Abstr.; Rev. Agric. Entomol.; SEA Abstr.; Soils Fert.; Soyabean Abstr.

LC HD9199.I4 A32 **ISSN** 0536-7093
DD 331.7 II
COFFEE STATISTICS. See Agriculture-Abstracting, Bibliographies and Statistics.

LC S590 **ISSN** 0227-0781
DD 631.5/84 CN
COGNITION (SCARBOROUGH). (COGNITION : THE NEWSLETTER OF THE CANADIAN ORGANIC GROWERS.). [Cognition]. **Added/Corp** Canadian Organic Growers. (1977)-. Newsletter. English. Four times a year. 19.20Can$. Canadian Organic Growers, Box 6408 Station J, Ottawa Ontario K2A 3A6 Canada. **Tel** (416)499-8418. **ED** Elizabeth Irving. **Bk Rev. Ad Acc. Circ:** 3,000 (ctrl). ***Continues*** *Newsletter (Organic Gardeners and Farmers Association).*
Desc: The newsletter of Canadian Organic Growers, a non-profit organization whose members are farmers, gardeners and consumers interested in safe food and a clean environment.

LC HB241 **ISSN** 0091-1267
DD 338 US
COLD STORAGE. [Cold storage]. **Added/Corp** United States. Crop Reporting Board. United States. Office of Marketing Services. United States. War Food Administration. United States. Agricultural Marketing Service. United States. Agricultural Statistics Board. United States. Office of Marketing Services. (Mar. 1945)-. Government Publication. English. Twelve times a year. $39.00. US Department of Agriculture, 14th Street and Independence Avenue SW, Washington DC 20250. **Tel** (202)720-5457. **(Subscription address:** Superintendent of Documents, US Government Printing Office, Washington DC 20402. **)** Documents available from Documents on Demand. ***Continues*** *Cold Storage Space and Holdings Report.*
Desc: Contain short articles on current production and market trends of agricultural commodities including tables and statistics on slaughtered poultry, areas planted and harvested, and stored supplies.
Ind/Abst Am. Stat. Index.

LC S **ISSN** 0279-389X
DD 630 US
COLORADO POTATO GROWER. Vol. 1-2, (June 1923)-. Periodical. English. Twelve times a year. Colorado Potato Growers Association, 2401 Larimer Street/Colorado Building, Denver CO 80205.

LC HB241 **ISSN** 1078-5612
DD 338 US
COLORADO WHEAT GROWER. [Colo. wheat grow.]. **Added/Corp** Colorado Association of Wheat Growers. (19??)-. Periodical. English. Fifty times a year. $20.00. National Association of Wheat Growers, 415 Second Street Northeast, Suite 300, Washington DC 20002. **Tel** (202)547-7800, FAX (303)740-4244. **Ad Acc. Circ:** 1,200. ***Continues*** *Report from Washington (Englewood, Colo.), 0882-8725.*

LC S **ISSN** 0538-9143
DD 631 US
COMBINED PROCEEDINGS / INTERNATIONAL PLANT PROPAGATORS' SOCIETY. See Gardening and Horticulture.

LC TP963
DD 631.8058 US
COMMERCIAL FERTILIZER AND PLANT FOOD INDUSTRY. (YEARBOOK.). English. One time a year. W W Brown Publishing Company, 75 3rd Avenue NW, Atlanta GA 30308.

LC S633.2 .A215
DD 631 US
COMMERCIAL FERTILIZERS. Added/Corp National Fertilizer Development Center (U.S.). Economics and Marketing Staff. National Fertilizer Development Center (U.S.). Economics and Marketing. National Fertilizer & Environmental Research Center (U.S.). **VFOAT** Commercial Fertilizer Consumption. (198?)-. Government Publication. English. One time a year. US Department of Agriculture / National Agricultural Statistics Service (NASS), Room 5829 South Building, Washington DC 20250. **Tel** (202)720-4020, FAX (314)875-5231.

Agriculture —Crop Production and Soil

Continues Commercial Fertilizer. Consumption for Year Ended June 30 ..., 0884-2000.
Ind/Abst Predicasts.

LC S633.2 .A215   **ISSN** 0884-2000
DD 631   US
    TITLE CHANGE
COMMERCIAL FERTILIZERS. CONSUMPTION.
(COMMERCIAL FERTILIZERS. CONSUMPTION FOR YEAR ENDED JUNE 30 ...). [Commer. fertil., Consum.]. **Added/Corp** United States. Crop Reporting Board. (June 30, 1977)-(198?). Government Publication. English. US Department of Agriculture / National Agricultural Statistics Service (NASS), Room 5829 South Building, Washington DC 20250. **Tel** (202)720-4020, FAX (314)875-5231. *Continues* Commercial Fertilizers. Final Consumption for the Year Ended June 30 ... . *Continued by* Commercial Fertilizers (Muscle Shoals, Ala.).
Ind/Abst Predicasts (?-?).

LC S
DD 630   UK
COMMERCIAL GROWER WEEKLY.
(1981)-. Periodical. English. One time a week. £25.00. Benn Electronics Publishing Ltd, Sovereign Way, Tonbridge, Kent TN9 1RW United Kingdom. **Tel** 011 44 1732 364422, telex 27844.

LC SB215
DD 633.6   UK
COMMITTEE PAPER. Added/Corp
Sugar Beet Research and Education Committee (Great Britain). No. 1509 (1976)-. Monographic series. English.
Ind/Abst Field Crop Abstr.; Plant Breed. Abstr.; Rev. Plant Pathol.; Sug. Indus. Abstr.; Weed Abstr.; Wheat Barley Trit. Abstr.

LC S590 .C54   **ISSN** 0010-3624
DD 631.4/05   US
    CCC
    CODEN CSOSA2
Pr Rev.
COMMUNICATIONS IN SOIL SCIENCE AND PLANT ANALYSIS.
[Commun. soil sci. plant anal.]. **VFOAT** Soil Science and Plant Analysis. Vol. 1 (Jan. 1970)-. Periodical. English. Twenty times a year. $1225.00. Marcel Dekker Inc., 270 Madison Avenue, New York NY 10016. **Tel** (212)696-9000, (800)228-1160, FAX (212)685-4540, telex 421419. **(Subscription address:** Marcel Dekker Inc., PO Box 5017, Monticello NY 12701. **Tel** (800)228-1160.) **ED** J. Benton Jones and Harry A. Mills. **Bk Rev. Ad Acc.** ctrl circ. available on microfiche. Documents available from The Genuine Article, BIOSIS Document Express, CASDDS.
Desc: Provides a rapid means of publication on important developments in soil science and crop production, with particular reference to elemental content of soils and plants, and plant nutrition. Topics examined include soil chemistry, mineralogy, fertility and testing of soils, soil-crop nutrition, plant analysis, interpretation of soil tests and plant analysis, liming and fertilization of soils, and techniques for correcting deficiencies. Its international coverage explores soils of all climates, including sub-tropical and tropical.
Ind/Abst AgBiotech News Inf.; AGRICOLA [Full Cov.]; Anal. Abstr.; BioBusiness; Biol. Abstr.; Chem. Abstr.; Chem. Titles; Coal Abstr.; Cot. Trop. Fibr. Abstr. Bibliogr.; Crop Physiol. Abstr.; Curr. Aware. Biol. Sci., CABS; Curr. Cit.; Curr. Contents Agric. Biol. Environ. Sci.; Ecol. Abstr.; EMBASE; Energy Res. Abstr. (Dec. 1975-); Environ. Period. Bibliogr.; Field Crop Abstr.; For. Prod. Abstr.; For. Abstr.; Geogr. Abstr. Phys. Geogr.; Geol. Abstr.; GeoRef; Grass. Forage Abstr.; Hortic. Abstr.; INIS Atomindex [Micro.]; Int. Dev. Abstr. (?-?); Irr. Drain. Abstr.; Maize Abstr.; Nematol. Abstr.; Nutr. Abstr. Rev., Ser. B, Live Feeds and Feed.; Ornamental Hort. (1991-); Life Sci. Collect.; Plant Breed. Abstr.; Plant Grow. Reg. Abstr.; Postharvest News Inf.; Potato Abstr.; Res. Alert [Full Cov.]; Rev. Plant Pathol.; Rice Abstr.; Sci. Cit. Index; SCISEARCH; Seed Abstr.; Soils Fert.; Sorghum Mill. Abstr.; Soyabean Abstr.; Weed Abstr.; Wheat Barley Trit. Abstr.

LC S
DD 630   US
COMPACT FRUIT TREE. Added/Corp
International Dwarf Fruit Tree Associaton. Dwarf Fruit Tree Association. Dwarf Fruit Tree Association. News Letter. Dwarf Fruit Tree Association. Dwarf Notes. Vol. 1 (Oct. 1958)-. Periodical. English. One time a year. $50.00 comes with membership. International Dwarf Fruit Tree Association, 14 S Main Street, Middleburg PA 17842. **Tel** (717)837-1551.
Ind/Abst Agric. Eng. Abstr. (1991-); Hortic. Abstr.; Irr. Drain. Abstr.; Plant Breed. Abstr.; Plant Grow. Reg. Abstr.; Soils Fert.

LC S
DD 630   FR
COMPTE RENDU ANNUEL DES TRAVAUX.
(19??)-. French. One time a year. 318.32F France; 325.00F other. Institut Technique Vigne Vin, 21 rue Francois I, 75008 Paris France. **Tel** 011 33 1 47234200, FAX 011 33 1 47205465.

LC S
DD 630   FR
COMPTE RENDU ANNUEL DES TRAVAUX.
(19??)-. French. One time a year. 318.32F France; 325.00F other. Institut Technique Vigne Vin, 21 rue Francois I, 75008 Paris France. **Tel** 011 33 1 47234200, FAX 011 33 1 47205465.

LC SB218 .C65   **ISSN** 0373-305X
DD 633.6/3/05   FR
COMPTE RENDU DES TRAVAUX EFFECTUES EN ... .
VFOAT Compte Rendu des Travaux. (19??)-. Periodical. French. 45 rue de Naples, 75008 Paris France.

LC S   **ISSN** 0100-8617
DD 630   BL
COMUNICADO TECNICO - UEPAE DE DOURADOS.
[Circ. tec. - UEPAE Dourados]. **VFOAT** Comunicado Tecnico - Unidade de Execucao de Pesquisa de Ambito Estadual de Dourados. (1978)-. Monographic series. Portuguese. Irregular. Price varies per volume. MS Unidade de Execucao de Pesquisa de Ambito Estadual, Dourados Brazil.
Ind/Abst Field Crop Abstr.; Soyabean Abstr.; Wheat Barley Trit. Abstr.

LC S   **ISSN** 0100-8765
DD 630   BL
    UDC 633/636
COMUNICADO TECNICO - UNIDADE DE EXECUCAO DE PESQUISA DE AMBITO TERRITORIAL DE PORTO VELLIO.
[Comun. tec. - Unidade Exec. Pesqui. Ambito Territ. Porto Vellio]. (1978)-. Monographic series. Portuguese. Irregular. Price varies per volume. Unidade de Execucao de Pesquisa de Ambito Territorial, Porto Vellio Brazil.
Ind/Abst Nutr. Abstr. Rev., Ser. B, Live Feeds and Feed.; Rice Abstr.

LC S590   **ISSN** 1056-9707
DD 631   US
CONSERVATION IMPACT.
(CONSERVATION IMPACT : A NEWSLETTER FROM THE CONSERVATION TECHNOLOGY INFORMATION CENTER.). [Conserv. impact]. **Added/Corp** Conservation Technology Information Center. Vol. 5, No. 9 (Sept. 1987)-. Newsletter. English. Eleven times a year. Free to members of the Conservation Technology Information Center. Conservation Technology Information Center, 1220 Potter Drive, Room 170, West Lafayette IN 47906. **Tel** (219)494-9555. *Continues* Conservation Tillage News, 8755-5719.

LC TP680   **ISSN** 0215-1162
DD 665.355   INT
CORD. COCONUT RESEARCH & DEVELOPMENT.
[CORD, Coconut res. dev.]. **VFOAT** Coconut Research & Development; CORD. Coconut Research and Development. (1985)-. Periodical. English. Two times a year (Jan. and July). $25.00. Asian & Pacific Coconut Community, PO Box 1343, Jakarta 10013 Indonesia. **Tel** 011 62 21 5250073, FAX 011 62 21 5205160, telex 62863. **ED** J. C. Suharto (editor's address: APCC, 3rd Floor, Wisma Bakrie, JL. H. R. Rasuna Said, PO Box 1343, Jakarta 10013 Indonesia). Index available.
Desc: Devoted exclusively to original articles on Coconut Research and Development while encouraging those involved in research and development to disseminate their findings also assists policy makers and planners to be aware of the latest development.

LC S   **ISSN** 0279-4217
DD 630   US
CORN GROWER.
(CORN GROWER : THE OFFICIAL PUBLICATION OF THE NATIONAL CORN GROWERS ASSOCIATION.). [Corn grower]. **Added/Corp** National Corn Growers Association. Vol. 1, No. 1 (April 1981)-. Periodical. English. Twelve times a year. Free to members of the National Corn Growers Association. National Corn Growers Association, 1000 Executive Parkway, Suite 105, St Louis MO 63141. **Tel** (314)275-9915. *Formed by the union of* Corn Talk *and* Farm Energy, 0274-8371.

LC S
DD 630   US
CORN ROW WIDTH, CORN PLANT POPULATION AND SOYBEAN ROW SPACING AND VARIETIES.
English. One time a year. The Service, Full Depository, 707 Savings and Loan Building, Des Moines IA 50309.
Desc: Counts and measurements from random plots in fields in selected states during the forecast period.

LC S
DD 630   IT
CORRIERE VINICOLO, IL. Added/Corp
Unione Italiana Vini. (19??)-. Periodical. Italian. One time a week. L163500. Unione Italiana Vinicolo, Via S Vittore Al Teatro 8, 20123 Milan Italy. **Tel** 011 39 2 801595.

LC HD1775.L8 L7 HD9066.U46 U46L6
DD 338.1/09763 S   US
COSTS AND RETURNS FOR RICE, SOUTHWEST LOUISIANA RICE AREA.
English. One time a year.

LC HD9220.U53 F63   **ISSN** 0149-0613
DD 338.1/3   US
COSTS AND RETURNS FROM VEGETABLE CROPS IN FLORIDA, WITH COMPARISONS. Main/Corp
University of Florida. Food and Resource Economics Dept. English. One time a year. Food and Resource Economics Department, Agricultural Experiment Station, Institute of Food and Agricultural Sciences, University of Florida, Gainesville FL 32611.

LC Z5071
DD 016.63   UK
COTTON AND TROPICAL FIBRES ABSTRACTS BIBLIOGRAPHY. See
Agriculture-Abstracting, Bibliographies and Statistics.

LC S
DD 630   US
COTTON CROP LETTER.
Periodical. English. Twelve times a year. *Continues* Southern Crop Letter.

LC S   **ISSN** 0746-8385
DD 630   US
COTTON FARMING.
[Cotton farm.]. Vol. 20, No. 1 (Jan. 1976)-. Periodical. English. Twelve times a year. $9.00. Little Publications, 6263 Popular Avenue, Suite 540, Memphis TN 38119. **Tel** (901)767-4020. *Continues in part* Cotton Farming and Supplemental Crops (Texas, Oklahoma Plains Edition).
Ind/Abst Text. Technol. Dig.

LC S   **ISSN** 0093-4313
DD 630   US
COTTON GINNINGS. A10.
(COTTON GINNINGS.). [Cotton ginning A10]. **Added/Corp** United States. Bureau of the Census. United States. Social and Economic Statistics Administration. United States. Agricultural Statistics Board. (19??)-. Thirteen times a year (published monthly with annual summary in May). $28.00. U.S. Department of Agriculture, ERS-NASS, 341 Victory Drive, Herndon VA 22070. **Tel** (800)999-6779, (703)834-0125. *Absorbed* Cotton Ginnings (A.20), 0093-4321; *Continues* Cotton Ginnings in the United States, 0093-433X.

LC SB249 .U545a   **ISSN** 0093-433X
DD 633/.51/6   US
    TITLE CHANGE
COTTON GINNINGS IN THE UNITED STATES.
[Cotton ginnings U. S.]. **Added/Corp** United States. Bureau of the Census. (1971)-(19??). Government Publication. English. US Department of Commerce / Bureau of the Census, Data User Services Division, Customer Services, Washington DC 20233-0800. **Tel** (301)763-4100. Documents available from Documents on Demand. *Continues* Cotton Production in the United States (Washington, D.C. : 1915), 0070-0681. *Continued by* Cotton Ginnings, 0093-4313.
Desc: Presents final figures for cotton ginnings and production in the US and includes comparative summary data on crops, by state, for a 10-year period.
Ind/Abst Am. Stat. Index.

LC HB241   **ISSN** 0194-9772
DD 338   US
    CCC
COTTON GROWER.
[Cotton grow.]. Vol. 15, No. 7 (July 1979)-. Trade Publication. English. Nine times a year. $24.00. Meister Publishing Company, 37733 Euclid Avenue, Willoughby OH 44094-5992. **Tel** (216)942-2000, (800)572-7740, FAX (216)942-0662. *Continues* American Cotton Grower, 0044-765X.
Desc: Serves the grower, ginner, and marketing side of the industry.
Ind/Abst Text. Technol. Dig.

LC S
DD 630   US
COTTON: MONTHLY REVIEW OF THE WORLD SITUATION. See
Fabrics and Textile Industries.

LC HD9093.U4 A32   **ISSN** 0010-9827
DD 338.1/3   US
COTTON PRICE STATISTICS. See
Agriculture-Abstracting, Bibliographies and Statistics.

LC TS1565.U6 C65   **ISSN** 0098-7026
DD 677/.21/30973   US
COTTON QUALITY CROP. See
Agriculture-Abstracting, Bibliographies and Statistics.

LC HD9093.U4 C68   **ISSN** 0565-2014
DD 338.4/7/6643630973   US
COTTONSEED QUALITY.
(COTTONSEED QUALITY CROP OF ...). **Added/Corp** United States. Agricultural Marketing Service. Cotton Division. United States. Consumer and Marketing Service. Cotton Divsion. (19??)-. English. One time a year. $6.00. US Department

of Agriculture / Tennessee, Agricultural Marketing Service, 4841 Summer Avenue, Memphis TN 38122. **Tel** (901)766-2934, 766-2931.
Desc: A report summarizing the quality of cottonseed, by quality factors, state and U.S.

LC S
DD 630 US

COTTONSEED REVIEW. **Added/Corp** United States. Agricultural Marketing Service. Cotton Division. Market News Branch. United States. Agricultural Marketing Service. Cotton Division. (19??)-. Periodical. English. One time a week. $16.00. US Department of Agriculture / Tennessee, Agricultural Marketing Service, 4841 Summer Avenue, Memphis TN 38122. **Tel** (901)766-2934, 766-2931.
Desc: A report during the harvest season showing prices, grade, and other quality factors by state.

LC SB249 .U46 **ISSN** 0498-1987
DD 633/.51/70973 US

COTTONSEED VARIETIES PLANTED. (COTTONSEED VARIETIES PLANTED CROP OF ...). **Added/Corp** United States. Agricultural Marketing Service. Cotton Division. United States. Production and Marketing Administration. Cotton Branch. United States. Consumer and Marketing Service. Cotton Division. (19??)-. English. One time a year. $6.00. US Department of Agriculture / Tennessee, Agricultural Marketing Service, 4841 Summer Avenue, Memphis TN 38122. **Tel** (901)766-2934, 766-2931. available on microfiche.
Desc: A report showing the percentage of cotton planted, by variety, on a county, state and national basis.

LC S590 **ISSN** 0885-8152
DD 631 US

COUNTRYMARK. [Countrymark]. **VFOAT** Countrymark. Vol. 1, No. 2 (Oct./Nov. 1985)-. Periodical. English. Six times a year. $3.00. Countrymark Inc., 35 East Chestnut Street, PO Box 479, Columbus OH 43216. **Tel** (614)221-1188. ***Continues*** *Countryside (Columbus, Ohio), 0885-5714.*

LC HD1401 **ISSN** 0011-0787
DD 338.1 US

CRANBERRIES (PORTLAND). (CRANBERRIES; THE NATIONAL CRANBERRY MAGAZINE.). [Cranberries]. (1936)-. Trade Publication. English. Eleven times a year (Monthly with Dec./Jan. combined). $20.00. Cranberries, PO Box 858, South Carver MA 02366. **Tel** (508)866-5055, FAX (508)866-2970. **ED** Carolyn Gilmore. Index available. cum. index. **Bk Rev. Ad Acc. Circ:** 800 (ctrl). available on an online database from DIALOG; available with charts; available with illustrations.
Desc: Cranberry industry news, including research, chemicals, grower profiles, economic data, growing information, weather, products, trends and marketing.

LC S **ISSN** 0196-884X
DD 630 US

CRANBERRIES (WASHINGTON). (CRANBERRIES.). [Cranberries]. **Added/Corp** United States. Crop Reporting Board. United States. Agricultural Statistics Board. (19??)-. Statistical Publication. English. One time a year (Aug.). $10.00. US Department of Agriculture / National Agricultural Statistics Service (NASS), Room 5829 South Building, Washington DC 20250. **Tel** (202)720-4020, FAX (314)875-5231. **(Subscription address:** ERS NASS, 341 Victory Drive, Herndon VA 22070. **Tel** (800)999-6779, (703)834-0125.**)**
Desc: Information of production, utilization, price, and value for the 1982-1984 of crops, by the states.

LC S451.P4 P4 S107 **ISSN** 0743-6572
DD 338.1/09748 US

CROP AND LIVESTOCK ANNUAL SUMMARY. [Crop livest. annu. summ.]. **Added/Corp** Pennsylvania Crop Reporting Service. United States. Dept. of Agriculture. Statistical Reporting Service. Pennsylvania. Dept. of Agriculture. (1970)-. English. One time a year. $5.00. US Department of Agriculture / National Agricultural Statistics Service (NASS), Room 5829 South Building, Washington DC 20250. **Tel** (202)720-4020, FAX (314)875-5231. ***Continues*** *Pennsylvania Crops and Livestock Annual Summary.*

LC S **ISSN** 0701-7065
DD 630 CN

CROP AND WEATHER REPORT. [Crop weather rep.]. **Added/Corp** Saskatchewan. Saskatchewan Agriculture. Statistics Branch. Saskatchewan. Saskatchewan Agriculture. Statistics Section. Saskatchewan. Saskatchewan Agriculture and Food. Statistics Section. (Apr. 1975)-. Periodical. English. Irregular. Free on request. Saskatchewan Agriculture Statistics Branch, 3085 Albert Street, Regina Saskatchewan S4S 0B1 Canada. **Tel** (306)787-5167. ***Continues*** *Crop Report, 0581-8028.*

LC S
DD 630 US

CROP CONDITION REPORT : A REPORT COMMENTING ON CROP CONDITIONS TRIBUTARY TO ELEVATORS IN MINNESOTA, NORTH DAKOTA, AND SOUTH DAKOTA, BASED PRIMARILY ON MANAGERS' AND SUPERINTENDENTS' REPORTS DATED ... . Periodical. English. One time a week.

LC S **ISSN** 0256-0933
DD 630 II

CROP IMPROVEMENT. [Crop improv.]. **Added/Corp** Crop Improvement Society of India. Vol. 1 (Dec. 1974)-. Periodical. English. Two times a year. $50.00. Crop Improvement Society of India, Ludhiana India.
Ind/Abst AGRICOLA; Agrofor. Abstr. (1991-); BioBusiness; Curr. Cit.; For. Abstr.; Genet. Abstr.; Irr. Drain. Abstr.; Maize Abstr.; Nematol. Abstr.; Life Sci. Collect.; Plant Breed. Abstr.; Plant Grow. Reg. Abstr.; Rice Abstr.; Seed Abstr.; Soils Fert.; Sorghum Mill. Abstr.; Soyabean Abstr.; Wheat Barley Trit. Abstr.

LC Z6662 **ISSN** 0306-7556
DD 016.61 UK

CROP PHYSIOLOGY ABSTRACTS. **See** Agriculture-Abstracting, Bibliographies and Statistics.

LC SB183
DD 633 US

CROP PRODUCTION / IOWA CROP AND LIVESTOCK REPORTING SERVICE. **VFOAT** Crop Production: Crop Report; Crops: Crop Production. Oct. 1, 1973-. Periodical. English. Irregular. ***Continues*** *Crop Report / Iowa.*
Desc: Estimated production of corn, wheat, soybeans, and other crops for Iowa and the United States; pasture conditions.

LC SB183 **ISSN** 1100-1186
DD 633 SW
CODEN CRSCE5

CROP PRODUCTION SCIENCE. [Crop prod. sci.]. **Added/Corp** Sveriges Lantbruksuniversitet. Institutionen for Vaxtodlingslara. (1988)-. Monographic series. English. Swedish University of Agricultural Sciences / Crop Production, Dept of Crop Production Science, PO Box 7043, S-750 07 Uppsala Sweden. Documents available from BIOSIS Document Express. ***Continues in part*** *Rapport (Sveriges Lantbruksuniversitet. Institutionen for Vaxtodlingslara), 0348-1034.*
Ind/Abst Biol. Abstr. (1988-); Field Crop Abstr.; Plant Breed. Abstr.; Potato Abstr.

LC SB192.U5 U54A
DD 338.1/731/0973 US

CROP PRODUCTION. SMALL GRAINS, ... ANNUAL SUMMARY AND .. CROP WINTER WHEAT AND RYE SEEDINGS. **VFOAT** Small Grains, ... Annual Summary and .. Crop Winter Wheat and Rye Seedings. Government Publication. English. One time a year. US Department of Agriculture, 14th Street and Independence Avenue SW, Washington DC 20250. **Tel** (202)720-5457. ***Continues*** *Small Grains.*

LC SB83 .C73 **ISSN** 0363-8561
DD 338.1/0973/021 US

CROP PRODUCTION (WASHINGTON, D.C.). (CROP PRODUCTION.). **Main/Corp** United States. Crop Reporting Board. **Added/Corp** United States. Crop Reporting Board. United States. Bureau of Agricultural Economics. United States. Agricultural Marketing Service. United States. Agricultural Statistics Board. (1941)-. Government Publication. English. Nineteen times a year (monthly and 5 annual reports). $59.00. Superintendent of Documents, US Government Printing Office, Washington DC 20402. **Tel** (202)275-3328, FAX (202)786-2377. available on an online database from DIALOG. Documents available from Documents on Demand. ***Absorbed*** *Farm Numbers (Washington, D.C.).*
Ind/Abst Am. Stat. Index.

LC S **ISSN** 1033-3967
DD 630 AT
CEASED

CROP PROTECTION BULLETIN. (1989)-(Jan./Feb. 1993). Bulletin. English. Institute of Plant Sciences, Swan Street, Burnley 3121 Australia. **Tel** 011 61 3 8101511, FAX 011 61 3 8195653. ***Continues*** *Crop Information Service Bulletin, 0815-922X.*

LC S
DD 630 UK

CROP PROTECTION DIRECTORY (UNITED KINGDOM ED.). (THE CROP PROTECTION DIRECTORY.). [Crop prot. dir.U.K. ed.]. (1988)-. Directory. English. Every 2 years. $220.00. Elaine Warrell Associates, 105 Lee Road, London SE3 9DZ United Kingdom. **Tel** 011 44 181 8526158, FAX 011 44 181 2970789. **ED** Elaine Warrell and Anne Kirkwood. Index available. **Circ:** 500.
Desc: Covers who does what for the many areas of crop protection which impinge on the UK's arable and horticultural crops, forestry and amenity areas. It also has a special section on organisations and individuals involved in environmental issues and crop protection.

LC SB761 **ISSN** 0261-2194
DD 635.97 UK
CCC
CODEN CRPTD6
Pr Rev.

CROP PROTECTION (GUILDFORD, SURREY). (CROP PROTECTION.). [Crop prot.]. Vol. 1, No. 1 (March 1982)-. Academic Scholarly Publication. English. Eight times a year. $621.00. Butterworth Heinemann Publishers, Linacre House Jordan Hill, Oxford OX2 8DP United Kingdom. **Tel** 011 44 1865 310366, FAX 011 44 1865 310898. **(Subscription address:** Elsevier Science Ltd. / Oxford Fulfillment Centre, PO Box 800, Kidlington OX5 1DX United Kingdom. **Tel** 011 44 865 843355.**) ED** G. E. Russell. Index available. **Bk Rev. Ad Acc.** available on microfilm and microfiche from University Microfilms International (UMI); available on an online database from Elsevier Electronic Subscriptions (EES). Documents available from The Genuine Article, BIOSIS Document Express, CASDDS, Documents on Demand.
Desc: Provides a vehicle for the exchange of information between the developers and the users of the whole spectrum of crop protection measures and brings into focus this diverse subject area.
Ind/Abst AgBiotech News Inf.; AGRICOLA [Full Cov.]; Agric. Eng. Abstr. (1991-); Agrofor. Abstr. (1991-); Biocont. News Inf. (19??-19??); Biodeter. Abstr. (19??-19??); Biol. Abstr. (1985-); Chem. Abstr.; Cot. Trop. Fibr. Abstr. Bibliogr.; Curr. Aware. Biol. Sci., CABS; Curr. Cit.; Curr. Contents Agric. Biol. Environ. Sci.; Ecol. Abstr.; EMBASE; Environ. Abstr.; Field Crop Abstr.; Food Sci. Technol. Abstr.; For. Abstr.; Geogr. Abstr. Phys. Geogr.; Geogr. Abstr. Human Geogr. (?-?); Grass. Forage Abstr.; Hortic. Abstr.; Int. Dev. Abstr.; Maize Abstr.; Nematol. Abstr.; Ornamental Hort. (19??-19??); PESTDOC; Plant Breed. Abstr.; Plant Genet. Resour. Abstr.; Plant Grow. Reg. Abstr.; Postharvest News Inf.; Potato Abstr.; Res. Alert [Full Cov.]; Rev. Agric. Entomol.; Rev. Plant Pathol.; Rice Abstr.; Sci. Cit. Index; SCISEARCH; Seed Abstr.; Soils Fert.; Sorghum Mill. Abstr.; Soyabean Abstr.; Weed Abstr.; Wheat Barley Trit. Abstr.; World Agric. Econ. Rural Sociol. Abstr.

LC SB761 **ISSN** 0260-485X
DD 635.97 UK

CROP PROTECTION IN NORTHERN BRITAIN. [Crop prot. North. Br.]. **Added/Corp** Great Britain. Dept. of Agriculture and Fisheries for Scotland. Scottish Colleges of Agriculture. Scottish Crop Research Institute. British Crop Protection Council. Association for Crop Protection in Northern Britain. (19??)-. English. Every 3 years.
Ind/Abst AGRICOLA [Full Cov.].

LC S
DD 630 UK

CROP PROTECTION MONTHLY. (19??)-. English. Twelve times a year. £595.00. British Sulphur Corporation Ltd, 31 Mount Pleasant, London WC1X 0AD United Kingdom. **Tel** 011 44 171 8375600, FAX 011 44 171 8370292, telex 918918 SULFEX G. **(Subscription address:** CRU International Ltd., 31 Mount Pleasant, London WC1X 0AD United Kingdom. **Tel** 011 44 171 8375600, FAX 011 44 171 8370292.**)**

LC SB599 **ISSN** 0225-5774
DD 632/.05 CN
CEASED

CROP PROTECTION NEWSLETTER. [Crop prot. newsl.]. **Added/Corp** Alberta Horticultural Research Center. Vol. 1 (Apr. 15, 1977)-(June 1993). Newsletter. English. Twelve times a year. Free on request. Alberta Special Crops and Horticulture Research Centre, Bag Service 200, Brooks Alberta T0J 0Y0 Canada. **Tel** (403)362-3391. **ED** D.A. Kaminski. Index available. **Circ:** 350 (ctrl).
Desc: Discusses plant diseases, insect pests and weeds in Southern Alberta and control recommendations for same. Lists new crop protection publication titles, meeting notices, etc.

LC SB950.A1 C76 **ISSN** 0733-2068
DD 632/.9 US

CROP PROTECTION RESEARCH. **See** Pest Control.

LC S
DD 630 CN
TITLE CHANGE

CROP REPORT / ALBERTA WHEAT POOL. **Added/Corp** Alberta Wheat Pool. (19??)-(19??). Periodical. English. Alberta Wheat Pool, Box 2700, 505 2nd Street Southwest, Calgary Alberta T2P 2P5 Canada. **Tel** (403)290-4648. **ED** D B McIntyre. **Bk Rev. Ad Acc. Circ:** 1,000 (ctrl). ***Merged into*** *Budget, 0843-2309.*
Desc: In-season report of crop conditions for Alberta and Northeast British Columbia. Approximately May - October.

LC S
DD 630 US
CROP REPORT OF IOWA. **VFOAT** Crop Production: Crop Report of Iowa; Crops: Crop Report of Iowa. (May 12, 1975)-. English. One time a year. ***Continues*** *Crop Report / Iowa.*
Desc: Winter wheat production forecasts for Iowa and the United States; pasture conditions, and hay stocks on farms.

LC SB188 **ISSN** 0843-6894
DD 633.1/097124 CN
CROP REPORT / SASKATCHEWAN WHEAT POOL. [Crop rep. - Sask. Wheat Pool]. **Added/Corp** Saskatchewan Wheat Pool. (May 23, 1975)-. Periodical. English. One time a week (during the growing season). 60.03Can$. Saskatchewan Wheat Pool, 2625 Victoria Avenue, Regina Saskatchewan S4T 7T9 Canada. **Tel** (306)569-4411, FAX (306)569-4885, telex 0712284. ***Continues*** *Farm Reporting Service. Crop and Weather Report., 0848-3302.*
Desc: Reports on weather conditions, crop development, pasture conditions, and more for the Saskatchewan area.

LC SB183 **ISSN** 0970-4884
DD 633 II
CODEN CROREU
CROP RESEARCH (HISAR). (CROP RESEARCH.). [Crop Res.]. **Added/Corp** Agricultural Research Information Centre (Hisar, India). Vol. 1 No. 1 (June 1988)-. Periodical. English. Two times a year. $100.00. Agricultural Research Information Centre, Managing Director, 49 Priti Nagar, Hisar-125001 India. **(Subscription address:** Prints India, 11 Darya Ganj, New Delhi 110002 India. **Tel** 011 91 11 3268645, FAX 011 91 11 3275542, telex 31-61087 PRIN-IN.) Documents available from BIOSIS Document Express.
Ind/Abst Biol. Abstr. (1991-); Crop Physiol. Abstr.; Field Crop Abstr.; Hortic. Abstr.; Ornamental Hort. (1991-); Plant Grow. Reg. Abstr.; Rev. Plant Pathol.; Seed Abstr.; Soils Fert.; Sorghum Mill. Abstr.; Soyabean Abstr.; Weed Abstr.; Wheat Barley Trit. Abstr.

LC S **ISSN** 0110-1978
DD 630 NZ
CODEN CPRSRV
CROP RESEARCH NEWS. (CROP RESEARCH NEWS - NEW ZEALAND. DEPT. OF SCIENTIFIC AND INDUSTRIAL RESEARCH. CROP RESEARCH DIVISION.). **Main/Corp** New Zealand. Dept. of Scientific and Industrial Research. Crop Research Division. Academic Scholarly Publication. English. Documents available from CASDDS.
Ind/Abst Chem. Abstr.

LC SB183 .C7 **ISSN** 0011-183X
DD 633.00 US
CCC
CODEN CRPSAY
Pr Rev.
CROP SCIENCE. [Crop sci.]. **Added/Corp** Crop Science Society of America. Vol. 1 (Jan./Feb. 1961)-. Periodical. English. Six times a year. $127.00. American Society of Agronomy, 677 South Segoe Road, Madison WI 53711. **Tel** (608)273-8080, FAX (608)273-2021. **ED** P. Steven Baenziger. Index available. cum. index. **Ad Acc. Circ:** 7,500. Documents available from The Genuine Article, BIOSIS Document Express, UMI Article Clearinghouse, CASDDS.
Desc: Reports on recent developments in crop breeding and genetics, crop physiology and biochemistry, ecology, cytology, crop and seed production, statistics, and weed control.
Ind/Abst AgBiotech News Inf.; AGRICOLA [Full Cov.]; Agric. Eng. Abstr. (1991-); BioBusiness; Biol. Agric. Index; Biol. Abstr.; Biol. Dig.; Biostatistica (19??-19??); Chem. Abstr.; Cot. Trop. Fibr. Abstr. Bibliogr.; Crop Physiol. Abstr.; Curr. Aware. Biol. Sci., CABS; Curr. Cit.; Curr. Contents Agric. Biol. Environ. Sci.; Energy Res. Abstr.; Expand. Acad. Index (1992-); Field Crop Abstr.; Food Sci. Technol. Abstr.; Genet. Abstr.; Grass. Forage Abstr.; Hortic. Abstr.; Index Vet.; INIS Atomindex [Micro.]; Irr. Drain. Abstr.; Maize Abstr.; Microbiol. Abstr. Sect. A; Microbiol. Abstr. Sect. C; Nematol. Abstr.; Newsp. Period. Abstr. (1989-); Nutr. Abstr. Rev., Ser. B, Live Feeds and Feed.; Nutr. Abstr. Rev., Ser. A, Hum. Exp.; Ornamental Hort. (19??-19??); Life Sci. Collect.; PESTDOC; Plant Breed. Abstr.; Plant Genet. Resour. Abstr.; Plant Grow. Reg. Abstr.; Potato Abstr.; Protozoolog. Abstr.; Ref. Upd. Deluxe Ed.; Res. Alert [Full Cov.]; Rev. Agric. Entomol.; Rev. Med. Vet. Mycology; Rev. Plant Pathol.; Rice Abstr.; Sci. Cit. Index; SCISEARCH; Seed Abstr.; Soils Fert.; Sorghum Mill. Abstr.; Soyabean Abstr.; Vitis Vitic. Enol. Abstr.; Weed Abstr.; Wheat Barley Trit. Abstr.

LC HD1751 .A5 HD9031
DD 338.1/0973 338.1/73/0973021 US
CROP VALUES, FINAL ESTIMATES BY STATES. **Added/Corp** United States. Crop Reporting Board. (1978-82)-. Government Publication. English. US Department of Agriculture / National Agricultural Statistics Service (NASS), Room 5829 South Building, Washington DC 20250. **Tel** (202)720-4020, FAX (314)875-5231. ***Continues*** *Field Crops, Production, Disposition, and Value by States.*

LC HD9001 .C76 **ISSN** 0884-2329
DD 338.1/3/0973021 US
CROP VALUES (WASHINGTON, D.C.). (CROP VALUES.). [Crop values]. Government Publication. English. One time a year. US Department of Agriculture / National Agricultural Statistics Service (NASS), Room 5829 South Building, Washington DC 20250. **Tel** (202)720-4020, FAX (314)875-5231. available on microfiche (Vols. for (1981/1983-) distributed to depository libraries).

LC SB87.A78 C75 **ISSN** 0519-5357
DD 338.1/09946 AT
CROPS AND PASTURES, TASMANIA. **Added/Corp** Australian Bureau of Statistics. (19??)-. Statistical Publication. English. One time a year. 2.10Aus$. Australian Bureau Statistics / Tasmanian Office, Commonwealth Government Centre, 188 Collins Street, Hobart GPO Box 66A, Hobart Tasmania 7001 Australia. **Tel** 011 61 2 205889.
Desc: Statistics covering area of agricultural establishments; area, production and yield per hectare for crops, vegetables, pastures, grasses, hay and seed; stocks of major grains and hay, etc.

LC SB183 **ISSN** 0279-9405
DD 633 US
CROPS (TOPEKA, KAN.). (CROPS.). **Added/Corp** Kansas. State Board of Agriculture. United States. Dept. of Agriculture. Kansas Crop & Livestock Reporting Service. (198?)-. Government Publication. English. Twelve times a year. $10.00. US Department of Agriculture / National Agricultural Statistics Service (NASS), Room 5829 South Building, Washington DC 20250. **Tel** (202)720-4020, FAX (314)875-5231. **ED** M.E. Johnson. **Circ:** 1,800. Documents available from Documents on Demand. ***Absorbed*** *Farm Numbers and Land in Farms.*
Desc: Acreage planted, acreage harvested, yield and production of Kansas crops; quality of wheat during growing season; wheat varieties; stocks on hand of major crops; farm income; farm land values.
Ind/Abst Environ. Abstr.

LC SB188 **ISSN** 0895-9978
DD 633 US
CCC
CSSA SPECIAL PUBLICATION - CROP SCIENCE SOCIETY OF AMERICA. (CSSA SPECIAL PUBLICATION.). [CSSA spec. publ. - Crop Sci. Soc. Am.]. **Added/Corp** Crop Science Society of America. **VFOAT** Special Publication. **VAT** Crop Science Society of America Special Publication. (1970)-. Monographic series. English. Irregular. Price varies per volume. American Society of Agronomy, 677 South Segoe Road, Madison WI 53711. **Tel** (608)273-8080, FAX (608)273-2021.
Ind/Abst BioBusiness; Soyabean Abstr.

LC S590 **ISSN** 0845-308X
DD 631.4/06/071 CN
CSSS NEWSLETTER. [CSSS newsl.]. **VAT** Canadian Society of Soil Science Newsletter. (July 1988)-. Newsletter. English. Canadian Society of Soil Science, 151 Slater Street, Suite 907 Ottawa, Ontario K1P 5H4 Canada. **Tel** (613)521-5444. ***Continues*** *Newsletter - Canadian Society of Soil Science, 0228-2178.*

LC S **ISSN** 0011-2720
DD 630 HU
CUKORIPAR. **Added/Corp** Mezogazdasagi es Elelmiszeripari Tudomanyos Egyesulet (Hungary). Cukoripari Szakosztaly. Magyar Elelmiszeripari Tudomanyos Egyesuelet. Cukoripari Szakosztaly. (1948)-. Periodical. Hungarian (summaries and/or abstracts in English, German and Russian). Four times a year. $21.00. **(Subscription address:** Kultura, PO Box 143, H-1300 Budapest 3 Hungary. **Tel** 011 36 1 2500194.) **ED** Albert Vigh. **Bk Rev. Circ:** 1,400. available on microfilm.
Ind/Abst Chem. Abstr.; Nutr. Abstr. Rev., Ser. B, Live Feeds and Feed.; Plant Genet. Resour. Abstr.; Sug. Indus. Abstr.

LC SB761 **ISSN** 0045-9216
DD 635.97 FR
CULTIVAR. No. 57 (Jan. 1974)-. Periodical. French. Twelve times a year. Documentation Agricole, 228 rue du Faubourg St. Martin, 75010 Paris France. **Tel** 011 33 1 40051818, 011 33 1 40380880. **Bk Rev. Ad Acc. Circ:** 66,000 (ctrl).
Desc: Contains articles, technical summaries, comparatives, tables, trial results, analysis and discussions about research projects.
Ind/Abst Agric. Eng. Abstr. (1991-); Anim. Breed. Abstr.; Dairy Sci. Abstr.; Field Crop Abstr.; Helminthol. Abstr. (1991-); Index Vet.; Maize Abstr.; Nutr. Abstr. Rev., Ser. B, Live Feeds and Feed.; PESTDOC; Plant Breed. Abstr.; Potato Abstr.; Rev. Agric. Entomol.; Rev. Med. Vet. Entomol.; Soils Fert.; Sug. Indus. Abstr.; Vet. Bull.; Weed Abstr.; Wheat Barley Trit. Abstr.; World Agric. Econ. Rural Sociol. Abstr.

LC SB111.A2 C8
DD 630/.913 CU
CULTIVOS TROPICALES : CT. **Added/Corp** Instituto de Ciencia Agricola (Cuba) Cuba. Ministerio de Educacion Superior. **VFOAT** CT; C.T.; Revista Cultivos Tropicales. Vol. 1, No. 1 (April 1979)-. Periodical. Spanish. Three times a year. $26.87 North and South America; $30.90 other. Instituto Nacional de Ciencias Agricolas, Gaveta Postal No. 1, San Jose de las Lajas, Havana 22700 Cuba. **Circ:** 400. available on CD-ROM and an online database.
Ind/Abst Agrofor. Abstr.; Crop Physiol. Abstr.; Field Crop Abstr.; For. Abstr.; Hortic. Abstr.; Irr. Drain. Abstr.; Maize Abstr.; Plant Breed. Abstr.; Plant Grow. Reg. Abstr.; Postharvest News Inf.; Potato Abstr.; Rev. Plant Pathol.; Rice Abstr.; Soils Fert.; Soyabean Abstr.; Sug. Indus. Abstr.; Weed Abstr.

LC S590 **ISSN** 0254-1092
DD 631.4 II
CODEN CUAGEG
CURRENT AGRICULTURE. [Curr. agric.]. **Added/Corp** Indian Society of Agricultural Research Scientists. Vol. 1 (Jan./June 1977)-. Academic Scholarly Publication. English. Four times a year. $70.00. Indian Society of Agricultural Research Scientists, Karnal India. **(Subscription address:** Prints India, 11 Darya Ganj, New Delhi 110002 India. **Tel** 011 91 11 3268645, FAX 011 91 11 3275542, telex 31-61087 PRIN-IN.) Documents available from CASDDS.
Ind/Abst AGRICOLA; Chem. Abstr.; Cot. Trop. Fibr. Abstr. Bibliogr.; Hortic. Abstr.; Irr. Drain. Abstr.; Plant Grow. Reg. Abstr.; Seed Abstr.

LC HD1775.O5 C8 **ISSN** 0030-1701
DD 338.1/09766 US
CURRENT FARM ECONOMICS (1984). (CURRENT FARM ECONOMICS.). [Curr. farm econ.]. **Added/Corp** Oklahoma Agricultural Experiment Station. Oklahoma State University. Dept. of Agricultural Economics and Extension Economics. (1984)-. Periodical. English. Four times a year. Free on request. Oklahoma State University / Agriculture, Department of Agricultural Economics, 313 AG Hall, Stillwater OK 74078. **Tel** (405)744-5398. available on microfilm and microfiche from University Microfilms International (UMI). ***Continues*** *Oklahoma Current Farm Economics, 0896-2626.*
Ind/Abst Postharvest News Inf.

LC S
DD 630 US
CURRENT INDUSTRIAL REPORTS. M22P, CONSUMPTION ON THE COTTON SYSTEM AND STOCKS [COMPUTER FILE]. (19??)-. Periodical. English. US Department of Commerce / Bureau of the Census, Data User Services Division, Customer Services, Washington DC 20233-0800. **Tel** (301)763-4100. **(Subscription address:** Superintendent of Documents, US Government Printing Office, Washington DC 20402.) ***Continues*** *Current Industrial Reports. M22P, Consumption on the Cotton System and Stocks.*
Desc: Presents data on consumption and stocks of cotton and manmade fiber staple, stocks of cotton held at public storage and at compresses, and stocks of cotton and manmade fiber staple held by consuming establishments by type of material.
Ind/Abst Am. Stat. Index.

LC SB621 **ISSN** 0924-1949
DD 581.2 NE
CODEN CPBAE2
Pr Rev.
CURRENT PLANT SCIENCE AND BIOTECHNOLOGY IN AGRICULTURE. [Curr. plant sci. biotechnol. agric.]. (1985)-. Monographic series. English. Price varies per volume. Martinus Nijhoff Publishers, Subsidiary of Kluwer Academic Publishers, Koraalrood 50, 2718 SC Zoetermeer Netherlands. **Tel** 011 31 79 684400.
Desc: Monographs and conference papers on state of the art research findings and techniques in plant science and biotechnolgy. Particular emphasis is placed on agricultural applications.
Ind/Abst GeoRef.

LC S **ISSN** 0011-4111
DD 630 US
CUSTOM APPLICATOR. (19??)-. Periodical. English. Nine times a year. Little Publications, 6263 Popular Avenue, Suite 540, Memphis TN 38119. **Tel** (901)767-4020.

LC HD9114.B7 S34
DD 338.17 BL
CUSTOS DE PRODUCAO E PERSPECTIVAS DA AGROINDUSTRIA DO ACUCAR E DO ALCOOL. **Main/Corp** Cooperativa Central dos Produtores de Acucar e Alcool do Estado de Sao Paulo. Divisoa Economica. (19??)-. Portuguese.

Agriculture —Crop Production and Soil

LC S
DD 630 US

DAILY SPOT COTTON QUOTATIONS.
Added/Corp United States. Agricultural Marketing Service. Cotton Division. United States. Agricultural Marketing Service. Cotton Division. Market News Branch. (197?)-. Periodical. English. Seven times a week. $123.00 US; $135.00 Canada; $177.00 other. US Department of Agriculture / Tennessee, Agricultural Marketing Service, 4841 Summer Avenue, Memphis TN 38122. **Tel** (901)766-2934, 766-2931. available via electronic mail. *Continues* Spot Cotton Quotations.
Desc: Released each trading day of the year. Includes price quotations in each designated spot cotton market, transactions, and daily closing and settlement prices for future contracts.

LC S ISSN 0273-8619
DD 630 US

DALLAS ORNAMENTAL CROPS MARKET NEWS.
[Dallas ornam. crops mark. news]. Vol. 10, No. 79 (Oct. 31, 1977)-. Periodical. English. Two times a week. Texas Department of Agriculture, 18th & Congress Street, PO Box 12847, Austin TX 78711. **Tel** (512)463-7435, FAX (512)463-7643. *Continues* Texas Ornamental Crops Market News, 0160-4864.

LC S ISSN 0252-3353
DD 630 IQ
CODEN DAPJD4

DATE PALM JOURNAL, THE. [Date palm j.].
Added/Corp FAO Regional Project for Palm & Dates Research Centre in the Near East & North Africa. **VFOAT** Nakhlat Al-Tamr. Vol. 1 (July 1981)-. Academic Scholarly Publication. English (Arabic and English). Two times a year. SC Res Council AGR Water R RCTR, PO Box 2416, Badghad Iraq. Documents available from BIOSIS Document Express, CASDDS.
Ind/Abst Abstr. Trop. Agric.; Biodeter. Abstr.; Biol. Abstr.; Chem. Abstr.; Food Sci. Technol. Abstr.; Nematol. Abstr.; Ornamental Hort.; Plant Breed. Abstr.; Plant Grow. Reg. Abstr.; Postharvest News Inf.; Rev. Agric. Entomol.

LC SB354 ISSN 0302-7074
DD 634 SA

DECIDUOUS FRUIT GROWER, THE.
[Decid. fruit grow.]. **Added/Corp** Deciduous Fruit Board (South Africa). **VFOAT** Die Sagtevrugteboer. Vol. 26, Pt. 3 (March 1976)-. Academic Scholarly Publication. English (Afrikaans). Twelve times a year. $35.78. Deciduous Fruit Board, Parc du Cap Mispel Road, PO Box 1801, Bellville 7530 South Africa. **Tel** 011 27 21 946-1040, FAX 011 27 21 946 1967. **ED** H. Wenhold. **Bk Rev**. **Ad Acc**. **Circ:** 5,000. *Formed by the union of* Delicious Fruit Grower *and* Sagtevrugteboer.
Desc: Scientific and technical reports on deciduous fruit growing and research. Also covers dried and canning, marketing, packaging and general information on cape fruit industry.
Ind/Abst AgBiotech News Inf.; AGRICOLA; Agrofor. Abstr. (19??-19??); Biocont. News Inf.; Biodeter. Abstr. (1991-); Crop Physiol. Abstr.; EMBASE; Hortic. Abstr.; Irr. Drain.; Nematol. Abstr.; Plant Breed. Abstr.; Plant Grow. Reg. Abstr.; Postharvest News Inf.; Rev. Plant Pathol.; Soils Fert.

LC SB183 US
DD 633
TITLE CHANGE

DEPARTMENTAL SERIES - DEPARTMENT OF AGRONOMY AND SOILS, AGRICULTURAL EXPERIMENT STATION, AUBURN UNIVERSITY.
Main/Corp Alabama. Agricultural Experiment Station. Dept. of Agronomy and Soils. **Added/Corp** Auburn University. Agronomy and Soils Dept. **VFOAT** Agronomy and Soils Departmental Series; Agronomy & Soils Departmental Series. No. 19 (Sept. 1974)-(19??). Monographic series. English. *Continued by* Agronomy and Soils Departmental Series.
Ind/Abst Soils Fert.

LC S ISSN 0378-519X
DD 630 NE
CODEN DCSCDC
Pr Rev.

DEVELOPMENTS IN CROP SCIENCE.
[Dev. crop sci.]. (1976)-. Monographic series. English. Irregular. Price varies per volume. Elsevier Science Publishers BV, PO Box 211, 1000 AE Amsterdam Netherlands. **Tel** 011 31 20 4853641, 011 31 20 4853642, FAX 011 31 20 4853598. Documents available from CASDDS.
Desc: Series on crop science with volumes covering topics such as plant physiology, breeding, and plant tissue culture.
Ind/Abst AGRICOLA [Full Cov.]; Chem. Abstr.

LC S590 ISSN 0167-840X
DD 631.4 NE
CODEN DVPSD8

DEVELOPMENTS IN PLANT AND SOIL SCIENCES.
[Dev. plant soil sci.]. Vol. 1 (1981)-. Monographic series. English. Martinus Nijhoff Publishers, Subsidiary of Kluwer Academic Publishers, Koraalrood 50, 2718 SC Zoetermeer Netherlands. **Tel** 011 31 79 684400. **(Subscription address:** Kluwer Academic Publishers / US Subscriptions, PO Box 253, Accord Station, Hingham MA 02018. **Tel** (617)871-6600.)
Ind/Abst Chem. Abstr.; Curr. Cit.

LC S590 ISSN 0166-0918
DD 631.4 NE
CODEN DSSCDM
Pr Rev.

DEVELOPMENTS IN SOIL SCIENCE. [Dev. soil sci.].
(1972)-. Monographic series. English. Irregular. Price varies per volume. Elsevier Science Publishers BV, PO Box 211, 1000 AE Amsterdam Netherlands. **Tel** 011 31 20 4853641, 011 31 20 4853642, FAX 011 31 20 4853598. **(Subscription address:** Elsevier Science Inc. / New York Books, 655 Avenue of the Americas, New York NY 10010. **Tel** (212)633-3650.) Documents available from BIOSIS Document Express, CASDDS.
Ind/Abst Biol. Abstr.; Chem. Abstr. (1972-1983); Curr. Cit.; For. Abstr.; GeoRef; Life Sci. Collect.; Pollut. Abstr. Indexes; Rice Abstr.; Soils Fert.

LC S ISSN 0364-2658
DD 630 US

DIGEST FOR REPORTERS. Main/Corp United
States. Crop Reporting Board. (19??)-. English. Twelve times a year. U.S. Department of Agriculture, ERS-NASS, 341 Victory Drive, Herndon VA 22070. **Tel** (800)999-6779, (703)834-0125.

LC SB307.C3 D57
DD 633/.83 II

DIRECTORY OF CARDAMOM PLANTERS.
1974-. Directory. English. Rs50.00. Cardamon Board, Chittoor Road, Ermakulam 682018 India.

LC S590 ISSN 0725-8526
DD 631.4 AT

DIVISION OF SOILS DIVISIONAL REPORT.
(DIVISIONAL REPORT / CSIRO, DIVISION OF SOILS.). [Div. Soils div. rep.]. **Added/Corp** Commonwealth Scientific and Industrial Research Organization (Australia). Division of Soils. No. 59 (1982)-. Monographic series. English. Price varies per volume. CSIRO Publications, PO Box 89, 314 Albert Street, East Melborne Victoria 3002 Australia. **Tel** 011 61 3 4187333, 4187217, FAX 011 61 3 4190459, telex AA 30236. *Continues* Division of Soils Divisional Report, 0725-8526.
Ind/Abst Geogr. Abstr. Phys. Geogr.; GeoRef.

LC S ISSN 0101-5494
DD 630 BL

DOCUMENTOS / EMPRESA BRASILEIRA DE PESQUISA AGROPECUARIA, VINCULADA AO MINISTERIO DA AGRICULTURA, CENTRO NACIONAL DE PESQUISA DE SOJA.
Added/Corp Centro Nacional de Pesquisa da Soja (Brazil). (198?)-. Monographic series. Portuguese. Embrapa, Dept. Dif. Tecnologiaogi, Caixa Postal 040315, 07770 901 Brasilia DF Brazil. **Tel** 011 55 61 2724241.
Ind/Abst Rev. Plant Pathol.; Seed Abstr.; Soyabean Abstr.

LC S
DD 630 GW

DUNGEMITTELVERSORGUNG. Main/Corp
Germany (Federal Republic). Statistisches Bundesamt. (Jan. 1962)-. Periodical. German. Twelve times a year. DM48.00. Metzler Poeschel Verlag Veroeffen, Statist Bundesamt Kernerstr 43, D-70182 Stuttgart Germany. **Tel** 011 49 7071 935350. **(Subscription address:** Metzler Poeschel H Leins GmbH, Postfach 1152, D 72125 Kusterdingen Germany. **Tel** 011 49 7071 935350.)

LC S ISSN 0951-1547
DD 630 UK

EDIBLE NUT MARKET REPORT. [Edible nut
mark. rep.]. (195?)-. Periodical. English. Two times a year. $200.00. Man-Producten Rotterdam BV, PO Box 253, 3000 AG Rotterdam Netherlands. **Tel** 011 31 10 4177377, FAX 011 31 10 4147550, telex 21171. **ED** Jan Arie Kampstee and Guus Debouille.
Desc: News and information on various kinds of nuts, such as groundnuts, cashews, almonds, brazils, hazelnuts and many more.

LC S590 .J63 ISSN 0302-6701
DD 631.4/05 UA
CODEN EJSSAF

EGYPTIAN JOURNAL OF SOIL SCIENCE.
[Egypt. j. soil sci.]. **Added/Corp** Jamiyah al-Misriyah li-Ulum al-Aradi. **VFOAT** Majallah Al-Misriyah Li-Ulum Al-Aradi. Vol. 12 (1972)-. English (summaries and/or abstracts in Arabic). Four times a year. $107.00. National Information & Documentation Center, A1-Tahrir St Dokki Awqaf PO, Cairo Egypt. **Tel** 011 20 2 701696, telex 93069. Documents available from CASDDS. *Continues* United Arab Republic Journal of Soil Science.
Ind/Abst Chem. Abstr.; EMBASE; Field Crop Abstr.; GeoRef; Grass. Forage Abstr.; Hortic. Abstr.; Irr. Drain. Abstr.; Potato Abstr.; Rice Abstr.; Seed Abstr.; Soils Fert.; Wheat Barley Trit. Abstr.

LC SB320
DD 635 JA

●ENGEI SHINCHISHIKI. YASAI GO.
Added/Corp Takki Shubyo Kaobushiki Kaisha. (1993)-. Japanese. Twelve times a year. Takii Shubyo K.K. Shuppanbu, (Takii & Co. Ltd.), 180 Inokuma Higashi Iru, Umekoki Shimogyoku, Kyotoshi Kyotofu 600-91 Japan. *Continues* Engei Shinchishiki. Yasai Saibai no Saishin Johoshi.

LC SB192.F7 E58
DD 338.1/7/31094435 FR

ENQUETE PAR SONDAGE SUR LES PRODUCTIONS DE CEREALES DANS L'OISE.
(1962)-. French. Direction Dept l'Agriculture de l'Oise, 29 boulevard Amyot d'Inville, Beauvars 60021 France.

LC TA760 .E76 ISSN 1073-7227
DD 631.4/5/05 US

●EROSION CONTROL (SANTA BARBARA, CALIF.).
(EROSION CONTROL : THE OFFICIAL JOURNAL OF THE INTERNATIONAL EROSION CONTROL ASSOCIATION.). [Eros. control]. **Added/Corp** International Erosion Control Association. Vol. 1, No. 1 (Mar./Apr. 1994)-. Periodical. English. Six times a year. $80.00. Forester Communications, 216 East Gutierrez Street, PO Box 3100, Santa Barbara CA 93101. **Tel** (805)681-1300. **ED** John Trotti. **Ad Acc**. **Circ:** 17,300 (ctrl).

LC S622 .E75
DD 631.45 YU

EROZIJA. **Added/Corp** Belgrad. Institut Za
Sumarstvo i Drvnu Industriju. Odeljenje Za Eroziju i Melioracije. (19??)-. English. Kneza Viseslava 3, Belgrad Yugoslavia.

LC SB354 ISSN 0014-0309
DD 634 GW
CCC

ERWERBSOBSTBAU. Vol. 1 (April 1979)-.
Periodical. German. Eight times a year. $244.12. Blackwell Wissenschafts-Verlag, Kurfuerstendamm 57, D-10707 Berlin Germany. **Tel** 011 49 30 32790623, 011 49 30 32790624, FAX 011 49 30 327 90610. **ED** E.L. Loewel. Index available. cum. index. **Bk Rev**. **Ad Acc**. **Circ:** 2,500.
Desc: Reports about fruit crops, research and field findings.
Ind/Abst Agric. Eng. Abstr. (1991-); Crop Physiol. Abstr.; Hortic. Abstr.; Irr. Drain. Abstr.; Leis., Rec., Tour. Abstr.; Plant Breed. Abstr.; Plant Grow. Reg. Abstr.; Postharvest News Inf.; Rev. Agric. Entomol.; Rev. Plant Pathol.; Rural Dev. Abstr.; Soils Fert.; Weed Abstr.; World Agric. Econ. Rural Sociol. Abstr.

LC S631 ISSN 0252-354X
DD 631.8 TH

ESCAP AGRICULTURE DIVISION, ARSAP/FADINAP, REGIONAL INFORMATION SUPPORT SERVICE (RISS).
See Agriculture-Abstracting, Bibliographies and Statistics.

LC S
DD 630 FR
UDC 63(443.83)

EST AGRICOLE ET VITICOLE, L'. (1967)-.
Periodical. French. (German). One time a week. *Continues in part* Journal Agricole d'Alsace et de Lorraine; Bas-Rhin Agricole.

LC S
DD 630 US

ESTIMATED GRADE AND STAPLE OF UPLAND COTTON GINNED IN THE UNITED STATES. Main/Corp United States.
Agricultural Marketing Service. Cotton Division. Market News Section. (19??)-. Periodical. English. Agricultural Marketing Service, 4841 Summer Avenue, Memphis TN 38122.

LC HF
DD 380.1 UK

EUROFRUIT. Vol. 4, No. 8 (Aug.1976)-. Trade
Publication. Multiple languages (French, Italian, Spanish, English and German). Eleven times a year (monthly with Jan./Dec. combined). $152.30. Market Intelligence Ltd., 440/441 Market Towers, 4th Floor, London SW8 5NQ United Kingdom. **Tel** 011 44 171 4986711, FAX 011 44 171 4986472, telex 8950975. **ED** Chris White. Index available (Bound in Dec. issue). cum. index. **Bk Rev**. **Ad Acc**; **Adv Mgr:** Erica Nicholson. **Circ:** 7,000 (ctrl).
Desc: The international marketing magazine for producers, exporters, importers and buyers of fruit and vegetables as well as associated service industries.

LC S ISSN 1161-0301
DD 630 FR
CCC

EUROPEAN JOURNAL OF AGRONOMY.
(EUROPEAN JOURNAL OF AGRONOMY : THE JOURNAL OF THE EUROPEAN SOCIETY FOR AGRONOMY.). [Eur. J. agron.].
Added/Corp European Society for Agronomy. (1993)-.

Periodical. English. Four times a year. $306.21. Gauthier-Villars, 15 rue Gossin, 92543 Montrouge Cedex France. **Tel** 33 1 40 92 65 00, FAX 33 1 40 92 65 97. **(Subscription address:** Centrale des Revues, 11 rue Gossin, 92543 Montrouge Cedex France. **Tel** 011 33 1 46565266.**) ED** R.B. Austin.
Desc: The official journal of the European Society of Agronomy, publishes papers in English describing experimental and theoretical contributions to crop science in the following fields: crop physiology, crop production and management, agroclimatology and modelling, plant-soil relationships, crop quality and post harvest physiology, farming and cropping systems, and agroecosystems and the environment.
Ind/Abst Curr. Aware. Biol. Sci., CABS.

LC QH84.8 .R47 **ISSN** 1164-5563
DD 574.909/4/8 FR
CCC
CODEN EJSBE2
•EUROPEAN JOURNAL OF SOIL BIOLOGY. [Eur. J. soil biol.]. Vol. 29, No. 1 (1993)-. Academic Scholarly Publication. English (summaries and/or abstracts in French). Four times a year. $218.73. Gauthier-Villars, 15 rue Gossin, 92543 Montrouge Cedex France. **Tel** 33 1 40 92 65 00, FAX 33 1 40 92 65 97. **(Subscription address:** Centrale des Revues, 11 rue Gossin, 92543 Montrouge Cedex France. **Tel** 011 33 1 46565266.**) ED** P. Trehen (Rennes, France). Documents available from CASDDS. ***Continues** Revue d'Ecologie et de Biologie du Sol, 0035-1822.*
Desc: Concerned with microbial and faunal ecology and activity in soils. the different aspects of their populations and communities behavior are covered, as well as their populations and processes of natural and disturbed environments. The whole field of environmental biology is also covered, such as the effect and the fate of pollutants.
Ind/Abst Chem. Abstr.; Curr. Aware. Biol. Sci., CABS; Curr. Cit.; Sci. Cit. Index.

LC S590 .J6 **ISSN** 1351-0754
DD 631.4 UK
CCC
CODEN ESOSES
•EUROPEAN JOURNAL OF SOIL SCIENCE. Added/Corp British Society of Soil Science. Vol. 45, No. 1 (Mar. 1994)-. Academic Scholarly Publication. English. Four times a year. $225.00. Blackwell Scientific Publications Ltd, Marston Book Services, PO Box 88, Oxford OX2 ONE United Kingdom. **Tel** 011 44 1865 206206, FAX 011 44 1865 206219, telex 837 515 MARDIS G. ***Formed by the union of** Journal of Soil Science, 0022-4588; Pedologie, 0079-0419 **and** Science du Sol (Plaisir, France : 1984), 0767-2853.*
Ind/Abst Curr. Cit.

LC HD9030.1 .F68 **ISSN** 0896-0216
DD 382/.4131/05 US
CEASED
EXPORT MARKETS FOR U.S. GRAIN AND PRODUCTS. [Export mark. U. S. grain prod.]. **Added/Corp** United States. Foreign Agricultural Service. United States. World Agricultural Outlook Board. **VFOAT** Export Markets for US Grain and Products. **VAT** Export Markets for United States Grain and Products. (Jan. 1987)-(Dec. 1993). Government Publication. English. Department of Agriculture / Foreign Agricultural Service, 14th Street and Independence Avenue SW, Washington DC 20250-1000. **Tel** (202)720-3935, FAX (202)720-7729. **Circ:** 1,132. available on microfiche (distributed to depository libraries). ***Continues** Foreign Agriculture Circular. Grains. Export Markets for U.S. Grain and Feed Commodities.*
Desc: Contains U.S. grain export forecast, shipments and sales. Covers world trade and market development activities.

LC S
DD 630 GW
F.O. LICHT'S INTERNATIONAL SUGAR AND SWEETENER REPORT. Added/Corp F.O. Licht. **VFOAT** World Sugar Balances. (1990)-. Periodical. English. Irregular (3 issues per month). $1078.55. F.O. Licht KG, PO Box 1220, D-23909 Ratzeburg Germany. **Tel** 011 49 4541 83403. ***Continues** F.O. Licht's International Sugar Report.*

LC S **ISSN** 0255-6448
DD 630 SY
CODEN FFBNE4
FABIS. (FABIS NEWSLETTER.). [Fabis]. **Added/Corp** International Center for Agricultural Research in Dry Areas. Faba Bean Information Service. **VFOAT** Faba (Broad) Bean Information Service Newsletter. No. 1 (June 1979)-. Newsletter. English (Arabic). Three times a year. International Center for Agricultural Research in the Dry Areas, PO Box 5466, Aleppo Syria. **Tel** 213433, telex 331206. **ED** Nihad F. Maliha. **Bk Rev. Ad Acc. Circ:** 1,000 (ctrl).
Desc: Faba beans, news, short communications, and reviews.
Ind/Abst AGRICOLA [Full Cov.]; Agrofor. Abstr. (1991-); Biodeter. Abstr. (1991-); Crop Physiol. Abstr.; Field Crop Abstr.; For. Abstr.; Grass. Forage Abstr.; Hortic. Abstr.; Irr. Drain. Abstr.; Maize Abstr.; Nematol. Abstr.; Plant Breed. Abstr.; Plant Genet. Resour. Abstr.; Plant Grow. Reg. Abstr.; Rev. Plant Pathol.; Seed Abstr.; Weed Abstr.

LC S631 .F24
DD 631.8 II
FAI ABSTRACT SERVICE. Added/Corp Fertiliser Association of India. **VFOAT** Abstract Service. (19??)-. English. Twelve times a year. $10.00. Fertilizer Association of India, New Delhi India. **(Subscription address:** Prints India, 11 Darya Ganj, New Delhi 110002 India. **Tel** 011 91 11 3268645, FAX 011 91 11 3275542, telex 31-61087 PRIN-IN.**)**

LC S
DD 630 IT
FAO FERTILIZER AND PLANT NUTRITION BULLETIN. Added/Corp Food and Agriculture Organization of the United Nations. **VAT** Food and Agriculture Organization of the United Nations Fertilizer and Plant Nutrition Bulletin. (1981)-. Bulletin. English. Irregular. Price varies per volume. Food Agriculture Organization (FAO) / Italy, GIPCI66 via Terme di Caracalla, 00100 Rome Italy. **Tel** 011 39 6 52252925, FAX 011 39 6 52253152. **(Subscription address:** UNIPUB, 4611 F Assembly Drive, Lanham MD 20706. **Tel** (800)274-4888, (301)459-7666.**)** ***Continues** FAO Fertilizer Bulletin.*

LC SB183 **ISSN** 0259-2525
DD 633 IT
FAO PLANT PRODUCTION AND PROTECTION SERIES. [FAO plant prod. prot. ser.]. **Added/Corp** Food and Agriculture Organization of the United Nations. **VFOAT** Plant Production and Protection Series. (1976)-. Monographic series. English. Irregular. Price varies per volume. Food Agriculture Organization (FAO) / Italy, GIPCI66 via Terme di Caracalla, 00100 Rome Italy. **Tel** 011 39 6 52252925, FAX 011 39 6 52253152.
Ind/Abst AGRICOLA; Field Crop Abstr.; Grass. Forage Abstr.; Nematol. Abstr.; Nutr. Abstr. Rev., Ser. B, Live Feeds and Feed.; Nutr. Abstr. Rev., Ser. A, Hum. Exp.; Plant Breed. Abstr.; Potato Abstr.

LC S **ISSN** 0253-2050
DD 630 IT
CODEN FSBUDD
FAO SOILS BULLETIN. [FAO soils bull.]. **Added/Corp** Food and Agriculture Organization of the United Nations. **VFOAT** Soils Bulletin. **VAT** Food and Agriculture Organization of the United Nations Soils Bulletin. No. 33 (1965)-. Bulletin. English. Irregular. Price varies per volume. Food Agriculture Organization (FAO) / Italy, GIPCI66 via Terme di Caracalla, 00100 Rome Italy. **Tel** 011 39 6 52252925, FAX 011 39 6 52253152. **(Subscription address:** Unipub, 4611 F Assembly Drive, Lanham MD 20706. **Tel** (800)274-8888, (301)459-7666.**)** Documents available from BIOSIS Document Express, CASDDS. ***Continues** Soils Bulletin, 0532-0437.*
Ind/Abst AGRICOLA [Full Cov.]; Biol. Abstr.; Chem. Abstr.; EMBASE; Life Sci. Collect.; Soils Fert.

LC S633 .A5 **ISSN** 0430-0750
DD 631.8 US
CCC
NLM S 631 F233 **CODEN** FMCHA2
FARM CHEMICALS HANDBOOK. [Farm chem. handb.]. (1951)-. Trade Publication. English. One time a year. $85.31. Meister Publishing Company, 37733 Euclid Avenue, Willoughby OH 44094-5992. **Tel** (216)942-2000, (800)572-7740, FAX (216)942-0662. ***Continues** American Fertilizer Hand Book.*
Desc: Reference source in crop protection.

LC S
DD 630 US
FEDERAL-STATE-PRIVATE COOPERATIVE SNOW SURVEYS. BASIC DATA SUMMARY OF SNOW SURVEY AND SOIL MOISTURE MEASUREMENTS FOR WESTERN UNITED STATES, INCLUDING COLUMBIA RIVER DRAINAGE IN CANADA. Added/Corp United States. Soil Conservation Service. California. Dept. of Water Resources. British Columbia. Dept. of Lands, Forests and Water Resources. **VFOAT** Snow Survey and Soil Moisture Measurements, Basic Data Summary for Western United States, Including Columbia River Drainage in Canada. (19??)-. English. West Technical Service Center, Room 111/511 NW Broadway, Portland OR 97209.

LC S **ISSN** 1241-3682
DD 630 FR
FEL ACTUALITES HEBDO : MARCHES EUROPEENS DES FRUITS ET LEGUMES. (19??)-. Bulletin. French. One time a week. $349.95. SIDEFEL, 115 rue Faubourg Poissonniere, 75009 Paris France. **Tel** 011 33 1 44 53 75 31, FAX 011 33 1 44 53 75 39. ***Continues** FEL Actualites : Marches Europeens des Fruits et Legumes.*

LC S
DD 630 FR
TITLE CHANGE
FEL ACTUALITES : MARCHES EUROPEENS DES FRUITS ET LEGUMES. Added/Corp Societe Interprofessionnelle pour l'Edition, la Documentation et l'Information Economique en Fruits et Legumes (France). **VAT** Fruits et Legumes Actualites. (March 1984)-(19??). Periodical. French. SIDEFEL, 115 rue Faubourg Poissonniere, 75009 Paris France. **Tel** 011 33 1 44 53 75 31, FAX 011 33 1 44 53 75 39. ***Continues** MFL.*
***Continued by** FEL Actualites Hebdo, 1241-3682.*

LC HD9483.I4 F47
DD 338.4/766862/09541 II
FERTILISER & ALLIED AGRICULTURAL STATISTICS, NORTHERN REGION. See Agriculture-Abstracting, Bibliographies and Statistics.

LC Z5071 **ISSN** 0430-327X
DD 016.63 II
FERTILISER STATISTICS. See Agriculture-Abstracting, Bibliographies and Statistics.

LC HD9483.A1F47
DD 331.7 UK
FERTILIZER FOCUS. Vol. 1, No. 1 (Feb. 1984)-. Periodical. English. Twelve times a year. $376.47. FMB Publications Ltd., FMB House 6, Windmill Road Hampton Hill, Middlesex TW12 1RH United Kingdom. **Tel** 011 44 181 9797866.
Desc: Information for those interested in the fertilizer industry.
Ind/Abst Agric. Eng. Abstr. (1991-); Maize Abstr.; Rice Abstr.; Soils Fert.

LC HD9483.A1 F39
DD 338.4/766862/021 FR
FERTILIZER INDICATORS. See Industry and Production.

LC S631 **ISSN** 0167-1731
DD 631.8 NE
CCC
CODEN FRESDF
Pr Rev.
FERTILIZER RESEARCH. (FERTILIZER RESEARCH; AN INTERNATIONAL JOURNAL ON FERTILIZER USE.). [Fertil. res.]. Vol. 1 (1980)-. Academic Scholarly Publication. English. Six times a year. $573.00. Kluwer Academic Publishers, Postbus 322, 3300 AH Dordrecht The Netherlands. **Tel** 011 31 78 524400, FAX 011 31 78 183273, telex 20083. **ED** P.L.G. Vlek. **Ad Acc. Acid Free. Circ:** 500. available on microfilm and microfiche from University Microfilms International (UMI). Documents available from The Genuine Article, CASDDS.
Desc: Provides a broad coverage of all topics of research concerned and connected with fertilizers and their use, in all areas of the world. Special issues are dedicated to the proceedings of symposia and workshop. Contributions are accepted in the fields of inorganic, organic and biofertilizers in relation to crop and forest production and quality, soil productivity as related to soil fertility, chemistry and microbiology, and the environmental and economic aspects of fertilizer adoption and use.
Ind/Abst AGRICOLA [Full Cov.]; Agric. Eng. Abstr.; Agrofor. Abstr.; BioBusiness; Chem. Abstr.; Crop Physiol. Abstr.; Curr. Aware. Biol. Sci., CABS; Curr. Cit.; Field Crop Abstr.; For. Abstr.; Hortic. Abstr.; Irr. Drain. Abstr.; Maize Abstr.; Plant Breed. Abstr.; Potato Abstr.; Res. Alert [Select. Cov.]; Rice Abstr.; SCISEARCH; Seed Abstr.; Soils Fert.; Sorghum Mill. Abstr.; Soyabean Abstr.; Wheat Barley Trit. Abstr.

LC S631 **ISSN** 0253-9616
DD 631.8 CH
CODEN FBSEDX
FFTC BOOK SERIES. [FFTC book ser.]. **Added/Corp** Asian and Pacific Council. Food & Fertilizer Technology Center. **VFOAT** F.F.T.C. Book Series. **VAT** Food and Fertilizer Technology Center Book Series. No. 1 (1978)-. Monographic series. English. ASPAC Food & Fertilizer Technology Center, Agriculture Building, 14 Wen Chow Street, Taipei Taiwan. Documents available from CASDDS.
Ind/Abst Biodeter. Abstr.; Chem. Abstr.; Maize Abstr.; Postharvest News Inf.; Rev. Agric. Entomol.

LC SB183 .F5 **ISSN** 0015-069X
DD 633/.05 UK
FIELD CROP ABSTRACTS. See Agriculture-Abstracting, Bibliographies and Statistics.

LC S133 .S75a **ISSN** 0575-8548
DD 338.1/0971 CN
FIELD CROP REPORTING SERIES. [Field crop rep. ser.]. **Main/Corp** Statistics Canada. Agriculture Division. Crops Section. **Added/Corp** Canada. Dominion Bureau of Statistics. Crops Section. Statistics Canada. Crops Section. Statistics Canada. Crops Section. Serie de Rapports sur les Grandes Cultures. **VFOAT** Crop Reporting Series; Serie de Rapports sur les Grandes Cultures; Serie de Rapport sur les Grandes Cultures.

VAT Serie de Rapports sur les Grandes Cultures (1974). (Aug. 11, 1971)-. English (French). Irregular. 102.00Can$. Statistics Canada Publications Sales and Services, R.H. Coats Building 6th Floor, Ottawa Ontario K1A 0T6 Canada. **Tel** (613)951-5078, (800)267-6677, FAX (613)951-1584, telex 053-3585. ***Absorbed*** *Serie de Rapports sur les Grandes Cultures;* ***Continues*** *Field Crop Reporting Series, 0575-8548.*
Desc: Provides reliable and current farm-level data for each of the principal Canadian field crops. Eight reports, released at strategic points in the year, contain forecasts and official estimates by province for stocks, area and production. Individual reports cover seeding intentions, seeded area, stocks at March 31 and crop year end, forecast and final production.

LC S21 .D85b **ISSN** 0147-457X
DD 338.1/7/300973 US
FIELD CROPS PRODUCTION, DISPOSITION, VALUE. [Field crops prod. dispos. value]. **Added/Corp** United States. Crop Reporting Board. (1975)-. English. One time a year. US Department of Agriculture / National Agricultural Statistics Service (NASS), Room 5829 South Building, Washington DC 20250. **Tel** (202)720-4020, FAX (314)875-5231. ***Continues*** *Field Crops (Washington, D.C.), 0892-8894.*

LC SB183
DD 633 US
FIELD CROPS : PRODUCTION, DISPOSITION, VALUE. (19??)-. English. One time a year. Full Depository, 707 Savings and Loan Building, Des Moines IA 50309.
Desc: Farm disposition of major farm products, showing estimated production, quantity used on farms where produced, quantity sold or to be sold, price, and value.

LC SB183 **ISSN** 0378-4290
DD 633 NE
CCC
CODEN FCREDZ
Pr Rev.
FIELD CROPS RESEARCH. [Field crops res.]. Vol. 1 (Feb. 1978)-. Academic Scholarly Publication. English. Fifteen times a year (5 volumes). $1210.00. Elsevier Science Publishers BV, PO Box 211, 1000 AE Amsterdam Netherlands. **Tel** 011 31 20 4853641, 011 31 20 4853642, FAX 011 31 20 4853598. **ED** G F Arkin and G L Wilson. available on microfilm and microfiche from University Microfilms International (UMI); available on an online database from Elsevier Electronic Subscriptions (EES). Documents available from The Genuine Article, BIOSIS Document Express, Documents on Demand.
Desc: Publishes research results of the scientific study of crop farming systems. The subject fields covered include agronomy, improvement, physiology, ecology and protection, soil and water management, and farming systems.
Ind/Abst AGRICOLA; Agrofor. Abstr. (19??-19??); Biol. Agric. Index; Biol. Abstr.; Cot. Trop. Fibr. Abstr. Bibliogr.; Crop Physiol. Abstr.; Curr. Aware. Biol. Sci., CABS; Curr. Cit.; Curr. Contents Agric. Biol. Environ. Sci.; Ecol. Abstr.; EMBASE; Environ. Abstr. (Sept. 30, 1991-); Environ. Period. Bibliogr.; Field Crop Abstr.; For. Abstr.; Geogr. Abstr. Human Geogr. (?-?); Grass. Forage Abstr.; Hortic. Abstr.; Int. Dev. Abstr.; Irr. Drain. Abstr.; Maize Abstr.; Nematol. Abstr.; Life Sci. Collect.; PESTDOC; Plant Breed. Abstr.; Plant Grow. Reg. Abstr.; Potato Abstr.; Res. Alert [Full Cov.]; Rev. Agric. Entomol.; Rice Abstr.; Sci. Cit. Index; SCISEARCH; Seed Abstr.; Soils Fert.; Sorghum Mill. Abstr.; Soyabean Abstr.; Wheat Barley Trit. Abstr.; World Agric. Econ. Rural Sociol. Abstr.

LC SB369.2.F6 F65a
DD 338.1/7/4309759 US
FLORIDA CITRUS TREE INVENTORY. **Main/Corp** Florida Crop and Livestock Reporting Service. **Added/Corp** Florida. Division of Plant Industry. (19??)-. English. USDA NASS Florida Agricultural Statistics Service, 1222 Woodward Street, Orlando FL 32803. **Tel** (407)648-6013.

LC SB320 **ISSN** 1064-6558
DD 635 US
FLORIDA GROWER'S ORNAMENTAL OUTLOOK. [Fla. grow. ornam. outlook]. **VFOAT** Ornamental Outlook. Vol. 1, No. 1 (Jan./Feb. 1992)-. Trade Publication. English. Twenty times a year (Publishes Outlook eight times and Foliage publishes twelve times). $48.00. FGR Incorporated, 1331 North Mills Avenue, Orlando FL 32803-7194. **Tel** (407)894-6522, FAX (407)894-6511.

LC S **ISSN** 0744-5997
DD 630 US
FLORIDA WATERMELON REPORT. Vol. 1, No. 1 (May 5, 1982)-. Periodical. English. One time a week (first week in May-last week in June). Federal-State Market News Service, 1220 N Street, Suite 216, Box 942871, Sacramento CA 94271-0001. **Tel** (916)654-0298, FAX (916)654-1046. ***Continues*** *Southeastern Watermelon Report, 0194-7621.*

LC S
DD 630 US
FLORIDA WEATHER AND CROP NEWS. (19??)-. English. One time a week. $15.00. US Department of Agriculture / National Agricultural Statistics Service (NASS), Room 5829 South Building, Washington DC 20250. **Tel** (202)720-4020, FAX (314)875-5231. ctrl circ.
Desc: Covers weather summary and precipitation; temperatures, crop and livestock conditions; movement of vegetable and citrus pasture condition.

LC HD **ISSN** 0885-0704
DD 331 US
FOOD AND JUSTICE. [Food justice]. **Added/Corp** United Farm Workers. (198?)-. Periodical. English. Twelve times a year. Free on request. United Farm Workers of America, PO Box 62, Keene CA 93570. **Tel** (805)822-5571, (805)845-2244.

LC HD9015.E8 S73a
DD 338.1/094 LU
FORSYNINGSBALANCER. VERSORGUNGSBILANZEN. SUPPLY BALANCE SHEETS. **Main/Corp** Statistical Office of the European Communities. **Added/Corp** Statistical Office of the European Communities. Versorgungsbilanzen. Statistical Office of the European Communities. Supply Balance Sheets. **VFOAT** Versorgungsbilanzen; Supply Balance Sheets. (19??)-. English (French). $11.50. Statistical Office of the European Communities, rue Alcide de Gasperi, BP 1907, Luxembourg Luxembourg.

LC SB123 .F74 **ISSN** 0301-2727
DD 631.5 GW
CODEN FSPZAR
FORTSCHRITTE DER PFLANZENZUCHTUNG. [Fortschr. Pflanzenzucht.]. **VFOAT** Advances in Plant Breeding. 1-1971. Monographic series. German (summaries and/or abstracts in English). Price varies per volume. Paul Parey Verlag, PO Box 106304, D 20043 Hamburg Germany. **Tel** 011 49 40 33969134. **Bk Rev**. Documents available from BIOSIS Document Express.
Desc: Journal publishes original papers and short communications by internationally recognized scientists, covering all areas of plant breeding, plant physiology, pathology, growth and development.
Ind/Abst Biol. Abstr.; Life Sci. Collect.; Plant Breed. Abstr.

LC SB183 **ISSN** 0301-2735
DD 633 GW
CODEN AACSE2
CEASED
FORTSCHRITTE IM ACKER- UND PFLANZENBAU. [Fortschr. Acker- Pflanzenbau]. **VFOAT** Advances in Agronomy and Crop Science. No. 1 (1973)-(19??). Monographic series. German (summaries and/or abstracts in English). Paul Parey Verlag, PO Box 106304, D 20043 Hamburg Germany. **Tel** 011 49 40 33969134. Documents available from BIOSIS Document Express.
Ind/Abst AGRICOLA; Biol. Abstr. (1986-).

LC SB761 **ISSN** 0395-8515
DD 635.97 FR
FOURRAGES ACTUALITES. [Fourrages actual.]. No. 1-. Periodical. French. Four times a year.
Ind/Abst AGRICOLA.

LC SB761 **ISSN** 0350-3615
DD 635.97 CI
CODEN FHJUDA
FRAMENTA HERBOLOGICA JUGOSLAVICA. [Fragm. herbol. Jugosl.]. (1971)-. Academic Scholarly Publication. Serbo-Croatian (Roman). Documents available from CASDDS.
Ind/Abst Biocont. News Inf.; Chem. Abstr. (1982-); Field Crop Abstr.; Hortic. Abstr.; Maize Abstr.; Soils Fert.; Weed Abstr.; Wheat Barley Trit. Abstr.

LC HF **ISSN** 0152-6790
DD 380.1 FR
FRANCE FRUITS ET LEGUMES. Periodical. French (German, Italian and Spanish).

LC HD1401 **ISSN** 0384-7322
DD 338.1/7/349105 CN
FRASER'S POTATO NEWSLETTER. (March 1967)-. Newsletter. English. Irregular (45 issues). 85.00Can$. J H Fraser, Rural Route 1, Charlottetown, Prince Edward Island C1A 7J6 Canada. **Tel** (902)569-2685. **ED** J. H. Fraser. **Ad Acc. Circ:** 2,000.
Desc: Potatoes acreage, production, holdings, trends. Written by potato growers.

LC HD9241 .W56 **ISSN** 0740-4735
DD 338.1/0973 338.1/34/0973021 US
FRESH FRUIT AND VEGETABLE PRICES. **Added/Corp** United States. Agricultural Marketing Service. United States. Agricultural Marketing Service. Fruit and Vegetable Division. Market News Branch. United States. Agricultural Marketing Service. Fruit and Vegetable Division. United States. Consumer and Marketing Service. Fruit and Vegetable Division. (1954)-. Government Publication. English. One time a year. $10.00. US Department of Agriculture / Agricultural Marketing Service / Washington, DC, Market News Branch, Fruit and Vegetable Division, Washington DC 20250. **Tel** (202)720-2745, (202)720-3343, FAX (202)720-7502. ***Continues*** *Wholesale Prices of Fresh Fruits and Vegetables, and Auction Prices of Fresh Fruits at New York City and Chicago, and F.O.B. Prices at Leading Shipping Points, by Months, 8755-5069.*

LC SB21 .C823 **ISSN** 0016-2167
DD 631/.05 US
CODEN FOPSAC
FRONTIERS OF PLANT SCIENCE. [Front. plant sci.]. **Added/Corp** Connecticut Agricultural Experiment Station. Vol. 1 (Nov. 1948)-. Periodical. English. Irregular. Free on request. Connecticut Agricultural Experiment Station, 123 Huntington Street, Box 1106, New Haven CT 06504-1106. **Tel** (203)789-7272, FAX (203)789-7232. **ED** Paul Gough. cum. index. **Circ:** 5,000. Documents available from BIOSIS Document Express, CASDDS.
Ind/Abst AGRICOLA [Full Cov.]; Biol. Abstr.; Chem. Abstr.; EMBASE; Field Crop Abstr.; For. Prod. Abstr.; For. Abstr.; Grass. Forage Abstr.; Hortic. Abstr.; Irr. Drain. Abstr.; Nematol. Abstr.; Plant Breed. Abstr.; Vitis Vitic. Enol. Abstr.

LC S **ISSN** 0429-7830
DD 630 GW
UDC 634.1/.8:339
FRUCHTHANDEL DUSSELDORF. [Fruchthandel Dusseld.]. (1961)-. Trade Publication. German. One time a week. DM275.00 Germany; DM415.75 other. Dr Rolf M. Wolf Verlag GmbH, Lindemannstr 12, D-40237 Duesseldorf Germany. **Tel** 011 49 211 991040, FAX 011 49 211 663162. **ED** Mrs. A. Weintz (editor's phone: 49 211 9910421). **Ad Acc, Adv Mgr:** M Tedet, **Tel** 49 211 9910420. **Circ:** 5,200.
Desc: Provides information on international matters affecting the German fresh produce trade including reports on major producing countries and individual products.

LC HD9254.C18 F18 **ISSN** 0383-008X
DD 338.1/7/40971 CN
FRUIT AND VEGETABLE PRODUCTION. [Fruit veg. prod.]. **Main/Corp** Statistics Canada. Agriculture Division. Crops Section. **Added/Corp** Statistics Canada. Crops Section. Statistics Canada. Horticultural Crops Unit. Statistics Canada. Crops Section. Production de Fruits et Legumes. **VFOAT** Production de Fruits et Legumes. Vol. 45, No. 1 (May 1976)-. English (French). Four times a year. 104.00Can$ Canada; $125.00 US; $146.00 other. Statistics Canada Publications Sales and Services, R.H. Coats Building 6th Floor, Ottawa Ontario K1A 0T6 Canada. **Tel** (613)951-5078, (800)267-6677, FAX (613)951-1584, telex 053-3585. ***Continues*** *Statistics Canada. Crops Section. Fruit and Vegetable Crop Reports.*
Desc: Contains annual estimates of planted acreage and production and value of commercially grown vegetables: mushroom statistics, tobacco, intentions to contract, contracted acreage and planted acreages of main processing crops; includes estimated production of principal commercial fruit crops and value of production. All data shown are on a provincial basis.

LC S **ISSN** 0016-2248
DD 630 BE
CODEN FRUBA7
FRUIT BELGE, LE. [Fruit Belge]. **Added/Corp** Ligues Pomologiques Wallonnes. (1933)-. Academic Scholarly Publication. French. Six times a year. $67.17. Fruit Belge, 69 rue du Village, B 4460 Velroux Belgium. **Tel** 011 33 41 792336. **ED** A. Sansdrap. Index available. **Bk Rev. Ad Acc. Circ:** 1,500 (ctrl). Documents available from CASDDS.
Desc: Contains all subjects related to fruit culture.
Ind/Abst Agric. Eng. Abstr. (1991-); Chem. Abstr. (1933-1976); Food Sci. Technol. Abstr.; Hortic. Abstr.; Plant Breed. Abstr.; Postharvest News Inf.; Rev. Agric. Entomol.; Weed Abstr.

LC SB354 **ISSN** 1054-8319
DD 634 US
FRUIT CROPS FACT SHEET. [Fruit crops fact sheet]. **Added/Corp** University of Florida. Agricultural Extension Service. Florida Cooperative Extension Service. No. 1 (1967)-. Monographic series. English (Spanish). Price varies per volume. University of Florida Agricultural Experiment Station, Gainesville FL 32601.
Ind/Abst AGRICOLA [Full Cov.].

LC SB354 **ISSN** 1049-4545
DD 634 US
FRUIT GARDENER, THE. [Fruit gard.]. **Added/Corp** California Rare Fruit Growers. Vol. 18, No. 3 (Third Quarter 1986)-. Periodical. English. Six times a year (Feb., Apr., June, Aug., Oct., Dec.). $16.00 US; $25.00 Canada and Mexico; $30.00 other Comes with California Rare Fruit Growers Membership. California Rare Fruit Growers Inc., PO Box W, El Cajon CA 92022. **Tel** (619)441-7395. **ED** Clytia Chambers, (phone: (818)762-0730). cum. index. **Bk Rev**, (Qty: 6). **Ad Acc. Circ:** 3,000. ***Continues*** *California Rare Fruit Growers Newsletter, 0742-8049.*

LC SB354 **ISSN** 0953-2188
DD 634 UK
FRUIT GROWER MAIDSTONE. (FRUIT GROWER.). [Fruit grow.Maidstone]. (1987)-. Trade Publication. English. Twelve times a year. $49.62. Anchris Publishing, Lamberhurst Road, Horsmonden, Kent TN12

8DP United Kingdom. **Tel** 011 44 189 2724277, FAX 011 44 189 2722516. **ED** John Jarrett. **Bk Rev. Ad Acc. Circ:** 3,000 (ctrl). ***Continues*** *Top Fruit Grower.*

LC SB354 .A54 **ISSN** 0091-3642
DD 634/.04/705 US
UDC 634.1
CODEN FVRJAA

Pr Rev.
FRUIT VARIETIES JOURNAL. [Fruit var. j.]. Vol. 27 (Jan. 1973)-. Periodical. English. Four times a year. $25.00. American Pomological Society, 103 Tyson Building, University Park PA 16802. **Tel** (814)863-6163, FAX (814)863-6139. **ED** David C Ferree. cum. index. **Bk Rev. Ad Acc. Circ:** 1,000 (ctrl). available on microfilm and microfiche from University Microfilms International (UMI). Documents available from The Genuine Article, BIOSIS Document Express. ***Continues*** *Fruit Varieties and Horticultural Digest, 0016-2272.*
Desc: Promotes fruit variety and rootstock improvement through breeding and testing. Publishes latest information on fruit variety introductions and performance of existing varieties.
Ind/Abst AgBiotech News Inf.; AGRICOLA [Full Cov.]; Biol. Abstr.; Curr. Aware. Biol. Sci., CABS; Curr. Cit.; Curr. Contents Agric. Biol. Environ. Sci.; Food Sci. Technol. Abstr.; Hortic. Abstr.; Irr. Drain. Abstr.; Nematol. Abstr.; Life Sci. Collect.; Plant Breed. Abstr.; Plant Grow. Reg. Abstr.; Postharvest News Inf.; Res. Alert [Select. Cov.]; Rev. Agric. Entomol.; Rev. Plant Pathol.; SCISEARCH; Seed Abstr.; Soils Fert.; Vitis Vitic. Enol. Abstr.

LC S **ISSN** 1256-5458
DD 630 FR
UDC 631/635
●**FRUITROP ENGLISH ED.** (FRUITROP.). (1994)-. Periodical. English. Eleven times a year. $131.23. CIRAD-FLHOR, Departement des Productions Fruitieres et Horticoles, rue Poncelet, 75017 Paris France. **Tel** 011 33 1 40537050.

LC SB354 **ISSN** 0016-2299
DD 634 FR
CODEN FRUIAS
FRUITS. **Added/Corp** Institut des Fruits et Agrumes Coloniaux. Institut Francais de Recherches Fruitieres Outre-mer. Institut de Recherches sur ls Fruits et Agrumes. Vol. 6, (1951)-. Academic Scholarly Publication. French (Spanish and English; summaries and/or abstracts in English, German and Spanish). Six times a year (1 special iss. included). $215.00. IRFA Inst Rech Fruits Agrumes, BP 5035, 34032 Montpellier France. **Tel** 011 33 1 45531692, telex 610992. **ED** Chantal Cabot. Index available. cum. index. **Bk Rev. Ad Acc. Circ:** 1,000. Documents available from CASDDS. ***Continues*** *Fruits d'Outre Mer, 0367-2816.*
Desc: Information on culture, plant protection, maturation, harvest, conservation and industrial transformation of tropical and subtropical fruits.
Ind/Abst AGRICOLA; Agrofor. Abstr.; Chem. Abstr.; Curr. Cit.; Field Crop Abstr.; Food Sci. Technol. Abstr.; For. Abstr.; Nematol. Abstr.; Life Sci. Collect.; PESTDOC; Plant Genet. Resour. Abstr.; Postharvest News Inf.; Rev. Agric. Entomol.; Rev. Plant Pathol.; Seed Abstr.; Soils Fert.

LC S **ISSN** 0016-2302
DD 630 NE
FRUITTEELT, DE. [Fruitteelt]. (1922)-. Trade Publication. Dutch. One time a week. Price varies. Nederlandse Fruittelers Organ, Postbus 90607, 2509 Hague Netherlands. **Tel** 011 31 70 3450600, FAX 011 31 70 3453902, telex 32185.
Ind/Abst AgBiotech News Inf.; Agric. Eng. Abstr.; Biocont. News Inf.; Hortic. Abstr.; Irr. Drain. Abstr.; Plant Breed. Abstr.; Plant Grow. Reg. Abstr.; Postharvest News Inf.; Rev. Agric. Entomol.; Rev. Plant Pathol.; Saf. Health Work; Soils Fert.; Weed Abstr.

LC S **ISSN** 0214-0578
DD 630 SP
UDC 634
FRUT. [Frut]. (1986)-. Periodical. Spanish. Six times a year. Ediciones y Textos, SA, Roger de Flor, 222 bis 1o 5a, 08013 Barcelona Spain. **Tel** 93 459 00 55, FAX 93 459 41 36.
Ind/Abst Postharvest News Inf.

LC QK **ISSN** 0148-9038
DD 581 US
CODEN FNETDO
FUNGICIDE AND NEMATICIDE TESTS. [Fungic. nematicide tests.]. **Added/Corp** American Phytopathological Society. Vol. 24 (1968)-. English. One time a year (May or June). $23.00. Louisiana State University / Department of Plant Pathology, 302 Life Sciences Building, Baton Rouge LA 70803. **Tel** (504)642-8150. **ED** David Ritchie. Index available. **Ad Acc. Circ:** 1,600 (ctrl). Documents available from CASDDS. ***Continues*** *Fungicide-Nematocide Tests, Results, 0196-2833.*
Desc: The effectiveness of various chemicals for control of fungal and nematode diseases occurring on a wide array of crops.
Ind/Abst Chem. Abstr.; Nematol. Abstr.; PESTDOC; Protozoolog. Abstr.; Rev. Med. Vet. Mycology; Rev. Plant Pathol.; Soils Fert.; Soyabean Abstr.

LC S18 .G37 **ISSN** 0378-8032
DD 630 PO
CODEN GOSADL
GARCIA DE ORTA : SERIE DE ESTUDOS AGRONOMICOS. [Garcia de Orta. ser. estud. agron.]. **Added/Corp** Portugal. Junta de Investigacoes Cientificas do Ultramar. Portugal. Junta de Investigacoes do Ultramar. **VFOAT** Serie de Estudos Agronomicos. Vol. 1 (1973)-. Academic Scholarly Publication. Multiple languages (French and Portuguese; summaries and/or abstracts in English). Two times a year. 1900$00. Instituto de Investigacao Cientifica Tropical, Centro de Documentacao e Informacao, rua Jau 47, 1 300 Lisbon Portugal. **Tel** 645321. Index available. **Circ:** 1,000 (ctrl). Documents available from CASDDS. ***Continues in part*** *Garcia de Orta.*
Desc: Publishes articles on agronomy (agriculture, forestry, fisheries and their products, soils, phytopathology, etc.) and on other directly-related sciences and technologies.
Ind/Abst AGRICOLA; Chem. Abstr.; Field Crop Abstr.; Grass. Forage Abstr.; Nutr. Abstr. Rev., Ser. B, Live Feeds and Feed.; Nutr. Abstr. Rev., Ser. A, Hum. Exp.; Plant Breed. Abstr.; Rev. Med. Vet. Mycology; Rev. Plant Pathol.; Seed Abstr.; Soils Fert.

LC TP375 .G3 **ISSN** 0016-5395
DD 664 PL
CODEN GACUA2
GAZETA CUKROWNICZA. [Gaz. cukr.]. **Added/Corp** Stowarzyszenie Technikow Cukrownikow. Zjednoczenie Przemyslu Cukrowniczego. (1893)-. Periodical. Polish (summaries and/or abstracts in English, German and Russian; table of contents in Russian, German and English). Twelve times a year. $60.00. **(Subscription address:** Ars Polona-Ruch, PO Box 1001, Krakowskie Przedmiescie 7, 00-068 Warsaw Poland. **Tel** 011 48 22 261201.) Documents available from CASDDS.
Ind/Abst AGRICOLA; Biodeter. Abstr. (1991-); Chem. Abstr.; Field Crop Abstr.; Food Sci. Technol. Abstr.; Grass. Forage Abstr.; Nutr. Abstr. Rev., Ser. B, Live Feeds and Feed.; Saf. Health Work; Soils Fert.; Sug. Indus. Abstr.

LC S **ISSN** 0016-6286
DD 630 GW
CCC
GEMUSE (MUNCHEN). (GEMUSE.). [Gemuse]. (1965)-. Trade Publication. German. Twelve times a year. $85.21. BLV Verlagsgesellschaft MBH, Lothstrasse 29, D80797 Munich Germany. **Tel** 011 49 89 12705214.
Ind/Abst AGRICOLA; Agric. Eng. Abstr. (1991-); Biodeter. Abstr. (19??-19??); Field Crop Abstr.; Hortic. Abstr.; Irr. Drain. Abstr.; Plant Breed. Abstr.; Postharvest News Inf.; Rev. Agric. Entomol.; Rev. Plant Pathol.; Seed Abstr.; Soils Fert.; Weed Abstr.; World Agric. Econ. Rural Sociol. Abstr.

LC S **ISSN** 1018-4899
DD 630 CE
UDC 63
●**GENERAL PUBLICATIONS CATALOG - INTERNATIONAL IRRIGATION MANAGEMENT INSTITUTE.** [Gen. publ. cat. - Int. Irrig. Manag. Inst.]. (1993)-. Catalog. English. Irregular. Free. International Irrigation Management Institute (IIMI), Digana Village via Kandy, Sri Lanka. **Circ:** 5,000.
Ind/Abst Postharvest News Inf.

LC S **ISSN** 0925-9864
DD 630 NE
CCC
CODEN GRCEE9

Pr Rev.
GENETIC RESOURCES AND CROP EVOLUTION. **VFOAT** GRACE. Vol. 39, No. 1 (1992)-. Periodical. English. Six times a year. $405.00. Kluwer Academic Publishers, Postbus 322, 3300 AH Dordrecht The Netherlands. **Tel** 011 31 78 524400, FAX 011 31 78 183273, telex 20083. **ED** P. Hanelt. **Bk Rev. Acid Free.** available on microfilm and microfiche from University Microfilms International (UMI). Documents available from BIOSIS Document Express.
Desc: Devoted to all aspects of plant genetic resources research. It publishes original articles in the fields of taxonomical, morphological, physiological, biochemical, genetical, cytological or ethnobotanical research of genetic resources and includes contributions to gene-bank management in a broad sense, that means collecting, maintenance, evaluation, storage and documentation.
Ind/Abst Biol. Abstr.; Curr. Aware. Biol. Sci., CABS.

LC SB183 **ISSN** 0159-6071
DD 633 AT
GENETIC RESOURCES COMMUNICATION. [Genet. resour. commun.]. **Added/Corp** Commonwealth Scientific and Industrial Research Organization. Division of Tropical Crops and Pastures. **VFOAT** GRC. No. 1 (1980)-. Monographic series. English.
Ind/Abst AGRICOLA [Full Cov.].

LC S
DD 630 XR
GENETIKA A SLECHTENI. **Added/Corp** Ceskoslovenska Akademie Zemedelska. Ustav Vedeckotechnickych Informaci Pro Zemedelstvi. **VFOAT** Sbornik UVTIZ. Genetika a Slechteni. Vol. 26, No. 2 (1990)-. Periodical. Czech (summaries and/or abstracts in English, German and Russian; table of contents in English, German and Russian). Four times a year. $60.20. **(Subscription address:** Artia Pegas Press Ltd., Palac Metro Narodni Trida 25, 11210 Prague 1 Czech Republic. **Tel** 011 42 2 24196265, 011 42 2 24196266.) ***Continues*** *Sbornik UVTIZ. Genetika a Slechteni, 0036-5378.*
Ind/Abst Irr. Drain. Abstr.; Plant Grow. Reg. Abstr.; Rev. Plant Pathol.; Soyabean Abstr.; Vitis Vitic. Enol. Abstr.

LC S590 **ISSN** 0016-7061
DD 631.4 NE
CCC
CODEN GEDMAB

Pr Rev.
GEODERMA. [Geoderma]. Vol. 1, No. 1 (Sept. 1967)-. Academic Scholarly Publication. English. Twenty-four times a year (6 vols.). $1482.00. Elsevier Science Publishers BV, PO Box 211, 1000 AE Amsterdam Netherlands. **Tel** 011 31 20 4853641, 011 31 20 4853642, FAX 011 31 20 4853598. **ED** R W Simonson. available on microfilm and microfiche from University Microfilms International (UMI); available on an online database from Elsevier Electronic Subscriptions (EES). Documents available from The Genuine Article, BIOSIS Document Express, CASDDS.
Desc: Helps stimulate wide interdisciplinary cooperation and understanding among workers in the different fields of pedology by bringing together papers from the entire field of soil research, rather than emphasizing any one subdiscipline.
Ind/Abst AGRICOLA; AQUAREF; Biol. Abstr.; Chem. Abstr.; Curr. Aware. Biol. Sci., CABS; Curr. Cit.; Curr. Contents Agric. Biol. Environ. Sci.; Ecol. Abstr.; Environ. Period. Bibliogr.; Field Crop Abstr.; Geogr. Abstr. Phys. Geogr.; Geogr. Abstr. Human Geogr. (?-?); Geol. Abstr.; GeoRef; Grass. Forage Abstr.; Hortic. Abstr.; Int. Dev. Abstr.; Irr. Drain. Abstr.; Leadscan; Maize Abstr.; Life Sci. Collect.; Res. Alert [Full Cov.]; Rev. Agric. Entomol.; Sci. Cit. Index; SCISEARCH; Seed Abstr.; Soils Fert.; Soyabean Abstr.; Weed Abstr.

LC SB188 **ISSN** 1186-0049
DD 633.1/17 CN
GERMINATOR (LETHBRIDGE). (GERMINATOR.). [Germinator]. **Added/Corp** Alberta Winter Wheat Producers Commission. (Winter 1990)-. Periodical. English. Four times a year. Limited free distribution. Alberta Winter Wheat Producers Commission, 1205 Michigan Pl. South, Lethbridge Alberta T1K 3P4 Canada.

LC S
DD 630 NE
GEWASBESCHERMING EN GROEIREGULATIE IN DE FRUITTEELT. (19??)-. Dutch. One time a year (February). Fl40.00. Nederlandse Fruittelers Organ, Postbus 90607, 2509 Hague Netherlands. **Tel** 011 31 70 3450600, FAX 011 31 70 3453902, telex 32185.

LC S **ISSN** 0748-6782
DD 630 US
GILMORE SUGAR MANUAL, THE. [Gilmore sugar man.]. (1981)-. Trade Publication. English. Every 2 years. $40.00 US; $45.00 other. Sugar Publications, Gilmore Sugar Manual Division, 503 Broadway, Fargo ND 58102. **Tel** (701)237-5747, FAX (701)235-0140. **ED** Don Lilleboe. **Ad Acc. Circ:** 700. ***Continues*** *Gilmore Louisiana-Florida- Hawaii-Texas-Puerto Rico Sugar Manual.*
Desc: Contains technical and general information on cane sugar mills in the United States and Puerto Rico.

LC S604.8 **ISSN** 1122-603X
DD 631.7 IT
GIORNALE DELL'IRRIGAZIONE. (1994)-. Trade Publication. Italian. Twelve times a year. L42.000. Edagricole, PO Box 2157, 40100 Bologna Italy. **Tel** 011 39 51 492211 Ext. 22, FAX 011 39 51 493660, telex 510336 EDAGRI. **Ad Acc.**

LC S **ISSN** 1321-0165
DD 630 AT
GOOD FRUIT AND VEGETABLES. (1990)-. Periodical. English. Twelve times a year. 39.00Aus$ (Australia); 58.00Aus$ (China, Papua, New Guinea, Fiji, Indonesia, Malaysia, India, China, and Japan); 66.50Aus$ (other). Rural Press / Victoria, PO Box 160, Port Melbourne Victoria 3207 Australia. **Tel** 11 61 3 2870900, telex 35668. **ED** Tony Biggs. Index available. **Bk Rev. Ad Acc. Circ:** 9,000. ***Continues*** *Commercial Horticulture, 0728-3814.*
Desc: Catered to fruit and vegetable growers. Provides technical and market information to growers.

LC SB354 **ISSN** 0046-6174
DD 634 US
GOODFRUIT GROWER, THE. [Goodfruit grow.]. **Added/Corp** Washington State Fruit Commission. **VAT** Good Fruit Grower. (1946)-. Periodical. English.

Seventeen times a year. $30.00. Washington State Fruit Commission, PO Box 9219, 1005 Tieton Drive, Yakima WA 98902. **Tel** (509)575-2315. **ED** Jim Black. Index available. **Ad Acc. Circ:** 12,600.
Desc: Covers Pacific Northwest tree fruit industry: production, handling, storage, packaging, marketing, promotion, research and economics of apples, pears, cherries, plums, nectarines and grapes.
Ind/Abst Hortic. Abstr.; Postharvest News Inf.

LC SB188 **ISSN** 0229-8090
DD 633.1/09712 CN
GRAINEWS. [Grainews]. **Added/Corp** United Grain Growers. Farm Information Services. (1975)-. Periodical. English. Sixteen times a year (plus a Spring Planning Manual in March). 23.56Can$. United Grain Growers, 2500-201 Portage Avenue, Box 6600, Winnipeg Manitoba R3C 3A7 Canada. **Tel** (204)944-5697, FAX (204)944-5416. **ED** John Clark. Index available. cum. index. **Bk Rev. Ad Acc. Circ:** 69,000.
Desc: Farm newspaper serving farm families on the prairies. Provides information on grain, oilseed, forage, grass seed, production and marketing, financial management, machinery management, and more.

LC S
DD 630 US
GRAPE ACREAGE. **VFOAT** Grape Acreage Survey. English. One time a year. $4.00 US; $8.00 other. California Agricultural Statistics Service, California Department of, Food and Agriculture, PO Box 1258, Sacramento CA 95812. **Tel** (916)551-1533.
Desc: Acreages of grapes by year planted, variety, and county.

LC SB354 **ISSN** 1049-670X
DD 634 US
GRAPE GROWER (FRESNO, CALIF.). (GRAPE GROWER.). [Grape grow.]. (1969)-. Trade Publication. English. Twelve times a year. $19.95. Western Agricultural Publishing Company, 1755 North Fine Avenue, Fresno CA 93727. **Tel** (209)252-7000, FAX (209)252-7387. **ED** Patrick Cavanaugh. ***Continues*** *California and Western States Grape Grower, 0092-2145.*

LC SB761 **ISSN** 0142-5242
DD 635.97 UK
CCC
CODEN GFSCDW
Pr Rev.
GRASS AND FORAGE SCIENCE. (GRASS AND FORAGE SCIENCE : THE JOURNAL OF THE BRITISH GRASSLAND SOCIETY.). [Grass forage sci.]. **Added/Corp** British Grassland Society. Vol. 34, No. 1 (March 1979)-. Academic Scholarly Publication. English. Four times a year. $282.00. Blackwell Scientific Publications Ltd, Marston Book Services, PO Box 88, Oxford OX2 ONE United Kingdom. **Tel** 011 44 1865 206206, FAX 011 44 1865 206219, telex 837 515 MARDIS G. **ED** R. J. Livingston. **Bk Rev. Ad Acc. Circ:** 2,010. available on microfilm and microfiche from University Microfilms International (UMI). Documents available from The Genuine Article, BIOSIS Document Express, CASDDS. ***Continues*** *Journal of the British Grassland Society, 0007-0750.*
Desc: Results of research and development in grass and forage production management and utilization. Includes material of a developmental nature.
Ind/Abst AGRICOLA [Full Cov.]; Biodeter. Abstr. (1991-); Biol. Abstr.; Chem. Abstr.; Crop Physiol. Abstr.; Curr. Aware. Biol. Sci., CABS; Curr. Cit.; Curr. Contents Agric. Biol. Environ. Sci.; Dairy Sci. Abstr.; Field Crop Abstr.; Grass. Forage Abstr.; Index Vet.; Int. Abstr. Oper. Res. [Select. Cov.]; Maize Abstr.; Nutr. Abstr. Rev., Ser. B, Live Feeds and Feed.; Nutr. Abstr. Rev., Ser. A, Hum. Exp.; Life Sci. Collect.; Plant Breed. Abstr.; Plant Grow. Reg. Abstr.; Postharvest News Inf.; Res. Alert [Full Cov.]; Rev. Agric. Entomol.; Rev. Med. Vet. Entomol.; Rev. Plant Pathol.; Sci. Cit. Index; SCISEARCH; Seed Abstr.; Soils Fert.; Soyabean Abstr.; Vet. Bull.; Weed Abstr.; Wheat Barley Trit. Abstr.

LC SB183 .H47 **ISSN** 1350-9837
DD 633.005/6 UK
•**GRASSLANDS AND FORAGE ABSTRACTS.** **See** Agriculture-Abstracting, Bibliographies and Statistics.

LC SB320 **ISSN** 1049-8494
DD 635 US
CODEN GLVNEL
GREAT LAKES VEGETABLE GROWERS NEWS, THE. [Great Lakes veg. grow. news]. **Added/Corp** Michigan Vegetable Council. **VFOAT** Vegetable Growers News. (19??)-. Trade Publication. English. Twelve times a year. $7.00. Great Lakes Publishing Company, 343 South Union, PO Box 128, Sparta MI 49345. **Tel** (616)887-9008, FAX (616)887-2666. **ED** Matt McCallum. **Ad Acc, Adv Mgr:** Dee Rau, **Tel** (616)887-9008. **Circ:** 13,250 (ctrl).
Desc: To inform vegetable and potato growers, bedding plant and greenhouse operators, and farm and roadside market operators about growing and marketing techniques, business management ideas, event, meetings, and other development important to the vegetable and greenhouse industries.
Ind/Abst BioBusiness (1990-).

LC HD9483.U5 F45 **ISSN** 0193-9106
DD 338.4/766862/0973 US
GREEN MARKETS FERTILIZER PRICE HANDBOOK. **See** Industry and Production.

LC SB320 **ISSN** 0848-6751
DD 635/.0483 CN
GREENHOUSE VEGETABLE PRODUCTION GUIDE (EDMONTON). (GREENHOUSE VEGETABLE PRODUCTION GUIDE.). [Greenh. veg. prod. guide]. **Added/Corp** Alberta. Alberta Agriculture. **VFOAT** Greenhouse Vegetable ... Production Guide for Commercial Growers. (1990)-. Periodical. English. ***Continues*** *Greenhouse Cucumber Production Guide., 0844-8140.*

LC SB183 **ISSN** 0903-0727
DD 633 DK
GRN VIDEN. LANDBRUG. **Added/Corp** Statens Planteavlsforsg (Denmark). **VFOAT** Landbrug. (19??)-. Monographic series. Danish. Irregular. Price varies per volume.
Ind/Abst Nematol. Abstr.; Ornamental Hort. (1991-); Potato Abstr.; Rev. Plant Pathol.; Seed Abstr.

LC S **ISSN** 0737-9935
DD 630 US
GROWER ADVISOR. [Grow. advis.]. Periodical. English. Twelve times a year. California Avocado Advisory Board, 4533-B Macarthur Blvd., Newport CA 92660.

LC S **ISSN** 0745-1784
DD 630 US
CCC
GROWER (SHAWNEE MISSION, KAN.), THE. (THE GROWER.). [Grower]. (19??)-. Periodical. English. Twelve times a year. $20.00. Vance Publishing Corporation, 400 Knightsbridge Parkway, Lincolnshire IL 60069. **Tel** (800)255-5113, (708)634-2600. **ED** David Ezell and Gwen Belmont. **Ad Acc. Circ:** 28,500 (ctrl).
Desc: Provides essential information on a wide variety of subjects: biotechnology, pest and disease control, irrigation, packing and new machinery.

LC S **ISSN** 1059-2563
DD 630 US
GROWER (STORRS, CONN.). (THE GROWER : VEGETABLE AND SMALL FRUIT NEWSLETTER.). [Grower]. **Added/Corp** United States. Dept. of Agriculture. University of Connecticut. Cooperative Extension Service. University of Connecticut. Cooperative Extension System. **VFOAT** Vegetable and Small Fruit Newsletter. (1986)-. Newsletter. English. Twelve times a year.
Ind/Abst AGRICOLA [Full Cov.].

LC S **ISSN** 0017-4777
DD 630 CN
GROWER (TORONTO). (THE GROWER.). **Added/Corp** Ontario Fruit and Vegetable Growers' Association. (Mar. 1952)-. Trade Publication. English. Twelve times a year. 24.01Can$. Ontario Fruit and Vegetable Grower's Association, 355 Elmira Road Unit 103, Guelph Ontario, N1K 1S5 Canada. **Tel** (519)763-8728, FAX (519)763-6604. **ED** Blair Adams. **Ad Acc, Adv Mgr:** James Shaw, **Tel** (416)463-0007. **Circ:** 11,600 (ctrl). ***Supersedes*** *Canadian Grower.*
Desc: Covers Ontario's fruit, vegetable and greenhouse industry. Includes research innovations, market trends, new products and upcoming events.
Ind/Abst Crop Physiol. Abstr.

LC S605 .G75 **ISSN** 0017-4904
DD 631.45 SW
GRUNDFOERBAETTRING. **Added/Corp** Kungl. Lantbrukshoegskolan (Sweden). Institutionen foer Agronomisk Hydroteknik. Saellskapet foer Agronomisk Hydroteknik. Lantbrukshoegskolan. Institutionen foer Lantbrukets Hydroteknik. Kungl. Tekniska Hogskolan. Institutionen foer Kulturteknik. Lantbrukshogskolan. Institutionen foer Markvetenskap. Avd. foer Lantbrukets Hydroteknik. Vol. 1 (1947)-. Periodical. Swedish (English). Irregular. Gunnar Hallgren, Department of Agricultural Hydrotech, Uppsala Sweden.

LC S **ISSN** 0420-0136
DD 630 GW
GRUNDLAGEN ZUR PFLANZENQUARANTAENE. **Main/Corp** Deutsche Akademie der Landwirtschaftswissenschaften, Berlin. 1- 1964-. Periodical. German. Deutsche Akademie der Landwirtschaftswissenschaften, Berlin Germany.

LC SB229.J33 N67a
DD 633.6 JA
GYOMU HOKOKU - NORINSHO SATOKIBIGEN GENSHU NOJO. **Main/Corp** Norinsho Satokibigen Genshu Nojo. (19??)-. Japanese. Kumage-gun Nakatane-cho, Satokibigen Genshu Nojo Yuku, 891-36 Kagoshima-ken Japan.

LC SB354
DD 634 HU
GYUMOLCSTERMESZTES. **Added/Corp** Gyumolcstermesztes, Feldolgozas es Tarolas Korszerusitese Kutatasi Celprogram. Kerteszeti Kutato Intezet. **VFOAT** Fruit Growing. Vol. 1 (1974)-. Periodical. Hungarian (summaries and/or abstracts in English, German, French and Russian).

LC SB183 .H36a
DD 633/.095195 KO
HANGUK CHANGMUL HAKHOE CHI. **Main/Corp** Han'guk Changmul Hakhoe. **Added/Corp** Han'guk Changmul Hakhoe. Journal. **VFOAT** Journal of the Korean Society of Crop Science. (19??)-. Periodical. Korean (English and Korean). Not for sale. Seoul National University College of Agriculture, Suweon Korea.
Ind/Abst Plant Breed. Abstr.; Plant Grow. Reg. Abstr.; Seed Abstr.; Soyabean Abstr.

LC SB197 .H36
DD 633 KO
HANGUK CHOJI YONGUHOE PO. **VFOAT** Journal of Korean Society of Grassland Science. (197?)-. Periodical. Korean (Korean). Two times a year.
Ind/Abst Agrofor. Abstr.; Crop Physiol. Abstr.; For. Abstr.; Maize Abstr.; Nutr. Abstr. Rev., Ser. B, Live Feeds and Feed.; Plant Breed. Abstr.; Plant Genet. Resour. Abstr.; Seed Abstr.; Soils Fert.; Sorghum Mill. Abstr.; Soyabean Abstr.; Weed Abstr.

LC SB183 **ISSN** 0252-9777
DD 633 KO
HANGUK JAKMUL HAKHOE CHI. **Added/Corp** Hanguk Jakmul Hakhoe. **VFOAT** Korean Journal of Crop Science. (19??)-. Periodical. Korean (English; summaries and/or abstracts in English). Four times a year.
Ind/Abst Biodeter. Abstr.; Crop Physiol. Abstr.; Curr. Cit.; Hortic. Abstr.; Irr. Drain. Abstr.; Maize Abstr.; Plant Breed. Abstr.; Plant Grow. Reg. Abstr.; Rev. Plant Pathol.; Rice Abstr.; Soils Fert.

LC S590 .H36A **ISSN** 0367-6315
DD 631.4 KO
CODEN HTBHAY
HAN'GUK TOYANG PIRYO HAKHOE CHI. **Main/Corp** Hanguk Toyang Piryo Hakhoe. **VFOAT** Journal of Korean Society of Soil Science and Fertilizer. Academic Scholarly Publication. Korean (summaries and/or abstracts in English). Four times a year. Hanguk Toyang Piryo Hakhoe, c/o Institute of Agricultural Sciences, Suweon 170 Korea. Documents available from CASDDS.
Ind/Abst Chem. Abstr.

LC Z5071 **ISSN** 0018-0602
DD 016.63 UK
TITLE CHANGE
HERBAGE ABSTRACTS. **See** Agriculture-Abstracting, Bibliographies and Statistics.

LC QK86 **ISSN** 0848-0753
DD 333.95/316 CN
HERITAGE SEED PROGRAM. (HERITAGE SEED PROGRAM : [NEWSLETTER].). [Herit. Seed Program]. **Added/Corp** Heritage Seed Program. Canadian Organic Growers. (1988)-. Periodical. English. Three times a year. 14.40Can$. Heritage Seed Program, RR3 Uxbridge Ontario, L9P 1R3 Canada. **Tel** (905)852-7965. **ED** Heather Apple (editor's phone: (908)852-5635). **Bk Rev. Circ:** 1,800.
Desc: Articles about preserving the genetic diversity of food crops, heritage gardens, heirloom varieties.

LC S
DD 630 US
HINTS TO POTATO GROWERS. **Added/Corp** New Jersey State Potato Association. (19??)-. Periodical. English. Irregular (2 to 4 per year). $10.00. New Jersey State Potato Association, Box 231, Blake 219, New Brunswick NJ 08903.

LC S **ISSN** 0018-3040
DD 630 PL
CODEN HRANAX
HODOWLA ROSLIN AKLIMTYZACJA I NASIENNICTWO. (HODOWLA ROSLIN AKLIMTYZACJA I NASIENNICTWO. SELEKTSIIA RASTENII, AKKLIMATIZATSIIA I SEMENOVODSTVO; PLANT BREEDING, ACCLIMATIZATION AND SEED PRODUCTION.). [Hod. rosl. aklim. nasienn.]. **Added/Corp** Warsaw. Instytut Hodowli i Aklimatyzacji Roslin. **VFOAT** Selektsiia Rastenii, Akklimatizatsiia I Semenovodstvo; Plant Breeding, Acclimatization and Seed Production. Vol. 1 (1957)-. Academic Scholarly Publication. Polish (summaries and/or abstracts in English and Russian; table of contents in English and Russian). Six times a year. $87.00. **(Subscription address:** Ars Polona-Ruch, PO Box 1001, Krakowskie Przedmiescie 7, 00-068 Warsaw Poland. **Tel** 011 48 22 261201.**)** Documents available from BIOSIS Document Express, CASDDS.
Ind/Abst AgBiotech News Inf.; Biol. Abstr.; Chem. Abstr.; Crop Physiol. Abstr.; EMBASE; Field Crop Abstr.; Food Sci. Technol. Abstr.; Grass. Forage Abstr.; Maize Abstr.; Plant Breed. Abstr.; Plant Grow. Reg. Abstr.; Potato Abstr.; Rev. Med. Vet. Mycology; Rev. Plant Pathol.; Seed Abstr.; Wheat Barley Trit. Abstr.

LC S
DD 630 US
HOP STOCKS. **Added/Corp** United States. Crop Reporting Board. (Mar. 1974)-. Government Publication. English. Two times a year (Mar. & Sept.). $14.00. US Department of Agriculture / National Agricultural Statistics Service (NASS), Room 5829 South Building, Washington DC 20250. **Tel** (202)720-4020, FAX (314)875-5231. **(Subscription address:** ERS NASS, 341 Victory Drive, Herndon VA 22070. **Tel** (800)999-6779, (703)834-0125.) ***Continues*** *Stocks of Hops.*
Desc: Shows the amount of hops in storage in the United States.

LC S
DD 630 GW
HOPFEN-RUNDSCHAU. (19??)-. Periodical. German. Twelve times a year (plus special issue in Aug.). DM75.00. Verlag Hopfen Rundschau, Postfach 229, D-85283 Wolnzach Germany. **Tel** 011 49 8442 3511.
Desc: Contains information about all aspects of the hop industry.
Ind/Abst Food Sci. Technol. Abstr.

LC S **ISSN** 0018-490X
DD 630 BE
HOPPLANTER, DE. **Added/Corp** Hopplantersvereniging van Belgie. (19??)-. Periodical. Dutch. Irregular.

LC S451.5 **ISSN** 0319-6038
DD 630/.9713/22 CN
HURON SOIL AND CROP NEWS (1964). (HURON SOIL AND CROP NEWS.). **Added/Corp** Huron Soil and Crop Improvement Association. (1964)-. Trade Publication. English. One time a year. Free on request. Exeter Times-Advocate, PO Box 850, Exeter Ontario Canada. **Tel** (519)235-1331, FAX (519)235-0766. **ED** Jim Beckett. **Ad Acc.** Full Page (B&W) $1242.00. Half Page (B&W) $621.00. **Circ:** 7,000 (ctrl). ***Supersedes*** *Huron County Soil and Crop News, 0319-602X.*

LC S **ISSN** 0815-7383
DD 630 AT
HYBRID GRAIN SORGHUM YIELD RESULTS. [Hybrid grain sorghum yield results]. **Added/Corp** New South Wales. Dept. of Agriculture. (1983/84)-. English. One time a year. New South Wales Department of Agriculture, Locked Bag 21, Orange NSW 2800 Australia. **Tel** 011 61 63 913197.

LC S
DD 630 US
HYDROCARBON CONTAMINATED SOILS AND GROUNDWATER. (1991)-. Periodical. English.

LC S **ISSN** 0018-8808
DD 630 US
ICASALS NEWSLETTER. [ICASALS newsl.]. **Main/Corp** International Center for Arid and Semi-Arid Land Studies. **VAT** International Center for Arid and Semi-Arid Land Studies Newsletter. (1967)-. Newsletter. English. Four times a year. Free on request. International Center for Arid and Semi Arid Land Studies, Texas Tech University, PO Box 41036, Lubbock TX 79409-1036. **Tel** (806)742-2218, FAX (806)742-1954. **ED** Kendra K. Ecton. **Circ:** 3,000 (ctrl).
Desc: Describes the arid land mission of Texas Tech University, the research and activities associated with ICASALS.
Ind/Abst GeoRef.

LC SB354.6.U5 I3
DD 634/.09796 US
IDAHO FRUIT TREE CENSUS. **Added/Corp** United States. Dept. of Agriculture. Economics and Statistics Service. Idaho. Dept. of Agriculture. Idaho Crop and Livestock Reporting Service. (19??)-. English. Every 2 years. Idaho Crop and Livestock Reporting Service, PO Box 1699, Boise ID 83701. **Tel** (208)554-1507. **ED** R.C. Max. **Bk Rev**. **Ad Acc. Circ:** 150 (ctrl).

LC S
DD 630 US
IDAHO WHEAT. English. Six times a year. Idaho State Wheat Growers Association, Owyhee Plaza/Suite M, Boise ID 83702.

LC S590 **ISSN** 1044-4521
DD 631 US
IFDC REPORT (FRENCH ED.). (IFDC REPORT.). [IFDC rep.]. **VAT** International Fertilizer Development Center Report. Periodical. English (Spanish and French). Four times a year. Free. IFDC, PO Box 2040, Muscle Shoals AL 35662. **Tel** (205)381-6600, FAX (205)381-7408, telex TWX 810 731 3970. **ED** Marie K Thompson. **Circ:** 700.
Desc: An update on the work and progress at IFDC.

LC S **ISSN** 0536-3683
DD 630 JA
CODEN IKZAAD
Pr Rev. **TITLE CHANGE**
IKUSHUGAKU ZASSHI. (IKUSHU-GAKU ZASSHI.). [Ikushugaku zasshi]. **Added/Corp** Nihon Ikushu Gakkai. **VFOAT** Japanese Journal of Breeding. Vol. 1 (1951)-Vol. 44 (1994). Periodical. Japanese (summaries and/or abstracts in English; table of contents in English). University of Tokyo Japan Society of Breeding, Yakyol 1 1 1 Bunkyo Ku, Agriculture Department, Tokyo 113 Japan. **Tel** 011 81 3 381222111. **ED** Kokushi Toriyama. Index available. **Ad Acc. Circ:** 2,000. Documents available from The Genuine Article, BIOSIS Document Express, CASDDS. ***Continued by*** *Breeding Science.*
Ind/Abst AGRICOLA; Biol. Abstr.; Chem. Abstr.; Crop Physiol. Abstr.; Curr. Aware. Biol. Sci., CABS; Curr. Cit.; Curr. Contents Agric. Biol. Environ. Sci.; Genet. Abstr.; Hortic. Abstr.; Maize Abstr.; Ornamental Hort. (1991-); Life Sci. Collect.; Plant Breed. Abstr.; Plant Genet. Resour. Abstr.; Plant Grow. Reg. Abstr.; Potato Abstr.; Res. Alert [Select. Cov.]; Rev. Agric. Entomol.; Rev. Plant Pathol.; Rice Abstr.; SCISEARCH; Seed Abstr.; Soc. Sci. Cit. Index [Select. Cov.]; Soyabean Abstr.; Weed Abstr.; Wheat Barley Trit. Abstr.

LC S
DD 630 UK
ILDIS NEWSLETTER. **Added/Corp** International Legume Database & Information Service. **VAT** International Legume Database and Information Service Newsletter. No. 1 (Feb. 1988)-. Newsletter. English. Three times a year. ILDIS Coordinating Centre, Biology Department, University of Southampton, Southampton SO9 5NH United Kingdom.

LC S **ISSN** 0920-8771
DD 630 NE
ILEIA NEWSLETTER. [ILEIA newsl.]. **Added/Corp** Informationcentre for Low External Input Agriculture. **VFOAT** I.L.E.I.A. Newsletter. **VAT** Informationcentre for Low External Input Agriculture Newsletter. (198?)-. Newsletter. English. Four times a year. $27.50. ILEIA / Information Centre for Low External Input and Sustainable Agriculture, Kastanjelaan 5, PO Box 64, 3830 AB Leusden Netherlands. **Tel** 011 31 33 943086, FAX 011 31 33 940791, telex 79380 ETC NL. **Bk Rev**. ctrl circ.
Ind/Abst Irr. Drain. Abstr.

LC S **ISSN** 0273-8635
DD 630 US
ILLINOIS WEATHER & CROPS. [Ill. weather crops]. **Added/Corp** Illinois Cooperative Crop Reporting Service. **VAT** Illinois Weather and Crops. No. 1 (Oct. 27, 1980)-. Government Publication. English. One time a week. $12.00. US Department of Agriculture / National Agricultural Statistics Service (NASS), Room 5829 South Building, Washington DC 20250. **Tel** (202)720-4020, FAX (314)875-5231.

LC SB113
DD 631.521 NE
INDEX SEMINUM. **Main/Corp** Botanische Tuinen Utrecht. **VFOAT** Index Seminum. No. 32 (1990)-. Periodical. English (Latin). ***Continues*** *Index Seminum Atque Sporarum Anno ... Collectorum.*

LC SB295.B5 I48 **ISSN** 0970-1184
DD 630 II
INDIAN COCOA, ARECANUT & SPICES JOURNAL. [Indian Cocoa arecanut Spices J.]. **Added/Corp** India. Directorate of Cocoa, Arecanut & Spices Development. **VFOAT** Indian Cocoa, Arecanut and Spices Journal. Vol. 3, No. 1 (July/Sept. 1979)-. Periodical. English. Four times a year. Division of Library Services, Department of Public Instruction, PO Box 7841, Madison WI 53707. **(Subscription address:** Prints India, 11 Darya Ganj, New Delhi 110002 India. **Tel** 011 91 11 3268645, FAX 011 91 11 3275542, telex 31-61087 PRIN-IN.) ***Continues*** *Indian Arecanut, Spices & Cocoa Journal, 0970-1176.*
Ind/Abst Agrofor. Abstr. (19??-19??); Field Crop Abstr.; Food Sci. Technol. Abstr.; For. Abstr.; Hortic. Abstr.; Nematol. Abstr.; Plant Breed. Abstr.; Rev. Agric. Entomol.; Rev. Med. Vet. Entomol.; Rev. Plant Pathol.; Seed Abstr.; Soils Fert.; Weed Abstr.; World Agric. Econ. Rural Sociol. Abstr.

LC S **ISSN** 0367-7281
DD 630 II
INDIAN COCONUT JOURNAL (COCHIN). (INDIAN COCONUT JOURNAL.). [Indian coconut j.]. **Added/Corp** India. Directorate of Coconut Development. Vol. 8 (May 1977)-. Periodical. English. Twelve times a year. $10.00. Coconut Development Board, Minister of Agriculture/Government of India, Cochin 682011 India. **(Subscription address:** Prints India, 11 Darya Ganj, New Delhi 110002 India. **Tel** 011 91 11 3268645, FAX 011 91 11 3275542, telex 31-61087 PRIN-IN.) ***Continues*** *Coconut Bulletin, 0970-4426.*
Ind/Abst AgBiotech News Inf.; AGRICOLA; Agrofor. Abstr. (19??-19??); Food Sci. Technol. Abstr.; Hortic. Abstr.; Irr. Drain. Abstr.; Plant Grow. Reg. Abstr.; Rev. Agric. Entomol.; Rev. Plant Pathol.; Rural Dev. Abstr.; Seed Abstr.; Sug. Indus. Abstr.; World Agric. Econ. Rural Sociol. Abstr.

LC S **ISSN** 0019-4549
DD 630 II
CODEN ICOFAJ
INDIAN COFFEE. (INDIAN COFFEE; BULLETIN OF THE INDIAN COFFEE BOARD.). [Indian coffee]. **Added/Corp** India. Coffee Board. India. Coffee Board. Bulletin of the Indian Coffee Board. (19??)-. Trade Publication. English. Twelve times a year. $25.00. Coffee Board, Box 5366, Bangalore 560001 India. **Tel** 24920. **(Subscription address:** Prints India, 11 Darya Ganj, New Delhi 110002 India. **Tel** 011 91 11 3268645, FAX 011 91 11 3275542, telex 31-61087 PRIN-IN.) **ED** N. Jayarami Reddy. Index available. **Bk Rev**. **Ad Acc. Circ:** 7,500. Documents available from BIOSIS Document Express, CASDDS.
Desc: Devoted to the growth and development of the Indian coffee industry. Contains information on the latest researches on Indian coffee.
Ind/Abst AgBiotech News Inf.; AGRICOLA; Biodeter. Abstr.; Biol. Abstr.; Chem. Abstr.; EMBASE; Food Sci. Technol. Abstr.; Hortic. Abstr.; Plant Grow. Reg. Abstr.; Postharvest News Inf.; Rev. Agric. Entomol.; World Agric. Econ. Rural Sociol. Abstr.

LC S590 **ISSN** 0970-3349
DD 631.4 II
INDIAN JOURNAL OF SOIL CONSERVATION. [Indian j. soil conserv.]. **Added/Corp** Indian Association of Soil & Water Conservationists. Vol. 6, No. 1 (Apr. 1978)-. Periodical. English. Two times a year. ***Continues*** *Soil Conservation Digest.*
Ind/Abst AGRICOLA; Ecol. Abstr.; Geogr. Abstr. Phys. Geogr.; Int. Dev. Abstr.

LC S
DD 630 II
INDIAN SUGAR CROPS JOURNAL, THE. Vol. 4, No. 2 (April/June (1977)-. Periodical. English. Four times a year. Direcorate of Sugarcane Development, C-196 Ramprastha Colony Delhi, Ghaziabad 201 011 India. ***Continues*** *Cane Grower's Bulletin.*
Ind/Abst Maize Abstr.

LC S **ISSN** 0442-817X
DD 630 US
INDIANA WEEKLY WEATHER CROP REPORT. **Added/Corp** Purdue University Dept. of Agricultural Statistics. United States. Dept. of Agriculture. Statistical Reporting Service. State Statistical Office. (19??)-. Statistical Publication. English. Thirty-five times a year. $12.00. US Department of Agriculture / National Agricultural Statistics Service (NASS), Room 5829 South Building, Washington DC 20250. **Tel** (202)720-4020, FAX (314)875-5231. **ED** Lee Brown and Ralph W. Gann. **Circ:** 1,300 (ctrl). ***Continues*** *Indiana Weekly Weather and Crop Report.*
Desc: Progress of crops and farm work.

LC SB183 **ISSN** 0216-8170
DD 633 IO
CODEN IJCSEH
INDONESIAN JOURNAL OF CROP SCIENCE. [Indones. j. crop sci.]. **Added/Corp** Indonesia. Badan Penelitian dan Pengembangan Pertanian. Australian Centre for International Agricultural Research. Vol. 1, No. 1 (Jan. 1985)-. Periodical. English. Two times a year. Agency for Agricultural Research & Development, JL IR H Juanda 20, Bogor 16122 Indonesia. **Tel** 011 62 251 321746. Documents available from BIOSIS Document Express.
Ind/Abst AGRICOLA [Full Cov.]; Biol. Abstr. (1986-); Cot. Trop. Fibr. Abstr. Bibliogr.; Field Crop Abstr.; Maize Abstr.; Plant Breed. Abstr.; Rev. Plant Pathol.; Rice Abstr.; SEA Abstr.; Seed Abstr.; Soils Fert.

LC S **ISSN** 0926-6690
DD 630 NE
CCC
CODEN ICRDEW
Pr Rev.
INDUSTRIAL CROPS AND PRODUCTS. Vol. 1, No. 1 (Sept. 1992)-. Academic Scholarly Publication. English. Four times a year (1 volume). $249.00. Elsevier Science Publishers BV, PO Box 211, 1000 AE Amsterdam Netherlands. **Tel** 011 31 20 4853641, 011 31 20 4853642, FAX 011 31 20 4853598. available on an online database from Elsevier Electronic Subscriptions (EES). Documents available from CASDDS.
Ind/Abst AGRICOLA; Chem. Abstr.

LC S
DD 630 IT
INFERMIERE : NOTIZIARIO AGGIORNAMENTI PROFESSIONALI, L'. Italian. Six times a year. L40000. Fed Naz Collegi Ipasvi, Via Depretis 86, 00184 Rome Italy. **Tel** 011 39 6 4817516.

LC S **ISSN** 0145-6288
DD 630 US
INFOLETTER - INTERNATIONAL PLANT PROTECTION CENTER. (INFOLETTER - INTERNATIONAL PLANT PROTECTION CENTER, OREGON STATE UNIVERSITY.). **Main/Corp** International Plant Protection Center. (1970)-. Periodical. English (Spanish and French). Free. International Plant Protection Center, Oregon State University, Corvallis OR 97331. **Tel** (503)754-3541. **ED** A E Deutsch. **Circ:** 8,500.

Agriculture —Crop Production and Soil

LC SB354
DD 634
FR

INFOS / CENTRE TECHNIQUE INTERPROFESSIONNEL DES FRUITS ET LEGUMES. Added/Corp Centre Technique Interprofessionnel des Fruits et Legumes (France). No. 1 (Apr. 1984)-. Periodical. French. Ten times a year. $108.27. Centre Technique Interprofessionnel des Fruits et Legumes, 22 rue Bergere, F-75009 Paris France. **Tel** 011 33 1 47701693. *Continues CTIFL-Documents.*
Ind/Abst Biodeter. Abstr.; Irr. Drain. Abstr.; Plant Grow. Reg. Abstr.; Postharvest News Inf.; Rev. Agric. Entomol.; Rev. Plant Pathol.; Soils Fert.; World Agric. Econ. Rural Sociol. Abstr.

LC SB354
DD 634
SA

INLIGHTINSBULLETIN - NAVORSINGSINSTITUUT VIR SITRUS EN SUBTROPIESE VRUGTE. Main/Corp Citrus and Subtropical Fruit Research Institute. **VFOAT** Information Bulletin - Citrus and Subtropical Fruit Research Institute. No. 1 (July 1972)-. Bulletin. English (Afrikaans). Twelve times a year. Institute of Tropical Subtropical Crop, Private Bag X11208, Nelspruit 1200 South Africa. **Tel** 011 27 1311 52071.
Ind/Abst Agric. Eng. Abstr. (1991-); Hortic. Abstr.; Nematol. Abstr.; Plant Breed. Abstr.; Plant Genet. Resour. Abstr.; Plant Grow. Reg. Abstr.; Postharvest News Inf.; Rev. Agric. Entomol.; Rev. Plant Pathol.; Soils Fert.

LC SB295.G5 I59
DD 633.88
KO

INSAM YONGU NONMUNJIP. VFOAT Research Papers of Korea Ginseng Science. Vol. 1 (1979/1980)-. Periodical. English (Korean). Hanguk Insam Yoncho Yonguso, 112 Inui-dong, Chongno-ku, Seoul South Korea.

LC SB950
DD 632.9
ISSN 1353-5226
UK
Pr Rev.

●**INTEGRATED PEST MANAGEMENT REVIEWS.** (1995-). Academic Scholarly Publication. English. Four times a year. $259.00. Chapman & Hall, 2-6 Boundary Row, London SE1 8HN United Kingdom. **Tel** 011 44 171 8650066, FAX 011 44 171 5229623, telex 290164 CHAPMA G. **(Subscription address:** International Thomson Publishing Services Ltd., North Way Andover, Hampshire SP10 5BE United Kingdom. **Tel** 011 44 1264 332424.) **ED** David Dent. **Ad Acc**.
Desc: Covers agricultural pest management.

LC S
DD 630
ISSN 1010-5824
II

INTERNATIONAL ARACHIS NEWSLETTER. VFOAT IAN. No. 1 (May 1987)-. Newsletter. English. Two times a year. Legumes Program, Icrisat, Patancheru, Andhra Pradesh 502 324 India.
Ind/Abst Agrofor. Abstr. (1991-); Biocont. News Inf.; Biodeter. Abstr.; Field Crop Abstr.; For. Prod. Abstr. (1991-); Nematol. Abstr.; Plant Breed. Abstr.; Plant Genet. Resour. Abstr.; Plant Grow. Reg. Abstr.; Rev. Agric. Entomol.; Rev. Plant Pathol.; Soils Fert.; Weed Abstr.

LC QK495.L52 I58
DD 582.13
ISSN 1023-4861
II

●**INTERNATIONAL CHICKPEA AND PIGEONPEA NEWSLETTER.** Added/Corp International Crops Research Institute for the Semi-Arid Tropics. No. 1 (1994)-. Newsletter. English. Pulse Improvement Program International, Crops Research Institute for the Semi-Arid Tropics, Patancheuru PO, Andhra Pradesh 502 324 India. *Formed by the union of International Chickpea Newsletter, 0257-2508 and International Pigeonpea Newsletter, 0255-786X.*

LC S
DD 630
II
TITLE CHANGE

INTERNATIONAL CHICKPEA NEWSLETTER. Added/Corp International Crops Research Institute for the Semi-Arid Tropics. VFOAT ICN. No. 1 (Dec. 1979)-No. 29 (Dec. 1993). Newsletter. English. Pulse Improvement Program International, Crops Research Institute for the Semi-Arid Tropics, Patancheuru PO, Andhra Pradesh 502 324 India. *Merged with International Pigeonpea Newsletter, 0255-786X to form International Chickpea and Pigeonpea Newsletter, 1023-4861.*
Ind/Abst Biocont. News Inf. (19??-19??); Field Crop Abstr.; Irr. Drain. Abstr.; Nematol. Abstr.; Plant Breed. Abstr.; Plant Grow. Reg. Abstr.; Rev. Agric. Entomol.; Rev. Plant Pathol.; Seed Abstr.; Soils Fert.; Weed Abstr.; Wheat Barley Trit. Abstr.

LC TA710.A1 I5197
DD 624.1/513/0151
ISSN 0363-9061
UK
CODEN IJNGDZ
Pr Rev.

INTERNATIONAL JOURNAL FOR NUMERICAL AND ANALYTICAL METHODS IN GEOMECHANICS. See Engineering-Civil Engineering.

LC S
DD 630
II
TITLE CHANGE

INTERNATIONAL PIGEONPEA NEWSLETTER. Added/Corp International Crops Research Institute for the Semi-Arid Tropics. Pulse Improvement Program (International Crops Research Institute for the Semi-Arid Tropics) Pulses Improvement Program (International Crops Research Institute for the Semi-arid Tropics) Legumes Program (International Crops Research Institute for the Semi-Arid Tropics). (1981)-(1993). Newsletter. English. Pulse Improvement Program, International Crops Research Institute for the Semi-Arid Tropics, Patancheuru PO, Andhra Pradesh 502 324 India. *Merged with International Chickpea Newsletter, 0257-2508 to form International Chickpea and Pigeonpea Newsletter, 1023-4861.*
Ind/Abst Agric. Eng. Abstr. (1991-); Field Crop Abstr.; Irr. Drain. Abstr.; Maize Abstr.; Nematol. Abstr.; Plant Breed. Abstr.; Rev. Agric. Entomol.; Rev. Plant Pathol.; Rice Abstr.; Seed Abstr.

LC SB191.R5 I616
DD 633.1
PH
CODEN IRNOEE

●**INTERNATIONAL RICE RESEARCH NOTES.** Added/Corp International Rice Research Institute. VFOAT IRRN. Vol. 18, No. 1 (Mar. 1993)-. Periodical. English. Four times a year. International Rice Research Institute, PO Box 933, 1099 Manila Philippines. **Tel** (011)63 2 8181926, FAX (011)63 2 8182087, telex 45365, 7425365. Index available. cum. index. **Bk Rev** (Qty: 4). **Circ:** 12,000 (ctrl). *Continues International Rice Research Institute. International Rice Research Newsletter, 0115-0944.*

LC S
DD 630
IS

●**INTERNATIONAL WATER & IRRIGATION REVIEW.** VFOAT International Water and Irrigation Review. Vol. 13, No. 1 (1993)-. Trade Publication. English (summaries and/or abstracts in Arabic and Spanish). Four times a year (Jan., Apr., July, Oct.). $60.00. Amir Cohen Advertising Company, Ltd., PO Box 21051, 55 Weizmann Street, Tel Aviv 61210 Israel. **Tel** 011 972-3-6953192, FAX 011 972-3-6956116. **ED** Joshua Jacobson. **Ad Acc, Adv Mgr:** Amir Cohen. **Circ:** 10,466 (ctrl). *Continues Water & Irrigation Review.*
Desc: This journal is concerned with water in all aspects - agriculture, supply, purification, recycling, desalination, with special emphasis on irrigation. Contains a products review section on manufacturers products, with articles by professional engineers and researchers.

LC S
DD 630
ISSN 0579-4005
UN

INTRODUKTSIIA TA AKLIMATYZATSIIA ROSLIN NA UKRAINI. [Introd. aklim. roslin Ukr.]. Added/Corp Akademiia Nauk URSR, Kiev. Botanichnii Sad. Vol. 1 (1968)-. Monographic series. Ukrainian (summaries and/or abstracts in Russian; table of contents in Russian). Price varies per volume. Izdatelstvo Naukova Dumka / Ukrainian Academy of Sciences, Yu. A. Khramov, Dir., Ul. Repina 3, 252 601 Kiev Ukraine. **Tel** 011 7 44 4303441, 011 7 44 2254182, telex 131376.
Ind/Abst AGRICOLA.

LC SB87.S64 I57
DD 631/.0946
ISSN 0213-5000
SP
CODEN IAPVES

INVESTIGACION AGRARIA. PRODUCCION Y PROTECCION VEGETALES. [Invest. agrar., prod. prot. veg.]. Added/Corp Instituto Nacional de Investigaciones Agrarias. VFOAT Produccion y Proteccion Vegetales. Vol. 1, (April 1986)-. Periodical. Spanish (summaries and/or abstracts in English and French). Three times a year. $84.38. Instituto Nacional de Investigaciones Agrarias, C. Jose Abascal 56, 28003 Madrid Spain. **Tel** 011 34 1 3473906, FAX (91)4423587, telex 48989 INIA E. **(Subscription address:** CIT / Inia Biblioteca, CRT Coruna KM 7, Jose L. Bernabe, 28040 Madrid Spain. **) Bk Rev. Circ:** 1,800 (ctrl). Documents available from BIOSIS Document Express, CASDDS. *Formed by the union of Anales del Instituto Nacional de Investigaciones Agrarias. Serie Agricola and Anales del Instituto Nacional de Investigaciones Agrarias. Serie, Forestal.*
Desc: This represents significant contribution to knowledge of concepts related to plant production, protection and natural resources.
Ind/Abst AGRICOLA; Agric. Eng. Abstr. (1991-); Biol. Abstr. (1986-); Chem. Abstr.; Cot. Trop. Fibr. Abstr. Bibliogr.; Crop Physiol. Abstr.; Field Crop Abstr.; For. Abstr.; GeoRef.; Grass. Forage Abstr.; Hortic. Abstr.; Irr. Drain. Abstr.; Maize Abstr.; Nutr. Abstr. Rev., Ser. B, Live Feeds and Feed.; Plant Breed. Abstr.; Plant Grow. Reg. Abstr.; Postharvest News Inf.; Rev. Agric. Entomol.; Rev. Med. Vet. Entomol.; Rev. Plant Pathol.; Seed Abstr.; Soils Fert.; Vitis Vitic. Enol. Abstr.; Weed Abstr.; Wheat Barley Trit. Abstr.

LC S
DD 630
ISSN 0745-0109
US

IOWA CROP REPORT. (19??)-. Government Publication. English. Eleven times a year. $10.00. US Department of Agriculture / National Agricultural Statistics Service (NASS), Room 5829 South Building, Washington DC 20250. **Tel** (202)720-4020, FAX (314)875-5231. *Continues Crops / Iowa.*
Desc: Highlights major acreage, Production and stock reports of concern to Iowa Producers marketings and number on feed in Iowa.

LC S
DD 630
ISSN 1041-9268
US

IOWA CROPS AND WEATHER. (Sept. 20, 1976)-. English. One time a week. The Service, Full Depository, 707 Savings and Loan Building, Des Moines IA 50309. *Continues Iowa Weekly Weather and Crop Report.*
Desc: Data on Iowa weather, and its effects on fields, crops, and livestock.

LC S612 .I73
DD 631.6/2/05
ISSN 0306-7327
UK

IRRIGATION AND DRAINAGE ABSTRACTS. See Engineering-Abstracting, Bibliographies and Statistics.

LC S
DD 630
UDC 631.67
ISSN 0394-9338
IT

IRRIGAZIONE E DRENAGGIO. (1989)-. Periodical. Italian. Four times a year. Edagricole, PO Box 2157, 40100 Bologna Italy. **Tel** 011 39 51 492211 Ext. 22, FAX 011 39 51 493660, telex 510336 EDAGRI.
Ind/Abst Agric. Eng. Abstr. (1991-); Field Crop Abstr.; Hortic. Abstr.; Irr. Drain. Abstr.; Plant Breed. Abstr.; Potato Abstr.; Seed Abstr.; Soils Fert.; Wheat Barley Trit. Abstr.

LC S
DD 630
ISSN 1130-6017
SP

ITEA. PRODUCCION VEGETAL. [ITEA, Prod. veg.]. Added/Corp Asociacion Interprofesional Para el Desarrollo Agrario. VFOAT Produccion Vegetal; Informacion Tecnica Economica Agraria. Vol. 86V, No. 1 (1990)-. Periodical. Spanish (summaries and/or abstracts in English). Three times a year. $31.08. AIDA, Carretera Montanana 176, 50016 Zaragoza Spain. **Tel** 011 34 76 576311. *Continues ITEA, 0212-2731.*
Ind/Abst Crop Physiol. Abstr.; Hortic. Abstr.; Plant Breed. Abstr.; Postharvest News Inf.; Seed Abstr.; Soils Fert.

LC S590
DD 631.4
ISSN 0202-7143
RU
CODEN ITPADT

ITOGI NAUKI I TEKHNIKI. POCHVOVEDENIE I AGROKHIMIIA. VFOAT Pochvovedenie i Agrokhimiia; Seriia Pochvovedenie i Agrokhimiia; Itogi Nauki i Tekhniki. Seriia Pochvovedenie i Agrokhimiia. Vol. 1 (1974)-. Academic Scholarly Publication. Russian. Irregular. Price varies per volume. VINITI - Vsesoyuznyi Institut Nauchno-Tekhnicheskoi Informatsii, All-Union Scientific and Technical Information Institute, Baltiiskaia ulitsa 14, 125219 Moscow Russia. **Tel** 011 7 95 2384600, FAX 011 7 95 9430060, telex 411160. Documents available from CASDDS.
Ind/Abst Chem. Abstr.

LC SB114.N4 R54A
DD 631.5/21/07204921
NE

JAARVERSLAG / RIJKSPROEFSTATION VOOR ZAADONDERZOEK. Main/Corp Rijksproefstation voor Zaadonderzoek (Netherlands). VFOAT Annual Report. Dutch. One time a year. Rijksproefstation voor Zaadonderzoek Binnenhaven 1, PO Box 9104, 6700 He Wageningen The Netherlands.

LC HD9490.S64 S687A
DD 354.680082/61385/06
SA

JAARVERSLAG VAN DIE OLIESADERAAD VIR DIE JAAR ... . Main/Corp South Africa. Oilseeds Board. VFOAT Annual Report of the Oilseeds Board for the Year ... . May 1, 1981 to May 31, 1982). English (Afrikaans). One time a year. Oliesaderaad, Posbus 211, Pretoria 0001 South Africa. *Continues Jaarverslag van die Oliesadebeheerraad vir die Jaar ... .*

LC HD9086.J3 J45
DD 331.7
ISSN 0447-5321
JA

JAPAN COTTON STATISTICS AND RELATED DATA, THE. See Agriculture-Abstracting, Bibliographies and Statistics.

LC HD9116.J2 J36
DD 338.4/7/66410942 JA
JAPAN SUGAR YEARBOOK. English. Mitsui Bussan K.K. Toshitsu Hakkobu, (Sugar & Fermented Products Div. Mitsui & Co. Ltd.), 2-1 Otemachi 1 Chome, Chiyodaku Tokyo 100 Japan.

LC S
DD 630 BL
JORNAL DA ARMAZENAGEM. **Added/Corp** Centro Nacional de Treinamento em Armazenagem. (June 1979)-. Periodical. Portuguese. Four times a year. Centro Nacional de Treinamento em Armazenagem, Caixa Postal 375, Campus da Ufv 36.570, Vicosa-Mg Brazil.
Ind/Abst Field Crop Abstr.; Grass. Forage Abstr.

LC TP **ISSN** 1075-6302
DD 664 US
JOURNAL - AMERICAN SOCIETY OF SUGAR CANE TECHNOLOGISTS. FLORIDA DIVISIONS. (JOURNAL / AMERICAN SOCIETY OF SUGAR CANE TECHNOLOGISTS, FLORIDA AND LOUISIANA DIVISIONS.). [J. - Am. Soc. Sugar Cane Technol., Fla. Div.]. **Main/Corp** American Society of Sugar Cane Technologists. Florida Division. **Added/Corp** American Society of Sugar Cane Technologists. Louisiana Division. Vol. 1 (July 1982)-. English. One time a year. $15.00. American Society of Sugar Cane Technologists, LSU/Knapp Hall, Baton Rouge LA 70803. **Tel** (504)388-6083. ctrl circ. ***Continues*** *American Society of Sugar Cane Technologists. Proceedings.*
Ind/Abst AGRICOLA; Biocont. News Inf. (1991-); Field Crop Abstr.; Hortic. Abstr.; Plant Breed. Abstr.; Rev. Agric. Entomol.; Rev. Plant Pathol.; Soils Fert.; Weed Abstr.

LC S **ISSN** 1151-0285
DD 630 FR
CODEN JISVE8
JOURNAL INTERNATIONAL DES SCIENCES DE LA VIGNE ET DU VIN. Vol. 24 No. 1 (1990)-. Periodical. French (summaries and/or abstracts in English). Four times a year. $102.80. Vigne et Vin Publications Internationales, Bordeaux Technopolis, Site Montesquieu, 33651 Martillac cedex France. **Tel** 011 33 56 648230, FAX 011 33 56 648205, telex 550 415F. Documents available from CASDDS. ***Continues*** *Connaissance de la Vigne et du Vin, 0010-577X.*
Ind/Abst Chem. Abstr.

LC S583 .J6 **ISSN** 0021-8561
DD 630.2405 US
CCC
NLM W1 JO534D **CODEN** JAFCAU
Pr Rev.
JOURNAL OF AGRICULTURAL AND FOOD CHEMISTRY. [J. agric. food chem.]. **Added/Corp** American Chemical Society. Books and Journals Division. **VFOAT** Agricultural and Food Chemistry. Vol. 1 (Apr. 1, 1953)-. Periodical. English. Twelve times a year. $483.00. American Chemical Society, 1155 Sixteenth Street Northwest, Washington DC 20036. **Tel** (800)333-9511, (800)227-5558, (614)447-3776, FAX (202)447-3671. **(Subscription address:** American Chemical Society / Ohio, Department L 0011, Columbus OH 43268-0011. **) ED** Irvin E. Liener. Index available (free). **Bk Rev. Ad Acc. Acid Free. Circ:** 4,400 (ctrl). available on microfilm and microfiche from University Microfilms International (UMI). Documents available from The Genuine Article, BIOSIS Document Express, CASDDS, Documents on Demand.
Desc: Includes pesticides, plant nutrients and regulators, chemistry of food and feed, biochemistry of nutrition, flavor chemistry, toxicants, wood, fertilizers and compounds isolated from food material.
Ind/Abst AgBiotech News Inf.; AGRICOLA [Full Cov.]; Agrofor. Abstr. (1991-); Anal. Abstr.; BioBusiness; Biocont. News Inf. (19??-19??); Biodeter. Abstr. (19??-19??); Biol. Agric. Index; Biol. Abstr.; Chem. Abstr.; Chem. Titles; Chemorecept. Abstr.; Coal Abstr.; Cot. Trop. Fibr. Abstr. Bibliogr.; Crop Physiol. Abstr.; CSA Neuro. Abstr. (?-?); Curr. Biotechnol.; Curr. Chem. React.; Curr. Cit.; Curr. Contents Agric. Biol. Environ. Sci.; Curr. Contents Life Sci.; Dairy Sci. Abstr.; EMBASE; Energy Inf. Abstr.; Energy Res. Abstr.; Environ. Abstr.; Environ. Period. Bibliogr. (?-?); Field Crop Abstr.; Food Sci. Technol. Abstr.; Foods Adlibra; For. Prod. Abstr.; Grass. Forage Abstr.; Helminthol. Abstr. (19??-19??); Hortic. Abstr.; Index Chem.; Index Med.; Index Vet.; INIS Atomindex [Micro.]; Int. Aerosp. Abstr.; Irr. Drain. Abstr.; Mass Spect. Bull.; Methods Organ. Synth.; Microbiol. Abstr. Sect. A; Microbiol. Abstr. Sect. C; NAPRALERT; Nat. Prod. Updates; Nutr. Abstr. Rev., Ser. B, Live Feeds and Feed.; Nutr. Abstr. Rev., Ser. A, Hum. Exp.; Ornamental Hort. (1991-); PESTDOC; Pig News Inf.; Plant Breed. Abstr.; Plant Grow. Reg. Abstr.; Postharvest News Inf.; Potato Abstr.; Protozoolog. Abstr.; Ref. Upd. Deluxe Ed.; Res. Alert [Full Cov.]; Rev. Agric. Entomol.; Rev. Med. Vet. Entomol.; Rev. Med. Vet. Mycology; Rev. Plant Pathol.; Rice Abstr.; Sci. Cit. Index; SCISEARCH; Seed Abstr.; Soils Fert.; Sorghum Mill. Abstr.; Soyabean Abstr.; Stat. Theory Method Abstr. (1959-1963); Vet. Bull.; Vitis Vitic. Enol. Abstr.; Weed Abstr.; Wheat Barley Trit. Abstr.

LC S19 .W4 **ISSN** 0368-1157
DD 630/.5 PK
CODEN JAGRBD
JOURNAL OF AGRICULTURAL RESEARCH (LAHORE). (JOURNAL OF AGRICULTURAL RESEARCH.). **Added/Corp** Punjab (Pakistan). Dept. of Agriculture. Vol. 8, No. 3 (Sept. 1970)-. Academic Scholarly Publication. English. Six times a year. $33.00. AYUB Agricultural Research Institute, Jhang Road, Research Information Section, Faisalabad Pakistan. **Tel** 0411 655293. **ED** A. G. Kausar. Index available. **Bk Rev. Circ:** 500. available on microfilm from University Microfilms International (UMI). Documents available from CASDDS. ***Continues*** *West Pakistan Journal of Agricultural Research.*
Desc: Deals with plant breeding agronomy, soils, plant protection, food technology, biochemistry, nutrition, crop physiology, agricultural economics and agricultural engineering.
Ind/Abst Chem. Abstr. (1970-1981); Field Crop Abstr.; Nematol. Abstr.; Plant Breed. Abstr.; Plant Grow. Reg. Abstr.; Rice Abstr.; Seed Abstr.; Soyabean Abstr.; Weed Abstr.; Wheat Barley Trit. Abstr.

LC S590 **ISSN** 8755-8750
DD 631 US
CODEN JSPDE9
Pr Rev.
JOURNAL OF APPLIED SEED PRODUCTION. [J. appl. seed prod.]. **Added/Corp** Oregon Seed Growers League. International Herbage Seed Production Research Group. Vol. 1 (1983)-. English. One time a year (Oct.). $60.00. Journal of Applied Seed Production, Massey University / Seed Tech Centreer, Palmerston North New Zealand. **Tel** 011 64 6 3569099 ext. 8493, FAX 011 64 6 3505649. **ED** Dr. J. G. Hampton. Index available (published each issue). **Bk Rev**, (Qty: 1). **Ad Acc, Adv Mgr:** J.G. Hampton. **Circ:** 500.
Desc: An international journal which publishes research papers and reviews on all aspects of seed production in agricultural, horticultural and silvicultural species.
Ind/Abst AGRICOLA [Full Cov.]; Biodeter. Abstr.; Crop Physiol. Abstr.; Field Crop Abstr.; Grass. Forage Abstr.; Irr. Drain. Abstr.; Nematol. Abstr.; Plant Grow. Reg. Abstr.; Rev. Plant Pathol.; Rice Abstr.; Seed Abstr.; Soils Fert.; Soyabean Abstr.; Weed Abstr.

LC TP **ISSN** 0733-5210
DD 664 UK
CCC
CODEN JCSCDA
Pr Rev.
JOURNAL OF CEREAL SCIENCE. [J. cereal sci.]. Vol. 1, No. 1 (Jan. 1983)-. Academic Scholarly Publication. English. Six times a year. $381.59. Academic Press Ltd., A Division of Harcourt Brace & Company Ltd., 24-28 Oval Road, London NW1 7DX United Kingdom. **Tel** 011 44 171 2674466, FAX 011 44 171 4822293, 011 44 171 4854752, telex 25775 ACPRES G. **(Subscription address:** Harcourt Brace & Company, Ltd., Foots Cray High Street, Sidcup Kent DA14 5HP United Kingdom. **Tel** 011 44 181 3003322, FAX 011 44 181 3090807, telex 896 377 ACADEM.**) ED** T. Galliard and J. D. Schofield. Documents available from The Genuine Article, BIOSIS Document Express, CASDDS.
Desc: Publishes research papers covering all aspects of cereal science related to the functional and nutritional quality of cereal grains and their products.
Ind/Abst AgBiotech News Inf.; AGRICOLA [Full Cov.]; Biodeter. Abstr.; Biol. Abstr. (1984-); Chem. Abstr. (1983-); Curr. Aware. Biol. Sci., CABS; Curr. Cit.; Ei Page One; Field Crop Abstr.; Food Sci. Technol. Abstr.; Foods Adlibra; Maize Abstr.; Nutr. Abstr. Rev., Ser. A, Hum. Exp.; Plant Breed. Abstr.; Plant Genet. Resour. Abstr.; Postharvest News Inf.; Res. Alert [Full Cov.]; Rice Abstr.; Sci. Cit. Index; SCISEARCH; Seed Abstr.; Sorghum Mill. Abstr.; Soyabean Abstr.; Wheat Barley Trit. Abstr.

LC SB354
DD 634 US
Pr Rev.
•**JOURNAL OF CITRICULTURE.** Vol. 1, No. 1 (1996)-. Academic Scholarly Publication. English. Two times a year. $60.00 US; $84.00 other. The Haworth Press Inc., 10 Alice Street, Binghamton NY 13904-1580. **Tel** (607)722-5857, (800)3-HAWORTH, FAX (607)722-1424. **ED** Robert J. McNeil. **Bk Rev. Ad Acc. Acid Free.** available on microfiche from University Microfilms International (UMI). Documents available from Haworth Document Delivery Service.
Desc: Aimed toward the needs of the citrus grower, worker, and researcher. The journal welcomes submission of research papers of an applied nature, and which have developed conclusions and recommendations which can be of immediate significance and usefulness to the citrus industry.

LC S **ISSN** 0374-8537
DD 630 II
CODEN JCFRBM
Pr Rev.
JOURNAL OF COFFEE RESEARCH. [J. coffee res.]. **Added/Corp** Central Coffee Research Institute. (1971)-. Academic Scholarly Publication. English. Two times a year (Jan. and July). $25.00. Central Coffee Research Institute, 577 117 Chikmagalur District, Karnataka India. **(Subscription address:** Prints India, 11 Darya Ganj, New Delhi 110002 India. **Tel** 011 91 11 3268645, FAX 011 91 11 3275542, telex 31-61087 PRIN-IN.) Index available (Bound in July issue). **Ad Acc. Circ:** 500. Documents available from BIOSIS Document Express, CASDDS.
Desc: Journal devoted to publishing scientific and technical papers covering nutrition, plant improvement, protection processing, marketing and other aspects of coffee.
Ind/Abst AGRICOLA; Agrofor. Abstr. (1991-); BioBusiness; Biocont. News Inf.; Biodeter. Abstr. (19??-19??); Biol. Abstr.; Chem. Abstr.; Crop Physiol. Abstr.; EMBASE; Food Sci. Technol. Abstr.; Hortic. Abstr.; Leis., Rec., Tour. Abstr.; Plant Breed. Abstr.; Plant Grow. Reg. Abstr.; Postharvest News Inf.; Rev. Med. Vet. Mycology; Rev. Plant Pathol.; Rural Dev. Abstr.; Seed Abstr.; Soils Fert.; World Agric. Econ. Rural Sociol. Abstr.

LC SB354 .J68
DD 634 PL
CODEN JFOREN
•**JOURNAL OF FRUIT AND ORNAMENTAL PLANT RESEARCH.** **Added/Corp** Instytut Sadownictwa i Kwiaciarstwa (Skierniewice, Poland). Vol. 1, No. 1 (1993)-. Periodical. English. Four times a year. $56.00. **(Subscription address:** Ars Polona-Ruch, PO Box 1001, Krakowskie Przedmiescie 7, 00-068 Warsaw Poland. **Tel** 011 48 22 261201.**)** ***Continues*** *Fruit Science Reports, 0137-1479.*
Ind/Abst Chem. Abstr.

LC S **ISSN** 0378-2395
DD 630 II
CODEN JMAUDA
JOURNAL OF MAHARASHTRA AGRICULTURAL UNIVERSITIES. [J. Maharashtra Agric. Univ.]. **Added/Corp** Mahatma Phule Krishi Vidyapeeth. Punjabrao Krishi Vidyapeeth. Marathwada Krishi Vidyapeeth. Konkan Krishi Vidyapeeth. Vol. 1 Jan./Feb. (1976)-. Academic Scholarly Publication. English. Six times a year. $50.00. Maharashtra Agricultural University, College of Agriculture, Pune 411 005 India. **Tel** 57033. **(Subscription address:** Prints India, 11 Darya Ganj, New Delhi 110002 India. **Tel** 011 91 11 3268645, FAX 011 91 11 3275542, telex 31-61087 PRIN-IN.) **ED** P. L. Patil. **Bk Rev. Circ:** 700. Documents available from BIOSIS Document Express, CASDDS. ***Formed by the union of*** *Research Journal of Mahatma Phule Agricultural University, 0378-6404* ***and*** *P.K.V. Research Journal.*
Desc: Covers soil, plant protection, crop husbandry, plant protection, microbiology, social sciences, food technology, agricultural engineering, animal sciences.
Ind/Abst AgBiotech News Inf.; AGRICOLA; Agrofor. Abstr. (1991-); Biocont. News Inf.; Biodeter. Abstr.; Biol. Abstr.; Chem. Abstr.; Cot. Trop. Fibr. Abstr. Bibliogr.; Crop Physiol. Abstr.; Field Crop Abstr.; For. Abstr.; Grass. Forage Abstr.; Hortic. Abstr.; Index Vet.; Irr. Drain. Abstr.; Maize Abstr.; Microbiol. Abstr. Sect. A; Microbiol. Abstr. Sect. C; Life Sci. Collect.; Plant Breed. Abstr.; Plant Genet. Resour. Abstr.; Plant Grow. Reg. Abstr.; Postharvest News Inf.; Potato Abstr.; Rev. Med. Vet. Mycology; Rev. Plant Pathol.; Rice Abstr.; Seed Abstr.; Soils Fert.; Sorghum Mill. Abstr.; Soyabean Abstr.; Sug. Indus. Abstr.; Vitis Vitic. Enol. Abstr.; Weed Abstr.; Wheat Barley Trit. Abstr.; World Agric. Econ. Rural Sociol. Abstr.

LC SB761 **ISSN** 0970-2776
DD 635.97 II
CODEN JOREES
JOURNAL OF OILSEEDS RESEARCH. [J. oilseeds res.]. **Added/Corp** Indian Society of Oilseeds Research. Directorate of Oilseeds Research. Vol. 1, No. 1 (June 1984)-. English. Two times a year. $100.00. Indian Society of Oilseeds Research, Rajendranagar Hyderabad India. **(Subscription address:** Prints India, 11 Darya Ganj, New Delhi 110002 India. **Tel** 011 91 11 3268645, FAX 011 91 11 3275542, telex 31-61087 PRIN-IN.) Documents available from CASDDS.
Ind/Abst Agrofor. Abstr. (1991-); Chem. Abstr. (1985-1988); Curr. Cit.; Field Crop Abstr.; Hortic. Abstr.; Irr. Drain. Abstr.; Nematol. Abstr.; Plant Genet. Resour. Abstr.; Plant Grow. Reg. Abstr.; Rev. Agric. Entomol.; Rev. Plant Pathol.; Seed Abstr.; Soils Fert.; Soyabean Abstr.; Weed Abstr.

LC SB111.A2 J65 **ISSN** 0304-5242
DD 631/.0913 II
CODEN JPCRDW
JOURNAL OF PLANTATION CROPS. [J. plant. crops]. **Added/Corp** Indian Society for Plantation Crops. Vol. 1 (1973)-. Periodical. English. Two times a year. $75.00. Indian Society of Plantation Crops, Kasarogod 670, 124 Kerala India. **Tel** 011 91 44 520094. **(Subscription address:** Prints India, 11 Darya Ganj, New Delhi 110002 India. **Tel** 011 91 11 3268645, FAX 011 91 11 3275542, telex 31-61087 PRIN-IN.) **ED** H.H. Khan. Index available. **Bk Rev. Ad Acc. Circ:** 600. Documents available from BIOSIS Document Express, CASDDS.
Desc: Original reviews, scientific papers, short scientific reports, and book reviews pertaining to plantation crops; including spices and condiments.
Ind/Abst AGRICOLA; Agric. Eng. Abstr. (1991-); Agrofor. Abstr. (1991-); Biocont. News Inf. (19??-19??); Biodeter. Abstr.; Biol. Abstr.; Chem. Abstr.; Crop Physiol. Abstr.; Curr. Cit.; Field Crop Abstr.; Food Sci. Technol. Abstr.; For. Prod. Abstr. (1991-); For. Abstr.; Hortic.

Abstr.; Irr. Drain. Abstr.; Nematol. Abstr.; Life Sci. Collect.; Plant Breed. Abstr.; Plant Grow. Reg. Abstr.; Postharvest News Inf.; Rev. Agric. Entomol.; Rev. Plant Pathol.; Soils Fert.; Weed Abstr.; World Agric. Econ. Rural Sociol. Abstr.

LC S590 **ISSN** 0257-4993
DD 631.4 II

JOURNAL OF POTASSIUM RESEARCH. **Added/Corp** Potash Research Institute of India. Vol. 1, No. 1 (Mar. 1985)-. Periodical. English. Four times a year. $100.00. Potash Research Institute of India, Gurgaon Haryana India. **(Subscription address:** Prints India, 11 Darya Ganj, New Delhi 110002 India. **Tel** 011 91 11 3268645, FAX 011 91 11 3275542, telex 31-61087 PRIN-IN.)
Ind/Abst AGRICOLA; Cot. Trop. Fibr. Abstr. Bibliogr.; Crop Physiol. Abstr.; Field Crop Abstr.; Maize Abstr.; Nematol. Abstr.; Plant Grow. Reg. Abstr.; Potato Abstr.; Rev. Agric. Entomol.; Rev. Plant Pathol.; Rice Abstr.; Seed Abstr.; Soils Fert.; Sorghum Mill. Abstr.; Wheat Barley Trit. Abstr.

LC S
DD 630 US
Pr Rev.

•**JOURNAL OF POTATO PRODUCTION & POSTHARVEST HANDLING.** (Aug. 1995)-. English. Two times a year. $75.00 US; $105.00 other. The Haworth Press Inc., 10 Alice Street, Binghamton NY 13904-1580. **Tel** (607)722-5857, (800)3-HAWORTH, FAX (607)722-1424. **ED** R. Gary Beaver,PhD. Documents available from Haworth Document Delivery Service.
Desc: Covers applied research, reviews of publications and other media concerned with the production of potatoes. Provides new information important to both growers and scientists, linking together their fields of work.

LC S590 **ISSN** 0890-8524
DD 631 US
CCC
CODEN JPRAEN

JOURNAL OF PRODUCTION AGRICULTURE. [J. prod. agric.]. **Added/Corp** American Society of Agronomy. Crop Science Society of America. Soil Science Society of America. Vol. 1, No. 1 (Jan./Mar. 1988)-. Periodical. English. Four times a year. $61.00. American Society of Agronomy, 677 South Segoe Road, Madison WI 53711. **Tel** (608)273-8080, FAX (608)273-2021. Documents available from The Genuine Article, BIOSIS Document Express.
Ind/Abst AgBiotech News Inf.; AGRICOLA [Full Cov.]; Agric. Eng. Abstr. (1991-); Anim. Breed. Abstr.; BioBusiness; Biol. Abstr. (1988-); Curr. Aware. Biol. Sci., CABS; Curr. Cit.; Curr. Contents Agric. Biol. Environ. Sci.; Dairy Sci. Abstr.; Field Crop Abstr.; Grass. Forage Abstr.; Hortic. Abstr.; Index Vet.; Irr. Drain. Abstr.; Maize Abstr.; Microbiol. Abstr. Sect. A; Microbiol. Abstr. Sect. C; Nematol. Abstr.; Nutr. Abstr. Rev., Ser. B, Live Feeds and Feed.; Pig News Inf.; Plant Breed. Abstr.; Plant Grow. Reg. Abstr.; Postharvest News Inf.; Res. Alert [Select. Cov.]; Rev. Agric. Entomol.; Rev. Med. Vet. Mycology; Rev. Plant Pathol.; Rice Abstr.; SCISEARCH; Seed Abstr.; Soc. Sci. Cit. Index [Select. Cov.]; Soils Fert.; Sorghum Mill. Abstr.; Soyabean Abstr.; Sug. Indus. Abstr.; Weed Abstr.; Wheat Barley Trit. Abstr.; World Agric. Econ. Rural Sociol. Abstr.

LC S **ISSN** 0378-2409
DD 630 II
CODEN JRCRDC

JOURNAL OF ROOT CROPS. [J. root crops]. **Added/Corp** Indian Society for Root Crops. Vol. 1 (1975)-. Periodical. English. Two times a year. $70.00. Indian Society for Root Crops, Central Tuber Crops Research Institute, Trivandrum 695017 India. **(Subscription address:** Prints India, 11 Darya Ganj, New Delhi 110002 India. **Tel** 011 91 11 3268645, FAX 011 91 11 3275542, telex 31-61087 PRIN-IN.) Documents available from CASDDS.
Ind/Abst Biocont. News Inf.; Chem. Abstr.; Crop Physiol. Abstr.; EMBASE; Field Crop Abstr.; Plant Breed. Abstr.; Postharvest News Inf.; Rev. Agric. Entomol.; Rev. Plant Pathol.; Soils Fert.; Weed Abstr.

LC SB114.A1 A7 **ISSN** 0146-3071
DD 631.5/21/05 US
CODEN JSTEDV
Pr Rev.

JOURNAL OF SEED TECHNOLOGY. [J. seed technol.]. **Added/Corp** Association of Official Seed Analysts. (1976)-. Academic Scholarly Publication. English. Two times a year. $25.00. Association Official Seed Analysts, 268 Plant Science Building, Lincoln NE 68583. **Tel** (402)472-1444. **ED** Dr Loren Wiesner. **Circ:** 500. Documents available from BIOSIS Document Express, CASDDS. ***Continues** Proceedings of the Association of Official Seed Analysts, 0097-1324.*
Desc: Scientific articles dealing with seed analysis, research and technique. Some articles deal with specific crops and specialized areas of research.
Ind/Abst AGRICOLA [Full Cov.]; Biol. Abstr. (-1986); Chem. Abstr.; Crop Physiol. Abstr.; Curr. Cit.; Field Crop Abstr.; Grass. Forage Abstr.; Hortic. Abstr.; Maize Abstr.; Ornamental Hort. (1991-); Postharvest News Inf.; Rev. Plant Pathol.; Seed Abstr.; Soyabean Abstr.; Weed Abstr.; Wheat Barley Trit. Abstr.

LC SB381 .J68 **ISSN** 1052-0015
DD 634/.7/05 US
CODEN JSFVED

JOURNAL OF SMALL FRUITS & VITICULTURE. [J. small fruit vitic.]. **VFOAT** Journal of Small Fruits and Viticulture. Vol. 1, No. 1 (1992)-. Periodical. English. Four times a year. $75.00. The Haworth Press Inc., 10 Alice Street, Binghamton NY 13904-1580. **Tel** (607)722-5857, (800)3-HAWORTH, FAX (607)722-1424. **ED** Robert E. Gough. **Acid Free.** Documents available from Haworth Document Delivery Service.
Desc: Deals with the whole plant systems in the field. Deals with agricultural science, instead of basic science. Covers the practical problems of growers and extension personnel today.
Ind/Abst Food Sci. Technol. Abstr.

LC QH183 .J68
DD 574.5/26404/0954 II

JOURNAL OF SOIL BIOLOGY & ECOLOGY. **Added/Corp** Indian Society of Soil Biology and Ecology. **VFOAT** Journal of Soil Biology and Ecology. (198?)-. Periodical. English. Two times a year. $30.00. Indian Society of Soil Biology and Ecology, Department of Entomology, University of Agricultural Sciences, Bangalore 560024 India. **(Subscription address:** Prints India, 11 Darya Ganj, New Delhi 110002 India. **Tel** 011 91 11 3268645, FAX 011 91 11 3275542, telex 31-61087 PRIN-IN.)
Ind/Abst Nematol. Abstr.; Life Sci. Collect.

LC TD878 .J68 **ISSN** 1058-8337
DD 628.5/5/05 US
CCC
CODEN JSOCEZ

JOURNAL OF SOIL CONTAMINATION. [J. soil contam.]. **Added/Corp** Association for the Environmental Health of Soils. Vol. 1, No. 1 (1992)-. Academic Scholarly Publication. English. Four times a year. $395.00. CRC Press Inc., 2000 Corporate Boulevard Northwest, Boca Raton FL 33431. **Tel** (407)994-0555, (800)272-7737, FAX (407)998-9784, (800)374-3401, telex 568689. **(Subscription address:** CRC Press Inc. / New York, PO Box 750, Pearl River NY 10965.) **ED** James Dragun. Documents available from CASDDS, Documents on Demand.
Desc: Considers all types of soil contamination.Sludges & petroleum contamination and their chemical constituents are recent concerns, however, the journal also discusses petrochemical, chlorinated hydrocarbon, pesticide, and heavy metal contamination.
Ind/Abst Chem. Abstr.; Environ. Abstr.; Environ. Period. Bibliogr.

LC S590 .J6 **ISSN** 0022-4588
DD 631.405 UK
CCC
CODEN JSSCAH
Pr Rev. **TITLE CHANGE**

JOURNAL OF SOIL SCIENCE, THE. [J. soil sci.]. **Added/Corp** British Society of Soil Science. Vol. 1 (Mar. 1949)-Vol. 44, No. 4 (Dec. 1993). Academic Scholarly Publication. English. Blackwell Scientific Publications Ltd, Marston Book Services, PO Box 88, Oxford OX2 ONE United Kingdom. **Tel** 011 44 1865 206206, FAX 011 44 1865 206219, telex 837 515 MARDIS G. **ED** David Crawford. **Ad Acc. Circ:** 2,400. available on microfilm and microfiche from University Microfilms International (UMI). Documents available from The Genuine Article, BIOSIS Document Express, CASDDS. ***Merged with** Science du Sol (Plaisir, France : 1984), 0767-2853; Pedologie, 0079-0419 **to form** European Journal of Soil Science.*
Desc: Science of the soil in its widest aspect.
Ind/Abst AGRICOLA [Full Cov.]; Biol. Agric. Index; Biol. Abstr.; Chem. Abstr.; Chem. Titles; Curr. Aware. Biol. Sci., CABS; Curr. Cit.; Curr. Contents Agric. Biol. Environ. Sci.; Ecol. Abstr.; EMBASE; For. Abstr.; Geogr. Abstr. Phys. Geogr.; Geogr. Abstr. Human Geogr. (?-?); Geol. Abstr.; Grass. Forage Abstr.; Int. Dev. Abstr. (?-?); Irr. Drain. Abstr.; Leadscan; Maize Abstr.; Life Sci. Collect.; Res. Alert [Full Cov.]; Rice Abstr.; Sci. Cit. Index; SCISEARCH; Soils Fert.; World Ceram. Abstr.

LC S
DD 630 II

JOURNAL OF SPICES AND AROMATIC CROPS. (1992)-. English. Two times a year. $40.00. Calicut Indian Society for Spices. **(Subscription address:** Prints India, 11 Darya Ganj, New Delhi 110002 India. **Tel** 011 91 11 3268645, FAX 011 91 11 3275542, telex 31-61087 PRIN-IN.)

LC SB215 .A57 **ISSN** 0899-1502
DD 633.6/3 US
CODEN JSBREF

JOURNAL OF SUGAR BEET RESEARCH. [J. sugar beet res.]. **Added/Corp** American Society of Sugar Beet Technologists. Vol. 25, No. 1 (Spring 1988)-. Periodical. English. Four times a year. $35.00. American Society of Sugar Beet Technologists / Denver, 90 Madison Street/Suite 208, Denver CO 80206-5411. **Tel** (303)321-1520, FAX (303)321-1558. available on microfilm from University Microfilms International (UMI). ***Continues** Journal of the American Society of Sugar Beet Technologists, 0003-1216.*
Ind/Abst AGRICOLA [Full Cov.]; Field Crop Abstr.; Food Sci. Technol. Abstr.; Nematol. Abstr.; Plant Breed. Abstr.; Plant Genet. Resour. Abstr.; Rev. Plant Pathol.; Seed Abstr.

LC SB608
DD 635.21 II

JOURNAL OF THE INDIAN POTATO ASSOCIATION : OFFICIAL JOURNAL OF THE INDIAN POTATO ASSOCIATION, CENTRAL POTATO RESEARCH INSTITUTE. **Added/Corp** Indian Potato Association. (198?)-. Periodical. English. Four times a year. $10.00. **(Subscription address:** Prints India, 11 Darya Ganj, New Delhi 110002 India. **Tel** 011 91 11 3268645, FAX 011 91 11 3275542, telex 31-61087 PRIN-IN.) ***Continues** JIPA.*

LC S **ISSN** 0970-308X
DD 630 II
UDC 633.51

JOURNAL OF THE INDIAN SOCIETY FOR COTTON IMPROVEMENT. [J. Indian Soc. Cotton Improv.]. (1976)-. Periodical. English. Two times a year.
Ind/Abst Field Crop Abstr.; Irr. Drain. Abstr.; Plant Genet. Resour. Abstr.; Rev. Plant Pathol.; Seed Abstr.; Soils Fert.; Weed Abstr.

LC S590 .I5 **ISSN** 0019-638X
DD 631.4/05 II
CODEN JINSA4
Pr Rev.

JOURNAL OF THE INDIAN SOCIETY OF SOIL SCIENCE. [J. Indian Soc. Soil Sci.]. **Main/Corp** Indian Society of Soil Science. Vol. 1 (June 1953)-. Periodical. English. Four times a year. $60.00. Indian Society of Soil Science Institute, New Delhi 110012 India. **Tel** 5720991. **(Subscription address:** Prints India, 11 Darya Ganj, New Delhi 110002 India. **Tel** 011 91 11 3268645, FAX 011 91 11 3275542, telex 31-61087 PRIN-IN.) **ED** T. D. Biswas. Index available. cum. index. **Bk Rev. Ad Acc. Circ:** 2,000. Documents available from BIOSIS Document Express, CASDDS.
Ind/Abst AgBiotech News Inf.; AGRICOLA; Agrofor. Abstr. (19??-19??); Biol. Abstr.; Ceram. Abstr.; Chem. Abstr.; Crop Physiol. Abstr.; Curr. Cit.; Field Crop Abstr.; For. Prod. Abstr. (1991-); For. Abstr.; GeoRef; Grass. Forage Abstr.; Hortic. Abstr.; Indian Geosci. Abstr.; Irr. Drain. Abstr.; Maize Abstr.; Nematol. Abstr.; Plant Breed. Abstr.; Potato Abstr.; Rev. Agric. Entomol.; Rice Abstr.; Seed Abstr.; Soils Fert.; Sorghum Mill. Abstr.; Soyabean Abstr.; Sug. Indus. Abstr.; Weed Abstr.; Wheat Barley Trit. Abstr.

LC S
DD 630 CE

JOURNAL OF THE NATIONAL INSTITUTE OF PLANTATION MANAGEMENT. Vol. 1, No. 1. Periodical. English. Two times a year.
Ind/Abst Agrofor. Abstr. (1991-); Hortic. Abstr.; Rural Dev. Abstr.; World Agric. Econ. Rural Sociol. Abstr.

LC S **ISSN** 1055-1387
DD 630 US
Pr Rev.

JOURNAL OF TREE FRUIT PRODUCTION. (1992)-. Trade Publication. English. Two times a year. $75.00. The Haworth Press Inc., 10 Alice Street, Binghamton NY 13904-1580. **Tel** (607)722-5857, (800)3-HAWORTH, FAX (607)722-1424. **ED** Robert E. Gough (editor's address: Ridge Road, PO Box 100, Oakfield, ME 04763). **Bk Rev. Ad Acc. Acid Free.** available on microfiche. Documents available from Haworth Document Delivery Service.
Desc: Disseminates results of current research that are immediately applicable to the grower. The focus is on new technologies and innovative approaches to the management and marketing of apples, pears, peaches, plums, cherries, nectarines, apricots and some subtropical fruits such as olives and dates.
Ind/Abst Food Sci. Technol. Abstr.

LC S **ISSN** 1049-6467
DD 630 US
Pr Rev.

•**JOURNAL OF VEGETABLE CROP PRODUCTION.** (1993)-. Periodical. English. Two times a year. $75.00. The Haworth Press Inc., 10 Alice Street, Binghamton NY 13904-1580. **Tel** (607)722-5857, (800)3-HAWORTH, FAX (607)722-1424. **ED** M. LeRon Robbins. **Bk Rev. Ad Acc. Acid Free.** available on microfiche. Documents available from Haworth Document Delivery Service.
Desc: This journal is aimed at those specialists and professionals who labor with the problems of vegetable crop management from land preparation to seeding and consumption. Articles will cover the wide spectrum of the vegetable industry including field-related problems, harvesting, shipping, final consumption, and scientific input about vegetables.
Ind/Abst Food Sci. Technol. Abstr.

LC TS1870 .R856b ISSN 0379-1130
DD 633.8/952/095493 CE
CODEN JRRLDZ

JOURNAL - RUBBER RESEARCH INSTITUTE OF SRI LANKA. (JOURNAL OF THE RUBBER RESEARCH INSTITUTE OF SRI LANKA.). [J. - Rubber Res. Inst. Sri Lanka]. **Main/Corp** Rubber Research Institute of Sri Lanka. Vol. 53 (1976)-. Periodical. English. Irregular. Comes with Rubber Research Institute of Sri Lanka membership. Rubber Research Institute of Sri Lanka, Dartonfield, Agalawatta Sri Lanka. **Tel** 034 71427. Documents available from CASDDS. ***Continues*** *Quarterly Journal - Rubber Research Institute of Sri Lanka, 0378-6390.*
Ind/Abst Abstr. Trop. Agric.; Chem. Abstr. (1976-1983); Crop Physiol. Abstr.; Hortic. Abstr.; Rev. Plant Pathol.

LC S ISSN 0350-2155
DD 630 YU

JUGOSLOVENSKO VOCARSTVO. JOURNAL OF YUGOSLAV POMOLOGY. **Added/Corp** Jugoslovensko Naucno Vocarsko Drustvo. Vol. 1 (1967)-. Periodical. Serbo-Croatian (Roman). Four times a year. Jugoslo Naucno Vocarsko Drust, Vojvode Stepe 9, Cacak Yugoslavia. Documents available from CASDDS.
Ind/Abst Chem. Abstr.; Hortic. Abstr.; Irr. Drain. Abstr.; Plant Genet. Resour. Abstr.; Plant Grow. Reg. Abstr.; Soils Fert.

LC SB950.3.J3 K3
DD 632.94 JA

KAJU BYOGAICHU BOJO HANDOBUKKU. Japanese. One time a year. Shiga-ken Kaju Kumiai Rengoki, c/o Shiga-Kencho Nosan-Fukyuka, 1-1 Kyomachi, 4-chome, Otsu 520 Japan. **Tel** 0775-24-1121, FAX 0775-23-1581.

LC SB29.J3 K34A
DD 630.9 JA

KAJU SHIKENJO NYUSU. **Main/Corp** Norinsho Kaju Shikenjo (Japan). No. 10- May 1978-. Japanese. Norinsho Kaju Shikenjo, 2-1 Fujimoto Yatabecho, Tsukuba-gun, Ibaraki-ken, Yatabecho Japan.

LC SB369.5.K7 K35
DD 634 KO

KAMGYUL. **Added/Corp** Cheju Kamgyul Hyoptong Chohap. (19??)-. Periodical. Korean. Six times a year. Cheju Kamgyul Hyoptong Chohap, 586-10 Sogi 3-Ni, Sogiup Korea.

LC S ISSN 0022-9148
DD 630 RU
CODEN KAOVA7

KARTOFEL I OVOSHCHI. [Kartofel i ovoshchi]. **Added/Corp** U.S.S.R., Ministerstvo Selskogo Khoziaistva. Vol. 5 (1960)-. Periodical. Russian. Six times a year. $89.95. Agropromizdat, Sadovo-Spasskaia 18, 107807 Moscow Russia. **(Subscription address:** East View Publications Inc., 3020 Harbor Lane North, Suite 110, Minneapolis MN 55447. **Tel** (800)477-1005, (612)550-0961, FAX (612)559-2931.) **Bk Rev.** ***Continues*** *Kartofel.*
Ind/Abst AGRICOLA; Agric. Eng. Abstr.; Field Crop Abstr.; Maize Abstr.; Nematol. Abstr.; Plant Breed. Abstr.; Postharvest News Inf.; Potato Abstr.; Rev. Plant Pathol.; Seed Abstr.; Soils Fert.

LC S ISSN 0022-9156
DD 630 GW

KARTOFFELBAU. [Kartoffelbau]. **Added/Corp** Deutsche Kartoffel-Union. Forderungsgemeinschaft der Kartoffelwirtschaft. Vol. 1 (June 1950)-. Trade Publication. German. Twelve times a year. $101.33. Verlag TH Mann OHG, Postfach 200254, W 45837 Gelsenkirchen Germany. **Tel** 011 49 209 9304184. available on microfilm and microfiche; available on CD-ROM; available on diskette; available on audiocassette; available on videocassette.
Desc: Pertains to potato growing, machinery, technology, economy and science.
Ind/Abst AGRICOLA; Agric. Eng. Abstr. (1991-); Field Crop Abstr.; Irr. Drain. Abstr.; Nematol. Abstr.; Plant Breed. Abstr.; Postharvest News Inf.; Potato Abstr.; Rev. Agric. Entomol.; Rev. Plant Pathol.; Soils Fert.

LC SB608
DD 635.21 RU

KARTOPLIARSTVO. **Added/Corp** Ukraine. Ministerstvo sil'Shskoho Hospodarstva. (19??)-. Periodical. Russian.
Ind/Abst Agric. Eng. Abstr.; Biocont. News Inf.; Postharvest News Inf.

LC S ISSN 1010-3481
DD 630 KE

KENYA COFFEE. [Kenya coffee]. **Added/Corp** Coffee Board of Kenya. (1959)-. Trade Publication. English. Twelve times a year. Coffee Board of Kenya, Coffee Plaza, Haile Selassie Avenue, Box 3056, Nairobi Kenya. ***Continues*** *Coffee Board of Kenya. Monthly Bulletin.*
Ind/Abst Agrofor. Abstr. (19??-19??); Biocont. News Inf.; Curr. Cit.; EMBASE; Food Sci. Technol. Abstr.; Hortic. Abstr.; PESTDOC; Plant Genet. Resour. Abstr.; Potato Abstr.; Rev. Agric. Entomol.; Rev. Plant Pathol.; Soils Fert.; Weed Abstr.; World Agric. Econ. Rural Sociol. Abstr.

LC S ISSN 0131-7482
DD 630 RU

KHLIBOROB UKRAINY. (KHLEBOROB UKRAINY). **Added/Corp** Ukraine, Ministerstvo Silskoho Hospodarstva. **VFOAT** Khleborob Ukrainy. (1???)-. Periodical. Ukrainian. Twelve times a year. $24.50. Vydavnitstvo Urozhai, Yaroslavov val 10, 242034 Kiev Ukraine. **(Subscription address:** Victor Kamkin, 4956 Boiling Brook Parkway, Rockville MD 20852. **Tel** (301)881-5973.)

LC S ISSN 0235-2567
DD 630 RU

KHLOPOK. **Added/Corp** Gosudarstvennyi Agropromyshlennyi Komitet SSSR. Soviet Union. Ministerstvo Melioratsii i Vodnogo Khoziaistva. Vol. 1 (1988)-. Periodical. Russian. Six times a year. $15.50. Agropromizdat, Sadovo-Spasskaia 18, 107807 Moscow Russia. **(Subscription address:** Victor Kamkin, 4956 Boiling Brook Parkway, Rockville MD 20852. **Tel** (301)881-5973.) Documents available from CASDDS. ***Continues*** *Khlopkovodstvo, 0023-1231.*
Ind/Abst AgBiotech News Inf.; Agric. Eng. Abstr. (1991-); Chem. Abstr.; Cot. Trop. Fibr. Abstr. Bibliogr.; Field Crop Abstr.; Irr. Drain. Abstr.; PESTDOC; Plant Breed. Abstr.; Rev. Agric. Entomol.; Rev. Plant Pathol.; Seed Abstr.; Sorghum Mill. Abstr.

LC SB950
DD 632.9 JA

KITA NIPPON BYOGAICHU KENKYUKAI HO = ANNUAL REPORT OF THE SOCIETY OF PLANT PROTECTION OF NORTH JAPAN. **Main/Corp** Kita Nippon Byogaichu Kenkyukai. **VFOAT** Annual Report of the Society of Plant Protection of North Japan. No. 17 (Sept. 1966)-. Periodical. Japanese (summaries and/or abstracts in English). One time a year. ***Continues*** *Kita Nippon Byogaichu Kenkyukai. Nenpo. Annual Report.*
Ind/Abst Biocont. News Inf.; Hortic. Abstr.; Index Vet.; Nematol. Abstr.; Plant Breed. Abstr.; Potato Abstr.; Rev. Agric. Entomol.; Rev. Med. Vet. Entomol.; Rev. Plant Pathol.; Rice Abstr.; Seed Abstr.; Soyabean Abstr.

LC SB108.J3 J35a
DD 630 JA

KOGEI NOSAKUBUTSU TOKEI NEMPO. **Main/Corp** Japan. Norinsho. Norin Keizaikyoku. Tokei Johobu. (19??)-. Periodical. Japanese. Norin Keizaikyoku / Tokei Johobu, 2-1 Kasumigaseki -1 Chiyoda-ku, Tokyo Japan.

LC SB191.R5 I527f
DD 633.1 IO

KOMPILASI DATA OUTPUT & [I.E. DAN] INPUT USAHA TANI PADI INTENSIFIKASI PER KABUPATEN DI JAWA-MADURA. **Main/Corp** Indonesia. Biro Pusat Statistik. **Added/Corp** Indonesia. Badan Pengendali Bimas. (19??)-. Periodical. Indonesian. Biro Pusat Statistik / Central Bureau of Statistics, 8 Jalan Dr. Sutomo No. 8, Box 3, Jakarta Pusat 10710 Indonesia. **Tel** 011 62 21 372808, 011 62 21 374908 ext.342.

LC S ISSN 0130-2515
DD 630 RU

KORMA. [Korma]. **Added/Corp** Soviet Union. Ministerstvo Selskogo Khoziaistva. No. 1 (Jan./Feb. 1972)-. Periodical. Russian. Six times a year. $18.00. Izdatelstvo Kolos, Sadovaia-Spasskaia 18, 107807 Moscow Russia. Index available in last issue of volume--attached. ***Continues*** *Luga i Pastbishcha.*
Ind/Abst AGRICOLA.

LC S
DD 630 II

KRISHI CHAYANIKA. (19??)-. Periodical. Hindi. Four times a year. Rs32.00. Indian Council of Agricultural Research, Mgr Krishi Anusandham Bhavan, New Delhi 110 012 India. **Tel** 011 91 11 5713657, telex 031-62249 ICAR IN.
Desc: Specialized information on agricultural research conducted in India and elsewhere.
Ind/Abst Agric. Eng. Abstr.; Soyabean Abstr.

LC S7 .K8 ISSN 0940-3507
DD 630 GW

KUHN-ARCHIV. **Added/Corp** Martin-Luther-Universitat Halle-Wittenberg. Landwirtschaftliche Fakultat. (1992)-. German. Landwirtschaftsverlag GmbH, Postfach 480249, D-48079 Muenster Hiltrup Germany. **Tel** 011 49 2501 8010, FAX 011 49 2501 801204, telex 892665 LANDV D. ***Continues*** *Archiv fuer Acker- und Pflanzenbau und Bodenkunde, 0365-0340.*

LC S
DD 630 RU
TITLE CHANGE

KUKURUZA. **Added/Corp** Soviet Union. Ministerstvo Selskogo Khoziaistva. (1956)-(19??). Periodical. Russian. **(Subscription address:** East View Publications Inc., 3020 Harbor Lane North, Suite 110, Minneapolis MN 55447. **Tel** (800)477-1005, (612)550-0961, FAX (612)559-2931.) ***Continued by*** *Kukuruza I Sorgo, 0233-7770.*

LC S ISSN 0233-7770
DD 630 RU

KUKURUZA I SORGO. **Added/Corp** Soviet Union. Ministerstvo Selskogo Khoziaistva. No. 1 (1985)-. Periodical. Russian. Six times a year. $79.95. Agropromizdat, Sadovo-Spasskaia 18, 107807 Moscow Russia. **(Subscription address:** East View Publications Inc., 3020 Harbor Lane North, Suite 110, Minneapolis MN 55447. **Tel** (800)477-1005, (612)550-0961, FAX (612)559-2931.) ***Continues*** *Kukuruza, 0023-5040.*
Ind/Abst Field Crop Abstr.; Grass. Forage Abstr.; Maize Abstr.; Plant Breed. Abstr.; Rev. Plant Pathol.; Seed Abstr.; Sorghum Mill. Abstr.; Weed Abstr.

LC S622 .L36 ISSN 0898-5812
DD 628/.5 UK
CCC
CODEN LDREE7

LAND DEGRADATION AND REHABILITATION. [Land degrad. rehabil.]. **VFOAT** Land Degradation and Rehabilitation. Vol. 1, No. 1 (July/Aug. 1989)-. Periodical. English. Four times a year. $265.00. John Wiley & Sons Ltd., Baffins Lane, Chichester, West Sussex PO19 1UD United Kingdom. **Tel** 011 44 1243 779777, FAX 011 44 1243 776128 BTG:JWP001, telex 86290 WIBOOKG. **(Subscription address:** John Wiley & Sons, Inc. / Philadelphia, PO Box 7247, Philadelphia PA 19170. **Tel** (212)850-6645, (800)225-5945.) **ED** C. J. Barrow. available on microfilm and microfiche from University Microfilms International (UMI). Documents available from The Genuine Article.
Desc: An international journal which seeks to promote rational study of the recognition, monitoring, control and rehabilitation of degradation in terrestrial environments.
Ind/Abst AgBiotech News Inf.; AGRICOLA [Full Cov.]; Agric. Eng. Abstr.; Curr. Aware. Biol. Sci., CABS; Curr. Cit.; Ecol. Abstr.; Environ. Period. Bibliogr.; Fluid Abstr., Civil Eng.; Fluid Abstr. Proc. Eng.; FLUIDEX (199?-); For. Abstr.; Geogr. Abstr. Phys. Geogr.; Geogr. Abstr. Human Geogr.; GeoRef; Grass. Forage Abstr.; Int. Dev. Abstr.; Irr. Drain. Abstr.; Pollut. Abstr. Indexes; Res. Alert [Select. Cov.]; Rural Dev. Abstr.; Soc. Sci. Cit. Index [Select. Cov.]; Soils Fert.; World Agric. Econ. Rural Sociol. Abstr.

LC HD9383.1 .L358
DD 331.7 GW

LAND- UND FORSTWIRTSCHAFT, FISCHEREI. REIHE 3.2.2, WEINERZEUGUNG. **Added/Corp** Germany (West). Statistisches Bundesamt. **VFOAT** Weinerzeugung; Fachserie 3. (1985)-. German. W. Kohlhammer Verlag GmbH, Postfach 800430, D-70549 Stuttgart Germany. **Tel** 011 49 711 78630, FAX 011 49 711 7863430, telex 7-255820. ***Continues in part*** *Land- und Forstwirtschaft, Fischerei. Reihe 3.2.2, Weinerzeugung und Bestand, Weinbestande und Lagerbehalter.*

LC HD2085.R5 I54A
DD 630 IO

LAPORAN TAHUNAN - INSPEKTORAT PERKEBUNAN BESAR DAERAH IV RIAU. **Main/Corp** Indonesia. Inspektorat Perkebunan Besar Daerah IV Riau. (19??)-. Indonesian. One time a year. Direktorat Jenderal Perkebunan, Jl Sumatra No 16, Pekanbaru Indonesia.

LC S ISSN 0828-1432
DD 630 CN

LENS : LENTIL EXPERIMENTAL NEWS SERVICE. [LENS, Lentil exp. news serv.]. **Added/Corp** University of Saskatchewan. Crop Development Centre. Lentil Research Association. **VFOAT** Lentil Experimental News Service. Vol. 1, (1974)-. Periodical. English. Two times a year. Free on request. International Center for Agricultural Research in the Dry Areas, PO Box 5466, Aleppo Syria. **Tel** 213433, telex 331206.
Ind/Abst Plant Breed. Abstr.; Rev. Agric. Entomol.; Rice Abstr.; Weed Abstr.; Wheat Barley Trit. Abstr.

LC S
DD 630 SY

LENS NEWSLETTER. **Added/Corp** University of Saskatchewan. International Center for Agricultural Research in the Dry Areas. Lentil Experimental News Service. (198?)-. Newsletter. English. Two times a year. Free on request. International Center for Agricultural Research in the Dry Areas, PO Box 5466, Aleppo Syria. **Tel** 213433, telex 331206.
Ind/Abst Plant Grow. Reg. Abstr.

LC SD207 .L47 ISSN 0130-9099
DD 634.9090 RU

LESOVODSTVO, LESNYE KULTURY I POCHVOVEDENIE. **See** Forests and Forestry.

LC S
DD 630 SP
LEVANTE AGRICOLA. Vol. 1, No. 1 (1962)-. Periodical. Spanish. Twelve times a year. 4.375ptas Spain; 5.715ptas (surface mail), 6.800ptas (airmail) other. Ediciones y Promociones Lav SL LA, 46022 Valencia Spain. **Tel** 011 96 3720261.

LC HD9254.M3 L5 **ISSN** 0270-2002
DD 338.17 US
LIBRO VERDE, EL. [Libro verde]. (1979)-. Periodical. English (Spanish). El Libro Verde, Inc, 5380 Poplar Boulevard, Los Angeles CA 90032.

LC Z5074.S7 L57 S599.A1
DD 016.6314/7/73 US
LIST OF PUBLISHED SOIL SURVEYS. **Added/Corp** United States. Soil Conservation Service. United States. Natural Resources Conservation Service. (19??)-. English. One time a year. US Department of Agriculture / Soil Conservation Service / Washington, DC, 14th Street & Independence Avenue SW, Room 5105A, Washington DC 20250. **Tel** (202)720-4525, FAX (202)720-7690.
Desc: Contains soil maps and general information about the agriculture and climate of the area and descriptions of each kind of soil. Includes a discussion of the formation and classification of the soils in the area and also laboratory data when available.
Ind/Abst AGRICOLA.

LC SB215
DD 633.6 XR
CODEN LCUREK
LISTY CUKROVARNICKE A REPARSKE. **Added/Corp** Cukrspol Praha Modrany, A.S. **VFOAT** LCaR; LCaR, Listy Cukrovarnicke a Reparske. Vol. 108, No. 1 (1992)-. Periodical. Czech (summaries and/or abstracts in English and German; table of contents in English and German). Twelve times a year. Kcs180. CKD Praha, U Kolbenky 159, Prague 8 Czech Republic. Documents available from The Genuine Article. ***Continues*** *Listy Cukrovarnicke.*
Ind/Abst Res. Alert; Soc. Sci. Cit. Index [Select. Cov.].

LC S590 **ISSN** 0954-1098
DD 631.4 UK
LIVING EARTH (BRISTOL). (THE LIVING EARTH : JOURNAL OF THE SOIL ASSOCIATION.). [Living earth]. **Added/Corp** Soil Association. **VFOAT** Living Earth and Soil Association News. (April/June 1988)-. Periodical. English. Six times a year. $34.23. Soil Association, 86 Colston Street, Bristol BS1 5BB United Kingdom. **Tel** 011 44 117 9290661. **ED** Charlotte Russell. **Bk Rev**, (Qty: 20). **Ad Acc.** ctrl circ. ***Continues*** *Review (Soil Association), 0951-2381;* ***Absorbed*** *Soil Association. Soil Association News.*
Desc: Covers organic food and farming.

LC S **ISSN** 0273-8848
DD 630 US
LOUISIANA CROP-WEATHER SUMMARY. (LOUISIANA CROP-WEATHER SUMMARY.). **Added/Corp** Louisiana Crop and Livestock Reporting Service. Louisiana. Dept. of Agriculture and Forestry. Louisiana Agricultural Statistics Service. **VAT** Louisiana Crop, Weather Summary. (1957)-. Government Publication. English. Irregular (March 1 through mid December). $12.00. US Department of Agriculture / National Agricultural Statistics Service (NASS), Room 5829 South Building, Washington DC 20250. **Tel** (202)720-4020, FAX (314)875-5231. **ED** Bergen A. Nelson. **Circ:** 250 (ctrl).
Desc: Crop progress and weather information.

LC S297 .B54A
DD 630 IO
LUAS TANAMAN, PRODUKSI, DAN PERSEDIAAN TANAMAN PERKEBUNAN YANG TERPENTING. **Main/Corp** Indonesia. Biro Pusat Statistik. **VFOAT** Planted Area, Production, and Stocks of Principle Estate Crops. English (Indonesian). One time a year. Rp1500 Indonesia; $1.00 US. Biro Pusat Statistik / Central Bureau of Statistics, 8 Jalan Dr. Sutomo No. 8, Box 3, Jakarta Pusat 10710 Indonesia. **Tel** 011 62 21 372808, 011 62 21 374908 ext.342. ctrl circ.

LC HF
DD 380.1 RM
LUCRARI STIINTIFICE - INSTITUTUL DE CERCETARI PENTRU VALORIFICAREA LEGUMELOR SI FRUCTELOR. **Main/Corp** Institutul de Cercetari Pentru Valorificarea Legumelor Si Fructelor. **Added/Corp** Romania. Ministerul Agriculturii, Industriei Alimentare si Apelor. Centrala Pentru Legume si Fructe. Centrul Special Pentru Perfectionarea Pregatirii Profesionale a Cadrelor din Agricultura. Vol. 6 (1975)-. Periodical. Romanian (summaries and/or abstracts in English, French and Russian; table of contents in English, French and Russian). One time a year. ***Continues*** *Lucrari Stiinsifice - Institutul de Studii, Cercetari si Proiectari Pentru Constructii Horticiticole.*
Ind/Abst Field Crop Abstr.; Seed Abstr.

LC S
DD 630 II
MADHYAPRADESA KA RTU EVAM PHASALA PRATIVEDANA. Hindi. One time a year.

LC S **ISSN** 1012-3482
DD 630 IQ
MAGALLAT AL-BUHUT AL-ZIRA'IYYAT WA-AL-MAWARID AL-MA'IYYAT. AL-TURBAT WA-MASADIR AL-MIYAH. **See** Water Resources.

LC Z5071 **ISSN** 0267-2987
DD 016.63 UK
MAIZE ABSTRACTS. **See** Agriculture-Abstracting, Bibliographies and Statistics.

LC SB191.M2 M327
DD 633.1/53 US
MAIZE GENETICS COOPERATION NEWS LETTER. **Added/Corp** Cornell University. Dept. of Plant Breeding. University of Illinois (Urbana-Champaign Campus). Dept. of Botany. Indiana University, Bloomington. Dept. of Botany. Indiana University, Bloomington. Dept. of Plant Sciences. University of Missouri--Columbia. Agricultural Experiment Station. University of Missouri--Columbia. Dept. of Agronomy. United States. Dept. of Agriculture. (1932)-. English. One time a year. $10.00. University of Missouri Columbia / Curtis Hall, 210 Curtis Hall, Columbia MO 65211. **Tel** (314)882-2674. cum. index.
Ind/Abst AgBiotech News Inf.; Crop Physiol. Abstr.; Curr. Cit.; Field Crop Abstr.; Irr. Drain. Abstr.; Maize Abstr.; Plant Breed. Abstr.; Plant Genet. Resour. Abstr.; Plant Grow. Reg. Abstr.; Postharvest News Inf.; Rev. Agric. Entomol.; Rev. Plant Pathol.; Seed Abstr.; Soyabean Abstr.; Sug. Indus. Abstr.; Weed Abstr.; Wheat Barley Trit. Abstr.

LC HD9049.C8 S617
DD 338.1/7315/0968 SA
TITLE CHANGE
MAIZE NEWS. **Added/Corp** South Africa. Maize Board. **VFOAT** Mielienuus. (19??)-(1995). Periodical. Afrikaans (English). Maize Board Mieliraad, PO Box 669, Pretoria 0001 South Africa. **Tel** 012 325-2133. ***Continues*** *Mielienuus.* ***Merged into*** *Mielies.*

LC S
DD 630 US
MARKETING LETTUCE FROM IMPERIAL VALLEY AND BLYTHE DISTRICTS. **Main/Corp** Federal-State Market News Service. . Periodical. English. One time a year. $8.00 North America; $16.00 other. Federal-State Market News Service, 1220 N Street, Suite 216, Box 942871, Sacramento CA 94271-0001. **Tel** (916)654-0298, FAX (916)654-1046.
Desc: Shipments by states and California, FOB Prices, wholesale market prices, arrivals in 22 US cities by state, some acreage and production information.

LC S **ISSN** 0747-301X
DD 630 US
MARYLAND AGRI-FACTS. **Added/Corp** Maryland-Delaware Crop Reporting Service. Maryland Agricultural Statistics Service. Maryland. Dept. of Agriculture. (19??)-. Periodical. English. Twenty-four times a year. $10.00. Maryland Delaware Agricultural Statistics Service, 50 Harry S Truman Parkway, Annapolis MD 21401. **Tel** (301)841-5740.

LC SB354 **ISSN** 0025-4223
DD 634 US
MARYLAND FRUIT GROWER, THE. [Md. fruit grow.]. **Added/Corp** Maryland State Horticultural Society. University of Maryland Cooperative Extension Service. Vol. 1 (1931)-. Periodical. English. Four times a year (Jan., Apr., July, Oct.). $10.00. Maryland State Horticultural Society, University of Maryland, Department of Horticulture, College Park MD 20742. **Tel** (301)454-3899. **ED** CS Walsh. **Circ:** 300 (ctrl).

LC SB354 **ISSN** 1052-6161
DD 634 US
MARYLAND GRAPEVINE, THE. [Md. grapevine]. **Added/Corp** Maryland Grape Growers Association. (Fall 1981)-. Periodical. English. Four times a year (Mar., June, Sep., Dec.). $15.00. Maryland Grape Growers Association, 185717 Kingshill Road, Germantown MD 20874. **Tel** (301)972-1325. **ED** James L Russell. **Bk Rev.** **Ad Acc, Adv Mgr:** Myra Novak. **Circ:** 200.
Desc: Provides articles of viticultural interest and news of the Maryland Grape Growers Association.

LC TC424.M3 M37a **ISSN** 8756-9205
DD 627/.5/09752 US
MARYLAND STANDARDS AND SPECIFICATIONS FOR SOIL EROSION AND SEDIMENT CONTROL. **Main/Corp** Maryland. Water Resources Administration. (19??)-. English. Irregular. Water Resources Administration, Tawes State Office Building, Annapolis MD 21401.

LC S590 **ISSN** 0074-0411
DD 631.6 NE
MEDEDELING - INSTITUUT VOOR CULTUURTECHNIEK EN WATERHUISHOUDING. **Main/Corp** Instituut voor Cultuurtechniek en Waterhuishouding. No. 1 (1958)-. Monographic series. Dutch (summaries and/or abstracts in English). Irregular. Price varies per volume. Institute for Land and Water Management Research (ICW), PO Box 35, 6700 AA Wageningen The Netherlands. **Tel** 011 31 8370 19100, FAX 011 31 8370 11524, telex 75230 VISI N. **ED** Ing Bram ten Cate. cum. index. **Circ:** 700 (ctrl).
Desc: Covers water management, plant-soil-water relationships, soil technology, groundwater and surface water quality, outdoor recreation, and planning rural areas.
Ind/Abst Geogr. Abstr. Human Geogr.

LC SB215
DD 633.6 NE
MEDEDELING (INSTITUUT VOOR RATIONELE SUIKERPRODUCTIE). (MEDEDELING.). **Added/Corp** Instituut voor Rationele Suikerproductie. No. 1 (1978)-. Periodical. Dutch.
Ind/Abst Rev. Plant Pathol.; Sug. Indus. Abstr.

LC S **ISSN** 0755-3617
DD 630 FR
CODEN MASDDW
MEMOIRES DE L'ACADEMIE DES SCIENCES, ARTS ET BELLES LETTRES DE DIJON. [Mem. Acad. sci., arts belles-lett. Dijon]. 1871-. French. One time a year. cum. index. ***Continues*** *Compte Rendu des Travaux (Dijon, France).*
Ind/Abst BHA : Biblio. Hist. Art; GeoRef.

LC S
DD 630 ES
MEMORIA ANUAL / INSTITUTO NACIONAL DEL CAFE, INCAFE. **Main/Corp** Instituto Nacional del Cafe (El Salvador). Spanish. ***Continues*** *Memoria / Instituto Nacional del Cafe, INCAFE, Unidad de Estudios Especiales.*

LC S **ISSN** 0125-9318
DD 630 IO
CODEN MPERA4
MENARA PERKEBUNAN. **Added/Corp** Balai Penelitian Perkebunan Bogor. Algemeen Landbouw Syndicaat. Bogor, Indonesia. Balai Penjelidikan Perkebunan Besar. Vol. 1 (July 3, 1926)-. Periodical. Indonesian (summaries and/or abstracts in English). Four times a year. Balai Penelitian Perkebunan Bogor, (Research Institute for Estate Crops), J1 Taman Kencana 1, Box 81, Bogor Indonesia. **Tel** telex 48369 AARD IA. available with charts; available on microfiche. Documents available from CASDDS.
Ind/Abst Agric. Eng. Abstr.; Agrofor. Abstr.; Chem. Abstr. (1958-1981); Grass. Forage Abstr.; Hortic. Abstr.; Plant Breed. Abstr.; Plant Genet. Resour. Abstr.; Postharvest News Inf.; Rev. Plant Pathol.; Seed Abstr.; Soils Fert.; Weed Abstr.; World Agric. Econ. Rural Sociol. Abstr.

LC S631 **ISSN** 0169-2267
DD 631.8 NE
MESTSTOFFEN. [Meststoffen]. **Added/Corp** Nederlands Meststoffen Instituut. (1985)-. Periodical. Dutch. One time a year. F35.00. Ned Meststoffen Institute, Agro Business Park 20, 6708 PW Wageningen Netherlands. **Tel** 011 31 8370 79620. ***Continues*** *Stikstof, 0585-3060.*
Ind/Abst Agric. Eng. Abstr.; Dairy Sci. Abstr.; Grass. Forage Abstr.

LC SB320 **ISSN** 0885-6060
DD 635 US
MICHIGAN DRY BEAN DIGEST. [Mich. dry bean dig.]. **Added/Corp** Michigan Bean Shippers Association. (19??)-. Trade Publication. English. Four times a year. $25.00 US; $35.00 other. Michigan Dry Bean Digest, PO Box 6008, Saginaw MI 48608. **Tel** (517)790-3010, FAX (517)790-3747. **ED** John A. McGill. **Ad Acc, Adv Mgr:** Ann M. Waters. Full Page (B&W) 1,250.00. Full Page (Color) 1,500.00. **Circ:** 14,000.
Ind/Abst AGRICOLA [Select. Cov.].

LC S **ISSN** 1012-6775
DD 630 SA
MIELIES PRETORIA. [Mielies Pretoria]. **VFOAT** Maize. (1980)-. Periodical. Multiple languages. Twelve times a year. $8.23. NAMPO, PO Box 88, 9660 Bothaville South Africa. **Tel** 011 27 565 2145. ***Absorbed*** *Maize News.*

LC SB183
DD 633 US
MISSISSIPPI WEEKLY WEATHER & CROP REPORT. **Added/Corp** Mississippi State University. Cooperative Extension Service. (1975)-. Government Publication. English. Forty times a year. $12.00. US Department of Agriculture / National Agricultural Statistics Service (NASS), Room 5829 South Building, Washington DC 20250. **Tel** (202)720-4020, FAX (314)875-5231. **Circ:** 450 (ctrl). ***Continues*** *Mississippi*

Weather Crop Report.
Desc: Weekly progress and general development, rainfall and temperature.

LC S590 .D48a **ISSN** 0343-107X
DD 631.4 GW

MITTEILUNGEN DER DEUTSCHEN BODENKUNDLICHE GESELLSCHAFT.

Main/Corp Deutsche Bodenkundliche Gesellschaft. (1???)-. Periodical. German.
Ind/Abst Agric. Eng. Abstr. (1991-); Biodeter. Abstr.; For. Abstr.; GeoRef; Maize Abstr.; Nematol. Abstr.; Rice Abstr.; Soils Fert.; Soyabean Abstr.

LC S **ISSN** 0007-5922
DD 630 AU
CODEN MIKLD4

MITTEILUNGEN KLOSTERNEUBURG : REBE UND WEIN, OBSTBAU UND FRUCHTEVERWERTUNG.

See Food and Food Industry-Beverage Industry.

LC SB599 **ISSN** 1052-6129
DD 632 US

MONOGRAPH SERIES OF THE WEED SCIENCE SOCIETY OF AMERICA.

[Monogr. ser. Weed Sci. Soc. Am.]. **Added/Corp** Weed Science Society of America. (19??)-. Monographic series. English. Weed Science Society of America, 1508 West University Avenue, Champaign IL 61821. **Tel** (217)352-4212, FAX (217)398-4114.
Ind/Abst AGRICOLA [Full Cov.].

LC S **ISSN** 0279-0394
DD 630 US

MONTANA CROP & LIVESTOCK REPORTER.

Added/Corp Montana Crop and Livestock Reporting Service. **VAT** Montana Crop and Livestock Reporter. (1979)-. Government Publication. English. Twenty-four times a year. $12.00. US Department of Agriculture / National Agricultural Statistics Service (NASS), Room 5829 South Building, Washington DC 20250. **Tel** (202)720-4020, FAX (314)875-5231. **Circ:** 4,000 (ctrl).
Desc: Reports on state and county crop and livestock estimates, farm income, prices, etc.

LC HD9093.U4 A334 **ISSN** 0027-0318
DD 338.1/7351/0973 US

MONTHLY COTTON LINTERS REVIEW.

See Fabrics and Textile Industries.

LC S590 .M618 **ISSN** 0147-6874
DD 631.4/05 US
CCC
CODEN MUSBDU

MOSCOW UNIVERSITY SOIL SCIENCE BULLETIN.

[Moscow Univ. soil sci. bull.]. **Main/Corp** Moskovskii gosudarstvennyi universitet im. M.V. Lomonosova. (1974)-. Bulletin. English (Russian). Four times a year. $820.00. Allerton Press Inc., 150 Fifth Avenue, New York NY 10011. **Tel** (212)924-3950, FAX (212)463-9684, telex 427441 ALPRES. Documents available from Article Express International, BIOSIS Document Express, CASDDS.
Ind/Abst AGRICOLA [Full Cov.]; Agric. Eng. Abstr. (1991-); Agrofor. Abstr.; Bioeng. Abstr.; Biol. Abstr. (-1983); Chem. Abstr.; Ei Page One; EMBASE; Eng. Index Annu.; Field Crop Abstr.; GeoRef; Hortic. Abstr.; Potato Abstr.; Rev. Plant Pathol.; Rice Abstr.; Soils Fert.; Weed Abstr.

LC HD9225.U53 C24 **ISSN** 0094-2790
DD 381/.41/409794 US

MOVEMENT OF CALIFORNIA FRUITS AND VEGETABLES BY RAIL, TRUCK, AND AIR.

See Transportation.

LC S **ISSN** 0144-0551
DD 630 UK
CODEN MUSJDK

MUSHROOM JOURNAL.

(THE MUSHROOM JOURNAL.). [Mushroom j.]. **Added/Corp** Mushroom Growers' Association. (1973)-. Trade Publication. English. Twelve times a year. $217.46 (non-trade), $453.05 (trade). Mushroom Growers Association, 2 St. Pauls Street Stamford, Lincolnshire PE39 2BE United Kingdom. **Tel** 011 44 1780 66888, FAX 011 44 1780 66558. **ED** K. I. James. Index available. **Ad Acc. Circ:** 1,000 (ctrl). Documents available from CASDDS. ***Supersedes*** *Mushroom Growers' Association. MGA Bulletin.*
Desc: Comprehensive news and information on all aspects of the industry.
Ind/Abst AgBiotech News Inf.; AGRICOLA [Full Cov.]; Agric. Eng. Abstr. (1991-); Biodeter. Abstr.; Chem. Abstr. (1973-1983); Food Sci. Technol. Abstr.; Hortic. Abstr.; Microbiol. Abstr. Sect. A; Microbiol. Abstr. Sect. C; Nematol. Abstr.; Life Sci. Collect.; Plant Breed. Abstr.; Postharvest News Inf.; World Agric. Econ. Rural Sociol. Abstr.

LC SB320 **ISSN** 0541-3869
DD 635 US

MUSHROOM NEWS.

[Mushroom news]. **Added/Corp** American Mushroom Institute. Vol. 1, (1955)-. Trade Publication. English. Twelve times a year. $275.00. American Mushroom Institute, 907 East Baltimore Pike, Kennett Square PA 19348. **Tel** (610) 388-7806, FAX (215)388-0243. **ED** Timothy A. King (phone: (215)296-9611). Index available (Dec. iss.). **Ad Acc, Adv Mgr:** Tim King, **Tel** (215)296-9611. **Circ:** 700 (ctrl).
Desc: Layman and scientific articles on the mushroom industry.
Ind/Abst Agric. Eng. Abstr.; Hortic. Abstr.

LC HD9235.M952 U54 **ISSN** 0197-6281
DD 338.1/758/0973021 US

MUSHROOMS.

[Mushrooms]. **Added/Corp** United States. Crop Reporting Board. United States. Agricultural Statistics Board. (1966)-. Government Publication. English. One time a year (published in Aug.). $9.00. US Department of Agriculture / National Agricultural Statistics Service (NASS), Room 5829 South Building, Washington DC 20250. **Tel** (202)720-4020, FAX (314)875-5231.
Desc: Area, production, price and value for selected states, utilization for U.S., July 1, 1983-June 30, 1994 and intentions for coming year.

LC S
DD 630 AU
Pr Rev.

MUTATION BREEDING NEWSLETTER.

Added/Corp Joint FAO/IAEA Division of Atomic Energy in Food and Agriculture. Joint FAO/IAEA Division of Isotope and Radiation Applications of Atomic Energy for Food and Agricultural Development. (197?)-. Newsletter. English. Two times a year. Plant Breeding and Genetics Section, Joint FAO / IAEA Division, A-1400 Vienna Austria. **Tel** FAX 431 234564, telex 1-12645. **ED** M. Maluszynski. **Bk Rev. Circ:** 1,500 (ctrl).
Desc: Contains papers related to the use of mutation techniques and biotechnology for crop improvement.
Ind/Abst Field Crop Abstr.; Grass. Forage Abstr.; Hortic. Abstr.; Ornamental Hort. (1991-); Plant Breed. Abstr.; Rev. Plant Pathol.; Rice Abstr.; Seed Abstr.; Sorghum Mill. Abstr.; Soyabean Abstr.; Weed Abstr.; Wheat Barley Trit. Abstr.

LC S590 **ISSN** 0110-2079
DD 631.4 NZ

N.Z. SOIL SURVEY REPORT.

[N.Z. soil surv. rep.]. **VFOAT** New Zealand Soil Survey Report. No. 1 (1973)-. Periodical. English. Irregular. New Zealand Soil Bureau, Department of Scientific and Industrial Research, Private Bag, Lower Hutt New Zealand. **Tel** 673 119.
Desc: Soil surveys of areas of New Zealand and Pacific relating to soil properties and their suitability for various land uses.
Ind/Abst AGRICOLA.

LC S
DD 630 US

NATIONAL APPLE NEWS.

Added/Corp International Apple Institute. Vol. 1 (July 1970)-. Periodical. English. Six times a year. International Apple Institute, 6707 Old Dominion Drive/Suite 210, PO Box 1137, McLean VA 22101. ***Continues*** *National Apple News.*

LC SB211.P8 N378 **ISSN** 8756-2626
DD 635/.2126 US

NATIONAL POTATO GERMPLASM EVALUATION AND ENHANCEMENT REPORT.

Added/Corp Beltsville Agricultural Research Center. (1982)-. English. One time a year. available on microfiche (Vols. for (1985-) distributed to depository libraries). ***Continues*** *National Potato Breeding Report.*
Ind/Abst AGRICOLA.

LC S
DD 630 US

NATIONAL SURVEY OF CONSERVATION TILLAGE PRACTICES (INCLUDING OTHER TILLAGE TYPES).

(1991)-. Periodical. English. Conservation Technology Information Center, 1220 Potter Drive, Room 170, West Lafayette IN 47906. **Tel** (219)494-9555.

LC S
DD 630 US

NATIVE CORN REPORT.

Added/Corp Cornell University. American Indian Agriculture Program. No. 1 (Summer 1991)-. Periodical. English. Four times a year.

LC S **ISSN** 0745-0117
DD 630 US

NEBRASKA WEATHER & CROPS.

Added/Corp Nebraska Crop and Livestock Reporting Service. Nebraska Agricultural Statistics Service. **VFOAT** Nebraska Weather and Crops. (19??)-. Periodical. English. Irregular (weekly April-Nov. and monthly Dec.-March). $15.00. Nebraska Department of Agriculture Division of Agricultural Statistics, Box 81069, Lincoln NE 68501. **Tel** (402)437-5541.

LC HF
DD 380.1 US

NEW ORLEANS, FRESH FRUIT AND VEGETABLE WHOLESALE MARKET PRICES.

Main/Corp Federal-State Market News Service. **Added/Corp** United States. Agricultural Marketing Service. Louisiana. State Market Commission. **VFOAT** Fresh Fruit and Vegetable Wholesale Market Prices, New Orleans; Wholesale Market Prices at New Orleans, La. (1976)-. Government Publication. English. One time a year. US Department of Agriculture / Agricultural Marketing Service / Washington, DC, Market News Branch, Fruit and Vegetable Division, Washington DC 20250. **Tel** (202)720-2745, (202)720-3343, FAX (202)720-7502.

LC SB320
DD 635 NZ

NEW ZEALAND COMMERCIAL GROWER : OFFICIAL JOURNAL OF THE NEW ZEALAND VEGETABLE AND PRODUCE GROWERS' FEDERATION.

Added/Corp New Zealand Vegetable and Produce Growers' Federation. (19??)-. Periodical. English. Ten times a year (Jan./Feb. & Nov./Dec. issues combined). $42.98. Vegetable Producers Publishers Limited, PO Box 10232, Wellington, New Zealand. **Tel** 011 64 4 723795. **ED** David Poterson. **Ad Acc. Circ:** 5,800.
Desc: The magazine is in research and education institutes, business houses, produce merchants, exporters, processing factories, government department and service organizations.
Ind/Abst Hortic. Abstr.; Plant Breed. Abstr.

LC SB320 **ISSN** 1171-7033
DD 635.099305 NZ

NEW ZEALAND GROWING TODAY.

[N.Z grow. today]. **VFOAT** Growing Today. (1992)-. Periodical. English. Twelve times a year. $33.12. New Zealand Growing Today, PO Box 100 436, NSMC Auckland New Zealand. **Tel** 011 64 9 4128822. ***Continues*** *Growing Today, 0112-1588.*

LC S **ISSN** 0114-0671
DD 630 NZ
CCC
CODEN NZJSEF
Pr Rev.

NEW ZEALAND JOURNAL OF CROP AND HORTICULTURAL SCIENCE.

See Gardening and Horticulture.

LC S599.75.A1 N46B **ISSN** 0304-1735
DD 631.4/05 NZ
CODEN NSBRAL

NEW ZEALAND SOIL BUREAU SCIENTIFIC REPORT.

[N.Z. Soil Bur. sci. rep.]. (1971)-. Monographic series. English. Price varies per volume. New Zealand Soil Bureau, Department of Scientific and Industrial Research, Private Bag, Lower Hutt New Zealand. **Tel** 673 119. Documents available from CASDDS.
Desc: Scientific reports contain detailed scientific information on a wide variety of soil related topics.
Ind/Abst Chem. Abstr.; Geogr. Abstr. Phys. Geogr. (?-?); GeoRef.

LC S599.75.A1 N47 **ISSN** 0545-7904
DD 631.4/9931 NZ
CCC

NEW ZEALAND SOIL NEWS.

[N. Z. soil news]. **Added/Corp** New Zealand Society of Soil Science. (1953)-. Periodical. English. Six times a year. $32.23. New Zealand Society of Soil Science, Department of Soil Science, PO Box 84, Lincoln University, Canterbury New Zealand. **Tel** FAX 011 64 3 3252944. **ED** A.S. Campbell. Index available. cum. index. **Bk Rev. Circ:** 400 (ctrl). Documents available.
Ind/Abst AGRICOLA.

LC S590 **ISSN** 0029-0610
DD 631.4 JA
CODEN NIDHAX

NIHON DOJO HIRYOGAKU ZASSHI.

[Nippon dojo hiryogaku zasshi]. **Added/Corp** Nihon DojÅo HiryÅo Gakkai. **VFOAT** Journal of the Science of Soil and Manure, Japan; Japanese Journal of Soil Science and Plant Nutrition; Nippon Dojohiryogaku Zasshi. (1927)-. Academic Scholarly Publication. Japanese (English). Six times a year. $195.00. **(Subscription address:** Maruzen Company Ltd., PO Box 5050, Import & Export Department, Tokyo 100 31 Japan. **Tel** 011 81 3 32789224.) Documents available from CASDDS.
Ind/Abst AGRICOLA; Chem. Abstr.; Hortic. Abstr.; Plant Breed. Abstr.; Rev. Plant Pathol.; Rice Abstr.; Soils Fert.

LC SB183 **ISSN** 0011-1848
DD 633 JA
CODEN NISAAJ
Pr Rev.

NIHON SAKUMOTSU GAKKAI KIJI.

Main/Corp Nihon Sakumotsu Gakkai. **VFOAT** Proceedings of the Crop Science Society of Japan; Japanese Journal of Crop Science. (1927)-. Academic Scholarly Publication. Japanese (English). Four times a year. $162.14. Nihon Sakumotsu Gakkai, (Crop Science Soc. of Japan), c/o Tokyo Daigaku Nogakubu, 1-1 Yayoi 1 Chome, Bunkyoku Tokyo 113 Japan. **ED** Takashi Ovitani. **Circ:** 2,300 (ctrl). Documents available from The Genuine Article, CASDDS.
Desc: An organ of the crop sciences society of Japan.
Ind/Abst Agric. Eng. Abstr.; Agrofor. Abstr.;

BioBusiness; Chem. Abstr.; Cot. Trop. Fibr. Abstr. Bibliogr.; Crop Physiol. Abstr.; Curr. Aware. Biol. Sci., CABS; Curr. Cit.; Curr. Contents Agric. Biol. Environ. Sci.; Food Sci. Technol. Abstr.; For. Abstr.; Hortic. Abstr.; Maize Abstr.; Plant Breed. Abstr.; Plant Grow. Reg. Abstr.; Potato Abstr.; Res. Alert [Select. Cov.]; Rice Abstr.; SCISEARCH; Seed Abstr.; Soils Fert.; Sorghum Mill. Abstr.; Soyabean Abstr.; World Agric. Econ. Rural Sociol. Abstr.

LC S590 **ISSN** 0285-3507
DD 631 JA

NIHON SAKUMOTSU GAKKAI KYUSHU SHIBUKAIHO. [Nihon Sakumotsu Gakkai Kyushu Shibukaiho]. **VFOAT** Report of the Kyushu Branch of the Crop Science Society of Japan. (1958)-. Periodical. Japanese. One time a year. Kyushu University / Department of Agriculture, Department of Agriculture, 33 Fukuoka 812 Japan. ***Continues*** *Kyushu Sakumotsu Danwakaiho, 0285-3493.*
Ind/Abst Crop Physiol. Abstr.; Hortic. Abstr.; Irr. Drain. Abstr.; Soyabean Abstr.

LC S590 **ISSN** 0911-7067
DD 631 JA

NIHON SAKUMOTSU GAKKAI TOHOKU SHIBU KAIHO. [Nihon Sakumotsu Gakkai Tohoku Shibu kaiho]. **VFOAT** Report of the Tohoku Branch, the Crop Science Society of Japan. (1958)-. Periodical. Japanese. One time a year. Nihon Sakumotsu Gakkai Tohoku Shibu, (Tohoku Branch Crop Science Soc. of Japan), Akita Kenritsu Nogyo Tanki Daigaku, 2-2 Minami Ogatamura, Minamiakitagun Akitaken 010-04, Japan.
Ind/Abst Agric. Eng. Abstr.; Crop Physiol. Abstr.; Field Crop Abstr.; Hortic. Abstr.; Plant Grow. Reg. Abstr.; Potato Abstr.; Rice Abstr.; Seed Abstr.; Sorghum Mill. Abstr.; Soyabean Abstr.; Weed Abstr.

LC S590 **ISSN** 0091-9993
DD 631 US
CCC

NO-TILL FARMER. [No-till farmer]. **Added/Corp** No-Till Farmer Association. (19??)-. Trade Publication. English. Seventeen times a year (Twice monthly Jan. to May, once a month June to Dec.). $36.95. No-Till Farmer Inc., PO Box 624, Brookfield WI 53008-0624. **Tel** (414)782-4480, FAX (414)782-1252. **ED** Frank Lessiter. **Ad Acc. Circ:** 7,000.
Desc: Gives information on machinery, tillage practices, weed control, planting tips, disease and insect control, planter modifications and adjustment, cover crops, chemicals, and new drills and planters.

LC S **ISSN** 0387-2335
DD 630 JA

NOGYO DOBOKU GAKKAI RONBUNSHU. (NOGYO DOBOKU GAKKAI RONBUNSHU. TRANSACTIONS OF THE JAPANESE SOCIETY OF IRRIGATION, DRAINAGE AND RECLAMATION ENGINEERING.). [Nogyo doboku gakkai ronbunshu]. **Main/Corp** Nogyo Doboku Gakkai. **VFOAT** Transactions of the Japanese Society of Irrigation, Drainage and Reclamation Engineering. (1965)-. Periodical. Japanese (English; summaries and/or abstracts in English). Six times a year. Nogyo Doboku Gakkai, (Japanese Society of Irrigation Drainage & Reclamation Engineering), Nogyo Doboku Kaikan, 34-4 Shinbashi 5 Chome, Minatoku Tokyo 105 Japan. ***Continues*** *Nogyo Doboku Kenkyu. Bessatsu.*
Ind/Abst Rice Abstr.; Soils Fert.

LC S631 **ISSN** 0077-4839
DD 631.8 JA
CODEN NGKBA2

NOGYO GIJUTSU KENKYUJO HOKOKU. RENZOKU B: DOJO HIRYO. (NOGYO GIJUTSU KENKYUJO HOKOKU. B : DOJO HIRYO.). [Nogyo Gijutsu Kenkyujo hokoku B]. **Main/Corp** Norinsho Nogyo Gijutsu Kenkyujo (Japan). **VFOAT** Bulletin of the National Institute of Agricultural Sciences. Soils and Fertilizers (On Cover, Parallel with Japanese Title, 1952-72). No. 1- ; 1952-. Academic Scholarly Publication. Japanese (summaries and/or abstracts in English). Documents available from CASDDS.
Ind/Abst AGRICOLA; Chem. Abstr. (1952-1984); EMBASE; GeoRef.

LC S **ISSN** 0021-8588
DD 630 JA
Pr Rev.

NOGYO KISHO. [Nogyo kisho]. **Main/Corp** Nihon Nogyo Kishogakkai. **VFOAT** Journal of Agricultural Meteorology. (1943)-. Academic Scholarly Publication. Japanese (English; table of contents in English). Four times a year. $86.48. Society of Agricultural Meteorology of Japan, University of Tokyo, Department of Agricultural Engineering, Tokyo 113 Japan. **Tel** 011 81 3 38122111 ext. 5355. **ED** Satoshi Iwakiri. cum. index. **Bk Rev. Ad Acc. Circ:** 1,300.
Desc: Micrometeorology, crop physiology, protected cultivation, climatological hazard yield estimation, meteorological instrumentation and climatological statistics boundary layer meteorology.
Ind/Abst EMBASE; Fluid Abstr., Civil Eng.; Fluid Abstr. Proc. Eng.; FLUIDEX (1973-); Hortic. Abstr.; Wheat Barley Trit. Abstr.

LC SB183 **ISSN** 0911-6575
DD 633 JA
CODEN NSSHEC

NOGYO SEIBUTSU SHIGEN KENKYUJO KENKYU HOKOKU. [Nogyo Seibutsu Shigen Kenkyujo kenkyu hokoku]. **VFOAT** Bulletin of the National Institute of Agrobiological Resources. (1985)-. Bulletin. English (Japanese). Documents available from BIOSIS Document Express.
Ind/Abst Biol. Abstr. (1985-); Plant Breed. Abstr.; Plant Grow. Reg. Abstr.; Rice Abstr.; Soils Fert.; Soyabean Abstr.

LC S
DD 630 AT

NON-TILLAGE CROP PRODUCTION IN NORTHERN NEW SOUTH WALES : PROCEEDINGS OF THE PROJECT TEAM MEETING. **Added/Corp** Agricultural Research Centre (N.S.W.). (19??)-. English. One time a year. New South Wales Department of Agriculture / Agricultural Research Centre, Tamworth NSW 2340 Australia.

LC SB183
DD 633 KO

NONGSA SIHOM YONGU NONMUNJIP. CHANGMULPYON. **VFOAT** Research Reports of the Rural Development Administration. (1985)-. Periodical. Korean (summaries and/or abstracts in English). Two times a year. Rural Development Administration of Crops, Suweon Korea. ***Continues in part*** *Nongsa Sihom Yongu Pogo.*

LC S
DD 630 KO

NONGSA SIHOM YONGU NONMUNJIP. SIKHWAN, KYUNI, NONGGAPYON. **VFOAT** Research Reports of the Rural Development Administration. (1985)-. Periodical. Korean (summaries and/or abstracts in English). Two times a year. Rural Development Administration, Plant Environment Mycology and Farm Products Utilization, Suweon 170 Korea. ***Continues in part*** *Nongsa Sihom Yongu Pogo.*
Ind/Abst Plant Grow. Reg. Abstr.

LC HD9483.U53 N85A
DD 338.4/766862/09756 US

NORTH CAROLINA FERTILIZER TONNAGE REPORT. **VFOAT** Fertilizer Tonnage Report. English. One time a year. North Carolina Crop and Livestock Reporting Service, PO Box 27767, 1 West Edenton Street, Raleigh NC 27611. ***Continues*** *North Carolina Fertilizer Tonnage Report, Mixed Fertilizer by Grades and by Counties.*

LC S
DD 630 US

NORTH DAKOTA WHEAT VARIETIES. **Added/Corp** North Dakota Crop and Livestock Reporting Service. North Dakota. State Wheat Commission. North Dakota Agricultural Experiment Station (Fargo) North Dakota Agricultural Statistics Service. United States. Dept. of Agriculture. Statistical Reporting Service. United States. Dept. of Agriculture. Economics and Statistics Service. United States. National Agricultural Statistics Service. North Dakota State University. Extension Service. (1973)-. Government Publication. English. Irregular. Free on request. US Department of Agriculture / National Agricultural Statistics Service (NASS), Room 5829 South Building, Washington DC 20250. **Tel** (202)720-4020, FAX (314)875-5231. ***Continues*** *North Dakota Crop and Livestock Reporting Service. Wheat Varieties, North Dakota, 0090-9815.*

LC SB354
DD 634 AT

NORTHERN VICTORIA FRUITGROWER. **Added/Corp** Northern Victoria Fruitgrowers' Association. Vol. 1, No. 1 (May 1977)-. Periodical. English. Twelve times a year. Northern Victoria Fruitgrowers' Association, Shepparton Victoria Australia. ***Continues*** *The Northern Victorian Fruitgrower.*

LC HD1521 .I75a
DD 331.7/63/05 SZ

NOTE ON THE PROCEEDINGS OF THE ... / INTERNATIONAL LABOUR ORGANISATION, PROGRAMME OF INDUSTRIAL ACTIVITIES, COMMITTEE ON WORK ON PLANTATIONS. **See** Business and Economics-Labor.

LC S590 **ISSN** 0712-6522
DD 631.4/071356 CN

NOTES AND NEWS. [Notes news - Durham East Soil Crop Improv. Assoc.]. Vol. 5, 1st Ed. (Jan. 15, 1982)-. Periodical. English. Irregular. Free. Notes and News, 234 King Street East, Bowmanville Ontario L1C 1P5 Canada. ***Continues*** *Notes and News from the Durham Soil & Crop Improvement Assoc., 0712-6514.*

LC S
DD 630 US

NOTES FROM THE NORTH. **Added/Corp** Minnesota Grape Growers Association. (1978)-. Periodical. English. Four times a year. Comes with Minnesota Grape Growers Association membership; $15.00 (membership). Minnesota Grape Growers Association, 35680 Highway 61 Boulevard, Lake City MN 55041. **Tel** (612)345-3531. ***Supersedes*** *Minnesota Grape Growers Association. Membership Newsletter - Minnesota Grape Growers Association.*

LC S **ISSN** 0546-8191
DD 630 HU
CODEN NOVEAK
Pr Rev.

NOVENYTERMELES. **See** Biology-Botany.

LC SB320 **ISSN** 1181-9820
DD 635.9/69/09711 CN

NURSERY CROP PRODUCTION GUIDE FOR COMMERCIAL GROWERS. [Nurs. prod. guide commer. grow.]. **Added/Corp** British Columbia. Ministry of Agriculture and Fisheries. (1992)-. English. Every 2 years. Ministry of Agriculture, Fisheries, and Food, Extension Systems Branch, Parliment Systems Branch, Victoria British Columbia, V8W 2Z7 Canada. ***Continues in part*** *Nursery, Greenhouse Vegetable & Ornamental Production Guide for Commercial Growers, 0840-8068.*

LC S **ISSN** 0745-3469
DD 630 US

NUT GROWER. Vol. 1 (Sept./Oct. 1982)-. Trade Publication. English. Twelve times a year. $19.95. Western Agricultural Publishing Company, 1755 North Fine Avenue, Fresno CA 93727. **Tel** (209)252-7000, FAX (209)252-7387. **ED** Harry Cline. **Ad Acc. Circ:** 12,000.

LC S **ISSN** 0738-596X
DD 630 US

NUT KERNEL, THE. **Added/Corp** Pennsylvania Nut Growers Association. Vol. 1 (1948)-. Periodical. English. Three times a year. $5.00 Comes with Pennsylvania Nut Growers Association membership. Pennsylvania Nut Growers Association, Tucker Hill, 654 Beinhower Road, Etters PA 17319. **Tel** (717)326-3669. **Bk Rev. Ad Acc. Circ:** 300 (ctrl).
Desc: Contains information on grafting techniques, practices, resources, diseases, insects, and nut using recipes.

LC HD1401 **ISSN** 0229-7191
DD 338.1/9/71 CN

OFA FOOD BASKET. [OFA food basket]. Dec. 1979-. Periodical. English. Twelve times a year. Free. Ontario Federation Agriculture, Suite 502, 387 Bloor Street East, Toronto Ontario M4W 1H9. ***Continues*** *Farmer Price Index, 0705-8632.*

LC S600.62.O3 O44 **ISSN** 0735-6811
DD 630/.2/5169771 US

OHIO CROP AND WEATHER. (OHIO CROP AND WEATHER : SUMMARY FOR ...). [Ohio crop weather]. (19??)-. English. One time a year. Ohio Agricultural Research and Development Center, Ohio State University, 1680 Madison Avenue, Wooster OH 44691. **Tel** (216)263-3775.

LC SB354
DD 634 US

OHIO FRUIT JOURNAL. **Added/Corp** Ohio Fruit Growers Society. Vol. 1 (Sept. 1979)-. Periodical. English. Four times a year. $15.00. Ohio Fruit Growers Society, PO Box 479, 35 East Chestnut Street, Columbus OH 43216.

LC SB113
DD 631.521 GW

OIL WORLD : THE WEEKLY FORECASTING AND INFORMATION SERVICE FOR OILSEEDS, OILS, FATS AND OILMEALS. **Added/Corp** International Seed Testing Association. (1982)-. Periodical. English. Fifty-one times per year (Fri. except between Christmas & New Year). ISTA Mielke GmBH., Langenberg 25, D-21077 Hamburg Germany. **Tel** 011 49 40 7610500. ***Continues*** *Oil World Digest.*

LC HD9490.C2 A26 **ISSN** 0527-5911
DD 338.4/76643/0971021 CN

OILS AND FATS. [Oils fats]. **Added/Corp** Canada. Dominion Bureau of Statistics. Animal Products Section. Canada. Dominion Bureau of Statistics. Industry and Merchandising Division. Canada. Dominion Bureau of Statistics. Industry Division. Canada. Dominion Bureau of Statistics. Manufacturing and Primary Industries Division. Statistics Canada. Manufacturing and Primary Industries Division. Statistics Canada. Industry Division. **VFOAT** Huiles et Corps Gras; Huiles et Matieres Grasses. Vol. 1, No. 1 (Jan./June 1950)-. Statistical Publication. English (French). Twelve times a year. 48.02Can$. Statistics Canada Publications Sales and Services, R.H. Coats Building 6th Floor, Ottawa Ontario K1A 0T6 Canada. **Tel** (613)951-5078, (800)267-6677, FAX (613)951-1584, telex 053-3585.
Desc: Domestic purchases and production of deodorized

oils. Manufacturers' sales of deodorized oils by type, packaged margarine, shortening and salad oils. Oilseed crushings; production and stocks of vegetable oils meal.

LC SB761
DD 635.97 AT
OILSEEDS - SITUATION AND OUTLOOK. **Added/Corp** Australia. Bureau of Agricultural Economics. **VFOAT** Situation and Outlook - Oilseeds. (1977)-. Periodical. English. Australian Government Publishing Service, GPO Box 84, Canberra ACT 2601 Australia. **Tel** 011 61 6 2954411, FAX 011 61 6 2954455.

LC SB320 **ISSN** 0892-578X
DD 635 US
ONION WORLD. [Onion world]. (Jan. 1985)- Vol. 9 & 10 (Jan. 1993-94)-. Trade Publication. English. Eight times a year (Jan., Feb., March/April, May/June, July/Aug., Sept., Oct./Nov., and Dec.). $15.00. Onion World, PO Box 1467, Yakima WA 98907. **Tel** (509)248-2452, (800)900-2452, FAX (509)248-4056. **ED** Brent Clement. **Ad Acc, Adv Mgr:** Mike Stoken. **Circ:** 6,109 (ctrl).
Desc: Includes information on onion production and marketing. Grower and shipper feature stories, onion research, from herbicide an a pesticide studies to promising new varieties, market reports, feedback from major onion meetings and conventions, spot reports on overseas production and marketing, and other key issues and trends of interest to U. S. and Canadian onion growers.

LC SB188 **ISSN** 0008-7297
DD 633.1 CN
ONTARIO CORN PRODUCER. [Ont. corn prod.]. **Added/Corp** Ontario Corn Producers' Association. **VFOAT** Corn Producer. Vol. 1, No. 1 (March 1985)-. Trade Publication. English. Ten times a year (monthly with combined July/Aug. and Oct./Nov.). 20.01Can$. Ontario Corn Producers Association, 90 Woodlawn Road West, Guelph Ontario N1H 1B2 Canada. **Tel** (519)837-1660, FAX (519)837-1674. **ED** Terry Boland. **Ad Acc. Circ:** 25,000 (ctrl). ***Continues*** *Cash Crop Farming, 1193-7440.*
Desc: Information on corn and the corn industry.

LC S **ISSN** 0380-6057
DD 630 CN
ONTARIO GRAPE GROWER, THE. **Added/Corp** Ontario Grape Growers' Marketing Board. Vol. 1 (Sept. 1968)-. Periodical. English. Four times a year. Free on request. Ontario Grape Growers' Marketing Board, PO Box 100 Vineland Station, St. Catharines Ontario L0R 2E0 Canada. **Tel** (416)688-0990, FAX (416)688-3211. **ED** Brian Leyden. **Circ:** 8,500 (ctrl).
Desc: Current data on Ontario's vineyards and on Ontario wines.

LC S **ISSN** 0923-0769
DD 630 NE
CEASED
OOGST. (19??)-(19??). Dutch. Hollandse Maatschappij Landb, Postbus 108, 2280 AC Rijswijk Netherlands.

LC SB354 **ISSN** 0110-6260
DD 634 NZ
CCC
ORCHARDIST OF NEW ZEALAND, THE. [Orchard. N. Z.]. **Added/Corp** New Zealand Fruitgrowers' Federation. **VFOAT** A.Orchardist of N.Z.; A.Orchardist. (1928)-. Periodical. English. Eleven times a year (monthly except Jan.). $93.12. New Zealand Fruitgrowers Federation Ltd, PO Box 2175, Wellington New Zealand. **Tel** 011 64 4 726559, FAX 011 64 4 726409, telex 7913537. **ED** E. Smith. Index available. cum. index. **Bk Rev. Ad Acc. Circ:** 8,000 (ctrl).
Ind/Abst AGRICOLA; Agric. Eng. Abstr. (1991-); Biodeter. Abstr.; Hortic. Abstr.; Irr. Drain. Abstr.; Plant Breed. Abstr.; Plant Grow. Reg. Abstr.; Postharvest News Inf.; Rev. Agric. Entomol.; Seed Abstr.

LC S
DD 631 US
ORNAMENTAL CROPS, NATIONAL MARKET TRENDS. (19??)-. Government Publication. English. One time a week (Fri.). $120.00 North America; $240.00 other. US Department of Agriculture / Federal-State Market News, 630 Sansome Street, Room 727, San Francisco CA 94111. **Tel** (415)705-1300, FAX (415)705-1301. **ED** F. Teensma.

LC S **ISSN** 0474-7615
DD 630 II
CODEN ORYZAS
ORYZA. [Oryza]. **Added/Corp** Association of Rice Research Workers. Vol. 1 (1962)-. Academic Scholarly Publication. English. Three times a year (Apr., Aug., Dec.). $3.00 (individuals), $5.00 (institutions). Association of Rice Research Workers, Central Rice Research Institute, Cuttack 6 India. Documents available from BIOSIS Document Express, CASDDS.
Ind/Abst AGRICOLA; Biocont. News Inf. (19??-19??); Biodeter. Abstr. (1991-); Biol. Abstr.; Chem. Abstr.; Crop Physiol. Abstr.; Curr. Cit.; Field Crop Abstr.; Irr. Drain. Abstr.; Maize Abstr.; Nematol. Abstr.; Plant Breed. Abstr.; Plant Genet. Resour. Abstr.; Plant Grow. Reg. Abstr.; Postharvest News Inf.; Rev. Agric. Entomol.; Rev. Plant Pathol.; Rice Abstr.; Seed Abstr.; Soils Fert.; Weed Abstr.; Wheat Barley Trit. Abstr.; World Agric. Econ. Rural Sociol. Abstr.

LC S
DD 630 IT
OSSERVATORIO SUL MERCATO ORTOFRUTTICOLO. (19??)-. Italian. Two times a year. L200000.00. Nomisma, Strada Maggiore 44, 40125 Bologna Italy. **Tel** 011 39 51 239422.

LC HD9247.H3 H38a **ISSN** 0160-4589
DD 338.1/35/09969 US
OUTER-ISLAND PRICES OF WHOLESALE FRESH FRUITS AND VEGETABLES. **Main/Corp** Hawaii. Market News Service Branch. (19??)-. Periodical. English. Hawaii State Dept of Agriculture / Market News Service, PO Box 22159, Honolulu HI 96822.

LC HD9086.P3 P33
DD 338.17 PK
PAKISTAN COTTONS, THE. **Added/Corp** Pakistan Central Cotton Committee. Vol. 1 (Sept./Oct. 1956)-. Periodical. English. Four times a year. Rs26.00. Pakistan Central Cotton Committee, Noulvi Tanizuddin Khan Road, Karachi 1 Pakistan. **Tel** 011 92 21 5241046. **ED** S. Zain Idris Mirza. Index available. **Ad Acc.** Documents available from BLDSC. ***Supersedes*** *Pakistan Cotton Bulletin, 0479-2327.*
Ind/Abst Cot. Trop. Fibr. Abstr. Bibliogr.; Nematol. Abstr.

LC HD9116.P2 P34
DD 338.1/7361/095491 PK
PAKISTAN SUGAR JOURNAL. (Jan./Mar. 1985)-. Periodical. English. Four times a year. M Asghar Qureshi, PO Box 471, Nishatabad Faisalabad.
Ind/Abst Field Crop Abstr.; Hortic. Abstr.; Plant Breed. Abstr.; Postharvest News Inf.; Rev. Plant Pathol.; Seed Abstr.; Sug. Indus. Abstr.; World Agric. Econ. Rural Sociol. Abstr.

LC S **ISSN** 0031-3610
DD 630 US
PEACH TIMES. **Added/Corp** National Peach Council. (1956)-. Newsletter. English. Four times a year. $20.00 (membership). National Peach Council, Box 11280, Columbia SC 29211. **Tel** (803)253-4036. **ED** Lillie Hoover-Largent. **Bk Rev. Ad Acc. Circ:** 1,800 (ctrl).
Desc: Published by the National Peach Council. Information relative to the fresh peach industry.

LC S **ISSN** 0031-3653
DD 630 US
PEANUT FARMER, THE. [Peanut farmer]. (19??)-. Periodical. English. Irregular (Jan.-July). $12.00. Specialized Agriculture Publications, 3000 Highwoods Boulevard, Suite 300, Raleigh NC 27625. **Tel** (919)872-5040. **(Subscription address:** Specialized Agricultural Publications, PO Box 95075, Raleigh NC 27625. **) ED** Dayton Matlick. **Ad Acc. Circ:** 20,000 (ctrl).
Desc: Serves the peanut industry, farmers, shellers and processors.
Ind/Abst AGRICOLA.

LC SB188 **ISSN** 1042-9379
DD 633 US
PEANUT GROWER, THE. [Peanut grow.]. (April 1989)-. Trade Publication. English. Seven times a year (seasonal monthly, Jan.-July). $15.00. Vance Publishing Corporation, 400 Knightsbridge Parkway, Lincolnshire IL 60069. **Tel** (800)255-5113, (708)634-2600. **(Subscription address:** Agri Publications, PO Box 83, Tifton GA 31793. **) ED** Catherine Andrews. **Ad Acc. Circ:** 28,000 (ctrl).
Desc: Covers peanut production practices, marketing, legislation, research and news important to peanut growers.

LC HD9235.P32 U49 **ISSN** 0273-4923
DD 338.1/73368/0973 US
PEANUT MARKETING SUMMARY CROP. [Peanut market. summ. crop]. **Added/Corp** Federal-State Market News Service. (19??)-. English. One time a year (Nov.). $20.00. United States Department of Agriculture / Georgia, PO Box 1447, Thomasville GA 31799. **Tel** (912)228-1208.
Desc: Contains market data, prices for cleaned shelled peanuts at major shipping sections, three year records of monthly peanut oil and meal F.O.B. prices, the four most recent crop production reports, and exports of peanuts and oil for the four most recent crop years.

LC S
DD 630 US
PEANUT REPORT. (19??)-. English. One time a week (usually on Friday). $120.00 US, Canada and Mexico; $240.00 other. United States Department of Agriculture / Georgia, PO Box 1447, Thomasville GA 31799. **Tel** (912)228-1208. available via fax ($222.00 through Sprint Fax).
Desc: Designed to report on F.O.B. shipping point prices for shelled and unshelled peanuts in the three production areas in addition to peanut oil and peanut meal markets in the Southeast. Also includes information of interest to the industry from other sources such as exports, production, peanut stocks and processing reports, cold storage, foreign markets, and production information from other countries.

LC SB183 **ISSN** 0479-7558
DD 633 US
Pr Rev.
PEANUT RESEARCH. [Peanut res.]. **Added/Corp** National Peanut Council. Georgia Agricultural Commodity Commission for Peanuts. American Peanut Research and Education Association. American Peanut Research and Education Society. (May 1963)-. Periodical. English. Four times a year (Mar., June, Sept., Dec.). $25.00 US; $37.50 Canada and Mexico; $50.00 other. American Peanut Research Education Association, 376 AG Hall, Oklahoma State University, Stillwater OK 74078. **Tel** (405)744-6421, (405)744-9634, FAX (405)744-5269. **ED** H. Thomas Stalker (editor's address: North Carolina State University, P.O. Box 7629, Raleigh, NC 27695-7629, phone: (919)515-3281).
Desc: Currents events in APRES and the peanut industry.

LC SB351.P3 P39 **ISSN** 0095-3679
DD 633/.368/05 US
CODEN PNTSBY
Pr Rev.
PEANUT SCIENCE. [Peanut sci.]. **Added/Corp** American Peanut Research and Education Association. American Peanut Research and Education Society. Vol. 1 (March 1974)-. Trade Publication. English. Two times a year (Jan. & July). $25.00 (individual and institutions) US; $37.50 (individual and institution) Canada and Mexico; $50.00 (individual and institution) other; $35.00 organizational membership, US; $47.50 organizational membership, Canada and Mexico; $60.00 organizational membership, other Comes with American Peanut Research and Education Society membership. American Peanut Research Education Association, 376 AG Hall, Oklahoma State University, Stillwater OK 74078. **Tel** (405)744-6421, (405)744-9634, FAX (405)744-5269. **ED** H. Thomas Stalker (editor's address: North Carolina State University, P.O. Box 7629, Raleigh, NC 27695-7629, phone: (919)515-3281). Index available (Bound in next issue.). **Circ:** 650 (ctrl). Documents available from CASDDS.
Desc: Articles on the research, teaching, or extension programs directly with or applicable to production, storage, processing, and marketing of peanuts.
Ind/Abst AGRICOLA [Full Cov.]; Agric. Eng. Abstr. (1991-); Biocont. News Inf. (1991-); Biodeter. Abstr. (19??-19??); Chem. Abstr.; Crop Physiol. Abstr.; Curr. Aware. Biol. Sci., CABS; Curr. Cit.; Field Crop Abstr.; Food Sci. Technol. Abstr.; Nematol. Abstr.; Plant Breed. Abstr.; Plant Grow. Reg. Abstr.; Postharvest News Inf.; Rev. Agric. Entomol.; Rev. Med. Vet. Mycology; Rev. Plant Pathol.; Seed Abstr.; Soils Fert.; Weed Abstr.

LC S **ISSN** 0499-0579
DD 630 US
PEANUT STOCKS AND PROCESSING. **Added/Corp** United States. Crop Reporting Board. United States. Agricultural Marketing Service. United States. Agricultural Statistics Board. (19??)-. Government Publication. English. Twelve times a year. $30.00. US Department of Agriculture, 14th Street and Independence Avenue SW, Washington DC 20250. **Tel** (202)720-5457. **(Subscription address:** Superintendent of Documents, US Government Printing Office, Washington DC 20402. **)** available on microfiche (Vols. (July 1986-) distributed to depository libraries). Documents available from Documents on Demand.
Desc: Stocks as of January 31st and July 31st; millings production and disappearance of milled products for previous six months. US season totals in September.
Ind/Abst Am. Stat. Index.

LC Z6915 .P43
DD 016.6314 IE
PEAT ABSTRACTS. **See** Agriculture-Abstracting, Bibliographies and Statistics.

LC S
DD 630 US
PECAN MARKETING SUMMARY ... CROP FOR THE STATES OF ALABAMA, FLORIDA, GEORGIA, LOUISIANA, NEW MEXICO, NORTH CAROLINA, OKLAHOMA, SOUTH CAROLINA, TEXAS. **Added/Corp** United States. Agricultural Marketing Service. Fruit and Vegetable Division. Federal-State Market News Service. (19??)-. Periodical. English. One time a year (Sept.). $10.00 US, Canada and Mexico; $20.00 other. United States Department of Agriculture / Georgia, PO Box 1447, Thomasville GA 31799. **Tel** (912)228-1208.
Desc: This summary contains market data including a brief review of the harvesting season in the major producing states with twice weekly prices paid to grower charts, the three most recent crop production reports, the four most recent years of monthly cold storage reports, and exports of pecans for the four most recent crop years.

LC S
DD 630 US
PECAN REPORT, THE. (19??)-. English. Thirty-four times a year (Published during Oct. thru Jan.). $44.00 US, Canada and Mexico; $88.00 other. United States Department of Agriculture / Georgia, PO Box 1447, Thomasville GA 31799. **Tel** (912)228-1208.
Desc: This report is designed to report on prices paid to growers in most major pecan producing states. It includes information of interest to the industry from other sources such as crop production reports, cold storage reports, and export data.

LC HB241 **ISSN** 8750-5797
DD 338 US
PECAN SOUTH INCLUDING PECAN QUARTERLY. [Pecan south incl. pecan q.]. **Added/Corp** Texas Pecan Growers Association. Federated Pecan Growers Association. **VFOAT** Pecan South. Vol. 18, No. 4 (Sept. 1984)-. Periodical. English. Twelve times a year. $15.00. Texas Pecan Growers Association, PO Drawer CC, College Station TX 77841. **Tel** (409)846-3285, FAX (409)846-1752. **ED** Cindy Loggins Wise. **Bk Rev**, (Qty: 2-3). **Ad Acc. Circ:** 5,000. ***Formed by the union of*** *Pecan South, 0192-0863* ***and*** *Pecan Quarterly, 0048-3117.*
Ind/Abst AGRICOLA [Select. Cov.].

LC S590 **ISSN** 0031-4056
DD 631.4 GW
CCC
CODEN PDBLAM
Pr Rev.
PEDOBIOLOGIA. [Pedobiologia]. Vol. 1, (1961)-. Academic Scholarly Publication. English (French, German and Russian). Six times a year. $390.00. Gustav Fischer Verlag Jena, Postfach 100537, D-07705 Jena Germany. **Tel** 011 49 3641 626444, FAX 011 49 3641 626500. **(Subscription address:** VCH Publishers Inc., 303 Northwest 12th Avenue, Journals Department, Deerfield FL 33442. **Tel** (800)367-8249, (305)428-5566.**)** **ED** E Von Torne. Index available. **Bk Rev. Ad Acc. Circ:** 570. Documents available from The Genuine Article, BIOSIS Document Express, CASDDS, Documents on Demand.
Desc: Aim of this international journal is to offer a comprehensive survey of the facts, problems and tasks of soil biology and to stimulate and facilitate the interchange of information both practical and theoretical. Gives preference to contributions to soil biology.
Ind/Abst AgBiotech News Inf.; AGRICOLA; Biol. Abstr.; Chem. Abstr.; Curr. Aware. Biol. Sci., CABS; Curr. Cit.; Curr. Contents Agric. Biol. Environ. Sci.; Ecol. Abstr.; Ecology Abstr.; EMBASE; Energy Inf. Abstr.; Entomol. Abstr.; Environ. Abstr.; For. Abstr.; Geogr. Abstr. Phys. Geogr. (?-?); Maize Abstr.; Microbiol. Abstr. Sect. A; Microbiol. Abstr. Sect. C; Nematol. Abstr.; Life Sci. Collect.; Potato Abstr.; Res. Alert [Full Cov.]; Rev. Agric. Entomol.; Rev. Med. Vet. Entomol.; Rice Abstr.; Sci. Cit. Index; SCISEARCH; Soils Fert.

LC S590 **ISSN** 0079-0419
DD 631.4 BE
CODEN PEDOAE
TITLE CHANGE
PEDOLOGIE. [Pedologie]. **Added/Corp** Societe Belge de Pedologie. Vol. 1 (1951)-Vol. 43, No. 5 (Dec. 1993). Academic Scholarly Publication. Dutch (summaries and/or abstracts in English and French). Societe Belge de Pedologie, Krijgslaan 281, B-9000 Gent Belgium. **Bk Rev.** ctrl circ. Documents available from CASDDS. ***Merged with*** *Science du Sol (Plaisir, France: 1984), 0767-2853; Journal of Soil Science, 0022-4588* ***to form*** *European Journal of Soil Science.*
Ind/Abst AGRICOLA; Agrofor. Abstr. (1991-); Chem. Abstr.; Ecol. Abstr.; EMBASE; Field Crop Abstr.; For. Abstr.; Geogr. Abstr. Phys. Geogr.; GeoRef; Int. Dev. Abstr.; Soils Fert.

LC S590
DD 631.4 CC
PEDOSPHERE. **Added/Corp** Chung-Kuo Ko Hsueh Yuan. Nan-Ching tu Jang Yen Chiu So. Chung-Kuo Ko Hsueh Yuan. Laboratory of Material Cycling in Pedosphere. Vol. 1, No. 1 (Feb. 1991)-. Periodical. English. Four times a year. $210.00 US; $230.00 other (institutions). Science Press, 16 Donghuangchenggen North Street, Beijing 100707, People's Republic of China. **Tel** 011 86 1 4019821, 011 86 1 4010642, FAX 011 86 1 4012180, 011 86 1 4019810, telex 210147.

LC SB87.I5 L44a **ISSN** 0216-9657
DD 630.9 IO
PEMBERITAAN PENELITIAN TANAMAN INDUSTRI. **Added/Corp** Pusat Penelitian dan Pengembangan Tanaman Industri (Indonesia). Vol. 7, No. 39 (Apr./June 1981)-. Periodical. Indonesian (summaries and/or abstracts in English). Four times a year. ***Continues*** *Lembaga Penelitian Tanaman Industri (Indonesia) Pemberitaan Lembaga Penelitian Tanaman Industri.*
Ind/Abst Cot. Trop. Fibr. Abstr. Bibliogr.; Field Crop Abstr.; Plant Grow. Reg. Abstr.; Rev. Plant Pathol.; Soils Fert.

LC SB354
DD 634 US
PENNSYLVANIA FRUIT NEWS. Vol. 1 (1924)-. Periodical. English. Twelve times a year. $30.00 fruit growers and commerical firms; $50.00 other; Comes with State Horticultural Association of Pennsylvania membership. State Horticultural Association of Pennsylvania, Loganville PA 17342. **Tel** (717)428-2070. **ED** Rob Crass Weller (editor's address: Department of Horticultural Science, Pennsylvania State University, University Park, PA 16802, phone: (814)863-6163). **Ad Acc.**
Ind/Abst Agric. Eng. Abstr.; Hortic. Abstr.; Irr. Drain. Abstr.; Nematol. Abstr.; Plant Breed. Abstr.; Postharvest News Inf.; Rev. Agric. Entomol.; Rev. Plant Pathol.; Weed Abstr.

LC SB761 **ISSN** 0399-8533
DD 635.97 FR
PERSPECTIVES AGRICOLES. **Added/Corp** Institut Technique des Cereales et des Fourrages. (1977)-. Periodical. French. Eleven times a year. $120.30. Edit-Publishing Agricoles Francaises, 3 rue des Freres-Perier, 75116 Paris France. **Tel** 33 1 47233602, FAX 33 1 47201059. Index available (Jan.). **Bk Rev. Ad Acc.**
Ind/Abst Rev. Agric. Entomol.; Weed Abstr.; Wheat Barley Trit. Abstr.

LC SB599 **ISSN** 1056-3431
DD 632 US
PEST MANAGEMENT & CROP DEVELOPMENT BULLETIN. [Pest manage. crop dev. bull.]. **Added/Corp** Illinois. Natural History Survey Division. University of Illinois (Urbana-Champaign campus). College of Agriculture. **VFOAT** Pest Management and Crop Development Bulletin. (Mar. 22, 1990)-. Bulletin. English. University of Illinois Ag Newsletter Service, 116 Mumford Hall, 1301 West Gregory Drive, Urbana IL 61801. ***Continues*** *Insect, Weed & Plant Disease Survey Bulletin.*

LC S **ISSN** 0079-1342
DD 630 GW
CODEN PFZNAQ
PFLANZENSCHUTZ NACHRICHTEN. [Pflanzenschutz-Nachr.]. **Added/Corp** Farbenfabriken Bayer Aktiengesellschaft. **VFOAT** Plant Production and Other Crop Production. (19??)-. Periodical. English. Bayer AG, Bayerwerk, W 5090 Leverkusen Germany. Documents available from BIOSIS Document Express. ***Continues*** *Pflanzenschutz-Nachrichten Bayer, 0170-0405.*
Ind/Abst Biol. Abstr.; PESTDOC; Weed Abstr.

LC HD1920.5 .A32 **ISSN** 0378-3588
DD 633 LU
PFLANZLICHE ERZEUGUNG. **Added/Corp** Statistical Office of the European Communities. **VFOAT** Crop Production. (198?)-. English (French and German). Four times a year. £56.80 UK; 61.60p Ireland. Office for Official Publications of the European Communities, 2 rue Mercier, 2985 Luxembourg Luxembourg. **Tel** 011 352 499281, FAX 011 352 292942763. ***Continues*** *Statistical Office of the European Communities. Vegetabilsk Produktion.*

LC SB183 **ISSN** 0115-2025
DD 633 PH
CODEN PJCSDP
PHILIPPINE JOURNAL OF CROP SCIENCE, THE. [Philipp. j. crop sci.]. **Added/Corp** Crop Science Society of the Philippines. Philippine Council for Agriculture and Resources Research. Vol. 1 (March 1976)-. Academic Scholarly Publication. English. Three times a year (Apr., Aug., & Dec.). $45.00. Philippine Journal Crop Science, PO Box 165 College, 3720 Laguna Philippines. **ED** Evelyn Mae T. Mendoza (editor's address: Institute of Plant Breeding UP Los Banos College Laguna Philippines, editor's phone number: 011 63 2 2298 local 212). Index available (Bound in 3rd issue). **Ad Acc. Circ:** 300. Documents available from BIOSIS Document Express, CASDDS.
Desc: The original research papers and reviews on all aspects of horticulture and field crops. These research papers have been review and prepared in the tropics.
Ind/Abst AgBiotech News Inf.; Agrindex; Agrofor. Abstr. (1991-); Biol. Abstr.; Chem. Abstr.; Cot. Trop. Fibr. Abstr. Bibliogr.; Crop Physiol. Abstr.; Curr. Aware. Biol. Sci., CABS; Field Crop Abstr.; Food Sci. Technol. Abstr.; Grass. Forage Abstr.; Hortic. Abstr.; Irr. Drain. Abstr.; Maize Abstr.; Nematol. Abstr.; Philip. Sci. Technol. Abstr.; Plant Breed. Abstr.; Plant Grow. Reg. Abstr.; Potato Abstr.; Rev. Agric. Entomol.; Rev. Plant Pathol.; Rice Abstr.; Seed Abstr.; Soils Fert.; Sorghum Mill. Abstr.; Soyabean Abstr.; Weed Abstr.

LC S
DD 630 PH
Pr Rev.
PHILIPPINE JOURNAL OF WEED SCIENCE. **Added/Corp** Weed Science Society of the Philippines. **VFOAT** Journal of Weed Science. Vol. 5 (Dec. 1978)-. Academic Scholarly Publication. English. One time a year. $10.00. Weed Science Society of Philippines, University of Philippines-Los Bands College, Laguna Philippines. **Tel** 011 63 63 3397. **ED** Juliana S. Manuel. **Ad Acc. Circ:** 500 (ctrl). Documents available from CASDDS. ***Continues*** *Philippine Weed Science Bulletin, 0115-0855.*
Desc: Original research on applied and basic weed science in the Philippines and Asian Pacific region.
Ind/Abst Chem. Abstr.

LC SB215
DD 633.6 PH
PHILIPPINE SUGAR COMMISSION QUARTERLY. Vol. 1, No. 1 (Oct./Dec. 1980)-. Periodical. English. Four times a year. ***Continues*** *Philippine Sugar Institute Quarterly.*
Ind/Abst Philip. Sci. Technol. Abstr.

LC S590
DD 631.4 SZ
PHYSIKALISCHE EIGENSCHAFTEN VON BODEN DER SCHWEIZ. Vol. 1 (Aug. 1978)-. Periodical. German (French, English and French).

LC S
DD 630 SP
PHYTOMA ESPANA. (19??)-. Periodical. Spanish. Ten times a year. 10.000ptas Spain; 12.500ptas Europe; 13.500ptas other. Agropubli Sl, Blasco Ibanlez 24, 2A, 46010 Valencia Spain. **Tel** 011 34 6 3933949, FAX 011 34 6 3605779.
Ind/Abst Chem. Bus. Bull.; Chem. Bus. NewsBase (1989-); Chem. Bus. Update.

LC S **ISSN** 1230-0462
DD 630 PL
Pr Rev.
PHYTOPATHOLOGIA POLONICA. **See** Biology-Botany.

LC S **ISSN** 0031-9511
DD 630 CN
CCC
CODEN PYTPAX
Pr Rev.
PHYTOPROTECTION. [Phytoprotection]. Vol. 44 No. 1 (June 1963)-. Periodical. English (French). Three times a year. 36.02Can$. Society for Protection of Plants, 430 Goul Gouin, St. Jean Richelin J3B3E6 Canada. **Tel** (514)346-4494, FAX (514)346-7740. **ED** Guy Boivin. **Bk Rev. Circ:** 600 (ctrl). Documents available from The Genuine Article, BIOSIS Document Express, CASDDS.
Desc: Scientific papers dealing with all aspects of crop protection, forestry included.
Ind/Abst AGRICOLA; BioBusiness; Biocont. News Inf.; Biol. Abstr.; Chem. Abstr.; Curr. Aware. Biol. Sci., CABS; Curr. Contents Agric. Biol. Environ. Sci.; Entomol. Abstr.; For. Abstr.; Grass. Forage Abstr.; Hortic. Abstr.; Irr. Drain. Abstr.; Environ.; Maize Abstr.; Microbiol. Abstr. Sect. A; Nematol. Abstr.; Life Sci. Collect.; Plant Breed. Abstr.; Postharvest News Inf.; Potato Abstr.; Res. Alert [Full Cov.]; Rev. Agric. Entomol.; Rev. Plant Pathol.; Rice Abstr.; Sci. Cit. Index; SCISEARCH; Soils Fert.; Sorghum Mill. Abstr.; Soyabean Abstr.

LC SB13 .P55 **ISSN** 0032-079X
DD 631.405 NE
CCC
CODEN PLSOA2
Pr Rev.
PLANT AND SOIL. [Plant soil]. (1948)-. Periodical. English (French and German). Irregular (20 issues per year). $2502.00. Kluwer Academic Publishers, Postbus 322, 3300 AH Dordrecht The Netherlands. **Tel** 011 31 78 524400, FAX 011 31 78 183273, telex 20083. **ED** J.T. Lambers. **Ad Acc. Acid Free. Circ:** 1,300. available on microfilm and microfiche from University Microfilms International (UMI). Documents available from The Genuine Article, BIOSIS Document Express, CASDDS, Documents on Demand.
Desc: Publishes original research articles dealing with fundamental and applied aspects of plant nutrition, soil fertility, plant-microbe associations, soil microbiology, soil-borne plant diseases, soil and plant ecology, agrochemistry and agrophysics.
Ind/Abst AgBiotech News Inf.; AGRICOLA; Agric. Eng. Abstr. (1991-); Agrofor. Abstr. (19??-19??); BioBusiness; Biocont. News Inf. (19??-19??); Biodeter. Abstr.; Biol. Agric. Index; Biol. Abstr.; Chem. Abstr.; Coal Abstr.; Crop Physiol. Abstr.; Curr. Aware. Biol. Sci., CABS; Curr. Cit.; Curr. Contents Agric. Biol. Environ. Sci.; Ecol. Abstr.; Ecology Abstr.; EMBASE; Environ. Abstr.; Environ. Period. Bibliogr.; Field Crop Abstr.; Food Sci. Technol. Abstr.; For. Prod. Abstr. (1991-); For. Abstr.; Geogr. Abstr. Phys. Geogr.; GeoRef; Grass. Forage Abstr.; Hortic. Abstr.; Int. Dev. Abstr.; Irr. Drain. Abstr.; Leadscan; Maize Abstr.; Microbiol. Abstr. Sect. B; Microbiol. Abstr. Sect. A; Microbiol. Abstr. Sect. C; Nematol. Abstr.; Nutr. Abstr. Rev., Ser. A, Hum. Exp.; Life Sci. Collect.; PESTDOC; Plant Breed. Abstr.; Plant Genet. Resour. Abstr.; Plant Grow. Reg. Abstr.; Pollut. Abstr. Indexes; Potato Abstr.; Ref. Upd. Deluxe Ed.; Res. Alert [Full Cov.]; Rev. Agric. Entomol.; Rev. Plant Pathol.; Rice Abstr.; Sci. Cit. Index; SCISEARCH; Seed Abstr.; Soils Fert.; Sorghum Mill. Abstr.; Soyabean Abstr.; Vitis Vitic. Enol. Abstr.; Weed Abstr.; Wheat Barley Trit. Abstr.

LC Z5071 **ISSN** 0032-0803
DD 016.63 UK
PLANT BREEDING ABSTRACTS. **See** Agriculture-Abstracting, Bibliographies and Statistics.

LC SB599 .P95 **ISSN** 0191-2917
DD 632 US
CCC
CODEN PLDIDE
Pr Rev.
PLANT DISEASE. [Plant dis.]. **Added/Corp** American Phytopathological Society. Vol. 64 (Jan. 1980)-. Academic Scholarly Publication. English. Twelve times a year. $270.00. American Phytopathological Society, 3340 Pilot Knob Road, St. Paul MN 55121. **Tel** (612)454-7250, (800)328-7560, FAX (612)454-0766, telex 6502439657 (MCI UW). **ED** C Wendell Horne. **Ad Acc. Circ:** 5,306. available on microfilm and microfiche from University Microfilms International (UMI). Documents available from The Genuine Article, BIOSIS Document Express, CASDDS. ***Continues** Plant Disease Reporter, 0032-0811;* ***Absorbed** Phytopathology News, 0031-9503.*
Desc: Journal of plant pathology for reports of new diseases and epidemics.
Ind/Abst Abstr. Bull. Inst. Pap. Sci. Tech.; AgBiotech News Inf.; AGRICOLA [Full Cov.]; BioBusiness; Biocont. News Inf. (19??-19??); Biodeter. Abstr. (19??-19??); Biol. Agric. Index; Biol. Abstr.; Biol. Dig.; Chem. Abstr.; Cot. Trop. Fibr. Abstr. Bibliogr.; Curr. Aware. Biol. Sci., CABS; Curr. Cit.; Curr. Contents Agric. Biol. Environ. Sci.; Field Crop Abstr.; Food Sci. Technol. Abstr.; For. Abstr.; Grass. Forage Abstr.; Hortic. Abstr.; Irr. Drain. Abstr.; Maize Abstr.; Microbiol. Abstr. Sect. B (19??-19??); Microbiol. Abstr. Sect. A; Microbiol. Abstr. Sect. C; Nematol. Abstr.; Ornamental Hort. (19??-19??); Life Sci. Collect.; PESTDOC; Plant Breed. Abstr.; Plant Genet. Resour. Abstr.; Plant Grow. Reg. Abstr.; Postharvest News Inf.; Potato Abstr.; Res. Alert [Full Cov.]; Rev. Agric. Entomol.; Rev. Med. Vet. Mycology; Rev. Plant Pathol.; Rice Abstr.; Sci. Cit. Index; SCISEARCH; Seed Abstr.; Soils Fert.; Sorghum Mill. Abstr.; Soyabean Abstr.; Vitis Vitic. Enol. Abstr.; Weed Abstr.; Wheat Barley Trit. Abstr.; World Agric. Econ. Rural Sociol. Abstr.

LC SD123.3 .P634 **ISSN** 0048-4334
DD 631.5/23/05 IT
PLANT GENETIC RESOURCES NEWSLETTER (ROME, ITALY : 1979). (PLANT GENETIC RESOURCES NEWSLETTER.). [Plant genet. resour. newsl.]. **Added/Corp** Food and Agriculture Organization of the United Nations. Crop Ecology and Genetic Resources Unit. International Board for Plant Genetic Resources. **VFOAT** Ressources Genetiques Vegetales Bulletin. (197?)-. Newsletter. English (French and Spanish). Four times a year. Food Agriculture Organization (FAO) / Italy, GIPCI66 via Terme di Caracalla, 00100 Rome Italy. **Tel** 011 39 6 52252925, FAX 011 39 6 52253152. ***Continues** Plant Genetic Resources.*
Ind/Abst AGRICOLA; Biol. Dig.; Cot. Trop. Fibr. Abstr. Bibliogr.; Field Crop Abstr.; Grass. Forage Abstr.; Hortic. Abstr.; Maize Abstr.; Ornamental Hort. (1991-); Plant Breed. Abstr.; Plant Genet. Resour. Abstr.; Plant Grow. Reg. Abstr.; Potato Abstr.; Rice Abstr.; Seed Abstr.; Sorghum Mill. Abstr.; Wheat Barley Trit. Abstr.

LC Z5071 **ISSN** 0305-9154
DD 016.63 UK
PLANT GROWTH REGULATOR ABSTRACTS. **See** Agriculture-Abstracting, Bibliographies and Statistics.

LC S **ISSN** 1031-7279
DD 630 AT
PLANT INDUSTRIES REPORT. (19??)-. English. New South Wales Department of Agriculture & Fisheries, Division of Agriculture Services, PMB 21, Orange S NSW 2800 Australia. **Tel** 011 61 63 913100, FAX 011 61 63 629059. ***Continues** Miscellaneous Bulletin / Division of Plant Industries, 0812-3861.*

LC SB183
DD 633 II
PLANT MATERIAL DESCRIPTION. **Added/Corp** International Crops Research Institute for the Semi-Arid Tropics. No. 1 (1987)-. Periodical. English.
Ind/Abst Field Crop Abstr.; Plant Breed. Abstr.; Seed Abstr.

LC SB761 **ISSN** 0815-2195
DD 635.97 AT
CODEN PPQUE8
Pr Rev.
PLANT PROTECTION QUARTERLY. [Plant prot. q.]. **VFOAT** Plant Protection. Vol. 1, No. 1 (1985)-. Periodical. English. Four times a year (Feb., May, Aug., Nov.). 64.13Aus$. R G Richardson, PO Box 1108, Frankston Victoria 3199 Australia. **Tel** 011 61 3 7873804, FAX 011 61 3 7852007. **ED** R.G. Richardson and F.J. Richardson. Index available. cum. index. **Bk Rev. Ad Acc. Circ:** 500 (ctrl). Documents available from BIOSIS Document Express. ***Continues** Australian Weeds, 0725-0150.*
Desc: Covering all aspects of plant protection, including the protection of economic plants from weeds, pests and diseases, and the protection and ecology of plants on public land.
Ind/Abst AgBiotech News Inf.; AGRICOLA [Full Cov.]; Biocont. News Inf. (19??-19??); Biodeter. Abstr.; Biol. Abstr. (1985-); Curr. Cit.; Field Crop Abstr.; For. Abstr.; Grass. Forage Abstr.; Hortic. Abstr.; Maize Abstr.; Nematol. Abstr.; Ornamental Hort.; Plant Breed. Abstr.; Plant Grow. Reg. Abstr.; Rev. Agric. Entomol.; Rev. Plant Pathol.; Rice Abstr.; Weed Abstr.; Wheat Barley Trit. Abstr.

LC SB761 **ISSN** 0952-3863
DD 635.97 UK
CODEN PVSEEC
Pr Rev.
PLANT VARIETIES & SEEDS. **See** Gardening and Horticulture.

LC S **ISSN** 1254-7670
DD 630 FR
•**PLANTATIONS, RECHERCHE, DEVELOPPEMENT = PLANTATIONS, RESEARCH, DEVELOPMENT.** [Plant. rech. dev.]. **Added/Corp** CIRAD (Organization). Department des Cultures Perennes. **VFOAT** Plantations, research, development; PRD. (1994)-. Periodical. French (English and Spanish). Six times a year. Centre de Cooperation International en Recherche Agronomique pour le Developpement CP - CIRAD CP, Department des Cultures Perennes, 12 Square Petrarque, 75116 Paris France. **Tel** 011 33 1 53702000, telex 620871. ***Formed by the union of** Oleagineux, 0030-2082* ***and** Cafe, Cacao, the, 0007-9510.*
Ind/Abst Curr. Cit.

LC S600.62.I8 I58A **ISSN** 0163-4976
DD 633/.001/55169777 US
PLANTING TO HARVEST; ANNUAL CROP WEATHER SUMMARY. **Main/Corp** Iowa Crop and Livestock Reporting Service. **VFOAT** Weather and Field Crops From Planting to Harvest. English. Iowa Department of Agriculture, 833 Federal Building, 210 Walnut Street, Des Moines IA 50309. **Tel** (515)284-4340.

LC S
DD 630 US
PLUMAS-SIERRA COUNTIES CROP REPORT. **Main/Corp** Plumas County, Calif. Dept. of Agriculture. **Added/Corp** Sierra County, Calif. Dept. of Agriculture. (1969/70)-. Periodical. English. One time a year. ***Continues** Agricultural Production Report.*

LC S590 .P6 **ISSN** 0032-180X
DD 631.4 RU
CODEN PVDEAZ
POCHVOVEDENIE. [Pocvovedenie]. **Added/Corp** International Society of Soil Science. Soviet Section. Akademiia Nauk SSSR. **VFOAT** Pedologie; Pedology. Vol. 1-32, (1899)-(1937); (1938)-. Academic Scholarly Publication. Russian (English and German; table of contents in English). Twelve times a year. $360.00. Izdatelstvo Nauka / Akademiia Nauk, (Publishing House of the Russian Academy of Sciences), Leninskii Porspekt 14, 117901 Moscow Russia. **Tel** 011 95 9542153, FAX 011 95 9382144, telex 411964. **(Subscription address:** East View Publications Inc., 3020 Harbor Lane North, Suite 110, Minneapolis MN 55447. **Tel** (800)477-1005, (612)550-0961, FAX (612)559-2931.) Documents available from BIOSIS Document Express, CASDDS.
Ind/Abst AGRICOLA; Biol. Abstr.; Chem. Abstr.; Field Crop Abstr.; Soils Fert.

LC S590
DD 631.4 RU
CODEN PCAKA7
POCHVOVEDENIE I AAGROKHIMIIA. **Added/Corp** Belorusskii Nauchno-Issledovatelskii Institut Pochvovedeniia i Agrokhimii. (19??)-. Academic Scholarly Publication. Russian. Twelve times a year. $114.00. Documents available from CASDDS. ***Continues** Svoistva Pochv i Ikh Plodorodie.*
Ind/Abst Chem. Abstr. (?-1982).

LC S590 .P63 **ISSN** 0079-2985
DD 631.4 PL
CODEN PJSOBN
POLISH JOURNAL OF SOIL SCIENCE. [Pol. j. soil sci.]. (1968)-. Periodical. English (summaries and/or abstracts in Russian and Polish). Irregular. Polska Akademia Nauk / Zaklad Narodowy im. Ossoliniskich, Ossolineum Publishing House of the Polish Academy of Sciences, Ulitsa Rynek 9, 50-106 Wroclaw Poland. **Tel** 011 48 71 38625, FAX 011 48 71 448103, telex 0712771. **(Subscription address:** Ars Polona-Ruch, PO Box 1001, Krakowskie Przedmiescie 7, 00-068 Warsaw Poland. **Tel** 011 48 22 261201.) Documents available from BIOSIS Document Express, CASDDS.
Ind/Abst Biol. Abstr.; Chem. Abstr.; Ecol. Abstr.; EMBASE; Geogr. Abstr. Phys. Geogr.; GeoRef; Irr. Drain. Abstr.; Maize Abstr.; Soils Fert.; Wheat Barley Trit. Abstr.

LC SB608 **ISSN** 0032-4159
DD 635.21 FR
POMME DE TERRE FRANCAISE, LA. Vol. 1 No. 1 (July 1938)-. Periodical. French. Six times a year. $73.27. Le Pomme de Terre Francaise, 2 rue de Seze, 75009 Paris France. **Tel** 011 33 1 42665163, telex 280831 PLANTEX. cum. index. **Circ:** 7,000.
Desc: Covers seed potatoes industry, ware potatoes industry, cultivation technics, economy and statistics and professional activities.
Ind/Abst AgBiotech News Inf.; Field Crop Abstr.; Plant Breed. Abstr.; Postharvest News Inf.; Potato Abstr.; Rev. Agric. Entomol.

LC S
DD 630 US
POPCORN. (19??)-. Periodical. English. Two times a year. The Service, Full Depository, 707 Savings and Loan Building, Des Moines IA 50309.
Desc: July issue reports acreage planted to popcorn, and January issue gives acreage harvested, yield per acre, price and values for selected states.

LC SB183
DD 633 PL
PORADNIK PLANTATORA. **Added/Corp** Zwiazek Plantatorow Roslin Okopowych. No. 7/8 (July/Aug. 1976)-. Periodical. Polish. Twelve times a year. **(Subscription address:** Ars Polona-Ruch, PO Box 1001, Krakowskie Przedmiescie 7, 00-068 Warsaw Poland. **Tel** 011 48 22 261201.)

LC SB129 .P66 **ISSN** 0925-5214
DD 631.5 NE
CCC
CODEN PBTEED
Pr Rev.
POSTHARVEST BIOLOGY AND TECHNOLOGY. Vol. 1, No. 1 (July 1991)-. Academic Scholarly Publication. English. Eight times a year (2 volumes). $488.00. Elsevier Science Publishers BV, PO Box 211, 1000 AE Amsterdam Netherlands. **Tel** 011 31 20 4853641, 011 31 20 4853642, FAX 011 31 20 4853598. available on an online database from Elsevier Electronic Subscriptions (EES).
Ind/Abst AGRICOLA; Crop Physiol. Abstr.; Food Sci. Technol. Abstr.; Hortic. Abstr.; Ornamental Hort. (1991-); Postharvest News Inf.

LC SB129 .P59 **ISSN** 0957-7505
DD 631.55 UK
Pr Rev.
POSTHARVEST NEWS AND INFORMATION. **See** Agriculture-Abstracting, Bibliographies and Statistics.

LC S **ISSN** 0032-5546
DD 630 SZ
POTASH REVIEW. Vol. 1 (1953)-. Periodical. English. Six times a year. $28.00. International Potash Institute Worblaufen Berne, Scheidergasses 27, PO Box 1609, Ch4001 Basel Switzerland. **Tel** 011 41 31 585373. **ED** A Von Peter and H Kuenzli. **Bk Rev. Ad Acc. Circ:** 6,000 (ctrl).
Desc: Covers crop fertilization, plant physiology, and soil science.
Ind/Abst Agrofor. Abstr.; Field Crop Abstr.; Maize Abstr.; Soils Fert.

LC Z5071 **ISSN** 0308-7344
DD 016.63 UK
POTATO ABSTRACTS. **See** Agriculture-Abstracting, Bibliographies and Statistics.

LC S
DD 630 US
POTATO-BREEDING PROGRAM, USDA, THE. **Main/Corp** United States. Plant Genetics and Germplasm Institute. Vegetable Laboratory. **VFOAT** Potato-Breeding Program, USA. 43rd (1972)-. Periodical. English. One time a year. ***Continues** The National Potato-Breeding Program.*

LC SB188 **ISSN** 0886-4780
DD 633 US
POTATO COUNTRY. [Potato ctry.]. **VFOAT** Washington Oregon Potato Country. (1985)-. Trade Publication. English. Nine times a year. $15.00. Columbia Publishing Company / Washington, 2809 A Fruitvale, Yakima WA 98907. **Tel** (509)248-2452, (800)788-2452, FAX (509)575-3080. **ED** D. Brent Clement. **Ad Acc, Adv Mgr:** Mike Stoken, **Tel** (509)248-2452. **Circ:** 7,319 (ctrl). ***Continues** AG Marketer, 0193-7901.*
Desc: Covers production, marketing and handling. Information for potato growers, packers and shippers in the western United States.

LC SB608 **ISSN** 0815-6514
DD 635.21 AT
POTATO GROWER. [Potato grow.]. Vol. 29, No. 5 (Jan. 1976)-. Periodical. English. Twelve times a year. 16.44Aus$. Potato Growers Association of West Perth Inc, 103 Outram Street, West Perth Western Australia 6005 Australia. **Tel** 011 61 9 4810834. **ED** Phil Lalor. **Bk Rev. Ad Acc. Circ:** 500 (ctrl).
Desc: Potato growing information particularly pertaining to Western Australian growers.
Ind/Abst AGRICOLA.

LC S
DD 630 US
•**POTATO GROWER : POTATO GROWER OF IDAHO MAGAZINE.** (1993)-. English. Twelve times a year (Special additional in Dec. iss. mail to Idaho residents only). $19.00. Harris Publishing Inc, 520 Park Avenue, Idaho Falls ID 83402. **Tel** (208)524-7000, FAX (208)522-5241. **Ad Acc.** ctrl circ.

LC SB608
DD 635.21 US
POTATO REFERENCE YEARBOOK.
Main/Corp Potato Growers Association of California. **VFOAT** Potato Reference Book. 25th- 1969-. Periodical. English. One time a year. ***Continues*** *Potato Growers Association of California. Yearbook.*

LC SB608 **ISSN** 0014-3065
DD 635.21 NE
CODEN PORHBW
POTATO RESEARCH. [Potato res.]. **Added/Corp** European Association for Potato Research. Vol. 13 (1970)-. Academic Scholarly Publication. English (French and German). Four times a year. $185.00. European Association for Potato Research, Postbus 20, 6700 AA Wageningen The Netherlands. **Tel** 011 31 8370 83041. **ED** P. C. Struik. Index available. **Bk Rev. Circ:** 1,200 (ctrl). Documents available from The Genuine Article, BIOSIS Document Express, CASDDS. ***Continues*** *European Potato Journal.*
Desc: Original contributions on fundamental and applied research on potatoes, subject surveys, and reviews.
Ind/Abst AgBiotech News Inf.; AGRICOLA [Full Cov.]; Biocont. News Inf.; Biodeter. Abstr. (19??-19??); Biol. Abstr. (-1980); Chem. Abstr.; Crop Physiol. Abstr.; Curr. Aware. Biol. Sci., CABS; Curr. Cit.; Curr. Contents Agric. Biol. Environ. Sci.; EMBASE; Field Crop Abstr.; Food Sci. Technol. Abstr.; Irr. Drain. Abstr.; Nematol. Abstr.; Life Sci. Collect.; PESTDOC; Plant Breed. Abstr.; Plant Genet. Resour. Abstr.; Plant Grow. Reg. Abstr.; Postharvest News Inf.; Potato Abstr.; Res. Alert [Full Cov.]; Rev. Plant Pathol.; Sci. Cit. Index; SCISEARCH; Soils Fert.

LC SB320 **ISSN** 0961-7655
DD 635.21 UK
POTATO REVIEW. [Potato review]. (1991)-. Periodical. English. Four times a year. $65.03. Aremi, Barnside, Nairdwood Way, Great Missend HP16 0QU United Kingdom. **Tel** 011 44 1240 64121, FAX 011 44 1240 68731. **ED** D. Mossman. Index available. cum. index. **Ad Acc, Adv Mgr:** G. Davidon, **Tel** 011 44 494 86412. **Circ:** 18,500.
Desc: Includes review articles on market trends, technical and scientific developments, and new products. European and world developments in the crop are monitored.

LC HD9235.P82 U67 **ISSN** 0739-0238
DD 338.1/7421/0973 US
POTATO STATISTICAL YEARBOOK. See Agriculture-Abstracting, Bibliographies and Statistics.

LC SB608
DD 635.21 US
POTATOES. Added/Corp United States. Agricultural Statistics Board. (198?)-. Government Publication. English. $9.00 US; $11.25 other. US Department of Agriculture, 14th Street and Independence Avenue SW, Washington DC 20250. **Tel** (202)720-5457. **(Subscription address:** Superintendent of Documents, US Government Printing Office, Washington DC 20402. **)** ***Continues*** *Potatoes and Sweet Potatoes (Annual), 0499-0587.*

LC S **ISSN** 0499-0587
DD 630 US
TITLE CHANGE
POTATOES AND SWEETPOTATOES.
Added/Corp United States. Crop Reporting Board. **VFOAT** Potatoes and Sweet Potatoes. (19??)-(19??). English. US Department of Agriculture, 14th Street and Independence Avenue SW, Washington DC 20250. **Tel** (202)720-5457. ***Continued by*** *Potatoes (Wshington, D.C.).*

LC SB608
DD 635.21 US
POTATOES (NEW YORK CROP REPORTING SERVICE). (POTATOES.). Periodical. English. Twelve times a year. Building 8, State Campus, Albany NY 12235. ***Continues*** *Potato Stocks.*

LC S **ISSN** 0032-6801
DD 630 GW
PRAKTISCHE SCHADLINGSBEKAMPFER, DER. [Prakt. schadlingsbekampf.]. **Added/Corp** Deutscher Schadlingsbekampfer-Verband. (1950). Trade Publication. German. Twelve times a year. $133.57. Verlag Eduard F Beckmann KG, Postfach 1120, Haus Heideck, D-31251 Lehrte Germany. **Tel** 011 49 5132 85910, FAX 011 49 5132 53100. **ED** Heiner Behre. **Bk Rev. Ad Acc. Circ:** 1,000.
Ind/Abst AGRICOLA; PESTDOC.

LC HD9017.M8 P74
DD 338.1/0964 MR
PRINCIPALES PRODUCTIONS VEGETALES. Added/Corp Morocco. Wizarat al-Filahah wa-al-Islah al-Zirai. Division des Affaires Economiques. Morocco. Wizarat al-Filahah wa-al-Islah al-Zirai. Service des Statistiques et de la Documentation. (19??)-. French. Direction de la Statistique, Boite Postale 178, Rabat Morocco. **Tel** 011 212 77 73606, FAX 011 212 77 73217, telex 32774.

LC HD1940.C69 Z37C
DD 630 CI
PRIRODI RANIH USJEVA I VOCA. (1979)-. Serbo-Croatian (Roman). One time a year. 70.00 Din. Republicki Zavod za Statistiku, Central Bureau of Statistics of the Republic of Croatia, Ilica 3, Zagreb Croatia. **Tel** 011 385 41 45 44 22, FAX 011 385 41 42 94 13, 011 385 41 42 37 11, telex 21130 DZSTAT RH. ***Continues*** *Rani Usjevi I Voce.*

LC SB183 **ISSN** 0254-7279
DD 633 RM
CODEN PATADR
PROBLEME DE AGROFITOTEHNIE TEORETICA SI APLICATA. [Probl. agrofitoteh. teor. apl.]. **Added/Corp** Institutul de Cercetari Pentru Cereale si Plante Tehnice Fundulea. Vol. 1, Nr. 1 (1979)-. Academic Scholarly Publication. Romanian. Four times a year. Documents available from CASDDS.
Ind/Abst Chem. Abstr. (-1979); Field Crop Abstr.; Grass. Forage Abstr.; Irr. Drain. Abstr.; Maize Abstr.; Soils Fert.; Soyabean Abstr.; Weed Abstr.; Wheat Barley Trit. Abstr.

LC S
DD 630 RM
PROBLEME DE GENETICA TEORETICA SI APLICATA. Added/Corp Institutul de Cercetari Pentru Cereale si Plante Tehnice. Sectia de Ameliorarea Plantelor. Institutul de Cercetari Pentru Cereale si Plante Tehnice. (19??)-. Periodical. Romanian (summaries and/or abstracts in English; table of contents in English).
Ind/Abst AgBiotech News Inf.; Field Crop Abstr.; Maize Abstr.; Plant Breed. Abstr.; Plant Grow. Reg. Abstr.; Rev. Plant Pathol.

LC SB761 **ISSN** 0254-2293
DD 635.97 RM
CODEN PPPLD9
PROBLEME DE PROTECTIA PLANTELOR. See Pest Control.

LC SB950.A2 B75 **ISSN** 0955-1514
DD 632 UK
CODEN PBCDDQ
PROC. - BRIGHTON CROP PROT. CONF., PESTS DIS. (PROCEEDINGS OF AN INTERNATIONAL CONFERENCE ORGANISED BY THE BRITISH CROP PROTECTION COUNCIL HELD AT ...). [Proceedings - Brighton Crop Protection Conference,Pests and Diseases]. **Added/Corp** British Crop Protection Council. Nov. 21/24 (1988)-. Proceedings. English. Every 2 years. £60.00 UK; £65.00 other. BCPC Publications Sales, Bear Farm, Binfield Bracknell, Berkshire RG12 5QE United Kingdom. **Tel** 011 44 1734 342727, FAX 011 44 1734 341998. Documents available from CASDDS. ***Continues*** *British Crop Protection Conference--Pes and Diseases. Proceedings of a Conference Held at ... .*
Ind/Abst Chem. Abstr.

LC SB188 **ISSN** 1059-2644
DD 633 US
PROCEEDINGS / BELTWIDE COTTON CONFERENCES. [Proc. - Beltwide Cotton Conf.]. **Added/Corp** National Cotton Council of America. (1991)-. Proceedings. English. One time a year. $50.00. National Cotton Council, PO Box 12285, Memphis TN 38112. **Tel** (901)274-9030. ***Formed by the union of*** *Proceedings of the ... Beltwide Cotton Production Conference, 1052-5351; Cotton Dust, 0897-5531* ***and*** *Proceedings, 0522-8786.*
Ind/Abst AGRICOLA [Select. Cov.].

LC S **ISSN** 0955-1506
DD 630 UK
PROCEEDINGS - BRIGHTON CROP PROTECTION CONFERENCE. PESTS AND DISEASES. (PROCEEDINGS.). [Proc. - Brighton Crop Prot. Conf., Pests Dis.]. (1988)-. English. Every 2 years. BCPC Publications Sales, Bear Farm, Binfield Bracknell, Berkshire RG12 5QE United Kingdom. **Tel** 011 44 1734 342727, FAX 011 44 1734 341998. ***Continues*** *Proceedings of the ... British Crop Protection Conference. Pests and Diseases, 0144-1612.*
Ind/Abst Curr. Cit.

LC S631 **ISSN** 0369-9277
DD 631.8 UK
CODEN PFRSAZ
PROCEEDINGS - FERTILISER SOCIETY. (PROCEEDINGS / THE FERTILISER SOCIETY.). [Proc. - Fert. Soc.]. **Added/Corp** Fertiliser Society of London. No. 5 (Jan. 20, 1949)-. Monographic series. English. Irregular. Price varies per volume. The Fertiliser Society, Greenhill House, Thrope Wood, Peterborough PE3 6GF United Kingdom. **Tel** 011 44 1733 331303, FAX 011 44 1733 33617. Documents available from CASDDS. ***Continues*** *Papers Read Before the Fertiliser Society in London on.*
Ind/Abst AGRICOLA [Full Cov.]; Chem. Abstr.; Maize Abstr.; Potato Abstr.; Soils Fert.

LC S **ISSN** 0197-8748
DD 630 US
CODEN PPESD9
Pr Rev.
PROCEEDINGS OF AMERICAN PEANUT RESEARCH AND EDUCATION SOCIETY, INC. Main/Corp American Peanut Research and Education Society. **VFOAT** Proceedings, American Peanut Research and Education Society; Proceedings, APRES; Proceedings. Vol. 11 (1979)-. Academic Scholarly Publication. English. One time a year. $25.00 (individual and institutions) US; $37.50 (individual and institution) Canada and Mexico; $50.00 (individual and institution) other; $35.00 organizational membership, US; $47.50 organizational membership, Canada and Mexico; $60.00 organizational membership, other Comes with American Peanut Research and Education Society membership. American Peanut Research Education Association, 376 AG Hall, Oklahoma State University, Stillwater OK 74078. **Tel** (405)744-6421, (405)744-9634, FAX (405)744-5269. **ED** H. Thomas Stalker (editor's address: North Carolina State University, P.O. Box 7629, Raleigh, NC 27695-7629, phone: (919)515-3281). **Bk Rev. Ad Acc. Circ:** 700 (ctrl). Documents available from CASDDS. ***Continues*** *Proceedings of American Peanut Research and Education Association, 0160-6719.*
Desc: Research results in peanut industry of interest to university researchers and individuals interested in any phase of the peanut industry.
Ind/Abst Chem. Abstr. (1979-1983); Crop Physiol. Abstr.; Nematol. Abstr.; Plant Breed. Abstr.; Postharvest News Inf.; Rev. Agric. Entomol.

LC SB215
DD 633.6 US
PROCEEDINGS OF ... ANNUAL CONFERENCE / HAWAIIAN SUGAR TECHNOLOGISTS. Main/Corp Hawaiian Sugar Technologists. Conference. 50th (1991)-. English. One time a year. $16.00. Hawaiian Sugar Planters Association, PO Box 1057, AIEA, Honolulu HI 96701. ***Continues*** *Hawaiian Sugar Technologists. Conference. Hawaiian Sugar Technologists ... Annual Conference Reports.*

LC SB608
DD 635.21 US
PROCEEDINGS OF ANNUAL WASHINGTON POTATO CONFERENCE AND TRADE FAIR. Main/Conf Washington State Potato Conference and Trade Fair. 14th-(1975)-. Proceedings. English. One time a year.

LC S **ISSN** 0912-1048
DD 630 JA
PROCEEDINGS OF JAPANESE SOCIETY OF SUGAR BEET TECHNOLOGISTS. Proceedings. Japanese.
Ind/Abst Agric. Eng. Abstr. (1991-); Food Sci. Technol. Abstr.; Irr. Drain. Abstr.; Plant Grow. Reg. Abstr.; Rev. Plant Pathol.; Soils Fert.; Sug. Indus. Abstr.; Wheat Barley Trit. Abstr.

LC TP963.A1 F4 **ISSN** 0071-4607
DD 668.62082 US
CODEN PFRWAD
PROCEEDINGS OF THE ANNUAL MEETING - FERTILIZER INDUSTRY ROUND TABLE. (PROCEEDINGS - FERTILIZER INDUSTRY ROUND TABLE, WASHINGTON, D.C.). [Proc. annu. meet. Fert. Ind. Round Table]. **Main/Corp** Fertilizer Industry Round Table, Washington, D.C. No. 1 (1951)-. Proceedings. English. One time a year. $35.00. Fertilizer Industry Round Table, PO Box 5036, Glen Arm MD 21057. **Tel** (301)592-6271, FAX (301)592-5796. **ED** Paul J Prosser. ctrl circ. Documents available from CASDDS.
Ind/Abst AGRICOLA [Select. Cov.]; Chem. Abstr.

LC TA710 .A8 **ISSN** 0067-1525
DD 624.15 NZ
PROCEEDINGS OF THE ... AUSTRALIA-NEW ZEALAND CONFERENCE ON SOIL MECHANICS AND FOUNDATION ENGINEERING.
Main/Conf Australia-New Zealand Conference on Soil Mechanics and Foundation Engineering. (June 1952)-. Proceedings. English. New Zealand Institute of Engineers, PO Box 12241, Wellington New Zealand.

LC SB215 **ISSN** 0726-0822
DD 633.6 AT
CODEN PAUTDL
PROCEEDINGS OF THE ... CONFERENCE OF THE AUSTRALIAN SOCIETY OF SUGAR CANE TECHNOLOGISTS. [Proc. Conf. Aust. Soc. Sugar Cane Technol.]. **Main/Conf** Conference of the Australian Society of Sugar Cane Technologists. **VFOAT** Proceedings of the Australian Society of Sugar Cane Technologists. (1979)-. Academic Scholarly Publication. English. One time a year (April). 49.34Aus$. Australian Society of Sugar Cane Technologists, c/o Box 5611,

Agriculture —Crop Production and Soil

Mackay Mail Centre, Queensland 4741 Australia. **Tel** 011 61 79 521511, FAX 011 61 79 521734. **ED** Brian Egan. Index available. **Bk Rev. Ad Acc. Circ:** 1,000 (ctrl). Documents available from BIOSIS Document Express, CASDDS.
Desc: Contains papers of a technical nature for discussion at annual conference including manufacturing, agricultural and administrative matters.
Ind/Abst AGRICOLA [Full Cov.]; Biol. Abstr.; Chem. Abstr.; Food Sci. Technol. Abstr.; Sug. Indus. Abstr.

LC SB608.C5 I6   ISSN 0074-7203
DD 634/.3598/05   US
Pr Rev.
PROCEEDINGS OF THE ... CONFERENCE OF THE INTERNATIONAL ORGANIZATION OF CITRUS VIROLOGISTS. **Main/Corp**
International Organization of Citrus Virologists. Conference. (1961)-. Proceedings. English. Irregular. $35.00 US; (add $5.00 surface mail), (add $15.00 airmail) other. IOCV Department of Plant Pathology, University of California, Riverside CA 92521. **Tel** (909)787-4140. **ED** R H Brlansky, R F Lee, and L W Timmer. **Circ:** 300.
Continues Proceedings of the Conference on Citrus Virus Diseases.
Desc: Research papers presented at IOCV conferences.

LC TA710 .I52   ISSN 0534-882X
DD 624/.15/0631   CN
    CODEN PCSMB2
PROCEEDINGS OF THE ... INTERNATIONAL CONFERENCE ON SOIL MECHANICS AND FOUNDATION ENGINEERING. (PROCEEDINGS.). [Proc. Int. Conf. Soil Mech. Found. Eng.]. 1st (1936)-. Multiple languages (English and French).
Ind/Abst Bioeng. Abstr.; Curr. Cit.; Eng. Index Annu.; GeoRef.

LC S590   ISSN 0263-9335
DD 631.4   UK
PROCEEDINGS OF THE NORTH OF ENGLAND SOILS DISCUSSION GROUP. [Proc. North Engl. Soils Discuss. Group]. No. 1 (1964)-. Proceedings. English. One time a year.
Ind/Abst Soils Fert.

LC SB193 .S665a   ISSN 0193-6425
DD 633.2/02   US
PROCEEDINGS OF THE SOUTHERN PASTURE AND FORAGE CROP IMPROVEMENT CONFERENCE. [Proc. South. Pasture Forage Crop Improv. Conf.]. **Main/Conf** Southern Pasture and Forage Crop Improvement Conference. **Added/Corp** United States. Agricultural Research Service. Southern Region. United States. Agricultural Research Service. United States. Science and Education Administration. Office of the Regional Administrator for Federal Research (Southern Region). (1974)-. Proceedings. English. One time a year. Agricultural Research Southern Region, US Department of Agriculture, PO Box 53326, New Orleans LA 70153.
Continues Southern Pasture and Forage Crop Improvement Conference. Report - Southern Pasture and Forage Crop Improvement Conference.
Ind/Abst AGRICOLA [Full Cov.].

LC S   ISSN 0071-2507
DD 630   NE
PROCEEDINGS OF THE TRIENNIAL CONFERENCE. **Main/Corp** European Association for Potato Research. (19??)-. Proceedings. Multiple languages (English, French and German). Every 3 years. European Association for Potato Research, Postbus 20, 6700 AA Wageningen The Netherlands. **Tel** 011 31 8370 83041.

LC S590
DD 631.4   AO
PROCEEDINGS - REGIONAL CONFERENCE FOR AFRICA. **Main/Conf**
Regional Conference for Africa. 1st- 1955-. Proceedings. English.

LC S590 .S65   ISSN 0096-4522
DD 631.4062759   US
    CODEN SCSFAD
Pr Rev.
PROCEEDINGS / THE SOIL AND CROP SCIENCE SOCIETY OF FLORIDA. [Proc. - Soil Crop Sci. Soc. Fla.]. **Main/Corp** Soil and Crop Science Society of Florida. Meeting. Vol. 16 (1956)-. English. One time a year (Sept.). $25.00. Soil & Crop Science Society of Florida, 5007 60th Street East, Bradenton FL 34203. **Tel** (813)751-7636, FAX (813)751-7639. **ED** W. G. Blue, J. M. Bennett and F. M. Rhoads. ctrl circ. Documents available from The Genuine Article, BIOSIS Document Express, CASDDS. **Continues** Soil Science Society of Florida. Meeting. Proceedings, 0096-8382.
Ind/Abst AgBiotech News Inf.; AGRICOLA [Full Cov.]; Biol. Abstr.; Chem. Abstr.; Crop Physiol. Abstr.; Curr. Cit.; Curr. Contents Agric. Biol. Environ. Sci.; EMBASE; Field

Crop Abstr.; GeoRef; Grass. Forage Abstr.; Irr. Drain. Abstr.; Maize Abstr.; Nematol. Abstr.; Nutr. Abstr. Rev., Ser. B, Live Feeds and Feed.; Life Sci. Collect.; Pig News Inf.; Plant Breed. Abstr.; Plant Genet. Resour. Abstr.; Plant Grow. Reg. Abstr.; Res. Alert [Select. Cov.]; Rev. Agric. Entomol.; Rev. Plant Pathol.; Seed Abstr.; Soc. Sci. Cit. Index [Select. Cov.]; Sorghum Mill. Abstr.; Soyabean Abstr.; Wheat Barley Trit. Abstr.

LC S
DD 630   BL
PRODUCAO DE CANA-DE-ACUCAR ALAGOAS; INFORME SAFRA/ASPLANA. **VFOAT** Informe Safra; Producao de Cana de Acucar Alagoas. Portuguese. Associacao dos Plantadores de Cana de Alagoas, rua Sa E Albuquerque 502, Jaragua - Maceio Alagoas Brazil.

LC SB187.I7 I522A
DD 630   IO
PRODUKSI TANAMAN BAHAN MAKANAN DI INDONESIA. **Main/Corp**
Indonesia. Biro Pusat Statistic. **VFOAT** Production of Food Crops in Indonesia. (19??)-. English (English and Indonesian). One time a year. Rp2,000 Indonesia; $1.85 US. Biro Pusat Statistik / Central Bureau of Statistics, 8 Jalan Dr. Sutomo No. 8, Box 3, Jakarta Pusat 10710 Indonesia. **Tel** 011 62 21 372808, 011 62 21 374908 ext.342. ctrl circ.

LC S   ISSN 0117-0880
DD 630   PH
UDC 633.18
PROGRAM REPORT - INTERNATIONAL RICE RESEARCH INSTITUTE. [Program rep. - Int. Rice Res. Inst.]. (1990)-. Periodical. English. One time a year. P266.00 Philippines; $47.30 (airmail), $40.30 (surface mail) North America; $20.50 (airmail), $13.50 (surface mail) other. International Rice Research Institute, PO Box 933, 1099 Manila Philippines. **Tel** (011)63 2 8181926, FAX (011)63 2 8182087, telex 45365, 7425365. **ED** S J Banta. **Circ:** 13,000. **Continues** Annual Report - International Rice Research Institute (Los Banos), 0116-4341.
Desc: Reports on progress in areas such as rice breeding for resistance to diseases, insects, drought, adverse soils, and cold and hot temperature, pest control, water treatment, soil and crop management, cropping systems, machinery development, finances, and other items.

LC HD9235.E442 .M66
DD 338.1/75646/0972   MX
PROGRAMA SIEMBRA-EXPORTACION DE BERENJENA. **Added/Corp** Mexico. Direccion General de Economia Agricola. **VFOAT** Programa Siembra Exportacion de Berenjena. (19??)-. Spanish. Secretaria de Agricultura y Recursos Hidraulicos, Direccion General de Economia, Agricola Carolina No 132 - 120, Piso Delegacion Benito, Juarez Codigo Postal 03720 Mexico DF.

LC SB320   ISSN 0258-3089
DD 635   CH
PROGRESS REPORT / ASIAN VEGETABLE RESEARCH AND DEVELOPMENT CENTER. [Prog. rep. - Asian Veg. Res. Dev. Cent.]. **Main/Corp** Ya-Chow Shu Ts'ai Yen Chiu Fa Chan Chung Hsin. **Added/Corp** Asian Vegetable Research and Development Center. **VFOAT** AVRDC Progress Report. (1975)-. Periodical. English. One time a year. $15.00. Asian Vegetable Research & Development Center, PO Box 42, Shanhua Tainan 74199 Taiwan. **Tel** (06)5837801, FAX 06-5830009, telex 73560 AVRDC. **Circ:** 1,000. **Continues** Asian Vegetable Research and Development Center. Annual Report.
Desc: Provides full details of all research projects and other institutional information is also presented.

LC SB320   ISSN 0258-3097
DD 635   CH
PROGRESS REPORT SUMMARIES - ASIAN VEGETABLE RESEARCH AND DEVELOPMENT CENTER. (AVRDC PROGRESS REPORT SUMMARIES.). [Prog. rep. summ. - Asian Veg. Res. Dev. Cent.]. **Added/Corp** Asian Vegetable Research and Development Center. **VFOAT** AVRDS [sic] Progress Report Summaries. VAT Asian Vegetable Research and Development Center Progress Report Summaries. (1983)-. English. **Continues** Progress Report Summaries (Asian Vegetable Research and Development Center).
Ind/Abst Plant Genet. Resour. Abstr.

LC SB183
DD 633   US
PROSPECTIVE PLANTINGS. (19??)-. Periodical. English. Irregular. Full Depository, 707 Savings and Loan Building, Des Moines IA 50309.
Desc: Planting intentions for corn, oats, soybeans, and sorghum in Iowa and the United States.

LC S
DD 630   CN
PROTECTOR. **See** Environmental Issues-Conservation and Natural Resources.

LC HB241   ISSN 0846-3204
DD 338.4/76333/097123   CN
PULSE CROP NEWS. (PULSE CROP NEWS : OFFICIAL NEWSLETTER OF THE ALBERTA PULSE GROWERS COMMISSION.). [Pulse crop news]. **Added/Corp** Alberta Pulse Growers Commission. Summer Ed. (1991)-. Newsletter. English. Four times a year. $30.00 Canada; $35.00 other. Alberta Pulse Growers Commission, Box 1837, Lethbridge Alberta T1J 4T4 Canada.

LC SB183
DD 633   RU
PUTI POVYSHENIIA UROZHAINOSTI POLEVYKH KULTUR. **Added/Corp** Belorusskii Nauchno-Issledovatelskii Institut Zemledeliia. (19??)-. Periodical. Russian. Belorusskii Nauchno-Issledovatelskii Institut Zemledeliia, Russia.
Ind/Abst Plant Breed. Abstr.

LC S
DD 630   US
QUALITY OF COTTON CLASSED UNDER SMITH-DOXEY ACT. UNITED STATES. **See** Fabrics and Textile Industries.

LC S
DD 630   US
QUALITY WHEAT FROM THE PACIFIC NORTHWEST--USA. Vol. 1- (Feb. 1971)-. Periodical. English. Four times a year. Pacific Northwest Grain Standards and Quality Committee, Box 400, Pendleton OR 97801.

LC S
DD 630   TH
QUARTERLY NEWSLETTER (FAO REGIONAL OFFICE FOR ASIAN AND THE PACIFIC. ASIA AND PACIFIC PLANT PROTECTION COMMISSION). (QUARTERLY NEWSLETTER / ASIA AND PACIFIC PLANT PROTECTION COMMISSION.). **Added/Corp** FAO Regional Office for Asia and the Pacific. Asia and Pacific Plant Protection Commission. Vol. 26, No. 1 (Jan./March 1983)-. Newsletter. English. Four times a year. FAO Regional Office for Asia & the Pacific, Phra Atit Road, Maliwan Mansion, Bangkok 10200 Thailand. **Tel** 011 66 2 281-7844, FAX 011 66 2 2800445, telex 82815 FOODAG. **Continues** Quarterly Newsletter (Food and Agriculture Organization of the United Nations. Plant Protection Committee for the South East Asia and Pacific Region).
Ind/Abst Biocont. News Inf. (1991-); Hortic. Abstr.; Nematol. Abstr.; Potato Abstr.; Rev. Plant Pathol.; Rice Abstr.; Soyabean Abstr.; Weed Abstr.

LC SB272.A29 T4b
DD 633/.72/09689   MW
QUARTERLY NEWSLETTER - TEA RESEARCH FOUNDATION OF CENTRAL AFRICA. **Main/Corp** Tea Research Foundation of Central Africa. (19??)-. Newsletter. English. Four times a year. K30.00 Malawi; K36.00 Western Hemisphere; K35.00 other. Tea Research Foundation of Central Africa, PO Box 51, Mulanje Malawi. **Tel** (462)261 271 255, telex 44458 MI TERIFIC. **ED** W.J. Grice. Index available. cum. index. **Circ:** 500 (ctrl).
Desc: News and reports on all research work undertaken in connection with tea culture and manufacture.
Ind/Abst Trop. Agric.; Hortic. Abstr.; Maize Abstr.; Rev. Agric. Entomol.

LC SB354   ISSN 0033-6122
DD 634   AT
QUEENSLAND FRUIT AND VEGETABLE NEWS. **Added/Corp** Queensland. Committee of Direction of Fruit Marketing. Vol. 1 (Nov. 3, 1950)-. Trade Publication. English. Twenty-three times a year. 32.88Aus$. Committee of Direction Fruit Marketing, PO Box 19, Brisbane Queensland 4106 Australia. **Tel** 11 61 7 2132463, telex AA 42111. **ED** Helen O'Brien. Index available. **Bk Rev. Ad Acc. Circ:** 11,500 (ctrl).
Desc: Trade journal for Queensland's fruit and vegetable growers.

LC SB290 .K8
DD 633.8/952/09595   MY
R.R.I.M. PLANTING MANUAL. **Main/Corp**
Rubber Research Institute of Malaya. (19??)-. Monographic series. English. Price varies per volume.
Continues Planting Manual.

LC SB   ISSN 1014-191X
DD 630   INT
UDC 63
    CODEN NU052
RAPA PUBLICATION. [RAPA publ.]. **VFOAT** Regional Office for Asia and the Pacific Publication. (1986)-. Periodical. English. Irregular. Food and Agriculture Organization of the United Nations, Regional Office for Asia and the Pacific, Maliwan Mansion, Phra

Atit Road, Bangkok 10200 Thailand. **Continues** RAPA Monograph, 1014-1928.
Ind/Abst For. Abstr.; Rev. Plant Pathol.; Weed Abstr.

LC HD9200.C18 S6a
DD 354.67/1130082333 CM
RAPPORT D'ACTIVITES / SO. DE. CAO.
See Industry and Production.

LC S590 **ISSN** 0434-6793
DD 631.4 NE
CODEN IBBRAH
RAPPORT / INSTITUUT VOOR BODEMVRUCHTBAARHEID. [Rapp. - Inst. bodemvruchtbaarheid, Groningen]. (1961)-. Academic Scholarly Publication. Dutch (English). Irregular. Price varies per volume. Documents available from CASDDS.
Ind/Abst AGRICOLA; Chem. Abstr. (-1987); For. Abstr.; Plant Grow. Reg. Abstr.; Potato Abstr.

LC S590 **ISSN** 0348-0976
DD 631.4 SW
CODEN RJSME8
RAPPORTER FRAN JORDEBEARBETNINGSAVDELNINGEN, SVERIGES LANTBRUKSUNIVERSITET.
(RAPPORTER FRAN JORDBEARBETNINGSAVDELNINGEN. REPORTS FROM THE DIVISION OF SOIL MANAGEMENT.). [Rapp. jordbearbetningsavd., sver. lantbruksuniv.]. **Main/Corp** Sveriges Lantbruksuniversitet. Institutionen for Markvetenskap. **VFOAT** Reports from the Division of Soil Management. No. 53 (1977)-. Periodical. Swedish (summaries and/or abstracts in English). Swedish University of Agricultural Sciences / Crop Production, Dept of Crop Production Science, PO Box 7043, S-750 07 Uppsala Sweden. Documents available from BIOSIS Document Express. **Continues** Uppsala. Lantbrukshogskolan. Avdelningen for Jordbearbetning. Rapporter ... Reports.
Desc: Information on soil research
Ind/Abst AGRICOLA; Agric. Eng. Abstr. (1991-); Biol. Abstr. (1983-); Potato Abstr.; World Agric. Econ. Rural Sociol. Abstr.

LC SB761 **ISSN** 0724-4606
DD 635.97 GW
RAPS : FACHZEITSCHRIFT FUER OL- UND EIWEISSPFLANZEN. (Aug. 1983)-. Trade Publication. German. Four times a year. $31.16. Verlag TH Mann OHG, Postfach 200254, W 45837 Gelsenkirchen Germany. **Tel** 011 49 209 9304184.

LC SB354 **ISSN** 1075-6108
DD 634 US
Pr Rev.
RARE FRUIT COUNCIL INTERNATIONAL'S TROPICAL FRUIT NEWS, THE. [Rare Fruit Counc. Int. trop. fruit news].
Added/Corp Rare Fruit Council International. **VFOAT** Tropical Fruit News. (199?)-. Periodical. English. Twelve times a year. $35.00 Comes with Rare Fruit Council International membership. Rare Fruit Council International Inc., PO Box 561914, Miami FL 33256. **Tel** (305)378-4457. **ED** Bob G. Cannon II (editor's address: 2011 Allen Street, Englewood, FL 34223-1720, phone: (813)474-6133). **Bk Rev**, (Qty: 15-20). **Ad Acc, Adv Mgr:** Bob Cannon, **Tel** (813)474-6133. **Circ:** 1,000. **Continues** Newsletter (Rare Fruit Council International), 0897-3148.
Desc: Articles on all aspects of tropical fruits, propagation, preservation and cultivation.

LC SB354 **ISSN** 0726-1470
DD 634.0994 AT
RARE FRUIT COUNCIL OF AUSTRALIA INC. NEWSLETTER. [Newsl. - Rare Fruit Counc. Aust.]. (1980)-. Newsletter. English. Six times a year (Jan., Mar. May, July, Sept., Nov.). 28.78Aus$. Rare Fruit Council of Australia Inc., PO Box 707, Cairns Queensland 4870 Australia. **Tel** 011 61 7 552824. **ED** Thea Verstegen. **Ad Acc.** ctrl circ.

LC HF5585.P7 P3 **ISSN** 0190-6070
DD 381/.414/02573 US
RED BOOK (CHICAGO), THE. See Business and Economics-Commerce.

LC S590
DD 631.4 RU
REFERATIVNYI ZHURNAL: ZEMLEPOLZOVANIE, ZEMLEUSTROISTVO, OKHRANA POCHV. **Added/Corp** Vsesoiuznyi Nauchno-Issledovatelskii Institut Informatsii i Tekhniko-Ekonomicheskikh Issledovanii po Selskomu Khoziaistvu. **VFOAT** Zemlepolzovanie, Zemleustroistvo, Okhrana Pochv. No. 1 (Jan. 1974)-. Periodical. Russian. Twelve times a year. VINITI - Vsesoyuznyi Institut Nauchno-Tekhnicheskoi Informatsii, All-Union Scientific and Technical Information Institute, Baltiiskaia ulitsa 14, 125219 Moscow Russia. **Tel** 011 7 95 2384600, FAX 011 7 95 9430060, telex 411160.

LC SB249 .U57A **ISSN** 0193-9513
DD 633.5/17/0973 US
REGIONAL COTTON VARIETY TESTS.
(1973)-. English. One time a year. Free. Fiber Quality Research Unit, Southern Regional Research Center, PO Box 19687, New Orleans LA 71079. **Tel** (504)286-4562. **ED** Robert J Miravalle.

LC S590 **ISSN** 1066-4106
DD 631 US
REMINERALIZE THE EARTH. [Reminer. earth]. Issue 1 (Winter 1991)-. Periodical. English. Three times a year. $25.00. Soil Reminerlization, 152 South Street, Northhampton MA 01060. **Tel** (413)586-4429. **ED** Joanna Campe. **Bk Rev. Ad Acc. Circ:** 1,000. **Continues** Soil Remineralization, 0896-7237.
Desc: Forum for the exchange of ideas, experiences and research of those concerned with the networking and implementation of soil remineralization, and the regeneration of soils with gravel and rock dust.

LC HD1471.I5 S93A
DD 338.16 IO
RENCANA KEGIATAN DAN RENCANA ANGGARAN PENDAPATAN DAN BELANJA. **Main/Corp** Sumatra Planters Association. Research Institute. (19??)-. Indonesian. Balai Penelitian Perkebunan, Kampung Baru Kotakpos 104, Medan Indonesia.

LC SB337 .C82 **ISSN** 1064-5594
DD 631 US
REPORT / CUCURBIT GENETICS COOPERATIVE. [Rep. - Cucurbit Genet. Coop.]. **Main/Corp** Cucurbit Genetics Cooperative. **Added/Corp** University of Wisconsin--Madison. Dept. of Horticulture. (197?)-. Periodical. English. One time a year (July). $12.00. Cucurbit Genetics Cooperative, 1122 Holzapfel Hall, College Park MD 20742. **Tel** (301)405-4345, FAX (301)314-9308. **ED** Timothy Ng. **Circ:** 300.
Desc: Presents research papers on the genetics and breeding of cucurbits (e.g. squash, melons, cucumbers, watermelon).
Ind/Abst AgBiotech News Inf.; Hortic. Abstr.; Plant Breed. Abstr.; Plant Grow. Reg. Abstr.; Rev. Agric. Entomol.; Rev. Plant Pathol.; Seed Abstr.

LC S540.A2 I57 **ISSN** 0955-9051
DD 630.7 UK
REPORT FOR ... - INSTITUTE OF ARABLE CROPS RESEARCH. (REPORT FOR ... / AGRICULTURAL AND FOOD RESEARCH COUNCIL, INSTITUTE OF ARABLE CROPS RESEARCH.). [Rep. - Inst. Arable Crops Res.]. **Main/Corp** Institute of Arable Crops Research (Great Britain). **VFOAT** IARC Report. (1988)-. Periodical. English. One time a year. Free on request. Rothamsted Experimental Station, Harpenden Hertfordshire AL5 2JQ United Kingdom. **Tel** 011 44 158 2763133. **ED** A. J. Abbott. Index available. **Circ:** 3,000. **Formed by the union of** Annual Report (Long Ashton Research Station), 0954-4968 **and** Report (Rothamsted Experimental Station), 0262-1215.

LC SB608
DD 635.21 US
REPORT - IDAHO POTATO COMMISSION. **Main/Corp** Idaho Potato Commission. (May 1973)-. Periodical. English. Twelve times a year. $10.00. Idaho Potato Commission, PO Box 1068, Boise ID 83701. **Tel** (208)334-2350. **Continues** Idaho Potato Commission. Idaho Potato News.

LC HD9199.I4 **ISSN** 0445-5738
DD 338.17373 II
REPORT - INDIA (REPUBLIC) COFFEE BOARD. **Main/Corp** India (Republic) Coffee Board. 1st- 1940/41-. English. Coffee Board, Box 5366, Bangalore 560001 India. **Tel** 24920.

LC SB187.U6 L62 **ISSN** 0456-5959
DD 630.72 US
REPORT OF PROJECTS / LOUISIANA AGRICULTURAL EXPERIMENT STATION. DEPT. OF AGRONOMY.
(REPORT OF PROJECTS.). [Rep. proj.-La. Agric. Exp. Stn., Dep. Agron.]. **Main/Corp** Louisiana Agricultural Experiment Station. Department of Agronomy. Periodical. English. Department of Agronomy, Box E, Agricultural Experiment Station, Baton Rouge LA 70893.
Ind/Abst AGRICOLA [Full Cov.]

LC S
DD 630 US
REPORT OF ... SOYBEAN SEED RESEARCH CONFERENCE. **Main/Conf** Soybean Seed Research Conference. **Added/Corp** American Seed Trade Association. Soybean Seed Division. **VFOAT** Proceedings of ... Soybean Seed Research Conference. (19??)-. English. One time a year. $10.00. American Seed Trade Association, 1030 15th Street NW, Suite 964, Washington DC 20005. **Tel** (202)223-4080.

LC HD9257.S7 S65c
DD 354/.68/008233 SA
REPORT OF THE AUDITOR-GENERAL ON THE ACCOUNTS OF THE DECIDUOUS FRUIT BOARD AND THE SOUTH AFRICAN PLANT IMPROVEMENT ORGANISATION. VERSLAG VAN DIE OUDITEUR-GENERAAL VOR DIE REKENINGEN VAN DIE SAGTEVRUGTERAAD EN DIE SUID-AFRIKAANSE PLANT-VERBETERINGSORGANISASIE.
See Public Administration.

LC HD9049.A5 S62
DD 338.17 SA
REPORT OF THE AUDITOR-GENERAL ON THE ACCOUNTS OF THE LUCERNE SEED BOARD FOR THE FINANCIAL YEAR ... . **Added/Corp** South Africa. Dept. of the Auditor-General. South Africa. Office of the Auditor-General. South Africa. Lucerne Seed Board. **VFOAT** Verslag Van Die Ouditeur-Generaal Oor Die Rekenings Van Die Lusernsaadraad Vir Die Boekjaar ... . Afrikaans (English). Government Printer / South Africa, Bosman Street, Private Bag X85, Pretoria 0001 South Africa. **Tel** 011 27 12 3239731 ext. 262. **Continues** Report of the Controller and Auditor-General on the Accounts of the Lucerne Seed Control Board.

LC S623 .U43
DD 631.450973 US
REPORT OF THE CHIEF OF THE SOIL CONSERVATION SERVICE. **Main/Corp** United States. Soil Conservation Service. **VFOAT** Annual Reports of Department of Agriculture Soil Conservation Service. (1937)-. Government Publication. English. US Department of Agriculture, 14th Street and Independence Avenue SW, Washington DC 20250. **Tel** (202)720-5457.

LC S590 **ISSN** 0839-6523
DD 631.47715 CN
REPORT OF THE NEW BRUNSWICK SOIL SURVEY. [Rep. N.B. Soil Surv.]. **Main/Corp** Canada. Dept. of Agriculture. Research Branch. **Added/Corp** New Brunswick. Dept. of Agriculture and Rural Development. Canada. Dept. of Agriculture. Research Branch. Canada. Experimental Farms Service. New Brunswick. Dept. of Agriculture. (1940)-. Monographic series. English. Price varies per volume. New Brunswick Department of Agriculture and Rural Development, PO Box 6000, Fredericton New Brunswick E3B 5H1 Canada. **Continues** Report of the New Brunswick Soil Survey.

LC S
DD 630 US
REPORT OF THE ... NORTH AMERICAN ALFALFA IMPROVEMENT CONFERENCE. 30th (1986)-. English. Every 2 years. **Continues** Alfalfa Improvement Conference. Report of the Alfalfa Improvement Conference, 0196-2167.
Ind/Abst Weed Abstr.

LC S
DD 630 IT
REPORT OF THE ... SESSION OF THE COMMISSION FOR CONTROLLING THE DESERT LOCUST IN NORTHWEST AFRICA. **Main/Corp** Food and Agriculture Organization of the United Nations. Commission for Controlling the Desert Locust in Northwest Africa. 2nd (May 1973)-. Periodical. English. Food Agriculture Organization (FAO) / Italy, GIPCI66 via Terme di Caracalla, 00100 Rome Italy. **Tel** 011 39 6 52252925, FAX 011 39 6 52253152.

LC S **ISSN** 0495-8306
DD 630 US
REPORT OF THE TOMATO GENETICS COOPERATIVE. **Main/Corp** Tomato Genetics Cooperative. **VFOAT** TGC Report. (Mar. 1951)-. English. One time a year. $5.00. Cornell University / Tomato Genetics Cooperative, 1017 Bradfield Hall, Ithaca NY 14853. **Tel** (607)255-4573. **ED** R.W. Zobel and M. Mutschler. cum. index. **Circ:** 400.

LC HD9259.N7 M37
DD 354/.689/7008233 CK
REPORT OF THE TREE NUT AUTHORITY. **Main/Corp** Tree Nut Authority. 1st- 1975/76-. English. **Supersedes** Tung Board. Final Report of the Tung Board; Tung Board. Final Report of the Tung Board.

Agriculture —Crop Production and Soil

LC S
DD 630
SA
REPORT ON MAIZE FOR THE FINANCIAL YEAR ... FOR SUBMISSION TO THE MINISTER OF AGRICULTURE. **Main/Corp** South Africa. Maize Board. **VFOAT** Annual Report. (May 1990/Apr. 1991)-. English (Afrikaans). Maize Board Mieliraad, PO Box 669, Pretoria 0001 South Africa. **Tel** 012 325-2133. **Continues** South Africa. Maize Board. Report on Maize and Buckwheat for the Financial Year ... .

LC SB608
DD 635.21
ISSN 0309-2240
UK
REPORT / POTATO MARKETING BOARD. **Added/Corp** Great Britain. Potato Marketing Board. (1976)-. Monographic series. English.
Ind/Abst Nematol. Abstr.; Potato Abstr.

LC SB251.N6 A37A
DD 633.5/1/09669
NR
REPORT TO THE BOARD OF GOVERNORS ON THE INSTITUTE'S WORK. **Main/Corp** Ahmadu Bello University, Zaria, Nigeria. Institute for Agricultural Research and Special Services. English. Institute for Agricultural Research Samaru, Ahmadu Bello University, PMB 1044, Zaria Nigeria.

LC HD9235.P82 I34A
DD 353.9/796/008233
ISSN 0097-8280
US
REPORT TO THE GOVERNOR OF IDAHO AND THE LEGISLATURE FROM THE IDAHO POTATO COMMISSION. (REPORT TO THE GOVERNOR OF IDAHO AND THE LEGISLATURE.). **Main/Corp** Idaho Potato Commission. (19??)-. English. Every 2 years. Idaho Potato Commission, PO Box 1068, Boise ID 83701. **Tel** (208)334-2350. **Continues** Report to the Governor of Idaho and the Legislature.

LC S590
DD 631.4
ISSN 0083-7938
UK
REPORT - WELSH SOILS DISCUSSION GROUP. [Rep. - Welsh Soils Discuss. Group]. **Main/Corp** Welsh Soils Discussion Group. **Added/Corp** University College of Wales (Aberystwyth, Wales). No. 1 (1960)-. Monographic series. English. Irregular. Price varies per volume. Welsh Soils Discussion Group, University College of North Wales, Bangor Gwynedd LL57 2UW United Kingdom. **Tel** 011 44 1248 351151 ext. 412.
Ind/Abst GeoRef.

LC SB354
DD 634
ISSN 0845-9630
CN
RESEARCH BRANCH REPORT - RESEARCH STATION, SUMMERLAND, BRITISH COLUMBIA. (RESEARCH BRANCH REPORT.). [Res. Branch rep. - Res. Stn., Summerland, B.C.]. **Main/Corp** Canada. Agriculture Canada. Research Station (Summerland, B.C.). **VAT** Rapport de la Direction de la Recherche - Research Station, Summerland, British Columbia. (19??)-. English. One time a year.
Ind/Abst Grass. Forage Abstr.

LC SB183
DD 633
ISSN 0257-8441
II
CODEN RBITDO
RESEARCH BULLETIN - INTERNATIONAL CROPS RESEARCH INSTITUTE FOR THE SEMI-ARID TROPICS. (RESEARCH BULLETIN.). [Res. bull. - Int. Crops Res. Inst. Semi-arid Trop.]. **Added/Corp** International Crops Research Institute for the Semi-Arid Tropics. (19??)-. Bulletin. English. Documents available from BIOSIS Document Express.
Ind/Abst Biol. Abstr. (-1984); Field Crop Abstr.; Plant Genet. Resour. Abstr.; Sorghum Mill. Abstr.

LC SB608
DD 635.21
II
RESEARCH HIGHLIGHTS (CENTRAL POTATO RESEARCH INSTITUTE (INDIA)). (RESEARCH HIGHLIGHTS.). **Added/Corp** Central Potato Research Institute (India). Periodical. English.

LC S
DD 630
ISSN 0090-8142
US
RESEARCH PROGRESS REPORT - WESTERN SOCIETY OF WEED SCIENCE. **Main/Corp** Western Society of Weed Science. **Added/Corp** Western Weed Control Conference. Research Progress Report. (1952)-. English. One time a year. $16.50. Western Society of Weed Science, PO Box 963, Newark CA 94560. **Tel** (510)793-4169. Index available. **Circ:** 350.
Desc: Results of current research on weeds and weed control in the western United States.
Ind/Abst AGRICOLA [Select. Cov.]; PESTDOC.

LC SB183
DD 633
US
RESEARCH REPORT. **Added/Corp** North Carolina State University. Dept. of Crop Science. (1964)-. Monographic series. English. Price varies per volume. **Continues** Research Report (North Carolina State College. Dept. of Crop Science).

LC [S93 .E223]
DD 630
ISSN 0548-5967
US
CODEN NEXRAX
RESEARCH REPORT - AGRICULTURAL EXPERIMENT STATION. (AGRICULTURAL EXPERIMENT STATION RESEARCH REPORT - NEW MEXICO.). [Res. rep. Agric. Exp. Stn.]. **Main/Corp** New Mexico State University. Agricultural Experiment Station. **Added/Corp** New Mexico State University. Agricultural Experiment Station. Vol. 1 (May 1, 1955)-. Monographic series. English. Irregular. Price varies per volume. New Mexico University, Box CC, University Park NM 88003. **Tel** (505)646-1175. **ED** Robert C Caughlie. Index available. **Circ:** 500 (ctrl). Documents available from BIOSIS Document Express, CASDDS. **Continues** Press Bulletin - New Mexico State University, Agricultural Experiment Station.
Desc: Reports of continuing research, or reports of smaller research projects. Also includes a final report of grant-funded research projects.
Ind/Abst Biol. Abstr.; Chem. Abstr.

LC S
DD 630
ISSN 0725-9492
AT
RESEARCH REPORT (TROPICAL FRUIT RESEARCH STATION (N.S.W.)). (RESEARCH REPORT / TROPICAL FRUIT RESEARCH STATION.). (19??)-. English. One time a year. New South Wales Department of Agriculture / Tropical Fruit Research Station, Alstonville NSW Australia.

LC SB270.B7 C65A
DD 633.7
BL
RESUMOS - CONGRESSO BRASILEIRO DE PESQUISAS CAFEEIRAS. **Main/Conf** Congresso Brasileiro de Pesquisas Cafeeiras. Portuguese. Setor de Programacao Visual e Grafica, Av Rodrigues Alves, 129 - 3 Po S Andar, Rio de Janeiro Brazil.

LC HD9049.C8 S63A
DD 338.1/7/3150968
SA
REVIEW OF THE MAIZE POSITION. **Main/Corp** South Africa. Maize Board. (19??)-. English. Maize Board Mieliraad, PO Box 669, Pretoria 0001 South Africa. **Tel** 012 325-2133. **Continues** Review of the Maize Position.

LC S590
DD 631.4
ISSN 0100-0683
BL
CODEN RBCSDP
REVISTA BRASILEIRA DE CIENCIA DO SOLO. [Rev. bras. cienc. solo]. **Added/Corp** Sociedade Brasileira de Ci‚encia do Solo. Vol. 1 (1977)-. Academic Scholarly Publication. Portuguese (summaries and/or abstracts in English). Three times a year (Apr., Aug., and Dec.). $50.00. Sociedade Brasileira de Ciencia do Solo, Caixa Postal 28, 13001 970 Campinas, Sao Paulo Brazil. **Tel** 011 55 192 315422, 011 55 192 328937, FAX 011 55 192 314943, telex (019)1059. **ED** Antonio Carlos Moniz. Index available (Bound in 7th iss.). cum. index. **Circ:** 1,800. Documents available from CASDDS.
Desc: Original papers or review articles on soil science, including soil mineralogy, classification, physics chemistry, fertility, management, biology, and methods matters.
Ind/Abst AgBiotech News Inf.; Agric. Eng. Abstr. (1991-); Agrofor. Abstr.; Biocont. News Inf. (1991-); Chem. Abstr.; Crop Physiol. Abstr.; Energy Res. Abstr. (July 1979-); Field Crop Abstr.; For. Abstr.; GeoRef; Grass. Forage Abstr.; Irr. Drain. Abstr.; Maize Abstr.; Potato Abstr.; Rev. Agric. Entomol.; Rev. Plant Pathol.; Rice Abstr.; Seed Abstr.; Soils Fert.; Sorghum Mill. Abstr.; Soyabean Abstr.; Wheat Barley Trit. Abstr.

LC S
DD 630
ISSN 0325-9250
AG
REVISTA DE LA FACULTAD DE AGRONOMIA. **Added/Corp** Universidad de Buenos Aires. Facultad de Agronomia. Vol. 1, No. 1 (1980)-. Periodical. Spanish. Three times a year. Universidad de Buenos Aires / Agronomia, Facultad de Agronomia, Buenos Aires Argentina.
Ind/Abst For. Abstr.; Rev. Plant Pathol.; Seed Abstr.; Soils Fert.; Weed Abstr.

LC S
DD 630
ISSN 1010-2752
CU
REVISTA DE PROTECCION VEGETAL. [Rev. prot. veg.]. (1986)-. Periodical. Spanish. Three times a year. Centro Nacional de Salud Animal, Apartado 10, San Jose de las Lajas La Habana, Cuba.
Ind/Abst Agric. Eng. Abstr.; Biocont. News Inf.; Crop Physiol. Abstr.; Field Crop Abstr.; Hortic. Abstr.; Plant Breed. Abstr.; Rev. Plant Pathol.; Soils Fert.; Sorghum Mill. Abstr.; Weed Abstr.

LC S187 .E6
DD 630/.982/43
ISSN 0370-5404
AG
CODEN RIATAU
REVISTA INDUSTRIAL Y AGRICOLA DE TUCUMAN. [Rev. ind. agric. Tucuman]. **Added/Corp** Estacion Experimental Agricola de Tucuman. Vol. 1 (June 1910)-. Periodical. Spanish. Irregular. $120.00. Estacion Experiment Agricola, Casilla Correos 71, Tucuman Argentina. **Tel** 011 54 81 266561. cum. index. Documents available from CASDDS.
Ind/Abst AGRICOLA; Chem. Abstr.; Crop Physiol. Abstr.; Field Crop Abstr.; Fish Rev. (Jan. 1989-July 1992); Hortic. Abstr.; Maize Abstr.; Nematol. Abstr.; Plant Breed. Abstr.; Seed Abstr.; Soils Fert.; Soyabean Abstr.; Sug. Indus. Abstr.; Wildl. Rev. (Jan. 1989-July 1992).

LC SB294.C9 R48
DD 633.8/8/097291
CU
SUSPENDED
REVISTA PLANTAS MEDICINALES. **VFOAT** Plantas Medicinales. Periodical. Spanish (summaries and/or abstracts in English). One time a year. Ediciones Cubanas, Obispo 527 Altos ESQ Bernaza, CP 10100 Havana Cuba.

LC S
DD 630
ISSN 0760-9868
FR
UDC 634.8
REVUE DES OENOLOGUES ET DES TECHNIQUES VITIVINICOLES ET OENOLOGIQUES. (1982)-. Periodical. French. Four times a year. $64.52. Bourgogne Publications, Chateau de Chaintre Cidex 453B, 71570 Chapelle Guinchay France. **Tel** 011 33 1 85374321, FAX 011 33 1 85371983.
Ind/Abst Food Sci. Technol. Abstr.

LC S
DD 630
FR
REVUE LE PAYSAN FRANCAIS. No. 775 (Sept. 1982)-. Periodical. French. Twelve times a year. 165.00F (one-year), 295.00F (two-year) France; 265.00F other. Le Paysan Francais, 10 rue Bellefonds, 16100 Cognac France. **Tel** 011 33 45 352817. **Continues** Revue le Paysan.

LC S
DD 630
ISSN 0257-3385
CM
CODEN RSTZED
REVUE SCIENCE ET TECHNIQUE. SERIE SCIENCES AGRONOMIQUES ET ZOOTECHNIQUES. [Rev. sci. tech., Ser. sci. agron. zootech.]. **Added/Corp** Institute of Agronomic Research (Cameroon) Institute of Animal Research (Cameroon). **VFOAT** Serie Sciences Agronomiques et Zootechniques; Agronomic and Animal Sciences Series; Science and Technology Review. Agronomic and Animal Sciences Series. Vol. 1, No. 1 (Dec. 1984)-. Periodical. French (English). Four times a year. Institute of Agronomic and Animal Research, Yaounde Republique du Cameroun. Documents available from CASDDS. **Continues in part** Revue Science et Technique, 0250-989X.
Ind/Abst AGRICOLA; Chem. Abstr. (1985-1986).

LC SB191.R5 U517A
DD 338.1/7/3180973
ISSN 0193-1032
US
RICE CROP QUALITY. **Main/Corp** United States. Federal Grain Inspection Service. Government Publication. English. US Department of Agriculture, 14th Street and Independence Avenue SW, Washington DC 20250. **Tel** (202)720-5457.

LC S
DD 630
ISSN 0194-0929
US
RICE FARMING AND RICE INDUSTRY NEWS. **VFOAT** Rice Farming. (19??)-. Periodical. English. Six times a year. $9.00. Little Publications, 6263 Popular Avenue, Suite 540, Memphis TN 38119. **Tel** (901)767-4020. **ED** Patrick Shepard. **Circ:** 12,000.

LC S590
DD 631
ISSN 0035-4961
US
RICE JOURNAL (1938), THE. (THE RICE JOURNAL.). [Rice j.]. (1938)-. Trade Publication. English. Six times a year. $12.00. Specialized Agricultural Publications, 3000 Highwoods Boulevard, Suite 300, Raleigh NC 27625. **Tel** (919)872-5040. **Continues** Rice and Sugar Journal.
Ind/Abst AGRICOLA; Food Sci. Technol. Abstr.; Life Sci. Collect.; PESTDOC (?-?); Rice Abstr.

LC HB241
DD 338
ISSN 8750-460X
US
RICE MARKET REPORT. [Rice mark. rep.]. **Added/Corp** Louisiana. State Market News Service. Louisiana. Dept. of Agriculture. (19??)-. Periodical. English. One time a week. Louisiana Department of Agriculture & Forestry Department, Box 25060, Baton Rouge LA 70894. **Tel** (504)342-7011. **ED** Diana Landry.

LC HD9066.T34 R5
DD 338.1/7318/0951249
CH
RICE REVIEW. **Added/Corp** Joint Commission on Rural Reconstruction. Rural Economics Division. Hsing Cheng Yuan Nung yeh fa Chan wei Yuan Hui (China).

Dept. of Economics & Planning. (19??)-. English. Two times a year. Joint Commission on Rural Reconstruction in China, Taipei Taiwan.

LC HB241 **ISSN** 1057-7920
DD 338 US
RICE STOCKS. [Rice stocks]. **Added/Corp** United States. Crop Reporting Board. United States. Agricultural Statistics Board. (19??)-. Government Publication. English. Four times a year. $16.50. US Department of Agriculture, 14th Street and Independence Avenue SW, Washington DC 20250. **Tel** (202)720-5457. **(Subscription address:** Superintendent of Documents, US Government Printing Office, Washington DC 20402. **)** available on microfiche (Vols. for (1986-) distributed to depository libraries). Documents available from Documents on Demand.
Ind/Abst Am. Stat. Index.

LC S
DD 630 US
RICE WORLD. (19??)-. English. Twelve times a year. $16.00. Rice World, Box 3083, Lake Charles LA 70602. **Tel** (713)621-8807, FAX (713)621-8817. **ED** John Hart. **Bk Rev. Ad Acc, Adv Mgr:** John Hart. ctrl circ. ***Continues** Rice World & Soybean News, 0738-5943.*

LC S **ISSN** 0304-0593
DD 630 IT
UDC 631.17
RIVISTA DI INGEGNERIA AGRARIA. [Riv. ing. agrar.]. (1969)-. Periodical. Italian. Four times a year. L51100. Edagricole, PO Box 2157, 40100 Bologna Italy. **Tel** 011 39 51 492211 Ext. 22, FAX 011 39 51 493660, telex 510336 EDAGRI.

LC S590 .P64 **ISSN** 0080-3642
DD 631.4 PL
CODEN ROGLAA
ROCZNIKI GLEBOZNAWCZE. [Rocz. glebozn.]. **Added/Corp** Polskie Towarzystwo Gleboznawcze. **VFOAT** Ezhegodnik Pahvovedeniia; Soil Science Annual. (1950)-. Academic Scholarly Publication. Polish (summaries and/or abstracts in English and Russian). Four times a year. $58.00. **(Subscription address:** Ars Polona-Ruch, PO Box 1001, Krakowskie Przedmiescie 7, 00-068 Warsaw Poland. **Tel** 011 48 22 261201.**)** Documents available from CASDDS.
Ind/Abst AGRICOLA; Agrofor. Abstr.; Chem. Abstr.; Crop Physiol. Abstr.; Maize Abstr.; Potato Abstr.

LC SB13 .R6 **ISSN** 0080-3650
DD 630 PL
ROCZNIKI NAUK ROLNICZYCH. SERIA A, PRODUKCJA ROSLINNA = ANNALY SELSKOKHOZIAISTVENNYKH NAUK = POLISH AGRICULTURAL ANNUAL.
Added/Corp Polska Akademia Nauk. Komitet Uprawy i Hodowli Roslin. Polska Akademia Nauk. Komitet Uprawy Roslin. **VFOAT** Produkcja Roslinna; Annaly Selskokhoziaistvennykh Nauk; Polish Agricultural Annual. (1969)-. Monographic series. Polish (summaries and/or abstracts in English and Russian; table of contents in English and Russian). Irregular. Price varies per volume. Panstwowe Wydawnictwo Naukowe / PWN, (Polish Scientific Publishers PWN Ltd.), Ul. Miodowa 10, PO Box 391, 00-251 Warsaw Poland. **Tel** 011 48 22 312738, FAX 011 48 22 267163. **(Subscription address:** Ars Polona-Ruch, PO Box 1001, Krakowskie Przedmiescie 7, 00-068 Warsaw Poland. **Tel** 011 48 22 261201.**) Circ:** 750. ***Continues** Roczniki Nauk Rolniczych. Seria A, Roslinna.*
Ind/Abst Maize Abstr.; Nutr. Abstr. Rev., Ser. B, Live Feeds and Feed.; Nutr. Abstr. Rev., Ser. A, Hum. Exp.; Plant Grow. Reg. Abstr.; Potato Abstr.; Seed Abstr.

LC SB599 .R68 **ISSN** 0080-3693
DD 632 PL
CODEN RNORAR
ROCZNIKI NAUK ROLNICZYCH. SERIA E : OCHRONA ROSLIN. **See** Biology-Botany.

LC S **ISSN** 0116-4325
DD 630 PH
ROOT CROPS DIGEST. (1985)-. Periodical. English.
Ind/Abst Agrofor. Abstr. (1991-); Philip. Sci. Technol. Abstr.

LC S13 .C47 **ISSN** 0370-663X
DD 630 XR
CODEN ROVYAM
ROSTLINNA VYROBA. [Rostl. vyroba]. **Added/Corp** Czechoslovakia. Ministerstvo Zemedelstvi a Lesniho Hospodarstvi. Ustav Vedeckotechnickych Informaci. Ustredi Zemedelskeho a Potravinarskeho Vyzkumu (Czechoslovakia). Ustav Vedeckotechnickych Informaci. Ceskoslovenska Akademie Zemedelska. Ustav Vedeckotechnickych Informaci. Ceskoslovenska Akakademie Zemedelska. Ustav Vedeckotechnickych Informaci Pro Zemedelstvi. Vol. 8, No. 4 (1962)-. Academic Scholarly Publication. Czech (summaries and/or abstracts in English, German and Russian). Twelve times a year. DM358.00. PNS Ustredna Expedice Tisku Oddeleni Vyvozu Tisku, Jindrisska Ulice 14, Prague 1 Czech Republic. **(Subscription address:** Kubon & Sagner, ABT Zeitschriftenimport, D 80328 Munich Germany. **Tel** 011 49 89 54218130.**)** Documents available from The Genuine Article, CASDDS. ***Continues** Sbornik Ceskoslovenske Akademie Zemedelskych Ved. Rostlinna Vyroba.*
Ind/Abst AgBiotech News Inf.; AGRICOLA; Biocont. News Inf. (19??-19??); Chem. Abstr.; Crop Physiol. Abstr.; Curr. Cit.; Curr. Contents Agric. Biol. Environ. Sci.; EMBASE; Field Crop Abstr.; Food Sci. Technol. Abstr.; Grass. Forage Abstr.; Hortic. Abstr.; Irr. Drain. Abstr.; Nematol. Abstr.; Nutr. Abstr. Rev., Ser. B, Live Feeds and Feed.; Ornamental Hort.; Life Sci. Collect.; Plant Breed. Abstr.; Plant Grow. Reg. Abstr.; Potato Abstr.; Res. Alert [Select. Cov.]; Rev. Agric. Entomol.; Rev. Plant Pathol.; Seed Abstr.; Soils Fert.; Soyabean Abstr.; Wheat Barley Trit. Abstr.; World Agric. Econ. Rural Sociol. Abstr.

LC SB215 **ISSN** 0379-5829
DD 633.6 PE
SACCHARUM. [Saccharum]. Vol. 3, No. 1 (1975)-. Periodical. Spanish (summaries and/or abstracts in English). Two times a year.
Ind/Abst AGRICOLA.

LC SB354 **ISSN** 0137-4788
DD 634 PL
SAD NOWOCZESNY. Added/Corp Panstwowe Wydawnictwo Rolnicze i Lesne. No. 10 (1973)-. Periodical. Polish. Twelve times a year. $51.00. **(Subscription address:** Ars Polona-Ruch, PO Box 1001, Krakowskie Przedmiescie 7, 00-068 Warsaw Poland. **Tel** 011 48 22 261201.**)** Index available in last issue of volume--attached.

LC SB319.3.S65 S25 **ISSN** 0235-2591
DD 635/.0947 RU
CODEN SAVIER
SADOVODSTVO I VINOGRADARSTVO.
Added/Corp Soviet Union. Gosudarstvennyi Agropromyshlennyi Komitet. (1988)-. Academic Scholarly Publication. Russian. Six times a year. $99.95. Agropromizdat, Sadovo-Spasskaia 18, 107807 Moscow Russia. **(Subscription address:** East View Publications Inc., 3020 Harbor Lane North, Suite 110, Minneapolis MN 55447. **Tel** (800)477-1005, (612)550-0961, FAX (612)559-2931.**)** Documents available from CASDDS. ***Formed by the union of** Sadovodstvo, 0131-3568 **and** Vinodelie i Vinogradarstvo SSSR, 0042-6318.*
Ind/Abst Agric. Eng. Abstr. (1991-); Agrofor. Abstr. (1991-); Biocont. News Inf. (1991-); Chem. Abstr.; Food Sci. Technol. Abstr.; Hortic. Abstr.; Irr. Drain. Abstr.; Plant Breed. Abstr.; Postharvest News Inf.; Rev. Agric. Entomol.; Rev. Plant Pathol.; Seed Abstr.; Soils Fert.; Weed Abstr.; Wheat Barley Trit. Abstr.; World Agric. Econ. Rural Sociol. Abstr.

LC SB187.J3 S25
DD 631 JA
SAKUMOTSU TOKEI. Added/Corp Japan. Norin Suisansho. Keizaikyoku. Tokei Johobu. Japan. Norinsho. Norin Keizaikyoku. Tokei Chosabu. Japan. Norinsho. Sakumotsu Tokeika. Japan. Norinsho. Norin Keizaikyoku. Tokei Johobu. Norin Tokei Kyokai. No. 1 (1958)-. Japanese. ¥8000. Norin Tokei Kyokai, (Association of Agriculture & Forestry Statistics), 11-14 Meguro 2 Chome, Meguroku Tokyo 153 Japan.

LC S **ISSN** 0273-6004
DD 631 US
SAN FRANCISCO WHOLESCALE ORNAMENTAL CROPS REPORT.
Added/Corp Federal-State Market News Service. California. Bureau of Market News. United States. Agricultural Marketing Service. Fruit and Vegetable Division. **VFOAT** Ornamental Crops Market News. (19??)-. English. One time a week. $120.00. US Department of Agriculture / Federal-State Market News, 630 Sansome Street, Room 727, San Francisco CA 94111. **Tel** (415)705-1300, FAX (415)705-1301. **ED** F. Teensma. **Circ:** 100 (ctrl).
Desc: Information on cut flowers on San Francisco's market.

LC SB761
DD 635.97 XR
CODEN SAFRE8
SBORNIK AGRONOMICKA FAKULTA V CESKYCH BUDEJOVICICH FYTOTECHNICKA RADA. Added/Corp Vysoka Skola Zemedelska v Praze. Agronomicka Fakulta v Ceskych Budejovicich. **VFOAT** Fytotechnicka Rada; Nauchnye Trudy Ekonomicheskogo Fakulteta v Shskobudeevitskogo Selskokhoziaistvennogo Instituta. Totekhnicheskaia Seriia; Fitotekhnicheskaia Seriia; Collection of Scientific Papers of the Economic Agricultural. Series for Phytotechnics; Versity in Ceske Budejovice. Series for Phytotechnics. (1986)-. Periodical. Czech (summaries and/or abstracts in English, German and Russian). Two times a year. Documents available from CASDDS. ***Continues** Sbornik Provozne Ekonomicke Fakulty v Ceskych Budejovicich. Fytotechnicka Rada.*
Ind/Abst Chem. Abstr.; Maize Abstr.; Potato Abstr.

LC SB354 **ISSN** 0371-4942
DD 634 SZ
CODEN SZOWAZ
SCHWEIZERISCHE ZEITSCHRIFT FUER OBST- UND WEINBAU. [Schweiz. Z. Obst-Weinb.]. (1892)-. Academic Scholarly Publication. German. Twenty-six times a year. 59.00F. Verlag Stutz & Company AG, Postfach, CH-8820 Waedenwil Switzerland. **Tel** 011 41 1 7800837. Documents available from CASDDS.
Ind/Abst AgBiotech News Inf.; AGRICOLA; Agric. Eng. Abstr.; Agrofor. Abstr.; Biocont. News Inf. (1991-); Chem. Abstr. (1892-1984); EMBASE; Food Sci. Technol. Abstr.; Hortic. Abstr.; PESTDOC; Plant Grow. Reg. Abstr.; Rev. Agric. Entomol.; Rev. Plant Pathol.; Weed Abstr.; World Agric. Econ. Rural Sociol. Abstr.

LC S590 **ISSN** 0767-2853
DD 631.4 FR
CODEN SSOLEP
TITLE CHANGE
SCIENCE DU SOL (1984). (SCIENCE DU SOL : BULLETIN DE L'ASSOCIATION FRANCAISE POUR L'ETUDE DU SOL.). [Sci. sol]. **Added/Corp** Association Francaise pour l'Etude du Sol. (1984)-(1993). Bulletin. French (summaries and/or abstracts in English; table of contents in English and German). AFES, Science du Sol, Route de Thiverval, F 78850 Thiverval Grig France. **Tel** 011 33 30 815406, FAX 011 33 30 815396. Documents available from BIOSIS Document Express, CASDDS. ***Continues** Association Francaise pour l'Etude du Sol. Bulletin de l'Association Francaise pour l'Etude du Sol, 0335-1653. **Merged with** Journal of Soil Science, 0022-4688; Pedologie, 0079-0419 **to form** European Journal of Soil Science.*
Ind/Abst Biol. Abstr.; Chem. Abstr.; GeoRef; Maize Abstr.

LC S
DD 630 FR
SCIENCES AGRONOMIQUES. PRODUCTIONS VEGETALES. T280. (19??)-. French. 1638.71F France; 1700.00F other. Institut de l'Information Scientique et Technique (INIST), 2 Allee du Parc de Brabois, 54514 Vandoeuvre Nancy Cedex France. **Tel** 011 33 83 504600, FAX 011 33 83 504650. ***Continues** Pascal Thema. T280: Sciences Agronomiques. Productions Vegetales.*

LC S622 .U552A **ISSN** 0270-9538
DD 631.4/05 US
SCS-TP (UNITED STATES. SOIL CONSERVATION SERVICE). (SCS-TP.). [SCS-TP]. **Main/Corp** United States. Soil Conservation Service. **VAT** Soil Conservation Service-Technical Publication. Government Publication. English. US Department of Agriculture / Soil Conservation Service / Washington, DC, 14th Street & Independence Avenue SW, Room 5105A, Washington DC 20250. **Tel** (202)720-4525, FAX (202)720-7690.
Ind/Abst GeoRef.

LC HD9259.P333 O75a **ISSN** 0091-567X
DD 338.1/7/413 US
SEASON SUMMARY - OREGON BARTLETT PEAR COMMISSION. (SEASON SUMMARY.). **Main/Corp** Oregon Bartlett Pear Commission. (19??)-. English. One time a year. Oregon Bartlett Pear Commission, 601 Woodlark Building, Portland OR 97205.

LC SB29.C2 O63 **ISSN** 0317-350X
DD 338.1/7/409713 CN
SEASONAL FRUIT & VEGETABLE REPORT (ANNUAL SUMMARY). (FRUIT AND VEGETABLE PRODUCTION IN ONTARIO, ANNUAL SUMMARY.). **Main/Corp** Ontario. Ministry of Agriculture and Food. Economics Branch. **Added/Corp** Ontario. Ministry of Agriculture and Food. Economics Branch. Seasonal Fruit & Vegetable Report. 0474-1560. **VAT** Fruit and Vegetable Production in Ontario (Annual Summary). (19??)-. Periodical. English. One time a year. Ontario Ministry of Agriculture and Food, 801 Bay Street, Toronto Ontario M7A 1B3 Canada. **Tel** (416)965-1064, (416)326-3400. ***Continues** Ontario. Dept. of Agriculture and Food. Farm Economics, Cooperatives and Statistics Branch. Fruit and Vegetable Production in Ontario, Annual Summary., 0317-350X.*

LC SB251.U65 C6A
DD 633/.51/096625 UV
UDC 633.51(662.5)
SECTEURS D'EXPERIMENTATION DE BOBO-DIOULASSO ET DE OUAGADOUGOU : CAMPAGNE COTONNIERE. Main/Corp Comite de la Recherche Agronomique de Haute-Volta. French. Comite de la Recherche Agronomique de Haute-Volta, BP 267, Bobo-Dioulasso Burkina Faso.

LC Z **ISSN** 0141-0180
DD 016.631 UK
SEED ABSTRACTS. **See** Agriculture-Abstracting, Bibliographies and Statistics.

LC SB114.U7 P45A **ISSN** 0149-1296
DD 631.5/21 US
SEED ANALYSIS REPORT. Main/Corp Pennsylvania. Bureau of Plant Industry. (19??)-. English. One time a year. Pennsylvania Department of Agriculture, 2301 North Cameron Street, Harrisburg PA 17110. **Tel** (717)772-2853, FAX (717)787-2387.

LC HB241 **ISSN** 1065-5980
DD 338 US
SEED & CROPS INDUSTRY. [Seed crops ind.]. **VFOAT** Seed and Crops Industry. Vol. 43, No. 7 (Aug./Sept. 1992)-. Trade Publication. English. Ten times a year. $30.00. Freiberg Publishing Company, PO Box 7, Cedar Falls IA 50613. **Tel** (319)277-3599, FAX (319)277-3783. ***Continues*** *Seed Industry Journal, 1061-6330.*
Ind/Abst AGRICOLA.

LC SB117 .U46 **ISSN** 0733-2726
DD 631.5/21/0973 US
UDC 631.53(73)
SEED CROPS. ANNUAL SUMMARY. Government Publication. English. One time a year. US Department of Agriculture / National Agricultural Statistics Service (NASS), Room 5829 South Building, Washington DC 20250. **Tel** (202)720-4020, FAX (314)875-5231.

LC S **ISSN** 0190-7948
DD 630 US
UDC 631.53
SEED CROPS. VEGETABLE SEED REPORT. **VFOAT** Vegetable Seed Report; Vegetable Seeds. Government Publication. English. Irregular. US Department of Agriculture / Statistical Reporting Service, 14th Street & Independence Avenue SW, Washington DC 20250.

LC SB113 **ISSN** 0379-5594
DD 631.521 II
CODEN SEREDM
SEED RESEARCH. [Seed res.]. **Added/Corp** Indian Society of Seed Technology. Vol. 1 (1973)-. Academic Scholarly Publication. English. Two times a year. $30.00. Indian Society of Seed Technology, Indian Agricultural Research Institute, New Delhi 110012 India. **Tel** 581701. **(Subscription address:** Prints India, 11 Darya Ganj, New Delhi 110002 India. **Tel** 011 91 11 3268645, FAX 011 91 11 3275542, telex 31-61087 PRIN-IN.**)** **ED** M. Dadlani. **Circ:** 700 (ctrl). Documents available from BIOSIS Document Express, CASDDS.
Desc: Publishes original work and reviews related to seed production, storage, the physiology of germination, processing, marketing, seed testing and quality control.
Ind/Abst Agric. Eng. Abstr. (1991-); Agrofor. Abstr. (1991-); Biodeter. Abstr. (1991-); Biol. Abstr.; Chem. Abstr.; Cot. Trop. Fibr. Abstr. Bibliogr.; Crop Physiol. Abstr.; Curr. Aware. Biol. Sci., CABS; Curr. Cit.; Field Crop Abstr.; For. Abstr.; Hortic. Abstr.; Irr. Drain. Abstr.; Maize Abstr.; Nematol. Abstr.; Nutr. Abstr. Rev., Ser. B, Live Feeds and Feed.; Nutr. Abstr. Rev., Ser. A, Hum. Exp.; Plant Breed. Abstr.; Plant Genet. Resour. Abstr.; Plant Grow. Reg. Abstr.; Postharvest News Inf.; Rev. Agric. Entomol.; Rev. Plant Pathol.; Rice Abstr.; Seed Abstr.; Soils Fert.; Sorghum Mill. Abstr.; Soyabean Abstr.; Weed Abstr.; Wheat Barley Trit. Abstr.

LC S **ISSN** 0080-8504
DD 630 US
SEED TRADE BUYERS' GUIDE. (19??)-. Consumer Publication. English. One time a year. Comes with Seed World subscription. Scranton Gillette Communications Inc., 380 East Northwest Highway, Des Plaines IL 60016-2282. **Tel** (708)298-6622, FAX (708)390-0408.

LC S **ISSN** 0037-0797
DD 630 US
CCC
CODEN SWORAX
SEED WORLD. [Seed world]. Vol. 1 (1915)-. Trade Publication. English. Twelve times a year. $25.00. Scranton Gillette Communications Inc., 380 East Northwest Highway, Des Plaines IL 60016-2282. **Tel** (708)298-6622, FAX (708)390-0408. **ED** Lynn Whitmore. Index available. **Ad Acc. Circ:** 7,400 (ctrl). available on microfilm and microfiche from University Microfilms International (UMI). ***Absorbed*** *American Seedsman; National Seedsman; Florist and Nursery Exchange.*
Desc: Edited for retailers, wholesalers, and growers of flower, vegetable, grass, and agricultural seeds. Crop market information; industry trends and developments and more.
Ind/Abst AGRICOLA [Select. Cov.].

LC S **ISSN** 0582-5075
DD 630 UN
CODEN SEMVAB
SELEKTSIIA I SEMENOVODSTVO (KIEV). (SELEKTSIIA I SEMENOVODSTVO.). [Sel. semenovod.]. **Added/Corp** Ukraine. Ministerstvo Silskoho Hospodarstva. Vol. 3 (1965)-. Monographic series. Russian. Six times a year. $69.95. **(Subscription address:** East View Publications Inc., 3020 Harbor Lane North, Suite 110, Minneapolis MN 55447. **Tel** (800)477-1005, (612)550-0961, FAX (612)559-2931.**)** ***Continues*** *Selektsiia I Nasinnytstvo.*
Desc: Information on the seed industry and trade.
Ind/Abst AGRICOLA; Nematol. Abstr.; Plant Breed. Abstr.; Plant Grow. Reg. Abstr.; Potato Abstr.; Rev. Plant Pathol.

LC S **ISSN** 0037-184X
DD 630 SP
CODEN SEVIAH
SEMANA VITIVINICOLA, LE. [Sem. vitivinic.]. (1945)-. Academic Scholarly Publication. Spanish. One time a week. La Semana Vitivinicola, Apartado 642, 46080 Valencia Spain. Documents available from CASDDS.
Ind/Abst Chem. Abstr. (1945-1983); Food Sci. Technol. Abstr.; Vitis Vitic. Enol. Abstr.

LC SB113 **ISSN** 0037-1890
DD 631.521 IT
CODEN SEELBA
SEMENTI ELETTE. **Added/Corp** Ente Nazionale Sementi Elette. (1955)-. Academic Scholarly Publication. Italian. Six times a year. L47010. Edagricole, PO Box 2157, 40100 Bologna Italy. **Tel** 011 39 51 492211 Ext. 22, FAX 011 39 51 493660, telex 510336 EDAGRI. Documents available from CASDDS.
Ind/Abst AgBiotech News Inf.; Chem. Abstr.; Field Crop Abstr.; Nematol. Abstr.; Ornamental Hort.; Plant Breed. Abstr.; Plant Grow. Reg. Abstr.; Seed Abstr.; Sorghum Mill. Abstr.; Wheat Barley Trit. Abstr.

LC Z6297 .C45A SB290
DD 016.63 BL
SERINGUEIRA: RESUMOS INFORMATIVOS. **Main/Corp** Centro Nacional de Pesquisa da Seringueira (Brazil). Portuguese. Embrapa, Dept. Dif. Tecnologiaogi, Caixa Postal 040315, 07770 901 Brasilia DF Brazil. **Tel** 011 55 61 2724241.

LC SB215
DD 633.6 II
SISSTA SUGAR JOURNAL. **Added/Corp** South Indian Sugarcane & Sugar Technologists' Association. **VFOAT** S.I.S.S.T.A. Sugar Journal; Sugar Journal. **VAT** South Indian Sugarcane & Sugar Technologists Association Sugar Journal. (19??)-. Periodical. English. Four times a year.
Ind/Abst Field Crop Abstr.; Hortic. Abstr.; Postharvest News Inf.; Rev. Agric. Entomol.; Sug. Indus. Abstr.; Weed Abstr.

LC HD9490.U5 A33 **ISSN** 1049-488X
DD 338.1/7385/0973021 US
CODEN OCSRE9
SITUATION AND OUTLOOK REPORT. OIL CROPS. **See** Petroleum and Natural Gas.

LC HD9220.U5 S58 **ISSN** 1049-3352
DD 338.1/75/0973021 US
CODEN VSSRES
SITUATION AND OUTLOOK REPORT. VEGETABLES AND SPECIALTIES. [Situat. outlook rep., Veg. spec.]. **VFOAT** Vegetables and Specialties; Situation and Outlook Yearbook. Vegetable and Specialities; Vegetables and Specialities, Situation and Outlook. TVS-244 (Feb. 1988)-. Government Publication. English. Three times a year. $8.00; $3.00 (single issues) US; $10.00; $3.75 (single issues) other. US Department of Agriculture, 14th Street and Independence Avenue SW, Washington DC 20250. **Tel** (202)720-5457. available on microfiche (Vols. for 1988 distributed to depository libraries). ***Continues*** *Situation and Outlook Report. Vegetable (Washington, D.C. : 1987).*
Desc: Reports, consisting chiefly of tables and statistics, containing information on supply, demand and price research.
Ind/Abst BioBusiness (1990-); Trade Ind. ASAP [Full Txt.]; Trade Ind. Index [Full Txt.]; World Agric. Econ. Rural Sociol. Abstr.

LC S631 **ISSN** 0038-0687
DD 631.8 NZ
CCC
SOIL AND HEALTH. (SOIL AND HEALTH : JOURNAL OF THE NEW ZEALAND ORGANIC COMPOST SOCIETY.). [Soil and health]. **Added/Corp** New Zealand Organic Compost Society. Soil Association of New Zealand. **VFOAT** Soil and Health Journal. Vol. 24, No. 4 (Aug./Sept. 1965)-. Periodical. English. Six times a year (Jan., Mar., May, July, Sep., Nov.). $27.23. Soil and Health Association of New Zealand, PO Box 36, 170 Northcote, Auckland New Zealand. **Tel** 011 64 9 4806650. ***Continues*** *Compost Journal.*

LC S590 **ISSN** 0167-1987
DD 631.4 NE
CCC
CODEN SOTRD5
Pr Rev.
SOIL & TILLAGE RESEARCH. [Soil tillage res.]. **Added/Corp** International Soil Tillage Research Organisation. **VFOAT** Soil and Tillage Research. Vol. 1, No. 1 (Nov. 1980)-. Academic Scholarly Publication. English. Sixteen times a year (4 volumes). $1000.00. Elsevier Science Publishers BV, PO Box 211, 1000 AE Amsterdam Netherlands. **Tel** 011 31 20 4853641, 011 31 20 4853642, FAX 011 31 20 4853598. **ED** W B Voorhees and A Hadas. **Bk Rev. Ad Acc.** available on microfilm and microfiche from University Microfilms International (UMI); available on an online database from Elsevier Electronic Subscriptions (EES). Documents available from The Genuine Article, BIOSIS Document Express, CASDDS, Documents on Demand.
Desc: Concerned with the changes in the physical, chemical and biological parameters of the soil environment brought about by soil tillage and field traffic, their effects on crop establishment, root development and plant growth, and their interactions.
Ind/Abst AGRICOLA; Agric. Eng. Abstr. (19??-19??); BioBusiness; Biol. Abstr.; Chem. Abstr. (-1988); Cot. Trop. Fibr. Abstr. Bibliogr.; Curr. Aware. Biol. Sci., CABS; Curr. Cit.; Curr. Contents Agric. Biol. Environ. Sci.; Ecol. Abstr. (?-?); EMBASE; Environ. Abstr.; Environ. Period. Bibliogr.; Field Crop Abstr.; For. Abstr.; Geogr. Abstr. Phys. Geogr.; Geogr. Abstr. Human Geogr.; GeoRef; Grass. Forage Abstr.; Int. Dev. Abstr.; Irr. Drain. Abstr.; Maize Abstr.; Nematol. Abstr.; Life Sci. Collect.; Potato Abstr.; Res. Alert [Full Cov.]; Rice Abstr.; Sci. Cit. Index; SCISEARCH; Seed Abstr.; Soc. Sci. Cit. Index [Full Cov.]; Soils Fert.; Sorghum Mill. Abstr.; Soyabean Abstr.; Weed Abstr.; Wheat Barley Trit. Abstr.; World Agric. Econ. Rural Sociol. Abstr.

LC S623 .U42 **ISSN** 0199-9060
DD 631.4/973/05 US
CEASED
SOIL & WATER CONSERVATION NEWS. [Soil water conserv. news]. **Added/Corp** United States. Soil Conservation Service. **VFOAT** Soil and Water Conservation News; Soil Water Conservation. Vol. 1, No. 1 (April 1980)- Vol. 13 No. 4 (19??)-. Government Publication. English. Superintendent of Documents, US Government Printing Office, Washington DC 20402. **Tel** (202)275-3328, FAX (202)786-2377. available on microfilm and microfiche from University Microfilms International (UMI). Documents available from UMI Article Clearinghouse, Documents on Demand. ***Continues*** *Soil Conservation, 0038-0725.*
Desc: Contains articles on new developments and happenings in the field of soil and water conservation.
Ind/Abst Acad. Abstr. Full Text Elite; Acad. Abstr.; Acad. Search; AGRICOLA [Full Cov.]; Biol. Agric. Index; Biol. Dig.; Environ. Abstr.; EP Collect.; Gen. Sci. Source; GeoRef; Homework Help.; INFO-SOUTH Abstr.; Mag. Artic. Summar. Elite; Mag. Artic. Summar. Select; Mag. Artic. Summar. CD-ROM; Mag. Search; MasterFile FullTEXT 1000; MasterFile FullTEXT 350; MasterFile FullTEXT 650; MasterFile FullTEXT (July 1990-Dec. 1992) [Full Txt.]; Newsp. Period. Abstr. (1992-); OCLC; Plant Genet. Resour. Abstr.; Pub. Lib. FullTEXT; Telebase; Vocat. Search.

LC S590 .S577 **ISSN** 0038-0717
DD 631.4/05 UK
CCC
NLM W1 SO8862K **CODEN** SBIOAH
Pr Rev.
SOIL BIOLOGY & BIOCHEMISTRY. [Soil biol. biochem.]. **VAT** Soil Biology and Biochemistry. Vol. 1 (April 1969)-. Academic Scholarly Publication. English. Twelve times a year. $1145.00. Pergamon Press, An Imprint of Elsevier Science Ltd., The Boulevard, Langford Lane, Kidlington, Oxford OX5 1GB United Kingdom. **Tel** 011 44 1865 843000, 011 44 1865 843699, FAX 011 44 1865 843010. **(Subscription address:** Elsevier Science Ltd. / Oxford Fulfillment Centre, PO Box 800, Kidlington OX5 1DX United Kingdom. **Tel** 011 44 865 843355.**)** **ED** John S. Waid. Index Available, published separately, free-automatically sent. available on microfilm and microfiche from University Microfilms International (UMI); available on microfiche from the publisher; available on an online database from Elsevier Electronic Subscriptions (EES). Documents available from The Genuine Article, BIOSIS Document Express, CASDDS.
Desc: A forum for research on soil organisms, their biochemical activities and their influence on the soil environment and plant growth. Publishes original work on the quantitative, analytical and experimental aspects of such research.
Ind/Abst AgBiotech News Inf.; AGRICOLA [Select. Cov.]; Agrofor. Abstr. (1991-); Aqualine Abstr.; AQUAREF; Biocont. News Inf. (19??-19??); Biodeter. Abstr. (1991-); Biol. Agric. Index; Biol. Abstr.; Biol. Dig.; Biotechnol. Res. Abstr.; Chem. Abstr.; Coal Abstr.; Crop Physiol. Abstr.; Curr. Aware. Biol. Sci., CABS; Curr. Biotechnol.; Curr. Cit.; Curr. Contents Agric. Biol. Environ. Sci.; Ecol. Abstr.; Ecology Abstr.; EMBASE; Environ. Period. Bibliogr.; Field Crop Abstr.; For. Abstr.; Geogr. Abstr. Phys. Geogr.; Geol. Abstr.; Grass. Forage Abstr.; Int. Aerosp. Abstr.; Irr. Drain. Abstr.; Maize Abstr.; Microbiol. Abstr. Sect. B; Microbiol. Abstr. Sect. A; Microbiol. Abstr. Sect. C; Nematol. Abstr.; Life Sci. Collect.; PESTDOC; Plant Breed. Abstr.; Plant Genet. Resour. Abstr.; Plant Grow. Reg. Abstr.; Pollut. Abstr. Indexes; Res. Alert [Full Cov.]; Rev. Agric. Entomol.; Rice Abstr.; Sci. Cit. Index; SCISEARCH; Seed Abstr.; Soils Fert.; Sorghum Mill. Abstr.; Soyabean Abstr.; Sug. Indus. Abstr.; Weed Abstr.

LC S
DD 630 JA
SOIL MECHANICS & FOUNDATION ENGINEERING. JAPAN TSUCHI TO KISO. (19??)-. Japanese. Twelve times a year. $375.00. Doshitsu Kogakkai, (Japanese Soc. of Soil Mechanics & Foundation Engineering), 2-23 Kanda Awajicho, Chiyodaku Tokyo 101 Japan. **(Subscription address:** Japan Publications Trading Company Ltd., PO Box 5030, Tokyo International, Tokyo 100-31 Japan. **Tel** 011 81 3 3292 3753.**)**

LC S590 ISSN 0811-2622
DD 631.4 AT

SOIL NOTE. [Soil note]. Vol. 1 (1982)-. Periodical. English. Irregular. Soil & Water Conservation Australia, 9 The Crest, Killara New South Wales 2071 Australia. **Tel** 011 61 2 4843703, FAX 011 61 2 9806728.

LC S590 ISSN 0254-5616
DD 631.4 CC
CODEN SRREEC

SOIL RESEARCH REPORT. [Soil res. rep.]. **Added/Corp** Chung-kuo ko Hsueh Yuan. Nan-ching tu Jang Chiu so. No. 1 (1980)-. Monographic series. English. Documents available from BIOSIS Document Express.
Ind/Abst Biol. Abstr.; Soils Fert.

LC S590 .S6 ISSN 0038-075X
DD 631.4/05 US
CCC
CODEN SOSCAK

Pr Rev.
SOIL SCIENCE. [Soil sci.]. **Added/Corp** Rutgers University. Vol. 1 (Jan. 1916)-. Academic Scholarly Publication. English. Twelve times a year. $164.00. Williams & Wilkins Company, 428 East Preston Street, Baltimore MD 21202-3993. **Tel** (410)528-4000, (800)638-6423, FAX (410)528-8596, telex 87669. **(Subscription address:** Williams & Wilkins, PO Box 64380, Baltimore MD 21264. **Tel** 800 638-6423.) **ED** F. E. Bear. cum. index. **Ad Acc. Circ:** 2,450. Documents available from , The Genuine Article, BIOSIS Document Express, CASDDS, , Documents on Demand, Quick Copies.
Desc: Research articles of interest to soil testing bureaus, soil scientists, agronomists, and environmentalists.
Ind/Abst Abstr. Bull. Inst. Paper Chem.; Abstr. Bull. Inst. Pap. Sci. Tech.; AGRICOLA [Select. Cov.]; Agric. Eng. Abstr. (1991-); Agrofor. Abstr. (1991-); AQUAREF; Biogr. Index; Biol. Agric. Index; Biol. Abstr.; Can. Environ.; Chem. Abstr.; Chem. Titles; Coal Abstr.; Crop Physiol. Abstr.; Curr. Aware. Biol. Sci., CABS; Curr. Cit.; Curr. Contents Agric. Biol. Environ. Sci.; Curr. Geogr. Publ. (199?-); Ecol. Abstr.; EMBASE; Energy Inf. Abstr.; Energy Res. Abstr.; Environ. Abstr.; Environ. Period. Bibliogr.; Field Crop Abstr.; For. Abstr.; Geogr. Abstr. Phys. Geogr.; Geol. Abstr.; GeoRef; Geotech. Abstr.; Grass. Forage Abstr.; Hortic. Abstr.; Int. Aerosp. Abstr.; Irr. Drain. Abstr.; Maize Abstr.; Nematol. Abstr.; Nucl. Sci. Abstr.; Life Sci. Collect.; PESTDOC; Plant Grow. Reg. Abstr.; Res. Alert [Full Cov.]; Rev. Agric. Entomol.; Rice Abstr.; Sci. Cit. Index; SCISEARCH; Seed Abstr.; Sel. Water Resour. Abstr.; Soils Fert.; Sorghum Mill. Abstr.; Soyabean Abstr.; Stat. Theory Method Abstr. (1959-1963); Weed Abstr.; World Ceram. Abstr.

LC S590 ISSN 0038-0768
DD 631.4 JA
CODEN SSPNAW

Pr Rev.
SOIL SCIENCE AND PLANT NUTRITION (TOKYO). (SOIL SCIENCE AND PLANT NUTRITION.). [Soil sci. plant nutr.]. **Added/Corp** Nihon Dojo Hiryo Gakkai. Vol. 1 (July 1961)-. Academic Scholarly Publication. English. Four times a year. $110.00. Nippon Dojo Hiryo Gakkai, (Japanese Soc. of Soil Science & Plant Nutrition), 26-10-202 Hongo 6 Chome, Bunkyoku Tokyo 113 Japan. **(Subscription address:** Maruzen Company Ltd., PO Box 5050, Import & Export Department, Tokyo 100 31 Japan. **Tel** 011 81 3 32789224.) Documents available from The Genuine Article, BIOSIS Document Express, CASDDS. ***Continues*** *Soil and Plant Food.*
Ind/Abst AgBiotech News Inf.; AGRICOLA; Agrofor. Abstr. (1991-); BioBusiness; Biodeter. Abstr. (1991-); Biol. Abstr.; Chem. Abstr.; Crop Physiol. Abstr.; Curr. Aware. Biol. Sci., CABS; Curr. Cit.; Curr. Contents Agric. Biol. Environ. Sci.; Ecology Abstr.; EMBASE; Field Crop Abstr.; For. Abstr.; Geogr. Abstr. Phys. Geogr. (?-?); GeoRef; Grass. Forage Abstr.; Hortic. Abstr.; Irr. Drain. Abstr.; Maize Abstr.; Microbiol. Abstr. Sect. B; Microbiol. Abstr. Sect. A; Nematol. Abstr.; Ornamental Hort.; Life Sci. Collect.; Plant Breed. Abstr.; Potato Abstr.; Res. Alert [Full Cov.]; Rev. Agric. Entomol.; Rev. Plant Pathol.; Rice Abstr.; Sci. Cit. Index; SCISEARCH; Soils Fert.; Sorghum Mill. Abstr.; Soyabean Abstr.; Weed Abstr.; Wheat Barley Trit. Abstr.

LC S590
DD 631.4 ET
UDC 631.4

SOIL SCIENCE BULLETIN. (197?)-. Bulletin. English. Price varies per volume.

LC S590.S64 A13 ISSN 0361-5995
DD 631.4/973 US
CCC
CODEN SSSJD4

Pr Rev.
SOIL SCIENCE SOCIETY OF AMERICA JOURNAL. [Soil Sci. Soc. Am. j.]. **Main/Corp** Soil Science Society of America. **Added/Corp** Soil Science Society of America. Journal. Vol. 40 (Jan./Feb. 1976)-. Periodical. English. Six times a year. $117.00. American Society of Agronomy, 677 South Segoe Road, Madison WI 53711. **Tel** (608)273-8080, FAX (608)273-2021. **ED** Davie E. Kissel. Index available. cum. index. **Bk Rev. Ad Acc. Circ:** 8,100 (ctrl). Documents available from Article Express International, The Genuine Article, BIOSIS Document Express, UMI Article Clearinghouse, CASDDS, Documents on Demand. ***Continues*** *Proceedings - Soil Science Society of America, 0038-0776.*
Desc: Publishes papers on new developments in soil physics, mineralogy, chemistry, microbiology, fertility and plant nutrition, soil genesis and classification, soil and water management, forest and range soils, and fertilizer use and technology.
Ind/Abst Abstr. Bull. Inst. Pap. Sci. Tech.; AgBiotech News Inf.; AGRICOLA [Full Cov.]; Agric. Eng. Abstr. (1991-); Agrofor. Abstr. (1991-); AQUAREF; Bioeng. Abstr.; Biol. Agric. Index; Biol. Abstr.; Chem. Abstr.; Coal Abstr.; Crop Physiol. Abstr.; Curr. Cit.; Curr. Contents Agric. Biol. Environ. Sci.; Ecol. Abstr.; Ei Page One; EMBASE; Energy Res. Abstr. (April 1977-); Eng. Index Annu.; Environ. Abstr.; Environ. Period. Bibliogr.; Expand. Acad. Index (1992-); Field Crop Abstr.; For. Prod. Abstr. (1991-); For. Abstr.; Gen. Sci. Index; Geogr. Abstr. Phys. Geogr.; Geogr. Abstr. Human Geogr. (?-?); Geol. Abstr.; GeoRef; Grass. Forage Abstr.; Hortic. Abstr.; Int. Dev. Abstr.; Irr. Drain. Abstr.; Newsp. Period. Abstr. (1989-); Life Sci. Collect.; PESTDOC; Plant Breed. Abstr.; Plant Grow. Reg. Abstr.; Potato Abstr.; Res. Alert [Full Cov.]; Rev. Agric. Entomol.; Rev. Plant Pathol.; Rice Abstr.; Sci. Cit. Index; SCISEARCH; Seed Abstr.; Soils Fert.; Sorghum Mill. Abstr.; Soyabean Abstr.; Weed Abstr.; Wheat Barley Trit. Abstr.

LC S590 ISSN 0727-9078
DD 631.4 AT

SOIL SURVEY BULLETIN (NEW SOUTH WALES). (SOIL SURVEY BULLETIN.). [Soil surv. bull.]. **Added/Corp** New South Wales. Dept. of Agriculture. (1980)-. Bulletin. English. Irregular. Price varies per volume. ***Continues*** *Bulletin (New South Wales. Dept. of Agriculture. Chemists Branch. Soil Survey Unit), 0545-3631.*

LC S590 ISSN 0584-0554
DD 631 US

SOIL SURVEY HORIZONS. [Soil surv. horiz.]. **Added/Corp** North Central Soil Survey. Newsletter Publication Committee. Soil Survey Horizion Publication Corporation. Soil Science Society of America. Vol. 1 (Spring 1960)-. Periodical. English. Four times a year. $13.00. American Society of Agronomy, 677 South Segoe Road, Madison WI 53711. **Tel** (608)273-8080, FAX (608)273-2021. available on microfiche.
Ind/Abst AGRICOLA [Select. Cov.]; For. Abstr.; Maize Abstr.; Soils Fert.

LC S599.A1 S64 ISSN 0083-3320
DD 631.4/7/73 US
CODEN SSIRA9

SOIL SURVEY INVESTIGATIONS REPORT. [Soil surv. invest. rep.]. **Main/Corp** United States. Soil Conservation Service. **Added/Corp** United States. Soil Conservation Service. (1966)-. Government Publication. English. Irregular. Free on request. US Department of Agriculture / Information & Public Affairs Staff, PO Box 2890, Washington DC 20013. Documents available from BIOSIS Document Express.
Ind/Abst Biol. Abstr.; GeoRef.

LC S590 ISSN 0933-3630
DD 631.4 GW
CCC
CODEN SOTEEZ

SOIL TECHNOLOGY. [Soil technol.]. Vol. 1, No. 1 (March 1988)-. Academic Scholarly Publication. English (French, German and Spanish). Four times a year (1 volume). $241.00. Elsevier Science Publishers BV, PO Box 211, 1000 AE Amsterdam Netherlands. **Tel** 011 31 20 4853641, 011 31 20 4853642, FAX 011 31 20 4853598. **ED** D Gabriels. **Bk Rev. Ad Acc. Circ:** 500. available on an online database from Elsevier Electronic Subscriptions (EES). Documents available from The Genuine Article, BIOSIS Document Express, Documents on Demand.
Desc: Applied research and field applications on soil physics, soil mechanics, soil erosion and conservation, soil pollution, soil restoration, drainage and irrigation and land evaluation.
Ind/Abst AGRICOLA [Full Cov.]; Agric. Eng. Abstr. (1991-); Agrofor. Abstr.; Biol. Abstr.; Curr. Cit.; Curr. Contents Agric. Biol. Environ. Sci.; Ecol. Abstr. (?-?); Environ. Abstr.; Geogr. Abstr. Phys. Geogr.; Irr. Drain. Abstr.; Maize Abstr.; Potato Abstr.; Res. Alert [Select. Cov.]; Rice Abstr.; Soils Fert.; Soyabean Abstr.; Wheat Barley Trit. Abstr.

LC S590 .S67 ISSN 0266-0032
DD 631.4 UK
CODEN SUMAEU

Pr Rev.
SOIL USE AND MANAGEMENT. [Soil use manage.]. **Added/Corp** British Society of Soil Science. Vol. 1, No. 1 (March 1985)-. Academic Scholarly Publication. English. Four times a year. $170.00. CAB International Centre, Wallingford, Oxfordshire OX10 8DE United Kingdom. **Tel** 011 44 1491 832111, FAX 011 44 1491 833508, telex 847964 COMAGG G. Index available. **Ad Acc. Circ:** 1,050. available on microfilm and microfiche from University Microfilms International (UMI). Documents available from The Genuine Article, BIOSIS Document Express, CASDDS. ***Absorbed*** *Soil Survey and Land Evaluation.*
Desc: Publishes articles on the thematic issues of land management; contains occasional review articles on general topics such as acid rain.
Ind/Abst AgBiotech News Inf.; AGRICOLA [Full Cov.]; Biol. Abstr. (1985-); Chem. Abstr. (1985-); Curr. Aware. Biol. Sci., CABS; Curr. Cit.; Curr. Contents Agric. Biol. Environ. Sci.; Ecol. Abstr.; Environ. Period. Bibliogr.; For. Abstr.; Geogr. Abstr. Phys. Geogr.; Geogr. Abstr. Human Geogr.; GeoRef; Int. Dev. Abstr.; Irr. Drain. Abstr.; Maize Abstr.; Res. Alert [Select. Cov.]; Soils Fert.; Soyabean Abstr.; Weed Abstr.; Wheat Barley Trit. Abstr.

LC S590 .S67 ISSN 0038-0792
DD 631.405 UK
CODEN SOFEAT

SOILS AND FERTILIZERS. See Agriculture-Abstracting, Bibliographies and Statistics.

LC S599.6.T28 S64 ISSN 0370-9779
DD 631.4/951/249 CH
CODEN SFTWAM

SOILS AND FERTILIZERS IN TAIWAN. [Soils fert. Taiwan]. **Added/Corp** Tai-wan Sheng tu Jang fei Liao Hsueh hui. (1952)-. English. One time a year. Society of Soil and Fertilizer Sciences, c/o Department of Soil Science, National Chung Hsing University, Taichung Taiwan.
Desc: Information on soil, soil fertility and fertilizers.
Ind/Abst Field Crop Abstr.; Rev. Agric. Entomol.; Soils Fert.; Weed Abstr.

LC TD878 .S67
DD 628.5/5/05 US

•**SOILS & GROUNDWATER CLEANUP.** **VFOAT** Soils and Groundwater Cleanup. (1995)-. Periodical. English. Six times a year. $24.00. Group III Communications, 10229 East Independence Avenue, Independence MO 64053. **Tel** (816)254-8735. ***Continues*** *Soils (Independence, Mo.), 1056-0157.*

LC S ISSN 0375-5754
DD 630 AT

SOILS AND LAND USE SERIES. Main/Corp Australia. Commonwealth Scientific and Industrial Research Organization. Division of Soils. No. 1 (1949)-. Monographic series. English. Irregular. Price varies per volume. CSIRO Publications, PO Box 89, 314 Albert Street, East Melbourne Victoria 3002 Australia. **Tel** 011 61 3 4187333, 4187217, FAX 011 61 3 4190459, telex AA 30236.
Ind/Abst AESIS Q.

LC TD878 .S67 ISSN 1056-0157
DD 628.5/5/05 US
TITLE CHANGE

SOILS (INDEPENDENCE, MO.). (SOILS : ANALYSIS, MONITORING, REMEDIATION.). [Soils]. **VFOAT** Soils Magazine. (19??)-(1995). Periodical. English. Group III Communications, 10229 East Independence Avenue, Independence MO 64053. **Tel** (816)254-8735. Documents available from Documents on Demand. ***Continued by*** *Soil & Groundwater Cleanup.*
Ind/Abst Environ. Abstr.; Field Crop Abstr.; Irr. Drain. Abstr.; Rice Abstr.; Soils Fert.

LC S
DD 630 AT

SOILS NEWS. (19??)-. English. Four times a year. 9.04Aus$. Australian Society of Soil Science Inc., CIIRO Division of Soil PMB 2, Glen Osmond SA 5064 Australia. **Tel** 011 61 09 222 3437, FAX 011 61 8 338 1636.

LC S590 ISSN 1182-7858
DD 631.4/97123 CN

SOILUTIONS (EDMONTON). (SOILUTIONS.). [SOILutions]. **Added/Corp** Alberta. Soils Branch. Vol. 1, No. 1 (July/Aug. 1990)-. Periodical. English. Four times a year.

LC S590 ISSN 0584-0821
DD 631.4 BL
CODEN SOLOAL

SOLO, O. Added/Corp Centro Academico "Luiz de Queiroz". (19??)-. Academic Scholarly Publication. Portuguese. Two times a year. Centro Academico "Luis de Queiroz", Rua Voluntarios de Piracicaba 429, 13400 Piracicaba SP Brazil. **Bk Rev. Ad Acc. Circ:** 26,000. Documents available from BIOSIS Document Express, CASDDS.
Ind/Abst Biol. Abstr. (?-1984); Chem. Abstr.

LC S590 ISSN 0038-1217
DD 631.4 FR

SOLS. VFOAT Soils. Vol. 1- (1-) 1962-. Periodical. Multiple languages (English and French). Editions Sols Soils, 16 Avenue Sadi Carnot, 91160 Longjumeau France.

LC SB354 ISSN 0704-5859
DD 634/.5/062713 CN

SONG NEWS. Main/Corp Society of Ontario Nut Growers. **VAT** Society of Ontario Nut Growers News. (Fall 1972)-. Periodical. English. Two times a year (January and July). comes with Society of Ontario Nut Growers membership. Society of Ontario Nut Growers, R R 3, Niagara-on-the-Lake Ontario L0S 1J0 Canada. **Tel** (905)935-9773. **ED** Douglas Campbell (editor's phone:

(905)262-4927). **Ad Acc. Circ:** 400.
Desc: Promotion of nut tree growing; nut production and marketing of nut products and nut tree timber.

LC S **ISSN** 0584-1321
DD 630 US
Pr Rev.
SORGHUM NEWSLETTER. See Agriculture-Feed Grain and Milling.

LC SB191.S7 S67
DD 633.1 BL
UDC 633.174(81)
SORGO, UMA ALTERNATIVA ECONOMICA. Vol. 1 (1974)-. Portuguese. One time a year. Fundacao de Economia e Estatistica, Rua Duque de Caixias 1691, 90010 Porto Alegre, Rio Grande do Sul Brazil. **Tel** 0512-259455, FAX 0512-25006, telex 0515042.

LC S590 **ISSN** 0257-1862
DD 631.4 SA
CCC
CODEN SAJSEV
SOUTH AFRICA JOURNAL OF PLANT AND SOIL. [S. Afr. j. plant soil]. **Added/Corp** Foundation for Education, Science, and Technology (South Africa). Bureau for Scientific Publications. South African Society of Crop Production. Soil Science Society of South Africa. Southern African Weed Science Society. **VFOAT** Suid-Afrikaanse Tydskrif Vir Plant en Grond; Plant and Soil; Plant en Grond. Vol. 1, No. 1 (Feb. 1984)-. Academic Scholarly Publication. English (Afrikaans). Four times a year. $31.61. Foundation for Education Science & Technology, PO Box 1758, Pretoria 0001 South Africa. **Tel** 011 27 12 3226404, FAX 011 27 12 3207803. Documents available from CASDDS. ***Absorbed*** *Agroplantae, 0302-7139.*
Ind/Abst AGRICOLA [Full Cov.]; Chem. Abstr. (1984-); Cot. Trop. Fibr. Abstr. Bibliogr.; Crop Physiol. Abstr.; Curr. Cit.; Food Sci. Technol. Abstr.; Hortic. Abstr.; Irr. Drain. Abstr.; Maize Abstr.; Ornamental Hort. (1991-); Life Sci. Collect.; PESTDOC; Plant Breed. Abstr.; Plant Genet. Resour. Abstr.; Plant Grow. Reg. Abstr.; Pollut. Abstr. Indexes; Rev. Plant Pathol.; Seed Abstr.; Soils Fert.; Sorghum Mill. Abstr.; Soyabean Abstr.; Weed Abstr.

LC SB215 .S6 **ISSN** 0038-2728
DD 633.6 SA
SOUTH AFRICAN SUGAR JOURNAL, THE. [S. Afr. sugar j.]. **VFOAT** S.A. Sugar Journal. Vol. 1, (1917)-. Periodical. English. Twelve times a year. $41.00. South African Sugar Journal, PO Box 1209, Durban 4000 Natal South Africa. **Tel** (031)3056161, FAX (031)3044939, telex 622215. **ED** Glen R. Dewey. Index available. **Bk Rev. Ad Acc. Circ:** 4,000 (ctrl).
Desc: This journal covers a wide spectrum of subjects devoted entirely to sugar affairs. Technical and semitechnical articles related to the agricultural production of sugarcane and the factory production of raw and refined sugar.
Ind/Abst AGRICOLA; Field Crop Abstr.; Hortic. Abstr.; Irr. Drain. Abstr.; Rev. Agric. Entomol.; Soils Fert.; Sug. Indus. Abstr.; Weed Abstr.; World Agric. Econ. Rural Sociol. Abstr.

LC S **ISSN** 0038-3694
DD 630 US
UDC 633.852.52(75); 634.58(75)
SOUTHEASTERN PEANUT FARMER. [Southeast. peanut farmer]. Periodical. English. Ten times a year (monthly except Oct. and Dec.). $1.00. Georgia Peanut Commission, PO Box 706, Tifton GA 31793. **Tel** (912)386-3470, FAX (912)386-3501. **ED** Harris C Blackwood. **Ad Acc. Circ:** 17,500 (ctrl).
Ind/Abst AGRICOLA.

LC S
DD 630 US
SOUTHWEST REFERENCE .... See Agriculture-Livestock.

LC S
DD 630 US
SOUTHWESTERN PEANUT GROWERS NEWS. Added/Corp Southwestern Peanut Growers' Association. **VFOAT** SWPGA News; S.W.P.G.A. News. **VAT** Southwestern Peanut Growers' Association News. (19??)-. Periodical. English. Four times a year. $3.00. Southwestern Peanut Growers Association, PO Box 338, Gorman TX 76454. **Tel** (817)734-2222.

LC HD9235.S62 U678 **ISSN** 0275-4509
DD 338.4/7664726 US
SOYA BLUEBOOK. [Soya blueb.]. **Added/Corp** American Soybean Association. (1980)-. English. One time a year (July). $58.00. Soyatech Inc., 318 Main Street, Bar Harbor ME 04609. **Tel** (207)288-4969, (800)424-SOYA, FAX (207)288-5264. **ED** Peter Golbtz. **Bk Rev**, (Qty: 10 per year). **Ad Acc, Adv Mgr:** Sharyn Kingma. **Circ:** 2,500. available on microfiche from CIS / Congressional Information Service, Inc. ***Continues*** *Soybean Digest Blue Book.*
Ind/Abst Stat. Ref. Index.

LC SB205.S7 A18 **ISSN** 0038-6014
DD 633.3405 US
SOYBEAN DIGEST. [Soybean dig.]. **Added/Corp** American Soybean Association. (Nov. 1940)-. Periodical. English. Irregular. $20.00. American Soybean Association, 540 Maryville Ctr. Dr., Suite 390, St. Louis MO 63141. **Tel** (314)576-1770, FAX (314)576-2786. **Ad Acc. Circ:** 200,000 (ctrl). available on microfilm and microfiche from University Microfilms International (UMI). ***Absorbed*** *Proceedings. Annual Meeting - American Soybean Association, 0097-2371.*
Desc: Production, marketing and management information for soybean growers.

LC S **ISSN** 1054-2116
DD 631 US
SOYBEAN GENETICS NEWSLETTER. [Soyb. genet. newsl.]. **Added/Corp** United States. Agricultural Research Service. Iowa State University. Dept. of Agronomy. Iowa State University. Dept. of Genetics. Vol. 1, (April, 1974)-. Newsletter. English. One time a year. $15.00. Iowa State University / Agronomy Department, G301, C/O Reid Palmer, Ames IA 50011. **Tel** (515)294-7378, FAX (515)294-2299. **ED** Reid G. Palmer. Index available. **Circ:** 500.
Desc: Serves as a means of communication at the international level, with emphasis on genetics and breeding of the soybean and immediate relatives. Areas include biochemistry, entomology, pathology, physiology, and taxonomy.
Ind/Abst AgBiotech News Inf.; Crop Physiol. Abstr.; Field Crop Abstr.; Irr. Drain. Abstr.; Maize Abstr.; Nematol. Abstr.; Plant Breed. Abstr.; Plant Genet. Resour. Abstr.; Plant Grow. Reg. Abstr.; Rev. Agric. Entomol.; Rev. Plant Pathol.; Rice Abstr.; Seed Abstr.; Soils Fert.; Soyabean Abstr.

LC S590 **ISSN** 0111-9184
DD 631.4 NZ
Pr Rev.
SPECIAL PUBLICATION / AGRONOMY SOCIETY OF NEW ZEALAND. [Spec. publ. - Agron. Soc. N.Z.]. **Added/Corp** Agronomy Society of New Zealand. New Zealand. Dept. of Scientific and Industrial Research. Crop Research Division. No. 1 (1982)-. English. Irregular. $20.00 (per copy). Agronomy Society of New Zealand, Private Bag 4704, Christchurch New Zealand. **Tel** 011 64 3 3256400, FAX 011 64 3 3252074. **Circ:** 225.
Ind/Abst AGRICOLA [Full Cov.].

LC S **ISSN** 0277-4305
DD 630 US
CODEN SPICDE
SPECIAL PUBLICATION IFDC. [Spec. publ. IFDC]. **Added/Corp** International Fertilizer Development Center. **VAT** Special Publication International Fertilizer Development Center. (19??)-. Periodical. English.
Ind/Abst Soils Fert.

LC S590 **ISSN** 1063-2565
DD 631 US
CCC
CODEN SSAPAV
SSSA SPECIAL PUBLICATION. [SSSA spec. publ.]. **Added/Corp** Soil Science Society of America. **VAT** Soil Science Society of America Special Publication. No. 8 (1979)-. Monographic series. English. Irregular. Price varies per volume. Soil Science Society of America, 677 South Segoe Road, Madison WI 53711. **Tel** (608)273-8080, FAX (608)273-2021. ***Continues*** *SSSA Special Publication Series, 0081-1904.*
Desc: Publishes papers on new developments in soil physics, mineralogy chemistry, microbiology, fertility and plant nutrition, soil genesis and classification, soil and water management, forest and range soils, and fertilizer use and technology.
Ind/Abst Curr. Cit.

LC HB241 **ISSN** 0279-3148
DD 338 US
STAPLREVIEW. [Staplreview]. **Added/Corp** Staple Cotton Cooperative Association. **VFOAT** Stapl Review. **VAT** Stapl Review. Vol. 1 (Sept. 1976)-. English. Four times a year. Free on request. Staple Cotton, PO Box 547, Greenwood MS 38930. **Tel** (601)453-6231. ***Continues*** *Staple Cotton Review, 0038-9838.*

LC S245 .E22 **ISSN** 0106-2581
DD 630 DK
STATENS PLANTEAVLSUDVALG BERETNING. Main/Corp Denmark. Statens Planteavlsudvalg. **VFOAT** Beretning. (1979)-. Danish. One time a year. ***Continues*** *Denmark. Statens Planteavlsudvalg. Beretning Fra Statens Planteavlsudvalg For Finansaaret ... .*
Ind/Abst Plant Breed. Abstr.

LC HD2082 .S78
DD 630 IO
STATISTIK PERKEBUNAN BESAR. 1982-. Indonesian. One time a year. Biro Pusat Statistik / Central Bureau of Statistics, 8 Jalan Dr. Sutomo No. 8, Box 3, Jakarta Pusat 10710 Indonesia. **Tel** 011 62 21 372808, 011 62 21 374908 ext.342. **Bk Rev. Ad Acc.** ctrl circ.

LC SB176.I5 S8
DD 630 IO
STATISTIK TANAMAN BAHAN MAKANAN. See Agriculture-Abstracting, Bibliographies and Statistics.

LC S **ISSN** 1382-0338
DD 630 NE
UDC 633+635.9
STATISTISCH BERICHT. [Stat. ber. - Prod.schap Siergewassen]. (1983)-. Periodical. Dutch. Twelve times a year. $96.96. PVS, Postbus 93099, 2509 AB Den Haag Netherlands. **Tel** 011 31 70 3041234, FAX 011 31 70 3838540.

LC S590 **ISSN** 0111-977X
DD 631.4 NZ
STREAMLAND. (1982)-. Periodical. English. Twelve times a year. Ministry of Works and Development, Water and Soil Division, Box 12041, Wellington North New Zealand.

LC SB111A2 S2 **ISSN** 0207-9224
DD 631.58 RU
CODEN SUKUA8
SUBTROPICHESKIE KULTURY. [Subtrop. kult.]. **Added/Corp** Makharadze, Russia. Vsesoiuznyi Nauchnoissledovatelskii Institut Chaia i Subtropicheskikh Kultur. No. 1 (1936)-. Academic Scholarly Publication. Multiple languages (Russian; summaries and/or abstracts in English; table of contents in English). Four times a year. $20.00. **(Subscription address:** Victor Kamkin, 4956 Boiling Brook Parkway, Rockville MD 20852. **Tel** (301)881-5973.) Documents available from BIOSIS Document Express, CASDDS.
Ind/Abst AGRICOLA; Agric. Eng. Abstr.; Agrofor. Abstr. (19??-19??); Biol. Abstr. (?-1986); Chem. Abstr.; Crop Physiol. Abstr.; For. Abstr.; Hortic. Abstr.; Ornamental Hort. (1991-); Plant Breed. Abstr.; Plant Genet. Resour. Abstr.; Plant Grow. Reg. Abstr.; Postharvest News Inf.; Rev. Plant Pathol.; Soils Fert.

LC S **ISSN** 0851-2582
DD 630 MR
UDC 664.11
SUCRERIE MAGHREBINE. [Sucr. maghreb.]. (1972)-. Periodical. French. Four times a year.
Ind/Abst Field Crop Abstr.; Hortic. Abstr.; Nutr. Abstr. Rev., Ser. A, Hum. Exp.; Sug. Indus. Abstr.

LC S596.7 .S84 **ISSN** 1130-796X
DD 631.4 SP
CCC
CEASED
SUELO Y PLANTA. [Suelo planta]. **Added/Corp** Consejo Superior de Investigaciones Cientificas (Spain). Vol. 1, No. 1 (1991)-(1993). Periodical. Spanish (English). Consejo Superior Investigacion Cientificas / CSIC, Vitruvio 8, 28006 Madrid Spain. **Tel** 011 34 1 5612833, FAX 011 34 1 4113077, telex 42182. ***Continues*** *Anales de Edafologia y Agrobiologia, 0365-1797.*
Ind/Abst Plant Genet. Resour. Abstr.

LC S591 .A75
DD 631.4/08 AG
UDC 633.413
SUELOS. Spanish. Instituto Nacional de Tecnologia Agropecuaria, Centro de Investigaciones de Recursos Naturales, Cervino 3101, Buenos Aires Argentina. ***Continues*** *Argentine Republic. Instituto de Suelos y Agrotecnia. Publicacion.*

LC SB215
DD 664.1 US
UDC 633.61
SUGAR BEET JOURNAL. Vol. 1 (Oct. 1935)-. Periodical. English. Twelve times a year. Farmers & Manufacturers Beet Sugar Association, 4800 Fashion Square Boulevard, Suite 740, Saginaw MI 48603.

LC SB226 .S83 **ISSN** 0265-7406
DD 633.6/1/05 UK
CODEN SUCAEE
SUGAR CANE (1983). (SUGAR CANE.). [Sugar cane]. Issue No. 1 (May/June 1983)-. Academic Scholarly Publication. English. Six times a year. $128.34. International Media Ltd., PO Box 26, Port Talbot, W Glamorgan SA13 1NX United Kingdom. **Tel** 011 44 639 887498, FAX 011 44 639 899830. **ED** Desmond Leighton. **Bk Rev. Ad Acc. Circ:** 2,000. ***Continues in part*** *International Sugar Journal, 0020-8841.*
Desc: Articles and abstracts on the growing of sugar cane, harvesting, breeding of varieties, pest and disease control and botany.
Ind/Abst Agric. Eng. Abstr. (1991-); Crop Physiol. Abstr.; EMBASE; Field Crop Abstr.; Hortic. Abstr.; Irr. Drain. Abstr.; Life Sci. Collect.; Plant Breed. Abstr.; Rev. Agric. Entomol.; Rev. Plant Pathol.; Sug. Indus. Abstr.

LC TP375 .T37 **ISSN** 0957-5022
DD 016.664/12 UK
SUGAR INDUSTRY ABSTRACTS. See Agriculture-Abstracting, Bibliographies and Statistics.

LC HD9101 .S92 **ISSN** 0039-4734
DD 338.4/7/6641 US
CODEN SUJOAJ

SUGAR JOURNAL. [Sugar j.]. Vol. 1 (June 1938)-. Academic Scholarly Publication. English. Twelve times a year. $33.00. Kriedt Enterprises LTD, 129 South Cortez Street, New Orleans LA 70119. **Tel** (504)482-3914, FAX (504)482-4205. **ED** W. H. Flanagan. cum. index (Dec. Issue). **Bk Rev. Ad Acc. Circ:** 3,300 (ctrl). Documents available from BIOSIS Document Express, CASDDS, Documents on Demand. ***Supersedes*** *Rice and Sugar Journal.*
Desc: Contains technical articles on topics of special interests: factory operations, agricultural production, experimental field programs, disease control and similar subjects of special interest.
Ind/Abst AGRICOLA; Biol. Abstr.; Chem. Abstr. (1938-1983); EMBASE; Energy Inf. Abstr.; Environ. Abstr.; Food Sci. Technol. Abstr.; Life Sci. Collect.; PESTDOC.

LC SB215 **ISSN** 0049-2477
DD 633.6 PH
UDC 633.61
SUSPENDED

SUGAR NEWS. Vol. 1 (Sept. 1919)-Suspended (Jan. 1985). Periodical. English. Twelve times a year. $15.00. Sugar News Press, PO Box 514, Manila Philippines.
Ind/Abst Philip. Sci. Technol. Abstr.

LC HD1401 **ISSN** 0229-737X
DD 338.1/7361/05 CN

SUGAR WORLD. (SUGAR WORLD : A NEWSLETTER ON ISSUES OF CONCERN TO SUGAR WORKER.). [Sugar world]. **Added/Corp** Gatt-Fly. No. 1 (Oct. 1, 1977)-. Newsletter. English (Spanish). Six times a year (Feb., Apr., Jun., Aug., Oct., Dec.). ICCSASW, 11 Madison Avenue, Toronto Ontario M5R 2S2 Canada. **Tel** (416)597-8454. Index available (free). cum. index. **Bk Rev**. ctrl circ.
Desc: A newsletter on issues of concern to sugar workers.
Ind/Abst Hum. Rights Intern. Rep.

LC SB188 **ISSN** 0039-4750
DD 633 US

SUGARBEET GROWER, THE. Added/Corp Western Sugarbeet Growers Association. Vol. 1 (May 1963)-. Trade Publication. English. Six times a year (Jan., Feb., Mar., Apr., May, Aug.). $9.00. Sugar Publications, Gilmore Sugar Manual Division, 503 Broadway, Fargo ND 58102. **Tel** (701)237-5747, FAX (701)235-0140. **ED** Donald Lilleboe. **Bk Rev**, (Qty: 2-3). **Ad Acc. Circ:** 13,000 (ctrl).
Desc: Information for the sugarbeet growers in the US and Canada, concentrating on legislation, industry news, and growing practices. Feature articles on growers and officials.
Ind/Abst AGRICOLA.

LC S **ISSN** 0039-4777
DD 630 PH
UDC 338.516:633.1(73)
CEASED

SUGARLAND. Vol. 1 (Feb. 1964)-(19??). Periodical. English. Sugarland Publications, Sugar Center Building, Room 207 209, Bacolod City Philippines. **Tel** 011 63 2 22643. **Bk Rev. Ad Acc. Circ:** 3,000 (ctrl).
Desc: Editorial, ideas and comments on all aspects of the sugarcane industry including production, fertilization, herbicides, farm labor, irrigation, soil, molasses, sugar trade, cane varieties, by-products, etc.
Ind/Abst Philip. Sci. Technol. Abstr.

LC S **ISSN** 0160-0680
DD 630 US
CODEN SUAGDL

SULPHUR IN AGRICULTURE. [Sulphur agric.]. Vol. 1 (1977)-. Academic Scholarly Publication. English. One time a year. Free (qualified personnel). Sulphur Institute, 1140 Connecticut Avenue NW, Washington DC 20036. **Tel** (202)331-9660, FAX (202)293-2940. **ED** Robert Morris, Robert Durieux, Donald Messick, Eliza Haskins. **Bk Rev. Circ:** 3,000 (ctrl). Documents available from CASDDS. ***Supersedes*** *Sulphur Institute Journal, 0039-4904.*
Desc: Articles pertaining to the role of sulphur as a nutrient, results of research into this, and quantitative nature of potential need for sulphur in crop applications.
Ind/Abst Chem. Abstr. (1977-1983); Field Crop Abstr.; Grass. Forage Abstr.; Maize Abstr.; Rice Abstr.; Soils Fert.

LC S478 **ISSN** 1037-5678
DD 630.9941 AT

SUMMARY OF CROPS, WESTERN AUSTRALIA. See Agriculture-Abstracting, Bibliographies and Statistics.

LC HD9031 .U16a **ISSN** 0277-2191
DD 633.1/072073 US

SUMMARY PROGRESS REPORT - U.S. GRAIN MARKETING RESEARCH LABORATORY. (SUMMARY PROGRESS REPORT / U.S. GRAIN MARKETING RESEARCH LABORATORY.). [Summ. prog. rep. - U.S. Grain Mark. Res. Lab.]. **Main/Corp** U.S. Grain Marketing Research Laboratory. (19??)-. English. One time a year. US Grain Marketing Research Laboratory, 1515 College Avenue, Manhattan KS 66502.

LC SB354 **ISSN** 0899-8809
DD 634 US

SUN-DIAMOND GROWER. [Sun-Diam. grow.]. **VFOAT** Sun Diamond Grower. Vol. 1, No. 1 (Oct./Nov. 1980)-. Trade Publication. English. Four times a year. $12.00 US; $45.00 other. Sun-Diamond Growers of California, 1050 South Diamond Street, Stockton CA 95205. **ED** Sandra J McBride. **Ad Acc. Circ:** 10,000 (ctrl). ***Continues*** *Diamond/Sunsweet News, 0899-8876.*
Desc: Key resource for California's agribusiness community, providing current information about production techniques and industry affairs for the walnut, hazelnut, raisin grapes, prune and fig industries.

LC S **ISSN** 0192-8988
DD 630 US

SUNFLOWER (FARGO), THE. (THE SUNFLOWER.). **Added/Corp** National Sunflower Association. Sunflower Association of America. Vol. 1 (Aug. 1975)-. Trade Publication. English. Six times a year. $9.00. National Sunflower Association, 4023 State Street, Bismarck ND 58501. **Tel** (701)328-5100, FAX (701)328-5101. **ED** Larry Kleingartner. Index available. cum. index. **Ad Acc. Circ:** 20,000.
Desc: Articles, mainly oriented toward sunflower growers, pertaining to the production, marketing and utilization of this crop.

LC S159 **ISSN** 0381-078X
DD 338.1/7/3009714 CN
UDC 332.334.4:63(714)

SUPERFICIE DES PRINCIPALES GRANDES CULTURES. VFOAT Area of the Principal Field Crops. English (French). One time a year. Bureau of Statistics / Quebec, Publications, 117 rue Saint Andre, Quebec Quebec G1K 3Y3 Canada. **Tel** (418)691-2401, (800)463-4090.

LC SB113 **ISSN** 0039-6990
DD 631.521 SW
UDC 63

SVERIGES UTSADESFORENINGS TIDSKRIFT. [Sver. utsadesforen. tidskr.]. **Main/Corp** Sveriges Utsadesforening. **VFOAT** Journal of the Swedish Seed Association. Vol. 1 (1891)-. Periodical. Swedish (English). Four times a year. $12.82. Sveriges Utsadesfoerening, Swedish Seed Association, S-268 00 Svaloev Sweden. **Tel** 011 46 418 62510, FAX 011 46 418 62383, telex 72476 SVALOEF S. **ED** A Hagberg. Index available. cum. index. **Circ:** 1,300 (ctrl).
Desc: Concerns plant breeding and husbandry.
Ind/Abst AgBiotech News Inf.; AGRICOLA; Field Crop Abstr.; Hortic. Abstr.; Maize Abstr.; Nematol. Abstr.; Plant Breed. Abstr.; Potato Abstr.; Rev. Agric. Entomol.; Rev. Plant Pathol.; Rice Abstr.; Seed Abstr.; Weed Abstr.; Wheat Barley Trit. Abstr.

LC TA775 .S78
DD 338.4/762415/0948505 SW

SWEDISH FOUNDATION. (19??)-. English. Every 2 years. Gem International AB, Sagvagen 12, S-184 40 Akersberga Sweden.

LC SB396.5 .V54 **ISSN** 0230-2241
DD 634 HU

SZOLOTERMEZTESES BORASZAT. (VINOGRADARSTVO I VINODELIE = SZOLOTERMEZTESES BORASZAT.). [Szolotermezt. borasz.]. **Added/Corp** Ukraine. Ministerstvo Silskoho Hospodarstva. No. 7 (1969)-. Russian. Four times a year. University of Horticulture, Research Institute for Viticulture and Enology, PO Box 25, Kisfai 182, Kecskemet 6000 Hungary. ***Continues*** *Vinogradarstvo.*
Ind/Abst AGRICOLA.

LC S
DD 630 CC

TA TOU KO HSUEH. VFOAT Soybean Science. (1982)-. Periodical. Chinese. Four times a year.
Ind/Abst Biocont. News Inf.; Crop Physiol. Abstr.; Field Crop Abstr.; Nematol. Abstr.; Plant Genet. Resour. Abstr.; Rev. Agric. Entomol.; Seed Abstr.

LC SB229.T25 **ISSN** 0372-2414
DD 338.1/7361/0951249 CH
CODEN TTYYBR

TAI-WAN TANG YEH YEN CHIU SOYYEN CHIU HUI PAO. (YEN CHIU HUI PAO = REPORT OF THE TAIWAN SUGAR RESEARCH INSTITUTE.). [Tai-wan tang yeh yen chiu so yen chiu hui pao]. **Added/Corp** Tai-wan Tang Yeh Yen Chiu So. **VFOAT** Report of the Taiwan Sugar Research Institute; Taiwan Tang Yeh Yen Chiu So Yen Chiu Hui Pao. (1973)-. Academic Scholarly Publication. English (Chinese). Four times a year. Taiwan Sugar Research Institute, 54 Sheng Chan Road, Tainan Taiwan. Documents available from BIOSIS Document Express, CASDDS. ***Continues*** *Yen Chiu Hui Pao (Taiwan Tang Yeh Shih Yen So).*
Ind/Abst AGRICOLA; Agric. Eng. Abstr.; Biol. Abstr.; Chem. Abstr.; EMBASE; Field Crop Abstr.; Hortic. Abstr.; Soils Fert.

LC HD9116.T3 T33 **ISSN** 0492-1712
DD 338.1/7/360951249 CH
CODEN TWSUA5

TAIWAN SUGAR. [Taiwan sugar]. (1954)-. Academic Scholarly Publication. English. Six times a year. $22.00. Taiwan Sugar Corporation, 25 Pao Ching Road/Room 606, Taipei 100 Taiwan. **Tel** 011 886 2 3110521. Documents available from CASDDS.
Ind/Abst AgBiotech News Inf.; AGRICOLA [Select. Cov.]; Chem. Abstr.; Food Sci. Technol. Abstr.; Maize Abstr.; Plant Breed. Abstr.; Rev. Plant Pathol.; Sug. Indus. Abstr.; Weed Abstr.

LC SB272.K45 T38
DD 633.7/2/096762 KE
UDC 633.72

TEA. Vol. 1, No. 1 (July 1980)-. Periodical. English. Two times a year. Tea Board of Kenya, PO Box 820, Kericho Kenya. ***Continues*** *Tea in East Africa, 0377-6034.*
Ind/Abst Agrofor. Abstr.; Biocont. News Inf.; Crop Physiol. Abstr.; Food Sci. Technol. Abstr.; Maize Abstr.; Plant Breed. Abstr.; Weed Abstr.

LC S590 **ISSN** 0710-9466
DD 631.4 CN
UDC 332.33; 631.4

TECH. MEMO. - UNIVERSITY OF GUELPH. DEPARTMENT OF LAND RESOURCE SCIENCE. (TECH. MEMO.). [Tech. memo - Univ. Guelph, Dep. Lnad Resour. Sci.]. **Added/Corp** Ontario Agricultural College. Dept. of Land Resource Science. **VAT** Tech. Memo. - University of Guelph. Ontario Agricultural College. Department of Land Resource Science. English. Tech Memo University of Guelph Science, Guelph Ontario N1G 2W1 Canada. **Tel** (518)824-4120, telex 069-56645. Index available. **Circ:** 60 (ctrl).
Desc: Research documents, Data Depository, and specialized research work.

LC S631 **ISSN** 0379-7627
DD 631.8 CH
CODEN APFBAX

TECHNICAL BULLETIN - ASPAC, FOOD & FERTILIZER TECHNOLOGY CENTER. (TECHNICAL BULLETIN - FOOD & FERTILIZER TECHNOLOGY CENTER.). [Tech. bull. - ASPAC Food Fertil. Tech. Cent.]. **Main/Corp** Asian and Pacific Council. Food & Fertilizer Technology Center. (1970)-. Bulletin. English. Irregular. Food and Fertilizer Technology Center for the Asian and Pacific Region, Agriculture Building, 114 Wen Chow Street, PO Box 22-149, Taipei Taiwan. Documents available from CASDDS.
Ind/Abst AGRICOLA; Chem. Abstr. (1970-1982); Crop Physiol. Abstr.; Field Crop Abstr.; For. Abstr.; Hortic. Abstr.; Plant Grow. Reg. Abstr.; Soils Fert.; Weed Abstr.

LC S590 .W13 **ISSN** 0074-042X
DD 631 NE
CODEN ILWBA8

TECHNICAL BULLETIN - INSTITUTE FOR LAND AND WATER MANAGEMENT RESEARCH. [Tech. bull. - Inst. Land Water Manage. Res.]. **Main/Corp** Instituut voor Cultuurtechniek en Waterhuishouding. (1958)-. Bulletin. English (summaries and/or abstracts in French). Irregular. Price varies per volume. Institute for Land and Water Management Research (ICW), PO Box 35, 6700 AA Wageningen The Netherlands. **Tel** 011 31 8370 19100, FAX 011 31 8370 11524, telex 75230 VISI N. **ED** Andre F.M. Schoots. cum. index. **Circ:** 1,600 (ctrl).
Desc: Covers water management, plant-soil-water relationships, soil technology, groundwater and surface water quality, land layout and farm economics, outdoor recreation, and planning rural areas.
Ind/Abst EMBASE; GeoRef.

LC SB761 **ISSN** 1014-3351
DD 635.97 TH

TECHNICAL DOCUMENT / FAO REGIONAL OFFICE FOR ASIA AND THE PACIFIC. ASIA AND PACIFIC PLANT PROTECTION COMMISSION. (TECHNICAL DOCUMENT.). (1983)-. Monographic series. English. Price varies per volume. FAO Regional Office for Asia and the Pacific, Maliwan Mansion/Phra Atit Road, Bangkok 10200 Thailand. ***Continues*** *Technical Document (Food and Agriculture Organization of the United Nations. Plant Protection Committee for the South East Asia and Pacific Region), 0428-9765.*
Ind/Abst AGRICOLA; Cot. Trop. Fibr. Abstr. Bibliogr.; Rev. Plant Pathol.; Soyabean Abstr.

LC SB110
DD 631.586 SY
CODEN TMIAEX

TECHNICAL MANUAL. Added/Corp International Center for Agricultural Research in the Dry Areas. **VFOAT** ICARDA Technical Manual. **VAT** International Center for Agricultural Research in the Dry Areas Technical Manual. (19??)-. Monographic series. English. International Center for Agricultural Research in the Dry Areas, PO Box 5466, Aleppo Syria. **Tel** 213433, telex 331206.
Ind/Abst Sorghum Mill. Abstr.

LC S590
DD 631.4 AT
CODEN TMCREK

TECHNICAL MEMORANDUM. **Added/Corp** Institute of Natural Resources and Environment (Australia). Division of Water Resources. (198?)-. Monographic series. English. Price varies per volume. CSIRO Publications, PO Box 89, 314 Albert Street, East Melborne Victoria 3002 Australia. **Tel** 011 61 3 4187333, 4187217, FAX 011 61 3 4190459, telex AA 30236. ***Continues*** *Technical Memorandum (Institute of Natural Resources and Environment (Australia). Division of Water Resources Research).*
Ind/Abst For. Abstr.; Geogr. Abstr. Phys. Geogr.; Geogr. Abstr. Human Geogr.; GeoRef; Irr. Drain. Abstr.

LC S590 **ISSN** 0072-7210
DD 631.4 UK
UDC 631.4(410)
CODEN SSTMDI

TECHNICAL MONOGRAPH - GREAT BRITAIN. SOIL SURVEY. [Tech. monogr. - Soil Surv.]. **Main/Corp** Soil Survey of England and Wales. **VFOAT** Soil Survey Technical Monograph. No. 1 (1969)-. Academic Scholarly Publication. English. Irregular. Price varies per volume. Soil Survey and Land Research Centre, Silsoe Campus, Silsoe Bedfordshire MK45 4DT United Kingdom. **ED** J M Hodgson. **Bk Rev. Ad Acc. Circ:** 1,000. Documents available from CASDDS.
Desc: Various aspects of soil survey and other soil studies.
Ind/Abst Chem. Abstr.; GeoRef.

LC S
DD 630 II

TECHNOLOGICAL REPORT - COTTON TECHNOLOGICAL RESEARCH LABORATORY. **Main/Corp** Cotton Technological Research Laboratory. (19??)-. English. One time a year (May or June). $65.00 India; $20.00 other. Indian Council of Agricultural Research, Mgr Krishi Anusandham Bhavan, New Delhi 110 012 India. **Tel** 011 91 11 5713657, telex 031-62249 ICAR IN.
Ind/Abst AGRICOLA; Field Crop Abstr.; Plant Breed. Abstr.

LC SB761 **ISSN** 0235-2559
DD 635.97 RU

TEKHNICHESKIE KULTURY. **Added/Corp** Gosudarstvennyi Agropromyshlennyi Komitet SSSR. Vol. 1 (Jan./Feb. 1988)-. Periodical. Russian. Four times a year. $69.95. Agropromizdat, Sadovo-Spasskaia 18, 107807 Moscow Russia. **(Subscription address:** East View Publications Inc., 3020 Harbor Lane North, Suite 110, Minneapolis MN 55447. **Tel** (800)477-1005, (612)550-0961, FAX (612)559-2931.) ***Formed by the union of*** *Tabak, 0039-873X* ***and*** *Len i Konoplia, 0024-418X.*
Ind/Abst Biocont. News Inf.; Field Crop Abstr.; Plant Breed. Abstr.; Postharvest News Inf.; Rev. Agric. Entomol.; Seed Abstr.; Soyabean Abstr.; Weed Abstr.; Wheat Barley Trit. Abstr.

LC S590 **ISSN** 0340-4927
DD 631.4 GW
CODEN TELMDR

TELMA. [Telma]. **Added/Corp** Deutsche Gesellschaft fuer Moor- und Torfkunde. Vol. 1 (1971)-. Periodical. German (summaries and/or abstracts in English). One time a year. DM55.00. Deutsche Gesellschaft fuer Moor und Torfkunde, Stilleweg 2, 30655 Hannover Germany. **Tel** 011 5 11 643 2241, 011 5 11 2459, FAX 011 5 11 2304. **Circ:** 600 (ctrl). Documents available from CASDDS.
Desc: Reports of the German peat society; geosciences; peat winning and peat utilization; agriculture, forestry and horticulture; chemistry, physics and biology; nature conservation and environmental planning; medicine and balneology.
Ind/Abst AGRICOLA; Chem. Abstr.; Coal Abstr.; Ecol. Abstr.; Geogr. Abstr. Phys. Geogr.; Geogr. Abstr. Human Geogr.; GeoRef; Grass. Forage Abstr.; Irr. Drain. Abstr.; Ornamental Hort.; Soils Fert.

LC S **ISSN** 0893-2891
DD 630 US
UDC 633(768)
SUSPENDED

TENNESSEE GROWER. **VFOAT** TN Grower. Suspended (Jan. 1987). Periodical. English. Four times a year. $10.00. Rural Cumberland Resources, Rt 6 Box 526, Crossville TN 38555. ***Continues*** *Tennessee Organic Grower.*

LC SB113.4 .T5 **ISSN** 0095-1927
DD 338.1/7 US

TEXAS CERTIFIED SEED DIRECTORY. 1971-. Directory. English. One time a year. Texas Department of Agriculture, 18th & Congress Street, PO Box 12847, Austin TX 78711. **Tel** (512)463-7435, FAX (512)463-7643. ***Continues*** *Texas Seed Directory.*

LC SB369.2.T4 T49 **ISSN** 0748-7746
DD 338.1/7435/09764 US
UDC 338.439.4:634.3(764)

TEXAS CITRUS TREE INVENTORY SURVEY. [Tex. citrus tree invent. surv.]. English. One time a year. Texas Crop and Livestock Reporting Service, PO Box 70, Austin TX 78767. **Tel** (512)482-5581.

LC S **ISSN** 0040-7135
DD 630 DK
Pr Rev. **CEASED**

TIDSSKRIFT FOR PLANTEAVL. **Main/Corp** Denmark. Statens Forsoegsvirksomhed i Plantekultur. **Added/Corp** Denmark. Statens Forsoegsvirksomhed i Plantekultur. Denmark. Statens Planteavlsudvalg. (1895)-Vol. 96 (Mar. 1993). Periodical. Danish (English). Landbrugsministeriet - Statens Planteavlsfoersog, Skovbrynet 18, DK-2800 Lyngby Denmark. **Tel** 011 45 45 930999. **ED** Ole Wagn. **Circ:** 900 (ctrl). ***Supersedes*** *Om Langsbrugets Kulturplanter of Dertil Hoerende Froeavl.*
Desc: Articles on crop production, crop protection and soil.
Ind/Abst Agric. Eng. Abstr. (1991-); Agrofor. Abstr.; Crop Physiol. Abstr.; Entomol. Abstr.; Field Crop Abstr.; Food Sci. Technol. Abstr.; Hortic. Abstr.; Maize Abstr.; Microbiol. Abstr. Sect. A; Nematol. Abstr.; Nutr. Abstr. Rev., Ser. A, Hum. Exp.; Ornamental Hort. (19??-19??); Plant Breed. Abstr.; Plant Grow. Reg. Abstr.; Postharvest News Inf.; Potato Abstr.; Rev. Agric. Entomol.; Rev. Plant Pathol.; Seed Abstr.; Soils Fert.; Wheat Barley Trit. Abstr.

LC S **ISSN** 1156-1602
DD 630 FR
CEASED

TOP CULTURES (FRANCE). (TOP CULTURES.). No. 1 (Nov. 1990)-(July 1995). Periodical. French. Nouvelles Editions Publs Agricoles, 8 Cite Paradis, F 75010 Paris Cedex 10 France. **Tel** 011 33 1 40227900, 011 33 1 40227974. ***Continues*** *Agri Decideur, 0992-8162.*

LC S **ISSN** 0387-6993
DD 630 JA
CODEN TYSHDH

TOTTORI-KEN YASAI SHIKENJO KENKYU HOKOKU. [Tottori-ken Yasai Shikenjo kenkyu hokoku]. **VFOAT** Bulletin of the Tottori Vegetable and Ornamental Crops Experiment Station. (1979)-. Academic Scholarly Publication. Japanese. One time a year. Tottoriken Engei Shikenjo, (Tottori Prefectural Horticultural Experiment Station), Yurashuku Daieimachi, Tohakugun Tottoriken 689-22, Japan. Documents available from CASDDS.
Ind/Abst Chem. Abstr. (-1985).

LC S **ISSN** 0412-6300
DD 630 US
UDC 634.3
CODEN TCECDG

TRANSACTIONS OF THE CITRUS ENGINEERING CONFERENCE. [Trans. Citrus Eng. Conf.]. **Main/Conf** Citrus Engineering Conference. (1955)-. Academic Scholarly Publication. English. One time a year. $15.00. Bailey Motor Equipment Company, PO Box 3386, Orlando FL 32802. **Tel** (407)422-8134. Documents available from Article Express International, CASDDS.
Ind/Abst AGRICOLA [Full Cov.]; Bioeng. Abstr.; Chem. Abstr.; Ei Page One; Eng. Index Annu.; Food Sci. Technol. Abstr.

LC SB111.A2 T75 **ISSN** 0041-3216
DD 630/.913 UK
CCC
CODEN TAGLA2TAGLA
Pr Rev.

TROPICAL AGRICULTURE. [Trop. agric.]. **Added/Corp** Imperial College of Tropical Agriculture (Trinidad and Tobago). (Jan. 1924)-. Periodical. English. Four times a year (Jan., April, July and Oct.). $272.09. University of the West Indies, The Bursar / St. Augustine, Trinidad and Tobago. **Tel** 011 809 6453351, 011 809 6624620 ext. 3328, FAX 011 809 6621182. **ED** Dr. F.A. Gumbs (editor's address: University of the West Indies, Faculty of Agriculture, St. Augustine, Trinidad and Tobago; phone: 809 6453640). Index available in last issue of volume--attached. **Bk Rev**, (Qty: 12-15 per year). **Ad Acc.** available on microfilm and microfiche from University Microfilms International (UMI). Documents available from The Genuine Article, BIOSIS Document Express, CASDDS, Documents on Demand.
Desc: Communicates ideas and research results concerning the topic of agriculture in tropical and semi-tropical countries.
Ind/Abst AGRICOLA [Full Cov.]; Agric. Eng. Abstr. (1991-); Agrofor. Abstr. (19??-19??); Anim. Breed. Abstr.; BioBusiness; Biocont. News Inf. (1991-); Biodeter. Abstr. (1991-); Biol. Agric. Index; Biol. Abstr.; Chem. Abstr.; Cot. Trop. Fibr. Abstr. Bibliogr.; Crop Physiol. Abstr.; Curr. Aware. Biol. Sci., CABS; Curr. Cit.; Curr. Contents Agric. Biol. Environ. Sci.; Dairy Sci. Abstr.; Ecol. Abstr.; Energy Inf. Abstr.; Environ. Abstr.; Environ. Period. Bibliogr.; Field Crop Abstr.; Food Sci. Technol. Abstr.; For. Abstr.; Geogr. Abstr. Phys. Geogr.; Geogr. Abstr. Human Geogr.; Grass. Forage Abstr.; Helminthol. Abstr. (1991-); Hortic. Abstr.; Int. Dev. Abstr.; Irr. Drain. Abstr.; Maize Abstr.; Microbiol. Abstr. Sect. A; Nematol. Abstr.; Nutr. Abstr. Rev., Ser. B, Live Feeds and Feed.; Life Sci. Collect.; PESTDOC; Plant Breed. Abstr.; Plant Genet. Resour. Abstr.; Plant Grow. Reg. Abstr.; Postharvest News Inf.; Potato Abstr.; Poult. Abstr.; Res. Alert [Full Cov.]; Rev. Agric. Entomol.; Rev. Plant Pathol.; Rice Abstr.; Sci. Cit. Index (19??-19??); SCISEARCH; Seed Abstr.; Soils Fert.; Sorghum Mill. Abstr.; Soyabean Abstr.; Sug. Indus. Abstr.; Weed Abstr.; World Agric. Econ. Rural Sociol. Abstr.

LC S **ISSN** 0388-9386
DD 630 JA
CODEN TARSDD

TROPICAL AGRICULTURE RESEARCH SERIES. [Trop. agric. res. ser.]. **Added/Corp** Nettai Nogyo Kenkyu Senta. No. 1 (1967)-. Academic Scholarly Publication. English (summaries and/or abstracts in English). One time a year. Price varies per volume. Tropical Agriculture Research Center, 1 2 Owashi Tsukubashi, Ibarakiken 305 Japan. Documents available from BIOSIS Document Express, CASDDS.
Ind/Abst AGRICOLA [Full Cov.]; Biol. Abstr.; Chem. Abstr.; Irr. Drain. Abstr.; Microbiol. Abstr. Sect. A; Life Sci. Collect.; Virol. AIDS Abstr.

LC SB202.A8 T76 **ISSN** 0049-4763
DD 633.2 AT
CODEN TRGRB4
Pr Rev.

TROPICAL GRASSLANDS. [Trop. grassl.]. **Added/Corp** Tropical Grassland Society of Australia. Vol. 1, No. 1 (May 1967)-. Periodical. English. Four times a year (Mar. June, Sept, Dec.). 73.99Aus$. Tropical Grassland Society of Australia, Cunningham Lab Carmody Road, St. Lucia Queensland 4067 Australia. **Tel** 011 61 7 3770209, FAX 011 61 7 3713946, telex 42159. **ED** Lyle Winks (editor's address: McNeils Road, MS825 Ipswichm Queensland 4306 Australia, phone: 011 074 672314). Index available. cum. index. **Bk Rev. Circ:** 700 (ctrl). available on microfilm and microfiche from University Microfilms International (UMI). Documents available from The Genuine Article, BIOSIS Document Express.
Desc: Findings of pasture research and development. General review articles, critical field observations and documented case studies of commercial pasture enterprises.
Ind/Abst AGRICOLA [Full Cov.]; Agrofor. Abstr. (19??-19??); Biol. Abstr.; Curr. Aware. Biol. Sci., CABS; Curr. Cit.; Curr. Contents Agric. Biol. Environ. Sci.; Dairy Sci. Abstr.; Field Crop Abstr.; For. Abstr.; Grass. Forage Abstr.; Irr. Drain. Abstr.; Maize Abstr.; Nematol. Abstr.; Nutr. Abstr. Rev., Ser. B, Live Feeds and Feed.; Life Sci. Collect.; Plant Breed. Abstr.; Plant Genet. Resour. Abstr.; Res. Alert [Full Cov.]; Rev. Agric. Entomol.; Rev. Plant Pathol.; Sci. Cit. Index; SCISEARCH; Seed Abstr.; Soils Fert.; Sorghum Mill. Abstr.; Weed Abstr.

LC HD9019.T76
DD 382/.417/0973021 US

•TROPICAL PRODUCTS, WORLD MARKETS AND TRADE. **Added/Corp** United States. Foreign Agricultural Service. United States. World Agricultural Outlook Board. (Apr. 1994)-. Statistical Publication. English. Four times a year. $22.00. US Department of Agriculture / Foreign Agricultural Service, 14th Street & Independence Avenue Southwest, Washington DC 20250. **Tel** (202)720-9445, FAX (202)720-7729. **(Subscription address:** NTIS, 5285 Port Royal Road, Springfield VA 22161. **Tel** (703)487-4630.) available on microfiche. ***Continues*** *World Coffee Situation.*

LC S590
DD 631.4 US

TROPSOILS TECHNICAL REPORT. (1985/86)-. English. Every 2 years. North Carolina State University / Tropsoils, TropSoils Management Entity, Raleigh NC 27650. ***Continues*** *TropSoils Triennial Technical Report.*

LC S590
DD 631.4 AI

TRUDY INSTITUTA POCHVOVEDENIIA I AGROKHIMII. **Added/Corp** Soviet Union. Ministerstvo Sel'Skogo Khoziaistva. Nauchno-Issledovatel'Skii Institut Pochvovedeniia i Agrokhimii. Vsesoiuznoe Obshchestvo Pochvovededov (Soviet Union) Armianskii Filial. (19??)-. Monographic series. Russian (Armenian). Irregular. Price varies per volume.

LC SB183 **ISSN** 0496-3490
DD 633 CC
CODEN TSHPA9

TSO WU HSUEH PAO. [Tso Wu Hsueh Pao]. **Added/Corp** Chung-kuo Tso Wu Hsueh Hui. **VFOAT** Zuowu Xuebao; Acta Agronomica Sinica. (1962)-. Periodical. Chinese (English; table of contents in English). Four times a year. Institute of Scientific and Technological Information of China, China Publications Centre, People's Republic of China. **(Subscription address:** China International Book Trading Corporation, PO Box 399, Library Service Department, Beijing 100044 People's Republic of China. **Tel** 011 86 1 8414284, FAX 011 86 1 8412023, telex 22496 CIBTC CN.) Documents available from BIOSIS Document Express.
Ind/Abst Biol. Abstr. (1988-); Plant Breed. Abstr.; Rev. Plant Pathol.; Rice Abstr.; Seed Abstr.; Soyabean Abstr.

LC SB123.3 .T76 ISSN 1000-6435
DD 631.5(2-36) CC
TSO WU PIN CHUNG TZU YUAN. **Added/Corp** Chung-kuo Nung Yeh ko Hsueh Yuan. Pin Chung Tzu Yuan Yen Chiu so. **VFOAT** Zuowupinzhongziyuan; Crop Genetic Resources. (19??)-. Academic Scholarly Publication. Chinese. Four times a year. $20.00. Zhongguo Nongye Kexueyuan / Zuowu Pinzhong Ziyuan Yanjiusuo, Chinese Academy of Agricultural Science, Institute of Crop Genetic Resources, 2826 Baishiqiao Lu, Beijing 100081 People's Republic of China. **Tel** 8314433. **ED** Li Shenglin. **Ad Acc**.
Ind/Abst Plant Breed. Abstr.; Seed Abstr.

LC QR ISSN 0912-2184
DD 576 JA
TSUCHI TO BISEIBUTSU. [Tsuchi to biseibutsu]. **VFOAT** Soil Microorganisms. (1960)-. Periodical. Multiple languages. Two times a year. Dojo Biseibutsu Kenkyukai, (Soil Microbiological Soc. of Japan), Nogyo Kankyo Gijutsu Kenkyujo, 1-1 Kannondai 3 Chome, Tsukubashi Ibarakiken 305, Japan. ***Continues*** *Dojo Biseibutsu Danwakai Koen Narabini Toron Kiroku.*
Ind/Abst Rev. Plant Pathol.

LC S599.6.C5 T83 ISSN 0253-9829
DD 631.4 CC
CODEN TUJADP
TU JANG. [Turang]. **VFOAT** Turang. Academic Scholarly Publication. Chinese. Six times a year. $0.25. Chiang-su Jen Min Chu Pan She, Post Office Nan-Ching Shin, Nan-Ching Shin, People's Republic of China. Documents available from CASDDS.
Ind/Abst Chem. Abstr.

LC S599.6.C5 T84 ISSN 0564-3945
DD 631.4/17/0951 CC
CODEN TUTOEG
TU JANG TUNG PAO. [Tu Jang Tung Pao]. **Added/Corp** Chung-kuo tu Jang Hsueh hui. **VFOAT** Turang Tongbao; Journal of Soil Science. (19??)-. Academic Scholarly Publication. Chinese. Six times a year. Documents available from CASDDS.
Ind/Abst Chem. Abstr. (1984-); Soyabean Abstr.

LC S590 .T8 ISSN 0564-3929
DD 631.4/05 CC
CODEN TJHPAE
TURANG XUEBAO. (TU JANG HSUEH PAO.). [Turang xuebao]. **Added/Corp** Chung-kuo tu Jang Hsueh Hui. **VFOAT** Acta Pedologica Sinica. (1953)-. Academic Scholarly Publication. Chinese (summaries and/or abstracts in English). Four times a year. $43.30. **(Subscription address:** China International Book Trading Corporation, PO Box 399, Library Service Department, Beijing 100044 People's Republic of China. **Tel** 011 86 1 8414284, FAX 011 86 1 8412023, telex 22496 CIBTC CN.**)** Documents available from CASDDS.
Ind/Abst Chem. Abstr.; EMBASE; Field Crop Abstr.; GeoRef; Irr. Drain. Abstr.; Rev. Plant Pathol.; Rice Abstr.; Soils Fert.

LC SB599 ISSN 1056-2648
DD 632 US
TURF & ORNAMENTAL CHEMICALS REFERENCE: T&OCR. [Turf ornam. chem. ref.]. **Added/Corp** Chemical and Pharmaceutical Press. **VFOAT** T&OCR; Turf and Ornamental Chemicals Reference. (1992)-. English. Irregular. $110.00. C & P Press, Building 3, Brooklyn Navy Yard, Brooklyn NY 11205. **Tel** 800 571-9851.

LC SB320
DD 635 CH
UDC 635.1/.8(213)
TVIS NEWS. **VFOAT** T.V.I.S. News. Vol. 1, No. 1 (Feb. 1985)-. Periodical. English. $8.00 Taiwan; $2.00 developing countries. Asian Vegetable Research & Development Center, PO Box 42, Shanhua Tainan 74199 Taiwan. **Tel** (06)5837801, FAX 06-5830009, telex 73560 AVRDC. **Circ:** 1,500.
Desc: Provides a platform for scientists working with mung bean, soybean and Chinese cabbage to exchange information.

LC S
DD 630 PH
UCAP WEEKLY BULLETIN. Bulletin. English. Fifty-one times per year. $200.00. United Coconut Association of the Philippines, 4th Floor, G&A 2303 Pasong Tamo Ex, Manila Philippines. **Tel** 011 63 2 8167495. **ED** Yvonne T.V. Agustin.
Desc: Covers news on developments affecting coconut trade and marketing and updated statistics on coconut products and competing substitutes, rainfall data, and inter alia.

LC S ISSN 0093-4429
DD 630 US
UNITED STATES COTTON QUALITY REPORT FOR GINNINGS. **Added/Corp** United States. Agricultural Marketing Service. Cotton Division. United States. Agricultural Marketing Service. Cotton Division. Market News Section. United States. Agricultural Marketing Service. Cotton Division. Market News Branch. (19??)-. English. Six times a year. $16.00. US Department of Agriculture / Tennessee, Agricultural Marketing Service, 4841 Summer Avenue, Memphis TN 38122. **Tel** (901)766-2934, 766-2931. Documents available from Documents on Demand.
Ind/Abst Am. Stat. Index.

LC S ISSN 0139-6013
DD 630 XR
UDC 633/635
URODA. [Uroda]. (1953)-. Periodical. Czech. Twelve times a year. DM112.00. **(Subscription address:** Kubon & Sagner, ABT Zeitschriftenimport, D 80328 Munich Germany. **Tel** 011 49 89 54218130.**)**

LC HF ISSN 0924-7165
DD 380.1 NE
VAKBLAD VOOR DE HANDEL IN AARDAPPELEN, GROENTEN EN FRUIT. **VFOAT** Vakblad. Vol. 32, No. 2 (Jan. 12, 1978)-. Periodical. Dutch. Four times a year. Fl258.75, $162.65 Netherlands; Fl278.25, $174.90 other. Stichting Vakblad, Bezuidenhoutseweg 82, 2594 Ax the Hague Netherlands. **Tel** 011 31 70 3850500. ***Continues*** *Vakblad voor de Export-, Import- en Groothandel in Aardappelen, Groenten en Fruit.*

LC S590
DD 631.4 XR
VEDECKE PRACE = NAUCHNYE TRUDY = SCIENTIFIC STUDIES. **Added/Corp** Vyzkumny Ustav pro Zurodneni Zemedelskych Pud. **VFOAT** Nauchnye Trudy; Scientific Studies. (1982)-. Periodical. Czech (summaries and/or abstracts in English and Russian; table of contents in English and Russian).
Desc: Information on soil science, underground water, soil moisture, and drainage.
Ind/Abst Agric. Eng. Abstr.

LC S
DD 630 XO
CODEN VPVODC
VEDECKE PRACE VYSKUMNEHO USTAVU RASTLINNEJ VYROBY V PIESTANOCH. OBILNINY - STRAKOVINY = SCIENTIFIC PAPERS OF THE RESEARCH INSTITUTE FOR PLANT PRODUCTION AT PIESTANY. CEREALS - LEGUMES. **Added/Corp** Vyskumny Ustav Rastlinnej Vyroby. **VFOAT** Scientific Papers of the Research Institute for Plant Production at Piestany. Cereals - Legumes. 15 (1978)-. Slovak (summaries and/or abstracts in English and Russian). Vyskumny Ustav Rastlinnej Vyroby, Priroda, Krizhova 9, 815 34 Bratislava Slovakia. Documents available from BIOSIS Document Express. ***Continues in part*** *Vyskumny Ustav Rastlinnej Vyroby. Vedecke Prace Vyskumneho Ustavu Rastlinnej Vyroby v Piestanoch.*
Ind/Abst Biol. Abstr.; Field Crop Abstr.

LC SB761
DD 635.97 XO
VEDECKE PRACE VYSKUMNEHO USTAVU RASTLINNEJ VYYROBY V PIESTANOCH. KRMOVINY = SCIENTIFIC PAPERS OF THE RESEARCH INSTITUTE FOR PLANT PRODUCTION AT PIESTANY. FORAGE CROPS. **Added/Corp** Vyskumny Ustav Rastlinnej Vyroby. **VFOAT** Scientific Papers of the Research Institute for Plant Production at Piestany. Forage Crops. (1978)-. Slovak (summaries and/or abstracts in English and Russian). Vyskumny Ustav Rastlinnej Vyroby, Priroda, Krizhova 9, 815 34 Bratislava Slovakia. ***Continues in part*** *Vyskumny Ustav Rastlinnej Vyroby. Vedecke Prace Vyskumneho Ustavu Rastlinnej Vroby v Piestanoch.*
Ind/Abst Grass. Forage Abstr.; Maize Abstr.; Soils Fert.; Sorghum Mill. Abstr.; Weed Abstr.

LC SB320
DD 635 II
VEGETABLE SCIENCE. **Added/Corp** Indian Society of Vegetable Science. (19??)-. Periodical. English. Two times a year. $50.00. Indian Society of Vegetable Science, New Delhi India. **(Subscription address:** Prints India, 11 Darya Ganj, New Delhi 110002 India. **Tel** 011 91 11 3268645, FAX 011 91 11 3275542, telex 31-61087 PRIN-IN.**)**
Ind/Abst Field Crop Abstr.; Hortic. Abstr.; Plant Breed. Abstr.; Plant Grow. Reg. Abstr.; Potato Abstr.; Seed Abstr.; Soils Fert.; Weed Abstr.

LC S
DD 630 US
VEGETABLES FOR THE HOT, HUMID TROPICS. **Main/Corp** United States. Agricultural Research Service. (1978)-. Periodical. English. Irregular. $11.50. National Technical Information Service - NTIS, Room 2027S, 5285 Port Royal Road, Springfield VA 22161. **Tel** (703)487-4630, (703)487-4660, (703)487-4650, FAX (703)321-8547, telex 89-9405.

LC SB320 ISSN 0193-6603
DD 635 US
VEGETABLES (WASHINGTON). (VEGETABLES.). [Vegetables]. **Added/Corp** United States. Crop Reporting Board. United States. Agricultural Statistics Board. (Jan. 1977)-. Government Publication. English. Irregular. $23.00. Superintendent of Documents, US Government Printing Office, Washington DC 20402. **Tel** (202)275-3328, FAX (202)786-2377. available on microfiche (Vols. for (1986-) distributed to depository libraries). Documents available from Documents on Demand. ***Formed by the union of*** *United States. Crop Reporting Board. Vegetables, Fresh Market* ***and*** *United States. Crop Reporting Board. Vegetables, Processing.*
Ind/Abst Am. Stat. Index (19??-).

LC S
DD 630 NE
VERSLAG / PROEFSTATION VOOR DE AKKERBOUW ON DE GROENTETEELT IN DE VOLLEGROND. **Added/Corp** Proefstation voor de Akkerbouw en de Groenteteelt in de Vollegrond. (19??)-. Monographic series. Dutch (summaries and/or abstracts in English).
Ind/Abst Agric. Eng. Abstr.

LC S599.45.A1 M68a ISSN 0137-0944
DD 631.4 RU
CODEN VMUPDN
VESTNIK MOSKOVSKOGO UNIVERSITETA. SERIA 17. POCHVOVEDENIE. (VESTNIK MOSKOVSKOGO UNIVERSITETA. SERIIA XVII: POCHVOVEDENIE.). [Vestn. Moskovskogo univ., Ser. 17, PoČcvoved.]. **Main/Corp** Moskovskii Gosudarstvennyi Universitet Im. M. V. Lomonosova. **VFOAT** Pochvovedenie; Vestnik Moskovskogo Universiteta. Pochvovedenie. **VAT** Vestnik Moskovskogo Universiteta. Seriia Semnadtsat. Pochvovedenie. (1977)-. Academic Scholarly Publication. Russian (summaries and/or abstracts in English; table of contents in English). Four times a year. $49.95. Izdatelstvo Moskovskogo Universiteta, K-9 Ulitsa Gertsena 5/7, 103009 Moscow Russia. **Tel** (301)881-5973. **(Subscription address:** East View Publications Inc., 3020 Harbor Lane North, Suite 110, Minneapolis MN 55447. **Tel** (800)477-1005, (612)550-0961, FAX (612)559-2931.**)** Documents available from CASDDS. ***Supersedes in part*** *Moskovskii Gosudarstvennyi Universitet im. M.V. Lomonosova. Vestnik Moskovskogo Universiteta. Seriia VI: Biologiia, 0579-9422.*
Ind/Abst AGRICOLA; Chem. Abstr.

LC SB320
DD 635 AT
VICTORIAN VEGETABLE GROWER, THE. Vol. 20, No. 1 (Feb. 1976)-. Periodical. English. Four times a year. $7.38 US. Vegetable Growers Association of Victoria, Box 403, 542 Footscray Road, Footscray Victoria 3011 Australia. **Tel** (03)689-3556. **Ad Acc. Circ:** 400 (ctrl).

LC SB387 .V634 ISSN 0390-0479
DD 634 IT
CODEN VIGNDL
VIGNEVINI. [Vignevini]. Vol. 1 (Nov./Dec. 1974)-. Academic Scholarly Publication. Italian. Twelve times a year. L54500. Edagricole, PO Box 2157, 40100 Bologna Italy. **Tel** 011 39 51 492211 Ext. 22, FAX 011 39 51 493660, telex 510336 EDAGRI. Index available in last issue of volume--attached. Documents available from CASDDS.
Ind/Abst AGRICOLA; Agric. Eng. Abstr. (1991-); Chem. Abstr.; Crop Physiol. Abstr.; Curr. Cit.; Food Sci. Technol. Abstr.; Hortic. Abstr.; Nematol. Abstr.; Life Sci. Collect.; Plant Breed. Abstr.; Soils Fert.; Vitis Vitic. Enol. Abstr.; Weed Abstr.; World Agric. Econ. Rural Sociol. Abstr.

LC TP557 .V55 ISSN 0276-4687
DD 641.2/22/05 US
VINEYARD ALMANAC & WINE GAZETTER, THE. **VFOAT** Vineyard Almanac and Wine Gazetteer. (19??)-. English. One time a year. $2.25. Vineyard Almanac and Wine Gazetteer, 960 North San Antonia Road, Suite 125, Los Altos CA 94022.

LC TP544 .V53 ISSN 1047-4951
DD 634.8/09 US
CODEN VWMAE9
VINEYARD & WINERY MANAGEMENT. [Vineyard winery manage.]. **VFOAT** A.Vineyard and winery management. Vol. 12, No. 2 (May/June 1986)-. Trade Publication. English. Six times a year. $25.00. Vineyard and Winery Management, PO Box 231, Watkins Glen NY 14891. **Tel** (607)535-7133, (800)535-5670, FAX (607)535-2998. **ED** J. William Moffett. cum. index. **Ad Acc, Adv Mgr:** Hope Merletti, **Tel** (800)535-5670. **Circ:** 3,500 (ctrl). ***Continues*** *Eastern Grape Grower & Winery News, 0194-5254.*
Desc: Bottom line resource for vineyard and winery owners and operators outlining basic how-tos of the grape industry.
Ind/Abst BioBusiness (1989-).

LC S ISSN 1131-5997
DD 630 SP
UDC 634.8
VINO Y GASTRONOMIA. (1991)-. Periodical. Spanish. Twelve times a year. $71.06. Vina y Vino, Santa Hortensia 27 IA, 28002 Madrid Spain. **Tel** 011 34 1 4151662. ***Continues*** *Vina, Vino y Gastronomia, 1130-2917.*

LC SB354 .V58 **ISSN** 0097-1782
DD 634/.1/09755 US
VIRGINIA FRUIT. **Added/Corp** Virginia State Horticultural Society. Virginia State Horticultural Society. Report. (19??)-. Periodical. English. Six times a year. $15.00. Virginia State Horticultural Society, PO Box 718, Staunton VA 76401. **Tel** (703)885-9046. **Ad Acc. Circ:** 500.

LC S **ISSN** 0399-3558
DD 630 FR
VITI. **VFOAT** Vititechnique. No. 64 (Dec./Jan. 1983)-. Periodical. French. Eleven times a year. 303.62F France; 366.00F other. Documentation Agricole, 228 rue du Faubourg St. Martin, 75010 Paris France. **Tel** 011 33 1 40051818, 011 33 1 40380880. **(Subscription address:** Revue Viti Service Abonnements, B P 210, 60732 S Genevieve, CDX 9 France. **)** ***Continues*** *Vititechnique, 0399-3558.*
Desc: Information on the cultivation or culture of grapes.

LC TP **ISSN** 0042-7500
DD 663.2 GW
CODEN VITIAY
VITIS. [Vitis]. **Added/Corp** Bundesforschungsanstalt fuer Rebenzuechtung Geilweilerhof. Forschungs-Institut fuer Rebenzuechtung Geilweilerhof. (1957)-. Academic Scholarly Publication. Multiple languages (English, French, German, Italian and Spanish). Four times a year. $70.62. Vitis / Bundesanstalt fuer Zuechtungsforschung, Forschung Wein Geilweilerhof, D-76833 Siebeldingen Germany. **Tel** 011 49 6345 410. Index available. **Bk Rev. Circ:** 800. available with charts; available with illustrations; available on an online database from STN International. Documents available from The Genuine Article, CASDDS. ***Continued in part by*** *Vitis, Viticulture and Enology Abstracts, 0175-8292.*
Desc: Covers viticulture, the breeding of vine wine.
Ind/Abst AGRICOLA; Chem. Abstr.; Chemorecept. Abstr.; Crop Physiol. Abstr.; Curr. Aware. Biol. Sci., CABS; Curr. Contents Agric. Biol. Environ. Sci.; EMBASE; Food Sci. Technol. Abstr.; Hortic. Abstr.; Nematol. Abstr.; Life Sci. Collect.; Plant Breed. Abstr.; Plant Grow. Reg. Abstr.; Res. Alert [Full Cov.]; Rev. Agric. Entomol.; Rev. Plant Pathol.; Vitis Vitic. Enol. Abstr.

LC Z7951 **ISSN** 0175-8292
DD 016.64122 GW
VITIS, VITICULTURE AND ENOLOGY ABSTRACTS. **See** Agriculture-Abstracting, Bibliographies and Statistics.

LC S590 **ISSN** 0110-4691
DD 631.4 NZ
WATER AND SOIL MANAGEMENT PUBLICATION. **VFOAT** Management Publication - Water and Soil. Periodical. English. New Zealand Ministry of Works & Development, PO Box 12041, Wellington New Zealand.
Ind/Abst Geogr. Abstr. Human Geogr. (?-?).

LC S590 **ISSN** 0110-4705
DD 631.4 NZ
WATER & SOIL MISCELLANEOUS PUBLICATION. [Water soil misc. publ.]. **Added/Corp** National Water and Soil Conservation Organization. New Zealand. Water and Soil Division. **VFOAT** Miscellaneous Publication - Water and Soil. No. 1 (1978)-. Monographic series. English. Irregular. Price varies per volume. Water and Soil Directorate, PO Box 12 041, Wellington North New Zealand. **Tel** 729 929.
Ind/Abst AGRICOLA (19??-); Agrofor. Abstr. (19??-); Ecol. Abstr. (?-?); Geogr. Abstr. Phys. Geogr. (?-?); Geol. Abstr. (19??-); GeoRef (?-1984); Wildl. Rev. (19??-199?).

LC SB611 .W35 **ISSN** 0043-1729
DD 632/.58 UK
WEED ABSTRACTS. **See** Agriculture-Abstracting, Bibliographies and Statistics.

LC S **ISSN** 0145-0360
DD 630 US
WEEKLY COTTON MARKET REVIEW. **Added/Corp** United States. Agricultural Marketing Service. Cotton Division. United States. Agricultural Marketing Service. Cotton Division. Market News Section. United States. Agricultural Marketing Service. Cotton Division. Market News Branch. (19??)-. Periodical. English. One time a week. $27.00. US Department of Agriculture / Tennessee, Agricultural Marketing Service, 4841 Summer Avenue, Memphis TN 38122. **Tel** (901)766-2934, 766-2931.
Desc: A weekly summary of developments and activity in cotton marketing. Presents a synopsis of market conditions for U.S. cotton. Includes information in tabular and narrative format.

LC QC983 .A41 **ISSN** 0043-1974
DD 630/.2/516973 US
WEEKLY WEATHER AND CROP BULLETIN. **Added/Corp** United States. Weather Bureau. United States. National Weather Service. United States. Environmental Data Service. United States. Environmental Data and Information Service. United States. Agricultural Marketing Service. United States. Dept. of Agriculture. Statistical Reporting Service. United States. Dept. of Agriculture. Economics, Statistics, and Cooperatives Service. United States. Dept. of Agriculture. Economics and Statistics Service. United States. World Food and Agricultural Outlook and Situation Board. United States. World Agricultural Outlook Board. United States. National Agricultural Statistics Service. **VFOAT** Weekly Weather & Crop Bulletin. (1924)-. Bulletin. English. One time a week. $45.00. Weekly Weather Crop Bulletin, Department Commerce, NOAA & USDA South Building, Washington DC 20250. **Tel** (202)720-7917. **ED** Fred Finger. **Ad Acc. Circ:** 3,000. available on microfilm and microfiche from University Microfilms International (UMI). Documents available from Documents on Demand. ***Absorbed*** *Snow and Ice Bulletin.*
Desc: Review of weather and how it affected crops nationally and internationally.
Ind/Abst Am. Stat. Index.

LC S **ISSN** 0375-8818
DD 630 GW
CCC
WEIN-WISSENSCHAFT, DIE. [Wein-Wiss.]. **VFOAT** Viticultural and Enological Sciences; DWW. (1954)-. Academic Scholarly Publication. German (English and French). Six times a year. $69.09. Fachverlag Dr Fraund GmbH, Postfach 1329, D-61364 Friedrichsdorf Germany. **Tel** 011 49 6172 71060. Documents available from CASDDS. ***Continues*** *Deutsche Weinbau. Wissenschaftliche Beihefte.*
Ind/Abst AGRICOLA; Chem. Abstr.; Food Sci. Technol. Abstr.; Vitis Vitic. Enol. Abstr.

LC S **ISSN** 0744-4508
DD 630 US
WESTERN AND CENTRAL NEW YORK FRUIT AND VEGETABLE REPORT. **Added/Corp** New York. Dept. of Agriculture and Markets. U.S. Agriculture Marketing Service. Fruit and Vegetable Division. Federal-State Market News Service. (19??)-. Trade Publication. English. Two times a week. US Department of Agriculture / Market News / Rochester, NY, 900 Jefferson Road/Room 120, Rochester NY 14623. **Tel** (716)424-2690.

LC HB241 **ISSN** 0043-3799
DD 338 US
WESTERN GROWER & SHIPPER. [West. grow. shipp.]. **VFOAT** Western Grower and Shipper. Vol. 1 (Dec. 1929)-. Trade Publication. English. Twelve times a year. $18.00. Western Grower Association, PO Box 2130, Newport Beach CA 92658. **Tel** (714)863-1000. **ED** Heather Flower. **Ad Acc, Adv Mgr Tel** (510)653-2122. **Circ:** 4,500 (ctrl).
Desc: Agriculture publication serving fruit and vegetable growers in Arizona and California.
Ind/Abst AGRICOLA (-1987).

LC HD **ISSN** 0814-9267
DD 338.173110994 AT
WHEAT AUSTRALIA INTERNATIONAL. **Added/Corp** Australian Wheat Board. (1985)-. Periodical. English. Six times a year. Free. Australian Wheat Board, 528 Lonsdale Street, Melbourne Victoria 3000 Australia. **Tel** 011 61 3 96051555, FAX 011 61 3 9602782, telex AA 130196. ctrl circ.

LC SB188 **ISSN** 0882-9691
DD 633 US
CEASED
WHEAT GROWER (WASHINGTON, D.C.), THE. (THE WHEAT GROWER.). [Wheat grow.]. **Added/Corp** National Association of Wheat Growers (U.S.). (1978)-(May/June 1995). Periodical. English. National Association of Wheat Growers, 415 2nd Street Northeast, Suite 300, Washington DC 20002. **Tel** (202)547-7800. **ED** Barry L. Jenkins. **Ad Acc. Circ:** 67,000. ***Absorbed*** *National Association of Wheat Growers. Proceedings of the Annual Meeting; Wheat Facts (Washington, D.C.).*
Desc: Helps keep readers informed of legislation, regulations, innovations and marketing information they need to be more efficient, profitable agricultural producers.
Ind/Abst Stat. Ref. Index.

LC HD1401 **ISSN** 0829-4763
DD 338.1/7311/0971 CN
WHEATGROWER (REGINA). (THE WHEATGROWER.). [Wheatgrower]. **Added/Corp** Western Canadian Wheat Growers Association. **VFOAT** Western Wheat Grower. (Jan. 1985)-. Periodical. English. Twelve times a year. 100.04Can$. Western Canadian Wheat Growers Association, 4401 Alberta Street 201, Regina Saskatchewan S4S 6B6 Canada. **Tel** (306)586-5866, FAX (306)586-2707. **ED** Stuart Holtby.

LC S **ISSN** 0043-5953
DD 630 AU
WINZER : FACHBLATT DES OESTERREICHISCHE WEINHAUS, DER. **Added/Corp** Bundesverband der Weinbautreibenden Osterreichs. (1954)-. Periodical. German. Twelve times a year. $91.10. Oesterreichischer Agrarverlag, Inkustr 1 7 Bueropark Donau, A 3400 Klosterneuberg Austria. **Tel** 011 43 2243 33300.

LC S
DD 630 IO
WORKING PAPER. **Added/Corp** ESCAP Regional Co-Ordination Centre for Research and Development of Coarse Grains, Pulses, Roots and Tuber Crops in the Humid Tropics of Asia and the Pacific. **VFOAT** Working Paper Series. (198?)-. Monographic series. English.
Ind/Abst Maize Abstr.; Nutr. Abstr. Rev., Ser. A, Hum. Exp.; Postharvest News Inf.; Potato Abstr.; Soyabean Abstr.; World Agric. Econ. Rural Sociol. Abstr.

LC S
DD 630 US
WORKING PAPERS ON COMMERCIALIZATION OF AGRICULTURE AND NUTRITION. **Added/Corp** International Food Policy Research Institute. No. 1 (1986)-. Monographic series. English. IFPRI, 1776 Massachusetts Avenue NW, Washington DC 20036. **Tel** (202)862-5600, FAX (202)467-4439, telex 440054.
Ind/Abst World Agric. Econ. Rural Sociol. Abstr.

LC S
DD 630 UK
WORLD FERTILIZER REVIEW. (19??)-. Periodical. English. Twelve times a year. $690.00 US. Fertecon Limited, 25 Copperfield Street, Suite B, London SE1 0EN United Kingdom. **Tel** 011 44 171 2619998, FAX 011 44 171 9287911. ***Continues*** *Fertcon Monthly Report.*

LC S590 **ISSN** 0532-0488
DD 631.4 IT
CODEN WSRRDX
WORLD SOIL RESOURCES REPORTS. [World soil resour. rep.]. **Added/Corp** Food and Agriculture Organization of the United Nations. United Nations Educational, Scientific and Cultural Organizations. Food and Agriculture Organization of the United Nations. World Soil Resources Office. **VFOAT** World Soil Resources Report. No. 1 (1961)-. Academic Scholarly Publication. English. Irregular. Price varies per volume. Food Agriculture Organization (FAO) / Italy, GIPCI66 via Terme di Caracalla, 00100 Rome Italy. **Tel** 011 39 6 52252925, FAX 011 39 6 52253152. **(Subscription address:** UNIPUB, 4611 F Assembly Drive, Lanham MD 20706. **Tel** (800)274-4888, (301)459-7666.**)** Documents available from CASDDS.
Ind/Abst Chem. Abstr.; GeoRef; Soils Fert.

LC QD
DD 547 UK
WORLDWIDE DIRECTORY OF AGROBIOLOGICALS, THE. **See** Chemistry and Chemicals-Organic Chemistry.

LC S **ISSN** 0916-6858
DD 630 JA
CODEN KHYCEJ
YASAI, CHAGYO SHIKENJO KENKYU HOKOKU. B, CHAGYO. (YASAI CHAGYO SHIKENJO KENKYU HOKOKU. B, CHAGYO = BULLETIN OF THE NATIONAL RESEARCH INSTITUTE OF VEGETABLES, ORNAMENTAL PLANTS AND TEA. SERIES B, TEA.). **Added/Corp** Norin Suisansho Yasai Chagyo Shikenjo (Japan). **VFOAT** Chagyo; Tea; Bulletin of the National Research Institute of Vegetables, Ornamental Plants and Tea. Series B, Tea. (Mar. 1991)-. Bulletin. Japanese (summaries and/or abstracts in English; table of contents in English). Norin Suisansho Yasai Chagyo Shikenjo, (National Research Institute of Vegetables Ornamental Plants & Tea Ministry of Agriculture Forestry & Fisheries), 360 Kusawa Anocho, Agegun Mieken 514-23 Japan. ***Continues*** *Yasai Chagyo Shikenjo Kenkyu Hokoku. B, Kanaya, 0914-6652.*
Ind/Abst Rev. Plant Pathol.

LC S **ISSN** 0068-5720
DD 630 US
YEARBOOK - CALIFORNIA MACADAMIA SOCIETY. [Yearb. - Calif. Macadamia Soc.]. **Main/Corp** California Macadamia Society. (19??)-. Periodical. English. One time a year. $17.50. California Macademia Society, PO Box 1298, Fallbrook CA 92088. **Tel** (619)743-0358. **ED** Jim Teeter. Index available. **Ad Acc. Circ:** 500 (ctrl).
Ind/Abst AGRICOLA [Select. Cov.].

LC SB379.A9 C3 **ISSN** 0096-5960
DD 634 US
YEARBOOK OF THE CALIFORNIA AVOCADO SOCIETY. (YEARBOOK OF THE CALIFORNIA AVOCADO SOCIETY FOR THE YEAR ...). [Yearb. Calif. Avocado Soc.]. **Main/Corp** California Avocado Society. (1941)-. English. One time a year (July). $50.00. California Avocado Society, PO Box 4816, Saticoy CA 93003. **Tel** (805)644-1184. **ED** J. S. Shepherd. **Bk Rev. Ad Acc. Circ:** 2,000. ***Continues*** *California Avocado Association. Yearbook of the California Avocado Association for the Year ... .*
Desc: Compendiums of information on every aspect of avocado industry: culture, marketing, pests and diseases, economics, basic research reports and applied research "how-to" articles, popular and technical.
Ind/Abst AGRICOLA; Biocont. News Inf.; Crop Physiol.

Abstr.; Hortic. Abstr.; Plant Breed. Abstr.; Postharvest News Inf.; Rev. Agric. Entomol.; Rev. Plant Pathol.; Seed Abstr.; Soils Fert.

LC S **ISSN** 0044-1864
DD 630 RU
CODEN ZSRSBX

ZASCITA RASTENIJ. (ZASCHITA RASTENII.). [Zasc. rast.]. **Added/Corp** Soviet Union. Ministerstvo Selskogo Khoziaistva. Vol. 11 (1966)-. Periodical. Russian. Twelve times a year. $91.95. Izdatelstvo Kolos, Sadovaia-Spasskaia 18, 107807 Moscow Russia. **(Subscription address:** East View Publications Inc., 3020 Harbor Lane North, Suite 110, Minneapolis MN 55447. **Tel** (800)477-1005, (612)550-0961, FAX (612)559-2931.**)** Index available in last issue of volume--attached. Documents available from BIOSIS Document Express. ***Continues*** *Zashchita Rastenii ot Vreditelei i Boleznei.*
Ind/Abst Biocont. News Inf.; Biol. Abstr. (?-1986); Hortic. Abstr.; Life Sci. Collect.; PESTDOC; Potato Abstr.; Rev. Agric. Entomol.; Rev. Plant Pathol.; Weed Abstr.; Wheat Barley Trit. Abstr.

LC S **ISSN** 0931-2250
DD 630 GW
CCC
CODEN ZAPFAR
Pr Rev.

ZEITSCHRIFT FUER ACKER- UND PFLANZENBAU. (JOURNAL OF AGRONOMY AND CROP SCIENCE = ZEITSCHRIFT FUER ACKER- UND PFLANZENBAU.). [Z. Acker- Pflanzenb.]. (1949)-. Academic Scholarly Publication. English (German). Ten times a year. $1077.78. Blackwell Wissenschafts-Verlag, Kurfuerstendamm 57, D-10707 Berlin Germany. **Tel** 011 49 30 32790623, 011 49 30 32790624, FAX 011 49 30 327 90610. **ED** Gerhard Geisler, Samuel Ch. Jutzi, Paul C. Struik. Index available. cum. index. **Bk Rev. Ad Acc. Circ:** 2,500. Documents available from The Genuine Article, BIOSIS Document Express, CASDDS. ***Continues*** *Journal fuer Landwirtschaft.*
Desc: Agricultural meteorology, plant production and crop rotation, soil cultivation and land improvement, soil physics and chemistry, nutrient supply and balances.
Ind/Abst AGRICOLA; Biol. Abstr.; Chem. Abstr.; Cot. Trop. Fibr. Abstr. Bibliogr.; Crop Physiol. Abstr.; Curr. Aware. Biol. Sci., CABS; Curr. Cit.; Curr. Contents Agric. Biol. Environ. Sci.; Environ. Period. Bibliogr.; Field Crop Abstr.; Food Sci. Technol. Abstr.; GeoRef; Grass. Forage Abstr.; Hortic. Abstr.; Index Vet.; Irr. Drain. Abstr.; Maize Abstr.; Nutr. Abstr. Rev., Ser. B, Live Feeds and Feed.; Life Sci. Collect.; Plant Breed. Abstr.; Plant Genet. Resour. Abstr.; Plant Grow. Reg. Abstr.; Potato Abstr.; Res. Alert [Full Cov.]; Rev. Agric. Entomol.; Rev. Plant Pathol.; Rice Abstr.; Sci. Cit. Index; SCISEARCH; Seed Abstr.; Soils Fert.; Sorghum Mill. Abstr.; Soyabean Abstr.; Weed Abstr.; Wheat Barley Trit. Abstr.; World Agric. Econ. Rural Sociol. Abstr.

LC S605 .Z4 **ISSN** 0934-666X
DD 630 GW
CCC
CODEN ZKLAEW

ZEITSCHRIFT FUER KULTURTECHNIK UND LANDENWICKLUNG. [Z. Kult.tech. Landentwickl.]. **VFOAT** Journal of Rural Engineering and Development. Vol. 30 (Jan./Feb. 1989)-. Periodical. German (summaries and/or abstracts in English; table of contents in English). Six times a year. DM418.00 Europe; DM416.00 other. Blackwell Wissenschafts-Verlag, Kurfuerstendamm 57, D-10707 Berlin Germany. **Tel** 011 49 30 32790623, 011 49 30 32790624, FAX 011 49 30 327 90610. **ED** B. Scheffer. Index available. cum. index. **Bk Rev. Ad Acc. Circ:** 500. Documents available from BIOSIS Document Express. ***Continues*** *Zeitschrift fuer Kultutechnik und Flurbereinigung, 0044-2984.*
Ind/Abst Agric. Eng. Abstr.; Biol. Abstr. (1989-); For. Abstr.; GeoRef; Grass. Forage Abstr.; World Agric. Econ. Rural Sociol. Abstr.

LC S13 .Z553 **ISSN** 0372-9893
DD 630 RU
CODEN ZRKZAB

ZERNOVOE HOZAJSTVO. (ZERNOVOE KHOZIAISTVO.). [Zern. hoz.]. **Added/Corp** Soviet Union. Ministerstvo Selskogo Khoziaistva. (1963)-. Academic Scholarly Publication. Russian. Four times a year. $28.00. Izdatelstvo Kolos, Sadovaia-Spasskaia 18, 107807 Moscow Russia. Index available. Documents available from CASDDS.
Ind/Abst AGRICOLA; Chem. Abstr. (1972-1982).

LC SB354-402 **ISSN** 1000-8047
DD 634 CC

ZHONGGUO GUOSHU. **VFOAT** China Fruits. (1959)-. Periodical. Chinese. Four times a year. Zhongguo Nongye Kexueyuan Guoshu Yanjiusuo, Chinese Academy of Agricultural Sciences, Fruit Tree Research Institute, Wenquan Xingcheng, Liaoning 121600 People's Republic of China. **ED** Lin Yan.
Ind/Abst Hortic. Abstr.; Plant Breed. Abstr.; Rev. Plant Pathol.

LC SB188 **ISSN** 1001-7216
DD 633.18 CH

ZHONGGUO SHUIDAO KEXUE. **See** Food and Food Industry.

LC SB317.B2 C4 **ISSN** 1000-6567
DD 633.5/8 CC

ZHUZI YANJIU HUIKAN. (CHU TZU YEN CHIU HUI KAN.). [Zhuzi yanjiu huikan]. **Added/Corp** Che-Chiang Sheng lin yeh ko Hsueh yen Chiu so. **VFOAT** Journal of Bamboo Research. (1982)-. Periodical. Chinese (summaries and/or abstracts in English). Two times a year. RMBY8.00. China National Publishing Import & Export Corporation, 16 Gongti E Rd., Chaoyang Dist., Beijing 100704, People's Republic of China. **Tel** 011 8601 50630169, 5066688, FAX 011 8601 5063101, 5063010, telex 22313.
Ind/Abst Biodeter. Abstr.; For. Prod. Abstr. (1991-); For. Abstr.; Rev. Agric. Entomol.

LC SB211.P8 I56a **ISSN** 0302-7716
DD 635 PL

ZIEMNIAK. [Ziemniak]. **Main/Corp** Instytut Ziemniaka Bonin. **VFOAT** Kartofel'; Potato. (1969)-. Multiple languages (Polish and German; summaries and/or abstracts in English and Russian). Panstwowe Wydawnictwo Rolnicze i Lesne, Al. Jerozolimskie 28, PO Box 374, 00 024 Warsaw Poland. **Tel** 011 48 22 266451, telex 642410 IUNG PL.
Ind/Abst Crop Physiol. Abstr.; Field Crop Abstr.; Postharvest News Inf.; Potato Abstr.

LC S
DD 630 GW

ZMP BILANZ. GEMUSE. (1976/77)-. Periodical. German. One time a year. ZMP Marktberichte Bonn, Rochusstrabe 2, D-53123 Bonn Germany. **Tel** 011 49 228 9777170. ***Continues*** *Die Agrarmarkte BR Deutschland, EWG und Weltmarkt: Obst und Gemuse.*

LC SB608
DD 635.21 GW

ZMP-BILANZ : KARTOFFELN. German. One time a year. ZMP Marktberichte Bonn, Rochusstrabe 2, D-53123 Bonn Germany. **Tel** 011 49 228 9777170. ***Continues*** *Jahresbericht Kartoffeln (Kartoffelbilanz).*

LC HF
DD 380.1 GW

ZMP. BILANZ. OBST. (1976/77)-. Periodical. German. One time a year. ZMP Marktberichte Bonn, Rochusstrabe 2, D-53123 Bonn Germany. **Tel** 011 49 228 9777170. ***Continues*** *Die Agrarmarkte BR Deutschland, EWG und Weltmarkt: Obst und Gemuse.*

LC TP375 .Z85 **ISSN** 0344-8657
DD 664 GW
CCC
CODEN ZUCKDI
Pr Rev.

ZUCKERINDUSTRIE. (ZUCKERINDUSTRIE. SUGAR INDUSTRY.). [Zuckerindustrie]. **Added/Corp** Verein der Zuckerindustrie. Verein Deutscher Zuckertechniker. Verein der Kaufleute der Deutschen Zuckerindustrie. **VFOAT** Sugar Industry. Vol. 28 (Jan. 1978)-. Trade Publication. German (summaries and/or abstracts in English, French and Spanish). Twelve times a year (subscription includes 2 Buyers Guides and 1 index). $259.47. Verlag Dr Albert Bartens, PO Box 380250, 14112 Berlin Germany, Lueckhoffstr 16, 14129 Berlin Germany. **Tel** 011 49 0 30 803-5678, FAX 011 49 0 30 803-2049. **ED** J Bruhns. Index available. **Bk Rev. Ad Acc. Circ:** 2,200. Documents available from The Genuine Article, CASDDS. ***Formed by the union of*** *Zeitschrift fur die Zuckerindustrie, 0044-2623* ***and*** *Zucker, 0044-538X.*
Desc: Covers beet and cane agriculture, beet and cane sugar technology, sugar trading, sweeteners, renewable raw materials.
Ind/Abst AGRICOLA; BioBusiness; Biodeter. Abstr. (1991-); Chem. Abstr.; Curr. Cit.; Curr. Contents Agric. Biol. Environ. Sci.; EMBASE; Field Crop Abstr.; Food Sci. Technol. Abstr.; Nutr. Abstr. Rev., Ser. A, Hum. Exp.; Life Sci. Collect.; Res. Alert [Full Cov.]; Rev. Plant Pathol.; Sci. Cit. Index; SCISEARCH; Seed Abstr.; Soc. Sci. Cit. Index [Select. Cov.]; Sug. Indus. Abstr.; World Agric. Econ. Rural Sociol. Abstr.

LC SB188 **ISSN** 0044-5398
DD 633 GW

ZUCKERRUEBE, DIE. **Added/Corp** Marktverband Rubenbau und Zuckerwirtschaft fuer das Land Niedersachsen. Vol. 1 (Mar. 1952)-. Trade Publication. German. Six times a year. $40.99. Verlag TH Mann OHG, Postfach 200254, W 45837 Gelsenkirchen Germany. **Tel** 011 49 209 9304184.
Ind/Abst Field Crop Abstr.; Potato Abstr.; Soils Fert.; Weed Abstr.

DAIRY INDUSTRY

ISSN 0950-3730
DD 637 UK

AGRA EUROPE. MILK PRODUCTS. [Agra Eur., Milk prod.]. **VFOAT** Milk Products. (1986)-. Trade Publication. English. Ten times a year. £265.00 UK; £285.00 Europe; £295.00 other. Agra Europe London Limited, 25 Frant Road, Tunbridge Wells, Kent TN2 5JT United Kingdom. **Tel** 011 44 1892 533813, FAX 011 44 1892 544895, telex 95114 AGRATW G. available on an online database from DIALOG.
Desc: A report on EC butter, cheese and milk production and markets, with graphs and tables covering principal dairying nations of Europe and the world.
Ind/Abst F&S Index Plus Text, Int. [Full Txt.] [Select. Cov.]; PROMT [Full Txt.].

ISSN 0141-223X
UK

AGRA EUROPE. PRESERVED MILK. [Agra Eur. Preserv. milk]. **VFOAT** Preserved Milk. (1964)-. Trade Publication. English. Ten times a year. $607.47. Agra Europe London Limited, 25 Frant Road, Tunbridge Wells, Kent TN2 5JT United Kingdom. **Tel** 011 44 1892 533813, FAX 011 44 1892 544895, telex 95114 AGRATW G. **ED** Guy Faulkner. available on an online database from DIALOG.
Desc: Reports on whole, skim, whey, condensed and casein. Latest figures on European and world production, stocks, exports, imports and prices.
Ind/Abst F&S Index Plus Text, Int. [Full Txt.] [Select. Cov.]; PROMT [Full Txt.].

GW

AGRARMARKTE BR DEUTSCHLAND, EWG UND WELTMARKT. MILCH UND MILCHERZEUGNISSE, DIE. **Added/Corp** Zentrale Markt und Preisberichtstelle fur Erzeugnisse der Land- und Erhahrungswirtschaft. 1966-. Periodical. German. ZMP Marktberichte Bonn, Rochusstrabe 2, D-53123 Bonn Germany. **Tel** 011 49 228 9777170.

ISSN 1148-5647
FR
UDC 31(44)

AGRESTE. CONJONCTURE, LAIT ET PRODUITS LAITIERS. (1990)-. Periodical. French. Twelve times a year. 160.00F France; 180.00F other. Ministere de l'Agriculture et de la Peche, Direction des Affaires Financieres et Economiques, Service Central des Enquetes et Etudes Statistiques, 4 Avenue de Saint-Mande, 75570 Paris Cedex 12 France. **Tel** 011 33 1 43444633, 16 61288305.

ISSN 1182-2015
DD 338.1/77/09714/05 CN

AGROPUR NOUVELLES. [Agropur nouv.]. **Added/Corp** Agropur, Cooperative Agro-Alimentaire. (Dec. 1983)-. Periodical. French. Twelve times a year. Agropur/Cooperative Agro-Alimentaire, 510 rue Principale, Granby Quebec J2G 7G2 Canada. ***Continues*** *Nouvelles (Agropur, Cooperative Agro-Alimentaire)., 0822-5648.*

ISSN 1194-9589
CN

•**ALBERTA DAIRYMAN.** (1993)-. Trade Publication. English. Two times a year. 3.50Can$ Canada; 5.00Can$ US; 10.00Can$ other. Bowes Publishers Ltd., 4504 61st Avenue, Leduc Alberta, T9E 2Y1 Canada. **Tel** (403)986-2271, FAX (403)986-6397. **ED** Susan Moscicki & Wendy Weir. **Ad Acc. Circ:** 2,000.

LC HD9425.E8 A54
DD 338.1/76/0094 LU

ANIMAL PRODUCTION. **See** Agriculture-Livestock.

ISSN 0271-9967
DD 636 US
CODEN AMNCDO

ANNUAL MEETING - NATIONAL MASTITIS COUNCIL, INC. (ANNUAL MEETING.). [Annu. meet. - Natl. Mastitis Counc. inc.]. **Main/Corp** National Mastitis Council (U.S.). Meeting. **VFOAT** Annual Report. (1962)-. Academic Scholarly Publication. English. One time a year (June). $14.95. NASCO, 901 Janesville Avenue, PO Box 901, Fort Atkinson WI 53538-0901. **Tel** (800)558-9595, (414)563-2446, FAX (414)563-8296, telex 26-5476. Documents available from CASDDS.
Ind/Abst AGRICOLA [Full Cov.]; Chem. Abstr.

LC WMLC L 83/3162 **ISSN** 0538-7078
BE

ANNUAL MEMENTO / INTERNATIONAL DAIRY FEDERATION. **Main/Corp** International Dairy Federation. **VFOAT** Memento Annuel; Memento. English. One time a year. International Dairy Federation, 41 Square Vergote, 1040 Brussels Belgium. **Tel** 011 32 2 7339888, FAX 011 32 2 7330413, telex 63818.
Desc: Contains reports of the federation's annual meetings.

US

ANNUAL PROGRESS REPORT - SOUTHEAST LOUISIANA DAIRY AND PASTURE EXPERIMENT STATION. **Main/Corp** Southeast Louisiana Dairy and Pasture Experiment Station. **Added/Corp** Louisiana State

University and Agricultural and Mechanical College. Center for Agricultural Sciences and Rural Development. (1974)-. Periodical. English. One time a year.

NZ

ANNUAL REPORT & ACCOUNTS / WAIKATO DAIRY CO-OPERATIVE LIMITED. **Main/Corp** Waikato Dairy Co-Operative Limited. **VFOAT** Report and Accounts; Annual Report and Accounts. (198?)-. Periodical. English. One time a year. ***Continues*** *Waikato Dairy Co-operative Limited. Annual Report.*

LC HD9275.A84 A872a
DD 338.177/0994/02 AT

ANNUAL REPORT / AUSTRALIAN DAIRY CORPORATION. **Main/Corp** Australian Dairy Corporation. (1976)-. English. One time a year. Dairy Industry House, PO Box 330, Prahran Victoria 3181 Australia. ***Continues*** *Annual Report / Australian Dairy Produce Board.*

AT

ANNUAL REPORT - AUSTRALIAN NATIONAL DAIRY COMMITTEE. **Main/Corp** Australian National Dairy Committee. (1976)-. English.

LC SF221 .S6
DD 354.680082/337/06 SA

ANNUAL REPORT FOR THE YEAR ENDED ... / DAIRY CONTROL BOARD (SOUTH AFRICA). **Main/Corp** South Africa. Dairy Control Board. **VFOAT** Jaarverslag vir die Jaar Geeindig. Afrikaans (English). One time a year. Free. Dairy Board, PO Box 1284, Pretoria 0001 South Africa. **Tel** (012)28-6400, FAX (012)323-1956, telex 3-22504SA. Index available. **Circ:** 1,000 (ctrl). ***Continues*** *South Africa. Dairy Board. Annual Report - Dairy Board, 0304-6923.*

LC KFM9272.D2 A825
DD 353.9/786/008233 US

ANNUAL REPORT - MONTANA. BOARD OF MILK CONTROL. **Main/Corp** Montana. Board of Milk Control. (19??)-. English. One time a year. Montana Board of Milk Control, 805 North Main, Helena MT 59601. **Tel** (406)444-2875. **ED** Manys Koontz. **Circ:** 525.
Desc: Statistical report of milk receipts and utilization in Montana.

LC HD9275.C18 C37a **ISSN** 0382-3229
DD 354.710082/337043/06 CN

ANNUAL REPORT / THE CANADIAN DAIRY COMMISSION / RAPPORT ANNUEL / LA COMMISSION CANADIENNE DU LAIT. **Main/Corp** Canadian Dairy Commission. **VFOAT** Rapport Annuel. (1968)-. Government Publication. English (French). One time a year. Free on request. Agriculture Canada, Communications Branch, Ottawa Ontario K1A 0C7 Canada.

FI
TITLE CHANGE

ANNUAL REPORT / VALIO, FINNISH CO-OPERATIVE DAIRIES' ASSOCIATION. **Main/Corp** Valio (Firm). (19??)-(198?). English. ***Continued by*** *Valio Finnish Cooperative Dairies Association.*

ISSN 0253-6595
II
CODEN AJDRDW
TITLE CHANGE

ASIAN JOURNAL OF DAIRY RESEARCH. [Asian j. dairy res.]. **Added/Corp** Agricultural Research Communication Centre (India). Vol. 1, No. 1 (March 1982)-(1993). Academic Scholarly Publication. English. Agricultural Research Communication Centre, Sadar Karnal 132001, Haryana India. **Tel** 011 91 3036. Documents available from CASDDS. ***Continued by*** *Journal of Dairying Foods & Home Sciences.*
Desc: Original research articles on all aspects of dairy production, processing and management by eminent dairy research workers.
Ind/Abst Anim. Breed. Abstr.; BioBusiness; Biodeter. Abstr. (1991-); Chem. Abstr.; Dairy Sci. Abstr.; Food Sci. Technol. Abstr.; Nutr. Abstr. Rev., Ser. B, Live Feeds and Feed.

AT

AUSTRALIAN DAIRY FOODS. **Added/Corp** Australian Institute of Dairy Factory Managers and Secretaries. (1979)-. Periodical. English. Six times a year. 53.44Aus$. Indigo Arch Pty, PO Box 114, Malvern 3144 Australia. **Tel** 011 61 3 5761275, FAX 011 61 3 5761276. **ED** Anne Burgi. **Ad Acc.** ctrl circ. ***Absorbed*** *Butter Fat & Solids.*

LC SF **ISSN** 1038-8923
DD 636.2340994 AT
TITLE CHANGE

AUSTRALIAN HOLSTEIN DAIRYMAN. [Aust. Holst. dairym]. (1992)-(1995). Periodical. English. Shepparton Printing Service, PO Box 1884, Shepparton Victoria 3630 Australia. **Tel** 011 61 58 315205. **ED** G. Phillips. Index available. **Bk Rev**. **Ad Acc. Circ:** 4,000 (ctrl). ***Continues*** *Australian Holstein - Friesian Dairyman, 1035-0004* ***and*** *Dairyman.* ***Continued by*** *Australian Holstein Journal.*

LC SF
DD 636.2340994 AT

•**AUSTRALIAN HOLSTEIN JOURNAL.** (1995)-. English. Twelve times a year. $65.00. Holstein Friesian Association / Australia, 504 Race Course Road, Flemington VIC 3031 Australia. **Tel** 011 61 3 93761811. ***Continues*** *Australian Holstein Dairyman.*

LC SF **ISSN** 1034-9553
DD 636.28 AT

AUSTRALIAN ILLAWARRA DAIRYMAN. [Aust. Illawarra Diarym.]. (1989)-. Periodical. English. Four times a year. Shepparton Printing Service, PO Box 1884, Shepparton Victoria 3630 Australia. **Tel** 011 61 58 315205. ***Continues*** *Dairyman, 0311-9653.*

LC SF250.5 **ISSN** 0004-9433
DD 637 AT
CODEN AJDTAZ
Pr Rev.

AUSTRALIAN JOURNAL OF DAIRY TECHNOLOGY, THE. [Aust. j. dairy technol.]. Vol. 1, (Jan./March 1946)-. Academic Scholarly Publication. English. Two times a year (May, Nov.). 41.11Aus$. Dairy Industry Association of Australia, PO Box 20, Dairy Research Lab, Highett Victoria 3190 Australia. **Tel** 011 61 3 5562211, FAX 011 61 3 5320003, telex 33766. **ED** H. C. Deeth (editor's address: Queensland Food Research Laboratories, 19 Hercules Street, Hamilton 4007 Queensland). Index available. cum. index. **Bk Rev**. **Ad Acc. Circ:** 2,000. available on microfilm; available on an online database (File nos. 50 & 53) from Knight-Ridder Information, Inc. Documents available from The Genuine Article, BIOSIS Document Express, CASDDS, BLDSC, The UnCover Company, SWETS, UMI Article Clearinghouse.
Desc: Articles and general information on dairy technology. Articles written by researchers and industry personnel aimed at dairy science and dairy processing, not milk production.
Ind/Abst AGRICOLA [Full Cov.]; Anim. Breed. Abstr.; BioBusiness; Biol. Abstr.; Chem. Abstr.; Curr. Aware. Biol. Sci., CABS; Curr. Biotechnol.; Curr. Cit.; Curr. Contents Agric. Biol. Environ. Sci.; Dairy Sci. Abstr.; EMBASE; Food Sci. Technol. Abstr.; Foods Adlibra; Index Vet.; Leis., Rec., Tour. Abstr.; Microbiol. Abstr. Sect. A; Nutr. Abstr. Rev., Ser. B, Live Feeds and Feed.; Nutr. Abstr. Rev., Ser. A, Hum. Exp.; Life Sci. Collect.; Res. Alert [Full Cov.]; Rural Dev. Abstr.; Sci. Cit. Index; SCISEARCH; Vet. Bull.; World Agric. Econ. Rural Sociol. Abstr.

ISSN 0005-2450
US

AYRSHIRE DIGEST. [Ayrsh. dig.]. **Added/Corp** Ayrshire Breeders Association. (19??)-. Trade Publication. English. Ten times a year (Publishes 6 issues of Digest and 4 issues of newsletters). $14.00. Ayrshire Digest Association, PO Box 1608, Brattleboro VT 05302. **Tel** (802)254-7460, FAX (802)254-8251. **ED** Jill Stare. **Ad Acc. Circ:** 3,000 (ctrl). ***Continues*** *Ayrshire Quarterly.*
Desc: This magazine deals with items of specific interest to Ayrshire breeders, focusing primarily on genetics.

US

BALANCED DAIRYING. ECONOMICS. **Added/Corp** Texas Agricultural Extension Service. **VFOAT** Economics. (1987)-. Periodical. English. ***Continues*** *Balanced Dairying Economics Letter.*
Ind/Abst Agric. Eng. Abstr.; Dairy Sci. Abstr.

UK

BETTER BREEDING. **Added/Corp** Great Britain. Milk Marketing Board. (19??)-. Periodical. English. Four times a year. Free on request. Milk Marketing Board, Giggs Hill Green / Thames Ditton, Surrey KT7 0EL United Kingdom. **Tel** 011 44 1270 535659, FAX 011 44 1270 536586. **ED** Rosemary Haggett. **Circ:** 95,000 (ctrl).
Desc: The main publication of the Milk Marketing Board's artificial insemination section and is sent to all dairy farmers and artificial insemination members to inform them of developments related to the Milk Marketing Board bull stud.

ISSN 0824-4774
DD 636.2/34 CN

BRITISH COLUMBIA HOLSTEIN NEWS. [B.C. Holst. news]. **Added/Corp** Holstein-Friesian Association of Canada. B.C. Branch. **VFOAT** B.C. Holstein News. (1979)-. Periodical. English. Six times a year. 10.00Can$ (one-year), 18.00Can$ (two-year) Canada; 12.00Can$ (one-year), 22.00Can$ (two-year) US; 25.00Can$ (one-year), 48.00Can$ (two-year) other. British Columbia Holstein News, British Columbia V0X 1J0 Canada. **Tel** (604)888-5142. **ED** Barbara D. Souter. **Ad Acc. Circ:** 2,300.
Desc: Focusing on British Columbia holsteins and breeders.

UK

BRITISH GOAT SOCIETY'S YEAR BOOK FOR..., THE. **Main/Corp** British Goat Society. (19??)-. English. One time a year. $14.55. British Goat Society, 34/36 Fore Street, Newton Abbot, Devon TQ13 9AD United Kingdom. **Tel** 011 44 1626 833168. **ED** R Goodwin and E Worthy. cum. index. **Circ:** 2,000.
Desc: Informative articles, photographs, breeders advertisement; all breeds of goats.

ISSN 0259-8434
BE

BULLETIN - INTERNATIONAL DAIRY FEDERATION. [Bull. - Int. Dairy Fed.]. **VFOAT** Bulletin of the International Dairy Federation. (1985)-. Bulletin. English. Irregular. ***Continues*** *Bulletin - Federation Internationale de Laiterie, 0250-5118.*
Ind/Abst Nutr. Abstr. Rev., Ser. B, Live Feeds and Feed.; Nutr. Abstr. Rev., Ser. A, Hum. Exp.; World Agric. Econ. Rural Sociol. Abstr.

LC SF221 .B83 **ISSN** 0250-5118
DD 637/.13 BE
CODEN BIDFDY
TITLE CHANGE

BULLETIN (INTERNATIONAL DAIRY FEDERATION). (BULLETIN / FEDERATION INTERNATIONAL DE LAITERIE.). **Added/Corp** International Dairy Federation. (1978)-(19??). Bulletin. English (French). International Dairy Federation, 41 Square Vergote, 1040 Brussels Belgium. **Tel** 011 32 2 7339888, FAX 011 32 2 7330413, telex 63818. Index available. cum. index. **Circ:** 1,000 (ctrl). Documents available from CASDDS. ***Continues*** *International Dairy Federation. Annual Bulletin - International Dairy Foundation.* ***Continued by*** *Bulletin - International Dairy Federation, 0259-8434.*
Desc: Covers dairy technology, science and economics.
Ind/Abst Agric. Eng. Abstr. (?-?); Biodeter. Abstr. (?-?); Chem. Abstr. (?-?); Curr. Cit.; Food Sci. Technol. Abstr. (?-?); Index Vet. (?-?); Vet. Bull. (?-?).

LC HD9275.U7 C25
US

CALIFORNIA DAIRY INDUSTRY STATISTICS: MANUFACTURED DAIRY PRODUCTS, MILK PRODUCTION, UTILIZATION AND PRICES. **Main/Corp** California Crop and Livestock Reporting Service. **VFOAT** Manufactured Dairy Products, Milk Production, Utilization and Prices. (1960)-. English. One time a year. $10.00. California Agricultural Statistics Service, California Department of, Food and Agriculture, PO Box 1258, Sacramento CA 95812. **Tel** (916)551-1533. ***Continues in part*** *Special Publications / California. Dept. of Agriculture.*
Desc: Historic and detailed data on milk and dairy products.

ISSN 0892-4406
DD 338 US

CALIFORNIA DAIRY INFORMATION BULLETIN. [Calif. dairy inf. bull.]. Vol. 43, No. 9 (Sept. 1986)-. Bulletin. English. Twelve times a year. $15.00. California Agricultural Statistics Service, California Department of, Food and Agriculture, PO Box 1258, Sacramento CA 95812. **Tel** (916)551-1533. ***Continues*** *Dairy Information Bulletin, 0279-2605.*
Desc: Production, utilization, and prices of milk and dairy products.

CN

•**CANADIAN DAIRY.** (Apr. 1995)-. Trade Publication. English. Five times a year. 19.45Can$. Maccan Publishing Company Ltd, 3269 Bloor Street West, Suite 205, Toronto Ontario M8X 1E2 Canada. **Tel** (416)239-8423. **ED** I. Macnab. **Ad Acc. Circ:** 2,000 (ctrl). ***Continues*** *Modern Dairy, 0026-7651.*
Desc: Canada's business magazine for dairy processors/distributors. Articles on processing, packaging, materials handling, distribution and marketing.
Ind/Abst BioBusiness; Biodeter. Abstr.; Dairy Sci. Abstr.; Food Sci. Technol. Abstr.; Life Sci. Collect.; Sug. Indus. Abstr.

ISSN 0831-3008
DD 636.2/24 CN
Pr Rev.

CANADIAN GUERNSEY JOURNAL. [Can. Guernsey j.]. **Added/Corp** Canadian Guernsey Association. **VFOAT** Canadian Guernsey Breeders' Journal. Vol. 60, No. 4 (June 1985)-. Periodical. English. Six times a year (Jan., Mar., May, July, Sept., Nov.). 28.01Can$. Canadian Guernsey Association, 368 Woolwich Street, Guelph Ontario N1H 3W6 Canada. **Tel** (519)836-2141. **ED** V. M. MacDonald. **Ad Acc. Circ:** 500 (ctrl). ***Continues*** *Canadian Guernsey Breeders' Journal, 0045-4907.*
Desc: This magazine covers dairy cattle in Canada and Guernsey cattle around the world.

ISSN 0008-3909
CN
UDC 636.224.3(71)
CANADIAN JERSEY BREEDER. See Agriculture-Livestock.

ISSN 0891-1509
DD 338 US
CCC
CODEN CHMNE6
CHEESE MARKET NEWS. [Cheese mark. news]. (198?)-. Trade Publication. English. One time a week. $70.00. Cahners Publishing Company, 249 West 17th Street, New York NY 10011. **Tel** (212)645-0067, FAX (212)242-6987. **(Subscription address:** Cahners Publishing Company / Colorado, Paid Subscription Service Center, PO Box 7610, Highlands Ranch CO 80126-7610. **Tel** (303)470-4466, FAX (303)470-4691.**)** available on an online database (file 648/Full-Text) from DIALOG. ***Continues** Dairy Foods the National Dairy News, 0888-2363.*
Desc: Contains news affecting the cheese industry, from processing to marketing to retailing. Provides information on trading prices, market analyses and predictions of the industry's future.
Ind/Abst BioBusiness.

ISSN 0009-2142
US
CHEESE REPORTER. Vol. 1 (1876)-. Periodical. English. One time a week. $70.00. Cheese Reporter, 4210 East Washington Avenue, Madison WI 53704. **Tel** (608)246-8430, FAX (608)246-8431. **ED** Richard Groves. **Bk Rev. Ad Acc, Adv Mgr:** Kevin Thome. **Circ:** 2,400 (ctrl).
Desc: Reports on technology, production, sales, promotion, merchandising and general cheese and dairy industry news.
Ind/Abst BioBusiness; Foods Adlibra.

ISSN 0896-9426
DD 334 US
COOPERATIVE PARTNERS. [Coop. partn.]. **Added/Corp** Land O'Lakes, Inc. Farmers Union Central Exchange (Saint Paul, Minn.). **VFOAT** Partners. (Nov./Dec. 1987)-. Periodical. English. Twelve times a year. $5.00. Land O'Lakes Inc, PO Box 64089, St Paul MN 55164. **Tel** (612)451-5035. ***Formed by the union of** Land O'Lakes Mirror, 0196-5840 **and** Co-Op Country News, 0889-2903.*

LC HD9282.U5 N796a **ISSN** 0737-6324
DD 338.1/371/09756 US
COST OF PRODUCING MILK ON N.C. GRADE A DAIRY FARMS, THE. (THE COST OF PRODUCING MILK ON NORTH CAROLINA GRADE A DAIRY FARMS : ANNUAL REPORT TO THE NORTH CAROLINA MILK COMMISSION / PREPARED BY THE DEPARTMENT OF ECONOMICS AND BUSINESS AND THE NORTH CAROLINA AGRICULTURAL EXTENSION SERVICE, NORTH CAROLINA STATE UNIVERSITY AT RALEIGH.). [Cost prod. milk N.C. grade A dairy farms]. **Added/Corp** North Carolina Milk Commission. North Carolina State University. Dept. of Economics and Business. North Carolina Agricultural Extension Service. North Carolina State University. Dept. of Agricultural and Resources Economics. **VFOAT** Cost of Producing Milk on N.C. Grade A Dairy Farms. (19??)-. English.

ISSN 0045-9259
US
CODEN CDPJDE
SUSPENDED
CULTURED DAIRY PRODUCTS JOURNAL OF THE AMERICAN CULTURED DAIRY PRODUCTS INSTITUTE. (CULTURED DAIRY PRODUCTS JOURNAL.). [Cult. dairy prod. j. Am. Cult. Dairy Prod. Inst.]. **Added/Corp** American Cultured Dairy Products Institute. **VFOAT** CDP. Vol. 1 (Aug. 1966)-Suspended (Nov. 1995). Periodical. English. Four times a year. $20.00. Milk Industry Foundation, 888 16th Street Northwest, Washington DC 20006. **Tel** (202)296-4250, FAX (202)331-7820. **Ad Acc.** Documents available from BIOSIS Document Express, CASDDS.
Ind/Abst AgBiotech News Inf.; AGRICOLA [Full Cov.]; Anim. Breed. Abstr.; BioBusiness; Biodeter. Abstr. (1991-); Biol. Abstr. (1987-); Chem. Abstr.; Curr. Cit.; Dairy Sci. Abstr.; Food Sci. Technol. Abstr.; Foods Adlibra; Index Vet.; Nutr. Abstr. Rev., Ser. B, Live Feeds and Feed.; Rev. Med. Vet. Mycology.

LC SF239 .D15
DD 636.213 US
UDC 636.2.034
DAIRY CATTLE FEEDING AND MANAGEMENT. 1st Ed.-. English. John Wiley & Sons, Inc., 605 Third Avenue, New York NY 10158-0012. **Tel** (212)850-6000, (212)850-6645, FAX (212)850-6088, telex 12-7063. **(Subscription address:** John Wiley & Sons / UK, Baffins Lane, Chichester, West Sussex PO19 1UD United Kingdom. **Tel** 011 44 1243 779777, FAX 011 44 243 776128, telex 86290 WIBOOKG.**) ED** H O Henderson and P M Reaves.

ISSN 0383-6207
DD 636.2/1/40971 CN
DAIRY CONTACT. Vol. 1, Apr. (1976)-. Periodical. English. Twelve times a year. 11.22Can$. Dairy Contact, 11802 124th Street, Suite 210, Edmonton Alberta T5L 0M3 Canada. **Tel** (403)455-4173. **Ad Acc. Circ:** 25,900.

ISSN 0011-5568
US
NLM W1 DA239 **CODEN** DACDAK
Pr Rev.
DAIRY COUNCIL DIGEST. [Dairy Counc. dig.]. **Main/Corp** National Dairy Council. (1929)-. Periodical. English. Six times a year. $12.00. National Dairy Council, 10255 West Higgins Road, Suite 900, Rosemont IL 60018. **Tel** (708)803-2000, FAX (708)803-2077. **ED** Lois McBean. Index available. **Circ:** 85,000 (ctrl). Documents available from CASDDS.
Desc: An interpretive review of current nutrition research information for professionals. Subjects relate to the nutritional importance of dairy products to a well-balanced diet.
Ind/Abst AGRICOLA [Full Cov.]; Chem. Abstr.; Consum. Health Nutr. Index (?-?); Dairy Sci. Abstr.; Foods Adlibra; Health Index (1989-); Health Period. Database; Health Ref. Cent. (Jan. 1989-) [Full Cov.]; Nutr. Abstr. Rev., Ser. B, Live Feeds and Feed.; Nutr. Abstr. Rev., Ser. A, Hum. Exp.

LC HD9000 **ISSN** 1032-9552
DD 338.177099405 AT
DAIRY ECONOMICS RESEARCH REPORT. [Dairy econ. res. rep.]. (1989)-. Monographic series. English. Irregular. Price varies per volume. University of New England / Armidale, Department of Agricultural and Resource Economics, Armidale New South Wales 2351 Australia. **Tel** 011 61 67 732232, FAX 011 61 67 711531.
Ind/Abst World Agric. Econ. Rural Sociol. Abstr.

ISSN 0111-915X
NZ
CCC
DAIRY EXPORTER. Vol. 57, No. 7 (Jan. 1982)-. Periodical. English. Twelve times a year. $35.82. New Zealand Diary Exporter, PO Box 38272, Petone New Zealand. **Tel** 011 64 4 5683475, FAX 011 64 4 5683474. **ED** Hedley Dunn. Index available (Bound in 2nd issue). **Bk Rev. Ad Acc, Adv Mgr:** C. Cook, **Tel** 09 358 8124. **Circ:** 21,700. ***Continues** New Zealand Dairy Exporter.*

ISSN 0011-5576
UK
DAIRY FARMER (IPSWICH, SUFFOLK). (DAIRY FARMER.). Vol. 32, No. 1 (Jan. 1985)-. Trade Publication. English. Twelve times a year. £34.00 UK; £24.00 Ireland; $63.00 other. Farming Press, Royal Sovereign House, 40 Beresford Street, Woolwich London SE18 6BO United Kingdom. **Tel** 011 44 181 8557777, FAX 011 44 181 3173938. **(Subscription address:** Morgan Grampian, 40 Beresford Street, London SE18 6BQ United Kingdom. **Tel** 011 44 171 8557777, FAX 011 44 181 8555548.**) ED** David Smead. ***Continues** Dairy Farmer and Dairy-Beef Producer.*
Ind/Abst Anim. Breed. Abstr.; Dairy Sci. Abstr.; EP Collect.; Homework Help.; Index Vet.; MasterFile FullTEXT 1000; MasterFile FullTEXT 350; MasterFile FullTEXT 650; MasterFile FullTEXT; Nutr. Abstr. Rev., Ser. B, Live Feeds and Feed.; OCLC; Telebase.

ISSN 1182-8900
DD 636.2/142/09713 CN
DAIRY FARMER (LONDON, ONT.). (DAIRY FARMER.). [Dairy farmer]. (Autumn 1990)-. Periodical. English. Four times a year. $1.75 per number. Ontario Dairy Farmer, Box 7400, Station E, London Ontario N5Y 4X3 Canada. ***Continues** Ontario Dairy Farmer., 0832-5162.*

ISSN 1055-0607
DD 637 US
CODEN DAFIEK
DAIRY FIELD (1991). (DAIRY FIELD.). [Dairy field]. Vol. 174, No. 1 (Jan. 1991)-. Trade Publication. English. Twelve times a year. $55.00 (US); $110.00 (other). Stagnito Publishing Company, 1935 Sherner Road, Suite 100, Northbrook IL 60062. **Tel** (708)205-5660, FAX (708)205-5680. ***Continues** Dairy Field Today, 1053-9425.*
Ind/Abst BioBusiness (1991-).

LC SF257 .D34 **ISSN** 1043-3546
DD 363 US
NLM W1; DA239F **CODEN** DFESEC
DAIRY, FOOD AND ENVIRONMENTAL SANITATION. (DAIRY, FOOD, AND ENVIRONMENTAL SANITATION : A PUBLICATION OF THE INTERNATIONAL ASSOCIATION OF MILK, FOOD AND ENVIRONMENTAL SANITARIANS.). [Dairy food environ. sanit.]. **Added/Corp** International Association of Milk, Food, and Environmental Sanitarians. Vol. 9, No. 1 (Jan. 1989)-. Trade Publication. English. Twelve times a year. $130.00. IAMFES, 6200 Aurora Avenue, Suite 200W, Des Moines IA 50322. **Tel** (515)276-3344, (800)369-6337, FAX (515)276-8655. available on microfilm and microfiche from University Microfilms International (UMI). ***Continues** Dairy and Food Sanitation, 0273-2866.*

Ind/Abst AgBiotech News Inf.; AGRICOLA [Full Cov.]; Agric. Eng. Abstr. (1991-); BioBusiness (1989-); Biodeter. Abstr. (1991-); Curr. Cit.; Dairy Sci. Abstr.; Food Sci. Technol. Abstr.; Index Vet.; Poult. Abstr.; Rev. Med. Vet. Mycology.

LC HD9275.U3 D33 **ISSN** 0888-0050
DD 338.1/77/0973 US
CCC
CODEN DAFOE4
DAIRY FOODS. [Dairy foods]. Vol. 87, No. 2 (Feb. 1986)-. Periodical. English. Twelve times a year. $89.00 US; $155.00 (surface mail), $250.00 (airmail) other. Cahners Publishing Company, 249 West 17th Street, New York NY 10011. **Tel** (212)645-0067, FAX (212)242-6987. **(Subscription address:** Cahners Publishing Company / Colorado, Paid Subscription Service Center, PO Box 7610, Highlands Ranch CO 80126-7610. **Tel** (303)470-4466, FAX (303)470-4691.**) ED** Wendy Kimbrell. Index available. **Ad Acc. Circ:** 20,000 (ctrl). available on microfilm and microfiche from University Microfilms International (UMI); available on an online database (file 648/Full-Text) from DIALOG. ***Continues** Dairy Record, 0011-5673.*
Desc: Provides credible information by analyzing and reporting on technologies, trends and industry issues in every product category in an easy-to-read format.
Ind/Abst AgBiotech News Inf.; BioBusiness (1989-); Bus. ASAP (1990-) [Full Txt.]; Bus. Index (1986-); Dairy Sci. Abstr.; F&S Index Plus Text, Int. [Select. Cov.]; Food Sci. Technol. Abstr.; Foods Adlibra; Gen. BusinessFile (1986-); Index Vet.; Int. Packag. Abstr.; Mark. Advert. Ref. Serv.; PROMT; Soyabean Abstr.; Trade Ind. ASAP [Full Txt.]; Trade Ind. Index [Full Txt.].

ISSN 1057-2619
DD 637 US
CCC
CODEN DFNEEF
DAIRY FOODS NEWSLETTER. [Dairy foods newsl.]. (19??)-. Trade Publication. English. One time a week (50 issues). $279.90. Cahners Publishing Company, 249 West 17th Street, New York NY 10011. **Tel** (212)645-0067, FAX (212)242-6987. **(Subscription address:** Cahners Publishing Company / Colorado, Paid Subscription Service Center, PO Box 7610, Highlands Ranch CO 80126-7610. **Tel** (303)470-4466, FAX (303)470-4691.**)** available on an online database (file 648/Full-Text) from DIALOG. ***Continues** Dairy Industry Newsletter (Arlington, Va. : 1975).*
Desc: Offers dairy processing and marketing executives easy-to-read, up-to-the-minute industry news. Topics include mergers and acquisitions, company earnings, industry pricing statistics, new products and legislative and regulatory news.

ISSN 0011-5592
DD 636 US
DAIRY GOAT JOURNAL. [Dairy goat j.]. Vol. 9, No. 6 (Aug. 1931)-. Periodical. English. Ten times a year. $19.00. Duck Creek, W 2997 Market Road, Helenville WI 53137. **Tel** (414)593-8385, FAX (414)593-8384. **ED** Ann Miller. Index available. **Bk Rev. Ad Acc. Circ:** 12,000. available on microfilm from University Microfilms International (UMI). ***Continues** International Dairy Goat Journal.*
Desc: Authoritative articles on all aspects of goat keeping from family milk supply to commercial dairying. Topics include buying, breeding, veterinary help, etc.

ISSN 0970-3438
II
UDC 637.1
DAIRY GUIDE. NEW DELHI. (1978)-. Periodical. English. Twelve times a year. $25.00. **(Subscription address:** Prints India, 11 Darya Ganj, New Delhi 110002 India. **Tel** 011 91 11 3268645, FAX 011 91 11 3275542, telex 31-61087 PRIN-IN.**)**

ISSN 0011-5614
US
CCC
DAIRY HERD MANAGEMENT. [Dairy herd manage.]. (Oct. 1965)-. Periodical. English. Twelve times a year. Free to qualified readers, $12.00 US; $17.00 other. Vance Publishing Corporation, 400 Knightsbridge Parkway, Lincolnshire IL 60069. **Tel** (800)255-5113, (708)634-2600. **(Subscription address:** Vance Publishing Corporation, PO Box 421, Lincolnshire IL 60069. **Tel** (708)634-4347.**)** available on microfilm and microfiche from University Microfilms International (UMI).
Ind/Abst AGRICOLA [Full Cov.]; Biol. Agric. Index.

LC SF233.I4 D326
DD 338.1/771/0954 II
DAIRY INDIA. See Agriculture-Abstracting, Bibliographies and Statistics.

LC SF221 .D37 **ISSN** 0308-8197
DD 637/.05 UK
CODEN DINIDD
Pr Rev.
DAIRY INDUSTRIES INTERNATIONAL. [Dairy ind. int.]. Vol. 40, No. 6 (June 1975)-. Academic Scholarly Publication. English. Twelve times a year. $212.00. Wilmington Publishing Ltd., PO Box 200, Field End Road, Ruislip Middlesex HA4 OSY United Kingdom. **Tel** 011 44 181 8413970, FAX 011 44 181 8419676. **ED** Pauline Russell. **Bk Rev. Ad Acc. Circ:** 6,000. available

on an online database (file 648/Full-Text) from DIALOG. Documents available from The Genuine Article, CASDDS. ***Continues*** *Dairy Industries, 0011-5622.*
Desc: Covers milk and dairy products such as processing, marketing, and new developments.
Ind/Abst BioBusiness (1984-); Biodeter. Abstr. (1991-); Chem. Abstr. (-1988); Curr. Contents Agric. Biol. Environ. Sci. (19??-); Curr. Technol. Index (19??-); Dairy Sci. Abstr. (19??-); EMBASE (19??-); EP Collect.; F&S Index Plus Text, Int. (19??-) [Select. Cov.]; Food Sci. Technol. Abstr. (19??-); Homework Help.; Infomat Int. Bus. (19??-); Int. Packag. Abstr. (19??-); Leis., Rec., Tour. Abstr.; MasterFile FullTEXT 1000; MasterFile FullTEXT 350; MasterFile FullTEXT 650; MasterFile FullTEXT (July 1994-); PROMT (19??-); Res. Alert (19??-) [Select. Cov.]; Rural Dev. Abstr. (19??-); SCISEARCH (19??-); Soc. Sci. Cit. Index [Select. Cov.]; Telebase; Trade Ind. ASAP (19??-) [Full Txt.]; Trade Ind. Index (19??-) [Full Txt.]; Vocat. Search; World Agric. Econ. Rural Sociol. Abstr. (19??-).

AT
DAIRY INDUSTRY LEADER. Added/Corp Dairy Industry Marketing Authority (Sydney, N.S.W.). No. 1 (Dec. 1982)-. Periodical. English. Six times a year. Free on request. New South Wales Dairy Corporation, 71-75 Regent Street, Sydney NSW 2000 Australia. **Tel** FAX 011 61 2 3194345. ***Continues*** *New South Wales Dairyman, 0310-3714.*

ISSN 0956-8131
DD 338.177 UK
DAIRY INDUSTRY NEWSLETTER. [Dairy ind. newsl.]. **VFOAT** Barry Wilson's Dairy Industry Newsletter. (1989)-. Periodical. English. Twenty-five times a year. $453.47. Eden Publishing, 13 Hertford Street, Cambridge CB4 3AE United Kingdom. **Tel** 011 44 1223 460478, FAX 011 44 1223 464109. **ED** Barry Wilson. **Bk Rev**, (Qty: 1-2).

US
•DAIRY, LIVESTOCK, AND POULTRY. DAIRY, WORLD MARKETS AND TRADE. Added/Corp United States. Foreign Agricultural Service. United States. World Agricultural Outlook Board. **VFOAT** Dairy, World Markets and Trade. (Mar. 1994)-. Government Publication. English. Two times a year. $14.00. US Department of Agriculture / Foreign Agricultural Service, 14th Street & Independence Avenue Southwest, Washington DC 20250. **Tel** (202)720-9445, FAX (202)720-7729. **(Subscription address:** NTIS, 5285 Port Royal Road, Springfield VA 22161. **Tel** (703)487-4630.**)** ***Continues*** *World Dairy Situation.*

US
•DAIRY, LIVESTOCK AND POULTRY, U.S. TRADE AND PROSPECTS. Added/Corp United States. Foreign Agricultural Service. United States. World Agricultural Outlook Board. **VFOAT** Dairy, Livestock and Poultry, US Trade and Prospects. (Mar. 1994)-. Government Publication. English. Twelve times a year. $78.00. US Department of Agriculture / Foreign Agricultural Service, 14th Street & Independence Avenue Southwest, Washington DC 20250. **Tel** (202)720-9445, FAX (202)720-7729. **(Subscription address:** NTIS, 5285 Port Royal Road, Springfield VA 22161. **Tel** (703)487-4630.**)** ***Continues*** *U.S. Dairy, Livestock, and Poultry Trade.*

ISSN 0744-1282
US
DAIRY MARKET NEWS. [Dairy mark. news]. **Added/Corp** Federal-State Market News Service. United States. Agricultural Marketing Service. Dairy Division. Wisconsin. Dept. of Agriculture. Vol. 99, No. 89-Vol. 100, No. 44; Vol. 42, No. 57 (July 30, 1974)-. Periodical. English. One time a week. $50.00. US Department of Agriculture / Wisconsin, PO Box 8911, Madison WI 53708. **Tel** (608)264-5254, FAX (608)264-5011. **Circ:** 2500. ***Continues*** *Dairy and Poultry Market News: Dairy Report.*
Desc: Provides information on milk and related dairy products, government programs, and miscellaneous items that affect the US dairy industry.

LC HD9275.U3 D315 **ISSN** 0098-6690
DD 338.1/77/0973 US
DAIRY MARKET STATISTICS, ANNUAL SUMMARY. See Agriculture-Abstracting, Bibliographies and Statistics.

ISSN 0957-8625
DD 338.177 UK
DAIRY MARKETS WEEKLY. [Dairy mark. wkly.]. **Added/Corp** Agra Europe (London). **VFOAT** Agra Europe Dairy Markets Weekly. (1989)-. Trade Publication. English. One time a week. $829.94. Agra Europe London Limited, 25 Frant Road, Tunbridge Wells, Kent TN2 5JT United Kingdom. **Tel** 011 44 1892 533813, FAX 011 44 1892 544895, telex 95114 AGRATW G.
Ind/Abst PROMT [Full Txt.].

US
DAIRY MONTHLY IMPORTS. Added/Corp United States. Foreign Agricultural Service. (Jan. 1991)-. Government Publication. English. Twelve times a year. $50.00. US Department of Agriculture / Foreign Agricultural Service, 14th Street & Independence Avenue Southwest, Washington DC 20250. **Tel** (202)720-9445, FAX (202)720-7729. ***Continues in part*** *Dairy, Livestock, and Poultry. Meat and Dairy Monthly Imports.*

FR
DAIRY PACKAGING NEWSLETTER. Added/Corp International Dairy Federation. (197?)-. Newsletter. English. Twelve times a year. International Dairy Federation, 41 Square Vergote, 1040 Brussels Belgium. **Tel** 011 32 2 7339888, FAX 011 32 2 7330413, telex 63818.
Ind/Abst Dairy Sci. Abstr.; Food Sci. Technol. Abstr.; Int. Packag. Abstr.; Rice Abstr.

LC SF261 .U54 **ISSN** 0565-2049
DD 353.008/24 US
DAIRY PLANTS SURVEYED AND APPROVED FOR USDA GRADING SERVICE. Government Publication. English. US Department of Agriculture, 14th Street and Independence Avenue SW, Washington DC 20250. **Tel** (202)720-5457. available on microfiche (Vols. for (1986-) distributed to depository libraries). ***Continues*** *Dairy Plants Surveyed and Approved for USDA Grading Service, 0565-2049.*

ISSN 0069-7699
UK
DAIRY PRODUCE; A REVIEW OF PRODUCTION, TRADE, CONSUMPTION AND PRICES RELATING TO BUTTER, CHEESE, CONDENSED MILK, MILK POWDER, CASEIN, EGGS AND EGG PRODUCTS. Main/Corp Commonwealth Secretariat. 1967-. English. Commonwealth Secretariat / London, Marlborough House, Pall Mall, London SW1Y 5HX United Kingdom. **Tel** 011 44 171 8393411, telex 27678. ***Continues*** *Dairy Produce.*

LC HD9275.U3 U543A
DD 338.1/77/0973021 US
DAIRY PRODUCTS ... SUMMARY / UNITED STATES DEPARTMENT OF AGRICULTURE, STATISTICAL REPORTING SERVICE, CROP REPORTING BOARD. VAT Dairy Products. 1983-. Statistical Publication. English. One time a year. US Department of Agriculture, 14th Street and Independence Avenue SW, Washington DC 20250. **Tel** (202)720-5457. ***Continues*** *Dairy Products Annual Summary, 0363-9657.*

ISSN 0093-1446
DD 637 US
DAIRY PRODUCTS (WASHINGTON, D.C.). (DAIRY PRODUCTS / CROP REPORTING BOARD, ECONOMICS, STATISTICS, & COOPERATIVES SERVICE. U.S. DEPARTMENT OF AGRICULTURE.). [Dairy prod.]. **Added/Corp** United States. Crop Reporting Board. United States. Agricultural Statistics Board. (April 1972)-. Government Publication. English. Thirteen times a year. $40.00. US Department of Agriculture, 14th Street and Independence Avenue SW, Washington DC 20250. **Tel** (202)720-5457. **(Subscription address:** Superintendent of Documents, US Government Printing Office, Washington DC 20402. **)** available on microfiche (Vols. for (1986-) distributed to depository libraries). Documents available from Documents on Demand. ***Formed by the union of*** *Evaporated, Condensed, and Dry Milk Report, 0093-1462; Milk Prices Paid by Creameries and Cheese Plants; Production of Cottage Cheese; Production of Creamery Butter and Cheese* ***and*** *Production of Ice Cream and Related Frozen Products.*
Ind/Abst Am. Stat. Index; Dairy Sci. Abstr.

ISSN 1182-5480
DD 636.2/142 CN
DAIRY RESEARCH REPORT (GUELPH). (DAIRY RESEARCH REPORT.). [Dairy res. rep.]. **Added/Corp** University of Guelph. Ontario Agricultural College. Dairy Research Program. Ontario. Ministry of Agriculture and Food. (1990)-. English. Limited free distribution. Department of Animal and Poultry Science, Ontario Agricultural College, University of Guelph, Guelph Ontario N1G 2W1 Canada. **Tel** (519)824-4120, (519)836-9873, telex 06956645. ***Continues*** *Guelph Dairy Research Report., 0828-7996.*

LC HD9275.E86 D35 **ISSN** 0142-422X
DD 338.17 UK
DAIRY REVIEW. Added/Corp Agra Europe (London) Limited. **VFOAT** Agra Europe ... Dairy Review. (19??)-. English. Irregular. £85.00. Agra Europe London Limited, 25 Frant Road, Tunbridge Wells, Kent TN2 5JT United Kingdom. **Tel** 011 44 1892 533813, FAX 011 44 1892 544895, telex 95114 AGRATW G.

ISSN 0300-0753
DD 338.1/77/0971 CN
DAIRY REVIEW, THE. See Agriculture-Abstracting, Bibliographies and Statistics.

LC HD1401 **ISSN** 0011-5681
DD 338.47637 UK
DAIRY SCIENCE ABSTRACTS. See Agriculture-Abstracting, Bibliographies and Statistics.

ISSN 0578-4875
DD 637 US
DAIRY SCIENCE EXTENSION LEAFLET. [Dairy sci. ext. leafl.]. **Added/Corp** United States. Dept. of Agriculture. Clemson University. Extension Service. Clemson University. Cooperative Extension Service. (Aug. 1964)-. English. Clemson University Extension Service, Department of Agriculture, Clemson SC 29634.
Ind/Abst AGRICOLA [Full Cov.].

LC HD9275.A1 M54
DD 338.1/77/021 FR
•DAIRY SECTOR INDICATORS = INDICATEURS DU SECTEUR LAITIER. Added/Corp Organisation for Economic Co-operation and Development. **VFOAT** Indicateurs du Secteur Laitier. (1994)-. English (French). OECD Publications and Information Center, 2 rue Andre-Pascal, 75775 Paris Cedex 16 France. **Tel** 011 33 1 49104262, US:(202)785-6323, FAX 011 33 1 45248500, 011 33 1 45248176, telex 620 160 OCDE. **(Subscription address:** OECD Publications Center, 2001 L Street, Suite 700, Washington DC 20036. **Tel** (202)822-3873, (202)785-6323.**)** ***Continues*** *Milk and Milk Products Balances in OECD Countries.*
Desc: Data on production, consumption, imports and exports of milk, butter, cheese, and eggs in OECD countries.

LC HD9275.Z55 D34
DD 338.1/77/096891 RH
DAIRY SITUATION AND OUTLOOK REPORT. Added/Corp Zimbabwe. Agricultural Marketing Authority. Economics Section. Zimbabwe. Agricultural Marketing Authority. (19??)-. English. One time a year.
Ind/Abst Predicasts Forecasts; World Agric. Econ. Rural Sociol. Abstr.

ISSN 0736-4962
US
DAIRY WORLD (MILLBURY, MASS.). (DAIRY WORLD.). [Dairy world]. (19??)-. English. Six times a year. $6.00. IBA Inc, 27 Providence Road, PO Box 31, Millbury MA 01527. **Tel** (617)865-2507. **ED** Diane Cowie. **Ad Acc. Circ:** 38,406 (ctrl). available on microfilm from University Microfilms International (UMI).
Desc: Provides updated information, including the results of original research. Also covers animal health, milk production and marketing, sanitation, farm operations, equipment and supplies.

LC SF232.W47 D34 **ISSN** 0011-572X
DD 637 US
TITLE CHANGE
DAIRYMAN (CORONA), THE. (DAIRYMAN.). [Dairyman]. **VAT** Dairy Man. Vol. 1, No. 1 (1922)-Vol. 75, No. 12 (Dec. 1994). Periodical. English. Holstein Friesian World, 8036 Lake Street, PO Box 299, Sandy Creek NY 13145. **Tel** (315)387-3441, (800)334-1904, FAX (315)387-3655. **ED** Dennis Halladay. **Ad Acc. Circ:** 32,500 (ctrl). ***Continued by*** *Western Dairyman, 1079-0578.*
Desc: Emphasis is on news about dairy farmers, dairy farming and related dairy industries.

ISSN 0894-1653
DD 338 US
DAIRYMEN'S DIGEST (MORNING GLORY FARMS ED.). (DAIRYMEN'S DIGEST.). [Dairym. dig.]. **Added/Corp** Associated Milk Producers. Morning Glory Farms Region. Vol. 18, No. 4 (Apr. 1987)-. Periodical. English. Twelve times a year. $3.00. Associated Milk Producers Inc., 116 North Main Street, Morning Glory Farms, Scawano WI 54166. **Tel** (715)526-2131. **ED** JoDee Sattler. **Ad Acc. Circ:** 6,000 (ctrl). ***Continues*** *Dairymen's Digest.; Mid-States Region [Ed]., 0745-5399.*
Desc: News related to our cooperative and its members.

ISSN 0745-9033
DD 338 US
DAIRYMEN'S DIGEST. NORTH CENTRAL REGION EDITION. (DAIRYMEN'S DIGEST.). [Dairym. dig.]. **Added/Corp** Associated Milk Producers. North Central Region. Vol. 3, No. 7 (July 1972)-. Trade Publication. English. Twelve times a year. $6.00. North Central Region Associated Milk Producers, PO Box 275, Spirit Lake IA 51360. **Tel** (712)336-2805. **ED** John E. Van Der Linden. **Bk Rev. Ad Acc. Circ:** 13,000 (ctrl). ***Continues*** *Dairymen Digest.*
Ind/Abst AGRICOLA.

ISSN 0011-5738
DD 637 US
DAIRYNEWS (PEARL RIVER, N.Y.). (DAIRYNEWS.). [Dairynews]. **Added/Corp** Dairylea Cooperative Incorporated. **VFOAT** Dairy News. Vol. 53, No. 20 (Oct. 22, 1969)-. Trade Publication. English. Four times a year. $8.00. Dairylea Cooperative Inc., PO Box 4844, Syracuse NY 13221. **Tel** (315)433-0100, FAX

(315)433-2345. **ED** Kris R. Green. **Ad Acc**, **Adv Mgr:** Monica Coleman. **Circ:** 5,200. ***Continues*** *Dairymen's League News.*
Desc: Designed for Northeastern dairy farmers. Communicates pertinent legislation, market analysis, quality control, management and financial issues.

ISSN 0904-4310
DK

DANISH DAIRY & FOOD INDUSTRY ... WORLDWIDE. [Dan. dairy & food ind.-worldwide]. **Added/Corp** Dansk Mejeristforening. Dansk Mejeriingenir Forening. **VFOAT** Danish Dairy & Food Industry Worldwide; Danish Dairy and Food Industry ... Worldwide. (Oct. 1988)-. English. Every 2 years. Danish Dairy Engineer's Association, Cikorievej 8, DK-5220 Odense SOe Denmark. **Tel** 011 66 124025, FAX 011 66 144026. ***Continues*** *Danish Dairy Industry ... Worldwide, 0105-1210.*
Ind/Abst Curr. Cit.

ISSN 0012-0480
GW
CODEN DMWSAB

DEUTSCHE MILCHWIRTSCHAFT (HILDESHEIM). (DEUTSCHE MILCHWIRTSCHAFT.). [Dtsch. Milchwirtsch.]. **Added/Corp** Zentralverband Deutscher Molkereifachleute und Milchwirtschaftler. Vol. 19, No. 40 (Oct. 2, 1968)-. Trade Publication. German. Twenty-six times a year. $379.53. Verlag TH Mann OHG, Postfach 200254, W 45837 Gelsenkirchen Germany. **Tel** 011 49 209 9304184. **ED** H Roland Sobua. **Bk Rev. Ad Acc. Circ:** 43,500. ***Continues*** *Molkerei- und Kaserei-Zeitung.*
Desc: Covers engineering, technology, the economy, science and social contributions of dairying.
Ind/Abst Curr. Cit.; Dairy Sci. Abstr.; Food Sci. Technol. Abstr.; Int. Packag. Abstr.; Leis., Rec., Tour. Abstr.; Rural Dev. Abstr.; World Agric. Econ. Rural Sociol. Abstr.

GW

DEUTSCHE ZUCKERRUEBENZEITUNG. Periodical. German. Six times a year. DM17.00 Germany; DM24.00 other. Deutsche Zuckerruebenzeitung, Simon Breu Strasse 52, 97074 Wuerzburg Germany. **Tel** 49 931 71054, FAX 49 931 884517, telex 680106.

LC SF253 .D44 **ISSN** 0264-8407
DD 637/.028/7 UK
CODEN DDCHDM
Pr Rev.

DEVELOPMENTS IN DAIRY CHEMISTRY. [Dev. dairy chem.]. (1982)-. Academic Scholarly Publication. English. Irregular. Price varies per volume. Elsevier Science Publishers BV, PO Box 211, 1000 AE Amsterdam Netherlands. **Tel** 011 31 20 4853641, 011 31 20 4853642, FAX 011 31 20 4853598. Documents available from CASDDS.
Ind/Abst Chem. Abstr.

ISSN 0938-9369
GW
CODEN LEMIEZ

DMZ, LEBENSMITTELINDUSTRIE UND MILCHWIRTSCHAFT. **VFOAT** DMZ; Magazine for Food and Dairy Industry; Journal d'Industrie Alimentaire et de Laiterie. **VAT** Deutsche Molkerei-Zeitung Lebensmittelindustrie und Milchwirtschaft. (Jan. 1990)-. Periodical. German. One time a week. DM438.75. VV-Gmbh / Volkswirtschaftlicher Verlag, Postfach 701920, D-81319 Munich Germany. **Tel** 011 49 89 7141013, FAX 011 49 89 7192753, telex 5212 287 VOVE D. ***Continues*** *Deutsche Molkerei-Zeitung (Munich, Germany : 1951).*
Ind/Abst Chem. Abstr.

BE

DOCUMENTS - INTERNATIONAL DAIRY FEDERATION. **Main/Corp** International Dairy Federation. No. 1 (1952)-. Monographic series. English (French). Irregular. 11500F. International Dairy Federation, 41 Square Vergote, 1040 Brussels Belgium. **Tel** 011 32 2 7339888, FAX 011 32 2 7330413, telex 63818. Index available. cum. index. **Circ:** 1,000.
Desc: Bulletin and standards on dairy economics, technology and science.
Ind/Abst AGRICOLA.

UK
SUSPENDED

EC DAIRY FACTS & FIGURES. **Added/Corp** Great Britain. Milk Marketing Board. **VFOAT** E.C. Dairy Facts & Figures; EC Dairy Facts and Figures. (1991)-Suspended (1994). Trade Publication. English. Milk Marketing Board, Giggs Hill Green / Thames Ditton, Surrey KT7 0EL United Kingdom. **Tel** 011 44 1270 535659, FAX 011 44 1270 536586. ***Continues*** *EEC Dairy Facts and Figures.*

ISSN 0226-3947
DD 338.1/371/097123 CN

ECONOMICS OF MILK PRODUCTION IN ALBERTA. [Econ. milk prod. Alta.]. Vol. 37 (1977)-. English. One time a year. Free. Production Economics Branch, Alberta Department of Agriculture, 7000 113 Street, Edmonton Alberta T6H 5T6 Canada. **Tel** (403)427-5397. **ED** R Susko. **Circ:** 2,000. ***Formed by the union of*** *Edmonton Dairy Farm Business Summary, 0383-5928; Calgary Dairy Farm Business Summary, 0383-5952; Lethbridge Dairy Farm Business Summary, 0383-5936* ***and*** *Peace River Dairy Farm Business Summary, 0383-5944.*
Desc: The report deals with the farm cost and price analysis and economic conditions encountered in the production of fluid milk in Alberta.

ISSN 0378-2700
UA
CODEN EJDSDB
Pr Rev.

EGYPTIAN JOURNAL OF DAIRY SCIENCE. [Egyptian j. dairy science]. **Added/Corp** Egyptian Society of Dairy Science. Vol. 1, (June 1973)-. Academic Scholarly Publication. English (summaries and/or abstracts in Arabic). Two times a year (June and December). $45.00. Egyptian Society of Dairy Science, National Research Center/Dokki, Cairo. **Tel** 011 20 2 701211 415, FAX 011 20 2 700931, telex 94022 NAREC ON. **ED** M. H. Abad El-Salam. **Bk Rev. Ad Acc. Circ:** 1000. Documents available from CASDDS.
Desc: Research papers in the areas of processing milk products and milk production.
Ind/Abst AGRICOLA; Anim. Breed. Abstr.; Biodeter. Abstr. (19??-19??); Chem. Abstr.; Curr. Cit.; Dairy Sci. Abstr.; Food Sci. Technol. Abstr.; Nutr. Abstr. Rev., Ser. B, Live Feeds and Feed.; Nutr. Abstr. Rev., Ser. A, Hum. Exp.; Poult. Abstr.; Rev. Agric. Entomol.; Rev. Med. Vet. Entomol.; Rice Abstr.; Soyabean Abstr.

GW

EUROPAMARKT : MILCH. **Added/Corp** Zentrale Markt- und Preisberichtstelle fur Erzeugnisse der Land,- Forst- und Ernahrungswirtschaft. No. 6 (June 1972)-. Periodical. German. Twelve times a year. DM73.00. Zentrale Market und Preisberichtstelle fur Erzeugnisse der Land, Forst und Ernahrungswirtschaft GmbH (ZMP), Godesberger Allee 142-148, 5300 Bonn 2 Germany. **Tel** 888-0, telex 88576759. **Bk Rev. Ad Acc. Circ:** 250. ***Continues*** *Europamarkt: Die Milchwirtschaftlichen Markte Westeuropas.*
Desc: Covers milk production and dairy markets. Butter and cheese production, dairy product stocks and prices are also covered.

GW

EUROPAMARKT: MILCH BUTTER KASE. German. Ten times a year. DM276.00 Germany; DM360.00 other. ZMP Marktberichte Bonn, Rochusstrabe 2, D-53123 Bonn Germany. **Tel** 011 49 228 9777170.

ISSN 0936-6318
GW

EUROPEAN DAIRY MAGAZINE. **VFOAT** EDM. (19??)-. Trade Publication. English (French and German). Four times a year. $58.73. Verlag TH Mann OHG, Postfach 200254, W 45837 Gelsenkirchen Germany. **Tel** 011 49 209 9304184.
Ind/Abst Dairy Sci. Abstr.; Index Vet.; Nutr. Abstr. Rev., Ser. A, Hum. Exp.; Soyabean Abstr.

LC HD9275.C3 S273
DD 338.1/77/097124 CN

FARM BUSINESS ANALYSIS ... DAIRY ENTERPRISE / SASKATCHEWAN AGRICULTURE, MARKETING AND ECONOMICS DIVISION. English. One time a year.

KE

FARMING TODAY (NAIROBI, KENYA). (FARMING TODAY.). (198?)-. Periodical. English. Twelve times a year. Sh400.00 Kenya; $30.00 other. News Publishers Ltd / Kenya, Norwich Union House/4th Floor, Mama Ngina Street, PO Box 30339, Nairobi Kenya. **ED** Mr. Wachira. Index available. **Bk Rev. Ad Acc. Circ:** 7,000. ***Continues*** *Kenya Dairy & Livestock Farmer.*

ISSN 1056-3210
DD 637 US
CEASED

FARMLIFE. [Farmlife]. **Added/Corp** Eastern Milk Producers Cooperative Association. **VFOAT** Farm Life; Eastern Milk Producers Farmlife. Vol. 70, No. 3 Mar. (1991)-(April 1995). Periodical. English. Twelve times a year. $12.00. Eastern Milk Producers Cooperative Association Inc, 2401 Burnet Avenue, PO Box 6966, Syracuse NY 13217-6966. **Tel** (315)463-0781, FAX (315)437-1225. ***Continues*** *Eastern Milk Producer, 8755-9544.*

LC HD1751 .A5 HD9282.U3A28 **ISSN** 0501-4670
DD 338.1/0973 S 381/.41/710973 US

FEDERAL MILK ORDER MARKET STATISTICS. **See** Agriculture-Abstracting, Bibliographies and Statistics.

BE

FLAVOUR NEWS. No. 1 (Aug. 1979)-. English. One time a year.

LC HD9282.U5 F55
DD 331.7 US

FLORIDA AGRICULTURAL STATISTICS. DAIRY SUMMARY. **See** Agriculture-Abstracting, Bibliographies and Statistics.

LC SF13.F6 F5
US

FLORIDA AGRICULTURAL STATISTICS. LIVESTOCK, DAIRY, AND POULTRY SUMMARY. **Added/Corp** Florida Agricultural Statistics Service. United States. Dept. of Agriculture. Florida. Dept. of Agriculture and Consumer Services. **VFOAT** Livestock, Dairy, and Poultry Summary; Livestock, Dairy, Poultry. (1991)-. English. USDA NASS Florida Agricultural Statistics Service, 1222 Woodward Street, Orlando FL 32803. **Tel** (407)648-6013. ***Formed by the union of*** *Florida Agricultural Statistics. Livestock Summary; Florida Agricultural Statistics. Dairy Summary* ***and*** *Florida Agricultural Statistics. Poultry Summary.*

LC TJ1480
DD 631.3 US

FURROW. DAIRYLAND EDITION, THE. **See** Agriculture-Agricultural Equipment.

PL

GOSPODARSKI CHOW ZWIERZAT. **See** Agriculture-Livestock.

LC SF221 **ISSN** 0253-2980
KO
CODEN HNAHDO

HANGUG RAGNON HAGHOI JI. (HANGUK NANGNONG HAKHOE CHI.). [Hangug ragnon haghoi ji]. **VFOAT** Korean Journal of Dairy Science. Academic Scholarly Publication. Korean (Korean). Hanguk Nangnong Hakhoe, Sodon-dong, Suwon-Si South Korea. Documents available from CASDDS.
Ind/Abst Chem. Abstr.; Maize Abstr.; Nutr. Abstr. Rev., Ser. B, Live Feeds and Feed.; Rice Abstr.

UK

HERD BOOK - BRITISH GOAT SOCIETY. **Main/Corp** British Goat Society. No. 1 (1875)-. Trade Publication. English. One time a year. £15.00 UK; £18.00 (surface mail) other. British Goat Society, 34/36 Fore Street, Newton Abbot, Devon TQ13 9AD United Kingdom. **Tel** 011 44 1626 833168. **ED** R Goodwin and E Worthy. Index available. **Bk Rev. Ad Acc. Circ:** 2,000.
Desc: Information on dairy goats registered and their milk yields.

ISSN 0018-2885
US

HOARD'S DAIRYMAN. Vol. 1 (1870)-. Periodical. English. Twenty times a year. $14.00. Hoard's Dairyman, PO Box 801, Fort Atkinson WI 53538. **Tel** (414)563-5551, FAX (414)563-7298. **ED** W. D. Knox. Index available. **Ad Acc. Circ:** 130,000. available on microfilm and microfiche from University Microfilms International (UMI).
Desc: Contains dairy farming information.
Ind/Abst AGRICOLA; Agric. Eng. Abstr. (1991-); Biogr. Index; Dairy Sci. Abstr.; Index Vet.; Leis., Rec., Tour. Abstr.; Rural Dev. Abstr.; Soyabean Abstr.; Vet. Bull.; World Agric. Econ. Rural Sociol. Abstr.

LC SF193.H7 H7
DD 636.2/34 US

HOLSTEIN-FRIESIAN HERD-BOOK. **Added/Corp** Holstein-Friesian Association of America. Holstein-Friesian Association of America. Advanced Register Year Book of the Holstein-Friesian Association of America. **VAT** Holstein-Friesian Herd Book. (1886)-. Trade Publication. English. One time a year. Holstein-Friesian Association of America, South Main Street, Battleboro VT 05301. ***Continues*** *Dutch-Friesian Herd Book.*

ISSN 0954-6219
UK
TITLE CHANGE

HOLSTEIN FRIESIAN JOURNAL (RICKMANSWORTH). (THE HOLSTEIN FRIESIAN JOURNAL.). [Holst. Friesian j.]. **Added/Corp** Holstein Friesian Society of Great Britain & Ireland. Vol. 70, No. 3 (June 1988)-(19??). Trade Publication. English. The Holstein Journal Group Inc., 333 Lesmill Road, Don Mills Ontario M3B 2V1 Canada. **Tel** (416)441-3030, FAX (416)441-3038. ***Continues*** *British Friesian Journal, 0007-0726.* ***Continued by*** *Holstein Journal.*
Desc: News, views and current information on pedigree Holstein Friesians. Includes practical and technical production and conformation achievements of top animals promoting the services of HFS.
Ind/Abst Anim. Breed. Abstr.

ISSN 0710-1309
DD 636.2/34 CN

HOLSTEIN JOURNAL. [Holst. j.]. Vol. 44, No. 1 (Apr. 1981)-. Trade Publication. English (French). Twelve times a year. 60.00Can$. The Holstein Journal Group Inc., 333 Lesmill Road, Don Mills Ontario M3B 2V1 Canada. **Tel** (416)441-3030, FAX (416)441-3038. **ED** Bonnie Cooper. **Ad Acc**, **Adv Mgr:** Peter English. **Circ:** 18,450. ***Continues*** *Holstein-Friesian Journal, 0018-3687* ***and*** *British Friesian Journal.*
Desc: News, views and current information on pedigree Holstein Friesians. Includes practical and technical production and conformation achievements of top animals promoting the services of HFS.

ISSN 0713-2050
DD 636.2/34 CN
HOLSTEIN SIRE CATALOGUE. [Holst. sire cat.]. 1981-. Periodical. English. Gouvernement du Quebec, 875 2nd Floor Grande Allee Est. Ed., Quebec G1R 4Y8 Canada. ***Continues in part*** *Dairy Sire Catalogue, 0713-2026.*

ISSN 0199-4239
DD 338 US
HOLSTEIN WORLD. [Holst. world]. Vol. 77 (Jan. 10, 1980)-. Periodical. English. Sixteen times a year (monthly plus bonus issues in Mar., Apr., Sept. & Oct.). $27.50. Holstein Friesian World, 8036 Lake Street, PO Box 299, Sandy Creek NY 13145. **Tel** (315)387-3441, (800)334-1904, FAX (315)387-3655. available on microfilm and microfiche from University Microfilms International (UMI). ***Continues*** *Holstein-Friesian World, 0018-3695.*

LC HD9298.U3 S26 ISSN 0898-9877
DD 338.1/771/0973021 US
IMS LIST, SANITATION COMPLIANCE AND ENFORCEMENT RATINGS OF INTERSTATE MILK SHIPPERS. [IMS list sanit. compliance enforc. rat. interstate milk shipp.]. **Added/Corp** United States. Food and Drug Administration. **VFOAT** Sanitation Compliance and Enforcement Ratings of Interstate Milk Shippers. **VAT** Interstate Milk Shippers List, Sanitation Compliance and Enforcement Ratings of Interstate Milk Shippers; IMS List. (198?)-. English. Four times a year. Free on request. Food and Drug Administration Milk Safety Board, 200 C Street Southwest, Washington DC 20204. **Tel** (202)485-0178. ***Continues*** *Sanitation Compliance and Enforcement Ratings of Interstate Milk Shippers, 0274-7103.*

LC SF221 ISSN 0019-4603
II
INDIAN DAIRYMAN. (INDIAN DAIRYMAN : JOURNAL OF THE INDIAN DAIRY SCIENCE ASSOCIATION.). [Indian dairyman]. **Added/Corp** Indian Dairy Science Association. Vol. 1 (July 1949)-. Periodical. English. Twelve times a year. $90.00. Indian Dairy Association, Ida House Sector IV, New Delhi 110022 India. **Tel** 011 91 11 674719. **(Subscription address:** Prints India, 11 Darya Ganj, New Delhi 110002 India. **Tel** 011 91 11 3268645, FAX 011 91 11 3275542, telex 31-61087 PRIN-IN.**)** **ED** R. S. Gill. **Bk Rev. Ad Acc. Circ:** 2,500 (ctrl). ***Absorbed*** *Monthly Bulletin of the Bangalore Dairy Cattle Society.*
Desc: Caters to the information needs of dairymen, professionals, policymakers, and scientists. Carries popular articles on production, processing, and management of the dairy industry.
Ind/Abst AgBiotech News Inf.; Anim. Breed. Abstr.; Biodeter. Abstr. (19??-19??); Chemorecept. Abstr.; Curr. Cit.; Dairy Sci. Abstr.; Food Sci. Technol. Abstr.; Grass. Forage Abstr.; Leis., Rec., Tour. Abstr.; Microbiol. Abstr. Sect. A; Nutr. Abstr. Rev., Ser. B, Live Feeds and Feed.; Nutr. Abstr. Rev., Ser. A, Hum. Exp.; Life Sci. Collect.; Postharvest News Inf.; Rural Dev. Abstr.; Soyabean Abstr.; World Agric. Econ. Rural Sociol. Abstr.

LC SF221 ISSN 0019-5146
DD 637/.05 II
NLM W1 IN207E CODEN IJDSAI
INDIAN JOURNAL OF DAIRY SCIENCE. [Indian j. dairy sci.]. **Added/Corp** Indian Dairy Science Association. Vol. 1 (1948)-. Periodical. English. Twelve times a year. $45.00. Indian Dairy Association, Ida House Sector IV, New Delhi 110022 India. **Tel** 011 91 11 674719. **(Subscription address:** Prints India, 11 Darya Ganj, New Delhi 110002 India. **Tel** 011 91 11 3268645, FAX 011 91 11 3275542, telex 31-61087 PRIN-IN.**)** **ED** H. Abichandami. Index available. **Bk Rev. Ad Acc. Circ:** 1,000 (ctrl). Documents available from BIOSIS Document Express, CASDDS.
Desc: Records the original scientific work of dairy scientists in the various facets of dairying. Publishes papers on dairy husbandry, technology, management, microbiology and animal health care.
Ind/Abst AgBiotech News Inf.; AGRICOLA; Agric. Eng. Abstr. (1991-); Agrofor. Abstr. (1991-); Anim. Breed. Abstr.; Biodeter. Abstr. (19??-19??); Biol. Abstr.; Chem. Abstr.; Chemorecept. Abstr.; Curr. Cit.; Dairy Sci. Abstr.; Field Crop Abstr.; Food Sci. Technol. Abstr.; For. Abstr.; Genet. Abstr.; Grass. Forage Abstr.; Helminthol. Abstr. (1991-); Leis., Rec., Tour. Abstr.; Maize Abstr.; Microbiol. Abstr. Sect. A; Nutr. Abstr. Rev., Ser. B, Live Feeds and Feed.; Nutr. Abstr. Rev., Ser. A, Hum. Exp.; Life Sci. Collect.; Potato Abstr.; Rev. Agric. Entomol.; Rev. Med. Vet. Entomol.; Rice Abstr.; Rural Dev. Abstr.; Soyabean Abstr.; Sug. Indus. Abstr.; World Agric. Econ. Rural Sociol. Abstr.

ISSN 0019-7513
IT
UDC 637
CODEN INLADZ
INDUSTRIA DEL LATTE. [Ind. latte]. (1965)-. Periodical. Multiple languages. Four times a year. Centro Sperimentale Del Latte, Via Salasco 4, 20136 Milan Italy. **Tel** 011 39 2 5451208. Documents available from CASDDS.
Ind/Abst Chem. Abstr.; Food Sci. Technol. Abstr.

ISSN 0046-9181
AG
INDUSTRIA LECHERA : ORGANO DEL CENTRO NACIONAL DE LA INDUSTRIA LECHERA, LA. **Added/Corp** Centro Nacional de la Industria Lechera. Vol. 1, No. 1, (August 1919)-. Periodical. Spanish. Six times a year. $100.00. Centro de la Industria Lechera, Mediana 281, Buenos Aires 1178 Argentina. **Tel** 011 54 1 9836149.
Ind/Abst Food Sci. Technol. Abstr.

II
INTEGRATED SAMPLE SURVEY FOR ESTIMATION OF ANIMAL PRODUCTS [MICROFORM] : MILK, WOOL, EGGS, AND MEAT / HIMACHAL PRADESH GOVERNMENT, ANIMAL HUSBANDRY DEPARTMENT. See Agriculture-Livestock.

ISSN 0958-6946
UK
CCC
CODEN IDAJE6
Pr Rev.
INTERNATIONAL DAIRY JOURNAL. [Int. dairy j.]. **Added/Corp** International Dairy Federation. Vol. 1, No. 1 (1991)-. Academic Scholarly Publication. English. Twelve times a year. $748.00. Elsevier Applied Science, An Imprint of Elsevier Science Ltd., The Boulevard, Langford Lane, Kidlington, Oxford OX5 1GB United Kingdom. **Tel** 011 44 1865 843000, 011 44 1865 843699, FAX 011 44 1865 843010. **(Subscription address:** Elsevier Science Ltd. / Oxford Fulfillment Centre, PO Box 800, Kidlington OX5 1DX United Kingdom. **Tel** 011 44 865 843355.**)** available on microfilm and microfiche from University Microfilms International (UMI); available on an online database from Elsevier Electronic Subscriptions (EES). Documents available from CASDDS.
Desc: Covers all aspects of dairy science and technology paying particular attention to applied research and to the interface of the dairy and food industries.
Ind/Abst AGRICOLA; Chem. Abstr.; Curr. Aware. Biol. Sci., CABS; Curr. Cit.; Dairy Sci. Abstr.; Food Sci. Technol. Abstr.; Foods Adlibra (1991-).

ISSN 0744-608X
US
IOWA DAIRY MARKETING NEWS. Periodical. English. Twelve times a year. Mid-America Dairymen Inc, Iowa Division, 1115 East 19th Street North, Newton IA 50208.

LC S ISSN 1056-9537
DD 630 US
JOURNAL - AGRI-MARK, INC. (JOURNAL.). [J. - Agri-Mark Inc.]. **Added/Corp** Agri-Mark, Inc. (1986)-. Periodical. English. Six times a year. Agri-Mark Inc, PO Box 5800, Lawrence MA 01842. **Tel** (508)689-4442. ***Continues*** *Agri-Mark Journal, 0274-9270.*

ISSN 0022-0299
UK
CCC
NLM W1 JO613 CODEN JDRSAN
Pr Rev.
JOURNAL OF DAIRY RESEARCH, THE. [J. dairy res.]. **Added/Corp** Great Britain. Empire Marketing Board. Dairy Research Committee. Vol. 1 (Nov. 1929)-. Academic Scholarly Publication. English. Four times a year. $340.00. Cambridge University Press, The Edinburgh Building, Shaftesbury Road, Cambridge CB2 2RU United Kingdom. **Tel** 011 44 1223 312393, FAX 011 44 1223 315052, telex 851-817256. **(Subscription address:** Cambridge University Press / North America, 110 Midland Avenue, Port Chester NY 10573. **Tel** (800)431-1580, (914)937-9600.**)** **ED** B. A. Rolls and M. L. Green. cum. index. available on microfilm and microfiche from University Microfilms International (UMI). Documents available from The Genuine Article, BIOSIS Document Express, CASDDS, Documents on Demand.
Desc: Publishes original research on all aspects of dairy science. These include: animal husbandry, the physiology, biochemistry and endocrinology of lactation, milk production, composition, preservation, processing and separation, biotechnology and studies in bacteriology, enzymology and immunology, dairy products such as cheese, fermented milks and spreads, the use of milk products in other foods, and the development of methods relevant to these subjects.
Ind/Abst AgBiotech News Inf.; AGRICOLA [Full Cov.]; Agric. Eng. Abstr. (1991-); Anal. Abstr.; Anim. Breed. Abstr.; BioBusiness; Biol. Agric. Index; Biol. Abstr.; Chem. Abstr.; Chemorecept. Abstr.; Curr. Aware. Biol. Sci., CABS; Curr. Cit.; Curr. Contents Agric. Biol. Environ. Sci.; Dairy Sci. Abstr.; Energy Inf. Abstr.; Environ. Abstr.; Field Crop Abstr.; Food Sci. Technol. Abstr.; Foods Adlibra; Grass. Forage Abstr.; Index Med.; Microbiol. Abstr. Sect. B (19??-19??); Microbiol. Abstr. Sect. A; Nutr. Abstr. Rev., Ser. B, Live Feeds and Feed.; Nutr. Abstr. Rev., Ser. A, Hum. Exp.; Nutr. Res. Newsl.; Life Sci. Collect.; PESTDOC; Pig News Inf.; Ref. Upd. Deluxe Ed.; Res. Alert [Full Cov.]; Sci. Cit. Index; SCISEARCH; Soyabean Abstr.

LC SF221 .J6 ISSN 0022-0302
DD 637 US
CCC
NLM W1 JO613E CODEN JDSCAE
Pr Rev.
JOURNAL OF DAIRY SCIENCE. [J. dairy sci.]. **Added/Corp** American Dairy Science Association. Vol. 1 (May 1917)-. Academic Scholarly Publication. English. Twelve times a year. $130.00. American Dairy Science Association, 1111 North Dunlap Avenue, Savoy IL 61874. **Tel** (217)356-3182, FAX (217)398-4119. **ED** J. W. Fuquay. Index available (bound in Dec. issue). cum. index. **Ad Acc. Circ:** 4,800 (ctrl). available on microfilm and microfiche from University Microfilms International (UMI). Documents available from The Genuine Article, BIOSIS Document Express, CASDDS, Documents on Demand.
Desc: Covers dairy cattle, mastitis, nutrition, disease, physiology, dairy goats, lactation, breeding, milk production, cheese chemistry, milk chemistry, enzymes, butter, yogurt, whey, starters and microbiology.
Ind/Abst AgBiotech News Inf.; AGRICOLA [Full Cov.]; Agric. Eng. Abstr. (1991-); Agrofor. Abstr. (1991-); BioBusiness; Biodeter. Abstr. (19??-19??); Biol. Agric. Index; Biol. Abstr.; Chem. Abstr.; Chemorecept. Abstr.; Curr. Biotechnol.; Curr. Cit.; Curr. Contents Agric. Biol. Environ. Sci.; Dairy Sci. Abstr.; EMBASE; Energy Res. Abstr.; Environ. Sci.; Field Crop Abstr.; Food Sci. Technol. Abstr.; Foods Adlibra; Genet. Abstr.; Grass. Forage Abstr.; Index Med.; INIS Atomindex [Micro.]; Leis., Rec., Tour. Abstr.; Microbiol. Abstr. Sect. B; Microbiol. Abstr. Sect. A; Nutr. Abstr. Rev., Ser. B, Live Feeds and Feed.; Nutr. Abstr. Rev., Ser. A, Hum. Exp.; Life Sci. Collect.; PESTDOC; Plant Breed. Abstr.; Postharvest News Inf.; Protozoolog. Abstr.; Res. Alert [Full Cov.]; Rev. Med. Vet. Mycology; Rev. Plant Pathol.; Rural Dev. Abstr.; Sci. Cit. Index; SCISEARCH; Soc. Sci. Cit. Index [Select. Cov.]; Sorghum Mill. Abstr.; Soyabean Abstr.; Stat. Theory Method Abstr. (1959-1963); World Agric. Econ. Rural Sociol. Abstr.

II
•**JOURNAL OF DAIRYING FOODS & HOME SCIENCES.** (1993)-. English. Four times a year. $50.00 one-year; $90.00 two-year; $125.00 three-year. Agricultural Research Communication Centre, Sadar Karnal 132001, Haryana India. **Tel** 011 91 3036. **(Subscription address:** Prints India, 11 Darya Ganj, New Delhi 110002 India. **Tel** 011 91 11 3268645, FAX 011 91 11 3275542, telex 31-61087 PRIN-IN.**)**

ISSN 0037-9840
UK
CODEN JSDTAR
JOURNAL OF THE SOCIETY OF DAIRY TECHNOLOGY. [J. Soc. Dairy Technol.]. **Main/Corp** Society of Dairy Technology. Vol. 1, (Oct. 1947)-. Academic Scholarly Publication. English. Four times a year. £150.00 (surface mail), £180.00 (airmail) US and Canada; £90.00 (surface mail), £110.00 (airmail) other. Society of Dairy Technology, 72 Ermine Street, Huntingdon Cambridgeshire, PE18 6EZ United Kingdom. **Tel** 011 44 1480 450741, FAX 011 44 1480 431800. Index available. cum. index. **Bk Rev. Ad Acc. Circ:** 2,500 (ctrl). Documents available from The Genuine Article, CASDDS.
Ind/Abst AgBiotech News Inf.; AGRICOLA [Full Cov.]; BioBusiness; Biodeter. Abstr. (19??-19??); Chem. Abstr.; Curr. Cit.; Curr. Contents Agric. Biol. Environ. Sci.; Dairy Sci. Abstr.; EMBASE; Food Sci. Technol. Abstr.; Foods Adlibra; Index Vet.; Int. Packag. Abstr.; Life Sci. Collect.; Res. Alert [Full Cov.]; Sci. Cit. Index; SCISEARCH; Soc. Sci. Cit. Index [Select. Cov.]; Vet. Bull.

LC WMLC L 83/1436
UK
KALENDARZ DZIENNIKA POLSKIEGO. **VFOAT** Kalendarz. Polish. One time a year. £3.60. Dziennik Polski, 9 Charleville Road, London W14 9JL United Kingdom. **Tel** 011 44 181 3859393, FAX 011 44 181 3859393. **ED** (editor's address: 9 Charleville Road, London W14 9JL England). Index available. cum. index. **Bk Rev. Ad Acc. Circ:** 1,000 (ctrl). ***Continues*** *Kalendarz Dziennika Polskiego w Wielkiei Brytanii.*

LC SF227.G3 K5 ISSN 0023-1347
GW
CODEN KMWFAF
KIELER MILCHWIRTSCHAFTLICHE FORSCHUNGSBERICHTE. [Kiel. Milchwirtsch. Forschungsber.]. **Added/Corp** Bundesanstalt fuer Milchforschung. Kollegium. (1949)-. Trade Publication. German (summaries and/or abstracts in English and French). Four times a year. $115.15. Verlag TH Mann OHG, Postfach 200254, W 45837 Gelsenkirchen Germany. **Tel** 011 49 209 9304184. Documents available from The Genuine Article, CASDDS.
Ind/Abst Chem. Abstr.; Curr. Biotechnol.; Curr. Cit.; Dairy Sci. Abstr.; EMBASE; Energy Res. Abstr.; Food Sci. Technol. Abstr.; Maize Abstr.; Nutr. Abstr. Rev., Ser. B, Live Feeds and Feed.; Nutr. Abstr. Rev., Ser. A, Hum. Exp.; Life Sci. Collect. (Jan. 1973-); Res. Alert [Select. Cov.]; Rev. Agric. Entomol.; Rev. Med. Vet. Mycology; SCISEARCH; Wheat Barley Trit. Abstr.

ISSN 0023-7302
FR
CCC
NLM W1 LA408 CODEN LAITAG
Pr Rev.

LAIT, LE. [Lait]. No. 1 (1921)-. Academic Scholarly Publication. French. Six times a year. $294.00. Editions Scientifique Elsevier, 141 rue de Javel, 75747 Paris Cedex 15 France. **Tel** 011 33 1 45589067, FAX 011 33 1 45589424. **(Subscription address:** Editions Scientifiques Elsevier / for North America, PO Box 7247-7576, Philadelphia PA 19170-7576. **) ED** J.L. Maubois. available on microfilm and microfiche from University Microfilms International (UMI); available on an online database from Elsevier Electronic Subscriptions (EES). Documents available from The Genuine Article, CASDDS. ***Continues** Revue Generale du Lait.*
Desc: Includes scientific articles in the microbiology, biochemistry, and physicochemistry of milk and its derivatives, or on transformation procedures.
Ind/Abst AGRICOLA; Biodeter. Abstr. (19??-19??); Chem. Abstr.; Curr. Biotechnol.; Curr. Cit.; Curr. Contents Agric. Biol. Environ. Sci.; Dairy Sci. Abstr.; EMBASE; Food Sci. Technol. Abstr.; Helminthol. Abstr. (1991-); Index Vet.; Int. Packag. Abstr.; Nutr. Abstr. Rev., Ser. B, Live Feeds and Feed.; Nutr. Abstr. Rev., Ser. A, Hum. Exp.; Res. Alert [Full Cov.]; Sci. Cit. Index; SCISEARCH; Vet. Bull.

ISSN 0770-2515
BE
SUSPENDED

LAIT ET NOUS, LE. [Lait nous]. **Added/Corp** Belgium. Office National du Lait et de Ses Derives. No. 4 (1976)-Suspended (Jan. 1995). Periodical. French (Dutch). Four times a year. Office National Lait et Ses Derives, rue Froissart 95 99, 1040 Brussels Belgium. **Tel** 011 32 2 2381611, FAX 011 32 2 2306503. **Ad Acc. Circ:** 35,000 (ctrl). ***Continues** Belgique Laitiere, 0005-8424.*
Desc: Contains information on all facets of the dairy industry.
Ind/Abst AGRICOLA; Agric. Eng. Abstr. (1991-); Dairy Sci. Abstr.; Food Sci. Technol. Abstr.; Nutr. Abstr. Rev., Ser. B, Live Feeds and Feed.; Rice Abstr.

ISSN 0392-6060
IT
UDC 637.1

LATTE (1976), IL. [Latte 1976]. (1976)-. Periodical. Italian. Twelve times a year. L126040. Tecniche Nuove SPA, Via Ciro Menotti 14, 20129 Milan Italy. **Tel** 011 39 2 75701, FAX 011 39 2 7570205, telex 334647 TECHS I.
Ind/Abst Food Sci. Technol. Abstr.

ISSN 0745-0842
US
UDC 338.439.4:636(781)

LIVESTOCK (TOPEKA, KAN.). See Agriculture-Livestock.

UK

M.R.S. REPORT. (No. 6- Nov. 1968)-. Periodical. English. Four times a year.

CN

•**MANITOBA DAIRYMAN.** (1993)-. English. Two times a year. 3.50Can$ Canada; 5.00Can$ US; 10.00Can$ other. Bowes Publishers Ltd., 4504 61st Avenue, Leduc Alberta, T9E 2Y1 Canada. **Tel** (403)986-2271, FAX (403)986-6397. **ED** Susan Moscicki & Wendy Weir. **Ad Acc. Circ:** 2,250.

LC SF250
DD 637 GW

MARKTBERICHT: MILCH. Added/Corp Zentrale Markt- und Preisberichtstelle der Deutschen Landwirtschaft. Vol. 14, No. 22 (May 30, 1965)-. Periodical. German. One time a week. DM345.60. ZMP Marktberichte Bonn, Rochusstrabe 2, D-53123 Bonn Germany. **Tel** 011 49 228 9777170.

ISSN 0025-8776
NO

MEIERIPOSTEN. Added/Corp Norske Meierifolks Landsforening. (1911)-. Trade Publication. Norwegian. Sixteen times a year. $101.16. Norwegian Association of Dairy Managers, Boks 398, Oslo 1 Norway. **Tel** 011 47 2 2422520, FAX 011 47 2 2413801. **ED** Steinar Husby (editor's telephone: 011 47 2 2422520). cum. index. **Bk Rev. Ad Acc. Circ:** 2,543 (ctrl).
Desc: Keeps the readers informed of the development in the field of technique, technology and economy in the dairy and ice cream industry and also other related foodstuff industries at home as well as abroad.
Ind/Abst AgBiotech News Inf.; AGRICOLA; Agric. Eng. Abstr. (1991-); Anim. Breed. Abstr.; Biodeter. Abstr. (19??-19??); Dairy Sci. Abstr.; Food Sci. Technol. Abstr.; Grass. Forage Abstr.; Index Vet.; Maize Abstr.; Nutr. Abstr. Rev., Ser. B, Live Feeds and Feed.; Nutr. Abstr. Rev., Ser. A, Hum. Exp.; Rev. Med. Vet. Mycology; Vet. Bull.; World Agric. Econ. Rural Sociol. Abstr.

NE

MELK. Dutch. Administratie Redaktie Melk, Postbus 222, 3440 AE Woerden Netherlands. **Tel** 03480/29531.

LC SF233.N4 H34
NE

MELKKOEIEN. Main/Corp Hague. Landbouw-Economisch Instituut. Afdeling Bedrijfseconomisch Onderzoek Landbouw. (19??)-. Dutch. Fl4.50. Landbouw-Economisch Instituut, Postbus 29703, 2502 LS Hague Netherlands. **Tel** 011 31 70 3308330, FAX 011 31 70 615624. **ED** M. N. de Groof. **Circ:** 300.
Desc: Outline of the development of prices, costs and profitability of dairy production.

MX

MEXICO HOLSTEIN. Added/Corp Holstein-Friesian de Mexico. (19??)-. Periodical. Spanish. BN Editores SA De CV, Genova 2 K Col Juarez, 06600 Mexico DF Mexico. **Tel** 5143415.

ISSN 0026-2315
US

MICHIGAN MILK MESSENGER. Added/Corp Michigan Milk Producers Association. Vol. 1 (June 1919)-. Trade Publication. English. Twelve times a year. $5.00. Michigan Milk Messenger, PO Box 8002, Novi MI 48050-8002. **Tel** (313) 474-6672, FAX (313)474-0924.

GW
Pr Rev.

MILCH-MARKETING. German. Twelve times a year. DM125.00. Milchwirtschaftlicher Verlag, Rheintalstrasse 6, D-53498 Bad Breisig Germany. **Tel** 011 49 2633 454000. **ED** Hans Wortelkamf.
Desc: Covers dairy marketing.

ISSN 0343-0200
GW

MILCH PRAXIX UND RINDERMAST, DIE. See Agriculture-Livestock.

ISSN 0544-1706
AU
CODEN MBWRAU

MILCHWIRTSCHAFTLICHE BERICHTE AUS DEN BUNDESANSTALTEN WOLFPASSING UND ROTHOLZ. [Milchwirtsch. Ber. Bundesanst. Wolfpassing Rotholz]. **Added/Corp** Verein der Forderer der Wissenschaftlichen Versuchstatigkeit der Milchwirtschaftlichen Bundesanstalten Wolfpassing und Rotholz. Vol. 1, (Jan. 1964)-. Academic Scholarly Publication. German. Four times a year (Jan., Apr., July, Oct.). S350.00. Verein Zur Foerderung Oesterr, Milchwirtschaft, A-3261 Steinakirchen Austria. **Tel** 011 43 07488 20224, FAX 07488 20211, telex 202 360. **ED** Ferdinand Becker. Index available. cum. index. **Ad Acc. Circ:** 1,000 (ctrl). Documents available from CASDDS. ***Supersedes** Milchwissenschaftliche Berichte, 0540-0651.*
Ind/Abst Chem. Abstr.; Dairy Sci. Abstr.; EMBASE; Food Sci. Technol. Abstr.; Maize Abstr.

LC SF221 .M33 ISSN 0026-3788
DD 637/.1/05 GW
CCC
CODEN MILCAD
Pr Rev.

MILCHWISSENSCHAFT. (MILCHWISSENSCHAFT. MILK SCIENCE INTERNATIONAL.). [Milchwissenschaft]. **Added/Corp** Deutsche Gesellschaft fuer Milchwissenschaft. **VFOAT** Milk Science International. Vol. 1 (Nov. 1946)-. Academic Scholarly Publication. German (English). Twelve times a year. $294.01. VV-Gmbh / Volkswirtschaftlicher Verlag, Postfach 701920, D-81319 Munich Germany. **Tel** 011 49 89 7141013, FAX 011 49 89 7192753, telex 5212 287 VOVE D. Index available. cum. index. **Bk Rev. Ad Acc. Circ:** 1,500 (ctrl). Documents available from The Genuine Article, CASDDS.
Desc: Journal of nutrition research and food science.
Ind/Abst AgBiotech News Inf.; AGRICOLA; Agric. Eng. Abstr. (1991-); Anim. Breed. Abstr.; BioBusiness; Biodeter. Abstr. (19??-19??); Chem. Abstr.; Chemorecept. Abstr.; Curr. Biotechnol.; Curr. Cit.; Curr. Contents Agric. Biol. Environ. Sci.; Dairy Sci. Abstr.; EMBASE; Energy Res. Abstr.; Food Sci. Technol. Abstr.; Foods Adlibra; Maize Abstr.; Microbiol. Abstr. Sect. B (19??-19??); Microbiol. Abstr. Sect. A; Nutr. Abstr. Rev., Ser. B, Live Feeds and Feed.; Nutr. Abstr. Rev., Ser. A, Hum. Exp.; Life Sci. Collect.; PESTDOC; Pig News Inf.; Res. Alert [Full Cov.]; Rev. Med. Vet. Entomol.; Rev. Med. Vet. Mycology; Rice Abstr.; Sci. Cit. Index; SCISEARCH; Soyabean Abstr.

LC HD9275.U8 M53 ISSN 0740-9222
DD 338.1/771/0973 US

MILK FACTS. [Milk facts]. **Added/Corp** Milk Industry Foundation (U.S.). (1940)-. Trade Publication. English. One time a year. $35.00. Milk Industry Foundation, 888 16th Street Northwest, Washington DC 20006. **Tel** (202)296-4250, FAX (202)331-7820. **ED** S. Wood.
Desc: Contains reference data on the production and consumption of dairy products.

LC HD9282.G69 M5 ISSN 0026-4172
DD 338.1771 UK
CODEN MIINAV
TITLE CHANGE

MILK INDUSTRY, THE. [Milk ind.]. **Added/Corp** National Dairymen's Association. (1920)-(1994). Trade Publication. English. Twelve times a year. National Dairymen's Association, 19 Cornwall Terrace, London NW1 EQP United Kingdom. **Tel** 011 44 171 9354562, FAX 011 44 171 4874734. **ED** Ron Jeffries. **Bk Rev. Ad Acc. Circ:** 6,000. available on microfilm from University Microfilms International (UMI). ***Continued by** Milk Industry International.*
Desc: Journal for dairy management. Dairy processing, manufacturing, products, research, and distribution are addressed.
Ind/Abst BioBusiness; Biodeter. Abstr. (1991-1994); Dairy Sci. Abstr.; Food Sci. Technol. Abstr.; Int. Packag. Abstr.; Life Sci. Collect.; Soyabean Abstr.

LC HD9282.G69 M5
DD 338.1771 UK

•**MILK INDUSTRY INTERNATIONAL. Added/Corp** National Dairymen's Association. **VFOAT** Milk Industry. Vol. 97, No. 1 (Jan. 1995)-. Trade Publication. English. Twelve times a year. £50.00 Europe; £65.00 other. National Dairymen's Association, 19 Cornwall Terrace, London NW1 EQP United Kingdom. **Tel** 011 44 171 9354562, FAX 011 44 171 4874734. **ED** Ron Jeffries. **Bk Rev. Ad Acc. Circ:** 5,100. available with charts; available with illustrations. ***Continues** Milk Industry, 0026-4172.*
Desc: Journal for dairy management. Dairy processing, manufacture, products, research, and distribution are addressed.

ISSN 0162-2781
DD 338 US
TITLE CHANGE

MILK MARKETER. [Milk mark.]. **Added/Corp** Milk Marketing, Inc. (1978)-(1995). Periodical. English. Milk Marketing Inc, PO Box 36050, 8257 Dow Circle, Strongsville OH 44136. **Tel** (216)826-4730. ***Supersedes in part** Milk Reporter; Cincinnati Gazette; Miami Valley Dairyman; Central Ohio Digest; Ft. Wayne Newsletter. **Continued by** MMI's Focus, 1084-7286.*

ISSN 0026-4180
UK
CEASED

MILK PRODUCER. Added/Corp Great Britain. Milk Marketing Board. Vol. 1 (Jan. 1954)-(19??). Trade Publication. English. Warner's Group Distribution Ltd, The Maltinigs Manor Lane, Bourne Lincolnshire, PE10 9PH United Kingdom. **Tel** 011 44 1778 393652, FAX 011 44 1778 393668. **ED** Vivienne Martin. Index available. **Bk Rev. Ad Acc. Circ:** 12,000 (ctrl). ***Supersedes** Home Farmer.*
Desc: Specialised articles related to dairy matters.
Ind/Abst Agric. Eng. Abstr. (1991-); Dairy Sci. Abstr.; Food Sci. Technol. Abstr.; Index Vet.; Nutr. Abstr. Rev., Ser. B, Live Feeds and Feed.

LC HD9282.U3 M487 ISSN 0026-4202
DD 338.1/771/0973021 US

MILK PRODUCTION (WASHINGTON). (MILK PRODUCTION.). [Milk prod.]. **Added/Corp** United States. Crop Reporting Board. United States. Agricultural Marketing Service. United States. Agricultural Statistics Board. **VFOAT** Special Milk Production. (19??)-. Government Publication. English. Twelve times a year. $33.00. US Department of Agriculture, 14th Street and Independence Avenue SW, Washington DC 20250. **Tel** (202)720-5457. **(Subscription address:** Superintendent of Documents, US Government Printing Office, Washington DC 20402. **)** available on microfiche (Vols. for (1986-) distributed to depository libraries). Documents available from Documents on Demand.
Ind/Abst Am. Stat. Index.

LC SF199.S56 J68 ISSN 1073-9394
DD 636 US

•**MILKING SHORTHORN JOURNAL (1993).** (MILKING SHORTHORN JOURNAL.). [Milk. Shorthorn j.]. **Added/Corp** American Milking Shorthorn Society. Vol. 74, No. 1 (Jan./Feb. 1993)-. Trade Publication. English. Six times a year. $15.00. American Milking Shorthorn, PO Box 449, Beloit WI 53511. **Tel** (417)862-6661. ***Continues** Journal of the Milking Shorthorn and Illawarra Breeds, 0145-8264.*

US

MILKING SHORTHORN YEAR BOOK. Main/Corp American Milking Shorthorn Society. **Added/Corp** Milking Shorthorn Society. Vol. 28 (1943)-. Trade Publication. English. One time a year. $6.00. American Milking Shorthorn, PO Box 449, Beloit WI 53511. **Tel** (417)862-6661. ***Continues** Milking Shorthorn Year Book.*

ISSN 0026-704X
CI
CODEN MLJEAU

MLJEKARSTVO. [Mljekarstvo]. (1951)-. Academic Scholarly Publication. Serbo-Croatian (Roman) (summaries and/or abstracts in English, French and German). Twelve times a year. Udruzenje Mlekarskih Radnika Republike Hrvatske, Association of Dairyman of

Agriculture —Dairy Industry

SR Croatia, Ilica 31-111, Zagreb Croatia. **Tel** 011 385 41 424420. Index available. **Bk Rev**. **Ad Acc**. **Circ:** 1,000. Documents available from CASDDS.
 Ind/Abst Chem. Abstr.; Soyabean Abstr.

LC HD28
DD 338
ISSN 1084-7286
US

● **MMI'S FOCUS.** [MMI's focus]. **Added/Corp** Milk Marketing, Inc. **VFOAT** Milk Marketing, Inc.'s Focus. Vol. 1, No. 1 (July/Aug. 1995)-. Periodical. English. Ten times a year. $5.00. Milk Marketing Inc, PO Box 36050, 8257 Dow Circle, Strongsville OH 44136. **Tel** (216)826-4730. **Continues** Milk Marketer, 0162-2781.

ISSN 0026-7651
DD 338.1/7/70971
CN
CODEN MDRYA6
TITLE CHANGE

MODERN DAIRY. [Mod. dairy]. Vol. 48 (Jan. 1969)-(19??). Trade Publication. English. Maccan Publishing Company Ltd, 3269 Bloor Street West, Suite 205, Toronto Ontario M8X 1E2 Canada. **Tel** (416)239-8423. **ED** I. Macnab. **Ad Acc**. **Circ:** 2,000 (ctrl). **Continues** Canadian Dairy and Ice Cream Journal, 0366-5658. **Continued by** Canadian Dairy.
 Desc: Canada's business magazine for dairy processors/distributors. Articles on processing, packaging, materials handling, distribution and marketing.
 Ind/Abst BioBusiness (1989-); Biodeter. Abstr.; Curr. Cit.; Dairy Sci. Abstr.; Food Sci. Technol.; Life Sci. Collect. (1989-); Sug. Indus. Abstr.

GW

MOLKEREI-ZEITUNG; WELT DER MILCH, DIE. **VFOAT** Welt der Milch. (1947)-. Periodical. German. Twenty-six times a year. $497.44. Heinrichs Verlag GmbH, Stephanstrasse 12, Postfach 100550, W-31105 Hildesheim F R Germany. **Tel** 011 49 5121 53279, FAX 011 49 5121 511385.
 Ind/Abst Dairy Sci. Abstr.; Food Sci. Technol. Abstr.

ISSN 0540-6021
GW
CEASED

MOLKEREITECHNIK. (1959)-(19??). Monographic series. German. Verlag Th Mann, Nordring 10, W-4650 Gelsenkirchen-Buer Germany. **Tel** (02) 09 137431, FAX 395398, telex 824727. ctrl circ.
 Ind/Abst Food Sci. Technol. Abstr.

LC SF221 .M74
RU

MOLOCHNAIA PROMYSHLENNOST. (1992)-. Periodical. Russian. Eight times a year. $79.95. Izdatelstvo Kolos, Sadovaia-Spasskaia 18, 107807 Moscow Russia. **(Subscription address:** East View Publications Inc., 3020 Harbor Lane North, Suite 110, Minneapolis MN 55447. **Tel** (800)477-1005, (612)550-0961, FAX (612)559-2931.) **Continues in part** Molochnaia i Miasnaia Promyshlennost, 0235-2575.
 Ind/Abst Soyabean Abstr.

ISSN 0026-9034
RU

MOLOCHNOE I MIASNOE SKOTOVODSTVO. See Agriculture-Livestock.

ISSN 0368-9210
IT
CODEN MDLAA6

MONDO DEL LATTE, IL. (IL MONDO DEL LATTE; IL LATTE NEL MONDO.). [Mondo latte]. **VFOAT** Latte Nel Mondo. Vol. 1 (1947)-. Academic Scholarly Publication. Italian (summaries and/or abstracts in English). Twelve times a year. L81750. Editoriale Il Mondo Del Latte, Corso di Porta Romana 2, 20122 Milan Italy. **Tel** 011 39 2 72021817, FAX 011 39 2 72021838. Index available. cum. index. **Bk Rev**. **Ad Acc**, **Adv Mgr:** Sede di Roma, **Tel** 06 4885648. **Circ:** 1,200 (ctrl). Documents available from CASDDS.
 Desc: Technical, economic, and legal information for the dairy industry.
 Ind/Abst AGRICOLA; Chem. Abstr. (1947-1981).

SP

MUNDO GANADERO. See Agriculture-Livestock.

XR

NAS CHOV. See Agriculture-Livestock.

LC SF15.G7 A33
DD 338.1771
UK
Pr Rev.

NATIONAL MILK RECORDS. ANNUAL REPORT, ENGLAND & WALES. **Main/Corp** Great Britain. Milk Marketing Board. (1???)-. Periodical. English. One time a year. £10.00. Milk Marketing Board, Giggs Hill Green / Thames Ditton, Surrey KT7 0EL United Kingdom. **Tel** 011 44 1270 535659, FAX 011 44 1270 536586. **ED** D.P. Cawthorn. **Ad Acc**. **Circ:** 16,000 (ctrl).
 Desc: Production records for herds of cows in England and Wales, including yield percentages of fat, lactose, PTN, and weights of CGI's for cows.

ISSN 0028-209X
NE
CODEN NMDJAX
Pr Rev.

NEDERLANDS MELK- EN ZUIVELTIJDSCHRIFT. (NETHERLANDS MILK AND DAIRY JOURNAL.). [Ned. Melk-Zuiveltijdschr.]. **Added/Corp** Genootschap ter Bevordering Van Melkkunde. Centrum Voor Landbouwpublikaties en Landbouwdocumentatie (Netherlands). **VFOAT** Nederlands Melk- en Zuiveltijdschrift. (1969)-. Academic Scholarly Publication. English. Four times a year (Mar., May., Oct., Dec.) $54.81. Netherlands Milk & Dairy, PO Box 8129, 6700 EV Wageningen Netherlands. **Tel** 011 31 8370 82289, FAX 011 31 8370 83669. **ED** A. Noomen. Index available (4th issue). **Circ:** 700. Documents available from The Genuine Article, BIOSIS Document Express, CASDDS. **Continues** Nederlands Melk- en Zuiveltijdschrift, 0028-209X.
 Desc: Contains original papers and abstracts on key issues and developments in all areas of dairy management, production and trade.
 Ind/Abst Biodeter. Abstr.; Biol. Abstr.; Chem. Abstr.; Curr. Aware. Biol. Sci., CABS; Curr. Cit.; Curr. Contents Agric. Biol. Environ. Sci.; Dairy Sci. Abstr.; EMBASE; Food Sci. Technol. Abstr.; Foods Adlibra; Index Vet.; Nutr. Abstr. Rev., Ser. B, Live Feeds and Feed.; Nutr. Abstr. Rev., Ser. A, Hum. Exp.; Life Sci. Collect.; Res. Alert [Full Cov.]; Sci. Cit. Index; SCISEARCH; Soyabean Abstr.; Vet. Bull.

LC HD9275.N45 N42
NZ

NEW ZEALAND DAIRY BOARD ANNUAL REPORT. **Main/Corp** New Zealand Dairy Board. (1989)-. English. One time a year. New Zealand Dairy Board, Pastoral House 25/The Terrace, PO BOX 417, Wellington New Zealand. **Tel** 011 64 4 718300, 011 64 4 723691. **Continues** Annual Report / New Zealand Dairy Board.

LC HD9275.N45 N422a
DD 338.1/7/709931
NZ

NEW ZEALAND DAIRY INDUSTRY; A SURVEY, THE. **Main/Corp** New Zealand. Dairy Board. Economics Section. (19??)-. English. Irregular. New Zealand Dairy Board, Pastoral House 25/The Terrace, PO BOX 417, Wellington New Zealand. **Tel** 011 64 4 718300, 011 64 4 723691. **ED** N.H. Martin. **Circ:** 5,000.
 Desc: Introductory and general information on New Zealand's dairy industry.

BE

NEWSLETTER OF THE INTERNATIONAL DAIRY FEDERATION. **VFOAT** Federation Internationale de Laiterie. Newsletter. Newsletter. English (French). 9400F. International Dairy Federation, 41 Square Vergote, 1040 Brussels Belgium. **Tel** 011 32 2 7339888, FAX 011 32 2 7330413, telex 63818.

SW

NORDISK MEJERIINDUSTRI. (1???)-. Periodical. Swedish. Eleven times a year (monthly except July). $83.35. Nordisk Mejeriindustri, PO Box 9083, S25009 Helsingborg Sweden. **Tel** 011 46 42 116370, FAX 011 46 42 113422.
 Ind/Abst Dairy Sci. Abstr.; Food Sci. Technol. Abstr.; Selec. Coop. Index Manage. Period.

ISSN 0145-9112
US

NORTHEAST IMPROVER, THE. **VFOAT** Improver. Vol. 57, No. 3 (May/June 1975)-. Periodical. English. Six times a year. $2.40 members, $3.00 nonmembers. Northeast Improver, Research Park/Building 1, Brown Road, Ithaca NY 14850. **Tel** (612)636-2117. **Bk Rev**. **Ad Acc**. **Circ:** 18,500 (ctrl). **Continues** NYDHIC Improver, 0300-6662.
 Desc: Official publication for participating Northeast Dairy Herd Improvement DHI Organizations in the northeast. We keep DHI dairymen posted on industry trends to increase productivity and profitability.

AT

NSW DAIRYMEN'S DIGEST. **Added/Corp** N.S.W. Dairy Farmer's Association. **VFOAT** N.S.W. Dairymen's Digest. Vol. 1, No. 1 (Oct. 1, 1972)-. Newspaper. English. Twelve times a year. 35.00Aus$ Australia; 45.00Aus$ other. New South Wales Dairy Association / DFA Newspapers Ltd., 491 Elizabeth Street, Surry Hills NSW 2010 Australia. **Tel** 011 61 2 3180688, FAX 011 61 2 3193349. **ED** Margaret Konemann. **Ad Acc**. **Continues** The Dairyman and Primary Producer.

LC HD9000
DD 338.176
AU

● **OESTERREICHISCHE MILCH- & LEBENSMITTELWIRTSCHAFT.** **Added/Corp** Oesterreichische Milchinformationsgesellschaft. **VFOAT** Oesterreichische Milch- und Lebensmittelwirtschaft; OEMW. (March 1995)-. Periodical. German. Twelve times a year. S1850.00 Austria; S2451.00 other.
Oesterreichischer Agrarverlag, Inkustr 1 7 Bueropark Donau, A 3400 Klosterneuberg Austria. **Tel** 011 43 2243 33300. **Continues** Oesterreichische Milchwirtschaft.

LC HD9000
DD 338.176
AU
TITLE CHANGE

OESTERREICHISCHE MILCHWIRTSCHAFT, DIE. **Added/Corp** Milchwirtschaftsfonds. Oesterreichische Milchinformationsgesellschaft. **VFOAT** Oesterreichische Lebensmittel- und Milchwirtschaft; OEMW. (Oct. 1950)-(Feb. 1995). Periodical. German. Oesterreichischer Agrarverlag, Inkustr 1 7 Bueropark Donau, A 3400 Klosterneuberg Austria. **Tel** 011 43 2243 33300. **Continues** Oesterreichische Milch- und Fettwirtschaft. **Continued by** Oesterreichische Milch- & Lebensmittelwirtschaft.
 Ind/Abst Dairy Sci. Abstr. (?-?); Int. Packag. Abstr. (?-?); Soyabean Abstr. (?-?).

LC SF191
DD 636.2
AT

OFFICIAL HERD RECORDING STATISTICS. See Agriculture-Abstracting, Bibliographies and Statistics.

LC SF221 .I5615
DD 637/.06/21
BE

OFFICIAL NEWS AND INFORMATION - INTERNATIONAL DAIRY FEDERATION. **Main/Corp** International Dairy Federation. **VFOAT** Nouvelles et Informations Officielles - Bulletin Annuel. 1973-. Bulletin. Multiple languages (English and French). One time a year.

AT

OFFICIAL PRODUCTION RECORDS OF PURE BRED REGISTERED DAIRY COWS IN NEW SOUTH WALES. See Agriculture-Livestock.

ISSN 0899-4862
DD 636
US

OHIO NEWS (WOOSTER, OHIO). (OHIO NEWS.). **Added/Corp** Ohio Holstein-Friesian Association. **VFOAT** Ohio Holstein News. Vol. 49, No. 1 (Jan./Feb. 1983)-. Trade Publication. English. Six times a year. $15.00. Ohio Holstein Association, 1375 Heyl Road, Box 479, Wooster OH 44691. **Tel** (216)264-9088, FAX (216)263-1653. **ED** Esther Welch. **Bk Rev**. **Ad Acc**. **Circ:** 3,000 (ctrl). **Continues** Ohio Holstein News, 0199-7580.
 Desc: Service to the members of the Ohio Holstein Association through new product advertising, farm advertising, and activity information. A forum for information about the dairy industry.

ISSN 0030-3038
CN

ONTARIO MILK PRODUCER. **Added/Corp** Ontario. Milk Marketing Board. (1925)-. Trade Publication. English (French). Twelve times a year. 19.20Can$. Ontario Milk Marketing Board, 6780 Campobello Road, Mississauga Ontario L5N 2L8 Canada. **Tel** (416)821-8970. **ED** Bill Dimmick. **Ad Acc**. **Circ:** 15,000 (ctrl).
 Desc: Information on developments in farm management and agricultural research as well as Ontario Milk Marketing Board and national dairy policies.

LC HD9282.U3 U52B
DD 381/.41/710973
ISSN 0148-3951
US

PACKAGED FLUID MILK SALES IN FEDERAL MILK ORDER MARKETS. (PACKAGED FLUID MILK SALES IN FEDERAL MILK ORDER MARKETS / UNITED STATES DEPARTMENT OF AGRICULTURE, AGRICULTURAL MARKETING SERVICE.). Government Publication. English. US Department of Agriculture, 14th Street and Independence Avenue SW, Washington DC 20250. **Tel** (202)720-5457.

ISSN 0164-6222
US

PENNSYLVANIA GOLDEN GUERNSEY NEWS. **Added/Corp** Pennsylvania Guernsey Breeders Association. (19??)-. Periodical. English. Twelve times a year. Pennsylvania Guernsey Breeder Assn, 2497 Lincoln Highway East, Lancastor PA 17602. **Tel** (717)299-8955.

ISSN 0998-6650
FR
UDC 637

PROCESS CESSON-SEVIGNE. (PROCESS.). (1989)-. Periodical. French. Eleven times a year. $124.67. Editions du Boisaudry, BP 6359, 35036

Agriculture —Dairy Industry

Rennes Cedex France. **Tel** 011 33 99 322121. *Continues* Technique Laitiere & Marketing, 0295-6268. **Ind/Abst** Curr. Cit.

FR

PROCESS MAGAZINE : LE MENSUEL DES TECHNIQUES LAITIERES ET ALIMENTAIRES. See Food and Food Industry.

ISSN 0228-1686
DD 637/.09714 CN
PRODUCTEUR DE LAIT QUEBECOIS, LE. **Added/Corp** Office des Producteurs de Lait du Quebec. Vol. 1, No. 1 (Sept. 1980)-. Periodical. French. Eleven times a year. 13.60Can$. L Union Producteurs Agricoles, 555 boulevard Roland Therrien, Longueuil Quebec J4H 9Z9 Canada. **Tel** (514)679-0530.

ISSN 1187-662X
DD 636.2/142/0971405 CN
TITLE CHANGE
PRODUCTEUR LAITIER (BEDFORD. 1990). (LE PRODUCTEUR LAITIER.). [Prod. lait.]. Vol. 11, No. 3 (Oct. 1990)-(199?). Periodical. French. SELC Publishing Inc., 2100 Guy Suite 200, Montreal Quebec H3H 2M8 Canada. **Tel** (514)248-3356, FAX (514)248-2195. *Separated from* Le Producteur Agricole., 0706-5264. *Merged into* Le Producteur Plus, 1183-9929.

ISSN 0705-551X
DD 338.1/7733/0971 CN
PRODUCTION AND INVENTORIES OF PROCESS CHEESE AND INSTANT MILK POWDER. (PRODUCTION AND INVENTORIES OF PROCESS CHEESE AND INSTANT SKIM MILK POWDER.). [Prod. invent. process cheese instant skim milk powder]. **Added/Corp** Statistics Canada. Manufacturing and Primary Industries Division. Statistics Canada. Industry Division. **VFOAT** Production et Stocks de Fromage Fondu et de Lait Ecreme Instantane en Poudre; Production et Stocks de Fromage Refait et de Lait Ecreme Instantane en Poudre; Production et Stocks de Fromage Fondu et de Poudre de Lait Ecreme Instantane. Vol. 7, No. 1 (Jan. 1978)-. Periodical. English (French). Twelve times a year. 48.02Can$. Statistics Canada Publications Sales and Services, R.H. Coats Building 6th Floor, Ottawa Ontario K1A 0T6 Canada. **Tel** (613)951-5078, (800)267-6677, FAX (613)951-1584, telex 053-3585. *Continues* Selected Dairy By-Products., 0705-4416.
Desc: Provides monthly and cumulative production and inventory of packaged instant skim milk powder and process cheese with previous year's comparative data.

ISSN 0791-3036
DD 637.09417 637.0212 IE
PRODUCTION OF MILK AND MILK PRODUCTS. See Agriculture-Abstracting, Bibliographies and Statistics.

ISSN 0886-702X
DD 637 US
PROGRAM - AMERICAN DAIRY SCIENCE ASSOCIATION. MEETING. (PROGRAM / AMERICAN DAIRY SCIENCE ASSOCIATION.). [Program - Am. Dairy Sci. Assoc., Meet.]. **Main/Corp** American Dairy Science Association. Meeting. **VFOAT** Program and Abstracts; ADSA Annual Meeting and Branch Abstracts; ASDA Annual Meeting and Divisional Abstracts; Combined Annual Meeting; ADSA Program; Program and Abstracts; ADSA/SAS Abstracts; Abstracts. 72nd (June 26-29, 1977)-. English. One time a year. $10.00. American Dairy Science Association, 1111 North Dunlap Avenue, Savoy IL 61874. **Tel** (217)356-3182, FAX (217)398-4119.
Ind/Abst AGRICOLA.

ISSN 0478-6599
PL
PRZEGLAD MLECZARSKI. [Prz. mlecz.]. **Added/Corp** Centralny Zwiazek Spodzielni Mleczarskich (Poland). (1953)-. Periodical. Polish. Twelve times a year. Price on request. Ars Polona-Ruch, PO Box 1001, Krakowskie Przedmiescie 7, 00-068 Warsaw Poland. **Tel** 011 48 22 261201.)
Ind/Abst AGRICOLA; Dairy Sci. Abstr.; Nutr. Abstr. Rev., Ser. A, Hum. Exp.

AU
QUEENSLAND DAIRY FARMER. (19??)-. English. Eleven times a year (monthly with Dec./Jan. combined). 35.00Aus$ Australia; 45.00Aus$ other. Queensland Dairyfarmers Association, PO Box 61, Brisbane Queensland 4003 Australia. **Tel** 011 61 7 2362955, FAX 011 61 7 2362956. **Ad Acc, Adv Mgr:** Morris Lake. **Circ:** 2,000 (ctrl).

AT
QUEENSLAND DAIRYFARMER, THE. **Added/Corp** Queensland Dairymen's Organisation. (19??)-. Periodical. English. Twelve times a year. Free to Queenslan dairyfarmers; $35.00 other. Queensland Dairyfarmers Association, PO Box 61, Brisbane Queensland 4003 Australia. **Tel** 011 61 7 2362955, FAX 011 61 7 2362956.

LC SF233.J3 R32 ISSN 0385-0218
JA
CODEN RKSKD8
RAKUNO KAGAKU, SHOKUHIN NO KENKYU = JAPANESE JOURNAL OF DAIRY AND FOOD SCIENCE. [Rakuno kagaku. Shokuhin no kenkyu]. **Added/Corp** Nihon Rakuno Kagakkai. **VFOAT** Japanese Journal of Dairy and Food Science. (1976)-. Academic Scholarly Publication. Japanese (English). Six times a year. $108.00. Nihon Rakuno Kagakkai, (Japanese Dairy Science Assoc.), 6-45 Kamisugi 4 Chome, Sendaishi Miyagiken 980, Japan. **(Subscription address:** Maruzen Company Ltd., PO Box 5050, Import & Export Department, Tokyo 100 31 Japan. **Tel** 011 81 3 32789224.**) ED** Takeo Nakanishi. **Circ:** 650 (ctrl). Documents available from BIOSIS Document Express, CASDDS. *Continues* Rakuno Kagaku No Kenkyu.
Desc: Organ papers of Japanese Daily Science Association.
Ind/Abst Biodeter. Abstr.; Biol. Abstr.; Chem. Abstr.; Curr. Biotechnol.; Food Sci. Technol. Abstr.; Nutr. Abstr. Rev., Ser. A, Hum. Exp.; Life Sci. Collect.; Pig News Inf.

LC SF253 .K65 ISSN 0107-8666
DK
RAPPORT OM KONTROLLEN MED KONSUMMLKPRODUKTER FOR ARET. (19??)-. Danish. One time a year. Frederiksgade 21, 1265 Koenhavn K Denmark. **Tel** 01 11 48 88, FAX 01 32 12 18, telex 22 4 73. *Continues* Kontrollen Med Konsummlkprodukter.

LC HD9275.A83 V59a ISSN 0157-5856
DD 354.9450082337042/06 AT
REPORT FOR YEAR ENDED 30TH JUNE ... / VICTORIAN DAIRY INDUSTRY AUTHORITY. **Main/Corp** Victorian Dairy Industry Authority. (19??)-. English. One time a year. Victorian Dairy Industry Authority, Dombille Avenue, Hawthorn Victoria 3122 Australia. **Tel** 03 819 400. ctrl circ.

ISSN 0301-6315
UK
CODEN HRIRAH
REPORT / HANNAH RESEARCH INSTITUTE. **Main/Corp** Hannah Research Institute. (1972)-. English. Documents available from BIOSIS Document Express. *Continues* Hannah Dairy Research Institute, Kirkhill. Annual Report, 0301-8393.
Ind/Abst Anim. Breed. Abstr.; Biol. Abstr.

AT
REPORT OF RESEARCH / COMMONWEALTH SCIENTIFIC AND INDUSTRIAL RESEARCH ORGANIZATION, AUSTRALIA, DIVISION OF FOOD RESEARCH. See Food and Food Industry.

LC HD9275.S5 S66B
DD 354.680082/337/05 SA
REPORT OF THE AUDITOR-GENERAL ON THE ACCOUNTS OF THE DAIRY BOARD FOR THE FINANCIAL YEAR ... . **VFOAT** Verslag van die Ouditeur-Generaal oor die Rekenings van die Suiwelraad vir die Boekjaar ... . Afrikaans (English). One time a year. Government Printer / South Africa, Bosman Street, Private Bag X85, Pretoria 0001 South Africa. **Tel** 011 27 12 3239731 ext. 262. *Continues* Report of the Controller and Auditor-General on the Accounts of the Dairy Board and the Balance Sheet.

LC HD9282.A8 W48a
DD 338.1/7/7109941 AT
REPORT ON THE MARKET MILK INDUSTRY IN WESTERN AUSTRALIA. See Industry and Production.

ISSN 0995-6492
FR
REUSSIR- LAIT ELEVAGE. **Added/Corp** REUSSIR. **VFOAT** REUSSIR- Technical and Economical Information About Dairy Farming. (19??)-. Periodical. French. Twelve times a year. 200.00F France; 250.00F other. GIE Reussir, 10 Quai du Juillet, BP 67, 14007, Caen Cedex France. **Tel** 31-70-88-00, FAX 31-82-29-63. **ED** Marc Jourdan. **Circ:** 82,000.

ISSN 0300-5550
SP
REVISTA ESPANOLA DE LECHERIA. [Rev. esp. leche.]. **Added/Corp** Sindicato Nacional de Ganaderia. Comite Nacional Lechero. No. 1 (June 1951)-. Trade Publication. Spanish. Ten times a year. $222.05. Comite Nacional Lechero, Ayala 10 1 IZD, 28001 Madrid Spain. **Tel** 011 34 1 7595715, FAX 011 34 1 3001593. **(Subscription address:** Rincon Publicaciones SA, Titania I5, 28043 Madrid Spain. **Tel** 011 34 1 3884610.) **Bk Rev** (Qty: varies). **Ad Acc, Adv Mgr:** Luis Rincon. **Tel** 011 34 1 759 57 15. **Circ:** 2,000.
Ind/Abst Agric. Eng. Abstr. (19??-19??); Dairy Sci. Abstr.; Food Sci. Technol. Abstr.; Nutr. Abstr. Rev., Ser. A, Hum. Exp.; Life Sci. Collect.; World Agric. Econ. Rural Sociol. Abstr.

ISSN 0821-770X
DD 636.2/34 CN
UDC 636.234.2
REVUE HOLSTEIN QUEBEC, LA. [Rev. Holst. Que.]. Vol. 1, No. 1-. Periodical. French. Irregular. Free. Revue Holstein Quebec, 432 - 89 Av Chomedey, Laval Quebec H7W 3H4 Canada. ctrl circ.

ISSN 0295-4303
FR
RIA, LE TECHNICIEN DU LAIT. **VFOAT** Technicien du Lait. (1985)-. French. Six times a year. $115.58 EEC Countries; $93.91 France; $137.25 other. Sepaic, 42 rue du Louvre, BP 551, 75001 Paris France. **Tel** 011 33 1 42335740.

ISSN 1101-2706
SW
CODEN SDINEW
SCANDINAVIAN DAIRY INFORMATION. (SCANDINAVIAN DAIRY INFORMATION : SDI.). [Scand. dairy inf.]. **VFOAT** SDI. (19??)-. Trade Publication. English. Four times a year (Mar., June, Sept., Dec.). $48.41. Nordisk Mejeriindustri, PO Box 9083, S25009 Helsingborg Sweden. **Tel** 011 46 42 116370, FAX 011 46 42 113422. **ED** Vlf Borgstrom. **Bk Rev**. **Ad Acc**. ctrl circ.
Ind/Abst Biodeter. Abstr. (1991-); Curr. Cit.; Dairy Sci. Abstr.; Food Sci. Technol. Abstr.; Index Vet.; Wheat Barley Trit. Abstr.

SW
SCANDINAVIAN DAIRY INFORMATION - SDI. Vol. 1 (1987)-. Trade Publication. English. Four times a year (Mar., June, Sept., Dec.). Kr295.00. Nordisk Mejeriindustri, PO Box 9083, S25009 Helsingborg Sweden. **Tel** 011 46 42 116370, FAX 011 46 42 113422. **ED** Vlf Borgstrom. **Bk Rev**. **Ad Acc**. ctrl circ.
Ind/Abst Biodeter. Abstr. (1991-); Dairy Sci. Abstr.; Food Sci. Technol. Abstr.; Index Vet.; Wheat Barley Trit. Abstr.

SZ
SCHWEIZER BRAUNVIEH. **Added/Corp** Schweiz. Braunviehzuchtverband. **VFOAT** Race Brune Suisse; Razza Bruna Svizzera. (Jan. 1982)-. Periodical. German (French and Italian). Twelve times a year. *Continues* Mitteilungen des Schweizerichen Braunviehzuchtverbandes.
Ind/Abst Index Vet.

SZ
SCHWEIZERISCHE MILCHZEITUNG. **Added/Corp** Schweizerischer Milchwirtschaftlicher Verein. Schweizerischer Milchkauferverband. Verband Schweizerischer Kaseri- und Milchwirtschaftlicher Betriebsleiter. (19??)-. Periodical. German. One time a week. $139.55. Fischer Druck AG, Satz Druck und Verlag, CH-3110 Muensingen Switzerland. **Tel** 011 41 31 7212211, FAX 011 41 31 7214617, telex 845/911600.

IT
SCIENZA E TECNICA LATTIERO-CASEARIA. [Sci. tec. latt.-casearia]. **VFOAT** Bolletino dell'Associazione Italiana Tecnici del Latte. (1961)-. Italian. Six times a year. L50000 (individuals), L100000 (institutions) Europe; $85.00 Americas and Asia; $82.00 Africa; $94.00 other Comes with Associazione Italiana Techici del Latte membership. Associazione Italiana Tecnici Latte, Via Torelli 17, 43100 Parma Italy. **Tel** 011 39 521 481209. *Continues* Tecnica del Latte, 0390-007X.
Ind/Abst Curr. Cit.

ISSN 0952-1380
DD 636.3142 UK
SHEEP DAIRY NEWS. See Agriculture-Livestock.

LC HD9275.U6 D25 ISSN 1050-9151
DD 338.1/77/0973 US
CODEN DSOREE
TITLE CHANGE
SITUATION AND OUTLOOK REPORT. DAIRY. (SITUATION AND OUTLOOK REPORT. DAIRY / UNITED STATES DEPARTMENT OF AGRICULTURE, ECONOMIC RESEARCH SERVICE.). [Situat. outlook rep., Dairy]. **Added/Corp** United States. Dept. of Agriculture. Economic Research Service. United States. World Agricultural Outlook Board. **VFOAT** Situation and Outlook Yearbook. Dairy; Dairy; Dairy Situation and Outlook Report; Dairy Situation and Outlook Yearbook. DS-405 (June 1986)-(1993). Government Publication. English. Superintendent of Documents, US Government Printing Office, Washington DC 20402. **Tel** (202)275-3328, FAX (202)786-2377. available on microfilm and microfiche from University Microfilms International (UMI). *Continues* Outlook and Situation Report. Dairy, 0889-9835. *Merged with* Livestock and Poultry Update, 1048-1605 *and* Situation and Outlook Oeport. Livestock and Poultry, 1054-0849 *to form* Livestock, Dairy, and Poultry Situation and Outlook, 1076-2183.
Ind/Abst AGRICOLA; BioBusiness (1990-?); F&S Index Plus Text, Int. [Select. Cov.]; Trade Ind. ASAP [Full Txt.]; Trade Ind. Index [Full Txt.].

Agriculture — Dairy Industry

LC SF84 **ISSN** 1340-2773
DD 338.1762142 JA
CODEN SBRRE7YNKHEO
●**SNOW BRAND R & D REPORTS.** (SNOW BRAND R&D REPORTS = YUKIJIRUSHI NYUGYO KENKYU HOKOKU.). [Snow brand R D rep.]. **Added/Corp** Yukijirushi Nyugyo Kabushiki Kaisha. Gijutsu Kikakubu. **VFOAT** Snow Brand R and D Reports; Yukijirushi Nyugyo Kenkyu Hokoku. No. 100 (Oct. 1993)-. Periodical. Japanese (English). Yukijirushi Nyugyo K.K. Kenkyujo, (Research Lab. Snow Brand Milk Products Co. Ltd.), 1-2 Minamidai 1 Chome, Kawagoeshi Saitamaken 350, Japan. **Continues** Yukijirushi Nyugyo Kenkyujo Hokoku, 0082-4763.

LC SF221 .S58
KO
SOUL UYY. **VFOAT** Seoul Milk Monthly. Periodical. Korean (Korean). Twelve times a year. Soul Uyu Hypotong Chohap, 137-7 Sangbong-dong, Tongdaemun-ku, Seoul South Korea.

ISSN 0049-1446
AT
SOUTH AUSTRALIAN DAIRY FARMER'S JOURNAL, THE. **Added/Corp** South Australian Dairyfarmers Association. Vol. 25, No. 4/5 (Jan./Apr. 1985)-. Periodical. English. Ten times a year. 24.67Aus$. South Australian Dairy Farmer's Association Inc, 13 Leigh Street, Adelaide South Australia 5000 Australia. **Tel** 011 61 8 2313752, **FAX** 011 61 8 2319799. **ED** T.W. Inglis. **Bk Rev**. **Ad Acc**. **Circ**: 950. **Continues** South Australian Dairymens Journal.
Desc: Technical, economic, industrial and political aspects of dairy farming in South Australia and Australia.

LC SF253 .A55 **ISSN** 8755-3554
DD 637/.028/7 US
STANDARD METHODS FOR THE EXAMINATION OF DAIRY PRODUCTS (1967). See Public Health and Safety.

LC HD9275.U3 D28A
DD 338.1/77/0973021 US
STATISTICAL ANALYSIS OF ... DAIRY PROCESSOR DIRECTORY. Statistical Publication. English. One time a year. **Continues** Statistical Analysis of Dairy Processor Market Guide.

ISSN 0527-6268
CN
STOCKS OF FOOD COMMODITIES IN COLD STORAGE AND OTHER WAREHOUSES. [Stocks food commod. cold storage other wareh.]. **Added/Corp** Canada. Dominion Bureau of Statistics. Live Stock Section. Canada. Dominion Bureau of Statistics. Livestock and Animal Products Section. Statistics Canada. Livestock and Animal Products Section. **VFOAT** Stocks de Produits Alimentaires Dans les Entrepots Frigorifiques et Autres. (1949)-. Periodical. English (French). One time a year. 28.81Can$. Statistics Canada Publications Sales and Services, R.H. Coats Building 6th Floor, Ottawa Ontario K1A 0T6 Canada. **Tel** (613)951-5070, (800)267-6677, **FAX** (613)951-1584, telex 053-3585. **Continues** Summary of Cold Storage Reports., 0318-2576.
Desc: Provides summary data on stocks of dairy products, poultry and red meats for Canada and the provinces (except Newfoundland).

LC HD9282.U5 P39
DD 381/.4171/09748 US
SUMMARY OF FINANCIAL OPERATIONS OF LICENSEES FOR THE YEAR ENDED ... . English. One time a year.

FI
SUOMEN OSUUSMEIJERIEN LIIKETILASTO = FINLANDS ANDELSMEJERIERS DRIFTSTATISTIK. **VFOAT** Finlands Andelsmejeriers Driftstatistik; Andelsmeijeriers i Finland Driftstatistik. Monographic series. Finnish (Swedish). One time a year. Price varies per volume.
Ind/Abst Dairy Sci. Abstr.

ISSN 0494-9900
HU
UDC 637.1
TEJIPAR. [Tejipar]. **VFOAT** Molocnaja Promyslennost'; Dairy Industry; Milchindustrie. (1956)-. Periodical. Hungarian. Four times a year. **Continues** Tejipari Tudosito, 0324-4849.
Ind/Abst Index Vet.

LC HD9275.U7 T28 **ISSN** 0748-4119
DD 338.1/77/09768 US
TENNESSEE DAIRY STATISTICS. See Agriculture-Abstracting, Bibliographies and Statistics.

ISSN 0358-0202
FI
TIEDONANTOJA / VALTION MAITOTALOUDEN TUTKIMUSLAITOS = COMMUNICATIONS / STATE INSTITUTE FOR DAIRY RESEARCH. **Added/Corp** Valtion Maitotalouden Tutkimuslaitos (Finland). **VFOAT** Communications. (19??)-. Monographic series. Finnish. Price varies per volume. **Continues** Tiedonantoja (Valtion Maitotalouskoelaitos (Finland)), 0355-1482.
Ind/Abst Dairy Sci. Abstr.; Fish Rev. (Jan. 1989-July 1992); Nutr. Abstr. Rev., Ser. A, Hum. Exp.; Wildl. Rev. (Jan. 1989-July 1992).

LC HD9275.U3 F67
DD 382/.416/00973021 US
TITLE CHANGE
U.S. DAIRY, LIVESTOCK, AND POULTRY TRADE / UNITED STATES DEPARTMENT OF AGRICULTURE, FOREIGN AGRICULTURAL SERVICE. **Added/Corp** United States. Foreign Agricultural Service. United States. World Agricultural Outlook Board. **VFOAT** US Dairy, Livestock, and Poultry Trade; Dairy, Livestock, and Poultry Trade. (19??)-(1994). Government Publication. English. US Department of Agriculture, Foreign Agricultural Service, Room 4644-S, Washington DC 20250. **Continues** U.S. Trade and Prospects, Dairy, Livestock, and Poultry Products. **Continued by** Dairy, Livestock, and Poultry, U.S. Trade and Prospects (Washington, D.C. : 1994).
Ind/Abst Am. Stat. Index (?-?).

US
TITLE CHANGE
U.S. TRADE AND PROSPECTS, DAIRY, LIVESTOCK, AND POULTRY PRODUCTS. **Added/Corp** United States. Foreign Agricultural Service. United States. World Agricultural Outlook Board. **VFOAT** US Trade and Prospects, Dairy, Livestock, and Poultry Products; Dairy, Livestock, and Poultry Products. (199?)-(199?). Government Publication. English. US Department of Agriculture / Foreign Agricultural Service, 14th Street & Independence Avenue Southwest, Washington DC 20250. **Tel** (202)720-9445, **FAX** (202)720-7729. Documents available from Documents on Demand. **Continues** Dairy, Livestock, and Poultry, U.S. Trade and Prospects. **Continued by** U.S. Dairy, Livestock, and Poultry trade.
Ind/Abst Am. Stat. Index (?-?).

LC HD9000 **ISSN** 0273-9992
DD 338.17 US
URNER BARRY'S PRICE-CURRENT. See Agriculture-Livestock.

ISSN 0270-4153
US
WEEKLY INSIDERS DAIRY & EGG LETTER. **Added/Corp** Urner Barry Publications. **VAT** Weekly Insiders Dairy and Egg Letter. (19??)-. English. One time a week. $149.00. Urner Barry Publications Inc., PO Box 389, Toms River NJ 08754. **Tel** (908)240-5330, (800)932-0617, **FAX** (908)341-0891. **ED** John Carter. **Circ**: 225. **Continues** Weekly Insiders Butter & Egg Letter.
Desc: Statistics for spotting trends or forecasting. Storage stocks, slaughter figures, consumption and retail prices.

LC SF232.W47 D34 **ISSN** 1079-0578
DD 637 US
●**WESTERN DAIRYMAN, THE.** [West. dairym.]. **VFOAT** Western Dairy Man. Vol. 76, No. 1 (Jan. 1995)-. Periodical. English. Twelve times a year. $29.00. Holstein Friesian World, 8036 Lake Street, PO Box 299, Sandy Creek NY 13145. **Tel** (315)387-3441, (800)334-1904, **FAX** (315)387-3655. **Continues** Dairyman, 0011-572X.

LC HD9275.G4 W47
DD 338.4/764137/0943021 GW
WESTERN GERMAN/EEC AND WORLD MARKETS. ANNUAL REVIEW. **VAT** Western German, EEC and World Markets. Annual Review. English. One time a year. Zentrale Markt und Ernahrungswirtschaft, Godesberger Allee 142-148, W-5300 Bonn 2 Germany.

LC SF232.W6 W58 **ISSN** 0092-0304
DD 338.1/77/09775 US
WISCONSIN DAIRY FACTS. **Added/Corp** Wisconsin Statistical Reporting Service. Wisconsin Agriculture Reporting Service. Wisconsin. Dept. of Agriculture. University of Wisconsin. Dept. of Dairy Science. Wisconsin Agricultural Statistics Service. **VFOAT** Dairy Facts. (1963)-. English. One time a year (Sept.). $4.00. Wisconsin Agricultural Statistics Service, PO Box 9160, Madison WI 53713. **Tel** (608)264-5317. **ED** Marvin Heiser. **Circ**: 2,000. **Absorbed** Annual Dairy Summary.
Desc: Current and historic information on Wisconsin dairying-milk cows, milk production, disposition, utilization and consumption, herd improvements, farm income and other related data.

LC SF84 **ISSN** 0194-4401
DD 338.176 214 2 US
WISCONSIN HOLSTEIN NEWS. **Added/Corp** Wisconsin Holstein Friesian Association. (19??)-. Periodical. English. Twelve times a year. $25.00. Wisconsin Holstein Publications, PO Box 10, 902 Eighth Avenue, Baraboo WI 53913. **Tel** (608)356-2114, **FAX** (608)356-6312. **ED** Mary Farrell-Stieve. Index available. **Ad Acc**. **Circ**: 5,200 (ctrl).
Desc: Advertising and editorial as it relates to the membership of the Wisconsin Holstein Association. Promotional material.

LC HD9275.A1 F69
DD 338.1/77/05 US
TITLE CHANGE
WORLD DAIRY SITUATION / UNITED STATES DEPARTMENT OF AGRICULTURE, FOREIGN AGRICULTURAL SERVICE. **Added/Corp** United States. Foreign Agricultural Service. United States. World Agricultural Outlook Board. **VFOAT** Dairy, Livestock and Poultry, World Dairy Situation. (Nov. 1987)-(1993). Government Publication. English. Department of Agriculture / Foreign Agricultural Service, 14th Street and Independence Avenue SW, Washington DC 20250-1000. **Tel** (202)720-3935, **FAX** (202)720-7729. **Continues** Foreign Agriculture Circular. Dairy, Livestock and Poultry. World Dairy Situation and Outlook, 0894-8224. **Continued by** Dairy, Livestock and Poultry. Dairy, World Markets and Trade.

LC HD9275.A1 W67 **ISSN** 0259-8213
DD 338.1/77/05 SZ
WORLD MARKET FOR DAIRY PRODUCTS, THE. (THE WORLD MARKET FOR DAIRY PRODUCTS AT ...). [World market dairy prod.]. **Added/Corp** General Agreement on Tariffs and Trade (Organization). (Oct. 1981)-. Trade Publication. English (French and Spanish). One time a year. 25.00F. General Agreement on Tariffs and Trade / GATT, Centre William Rappard, 154 rue de Lausanne, 1211 Geneva 21 Switzerland. **Tel** 011 41 22 7395111, 011 41 22 7395019, **FAX** 011 41 22 7395458. **Circ**: 3,000. **Continues** Status Report on World Market for Dairy Products.
Desc: Examines trends in production, consumption and trade of dairy products. The report provides a comprehensive analysis per product category and contains detailed statistics and charts.

ISSN 0082-4763
JA
CODEN YNKHEO
TITLE CHANGE
YUKIJIRUSHI NYUGYO KENKYUJO HOKOKU = REPORTS OF RESEARCH LABORATORY. **Added/Corp** Yukijirushi Nyugyo Kabushiki Kaisha. Gijutsu Kenkyujo. **VFOAT** Reports of Research Laboratory. (198?)-(1993). Periodical. Japanese (English). Yukijirushi Nyugyo K.K. Kenkyujo, (Research Lab. Snow Brand Milk Products Co. Ltd.), 1-2 Minamidai 1 Chome, Kawagoeshi Saitamaken 350, Japan. Documents available from CASDDS. **Continues** Yukijirushi Nyuguo Gijutsu Kenkyujo Hokoku, 0082-4763. **Continued by** Snow Brand R&D Reports, 1340-2773.
Ind/Abst Chem. Abstr.

AU
ZEITGEMASSE SCHAFHALTUNG : MIT EINEM KAPITEL UEBER MILCHSCHAFHALTUNG. German. Four times a year. S88.00 Austria; S96.00 other. Der Fortschrittliche Landwirt, Hofgasse 5, A-8011 Graz Austria. **Tel** 011 43 316 821636. Index available. **Bk Rev**, (Qty: 70). **Ad Acc**, **Adv Mgr**: J. Tritscher. Acid Free. **Circ**: 35,000 (ctrl).

LC HD9275.N2 A3 **ISSN** 0168-518X
NE
ZUIVELINDUSTRIE. **VFOAT** Dairy Industry. Dutch (summaries and/or abstracts in English). One time a year. Fl15.00. Centraal Bureau voor de Statistiek, AFD ALG Zaken, Postbus 959, 2270 AZ Voorburg Netherlands. **Tel** 011 31 70 3373800, **FAX** 011 31 70 0387429, telex 32692 CBS NL. **Continues** Netherlands. Centraal Bureau voor de Statistiek Produktiestatistieken : Zuivelindustrie.

ISSN 0165-8573
NE
ZUIVELZICHT. [Zuivelzicht]. **Added/Corp** Koninklijke Nederlandse Zuivelbond. (1975)-. Periodical. Dutch. Twenty-six times a year. $119.91. Koninklijke Ned Zuivelbond, PO Box 5831, 2280 HV Rijswijk Netherlands. **Tel** 011 31 70 3953100. **Continues** Koninklijke Nederlandse Zuivelbond. Officieel Orgaan - Koninklijke Nederlandse Zuivelbond.

Agriculture —Feed Grain and Milling

FEED GRAIN AND MILLING

ISSN 0936-2975
GW

UDC 636.085 :338.45
ADVANCES IN FEED TECHNOLOGY.
[Adv. feed technol.]. (1989)-. Periodical. English (German and Spanish). Two times a year. DM59.00. Verlag Moritz Schaefer, Paulinenstr 43, Postfach 2254, W-4930 Detmold Germany. **Tel** (49)523 11 24637, FAX (49)5231 1 35896. Index available. cum. index. **Ad Acc. Circ:** 3,000.
Desc: Technical library for the practicing feed technologist.

LC S583
DD 631
UK
●ADVISOR, THE. See Agriculture-Crop Production and Soils.

ISSN 0228-5584
CN
DD 388.1/0971
CCC
AGRIWEEK. [Agriweek]. Added/Corp Corpus Publishers Services Limited. (1967)-. Periodical. English. Fifty times a year (weekly except 2 weeks during Christmas vacation). Century Publishing Company / Canada, PO Box 444, Winnipeg Manitoba R3C 2H6 Canada. **Tel** (204)943-8861. **Absorbed** Farmland Canada, 0713-0538.
Desc: Newsletter on Canadian agribusiness and agriculture.

ISSN 0377-8401
NE
CCC
CODEN AFSTDH
Pr Rev.
ANIMAL FEED SCIENCE AND TECHNOLOGY. [Anim. feed sci. technol.]. Vol. 1 (April 1976)-. Academic Scholarly Publication. English. Twenty times a year (5 volumes). $1361.00. Elsevier Science Publishers BV, PO Box 211, 1000 AE Amsterdam Netherlands. **Tel** 011 31 20 4853641, 011 31 20 4853642, FAX 011 31 20 4853598. **ED** J F D Greenhalgh and P J van Soest. available on microfilm and microfiche from University Microfilms International (UMI); available on an online database from Elsevier Electronic Subscriptions (EES). Documents available from The Genuine Article, BIOSIS Document Express, CASDDS, Documents on Demand.
Desc: Covers such areas as the nutritive value of feeds, methods of conserving, processing and manufacturing feeds, utilization of feeds and the improvement of such, and the environmental effects of feeds.
Ind/Abst AgBiotech News Inf.; AGRICOLA; Agric. Eng. Abstr. (1991-); Agrofor. Abstr. (1991-); BioBusiness; Biodeter. Abstr. (19??-19??); Biol. Abstr.; Chem. Abstr.; Curr. Cit.; Curr. Contents Agric. Biol. Environ. Sci.; Dairy Sci. Abstr.; Energy Inf. Abstr.; Environ. Abstr.; Field Crop Abstr.; Fish Rev. (Jan. 1989-July 1992); Food Sci. Technol. Abstr.; For. Prod. Abstr. (1991-); For. Abstr.; Grass. Forage Abstr.; Hortic. Abstr.; Index Vet.; Maize Abstr.; Nutr. Abstr. Rev., Ser. B, Live Feeds and Feed.; Nutr. Abstr. Rev., Ser. A, Hum. Exp.; Life Sci. Collect.; Pig News Inf.; Plant Breed. Abstr.; Postharvest News Inf.; Poult. Abstr.; Protozoolog. Abstr.; Res. Alert [Full Cov.]; Rev. Agric. Entomol.; Rev. Med. Vet. Mycology; Rice Abstr.; Sci. Cit. Index; SCISEARCH; Seed Abstr.; Soils Fert.; Sorghum Mill. Abstr.; Soyabean Abstr.; Sug. Indus. Abstr.; Vet. Bull.; Wheat Barley Trit. Abstr.; Wildl. Rev. (Jan. 1989-July 1992).

ISSN 0115-5784
DD 636
PH
ANIMAL FEED SERVICE BULLETIN.
[Anim. feed serv. bull.]. (1976)-. Periodical. English. Four times a year. Free on request. Bureau of Animal Industry, Visayas Avenida, Animal Feed Control, Dilimon Quezon City Philippines.
Desc: Contains information on animal feed.

IT
CEASED
ANNALI DELL ISTITUTO SPERIMENTALE PER LA CEREALICOLTURA. (19??)-(19??). Italian. Istituto Sperimentale Cerealicoltura, Via Cassia 176, 00191 Rome Italy. **Tel** 011 39 6 3295705.

LC HD9049.W5 C16
DD 354.710082/333
CN
ANNUAL REPORT / THE CANADIAN WHEAT BOARD. Main/Corp Canadian Wheat Board. VFOAT Canadian Wheat Board Annual Report. (1970/1971)-. Government Publication. English. Free on request. Agriculture Canada, Communications Branch, Ottawa Ontario K1A 0C7 Canada. **Continues** Canadian Wheat Board. Report of the Canadian Wheat Board.

LC HD1401
DD 338.1/731/0971021
ISSN 1190-8548
CN
●ANNUAL STATISTICAL TABLES (WINNIPEG). (ANNUAL STATISTICAL TABLES.). [Annu. stat. tables]. Added/Corp Canadian Grain Commission. VFOAT Tableaux Statistiqes Annuels. (1992/1993)-. English (French). Agriculture Canada, Communications Branch, Ottawa Ontario K1A 0C7 Canada. **Continues** Canadian Grain Commission. Annual Report - Canadian Grain Commission, 0706-2575.

DK
ARSBERETNING. Added/Corp Statens Foderstofkontrol (Denmark) Denmark. Plantedirektoratet. (1988)-. Danish. **Continues** Beretning Fra Statens Foderstofkontrol, 0901-134X.

ISSN 1043-5174
DD 630
US
BARLEY GENETICS NEWSLETTER.
[Barley genet. newsl.]. **Added/Corp** Colorado State University. Dept. of Agronomy. Vol. 1 (1971)-. Newsletter. English. Free on request. American Malting Barley Association, 735 North Waters Street, Milwaukee WI 53202. **Tel** (414)272-4640.
Ind/Abst AgBiotech News Inf.; AGRICOLA [Full Cov.]; Nematol. Abstr.; Plant Breed. Abstr.; Rev. Agric. Entomol.; Rev. Plant Pathol.; Seed Abstr.; Wheat Barley Trit. Abstr.

LC HD9043.1 .Z45a
GW
BILANZ GETREIDE-FUTTERMITTEL : BR DEUTSCHLAND, EG UND WELTMARKT. Main/Corp Zentrale Markt- und Preisberichtelle fur Erzeugnisse der Land-, Forst- und Ernahrungswirtschaft. VFOAT ZMP Bilanz Getreide-Futtermitte. VAT Bilanz Getreide-Futtermittel: Bundesrepublik Deutschland, Europaische Gemeinschaft und Weltmarkt. (1975/1976)-. Trade Publication. German. One time a year. DM18.00. Zentrale Market und Preisberichtstelle fur Erzeugnisse der Land, Forst und Ernahrungswirtschaft GmbH (ZMP), Godesberger Allee 142-148, 5300 Bonn 2 Germany. **Tel** 888-0, telex 88576759.

ISSN 0321-026X
RU
BIULLETIN NAUCHNO-TEKHNICHESKOI INFORMATSII VSESOIUZNOGO NAUCHNO-ISSLEDOVATELSKOGO INSTITUTA ZERNOBOBOVYKH I KRUPIANYKH KULTUR. [Biull. nauchno-tek. inf. Vses. nauchno-issled. inst. zernobobovykh krupianykh kul't.]. Main/Corp Vsesoiuznyi Nauchno-Issledovatelskii Institut Zernobobovykh i Krupianykh Kultur. **Added/Corp** Vsesoiuznaia Akademiia Selskokhoziaistvennykh Nauk. Vol. 8, (1974)-. Bulletin. Russian. All-Union Scientific Research Institute for Legumes and Groats, Moscow Russia.
Ind/Abst AGRICOLA.

ISSN 0102-0048
DD 633
BL
BOLETIM DE PESQUISA - UEPAE DOURADOS. [Bol. pesqui. Res. - UEPAE Dourados]. VFOAT Boletim de Pesquisa - Unidade de Execucfao de Pesquisa de Ambito Estadual de Dourados. (1979)-. Monographic series. Portuguese. Irregular. Price varies per volume. MS Unidade de Execucao de Pesquisa de Ambito Estadual, Dourados Brazil.
Ind/Abst Wheat Barley Trit. Abstr.

LC SB183 .B85
ISSN 0007-4896
II
CODEN BUGTA2
BULLETIN OF GRAIN TECHNOLOGY.
[Bull. grain technol.]. **Added/Corp** Foodgrain Technologists' Research Association of India. Vol. 1 (1963)-. Bulletin. English. Three times a year. $75.50. SEC Foodgrain Technologists, Research Association of India, Hapur 245 101 U P India. **Tel** 2496. (Subscription address: Prints India, 11 Darya Ganj, New Delhi 110002 India. **Tel** 011 91 11 3268645, FAX 011 91 11 3275542, telex 31-61087 PRIN-IN.) **ED** N. S. Agarwal, R. B. Doharey, and G. N. Bhardwaj. **Bk Rev. Ad Acc. Circ:** 500. Documents available from CASDDS.
Ind/Abst Agric. Eng. Abstr. (1991-); Chem. Abstr. (1963-1977); EMBASE; Field Crop Abstr.; Food Sci. Technol. Abstr.; Grass. Forage Abstr.; Nutr. Abstr. Rev., Ser. B, Live Feeds and Feed.; Nutr. Abstr. Rev., Ser. A, Hum. Exp.; Postharvest News Inf.; Rice Abstr.; Soils Fert.

LC HD9044.C2 A355
DD 338.1/7/310971
CN
CANADIAN GRAIN POSITION. Main/Corp Canada. Grain Commission. Economics and Statistics Division. (19??)-. English. One time a week. Receiver General of Canada CDN Grain Commission, 600 303 Main Street, Winnipeg Manitoba R3C 3G8 Canada. **Tel** (204)983-1570, FAX (204)983-0248. **Continues** Canada. Board of Grain Commissioners. Canadian Grain Position.

CN
CANADIAN GRAINS INDUSTRY; STATISTICAL HANDBOOK. See Agriculture-Abstracting, Bibliographies and Statistics.

ISSN 0133-3720
HU
CODEN CRCMCL
Pr Rev.
CEREAL RESEARCH COMMUNICATIONS. [Cereal res. commun.]. Vol. 1 (1973)-. Academic Scholarly Publication. English (Russian). Four times a year. Free. Cereal Research Institute, PO Box 391, 6701 Szeged Hungary. **Tel** (62)54-555, FAX 36-62-54-588, telex 82450. **ED** Zoltan Barabas. Index available. cum. index. **Bk Rev. Ad Acc. Circ:** 1,000. Documents available from The Genuine Article, CASDDS.
Desc: Covers cereal, plant breeding, genetics, agrotechnic, physiology, pathology, milling, bread making quality, tissue culture, wheat, barley, oats, sorghum, maize, and triticale.
Ind/Abst AgBiotech News Inf.; Chem. Abstr.; Crop Physiol. Abstr.; Curr. Aware. Biol. Sci., CABS; Curr. Cit.; Curr. Contents Agric. Biol. Environ. Sci.; Field Crop Abstr.; Food Sci. Technol. Abstr.; Grass. Forage Abstr.; Irr. Drain.; Maize Abstr.; Plant Breed. Abstr.; Plant Grow. Reg. Abstr.; Res. Alert [Select. Cov.]; Rev. Agric. Entomol.; Rev. Med. Vet. Mycology; Rev. Plant Pathol.; Rice Abstr.; SCISEARCH; Seed Abstr.; Soils Fert.; Sorghum Mill. Abstr.; Wheat Barley Trit. Abstr.

US
CEREALIST / THE KUSA SOCIETY, THE.
Added/Corp KUSA Society. KUSA Research Foundation. No. 1 (Spring/Summer '89-). Periodical. English. Two times a year.

LC HD9044.C2 C47
ISSN 0820-9030
DD 338.1/731/0971
CN
CEREALS AND OILSEEDS REVIEW.
[Cereals oilseeds rev.]. **Added/Corp** Statistics Canada. Agriculture Statistics Division. Statistics Canada. Crops Section. **VFOAT** Revue des Cereales et des Graines Oleagineuses. Vol. 6, No. 1 (Jan. 1983)-. Periodical. English (French). Twelve times a year. 173.00Can$. Statistics Canada Publications Sales and Services, R.H. Coats Building 6th Floor, Ottawa Ontario K1A 0T6 Canada. **Tel** (613)951-5078, (800)267-6677, FAX (613)951-1584, telex 053-3585. **Continues** Grains and Oilseeds Review, 0706-3555.
Desc: Reports on supply and disposition of the four traditional major wheat exporters, Canada, Australia, United States and Argentina.

ISSN 0304-5439
MX
CIMMYT REPORT ON WHEAT IMPROVEMENT. 1973-. English. One time a year. Centro Internacional de Mejoramiento de Maiz y Trigo, Apartado 6, 641 Londres 40, 06600 Mexico City DF Mexico. **Supersedes in part** CIMMYT Annual Report on Maize and Wheat Improvement.

ISSN 0100-8625
BL
UDC 633.110981
CIRCULAR TECNICA - CENTRO NACIONAL DE PESQUISA DE TRIGO.
(CIRCULAR TECNICA.). [Circ. tec. - Cent. Nac. Pesqui. Trigo]. (1979)-. Monographic series. Portuguese. Irregular. Price varies per volume. Centro Nacional de Pesquisa de Trigo, RS CNPT, Passo Fundo Brazil.
Ind/Abst Wheat Barley Trit. Abstr.

US
CORN FOR GRAIN : HARVESTING, HANDLING AND DRYING METHODS / IOWA CROP AND LIVESTOCK REPORTING SERVICE. English. One time a year. The Service, Full Depository, 707 Savings and Loan Building, Des Moines IA 50309.
Desc: Statistics on harvesting, handling, and drying of corn in the districts of Iowa, and comparisons with selected other states.

ISSN 0101-6644
BL
UDC 63
DOCUMENTOS - CENTRO NACIONAL DE PESQUISA DE TRIGO. (DOCUMENTOS.).
[Doc. - Cent. Nac. Pesqui. Trigo]. **VFOAT** Documentos - CNPT. (1978)-. Monographic series. Portuguese. Irregular. Price varies per volume. Centro Nacional de Pesquisa de Trigo, RS CNPT, Passo Fundo Brazil.
Ind/Abst Wheat Barley Trit. Abstr.

CN
EASTERN NUTRITION CONFERENCE PROCEEDINGS. (19??)-. Proceedings. English. One time a year (May). 18.00Can$. Canadian Feed

Industry Association, 325 Dalhousie Street, Suite 625, Ottawa Ontario K1N 7G2 Canada. **Tel** (613)238-6421, FAX (613)238-6620.

ISSN 0832-6215
DD 382/.4131/0971021 CN
EXPORTS OF CANADIAN GRAIN AND WHEAT FLOUR. [Exports Can. grain wheat flour]. **Added/Corp** Canadian Grain Commission. Economics and Statistics Division. **VFOAT** Exportations de Grain Canadien et de Farine de Ble. (March 1971)-. Periodical. English (French). Twelve times a year. 48.00Can$. Receiver General of Canada CDN Grain Commission, 600 303 Main Street, Winnipeg Manitoba R3C 3G8 Canada. **Tel** (204)983-1570, FAX (204)983-0248.

ISSN 0071-450X
DD 664 US
FEED ADDITIVE COMPENDIUM (1966). (FEED ADDITIVE COMPENDIUM.). [Feed addit. comp.]. **Added/Corp** Animal Health Institute. Vol. 4 (1966)-. Periodical. English. Eleven times a year. $189.00. Miller Publishing Company, 12400 Whitewater Drive, Suite 160, Minnetonka MN 55343. **Tel** (612)931-0211. **(Subscription address:** Feed Additive Compendium, 191 South Gary Avenue, Carol Stream IL 60188. **)** ***Continues*** *Feedstuffs Feed Additive Compendium.*
Ind/Abst AGRICOLA.

ISSN 0886-5884
DD 636 US
FEED & FEEDING DIGEST. [Feed feed. dig.]. **VFOAT** Feed and Feeding Digest. (19??)-. Trade Publication. English. Irregular. National Grain and Feed Association, 1201 New York Avenue, Suite 830, Washington DC 20005. **Tel** (202)289-0873. ***Continues*** *The Feed Trader and Retailer.*
Ind/Abst AGRICOLA.

ISSN 1055-3223
DD 338 US
FEED & GRAIN. [Feed grain]. **VFOAT** Feed and Grain. (1991)-. Trade Publication. English. Seven times a year. $40.00. Johnson Hill Press Inc., (A Division of PTN Publishing Co.), 1233 Janesville Avenue, PO Box 803, Fort Atkinson WI 53538-0803. **Tel** (414)563-6388, FAX (414)563-1704. **ED** Kay Jensen. **Ad Acc.** Full Page (B&W) $3320.00. Full Page (Color) $4220.00 (4-color). **Circ:** 19,227 (ctrl). ***Continues*** *Feed & Grain Times, 0163-4119.*
Desc: Serves owners and operators of feed, grain, and allied grain handling and processing facilities. Features address the business management and operational issues that impact profitability.

ISSN 1085-0813
DD 338 US
TITLE CHANGE
FEED & GRAIN DE MEXICO. [Feed grain Mex.]. **VFOAT** Feed and Grain de Mexico. (199?)-(199?). Periodical. English. Four times a year. Johnson Hill Press Inc., (A Division of PTN Publishing Co.), 1233 Janesville Avenue, PO Box 803, Fort Atkinson WI 53538-0803. **Tel** (414)563-6388, FAX (414)563-1704. ***Continues*** *Feed & Grain (Special Mexican Ed.), 1079-0411.* ***Continued by*** *Feed & Grain para America Latina, 1085-0503.*

ISSN 1085-0503
DD 338 US
●**FEED & GRAIN PARA AMERICA LATINA.** [Feed grain Am. Lat.]. **VFOAT** Feed and Grain para America Latina. Vol. 3, No. 4 (Oct. 1995)-. Periodical. Spanish. Four times a year. Johnson Hill Press Inc., (A Division of PTN Publishing Co.), 1233 Janesville Avenue, PO Box 803, Fort Atkinson WI 53538-0803. **Tel** (414)563-6388, FAX (414)563-1704. ***Continues*** *Feed & Grain de Mexico, 1085-0813.*

ISSN 1079-0411
DD 338 US
TITLE CHANGE
FEED & GRAIN (SPECIAL MEXICAN ED.). (FEED & GRAIN.). [Feed grain]. **VFOAT** Feed and Grain. (993)-(199?). Trade Publication. Spanish. Four times a year (Jan., April, July, Oct.). $25.00 US; $30.00 Canada and Mexico; $40.00 other. Johnson Hill Press Inc., (A Division of PTN Publishing Co.), 1233 Janesville Avenue, PO Box 803, Fort Atkinson WI 53538-0803. **Tel** (414)563-6388, FAX (414)563-1704. ***Continued by*** *Feed & Grain de Mexico, 1085-0813.*
Desc: Serves as a complement of the North American version, but published in Spanish, serving owners and operators of feed, grain and allied grain handling and processing facilities.

ISSN 0950-771X
DD 636.08 UK
FEED COMPOUNDER. [Feed compd.]. (1981)-. Trade Publication. English. Eleven times a year (Jun/Jul combined). $71.87. HGM Publications, Abney House Baslow, Bakewell Derbyshire, DE45 1RZ United Kingdom. **Tel** 011 44 1246 582470, 1246 582329, FAX 011 44 1246 582425. **ED** Howard Mounsey. **Bk Rev. Ad Acc, Adv Mgr:** Simon Mounsey. **Circ:** 3,200.
Desc: Technical journal for feed and feed supplement companies and their suppliers covering nutrition, animal health, legislation, and feed production equipment.
Ind/Abst Biodeter. Abstr. (1991-); Curr. Cit.; Dairy Sci. Abstr.; Index Vet.; Nutr. Abstr. Rev., Ser. B, Live Feeds and Feed.; Pig News Inf.; Potato Abstr.; Poult. Abstr.; Rev. Med. Vet. Mycology; Rice Abstr.; Sug. Indus. Abstr.

LC HD1751 .A9322H **ISSN** 0193-984X
DD 338.1/873 US
FEED GRAIN, WHEAT, UPLAND COTTON AND RICE PROGRAMS, DISASTER AND DEFICIENCY PROVISIONS. (FEED GRAIN, WHEAT, UPLAND COTTON AND RICE PROGRAMS.). (1976)-. Government Publication. English. One time a year. US Department of Agriculture, 14th Street and Independence Avenue SW, Washington DC 20250. **Tel** (202)720-5457. ***Formed by the union of*** *Feed Grain, Wheat and Upland Cotton Program Disaster Provisions, 0360-8948* ***and*** *Rice Programs, Disaster and Deficiency.*

US
FEED INDUSTRY RED BOOK. (1938)-. English. One time a year. $36.00. Communications Marketing Inc., 9995 West 69th Street, Suite 201, Eden Prairie MN 55344. **Tel** (612)941-5820.

US
FEED INGREDIENT ANALYSES FOR OFFICIAL SAMPLES. Added/Corp Florida. Dept. of Agriculture and Consumer Services. Feed Laboratory. (1974)-. Periodical. English. One time a year.

ISSN 0274-5771
DD 664 US
CCC
CODEN FEINEW
FEED INTERNATIONAL. [Feed int.]. Vol. 1 (May/June 1980)-. Periodical. English (Spanish, German, French, Japanese, Chinese and Arabic). Twelve times a year. $48.00. Watt Publishing Company, 122 South Wesley Avenue, Mount Morris IL 61054. **Tel** (815)734-4171, FAX (815)734-7021, telex TWX 910-642-2891. **ED** Clay Gill and Roger Gilbert. **Ad Acc. Circ:** 16,000 (ctrl).
Desc: For the worldwide feed industry.
Ind/Abst BioBusiness (1990-); Nutr. Abstr. Rev., Ser. B, Live Feeds and Feed.

ISSN 0937-9134
GW
TITLE CHANGE
FEED MAGAZINE. [Feed mag.]. (March/April 1989)-(Mar. 1993). Periodical. English (summaries and/or abstracts in German and Spanish). Deutscher Fachverlag GmbH, Verlagsgruppe, D-60264 Frankfurt Germany. **Tel** 011 49 69 75951001, telex 411 862. ***Continues*** *Feed Magazine International, 0933-9744.* ***Merged into*** *Kraftfutter, 0023-4427.*

ISSN 0014-956X
DD 633 US
CCC
CODEN FEMAA9
FEED MANAGEMENT. [Feed manage.]. (1977)-. Periodical. English. Twelve times a year. $48.00. Watt Publishing Company, 122 South Wesley Avenue, Mount Morris IL 61054. **Tel** (815)734-4171, FAX (815)734-7021, telex TWX 910-642-2891. **ED** Clay Gill. **Bk Rev. Ad Acc. Circ:** 24,000 (ctrl). available on microfilm and microfiche from University Microfilms International (UMI). ***Formed by the union of*** *Feed Management. Central Edition* ***and*** *Feed Management. Eastern Edition.*
Desc: Serves feed manufacturers and mixers.
Ind/Abst AGRICOLA; Fish Rev. (Jan. 1989-July 1992); Wildl. Rev. (Jan. 1989-July 1992).

ISSN 0928-124X
NE
UDC 636.084.4
FEED MIX. [Feed mix]. (1992)-. Periodical. English. Eight times a year. $125.00. Misset Uitgeverij BV / Doetinchem, Postbus 4, 7000 BA Doetinchem Netherlands. **Tel** 011 31 8340 49911, 011 31 8340 49562, FAX 011 31 8340 43839, 011 31 8340 40515.

ISSN 0961-978X
UK
CEASED
FEEDS & FEEDING. [Feed. feed.]. **VFOAT** Feeds and Feeding. (1991)-(Feb. 1993). Trade Publication. English. HGM Publications, Abney House Baslow, Bakewell Derbyshire, DE45 1RZ United Kingdom. **Tel** 011 44 1246 582470, 1246 582329, FAX 011 44 1246 582425. **ED** Howard Mounsey. **Bk Rev. Ad Acc. Circ:** 10,500 (ctrl). ***Continues*** *Home Mixer.*
Desc: Magazine about feed and feeding for dairy, beef, sheep, pig and poultry farmers.

LC HD9052.U5 F4 **ISSN** 0014-9624
DD 338.4/766476/0973 US
CCC
CODEN FDSTAL
FEEDSTUFFS. [Feedstuffs]. (May 18, 1929)-. Trade Publication. English. One time a week. $95.00. Miller Publishing Company, 12400 Whitewater Drive, Suite 160, Minnetonka MN 55343. **Tel** (612)931-0211. **(Subscription address:** CDS / SIFD Agency Control, 1901 Bell Avenue, Des Moines IA 50315. **Tel** (515)246-6812.**)** available on microfilm and microfiche from University Microfilms International (UMI). Documents available from CASDDS, Documents on Demand. ***Continues*** *Farm Store.*
Ind/Abst AgBiotech News Inf.; AGRICOLA [Select. Cov.]; Agric. Eng. Abstr. (1991-); BioBusiness (1981-); Biodeter. Abstr. (19??-19??); Bus. Index (1985-); Chem. Abstr.; Dairy Sci. Abstr.; Energy Inf. Abstr.; Environ. Abstr.; F&S Index Plus Text, Int. [Select. Cov.]; Field Crop Abstr.; Foods Adlibra; Gen. BusinessFile (1985-); Grass. Forage Abstr.; Helminthol. Abstr. (1991-); Index Vet.; Irr. Drain. Abstr.; Leis., Rec., Tour. Abstr.; Maize Abstr.; Nutr. Abstr. Rev., Ser. B, Live Feeds and Feed.; Nutr. Abstr. Rev., Ser. A, Hum. Exp.; PESTDOC; Pig News Inf.; Postharvest News Inf.; Poult. Abstr.; PROMT; Protozoolog. Abstr.; Rev. Med. Vet. Mycology; Rural Dev. Abstr.; Soyabean Abstr.; Sug. Indus. Abstr.; Vet. Bull.; Trade Ind. Index (1981-); Wheat Barley Trit. Abstr.; World Agric. Econ. Rural Sociol. Abstr.

US
FEEDSTUFFS INDEX, THE. (Jan./March 1976)-. Periodical. English. Four times a year. available on request. Miller Publishing Company, 12400 Whitewater Drive, Suite 160, Minnetonka MN 55343. **Tel** (612)931-0211.

LC SF95 .S79A
LU
FODERBALANCER : RESSOURCER. Main/Corp Statistical Office of the European Communities. **VFOAT** Futterbilanz : Aufkommen; Feed Balance Sheet : Resources. 1976-. French (German). $8.60. Statistical Office of the European Communities, rue Alcide de Gasperi, BP 1907, Luxembourg Luxembourg.

FR
Pr Rev.
FOURRAGES. Added/Corp Association Francaise Pour la Production Fouragere. (19??)-. Periodical. French (summaries and/or abstracts in English). Four times a year (Mar., June, Sept., Dec.). $109.36. Association Francaise pour la Production Fourragere, Domaine INRA, CNRA / Route St. Cyrille, 78000 Versailles France. **Tel** 011 33 1 30219959, FAX 011 33 1 30833393, telex 695269F. **ED** Violette Allezard (Editor's Address: Le Bourg, Boyeux St. Jerome 01640 Jujurieux France, Telephone 74-36-90-88). Index available. cum. index. **Circ:** 1,200 (ctrl).
Desc: Syntheses of research and experimentations on animal feeds and forage plants..
Ind/Abst Agric. Eng. Abstr. (1991-); Dairy Sci. Abstr.; Field Crop Abstr.; Grass. Forage Abstr.; Leis., Rec., Tour. Abstr.; Maize Abstr.; Nutr. Abstr. Rev., Ser. B, Live Feeds and Feed.; Plant Breed. Abstr.; Postharvest News Inf.; Rural Dev. Abstr.; Soils Fert.; Soyabean Abstr.; World Agric. Econ. Rural Sociol. Abstr.

LC TS2120 .M34 **ISSN** 0133-0918
HU
CODEN GABODG
GABONAIPAR. [Gabonaipar]. Vol. 22- ; 1975-. Academic Scholarly Publication. Hungarian (English, German and Russian). Four times a year. $15.00. Lapkiado Vallalat, Lenin Korut 9-11, 1073 Budapest 7 Hungary. **Tel** 011 36 1 222408. **ED** Karoly Kalamar. Index available. cum. index. **Bk Rev. Ad Acc.** ctrl circ. Documents available from CASDDS. ***Continues*** *Malomipar es Termenyforgalom.*
Ind/Abst Chem. Abstr.; Pig News Inf.

LC TX761 .G43 **ISSN** 0367-4177
DD 641.8 GW
CCC
CODEN GEMBANGLMBAN
GETREIDE, MEHL UND BROT (1972). (GETREIDE, MEHL UND BROT.). [Getreide Mehl Brot]. **Added/Corp** Arbeitsgemeinschaft Getreideforschung. (1972)-. Trade Publication. German. Six times a year. $264.11. Deutscher Backer-Verlag GmbH, Bergstrabe 79-81 Postfach 102050, 44791 Bochum Germany. **Tel** 011 49 0234 51841, FAX 011 49 0234 582630. Documents available from BIOSIS Document Express, CASDDS. ***Formed by the union of*** *Getreide und Mehl, 0046-5879* ***and*** *Brot und Geback, 0007-2419.*
Ind/Abst AGRICOLA; Biol. Abstr.; Chem. Abstr.; Curr. Cit.; Field Crop Abstr.; Food Sci. Technol. Abstr.; Grass. Forage Abstr.; Int. Packag. Abstr.; Plant Breed. Abstr.; Soils Fert.; Soyabean Abstr.; Wheat Barley Trit. Abstr.

ISSN 0017-3029
DD 631 US
SUSPENDED
GRAIN AGE. [Grain age]. (1960)-Suspended (19??). Periodical. English. Six times a year. $15.00 US; $16.00 Canada; $19.00 other. Communications Marketing Inc., 9995 West 69th Street, Suite 201, Eden Prairie MN 55344. **Tel** (612)941-5820. ***Absorbed*** *Grain and Feed Review.*

ISSN 0164-3681
US
GRAIN & FEED JOURNALS (1978). (GRAIN & FEED JOURNALS.). Vol. 135, No. 10 (Oct. 1978)-. Periodical. English. Twenty-four times a year. $60.00. Grain and Feed Journals, 8440 N Waukegan

Road, Morton Grove IL 60053. **Tel** (312)675-7400. ***Continues*** *Grain & Farm Service Centers, 0091-0198;* ***Absorbed*** *Grain Industries Plants.*

US

GRAIN AND FEED MARKET NEWS.
Added/Corp United States. Agricultural Marketing Service. Livestock, Meat, Grain & Seed Division. United States. Agricultural Marketing Service. Livestock Division. United States. Agricultural Marketing Service. Livestock & Seed Division. Vol. 30, No. 1 (Jan. 8, 1982)-. Government Publication. English. One time a week. $70.00. US Department of Agriculture / Livestock and Seed Division, AMS/LMGS S Agr Building/Room 2623, PO Box 96456, Washington DC 20090. **Tel** (202)720-1050, (202)720-6231. **ED** Jim Beard. **Circ:** 700. Documents available from Documents on Demand. ***Formed by the union of*** *Grain Market News (Independence, Mo.), 0364-099X* ***and*** *Feed Market News (Independence, Mo.), 0364-2046.*
Desc: Grain prices, feed prices, grain export statistics.
Ind/Abst Am. Stat. Index.

ISSN 1047-4978
DD 338 US
CODEN GFEMER

GRAIN & FEED MARKETING. [Grain feed mark.]. **VFOAT** Grain and Feed Marketing. (198?)-. Trade Publication. English. Four times a year. $8.00. KR Publishing, PO Box 1036, Mercer Island WA 98040. **Tel** (206)236-2353.
Desc: Provides information on grain as feed and the grain trade.
Ind/Abst BioBusiness (1988-).

ISSN 0199-2287
US

GRAIN & FEED MERCHANT, THE.
Added/Corp Nebraska Grain & Feed Dealers Association. **VFOAT** Grain and Feed Merchant. (19??)-. Periodical. English. Twelve times a year. $40.00 nonmembers; $20.00 members. Nebraska Grain & Feed Dealers Association, 1620 M Street, Lincoln NE 68508. **Tel** (402)476-6174. **ED** Richard D. Sanne. **Ad Acc. Circ:** 1,000 (ctrl).
Desc: Features association activities, trade news and topics of interest to the Nebraska grain and feed trades.

ISSN 0191-5959
US

GRAIN & FEED REVIEW (DES MOINES, IOWA). (GRAIN & FEED REVIEW.). **VAT** Grain and Feed Review. Vol. 39 (Jan./Feb. 1978)-. Periodical. English. Six times a year. IGFA Services Inc, 2882 106th Street, Des Moines IA 50322. ***Continues*** *Iowa Grain and Feed Review.*

LC Z7164.G8 G7 TH9445.G7
DD 016.6331/0468/0289 US

GRAIN DUST ABSTRACTS . (1977)-. English. One time a year. National Agriculture Library, 10301 Baltimore Boulevard, Beltsville MD 20705. **Tel** (301)344-3937.

ISSN 0410-7470
CN

GRAIN ELEVATORS IN CANADA. (GRAIN ELEVATORS IN CANADA. SILOS A GRAIN DU CANADA.). **Added/Corp** Board of Grain Commissioners for Canada. Canadian Grain Commission. **VFOAT** Silos a Grain du Canada. (1953/1954)-. English (French). One time a year (Aug.). 12.01Can$. Receiver General of Canada CDN Grain Commission, 600 303 Main Street, Winnipeg Manitoba R3C 3G8 Canada. **Tel** (204)983-1570, FAX (204)983-0248. ***Continues*** *List of Grain Elevators in the Western and Eastern Divisions., 0317-4042.*

ISSN 0274-7138
US

GRAIN JOURNAL (DECATUR, ILL.).
(GRAIN JOURNAL.). [Grain j.]. Vol. 8, No. 12 (July 1980)-. Trade Publication. English. Six times a year (Feb., Apr., June, Aug., Oct., Dec.). $25.00. Country Journal Publications, 2490 North Water Street, Decatur IL 62526. **Tel** (217)877-9660, FAX (217)877-6647. **ED** Ed Zdrojewski. **Ad Acc, Adv Mgr:** Mark Avery. **Circ:** 11,000 (ctrl). ***Continues*** *Country Journal.*
Desc: Trade magazine for grain elevators.

LC HD9044.C3 G7 **ISSN** 0383-4417
DD 380.1/4131/0971 CN

GRAIN MATTERS. (GRAIN MATTERS : A LETTER FROM THE CANADIAN WHEAT BOARD.). **Added/Corp** Canadian Wheat Board. (Sept./Oct. 1975)-. Newsletter. English. Eight times a year. Free on request. Canadian Wheat Board, 423 Main Street, Winnipeg Manitoba R3L 1W5 Canada. **Tel** (204)983-3421, FAX (204)983-3841. ctrl circ.

US

GRAIN SORGHUM RESEARCH AND UTILIZATION CONFERENCE. Main/Conf Grain Sorghum Research and Utilization Conference. **Added/Corp** Grain Sorghum Producers Association. Texas Grain Sorghum Producers Board. Kansas Grain Sorghum Producers Association. (1977)-. Periodical. English. Every 2 years. $15.00. Grain Sorghum Promotion Federation, PO Box 530, Abernathy TX 79311. **Tel** (806) 298-2543, FAX (806) 298-4234.

ISSN 0381-3010
CN

GRAIN STATISTICS WEEKLY. See Agriculture-Abstracting, Bibliographies and Statistics.

LC HD9034 .U56a **ISSN** 0193-5585
DD 338.1/731/0973021 US

GRAIN STOCKS (WASHINGTON, D.C.).
(GRAIN STOCKS.). **Added/Corp** United States. Agricultural Statistics Board. United States. Crop Reporting Board. (Oct. 1975)-. Government Publication. English. Four times a year. $18.50. US Department of Agriculture, 14th Street and Independence Avenue SW, Washington DC 20250. **Tel** (202)720-5457. **(Subscription address:** Superintendent of Documents, US Government Printing Office, Washington DC 20402.) available on microfiche (Vols. for (1986-) distributed to depository libraries). Documents available from Documents on Demand. ***Continues*** *Grain Stocks in all Positions, 0094-1301.*
Ind/Abst Am. Stat. Index.

LC SB190 .G64 **ISSN** 0199-4336
DD 633.1/0468 US

GRAIN STORAGE & HANDLING. [Grain storage handl.]. **VAT** Grain Storage and Handling. Periodical. English. Six times a year. Grain Storage & Handling, PO Box 29155, Shawnee Mission KS 66201.

US

GRAIN STORAGE, PROCESSING AND MARKETING. RESEARCH REPORT.
Added/Corp U.S. Agency for International Development. Kansas State University. Food and Feed Grain Institute. No. 6 (May 1974)-. Monographic series. English. Price varies per volume. Food and Feed Grain Institute / Kansas State University, Manhattan KS 66506.
Ind/Abst Postharvest News Inf.

LC HD9044.C2 A3 **ISSN** 0072-5358
DD 338.1/731/0971 338.1/7/31 CN

GRAIN TRADE OF CANADA. [Grain trade Can.]. **Main/Corp** Statistics Canada. Crops Section. Crops Section. **Added/Corp** Canada. Dominion Bureau of Statistics. Agriculture Division. Board of Grain Commissioners for Canada. Statistics Branch. Canada. Dominion Bureau of Statistics. Crops Section. Statistics Canada. Crops Section. Canadian Grain Commission. Economics and Statistics Division. Board of Grain Commissioners for Canada. Statistics Division. **VFOAT** Commerce des Grains au Canada. (1948/1949)-. Periodical. English (French). One time a year. 51.00Can$. Statistics Canada Publications Sales and Services, R.H. Coats Building 6th Floor, Ottawa Ontario K1A 0T6 Canada. **Tel** (613)951-5078, (800)267-6677, FAX (613)951-1584, telex 053-3585. ***Continues*** *Report on the Grain Trade of Canada.*
Desc: Provides information on area and production of grains, marketing and inspections; reports on the receipts and shipments of grain by rail and lake, and the exports of grain products by country of destination. Also reports on oilseed crushings and milling.

US

GRAIN TRANSPORTATION. Added/Corp United States. Dept. of Agriculture. Office of Transportation. (1990)-. Government Publication. English. Fifty times a year. Free on request. US Department of Agriculture, 14th Street and Independence Avenue SW, Washington DC 20250. **Tel** (202)720-5457. Documents available from Documents on Demand. ***Continues*** *Grain Transportation Situation.*
Ind/Abst Am. Stat. Index.

LC HD9030.1 .G753 **ISSN** 1076-3929
DD 382/.4131/05 US

•**GRAIN, WORLD MARKETS AND TRADE.**
(GRAIN, WORLD MARKETS AND TRADE / UNITED STATES DEPARTMENT OF AGRICULTURE, FOREIGN AGRICULTURAL SERVICE.). [Grain world mark. trade]. **Added/Corp** United States. Foreign Agricultural Service. United States. World Agricultural Outlook Board. (Jan. 1994)-. Government Publication. English. Twelve times a year. $70.00. Department of Agriculture / Foreign Agricultural Service, 14th Street and Independence Avenue SW, Washington DC 20250-1000. **Tel** (202)720-3935, FAX (202)720-7729. **(Subscription address:** NTIS, 5285 Port Royal Road, Springfield VA 22161. **Tel** (703)487-4630.**) Circ:** 1,710. ***Formed by the union of*** *World Grain Situation and Outlook, 0898-3399* ***and*** *Export Markets for U.S. Grain and Products, 0896-0216.*
Ind/Abst Am. Stat. Index.

LC SB192.P5 G7 **ISSN** 0115-222X
DD 633/.1/09599 PH

GRAINS JOURNAL. [Grains j.]. Vol. 1 (Feb. 1976)-. Periodical. English. Six times a year.
Ind/Abst AGRICOLA; Philip. Sci. Technol. Abstr.

LC HD9031 .G78 **ISSN** 8756-8845
DD 338.1/731/0973 US

HARVEST STATES JOURNAL. [Harvest States j.]. **Added/Corp** Harvest States Cooperatives (Minn.). Vol. 3, No. 3 (June/July 1983)-. Periodical. English. Six times a year. Free on request. Harvest States Cooperatives, 1667 North Snelling Avenue, St Paul MN 55108. **Tel** (612)646-9433. ***Continues*** *GTA Journal, 0731-4477.*

ISSN 0891-5946
DD 338 US
CCC

HAY & FORAGE GROWER. [Hay forage grow]. **VFOAT** Hay and Forage Grower. (1986)-. Trade Publication. English. Two times a year. $10.00. Intertec Publishing Corporation, 9800 Metcalf, Overland Park KS 66212. **Tel** (913)341-1300. **(Subscription address:** Intertec Publishing Corporation, PO Box 2901, Overland Park KS 66282. **Tel** 800 441-0294.**)** ***Continues*** *Forage and Grassland Progress, 0015-6906.*

ISSN 0744-1517
US

HAY MARKET NEWS (BELL, CALIF.). See Business and Economics-Marketing and Purchasing.

UK

HOME-GROWN CEREALS AUTHORITY BULLETIN & DIGEST. (1966)-. Bulletin. English. One time a week. £45.00 England; £70.00 other. Home-Grown Cereals Authority, Hamlyn House, Highgate Hill, London N19 5PR United Kingdom. **Tel** 011 44 171 2633391, 011 44 171 2813072, FAX 011 44 171 2810884, telex 27615, 267828. **ED** Stephen Thornhill. Index available. **Circ:** 2,500.

AU

ICC STANDARDS METHODS. See Food and Food Industry.

ISSN 0745-8525
US

ILLINOIS GRAIN & LIVESTOCK MARKET NEWS. [Ill. grain livest. mark. news]. **VFOAT** Market News. **VAT** Illinois Grain and Livestock Market News. Periodical. English. Twelve times a year. Free. Illinois Department of Agriculture, PO Box 19281, Springfield IL 62794. **Tel** (217)782-2172, FAX (217)785-4505. **Circ:** 2,000.
Desc: Market summaries of Illinois direct cattle, direct hog, and direct sheep prices and volume, terminal sales, transportation situation report, hay market news report and other pertinent grain and livestock marketing information in Illinois.

LC TS2135.I4 I5 **ISSN** 0376-9887
DD 338.4/7/6647220954 II

INDIAN MILLER. Added/Corp Roller Flour Millers' Federation of India. (19??)-. Periodical. English. Six times a year. Roller Flour Millers Federation of India, 6 Todar Mal Lane Bengali Market, New Delhi 110001 India.
Ind/Abst Food Sci. Technol. Abstr.

ISSN 0245-4505
FR
CODEN ICRLDL

INDUSTRIES DES CEREALES.
(INDUSTRIES DES CEREALES : REVUE DE L'APIC-ASSOCIATION POUR LE PROGRES DES INDUSTRIES DE CEREALES.). [Ind. cereales]. **Added/Corp** Association pour le Progres des Industries de Cereales. No. 1 (Jan./Feb. 1980)-. Academic Scholarly Publication. French. Six times a year. $109.36. AGP Editions, 1 rue du Coq Heron, 75001 Paris France. **Tel** 011 33 1 40265708. **Bk Rev. Ad Acc. Circ:** 3,000. Documents available from CASDDS. ***Formed by the union of*** *Technique des Industries Cerealieres, 0397-734X; Meunerie Francaise* ***and*** *Bulletin des Anciens Eleves de l'Ecole de Meunerie.*
Ind/Abst Biodeter. Abstr. (1991-); Chem. Abstr. (1980-1983); Curr. Cit.; Food Sci. Technol. Abstr.; Postharvest News Inf.; Rev. Plant Pathol.; Wheat Barley Trit. Abstr.

US

INSPECTION & WEIGHING UPDATE. VAT Inspection and Weighing Update. Periodical. English. Federal Grain Inspection Service, US Department of Agriculture, Washington DC 20255.

UK

INTERNATIONAL MILLING FLOUR & FEED. VFOAT International Milling Flour and Feed. Vol. 184, No. 7 (July 1991)-. Trade Publication. English. Twelve times a year. $195.08. Turret Group, 177 Hagden Lane, Watford Hertfordshire WD1 8LN United Kingdom. **Tel** 011 44 1923 228577, FAX 011 44 1923 221346. available on an online database (file 648/Full-Text) from DIALOG. ***Continues*** *Milling Flour and Feed, 0954-4860.*
Ind/Abst Infomat Int. Bus.; PROMT.

LC HD9049.W5 S645
SA

JAARVERSLAG - KORINGRAAD.
Main/Corp South Africa. Wheat Board. Afrikaans. 2.00. Wheat Board, PO Box 908, Pretoria South Africa. ***Continues*** *South Africa. Wheat Industry Control Board. Jaarverslag.*

Agriculture — Feed Grain and Milling

KANSAS CITY GRAIN MARKET REVIEW. (19??)-(Sept. 1993). Periodical. English. Board of Trade of Kansas City, 4800 Main Street/Suite 303, Kansas City MO 64112. Tel (816)753-7367. **ED** Ron Johnson. Index available. cum. index. **Bk Rev. Ad Acc. Circ:** 980 (ctrl). *Supersedes Kansas City Grain Reporter.*
Desc: Grain market futures and cash market prices, statistics and news relevant to supply and demand and values.
ISSN 0738-7296
US CEASED

KOMBIKORMOVAIA PROMYSHLENNOST. Added/Corp Soviet Union. Ministerstvo Khleboproduktov. Gosudarstvennyi Agropromyshlennyi Komitet SSSR. Soiuz Nauchnykh i Inzhenernykh Obshchestv SSSR. Gosudarstvennaia Komissiia Soveta Ministrov SSSR po Prodovolstviiu i Zakupkam. Russia (Federation). Ministerstvo Selskogo Khoziaistva. Assotsiatsiia Sovetskikh Kombikormovykh Predpriiatii. VNPO "Kombikorm.". (1988)-. Periodical. Russian. Six times a year. $99.95. Agropromizdat, Sadovo-Spasskaia 18, 107807 Moscow Russia. **(Subscription address:** East View Publications Inc., 3020 Harbor Lane North, Suite 110, Minneapolis MN 55447. **Tel** (800)477-1005, (612)550-0961, FAX (612)559-2931.) *Continues Mukomolno-Elevatornaia i Kombikormovaia Promyshlennost, 0131-2413.*
Desc: Information on the flour and feed trade.
ISSN 0235-2605
RU

KORMOVYE KULTURY. Added/Corp Gosudarstvennyi Agropromyshlennyi Komitet SSSR. (1988)-. Periodical. Russian. Six times a year. Agropromizdat, Sadovo-Spasskaia 18, 107807 Moscow Russia. *Continues Kormoproizvodstvo, 0206-5711.*
Ind/Abst Agric. Eng. Abstr.; Grass. Forage Abstr.; Maize Abstr.; Nutr. Abstr. Rev., Ser. B, Live Feeds and Feed.; Postharvest News Inf.; Seed Abstr.; Soils Fert.; Sug. Indus. Abstr.; Weed Abstr.; Wheat Barley Trit. Abstr.
ISSN 0235-2540
RU

KRAFTFUTTER. [Kraftfutter]. (1953)-. Trade Publication. German (English). Twelve times a year. DM188.80. Deutscher Fachverlag GmbH, Verlagsgruppe, D-60264 Frankfurt Germany. **Tel** 011 49 69 75951001, telex 411 862. **Bk Rev. Ad Acc. Circ:** 3,100 (ctrl). Documents available from CASDDS. *Absorbed Feed Magazine, 0937-9134.*
Desc: Covers all questions pertaining to the manufacture of mixed fodder and informs about animal nutrition, marketing and sale of mixed fodder, as well as social and legal questions in the farming business.
Ind/Abst AGRICOLA; Agrofor. Abstr. (1991-); Biodeter. Abstr.; Chem. Abstr.; Dairy Sci. Abstr.; EMBASE; Energy Res. Abstr. (Oct. 1972-); Maize Abstr.; Nutr. Abstr. Rev., Ser. B, Live Feeds and Feed.; PESTDOC; Pig News Inf.; Poult. Abstr.
ISSN 0023-4427
GW CODEN KFFUAS

KRMIVARSTVI A SLUZBY. Added/Corp Vyzkumny Ustav Krmivarskeho Prumyslu a Sluzeb. (1973)-. Periodical. Czech. Twelve times a year. Documents available from CASDDS.
Ind/Abst Chem. Abstr.; Index Vet.; Maize Abstr.; Nutr. Abstr. Rev., Ser. B, Live Feeds and Feed.; Nutr. Abstr. Rev., Ser. A, Hum. Exp.; Pig News Inf.; Poult. Abstr.; Soyabean Abstr.; Wheat Barley Trit. Abstr.
XR
LC HD9041.1 .L6
DD 338.1
UK

LONDON CORN CIRCULAR, THE. (1843)-. English. One time a week. £45.00. London Corn Circular, 54 Wentworth Crescent, Ash Vale NR, Aldershot Hampshire GU12 5LF United Kingdom. **Tel** 011 44 1252 29082. **ED** D.S. Alexander. **Bk Rev. Ad Acc.**
Desc: Agricultural comments, views, prices and news.
LC HD9056.N4 A3
ISSN 0168-5066
NE

MEELFABRIEKEN, GORT- EN RIJSTPELLERIJEN E.D. / CENTRAAL BUREAU VOOR DE STATISTIEK, HOOFDAFDELING STATISTIEKEN VAN INDUSTRIE EN BOUWNIJVERHEID.
VFOAT Meelfabrieken, Gort- en Rijstpellerijen en Dergelijke; Flour Manufacturing, Grain Milling, and Husking. 1981-. Dutch (summaries and/or abstracts in English). One time a year. Fl7.00. Centraal Bureau voor de Statistiek, AFD ALG Zaken, Postbus 959, 2270 AZ Voorburg Netherlands. **Tel** 011 31 70 3373800, FAX 011 31 70 0387429, telex 32692 CBS NL. *Continues Netherlands. Centraal Bureau voor de Statistiek. Produktiestatistieken: Maelfabrieken.*
LC HD9056.U4 M676
DD 338.4/7/6647200973
ISSN 0091-4843
US CODEN MBNEDH

MILLING AND BAKING NEWS. [Milling baking news]. Vol. 51, No. 32 (Oct. 1972)-. Trade Publication. English. One time a week. $99.00. Sosland Publishing Company / Missouri, 4800 Main Street, Suite 100, Kansas City MO 64112. **Tel** (816)756-1000, FAX (816)756-0494, telex 820182. **ED** Morton Sosland. Index available. **Ad Acc. Circ:** 4,200. available on an online database (file 648/Full-Text) from DIALOG. *Continues Southwestern Miller. Continued in part by Milling Directory Buyer's Guide, 1045-9030.*
Desc: Overview of events in milling and baking industry.
Ind/Abst BioBusiness; F&S Index Plus Text, Int. [Select. Cov.]; PROMT; Stat. Ref. Index; Trade Ind. ASAP [Full Txt.]; Trade Ind. Index [Full Txt.].
LC HD9056..U4 M73
DD 338.4/766472/002573
ISSN 1045-9030
US TITLE CHANGE

MILLING DIRECTORY BUYER'S GUIDE. [Milling dir. buy. guide]. **VFOAT** Milling Directory and Buyer's Guide; Milling Directory & Buyer's Guide; Milling Directory. (1987)-(1993). Trade Publication. English. Sosland Publishing Company / Missouri, 4800 Main Street, Suite 100, Kansas City MO 64112. **Tel** (816)756-1000, FAX (816)756-0494, telex 820182. *Continues in part Milling and Baking News, 0091-4843. Merged with Grain Guide, 1049-4073 to form North American Grain & Milling Annual.*
NE

MOLENAAR, DE. Added/Corp Stichting Maalderijbelangen. (19??)-. Periodical. Dutch. Twenty-five times a year. $123.33. Uitgeverij Eisma BV, Postbus 340, 8901 BC Leeuwarden Netherlands. **Tel** 011 31 58 152545.
ISSN 0026-9018
IT Pr Rev.

MOLINI D'ITALIA. [Molini Ital.]. (April 1950)-. Periodical. Italian. Eleven times a year (monthly except Aug.). L40880. Avenue Media, via Riva Reno 61, 40122 Bologna Italy. **Tel** 011 39 51 227597, FAX 011 39 51 262203. **Bk Rev,** (Qty: 30). **Ad Acc. Circ:** 3,000.
Ind/Abst AGRICOLA.
DD 631
ISSN 1046-6088
US Pr Rev.

MONTANA GRAIN NEWS. [Mont. grain news]. **Added/Corp** Montana Grain Growers Association. Periodical. English. Every 2 years. Montana Grain Growers Association, PO Box 1165, 750 6th Street SW, Great Falls MT 59403. **Tel** (406)761-4596, FAX (406)761-4606. **ED** Randy Johnson. **Ad Acc, Adv Mgr:** Nancy Anderson. **Circ:** 3100 (ctrl). *Continues MGGA Report, 0744-5113.*
LC TS2120 .M87
ISSN 0027-2949
GW

MUEHLE + MISCHFUTTERTECHNIK, DIE. (DIE MUEHLE + [I.E. UND] MISCHFUTTERTECHNIK.). [Muehle + Mischfuttertech.]. (1965)-. Trade Publication. German (summaries and/or abstracts in English, French and Spanish). One time a week. $301.23. Wochenschrift die Muehle, Postfach 2254, D-32712 Detmold Germany. **Tel** 011 49 5231 24637, FAX 011 49 5231 35896, telex 935803. **Bk Rev. Ad Acc. Circ:** 3,500. *Continues Muehle.*
Desc: International magazine for grain processing, feed grain manufacturing and related areas.
Ind/Abst AGRICOLA; Agric. Eng. Abstr. (1991-); Biodeter.; Energy Res. Abstr. (Oct. 1974-); Food Sci. Technol. Abstr.; Maize Abstr.; Nutr. Abstr. Rev., Ser. B, Live Feeds and Feed.; Pig News Inf.; Postharvest News Inf.; Poult. Abstr.; Saf. Health Work; Soyabean Abstr.
DD 338
ISSN 0882-5149
US

NATIONAL CATTLE FEEDLOT, MEAT PACKER AND GRAIN DEALERS DIRECTORY. See Agriculture-Livestock.
LC HD9030.5 .F6
DD 338.1731
ISSN 0071-710X
US

NATIONAL GRAIN POLICIES. Main/Corp Food and Agriculture Organization of the United Nations. (1959)-. Periodical. English. One time a year. Food Agriculture Organization (FAO) / Italy, GIPCl66 via Terme di Caracalla, 00100 Rome Italy. **Tel** 011 39 6 52252925, FAX 011 39 6 52253152. **(Subscription address:** UNIPUB, 4611 F Assembly Drive, Lanham MD 20706. **Tel** (800)274-4888, (301)459-7666.)
DD 338.1/731/0971
ISSN 0848-7162
CN

NATIONAL GRAINS UPDATE (EASTERN ED.). (NATIONAL GRAINS UPDATE.). [Natl. grains update]. **Added/Corp** Canada. National Grains Bureau. (Mar. 1990). Periodical. English. Four times a year. *Continues in part Situation Report to Canadian Grain Producers., 0839-6841.*
DD 338.1/731/0971
ISSN 0848-7170
CN

NATIONAL GRAINS UPDATE (WESTERN ED.). (NATIONAL GRAINS UPDATE.). [Natl. grains update]. **Added/Corp** Canada. National Grains Bureau. (Mar. 1990). Periodical. English. Four times a year. *Continues in part Situation Report to Canadian Grain Producers., 0839-6841.*
LC SB193
DD 633.2
ISSN 0447-5933
JA CODEN NPSGAI

NIPPON SOCHI GAKKAISHI. (NIHON SOCHI GAKKAI SHI.). [Nippon Sochi Gakkaishi]. **Main/Corp** Nihon Sochi Gakkai. **Added/Corp** Nihon Sochi Gakki. Kaishi. Nihon Sochi Gakki. Journal. **VFOAT** Journal of Japanese Society of Grassland Science. Vol. 1 (Dec. 1955)-. Academic Scholarly Publication. Japanese (summaries and/or abstracts in English; table of contents in English). Four times a year. ¥11000. Nihon Sochi Gakkai, (Japanese Soc. of Grassland Science), c/o Norin Suisansho Sochi Shikenjo, 768 Senbonmatsu Nishinasunomachi, Nasugun Tochigiken 329-27 Japan. **(Subscription address:** Maruzen Company Ltd., PO Box 5050, Import & Export Department, Tokyo 100 31 Japan. **Tel** 011 81 3 32789224.) **ED** M Ohshima. ctrl circ. Documents available from BIOSIS Document Express, CASDDS.
Desc: Monographs of grasses and fodder crops.
Ind/Abst AGRICOLA; Agric. Eng. Abstr.; Biol. Abstr.; Chem. Abstr.; Crop Physiol. Abstr.; Hortic. Abstr.; Maize Abstr.; Nutr. Abstr. Rev., Ser. B, Live Feeds and Feed.; Plant Breed. Abstr.; Plant Grow. Reg. Abstr.; Postharvest News Inf.; Rev. Med. Vet. Entomol.; Seed Abstr.; Soils Fert.; Sorghum Mill. Abstr.; Soyabean Abstr.
LC HD9052.J3 N64
JA

NOKO SHIRYO TOKEI NEMPO. Added/Corp Japan. Norinsho. Chikusankyoku. Shiryoka. Japan. Norinsho. Chikusankyoku. Ryutsu Shiryoka. (19??)-. Periodical. Japanese. ¥7500. Nihon Shiryo Kyokai, (Japan Feed Council), Shiryo Kaikan 2-1, Azabudai 2 chome, Minatoku Tokyo 106 Japan.
DD 633
ISSN 1082-1740
US

●**NORTH AMERICAN GRAIN & MILLING ANNUAL.** [North Am. grain milling annu.]. **VFOAT** North American Grain and Milling Annual; Grain & Milling Annual; A.Grain and milling annual. (1994)-. English. One time a year. $90.00. Sosland Publishing Company / Missouri, 4800 Main Street, Suite 100, Kansas City MO 64112. **Tel** (816)756-1000, FAX (816)756-0494, telex 820182. *Formed by the union of Grain Guide, 1049-4073 and Milling Directory Buyer's Guide, 1045-9030.*
AG

NUMERO ESTADISTICO. Added/Corp Bolsa de Cereales de Buenos Aires. **VFOAT** Bolsa de Cereales de Buenos Aires. Numero Estadistico. (1983)-. Spanish. Bolsa de Cereales, Corrientes 123, Buenos Aires Argentina. *Continues Bolsa de Cereales. Revista Institucional. Numero Estadistico.*
LC SF95 .N867
DD 636.08/5/05
ISSN 0309-135X
UK

NUTRITION ABSTRACTS AND REVIEWS. SERIES B. LIVESTOCK FEEDS AND FEEDING. See Agriculture-Abstracting, Bibliographies and Statistics.
LC SF97 .A545
DD 636.08/55
ISSN 0569-2628
US CODEN OPFMAG

OFFICIAL PROCEEDINGS, ANNUAL MEETING - AMERICAN ASSOCIATION OF FEED MICROSCOPISTS. [Off. proc. Annu. meet. - Amer. Assoc. Feed Microsc.]. **Main/Corp** American Association of Feed Microscopists. (19??)-. Academic Scholarly Publication. English. One time a year. $25.00. American Association of Feed Microscopists, 1118 Apple Drive, Mechanicsburg PA 17055. **Tel** (717)766-6039. Documents available from CASDDS.
Ind/Abst Chem. Abstr.
US

OFFICIAL PUBLICATION - ASSOCIATION OF AMERICAN FEED CONTROL OFFICIALS. Main/Corp Association of American Feed Control Officials. (19??)-. One time a year. $25.00. Georgia Department of Agriculture, 19 Martin Luther King Drive, Room 226, Capitol Square, Atlanta GA 30334-4250. **Tel** (404)656-3600, (404)656-3722, FAX (404)656-9380, (404)651-7957. **ED** Earl M. Haas. **Circ:** 2,500.
Desc: Contains official feed terms, model legislation, control official's directory and proceedings.
LC TJ859 .O43
DD 621.2/1/0973
ISSN 0276-3338
US

OLD MILL NEWS. See Architecture.

Agriculture —Feed Grain and Milling

DD 338   **ISSN** 0897-5051   US
OREGON WHEAT. See Industry and Production.

BE
PANORAMA. (19??)-. French (English, German and Italian). Twelve times a year. 15.000F. European Feed Manufacture Federation, rue de la Loi 223 Bte 3, 1040 Brussels Belgium. **Tel** 011 32 2 2308715, FAX 011 32 2 2305722. **Circ**: 150.
Desc: Information on monthly events.
Ind/Abst Int. Packag. Abstr.; Repere.

LC HD9066.I6 I53b   IO
PEDOMAN PELAKSANAAN PENGADAAN DALAM NEGERI. **Main/Corp** Indonesia. Badan Urusan Logistik. (19??)-. Indonesian. Baden Urusan Logistik, JL Teuku Umar 10-12, Jakarta Indonesia.

DD 338.1/731/0971   **ISSN** 0848-7189
POINT, SECTEUR DES GRAINS (ED. DE L'EST). (LE POINT, SECTEUR DES GRAINS.). [Point sect. grains]. **Added/Corp** Canada. Bureau National des Grains. (Mar. 1990)-. Periodical. French. Four times a year. **Continues in part** Rapport de Situation a l'Intention des Producteurs Canadiens de Cereales.

DD 338.1/731/0971   **ISSN** 0848-7197   CN
POINT, SECTEUR DES GRAINS (ED. DE L'OUEST). (LE POINT, SECTEUR DES GRAINS.). [Point sect. grains]. **Added/Corp** Canada. Bureau National des Grains. (Mar. 1990)-. Periodical. French. Four times a year. **Continues in part** Rapport de Situation a l'Intention des Producteurs Canadiens de Cereales.

UK
PRESS RELEASE - INTERNATIONAL WHEAT COUNCIL. **Main/Corp** International Wheat Council. Trade Publication. English. International Wheat Council, One Canada Square, Canary Wharf, London E14 5AE United Kingdom. **Tel** 011 44 171 5131122, FAX 011 44 171 7120071, telex 8813241.

DD 636   **ISSN** 0885-7687   US
PROCEEDINGS / CORNELL NUTRITION CONFERENCE FOR FEED MANUFACTURERS. [Proc. Cornell Nutr. Conf. Feed Manuf.]. **Added/Corp** New York State College of Agriculture. Dept. of Poultry Husbandry. New York State College of Agriculture. Dept. of Animal Husbandry. New York State College of Agriculture. Dept. of Biochemistry and Nutrition. Cornell University. Graduate School of Nutrition. American Feed Manufacturers' Association. New York State College of Agriculture. Dept. of Biochemistry. New York State College of Agriculture. Dept. of Poultry Science. New York State College of Agriculture. Dept. of Animal Science. New York State College of Agriculture and Life Sciences. Dept. of Animal Science. New York State College of Agriculture and Life Sciences. Dept. of Poultry Science. New York State College of Agriculture and Life Sciences. Dept. of Poultry and Avian Sciences. (1957)-. Proceedings. English. One time a year. $10.00. Cornell University Department of Animal Science, 272 Morrison Hall, Ithaca NY 14853. **Tel** (607)255-4478, FAX (607)255-9829. **Continues** Cornell Nutrition Conference for Feed Manufacturers. Proceedings of the ... Cornell Nutrition Conference for Feed Manufacturers, 0885-7687.
Ind/Abst Bibliogr. Agric.

DD 636   **ISSN** 0542-8386   US
PROCEEDINGS - MARYLAND NUTRITION CONFERENCE FOR FEED MANUFACTURERS. [Proc. - Md. Nutr. Conf. Feed Manuf.]. **Main/Corp** Maryland Nutrition Conference for Feed Manufacturers. Proceedings. English. One time a year. $7.50. Maryland Feed Industry Council, University of Maryland, Poultry Science Department, 3129 Animal Science Center, College Park MD 20742. **Tel** (301)314-9557. **Circ**: 1,000.
Desc: Covers animal nutrition.
Ind/Abst AGRICOLA [Full Cov.].

CN
TITLE CHANGE
PROCEEDINGS OF THE ... ANNUAL UNIVERSITY OF GUELPH NUTRITION CONFERENCE FOR FEED MANUFACTURERS. **Main/Conf** University of Guelph Nutrition Conference for Feed Manufacturers. (1965)-(19??). Proceedings. English. Canadian Feed Industry Association, 325 Dalhousie Street, Suite 625, Ottawa Ontario K1N 7G2 Canada. **Tel** (613)238-6421, FAX (613)238-6620. ctrl circ. **Continued by** Eastern Nutrition Conference Proceedings.
Desc: Papers presented by scientists at the Guelph Nutrition Conference.

LC SB189 .P77   **ISSN** 0033-2461   PL
PRZEGLAD ZBOZOWO-MYNARSKI. [Przegl. zboz.-myn.]. Vol. 1 (April 1957)-. Periodical. Polish (table of contents in English, Russian and Multiple languages). Twelve times a year. $120.00. **(Subscription address:** Ars Polona-Ruch, PO Box 1001, Krakowskie Przedmiescie 7, 00-068 Warsaw Poland. **Tel** 011 48 22 261201.)
Ind/Abst AGRICOLA; Food Sci. Technol. Abstr.

AT
QUEENSLAND GRAINGROWER, THE.
Added/Corp Queensland Graingrowers Association. (Nov. 24, 1976)-. Periodical. English. Fifty-one times per year. 64.13Aus$. Western Publishers Pty Ltd, PO Box 656, Toowoomba Queensland 4350 Australia. **Tel** 011 61 7 2865688. **ED** S. Darracott. **Bk Rev**. **Ad Acc**. **Circ**: 10,000 (ctrl).
Desc: Grain growing (all types) plus associated industries, motoring and general farm living.

UK
REPORT FOR THE FISCAL YEAR.
Main/Corp International Wheat Council. (1991/1992)-. English. £30.00 UK / $50.00 other. International Wheat Council, One Canada Square, Canary Wharf, London E14 5AE United Kingdom. **Tel** 011 44 171 5131122, FAX 011 44 171 7120071, telex 8813241. **Continues** International Wheat Council. Report for the Crop Year.

LC SB191.W5 A77   AT
REPORT FOR THE YEAR ... . **Main/Corp** Commonwealth Scientific and Industrial Research Organization (Australia). Grain Quality Research Laboratory. **VFOAT** Annual Report. (1991/1992)-. English. CSIRO Publications, PO Box 89, 314 Albert Street, East Melbourne Victoria 3002 Australia. **Tel** 011 61 3 4187333, 4187217, FAX 011 61 3 4190459, telex AA 30236. **Continues** Commonwealth Scientific and Industrial Research Organization (Australia). Wheat Research Unit. Report for the Year... .

LC HD9049.W4S58   SA
DD 354.680082/333
REPORT OF THE AUDITOR-GENERAL ON THE ACCOUNTS OF THE WHEAT BOARD FOR THE FINANCIAL YEAR ... . **VFOAT** Verslag van die Ouditeur-Generaal oor die Rekenings van die Koringraad vir die Boekjaar ... . (1976)-. Afrikaans (English). One time a year. R1.00. Staatsdrukker, Bosmanstraat, Privaatsak X85, Pretoria 0001 South Africa. **Continues** Verslag van die Kontroleur en Ouditeur-Generaal oor die Rekenings van die Koringraad.

SA
REPORT ON GRAIN SORGHUM FOR THE FINANCIAL YEAR ... / MAIZE BOARD. **Main/Corp** South Africa. Maize Board. **VFOAT** Report on Grain Sorghum. (198?)-. Periodical. English. Maize Board, PO Box 669, Pretoria South Africa. **Continues** South Africa. Maize Board. Report on Grain Sorghum and Buckwheat for the Financial Year.

LC HD9235.B42 S65   SA
DD 354/.68/008233
REPORT - SOUTH AFRICA. DRY BEAN BOARD. **Main/Corp** South Africa. Dry Bean Board. **VFOAT** Verslag. Multiple languages (English and Afrikaans). Arcadia Telegrams Boneraad, 45 Hamilton Street, PO Box 678, Pretoria South Africa.

LC SB191.O2 R44   **ISSN** 0733-9283
DD 633.1/33/0973
RESULTS FROM THE COOPERATIVE COORDINATED OAT BREEDING NURSERIES, AND THE UNIFORM WINTER-HARDINESS NURSERIES. (RESULTS FROM THE COOPERATIVE COORDINATED OAT BREEDING NURSERIES FOR ... AND THE UNIFORM WINTER-HARDINESS NURSERIES FOR ...). (19??)-. Government Publication. English. One time a year. US Department of Agriculture, 14th Street and Independence Avenue SW, Washington DC 20250. **Tel** (202)720-5457.

UK
SECRETARIAT PAPER - INTERNATIONAL WHEAT COUNCIL.
Main/Corp International Wheat Council. No. 1 (1961)-. Monographic series. English (summaries and/or abstracts in Russian, Spanish and French). Price varies per volume. International Wheat Council, One Canada Square, Canary Wharf, London E14 5AE United Kingdom. **Tel** 011 44 171 5131122, FAX 011 44 171 7120071, telex 8813241.
Desc: A survey of port capacities and internal transportation facilities for grain in over 60 developing countries.

LC SF97 .S53   JA
CODEN SHTKD3
SHIRYO KENKYU HOKOKU. [Shiryo kenkyu hokoku]. **Added/Corp** Norin Suisansho Tokyo Hishiryo Kensajo. (1966)-. Academic Scholarly Publication. Japanese. Norin Suisansho Tokyo Hishiryo Kensajo, (Tokyo Fertilizer & Feed Inspection Station Ministry of Agriculture Forestry & Fisheries), Otemachi Godo Chosha Dai 3 Gokan, 3-3 Otemachi 1 Chome, Chiyodaku Tokyo 100 Japan. Documents available from CASDDS.
Ind/Abst Chem. Abstr.

LC HD9052.U5 A3   **ISSN** 1050-9143
DD 338.1/7325/0973   US
CODEN FESREQ
CEASED
SITUATION AND OUTLOOK REPORT. FEED. [Situat. outlook rep., Feed]. **Added/Corp** United States. Dept. of Agriculture. Economic Research Service. United States. World Agricultural Outlook Board. **VFOAT** Feed; Situation and Outlook Yearbook. Feed; Feed Situation and Outlook Report; Feed Situation and Outlook. FDS-300 (Aug. 1986)-(Oct. 1994). Periodical. English. Economic Research Service USDA, 341 Victory Drive, Herndon VA 22070. **Tel** (800) 999-6779. available on microfiche (Vols. for 1986- distributed to depository libraries). Documents available from Documents on Demand. **Continues** Feed Outlook and Situation Report, 8755-853X.
Desc: Reports, consisting chiefly of tables and statistics, which contain information on supply, demand, and price research.
Ind/Abst AGRICOLA; Am. Stat. Index; BioBusiness; F&S Index Plus Text, Int. [Select. Cov.]; Maize Abstr.; Nutr. Abstr. Rev., Ser. B, Live Feeds and Feed.; Predicasts Forecasts; Trade Ind. ASAP [Full Txt.]; Trade Ind. Index [Full Txt.].

LC S   **ISSN** 0584-1321
DD 630   US
Pr Rev
SORGHUM NEWSLETTER. [Sorghum newsl.]. **Added/Corp** Sorghum Improvement Conference of North America. Vol. 17 (1974)-. Newsletter. English. One time a year (Nov.). $15.00. University of Georgia / Department of Crop & Soil, Griffin GA 30223. **Tel** (404)228-7326, FAX (404)229-3215. **ED** R.R. Duncan. Index available. cum. index (Vol. 1 - Vol. 32 only). **Bk Rev**. available on microfilm from University Microfilms International (UMI). **Continues** Sorghum Newsletter, 0584-1321.
Desc: International exchange of research information, ideas, research techniques, and problems of the sorghum and millets industry.
Ind/Abst Biocont. News Inf.; Crop Physiol. Abstr.; Nematol. Abstr.; Plant Breed. Abstr.; Plant Genet. Resour. Abstr.; Plant Grow. Reg. Abstr.; Sorghum Mill. Abstr.

ISSN 0736-1092
US
STATISTICAL ANNUAL - MINNEAPOLIS GRAIN EXCHANGE. See Agriculture-Abstracting, Bibliographies and Statistics.

ISSN 0889-0471
US
STOCKS OF GRAIN AT SELECTED TERMINAL & ELEVATOR SITES. WEEKLY ED. (STOCKS OF GRAIN AT SELECTED TERMINAL & ELEVATOR SITES / LIVESTOCK & GRAIN MARKET NEWS BRANCH, LIVESTOCK, MEAT, GRAIN & SEED DIVISION, U.S. DEPARTMENT OF AGRICULTURE.). **Added/Corp** United States. Livestock & Grain Market News Branch. (1982)-. Periodical. English. One time a week. $55.00. US Department of Agriculture / Portland, 1220 Southwest Ave Room 1772, Portland OR 97204. **Tel** (503)326-2237, FAX (503)326-5140. ctrl circ. **Continues** National Stocks of Grain Report.
Desc: Amount of grain stored in selected terminal and elevator sites.

LC SB114.U7 O53A   **ISSN** 0193-8592
DD 353.97660082/33   US
SUMMARY INSPECTION REPORT OF OFFICIAL SAMPLES ON SEED, FEED, FERTILIZER & AG-LIME. **Main/Corp** Oklahoma. Plant Industry Division. English. One time a year. Oklahoma State Department of Agriculture, 2800 North Lincoln Boulevard, Oklahoma City OK 73105. **Tel** (405)521-3864, FAX (405)521-4912. ctrl circ.

LC TS2120 .T4   **ISSN** 0040-1862
IT
CCC
CODEN TEMOAZ
TECNICA MOLITORIA. [Tec. molit.]. Vol. 12 No. 1 (Jan. 1961)-. Trade Publication. Italian. Twelve times a year. L95380. Chiriotti Editori, PO Box 66, 10064 Pinerolo Italy. **Tel** 121 794493, FAX 121/794480, telex 211 820 CHIED I. Index available. **Bk Rev**. **Ad Acc**. **Circ**: 4,000. Documents available from CASDDS. **Continues**

Selezione di Tecnica Nolitoria.
Desc: Magazine specializing in pasta production, flour and feed milling, cereal chemistry, silos, etc.
Ind/Abst AGRICOLA; Agric. Eng. Abstr. (1991-); BioBusiness (1990-); Biodeter. Abstr. (1991-); Chem. Abstr. (1961-1983); Curr. Cit.; Food Sci. Technol. Abstr.; Maize Abstr.; Nutr. Abstr. Rev., Ser. B, Live Feeds and Feed.; Postharvest News Inf.; Rev. Med. Vet. Mycology; Rice Abstr.; Weed Abstr.; Wheat Barley Trit. Abstr.

LC SB188 **ISSN** 0138-4309
DD 633.1 GW
NLM W1 TI362 **CODEN** TIFUDF

TIERERNAEHRUNG UND FUETTERUNG. [Tierernaehr. Fuetter.]. (1975)-. Periodical. German (summaries and/or abstracts in English and Russian). Deutscher Landwirtschaftsverlag, Grabbaallee 41, D-13156 Berlin Germany. **Tel** 011 49 30 48320311. Documents available from CASDDS. ***Continues*** *Jahrbuch fure Tierernaehrung und Fuetterung.*
Ind/Abst Biodeter. Abstr.; Chem. Abstr.; Dairy Sci. Abstr.; Grass. Forage Abstr.; Index Vet.; Maize Abstr.; Nutr. Abstr. Rev., Ser. B, Live Feeds and Feed.; Pig News Inf.; Postharvest News Inf.; Potato Abstr.; Small Anim. Abstr. Bibliogr.; Sug. Indus. Abstr.; Wheat Barley Trit. Abstr.

LC TS2120 .A74A **ISSN** 0342-572X
GW
CODEN VAGED6

VEROFFENTLICHUNGEN DER ARBEITSGEMEINSCHAFT GETREIDEFORSCHUNG E.V., DETMOLD. [Veroff. Arb. gem. Getreideforsch. e. V., Detm.]. (1946)-. Academic Scholarly Publication. German. Irregular. Price varies per volume. Granum-Verlag, Postfach 23, Detmold Germany. Documents available from CASDDS.
Ind/Abst Chem. Abstr.; Food Sci. Technol. Abstr.

LC HD9044.C2 C34A **ISSN** 0380-8718
DD 338.1/7/310971 CN

VISIBLE GRAIN SUPPLIES AND DISPOSITION. [Visible grain supplies dispos.]. **Main/Corp** Canadian Grain Commission. Economics and Statistics Division. (1970/71)-. Periodical. English. One time a year. Free (with subscription to Grain Statistics Weekly) US, 11.00Can$ other. Receiver General of Canada CDN Grain Commission, 600 303 Main Street, Winnipeg Manitoba R3C 3G8 Canada. **Tel** (204)983-1570, FAX (204)983-0248. ***Supersedes*** *Marketings, Distribution & Visible Carry-Over of Canadian Grain In and Through Licensed Elevators, 0068-7065.*

LC Z5071 **ISSN** 0265-7880
DD 016.63 UK

WHEAT, BARLEY AND TRITICALE ABSTRACTS. **See** Agriculture-Abstracting, Bibliographies and Statistics.

UK

WHEAT MARKET REPORT. PMR.
Main/Corp International Wheat Council. No. 56, (Nov. 1976)-. Periodical. English (French and Spanish). Twelve times a year. £250.00 Europe; £400.00 other. International Wheat Council, One Canada Square, Canary Wharf, London E14 5AE United Kingdom. **Tel** 011 44 171 5131122, FAX 011 44 171 7120071, telex 8813241. **ED** A. W. DeMaria. Index available. **Circ:** 2,300.
Desc: Current assessment supply and demand outlook for grain. Prices, freight rates, and national policies.

LC HD1491 **ISSN** 1185-2194
DD 338.1/73 CN

WILD OATS (WINNIPEG). (WILD OATS.). [Wild oats]. Vol. 1, No. 1 (Sept. 4, 1990)-. Periodical. English. Forty times a year. 156.07Can$. Wild Oats Publishing, 703-167 Lombard Avenue, Winnipeg Manitoba R3B 0V3 Canada. **Tel** (204)942-1459, FAX (204)942-7652. **ED** John Duvenaud. ctrl circ. available via fax. ***Continues*** *Farm Market Week., 0833-0956.*
Desc: Grain market advisory for western Canadian grains, oilseeds and special crops.

LC HD9030.1 .W67 **ISSN** 0745-8991
DD 338.1/731/05 US
CODEN WOGREJ

WORLD GRAIN. [World grain]. Vol. 1, No. 1 (Oct. 1982)-. Periodical. English. Nine times a year. $32.00. Sosland Publishing Company / Missouri, 4800 Main Street, Suite 100, Kansas City MO 64112. **Tel** (816)756-1000, FAX (816)756-0494, telex 820182.
Ind/Abst Food Sci. Technol. Abstr.; Foods Adlibra; Nutr. Abstr. Rev., Ser. B, Live Feeds and Feed.; Sug. Indus. Abstr.

ISSN 0898-3399
DD 338 US
TITLE CHANGE

WORLD GRAIN SITUATION AND OUTLOOK. [World grain situat. outlook]. **Added/Corp** United States. Foreign Agricultural Service. Grain and Feed Division. United States. World Agricultural Outlook Board. (Jan. 1987)-(1993). Government Publication. English. Department of Agriculture / Foreign Agricultural Service, 14th Street and Independence Avenue SW, Washington DC 20250-1000. **Tel** (202)720-3935, FAX (202)720-7729. **Circ:** 1,710. available on microfiche. Documents available from Documents on Demand. ***Continues*** *Foreign Agriculture Circular. Grains. World Grain Situation and Outlook.* ***Merged with*** *Export Markets for U.S. Grain and Products, 0896-0216* ***to form*** *Grain, World Markets and Trade.*
Desc: Report contains latest information on world grain production, consumption, trade, market development, prices and economic indicators.
Ind/Abst Am. Stat. Index (?-?); F&S Index Plus Text, Int. (?-?) [Select. Cov.]; Predicasts Forecasts (?-?); Trade Ind. ASAP (?-?) [Full Txt.]; Trade Ind. Index [Full Txt.].

UK

WORLD GRAIN STATISTICS. **Added/Corp** International Wheat Council. (1991)-. Trade Publication. English. One time a year. £80.00 UK; $125.00 US. International Wheat Council, One Canada Square, Canary Wharf, London E14 5AE United Kingdom. **Tel** 011 44 171 5131122, FAX 011 44 171 7120071, telex 8813241. ***Continues*** *World Wheat Statistics, 0512-3844.*

ISSN 0170-7809
GW

ZMP BILANZ. GETREIDE-FUTTERMITTEL. **Added/Corp** Zentrale Markt- und Preisberichtstelle fuer Erzeugnisse der Land-, Forst- und Ernaehrungswirtschaft. **VFOAT** Bilanz. Getreide-Futtermittel. (19??)-. Trade Publication. German. One time a year (Feb. or Mar.). $115.15. ZMP Marktberichte Bonn, Rochusstrabe 2, D-53123 Bonn Germany. **Tel** 011 49 228 9777170.

LIVESTOCK

LC S
DD 630 US

ABOUT COWS [COMPUTER FILE]. (19??)-. English. $17.96 (schools and libraries), $19.95 (all except schools and libraries) US; $32.96 (schools and libraries), $34.95 (all except schools and libraries) other. Quanta Press, Inc., 1313 Fifth Street Southeast, Suite 208C, Minneapolis MN 55414. **Tel** (612)379-3956, FAX (612)623-4570.

ISSN 1068-8021
DD 636 US

ACJ (PLATTE CITY, MO.). (ACJ : THE OFFICIAL PUBLICATION OF THE ACA.). [ACJ]. **Added/Corp** American Chianina Association. **VAT** American Chianina journal. (19??)-. Periodical. English. Eleven times a year (monthly except June). $24.00 North America; $50.00 Central America, Panama, Costa Rica, Bahamas, Bermuda, El Salvador, Nicaragua, St. Pierre, Miquelon, Guatemala and Colombia; $65.00 Europe, (except Estonia, Latvia, Lithuania and USSR) North Africa, Meditteranean, Brazil, Argentina, Venezuela, Ecuador, Uruguay, Great Britain; $80.00 other. American Chianina Journal, PO Box 890, Platte City MO 64079. **Tel** (816)431-2808, FAX (816)431-5381. **ED** Mary Kathryn McFarland. Index available. **Ad Acc. Circ:** 2,000 (ctrl). ***Continues*** *American Chianina journal, 0198-8816.*
Desc: Featuring the Chianina breed, its achievements, and the people involved.

ISSN 0138-6247
CU
SUSPENDED

ACPA. **Added/Corp** Asociacion Cubana de Produccion Animal. **VFOAT** Revista ACPA; Revista A.C.P.A. **VAT** Asociacion Cubana de Produccion Animal; Revista Asociacion Cubana de Produccion Animal. No. 1 (July/Sept. 1982)-Suspended (1992). Periodical. Spanish. Two times a year. Ediciones Cubanas, Obispo 527 Altos ESQ Bernaza, CP 10100 Havana Cuba.
Ind/Abst Anim. Breed. Abstr.; Dairy Sci. Abstr.; Pig News Inf.; Poult. Abstr.; Sug. Indus. Abstr.

ISSN 0860-2603
PL
CODEN AATZE6

ACTA ACADEMIAE AGRICULTURAE AC TECHNICAE OLSTENENSIS. ZOOTECHNICA. (ZOOTECHNICA.). [Acta Acad. Agric. Tech. Olst., Zootech.]. (1985)-. Academic Scholarly Publication. Polish. Wydawnictwo Akademia Rolniczo-Techniczna w Olsztynie / Agricultural and Technical Academy in Olsztyn, Blok 21, 10-957 Olsztyn-Kortowo Poland. **Tel** 011 48 89 273310. Documents available from CASDDS. ***Continues*** *Zeszyty Naukowe Akademii Rolniczo-Technicznej w Olsztynie. Zootechnika, 0324-9239.*
Ind/Abst AGRICOLA; Agric. Eng. Abstr.; Chem. Abstr. (1985-); Field Crop Abstr.; Nutr. Abstr. Rev., Ser. B, Live Feeds and Feed.; Postharvest News Inf.; Potato Abstr.; Poult. Abstr.; Soils Fert.

LC SF1 .P582 **ISSN** 0065-0935
PL
CODEN AASZBW

ACTA AGRARIA ET SILVESTRIA. SERIES ZOOTECHNICA. [Acta agrar. silv., ser. zootech.]. **Added/Corp** Polska Akademia Nauk. Komisja Nauk Rolniczych I Lesnych. **VFOAT** Acta Agraria et Silvestria. Series Zootechnica. Vol. 1 (1961)-. Periodical. Polish (summaries and/or abstracts in English and Russian; table of contents in Polish, English and Russian). Irregular. **(Subscription address:** Ars Polona-Ruch, PO Box 1001, Krakowskie Przedmiescie 7, 00-068 Warsaw Poland. **Tel** 011 48 22 261201.) Documents available from BIOSIS Document Express, CASDDS.
Ind/Abst Biol. Abstr.; Chem. Abstr. (-1989); Dairy Sci. Abstr.; EMBASE; Index Vet.; Nutr. Abstr. Rev., Ser. B, Live Feeds and Feed.; Pig News Inf.; Poult. Abstr.

LC SF1 .A26 **ISSN** 0906-4702
DK
CCC
CODEN ASSAEI

ACTA AGRICULTUR SCANDINAVICA. SECTION A, ANIMAL SCIENCE.
Added/Corp Kungl. Skogs- och Lantbruksakademien (Sweden) Scandinavian Agricultural Research Workers' Association. **VFOAT** Animal Science. Vol. 42, No. 1 (Feb. 1992)-. Periodical. English. Four times a year. $150.00. Scandinavian University Press, PO Box 2959 Toeyen, N 0608 Oslo 6 Norway. **Tel** 011 47 2 2575400, FAX 011 47 2 2575353, telex 71896 UROR N. **(Subscription address:** Scandinavian University Press, 200 Meacham Ave., Elmont NY 11003. **Tel** (516)352-7300, FAX (516)352-7377.) **ED** Ake Barklund. Documents available from The Genuine Article. ***Continues in part*** *Acta Agricultur Scandinavica, 0001-5121.*
Desc: Original articles concerning agricultural research of relevance to Scandinavian conditions. Covers a broad spectrum of research in animal science and its applications related to animal breeding and genetics; animal physiology; nutrition and feeding; general animal husbandry, including its economic and technical aspects; animal behaviour and hygiene and qualitative aspects of animal products.
Ind/Abst Curr. Aware. Biol. Sci., CABS; Leadscan; Res. Alert [Full Cov.]; Sci. Cit. Index; SCISEARCH.

LC HD9422.1 .A32 **ISSN** 0243-6566
DD 338.4/76649/00944 FR
UDC 338.43:637.5(44)

ACTIVITE DES ABATTOIRS EN ... / REPUBLIQUE FRANCAISE, MINISTERE DE L'AGRICULTURE, DIRECTION GENERALE DE L'ADMINISTRATION ET DU FINANCEMENT, SERVICE DES ENQUETES ET ETUDES STATISTIQUES. French. Republique Francaise Ministere de l'Agriculture Direction Generale de l'Administration et du Financement, Service des Enquetes et Etudes Statistiques, 4 Avenue de Saint Mande, 75570 Paris France.

II

ADMINISTRATION REPORT OF THE ANIMAL HUSBANDRY DEPARTMENT FOR THE YEAR ... . **Main/Corp** Kerala (India). Animal Husbandry Department. Periodical. English. One time a year.

LC HA1248.L69 S73
DD 338.1/76/0094359 GW
UDC 338.43:637.5(430-317)

AGRARBERICHTERSTATTUNG. HEFT 4, VIEHHALTUNG. **See** Agriculture-Abstracting, Bibliographies and Statistics.

GW

AGRARMARKTE BR DEUTSCHLAND, EWG UND WELTMARKT. VIEH UND FLEISCH, DIE. (1966)-. Trade Publication. German. One time a year. ZMP Marktberichte Bonn, Rochusstrabe 2, D-53123 Bonn Germany. **Tel** 011 49 228 9777170. ***Continues*** *Die Agrarmarkte in der Bundesrepublik und im Ausland.*

ISSN 1148-5612
FR
UDC 31(44)

AGRESTE. CONJONCTURE, PRODUCTIONS ANIMALES. (1990)-. Periodical. French. Irregular. 130.00F France; 150.00F other. Ministere de l'Agriculture et de la Peche, Direction des Affaires Financieres et Economiques, Service Central des Enquetes et Etudes Statistiques, 4 Avenue de Saint-Mande, 75570 Paris Cedex 12 France. **Tel** 011 33 1 43444633, 16 61288305.

ISSN 1155-4487
FR
UDC 31(44)

AGRESTE. SERIES, ANIMAUX HEBDO. (1991)-. Periodical. French. One time a week. 420.00F France; 530.00F other. Ministere de l'Agriculture et de la

Peche, Direction des Affaires Financieres et Economiques, Service Central des Enquetes et Etudes Statistiques, 4 Avenue de Saint-Mande, 75570 Paris Cedex 12 France. **Tel** 011 33 1 43444633, 16 61288305.

ISSN 1150-1529
FR
UDC 31(44)
AGRESTE. SERIES, AVICULTURE.
(1990)-. Periodical. French. Twelve times a year. 320.00F France; 350.00F other. Ministere de l'Agriculture et de la Peche, Direction des Affaires Financieres et Economiques, Service Central des Enquetes et Etudes Statistiques, 4 Avenue de Saint-Mande, 75570 Paris Cedex 12 France. **Tel** 011 33 1 43444633, 16 61288305.

LC SB23 **ISSN** 0791-3524
DD 630.9417 630.20112 IE
AGRICULTURAL STATISTICS, JUNE ..., LAND UTILISATION AND NUMBERS OF LIVESTOCK, REGIONAL ANALYSIS.
See Agriculture-Abstracting, Bibliographies and Statistics.

LC SF **ISSN** 0989-2648
DD 636 FR
UDC 631
AGRO PERFORMANCES.
(1987)-. Periodical. French. Six times a year. $54.68. Sepco, 83 85 Ave de la Grande Armee, 75782 Paris Cedex 16 France. **Tel** 011 33 1 40662171.

ISSN 0516-3889
US
ALABAMA CATTLEMAN.
[Ala. cattlem.]. **Added/Corp** Alabama Cattlemen's Association. Vol. 1 (June 1958)-. Trade Publication. English. Twelve times a year. $15.00. Alabama Cattleman, PO Box 1746, Montgomery AL 36103. **Tel** (334)265-1867, FAX (334)269-1927. **ED** W. Powell. **Ad Acc. Circ:** 16,000 (ctrl).
Desc: Trade news magazine for Alabama's beef cattle industry.

ISSN 1187-0761
DD 338.1 CN
ALBERTA BEEF (1991).
(ALBERTA BEEF.). [Alta. beef]. Vol. 1, No. 1 (Feb. 1991)-. Trade Publication. English. Twelve times a year. 19.45Can$. Creative Motion Publishing, #202-2915 19th Street Northeast, Calgary Alberta T2E 7A2 Canada. **Tel** (403)250-1090, FAX (403)291-9546. **ED** Cindy McCreath. ***Continues** World of Beef Magazine., 0848-8142.*

ISSN 0226-6075
DD 338.1/76213/097123 CN
UDC 338.43:636.2(712)
ALBERTA CATTLEMAN, THE.
[Alta. cattlem.]. Vol. 1 (March 1977)-. Periodical. English. Irregular. Free. Consolidated Communications, 807 Manning Road Northeast, Suite 200, Calgary Alberta T2E 7M8 Canada. **Tel** (403)569-9520, FAX (403)569-9590. ctrl circ.

LC SF **ISSN** 1075-0487
DD 636 US
•ALIMENTOS BALANCEADOS PARA ANIMALES.
[Alimentos balanc. animales]. Vol. 1, No. 1 (May 1994)-. Trade Publication. Spanish (table of contents in English). Four times a year. $30.00. Watt Publishing Company, 122 South Wesley Avenue, Mount Morris IL 61054. **Tel** (815)734-4171, FAX (815)734-7021, telex TWX 910-642-2891. **ED** Clayton Gill. **Ad Acc, Adv Mgr:** Mirdza Kalnins, **Tel** (815)734-4171. Full Page (B&W) $2,480.00. **Circ:** 9,000.
Desc: For feed industry people in Latin American countries.

ISSN 0230-1814
HU
CODEN ATAKDW
ALLATTENYESZTES ES TARKARMANYOZAS.
[Allatteny. takarm.]. **Added/Corp** Agrartudomanyi Egyetem (Budapest, Hungary). **VFOAT** Animal Breeding and Feeding. Vol. 30, No. 1 (1981)-. Academic Scholarly Publication. Hungarian (summaries and/or abstracts in English; table of contents in English, German and Russian). Six times a year. $35.00. **(Subscription address:** Kultura, PO Box 143, H-1300 Budapest 3 Hungary. **Tel** 011 36 1 2500194.) Documents available from BIOSIS Document Express, CASDDS. ***Continues** Allattenyesztes, 0365-4052.*
Ind/Abst Biodeter. Abstr.; Biol. Abstr.; Chem. Abstr.; Dairy Sci. Abstr.; Index Vet.; Maize Abstr.; Nutr. Abstr. Rev., Ser. B, Live Feeds and Feed.; Postharvest News Inf.; Poult. Abstr.; Soils Fert.; Soyabean Abstr.; Vet. Bull.; Wheat Barley Trit. Abstr.

ISSN 1064-1599
DD 636 US
TITLE CHANGE
AMBC NEWS.
(AMBC NEWS : THE NEWSLETTER OF THE AMERICAN MINOR BREEDS CONSERVANCY.). [AMBC news]. **Added/Corp** American Minor Breeds Conservancy. **VAT** American Minor Breeds Conservancy News. Vol. 1, No. 1 (Fall 1982)-(1993). Newsletter. English. American Livestock Breeds Conservancy, PO Box 477, Pittsboro NC 27312. **Tel** (919)542-5704. **ED** Carolyn Christman and Cynthia Ehrman. **Bk Rev**, (Qty: 3 or 4). **Ad Acc, Adv Mgr:** C. Ehrman, **Tel** (919)542-5704. **Circ:** 4,500 (ctrl). ***Continues** American Minor Breeds Conservancy Newsletter. **Continued by** American Livestock Breeds Conservancy News.*

ISSN 1079-9737
DD 636 US
AMERICAN ASSOCIATION OF BOVINE PRACTITIONERS CONFERENCE.
(AMERICAN ASSOCIATION OF BOVINE PRACTITIONERS CONFERENCE : [PROCEEDINGS].). [Am. Assoc. Bovine Pract. Conf.]. **Main/Corp** American Association of Bovine Practitioners. Conference. 25th (1992)-. Proceedings. English (French, German and Spanish). One time a year. $20.00. American Association of Bovine Practitioners, PO Box 2319, West Lafayette IN 47906. **Tel** (317)494-8560. ***Continues** American Association of Bovine Practitioners. Convention Proceedings of the ... Annual Convention, 0743-0450.*
Ind/Abst Bibliogr. Agric.

ISSN 0002-872X
US
AMERICAN HEREFORD JOURNAL.
Added/Corp American Hereford Association. Vol. 1 (1910)-. Periodical. English. Eleven times a year (monthly except June). $15.00. Hereford Publications Inc, 1501 Wyandotte, Box 014059, Kansas City MO 64101. **Tel** (816)842-8878, telex 42344 AHA KSC. **ED** Lovell Kuykendall. **Circ:** 7,500.
Desc: Published for breeders of Hereford beef cattle. Official publication of the American Hereford Association.

US
•AMERICAN LIVESTOCK BREEDS CONSERVANCY NEWS.
Added/Corp American Livestock Breeds Conservancy. **VFOAT** ALBC News. (1993)-. Periodical. English. Six times a year. Comes with membeship. American Livestock Breeds Conservancy, PO Box 477, Pittsboro NC 27312. **Tel** (919)542-5704. ***Continues** AMBC News, 1064-1599.*

ISSN 0886-4357
DD 636 US
AMERICAN RED ANGUS.
(AMERICAN RED ANGUS : THE OFFICIAL PUBLICATION OF THE RED ANGUS ASSOCIATION OF AMERICA.). [Am. Red Angus]. **Added/Corp** Red Angus Association of America. (July 1964)-. Trade Publication. English. Eleven times a year (June/July issues combined). $15.00. American Red Angus, 4201 I 35 North, Denton TX 76201. **Tel** (817)387-3502. **ED** Susan Ramsay. **Ad Acc.** ctrl circ.
Ind/Abst Bibliogr. Agric.

RM
ANALELE INSTITUTULUI DE BIOLOGIE SI NUTRITIE ANIMALA BALOTESTI.
Added/Corp Institutul de Biologie si Nutritie Animala Balotesti. **VFOAT** Analele I.B.N.A.; Analele IBNA. Vol. 13 (1988)-. Romanian (summaries and/or abstracts in English, German and Russian). One time a year. ***Continues** Lucrarile Stiintifice ale Institutului de Cercetari pentru Nutritia Animalelor.*
Ind/Abst Grass. Forage Abstr.; Nutr. Abstr. Rev., Ser. B, Live Feeds and Feed.

SP
ANAPORC.
(19??)-. Spanish. Twelve times a year. 6000ptas Spain; 8000ptas other. Asociacion de Porcinocultura Anaporc, Avanida de Selva SN, 17170 Amer Gerona Spain. **Tel** 011 34 72 430828.

ISSN 0003-3464
SA
ANGORABOT & SYBOTHAAR -BLAD.
(THE ANGORA GOAT & MOHAIR JOURNAL.). [Angorabot. sybothaar -bl.]. **Added/Corp** Angora Goat Stud Breeders' Society of South Africa. South African Mohair Growers' Association. South Africa Ram Breeders' Society. South Africa. Mohair Board. **VFOAT** Angorabok-en Sybokhaar-Blad.; Angora Goat and Mohair Journal. (1959)-. Periodical. English (Afrikaans). Two times a year (March and September). $8.95. Angora Goat Stud Breeders Society of South Africa, Box 2243, PT Elizabeth 6056 South Africa. **Tel** 011 27 41 14923. **ED** J. Engelbrecht. **Ad Acc. Circ:** 3,000 (ctrl).

ISSN 0194-9543
US
ANGUS JOURNAL.
Added/Corp American Angus Association. Vol. 1, No. 1 (July 1979)-. Trade Publication. English. Eleven times a year (June/July issue combined). $20.00. American Angus Association, 3201 Frederick Boulevard, St Joseph MO 64501. **Tel** (816)233-0508, (816)233-0563 evening, FAX (816)233-0508, ext 112. **ED** Greg Garwood. **Ad Acc. Circ:** 22,000. available on microfilm and microfiche from University Microfilms International (UMI). ***Supersedes** Aberdeen-Angus Journal, 0001-3161.*
Desc: Official publication of the purebred Angus cattle registry. Contains breeder features, sale reports, market trends and up-to-date genetic research.

ISSN 0849-6188
DD 636.2/23 CN
CEASED
ANGUS TIMES.
[Angus times]. **Added/Corp** Canadian Aberdeen-Angus Association. **VFOAT** Canadian Angus Times. (Oct. 1989)-(March 1994). Periodical. English. Canadian Aberdeen Angus Association, 2352 Smith Street, Regina Saskatchewan S4P 2P6 Canada. **Tel** (306)757-5539, FAX (306)522-5363. **ED** Catherine Vance. Index available. **Ad Acc, Adv Mgr:** L Reich. **Circ:** 3500 (ctrl).
Desc: Features articles and news highlighting activities of interest to breeders of Aberdeen Angus cattle.

ISSN 0402-4265
US
ANGUS TOPICS.
(1955)-. Periodical. English. Eleven times a year (monthly except Jan.). $12.00. Angus Topics Inc., 3 Smith Street, Carmi IL 62821. **Tel** (618)382-8553, FAX (618)382-3394. **ED** Ernest & Judy Bingman. **Ad Acc, Adv Mgr:** Ernest Bingham. **Circ:** 8,000 (ctrl).
Desc: Devoted to the improvement and promotion of the Aberdeen-Angus breed of beef cattle.

LC SF1 .A63 **ISSN** 0003-3499
DD 636.05 UK
NLM ZW 1 A573
ANIMAL BREEDING ABSTRACTS.
See Agriculture-Abstracting, Bibliographies and Statistics.

US
ANIMAL FINDERS' GUIDE.
See Animal Welfare-Pets.

CC
ANIMAL HUSBANDRY & VETERINARY MEDICINE.
See Veterinary Sciences.

LC HD9425.E8 A54
DD 338.1/76/0094 LU
ANIMAL PRODUCTION.
Added/Corp Statistical Office of the European Communities. **VFOAT** Production Animale. Vol. 1 (1987)-. Trade Publication. English (French). Four times a year. £74.00. Office for Official Publications of the European Communities, 2 rue Mercier, 2985 Luxembourg Luxembourg. **Tel** 011 352 499281, FAX 011 352 292942763. **(Subscription address:** Her Majesty's Stationery Office, PO Box 276, Public Centre, London SW8 5DT United Kingdom. **Tel** 011 44 171 8738499, 011 44 171 8738456.) ***Continues** Animalsk Produktion, 0250-6580.*
Desc: Statistics on production and external trade in meat, eggs and poultry, and the production of milk and dairy products. Also includes supply balance sheets, results of surveys, and forecasts.

ISSN 0003-3561
UK
CCC
CODEN ANIPA8
TITLE CHANGE
ANIMAL PRODUCTION.
[Anim. prod.]. **Added/Corp** British Society of Animal Production. Vol. 1 (March 1959)-(19??). Periodical. English. Durrant Periodicals, Winton LEA Pencaitland, East Lothian EH34 5AY United Kingdom. **Tel** 011 44 875 340354. **ED** TCJ Lawrence. Index available. cum. index. **Bk Rev. Ad Acc.** ctrl circ. Documents available from The Genuine Article, BIOSIS Document Express, CASDDS. ***Supersedes** Report of Proceedings - British Society of Animal Production. **Continued in part by** British Society of Animal Production. Proceedings; **Continued by** Animal Science.*
Ind/Abst AGRICOLA [Full Cov.]; Agric. Eng. Abstr.; Agrofor. Abstr.; Anim. Breed. Abstr.; BioBusiness; Biol. Agric. Index; Biol. Abstr.; Biotechnol. Res. Abstr.; Chem. Abstr.; Curr. Cit.; Curr. Contents Agric. Biol. Environ. Sci.; Dairy Sci. Abstr.; EMBASE; Field Crop Abstr.; Food Sci. Technol. Abstr.; Grass. Forage Abstr.; Index Vet.; Leis., Rec., Tour. Abstr.; Maize Abstr.; Nutr. Abstr. Rev., Ser. B, Live Feeds and Feed.; Nutr. Abstr. Rev., Ser. A, Hum. Exp.; Life Sci. Collect.; PESTDOC; Pig News Inf.; Plant Breed. Abstr.; Postharvest News Inf.; Poult. Abstr.; Protozoolog. Abstr.; Res. Alert [Full Cov.]; Rice Abstr.; Rural Dev. Abstr.; Sci. Cit. Index (19??-19??); SCISEARCH; Soils Fert.; Soyabean Abstr.; Sug. Indus. Abstr.; Vet. Bull.; Wheat Barley Trit. Abstr.; Wildl. Rev.; World Agric. Econ. Rural Sociol. Abstr.

LC SF1 .A598 **ISSN** 1357-7298
UK
CODEN ANSCFO
•ANIMAL SCIENCE : AN INTERNATIONAL JOURNAL OF FUNDAMENTAL AND APPLIED RESEARCH.
Added/Corp British Society of Animal Science. Vol. 60, Pt. 1 (Feb. 1995)-. Periodical. English. Six times a year. $270.00. Durrant Periodicals, Winton LEA Pencaitland, East Lothian EH34 5AY United Kingdom. **Tel** 011 44 875 340354. ***Continues** Animal Production, 0003-3561.*
Ind/Abst AGRICOLA; Chem. Abstr.; Curr. Cit.

Agriculture — Livestock

ISSN 0860-4037
PL
CODEN ANPREJ

ANIMAL SCIENCE PAPERS AND REPORTS. See Zoology.

US

ANIMAL SCIENCE RESEARCH REPORT. [Anim. sci. res. rep.]. **Added/Corp** Oklahoma Agricultural Experiment Station. (1977)-. Periodical. English. One time a year. $7.50. Oklahoma State University / Animal Science Research Report, 206 Animal Science Building, Stillwater OK 74078. **Tel** (405)744-5000. Documents available from BIOSIS Document Express. **Continues** Oklahoma Agricultural Experiment Station. Animal Sciences and Industry Research Report.
Ind/Abst Anim. Breed. Abstr.; Biol. Abstr.; Dairy Sci. Abstr.; Index Vet.; Maize Abstr.; Nutr. Abstr. Rev., Ser. B, Live Feeds and Feed.; Pig News Inf.; Soyabean Abstr.

ISSN 0208-5739
PL

ANNALS OF WARSAW AGRICULTURAL UNIVERSITY, SGGW-AR. ANIMAL SCIENCE. **VFOAT** Animal Science. Academic Scholarly Publication. English (Polish). One time a year. $14.00, $6.00 per issue. Akademia Rolnicza w Warszawie, Ul. Rakowiecka 41, Warsaw Poland. **Tel** telex 81 47 90 SGGW-AR PL. **ED** Henryk Sandner. **Ad Acc.** Documents available from CASDDS.
Desc: Poultry, animal production, animal breeding, animal nutrition, feed management and silkworm hygiene.
Ind/Abst Anim. Breed. Abstr.; Chem. Abstr.; Dairy Sci. Abstr.; Poult. Abstr.

CN

... ANNUAL FEEDER'S DAY REPORT, THE. **VFOAT** Feeder's Day Report. English. One time a year.

ISSN 1057-3216
US
DD 630

ANNUAL PROGRESS REPORT / SOUTHEAST RESEARCH STATION, LOUISIANA AGRICULTURAL EXPERIMENT STATION. [Annu. progr. rep. - La. Agric. Exp. Stn., Southeast Res. Stn.]. **Main/Corp** Louisiana Agricultural Experiment Station. Southeast Research Station. (198?)-. English. **Continues** Southeast Louisiana Dairy and Pasture Experiment Station. Annual Progress Report.
Ind/Abst AGRICOLA [Full Cov.].

ISSN 0951-0257
UK

ANNUAL REPORT / ANIMAL AND GRASSLAND RESEARCH INSTITUTE. **Main/Corp** Animal and Grassland Research Institute (Hurley, Berkshire). (1985/86)-. English. One time a year. Animal and Grassland Research Institute, Hurley Maidenhead, Berkshire SL6 5LR United Kingdom. **Continues** Annual Report / Grassland Research Institute (Hurley, Berkshire).
LC S584.7.A8A47

AT

●ANNUAL REPORT / AVCARE, NATIONAL ASSOCIATION FOR CROP PROTECTION AND ANIMAL HEALTH. **Main/Corp** Avcare Limited. (1993)-. English. Agricultural and Veterinary Chemicals Association of Australia Ltd, Private Bag 938, Sydney New South Wales 2059 Australia. **Tel** 011 61 02 9637 690. **Continues** Agricultural & Veterinary Chemicals Association of Australia. Annual Report.
LC SF15.R48 R48A
DD 636/.0096891
UDC 636(047.1)(689.1)

RH

ANNUAL REPORT FOR THE YEAR ENDED - ZIMBABWE. DIVISION OF LIVESTOCK AND PASTURES. **Main/Corp** Zimbabwe. Division of Livestock and Pastures. English. One time a year. **Continues** Annual Report / Southern Rhodesia. Division of Livestock and Pastures.
Ind/Abst Anim. Breed. Abstr.

ISSN 0837-2535
CN
DD 354.710082/656649

ANNUAL REPORT OF OPERATIONS UNDER THE MEAT IMPORT ACT. [Annu. rep. oper. Meat Import Act]. **Main/Corp** Canada. Agriculture Canada. **VFOAT** Rapport Annuel des Operations Effectue[e]s en Vertu de la Loi sur l'Importation de la Viande. (1982)-. Government Publication. English (French). Free on request. Agriculture Canada, Communications Branch, Ottawa Ontario K1A 0C7 Canada.

LC J905 .L3 HD9435.A8
DD 300/.994 S 354.940082/656649

AT

ANNUAL REPORT OF THE PIG MEAT PROMOTION ADVISORY COMMITTEE FOR THE YEAR ENDED 30 JUNE ... / DEPARTMENT OF PRIMARY INDUSTRY. **Main/Corp** Australia. Pig Meat Promotion Advisory Committee. English. One time a year. $1.00. Pig Meat Promotion Advisory Committee, Department of Primary Industry, Canberra Australian Capitol Territory 2600 Australia.

ISSN 0837-6875
CN
DD 354.71240082/65/0005

ANNUAL REPORT OF THE SASKATCHEWAN PORK PRODUCERS MARKETING BOARD FOR THE YEAR. [Annu. rep. Sask. Pork Prod. Mark. Board]. **Main/Corp** Saskatchewan Pork Producers Marketing Board. (1984)-. English. One time a year. Saskatchewan Pork Producers Marketing Board, 502-45th Street West, Saskatoon Saskatchewan S7L 6H2 Canada. **Tel** (306)653-3014, FAX (306)244-2918, telex 074-2764. **ED** Jack McClung. **Continues** Annual Report - Saskatchewan Hog Marketing Commission, 0228-6114.

CN

ANNUAL REPORT ON ARTIFICIAL INSEMINATION IN CANADA, YEAR ENDING DECEMBER 31ST ... . English. One time a year.
LC SF15.E85 Y34A
DD 338.1/7/60963
UDC 338.439.4:637.5(63)

ET

ANNUAL REPORT - PROVISIONAL MILITARY GOVERNMENT OF SOCIALIST ETHIOPIA, LIVESTOCK AND MEAT BOARD. **Main/Corp** Ethiopia. Yakabterbatana Yasega Bord. (19??)-. English. Provincial Military Government of Socialist Ethiopia, Livestock and Meat Board, Addis Ababa Ethiopia.

LC S389 .A3
DD 354/.943/00823305
ISSN 0480-9696
AT

ANNUAL REPORT - QUEENSLAND DEPARTMENT OF PRIMARY INDUSTRIES. [Annu. rep. - Dep. Prim. Ind., Qld.]. **Main/Corp** Queensland. Dept. of Primary Industries. (1963/1964)-. English. One time a year. Department of Primary Industries / Queensland Australia, GPO Box 46, Brisbane Queensland 4001 Australia. **Tel** 011 61 7 2393111, FAX 011 61 7 2212490, telex AA41620. **ED** A. J. Barker. **Circ:** 2,400 (ctrl). **Continues** Queensland. Dept. of Agriculture and Stock. Annual Report of the Department of Agriculture and Stock for the Year ... . **Continued in part by** Queensland. Dept. of Primary Industries. Botany Branch. Annual Report.
Desc: Corporate report (48 pages) covering significant achievements, developments, activities or changes in research, regulation and extension for the year reported.
Ind/Abst Anim. Breed. Abstr.; Hortic. Abstr.; Rev. Med. Vet. Mycology; Vet. Bull.

LC HD9435.C2 S27A
DD 338.1/7/640097124
ISSN 0228-6114
CN

ANNUAL REPORT - SASKATCHEWAN HOG MARKETING COMMISSION. [Annu. rep. - Sask. Hog Mark. Comm.]. **Main/Corp** Saskatchewan. Hog Marketing Commission. 1973-. English. One time a year. Saskatchewan Hog Marketing Commission, 1402 Quebec Avenue, Saskatoon Saskatchewan Canada. **Tel** (306)653-3014, FAX (306)653-3014, telex 074-2764. **ED** Jack McClung.

ISSN 1191-0321
CN
DD 354.71240082

ANNUAL REPORT - SASKATCHEWAN. TRIPARTITE BEEF ADMINISTRATION BOARD. (ANNUAL REPORT / TRIPARTITE BEEF ADMINISTRATION BOARD.). [Annu. rep. - Sask., Tripart. Beef Adm. Board]. **Main/Corp** Saskatchewan. Tripartite Beef Administration Board. (1991)-. English.

CN

ANNUAL REPORT / SPI MARKETING GROUP. **Main/Corp** SPI Marketing Group (Sask.). (19??)-. English. One time a year. Saskatchewan Pork Producers Marketing Board, 502-45th Street West, Saskatoon Saskatchewan S7L 6H2 Canada. **Tel** (306)653-3014, FAX (306)244-2918, telex 074-2764. **Continues** Saskatchewan Pork Producers Marketing Board. Annual Report of the Saskatchewan Pork Producers Marketing Board, 0837-6875.

ISSN 0816-2816
AT

ANNUAL REPORT / THE LIVESTOCK AND MEAT AUTHORITY OF QUEENSLAND. [Ann. rep. - Livest. Meat Auth. Qld.]. **Main/Corp** Livestock and Meat Authority of Queensland. English. One time a year. **Continues** Annual Report / Queensland Meat Industry Organization and Marketing Authority.

ISSN 0112-739X
NZ

ANNUAL REVIEW OF THE NEW ZEALAND SHEEP AND BEEF INDUSTRY. [Annu. rev. N.Z. sheep beef ind.]. **Added/Corp** New Zealand Meat and Wool Boards' Economic Service. **VFOAT** Annual Review of the Sheep & Beef Industry. (1985-86)-. English. New Zealand Meat and Wool Board's Economic Service, PO Box 5179, Wellington New Zealand. **Tel** 011 64 4 722178, FAX 011 64 4 712173. **Continues** Annual Review of the Sheep and Beef Industry.
LC SF55.J3 A57

JA

AOMORI-KEN CHIKUSAN SHIKENJO HOKOKU. **VFOAT** Bulletin of the Aomori Zootechnical Experiment Station. Bulletin. Japanese (summaries and/or abstracts in English). Aomori-Ken Chikusan Shikenjo, 51 Oaza Noheji Aza Biwano Noheji-machi Kamikita-gun, Aomori-ken 039-31 Japan.
LC SB981 .A334
DD 353/.008/233
US

APHIS 82. **Main/Corp** United States. Animal and Plant Health Inspection Service. **Added/Corp** United States. Animal and Plant Health Inspection Service. Plant Protection and Quarantine Programs. (19??)-. Monographic series. English. US Department of Agriculture / Animal & Plant Health Inspection Service, 741 Federal Building 1, 6505 Belcres Road, Hyattsville MD 20782. **Tel** (301)436-7817.

ISSN 0003-9438
GW
CODEN ARTZAJ
Pr Rev.

ARCHIV FUER TIERZUCHT. [Arch. Tierz.]. **Added/Corp** Deutsche Akademie der Landwirtschaftswissenschaften zu Berlin Deutsche Akademie der Landwirtschaftswissenschaften zu Berlin. Vol. 1 (1958)-. Periodical. German (summaries and/or abstracts in English and Russian; table of contents in English and Russian). Six times a year. DM210.00 (add DM9.00 for postage). Archiv fuer Tierzucht Redaktion, Wilhelm Stahl Allee 2, D-18196 Dummerstorf Germany. **Tel** 011 49 38208 7528. Index Available, published separately, free-automatically sent. Documents available from The Genuine Article, BIOSIS Document Express, CASDDS.
Ind/Abst AgBiotech News Inf.; Anim. Breed. Abstr.; Biol. Abstr.; Chem. Abstr. (1958-1982); Curr. Cit.; Curr. Contents Agric. Biol. Environ. Sci.; Dairy Sci. Abstr.; Food Sci. Technol. Abstr.; Index Vet.; Nutr. Abstr. Rev., Ser. B, Live Feeds and Feed.; Nutr. Abstr. Rev., Ser. A, Hum. Exp.; Life Sci. Collect.; Pig News Inf.; Plant Breed. Abstr.; Poult. Abstr.; Res. Alert [Select. Cov.]; SCISEARCH; Vet. Bull.

LC SF1 .A74
DD 636/.005
ISSN 0004-0592
SP
CCC
NLM W1 AR712C
CODEN AZOTAW
CEASED

ARCHIVOS DE ZOOTECNIA. [Arch. zootec.]. **Added/Corp** Patronato Alfonso el Sabio. Instituto de Zootecnia. Patronato Santiago Ramon y Cajal. Departamento de Zootecnia. Vol. 1, No. 1, (1952)-No. 4 (1993). Academic Scholarly Publication. Spanish (English; summaries and/or abstracts in English). Consejo Superior Investigacion Cientificas / CSIC, Vitruvio 8, 28006 Madrid Spain. **Tel** 011 34 1 5612833, FAX 011 34 1 4113077, telex 42182. Documents available from CASDDS.
Desc: The content of this scientific journal is zootechnology, especially animal nutrition and genetics, economics of cattle breeding and production of feed grain for livestock.
Ind/Abst AgBiotech News Inf.; Anim. Breed. Abstr.; Chem. Abstr.; Dairy Sci. Abstr.; EMBASE; Field Crop Abstr.; Fish Rev.; Food Sci. Technol. Abstr.; Grass. Forage Abstr.; Index Vet.; Nutr. Abstr. Rev., Ser. B, Live Feeds and Feed.; Ornamental Hort.; Life Sci. Collect.; Pig News Inf.; Poult. Abstr.; Protozoolog. Abstr.; Soyabean Abstr.; Sug. Indus. Abstr.; Vet. Bull.; Wheat Barley Trit. Abstr.; Wildl. Rev.

ISSN 8750-8281
US
DD 636

ARIZONA CATTLELOG (1985). (ARIZONA CATTLELOG : OFFICIAL PUBLICATION OF THE ARIZONA CATTLE GROWERS' ASSOCIATION.). **Added/Corp** Arizona Cattle Growers' Association. **VFOAT** Cattlelog. Vol. 41, No. 2 (Feb. 1985)-. Periodical. English. Twelve times a year. $15.00. Arizona Cattle Growers Association, 1401 North 24th Street, Suite 4, Phoenix AZ 85008. **Tel** (602)267-1129, FAX (602)220-9833. **ED** Robin Darrow. Index available. **Ad Acc.** **Circ:** 1,600. **Continues** Arizona Cattle Growers' Outlook.
Desc: Pertaining to the livestock industry, current issues on lands, grazing and anything affecting the industry as a whole.

Agriculture — Livestock

ISSN 8750-6432
US
TITLE CHANGE

ARIZONA FARMER-STOCKMAN. VFOAT Arizona Farmer Stockman. Vol. 64, No. 1 (Jan. 1985)-(19??). Periodical. English. Farm Progress Publishing, 191 South Gary Avenue, Carol Stream IL 60188-2089. **Tel** (708)462-2890 or 2891. **ED** Thomas D. Henry. **Circ:** 3,050. *Continues* Arizona Farmer-Ranchman, 0004-1491. *Continued by* Arizona Farmer (Spokane, Wash. : 1993), 1071-6521; *Merged into* California Farmer.
Ind/Abst Bibliogr. Agric. (-1987).

ISSN 0004-1750
US

ARKANSAS CATTLE BUSINESS. [Ark. cattle bus.]. **Added/Corp** Arkansas Cattlemen's Association. (19??)-. Trade Publication. English. Twelve times a year. $20.00. Arkansas Cattlemen's Association, 310 Executive Court, Little Rock AR 72205. **Tel** (501)224-2114, FAX (501)224-5377. **ED** Mark Cowan. **Ad Acc, Adv Mgr Tel** (501)224-2114. **Circ:** 7,200 (ctrl).
Desc: Deals with beef cattle production and subjects relating to beef cattle such as forage crops, grain crops, cattle feeding, disease, insect control, and pasture management. Some space is devoted to the activities of the Arkansas Cattlemen's Association and affiliated local cattlemen's organizations. In addition to those subjects mentioned above, it also deals with legislation.

US

ASI LAMB AND WOOL MARKET NEWS. (19??)-. English. Fifty times a year. $35.00. American Sheep Industry Association, 6911 South Yosemite Street, Englewood CO 80112. **Tel** (303)771-3500, FAX (303)771-8200. **ED** Laura Gerhard. **Circ:** 1,000.
Desc: Market newsletter with regional prices, marketing information, graphs and industry news.

TH

ASIAN LIVESTOCK : MONTHLY PUBLICATION OF THE ANIMAL PRODUCTION AND HEALTH COMMISSION FOR ASIA, THE FAR EAST AND THE SOUTH-WEST PACIFIC. **Added/Corp** Animal Production and Health Commission for Asia, the Far East and the South-West Pacific. Animal Production and Health Commission for Asia, the Far East and the South-West Pacific. Secretariat. VFOAT Asian Livestock Newsletter. (Oct. 1976)-. Periodical. English. Twelve times a year. $10.00. Food & Agricultural Organization of the UN / Pacific, 39 Phra A Thit, Bangkok Thailand. **Tel** 011 61 2 281 7844, FAX 011 66 2 280 0445, telex 82815 FOODAG TH. **ED** Balbir K. Soni, Masao Sasaki and Vishnu Songkitti. Index available. **Bk Rev. Circ:** 3,500 (ctrl).
Desc: Published to support the development of livestock as an integral part of agriculture in Asia.
Ind/Abst Anim. Breed. Abstr.; Dairy Sci. Abstr.

ISSN 1184-0021
CN
DD 636.2/13/09715

ATLANTIC BEEF. [Atl. beef]. VFOAT Atlantic Beef Quarterly. Vol. 1, No. 1 (Spring 1990)-. Periodical. English. Four times a year. 8.00Can$ Canada; 12.00Can$ US. DVL Publishing Inc, PO Box 1509, Liverpool Nova Scotia B0T 1K0 Canada. **Tel** (902)683-2763. **ED** Dirk van Loon. **Circ:** 4,000.

AT

AUSTRALIAN CATTLE MAGAZINE, THE. (Dec. 1976/Jan. 1977)-. Periodical. English. Twelve times a year. Australian Pastoral Press Pty. Ltd, 8 White Street Tamworth, New South Wales, 2340 Australia. *Continues* Cattle.

AT

AUSTRALIAN CHAROLAIS NEWS. **Added/Corp** Charolais Society of Australia. (Sept. 1979)-. Newsletter. English. Six times a year. Charolais Society of Australia, PO Box 861, Sydney New South Wales 2060 Australia. **ED** Board. **Bk Rev. Ad Acc. Circ:** 2,000. *Continues* Charolais Newsletter.

ISSN 1034-6171
AT
DD 636.294

AUSTRALIAN DEER FARMING. [Aust. deer farming]. **Added/Corp** Australian Deer Breeder's Federation. (1990)-. Periodical. English. Six times a year (Feb., April, June, Aug., Oct., Dec.). 49.34Aus$. Australian Deer Farming, GPO Box 473, Margaret River WA 6285 Australia. **Tel** 011 61 97 573110, FAX 011 61 97 573114. **ED** A. J. Roberts. Index available. **Bk Rev,** (Qty: 20+). **Ad Acc. Circ:** 1,000. *Continues* The Federal Deerbreeder, 0813-7765.
Desc: News and information on deerfarming and deerbreeding.

LC SF380
ISSN 0818-8203
DD 636.3900994
AT

AUSTRALIAN GOAT FARMER. [Aust. goat farmer]. (1986)-. Periodical. English. Six times a year (Feb., April, June, Aug., Oct., Dec.). 30.00Aus$ Australia; 38.00Aus$ New Zealand; 55.00Aus$ other. Australian Goat Farmer, PO Box 392, Baulkham Hills, New South Wales 2153 Australia. **Tel** 011 61 2 6862033, FAX 011 61 2 6861939.

AT

AUSTRALIAN GOAT WORLD, THE. **Added/Corp** Goat Society of Australia. (19??)-. Periodical. English. Six times a year. 14.79Aus$. Dairy Goat Society Australia, PO Box 189, Kiama New South Wales 2533 Australia. **Tel** 11 61 42 323333. **ED** Nel Matthews. **Bk Rev. Ad Acc. Circ:** 800 (ctrl).
Desc: All matters connected with dairy goats-research disease, husbandry and personal experiences.

AT

AUSTRALIAN JERSEY JOURNAL. **Added/Corp** Australian Jersey Herd Society (New South Wales). Vol. 9, No. 1 (Jan 1976)-. Periodical. English. Twelve times a year. 9.86Aus$. Australian Jersey Breeders Association, PO Box 292, Ascot Vale Victoria 3032 Australia. **Tel** 03 376 9161.

ISSN 0156-2681
AT

AUSTRALIAN MEAT INDUSTRY BULLETIN, THE. **Added/Corp** Meat & Allied Trades Federation of Australia. Vol. 1, No. 1 (August, 1981)-. Trade Publication. English. Six times a year. 27.13Aus$. Meat & Allied Trades Federation of Australia, PO Box 1208, Crows Nest New South Wales, 2065 Australia. **Tel** 011 61 2 9067767, FAX 011 61 2 9068022, telex AA22480. **ED** J. Noble. **Bk Rev. Ad Acc. Circ:** 8,000 (ctrl). *Continues* Meat Trades Journal of Australia.
Desc: News stories and features on Australian meat industry.

AT

AUSTRALIAN POLL DORSET JOURNAL. **Added/Corp** Australian Poll Dorset Association. Vol. 5, No. 1 (Jan/Feb 1975)-. Periodical. English. Four times a year. 20.55Aus$. Australian Poll Dorset Journal, Box 75B GPO Weston Studstock, Melbourne 3001 Australia. **Tel** 011 61 3 859 8671. **ED** Tricia Williams. **Bk Rev. Ad Acc. Circ:** 1,900 (ctrl).
Desc: Journal of Poll Dorset activities, including shows and sales for the year.

SP
Pr Rev.

AVANCES EN ALIMENTACION Y MEJORA ANIMAL. (1???)-. Periodical. Spanish. Six times a year. $50.00. AYMA, Cristobal Bordiu 35, 28003 Madrid Spain. **ED** Amalio de Juana. Index available. **Bk Rev. Ad Acc. Circ:** 2,000.
Desc: Advances in animal feeding, poultry, cows, goats, farm animals and related sciences.
Ind/Abst AgBiotech News Inf.; Anim. Breed. Abstr.; Dairy Sci. Abstr.; Grass. Forage Abstr.; Index Vet.; Maize Abstr.; Nutr. Abstr. Rev., Ser. B, Live Feeds and Feed.; Nutr. Abstr. Rev., Ser. A, Hum. Exp.; Pig News Inf.; Potato Abstr.; Poult. Abstr.; Soils Fert.

ISSN 0150-939X
FR
TITLE CHANGE

AVICULTEUR, L'. [Aviculteur]. (1962)-(19??). Periodical. French. Editions du Boisbaudry, BP 6359, 35036 Rennes Cedex France. **Tel** 011 33 99 322121. *Continued by* Filieres Avicoles.
Ind/Abst AGRICOLA.

ISSN 0005-2442
UK

AYRSHIRE CATTLE SOCIETY'S JOURNAL, THE. VFOAT Ayrshire Journal. Vol. 1 (March 1929)-. Trade Publication. English. Two times a year. $30.00. Ayrshire Cattle Society, 1 Racecourse Road, Ayr United Kingdom. **Tel** 011 44 1292 611973. **ED** Stuart Thomson. **Bk Rev. Ad Acc. Circ:** 4,000. available with illustrations.
Desc: Covers genetic improvement, promotion, show, and sales of the Ayrshire dairy cow.
Ind/Abst Dairy Sci. Abstr.

ISSN 0005-2450

AYRSHIRE DIGEST. See Agriculture-Dairy Industry.

ISSN 1182-557X
DD 636.3/9/009711
CN

B.C. GOAT NEWS. (B.C. GOAT NEWS : OFFICIAL PUBLICATION OF THE B.C. GOAT BREEDERS ASSOCIATION.). [B.C. goat news]. **Added/Corp** British Columbia Goat Breeders' Association. VFOAT British Columbia Goat News. Issue 2 (Mar./Apr. 1990)-. Periodical. English. Dairy Goat News, 5727 Ross Road, Mt Lehman British Columbia V0X 1V0 Canada. *Continues* B. C. Dairy Goat News., 0319-292X.

ISSN 1075-0096
DD 636
US

●**BANNER (CUBA, ILL.), THE.** (THE BANNER.). [Banner]. Vol. 17, No. 1 (Feb. 1994)-. Periodical. English. Nine times a year (monthly with combined Jan./Feb., Aug./Sept., Oct./Nov.). $20.00. Banner Publications / Illinois, PO Box 500, Cuba IL 61427. **Tel** (309)785-5058, FAX (309)785-5050. *Formed by the union of* Suffolk Banner, 0194-7230 *and* Hampshire World (Cuba, Ill. : 1989).

ISSN 0154-5752
FR
UDC 63

BAROMETRE PORC. (1977)-. Periodical. French. Fourteen times a year (Monthly with two special issues). $59.06. Institut Technique du Porc, 34 boulevard de la Gare, F 31500 Toulouse France. **Tel** 011 33 61 800588, FAX 011 33 61 543263.

LC HD9425.N4 E26a

NE

BEDRIJFSGEGEVENS VOOR HET SLAGERSBEDRIJF, BEDRIJFSRESULTATEN IN- EN VERKOOPBELEID, VESTIGINGSPLAATS EN RESULTAAT. **Main/Corp** Economisch Instituut Voor Het Midden- en Kleinbedrijf. (19??)-. Dutch. Economisch Instituut voor het Midden- en Kleinbedrijf, Talielaan 33, Postbus 7001, 2701 AA Zoetermeer Netherlands.

ISSN 0744-253X
DD 338
US

BEEF BUSINESS BULLETIN. [Beef bus. bull.]. Trade Publication. English. One time a week. National Cattlemen's Association, 5420 South Quebec Street, Englewood CO 80111. **ED** Roger Berglund. **Circ:** 24,000.
Desc: Beef business management.

US

BEEF CATTLE RESEARCH IN TEXAS. **Main/Corp** Texas. Agricultural Experiment Station. (1???)-. English. One time a year. $4.25. Texas A & M University / Agriculture Communication, Bulletin Room, Department of Agriculture Communication, College Station TX 77843. **Tel** (409)845-2830. **Circ:** 1,500 (ctrl).
Desc: Annual compilation of beef cattle research being done by Texas Agriculture Experiment Station.
Ind/Abst Anim. Breed. Abstr.; Index Vet.; Rev. Med. Vet. Entomol.

ISSN 0195-0444
US
SUSPENDED

BEEF DIGEST. (1975)-Suspended (19??). Periodical. English. Six times a year. $12.00. Rawson Publication, PO Box 30109, Columbia MO 65205. **Tel** (314)474-2646.

UK

BEEF SHORTHORN RECORD. New Series, No. 1 (June 1959)-. Periodical. English. Two times a year. *Continues* Shorthorn Record.

ISSN 0005-7738
DD 338
CCC

BEEF (ST. PAUL, MINN.). (BEEF.). [Beef]. (19??)-. Trade Publication. English. Thirteen times a year. $24.71. Intertec Publishing Corporation, 9800 Metcalf, Overland Park KS 66212. **Tel** (913)341-1300. (**Subscription address:** Intertec Publishing Corporation, PO Box 2901, Overland Park KS 66282. **Tel** 800 441-0294.) **ED** Paul Andre. **Ad Acc. Circ:** 120,000 (ctrl). available on microfilm and microfiche from University Microfilms International (UMI).
Desc: For commercial feed lots, farmer feeders, cow-calf operators, stocker-growers, backgrounders and NCA members in the US.

ISSN 0747-010X
US

BEEFALO NICKEL. (BEEFALO NICKEL : OFFICIAL PUBLICATION, AMERICAN BEEFALO WORLD REGISTRY.). Vol. 1, No. 1 (Dec. 1983/Jan. 1984)-. Trade Publication. English. Six times a year. Badlands Photo and Advertising Grafton ND 58237.

ISSN 0194-4282
US

BEEFMASTER COWMAN, THE. **Added/Corp** Beefmaster Breeders Universal. (19??)-. Trade Publication. English. Twelve times a year. $20.00. Gulf Coast Publishing Corporation, 11201 Morning Court, San Antonio TX 78213. **Tel** (210)344-8300, FAX (512)344-4258. **Ad Acc. Circ:** 8,500 (ctrl).

ISSN 0106-1542
DK
CODEN FSMHAQ

BERETNING - FAELLESUDVALGET FOR STATENS MEJERI- OG HUSDYRBRUGSFORSG. **Main/Corp** Faellesudvalget for Statens Mejeri-Og Husdyrbrugsforsg. 1-. Academic Scholarly Publication. Danish. Price varies per volume. Documents available from CASDDS.
Ind/Abst Chem. Abstr. (1974-1976).

Agriculture —Livestock

ISSN 0523-1051
US
SUSPENDED

BETTER BEEF BUSINESS. (196?)-Suspended (Nov. 1985). Periodical. English. Six times a year. Better Beef Business, PO Box 4173, Kansas City KS 66104. **Tel** (913)334-0405. **Ad Acc.** available with charts; available with illustrations. *Continues Magic Circle Stockman.*

ISSN 1034-9219
AT

BIENNIAL REPORT / CSIRO AUSTRALIAN ANIMAL HEALTH LABORATORY. **Added/Corp** Australian Animal Health Laboratory. (1987/1989)-. English. Every 2 years. CSIRO Publications, PO Box 89, 314 Albert Street, East Melborne Victoria 3002 Australia. **Tel** 011 61 3 4187333, 4187217, FAX 011 61 3 4190459, telex AA 30236. *Continues Australian Animal Health Laboratory. Annual Report, 0818-643X.*

ISSN 1056-2400
US
DD 636

BISON WORLD. (BISON WORLD : OFFICIAL PUBLICATION OF THE AMERICAN BISON ASSOCIATION.). [Bison world]. **Added/Corp** American Bison Association. (19??)-. Periodical. English. Six times a year (Jan., Mar., May, July, Sept., Nov.). $50.00. National Bison Association, 4701 Marion, Suite 301, Denver CO 80216. **Tel** (303)292-2833. **ED** Kim Dowling. Index available. **Bk Rev. Ad Acc. Circ:** 1,200 (ctrl). *Absorbed Buffalo.*
Desc: Contents include articles on buffalo management, marketing and husbandry, as well as history, collecting, art and human interest stories.

LC SF55.P7 I57a
DD 636/.009438

ISSN 0209-2492
PL

BIULETYN INFORMACYJNY - INSTYTUT ZOOTECHNIKI. (BIULETYN INFORMACYJNY - INSTYTUT ZOOTECHNIKI, ZAKLAD INFORMACJI ZOOTECHNICZNEJ.). [Biul. Inf. - Inst. Zootech.]. **Main/Corp** Instytut Zootechniki (Poland). Zaklad Informacji Zootechnicznej. (19??)-. Periodical. Polish (summaries and/or abstracts in English, Russian and German). Six times a year. Instytut Zootechniki / Institute of Animal Production, Ul. Sarego 2, 31-047 Krakow Poland. **Tel** 011 48 12 227333, FAX 011 48 12 228065. **Circ:** 1,000.
Ind/Abst Dairy Sci. Abstr.; Index Vet.; Maize Abstr.; Nutr. Abstr. Rev., Ser. B, Live Feeds and Feed.; Pig News Inf.; Poult. Abstr.

ISSN 0711-1797
CN
DD 636.2/42
UDC 636.242

BLONDE COUNTRY / ANNUAL HEARD REFERENCE ED. [Blonde ctry., Annu. herd ref. ed.]. **VFOAT** Canadian Blonde d'Aquitaine Herd Reference Issue.; Herd Reference Issue. 1980/81-. English. One time a year. Canadian Blonde d'Aquitaine Association, 207-1606 Centre Street North, Calgary Alberta T2E 2R9 Canada. **Tel** (403)276-5771. **Ad Acc. Circ:** 800 (ctrl).

ISSN 0067-9615
BL
NLM W1 BO164P

BOLETIM DE INDUSTRIA ANIMAL. [Bol. ind. anim.]. **Added/Corp** Sao Paulo, Brazil (State). Directoria de Industria Animal. Sao Paulo, Brazil (State). Departmento da Producao Animal. Sao Paulo, Brazil (State). Departmento de Industria Animal. Instituto de Zootecnia (Sao Paulo, Brazil). New Series Vol. 4, No. 1 (Jan. 1941)-. Bulletin. Portuguese (summaries and/or abstracts in English). Two times a year. $18.00 (latest edition). Instituto de Zootecnia, Caixa Postal 60, 13460 Nova Odessa Sao Paulo Brazil. **Tel** 011 55 194 661410. **ED** Nils Ferdinand Sabey. Index available. **Bk Rev. Ad Acc. Circ:** 2,400. *Continues Revista de Industria Animal.*
Desc: Concerned with animal science ruminants and forage crops.
Ind/Abst Abstr. Trop. Agric.; Anim. Breed. Abstr.; Dairy Sci. Abstr.; Field Crop Abstr.; Food Sci. Technol. Abstr.; Grass. Forage Abstr.; Index Vet.; Nutr. Abstr. Rev., Ser. B, Live Feeds and Feed.; Nutr. Abstr. Rev., Ser. A, Hum. Exp.; Pig News Inf.; Poult. Abstr.; Rev. Med. Vet. Entomol.; Vet. Bull.

ISSN 0524-1685
US
CODEN BOVPBO

BOVINE PRACTITIONER, THE. See Veterinary Sciences.

ISSN 0192-6764
US

BRAHMAN JOURNAL, THE. **Added/Corp** American Brahman Breeders Association. Vol. 1 (1971)-. Periodical. English (Spanish). Twelve times a year. $15.00. Brahman Journal, Box 220, Eddy TX 76524. **Tel** (817)859-5451. **ED** Joe Brockett. Index available. **Ad Acc. Circ:** 4,188.
Desc: Information about and pertaining to the American Brahman breed of cattle.

ISSN 0006-9132
US
DD 636

BRANGUS JOURNAL. [Brangus j.]. **Added/Corp** International Brangus Breeders Association. American Brangus Breeders Association. Vol. 1 (1953)-. Trade Publication. English. Eleven times a year (monthly except June). $20.00. M. A. Brooks, PO Box 503, Mossvale New South Wales, 2577 Australia. **Tel** 011 61 4 8681338, FAX 011 61 4 8691438. **ED** Ellen H. Godwin. **Bk Rev. Ad Acc. Circ:** 3,500 (ctrl).
Desc: International news magazine serving the Brangus breed of beef cattle including Brangus crossbreds and Brahman and Angus stock necessary to produce Brangus cattle.

US

BRAYER, THE. **Added/Corp** American Donkey and Mule Society. (19??)-. Periodical. English. Four times a year. $14.00. American Donkey & Mule Society, 2901 North Elm Street, Denton TX 76201. **Tel** (817)382-6845.

LC HD9424.B7 B73
DD 381/.025/81
UDC 338.439.4:636.2(81)

BL

BRAZIL SELLING : CATTLE BREEDING & AGRO INDUSTRIES. **VAT** Brazil Selling: Cattle Breeding and Agro Industries. (1974)-. English. Editora de Guias, PO Box 4724, 01310 Sao Paulo Brazil. **Tel** 288-7667.

ISSN 0712-5291
CN
DD 338.1/76213/09713

BREEDER AND FEEDER. (BREEDER AND FEEDER / ONTARIO BEEF IMPROVEMENT ASSOCIATION.). **Added/Corp** Ontario Beef Improvement Association. Ontario Cattlemen's Association. **VAT** Breeder & Feeder. (1963)-. Periodical. English. Seven times a year. $25.00 Comes with Ontario Cattlemen's Association membership. Ontario Cattlemen's Association, 50 Dovercliffe Road, Unit 6, Guelph Ontario N1G 3A6 Canada. **Tel** (519)824-0334. **ED** Jean Szkotnicki. **Bk Rev. Ad Acc.**
Desc: News and information is pertinent to cow-calf, background and feedlot operators. Also includes the events and activities of the OCA.

JA

●**BREEDING SCIENCE.** (1994)-. Periodical. Japanese. Four times a year. ¥8000.00. University of Tokyo Japan Society of Breeding, Yakyol 1 1 1 Bunkyo Ku, Agriculture Department, Tokyo 113 Japan. **Tel** 011 81 3 381222111. *Continues Japanese Journal of Breeding.*
Ind/Abst Curr. Cit.

LC SF961.B71
DD 636.0896(1-9)

UK

BRITISH CATTLE VETERINARY ASSOCIATION PROCEEDINGS FOR ... . See Veterinary Sciences.

UK

BRITISH CHAROLAIS HERD BOOK, CONTAINING THE AGES AND PEDIGREES OF BRITISH CHAROLAIS CATTLE WITH SUPPLEMENTARY REGISTER, THE. **Main/Corp** British Charolais Cattle Society. **VFOAT** Herd Book of British Charolais Cattle. Vol. 1 (1966)-. Trade Publication. English. One time a year.

UK

BRITISH FARMER AND STOCK BREEDER. YEARBOOK AND FARM DIARY. (1971)-. English. Twenty-four times a year. Reed Business Publishing / West Sussex, England, Perrymount Road, Haywards Heath, West Sussex RH16 3DH United Kingdom. **Tel** 011 44 1444 441212, FAX 011 44 1444 445447.

UK

BRITISH GOAT SOCIETY'S YEAR BOOK FOR..., THE. See Agriculture-Dairy Industry.

LC SF55.Y8 B76
CI

BROJ STOKE I STOCNA PROIZVODNJA. (1980)-. Periodical. Serbo-Croatian (Roman). One time a year. 70.00. Republicki Zavod za Statistiku, Central Bureau of Statistics of the Republic of Croatia, Ilica 3, Zagreb Croatia. **Tel** 011 385 41 45 44 22, FAX 011 385 41 42 94 13, 011 385 41 42 37 11, telex 21130 DZSTAT RH. *Continues Broj Stoke I Stocna Proizvodnja U Sr Hrvatskoj.*

ISSN 0007-2516
US

BROWN SWISS BULLETIN, THE. **Main/Corp** Brown Swiss Cattle Breeders' Association. Vol. 1 (July 1922)-. Trade Publication. English. Twelve times a year. $15.00. Brown Swiss Cattle Breeders Association, PO Box 1038, Beloit WI 53521. **Tel** (608)365-4474, FAX (608)365-5577, telex 508331. **ED** Connie Gritton. **Ad Acc. Circ:** 2,800 (ctrl).
Desc: Information on Brown Swiss breed meetings, production, type, sales, shows, performance information, breeder and commercial advertising.

ISSN 0196-9137
US
TITLE CHANGE

BUFFALO (CUSTER). (BUFFALO!). [Buffalo]. **Added/Corp** National Buffalo Association. (19??)-(19??). Periodical. English. National Buffalo Association, 4 East Main Street, PO Box 580, Ft. Pierre SD 57532. **Tel** (605)223-2829. **ED** Kim Dowling. Index available. **Bk Rev. Ad Acc. Circ:** 1,200 (ctrl). *Merged into Bison World, 1056-2400.*
Desc: Contents include articles on buffalo management, marketing and husbandry, as well as history, collecting, art and human interest stories.

LC SF191
DD 636.293

ISSN 0857-1554
TH

BUFFALO JOURNAL. [Buffalo J.]. (1985)-. Periodical. English. Three times a year (Apr., Aug., Dec.). $65.00. Research Centre for Bioscience in Animal Reproduction, Chulalongkorn University, Bangkok 10500 Thailand. **Tel** 011 66 2518936, FAX 011 66 2553910, telex 20217. **ED** Maneewan Kamonpatana. Index available. cum. index. **Circ:** 100 (ctrl).
Desc: Information related to buffalo science.
Ind/Abst Helminthol. Abstr. (1991-); Index Vet.; Sug. Indus. Abstr.; Vet. Bull.

ISSN 0557-4668
RM
CODEN BIAVDX
TITLE CHANGE

BULETINUL INSTITUTUL AGRONOMIC CLUJ-NAPOCA. SERIA ZOOTEHNIE SI MEDICINA VETERINARA. [Bul. Inst. Agron. Cluj-Napoca, Ser. zooteh. med. vet.]. **Main/Corp** Institutul Agronomic Dr. Petru Groza. **VFOAT** Seria Zootehnie si Medicina Veterinara; Buletin IACN-ZMV. Vol. 32 (1978)-(19??). Academic Scholarly Publication. Romanian (English; summaries and/or abstracts in English). Universitatea de Stiinte Agricole, Str. Manastur Nr. 3, Cluj-Napoca Romania. **Tel** 011 40 951 193792. **ED** Alexandru Salontai. **Circ:** 500 (ctrl). Documents available from CASDDS. *Continues in part Institutul Agronomic "Dr. Petru Groza." Buletinul Institutului Agronomic Cluj-Napoca, 0378-0554. Continued by Buletinul Universitatii de Stiinte Cluj-Napoca Seria Zootehnie si Medicina Veterinara., 1221-3594.*
Ind/Abst Agric. Eng. Abstr.; Anim. Breed. Abstr.; Chem. Abstr. (1978-1980); Dairy Sci. Abstr.; Fish Rev.; Helminthol. Abstr.; Index Vet.; Nutr. Abstr. Rev., Ser. B, Live Feeds and Feed.; Poult. Abstr.; Protozoolog. Abstr.; Refer. Z.; Vet. Bull.; Wildl. Rev.

ISSN 1221-3594
RM
UDC 636

BULETINUL UNIVERSITATII DE STIINTE AGRICOLE CLUJ-NAPOCA. SERIA ZOOTEHNIE SI MEDICINA VETERINARA. (1993)-. Bulletin. Multiple languages. One time a year. Universitatea de Stiinte Agricole, Str. Manastur Nr. 3, Cluj-Napoca Romania. **Tel** 011 40 951 193792. **ED** Leon Muntean. **Circ:** 200 (ctrl).

ISSN 0398-091X
FR

BULLETIN DE L'ELEVAGE FRANCAIS. [Bull. elev. fr.]. (1974)-. Periodical. Multiple languages. Association pour la Diffusion a l'Etranger des Techniques de l'Elevages Francais, Paris France.
Ind/Abst Pig News Inf.

FR

BULLETIN DE SNIA. (19??)-. Bulletin. French. Twelve times a year. Free to members. Syndicat National des Industriels de la Nutrition Animale, 41 bis boulevard Latour Maubourg, 75007 Paris France. **Tel** 011 31 1 44186346.

ISSN 0194-3707
US

BULLETIN FROM WISCONSIN LIVE STOCK BREEDERS' ASSOCIATION, THE. **Main/Corp** Wisconsin Live Stock Breeders' Association. (19??)-. Bulletin. English. Twelve times a year. The Wisconsin Live Stock Breeders Association, 801 West Badger Road, Madison WI 53713.

ISSN 0125-9660
IO

BULLETIN (LEMBAGA PENELITIAN PETERNAKAN (INDONESIA)). (BULLETIN / LEMBAGA PENELITIAN PETERNAKAN.). **Added/Corp** Lembaga Penelitian Peternakan (Indonesia). (196?)-. Bulletin. Indonesian (summaries and/or abstracts in English). Irregular. Lembaga Penelitian, Institut Pertanian Bogor, JL Raya Pajajaran, Bogor Indonesia. **Tel** (0251) 28105.

ISSN 0378-9721
KE
NLM W1 BU755V CODEN BAHADH
BULLETIN OF ANIMAL HEALTH AND PRODUCTION IN AFRICA. [Bull. anim. health prod. Afr.]. **Added/Corp** Inter-African Bureau for Animal Resources. East African Literature Bureau. **VFOAT** Bulletin des Sante et Production Animales en Afrique; Bulletin - Inter-African Bureau for Animal Resources. Vol. 23 (March 1975)-. Bulletin. English (French). Four times a year. $20.00. Interafrican Bureau of Animal Resources, PO Box 30786, Nairobi Kenya. **Tel** 011 254 2 338544, telex 22893. **ED** W.N. Masiga. cum. index. **Bk Rev. Circ:** 1,000 (ctrl). Documents available from BIOSIS Document Express, CASDDS. ***Continues*** *Bulletin of Epizootic Diseases of Africa, 0007-487X.*
Desc: Articles of original research, relevant to animal health and production activities which may lead to the improvement of livestock and animal resources in Africa.
Ind/Abst AGRICOLA [Full Cov.]; Agrofor. Abstr. (1991-); Anim. Breed. Abstr.; Biodeter. Abstr.; Biol. Abstr.; Chem. Abstr. (1975-1981); Dairy Sci. Abstr.; Fish Rev. (Jan. 1989-July 1992); For. Prod. Abstr. (1991-); For. Abstr.; Grass. Forage Abstr.; Helminthol. Abstr. (1991-); Index Vet.; Nutr. Abstr. Rev., Ser. B, Live Feeds and Feed.; Life Sci. Collect. (?-1987); PESTDOC (1975-1981); Pig News Inf.; Poult. Abstr.; Protozoolog. Abstr.; Rev. Agric. Entomol.; Rev. Med. Vet. Entomol.; Rev. Med. Vet. Mycology; Small Anim. Abstr. Bibliogr.; Vet. Bull.; Trop. Dis. Bull.; Wheat Barley Trit. Abstr.; Wildl. Rev. (Jan. 1989-July 1992).

LC HD9017.T3 B84
DD 338.1/09678 TZ
BULLETIN OF CROP AND LIVESTOCK STATISTICS. See Agriculture-Abstracting, Bibliographies and Statistics.

ISSN 0989-1994
FR
UDC 01
BULLETIN SIGNALETIQUE - DOC MNE. (BULLETIN SIGNALETIQUE.). **VFOAT** Bulletin Signaletique - Documentation Maison Nationale des Eleveurs. (1988)-. Bulletin. French. Eleven times a year. 979.32F France; 1300.00F other. Maison Nationale des Eleveurs, Service Doc, 149 rue de Bercy, 75595 Paris Cedex 12 France. **Tel** 011 33 1 40045176. Index available. **Ad Acc. Circ:** 850. available on microfiche. ***Continues*** *Bulletin Signaletique - M.N.E, 0241-8088.*

ISSN 0153-6281
FR
UDC 63
BULLETIN TECHNIQUE DE L'INSEMINATION ARTIFICIELLE. See Veterinary Sciences.

UK
UDC 636.2
BULLS (OTHER THAN FRIESIAN) WITH IMPROVED CONTEMPORARY COMPARISONS. **Main/Corp** Great Britain. Breeding and Production Organisation. Periodical. English. One time a year. ***Continues*** *Bulls other than Friesian with Contemporary Comparisons.*

ISSN 0007-7194
NO
UDC 636 CCC
BUSKAP OG AVDRATT. Vol. 1 (1949)-. Periodical. Norwegian. Four times a year. $6.66. Norske Husdyrtidskrifter, Storgaten 1, 2800 Gjoevik Norway. ***Absorbed*** *Avlsleget for Norsk Rdt fe. Avlsleget for Norsk Rdt fe Medlemsblad.*
Ind/Abst Anim. Breed. Abstr.; Dairy Sci. Abstr.; Field Crop Abstr.; Grass. Forage Abstr.; Index Vet.; Vet. Bull.

ISSN 1351-6175
UK
●**BUTCHERS' NEWSLETTER.** (1993)-. Newsletter. English. Five times a year. Free to Meat Trader subscribers. National Federation of Meat Traders, 1 Belgrave, Tunbridge Kent PN1 1YW United Kingdom. **Tel** 011 44 1892 541412, FAX 011 44 1892 535462.

LC S530.52.B6 C3
BL
CADASTRO DAS INSTITUICOES DE PESQUISA, PESQUISADORES E SUAS ATIVIDADES NO RIO GRANDE DO SUL : II. AGRONOMIA E ZOOTECNIA. **Added/Corp** Fundacao de Amparo a Pesquisa do Estado do Rio Grande do Sul. **VAT** Cadastro das Instituicoes de Pesquisa, Pesquisadores e Suas Atividades No Rio Grande do Sul: Dois: Agronomia e Zootecnia. (1975)-. Portuguese. Medicina Veterinaria, Caixa Postal 1646 90.000, Porto Alegre Brazil.

ISSN 0007-7798
DD 636 US
CALF NEWS. [CALF news]. **VAT** Concerning America's Livestock Feeders News. (1963)-. Periodical. English. Twelve times a year. $24.00. CALF News Magazine, 11477 Hungate Road, Colorado Springs CO 80908. **Tel** (719)495-0303, FAX (719)495-9204. **ED** Steve Dittmer. **Circ:** 4,200.
Desc: Only magazine devoted specifically to large (1,000 herd and over) cattle feeding. Special emphasis: people, business management, animal health and nutrition, feedlot profiles, new marketing concepts.

ISSN 0008-0942
US
CALIFORNIA CATTLEMAN. [Calif. cattlem.]. **Added/Corp** California Cattlemen's Association. Vol. 1-5, No. 3. (July 1919)-. Periodical. English. Eleven times a year (Combined July/August). $20.00. California Cattlemen's Association, PO Box 613, Fair Oaks CA 95628. **Tel** (916)965-6122. **ED** Kimberly Bradley, (phone: (916)444-0845). Index available. **Ad Acc, Adv Mgr:** J. Danekas, **Tel** (916)965-6122. **Circ:** 4,300 (ctrl).
Desc: Deals with the cattle industry - focusing in California.
Ind/Abst Calif. Period. Index (19??-); Calif. Period. Microfi. (19??-).

ISSN 0279-2621
US
CEASED
CALIFORNIA LIVESTOCK REVIEW. Vol. 1, No. 1 (Sept. 19, 1979)-(April 1994). English. California Agricultural Statistics Service, California Department of, Food and Agriculture, PO Box 1258, Sacramento CA 95812. **Tel** (916)551-1533. ***Formed by the union of*** *Cattle on Feed (Sacramento, Calif.); Pasture and Range* ***and*** *Livestock Slaughter (Sacramento, Calif.).*
Desc: Livestock inventories, intentions, and values; pasture, slaughter, and on-feed data for cattle and sheep.

ISSN 0008-3739
CN
CANADIAN HEREFORD DIGEST. (THE CANADIAN HEREFORD DIGEST.). (1943)-. Periodical. English (French). Eleven times a year (monthly except Jan.). 50.00Can$. Gilmore Publications Ltd., 5160 Skyline Way Northeast, Calgary Alberta T2E 6V1 Canada. **Tel** (403)274-1734, FAX (403)275-4999. **ED** Kurt Gilmore. **Ad Acc, Adv Mgr:** Janice McCurdie. **Circ:** 3,300 (ctrl).

ISSN 0008-3909
CN
UDC 636.224.3(71)
CANADIAN JERSEY BREEDER. Vol. 1 (Dec. 1945)-. Periodical. English (French). Twelve times a year. 20.01Can$. Canadian Jersey Breeder, 343 Waterloo Avenue, Guelph Ontario N1H 3K1 Canada. **Tel** (519)821-9150. **ED** Russell Gammon. **Ad Acc. Circ:** 1,800 (ctrl).
Desc: The official publication for breeders of purebred Jersey cattle in Canada. Vitally concerned with profitable dairying.

ISSN 0008-3984
CN
CCC
CODEN CNJNAT
Pr Rev.
CANADIAN JOURNAL OF ANIMAL SCIENCE. [Can. j. anim. sci.]. **Added/Corp** Canadian Society of Animal Production. Agricultural Institute of Canada. Canadian Society of Animal Science. National Committee on Agricultural Services. **VFOAT** Revue Canadienne de Zootechnie. Vol. 37 (June 1957)-. Periodical. English (summaries and/or abstracts in French). Four times a year. 72.02Can$. Agricultural Institute of Canada, 151 Slater Street, Suite 907, Ottawa Ontario K1P 5H4 Canada. **Tel** (613)232-9459, (613)238-2271, FAX (613)594-5190. **ED** J. Buchanan-Smith. **Ad Acc. Circ:** 1,600. available on microfilm and microfiche from University Microfilms International (UMI). Documents available from The Genuine Article, BIOSIS Document Express, CASDDS, Documents on Demand. ***Continues in part*** *Canadian Journal of Agricultural Science, 0366-6557.*
Desc: Publishes original research on all aspects of domestic livestock and their products.
Ind/Abst AgBiotech News Inf.; AGRICOLA [Full Cov.]; Agric. Eng. Abstr. (1991-); Anim. Breed. Abstr.; BioBusiness; Biol. Agric. Index; Biol. Abstr.; Chem. Abstr.; CSA Neuro. Abstr. (?-?); Curr. Aware. Biol. Sci., CABS; Curr. Biotechnol.; Curr. Cit.; Curr. Contents Agric. Biol. Environ. Sci.; Dairy Sci. Abstr.; Environ. Abstr.; Field Crop Abstr.; Food Sci. Technol. Abstr.; Grass. Forage Abstr.; Index Vet.; Leadscan; Maize Abstr.; Nutr. Abstr. Rev., Ser. B, Live Feeds and Feed.; Nutr. Abstr. Rev., Ser. A, Hum. Exp.; Life Sci. Collect.; PESTDOC; Pig News Inf.; Plant Breed. Abstr.; Potato Abstr.; Poult. Abstr.; Protozoolog. Abstr.; Res. Alert [Full Cov.]; Rev. Med. Vet. Mycology; Sci. Cit. Index; SCISEARCH; Soc. Sci. Cit. Index [Select. Cov.]; Soyabean Abstr.; Vet. Bull.; Wheat Barley Trit. Abstr.; Wildl. Rev.

CN
CANFAX. See Veterinary Sciences.

CK
CARTA GANADERA. **Added/Corp** Banco Ganadero. (19??)-. Periodical. Spanish. Twelve times a year. $52.00. Banco Ganadero, Cra 9A, 72-21 Piso 50, Bogota Colombia. **Tel** 011 57 1 2170100 ext 314766.

ISSN 0310-8279
AT
CATTLE. Vol. 5, No. 4 (Feb./March 1976)-. Periodical. English. Twelve times a year (2 semiannual reports). $18.00 US; $22.50 other.
Desc: Short articles on current production and market trends.

ISSN 0897-2737
DD 636 US
CATTLE BUSINESS IN MISSISSIPPI. [Cattle bus. Miss.]. **Added/Corp** Mississippi Cattlemen's Association. **VFOAT** Cattle Business. (198?)-. Periodical. English. Ten times a year. $30.00. Mississippi Cattlemans Association, 121 North Jefferson Street, Jackson MS 39202. **Tel** (601)354-8951. ***Continues*** *Cattle Business.*

ISSN 1182-8765
DD 636.2/084/05 CN
CATTLE FEEDER, THE. [Cattle feed.]. **Added/Corp** Saskatchewan Cattle Feeders Association. **VFOAT** Cattlefeeder. Vol. 1, No. 1 (Oct. 1990)-. Periodical. English. Six times a year. Free to members. Saskatchewan Cattle Feeders Association, 201-4401 Albert Street, Regina Saskatchewan S4S 6B6 Canada.

ISSN 0411-289X
US
CATTLE GUARD. [Cattle guard]. **Added/Corp** Colorado Cattlemen's Association. Vol. 1 (Nov. 1955)-. Periodical. English. Eleven times a year. $20.00. Colorado Cattlemens Association, 8833 Ralston Road, Arvada CO 80002. **Tel** (303)431-6422. **ED** Larry Kerr. **Ad Acc. Circ:** 3,500 (ctrl).
Desc: Published and edited for beef cattle producers in Colorado, with editorial material on beef cattle reproduction.

ISSN 0364-202X
US
CATTLE ON FEED (WASHINGTON, D.C.). (CATTLE ON FEED.). **Added/Corp** United States. Crop Reporting Board. United States. Agricultural Statistics Board. (1963)-. Government Publication. English. Twelve times a year. $22.00. US Department of Agriculture, 14th Street and Independence Avenue SW, Washington DC 20250. **Tel** (202)720-5457. **(Subscription address:** ERS NASS, 341 Victory Drive, Herndon VA 22070. **Tel** (800)999-6779, (703)834-0125.**)** available on microfiche (Vols. for (1986-) distributed to depository libraries). Documents available from Documents on Demand. ***Continues*** *Cattle and Calves on Feed.*
Ind/Abst Am. Stat. Index.

ISSN 0969-1251
UK
●**CATTLE PRACTICE.** See Veterinary Sciences.

ISSN 0094-3819
US
CATTLE (WASHINGTON). (CATTLE.). **Added/Corp** United States. Dept. of Agriculture. Statistical Reporting Service. United States. Crop Reporting Board. United States. Agricultural Statistics Board. (Feb. 1973)-. Government Publication. English. Fourteen times a year (including two semi-annual reports in Jan. and July). $39.00. Superintendent of Documents, US Government Printing Office, Washington DC 20402. **Tel** (202)275-3328, FAX (202)786-2377. ***Continues in part*** *Cattle, Sheep and Goat Inventory, 0094-3827.*

ISSN 0008-8552
US
UDC 636.282(764)
CATTLEMAN. [The Cattleman]. (19??)-. Periodical. English. Twelve times a year. $25.00. Texas & Southwestern Cattle, 1301 West 7th, Ft Worth TX 76102. **Tel** (817)332-7155. **ED** Dale Segraves. **Bk Rev. Ad Acc. Circ:** 19,169 (ctrl). available on microfilm and microfiche from University Microfilms International (UMI).
Desc: Focuses on beef industry in Texas and Southwest. Articles on beef production, breeding, grasses, feedlots, brush control, and Western history.

ISSN 0008-3143
DD 636.2/00971 CN
CATTLEMEN. [Cattlemen]. **Added/Corp** Canadian Cattlemen's Association. Vol. 32, No. 6 (June 1969)-. Periodical. English. Ten times a year. 17.95Can$. United Grain Growers, 2500-201 Portage Avenue, Box 6600, Winnipeg Manitoba R3C 3A7 Canada. **Tel** (204)944-5697, FAX (204)944-5416. **Ad Acc. Circ:** 40,636. ***Continues*** *Canadian Cattlemen, 0319-504X;* ***Absorbed*** *Hereford Bulletin, 0703-7872.*
Desc: Edited for commercial and purebred cattle producers across Canada who are interested in increasing the efficiency and profitability of their operations.

ISSN 0008-8668
AG
CEBU Y DERIVADOS. Periodical. Spanish. Twelve times a year. Cebu y Derivados, Arenales 2777, Buenos Aires Argentina.

Agriculture —Livestock

LC SF55.R5 R53A   **ISSN** 0376-5822
DD 636/.009689/1   RH
CENSUS OF LIVESTOCK IN EUROPEAN AREAS.
Main/Corp Southern Rhodesia. Central Statistical Office. English. $0.25 single issue. Central Statistical Office / Zimbabwe, PO Box 8063, Causeway Salisbury Harare, Zimbabwe. **Tel** 011 263 0 706681.

ISSN 0824-1767
DD 636.2/42   CN
CHAROLAIS BANNER. [Charolais banner].
Added/Corp Canadian Charolais Association. Vol. 18, No. 9 (June 1984)-. Periodical. English. Eleven times a year. 24.01Can$. Charolais Banner, 1120 53rd Avenue NE, Suite 101A, Calgary Alta T2E 6N9 Canada. **Tel** (403)295-2292, FAX (403)275-3084. **ED** Mark Kihn. Index available. cum. index. **Ad** Acc, **Adv Mgr:** Rob Pek. ctrl circ. **Continues** Canadian Charolais Banner, 0008-5499.
Desc: Publication concentrating on Charolais cattle.

ISSN 0828-7600
DD 636.2/42   CN
CHAROLAIS CONNECTION. [Charolais connect.].
Added/Corp Canadian Charolais Association. Vol. 1, No. 1 (Oct. 1984)-. Periodical. English. Four times a year. 12.01Can$. Charolais Banner, 1120 53rd Avenue NE, Suite 101A, Calgary Alta T2E 6N9 Canada. **Tel** (403)295-2292, FAX (403)275-3084. **ED** Mark Kihn. **Ad Acc, Adv Mgr:** Rob Pek. ctrl circ.
Desc: Tabloid-type newspaper about Charolais cattle and the cattle industry.

ISSN 0191-5444
US
CHAROLAIS JOURNAL. Added/Corp
American-International Charolais Association. Vol. 1, (1978)-. Periodical. English. Twelve times a year. $20.00. Charolais Publications, PO Box 20247, Kansas City MO 64195. **Tel** (816)464-5977. **ED** Nancy Gingrich. **Ad** Acc. Circ; 5,000 (ctrl).
Desc: Articles relating to feedlot management, spouse, estate planning and hay fencing. Includes shows, relative breeders and sales reports.

AT
CHAROLAIS NEWSLETTER, THE.
Added/Corp Charolais Society of Australia. (April 1976)-. Newsletter. English. Twelve times a year. Charolais Society of Australia, PO Box 861, Sydney New South Wales 2060 Australia.

ISSN 1184-1575
DD 636.2/42   CN
CHAROLAIS ROUNDUP. (CHAROLAIS ROUNDUP / ONTARIO CHAROLAIS ASSOCIATION.). [Charolais roundup].
Added/Corp Ontario Charolais Association. **VFOAT** Ontario Charolais Association Roundup. Vol. 10 (July 1990)-. Periodical. English. Four times a year. Free to members. Ontario Charolais Association, Rural Route 2, Beaverton Ontario L0K 1A0 Canada. **Continues** Roundup (Allenford, Ont.), 0845-2946.

ISSN 0009-3386
DD 636   US
TITLE CHANGE
CHESTER WHITE JOURNAL. [Chester White j.].
Added/Corp Chester White Swine Record Association. Vol.9 No.5 (July 1918)-(199?). English. Chester White Swine Record Association, 1803 West Detweiller Drive, PO Box 9758, Peoria IL 61612. **Tel** (309)691-0151. **ED** Daniel Parish. **Continues** White Breeders' Companion. **Merged with** Chester White Journal and Spotted News, 1075-0177 **to form** Spotted News, 0038-8432.

ISSN 1075-0177
US
●CHESTER WHITE JOURNAL, POLAND CHINA ADVANTAGE, SPOTTED NEWS.
Added/Corp Chester White Swine Record Association. National Spotted Swine Record. Poland China Record Association. **VFOAT** CWJ/Spotted/PC; Chester White Journal, Spotted News, Poland ID SID: 03756 Olhina Advantage; C.W.J./Spotted/P.C. Vol. 1 No. 1 (Feb.-Mar., 1995)-. English. Six times a year (Feb., Apr., June, Aug., Oct., Dec.). $10.00. Chester White Swine Record Association, 1803 West Detweiller Drive, PO Box 9758, Peoria IL 61612. **Tel** (309)691-0151. **Continues** Chester White Journal and Spotted News, 1075-0177; **Absorbed** Spotted News, 0038-8432.

ISSN 0714-3621
DD 636.3/009714   CN
CHEVRE QUEBEC. Added/Corp
Federation des Producteurs Caprins du Quebec. **VFOAT** Chevre. Vol. 1 (Feb. 1982)-. Periodical. French. Four times a year. $15.00. Federation Des Producteurs Caprins, Du Quebec 515 AV. Vigeur, Montreal Quebec H2L 2P2 Canada.

ISSN 0045-6608
FR
UDC 636.39
CHEVRE TOURS, LA. (CHEVRE). (1958)-.
Periodical. French. Six times a year. $69.99. Societe de Presse et d Edition Ovine et Caprine, 19 Quai de Juillet, BP 67, 14007 CAEN Cedex France. **Tel** 011 33 31356507.
Ind/Abst AgBiotech News Inf.; Anim. Breed. Abstr.; Dairy Sci. Abstr.; Index Vet.

LC SF553. J3 C47A
JA
CHIBA-KEN SANGYO SHIKENJO TOKUBETSU HOKOKU. Main/Corp
Chiba-ken Sangyo Shikenjo. No. 1- ; 1978-. Japanese. Chiba-Ken Sangyo Shikenjo, 1055 Aburai, Togane-Shi 283, Togane Japan.

US
CHICKENS AND EGGS, FINAL ESTIMATES FOR ... .
Government Publication. English. US Department of Agriculture / Economics and Statistics Service, Washington DC 20250. available on microfiche (Vols. for (1980-83-) distributed to depository libraries).

LC SF15.J3 N67a
DD 636   JA
CHIKUSAMBUTSU SEISANHI CHOSA HOKOKU. Main/Corp
Japan. Norinsho. Norin Keizaikyoku. Tokei Johobu. (1971)-. Japanese. Norin Tokei Kyokai, (Association of Agriculture & Forestry Statistics), 11-14 Meguro 2 Chome, Meguroku Tokyo 153 Japan. **Continues** Japan. NorinshAo. Norin Keizaikyoku. Tokei Chosabu. Chikusambutsu Seisanhi Chosa Hokoku.

JA
CODEN CKNKAJ
CHIKUSAN NO KENKYU. ANIMAL HUSBANDRY. See Veterinary Sciences.

ISSN 0577-7658
JA
CODEN CSKKAQ
CHIKUSAN SHIKENJO KENKYU HOKOKU. [Chikusan Shikenjo kenkyu hokoku].
Main/Corp Chikusan Shikanjo (Chiba, Japan). **VFOAT** Bulletin of National Institute of Animal Industry; Hokoku. No. 1 (Feb. 1963)-. Academic Scholarly Publication. Japanese (summaries and/or abstracts in English; table of contents in English). National Institute of Animal Husbandry, Tsukuba Norindanci, PO Box 5, Ibaraki 305 Japan. Documents available from CASDDS. **Supersedes** Nogyo Gijutsu Kenkyujo Tosan Nogyo: G (Chikusan); **Supersedes in part** Kanto Tosan Nogyo Shikenjo Kenkyu Hokoku.
Ind/Abst Chem. Abstr.; Food Sci. Technol. Abstr.; Index Vet.; Nutr. Abstr. Rev., Ser. B, Live Feeds and Feed.; Nutr. Abstr. Rev., Ser. A, Hum. Exp.; Pig News Inf.; Poult. Abstr.; Rev. Agric. Entomol.; Rice Abstr.; SEA Abstr.; Sug. Indus. Abstr.

XR
CHOVATEL. (19??)-.
Periodical. Czech. Twelve times a year. DM107.00. (**Subscription address:** Kubon & Sagner, ABT Zeitschriftenimport, D 80328 Munich Germany. **Tel** 011 49 89 54218130.)
Ind/Abst Anim. Breed. Abstr.; Poult. Abstr.

LC HD9426.K6 C47
KO
CHUKHYOP CHOSA KYEBO = QUARTERLY REVIEW. Added/Corp
Chuksanop Hyoptong Chohap Chunganghoe (Korea). **VFOAT** Quarterly Review. (April 1981)-. Periodical. English (Korean). Four times a year. Chuksanop Hyoptong Chohap Chunganghoe, 1-426 Youido-dong Korea.

LC SF55.K6 C46
KO
CHUKSAN CHINHUNG.
Periodical. Korean. Twelve times a year. Chuksanop Hyoptong Chohap Chunganghoe, 1-426 Youido-dong Korea.

ISSN 0253-9187
CC
NLM W1; CH9874
CHUNG-KUO HSU MU HSUEH HUI HUI CHI = JOURNAL OF THE CHINESE SOCIETY OF ANIMAL SCIENCE. Main/Corp
Chung-Kuo Hsu Mu Hueh Hi. **Added/Corp** Chung-Kuo Hsu mu Hsueh Hui (Taipei, Taiwan). **VFOAT** Journal of the Chinese Society of Animal Science. (197?)-. Periodical. Chinese (summaries and/or abstracts in English; table of contents in English). Four times a year.
Ind/Abst Index Vet.; Soyabean Abstr.

ISSN 0259-2932
CU
CODEN CAGPDY
CIENCIA Y TECNICA EN LA AGRICULTURA. GANADO PORCINO. [Cienc. tec. agric., Ganado porc.].
Added/Corp Centro de Informacion y Documentacion Agropecuario (Cuba) Centro de Investigaciones Porcinas (Cuba). **VFOAT** Ganado Porcino. (1978)-. Spanish (summaries and/or abstracts in English; table of contents in English). Every 2 years. Ediciones Cubanas, Obispo 527 Altos ESQ Bernaza, CP 10100 Havana Cuba.
Ind/Abst Index Vet.; Pig News Inf.

US
COMPARATIVE RECEIPTS AND SHIPMENTS OF LIVE STOCK FOR MONTHS ENDING ... / OKLAHOMA NATIONAL STOCK YARDS CO. Main/Corp
Oklahoma National Stock Yards Co. Periodical. English. Twelve times a year.

ISSN 0010-5929
IT
CONIGLICOLTURA. (RIVISTA DI CONIGLICOLTURA.). [Coniglicoltura.]. Vol. 15 No. 1 (1964)-.
Periodical. Italian. Twelve times a year. L42240. Edagricole, PO Box 2157, 40100 Bologna Italy. **Tel** 011 39 51 492211 Ext. 22, FAX 011 39 51 493660, telex 510336 EDAGRI.
Ind/Abst AGRICOLA; Agric. Eng. Abstr. (1991-); Anim. Breed. Abstr.; Dairy Sci. Abstr.; Helminthol. Abstr.; Index Vet.; Nutr. Abstr. Rev., Ser. B, Live Feeds and Feed.; Protozoolog. Abstr.; Soyabean Abstr.; Vet. Bull.; Wheat Barley Trit. Abstr.

ISSN 8750-7595
DD 636   US
COUNTRYSIDE AND SMALL STOCK JOURNAL (1985). (COUNTRYSIDE AND SMALL STOCK JOURNAL.). [Countrys. small stock j.]. VFOAT
Countryside; Countryside & Small Stock Journal. Vol. 69, No. 2, (Feb. 1985)-. Periodical. English. Six times a year. $18.00. Countryside Publications Ltd, N2601 Winter Sports Road, Withee WI 54498. **Tel** (715)785-7979, (800)551-5691. **ED** Jerome D. Belanger. Index available. **Bk Rev. Ad Acc.** Circ: 14,000. available on microfilm and microfiche from University Microfilms International (UMI). Documents available from UMI Article Clearinghouse, Magazine Collection. **Formed by the union of** Countryside, 0363-8723; Dairy Goat Guide, 0164-6519 **and** Backyard Poultry, 0194-9462.
Desc: Devoted to simple county living and small scale livestock raising.
Ind/Abst Acad. Abstr. Full Text Elite; Acad. Abstr.; EP Collect.; Gen. Period. Index (1985-); Homework Help.; Mag. Artic. Summar. Elite; Mag. Artic. Summar. Select; Mag. Artic. Summar. CD-ROM; Mag. Index Plus (1989-); Mag. Search; MasterFile FullTEXT 1000; MasterFile FullTEXT 350; MasterFile FullTEXT 650; MasterFile FullTEXT (July 1990-); Newsp. Period. Abstr. (1989-); OCLC; Pub. Lib. FullTEXT; Telebase; Mag. Index; Vocat. Search.

ISSN 0279-8204
US
COW COUNTRY. [Cow ctry.]. Added/Corp
Wyoming Stock Growers Association. (1951)-. Periodical. English. Eleven times a year (monthly except combined July/Aug.). $20.00. Wyoming Stock Growers Association, 113 East 20th Street, Box 206, Cheyenne WY 82003. **Tel** (307)638-3942. **ED** Cindy Garretson. **Ad Acc.** Circ: 1,650 (ctrl).
Desc: Focus on Wyoming issues involving cattle industry, as well as national and international issues that affect day-to-day management of ranching business.

LC S451.P4 P4 S107   **ISSN** 0743-6572
DD 338.1/09748   US
CROP AND LIVESTOCK ANNUAL SUMMARY. See Agriculture-Crop Production and Soils.

ISSN 0714-8240
DD 636/.006/071   CN
CSAS NEWSLETTER. [CSAS newsl.].
Added/Corp Canadian Society of Animal Science. (197?)-. Newsletter. English. Irregular. Free to members of the Canadian Society of Animal Science. Agricultural Institute of Canada, 151 Slater Street, Suite 907, Ottawa Ontario K1P 5H4 Canada. **Tel** (613)232-9459, (613)238-2271, FAX (613)594-5190. **Bk Rev. Ad Acc.** Circ: 500 (ctrl).

ISSN 0210-1912
SP
UDC 636.5
CUNICULTURAL. [Cunicultura]. (1976)-.
Periodical. Spanish. Six times a year (Feb., Apr., June, Aug., Oct., Dec.). 5500ptas. Real Escuela Oficial Superior de Avicultura, Plana de Paraiso 14, 08350 Barcelona Spain. **Tel** 011 34 3 7921137, FAX 011 34 3 7923141. **ED** Jose Castello. **Bk Rev. Ad Acc.** Circ: 2,800.
Desc: Articles on rabbit raising: management, nutrition, diseases and genetics.

ISSN 0152-3058
FR
UDC 57
CODEN 59
CUNICULTURE (PARIS). (1974)-.
Periodical. French. Six times a year. $76.11. Assn Francaise de Cuniculture, BP 50, 63370 Lempdes France. **Tel** 011 33 73 920152, FAX 011 33 73 928580. Circ: 5,000.
Ind/Abst Agric. Eng. Abstr. (1991-); Anim. Breed. Abstr.; Index Vet.; Nutr. Abstr. Rev., Ser. B, Live Feeds and Feed.; Soils Fert.; Vet. Bull.; Wheat Barley Trit. Abstr.

Agriculture —Livestock

DD 636.2/142 ISSN 0821-7440 CN
UDC 636.2.034
DAIRY CATTLE. (DAIRY REPORT / ANIMAL & POULTRY SCIENCE DEPARTMENT, UNIVERSITY OF SASKATCHEWAN.). [Dairy rep.]. **Main/Corp** University of Saskatchewan. Animal & Poultry Science Dept. **VFOAT** Dairy Cattle Management Feeding and Research Results. English. One time a year. Free. Animal & Poultry Science Department, University of Saskatoon, Saskatoon Saskatchewan S7N 0W0 Canada. ctrl circ. **Continues** University of Saskatchewan. Dept. of Animal Science. Dairy Report, 0821-7440.

DD 636 ISSN 0011-5592 US
DAIRY GOAT JOURNAL. See Agriculture-Dairy Industry.

ISSN 0110-7992 NZ
DEER FARMER, THE. [Deer farm.]. (19??)-. Periodical. English. Ten times a year. $150.00. Deer Farmer, PO Box 11092, Wellington New Zealand. **Tel** 011 64 4 4739243, FAX 011 64 4734530. **ED** B. Hutching. **Bk Rev. Ad Acc. Circ:** 4,000. **Continues** Deerfarming Annual.
 Desc: Carries articles on topics of interest to deer farmers and others in the industry.
 Ind/Abst AGRICOLA; Leis., Rec., Tour. Abstr.; Rural Dev. Abstr.; World Agric. Econ. Rural Sociol. Abstr.

ISSN 0340-3858 GW
UDC 338.439.4:636.4/.5(430.1) CCC
DGS, DEUTSCHE GEFLUGELWIRTSCHAFT UND SCHWEINEPRODUKTION. [DGS. Dtsch. Geflugelwirtsch. Schweineprod.]. **VFOAT** DGS. Vol. 24 (Jan. 1, 1974)-. Trade Publication. German. One time a week. $236.60. Verlag Eugen Ulmer, Postfach 700561, D-70574 Stuttgart Germany. **Tel** 011 49 711 4507108, FAX 011 49 711 4507120, telex 7-23634. **ED** Roland Ulmer. **Continues** Deutsche Geflugelwirtschaft und Schweineproduktion.
 Ind/Abst Leis., Rec., Tour. Abstr.; Rural Dev. Abstr.; World Agric. Econ. Rural Sociol. Abstr.

ISSN 0521-0097 UK
DIGEST - BRITISH CATTLE BREEDERS' CLUB. **Main/Corp** British Cattle Breeders' Club. (1???)-. English. Four times a year.
 Ind/Abst Index Vet.; World Agric. Econ. Rural Sociol. Abstr.

ISSN 0100-9443 BL
DOCUMENTOS (CENTRO NACIONAL DE PESQUISA DE GADO DE CORTE (BRAZIL)). (DOCUMENTOS / EMBRAPA-CNPGC.). [Doc. - Cent. Nac. Pesqui. Gado Corte]. (1977)-. Monographic series. Portuguese. Irregular. Price varies per volume.
 Ind/Abst Biocont. News Inf.; Plant Genet. Resour. Abstr.

ISSN 0012-6454 US
DD 328 CCC
DROVER'S JOURNAL (SHAWNEE MISSION, KAN.). (DROVER'S JOURNAL.). **VFOAT** Drovers Journal. Vol. 89, (Jan. 4, 1961)-. Periodical. English. Twelve times a year. Vance Publishing Corporation, 400 Knightsbridge Parkway, Lincolnshire IL 60069. **Tel** (800)255-5113, (708)634-2600. **ED** Fred Knap. **Circ:** 47,000. available on microfilm from University Microfilms International (UMI). **Continues** Chicago Daily Drovers' Journal; **Absorbed** Drovers Telegram; Stockman's Journal; Livestock Reporter.
 Desc: Beef cattle publication.

LC SF1 .E8 ISSN 0259-322X NE
EAAP PUBLICATION. [EAAP publ.]. **Added/Corp** European Association for Animal Production. **VAT** European Association for Animal Production Publications. (19??)-. Monographic series. English. Irregular. PUDOC, PO Box 4, 6700 AA Wageningen Netherlands. **Tel** 011 31 8370 84541, FAX 31 8370 84761, telex 45015 BLUWG NL. **Continues** Publication (European Association for Animal Production), 0071-2477.
 Desc: Examines livestock.

US
EASTERN ARTIFICIAL BREEDERS' CO-OPERATOR. **Added/Corp** Eastern Artificial Insemination Cooperative. New York Artificial Breeders Cooperative. Vol. 1 (June 1944)-. Periodical. English. Twelve times a year. Eastern Artificial Insemination Cooperative, PO Box 518, Ithaca NY 14850.

DD 637/.541/0971 ISSN 0821-4689 CN
TITLE CHANGE
EGG PRODUCER, THE. [Egg prod.]. **Added/Corp** Canadian Egg Marketing Agency. Vol. 1, No. 1 (Feb. 1982)-(1993). Trade Publication. English (French). Canadian Egg Marketing Agency, 320 Queen Street, Suite 1900, Place de Ville, Ottawa Ontario K1R 5A3 Canada. **Tel** (613)238-2514, FAX (613)238-1967. **ED** Ian Elliott. **Circ:** 3,500 (ctrl). **Continued by** Today's Egg Producer, 1195-1877.
 Desc: News, commentary and features of interest to Canadian egg producers.

ISSN 0302-4520 UA
CODEN EGAPBW
EGYPTIAN JOURNAL OF ANIMAL PRODUCTION. [Egypt. j. anim. prod.]. **Added/Corp** al-Jamiyah al-Misriyah lil-Intaj al-Hayawani. Vol. 12 (1972)-. Academic Scholarly Publication. English (summaries and/or abstracts in Arabic). Two times a year. $57.00. National Information & Documentation Center, A1-Tahrir St Dokki Awqaf PO, Cairo Egypt. **Tel** 011 20 2 701696, telex 93069. Documents available from CASDDS. **Continues** United Arab Republic Journal of Animal Production.
 Ind/Abst AGRICOLA; Anim. Breed. Abstr.; Chem. Abstr.; Dairy Sci. Abstr.; Food Sci. Technol. Abstr.; Helminthol. Abstr.; Index Vet.; Nutr. Abstr. Rev., Ser. B, Live Feeds and Feed.; Nutr. Abstr. Rev., Ser. A, Hum. Exp.; Poult. Abstr.; Vet. Bull.; Wheat Barley Trit. Abstr.

AT
ELDERS WEEKLY. English. Irregular (102 issues per year). 82.50 Aus$. Western Farmer & Grazier, PO Box 1268, Victoria Park East, 6101 Australia. **Tel** 011 61 9 3560356. **ED** Graham Greenwood. **Ad Acc, Adv Mgr:** Pete Maye & Margaret Green, **Tel** 356-0320. **Circ:** 13,000. **Absorbed** Farm Weekly.

FR
ELEVAGE BOVIN, L'. No. 113 (Jan. 1982)-. Periodical. French. Twelve times a year. Compagnie Gen Developpement, 11 rue Godefroy Cavaignac, 75541 Paris Cedex 11 France. **Tel** 011 33 1 43790630, FAX 011 33 1 43791775, telex 211351. **Continues** Elevage. Bovin, Ovin, Caprin.

ISSN 0422-9703 FR
NLM W1 EL454B
ELEVAGE ET INSEMINATION. (ELEVAGE INSEMINATION.). [Elev. insemin.]. **Added/Corp** Union Nationale des Cooperatives d'Elevage et d'Insemination Artificielle. (1950)-. Periodical. French. Six times a year. $80.93. Selia, 149 rue de Bercy, 75595 Paris Cedex 12 France. **Tel** 011 33 1 40045381. **Bk Rev.** ctrl circ.
 Ind/Abst AGRICOLA; Anim. Breed. Abstr.

FR
ELEVAGE OVIN. French. Elevage Ovin, 11 rue Pierre Leroux, 87003 Limoges Cedex France.

BE
ELEVAGES BELGES, LES. **Added/Corp** Association Nationale des Eleveurs et Detenteurs de Betail Bovin. (19??)-. Periodical. French. Twelve times a year.
 Ind/Abst World Agric. Econ. Rural Sociol. Abstr.

FR
ELEVEUR DE LAPINS, L'. (1978)-. Periodical. French. Five times a year. $74.36. Editions du Boisbaudry, BP 6359, 35036 Rennes Cedex France. **Tel** 011 33 99 322121.

LC SF ISSN 0709-8510 CN
DD 636.2/009714
ENTRE-NOUS - SOCIETE DES ELEVEURS DE BOVINS CANADIENS. (ENTRE-NOUS.). **Added/Corp** Societe des Eleveurs de Bovins Canadiens. (1970)-. Periodical. French. Four times a year. 12.01Can$. Societe des Eleveurs de Bovins Canadiens, 468 Dolbeau, Sherbrooke Quebec J1G 2Z7 Canada. **Tel** (819)346-1258. **ED** Jean-Guiy Bernier. **Ad Acc:** 220 (ctrl). **Continues in part** Entre-Nous, 0046-2144.

SP
ESPANA AGRICOLA Y GANADERA. See Fish and Fisheries.

GT
ESTADISTICAS AGROPECUARIAS CONTINUAS. **Added/Corp** Instituto Nacional de Estadistica (Guatemala). (1984)-. Statistical Publication. Spanish. **Continues** Estadisticas Agricolas Continuas.

ISSN 0297-4444 FR
UDC 619:614.23(213)
ETUDES ET SYNTHESES DE L'I.E.M.V.T. See Veterinary Sciences.

LC Discard UK
EUROPEAN WEEKLY MARKET SURVEY. (19??)-. Periodical. English. Fifty times a year. $256.68. Meat & Livestock Commission / Economic Service Department, PO Box 44, Winterhill House, Milton Keynes MK6 1AX United Kingdom. **Tel** 011 44 1908 677577, FAX 011 44 1908 609221, telex 82227. **Circ:** 1,000.
 Desc: Provides information on market developments and EEC policy which affect the meat and livestock sector.

ISSN 0882-3022 US
DD 636
FACT SHEET (FOOD ANIMAL CONCERNS TRUST). (FACT SHEET.). [FACT sheet - Food Anim. Concerns Trust.]. **Added/Corp** Food Animal Concerns Trust. (19??)-. Periodical. English. Irregular. Free. Fact Inc, PO Box 14599, Chicago IL 60614. **Tel** (312)525-4952. **ED** Robert A. Brown. Index available. **Bk Rev. Circ:** 15,000.
 Desc: Describes husbandry methods and problems.

LC SF ISSN 0254-6019 IT
DD 636 CODEN FAPPDA
FAO ANIMAL PRODUCTION AND HEALTH PAPER. [FAO anim. prod. health pap.]. **Main/Corp** Food and Agriculture Organization of the United Nations. **VFOAT** Animal Production and Health Paper. (1977)-. Monographic series. English. Irregular. Price varies per volume. Food Agriculture Organization (FAO) / Italy, GIPCI66 via Terme di Caracalla, 00100 Rome Italy. **Tel** 011 39 6 52252925, FAX 011 39 6 52253152. **(Subscription address:** UNIPUB, 4611 F Assembly Drive, Lanham MD 20706. **Tel** (800)274-4888, (301)459-7666.) Documents available from CASDDS.
 Ind/Abst Agrofor. Abstr.; Anim. Breed. Abstr.; Biodeter. Abstr.; Chem. Abstr.; Dairy Sci. Abstr.; Index Vet.; Nutr. Abstr. Rev., Ser. B, Live Feeds and Feed.; Pig News Inf.; Poult. Abstr.; World Agric. Econ. Rural Sociol. Abstr.

IT
FAO ANIMAL PRODUCTION AND HEALTH SERIES. **Main/Corp** Food and Agriculture Organization of the United Nations. **VFOAT** Animal Production and Health Series. (19??)-. Monographic series. English. Irregular. Price varies per volume. Food Agriculture Organization (FAO) / Italy, GIPCI66 via Terme di Caracalla, 00100 Rome Italy. **Tel** 011 39 6 52252925, FAX 011 39 6 52253152.
 Ind/Abst Index Vet.; Sug. Indus. Abstr.; Vet. Bull.

LC S ISSN 0739-9235 US
DD 630
FARMER STOCKMAN OF THE MIDWEST. See Agriculture.

KE
FARMING TODAY (NAIROBI, KENYA). See Agriculture-Dairy Industry.

ISSN 0380-352X CN
FEATHER FANCIER. (1945)-. Periodical. English. Eleven times a year (Jul./Aug. issue combined). 20.00Can$. Feather Fancier, Rural Route 5, Forest Ontario N0N 1J0 Canada. **Tel** (519)899-2364.

ISSN 1030-8474 AT
FEEDBACK (SYDNEY, N.S.W.). (FEEDBACK.). **Added/Corp** Aus-Meat (Firm). **VFOAT** Aus-Meat Feedback. Vol. 1, No. 4 (Aug. 1988)-. Trade Publication. English. Six times a year. Aus-Meat, Sydney NSW Australia. **Continues** Aus-Meat Feedback, 1030-8474.

ISSN 0961-978X UK
CEASED
FEEDS & FEEDING. See Agriculture-Feed Grain and Milling.

FR
FILIERES AVICOLES. (19??)-. Periodical. French. Eleven times a year. 440.74F France; 538.69F European Union; 550.00F other. Editions du Boisbaudry, BP 6359, 35036 Rennes Cedex France. **Tel** 011 33 99 322121. **Continues** L'Aviculteur.

ISSN 0430-6465 GW
FLEISCHFORSCHUNG UND PRAXIS. (1969)-. Periodical. German. Irregular. Verlag der Rheinhessischen, Druckwerkstatte Wormser, D-55232 Alzey Germany.

ISSN 0015-363X GW
CODEN FLEIA8
Pr Rev.
FLEISCHWIRTSCHAFT, DIE. [Fleischwirtschaft]. (1939)-. Trade Publication. German (English, French, Italian and Spanish). Twelve times a year. DM407.65. Deutscher Fachverlag GmbH, Verlagsgruppe, D-60264 Frankfurt Germany. **Tel** 011 49

Agriculture — Livestock

69 75951001, telex 411 862. Documents available from The Genuine Article, BIOSIS Document Express, CASDDS. **Continues** Fleischwarenindustrie.
Ind/Abst AGRICOLA; Anim. Breed. Abstr.; BioBusiness; Biocont. News Inf. (1991-); Biodeter. Abstr. (1991-); Biol. Abstr.; Chem. Abstr.; Curr. Cit.; Curr. Contents Agric. Biol. Environ. Sci.; Dairy Sci. Abstr.; EMBASE; Energy Res. Abstr.; Food Sci. Technol. Abstr.; Helminthol. Abstr. (19??-19??); Index Vet.; Int. Aerosp. Abstr.; Int. Packag. Abstr.; Key Word Index Wildl. Res.; Leis., Rec., Tour. Abstr.; Nutr. Abstr. Rev., Ser. B, Live Feeds and Feed.; Nutr. Abstr. Rev., Ser. A, Hum. Exp.; Pig News Inf.; Poult. Abstr.; Protozoolog. Abstr.; Res. Alert [Select. Cov.]; Rev. Med. Vet. Mycology; Rural Dev. Abstr.; SCISEARCH; Soc. Sci. Cit. Index [Select. Cov.]; Soyabean Abstr.; Vet. Bull.; World Agric. Econ. Rural Sociol. Abstr.

UK

UDC 636.323.3; 636.324.1
FLOCK BOOK OF DORSET HORN AND POLL DORSET SHEEP, THE. Main/Corp Dorset Horn and Poll Dorset Sheep Breeders' Association. **VFOAT** Dorset Horn and Poll Dorset Flock Book; Dorset Horn and Poll Dorset Sheep Breeders' Association Flock Book. English. One time a year. **Continues** Flock Book of Dorset Horn Sheep.

LC HD9433.U5 F55
DD 331.7

US

FLORIDA AGRICULTURAL STATISTICS. LIVESTOCK SUMMARY. See Agriculture-Abstracting, Bibliographies and Statistics.

ISSN 0015-3958
DD 637

US

FLORIDA CATTLEMAN AND LIVESTOCK JOURNAL, THE. [Fla. cattlem. livest.]. **Added/Corp** Florida State Cattlemen's Association. Florida Cattlemen's Association. (19??)-. Trade Publication. English. Twelve times a year. $5.00. Florida Cattlemens Association, PO Box 1403, Kissimmee FL 32742-1403. **ED** Donald E. Berry. **Ad Acc. Circ:** 7,231 (ctrl). **Continues** Florida Cattleman and Dairy Journal.
Desc: Provides information concerning cow-calf operations and other related livestock concerns.
Ind/Abst AGRICOLA.

LC S
ISSN 0015-4091
DD 630

US
CODEN FGRAAE

FLORIDA GROWER & RANCHER. See Agriculture.

US

FLORIDA LIVESTOCK ROUNDUP. Vol. 1 (1961)-. Government Publication. English. US Department of Agri Nass Publ Unt, 14th Independence Avenue SW/Room 5829, Washington DC 20250. **Tel** (202)447-4020.

ISSN 0225-0888
DD 381/.4163/0097123

CN

FOOT NOTES - BEEF AND SHEEP BRANCH (EDMONTON). See Business and Economics-Commerce.

LC HD9411 .U54A
ISSN 0164-1824
DD 664/.907/0973
UDC 637.5.04/.07

US

FOREIGN MEAT INSPECTION. Main/Corp United States. Dept. of Agriculture. Office of the Secretary. Government Publication. English. One time a year. Department of Agriculture / Foreign Agricultural Service, 14th Street and Independence Avenue SW, Washington DC 20250-1000. **Tel** (202)720-3935, FAX (202)720-7729.

LC SF967.B7 T49A
ISSN 0748-7754
DD 636.2/0894565

US

FOURTH QUARTER AND ANNUAL REPORT ON THE TEXAS BOVINE BRUCELLOSIS PROGRAM. Main/Corp Texas Animal Health Commission. **VFOAT** Annual Report on the Texas Bovine Brucellosis Program; Texas Bovine Brucellosis Program. (19??)-. English. One time a year. Texas Animal Health Commission, Sam Houston State Office Building, PO Box 12966, Austin TX 78711. **Tel** (512)475-4111. **ED** Joe Morris. **Circ:** 50 (ctrl).
Desc: Statistics on the current fiscal year Brucellosis program in the state of Texas. Includes relevant statistical data on each individual county in Texas.

ISSN 0532-582X

CN

FRANK GERSTEIN LECTURES, THE. Added/Corp York University (Toronto, Ont.). (1962)-. Monographic series. English. Irregular. Price varies per volume. CTR Publications, York University, 4700 Keele Street, Downsview Ontario M3J 1P3 Canada. **Tel** (416)889-6703.

ISSN 0164-3711
DD 598

US

GAME BIRD BREEDERS, AVICULTURISTS, ZOOLOGISTS AND CONSERVATIONISTS GAZETTE. [Game bird breed. avic. zool. conserv. gaz.]. **Added/Corp** Pheasant Trust, England. American Game Bird Breeders' Federation. **VFOAT** Gazette. Jan. (1970)-. Periodical. English. Twelve times a year. $20.00. Gazette, 1155 East 4780 South, Salt Lake City UT 84117. **Tel** (801)262-4852. **Continues** Game Bird Breeders, Aviculturists and Conservationists' Gazette.

LC SF15.C7 M55A

CK

GANADERIA. Main/Corp Colombia. Ministerio de Agricultura. 1976/78-. Spanish. Ministerio de Agricultura, Oficina de Comunicaciones, Carrera 10 No 20-30, Bogota de Colombia.

ISSN 0433-1818
SZ
UDC 636.53
GARTEN UND KLEINTIERZUCHT. B : RASSEGEFLUGELZUCHTER. [Gart. Kleintierzucht. Ausg. B. Rassegeflugelzuchter.]. Vol. 1 (Oct. 1962)-. Periodical. German. Twenty-six times a year. Deutscher Judo Verband, Redaktion Ippon Segewaldweg 40, D-12557 Berlin Germany. **Tel** 011 49 711 210770, telex 051 678.

ISSN 0433-1834
SZ
UDC 636.5/.6
GARTEN UND KLEINTIERZUCHT. D : KLEINTIERZUCHTER. [Gart. Kleintierzucht. Ausg. D Kleintierzucht.]. Periodical. German. Twenty-six times a year. Deutscher Judo Verband, Redaktion Ippon Segewaldweg 40, D-12557 Berlin Germany. **Tel** 011 49 711 210770, telex 051 678.

LC SF
ISSN 1157-4569
DD 636
FR
UDC 63
GDS INFO PARIS. (GDS INFO.). **VFOAT** Groupements de Defense Sanitaire du Betail Info (Paris). (1990)-. Periodical. French. **Continues** GDS Informations Sanitaires, 0295-5083.
Ind/Abst Index Vet.; Vet. Bull.

NE

UDC 636.39(492)
GEITEHOUDER, DE. Vol. 20, No. 2 (Feb. 1957)-. Periodical. Dutch. Twelve times a year. DE Geitehouder, Markt 19 PO Box 6, Kruiningen Netherlands. **Tel** (0)1130-2110. **ED** M A C Zwetslsot. Index available. cum. index. Bk Rev. **Ad Acc. Circ:** 2,100 (ctrl).
Desc: Journal of the Dutch organization for goatbreeding.

ISSN 0703-8356
DD 636.2/32
CN
UDC 636.234(71)
GELBVIEH EYEOPENER. Vol. 1 (July 1976)-. Periodical. English. Six times a year. Free. Canadian Gelbvieh Association, 120 310 Ninth Avenue SW, Calgary Alta T2P 1K5. ctrl circ.

LC SF105 .A66
DD 636.08/2/05
FR
NLM W1; GE293T **CODEN** GSEVE9
Pr Rev.
GENETICS, SELECTION, EVOLUTION.
See Biology-Genetics.

ISSN 0744-4451
US
GEORGIA CATTLEMAN. [Georgia cattlem.]. **Added/Corp** Georgia Cattlemen's Association. (19??)-. Periodical. English. Twelve times a year. $20.00. Georgia Cattlemens Association, PO Box 11307, Macon GA 31212. **Tel** (912)474-6560.
Ind/Abst AGRICOLA [Select. Cov.].

ISSN 0367-4916
PL
CODEN GOMIAC
GOSPODARKA MIESNA. [Gosp. mies.]. Academic Scholarly Publication. Polish. Twelve times a year. $90.00. (**Subscription address:** Ars Polona-Ruch, PO Box 1001, Krakowskie Przedmiescie 7, 00-068 Warsaw Poland. **Tel** 011 48 22 261201.) Documents available from CASDDS.
Ind/Abst AGRICOLA; Chem. Abstr.

PL

GOSPODARSKI CHOW ZWIERZAT. No. 1 (Jan. 1976)-. Periodical. Polish. Twelve times a year. (**Subscription address:** Ars Polona-Ruch, PO Box 1001, Krakowskie Przedmiescie 7, 00-068 Warsaw Poland. **Tel** 011 48 22 261201.)

SA

UDC 636.38(680)
GOUE VAG. VFOAT Golden Fleece. Vol. 1, No. 3 (May 1971)-. Periodical. Afrikaans (English). Twelve times a year. R9.60 South Africa; $4.76 US. South Africa Wool Board, Private Bag X245, Pretoria 0001 South Africa. **Tel** 011 44 12 281711, FAX 011 44 12 284616, telex 322151. **ED** Ona Viljoen. **Ad Acc. Circ:** 32,244 (ctrl).
Desc: Main purpose is to keep South African woolgrowers informed on sheep and wool matters-locally and internationally.
Ind/Abst Text. Technol. Dig.

ISSN 0744-5008
DD 636
US
UDC 636.2
GREAT AMERICAN COW TRADER, THE. [Great Am. cow trader]. **VFOAT** Cow Trader. (19??)-. Periodical. English. One time a week. $4.00. The Great American Cow Trader, 108 North Reed Street, Columbia KY 42728.

ISSN 0017-5110
DD 338
US
GUERNSEY BREEDERS' JOURNAL. [Guernsey breed. j.]. **Added/Corp** American Guernsey Cattle Club. American Guernsey Association. Vol. 1, (Jan. 1910)-. Trade Publication. English. Ten times a year (monthly except Jan. and July). $15.00. American Guernsey Association, PO Box 666, 7614 State Ridge Boulevard, Reynoldsburg OH 43068. **Tel** (614)864-2409. **ED** Sheri Spelman and Becky Goodwin. **Ad Acc. Circ:** 1900. available on microfilm and microfiche from University Microfilms International (UMI).
Desc: Production, management, shows, and sales of Guernsey cattle.

UK

GUERNSEY BREEDERS' JOURNAL. Added/Corp English Guernsey Cattle Society. Vol. 1, No. 1 (New Series) (Summer 1947)-. Periodical. English. Two times a year. English Guernsey Cattle Society, Bury Farm Pednor Road Chesham, Buckinghamshire HP5 2LA United Kingdom. **Tel** CHESHAM 774114. **ED** M. James. **Ad Acc. Circ:** 2,000 (ctrl).
Desc: Breed Society members and interested parties. Journal giving information on the Guernsey breed.

ISSN 0017-5552
DD 636
US
GULF COAST CATTLEMAN. [Gulf coast cattlem.]. **Added/Corp** Louisiana Cattlemen's Association. Vol. 14, No. 4 (June 1948)-. Trade Publication. English. Twelve times a year. Free on request. Gulf Coast Publishing Corporation, 11201 Morning Court, San Antonio TX 78213. **Tel** (210)344-8300, FAX (512)344-4258. **ED** Ralph Means (512)344-8300. **Ad Acc. Circ:** 14,500 (ctrl). **Separated from** Coastal Cattleman.
Desc: Devoted to the improvement of breeding, feeding and marketing of livestock in the southern United States.

LC SF83.J32 Y358a
ISSN 0389-0724
JA
GYOMU HOKOKU. Main/Corp Yamaguchi-Ken Chikusan Shikenjo. (19??)-. Japanese. Yamaguchi-ken Chikusan, Shikenjo Isa-Cho Mine-shi, Yamaguchi-ken 759-22 Japan.

LC SF1 .H36a
ISSN 0367-5807
KO
CCC
CODEN HGCHAG
Pr Rev.
HAN'GUK CHUKSAN HAKHOE CHI. See Zoology.

LC SF1 .H37
KO
HANGUK CHUKSAN KWAHAK YONGU POGO. VFOAT Annual Research Reports of the Korea Institute of Animal Sciences. Vol. 1 (1981)-. Periodical. English (Korean). One time a year. Hanguk Chuksan Kwahak Yonguso, 129 Ami-ri Pubal-Myon Ich On-gun, Kyonggi-do Korea 172-18.

ISSN 0846-4782
CN
DD 354.710082/336
HEALTH OF ANIMALS. [Health anim.]. **Added/Corp** Agriculture Canada. Canada. Health of Animals Directorate. **VFOAT** Hygiene Veterinaire. (1987)-. Government Publication. English (French). Free on request. Agriculture Canada, Communications Branch, Ottawa Ontario K1A 0C7 Canada. **Continues** National Animal Health Program (Canada) Annual Review., 0839-8143.

US

HEIFER INTERNATIONAL EXCHANGE, THE. Added/Corp Heifer Project. **VFOAT** Exchange; Heifer Project Exchange. (19??)-. Periodical. English. Four times a year (Jan., Apr., July, Oct.). Heifer Project International, PO Box 808, Little Rock AR 72203. **Tel** (501)376-6836. **ED** Jerry Aaker. ctrl circ.
Desc: Technical articles and resources for livestock development field workers and planners.

SP

HENS REVISTA TECHNICO-GANADERA. Added/Corp Piensos Hens, S.A. **VFOAT** Revista Technico-Ganadera. **VAT**

Agriculture — Livestock

Revista Tecnico Ganadera. Vol. 11, No. 112 (Feb. 1970)-. Periodical. Spanish. Twelve times a year. **Continues** *El Avicultur Hens.*

UK
HERD BOOK - BRITISH GOAT SOCIETY.
See Agriculture-Dairy Industry.

NZ
HERD BOOK OF THE NEW ZEALAND HEREFORD CATTLE BREEDERS' ASSOCIATION, THE. Main/Corp New Zealand
Hereford Cattle Breeders' Association. **VFOAT** Hereford Herd Book, N.Z. Vol. 1 (1899)-. Trade Publication. English. One time a year (Nov/Dec). 39.38NZ$. New Zealand Hereford Association Inc, PO Box 503, Fielding New Zealand. **Tel** 011 64 6 3234484, FAX 011 64 6 3233878. **Circ:** 450 (ctrl).

ISSN 0195-1947
US

UDC 636.481

SUSPENDED
HOG DIGEST. Periodical. English. Six times a year.
$12.00. Beef Digest Rawson Publication, PO Box 30109, Columbia MO 65205. **Tel** (314)474-2646.

ISSN 0380-3651
CN
DD 380.1/41/6400971
HOG MARKET PLACE QUARTERLY.
Added/Corp Ontario Pork Producers Marketing Board. **VFOAT** Market Place Quarterly; Market Place. (1???)-. Periodical. English. Four times a year (Mar., June, Sept., Dec.). 11.21Can$. Agricultural Publishing Company Ltd, 100 Broadview Avenue, Suite 402, Toronto Ontario M4M 3H3 Canada. **Tel** (416)463-8306. **ED** John Phillips. **Ad Acc. Circ:** 20,000.
Desc: A hog magazine for Ontario pork producers.

US
HOGS AND PIGS / IOWA CROP AND LIVESTOCK REPORTING SERVICE.
Added/Corp Iowa Crop and Livestock Reporting Service. United States. Dept. of Agriculture. Economics, Statistics and Cooperatives Service. Iowa. Agricultural Statistics Division. (Dec. 1942)-. Periodical. English. Four times a year. Free. The Service, Full Depository, 707 Savings and Loan Building, Des Moines IA 50309.
Desc: Hogs and pigs on farms, sows farrowing and pigs saved, in Iowa, with summaries for surrounding states.

LC WMLC L 83/1169
ISSN 0565-2189
DD 636
HOGS AND PIGS (WASHINGTON, D.C.).
(HOGS AND PIGS.). [Hogs pigs]. **Added/Corp** United States. Crop Reporting Board. United States. Agricultural Statistics Board. (1968)-. Government Publication. English. Four times a year. $20.00. US Department of Agriculture, 14th Street and Independence Avenue SW, Washington DC 20250. **Tel** (202)720-5457. (**Subscription address:** Superintendent of Documents, US Government Printing Office, Washington DC 20402.) Documents available from Documents on Demand. **Continues** *Pig Crop Report.*
Ind/Abst Am. Stat. Index.

ISSN 1056-1374
DD 636
US
HOGS TODAY. [Hogs today]. (198?)-. Periodical.
English. Ten times a year. Farm Journal Inc, 230 West Washington Square, Philadelphia PA 19106. **Tel** (215)829-4700, (800)331-9310. **ED** Dean Houghton. **Ad Acc, Adv Mgr:** Ray Evans, **Tel** (215) 829-4736. **Circ:** 101,000. **Continues** *Hog Extra.*
Desc: Provides production, pricing, regulation, health and nutrition information and other information to pork producers.

LC SF198
ISSN 1380-2879
DD 636.2
NE
UDC 636.2
●HOLSTEIN INTERNATIONAL NEDERLANDSE ED. (HOLSTEIN
INTERNATIONAL). [Holstein int. Ned. ed.]. (1994)-. Periodical. Dutch. Twelve times a year. Holstein International BV, Witewei 2, 9051 TB Stiens Netherlands. **Tel** 011 31 51094100, FAX 011 31 18333967. **Ad Acc**.

ISSN 0823-6410
CN
DD 636.2/006/071233
UDC 636.2(71)
HOME QUARTER. [Home quart.]. Vol. 1, No. 1
(Autumn '81)-. Periodical. English. Four times a year. $25.00. Stockmen's Memorial Foundation, Alberta T2E 7A6 Canada. **Tel** (403)250-7529. **ED** Donna J Wallace. **Circ:** 1,200 (ctrl).
Desc: Newsletter of the Stockmen's Memorial Foundation. Emphasizes the history, economics and techniques of the livestock industry in Western Canada.

CH
HSU CHAN YEN CHIU. JOURNAL OF THE TAIWAN LIVESTOCK RESEARCH.
Added/Corp Tai-wan Sheng hsu Chan Shih yen so. **VFOAT** Journal of the Taiwan Livestock Research. Vol. 7, No. 2 (Dec. 1974)-. Periodical. Multiple languages (Chinese and English). Two times a year. Livestock Research Institute, Tainan Taiwan.
Ind/Abst Field Crop Abstr.; Maize Abstr.; Nutr. Abstr. Rev., Ser. B, Live Feeds and Feed.; Pig News Inf.; Plant Breed. Abstr.; Plant Grow. Reg. Abstr.; Postharvest News Inf.; Poult. Abstr.

LC SF604 .H75
ISSN 0529-5127
DD 636.089/05
CC
HSU MU SHOU I HSUEH PAO = ACTA VETERINARIA ET ZOOTECHNICA SINICA. See Veterinary Sciences.

ISSN 0046-8339
SW
HUSDJUR : SVENSK HUSDJURSSKOTSEL, LADUGARDEN.
Added/Corp Svensk HusdjursskËotsel. (1968)-. Periodical. Swedish. Twelve times a year. $33.66. Tidningen Husdjur, S 631 84 Eskilstuna Sweden. **Continues** *Svensk Husdjursskotel, Ladugarden.*
Ind/Abst Anim. Breed. Abstr.; Dairy Sci. Abstr.; Nutr. Abstr. Rev., Ser. B, Live Feeds and Feed.; Pig News Inf.; Poult. Abstr.

ISSN 1041-1682
DD 630
US
IDAHO FARMER-STOCKMAN. [Ida.
farmer-stockm.]. **VFOAT** Idaho Farmer Stockman. Vol. 89, No. 13 (July 1, 1971)-. Trade Publication. English. Eleven times a year. $19.95. Western Farmer Stockman, Box 2160, Spokane WA 99210. **Tel** (509)459-5361, FAX (509)459-5102. **ED** T. D. Henry. **Ad Acc. Circ:** 16,752 (ctrl). **Continues** *Idaho Farmer.*
Desc: General news and information for farmers, ranchers, and agriculture-oriented businesses.

US
IDAHO WOOL GROWER'S BULLETIN.
(19??)-. Bulletin. English. Twelve times a year. Free to members; $20.00 membership. Idaho Wool Growers Association, Box 2596, Boise ID 83701. **Tel** (208)344-2271. **Ad Acc. Circ:** 1,300 (ctrl).

LC SF83.A35 I57
ISSN 1014-9015
ET
ILCA ... ANNUAL REPORT AND PROGRAMME HIGHLIGHTS. [ILCA ...: annu.
rep. programme highlights]. **Main/Corp** International Livestock Centre for Africa. **VFOAT** ILCA Annual Report and Programme Highlights. (1990)-. English. One time a year. Free. International Livestock Centre for Africa, PO Box 5689, Addis Ababa Ethiopia. **Circ:** 7,500. **Continues** *International Livestock Centre for Africa. ILCA Annual Report, 0255-0040.*

ISSN 0255-0008
ET
ILCA BULLETIN. [ILCA bull.]. VFOAT International
Livestock Centre for Africa Bulletin. (1978)-. Bulletin. English. Four times a year.
Ind/Abst For. Abstr.; Helminthol. Abstr. (1991-).

ISSN 0257-8409
ET
ILCA RESEARCH REPORT. [ILCA res. rep.].
Added/Corp International Livestock Centre for Africa. **VAT** International Livestock Centre for Africa Research Report. (198?)-. Monographic series. English (French). Irregular. Price varies per volume. ILCA Research Report, PO Box 5689, Addis Ababa Ethiopia. **Ad Acc. Circ:** 1,000 (ctrl). available on microfiche. **Formed by the union of** *ILCA Systems Study* **and** *ILCA Monograph.*
Desc: Related major research findings in the field of agriculture, especially in livestock farming in Africa south of the Sahara.
Ind/Abst Agrofor. Abstr.; Anim. Breed. Abstr.; Helminthol. Abstr.; Index Vet.; Maize Abstr.; World Agric. Econ. Rural Sociol. Abstr.

ISSN 0745-8525
US
ILLINOIS GRAIN & LIVESTOCK MARKET NEWS. See Agriculture-Feed Grain and
Milling.

LC Z5071
ISSN 0568-2800
DD 016.63
UK
INDEX OF CURRENT RESEARCH ON PIGS. Added/Corp Commonwealth Agricultural
Bureaux. National Institute for Research in Dairying (Great Britain) Agricultural Research Council (Great Britain). (19??)-. Abstracting/Indexing Service. English. One time a year (published in Feb.) $53.00. CAB International Centre, Wallingford, Oxfordshire OX10 8DE United Kingdom. **Tel** 011 44 1491 832111, FAX 011 44 1491 833508, telex 847964 COMAGG G. **Ad Acc**. available on an online database from Knight-Ridder Information, Inc.; Ovid Technologies, Inc.; European Space Agency; DIALOG; DIMDI; CISTI; and BRS. Documents available from BLDSC.
Desc: Contains a list of research projects currently in progress and a list of publications which appeared during the previous year.
Ind/Abst Anim. Breed. Abstr.; Nutr. Abstr. Rev., Ser. B, Live Feeds and Feed.; Nutr. Abstr. Rev., Ser. A, Hum. Exp.; Protozoolog. Abstr.

ISSN 0970-3209
II
CODEN IJNUEA
INDIAN JOURNAL OF ANIMAL NUTRITION. [Indian j. anim. nutr.]. Added/Corp
Animal Nutrition Society of India. (1984)-. Periodical. English. Four times a year. $70.00 one-year; $120.00 two-year; $160.00 three-year. Agricultural Research Communication Centre, Sadar Karnal 132001, Haryana India. **Tel** 011 91 3036. Documents available from BIOSIS Document Express.
Desc: Publishes original research papers and short notes on all aspects of animal nutrition.
Ind/Abst AGRICOLA; Agrofor. Abstr. (1991-); Anim. Breed. Abstr.; Biodeter. Abstr. (1991-); Biol. Abstr. (1987-); Dairy Sci. Abstr.; Field Crop Abstr.; Food Sci. Technol. Abstr.; For. Prod. Abstr. (1991-); For. Abstr.; Grass. Forage Abstr.; Hortic. Abstr.; Index Vet.; Indian Sci. Abstr.; Maize Abstr.; Nutr. Abstr. Rev., Ser. B, Live Feeds and Feed.; Pig News Inf.; Plant Breed. Abstr.; Postharvest News Inf.; Poult. Abstr.; Protozoolog. Abstr.; Rev. Agric. Entomol.; Rev. Med. Vet. Mycology; Rice Abstr.; Seed Abstr.; Soils Fert.; Sorghum Mill. Abstr.; Soyabean Abstr.; Sug. Indus. Abstr.; Weed Abstr.; Wheat Barley Trit. Abstr.

II
INDIAN JOURNAL OF ANIMAL PRODUCTION AND MANAGEMENT. Vol.
1, No. 1 (Jan. 1985)-. Periodical. English. Four times a year. $50.00. Indian Society of Animal Production and Managament, Hisar India. (**Subscription address:** Prints India, 11 Darya Ganj, New Delhi 110002 India. **Tel** 011 91 11 3268645, FAX 011 91 11 3275542, telex 31-61087 PRIN-IN.)
Ind/Abst Anim. Breed. Abstr.; Curr. Cit.; Dairy Sci. Abstr.; Helminthol. Abstr. (1991-); Index Vet.; Nutr. Abstr. Rev., Ser. B, Live Feeds and Feed.; Pig News Inf.; Poult. Abstr.; Protozoolog. Abstr.; Rev. Med. Vet. Entomol.; Vet. Bull.; World Agric. Econ. Rural Sociol. Abstr.

LC SF1 .I54
ISSN 0367-6722
DD 636/.005
II
CODEN IALRBR
INDIAN JOURNAL OF ANIMAL RESEARCH. See Veterinary Sciences.

ISSN 0325-3414
AG
Pr Rev.
INDUSTRIA CARNICA LATINOAMERICANA, LA. (19??)-. Periodical.
Spanish. Four times a year. $45.00. Publitec S A E C, Y M Corrientes 1485-3-C, 1042 Buenos Aires Argentina. **Tel** FAX 054-1-401584, telex 24568 BIOSUR AR. **ED** Ana M Galibert. **Bk Rev. Ad Acc. Adv Mgr:** Nestor Galibert. **Circ:** 5,000 (ctrl).
Desc: Science and technology of the meat industry.

ISSN 0279-7771
US
Pr Rev.
INDUSTRIA PORCINA. Vol. 1, No. 1 (Jan.-Feb.
1981)-. Periodical. Spanish. Six times a year. $36.00. Watt Publishing Company, 122 South Wesley Avenue, Mount Morris IL 61054. **Tel** (815)734-4171, FAX (815)734-7021, telex TWX 910-642-2891. **ED** Peter Best (editor's phone: 44-730-261951). **Ad Acc, Adv Mgr:** Clay Schreiber. **Circ:** 9,000 (ctrl). **Continues in part** *Pig International, 0191-8834.*
Desc: Emphasis on the areas of production, disease control, husbandry and marketing.

LC S671 .K8 SF1
GW
UDC 636
INFORMATIONEN. Main/Corp
Arbeitsgemeinschaft Technik und Bau in der Tierhaltung. German.

ISSN 0020-0778
IT
INFORMATORE ZOOTECNICO. [Inf.
zootec.]. **Added/Corp** Italy. Direzione Generale della Produzione Agricola. Vol. 1 (1954)-. Periodical. Italian. Twelve times a year. L47010. Edagricole, PO Box 2157, 40100 Bologna Italy. **Tel** 011 39 51 492211 Ext. 22, FAX 011 39 51 493660, telex 510336 EDAGRI.
Ind/Abst AGRICOLA; Nutr. Abstr. Rev., Ser. B, Live Feeds and Feed.; Nutr. Abstr. Rev., Ser. A, Hum. Exp.

US
INSTITUTIONAL MEAT PURCHASE SPECIFICATIONS. Main/Corp United States.
Agricultural Marketing Service. Livestock Division. (1???)-. Government Publication. English. Irregular. $25.00. US Department of Agriculture, 14th Street and Independence Avenue SW, Washington DC 20250. **Tel** (202)720-5457.

II
INTEGRATED SAMPLE SURVEY FOR ESTIMATION OF ANIMAL PRODUCTS [MICROFORM] : MILK, WOOL, EGGS, AND MEAT / HIMACHAL PRADESH GOVERNMENT, ANIMAL HUSBANDRY DEPARTMENT. Added/Corp Himachal Pradesh
(India). Animal Husbandry Dept. (1992)-. English (Hindi).

US
UDC 636.39
INTERNATIONAL GOAT ASSOCIATION NEWSLETTER. Vol. 1, No. 1 (Sept. 1984)-. Newsletter. English. $5.00. International Goat Association, 11211 North 84th Street, Scottsdale AZ 85260. **Tel** (602)991-0821. **ED** George F W Haenlein (editor's address: 028 Agriculture Hall, Department of Animal Science, University of Delaware, Newark DE 19711).

ISSN 0970-2857
II
CCC
NLM W1; IN7654J **CODEN** IASCEK
INTERNATIONAL JOURNAL OF ANIMAL SCIENCES. [Int. J. Anim. Sci.]. Vol. 2, No. 2 (July 1987)-. Periodical. English. Two times a year. $100.00. Nitasha Publications, Sonepat, Haryana India. **(Subscription address:** Prints India, 11 Darya Ganj, New Delhi 110002 India. **Tel** 011 91 11 3268645, FAX 011 91 11 3275542, telex 31-61087 PRIN-IN.) Documents available from CASDDS. ***Continues*** *Farm Animals, 0970-0803.*
Ind/Abst Agrofor. Abstr.; Anim. Breed. Abstr.; Biodeter. Abstr.; Chem. Abstr. (1987-1988); Curr. Cit.; Dairy Sci. Abstr.; Grass. Forage Abstr.; Helminthol. Abstr. (1991-); Index Vet.; Nutr. Abstr. Rev., Ser. B, Live Feeds and Feed.; PESTDOC; Poult. Abstr.; Protozoolog. Abstr.; Rev. Med. Vet. Entomol.; Rice Abstr.; Vet. Bull.; Wheat Barley Trit. Abstr.

ISSN 0744-3951
US
UDC 636.342.5
INTERNATIONAL LIMOUSIN JOURNAL. [Int. Limousin j.]. Vol. 1 (May 1941)-. Periodical. English. Twelve times a year. Limousin World Inc, 1241 South 11th Street, Yukon OK 73099-5305.

ISSN 0263-2217
UK
INTERNATIONAL MEAT MARKET REVIEW. **Added/Corp** MLC Economic Information Service. **VFOAT** Meat Market Review. No. 1 (May 1987)-. Trade Publication. English. Two times a year. $136.89. Meat & Livestock Commission / Economic Service Department, PO Box 44, Winterhill House, Milton Keynes MK6 1AX United Kingdom. **Tel** 011 44 1908 677577, FAX 011 44 1908 609221, telex 82227. **Circ:** 800. ***Continues*** *International Market Review.*
Ind/Abst World Agric. Econ. Rural Sociol. Abstr.

ISSN 0963-5866
DD 636.4 UK
INTERNATIONAL PIG TOPICS. [Int. pig top.]. (1990)-. Trade Publication. English. Eight times a year. $50.00. Positive Action Publishers Ltd., PO Box 4, Driffield, North Humberside YO25 9DJ United Kingdom. **Tel** 011 44 1377 241724, FAX 011 44 1377 241910. **ED** Brent Roach. **Circ:** 20,000.
Desc: Technical magazine for pig producers and breeders.

US
INTERNATIONAL PIGLETTER. **Added/Corp** Pig World, Inc. **VFOAT** Pigletter; International Piglitter. Vol. 1, No. 1 (Mar. 1981)-. Periodical. English. Twelve times a year. $85.00. Pig World Inc., PO Box 21505, St Paul MN 55121-0505. **Tel** (612)454-5928, FAX (612)688-7602. Index available.

ISSN 0213-5035
SP
CODEN IAPAEX
INVESTIGACION AGRARIA. PRODUCCION Y SANIDAD ANIMALES. [Investig. agrar., Prod. Sanid. anim.]. **Added/Corp** Instituto Nacional de Investigaciones Agrarias. **VFOAT** Produccion y Sanidad Animales. Vol. 1 (April/Aug. 1986)-. Periodical. Spanish (summaries and/or abstracts in English and French). Three times a year. $84.38. Instituto Nacional de Investigaciones Agrarias, C. Jose Abascal 56, 28003 Madrid Spain. **Tel** 011 34 1 3473906, FAX (91)4423587, telex 48989 INIA E. **(Subscription address:** CIT / Inia Biblioteca, CRT Coruna KM 7, Jose L. Bernabe, 28040 Madrid Spain.) **Bk Rev. Circ:** 1,750 (ctrl). Documents available from BIOSIS Document Express. ***Continues*** *Anales del Instituto Nacional de Investigaciones Agrarias. Serie Ganadera.*
Ind/Abst AgBiotech News Inf.; Agric. Eng. Abstr. (1991-); Anim. Breed. Abstr.; Biol. Abstr.; Dairy Sci. Abstr.; Index Vet.; Nutr. Abstr. Rev., Ser. B, Live Feeds and Feed.; Soyabean Abstr.; Vet. Bull.

ISSN 0134-2681
RU
NLM W1 ZH323 **CODEN** INTVD2
ITOGI NAUKI I TEHNIKI - VSESOUZNYJ INSTITUT NAUCNOJ I TEHNICESKOJ INFORMACII. SERIA ZIVOTNOVODSTVO I VETERINARIJA. See Veterinary Sciences.

LC SF95 .N47A
NE
JAARSTATISTIEK VAN DE VEEVOEDERS. **Main/Corp** Netherlands (Kingdom, 1815-). Ministerie Van Landbouw en Visserij. Directie Algemene Zaken. Afdeling Statistiek en Documentatie. (19??)-. Dutch. Ministere Van Landbouw en Visserij, 1E Van Den Boschstraat 4, S-Gravenhage Netherlands.

GW
JAHRBUCH FUER DIE GEFLUGELWIRTSCHAFT. German. One time a year. Verlag Eugen Ulmer, Postfach 700561, D-70574 Stuttgart Germany. **Tel** 011 49 711 4507108, FAX 011 49 711 4507120, telex 7-23634.

DD 343/.436/076 AU
JAHRESBERICHT DER VIEH- UND FLEISCHKOMMISSION BEIM BUNDESMINISTERIUM FUER LAND- UND FORSTWIRTSCHAFT. See Food and Food Industry.

JA
JAPANESE JOURNAL OF SWINE HUSBANDRY RESEARCH. (19??)-. English. Japanese Society of Swine Husbandry, 1 37 20 Yoyogi, Shibuya Ku Tokyo 151 Japan.

ISSN 0021-5953
DD 637 US
JERSEY JOURNAL. [Jersey j.]. **Added/Corp** American Jersey Cattle Club. National All-Jersey Inc. Vol. 1 (Oct. 5, 1953)-. Trade Publication. English. Twelve times a year. $15.00. American Jersey Cattle Association, 6486 East Main Street, Reynoldsburg OH 43068-2362. **Tel** (614)861-3636, FAX (614)861-8040. **ED** Lynn G. Bell. Index available (bound in issue). cum. index. **Ad Acc, Adv Mgr:** Kim Billman, **Tel** (614)861-3636. **Circ:** 4,200 (ctrl). available on microfilm from University Microfilms International (UMI). ***Absorbed*** *Jersey Bulletin (1937).*
Desc: Articles and advertisements relating to the Jersey dairy cattle industry.

UK
UDC 636.224.3(410)
JERSEY / THE JERSEY CATTLE SOCIETY OF THE UNITED KINGDOM, THE. No. 107 (New Series)- Winter 1970/71. Periodical. English. Four times a year.
Ind/Abst Dairy Sci. Abstr.

ISSN 0332-0588
DD 630 IE
JOURNAL - IRISH GRASSLAND AND ANIMAL PRODUCTION ASSOCIATION. [J. - Ir. Grassl. Anim. Prod. Assoc.]. **VFOAT** Irish Grassland & Animal Production Association Journal. (1962)-. English. One time a year.
Ind/Abst Nutr. Abstr. Rev., Ser. B, Live Feeds and Feed.

ISSN 1230-1388
PL
CODEN JFESEA
JOURNAL OF ANIMAL AND FEED SCIENCES. [J. Amim. Feed Sci.]. **Added/Corp** Kielanowski Instytut Fizjologii i Zywienia Zwierzat. Vol. 1, No. 1 (1992)-. Periodical. English (summaries and/or abstracts in Polish). Four times a year. $40.00. Polska Akademia Nauk / Instytut Fizjologii i Zywienia Zwierzat im. Jana Kielanowskiego, (Polish Academy of Science / Kielanowski Institute of Animal Physiology and Nutrition), 00-110 Jablonna Poland. **Tel** 011 48 22 743222, FAX 011 48 22 742038. **(Subscription address:** Ars Polona-Ruch, PO Box 1001, Krakowskie Przedmiescie 7, 00-068 Warsaw Poland. **Tel** 011 48 22 261201.) ***Continues*** *Roczniki Nauk Rolniczych. Seria B. Zootechniczna, 0080-3669.*

ISSN 0189-0514
NR
JOURNAL OF ANIMAL PRODUCTION RESEARCH. **Added/Corp** National Animal Production Research Institute (Nigeria). Vol. 1, No. 1 (Jan. 1981)-. Periodical. English. Two times a year. $30.00. National Animal Production Research Institute, PMB 1096, Zaria Nigeria. **Tel** 011 234 69 50596.
Ind/Abst AGRICOLA [Full Cov.]; Anim. Breed. Abstr.; Food Sci. Technol. Abstr.; Index Vet.; Nutr. Abstr. Rev., Ser. B, Live Feeds and Feed.; Nutr. Abstr. Rev., Ser. A, Hum. Exp.; Pig News Inf.; Poult. Abstr.; Rev. Agric. Entomol.; Sorghum Mill. Abstr.; Sug. Indus. Abstr.

LC SF1 .J6 **ISSN** 0021-8812
DD 636.05 US
NLM W1 JO536H **CODEN** JANSAG
Pr Rev.
JOURNAL OF ANIMAL SCIENCE. [J. anim. sci.]. **Added/Corp** American Society of Animal Science. American Society of Animal Production. American Society of Animal Science. Abstracts. American Dairy Science Association. Combined annual meeting. American Society of Animal Science. ASAS section abstracts. Vol. 1 (Feb. 1942)-. Academic Scholarly Publication. English. Twelve times a year. $175.00. American Society of Animal Science, 309 West Clark Street, Champaign IL 61820-4690. **Tel** (217)356-3182, FAX (217)398-4119. **ED** Austin J. Lewis. Index available. cum. index. **Circ:** 7,500. available on microfilm and microfiche from University Microfilms International (UMI). Documents available from The Genuine Article, BIOSIS Document Express, UMI Article Clearinghouse, CASDDS. ***Supersedes*** *Record of Proceedings of the Annual Meeting - American Society of Animal Production, 0096-0837.*
Desc: Increases knowledge and understanding of animals, especially farm animals, and to improve care and productivity of animals, both commercially and in research.
Ind/Abst AgBiotech News Inf.; AGRICOLA [Full Cov.]; Agric. Eng. Abstr. (1991-); Agrofor. Abstr. (1991-); Anim. Behav. Abstr.; Anim. Breed. Abstr.; BioBusiness; Biol. Agric. Index; Biol. Abstr.; Chem. Abstr.; Chemorecept. Abstr.; Cot. Trop. Fibr. Abstr. Bibliogr.; CSA Neuro. Abstr.; Curr. Biotechnol.; Curr. Cit.; Curr. Contents Agric. Biol. Environ. Sci.; Dairy Sci. Abstr.; EMBASE; Energy Res. Abstr.; Environ. Period. Bibliogr. (?-?); Expand. Acad. Index (1992-); Fish Rev. (Jan. 1989-July 1992); Food Sci. Technol. Abstr.; For. Abstr.; Genet. Abstr.; Grass. Forage Abstr.; Helminthol. Abstr.; Index Med.; INIS Atomindex [Micro.]; Int. Aerosp. Abstr.; Maize Abstr.; Microbiol. Abstr. Sect. B (19??-19??); Newsp. Period. Abstr. (1992-); Nutr. Abstr. Rev., Ser. B, Live Feeds and Feed.; Nutr. Abstr. Rev., Ser. A, Hum. Exp.; Life Sci. Collect.; PESTDOC; Pig News Inf.; Plant Breed. Abstr.; Poult. Abstr.; Protozoolog. Abstr.; Ref. Upd. Basic Ed.; Ref. Upd. Deluxe Ed.; Res. Alert [Full Cov.]; Rev. Med. Vet. Entomol.; Rev. Med. Vet. Mycology; Rice Abstr.; Sci. Cit. Index; SCISEARCH; Small Anim. Abstr. Bibliogr.; Soc. Sci. Cit. Index [Select. Cov.]; Soils Fert.; Sorghum Mill. Abstr.; Soyabean Abstr.; Stat. Theory Method Abstr. (1959-1963); Sug. Indus. Abstr.; Wildl. Rev. (Jan. 1989-July 1992); World Agric. Econ. Rural Sociol. Abstr.

ISSN 0767-9874
FR
CODEN JRPRD9
JOURNEES DE LA RECHERCHE PORCINE EN FRANCE. [Journ. rech. porc. Fr.]. **Main/Corp** Institut National de la Recherche Agronomique. **Added/Corp** Institut Technique du Porc. (19??)-. Periodical. French. INRA Editions / Institut National de la Recherche Agronomique, Route de Saint-Cyr, 78026 Versailles Cedex France. **Tel** 011 33 1 30833406, FAX 011 33 1 30833449, telex INRAPUB 699 368 F.
Ind/Abst Dairy Sci. Abstr.; Nutr. Abstr. Rev., Ser. B, Live Feeds and Feed.; Pig News Inf.; Soyabean Abstr.; Wheat Barley Trit. Abstr.

ISSN 0022-8826
US
KANSAS STOCKMAN, THE. **Added/Corp** Kansas Livestock Association. (19??)-. Periodical. English. Ten times a year. $100.00. Kansas Livestock Association, 6031 Southwest 37th Street, Topeka KS 66614. **Tel** (913)273-5115, FAX (913)273-3399. **ED** Todd Domer. **Ad Acc, Adv Mgr:** Tammy Jauker. **Circ:** 6,900 (ctrl).
Desc: A news and feature magazine for the members of the Kansas Livestock Association. Articles provide information of interest to Kansas seedstock breeders, commerical cow-calf producers, stockers operators, cattle feeders and feedyards.

ISSN 0889-2857
DD 637 US
KETCH PEN, THE. [Ketch pen]. **Added/Corp** Washington Cattlemen's Association. (198?)-. Periodical. English. Nine times a year. Free to members. Washington Cattlemen's Association, 1720 Canyon Road, Ellensburg WA 98926. **Tel** (509) 925-9871, FAX (509) 925-3004. **ED** kent Labseck. **Ad Acc. Circ:** 2,800.
Desc: Informs beef cattle producers in Washington state of news and events of the Washington Cattlemen's Association.

TU
LALAHAN HAYVANCILIK ARASTIRMA ENSTITUSU DERGISI. **Added/Corp** Tarim Orman ve Koyisleri Bakanligi. Hayvancilik Arastirma Enstitusu Mudurlugu. **VFOAT** Journal of Lalahan Livestock Research Institute. (19??)-. Periodical. Turkish.
Ind/Abst Index Vet.; Nutr. Abstr. Rev., Ser. B, Live Feeds and Feed.; Vet. Bull.

LC HD9890.1 .N3
DD 338.1/763145 US
•**LAMB & WOOL GROWER.** See Fabrics and Textile Industries.

US
LAMB CROP & WOOL / IOWA CROP AND LIVESTOCK REPORTING SERVICE. **Added/Corp** Iowa Crop and Livestock Reporting Service. United States. Dept. of Agriculture. Economics, Statistics and Cooperatives Service. Iowa. Agricultural Statistics Division. (1976)-. Government Publication. English. Irregular. Free. US Department of Agriculture / National Agricultural Statistics Service (NASS), Room 5829 South Building, Washington DC

Agriculture —Livestock

20250. **Tel** (202)720-4020, FAX (314)875-5231. *Continues* Lamb Crop.
Desc: Gives figures for lamb crops and wool shorn for selected states. Some years include Iowa sheep inventory and marketing.

ISSN 0738-730X
US

LANCASTER LIVESTOCK REPORTER.
(1950)-. Periodical. English. Fifty times a year. $30.00. Lancaster Livestock Reporter, PO Box 4632, Lancaster PA 17604. **Tel** (717)569-7901, FAX (717)569-7901. **ED** Mildred M. Bunting. **Ad Acc. Circ:** 1,600.
Desc: Current livestock and dressed beef prices, market analysis, weekly average prices for livestock sold on Lancaster County markets and trend guide for eastern United States.

LC HD9433.G34 G47a
DD 338.1/762/00943
GW

●**LAND- UND FORSTWIRTSCHAFT, FISCHEREI. REIHE 4.2.1, SCHLACHTUNGEN UND FLEISCHERZEUGUNG. Added/Corp**
Germany. Statistisches Bundesamt. **VFOAT** Schlachtungen und Fleischerzeugung; Fachserie 3. (1993)-. German. Four times a year. W. Kohlhammer Verlag GmbH, Postfach 800430, D-70549 Stuttgart Germany. **Tel** 011 49 711 78630, FAX 011 49 711 7863430, telex 7-255820. *Continues* tLand- und Forstwirtschaft, Fischerei. Reihe 4.2.1, Schlachtungen und Fleischgewinnung.

ISSN 1069-1774
US

LARGE ANIMAL VETERINARY REPORT.
See Veterinary Sciences.

LC SF487.8.A1 L39
DD 338.1/77541/0973021
ISSN 1057-7866
US

LAYERS AND EGG PRODUCTION. [Layers egg prod.]. **Added/Corp** United States. Agricultural Statistics Board. **VFOAT** Eggs, Chickens, and Turkey Series Annual Summary ... By Months December 1 ... Inventory Numbers. (1984/1985)-. Government Publication. English. One time a year (January). $1.75. US Department of Agriculture / National Agricultural Statistics Service (NASS), Room 5829 South Building, Washington DC 20250. **Tel** (202)720-4020, FAX (314)875-5231. available on microfiche (Vols. for 1984/85- distributed to depository libraries). *Continues* Eggs, Chickens, and Turkey Series. Layers and Egg Production.

ISSN 0245-7695
FR

UDC 636
LIMOUSIN ELEVAGE. (1971)-. Periodical. French. Twelve times a year. Nouvelle Societe de Presse, La Valeyrie, 19330 St. Germain Vrgnes France. **Tel** 011 33 1 55295999.

ISSN 0381-5552
CN

DD 636.2/42
LIMOUSIN LEADER, THE. [Limousin lead.]. Vol. 1 (April 1974)-. Trade Publication. English. Ten times a year (July/Aug. & Sept./Oct. issues combined). 20.01Can$. Limousin Leader, 221 18th Street Southeast, North Entrance, Calgary Alberta T2E 6J5 Canada. **Tel** (403)291-6770. Index available. **Bk Rev. Ad Acc. Circ:** 3,000 (ctrl).
Desc: The national voice of the Canadian Limousin breeder. It carries news, advertising, and editorials on the breed.

ISSN 8750-2127
US

DD 636
LIMOUSIN WORLD. Added/Corp North American Limousin Foundation. **VFOAT** World. Vol. 1, No. 1 (Oct. 1983)-. Periodical. English. Eleven times a year (monthly except June). $22.00. Limousin World Inc, 1241 South Eleventh Street, Yukon OK 73099-5305. **Tel** (405)350-0040. **ED** Wes Ishmael. **Circ:** 10,500.
Desc: Devotes to the promotion and advancement of the Limousin breed of cattle.

UK

UDC 636.321.38
LISCOMBE SHEEP BULLETIN. No. 1-. Bulletin. English. Price varies per volume.

ISSN 0970-3004
II

LIVESTOCK ADVISER. [Livest. advis.]. Vol 1 (Jan. 1976)-. Periodical. English. Twelve times a year. $30.00. Livestock Adviser, Bangalore India. **(Subscription address:** Prints India, 11 Darya Ganj, New Delhi 110002 India. **Tel** 011 91 11 3268645, FAX 011 91 11 3275542, telex 31-61087 PRIN-IN.)
Ind/Abst Agrofor. Abstr. (1991)-; Anim. Breed. Abstr.; Curr. Cit.; Dairy Sci. Abstr.; Food Sci. Technol. Abstr.; For. Prod. Abstr. (1991)-; For. Abstr.; Grass. Forage Abstr.; Helminthol. Abstr. (1991)-; Maize Abstr.; Nutr. Abstr. Rev.; Ser. B, Live Feeds and Feed.; Life Sci. Collect. (1985-); Pig News Inf.; Rev. Med. Vet. Entomol.; Soils Fert.; Sug. Indus. Abstr.; Wheat Barley Trit. Abstr.; World Agric. Econ. Rural Sociol. Abstr.

LC Z5071
DD 016.63
ISSN 0812-2598
AT

LIVESTOCK AND LIVESTOCK PRODUCTS, AUSTRALIA. See Agriculture-Abstracting, Bibliographies and Statistics.

AT

LIVESTOCK AND LIVESTOCK PRODUCTS : SOUTH AUSTRALIA. See Agriculture-Abstracting, Bibliographies and Statistics.

LC HD9428.A83 W465
DD 338.1/76/009941
AT

LIVESTOCK AND LIVESTOCK PRODUCTS, WESTERN AUSTRALIA / AUSTRALIAN BUREAU OF STATISTICS, WESTERN AUSTRALIAN OFFICE. See Agriculture-Abstracting, Bibliographies and Statistics.

US

LIVESTOCK FACT SHEET. Main/Corp
California. University, Berkeley. Agricultural Extension Service. No. 18 (April 1974)-. Periodical. English. University of California at Berkeley / Agriculture, Agriculture Extension Service, Berkeley CA 94720.

ISSN 0024-5208
US

DD 338
LIVESTOCK MARKET DIGEST. [Livest. mark. dig.]. (1950). Periodical. English. One time a week. $20.00 (one-year); $30.00 (two-year). Livestock Market Digest Inc, PO Box 7458, Albuquerque NM 87104. **Tel** (505)243-9515. **ED** Carol Wilson. **Bk Rev. Ad Acc. Circ:** 48,500 (ctrl).
Desc: National journal for livestock producers and grassroots stockmen involved in production of forage, or the feeding and marketing of livestock and other agricultural related activities.

ISSN 1061-4001
US

LIVESTOCK MARKET NEWS (AUSTIN, TEX.). (LIVESTOCK MARKET NEWS.). **Added/Corp**
Texas. Dept. of Agriculture. (19??)-. Periodical. English. One time a week. $20.00. Texas Department of Agriculture, 18th & Congress Street, PO Box 12847, Austin TX 78711. **Tel** (512)463-7435, FAX (512)463-7643. *Continues* Texas. Dept. of Agriculture. Texas Livestock Market News, 0199-7041.

ISSN 0068-7324
CN

DD 338.1/76/00971
LIVESTOCK MARKET REVIEW (ANNUAL ED.). (LIVESTOCK MARKET REVIEW / REVUE DU MARCHE DES BESTIAUX.). [Livest. mark. rev.]. **Added/Corp** Canada. Dept. of Agriculture. Markets Information Section. Canada. Livestock Division. **VFOAT** Revue du Marche des Bestiaux. 31st (1950)-. Government Publication. English (French). One time a year. Free on request. Agriculture Canada, Communications Branch, Ottawa Ontario K1A 0C7 Canada. *Continues* Canada. Dept. of Agriculture. Marketing Service. Annual Market Review.

US

LIVESTOCK, MEAT, WOOL MARKET NEWS. Added/Corp United States. Agricultural Marketing Service. Livestock, Poultry, Grain, and Seed Division. United States. Agricultural Marketing Service. Livestock Division. (1932)-. Government Publication. English. One time a week. $70.00. US Department of Agriculture / Livestock and Seed Division, AMS/LMGS S Agr Building/Room 2623, PO Box 96456, Washington DC 20090. **Tel** (202)720-1050, (202)720-6231. **Circ:** 800. available on microfiche (Vols. for (1986-) distributed to depository libraries). Documents available from Documents on Demand. *Continues* United States. Agricultural Marketing Service. Livestock Division. Livestock, Meat, Wool Market News.
Desc: Information on livestock, meat, wool prices and livestock slaughter.
Ind/Abst Am. Stat. Index.

ISSN 0301-6226
NE
CCC
CODEN LPSCDL

Pr Rev.
LIVESTOCK PRODUCTION SCIENCE.
[Livest. prod. sci.]. **Added/Corp** European Association for Animal Production. Vol. 1 (Feb. 1974)-. Academic Scholarly Publication. English (French and German). Twelve times a year (4 vols.). $883.00. Elsevier Science Publishers BV, PO Box 211, 1000 AE Amsterdam Netherlands. **Tel** 011 31 20 4853641, 011 31 20 4853642, FAX 011 31 20 4853598. **ED** H. de Boer. Index available in last issue of volume--attached. available on microfilm and microfiche from University Microfilms International (UMI); available on an online database from Elsevier Electronic Subscriptions (EES). Documents available from The Genuine Article, BIOSIS Document Express, CASDDS.
Desc: Promotes sound development of livestock production by the international exchange and synthesis of research results.
Ind/Abst AgBiotech News Inf.; Anim. Breed. Abstr.; BioBusiness; Biol. Abstr.; Chem. Abstr.; Curr. Cit.; Curr. Contents Agric. Biol. Environ. Sci.; Dairy Sci. Abstr.; Fish Rev. (Jan. 1989-July 1992); Food Sci. Technol. Abstr.; Grass. Forage Abstr.; Helminthol. Abstr. (1991-); Index Vet.; Maize Abstr.; Nutr. Abstr. Rev., Ser. B, Live Feeds and Feed.; Life Sci. Collect.; Pig News Inf.; Poult. Abstr.; Protozoolog. Abstr.; Res. Alert [Full Cov.]; Rev. Med. Vet. Entomol.; Rice Abstr.; Sci. Cit. Index; SCISEARCH; Soc. Sci. Index [Select. Cov.]; Sorghum Mill. Abstr.; Soyabean Abstr.; Vet. Bull.; Wildl. Rev. (Jan. 1989-July 1992).

LC SF
DD 636
AT

LIVESTOCK PRODUCTS, AUSTRALIA / AUSTRALIAN BUREAU OF STATISTICS.
See Agriculture-Abstracting, Bibliographies and Statistics.

US

LIVESTOCK RESEARCH FOR RURAL DEVELOPMENT [COMPUTER FILE].
(1989)-. Periodical. English. Four times a year.
Ind/Abst Agrofor. Abstr.; Anim. Breed. Abstr.; Dairy Sci. Abstr.; For. Prod. Abstr. (1991-); Maize Abstr.; Nutr. Abstr. Rev., Ser. B, Live Feeds and Feed.; Pig News Inf.; Sug. Indus. Abstr.; Wheat Barley Trit. Abstr.; World Agric. Econ. Rural Sociol. Abstr.

US

LIVESTOCK REVIEW / WISCONSIN. Trade Publication. English. Twelve times a year. $10.00. Wisconsin Agricultural Statistics Service, PO Box 9160, Madison WI 53713. **Tel** (608)264-5317.
Desc: Summary of livestock information including hogs, cattle, sheep, honey production, cold storage holdings and prices.

US

UDC 338.439.4:637.5(777)
LIVESTOCK SLAUGHTER. (Feb. 1950)-. Periodical. English. Twelve times a year. The Service, Full Depository, 707 Savings and Loan Building, Des Moines IA 50309.
Desc: Slaughter of cattle, calves, and hogs in Iowa and the United States.

ISSN 1057-7874
US

DD 338
LIVESTOCK SLAUGHTER. SUMMARY.
(LIVESTOCK SLAUGHTER. SUMMARY.). [Livest. slaught., Summ.]. **Added/Corp** United States. Crop Reporting Board. United States. Agricultural Statistics Board. **VFOAT** Annual Livestock Slaughter. (1983)-. Periodical. English. One time a year. U.S. Department of Agriculture, ERS-NASS, 341 Victory Drive, Herndon VA 22070. **Tel** (800)999-6779, (703)834-0125. available on microfiche (Vols. for (1983) distributed to depository libraries). *Continues* Livestock Slaughter (Washington, D.C.). Annual Summary, 0276-7171.

ISSN 0499-0544
US

DD 338
LIVESTOCK SLAUGHTER (WASHINGTON, D.C.). (LIVESTOCK SLAUGHTER.). [Livest. slaught.]. **Added/Corp** United States. Crop Reporting Board. United States. Agricultural Statistics Board. (196?)-. Government Publication. English. Twelve times a year. $45.00. US Department of Agriculture, 14th Street and Independence Avenue SW, Washington DC 20250. **Tel** (202)720-5457. **(Subscription address:** Superintendent of Documents, US Government Printing Office, Washington DC 20402.) available on microfiche (Vols. for 1986- distributed to depository libraries). Documents available from Documents on Demand. *Continues* Commercial Livestock Slaughter and Meat Production.
Ind/Abst Am. Stat. Index.

CN

●**LIVESTOCK STATISTICS.** See Agriculture-Abstracting, Bibliographies and Statistics.

LC Z5071
DD 016.63
AT

LIVESTOCK STATISTICS, TASMANIA / THE AUSTRALIAN BUREAU OF STATISTICS. See Agriculture-Abstracting, Bibliographies and Statistics.

Agriculture —Livestock

ISSN 0745-0842
US
UDC 338.439.4:636(781)
LIVESTOCK (TOPEKA, KAN.).
(LIVESTOCK.). [Livest.]. Periodical. English. Twelve times a year. Kansas Crop & Livestock Reporting Service, 444 SE Quincy/Room 290, Topeka KS 66683. **Tel** (913)295-2600.
Desc: Inventory of livestock on farms, including cattle by classes.

ISSN 0162-5047
US
LIVESTOCK WEEKLY (SAN ANGELO).
(LIVESTOCK WEEKLY.). Vol. 29, No. 4 (Feb. 10, 1977)-. Newspaper. English. Fifty times a year (weekly on Thurs. except last week in Dec. and first week of Jan.). $25.00. Livestock Weekly, 2601 Sherwood Way, PO Box 3306, San Angelo TX 76902. **Tel** (915)949-4611. **ED** Stanley R. Frank. **Bk Rev. Ad Acc. Circ:** 18,100 (ctrl).
Continues West Texas Livestock Weekly.
Desc: A newspaper featuring stories and columns on cattle, sheep and wool markets.

ISSN 1043-0830
DD 636 US
LLAMA LIFE. [LLama life]. (198?)-. Periodical. English. Four times a year (Mar., June, Sept., Dec.). $16.00. Llama Life, 2259 Country Road, #220, Durango CO 81301. **Tel** (303) 259-0002.

ISSN 0731-8901
US
LLAMA WORLD. (LLAMA WORLD : MAGAZINE OF THE INTERNATIONAL LLAMA ASSOCIATION.). [Llama world]. **Added/Corp** International Llama Association. Andes Llamas Ranch. (1982)-. Periodical. English. Four times a year. Llama World Magazine, 120 South Park, Walla Walla WA 99362. **Continues** Llama Newsletter, 0730-7802.

ISSN 1065-7444
DD 658 US
LMA BUSINESSLETTER, THE. (THE LMA BUSINESSLETTER / LMA.). [LMA bus.lett.]. **Added/Corp** Livestock Marketing Association. **VFOAT** LMA Business Letter. **VAT** Livestock Marketing Association Businessletter. (19??)-. Periodical. English. One time a week. Livestock Marketing Association, 7509 Tiffany Spring Parkway, Kansas City MO 64153-2315. **Continues** Businessletter (Livestock Marketing Association), 0883-2552.

ISSN 0823-4604
DD 338.1/76242 CN
MAINE-ANJOU INTERNATIONAL.
[Maine-Anjou int.]. **Added/Corp** Canadian Maine-Anjou Association. American Maine-Anjou Association. (1982)-. Trade Publication. English. Six times a year. 20.00Can$. Canadian Maine-Anjou Association, 110 3016 19th Street Northeast, Calgary Alberta T2E 6Y9 Canada. **Tel** (403)291-7081. **Continues** Maine-Anjou Canada, 0229-6578.

ISSN 0164-7997
US
MAINE-ANJOU MARK. Added/Corp
International Maine-Anjou Association. Canadian Maine-Anjou Association. American Maine-Anjou Association. (1972)-. Periodical. English. Twelve times a year. $10.00. Maine-Anjou Publications, 564 Livestock Exchange Building, Kansas City MO 64102.

ISSN 0316-8581
DD 636.2/42 CN
MAINELINE. Vol. 1 (July 1974)-. Periodical. English. Twelve times a year. $5.00 North America; $10.00 other. Canadian Maine-Anjou Association, 110 3016 19th Street Northeast, Calgary Alberta T2E 6Y9 Canada. **Tel** (403)291-7081.

ISSN 0747-4121
DD 636 US
MARKET REPORT & NEWSLETTER.
[Mark. rep. newsl.]. **Added/Corp** Arizona Cattle Growers' Association. **VFOAT** Market Report and Newsletter. (19??)-. Newsletter. English. One time a week. comes with Arizona Cattle Growers Association Membership. Arizona Cattle Growers Association, 1401 North 24th Street, Suite 4, Phoenix AZ 85008. **Tel** (602)267-1129, **FAX** (602)220-9833. **ED** Renee Hamill. **Ad Acc. Circ:** 1,100 (ctrl).
Desc: News about the Arizona Cattle Grower's Association and its membership.

AT
MEAT & LIVESTOCK REVIEW. Added/Corp
Australian Meat and Live-stock Corporation. Market Intelligence Unit. **VFOAT** Meat and Livestock Review. (Jan. 1992)-. Periodical. English. Twelve times a year. Free on request. Australian Meat & Livestock Corporation, GPO 4129, Sydney 2001 Australia. **Tel** 011 61 2 260-3111, **FAX** 011 61 02 2676620, telex AA22887.
Continues In Brief (Sydney, N.S.W.).
Desc: Covers domestic and overseas markets for cattle, sheep, and goats.

US
MEAT AND POULTY INSPECTION REGULATIONS. Main/Corp United States. Meat and Poultry Inspection Program. (1977)-. Government Publication. English. Irregular. $232.00 domestic/ $290.00 other. Superintendent of Documents, US Government Printing Office, Washington DC 20402. **Tel** (202)275-3328, **FAX** (202)786-2377. **Continues** Meat and Poultry Inspection Regulations.
Desc: Contains regulations for slaughter and processing of livestock and poultry, as well as for certain voluntary services and humane slaughter.
LC HD9414 .U53a

ISSN 0748-0318
US
MEAT ANIMALS, PRODUCTION, DISPOSITION, AND INCOME. (MEAT ANIMALS, PRODUCTION, DISPOSITION, AND INCOME / UNITED STATES DEPARTMENT OF AGRICULTURE, STATISTICAL REPORTING SERVICE, CROP REPORTING BOARD.). [Meat anim. prod. dispos. income]. **Added/Corp** United States. Crop Reporting Board. United States. Agricultural Statistics Board. **VFOAT** Meat Animals. (1983)-. Statistical Publication. English. One time a year (Apr.). $10.00. US Department of Agriculture / National Agricultural Statistics Service (NASS), Room 5829 South Building, Washington DC 20250. **Tel** (202)720-4020, **FAX** (314)875-5231. **(Subscription address:** ERS NASS, 341 Victory Drive, Herndon VA 22070. **Tel** (800)999-6779, (703)834-0125.)
Continues Meat Animals, Production, Disposition, Income, 0094-7385.
LC HD9410.4 .O73a
DD 338.4/76649/0021 FR
MEAT BALANCES IN OECD COUNTRIES = BILANS DE LA VIANDE DANS LES PAYS DE L'OCDE. Added/Corp
Organisation for Economic Co-Operation and Development. **VFOAT** Bilans de la Viande dans les Pays de l'OCDE. (1982)-. English (French). One time a year. $36.00. OECD Publications and Information Center, 2 rue Andre-Pascal, 75775 Paris Cedex 16 France. **Tel** 011 33 1 49104262, US:(202)785-6323, **FAX** 011 33 1 45248500, 011 33 1 45248176, telex 620 160 OCDE. **(Subscription address:** OECD Publications Center, 2001 L Street, Suite 700, Washington DC 20036. **Tel** (202)822-3873, (202)785-6323.) **Continues** Organisation for Economic Co-operation and Development. Meat Balances in OECD Member Countries.

ISSN 0025-6358
US
MEAT BOARD REPORTS [ANNUAL REPORT]. See Food and Food Industry.

ISSN 0961-2076
UK
MEAT FOCUS INTERNATIONAL. [Meat focus int.]. (1992)-. English. Twelve times a year. $205.00. CAB International Centre, Wallingford, Oxfordshire OX10 8DE United Kingdom. **Tel** 011 44 1491 832111, **FAX** 011 44 1491 833508, telex 847964 COMAGG G.

AT
MEAT INDUSTRY BULLETIN, THE.
Added/Corp Meat and Allied Trades' Federation of Australia. New South Wales Division. (19??)-. Bulletin. English. Twelve times a year. Meat & Allied Trades Federation of Australia, PO Box 1208, Crows Nest New South Wales, 2065 Australia. **Tel** 011 61 2 9067767, **FAX** 011 61 2 9068022, telex AA22480.

ISSN 0924-7068
NE
UDC 637.5
MEAT INTERNATIONAL. See Food and Food Industry.

ISSN 0747-6019
DD 338 US
MEAT PRICE OUTLOOK. [Meat price outlook]. **Added/Corp** Price Analysis Systems, Inc. (19??)-. Periodical. English. One time a week. $429.00. Price Analysis Systems / Tennessee, 889 Ridge Lake Boulevard, Suite 301, Memphis TN 38120. **Tel** (800)223-4412, (901)766-4499.

US
●**MEAT PROCESSING INTERNATIONAL.**
(19??)-. Periodical. English. Six times a year. $27.00. Watt Publishing Company, 122 West Sydney Avenue, Mount Morris IL 61054. **Tel** (815)734-4171, **FAX** (815)734-7021, telex TWX 910-642-2891.
Desc: News for processors, marketers, and distributors of meat products in Europe, Africa, and Latin America and Asia / Pacific countries.

US
MEAT REPORT FROM THE UNIVERSITY OF ILLINOIS AT URBANA-CHAMPAIGN.
See Food and Food Industry.

ISSN 0815-676X
AT
MEAT RESEARCH NEWSLETTER. (MEAT RESEARCH NEWS LETTER.). [Meat res. newsl.]. **Added/Corp** Commonwealth Scientific and Industrial Research Organization (Australia). Meat Research Laboratory. No. 1 (Jan. 1976)-. Periodical. English. Six times a year. CSIRO Publications, PO Box 89, 314 Albert Street, East Melbourne Victoria 3002 Australia. **Tel** 011 61 3 4187333, 4187217, **FAX** 011 61 3 4190459, telex AA 30236.
Ind/Abst AGRICOLA.

ISSN 0309-1740
UK
CCC
CODEN MESCDN
Pr Rev.
MEAT SCIENCE. [Meat sci.]. Vol. 1 (Jan. 1977)-. Academic Scholarly Publication. English. Twelve times a year. $1090.00. Elsevier Applied Science, An Imprint of Elsevier Science Ltd., The Boulevard, Langford Lane, Kidlington, Oxford OX5 1GB United Kingdom. **Tel** 011 44 1865 843000, 011 44 1865 843699, **FAX** 011 44 1865 843010. **(Subscription address:** Elsevier Science Ltd. / Oxford Fulfillment Centre, PO Box 800, Kidlington OX5 1DX United Kingdom. **Tel** 011 44 865 843355.) **ED** R. A. Lawrie. **Bk Rev. Ad Acc.** available on microfilm and microfiche from University Microfilms International (UMI); available on an online database from Elsevier Electronic Subscriptions (EES). Documents available from The Genuine Article, BIOSIS Document Express, CASDDS.
Desc: Provides an appropriate medium for the dissemination of interdisciplinary and international knowledge on all the factors which influence the property of meat.
Ind/Abst AgBiotech News Inf.; AGRICOLA [Full Cov.]; BioBusiness; Biodeter. Abstr. (19??-19??); Biol. Abstr. (1985-); Chem. Abstr.; Chemorecept. Abstr.; Curr. Cit.; Curr. Contents Agric. Biol. Environ. Sci.; EMBASE; Food Sci. Technol. Abstr.; Index Vet.; Int. Packag. Abstr.; Nutr. Abstr. Rev., Ser. B, Live Feeds and Feed.; Nutr. Abstr. Rev., Ser. A, Hum. Exp.; Life Sci. Collect.; Pig News Inf.; Res. Alert [Full Cov.]; Sci. Cit. Index; SCISEARCH; Vet. Bull.

RM
MEDICINA VETERINARA SI CRESTEREA ANIMALELOR. See Veterinary Sciences.

ISSN 1061-6586
DD 636 US
MIDWEST PUREBRED DOGPOST!, THE.
[Midwest purebred DOGPosT!]. (1992)-. Periodical. English. Twelve times a year. $14.00. The Midwest Purebred Dogpost, PO Box 845, Wisconsin Rapids WI 54495-0845.

ISSN 0343-0200
GW
MILCH PRAXIX UND RINDERMAST, DIE.
[Milch prax. rindermast]. (1965)-. Trade Publication. German. Four times a year. DM32.53 Germany; DM38.60 other. Verlag TH Mann OHG, Postfach 200254, W 45837 Gelsenkirchen Germany. **Tel** 011 49 209 9304184. **ED** HU Wiesner. **Bk Rev. Ad Acc. Circ:** 3,500. available with charts.
Desc: Dairy, dairy cattle, feed, feeding stuff, cow shed, milking machines, horned cattle, calves and milk hygienics.
Ind/Abst AGRICOLA.

ISSN 0941-1348
GW
MILCHRIND. [Milchrind]. **Added/Corp** Verband Deutscher Schwarzbuntzuechter. Verband Deutscher Rotbuntzuechter. (1992)-. Trade Publication. German. Four times a year. $34.54. Landwirtschaftsverlag GmbH, Postfach 480249, D-48079 Muenster Hiltrup Germany. **Tel** 011 49 2501 8010, **FAX** 011 49 2501 801204, telex 892665 LANDV D. **Continues** Deutsche Schwarzbunte, 0343-3145.

LC SF199.S56 J68
ISSN 1073-9394
DD 636 US
●**MILKING SHORTHORN JOURNAL (1993).** See Agriculture-Dairy Industry.

ISSN 1037-0641
DD 636.213099405 AT
MILNE'S PRIME BEEF. [Milne's prime beef]. **VFOAT** Prime Beef. (1990)-. Periodical. English. Ten times a year (monthly with combined Jan./Feb. and Nov./Dec.). 19.74Aus$. Richard Milne Pty Ltd., PO Box 113, Pyrmont NSW 2009 Australia. **Tel** 011 61 2 8197322, **FAX** 011 61 2 8197650. **Continues** Milne's Prime Beef Producer, 1033-7911.

Agriculture—Livestock

ISSN 0192-3056
US
MISSOURI BEEF CATTLEMAN.
Added/Corp Missouri Cattlemen's Association. **VFOAT** Mo Beef. (19??)-. Periodical. English. Twelve times a year. Missouri Beef Cattleman Inc, PO Box 16050, Kansas City MO 64112. **Tel** (913)384-1918.

GW
MITTEILUNGEN FUER DIE VIEH- UND FLEISCHWIRTSCHAFT. (19??)-. Trade Publication. German. Four times a year. DM48.00. Verkehrs- und Wirtschafts- Verlag, Hohestr 39, PF100555, W-4600 Dortmund 1 Germany. **Tel** 0231/128048, FAX 0231/125640, telex 17231329. **ED** Dieter Callum. **Bk Rev. Ad Acc, Adv Mgr:** Christel Adam. **Circ:** 1,340.
Desc: Information for traders of beef cattle.

ISSN 0721-099X
GW
MITTEILUNGSBLATT DER BUNDESANSTALT FUER FLEISCHFORSCHUNG, KULMBACH.
[Mitteilungsbl. Bundesanst. Fleischforsch. Kulmb.]. (1974)-. Periodical. German. Four times a year.
Ind/Abst Biodeter. Abstr.; Curr. Cit.; Index Vet.; Nutr. Abstr. Rev., Ser. B, Live Feeds and Feed.; Pig News Inf.; Rev. Med. Vet. Mycology; Vet. Bull.

ISSN 0140-6388
UK
MLC ECONOMIC INFORMATION SERVICE. MEAT DEMAND TRENDS. [MLC Econ. Inf. Serv., Meat demand trends]. **VFOAT** Meat and Livestock Commission. Economic Information Service. Meat Demand trends; Meat Demand Trends (Milton Keynes). (1976)-. Periodical. English. Three times a year (Jan., May, Sept.). £115.00 UK; £95.00 other. Meat & Livestock Commission / Economic Service Department, PO Box 44, Winterhill House, Milton Keynes MK6 1AX United Kingdom. **Tel** 011 44 1908 677577, FAX 011 44 1908 609221, telex 82227.
Ind/Abst Pig News Inf.

NE
MOLENAAR, DE. See Agriculture-Feed Grain and Milling.

ISSN 0026-9034
RU
MOLOCHNOE I MIASNOE SKOTOVODSTVO. Added/Corp Russia (1923-U.S.S.R.) Ministerstvo Selskogo Khoziaistva. (1960)-. Periodical. Russian. Four times a year. $79.95. Izdatelstvo Kolos, Sadovaia-Spasskaia 18, 107807 Moscow Russia. **(Subscription address:** East View Publications Inc., 3020 Harbor Lane North, Suite 110, Minneapolis MN 55447. **Tel** (800)477-1005, (612)550-0961, FAX (612)559-2931.) Continues Molochnoe i Miasnoe Zhivotnovodstvo; Absorbed Obmen Opytom v Selskom Khoziaistve. Molochnaia Ferma.
Ind/Abst Index Vet.

LC S
ISSN 0279-0394
DD 630
US
MONTANA CROP & LIVESTOCK REPORTER. See Agriculture-Crop Production and Soils.

ISSN 1073-1458
DD 630
US
●**MONTANA FARMER (1993).** (MONTANA FARMER.). [Mont. farmer.]. Vol. 80, No. 11 (July 1993)-. Periodical. English. Twelve times a year. Western Farmer Stockman, Box 2160, Spokane WA 99210. **Tel** (509)459-5361, FAX (509)459-5102. Continues Montana Farmer-Stockman, 1041-1674.

ISSN 0027-0024
US
CODEN MWOGA
MONTANA WOOLGROWER. Added/Corp Montana Wool Growers Association. **VFOAT** Montana Wool Grower. (1928)-. Trade Publication. English. Six times a year. $35.00. Montana Wool Growers Association, PO Box 1693, Helena MT 59624. **Tel** (406)442-1330, FAX (406)449-8606. **ED** Bob Gilbert. **Ad Acc. Circ:** 2,500 (ctrl).
Desc: Received by 90 percent of those raising sheep in Montana. Articles of importance to the sheep producer, education, information, politics.

ISSN 0744-2998
US
UDC 339.13:637.1/.4(73)
MONTHLY COLDS STORAGE REPORT (CHICAGO, ILL.). (MONTHLY COLD STORAGE REPORT / FEDERAL-STATE MARKET NEWS SERVICE.). Periodical. English. Twelve times a year. $84.00. Monthly Cold Storage Report, 536 South Clark Street Room 936, Chicago IL 60605. **Circ:** 55.

Desc: Cold storage holdings of poultry and eggs, monthly average prices, export tables and general market information.

SP
MUNDO GANADERO. (19??)-. Spanish. Eleven times a year. 6000.00ptas Spain; 11.000ptas other. Edagricole Espana SA, Castello 32, 28001 Madrid Spain. **Tel** 011 34 1 5780534, 011 34 1 5780820. **Ad Acc.** ctrl circ.
Desc: Contains news and technology on companies and new products in the industry.
Ind/Abst Nutr. Abstr. Rev., Ser. B, Live Feeds and Feed.

UK
N.P.B.A. GAZETTE. VFOAT NPBA Gazette. **VAT** National Pig Breeders' Association Gazette. No. 1 (Nov. 1927)-. Trade Publication. English.

XR
NAS CHOV. Added/Corp Jednota Svaz Ceskych Zemedelou. (19??)-. Periodical. Czech. Twelve times a year. DM148.00. **(Subscription address:** Kubon & Sagner, ABT Zeitschriftenimport, D 80328 Munich Germany. **Tel** 011 49 89 54218130.)
Ind/Abst AgBiotech News Inf.; Anim. Breed. Abstr.; Dairy Sci. Abstr.; Pig News Inf.; Poult. Abstr.

ISSN 0882-5149
DD 338
US
NATIONAL CATTLE FEEDLOT, MEAT PACKER AND GRAIN DEALERS DIRECTORY. (1970)-. Periodical. English. Every 2 years. $45.00. Tara National Directory, PO Box 3614, 2143 50th Street, Lubbock TX 79412. **Tel** (806)762-3407. **ED** Trina Caranfa Garcia. **Circ:** 5,000 (ctrl).
Desc: National listings of cattle feedlots 1,000-plus head, interstate meat packers, grain dealers 100,000-plus bushels. Contains 11,500-plus listings by state, city, region name, address and telephone.

ISSN 0885-7679
DD 338
US
NATIONAL CATTLEMEN. (NATIONAL CATTLEMEN : THE MONTHLY PUBLICATION OF THE NATIONAL CATTLEMEN'S ASSOCIATION.). [Natl. cattlem.]. **Added/Corp** National Cattlemen's Association (U.S.). Vol. 1, No. 1 (Sept. 1985)-. Trade Publication. English. Eleven times a year. Free to members of the National Cattlemens Association; $100.00 (individuals) membership. National Cattlemens Association, PO Box 3469, Englewood CO 80155. **Tel** (303)694-0305. **ED** Kendal Frazier and Cheryl Burke. **Ad Acc. Circ:** 36,905.
Desc: Covers cattle business management.

AT
NATIONAL COUNTRY LIFE. LIVESTOCK FARMING EDITION. VFOAT Livestock Farming Edition. Vol. 89, No. 43 (June 1978)-. Periodical. English. Four times a year. 8.00Aus$. Rural Press Group / New South Wales, Edgecliff Centre, PO Box 299, Windsor NSW 2756 Australia. Continues in part Country Life.

ISSN 0027-9447
DD 338
US
CODEN NAHFAP
NATIONAL HOG FARMER. [Nat. hog farmer]. (1956)-. Trade Publication. English. Fourteen times a year. $24.71. Intertec Publishing Corporation, 9800 Metcalf, Overland Park KS 66212. **Tel** (913)341-1300. **(Subscription address:** Intertec Publishing Corporation, PO Box 2901, Overland Park KS 66282. **Tel** 800 441-0294.) **ED** Bill Fleming. **Ad Acc. Circ:** 110,000 (ctrl) available on microfilm and microfiche from University Microfilms International (UMI). Continues National Hog Farmer Newsletter.
Desc: Information for hog producers.
Ind/Abst BioBusiness (1990-).

LC HD9890.1 .N3
ISSN 1075-0231
DD 338.1/763145
US
CODEN NLWGEE
TITLE CHANGE
NATIONAL LAMB & WOOL GROWER.
See Fabrics and Textile Industries.

LC TS1971.U6 N37
ISSN 0743-3956
DD 664/.9/0029473
US
NATIONAL MEAT PACKER REFERENCE GUIDE. [Natl. meat pack. ref. guide]. **VFOAT** National Meat Packer. (19??)-. English. $19.95. Agriscan Corporation, Box 398, Llano TX 78643. **Tel** (915)247-3022. **ED** Brad Bradley. **Circ:** 5,200 (ctrl).
Desc: Listed by category of livestock slaughtered (bulls, cows, veal calves, fed steers, heifers, hogs, sows, boars, lambs, goats), cross-indexed by state, with plant name, address and phone numbers.

ISSN 0028-0267
US
NATIONAL STOCK DOG MAGAZINE.
[Natl. stock dog mag.]. (19??)-. Periodical. English. Six times a year. $18.00. National Stock Dog Registry, PO Box 402, Butler IN 46721-0402. **Tel** (219)868-2670. **ED** J.R. Russell. Index available. cum. index. **Bk Rev. Ad**

Acc. Circ: 5,000.
Desc: For the preservation and advancement of the livestock working breeds of America and the world.

ISSN 0130-9803
BW
CODEN NORZAT
NAUCNYE OSNOVY RAZVITIA ZIVOTNOVODSTVA V BELORUSSII.
(NAUCHNYE OSNOVY RAZVITIIA ZHIVOTNOVODSTVA V BELORUSSII.). [Naucn. osn. razvit. zivotnovod. Beloruss.]. **Added/Corp** Belaruski Navukova-Dasledchy Instytut Zhyviolahadouli. **VFOAT** Nauchnye Osnovy Razvitiia Zhivotnovodstva v Respublike Belarus. (1970)-. Periodical. Russian. Nauka i Tekhnika / Byelarus, Science & Technology Publishing House, Ulitsa Zhodinskaya 18, 220067 Minsk Byelarus. **Tel** 0172 63-76-18.
Ind/Abst Index Vet.; Postharvest News Inf.

ISSN 1062-8274
US
NEBRASKA CATTLEMAN. (THE NEBRASKA CATTLEMAN : OFFICIAL PUBLICATION OF THE NEBRASKA STOCK GROWERS ASSOCIATION.). **Added/Corp** Nebraska Stock Growers Association. (1944)-. Periodical. English. Eleven times a year. $30.00. Nebraska Stock Growers Association, PO Drawer 40, Alliance NE 69301. **Tel** (308)762-3005. **ED** Troy E. Smith. **Bk Rev. Ad Acc. Circ:** 7,000.
Desc: Published for Nebraska beef cattle raisers and related occupations. Information on cattle health and management and contains special features that vary.

ISSN 0047-9489
US
NEVADA RANCHER, THE. Added/Corp
Nevada Cattlemen's Association. (19??)-. Periodical. English. Twelve times a year. $10.75. Jay Publishing, PO Box 1465, Sparks NV 89432. **Tel** (702)358-2681.

US
NEW ENGLAND POULTRY LETTER / COOPERATIVE EXTENSION SERVICES. Added/Corp University of Maine at Orono. Cooperative Extension Service. University of Maine at Orono. Cooperative Extension. University of Connecticut. Cooperative Extension System. New England Cooperative Extension Consortium. United States. Dept. of Agriculture. **VFOAT** Poultry Letter. (1987?)-. Periodical. English. Six times a year. $5.00. University of Maine Cooperative Ext., 5735 Hichner Hall, Orono ME 04469. **Tel** (207)581-2790. Continues New England Poultry Newsletter.
Ind/Abst Bibliogr. Agric.

AT
NEW SOUTH WALES PRODUCTION & MARKETING REPORT. PIGS. Added/Corp
New South Wales. Dept. of Agriculture. Division of Marketing and Economic. **VFOAT** New South Wales Production and Marketing Report. Pigs; Pigs. (19??)-. Periodical. English. New South Wales Department of Agriculture / Division of Marketing and Economics, Orange NSW 2800 Australia.

ISSN 0279-8611
US
NEW YORK HOLSTEIN NEWS. Added/Corp
New York Holstein-Friesian Association. **VFOAT** NYN. (19??)-. Periodical. English. Twelve times a year. $15.00 with free index. New York Holstein News, PO Box 190, Ithaca NY 14851. **Tel** (607)273-7591, FAX (607)273-7612. **ED** Jennifer Kelly. Index available (free). **Ad Acc.** Full Page (B&W) $500.00. Half Page (B&W) $325.00. **Circ:** 4,500. Continues New York Holstein-Friesian News, 0028-727X.
Desc: Focused on supporting high breed standards, modern herd practices, and efficient dairy herd practices.

ISSN 0715-4526
DD 636.08/245
CN
NEWSLETTER / B.C.A.I. CENTRE. [Newsl. - B.C.A.I. Cent.]. **Main/Corp** B.C. Artificial Insemination Centre. **VAT** Newsletter - British Columbia Artificial Insemination Centre. Newsletter. English. Four times a year. Newsletter British Columbia Artificial Insemination Centre Milner, British Columbia V0X 1T0 Canada.

LC HF5681.V3 J36a
DD 657
JA
NO-CHIKUSANGYOYO KOTEI SHISAN HYOKA HYOJUN. See Business and Economics-Accounting.

KO
NONGSA SIHOM YONGU POGO. CHUKSAN, KAWI. VFOAT Research Reports of the Office of Rural Development. Vol. 22 (Dec. 1980)-. Korean (summaries and/or abstracts in English). One time a year. Office of Rural Development, Ministry of Agriculture and Fisheries, Suweon South Korea. Formed by the union of Nongsa Sihom Yongu Pogo - and Chuksan Pyon and Nongsa Sihom Yongu Pogo. Kachuk Wiseng, Jamop Pyon.
Ind/Abst Poult. Abstr.

Agriculture —Livestock

UDC 636
ISSN 0210-5659
SP
NUESTRA CABANA. [Nuestra cabana]. (1972)-. Periodical. Spanish. Twelve times a year. $56.00. Tecnipublicaciones SA, C Fernando VI No 27, 28004 Madrid Spain. **Tel** 011 34 1 3197889, **FAX** 011 34 1 4101069, telex 43905 YEBE E.

UDC 631.52
ISSN 0250-3360
KO
NYNGJON-HAG HOI JI. [Nyngjon-hag hoi ji]. **VFOAT** Korean Journal of Breeding. (1969)-. Periodical. Korean (summaries and/or abstracts in English). Four times a year (Jan., Apr., July, Oct.). $30.00. Korean Breeding Society, Upland Crop Division, I CR EX ST RDA, Suwon 441 100 Korea. **Tel** 011 82 331 2902823.

LC SF1 .O37
KO
OEGUK KWAHAK KISUL TONGBO. SUUI CHUKSAN. VFOAT Zhivotnovodstvo I Veterinariia. Periodical. Korean.

AU
OESTERREICHISCHE RINDERZUCHT. CATTLE BREEDING IN AUSTRIA. L'ALLEVAMENTO BOVINO IN AUSTRIA, DIE. VFOAT Cattle Breeding in Austria; L'Allevamento Bovino in Austria. (19??)-. Periodical. German (English and Italian). Irregular.

AT
OFFICIAL PRODUCTION RECORDS OF PURE BRED REGISTERED DAIRY COWS IN NEW SOUTH WALES. Main/Corp New South Wales. Dept. of Agriculture. Division of Dairying. **VFOAT** Recording of Pure Bred Registered Dairy Cattle in New South Wales. No. 38 (1972/73)-. Periodical. English. New South Wales Department of Agriculture / Division of Dairying, NSW Australia. **Continues** Recording of Pure Bred Registered Dairy Cattle in New South Wales ... and Register of Merit Awards.

LC SF
DD 636
ISSN 1068-0195
US
OHIO BEEF CATTLE RESEARCH & INDUSTRY REPORT. [Ohio beef cattle res. ind. rep.]. **Added/Corp** Ohio Agricultural Research and Development Center. Ohio State University. Cooperative Extension Service. **VFOAT** Ohio Beef Cattle Research and Industry Report. (March 1990)-. English. One time a year. Ohio Agricultural Research and Development Center, Ohio State University, 1680 Madison Avenue, Wooster OH 44691. **Tel** (216)263-3775. **Continues** Beef Cattle Research Report (Wooster, Ohio), 1053-167X. **Ind/Abst** AGRICOLA.

ISSN 0030-1698
US
OKLAHOMA COWMAN. Added/Corp Oklahoma Cattlemen's Association. **VFOAT** Cowman. (1961)-. Periodical. English. Twelve times a year. $50.00. Oklahoma Cattlemens Association, Box 82395, Oklahoma City OK 73148. **Tel** (405)235-4391. **ED** A.J. Smith. **Ad Acc. Circ:** 5,200 (ctrl).
Desc: Current trends of the beef cattle industry in Oklahoma.

LC S
DD 630
ISSN 0145-9392
US
OKLAHOMA FARMER-STOCKMAN, THE. See Agriculture.

DD 636.3/009713
ISSN 0844-5303
CN
ONT. SHEEP NEWS. [Ont. sheep news]. **Added/Corp** Ontario Sheep Marketing Agency. **VFOAT** Ontario Sheep News; Sheep News; OSMA Sheep News. **VAT** Ontario Sheep Marketing Agency Sheep News. Vol. 1, Issue 1 (July/Aug. 1987)-. English. Six times a year (Jan., March, May, July, Sept., Nov.). 9.61Can$. Ontario Sheep Marketing Agency, 130 Malcolm Road, Guelph Ontario N1K 1B1 Canada. **Tel** (519)836-0043, **FAX** (519)824-9101. **ED** Kelly Maloney. **Ad Acc.** ctrl circ.

LC WMLC L 83/8854
DD 636
ISSN 1067-7712
US
OSTRICH NEWS. [Ostrich news]. Vol. 1, No. 1 (Oct. 1988)-. Periodical. English. Twelve times a year. $48.00. Ostrich News Inc, 5th and C Streets, PO Box 860, Cache OK 73527-0860. **Tel** (405)429-3765, (800)242-7222, **FAX** (405)429-3935.

ISSN 0030-7572
RU
OVTSEVODSTVO. (Oct. 1955)-. Periodical. Russian. Six times a year. $79.95. **(Subscription address:** East View Publications Inc., 3020 Harbor Lane North, Suite 110, Minneapolis MN 55447. **Tel** (800)477-1005, (612)550-0961, **FAX** (612)559-2931.)

Absorbed in part Karakulevodstvo i Zverovodstvo.
Ind/Abst Agric. Eng. Abstr.; Index Vet.; Nutr. Abstr. Rev., Ser. B, Live Feeds and Feed.

US
PACKERS AND STOCKYARDS RESUME. Vol. 1, No. 1 (1963)-. Government Publication. English. Irregular. US Department of Agriculture / Agricultural Marketing Service / Washington, DC, Market News Branch, Fruit and Vegetable Division, Washington DC 20250. **Tel** (202)720-2745, (202)720-3343, **FAX** (202)720-7502. Documents available from Documents on Demand. **Continues** P & S Docket.
Ind/Abst Am. Stat. Index.

ISSN 0253-8318
PK
CODEN PVJODU
PAKISTAN VETERINARY JOURNAL. See Veterinary Sciences.

LC SF15.I42 U79A
II
PASU PALANA PRAGATI. Main/Corp Uttar Pradesh (India). Hindi (Hindi).

FR
PATRE. (19??)-. Periodical. French. Ten times a year. $83.11. Societe de Presse et d Edition Ovine et Caprine, 19 Quai de Juillet, BP 67, 14007 CAEN Cedex France. **Tel** 011 33 31356507. **ED** Philippe Pelzer. Index available. **Bk Rev**, (Qty: 10/yr). **Ad Acc. Circ:** 5,500 (ctrl).
Desc: Provides information about sheep production for farmers and advisers.

LC SF604 .A77a
DD 354.54/1620082336
II
PERFORMANCE BUDGET ON ANIMAL HUSBANDRY & VETERINARY. See Veterinary Sciences.

LC SF15.I5 B57A
IO
UDC 636
PETERNAKAN DAN UNGGAS. Main/Corp Indonesia. Biro Pusat Statistik. **VFOAT** Livestock and Poultry. Multiple languages (English and Indonesian). $2.00. Biro Pusat Statistik / Central Bureau of Statistics, 8 Jalan Dr. Sutomo No. 8, Box 3, Jakarta Pusat 10710 Indonesia. **Tel** 011 62 21 372808, 011 62 21 374908 ext.342.

LC SF1 .P45
DD 636.05
ISSN 0048-3761
PH
CODEN PJAIAG
PHILIPPINE JOURNAL OF ANIMAL INDUSTRY, THE. [Philipp. J. Anim. Ind.]. Vol. 1 (Jan.-Feb. 1934)-. Periodical. English. Four times a year. cum. index. Documents available from CASDDS. **Supersedes** Gazette / Philippines. Bureau of Animal Industry.
Ind/Abst Chem. Abstr. (1934-1982); Philip. Sci. Technol. Abstr.

ISSN 0115-2173
PH
CODEN PJVSDI
Pr Rev.
PHILIPPINE JOURNAL OF VETERINARY AND ANIMAL SCIENCES. See Veterinary Sciences.

ISSN 0031-9759
UK
UDC 636.4
PIG FARMING. [Pig farming]. Vol. 1 (1953)-. Periodical. English. Twelve times a year. $63.00. Farming Press, Royal Sovereign House, 40 Beresford Street, Woolwich London SE18 6BO United Kingdom. **Tel** 011 44 181 8557777, **FAX** 011 44 181 3173938. **(Subscription address:** Morgan Grampian, 40 Beresford Street, London SE18 6BQ United Kingdom. **Tel** 011 44 171 8557777, **FAX** 011 44 181 8555548.) **ED** Bryan Kelly. **Ad Acc. Circ:** 13,000 (ctrl).
Desc: Information which helps improve the efficiency and therefore profitability of pig producers in the UK and overseas.
Ind/Abst AGRICOLA; EMBASE; Index Vet.; PESTDOC; Pig News Inf.

ISSN 0191-8834
US
CCC
PIG INTERNATIONAL (EUROPE, ASIA, AFRICA, LATIN AMERICA AND OCEANIA EDITION.) (PIG INTERNATIONAL.). [Pig int.]. (19??)-. Periodical. English (French, German, Italian, Japanese and Spanish; summaries and/or abstracts in French, German, Italian, Japanese and Spanish). Thirteen times a year (monthly except semimonthly in Dec.). Watt Publishing Company, 122 South Wesley Avenue, Mount Morris IL 61054. **Tel** (815)734-4171, **FAX** (815)734-7021, telex TWX 910-642-2891. **ED** Peter Best. **Ad Acc. Circ:** 16,000 (ctrl). available on microfilm from University Microfilms

International (UMI). **Continued in part by** Industria Porcina, 0279-7771.
Desc: Covers aspects of pig production and marketing for pig businessmen in Europe, Asia, and Africa.
Ind/Abst Anim. Breed. Abstr.; Curr. Cit.; Dairy Sci. Abstr.; Index Vet.; PESTDOC; Pig News Inf.

ISSN 1352-9749
UK
●**PIG JOURNAL, THE.** [Pig j.]. **Added/Corp** Pig Veterinary Society. Vol. 32 (1994)-. English. Two times a year. $37.64. Pig Veterinary Society, Grove House, Corston, Malmesbury Wiltshire SN16 0HL United Kingdom. **Tel** 011 44 1666 822967, **FAX** 011 44 1666 822970, telex 46624. **Continues** Pig Veterinary Journal, 0956-0939.
Ind/Abst Curr. Cit.

LC S217 .Z3 SF396.G7
DD 338.1/0941 S 338.1/764/00941
UK
UDC 338.3:636.4(410)
PIG MANAGEMENT SCHEME RESULTS. Main/Corp University of Cambridge. Agricultural Economics Unit. English. One time a year. £3.00. Agricultural Economics Unit, Department of Land Economy, 16-21 Silver Street, Cambridge CB3 9EP United Kingdom. **Tel** 011 44 1223 337147. Index available. **Circ:** 1,500.
Desc: Survey of financial and physical results of pig production on about 150 farms in the eastern region of England.

LC Z5074
DD 016.63
ISSN 0143-9014
UK
CODEN PNINEZ
PIG NEWS AND INFORMATION. See Agriculture-Abstracting, Bibliographies and Statistics.

ISSN 0791-3044
IE
DD 636.4
PIG STATISTICS, NUMBER AND WEIGHT OF PIGS SLAUGHTERED AT BACON FACTORIES. See Agriculture-Abstracting, Bibliographies and Statistics.

ISSN 0791-3095
IE
DD 636.4
PIG SURVEY AUGUST DUBLIN. See Agriculture-Abstracting, Bibliographies and Statistics.

ISSN 0168-9533
NE
CODEN PIGSE5
PIGS. [Pigs]. (Oct. 1984)-. Periodical. English. Eight times a year. $78.00. Misset Uitgeverij BV / Doetinchem, Postbus 4, 7000 BA Doetinchem Netherlands. **Tel** 011 31 8340 49911, 011 31 8340 49562, **FAX** 011 31 8340 43839, 011 31 8340 40515. **ED** Adrian Bal. Index available. **Bk Rev. Ad Acc. Circ:** 11,300 (ctrl).
Desc: Providing trade information about pig farming throughout the world.
Ind/Abst Agric. Eng. Abstr. (1991)-; Anim. Breed. Abstr.; BioBusiness; Food Sci. Technol. Abstr.; Index Vet.; Pig News Inf.

ISSN 0710-0361
CN
DD 636.4/002/07
PLAYBOAR MAGAZINE. [Playboar mag.]. Periodical. English. Four times a year. $2.50 per no. Pigskin Productions, PO Box 353 Station A, Kingston Ontario K7M 6R7 Canada.

NE
UDC 636.5
PLUIMVEEHOUDERIJ, DE. 1.- Yearly volume; Jan. 1971-. Trade Publication. Dutch. One time a week. $195.27. Misset Uitgeverij BV / Doetinchem, Postbus 4, 7000 BA Doetinchem Netherlands. **Tel** 011 31 8340 49911, 011 31 8340 49562, **FAX** 011 31 8340 43839, 011 31 8340 40515. **ED** W Wisman. Index available. **Ad Acc. Circ:** 7,500 (ctrl). **Supersedes** Nederlandse Pluimveehouderij; Bedrijfspluimveehouder.
Desc: Specialized Dutch trade journal on all aspects of poultry farming.

ISSN 0162-7953
US
UDC 636.222.7
POLLED HEREFORD WORLD (1965). (POLLED HEREFORD WORLD.). **VFOAT** Polled Hereford World, Guide Edition. Vol. 19, No. 18 (Sept. 15, 1965)-. Periodical. English. Twelve times a year. $20.00. American Polled Hereford Publications Inc, 11020 Northwest Ambassador Drive, Kansas City MO 64153. **Tel** (816)891-8400. **ED** Ed Bible. **Ad Acc. Circ:** 11,500 (ctrl). **Formed by the union of** Polled Hereford World Magazine, 0032-3608 **and** Polled Hereford Guide.
Desc: Features industry information and breed reports for breeders of Polled Hereford cattle.

ISSN 1182-851X
CN
DD 338.1/764/00971405
PORC EXPRESS. (PORC EXPRESS : BULLETIN D'INFORMATION DE LA F.P.P.Q.). [Porc express]. **Added/Corp** Federation des Producteurs de Porcs du Quebec. Vol. 1, No 1 (1990)-. Bulletin. French. Four times

Agriculture —Livestock

a year. Free for members. Federation des Producteurs de Porcs du Quebec, 555 boulevard Roland Therrien, Longueil Quebec J4H 3Y9 Canada.

FR

PORC MAGAZINE. French. Eleven times a year (monthly with Aug. & Sept. combined). 328.00F France; 428.00F other (one-year). 590.40F France; 790.40F other (two-year). Editions du Boisdaudry, BP 6359, 35036 Rennes Cedex France. **Tel** 011 33 99 322121.

ISSN 1182-1000
DD 338.1/764/0971405 CN

PORC QUEBEC. (PORC QUEBEC : LE MAGAZINE DE LA FEDERATION DES PRODUCTEURS DE PORCS DU QUEBEC.). [Porc Que.]. **Added/Corp** Federation des Producteurs de Porcs du Quebec. Vol. 1, No. 1 (May 1990)-. Periodical. French. Four times a year. 10.46Can$. Federation des Producteurs de Porcs du Quebec, 555 boulevard Roaland Therrien, Longueuil Quebec J4H 3Y9 Canada. **Tel** (514)679-0530.

ISSN 0481-2468
CN

PORCS. **Main/Corp** Quebec (Province) Bureau of Statistics. **VFOAT** Hogs. English (French). Two times a year. Bureau of Statistics / Quebec, Publications, 117 rue Saint Andre, Quebec Quebec G1K 3Y3 Canada. **Tel** (418)691-2401, (800)463-4090.

ISSN 0745-3787
DD 636 US
CCC

PORK. [Pork]. (198?)-. Periodical. English. Twelve times a year. $10.00. Vance Publishing Corporation, 400 Knightsbridge Parkway, Lincolnshire IL 60069. **Tel** (800)255-5113, (708)634-2600. available on microfilm from University Microfilms International (UMI). **Continues** Pork Producers Reference, 0279-6813.

US

PORK 92. (19??)-. Periodical. English. Twelve times a year. Vance Publishing Corporation, 400 Knightsbridge Parkway, Lincolnshire IL 60069. **Tel** (800)255-5113, (708)634-2600. **Continues** Pork Money II.

LC SF391 .P67 ISSN 1032-3759
AT

PORK JOURNAL. **VFOAT** Milne's Pork Journal. (19??)-. Trade Publication. English. Twelve times a year. 35.35Aus$. Richard Milne Pty Ltd., PO Box 113, Pyrmont NSW 2009 Australia. **Tel** 011 61 2 8197322, FAX 011 61 2 8197650. **ED** Brian McErlane. **Bk Rev**. **Ad Acc**, **Adv Mgr:** Tracie Murray. **Circ:** 3,000. **Absorbed** Pig Farmer, 0031-9740.
 Desc: Contains management information for pork producers.

US
TITLE CHANGE

PORK MONEY II. (19??)-(19??). Periodical. English. Vance Publishing Corporation, 400 Knightsbridge Parkway, Lincolnshire IL 60069. **Tel** (800)255-5113, (708)634-2600. **Continues** Hog Farm Management. **Continued by** Pork 92.

ISSN 1197-1363
DD 338.1 CN

●**PORK PRODUCER.** [Pork prod.]. **Added/Corp** Ontario Pork Producers Marketing Board. (1993)-. Periodical. English. Four times a year. Agricultural Publishing Company Ltd, 100 Broadview Avenue, Suite 402, Toronto Ontario M4M 3H3 Canada. **Tel** (416)463-8306. **Continues** Hog Market Place Quarterly, 0380-3651.

ISSN 0745-1776
US

PORT CHALLENGER. (PORK CHALLENGER : THE NATIONAL PORK PRODUCERS COUNCIL MAGAZINE.). **Added/Corp** National Pork Producers Council (U.S.). (Mar. 1982)-. Periodical. English. Four times a year. free. Pork Publication, National Pork Producers Council, PO Box 10383, Des Moines IA 50306. **Tel** (515)223-2600.

ISSN 0137-1649
PL

PRACE I MATERIALY ZOOTECHNICZNE = POLSKII NAUCHNYI ZHURNAL PO ZOOTEKHNII. See Zoology.

ISSN 8750-5673
DD 636 US

PREMIER HOG PRODUCER. (19??)-. Trade Publication. English. Six times a year. Premier Hog Producer, PO Box 843, Franklin TN 37064. **Continues** Southern Hog Producer, 0194-4835.

US

PROCEEDINGS / LIVESTOCK CONSERVATION INSTITUTE. **Main/Corp** Livestock Conservation Institute. Meeting. (1988)-. Proceedings. English. Livestock Conservation Inst, 6414 Copps Avenue/Suite 116, Madison WI 53716. **Tel** (608)221-4848. **Continues** Livestock Conservation Institute. Meeting.; Official Proceedings.

US

PROCEEDINGS OF ANNUAL CONVENTION OF THE NATIONAL ASSOCIATION OF ANIMAL BREEDERS. **Main/Corp** National Association of Animal Breeders. **Added/Corp** National Association of Artificial Breeders. (1948)-. English. One time a year. National Association of Animal Breeders, 401 Bernadette Drive PO Box 1033, Columbia MO 65205. **Tel** (314)445-4406, FAX (314)446-2279, telex 7401040 NAAB.

ISSN 0198-8999
US
CODEN PRMCAC

PROCEEDINGS OF THE ANNUAL RECIPROCAL MEAT CONFERENCE OF THE AMERICAN MEAT SCIENCE ASSOCIATION. [Proc. annu. Recipr. Meat Conf. Am. Meat Sci. Assoc. coop. Natl. Live Stock Meat Board]. **Main/Corp** Reciprocal Meat Conference of the American Meat Science Association. **Added/Corp** American Meat Science Association. National Live Stock and Meat Board. **VFOAT** Proceedings, Annual Reciprocal Meat Conference of the American Meat Science Association in Cooperation with the National Live Stock and Meat Board; Reciprocal Meat Conference. (19??)-. Academic Scholarly Publication. English. One time a year. $30.00. National Livestock & Meat Board, 444 North Michigan Avenue, Chicago IL 60611. **Tel** (312)467-5520, FAX (312)467-9729. Index available. Documents available from CASDDS. **Continues** Reciprocal Meat Conference. Report of Proceedings.
 Ind/Abst AGRICOLA [Full Cov.]; Chem. Abstr.; Food Sci. Technol. Abstr.

LC SF ISSN 0067-2149
DD 636 AT
CODEN PAANA2

PROCEEDINGS OF THE AUSTRALIAN SOCIETY OF ANIMAL PRODUCTION. (PROCEEDINGS OF THE AUSTRALIAN SOCIETY OF ANIMAL PRODUCTION ... BIENNIAL CONFERENCE.). [Proc. Aust. Soc. Anim. Prod.]. **Main/Corp** Australian Society of Animal Production. Conference. Vol. 1 (1956)-. Proceedings. English. Every 2 years. 53.44Aus$. ASAP Publications / Australia, University of New England, Animal Science Department, Armidale New South Wales 2351 Australia. **ED** G Judson. **Circ:** 3,000. Documents available from BIOSIS Document Express, CASDDS.
 Desc: Covers the animal production of sheep, cattle, pigs and poultry.
 Ind/Abst AgBiotech News Inf.; AGRICOLA [Select. Cov.]; Agrofor. Abstr. (19??-19??); Anim. Breed. Abstr.; Biol. Abstr.; Chem. Abstr.; Curr. Cit.; Dairy Sci. Abstr.; Grass. Forage Abstr.; Helminthol. Abstr. (1991-); Index Vet.; Maize Abstr.; Nutr. Abstr. Rev., Ser. B, Live Feeds and Feed.; Nutr. Abstr. Rev., Ser. A, Hum. Exp.; Life Sci. Collect.; Pig News Inf.; Postharvest News Inf.; Poult. Abstr.; Protozoolog. Abstr.; Rev. Med. Vet. Mycology; Rice Abstr.; Sorghum Mill. Abstr.; Soyabean Abstr.; Sug. Indus. Abstr.; Vet. Bull.; Wheat Barley Trit. Abstr.; World Agric. Econ. Rural Sociol. Abstr.

ISSN 0370-2731
NZ
CODEN PZAPAD
Pr Rev.

PROCEEDINGS OF THE NEW ZEALAND SOCIETY OF ANIMAL PRODUCTION. [Proc. N. Z. soc. anim. prod.]. **Main/Corp** New Zealand Society of Animal Production. (1951)-. Proceedings. English. One time a year. $32.95. New Zealand Society Animal Product/Genetics, Ruakura Agriculture Research Centre, Private Bag, Hamilton New Zealand. **Tel** 011 64 7 8569157, FAX 011 64 7 8569150. **ED** T. Rearden. Index available. cum. index. **Bk Rev**. **Ad Acc**. **Circ:** 1,000 (ctrl). Documents available from CASDDS.
 Desc: Animal production research undertaken in New Zealand covering: sheep, cattle, deer and goats including genetics, reproduction, nutrition, management and diseases.
 Ind/Abst AgBiotech News Inf.; AGRICOLA; Agrofor. Abstr. (1991-); Anim. Breed. Abstr.; Chem. Abstr.; Curr. Cit.; Dairy Sci. Abstr.; Fish Rev. (Jan. 1989-July 1992); Food Sci. Technol. Abstr.; Grass. Forage Abstr.; Helminthol. Abstr. (1991-); Index Vet.; Nutr. Abstr. Rev., Ser. B, Live Feeds and Feed.; Pig News Inf.; Rev. Med. Vet. Mycology; Soyabean Abstr.; Vet. Bull.; Wildl. Rev. (Jan. 1989-July 1992).

LC SF105.5 .T4 ISSN 0190-4531
DD 636.08/245 US

PROCEEDINGS OF THE TECHNICAL CONFERENCE ON ARTIFICIAL INSEMINATION AND REPRODUCTION. **Main/Conf** Technical Conference on Artificial Insemination and Reproduction. **Added/Corp** National Association of Animal Breeders. (19??)-. Proceedings. English. Every 2 years. $15.00. National Association of Animal Breeders, 401 Bernadette Drive PO Box 1033, Columbia MO 65205. **Tel** (314)445-4406, FAX (314)446-2279, telex 7401040 NAAB.

ISSN 0114-4553
DD 636.305 NZ

PROCEEDINGS OF THIS SOCIETY'S SEMINAR - SHEEP & BEEF CATTLE SOCIETY OF THE NEW ZEALAND VETERINARY ASSOCIATION. (PROCEEDINGS OF THIS SOCIETY'S SEMINAR.). [Proc. Soc. Semin. - Sheep Beef Cattle Soc. N.Z. Vet. Assoc.]. (1978)-. Proceedings. English. One time a year. New Zealand Veterinary Association, PO Box 27499, Wellington New Zealand. **Tel** 011 64 4 843632.
 Ind/Abst Protozoolog. Abstr.

LC SF
DD 636 US

PROCEEDINGS / WESTERN SECTION, AMERICAN SOCIETY OF ANIMAL SCIENCE. **Main/Corp** American Society of Animal Science. Western Section. Meeting. **Added/Corp** Canadian Society of Animal Science. Western Branch. **VFOAT** Proceedings, Annual Meeting; Proceedings from Annual Meeting; WSASAS Proceedings. Vol. 33 (1982)-. Proceedings. English. One time a year. University of Nevada Animal Science Department, Reno NV 89507. **Continues** American Society of Animal Science. Western Section. Meeting. American Society of Animal Science, Western Section Meeting.
 Ind/Abst Rev. Med. Vet. Mycology; Soyabean Abstr.; World Agric. Econ. Rural Sociol. Abstr.

UY

PRODUCCION OVINA. **Added/Corp** Uruguay. Depto de Investigacion de la Produccion Ovina. Vol. 1, No. 1 (1988)-. Periodical. Spanish (summaries and/or abstracts in English).
 Ind/Abst Grass. Forage Abstr.; Nutr. Abstr. Rev., Ser. B, Live Feeds and Feed.

ISSN 0229-7876
DD 338.1/764/009714 CN
TITLE CHANGE

PRODUCTEUR DE PORC QUEBECOIS. (LE PRODUCTEUR DE PORC QUEBECOIS.). [Prod. porc que.]. Vol. 3, No. 1 (May 1981)-(199?). Periodical. French. SELC Publishing Inc., 2100 Guy Suite 200, Montreal Quebec H3H 2M8 Canada. **Tel** (514)248-3356, FAX (514)248-2195. **ED** Mario Martel. Index available. **Ad Acc**. **Circ:** 5,800. **Continues** Producteur de Porc, 0709-8294. **Merged into** Le Producteur Plus, 1183-9929.
 Desc: Farm management publication for pork producers.

ISSN 1183-7500
DD 636.5 CN

PROVOQUE (LONGUEUIL). (PROVOQUE.). [Provoque]. **Added/Corp** Federation des Producteurs de Volailles du Quebec. **VAT** Producteurs de Volailles du Quebec (Longueuil). Vol. 2, No 3 (May/June 1991)-. Periodical. French. Six times a year. Limited free distribution. Federation des Producteurs de Volailles du Quebec, 555 boulevard Roland-Therrien, Longueuil Quebec J4H 3Y9 Canada. **Continues** Bulletin (Federation des Producteurs de Volailles du Quebec), 1186-7779.

ISSN 0137-4214
PL

PRZEGLAD HODOWLANY. **Added/Corp** Polskie Towarzystwo Zootechniczne. (19??)-. Periodical. Polish. Twelve times a year. $57.00. (**Subscription address:** Ars Polona-Ruch, PO Box 1001, Krakowskie Przedmiescie 7, 00-068 Warsaw Poland. **Tel** 011 48 22 261201.)
 Ind/Abst AgBiotech News Inf.; Anim. Breed. Abstr.; Dairy Sci. Abstr.; Nutr. Abstr. Rev., Ser. B, Live Feeds and Feed.; Pig News Inf.; Plant Breed. Abstr.

NE
UDC 636.2

PUBLIKATIE - PROEFSTATION VOOR DE RUNDVEEBOUDERIJ. **Main/Corp** Proefstation Voor de Rundveenouderij. N.3- July 1974-. Monographic series. Dutch. Price varies per volume.
 Ind/Abst Dairy Sci. Abstr.; Maize Abstr.; Nutr. Abstr. Rev., Ser. B, Live Feeds and Feed.

NE

PUBLIKATIE / PROEFSTATION VOOR DE RUNDVEEHOUDERIJ, SCHAPENHOUDERIJ EN PAARDENHOUDERIJ. **Added/Corp** Proefstation voor de Rundveehouderij, Schapenhouderij en Paardenhouderij. (1983)-. Monographic series. Dutch (summaries and/or abstracts in English; table of contents in English). **Continues** Publikatie (Proefstation voor de Rundveehouderij).
 Ind/Abst Agric. Eng. Abstr.; Dairy Sci. Abstr.; Nutr. Abstr. Rev., Ser. B, Live Feeds and Feed.

ISSN 8750-1880
DD 636 US
CEASED

PUREBRED PICTURE, THE. (THE PUREBRED PICTURE / OFFICIAL PUBLICATION OF THE AMERICAN BERKSHIRE [AND] AMERICAN LANDRACE.). **Added/Corp** Poland China Record Association. American Berkshire Association. American

Agriculture —Livestock

Landrace Association. (Aug./Sept. 1984)-(Dec. 1994). Trade Publication. English. Poland China Record Association, PO Box 9758, Peoria IN 61612. **Tel** (309)691-6301. **ED** Ernie Barnes and Jack Wall. **Ad Acc**. **Circ:** 5,000 (ctrl). *Continues* Berkshire News, 0005-9196.
 Desc: Promotions of Purebred Berkshire, Poland and Landrace swine breeds. Serves to form the memberships of the 3 organizations of important happenings.

ISSN 0708-9570
DD 636.3/9/006271   CN
QUARTERLY - CANADIAN GOAT SOCIETY. **Main/Corp** Canadian Goat Society. **VAT** Canadian Goat Society. No. 1 (Summer 1978)-. Periodical. English (French; summaries and/or abstracts in French). Four times a year (Published on 15th on the month). 12.01Can$. Canadian Goat Society, PO Box 357, Fergus Ontario N1M 3E2 Canada. **Tel** (519)843-3294.

ISSN 0821-6924
DD 338.1/765142/0971   CN
UDC 339.1:637.4(71)
QUOI DE N'OEUF. Vol. 1, No. 1 (Feb. 1982)-. Periodical. French (English). Twelve times a year. $15.00. Canadian Egg Marketing Agency, 320 Queen Street, Suite 1900, Place de Ville, Ottawa Ontario K1R 5A3 Canada. **Tel** (613)238-2514, FAX (613)238-1967. **ED** Ian Elliott. **Circ:** 3,000 (ctrl).
 Desc: Articles covering agriculture.

ISSN 0827-4053
DD 636.3/13/05   CN
RAM'S HORN (SCOTSBURN). (THE RAM'S HORN.). [Ram's horn]. No. 1 (Nov. 1981)-. Periodical. English. Eleven times a year. 20.01Can$. Ram's Horn, 125 Highfield Road, Toronto Ontario M4L 2V4 Canada. **Tel** (416)469-8414, FAX (416)469-8414. **ED** Brewster Kneen and Cathleen Kneen. **Bk Rev**, (Qty: 4). **Circ:** 600 (ctrl). available on an online database from WEB.
 Desc: Food system analysis, from production to distribution, with emphasis on structure and ideology.

LC SF371 .S44   **ISSN 1084-5402**
DD 636.3/005   US
RANCH & RURAL LIVING. [Ranch rural living]. **Added/Corp** Texas Sheep and Goat Raisers' Association. **VFOAT** Ranch and Rural Living; Ranch Magazine. Vol. 73, No. 4 (Jan. 1992)-. Periodical. English. Twelve times a year. $22.00 (one-year), $40.00 (two-year). Ranch & Rural Living Magazine, PO Box 2678, San Angelo TX 76902. **Tel** (915)655-4434. *Continues* Ranch Magazine, 0145-8515.
 Ind/Abst AGRICOLA.

LC SF371 .S44   **ISSN 0145-8515**
DD 636.3/005   US
    TITLE CHANGE
RANCH MAGAZINE, THE. [Ranch mag.]. **Added/Corp** Texas Sheep and Goat Raisers' Association. (Oct. 1971)-(19??). Periodical. English. Texas Sheep and Goat Raisers Association, PO Box 2678, San Angelo TX 76902. **Tel** (915)655-4434, FAX (915)655-2255. **ED** Scott Campbell. **Ad Acc. Circ:** 7,000 (ctrl). available on microfilm and microfiche from University Microfilms International (UMI). *Continues* Sheep and Goat Raiser, 0037-3397. *Continued by* Ranch & Rural Living, 1084-5402.
 Desc: Sheep, Angora goat, Cashmere goat and cattle raiser information, market updates, wool and Mohair fashions, ranch profiles, and general and detailed agriculture information.
 Ind/Abst AGRICOLA (?-?); Wildl. Rev. (?-?).

LC S   **ISSN 0922-3282**
DD 630   NE
RAPPORT - INSTITUUT VOOR VEEVOEDINGSONDERZOEK. (IVVO RAPPORT.). [Rapp. - Inst. Veevoed. onderz.]. **Added/Corp** Instituut voor Veevoedingsonderzoek "Hoorn". **VFOAT** Rapport IVVO. (19??)-. Monographic series. Dutch (summaries and/or abstracts in English). *Continues* nstituut voor Veevoedingsonderzoek "Hoorn". Intern Rapport.
 Ind/Abst Potato Abstr.

NE
RAPPORT / PROEFSTATION VOOR DE RUNDVEEHOUDERIJ, SCHAPENHOUDERIJ EN PAARDENHOUDERIJ. **Added/Corp** Proefstation Voor de Rundveehouderij, Schapenhouderij en Paardenhouderij (Netherlands). (1982)-. Monographic series. Dutch (summaries and/or abstracts in English; table of contents in English). *Continues* Rapport (Proefstation Voor de Rundveehouderij (Netherlands)).
 Ind/Abst Agric. Eng. Abstr.; Dairy Sci. Abstr.; Nutr. Abstr. Rev., Ser. B, Live Feeds and Feed.; Plant Genet. Resour. Abstr.; Sug. Indus. Abstr.

ISSN 0347-9838
SW
RAPPORT - SVERIGES LANTBRUKSUNIVERSITET, INSTITUTIONEN FOR HUSDJURS UTFODRING OCH VARD. (RAPPORT / INSTITUTIONEN FOR HUSDJURENS UTFODRING OCH VARD.). [Rapp. - Sver. lantbruksuniv. Inst. husdjurens utfodr. vard.]. (1978)-. Monographic series. Swedish (English). Price varies per volume. Swedish University of Agricultural Sciences / Animal Husbandry, Department of Animal Husbandry, Uppsala Sweden. *Continues* Rapport (Lantbrukshogskolan. Institutionen for Husdjurens Utfodring Och Vard), 0346-766X.
 Ind/Abst Dairy Sci. Abstr.; Nutr. Abstr. Rev., Ser. B, Live Feeds and Feed.; Poult. Abstr.; Rice Abstr.

LC S
DD 630   US
RECEIPTS AND SHIPMENTS OF LIVESTOCK FOR THE YEAR. **Main/Corp** Chicago. Union Stock Yard and Transit Company. (19??)-. English.

ISSN 0034-1614
US
RECORD STOCKMAN, THE. (19??)-. Periodical. English. One time a week. $35.00. Record Stockman, PO Box 1209, Wheat Ridge CO 80034. **Tel** (303)425-5777. **ED** Dan Green. **Ad Acc**.
 Desc: Deals with livestock news and information.

US
●RED MEATS YEARBOOK. **Added/Corp** United States. Dept. of Agriculture. Economic Research Service. (1994)-. English. One time a year (July). $12.00. U.S. Department of Agriculture, ERS-NASS, 341 Victory Drive, Herndon VA 22070. **Tel** (800)999-6779, (703)834-0125. *Continues* Livestock and Meat Statistics.

RU
REFERATIVNYI ZHURNAL. MOLOCHNOE I MIASNOE SKOTOVODSTVO. **Added/Corp** Soviet Union. Ministerstvo Selskogo Khoziaistva. Vsesoiuznyi Nauchno-Issledovatelskii Institut Informatsii i Tekhniko-Ekonomicheskikh Issledovanii po Selskomu Khoziaistvu. **VFOAT** Molochnoe i Miasnoe Skotovodstvo. No. 1 (1972)-. Abstracting/Indexing Service. Russian. Six times a year. $26.00. VINITI - Vsesoyuznyi Nauchno-Tekhnicheskoi Informatsii, All-Union Scientific and Technical Information Institute, Baltiiskaia ulitsa 14, 125190 Moscow Russia. **Tel** 011 7 95 2384600, FAX 011 7 95 9430060, telex 411160. **(Subscription address:** Victor Kamkin, 4956 Boiling Brook Parkway, Rockville MD 20852. **Tel** (301)881-5973.)
 Ind/Abst Anim. Breed. Abstr.; Dairy Sci. Abstr.; Food Sci. Technol. Abstr.; Nutr. Abstr. Rev., Ser. B, Live Feeds and Feed.

ISSN 0899-3572
DD 636   US
REGISTER (KANSAS CITY, MO.), THE. (THE REGISTER.). [Register]. **Added/Corp** American Simmental Association. (1987)-. Periodical. English. Twelve times a year. $25.00. American Simmental Association, 2 Simmental Way, Bozeman MT 59715. **Tel** (800)338-8827. **ED** Jeff Thomas, (phone: (406)587-2778). **Ad Acc.** ctrl circ.

US
REGISTERED HOLSTEIN TYPE-PRODUCTION SIRE SUMMARIES. **Added/Corp** Holstein-Friesian Association of America. **VFOAT** Sire Summaries; Sire Summaries ... with Linear Descriptive Type Proofs. **VAT** Registered Holstein Type Production Sire Summaries. (1987)-. English. Two times a year. Holstein Association, 1 Holstein Place, Brattleboro VT 05302. **Tel** (802)254-4551. *Continues* Registered Holstein Total Performance Sire Summaries.

US
REPORT TO FARMERS ... ANNUAL SWINE FIELD DAY. **Main/Corp** Florida. University, Gainesville. Agricultural Extension Service. 5th Ed. (1960)-. Periodical. English. One time a year. University of Florida Agricultural Experiment Station, Gainesville FL 32601.
 Ind/Abst Nutr. Abstr. Rev., Ser. B, Live Feeds and Feed.; Pig News Inf.

LC S494 .Z8 SF871 .Z8   **ISSN 0936-6768**
DD 631/.53/05   GW
    CCC
NLM W1; RE213KL   **CODEN RDANEF**
REPRODUCTION IN DOMESTIC ANIMALS 1990. **See** Veterinary Sciences.

ISSN 0155-7742
AT
RESEARCH REPORT - CSIRO DIVISION OF ANIMAL PRODUCTION. **Main/Corp** Commonwealth Scientific and Industrial Research Organization (Australia). Division of Animal Production. (1977)-. English. Irregular. CSIRO Publications, PO Box 89, 314 Albert Street, East Melborne Victoria 3002 Australia. **Tel** 011 61 3 4187333, 4187217, FAX 011 61 3 4190459, telex AA 30236.

LC SF196.F7 F75a
DD 338.1/76200944   FR
RESULTATS DEFINITIFS DE L'ENQETE SUR LE CHEPTEL BOVIN. **Main/Corp** France. Service Central des Enquetes et Etudes Statistiques. (19??)-. French. **SCEES** - Service Central des Enquetes et Etudes Statistiques, 4 Avenue de Saint-Mande, 75570 Paris Cedex 12 France. **Tel** 011 33 1 49558576.

LC S   **ISSN 0326-0550**
DD 630   AG
UDC 636.082.4.001.5
REVISTA ARGENTINA DE PRODUCCION ANIMAL. [Rev. argent. prod. anim.]. (1980)-. Periodical. Spanish. Six times a year. Asociacion Argentina de Produccion Animal, Casilla de Correo 276 Balcaire, Buenos Aires Argentina.
 Ind/Abst Field Crop Abstr.; Index Vet.; Nutr. Abstr. Rev., Ser. B, Live Feeds and Feed.; Pig News Inf.; Plant Breed. Abstr.; Poult. Abstr.; Seed Abstr.; Soils Fert.; Sorghum Mill. Abstr.; Soyabean Abstr.; Vet. Bull.; World Agric. Econ. Rural Sociol. Abstr.

ISSN 0258-6495
CU
CODEN RCRADJ
    CEASED
REVISTA CUBANA DE REPRODUCCION ANIMAL. [Rev. cuba reprod. anim.]. (19??)-(19??). Academic Scholarly Publication. Spanish. Ediciones Cubanas, Obispo 527 Altos ESQ Bernaza, CP 10100 Havana Cuba. Documents available from CASDDS.
 Ind/Abst Anim. Breed. Abstr.; Chem. Abstr.; Dairy Sci. Abstr.; Nutr. Abstr. Rev., Ser. B, Live Feeds and Feed.; Pig News Inf.

ISSN 0397-6866
UDC 63   FR
REVUE CHIEN 2000. [Rev. chien]. **VFOAT** Revue Chien Deux Mille; Revue Chiens 2000. (1976)-. Periodical. French. Eleven times a year. $54.89. Revue Chien 2000, 8 10 rue Pierre Brossolette, 92300 Levallois Perr France. **Tel** 011 33 1 40874015. *Continues* Revue du Chien, Chiens 2000, 0397-6874.

ISSN 0242-6595
FR
CODEN REAADG
REVUE DE L'ALIMENTATION ANIMALE. [Rev. aliment. anim.]. No. 341 (Mar. 1981)-. Academic Scholarly Publication. French. Ten times a year. $168.42. Nouvelles Editions Publs Agricoles, 8 Cite Paradis, F 75010 Paris Cedex 10 France. **Tel** 011 33 1 40227900, 011 33 1 40227974. Index available. cum. index. **Bk Rev. Ad Acc. Circ:** 2,500. Documents available from BIOSIS Document Express, CASDDS. *Continues* Industries de l'Alimentation Animale.
 Desc: News, information studies and reports concerning feedstuff industries and animal products.
 Ind/Abst Biol. Abstr. (1987-); Chem. Abstr.

LC SF221 .I42   **ISSN 0035-3590**
DD 338.1/7/705   FR
CODEN RLAFA9
REVUE LAITIERE FRANCAISE. [Rev. lait. fr.]. **VFOAT** RLF. (19??)-. Academic Scholarly Publication. French. Eleven times a year. $100.61. Revue Laitiere Francaise, BP 10, 76231 BOIS GIlaume CDX France. **Tel** 011 33 16 35594, 500. **Ad Acc. Circ:** 8,000 (ctrl). *Continues* Industrie Laitiere.
 Ind/Abst AGRICOLA; BioBusiness (1990-); EMBASE; Food Sci. Technol. Abstr.; Int. Packag. Abstr.

FR
REVUE TECHNIQUE DE LA VIANDE ET DES ABATTOIRS. French. Twelve times a year. 315.00F. Sepaic, 42 rue du Louvre, BP 551, 75001 Paris France. **Tel** 011 33 1 42335740.

LC SF55.A39 C65A
DD 338.1/7/608830966   UV
UDC 338.3:636.2(71)
REVUE TRIMESTRIELLE D'INFORMATION TECHNIQUE ET ECONOMIQUE. **Main/Corp** Communaute Economique du Betail et de la Viande. Secretariat Executif. Periodical. French. Communaute Economique du Betail et de la Viande Secretariat Executif, BP 638, Ouagadougou Burkina Faso.

Agriculture —Livestock

LC HA1173 .A27 SF196.A8
DD 314.36
UDC 338.3:636.2(436)
AU
RINDERRASSENERHEBUNG. See Agriculture-Abstracting, Bibliographies and Statistics.

IT
RIVISTA DI SUINICOLTURA. VFOAT Suinicoltura. Vol. 12, No. 1 (Jan. 1971)-. Periodical. Italian. Twelve times a year. L42240. Edagricole, PO Box 2157, 40100 Bologna Italy. **Tel** 011 39 51 492211 Ext. 22, FAX 011 39 51 493660, telex 510336 EDAGRI. **Continues** Suinicoltura.
Ind/Abst AGRICOLA; Anim. Breed. Abstr.; Biodeter. Abstr. (1991-); Dairy Sci. Abstr.; Helminthol. Abstr. (19??-19??); Index Vet.; Irr. Drain. Abstr.; Nutr. Abstr. Rev., Ser. B, Live Feeds and Feed.; Nutr. Abstr. Rev., Ser. A, Hum. Exp.; Pig News Inf.; Rev. Med. Vet. Entomol.; Soils Fert.; Vet. Bull.

ISSN 1072-5636
DD 636
US
•**ROCKY MOUNTAIN LIVESTOCK JOURNAL.** [Rocky Mt. livest. j.]. Vol. 20, No. 196 (Oct. 1993)-. Trade Publication. English. Twelve times a year. Twin Publishing Co., 425 West Griggs, Las Cruces NM 88005. **Tel** (800)524-0070, FAX (505)524-1702. **ED** Janet Sands. **Ad Acc. Circ:** 6,000. **Continues** Rocky Mountain Feed and Livestock Journal, 1070-0927.
Desc: Articles included pertain to governmental legislation concerning the livestock industry and related fields.

LC SF1 .A355a
PL
ROCZNIKI AKADEMII ROLNICZEJ W POZNANIU - WYDZIAL ZOOTECHNICZNY. Main/Corp Akademia Rolnicza w Poznaniu. Wydzial Zootechniczny. (1973)-. Polish (summaries and/or abstracts in English and Russian). One time a year. $12.00 US. Wydawnictwo Akademii Rolniczej w Poznaniu, Ul. Witosa 45, 60-667 Poznan Poland. **Tel** 011 48 61 487809, FAX 011 48 61 487802. **Ad Acc. Circ:** 200 (ctrl). **Continues** Wyzsza Szkola Rolnicza. Wydzial Zootechniczny. Roczniki Wyzszej Szkoly Rolniczej w Poznaniu - Wydzial Zootechniczny.
Desc: Scientific papers in the 13 specialist series are published; each paper contains explanations of tables and figures in English.
Ind/Abst For. Prod. Abstr. (1991-).

ISSN 0137-1657
PL
CODEN RNZOD8
ROCZNIKI NAUKOWE ZOOTECHNIKI = ANNALS OF ANIMAL SCIENCE. [Rocz. nauk. zootech.]. **Added/Corp** Instytut Zootechniki (Poland). **VFOAT** Polish Journal of Animal Science and Technology.; Pol'skii Zhurnal Zootekhniki i Tekhnologii. Vol. 1 (1974)-. Academic Scholarly Publication. Polish (summaries and/or abstracts in English, Russian, Polish and French; table of contents in English and Russian). Two times a year. Instytut Zootechniki / Institute of Animal Production, Ul. Sarego 2, 31-047 Krakow Poland. **Tel** 011 48 12 227333, FAX 011 48 12 228065. **Circ:** 800. available on an online database; available on CD-ROM. Documents available from CASDDS.
Desc: Breeding, feed science, and animal production economics.
Ind/Abst AGRICOLA; Chem. Abstr.; Fish Rev. (Jan. 1989-July 1992); Food Sci. Technol. Abstr.; Wildl. Rev. (Jan. 1989-July 1992).

ISSN 0137-1665
PL
ROCZNIKI NAUKOWE ZOOTECHNIKI. MONOGRAFIE I ROZPRAWY. [Rocz. naukowe zootech., monogr. rozpr.]. **VFOAT** Roczniki Naukowe Zootechniki. (1975)-. Periodical. Polish (summaries and/or abstracts in English and Russian). Panstwowe Wydawnictwo Naukowe / PWN, (Polish Scientific Publishers PWN Ltd.), Ul. Miodowa 10, PO Box 391, 00-251 Warsaw Poland. **Tel** 011 48 22 312738, FAX 011 48 22 267163. **Supersedes** Zeszyty Naukowe. Seria A.
Ind/Abst AGRICOLA; Food Sci. Technol. Abstr.; Grass. Forage Abstr.; Nutr. Abstr. Rev., Ser. B, Live Feeds and Feed.; Pig News Inf.; Postharvest News Inf.; Potato Abstr.; Poult. Abstr.

ISSN 0318-6806
DD 636.3/908/20627123
CN
UDC 636.393
S. L. A. N. T. : SAANEN, LAMANCHA, ALPINE, NUBIAN, TOGGENBURG. VFOAT SLANT. Jan. 1974-. Periodical. English. Irregular. $2.50. SLANT, RR 6 Suite 6, PO Box 16 Canada.

ISSN 0036-455X
DD 636
US
CEASED
SANTA GERTRUDIS JOURNAL, THE. (1959/1960)-Vol. 36 (1995). Trade Publication. English. Santa Gertrudis Journal, PO Box 938, Keller TX 76248. **Tel** (817)831-4468. **ED** Jeff Dunklin. Index available. **Bk Rev. Ad Acc. Circ:** 5,000 (ctrl).
Desc: Dedicated to the Santa Gertrudis breed of beef cattle and breeders, both purebred and commercial.

ISSN 8750-3743
US
UDC 636.282
SANTA GERTRUDIS TRIBUNE. (198?)-. Periodical. English. Twenty-four times a year. $10.00 (one-year), $25.00 (three-year). Santa Gertrudis Tribune, PO Box 158, Valley Mills TX 76689. **Tel** (817)932-6364. **ED** Kay Barrett. **Ad Acc. Circ:** 4,800.
Desc: Contains current events in Santa Gertrudis breeds and general information of beef industry.

ISSN 0136-3751
RU
SBORNIK NAUCHNYKH TRUDOV (VSESOIUZNYI NAUCHNO-ISSLEDOVATELSKII INSTITUT FIZIOLOGII, BIOKHIMII I PITANIIA). See Veterinary Sciences.

BW
SBORNIK TRUDOV - BELORUSSKII NAUCHNO-ISSLEDOVATEL'SKII INSTITUT ZHIVOTNOVODSTVA. Main/Corp Belorusskii Nauchno-Issledovatel'skii Institut Zhivotnovodstva. Vol. 16 (1975)-. Monographic series. Russian. Price varies per volume. **Continues** Nauchnye Trudy / Beloruskii Nauchno-Issledovateskii Institut Zhivotnovodstva.
Ind/Abst Nutr. Abstr. Rev., Ser. B, Live Feeds and Feed.; Pig News Inf.

XR
CODEN SVSBDZ
SBORNIK VYSOKE SKOLY ZEMEDELSKE V PRAZE, FAKULTA AGRONOMICKA. RADA B. ZIVOCISNA VYROBA. [Sb. vys. sk. zemed. Praze, Fak. agron. Rada B., Zivoc vyroba]. **Added/Corp** Vysoka Skola Zemedelska v Praze. Agronomicka Fakulta. **VFOAT** Zivocisna Vyroba. (1966)-. Academic Scholarly Publication. Czech (summaries and/or abstracts in English, German and Russian; table of contents in English, German and Russian). One time a year. Vysoka Skola Zemedelska, Zemedelska 1, 61300 Brno Czech Republic. **Tel** FAX 42 05 452 11128. Documents available from CASDDS. **Continues in part** Sbornik Vysoke Skoly Zemedelske v Praze, Fakulta Agronomicka.
Ind/Abst AGRICOLA; Agric. Eng. Abstr. (1991-); Chem. Abstr.; EMBASE; Field Crop Abstr.; Food Sci. Technol. Abstr.; Index Vet.; Plant Genet. Resour. Abstr.; Poult. Abstr.; Rev. Med. Vet. Mycology.

ISSN 1079-7963
DD 636
US
•**SEEDSTOCK EDGE.** See Veterinary Sciences.

SP
SERIE: PRODUCCION ANIMAL.
Added/Corp Instituto Nacional de Investigaciones Agrarias. **VFOAT** Produccion Animal. No. 1 (1971)-. Spanish (summaries and/or abstracts in English). Four times a year. 3,000ptas. Instituto Nacional de Investigaciones Agrarias, C. Jose Abascal 56, 28003 Madrid Spain. **Tel** 011 34 1 3473906, FAX (91)4423587, telex 48489 INIA E. **Bk Rev. Circ:** 1,500. **Supersedes in part** Spain. Instituto Nacional de Investigaciones Agronomicas. Anales; Spain. Instituto Nacional de Investigaciones Agronomicas. Boletin.
Desc: Original scientific papers that represent a significant contribution to knowledge of concepts related to animal production and animal health.

ISSN 0037-3338
CN
UDC 636.5
SHAVER NEWS. Vol. 1 (March 1964)-. Periodical. English (Spanish). Irregular. Free. Shaver Poultry Breeding Farms, Cambridge Galt Ontario N1R 5V9 Canada. **Tel** (519)621-5191, telex 069-59337. **Circ:** 6,000.

US
•**SHEEP & GOAT RESEARCH JOURNAL.**
Added/Corp American Sheep Industry Association. **VFOAT** Sheep and Goat Research Journal. Vol. 10, No. 2 (1994)-. Periodical. English. Three times a year. American Sheep Industry Association, 6911 South Yosemite Street, Englewood CO 80112. **Tel** (303)771-3500, FAX (303)771-8200. **Continues** Sheep Research Journal, 1057-1809.
Ind/Abst Bibliogr. Agric.

ISSN 0895-1500
US
DD 677
SHEEP AND GOAT, WOOL AND MOHAIR. [Sheep goat wool mohair]. **Added/Corp** Texas Agricultural Experiment Station. (197?)-. English.
Ind/Abst AGRICOLA [Full Cov.].

LC SF375.4.A1 U54a
ISSN 0094-3851
US
SHEEP AND GOATS. Added/Corp United States. Crop Reporting Board. United States. Agricultural Statistics Board. (1973)-. Government Publication. English. One time a year (Feb.). $19.00. US Department of Agriculture / National Agricultural Statistics Service (NASS), Room 5829 South Building, Washington DC 20250. **Tel** (202)720-4020, FAX (314)875-5231. **Continues** Cattle, Sheep and Goat Inventory, 0094-3827.
Desc: List number of operations keeping sheep by states and total for U.S.

US
UDC 636.38(777)
SHEEP AND LAMBS ON FEED / IOWA CROP AND LIVESTOCK REPORTING SERVICE. Periodical. English. Two times a year. The Service, Full Depository, 707 Savings and Loan Building, Des Moines IA 50309.
Desc: Statistics on placements, marketings, inventories; weight groups; stock sheep and lambs in selected states and United States.

US
SHEEP AND WOOL. Added/Corp Iowa Crop and Livestock Reporting Service. United States. Dept. of Agriculture. Economics, Statistics and Cooperatives Service. Iowa. Agricultural Statistics Division. (19??)-. English. One time a year. The Service, Full Depository, 707 Savings and Loan Building, Des Moines IA 50309.

ISSN 0037-3400
US
SHEEP BREEDER AND SHEEPMAN MAGAZINE. Added/Corp American Cheviot Sheep Society. American Corriedale Assn. American Oxford Down Record Assn. American Oxford Sheep Assn. American & Delaire-Merino Assn. American Lincoln Assn. Vol. 100, No. 11 (Nov. 1980)-. Periodical. English. Ten times a year. $18.00. Livestock Publishing Inc., PO Box 796, Columbia MO 65201. **Tel** (314)442-8257. **ED** Larry Mead. Index available. **Ad Acc. Circ:** 8,500 (ctrl). **Continues** Sheep Breeder and Sheepman.

ISSN 0702-8881
DD 636.3/00971
CN
SHEEP CANADA MAGAZINE. (SHEEP CANADA.). (July/Aug. 1976)-. Periodical. English. Four times a year. 12.01Can$. Consolidated Communications, 807 Manning Road Northeast, Suite 200, Calgary Alberta T2E 7M8 Canada. **Tel** (403)569-9520, FAX (403)569-9590. **ED** Pat Ottmann. **Ad Acc. Circ:** 1,500 (ctrl).
Desc: Information concerning lamb and wool production and marketing, book reviews, advertising, reviews on new technology in sheep industry from around the world.

ISSN 0952-1380
DD 636.3142
UK
SHEEP DAIRY NEWS. [Sheep dairy news]. (1984)-. Periodical. English. Three times a year. $11.98. British Sheep Dairying Association, Wield Wood, Alresford SO24 9RU United Kingdom. **Tel** 011 44 1420 563151, FAX 011 44 1420 561018.
Ind/Abst Index Vet.; Nutr. Abstr. Rev., Ser. B, Live Feeds and Feed.; Vet. Bull.

ISSN 0141-2434
UK
SHEEP FARMER. [Sheep Farmer]. (1974)-. Periodical. English. Four times a year. comes with National Sheep Association Membership. National Sheep Association, Sheep Center, Malvern Worcester, WR13 6PH United Kingdom. **Tel** 011 44 1684 892661, FAX 011 44 1684 892663.

ISSN 0228-2933
DD 636.3/11/0971
CN
UDC 636.3/.38(71)
SHEEP FOCUS "N" FACTS. [Sheep focus facts]. **VAT** Focus and Facts. No. 1- July 1980-. Periodical. English (summaries and/or abstracts in French). Six times a year. $7.74. Sheep Focus and Facts, PO Box 1000, Mountain Ontario K0E 1S0 Canada. **Tel** (613)989-2645.

AT
SHEEP INDUSTRY REVIEW VICTORIA. Main/Corp Victoria, Australia. Dept. of Agriculture. Sheep Industry Branch. (1973)-. Periodical. English. Victoria Department of Agriculture / Sheep Industry Branch, Victoria Australia.

ISSN 0279-9200
DD 636
US
SHEEP MAGAZINE. [Sheep mag.]. **VFOAT** Sheep. (19??)-. Periodical. English. Ten times a year (monthly with April-May and Aug-Sept. combined). $19.00. Duck Creek Publications, West 2997 Markert Road, Helenville WI 53137. **Tel** (414)593-8385, FAX (414)593-8384. **ED** D E Thompson. **Bk Rev. Ad Acc. Circ:** 12,000.
Desc: For those interested in raising sheep for fun and profit.

Agriculture — Livestock

DD 636
ISSN 1057-1809
US
TITLE CHANGE
SHEEP RESEARCH JOURNAL. (SHEEP RESEARCH JOURNAL / SID, SHEEP INDUSTRY DEVELOPMENT PROGRAM, INC.). [Sheep res. j.]. **Added/Corp** Sheep Industry Development Program. **VFOAT** SID Sheep Research Journal; SID Research Journal. **VAT** Sheep Industry Development Research Journal; Sheep Industry Development Sheep Research Journal. (1989)-(1994). Periodical. English. American Sheep Industry Association, 6911 South Yosemite Street, Englewood CO 80112. **Tel** (303)771-3500, FAX (303)771-8200. **Continues** Research Journal (Sheep Industry Development Program). **Continued by** Sheep & Goat Research Journal.
Ind/Abst Field Crop Abstr.; Grass. Forage Abstr.; Index Vet.; Nutr. Abstr. Rev., Ser. B, Live Feeds and Feed.; Protozoolog. Abstr.; Vet. Bull.; World Agric. Econ. Rural Sociol. Abstr.

LC SF375.5.N4 A3
DD 338.1/7/63009931
NZ
SHEEP RETURNS. Main/Corp New Zealand. Dept. of Statistics. (19??)-. English. One time a year. 31.35NZ$. Department of Statistics / New Zealand, PO Box 2922, Wellington New Zealand. **Tel** 011 64 4 4954600. **ED** K Sullivan. **Bk Rev. Circ:** 450 (ctrl). **Continues** Annual Sheep Returns.

ISSN 8750-7897
US
SHEPHERD (NEW WASHINGTON, OHIO), THE. (THE SHEPHERD.). [Shepherd]. **VFOAT** Shepherd Magazine. Vol. 30, No. 1 (Jan. 1985)-. Trade Publication. English. Twelve times a year. $20.00. Sheep and Farm Life, 5969 Johnston Road, New Washington OH 44854. **Tel** (419)492-2364. **ED** Guy and Pat Flora (editor's address: PO Box 97, Cardington, OH 43315-0097; phone: (419)947-9289). Index Bound in First Issue (Free). **Bk Rev**, (Qty: 2). **Ad Acc, Adv Mgr:** Ken Kark, **Tel** (419)492-2364. **Circ:** 6,000. **Formed by the union of** Shepherd (Sheffield, Mass.) **and** Sheep and Farm Life, 0199-3054.
Desc: Serves those interested and involved in any aspect of the sheep and wool industry.

UDC 636.32/.38
US
SHEPHERD'S FRIEND : FOR THOSE WHO CARE FOR SHEEP, THE. Vol. 1, No. 1 (April 1985)-. Periodical. English. Twelve times a year. Graphicom Inc, PO Box 8246, Madeira Beach FL 33738. **Tel** (606)986-1495. **Formed by the union of** Sheep Tales **and** Lamb & Wool Production.

DD 636
ISSN 0149-9319
US
SHORTHORN COUNTRY. [Shorthorn ctry.]. **Added/Corp** American Shorthorn Association. Vol. 1, (May 1, 1974)-. Trade Publication. English. Eleven times a year (monthly except June). $24.00. American Shorthorn Association, 8288 Hascall Street, Omaha NE 68124. **Tel** (402)393-7200, FAX (402)393-7203. **ED** L. Jess Asher. **Ad Acc, Adv Mgr:** A. K. Sears, **Tel** (402)393-7051. **Circ:** 4,950 (ctrl).
Desc: Official breed publication of the American Shorthorn Association.

DD 636.2/22
ISSN 0037-427X
CN
SHORTHORN NEWS. [Shorthorn news]. **Added/Corp** Canadian Shorthorn Associaion. **VFOAT** Canadian Shorthorn News. (1???)-. Periodical. English (French). Eight times a year. 25.00Can$. Canadian Shorthorn Association, 5 Douglas Street Gummer Building, Guelph Ontario N1H 2S8 Canada. **Tel** (519)822-6841. **ED** Craig Andrew. **Ad Acc. Circ:** 1,800 (ctrl).
Desc: Includes Shorthorn show and sale reports, promotion of Shorthorn breed and editorials on Shorthorn breeds.

UDC 636.2
ISSN 0195-2463
US
SHOW STEER, THE. Vol. 1 (Sept. 1979)-. Periodical. English. Irregular. $15.00. Show Steer, PO Box 111, Eagleville MO 64442. **Tel** (816)867-3316. **ED** Eldon L Miller. **Ad Acc. Circ:** 8,000 (ctrl).
Desc: Livestock publication. Cattle show results.

US
SID RESEARCH JOURNAL. Added/Corp Sheep Industry Development Program. **VFOAT** Research Journal. **VAT** Sheep Industry Development Research Journal. Vol. 4, No. 2 (Spring 1988)-. Periodical. English. Three times a year (published Spring, Summer and Fall). $30.00 US; $45.00 other. American Sheep Industry Association, 6911 South Yosemite Street, Englewood CO 80112. **Tel** (303)771-3500, FAX (303)771-8200. **Continues** SID Research Digest.
Desc: For progressive producers, researchers, and educators.

DD 636.2'36
ISSN 0225-7211
CN
SIMMENTAL COUNTRY. Added/Corp Canadian Simmental Association. Vol. 1 (Oct. 1979)-. Trade Publication. English. Twelve times a year. 28.42Can$. Pritchett Publications, Simmental Country, #13-4101 19th Street North East, Calgary Alberta T2E 7C4 Canada. **Tel** (403)250-5255. **Supersedes** Simmental Scene, 0318-0913.

US
SIMMENTAL JOURNAL. No. 1 (April 15, 1975)-. Periodical. English. Twenty-four times a year.

UDC 636.237.23
US
SIMMENTAL SHIELD UPDATE. VFOAT Update. Vol. 1, No. 1 (Aug. 1977)-. Periodical. English. Twelve times a year.
Ind/Abst Life Sci. Collect.

AG
SINTESIS ESTADISTICA - MINISTERIO DI ECONOMIA, JUNTA NACIONAL DE CARNES DE LA REPUBLICA ARGENTINA. See Agriculture-Abstracting, Bibliographies and Statistics.

SO
SOMALI JOURNAL OF RANGE SCIENCE : PUBLICATION OF THE DEPARTMENT OF BOTANY AND RANGE SCIENCE, FACULTY OF AGRICULTURE, SOMALI NATIONAL UNIVERSITY. Added/Corp Universita Nazionale della Somalia. Dept. of Botany and Range Science. Vol. 1, No. 1 (Apr. 1986)-. Periodical. English. Two times a year.
Desc: Focuses on the Somali rangelands, the management of the rangelands, and livestock of the area.
Ind/Abst Seed Abstr.

ISSN 0375-1589
SA
CCC
CODEN SAJAC9
Pr Rev.
SOUTH AFRICAN JOURNAL OF ANIMAL SCIENCE. [S. Afr. j. anim. sci.]. **Added/Corp** South African Society of Animal Production. **VFOAT** Suid-Afrikaanse Tydskrif vir Veekunde. Vol. 1 (1971)-. Academic Scholarly Publication. English (Afrikaans; summaries and/or abstracts in English and Afrikaans). Four times a year. $38.77. Foundation for Education Science & Technology, PO Box 1758, Pretoria 0001 South Africa. **Tel** 011 27 12 3226404, FAX 011 27 12 3207803. **ED** R. I. Mackie. Index available. **Bk Rev. Ad Acc. Circ:** 1,000 (ctrl). Documents available from The Genuine Article, BIOSIS Document Express, CASDDS. **Supersedes** South African Society of Animal Production. Proceedings; **Absorbed** Agroanimalia, 0302-7104.
Desc: Original research in animal science.
Ind/Abst Abstr. Anthropol.; AgBiotech News Inf.; AGRICOLA [Full Cov.]; Anim. Breed. Abstr.; Biodeter. Abstr. (1991-); Biol. Abstr.; Chem. Abstr.; Curr. Cit.; Curr. Contents Agric. Biol. Environ. Sci.; Dairy Sci. Abstr.; Field Crop Abstr.; Fish Rev. (19??-199?); Food Sci. Technol. Abstr.; Grass. Forage Abstr.; Index Vet.; Maize Abstr.; Nutr. Abstr. Rev., Ser. B, Live Feeds and Feed.; Life Sci. Collect.; PESTDOC; Pig News Inf.; Plant Breed. Abstr.; Postharvest News Inf.; Poult. Abstr.; Res. Alert [Select. Cov.]; Seed Abstr.; Soyabean Abstr.; Vet. Bull.; Wheat Barley Trit. Abstr.; Wildl. Rev. (19??-199?).

US
SOUTH CAROLINA EGGSAMINER. Added/Corp South Carolina Egg Board. Vol. 6, No.8 (Sept. 1978)-. Periodical. English. Twelve times a year. South Carolina Egg Board, PO Box 11280, Columbia SC 29211.

LC S
DD 630
US
SOUTHWEST REFERENCE ... . 1981-. English. One time a year. $12.00. The Weekly Livestock Reporter, 120 No Rayner, PO Box 7796, Fort Worth TX 76111. **Tel** (817)831-3147. **ED** Ted Goudly. **Ad Acc. Circ:** 20,000.
Desc: Livestock production and marketing, both registered and commercial, general markets, feed grains and livestock, legislation and events affecting farmers and ranchers.

DD 636
ISSN 1050-9526
US
SOUTHWEST STOCKMAN. [Southwest stockm.]. (1990)-. Periodical. English. Fifty-one times per year. $30.00. Record Stockman, PO Box 1209, Wheat Ridge CO 80034. **Tel** (303)425-5777. **Continues** Texas Farm & Ranch News, 0049-3511.

US
TITLE CHANGE
SPOTTED NEWS. (1926)-(1995). Periodical. English. National Spotted Swine Record Inc., 1803 West Detweiller Drive, PO Box 9758, Peoria IL 61615. **Tel** (309)693-1804, (309)693-1804. **Merged into** Chester White Journal Spotted News.

ISSN 0239-5096
PL
STAN HODOWLI I WYNIKI OCENY SWIN W ROKU ... = REPORT ON PIG BREEDING IN POLAND IN ... . Added/Corp Instytut Zootechniki (Poland) Centralna Stacja Hodowli Zwierzat (Poland). **VFOAT** Report on Pig Breeding in Poland in ... . (1982)-. Polish (summaries and/or abstracts in English). One time a year. Instytut Zootechniki / Institute of Animal Production, Ul. Sarego 2, 31-047 Krakow Poland. **Tel** 011 48 12 227333, FAX 011 48 12 228065. **Continues** Wyniki Oceny Swin na Podstawie Badan Przeprowadzonych w Stacjach Kontroli Uzytkowosci Rzeznej Trzody Chlewnej Instytutu Zootechniki za Rok ... .
Ind/Abst Pig News Inf.

LC SF55.I8 A56
DD 338.1/76/00945021
IT
STATISTICHE DELLA ZOOTECNIA, PESCA E CACCIA. Added/Corp Istituto Centrale di Statistica (Italy). Vol. 26 (1984)-. Italian. One time a year. Istituto Nazionale Statistica, GBP SEZ4 Via Cesare Balbo 16, 00184 Rome Italy. **Tel** 011 39 6 46735118. **Continues** Annuario Statistico della Zootecnia, Pesca e Caccia, 0390-6426.

LC S235 .A8193
DD 338.1/0945/021
ISSN 1120-8945
IT
CEASED
STATISTICHE DELL'AGRICOLTURA, ZOOTECNIA E MEZZI DI PRODUZIONE. [Stat. agric. zootec. mezzi prod.]. **Added/Corp** Istituto Centrale di Statistica (Italy) Istituto Nazionale di Statistica (Italy). No. 33 (1985)-(June 1994). Italian. Istituto Nazionale Statistica, GBP SEZ4 Via Cesare Balbo 16, 00184 Rome Italy. **Tel** 011 39 6 46735118. **(Subscription address:** Superintendent of Documents, US Government Printing Office, Washington DC 20402. **) Continues** Statistiche Agrarie, 1120-8937.

AT
STOCK JOURNAL (ADELAIDE, S. AUST.). (STOCK JOURNAL.). **Added/Corp** Adelaide Woolbrokers' Association. South Australian Stock Salesmen's Association. (1967)-. Periodical. English. One time a week. 78.10Aus$. Stock Journal Publishers, 213 Greenhill Road, Unley SA 5061 Australia. **Tel** 011 61 8 3725222. **Continues** Adelaide Stock & Station Journal.

DD 338.1/76213/097124
ISSN 0820-4683
CN
STOCKGROWER DIGEST, THE. [Stockgrow. dig.]. Vol. 16, No. 2 IE Vol. 1, No. 1 (Feb. 1987)-. Periodical. English. Twelve times a year. Focus Publications Inc, PO Box 4752, Regina Saskatchewan S4P 3Y4 Canada. **Continues** The Saskatchewan Stockgrower Magazine, 0820-4675.

DD 636
ISSN 0899-1057
US
STOCKMAN GRASS FARMER, THE. [Stockman grass farmer.]. **VFOAT** Grass Farmer. Vol. 44, No. 2 (Feb. 1987)-. Periodical. English. Twelve times a year. $24.50 (one-year), $40.00 (two-year) US; $50.00 (one-year), $80.00 (two-year) other. Stockman Magazine, PO Box 9607, Jackson MS 39211. **Tel** (601)981-4805. **Continues** Stockman.

DD 338.4/7664/00971
ISSN 0527-6268
CN
STOCKS OF FOOD COMMODITIES IN COLD STORAGE AND OTHER WAREHOUSES. See Agriculture-Dairy Industry.

UDC 637
ISSN 1016-5711
SJ
SUDAN JOURNAL OF ANIMAL PRODUCTION, THE. [Sudan j. anim. prod.]. (1988)-. Periodical. English. Two times a year. Veterinary Research Administration, PO Box 8067 El Amarat, Khartoum Sudan.
Ind/Abst Index Vet.; Nutr. Abstr. Rev., Ser. B, Live Feeds and Feed.; Poult. Abstr.; Sorghum Mill. Abstr.; Sug. Indus. Abstr.; Wheat Barley Trit. Abstr.

NLM W1 SU161
ISSN 0562-5084
SJ
CODEN SJVSAE
SUDAN JOURNAL OF VETERINARY SCIENCE AND ANIMAL HUSBANDRY, THE. See Veterinary Sciences.

Agriculture —Livestock

DD 636
ISSN 0194-7230
US

SUFFOLK BANNER, THE. [Suffolk banner]. (19??)-(1993). Periodical. English. Banner Publications / Illinois, PO Box 500, Cuba IL 61427. **Tel** (309)785-5058, FAX (309)785-5050. **ED** Gregory A. Deakin. **Ad Acc.** Circ: 3,000. **Merged with** Hampshire World (Cuba, Ill. : 1989) **to form** Banner (Cuba, Ill.), 1075-0096.
Desc: Devoted solely to suffolk sheep.

LC HD9428.A83 W4686A
DD 354.9410082/42
AT

SUMMARY OF ACTIVITIES OF THE WESTERN AUSTRALIAN MEAT INDUSTRY AUTHORITY FOR THE YEAR ENDED ... . **Main/Corp** Western Australian Meat Industry Authority. English. One time a year. Western Australian Meat Industry Authority, PO Box 56, Victoria Park 6100 Perth Western Australia.

LC WMLC L 83/6650
AT

SUPPLEMENTARY SHEEP BRANDS AND MARKS DIRECTORY OF NEW SOUTH WALES. (19??)-. Directory. English. Irregular.

ISSN 0274-5410
US

SURVEY ANNOUNCEMENT - KENTUCKY CROP & LIVESTOCK REPORTING SERVICE. **Main/Corp** Kentucky Crop & Livestock Reporting Service. Vol. 1 (May 27, 1980)-. Periodical. English. Six times a year. Kentucky Crop & Livestock Reporting Service, PO Box 1120, 645 Post Office Building, Louisville KY 40201.

ISSN 0039-713X
RU
CODEN SVINAI

SVINOVODSTVO (MOSKVA). (SVINOVODSTVO.). [Svinovodstvo]. **Added/Corp** Soviet Union. Ministerstvo Selskogo Khoziaistva. (1930)-. Academic Scholarly Publication. Russian. Six times a year. $79.95. **(Subscription address:** East View Publications Inc., 3020 Harbor Lane North, Suite 110, Minneapolis MN 55447. **Tel** (800)477-1005, (612)550-0961, FAX (612)559-2931.**)** Documents available from CASDDS.
Ind/Abst Anim. Breed. Abstr.; Chem. Abstr. (1930-1983); Maize Abstr.; Pig News Inf.; Wheat Barley Trit. Abstr.

ISSN 1066-4963
US

●**SWINE HEALTH AND PRODUCTION.** (SWINE HEALTH AND PRODUCTION : THE OFFICIAL JOURNAL OF THE AMERICAN ASSOCIATION OF SWINE PRACTITIONERS.). **Added/Corp** American Association of Swine Practitioners. (1993)-. Periodical. English. Six times a year. $75.00. American Association of Swine Practitioners, 5921 Fleur Drive, Des Moines IA 50321. **Continues** Newsletter (American Association of Swine Practitioners).

ISSN 0181-6764
FR

TECHNI-PORC. (Jan./Feb. 1978)-. Periodical. French. Six times a year. $69.99. Institut Technique de Porc, 149 rue de Bercy, 75579 Paris Cedex 12 France. **Tel** 011 33 1 40045362, FAX 011 33 1 40045377. **ED** J. G. Povlenc. cum. index. **Bk Rev**, (Qty: 6). **Ad Acc. Circ:** 1,000. **Continues** Institut Technique du Porc. Bulletin.
Ind/Abst Anim. Breed. Abstr.; Pig News Inf.; World Agric. Econ. Rural Sociol. Abstr.

LC S
DD 630
ISSN 0279-165X
US

TEXAS FARMER STOCKMAN. See Agriculture.

ISSN 0744-4761
US

TEXAS HEREFORD. **Added/Corp** Texas Hereford Assocation. Vol. 1 (1951/52)-. Periodical. English. Eleven times a year (monthly except July). $10.00. Texas Hereford Association, 4609 Airport Freeway, Fort Worth TX 76117. **Tel** (817)831-3161, FAX (817)831-3162. **ED** Jack Chastain. **Ad Acc. Circ:** 2,100.
Desc: Information on health, feeding and other information on cattle specifically Hereford breed.

LC HD9417.T4 T49a
DD 338.1/7/6009764
ISSN 0091-1550
US
TITLE CHANGE

TEXAS LIVESTOCK STATISTICS. See Agriculture-Abstracting, Bibliographies and Statistics.

ISSN 0747-1556
DD 636
US

TEXAS LONGHORN JOURNAL. (TEXAS LONGHORN JOURNAL : THE BUSINESS PUBLICATION OF THE TEXAS LONGHORN INDUSTRY.). [Tex. longhorn j.]. (19??)-. Periodical. English. Six times a year. Texas Longhorn Journal, PO Box 1609, Monument CO 80132. **Tel** (719)488-0700.

II

THESIS ABSTRACTS (INDIAN AGRICULTURAL UNIVERSITIES ASSOCIATION). (THESIS ABSTRACTS.). **Added/Corp** Indian Agricultural Universities Association. Haryana Agricultural University. Directorate of Publications. (19??)-. English. Four times a year. $40.00. Haryana Agricultural University / Publications, Directorate of Publications, Hissar, Haryana India. **(Subscription address:** Prints India, 11 Darya Ganj, New Delhi 110002 India. **Tel** 011 91 11 3268645, FAX 011 91 11 3275542, telex 31-61087 PRIN-IN.**)**

ISSN 0906-1746
DD 636.309 489
DK

TIDSSKRIFT FOR DANSK FAAREAVL. [Tidsskr. dan. fareavl]. (1991)-. Periodical. Danish. Ten times a year. Dansk Faareavl, Landbrugets Raadgivningscenter, Udkaersvej 15, DK 8200 Aarhus N Denmark. **Tel** 011 45 86 109088, FAX 011 45 86 109700. **Continues** Tidsskrift for Fareavl, 0040-7038.
Ind/Abst Nutr. Abstr. Rev., Ser. B, Live Feeds and Feed.

SZ

TIERHALTUNG. **VFOAT** Animal Management. (1977)-. Monographic series. German (English; summaries and/or abstracts in English). Irregular. Price varies per volume. Birkhaeuser Verlag Ag, Klosterberg 23, PO Box 133, CH-4010 Basel Switzerland. **Tel** 011 41 61 2717400, FAX 011 41 61 2717666, telex 963475 birk ch.
Ind/Abst AgBiotech News Inf.; Anim. Breed. Abstr.; Dairy Sci. Abstr.; Index Vet.; Life Sci. Collect.; Pig News Inf.

ISSN 0040-7364
GW

TIERZUCHTER, DER. [Tierzuchter]. **Added/Corp** Arbeitsgemeinschaft Deutscher Tierzuchter. Vol. 1 (Jan. 1949)-. Trade Publication. German. Twelve times a year. $117.45. Deutsche Landwirtschafts Gesellschaft, Verlags GmbH, Eschborner Landstr 122, D-60489 Frankfurt Germany. **Tel** 011 49 69 247880, FAX 011 49 69 24788580.
Ind/Abst AgBiotech News Inf.; AGRICOLA; Dairy Sci. Abstr.; Index Vet.; Nutr. Abstr. Rev., Ser. B, Live Feeds and Feed.; Pig News Inf.; Soyabean Abstr.; Vet. Bull.

ISSN 1034-6147
DD 636.2085
AT

TODAY'S FEED LOTTING. [Today's feed lotting]. (1990)-. Periodical. English. Four times a year (Jan., Apr., July, Oct.). 40.00Aus$. Peter Buffey Media, PO Box 6337 Toowoomba, West Queensland, 4350 Australia. **Tel** 011 61 76 333 262, FAX 011 61 76 333 285. **ED** Peter Buffey. **Bk Rev. Ad Acc. Circ:** 1,463 (ctrl).

US

TRI STATE LIVESTOCK NEWS. English. One time a week (published Saturdays). 427.50 (one-year), $52.00 (two-year). Tri-State Livestock News, PO Box 719, Sturgis SD 57785. **Tel** (605)347-2585. **ED** George Thompson. **Ad Acc. Circ:** 11,500.

PL

TRZODA CHLEWNA. **VFOAT** Biblioteczka Producenta Trzody Chlewnej. (1968)-. Periodical. Polish. Twelve times a year. $24.00. **(Subscription address:** Ars Polona-Ruch, PO Box 1001, Krakowskie Przedmiescie 7, 00-068 Warsaw Poland. **Tel** 011 48 22 261201.**) Continues** Biblioteczka Producenta Trzody Chlewnej.

LC SF55.T28 T85
DD 636.09
CH

TUNG HAI HSU MU. **Added/Corp** Tung Hai ta Hsueh Hsu Mu Hui. Tung Hai ta Hsueh. Hsu Mu Hsi. **VFOAT** Hsu Mu Hsi Hsi Kan. June (1978)-. Chinese. Tung Hai Ta Hsueh, Hsu Mu Hsueh Hsi, PO Box 884, Taichung Taiwan.

US

TURKEY HATCHERY (WASHINGTON, D.C.). (TURKEY HATCHERY.). Government Publication. English. Twelve times a year. US Department of Agriculture / National Agricultural Statistics Service (NASS), Room 5829 South Building, Washington DC 20250. **Tel** (202)720-4020, FAX (314)875-5231. available on microfiche (Vols. for 1986-) distributed to depository libraries). Documents available from Documents on Demand.
Ind/Abst Am. Stat. Index.

LC SF507 .T87
DD 338.1/76592/00973021
ISSN 1057-7858
US

TURKEYS (1985). (TURKEYS.). [Turkeys]. **Added/Corp** United States. Crop Reporting Board. United States. Agricultural Statistics Board. **VFOAT** Turkey Inventory. (1985)-. Trade Publication. English. One time a year. $25.00 US; $31.50 (6 issues plus 1 annual and 1 special report) other. US Department of Agriculture / Statistical Reporting Service, 14th Street & Independence Avenue SW, Washington DC 20250. **Continues** Eggs, Chickens & Turkeys. Turkeys.

LC HD9275.U3 F67
DD 382/.416/00973021
US
TITLE CHANGE

U.S. DAIRY, LIVESTOCK, AND POULTRY TRADE / UNITED STATES DEPARTMENT OF AGRICULTURE, FOREIGN AGRICULTURAL SERVICE. See Agriculture-Dairy Industry.

ISSN 0229-6756
DD 636.2/082/05
CN

UB NEWS. [UB news]. **VAT** United Breeder News. Vol. 12, No. 4 (July/Aug. 1980)-. Periodical. English. Six times a year. United Breeders, RR 5, Guelph Ontario N1H 6J2 Canada. **Continues** United News, 0566-7712.

ISSN 0164-9353
US

UNITED CAPRINE NEWS. (197?)-. Periodical. English. Twelve times a year. $15.00. Hoegger Supply Company, PO Box 331, Fayetteville GA 30214. **Tel** (404)461-4129.

ISSN 0954-5875
UK

UNITED KINGDOM MEAT MARKET REVIEW. [U.K. meat mark. rev.]. (1988)-. English. Two times a year. $128.34. Meat & Livestock Commission / Economic Service Department, PO Box 44, Winterhill House, Milton Keynes MK6 1AX United Kingdom. **Tel** 011 44 1908 677577, FAX 011 44 1908 609221, telex 82227. **Continues** MLC UK Market Review, 0264-1525.
Ind/Abst World Agric. Econ. Rural Sociol. Abstr.

LC HD9000
DD 338.17
ISSN 0273-9992
US

URNER BARRY'S PRICE-CURRENT. **VFOAT** Urner Barry's Price Current; Price-Current; Price Current. **VAT** Urner Barry's Price Current. (Dec. 1, 1980)-. Periodical. English. Five times a week (daily except Sat. and Sun.) $121.00. Urner Barry Publications Inc., PO Box 389, Toms River NJ 08754. **Tel** (908)240-5330, (800)932-0617, FAX (908)341-0891. **Continues** Producers' Price-Current, 0032-9711.
Desc: Current trading prices for poultry, dairy and eggs. Synopsis of trends for chicken, turkeys and eggs.

NE

VARKENS : MAANDBLAD VOOR FOKKERIJ & MESTERIJ. Periodical. Dutch. Twelve times a year. Centraal Bureau Voor de Varkensfokkerij in Nederland, PO Box 1159, 6501 BD Nijmegen Netherlands. **Continues** Varkens Fokkerijmesterij.

ISSN 0749-6664
DD 338
US

VEALER, THE. **Added/Corp** American Veal Association. (198?)-. Periodical. English. Twelve times a year. $20.00 US; $30.00 Canada; $40.00 other. Graphicom Inc, PO Box 8246, Madeira Beach FL 33738. **Tel** (606)986-1495. **ED** Lea Schultz. **Bk Rev. Ad Acc. Circ:** 2,000 (ctrl).
Desc: Directed to the growers and producers of milk-fed veal meat.

ISSN 0168-7565
NE

VEETEELT. [Veeteelt]. **Added/Corp** Koninlijk Nederlands Rundvee Syndicaat. (1984)-. Periodical. Dutch (summaries and/or abstracts in English). Irregular. Veeteelt, PO Box 454, 6800 AL Arnhem Netherlands. **Tel** 011 31 85 862 426. Index available (Free). **Continues** Friese Veefokkerij & Veeverbetering.

LC SF98.P7 V47
GW

VERBESSERUNG DER EIWEISSVERSORGUNG DER LANDWIRTSCHAFTLICHEN NUTZTIERE. Periodical. German (summaries and/or abstracts in English and Russian). 22.10. Akademie-Verlag GmbH, Postfach, D-13162 Berlin Germany. **Tel** 011 49 30 47889300, FAX 011 49 30 47889357. **(Subscription address:** VCH Publishers Inc., 303 Northwest 12th Avenue, Journals Department, Deerfield FL 33442. **Tel** (800)367-8249, (305)428-5566.**)**

ISSN 1059-8456
DD 636
US
CEASED

VETERINARY UPDATE (LARGE ANIMALS). See Veterinary Sciences.

SA

VLEIS = MEAT. **VFOAT** Meat. (19??)-. Periodical. Afrikaans (English). Twelve times a year. Vleis, 22 Melle Street, Braamfontein, PO Box 6692, Johannesburg South Africa.

SA

VLEISRAADFOKUS. **VFOAT** Meat Board Focus. Apr. 1978-. Periodical. Afrikaans (English). Twelve times a year. Vleisraad, PO Box 1357, Pretoria 0001 South Africa. **Supersedes** Vleisnywerheid.

Agriculture — Livestock

ISSN 0043-1842
US
WEEKLY LIVESTOCK REPORTER, THE. (19??)-. Periodical. English. One time a week. $18.00. Weekly Livestock Reporter, 120 N Rayner, PO Box 7655, Fort Worth TX 76111. **Tel** (817)831-3147, FAX (817)831-3117. **ED** Ted Gouldy. **Ad Acc. Circ:** 12,000.
 Desc: Covers both registered and commercial cattle, plus all items of interest to agri-business.

ISSN 0225-3488
DD 338.1/764183/09712
CN
WESTERN HOG JOURNAL. [West. hog j.].
Added/Corp Alberta. Pork Producers Marketing Board. Saskatchewan. Hog Marketing Commission. Manitoba Hog Producers' Marketing Board. British Columbia Hog Marketing Commission. Vol. 1 (Summer 1979)-. Trade Publication. English. Four times a year. Free on request. Alberta Pork Producers Development Corporation, 10319 Princess Elizabeth Avenue, Edmonton Alberta T5G 0Y5 Canada. **Tel** (403)474-8288, FAX (403)471-8065, telex 037 3367. **ED** W.W. Toma. **Bk Rev. Ad Acc, Adv Mgr:** W. Toma. **Circ:** 10,000 (ctrl). **Supersedes** Alberta Hog Journal, 0315-3800.
 Desc: Pork industry information from marketing through production and management in all its aspects.

ISSN 0094-6710
US
WESTERN LIVESTOCK JOURNAL. CENTRAL EDITION. (WESTERN LIVESTOCK JOURNAL.). Vol. 51, No. 35 (May 21, 1973)-. Periodical. English. One time a week. $30.00. Nelson R Crow, 650 South Lipan Street, Denver CO 80223. **Tel** (303)722-7600. **Continues** Western Livestock Journal. Mountain Plains & Southwest Weekly Ed., 0094-6729.

US
WESTERN LIVESTOCK REPORTER. Vol. 1, No. 1 (Sept. 6, 1940)-. English. One time a week. $28.00. Western Livestock Reporter, PO Box 60758, Billings MT 59107. **Tel** (406)259-4589.

UDC 63(78)
US
WESTERN LIVESTOCK ROUND-UP. Periodical. English. Twelve times a year. $35.00. Western Livestock Marketing, 2490 West 26th Avenue/Room 240, Denver CO 80211. **Tel** (303)964-0180.
 Desc: Publishes situations and outlooks of supplies and demand of livestock and feedgrains particularly as pertains to western agriculture.

CN
WHO'S WHO IN CANADIAN HOLSTEIN SIRES. French (English). Two times a year (Mar. & Sept.). 35.00Can$ (Canada and US); 50.00Can$ (other). Holstein Association of Canada, PO Box 610, Brantford Ontario, N3T 5R4 Canada. **Tel** (519) 756-8300, FAX (519) 756-5878, (519)756-3502, telex 06181139.

LC HE9788.4.A55 W48
ISSN 1042-2633
DD 387.7/44
US
WHO'S WHO IN LIVE ANIMAL TRADE & TRANSPORT. [Who's who live anim. trade transp.]. 3rd Ed. (1989)-. English. Every 2 years. $28.50. Silesia Companies Inc, PO Box 441110, Fort Washington MD 20744. **Tel** (301)292-1970, FAX (301)292-1787, telex 4997385. **ED** Dale L. Anderson. Index available. **Ad Acc. Circ:** 1,600. **Continues** Who's Who in Animal Transportation, 8755-688X.
 Desc: Primarily contains listings plus some general articles in the field.

ISSN 0049-7711
GW
CCC
CODEN WIFUAB
WIRTSCHAFTSEIGENE FUTTER. (DAS WIRTSCHAFTSEIGENE FUTTER.). [Wirtschaftseigene Futter]. **Added/Corp** Deutsche Landwirtschafts-Gesellschaft (Germany : West). Vol. 8, No. 1 (June 1962)-. Trade Publication. German (summaries and/or abstracts in English). Three times a year. $115.92. Deutsche Landwirtschafts Gesellschaft, Verlags GmbH, Eschborner Landstr 122, D-60489 Frankfurt Germany. **Tel** 011 49 69 247880, FAX 011 49 69 24788580. **ED** Walter Staudacher (editor's address: Zimmerweg 16, W-6000 Frankfurt 1 Germany). Index available. cum. index. **Bk Rev.** ctrl circ. Documents available from BIOSIS Document Express, CASDDS. **Continues** Futterkonservierung.
 Desc: Provides latest information on production, storage and utilization of various fodders, principally relating to dairy cattle. Covers biological and technique topics.
 Ind/Abst AGRICOLA; Agric. Eng. Abstr. (1991-); BioBusiness; Biodeter. Abstr. (1991-); Biol. Abstr.; Chem. Abstr. (1962-1983); Grass. Forage Abstr.; Maize Abstr.; Nutr. Abstr. Rev., Ser. B, Live Feeds and Feed.; Pig News Inf.; Postharvest News Inf.; Protozoolog. Abstr.; Rev. Med. Vet. Mycology; Soyabean Abstr.; Sug. Indus. Abstr.; Wheat Barley Trit. Abstr.

ISSN 0043-7840
US
WOOL SACK, THE. Added/Corp North Central Wool Marketing Corp. (197?)-. Periodical. English. Two times a year (Jan., Jun.). Free on request. Wool Growers Association, 315 5th Street, PO Box 328, Brookings SD 57006. **Tel** (605)692-2324. **ED** Dick Boniface. **Ad Acc. Circ:** 10,000 (ctrl). **Continues** Wool News.
 Desc: Covers sheep production and wool marketing, all facets of sheep and lamb raising. Production deals strictly with sheep.
 Ind/Abst Text. Technol. Dig.

LC SF1 .W893
ISSN 1014-6954
IT
CODEN WARVAI
WORLD ANIMAL REVIEW = REVUE MONDIALE DE ZOOTECHNIE = REVISTA MUNDIAL DE ZOOTECNIA.
Added/Corp Food and Agriculture Organization of the United Nations. **VFOAT** Revue Mondiale de Zootechnie; Revista Mundial de Zootecnia. (1991)-. Periodical. English (French and Spanish). Four times a year. L26000. Food Agriculture Organization (FAO) / Italy, GIPCI66 via Terme di Caracalla, 00100 Rome Italy. **Tel** 011 39 6 52252925, FAX 011 39 6 52253152. Documents available from CASDDS. **Formed by the union of** World Animal Review, 0049-8025; Revue Mondiale de Zootechnie, 0252-0176 **and** Revista Mundial de Zootecnia, 0252-0184.
 Ind/Abst AgBiotech News Inf.; AGRICOLA; Agrofor. Abstr.; Anim. Breed. Abstr.; Biol. Abstr.; Chem. Abstr.; Dairy Sci. Abstr.; Int. Dev. Abstr.; Life Sci. Collect.; Protozoolog. Abstr.; Wildl. Rev.

ISSN 0239-4715
PL
CODEN WOSZDY
WYNIKI OCENY SWIN NA PODSTAWIE BADAN PRZEPROWADZONYCH W STACJACH KONTROLI UZYTKOWOSCI RZEZNEJ TRZODY CHLEWNEJ INSTYTUTU ZOOTECHNIKI ZA ROK ... = RESULTS OF EVALUATION IN PIG TESTING STATIONS OF THE INSTITUTE OF ANIMAL PRODUCTION IN ... INSTYTUT ZOOTECHNIKI W POLSCE, ZAKLAD INFORMACJI ZOOTECHNICZNEJ. Added/Corp Instytut Zootechniki w Polsce. Zaklad Informacji Zootechnicznej. **VFOAT** Results of Evaluation in Pig Testing Stations of the Institute of Animal Production. (1976)-. Polish (summaries and/or abstracts in English). One time a year. Panstwowe Wydawnictwo Rolnicze i Lesne, Al. Jerozolimskie 28, PO Box 374, 00 024 Warsaw Poland. **Tel** 011 48 22 266451, telex 642410 IUNG PL. Documents available from BIOSIS Document Express.
 Ind/Abst Biol. Abstr. (?-1983).

ISSN 0043-9827
US
CEASED
WYOMING WOOL GROWER. Added/Corp Wyoming Wool Growers Association. (19??)-(1993). Periodical. English. Wyoming Wool Grower, Box 115, Casper WY 82602. **Tel** (307)265-5250. **ED** Carolyn Paseneaux. **Bk Rev. Ad Acc. Circ:** 1,150.
 Desc: Education and information about the sheep industry.

ISSN 0065-8456
US
YEARBOOK / AMERICAN GOAT SOCIETY. Main/Corp American Goat Society. (19??)-. English. Irregular. American Goat Society Inc, Route 2 Box 112, Deleon TX 76444.

LC SF55.T28 T33A
CH
YEN CHIU SHIH YEN PAO KAO - TAI-WAN TANG YEH KU FEN YU HSIEN KUNG SSU HSU CHAN YEN CHIU SO.
Main/Corp Tai-Wan Tang Yeh Ku Fen Yu Hsien Kung Ssu. Hsu Chan Yen Chiu So. **VFOAT** Annual Research Report - Animal Industry Research Institute, Taiwan Sugar Corporation. Chinese (summaries and/or abstracts in English). Animal Industry Research Institute, Taiwan Sugar Corporation Chunan, Miaoli Taiwan.

ISSN 1079-6037
DD 636
US
●**YOUNG RIDER.** [Young rider]. (Jan. 1994)-. Periodical. English. Six times a year. $13.00. Young Rider, PO Box 725, Williamsburg VA 23187. **Tel** (804)229-6294.

LC SF396.G3 Z3
DD 338.1/764/00943021
GW
ZAHLEN AUS DER DEUTSCHEN SCHWEINEPRODUKTION. Added/Corp Arbeitsgemeinschaft Deutscher Schweineerzeuger. **VFOAT** Schweineproduktion in der Bundesrepublik Deutschland. (19??)-. Trade Publication. German (English and French). One time a year. DM20.00. Zentralverband der Deutschen Schweineproduktion e.V., Adenauerallee 174, D53113 Bonn Germany. **Tel** 02 28 21 10 09, FAX 02 28 21 17 77. **ED** K. Schulr, J. Iugwersen. **Acid Free. Circ:** 1,000 (ctrl).
 Desc: Covers the pork industry in Germany.

ISSN 0350-8005
UDC 636
YU
ZBORNIK RADOVA - POLJOPRIVREDNI FAKULTET. INSTITUT ZA STOCARSTVO, NOVI SAD. (ZBORNIK RADOVA.). [Zb. rad. - Poljopr. fak., Inst. stoc. Novi Sad]. **VFOAT** Review of Research Work - Faculty of Agriculture. Livestock Research Institute, Novi Sad. (19??)-. Multiple languages. One time a year.
 Ind/Abst Pig News Inf.; Postharvest News Inf.

LC SF1 .Z4
ISSN 0044-3581
DD 636.08/2/05
GW
CCC
NLM W1 ZE625R
CODEN ZTZBAS
Pr Rev.
ZEITSCHRIFT FUER TIERZUCHTUNG UND ZUCHTUNGSBIOLOGIE (HAMBURG, GERMANY : 1939).
(ZEITSCHRIFT FUER TIERZUCHTUNG UND ZUCHTUNGSBIOLOGIE.). [Z. tierz. zuchtungsbiol.]. **Added/Corp** Reichsarbeitsgemeinschaft Tierzucht (Germany). **VFOAT** Journal of Animal Breeding and Genetics. Vol. 41 (1938)-. Academic Scholarly Publication. German (English). Six times a year. DM909.00 Europe; DM906.00 other. Blackwell Wissenschafts-Verlag, Kurfuerstendamm 57, D-10707 Berlin Germany. **Tel** 011 49 30 32790623, 011 49 30 32790624, FAX 011 49 30 327 90610. **ED** Franz Pirchner. Index available. cum. index. **Bk Rev. Ad Acc. Circ:** 2,500. Documents available from BIOSIS Document Express, CASDDS. **Continues** Zeitschrift fuer Zuchtung. Reihe B, Tierzuchtung und Zuchtungsbiologie.
 Desc: Publishes articles on research in animal production, quantitative genetics, biology and evolution of domestic animals.
 Ind/Abst AGRICOLA; Biol. Abstr.; Chem. Abstr. (1924-); Curr. Contents Agric. Biol. Environ. Sci.; Genet. Abstr.; Index Vet.; Life Sci. Collect.; Plant Breed. Abstr.; Poult. Abstr.; Small Anim. Abstr. Bibliogr.; Vet. Bull.

LC SF757 .Z45
JA
ZENKOKU KACHIKU HOKEN EISEI GYOSEKI SHOROKU. Added/Corp Japan. Norinsho. Chikusankyoku. Eiseika. Dobutsuyo Seibutsugakuteki Seizai Kyokai. (1969)-. Periodical. Japanese. One time a year. Dobutsuyo Seibutsugakuteki Seizai Kyokai, (Japanese Association of Veterinary Biologics), 11 Kanda Mikuracho, Chiyodaku Tokyo 101 Japan.

ISSN 0137-1916
PL
ZESZYTY NAUKOWE. AKADEMIA ROLNICZA W KRAKOWIE, ZOOTECHNIKA. (ZESZYTY NAUKOWE. ZOOTECHNIKA.). [Zesz. nauk. Akad. Roln. Krak., Zootech.]. **Main/Corp** Akademia Rolnicza w Krakowie. No. 13 (1974)-. Periodical. Polish. Panstwowe Wydawnictwo Naukowe / PWN, PWN Scientific Publishers PWN Ltd.), Ul. Miodowa 10, PO Box 391, 00-251 Warsaw Poland. **Tel** 011 48 22 312738, FAX 011 48 22 267163. **Continues** Zootechnika.
 Ind/Abst AGRICOLA; Poult. Abstr.

LC SF1 .Z46
ISSN 0514-7441
BU
CODEN ZHVNAS
ZHIVOTNOVUDNI NAUKI. See Veterinary Sciences.

ISSN 0044-4847
XR
CODEN ZIVYAY
ZIVOCISNA VYROBA. [Zivoc. vyroba]. Vol. 7, No. 4 (1962)-. Academic Scholarly Publication. Czech (summaries and/or abstracts in English, German and Russian; table of contents in English, German and Russian). Twelve times a year. $123.00. **(Subscription address:** Kubon & Sagner, ABT Zeitschriftenimport, D 80328 Munich Germany. **Tel** 011 49 89 54218130.) **ED** Ing. Marie Cern (Editor in Chief). Documents available from The Genuine Article, BIOSIS Document Express, CASDDS. **Continues** Ceskoslovenska Akademie Zemedelskych Ved. Sbornik. Zivocisna Yvroba.
 Ind/Abst AgBiotech News Inf.; AGRICOLA; Anim. Breed. Abstr.; Biol. Abstr.; Chem. Abstr.; Curr. Cit.; Curr. Contents Agric. Biol. Environ. Sci.; Dairy Sci. Abstr.; EMBASE; Food Sci. Technol. Abstr.; Helminthol. Abstr.; Index Vet.; Maize Abstr.; Nutr. Abstr. Rev., Ser. B, Live Feeds and Feed.; Nutr. Abstr. Rev., Ser. A, Hum. Exp.; Life Sci. Collect.; Pig News Inf.; Res. Alert [Select. Cov.]; Soc. Sci. Cit. Index [Select. Cov.]; Soyabean Abstr.; Vet. Bull.; Wheat Barley Trit. Abstr.

GW
ZMP MARKTBERICHT: SCHLACHTVIEH. Added/Corp Zentrale Markt- und Preisberichtstelle fur Erzeugnisse der Land-, Forst-

Agriculture —Poultry and Poultry Products

und Ernahrungswirtschaft. (19??)-. Periodical. German. Two times a week (104 per year). $396.11. ZMP Marktberichte Bonn, Rochusstrasse 2, D-53123 Bonn Germany. **Tel** 011 49 228 9777170. *Continues Europemarkt: die Markte fur Schlachtrinder und Schweine Westeuropas.*

LC SF1 .Z66   **ISSN** 0137-1940
PL

ZOOTECHNIKA / AKADEMIA ROLNICZA W SZCZECINIE. **Added/Corp**
Akademia Rolnicza w Szczecinie. (1973)-. Academic Scholarly Publication. Polish (summaries and/or abstracts in English, German and Russian). One time a year. Price varies per volume. Akademia Rolnicza w Szczecinie / Agricultural University in Szczecin, Dzial Wydawnictwo, Ul. Doktora Judyma 22, 71-460 Szczecin Poland. **Tel** 011 48 91 541639, FAX 011 48 91 541642. *Continues Zootechnika (Wyzsza Szkola Rolnicza w Szczecinie).*
Ind/Abst Index Vet.

VE

ZOOTECNIA TROPICAL. **Added/Corp**
Fondo Nacional de Investigaciones Agropecuarias (Venezuela). No. 1 (1983)-. Periodical. Spanish (summaries and/or abstracts in English). Two times a year.
Ind/Abst Pig News Inf.

ISSN 0390-0487
IT
CODEN ZNAND2

ZOOTECNICA E NUTRIZIONE ANIMALE.
[Zootec. nutr. anim.]. **Added/Corp** Associazione Scientifica di Produzione Animale. Vol. 1, No. 1 (Mar. 1975)-. Periodical. Italian (summaries and/or abstracts in English and Italian). Six times a year. L51100. Edagricole, PO Box 22, 40100 Bologna Italy. **Tel** 011 39 51 492211 Ext. 22, FAX 011 39 51 493660, telex 510336 EDAGRI. Index available in last issue of volume--attached. Documents available from CASDDS.
Ind/Abst AgBiotech News Inf.; AGRICOLA; Agric. Eng. Abstr. (1991-); Agrofor. Abstr. (19??-19??); Anim. Breed. Abstr.; Biodeter. Abstr. (1991-); Chem. Abstr.; Dairy Sci. Abstr.; For. Abstr.; Index Vet.; Maize Abstr.; Nutr. Abstr. Rev., Ser. B, Live Feeds and Feed.; Life Sci. Collect.; Pig News Inf.; Postharvest News Inf.; Poult. Abstr.; Rev. Med. Vet. Mycology; Sorghum Mill. Abstr.; Soyabean Abstr.; Sug. Indus. Abstr.; Vet. Bull.; Wheat Barley Trit. Abstr.

IT

ZOOTECNICA INTERNATIONAL. (19??)-.
Periodical. Multiple languages (Arabic, English, French and German; summaries and/or abstracts in Arabic, English, French and German). Twelve times a year. L65000. Zootecnica International, Via Ugo Foscolo 35, 50018 Scandicci Italy. **Tel** 011 39 55 251891.
Ind/Abst Anim. Breed. Abstr.; Nutr. Abstr. Rev., Ser. B, Live Feeds and Feed.; Poult. Abstr.

ISSN 0235-2478
RU

ZOOTEKHNIIA. **Added/Corp**
Soviet Union. Gosudarstvennyi Agropromyshlennyi Komitet. (Jan. 1988)-. Periodical. Russian. Twelve times a year. $119.95. Agropromizdat, Sadovo-Spasskaia 18, 107807 Moscow Russia. **(Subscription address:** East View Publications Inc., 3020 Harbor Lane North, Suite 110, Minneapolis MN 55447. **Tel** (800)477-1005, (612)550-0961, FAX (612)559-2931.**)** *Continues Zhivotnovodstvo, 0044-4480.*
Ind/Abst Agric. Eng. Abstr.; Index Vet.; Maize Abstr.; Nutr. Abstr. Rev., Ser. B, Live Feeds and Feed.; Potato Abstr.; Rev. Med. Vet. Entomol.; Sug. Indus. Abstr.; Vet. Bull.

POULTRY AND POULTRY PRODUCTS

LC HD9284.G3 Z45A
GW
UDC 338.43:636.5(430.1); 338.4:637.4(430.1)

AGRARMARKTE BR DEUTSCHLAND, EWG UND WELTMARKT : EIER UND GEFLUGEL, DIE. **Main/Corp**
Zentrale Markt- und Preisberichtstelle fur Erzeugnisse der Land-, Forst- und Ernahrungswirtschaft. German. 1 Kolner Strasse 142-148, 53 Bonn-Bad Godesberg Germany.

LC HD9424.C2 C35A
DD 338.1/7/608830971   CN
UDC 338.439.4:636/637(71)

ANIMAL AND ANIMAL PRODUCTS; OUTLOOK. **Main/Corp**
Canada. Marketing and Trade Division. English. Marketing and Trade Division, Ottawa Ontario K1A 0C5 Canada.

US

ANIMAL SCIENCE RESEARCH REPORT. See Agriculture-Livestock.

ISSN 0003-9098
GW
UDC 636.5   **CODEN** AGEFAB
Pr Rev.

ARCHIV FUER GEFLUGELKUNDE. [Arch. gefluegelkd.]. Vol. 1- July 1927-.
Periodical. German (summaries and/or abstracts in English, English and French). Six times a year. $514.02. Verlag Eugen Ulmer, Postfach 700561, D-70574 Stuttgart Germany. **Tel** 011 49 711 4507108, FAX 011 49 711 4507120, telex 7-23634. **ED** Roland Ulmer. Documents available from The Genuine Article, CASDDS.
Ind/Abst Anim. Breed. Abstr.; Biodeter. Abstr.; Chem. Abstr.; Curr. Cit.; Curr. Contents Agric. Biol. Environ. Sci.; Energy Res. Abstr.; Food Sci. Technol. Abstr.; Maize Abstr.; Nutr. Abstr. Rev., Ser. B, Live Feeds and Feed.; Nutr. Abstr. Rev., Ser. A, Hum. Exp.; Life Sci. Collect.; PESTDOC; Poult. Abstr.; Protozoolog. Abstr.; Res. Alert [Full Cov.]; Sci. Cit. Index; SCISEARCH.

ISSN 0970-1273
II
UDC 636.585(540)   **CODEN** AVREDB

AVIAN RESEARCH : OFFICIAL JOURNAL OF THE INDIAN POULTRY CLUB. [Avian res.]. (1982)-.
Academic Scholarly Publication. English. Four times a year. Treasurer Cum Business Manager Avian Research, C A R I, Izatnagar-243 1222 India. Documents available from CASDDS. *Continues Indian Poultry Gazette, 0019-6142.*
Ind/Abst Chem. Abstr. (1983-); Food Sci. Technol. Abstr.

ISSN 0133-011X
HU

BAROMFITENYESZTES ES FELDOLGOZAS. [Baromfiteny. feldolg.]. Vol. 25, No. 5- 1976-.
Periodical. Hungarian (German and Russian; table of contents in English, German and Russian). Six times a year. Lapkiado Vallalat, Lenin Korut 9-11, 1073 Budapest 7 Hungary. **Tel** 011 36 1 222408. *Continues Baromfiipar, 0005-6049.*
Ind/Abst Anim. Breed. Abstr.; Energy Res. Abstr. (Aug. 1982-); Food Sci. Technol. Abstr.; Index Vet.; Leis., Rec., Tour. Abstr.; Nutr. Abstr. Rev., Ser. B, Live Feeds and Feed.; Poult. Abstr.; Protozoolog. Abstr.; Rural Dev. Abstr.; Vet. Bull.; World Agric. Econ. Rural Sociol. Abstr.

ISSN 0007-1668
UK
NLM W1 BR747L   **CODEN** BPOSA4
Pr Rev.

BRITISH POULTRY SCIENCE. [Br. poult. sci.]. **Added/Corp**
Poultry Education Association (Great Britain). Vol. 1 (Apr. 1960)-. Periodical. English. Five times a year. $260.00. Carfax Publishing Company, PO Box 25, Abingdon, Oxfordshire OX14 3UE United Kingdom. **Tel** 011 44 1235 555335, FAX 011 44 1235 553559, telex 817484. **ED** B.O. Hughes. **Bk Rev**. **Ad Acc**. available on microfiche. Documents available from The Genuine Article, CASDDS.
Desc: Reports the results of studies with an experimental and biological framework in the poultry industry.
Ind/Abst AgBiotech News Inf.; AGRICOLA [Full Cov.]; Agric. Eng. Abstr. (1991-); Agrofor. Abstr. (1991-); Anim. Breed. Abstr.; BioBusiness; Chem. Abstr.; Curr. Cit.; Curr. Contents Agric. Biol. Environ. Sci.; Fish Rev.; Food Sci. Technol. Abstr.; Index Med.; Index Vet.; Leis., Rec., Tour. Abstr.; Maize Abstr.; Nutr. Abstr. Rev., Ser. B, Live Feeds and Feed.; Nutr. Abstr. Rev., Ser. A, Hum. Exp.; Life Sci. Collect.; PESTDOC; Poult. Abstr.; Protozoolog. Abstr.; Res. Alert [Full Cov.]; Rev. Med. Vet. Mycology; Rice Abstr.; Sci. Cit. Index; SCISEARCH; Sorghum Mill. Abstr.; Soyabean Abstr.; Vet. Bull.; Wheat Barley Trit. Abstr.; Wildl. Rev.

ISSN 0007-2176
US
DD 338   CCC

BROILER INDUSTRY. [Broiler ind.]. (Sept. 1957)-.
Periodical. English. Twelve times a year. $54.00. Watt Publishing Company, 122 South Wesley Avenue, Mount Morris IL 61054. **Tel** (815)734-4171, FAX (815)734-7021, telex TWX 910-642-2891. **ED** David Amey. **Ad Acc**. **Circ:** 14,000 (ctrl). available on microfilm and microfiche from University Microfilms International (UMI). *Continues Eastern Breeder and Boiler Grower; Absorbed Poultry Processing & Marketing.*
Desc: Devoted to the production, processing, and marketing of broilers.
Ind/Abst PESTDOC.

FR

BULLETIN DE SNIA. See Agriculture-Livestock.

FR

BULLETIN D'INFORMATION / STATION EXPERIMENTALE D'AVICULTURE DE PLOUFRAGAN. **Added/Corp**
Station Experimentale d'Aviculture de Ploufragan. (19??)-. Bulletin. French. Four times a year. Station Experimentale d'Aviculture de Ploufragan, France.

Ind/Abst Food Sci. Technol. Abstr.; Index Vet.; Nutr. Abstr. Rev., Ser. B, Live Feeds and Feed.; Poult. Abstr.; Vet. Bull.

ISSN 0744-6160
US

CALIFORNIA POULTRY REPORT.
Periodical. English. Twelve times a year. $15.00. California Agricultural Statistics Service, California Department of, Food and Agriculture, PO Box 1258, Sacramento CA 95812. **Tel** (916)551-1533. *Continues Weekly Poultry Report, 0279-2532.*
Desc: Chicken and turkey settings, hatchings, eggs produced, inventory, value, and cold storage.

ISSN 0008-2732
CN

CANADA POULTRYMAN. **Added/Corp**
Canadian Egg Producers Council. Canadian Broiler Council. Canadian Turkey Marketing Agency. (1929)-. Trade Publication. English (French). Twelve times a year (Includes a supplement to June issue.). 15.21Can$. Farm Papers Ltd, 9547 152nd Street, Suite 105A, Surrey BC V3R 5Y5 Canada. **Tel** (604)585-3131, FAX (604)585-1504. **ED** Anthony Greaves. **Ad Acc, Adv Mgr:** C. Greaves, **Tel** (604)585-3131. **Circ:** 9,000 (ctrl).
Desc: Industry administration, disease control, finance topics, poultry management and profiles of industry people for the Canadian egg, chicken and turkey producers.

ISSN 1185-1708
CN
DD 338.1

CHICKEN FORUM. (COUP D'OEIL SUR LE POULET.). [Chick. forum]. **Added/Corp**
Office Canadien de Commercialisation des Poulets. **VFOAT** Chicken Forum. Vol. 1, No 1 (Feb. 1991)-. Periodical. French (English). Six times a year. Limited Free Distribution. Office Canadien de Commercialisation de Poulets, Bureau 300, 377 rue Dalhousie, Ottawa Ontario K1N 9N8 Canada.

ISSN 1185-1708
CN
DD 338.1

CHICKEN FORUM. [Chick. forum]. **Added/Corp**
Canadian Chicken Marketing Agency. **VFOAT** Coup d'Oeil sur le Poulet. Vol. 1, No. 1 (Feb. 1991)-. Periodical. English (French). Six times a year. Limited free distribution. Canadian Chicken Marketing Agency, Suite 300, 377 Dalhousie Street, Ottawa Ontario K1N 9N8 Canada.

ISSN 1076-3945
US
DD 636   **CODEN** CHEGED

●CHICKENS AND EGGS (WASHINGTON, D.C. 1994). (CHICKENS AND EGGS.). [Chick. eggs]. **Added/Corp**
United States. National Agricultural Statistics Service. United States. Agricultural Statistics Board. (Jan. 1994)-. Government Publication. English. Twelve times a year. $46.00. US Department of Agriculture, 14th Street and Independence Avenue SW, Washington DC 20250. **Tel** (202)720-5457. **(Subscription address:** Superintendent of Documents, US Government Printing Office, Washington DC 20402. **)** available on microfiche. *Continues Eggs, Chickens and Turkeys, 0093-013X.*
Ind/Abst Am. Stat. Index; BioBusiness.

JA
CODEN CKNKAJ

CHIKUSAN NO KENKYU. ANIMAL HUSBANDRY. See Veterinary Sciences.

US

COMPILATION OF MEAT AND POULTRY INSPECTION ISSUANCES. **Added/Corp**
United States. Food Safety and Inspection Service. (Feb. 1984)-. Government Publication. English. Irregular. $112.00 US; $140.00 other. US Department of Agriculture / Food Safety and Inspection Service, Washington DC 20250. available on microfiche (Vols. for (1986-) distributed to depository libraries). *Continues Issuances of the Meat and Poultry Inspection Program, 0364-1368.*
Desc: An official publication of procedural guidelines and instructions to aid all Meat and Poultry Inspection employees in enforcing laws and regulations in the area of Federal meat and poultry inspection.

US

●DAIRY, LIVESTOCK AND POULTRY, U.S. TRADE AND PROSPECTS. See Agriculture-Dairy Industry.

US

DELMARVA BROILER CHICKS. **Added/Corp**
Maryland-Delaware Crop Reporting Service. United States. Crop Reporting Board. **VFOAT** Broiler Chicks. Oct. 16, (1976)-. Periodical. English. One time a week. $15.00. Maryland Delaware Agricultural Statistics Service, 50 Harry S Truman Parkway, Annapolis MD 21401. **Tel** (301)841-5740. *Continues Delmarva Broiler Chick Report.*

Agriculture —Poultry and Poultry Products

DD 338   **ISSN** 0896-2804   US
EGG INDUSTRY (MOUNT MORRIS, ILL. : 1987). (EGG INDUSTRY.). [Egg ind.]. Vol. 93, No. 10 (Oct. 1987)-. Newsletter. English. Twelve times a year. $36.00. Watt Publishing Company, 122 South Wesley Avenue, Mount Morris IL 61054. **Tel** (815)734-4171, FAX (815)734-7021, telex TWX 910-642-2891. available on microfilm and microfiche from University Microfilms International (UMI). **Continues** Poultry Tribune (Mount Morris, Ill. : 1969), 0032-5805.
  Desc: Articles on management, production, and marketing of eggs.
  Ind/Abst AGRICOLA.

ISSN 0744-303X   US
EGG MARKET NEWS REPORT (CHICAGO, ILL.). (EGG MARKET NEWS REPORT.). **Added/Corp** Illinois. Dept. of Agriculture. United States. Agricultural Marketing Service. Poultry Division. Federal-State Market News Service. (19??)-. Periodical. English. Two times a week. $125.00. USDA AMS Poultry Market, 800 Roosevelt Road, Building A Suite 310, Glen Ellyn IL 60137. **Tel** (708)790-6910, FAX (708)790-6948. **Circ:** 110.
  Desc: Supply, demand, price and statistical information pertaining to egg and egg products marketing on a current basis.

ISSN 0145-3904   US
EGG PRODUCTS. Main/Corp United States. Crop Reporting Board. **Added/Corp** United States. Agricultural Marketing Service. Production of Liquid Eggs by Egg-Breaking Plants. United States. Agricultural Marketing Service. Liquid, Frozen, and Dried Egg Production. United States. Bureau of Agricultural Economics. Liquid, Frozen, and Dried Egg Production. (19??)-. Government Publication. English. Twelve times a year. $30.00. Superintendent of Documents, US Government Printing Office, Washington DC 20402. **Tel** (202)275-3328, FAX (202)786-2377. Documents available from Documents on Demand.
  Desc: Current production and market trends of agricultural commodities, including tables and statistics on slaughtered poultry, areas planted and harvested, and stored supplies.
  Ind/Abst Am. Stat. Index.

ISSN 0093-013X   US
CODEN ECTUEF
TITLE CHANGE
EGGS, CHICKENS AND TURKEYS. (EGGS, CHICKENS AND TURKEYS.). [Eggs chick. turk.]. **Added/Corp** United States. Crop Reporting Board. United States. Agricultural Statistics Board. **VFOAT** Eggs, Chickens & Turkeys. (Dec. 1969)-(Dec. 22, 1993). Trade Publication. English. Superintendent of Documents, US Government Printing Office, Washington DC 20402. **Tel** (202)275-3328, FAX (202)786-2377. Documents available from Documents on Demand. **Formed by the union of** Pullet Chicks for Broiler Hatchery Supply Flocks; Turkeys and Chickens Tested and Hatchery Production, 0093-0121. **Continued by** Chickens and Eggs.
  Desc: Short articles on current production and market trends of agricultural commodities, including tables and statistics on slaughtered poultry, areas planted and harvested, and stored supplies.
  Ind/Abst Am. Stat. Index; BioBusiness (1990-).

LC SF13.F6 F5   US
FLORIDA AGRICULTURAL STATISTICS. LIVESTOCK, DAIRY, AND POULTRY SUMMARY. See Agriculture-Dairy Industry.

ISSN 1049-3336   US
FOOD PRODUCTS PRESS SERIES IN POULTRY & EGG PRODUCTS, PRODUCTION AND MARKETING. VFOAT FPP Series in Poultry & Egg Products, Production and Marketing. (1990)-. Monographic series. English. One time a year. Price varies per volume. The Haworth Press Inc., 10 Alice Street, Binghamton NY 13904-1580. **Tel** (607)722-5857, (800)3-HAWORTH, FAX (607)722-1424.

ISSN 0016-4313   US
GAMECOCK, THE. (GAMECOCK.). (1935)-. Periodical. English. Twelve times a year. $20.00. The Gamecock, PO Box 158, Hartford AR 72938-0158. **Tel** (501)639-2324. **ED** J. G. Griffiths. **Ad Acc. Circ:** 16,000 (ctrl).
  Desc: Articles on gamefowl, poultry diseases, sport results, advertising of supplies for proper care of gamefowl and some history of gamefowl.

ISSN 0017-1506   US
GOBBLES. Added/Corp Minnesota Turkey Growers Association. (1945)-. Trade Publication. English. Twelve times a year. $25.00. Minnesota Turkey Growers Association, 2380 Wycliff Street, St Paul MN 55114. **Tel** (612)646-4553, FAX (612)646-4554. **ED** Kristine Claussen. **Ad Acc. Circ:** 1,025.
  Desc: For turkey growers, processors and hatchers.

LC HD9437.U6 H37   **ISSN** 8755-2973
DD 338.1/765/00973   US
HATCHERY PRODUCTION. SUMMARY. (HATCHERY PRODUCTION ... SUMMARY.). [Hatch. prod., Summ.]. (1983)-. Statistical Publication. English. One time a year. US Department of Agriculture / National Agricultural Statistics Service (NASS), Room 5829 South Building, Washington DC 20250. **Tel** (202)720-4020, FAX (314)875-5231. **Continues** Eggs, Chickens & Turkeys. Hatchery Production.

CN
HATCHERY REVIEW / REVUE SUR LES COUVOIRS. Added/Corp Canada. Agriculture Canada. **VFOAT** Revue sur les Couvoirs. (19??)-. Government Publication. English (French). One time a year. Free on request. Agriculture Canada, Communications Branch, Ottawa Ontario K1A 0C7 Canada.

US
HAWAII CHICKENS & EGGS. Main/Corp Hawaii Agricultural Statistics Service. **Added/Corp** Hawaii Agricultural Statistics Service. Hawaii. Dept. of Agriculture. United States. Dept. of Agriculture. **VFOAT** Hawaii Chickens and Eggs. (August 29, 1991)-. Periodical. English. Twelve times a year. **Continues** Hawaii Chickens.

ISSN 0139-8822   XO
CODEN HYDIDH
HYDINARSTVO. (HYDINARSTVO; VEDECKE PRACE VYSKUMNEHO USTAVU CHOVU A SLACHTENIA HYDINY V IVANKE PRI DUNAJI.). [Hydinarstvo]. **Main/Corp** Vyskumny Ustav Chovu a Slachtenia Hydiny. **Added/Corp** Vyskumny Ustav Chovu a Slachtenia Hydiny. Vedecke Prace. (1973)-. Academic Scholarly Publication. Czech (summaries and/or abstracts in English and Russian; table of contents in English and Russian). Irregular. Priroda Vydavatelstvo Knih a Casopisov n.p., Bratislava Slovakia. Documents available from BIOSIS Document Express, CASDDS. **Continues** Vyskumny Ustav Pre Chov Hydiny. Vedecke Prace.
  Ind/Abst Biol. Abstr. (?-1986); Chem. Abstr.; Nutr. Abstr. Rev., Ser. B, Live Feeds and Feed.; Poult. Abstr.; Rev. Med. Vet. Mycology; Soyabean Abstr.

ISSN 0019-5529   II
CODEN IJPOAW
INDIAN JOURNAL OF POULTRY SCIENCE. (INDIAN JOURNAL OF POULTRY SCIENCE : OFFICIAL JOURNAL OF THE INDIAN POULTRY SCIENCE ASSOCIATION.). [Indian j. poult. sci.]. **Added/Corp** Indian Poultry Science Association. Vol. 1 (Sept. 1966)-. Periodical. English. Three times a year. $75.00. (**Subscription address:** Prints India, 11 Darya Ganj, New Delhi 110002 India. **Tel** 011 91 11 3268645, FAX 011 91 11 3275542, telex 31-61087 PRIN-IN.) Documents available from BIOSIS Document Express, CASDDS.
  Ind/Abst AGRICOLA; Agrofor. Abstr. (1991-); Anim. Breed. Abstr.; Biodeter. Abstr. (1991-); Biol. Abstr.; Chem. Abstr.; Food Sci. Technol. Abstr.; Index Vet.; Leis. Rec., Tour. Abstr.; Maize Abstr.; Nutr. Abstr. Rev., Ser. B, Live Feeds and Feed.; Nutr. Abstr. Rev., Ser. A, Hum. Exp.; Poult. Abstr.; Protozoolog. Abstr.; Rev. Med. Vet. Entomol.; Rev. Med. Vet. Mycology; Rice Abstr.; Rural Dev. Abstr.; Soyabean Abstr.; Vet. Bull.; World Agric. Econ. Rural Sociol. Abstr.

II
INDIAN POULTRY INDUSTRY YEARBOOK. (1974)-. English. One time a year. Price varies. (**Subscription address:** Prints India, 11 Darya Ganj, New Delhi 110002 India. **Tel** 011 91 11 3268645, FAX 011 91 11 3275542, telex 31-61087 PRIN-IN.)

ISSN 0019-6150   II
CODEN IPRWD9
INDIAN POULTRY REVIEW. [Indian poult. rev.]. Vol. 6, No. 11 (1969)-. Periodical. English. Twenty-six times a year. Rs50.00. Indian Poultry Lovers Association, 57-B Towsend Road, Calcutta 700025 India. Documents available from CASDDS.
  Ind/Abst AGRICOLA; Chem. Abstr. (1969-1981).

ISSN 0019-7467   US
INDUSTRIA AVICOLA. (19??)-. Periodical. Spanish (English). Twelve times a year. $54.00. Watt Publishing Company, 122 South Wesley Avenue, Mount Morris IL 61054. **Tel** (815)734-4171, FAX (815)734-7021, telex TWX 910-642-2891. **ED** Robert Tuten. **Ad Acc. Circ:** 16,000 (ctrl).
  Desc: Poultry husbandry, management, marketing, processing for poultry producers in Latin America.

UK
INTERNATIONAL HATCHERY PRACTICE. (1986)-. Trade Publication. English. Eight times a year. $50.00. International Hatchery, PO Box 4, Driffield North Humberside YO25 9DJ, United Kingdom. **Tel** 011 44 1377 241724, FAX 011 44 1377 241910. **ED** Nigel Horrox. **Circ:** 14,500.
  Desc: Technical publication which covers all areas of poultry breeding and rearing.
  Ind/Abst Biodeter. Abstr.; Index Vet.; Nutr. Abstr. Rev., Ser. B, Live Feeds and Feed.; Poult. Abstr.

LC HD9433.A1 S7   **ISSN** 0259-8183
DD 382/.4160883/05   SZ
INTERNATIONAL MARKETS FOR MEAT, THE. [Int. markets meat]. **Added/Corp** General Agreement on Tariffs and Trade (Organization). (1985)-. English (French and Spanish). One time a year. 25.00F. General Agreement on Tariffs and Trade / GATT, Centre William Rappard, 154 rue de Lausanne, 1211 Geneva 21 Switzerland. **Tel** 011 41 22 7395111, 011 41 22 7395019, FAX 011 41 22 7395458. **Continues** World Market for Bovine Meat at ... .
  Desc: Examines trends in the production, consumption and trade of Bovine meat and describes major trade policy developments. Provides comprehensive statistical analyses and contains detailed tables and charts by product category.
  Ind/Abst F&S Index Plus Text, Int. [Select. Cov.]; Predicasts Forecasts.

ISSN 1230-1388   PL
CODEN JFESEA
JOURNAL OF ANIMAL AND FEED SCIENCES. See Agriculture-Livestock.

LC SF481 .J68   **ISSN** 1056-6171
DD 636   US
Pr Rev.
JOURNAL OF APPLIED POULTRY RESEARCH. [J. appl. poult. res.]. **Added/Corp** Applied Poultry Science, Inc. **VFOAT** JAPR. Vol. 1 No. 1 (Mar. 1992)-. Periodical. English. Four times a year (Mar., June, Sept., Dec.). $40.00. Applied Poultry Science, Inc., PO Box 5486, Athens GA 30604. **Tel** (706)542-9149. **ED** Cynthia E. Walker. Index available (Index yearly in 4th issue.). **Bk Rev. Circ:** 800.

LC HD9410.9.G3 L36   GW
LAND- UND FORSTWIRTSCHAFT, FISCHEREI. REIHE 4.3, FLEISCHUNTERSUCHUNG. See Industry and Production.

LC HD9437.U6 U54B   **ISSN** 0195-4776
DD 338.1/76513/0973   US
UDC 636.439.4:637.4(73)
LIST OF PLANTS OPERATING UNDER USDA POULTRY AND EGG GRADING AND EGG PRODUCTS INSPECTION PROGRAMS. (LIST OF PLANTS OPERATING UNDER USDA POULTRY AND EGG GRADING AND EGG PRODUCTS INSPECTION PROGRAMS / UNITED STATES DEPARTMENT OF AGRICULTURE, AGRICULTURAL MARKETING SERVICE, POULTRY AND DAIRY QUALITY DIVISION). Government Publication. English. One time a year. US Department of Agriculture / Agricultural Marketing Service / Washington, DC, Market News Branch, Fruit and Vegetable Division, Washington DC 20250. **Tel** (202)720-2745, (202)720-3343, FAX (202)720-7502. available on microfiche (Vols. for (May 1983) - distributed to depository libraries). **Continues** List of Plants Operating under USDA Poultry and Egg Inspection and Grading Programs, 0565-2138.

US
LIVESTOCK & POULTRY INVENTORY, VALUE / IOWA CROP AND LIVESTOCK REPORTING SERVICE. 1977-. English. One time a year. The Service, Full Depository, 707 Savings and Loan Building, Des Moines IA 50309. **Continues** Livestock and Poultry : Number and Value.
  Desc: Number and value of hogs and pigs, chickens and turkeys, cattle and calves, sheep and lambs on Iowa farms.

LC HD9411 .L59   **ISSN** 1048-1605
DD 338.1/76/00973021   US
TITLE CHANGE
LIVESTOCK AND POULTRY UPDATE. [Livest. poult. update]. **Added/Corp** United States. Dept. of Agriculture. Economic Research Service. United States. World Agricultural Outlook Board. (1988)-(199?). Periodical. English. U.S. Department of Agriculture, ERS-NASS, 341 Victory Drive, Herndon VA 22070. **Tel** (800)999-6779, (703)834-0125. **Merged with** Situation and Outlook Report. Livestock and Poultry, 1054-0849

Agriculture —Poultry and Poultry Products

and Situation and Outlook Report. Dairy, 1050-9151 to form Livestock, Dairy, and Poultry Situation and Outlook, 1076-2183.

LC HD9411 .W4   ISSN 0892-6077
DD 338.4/76649/00973   US
CODEN MEAPE7

MEAT & POULTRY. See Food and Food Industry.

US
MEAT & POULTRY FACTS. Added/Corp American Meat Institute. **VFOAT** Meat and Poultry Facts. (1992)-. Periodical. English. One time a year. $12.00 (members of American Meat Institute), $32.00 (nonmembers). American Meat Institute, PO Box 3556, Washington DC 20007. **Tel** (703)841-2400. *Continues Meat Facts, 1062-5933.*

LC HD9410.9.U5 D46a   ISSN 0093-4364
DD 353.0082/336043   US
MEAT AND POULTRY INSPECTION. (MEAT AND POULTRY INSPECTION : REPORT OF THE SECRETARY OF AGRICULTURE TO THE U.S. CONGRESS.). [Meat poult. insp.]. **Main/Corp** United States. Food Safety and Inspection Service. (1981)-. English. One time a year. US Department of Agriculture / Food Safety and Inspection Service, Washington DC 20250. available on microfiche (Vols. for (1982-) distributed to depository libraries). *Continues United States. Food Safety and Quality Service. Meat and Poultry Inspection.*

ISSN 0740-8609
DD 614   US
MEAT AND POULTRY INSPECTION DIRECTORY. (MEAT AND POULTRY INSPECTION DIRECTORY.). [Meat poult. insp. dir.]. Added/Corp United States. Meat and Poultry Inspection Operations. United States. Meat and Poultry Inspection Program. United States. Food Safety and Inspection Service. Inspection Operations. (July/Dec. 1977)-. Government Publication. English. Two times a year. $36.00. US Department of Agriculture, 14th Street and Independence Avenue SW, Washington DC 20250. **Tel** (202)720-5457. (**Subscription address:** Superintendent of Documents, US Government Printing Office, Washington DC 20402.) available on depository microfiche (Vols. for (July 1985-) distributed to depository libraries). *Continues APHIS Program Services Directory.*

US
UDC 637.5.071(73)
MEAT AND POULTRY INSPECTION MANUAL. **Main/Corp** United States. Meat and Poultry Inspection Program. (19??)-. Government Publication. English. Irregular. US Department of Agriculture, 14th Street and Independence Avenue SW, Washington DC 20250. **Tel** (202)720-5457. *Continues Meat and Poultry Inspection Manual.*

ISSN 0924-7068
UDC 637.5   NE
MEAT INTERNATIONAL. See Food and Food Industry.

LC HD9411 .M4   ISSN 0882-3065
DD 338.4/36649/00973021   US
MEAT PRICE RELATIONSHIPS. See Industry and Production.

ISSN 1032-3767
DD 636.5080994   AT
MILNE'S POULTRY DIGEST. [Milne's poult. dig.]. (1988)-. Trade Publication. English. Six times a year. 22.20Aus$. Richard Milne Pty Ltd., PO Box 113, Pyrmont NSW 2009 Australia. **Tel** 011 61 2 8197322, FAX 011 61 2 8197650. **ED** Brian McErlane. **Bk Rev. Ad Acc, Adv Mgr:** Tracie Murray. **Circ:** 2,000. *Continues Australian Poultry Digest, 0815-9297.*
Desc: Features management advice for poultry, meat and egg farmers.
Ind/Abst Anim. Breed. Abstr.; Maize Abstr.; Poult. Abstr.

NE
CODEN MWPOEZ
MISSET WORLD POULTRY. **VFOAT** World Poultry; Misset-World Poultry. Vol. 6, No. 4 (Aug./Sept. 1990)-. Periodical. English. Twelve times a year. $97.00. Misset Uitgeverij BV / Doetinchem, Postbus 4, 7000 BA Doetinchem Netherlands. **Tel** 011 31 8340 49911, 011 31 8340 49562, FAX 011 31 8340 43839, 011 31 8340 40515. *Formed by the union of Poultry (Doetinchem, Netherlands), 0169-4405 and World Poultry.*
Ind/Abst Index Vet.

US
MONTHLY POULTRY SUGGESTIONS / DEPARTMENT OF ANIMAL SCIENCE, COLLEGE OF AGRICULTURE, UNIVERSITY OF ILLINOIS AT URBANA-CHAMPAIGN. Added/Corp University of Illinois at Urbana Champaign. Dept. of Animal Science.

(19??)-. Periodical. English. Twelve times a year. $6.00. Agricultural Newsletter Service, University of Illinois, 116 Mumford Hall, Urbana IL 61801. **Tel** (217)333-2666.

LC SF481.25 .N37   ISSN 0271-793X
DD 635.5/0025/73   US
UDC 636.5.082(73)
NATIONAL POULTRY IMPROVEMENT PLAN. DIRECTORY OF PARTICIPANTS HANDLING EGG-TYPE AND MEAT-TYPE CHICKENS AND TURKEYS. [Natl. poult. improv. plan dir. particip. handl. egg-type meat-type chick. turk.]. Trade Publication. English. One time a year. US Department of Agriculture / Animal & Plant Health Inspection Service, 741 Federal Building 1, 6505 Belcres Road, Hyattsville MD 20782. **Tel** (301)436-7817. available on microfiche (Vols. for (1984-) distributed to depository libraries). *Continues Directory of Participants Handling Egg-Type and Meat-Type Chickens and Turkeys.*

LC SF481.25 .N374   ISSN 0271-7948
DD 636.5/0025/73   US
UDC 636.5.082(73)
NATIONAL POULTRY IMPROVEMENT PLAN. DIRECTORY OF PARTICIPANTS HANDLING WATERFOWL, EXHIBITION POULTRY, AND GAME BIRDS. [Natl. poult. improv. plan dir. particip. handl. waterfowl exhib. poult. game birds]. **VFOAT** Directory of Participants Handling Waterfowl, Exhibition Poultry, and Game Birds. Directory. English. One time a year. Free. US Department of Agriculture / Animal & Plant Health Inspection Service, 741 Federal Building 1, 6505 Belcres Road, Hyattsville MD 20782. **Tel** (301)436-7817. **ED** Irvin L Peterson. **Circ:** 3,000 (ctrl). available on microfiche (Vols. for (1981, 1984-) distributed to depository libraries). *Continues Directory of Participants Handling Egg-Type and Meat-Type Chickens and Turkeys.*

ISSN 0029-0254
JA
CODEN NKKGABUKKGAB
NIHON KAKIN GAKKAISHI. (NIHON KAKIN GAKKAISHI. JAPANESE POULTRY SCIENCE.). [Nihon Kakin Gakkaishi]. Added/Corp Japan Poultry Science Association. Nihon Bankoku Kakkim Gakkai. **VFOAT** Japanese Poultry Science. Vol. 1 (Oct. 1964)-. Academic Scholarly Publication. Japanese (summaries and/or abstracts in English; table of contents in English). Six times a year. $172.00. Nihon Kakin Gakkai, (Japanese Poultry Science Assoc.), Norin Suisansho Chikusan, Shikenjo Kukizakimachi, Inashikigun Ibarakiken 305, Japan. Documents available from BIOSIS Document Express, CASDDS.
Ind/Abst AGRICOLA; Biol. Abstr.; Chem. Abstr.; Food Sci. Technol. Abstr.; Index Vet.; Nutr. Abstr. Rev., Ser. B, Live Feeds and Feed.; PESTDOC; Poult. Abstr.; Protozoolog. Abstr.; Vet. Bull.; Wheat Barley Trit. Abstr.; World Agric. Econ. Rural Sociol. Abstr.

LC QL671
DD 598.61   JA
CODEN NNKEDT
NIWATORI NO KENKYU; THE NIWATORI-NO-KENKYU. **VFOAT** Niwatori-no-Kenkyu. Vol. 1 (Mar. 1924)-. Academic Scholarly Publication. Japanese. Twelve times a year. Niwatori No Kenkyusha, 4-1-623 Marunochi 2 Chome, Chiyodaku Tokyo 100 Japan. Documents available from CASDDS.
Ind/Abst Chem. Abstr.

ISSN 1040-2365
DD 630   US
P / PURDUE UNIVERSITY, COOPERATIVE EXTENSION SERVICE. [P]. Added/Corp United States. Dept. of Agriculture. Purdue University. Cooperative Extension Service. **VFOAT** Poultry. (196?)-. Monographic series. English. *Continues Mimeo P.*
Ind/Abst AGRICOLA [Full Cov.].

ISSN 0306-1582
UK
POULTRY ABSTRACTS. See Agriculture-Abstracting, Bibliographies and Statistics.

ISSN 0970-1958
II
POULTRY ADVISER. [Poult. advis.]. Vol. 7, No. 9, (Feb. 1975)-. Periodical. English. Twelve times a year. $40.00. Poultry Adviser, 97 St Johns Church Road, Bangalore 560 005 India. **Tel** 011 91 812-561627. (**Subscription address:** Prints India, 11 Darya Ganj, New Delhi 110002 India. **Tel** 011 91 11 3268645, FAX 011 91 11 3275542, telex 31-61087 PRIN-IN.)
Ind/Abst Agric. Eng. Abstr. (1991-); Anim. Breed. Abstr.; Biodeter. Abstr. (1991-); Curr. Cit.; Maize Abstr.; Nutr. Abstr. Rev., Ser. B, Live Feeds and Feed.; Nutr. Abstr. Rev., Ser. A, Hum. Exp.; Life Sci. Collect.; Poult. Abstr.;

Protozoolog. Abstr.; Rev. Med. Vet. Entomol.; Rev. Med. Vet. Mycology; Rice Abstr.; Rural Dev. Abstr.; World Agric. Econ. Rural Sociol. Abstr.

UK
●POULTRY AND AVIAN BIOLOGY REVIEWS. (1995)-. Periodical. English. Four times a year. $234.00. Science and Technology Letters, PO Box 81, Northwood Middlesex HA6 3DN United Kingdom. **Tel** 011 44 19238 23586, FAX 011 44 19238 25066. (**Subscription address:** Henchek & Associates, 68 East Wacker Place, Suite 800, Chicago IL 60601.) *Continues Poultry Science Reviews, 0964-6604.*

ISSN 0032-5716
DD 636   US
POULTRY AND EGG MARKETING. [Poult. egg mark.]. **VFOAT** Poultry & Egg Marketing. Vol. 48, No. 45 (Nov. 2, 1968)-. Trade Publication. English. Six times a year (Jan., Mar., May, July, Sept., Nov.). $12.00. Poultry and Egg News, PO Box 1338, Gainesville GA 30503. **Tel** (404)536-2476, FAX (404)532-4894. **ED** Jim Mathis. **Ad Acc. Circ:** 10,000. *Continues Poultry & Eggs Weekly.*
Desc: Covers processing and marketing operations as well as marketing factors including wholesalers, distributors and retailers.

UK
POULTRY BOOKLET. Periodical. English. One time a year.

ISSN 0032-5724
US
CCC
POULTRY DIGEST (MT. MORRIS, ILL.). (POULTRY DIGEST.). (April 1947)-. Periodical. English. Twelve times a year. $54.00. Watt Publishing Company, 122 South Wesley Avenue, Mount Morris IL 61054. **Tel** (815)734-4171, FAX (815)734-7021, telex TWX 910-642-2891. **ED** Charles Perry. Index available. cum. index. **Ad Acc. Circ:** 20,000 (ctrl). available on microfilm and microfiche from University Microfilms International (UMI). *Continues National Poultry Digest.*
Desc: For owners and supervisors of production of eggs, broilers, and turkeys.
Ind/Abst Agric. Eng. Abstr.; BioBusiness; Index Vet.

UK
POULTRY FORUM : OFFICIAL POULTRY JOURNAL OF THE NATIONAL FARMERS' UNION. Added/Corp National Farmers' Union. (Great Britain). (19??)-. Periodical. English. Six times a year. $128.34. National Farmers Union, 22 Long Acre, London WX2F 9LY United Kingdom. **Tel** 011 44 171 2355077.

ISSN 0032-5740
II
CODEN POGUEJ
POULTRY GUIDE (ENGLISH ED.). (POULTRY GUIDE.). [Poult. guide]. Vol. 1 (1964)-. Trade Publication. English. Twelve times a year. $70.00. C.P. Narang Pvt. Ltd., New Delhi India. (**Subscription address:** Prints India, 11 Darya Ganj, New Delhi 110002 India. **Tel** 011 91 11 3268645, FAX 011 91 11 3275542, telex 31-61087 PRIN-IN.)
Ind/Abst Anim. Breed. Abstr.; BioBusiness; Food Sci. Technol. Abstr.; Nutr. Abstr. Rev., Ser. B, Live Feeds and Feed.; Poult. Abstr.; Rice Abstr.

ISSN 0032-5767
DD 636   US
CCC
CODEN POINE8
POULTRY INTERNATIONAL. [Poult. int.]. Vol. 1 (Jan. 1962)-. Periodical. English (summaries and/or abstracts in French, German, Italian and Spanish). Fourteen times a year (monthly plus Sept. directory and July yearbook). $63.00. Watt Publishing Company, 122 South Wesley Avenue, Mount Morris IL 61054. **Tel** (815)734-4171, FAX (815)734-7021, telex TWX 910-642-2891. **ED** Terry Evans. **Ad Acc. Circ:** 19,000 (ctrl). available on microfilm from University Microfilms International (UMI).
Desc: Articles on production, processing, and marketing of poultry.
Ind/Abst Agric. Eng. Abstr. (1991-); Anim. Breed. Abstr.; BioBusiness; Curr. Cit.; Food Sci. Technol. Abstr.; Index Vet.; Nutr. Abstr. Rev., Ser. B, Live Feeds and Feed.; PESTDOC; Pig News Inf.; Poult. Abstr.; Protozoolog. Abstr.

US
POULTRY / IOWA CROP AND LIVESTOCK REPORTING SERVICE. July 1976-. Periodical. English. Twelve times a year. Full Depository, 707 Savings and Loan Building, Des Moines IA 50309. *Formed by the union of Egg Production and Hatchery Production.*
Desc: Statistics and projections for egg production, and chicken and poultry production in Iowa and the United States.

ISSN 0744-298X
US

POULTRY MARKET NEWS REPORT (CHICAGO, ILL.). (POULTRY MARKET NEWS REPORT / FEDERAL-STATE MARKET NEWS SERVICE.). **Added/Corp** Illinois. Dept. of Agriculture. United States. Agricultural Marketing Service. Poultry Division. Federal-State Market News Service. (19??)-. Periodical. English. Three times a week. $145.00. USDA AMS Poultry Market, 800 Roosevelt Road, Building A Suite 310, Glen Ellyn IL 60137. **Tel** (708)790-6910, FAX (708)790-6948.

ISSN 0381-3649
CN

POULTRY MARKET REPORT. (POULTRY MARKET REPORT = RAPPORT SUR LE MARCHE DES VOLAILLES.). **Added/Corp** Canada. Poultry Division. Canada. Dept. of Agriculture. Market Information Service. Canada. Agriculture Canada. Market Information Service. **VFOAT** Rapport sur le Marche des Volailles. (Apr. 21, 1961)-. Government Publication. Multiple languages (English and French). Twelve times a year. Free on request. Agriculture Canada, Communications Branch, Ottawa Ontario K1A 0C7 Canada. ***Supersedes*** *Canada. Dept. of Agriculture. Market Information Service. Poultry Products Market Report., 0381-3630;* ***Absorbed*** *Marche des Volailles., 0381-3665* ***and*** *Canada. Agriculture Canada. Production and Marketing Branch. Poultry Market Review., 0032-5775.*

LC HD9437.C2 A34
DD 380.1/4165/00971 CN
UDC 339.13:636.5(73)

POULTRY MARKET REVIEW. **VFOAT** Revue Annuelle du Marche Avicole. (1981)-. Government Publication. English (French). One time a year. Free on request. Agriculture Canada, Communications Branch, Ottawa Ontario K1A 0C7 Canada. ***Continues*** *Annual Poultry Market Review, 0527-6659.*

LC HD1751 .A5 HD9437.U6 **ISSN** 0565-1980
DD 338.1/0973 S 338.1/7/6500973 US
UDC 338.3:636.5(73)

POULTRY MARKET STATISTICS. **See** Agriculture-Abstracting, Bibliographies and Statistics.

US

POULTRY MARKET STATISTICS ... ANNUAL SUMMARY / UNITED STATES DEPARTMENT OF AGRICULTURE, AGRICULTURAL MARKETING SERVICE. **See** Agriculture-Abstracting, Bibliographies and Statistics.

ISSN 1079-2155
DD 338 US

•**POULTRY MARKETING & TECHNOLOGY.** [Poult. mark. technol.]. **VFOAT** Poultry Marketing and Technology; Poultry. (1993)-. Periodical. English. Six times a year. Marketing & Technology Group, 1415 North Dayton Street, Chicago IL 60622. **Tel** (312)266-3311, FAX (312)266-3363. **ED** Pamela Bowers. **Circ:** 11,000.
Desc: Focuses on technological innovations and new marketing strategies related to the poultry industry.

ISSN 0032-5783
US

POULTRY PRESS. (1914)-. Trade Publication. English. Twelve times a year. $14.00. Poultry Press, PO Box 542, Connersville IN 47331-0542. **Tel** (317)827-0932. **ED** William F. Wulff. **Bk Rev. Ad Acc. Circ:** 5,800 (ctrl).
Desc: Features poultry show reports and the rarer breeds of fancy poultry.

ISSN 0898-4565
DD 664 US
CODEN POPREL

POULTRY PROCESSING. [Poult. process.]. (19??)-. Trade Publication. English. Six times a year. $20.00 US and possessions; $25.00 other. Advanstar Communications Inc., 131 West First Street, Duluth MN 55802. **Tel** (218)723-9477, (800)346-0085, FAX (218)723-9437.
Ind/Abst BioBusiness (1989-).

LC SF481 .P77 **ISSN** 0032-5791
DD 636.5005 US
NLM W1 PO968 **CODEN** POSCAL
Pr Rev.

POULTRY SCIENCE. [Poultry sci.]. **Added/Corp** Poultry Science Association. American Association of Instructors and Investigators in Poultry Husbandry. Vol. 1, (Oct. 1921)-. Academic Scholarly Publication. English. Twelve times a year. $125.00. Poultry Science Association, 309 West Clark Street, Champaign IL 61820. **Tel** (217)356-3182, FAX (217)398-4119. Index available (1986-1993 ($11.00 per iss.) or ($132.00 per vol.)). cum. index. available on microfilm and microfiche from University Microfilms International (UMI). Documents available from The Genuine Article, BIOSIS Document Express, CASDDS, Documents on Demand. ***Supersedes*** *American Association of Instructors and Investigators in Poultry Husbandry. Journal.*
Ind/Abst AgBiotech News Inf.; AGRICOLA [Full Cov.]; Agric. Eng. Abstr. (1991-); Anim. Breed. Abstr.; BioBusiness; Biodeter. Abstr. (19??-19??); Biol. Agric. Index; Biol. Abstr.; Chem. Abstr.; Curr. Biotechnol.; Curr. Cit.; Curr. Contents Agric. Biol. Environ. Sci.; Dairy Sci. Abstr.; EMBASE; Energy Inf. Abstr.; Environ. Abstr.; Food Sci. Technol. Abstr.; Index Med.; Index Vet.; Maize Abstr.; Nucl. Sci. Abstr.; Nutr. Abstr. Rev., Ser. B, Live Feeds and Feed.; Nutr. Abstr. Rev., Ser. A, Hum. Exp.; Life Sci. Collect.; PESTDOC; Poult. Abstr.; Protozoolog. Abstr.; Ref. Upd. Deluxe Ed.; Res. Alert [Full Cov.]; Rev. Agric. Entomol.; Rev. Med. Vet. Entomol.; Rev. Med. Vet. Mycology; Rice Abstr.; Sci. Cit. Index; SCISEARCH; Sorghum Mill. Abstr.; Soyabean Abstr.; Stat. Theory Method Abstr. (1959-1963); Sug. Indus. Abstr.; Vet. Bull.; Weed Abstr.; Wheat Barley Trit. Abstr.; Wildl. Rev.

ISSN 0964-6604
UK
CCC
CODEN PCIRE4
TITLE CHANGE

POULTRY SCIENCE REVIEWS. Vol. 4, No. 1 (1992)-Vol. 5 (1994). Academic Scholarly Publication. English. Elsevier Applied Science, An Imprint of Elsevier Science Ltd., The Boulevard, Langford Lane, Kidlington, Oxford OX5 1GB United Kingdom. **Tel** 011 44 1865 843000, 011 44 1865 843699, FAX 011 44 1865 843010. ***Continues*** *Critical Reviews in Poultry Biology, 0889-4434.* ***Continued by*** *Poultry and Avian Biology Reviews.*
Ind/Abst AGRICOLA (?-?).

ISSN 0306-7610
UK

POULTRY SCIENCE SYMPOSIUM. [Poult. sci. symp.]. **Added/Corp** British Poultry Science Ltd. No. 8 (1971)-. Monographic series. English. One time a year. Price varies per volume. ***Continues*** *British Egg Marketing Board Symposium.*
Ind/Abst AGRICOLA [Full Cov.].

ISSN 0966-7318
UK
CCC

POULTRY SCIENCE SYMPOSIUM SERIES. (19??)-. English. One time a year. $156.00. Carfax Publishing Company, PO Box 25, Abingdon, Oxfordshire OX14 3UE United Kingdom. **Tel** 011 44 1235 555335, FAX 011 44 1235 553559, telex 817484.

LC HD9437.U6 P72 **ISSN** 0364-2682
DD 338.4/766493 US

POULTRY SLAUGHTER. **Added/Corp** United States. Crop Reporting Board. United States. Agricultural Statistics Board. Vol. 1, (Dec. 1973)-. Government Publication. English. Twelve times a year. $34.00. US Department of Agriculture, 14th Street and Independence Avenue SW, Washington DC 20250. **Tel** (202)720-5457. **(Subscription address:** Superintendent of Documents, US Government Printing Office, Washington DC 20402. **)** available on microfiche (Vols. for 1986- distributed to libraries). Documents available from Documents on Demand. ***Continues*** *Poultry Slaughtered Under Federal Inspection.*
Ind/Abst Am. Stat. Index.

ISSN 0885-3371
DD 636 US

POULTRY TIMES (NATIONAL ED.). (POULTRY TIMES.). [Poult. times]. (19??)-. Periodical. English. Twenty-six times a year. $19.00. Poultry Times, PO Box 1338, Gainesville GA 30503. **Tel** (404)536-2476, FAX (404)532-4894. **ED** Jim Mathis, 345 Green Street, Gainsville, GA 30501 USA. **Ad Acc. Circ:** 13,500.
Desc: News articles reporting on research, technical development and current trends in production, marketing, and pricing. Activities of industry organizations are reported, with an emphasis placed on regional news. Also includes coverage of legislative activity, new products, research findings, market conditions, and disease control, as well as editorials, reader opinions, statistical data, and management advice.

ISSN 0971-0752
II

POULTRY TODAY & TOMORROW. [Poult. Today Tomorrow]. **Added/Corp** Agricultural Research Information Centre (Hisar, India). **VFOAT** Poultry Today and Tomorrow. (1991)-. Periodical. English (Hindi). Four times a year. $30.00. Agricultural Research Information Centre, Managing Director, 49 Priti Nagar, Hisar-125001 India. **(Subscription address:** Prints India, 11 Darya Ganj, New Delhi 110002 India. **Tel** 011 91 11 3268645, FAX 011 91 11 3275542, telex 31-61087 PRIN-IN.**)**
Ind/Abst Anim. Breed. Abstr.

ISSN 0032-5813
UK
UDC 636.5

POULTRY WORLD. [Poult. world]. Vol. 1 New Ser. Vol. 1 (1907)-. Trade Publication. English. One time a week. $72.03. Reed Business Publishing / West Sussex, England, Perrymount Road, Haywards Heath, West Sussex RH16 3DH United Kingdom. **Tel** 011 44 1444 441212, FAX 011 44 1444 445447. available on microfilm and microfiche from University Microfilms International (UMI). ***Absorbed*** *Poultry Farmer.*
Ind/Abst AGRICOLA; Nutr. Abstr. Rev., Ser. B, Live Feeds and Feed.

LC HD9284.U45 C33
DD 338.1/7/65009794 US
UDC 339.13:636.5(794); 338.3:636.5(794)

PRODUCTION AND MARKETING EGGS, CHICKENS AND TURKEYS, CALIFORNIA. **Main/Corp** California. Crop and Livestock Reporting Service. Trade Publication. English. California Crop and Livestock Reporting Service, PO Box 1258, Sacramento CA 95806. **Tel** (916)445-6076.

CN

•**PRODUCTION OF EGGS.** (1993)-. Periodical. English (French). Twelve times a year. Statistics Canada Publications Sales and Services, R.H. Coats Building 6th Floor, Ottawa Ontario K1A 0T6 Canada. **Tel** (613)951-5078, (800)267-6677, FAX (613)951-1584, telex 053-3585. ***Continues*** *Production and Stocks of Eggs and Poultry.*

LC HD9437.C2 A32 **ISSN** 0068-7189
DD 338.1/765/00971 CN

PRODUCTION OF POULTRY AND EGGS. [Prod. poult. eggs]. **Added/Corp** Statistics Canada. Agriculture Division. Canada. Dominion Bureau of Statistics. Canada. Dominion Bureau of Statistics. Agriculture Division. Canada. Dominion Bureau of Statistics. Livestock and Animal Products Division. Statistics Canada. Agriculture Statistics Division. Statistics Canada. Livestock and Animal Products Division. Canada. Dominion Bureau of Statistics. Live Stock Section. **VFOAT** Production of Poultry and Eggs in Canada; Production de Volaille et Oeufs. (1946)-. English (French). One time a year. 36.00Can$ Canada; $44.00 US; $51.00 other. Statistics Canada Publications Sales and Services, R.H. Coats Building 6th Floor, Ottawa Ontario K1A 0T6 Canada. **Tel** (613)951-5078, (800)267-6677, FAX (613)951-1584, telex 053-3585. ***Continues*** *Canada. Dominion Bureau of Statistics. Poultry and Egg Production in Canada.*
Desc: This publication annually assembles charts and tables which present current and historical data on the turkey, chicken, stewing hen and egg industries in Canada.

LC SF488.R8 P8 **ISSN** 0033-3239
DD 636.5 RU

PTITSEVODSTVO. **Added/Corp** Russia (1923-U.S.S.R.). Ministerstvo Selskogo Khoziaistva. Russia (1923-U.S.S.R.). Ministerstvo Selskogo Khoziaistva i Zagotovok. Vol. 1 (1951)-. Periodical. Russian. Six times a year. $79.95. Izdatelstvo Kolos, Sadovaia-Spasskaia 18, 107807 Moscow Russia. **(Subscription address:** East View Publications Inc., 3020 Harbor Lane North, Suite 110, Minneapolis MN 55447. **Tel** (800)477-1005, (612)550-0961, FAX (612)559-2931.**)**
Ind/Abst Anim. Breed. Abstr.; For. Prod. Abstr. (1991-); Potato Abstr.; Poult. Abstr.

UK

QUARTERLY JOURNAL - AGRICULTURAL DEVELOPMENT AND ADVISORY SERVICE, POULTRY SECTION. ABSTRACTS SECTION. **Main/Corp** Great Britain. Agricultural Development and Advisory Service. Poultry Section. **VFOAT** Poultry Quarterly Journal; Poultry Section B Quarterly Journal; PQJ. (19??)-. Periodical. English. Four times a year.

ISSN 0347-9838
SW

RAPPORT - SVERIGES LANTBRUKSUNIVERSITET, INSTITUTIONEN FOR HUSDJURS UTFODRING OCH VARD. **See** Agriculture-Livestock.

LC S21.R44 A174 SF487 **ISSN** 0098-6836
DD 630/.8 S 636.5/1/4 US

REPORT OF RANDOM SAMPLE EGG PRODUCTION TESTS, UNITED STATES AND CANADA. **Main/Corp** Animal Improvement Programs Laboratory. (1972)-. English. ***Continues*** *Report of Egg Production Tests, United States and Canada.*

ISSN 0307-4927
UK
UDC 636.5

REPORT OF THE HOUGHTON POULTRY RESEARCH STATION. **Main/Corp** Houghton Poultry Research Station. . Periodical. English. Every 2 years.

ISSN 0257-9162
CU
CODEN REAVDB

REVISTA AVICULTURA. [Rev. avic.]. Vol. 17, No. 2/3 (Aug. 1973)-. Academic Scholarly Publication. Spanish. Four times a year. $13.00. Ediciones Cubanas, Obispo 527 Altos ESQ Bernaza, CP 10100 Havana Cuba. **Bk Rev. Ad Acc. Circ:** 20,000. Documents available from CASDDS. ***Continues*** *Avicultura.*
Desc: Contains a review of world literature on various topics in the form of summaries, plus complete original

papers, with the most recent advances made in Cuba and the rest of the world in the fields of zootechnology, pathology and nutrition.
Ind/Abst Anim. Breed. Abstr.; Chem. Abstr.; Helminthol. Abstr.; Index Vet.; Poult. Abstr.; Protozoolog. Abstr.; Rev. Med. Vet. Entomol.; Vet. Bull.

ISSN 0303-5239
CU
NLM W1 RE539D CODEN RCCADC
REVISTA CUBANA DE CIENCIA AVICOLA. **Added/Corp** Combinado Avicola Nacional. Vol. 1 (Nov. 1972)-. Periodical. Spanish (summaries and/or abstracts in English). Three times a year. $35.00. Ediciones Cubanas, Obispo 527 Altos ESQ Bernaza, CP 10100 Havana Cuba. **Circ:** 20,000 (ctrl). Documents available from CASDDS.
Desc: Related to investigations made in Cuba in the field of livestock and poultry and their applications in zootechnology, genetics, pathology, nutrition, economics and others.
Ind/Abst Anim. Breed. Abstr.; Chem. Abstr.; Helminthol. Abstr. (1991-); Index Vet.; Maize Abstr.; Poult. Abstr.; Protozoolog. Abstr.; Rev. Med. Vet. Mycology; Vet. Bull.

IT
RIVISTA DI AVICOLTURA. **VFOAT** A.V.; AV. Vol. 47, Jan. (1978)-. Periodical. Italian (summaries and/or abstracts in English). Twelve times a year. L40200. Edagricole, PO Box 2157, 40100 Bologna Italy. **Tel** 011 39 51 492211 Ext. 22, FAX 011 39 51 493660, telex 510336 EDAGRI. Index available in last issue of volume--attached. **Continues** Avicoltura.
Ind/Abst Agric. Eng. Abstr. (1991-); Anim. Breed. Abstr.; Helminthol. Abstr.; Index Vet.; Maize Abstr.; Nutr. Abstr. Rev., Ser. B, Live Feeds and Feed.; Nutr. Abstr. Rev., Ser. A, Hum. Exp.; Poult. Abstr.; Soyabean Abstr.; Vet. Bull.

ISSN 0137-1657
PL
CODEN RNZOD8
ROCZNIKI NAUKOWE ZOOTECHNIKI = ANNALS OF ANIMAL SCIENCE. See Agriculture-Livestock.

ISSN 0582-4818
SP
SELECCIONES AVICOLAS. **Added/Corp** Real Escula Oficial y Superior de Avicultura (Spain). Vol. 1 (1959)-. Periodical. Spanish. Twelve times a year. $50.00. Real Escuela Oficial Superior de Avicultura, Plana de Paraiso 14, 08350 Barcelona Spain. **Tel** 011 34 3 7921137, FAX 011 34 3 7923141. Index available. **Bk Rev. Ad Acc. Circ:** 3,000.
Desc: Original articles on poultry management, nutrition, diseases, economics, as well as articles reproduced from other sources.

LC HD9411 .L58 ISSN 1054-0849
DD 338.1/76/00973021 US
TITLE CHANGE
SITUATION AND OUTLOOK REPORT. LIVESTOCK AND POULTRY. (SITUATION AND OUTLOOK REPORT. LIVESTOCK AND POULTRY / UNITED STATES DEPARTMENT OF AGRICULTURE, ECONOMIC RESEARCH SERVICE.). [Situat. outlook rep., Livest. poult.]. **Added/Corp** United States. Dept. of Agriculture. Economic Research Service. United States. World Agricultural Outlook Board. **VFOAT** Livestock and Poultry; Livestock and Poultry Situation and Outlook Report. LPS-20 (May 1986)-(Nov. 1993). Government Publication. English. Superintendent of Documents, US Government Printing Office, Washington DC 20402. **Tel** (202)275-3328, FAX (202)786-2377. available on microfiche (Vols. for 1987- distributed to depository libraries). **Continues** Outlook and Situation Report. Livestock and Poultry. **Merged with** Situation and Outlook Report. Dairy, 1050-9151 **and** Livestock and Poultry Update, 1048-1605 **to form** Livestock, Dairy, and Poultry Situation and Outlook.
Desc: Reports, consisting chiefly of tables and statistics, contains information on supply, demand and price research.
Ind/Abst F&S Index Plus Text, Int. [Select. Cov.]; Poult. Abstr.; Predicasts Forecasts; Trade Ind. ASAP [Full Txt.]; Trade Ind. Index [Full Txt.]; World Agric. Econ. Rural Sociol. Abstr.

SA
SOUTH AFRICAN POULTRY ASSOCIATION BULLETIN. **Main/Corp** South African Poultry Association. **VFOAT** Poultry Bulletin. (1937)-. Bulletin. Multiple languages (Afrikaans and English). Twelve times a year. R75.00 other. R120.00 other. Promass Pty Ltd., PO Box 1192, Honedew 2040 South Africa. **Tel** 011 27 11 7952051, 011 27 11 7952052.

ISSN 0263-5178
UK
TECHNICAL BULLETIN (EGGS AUTHORITY). (TECHNICAL BULLETIN / THE EGGS AUTHORITY.). (1977)-. Bulletin. English.

ISSN 0040-1889
MX
NLM W1 TE219 CODEN TPMXA3
TECNICA PECUARIA EN MEXICO. [Tec. pecu. Mex.]. **Added/Corp** Instituto Nacional de Investigaciones Pecuarias. (1963)-. Periodical. Spanish (summaries and/or abstracts in English, French and German). Four times a year. Instituto Nacional de Investigaciones Pecuarias, 1 Beechfield Avenue Urmston, Palo Alto 10 DF Mexico. Documents available from CASDDS.
Ind/Abst Chem. Abstr. (-1984); Field Crop Abstr.; Helminthol. Abstr. (1991-); Life Sci. Collect.; Pig News Inf.; Plant Breed. Abstr.; Rev. Med. Vet. Mycology; Seed Abstr.; Sorghum Mill. Abstr.

ISSN 1195-1877
DD 637 CN
●**TODAY'S EGG PRODUCER.** [Today's egg prod.]. **Added/Corp** Canadian Egg Marketing Agency. (Between Dec. 1992-June 1993)-. Trade Publication. English. Twelve times a year. Free. Canadian Egg Marketing Agency, 320 Queen Street, Suite 1900, Place de Ville, Ottawa Ontario K1R 5A3 Canada. **Tel** (613)238-2514, FAX (613)238-1967. **Continues** The Egg Producer., 0821-4689.

ISSN 0041-4271
US
CCC
TURKEY WORLD (1968). (TURKEY WORLD.). (1968)-. Periodical. English. Six times a year. $28.00. Watt Publishing Company, 122 South Wesley Avenue, Mount Morris IL 61054. **Tel** (815)734-4171, FAX (815)734-7021, telex TWX 910-642-2891. **ED** Bernard Heffernan. **Ad Acc. Circ:** 10,000 (ctrl). **Continues** Poultry Meat (Broiler and Turkey Edition).
Desc: Serves individuals and firms engaged in producing, processing, and marketing turkeys.
Ind/Abst Index Vet.

ISSN 0041-428X
UK
TURKEYS. Vol. 1 (Nov. 1952)-. Trade Publication. English. Six times a year (Feb., Apr., June, Aug., Oct., Dec.). $34.23. Fancy Fowl Publications Ltd., Andover Road Highclere, Newbury Berkshire RG15 9PH United Kingdom. **Tel** 011 44 1635 253239, telex 848507 HJULPH G. **ED** Shirley Murdoch. **Bk Rev. Ad Acc. Circ:** 6,000 (ctrl).
Desc: All aspects of turkey breeding, growing, processing and marketing.

US
TURKEYS, FINAL ESTIMATES FOR ... . (1975)-. Government Publication. English. US Department of Agriculture / Statistical Reporting Service, 14th Street & Independence Avenue SW, Washington DC 20250. **Continues** Turkeys, Revised Estimates.

US
U.S. DIRECTORY OF POULTRY & EGG PROCESSING PLANTS. (1976)-. Directory. English.

US
TITLE CHANGE
U.S. TRADE AND PROSPECTS, DAIRY, LIVESTOCK, AND POULTRY PRODUCTS. See Agriculture-Dairy Industry.

LC HD9413 .U76 ISSN 0738-6745
DD 381/.4566492/02573 US
URNER BARRY'S MEAT & POULTRY DIRECTORY. [Urner Barry's Meat poult. dir.]. **VFOAT** Urner Barry's Meat and Poultry Directory; Meat & Poultry Directory; Meat and Poultry Directory. (1984)-. Directory. English. Twelve times a year. $95.00. Urner Barry Publications Inc., PO Box 389, Toms River NJ 08754. **Tel** (908)240-5330, (800)932-0617, FAX (908)341-0891. **ED** Paul B. Brown Jr. **Bk Rev. Ad Acc. Circ:** 2,200 (ctrl).
Desc: A national directory of meat and poultry traders with over 8,500 listings of current, relative information. Many listings contain phone numbers, key personnel, sales territory, products handled, and product form.

UK
VETMARK INTERNATIONAL POULTRY PRACTICE. (19??)-. English. Four times a year. Free. International Poultry Practice, PO Box 237, Cambridge CB4 3AW United Kingdom. **Tel** 011 44 1223 316555, FAX 011 44 1223 357389, telex 8950511 ONEONE G. **Continues** International Poultry Practice, 0951-9157.

ISSN 0042-6733
US
VIRGINIA POULTRYMAN, THE. **Added/Corp** Virginia Poultry Federation. Virginia Poultry Products Commission. West Virginia Poultry Association. Virginia State Feed Association. West Virginia Farm Supply Association. Virginia State Poultry Federation. (1947)-. Periodical. English. Twelve times a year. $4.00. Virginia Poultry Federation, Box 552, Harrisonburg VA 22801. **Tel** (703)433-2451. **ED** Richard W Moyers. **Bk Rev. Ad Acc. Circ:** 2,100 (ctrl).

ISSN 1052-4843
LC HD9437.U6 W38 US
DD 338.1/765/0097305
WATT POULTRY YEARBOOK. [Watt poult. yearb.]. **VFOAT** Watt Poultry Year Book; Poultry Yearbook; A.Poultry year book. (Fall 1990)-. Periodical. English. One time a year. $35.00. Watt Publishing Company, 122 South Wesley Avenue, Mount Morris IL 61054. **Tel** (815)734-4171, FAX (815)734-7021, telex TWX 910-642-2891.

ISSN 0160-4872
US
WEEKLY INSIDERS POULTRY REPORT. See Agriculture-Abstracting, Bibliographies and Statistics.

ISSN 0160-4910
US
WEEKLY INSIDERS TURKEY LETTER. See Agriculture-Abstracting, Bibliographies and Statistics.

LC HD9284.U4 W5 ISSN 1044-5528
DD 338.7/665/0029473 US
WHO'S WHO IN THE EGG AND POULTRY INDUSTRIES IN THE UNITED STATES AND CANADA. [Who's who egg poult. ind. U. S. A. Can.]. **VFOAT** Who's Who in the Egg and Poultry Industries; Who's Who Buyers Guide; Who's Who in the Egg & Poultry Industries. (1987)-. Directory. English. One time a year. $75.00. Watt Publishing Company, 122 South Wesley Avenue, Mount Morris IL 61054. **Tel** (815)734-4171, FAX (815)734-7021, telex TWX 910-642-2891. **Continues** Who's Who in the Egg and Poultry Industries, 0510-4130.

UK
WORLD POULTRY INDUSTRY. (May 1980)-. Periodical. English. Twelve times a year. Reed Business Publishing / West Sussex, England, Perrymount Road, Haywards Heath, West Sussex RH16 3DH United Kingdom. **Tel** 011 44 1444 441212, FAX 011 44 1444 445447. **Continues** Poultry Industry.

LC SF481 .W75 ISSN 0043-9339
DD 636.505 UK
CCC
NLM W1 WO905 CODEN WPSJAO
Pr Rev.
WORLD'S POULTRY SCIENCE JOURNAL. [World's poult. sci. j.]. **Added/Corp** World's Poultry Science Association. Vol. 1 (Spring 1945)-. Periodical. English. Three times a year. $130.00. Watt Publishing Company, 122 South Wesley Avenue, Mount Morris IL 61054. **Tel** (815)734-4171, FAX (815)734-7021, telex TWX 910-642-2891. cum. index. **Bk Rev. Ad Acc. Circ:** 6,000 (ctrl). available on microfilm and microfiche from University Microfilms International (UMI). Documents available from The Genuine Article, BIOSIS Document Express.
Desc: All aspects of poultry science: veterinary nutrition, husbandry, genetics, lighting, etc. association news.
Ind/Abst AGRICOLA [Full Cov.]; Agric. Eng. Abstr. (1991-); Anim. Breed. Abstr.; BioBusiness; Biol. Abstr.; Curr. Cit.; Food Sci. Technol. Abstr.; Index Vet.; Nutr. Abstr. Rev., Ser. B, Live Feeds and Feed.; Life Sci. Collect.; PESTDOC; Poult. Abstr.; Res. Alert [Full Cov.]; Rev. Med. Vet. Entomol.; Sci. Cit. Index; SCISEARCH; Wildl. Rev.

ANIMAL WELFARE

ISSN 1032-3945
AT
ACCART NEWS. [ACCART news]. **Added/Corp** Australian Council for the Care of Animals in Research and Teaching. **VAT** Australian Council for the Care of Animals in Research and Teaching News. Vol. 1, No. 1 (Spring 1988)-. Periodical. English. Four times a year.
Ind/Abst Index Vet.

LC WMLC 93/214 ISSN 1040-2225
DD 179 US
ADVOCATE (DENVER, COLO.). (ADVOCATE.). [Advocate]. **Added/Corp** American Humane Association. American Humane Association. Animal Protection Division. Vol. 1 No. 1 (Nov. 1983)-. Periodical. English. Four times a year. $15.00. American Humane Association, 63 Inverness Drive East, Englewood CO 80112. **Tel** (303)792-9900, FAX (303)695-6348. **ED** Susan W Halberstandt. **Bk Rev. Circ:** 28,500 (ctrl). **Continues in part** National Animal Protection Newsletter, 0738-582X.
Desc: Reports American Humane Association's animal protection activities and legislative activities from the Washington DC office. Includes reviews concerning the treatment of animals in entertainment as well as pet care and health topics.
Ind/Abst AGRICOLA [Select. Cov.].

LC WMLC 93/1358 ISSN 0199-543X
DD 636 US
CODEN AFAWE5

AFA WATCHBIRD, THE. [A.F.A. watchb.]. **Main/Corp** American Federation of Aviculture. **VFOAT** Watchbird. **VAT** American Federation of Aviculture Watchbird. Vol. 1 (1974)-. Periodical. English. Six times a year. $24.00 Comes with American Federation Aviculture membership. American Federation Aviculture, PO Box 56218, Phoenix AZ 85073-6218. **Tel** (602)484-0931, FAX (602)484-0109. **ED** Jerry Jennings. Index available. cum. index. **Bk Rev**. **Ad Acc**. **Circ:** 10,100 (ctrl).

LC HV4763 .A443 ISSN 0147-4383
DD 179/.3/02573 US

AGENCY DIRECTORY - AMERICAN HUMANE. **Main/Corp** American Humane Association. **Added/Corp** American Humane Association. American Humane Agency Directory. **VFOAT** American Humane Agency Directory. (19??)-. Directory. English. American Humane, 5351 South Roslyn Street, Englewood CO 80110.

UK

AGSCENE (PETERSFIELD, HAMPSHIRE). (AGSCENE : NEWS & COMMENT ON AGRICULTURE AND THE ENVIRONMENT.). **Added/Corp** Compassion in World Farming (Organization). **VFOAT** Ag; Ag Scene. (19??)-. Periodical. English. Four times a year (Mar., June, Sept., Dec.). $17.11. Compassion In The World of Farming, 20 Lavant St Petersfield, Hampshire GU32 3EW United Kingdom. **Tel** 011 44 1730 64208.

US

AHPA NEWS. **See** Horses and Horsemanship.

LC SF481 .A76 ISSN 1083-0553
DD 636.59605 US

•**AMERICAN PIGEON NEWS.** [Am. pigeon news]. Vol. 111, No. 1 (Jan. 1995)-. Periodical. English. Twelve times a year. American Racing Pigeon News, 34 East Franklin Street, BellBrook OH 45305. **Tel** (513)848-4972, FAX (513)848-3012. ***Continues*** *American Racing Pigeon News, 0003-0686.*

LC SF481 .A76 ISSN 0003-0686
DD 636.59605 US
TITLE CHANGE

AMERICAN RACING PIGEON NEWS, THE. [Am. racing pigeon news]. (19??)-(199?). Periodical. English. American Racing Pigeon News, 34 East Franklin Street, BellBrook OH 45305. **Tel** (513)848-4972, FAX (513)848-3012. ***Continues*** *Homing Exchange.* ***Continued by*** *American Pigeon News, 1083-0553.*

US

ANIMAL BEHAVIOR CONSULTANT NEWSLETTER. (19??)-. Newsletter. English. Four times a year (Jan., Apr., July, Oct.). $5.00. Animal Behavior Consultant, PO Box 180, Mercer University, Macon GA 31207. **Tel** (912)752-2973. **ED** John C. Wright and Peter L. Borchett. **Bk Rev**. **Circ:** 350.

LC BJ1518
DD 179.3 UK

•**ANIMAL CONCERN UPDATE.** (1994)-. Bulletin. English. Four times a year. £10.00 (Comes with membership). Animal Concern Ltd., 62 Old Dumbarton Road, Glasgow G3 8RE United Kingdom. **Tel** 011 44 141 3346014, FAX 011 44 141 4456470. **ED** John F. Robins. available with illustrations.
Desc: Includes information on events and political action regarding animal welfare.

US
CEASED

ANIMAL LAW NEWSLETTER / ANIMAL PROTECTION COMMITTEE, YOUNG LAWYER'S DIVISION, AMERICAN BAR ASSOCIATION. (19??)-(Jan. 1995). Newsletter. English. American Bar Association, 750 North Lake Shore Drive, Chicago IL 60611. **Tel** (312)988-5500, (312)988-5241, FAX (312)988-6014, telex 270593. ***Continues*** *Animal Law Report.*

ISSN 0816-486X
DD 179.30994 AT
CEASED

ANIMAL LIBERATION. [Anim. Lib.]. **Added/Corp** Animal Liberation (Australia). (1985)-(1993). Periodical. English. Animal Liberation Action, PO Box 15, Elwood 3184 Australia. **Tel** 011 61 3 328 3603. **ED** Patty Mark. Index available. cum. index. **Bk Rev**. **Ad Acc**. **Circ:** 500 (ctrl). ***Continues*** *Outcry (Glen Iris), 0725-9700.*
Desc: Contains Australian animal rights information. Includes interviews, profiles, and features all aspects of the animal rights & welfare movement.

ISSN 1071-0035
DD 179 US

ANIMAL PEOPLE. [Anim. people]. **Added/Corp** Animal People, Inc. (199?)-. Periodical. English. Ten times a year (monthly except Feb. & Aug.). $18.00. Animal People, PO Box 205, Shushan NY 12873. **Tel** (518)854-9436, FAX (518)854-9601. **ED** Merritt Clifton. **Bk Rev**, (Qty: 36). **Ad Acc**. **Circ:** 15,000.
Desc: Covers all events and news concerning the animal protection community.

LC SF25 .A54 ISSN 0733-4710
DD 636/.0025/73 US

ANIMAL PEOPLE'S DIRECTORY, THE. (THE ANIMAL PEOPLE'S DIRECTORY : APD.). **VFOAT** APD; A.P.D. (1982)-. English. One time a year. $9.50. APD Publications, PO Box 462, Logandale NV 89021.

LC KF390.5.A5 A132 ISSN 0730-6792
DD 346.73/046954 347.30646954 US

ANIMAL RIGHTS LAW REPORTER. **Added/Corp** Society for Animal Rights (U.S.). (Jan. 1980)-. Periodical. English. Twelve times a year. $15.00 Comes with Society for Animal Rights membership. Society for Animal Rights, 421 South State Street, Clark Summit PA 18411. **Tel** (717)586-2200.
Desc: An objective analysis of the animal rights movement. Examines issues tactics, personalities, new regulations and literature.

ISSN 1192-4861
DD 179 CN

ANIMAL TALK. [Anim. talk]. **Added/Corp** Toronto Humane Society. (1990)-. Periodical. English. Four times a year. 20.00Can$. Toronto Humane Society, Education Department, 11 River Street, Toronto Ontario M5A 4C2 Canada. **Tel** (416)392-2273. ***Continues*** *Society News (Toronto Humane Society)., 0845-5082.*

LC HV4905 .A18
DD 636.08/3 UK

ANIMAL WELFARE. (Jan./Feb. 1976)-. English. £0.10. British Union for the Abolition of Vivisection, 47 Whitehall, London SW1 United Kingdom. ***Continues*** *A V Times.*

ISSN 0962-7286
UK

NLM W1; AN2282

ANIMAL WELFARE. **Added/Corp** Universities Federation for Animal Welfare. Vol. 1, No. 1 (1992)-. Periodical. English. Four times a year. $94.11. Universities Federation for Animal Welfare, 8 Hamilton Close, South Mimms, Hertfordshire EN6 3QD United Kingdom. **Tel** 011 44 1707 58202, FAX 011 44 1707 49279. **ED** Roger Ewbank. Index available. cum. index. **Bk Rev**.
Desc: Brings together the results of scientific research and technical studies related to the welfare of animals kept on farms, in laboratories, and in zoos, as companions or living in the wild. Designed for use by all concerned with the management, care and welfare of animals, from administrators to zoologists.
Ind/Abst Soc. Sci. Cit. Index [Select. Cov.].

ISSN 1050-561X
DD 179 US

ANIMAL WELFARE INFORMATION CENTER NEWSLETTER. [Animal Welf. Inf. Cent. newsl.]. **Added/Corp** Animal Welfare Information Center (U.S.). Vol. 1, No. 1 & 2 (Spring/Summer 1990)-. Newsletter. English. Four times a year. National Agricultural Library, 10301 Baltimore Boulevard, Beltsville MD 20705.
Ind/Abst AGRICOLA [Full Cov.].

LC QL76.5.U6 A54 ISSN 0747-5128
US

ANIMAL WELFARE. LIST OF LICENSED EXHIBITORS. (ANIMAL WELFARE. LIST OF LICENSED EXHIBITORS / UNITED STATES DEPARTMENT OF AGRICULTURE, ANIMAL AND PLANT HEALTH INSPECTION SERVICE, VETERINARY SERVICES.). [Anim. welf., List licens. exhib.]. **Added/Corp** United States. Animal and Plant Health Inspection Service. Veterinary Services. United States. Animal and Plant Health Inspection Service. Regulatory Enforcement and Animal Care. **VFOAT** List of Licensed Exhibitors. (19??)-. English. One time a year. US Department of Agriculture / Animal & Plant Health Inspection Service, 741 Federal Building 1, 6505 Belcres Road, Hyattsville MD 20782. **Tel** (301)436-7817.

ISSN 0747-5144
US

ANIMAL WELFARE. LIST OF REGISTERED RESEARCH FACILITIES. [Anim. welf., List regist. res. facil.]. **Added/Corp** United States. Animal and Plant Health Inspection Service. Veterinary Services. **VFOAT** List of Registered Research Facilities. (19??)-. Periodical. English. One time a year. US Department of Agriculture / Animal & Plant Health Inspection Service, 741 Federal Building 1, 6505 Belcres Road, Hyattsville MD 20782. **Tel** (301)436-7817.

ISSN 0968-2147
UK

ANIMAL WORLD HORSHAM. (ANIMAL WORLD.). [Anim. world Horsham]. (1981)-. Periodical. English. Six times a year (Feb., Apr., June, Aug., Oct., Dec.). $6.84. Royal Society for the Prevention of Cruelty to Animals, Causeway, Horsham WS RH12 1HG United Kingdom. **Tel** 011 44 1403 264181, FAX 011 44 1403 241048. **ED** Michael Miller. **Circ:** 70,000. ***Continues*** *Animal Ways.*
Desc: Animal World is the youth membership magazine of the RSPA; covers animal welfare related features, new items, puzzles, and pictures.

US

ANIMALS' ADVOCATE : THE QUARTERLY NEWSLETTER OF THE ANIMAL LEGAL DEFENSE FUND, THE. **Added/Corp** Animal Legal Defense Fund. (Summer 1989)-. Periodical. English. Four times a year. Comes with Animal Legal Defense Fund membership; $15.00 (membership). Animal Legal Defense Fund, 1363 Lincoln Avenue, San Rafael CA 94901. ***Continues*** *Newsletter (Animal Legal Defense Fund).*

ISSN 0892-8819
US

ANIMALS' AGENDA, THE. [Anim. agenda]. **Added/Corp** Animal Rights Network. Vol. 5, No. 1 (Jan./Feb. 1985)-. Periodical. English. Six times a year (Jan., Mar., May, July, Sept., Nov.). $22.00. Animal Rights Network, PO Box 25881, Baltimore MD 21224. **Tel** (410)675-4566, FAX (410)675-0066. **(Subscription address:** The Animal's Agenda, PO Box 6809, Syracuse NY 13217. **Tel** (800)825-0061.) **ED** Kim Bartlett. Index available. cum. index. **Bk Rev**, (Qty: 40 per year). **Ad Acc**, **Adv Mgr:** David Patrice Greanville, **Tel** (203)452-0446. **Circ:** 30,000. available on an online database, CD-ROM, magnetic tape, and microfilm. Documents available from UMI Article Clearinghouse. ***Continues*** *Agenda (Westport, Conn.), 0741-5044.*
Desc: A comprehensive magazine in the field of animal protection. Features a wide range of subjects relating to humanity's exploitation of animals and the environment. The writers often discuss matters relating to the ethical and health aspects of vegetarianism and a cruelty-free lifestyle.
Ind/Abst AGRICOLA; Altern. Press Index; Gen. Period. Index (1989-); Mag. Index Plus (1989-); Newsp. Period. Abstr. (1988-); Mag. Index (1989-).

LC HV4701 .O8 ISSN 0030-6835
DD 179/.3/05 US

ANIMALS (BOSTON). (ANIMALS.). [Animals]. **Added/Corp** Massachusetts Society for the Prevention of Cruelty to Animals. Vol. 103, No. 4 (April 1970)-. Periodical. English. Six times a year. $19.00. Massachusetts Society for the Prevention of Cruelty to Animals, 350 South Huntington, Boston MA 02130. **Tel** (617)522-7400, FAX (617)522-4885. **(Subscription address:** Kable Publishers Aide / Illinois, 308 East Hitt Street, Subscription Department, Mt. Morris IL 61054-1473. **Tel** (815)734-1261.) **ED** Joni Praded and Paula Abend. **Bk Rev**. **Circ:** 70,000. available on microfilm and microfiche from University Microfilms International (UMI). Documents available from UMI Article Clearinghouse. ***Continues*** *Our Dumb Animals, 0275-2476.*
Desc: Covers the diversity of the animal world; articles and photography on animal issues and controversies, the latest pet topics, and wild and domestic animals.
Ind/Abst Acad. Search; EP Collect.; Homework Help.; Key Word Index Wildl. Res.; Mag. Search; MasterFile FullTEXT 1000; MasterFile FullTEXT 350; MasterFile FullTEXT 650; MasterFile FullTEXT (July 1993-) [Full Txt.]; Newsp. Period. Abstr. (1988-); OCLC; Prim. Search; Pub. Lib. FullTEXT; Telebase.

ISSN 0254-3923
DD 636 UK

ANIMALS INTERNATIONAL. [Anim. int.]. **Added/Corp** World Society for the Protection of Animals. Vol. 1, No. 1 (Jan.-March 1981)-. Periodical. English. Four times a year. World Society for the Protection of Animals, 106 Jermyn Street, London SW1Y 6EE United Kingdom. ***Formed by the union of*** *Animalia* ***and*** *ISPA News.*
Ind/Abst AGRICOLA [Select. Cov.].

ISSN 0700-8392
CN

ANIMALS' VOICE. Vol. 1 (March 1960)-. English. Ontario Humane Society, 969 Yonge Street, Toronto M4Y 2A7 Canada.

ISSN 1062-2942
DD 179 US

ANIMALS' VOICE MAGAZINE, THE. [Anim. voice mag.]. **Added/Corp** Compassion for Animals Foundation. **VFOAT** Animals' Voice. (1988)-. Periodical. English. Four times a year. $20.00. Compassion for Animals Foundation Inc., PO Box 341347, Los Angeles CA 90034. **Tel** (213)204-2323. **(Subscription address:** Animal's Voice Magazine, PO Box 16955, North Hollywood CA 91615. **Tel** (818)760-8983.) **Circ:** 30,000. ***Continues*** *Animals' Voice (Chico, Calif.), 0889-6712.*
Desc: Magazine of the animal defense movement. It features news coverage of animal defense issues as well as editorial, photography, commentary, profiles, art, poetry and a section about what one can do to help animals.

ISSN 1039-9089
AT

•**ANZCCART NEWS / AUSTRALIAN AND NEW ZEALAND COUNCIL FOR THE CARE OF ANIMALS IN RESEARCH AND TEACHING.** **Added/Corp** Australian and New Zealand Council for the Care of Animals in Research and

Animal Welfare

Teaching. **VAT** Australian and New Zealand Council for the Care of Animals in Research and Teaching News. Vol. 6, No. 1 (Autumn 1993)-. Periodical. English. Four times a year. Free on request. Dr. R.M. Baker, PO Box 19, Glen Osmond SA 5064 Australia. **Tel** 011 61 8 3037393. **Continues** ACCART News, 1032-3945.

AT

●**ANZSLAS NEWSLETTER.** (1995)-. Newsletter. English. Four times a year. 40.00Aus$. ANZSLAS Animal Resource Center, PO Box 1180, Canning Vale WA 6155 Australia. **Tel** 011 09 3325033. **Absorbed** ASLAS Newsletter.

ISSN 0887-7386
US
CCC
CODEN AHPDE3
Pr Rev.

●**APIS, THE.** **VFOAT** Animal Health Products. (1993)-. Periodical. English. Four times a year. $275.00. CITA International, Industrial Publ Division, PO Box 70, Phoenix AZ 85001. **Tel** (602)447-0480, FAX (602)447-0305. **ED** E. Morsy. Index available. cum. index. **Ad Acc. Circ:** 750 (ctrl).

UK

ARK. No. 54 (1978)-. English. Three times a year. $8.55. Catholic Study Circle for Animal Welfare, 39 Onslow Gardens, South Woodford London E18 1ND United Kingdom. **Tel** 011 44 181 9890478. **ED** Kevin Daley. **Bk Rev. Ad Acc. Circ:** 2,000. **Continues** Journal from the Royal College of Art.
 Desc: Promotes concern and respect for animals by prayer, example and propaganda; embraces the Christian tradition of care for animals.
 Ind/Abst AgBiotech News Inf.; Anim. Breed. Abstr.; Br. Archaeol. Bibliogr.; Libr. Inf. Sci. Abstr.; Pig News Inf.; Poult. Abstr.

ISSN 0969-207X
DD 179.3
UK

ARKANGEL LONDON. [Arkangel Lond.]. (1989)-. Periodical. English. Catholic Study Circle for Animal Welfare, 39 Onslow Gardens, South Woodford London E18 1ND United Kingdom. **Tel** 011 44 181 9890478.

ISSN 1039-0154
AT
TITLE CHANGE

ASLAS NEWSLETTER. **VFOAT** Australian Society for Laboratory Animal Science Newsletter. (1989)-(1995). Newsletter. English. ANZSLAS Animal Resource Center, PO Box 1180, Canning Vale WA 6155 Australia. **Tel** 011 09 3325033. **Continues** Australian Society for Laboratory Animal Science Newsletter, 0817-4881. **Merged into** ANZSLAS Newsletter.

LC HV4701 .S7
DD 179./3/05
NLM W1 A164
ISSN 0274-7774
US

AV MAGAZINE, THE. [AV mag.]. **Added/Corp** American Anti-Vivisection Society. **VAT** Anti-Vivisection Magazine. Vol. 85 (Jan. 1977)-. Periodical. English. Eleven times a year (monthly except Aug.). $15.00. American Anti-Vivisection Society, 801 Old York Road, Noble Plaza, Jenkintown PA 19046. **Tel** (215)887-0816, FAX (215)887-2088. **ED** B. G. Kelly. **Bk Rev,** (Qty: 5). **Circ:** 9,000. **Continues** A-V, 0001-2831.
 Desc: Intended to abolish painful experiments on animals through appropriate legislation; concerns animals' rights and allied subjects.

ISSN 1071-1384
DD 179
NLM W1; A169L
US

AWI QUARTERLY. [AWI q.]. **Added/Corp** Animal Welfare Institute. **VAT** Animal Welfare Institute Quarterly. Vol. 41, No. 3 (Summer 1992)-. Periodical. English. Four times a year (Jan., April, July, Oct.). Free on request. Animal Welfare Institute, PO Box 3650, Washington DC 20007. **Tel** (202)337-2332, FAX (202)338-9478. **ED** Christine Stevens. **Bk Rev. Circ:** 16,000. **Continues** Animal Welfare Institute Quarterly, 0743-0841.
 Desc: Dealing with current animal welfare issues, including treatment of captive animals in laboratories, commercial trade, factory farms, and traplines, summaries of international meetings, laws and treaties affecting animals, articles by undercover investigators, and book reviews.
 Ind/Abst Bibliogr. Agric.

SP

BARRUTIK. (19??)-. Spanish. Four times a year. Free. Asociacion Apoyo Presos Presas, Calle Uribarri 2-3, 48007 Bilbao Spain. **Tel** 011 34 4 4464100.

UK

NLM W1; CA456P
CAMPAIGNER. **Added/Corp** National Anti-Vivisection Society (Great Britain). (Jan./Feb./Mar. 1990)-. Periodical. English. Four times a year. National Anti-Vivisection Society, 51 Harley Street, London W1N 1DD United Kingdom. **Tel** 011 44 171 5804034. **Continues** Campaigner and Animals' Defender, 0954-321X.

ISSN 0825-1711
DD 636.08/85
CN

CARING FOR ANIMALS (OTTAWA, ONT.). (CARING FOR ANIMALS.). [Caring anim.]. **Added/Corp** Canadian Federation of Humane Societies. Experimental Animals Committee. Vol. 1, No. 1 (Spring 1984)-. Periodical. English. Two times a year. Free on request. Canadian Federation of Humane Societies / Nepean, 30 Concourse Gate, Suite 102, Nepean Ontario K2E 7V7 Canada. **Tel** (613)224-8072, FAX (613)723-0252. **ED** Stephanie Brown. **Bk Rev. Circ:** 2,500 (ctrl).
 Desc: News, philosophy and editorial information on the alternatives of live animals used in research, teaching and testing. Directed to animal care, welfare of the animals, laboratory and used committees.

US
CODEN ESUPEF

ENDANGERED SPECIES UPDATE. See Environmental Issues-Conservation and Natural Resources.

ISSN 0268-4306
UK

FRAME NEWS. (FRAME NEWS : NEWSLETTER OF THE FUND FOR THE REPLACEMENT OF ANIMALS IN MEDICAL EXPERIMENTS.). [FRAME news]. **Added/Corp** Fund for the Replacement of Animals in Medical Experiments. **VAT** Fund for the Replacement of Animals in Medical Experiments News. (1984)-. Newsletter. English. Three times a year. $25.67. FRAME, Eastgate House, 34 Stoney Street, Nottingham NG1 1NB United Kingdom. **Tel** 011 44 115 9584740, FAX 011 44 115 9503570. **ED** Gilly Griffin. **Bk Rev,** (Qty: 6-10). **Circ:** 2,265 (ctrl). **Continues** Fund for the Replacement of Animals in Medical Experiments. Progress Report; FRAME Technical News, 0143-8352.
 Desc: Provides general information on laboratory animal experimentation, alternative methods and their development, current legislation, and the work of FRAME itself.
 Ind/Abst AGRICOLA.

ISSN 0715-5891
DD 179/.3/060711
CN

FUR-BEARERS, THE. [Fur-bearers]. **Added/Corp** Association for the Protection of Fur-Bearing Animals. (19??)-. Periodical. English. Four times a year. 4.01Can$. Association for the Protection of Fur-Bearing Animals, 2235 Commerical Drive, Vancouver British Columbia, V5N 4B6 Canada. **Tel** (604)255-0411, FAX (604)255-1491.
 Desc: News and information on the welfare of fur-bearing animals.

LC HD9426.I53 J344a
IO

HASIL PENELITIAN USAHA PETERNAKAN DI D.K.I. JAKARTA. See Industry and Production.

LC HV4702 .H8514
DD 636.08/3
ISSN 1059-1621
US

HSUS NEWS. [HSUS news]. **Added/Corp** Humane Society of the United States. **VFOAT** Humane Society News. **VAT** Humane Society of the United States News. Vol. 34, No. 1 (Winter 1989)-. Periodical. English. Four times a year. Humane Society of the United States, 2100 L Street NW, Washington DC 20037. **Tel** (202)452-1100. **Continues** Humane Society of the United States. Humane Society of the United States News.

LC QL55 .H85 WMLC 93/1440
DD 179
NLM W1; HU479H
ISSN 1062-4805
US
Pr Rev.
CEASED

HUMANE INNOVATIONS AND ALTERNATIVES. [Hum. innov. altern.]. **Added/Corp** Psychologists for the Ethical Treatment of Animals. Vol. 5 (1991)-Vol. 8 (1994). English. (August). Psychologists for the Ethical Treatment of Animals, PO Box 1297, Washington Grove MD 20880. **Tel** (301)963-4751. **ED** E. Bernstein. Index available. cum. index. **Circ:** 500. **Continues** Humane Innovations and Alternatives in Animal Experimentation, 0893-9535.
 Desc: Covers laboratory animals, animal experimentation, animal welfare, and animal testing alternatives.
 Ind/Abst Bibliogr. Agric.

ISSN 1184-1524
DD 639/.11
CN

HUMANE TRAPPING PROGRAM ANNUAL REPORT. [Hum. Trapp. Program annu. rep.]. **Main/Corp** Humane Trapping Program. **Added/Corp** Alberta Research Council. Forestry Dept. (1989/1990)-. English.

LC BJ
DD 179.3
US

IIFARSIGHTED REPORT. **Added/Corp** Incurably Ill for Animal Research (Organization). **VAT** Incurably Ill for Animal Research Sighted Report. (198?)-. Periodical. English. Four times a year. $25.00. Incurable Ill Animal Research, PO Box 27454, Lansing MI 48909. **Tel** (517)887-1141, FAX (517)887-1550. **ED** Greg Maas. **Circ:** 2,500 (ctrl).

LC QL85 .I53
DD 591.51
NLM Z 7993; I61
ISSN 1062-7278
US

INTERACTIONS BIBLIOGRAPHY, THE. See Animal Welfare-Abstracting, Bibliographies and Statistics.

ISSN 1058-112X
DD 179
NLM W1; JO14R
US

JOHNS HOPKINS CENTER FOR ALTERNATIVES TO ANIMAL TESTING : NEWSLETTER, THE. [Johns Hopkins Cent. Altern. Anim. Test.]. **Added/Corp** Johns Hopkins Center for Alternatives to Animal Testing. Vol. 1, No. 1 (Fall 1982)-. Newsletter. English. Three times a year. Free, US; $30.00 other. Johns Hopkins University Press, 2715 North Charles Street, Baltimore MD 21218-4319. **Tel** (410)516-6987, FAX (410)516-6968.
 Ind/Abst AGRICOLA [Select. Cov.].

ISSN 1048-0706
DD 351
US
CCC
NLM W1; LA231HG
CODEN LRENEX
TITLE CHANGE

LABORATORY REGULATION NEWS. [Lab. regul. news]. **Added/Corp** Bureau of National Affairs (Washington, D.C.). Vol. 1, No. 1 (Jan. 23, 1990)-(1993). Periodical. English. Buraff Publications Inc., 714 Church Street, Alexandria VA 22314. **Tel** (800)333-1291, (703)739-8500. **Continued by** Environmental Laboratory Washington Report, 1070-2504.

ISSN 1043-1039
DD 382
US

LIVE ANIMAL TRADE & TRANSPORT MAGAZINE. See Business and Economics-Commerce.

ISSN 0891-088X
DD 591
US

MAINSTREAM (SACRAMENTO, CALIF.). (MAINSTREAM / ANIMAL PROTECTION INSTITUTE OF AMERICA.). [Mainstream]. **Added/Corp** Animal Protection Institute of America. (19??)-. Periodical. English. Four times a year (Jan., Apr., July, Oct.). $25.00. Animal Protection Institute of America, PO Box 22505, Sacramento CA 95822. **Tel** (916)731-5521. **ED** Gil Lamont. **Bk Rev,** (Qty: 1-2). **Circ:** 32,000 (ctrl). available on an online database from Internet; and AOL.
 Desc: To inform and educate readers about major animal welfare problems of the day and current events in the humane movement.
 Ind/Abst AGRICOLA; GeoRef.

ISSN 0725-8739
DD 636.7
AT

MERIGAL. [Merigal]. (1980)-. Periodical. English. Four times a year. 12.33Aus$. Australia Native Dog Conservation Ltd., PO Box 91, Bargo New South Wales 2574 Australia. **Tel** 011 61 46 841156. **Continues** Warrigal, 0725-8720.

US
Pr Rev.

NACA NEWS. (19??)-. Periodical. English. Six times a year. $20.00. National Animal Control Association, PO Box 480851, Kansas City MO 64148-0851. **Tel** (800)828-6474, FAX (913)768-0607. **ED** John Mays. **Bk Rev,** (Qty: 10-12). **Ad Acc. Circ:** 4,000.

ISSN 0044-829X
CN
Pr Rev.

NEWS BULLETIN - ANIMAL DEFENCE LEAGUE OF CANADA. **Main/Corp** Animal Defence League of Canada. (1???)-. Bulletin. English. Two times a year (Sept.). Free on request. Animal Defence League Canada, PO Box 3880, Station C, Ottawa Ontario K1Y 4M5 Canada. **Tel** (613)233-6117. **Circ:** 3,500. **Continues** Anti-Vivisection Council of Ottawa. Monthly Bulletin., 0382-5256.

ISSN 0712-2950
DD 179/.3/06071383
CN

NEWSLETTER (HUMANE SOCIETY OF OTTAWA-CARLETON). (NEWSLETTER / THE HUMANE SOCIETY OF OTTAWA-CARLETON.). (1978)-. Newsletter. English. Three times a year. Free to Members. Humane Society of Ottawa-Carleton, 101 Champagne Avenue South, Ottawa Ontario K1S 4P3 Canada.

AT
CEASED

NEWSLETTER / THE AUSTRALIAN FEDERATION FOR THE WELFARE OF ANIMALS. **Added/Corp** Australian Federation for the Welfare of Animals. (19??)-(Oct. 1994). Newsletter. English. Australian Federation for the Welfare of Animals,

Animal Welfare

PO Box 114, Walkerville SA 5081 Australia. **Tel** 011 61 8 3446337, FAX 011 61 8 3449227. **ED** Dr. A. Blackshaw. **Circ:** 200 (ctrl).
Desc: Newsletter for AFWA, an independent national body of people who wish to put common sense into animal welfare.

ISSN 1199-7826
DD 636.088 **CN**
●**PET TALK (DARTMOUTH).** (PET TALK.). [Pet talk]. (1993)-. Periodical. English. Six times a year. 12.00Can$. K & J Desktop Publishing, PO Bos 2877, Dartmouth, Nova Scotia B2W 4Y2 Canada.

LC HV4763 .P48 **ISSN** 0899-9708
DD 179 **US**
NLM W1; PE942
TITLE CHANGE
PETA NEWS. (PETA NEWS / PEOPLE FOR THE ETHICAL TREATMENT OF ANIMALS.). [PETA News]. **Added/Corp** People for the Ethical Treatment of Animals. **VAT** People for the Ethical Treatment of Animals News. (1981)-(1994). Periodical. English (Dutch and German). People for the Ethical Treatment of Animals, PO Box 42516, Washington DC 20015. **Tel** (415)431-9886. **ED** Kathy Guillermo (phone: (301)770-PETA). **Ad Acc. Circ:** 203,000. **Continued by** PETA's Animal Times.
Desc: Newsletter covering animal rights issues including vivisection, vegetarianism, fur trade, animals in entertainment, PETA's programs, and tips for activists.

LC HV4763 .P48
US
●**PETA'S ANIMAL TIMES. Added/Corp** People for the Ethical Treatment of Animals. **VFOAT** People for the Ethical Treatment of Animals' Animal Times; Animal Times. (1994)-. Periodical. English (Dutch and German). Six times a year (Feb., Apr., June, Aug., Oct., Dec.). $15.00. People for the Ethical Treatment of Animals, PO Box 42516, Washington DC 20015. **Tel** (415)431-9886. **ED** Kathy Guillermo (phone: (301)770-PETA). **Ad Acc. Circ:** 203,000. **Continues** PETA News, 0899-9708.

ISSN 1048-8030
DD 598 **US**
RAPTOR REPORT. See Zoology-Ornithology.

SZ
RED DATA BOOK. See Environmental Issues-Conservation and Natural Resources.

LC QL55 .R47 **ISSN** 0229-1223
DD 636.08/85/02571 **CN**
RESEARCH ANIMALS IN CANADA. [Res. Anim. Can.]. **Added/Corp** Canadian Council on Animal Care. (July 1980)-. English. Every 2 years. Free on request. Canadian Council on Animal Care, 151 Slater Street, Suite 1105, Ottawa Ontario K1P 5H3 Canada. **Tel** (613)563-3505. **ED** Ann McWilliam. **Bk Rev.**
Desc: Focuses on animal care, recent contributions of biomedical research to human and animal health, replacement techniques and animal-related issues on a global basis.

ISSN 0700-5237
DD 636.08/85/0971 **CN**
RESOURCE (OTTAWA). (RESOURCE.). **Added/Corp** Canadian Council on Animal Care. Vol. 1, Sept. (1975-). Periodical. English (French). Every 2 years. Free. Canadian Council on Animal Care, 151 Slater Street, Suite 1105, Ottawa Ontario K1P 5H3 Canada. **Tel** (613)563-3505. **ED** Ann McWilliam. **Bk Rev. Circ:** 7,700 (ctrl).
Desc: Focuses on animal care, recent contributions of biomedical research to human and animal health, replacement techniques and animal-related issues on a global basis.

ISSN 1052-7559
DD 636 **US**
NLM W1; SC162L
SCAW NEWSLETTER. [SCAW newsl.]. **Added/Corp** Scientists Center for Animal Welfare (Washington, D.C.). **VAT** Scientists Center for Animal Welfare Newsletter. Vol. 10, No. 4 (Winter 1989)-. Newsletter. English. Four times a year. $40.00. Scientists Center for Animal Welfare, 7833 Walker Drive, Suite 340, Greenbelt MD 20770. **Tel** (301)345-3500, FAX (301)345-3503. **Continues** Newsletter (Scientists Center for Animal Welfare (Washington, D.C.)), 0742-5260.
Ind/Abst AGRICOLA.

ISSN 0734-3078
US
SHELTER SENSE. Added/Corp Humane Society of the United States. National Humane Education Center. (April 1978)-. Periodical. English. Ten times a year. $8.00. Humane Society of the United States, 2100 L Street NW, Washington DC 20037. **Tel** (202)452-1100. **ED** Susan Bury Stauffer. **Bk Rev. Circ:** 3,000.
Desc: A newsletter for humane and animal control workers that helps them increase their professionalism, reduce animal suffering, and solve community animal problems.
Ind/Abst Urban Aff. Abstr.

LC WMLC 93/2540
US
●**SOUL OF THE WOLF.** (1994)-. Periodical. English. Four times a year. $25.00. Soul of the Wolf, PO Box 1026, Agoura CA 91301. **Tel** (805)379-3803. **Continues** Wolves and Other Canids.

ISSN 1044-2618
DD 639 **US**
WILDLIFE REHABILITATION TODAY. [Wildl. rehabil. today]. Vol. 1, No. 1 (Summer 1989)-. Trade Publication. English. Four times a year. $15.00. Coconut Creek Publishing Co., 2201 NW 40th Terrace, Coconut Creek FL 33066. **Tel** (305)972-6092, FAX (305)972-6092. **ED** Don Mackey. Index available (June). cum. index. **Bk Rev**, (Qty: minimum 4/year). **Ad Acc. Circ:** 8-10,000. Documents available from Documents on Demand.
Desc: Published for people who care about and for injured and orphaned wild animals. Articles describe the latest rescue, treatment, breeding and release techniques and issues regarding wildlife rehabilitation and endangered wildlife conservation.
Ind/Abst Environ. Abstr.

ABSTRACTING, BIBLIOGRAPHIES AND STATISTICS

LC QL85 .I53 **ISSN** 1062-7278
DD 591.51 **US**
NLM Z 7993; I61
INTERACTIONS BIBLIOGRAPHY, THE. [Interact. bibliogr.]. **VFOAT** TIB. Vol. 3, No. 1 (Mar. 1992)-. Bibliography. English. Four times a year. $60.00. Rockydell Resources, 8732 Rock Springs Road, Penryn CA 95663-9622. **Tel** (916)663-3294. **Continues** Interactions of Man & Animals, 1056-991X.

PETS

ISSN 0744-9631
US
ACFA BULLETIN. (ACFA BULLETIN : OFFICIAL PUBLICATION OF THE AMERICAN CAT FANCIERS ASSOCIATION.). **Added/Corp** American Cat Fanciers Association. **VFOAT** A.C.F.A. Bulletin. **VAT** American Cat Fanciers Association Bulletin. (19??)-. Bulletin. English. Twelve times a year. American Cat Fanciers Association, PO Box 203, Point Lookout MO 65726.

LC SF421 .A33
KO
AEGYON UI OL. Added/Corp Taehan Kunyonggyon Hyophoe. (19??)-. Periodical. Korean. Taehan Kunyonggyon Hyophoe, 108-1 4-ka Chungmu-ro, Chung-ku Seoul Korea.

LC SF429.A4 A35 **ISSN** 8750-9776
DD 636.7/53 **US**
AFGHAN HOUND REVIEW, THE. [Afghan hound rev.]. (19??)-. Periodical. English. Six times a year (Feb., Apr., June, Aug., Oct., Dec.). $40.00. The Afghan Hound Review, PO Box 30430, Santa Barbara CA 93130. **Tel** (805)966-7270, FAX (805)682-1771. **ED** Bo N. Bengtson. **Bk Rev**, (Qty: 2-3). **Ad Acc. Circ:** 2,000.
Desc: News and information for the hounds such as show racing, obedience, grooming, care and other news.

LC SF421 .A52 SF421 .A523
DD 636.7/0973 **US**
●**AKC GAZETTE. Added/Corp** American Kennel Club. **VFOAT** American Kennel Club Gazette; Gazette. Vol. 112, No. 1 (Jan. 1995)-. Periodical. English. Twelve times a year. $28.00. American Kennel Club, 5580 Center View Drive, Raleigh NC 27606. **Tel** (919)233-9780. **Continues** Pure-Bred Dogs, American Kennel Gazette, 0033-4561.

LC SF456 .A37
DD 639.3/4/05 **XR**
AKVARIUM, TERARIUM. (19??)-. Periodical. Czech. Twelve times a year. $130.00. PNS-Ustredni Expedice A, Dovoz Tisku Kafkova 19, 160 00 Prague 6 Czech Republic. **(Subscription address:** Kubon & Sagner, ABT Zeitschriftenimport, D 80328 Munich Germany. **Tel** 011 49 89 54218130.) **Continues** Akvarium a Terarium.

LC WMLC 91/3430 **ISSN** 1059-4477
DD 636 **US**
AMERICAN AIREDALE, THE. (THE AMERICAN AIREDALE : OFFICIAL NEWSLETTER OF THE AIREDALE TERRIER CLUB OF AMERICA, INC.). [Amer. Airedale]. **Added/Corp** Airedale Terrier Club of America. No. 5 (Oct.-Nov. 1991)-. Newsletter. English. Six times a year. Airedale Terrier Club of America, Phyllis Madaus Assistant Secretary, 205 Satsuma Drive, Sanford FL 32771. **Continues** ATCA Newsletter.

LC SF429.B86 A44 **ISSN** 0002-774X
DD 636.7/3 **US**
AMERICAN BULLMASTIFF, THE. (19??)-. Periodical. English. Four times a year. The Greeleys, Box 13201, Syracuse NY 13261.

LC SF461.A1 N3 **ISSN** 0002-7782
DD 636.68605 **US**
TITLE CHANGE
AMERICAN CAGE-BIRD MAGAZINE. [Am. cage-bird mag.]. **VFOAT** American Cage Bird Magazine. (1951)-(Feb. 1994). Periodical. English. Audubon Publishing Company, One Glamore Court, Smithtown NY 11787. **Tel** (516)979-7962, FAX (516)979-8681. **ED** Arthur Freud. Index available. **Bk Rev. Ad Acc. Circ:** 50,000. **Continues** American Canary Magazine. **Continued by** Bird Breeder, 1073-5186.
Desc: Information by internationally known authors on the breeding, feeding, maintenance, taming and health care of parrots, cockatiels, budgies, canaries, finches and other pet birds.
Ind/Abst Fish Rev.; Wildl. Rev.

US
AMERICAN HEARTWORM SOCIETY BULLETIN. See Veterinary Sciences.

ISSN 0888-627X
DD 636 **US**
AMERICAN KENNEL CLUB AWARDS. [Am. Kennel Club awards]. **Added/Corp** American Kennel Club. Vol. 6, No. 7 (July 1986)-. Periodical. English. Twelve times a year. $40.00. American Kennel Club, 5580 Center View Drive, Raleigh NC 27606. **Tel** (919)233-9780. **Ad Acc. Circ:** 12,800. **Continues** American Kennel Club Show, Obedience and Field Trial Awards, 0272-4383.

LC SF423 .A5 **ISSN** 0162-2013
US
AMERICAN KENNEL CLUB STUD BOOK REGISTER. Added/Corp National American Kennel Club. American Kennel Club. Vol. 1 (1879)-. Periodical. English. Twelve times a year. $75.00. American Kennel Club, 5580 Center View Drive, Raleigh NC 27606. **Tel** (919)233-9780. **Circ:** 500. available on microfilm and microfiche from University Microfilms International (UMI).

ISSN 0824-8494
DD 636/.009714 **CN**
AMI DES BETES, L'. [Ami betes]. Vol. 1, No. 1 (Jan. 1984)-. Periodical. French. Twelve times a year. $1.00.

ISSN 0709-4116
DD 636.08/87/05 **CN**
ANIMAG. Vol. 1 (June 1978)-. Periodical. French. Three times a year. 35.00Can$. Animag, CP 2024 Succ, Sherbrooke Quebec J1J 3Y1 Canada.

US
ANIMAL FINDERS' GUIDE. (198?)-. Periodical. English. Eighteen times a year. $25.00. Animal Finders Guide, PO Box 99, Prairie Creek IN 47869. **Tel** (812)898-2701. **ED** Patrick D. Hoctor (phone: (812)898-2678). **Bk Rev**, (Qty: varies). **Ad Acc, Adv Mgr:** Sharon Hoctor, **Tel** (812)898-2678. **Circ:** 5,000.
Desc: Articles, classified ads, and display ads pertaining to exotic animals and alternative livestock.

ISSN 0710-9148
DD 636.08/87/05 **CN**
ANIMAL MAGAZINE, L'. [Anim. mag.]. Vol. 1, No. 1 (March 1981)-. Periodical. French. Six times a year. $10.00. L'Animal Magazine, CP 388 Succursale A, Longueuil Quebec J4H 3Z2 Canada.

ISSN 0214-3151
SP
ANIMALIA (BARCELONA). (ANIMALIA.). [Animalia]. (1988)-. Periodical. Spanish. Eleven times a year. $100.00. Elsevier Prensa SA, Avenida Paral Lel 180, 08015 Barcelona Spain. **Tel** 011 34 3 3255350, FAX 011 34 3 4252880. **Ad Acc.** Full Page (B&W) 160000ptas. Half Page (B&W) 10000ptas. Full Page (Color) 20000ptas. Half Page (Color) 130000ptas. **Circ:** 7,000.
Desc: Dedicated to pets, including health care, medicine, diet, and show activities.

LC SF409
DD 636 **US**
●**ANIMALTOWN NEWS.** (1994)-. Consumer Publication. English. Twelve times a year. $6.00. Killian Graphics, Box 91, Chatham NJ 07928. **ED** Judy Killian. **Bk Rev.** available with illustrations.
Desc: Aimed at all pet lovers; contains articles on specific breeds of pets, ways to deal with the death of a pet, keeping pets healthy, etc.

LC SF456 .A76 **ISSN** 0151-6981
DD 639/.34/05 **FR**
Pr Rev.
AQUARAMA. Added/Corp Association pour la Vulgarisation de l'Aquariophilie et Terrariophilie. (19??)-. Periodical. French. Six times a year. $53.81. Aquarama, 24 rue de Verdun, 67000 Strasbourg France. **Tel** 011 33 88 619608, FAX 011 33 88 411074. **ED** Didie Prevot.

Animal Welfare —Pets

Index available. cum. index. **Bk Rev.** **Ad Acc, Adv Mgr:** A. Saegel. **Circ:** 10,000 (ctrl).
Ind/Abst Aquat. Sci. Fish. Abstr. [CD-ROM Ed.].

ISSN 0899-045X
DD 639 US
AQUARIUM FISH MAGAZINE. [Aquar. fish mag.]. **VFOAT** Aquarium Fish. (1988)-. English. Six times a year. $24.97. Fancy Publications, PO Box 6050, Mission Viejo CA 92690. **Tel** (714)855-8822, (800)426-2516, FAX (714)855-3045. **(Subscription address:** Neodata / Colorado, PO Box 2606, Boulder CO 80322. **)**

LC SF600 **ISSN** 1043-0849
DD 636 US
Pr Rev.
BARKER (KANSAS CITY, MO.), THE. See Veterinary Sciences.

LC SF429.B15 B36 **ISSN** 0094-9744
DD 636.7/53 US
BASENJI. (THE BASENJI.). [Basenji]. (19??)-. Periodical. English. Twelve times a year. The Basenji, 789 Linton Hill Road, Newtown PA 18940. **Tel** (215)860-8254. **Bk Rev.** **Ad Acc.** **Circ:** 1,500.
Desc: Publication for Basenji (dog) breeders, fanciers and pet owners.

ISSN 0736-9743
US
BETTER BEAGLING MAGAZINE. VFOAT Better Beagling. (1982)-. Periodical. English. Twelve times a year. $12.00 (one-year), $24.00 (two-year). Better Beagling, PO Box 142, Essex VT 05451. ***Continues*** *Large Pack.*

ISSN 0199-8315
DD 636 US
BICHON FRISE REPORTER, THE. [Bichon frise report.]. Vol. 1 (Oct./Nov. 1979)-. Periodical. English. Four times a year. The Bichon Frise Reporter, PO Box 827, Culver City CA 90232.

LC SF **ISSN** 1073-5186
DD 636 US
●**BIRD BREEDER.** [Bird breed.]. Vol. 66, No. 3/4 (March/Apr. 1994)-. Periodical. English. Twelve times a year. $29.97. Fancy Publications, PO Box 6050, Mission Viejo CA 92690. **Tel** (714)855-8822, (800)426-2516, FAX (714)855-3045. **(Subscription address:** Palm Coast Data, PO Box 420163, Agency Department, Palm Coast FL 32142. **Tel** (904)445-4662 ext. 669, (800)829-5475.) Index Available in first issue of next volume--attached. **Ad Acc.** available with illustrations. ***Continues*** *American Cage-Bird Magazine, 0002-7782.*
Desc: Information on the breeding, feeding, maintenance, taming and health care of parrots, cockatiels, budgies, canaries, finches and other pet birds.

LC WMLC L 83/2744 **ISSN** 0891-771X
DD 636 US
BIRD TALK. [Bird talk]. (198?)-. Periodical. English. Twelve times a year. $26.97. Fancy Publications, PO Box 6050, Mission Viejo CA 92690. **Tel** (714)855-8822, (800)426-2516, FAX (714)855-3045. **(Subscription address:** Neodata / Colorado, PO Box 2606, Boulder CO 80322. **) ED** Linda Lewis. **Circ:** 72,000. ***Continues*** *International Bird Talk, 0742-8359.*
Ind/Abst Fish Rev.; Wildl. Rev.

LC SF460 .B57 **ISSN** 0199-5979
DD 636.6/86 US
BIRD WORLD (NORTH HOLLYWOOD). See Zoology-Ornithology.

LC SF411-459 **ISSN** 0890-8923
DD 636 US
BLOODLINES. (BLOODLINES : DOG AND PET STOCK JOURNAL.). [Bloodlines]. **Added/Corp** United Kennel Club. (1913)-. Periodical. English. Six times a year (Jan., March, May, July, Sept., Nov.). $15.00. United Kennel Club Inc, 100 East Kilgore Road, Kalamazoo MI 49001. **Tel** (616)343-9020, FAX (616)343-7037. **ED** Kerry Knudsen. Index available (Bound in next issue.). **Bk Rev.** **Ad Acc, Adv Mgr:** T. Birdsong, **Tel** (616)343-9020. **Circ:** 4,000.
Desc: Devoted principally to working and show dogs, obedience training and trials. Includes information on health care, training and events.

LC SF428 .B6 **ISSN** 0190-0226
DD 646.7/08 US
BOARDING KENNEL PROPRIETOR. Periodical. English. Twelve times a year. $12.50. Boarding Kennel Proprietor, 2785 North Speer Blvd., Denver CO 80211.

ISSN 0746-2875
DD 636 US
BORZOI QUARTERLY (WHEAT RIDGE, COLO.), THE. (THE BORZOI QUARTERLY.). [Borzoi q.]. (19??)-. Periodical. English. Six times a year. $40.00. Hoflin Publishing Ltd., 4401 Zephyr Street, Wheat Ridge CO 80033-3299. **Tel** (303)934-5656, FAX (303)422-7000. **ED** Donald R. Hoflin. **Ad Acc, Adv Mgr:** Cindy Kerstiens. **Circ:** 398.

ISSN 1059-0625
DD 636 US
BREEDER FORUM. [Breed. forum]. **Added/Corp** Kal Kan Foods. Vol. 1, No. 1 (1991)-. Periodical. English. Four times a year. Free on request. Kal Kan Foods Inc. Professional Services, 3250 East 44th Street, PO Box 58853, Vernon CA 90058. **Tel** (213)587-3663. ***Formed by the union of*** *Pedigree Forum, 1042-9107* ***and*** *Kal Kan Forum (Vernon, Calif. : 1988), 1043-1772.*

ISSN 0746-1410
US
CANINE CHRONICLE. (19??)-. Periodical. English. Twelve times a year. $80.00. Canine Chronicle, 605 2nd Avenue North, Columbus MS 39701. **Tel** (601)327-1124.

ISSN 0069-1003
US
CAT FANCIERS' NEWS. (1984)-. Periodical. English. One time a year. $84.50. Cat Fancier's Association, 1309 Allaire Avenue, Ocean NJ 07712. **Tel** (201)531-2390. **ED** Marna Fogarty. **Ad Acc.** **Circ:** 2,000.
Desc: Articles on cats and cat shows.

LC SF441 .I57 **ISSN** 0892-6514
DD 636.8/005 US
CAT FANCY (SAN JUAN CAPISTRANO, CALIF.). (CAT FANCY.). **VFOAT** Cat Fancy Magazine. Vol. 29, No. 1 (Jan. 1986)-. Periodical. English. Twelve times a year. $25.97. Fancy Publications, PO Box 6050, Mission Viejo CA 92690. **Tel** (714)855-8822, (800)426-2516, FAX (714)855-3045. **(Subscription address:** Neodata / Colorado, PO Box 2606, Boulder CO 80322. **) ED** Linda Lewis. **Bk Rev.** **Ad Acc.** **Circ:** 237,528. ***Continues*** *International Cat Fancy.*

ISSN 1074-7788
DD 636 US
CAT INDUSTRY NEWSLETTER. [Cat ind. newsl.]. Vol. 1, No. 1 (July 25, 1992)-. Newsletter. English. Twelve times a year. $295.00. Good Communications, Inc., PO Box 10069, Austin TX 78766-1069. **Tel** (512)454-6090, FAX (512)454-3420. **ED** Becki Reynolds (editor's address: PO Box 1528, Charleston, SC 29401, phone: (803)577-2987).
Desc: Covers new products and marketing and products for cats. Special emphasis is given to cat food and cat litter, both supermarket and specialty brands.

ISSN 1055-8438
DD 636 US
CAT LOVERS : THE OFFICIAL CLA CLUB MAGAZINE. [Cat lovers]. **Added/Corp** Cat Lovers of America. **VFOAT** Cat Lovers Magazine. Vol. 1, No. 1 (Fall 1991)-. Periodical. English. Four times a year. $29.00 (membership included). Cat Lovers of America, PO Box 5050, El Toro CA 92630.

ISSN 0163-1926
US
CAT WORLD. (197?)-. Periodical. English. Six times a year. Cat World, PO Box 35635, Phoenix AZ 85069.

US
CATEGORY REPORT - HOUSEHOLD, PETS, AND MISCELLANEOUS PRODUCTS / CRO. (19??)-. English. Twelve times a year. $1040.00 US and Canada; $1070.00 Europe and Pan America; $1095.00 other. Marketing Intelligence Service Ltd., 6473D Route 64, Naples NY 14512. **Tel** (716)374-6326, (800)836-5710, FAX (714)374-5217, telex 469979.
Desc: Combines domestic and foreign new product information for the household, pet, and various other industries. Includes product and packaging descriptions with illustrations, manufacturing and marketing innovations, emerging trends, and other background information.

ISSN 0008-8544
US
CATS MAGAZINE. [Cats mag.]. **VFOAT** Cats. (1945)-. Periodical. English. Twelve times a year. $21.97. Cats Magazine, PO Box 290037, Port Orange FL 32129. **Tel** (904)788-2770. **ED** Linda J. Walton. **Bk Rev.** **Ad Acc.** **Circ:** 189,697. available on microfilm and microfiche from University Microfilms International (UMI). Documents available from UMI Article Clearinghouse.
Desc: Includes articles, care and health information, poems, photos, and columns.
Ind/Abst Newsp. Period. Abstr. (1988-).

AT
CLUMBER SPANIEL CORRESPONDENCE. English. Twelve times a year. 24Aus$ Australia; 36Aus$ other. Erinrac Enterprises, Foott Road, Upper Beaconsfield Victoria 3808 Australia. **Tel** (059)44 3383, FAX (059)44 3384. **ED** Jan Irving. **Bk Rev**, (Qty: 6-12). **Ad Acc.** **Circ:** 5000.
Desc: Includes information from specialists on the breed worldwide.

ISSN 0744-0731
US
COLLIE REVIEW. (19??)-. Periodical. English. Twelve times a year. $30.00. Drucker Publications, 8760 Appian Way, Los Angeles CA 90046. **Tel** (310)553-9277. **ED** M D Drucker. **Bk Rev.** **Ad Acc.** **Circ:** 5,000. ***Continues*** *Collie & Shetland Sheepdog Review.*
Desc: Includes news of show wins, new champions, litters, etc.

ISSN 0317-1965
DD 636.7/006/2714281 CN
CYNOMAG. Added/Corp Club Canin de Montreal. Vol. 1, No. 3 (May 1973)-. French. Club Canin de Montreal, 12337 Charles Renard, Riviere des Prairies Quebec Canada. ***Continues*** *Information, 0317-1973.*

LC SF429.D6 D64 **ISSN** 1045-1757
DD 636.7/3 US
DOBERMAN QUARTERLY : DQ. [Doberman q.]. **VFOAT** DQ. (19??)-. Periodical. English. Four times a year. Doberman Quarterly, 739 Edgemar, Pacifica CA 94044.

LC SF421 .D625 **ISSN** 0892-6522
DD 636 US
DOG FANCY (LOS ANGELES, CALIF.). (DOG FANCY.). [Dog fancy]. **VFOAT** Dog Fancy Magazine; Dogfancy. Vol. 17, No. 1 (Jan. 1986)-. Periodical. English. Twelve times a year. $25.97. Fancy Publications, PO Box 6050, Mission Viejo CA 92690. **Tel** (714)855-8822, (800)426-2516, FAX (714)855-3045. **(Subscription address:** Neodata / Colorado, PO Box 2606, Boulder CO 80322. **) ED** Linda Lewis. **Bk Rev.** **Ad Acc.** **Circ:** 135,320. ***Continues*** *International Dog Fancy.*

ISSN 1074-777X
DD 636 US
DOG INDUSTRY NEWSLETTER. [Dog ind. newsl.]. (199?)-. Newsletter. English. Twelve times a year. $295.00. Good Communications, Inc., PO Box 10069, Austin TX 78766-1069. **Tel** (512)454-6090, FAX (512)454-3420. **ED** Becki Reynolds (editor's address: PO Box 1528, Charleston, SC 29401, phone: (803)577-2987).
Desc: Covers new products and the business of marketing products for dogs. Special emphasis is given to dog food, both supermarket and specialty brands.

LC WMLC 91/3373 **ISSN** 1062-0699
DD 636 US
DOG WATCH (STUDIO CITY, CALIF.). (DOG WATCH : A WEEKLY NEWSPAPER FOR THE PUREBRED DOG FANCY.). [Dog watch]. Vol. 1, Issue 1 (Oct. 4, 1991)-. Periodical. English. One time a week. $120.00. Dog Watch, 11331 Ventura Boulevard, Suite 301, Studio City CA 91604-3155.

ISSN 0012-4893
DD 636 US
DOG WORLD. (DOG WORLD; THE COMPLETE ALL-BREED MAGAZINE.). [Dog world]. **VFOAT** Dog World Magazine. Vol. 1 (Jan. 1916)-. Periodical. English. Twelve times a year. $28.00. Intertec Publishing Corp, 29 North Wacker Drive, Chicago IL 60606-3298. **Tel** (312)726-2802, FAX (312)726-3091. **ED** Enid S. Bergstrom. **Bk Rev.** **Ad Acc.** **Circ:** 63,000. available on microfilm and microfiche from University Microfilms International (UMI). Documents available from UMI Article Clearinghouse.
Desc: For breeders, exhibitors, hobbyists and professionals in kennel operations, grooming, veterinarians, animal hospitals/clinics and pet supplies. Includes articles on health care, veterinary medical research, grooming, legislation show awards, training, show schedules, junior showmanship, kennel operations, breed qualities and histories.
Ind/Abst Newsp. Period. Abstr. (1988-).

UK
DOG WORLD. English. One time a week. $165.50. Press House, 9 Tufton Street, Ashford Kent TN23 1QN United Kingdom. **Tel** 011 44 1233 621877.
Desc: Covers everything about dogs including dog sport news (including showing), training and breed history.

ISSN 0012-4915
CN
DOGS IN CANADA. [Dogs Can.]. Vol. 28, No. 6 (March 1940)-. Periodical. English. Thirteen times a year. 28.01Can$. Dogs in Canada, 43 Railside Road, Don Mills Ontario M3A 3L9 Canada. **Tel** (416)441-3228. **Bk Rev.** **Ad Acc.** **Circ:** 21,000. ***Continues*** *Kennel and Bench;* ***Absorbed*** *Dogs Annual, 0317-1485.*
Desc: For breeders, exhibitors and people with a serious interest in dogs. Covers choosing a breed, training, health, grooming and includes color photos and articles.
Ind/Abst Can. Index (?-?).

GW
DU UND DAS TIER. Added/Corp Deutscher Tierschutzbund. (1971)-. Periodical. German. Six times a year. DM29.50 Germany; DM43.40 other. Verlag M & H Schaper GmbH & Co, Postfach 1642, D-31046 Alfeld

Animal Welfare —Pets

Leine Germany. **Tel** 011 49 5181 80090, FAX 011 49 5181 800933. *Supersedes* Tier-Illustrierte.
Ind/Abst Index Vet.; Pig News Inf.; Vet. Bull.

FR

EUROPEAN JOURNAL OF COMPANION ANIMAL PRACTICE, THE.
Added/Corp Federation of European Companion Animal Veterinary Associations. **VFOAT** EJCAP. Vol. 1 (Sept. 1990)-. Periodical. English. Two times a year. $40.00. Fecava, Torenstraatje, 5301 KE Zaltbommel Netherlands. **Tel** 011 31 4180 15839.
Ind/Abst Index Vet.; Small Anim. Abstr. Bibliogr.; Vet. Bull.

ISSN 0849-3405
DD 636/.0097123/05 CN

FANCIERS DIGEST, THE. [Fanciers dig.].
VFOAT Fancier's Digest. (Jan. 1990)-. Periodical. English. Twelve times a year. Limited free distribution. Real Press, 97-53431 Range Road 221, Androssan Alberta T0B 0E0 Canada. *Continues* Western Canada Rabbit News., 0844-5419.

US

FRONT AND FINISH. (19??)-. English. Twelve times a year. $24.00. Front and Finish, PO Box 333, Galesburg IL 61402. **ED** Robert T. Self.
Ind/Abst Mag. Search; MasterFile FullTEXT (July 1993-).

ISSN 0746-5483
US

GORDON QUARTERLY, THE. (THE GORDON QUARTERLY : GQ.). [Gordon q.]. **VFOAT** GQ; G.Q. Vol. 1, No. 1 (Fall 1983)-. Periodical. English. Four times a year. $36.00 US/ $40.00 other. The Gordon Quarterly, 4401 Zephyr Street, Wheat Ridge CO 80033-3299. **Tel** (303)420-2222, FAX (303)422-7000. **Circ:** 480.
Desc: Publication about Gordon Setters.

LC SF429.G8 G8 **ISSN** 0191-7633
US

GREYHOUND BREEDER'S JOURNAL.
Vol. 1 (1977)-. English. Greyhound Breeder's Journal, 304 Northwest 17th Street, Abilene KS 67410.

LC SF427.5 .G76 **ISSN** 0199-8366
DD 636.7/083/05 US

GROOM & BOARD. [Groom board]. **VFOAT** Groom and Board. Vol. 1, No. 1 (Jan./Feb. 1980)-. Trade Publication. English. Nine times a year. $25.00. H. H. Backer Associates Inc, 20 East Jackson Boulevard, Chicago IL 60604. **Tel** (312)663-4040, FAX (312)663-5676. **ED** Karen Long Machead. **Ad Acc. Circ:** 16,000 (ctrl).
Desc: National magazine for professional groomers and kennel operators, with news, technical articles and money-making ideas.

LC SF415.5 .A54 **ISSN** 0747-5136
DD 380.5/24 US

HANDLERS. (ANIMAL WELFARE. LIST OF REGISTERED CARRIERS AND INTERMEDIATE HANDLERS.). [Anim. welf., List regist. carriers intermed. handl.]. **Added/Corp** United States. Animal and Plant Health Inspection Service. Veterinary Services. **VFOAT** List of Registered Carriers and Intermediate Handlers. (19??)-. English. One time a year. US Department of Agriculture / Animal & Plant Health Inspection Service, 741 Federal Building 1, 6505 Belcres Road, Hyattsville MD 20782. **Tel** (301)436-7817.

ISSN 0018-6384
US

HOUNDS AND HUNTING. (1903)-. Periodical. English. Twelve times a year. $14.00. Hounds and Hunting, Box 372, Bradford PA 16701. **Tel** (814)368-6154, 368-6155, FAX (814)368-3522. **ED** R.F. Slike. **Bk Rev. Ad Acc. Circ:** 12,000 (ctrl).
Desc: Devoted to field trial beagling and gun-dog trials and the beagle hound.

ISSN 0899-9570
DD 636 US

I LOVE CATS. [I love cats]. Vol. 1, Issue 1 (Jan./Feb. 1989)-. Periodical. English. Six times a year. $24.00. Hochman Associates, 950 Third Avenue, 16th Floor, New York NY 10022. **Tel** (212)371-4932.
(Subscription address: CDS Agency Hard Copy, PO Box 4966, Des Moines IA 50340. **Tel** (515)247-7569.)

US

NLM W1; IN6545

INTERACTIONS / DELTA SOCIETY.
Added/Corp Delta Society. (1992)-. Periodical. English. Four times a year. $35.00. Delta Society, 321 Burnett Avenue South, Suite 303, Renton WA 98055-2569. **Tel** (206)226-7357, FAX (206)235-1076. *Continues* People, Animals, Environment, 8755-5875.

ISSN 1074-780X
DD 636 US

● **INTERNATIONAL PET INDUSTRY NEWSLETTER.** See Veterinary Sciences.

LC SF429.I89 I87 **ISSN** 0735-8504
DD 636.7/6 US

ITALIAN GREYHOUND, THE. (19??)-. Periodical. English. Six times a year. The Italian Greyhound, 8414 Kingsgate Road, Potomac MD 20854. **Tel** (301)299-6269. **ED** William Cooper, Joan Cooper and Annette Norton. Index available. **Bk Rev. Ad Acc. Circ:** 800.

ISSN 0022-4510
UK
CCC
NLM W1 JO877L **CODEN** JAPRAN
Pr Rev.

JOURNAL OF SMALL ANIMAL PRACTICE, THE. See Veterinary Sciences.

US
CODEN JSEMEF
JOURNAL OF SMALL EXOTIC ANIMAL MEDICINE. See Veterinary Sciences.

UK
KENNEL GAZETTE, THE. (19??)-. Periodical. English. Twelve times a year. £30.00 overseas surface mail; £36.00 (Europe), £50.00 (other) airmail. Kennel Club, 1-5 Charles Strasse/Piccadilly, London W1Y 8AB United Kingdom. **Tel** 011 44 171 4936651.

LC SF425.15 .K46 **ISSN** 0164-4289
DD 636.7/08/1105

KENNEL REVIEW. [Kennel rev.]. (Jan. 1898)-. Periodical. English. Twelve times a year. $45.00 (second class), $75.00 (first class) US; $65.00 (second class), $105.00 (first class) Canada and Mexico; $75.00 (second class), $165.00 (first class) other. B & E Publications, 11331 Ventura Boulevard, Studio City CA 91604. **Tel** (818)761-3647. **ED** Richard Beauchamp. **Bk Rev. Ad Acc. Circ:** 10,000 (ctrl). *Absorbed* Collie; Dogology.

ISSN 8750-3557

LABRADOR QUARTERLY : LQ, THE.
[Labrador q.]. **VFOAT** LQ. Vol. 1, No. 1; Summer 1984-. Periodical. English. Four times a year. $40.00. Hoflin Publishing Ltd., 4401 Zephyr Street, Wheat Ridge CO 80033-3299. **Tel** (303)934-5656, FAX (303)422-7000. **ED** Donald R. Hoflin. **Ad Acc, Adv Mgr:** Cindy Kerstiens. **Circ:** 2,678.

ISSN 1071-2593
DD 022 US

LIBRARY CAT NEWSLETTER, THE. [Libr. cat newsl.]. **Added/Corp** Library Cat Society (Sauk Centre, Minn.). Vol. 2, No. 1 (Jan./Feb. 1988)-. Newsletter. English. Four times a year. $6.00. Library Cat Society, PO Box 274, Morhead MN 56560. **Tel** (618)236-7205. *Continues* Newsletter (Library Cat Club of America).

ISSN 0746-4002
US

MALAMUTE QUARTERLY, THE. [Malamute q.]. (19??)-. Periodical. English. Four times a year. $40.00. Hoflin Publishing Ltd., 4401 Zephyr Street, Wheat Ridge CO 80033-3299. **Tel** (303)934-5656, FAX (303)422-7000. **ED** Donald R. Hoflin. **Ad Acc, Adv Mgr:** Cindy Kerstiens. **Circ:** 916.

ISSN 1050-8457
DD 636 US

NATIONAL DOG REVIEW. [Natl. dog rev.]. Vol. 1, No. 1 (Dec. 1991)-. Periodical. English. Twelve times a year. $45.00. National Dog Review, PO Box 568, Rochester PA 15074.

LC SF **ISSN** 1080-3076
DD 636 US
NLM W1; NA805EM

NATURAL PET. (NATURAL PET : ALTERNATIVE LIFESTYLES FOR OUR PETS.). [Nat. pet]. **VFOAT** Naturalpet. Vol. 1, No. 1 (Oct. 1992)-. Periodical. English. Six times a year. $15.00. Pet Publications, Melbourne FL.

LC SF429.S65 S52a **ISSN** 0583-1776
DD 636.7/3 US

NEWSLETTER - SIBERIAN HUSKY CLUB OF AMERICA. (NEWSLETTER.). [Newsl. - Sib. Husky Club Am.]. **Main/Corp** Siberian Husky Club of America. (19??)-. Newsletter. English. Six times a year. Cingel, 118 Young Street, East Hampton Ct 06424-1844.

US

NORTH AMERICAN DIRECTORY OF EXOTIC ANIMAL & BIRD OWNERS.
VFOAT North American Directory of Exotic Animal and Bird Owners. (1990)-. Directory. English. $30.00. Pat and Connie Corbett, Department NA, Skaar Route, Box 4028, Sidney MT 59270. *Continues* Directory of North American Exotic Animal and Bird Owners.

LC SF431 .O35 **ISSN** 0094-0186 #y 0094-0816
DD 636.7/08/3 US

OFF-LEAD. VAT Off Lead. (1971)-. Periodical. English. Twelve times a year. $20.00. Arner Publications, 100 Bouck Street, Rome NY 13440. **Tel** (315)339-2033.

ED Lorenz D Arner. Index available. **Bk Rev. Ad Acc. Circ:** 5,000 (ctrl).
Desc: Includes more than 10,000 dog owners actively engaged in dog care and training, including professional trainers, dog training clubs, sportsmen, government agencies, individual competitors, and house pet owners.

ISSN 0955-9469
UK

OUR DOGS MANCHESTER. (1895)-. Newspaper. English. One time a week. £65.00 UK; £90.00 Europe;. Our Dogs Publishing, 5 Oxford Road Station Approach, Manchester M60 1SX United Kingdom. **Tel** 011 44 161 23262660, FAX 011 44 161 2365534.

ISSN 0030-6851
US

OUR FOURFOOTED FRIENDS. Added/Corp Animal Rescue League of Boston. (19??)-. Periodical. English. Four times a year. $4.00. Animal Rescue League of Boston, PO Box 265, Boston MA 02117. **Tel** (617)426-9170.

LC SF414.7 .P45 **ISSN** 0098-5406
DD 381/.41/6088705 US

PET AGE. Vol. 1 (July 1971)-. Trade Publication. English. Twelve times a year. $25.00. H. H. Backer Associates Inc, 20 East Jackson Boulevard, Chicago IL 60604. **Tel** (312)663-4040, FAX (312)663-5676. **ED** Karen M. Long. **Ad Acc. Circ:** 17,000 (ctrl).
Desc: A magazine for pet shop owners, managers, distributors and manufacturers. Focuses on management and sales techniques, animal care and industry issues through news and features.

ISSN 0731-468X
US

PET ANIMAL HEALTH LETTER, THE. See Veterinary Sciences.

ISSN 0191-4766
DD 338 US

PET BUSINESS. [Pet bus.]. **Added/Corp** Western World Pet Supply Association. **VFOAT** Pet Business Magazine. (March 1978)-. Trade Publication. English. Thirteen times a year (monthly except twice in March). $24.00. Pet Business Inc, 5400 Northwest 84th Avenue, Miami FL 33166. **Tel** (305)592-9890, FAX (305)592-9726. **ED** Rita Davis. Index available. **Ad Acc. Circ:** 25,000 (ctrl). *Continues* Aquarium Industry.
Desc: News magazine for the pet industry.

LC SF411 .P3 **ISSN** 0553-8572
DD 658.896366 US

PET DEALER. Vol. 1 (Feb. 1927)-. Trade Publication. English. Twelve times a year. $25.00. PTN Publishing Company, 445 Broad Hollow Road, Melville NY 11747. **Tel** (516)845-2700, FAX (516)845-7109. **Bk Rev. Ad Acc. Circ:** 15,500 (ctrl). *Absorbed* Pet Shop.
Desc: Geared to the pet shop retailer/buyer of supplies and/or livestock.

ISSN 1046-2112
DD 636 US

PET FOCUS. See Veterinary Sciences.

ISSN 0742-9746
US

PET LOVERS' GAZETTE. VFOAT Pet Lovers'. (19??)-. Periodical. English. Six times a year. $10.00. Pet Lovers Gazette, 31 West Main Street, Marlton NJ 08053. **Tel** (609)983-0863.

ISSN 0031-6245
DD 338 US
CCC
CODEN PEINE6

PETFOOD INDUSTRY. [Petfood ind.]. **VFOAT** Pet Food Industry. Vol. 1 (1959)-. Trade Publication. English. Six times a year. $36.00. Watt Publishing Company, 122 South Wesley Avenue, Mount Morris IL 61054. **Tel** (815)734-4171, FAX (815)734-7021, telex TWX 910-642-2891. **ED** Marcella Sadler. **Ad Acc. Circ:** 5,000 (ctrl). available on microfilm from University Microfilms International (UMI).
Desc: Serves individuals and firms manufacturing pet foods.
Ind/Abst BioBusiness.

AG

PET'S. See Veterinary Sciences.

CN

PETS CARE GUIDE FOR THE OLDER PET. (19??)-. Consumer Publication. English. One time a year (December). Moorshead Magazines Ltd., 10 Gateway Boulevard, Suite 490, North York Ontario M3C 3T4 Canada. **Tel** (416)696-5488, FAX (416)696-7395.

ISSN 0831-2621
DD 636.08/87/05 CN

PETS MAGAZINE (1985). (PETS MAGAZINE.). [Pets mag.]. Vol. 2, No. 6 (May/June 1985)-. Consumer Publication. English. Six times a year. 8.18Can$. Moorshead Magazines Ltd., 10 Gateway Boulevard, Suite 490, North York Ontario M3C 3T4 Canada. **Tel** (416)696-5488, FAX (416)696-7395. **ED** Ed Zapletal. **Ad Acc. Circ:** 50,000. *Continues* Pets (Toronto, Ont.),

Animal Welfare —Pets

0715-8947.
Desc: Information of healthcare, behavior, nutrition and human/animal bonding for pet owners.

DD 636.08/87/05   **ISSN** 0840-5719 CN

PETS MAGAZINE. CARE GUIDE FOR PUPPIES & KITTENS & OTHER THINGS, TOO. [Pets mag., Care guide puppies kittens other things]. **VFOAT** Care Guide for Puppies & Kittens & Other Things, Too; Puppies & Kittens. **VAT** Pets Magazine. Care Guide for Puppies and Kittens and Other Things, Too. (1988)-. Consumer Publication. English. One time a year (September). Moorshead Magazines Ltd., 10 Gateway Boulevard, Suite 490, North York Ontario M3C 3T4 Canada. **Tel** (416)696-5488, FAX (416)696-7395.

DD 636.8/005   **ISSN** 0832-4786 CN

PETS MAGAZINE. CAT CARE GUIDE. [Pets mag., Cat care guide]. **VFOAT** Cat Care Guide. (Summer 1987)-. Consumer Publication. English. One time a year (April). Moorshead Magazines Ltd., 10 Gateway Boulevard, Suite 490, North York Ontario M3C 3T4 Canada. **Tel** (416)696-5488, FAX (416)696-7395.

DD 636.7/005   **ISSN** 0820-585X CN

PETS MAGAZINE. DOG CARE GUIDE. [Pets mag., Dog care guide]. **VFOAT** Dog Care Guide. (Summer 1987)-. Consumer Publication. English. One time a year (January). Moorshead Magazines Ltd., 10 Gateway Boulevard, Suite 490, North York Ontario M3C 3T4 Canada. **Tel** (416)696-5488, FAX (416)696-7395.

DD 636   **ISSN** 1067-0947 US

●**POINTING DOG JOURNAL, THE.** [Pointing dog j.]. Vol. 1, No. 1 (Jan./Feb. 1993)-. Periodical. English. Six times a year. $21.95. Wildwood Press, 2779 Aero Park Drive, Box 968, Traverse City MI 49685. **Tel** (616)946-3712.

DD 636   **ISSN** 1058-3637 US

POMERANIAN REGISTRY, THE. (1990)-. Periodical. English. Six times a year. $25.00. The Pomerian Registry, 6902 East 1st Street, Tucson AZ 85710-1221.

    ISSN 0744-8546 US

POMERANIAN REVIEW. Added/Corp American Pomeranian Club. **VFOAT** Pomeranian Review of the American Pomeranian Club, Inc. (19??)-. Periodical. English. Four times a year. American Pomeranian Club, PO Box 31927, Tucson AZ 85711.

LC SF429.P85 P67   **ISSN** 0477-5449
DD 636.7/2   US

POODLE REVIEW, THE. [Poodle rev.]. (19??)-. Periodical. English. Six times a year. $42.00 (one-year), $80.00 (two-year). Poodle Review, 4401 Zephyr Street, Wheat Ridge CO 80033-3299. **ED** Donald R. Hoflin & Cindy Kerstiens. **Ad Acc. Circ:** 1,739.

DD 636   **ISSN** 0882-2816 US

POODLE VARIETY. (19??)-. Trade Publication. English. Five times a year. $40.00 US; $48.00 other. Poodle Variety, PO Box 30430, Santa Barbara CA 93130. **Tel** (805)966-7270. **ED** Bo N. Bengtson. **Bk Rev**, (Qty: 1). **Ad Acc. Circ:** 2,000.
Desc: Specialist interest magazine for poodle fanciers interested in breeding, showing, obedience, etc.

DD 636   **ISSN** 0262-5849 UK

PPM. PET PRODUCT MARKETING. [PPM. Pet prod. mark.]. **VFOAT** Pet Product Marketing. (1980)-. Periodical. English. Twelve times a year. EMAP National Publications Ltd, Farndon Road, Market Harborough, Leicestershire, LE16 9NR United Kingdom. **Tel** 011 44 116 2555161. **Continues** Pet Product Marketing and Garden Supplies, 0031-6202.
Ind/Abst Infomat Int. Bus.

    UK

PRACTICAL FISHKEEPING. (Dec. 1978)-. English. Twelve times a year. £25.00UK; £32.00 other. EMAP National Publications Ltd, Farndon Road, Market Harborough, Leicestershire, LE16 9NR United Kingdom. **Tel** 011 44 116 2555161. **Continues** Petfish Monthly.

LC HV4746 .P76   **ISSN** 1045-2044
DD 636.7/083   US

PROJECT BREED DIRECTORY : A NATIONWIDE SOURCE BOOK FOR RESCUE AND ADOPTION OF ALL BREEDS OF DOGS. Added/Corp Network for Ani-males & Females, Inc. **VFOAT** Project BREED (Breed Rescue Efforts & EDucation) Directory. Vol. 1, No. 1 (1989)-. Directory. English. Irregular. $15.95. Network for ANI-Males & Females Inc, 18707 Curry Powder Lane, Germantown MD 20874. **ED** Shirley Weber.
Desc: Sources of rescue assistance in the US and Canada for 72 breeds.

LC SF421 .A52   **ISSN** 0033-4561
DD 636.7/0973   US
    TITLE CHANGE

PURE-BRED DOGS, AMERICAN KENNEL GAZETTE. [Pure bred dogs Am. kennel gaz.]. **Added/Corp** American Kennel Club. **VFOAT** Pure-Bred Dogs/American Kennel Gazette. **VAT** Pure Bred Dogs, American Kennel Gazette. (1952)-(1994). Periodical. English. American Kennel Club, 5580 Center View Drive, Raleigh NC 27606. **Tel** (919)233-9780. **ED** Diane Vesey, (editor's address: 51 Madison Avenue, New York, NY 10010, phone: (212)696-8291. Index available (Bound in Mar. issue). **Bk Rev**, (Qty: 12). **Ad Acc**, **Adv Mgr Tel** (212)696-8261. **Circ:** 53,500. available on microfilm and microfiche from University Microfilms International (UMI). **Continues** American Kennel Gazette, Pure-Bred Dogs, 0737-8807. **Continued in part by** American Kennel Club Show, Obedience and Field Trial Awards, 0272-4383; **Continued by** AKC Gazette.
Desc: Contains articles of interest to the pure-bred dog fancier. Reports information in all areas of pure-bred dog breeding and showing.

LC SF441   **ISSN** 0731-0366
DD 636.8   US

PURRRRR!. Vol. 1, No. 1 (Apr. 1982)-. Periodical. English. Twelve times a year. $18.00. Meow Company, 118 Massachusetts Avenue, Suite 187, Boston MA 02115.

DD 636.8/006/071   **ISSN** 0828-4865 CN

QUARTERLY - CANADIAN CAT ASSOCIATION. (THE QUARTERLY / CCA.). [Q. - Can. Cat. Assoc.]. **Added/Corp** Canadian Cat Association. **VAT** CCA Quarterly (1984); Canadian Cat Association Quarterly (1984). Vol. 21, No. 1 (Winter 1984)-. Periodical. English (French). Four times a year. Canadian Cat Association, 3 Greenside Avenue, London Ontario N6J 2X5 Canada. **Tel** (519)433-2947. **ED** Elaine Gleason. Index available. cum. index. **Bk Rev**. **Ad Acc. Circ:** 1,000 (ctrl). **Continues** CCA Quarterly, 0711-074X.
Desc: Contains articles of interest for all cat fanciers; proper care, grooming and health of cats, as well as poetry and stories about cats.

    ISSN 1068-1965 US

●**REPTILES (IRVINE, CALIF.).** (REPTILES : GUIDE TO KEEPING REPTILES AND AMPHIBIANS.). (1993)-. Periodical. English. Twelve times a year. $27.97. Fancy Publications, PO Box 6050, Mission Viejo CA 92690. **Tel** (714)855-8822, (800)426-2516, FAX (714)855-3045. (**Subscription address:** Neodata / Colorado, PO Box 2606, Boulder CO 80322.)

LC SF   **ISSN** 1084-4198
DD 636   US

●**RETRIEVER JOURNAL, THE.** [Retriev. j.]. Vol. 1, No. 1 (Oct./Nov. 1995)-. Periodical. English. Six times a year. $21.95. Wildwood Press, 2779 Aero Park Drive, Box 968, Traverse City MI 49685. **Tel** (616)946-3712.

    ISSN 8750-3549 US

RHODESIAN RIDGEBACK QUARTERLY, THE. **VFOAT** RRQ. Vol. 1, No. 1 (Fall 1984)-. Periodical. English. Four times a year. Hoflin Publishing Ltd., 4401 Zephyr Street, Wheat Ridge CO 80033-3299. **Tel** (303)934-5656, FAX (303)422-7000.

LC SF429.S35 S25   **ISSN** 0161-0651
DD 636.7/3   US

SAMOYED QUARTERLY, THE. (1977)-. Periodical. English. Four times a year. $40.00 (one-year), $76.00 (two-year). Hoflin Publishing Ltd., 4401 Zephyr Street, Wheat Ridge CO 80033-3299. **Tel** (303)934-5656, FAX (303)422-7000. **ED** Donald R. Hoflin and Cindy Kerstiens. **Ad Acc, Adv Mgr:** Cindy Kerstiens. **Circ:** 1,100.
Desc: Articles on all areas of interest to the Samoyed fancier.

    ISSN 0276-1521 US
Pr Rev.

SCHNAUZER SHORTS. (19??)-. Periodical. English. Seven times a year. $30.00. Dan Kiedrowski Company, Drawer A, La Honda CA 94020. **Tel** (415)747-0549. **Ad Acc, Adv Mgr:** Dan Kiedrowski. **Circ:** 900.
Desc: Reports on show results on miniature Schnauzers and breeding, litters available, health interests, and profiles of particular dogs.

    ISSN 0747-3532 US

SCOTTISH TERRIER QUARTERLY, THE. Vol. 1, No. 1 (Spring 1984)-. Periodical. English. Six times a year. Hoflin Publishing Ltd., 4401 Zephyr Street, Wheat Ridge CO 80033-3299. **Tel** (303)934-5656, FAX (303)422-7000.

    ISSN 0164-372X US

SETTER MAGAZINE, THE. Periodical. English. Six times a year. $12.50. Gerry Roberts, 2254 Wyandotte Street, Mountain View CA 94043.

LC WMLC L 83/9704   **ISSN** 0745-2012
DD 636   US

SHELTIE INTERNATIONAL. [Sheltie int.]. (1982)-. Periodical. English. Six times a year (Feb., Apr., June, Aug., Oct., Dec.). $43.00. Sheltie International, PO Box 6369, Los Osos CA 93412. **Tel** (805)528-2007. **ED** Jean Fergus (editor's address: 1456 14th Street, Slo, CA 93402). Index available. cum. index. **Bk Rev**, (Qty: 2). **Ad Acc. Circ:** 1,700.
Desc: A magazine about the care, training, showing and betterment of the Shetland Sheepdog.

LC WMLC L 83/8847   **ISSN** 0744-6608
    US

SHELTIE PACESETTER. (19??)-. Periodical. English. Six times a year. $44.00. Sheltie Pacesetter, PO Box 3310, Palos Verdes CA 90274. **Tel** (213)541-7820. **ED** Nancy Lee Marshall. Index available. cum. index. **Bk Rev**. **Ad Acc. Circ:** 3,500 (ctrl).

    ISSN 1040-5801 US

SHIH TZU REPORTER, THE. [Shih tzu report.]. (19??)-. Periodical. English. Six times a year (Jan., Mar., May, July, Sept., Nov.). $42.00 US; $52.00 Canada and Mexico; $60.00 other. Reporter Publications, PO Box 6369, Los Osos CA 93412. **ED** Jean Fargus (editor's address: 1456 14th Street, Slo, CA 93402, phone: (805)528-7229). **Bk Rev**. **Ad Acc**.

DD 636.7/08/88   **ISSN** 0701-0001 CN

SHOW RING. (July/Aug. 1976)-. Periodical. English. Six times a year. Show Ring Publications, PO Box 2077, New Westminster British Columbia V3L 5A3 Canada.

    ISSN 0274-7286 US

SIBERIAN QUARTERLY, THE. [Sib. q.]. (1980)-. Periodical. English. Four times a year. $40.00. Hoflin Publishing Ltd., 4401 Zephyr Street, Wheat Ridge CO 80033-3299. **Tel** (303)934-5656, FAX (303)422-7000. **ED** Donald R. Hoflin. **Ad Acc, Adv Mgr:** Cindy Kerstiens. **Circ:** 1,350.

    ISSN 8750-1953 US

SIGHTHOUND REVIEW. [Sighthound rev.]. Vol. 1, No. 1 (May/June 1984)-. Trade Publication. English. Six times a year. $40.00. The Afghan Hound Review, PO Box 30430, Santa Barbara CA 93130. **Tel** (805)966-7270, FAX (805)682-1771. **ED** Bo N. Bengtson. **Bk Rev**. **Ad Acc. Circ:** 2,000. **Continues** Sighthound, 0744-3323.
Desc: For Sighthound/Greyhound type breed fanciers. Covers showing, racing, coursing, obedience, care, training, etc.

DD 636   **ISSN** 1083-0111 US

●**SOUTHERN CALIFORNIA DOG MAGAZINE.** [South. Calif. dog mag.]. (1995)-. Periodical. English. Twelve times a year. $12.95. Southern California Dog Magazine, PO Box 900069, San Diego CA 92190. **Tel** (619)286-6280.

LC SF421 .S48   **ISSN** 0561-1245
DD 636.7/005   US

SOUTHERN DOG LOVERS DIGEST. Vol. 1, (Fall 1964)-. Periodical. English. Southern Dog Lover's Digest, PO Box 9270, Shreveport LA 71139.

    ISSN 0163-7649 US

STABLE & KENNEL NEWS OF THE SOUTH. See Horses and Horsemanship.

DD 639   **ISSN** 1062-6425 US

TALKING BETTAS. [Talking bettas]. **Added/Corp** Betta Buffs of Pittsburgh (Organization). (1991)-. Periodical. English. Twelve times a year. $12.00 (members). Beta Buffs of Pittsburgh, 146 Willow Drive, Freedom PA 15042.

DD 636   **ISSN** 1074-7796 US

●**VET. INDUSTRY NEWSLETTER.** [Vet. ind. newsl.]. **VFOAT** Veterinary Industry Newsletter. Vol. 1, No. 1 (Mar. 1, 1993)-. Periodical. English. Twelve times a year. $295.00. Good Communications, Inc., PO Box 10069, Austin TX 78766-1069. **Tel** (512)454-6090, FAX (512)452-3420. **ED** Becki Reynolds (editor's address: PO Box 1528, Charleston, SC 29401, phone: (803)577-7991).
Desc: Covers food and products for pets sold by the veterinarians.

Animal Welfare —Pets

LC WMLC 93/4140   **ISSN** 0747-4636
US
VIZSLA NEWS, THE. Added/Corp Vizsla Club of America. (19??)-. Periodical. English. Twelve times a year. Vizsla Club of America / VCA, 5425 Via Serena, Alta Loma CA 91701.

ISSN 0164-6478
US
WHIPPET, THE. [Whippet]. (1978)-. Periodical. English. Six times a year. $12.00. The Whippet, 3967 Anastasia Street, San Diego CA 92111.

ISSN 0883-7686
DD 636   US
YORKIE TALES. (19??)-. Periodical. English. Four times a year. $28.00. Yorkie Tales, 731 Paso Robles Street, Unit D, Paso Robles CA 93446. **Tel** (805)239-8406.

LC SF429.Y6 Y67
DD 636.7/55   US
YORKSHIRE TERRIER QUARTERLY, THE. Vol. 1 (May 1968)-. Periodical. English. Yorkshire Terrier Quarterly, Box 256, Times Square Station, New York NY 10036.

LC SF441   **ISSN** 1353-260X
DD 636.8   UK
●**YOUR CAT.** [Your cat]. (1994)-. Consumer Publication. English. Twelve times a year. EMAP Pursuit Publishing, Apex House 7th Fl. Oundle Road, Peterborough PE2 9NP United Kingdom. **Tel** 011 44 1733 264666. **(Subscription address:** Tower Publishing, Tower House, Sovereign Park, Market Harborough, Leicester LE16 9EF United Kingdom. **Tel** 011 44 1858 468811, FAX 011 44 1858 432164.**)**

LC SF421   **ISSN** 1353-260X
DD 636.7   UK
●**YOUR DOG.** (1995)-. Consumer Publication. English. Six times a year. EMAP Pursuit Publishing, Apex House 7th Fl. Oundle Road, Peterborough PE2 9NP United Kingdom. **Tel** 011 44 1733 264666. **(Subscription address:** Tower Publishing, Tower House, Sovereign Park, Market Harborough, Leicester LE16 9EF United Kingdom. **Tel** 011 44 1858 468811, FAX 011 44 1858 432164.**) Ad Acc.**

LC SF421   **ISSN** 1078-0343
DD 636.7   US
●**YOUR DOG.** (YOUR DOG / TUFTS UNIVERSITY SCHOOL OF MEDICINE.). [Your dog]. **Added/Corp** Tufts University School of Medicine. (July 1994)-. Newsletter. English. Twelve times a year. $16.00. Tufts University / School of Veterinary Medicine, North Grafton MA 01536. **Tel** (508)839-5302, (800)829-0926. **(Subscription address:** Your Dog, PO Box 420285, Palm Coast FL 32142. **Tel** (904)445-4662 ext. 818, (800)829-5475.**)**
Desc: Advice for dog owners.

LC SF411 .Y68   **ISSN** 0278-744X
DD 636.08/87/05   US
CEASED
YOUR FAMILY PET. VFOAT Family Pet. (19??)-(19??). Periodical. English. Meredith Publications / Special Interest Section, 1716 Locust Street, Des Moines IA 50309. **Tel** (515)284-3000.

LC SF411 .Y68
DD 636.08/87/05   US
●**YOUR PET.** (1994)-. English. Four times a year. $12.00. Your Pet Magazine, 30 Lincoln Plaza, Suite 6D, New York NY 10023. **Tel** (212)489-1416. **ED** Dominique Davis. **Ad Acc.**

ANTHROPOLOGY

US
AAA GUIDE. Main/Corp American Anthropological Association. 28th Ed. (1989-90)-. English. One time a year. $50.00. American Anthropological Association, 4350 North Fairfax Dr, Suite 640, Arlington VA 22203. **Tel** (703)528-1902 ext. 3031, FAX (703)528-3546.
Continues Guide to Departments of Anthropology, 0090-9939.
Desc: Lists information on academic departments of anthropology, museum and research institutions, and related government organizations.

LC AM101
ER
AASTARAAMAT. Main/Corp Eesti NSV Riiklik Etnograafiamuuseum. (1925)-. Periodical. Estonian (summaries and/or abstracts in German, English, French and Russian).

LC GN665 .A627   **ISSN** 0314-8769
DD 306/.0899915   AT
ABORIGINAL HISTORY. [Aborig. hist.]. **Added/Corp** Australian National University. Dept. of Pacific and Southeast Asian History. Vol. 1, Pt. 1-2 (1977)-. Periodical. English. One time a year (Nov.). 14.79Aus$. Anutech Pty. Limited, GPO Box 4, Canberra ACT 2601 Australia. **Tel** 011 61 6 2492479, FAX 011 61 6 2575088. **(Subscription address:** Aboriginal History, Box 2837 GPO, Canberra ACT 2601 Australia. **Tel** 011 61 6 2494685.**) ED** Peter Read. cum. index. **Bk Rev. Circ:** 300.
Desc: Aims to present articles and information in the field of Australian ethnohistory, particularly in the post-contact history of Aborigines and Torres Strait Islanders.
Ind/Abst Am. Hist. Life (1987-); Anthropol. Lit.; APAIS, Aust. Public Aff. Inf. Ser. (1978-).

LC GN665 .A64   **ISSN** 0310-723X
DD 301.45/19/91094   AT
ABORIGINAL NEWS (CANBERRA). See Ethnic Interests.

LC GN1 .A155   **ISSN** 0173-2986
DD 301/.0943/05   GW
ABSTRACTS IN GERMANY ANTHROPOLOGY. See Anthropology-Abstracting, Bibliographies and Statistics.

LC GN3 .A37a   **ISSN** 0160-1873
DD 301.2/08   US
NLM W1 AB889
ABSTRACTS OF THE ANNUAL MEETING - AMERICAN ANTHROPOLOGICAL ASSOCIATION. [Abstr. annu. meet. - Am. Anthropol. Assoc.]. **Main/Corp** American Anthropological Association. (19??)-. English. One time a year. $15.00. American Anthropological Association, 4350 North Fairfax Dr, Suite 640, Arlington VA 22203. **Tel** (703)528-1902 ext. 3031, FAX (703)528-3546.
Ind/Abst Anthropol. Index; GeoRef.

ISSN 1064-6981
DD 305   US
ACCENT (MARLBORO, MASS.). See Ethnic Interests.

LC GN289. A25   **ISSN** 0258-0357
DD 573.2/05   II
NLM W1 AC7524   **CODEN** ACANDO
ACTA ANTHROPOGENETICA. [Acta anthropog.]. Vol. 1 (1977)-. Academic Scholarly Publication. English. Four times a year (Jan., Apr., July, Oct.). $100.00. Saraswati Library, 206 Bidhan Sarani, Calcutta 700 006 India. **Tel** 011 91 33 345492. Documents available from BIOSIS Document Express, CASDDS.
Ind/Abst Biol. Abstr.; Chem. Abstr. (1976/77-1983-); EMBASE; Index Med. (1980-).

LC GN1 .A25   **ISSN** 1216-9803
HU
ACTA ETHNOGRAPHICA HUNGARICA. Added/Corp Magyar Tudomanyos Akademia. **VFOAT** Acta Ethnographica. Vol. 37, No. 1-4 (1992)-. Academic Scholarly Publication. English (French, German and Russian). Four times a year. $88.00. Akademiai Kiado, Publishing House of the Hungarian Academy of Sciences, Prielle Kornelia u. 19-35, H-1117 Budapest Hungary. **Tel** 011 36 1 1811991, FAX 011 36 1 1811991, telex 22-6228 AKNYO H. **Continues** Acta Ethnographica Academiae Scientiarum Hungaricae, 0001-5628.

LC GN1 .A3   **ISSN** 1230-0519
PL
●**ACTA UNIVERSITATIS LODZIENSIS. FOLIA ANTHROPOLOGICA. Added/Corp** Uniwersytet Lodzki. **VFOAT** Folia Anthropologica. (1993)-. Monographic series. Polish (summaries and/or abstracts in English). Irregular. Price varies per volume. Wydawnictwo Uniwersytetu Lodzkiego, Ul. Jaracza 34, Lodz Poland. **Tel** 011 48 42 331671, 011 48 42 336541. **(Subscription address:** Ars Polona-Ruch, PO Box 1001, Krakowskie Przedmiescie 7, 00-068 Warsaw Poland. **Tel** 011 48 22 261201.**) Continues in part** Acta Universitatis Lodziensis. Folia Zoologica et Anthropologica, 0208-6166.

ISSN 0208-6042
PL
ACTA UNIVERSITATIS LODZIENSIS. FOLIA ETHNOLOGICA. Added/Corp Uniwersytet Lodzki. **VFOAT** Folia Ethnologica. (1982)-. Monographic series. Polish (English and Russian). Irregular. Price varies per volume. Wydawnictwo Uniwersytetu Lodzkiego, Ul. Jaracza 34, Lodz Poland. **Tel** 011 48 42 331671, 011 48 42 336541. **(Subscription address:** Ars Polona-Ruch, PO Box 1001, Krakowskie Przedmiescie 7, 00-068 Warsaw Poland. **Tel** 011 48 22 261201.**) Continues in part** Acta Universitatis Lodziensis. Zeszyty Naukowe Uniwersytetu Lodzkiego. Seria 1 : Nauki Humanistyczno-Spoleczne, 0137-4591.

LC F2301
DD 970.05   VE
ACTA VENEZOLANA. Vol. 1 (July/Sept. 1945)-. Periodical. Spanish. Four times a year. Sociedad Interamericana de Antropologa Geografia, Apartado Postal 47286, Caracas 1041 Venezuela.

LC PL8000 .A29   **ISSN** 0954-416X
DD 496/.05   UK
CCC
CODEN ALCUEH
Pr Rev.
AFRICAN LANGUAGES AND CULTURES. See Linguistics.

LC DT751 .A4   **ISSN** 0002-0184
DD 572.968   SA
Pr Rev.
AFRICAN STUDIES (JOHANNESBURG). (AFRICAN STUDIES.). [Afr. stud.]. **Added/Corp** University of the Witwatersrand. Dept. of Bantu Studies. Vol. 1 (Mar. 1942)-. Periodical. English (Portuguese and French). Two times a year (June, & Dec.). $32.51. Witwatersrand University Press, PO Wits, Education Department, Johannesburg 2050 South Africa. **Tel** 011 27 11 4845906, FAX 011 27 11 40319263394386, telex 4-27125 SA. **ED** W. D. Hammond-Tooke. Index available. **Bk Rev. Ad Acc. Circ:** 700. Documents available from The Genuine Article. **Supersedes** Bantu Studies.
Desc: Devoted to the study of African anthropology, history, linguistics and other related fields.
Ind/Abst Abstr. Anthropol.; Am. Hist. Life (1963-1978); Anthropol. Index; Anthropol. Lit.; Appl. Soc. Sci. Index Abstr.; Arts Humanit. Citation Index [Select. Cov.]; Curr. Contents Soc. Behav. Sci.; Curr. Geogr. Publ. (199?-); Geogr. Abstr. Human Geogr. (?-?); Int. Bibliogr. Sociol.; Int. Dev. Abstr.; Int. Polit. Sci. Abstr.; Linguist. Lang. Behav. Abstr.; Middle East Abstr. Index; MLA Int. Bibl. Books Artic. Mod. Lang. Lit.; Res. Alert [Full Cov.]; Soc. Plann. Policy Dev. Abstr.; Soc. Sci. Cit. Index [Full Cov.]; Sociol. Abstr.

LC GN643 .A35
DD 305.80096   RU
AFRICANA. AFRIKANSKII ETNOGRAFICHESKII SBORNIK. Added/Corp Institut Etnografii Imeni N.N. Miklukho-Maklaia. **VFOAT** Afrikanskii Etnograficheskii Sbornik. Vol. 6 (1966)-. Russian (summaries and/or abstracts in English and French). One time a year. Institut Etnografii Imeni N.N. Miklukho-Maklaia., Russia. **(Subscription address:** Victor Kamkin, 4956 Boiling Brook Parkway, Rockville MD 20852. **Tel** (301)881-5973.**) Continues** Afrikanskii Etnograficheskii Sbornik.

LC GN671.P5 A36
DD 306/.09599   PH
AGHAM-TAO. VFOAT AghamTao. Vol. 1, No. 1 (Dec. 1978)-. Periodical. English. University of Philippines Department of Anthropology, Palma Hall, Diliman Quezon City Philippines.

ISSN 0711-382X
DD 497/.3/05   CN
CODEN AIRLEA
ALGONQUIAN AND IROQUOIAN LINGUISTICS. See Linguistics.

PE
AMAZONIA INDIGENA / COPAL, SOLIDARIDAD CON LOS GRUPOS NATIVOS. Vol. 1, No. 1 (July 1980)-. Periodical. Spanish. Three times a year. $9.00. Copal, Los Alamos 431, Lima 27 Peru.
Ind/Abst Hisp. Am. Period. Index, HAPI; Hum. Rights Intern. Rep.

LC E51 .A45   **ISSN** 0185-1179
DD 970.1   MX
NLM W1 AM109
AMERICA INDIGENA. See History-History of North and South America.

LC GN1 .A5   **ISSN** 0002-7294
DD 301.2   US
CCC
NLM W1 AM154   **CODEN** AMATA7
Pr Rev.
AMERICAN ANTHROPOLOGIST. [Am. anthropol.]. **Added/Corp** American Anthropological Association. Anthropological Society of Washington (Washington, D.C.) American Ethnological Society. Vol. 1 (Jan. 1888)-. Periodical. English. Four times a year. $105.00. American Anthropological Association, 4350 North Fairfax Dr, Suite 640, Arlington VA 22203. **Tel** (703)528-1902 ext. 3031, FAX (703)528-3546. **ED** H. Russell Bernard and Susan Valenza. cum. index. **Bk Rev. Ad Acc. Circ:** 12,000 (ctrl). available on microfilm and microfiche from University Microfilms International (UMI). Documents available from The Genuine Article, BIOSIS Document Express, UMI Article Clearinghouse. **Supersedes** Anthropological Society of Washington (Washington, D.C.). Transactions of the Anthropological Society of Washington.
Desc: Contains articles, reports, comments, film reviews, directed to a general anthropological audience.
Ind/Abst Abstr. Anthropol.; Acad. Abstr. Full Text Elite; Acad. Ind. [Computer File] (1987-); Acad. Search; Am. Hist. Life (1963-1972),(1982-); Am. Bibliogr. Slavic East Europ. Stud.; Annu. Bibliogr. Engl. Lang. Lit.; Anthropol. Index; Anthropol. Lit.; Appl. Soc. Sci. Index Abstr.; Arts Humanit. Citation Index [Select. Cov.];

Bibliogr. Mission.; Biol. Abstr.; Book Rev. Index; Br. Archaeol. Bibliogr.; Ceram. Abstr. (19??-); Curr. Cit.; Curr. Contents Soc. Behav. Sci.; Curr. Geogr. Publ. (199?-); Ecol. Abstr.; EMBASE; EP Collect.; Ethnoarts Index; Expand. Acad. Index (1987-); Film Lit. Index; Gen. Sci. Index; Gen. Sci. Source; Geogr. Abstr. Phys. Geogr. (19??-19??); Geogr. Abstr. Human Geogr.; GeoRef; Hist. Source (July 1990-); Homework Help.; Hum. Resour. Abstr.; Humanit. Source; Index Book Rev. Relig.; Index Period. Artic. Relat. Law (19??-19??); INFO-SOUTH Abstr.; Int. Bibliogr. Sociol.; Int. Dev. Abstr.; Int. Polit. Sci. Abstr.; Linguist. Lang. Behav. Abstr.; Mag. Search; MasterFile FullTEXT 1000; MasterFile FullTEXT 350; MasterFile FullTEXT 650; MasterFile FullTEXT (July 1990-); Med. Rev. Dig.; Middle East Abstr. Index; MLA Int. Bibl. Books Artic. Mod. Lang. Lit.; Multicult. Educ. Abstr.; Newsp. Period. Abstr. (1988-); OCLC; Peace Res. Abstr. J. (1964-); Popul. Index; Psychol. Abstr. (1928-); PsycINFO; PsycLit; Ref. Sources; Res. Alert [Full Cov.]; Sage Fam. Stud. Abstr.; Soc. Plann. Policy Dev. Abstr.; Soc. Sci. Source; Soc. Sci. Cit. Index [Full Cov.]; Soc. Sci. Index; Soc. Sci. Index Fulltext (Dec. 1988-) [Full Txt.]; Sociol. Abstr.; SportSearch; Stud. Women Abstr.; Telebase; U.S. Polit. Sci. Doc.; West. Hist. Q.; Women Stud. Abstr.

LC GN1 .A53 **ISSN** 0094-0496
DD 301.2/05 US
CCC
Pr Rev.

AMERICAN ETHNOLOGIST. [Am. ethnol.]. **Added/Corp** American Ethnological Society. Vol. 1, (Feb. 1974)-. Periodical. English. Four times a year. $70.00. American Anthropological Association, 4350 North Fairfax Dr, Suite 640, Arlington VA 22203. **Tel** (703)528-1902 ext. 3031, FAX (703)528-3546. **ED** Shirley Lindenbaum, Medea Ranck. **Bk Rev. Ad Acc. Circ:** 3,500 (ctrl). available on microfilm and microfiche from University Microfilms International (UMI). Documents available from The Genuine Article, UMI Article Clearinghouse.
Desc: Broad range of topical papers, review articles, comments, reflections and reviews on ecology, economy, social organization, ethnicity, politics, ideology, personality, cognition, ritual and symbolism.
Ind/Abst Abstr. Anthropol.; Acad. Abstr.; Acad. Search; Anthropol. Index; Anthropol. Lit.; Appl. Soc. Sci. Index Abstr.; Arts Humanit. Citation Index [Select. Cov.]; Bibliogr. Mission.; Book Rev. Index; Curr. Cit.; Curr. Contents Soc. Behav. Sci.; EP Collect.; Ethnoarts Index; Expand. Acad. Index (1989-); Hist. Source (Jan. 1992-); Homework Help.; Humanit. Source; Index Islam. Lit.; Index Book Rev. Relig.; INFO-SOUTH Abstr.; Int. Bibliogr. Sociol.; Mag. Search; MasterFile FullTEXT 1000; MasterFile FullTEXT 350; MasterFile FullTEXT 650; MasterFile FullTEXT (Jan. 1992-); Middle East Abstr. Index; Newsp. Period. Abstr. (1991-); OCLC; Peace Res. Abstr. J. (1976-1978); Psychol. Abstr. (1974-); PsycINFO; PsycLit; Recent. Publ. Artic.; Res. Alert [Full Cov.]; Rural Dev. Abstr.; Soc. Sci. Source; Soc. Sci. Cit. Index [Full Cov.]; Soc. Sci. Index; Soc. Sci. Index Fulltext (Nov. 1988-) [Full Txt.]; Telebase; World Agric. Econ. Rural Sociol. Abstr.

LC GN1 .A55 **ISSN** 0002-9483
DD 573.05 US
CCC
NLM W1 AM499 **CODEN** AJPNA9
Pr Rev.

AMERICAN JOURNAL OF PHYSICAL ANTHROPOLOGY. [Am. j. phys. anthropol.]. **Added/Corp** Wistar Institute of Anatomy and Biology. American Association of Physical Anthropologists. American Association of Physical Anthropologists. Proceedings of the Annual Meeting. Vol. 1 (Jan./March 1918-Dec. 1942); New Series, Vol. 1 (March 1943)-. Academic Scholarly Publication. English. Twelve times a year (plus 2 supplements). $1652.00. John Wiley & Sons, Inc., 605 Third Avenue, New York NY 10158-0012. **Tel** (212)850-6000, (212)850-6645, FAX (212)850-6088, telex 12-7063. **(Subscription address:** John Wiley & Sons / UK, Baffins Lane, Chichester, West Sussex PO19 1UD United Kingdom. **Tel** 011 44 1243 779777, FAX 011 44 243 776128, telex 86290 WIBOOKG.) **ED** Matt Cartmill. cum. index. available on microfilm. Documents available from The Genuine Article, BIOSIS Document Express, UMI Article Clearinghouse.
Desc: Publishes original articles on human evolution and variation-past and present-including primate morphology, physiology, genetics, adaptation, growth, development and behavior.
Ind/Abst ASTIS Curr. Aware. Bull. (1978-); Acad. Abstr.; Acad. Search; Annals Behav. Med.; Anthropol. Index; Anthropol. Lit.; Art Archaeol. Tech. Abstr.; ASTIS Bibliogr. (1978-); Biol. Abstr.; Br. Archaeol. Bibliogr.; Curr. Cit.; Curr. Contents Life Sci.; Curr. Contents Soc. Behav. Sci.; Curr. Primate Ref.; Curr. Titles Dent.; Dev. Med. Child Neurol. (-1990); EMBASE; EP Collect.; Expand. Acad. Index (1989-); GeoRef; Health Plan. Adminis.; Helminthol. Abstr. (1991-); Hist. Source (July 1993-); Homework Help.; Humanit. Source; Index Med.; Index Vet.; INFO-SOUTH Abstr.; Int. Bibliogr. Sociol.; Mag. Search; MasterFile FullTEXT 1000; MasterFile FullTEXT 350; MasterFile FullTEXT 650; MasterFile FullTEXT (July 1993-); Middle East Abstr. Index; Multicult. Educ. Abstr.; Newsp. Period. Abstr. (1989-); OCLC; Life Sci. Collect.; Protozoolog. Abstr.; Ref. Upd. Deluxe Ed.; Res. Alert [Full Cov.]; Sci. Cit. Index; SCISEARCH; Soc. Sci. Source; Soc. Sci. Cit. Index [Full Cov.]; Soc. Sci. Index; Soc. Sci. Index Fulltext (Nov. 1988-) [Full Txt.]; Stud. Women Abstr.; Telebase.

ISSN 0895-0482
DD 306 US

AMERICAN UNIVERSITY STUDIES. SERIES XXI, REGIONAL STUDIES. [Am. univ. stud., XXI Reg. stud.]. **VFOAT** American University Studies. Series 21, Regional Studies; Regional Studies. (1988)-. Academic Scholarly Publication. English. Irregular. Price varies per volume. Peter Lang Publishing, 62 West 45th Street, 4th Floor, New York NY 10036. **Tel** (212)764-1471, (800)770-5264, FAX (212)302-7574, telex 6973364 PLNY.

ISSN 0738-064X
US

AMS STUDIES IN ANTHROPOLOGY. [AMS stud. anthropol.]. **VFOAT** A.M.S. Studies in Anthropology; Studies in Anthropology. No. 1 (1983)-. Monographic series. English. Irregular. Price varies per volume. AMS Press Inc., 56 East 13th Street, New York NY 10003. **Tel** (212)777-4700, FAX (212)995-5413, telex 710 581 2302.
Desc: Monographic series covering anthropology. Contains volumes on subjects such as the rise to supremacy of Zoroastrianism in Persia from 1200 BC and the work and lives of underground coal miners in the northern Appalachian region of the United States.

ISSN 0101-451X
BL

ANAIS DO MUSEU DE ANTROPOLOGIA. (ANAIS DO MUSEU DE ANTROPOLOGIA DA UFSC.). [An. Mus. Antropol.]. Vol. 7-9, Nos. 9-10 (1977)-. Portuguese. One time a year. Secretaria do Museu de Antropologia, Caixa Postal 476, 88.000 Florianopolis Santa Catarina Brazil. ***Continues*** *Anais do Museu de Antropologia, 0101-451X.*
Ind/Abst Anthropol. Lit.

MX

ANALES ANTROPOLOGICOS / FACULTAD DE ANTROPOLOGIA DE LA UNIVERSIDAD VERACRUZANA. **Added/Corp** Universidad Veracruzana. Facultad de Antropologia. (1986)-. Spanish. ***Continues*** *Anuario Antropologico.*
Ind/Abst Am. Hist. Life.

LC GN560.M6 A5 **ISSN** 0185-1225
MX

ANALES DE ANTROPOLOGIA. Vol. 21 (1984)-. Monographic series. Spanish. Irregular. Price varies per volume. UNAM Inst Invest Antropologica, Ciudad Universitaria Coyoacan, 04510 Mexico DF Mexico. ***Formed by the union of*** *Anales de Antropologia. I, Arqueologia y Antropologia Fisica* ***and*** *Anales de Antropologia. II, Etnologia y Linguistica.*
Ind/Abst Anthropol. Lit.; Hisp. Am. Period. Index, HAPI.

ISSN 0325-0288
DD 970.1 AG

ANALES DE ARQUEOLOGIA Y ETNOLOGIA / UNIVERSIDAD NACIONAL DE CUYO, FACULTAD DE FILOSOFIA Y LETRAS. **See** Archaeology.

LC F1461 .S67 **ISSN** 0252-337X
DD 972.81/005 GT

ANALES DE LA ACADEMIA DE GEOGRAFIA E HISTORIA DE GUATEMALA. **Main/Corp** Academia de Geografia e Historia de Guatemala. Vol. 53 (Jan./Dec. 1980)-. Spanish. Four times a year. $20.00. Academia de Geografia e Historia de Guatemala, 3A Avenida 8-35 Zona A, 01001 Guatemala Guatemala. **Tel** 011 502 2 535141 23544, FAX 011 502 2 23544. **ED** Licda Alcira Goicolea V. Index available. cum. index. **Bk Rev. Circ:** 1,000. ***Continues*** *Sociedad de Geografia e Historia de Guatemala. Anales de la Sociedad de Geografia e Historia.*
Desc: Covers several disciplines including, anthropology, archaeology, bibliography, ethnology, folklore, geography, history, linguistics, and among other related issues.
Ind/Abst Am. Hist. Life (1980-); Anthropol. Lit.

LC DT641 .A63 **ISSN** 0254-4296
DD 967.5/1/005 CG

ANNALES AEQUATORIA. [Ann. aequat.]. **Added/Corp** Missionaries of the Sacred Heart (Mbandaka, Zaire) Centre Aequatoria (Mbandaka, Zaire). Vol. 1 (1980)-. Periodical. French (English and German). One time a year. $20.00. Aequatoria Center de Recherches, BP 276, Mbandaka Zaire. **ED** Honore Vinck. Index available. **Bk Rev. Circ:** 550. ***Continues*** *Aequatoria.*
Desc: Promotes scientific research in matters of Zairian cultures, history and languages more particularly to the mongo people.
Ind/Abst Anthropol. Index; Anthropol. Lit.; Bibliogr. Mission.

ISSN 0980-157X
FR

ANNALES DE LA FOUNDATION FYSSEN. **Added/Corp** Fondation Fyssen. No. 1 (1985)-. Periodical. French. One time a year. 194 rue de Rivoli, Paris France.

LC GN655.I9 A25a **ISSN** 0587-4149
IV

ANNALES DE L'UNIVERSITE D'ABIDJAN. SERIE F: ETHNOSOCIOLOGIE. **Main/Corp** Universite d'Abidjan. **Added/Corp** Universite d'Abidjan. Institut d'Ethnosociologie. (1969)-. French. Price varies. Universite Nationale de Cote d'Ivoire Institut d'Ethnosociologie, BP 865, Abidjan 08 Ivory Coast. **Tel** 011 225 439000. **Bk Rev. Circ:** 1,000.
Ind/Abst Anthropol. Lit.

ISSN 0287-8429
JA
NLM W1; AN62H **CODEN** APANEE
TITLE CHANGE

ANNALS OF PHYSIOLOGICAL ANTHROPOLOGY, THE. [Ann. physiol. anthropol.]. **Added/Corp** Seiri Jinruigaku Kenkyukai (Japan). **VFOAT** Serii Jinruishi; Seiri Jinruigaku Kenkyukai Kaishi. (198?)-(1994). Periodical. English (Japanese). Research Society of Physiological Anthropology, Department of Ergonomics, Faculty of Engineering, Chiba University 1-33 Yayoi-Cho, Chiba 260 Japan. **(Subscription address:** Japan Publications Trading Company Ltd., PO Box 5030, Tokyo International, Tokyo 100-31 Japan. **Tel** 011 81 3 3292 3753.) Documents available from BIOSIS Document Express. ***Continued by*** *Applied Human Science, 0287-8429.*
Ind/Abst Biol. Abstr. (1984-); Curr. Cit.; Ergon. Abstr.; Health Plan. Adminis.; Index Med. (Vol. 3, No. 1, 1984-).

LC GN1 .A614
SA

ANNALS OF THE CAPE PROVINCIAL MUSEUMS. HUMAN SCIENCES. **VFOAT** Human Sciences. Vol. 1, Pt. 1 (March 20, 1979)-. Periodical. English. Irregular. Albany Museum, Somerset Street, Grahamstown 6140 South Africa. ***Continues in part*** *Annals of the Cape Provincial Museums.*

US

ANNOTATED BIBLIOGRAPHIES FOR ANTHROPOLOGISTS. **VFOAT** ABA. Vol. 1 , No. 1 (Fall 1991)-. Periodical. English. Two times a year.

LC GN1 .A62 **ISSN** 0570-2259
DD 301 RM
CODEN ARNAAG

ANNUAIRE ROUMAIN D'ANTHROPOLOGIE. [Annu. roum. anthropol.]. Vol. 1 (1964)-. French. One time a year. DM191.00. **(Subscription address:** Kubon & Sagner, ABT Zeitschriftenimport, D 80328 Munich Germany. **Tel** 011 49 89 54218130.) Documents available from BIOSIS Document Express.
Desc: Publishes articles of contemporary paleontology and anthropology.
Ind/Abst Anthropol. Index; Anthropol. Lit.; Biol. Abstr.; EMBASE.

LC GN36.H82 B826a
DD 306/.074/04391 HU

ANNUAL REPORT / ETHNOGRAPHICAL MUSEUM. **Main/Corp** Neprajzi Muzeum (Hungary). (19??)-. English. One time a year. Ethnographical Museum, 1055 Kossuth Lajor Ter 12, Budapest Hungary. **Tel** 00361/315 996. ctrl circ.

LC GN1 .A623 **ISSN** 0084-6570
DD 301.2/05 US
CCC
NLM W1 AN769L **CODEN** ARAPCW
Pr Rev.

ANNUAL REVIEW OF ANTHROPOLOGY. [Annu. rev. anthropol.]. Vol. 1 (1972)-. English. One time a year (October). $49.00. Annual Reviews Inc., 4139 El Camino Way, PO Box 10139, Palo Alto CA 94303-0139. **Tel** (415)493-4400, (800)523-8635, FAX (415)855-9815. **ED** William Durham. Index available. cum. index. ctrl circ. available on microfilm from University Microfilms International (UMI). Documents available from The Genuine Article, BIOSIS Document Express. ***Continues*** *Biennial Review of Anthropology, 0067-8503.*
Desc: Reviews in the biological, physical, medical, and social sciences.
Ind/Abst Acad. Search; Anthropol. Index; Anthropol. Lit.; Arts Humanit. Citation Index [Select. Cov.]; Biol. Abstr.; Br. Archaeol. Bibliogr.; Curr. Cit.; Curr. Contents Soc. Behav. Sci.; EP Collect.; Homework Help.; Int. Bibliogr. Sociol.; Int. Polit. Sci. Abstr.; Linguist. Lang. Behav. Abstr.; MasterFile FullTEXT 1000; MasterFile FullTEXT 350; MasterFile FullTEXT 650; MasterFile FullTEXT (July 1992-); Nutr. Abstr. Rev., Ser. A, Hum. Exp.; OCLC; Life Sci. Collect.; Psychol. Abstr. (1976-); PsycINFO; PsycLit; Res. Alert [Full Cov.]; Rural Dev. Abstr.; Soc. Plann.

Policy Dev. Abstr.; Soc. Sci. Source; Soc. Sci. Cit. Index [Full Cov.]; Sociol. Abstr.; Telebase; World Agric. Econ. Rural Sociol. Abstr.

NE
CEASED

ANTHROPOLGISCHE VERKENNINGEN. [Antropol. verkenn.]. (1982)-(1994). Periodical. Dutch. Coutinho BV, Slochterlaan 7, 1405 AL Bussum Netherlands. **Tel** 011 31 2159 49991, FAX 011 31 2159 47165. **ED** Kootje Willemse. **Bk Rev**, (Qty: 40). **Ad Acc**, **Adv Mgr:** M. Brandt, **Tel** 2159-49991. **Circ:** 600.
Ind/Abst Soc. Plann. Policy Dev. Abstr.

LC GN1 .B7 **ISSN** 0524-2304
XO

ANTHROPOLOGIA. **Main/Corp** Univerzita Komenskeho V Bratislave. Prirodovedecka Fakulta. (1959)-. Periodical. Czech (Slovak, English and German; summaries and/or abstracts in Russian). Slovenske Pedagogicke Nakladetelstvo, Sasinkova 5, 891 12 Bratislava, Slovakia.
Ind/Abst Abstr. Anthropol. (19??-).

LC GN1 .A63 **ISSN** 0003-5440
HU
NLM W1 AN846G

ANTHROPOLOGIAI KOZLEMENYEK. [Anthropol. koezl.]. **Added/Corp** Magyar Biologiai Tarsasag. Anthropologiai Szakosztaly. Vol 1, (1957)-. Academic Scholarly Publication. Hungarian (German and French; summaries and/or abstracts in English, French, German and Russian). Two times a year. $30.00. Akademiai Kiado, Publishing House of the Hungarian Academy of Sciences, Prielle Kornelia u. 19-35, H-1117 Budapest Hungary. **Tel** 011 36 1 1811991, FAX 011 36 1 1811991, telex 22-6228 AKNYO H. **(Subscription address:** Kultura, PO Box 143, H-1300 Budapest 3 Hungary. **Tel** 011 36 1 2500194.**)** **ED** O. Eiben. **Circ:** 400. ***Supersedes in part*** *Biologiai Kozlemenyek, 0006-3142.*
Ind/Abst Anthropol. Index; EMBASE.

LC BD450 .A55 **ISSN** 0301-6587
SP

ANTHROPOLOGICA (BARCELONA). (ANTHROPOLOGICA.). [Anthropologica]. **Added/Corp** Instituto de Antropologia de Barcelona. No. 1 (1973)-. Periodical. Spanish (summaries and/or abstracts in English, French and German). Three times a year.

LC F3429 .A554 **ISSN** 0254-9212
DD 985/.00498 PE

ANTHROPOLOGICA DEL DEPARTAMENTO DE CIENCIAS SOCIALES. [Anthropol. Dep. cienc. soc.]. **Added/Corp** Pontificia Universidad Catolica del Peru. Departamento de Ciencias Sociales. **VFOAT** Anthropologica; Revista Anthropologica. Vol. 1, No. 1 (1983)-. Periodical. Spanish. One time a year. $26.50. Pontificia Universidad Catolica del Peru, Fondo Editorial, Apartado 1761, Lima 1 Peru. **Tel** 011 51 14 622540. **ED** Alejandro Ortiz Rescaniere. ***Continues*** *Debates en Antropologia.*
Ind/Abst Anthropol. Lit.

LC E78.C2 A53 **ISSN** 0003-5459
DD 306/.05 CN
CCC
NLM W1 AN846K **CODEN** ATRPBS
Pr Rev.

ANTHROPOLOGICA (OTTAWA). (ANTHROPOLOGICA.). [Anthropologica]. **Added/Corp** University of Ottawa. Research Center for Amerindian Anthropology. University of Ottawa. Canadian Research Centre for Anthropology. Saint Paul University (Ottawa, Ont.). Canadian Research Centre for Anthropology. No. 1-8 (1955-1959); New Series Vol. 1 (1959)-. Periodical. English (French). Two times a year (Spring and Fall). 40.00Can$. Wilfrid Laurier University Press, 75 University Avenue West, Waterloo Ontario N2L 3C5 Canada. **Tel** (519)884-1970 ext. 6124, FAX (519)725-1399. **ED** Andrew P. Lyons and Jean-Marc Philibert. Index available. **Bk Rev**. **Ad Acc**. **Circ:** 400. available on microfiche from Micromedia Limited; available in microform from Micromedia Limited. Documents available from BIOSIS Document Express.
Desc: Articles and reviews in all areas of cultural and social anthropology.
Ind/Abst ASTIS Curr. Aware. Bull. (1978-); Abstr. Anthropol. (19??-); Am. Hist. Life (1978-); Anthropol. Index; Anthropol. Lit.; ASTIS Bibliogr. (1978-); Biol. Abstr.; Can. Index; Int. Bibliogr. Zeitschriftenliteratur Allen Gebieten Wissens; Linguist. Lang. Behav. Abstr.; Middle East Abstr. Index; MLA Int. Bibl. Books Artic. Mod. Lang. Lit.; Psychol. Abstr. (1968-); PsycINFO (1990-); PsycLit; Repere (1983-); Soc. Plann. Policy Dev. Abstr.; Sociol. Abstr.

US

ANTHROPOLOGICAL FIELD STUDIES / OFFICE OF CULTURAL RESOURCE MANAGEMENT, DEPARTMENT OF ANTHROPOLOGY, ARIZONA STATE UNIVERSITY. **Added/Corp** Arizona State University. Office of Cultural Resource Management. No. 1 (1980)-. Monographic series. English. Irregular. Price varies per volume. Arizona State University / Department of Anthropology, Tempe AZ 85287. **Tel** (602)965-7596.

LC GN1 .A652 **ISSN** 0066-4677
DD 301.2 AT
Pr Rev. **CEASED**

ANTHROPOLOGICAL FORUM. **Added/Corp** University of Western Australia. Dept. of Anthropology. (1963)-(Feb. 1995). English. University Bookshop, PO Box 656, Nedlands WA 6009 Australia. **Tel** 011 61 9 3802069. **Bk Rev**. **Ad Acc**. **Circ:** 600.
Desc: Social and cultural anthropology and comparative sociology. General disciplinary coverage specializing in aboriginal Australia, multi-cultural Australia, Papua New Guinea, South-East Asia.
Ind/Abst Anthropol. Index; Anthropol. Lit.; APAIS, Aust. Public Aff. Inf. Ser. (19??-); Ethnoarts Index.

LC GN1 .A7433 **ISSN** 0960-0604
DD 301/.05 UK
CODEN AJECER

ANTHROPOLOGICAL JOURNAL ON EUROPEAN CULTURES. **Added/Corp** European Centre for Traditional and Regional Cultures. **VFOAT** AJEC. Vol. 1, No. 1 (1990)-. Periodical. English. Two times a year. $51.86. Seminaire d'Ethnologie, Univ de Fribourg Misericorde, CH 1700 Fribourg Switzerland. **Tel** 011 41 37 219111.
Ind/Abst Soc. Plann. Policy Dev. Abstr.

ISSN 0003-5483
DD 401 US
Pr Rev.

ANTHROPOLOGICAL LINGUISTICS. **See** Linguistics.

LC Z5112 .A573 GN1 **ISSN** 0190-3373
DD 016.306/05 US

ANTHROPOLOGICAL LITERATURE. **See** Anthropology-Abstracting, Bibliographies and Statistics.

LC E78.N4 A65 **ISSN** 0077-7897
DD 970.4/9 US

ANTHROPOLOGICAL PAPERS (CARSON CITY). (ANTHROPOLOGICAL PAPERS.). **Added/Corp** Nevada State Museum. Nevada Archaeological Survey. **VFOAT** Nevada State Museum Anthropological Papers. No. 1 (1959)-. Monographic series. English. Irregular. Price varies per volume. Nevada State Museum, Capitol Complex, Carson City NV 89710. **Tel** (702)885-4810. **ED** Donald R. Tuohy.
Desc: Anthropological and archaeological papers pertaining to the Great River Basin.

LC GN2 .A27 **ISSN** 0065-9452
US
CODEN APNHAN

ANTHROPOLOGICAL PAPERS OF THE AMERICAN MUSEUM OF NATURAL HISTORY. [Anthropol. pap. Am. Mus. Nat. Hist.]. **VFOAT** Anthropological Papers, American Museum of Natural History. Vol. 1, Pt. 1 (Jan. 1907)-. Monographic series. English. Irregular. Price varies per volume. American Museum of Natural History, Central Park West at 79th Street, New York NY 10024. **Tel** (212)769-5500, (800)234-5252, telex 910 240 8933 MICRO PRESS VQ. **ED** Brenda Jones. **Circ:** 1,500 (ctrl). available on microfilm from University Microfilms International (UMI). Documents available from BIOSIS Document Express.
Desc: Each issue devoted exclusively to one report in the field of anthropology or archaeology.
Ind/Abst Am. Hist. Life (1963-1970); Art Archaeol. Tech. Abstr.; Biol. Abstr.

ISSN 0041-9354
US
Pr Rev.

ANTHROPOLOGICAL PAPERS OF THE UNIVERSITY OF ALASKA. [Anthropol. pap. Univ. Alsk.]. **Main/Corp** University of Alaska, Fairbanks. Vol. 16 (July 1974)-. English. Irregular. University of Alaska / Anthropology, Box 95212, Department of Anthropology, Fairbanks AK 99701. **Tel** (907)474-8288. **ED** Linda Ellanna. Index available. cum. index. **Circ:** 330. ***Continues*** *Anthropological Papers of the University of Alaska, 0041-9354.*
Desc: Publishes papers on any phase of arctic or subarctic anthropology.
Ind/Abst ASTIS Curr. Aware. Bull. (1978-); ASTIS Bibliogr. (1978-); Linguist. Lang. Behav. Abstr.; Soc. Plann. Policy Dev. Abstr.; Sociol. Abstr.; West. Hist. Q.

ISSN 0066-7501
US

ANTHROPOLOGICAL PAPERS OF THE UNIVERSITY OF ARIZONA. **Added/Corp** University of Arizona. Vol. 1 (1959)-. Monographic series. English. Irregular. Price varies per volume. University of Arizona Press, 1230 North Park Avenue, Suite 102, Tucson AZ 85719. **Tel** (602)882-3065, (800)426-3797, FAX (602)621-8899.
Ind/Abst Geogr. Abstr. Human Geogr. (?-?).

LC GN2 .M5 **ISSN** 0076-8367
DD 572 US

ANTHROPOLOGICAL PAPERS (UNIVERSITY OF MICHIGAN. MUSEUM OF ANTHROPOLOGY). (ANTHROPOLOGICAL PAPERS.). [Anthropol. pap. - Univ. Mich., Mus. Anthr.]. **Main/Corp** University of Michigan. Museum of Anthropology. **Added/Corp** University of Michigan. Museum of Anthropology. No. 1 (1949)-. Monographic series. English. Irregular. Price varies per volume. Museum of Anthropology / Michigan, University of Michigan, 4009 Museums, Ann Arbor MI 48109. **Tel** (313)764-0485.

US

ANTHROPOLOGICAL PAPERS / UNIVERSITY OF UTAH. **Added/Corp** University of Utah. **VFOAT** University of Utah Press Anthropological Papers. (1968)-. Monographic series. English. Irregular. $27.50 (latest edition). University of Utah Press, 101 University Services Building, Salt Lake City UT 84112. **Tel** (801)581-6771. ***Continues*** *Anthropological Papers (University of Utah. Dept. of Anthropology), 0083-4947.*

LC GN1 .P7 **ISSN** 0003-5491
DD 572.05 US
CCC
NLM W1 AN847M
Pr Rev.

ANTHROPOLOGICAL QUARTERLY. [Anthropol. q.]. **Added/Corp** Catholic Anthropological Conference. Catholic University of America. Dept. of Anthropology. Vol. 26 (Jan. 1953)-. Periodical. English. Four times a year. $32.00. Catholic University of America Press, 620 Michigan Avenue Northeast, Administration Building/Room 303, Washington DC 20064. **Tel** (202)319-5052, FAX (202)319-5802. **ED** Phyllis Pease Chock. (bound in Oct. issue). cum. index. **Bk Rev**. **Ad Acc**. **Circ:** 950. available on microfilm and microfiche from University Microfilms International (UMI). Documents available from The Genuine Article, UMI Article Clearinghouse. ***Continues*** *Primitive Man, 0887-3925.*
Desc: Contains articles on all areas of socio-cultural anthropology.
Ind/Abst Abstr. Anthropol.; Acad. Abstr.; Acad. Search; Am. Bibliogr. Slavic East Europ. Stud.; Annu. Bibliogr. Engl. Lang. Lit.; Anthropol. Index; Anthropol. Lit.; Arts Humanit. Citation Index [Select. Cov.]; Curr. Contents Soc. Behav. Sci.; Educ. Adm. Abstr. (?-?); EP Collect.; Ethnoarts Index; Expand. Acad. Index (1989-); Gen. Sci. Source; Geogr. Abstr. Human Geogr.; Homework Help.; Hum. Resour. Abstr. (?-?); INFO-SOUTH Abstr.; Int. Bibliogr. Sociol.; Int. Dev. Abstr.; Linguist. Lang. Behav. Abstr.; Mag. Search; MasterFile FullTEXT 1000; MasterFile FullTEXT 350; MasterFile FullTEXT 650; MasterFile FullTEXT (July 1990-); Middle East Abstr. Index; MLA Int. Bibl. Books Artic. Mod. Lang. Lit.; Multicult. Educ. Abstr.; Newsp. Period. Abstr. (1990-); OCLC; PsycINFO; PsycLit; Pub. Lib. FullTEXT; Res. Alert [Full Cov.]; Soc. Plann. Policy Dev. Abstr.; Soc. Sci. Source; Soc. Sci. Cit. Index [Full Cov.]; Soc. Sci. Index; Soc. Sci. Index Fulltext (April 1988-) [Full Txt.]; Sociol. Abstr.; Sociol. Educ. Abstr.; Spec. Educ. Needs Abstr.; Stud. Women Abstr.; Telebase; Women Stud. Abstr.

LC UNC GN1 .A77 **ISSN** 0271-0641
DD 301 US

ANTHROPOLOGICAL RESEARCH PAPER. [Antropol. res. pap.]. **Added/Corp** Arizona State University. **VFOAT** Anthropological Research Papers; ARP. No. 1 (1969)-. Monographic series. English (Spanish and French). Irregular (1 to 3 per year). Price varies per volume. Arizona State University / Department of Anthropology, Tempe AZ 85287. **Tel** (602)965-7596. **ED** GA Clark. cum. index. **Circ:** 1,000.

ISSN 0918-7960
JA

●**ANTHROPOLOGICAL SCIENCE : JOURNAL OF THE ANTHROPOLOGICAL SOCIETY OF NIPPON.** **Added/Corp** Nihon Jinrui Gakkai. **VFOAT** Journal of the Anthropological Society of Nippon; Jinruigaku Zasshi. Vol. 101, No. 1 (Jan. 1993)-. Periodical. English (Japanese). Four times a year. $150.00. Nippon Jinrui Gakkai, (Anthropological Soc. of Nippon), Nihon Gakkai Jimu Senta, 4-16 Yayoi 2 Chome, Bunkyoku Tokyo 113 Japan. **(Subscription address:** Japan Publications Trading Company Ltd., PO Box 5030, Tokyo International, Tokyo 100-31 Japan. **Tel** 011 81 3 3292 3753.**)** ***Continues*** *Jinruigaku Zasshi.*
Ind/Abst Anthropol. Lit.; Soc. Sci. Cit. Index [Full Cov.].

US

ANTHROPOLOGICAL SERIES. **Main/Corp** Pennsylvania. Historical and Museum Commission. No. 1 (1971)-. Monographic series. English. Price varies per volume. Pennsylvania Historical and Museum Commission, Box 1026, Harrisburg PA 17108. **Tel** (717)787-9123, FAX (717)783-1073. Index available.
Desc: Study on anthology of Pennsylvania anthropology, archaeology or Indian history.

LC GN301 .C34 ISSN 0702-8997
DD 301/.05 CN

ANTHROPOLOGIE ET SOCIETES.

[Anthropol. soc.]. **Added/Corp** Universite Laval. Departement d'Anthropologie. Vol. 1, No 2 (1977)-. Monographic series. French (English). Irregular. 56.02Can$. Anthropologie et Societes, University of Laval, Department d'Anthropologie, Sainte-Foy Quebec G1K 7P4 Canada. **Tel** (418)656-3027, (416)656-3700, FAX (418)656-3284. Index available. cum. index. **Bk Rev**. **Ad Acc**. **Circ:** 1,200. ***Continues*** *Cahiers d'Anthropologie de l'Universite Laval, 0704-7967.*
Desc: A journal open to all approaches in general anthropology whose main objective is to represent Quebec interests in anthropology.
Ind/Abst Anthropol. Index; Anthropol. Lit.; Curr. Contents Soc. Behav. Sci.; Ethnoarts Index; Repere (1983-).

ISSN 0003-553X
SZ

ANTHROPOLOGIE : INTERNATIONAL JOURNAL FOR THE SCIENCE OF MAN.

(19??)-. Academic Scholarly Publication. English (French). Three times a year. $108.00. **(Subscription address:** Karger Libri AG, Petersgraben 31, CH 4009 Basel 11 Switzerland. **Tel** 011 41 61 3061500.**)** Documents available from The Genuine Article.
Ind/Abst Anthropol. Lit.; Arts Humanit. Citation Index [Select. Cov.]; Res. Alert [Full Cov.]; Soc. Sci. Cit. Index [Full Cov.].

ISSN 0758-5683
FR

ANTHROPOLOGIE MARITIME.

(ANTHROPOLOGIE MARITIME / CENTRE D'ETHNO-TECHNOLOGIE EN MILIEUX AQUATIQUES.). [Anthropol. marit.]. Bulletin No. 1 (1984)-. Periodical. French.
Ind/Abst Anthropol. Lit.

ISSN 0003-5521
FR
CCC
NLM W1 AN849B CODEN ATRPAR
Pr Rev.

ANTHROPOLOGIE (PARIS).

(L'ANTHROPOLOGIE.). [Anthropologie]. Vol. 1 (1890)-. Periodical. French. Four times a year. $301.00. Masson Editeur, BP 22, 41354 Vineuil Cedex France. **Tel** 011 33 54 504612, FAX 011 33 54 504611. cum. index. **Bk Rev**. **Circ:** 30 (ctrl). available on microfilm and microfiche from University Microfilms International (UMI). Documents available from BIOSIS Document Express. ***Formed by the union of*** *Materiaux pour l'Histoire Primitive et Naturelle de l'Homme; Revue d'Anthropologie* ***and*** *Revue d'Ethnographie.*
Desc: Presents original works from outstanding French and foreign specialists on all the subjects of modern anthropology science.
Ind/Abst Abstr. Anthropol.; Anthropol. Lit.; Biol. Abstr.; EMBASE; GeoRef.

ISSN 0993-4871
FR
UDC 572

ANTHROPOLOGIE VISUELLE.

(1988)-. Monographic series. French. Irregular. 130.00F France; 205.00F other (latest issue). Editions de l'Ecole des Hautes Edude en Sciences Sociales, 131 Bd St. Michel, 75005 Paris France. **Tel** 011 33 1 43544715, FAX 011 33 1 43548073. **ED** Marc Auge and Jean-Paul Colleyn. **Circ:** 1,000.

LC GN1 .A69 ISSN 0003-5548
DD 573 GW
CCC
NLM Z 5112 A628

ANTHROPOLOGISCHER ANZEIGER.

[Anthropol. Anz.]. Vol. 1 (March 1924)-. Periodical. German. Four times a year. $245.00. E. Schweizerbartische Verlagsbuchhandlung, Johannesstrasse 3A, D-70176 Stuttgart Germany. **Tel** 011 49 711 625001, FAX 011 49 711 625005, telex 723363 SCHB D. **ED** H Walter and G Hauser. **Bk Rev**. **Ad Acc**. available on microfilm and microfiche from University Microfilms International (UMI).
Desc: Contains information on anthropology.
Ind/Abst Anthropol. Index; Anthropol. Lit.; EMBASE; Health Plan. Adminis.; Index Med.

LC GN1 .S66 ISSN 1061-1959
DD 301 US
CCC

ANTHROPOLOGY & ARCHEOLOGY OF EURASIA.

[Anthropol. archeol. Eurasia]. **VFOAT** Anthropology and Archeology of Eurasia. Vol. 31, No. 1 (Summer 1992)-. Periodical. English (translations available in Russian). Four times a year. $381.00 US; $421.00 other. M. E. Sharpe Inc., 80 Business Park Drive, Armonk NY 10504. **Tel** (914)273-1800, (800)541-6563, FAX (914)273-2106. ***Continues*** *Soviet Anthropology and Archeology, 0038-528X.*
Ind/Abst Anthropol. Index; Curr. Contents Soc. Behav. Sci.; Soc. Sci. Cit. Index [Full Cov.].

ISSN 0161-7761
US
Pr Rev.

ANTHROPOLOGY & EDUCATION QUARTERLY.

[Anthropol. educ. q.]. **Added/Corp** Council on Anthropology and Education. **VAT** Anthropology and Education Quarterly. Vol. 7, No. 3 (Aug. 1976)-. Periodical. English. Four times a year. $60.00. American Anthropological Association, 4350 North Fairfax Dr, Suite 640, Arlington VA 22203. **Tel** (703)528-1902 ext. 3031, FAX (703)528-3546. **ED** Henry T. Trueba and Lyle Green. **Bk Rev**. **Ad Acc**. **Circ:** 1,400 (ctrl). available on microfilm and microfiche from University Microfilms International (UMI). Documents available from The Genuine Article. ***Continues*** *Council on Anthropology and Education Quarterly, 0098-2881;* ***Absorbed*** *Newsletter - Council on Anthropology and Education.*
Desc: Articles on anthropological research in education as well as discussions of educational development and the teaching of anthropology.
Ind/Abst Abstr. Anthropol.; Acad. Search; Anthropol. Index; Anthropol. Lit.; Arts Humanit. Citation Index [Select. Cov.]; Contents Pages Educ.; Curr. Cit.; Curr. Contents Soc. Behav. Sci.; Curr. Index J. Educ.; Educ. Index; EP Collect.; Gen. Sci. Source; Homework Help.; INFO-SOUTH Abstr.; Linguist. Lang. Behav. Abstr.; Mag. Search; MasterFile FullTEXT 1000; MasterFile FullTEXT 350; MasterFile FullTEXT 650; MasterFile FullTEXT (Jan. 1994-); Middle East Abstr. Index; Multicult. Educ. Abstr.; OCLC; Psychol. Abstr. (1985-); PsycINFO; PsycLit; Res. Alert [Full Cov.]; School Organ. Manage. Abstr.; Soc. Plann. Policy Dev. Abstr.; Soc. Sci. Cit. Index [Full Cov.]; Sociol. Abstr.; Sociol. Educ. Abstr.; Spec. Educ. Needs Abstr.; Telebase.

LC GN1 .A6955
US

•ANTHROPOLOGY AND HUMANISM.

Added/Corp Society for Humanistic Anthropology. Vol. 18, No. 1 (June 1993)-. Periodical. English. Two times a year. American Anthropological Association, 4350 North Fairfax Dr, Suite 640, Arlington VA 22203. **Tel** (703)528-1902 ext. 3031, FAX (703)528-3546. **ED** Miles Richardson. cum. index. **Bk Rev**. **Ad Acc**. **Circ:** 179. available on microfilm and microfiche. ***Continues*** *Anthropology and Humanism Quarterly, 0193-5615.*

LC Z5112 .I57 ISSN 0960-1511
UK
CEASED

ANTHROPOLOGY AND RELATED DISCIPLINES / INTERNATIONAL CURRENT AWARENESS SERVICES.

Added/Corp International Current Awareness Services. British Library of Political and Economic Science. **VFOAT** Anthropology. Vol. 1, No. 1 (Nov. 1990)-(March 1994). English. Routledge, 11 New Fetter Lane, London EC4P 4EE United Kingdom. **Tel** 011 44 171 5839855, FAX 011 44 171 5830701. **(Subscription address:** Kinokuniya Company Ltd., 38-1 Sakuragaoka 5, chome Setagaya-ku, Tokyo 156 Japan. **Tel** FAX 011 03 3439 0136.**)**

LC GN325 .A53
DD 306 US

ANTHROPOLOGY (GUILFORD, CONN.).

(ANTHROPOLOGY.). **VFOAT** Annual Editions. (1982)-. Periodical. English. One time a year. $12.95. Dushkin Publishing Group Inc., Sluice Dock, Guilford CT 06437. **Tel** (203)453-4351, (800)243-6532, FAX (203)453-6000. **ED** Elvio Angeloni. ***Continues*** *Annual Editions. Readings in Anthropology, 0095-5582.*
Desc: Collection of articles providing anthropological perspectives on a range of world cultures.
Ind/Abst Middle East Abstr. Index.

LC GN2 .A227 ISSN 0098-1605
DD 301.2/05 US

ANTHROPOLOGY NEWSLETTER.

Added/Corp American Anthropological Association. American Anthropological Association. Newsletter. **VFOAT** Newsletter - American Anthropological Association. Vol. 15, No. 7, Sept. (1974)-. Newsletter. English. Irregular (9 issues). $75.00. American Anthropological Association, 4350 North Fairfax Dr, Suite 640, Arlington VA 22203. **Tel** (703)528-1902 ext. 3031, FAX (703)528-3546. **ED** David Givens. **Ad Acc**. **Circ:** 10,000 (ctrl). ***Continues*** *American Anthropological Association Newsletter of the American Anthropological Association.*
Desc: News on association affairs, departments and people, jobs, grants, brief research reports, announcements, a meeting and seminar calendar, and the Association's annual report.

ISSN 1053-4202
DD 128 US

ANTHROPOLOGY OF CONSCIOUSNESS.

(ANTHROPOLOGY OF CONSCIOUSNESS / SOCIETY FOR THE ANTHROPOLOGY OF CONSCIOUSNESS.). [Anthropol. conscious.]. **Added/Corp** American Anthropological Association. Society for the Anthropology of Consciousness (U.S.). Vol. 1, No. 1-2 (Mar./June 1990)-. Periodical. English. Four times a year. $40.00 (institutions), $38.00 (individuals). American Anthropological Association, 4350 North Fairfax Dr, Suite 640, Arlington VA 22203. **Tel** (703)528-1902 ext. 3031, FAX (703)528-3546. ***Continues*** *AASC Quarterly, 1045-4330.*
Ind/Abst Except. Hum. Exp.

ISSN 0066-4715
CN

ANTHROPOLOGY OF THE NORTH.

(ANTHROPOLOGY OF THE NORTH : TRANSLATIONS FROM RUSSIAN SOURCES.). **Added/Corp** Arctic Institute of North America. No. 1 (1961)-. Monographic series. English. Irregular. Price varies per volume. Arctic Institute of North America, University of Calgary, 2500 University Drive Northwest, Calgary Alberta T2N 1N4 Canada. **Tel** (403)220-7515, FAX (403)282-4609.

LC GN448.5 .A57 ISSN 0883-024X
DD 306.3/05 US
CODEN AWORE9

ANTHROPOLOGY OF WORK REVIEW.

(ANTHROPOLOGY OF WORK REVIEW : AWR.). [Anthropol. work rev.]. **Added/Corp** Society for the Anthropology of Work (U.S.). **VFOAT** AWR; National Directory of Work Anthropologists. Vol. 4, No. 1 (Feb. 1983)-. Periodical. English. Four times a year. $18.00. American Anthropological Association, 4350 North Fairfax Dr, Suite 640, Arlington VA 22203. **Tel** (703)528-1902 ext. 3031, FAX (703)528-3546. **ED** Mika and Herbert Applebaum. **Bk Rev**. **Ad Acc**. **Circ:** 325. ***Continues*** *Anthropology of Work Newsletter.*
Desc: Devoted to the study and research on the subject of work, from a cross-cultural, anthropological perspective.

IS

ANTHROPOLOGY OF YIDDISH FOLKSONGS.

See Music.

LC GN1 .R69 ISSN 0268-540X
DD 306/.05 UK
Pr Rev.

ANTHROPOLOGY TODAY.

[Anthropol. today]. **Added/Corp** Royal Anthropological Institute of Great Britain and Ireland. Vol. 1, No. 1 (Feb. 1985)-. Periodical. English. Six times a year (Feb., Apr., June, Aug., Oct., Dec.). $49.00. Royal Anthropological Institute, 50 Fitzroy Street, London W1P 5HS United Kingdom. **Tel** 011 44 171 3870455. **(Subscription address:** Turpin Distribution Services Limited, Blackhorse Road, Letchworth, Hertfordshire SH6 1HN United Kingdom. **Tel** 011 44 1462 672555, FAX 011 44 1462 480947.**) ED** Jonathan Benthall and Gustaaf Houtman. **Ad Acc**. **Circ:** 2,300. available on microfilm and microfiche from University Microfilms International (UMI). ***Continues*** *Royal Anthropological Institute News, 0307-6776.*
Desc: Aims for the professional anthropologist, with special emphasis on public and topical aspects of anthropology. Reviews of conferences, correspondence and news sections are included.
Ind/Abst Anthropol. Index; Br. Archaeol. Bibliogr.; Curr. Cit.; Geogr. Abstr. Human Geogr. (?-?); Linguist. Lang. Behav. Abstr.; Soc. Plann. Policy Dev. Abstr.; Sociol. Abstr.

ISSN 0003-5564
DD 301 US

ANTHROPOLOGY UCLA.

[Anthropol. UCLA]. **Added/Corp** University of California, Los Angeles. Anthropology Graduate Students Association. University of California, Los Angeles. Dept. of Anthropology. University of California, Los Angeles. Dept. of Anthropology. Graduate Students Association. **VFOAT** Anthropology UCLA. **VAT** Anthropology University of California, Los Angeles. Vol. 1, No. 1 (Jan. 1969)-. Monographic series. English. Irregular (1 or 2 per year). $15.00. Anthropology UCLA, Haines Hall Room 341, University of California, Los Angeles, Los Angeles CA 90024. **Tel** (310)825-2055. **ED** Ari Nave. **Circ:** 300.
Desc: Devoted to the scholarly writings of UCLA anthropology graduate students and faculty in all subfields of anthropology.
Ind/Abst Abstr. Anthropol. (19??-); Anthropol. Lit. (-Vol. 10, 1988); Int. Bibliogr. Sociol.; Middle East Abstr. Index.

LC GN1 .A698
GR

ANTHROPOS.

Vol. 1, No. 1 (1974)-. English (Greek, Modern). Irregular. $50.00. Anthropologike Hetaireia/Tes Hellados/ Greece Anthropological Society, Daphnomili 5, Athens 114 71 Greece. **Tel** 011 30 1 3610251. **ED** Aris N. Poulianos. Index available. cum. index. **Bk Rev**. **Circ:** 2,000. Documents available from The Genuine Article.
Desc: Emphasis is mainly on physical anthropology, world ethnography and prehistoric archaeology.
Ind/Abst Anthropol. Lit.; Appl. Soc. Sci. Index Abstr.; Arts Humanit. Citation Index [Select. Cov.]; Bibliogr. Mission.; Curr. Contents Soc. Behav. Sci.; Index Book Rev. Relig.; Int. Dev. Abstr. (?-?); Res. Alert [Full Cov.]; Soc. Sci. Cit. Index [Full Cov.].

LC GN1 .A7
AU

ANTHROPOS.

See Linguistics.

ISSN 0257-9774
SZ
Pr Rev.

ANTHROPOS FRIBOURG.

(1906)-. Miscellaneous (English, French and German). Two times a year. $197.94. Editions Saint Paul Paulus Verlag,

Anthropology

Boulevard de Perolles 42, CH-1700 Fribourg Switzerland. **Tel** 011 41 37 864331, **FAX** 011 41 37 864330. Index available. **Bk Rev. Ad Acc. Circ:** 800.
 Desc: Articles on anthropology, ethnographie, linguistics, and the science of religion.

DD 572   **ISSN** 0503-8413
VE
ANTROPOLOGIA. Main/Corp Venezuela. Universidad Central, Caracas. Instituto de Antropologia e Historia. Vol. 1 (1954)-. Spanish. Irregular. Instituto Caribe de Antropologia y Geografia, Apartado Postal 1930, Caracas 1010-A Venezuela. **Continues** *Venezuela. Universidad Central, Caracas. Instituto de Antropologia y Geografia.*

ISSN 1131-5814
SP
ANTROPOLOGIA. Added/Corp Asociacion Madrilena de Antropologia. No. 1 (Oct. 1991)-. Periodical. Spanish (summaries and/or abstracts in English). Two times a year. 5000ptas Spain; 7700ptas other Europe; 8200ptas other. Grupo Antropologia, Duque de Osuna, 8 Int 3 Izda, 28015 Madrid Spain. **Tel** 011 34 1 5592654.

LC F3319 .A56
DD 985/.005   BO
ANTROPOLOGIA. VFOAT Revista del Instituto Nacional de Antropologia. Vol. 1 (1979)-. Periodical. Spanish. Instituto Nacional De Antropologia, La Paz Bolivia.

LC GN1 .A73
DD 306/.05   IT
Pr Rev.
ANTROPOLOGIA CONTEMPORANEA.
Added/Corp Unione Antropologica Italiana. Federazione delle Istituzioni Antropologiche Italiane. **VFOAT** Italian Journal of Anthropology. Vol. 1, No. 1 (1978)-. Periodical. Italian (summaries and/or abstracts in English). Four times a year. L75000. Karta Sas, Via Slataper 10, 50134 Florence Italy. **Tel** 011 39 55 496502. Index available in last issue of volume-attached. **Bk Rev. Circ:** 500.
 Desc: Provides information on anthropology and physical anthropology.
 Ind/Abst Anthropol. Lit.

ISSN 0518-0678
CL
ANTROPOLOGIA FISICA CHILENA / UNIVERSIDAD DE CHILE, CENTRO DE ESTUDIOS ANTROPOLOGICOS.
Added/Corp Universidad de Chile. Centro de Estudios Antropol,ogicos. (No. 1, 1960)-. Periodical. Spanish.

ISSN 0393-9081
IT
NLM W1; AN897UD
ANTROPOLOGIA MEDICA : AM. [Antropol. med.]. **VFOAT** AM. Vol. 1 (May 1986)-. Periodical. Italian (English and French). Two times a year. Grafo Edizioni, Via A Bassi 10, 25123 Brescia Italy. **Tel** 011 39 30 393221, FAX 011 39 30 307397.
 Ind/Abst Anthropol. Lit.

LC F1219 .M6248
MX
ANTROPOLOGIA (MEXICO CITY, MEXICO). (ANTROPOLOGIA : BOLETIN OFICIAL DEL INSTITUTO NACIONAL DE ANTROPOLOGIA E HISTORIA.). No. 1 (Jan./Feb. 1985)-. Periodical. Spanish. Six times a year. Direccion de Publicaciones, Cordoba 45, Col Roma, Mexico City Mexico. **Continues** *Antropologia e Historia, 0185-142X.*

LC GN1 .A733   **ISSN** 0870-0990
DD 306   PO
ANTROPOLOGIA PORTUGUESA.
[Antropol. port.]. Vol. 1 (1983)-. Portuguese (summaries and/or abstracts in English). One time a year. Instituto de Antropologia, Universidade de Coimbra, 3000 Coimbra Portugal. **Continues** *Contribuicoes Para o Estudo da Antropologia Portuguesa, 0374-6836.*
 Ind/Abst Anthropol. Lit.

LC GN1 .A735
SP
CEASED
ANTROPOLOGIA Y ETNOLOGIA.
Added/Corp Spain. Consejo Superior de Investigaciones Cientificas. Instituto Bernardino de Sahagun. (1949)-(1995). Spanish. Consejo Superior Investigacion Cientifica / CSIC, Vitruvio 8, 28006 Madrid Spain. **Tel** 011 34 1 5612833, FAX 011 34 1 4113077, telex 42182.
 Desc: Information on anthropology and ethnology.

LC GN1 .A628
SP
ANTROPOLOGIA Y PALEOECOLOGIA HUMANA / LABORATORIO DE ANTROPOLOGIA, UNIVERSIDAD DE GRANADA Y PATRONATO CUEVA DEL AGUA, EXCMA. DIPUTACION PROVINCIAL. No. 1 (1979)-. Periodical. Spanish (Spanish). Universidad de Granada y Patronato Cueva del Agua, Laboratorio de Antropologia, Granada Spain.
 Ind/Abst Anthropol. Lit.

ISSN 0186-9787
MX
ANTROPOLOGIA Y TECNICA. (1981)-.
Periodical. Spanish (English). Irregular. UNAM - Universidad Nacional Autonoma de Mexico / Filosofia, Facultad de Filosofia y Letras, Apartado 70 447, 04510 Mexico DF Mexico. **Tel** 011 52 5 5505215, FAX 011 52 5 6654991.
 Ind/Abst Anthropol. Lit.

LC F2229 .A65   **ISSN** 0003-6110
DD 306/.08998   VE
Pr Rev.
ANTROPOLOGICA. No. 1 (Sept. 1956)-.
Periodical. Spanish (English and French). Two times a year. Bs200.00 Venezuela; $25.00 other. Instituto Caribe de Antropologia Sociologia, Apartado Postal 1930, Caracas 1010-A Venezuela. **Tel** 782.87.11, FAX 781 5732, telex 21553 FLASA VC. **ED** Werner Wilbert. Index available (No. 1-62). cum. index (No. 1-62). **Bk Rev. Ad Acc. Circ:** 1,000.
 Desc: Original contributions on the anthropology of Venezuela and neighbouring countries (Columbia, Brazil, Guyana, Meso America to the Equator).
 Ind/Abst Abstr. Anthropol.; Anthropol. Index; Ethnoarts Index; Hisp. Am. Period. Index, HAPI.

LC GN301 .A577   **ISSN** 0345-0902
DD 306/.05   SW
ANTROPOLOGISKA STUDIER. Added/Corp
Antropologforeningen (Stockholms Universitet). (1971)-. Periodical. English (Swedish). Four times a year. Kr60.00. Socialantropologiska Institutionen, Stockholms Universitet, Stockholm Sweden. **Continues** *Antropologynytt.*
 Ind/Abst Anthropol. Lit.

LC GN301 .A58
DD 301.2/05   BL
ANUARIO ANTROPOLOGICO. (1976)-.
Portuguese. One time a year. $150.00. Edicoes Tempo Brasileiro Ltd, R Gago Coutinho 61/Laranjeiras, Rio de Janeiro RJ Brazil. **Tel** 011 55 21 2055949. **ED** Franco Portella. cum. index. **Ad Acc. Circ:** 2,000 (ctrl).
 Ind/Abst Anthropol. Lit.

US
APLA NEWSLETTER. See Law.

LC GN   **ISSN** 0287-8429
DD 301   JA
NLM W1; AN62H
●**APPLIED HUMAN SCIENCE : JOURNAL OF PHYSIOLOGICAL ANTHROPOLOGY.**
Added/Corp Nihon Seiri Jinruigakkai. **VFOAT** Journal of Physiological Anthropology. Vol. 14, No. 1 (Jan. 1995)-. Periodical. English. Research Society of Physiological Anthropology, Department of Ergonomics, Faculty of Engineering, Chiba University 1-33 Yayoi-Cho, Chiba 260 Japan. **Continues** *Annals of Physiological Anthropology, 0287-8429.*
 Ind/Abst Index Med. (1995-).

SZ
ARBEITSBLATTER / SEMINAR FUER ETHNOLOGIE, UNIVERSITAET BERN.
Added/Corp Universitat Bern. Institut fuer Ethnologie. Universitat Bern. Seminar fuer Ethnologie. (1988)-. Monographic series. German. Irregular. Price varies per volume. Institut fuer Ethnologie / Universitat Bern, Langabstr 49A, CH-3000 Bern 9 Switzerland. **Tel** 011 41 31 658995.

LC CC75 .A66   **ISSN** 0003-813X
DD 930/.1/028   UK
    CODEN ARCHAG
Pr Rev.
ARCHAEOMETRY. See Archaeology.

GW
ARCHAOLOGISCHE BERICHTE / HERAUSGEGEBEN VON DER DEUTSCHEN GESELLSCHAFT FUER UR- UND FRUHGESCHICHTE. See
Archaeology.

LC WMLC 93/3209 CC75.7 .A72   **ISSN** 0891-2920
DD 930   US
    CODEN ARCMEZ
Pr Rev.   CEASED
ARCHEOMATERIALS. See Archaeology.

LC GR1 .A59   **ISSN** 0066-6513
AU
ARCHIV FUER VOLKERKUNDE.
Added/Corp Museum fuer Voelkerkunde (Austria) Verein "Freunde der Voelkerkunde" (Austria). Vol. 1 (1946)-. Periodical. German (English and Spanish). One time a year. S415.00. Verein Freunde der Volkerkunde, Museum fuer Volkerkunde, Neue Hofburg A-1014 Vienna Austria. **Tel** 011 43 1 521770. **ED** Christian F. Feest and Alfred Janata. **Bk Rev. Ad Acc. Circ:** 400.
 Desc: Material culture, non-European art and museum studies.
 Ind/Abst Anthropol. Index; Anthropol. Lit.; Ethnoarts Index.

LC GN1 .A8   **ISSN** 0373-3009
IT
NLM W1 AR596S
ARCHIVIO PER L'ANTROPOLOGIA E LA ETNOLOGIA. Vol. 1 (1871)-. Italian (English). One time a year. L140000 Italy; L180000 other. Soc Italiana Antropologia Ftno, via del Proconsolo 12, 50128 Firenze Italy. **Tel** 055/2396449. **Bk Rev. Ad Acc.** ctrl circ.
 Ind/Abst Anthropol. Index; Anthropol. Lit.

LC F1221.N3 A73
DD 972/.005   MX
ARCHIVOS DE INFORMACION SOBRE EL IDIOMA Y LA CULTURA DE LOS NAHUAS. Spanish.

LC DU122.L3 .A73   **ISSN** 0570-720X
AT
    CEASED
ARCHIVS. [Archivs]. **Added/Corp** Latviesu Apvieniba Australija. Zinatnes Nozare. Karla Zarina Fonds. Australijas Latviesu Centralais Archivs. Pasaules Brivo Latviesu Apvieniba. (1960)-Vol. 31 (1993). Latvian. World Federation of Free Latvians, Karla Zarina Fonds, 3 Dickens Street, Elwood Victoria 3184 Australia.
 Ind/Abst MLA Int. Bibl. Books Artic. Mod. Lang. Lit.

LC G600 .A6955   **ISSN** 0066-6939
US
    CCC
    CODEN ARANBP
Pr Rev.
ARCTIC ANTHROPOLOGY. [Arct. anthropol.].
Vol. 1 (1962)-. Periodical. English. Two times a year. $87.00. University of Wisconsin Press, Journal Division, 114 North Murray Street, Madison WI 53715. **Tel** (608)262-4952, FAX (608)262-8909. **Ad Acc, Adv Mgr Tel** (608)262-5839. available on microfilm and microfiche from University Microfilms International (UMI). Documents available from The Genuine Article, BIOSIS Document Express.
 Desc: Publishes all aspects of the science of man in the arctic, subarctic and continuous regions of the world.
 Ind/Abst ASTIS Curr. Aware. Bull. (1978-); Abstr. Anthropol.; Acad. Search; Am. Hist. Life (1970-1972, 1982-); Am. Bibliogr. Slavic East Europ. Stud.; Anthropol. Index; Anthropol. Lit.; ASTIS Bibliogr. (1978-); Biol. Abstr.; Curr. Contents Soc. Behav. Sci.; EP Collect.; Ethnoarts Index; Geogr. Abstr. Phys. Geogr.; Geogr. Abstr. Human Geogr.; GeoRef; Homework Help.; INFO-SOUTH Abstr.; Int. Dev. Abstr.; Mag. Search; MasterFile FullTEXT 1000; MasterFile FullTEXT 350; MasterFile FullTEXT 650; MasterFile FullTEXT (July 1993-); OCLC; Res. Alert [Full Cov.]; Soc. Sci. Cit. Index [Full Cov.]; Telebase.

LC DK511.L15 A7   **ISSN** 0570-6343
DD 947   LV
ARHEOLOGIJA UN ETNOGRAFIJA. See
Archaeology.

ISSN 1062-1601
DD 301   US
Pr Rev.
ARIZONA ANTHROPOLOGIST. (ARIZONA ANTHROPOLOGIST : PAPERS OF THE UNIVERSITY OF ARIZONA DEPARTMENT OF ANTHROPOLOGY.). [Ariz. anthropol.]. **Added/Corp** University of Arizona. Dept. of Anthropology. University of Arizona. Anthropology Students Assoc. No. 7 (1991)-. Periodical. English. One time a year (fall). $10.00. University of Arizona / Arizona Anthropologist, Department of Anthropology, Building 30, Tuscon AZ 85721. **Tel** (602)621-2796, (602)621-1955, FAX (602)621-3816, telex 1561507 ARID UT. **ED** Louise M. Senior. **Bk Rev**, (Qty: 2). **Circ:** 200. **Continues** *Atlatl, 0275-3553.*
 Desc: Contains papers written on theoretical concerns by members of the Department of Anthropology at the University of Arizona and original research in anthropology, archaeology, and related disciplines.
 Ind/Abst Abstr. Anthropol.

ISSN 0518-6617
US
ARKANSAS AMATEUR, THE. See
Archaeology.

LC GN301 .G68A   **ISSN** 0436-2020
SW
ARSTRYCK - GOTEBORGS ETNOGRAFISKA MUSEUM. Main/Corp
Goteborgs Ethografiska Museum. **VFOAT** Annual Report - Ethnographical Museum, Gothenburg, Sweden. Swedish (English and Spanish). One time a year. Kr10.00. Goteborgs Etnografiska Museum, Norra Hamngatan 12, S411 14 Goteborg Sweden. **Tel** 011 46 31 612776, FAX 011 46 31 741059.
 Ind/Abst Anthropol. Lit.; Ethnoarts Index.

Anthropology

Pr Rev.
ISSN 0044-9075
AT
ARTEFACT, THE. See Archaeology.

ISSN 0212-0372
SP
ARXIU D'ETNOGRAFIA DE CATALUNYA. **Added/Corp** Facultad de Filosofia y Letras de Tarragona. Departament d'Antropologia Cultural. Institut Catala d'Antropologia. (1982)-. Periodical. Catalan (Spanish, French and English). One time a year. $15.55. Universitat Rovira i Virgili, Placa Imperial Tarraco 1, 43071 Tarragona Spain. **Tel** 011 34 77 559770.

US
ASA MONOGRAPHS. (19??)-. English. Irregular. Routledge Chapman & Hall Inc., 29 West 35th Street, New York NY 10001. **Tel** (212)244-3336, (212)244-6412.
 Ind/Abst Leis., Rec.; Tour. Abstr.; Rural Dev. Abstr.; World Agric. Econ. Rural Sociol. Abstr.

ISSN 0272-0566
US
ASA STUDIES. [ASA stud.]. **Main/Corp** Association of Social Anthropologists of the Commonwealth. **VAT** Association of Social Anthropologists of the Commonwealth Studies. Monographic series. English. Price varies per volume. John Wiley & Sons, Inc., 605 Third Avenue, New York NY 10158-0012. **Tel** (212)850-6000, (212)850-6645, FAX (212)850-6088, telex 12-7063. **(Subscription address:** John Wiley & Sons / UK, Baffins Lane, Chichester, West Sussex PO19 1UD United Kingdom. **Tel** 011 44 1243 779777, FAX 011 44 243 776128, telex 86290 WIBOOKG.**)**

ISSN 0587-1964
US
ASAO MONOGRAPH. **Main/Corp** Association for Social Anthropology in Oceania. **VFOAT** Monograph Series - Association for Social Anthropology in Oceania. **VAT** Association for Social Anthropology in Oceania Monograph. No. 1-. Monographic series. English. Irregular. Price varies per volume. University of Pittsburgh Press, 127 North Bellefield Avenue, Pittsburgh PA 15260. **Tel** (412)624-4110.
 Ind/Abst Soc. Plann. Policy Dev. Abstr.; Sociol. Abstr. (?-?).

LC DS514 .A78
DD 950/.05
ISSN 0066-8435
US
ASIAN PERSPECTIVES (HONOLULU). See Archaeology.

LC DU744 .A75
DD 301.29/95/1
US
ASMAT SKETCH BOOK, AN. (1970)-. English. Irregular. $3.50. Asmat Museum of Culture & Progress, 3204 East 43rd Street, Minneapolis MN 55406. **Tel** (612)722-2223. **ED** Frank Trenkenshuh. ctrl circ.
 Desc: Focuses on the Asmat people.

ISSN 0993-538X
FR
UDC 3
ATELIER ASEMI. **VFOAT** Atelier Asie du Sud-Est et le Monde Insulindien. (1988)-. Monographic series. French. Irregular. CID, 131 boulevard Saint Michel, 75005 Paris France. **Tel** 011 33 1 43544715, FAX 011 33 1 43548073. **Circ:** 500.

LC GN1 .A96
DD 301/.05
ISSN 1035-8811
AT
CODEN AJANE6
AUSTRALIAN JOURNAL OF ANTHROPOLOGY, THE. **Added/Corp** Anthropological Society of New South Wales. **VFOAT** TAJA; T.A.J.A. (1990)-. Periodical. English. Three times a year (Apr., Aug., Sept). 80.00Aus$ Australia; 90.00Aus$ other. Anthropological Society of New South Wales, University of Sydney, Department of Anthropology, Sydney New South Wales 2006, Australia. **Tel** 61 2 6922360. **ED** Prof. M Allan. **Bk Rev**, (Qty: each issue). **Ad Acc. Circ:** 700 (ctrl). available on microfilm and microfiche from University Microfilms International (UMI). Documents available from UMI Article Clearinghouse. **Continues** Mankind, 0025-2328.
 Ind/Abst Acad. Search; Anthropol. Lit.; APAIS, Aust. Public Aff. Inf. Ser. (1990-); EP Collect.; Expand. Acad. Index (1990-); Homework Help.; Humanit. Source; Linguist. Lang. Behav. Abstr.; MasterFile FullTEXT 1000; MasterFile FullTEXT 350; MasterFile FullTEXT 650; MasterFile FullTEXT (Jan. 1992-); Newsp. Period. Abstr. (1991-); OCLC; Soc. Plann. Policy Dev. Abstr.; Soc. Sci. Source; Soc. Sci. Index; Soc. Sci. Index Fulltext (1990-) [Full Txt.]; Sociol. Abstr.; Telebase; World Mag. Bank.

LC GN1 .B3
DD 573
ISSN 0005-3856
GW
CCC
BAESSLER-ARCHIV. **Added/Corp** Baessler Institut. Museum fuer Voelkerkunde (Germany). Museum fuer Voelkerkunde (Germany : West). (1910)-. Periodical. German. Two times a year (semiannual). DM158.00. Dietrich Reimer Verlag, Unter den Eichen 57, D-12203 Berlin Germany. **Tel** 011 49 30 8314081, FAX 011 49 30 831623.

GW
BAESSLER-ARCHIV; BEITRAEGE ZUR VOELKERKUNDE. BEIHEFT. (1911)-. Monographic series. German (English, French and Spanish). Irregular. Price varies per volume. Dietrich Reimer Verlag, Unter den Eichen 57, D-12203 Berlin Germany. **Tel** 011 49 30 8314081, FAX 011 49 30 831623. **ED** D. Eisleb and K. Helfrich. cum. index. **Ad Acc.**
 Ind/Abst Anthropol. Index; Anthropol. Lit.; Ethnoarts Index.

LC GN836.A73 B35
DD 936.6/01/05
SP
BAJO ARAGON, PREHISTORIA. **Added/Corp** Grupo Cultural Caspolino. (1979)-. Periodical. Spanish. Grupa Cultural Caspolino, Spain.
 Ind/Abst Anthropol. Lit.

US
BALLENA PRESS ANTHROPOLOGICAL PAPERS. **VFOAT** Anthropological Papers. No. 1 (1973)-. Monographic series. English. Price varies per volume. Ballena Press, PO Box 3914, San Rafael CA 94902.

ISSN 0522-0033
GW
BAR VON BERLIN, DER. (DER BAR VON BERLIN : JAHRBUCH DES VEREINS FUER DIE GESCHICHTE BERLINS.). [Bar Berl.]. **Added/Corp** Verein Fur die Geschichte Berlins. Verein Fur die Geschichte Berlins. Jahrbuch. (1954)-. German. One time a year. **Continues** Jahrbuch des Vereins Fur die Geschichte Berlins.
 Ind/Abst BHA : Biblio. Hist. Art.

ISSN 0067-4478
DD 572
SZ
BASLER BEITRAEGE ZUR ETHNOLOGIE. Vol. 1 (1964)-. Monographic series. German. Irregular. Wepf and Company, Eisengasse 5, CH-4001 Basel Switzerland. **Tel** 011 41 61 257574, FAX 011 41 61 253597, telex 965532.

LC GN585.G4 B34
ISSN 0720-8006
GW
BAYERISCHE BLATTER FUER VOLKSKUNDE. **Added/Corp** Bayerische Julius-Maximilians-Universitat Wurzburg. Bayerisches Nationalmuseum. Arbeitsgruppe fuer Volkskunde und Kulturgeschichte. Bayerisches Nationalmuseum. **VFOAT** BBV. Vol. 1, No. 1 (April 1974)-. Periodical. German. Four times a year. DM30.00. Bayerische Blatter fuer Volkskunde, c/o Institut fuer Deutsche Philologie, Volkskundliche Abteilund, Universitaet Wuerzburg AmHubland, D-97074 Wuerzburg Germany. **Tel** 011 49 931 8885607, 011 49 931 8885608, FAX 011 49 931 8884616. **ED** Wolfgang Brueckner. **Bk Rev**, (Qty: 5-10). **Circ:** 900.

ISSN 0438-4679
GW
UDC 908.728
BEITRAEGE ZUR MITTELAMERIKANISCHEN VOLKSKUNDE. **Main/Corp** Hamburg. Museum fur Volkerkunde und Vorgeschichte. (1953)-. Monographic series. German. Irregular. Price varies per volume. Klaus Renner Fachbuchhdlg Verlag, Am Sonnenhang 8, D-82069 Hohenschftlrn Germany.

SZ
BERICHT UEBER DAS BASLER MUSEUM FUER VOLKERKUNDE UND SCHWEIZERISCHE MUSEUM FUER VOLKSKUNDE FUER DAS JAHR ... . **Main/Corp** Museum fuer Volkerkunde und Schweizerische Museum fuer Volkskunde Basel. (194?)-. Irregular. Birkhaeuser Verlag Ag, Klosterberg 23, PO Box 133, CH-4010 Basel Switzerland. **Tel** 011 41 61 2717400, FAX 011 41 61 2717666, telex 963475 birk ch. **Continues** Museum fuer Volkerkunde und Schweizerisches Museum fuer Volkskunde. Bericht Uber das Basler Museum fuer Volkerkunde.
 Ind/Abst Anthropol. Lit.

LC GN49 .B47
ISSN 0216-7204
IO
BERKALA BIOANTHROPOLOGI INDONESIA. **VFOAT** Indonesian Journal of Bioanthropology. 1 (Dec. 1980)-. Periodical. English (Indonesian). Three times a year. Laboratorium Anthropologi Ragawi, Jurusan Ilmu-Ilmu Anatomi Fakultas Kedokteran, Universitas Gajah Mada Yogyakarta Indonesia.

LC Z7111 .B47 GN25
DD 016.301/05
ISSN 0896-8101
US
BIBLIOGRAPHIC GUIDE TO ANTHROPOLOGY AND ARCHAEOLOGY. See Archaeology.

DD 016
ISSN 0742-6844
US
BIBLIOGRAPHIES AND INDEXES IN ANTHROPOLOGY. See Anthropology-Abstracting, Bibliographies and Statistics.

LC GN585.R7 M86a
RM
BIHAREA. **Main/Corp** Muzeul Tarii Crisurilor. (19??)-. Romanian (summaries and/or abstracts in English and German). Muzeul Tarii Crisurilor, St. Stadionului Nr 2, Oradea Romania.
 Ind/Abst BHA : Biblio. Hist. Art.

LC DS611 .B5
ISSN 0006-2294
NE
CODEN BTTVE2
Pr Rev.
BIJDRAGEN TOT DE TAAL-, LAND- EN VOLKENKUNDE. [Bijdr. taal-, land- volkenkd.]. **Added/Corp** Koninklijk Instituut voor Taal-, Land- en Volkenkunde (Netherlands). **VFOAT** Anthropologica. Vol. 105 (1949)-. Periodical. Multiple languages (Dutch and English). Four times a year. $92.49. Royal Institute of Linguistics and Anthropology, PO Box 9515, 2300 RA Leiden, The Netherlands. **Tel** 011 31 71 272372, FAX 011 31 71 272638. **ED** H.J.M. Claessen. cum. index. **Bk Rev Circ:** 1,800. Documents available from The Genuine Article. **Continues** Bijdragen Tot de Taal-, Land- en Volkenkunde van Nederlandsch--Indie, 0006-2294.
 Desc: Focused mainly on the linguistics, anthropology and history of Southeast Asia (especially Indonesia).
 Ind/Abst Am. Hist. Life (1971-); Anthropol. Index; Anthropol. Lit.; Arts Humanit. Citation Index [Select. Cov.]; Curr. Contents Soc. Behav. Sci.; MLA Int. Bibl. Books Artic. Mod. Lang. Lit.; Res. Alert [Full Cov.]; Soc. Sci. Cit. Index [Full Cov.].

DD 301
ISSN 0893-3111
US
BISHOP MUSEUM BULLETIN IN ANTHROPOLOGY. [Bishop Mus. bull. anthropol.]. **Added/Corp** Bernice Pauahi Bishop Museum. **VFOAT** Bishop Museum Bulletins in Anthropology. Vol. 1 (1987)-. Bulletin. English. Irregular. Price varies per volume. Bishop Museum Press, 1525 Bernice Street, Honolulu HI 96817. **Tel** (808)847-3511, FAX (808)841-8968. **Continues in part** Bernice Pauahi Bishop Museum. Bernice P. Bishop Museum Bulletin, 0005-9439.

LC QH198.H3 B45
DD 996.9/005
ISSN 0893-1348
US
CODEN BMOPEC
BISHOP MUSEUM OCCASIONAL PAPERS. See Biology-Botany.

ISSN 0812-8405
AT
CEASED
BLACK VOICES. (1984)-(19??). English. James Cook University Social & Cultural Studies Department, Townsville Queensland 4811 Australia. **Tel** 011 61 77 814652.
 Ind/Abst APAIS, Aust. Public Aff. Inf. Ser. (1988-).

LC WMLC L 83/7785
ISSN 0532-260X
BL
BOLETIM DE ANTROPOLOGIA. **Added/Corp** Universidade do Ceara. Instituto de Antropologia. Vol. 1, No. 1 (1957)-. Bulletin. Portuguese. Universidade do Ceara / Instituto de Antropologia, 60000 Fortaleza Ceara Brazil.
 Ind/Abst Anthropol. Lit.

ISSN 0522-7291
BL
CODEN BMPAE6
BOLETIM DO MUSEU PARAENSE EMILIO GOELDI. SERIE ANTROPOLOGIA. [Bol. Mus. Para. Emilio Goeldi, Antropol.]. **VFOAT** Serie Antropologia. Vol. 1, No. 1 (June 1984)-. Bulletin. Portuguese. Two times a year. Documents available from BIOSIS Document Express. **Continues** Boletim do Museu Paraense Emilio Goeldi. Nova Serie, Antropologia, 0522-7291.
 Ind/Abst Anthropol. Lit.; Biol. Abstr.

LC GN2 .M4
DD 301.2/05
NLM W1 BO211
ISSN 0120-2510
CK
BOLETIN DE ANTROPOLOGIA. [Bol. antropol.]. **Added/Corp** Universidad de Antioquia. Universidad de Antioquia. Departamento de Antropologia. **VFOAT** Antropologia. (Sept. 1969)-. Periodical. Spanish. Universidad de Antioquia / Departamento de Publicaciones, Apartado 1226, Medellin Colombia. **Tel** 011 57 4 2631311, 011 57 4 2630011, FAX 011 57 4 2638282. **Bk Rev. Ad Acc. Circ:** 1,000 (ctrl). **Continues** Boletin del Instituto de Antropologia, 0374-6283.
 Desc: Publishes anthropological studies and news from

Anthropology

Colombia.
Ind/Abst Am. Hist. Life (1970-); Anthropol. Index; Anthropol. Lit.

LC E51 .B59   **ISSN** 0252-841X
DD 980/.005   MX
Pr Rev.
BOLETIN DE ANTROPOLOGIA AMERICANA. [Bol. antropol. am.]. **Added/Corp** Pan American Institute of Geography and History. (June 1980)-. Periodical. Spanish (English, Portuguese and French). Two times a year. $38.00. Instituto Panamericano de Geographico Historia, APDO 18879 Secretaria General, 11870 Mexico DF Mexico. **Tel** 011 52 5 2775888, 011 52 5 2775791, **FAX** 011 52 5 2716172. **ED** Felipe Bate. Index available. **Circ**: 1,000.
Supersedes Boletin Bibliografico de Antropologia Americana.
Desc: Publishes essays, studies and classical documents related to anthropology, archaeology, ethnohistory and ethnolinguistics in Latin America.
Ind/Abst Am. Hist. Life (1982-1986); Anthropol. Index; Anthropol. Lit.; Ethnoarts Index; Hisp. Am. Period. Index, HAPI; Int. Bibliogr. Sociol.

LC GN1 .M46A
    MX
BOLETIN DE LA ESCUELA DE CIENCIAS ANTROPOLOGICAS DE LA UNIVERSIDAD DE YUCATAN. **Main/Corp** Merida, Mexico. Universidad de Yucatan. Escuela de Ciencias Antropologicas. Year 1, No. 1- ; July 1973-. Periodical. Spanish. $15.00 US, $20.00 Europe. Calle 76 No 455-LL Por 41 Y, 43 Merida Yucatan Mexico. **Tel** 5-45-23. **ED** Alfredo Barrera Rubie. **Bk Rev**. **Ad Acc**. **Circ**: 1,000 (ctrl).
Desc: A journal related with prehispanic and modern Mayan culture of Yucatan and related areas.

LC QH301
DD 574   SP
BOLETIN DE LA SOCIEDAD ESPANOLA DE ANTROPOLOGIA BIOLOGICA.
Added/Corp Sociedad Espanola de Antropologia Biologica. (1980)-. Periodical. Spanish (English and French). One time a year. $14.70 Spain; $16.20 Europe and Pan-America; $16.70 other. Sociedad Espanola de Antropologia Biologica, Universidad Complutense, Departamento de Biologia, Madrid 28040 Spain. **Tel** 011 34 91 2439775. ctrl circ.
Desc: Covers physical anthropology, human evolution, prehistorical and historical anthropology, growth and development, biodemography, somatology, seric polymorphisms, dermatoglyphics, etc.
Ind/Abst Anthropol. Lit.

LC F2230.1.A7 B65   **ISSN** 0716-1530
DD 709/.8   CL
BOLETIN DEL MUSEO CHILENO DE ARTE PRECOLOMBINO. [Bol. Mus. Chil. Arte Precolomb.]. **Added/Corp** Museo Chileno de Arte Precolombino. No 1 (1986)-. Periodical. Spanish. One time a year. Price varies. Museo Chileno Arte Precolumbin, Casilla 3687, Bandera 361, Santiago Chile. **Tel** 011 56 2 6953851 6953627.
Ind/Abst Anthropol. Lit.

    MX
BOLETIN INFORMATIVO. **VFOAT** Boletin Informativo del Instituto de Antropologia. (19??)-. Periodical. Spanish. Instituto Nacional de Antropologia e Historia, Cordoba 4J 7DF Mexico.
Ind/Abst Anthropol. Lit.

    BO
BOLETIN LURATHA / INSTITUTO NACIONAL DE ANTROPOLOGIA. Vol. 4, No. 1 (July/Sept. 1982)-. Periodical. Spanish. Four times a year. Casilla de Correos, 7543 La Paz Bolivia.
Continues Luratha.

ISSN 0922-1433
NLM W1; BO707F   NE
BONES. See Archaeology.

LC DS646.3 .B69   **ISSN** 0006-7806
DD 915.98/3/033   US
BORNEO RESEARCH BULLETIN. See History-History of Asia.

ISSN 1055-7792
    US
BORNEO RESEARCH COUNCIL MONOGRAPH SERIES. **Added/Corp** Borneo Research Council. **VFOAT** BRC Monograph Series. (1991)-. Monographic series. English. Price varies per volume. Borneo Research Council, Inc, Department of Anthropology, College of William and Mary, Williamsburg VA 23185.

LC GN2 .G473
DD 306   SZ
BULLETIN ANNUEL / MUSEE D'ETHNOGRAPHIE DE LA VILLE DE GENEVE. **Added/Corp** Musee d'Ethnographie de la Ville de Geneve. **VFOAT** Bulletin du Musee d'Ethnographie; Bulletin. No. 12 (1969)-. Bulletin. French. One time a year. 18.00F Europe; 20.00F other. Musee d'Ethnographie, 65 67 boulevard Carl Vogt, CH-1205 Geneva Switzerland. **Tel** 011 41 22 3281218. **Continues** Bulletin Annuel (Musee et Institut d'Ethnographie de la Ville de Geneve).
Ind/Abst Anthropol. Lit.

LC GN   **ISSN** 1187-0826
DD 301   CN
BULLETIN / CASCA, CANADIAN ANTHROPOLOGY SOCIETY. [Bull. - Can. Anthropol. Soc.]. **Added/Corp** Canadian Anthropology Society. **VFOAT** CASCA Bulletin. **VAT** Bulletin - Societe Canadienne d'Anthropologie. (Fall 1989)-. Bulletin. English (French). Two times a year (Spring and Fall). 4.01Can$. Canadian Anthropology Society / CASCA, Department of Anthropology, 1455 Maisonneuve Boulevard West, Montreal Quebec LB617 1 Canada. **Tel** (514)848-4508. **Continues** Canadian Ethnology Society. Bulletin, 0704-0326.

LC GN1 .B79   **ISSN** 0577-0963
DD 301/.06/077 572   US
BULLETIN - CENTRAL STATES ANTHROPOLOGICAL SOCIETY (U.S.). (BULLETIN / CENTRAL STATES ANTHROPOLOGICAL SOCIETY.). [Bull. - Cent. States Anthropol. Soc. (U. S.)]. **Main/Corp** Central States Anthropological Society. **Added/Corp** Central States Anthropological Society (U.S.). **VFOAT** CSAS Bulletin. (1966)-. Bulletin. English. Irregular. $15.00 (comes with membership). American Anthropological Association, 4350 North Fairfax Dr, Suite 640, Arlington VA 22203. **Tel** (703)528-1902 ext. 3031, **FAX** (703)528-3546. **Continues** Central States Bulletin.

LC DU510.A1 S6
DD 920/.05   FP
BULLETIN DE LA SOCIETE DES ETUDES OCEANIENNES (POLYNESIE ORIENTALE). See History-History of Australia and Oceania.

    BE
BULLETIN DU CENTRE GENEVOIS D'ANTHROPOLOGIE / MUSEE D'ETHNOGRAPHIE, DEPARTEMENT D'ANTHROPOLOGIE. **Added/Corp** Centre Genevois d'Anthropologie. Musee d'Ethnographie de la Ville de Geneve. Departement d'Anthropologie. **VFOAT** BCGA. (1988)-. Bulletin. French (summaries and/or abstracts in English and Italian). One time a year. 1500F. Editions Peeters SA, Bondgenotenlaan 153, BP 41, B-3000 Leuven Belgium. **Tel** 011 32 16 235170, **FAX** 011 32 16 228500, telex 65987 PUL B. **ED** L. Necker and A. Gallay. Index available. **Bk Rev**. **Ad Acc**.
Ind/Abst Anthropol. Lit.

ISSN 0544-7631
    MC
CODEN MAPBA8
BULLETIN DU MUSEE D'ANTHROPOLOGIE PREHISTORIQUE DE MONACO. [Bull. Mus. anthropol. prehist. Monaco]. **Added/Corp** Musee d'Anthropologie Prehistorique (Monaco). No. 2 (1955)-. Bulletin. French (English and Italian). One time a year. $17.50. Musee Anthropologie Prehistorique, boulevard du Jardin Exotique, Principaute de Monaco. **Tel** 011 33 93 158006. Index available. cum. index. **Continues** Publications du Musee d'Anthropologie Prehistorique de Monaco.
Desc: Prehistory, anthropology, geology of the quaternary, paleontology.
Ind/Abst Anthropol. Lit.; Art Archaeol. Tech. Abstr.; GeoRef.

LC GN1 .D47a
DD 301.2/05   II
BULLETIN OF THE DEPARTMENT OF ANTHROPOLOGY, DIBRUGARH UNIVERSITY, THE. **Main/Corp** Dibrugarh University. Dept. of Anthropology. Vol. 1 (1972)-. Bulletin. English. Irregular. Price varies per volume. Dibrugarh University, Department of Anthropology, Dibrugarh Pin 786004 India.
Ind/Abst Anthropol. Lit.

ISSN 0538-5865
    AU
BULLETIN OF THE INTERNATIONAL COMMITTEE ON URGENT ANTHROPOLOGICAL AND ETHNOLOGICAL RESEARCH. **Main/Corp** International Committee on Urgent Anthropological and Ethnological Research. No. 1 (1958)-. Bulletin. English. One time a year. $21.82. Verlag E Stiglmayr, Wienerstrasse 141, A 2822 Foehrenau Austria. **Tel** 011 43 2627 6236.

LC GN1 .K64A   **ISSN** 0385-3039
DD 301.2/05   JA
CODEN BNSADR
BULLETIN OF THE NATIONAL SCIENCE MUSEUM. SERIES D, ANTHROPOLOGY.
[Bull. Natl. Sci. Mus. Ser. D]. **Main/Corp** Kokuritsu Kagaku Hakubutsukan (Japan). **VFOAT** Kokuritsu Kagaku Hakubutsukan Kenkyu Hokoku. Jinruigaku. Vol. 1 (1975)-. Bulletin. English. One time a year. National Science Museum, Ueno Park, Tokyo 110 Japan. Documents available from BIOSIS Document Express.
Supersedes in part Bulletin of the National Science Museum.
Ind/Abst Anthropol. Index; Anthropol. Lit.; Biol. Abstr.

LC E78.O45 O47   **ISSN** 0078-432X
DD 970.1/05   US
BULLETIN OF THE OKLAHOMA ANTHROPOLOGICAL SOCIETY. [Bull. Okla. Anthropol. Soc.]. **Main/Corp** Oklahoma Anthropological Society. Vol. 1 (1953)-. Bulletin. English. One time a year. Oklahoma Anthropological Society, Route 1 Box 62B, Cheyenne OK 73628-9729. **Tel** (405)497-2566, **FAX** (405)497-2662.
Desc: Information on the Indians of North America.
Ind/Abst Anthropol. Lit.; Ethnoarts Index.

LC E51 .S41   **ISSN** 0582-1592
    SZ
BULLETIN / SOCIETE SUISSE DES AMERICANISTES. **Added/Corp** Societe Suisse des Americanistes. Musee et Institut d'Ethnographie de la Ville de Geneve. Musee d'Ethnographie de la Ville de Geneve. No. 1 (Sept. 1950)-. Bulletin. French (German, English and Spanish). One time a year. $33.00. Musee d'Ethnographie, 65 67 boulevard Carl Vogt, CH-1205 Geneva Switzerland. **Tel** 011 41 22 3281218. cum. index.
Ind/Abst Anthropol. Index.

ISSN 0037-8984
    FR
NLM W1 BU936K   **CODEN** BSANA8
BULLETINS ET MEMOIRES DE LA SOCIETE D'ANTHROPOLOGIE DE PARIS. [Bull. mem. Soc. anthropol. Paris].
Added/Corp Societe d'Anthropologie de Paris. Centre de Recherches Anthropologiques. Vol. 1, (1900)-. Bulletin. French. Four times a year. $96.23. Societe d'Anthropologie, Musee L Homme, 17 PL Trocadero, 75116 Paris France. **Tel** 011 33 1 47046311. Documents available from BIOSIS Document Express. **Continues** Societe d'Anthropologie de Paris. Bulletins de la Societe d'Anthropologie de Paris, 0301-8644; **Absorbed** Societe d'Anthropologie de Paris. Memoires de la Societe d'Anthropologie de Paris.
Ind/Abst Anthropol. Lit.; Biol. Abstr.; EMBASE; GeoRef.

LC GN301 .C332
DD 301/.0   BL
CADERNOS DE CAMPO : REVISTA DOS ALUNOS DE POS-GRADUACAO EM ANTROPOLOGIA. **Added/Corp** Universidade de Sao Paulo. Programa de Pos-Graduacao em Antropologia Social. **VFOAT** Revista Dos Alunos de Pos-Graduacao em Antropologia. Vol. 1, No. 1 (1991)-. Periodical. Portuguese. Two times a year. Universidade de Sao Paulo / Department of Anthropology, Programa de Pos-Graduacao em Antropologia Social, USP Caixa Postal 8105, 05508 Sao Paulo SP Brazil.

LC GN51 .C33   **ISSN** 0758-2714
DD 573/.6/05   FR
NLM W1; CA134H
CAHIERS D'ANTHROPOLOGIE ET BIOMETRIE HUMAINE. [Cah. anthropol. biom. hum.]. **Added/Corp** Societe de Biometrie Humaine (France) Centre National de la Recherche Scientifique (France). No. 1 (1983)-. Academic Scholarly Publication. French (summaries and/or abstracts in English). Four times a year. $49.21. Societe de Biometrie Humaine, 41 rue Gay-Lussac, 75005 Paris France. **Tel** 33 1 46330596. **Bk Rev**. **Ad Acc**. **Circ**: 450. Formed by the union of Cahiers d'Anthropologie, 0398-6675 and Biometrie Humaine, 0183-5688.
Desc: Topics include human anatomy, biology, biometry, biostereometry, psychology, primatology, anthropology - normal and medical.
Ind/Abst Anthropol. Lit.; EMBASE; Nutr. Abstr. Rev., Ser. A, Hum. Exp.; Psychol. Abstr. (1983-); PsycINFO.

LC GN502 .E73   **ISSN** 0761-9871
DD 306/.05   FR
Pr Rev.
CAHIERS DE SOCIOLOGIE ECONOMIQUE ET CULTURELLE, ETHNOPSYCHOLOGIE. See Sociology.

ISSN 0249-5635
    FR
Pr Rev.
CAHIERS ETHNOLOGIQUES. (CAHIERS ETHNOLOGIQUES : REVUE DE CENTRE D'ETUDES ETHNOLOGIQUES.). [Cah. ethnol.]. **Added/Corp** Universite de Bordeaux II. Centre d'Etudes Ethnologiques. (1980)-. Periodical. French. Two times a year. $43.74. Bibliotheque Interuniversitaire de Bordeaux,

Lettres et Sciences Humaines, 3 Ter Place de la Victoire, 33076 Bordeaux Cedex France. **Tel** 011 33 56 913424, FAX 011 33 56 990380, telex 572237. Index Bound in First Issue. **Bk Rev**, (Qty: 2). **Circ:** 300. ***Continues*** *Cahiers du Centre d'Etudes et de Recherches Ethnologiques, 0397-9083.*
Desc: Information on ethnology.
Ind/Abst Anthropol. Lit.

LC GN1 .C25 **ISSN** 0272-5452 US

CALIFORNIA ANTHROPOLOGIST. [Calif. anthropol.]. **Added/Corp** California. State College, Los Angeles. Anthropological Society. California State University, Los Angeles. Vol.1 (Spring 1971)-. Periodical. English. Two times a year. Free on request. California State University / Department of Anthropology, 5151 State University Drive, Los Angeles CA 90032. **Tel** (310)224-2440. **ED** Kathy Hall. **Circ:** 200.
Desc: Anthropology and archaeology related studies submitted by students and faculty of the university.
Ind/Abst Anthropol. Lit.; Art Archaeol. Tech. Abstr.

LC GN1 .C34 UK

CAMBRIDGE ANTHROPOLOGY. **Added/Corp** University of Cambridge. Dept. of Social Anthropology. Vol. 1 (1973)-. Periodical. English. Three times a year. $51.33. Cambridge University Department of Social Anthropology, Cambridge CB2 3RF United Kingdom. Index available. cum. index. **Bk Rev. Ad Acc.**
Desc: Articles of interest in social anthropology.
Ind/Abst Anthropol. Lit.; Int. Bibliogr. Sociol.

ISSN 0068-6719
DD 572 UK
CEASED

CAMBRIDGE PAPERS IN SOCIAL ANTHROPOLOGY. **Added/Corp** University of Cambridge. Dept,. of Archaeology and Anthropology. No. 1 (1958)-(19??). Academic Scholarly Publication. English. Cambridge University Press, The Edinburgh Building, Shaftesbury Road, Cambridge CB2 2RU United Kingdom. **Tel** 011 44 1223 312393, FAX 011 44 1223 315052, telex 851-817256.

ISSN 0957-0306 UK
CODEN CSBAEN

CAMBRIDGE STUDIES IN BIOLOGICAL ANTHROPOLOGY. [Camb. stud. biol. anthropol.]. (1985)-. Monographic series. English. Irregular. Price varies per volume. Cambridge University Press / New York, 40 West 20th Street, New York NY 10011-4211. **Tel** (212)924-3900, (800)221-4512, FAX (212)691-3239. **(Subscription address:** Cambridge University Press / Outside of North America, United Kingdom. **Tel** 011 44 223 312 393, FAX 011 44 223 325 959.) Documents available from BIOSIS Document Express.
Ind/Abst Biol. Abstr. (1985-).

UK

CAMBRIDGE STUDIES IN SOCIAL AND CULTURAL ANTHROPOLOGY. (1990)-. Monographic series. English. Irregular. Price varies per volume. Cambridge University Press, The Edinburgh Building, Shaftesbury Road, Cambridge CB2 2RU United Kingdom. **Tel** 011 44 1223 312393, FAX 011 44 1223 315052, telex 851-817256. **(Subscription address:** Cambridge University Press / North America, 110 Midland Avenue, Port Chester NY 10573. **Tel** (800)431-1580, (914)937-9600.) ***Continues*** *Cambridge Studies in Social Anthropology, 0068-6794.*
Desc: Series covering anthropology, ethnology and cultural change.

CN

CANADIAN ASSOCIATION OF PHYSICAL ANTHROPOLOGY NEWSLETTER. **Added/Corp** Canadian Association for Physical Anthropology. **VFOAT** Bulletin. (19??)-. Newsletter. English (French). One time a year. $25.00. Canadian Association for Physical Anthropology, c/o Department of Anatomy, Queen's University Canada. **ED** Hermann Helmut. **Bk Rev. Circ:** 100. ***Continues*** *Canadian Review of Physical Anthropology.*
Desc: Covers the business of the Association and news of members, research, and political issues.

LC E78.C2 C483 **ISSN** 0715-3244
DD 971/.00497/005 CN
CODEN CJNSF7

CANADIAN JOURNAL OF NATIVE STUDIES. See History-History of North and South America.

ISSN 0008-4948 CN

NLM W1 CA66
Pr Rev.
CANADIAN REVIEW OF SOCIOLOGY AND ANTHROPOLOGY, THE. [Can. rev. sociol. anthropol.]. **Added/Corp** Canadian Political Science Association. Anthropology and Sociology Chapter. Canadian Sociology and Anthropology Association. **VFOAT** Revue Canadienne de Sociologie et d'Anthropologie. Vol. 1, Feb. (1964)-. Periodical. English (summaries and/or abstracts in French). Four times a year. 70.00Can$ Canada; 75.00Can$ other. Concordia University CSAA, 1455 de Maisonneuve Ouest, Room 317-1, Montreal Quebec H3G 1M8 Canada. **Tel** (514)848-8780, FAX (514)848-3494. **ED** Jim E. Curtis. Index available. cum. index. **Bk Rev. Ad Acc. Circ:** 1,800. available on microfilm and microfiche from University Microfilms International (UMI). Documents available from The Genuine Article, UMI Article Clearinghouse.
Desc: Carries updated articles, commentaries and book reviews on key research findings, and on the current theoretical debates in the social sciences.
Ind/Abst ASTIS Curr. Aware. Bull. (1978-); Abstr. Anthropol.; Acad. Abstr.; Acad. Search; Am. Hist. Life (1969-); Am. Bibliogr. Slavic East Europ. Stud.; Anthropol. Index; Anthropol. Lit.; Appl. Soc. Sci. Index Abstr.; Arts Humanit. Citation Index [Select. Cov.]; ASTIS Bibliogr. (1978-); Can. Index (?-?); Can. Period. Index; Commun. Abstr. (?-?); Crim. Justice Abstr.; Curr. Cit.; Curr. Contents Soc. Behav. Sci.; EP Collect.; Expand. Acad. Index (1989-); Geogr. Abstr. Human Geogr. (?-?); Homework Help.; Hum. Resour. Abstr. (?-?); INFO-SOUTH Abstr.; Int. Bibliogr. Sociol.; Int. Dev. Abstr. (?-?); Int. Polit. Sci. Abstr.; Leis., Rec., Tour. Abstr.; Mag. Search; MasterFile FullTEXT 1000; MasterFile FullTEXT 350; MasterFile FullTEXT 650; MasterFile FullTEXT (Jan. 1992-); Middle East Abstr. Index; Multicult. Educ. Abstr.; Newsp. Period. Abstr. (1991-); OCLC; Psychol. Abstr. (1984-); PsycINFO; PsycLit; Res. Alert [Full Cov.]; Rural Dev. Abstr.; Sage Fam. Stud. Abstr. (?-?); Sage Race Relat. Abstr.; Soc. Plann. Policy Dev. Abstr.; Soc. Sci. Source; Soc. Sci. Cit. Index [Full Cov.]; Soc. Sci. Index; Soc. Sci. Index Fulltext (Nov. 1988-) [Full Txt.]; Sociol. Abstr. (?-?); Sociol. Educ. Abstr.; Stud. Women Abstr.; Telebase; Women Stud. Abstr.; World Agric. Econ. Rural Sociol. Abstr.

LC GN1 .C34 **ISSN** 0314-9099
DD 306/.05 AT

CANBERRA ANTHROPOLOGY. **Added/Corp** Australian National University. Research School of Pacific Studies. Dept. of Anthropology. Australian National University. Faculty of Arts. Dept. of Prehistory and Anthropology. (Oct. 1977)-. Periodical. English. Two times a year. 24.67Aus$. Australian National University, GPO Box 4, Department of Anthropology, Canberra ACT 2601 Australia. **Tel** 011 61 6 2492123. Index available (Author title index bound with Vol. 16, No.1). **Bk Rev. Ad Acc. Circ:** 400.
Desc: Provides a forum for the publication of research in all branches of anthropology.
Ind/Abst Anthropol. Lit.

LC DS432.A2 C38 II

UDC 958
CAUMASA. Vol. 1, No. 1 (Feb. 1983)-. Periodical. Hindi (Hindi). Three times a year. Rs12.00. Madhyapradesh Adivasi Lokakala Parishad, R14 Guru Tech Bahadur Complex, Bhopal India.

LC GN1 .C44 **ISSN** 0739-7917
DD 306/.05 US
CEASED

CENTRAL ISSUES IN ANTHROPOLOGY. (CENTRAL ISSUES IN ANTHROPOLOGY : A JOURNAL OF THE CENTRAL STATES ANTHROPOLOGICAL SOCIETY.). [Cent. issues anthropol.]. **Added/Corp** Central States Anthropological Society (U.S.). Vol. 1, No. 1 (Mar. 1979)-Vol. 10. Periodical. English. American Anthropological Association, 4350 North Fairfax Dr, Suite 640, Arlington VA 22203. **Tel** (703)528-1902 ext. 3031, FAX (703)528-3546. ***Continues*** *Central States Anthropological Society (U.S.). Proceedings of the Central States Anthropological Society, Selected Papers.*
Ind/Abst Abstr. Anthropol.; Anthropol. Index; Anthropol. Lit. (?-Vol. 10, 1988); Linguist. Lang. Behav. Abstr.; Soc. Plann. Policy Dev. Abstr.; Sociol. Abstr.

ISSN 0577-3334 US

CERAMICA DE CULTURA MAYA ET AL. See Archaeology.

LC DB191 .C45 **ISSN** 0009-0794 XR

CESKY LID. See History-History of Europe.

FR

CHASSE MAREE. (1981)-. French. Eight times a year. $170.60. Scop Le Chasse Maree, Abri du Marin/BP 159, 29100 Douarenez France. **Tel** 98 92 09 19, FAX 98 92 80 01. **ED** Bernard Cadoret. Index available. **Bk Rev**, (Qty: 20). **Circ:** 25,000 (ctrl).

ISSN 8756-0011
DD 301 US

CHICAGO ANTHROPOLOGY EXCHANGE. [Chic. anthropol. exch.]. Periodical. English. One time a year. $10.00 US; $14.00 other. Chicago Anthropology Exchange, Department of Anthropology, University of Chicago, 1126 East 59th Street, Chicago IL 60637.
Ind/Abst Anthropol. Lit. (-Vol. 11, 1989).

LC GN1 .G46 **ISSN** 1053-7589
DD 306 US

CHICO ANTHROPOLOGICAL SOCIETY PAPERS. [Chico Anthropol. Soc. pap.]. **Added/Corp** California State University, Chico. Chico Anthropological Society. **VFOAT** Chico Anthropology Society Papers. No. 12 (1990)-. Periodical. English. Irregular. $10.00. Chico Anthropological Society, Dept. of Anthropology, California State University-Chico, Chico CA 95929. **Tel** (916)895-6192. ***Continues*** *Genetic Drift, 0278-4106.*

LC HM1 .C45 **ISSN** 0009-4625 US
CCC

Pr Rev.
CHINESE SOCIOLOGY AND ANTHROPOLOGY. See Sociology.

LC BV **ISSN** 1064-1602
DD 253 US

CHRISTIAN ANTHROPOLOGY. See Religions and Theology.

ISSN 0244-9277 FR

CIVILISATIONS (UNIVERSITE DE PARIS IV : PARIS-SORBONNE). (CIVILISATIONS.). **Added/Corp** Universite de Paris IV : Paris-Sorbonne. (1980)-. Monographic series. English. Irregular. Price varies per volume. Presses de l'Universite de Paris-Sorbonne, 18 rue de la Sorbonne, 75005 Paris France.

SP

COLECCION ANTROPOLOGIA E HISTORIA / ADMINISTRACION DEL PATRIMONIO CULTURAL. **VFOAT** Antropologia e Historia. (1976)-. Monographic series. Spanish. Irregular. Price varies per volume. ***Continues*** *Coleccion Antropologia (El Salvador. Direccion del Patrimonio Cultural. Departamento de Etnografia).*

MX

COLECCION BREVE. **Main/Corp** Mexico (City). Museo Nacional de Antropologia. Servicios Educativos. 1- 1968-. Monographic series. Spanish. Irregular. Price varies per volume. Inst Nacional Anthrop Historia, Cordoba 4J, Mexico 7DF Mexico.

MX

COLECCION INI. **Added/Corp** Instituto Nacional Indigenista (Mexico). **VFOAT** INI. No. 1 (1977)-. Monographic series. Spanish. Price varies per volume. Inst Nacional Anthrop Historia, Cordoba 4J, Mexico 7DF Mexico. ***Continues*** *Coleccion SEP-INI.*

GW

COLLECTANEA INSTITUTI ANTHROPOS. **Main/Corp** Anthropos Institute. Vol. 1 (1967)-. Monographic series. Multiple languages (English, French and German). Irregular. Price varies per volume. Academia Verlag Richarz GmbH, Postfach 1163, D-53734 St. Augustin Germany. **Tel** 011 49 2241 333349.

LC QH301 **ISSN** 0078-1053
DD 574 CN
CODEN CNORE2

COLLECTION NORDICANA. See Biology.

ISSN 0350-6134 CI

NLM W1 CO204L
COLLEGIUM ANTROPOLOGICUM. [Coll. antropol.]. (1977)-. Academic Scholarly Publication. Multiple languages (English, French, German and Spanish). Two times a year. $13.00 (individuals), $53.00 (institutions). Institute for Anthropological Research, University of Zagreb, Jurjevska 31 1A, 41000 Zagreb Croatia. **Tel** 011 38 41 432186. Documents available from The Genuine Article, BIOSIS Document Express, CASDDS.
Ind/Abst Anthropol. Lit.; Art Archaeol. Tech. Abstr.; Biol. Abstr.; Chem. Abstr.; Curr. Contents Soc. Behav. Sci.; EMBASE; Geogr. Abstr. Human Geogr. (?-?); Int. Bibliogr. Sociol.; Res. Alert [Full Cov.]; Soc. Sci. Cit. Index [Full Cov.].

ISSN 0366-7634 FR
CODEN COINAV

COLLOQUES INTERNATIONAUX DU CENTRE NATIONAL DE LA RECHERCHE SCIENTIFIQUE. (COLLOQUES INTERNATIONAUX.). [Colloq. int. Cent. Natl. Rech. Sci.]. **Main/Corp** Centre National de la Recherche Scientifique (France). (1946)-. Monographic series. French. Irregular. Price varies per volume. Editions du CNRS, 22 rue Saint Armand, F 75015 Paris France. **Tel** 011 33 1 45075050, telex 200 356 F. Documents available from BIOSIS Document Express, CASDDS.
Desc: International studies and contributions to ethnology

Anthropology

and history.
Ind/Abst Biol. Abstr. (-1978); Chem. Abstr. (1946-1980); GeoRef; Zentralbl. Math. Ihre Grenzgeb.

US
COLUMBIA STUDIES IN ARCHAEOLOGY AND ETHNOLOGY. See Archaeology.

ISSN 0162-8216
US
COMMUNICATION THEORY IN THE CAUSE OF MAN. Periodical. English. Irregular. Communication Theory in the Cause of Man, PO Box 5095, San Jose CA 95150.

ISSN 1059-5422
DD 301 US
COMPETITIVENESS REVIEW. See Sociology.

ISSN 0871-178X
PO
COMUNICACOES. SERIE DE CIENCIAS ETNOLOGICAS E ETNO-MUSEOLOGICAS / INSTITUTO DE INVESTIGACAO CIENTIFICA TROPICAL. **Added/Corp** Instituto de Investigacao Cientifica Tropical (Portugal). **VFOAT** Serie de Ciencias Etnologicas e Etno-Museologicas. (1992)-. Monographic series. Portuguese. Irregular. Price varies per volume. Instituto de Investigacao Cientifica Tropical, Centro de Documentacao e Informacao, rua Jau 47, 1 300 Lisbon Portugal. **Tel** 645321. **Circ:** 1,000 (ctrl).

US
CONTRIBUTIONS. ANTHROPOLOGY AND HISTORY. **Main/Corp** Florida. University, Gainesville. State Museum. (1971)-. English.

ISSN 0737-6448
US
CONTRIBUTIONS IN ANTHROPOLOGY AND HISTORY. (CONTRIBUTIONS IN ANTHROPOLOGY AND HISTORY / MILWAUKEE PUBLIC MUSEUM.). [Contrib. anthropol. hist.]. **Added/Corp** Milwaukee Public Museum. No. 1 (1980)-. Monographic series. English. Irregular. Price varies per volume. Milwaukee Public Museum, 800 West Wells Street, Milwaukee WI 53233. **Tel** (414)278-2702.
Desc: Includes original research in anthropology, archaeology, and history. Titles on the study of American Indian culture may be included.

ISSN 0070-8232
US
CONTRIBUTIONS IN ANTHROPOLOGY (PORTALES, N.M.). (CONTRIBUTIONS IN ANTHROPOLOGY / EASTERN NEW MEXICO UNIVERSITY.). [Contrib. anthropol.]. **Added/Corp** Eastern New Mexico University. Vol. 1, No. 1 (Feb. 1968)-. Monographic series. English. Irregular. Price varies per volume. Eastern New Mexico University / Paleo Indian Institute, Portales NM 88130. **Tel** (515)562-2180. **ED** John L. Montgomery. **Circ:** 300 (ctrl).
Desc: Anthropology and archaeology of the southern high plains and the Southwest.
Ind/Abst GeoRef.

ISSN 0832-8609
DD 971.1/01 CN
CEASED
CONTRIBUTIONS TO HUMAN HISTORY. [Contrib. hum. hist.]. **Added/Corp** British Columbia Provincial Museum. No. 1 (Mar. 2, 1987)-(19??). Monographic series. English.

ISSN 0217-2992
SI
CONTRIBUTIONS TO SOUTHEAST ASIAN ETHNOGRAPHY. No. 1 (Sept. 1982)-. Monographic series. English (Malay). Irregular. Price varies per volume. Ohio State University / Department of Anthropology, 208 Lord Hall, 124 West 17th Avenue, Columbus OH 43210-1364. **Tel** (614)292-4149.
Ind/Abst Anthropol. Lit.

ISSN 0890-9377
DD 301 US
CONTRIBUTIONS TO THE STUDY OF ANTHROPOLOGY. [Contrib. study anthropol.]. No. 1 (1987)-. Monographic series. English. Irregular. Price varies per volume. Greenwood Press Inc., PO Box 5007, Westport CT 06881-5007. **Tel** (203)226-3571, FAX (203)222-1502.

LC DT2871 .C66 ISSN 0250-2992
DD 968.9105 RH
COOKEIA : SERIES OF MISCELLANEOUS PUBLICATIONS IN THE HUMAN SCIENCES BY THE NATIONAL MUSEUMS AND MONUMENTS OF ZIMBABWE. See History-History of Africa.

ISSN 0304-3134
UDC 341.16:001 IT
CODEN NU053
CORRIERE UNESCO. [Corr. Unesco Ed. ital.]. (1947)-. Periodical. Italian. Eleven times a year. L32700. Editalia Edizioni D Italia, Via di Palla Corda 7, 00186 Rome Italy. **Tel** 011 39 6 6541592, FAX 011 39 6 6869561.

LC GN1 .C73 ISSN 0308-275X
DD 301/.05 UK
CRITIQUE OF ANTHROPOLOGY. [Crit. anthropol.]. Vol. 1 (Spring 1974)-. Periodical. English. Four times a year. $152.00. Sage Publications Ltd., 6 Bonhill Street, London EC2A 4PU United Kingdom. **Tel** 011 44 181 3740645, FAX 011 44 181 3748741, telex 296207 SAGE G. **Ad Acc**. **Acid Free.** Documents available from The Genuine Article.
Desc: Dedicated to development of anthropology as a discipline that subjects social reality to critical analysis.
Ind/Abst Abstr. Anthropol.; Altern. Press Index; Anthropol. Lit.; Curr. Contents Soc. Behav. Sci.; Int. Bibliogr. Sociol.; Left Index; Linguist. Lang. Behav. Abstr.; Middle East Abstr. Index; Res. Alert [Full Cov.]; Soc. Plann. Policy Dev. Abstr.; Soc. Sci. Cit. Index [Full Cov.]; Sociol. Abstr.

ISSN 1053-9778
DD 301 US
Pr Rev.
CROSSCURRENTS (NEW BRUNSWICK, N.J.). (CROSSCURRENTS.). [Crosscurrents]. **Added/Corp** Rutgers University. Graduate Program of Anthropology. Vol. 1 (Sept. 1987)-. English. One time a year (Autumn). $20.00. Rutgers University / Anthropology, PO Box 270, Department of Anthropology, New Brunswick NJ 08901. **Tel** (908)932-9790, (908)932-9886. **ED** Debra L. Wallace. **Bk Rev**. **Circ:** 500.
Desc: Anthropological articles by graduate students along with commentaries by anthropologists.

ISSN 0590-160X
DD 572 GT
NLM W1 CU122
CUADERNOS DE ANTROPOLOGIA (CIUDAD DE GUATEMALA). (CUADERNOS DE ANTROPOLOGIA.). [Cuad. antropol.]. **Added/Corp** Universidad de San Carlos de Guatemala. Facultad de Humanidades. Departamento de Publicaciones. Universidad de San Carlos de Guatemala. Instituto de Investigaciones Historicas. Vol. 1 (May 1962)-. Periodical. Spanish. Four times a year. Universidad de San Carlos de Guatemala, Facultad de Humanidades, Departamento de Publicaciones, Guatemala 12 Guatemala.
Ind/Abst Am. Hist. Life (1965-1966); Anthropol. Index.

LC GN585.S7 C83 ISSN 0590-1871
DD 305.8/00946/52 SP
Pr Rev.
CUADERNOS DE ETNOLOGIA Y ETNOGRAFIA DE NAVARRA. [Cuad. etnol. etnogr. Navarra]. **Added/Corp** Institucion Principe de Viana. Navarre (Spain). Departamento de Educacion y Cultura. (1969)-. Periodical. Spanish (Basque and French). Two times a year. 1800ptas. Gobierno de Navarra, Navas de Tolosa 21, 31002 Pamplona Spain. **Tel** 34 948 107121, FAX 34 948 227673. Index available. cum. index. **Circ:** 1,200.
Ind/Abst Anthropol. Lit.; BHA : Biblio. Hist. Art.

LC GN835.A1 C8
DD 936.6 SP
CUADERNOS DE PREHISTORIA DE LA UNIVERSIDAD DE GRANADA. **Added/Corp** Universidad de Granada. Departamento de Prehistoria. **VFOAT** C. de Prehistoria, Universidad de Granada. No. 1 (1976)-. Periodical. Spanish. One time a year. 4500ptas Spain; 4369ptas other. Universidad de Granada, Campus Universidad de Cartuja, 18071 Granada Spain. **Tel** 011 34 58 243930, 011 34 58 243931.

LC GN1 .C786 ISSN 0185-1659
MX
CUICUILCO. (CUICUILCO : REVISTA DE LA ESCUELA NACIONAL DE ANTROPOLOGIA.). [Cuicuilco]. (1980)-. Periodical. Spanish. Irregular. Oficina de Difusion Cultural, Escuela Nacional de Antropologia e Historia, Periferico sur y Calle del Zapote, Mexico City 22 Mexico.
Ind/Abst Ethnoarts Index.

LC GN301 .C85 ISSN 0886-7356
DD 306/.05 US
CULTURAL ANTHROPOLOGY. (CULTURAL ANTHROPOLOGY : JOURNAL OF THE SOCIETY FOR CULTURAL ANTHROPOLOGY.). [Cult. anthropol.]. Vol. 1, No. 1 (Feb. 1986)-. Periodical. English. Four times a year. $50.00. American Anthropological Association, 4350 North Fairfax Dr, Suite 640, Arlington VA 22203. **Tel** (703)528-1902 ext. 3031, FAX (703)528-3546. **ED** George E. Marcus and Lyle Green. **Ad Acc**. **Circ:** 1,200 (ctrl). available on microfilm and microfiche from University Microfilms International (UMI). Documents available from The Genuine Article.
Desc: A forum for discussion and debate in the study of culture as it is developing in anthropology and all other relevant disciplines. Publishes articles, reviews and interviews.
Ind/Abst Anthropol. Lit.; Arts Humanit. Citation Index [Select. Cov.]; Curr. Cit.; Curr. Contents Soc. Behav. Sci.; Ethnoarts Index; Int. Bibliogr. Sociol.; Linguist. Lang. Behav. Abstr.; Res. Alert [Full Cov.]; Soc. Plann. Policy Dev. Abstr.; Soc. Sci. Cit. Index [Full Cov.]; Sociol. Abstr.

LC CB158 .C83 ISSN 0748-772X
DD 303.4/9/05 US
Pr Rev. SUSPENDED
CULTURAL FUTURES RESEARCH. [Cult. futures res.]. **VFOAT** C.F.R.; CFR. Vol. 7, No. 1 (Autumn 1982)-?. Periodical. English. Four times a year. $30.00. North Arizona University, Cultural Futures Research, Box 15200, Flagstaff AZ 86011. **Tel** (602)523-3180. **ED** Reed D Riner. **Bk Rev**. **Ad Acc**. **Circ:** 128. **Formed by the union of** Anthro-Tech **and** Cultural & Educational Futures.
Desc: Refereed papers on the history, theories and methodologies of holistic and cross-cultural futures. Also includes research and applications of those findings.
Ind/Abst Abstr. Anthropol.

LC GN301 .C86 ISSN 0902-7521
DD 301/.05 DK
CULTURE & HISTORY (COPENHAGEN). (CULTURE & HISTORY.). [Cult. hist.]. **Added/Corp** Center for Comparative Cultural Research (Copenhagen, Denmark) Center for Research in the Humanities (Copenhagen, Denmark). **VFOAT** Culture and History. (1987)-. English. Irregular. Price varies per volume. Scandinavian University Press, PO Box 2959 Toeyen, N 0608 Oslo 6 Norway. **Tel** 011 47 2 2575400, FAX 011 47 2 2575353, telex 71896 UROR N. **(Subscription address:** Scandinavian University Press, 200 Meacham Ave., Elmont NY 11003. **Tel** (516)352-7300, FAX (516)352-7377.**)** **ED** Michael Harbsmeier, Mogens Trolle Larsen and Uffe Ostgard.
Desc: Functions as an international forum for debate in the general field of cultural historical studies. Founded by scholars attached to Danish research concerned with comparative cultural studies, the serial has roots in a Danish or Scandinavian tradition.
Ind/Abst Am. Hist. Life (1989-); Anthropol. Lit.; Linguist. Lang. Behav. Abstr.; Soc. Plann. Policy Dev. Abstr.; Sociol. Abstr.

LC BF GN ISSN 1354-067X
DD 150 301 UK
NLM W1; CU443 CODEN CUPSFQ
●**CULTURE & PSYCHOLOGY.** See Psychology.

LC GR113 .C84 ISSN 0701-0184
DD 398/.042/0971 CN
Pr Rev.
CULTURE & TRADITION. See Folklore.

FR
CULTURE KHMERE. **Added/Corp** Centre de Documentation et de Recherche Sur la Civilisation Khmere. **VFOAT** Vappadham Khmaer. No. 1 (April/Sept. 1981)-. Periodical. French (Khmer). Two times a year.

LC RC455.4.E8 C85 ISSN 0165-005X
DD 616.8/9/005 NE
CCC
NLM W1 CU446 CODEN CMPSD2
Pr Rev.
CULTURE, MEDICINE AND PSYCHIATRY. See Medical Sciences-Psychiatry.

LC GN301 .C844 ISSN 0229-009X
DD 306/.05 CN
CULTURE (QUEBEC. 1981). (CULTURE.). [Culture]. **Added/Corp** Canadian Anthropology Society. Vol. 9, No. 1 (1989)-. Periodical. English (French). Two times a year (Mar., & Oct.). 60.00Can$ Comes with Canadian Anthropology Society membership. Canadian Anthropology Society / CASCA, Department of Anthropology, 1455 Maisonneuve Boulevard West, Montreal Quebec LB617 1 Canada. **Tel** (514)848-4508. **Continues** Culture (Canadian Ethnology Society), 0229-009X.
Ind/Abst Anthropol. Lit.

LC DT641 .C84 ISSN 0302-5640
DD 916.75/1/0305 CG
CULTURES AU ZAIRE ET EN AFRIQUE. [Cult. Zaire Afr.]. 1973-. Periodical. French. Four times a year. $16.00. Office National de la Recherche et du Development, BP 16706, 1 Kinshasa Congo Zaire. **Supersedes** Dombi.

LC GN1 .C8 ISSN 0011-3204
DD 301.2/05 CCC
NLM W1 CU686 CODEN CUANAX
Pr Rev.
CURRENT ANTHROPOLOGY. [Curr. anthropol.]. **Added/Corp** Wenner-Gren Foundation for Anthropological Research. Vol. 1 (Jan. 1960)-. Periodical. English. Five times a year. $120.00. University of Chicago Press / Journals Division, PO Box 37005, 5720 South Woodlawn, Chicago IL 60637. **Tel** (312)753-3347, FAX (312)753-0811. **ED** Richard G. Fox. cum. index. **Acid Free.** available on microfilm from University Microfilms International (UMI). Documents available from The

Genuine Article, UMI Article Clearinghouse. ***Continues*** *Yearbook of Anthropology.*
Desc: An international forum publishing research, theory, and critical analyses in anthropology and its related areas. The journal features papers in a wide variety of areas, including social, cultural, and physical anthropology, ethnology, and ethnohistory, archaeology and prehistory, folklore and linguistics.
Ind/Abst Abstr. Anthropol. (19??-); Acad. Abstr.; Acad. Ind. [Computer File] (1987-); Acad. Search; Am. Hist. Life (1971-1974, 1980-); Anthropol. Index; Anthropol. Lit.; Appl. Soc. Sci. Index Abstr.; Arts Humanit. Citation Index [Select. Cov.]; Br. Archaeol. Bibliogr.; Curr. Cit.; Curr. Contents Soc. Behav. Sci.; Curr. Geogr. Publ. (199?-); Ecol. Abstr. (?-?); EP Collect.; Ethnoarts Index; Expand. Acad. Index (1987-); Gen. Sci. Source; Geogr. Abstr. Human Geogr. (?-?); GeoRef; Homework Help.; Hum. Resour. Abstr. (?-?); INFO-SOUTH Abstr.; Int. Dev. Abstr. (?-?); Int. Polit. Sci. Abstr.; Linguist. Lang. Behav. Abstr.; Mag. Search; MasterFile FullTEXT 1000; MasterFile FullTEXT 350; MasterFile FullTEXT 650; MasterFile FullTEXT (July 1990-); Middle East Abstr. Index; MLA Int. Bibl. Books Artic. Mod. Lang. Lit.; Newsp. Period. Abstr. (1990-); OCLC; Peace Res. Abstr. J. (1960-1978); Psychol. Abstr. (1971-); PsycINFO; PsycLit; Pub. Lib. FullTEXT; Res. Alert [Full Cov.]; Sage Fam. Stud. Abstr. (?-?); Soc. Plann. Policy Dev. Abstr.; Soc. Sci. Source; Soc. Sci. Cit. Index [Full Cov.]; Soc. Sci. Index; Soc. Sci. Index Fulltext (Dec. 1988-) [Full Txt.]; Sociol. Abstr.; Stud. Women Abstr.; Telebase; West. Hist. Q.

LC GN289 .C88 **ISSN** 0748-7819
DD 573.2 US
CURRENT DEVELOPMENTS IN ANTHROPOLOGICAL GENETICS. **See** Biology-Genetics.

LC E61 .C96 **ISSN** 8755-898X
DD 970.01/1 US
CURRENT RESEARCH IN THE PLEISTOCENE. **Added/Corp** University of Maine at Orono. Center for the Study of Early Man. Vol. 2 (1985)-. English (Chinese, Spanish and Russian). One time a year. $20.00. Oregon State University / Corvallis, CSFA Weniger 355, Corvallis OR 97331. **Tel** (503)737-3854, (503)737-4595. **ED** Jim I. Mead. **Circ:** 600 (ctrl). ***Continues*** *Current Research (Orono, Me.), 0743-426X.*
Desc: Journal of quaternary sciences. Topics include anthropology, archaeology, taphonomy and bone modification, physical anthropology, and paleoenvironments.
Ind/Abst Abstr. Anthropol.; Anthropol. Lit.; GeoRef.

DD 572 US
NLM W1 CU82A
CURRENT TOPICS IN ANTHROPOLOGY. Vol. 1 (1971)-. Periodical. English. Two times a year. Addison Wesley Publishing Company, 350 Bridge Parkway, Suite 208, Redwood City CA 94065. **Tel** (415)594-4423, (800)447-2226.

DK
CVA NEWSLETTER / COMMISSION ON VISUAL ANTHROPOLOGY / BULLETIN DE LA COMMISSION D'ANTHROPOLOGIE VISUELLE / COMMISSION D'ANTHROPOLOGIE VISUELLE. **Added/Corp** Commission on Visual Anthropology. International Union of Anthropological and Ethnological Sciences. Institut fuer den Wissenschaftlichen Film (Gottingen, Germany) Istituto Superiore Regionale Etnografico (Nuoro, Italy). **VFOAT** Bulletin de la Commission d'Anthropologie Visuelle; CVA Review. (Spring 1992)-. Newsletter. English (French and Spanish). Two times a year. kr160.00 Denmark, $16.00 US, $24.00 other, £21.50 ECU (institutions); kr130.00 Denmark, $20.00 US, £17.25 ECU (standard). Commission on Visual Anthropology Newsletter, Intervention Press, Castenschioldsvej 7, DK 8270 Hoejbjerg Denmark. **Tel** 011 45 86 272333, FAX 011 45 86 275133. **ED** Peter Ian Crawford. **Bk Rev**, (Qty: 10-15). **Ad Acc, Adv Mgr:** Peter Crawford. Full Page (B&W) $250.00. Half Page (B&W) $170.00. **Circ:** 1,200 (ctrl). ***Continues*** *CVA Review, 0846-8648.*
Desc: This publication comes with global coverage of the development within visual anthropology. Contain reports and review articles as well as general news and information on recent development and events. Gives special emphasis to reports on ongoing research projects and development projects and to activities taking place in the Third World countries and indigenous communities. Other features are reviews of ethnographic films and videos.

ISSN 0846-8648
DD 306/.0208 CN
CVA REVIEW. **See** Motion Picture.

LC HM **ISSN** 0822-6733
DD 301 CN
DEPARTMENTAL WORKING PAPER - CARLETON UNIVERSITY. DEPARTMENT OF SOCIOLOGY AND ANTHROPOLOGY. (DEPARTMENTAL WORKING PAPER.). [Dep. work. pap. - Carleton Univ., Dep. Sociol. Anthropol.]. (197?)-. Monographic series. English. Six times a year. Price varies per volume. Department of Sociology and Anthropology, Carleton University, Ottawa Ontario K1S 5B6 Canada. **Tel** (613)788-2582. **ED** Bruce A. Cox. **Circ:** 30.
Desc: Contains articles on anthropology and sociology.

ISSN 8756-0488
DD 306 US
DEVELOPMENT ANTHROPOLOGY NETWORK. **See** Business and Economics-Economic Assistance and Development.

LC GN2 .D423
GW
DGV INFORMATIONEN. **See** Folklore.

LC HX550.A56 D53 **ISSN** 0304-4092
DD 335.43/8/3012 NE
CCC
CODEN DIAAER
Pr Rev.
DIALECTICAL ANTHROPOLOGY. [Dialect. anthropol.]. Vol. 1 (Nov. 1975)-. Periodical. English. Four times a year. $248.00. Kluwer Academic Publishers, Postbus 322, 3300 AH Dordrecht The Netherlands. **Tel** 011 31 78 524400, FAX 011 31 78 183273, telex 20083. **ED** Stanley Diamond. **Bk Rev. Ad Acc. Acid Free.** available on microfilm and microfiche from University Microfilms International (UMI). Documents available from The Genuine Article.
Desc: An independent international journal in the critical tradition committed to the transformation of our society and the humane union of theory and practice of anthropology.
Ind/Abst Abstr. Anthropol.; Anthropol. Index; Anthropol. Lit.; Arts Humanit. Citation Index [Select. Cov.]; Curr. Contents Soc. Behav. Sci.; Left Index; Linguist. Lang. Behav. Abstr.; Middle East Abstr. Index; Philos. Index; Res. Alert [Full Cov.]; Soc. Plann. Policy Dev. Abstr.; Soc. Sci. Cit. Index [Full Cov.]; Sociol. Abstr.

ISSN 0095-2907
DD 970.1 US
DICKSON MOUNDS MUSEUM ANTHROPOLOGICAL STUDIES. **Main/Corp** Dickson Mounds Museum. **Added/Corp** Illinois State Museum. No. 1 (1971)-. Monographic series. English. Irregular. Price varies per volume. Illinois State Museum, Spring and Edwards Street, Springfield IL 62706. **Tel** (217)782-7386, FAX (217)782-1254.

US
●**DISCOVERING MULTICULTURAL AMERICA. [CD-ROM].** (May 1995)-. English. One time a year. $895.00. Gale Research Inc., 835 Penobscot Building, 645 Griswold Street, Detroit MI 48226. **Tel** (800)877-GALE, (313)961-2242, FAX (313)961-6083, (800)414-5043, telex TWX 810-221-7086.
Desc: Access to data on African Americans, Hispanic Americans, Asian Americans, and Native North Americans. Multimedia format with biographical sketches on contemporary and historical figures, statistical data, full-text periodical articles, contact information for cultural and ethnic organizations, and texts of historical documents and speeches.

FR
Pr Rev.
DROIT ET CULTURES / REVUE SEMESTRIELLE ANTHROPOLOGIE ET D'HISTOIRE. French (English). Two times a year. 270.00F. Editions L'Harmattan, 5 rue de l Ecole Polytechnique, 75005 Paris France. **Tel** 33 1 43547910, FAX 33 1 43258203.
Desc: Topics on anthropology and law.

ISSN 0332-5784
NO
DUGNAD. (DUGNAD. UTGIS AV MAGISTRE OG MAGISTERGRADSSTUDENTER I ETNOLOGI].). [Dugnad]. **Added/Corp** Universitetet I Oslo. Institutt for Etnologi. (1975)-. Periodical. Norwegian (summaries and/or abstracts in English). Four times a year (Mar., June, Sept., Dec.). $57.00 (institutions); $34.00 (individuals). Novus Press, PO Box 748 Sentrum, N-0106 Oslo Norway. **Tel** 011 47 22 717450, FAX 011 47 22 718107.
Ind/Abst Anthropol. Lit.

TZ
CEASED
EACROTANAL INFORMATION. **Added/Corp** Eastern African Centre for Research on Oral Traditions and African National Languages. International Fund for the Promotion of Culture. Vol. 1 No.1 (1980)-(1993). Periodical. English (French). Accountant Eacrotanal, PO Box 600, Zanzibar Tanzania. **Tel** 32011. **ED** Didier Rapanoel. **Bk Rev. Circ:** 500.

LC GN1 .E15 **ISSN** 0012-8686
DD 572.05 II
NLM W1 EA839 **CODEN** EAANAH
EASTERN ANTHROPOLOGIST, THE. [East. anthropol.]. **Added/Corp** Ethnographic and Folk-Culture Society (Uttar Pradesh, India). Vol. 1 (Sept. 1947)-. Periodical. English. Four times a year. $80.00. Scientific Publishers, PO Box 91, Ratanada Road, Jodhpur 342011 India. **(Subscription address:** Prints India, 11 Darya Ganj, New Delhi 110002 India. **Tel** 011 91 11 3268645, FAX 011 91 11 3275542, telex 31-61087 PRIN-IN.) **ED** K N Sharma and J S Bhamdari. Index available. cum. index. **Bk Rev. Ad Acc. Circ:** 1,100. Documents available from BIOSIS Document Express.
Desc: Publishes research papers, communications and book reviews of interest to professional anthropologists and other scientists. International in character, contents and coverage.
Ind/Abst Anthropol. Index; Anthropol. Lit.; Biol. Abstr.; Int. Polit. Sci. Abstr.; Middle East Abstr. Index; Soc. Plann. Policy Dev. Abstr.; Sociol. Abstr. (?-?).

LC GN301 .E35 **ISSN** 0953-2919
DD 305.8/005 UK
EDINBURGH ANTHROPOLOGY. [Edinb. anthropol.]. (1987)-. English. The Secretary / Scotland, Department of Social Anthropology, Adam Ferguson Building, George Square, Edinburgh EH8 9LL United Kingdom.
Ind/Abst Anthropol. Lit.

LC F2229 .D67 **ISSN** 0095-165X
DD 980/.004/98 US
EL DORADO. [Dorado]. **VFOAT** Relaciones Antropologicas. Vol. 1 (Aug. 1973)-. Periodical. English. G E Fay, Greeley CO 80639.
Ind/Abst Ethnoarts Index.

ISSN 0013-9645
FR
EPISTEMOLOGIE SOCIOLOGIQUE. No. 1 (1964)-. Periodical. French. Two times a year. Centre National de la Recherche Scientifique, Informascience, 26 rue Boyer, 75971 Paris France. **Tel** 011 33 1 61411105, telex CNRSDOC 220880 F.

LC GN301 **ISSN** 0871-3332
DD 306 PO
ESTUDIOS REGIONAIS. (VIANA DO CASTELO, PORTUGAL). **Added/Corp** Centro de Estudos Regionais (Viana do Castelo, Portugal). (June 1989)-. Periodical. Portuguese. One time a year. $5.00. Centro de Estudos Regionais, Largo 9 de Abril, 4900 Viana do Castelo Portugal. ***Continues*** *Boletim Cultural (Viana do Castelo, Portugal).*

ISSN 0870-4457
PO
UDC 572.9(05)
ESTUDOS DE ANTROPOLOGIA CULTURAL E SOCIAL. [Estud. antropol. cult. soc.]. (1988)-. Monographic series. Portuguese. Irregular. Price varies per volume. Instituto de Investigacao Cientifica Tropical, Centro de Documentacao e Informacao, rua Jau 47, 1 300 Lisbon Portugal. **Tel** 645321. **Circ:** 1,000 (ctrl). ***Continues*** *Estudos de Antropologia Cultural, 0870-6891.*

ISSN 0870-6344
PO
ESTUDOS DE CASTELO BRANCO. **See** History.

CE
ETHNIC STUDIES REPORT. **Added/Corp** International Centre for Ethnic Studies. Vol. 1, No. 1 (May 1983)-. Periodical. English. Two times a year. $18.00. International Centre for Ethnic Studies, 554 1 Peradeniya Road, Kandy Sri Lanka. **Tel** 011 94 8 23095.
Ind/Abst Hum. Rights Intern. Rep.

LC E78.C15 E8 **ISSN** 0071-1799
DD 970.4/94 US
ETHNIC TECHNOLOGY NOTES. **Added/Corp** San Diego Museum of Man. No. 1 (1967)-. Monographic series. English. Irregular. Price varies per volume. San Diego Museum of Man, 1350 El Prado Balboa Park, San Diego CA 92101. **Tel** (619)239-2001. **ED** Ken Hedges. **Circ:** 500.
Desc: Papers on anthropological and archaeological subjects of the Western Hemisphere.

ISSN 0014-1798
HU
ETHNOGRAPHIA (BUDAPEST. 1949). (ETHNOGRAPHIA / NEPELET : A MAGYAR NEPRAJZI TARSASAG KOZLONYE.). [Ethnographia]. **Added/Corp** Magyar Neprajzi Tarsasag. **VFOAT** Nepelet. (1926)-. Periodical. Hungarian (summaries and/or abstracts in English, German and Russian). Two times a year. $14.00. **(Subscription address:** Kultura, PO Box 143, H-1300 Budapest 3 Hungary. **Tel** 011 36 1 2500194.) cum. index. ***Continues*** *Nepelet.*
Ind/Abst Anthropol. Index; BHA : Biblio. Hist. Art; MLA Int. Bibl. Books Artic. Mod. Lang. Lit.

ISSN 0336-1438
FR
ETHNOGRAPHIE, L'. **Added/Corp** Societe d'Ethnographie de Paris. (1860)-. French. Two times a year. $59.06. Societe d Ethnographie de Paris, 6 rue Champfleury, 75007 Paris France. **Tel** 011 33 1 47345788. Index available. cum. index. **Bk Rev.**
Ind/Abst Anthropol. Lit.; Ethnoarts Index.

LC GN700 .E752 ISSN 0012-7477
GW

ETHNOGRAPHISCH-ARCHAOLOGISCHE ZEITSCHRIFT : EAZ. See Archaeology.

CN

ETHNOGRAPHY MONOGRAPH. 1- Sept. 1973-. Monographic series. English. Irregular. Price varies per volume. Royal Ontario Museum Publications Service, 100 Queen's Park, Toronto Ontario M5S 2C6 Canada. **Tel** (416)586-5590, FAX (416)586-5827.

ISSN 0425-4597
DK

ETHNOLOGIA EUROPAEA. [Ethnol. Eur.]. Vol. 1 (1967)-. English (French and German). Irregular (2 issues). Kr280.00. AIO Print Ltd., Cikorie Vej 8, DK-5220 Odense Denmark. **Tel** 011 45 66121030. **ED** Bjarne Stoklund (editor's address: Department of European Ethnology, Brede alle 69, DK-2800 Lyngby Denmark). **Ad Acc. Circ:** 600.
Desc: Covers the field of European ethnology, anthropology, folk life studies in presenting studies from all parts of Europe as well as methodological contributions.
Ind/Abst Anthropol. Index; Anthropol. Lit.; MLA Int. Bibl. Books Artic. Mod. Lang. Lit.

LC GN301 .E7 ISSN 0355-1776
FI

ETHNOLOGIA FENNICA. [Ethnol. fenn.]. **Added/Corp** Seurasaarisaatio. **VFOAT** Finnish Studies in Ethnology. (1971)-. Periodical. English (Finnish and German). Irregular. Fmk60.00. Ethnologia Fennica, Ethnos Ry Museovirasto PL913, 00101 Helsinki Finland. **Tel** 011 358 0 4050241. **(Subscription address:** Bookstore Tiedekirja, Kirkkokatu 14, SF 00170 Helsinki Finland. **Tel** 011 358 0 635177.) **ED** Pekka Leimu. **Bk Rev. Circ:** 300 (ctrl).
Ind/Abst Anthropol. Lit.; MLA Int. Bibl. Books Artic. Mod. Lang. Lit.

LC GN549
DD 572 XO
•**ETHNOLOGIA SLOVACA ET SLAVICA.** (1992/1993)-. Periodical. English (German; summaries and/or abstracts in Czech, Polish, Russian, Slovak and Sorbian languages). Department of Ethnology, Comenius University, 81801 Bratislava Slovakia. ***Continues*** *Ethnologia Slavica, 0083-4106.*

LC GN301 .E76
DD 301 RM
ETHNOLOGICA. **Added/Corp** Association d'Histoire Comparative des Institutions et du Droit de la Republique Socialiste de Roumanie. Association d'Histoire Comparative des Institutions et du Droit de la Republique Socialiste de Roumanie. Recherches sur l'Histoire des Institutions et du Droit. (19??)-. Periodical. English (French and German). One time a year. Ethonologica Bucuresti, Calea Victoriei 125, Sectorul I, Casuta Postala 298, Bucharest Romania.

LC GN1 .E86 ISSN 0014-1828
DD 390.06 US
NLM W1 ET445 CODEN ETNLB6
Pr Rev.
ETHNOLOGY. [Ethnology]. **Added/Corp** University of Pittsburgh. Vol. 1 (Jan. 1962)-. Periodical. English. Four times a year (Feb., May, Aug., Nov.). $40.00. Ethnology, Department Anthropology, University of Pittsburgh, Pittsburgh PA 15260. **Tel** (412)648-7503, FAX (412)648-5911. **ED** Leonard Plotnicov and Stacy Hoffman. Index available. cum. index. **Circ:** 2,200. available on microfilm and microfiche from University Microfilms International (UMI). Documents available from The Genuine Article, BIOSIS Document Express, UMI Article Clearinghouse.
Desc: An international journal of cultural and social anthropology.
Ind/Abst Acad. Ind. [Computer File] (1992-); Acad. Search; Am. Hist. Life (1969-1972, 1983-); Anthropol. Lit.; Appl. Soc. Sci. Index Abstr.; Biol. Abstr.; Curr. Contents Arts Humanit.; Curr. Geogr. Publ. (199?-); EP Collect.; Ethnoarts Index; Expand. Acad. Index (1989-); Homework Help.; Hum. Resour. Abstr.; Int. Bibliogr. Sociol.; Int. Dev. Abstr. (?-?); Int. Polit. Sci. Abstr.; Mag. Search; MasterFile FullTEXT 1000; MasterFile FullTEXT 350; MasterFile FullTEXT 650; MasterFile FullTEXT (July 1993-); Middle East Abstr. Index; MLA Int. Bibl. Books Artic. Mod. Lang. Lit.; Newsp. Period. Abstr. (1991-); OCLC; Res. Alert [Full Cov.]; Sage Fam. Stud. Abstr.; Soc. Plann. Policy Dev. Abstr.; Soc. Sci. Source; Soc. Sci. Cit. Index [Full Cov.]; Soc. Sci. Index; Soc. Sci. Index Fulltext (Oct. 1988-) [Full Txt.]; Soc. Work Abstr. [Select. Cov.]; Sociol. Abstr.; Telebase; U.S. Polit. Sci. Doc.; West. Hist. Q.; Women Stud. Abstr.

LC GN1 .E88 ISSN 0014-1844
DD 572.05 SW
NLM W1 ET447 CODEN ESEMBP
ETHNOS. [Ethnos]. **Added/Corp** Statens Etnografiska Museum (Sweden) Etnografiska Museet (Stockholm, Sweden) Folkens Museum Etnografiska. Vol. 1 (Jan. 1936)-. Periodical. English (French, German and Swedish). Two times a year. $71.00. Scandinavian University Press, PO Box 2959 Toeyen, N 0608 Oslo 6 Norway. **Tel** 011 47 2 2575400, FAX 011 47 2 2575353, telex 71896 UROR N. **(Subscription address:** Scandinavian University Press, 200 Meacham Ave., Elmont NY 11003. **Tel** (516)352-7300, FAX (516)352-7377.) **ED** Ulla Wagner and Gudrun Dahl. Index available. cum. index. **Bk Rev. Circ:** 800 (ctrl). Documents available from BIOSIS Document Express.
Desc: Devoted to articles and book reviews on anthropology, ethnography and archaeology.
Ind/Abst Abstr. Anthropol. (19??-); Am. Hist. Life (1965-1970); Anthropol. Index; Anthropol. Lit. (1971-); Biol. Abstr.; Curr. Contents Soc. Behav. Sci.; Ethnoarts Index; Geogr. Abstr. Human Geogr. (1971-); Hisp. Am. Period. Index, HAPI; Int. Dev. Abstr. (1971-); Int. Labour Doc.; Middle East Abstr. Index; Soc. Plann. Policy Dev. Abstr.; Sociol. Abstr.; Middle East J. (1971-).

LC DP48 .E87 ISSN 0211-772X
SP

ETNOGRAFIA ESPANOLA. [Etnogr. esp.]. **Added/Corp** Spain. Subdireccion General de Arqueologia. Spain. Subdireccion General de Arqueologia y Etnografia. (1980)-. Spanish.
Ind/Abst Anthropol. Lit.

LC GN585.P6 E8 ISSN 0071-1861
PL

ETNOGRAFIA POLSKA. [Etnogr. pol.]. **Added/Corp** Instytut Historii Kultury Materialnej (Polska Akademia Nauk). Dzia IV. Etnografia. Instytut Historii Kultury Materialnej (Polska Akademia Nauk). (1958)-. Periodical. Polish (table of contents in Russian and English). Two times a year. $40.00. **(Subscription address:** Ars Polona-Ruch, PO Box 1001, Krakowskie Przedmiescie 7, 00-068 Warsaw Poland. **Tel** 011 48 22 261201.)
Ind/Abst Am. Hist. Life (1959-); Anthropol. Index; MLA Int. Bibl. Books Artic. Mod. Lang. Lit.; Numis. Lit. (1959-).

LC GN1 .S5 ISSN 0354-0316
DD 305.8 XV
ETNOLOG : GLASNIK SLOVENSKEGA ETNOGRAFSKEGA MUZEJA. **Added/Corp** Slovenski etnografski muzej. (1991)-. Periodical. Slovenian (summaries and/or abstracts in English). Narodni Muzej, Presernova 20, Ljubljana Slovenia. **Tel** 061-218-886. ***Continues*** *Slovenski Etnograf.*
Ind/Abst BHA : Biblio. Hist. Art.

LC GN2 .G6
DD 572.05 SW
ETNOLOGISKA STUDIER. **Main/Corp** Goteborgs Etnografiska Museum. **VFOAT** Etnologiska Studier. Vol. 1 (1935)-. Monographic series. English (German and Swedish). Irregular. Price varies per volume. Goteborgs Etnografiska Museum, Norra Hamngatan 12, S411 14 Goteborg Sweden. **Tel** 011 46 31 612776, FAX 011 46 31 741059. **ED** Kjell Zetterstrom. **Circ:** 1,200.
Desc: South American ethnology and archaeology.
Ind/Abst Ethnoarts Index.

LC DR1523 .E87 ISSN 0351-4323
DD 306/.094972 CI
ETNOLOSKA ISTRAZIVANJA / ETNOGRAFSKI MUZEJ U ZAGREBU. **Added/Corp** Etnografski Muzej u Zagrebu. **VFOAT** Ethnological Researches. (1981)-. Periodical. Serbo-Croatian (Roman) (summaries and/or abstracts in English). One time a year. Etnografski Muzej Zagreb, Mazuranicev TRG 14, Zagreb Croatia. **Tel** 385 0 41 458-544, 385 0 41 444-011, FAX 385 0 41 444-011. **ED** Damodar Frlan. ***Formed by the union of*** *Etnografska Istrazivanja I Graa* ***and*** *Vjesnik Ethografskog Muzeja u Zagrebu.*
Desc: Covers a wide spector of ethnological research.

LC E99.E7 E83 ISSN 0701-1008
DD 970/.004/97 CN
ETUDES INUIT. [Etud. Inuit]. **Added/Corp** Inuksiutiit Katimajiit. **VFOAT** Inuit Studies. Vol. 1 (1977)-. Periodical. English (French). Two times a year. 47.00Can$. Laval University / Pavillion Alexandre Vachon, Sainte-Foy Quebec G1K 7P4 Canada. **Tel** (418)656-2352. **ED** Francois Therien. Index available. cum. index. **Bk Rev. Ad Acc. Circ:** 600 (ctrl).
Desc: Research studies on Inuit culture and the language of Siberia, Canada and Greenland and Alaska in the perspective of social sciences and humanities.
Ind/Abst ASTIS Curr. Aware. Bull. (1978-); Abstr. Anthropol.; Am. Hist. Life (1985-); Anthropol. Lit.; ASTIS Bibliogr. (1978-); MLA Int. Bibl. Books Artic. Mod. Lang. Lit.; Repere (1983-); Soc. Plann. Policy Dev. Abstr.

LC GN812.L63 E78
DD 936.4 FR
ETUDES PREHISTORIQUES ET HISTORIQUES DES PAYS DE LA LOIRE. **Added/Corp** Association d'Etudes Prehistoriques et Historiques des Pays de la Loire. Vol. 8 (1985)-. Monographic series. French. Price varies per volume. Assn. Etudes Prehistoriques et Protohistoriques, 2 Allee du Commandant Charcot, 44035 Nantes France. ***Continues*** *Etudes Prehistoriques et Protohistoriques des Pays de la Loire, 0299-2760.*
Ind/Abst Anthropol. Lit.

ISSN 1060-1538
DD 301 US
CCC
EVOLUTIONARY ANTHROPOLOGY / ISSUES, NEWS AND REVIEWS. [Evol. anthropol.]. Vol. 1 (1992)-. Periodical. English. Six times a year. $175.00. John Wiley & Sons, Inc., 605 Third Avenue, New York NY 10158-0012. **Tel** (212)850-6000, (212)850-6645, FAX (212)850-6088, telex 12-7063. **(Subscription address:** John Wiley & Sons Inc / New Jersey, PO Box 2575, Secaucus NJ 07096-2575.) **ED** John Fleagle.
Desc: Focuses on issues of current interest in biological anthropology, paleoanthropology, archaeology, functional morphology, social biology, and bone biology, including dentition and osteology as well as human biology, genetics, and ecology. The journal is a source of information for classroom teaching and research activities in evolutionary anthropology.

LC QH366.A1 E9 ISSN 0071-3260
DD 575/.005 US
CCC
NLM W1 EV64 CODEN EVBIAI
EVOLUTIONARY BIOLOGY. See Biology-Genetics.

LC QH359 .E94
DD 575 US
CODEN ETREE8
Pr Rev.
EVOLUTIONARY THEORY & REVIEW. **Added/Corp** University of Chicago. Dept. of Ecology and Evolution. **VFOAT** Evolutionary Theory and Review; Evolutionary Theory. Vol. 10, No. 1 (Jan. 1991)-. Periodical. English. Irregular. $28.00 (institutions), $22.00 (individuals). University of Chicago Department of Ecology and Evolution, 1101 East 57th Street, Chicago IL 60637. **Tel** (312)702-9475. **ED** L.M. van Valen. **Bk Rev**, (Qty: 100). **Circ:** 650. ***Continues*** *Evolutionary Theory, 0093-4755.*
Desc: Deals with the evolutionary half of biology where the center of interest is on organisms and populations. Book reviews are also contained.

LC GN1 .E9 ISSN 0014-4738
DD 301.2/05 US
Pr Rev.
EXPEDITION. See Archaeology.

LC DL1 .N4 ISSN 0348-971X
SW

FATABUREN. [Fataburen]. **Added/Corp** Nordiska Museet (Stockholm, Sweden). (1906)-. Swedish. One time a year. Kr200.00. Nordiska Museet, Box 27870, S0115 93 Stockholm Sweden. **Tel** 46 8 224120. ***Continues*** *Meddelanden Fran Nordiska Museet.*
Ind/Abst Anthropol. Index; BHA : Biblio. Hist. Art; MLA Int. Bibl. Books Artic. Mod. Lang. Lit.

LC GN2 .F4 ISSN 0071-4739
DD 301 US
CODEN FIEAAV
FIELDIANA. ANTHROPOLOGY. [Fieldiana, Anthropol.]. (1945)-. Monographic series. English. One time a year. Price varies per volume. Field Museum of Natural History, Roosevelt Road at Lake Shore Drive, Chicago IL 60605-2496. **Tel** (312)922-9410 ext. 402, FAX (312)922-0671. **ED** James S Ashe. **Circ:** 450. Documents available from BIOSIS Document Express. ***Continues*** *Anthropological Series (Chicago, Ill.), 0894-8380.*
Desc: This publicaiton contains studies, descriptions, and catalogs of Field Museum collections and of research in the field.
Ind/Abst ASTIS Curr. Aware. Bull. (1978-); ASTIS Bibliogr. (1978-); Biol. Abstr. (1985-); Geogr. Abstr. Human Geogr.; GeoRef.

LC E78.F6 F58 ISSN 0015-3893
DD 913.759 US
CODEN FANTA9
FLORIDA ANTHROPOLOGIST, THE. [Fla. anthropol.]. **Added/Corp** Florida Anthropological Society. Vol. 1 (May 1948)-. Periodical. English. Four times a year. (comes with Florida Anthropological Society membership). Florida Anthropological Society, 5822 Dory Way, Tampa FL 33615. **Tel** (904)487-2333. **ED** Brent Weisman (editor's address: 714 NE 7th Avenue, Gainesville FL 32601). Index available. cum. index. **Bk Rev. Ad Acc. Circ:** 700-800. Documents available from BIOSIS Document Express.
Desc: Contains papers of the Annual Conference on Historic Site Archeology.
Ind/Abst Abstr. Anthropol. (19??-); Anthropol. Lit.; Biol. Abstr.; Ethnoarts Index.

LC GN1 .F57 ISSN 0164-1662
DD 301.2/05 US
CODEN FJANER
FLORIDA JOURNAL OF ANTHROPOLOGY, THE. **Added/Corp** University of Florida Anthropology Student Association. Vol. 1 (Winter 1976)-. Academic Scholarly Publication. English. One time a year (Oct.). $19.00. University of Florida / Anthropology, 1350 Turlington Hall, Gainesville FL 32611. **Tel** (904)392-2031. **ED** Susan E. Stans. **Bk**

Anthropology

Rev. Circ: 60 (ctrl).
 Desc: Anthropology and related fields are the topics that this journal are dedicated to publish. Articles, book reviews and discussions of interest are welcome for consideration.

US

FLORIDA STATE UNIVERSITY NOTES IN ANTHROPOLOGY. Vol. 15 (1976)-. Monographic series. English. Irregular. Price varies per volume. University of Florida Press, 15 Northwest 15th Street, Gainesville FL 32611. **Tel** (904)392-5717, (800)226-3822. *Continues Notes in Anthropology.*

LC GN301 4.F63

JA

FOKUROA. Added/Corp Minzoku no Shiso o Kangaeru Kai. 1 (July 1977)-. Periodical. Japanese. Six times a year. Dai N, Dempa Building, 14-10 Soto Kanda 2, Chiyoda-ku Tokyo Japan.

LC GN1 .F59   ISSN 0085-0756
DK

FOLK (KBENHAVN). (FOLK.). **Added/Corp** Dansk Etnografisk Forening. Vol. 1 (1952)-. Danish (English, French and German). One time a year. kr280.00. Danish Ethnographical Association, Frederiksholms Kanal 4, DK 1220 Copenhagen K Denmark. **Tel** 011 45 1 33121716. **ED** Kirsten Hastrup, Ida Nicolaisen, Susan R. Whyte and Inger Wulff. Index available. **Bk Rev. Circ:** 1,000.
 Desc: International journal containing articles on social and cultural anthropology, reflecting the regional and theoretical diversity of the field.
 Ind/Abst Anthropol. Index; Anthropol. Lit.

ISSN 0429-1530
GW

FORSCHUNGEN ZUR ETHNOLOGIE UND SOZIALPSYCHOLOGIE. Vol. 1 (1953)-. Monographic series. German. Irregular. Price varies per volume. Duncker und Humblot Verlag, Postfach 410329, D-12113 Berlin Germany. **Tel** 011 49 30 79000612, 011 49 30 79000613.

LC Z5118.A6 B8   ISSN 1157-3759
DD 016.301   FR

FRANCIS BULLETIN SIGNALETIQUE. 525, PREHISTOIRE ET PROTOHISTOIRE. Added/Corp Institut de l'Information Scientifique et Technique (France). Sciences Humaines et Sociales. **VFOAT** Prehistoire et Protohistoire; Prehistory and Protohistory. Vol. 45, No. 1 (1991)-. Bulletin. French. Four times a year. CNRS / Institut d'Information Scientifique et Technique, (Centre National de la Recherche Scientifique), 15 Quai Anatole France, 75700 Paris France. **Tel** 011 33 1 47531515, FAX 011 33 1 45517307, telex 260034. **(Subscription address:** Institut d'Information Scientifique et Technique Diffusion, 2 Allee du Parc de Brabois, 54514 Vandoeuvre Nancy France. **Tel** 011 33 83 504664, FAX 011 33 83 504666, telex 961942.) Index available (free). available on CD-ROM. *Continues Bulletin Signaletique. 525, Prehistoire et Protohistoire.*

LC GN301 .B85   ISSN 1157-3791
DD 305.8   FR
CEASED

FRANCIS BULLETIN SIGNALETIQUE. 529, ETHNOLOGIE. Added/Corp Institut de l'Information Scientifique et Technique (France). Sciences Humaines et Sociales. **VFOAT** Ethnologie; Bulletin Signaletique; Ethnology. Vol. 45, No. 1 (1991)-Vol. 48, No. 4 (1994). Bulletin. French. Four times a year. CNRS / Institut d'Information Scientifique et Technique, (Centre National de la Recherche Scientifique), 15 Quai Anatole France, 75700 Paris France. **Tel** 011 33 1 47531515, FAX 011 33 1 45517307, telex 260034. **(Subscription address:** Institut d'Information Scientifique et Technique Diffusion, 2 Allee du Parc de Brabois, 54514 Vandoeuvre Nancy France. **Tel** 011 33 83 504664, FAX 011 33 83 504666, telex 961942.) Index available (free). available on CD-ROM. *Continues Bulletin Signaletique. 529, Ethnologie, 0765-1473.*

PO

UDC 576.2

GARCIA DE ORTA : SERIE DE ANTROPOBIOLOGIA : REVISTA DA JUNTA DE INVESTIGACOES CIENTIFICAS DO ULTRAMAR. Added/Corp Portugal. Junta de Investigacoes Cientificas do Ultramar. **VFOAT** Serie de Antropobiologia. Vol. 1, No. 1 and 2 (1982)-. Periodical. Portuguese (English, French, Spanish, Italian and German; summaries and/or abstracts in English). Two times a year. 1400$00. Instituto de Investigacao Cientifica Tropical, Centro de Documentacao e Informacao, rua Jau 47, 1 300 Lisbon Portugal. **Tel** 645321. **Circ:** 1,000 (ctrl).
 Desc: Publishes articles on biological anthropology in a broad sense (physical anthropology, human ecology, evolution and development, genetics and physiology of populations, etc.).
 Ind/Abst Anthropol. Lit.

LC GN1 .G47   ISSN 0293-0277
DD 569/.9   FR

GENRE HUMAIN, LE. [Genre humain]. (1981)-. Periodical. French. Four times a year. $69.99. Altek Data, 49 rue de la Vanne, 92120 Montrouge Cedex France. **Tel** 011 33 1 41171393.

LC G1 .G42   ISSN 0256-7253
PN

GEOMUNDO. See Geography.

ISSN 0072-1395
US
CODEN GSCMA2

Pr Rev.

GEOSCIENCE AND MAN. See Geography.

LC GN1 .C542
DD 301.05   YU

GLASNIK CETINJSKIH MUZEJA. BULLETIN DES MUSEES DE CETIGNE. VFOAT Bulletin des Musees de Cetigne. (1968)-. Bulletin. Serbo-Croatian (Cyrillic) (summaries and/or abstracts in English, French and Russian). *Supersedes Glasnik Etnografskog Muzeja na Cetinja.*
 Ind/Abst BHA : Biblio. Hist. Art.

ISSN 0350-0861
YU

GLASNIK ETNOGRAFSKOG INSTITUTA. Added/Corp Etnografski Institut (Srpska Akademija Nauka) Etnografski Institut (Srpska Akademija Nauka i Umetnosti). **VFOAT** Bulletin de l'Institut Ethnographique; Glasnik Etnografskog Instituta Srpske Akademije Nauka i Umetnosti; Glasnik Etnografskog Instituta SAN; Glasnik Etnografskog Instituta SANU. (1955/1957)-. Bulletin. Serbo-Croatian (Cyrillic) (summaries and/or abstracts in English and French; table of contents in Multiple languages). *Continues Glasnik Etnografskog Instituta SAN.*
 Ind/Abst Anthropol. Lit.

LC GN301 .S58A   ISSN 0351-2908
XV

GLASNIK SLOVENSKEGA ETNOLOSKEGA DRUSTVA. Main/Corp Slovensko Etnolosko Drustvo. **VFOAT** Bulletin of Slovene Ethnological Society. Vol. 5 (1976)-. Bulletin. Slovenian (English). Four times a year. $20.00. Filozofska Fakulteta, Askerceva 12, 61000 Ljubljana Slovenia. **Tel** (061)332-611. **ED** Nasko Kriznar. **Bk Rev. Ad Acc. Circ:** 700 (ctrl). *Continues Slovensko Etnologsko Drustvo. Glasnik.*
 Desc: Publishes dissertations and book reviews, concerning Slovenian and partially world ethnology.
 Ind/Abst Anthropol. Lit.

LC BV4800   ISSN 1045-9731
DD 242   US

GLOBAL PRAYER DIGEST. [Glob. pray. dig.]. **Added/Corp** Frontier Fellowship. U.S. Center for World Mission. **VFOAT** Frontier Fellowship Global Prayer Digest. (1982)-. Periodical. English. Twelve times a year. $9.00. US Center for World Mission, 1605 East Elizabeth Street, Pasadena CA 91104. **Tel** (818)797-1111, (818)398-2317. **Circ:** 19,000 (ctrl).

US
SUSPENDED

GLOBAL REPORTER, THE. Added/Corp Anthropology Resource Center (Washington, D.C.). Vol. 1 No. 1 (March 1983)-. Periodical. English. Four times a year. Anthropology Resource Center, 37 Temple Place, Room 521, Boston MA 02111. *Continues Bulletin (Anthropology Resource Center (Boston, Mass.)); ARC Newsletter (Cambridge, Mass.).*
 Ind/Abst Hum. Rights Intern. Rep.

LC F1465 .G85   ISSN 0017-5056
GT

GUATEMALA INDIGENA. Added/Corp Instituto Indigenista Nacional, Guatemala. Vol. 1 (1961)-. Periodical. Spanish. Four times a year. $12.00. Instituto Indigenista Nacional, Ciudad de Guatemala, Guatemala.
 Desc: Explains the history of the indigenous movement internationally, covers methodology used in the congress, lists calendar of events and supplies technical references for students of linguistic science and culture.
 Ind/Abst AGRICOLA; Anthropol. Index; Hisp. Am. Period. Index, HAPI (19??-).

UK

GYPSY. Added/Corp Gypsy and Folk-Lore Club. Vol. 3, No. 3 (1916)-. Periodical. English. *Continues Gypsy and Folk-Lore Gazette.*
 Ind/Abst Am. Humanit. Index (199?-).

ISSN 0820-2893
DD 971.23/004   CN

HERITAGE LINK. See History-History of North and South America.

ISSN 0882-4894
DD 301   US
Pr Rev.

HIGH PLAINS APPLIED ANTHROPOLOGIST. [High plains appl. anthropol.]. Periodical. English. Two times a year. $25.00. High Plains Society for Applied Anthropologist, 4777 South Oak Court, Littleton CO 80127-1217. **Tel** (303)969-2255. **ED** Larry Van Horn, Judith Van Horn. **Bk Rev. Ad Acc. Circ:** 150.
 Desc: Emphasizes a holistic approach to anthropology. Publishes articles, brief communications and book reviews in applied and practicing anthropology.

LC CB251 .H54
JA

HIKAKU BUNKA ZASSHI. See History.

ISSN 0073-2486
PE

HISTORIA Y CULTURA (LIMA). See History.

LC GN301 .H57   ISSN 0942-8704
GW

●**HISTORISCHE ANTHROPOLOGIE.** See Social Sciences.

LC GN1 .H57   ISSN 0275-7206
DD 306   SZ
CCC
CODEN HIAND7

HISTORY AND ANTHROPOLOGY. [Hist. anthropol.]. Vol. 1, Pt. 1 (Nov. 1984)-. Monographic series. English. Two times a year (2 issues per volume). $255.00 (academic institutions), $397.00 (corporate institutions). Harwood Academic Publishers, PO Box 90, Reading RG1 8JL United Kingdom. **Tel** 011 44 1734 560080, FAX 011 44 1734 568211. **ED** Francois Hartog. **Bk Rev. Ad Acc.**
 Ind/Abst Am. Hist. Life (1984-); Anthropol. Lit.

ISSN 0362-9074
US

NLM W1 HI82

HISTORY OF ANTHROPOLOGY NEWSLETTER. [Hist. anthropol. newsl.]. **VFOAT** HAN. (1973)-. Newsletter. English. Two times a year. $6.00. University of Chicago Department of Anthropology, 1126 East 59th Street, Chicago IL 60637. **Tel** (312)702-7702, FAX (312)702-4503. **ED** George W. Stocking Jr. **Circ:** 350. *Continues Newsletter, History of Anthropology, 0735-4320.*
 Desc: Documents, sources, bibliography, and short reviews of literature in the history of anthropology.
 Ind/Abst Am. Hist. Life.

LC GN1 .H68   ISSN 0339-543X
FR
Pr Rev.

HOMME (PARIS, 1975), L'. (L'HOMME : REVUE FRANCAISE D'ANTHROPOLOGIE.). [Homme]. **Added/Corp** Ecole des Hautes Etudes en Sciences Sociales. Centre National de la Recherche Scientifique (France). Vol. 15, No. 1 (Jan.-Mar. 1975)-. Periodical. French (summaries and/or abstracts in Spanish and English). Four times a year. 411.36F (institutions) France; 480.00F (institutions) other; 264.45F (individuals) France; 270.00F (individuals) other. Editions EHESS, 131 boulevard Saint Michel, 75005 Paris France. **Tel** 011 33 1 43544715, FAX 011 33 1 43548073. **(Subscription address:** Centrale des Revues, 11 rue Gossin, 92543 Montrouge Cedex France. **Tel** 011 33 1 46565266.) **ED** Jean Pouillon. Index available. cum. index. **Bk Rev. Ad Acc. Circ:** 1,000. *Continues Homme (Ecole Pratique des Hautes Etudes (France). Section des Sciences Economiques et Sociales), 0439-4216.*
 Desc: Covers anthropology.
 Ind/Abst Abstr. Anthropol.; Anthropol. Index; Anthropol. Lit.; Arts Humanit. Citation Index; Ethnoarts Index; Int. Bibliogr. Sociol.; Int. Polit. Sci. Abstr.; Lang. Lang. Behav. Abstr.; Math. Rev.; MLA Int. Bibl. Books Artic. Mod. Lang. Lit.; Res. Alert; Soc. Plann. Policy Dev. Abstr.; Soc. Sci. Cit. Index; Soc. Welf. Soc. Plan./Policy Soc. Dev.; Sociol. Abstr.; Women Stud. Abstr.

LC GN1 .H75   ISSN 0018-442X
GW
CCC
NLM W1 HO521   CODEN HOMOA7
Pr Rev.

HOMO. [Homo]. **Added/Corp** Deutsche Gesellschaft fuer Anthropologie. Vol. 1 (1949)-. Periodical. German (English). Three times a year. $354.00. Gustav Fischer Verlag Stuttgart, Postfach 720143, D-70577 Stuttgart Germany. **Tel** 011 49 711 458030, FAX 011 49 711 4580334, telex 2627-7111488. **(Subscription address:** VCH Publishers Inc., 303 Northwest 12th Avenue, Journals Department, Deerfield FL 33442. **Tel** (800)367-8249, (305)428-5566.) **ED** Ilse Schwidetzky. Index available. **Bk Rev. Ad Acc.** Documents available from BIOSIS Document Express.
 Desc: Research journal on human history. Official journal of the German anthropological society with original contributions in English.
 Ind/Abst Anthropol. Index; Anthropol. Lit.; Arts Humanit. Citation Index [Select. Cov.]; Biol. Abstr.; Curr. Contents Soc. Behav. Sci.; Soc. Sci. Cit. Index [Full Cov.].

Anthropology

LC DS793.S6445 H67
DD 951/.3004
CC
HSI NAN MIN TSU YEN CHIU. Added/Corp Chung-kuo Hsi Nan Min Tsu Yen Chiu Hui. 1 (June 1983)-. Periodical. Chinese. Ssu-Chuan Sheng Hsin Hua Shu Tien, Cheng-tu, People's Republic of China.

LC GN1 .H8
DD 570.5
NLM W1 HU444U
Pr Rev.
ISSN 0018-7143
US
CODEN HUBIAA
HUMAN BIOLOGY. See Biology.

ISSN 0018-716X
SZ
CCC
NLM W1 HU446C
Pr Rev.
CODEN HUDEA8
HUMAN DEVELOPMENT. See Psychology.

DD 304
ISSN 1074-4827
US
●**HUMAN ECOLOGY REVIEW.** [Hum. ecol. rev.]. Added/Corp Society for Human Ecology. VFOAT Human Ecology. Vol. 1, No. 1 (Winter/Spring 1993/94)-. Periodical. English. Two times a year. $60.00. Society for Human Ecology, 105 Elden Street, College Atlantic, Bar Harbor ME 04609. Tel (207)288-5015.

LC GN537
DD 572
ISSN 0739-2036
US
HUMAN ETHOLOGY NEWSLETTER. [Hum. ethol. newsl.]. Added/Corp International Society for Human Ethology. (19??)-. Newsletter. English. Four times a year (Mar., June, Sept., Dec). $25.00. Wayne State University / Psychology, Department of Psychology, C/O Glenn E. Weisfeld PH.D., Detroit MI 48202. Tel (313)577-2835, FAX (313)577-7636. ED Glenn E. Weisfeld PH.D. Bk Rev. (Qty: 12). Circ: 500.
Desc: Contains book reviews, articles, announcements and commentary on human behavior in evolutionary perspective.
Ind/Abst Int. Bibliogr. Sociol.

LC GN281 .H8474
DD 573.2/05
NLM W1; HU446L
Pr Rev.
ISSN 0393-9375
IT
HUMAN EVOLUTION. Vol. 1, No. 1 (Feb. 1986)-. Periodical. English. Six times a year. L150000. Karta Sas, Via Slataper 10, 50134 Florence Italy. Tel 011 39 55 496502. ED A.B. Chiarelli. Index available in last issue of volume--attached. Bk Rev. Ad Acc. Circ: 700.
Desc: Forum for the study of human evolution.
Ind/Abst Anthropol. Lit.; Curr. Primate Ref.

LC GN1 .H82
DD 300/.5
ISSN 0018-7240
US
HUMAN MOSAIC. See Sociology.

LC GN1 .H83
DD 305
ISSN 0018-7259
US
CCC
NLM W1 HU456
Pr Rev.
CODEN HUORAY
HUMAN ORGANIZATION. (HUMAN ORGANIZATION : JOURNAL OF THE SOCIETY FOR APPLIED ANTHROPOLOGY.). [Human organ.]. Added/Corp Society for Applied Anthropology. Vol. 8, No. 1 (Winter 1949)-. Periodical. English. Four times a year. $65.00 US; $70.00 other. Society for Applied Anthropology, Box 24083, Oklahoma City OK 73124. Tel (405)843-5113. ED Michael Angrosino. Index available in last issue of volume--attached. cum. index. Bk Rev. Ad Acc. Circ: 3,800 (ctrl). available on microfilm and microfiche from University Microfilms International (UMI). Documents available from The Genuine Article, BIOSIS Document Express, UMI Article Clearinghouse.
Continues Applied Anthropology, 0093-2914.
Desc: Scientific investigation of "the principles controlling the relations of human beings to one another... and the wide application of these principles to practical problems." Includes sections on government and industry, health and medical care, and international affairs.
Ind/Abst ABI/INFORM Glob. Ed.; ABI/INFORM [Computer File] (Fall 1972-Fall 1973); Abstr. Anthropol.; Acad. Abstr.; Acad. Ind. [Computer File] (1987-); Acad. Search; Agrofor. Abstr.; Am. Hist. Life (1963-); Anthropol. Lit.; Appl. Soc. Sci. Index Abstr.; Arts Humanit. Citation Index [Select. Cov.]; Biol. Abstr. (1985-); Curr. Cit.; Curr. Contents Soc. Behav. Sci.; Curr. Geogr. Publ. (199?-); Curr. Index J. Educ.; Educ. Adm. Abstr. (?-); EP Collect.; Expand. Acad. Index (1987-); Gen. Period. Index (198?-); Geogr. Abstr. Human Geogr. (?-?); Health Plan. Adminis.; Homework Help.; Hosp. Health Admin. Index; Hum. Resour. Abstr.; INFO-SOUTH Abstr.; Int. Bibliogr. Sociol.; Int. Dev. Abstr. (?-?); Int. Polit. Sci. Abstr.; Irr. Drain. Abstr.; Leis., Rec., Tour. Abstr.; Mag. Search; Maize Abstr.; MasterFile FullTEXT 1000; MasterFile FullTEXT 350; MasterFile FullTEXT 650; MasterFile FullTEXT (Jan. 1990-); Middle East Abstr. Index; Multicult. Educ. Abstr.; Newsp. Period. Abstr. (1991-); OCLC; Peace Res. Abstr. J. (1963-1968; 1970-1972; 1975-1977); Potato Abstr.; Psychol. Abstr. (1987-); PsycINFO (1990-); PsycLit; Pub. Lib. FullTEXT; Res. Alert [Full Cov.]; Rice Abstr.; Rural Dev. Abstr.; Sage Fam. Stud. Abstr.; Sage Public Adm. Abstr. (?-?); Sage Urban Stud. Abstr (?-?); Soc. Plann. Policy Dev. Abstr.; Soc. Sci. Source; Soc. Sci. Cit. Index [Full Cov.]; Soc. Sci. Index; Soc. Sci. Index Fulltext

(Winter 1988-) [Full Txt.]; Soc. Work Abstr. [Select. Cov.]; Sociol. Abstr.; Telebase; Women Stud. Abstr.; Work Relat. Abstr.; World Agric. Econ. Rural Sociol. Abstr.

LC DG576 .I34
DD 945.092
ISSN 0019-1280
IT
IDEA (ROME). See History.

ISSN 0073-5167
CCC
CODEN ISANBI
ILLINOIS STUDIES IN ANTHROPOLOGY. [Ill. stud. anthropol.]. No. 1 (1961)-. English. Irregular. Price varies. University of Illinois Press, 1325 South Oak Street, Champaign IL 61820. Tel (217)333-0950, FAX (217)244-8082. (Subscription address: University of Illinois Press, PO Box 4856, Hampden Station, Baltimore MD 21211. Tel (800)545-4703.) Documents available from BIOSIS Document Express.
Ind/Abst Biol. Abstr.

LC GN635.I4 I54
DD 301.2/0954
II
INDIAN ANTHROPOLOGIST. (INDIAN ANTHROPOLOGIST : JOURNAL OF THE INDIAN ANTHROPOLOGICAL ASSOCIATION.). Vol. 1, No. 1, (1971)-. Periodical. English. Two times a year (June, Dec). $52.00. Indian Anthropological Association, University of Delhi, Department of Anthropology, Delhi 7 India. Tel 2515329. ED B. K. Roy Burman. Bk Rev. Ad Acc. Circ: 1,100.
Desc: Research papers, both empirical and theoretical, on themes and problems of interest to professional anthropologists in all branches of anthropology.
Ind/Abst Anthropol. Index; Anthropol. Lit.

LC GN49 .I53
DD 573/.05
NLM W1 IN2255
ISSN 0378-8156
II
CODEN IJPGDB
INDIAN JOURNAL OF PHYSICAL ANTHROPOLOGY AND HUMAN GENETICS. See Biology-Genetics.

LC E51 .I37
DD 970.004/97
GW
INDIANA (BERLIN, GERMANY). See History-History of North and South America.

DK
INDIGENOUS AFFAIRS. (19??)-. English. Four times a year. $35.00. International Work Group for Indigenous Affairs, Fiolstraede 10, DK-1171 Copenhagen K Denmark. Tel 011 45 1 33124724. **Continues** IWGIA Newsletter, 0105-6387.

ISSN 0928-1460
NE
●**INDIGENOUS KNOWLEDGE & DEVELOPMENT MONITOR.** Added/Corp Centre for International Research and Advisory Networks. Centre for Indigenous Knowledge for Agriculture and Rural Development. Indigenous Knowledge Resource Centres. VFOAT Indigenous Knowledge and Development Monitor. Vol. 1, No. 1 (1993)-. Periodical. English. Three times a year. $27.41. Nuffic, PO Box 29777, 2502 LT The Hague Netherlands. Tel 011 31 70 4260260. Absorbed Cikard News.

LC F2269 .I54
DD 986.1/01/05
ISSN 0121-2079
CK
INFORMES ANTROPOLOGICOS. Added/Corp Instituto Colombiano de Antropologia. No. 1 (1985)-. Periodical. Spanish.
Ind/Abst Anthropol. Lit.

US
INTERNATIONAL BIBLIOGRAPHY OF SOCIAL SCIENCES: ANTHROPOLOGY. See Anthropology-Abstracting, Bibliographies and Statistics.

ISSN 0393-9383
IT
INTERNATIONAL JOURNAL OF ANTHROPOLOGY. [Int. j. anthropol.]. Added/Corp European Anthropological Association. Vol. 1, No. 1 (March 1986)-. Periodical. English. Four times a year (Mar., June, Sept., Dec). L115000. Karta Sas, Via Slataper 10, 50134 Florence Italy. Tel 011 39 55 496502.
Ind/Abst Anthropol. Lit.; Curr. Primate Ref.

ISSN 0074-8684
NE
INTERNATIONAL STUDIES IN SOCIOLOGY AND SOCIAL ANTHROPOLOGY. See Sociology.

LC PS536.2 .I56
DD 810/.8/005
ISSN 0021-0331
US
IO. No. 6 (1969)-. Monographic series. English. Irregular. Price varies per volume. North Atlantic Books, PO Box 12327, Berkeley CA 94701. Tel (510)644-2116, FAX (510)644-2136. ED Richard Grossinger. Circ: 3,000. **Continues** IO Magazine.

Desc: A series of issues on geography, alchemy, dreams, baseball, history of science, internal martial arts, aesthetics of literature and film, native thought, anthropology, and psychology.

LC GN635.I65 I74
DD 306/.09598/2
ISSN 0304-2189
IO
CEASED
IRIAN. [Irian]. Added/Corp Universitas Cenderawasih. Lembaga Anthropologi. (1972)- Vol. 21 (1993). Periodical. English (Indonesian). Irian, PO Box 1800, Jayapura Irian Jaya Indonesia. Tel 011 62 967 81281. ED Daniel C. Alamiseba. Circ: 460.
Desc: Linguistic and anthropological articles about the people and languages of Irian Jaya.
Ind/Abst Anthropol. Index; Ethnoarts Index; MLA Int. Bibl. Books Artic. Mod. Lang. Lit.; Rural Dev. Abstr.; World Agric. Econ. Rural Sociol. Abstr.

LC DU500 .I85
DD 996.5
ISSN 1054-9390
GU
CODEN ISLAE3
Pr Rev.
ISLA (MANGILAO, GUAM). (ISLA : A JOURNAL OF MICRONESIAN STUDIES.). [Isla]. Added/Corp University of Guam. (1992)-. Periodical. English (Truk). Two times a year (Jan., July). $35.00. University of Guam Press / Office of Graduate School and Research, UOG Station, Mangilao 96923 Guam. Tel (671)73-9401, FAX (671)734-3676, telex 7216275. ED Donald H. Rubinstein and J. Jennison-Williams. Bk Rev. (Qty: 12). Ad Acc. Adv Mgr: J.Jennison-Williams. Circ: 300 (ctrl).
Desc: Covers the Micronesian region of the Pacific Ocean.

ISSN 0105-4503
DK
IWGIA DOCUMENTS. Main/Corp International Work Group for Indigenous Affairs. VFOAT IWGIA Documentation. No. 1, (Jan. 1971)-. Periodical. English. Irregular. $70.00 (institutions); $50.00 (individuals). International Work Group for Indigenous Affairs, Fiolstraede 10, DK-1171 Copenhagen K Denmark. Tel 011 45 1 33124724. Ad Acc.
Ind/Abst Hum. Rights Intern. Rep.

DK
TITLE CHANGE
IWGIA NEWSLETTER. Added/Corp International Work Group for Indigenous Affairs. VFOAT Newsletter. No. 1 (July/Aug. 1991)-(199?). Newsletter. English. International Work Group for Indigenous Affairs, Fiolstraede 10, DK-1171 Copenhagen K Denmark. Tel 011 45 1 33124724. **Continues** IWGIA Newsletter, 0105-6387. **Continued by** Indigenous Affairs.
Desc: Reports and interviews about the race discrimination rights.
Ind/Abst Hum. Rights Intern. Rep.

LC GN
DD 301/573
GW
JAHRESBERICHT / BAYERISCHE STAATSGEMAELDESAMMLUNGEN. Main/Corp Bayerische Staatsgemaeldesammlungen. (19??)-. Periodical. German. One time a year.
Ind/Abst BHA : Biblio. Hist. Art.

ISSN 0044-8370
UK
CODEN JJAOE6
JASO : JOURNAL OF THE ANTHROPOLOGICAL SOCIETY OF OXFORD. Added/Corp Anthropological Society of Oxford. VAT Journal of the Anthropological Society of Oxford. Vol. 10, No. 3 (1979)-. Periodical. English. Three times a year (Apr., July, Dec). £13.50 (individuals); £24.00 (institutions). Institute of Social Anthropology, 51 Banbury Road, Oxford OX2 6PE United Kingdom. Tel 011 44 1865 274682. ED Jeremy Coote. Index available. cum. index. Bk Rev. Ad Acc. **Continues** Anthropological Society of Oxford. Journal of the Anthropological Society of Oxford, 0044-8370.

ISSN 0003-5505
JA
JINRUIGAKU ZASSHI. JOURNAL OF THE ANTHROPOLOGICAL SOCIETY OF NIPPON. Added/Corp Nippon Jinruigaku Kai. Hokoku. Nippon Jinruigaku Kai. Zasshi. Nippon Jinruigaku Kai. Bulletin. Nippon Jinruigaku Kai. Journal. Tokyo Jinrui Gakkai. Nippon Jinruigaku Kai. VFOAT Journal of the Anthropological Society of Nippon; Zinruigaku. Vol. 1, No. 1 (Feb. 1886)-. Periodical. Japanese (English, German and French). Four times a year. $150.00. (Subscription address: Japan Publications Trading Company Ltd., PO Box 5030, Tokyo International, Tokyo 100-31 Japan. Tel 011 81 3 3292 3753.) Documents available from The Genuine Article.
Ind/Abst Anthropol. Lit.; Curr. Contents Soc. Behav. Sci.; Res. Alert [Full Cov.]; Soc. Sci. Cit. Index [Full Cov.].

LC E51 .S68
DD 970.01
ISSN 0037-9174
FR
JOURNAL DE LA SOCIETE DES AMERICANISTES. See Archaeology.

LC DU1 .S553 ISSN 0300-953X
DD 990/.05 FR
JOURNAL DE LA SOCIETE DES OCEANISTES. [J. Soc. ocean.]. **Main/Corp** Societe des Oceanistes. **Added/Corp** Societe des Oceanistes. Musee de l'Homme (Museum National d'Histoire Naurelle). No. 1 (Dec. 1945)-. Periodical. French (English). Two times a year. 300.00F. Societe des Oceanistes, Musee de l'Homme, 75116 Paris France. **Tel** 011 33 1 47046340. Index available (free). cum. index. ***Continues** Societe des Oceanistes. Bulletin de la Societe des Oceanistes.*
Ind/Abst Am. Hist. Life (1986-); Anthropol. Lit.; Bibliogr. Mission.; Curr. Geogr. Publ. (199?-); Ethnoarts Index; MLA Int. Bibl. Books Artic. Mod. Lang. Lit.

LC DT1 .S65 ISSN 0399-0346
DD 960/.05 FR
Pr Rev.
JOURNAL DES AFRICANISTES.
Added/Corp Societe des Africanistes (France). Vol. 46, (1976)-. Periodical. French (summaries and/or abstracts in English). Two times a year (July, Dec.). $91.86. Musee de l'Homme, Pal Chaillot place Trocadero, 75116 Paris France. **Tel** 011 33 1 44057336. **ED** Ariane Deluz. Index available. cum. index. **Bk Rev**, (Qty: 2). **Circ:** 700 (ctrl). ***Continues** Journal de la Societe des Africanistes, 0037-9166.*
Desc: Presents original articles on anthropology: physical, social and cultural sociology; linguistics; and the prehistoric archaeology of Africa. Includes bibliographic information.
Ind/Abst Anthropol. Lit.; Ethnoarts Index.

LC GV1588.6 .J68 ISSN 0891-7124
DD 793.3/1 US
Pr Rev.
JOURNAL FOR THE ANTHROPOLOGICAL STUDY OF HUMAN MOVEMENT AT NEW YORK UNIVERSITY. [J. anthropol. study hum. mov. N.Y. Univ.]. **VFOAT** JASHM. Vol. 1, No. 1 (Spring 1980)-. Periodical. English. Two times a year (Spring & Autumn). $40.00. JASHM, Anthropology Department, McBride Hall, University of Iowa, Iowa City IA 52242. **Tel** (812)855-2301. **ED** D. Williams, B. Farnell (Editors telephone: (319)335-0522). Index available. **Bk Rev**, (Qty: 4).
Desc: Information on anthropology, movement studies and dance.
Ind/Abst Anthropol. Lit.

LC CC79.E85 J68 ISSN 0278-4165
DD 306/.072 US
CCC
Pr Rev.
JOURNAL OF ANTHROPOLOGICAL ARCHAEOLOGY. **See** Archaeology.

LC GN1 .S64 ISSN 0091-7710
DD 301.2/05 US
NLM W1 JO536L **CODEN** JAPRCP
Pr Rev.
JOURNAL OF ANTHROPOLOGICAL RESEARCH. [J. anthropol. res.]. (Spring 1973)-. Periodical. English. Four times a year. $40.00. Journal of Anthropological Research, University of New Mexico, Anthropology, Albuquerque NM 87131. **Tel** (505)277-4544. **ED** Philip K Bock. **Bk Rev. Circ:** 1,700. available on microfilm and microfiche from University Microfilms International (UMI). Documents available from The Genuine Article, BIOSIS Document Express, UMI Article Clearinghouse. ***Continues** Southwestern Journal of Anthropology, 0038-4801.*
Ind/Abst Abstr. Anthropol.; Acad. Abstr.; Acad. Search; Am. Hist. Life (1963-1969,1984-); Am. Bibliogr. Slavic East Europ. Stud.; Annu. Bibliogr. Engl. Lang. Lit.; Anthropol. Index; Anthropol. Lit.; Arts Humanit. Citation Index [Select. Cov.]; Biol. Abstr.; Br. Archaeol. Bibliogr.; Ceram. Abstr. (199?-); Curr. Contents Soc. Behav. Sci.; EP Collect.; Ethnoarts Index; Expand. Acad. Index (1989-); Gen. Sci. Source; Homework Help.; INFO-SOUTH Abstr.; Mag. Search; MasterFile FullTEXT 1000; MasterFile FullTEXT 350; MasterFile FullTEXT 650; MasterFile FullTEXT (Jan. 1992-); Middle East Abstr. Index; MLA Int. Bibl. Books Artic. Mod. Lang. Lit.; Newsp. Period. Abstr. (1991-); OCLC; Pub. Lib. FullTEXT; Res. Alert [Full Cov.]; Soc. Plann. Policy Dev. Abstr.; Soc. Sci. Source; Soc. Sci. Cit. Index [Full Cov.]; Soc. Sci. Index; Soc. Sci. Index Fulltext (Fall 1988-) [Full Txt.]; Sociol. Abstr.; Telebase.

LC E78.C15 J62 ISSN 0191-3557
DD 979/.005 US
CODEN JGBAEG
Pr Rev.
JOURNAL OF CALIFORNIA AND GREAT BASIN ANTHROPOLOGY. [J. Calif. Gt. Basin anthropol.]. **Added/Corp** Malki Museum. University of California, Riverside. Dept. of Anthropology. Vol. 1 (Summer 1979)-. Periodical. English. Two times a year. $25.00. Department Sociology and Anthropology / Bakersfield, California State University, 9001 Stockdale Highway, Bakersfield CA 93311. **Tel** (805)664-3153. **ED** Mark Q. Sutton. Index available. cum. index. **Bk Rev**, (Qty: varies). **Ad Acc. Circ:** 600 (ctrl). ***Supersedes** Journal of California Anthropology, 0361-7181.*
Desc: Anthropological studies of native peoples and culture of California, Baja and the Great Basin.
Ind/Abst Am. Hist. Life (1974-);(1979-); Anthropol. Lit.; Ethnoarts Index.

LC HT101 .U677 ISSN 0891-2416
DD 307.7/6/05 US
CCC
NLM W1; JO595S
Pr Rev.
JOURNAL OF CONTEMPORARY ETHNOGRAPHY. [J. contemp. ethnogr.]. **VFOAT** Contemporary Ethnography; JCE. Vol. 16, No. 1 (April 1987)-. Periodical. English. Four times a year (Jan., Apr., July, Oct.). $191.00. SAGE Periodical Press, 2455 Teller Road, Thousand Oaks CA 91320. **Tel** (805)499-0721, FAX (805)499-0871, telex 100799. **ED** Patricia A. Adler and Peter Adler. **Acid Free.** available on microfilm and microfiche from University Microfilms International (UMI). Documents available from The Genuine Article, UMI Article Clearinghouse. ***Continues** Urban Life, 0098-3039.*
Desc: Interdisciplinary journal of ethnography and qualitative research. Advances sociological knowledge through intensive, in-depth studies of human behavior in natural settings.
Ind/Abst Abstr. Anthropol.; Acad. Search; Anthropol. Index; Appl. Soc. Sci. Index Abstr.; Crim. Justice Abstr.; Curr. Cit.; Curr. Contents Soc. Behav. Sci.; Curr. Index J. Educ.; Educ. Adm. Abstr.; EP Collect.; Expand. Acad. Index (1989-); Homework Help.; Hum. Resour. Abstr. (?-?); INFO-SOUTH Abstr.; Mag. Search; MasterFile FullTEXT 1000; MasterFile FullTEXT 350; MasterFile FullTEXT 650; MasterFile FullTEXT (July 1993-); Newsp. Period. Abstr. (1991-); OCLC; Psychol. Abstr.; Res. Alert [Full Cov.]; Sage Fam. Stud. Abstr. (?-?); Sage Urban Stud. Abstr (?-?); Soc. Plann. Policy Dev. Abstr.; Soc. Sci. Source; Soc. Sci. Cit. Index [Full Cov.]; Soc. Sci. Index; Soc. Sci. Index Fulltext (Oct. 1988-) [Full Txt.]; Sociol. Abstr.; Soc. Res. Methodol. Abstr. (1992-); Telebase.

LC BF728 .J65 ISSN 0022-0221
DD 155.8/05 US
CCC
NLM W1 JO612A **CODEN** JCPGB5
Pr Rev.
JOURNAL OF CROSS-CULTURAL PSYCHOLOGY. **See** Psychology.

LC GN476.7 .J68 ISSN 0278-0771
DD 574.6 US
CODEN JOUEE9
Pr Rev.
JOURNAL OF ETHNOBIOLOGY. [J. ethnobiol.]. **Added/Corp** Center for Western Studies (Flagstaff, Ariz.). Vol. 1, No. 1 (May 1981)-. Periodical. English (Spanish). Two times a year. $60.00 (institutions) US, Canada, and Latin America; $35.00 (individuals) US and Canada; $25.00 (individuals) Latin America; $68.00 (institutions) other; $43.00 other. Society of Ethnobiology, Center Plant Conservation, PO Box 299, St. Louis MO 63166. **Tel** (314)577-9450. **ED** Willard van Asdall. Index available. cum. index. **Bk Rev. Ad Acc. Circ:** 400 (ctrl). Documents available from BIOSIS Document Express.
Desc: Research publication on multidisciplinary studies in anthropology and biology including archaeozoology, ethnobotany, ethnomedicine, folk classification, and ethnozoology.
Ind/Abst Abstr. Anthropol.; Anthropol. Lit.; Biol. Abstr. (1989-); Br. Archaeol. Bibliogr.; Fish Rev. (Jan. 1989-July 1992); Wildl. Rev. (Jan. 1989-July 1992).

LC QL750 .J68 ISSN 0289-0771
JA
CODEN JOETE8
Pr Rev.
JOURNAL OF ETHOLOGY. [J. ethol.]. **Added/Corp** Nihon Dobutsu Kodo Gakkai. Vol. 1, No. 1-2 (Nov. 1983)-. Periodical. English. Two times a year (June & Dec.). $80.00. Japan Ethological Society, Kyoto University, Department of Zoology, Sakyo-ku Kyoto 606-01 Japan. **Tel** 011 81 75 7512111, FAX 011 81 75 7516149, telex 5422302. **ED** Dr. Takeji Kimura (editor's address: Department of Biology, College of Arts and Sciences, University of Tokyo Komaba, Meguro, Tokyo 453, Japan, phone: 81-3-3467-1171 Ext. 423 or 81 3-3467-9145 Fax). Documents available from The Genuine Article, BIOSIS Document Express.
Ind/Abst AGRICOLA [Select. Cov.]; Anim. Behav. Abstr.; Biocont. News Inf.; Biol. Abstr. (1986-); Curr. Aware. Biol. Sci., CABS; Curr. Contents Agric. Biol. Environ. Sci.; Ecology Abstr.; Fish Rev. (Jan. 1989-July 1992); Life Sci. Collect.; Res. Alert [Select. Cov.]; SCISEARCH; Wildl. Rev. (Jan. 1989-July 1992).

LC GN281 .J63 ISSN 0047-2484
DD 573.2 UK
CCC
NLM W1 JO673VE **CODEN** JHEVAT
Pr Rev.
JOURNAL OF HUMAN EVOLUTION. [J. hum. evol.]. Vol. 1 (Jan. 1972)-. Academic Scholarly Publication. English. Twelve times a year. $581.81. Academic Press Ltd., A Division of Harcourt Brace & Company Ltd., 24-28 Oval Road, London NW1 7DX United Kingdom. **Tel** 011 44 171 2674466, FAX 011 44 171 4822293, 011 44 171 4854752, telex 25775 ACPRES G. **(Subscription address:** Harcourt Brace & Company, Ltd., Foots Cray High Street, Sidcup Kent DA14 5HP United Kingdom. **Tel** 011 44 181 3003322, FAX 011 44 181 3090807, telex 896 377 ACADEM.**)** **ED** P. Andrews and W. Jungers. Documents available from The Genuine Article, BIOSIS Document Express.
Desc: Concentrates on publishing the highest quality papers covering all aspects of human evolution. The central focus is aimed jointly at palaeoanthropological work, covering human and primate fossils, and at comparative studies of living species, including both morphological and molecular evidence. These include descriptions of new discoveries, interpretative analysis of new and previously described material, and assessments of the phylogeny and palaeobiology of primate species.
Ind/Abst Abstr. Anthropol.; Anthropol. Index; Anthropol. Lit.; Art Archaeol. Tech. Abstr.; Biol. Abstr.; Biostatistica; Br. Archaeol. Bibliogr.; Curr. Cit.; Curr. Contents Soc. Behav. Sci.; Curr. Primate Ref.; Ecol. Abstr.; Ecology Abstr.; EMBASE; Geol. Abstr.; GeoRef; Life Sci. Collect.; Res. Alert [Full Cov.]; Sci. Cit. Index; SCISEARCH; Soc. Sci. Cit. Index [Full Cov.].

LC CB201 .J68 ISSN 0092-2323
DD 910/.03 US
JOURNAL OF INDO-EUROPEAN STUDIES, THE. **See** Linguistics.

LC CB251 .J69 ISSN 0388-0508
DD 905 JA
JOURNAL OF INTERCULTURAL STUDIES (HIRAKATA, OSAKA). (THE JOURNAL OF INTERCULTURAL STUDIES.). [J. intercult. stud.]. **Added/Corp** Kansai Gaikokugo Daigaku. Kokusai Bunka Kenkyujo. No. 1 (1974)-. Periodical. English. One time a year. $51.00. Kansai Gaidai University, IRI 16 1 Kitakatahoko Cho, Hirakata City Osaka 573 Japan. **Tel** 011 81 720 555552. **ED** Haruo Kozu. **Bk Rev. Circ:** 1,000.
Desc: Covers the field of cultural anthropology.

LC P35 .J66 ISSN 1055-1360
DD 306.4/4/089 US
CODEN JLIAEI
JOURNAL OF LINGUISTIC ANTHROPOLOGY. (JOURNAL OF LINGUISTIC ANTHROPOLOGY : A PUBLICATION OF THE SOCIETY FOR LINGUISTIC ANTHROPOLOGY, A UNIT OF THE AMERICAN ANTHROPOLOGICAL ASSOCIATION.). [J. linguist. anthr.]. **Added/Corp** Society for Linguistic Anthropology (U.S.). **VFOAT** JLA. Vol. 1, No. 1 (June 1991)-. Periodical. English. Two times a year. $40.00. American Anthropological Association, 4350 North Fairfax Dr, Suite 640, Arlington VA 22203. **Tel** (703)528-1902 ext. 3031, FAX (703)528-3546. available on microfilm and microfiche from University Microfilms International (UMI).
Ind/Abst Anthropol. Lit.

ISSN 1064-7554
DD 599 US
NLM W1; JO748DES **CODEN** JMEVEY
•**JOURNAL OF MAMMALIAN EVOLUTION.** [J. mamm. evol.]. Vol. 1, No. 1 (Mar. 1993)-. Periodical. English. Four times a year. $135.00. Plenum Press, 233 Spring Street, New York NY 10013-1578. **Tel** (212)620-8000, (800)221-9369, FAX (212)463-0742, (212)807-1047, telex 23/421139.

LC HM ISSN 1359-1835
DD 301 UK
•**JOURNAL OF MATERIAL CULTURE.** **See** Sociology.

LC DE1 .J68 ISSN 0253-6625
DD 930/.0982/2 GR
CODEN JMAADI
JOURNAL OF MEDITERRANEAN ANTHROPOLOGY & ARCHAEOLOGY. [J. Medit. anthropol. archaeol.]. **VFOAT** JMAA. Vol. 1, No. 1 (1981)-. Periodical. English (French and German). Two times a year. Dr Nikolaus Xirotiris, Institut F Anthropologie, Goeth Universitat Frankfurt Main, Siesmayerstrasse 70, 6000 Frankfurt Germany. Documents available from BIOSIS Document Express.
Ind/Abst Biol. Abstr. (-1982).

LC R134.8 .J68
DD 616.07 IT
NLM W1; JO826R
JOURNAL OF PALEOPATHOLOGY. **See** Medical Sciences-Pathology.

LC GN33 .J65 ISSN 0922-2995
DD 306/.01 NE
CCC
NLM W1; JO863J **CODEN** JQANEI
Pr Rev.
JOURNAL OF QUANTITATIVE ANTHROPOLOGY. (JOURNAL OF QUANTITATIVE ANTHROPOLOGY : QA.). [J. quant. authropol.]. **VFOAT** QA. Vol. 1, No. 1/2 (1989)-. Periodical. English. Four times a year. $183.00. Kluwer Academic Publishers, Postbus 322, 3300 AH Dordrecht The Netherlands. **Tel** 011 31 78 524400, FAX 011 31 78 183273, telex 20083. **ED** Jeffrey C Johnson and Clyde Mitchell. Index available. **Bk Rev. Ad Acc. Acid Free. Circ:** 70. available on microfilm and microfiche from University Microfilms International (UMI).
Desc: The primary purpose is the advancement of

quantitative research in anthropology. The journal provides a forum for scientific research, methodological developments, computer applications and other subjects of interest to anthropologists in the traditional subdisciplines of biological/physical anthropology, archaeology and social/cultural anthropology, including linguistic anthropology. The journal highlights new developments in quantitative methods and modeling and computer applications in anthropology. Qualitative discussions of fundamental analytical problems and theoretical issues are also published.
Ind/Abst Anthropol. Lit.

LC GN1 .J6 **ISSN** 0449-315X
II

Pr Rev.
JOURNAL OF SOCIAL RESEARCH (RANCHI). (JOURNAL OF SOCIAL RESEARCH.). [J. soc. res.]. **Added/Corp** Council of Social and Cultural Research, Bihar. Ranchi, India (City) University Dept. of Anthropology. Vol. 1 (1958)-. Periodical. English. Two times a year. $24.00. Ranchi University / Anthropology, Department of Anthropology, Ranchi 834001 Bihar India. **Tel** 23695. **(Subscription address:** Prints India, 11 Darya Ganj, New Delhi 110002 India. **Tel** 011 91 11 3268645, FAX 011 91 11 3275542, telex 31-61087 PRIN-IN.) **ED** A B Saran, K N Sahay, A K Singh. Index available. cum. index. **Bk Rev**.
Desc: Publishes original papers of theoretical interest or those based on field work done preferably in India.
Ind/Abst Anthropol. Lit.; Appl. Soc. Sci. Index Abstr.; Middle East Abstr. Index; Rural Dev. Abstr.; Soc. Plann. Policy Dev. Abstr.; Sociol. Abstr. (?-?).

LC DS430 .B84 **ISSN** 0970-3411
II

JOURNAL OF THE ANTHROPOLOGICAL SURVEY OF INDIA, THE. **Added/Corp** Anthropological Survey of India. Vol. 39, No. 1 (Mar. 1990)-. Periodical. English. Four times a year. $106.00. Anthropological Survey of India, Jawaharlal Nehru Road, Calcutta 700016 India. **(Subscription address:** UBS Publishers Distributors, 5 Ansari Road, PO Box 7015, New Delhi 110002 India. **Tel** 011 91 11 3273601, 011 91 11 3266645.) ***Continues*** *Human Science, 0970-3411.*

ISSN 0373-4722
JA

NLM W1 JO922H
JOURNAL OF THE FACULTY OF SCIENCE, UNIVERSITY OF TOKYO. SECTION V, ANTHROPOLOGY.
Added/Corp Tokyo Daigaku. Rigakubu. **VFOAT** Anthropology. Vol. 2, Pt. 1 (Mar. 1959)-. English. Price varies. **(Subscription address:** Maruzen Company Ltd., PO Box 5050, Import & Export Department, Tokyo 100 31 Japan. **Tel** 011 81 3 32789224.) ***Continues*** *Journal of the Faculty of Science, Imperial University of Tokyo. Section 5, Anthropology.*
Ind/Abst Anthropol. Index; Anthropol. Lit.

LC GN2 .T6 **ISSN** 0373-4722
JA

JOURNAL OF THE FACULTY OF SCIENCE, UNIVERSITY OF TOKYO. SECTION V, ANTHROPOLOGY = TOKYO DAIGAKU RIGAKUBU KIYO. DAI 5-RUI, JINRUIGAKU. **Added/Corp** Tokyo Daigaku. Rigakubu. **VFOAT** Anthropology; Tokyo Daigaku Rigakubu Kiyo. Dai 5-rui, Jinruigaku. Vol. 2, Pt. 1 (1959)-. English. One time a year. Price varies. Tokyo Daigaku Rigakubu, (Faculty of Science University of Tokyo), 3-1 Hongo 7 Chome, Bunkyoku Tokyo 113 Japan. **Tel** 03 3812 2111. **(Subscription address:** Maruzen Company Ltd., PO Box 5050, Import & Export Department, Tokyo 100 31 Japan. **Tel** 011 81 3 32789224.) ***Continues*** *Journal of the Faculty of Science Imperial University of Tokyo. Section 5, Anthropology.*

LC GN1 .I5 **ISSN** 0019-4387
II
CODEN JIASDA

JOURNAL OF THE INDIAN ANTHROPOLOGICAL SOCIETY. [J. Indian Anthropol. Soc.]. **Added/Corp** Indian Anthropological Society. Vol. 1, No. 1 (Mar. 1966)-. Periodical. English. Three times a year. $50.00. Indian Anthropological Society Calcutta 700016 India, Calcutta India 700016. **Tel** 239627. **(Subscription address:** Prints India, 11 Darya Ganj, New Delhi 110002 India. **Tel** 011 91 11 3268645, FAX 011 91 11 3275542, telex 31-61087 PRIN-IN.) **ED** Surajit Sinha and Arabinda Basu. **Circ:** 700. Documents available from BIOSIS Document Express.
Desc: Devoted to all aspects of the science of man. It is designed to include original and significant articles in all branches of anthropology in any region.
Ind/Abst Anthropol. Index; Anthropol. Lit.; Biol. Abstr.; Middle East Abstr. Index; Soc. Plann. Policy Dev. Abstr.

LC GN2 .P7 **ISSN** 0032-4000
DD 996/.005 NZ
Pr Rev.
JOURNAL OF THE POLYNESIAN SOCIETY. **See** Linguistics.

LC GN1 .J68 **ISSN** 1359-0987
UK

•**JOURNAL OF THE ROYAL ANTHROPOLOGICAL INSTITUTE, THE.**
Added/Corp Royal Anthropological Institute of Great Britain and Ireland. Vol. 1, No. 1 (Mar. 1995)-. Periodical. English. Four times a year. $144.00 US; £90.00 other. Royal Anthropological Institute, 50 Fitzroy Street, London W1P 5HS United Kingdom. **Tel** 011 44 171 3870455. **(Subscription address:** Turpin Distribution Services Limited, Blackhorse Road, Letchworth, Hertfordshire SH6 1HN United Kingdom. **Tel** 011 44 1462 672555, FAX 011 44 1462 480947.) ***Absorbed*** *Man, 0025-1496.*
Ind/Abst Curr. Cit.; MasterFile FullTEXT (Jan. 1995-).

LC GN2 .S948 **ISSN** 0039-1344
DD 573/.06 US
Pr Rev.
JOURNAL OF THE STEWARD ANTHROPOLOGICAL SOCIETY. **Main/Corp** Steward Anthropological Society. Vol. 1 (Fall 1969)-. Periodical. English (Spanish). Two times a year. $22.00. Steward Anthropological Society, 109 Davenport Hall, University of Illinois, Anthropology Department, Urbana IL 61801. **Tel** (217)333-3616, (217)244-0183, FAX (217)244-3490. **ED** Ari Zighelboim, (phone: (217)328-4803). Index available. cum. index. **Circ:** 500.
Desc: Anthropological journal publishing high quality and theoretical papers from all fields of anthropology. Primarily a student run publication. Brief communications welcome.
Ind/Abst Anthropol. Index; Anthropol. Lit.; Ethnoarts Index; Middle East Abstr. Index.

LC F2379 .J68
DD 988/.101/05 GY
JOURNAL OF THE WALTER ROTH MUSEUM OF ANTHROPOLOGY.
Added/Corp Walter Roth Museum of Anthropology. **VFOAT** Archaeology and Anthropology. (198?)-. English. One time a year (Aug.). $20.00. Walter Roth Museum of Anthropology, PO Box 73, 61 Main Street, Georgetown Guyana. **Tel** 011 592 2 69434. **ED** Denis Williams. cum. index. **Bk Rev**. **Ad Acc**. **Circ:** 100 (ctrl). ***Continues*** *Journal of the Walter Roth Museum of Archaeology and Anthropology.*
Desc: A journal of the archaeology and anthropology of Northern Amazonia and The Antilles.

LC DS591 .J55 **ISSN** 0126-5016
DD 301 MY
JURNAL ANTROPOLOGI DAN SOSIOLOGI. [J. antropol. sosiologi]. **Added/Corp** Universiti Kebangsaan Malaysia. Jabatan Antropologi dan Sosiologi. Vol. 5 (1977)-. Periodical. Malay (English). One time a year. National University of Malaysia, Penerbit Universiti Kebangsan Malaysia, 43600 UKM Bangi, Selangor Malaysia. **Tel** telex UNIKEB MA 31496. **Bk Rev**. ***Continues*** *Jernal Antropoloji dan Sosioloji, 0303-318X.*
Ind/Abst Int. Bibliogr. Sociol.

LC DS485.H6 K26 **ISSN** 0377-7499
DD 954/.005 NP
KAILASH. [Kailash]. Vol. 1 (1973)-. Periodical. English (French and Nepali). Four times a year. $22.00. Ratna Pustak Bhandar, Post Box 98, Bhotahity, Kathmandu Nepal. **Tel** 011 977 1 223026. **ED** John F. Luck. cum. index. **Bk Rev**. **Ad Acc**. **Circ:** 1,200.
Desc: Anthropology journal on Himalayan studies.
Ind/Abst Anthropol. Lit.

LC GN **ISSN** 1069-0379
DD 301 US
Pr Rev.
KANSAS ANTHROPOLOGIST, THE. (THE KANSAS ANTHROPOLOGIST : JOURNAL OF THE KANSAS ANTHROPOLOGICAL ASSOCIATION.). [Kans. anthropol.]. **Added/Corp** Kansas Anthropological Association. Vol. 1O, No. 1 and 2 (1989)-. Periodical. English. Two times a year. Free to members; $25.00 (institutions), $22.00 (individuals) membership. Kansas Anthropological Association, Kansas State Historical Society, 6425 Southwest 6th Street, Topeka KS 66615-1099. **Tel** (913)272-8681. **ED** Virginia A. Wulfkuhle. **Bk Rev**, (Qty: 2). **Circ:** 450 (ctrl). ***Continues*** *Journal of the Kansas Anthropological Association.*
Desc: Contains original articles related to Kansas anthropology. Covers , ethnography, ethnohistory, cultural/social anthropology, and more.

LC DK445 .S63 **ISSN** 0355-1830
DD 914.71 FI
KANSATIETEELLINEN ARKISTO. [Kansatiet. ark.]. **Main/Corp** Suomen Muinaismuistoyhdistys. (1934)-. Academic Scholarly Publication. Finnish (English and German). One time a year. Price varies per volume. Suomen Muinaismuistoyhdistys, Finnish Antiquarian Society, Box 913, FIN-00101 Helsinki 10 Finland. **ED** Leena Sammallahti. **Circ:** 800.
Ind/Abst MLA Int. Bibl. Books Artic. Mod. Lang. Lit.

LC GN17.3.T28 K36 **ISSN** 0077-5843
DD 301/.0951/249 CH
KAO KU JEN LEI HSUEH KAN / KUO LI TAIWAN TA HSUEH. **Added/Corp** Kuo li Taiwan ta Hsueh. Kao ku Jen Lei Hsueh Hsi. **VFOAT** Bulletin of the Department of Archaeology and Anthropology. (1953)-. Bulletin. Chinese (English). National Taiwan University / Department of Anthropology, Taipei Taiwan. **Tel** 02-363-1658. **Bk Rev**. **Circ:** 1,000.

LC GN814.K3 A26
GW
KASSELER BEITRAEGE ZUR VOR- UND FRUHGESCHICHTE. **Added/Corp** Kassel. Staatliche Kunstsammlungen. Vol. 1 (1969)-. Monographic series. German. Irregular. Price varies per volume. N.G. Elwert Verlag, Postfach 1128, Reitgasse 7-9, W-3550 Marburg Germany. **Tel** 011 49 6421 25023, FAX 011 49 6421 15487.

LC F3722 .K54
DD 986.6/00498 EC
KIPU. **See** Sociology.

LC GN301 .K64a **ISSN** 0385-180X
JA
KOKURITSU MINZOKUGAKU HAKUBUTSUKAN KENKYU HOKOKU.
Main/Corp Kokuritsu Minzokugaku Hakubutsukan. **Added/Corp** Kokuritsu Minzokugaku Hakubutsukan. Bulletin of the National Museum of Ethnology. **VFOAT** Bulletin of the National Museum of Ethnology. (1976)-. Bulletin. Japanese (summaries and/or abstracts in English). Four times a year. National Museum of Ethnology, 10-1 Banpakukoen Senri, Suitashi Osaka 565 Japan. **Tel** 011 81 6 8762151, FAX 011 81 6 8750401.

LC GN301 .K643
JA
KOKURITSU MINZOKUGAKU HAKUBUTSUKAN KENKYU HOKOKU. BESSATSU. **Added/Corp** Kokuritsu Minzokugaku Hakubutsukan. Kokuritsu Minzokugaku Hakubutsukan. Kokuritsu Minzokugaku Hakubutsukan Kenkyu Hokoku. **VFOAT** Bulletin of the National Museum of Ethnology. Special Issue. (1983)-. Bulletin. Japanese. Kokuritsu Minzoku Hakubutsukan, Senri Banpaku Koen, Suita-Shi Osaka-Fu, 565 Japan.

LC NK7 .P6 **ISSN** 1230-6142
DD 745.05 PL
KONTEKSTY : POLSKA SZTUKA LUDOWA : ANTROPOLOGIA KULTURY, ETNOGRAFIA, SZTUKA. **See** The Arts-Art.

ISSN 0047-3928
US
Pr Rev.
LAMBDA ALPHA JOURNAL OF MAN. [Lambda Alpha j. man]. **Added/Corp** Wichita State University. Lambda Alpha. Alpha Chapter. **VFOAT** Journal of Man. Vol. 1 (Jan. 1969)-. Academic Scholarly Publication. English. One time a year (Jan.). $10.00. Lambda Alpha Journal of Man, Wichita State University, Lambda Alpha, Wichita KS 67208. **Circ:** 100.
Desc: Publishes scholarly papers by anthropology students and faculty.

LC GR175 .L36
IT
LARES (FIRENZE). (LARES.). **Added/Corp** Comitato Nazionale per le Tradizioni Popolari. Comitato Nazionale Italiano per le Arti Popolari. Societa di Etnografia Italiana. Universita di Roma. Istituto di Storia delle Tradizioni Popolari. Universita di Bari. Istituto di Storia delle Tradizioni Popolari. Federazione Italiani Arti e Tradizioni Popolari. Vol. 1 (1930)-. Periodical. Italian. Four times a year. L57160. Casa Editrice Leo S. Olschki, Viuzzo del Pozzetto, Casella Postale 66, 50126 Florence Italy. **Tel** 011 39 55 6530684, FAX 011 39 55 6530214. ***Supersedes*** *Lares (Rome).*
Ind/Abst MLA Int. Bibl. Books Artic. Mod. Lang. Lit.

SP
LAROUCO / GRUPO ARQUEOLOXICO LAROUCO. **See** Archaeology.

LC GN17.3.L29 L37 **ISSN** 1045-7577
DD 306/.098/05 US
LATIN AMERICAN ANTHROPOLOGY REVIEW, THE. [Lat. Am. anthr. rev.]. **Added/Corp** Society for Latin American Anthropology. Vol. 1, No. 1 (Spring 1989)-. Periodical. English. Two times a year. $30.00. American Anthropological Association, 4350 North Fairfax Dr, Suite 640, Arlington VA 22203. **Tel** (703)528-1902 ext. 3031, FAX (703)528-3546.
Desc: Features articles, research reports, and news briefs concerning Latin American current affairs, activities, academic programs, etc. of interest to both Latin American anthropologists and those concerned with Latin American issues.

LC K12 .A855 **ISSN** 0259-0816
DD 340/.115 AU
LAW & ANTHROPOLOGY. See Law.

US
LEADERS OF MODERN ANTHROPOLOGY SERIES. Monographic series. English. Irregular. Price varies per volume. Columbia University Press, 136 South Broadway, Irvington NY 10533. **Tel** (914)591-9111.

ISSN 0141-1012
US
LIBRARY OF ANTHROPOLOGY. [Libr. anthropol.]. Monographic series. English. Irregular. Price varies per volume. Gordon & Breach Science Publishers, Inc., PO Box 786, Cooper Station, New York NY 10276. **Tel** (212)206-8900, FAX (212)645-2459.

UK
LONDON SCHOOL OF ECONOMICS MONOGRAPHS ON SOCIAL ANTHROPOLOGY. (19??)-. English. Humanities Press, 165 1st Avenue, Atlantic Highlands NJ 07716. **Tel** (908)872-1441, (800)221-3845, FAX (908)872-0717, telex 752233. Index available.

LC GR1 .L8 **ISSN** 0076-1435
PL
LUD. See Folklore.

LC GT **ISSN** 1101-9948
DD 390 SW
UDC 39
LUND MONOGRAPHS IN SOCIAL ANTHROPOLOGY. [Lund monogr. soc. anthropol.]. (1991)-. Monographic series. English (Swedish). Irregular. Price varies per volume. Lund University Press, Box 141, S-22100 Lund Sweden. **Tel** 011 46 46 312000, FAX 011 46 46 305338, telex 33345 EDUCATE S. **ED** K. Ekholm-Friedman, J. Friedman.

ISSN 8755-8874
DD 301 US
MADISON INSTITUTE NEWSLETTER, THE. [Madison Inst. newsl.]. Vol. 4, Issue 1 (Spring Issue 1984)-. Newsletter. English. Four times a year. $12.00. Madison Institute, 5723 20th Avenue NW, Seattle WA 98107.

LC GN1 .M18 **ISSN** 0120-3045
DD 986 CK
MAGUARE : REVISTA DEL DEPARTAMENTO DE ANTROPOLOGIA DE LA UNIVERSIDAD NACIONAL DE COLOMBIA. Vol. 1, No. 1 (June 1981)-. Periodical. Spanish.

LC DS401 .M28 **ISSN** 0542-092X
IO
MAHARDDHIKA PRADIPTA. Vol. 1- 1963-. Indonesian (Indonesian). Balai Pustaka, Jl Dr Wahidin 1, Jakarta Indonesia.

LC E61 .M25 **ISSN** 8755-6898
DD 970.01 US
MAMMOTH TRUMPET. See Archaeology.

JA
MAN AND CULTURE IN OCEANIA. See Ethnic Interests.

LC GN855.I4 M34 **ISSN** 0258-0446
DD 954 II
MAN & ENVIRONMENT. See Earth Sciences-Geology.

LC GN301 .M36
DD 301.2/05 II
MAN AND LIFE. **Added/Corp** Institute of Social Research and Applied Anthropology. Vol. 1 (Jan./Dec. 1975)-. Periodical. English. One time a year. $15.00. Department of Anthropology of Calcutta University, 35 Ballygunge Circular Road, Calcutta 700019 India. **(Subscription address:** Prints India, 11 Darya Ganj, New Delhi 110002 India. **Tel** 011 91 11 3268645, FAX 011 91 11 3275542, telex 31-61087 PRIN-IN.**)**
Ind/Abst Anthropol. Lit.

LC GN1 .M3 **ISSN** 0025-1569
II
NLM W1 MA57E **CODEN** MANIAJ
Pr Rev.
MAN IN INDIA. [Man India]. Vol. 1 (March 1921)-. Periodical. English. Four times a year. $32.00. Man in India, 18 Church Road, Ranchi 834001 Bihar India. **(Subscription address:** Prints India, 11 Darya Ganj, New Delhi 110002 India. **Tel** 011 91 11 3268645, FAX 011 91 11 3275542, telex 31-61087 PRIN-IN.**)** **Bk Rev.** Documents available from The Genuine Article, BIOSIS Document Express.
Ind/Abst Abstr. Anthropol. (1971-1972); Am. Hist. Life (1971-1972); Anthropol. Index; Anthropol. Lit.; Biol. Abstr.; Curr. Contents Soc. Behav. Sci.; Curr. Geogr. Publ. (199?-); Int. Bibliogr. Sociol.; Int. Dev. Abstr. (?-?); Res. Alert [Full Cov.]; Soc. Plann. Policy Dev. Abstr.; Soc. Sci. Cit. Index [Full Cov.]; Sociol. Abstr. (?-?).

ISSN 0580-5287
AT
MAN IN SOUTHEAST ASIA. **Added/Corp** University of Queensland. Dept. of Anthropology and Sociology. University of Queensland. Dept. of Geography. No. 1 (Feb. 1968)-. Periodical. English. Two times a year. $3.00. University of Queensland / Anthropology and Sociology Department, St. Lucia RE Brisbane Australia. **Tel** 011 61 7 3773111, FAX 011 61 7 3651544, telex 40315.

LC E78.E2 M35 **ISSN** 0191-4138
DD 974/.01 US
CODEN MNOREA
Pr Rev. **TITLE CHANGE**
MAN IN THE NORTHEAST. **Added/Corp** Anthropological Research Center of Northern New England. Franklin Pierce College. Dept. of Anthropology. State University of New York at Albany. State University of New York at Albany. Institute for Northeast Anthropology. State Universtiy of New York at Albany. Institute for Archaeological Studies. No. 1 (Mar. 1971)-No. 45 (Spring 1993). Periodical. English. Institute for Archaeological Studies, University at Albany, SUNY SS 263, Albany NY 12222. **Tel** (518)442-4721. **ED** Dean R. Snow. cum. index. **Bk Rev. Ad Acc. Circ:** 325 (ctrl).
***Continued by** Northeast Anthropology, 1068-9982.*
Desc: The journal publishes articles and reviews covering anthropological subjects from Northeastern North America.
Ind/Abst Abstr. Anthropol.; Anthropol. Lit.; Ceram. Abstr. (199?-); Ethnoarts Index.

LC GN1 .M252 **ISSN** 0025-1496
UK
NLM W1 MA558R **CODEN** MANJCO
Pr Rev. **TITLE CHANGE**
MAN (LONDON). (MAN.). [Man]. **Added/Corp** Anthropological Institute of Great Britain and Ireland. Royal Anthropological Institute of Great Britain and Ireland. Vol. 1 (1901)-(1994). Periodical. English (French). Royal Anthropological Institute, 50 Fitzroy Street, London W1P 5HS United Kingdom. **Tel** 011 44 171 3870455. **ED** Dr. Hastings Donnan. Index available. **Bk Rev**, (Qty: 60/yr). **Ad Acc. Circ:** 3,300. available on microfilm and microfiche from University Microfilms International (UMI). Documents available from The Genuine Article, BIOSIS Document Express, UMI Article Clearinghouse.
***Absorbed** Journal of the Royal Anthropological Institute of Great Britain and Ireland, 0307-3114. **Absorbed by** The Journal of the Royal Anthropological Institute.*
Desc: Each issues contains several articles, followed by correspondence, a review section, and a list of books received. Title page and index are bound in with the final issue each year.
Ind/Abst Acad. Abstr.; Acad. Search; Am. Hist. Life (1971-1972); Anthropol. Index (19??-19??); Anthropol. Lit. (19??-19??); Arts Humanit. Citation Index [Select. Cov.]; Bibliogr. Mission. (19??-19??); Biol. Abstr. (?-1978); Br. Archaeol. Bibliogr. (19??-19??); Br. Humanit. Index (19??-19??); Crim. Penol. Police Sci. Abstr. (19??-19??); Curr. Cit.; Curr. Geogr. Publ. (199?-199?); EP Collect.; Ethnoarts Index (19??-19??); Expand. Acad. Index (1989-199?); Geogr. Abstr. Human Geogr. (19??-19??); Homework Help.; Index Book Rev. Relig. (-19??); INFO-SOUTH Abstr. (19??-19??); Int. Bibliogr. Sociol. (19??-19??); Int. Dev. Abstr. (19??-19??); Mag. Search (19??-19??); MasterFile FullTEXT 1000; MasterFile FullTEXT 350; MasterFile FullTEXT 650; MasterFile FullTEXT (Jan. 1992-1994); Middle East Abstr. Index (19??-19??); MLA Int. Bibl. Books Artic. Mod. Lang. Lit. (19??-19??); Multicult. Educ. Abstr. (19??-19??); Newsp. Period. Abstr. (1991-199?); OCLC; Pub. Lib. FullTEXT; Res. Alert (19??-19??) [Full Cov.]; Soc. Plann. Policy Dev. Abstr. (19??-19??); Soc. Sci. Source; Soc. Sci. Cit. Index [Full Cov.]; Soc. Sci. Index (19??-19??); Soc. Sci. Index Fulltext (Sept. 1988-19??) [Full Txt.]; Sociol. Abstr. (?-?); Stud. Women Abstr. (19??-19??); Telebase; World Mag. Bank.

LC GN1 .M32
DD 306/.094/13 II
MANAV. Vol. 1, No. 1 (1982/83)-. English. One time a year. Department of Anthropology / Utal University, Utal University Vani Vihar, Bhubaneswar-7510 India.
Ind/Abst Anthropol. Lit.

LC GN1 .M36 **ISSN** 0025-2344
DD 572/.05 US
NLM W1 MA616 **CODEN** MKQUA4
Pr Rev.
MANKIND QUARTERLY. (THE MANKIND QUARTERLY.). [Mank. q.]. Vol. 1 (July 1960)-. Periodical. English. Four times a year. $80.00. Council on Social and Economic Studies, PO Box 34070, Washington DC 20043. **Tel** (202)371-2700. **ED** R. Lynn, E. Polome, Hans Jurgens, and B. Chiarells. Index available. **Bk Rev. Ad Acc. Circ:** 1,150. available on microfilm and microfiche from University Microfilms International (UMI). Documents available from The Genuine Article, BIOSIS Document Express.
Desc: Includes anthropology (physical and cultural), linguistics, mythology, psychology, ethnography, cultural history and human evolution.
Ind/Abst Abstr. Anthropol.; Acad. Abstr.; Acad. Search; Am. Hist. Life (1972-1977); Anthropol. Index; Anthropol. Lit. (19??-1989); Appl. Soc. Sci. Index Abstr.; Arts Humanit. Citation Index [Select. Cov.]; Biol. Abstr.; Curr. Contents Soc. Behav. Sci.; EP Collect.; Homework Help.; INFO-SOUTH Abstr.; Int. Bibliogr. Sociol.; Int. Polit. Sci. Abstr.; Mag. Search; MasterFile FullTEXT 1000; MasterFile FullTEXT 350; MasterFile FullTEXT 650; MasterFile FullTEXT (Jan. 1992-); MLA Int. Bibl. Books Artic. Mod. Lang. Lit.; OCLC; Res. Alert [Full Cov.]; Soc. Plann. Policy Dev. Abstr.; Soc. Sci. Source; Soc. Sci. Cit. Index [Full Cov.]; Sociol. Abstr.; Telebase; Women Stud. Abstr.

LC GN635.M4 M27 **ISSN** 0303-3171
DD 301.29/59 MY
MANUSIA DAN MASYARAKAT. [Manus. masyarakat]. Vol. 1 (1972)-. English (Malay). One time a year. National University of Malaysia, Penerbit Universiti Kebangsan Malaysia, 43600 UKM Bangi, Selangor Malaysia. **Tel** telex UNIKEB MA 31496.

LC GN635.I65 M36
DD 572 IO
MANUSIA INDONESIA. **Added/Corp** Ikatan Karyawan Museum. Museum Pusat. (1966)-. Periodical. English (Indonesian). Museum Dausat, Jalan Merdeka Barat 12, Jakarta Indonesia.

ISSN 0922-1476
NE
Pr Rev. **CEASED**
MARITIME ANTHROPOLOGICAL STUDIES : MAST. **Added/Corp** Universiteit van Amsterdam. Antropologisch-Sociologisch Centrum. Vakgroep EUROMED. **VFOAT** MAST. Vol. 1, No. 1 (1988)-(Jan. 1995). Periodical. English. University of Amsterdam, Anthropological/Sociological Center, O Z Achterburgwal 185, 1012 DK Amsterdam The Netherlands. **Tel** 011 31 20 6252627. **ED** Jojada Verrips and Rob Van Ginkel. **Bk Rev. Ad Acc. Circ:** 250.
Desc: A international journal of anthropology on fishing and maritime communities. Aims to disseminate knowledge of contemporary and historical societies and cultures of people exploring the maritime environment.
Ind/Abst Anthropol. Lit.; Int. Bibliogr. Sociol.

ISSN 0106-5173
DK
MARXISTISK ANTROPOLOGI. **Added/Corp** International Movement of Radical Anthropologists. (1974)-. Periodical. English. Irregular. Intl Movement Radical Anthrop, Etnografisk AFD Moesgard, DK-8270 Hjbjerg Denmark.

LC E179.5 .P46 **ISSN** 0883-3680
DD 973/.05 US
Pr Rev.
MATERIAL CULTURE. [Mater. cult.]. **Added/Corp** Pioneer America Society. Vol. 16, No. 1 (Spring 1984)-. Periodical. English. Three times a year (Spring, Summer, Fall). $30.00 (institutions); $20.00 (individals). Pioneer America Society, 601 South College Road, Wilmington NC 28403. **Tel** (910)395-3493. **ED** William D. Walters, (309)438-7679. Index available. cum. index. **Bk Rev**, (Qty: 3-5). **Ad Acc. Circ:** 450. available on microfilm and microfiche from University Microfilms International (UMI). ***Continues** Pioneer America, 0032-0005.*
Desc: Diversified historical geographical and folklife material.
Ind/Abst Am. Hist. Life (1971-?, 1984-); Avery Index Archit. Period. Suppl. Colum. Univ. (1989-); Geogr. Abstr. Human Geogr.; MLA Int. Bibl. Books Artic. Mod. Lang. Lit.

ISSN 0076-521X
PL
CODEN MPANA6
MATERIALY I PRACE ANTROPOLOGICZNE. [Mater. pr. antropol.]. **Added/Corp** Polska Akademia Nauk. Zaklad Antropologii. Polskie Towarzystwo Antropologiczne. (1953)-. Monographic series. Polish (English; summaries and/or abstracts in English and German). Irregular. Price varies per volume. Polska Akademia Nauk / Zaklad Antropologii, Ul. Kuznicza 35, 50-951 Wroclaw Poland. **ED** E. Piasecki. available with illustrations. Documents available from BIOSIS Document Express.
Ind/Abst Anthropol. Index; Anthropol. Lit.; Biol. Abstr.

LC GN296 .M42 **ISSN** 0145-9740
DD 362.1 US
CCC
NLM W1 ME2057 **CODEN** MDANES
MEDICAL ANTHROPOLOGY. Vol. 1 (Winter 1977)-. Periodical. English. Four times a year. $233.00 university and hospital libraries; $363.00 other. Gordon & Breach Science Publishers, Inc., PO Box 786, Cooper Station, New York NY 10276. **Tel** (212)206-8900, FAX (212)645-2459. **ED** Lawrence S. Greene. Index available. **Ad Acc. Circ:** 1,000.
Desc: Explores the relationships among health, disease, treatment, and human social life with an emphasis on the cross-cultural similarities and differences in the way people cope with health problems. Provides important biosocial and cross-cultural perspectives on health, disease, illness and treatment for nurses, physicians, biologists, social scientists and other professionals in health-related fields.

Anthropology

Ind/Abst Abstr. Anthropol.; Annals Behav. Med.; Anthropol. Lit.; Curr. Cit.; Curr. Contents Soc. Behav. Sci. (Vol. 8 No. 1, 1984-); Index Med. (Vol. 8, No. 1, 1984-); Middle East Abstr. Index; NAPRALERT; Psychol. Abstr. (1985-); PsycINFO; PsycLit.

LC GN296 .M44   **ISSN** 0745-5194
DD 306/.45   US
NLM W1; ME206D   **CODEN** MAQUD5
MEDICAL ANTHROPOLOGY QUARTERLY.
[Med. anthropol. q.]. **Added/Corp** Society for Medical Anthropology. Vol. 14, No. 2 (Feb. 1983)-. Periodical. English. Four times a year. $80.00. American Anthropological Association, 4350 North Fairfax Dr, Suite 640, Arlington VA 22203. **Tel** (703)528-1902 ext. 3031, FAX (703)528-3546. **ED** Alan Harwood and Medea Ranck. **Bk Rev**. **Ad Acc**. **Circ**: 2,200 (ctrl). available on microfilm and microfiche from University Microfilms International (UMI). Documents available from The Genuine Article, BIOSIS Document Express. *Continues* Medical Anthropology Newsletter, 0543-2499.
Desc: Articles and reviews cover fields encompassing ethnomedicine, comparative medical systems, human ecology, transcultural psychiatry, human population dynamics and cultural epidemiology.
Ind/Abst Anthropol. Lit.; Biol. Abstr. (1987-); Curr. Cit.; Int. Bibliogr. Sociol.; Middle East Abstr. Index; PsycINFO; Res. Alert [Full Cov.]; Soc. Plann. Policy Dev. Abstr.; Soc. Sci. Cit. Index [Full Cov.]; Sociol. Abstr.

    US
MEMBERSHIP DIRECTORY - GYPSY LORE SOCIETY. See Folklore.

LC DX101 .G765   **ISSN** 0193-1598
DD 909/.04/91497   US
    TITLE CHANGE
MEMBERSHIP DIRECTORY - GYPSY LORE SOCIETY, NORTH AMERICAN CHAPTER. See Folklore.

    ISSN 0536-6712
    II
MEMOIR (ANTHROPOLOGICAL SURVEY OF INDIA).
(MEMOIR.). **Added/Corp** Anthropological Survey of India. (1960)-. Monographic series. English. One time a year. $100.00. Indian Books & Periodicals, 2429 Tilak Street, Phar Ganj, New Delhi 110005 India. **Tel** 011 91 11 735574. **Bk Rev**. *Continues* Memoir (India. Dept. of Anthropology).

    ISSN 0076-8375
    US
MEMOIRS OF THE MUSEUM OF ANTHROPOLOGY, UNIVERSITY OF MICHIGAN.
Main/Corp University of Michigan. Museum of Anthropology. No. 1 (1969)-. Monographic series. English. Irregular. Price varies per volume. Museum of Anthropology / Michigan, University of Michigan, 4009 Museums, Ann Arbor MI 48109. **Tel** (313)764-0485.

    ISSN 0327-5752
    AG
MEMORIA AMERICANA.
(1991)-. Spanish. Two times a year. Universidad de Buenos Aires / Antropologia, Instituto de Antropologia, 25 de Mayo 217, 1002 Buenos Aires Argentina. **Tel** 011 54 1 4320537, 011 54 1 4328696. **ED** Ana Maria Lorandi.

    GR
METIS : REVUE D'ANTHROPOLOGIE DU MONDE GREC ANCIEN.
French. Two times a year. Dr280.00 Europe; Dr320.00 other. Dedalus i Zaharopoulos SA, Arsaki 6, 105 64 Athens Greece. **Tel** 011 30 1 3233271 OR 3247791, FAX 011 30 1 3247791.

LC GN1 .M52   **ISSN** 0193-7804
DD 301   US
MICHIGAN DISCUSSIONS IN ANTHROPOLOGY.
[Mich. discuss. anthr.]. **Added/Corp** University of Michigan. Dept. of Anthropology. Vol. 1 (Fall 1975)-. Periodical. English. Irregular. $14.00 (individuals) and institutions; $12.00 students. University of Michigan Department of Anthropology, Ann Arbor MI 48109-1382. **Tel** (313)764-7274, FAX (313)763-6077. **Bk Rev**. **Circ**: 1,000.
Desc: Publishes a broad spectrum of articles from the fields of anthropology.

LC GN635.C5 M56
DD 951/.004   CC
MIN TSU HSUEH YEN CHIU. Added/Corp
Chung-kuo min tsu Hsueh yen Chiu hui. Vol. 1 (Aug. 8, 1981)-. Periodical. Chinese. Irregular. RMBY1.25. Hsin Hua Shu Tien, Beijing, People's Republic of China. **Tel** 011 89 1 551253.

LC DS730 .M523
DD 951/.004   CC
MIN TSU WEN HUA. VFOAT Minzuwenhua.
(19??)-. Periodical. Chinese. Six times a year. RMBY0.30. Science Press, 16 Donghuangchenggen North Street, Beijing 100707, People's Republic of China. **Tel** 011 86 1 4019821, 011 86 1 4010642, FAX 011 86 1 4012180, 011 86 1 4019810, telex 210147.

    JA
MINZOKUGAKU KENKYU. Added/Corp
Nihon Minzokugakkai. Minzokugaku Kyokai (Japan). Nihon Minzokugaku Kyokai. **VFOAT** Japanese Journal of Ethnology. (1935)-. Periodical. Japanese (summaries and/or abstracts in English and German; table of contents in English and German). Four times a year. $150.50. (**Subscription address:** Japan Publications Trading Company Ltd., PO Box 5030, Tokyo International, Tokyo 100-31 Japan. **Tel** 011 81 3 3292 3753.) cum. index.
Ind/Abst Anthropol. Lit.

    ISSN 0001-3935
DD 572   CH
UDC 572.9
MINZUXUE YANJIUSUO JIKAN, ZHONGYANG YANJIUYUAN.
(CHUNG YANG YEN CHIU YUAN MIN TSU HSUEH YEN CHIU SO CHI KAN.). [Minzuxue yanjiusuo jikan Zhongyang yanjiuyuan]. **Added/Corp** Chung Yang Yen Chiu Yuan. Min Tsu Hsueh Yen Chiu So. **VFOAT** Min Tsu Hsueh Yen Chiu So Chi Kan; Bulletin of the Institute of Ethnology, Academia Sinica. Vol. 1 No. 45 (1956)-. Bulletin. Chinese (English). Two times a year. $10.00. National Academy Institute of Ethnology, Nankang, Taipei Taiwan. **Tel** (02)7899325, FAX (02)7855636. (**Subscription address:** China Jen Books, World Building, Room 1011, 99 Chung Ching S Road, Taipei Taiwan.) **ED** Ying-Chang Chuang. **Circ**: 1,500 (ctrl).
Desc: Features research on Taiwan aborigines, social change in Taiwan, overseas Chinese research, behavioral science and religion and folklore in Taiwan.
Ind/Abst Anthropol. Index; Anthropol. Lit.; Int. Bibliogr. Sociol.; Linguist. Lang. Behav. Abstr.; Soc. Plann. Policy Dev. Abstr.; Sociol. Abstr. (?-?).

LC F3721 .M57   **ISSN** 0254-7678
DD 986.6/01   EC
MISCELANEA ANTROPOLOGICA ECUATORIANA.
(MISCELANEA ANTROPOLOGICA ECUATORIANA : BOLETIN DE LOS MUSEOS DEL BANCO CENTRAL DEL ECUADOR.). [Misc. antropol. Ecuat.]. **Added/Corp** Banco Central del Ecuador. No. 1 (1981)-. Monographic series. Spanish. One time a year. Price varies per volume. Museo Antropologico, Banco Central de Ecuador, Secretaria General, PO Box 1331, Guayaquil Ecuador. **Tel** 011 593 4 517717, telex 043257 BCOCNG ED MUSEO. Index available. **Circ**: 1,500.
Desc: Unpublished articles, in Spanish, by Ecuadorian or foreign authors on all subjects related to Ecuadorian anthropological investigations. Emphasis on Indians of South America.
Ind/Abst Anthropol. Lit.

    ISSN 0233-2493
    GW
MITTEILUNGEN AUS DEM MUSEUM FUER VOELKERKUNDE ZU LEIPZIG.
Added/Corp Museum fuer Voelkerkunde zu Leipzig. Leipzig. Stadtisches Museum fuer Voelkerkunde. (1960)-. Periodical. English. One time a year. Museum fuer Volkerkunde, Taeubchenweg 2, Postfach 969, 0 04009 Leipzig F R Germany. **Tel** 011 49 341 2142226, 011 49 341 2142256.
Ind/Abst Anthropol. Lit.

LC GN2 .H3   **ISSN** 0072-9469
    GW
MITTEILUNGEN AUS DEM MUSEUM FUER VOLKERKUNDE HAMBURG.
(MITTEILUNGEN AUS DEM MUSEUM FUER VOLKERKUNDE IN HAMBURG.). [Mitt. Mus. Volkerkd. Hambg.]. **Main/Corp** Hamburg. Museum fur Volkerkunde und Vorgeschichte. **Added/Corp** Hamburgisches Museum fur Volkerkunde und Vorgeschichte. Hamburgisches Museum fur Volkerkunde und Vorgeschichte. **VFOAT** Mitteilungen aus dem Museum fur Volkerkunde Hamburg. Vol. 1 (1906)-. German. Irregular. Klaus Renner Fachbuchhdlg Verlag, Am Sonnenhang 8, D-82069 Hohenschftlrn Germany. *Separated from* Jahrbuch der Hamburgischen Wissenschaftlichen Anstalten.
Ind/Abst Anthropol. Lit.

    ISSN 0066-4693
    AU
NLM W1 AN849H
MITTEILUNGEN DER ANTHROPOLOGISCHEN GESELLSCHAFT IN WIEN. Main/Corp
Anthropologische Gesellschaft in Wien. **Added/Corp** Gesellschaft fuer Anthropologie, Ethnologie und Praehistorie. Vol. 1-30 (Mar. 1870)-. German. One time a year. S1000.00 (latest volume). Verlag Ferdinand Berger & Soehne, Wienerstrasse 21-23, A-3580 Horn Austria. **Tel** 011 43 2982 4161232. cum. index. **Bk Rev**.
Ind/Abst Am. Hist. Life (1960-1973); Anthropol. Index; Anthropol. Lit.; Br. Archaeol. Bibliogr.

LC GN2 .B56   **ISSN** 0178-7896
DD 570   GW
MITTEILUNGEN DER BERLINER GESELLSCHAFT FUER ANTHROPOLOGIE, ETHNOLOGIE UND URGESCHICHTE.
[Mitt. Berl. Ges. Anthropol. Ethnol. Urgesch.]. **Added/Corp** Berliner Gesellschaft fuer Anthropologie, Ethnologie und Urgeschichte. (1965)-. Periodical. German. One time a year. Museum fuer Fruh und Vorgeschic, Schloss Charlottenburg Langhan, D-14059 Berlin Germany. **Tel** 011 49 30 32091233.
Ind/Abst Anthropol. Lit.

    IT
MONDO LADINO : BOLLETTINO DELL'ISTITUTO CULTURALE LADINO.
Added/Corp Istituto Culturale Ladino (Vigo di Fassa, Italy). (19??)-. Periodical. Italian (German and Ladino). Two times a year. L20440. Istituto Culturale Ladino, Loc San Giovanni, 38039 Vigo di Fassa Italy. **Tel** 011 39 462 64267, FAX 011 39 462 64909. **Bk Rev**. ctrl circ.
Desc: Covers arguments about history, geography, folklore, ethnology, linguistics, literature, archaeology, and architecture of the Ladin minority of the Dolomite area.

    ISSN 0326-7903
    AG
UDC 572
MONOGRAFIAS - MUSEO ETNOGRAFICO MUNICIPAL "DAMASO ARCE".
[Monogr. - Mus. Etnogr. Munic. "Damaso Arce"]. (1966)-. Monographic series. Spanish. Irregular. Price varies per volume.
Ind/Abst Anthropol. Lit.

    ISSN 0440-1522
    GW
MONOGRAPHIEN ZUR VOLKERKUNDE. Main/Corp
Hamburg. Museum fur Volkerkunde und Vorgeschichte. No. 1 (1943)-. Monographic series. German. Irregular. Price varies per volume. Klaus Renner Fachbuchhdlg Verlag, Am Sonnenhang 8, D-82069 Hohenschftlrn Germany.

    US
MONOGRAPHS IN DEVELOPMENT ANTHROPOLOGY.
(19??)-. Monographic series. English. Irregular. Price varies per volume. Institute for Development Anthropology, PO Box 2207, Binghamton NY 13902. **Tel** (607)772-6244. available with illustrations.
Desc: Provides information on anthropology in Africa and the Middle East.

    ISSN 0895-9994
DD 306   US
MONOGRAPHS IN ECONOMIC ANTHROPOLOGY.
[Monogr. econ. anthropol.]. **Added/Corp** Society for Economic Anthropology (U.S.). No. 1 (1983)-. Monographic series. English. Irregular. Price varies per volume. University Press of America, 4720 A Boston Way, Lanham MD 20706. **Tel** (301)459-3366, (800)462-6420.

    ISSN 0740-9729
DD 599.8   US
    CCC
NLM W1 MO568N   **CODEN** MONPD5
MONOGRAPHS IN PRIMATOLOGY. See Zoology.

LC GB500 .M68   **ISSN** 0276-4741
DD 304.2/0914/3   US
    CCC
Pr Rev.
MOUNTAIN RESEARCH AND DEVELOPMENT.
[Mt. res. dev.]. **Added/Corp** International Mountain Society. United Nations University. Vol. 1, No. 1 (May 1981)-. Academic Scholarly Publication. English (French, German and Spanish; summaries and/or abstracts in French and German). Four times a year (Feb., May, Aug., Nov.). $86.00. University of California Press, 2120 Berkeley Way, Berkeley CA 94720. **Tel** (510)642-4191, (510)642-3907, FAX (510)642-9917. **ED** Jack D. Ives. Index available. cum. index. **Bk Rev**. **Circ**: 960 (ctrl). available on microfilm and microfiche from University Microfilms International (UMI). Documents available from The Genuine Article.
Desc: Scholarly, interdisciplinary papers in natural and human sciences, assessments and analyses of developments affecting mountain peoples worldwide, commentaries and reviews.
Ind/Abst AGRICOLA [Select. Cov.]; Agrofor. Abstr. (1991-); Anthropol. Lit.; Curr. Aware. Biol. Sci., CABS; Curr. Cit.; Curr. Contents Agric. Biol. Environ. Sci.; Ecol. Abstr.; For. Abstr.; Geogr. Abstr. Phys. Geogr.; Geogr. Abstr. Human Geogr.; GeoRef; Int. Dev. Abstr.; Meteorol. Geoastrophys. Abstr. (199?-); Res. Alert [Full Cov.]; Risk Abstr.; Soc. Sci. Cit. Index; SCISEARCH; Soc. Sci. Cit. Index [Select. Cov.]; Soils Fert.; Wildl. Rev.

LC GN35 .C68a   **ISSN** 0892-8339
DD 306/.074   US
MUSEUM ANTHROPOLOGY.
[Mus. anthropol.]. **Added/Corp** Council for Museum Anthropology (U.S.). Vol. 10, No. 4 (Nov. 1986)-.

Periodical. English. Three times a year. $45.00. American Anthropological Association, 4350 North Fairfax Dr, Suite 640, Arlington VA 22203. **Tel** (703)528-1902 ext. 3031, FAX (703)528-3546. **ED** Linda B. Robertson. Index available. cum. index. **Circ:** 300. ***Continues*** *Council for Museum Anthropology (U.S.). Council for Museum Anthropology Newsletter, 0199-1450.*
Desc: Articles and information of interest to anthropologists that work in museums, with news on current research, exhibits and topical matters.
Ind/Abst Anthropol. Lit.; Ethnoarts Index.

ISSN 0895-7606
DD 970 US
NATIVE PEOPLES. See History-History of North and South America.

LC E76.6 .O58a **ISSN** 0381-4580
DD 301.2/07/11713 CN
NATIVE STUDIES IN COLLEGES AND UNIVERSITIES. See Education.

LC GN656 .B5 **ISSN** 0067-9208
DD 930.1 SA
CODEN NVNMAJ
NAVORSINGE VAN DIE NASIONALE MUSEUM. (NAVORSINGE VAN DIE NASIONALE MUSEUM = RESEARCHES OF THE NASIONALE MUSEUM.). [Navors. Nas. Mus.]. **Added/Corp** South Africa. National Museum. **VFOAT** Researches of the Nasionale Museum. Vol. 1, No. 1 (1952)-. Periodical. Afrikaans (English). South African National Museum, PO Box 52090, Saxonwold 2132 South Africa. **Tel** 011 27 11 6465513. ***Formed by the union of*** *South Africa. National Museum. Argeologiese Navorsing; Paleontologiese Navorsing van die Nasionale Museum, Bloemfontein, 0258-1493* ***and*** *South Africa. National Museum. Soologiese Navorsing.*
Ind/Abst Fish Rev. (Jan. 1989-July 1992); GeoRef; Wildl. Rev. (Jan. 1989-July 1992).

HU
NEPRAJZI ERTESITO : NEPRAJZI MUZEUM EVKONYVE. See Ethnic Interests.

ISSN 0381-7253
DD 301.43/4/062713541 CN
NEW HORIZONS. **VFOAT** Uj Latohatar. Vol. 1 (1974)-. Periodical. English (Hungarian). New Horizons Day Centre, 14 Viewmount Avenue, Toronto Ontario M6B 1T3 Canada.

ISSN 0727-3134
AT
NEWSLETTER - AUSTRALIAN ANTHROPOLOGICAL SOCIETY. (1928)-. Newsletter. English. Four times a year. 21.37Aus$. Australian Anthropological Society, Inc., Berndt Museum of Anthropology, University of Western Australia, Nedlands WA 6009 Australia. **Tel** 011 61 9 3803854, FAX 011 61 9 3801062. **ED** Dr. J.L. Gordon (editor's phone: 011 61 9 380 2850). **Bk Rev**, (Qty: approx 20/year). **Circ:** 300.
Desc: International journal of social anthropology and comparative sociology.

LC GN667.W5 W43A
DD 994.1/004/991 AT
NEWSLETTER - DEPARTMENT OF ABORIGINAL AFFAIRS, WESTERN AUSTRALIA. **Main/Corp** Australia. Dept. of Aboriginal Affairs. Western Australia. Vol. 1, No. 7 (July 1974)-. Newsletter. English. Department of Aboriginal Affairs, 600 Murray Street, Perth Western Australia 6005 Australia. ***Continues*** *Western Australia. Aboriginal Affairs Planning Authority. Newsletter.*

LC GN **ISSN** 1069-0360
DD 301 US
NEWSLETTER - KANSAS ANTHROPOLOGICAL ASSOCIATION (1989). (NEWSLETTER / KANSAS ANTHROPOLOGICAL ASSOCIATION.). [Newsl. - Kans. Anthropol. Assoc.)]. **Added/Corp** Kansas Anthropological Association. **VFOAT** Kansas Anthropological Association Newsletter. New Ser., Vol. 1, No. 1 (Sept. 1989)-. Newsletter. English. Six times a year. Free to members; $15.00 (institutions), $12.00 (individuals) membership. Kansas Anthropological Association, Kansas State Historical Society, 6425 Southwest 6th Street, Topeka KS 66615-1099. **Tel** (913)272-8681. **ED** Virginia Wulfkuhle. **Circ:** 450 (ctrl). ***Continues in part*** *Journal of the Kansas Anthropological Association.*
Desc: Contains Association news, announcements, current research notes, and brief articles related to Kansas anthropology.

ISSN 0278-2871
US
Pr Rev.
NEWSLETTER OF THE AMERICAN COMMITTEE TO ADVANCE THE STUDY OF PETROGLYPHS AND PICTOGRAPHS. Newsletter. English. Two times a year. $30.00 US, Canada and Mexico; $35.00 other countries. Snyder, PO Box 158, Shepherdstown WV 25443-0153. **Tel** (304)876-9431. **ED** Joseph J Snyder. cum. index. **Bk Rev. Ad Acc. Circ:** 500 (ctrl).
Desc: To facilitate and encourage the description, analysis, conservation, and preservation of prehistoric pictography in every form, in the Americas primarily, but additionally in every country and locality where these expressions of prehistoric intellect and information are found.

US
NEWSLETTER (SOUTHWESTERN ANTHROPOLOGICAL ASSOCIATION). (NEWSLETTER.). **Added/Corp** Southwestern Anthropological Association. **VFOAT** SWAA Newsletter. (19??)-. Newsletter. English. Four times a year. Southwestern Anthropological, PO Box 4552, Glendale CA 91202. **Tel** (202)224-3229. **ED** Sandra Brizee-Bowen. **Circ:** 600.
Desc: News, letters, essays, and other features.

ISSN 0196-0377
US
NEWSLETTER - TENNESSEE ANTHROPOLOGICAL ASSOCIATION. **Main/Corp** Tennessee Anthropological Association. Vol. 1 (Jan. 1976)-. Newsletter. English. Four times a year. Comes with Tennessee Anthropologist Association memberhship. Tennessee Anthropological Association, Department of Anthropology, University of Tennessee, 252 South Stadium Hall, Knoxville TN 37996-0720. **Tel** (615)974-4408. **ED** Charles H. Faulkner and Phil Carr. **Circ:** 300 (ctrl).
Desc: Strives to preserve the anthropological/archaeological resources and data in Tennessee by the encouragement of research, publication of the results of this research, and the support of historic preservation laws.
Ind/Abst Anthropol. Index; Anthropol. Lit.; Ethnoarts Index.

ISSN 0711-5342
DD 301/.05 CN
Pr Rev.
NEXUS (HAMILTON, ONT.). (NEXUS : THE CANADIAN STUDENT JOURNAL OF ANTHROPOLOGY : LE JOURNAL DES ETUDIANTS CANADIENS.). [Nexus]. **Added/Corp** McMaster University. Dept. of Anthropology. Vol. 1, No. 1 (Autumn 1980)-. Periodical. English (French; summaries and/or abstracts in French). One time a year. 20.00Can$. McMaster University / Department of Anthropology, 1280 Main Street West, Hamilton Ontario L8S 4L9 Canada. **Tel** (416)525-9140. **ED** Gwen Reimer and Douglass St. Christian. Index available. **Bk Rev. Ad Acc. Circ:** 150 (ctrl). ***Continues*** *Journal of Anthropology at McMaster, 0707-3771.*
Desc: Publishes papers of anthropological interest written by graduate and undergraduate students at Canadian universities and abroad. Occasional special topics.

LC GN387 .N594 **ISSN** 0822-7942
DD 305.9/0693 CN
CODEN NOPEES
NOMADIC PEOPLES. **Added/Corp** International Union of Anthropological and Ethnological Sciences. Commission on Nomadic Peoples. **VFOAT** Newsletter. No. 5 (Jan. 1980)-. Periodical. English (French). Two times a year. $52.00. Nordiska Afrikainstitutet, Sturegatan 9 1 TR EPOS, S 753 14 Uppsala Sweden. **Tel** 011 46 18 1833325. **ED** Philip Carl Salzman. **Bk Rev. Circ:** 500 (ctrl). ***Continues*** *Newsletter (Commission on Nomadic Peoples), 0822-7934.*
Desc: Contains material relevant to Third World studies. Covers anthropology, human ecology, cultural studies, livestock and range management agricultural economics.
Ind/Abst Abstr. Anthropol.; Anthropol. Lit.; Dairy Sci. Abstr.; Geogr. Abstr. Human Geogr.; Int. Dev. Abstr.; Int. Labour Doc.; Soc. Plann. Policy Dev. Abstr.

LC GN **ISSN** 0802-7285
DD 301 NO
Pr Rev.
NORSK ANTHROPOLOGISK TIDSSKRIFT. [Nor. intropol. tidsskr.]. **Added/Corp** Sosial Antropologisk Forening. Norges Almenvitenskapelige Forskaingsrad. (1990)-. Periodical. Norwegian. Four times a year. Kr255.00, $44.00. Scandinavian University Press, PO Box 2959 Toeyen, N 0608 Oslo 6 Norway. **Tel** 011 47 2 2575400, FAX 011 47 2 2575353, telex 71896 UROR N. **(Subscription address:** Scandinavian University Press, 200 Meacham Ave., Elmont NY 11003. **Tel** (516)352-7300, FAX (516)352-7377.) **ED** Jan Broegger. **Bk Rev. Ad Acc. Circ:** 300.
Desc: Journal of the Norwegian Association of Social Anthropology.

LC E78.E2 M35 **ISSN** 1068-9982
DD 974/.01 US
●**NORTHEAST ANTHROPOLOGY.** [Northeast anthr.]. **Added/Corp** State University of New York at Albany. Institute for Archaeological Studies. No. 46 (Fall 1993)-. Periodical. English. Two times a year. $55.00. Institute for Archaeological Studies, University at Albany, SUNY SS 263, Albany NY 12222. **Tel** (518)442-4721. ***Continues*** *Man in the Northeast, 0191-4138.*

LC E78.N77 N67 **ISSN** 0029-3296
DD 979.5 US
CODEN NARNAV
Pr Rev.
NORTHWEST ANTHROPOLOGICAL RESEARCH NOTES. [Northwest anthropol. res. notes]. **Added/Corp** University of Idaho. Dept. of Sociology/Anthropology. **VFOAT** NARN. Vol. 1 No. 1 (Fall 1967)-. Periodical. English. Two times a year. $40.00. Northwest Anthropological Research Notes, Laboratory of Anthropology, University of Idaho, Moscow ID 83843. **Tel** (208)885-6123. **ED** Roderick Sprague. Index available. **Circ:** 300. Documents available from BIOSIS Document Express.
Desc: Devoted to all branches of anthropology in the Pacific Northwest. Emphasis on new research and works that will encourage research such as bibliographies.
Ind/Abst Abstr. Anthropol. (19??-); Am. Hist. Life (1970-1971); Anthropol. Index; Anthropol. Lit.; Biol. Abstr.; Ethnoarts Index (1970-1971); Indice Hist. Esp. (1970-1971).

LC DL401 .N83 **ISSN** 0029-3601
NO
NORVEG. **VFOAT** Journal of Norwegian Ethnology. Vol. 1, (1951)-. Norwegian (English; summaries and/or abstracts in English). Two times a year. $39.00. Novus Press, PO Box 748 Sentrum, N-0106 Oslo Norway. **Tel** 011 47 22 717450, FAX 011 47 22 718107. **ED** Asbjoern Klepp. Each issue contains an index to its own contents (no volume index)--loose. **Bk Rev. Ad Acc. Circ:** 900. ***Supersedes*** *Ord og Sed.*
Desc: Norwegian journal of ethnology research.

ISSN 1044-0410
DD 306 US
NOTES ON ANTHROPOLOGY AND INTERCULTURAL COMMUNITY WORK. [Notes anthr. intercult. community work]. **VFOAT** NOA. (1985)-. Periodical. English. Four times a year. $1.80 (institute members), $2.25 (nonmembers) single issue. Summer Institute of Linguistic, 7500 West Camp Wisdom Road, Dallas TX 75236. **Tel** (214)709-2404, FAX (214)709-2433, telex 9108614123.

MX
NOTICIAS INDIGENISTAS DE AMERICA. See Ethnic Interests.

ISSN 0762-6819
FR
NLM W1; NO834GN
NOUVELLE REVUE D'ETHNOPSYCHIATRIE. **VFOAT** NRE. (1983)-. Periodical. French. Four times a year. Editions la Pensee Sauvage, BP 141, 38002 Grenoble Cedex France. **Tel** 011 33 76 871303. ***Continues*** *Ethnopsychiatrica, 0184-3796.*
Ind/Abst Anthropol. Lit.

LC GN301 .N83
DD 301/.05 MX
NUEVA ANTROPOLOGIA. **Added/Corp** Escuela Nacional de Antropologia e Historia (Mexico). Vol. 1 (July 1975)-. Periodical. Spanish. Four times a year. $12.25. Distr Cultural Especial SA CV, Av Popocatepetl 510, 03330 Mexico DF Mexico. **Tel** 011 52 5 6889831, 011 52 5 6889965.
Ind/Abst Chicano Index; Hisp. Am. Period. Index, HAPI.

ISSN 0078-3005
US
OCCASIONAL PAPERS IN ANTHROPOLOGY. **Added/Corp** Pennsylvania State University. Dept. of Anthropology. (1968)-. Monographic series. English. Irregular. Price varies per volume. Pennsylvania State University / Occasional Papers in Anthropology, 409 Carpenter Building, University Park PA 16802. **Tel** (814)865-2509.

ISSN 0276-8607
DD 974 US
OCCASIONAL PUBLICATIONS IN NORTHEASTERN ANTHROPOLOGY. [Occas. publ. northeast. anthropol.]. **Added/Corp** Man in the Northeast, Inc. Franklin Pierce College. Dept. of Anthropology. No. 1 (1976)-. Monographic series. English. Irregular. Price varies per volume. Archaeological Services, PO Box 386, Bethlehem CT 06751. **Tel** (203)266-7741. **ED** Howard R. Sargent and Evelyn A. Sargent. **Ad Acc. Circ:** 500.
Desc: This series provides monographs relating to northeastern North American anthropology.

LC GN665 .O25 **ISSN** 1030-6412
AT
OCEANIA MONOGRAPHS, THE. **Added/Corp** Australian National Research Council. University of Sydney. **VFOAT** Oceania Monograph. (1931)-. Monographic series. English. Irregular. Price varies per volume. University of Sydney, 116 Darlington Road / H42, Sydney NSW 2006 Australia. **Tel** 011 61 2 6922666, FAX 011 61 2 6922666. ***Absorbed*** *Oceania Linguistic Monographs.*

LC GN2 .A2142 GN301

RU

OCHERKI ISTORII RUSSKOI ETNOGRAFII, FOLKLORISTIKI I ANTROPOLOGII. (1956)-. Russian. Biblioteka Akademiia Nauk / Library of the Russian Academy of Sciences, Birzhevaia Liniia 1, 199034 St. Petersburg Russia. **Tel** 011 7 95 2183592, FAX 011 7 95 2187436.

ISSN 0211-5905
SP

UDC 39
OHITURA. [Ohitura]. **VFOAT** Estudios de Etnografia Alavesa. (1981)-. Spanish. One time a year.
Ind/Abst Anthropol. Lit.

ISSN 1071-6610
DD 301 US
●**OKLAHOMA ANTHROPOLOGICAL SOCIETY.** (OKLAHOMA ANTHROPOLOGICAL SOCIETY : [NEWSLETTER].). [Okla. Anthropol. Soc.]. **Added/Corp** Oklahoma Anthropological Society. Vol. 41, No. 1 (Jan. 1993)-. Newsletter. English. Six times a year. Free to members of the Oklahoma Anthropological Society. Oklahoma Anthropological Society, Route 1 Box 62B, Cheyenne OK 73628-9729. **Tel** (405)497-2566, FAX (405)497-2662. **ED** Frieda Vereecken Odell. **Bk Rev**, (Qty: 6). **Circ:** 550. ***Continues*** *Oklahoma Anthropological Society Newsletter.*
Desc: Newsletter reporting current events and research in the fields of anthropology, archaeology, geomorphology and related earth sciences.

AT
OLIVE PINK SOCIETY BULLETIN, THE. **Added/Corp** Olive Pink Society. **VFOAT** Bulletin of the Olive Pink Society. Vol. 1, No. 1 (Feb. 1989)-. Bulletin. English. Two times a year. Comes with Olive Pink Society Membership. Olive Pink Society, PO Box 1005, Albury, New South Wales, 2640 Australia. **Tel** 011 60 6 214228.

IT
OSSIMORI. (1992)-. Periodical. Italian. Four times a year. L50000. Protagon Editori Toscani, Via Di Ficareto 29, 53100 Siena Italy. **Tel** 011 39 577 55359.

ISSN 0078-740X
US
CEASED
PACIFIC ANTHROPOLOGICAL RECORDS. **Added/Corp** Bernice Pauahi Bishop Museum. Dept. of Anthropology. (1968)-No. 39. Monographic series. English. Bishop Museum Press, 1525 Bernice Street, Honolulu HI 96817. **Tel** (808)847-3511, FAX (808)841-8968.
Desc: Covers aspects of pacific anthropology, including archaeology, ethnology, linguistics, social and physical anthropology, ethnohistory, and ethnomusicology.

ISSN 0393-0149
IT
PADUSA. **See** Archaeology.

ISSN 0078-7809
GW
PAIDEUMA (WIESBADEN). (PAIDEUMA, MITTEILUNGEN ZUR KULTURKUNDE.). [Paideuma]. **Added/Corp** Universitat Frankfurt am Main. Frobenius-Institut. Deutsche Gesellschaft fur Kulturmorphologie. Frobenius Gesellschaft. Vol. 1 (1938)-. German (English and French). One time a year. DM80.00. Franz Steiner Verlag GmbH, Postfach 101061, D-70009 Stuttgart Germany. **Tel** 011 49 711 2582372, FAX 011 49 711 2582290, telex 723636 daz d. **ED** Beatrix Heintze. cum. index. **Ad Acc. Circ:** 500.
Desc: Contains essays and reviews in the field of ethnology (mostly African) and African economy, civilization and art.
Ind/Abst Am. Hist. Life (1977-); Anthropol. Index.

ISSN 0148-4737
US
NLM W1 PA361V
Pr Rev.
PALEOPATHOLOGY NEWSLETTER. **See** Archaeology.

CN
PAPERS FROM THE ... ANNUAL CONGRESS / CANADIAN ETHNOLOGY SOCIETY. **Main/Corp** Canadian Ethnology Society. English (French). One time a year. ***Continues*** *Canadian Ethnology Society. Proceedings of the ... Congress.*

ISSN 0581-6165
DD 572 US
PAPERS IN ANTHROPOLOGY (MUSEUM OF NEW MEXICO). (PAPERS IN ANTHROPOLOGY.). **VFOAT** Museum of New Mexico Paper in Anthropology. No. 1 (1958)-. Monographic series. English. Price varies per volume. Museum of New Mexico Foundation, PO Box 2087, Santa Fe NM 87504-2087. **Tel** (505)827-6476.
Ind/Abst Abstr. Anthropol.; Middle East Abstr. Index.

LC GN2 .K76 **ISSN** 0023-4869
DD 572.062794 US
PAPERS - KROEBER ANTHROPOLOGICAL SOCIETY. (PAPERS.). [Pap. - Kroeber Anthropol. Soc.]. **Main/Corp** Kroeber Anthropological Society. **VFOAT** Kroeber Anthropological Society Papers. No. 1 (1950)-. English. Two times a year. $24.00. University of California Kroeber Society, Anthropology Department, Berkeley CA 94720. **Tel** (510)642-6932. **ED** Scott Morgan. **Circ:** 400 (ctrl).
Ind/Abst Am. Hist. Life (1963-1964); Anthropol. Index; Anthropol. Lit.

LC E51 .H337 **ISSN** 0079-0303
DD 913 US
CODEN HPAEAQ
PAPERS OF THE PEABODY MUSEUM OF ARCHAEOLOGY AND ETHNOLOGY, HARVARD UNIVERSITY. **See** Archaeology.

LC GN1 .P37 **ISSN** 0938-0116
DD 573.05 GW
PARAGRANA. **Added/Corp** Freie Universitat Berlin. Forschungszentrum fuer Historische Anthropologie. (1992)-. Periodical. German. Two times a year. $39.00. Akademie-Verlag GmbH, Postfach, D-13162 Berlin Germany. **Tel** 011 49 30 47889300, FAX 011 49 30 47889357. **(Subscription address:** VCH Publishers Inc., 303 Northwest 12th Avenue, Journals Department, Deerfield FL 33442. **Tel** (800)367-8249, (305)428-5566.)

ISSN 0090-0745
US
NLM W1 PE872G **CODEN** PVHEA
PERSPECTIVES ON HUMAN EVOLUTION. [Perspect. hum. evol.]. 1- 1968-. English. Irregular. Holt Rinehart & Winston, 1st Anne's Road Eastbourne, East Sussex BN21 3UN United Kingdom. **Tel** (212)688-9100. **ED** S L Washbourn and Phyllis C Jay.

LC F2519.1.R6 P4 **ISSN** 0553-8467
DD 981/.00498/005 BL
PESQUISAS. ANTROPOLOGIA. **Added/Corp** Instituto Anchietano de Pesquisas. **VFOAT** Antropologia. No. 6 (1960)-. Monographic series. Portuguese (Multiple languages). Irregular. Price varies per volume. Sao Leopoldo, Praca Tiradentes, 35 Rio Grande Do Sul Brazil 93010-020. **Tel** FAX 051 5921035. Index available. cum. index. **Circ:** 500 (ctrl). Documents available from FAXON Xpress. ***Continues in part*** *Pesquisas (Instituto Anchietano de Pesquisas).*

LC GN1 .P47 **ISSN** 0195-8593
DD 306/.05 US
PHOENIX (STANFORD, CALIF.). (PHOENIX.). [Phoenix]. **VFOAT** Phoenix: New Directions in the Study of Man. Vol. 1 (Summer 1977)-. Periodical. English. Two times a year. Free to members, $10.00 students, $20.00 institutions, $15.00 other. ATAI, 2001 Tibbits Avenue, Troy NY 12180.

ISSN 1055-6443
DD 573 US
PHYSICAL ANTHROPOLOGY NEWS. (PHYSICAL ANTHROPOLOGY NEWS : PAN.). [Phys. anthropol. news]. **Added/Corp** American Association of Physical Anthropologists. Queens College (New York, N.Y.). Dept. of Anthropology. **VFOAT** PAN. Vol. 1, No. 1 (Spring 1982)-. Periodical. English. Two times a year. $6.00. International Institute of Human Evolution Research, Central Oregon University Center, 2600 Northwest College Way, Bend OR 97701-5998. **ED** Noel T. Boaz. **Circ:** 300.

LC E78.G73 P52 **ISSN** 0032-0447
US
NLM W1 PL101F **CODEN** PLNAA3
Pr Rev.
PLAINS ANTHROPOLOGIST. [Plains anthropol.]. **Added/Corp** Plains Anthropological Society. Vol. 1, No. 1 (May 1954)-. Periodical. English. Four times a year. comes with membership, $35.00 institution, $20.00 individual (membership). Plains Anthropological Society, 410 Wedgewood Drive, Lincoln NE 68510. **Tel** (402)488-3813. **ED** Patricia J O'Brien and Danny Walker. Index available. cum. index. **Bk Rev. Circ:** 1,200 (ctrl). available on microfilm and microfiche from University Microfilms International (UMI). Documents available from The Genuine Article, BIOSIS Document Express, UMI Article Clearinghouse. ***Supersedes*** *Plains Conference. News Letter.*
Desc: Publishes original papers on the anthropology of plains and adjacent areas of North America.
Ind/Abst Abstr. Anthropol. (19??-); Am. Hist. Life (1963-); Anthropol. Lit. (1963-); Arts Humanit. Citation Index [Select. Cov.]; Biol. Abstr.; Br. Archaeol. Bibliogr.; Curr. Contents Soc. Behav. Sci.; Ethnoarts Index (1963-); Expand. Acad. Index (1992-); Newsp. Period. Abstr. (1992-); Res. Alert [Full Cov.]; Soc. Sci. Cit. Index [Full Cov.].

LC GN585.R9 A42a

RU
POLEVYE ISSLEDOVANIIA INSTITUTA ETNOGRAFII. **Main/Corp** Institut Etnografii Imeni N.N. Miklukho-Maklaia. **Added/Corp** Institut Etnografii Imeni N.N. Miklukho-Maklaia. Institut Etnologii i Antropologii Im. N.N. Miklukho-Maklaia. **VFOAT** Polevye Issledovaniia. (1974)-. Russian. Irregular. Izdatelstvo Nauka / Akademiia Nauk, (Publishing House of the Russian Academy of Sciences), Leninskii Porspekt 14, 117901 Moscow Russia. **Tel** 011 95 9542153, FAX 011 95 9382144, telex 411964. ***Continues*** *Itogi Polevykh Rabot Instituta Etnografii V ... Godu.*

ISSN 1067-9847
DD 950 US
●**POSITIONS (DURHAM, N.C.).** (POSITIONS : EAST ASIA CULTURES CRITIQUE.). [Positions]. Vol. 1, No. 1 (Spring 1993)-. Periodical. English. Three times a year. $54.00. Duke University Press, PO Box 90660, Durham NC 27708-0660. **Tel** (919)687-3600, (919)688-5134 (orders), FAX (919)688-4574, telex 802829. **ED** Tani E. Barlow.
Ind/Abst Acad. Search; EP Collect.; Homework Help.; MasterFile FullTEXT 1000; MasterFile FullTEXT 350; MasterFile FullTEXT 650; MasterFile FullTEXT (July 1994-); OCLC; Telebase.

PL
PRACE KOMITETU NAUK ETNOLOGICZNYCH PAN. (1979)-. Monographic series. Polish. Price varies per volume. Panstwowe Wydawnictwo Naukowe / PWN, (Polish Scientific Publishers PWN Ltd.), Ul. Miodowa 10, PO Box 391, 00-251 Warsaw Poland. **Tel** 011 48 22 312738, FAX 011 48 22 267163.

LC GN397 .P7 **ISSN** 0888-4552
DD 301/.05 US
CCC
PRACTICING ANTHROPOLOGY. [Pract. anthropol.]. **Added/Corp** Society for Applied Anthropology. Vol. 1 (Sept. 1978)-. Periodical. English. Four times a year. $30.00. Society for Applied Anthropology, Box 24083, Oklahoma City OK 73124. **Tel** (405)843-5113. **ED** Benita Howell. **Bk Rev. Ad Acc. Circ:** 2,500 (ctrl). available on microfilm.
Desc: Provides career information for anthropologists working outside academia, encourages bridge between practice inside and outside the university and explores the uses of anthropology in policy research and implementation.
Ind/Abst Rural Dev. Abstr.

ISSN 0032-6534
AU
PRAEHISTORISCHE FORSCHUNGEN / HERAUSGEGEBEN VON DER ANTHROPOLOGISCHEN GESELLSCHAFT IN WIEN. **Added/Corp** Anthropologische Gesellschaft in Wien. (19??)-. Monographic series. German. Price varies per volume. Verlag Ferdinand Berger & Soehne, Wienerstrasse 21-23, A-3580 Horn Austria. **Tel** 011 43 2982 4161232. **Bk Rev.**

LC GN700 .P825 **ISSN** 0079-4848
DD 913.05 GW
CCC
PRAEHISTORISCHE ZEITSCHRIFT. **Added/Corp** Berliner Gesellschaft fuer Anthropologie, Ethnologie und Urgeschihte. Vol. 1 (1909)-. Periodical. German. Two times a year. $154.50. Walter de Gruyter Inc., PO Box 303421, D-10728 Berlin Germany. **Tel** 011 49 30 260050, FAX 011 49 30 26005251, telex 184027. cum. index.
Ind/Abst Anthropol. Index; Anthropol. Lit.; BHA : Biblio. Hist. Art; Br. Archaeol. Bibliogr.

LC GN848 .P72 GN1 .P74 **ISSN** 1167-492X
DD 301 FR
PREHISTOIRE ANTHROPOLOGIE MEDITERRANEENNES. **Added/Corp** Laboratoire d'Anthropologie et de Prehistoire des Pays de la Mediterranee Occidentale (France). (1992)-. Periodical. French. Universite de Provence, Centre de Aix 29, Robert Schuman, 13621 Aix Provence France. ***Continues*** *Travaux du Laboratoire d'Anthropologie, de Prehistoire et d'Ethnologie des Pays de la Mediterranee Occidentale.*

ISSN 0731-4108
DD 572 US
PROCEEDINGS OF THE AMERICAN ETHNOLOGICAL SOCIETY. [Proc. Am. Ethnol. Soc.]. **Added/Corp** American Ethnological Society. (1973)-. Proceedings. English. One time a year. American Ethnological Society, 1703 New Hampshire Avenue NW, Washington DC 20009. **Tel** (202)232-8800. **Bk Rev. Ad Acc.** ctrl circ. ***Continues*** *Proceedings of the ... Annual Spring Meeting of the American Ethnological Society, 0748-6995.*
Ind/Abst Anthropol. Index.

LC GN700 .P84a **ISSN** 0079-497X
DD 930 UK
Pr Rev.
PROCEEDINGS OF THE PREHISTORIC SOCIETY. **Main/Corp** Prehistoric Society (London, England). Vol. 1 (1935)-. Proceedings. English. One time a year (published in March). £30.00 (institutions), £20.00 (individuals). Prehistoric Society, Institute of Archaeology, Gordon Square, London WC1 United Kingdom. **Tel** 011 44 171 3877050, FAX 011 44 171 3832572. **Ad Acc. Circ:** 2,000. ***Continues*** *Proceedings of the Prehistoric Society of East Anglia.*
Ind/Abst Anthropol. Index; Anthropol. Lit.; Art Archaeol. Tech. Abstr.; Br. Archaeol. Bibliogr.; Br. Humanit. Index; Geogr. Abstr. Human Geogr.; Numis. Lit.

Anthropology

ISSN 0227-4523
DD 301/.09714
CN
PROFANE. (LE PROFANE : REVUE COMMUNAUTAIRE DES ETUDIANTS EN ANTHROPOLOGIE U.L.). [Profane]. No. 1-. Periodical. French. $1.25 per no. Le Profane, 2-520 St. Gabriel, Quebec Quebec G1R 1W3 Canada.

LC GN2 .P65
DD 573
NLM W1 PR92
ISSN 0033-2003
PL
CODEN PZANA7
PRZEGLAD ANTROPOLOGICZNY. [Prz. antropol.]. **Added/Corp** Polskie Towarzystwo Antropologiczne. Polskie Zaklady Antropologii. **VFOAT** Revue Anthropologique; Anthropological Review; Antropologicheskii Obzor. Vol. 1 (1926)-. Periodical. Polish (Russian and English; summaries and/or abstracts in English, French and Russian; table of contents in French, Russian and English). Irregular. Price varies per volume. (**Subscription address:** Ars Polona-Ruch, PO Box 1001, Krakowskie Przedmiescie 7, 00-068 Warsaw Poland. **Tel** 011 48 22 261201.) Documents available from BIOSIS Document Express.
Ind/Abst Anthropol. Index; Biol. Abstr.

ISSN 0327-6627
AG
PUBLICAR EN ANTROPOLOGIA Y CIENCIAS SOCIALES. Added/Corp Colegio de Graduados en Antropologia (Buenos Aires, Argentina). **VFOAT** Publicar. Vol. 1, No. 1 (May 1992)-. Periodical. Spanish. Two times a year. Colegio de Graduados en Antropologia, 25 de Mayo 217, 1002 Buenos Aires Argentina. **ED** Marcelo Alvarez.

DD 390
ISSN 8756-7245
US
PUBLICATIONS / GYPSY LORE SOCIETY, NORTH AMERICAN CHAPTER. See Folklore.

UDC 572.1
ISSN 0393-1099
IT
QUADERNI DI SCIENZE ANTROPOLOGICHE. [Quad. sci. antropol.]. (1978)-. Periodical. Italian. One time a year. Free upon request. Quaderni di Scienze, Corrain, Dip. Biologia, Univ. r Trieste 75, 35121 Padua Italy.
Ind/Abst Anthropol. Lit.

ISSN 0211-5557
SP
QUADERNS DE L'INSTITUT CATALA D'ANTROPOLOGIA. [Quad. Inst. Catala Antropol.]. No. 1 (1980)-. Periodical. Spanish. Two times a year. Quaderns, Urgell 259, SS 3, Barcelona 35 Spain.
Ind/Abst Anthropol. Lit.

LC HM
DD 301
ISSN 1077-8004
US
●**QUALITATIVE INQUIRY. See** Social Sciences.

LC DT450.63 .Q4
DD 967/.572/005
BD
QUE VOUS EN SEMBLE?. Added/Corp Cercle Saint-Paul. (19??)-. Periodical. French. Four times a year. $28.00. Que Vous en Semble, Grand Seminaire de Burasira, DS 17 Bujumbura Burundi.

LC HQ
DD 306
UK
CEASED
QUEEN'S UNIVERSITY PAPERS IN SOCIAL ANTHROPOLOGY, THE.
Main/Corp Queen's University (Belfast, Northern Ireland). **Added/Corp** Belfast. Queen's University. Dept. of Social Anthropology. Vol. 1 (1976)-Series complete. Periodical. English. Queens University of Belfast Department of Social Anthropology, Belfast BT7 1NN United Kingdom. **Tel** 011 44 1232 245133 ext. 3700. **ED** Reginald Byron. **Circ:** 400 (ctrl).
Desc: Contains results of research related to specific theoretical issues in social anthropology.

LC E78.Q3 R4
DD 971.4/00497
UDC 971.4(=97)
ISSN 0318-4137
CN
RECHERCHES AMERINDIENNES AU QUEBEC. VFOAT Bulletin d'Information. Vol. 1, No. 1-. Bulletin. French (English). Four times a year. 40.75 Can$ (one-year), 110.00 Can$ (three-year) (institutions), Canada; 50.00 Can$ (one-year), 130.00 Can$ (three-year) institutions other; 35.00 Can$ (one-year), 90.00 Can$ (three-year) individuals, Canada; 40.00 Can$ (one-year), 110.00 Can$ (three-year) individuals, other. Recherches Amerindiennes AU Quebec, 6742 rue St. Denis, Montreal Quebec H2S 2S2 Canada. **Tel** (514)277-6178. **Circ:** 1,000.
Desc: Each issue concerns a specific theme usually relative to Northeast American indians, plus commentaries, current news, book reviews, film reviews, and book updates. Modern presentations with maps, graphics, and pictures.
Ind/Abst Abstr. Anthropol.; Am. Hist. Life (1985-); Anthropol. Lit.; Ethnoarts Index; Repere.

ISSN 0812-7387
AT
CODEN RAMSEZ
RECORDS OF THE AUSTRALIAN MUSEUM. SUPPLEMENT. See Zoology.

AG
RELACIONES. Vol. 1 (March/April 1964)-. Periodical. Spanish. Irregular. Fundacion Para La Education, Defensa 251, 1065 Buenos Aires Argentina.
Ind/Abst Anthropol. Lit.

LC F2821 .S64
DD 913.82
AG
RELACIONES DE LA SOCIEDAD ARGENTINA DE ANTROPOLOGIA.
Main/Corp Sociedad Argentina de Antropologia, Buenos Aires. Vol. 1 (1937)-. Spanish. One time a year. $25.00 (latest edition). Editorial Facultar Filosofia, Letras Casilla de Correo 345, 5500 Mendoza Argentina. **Tel** 011 54 61 253010, 234571. (**Subscription address:** Fernando Garcia Cambeiro, 7331 Northwest 35th Street, PO Box 014, Miami FL 33122.) **Ad Acc. Circ:** 500.
Desc: Argentina and Latin America anthropology.

DD 621
ISSN 0894-5217
US
REMOTE SENSING NEWSLETTER IN ANTHROPOLOGY AND ARCHAEOLOGY. [Remote sens. newsl. anthropol. archaeol.]. **Added/Corp** American Association for the Advancement of Science. Section H--Anthropology. Vol. 1, Issue 1 (Jan. 1987)-. Newsletter. English. Four times a year. Remote Sensing Newsletter in Anthropology and Archaeology, 113 North Randall Road, Slidell LA 70458.

LC GN1 .J4
DD 301/.05
ISSN 1000-3193
CC
RENLEIXUE XUEBAO. (JEN LEI HSUEH HSUEH PAO = ACTA ANTHROPOLOGICA SINICA.). **Added/Corp** Chung-kuo ko Hsueh Yuan. Ku chi Chui Tung wu Yu ku jen lei Yen Chiu so. **VFOAT** Acta Anthropologica Sinica. Vol. 1, Aug. (1982)-. Academic Scholarly Publication. Chinese (summaries and/or abstracts in English). Four times a year. $91.60. Science Press, 16 Donghuangchenggen North Street, Beijing 100707, People's Republic of China. **Tel** 011 86 1 4019821, 011 86 1 4010642, FAX 011 86 1 4012180, 011 86 1 4019810, telex 210147. **Bk Rev. Ad Acc. Circ:** 40,000.
Desc: All kinds of articles and papers concerning population and its relationship with economic social factors and so forth are acceptable.
Ind/Abst Anthropol. Lit.; Life Sci. Collect.

LC J905 .L3 GN666
DD 328/.94/01 S 354/.94/008484
AT
REPORT - DEPARTMENT OF ABORIGINAL AFFAIRS. Main/Corp Australia. Dept. of Aboriginal Affairs. 1972/74-. English. $2.65. Australian Department of Aboriginal Affairs, M L C Tower/Woden Town Centre, Canberra Australian Capital Territory Australia.

ISSN 0284-9232
SW
REPORT - DEVELOPMENT STUDY UNIT, DEPARTMENT OF SOCIAL ANTHROPOLOGY, UNIVERSITY OF STOCKHOLM. (REPORT.). **VFOAT** Rapport - Stockholms Universitet, Socialantropologiska Institutionen, Sektionen for Utvecklingsstudier; Relatorio - Seccao de Estudos do Desenvolvimento, Instituto de Antropologia Social, Universidade de Estocolmo. (1980)-. Monographic series. Multiple languages. Irregular.
Ind/Abst Agrofor. Abstr.

US
REPORT OF THE COMMISSION ON HUMAN SETTLEMENTS. Main/Corp United Nations. Commission on Human Settlements. 1st (1978)-. Government Publication. English. Six times a year. United Nations Publications, 2 United Nations Plaza, Room DC2 0853, Department 007C, New York NY 10017. **Tel** (212)963-8303, (800)253-9646. **Continues** Report of the Session.

DD 550 572 574
ISSN 0885-8373
US
CODEN RISMDY
REPORTS OF INVESTIGATIONS - SOUTHERN METHODIST UNIVERSITY. INSTITUTE FOR THE STUDY OF EARTH AND MAN. See Earth Sciences.

LC N5310.7 .R47
DD 709/.01/1
ISSN 0277-1322
US
RES (CAMBRIDGE, MASS.). (RES.). [Res]. **Added/Corp** Peabody Museum of Archaeology and Ethnology. Universite de Paris X: Nanterre. Laboratoire d'Ethnologie et de Sociologie Comparative. J. Paul Getty Center for the History of Art and the Humanities. (Spring 1981)-. Academic Scholarly Publication. English (French). Two times a year. $53.00. Cambridge University Press / New York, 40 West 20th Street, New York NY 10011-4211. **Tel** (212)924-3900, (800)221-4512, FAX (212)691-3239. (**Subscription address:** Cambridge University Press / Outside of North America, United Kingdom. **Tel** 011 44 223 312 393, FAX 011 44 223 325 959.) **ED** Francesco Pellizzi.
Desc: Contains information about anthropology and comparative aesthetics dedicated to the study of the object, in particular cult and belief objects and objects of art.

LC GN635.I4 R45A
DD 301.2/05
II
RESEARCH BULLETIN - RESEARCH ASSOCIATION (ANTHROPOLOGY).
Main/Corp Research Association (Anthropology). Bulletin. English. Four times a year. $5.00. Lucknow University / Anthropology Research Association, C 239 Indira Nagar, Lucknow 226 016 India.

LC GN448 .R47
DD 306.3/05
ISSN 0190-1281
US
CCC
CODEN REANEM
RESEARCH IN ECONOMIC ANTHROPOLOGY. [Res. econ. anthropol.]. Vol. 1 (1978)-. English. Irregular. $73.25. JAI Press Inc., 55 Old Post Road, Suite 2, PO Box 1678, Greenwich CT 06836-1678. **Tel** (203)661-7602, FAX (203)661-0792. **ED** Barry L. Isaac.
Ind/Abst Anthropol. Lit.; Br. Archaeol. Bibliogr. (?-?); Ethnoarts Index; Int. Bibliogr. Sociol.; Int. Labour Doc.; Soc. Plann. Policy Dev. Abstr.

LC GN671.N5 R45
DD 995
ISSN 0254-0665
PP
RESEARCH IN MELANESIA. [Res. Melanes.]. **Added/Corp** University of Papua New Guinea. Dept. of Anthropology and Sociology. Vol. 1 (Apr. 1975)-. Periodical. English. Two times a year. $18.00. Research in Melanesia, Anthropology and Sociology Department, University Box 320, Papua New Guinea. **Tel** 011 675 267163, FAX 011 675 267187. **Bk Rev,** (Qty: 2). ctrl circ. **Continues** Man in New Guinea.
Ind/Abst Anthropol. Index; Anthropol. Lit.; Int. Bibliogr. Sociol.

US
RESEARCH MANUSCRIPT SERIES - INSTITUTE OF ARCHEOLOGY AND ANTHROPOLOGY, UNIVERSITY OF SOUTH CAROLINA. See Archaeology.

US
RESEARCH REPORTS / DEPARTMENT OF ANTHROPOLOGY, UNIVERSITY OF MASSACHUSETTS, AMHERST. Main/Corp University of Massachusetts at Amherst. Dept. of Anthropology. **Added/Corp** University of Massachusetts at Amherst. Dept. of Anthropology. No. 7 (May 1971)-. Monographic series. English. Irregular. Price varies per volume. University of Massachusetts at Amherst / Anthropology, 215 Machmer Hall, Department of Anthropology, Amherst MA 01003. **Tel** (413)545-2221. **Bk Rev. Ad Acc. Circ:** 600 (ctrl). **Continues** Research Reports - Department of Anthropology, University of Massachusetts, 0076-5066.
Desc: Current research in all sub-fields of anthropology; monographs and collections.

DD 975
Pr Rev.
ISSN 0882-2042
US
RESEARCH SERIES. See Archaeology.

LC Z5111 .R47
DD 301.2
ISSN 0093-8157
US
CCC
CODEN REVAEK
REVIEWS IN ANTHROPOLOGY. [Rev. anthropol.]. Vol. 1 (Feb. 1974)-. Academic Scholarly Publication. English. Four times a year. Price varies. Gordon & Breach Science Publishers, Inc., PO Box 786, Cooper Station, New York NY 10276. **Tel** (212)206-8900, FAX (212)645-2459. (**Subscription address:** Gordon & Breach Science Publishers / England, PO Box 90 Reading, Berkshire RG1 8JL United Kingdom. **Tel** 011 44 734 560080.) **ED** Nina L. Etkin. Index available. **Bk Rev. Ad Acc. Circ:** 1,000.
Desc: Reviews both scholarly and trade publications in anthropology, published in the U.S. and abroad. Extended review-essays are often state-of-the-art discussions of current knowledge and practice in the various fields of anthropology.
Ind/Abst Book Rev. Index (?-March 1989).

LC GN1 .R34
DD 572
ISSN 0486-6525
CK
REVISTA COLOMBIANA DE ANTROPOLOGIA. [Rev. colomb. antropol.]. **Added/Corp** Instituto Colombiano de Antropologia. Instituto Colombiano de Cultura. Vol. 1 (June 1953)-. Periodical. Spanish. One time a year. Instituto Columbiano de Antropologia, Carrera 7A No 28, 66 Bogota Colombia. **Continues** Revista del Instituto

Anthropology

Etnologico Nacional; Boletin de Arqueologia.
Ind/Abst Am. Hist. Life (1962-1965); Anthropol. Index; Anthropol. Lit.; Hisp. Am. Period. Index, HAPI.

LC GN1

EC

REVISTA DE ANTROPOLOGIA. No. 1 (Dec. 1969)-. Periodical. Spanish. University De Los Andes, Apartado Aereo 4976, Bogota Colombia.
Ind/Abst Anthropol. Lit.

LC GN1 .R355   **ISSN** 0034-7701
BL

REVISTA DE ANTROPOLOGIA (SAO PAULO). (REVISTA DE ANTROPOLOGIA.). [Rev. antropol.]. **Added/Corp** Associacao Brasileira de Antropologia. Universidade de Sao Paulo. Faculdade de Filosofia, Ciencias e Letras. Vol. 1 (June 1953)-. English (Portuguese, Spanish and French). One time a year. $15.00. Universidade de Sao Paulo / Faculdade de Filosofia, Ciencias e Letras, Secao de Publicacoes, Caixa Postal 8105, 05508 Butanta Sao Paulo SP Brazil. **Tel** 011 55 11 8133222 ext. 2191.
Ind/Abst Am. Hist. Life (1956-1966); Anthropol. Index; Hisp. Am. Period. Index, HAPI.

ISSN 1131-558X
SP

REVISTA DE ANTROPOLOGIA SOCIAL / DEPARTAMENTO DE ANTROPOLOGIA SOCIAL, FACULTAD DE CIENCIAS POLITICAS Y SOCIOLOGIA, UNIVERSIDAD COMPLUTENSE DE MADRID. **Added/Corp** Universidad Complutense de Madrid. Departamento de Antropologia Social. (1991)-. Periodical. Spanish. One time a year. Editorial Complutense, Donoso Cortes 65, Primera Planta, 28015 Madrid Spain. **Tel** 011 34 1 3946372, 011 34 1 3946373, 011 34 1 3946374.
Ind/Abst Am. Hist. Life (1955-1958, 1962-1978).

CK

REVISTA DE ANTROPOLOGIA Y ARQUEOLOGIA. **Added/Corp** Universidad de los Andes (Bogota, Colombia). Departamento de Antropologia. Vol. 6, No. 1 (1990)-. Spanish. Universidad de Los Andes / Colombia, Apartado Aereo 4976, Bogota Colombia. **Tel** 011 57 1 282-4066 Ext 2461. *Continues Revista de Antropologia (Bogota, Colombia), 0120-6613.*
Ind/Abst Anthropol. Lit.

LC GR257 .R4   **ISSN** 0034-8198
DD 398/.05
RM

REVISTA DE ETNOGRAFIE SI FOLCLOR. [Rev. etnogr. folclor]. **Added/Corp** Academia Republicii Populare Romine. **VFOAT** Review of Ethnography and Folklore. (1964)-. Periodical. Romanian (summaries and/or abstracts in English). Six times a year. DM384.00. **(Subscription address:** Kubon & Sagner, ABT Zeitschriftenimport, D 80328 Munich Germany. **Tel** 011 49 89 54218130.**)** *Continues Revista de Folclor, 1015-4779.*
Desc: Studies and materials on ethnography and folklore.
Ind/Abst MLA Int. Bibl. Books Artic. Mod. Lang. Lit.; RILM Abstr.

LC F3401 .L56   **ISSN** 0304-2367
DD 913.85
PE
SUSPENDED

REVISTA DEL MUSEO NACIONAL (LIMA). (REVISTA DEL MUSEO NACIONAL.). [Rev. Mus. Nac.]. **Main/Corp** Peru. Museo Nacional. Vol. 1 (1932)-Vol. 48 (1988). Academic Scholarly Publication. Spanish. One time a year. Museo Nacional Cultura Peruana, Av Alfonso Ugarte 650, Casilla Post 3048, Lima 1 Peru. **Tel** 011 51 14 235892. **ED** L. E. Valcarcel. cum. index. **Circ:** 1,000.
Desc: Articles on architecture, painting, paleography and the arts past and present in Peru. Covers historical and archaeological topics in scholarly essays.
Ind/Abst Am. Hist. Life (1954-); Anthropol. Index; Anthropol. Lit.; Ethnoarts Index; Hisp. Am. Period. Index, HAPI.

LC E51 .R46   **ISSN** 0556-6533
DD 306/.08997073
SP

REVISTA ESPANOLA DE ANTROPOLOGIA AMERICANA. [Rev. esp. antropol. am.]. **Added/Corp** Universidad Complutense de Madrid. Departamento de Antropologia y Enologia de America. **VFOAT** REAA. Vol. 4 (1969)-. Spanish. One time a year. 22.00ptas. Editorial Complutense, Donoso Cortes 65, Primera Planta, 28015 Madrid Spain. **Tel** 011 34 1 3946372, 011 34 1 3946373, 011 34 1 3946374. **ED** Miguel Rivera Dorado. **Bk Rev. Circ:** 1,500. *Continues Trabajos y Conferencias.*
Desc: General anthropology of the American continent, especially Latin America.
Ind/Abst Am. Hist. Life (1969-1972); Anthropol. Lit.; Hisp. Am. Period. Index, HAPI.

PN

REVISTA PANAMENA DE ANTROPOLOGIA : PUBLICACION DE LA ASOCIACION PANAMENA DE ANTROPOLOGIA. **Added/Corp** Asociacion Panamena de Antropologia. Vol. 1, No. 1 (Dec. 1975)-. Periodical. Spanish.
Ind/Abst Anthropol. Lit.

LC P   **ISSN** 0778-8118
DD 410
UDC 372.6
BE

REVUE D'ETHNOLINGUISTIQUE. See Linguistics.

ISSN 0892-6255
DD 301   US
SUSPENDED

RING OF FIRE. (RING OF FIRE : NEWSLETTER OF THE GREAT BASIN FOUNDATION, CENTER FOR ANTHROPOLOGICAL RESEARCH.). [Ring fire]. Newsletter. English. Two times a year. Free to members, $3.00 nonmembers. Great Basin Foundation, 1236 Concord Street, San Diego CA 92106.

ISSN 0271-6925
US

RIPLEY P. BULLEN MONOGRAPHS IN ANTHROPOLOGY AND HISTORY. [Ripley P. Bullen monogr. anthropol. hist.]. **Added/Corp** Florida State Museum. **VFOAT** Monographs in Anthropology and History. No. 1 (1978)-. Monographic series. English. Irregular. Price varies per volume. University of Florida Press, 15 Northwest 15th Street, Gainesville FL 32611. **Tel** (904)392-5717, (800)226-3822.
Desc: Scholarly studies in Southeastern United States anthropology and history.

IT

RIVISTA DI ANTROPOLOGIA. **Added/Corp** Istituto Italiano di Antropologia. Istituto Italiano di Antropologia. Atti della Societa Romana di Antropologia. Vol. 1 (1893/94)-. Italian (French and English). Irregular. L70000.00. Libreria Gia Nardecchia, Via Tor di Nona 39, 00186 Rome Italy. **Tel** 011 39 6 6830010, 6877617. **Bk Rev.**
Ind/Abst Anthropol. Index; Anthropol. Lit.

LC GN36.P72 K74a
PL

ROCZNIK MUZEUM ETNOGRAFICZNEGO W KRAKOWIE.
Main/Corp Muzeum Etnograficzne w Krakowie. (1966)-. Periodical. Polish (summaries and/or abstracts in English, French, German and Russian). One time a year.
Ind/Abst BHA : Biblio. Hist. Art.

LC DK4600.L8242 Z17
PL

ROCZNIK MUZEUM WSI LUBELSKIEJ. See History-History of Europe.

LC GN1 .R77   **ISSN** 0325-1217
DD 572.058
AG

RUNA. (RUNA; ARCHIVO PARA LAS CIENCIAS DEL HOMBRE.). [Runa]. **Added/Corp** Universidad de Buenos Aires. Instituto de Antropologia. Universidad de Buenos Aires. Instituto de Ciencias Antropologicas. Vol. 1 (1948)-. Academic Scholarly Publication. Spanish. One time a year. Universidad de Buenos Aires / Antropologia, Instituto de Antropologia, 25 de Mayo 217, 1002 Buenos Aires Argentina. **Tel** 011 54 1 4320537, 011 54 1 4328696.
Ind/Abst Am. Hist. Life (1958-1965, 1969-1970); Anthropol. Lit.; Hisp. Am. Period. Index, HAPI.

ISSN 1066-0127
DD 947   US

RUSSIA AND HER NEIGHBORS. See Social Sciences.

ISSN 0080-5180
GW

SAARBRUCKER BEITRAEGE ZUR ALTERTUMSKUNDE. Vol. 1 (1964)-. Monographic series. German. Irregular. Price varies per volume. Dr. Rudolf Habelt GmbH, Postfach 150104, D-53040 Bonn Germany. **Tel** 011 49 228 232015. **ED** V. R. Hachmann, J. Lichardus, W. Schmitthenner, F. Stein.
Ind/Abst Br. Archaeol. Bibliogr. (?-?).

LC F869.S22 S36
DD 913.794 979.49   US

SAN DIEGO MUSEUM PAPERS.
Added/Corp San Diego Museum. San Diego Museum of Man. No. 2 (1936)-. Monographic series. English. Irregular. Price varies per volume. San Diego Museum of Man, 1350 El Prado Balboa Park, San Diego CA 92101. **Tel** (619)239-2001. **ED** Ken Hedges. **Circ:** 500. *Continues Archaeology.*
Desc: Papers on anthropological and archaeological topics of the West Hemisphere.

ISSN 0833-8590
DD 362.1/09714   CN

SANTE CULTURE. (SANTE CULTURE / CULTURE HEALTH.). [Sante cult.]. **Added/Corp** GIRAME. **VFOAT** Culture Health. Vol. 3, No. 1 (1985)-. Periodical. French (English). Two times a year. 48.02Can$. Universite de Montreal / SOCP, PO Box 6128, Stn Centre-Ville, Montreal Quebec H3C 3J7 Canada. **Tel** (514)343-6853, FAX (514)343-2479. *Continues Bulletin d'Information en Anthropologie Medicale et en Psychiatrie Transculturelle, 0715-9358.*

LC GN1 .S12
DD 301/.05   II

SAP, SPECTRA OF ANTHROPOLOGICAL PROGRESS.
VFOAT Spectra of Anthropological Progress. Vol. 1 (1978)-. English. One time a year. $14.00. University of Delhi Department of Anthropology, Delhi 7 India. **Bk Rev. Ad Acc. Circ:** 100.
Desc: Covers growth and development, forensic anthropology, urban anthropology, social anthropology, ecology and society caste and kinship religion.
Ind/Abst Anthropol. Lit.

ISSN 0997-5373
FR

UDC 50
SAVOIRS LASALLE. (SAVOIRS.). (1988)-. Periodical. French. Irregular (5 to 6 issues per year). 122.00F. Fondation Nemo, Filature du Pont de Fer, 30460 LaSalle France. **Tel** 66 852567. *Continues Le Courrier des Medicinales en Montagne (Saint-Louis et Parahou), 0765-5045.*

LC GN2 .A215   **ISSN** 0131-3703
RU

SBORNIK MUZEIA ANTROPOLOGII I ETNOGRAFII / AKADEMIIA NAUK SOUIUZA SOVETSKIKH SOTSIALISTICHESKIKH RESPUBLIK.
Added/Corp Muzei Antropologii i Etnografii Imeni Imperatora Petra Velikogo. Muzei Antropologii i Etnografii (Akkademiia Nauk SSSR) Institut Etnografii Imeni N.N. Miklukho-Maklaia. **VFOAT** Sbornik; Publications du Musee d'Anthropologie et d'Ethnographie. (1927)-. Monographic series. Russian. Irregular. Price varies per volume. Izdatelstvo Nauka St. Petersburg, Mendeleevskaia Liniia 1, 199034 St. Petersburg, B-34 Russia. **Tel** 011 7 812 2182612. *Continues Sbornik Muzeia Antropologii i Etnografii Imeni Petra Velikogo pri Akademii Nauk Soiuza Sovetskikh Sotsialisticheskikh Respublik.*
Desc: Information on anthropology and ethnology.
Ind/Abst Ethnoarts Index.

LC F2822 .S4
DD 982/.004/98005   AG

SCRIPTA ETHNOLOGICA. (SCRIPTA ETHNOLOGICA : ORGANO DEL CENTRO ARGENTINO DE ETNOLOGIA AMERICANA.). (1973)-. Spanish (summaries and/or abstracts in English). One time a year.
Ind/Abst Anthropol. Lit.

LC GN303 .S47   **ISSN** 0387-6004
DD 306   JA

SENRI ETHNOLOGICAL STUDIES.
Added/Corp Kokuritsu Minzokugaku Hakubutsukan. (1978)-. Periodical. English (French and Spanish). National Museum of Ethnology, 10-1 Banpakukoen Senri, Suitashi Osaka 565 Japan. **Tel** 011 81 6 8726151, FAX 011 81 6 8750401.
Ind/Abst Int. Bibliogr. Sociol.

LC GN301 .S53
JA

SHAKAI JINRUIGAKU NENPO. **Added/Corp** Tokyo Toritsu Daigaku. Shakai Jinrui Gakkai. Vol. 1 (1975)-. Periodical. Japanese. One time a year. ¥3200. Kobundo, 1-7-13 Kanda Surugadai, Chiyoda-ku, Tokyo Japan. **Tel** FAX 03 294 7542.

LC DS894.49.S244 S27a
JA

SHOHO. **Main/Corp** Saitama Kenritsu Minzoku Bunka Senta. **VFOAT** Saitama Kenritsu Minzoku Bunka Senta Shoho. (1982)-. Academic Scholarly Publication. Japanese. Saitama Kenritsu Minzoku Bunka Senta, 10068-2 Aza Nakajima, Oaaz Kakura, Iwatsuki-shi 339 Japan. Documents available from CASDDS.
Ind/Abst Chem. Abstr.

ISSN 0037-7023
XO

SLOVENSKY NARODOPIS. (SLOVENSKY NARODOPIS : CASOPIS SLOVENSKEJ AKADEMIE VIED.). [Slov. narodop.]. **Added/Corp** Slovenska Akademia Vied. Vol. 1 (1953)-. Periodical. Slovak (German and English; summaries and/or abstracts in English, German and Russian; table of contents in English, German and Russian). Four times a year. $107.47. **(Subscription address:** Slovart GTG Ltd., Krupinska 4, 852 99 Bratislava Slovakia. **Tel** 011 42 7 839471 2.**) Bk Rev. Ad Acc. Circ:** 1,500 (ctrl).
Desc: Results and findings in ethnography and folklore of

the most outstanding Slovak scholars.
Ind/Abst Anthropol. Index; BHA : Biblio. Hist. Art; MLA Int. Bibl. Books Artic. Mod. Lang. Lit.

LC GN1 .S54   **ISSN** 0081-0223
DD 301/.05   US
NLM W1 SM454   **CODEN** SMCAAM
SMITHSONIAN CONTRIBUTIONS TO ANTHROPOLOGY. [Smithson. contrib. anthropol.]. **Added/Corp** Smithsonian Institution. Vol. 1 (1965)-. Monographic series. English. Irregular. Price varies per volume. Superintendent of Documents, US Government Printing Office, Washington DC 20402. **Tel** (202)275-3328, FAX (202)786-2377. **ED** Barbara Spann. cum. index. **Circ**: 2,000 (ctrl). available on microfilm; available on microfiche; available in microform. Documents available from BIOSIS Document Express. **Continues** Bulletin (Smithsonian Institution. Bureau of American Ethnology), 0082-8882.
Desc: Monographs that report the research of Smithsonian staff in the field of physical and cultural anthropology.
Ind/Abst Biol. Abstr.; GeoRef.

LC HM1 .S616   **ISSN** 0155-977X
DD 301/.05   AT
Pr Rev.
SOCIAL ANALYSIS (ADELAIDE, S. AUST.). See Social Sciences.

LC GN575 .S63   **ISSN** 0964-0282
DD 306   UK
    CCC
    CODEN SNTHE3
SOCIAL ANTHROPOLOGY : THE JOURNAL OF THE EUROPEAN ASSOCIATION OF SOCIAL ANTHROPOLOGISTS. **Added/Corp** European Association of Social Anthropologists. Vol. 1, Pt. 1A (Aug. 1992)-. Academic Scholarly Publication. English (French). Three times a year. $98.00. Cambridge University Press, The Edinburgh Building, Shaftesbury Road, Cambridge CB2 2RU United Kingdom. **Tel** 011 44 1223 312393, FAX 011 44 1223 315052, telex 851-817256. **(Subscription address:** Cambridge University Press in North America, 110 Midland Avenue, Port Chester NY 10573. **Tel** (800)431-1580, (914)937-9600.**) ED** Jean-Claude Galey.
Bk Rev.
Desc: Forum for debate about key issues and concepts in the field of social anthropology. Challenges preconceptions and re-examines the boundaries of discipline. Includes: book reviews, review articles, book notes, topics of current interest and reviews and reports on ethnographic and archival collections.
Ind/Abst Curr. Cit.

DD 302   **ISSN** 1041-9861
    US
SOCIOCRITICISM. See Sociology.

    ET
SOCIOLOGY ETHNOLOGY BULLETIN. **Added/Corp** Addis Ababa University. Dept. of Sociology and Social Administration. Addis Ababa University. Institute of Ethiopian Studies. **VFOAT** Sociology Ethnology Bulletin of Addis Ababa University; SEB. Vol. 1, No. 1 (Mar. 1991)-. Bulletin. English. Institute Ethiopian Studies, Addis Ababa University, PO Box 1176, Addis Ababa Ethiopia. **Tel** 011 251 1 110844. **Continues** Ethnological Society Bulletin.

LC F211 .S58   **ISSN** 1056-5299
DD 976/.01/05   US
SOTO STATES ANTHROPOLOGIST, THE. [Soto states anthropol.]. **Added/Corp** Waypoint Foundation. Point Foundation (Tallahassee, Fla.). **VFOAT** Anthropologist. Vol. 90, No. 1 (July 1990)-. Periodical. English. Four times a year (Jan., Apr., July, Oct.). $25.00 Comes with Soto States Anthropologist membership. The Point Foundation, Inc., PO Box 880, Live Oak FL 32060-0880. **Tel** (904)963-4918.

    SA
SOUTH AFRICAN JOURNAL OF CULTURAL HISTORY. See History-History of Africa.

LC GN1 .S63   **ISSN** 0257-7348
DD 306/.0954   II
SOUTH ASIAN ANTHROPOLOGIST. [South Asian anthropol.]. **Added/Corp** Sarat Chandra Roy Institute of Anthropological Studies. **VFOAT** S.A.A.N.; SAAN. Vol. 1, No. 1 (March 1980)-. Periodical. English. Two times a year. $18.00. Sarat Chandra Roy Institute of Anthropological Studies, H1/98 Harmu Housing Colony, Ranchi 834012 Bihar India. **(Subscription address:** Prints India, 11 Darya Ganj, New Delhi 110002 India. **Tel** 011 91 11 3268645, FAX 011 91 11 3275542, telex 31-61087 PRIN-IN.**) ED** P Dash Sharma. cum. index. **Bk Rev. Ad Acc. Circ:** 500 (ctrl).
Desc: Publishes articles on anthropology relevant to South Asia.
Ind/Abst Anthropol. Lit.; Int. Bibliogr. Sociol.; Rural Dev. Abstr.

LC GN2 .S9243   **ISSN** 0081-2994
DD 301.2/05   US
NLM W1 SO93K
SOUTHERN ANTHROPOLOGICAL SOCIETY PROCEEDINGS. **Added/Corp** Southern Anthropological Society. No. 1 (1968)-. Proceedings. English. Irregular. Price varies per volume. University of Georgia Press, 330 Research Drive, Suite B 100, Athens GA 60602. **Tel** (706)369-6132, FAX (706)369-6131.
Desc: Proceedings of the Southern Anthropological Society.

    ISSN 0069-9632
    US
SOUTHERN METHODIST UNIVERSITY CONTRIBUTIONS IN ANTHROPOLOGY. **Main/Corp** Southern Methodist University. **Added/Corp** Institute for the Study of Earth and Man. Dallas. Southern Methodist University. Dept. of Anthropology. No. 1 (1965)-. Monographic series. English. Irregular. Price varies per volume. Southern Methodist University, Department of English, Dallas TX 75275. **Tel** (214)692-2945.

    ISSN 0076-0994
    US
SOUTHWEST MUSEUM PAPERS. See Archaeology.

    ISSN 0932-5476
    GW
SOZIALANTHROPOLOGISCHE ARBEITSPAPIERE. (1987)-. Monographic series. German (English and French). Price varies per volume. Institut d'Ethnologie Musee de l'Homme, Palais de Chaillot, place du Trocadero 75116 Paris France. **Tel** 011 33 1 45538215.

    ISSN 0065-6941
    US
SPECIAL PUBLICATION OF THE AMERICAN ANTHROPOLOGICAL ASSOCIATION, A. **Main/Corp** American Anthropological Association. (19??)-. Monographic series. English. Irregular. Price varies per volume. American Anthropological Association, 4350 North Fairfax Dr, Suite 640, Arlington VA 22203. **Tel** (703)528-1902 ext. 3031, FAX (703)528-3546.

LC GN2 .K763   **ISSN** 0454-5419
DD 390   US
SPECIAL PUBLICATIONS - KROEBER ANTHROPOLOGICAL SOCIETY. **Main/Corp** Kroeber Anthropological Society. No. 1 (1967)-. English. Irregular. University of California Kroeber Society, Anthropology Department, Berkeley CA 94720. **Tel** (510)642-6932.
Ind/Abst GeoRef.

LC E78.A28 S86   **ISSN** 0585-3699
    US
    TITLE CHANGE
STONES & BONES NEWSLETTER. **Added/Corp** Alabama Archaeological Society. **VFOAT** Stones and Bones Newsletter; Stones & Bones; Stones and Bones. **VAT** Stones and Bones Newsletter. (1961)-(1994). Newsletter. English. Alabama Archaeological Society, 13075 Moundville Park, Moundville AL 35474. **Tel** (205)371-2266. **ED** Amos J. Wright. **Bk Rev. Circ:** 500 (ctrl). **Continued by** Stones & Bones.
Desc: Presents current anthropological and archaeological activities in Southeast, especially Alabama, with book reviews by both professionals and avocational writers, and professional articles.

    IT
STUDI ETNO-ANTROPOLOGICI E SOCIOLOGICI / PUBBLICATA SOTTO GLI AUSPICI DEL CONSIGLIO NAZIONALE DELLE RICHERCHE. Vol. 13 (1986)-. Italian (summaries and/or abstracts in English and French). One time a year. L23850. Studi Etno Antropologici, Corso Vittorio Emanuele 110, 80121 Naples Italy. **Tel** 011 39 81 681629, FAX 011 39 81 668264. cum. index. **Bk Rev. Ad Acc.** ctrl circ. **Continues** Etnologia, Antropologia Culturale.
Ind/Abst Anthropol. Lit.; Int. Bibliogr. Sociol.

    SZ
STUDIA ETHNOGRAPHICA FRIBURGENSIA. (1972)-. Monographic series. German (English). Irregular. Price varies per volume. Editions Universitaires, boulevard de Perolles 42, CH-1700 Fribourg Switzerland. **Tel** 011 41 37 246812, FAX 011 41 37 249147. **Circ:** 450 (ctrl).
Desc: Monograph series on ethnology.

LC GN585.F53 S76
    FI
STUDIA FENNICA. ETHNOLOGICA. **Added/Corp** Suomalaisen Kirjallisuuden Seura. **VFOAT** Ethnologica. (1992)-. English. Irregular. Fmk168.00 (Vol. 1). Finnish Literature Society, Hallituskatu 1, PB 259, 00171 Helsinki Finland. **Tel** 011 358 0 131231.
Continues in part Studia Fennica, 0085-6835.

DD 306   **ISSN** 1055-2464
    SW
STUDIES IN ANTHROPOLOGY AND HISTORY. [Stud. anth. hist.]. Vol. 1 (1991)-. Monographic series. English. Harwood Academic Publishers, PO Box 90, Reading RG1 8JL United Kingdom. **Tel** 011 44 1734 560080, FAX 011 44 1734 568211.

LC CB411 .S8   **ISSN** 0360-2370
DD 081   US
Pr Rev.
STUDIES IN EIGHTEENTH-CENTURY CULTURE. See History.

LC GN4 .S74   **ISSN** 0324-8666
DD 573   PL
NLM W1 ST92R
STUDIES IN HUMAN ECOLOGY. **Added/Corp** Instytut Ekologii (Polska Akademia Nauk). Vol. 1 (1973)-. English (summaries and/or abstracts in Polish). Irregular. $24.00. **(Subscription address:** Ars Polona-Ruch, PO Box 1001, Krakowskie Przedmiescie 7, 00-068 Warsaw Poland. **Tel** 011 48 22 261201.**)**
Ind/Abst Index Med.

DD 853   **ISSN** 1043-5794
    US
STUDIES IN ITALIAN CULTURE. LITERATURE IN HISTORY. [Stud. Ital. cult., Lit. hist.]. (1990)-. Monographic series. English. Irregular. Price varies per volume. Peter Lang Publishing, 62 West 45th Street, 4th Floor, New York NY 10036. **Tel** (212)764-1471, (800)770-5264, FAX (212)302-7574, telex 6973364 PLNY.

LC GN49 .S8   **ISSN** 0324-8291
DD 573/.05   PL
    CEASED
STUDIES IN PHYSICAL ANTHROPOLOGY. [Stud. phys. anthropol.]. **Added/Corp** Zaklad Antropologii (Polska Akademia Nauk). (1975)-Vol. 10 (19??). Periodical. English (summaries and/or abstracts in Polish). **(Subscription address:** Ars Polona-Ruch, PO Box 1001, Krakowskie Przedmiescie 7, 00-068 Warsaw Poland. **Tel** 011 48 22 261201.**)**
Ind/Abst Anthropol. Index; Anthropol. Lit.; EMBASE.

LC GN58.R8 A6
    RM
    CODEN SCANCH
STUDII SI CERCETARI DE ANTROPOLOGIE. (19??)-. Periodical. Romanian (summaries and/or abstracts in French). One time a year. $42.00. Editura Academia Republicii Socialiste Romania, Calea Victoriei Nr 125, R-79717 Bucuresti Romania. **Tel** telex 10376 PRSFI R. **ED** Olga Necrasov. Index available. **Bk Rev.** available with charts; available with illustrations. Documents available from BIOSIS Document Express. **Continues** Academia Republicii Populare Romine. Studii si Cercetari de Antropologie.
Desc: Publishes studies on contemporary paleontology and anthropology.
Ind/Abst Biol. Abstr. (?-1988).

LC GN301 .S85   **ISSN** 0379-8860
    SA
    CCC
SUID-AFRIKAANSE TYDSKRIF VIR ETNOLOGIE. **Added/Corp** Association of Afrikaans Ethnologists. Foundation for Education, Science, and Technology (South Africa). Bureau for Scientific Publications. Council for Scientific Publications (South Africa) South Africa. Dept. of National Education. **VFOAT** South African Journal of Ethnology; Etnologie; Ethnology. Vol. 1, No. 1 (1978)-. Periodical. Afrikaans (English). Four times a year. $31.61. Foundation for Education Science & Technology, PO Box 1758, Pretoria 0001 South Africa. **Tel** 011 27 12 3226404, FAX 011 27 12 3207803.
Ind/Abst Abstr. Anthropol. (19??-); EP Collect.; Homework Help.; MasterFile FullTEXT 1000; MasterFile FullTEXT 350; MasterFile FullTEXT 650; MasterFile FullTEXT; OCLC; Spec. Educ. Needs Abstr.; Telebase.

    FI
SUOMEN ANTROPOLOGI : SUOMEN ANTROPOLOGISEN SEURAN JULKAISU. (1976)-. Periodical. Finnish. Four times a year.
Ind/Abst Anthropol. Index; Anthropol. Lit.; MLA Int. Bibl. Books Artic. Mod. Lang. Lit.

LC F2679 .S75   **ISSN** 0378-9896
DD 980.1/05   PY
SUPLEMENTO ANTROPOLOGICO - UNIVERSIDAD CATOLICA. (SUPLEMENTO ANTROPOLOGICO.). [Supl. antropol. - Univ. Catol.]. **Added/Corp** Universidad Catolica Nuestra Senora de la Asuncion. Universidad Catolica Nuestra Senora de la Asuncion. Centro de Estudios Antropologicos. Vol. 5 (1970)-. Spanish (Portuguese and English). Two times a

Anthropology

year (June & Dec.). $25.00. Universidad Catolica Antropologicos, Casilla Correo 1718, Asuncion Paraguay. **Tel** 011 595 21 446251. **ED** Adriano Irala Burgos. Index available. cum. index. **Bk Rev. Ad Acc. Circ:** 1,000. *Continues Suplemento Antropologico de la Revista del Ateneo Paraguayo, 0084-6937.*
Desc: We concentrate on the Paraguayan and river plate areas with emphasis on the Indian cultures in those areas.
Ind/Abst Am. Hist. Life (1980-); Anthropol. Index; Anthropol. Lit.

UK
SURVIVAL INTERNATIONAL ANNUAL REVIEW. See Political Science-Civil Rights.

UK
SURVIVAL : THE INTERNATIONAL NEWSLETTER OF SURVIVAL INTERNATIONAL. See Political Science-Civil Rights.

ISSN 0889-7425
DD 301   US
SYMBOLS. (SYMBOLS : A PUBLICATION OF THE PEABODY MUSEUM AND THE DEPARTMENT OF ANTHROPOLOGY, HARVARD UNIVERSITY.).
[Symbols]. (Winter 1980)-. Periodical. English. Two times a year. $4.50. Symbols, Peabody Museum, Harvard University, Cambridge MA 02138. **Tel** (617)495-2269. **ED** Martha Lamberg-Karlovsky. **Bk Rev. Ad Acc. Circ:** 2,000 (ctrl). *Continues Newsletter of the Peabody Museum and the Department of Anthropology.*
Desc: Articles by anthropology faculty and Peabody curators, biographies of new faculty and curatorial appointments; photographs; writings on research and curatorial activities, visiting scholars and exhibitions.
Ind/Abst Ethnoarts Index.

LC DS493.9.G84 T35

NP
TAMU. Vol. 1, No. 1 (1981)-. Periodical. Nepali (Nepali). 5.00.

ISSN 0196-8297
US
TECHNICAL REPORTS (UNIVERSITY OF MICHIGAN. MUSEUM OF ANTHROPOLOGY). See Museums and Galleries.

MX
TECNOLOGIA. Main/Corp Mexico. Instituto Nacional de Antropologia e Historia. Departamento de Prehistoria. Spanish. Irregular. Instituto Nacional de Antropologia e Historia, Cordoba 4J 7DF Mexico.
Ind/Abst Food Sci. Technol. Abstr.; Rice Abstr.

ISSN 0040-2184
UK
CEASED
TEILHARD REVIEW, THE. Added/Corp
Teilhard Centre for the Future of Man. **VFOAT** Journal for Cosmic Convergence. Vol. 24, No. 1 (Spring 1989)-(Nov. 1994). Periodical. English. Teilhard Centre, 24 St. Martins Close, Stratford-on-Avon CV37 9QW United Kingdom. **Tel** 011 44 171 9375372. **ED** Tom Baxter (editor's telephone: 011 44 789 298178). **Bk Rev. Ad Acc, Adv Mgr:** T. Baxter. **Circ:** 850. available on microfilm and microfiche from University Microfilms International (UMI). *Continues Teilhard Review and Journal of Creative Evolution, 0952-6471.*

SP
TEMAS DE ANTROPOLOGIA ARAGONESA. Spanish. One time a year.
476.30ptas. Instituto Aragones de Antropologia, Apartado 159, Huesca Spain.

LC GN1 .T45   **ISSN** 0892-7979
DD 301/.05   US
TENNESSEE ANTHROPOLOGIST. [Tenn. anthropol.]. Added/Corp Tennessee Anthropological Association. (Spring 1976)-. Periodical. English. Two times a year (Apr. and Oct.). comes with membership. Tennessee Anthropological Association, Department of Anthropology, University of Tennessee, 252 South Stadium Hall, Knoxville TN 37996-0720. **Tel** (615)974-4408.
Desc: Covers anthropological topics in the Southeast including prehistoric archaeology, historic archaeology, Native American studies, Afro-American studies, and Southern Appalachian folk culture.
Ind/Abst Abstr. Anthropol.; Anthropol. Index; Anthropol. Lit.; Ethnoarts Index.

LC DC34 .T47   **ISSN** 0760-5668
FR
TERRAIN (PARIS, 1983). (TERRAIN : CARNETS DU PATRIMOINE ETHNOLOGIQUE.).
[Terrain]. **Added/Corp** France. Mission du Patrimoine Ethnologique. No. 1 (Oct. 1983)-. Periodical. French. Two times a year. $33.18. Caisse Nationale des Monuments Historiques, 62 rue St. Antoine, 75004 Paris France. **Tel** 011 33 1 44612000.
Ind/Abst Anthropol. Lit.; Int. Bibliogr. Sociol.

LC D848 .T47   **ISSN** 0040-392X
DD 905   IT
Pr Rev.
TERZO MONDO. See Sociology.

LC GN   **ISSN** 1024-5804
DD 301   AU
UDC 571/572
●THEORETICAL ANTHROPOLOGY. [Theor. anthropol.]. (1994)-. Periodical. English. Irregular. Institut fuer Volkerkunde, University of Vienna, Universitaetsstrasse 7, 4A 1010 Vienna Austria. available via Internet (http://www.univie.ac.at/voelkerkunde/theoretical-anthropology/).
Desc: Covers all aspects of anthropology.

DK
TIDSSKRIFTIE ANTROPOLOGI.
Added/Corp Foreningen Stotskifte. Nr. 21/22 (1990)-. Periodical. Danish. *Continues Stotskifte, 0108-1012.*
Ind/Abst Anthropol. Lit.

LC F1219.3.C9 T6   **ISSN** 0185-0989
DD 970.4   MX
SUSPENDED
TLALOCAN. [Tlalocan]. **Added/Corp** San Jacinto Museum of History. Instituto Nacional de Antropologia e Historia (Mexico) Universidad Nacional Autonoma de Mexico. Instituto de Investigaciones Historicas. Universidad Nacional Autonoma de Mexico. Instituto de Investigaciones Antropologicas. Vol. 1 (1943)-Suspended (1991). Periodical. Spanish (English). La Casa de Tlaloc, Madrid 5 301, Mexico 4 DF Mexico.
Ind/Abst Anthropol. Lit.; Hisp. Am. Period. Index, HAPI; MLA Int. Bibl. Books Artic. Mod. Lang. Lit.

ISSN 1066-2227
DD 306   US
●TOGETHER FOREVER. [Together forever]. Vol. 1, No. 1 (June 1993)-. Periodical. English. Twelve times a year. $48.00. T J Walker, 406 Rucker Place, PO Box 2492, Alexandria VA 22301.

PO
TRABALHOS DE ANTROPOLOGIA E ETNOLOGIA. Main/Corp Sociedade Portuguesa de Antropologia e Etnologia. Vol. 1 (1919)-. Periodical. Portuguese. cum. index.
Ind/Abst Anthropol. Lit.

LC DR381.S64 T72
XV
TRADITIONES. Added/Corp Slovenska Akademija Znanosti in Umetnosti. Razred za Filoloske in Literarne Vede. Institut za Slovensko Narodopisje (Slovenska Akademija Znanosti in Umetnosti). (1972)-. Slovenian (summaries and/or abstracts in English, French, German and Italian). One time a year. Slovenska Akademija Znanosti in Umetnosti, Razred za Filoloske in Literarne Vede, Novi Trg 5-1 Ljubljana Slovenia. **Tel FAX** 011 38 61 155232. **ED** Mojca Ravnik. **Circ:** 1,000.
Desc: Communications from the Slovenie Academy of Arts and Sciences.
Ind/Abst MLA Int. Bibl. Books Artic. Mod. Lang. Lit.

LC GN1 .T67   **ISSN** 1051-0559
DD 301/.05   US
TRANSFORMING ANTHROPOLOGY : A PUBLICATION OF THE ASSOCIATION OF BLACK ANTHROPOLOGISTS.
[Transform. anthropol.]. **Added/Corp** Association of Black Anthropologists. (1990)-. Periodical. English. Two times a year. $25.00. American Anthropological Association, 4350 North Fairfax Dr, Suite 640, Arlington VA 22203. **Tel** (703)528-1902 ext. 3031, **FAX** (703)522-3546.
Desc: Articles seek to advance the understanding of all forms of human diversity and commonality.

ISSN 0890-1562
DD 301   US
TRANSWORLD IDENTITY SERIES.
Added/Corp European Research Association (Bloomington, Ind.). Vol. 1 (1982)-. Monographic series. English. Price varies per volume. Eurolingua / Eurasian Linguistic Association, PO Box 101, Bloomington IN 47402. **Tel** (812)332-8918. **ED** Gyula Decsy.

LC GN705 .T65a
DD 913/.031   FR
TRAVAUX DE L'INSTITUT D'ART PREHISTORIQUE. Added/Corp Universite de Toulouse. Institut d'Art Prehistorique. Universite de Toulouse-Le Mirail. Institut d'Art Prehistorique. VFOAT Prehistoire 1965. Vol. 1 (1958)-. Periodical. French. One time a year. Regisseur Service Des Publications, 56 rue du Taur U Toulouse Mira, 31069 Toulouse Cedex France. **Tel** 011 33 61 225831.
Ind/Abst Anthropol. Lit.

FR
TRAVAUX ET MEMOIRES DE L'INSTITUT D'ETHNOLOGIE. See Social Sciences.

US
TREGANZA ANTHROPOLOGY MUSEUM PAPERS. Main/Corp Treganza Anthropology Museum. No. 6 (1970)-. Monographic series. English. Irregular. Price varies per volume. AE Treganza Anthropology Museum, San Francisco State University, 1600 Holloway Avenue, San Francisco CA 94132. **Tel** (415)469-1642. *Continues Occasional Papers / California. State College, San Francisco. Anthropology Museum.*

LC GN1 .T7   **ISSN** 0082-6413
GW
TRIBUS. Added/Corp Stuttgart. Museum fuer Lander- und Volkerkunde. Wurttembergischer Verein fuer Handelsgeographie und Forderung Deutscher Interessen im Auslande, (e. V.) Stuttgart. Stuttgart. Museum fuer Lander- und Volkerkunde. Jahrbuch des Linden-Museums. (1951)-. German. One time a year. DM30.00. Linden-Museum Stuttgart, Staatliches Museum fuer Volkerkunde, Hegelplatz 1, W-7000 Stuttgart 1 Germany. **Tel** 011 49 711 1231242. **ED** Klaus J. Brandt and Peter Thiele. **Bk Rev. Circ:** 800 (ctrl).
Ind/Abst Anthropol. Index; Anthropol. Lit.; Ethnoarts Index; Int. Bibliogr. Sociol.

ISSN 0121-2354
DD 301.7   CK
UNIDAD INDIGENA. [Unidad indig.]. (1975)-. Periodical. Spanish. Six times a year. Organizacion Nacional Indigena de Colombia, Bogota Colombia.
Ind/Abst Hum. Rights Intern. Rep.

ISSN 0068-6379
DD 301   US
UNIVERSITY OF CALIFORNIA PUBLICATIONS IN ANTHROPOLOGY.
[Univ. Calif. publ. anthropol.]. **Added/Corp** University of California, Berkeley. **VFOAT** Publications in Anthropology. (1964)-. Monographic series. English. Irregular. Price varies per volume. Regents University of California Press, 2120 Berkeley Way, Berkeley CA 94720. **Tel** (510)642-4191. **Circ:** 1,100 (ctrl).

ISSN 0227-0072
DD 301   CN
UNIVERSITY OF MANITOBA ANTHROPOLOGY PAPERS. Added/Corp
University of Manitoba. Dept. of Anthropology. (1970)-. Monographic series. English. Irregular. Price varies per volume. University of Manitoba Department of Anthropology, 432 Fletcher Argue Building, Winnipeg Manitoba R3T 2N2 Canada. **Tel** (204)474-9423. **ED** Board. **Circ:** 100.

ISSN 0077-118X
DD 301   US
UNIVERSITY OF MONTANA CONTRIBUTIONS TO ANTHROPOLOGY.
Main/Corp Montana. University, Missoula. Dept. of Anthropology. **Added/Corp** University of Montana (Missoula). Dept. of Anthropology. Contributions to Anthropology. **VFOAT** Contributions to Anthropology. (1967)-. Monographic series. English. Irregular. Price varies per volume. Department of Anthropology / Missoula, University of Montana, Missoula MT 59801. **Tel** (406)243-0211. **ED** Carling Malouf. *Supersedes in part Anthropology and Sociology Papers, 0544-8824.*

ISSN 0078-6071
US
UNIVERSITY OF OREGON ANTHROPOLOGICAL PAPERS. [Univ. Or. anthropol. pap.]. Main/Corp University of Oregon. Added/Corp University of Oregon. Dept. of Anthropology. VFOAT Anthropological Papers. (1971)-. Monographic series. English. Irregular. Price varies per volume. Anthropology Publications, Department of Anthropology, University of Oregon, Eugene OR 97403. **Tel** (503)686-5102. **ED** C. Melvin Aikens. **Circ:** 500.
Desc: Monographs in anthropology: archaeology, physical and cultural, with emphasis on northwest archaeology.

DD 306/.09931   NZ
UNIVERSITY OF OTAGO STUDIES IN PREHISTORIC ANTHROPOLOGY.
Added/Corp University of Otago. Dept. of Anthropology. (19??)-. Monographic series. English. Irregular. Price varies per volume. University of Otago Press, PO Box 56, Dunedin New Zealand. **Tel** 011 64 24 791000.
Continues Otago University Studies in Prehistoric Anthropology.

Anthropology

LC GN301 .U58 **ISSN** 0391-2876
DD 305.8 IT
UOMO, L'. [Uomo]. **Added/Corp** Universita Degli Studi di Roma "La Sapienza.". (1977)-. Periodical. Italian (English, French, German and Spanish). Two times a year. L110000. Giardini Editori Stampatori, Via Santa Bibbiana 28, 56127 Pisa Italy. **Tel** 011 39 50 934242.
Ind/Abst Anthropol. Lit.; Bibliogr. Mission.

ISSN 0566-8794
IT
UOMO & CULTURA. **VFOAT** U E C; Uomo E Cultura; U & C. (1968)-. Italian. Every 2 years. Libreria S F Flaccovio, Via Ruggiero Settimo 37, 90139 Palermo Italy. **Tel** 011 39 91 334323, or 334249, **FAX** 011 39 91 6112750.
Ind/Abst Anthropol. Lit.

IT
UOMO LIBERO, L'. (Jan. 1980)-. Periodical. Italian. Four times a year. L40880. Edizioni dell Uomo Libero, Via Pradaccio 8, 21014 Laveno Mombello Va Italy. **Tel** 011 39 332 667220.

LC HM219 **ISSN** 0906-7272
DD 306.6 DK
UPDATE & DIALOG DANISH ED. (UPDATE & DIALOG.). [Update dialog Dan. ed.]. **VFOAT** Update and Dialog (Danish Ed.). (1991)-. Periodical. Danish (English and Latvian). Two times a year. $19.76. Dialog Centre International, Katrinebjergvej 46, DK 8200 Arhus N Denmark. **Tel** 011 45 86169202, **FAX** 011 45 86105416. **ED** Johannes Aagaard. cum. index. **Bk Rev**. **Ad Acc**. **Circ**: 200 (ctrl).
Desc: Covers new and emerging religions worldwide with a special interest into paganism, cults, and new age movements.

ISSN 0348-9507
SW
UPPSALA RESEARCH REPORTS IN CULTURAL ANTHROPOLOGY. (19??)-. English (Swedish). Irregular. University of Uppsala / Department of Cultural Anthropology, Tradgardsgatan 18, S-752 20 Uppsala Sweden. **Circ**: 500.

ISSN 0348-5099
SW
UPPSALA STUDIES IN CULTURAL ANTHROPOLOGY. 1-. Monographic series. English (French). Irregular. Price varies per volume. University of Uppsala / Department of Cultural Anthropology, Tradgardsgatan 18, S-752 20 Uppsala Sweden. **ED** Anita Jacobson-Widding.
Desc: A series in which publications in the field of cultural and social anthropology.

LC GN **ISSN** 0894-6019
DD 301 US
Pr Rev.
URBAN ANTHROPOLOGY AND STUDIES OF CULTURAL SYSTEMS AND WORLD ECONOMIC DEVELOPMENT. [Urban anthropol. stud. cult. syst. world econ. dev.]. **Added/Corp** Institute for the Study of Man (Brockport, N.Y.). **VFOAT** Urban Anthropology. Vol. 14, No. 1-3 (Spring/Summer/Fall 1985)-. Periodical. English. Four times a year. $60.00. The Institute Incorporated, 56 Centennial Avenue, Brockport NY 14420. **Tel** (716)637-6531. **ED** Jack R. Rollwagen. cum. index. **Ad Acc**. **Continues** Urban Anthropology, 0363-2024.
Desc: Information on urban anthropology including world processes: urbanization, development and underdevelopment, colonialism and neocolonialism, and social and behavioral patterns as they relate to anthropology.
Ind/Abst Abstr. Anthropol.; Acad. Abstr.; Acad. Search; Curr. Contents Soc. Behav. Sci.; EP Collect.; Homework Help.; INFO-SOUTH Abstr.; Int. Bibliogr. Sociol.; Mag. Search; MasterFile FullTEXT 1000; MasterFile FullTEXT 350; MasterFile FullTEXT 650; MasterFile FullTEXT (Jan. 1992-); MLA Int. Bibl. Books Artic. Mod. Lang. Lit.; OCLC; Pub. Lib. FullTEXT; Refer. Z.; Sage Urban Stud. Abstr; Soc. Sci. Source; Soc. Sci. Index; Soc. Sci. Index Fulltext (Winter 1988-) [Full Txt.]; Sociol. Abstr.; Telebase.

US
VANDERBILT UNIVERSITY PUBLICATIONS IN ANTHROPOLOGY. No. 1-. Monographic series. English. Four times a year. Price varies per volume. Vanderbilt University / Department of Anthropology, Box 1532B, Nashville TN 37203. **Tel** (615)322-7522. **ED** Ronald Spores and Judith Gorodetzky. **Circ**: 1,500 (ctrl).
Desc: Monograph series publishing scholarly research in anthropology primarily on Mesoamerica but with no specific restrictions on geographic concentration; archaeology, ethnography and ethnohistory.

SW
VARIA (LUND, SWEDEN). (VARIA.). 1-. English (French). Irregular. Pontificio Istituto Orientale, Piazza S, Maria Maggiore 7, 00185 Rome Italy. **Tel** 011 39 6 4465589. **Circ**: 1,000.
Desc: A serial accomplished: concilium florentinum two serials in progress: Orientalia Christiana Analecta (monographies on Christian East) and Anaphorae Syriacae (on Syriac Liturgy).

LC GN4 .W5
DD 301 AU
VIENNA CONTRIBUTIONS TO ETHNOLOGY AND ANTHROPOLOGY = WIENER BEITRAEGE ZUR ETHNOLOGIE UND ANTHROPOLOGIE.
Added/Corp Universitaet Wien. Institut fuer Voelkerkunde. **VFOAT** Wiener Beitraege zur Ethnologie und Anthropologie. (1984)-. Monographic series. English (German). Verlag Ferdinand Berger & Soehne, Wienerstrasse 21-23, A-3580 Horn Austria. **Tel** 011 43 2982 4161232. **Continues** Wiener Beitraege zur Kulturgeschichte und Linguistik, 0083-9922.

LC F1545 .V55 **ISSN** 0304-3703
CR
VINCULOS. [Vinculos]. Vol. 1 (1975)-. Spanish (English). Two times a year. $18.00. Museo Nacional de Costa Rica, Biblioteca Apartado 749, San Jose 1000 Costa Rica. **Tel** 011 506 571433. **ED** Juan Vicente Guerrero. **Bk Rev**. **Circ**: 1,000 (ctrl).
Desc: Magazine specialized in anthropology and archaeology of Costa Rica and Central America.
Ind/Abst Anthropol. Index (19??-); Anthropol. Lit. (19??-); Avery Index Archit. Period. Suppl. Colum. Univ. (19??-199?); Ethnoarts Index (19??-); Hisp. Am. Period. Index, HAPI (19??-).

LC GN347 .V57 **ISSN** 0894-9468
DD 306/.0208 UK
CCC
CODEN VIANEQ
VISUAL ANTHROPOLOGY (JOURNAL).
(VISUAL ANTHROPOLOGY.). [Vis. anthropol.].
Added/Corp Commission on Visual Anthropology. Vol. 1, No. 1 (Nov. 1987)-. Periodical. English. Irregular. $255.00 (academic institutions), $397.00 (corporate institutions). Harwood Academic Publishers, PO Box 90, Reading RG1 8JL United Kingdom. **Tel** 011 44 1734 560080, **FAX** 011 44 1734 568211. **ED** J. Ruby. available. cum. index. **Bk Rev**. available on microfilm; available on microfiche.
Ind/Abst Abstr. Anthropol. (19??-); Anthropol. Lit. (19??-).

LC GN347 .S85 **ISSN** 1058-7187
DD 306 US
VISUAL ANTHROPOLOGY REVIEW.
(VISUAL ANTHROPOLOGY REVIEW : JOURNAL OF THE SOCIETY FOR VISUAL ANTHROPOLOGY.). [Vis. anthropol. rev.]. **Added/Corp** Center for Visual Anthropology. Society for Visual Anthropology (U.S.). **VFOAT** Journal of the Society for Visual Anthropology. Vol. 7, No. 1 (Spring 1991)-. Periodical. English. Two times a year. $25.00. American Anthropological Association, 4350 North Fairfax Dr, Suite 640, Arlington VA 22203. **Tel** (703)528-1902 ext. 3031, **FAX** (703)528-3546. **Continues** Society for Visual Anthropology Review, 1053-7147.
Desc: Information on motion picture, photography as related to ethnology.
Ind/Abst Anthropol. Lit.

LC GN865.W45 W46 **ISSN** 0083-8160
DD 916.6/03 NR
WEST AFRICAN JOURNAL OF ARCHAEOLOGY. See Archaeology.

AU
WIENER ETHNOHISTORISCHE BLAETTER. BEIHEFT. **Added/Corp** Vienna. Universitaet. Institut fuer Voelkerkunde. (1972)-. Monographic series. German. Price varies per volume. Wiener Ethnohistorische, Institut fuer Volkerkunde, Universitaet of Wiener, A 1010 Vienna Austria.
Ind/Abst Anthropol. Lit.

AU
WIENER ETHNOHISTORISCHE BLATTER. **Added/Corp** Universitat Wien. Institut fur Volkerkunde. (1970)-. Periodical. German. Irregular. Wiener Ethnohistorische, Institut fuer Volkerkunde, Universitaet of Wiener, A 1010 Vienna Austria.
Ind/Abst Anthropol. Lit.

LC GN1 .W5 **ISSN** 0084-0068
AU
WIENER VOLKERKUNDLICHE MITTEILUNGEN. **Added/Corp** Osterreichische Ethnologische Gesellschaft. Volkerkundliche Arbeitsgemeinschaft in der Anthropologischen Gesellschaft in Wien. Osterreichische Ethnologische Expeditions- und Forschungsgesellschaft. (1953)-. German (English and French). One time a year. Verein Freunde der Volkerkunde, Museum fuer Volkerkunde, Neue Hofburg A-1014 Vienna Austria. **Tel** 011 43 1 521770. **Ad Acc**. **Circ**: 450.
Ind/Abst Anthropol. Index; Anthropol. Lit.; Ethnoarts Index.

ISSN 0284-9224
SW
WORKING PAPER - DEVELOPMENT STUDY UNIT, DEPARTMENT OF SOCIAL ANTHROPOLOGY, UNIVERSITY OF STOCKHOLM. (WORKING PAPER.). **VFOAT** Arbetsrapport - Sektionen for Utvecklingsstudier, Socialantropologiska Institutionen, Stockholms Universitet; Informe de Trabajo - Seccion de Estudios para el Desarrollo, Departemento de Antropologia Social, Universidad de Estocolmo. (1984)-. Monographic series. Multiple languages. Irregular.
Ind/Abst Agrofor. Abstr.

LC AS36 .W95 GN1 **ISSN** 0196-1500
DD 081 S 301/.05 US
WYOMING CONTRIBUTIONS TO ANTHROPOLOGY. [Wyo. contrib. anthropol.].
Added/Corp University of Wyoming. Department of Anthropology. Vol. 1 (Spring 1978)-. English. Irregular. $5.00. University Wyoming, Department of Anthropology, Box 3431, Laramie WY 82071. **Tel** (307)766-5136.
Ind/Abst GeoRef.

LC E77 .Y3 GN2 .Y3
DD 572.082 US
YALE UNIVERSITY PUBLICATIONS IN ANTHROPOLOGY. **Main/Corp** Yale University. Department of Anthropology. **Added/Corp** Yale University. Institute of Human Relations. Peabody Museum of Natural History. No. 17 (1938)-. English. Irregular. Yale University Press, PO Box 209040, New Haven CT 06520. **Tel** (203)432-0940, (800)987-7323, **FAX** (203)432-0948. **Continues** Yale University Publications in Anthropology.

LC QH
DD 574 UZ
YASHLIK. See Biology.

ISSN 0096-848X
US
CCC
NLM W1 YE312 **CODEN** YANTAE
Pr Rev.
YEARBOOK OF PHYSICAL ANTHROPOLOGY (WASHINGTON).
(YEARBOOK OF PHYSICAL ANTHROPOLOGY.).
(1945)-. English. Irregular. $50.00. American Association of Physical Anthropologists, 1703 New Hampshire Avenue NW, Washington DC 20009. **Tel** (212)475-7700. Documents available from The Genuine Article, BIOSIS Document Express, UMI Article Clearinghouse.
Desc: Vol. 9 called also: Physical Anthropology 1953-1961.
Ind/Abst Anthropol. Index; Anthropol. Lit.; Biol. Abstr.; Expand. Acad. Index (1989-); INFO-SOUTH Abstr.; Mag. Search; MasterFile FullTEXT (Jan. 1992-); Newsp. Period. Abstr. (1989-); Ref. Upd. Deluxe Ed.; Res. Alert [Full Cov.]; Sci. Cit. Index (19??-19??); SCISEARCH.

LC GN1 .Y52 **ISSN** 0044-0477
DD 301 SW
CODEN YMERAD
YMER. [Ymer]. **Added/Corp** Svenska Sallskapet for Antropologi och Geografi. (1966)-. Swedish. Stockholm University Department of Geography, S-106 91, Stockholm Sweden. **Supersedes** Ymer, 0044-0477.
Ind/Abst Anthropol. Index; Bibliogr. Carto.; Ecol. Abstr.; Geogr. Abstr. Phys. Geogr.; GeoRef.

LC GN549.S6 E8 **ISSN** 0083-4106
DD 305.8 XO
Pr Rev. **TITLE CHANGE**
ZBORNIK FILOZOFICKEJ FAKULTY UNIVERZITY KOMENSKEHO. ETHNOLOGIA SLAVICA. (ETHNOLOGIA SLAVICA.). [Zb. filoz. fak. Univ. Komenskeho, Ethnol. Slav.]. **Added/Corp** Univerzita Komenskeho v Bratislave. Filozoficka Fakulta. Vol. 1 (1969)-(199?). Multiple languages (English, French and German; summaries and/or abstracts in Bulgarian, Czech, Russian, Serbian, Slovak and Sorbian languages). Department of Ethnology, Comenius University, 81801 Bratislava Slovakia. **ED** Jan Podolak. **Bk Rev**. **Circ**: 1,000 (ctrl).
Continued by Ethnologia Slovaca et Slavica.
Desc: An international review of Slavic ethnography, ethnology, and folklore.
Ind/Abst Anthropol. Lit.; MLA Int. Bibl. Books Artic. Mod. Lang. Lit.

LC GN301 .S68a
YU
ZBORNIK RADOVA ETNOGRAFSKOG INSTITUTA. **Main/Corp** Etnografski Institut (Srpska Akademija Nauka i Umetnosti). (1950)-. Serbo-Croatian (Cyrillic) (Serbo-Croatian (Roman); summaries and/or abstracts in French).
Ind/Abst BHA : Biblio. Hist. Art.

ISSN 0044-2666
GW
CCC
ZEITSCHRIFT FUER ETHNOLOGIE.
Added/Corp Berliner Gesellschaft fuer Anthropologie, Ethnologie, und Urgeschichte. Deutsche Gesellschaft fuer

Anthropology

Anthropologie, Ethnologie, und Urgeschichte. Deutsche Gesellschaft fuer Volkerkunde. (1869)-. Periodical. German (English). Two times a year. DM175.00. Dietrich Reimer Verlag, Unter den Eichen 57, D-12203 Berlin Germany. **Tel** 011 49 30 8314081, FAX 011 49 30 831623. **ED** Ulla Johansen and Claudius Muller. cum. index. **Bk Rev. Ad Acc.**
Ind/Abst Anthropol. Index; Anthropol. Lit.; Ethnoarts Index.

ISSN 0379-4458
AU

ZEITSCHRIFT FUER MENSCHENKUNDE. [Z. Menschenkd.]. (1925)-.
Periodical. German. Four times a year. $54.55. Wilhelm Braumueller, Servitengasse 5, A-1092 Vienna Austria. **Tel** 011 43 1 3191482, 3191159, FAX 011 43 1 3102805.

LC QM1 .Z4 ISSN 0044-314X
DD 611/.005 GW
        CCC
NLM W1 ZE468R CODEN ZMOAAN

ZEITSCHRIFT FUER MORPHOLOGIE UND ANTHROPOLOGIE. [Z. Morphol. Anthropol.]. (1899)-. Periodical. German (summaries and/or abstracts in English). Three times a year. $291.00. E. Schweizerbartische Verlagsbuchhandlung, Johannesstrasse 3A, D-70176 Stuttgart Germany. **Tel** 011 49 711 625001, FAX 011 49 711 625005, telex 723363 SCHB D. **ED** Hans W Juergens. Index available in last issue of volume--attached. **Bk Rev. Ad Acc.** Documents available from BIOSIS Document Express. *Supersedes* Morphologische Arbeiten (Jena, Germany).
Desc: Concerns morphology and physical anthropology.
Ind/Abst Anthropol. Index; Anthropol. Lit.; Biol. Abstr.; Index Med.

LC DT962.3 .Z55 ISSN 0250-3018
DD 968.91/01/05 RH

ZIMBABWEA. See History-History of Africa.

LC GN865.Z55 R46
DD 968.9/01/05 RH

ZIMBABWEAN PREHISTORY : JOURNAL OF THE PREHISTORY SOCIETY OF ZIMBABWE. Added/Corp
Prehistory Society of Zimbabwe. **VFOAT** Zimbabwe Prehistory. No. 19 (Dec. 1983)-. Periodical. English. The Prehistory Society of Zimbabwe, Harare Zimbabwe.
Continues Rhodesian Prehistory.
Ind/Abst Anthropol. Lit.; Ethnoarts Index.

LC DK511.L162 L37a
LV

ZINATNISKAS ATSKAITES SESIJAS MATERIALI PAR ARHEOLOGU UN ETNOGRAFU PETIJUMU REZULTATIEM.
Main/Corp Vestures Instituts (Latvijas PSR Zinatnu Akademija). (19??)-. Latvian. One time a year. Zinatne / Science Publishing House, Turgeneva Iela 19, Riga Latvia 1530. **Tel** 3712 212 797. **ED** E. Mugurevics. **Circ:** 800.
Desc: Contains short reviews of scientific studies about archaeologists and ethnographers; shows the results of investigations of archaeological and ethnographical expeditions, with information about the deliberation of archaeological monuments and their protection in Soviet Latvia. Materials supplemented with illustrations.

ABSTRACTING, BIBLIOGRAPHIES AND STATISTICS

LC GN1 .A15 ISSN 0001-3455
DD 306/.05 US
NLM Z 5112 A164

ABSTRACTS IN ANTHROPOLOGY. Vol. 1 (Feb. 1970)-. Abstracting/Indexing Service. English. Eight times a year. $288.00. Baywood Publishing Company Inc., 26 Austin Avenue, PO Box 337, Amityville NY 11701. **Tel** (516)691-1270, (800)638-7819, FAX (516)691-1770. **ED** Roger Moeller, Jay Custer. Index available.
Desc: Abstracts covering archaeology and physical and cultural anthropology linguistics. Includes full author and subject indices.
Ind/Abst Anthropol. Index; Br. Archaeol. Bibliogr.

LC GN1 .A155 ISSN 0173-2986
DD 301/.0943/05 GW

ABSTRACTS IN GERMANY ANTHROPOLOGY. Added/Corp Association for International Scientific Communication. No. 1 (Autumn 1980)-. Abstracting/Indexing Service. English. Two times a year. $36.85. Edition RE, Wolfgang Doering Strasse 4, D-37077 Goettingen Germany. **ED** Rolf Husmann.

LC Z ISSN 0003-5467
DD 016.572 UK
NLM Z 5111; M986a

ANTHROPOLOGICAL INDEX TO CURRENT PERIODICALS IN THE LIBRARY OF THE ROYAL ANTHROPOLOGICAL INSTITUTE.
(ANTHROPOLOGICAL INDEX.). [Anthropol. index curr. period. Libr. R. Anthropol. Inst.]. **Main/Corp** Museum of Mankind. Library. **Added/Corp** Museum of Mankind. Library. International Union of Anthropological and Ethnological Sciences. Commission on Documentation. Royal Anthropological Institute of Great Britain and Ireland. Vol. 21, Pt. 1 (Jan. 1/March 31, 1983)-. Abstracting/Indexing Service. English. Four times a year. $132.00. Royal Anthropological Institute, 50 Fitzroy Street, London W1P 5HS United Kingdom. **Tel** 011 44 171 3870455. **(Subscription address:** Turpin Distribution Services Limited, Blackhorse Road, Letchworth, Hertfordshire SH6 1HN United Kingdom. **Tel** 011 44 1462 672555, FAX 011 44 1462 480947.**) ED** Karen Godden. **Ad Acc. Circ:** 500. available on microfilm from University Microfilms International (UMI).
Continues Anthropological Index to Current Periodicals in the Museum of Mankind (Library Incorporating the Royal Anthropological Institute Library), 0003-5467.
Desc: Covers most of the periodical literature received by the Museum of Mankind Library in London. The index is arranged geographically with subdivisions by broad subjects. Entry is alphabetical by author.
Ind/Abst Hum. Rights Intern. Rep.

LC Z5112 .A573 GN1 ISSN 0190-3373
DD 016.306/05 US

ANTHROPOLOGICAL LITERATURE.
[Anthropol. lit.]. **Added/Corp** Tozzer Library. Vol. 11, No. 1 (1989)-. Abstracting/Indexing Service. English (Slavic, Scandinavian and German). Four times a year (Mar., June, Sept., Dec.). $200.00. Tozzer Library- Harvard University, 21 Divinity Avenue, Cambridge MA 02138. **Tel** (617)495-2253, FAX (617)495-0403. **ED** Julia A. Hendon and Lynne M. Schmelz (phone: (617)495-2292). cum. index. **Circ:** 300. available on an online database from Research Libraries Group Information Network.
Continues Anthropological Literature (Cambridge, Mass. : 1984), 0190-3373.
Desc: Author and subject index to articles from serials and edited works received annually by Tozzer Library. Articles are primarily focused on the fields of archaeology, biological and physical anthropology, cultural and social anthropology, and linguistics. Coverage is international with emphasis on materials published in European languages. This title has been continually published since 1979. It began with a print edition from (1979-1983), then to microfiche (1984-1988), and back to print (1989) - to present.

ISSN 0742-6844
DD 016 US

BIBLIOGRAPHIES AND INDEXES IN ANTHROPOLOGY. [Bibliogr. indexes anthropol.].
(1985)-. Monographic series. English. Irregular. Price varies per volume. Greenwood Press Inc., PO Box 5007, Westport CT 06881-5007. **Tel** (203)226-3571, FAX (203)222-1502.

US

INTERNATIONAL BIBLIOGRAPHY OF SOCIAL SCIENCES: ANTHROPOLOGY.
(19??)-. Bibliography. English. Irregular. $150.00 US; $187.50 Canada. Routledge Chapman & Hall Inc., 29 West 35th Street, New York NY 10001. **Tel** (212)244-3336, (212)244-6412.
Desc: Covers over 1,500 journals published throughout the world in 30 languages and stands as the long-term reference resource in the social sciences.

ANTIQUES

ISSN 0164-7008
US

AMERICAN COLLECTOR'S JOURNAL, THE. (19??)-. Periodical. English. Six times a year (Jan., Mar., May, July, Sept., Nov.). $4.25. American Collector's Journal, PO Box 407, Kewanee IL 61443. **Tel** (309)853-8441. **ED** Carol A. Savidge; (phone: (309)852-2602). **Bk Rev. Ad Acc. Circ:** 51,000 (ctrl).
Desc: Deals with stories and advertising on collectables and antiques.

LC NK805 .A684 ISSN 0161-5203
DD 745.1/0973 US

AMERICAN HOME'S TREASURY OF AMERICANA. VFOAT Treasury of Americana. Vol. 1 (1977)-. Periodical. English. $1.75. American Home Publishing Co., 641 Lexington Avenue, New York NY 10022.

LC NK1125 .A25 ISSN 0003-5653
DD 745/.05 NE

ANTIEK. See The Arts-Art.

IT

ANTIQUARIATO. (19??)-. Periodical. Italian. Eleven times a year. L51100. Giorgio Mondadori Intl, Via A Ponti 10, 20143 Milan Italy. **Tel** 011 39 2 891661.

LC TL
DD 629 US

ANTIQUE AIRPLANE DIGEST. See Aeronautics, Astronautics.

LC NK1125 .A26
DD 745.1/05 UK

ANTIQUE & COLLECTORS FAYRE.
VFOAT Antique and Collectors Fayre; Antique & Collectors Fair. (July 1986)-. Periodical. English. Twelve times a year. Browcom Group, Browcom House, Browells Lane, Feltham Middlesex TW13 7EQ United Kingdom.

LC NK1128 .A58 ISSN 1065-3694
DD 745.1/028/7 US

ANTIQUE & COLLECTORS REPRODUCTION NEWS. [Antiq. collect. reprod. news]. VFOAT Antique and Collectors Reproduction News. (Apr. 1992)-. Periodical. English. Twelve times a year. $32.00. Antique Coast to Coast, 8811 Sunny Hill Drive, Des Moines IA 50325. **Tel** (515)270-8994.

LC TL1 .A472 ISSN 0003-5831
DD 629.2/222/075 US

ANTIQUE AUTOMOBILE, THE. See Transportation-Automobiles.

ISSN 8750-1481
US

ANTIQUE BOTTLE & GLASS COLLECTOR. [Antiq. bottle glass collect.]. VFOAT
Antique Bottle and Glass Collector. Vol. 1, No. 1 (May 1984)-. Periodical. English. Twelve times a year. $19.00. Antique Bottle & Glass Collector, 102 Jefferson Street, Box 180, East Greenville PA 18041. **Tel** (312)777-0443. **ED** James Hagenbuch (editor's address: 102 Jefferson Street, East Greenville, PA 18041.) Telephone: (215)679-5849). **Bk Rev. Ad Acc. Circ:** 4,200 (ctrl).
Continues Antique Bottle World.

ISSN 0164-7237
US

ANTIQUE CAR TIMES. See Transportation-Automobiles.

UK

ANTIQUE COLLECTING. Added/Corp Antique Collectors' Club. (19??)-. Periodical. English. Ten times a year (monthly except Jan. and Aug.). $40.00. Antique Collectors Club, 5 Church Street, Woodbridge Suffolk 1P12 1DS United Kingdom. **Tel** 011 44 1394 385501, FAX 011 44 1394 334434, telex 987271. **ED** Susan Wilson. **Ad Acc. Circ:** 12,500.
Desc: Articles on collecting antiques including current price trends, written by experts on subjects not discussed elsewhere.
Ind/Abst BHA : Biblio. Hist. Art.

US

ANTIQUE COLLECTING (EPHRATA (PA.). (ANTIQUE COLLECTING.). (19??)-. Periodical. English. Twelve times a year. American Antique Collector, Box 327, Ephrata PA 17522.
Ind/Abst ARTbibliogr. Mod.

LC NK1125 .A28 ISSN 0003-5858
DD 708.051 UK

ANTIQUE COLLECTOR, THE. [Antiq. collect.]. (1930)-. Periodical. English. Six times a year. $39.50. Orpheus Publications, 7 St. Johns Road, Harrow Middlesex HA1 2EE United Kingdom. **Tel** 011 44 181 8634040, FAX 011 44 181 4249945. **(Subscription address:** Orpheus Publications Ltd., PO Box 648, Harrow Middlesex HA1 2NW United Kingdom. **Tel** 011 44 181 8634040, FAX 011 44 181 4249945.**) ED** David Coombs. **Bk Rev. Ad Acc. Circ:** 16,555. available on microfilm and microfiche from University Microfilms International (UMI).
Desc: Features artifacts, paintings, fairs and exhibitions, profiles, buying advice, and new discoveries.
Ind/Abst Archit. Period. Index (Vol. 55 No. 10, Oct. 1984-); Art Archaeol. Tech. Abstr.; ARTbibliogr. Mod.; BHA : Biblio. Hist. Art; Br. Humanit. Index; EP Collect.; Homework Help.; MasterFile FullTEXT 1000; MasterFile FullTEXT 350; MasterFile FullTEXT 650; MasterFile FullTEXT; OCLC; Telebase; World Mag. Bank.

LC NK1125 .A283 ISSN 0003-5866
UK
CCC

ANTIQUE DEALER AND COLLECTORS' GUIDE. (THE ANTIQUE DEALER AND COLLECTORS' GUIDE.). [Antiq. deal. collect. guide]. VFOAT Antique Dealer & Collectors Guide; Collector's Guide. Vol. 1 (July 1946)-. Periodical. English. Twelve times a year. $70.00. Reed Business Publishing / West Sussex, England, Perrymount Road, Haywards Heath, West Sussex RH16 3DH United Kingdom. **Tel** 011 44 1444 441212, FAX 011 44 1444 445447. *Continues* Antique Dealers' Weekly and Collectors' Guide.
Ind/Abst Art Archaeol. Tech. Abstr.; ARTbibliogr. Mod.; BHA : Biblio. Hist. Art.

Antiques

ISSN 1069-5141
US
●**ANTIQUE DOLL WORLD.** (1993)-. Periodical. English. Six times a year. $19.95. Inside Collector Holdings Inc., 225 Main Street, Suite 300, Northport NY 11768. **Tel** (516)261-8337, FAX (516)261-8235. **ED** Donna C. Kaonis. **Circ:** 7,000.
Desc: Includes articles on antique dolls, doll clothes, and accessories. Also contains information on other children's toys such as paper dolls and tea sets.

US
ANTIQUE GAZETTE. (19??)-. English. Twelve times a year. $14.00. Turner Publishing Company, 6949 Charlotte Pike / Suite 106, Nashville TN 37209. **Tel** (615)352-0941. **ED** Catherine Turner. **Bk Rev. Ad Acc. Circ:** 10,000 (ctrl).
Desc: Trade publication for collectors and dealers of antiques. Articles on antiques, shows and historic places. Each issue includes an antique locator and mall locator section.

LC NK **ISSN 0951-6913**
DD 745.1 UK
ANTIQUE (LONDON). (ANTIQUE.). [Antique]. (1986)-. Periodical. English. Four times a year. $36.00. Antique, 10-11 Lower John Street, London W1R 3PE United Kingdom. **Tel** 011 44 171 4349180, FAX 011 44 171 2875488.

LC TL440 .A58 **ISSN 0364-6963**
DD 629.22/75/075 US
ANTIQUE MOTORCYCLE, THE. See Motorcycles.

LC TS2301.P3 A67 **ISSN 0361-2147**
DD 621.389/33 US
ANTIQUE PHONOGRAPH MONTHLY, THE. Vol. 1, (Jan. 1973)-. Periodical. English. Ten times a year. $15.00. Allen Koenigsberg, 502 East 17th Street, Brooklyn NY 11226. **Tel** (718)941-6835. **ED** Allen Koenigsberg. Index available. cum. index. **Bk Rev. Ad Acc. Circ:** 2,000.
Desc: Covers history of recorded sound, from 1930-1977. Development of records and phonographs; scientific, cultural, musical, political, and historical background.

ISSN 1042-7392
DD 629 US
ANTIQUE POWER MAGAZINE. [Antiq. power mag.]. **Added/Corp** International Antique Power Association. **VFOAT** Antique Power. (1988)-. Periodical. English. Six times a year. $20.00. Antique Power Inc., PO Box 562, Yellow Springs OH 45387. **Tel** (513)767-1433, FAX (513)767-2726. **ED** Patrick Ertu. **Bk Rev,** (Qty: 6). **Ad Acc.** ctrl circ.

LC ML5 .A5965
DD 789.9/12/075 UK
ANTIQUE RECORDS. See Sound Recordings and Systems.

ISSN 0883-833X
DD 745 US
ANTIQUE REVIEW. [Antiq. rev.]. Vol. 11, No. 2 (Feb. 1990)-. Trade Publication. English. Twelve times a year. $20.00. Ohio Antique Review Inc, PO Box 538, Worthington OH 43085. **Tel** (614)885-9757, FAX (614)885-9762. **ED** Charles R. Muller. Index available (Bound in Jan. issue). **Bk Rev,** (Qty: 70-100). **Ad Acc, Adv Mgr:** JoAnne Geiger, **Tel** (614)885-9758. **Circ:** 9,500 (ctrl). **Continues** Ohio Antique Review, 0192-6721.
Desc: Focus on early american antiques price to 1900, and the buying and selling of now.

LC NK1127 .T74 **ISSN 0149-0192**
DD 380.1/45/745102573 US
ANTIQUE SHOP GUIDE. English. One time a year. $1.50. Tri-State Trade, PO Box 90, Knightstown IN 46148. **Continues** Tri-State Trader Antique Shop Guide to Over 3,000 Listings of Antique Shops, 0364-393X.

ISSN 0713-6315
DD 745.1/075/09713 CN
ANTIQUE SHOWCASE. [Antiq. showcase]. Vol. 17, No. 6 (Dec. 1981)-. Periodical. English. Nine times a year. 22.41Can$. Amis Gibbs Publications Limited, Highway 169 PO Box 260, Bala Ontario P0C 1A0 Canada. **Tel** (705)762-5631, FAX (705)762-5640. **ED** Barbara D.E. Sutton Smith. **Bk Rev. Ad Acc. Circ:** 8,500. **Continues** Ontario Showcase, 0030-3119.
Desc: Aimed at antique lovers and collectors. Articles, each written by specialists, focus on providing information to collectors. Museum exhibitions and acquisitions, and a show calendar are regular features. Upcoming trends, both national and international, are followed.

LC NK9509 .A57 **ISSN 0742-0420**
DD 688.7/2 US
ANTIQUE TOY WORLD. See Gifts, Toys.

LC NK1125 .A594 **ISSN 0882-6897**
DD 745.1/075 US
ANTIQUE TRADER ANTIQUES & COLLECTIBLES PRICE GUIDE, THE. [Antiq. trader antiq. collect. price guide]. **VFOAT** Antique Trader Antiques and Collectibles Price Guide; Antiques & Collectibles Price Guide; Antiques and Collectibles Price Guide. (1984)-. English. One time a year (Oct.). $12.95. Antique Trader Publications, PO Box 1050, Debuque IA 52004. **Tel** (319)588-2073, (800)334-7165. **ED** Mitzie Murrhy. Index available (Free). **Bk Rev. Circ:** 105,000.
Desc: Price guide to antiques and collectibles. Each issue has photos and description of items.

ISSN 0161-8342
US
ANTIQUE TRADER WEEKLY, THE. VFOAT Antique Trader. (1957)-. Trade Publication. English. Fifty-two times a year. $35.00. Antique Trader Publications, PO Box 1050, Debuque IA 52004. **Tel** (319)588-2073, (800)334-7165. **ED** Kyle Husfloen. **Bk Rev. Ad Acc. Circ:** 70,000. **Continues** Antique Trader.
Desc: A tabloid newspaper for the antiques and collectibles hobby. Thousands of antiques and collectibles for sale in each issue. Contains news and articles on antiques.

IT
ANTIQUES. (May 1991)-. Periodical. Italian. Edizioni Conde Nast Spa, Piazza Castello 27, 20121 Milan Italy. **Tel** 011 39 2 85611. **Continues** Casa Vogue Antiques.

ISSN 0260-9606
UK
ANTIQUES ACROSS THE WORLD. [Antiques world]. (1977)-. Periodical. English. Six times a year. £3.00. Michael Davlis (Shipping) Ltd., 111 Mortlake Road Kew, London TW9 471 United Kingdom.

ISSN 1059-8537
US
ANTIQUES ADVERTISER, THE. VFOAT Antiques Directory. (1992)-. Periodical. English. Twelve times a year. $19.95. Brimfield Publishing, Box 273, Brimfield MA 01010. **Tel** (413)267-3813.

ISSN 0274-6085
US
ANTIQUES & COLLECTIBLES (GREENVALE, N.Y.). (ANTIQUES & COLLECTIBLES.). **VFOAT** Antiques and Collectibles. (1980)-. Periodical. English. Twenty-six times a year. Antiques and Collectibles, Box 33, Westbury NY 11590. **Tel** (516)334-9650, FAX (516)334-5740. **ED** Rich Branciforte. **Bk Rev,** (Qty: 50-100). **Ad Acc. Circ:** 10,000 (ctrl).
Desc: Covering antiques, art, history restoration, travel, dolls, crafts.

LC AM201 .H6 **ISSN 0884-6294**
DD 790.1/3 US
TITLE CHANGE
ANTIQUES & COLLECTING HOBBIES. [Antiq. collect. hobbies]. **VFOAT** Antiques and Collecting Hobbies. Vol. 90, No. 1 (March 1985)-(1993). Periodical. English. Lightner Publishing Corporation, 1006 South Michigan Avenue, Chicago IL 60605. **Tel** (312)939-4767, FAX (312)939-0053. **ED** Frances L. Graham. **Bk Rev. Ad Acc. Circ:** 25,000 (ctrl). available on microfilm and microfiche from University Microfilms International (UMI). Documents available from UMI Article Clearinghouse. **Continues** Hobbies, 0018-2907. **Continued by** Antiques & Collecting Magazine.
Desc: Covers the field of antiques for novice or connoisseur with informative articles and advertising for buying and selling.
Ind/Abst Acad. Abstr. Full Text Elite; Acad. Abstr.; Acad. Search; Book Rev. Index; EP Collect.; Gen. Period. Index (1985-); Homework Help.; Mag. Artic. Summar. Elite; Mag. Artic. Summar. Select; Mag. Artic. Summar. CD-ROM; Mag. Index Plus (1989-); Mag. Index. Sel. (1986-); Mag. Search; MasterFile FullTEXT 1000; MasterFile FullTEXT 350; MasterFile FullTEXT 650; MasterFile FullTEXT (Jan. 1986-Sept. 1993); Music Index (-19??); Newsp. Period. Abstr. (1988-); OCLC; Pub. Lib. FullTEXT; Read. Guide Abstr. Select Ed.; Read. Guide Period. Lit.; Telebase; Mag. Index (1985-); Vocat. Search.

LC AM201 .H6
DD 790.1/3 US
●**ANTIQUES & COLLECTING MAGAZINE.** **VFOAT** Antiques and Collecting Magazine; Antiques & Collecting; Antiques and Collecting. Vol. 98, No. 8 (Oct. 1993)-. Periodical. English. Twelve times a year. $28.00. Lightner Publishing Corporation, 1006 South Michigan Avenue, Chicago IL 60605. **Tel** (312)939-4767, FAX (312)939-0053. **Continues** Antiques & Collecting Hobbies, 0884-6294.
Desc: Broad reference source for antique buffs and collectors.
Ind/Abst MasterFile FullTEXT (Oct. 1993-).

US
ANTIQUES AND THE ARTS WEEKLY. **VFOAT** Antiques & the Arts Weekly. (19??)-. Periodical. English. One time a week. $40.00. Bee Publishing Company, 5 Church Hill Road, Newtown CT 06470. **Tel** (203)426-3141, FAX (203)426-1394. **ED** R Scudder Smith. **Bk Rev. Ad Acc. Circ:** 24,000. available in microform.

ISSN 1198-8258
DD 745.1/05 CN
●**ANTIQUES! (TORONTO).** (ANTIQUES!). [Antiques]. No. 1 (May/June 1993)-. Periodical. English. Six times a year. 22.41Can$. Antiques, 20 Bloor Street East, Toronto ONT M4W 3T3 Canada. **Tel** (416)944-3880. **(Subscription address:** Antiques, PO Box 75114, Toronto ONT M4W 3T3 Canada. **)**

LC NK818 .A58 **ISSN 0888-5451**
DD 381/.457451/02577 US
ANTIQUEWEEK. [AntiqueWeek]. **VFOAT** Antique Week. Vol. 19, No. 2 (Apr. 14, 1986)-. Periodical. English. One time a week. $27.45. Mayhill Publications Inc, PO Box 90, Knightstown IN 46148. **Tel** (800)876-5133, FAX (317)345-5133. **Continues** Antique Week--Tri-State Report, 0746-4118.

ISSN 1067-0912
DD 745 US
CEASED
ANTIQUING AMERICA. [Antiq. Am.]. **VFOAT** Antiquing America and Antique Market Report; Antiquing America & Antique Market Report. Vol. 11, No. 5 (Dec. 1992)-(1994). Periodical. English. Web Publications Inc., 650 Westdale Drive, PO Box 12830, Wichita KS 67277. **Tel** (316)946-0600. **Continues** Antique Market Report, 8750-9024.

LC N9 .A377 **ISSN 0743-5517**
DD 700 US
ARCHITECTURAL DIGEST. THE ... ART AND ANTIQUES ANNUAL. See Architecture.

LC N6505 .A55 **ISSN 0195-8208**
DD 705 US
ART & ANTIQUES (NEW YORK, N.Y. : 1984). See The Arts-Art.

LC N8602 .A83 **ISSN 0197-1093**
DD 700/.75 US
ART & AUCTION (NEW YORK, N.Y.). (ART & AUCTION.). [Art auction]. **VAT** Art and Auction. Vol. 1 (May 1979)-. Periodical. English. Eleven times a year (monthly with July/Aug. issues combined). $42.00. Art and Auction, 440 Park Avenue South, 14th Floor, New York NY 10016. **Tel** (212)447-9555. **(Subscription address:** CDS / SIFD Agency Control, 1901 Bell Avenue, Des Moines IA 50315. **Tel** (515)246-6812.**) ED** Lin Smith. **Bk Rev. Ad Acc. Circ:** 22,000 (ctrl).
Desc: Covers the international art markets, from antiques to contemporary art. Articles include information on the artists, schools of art, furniture, analyses of trends in the markets, auction reviews and previews, a monthly calendar of gallery exhibitions, and auctions and antiques shows throughout the United States and Europe.

LC N8600 .A73 **ISSN 0161-1232**
DD 332.6/78 US
ART-ANTIQUES INVESTMENT REPORT, THE. See The Arts-Art.

ISSN 0831-2133
DD 759.11 CN
ART IMPRESSIONS. See The Arts-Art.

AG
ARTE AL DIA : REVISTA QUINCENAL DE INFORMACIONES DEL MERCADO DE ARTE Y ANTIGUEDADES. See The Arts-Art.

AT
TITLE CHANGE
AUSTRALIAN ANTIQUE BOTTLE COLLECTOR. VFOAT ABC. (1982)-(19??). Periodical. English. Crown Castleton, Box 235, Golden Square 3555 Australia. **Tel** 011 61 54 418070. **ED** Ken Arnold. **Bk Rev. Ad Acc. Circ:** 2,000 (ctrl). **Continues** Australian Bottle Review. **Continued by** Australian Antique Bottles & Collectables.
Desc: History of factories, show reports, bottles excavated, advertising, general news, bottle collecting and associated collectables auction reports.

AT
AUSTRALIAN ANTIQUE BOTTLES & COLLECTABLES. (19??)-. Periodical. English. Six times a year (published Jan., Mar., May, July, Sept., Nov.). 25.00Aus$ Australia; 40.00Aus$ UK; 39.00Aus$ other. Crown Castleton, Box 235, Golden Square 3555 Australia. **Tel** 011 61 54 418070. **Continues** Australian Antique Bottle Collector.

AT
AUSTRALIAN ANTIQUE COLLECTOR, THE. (198?)-. Periodical. English. Two times a year (Jan. July). 16.44Aus$. Reed Business Publishing Pty Ltd. / Australia, PO Box 5487, W Chatswood New South Wales 2057, Australia. **Tel** 011 61 2 3725222, FAX 011 61 2 4197533. **Continues** Australasian Antique Collector, 0004-8704.

Antiques

LC Z1000 .B74   **ISSN** 0068-0141
DD 018/.4   US
NLM Z 1000.5 B724
BOOKMAN'S PRICE INDEX. See
Antiques-Abstracting, Bibliographies and Statistics.

ISSN 0963-7443
UK
BRITISH BOTTLE REVIEW. [Br. bottle rev.].
(1978)-. Periodical. English. Four times a year (Mar., June, Sept., Dec.). $20.00. BBR Publishing, 2 Strafford Avenue, Elsecar NR, Barnsley Yorkshire S74 8AA United Kingdom. **Tel** 011 44 1226 745156. **ED** Alan Blakeman. **Bk Rev**. **Ad Acc**. **Circ:** 5,000.
Desc: News of events and coverage on antiques bottles, pots and lids.

ISSN 1168-108X
FR
UDC 902(448.3)
BULLETIN ANNUEL - ECOLE ANTIQUE DE NIMES. **VFOAT** Bulletin de l'Ecole Antique de Nimes; Bulletin - Ecole Antique de Nimes. (1966)-. Bulletin. French. One time a year. Price varies per volume. Musee Archaeologique, 13 Boulevard Amiral Courbet, 30000 Nimes France. **Tel** 011 33 66 672557. **Continues** Ecole Antique de Nimes, 0755-916X.

LC DC2 .F81   **ISSN** 0071-8394
FR
TITLE CHANGE
BULLETIN ARCHEOLOGIQUE DU COMITE DES TRAVAUX HISTORIQUES ET SCIENTIFIQUES. See Archaeology.

LC DC30 .B85   **ISSN** 0997-5322
DD 944/.01/05   FR
BULLETIN ARCHEOLOGIQUE DU COMITE DES TRAVAUX HISTORIQUES ET SCIENTIFIQUES. FASCICULE A, ANITQUITES NATIONALES. See Archaeology.

DD 629.225/0971/05   **ISSN** 1198-5011
CN
●**CANADIAN ANTIQUE POWER.** [Can. antique power]. Vol. 1, No. 1 (May/June 1993)-. Periodical. English. Six times a year. 15.97Can$. Canadian Antique Power, PO Box 120, Teeswater, Ontario N0G 2S0 Canada. **Tel** (519)392-6733.

LC TL1 .C3116
DD 629.2   US
●**CAR COLLECTOR & CAR CLASSICS.** See Transportation-Automobiles.

ISSN 0892-9769
US
Pr Rev.
CAROUSEL NEWS & TRADER, THE. **VFOAT** Carousel News and Trader; Carousel Trader. Vol. 3, No. 2 (Feb. 1987)-. Periodical. English. Twelve times a year. $25.00. Carousel News and Trader, 87 Park Avenue West, Suite 206, Mansfield OH 44902. **Tel** (419)529-4999, FAX (419)529-2321. **ED** Walter L. Loucks. **Bk Rev**. **Ad Acc**. **Circ:** 6,000. **Continues** Carousel Trader, 0892-9750.
Desc: News and stories about carousel history, restoration, buying and selling, auctions and events.

ISSN 0740-0780
DD 731   US
CARROUSEL ART. See The Arts-Crafts and Decorative Arts.

US
CATALOG OF FINE ANTIQUE CAMERAS & PHOTOGRAPHIC IMAGES. **Main/Corp** Allen & Hilary Weiner, firm, New York. No. 1 (June 1974)-. Catalog. English. Irregular. Allen & Hilary Weiner, 80 Central Park West, New York NY 10023. **Tel** (212)787-8357.

IE
CATALOG OF ... - SOTHEBY'S IN IRELAND. See The Arts-Art.

LC N8610 .C37
IT
CATALOGO INTERNAZIONALE BOLAFFI D'ARTE ANTICA E DI ANTIQUARIATO. See The Arts-Art.

ISSN 0383-7890
CN
CIRCA 76. Vol. 1 (July 1976)-. Periodical. English. Irregular. $7.50. Calico Publishing Company Ltd, PO Box 924, Barrie Ontario L4M 4Y6 Canada.
Desc: A journal of antiques & arts in Canada, Aug. 1976.

LC NK1127 .C58   **ISSN** 0094-1182
DD 745.1/025/73   US
CIVIL WAR COLLECTORS' DEALER DIRECTORY, THE. 1st- Ed.; 1974/75-. Directory. English. Three times a year. $4.95. C L Batson, 607 San Fedro Drive, Chesapeake VA 23320-8058. **Tel** (703)631-0884. **ED** C L Batson No. **Ad Acc**.
Desc: Alpha listing of all known dealers of memorabilia and books on American Civil War. Listings include categories of goods sold; also collectors' shows and publications.

LC NK1127 .C62   **ISSN** 0272-0175
DD 745.1/025/73   US
CLARK'S GUIDE TO AMERICA'S ANTIQUE SHOPS. 1st- Ed.; Jan. 1980-. English. Two times a year. $9.00. Clark Publications, RT. 1 Box 470, Cantonment FL 32533.

LC TL7 .C5   **ISSN** 0009-8310
DD 629.2074   US
CLASSIC CAR. See Transportation-Automobiles.

LC TL1 .C56   **ISSN** 0740-4794
DD 629.222   US
CLASSIC CAR BIMONTHLY. See Transportation-Automobiles.

ISSN 0745-8533
DD 688   US
COIN SLOT (LUZERNE, PA.), THE. (THE COIN SLOT : THE NEWLETTER FOR COLLECTORS OF ANTIQUE MECHANICAL DEVICES.). [Coin slot]. Issue 1 (Sept. 1974)-Vol. 1, No. 1 (Fall 1984)-. Periodical. English. Four times a year. $32.00. The Coin Slot, 4401 Zephyr Street, Wheat Ridge CO 80033-3299. **Tel** (303)420-2222. **ED** Donald Hoflin. **Bk Rev**. **Ad Acc**.

US
COLLECTOR MAGAZINE & PRICE GUIDE. (19??)-. Trade Publication. English. Twelve times a year. $13.50 US; $18.50 other (surface mail). Antique Trader Publications, PO Box 1050, Debuque IA 52004. **Tel** (319)588-2073, (800)334-7165. **Continues** The Antique Trader Price Guide to Antiques and Collectors' Items, 0556-5367.

ISSN 0162-1033
US
COLLECTORS NEWS & THE ANTIQUE REPORTER. (COLLECTORS NEWS AND THE ANTIQUE REPORTER: COVERING THE WONDERFUL WORLD OF COLLECTION--ANTIQUES TO MODERN.). Vol. 1 (May 1960)-. Periodical. English. Twelve times a year. $24.00. Collectors News, PO Box 156, Grundy Center IA 50638. **Tel** (319)824-6981. Index available (bound in Dec. issue).

LC NK805 .C64   **ISSN** 0744-5989
DD 745.1/0973/075   US
COLLECTORS' SHOWCASE (SAN DIEGO, CALIF.). (COLLECTORS' SHOWCASE.). [Collect. showc.]. Vol. 1, No. 1 (Sept./Oct. 1981)-. Periodical. English. Six times a year. $19.95. Collectors' Showcase, 4099 McEwen, Suite 350, Dallas TX 75244. **Tel** (214)851-1729, (800)477-2524. **ED** Donna Kaonis. **Bk Rev**. **Ad Acc**. **Circ:** 18,000.
Desc: Full-color magazine about antique toys, dolls and advertising, with news, reviews and auction reports.

ISSN 0738-9981
US
CEASED
COLLECTRIX. [Collectrix]. (Fall 1982)-(19??). English. Collectrix, 200 North Village Avenue #4c, Rockville MD 11570. **Tel** (516)766-0554.

US
DUMP DIGGERS GAZETTE. **Added/Corp** Antique Bottle Collectors of Colorado. (19??)-. Periodical. English. Irregular. $10.00. Antique Bottle Collectors of Colorado, PO Box 245, Littleton CO 80160.

ISSN 1062-9645
DD 681   US
ETCETERA (LOS ANGELES, CALIF.). (ETCETERA : MAGAZINE OF THE EARLY TYPEWRITER COLLECTORS ASSOCIATION.). [ETCetera]. **Added/Corp** Early Typewriter Collectors Association. (1987)-. Periodical. English. Four times a year. $20.00 North America; $25.00 other. Early Typewriter Collectors Association, 2591 Military Avenue, Los Angeles CA 90064. **Tel** (310)477-5229, FAX (310)268-8420. **ED** Darryl Rehr. Index available. **Bk Rev**. **Ad Acc**. **Circ:** 1,000.

ISSN 8756-775X
DD 332   US
EVALUATOR (RIVER FOREST, ILL.). See The Arts.

ISSN 0391-7517
IT
FELIX RAVENNA. See Archaeology.

ISSN 1053-136X
DD 745   US
FIELD GUIDES TO COLLECTING SHAKER ANTIQUES. [Field guides collect. Shak. antiq.]. (1991)-. Monographic series. English. $12.95 (single issue). Berkshire House, PO Box 915, Great Barrington MA 01230.

LC WMLC 93/3101   **ISSN** 1071-1015
DD 709   US
CEASED
FINE ART & ANTIQUES INTERNATIONAL. See The Arts.

ISSN 0745-6824
DD 621   US
FINE TOOL JOURNAL, THE. [Fine tool j.]. **Added/Corp** Iron Horse Antiques (Firm). (19??)-. Periodical. English. Four times a year (Feb., May, Aug., Nov.). $27.00. Antique & Collectible Tools, 27 Fickett Road, Pownal NE 04069. **Tel** (207)688-4962, FAX (207)688-4052. **ED** Clarence Blanchard. **Bk Rev**, (Qty: 40). **Ad Acc**, **Adv Mgr:** S. Ward. **Circ:** 2,000.
Desc: Specialty magazine that includes antique tools, implements, and utensils.

LC NK2528 .F8   **ISSN** 0016-3058
DD 749.2205   UK
FURNITURE HISTORY. See Interior Design and Decoration-Home Furnishings.

ISSN 0016-559X
IT
UDC 7
GAZZETTA ANTIQUARIA. [Gazz. antiq.]. (1963)-. Periodical. Italian. Four times a year. L23850. Polistampa, Via Del Serragli 190R, 50124 Florence Italy. **Tel** 011 39 55 233-7702.

LC NK1127 .A135a
DD 380.1/45/754102541   UK
GUIDE TO THE ANTIQUE SHOPS OF BRITAIN. **Main/Corp** Antique Collectors' Club. (1972)-. Directory. English. $29.50 North America; £14.50 other. Antique Collectors Club, 5 Church Street, Woodbridge Suffolk 1P12 1DS United Kingdom. **Tel** 011 44 1394 385501, FAX 011 44 1394 334434, telex 987271. **ED** Carol Adams. **Bk Rev**. **Ad Acc**. **Adv Mgr:** Jean Johnson. **Circ:** 10,000.
Desc: Over 7,000 entries for antique shops, markets, centres and galleries across Britain listed by area and indexed by specialty. Also lists auctioneers, packers, shippers and restores.

ISSN 0017-5617
US
GUN REPORT. (June 1955)-. Trade Publication. English. Twelve times a year. $33.00. World Wide Gun Report Inc., PO Box 38, 110 South College Avenue, Aledo IL 61231. **Tel** (309)582-5311, FAX (309)582-5555. **ED** Kandy Harrison. Index available. cum. index. **Bk Rev**, (Qty: 12). **Ad Acc**. **Circ:** 6,500 (ctrl).
Desc: Factual and original articles on antique guns, cartridges and accoutrements and the history of their times. A guide to meetings and shows promoted by gun enthusiasts. Book reviews, questions and answers.

US
HEMMINGS MOTOR NEWS. See Transportation-Automobiles.

ISSN 0738-8829
US
HERITAGE WEST (SACRAMENTO, CALIF.). (HERITAGE WEST.). Vol. 2, No. 5 (June 1983)-. Periodical. English. Six times a year. $12.00. Heritage West, 7723 Billings Way, Sacramento CA 95832-9990. **Tel** (916)392-8463. **ED** James Harold Leach. **Circ:** 12,000. **Continues** Antiques and Collectibles Magazine.

LC TL1 .H83   **ISSN** 0018-5213
DD 388.3/21/09   US
HORSELESS CARRIAGE GAZETTE. See Transportation-Automobiles.

LC NK1125 .I57   **ISSN** 1052-861X
DD 745.1/075   US
INSIDE COLLECTOR, THE. [Inside collect.]. (June 1990)-. Periodical. English. Nine times a year (Approx. every 6 weeks). $29.95. Inside Collector, 225 Main Street, Suite 300, Northport NY 11768. **Tel** (516)261-8337, FAX (516)261-8235. **ED** Donna Kaonis. **Bk Rev**. **Ad Acc**, **Adv Mgr:** Keith Kaonis. **Circ:** 58,000.
Desc: An indispensable guide to popular antiques and collectibles. It focuses on toys, dolls, antique advertising, comic and pop culture memborabilia.

ISSN 0836-5873
DD 707/.5/0971   CN
TITLE CHANGE
INSIGHT ON COLLECTABLES (1987). (INSIGHT ON COLLECTABLES.). [Insight collect.]. **VFOAT** Insight on Collectibles. Vol. 6, No. 6 (Sept. 1987)-(1993). Periodical. English. Trajan Publishing Corporation, 103 Lakeshore RE, Suite 202, Saint Catherine Ontario, L2N 2T6 Canada. **Tel** (905)646-6774, FAX (905)646-0995. **ED** John Elvidge, Lise Mollow, Leslie Grove. **Bk Rev**. **Ad Acc**. **Circ:** 20,000 (ctrl).
Continues Insight (Durham, Ont.), 0833-4447.
Continued by Collectibles Canada.

Antiques

LC NK9507 .J68 ISSN 0734-5534
DD 730/.0951 US
JOURNAL - INTERNATIONAL CHINESE SNUFF BOTTLE SOCIETY. (JOURNAL.). [J. - Int. Chin. Snuff Bottle Soc.]. **Added/Corp** International Chinese Snuff Bottle Society. (197?)-. Periodical. English. Four times a year (Mar., Jun., Sept., Dec.). Comes with International Chinese Snuff Bottle Society membership; $95.00 (membership). International Chinese Snuff Bottle Society, 2601 North Charles Street, Baltimore MD 21218. **Tel** (301)467-9400, FAX (301)243-3451. **ED** Berthe H. Ford and Elsa Graser. Index available. cum. index. **Bk Rev. Ad Acc. Circ:** 650 (ctrl). **Continues** Newsletter (Chinese Snuff Bottle Society of America).
Desc: Scholarly articles on snuff, snuff bottles and their history. Dealer lists, convention reviews and other related reviews are also included.

LC NK2668 .J68 ISSN 1054-9080
DD 749.2951 US
JOURNAL OF THE CLASSICAL CHINESE FURNITURE SOCIETY. See Interior Design and Decoration-Home Furnishings.

 ISSN 0738-9736
 US
KANHISTIQUE. See History-History of North and South America.

LC DS820.8 .K62 ISSN 0368-6272
 JA
 CODEN KNKAAF
KOBUNKAZAI NO KAGAKU. See The Arts-Art.

LC NK1125 .A39 ISSN 0738-2405
DD 745.1/075 US
KOVELS' ANTIQUES & COLLECTIBLES PRICE LIST, THE. VFOAT Antiques & Collectibles Price List; Kovels' Antiques and Collectibles Price List; Antiques and Collectibles Price List. 15th Ed. (1982-83)-. English. One time a year. $16.90. Random House Inc., 400 Hahn Road, Westminster MD 21157. **Tel** (800)726-0600, (800)733-3000, FAX (800)659-2436, (410)386-7013. **ED** Ralph and Terry Kovel. **Continues** Kovel, Ralph M. Kovels' Antiques Price List.

LC NK1125 .A39 ISSN 0741-6091
DD 745.1/075/0973 US
KOVELS ON ANTIQUES AND COLLECTIBLES. [Kovels antiq. collect.]. Vol. 7, No. 10 (June 15, 1981)-. Periodical. English. Twelve times a year. $27.00. Antiques Inc, Box 22200, Beachwood OH 44122. **Tel** (216)752-2252. **(Subscription address:** Palm Coast Data, PO Box 420163, Agency Department, Palm Coast FL 32142. **Tel** (904)445-4662 ext. 669, (800)829-5475.) Index available. **Continues** Kovels, Ralph M. Kovels on Antiques and Collectables, 0741-6091.

 ISSN 0192-5458
 US
KRUSE REPORT. See Transportation-Automobiles.

 ISSN 0459-2980
 LY
LIBYA ANTIQUA. See Archaeology.

 ISSN 0309-3700
 UK
LIVERPOOL CLASSICAL MONTHLY : LCM. [Liverp. class. mon. LCM]. **VFOAT** LCM; L.C.M. Vol. 1, No. 1 (Jan. 1976)-. Periodical. English (French, German, Italian and Greek, Modern). Ten times a year (monthly except Aug. and Sept.). $35.00. University of Liverpool / Department of Public Health, PO Box 147, Liverpool L69 3BX United Kingdom. **Tel** 011 44 151 7945581, FAX 011 44 151 7945588. **(Subscription address:** University of Liverpool, Classics Department, PO Box 147, Liverpool L69 3BX United Kingdom. **Tel** 011 44 151 7945581.) **Bk Rev. Circ:** 475.

LC NK1133 .L9
DD 745.1 US
LYLE OFFICIAL ANTIQUES REVIEW, THE. (1971/1972)-. English. One time a year (Sept.). The Putnam Publishing Group, 390 Murray Hill Parkway East, Rutherford NJ 07073. **Tel** (800)631-8571.

LC NK1125 .A3 ISSN 0161-9284
DD 745 US
MAGAZINE ANTIQUES (1971), THE. (THE MAGAZINE ANTIQUES.). [Mag. antiq.]. **VFOAT** Antiques. Vol. 99 No. 3 (March 1971)-. Periodical. English. Twelve times a year. $39.95. Brant Publishing, 575 Broadway, New York NY 10012. **Tel** (212)941-2800. **(Subscription address:** CDS / SIFD Agency Control, 1901 Bell Avenue, Des Moines IA 50315. **Tel** (515)246-6812.) available on microfilm and microfiche from University Microfilms International (UMI). Documents available from The Genuine Article, UMI Article Clearinghouse. **Continues** Antiques (New York, N.Y. : 1952), 0003-5939.
Desc: For all who seriously seek an expanded, definitive knowledge of our creative heritage. Every issue is an excursion into our nation's past and a unique visual experience.
Ind/Abst Acad. Abstr. Full Text Elite; Acad. Abstr.; Acad. Search; Am. Hist. Life (1983-); Art Archaeol. Tech. Abstr.; Art Index; ARTbibliogr. Mod.; Arts Humanit. Citation Index [Full Cov.]; Avery Index Archit. Period. Suppl. Colum. Univ. (1990-); BHA : Biblio. Hist. Art; Curr. Contents Arts Humanit.; EP Collect.; Gen. Period. Index (1985-); Homework Help.; Mag. Artic. Summar. Elite; Mag. Artic. Summar. Select; Mag. Artic. Summar. CD-ROM; Mag. Index Plus (1989-); Mag. Index. Sel. (1986-); Mag. Search; MasterFile FullTEXT 1000; MasterFile FullTEXT 350; MasterFile FullTEXT 650; MasterFile FullTEXT (Jan. 1984-); Newsp. Period. Abstr. (1988-); OCLC; Pub. Lib. FullTEXT; Read. Guide Abstr. Select Ed.; Read. Guide Period. Lit.; Res. Alert [Full Cov.]; Telebase; Mag. Index (1977-); Vocat. Search.

LC NX ISSN 0147-0639
DD 705 US
MAINE ANTIQUE DIGEST. (1973)-. Trade Publication. English. Twelve times a year. $37.00. Maine Antique Digest, PO Box 1429, Waldoboro ME 04572. **Tel** (207)832-7534, FAX (207)832-7341. **ED** Samuel Pennington. **Bk Rev. Ad Acc. Adv Mgr:** Alice Greene, **Tel** (207)832-4888. **Circ:** 27,000. available on microfilm from University Microfilms International (UMI); available via Internet (http://gray.maine.com/mad/).
Desc: Presents coverage of the marketplace in American art, antiques and accessories.

LC NK1127 .M36
DD 745.1/025/73 US
●**MALONEY'S ANTIQUES & COLLECTIBLES RESOURCE DIRECTORY. VFOAT** Maloney's Antiques and Collectibles Resource Directory; Antiques & Collectibles Resource Directory; Antiques and Collectibles Resource Directory. 2nd Ed. (1994/1995)-. Directory. English. Every 2 years (every two years). $25.45. Chilton Book Company, 1 Chilton Way, Radnor PA 19089. **Tel** (610)964-4000, (800)695-1214, FAX (215)964-4273, telex 6851035 CHILTON UW.

 ISSN 0883-6949
 US
MANNLICHER COLLECTOR, THE. No. 1 (1985)-. Periodical. English. Four times a year. $10.00. Mannlicher Collectors Association, Box 7144, Salem OR 97303.

MASS BAY ANTIQUES. (19??)-. Periodical. English. Twelve times a year. $15.00. North Shore Weeklies, 2 Washington Street, Box 192, Ipswich MA 01938. **Tel** (508)356-5141, FAX (508)356-9188.

 ISSN 0714-8569
DD 629.2/222 CN
MEMBERS & CARS. See Transportation-Automobiles.

 IT
MISCELLANEA GRECA E ROMANA. **Added/Corp** Istituto Italiana per la Storia Antica. (1965)-. Periodical. Italian. One time a year. Price varies per volume.

LC ML5 .M643
DD 789.7/05 UK
MUSIC BOX, THE. See Music.

LC AM303 .N37 ISSN 0899-6172
DD 700/.25/73 US
NATIONAL DIRECTORY OF ART & ANTIQUE BUYERS & SPECIALISTS. [Natl. dir. art antiq. buy. spec.]. **VFOAT** National Directory of Art and Antique Buyers and Specialists. 1988 Ed.-. Directory. English. Every 2 years. $75.00. Merit Agencies Inc, Box 342, Englewood CO 80110. **Tel** (303)986-8131. **ED** William D'Angelo. **Circ:** 500.

LC NK11 .N37
DD 681.1/1/06073 US
NAWCC BULLETIN. Added/Corp National Association of Watch and Clock Collectors. **VFOAT** Bulletin of the National Association of Watch and Clock Collectors, Inc. Vol. 28, (Feb. 1986)-. Bulletin. English. Six times a year (Feb., Apr., June, Aug., Oct., Dec.). $25.00 (Comes with National Association of Watch and Clock Collectors and Bulletin of NAWCC membership). National Association Watch & Clock Collectors, 514 Poplar Street, Columbia PA 17512. **Tel** (717)684-8261, FAX (717)684-0878. **ED** Kathy Everett. **Continues** Bulletin of the National Association of Watch and Clock Collectors.

 ISSN 0897-5795
DD 745 US
NEW ENGLAND ANTIQUES JOURNAL. [N. Engl. antiq. j.]. **VFOAT** Antiques Journal. (19??)-. Periodical. English. Twelve times a year. $19.95. Turely Publications, 4 Church Street, Ware MA 01082. **Tel** (413)967-3505, FAX (413)967-6009. **ED** Rufus Foshee and Jody Young. **Bk Rev. Ad Acc. Circ:** 20,000 (ctrl).
Desc: Provides in-depth coverage of the antiques market in the Northeast.

 ISSN 0738-8365
 US
NEW YORK ANTIQUE ALMANAC OF ART, ANTIQUES, INVESTMENTS & YESTERYEAR, THE. VFOAT New York Antique Almanac; Antique Almanac of Art, Antiques, Investments & Yesteryear. (19??)-. Trade Publication. English. Twelve times a year. $10.00. New York Eye Publishing Company, PO Box 335, Lawrence NY 11559.

 ISSN 0583-9181
 US
NEWSLETTER - SOCIETY FOR THE PRESERVATION OF LONG ISLAND ANTIQUITIES. Main/Corp Society for the Preservation of Long Island Antiquities. (19??)-. Newsletter. English. One time a year. Society for the Preservation of Long Island Antiquities, 93 North Country Road, Setauket NY 11733.

 SZ
NUMISMATICA E ANTICHITA. See Hobbies-Numismatics.

 ISSN 0346-9212
 SW
NYA ANTIK & AUKTION. VAT Nya Antik Och Auktion. (19??)-. Periodical. Swedish. Eleven times a year (monthly except Aug.). Allers Forlag AB, Pren Avd Stina Wiberg, S251 85 Helsingborg Sweden. **Tel** 011 46 42 173500. **ED** Christian Wollin. **Bk Rev. Ad Acc. Circ:** 45,000 (ctrl).
Desc: Concerns art, antiques and collectables with emphasis on Sweden and Scandinavia.

LC NK ISSN 8756-047X
DD 745 US
OCCASIONAL PAPERS ON ANTIQUITIES. [Occas. pap. antiq.]. Vol. 1-. Monographic series. English. One time a year. Price varies per volume. The J Paul Getty Museum, 17985 Pacific Highway, Malibu CA 90265. **Bk Rev. Circ:** 500 (ctrl).

LC HF5482 .O37
DD 381/.1 US
OFFICIAL DIRECTORY TO U.S. FLEA MARKETS / FROM THE EDITORS OF THE HOUSE OF COLLECTIBLES, THE. Added/Corp House of Collectibles. Editorial Dept. **VFOAT** Official Directory to US Flea Markets. 1st Ed. (1987)-. Directory. English. Irregular. Random House Inc., 400 Hahn Road, Westminster MD 21157. **Tel** (800)726-0600, (800)733-3000, FAX (800)659-2436, (410)386-7013.

LC NK30 .O36 ISSN 0743-8729
DD 745.1/03/21 US
OFFICIAL ENCYCLOPEDIA OF ANTIQUES AND COLLECTIBLES, THE. (THE OFFICIAL ENCYCLOPEDIA OF ANTIQUES AND COLLECTIBLES.). [Off. encycl. antiq. collect.]. **Added/Corp** House of Collectibles. **VFOAT** Official Encyclopedia, Antiques and Collectibles; Antiques Encyclopedia. 1st Ed. (1983)-. English. Irregular. $14.00. Random House Inc., 400 Hahn Road, Westminster MD 21157. **Tel** (800)726-0600, (800)733-3000, FAX (800)659-2436, (410)386-7013.

LC NK4893 .O33 ISSN 1046-7289
DD 688.7/221/075 US
OFFICIAL IDENTIFICATION AND PRICE GUIDE TO ANTIQUE & MODERN DOLLS, THE. [Off. identif. price guide antiq. mod. dolls]. **Added/Corp** House of Collectibles. **VFOAT** Antique & Modern Dolls; Antique and Modern Dolls; Dolls. **VAT** Official Identification and Price Guide to Antique and Modern Dolls. (1989)-. English. Irregular. $12.95. Random House Inc., 400 Hahn Road, Westminster MD 21157. **Tel** (800)726-0600, (800)733-3000, FAX (800)659-2436, (410)386-7013. **ED** Julie Collier. **Continues** Official Price Guide to Antique & Modern Dolls.

LC NK805 .O35 ISSN 1050-6144
DD 745.1/075 US
OFFICIAL ... IDENTIFICATION AND PRICE GUIDE TO ANTIQUES AND COLLECTIBLES, THE. [Off. identif. price guide antiq. collect.]. **Added/Corp** House of Collectibles. **VFOAT** Antiques and Collectibles; Antiques. 10th Ed. (1990)-. English. Irregular. $16.90. Random House Inc., 400 Hahn Road, Westminster MD 21157. **Tel** (800)726-0600, (800)733-3000, FAX (800)659-2436, (410)386-7013. **Continues** Official Price Guide to Antiques and Other Collectibles, 0747-5349.

LC NK7492 .O37 ISSN 0743-9571
DD 681.1/13/09730750973 US
OFFICIAL PRICE GUIDE TO ANTIQUE CLOCKS, THE. See Jewelry-Clocks and Watches.

Antiques

LC NK7312 .O35
DD 739.27/075
ISSN 0742-5805
US
OFFICIAL PRICE GUIDE TO ANTIQUE JEWELRY, THE. See Jewelry.

LC NK1068 .O37
DD 745.1/0951/075
ISSN 0747-5365
US
OFFICIAL PRICE GUIDE TO ORIENTAL COLLECTIBLES, THE. See Hobbies.

DD 745
ISSN 1045-8182
US
OLD NEWS IS GOOD NEWS ANTIQUES GAZETTE, THE. [Old news is good news antiq. gaz.]. VFOAT Antiques Gazette. Periodical. English. Twelve times a year. $10.00. Alexander Publishing Company, 4928 Government Street, PO Box 65292, Baton Rouge LA 70896. **Continues** Old News is Good News Gazette.

ISSN 0229-6993
CN
DD 745.1/075/09715
PASTIMES (ARMDALE). (PASTIMES : A PUBLICATION ABOUT ANTIQUES AND COLLECTIBLES OF ATLANTIC CANADA). Vol. 1, No. 1 (June, 1980)-. Periodical. English. Irregular. $4.00 Canada; $6.00 other. Pastimes, PO Box 75, Armdale Nova Scotia B3L 4J7 Canada.

GW
PAULY'S REALENCYCLOPADIE. (19??)-. German. Alfred Druckenmuller Verlag, Postfach 4, Martiusstr 8, W-8 Munich 44 Germany.
Desc: Dealer encyclopedia of the classical studies of antiques.

LC NK805 .P56
DD 745.1/0973/075
US
PICTORIAL PRICE GUIDE TO AMERICAN ANTIQUES AND OBJECTS MADE FOR THE AMERICAN MARKET. (1977)-. Periodical. English. One time a year. New American Library, 120 Woodbine Street, Bergenfield NJ 07621. Tel (201)387-0600.

DD 749.22
ISSN 0953-0800
UK
REGIONAL FURNITURE. [Reg. furnit.]. (1987)-. Periodical. English. One time a year. Regional Furniture Society, Trouthouse, Warrens Cross / Secy, Lechlade Gloucester GL7 3DR United Kingdom. Tel 011 44 1367 252880.
Ind/Abst BHA : Biblio. Hist. Art.

US
RENNINGER'S ANTIQUE GUIDE. (1979)-. Periodical. English. Twenty-six times a year. $12.00. Renningers Antique Guide, PO Box 495, Lafayette Hill PA 19444. Tel (610)828-4614. **Bk Rev**. **Ad Acc**. **Circ:** 60,000. **Continues** Rennigerr's Guide.
Desc: Information on antiques and collectibles, antique shows, etc.

ISSN 0736-5934
US
SUSPENDED
RESTORATION (TUCSON, ARIZ.). See Transportation-Automobiles.

ISSN 0048-8771
US
RUNNING BOARD, THE. See Transportation-Automobiles.

LC WMLC 93/4080
DD 636
ISSN 0889-2970
US
RURAL HERITAGE. [Rural herit.]. Vol. 11, No. 2 (Summer 1986)-. Periodical. English. Six times a year (Jan., March, May, July, Sept., Nov.). $19.00. Rural Heritage, 281 Dean Ridge Lane, Gainesboro TN 38562. Tel (615)268-0655. **ED** Gail Damerow. Index available (bound in May issue). cum. index. **Bk Rev**, (Qty: 30-40). **Ad Acc**. **Circ:** 3,000. **Continues** Evener, 0164-6613.
Desc: Focus on traditional rural skills with emphasis on present day farming with mules, oxen and horses.
Ind/Abst Bibliogr. Agric.

LC NK1125 .S327
DD 745.1/075
US
SCHROEDER'S ANTIQUES PRICE GUIDE. VFOAT Antiques Price Guide. 1st Ed. (1983)-. English. One time a year. $12.95. Collector Books, PO Box 3009, Paducah KY 42002. Tel (502)898-6211, (800)626-5420. **ED** Sharon and Bob Huxford.

LC NK1127 .S55
DD 381/.457451/02574
US
●**SLOAN'S GREEN GUIDE, ANTIQUING IN NEW ENGLAND.** VFOAT Antiquing in New England; Sloan's Antiquing in New England. (1993)-. Periodical. English. Irregular. The Antique Press, 9 Brimmer Street, Boston MA 02114. Tel (617)723-3001. **Continues** Sloan's Green Guide to Antiquing in New England, 1051-6719.

DD 745
ISSN 1051-6719
US
SLOAN'S GREEN GUIDE TO ANTIQUING IN NEW ENGLAND. [Sloan's green guide antiq. N. Engl.]. VFOAT Sloan's Green Guide, Antiquing in New England. (1992)-. English. $14.95. The Antique Press, 9 Brimmer Street, Boston MA 02114. Tel (617)723-3001. **Continues** Sloan's Green Guide to Antiques Dealers. New England, 0898-090X.

US
SOUND WAVES : MONTHLY NEWSLETTER. (19??)-. Newsletter. English. Twelve times a year. Free to major libraries. VRPS Inc, POB 165345, Irving TX 75016. **ED** George J Potter and Ken Deibel. **Bk Rev**. **Ad Acc**. **Circ:** 450.
Desc: Articles, ads, technical reviews, book reviews on antique radio and phonograph collecting.

DD 629.222
ISSN 0846-1333
CN
CEASED
SPORTING CLASSICS (OTTAWA). See Transportation-Automobiles.

DD 338
ISSN 1047-885X
US
STEWART'S GUIDE TO ANTIQUE & COLLECTIBLE SHOPS COVERING LOS ANGELES COUNTY. [Stewart's guide antique collect. shops cover. Los Angel. Cty.]. VFOAT Stewarts' Antique & Collectibles Guide, LA; County Stewarts' Antique and Collectibles Guide, LA County. (1991)-. English. One time a year. $5.95. Stewart Publications, 7510 Sunset Boulevard, Suite 244, Los Angeles CA 90046.

DD 381
ISSN 1053-5918
US
STEWART'S GUIDE TO ANTIQUE & COLLECTIBLES SHOPS. [Stewart's guide antique collect. shops]. VFOAT Stewart's Guide to Antique and Collectibles Shops; Guide to Antique & Collectibles Shops; Antique & Collectibles Shops; Antique and Collectibles Shops. (1990/91)-. English. $6.95. Stewart Publications, 7510 Sunset Boulevard, Suite 244, Los Angeles CA 90046.

DD 790
ISSN 1073-5992
US
●**TOY TRADER (DUBUQUE, IOWA).** See Gifts, Toys.

DD 790
ISSN 0897-814X
US
TREASURE CHEST (NEW YORK, N.Y). (TREASURE CHEST.). [Treasure chest]. (1988)-. Trade Publication. English. Twelve times a year. $25.00. Venture Publishing Company, 212 Broadway, Suite 414, New York NY 10023. Tel (212)496-2234. **ED** Howard Fischer. Index available. **Bk Rev**. **Ad Acc**. **Circ:** 50,000 (ctrl).
Desc: The information source and marketplace for collectors and dealers of antiques and collectibles.

DD 745.1/0971
ISSN 0315-2383
CN
UNITT'S CANADIAN PRICE GUIDE TO ANTIQUES & COLLECTABLES. VFOAT Canadian Price Guide to Antiques and Collectables. (1968)-. Periodical. English. One time a year. 14.36Can$. Fitzhenry & Whiteside, 195 Allstate Parkway, Markham Ontario L3R 4T8 Canada. Tel (800)387-9776, (905)477-9700.

DD 745.1/075/09713
ISSN 0711-0081
CN
UPPER CANADIAN, THE. [Upper Can.]. (Sept./Oct. 1980)-. Periodical. English (French). Six times a year. 18.70Can$. Upper Canadian Company Ltd, PO Box 653, Smiths Falls Ontario K7A AT6 Canada. Tel (613)283-1168. **ED** Bill Dobson. Index available (included). **Bk Rev**, (Qty: 12). **Ad Acc**, **Adv Mgr:** Bill Dobson. **Circ:** 5,000.
Desc: Current trends in Canadian antiques, show coverage, book reviews, price guide, and show listings.

DD 707/.471428
ISSN 0849-0465
CN
VENTES AUX ENCHERES PUBLIQUES. See The Arts-Art.

LC TL506.A1 V55
DD 629.133/34/05
ISSN 0091-6943
US
VINTAGE AIRPLANE, THE. See Aeronautics, Astronautics.

ISSN 0042-9945
GW
WAFFEN- UND KOSTUMKUNDE. (WAFFEN- UND KOSTUMKUNDE : ZEITSCHRIFT DER GESELLSCHAFT FUER HISTORISCHE WAFFEN- UND KOSTUMKUNDE.). [Waffen- Kostumkd.]. VFOAT Zeitschrift der Gesellschaft fur Historische Waffen- und Kostumkun. (1959)-. German (English, French and Italian). Irregular. DM35.00. Verlag Otto Schwartz & Company, Annastrasse 7, D-37075 Goettingen Germany. Tel 011 49 551 31051, 011 49 551 31052, FAX 011 49 551 372812. **ED** Ruth Bleckwenn, Peter Krenn, H U Haedeke. **Bk Rev**. **Circ:** 500. Documents available from The Genuine Article. **Continues** Mitteilungen der Gesellschaft fur Historische Kostum- und Waffenkunde.
Desc: Historical weapons, and historical costumes.
Ind/Abst ARTbibliogr. Mod. (19??-) ; Arts Humanit. Citation Index (19??-) [Full Cov.] ; BHA : Biblio. Hist. Art (19??-) ; Curr. Contents Arts Humanit. (19??-) ; Res. Alert (19??-) [Full Cov.].

LC NK1133 .W33
DD 745.1/075
ISSN 1076-1985
US
●**WARMAN'S ANTIQUES AND COLLECTIBLES PRICE GUIDE.** [Warman's antiq. collect. price guide]. VFOAT Antiques and Collectibles Price Guide. 28th Ed. (1994)-. English. Irregular. $14.95 per copy. Chilton Book Company, 1 Chilton Way, Radnor PA 19089. Tel (610)964-4000, (800)695-1214, FAX (215)964-4273, telex 6851035 CHILTON UW. **Continues** Warman's Antiques and their Prices, 0196-2272.

LC NK1133 .W33
DD 745.1/075
ISSN 0196-2272
US
TITLE CHANGE
WARMAN'S ANTIQUES AND THEIR PRICES. VFOAT Antiques and Their Prices. (1976)-(1993). English. Warman Publishing Company, PO Box 1112, Willow Grove PA 19090-0703. Tel (215)657-1812. **Continues** Warman's Antiques and Their Current Prices. **Continued by** Warman's Antiques and Collectibles Price Guide, 1076-1985.

LC NK
DD 745.13
ISSN 0043-261X
GW
WELTKUNST, DIE. See The Arts-Art.

LC NX
DD 381/.45/7451025712
ISSN 0705-310X
CN
WESTERN CANADIAN ANTIQUE & ART DEALERS YEARBOOK. VAT Western Canadian Antique and Art Dealers Yearbooks. (1976)-. English. One time a year. $1.25 per no. Left Bank Publications, 148 East 1st Avenue, Vancouver BC V5T 1A4. **Formed by the union of** B.C. Antique Dealers Yearbook **and** 'Where-to-Find' on B.C. Art Dealers, 0714-8968.

LC NK1127 .W47
DD 745.1/025/73
ISSN 1043-8173
US
WHO'S WHO IN COLLECTIBLES AND ANTIQUES. [Who's who collect. antiq.]. VFOAT Who's Who in Collecting and Antiques. 1st Ed. (1989)-. Periodical. English. One time a year. $4.95. Collectors Connection and Registry, PO Box 54, South San Francisco CA 94083-0054.

LC NK1127 .E66
DD 381/.45/745102573
ISSN 0192-8821
US
Y-NOT ANTIQUE & FLEA MARKET DIRECTORY, THE. VAT Y-Not Antique and Flea Market Directory; Why-Not Antique and Flea Market Directory. Directory. English. One time a year. $3.00. Flea Market Directory, PO Box 8561, Fort Lauderdale FL 33310.

ISSN 0194-9349
US
YESTERYEAR (PRINCETON). (YESTERYEAR.). (19??)-. Periodical. English. Twelve times a year. $17.00. Yesteryear, PO Box 2, Princeton WI 54968. Tel (414)787-4808. **ED** Michael Jacobi. **Bk Rev**, (Qty: 60). **Ad Acc**. **Circ:** 8,000 (ctrl).
Desc: Antique and collectible news for the Northcentral states. Question and answer columns, features, photos and extensive calendar of upcoming events.

ABSTRACTING, BIBLIOGRAPHIES AND STATISTICS

LC Z1000 .B74
DD 018/.4
NLM Z 1000.5 B724
ISSN 0068-0141
US
BOOKMAN'S PRICE INDEX. [Bookman's price index]. **Added/Corp** Gale Research Company. VFOAT BPI. Vol. 1, (1964)-. English. Two times a year. $230.00. Gale Research Inc., 835 Penobscot Building, 645 Griswold Street, Detroit MI 48226. Tel (800)877-GALE, (313)961-2242, FAX (313)961-6083, (800)414-5043, telex TWX 810-221-7086. **ED** Anne McGrath.
Desc: Consolidates descriptions found in catalogs of American and foreign antiquarian dealers. Entries provide price, author, title, publication date and place, condition, and dealer.

ARCHAEOLOGY

ISSN 0747-9646
DD 930
US
A.S.A. BULLETIN (REDLANDS, CALIF.). (A.S.A. BULLETIN.). [A.S.A. bull.]. **Main/Corp** Archaeological Survey Association of Southern California. **Added/Corp** Archaeological Survey Association of Southern California. **VFOAT** Special Bulletin; ASA Bulletin. **VAT** Archaeological Survey Association Bulletin. (19??)-. Bulletin. English. Four times a year. comes with membership. Archaeological Survey Association of Southern California Inc., San Bernardino County Museum, 2024 Orange Tree Lane, Redlands CA 92374. **Tel** (714)798-8570. **ED** Michelle Baty. **Continues** ASA Newsletter; **Absorbed** ASA Journal.
Desc: Promotes responsible archaeology.

LC DL1 .N6
DK
AARBGER FOR NORDISK OLDKYNDIGHED OG HISTORIE / UDGIVNE AF DET KONGELIGE NORDISKE OLDSKRIFT-SELSKAB. See History-History of Europe.

ISSN 0417-2442
DD 939
GW
ABHANDLUNGEN DER DEUTSCHEN ORIENT-GESELLSCHAFT. Main/Corp Deutsche Orient-Gesellschaft. **Added/Corp** Deutsche Orient-Gesellschaft. No. 1 (1956)-. Monographic series. German. Irregular. Price varies per volume. Gebrueder Mann Verlag, Lindenstrasse 76, D-10969 Berlin Germany. **Tel** 011 49 30 25913589, telex 183723. **(Subscription address:** Gebrueder Mann Verlag / KNO, Postfach 800620, Koch, Neff & Oetinger, D-70506 Stuttgart Germany. **Tel** 011 49 711 78992022.) Index available. **Circ:** 500.
Desc: Accounts of digs by the German Orient Society.

LC DS61
ISSN 0418-9728
DD 956
GW
ABHANDLUNGEN. ISLAMISCHE REIHE. [Abh. Dtsch. Archaol. Inst. Kairo, Islam. Reihe]. **Main/Corp** Deutsches Archaologisches Institut. Abteilung Kairo. **VFOAT** Islamische Reihe. Vol. 1 (1959)-. Periodical. German. J J Augustin Inc, PO Box 311, Locust Valley NY 11560. **Tel** (516)676-1510.
Ind/Abst Avery Index Archit. Period. Suppl. Colum. Univ. (19??-199?).

ISSN 0417-3341
GW
ABHANDLUNGEN. KOPTISCHE REIHE. [Abh. Dtsch. Archaol. Inst. Kairo, Kopt. Reihe]. **Main/Corp** Deutsches Archaologisches Institut. Abteilung Kairo. Vol. 1 (1962)-. Periodical. German. Deutsches Archaologisches Institut, Wiesbaden Germany.
Ind/Abst Avery Index Archit. Period. Suppl. Colum. Univ.

ISSN 0743-4251
US
ABSTRACTS IN MARYLAND ARCHAEOLOGY. [Abstr. Md. Archeol.]. **Added/Corp** Council for Maryland Archeology. Vol. 1, No. 1 (Jan. 1983)-. English. Two times a year. $6.00 (includes membership). Council for Maryland Archeology, 100 Community Place, Room 3-209, Crownsville MD 21032-2023. **Tel** (410)514-7665, FAX (410)987-4071. **ED** James D. Sorenson. **Bk Rev. Ad Acc. Circ:** 100 (ctrl).
Desc: Includes descriptive summaries of recent reports, articles, and other publications relating to Maryland archaeology.

LC N1.A1 A25
ISSN 0065-0900
DD 709
IT
ACTA AD ARCHAEOLOGIAM ET ARTIUM HISTORIAM PERTINENTIA. See The Arts-Art.

LC CC1 .A2
ISSN 0065-101X
DD 913.05
DK
CCC
ACTA ARCHAEOLOGICA. [Acta archaeol.]. Vol. 1 (1930)-. English (French and German). One time a year. $100.74. Munksgaard International Publishers Ltd, PO Box 2148, DK-1016 Copenhagen K Denmark. **Tel** 011 45 33 127030, FAX 011 45 33 129431 MUNKS DK. **ED** Klavs Randsborg. Index available. **Circ:** 500 (ctrl).
Desc: Archaeology, anthropology and history.
Ind/Abst Anthropol. Index; Anthropol. Lit.; Avery Index Archit. Period. Suppl. Colum. Univ. (19??-199?); BHA : Biblio. Hist. Art; Br. Archeol. Bibliogr.; Numis. Lit.

LC DB920 .A15
ISSN 0001-5210
HU
CCC
CODEN ACGCBJ
ACTA ARCHAEOLOGICA ACADEMIAE SCIENTIARUM HUNGARICAE. [Acta archaeol. Acad. Sci. Hung.]. **Added/Corp** Magyar Tudomanyos Akademia. Vol. 1, Issue No. 1/2 (1951)-. Academic Scholarly Publication. Hungarian (English, Russian, French and German). Four times a year. $128.00. Akademiai Kiado, Publishing House of the Hungarian Academy of Sciences, Prielle Kornelia u. 19-35, H-1117 Budapest Hungary. **Tel** 011 36 1 1811991, FAX 011 36 1 1811991, telex 22-6228 AKNYO H. **ED** Denes Gabler (editor's address: Acta Archaeologica, H-1014 Budapest, Uri u 49, Hungary). Index available. cum. index. **Bk Rev. Ad Acc. Circ:** 900. Documents available from BIOSIS Document Express.
Desc: Devoted to the results achieved by Hungarian archaeologists. It covers studies of the most important excavations, finds and problems of the period from the Paleolithic to the Middle Ages. It contains, further, short papers on individual finds, comprehensive reports on the single fields of research, as well.
Ind/Abst Anthropol. Lit.; BHA : Biblio. Hist. Art; Biol. Abstr.; Br. Archeol. Bibliogr.; GeoRef; Numis. Lit.

LC DB350 .A22
ISSN 0001-5229
PL
ACTA ARCHAEOLOGICA CARPATHICA. [Acta archaeol. Carpath.]. **Added/Corp** Polska Akademia Nauk. Oddzial w Krakowie. Polska Akademia Nauk. Oddzial w Krakowie. Komisja Archeologiczna. Vol. 1 (1958)-. Academic Scholarly Publication. Polish (summaries and/or abstracts in French, English, German and Polish; table of contents in French and Russian). One time a year. $18.00. Polska Akademia Nauk, Oddzial w Krakowie / Komisja Archeologiczna, Ul. Slawkowska 17, 31-016 Krakow Poland. **Tel** 011 48 12 224853, FAX 011 48 12 222791. **(Subscription address:** Ars Polona-Ruch, PO Box 1001, Krakowskie Przedmiescie 7, 00-068 Warsaw Poland. **Tel** 011 48 22 261201.) cum. index.
Desc: Covers early Middle Ages and prehistory of the Carpathian countries; also mountain archaeology.
Ind/Abst Anthropol. Lit.; BHA : Biblio. Hist. Art; Br. Archeol. Bibliogr. (?-?); GeoRef; Numis. Lit.

ISSN 0065-0986
PL
ACTA ARCHAEOLOGICA LODZIENSIA. 11 (1962)-. Monographic series. Polish. One time a year. Price varies per volume. Lodzkie Towarzystwo Naukowe / Lodz Scientific Society, Ul. Piotrowska 179, 90-447 Lodz Poland. **Tel** 011 48 42 361026, FAX 011 48 42 362415. **(Subscription address:** Ars Polona-Ruch, PO Box 1001, Krakowskie Przedmiescie 7, 00-068 Warsaw Poland. **Tel** 011 48 22 261201.) **Continues** Acta Archaeologica Universitatis Lodziensis.
Ind/Abst Numis. Lit.

ISSN 0776-2984
BE
UDC 378 :930
ACTA ARCHAEOLOGICA LOVANIENSIA. [Acta archaeol. lovan.]. (1969)-. Periodical. Dutch. One time a year. Editions Peeters SA, Bondgenotenlaan 153, BP 41, B-3000 Leuven Belgium. **Tel** 011 32 16 235170, FAX 011 32 16 228500, telex 65987 PUL B.
Ind/Abst Anthropol. Lit.; BHA : Biblio. Hist. Art; Numis. Lit.

LC D111 .A3
ISSN 0212-2960
DD 940.1/05
SP
ACTA HISTORICA ET ARCHAEOLOGICA MEDIAEVALIA / DEPARTAMENTO DE HISTORIA MEDIEVAL, INSTITUTO DE HISTORIA MEDIEVAL. Added/Corp Universidad de Barcelona. Departamento de Historia Medieval. Universidad de Barcelona. Instituto de Historia Medieval. **VFOAT** Acta Mediaevalia. Vol. 1, No. 1 (1980)-. Periodical. Catalan (Spanish, French, Italian and English). One time a year. 2500ptas. Universidad de Barcelona, Departamento de Historia Medieval, Paleografia y Diplomatica, Facultad de Geografia e Historia, Torre B, Planta 6A, 08028 Barcelona Spain. **Tel** 011 34 3 3184266, FAX 011 34 3 4498510. **(Subscription address:** Universidad de Barcelona, Edificio Central, Avenida Cortes Catalanas, 585, 08007 Barcelona Spain.) **ED** Manuel Riu and Salvador Claramunt. **Bk Rev. Ad Acc. Circ:** 1,000.

LC CC1
GW
ACTA PRAEHISTORICA ET ARCHAEOLOGICA. No. 1 (1970)-. English (French and German). One time a year. Potsdamer Str 199, W-1000 Berlin 30 Germany. **Continues in part** Berliner Jahrbuch fur Vor und Fruhgeschichte.
Ind/Abst Anthropol. Lit.; Numis. Lit.

LC DK4088 .A28
ISSN 0208-6034
PL
ACTA UNIVERSITATIS LODZIENSIS. FOLIA ARCHAEOLOGICA. Added/Corp Uniwersytet Lodzki. **VFOAT** Folia Archaeologica. (1980)-. Monographic series. Polish (summaries and/or abstracts in English and German). Irregular. Price varies per volume. Wydawnictwo Uniwersytetu Lodzkiego, Ul. Jaracza 34, Lodz Poland. **Tel** 011 48 42 331671, 011 48 42 336541. **(Subscription address:** Ars Polona-Ruch, PO Box 1001, Krakowskie Przedmiescie 7, 00-068 Warsaw Poland. **Tel** 011 48 22 261201.) **Continues in part** Acta Universitatis Lodziensis. Seria I, Nauki Humanistyczno-Spoleczne, 0137-4591.
Ind/Abst Anthropol. Lit.

ISSN 0137-6616
PL
UDC 903
CODEN 902
ACTA UNIVERSITATIS NICOLAI COPERNICI. NAUKI HUMANISTYCZNO-SPOLECZNE. ARCHEOLOGIA. (1974)-. Monographic series. Multiple languages. Irregular. Price varies per volume. Uniwersytet Mikolaja Kopernika, Biblioteka Uniwersytecka, Ul. Gagarina 13, 87-100 Torun Poland. **Tel** 011 48 56 23352.
Ind/Abst Anthropol. Lit.

LC PA3339 .A4
ISSN 0001-9046
IT
AEGYPTUS. [Aegyptus]. **Added/Corp** R. Accademia Scientifico-Letteraria (Milan, Italy). Scuola Papirologica. Universita Cattolica del Sacro Cuore. Scuola di Papirologia. Vol. 1 (Jan. 1920)-. Periodical. Italian (English, German and French). Two times a year. L186000. Vita e Pensiero Publlic University, Largo Gemelli 1, 20123 Milan Italy. **Tel** 011 39 2 72342310, 011 39 2 72342370. **Supersedes in part** R. Accademia Scientifico-Letteraria (Milan, Italy). Scuola Papirologica. Pubblicazioni.
Ind/Abst BHA : Biblio. Hist. Art; MLA Int. Bibl. Books Artic. Mod. Lang. Lit.; New Testam. Abstr.; Numis. Lit.; Old Testam. Abstr.

LC DA670.E13 A37
ISSN 0140-9220
DD 930.1/028
UK
SUSPENDED
AERIAL ARCHAEOLOGY. Added/Corp Aerial Archaeology Foundation (Great Britain) Committee for Archaeological Air Photography (Anglian Region). Vol. 1 (1977)-Suspended (1995). Periodical. English. Irregular. Aerial Archaeology Publication, 15 Colin McLean Road, Norfolk NR19 2RY United Kingdom.

LC DT251 .A45
DD 930
TI
AFRICA (TUNIS). (AFRICA / INSTITUT NATIONAL D'ARCHEOLOGIE ET D'ART.). **Added/Corp** Mahad al-Qawmi Lil-Athar Wa-al-Funun bi-Tunis. **VFOAT** Afriqiyah. (1966)-. Periodical. English (Arabic and French). Institut National d'Archeologie et d'Art.Fashion Newsletter, Tunisia.
Ind/Abst BHA : Biblio. Hist. Art.

ISSN 1060-0671
DD 301
US
AFRICAN-AMERICAN ARCHAEOLOGY. (AFRICAN-AMERICAN ARCHAEOLOGY : NEWSLETTER OF THE AFRICAN-AMERICAN ARCHAEOLOGY NETWORK.). [Afr.-Am. archaeol.]. **Added/Corp** African-American Archaeology Network. National Museum of Natural History (U.S.). Dept. of Anthropology. **VFOAT** African American Archaeology. No. 1 (Spring 1990)-. Newsletter. English. Three times a year. Free on request. Smithsonian Institution Press, 470 L'Enfant Plaza, Suite 7100, Washington DC 20560. **Tel** (202)287-3738, (800)782-4612, FAX (202)287-3184. **(Subscription address:** Smithsonian Institute, Department of Anthropology, Washington DC 20560.)

LC DT13 .A35
ISSN 0263-0338
DD 960/.1/05
UK
AFRICAN ARCHAEOLOGICAL REVIEW, THE. Vol. 1 (1983)-. Periodical. English. Four times a year. $100.00. Plenum Press, 233 Spring Street, New York NY 10013-1578. **Tel** (212)620-8000, (800)221-9369, FAX (212)463-0742, (212)807-1047, telex 23/421139. **ED** David Phillipson. **Bk Rev. Ad Acc. Circ:** 300. available on microfilm from University Microfilms International (UMI).
Desc: An international annual publication covering the archaeology of Africa and neighboring islands. The emphasis is on new data from the field and studies of wider than regional significance. Includes articles, reports on research in progress, review articles on major new publications, annotated bibliographies, brief editorial comment and a list of publications received.
Ind/Abst Abstr. Anthropol.; Anthropol. Lit.; Ethnoarts Index; Geogr. Abstr. Phys. Geogr.; Geogr. Abstr. Human Geogr.; Geol. Abstr.

ISSN 0309-0051
UK
TITLE CHANGE
AIA BULLETIN. Added/Corp Association for Industrial Archaeology. **VFOAT** Bulletin. **VAT** Association for Industrial Archaeology Bulletin. (19??)-(19??). Bulletin. English. Association for Industrial Archaeology, Wharfage Ironbridge Telford, Shropshire TF8 7AW United Kingdom. **Tel** 011 44 1952 433522. **Continued by** Industrial Archaeology News.

LC DK445

FI

AIKAKAUSKIRJA. **Main/Corp** Suomen Muinaismuistoyhdistys. **VFOAT** Tidskrift. 1- 1874-. Finnish (Swedish, German, English and French). cum. index.

LC F1076.9 .A57 **ISSN** 0701-1776
DD 971.23/01/05 CN

ALBERTA ARCHAEOLOGICAL REVIEW, THE. **Added/Corp** Archaeological Society of Alberta. No. 1 (Mar. 1977)-. Periodical. English. Two times a year (Spring and Fall). 12.00Can$. Alberta Archaeological Review, 314-4516 Valiant Drive Northwest, Galgary Alta T3A OY1 Canada. **Tel** (403)288-1837. **ED** Michael Wilson. **Bk Rev**, (Qty: varies). **Circ:** 350. ***Continues*** *Newsletter (Archaeological Society of Alberta).*
Desc: Review of Archaeological Report by the professionals and vocational archaeologists in Alberta.
Ind/Abst Am. Hist. Life (1985-); Anthropol. Index; Ethnoarts Index.

LC GN836.C3 A65

AU
TITLE CHANGE

ALMOGAREN. **Added/Corp** Kanareninstitut. Gesellschaft fuer Interdisziplinare Saharaforschung. (1970)-(19??). English (summaries and/or abstracts in French and Spanish). Dr Hans Biedermann, Leechgasse 2, A-8010 Graz Austria. ***Continued by*** *Institutum Canarium Yearbook. Alamogaren.*

LC DD801.T46 A7 **ISSN** 0065-6585
GW

ALT-THURINGEN. **See** History-History of Europe.

LC CC1 .A58 **ISSN** 0363-969X
DD 930/.1 US

AMATEUR ARCHAEOLOGIST. Vol. 1 Issue 1 (July 1976)-. Periodical. English. Four times a year. $6.50 (institutions); $8.50 (individuals). Amateur Archaeologist, 3261 Guail Avenue N, Golden Valley NM 55422.

LC E51 .A52 **ISSN** 0002-7316
US
CCC
CODEN AANTAM

Pr Rev.

AMERICAN ANTIQUITY; A QUARTERLY REVIEW OF AMERICAN ARCHAEOLOGY. [Am. antiq.]. **Added/Corp** Society for American Archaeology. Vol. 1, No. 1 (July 1935)-. Periodical. English. Four times a year. $150.00. Society for American Archaeology, 900 Second Street NE, Suite 12, Washington DC 20002. **Tel** (202)789-8200, FAX (202)789-0284. **(Subscription address:** Society for American Archaology, Department 0123, Washington DC 20073. **Tel** (202)789-8200.) **ED** J. Jefferson Reid. Index available. cum. index. **Bk Rev**. **Ad Acc**. **Acid Free. Circ:** 6,000 (ctrl). available on microfilm and microfiche from University Microfilms International (UMI). Documents available from The Genuine Article, UMI Article Clearinghouse.
Desc: Covers the archaeology of the Western Hemisphere. Complementing the several theoretical papers per issue are a number of shorter reports treating artifact analysis, dating and reports of excavations. Includes detailed obituaries and a regular column on current research.
Ind/Abst ASTIS Curr. Aware. Bull. (1978-); Abstr. Anthropol.; Acad. Search; Am. Hist. Life (1969-1971),(1982-); Anthropol. Index; Anthropol. Lit.; Art Archaeol. Tech. Abstr.; Art Index; Arts Humanit. Citation Index [Full Cov.]; ASTIS Bibliogr. (1978-); Book Rev. Index; Ceram. Abstr.; Curr. Cit.; Curr. Contents Arts Humanit.; Curr. Contents Soc. Behav. Sci.; Curr. Geogr. Publ. (199?-); EP Collect.; Ethnoarts Index; Expand. Acad. Index (1987-); Geogr. Abstr. Human Geogr.; GeoRef; Hisp. Am. Period. Index, HAPI; Hist. Source (July 1993-); Homework Help.; Humanit. Index; Humanit. Source; INFO-SOUTH Abstr.; Mag. Search; MasterFile FullTEXT 1000; MasterFile FullTEXT 350; MasterFile FullTEXT 650; MasterFile FullTEXT (July 1993-); Middle East Abstr. Index; Newsp. Period. Abstr. (1991-); OCLC; Res. Alert [Full Cov.]; Soc. Sci. Cit. Index [Full Cov.]; SportSearch; Telebase.

LC F
DD 970 US

AMERICAN ARCHEOLOGIST, THE. (THE AMERICAN ARCHEOLOGIST : "A QUARTERLY JOURNAL OF THE PREHISTORY OF THE UNITED STATES".). Vol. 1 (Summer 1974)-. Periodical. English. Four times a year. Popular Archeology, Arlington VA.

ISSN 0740-8358
US
SUSPENDED

AMERICAN ARCHEOLOGY. [Am. archeol.]. (198?)-Suspended with Vol. 7, No. 2 (19??). Periodical. English. Three times a year. Atechiston Inc., 81 West Mountain Road, Ridgefield CT 06877. **Tel** (203)431-6819. **ED** Michael J. O'Brien. **Bk Rev**. ***Absorbed*** *Contract Abstracts and CRM Archeology.*
Ind/Abst Am. Hist. Life (1985-); Anthropol. Lit.

US

AMERICAN BOTTOM ARCHAEOLOGY : FAI-270 SITE REPORTS. **Added/Corp** Illinois. Dept. of Transportation. United States. Federal Highway Administration. United States. National Park Service. Illinois Archaeological Survey. **VFOAT** FAI-270 Site Reports. Vol. 1 (1983)-. Monographic series. English. Irregular. Price varies per volume. University of Illinois Press, 1325 South Oak Street, Champaign IL 61820. **Tel** (217)333-0950, FAX (217)244-8082. **(Subscription address:** University of Illinois Press, PO Box 4856, Hampden Station, Baltimore MD 21211. **Tel** (800)545-4703.) **ED** Charles J. Bareis and James W. Porter.

LC CC1 .A6 **ISSN** 0002-9114
DD 930 US

AMERICAN JOURNAL OF ARCHAEOLOGY. (AMERICAN JOURNAL OF ARCHAEOLOGY : THE JOURNAL OF THE ARCHAEOLOGICAL INSTITUTE OF AMERICA.). [Am. j. archaeol.]. **Added/Corp** Archaeological Institute of America. American School of Classical Studies at Athens. American School of Classical Studies in Rome. American School for Oriental Study and Research in Palestine. Vol. 1 No. 1 (1897)-. Academic Scholarly Publication. English. Four times a year. $120.00. Archaeological Institute of America, Boston University, 675 Commonwealth Avenue, Boston MA 02215-1401. **Tel** (617)353-9361, FAX (617)353-6550. **ED** Fred S. Kleiner. Index available (bound in last issue). cum. index. **Bk Rev**. **Circ:** 3,400 (ctrl). available on microfilm and microfiche from University Microfilms International (UMI). Documents available from The Genuine Article, UMI Article Clearinghouse. ***Continues*** *American Journal of Archaeology and of the History of the Fine Arts.* ***Continued in part by*** *Bulletin of the Archaeological Institute of America.*
Desc: Scholarly articles dealing with Mediterranean archaeology, art, architecture, literature, and history from prehistoric times to the late antique.
Ind/Abst Acad. Ind. [Computer File] (1992-); Acad. Search; Anthropol. Index; Anthropol. Lit.; Art Index; Arts Humanit. Citation Index [Full Cov.]; Avery Index Archit. Period. Suppl. Colum. Univ. (1990-1992); BHA : Biblio. Hist. Art; Book Rev. Index; Br. Archaeol. Bibliogr.; Ceram. Abstr.; Curr. Contents Arts Humanit.; Curr. Contents Soc. Behav. Sci.; EP Collect.; Expand. Acad. Index (1989-); Hist. Source (July 1993-); Homework Help.; Humanit. Index; Humanit. Source; Index Book Rev. Relig.; INFO-SOUTH Abstr.; Mag. Search; MasterFile FullTEXT 1000; MasterFile FullTEXT 350; MasterFile FullTEXT 650; MasterFile FullTEXT (July 1993-); Middle East Abstr. Index; New Testam. Abstr.; Newsp. Period. Abstr. (1989-); Numis. Lit.; OCLC; Old Testam. Abstr.; Relig. Index One Period.; Res. Alert [Full Cov.]; Soc. Sci. Cit. Index [Full Cov.]; Soc. Sci. Index; SportSearch; Telebase.

ISSN 0778-4287
BE

UDC 930.26(493)

AMPHORA BRAINE-L'ALLEUD. [Amphora Braine-l'Alleud]. (1983)-. Periodical. French. Four times a year. ***Continues*** *Bulletin du Club Archeologique Amphora, 0770-5182.*
Ind/Abst Numis. Lit.

ISSN 0066-1392
DD 930 DK

ANALECTA ROMANA INSTITUTI DANICI. [Analecta Rom. Inst. Dan.]. **Added/Corp** Danske selskab (Copenhagen, Denmark). **VFOAT** Analecta Romana. (1960)-. Monographic series. English (French and Italian). Irregular. Price varies per volume. L'Erma di Bretschneider SPA, via Cassiodoro 19, 00193 Rome Italy. **Tel** 011 39 6 6874127, 011 39 6 6874129, FAX 011 39 6 6874129.
Desc: Presents contributions within the fields of classical and medieval archaeology.
Ind/Abst Avery Index Archit. Period. Suppl. Colum. Univ. (19??-199?); BHA : Biblio. Hist. Art.

ISSN 0066-1406
DK

ANALECTA ROMANA INSTITUTI DANICI. SUPPLEMENTUM. [Analecta rom. inst. dan., Suppl.]. (1960)-. Monographic series. Multiple languages (Danish, English, French, German and Italian). Irregular. Price varies per volume. L'Erma di Bretschneider SPA, via Cassiodoro 19, 00193 Rome Italy. **Tel** 011 39 6 6874127, 011 39 6 6874129, FAX 011 39 6 6874129.
Desc: Presents contributions within the fields of classical and medieval archaeology.
Ind/Abst Avery Index Archit. Period. Suppl. Colum. Univ. (19??-199?).

ISSN 0325-0288
DD 970.1 AG

ANALES DE ARQUEOLOGIA Y ETNOLOGIA . [An. arqueol. etnol.]. Vol. 8 (1947)-. Spanish. One time a year. Centro Universitario, 5550 Casilla Correo 345, Mendoza Argentina. ***Continues*** *Anales del Instituto de Etnologia Americana.*
Ind/Abst Am. Hist. Life (1961-1971); Anthropol. Index; Anthropol. Lit.; Ethnoarts Index.

ISSN 0213-5663
SP

ANALES DE PREHISTORIA Y ARQUEOLOGIA. [An. prehist. arqueol.]. **Added/Corp** Universidad de Murcia. Secretariado de Publicaciones e Intercambio Cientifico. (1985)-. Periodical. Spanish. Price varies. Universidad de Murcia, Apartado 4021, 30380 Murcia Spain. **Tel** 011 34 68 363013, 011 34 68 363014.
Ind/Abst Anthropol. Lit.

LC DS56 .A66 **ISSN** 0066-1546
DD 956.1/005 UK

ANATOLIAN STUDIES. [Anatol. stud.]. **Added/Corp** British Institute of Archaeology at Ankara. Vol. 1 (1951)-. English (German and French). One time a year (Dec.). $54.76. British Institute of Archaeology at Ankara, 31-34 Gordon Square, London WC1H 0PY United Kingdom. **Tel** 011 44 171 3882361, FAX 011 44 171 3882361. **ED** O. R. Gurney. Index available. cum. index. **Ad Acc**. **Circ:** 850 (ctrl).
Desc: All aspects of Turkish archaeology and ancillary subjects. Also discusses archaeology of neighboring areas.
Ind/Abst Art Archaeol. Tech. Abstr.; Avery Index Archit. Period. Suppl. Colum. Univ. (19??-199?); BHA : Biblio. Hist. Art; Middle East Abstr. Index; Numis. Lit.

ISSN 0929-077X
NE

•ANCIENT CIVILIZATIONS FROM SCYTHIA TO SIBERIA. **See** History-History of Europe.

LC F1435 .A24 **ISSN** 0956-5361
DD 940 US
CCC
CODEN ANMSE7

ANCIENT MESOAMERICA. Vol. 1, No. 1 (Spring 1990)-. Academic Scholarly Publication. English (summaries and/or abstracts in Spanish). Two times a year (April and October). $119.00. Cambridge University Press / New York, 40 West 20th Street, New York NY 10011-4211. **Tel** (212)924-3900, (800)221-4512, FAX (212)691-3239. **(Subscription address:** Cambridge University Press / Outside of North America, United Kingdom. **Tel** 011 44 223 312 393, FAX 011 44 223 325 959.) **ED** William H. Fowler, Jr. and Stephen D. Houston. available on microfilm and microfiche from University Microfilms International (UMI).
Desc: An international forum for the method, theory, substance and interpretation of Mesoamerican archaeology, art history and ethnohistory.
Ind/Abst Anthropol. Lit.; Ethnoarts Index; Geogr. Abstr. Human Geogr.; Hisp. Am. Period. Index, HAPI (199?-).

ISSN 0735-1348
UK

Pr Rev.

ANCIENT TL. [Anc. TL]. **Added/Corp** TL Laboratory (Durham, England). **VAT** Ancient Thermoluminescence. No. 1 (Autumn 1977)-. Periodical. English. Three times a year (Mar., July, Oct.). $15.93 (individuals); $23.90 (institutions). Durham University, TL Laboratory, Archaeology II, TL Laboratory, Woodside Building, South Road, Durham DH1 3LE United Kingdom. **Tel** 011 44 191 3743624, FAX 011 44 191 3743741, telex 537351. **ED** I. K. Bailiff. Index available. **Ad Acc**. **Circ:** 150 (ctrl). available on diskette (Apple Macintosh).
Desc: For scientists engaged in the application of thermoluminescence and ESR dating techniques in archaeology and geology. Includes short research papers and date lists.
Ind/Abst Br. Archaeol. Bibliogr.

LC DE1 .A375 **ISSN** 0160-9645
DD 930/.005 US
Pr Rev.

ANCIENT WORLD, THE. [Anc. world]. Vol. 1, (Mar. 1978)-. Academic Scholarly Publication. English (Latin and Greek, Modern). Two times a year (June, Dec.). $30.00. Ares Publishers Inc., 7406 North Sheridan Road, Chicago IL 60626. **Tel** (312)743-1405. **ED** T. Miller, (phone: (312)743-1907). cum. index (After Vol. 25). **Bk Rev**, (Qty: 4-12). **Ad Acc**, **Adv Mgr:** J. Remer, **Tel** (312)743-1907. **Circ:** 1,000 (ctrl). Documents available from The Genuine Article.
Desc: A scholarly journal forming a current-research library on the history and archaeology of the ancient world with special thematic issues. Emphasis on new discoveries.
Ind/Abst Arts Humanit. Citation Index (19??-19??) [Full Cov.]; Curr. Contents Arts Humanit.; Middle East Abstr. Index; Old Testam. Abstr.; Res. Alert [Full Cov.].

LC F2229 .A565 **ISSN** 1055-8756
DD 980/.01/05 US

ANDEAN PAST. [Andean past]. **Added/Corp** Cornell University. Latin American Studies Program. Vol. 1 (1987)-. Monographic series. English. Irregular. Price varies per volume. Latin American Studies, Cornell University, 190 Uris Hall, Ithaca NY 14853. **Tel** (607)255-2080.
Ind/Abst Anthropol. Lit.; Ethnoarts Index.

LC DS485.A55 A684 **ISSN** 0258-0373
DD 934 II

Archaeology

ANDHRA PRADESH JOURNAL OF ARCHAEOLOGY, THE. [Andhra Pradesh j. archaeol.]. **Added/Corp** Andhra Pradesh (India). Director of Archaeology and Museums. (1979)-. Periodical. English.
Ind/Abst Anthropol. Lit.; Avery Index Archit. Period. Suppl. Colum. Univ. (19??-199?).

LC DA155 .A65   ISSN 0264-5254
DD 941.01/05   UK

ANGLO-SAXON STUDIES IN ARCHAEOLOGY AND HISTORY. See History-History of Europe.

LC Q60 .H53   ISSN 0066-2011
   FI

ANNALES ACADEMIAE SCIENTIARUM FENNICAE. SERIES B. (SUOMALAISEN TIEDEAKATEMIAN TOIMITUKSIA. SARJA B; ANNALES ACADEMI SCIENTIARUM FENNIC. SER. B.). [Ann. Acad. Sci. Fenn., Ser. B]. **Main/Corp** Suomalainen Tiedeakatemia. **Added/Corp** Suomalainen Tiedeakatemia. Annales Academiae Scientiarum Fennicae. Ser. B. **VFOAT** Suomalainen Tiedeakatemia. Annales Academiae Scientiarum Fennicae. Series B. (1909)-. Multiple languages (English, German and French). Suomalainen Tiedeakatemia / Academia Scientiarum Fennica, Mariankatu 5, SF-00170 Helsinki Finland. cum. index.
Ind/Abst MLA Int. Bibl. Books Artic. Mod. Lang. Lit.; Soc. Plann. Policy Dev. Abstr.

LC DS94.5 .A75   ISSN 0570-1554
   SY

ANNALES ARCHEOLOGIQUES ARABES SYRIENNES. Added/Corp Syria. Mudiriyah al-Ammah lil-Athar Wa-al-Matahif. **VFOAT** Hawliyat al-AtharAiyah al-Arabiyah al-Suriyah; Majallat al-Hawliyat al-Athariyah al-Suriyah. Vol. 16, No. 1 (1966)-. Monographic series. French (Arabic, English and German). One time a year. Price varies per volume. Direction General Antiquites et des Musees, Rep Arabe Syrien, Damascus Syria. **Tel** 011 963 11 214855, telex 412491. **Bk Rev**. **Circ**: 1,000. Continues Annales Archeologiques de Syrie, 0570-1554.
Desc: Reports of current excavations covering Neolithic and Early, Middle and Late Bronze periods. Includes the Iron Age and the Hellinistic, Roman Byzantine and Islamic periods reports on restoration of historic monuments and sites in Syria.
Ind/Abst Anthropol. Lit.; BHA : Biblio. Hist. Art.

LC DH801.N2 S6
DD 949.3/4   BE

ANNALES DE LA SOCIETE ARCHEOLOGIQUE DE NAMUR. Main/Corp Societe Archeologique de Namur. (1849)-. French. One time a year. Free on request. Societe Archeologique de Namur, 24 rue de Fer, 5000 Namur Belgium. **Tel** 011 32 81 224362.
Ind/Abst BHA : Biblio. Hist. Art; Numis. Lit.

LC CC   ISSN 0373-7039
DD 930.1   FR
UDC 57

ANNALES DE LA SOCIETE DES SCIENCES NATURELLES ET D'ARCHEOLOGIE DE TOULON ET DU VAR. See Natural History.

   BE

ANNALES DE LA SOCIETE ROYALE D'ARCHEOLOGIE DE BRUXELLES.
Main/Corp Societe Royale d'Archeologie de Bruxelles. Vol. 1 (1887)-. French. Irregular. 1000F. Societe Royale d'Archeologie de Bruxelles, Avenue Penelope 21, B 1190 Brussels Belgium. **Tel** 011 32 2 3439568. cum. index.
Ind/Abst BHA : Biblio. Hist. Art.

LC CC110   ISSN 0776-1244
DD 930.26   BE
UDC 930.26

ANNALES DE L'INSTITUT ARCHEOLOGIQUE DU LUXEMBOURG. [Ann. Inst. archeol. Luxemb.]. (1847)-. Periodical. French. One time a year. Institut Archeologique du Luxembourg, rue des Martyrs 13, B 6700 Arlon Belgium. **Tel** 011 32 63 221236.
Ind/Abst BHA : Biblio. Hist. Art.

LC DC611.N841 A74   ISSN 0003-4134
   FR

ANNALES DE NORMANDIE. See History-History of Europe.

   ISSN 0771-2723
   BE

ANNALES D'HISTOIRE DE L'ART ET D'ARCHEOLOGIE. See The Arts-Art.

LC DS56 .A68
DD 935/.005   LE
UDC 930

ANNALES D'HISTOIRE ET D'ARCHEOLOGIE. See History-History of the Near East.

   ISSN 0776-135X
   BE

UDC 930.26
ANNALES DU CERCLE ARCHEOLOGIQUE DE MONS. [Ann. Cercle archeol. Mons]. (1856)-. Periodical. French. One time a year. 1150.00F. Cercle Archeologique de Mons, rue de l'Amitie 32, 7080 Frameries Belgium. **Tel** 011 32 65 674273. (**Subscription address:** Libr l'Oiseau Lire, rue de la Clef 32, 7000 Mons Belgium.)
Ind/Abst BHA : Biblio. Hist. Art.

   ISSN 0776-1252
   BE

UDC 930.26
ANNALES DU CERCLE ARCHEOLOGIQUE D'ENGHIEN. [Ann. Cercle archeol. Enghien]. (1880)-. Periodical. French. One time a year. 800.00F (also comes with Cercle Archeologique d'Enghien membership). Cercle Archeologique d'Enghien, 409 Chaussee de Bruxelles, 7850 Enghien Belgium. **Tel** 011 32 2 3954645.
Ind/Abst BHA : Biblio. Hist. Art.

LC DC607.1 .A6   ISSN 0003-4398
   FR

ANNALES DU MIDI. [Ann. Midi]. **Added/Corp** Universite de Toulouse. Vol. 1 (1889)-. French. Four times a year. $103.90. Editions Privat, 14 rue des Arts, 31000 Toulouse Cedex France. **Tel** 011 33 61 230926. (**Subscription address:** Centrale des Revues, 11 rue Gossin, 92543 Montrouge Cedex France. **Tel** 011 33 1 46565266.)
Ind/Abst Am. Hist. Life (1967-); BHA : Biblio. Hist. Art; MLA Int. Bibl. Books Artic. Mod. Lang. Lit.; Romant. Move.

   UA

ANNALES DU SERVICE DES ANTIQUITES DE L'EGYPTE. Main/Corp Egypt. Service des Antiquites. **Added/Corp** Egypt. Ministry of Public Works. Vol. 1 (1900)-. French (English). Institut Francais d'Archeologie Orientale du Caire, 37 Mounira Street, Cairo Rae Egypt. (**Subscription address:** Leila Bookshop, PO Box 31 El Daher, 11271 Cairo Egypt. **Tel** 011 202 3924475, 011 202 3507399.) cum. index.
Ind/Abst BHA : Biblio. Hist. Art.

   ISSN 0990-2473
   FR

ANNUAIRE DE LA SOCIETE D'HISTOIRE ET D'ARCHEOLOGIE DE DAMBACH-LA-VILLE, BARR, OBERNAI. See History-History of Europe.

   ISSN 0766-5911
   FR

ANNUAIRE - SOCIETE D'HISTOIRE ET D'ARCHEOLOGIE DE COLMAR. See History-History of Europe.

   FR

ANNUAIRE / SOCIETE D'HISTOIRE ET D'ARCHEOLOGIE DE MOLSHEIM ET ENVIRONS. See History-History of Europe.

LC Z3656.A2 A6
DD 016.932   NE

ANNUAL EGYPTOLOGICAL BIBLIOGRAPHY. See Archaeology-Abstracting, Bibliographies and Statistics.

LC DS101 .A45   ISSN 0066-0035
   US

ANNUAL OF THE AMERICAN SCHOOLS OF ORIENTAL RESEARCH, THE.
Main/Corp American Schools of Oriental Research. Vol. 4 (1922/1923)-. Monographic series. English. Irregular. Price varies per volume. Scholars Press Customer Service, PO Box 6996, Alpharetta GA 30239. **Tel** (800)437-6692, (404)442-8633, FAX (404)442-9742. **ED** Eric M. Meyers. **Bk Rev. Ad Acc.** available on microfilm and microfiche from University Microfilms International (UMI). Continues Annual of the American School of Oriental Research in Jerusalem.
Desc: Monographs on subjects in ancient Near Eastern archaeology and history.

LC F1 .D82   ISSN 0888-3165
DD 974   US

ANNUAL PROCEEDINGS / DUBLIN SEMINAR FOR NEW ENGLAND FOLKLIFE. [Annu. proc. - Dublin Semin. N. Engl. Folklife]. **Added/Corp** Dublin Seminar for New England Folklife. Boston University. American and New England Studies Program. Dublin School (Dublin, N.H.). Vol. 1 (1976)-. Proceedings. English. Irregular (published 2-3 years after conference). $12.00. Boston University Scholarly Publications, 985 Commonwealth Avenue, Boston MA 02215. **Tel** (617)353-4106. **ED** Peter Benes. **Circ**: 2,000.
Desc: An edited publication of the professional conference dealing, each year, with a specific area of New England folk culture.
Ind/Abst Am. Hist. Life (1985-); Avery Index Archit. Period. Suppl. Colum. Univ. (1984-199?).

LC DS54.3 .C93B
DD 939/.37/005   CY

ANNUAL REPORT OF THE DEPARTMENT OF ANTIQUITIES FOR THE YEAR ... / REPUBLIC OF CYPRUS, MINISTRY OF COMMUNICATIONS WORKS. Main/Corp Cyprus. Tmema Archaioteton. 1980-. English (English, Greek, Modern and French, German). One time a year. £2.00. Department of Antiquities / Cyprus, Ministry of Communications Works, Nicosia Cyprus. **Tel** 011 357 21 7225507. **Circ**: 1,000 (ctrl). Continues Annual Report of the Director of the Department of Antiquities for the Year ... .

LC CN1170 .A34   ISSN 0970-0617
DD PL480:I-E-E-339   II

ANNUAL REPORT ON INDIAN EPIGRAPHY FOR... / DEPARTMENT OF ARCHAEOLOGY. Main/Corp India (Republic). Archaeological Survey. **Added/Corp** India. Dept. of Archaeology. Archaeological Survey of India. (1947/48)-. English. One time a year. Price varies. Archeological Survey, Manager of Publications, New Delhi 6 India. (**Subscription address:** Prints India, 11 Darya Ganj, New Delhi 110002 India. **Tel** 011 91 11 3268645, FAX 011 91 11 3275542, telex 31-61087 PRIN-IN.) Continues India (Republic). Dept. of Archaeology. Report on South-Indian Epigraphy.

LC DF11 .A85   ISSN 0067-0081
   IT

ANNUARIO DELLA SCUOLA ARCHEOLOGICA DI ATENE E DELLE MISSIONI ITALIANE IN ORIENTE. [Annu. Sc. archeol. Atene Mission. ital. Oriente]. **Main/Corp** Scuola Archeologica Italiana di Atene. Vol. 1-15 (1914-1932-1933)-Vol. 16 (1939/1940)-. Proceedings. Italian. Prive varies per volume. L'Erma di Bretschneider SPA, via Cassiodoro 19, 00193 Rome Italy. **Tel** 011 39 6 6874127, 011 39 6 6874129, FAX 011 39 6 6874129. **Circ**: 600.
Desc: The proceedings of seminars or round tables, acts, and archaeological reports.
Ind/Abst Art Index; Avery Index Archit. Period. Suppl. Colum. Univ. (19??-199?).

LC GN2 .A27   ISSN 0065-9452
   US
   CODEN APNHAN

ANTHROPOLOGICAL PAPERS OF THE AMERICAN MUSEUM OF NATURAL HISTORY. See Anthropology.

LC GN1 .S66   ISSN 1061-1959
DD 301   US
   CCC

ANTHROPOLOGY & ARCHAEOLOGY OF EURASIA. See Anthropology.

LC CC13.R9 A5   RU

ANTICHNAIA DREVNOST I SREDNIE VEKA. Added/Corp Sverdlovsk, Russia. Ural'skii Gosudarstvennyi Universitet. Kafedra Istorii Drevnego Mira i Srednikh Vekov. (19??)-. Russian. Ural'skii Gosudarstvennyi Universitet, Pr. Lenina 51, Sverdlovsk Russia. **Tel** 011 7 557543. **ED** M.A. Poljakovskaja, S.P. Karpov, A.S. Kozlov, A.I. Romanchuk. **Circ**: 1,000.

LC DE1 .A378   RU

ANTICHNYI MIR I ARKHEOLOGIIA. (1972)-. Periodical. Russian. Irregular. 1.13rub. Saratov N.G. Chernyshevskii State University, Astrakhanskaya Ulitsa 83, 410071 Saratov Russia. **Tel** 011 7 241696, FAX 011 7 240446, telex 241125.

LC N5320 .A55   ISSN 0003-5688
DD 709/.01   SZ

ANTIKE KUNST. [Antike Kunst]. **Added/Corp** Vereinigung der Freunde Antiker Kunst (Switzerland). (1958)-. Periodical. German (French and English). Two times a year (April and October). $105.60. Vereinigung der Freunde Antiker Kunst, Archaologisches Seminar der Universitat, Schonbeinstrasse 20, CH-4056 Basel Switzerland. cum. index. **Bk Rev. Circ**: 1,100 (ctrl).
Desc: Classical archaeology.
Ind/Abst Art Index; Avery Index Archit. Period. Suppl. Colum. Univ. (19??-199?); Numis. Lit.

   ISSN 0066-4782
   SZ

ANTIKE KUNST. BEIHEFT. Added/Corp Vereinigung der Freunde Antiker Kunst (Switzerland). Vol. 1 (1963)-. Multiple languages (German, French and

English). Irregular. Vereinigung der Freunde Antiker Kunst, Archaologisches Seminar der Universitat, Schonbeinstrasse 20, CH-4056 Basel Switzerland.

ISSN 0518-018X
GW

ANTIKE PLASTIK. See The Arts-Art.

ISSN 1015-9274
GW

UDC 902/903

ANTIKE WELT SONDERNUMMER. See History.

LC DG11 .A57
DD 937/.005 IT

ANTIQUA (ARCHEOCLUB D'ITALIA). (ANTIQUA.). **Added/Corp** Archeoclub d'Italia. (June 1976)-. Academic Scholarly Publication. Italian. Six times a year. Free to members; L50000 (institutions), L60000 (institutions) membership. Archeoclub d'Italia, Via Arco dei Banchi 8, 00186 Rome Italy. **Tel** 011 39 6 6875838. **ED** Ettore Feliciani. Index available. **Bk Rev. Ad Acc.**
Desc: Contains scholarly articles on techniques and discoveries in the field of Italian archaeology.

LC DA20 .S612 **ISSN** 0003-5815
DD 930.1/05 UK
CCC

ANTIQUARIES JOURNAL. (THE ANTIQUARIES JOURNAL.). [Antiq. j.]. **Added/Corp** Society of Antiquaries of London. Vol. 1 (Jan. 1921)-. Periodical. English. One time a year. $84.00. Oxford University Press / UK, Walton Street, Oxford OX2 6DP United Kingdom. **Tel** 011 44 1865 56767, FAX 011 44 1865 267773, telex 851/837330 OXPRES G. **(Subscription address:** Oxford University Press / USA, Journals Marketing Department, Oxford University Press, 2001 Evans Road, Cary NC 27513. **Tel** (800)451-7556, (919)677-0977, FAX (919)677-1714.**)** **ED** H. Chapman. Index available (free). cum. index. **Bk Rev. Circ:** 325. available on microfilm and microfiche from University Microfilms International (UMI). ***Continues*** *Society of Antiquaries of London. Proceedings of the Society of Antiquaries of London.* ***Continued in part by*** *Society of Antiquaries of London. Library. Bibliography of Periodicals Literature.*
Desc: Reports of excavations in Britain and abroad, descriptions of finds, surveys of archaeological history in special fields and studies in ancient and medieval art, crafts, heraldry and social and economic life.
Ind/Abst Am. Hist. Life (1990-); Anthropol. Index; Anthropol. Lit.; Archit. Period. Index (1973-); Art Archaeol. Tech. Abstr.; Arts Humanit. Citation Index (19??-19??) [Full Cov.]; Avery Index Archit. Period. Suppl. Colum. Univ. (1988/1989-); BHA : Biblio. Hist. Art; Book Rev. Index; Br. Archaeol. Bibliogr.; Br. Humanit. Index; Geogr. Abstr. Human Geogr.; Numis. Lit.

LC CC **ISSN** 0066-4855
DD 930.1 GW

ANTIQUITAS. REIHE 3. ABHANDLUNGEN ZUR VOR-UND FRUHGESCHICHTE, ZUR KLASSISCHEN UND PROVINZIAL-ROMANISC HEN ARCHAEOLOGIE. Vol. 1 (1960)-. Monographic series. German. Irregular. Price varies per volume. Dr. Rudolf Habelt GmbH, Postfach 150104, D-53040 Bonn Germany. **Tel** 011 49 228 232015. **ED** G.A. Refoldy, N. Himmelmann-Wildschutz, W. Janssen, and J. Straub.
Desc: Essays in the fields of prehistory and early history, classical archaeology and the archaeology of the Roman provinces and the history of the ancient world.

LC CC1 .A7 **ISSN** 0003-598X
DD 930/.05 UK
CCC
CODEN ATQYAF

Pr Rev.

ANTIQUITY. [Antiquity]. Vol. 1 (Mar. 1927)-. Periodical. English. Four times a year. $106.00. Oxford University Press / UK, Walton Street, Oxford OX2 6DP United Kingdom. **Tel** 011 44 1865 56767, FAX 011 44 1865 267773, telex 851/837330 OXPRES G. **(Subscription address:** Oxford University Press / USA, Journals Marketing Department, Oxford University Press, 2001 Evans Road, Cary NC 27513. **Tel** (800)451-7556, (919)677-0977, FAX (919)677-1714.**)** **ED** Christopher Chippindale and Timothy Taylor. Index available. cum. index. **Bk Rev. Ad Acc.** available on microfilm and microfiche from University Microfilms International (UMI). Documents available from The Genuine Article, UMI Article Clearinghouse.
Desc: Internationally recognized within the field of archaeology, reporting specialist work to the wider readership and larger issues that concern every archaeologist.
Ind/Abst Abstr. Anthropol. (19??-); Acad. Abstr.; Acad. Ind. [Computer File] (1987-); Acad. Search; Am. Hist. Life (1968-1970); Anthropol. Index; Anthropol. Lit. (1968-1970); Art Archaeol. Tech. Abstr.; Art Index; Arts Humanit. Citation Index [Full Cov.]; Avery Index Archit. Period. Suppl. Colum. Univ. (19??-199?); BHA : Biblio. Hist. Art; Br. Archaeol. Bibliogr.; Br. Humanit. Index; Ceram. Abstr. (19??-); Curr. Cit.; Curr. Contents Arts Humanit.; Curr. Contents Soc. Behav. Sci.; Curr. Geogr. Publ. (199?-); Ecol. Abstr. (1968-1970); EP Collect.; Ethnoarts Index; Expand. Acad. Index (1987-); Geogr. Abstr. Phys. Geogr.; Geogr. Abstr. Human Geogr.; GeoRef; Hist. Source (July 1990-); Homework Help.; Humanit. Index; Humanit. Source; INFO-SOUTH Abstr.; Mag. Search; MasterFile FullTEXT 1000; MasterFile FullTEXT 350; MasterFile FullTEXT 650; MasterFile FullTEXT (July 1990-); Middle East Abstr. Index (1968-1970); MLA Int. Bibl. Books Artic. Mod. Lang. Lit.; Newsp. Period. Abstr. (1990-); Numis. Lit.; OCLC; Pub. Lib. FullTEXT; Res. Alert [Full Cov.]; Soc. Sci. Source; Soc. Sci. Cit. Index [Full Cov.]; Telebase.

ISSN 0074-039X
RM

ANUARUL INSTITUTULUI DE ISTORIE SI ARHEOLOGIE A. D. XENOPOL. **Main/Corp** Academia Republicii Socialiste Romania. Institutul de Istorie Si Arheologie A. D. Xenopol. **Added/Corp** Academia Republicii Populare Romine. Institutul de Istorie si Arheologie. Anuarul. Academia Republicii Socialiste Romania. Institutul de Istorie si Arheologie. Anuarul. Vol. 1 (1964)-. Periodical. Romanian. One time a year. **(Subscription address:** Ilexim Press Department, PO Box 1, 136-1-137, Bucharest, Romania. **Tel** 011 40 1 173836.**)** ***Supersedes*** *Academia Republicii Populare Romine. Filiala Iasi. Studii si Cercetari Stiintifice. Istorie.*
Ind/Abst Am. Hist. Life (1964-1976, 1979-); BHA : Biblio. Hist. Art.

LC CC5 .A55 **ISSN** 0003-6293
DD 930.1/005 AU

ANZEIGER FUER DIE ALTERTUMSWISSENSCHAFT. [Anz. Altertwiss.]. Vol. 1 (March 1948)-. Periodical. German. Four times a year. S475.00. Universitaetsverlag Wagner GmbH, Andreas Hofer Str. 13, Postfach 165, A 6010 Innsbruck Austria. **Tel** 011 43 512 587721, FAX 011 43 512 582209. **ED** Sebastian Posch.
Ind/Abst Am. Hist. Life (1964-1972).

GT

APUNTES ARQUEOLOGICOS. (1991)-. Spanish. Two times a year. Universidad de San Carlos de Guatemala, Escuela de Historia, Area de Arqueologia, Ciudad Universitaria, Guatemala 12 Guatemala.

LC DG11 .A67
DD 937/.005 IT

AQUILEIA NOSTRA. Added/Corp Museo Archeologico di Aquileia. Associazione Nazionale per Aquileia. (1930)-. Multiple languages (English, French, German and Italian). One time a year. Associazione Nazionale per Aquileia, Via Patriarca Poppone 6, 33051 Aquileia Italy. **Tel** 011 39 431 91113.
Ind/Abst BHA : Biblio. Hist. Art.

LC DC611.A652 A57 **ISSN** 0758-9670
DD 936.4 FR

AQUITANIA. See History-History of Europe.

ISSN 0905-7196
DK
CCC

ARABIAN ARCHAEOLOGY AND EPIGRAPHY. Vol. 1, No. 1 (Oct. 1990)-. Periodical. English. Four times a year. $339.74. Munksgaard International Publishers Ltd, PO Box 2148, DK-1016 Copenhagen K Denmark. **Tel** 011 45 33 127030, FAX 011 45 33 129387, telex 19431 MUNKS DK.
Desc: Serves as a forum for the publication of studies in the archaeology, epigraphy, numismatics and early history of Bahrain, Kuwait, Oman, Qatar, Saudi Arabia, the United Arab Emirates, the Yemen Arab Republic and the People's Democratic Republic of Yemen.
Ind/Abst Anthropol. Lit.; Arts Humanit. Citation Index [Full Cov.]; Geogr. Abstr. Human Geogr.; Soc. Sci. Cit. Index [Select. Cov.].

LC N8555 .A7 **ISSN** 0066-5738
GW

ARBEITSBLAETTER FUER RESTAURATOREN. See Museums and Galleries.

LC DL301 .I8 **ISSN** 0256-8462
IC

ARBOK HINS ISLENZKA FORNLEIFAFELAGS. Added/Corp Islenska Fornleifafelag. **VFOAT** Arbok Fornleifafelagsins. (1881)-. Icelandic. One time a year.
Ind/Abst BHA : Biblio. Hist. Art.

LC GN826.N8 O65
NO

ARBOK - UNIVERSITETETS OLDSAKSAMLING. Main/Corp Universitetet I Oslo. Universitetets Oldsaksamling. (1927)-. Periodical. Norwegian (English; summaries and/or abstracts in English). One time a year. Kr150.00. Universitetets Oldsaksamling, Frederiks GT 3, 0164 Oslo 1 Norway. **Tel** (02)416300. ***Continued in part by*** *Universitetet i Oslo. Universitetets Oldsaksamling. Universitetets Oldsaksamlings Arsberetning; Universitetet i Oslo. Universitetets Oldsaksamling. Universitetets Oldsaksamlings Tilvekst.*
Desc: Articles cover Norwegian archaeology.
Ind/Abst Art Archaeol. Tech. Abstr.; Br. Archaeol. Bibliogr.

ISSN 0048-1742
CN

ARCH NOTES. Added/Corp Ontario Archaeological Society. Vol. 1 (March 1962)-. Periodical. English. Six times a year. 55.00Can$ Comes with Ontario and Archaeological Society membership. Ontario Archaeological Society, 126 Willowdale Avenue, North York Ontario M2N 4Y2 Canada. **Tel** (416)730-0797, FAX (416)730-0797. **Circ:** 800.
Ind/Abst Anthropol. Lit.

GW

ARCHAEO-PHYSIKA. Added/Corp Gesellschaft der Freunde und Forderer des Rheinischen Landesmuseums in Bonn. Rheinisches Landesmuseum Bonn. Vol. 1 (1965)-. Monographic series. English (German). Irregular. Price varies per volume. Dr. Rudolf Habelt GmbH, Postfach 150104, D-53040 Bonn Germany. **Tel** 011 49 228 232015.
Ind/Abst Br. Archaeol. Bibliogr.

LC GN799.A8 A72 **ISSN** 0142-7253
DD 520/.9/01 UK
CCC
CODEN ARHADN

Pr Rev.

ARCHAEOASTRONOMY. [Archaeoastronomy]. (1979)-. Periodical. English. One time a year. $36.00. Science History Publications Ltd., 16 Rutherford Road, Cambridge CB2 2HH United Kingdom. **Tel** 011 44 1223 565532, FAX 011 44 1223 565532. **ED** C.L.N. Ruggles. Index available. cum. index. **Bk Rev. Ad Acc. Circ:** 700. Documents available from Ask*IEEE.
Desc: Research articles on astronomical aspects of archaeology.
Ind/Abst Am. Hist. Life; Anthropol. Lit.; Astron. Astrophys. Abstr.; Br. Archaeol. Bibliogr.; INSPEC (1979-); Math. Rev.

LC E59.A8 A684 **ISSN** 1062-189X
DD 930 US

ARCHAEOASTRONOMY & EHNOASTRONOMY NEWS. See Astronomy.

LC E59.A8 A68 **ISSN** 0190-9940
DD 520/.93 US

ARCHAEOASTRONOMY (COLLEGE PARK). (ARCHAEOASTRONOMY.). [Archaeoastron.]. **Added/Corp** University of Maryland. Center for Archaeoastronomy. Vol. 2, No. 2 (Spring 1979)-. Periodical. English. One time a year. $60.00. The Center for Archaeoastronomy, PO Box X, College Park MD 20740. **Tel** (301)864-6637. **ED** John B Carlson. **Bk Rev. Ad Acc. Circ:** 1,300. ***Continues*** *Archaeoastronomy Bulletin, 0272-5436.*
Desc: Astronomical practices, celestial lore and mythology and cosmologies of ancient cultures and the native peoples of today.
Ind/Abst Astron. Astrophys. Abstr.; Br. Archaeol. Bibliogr.; Ethnoarts Index.

LC DA670.N79 A6 **ISSN** 0261-3417
UK

ARCHAEOLOGIA AELIANA. (ARCHAEOLOGIA AELIANA, OR, MISCELLANEOUS TRACTS RELATING TO ANTIQUITY.). [Archaeol. aeliana]. **Added/Corp** Society of Antiquaries of Newcastle upon Tyne. Society of Antiquaries of Newcastle upon Tyne. Annual Report. **VFOAT** Archaeologia Aeliana; Miscellaneous Tracts Relating to Antiquity. Vol. 1 (1822)- Vol. 4; 2nd Ser., Vol. 1- Vol. 25; 3rd Ser., Vol. 1- Vol. 21; 4th Ser., Vol. 1 (1925)-. English. One time a year. $26.78. Soc Antiquaries Newcastle Tyne, Black Gate, Newcastle Upon Tyne United Kingdom. cum. index.
Ind/Abst Art Archaeol. Tech. Abstr.; Avery Index Archit. Period. Suppl. Colum. Univ.; BHA : Biblio. Hist. Art; Numis. Lit.

ISSN 0720-2156
DD 930/.05 GW

ARCHAEOLOGIA ATLANTICA. Vol. 1 (1975)-. Periodical. English (German). One time a year. Moreland Editions, D-2357 Bad Bramstedt 1120, Federal Republic of Germany, Bad Bramstedt.

LC DB1 .A7 **ISSN** 0003-8008
DD 936.4/005 AU

ARCHAEOLOGIA AUSTRIACA. **Added/Corp** Universitaet Wien. Anthropologisches Institut. Universitaet Wien. Institut fuer Ur- und Fruehgeschichte. Universitaet Wien. Urgeschichtliches Institut. Oesterreichische Arbeitsgemeinschaft fuer Ur- und Fruehgeschichte. No. 1 (1948)-. Periodical. German. One time a year. S1980.00. Oesterreichischer Bundesverlag, Schwarzenbergstr 5, Postfach 79, A-1015 Vienna Austria. **Tel** 011 43 1 51405. cum. index.
Ind/Abst Anthropol. Index; Anthropol. Lit.; BHA : Biblio. Hist. Art; Br. Archaeol. Bibliogr.

Archaeology

LC DA700 .A66
ISSN 0306-6924
UK
ARCHAEOLOGIA CAMBRENSIS. [Archaeol. cambrensis]. **Added/Corp** Cambrian Archaeological Association. Vol. 1, No. 1 (Jan. 1846)-. English. One time a year. Comes with membership. Cambrian Archaeological Association, Laurels Westfield Road, Newport Gwent NP9 4ND United Kingdom. **Tel** 011 44 1222 763777. available on microfilm from University Microfilms International (UMI).
Ind/Abst Avery Index Archit. Period. Suppl. Colum. Univ.; BHA : Biblio. Hist. Art; Numis. Lit.

LC DA670.K2 A7
ISSN 0066-5894
UK
ARCHAEOLOGIA CANTIANA. [Archaeol. cantiana.]. **Added/Corp** Kent Archaeological Society. Vol. 1, (1858)-. English. One time a year. $42.78. Kent Archaeological Society, Barnfield Church Lane, East Peckham, Tonbridge KT TN12 5JJ United Kingdom. **Tel** 011 44 1622 871945. **ED** A. Detsicas. Index available. cum. index. **Bk Rev. Circ:** 1,500 (ctrl).
Desc: Concerned with the archaeology and history of Kent in the widest terms.
Ind/Abst Avery Index Archit. Period. Suppl. Colum. Univ. (1988); BHA : Biblio. Hist. Art; Br. Archaeol. Bibliogr.; Br. Humanit. Index; Numis. Lit.

ISSN 0231-5823
XR
UDC 902
ARCHAEOLOGIA HISTORICA. [Archaeol. hist.]. (19??)-. Multiple languages. Irregular.
Ind/Abst BHA : Biblio. Hist. Art.

LC DA20 .A64
ISSN 0261-3409
UK
ARCHAEOLOGIA, OR MISCELLANEOUS TRACTS RELATING TO ANTIQUITY. [Archaeologia]. **Added/Corp** Society of Antiquaries of London. **VFOAT** Archaeologia; Miscellaneous Tracts Relating to Antiquity. Vol. 1 (1770)-. English. Irregular (published every 3-4 years). £42.00. Society of Antiquaries of London, Burlington House, Piccadilly, London W1V 0HS United Kingdom. **Tel** 011 44 171 7340193, FAX 011 44 171 2876967. **(Subscription address:** David Brown Book Company, PO Box 511, Oakville CT 06779. **Tel** (203)945-9329, FAX (203)945-9468.**) ED** Elizabeth Nichols. Index available. cum. index. **Ad Acc. Circ:** 2,000. available on microfilm from University Microfilms International (UMI).
Desc: Covers prehistoric to medieval archaeology and history of arts and crafts, and architecture.
Ind/Abst Anthropol. Index; Art Index; Avery Index Archit. Period. Suppl. Colum. Univ.; BHA : Biblio. Hist. Art; Numis. Lit.

LC GN845.P7 A75
DD 571 943.8
ISSN 0066-5924
PL
ARCHAEOLOGIA POLONA / POLSKA AKADEMIA NAUK, INSTYTUT HISTORII KULTURY MATERIALNEJ. **Added/Corp** Instytut Historii Kultury Materialnej (Polska Akademia Nauk). Vol. 1 (1958)-. English (French, German, Italian and Russian). One time a year. $25.00. **(Subscription address:** Ars Polona-Ruch, PO Box 1001, Krakowskie Przedmiescie 7, 00-068 Warsaw Poland. **Tel** 011 48 22 261201.)
Ind/Abst Anthropol. Index; Anthropol. Lit.; BHA : Biblio. Hist. Art; Br. Archaeol. Bibliogr.; Numis. Lit.

LC DT963.3 .A73
DD 968.9/4
ZA
Pr Rev.
ARCHAEOLOGIA ZAMBIANA. **Added/Corp** Zambia. National Monuments Commission. No. 1 (Nov. 1964)-. Newsletter. English. Irregular. Free on request. National Heritage Conservation Committee, PO Box 60124, Livingstone Zambia. **Tel** 011 260 3 320481, FAX 011 260 3 324509. **ED** Lawrence Sumpa (phone: 011 260 3 32488). **Bk Rev.** (Qty: 1). **Ad Acc. Circ:** 500 (ctrl).
Desc: News and information about archaeology in Zambia.

LC DB2621 .A73
DD 943.7/12/005
XR
ARCHAEOLOGICA PRAGENSIA : ARCHEOLOGICKY SBORNIK MUZEA HLAVNIHO MESTA PRAHY. **Added/Corp** Muzeum Hlavniho Mesta Prahy. (1980)-. Czech (summaries and/or abstracts in German). One time a year. kcs40.00. Muzeum Hlavniho Mesta Prahy, Kozna 1/475, 110 01 Prague 1 Czech Republic. **ED** Jiri Hrala. **Circ:** 500 (ctrl).
Ind/Abst Anthropol. Lit.

ISSN 0952-3332
UK
Pr Rev.
ARCHAEOLOGICAL COMPUTING NEWSLETTER. [Archaeol. comput. newsl.]. **Added/Corp** North Staffordshire Polytechnic. Dept. of Computing. University of Oxford. Institute of Archaeology. **VFOAT** ACN. No. 1 (Dec. 1984)-. Newsletter. English. Four times a year (Mar., June, Sept., Dec.). $15.41. Archaeological Computing Newsletter, 36 Beaumont Street, University of Oxford, Oxford OX1 2PG United Kingdom. **Tel** 011 44 1865 278240, FAX 011 44 1865 278254. **ED** Dr. Gary Lock. Index available. cum. index. **Bk Rev. Ad Acc. Circ:** 300.

ISSN 1380-2038
NE
●**ARCHAEOLOGICAL DIALOGUES.**
Added/Corp Archaeological Dialogues Foundation. Vol. 1, No. 1 (Jan. 1994)-. Periodical. English. Two times a year (Jan. and Aug.). $75.60 (institutions), $54.00 (individuals). Van Gorcum & Company BV, PO Box 43, NL 9400 AA Assen Netherlands. **Tel** 011 31 5920 46846, FAX 011 31 5920 72064. **(Subscription address:** David Brown Book Company, PO Box 511, Oakville CT 06779. **Tel** (203)945-9329, FAX (203)945-9468.**)**

LC CC76 .A73
DD 930.1
ISSN 1061-8961
US
ARCHAEOLOGICAL FIELDWORK OPPORTUNITIES BULLETIN. [Archaeol. fieldwork oppor. bull.]. **Added/Corp** Archaeological Institute of America. **VFOAT** Archaeological Fieldwork Opportunities Bulletin. (19??)-. Bulletin. English. One time a year. $15.00. Kendall/Hunt Publishing Co., 2460 Kerper Boulevard, Dubuque IA 52001. **Tel** (319)589-1000. **ED** Galina Gorokhoff. **Circ:** 2,500. **Continues** Archaeological Fieldwork and Opportunities Bulletin.
Desc: Listing of worldwide excavations seeking volunteers.

LC DA20 .R86
ISSN 0066-5983
UK
ARCHAEOLOGICAL JOURNAL, THE. [Archaeol. j.]. **Added/Corp** British Archaeological Association. Central Committee. Royal Archaeological Institute of Great Britain and Ireland. Central Committee. Royal Archaeological Institute of Great Britain and Ireland. Central Committee. Royal Archaeological Institute of Great Britain and Ireland. Council. Royal Archaeological Institute (Great Britain). Vol. 1, No. 1 (March 1844)-. Periodical. English. One time a year. $47.92. Royal Archaeological Institute, Society of Antiquaries, Burlington House, Piccadilly London W1V 0HS United Kingdom. **Tel** 011 44 171 7340193. **ED** R.T. Schadla-Hall. Index available. cum. index. **Bk Rev. Circ:** 2,000 (ctrl). available on microfiche.
Desc: Contains archaeological and architectural articles fully illustrated together and reviews of recent publications.
Ind/Abst Anthropol. Index; Anthropol. Lit.; Archit. Period. Index (March 1844-); Art Index; Avery Index Archit. Period. Suppl. Colum. Univ. (1988-); BHA : Biblio. Hist. Art; Br. Archaeol. Bibliogr. Mar. 1844-; Br. Humanit. Index; Numis. Lit.

LC CC75 .A65
DD 930.1/028
ISSN 1043-1691
US
CODEN AMTHE2
TITLE CHANGE
ARCHAEOLOGICAL METHOD AND THEORY. [Archaeol. method theory]. Vol. 1 (1989)-Vol. 5 (1993). Periodical. English. University of Arizona Press, 1230 North Park Avenue, Suite 102, Tucson AZ 85719. **Tel** (602)882-3065, (800)426-3797, FAX (602)621-8899. **Continues** Advances in Archaeological Method and Theory, 0162-8003. **Continued by** Journal of Archaeological Method and Theory.
Ind/Abst Anthropol. Lit. (?-?).

ISSN 0194-3413
US
ARCHAEOLOGICAL NEWS. [Archaeol. news]. Vol. 1 (Winter 1972)-. Academic Scholarly Publication. English. One time a year. $22.50. Department of Classics, Park Hall, University of Georgia, Athens GA 30602. **Tel** (706)542-2187. **ED** Nancy T. de Grummard, Naomi Norman. **Bk Rev. Ad Acc. Circ:** 500.
Desc: A journal containing scholarly articles, news and reviews of interest to archaeologists, anthropologists, art historians and classicists.

LC D51
DD 930
ISSN 1075-2196
UK
CODEN ARPOE4
Pr Rev.
●**ARCHAEOLOGICAL PROSPECTION.** [Archaeol. prospect.]. Vol. 1, No. 1 (Nov. 1994)-. Academic Scholarly Publication. English. Four times a year. $225.00. John Wiley & Sons Ltd., Baffins Lane, Chichester, West Sussex PO19 1UD United Kingdom. **Tel** 011 44 1243 779777, FAX 011 44 1243 776128 BTG:JWP001, telex 86290 WIBOOKG. **(Subscription address:** John Wiley & Sons, Inc. / Philadelphia, PO Box 7247, Philadelphia PA 19170. **Tel** (212)850-6645, (800)225-5945.**)** Documents available from BLDSC.

UK
ARCHAEOLOGICAL REVIEW FROM CAMBRIDGE. [Archaeol. rev. Camb.]. **Added/Corp** University of Cambridge. Dept. of Archaeology. **VFOAT** ARC; A.R.C. Vol. 2, No. 1 (Spring 1983)-. Academic Scholarly Publication. English. Two times a year. $27.37. University of Cambridge / Department of Archaeology, Downing Street, Cambridge CB2 3DZ United Kingdom. **Bk Rev. Circ:** 300. **Continues** Archaeological Reviews from Cambridge, 0261-4332.
Ind/Abst Anthropol. Lit.; BHA : Biblio. Hist. Art; Br. Archaeol. Bibliogr.

ISSN 0196-5409
US
ARCHAEOLOGICAL SERIES (TUCSON). (ARCHAEOLOGICAL SERIES.). No. 1-. Monographic series. English. Price varies per volume. University of Arizona / Museum, Arizona State Museum, Cultural Resource Management Section, Tucson AZ 85721. **Tel** (602)621-4794. cum. index. **Bk Rev. Ad Acc. Circ:** 150 (ctrl).
Desc: Results of archaeological survey, testing, and mitigation projects in Arizona. Conducted under contract to various government and private sponsors.

DD 978.3
ISSN 0561-0478
US
ARCHAEOLOGICAL STUDIES. CIRCULAR (PIERRE. 1948). (ARCHAEOLOGICAL STUDIES : CIRCULAR.). **Added/Corp** South Dakota Archaeological Commission. South Dakota State Archaeological Commission. No. 1 (1948)-. Monographic series. English. Price varies per volume. South Dakota Archaeological Commission, 500 East Capitol, Pierre SD 57501. **Continues** Archaeological Studies.

ISSN 0307-5117
UK
ARCHAEOLOGICAL SURVEY OF EGYPT. MEMOIR. (ARCHAEOLOGICAL SURVEY OF EGYPT.). [Archaeol. surv. Egypt, Memoir]. (19??)-. Monographic series. English. Price varies per volume. Egypt Exploration Society, 3 Doughty Mews, Longon WC1N 2PG United Kingdom. **Tel** 011 44 171 2421880.

US
ARCHAEOLOGICAL SURVEY REPORT (SAN ANTONIO, TEX.). (ARCHAEOLOGICAL SURVEY REPORT / CENTER FOR ARCHAEOLOGICAL RESEARCH, THE UNIVERSITY OF TEXAS AT SAN ANTONIO.). Monographic series. English. Irregular. Price varies per volume. Center for Archaeological Research, University of Texas at San Antonio, San Antonio TX 78285.

LC Z5132 .A67
ISSN 0341-8308
GW
CEASED
ARCHAEOLOGISCHE BIBLIOGRAPHIE. See Archaeology-Abstracting, Bibliographies and Statistics.

LC CC5 .A73
ISSN 0341-2873
GW
ARCHAEOLOGISCHE INFORMATIONEN. **Added/Corp** Deutsches Gesellschaft fuer Ur- und Fruehgeschichte. Vol. 1 (1972)-. Monographic series. German. Irregular. $21.41. Dr. Rudolf Habelt GmbH, Postfach 150104, D-53040 Bonn Germany. **Tel** 011 49 228 232015.
Ind/Abst Anthropol. Lit.; BHA : Biblio. Hist. Art.

LC DS261 .A72
DD 935
ISSN 0066-6033
US
CCC
ARCHAEOLOGISCHE MITTEILUNGEN AUS IRAN. (1929)-. Monographic series. German (English). One time a year. Price varies per volume. Dietrich Reimer Verlag, Unter den Eichen 57, D-12203 Berlin Germany. **Tel** 011 49 30 8314081, FAX 011 49 30 831623. **Ad Acc.**
Ind/Abst Anthropol. Lit.; Avery Index Archit. Period. Suppl. Colum. Univ. (19??-199?); BHA : Biblio. Hist. Art.

LC DD51 .A7
DD 913.363
ISSN 0342-734X
GW
ARCHAEOLOGISCHES KORRESPONDENZBLATT. [Archaeol. Korrespondenzbl.]. **Added/Corp** Roemisch-Germanisches Zentralmuseum. Nordwestdeutscher Verband fuer Altertumsforschung. West- und Sueddeutscher Verband fuer Altertumsforschung. Vol. 1 (1971)-. German (English and French). Four times a year. $65.25. Roemisch Germanisches Zentral, Ernst Ludwig Platz 2, D-55116 Mainz Germany. **Tel** 011 49 6131 232231, FAX 011 49 6131 232235.
Desc: Short studies on archaeological subjects. Publication of recent finds and discoveries.
Ind/Abst Art Archaeol. Tech. Abstr.; Avery Index Archit. Period. Suppl. Colum. Univ. (1989-); BHA : Biblio. Hist. Art; Br. Archaeol. Bibliogr.

GW
●**ARCHAEOLOGISCHES NACHRICHTENBLATT.** (1995)-. German. Six times a year. $45.00. Akademie-Verlag GmbH, Postfach, D-13162 Berlin Germany. **Tel** 011 49 30 47889300, FAX 011 49 30 47889357. **Continues** Ausgrabungen und Funde.

LC GN700 .A725 **ISSN** 0003-8113
DD 913 US
Pr Rev.
ARCHAEOLOGY. [Archaeology]. **Added/Corp** Archaeological Institute of America. Vol. 1 (Mar. 1948)-. Periodical. English. Six times a year. $19.97. Archaeology Institute of America, 135 William Street, New York NY 10038. **Tel** (212)732-5154. **(Subscription address:** Palm Coast Data, PO Box 420163, Agency Department, Palm Coast FL 32142. **Tel** (904)445-4662 ext. 669, (800)829-5475.) **ED** Peter Young. cum. index. **Bk Rev. Ad Acc. Circ:** 140,000. available on microfilm and microfiche from University Microfilms International (UMI). Documents available from The Genuine Article, UMI Article Clearinghouse.
Desc: Articles by archaeologists and feature reports of current excavations, recent discoveries, and special studies of ancient kingdoms.

Ind/Abst Abstr. Anthropol.; Acad. Abstr. Full Text Elite; Acad. Abstr.; Acad. Ind. [Computer File] (1987-); Acad. Search; Am. Hist. Life (1971-1972); Anthropol. Lit. (-Vol. 11, 1989); Art Archaeol. Tech. Abstr.; Art Index; Arts Humanit. Citation Index [Full Cov.]; Avery Index Archit. Period. Suppl. Colum. Univ. (1989-); Book Rev. Digest; Book Rev. Index; Br. Archaeol. Bibliogr.; Ceram. Abstr.; Curr. Geogr. Publ. (199?-); EP Collect.; Ethnoarts Index; Expand. Acad. Index (1987-); GeoRef; Hist. Source (May 1984-); Homework Help.; Humanit. Index; Humanit. Source; Index Book Rev. Relig.; INFO-SOUTH Abstr.; INIS Atomindex [Micro.]; Mag. Artic. Summar. Elite; Mag. Artic. Summar. Select; Mag. Artic. Summar. CD-ROM; Mag. Search; MasterFile FullTEXT 1000; MasterFile FullTEXT 350; MasterFile FullTEXT 650; MasterFile FullTEXT (May 1984-); Middle East Abstr. Index; Newsp. Period. Abstr. (1988-); Numis. Lit.; OCLC; Old Testam. Abstr.; Pop. Period. Index; Pub. Lib. FullTEXT; Read. Guide Period. Lit.; Relig. Index One Period.; Res. Alert [Full Cov.]; Sage Urban Stud. Abstr (?-?); Soc. Sci. Cit. Index [Full Cov.]; Telebase; Vocat. Search; West. Hist. Q.

ISSN 1071-0507
DD 220 US
TITLE CHANGE
ARCHAEOLOGY AND BIBLICAL RESEARCH. [Archaeol. Biblic. res.]. **Added/Corp** Associates for Biblical Research. Vol. 1, No. 1 (Winter 1988)-(19??). Periodical. English. Associates for Biblical Research, PO Box 125, Ephrata PA 17522. **Tel** (717)733-3585, FAX (717)733-3585. ***Continues*** *Bible and Spade, 0162-9301.* ***Changed back to*** *Bible and Spade.*
Desc: Reports of ABR ministries, news items on both archaeology and creation-science, and notices of audio and video tapes, as well as books available from ABR.

ISSN 0281-5877
SW
UDC 901
ARCHAEOLOGY AND ENVIRONMENT. [Archaeol. environ.]. (1983)-. Monographic series. English. Irregular. Price varies per volume.
Ind/Abst Numis. Lit.

LC DT510.3 .A72
DD 966.7/01/05 GH
ARCHAEOLOGY IN GHANA. 1978/79-. Periodical. English. University of Ghana Department of Archaeology, Legon Ghana. ***Supersedes*** *Sankofa.*

ISSN 0044-8591
US
ARCHAEOLOGY IN MONTANA. VFOAT Archeology in Montana. (Summer 1958)-. Periodical. English. Three times a year. $15.00. Montana Archaeological Society, Montana State University, PO Box 2123, Billings MT 59103.
Ind/Abst Am. Hist. Life (1983-); Anthropol. Lit.; Ethnoarts Index.

LC DU416 .A73 **ISSN** 0113-7832
DD 993.01/05 NZ
ARCHAEOLOGY IN NEW ZEALAND. [Archaeol. N.Z.]. **Added/Corp** New Zealand Archaeological Association. Vol. 31, No. 1 (Mar. 1988)-. Periodical. English. Four times a year (Mar., June, Sep., Dec.). $42.97. New Zealand Archaeology Association, Private Bag 92018, Auckland 1 New Zealand. **Tel** 011 64 3 4798751, FAX 011 64 3 4741607. **ED** Joan Lawrence. ***Continues*** *Newsletter (New Zealand Archaeological Association), 0028-7962.*
Ind/Abst Anthropol. Index; Anthropol. Lit.

LC F1122.9 .A73 **ISSN** 0715-2086
DD 971.8/201/05 CN
ARCHAEOLOGY IN NEWFOUNDLAND & LABRADOR. [Archaeol. Nfld. Labrador]. **VFOAT** Archaeology in Newfoundland and Labrador. Annual Report No. 1 (1980)-. English. One time a year. Government of Newfoundland & Labrador, Historic Resources Division, St. John's Newfoundland A1C 5T7 Canada.
Ind/Abst Anthropol. Lit.

ISSN 0728-4896
AT
CCC
NLM W1 AR159P **CODEN** AOCEDN
Pr Rev.
ARCHAEOLOGY IN OCEANIA. [Archaeol. Oceania]. **Added/Corp** University of Sydney. Vol. 16, No. 1 (April 1981)-. Periodical. English. Irregular (3 issues per year). 48.00Aus$. University of Sydney, 116 Darlington Road / H42, Sydney NSW 2006 Australia. **Tel** 011 61 2 6922666, FAX 011 61 2 6922666. **ED** J. Peter White. **Bk Rev**, (Qty: 20). **Ad Acc, Adv Mgr:** D. Koller, **Tel** (02)692-2666. **Circ:** 600. available on microfilm and microfiche from University Microfilms International (UMI). Documents available from BIOSIS Document Express. ***Continues*** *Archaeology & Physical Anthropology in Oceania, 0003-8121.*

Ind/Abst Abstr. Anthropol.; Anthropol. Index; Anthropol. Lit. (1981-); APAIS, Aust. Public Aff. Inf. Ser. (1981-); Biol. Abstr.; Ethnoarts Index; GeoRef (1981-).

ISSN 1058-2673
DD 220 US
ARCHAEOLOGY IN THE BIBLICAL WORLD. [Archaeol. biblic. world]. **Added/Corp** Near East Archaeological Society (U.S.). Vol. 1, No. 1 (Spring 1991)-. English. One time a year. Comes with Near East Archaeological Society Bulletin. Near East Archaeological Society, 2313 East 20th Street, Joplin MO 64804. **Tel** (417)623-7573.

ISSN 0790-892X
IE
ARCHAEOLOGY IRELAND. Vol. 1, No. 1 (Sept. 1987)-. Periodical. English. Four times a year.
Ind/Abst BHA : Biblio. Hist. Art.

JM
ARCHAEOLOGY JAMAICA. Added/Corp Archaeological Society of Jamaica. **VFOAT** AJ. (19??)-. Periodical. English. Four times a year. $10.00 Comes with Archaeological Society of Jamaica membership. Archaeological Society of Jamaica, PO Box 45, 1 Hillview Avenue, Kingston 10 Jamaica. **Tel** (809)929-1802.

ISSN 0316-1285
DD 930/.1 CN
ARCHAEOLOGY MONOGRAPH. Added/Corp Royal Ontario Museum. **VFOAT** Royal Ontario Museum Archaeology Monograph. (1974)-. Monographic series. English. Irregular. Price varies per volume. Royal Ontario Museum Publications Service, 100 Queen's Park, Toronto Ontario M5S 2C6 Canada. **Tel** (416)586-5590, FAX (416)586-5827.

LC E77.8 .A7 **ISSN** 0360-1021
DD 974/.006 US
Pr Rev.
ARCHAEOLOGY OF EASTERN NORTH AMERICA. [Archaeol. East. North Am.]. **Added/Corp** Eastern States Archeological Federation (U.S.). Vol. 1 No. 1 (1973)-. English. One time a year. $30.00 (institutions), $20.00 (individuals) Comes with Eastern States Archaeology Federation membership. Eastern States Archaeology Federation, PO Box 386, Bethlehem CT 06751. **Tel** (203)266-7741. **ED** Dennis Curry. **Circ:** 500. ***Absorbed*** *Bulletin - Eastern States Archaeological Federation, 0160-3523.* ***Continued in part by*** *Bulletin - Eastern States Archeological Federation (U.S.) Meeting, 0749-0100.*
Desc: The journal of Eastern States Archaeological Federation.
Ind/Abst Abstr. Anthropol.; Anthropol. Lit.; Ethnoarts Index.

ISSN 0106-0880
DK
ARCHAEOLOGY OF SVENDBORG, DENMARK, THE. (1978)-. Monographic series. English. Irregular. Price varies per volume. Odense University Press, 55 Campusvej, DK-5230 Odense M Denmark. **Tel** 011 45 7 66157999, FAX 011 45 7 66158126.

LC CC75 .A66 **ISSN** 0003-813X
DD 930/.1/028 UK
CODEN ARCHAG
Pr Rev.
ARCHAEOMETRY. [Archaeometry]. **Added/Corp** University of Oxford. Research Laboratory for Archaeology and the History of Art. Vol. 1 (June 1958)-. Periodical. English (French). Two times a year (Feb./Aug.). $90.00. Research Laboratory of Archaeology, 6 Keble Road, Oxford OX1 3QJ United Kingdom. **Tel** 011 44 1865 515211, FAX 011 44 1865 273932. **ED** M. J. Aitken and E. T. Hall. Index available. cum. index. **Ad Acc. Circ:** 950. Documents available from The Genuine Article, Ask*IEEE, CASDDS.
Desc: Archaeometry is a research journal concerned with the involvement of the physical sciences in archaeology and art history. Because of the interdisciplinary nature of this field, authors are encouraged to write with the non-specialist in mind.
Ind/Abst Abstr. Anthropol. (July 1973-); Anthropol. Index; Anthropol. Lit.; Art Archaeol. Tech. Abstr.; Arts Humanit. Citation Index [Full Cov.]; Br. Archaeol. Bibliogr.; Ceram. Abstr.; Chem. Abstr.; Curr. Cit.; Curr. Contents Arts Humanit.; Curr. Contents Soc. Behav. Sci.; Ethnoarts Index (July 1973-); INSPEC (July 1973-); Numis. Lit. (July 1973-); Plant Breed. Abstr.; Res. Alert [Full Cov.]; Soc. Sci. Cit. Index [Full Cov.]; Stat. Theory Method Abstr. (1974-1975).

LC CC77.U5 A73
DD 930.1/028/04 FR
ARCHAEONAUTICA. Added/Corp Centre National de la Recherche Scientifique (France) France. Service des Fouilles et Antiquites. (1977)-. French. Irregular. 312.00F. CNRS / Institut d'Information Scientifique et Technique, (Centre National de la Recherche Scientifique), 15 Quai Anatole France, 75700 Paris France. **Tel** 011 33 1 47531515, FAX 011 33 1 45517307, telex 260034.
Desc: Articles on archaeological discoveries from shipwrecks, various strata and their importance, and the effect of modern technologies on archaeological issues.
Ind/Abst Br. Archaeol. Bibliogr. (?-?).

LC DF10 .A687
DD 938.005 GR
ARCHAIOLOGIA. Vol. 1 (Nov. 1981)-. Academic Scholarly Publication. Greek, Modern (summaries and/or abstracts in English). Four times a year. $27.00. Lambrakis Press SA, 3 Christou Lada, 102 37 Athens Greece. **Tel** 011 30 1 3237283, 011 30 1 3230221. **ED** Anna Lambraki. Index available. cum. index. **Bk Rev. Ad Acc. Circ:** 7,500.
Desc: Archaeological publication catering to a wide audience; of interest to the general public as well as the archaeological specialist; of special interest to the young.
Ind/Abst Numis. Lit.

LC DF10 .A69 **ISSN** 0004-6604
GR
ARCHAIOLOGIKA ANALEKTA EX ATHENON. ATHENS ANNALS OF ARCHAEOLOGY. Added/Corp Greece. Genike Epitheoresis Archaioteton kai Anasteloseos. Greece. Genike Dieuthynsis Archaioteton kai Anasteloseos. **VFOAT** Athens Annals of Archaeology. Vol. 1 (1968)-. Periodical. Greek, Modern (summaries and/or abstracts in French, German, English and Italian). Two times a year. Price varies. Ministry of Culture, 57 Panepiatimiou Street, Athens GR 105 64 Greece. **Tel** 011 30 1 32539016.
Ind/Abst Art Archaeol. Tech. Abstr.; BHA : Biblio. Hist. Art; Numis. Lit.

LC DF10 .A7 **ISSN** 1105-0950
GR
ARCHAIOLOGIKE EPHEMERIS : EKDIDOMENE TES ARCHAIOLOGIKES HETAIREIAS. Added/Corp Archaiologike Hetaireia. **VFOAT** AE. (1910)-. Periodical. Greek, Modern (English, French, German and Italian). One time a year. $120.00. Wasmuth KG, Hardenbergstrasse 9A, D-10623 Berlin Germany. **Tel** 011 49 30 3131920. available on microfilm. ***Continues*** *Ephemeris Archaiologike (Athens, Greece : 1883).*
Ind/Abst Anthropol. Index; BHA : Biblio. Hist. Art; Numis. Lit.

LC DF10 .A73
GR
ARCHAIOLOGIKON DELTION. Added/Corp Greece. Hypourgeio Politismou. Greece. Hypourgeion ton Ekklesiastikon kai tes Demosias Ekpaideuseos. Greece. Hypourgeion ton Threskeumaton kai Paideias. Greece. Hypourgeion ton Threskeumaton kai tes Ethnikes Paideias. **VFOAT** Deltion Arkhaiologikon. Vol. 1 (1915)-. Periodical. Greek, Modern (English, German and French). One time a year (irregular). DM460.00. Wasmuth KG, Hardenbergstrasse 9A, D-10623 Berlin Germany. **Tel** 011 49 30 3131920. **Circ:** 1,200 (ctrl).
Desc: Reports on activities of Greek archaeological service and foreign archaeological schools working in Greece.
Ind/Abst Avery Index Archit. Period. Suppl. Colum. Univ. (19??-199?); Numis. Lit.

LC DQ30 .A7
DD 936.4 SZ
ARCHAOLOGIE DER SCHWEIZ. Added/Corp Schweizerische Gesellschaft fuer Ur- und Fruhgeschichte. Verband Schweizerischer Kantonsarchaologen. **VFOAT** Archeologie Suisse. (1978)-. Periodical. French (German and Italian). Four times a year (Mar., June, Sept., Dec.). $34.89. Schweiz Gesellschaft Fruhgesch, Petersgraben 9-11, Postfach, CH-4001 Basel Switzerland. **Tel** 011 41 61 2613078, FAX 011 41 61 2612602. **ED** S. Martin-Kilcher. **Ad Acc. Circ:** 3,500 (ctrl). ***Continues*** *Mitteilungsblatt der Schweizerischen Gesellschaft fuer Ur- und Fruhgeschichte.*
Desc: New results of scientific researches in archaeology in Switzerland.
Ind/Abst Anthropol. Lit.; BHA : Biblio. Hist. Art.

LC DD801.B2345 A73 **ISSN** 0724-8954
DD 936.3 GW
ARCHAOLOGISCHE AUSGRABUNGEN IN BADEN-WURTTEMBERG. [Archaol. Ausgrab. Baden-Wurtt.]. **Added/Corp** Landesdenkmalamt Baden-Wurttemberg. Forderkreis

Archaeology

fuer die Ur- und Fruhgeschichtliche Forschung in Baden. Gesellschaft fuer Vor- und Fruhgeschichte in Wurttemberg und Hohenzollern. (1981)-. Periodical. Lit.; German. One time a year. DM39.00. Konrad Theiss Verlag GmBH & Company, 70190 Stuttgart - Villastrasse 11, Postfach 10 42 52, 70037 Stuttgart 1 Germany. **Tel** 0711 2686101, FAX 0711 2686115. **Acid Free. Circ:** 1,000.
 Desc: Presents archaeological finds.
 Ind/Abst Anthropol. Lit.; BHA : Biblio. Hist. Art.

LC DS247.Y43 A72
DD 939.4

GW
ARCHAOLOGISCHE BERICHTE AUS DEM YEMEN. Added/Corp Deutsches Archaologisches Institut Sana. No. 1 (1982)-. Periodical. German.
 Ind/Abst Anthropol. Lit.

GW
ARCHAOLOGISCHE BERICHTE / HERAUSGEGEBEN VON DER DEUTSCHEN GESELLSCHAFT FUER UR- UND FRUHGESCHICHTE. (1987)-.
Monographic series. German. Price varies per volume. Computational Mechanics, Ashurst Lodge, Ashurst, Southampton SO4 2AA, United Kingdom. **Tel** 011 44 1703 293223, FAX 011 44 1703 292853. **(Subscription address:** Computational Mechanics, 25 Bridge Street, Billerica MA 01821. **Tel** (508)667-5841.**)**
 Ind/Abst Anthropol. Lit.

GW
ARCHAOLOGISCHE FORSCHUNGEN.
Added/Corp Deutsches Archaologisches Institut. **VFOAT** AF. Vol. 1 (1975)-. Monographic series. German. Irregular. Price varies per volume. Gebrueder Mann Verlag, Lindenstrasse 76, D-10969 Berlin Germany. **Tel** 011 49 30 25913589, telex 183723. **(Subscription address:** Gebrueder Mann Verlag / KNO, Postfach 800620, Koch, Neff & Oetinger, D-70506 Stuttgart Germany. **Tel** 011 49 711 78992022.**)** Index available. **Ad Acc. Circ:** 800.
 Desc: Monographs on subjects of classical archaeology.

ISSN 0721-2399
GW
UDC 902/904(430.1-43.6)

CODEN 571
ARCHAOLOGISCHE JAHR IN BAYERN, DAS. (1981)-. Periodical. German. One time a year.
 Ind/Abst BHA : Biblio. Hist. Art.

ISSN 0170-5814
GW
ARCHAOLOGISCHE MITTEILUNGEN AUS IRAN. ERGANZUNGSBAND.
Added/Corp Deutsches Archaologisches Institut. Abteilung Teheran. (1938)-. Monographic series. German. Dietrich Reimer Verlag, Unter den Eichen 57, D-12203 Berlin Germany. **Tel** 011 49 30 8314081, FAX 011 49 30 831623.
 Ind/Abst BHA : Biblio. Hist. Art.

ISSN 0178-045X
GW
UDC 902
ARCHAOLOGISCHE NACHRICHTEN AUS BADEN. [Archaol. Nachr. Baden]. (1968)-. Periodical. German. Two times a year.
 Ind/Abst BHA : Biblio. Hist. Art; Numis. Lit.

LC CC5 .A74 ISSN 0003-8105
GW
ARCHAOLOGISCHER ANZEIGER.
[Archaol. Anz.]. **Added/Corp** Deutsches Archaologisches Institut. No. 1 (1963)-. Periodical. German (English). Four times a year. $182.70. Walter de Gruyter Inc., PO Box 303421, D-10728 Berlin Germany. **Tel** 011 49 30 260050, FAX 011 49 30 26005251, telex 184027.
 Ind/Abst Anthropol. Lit.; Art Index; BHA : Biblio. Hist. Art; Br. Archaeol. Bibliogr. (?-19??); Numis. Lit.

GR
ARCHEION EUVOIKON MELETON. See History-History of Europe.

IT
ARCHEO. Added/Corp Istituto Geografico De Agostini. No. 1 (Mar. 1985)-. Periodical. Italian. Twelve times a year. L55590. RCS Rizzoli Periodici, Via A Rizzoli 2, 20132 Milan Italy. **Tel** 011 39 2 27200720. cum. index.

FR
ARCHEO-LOG / EDITEE PAR LE GROUPE DIAPRE EN COLLABORATION AVEC LE CENTRE D'INFORMATIQUE DE LA PHILOSOPHIE ET LETTRES. Vol. 1 (May 1986)-. Periodical. French.
 Ind/Abst Anthropol. Lit.

LC CC3 .A65 ISSN 0570-6270
DD 930.1/05 FR
ARCHEOLOGIA. (ARCHEOLOGIA.).
[Archeologia]. No. 1 (Nov./Dec. 1964)-. Periodical. French. Eleven times a year. $101.70. Editions Faton, BP90, 21803 Quetigny Cedex France. **Tel** 011 33 80 469393, FAX 011 33 80 469350. cum. index.
 Ind/Abst Anthropol. Lit.; Archit. Period. Index (April 1980-)(Apr. 1980-); Art Archaeol. Tech. Abstr.; Avery Index Archit. Period. Suppl. Colum. Univ. (1989-); Br. Archaeol. Bibliogr.; Energy Res. Abstr. (Aug. 1982-).

LC DE1 .A65 ISSN 0391-8165
IT
ARCHEOLOGIA CLASSICA. (ARCHEOLOGIA CLASSICA : RIVISTA DELL'ISTITUTO DI ARCHEOLOGIA DELLA UNIVERSITA DI ROMA.).
[Archeol. class.]. **Added/Corp** Universita di Roma. Istituto di Archeologia. Universita di Roma. Istituto di Archeologia e Storia dell'Arte Greca e Romana. Universita di Roma. Istituto di Etruscologia e Antichita Italiche. Scuola Nazionale i Archeologia (Italy) Universita Degli Studi di Roma "La Sapienza." Sezione di Archeologia e Storia dell'Arte Greca, Romana e Tardo-Antica. Universita Degli Studi di Roma "La Sapienza." Sezione di Etruscologia e Antichita Italiche. Universita Degli Studi di Roma "La Sapienza." Istituto di Archeologia e Storia dell'Arte Greca e Romana. Universita Degli Studi di Roma "La Sapienza." Istituto di Etruscologia e Antichita Italiche. (Mar. 1949)-. Italian (German and French). Irregular. Price varies per volume. L'Erma di Bretschneider SPA, via Cassiodoro 19, 00193 Rome Italy. **Tel** 011 39 6 6874127, 011 39 6 6874129, FAX 011 39 6 6874129.
 Ind/Abst Avery Index Archit. Period. Suppl. Colum. Univ.; MLA Int. Bibl. Books Artic. Mod. Lang. Lit.; Numis. Lit.

LC CC ISSN 0154-2656
DD 930.1 FR
ARCHEOLOGIA CORSA. [Archeol. corsa].
VFOAT Etudes et Memoires. (1976)-. French.
 Ind/Abst BHA : Biblio. Hist. Art.

LC DG431 .A76
DD 937 IT
ARCHEOLOGIA MEDIEVALE. (1974)-. Italian.
One time a year (Dec.). L54500. Edizioni All Insegna del Giglio, via R Giuliana 152 R, 50141 Florence Italy. **Tel** 011 39 55 451593.
 Ind/Abst BHA : Biblio. Hist. Art; Br. Archaeol. Bibliogr.; Geogr. Abstr. Phys. Geogr. (?-?).

IT
ARCHEOLOGIA MEDIOEVO. Added/Corp
Gruppo Archeologico Romano. No. 1 (1980)-. Italian.
 Ind/Abst Numis. Lit.

ISSN 0003-8180
PL
ARCHEOLOGIA POLSKI. Added/Corp Polska Akademia Nauk. Instytut Historii Kultury Materialnej.
(1957)-. Academic Scholarly Publication. Polish (summaries and/or abstracts in English, German and Multiple languages). Two times a year. Price varies per volume. Polska Akademia Nauk / Instytut Historii Kultury Materialnej, Al. Solidarnosci 105, 00-140 Warsaw Poland. **(Subscription address:** Ars Polona-Ruch, PO Box 1001, Krakowskie Przedmiescie 7, 00-068 Warsaw Poland. **Tel** 011 48 22 261201.**)**
 Desc: Studies on archaeological elements and methodology.
 Ind/Abst Anthropol. Index; BHA : Biblio. Hist. Art; Numis. Lit.

ISSN 0003-8164
IT
ARCHEOLOGIA (ROMA). (ARCHEOLOGIA.).
[Archeologia]. Vol. 1, No. 1 (Oct. 1962)-. Italian. Six times a year.
 Ind/Abst BHA : Biblio. Hist. Art.

LC DG55.V45 A73 ISSN 0392-9876
DD 937/.3 IT
ARCHEOLOGIA VENETA. Added/Corp
Societa Archeologica Veneta. No. 1 (1978)-. Periodical. Italian. One time a year. Libraccio San Zielo & C, Via del Portello 42, 35129 Padua Italy. **Tel** 011 39 49 8075035.
 Ind/Abst BHA : Biblio. Hist. Art; Numis. Lit.

LC CC9 .A74 ISSN 0392-9485
DD 930.1/05 IT
ARCHEOLOGIA VIVA. Vol. 1, No. 1 (March 1982)-. Periodical. Italian. Six times a year. L23160.
Giunti Gruppo Editore, Via Bolognese 165, 50139 Florence Italy. **Tel** 011 39 55 6679267, 011 39 55 6679257, FAX 011 39 55 268312, telex 571438.
 Ind/Abst Numis. Lit.

LC CC13.P6 A72 ISSN 0066-605X
DD 930.105 PL
ARCHEOLOGIA (WARSAW. 1947).
(ARCHEOLOGIA : ROCZNIK PANSTWOWEGO MUZEUM ARCHEOLOGICZNEGO W WARSZAWIE I POLSKIEGO TOWARZYSTWA ARCHEOLOGICZNEGO.). [Archeologia]. **Added/Corp** Panstwowe Muzeum Archeologiczne (Poland) Polskie Towarzystwo Archeologiczne. Instytut Historii Kultury Materialnej (Polska Akademia Nauk). Vol. 1 (1947)-. Polish. One time a year. $40.00. **(Subscription address:** Ars Polona-Ruch, PO Box 1001, Krakowskie Przedmiescie 7, 00-068 Warsaw Poland. **Tel** 011 48 22 261201.**)**
 Ind/Abst BHA : Biblio. Hist. Art; Numis. Lit.

ISSN 0749-9116
DD 353 US
ARCHEOLOGICAL AND HISTORICAL DATA RECOVERY PROGRAM. Main/Corp
United States. Interagency Archaeological Services Division. (1979)-. Government Publication. English. One time a year. US Department of the Interior / National Park Service, 1849 C Street NW, Room 3104, Washington DC 20240. **Tel** (202)208-4621, FAX (202)208-7520. **Circ:** 1,000. **Continues** United States. Heritage Conservation and Recreation Service. Archeological and Historical Data Recovery Program, 0749-9116.

ISSN 0526-9938

DD 979.4 571 US
ARCHEOLOGICAL REPORT. Added/Corp
California. Resources Agency. Division of Beaches and Parks. Interpretive Services Section. California. Resources Agency. Department of Parks and Recreation. (1961)-. Monographic series. English. Irregular. Price varies per volume. California Department of Parks & Recreation, PO Box 9422896, Sacramento CA 94296. **Tel** (916)445-9663.

LC DB200 .A7 ISSN 0044-8605
XR
ARCHEOLOGICKE ROZHLEDY.
Added/Corp Statni Archeologicky Ustav (Czechoslovakia) Ceskoslovenska Akdemie Ved. **VFOAT** Arkheologicheskie Novosti; Nouvelles Archeologiques. Vol. 1 (1949)-. Periodical. Czech (summaries and/or abstracts in Russian, French and German; table of contents in French and Russian). Four times a year. DM248.00 Germany; DM298.00 other. Archaeological Institute of the Czech Academy of Sciences, Prague Czech Republic. **(Subscription address:** Kubon & Sagner, ABT Zeitschriftenimport, D 80328 Munich Germany. **Tel** 011 49 89 54218130.**)** **ED** Josef Poulik and Jiri Hrala. **Bk Rev. Circ:** 1,400 (ctrl). **Continues** Statni Archeologicky Ustav (Czechoslovakia). Information Bulletin.
 Ind/Abst Anthropol. Lit.; Art Archaeol. Tech. Abstr.; BHA : Biblio. Hist. Art; Br. Archaeol. Bibliogr.; Numis. Lit.

ISSN 0758-7708
FR
ARCHEOLOGIE DU MIDI MEDIEVAL.
[Archeol. Midi mediev.]. **Added/Corp** Centre d'Archeologie Medievale du Languedoc. (1983)-. French. Eleven times a year. $43.74. Centre de Archeologie Medieval, Cite de Carcassonne, 11000 Carcassonne France. **Tel** 011 33 68 712117.
 Ind/Abst BHA : Biblio. Hist. Art.

ISSN 0293-9134
UDC 9 SUSPENDED
ARCHEOLOGIE EN BRETAGNE. SUPPLEMENT. [Archeol. Bretagne, Suppl.].
(1979)-Suspended (19??). Monographic series. French. Faculte de Lettres Sciences, Sociales PB 813, 29285 Brest Cedex France. **Tel** 011 33 98 445273.
 Ind/Abst BHA : Biblio. Hist. Art.

ISSN 0221-4792
FR
ARCHEOLOGIE EN LANGUEDOC.
Added/Corp Federation Archeologique de l'Herault. Vol. 1 (1978)-. French. One time a year.
 Ind/Abst Anthropol. Lit.; BHA : Biblio. Hist. Art.

ISSN 0335-5233
FR SUSPENDED
ARCHEOLOGIE ET BRETAGNE.
(1974)-(19??). Periodical. French. Four times a year. Faculte de Lettres Sciences, Sociales PB 813, 29285 Brest Cedex France. **Tel** 011 33 98 445273.
 Ind/Abst BHA : Biblio. Hist. Art.

ISSN 0778-2837
BE
UDC 430.26
ARCHEOLOGIE IN VLAANDEREN.
[Archeol. Vlaan.]. **VFOAT** Archaeology in Flanders. (1991)-. Periodical. Multiple languages. One time a year. 990.00F. Instituut voor het Archeologisch Patrimonium, Doornveld 1 bus 30, 1731 Asse Zellik Belgium. **ED** Guy de Boe. **Continues** Archaeologia Belgica, 0772-7488.
 Ind/Abst BHA : Biblio. Hist. Art.

ISSN 1156-7198
FR
ARCHEOLOGIE ISLAMIQUE. (1990)-.
Periodical. French. One time a year. 187.68F France; 198.00F other. Editions Maisonneuve et Larose, 15 rue Victor Cousin, 75005 Paris France. **Tel** 011 33 1 44414930.
 Ind/Abst BHA : Biblio. Hist. Art.

LC CC3 .A66 ISSN 0153-9337
DD 930.1 FR
ARCHEOLOGIE MEDIEVALE. [Archeol. mediev.]. Vol. 1 (1971)-. French. One time a year. $34.99. Editions du CNRS, 22 rue Saint Armand, F 75015 Paris France. **Tel** 011 33 1 45075050, telex 200 356 F. **Circ:** 1,500.
 Desc: Chronicle of each archaeological site begun in

Archaeology

France.
Ind/Abst Art Archaeol. Tech. Abstr.; Avery Index Archit. Period. Suppl. Colum. Univ.; BHA : Biblio. Hist. Art.

ISSN 1190-9110
DD 971.4/005 CN
ARCHEOLOGIQUES (QUEBEC). See
History-History of North and South America.

LC CC75.7 .A72 **ISSN** 0891-2920
DD 930 US
CODEN ARCMEZ
Pr Rev. **CEASED**
ARCHEOMATERIALS. [Archeomaterials]. Vol. 1, No. 1 (Fall 1986)-Vol. 7, No. 1 (Winter 1993). Academic Scholarly Publication. English. Archeomaterials, 3333 East 143rd Avenue, Burnham IL 60633. **ED** Tamara Stech, JoAnna Carrol. cum. index. **Bk Rev**. **Ad Acc**. **Circ:** 200. Documents available from CASDDS.
Ind/Abst Anthropol. Lit.; Art Archaeol. Tech. Abstr.; Ceram. Abstr. (19??-); Chem. Abstr. (1986-).

ISSN 0339-7890
UDC 73 FR
ARCHEONUMIS. [Archeonumis]. (1972)-.
Periodical. French.
Ind/Abst Numis. Lit.

FR
ARCHITECTURAL HERITAGE. VFOAT Architectural Heritage, Reports and Studies. 1984-. English. Irregular. Manhattan Publishing Company, PO Box 650, Croton-on-Hudson NY 10520. **Tel** (914)271-5194.

LC NA **ISSN** 1066-6516
DD 720 US
Pr Rev.
ARCHITRONIC (KENT, OHIO).
(ARCHITRONIC [COMPUTER FILE] : THE ELECTRONIC JOURNAL OF ARCHITECTURE.). [Architronic]. **Added/Corp** Kent State University. School of Architecture and Environmental Design. **VFOAT** Arcitron. Vol. 1, No. 1 (1992)-. Periodical. English. Three times a year. Free. Kent State University School of Architecture and Environmental Design, PO Box 5190, Kent OH 44242-0001. **Tel** (216)672-2869, FAX (216)672-3809. **ED** E Robinson. available via Internet (gopher.kent.edu).
Desc: Disseminates articles on all aspects of architecture.

LC DP44 .A7 **ISSN** 0066-6742
SP
ARCHIVO ESPANOL DE ARQUEOLOGIA. [Arch. esp. arqueol.].
Added/Corp Instituto Diego Velazquez. Instituto Espanol de Arqueologia "Rodrigo Caro.". Vol. 14, No. 40 (1940)-. Periodical. Spanish (English, French, Italian and Portuguese). Two times a year. 3000ptas Spain; 4500ptas other. Consejo Superior Investigacion Cientificas / CSIC, Vitruvio 8, 28006 Madrid Spain. **Tel** 011 34 1 5612833, FAX 011 34 1 4113077, telex 42182. **Supersedes in part** Archivo Espanol de Arte y Archeologia.
Desc: Studies on archaeology and ancient history; epigraphics and numismatics.
Ind/Abst Anthropol. Index; Avery Index Archit. Period. Suppl. Colum. Univ. (1988-); BHA : Biblio. Hist. Art; Numis. Lit.

LC DB920 .A2 **ISSN** 0003-8032
DD 943.6 HU
Pr Rev.
ARCHOLOGIAI ERTESITO. [Archol. ert.].
Added/Corp Magyar Tudomanyos Akademia. Archaeologiai Bizottsag. Orszagos Regeszeti es Embertani Tarsulat (Hungary) Magyar Regeszeti, Muveszettorteneti es Eremtani Tarsulat. Magyar Regeszeti es Muveszettorteneti Tarsulat. (1868)-. Academic Scholarly Publication. Hungarian. Two times a year. $28.00. Magyar Nemzeti Muzeum, PF 364, H-1370 Budapest Hungary. **Tel** 011 36 1 1382662, FAX 011 36 1 1177806. (**Subscription address:** Kultura, PO Box 143, H-1300 Budapest 3 Hungary. **Tel** 011 36 1 2500194.) **ED** Istvan Fodor. **Bk Rev**, (Qty: 20). **Circ:** 900 (ctrl).
Desc: Covers the archaeology of Hungary.
Ind/Abst Anthropol. Index; Avery Index Archit. Period. Suppl. Colum. Univ.; BHA : Biblio. Hist. Art.

LC CC79.5.A5 A7 **ISSN** 0299-3600
DD 930.1 FR
ARCHOZOOLOGIA. [Archaeozoologia]. **VFOAT** Archo Zoologia; ArchaeoZoologia. Vol. 1 (1987)-. Periodical. English (French). Two times a year. $122.48. Editions la Pensee Sauvage, BP 141, 38002 Grenoble Cedex France. **Tel** 011 33 76 871303. **ED** Peusee Sauvage.
Desc: Contain the acts of the International Conference of Archaeozoology.
Ind/Abst Anthropol. Lit.

ISSN 0980-7527
UDC 930.26 (448.2) FR
ARDECHE ARCHEOLOGIE. (1984)-.
Periodical. French.
Ind/Abst BHA : Biblio. Hist. Art.

ISSN 0570-622X
GR
ARHAIOLOGIKON DELTION. [Arhaiol. delt.].
(19??)-. Periodical. Greek, Modern.
Ind/Abst BHA : Biblio. Hist. Art.

LC WMLC L 83/66 **ISSN** 0066-7358
DD 949.8 571 RM
ARHEOLOGIA MOLDOVEI. **Added/Corp** Academia Republicii Populare Romine. Filiala Iasi. Institutul de Istorie si Filologie. Sectia de Istorie Veche si Arheologie. Academia Republicii Populare Romine. Filiala Iasi. Institutul de Istorie si Arheologie. Sectia de Istorie Veche si Arheologie. Academia de Stiinte Sociale si Politice a Republicii Socialiste Rpmania. Sectia de Istorie si Arheologie. Institutul de Istorie si Arheologie "A.D. Xenopol". (1961)-. Romanian (summaries and/or abstracts in French and Russian). One time a year. $35.00 Europe; $38.00 US. Editura Academia Republicii Socialiste Romania, Calea Victoriei Nr 125, R-79717 Bucuresti Romania. **Tel** telex 10376 PRSFI R.
(**Subscription address:** Rodipet SA, Societatea Romana de Difuzare a Presei si Tiparurilor, Bucuresti Piata Pressei Libere Nr. 1 Sector 1, PO Box 33-57, Bucharest Romania. **Tel** 011 40 1 6172142, FAX 011 40 1 3129432, 011 40 1 3129433, telex 11995.)
Ind/Abst Anthropol. Index; BHA : Biblio. Hist. Art; Numis. Lit.

LC CC13.R9 A7 **ISSN** 0324-1203
BU
CODEN ARKHDP
ARHEOLOGIJA. (ARKHEOLOGIIA.). [Arheologija].
Added/Corp Arkheologicheski Institut i Muzei (Bulgarska Akademiia na Naukite). (1959)-. Periodical. Bulgarian. Four times a year. Free on request. Haventa Limited, 51 Union Street, Brunswick ME 04011. **Tel** (207)729-1826.
(**Subscription address:** Kubon & Sagner, ABT Zeitschriftenimport, D 80328 Munich Germany. **Tel** 011 49 89 54218130.) Documents available from CASDDS.
Ind/Abst Anthropol. Index; Anthropol. Lit.; Avery Index Archit. Period. Suppl. Colum. Univ.; BHA : Biblio. Hist. Art; Chem. Abstr.; Numis. Lit.

LC DK511.L15 A7 **ISSN** 0570-6343
DD 947 LV
ARHEOLOGIJA UN ETNOGRAFIJA.
Added/Corp Latvijas Padomju Socialistiskas Republikas Zinatnu Akademija. Vestures Instituts. (1957)-. Monographic series. Latvian (summaries and/or abstracts in Russian). Irregular.
Ind/Abst MLA Int. Bibl. Books Artic. Mod. Lang. Lit.

LC CC **ISSN** 0350-2503
DD 930.1 YU
ARHEOLOSKI PREGLED. **Main/Corp** Savez Arheoloskih Drustava Jugoslavije. Beograd. Vol. 17 (1975)-. Periodical. Serbo-Croatian (Roman). **Continues** Savez Arheoloskih Drustava Jugoslavije. Arheoloski Pregled.

LC GN700 .A73 **ISSN** 0570-8958
DD 573.3 CI
ARHEOLOSKI RADOVI I RASPRAVE.
Added/Corp Jugoslovenska Akademija Znanosti i Umjetnosti. **VFOAT** Acta et Dissertationes Archaeologicae. (1959)-. Serbo-Croatian (Roman) (summaries and/or abstracts in French and German). **Ind/Abst** Anthropol. Lit.; Avery Index Archit. Period. Suppl. Colum. Univ. (19??-199?); BHA : Biblio. Hist. Art.

ISSN 0570-8966
XV
ARHEOLOSKI VESTNIK. **Added/Corp** Slovenska Akademija Znanosti in Umetnosti, Ljubljana. Sekcija za Arheologijo. **VFOAT** Acta Archaeologica. (1950)-. Slovenian (English, French and German). Slovenska Akademija Znanosti in Umetnosti, Razred za Filoloske in Literarne Vede, Novi Trg 5-1 Ljubljana Slovenia. **Tel** FAX 011 38 61 155232.
Ind/Abst Anthropol. Index; Avery Index Archit. Period. Suppl. Colum. Univ.; BHA : Biblio. Hist. Art; Numis. Lit.

ISSN 0890-1333
DD 979 US
ARIZONA ARCHAEOLOGICAL COUNCIL NEWSLETTER. [Ariz. Archaed. Counc. newsl.]. **Added/Corp** Arizona Archaeological Council. (197?)-. Newsletter. English. Four times a year. $15.00. Arizona Archaeological Council, 3900 East Old Highway 66, Suite 6, Flagstaff AZ 86004. **Tel** (602)526-1928, FAX (602)526-2202. **ED** Teresa Hoffman. **Circ:** 180.
Desc: Issues dealing with archaeology on both the state and federal level.

ISSN 0518-6617
US
ARKANSAS AMATEUR, THE. **VFOAT** Amateur. Vol. 1 (Jan. 1962)-. Periodical. English. Six times a year. $12.00. NWAAS, PO Box 1154, Fayetteville AR 72702-1154. **Tel** (501)443-2139. **ED** Irlene Shoemaker. **Bk Rev**. **Circ:** 450 (ctrl).
Ind/Abst Ethnoarts Index.

LC E78.A8 A72 **ISSN** 0004-1718
US
ARKANSAS ARCHAEOLOGIST, THE.
(THE ARKANSAS ARCHAEOLOGIST : BULLETIN OF THE ARKANSAS ARCHEOLOGICAL SOCIETY.). [Ark. arch.]. **Added/Corp** Arkansas Archeological Society. Vol. 3, No. 1 (Jan. 1962)-. Bulletin. English. One time a year. $8.00 membership. Arkansas Archeological Survey, PO Box 1249, Fayetteville AR 72702. **Tel** (501)575-3556. **Continues** Newsletter (Arkansas Archeological Society); **Absorbed** Arkansas Archeology.
Ind/Abst Am. Hist. Life (1970-); Anthropol. Lit.; Ethnoarts Index.

ISSN 0277-6308
US
ARKANSAS ARCHEOLOGICAL SURVEY RESEARCH REPORT. **Main/Corp** Arkansas Archeological Survey. **Added/Corp** Arkansas Archeological Survey. Research Report. No. 15 (1977)-. Monographic series. English. Irregular. Price varies per volume. Arkansas Archeological Survey, PO Box 1249, Fayetteville AR 72702. **Tel** (501)575-3556. **ED** W. Fredrick Limp. **Continues** Research Report - Arkansas Archeological Survey.

ISSN 0882-5491
DD 976 US
ARKANSAS ARCHEOLOGICAL SURVEY RESEARCH SERIES. [Ark. Archeol. Surv. res. ser.]. **Added/Corp** Arkansas Archeological Survey. **VFOAT** Research Series (Arkansas Archeological Survey). No. 12 (1981)-. Monographic series. English. Irregular. Price varies per volume. Arkansas Archeological Survey, PO Box 1249, Fayetteville AR 72702. **Tel** (501)575-3556. **ED** Hester A. Davis. **Circ:** 500 (ctrl). **Continues** Research Series (Arkansas Archeological Survey).

ISSN 0882-5483
DD 976 US
ARKANSAS ARCHEOLOGICAL SURVEY TECHNICAL PAPER. [Ark. Archeol. Surv. tech. pap.]. **Added/Corp** Arkansas Archeological Survey. **VFOAT** Technical Paper. (198?)-. Monographic series. English. Irregular. Price varies per volume. Arkansas Archeological Survey, PO Box 1249, Fayetteville AR 72702. **Tel** (501)575-3556. **ED** Hester A. Davis. **Circ:** 100 (ctrl).

LC DL1016 .A74 **ISSN** 0784-235X
FI
ARKEOLOGIA SUOMESSA. **Added/Corp** Finland. Museovirasto. (19??)-. Finnish. One time a year. Arkeologia Suomessa, Ethnos Ry Museovirasto PL913, 00101 Helsinki Finland.

LC CC75.7 .A74
DD 930/.1 NO
ARKEOLOGISKE SKRIFTER. (1975)-.
English (Norwegian). Universitetet i Bergen, Historisk Museum, N-5065 Blomsterndalen Norway.
Ind/Abst Anthropol. Lit.

LC DK3 .A2773 **ISSN** 0571-0626
RU
ARKHEOGRAFICHESKII EZHEGODNIK.
Added/Corp Akademiia Nauk SSSR. Arkheograficheskaia Komissiia. (1957)-. Russian. (**Subscription address:** East View Publications Inc., 3020 Harbor Lane North, Suite 110, Minneapolis MN 55447. **Tel** (800)477-1005, (612)550-0961, FAX (612)559-2931.)
Ind/Abst Numis. Lit.

LC DK511.M55 A848
MV
ARKHEOLOGICHESKIE ISSLEDOVANIIA V MOLDAVII V ... GG. .
Added/Corp Akademiia de Shtiintse a RSSM. Sektsiia de Etnografie shi Studiere a Artelor. Institutul de Istorie (Akademiia de Shtiintse a RSSM). (19??)-. Russian. One time a year. 2.40rub. Moldovan Academy of Sciences, Bul Stefan cel Mare 1, 277001 Chisinau Moldova. **Tel** 011 373 2 261478, FAX 011 373 2 262091. **Circ:** 600.

RU
ARKHEOLOGICHESKIE OTKRYTIIA NA NOVOSTROIKAKH. **Added/Corp** Institut Arkheologii (Akademiia Nauk SSSR). (1986)-. Monographic series. Russian (Russian; summaries and/or abstracts in English). Irregular. Price varies per volume.
Ind/Abst Numis. Lit.

LC DK508.3 .A76 **ISSN** 0235-3490
UN
ARKHEOLOHIIA. Vol. 1 (1989)-. Periodical. Ukrainian. Four times a year. Izdatelstvo Naukova Dumka / Ukrainian Academy of Sciences, Yu. A. Khramov, Dir., Ul. Repina 3, 252 601 Kiev Ukraine. **Tel** 011 7 44 4303441, 011 7 44 2254182, telex 131376. **Continues** Arkheolohiia (Kiev, Ukraine : 1971).
Ind/Abst Anthropol. Lit.; BHA : Biblio. Hist. Art; Numis. Lit.

Archaeology

ISSN 0901-0815
DK

ARKOLOGISKE UDGRAVNINGER I DANMARK / RIGSANTIKVARENS ARKOLOGISKE SEKRETARIAT.
Added/Corp Rigsantikvarens Arkologiske Sekretariat (Denmark) Arkologiske Nvn (Denmark). (1984)-. Danish. One time a year. Free. Danmark National Museet, Museumstjenesten Sjoerupvej 1, DK-8800 Lysgaard Denmark.

LC CC13.S66 A77 **ISSN** 0187-6074
DD 972/.01/05 MX

ARQUEOLOGIA. **Added/Corp** Instituto Nacional de Antropologia e Historia (Mexico). Direccion de Monumentos Prehispanicos. (1989)-. Periodical. Spanish. Two times a year (Jan. & June). Direccion de Monumentos Prehispanicos, Instituto Nacional de Antropologia e Historia, Cordoba No. 45, Col. Roma Mexico DF Mexico.
Ind/Abst Anthropol. Lit.

LC F1219 .A7633 **ISSN** 0188-8218
MX

●**ARQUEOLOGIA MEXICANA.** **Added/Corp** Instituto Nacional de Antropologia e Historia (Mexico). Vol. 1, No. 1 (Apr./May 1993)-. Periodical. Spanish. Six times a year. $40.00 North America, Central America and Carribean; $47.00 Europe and South America; $54.00 other. Editorial Raices, Avenue Taxquena 1798, 04250 69 Mexico DF Mexico. **Tel** 011 52 5 5818333.

LC CC13.P8 A76 **ISSN** 0870-2306
PO

ARQUEOLOGIA (PORTO).
(ARQUEOLOGIA.). [Arqueologia]. **Added/Corp** Grupo de Estudos Arqueologicos do Porto (Portugal). No. 1 (June 1980)-. Periodical. Portuguese (English). Two times a year. Grupo de Estudos Arqueologicos do Porto, R Antonio Cardoso 175, 4100 Porto Portugal.
Ind/Abst Anthropol. Lit.; Ethnoarts Index.

PO
ARQUEOLOGO PORTUGUES, O.
Added/Corp Lisbon. Museu Etnologico do Dr. Leite de Vasconcellos. Vol. 1-30 (1895/1938)-. Portuguese. One time a year. 2500$00. Museu Nacional de Arqueologia, Placa do Imperio, P-1400 Lisbon Portugal. cum. index.
Bk Rev.
Ind/Abst Anthropol. Lit.; Numis. Lit.

LC N5310 .A67
DD 709/.01/1 SP

ARS PRAEHISTORICA. Vol. 1, (1982)-. English (French, German, Italian and Spanish). Apartado de Correos 101, Sabadell (Barcelona) Spain.
Ind/Abst Br. Archaeol. Bibliogr.

ISSN 0044-9075
AT
Pr Rev.
ARTEFACT, THE. [Artefact]. **Added/Corp** Archaeological Society of Victoria. No. 1-39, (1965-Nov. 1975); New Series, Vol. 1 (March 1976)-. Periodical. English. One time a year. 16.44Aus$. Archaeological & Anthropological Society, PO Box 328c, Melbourne Victoria 3001 Australia. **Tel** 011 81 3 5230549. **ED** Robert G. Bednarik. **Bk Rev. Ad Acc. Circ:** 400 (ctrl).
Desc: Archaeology, anthropology and ethnohistory of the Pacific region.
Ind/Abst Anthropol. Lit.; APAIS, Aust. Public Aff. Inf. Ser. (1980-); Br. Archaeol. Bibliogr.

LC N8 .A75 **ISSN** 0004-3648
DD 705 SZ
ARTIBUS ASIAE. See The Arts-Art.

SZ
ARTIBUS ASIAE. SUPPLEMENTUM. See The Arts-Art.

LC E78.S7 A74 **ISSN** 0004-3680
DD 917.9/03 US
ARTIFACT, THE. **Added/Corp** El Paso Archaeological Society. Vol. 1 (1963)-. Periodical. English. Four times a year. $20.00. El Paso Archaeological Society Inc, PO Box 4345, El Paso TX 79914. **Tel** (915)751-3295. **ED** P. Baker and C. Hedrick. **Bk Rev. Circ:** 215 (ctrl).
Desc: Contributed to by amateur and professional archaeologists. Covers archaeology in the El Paso area in particular and the Southwest in general.
Ind/Abst Anthropol. Lit.; Ethnoarts Index.

LC DR431 .A8
TU
ASAG FRAT HAVZAS ... YUZEY ARASTRMALAR. **VFOAT** Asag Frat. (1975)-. Turkish.

ISSN 0066-829X
US
ASIAN AND PACIFIC ARCHAEOLOGY SERIES. **Added/Corp** Hawaii. University, Honolulu. Social Science Research Institute. No. 1 (1967)-. Monographic series. English. Irregular. Price varies per volume. University of Hawaii Press, 2840 Kolowalu Street, Honolulu HI 96822. **Tel** (808)956-8833, (808)948-8697, FAX (808)988-6052.
Desc: A series of books on archaeology.

LC DS514 .A78 **ISSN** 0066-8435
DD 950/.05 US
ASIAN PERSPECTIVES (HONOLULU).
(ASIAN PERSPECTIVES.). **Added/Corp** Far-Eastern Prehistory Association. American Branch. Vol. 1 (1957)-. English. Two times a year (July & Nov.). $33.00. University of Hawaii Press, 2840 Kolowalu St., Honolulu HI 96822. **Tel** (808)956-8833, (808)948-8697, FAX (808)988-6052. **ED** Michael W. Graves. cum. index.
Bk Rev. Ad Acc. Circ: 500. available on microfilm and microfiche from University Microfilms International (UMI).
Desc: Deals with the archaeology and prehistory of Asia and the Pacific, covering island areas from Madagascar to Hawaii and Easter Island, and continental areas from Pakistan to Siberia to Vietnam.
Ind/Abst Abstr. Anthropol.; Anthropol. Index; Anthropol. Lit.; Ceram. Abstr. (19??-); Curr. Geogr. Publ. (199?-).

LC DS211 .A84
SU
SUSPENDED
ATLAL. **Added/Corp** Saudi Arabia. Idarat al-Athar wa-al-Matahif. **VFOAT** Journal of Saudi Arabian Archaeology. (1977)-Suspended Vol. 13 (19??). Periodical. Arabic (English). One time a year. $12.00 Saudi Arabia; $24.00 other. Director General Department of Antiques and Museums, POB 3734, Riyadh 11481 Saudi Arabia. **Tel** 011 966 1 4115777, FAX 011 966 1 4112051. **ED** Hamid Abu Duruk. cum. index. **Bk Rev. Ad Acc. Circ:** 4,000.
Desc: Archaeological reports on the ongoing survey, excavation programs in Saudi Arabia. Also, recent exploration and research, etc.
Ind/Abst Anthropol. Lit.; Middle East Abstr. Index.

IT
ATTI DELLA PONTIFICIA ACCADEMIA ROMANA DI ARCHEOLOGIA. MEMORIE.
Added/Corp Pontificia Accademia Romana di Archeologia. Ser. 3, Vol. 1 (1923/1924)-. Italian. L'Erma di Bretschneider SPA, via Cassiodoro 19, 00193 Rome Italy. **Tel** 011 39 6 6874127, 011 39 6 6874129, FAX 011 39 6 6874129. **Continues in part** Dissertazione Della Pontificia Accademia Romana di Archeologia.
Ind/Abst BHA : Biblio. Hist. Art.

LC CC31 .P72

IT
ATTI DELLA PONTIFICIA ACCADEMIA ROMANA DI ARCHEOLOGIA. SERIE III, RENDICONTI. **Added/Corp** Pontificia Accademia romana di archeologia. **VFOAT** Rendiconti della Pont. Accad. Romana di Archeologia; Rend. della Pont. Accad. Rom. d'Arch. Vol. 1 (1923)-. Italian. Irregular. 16000000L. L'Erma di Bretschneider SPA, via Cassiodoro 19, 00193 Rome Italy. **Tel** 011 39 6 6874127, 011 39 6 6874129, FAX 011 39 6 6874129. cum. index. **Continues in part** Dissertazione della Pontificia Accademia Romana di Archeologia.
Ind/Abst Avery Index Archit. Period. Suppl. Colum. Univ. (19??-199?); BHA : Biblio. Hist. Art.

LC WMLC L 83/7545
IT
ATTI E MEMORIE DELLA SOCIETA ISTRIANA DI ARCHEOLOGIA E STORIA PATRIA. **Main/Corp** Societa Istriana di Archeologia e Storia Patria. **VFOAT** Atti e Memorie. Vol. 1 (1884)-. Periodical. Italian. One time a year (One volume & one supplement per year). L20440. Societa Istriana di Archeologia e Storia Patria, Via Lamarmora 17, 34139 Trieste Italy. **Bk Rev. (Qty: 5). Circ:** 500 (ctrl).
Desc: Contains information on archaeology history and folklore of the Istria region.
Ind/Abst BHA : Biblio. Hist. Art.

ISSN 0004-8127
GW
UDC 930.26
TITLE CHANGE
AUSGRABUNGEN UND FUNDE.
(1956)-(Jan. 1996). Periodical. German. Akademie-Verlag GmbH, Postfach, D-13162 Berlin Germany. **Tel** 011 49 30 47889300, FAX 011 49 30 47889357. **(Subscription address:** VCH Publishers Inc., 303 Northwest 12th Avenue, Journals Department, Deerfield FL 33442. **Tel** (800)367-8249, (305)428-5566.) Documents available from The Genuine Article. **Continued by** Archaeologisches Nachrichtenblatt.
Desc: Reports recent excavations and finds from pre- and early history, as well as medieval archaeology, from Central and Eastern Germany.
Ind/Abst Anthropol. Index; Arts Humanit. Citation Index [Full Cov.]; BHA : Biblio. Hist. Art; Numis. Lit.; Res. Alert [Full Cov.]; Soc. Sci. Cit. Index [Full Cov.].

LC DD801.W5445 A87 **ISSN** 0175-6133
DD 936.3 GW
AUSGRABUNGEN UND FUNDE IN WESTFALEN-LIPPE / IM AUFTRAG DES LANDSCHAFTSVERBANDES WESTFALEN-LIPPE HERAUSGEGEBEN VON WESTFALISCHES MUSEUM FUER ARCHAOLOGIE, AMT FUER BODENDENKMALPFLEGE. See History-History of Europe.

ISSN 0312-2417
AT
Pr Rev.
AUSTRALIAN ARCHAEOLOGY.
(AUSTRALIAN ARCHAEOLOGY : AA). [Aust. archaeol.]. **Added/Corp** Australian Archaeological Association. Australian Archaeological Association. Newsletter. **VFOAT** AA; Newsletter. No. 1 (Nov. 1974)-. Periodical. English. Two times a year. 34.53Aus$. University of Western Australia, Department of Archaeology, Membership Secretary AAA Inc, Nedlands Western Australia 6009 Australia. **Tel** 011 61 9 3802868, FAX 011 61 9 3801023. **ED** Dr. Betty Meehan. cum. index. **Bk Rev. Ad Acc. Circ:** 400 (ctrl).
Desc: All fields of archaeology and other subjects relevant to archaeological research and practice in Australia and nearby areas.
Ind/Abst Anthropol. Lit.; APAIS, Aust. Public Aff. Inf. Ser. (1982-); Ethnoarts Index.

LC DU106 .A94 **ISSN** 0810-1868
DD 994/.01 AT
AUSTRALIAN JOURNAL OF HISTORICAL ARCHAEOLOGY, THE.
Added/Corp Australian Society for Historical Archaeology. Vol. 1 (Jan. 1983)-. English. One time a year. Free to members of the Australian Society for Archaeology. Australian Society for Historical Archaeology, Box 220, Holme Building, University of Sydney, Sydney New South Wales 2006 Australia. **Tel** 011 61 2 6922763. **ED** N. Ritchie. **Bk Rev. Circ:** 430 (ctrl).
Desc: Historical archaeology and the study of the material remains of European settlement in Australia, and New Zealand, comparative material and techniques worldwide.
Ind/Abst Anthropol. Lit.; APAIS, Aust. Public Aff. Inf. Ser.

ISSN 0749-1816
DD 978 US
AWANYU. [Awanyu]. **Added/Corp** Archaeological Society of New Mexico. (Mar. 1, 1973)-. Periodical. English. Four times a year (also volume of papers). $15.00 (individual memberships), $20.00 (institutional memberships), $30.00 (sustaining family memerships). Archaeological Society of New Mexico, PO Box 3485, Albuquerque NM 87110. **ED** Karl and Nancy Olsen, 1517 Dartmouth NE, Albuquerque, NM 87106 USA; Telephone: (505)255-7719. **Circ:** 450. **Supersedes** Newsletter - Archaeological Society of New Mexico.
Desc: News items of general interest on New Mexico archaeology, ethnology or anthropology. News of the society or of its affiliated local chapters.
Ind/Abst Ethnoarts Index.

UK
AYRSHIRE MONOGRAPHS. (19??)-. Monographic series. English. Two times a year. Price varies per volume. Ayrshire Archaeological and Natural History Society, Ronald W. Brash, 10 Robsland Avenue, Ayr KA7 2RW United Kingdom. **Tel** 011 44 1292 266745. **ED** John Strawhorn, Trevor Mathews, David Reid. **Circ:** 500. **Continues** Ayrshire Collections.

LC DT365.3 .A94 **ISSN** 0067-270X
DD 967/.001 KE
AZANIA. [Azania]. **Added/Corp** British Institute in Eastern Africa. British Institute of History and Archaeology in East Africa. Vol. 1 (1966)-. English (French, German and Italian). One time a year. $33.00. British Institute in Eastern Africa, PO Box 30710, Nairobi Kenya. **Tel** 011 254 2 43721, 011 254 2 43330. **ED** J. E. G. Sutton. Index available. cum. index. **Bk Rev. (Qty: 10). Circ:** 750.
Desc: Research articles on prehistory, ethnography and linguistics which concentrate on the Eastern African region; similar studies on other parts of the continent also published.
Ind/Abst Anthropol. Lit.; Ethnoarts Index; GeoRef; Int. Bibliogr. Sociol.

LC DS69.5 .B25 **ISSN** 0418-9698
GW
BAGHDADER MITTEILUNGEN. [Baghdad. Mitt.]. **Added/Corp** Deutsches Archaologisches Institut. Abteilung Baghdad. Vol. 1 (1960)-. German. One time a year. DM174.00. Gebrueder Mann Verlag, Lindenstrasse 76, D-10969 Berlin Germany. **Tel** 011 49 30 25913589, telex 183723. Index available. **Circ:** 600.
Desc: Scientific works concerning archeological themes and studies on languages of the Two-River area starting with prehistoric times and ending with the Islamic period.
Ind/Abst Avery Index Archit. Period. Suppl. Colum. Univ. (19??-199?); BHA : Biblio. Hist. Art.

LC DS67 .B3

GW

BAGHDADER MITTEILUNGEN. BEIHEFT. **Added/Corp** Deutsches Archaologisches Institute. Abteilung Baghdad. (1968)-. Periodical. German. Irregular. Price varies per volume. Gebrueder Mann Verlag, Lindenstrasse 76, D-10969 Berlin Germany. **Tel** 011 49 30 25913589, telex 183723. **(Subscription address:** Gebrueder Mann Verlag / KNO, Postfach 800620, Koch, Neff & Oetinger, D-70506 Stuttgart Germany. **Tel** 011 49 711 78992022.**)** Index available. **Circ:** 600.
Desc: Scientific works concerning archeological themes and studies on languages of the Two-River area from prehistoric times to the Islamic period.
Ind/Abst Avery Index Archit. Period. Suppl. Colum. Univ. (19??-199?).

LC CC **ISSN** 0143-3032
DD 930.1 UK

BAR BRITISH SERIES. **VAT** British Archaeological Reports, British Series. (1978)-. Monographic series. English. Irregular. Price varies per volume. British Archaeological Reports, 5 Centremead Osney Mead, Oxford 0X2 0E5 United Kingdom. ***Continues** British Archaeological Report, 0306-1205.*
Ind/Abst Annu. Bibliogr. Engl. Lang. Lit.; Avery Index Archit. Period. Suppl. Colum. Univ. (1988-); Curr. Cit.; GeoRef.

ISSN 0143-3067
UK

BAR INTERNATIONAL SERIES. [BAR int. ser.]. **VFOAT** B.A.R. International Series. (1978)-. Monographic series. English. Irregular. Price varies per volume. Tempus Repartum, 29 Beaumont Street, Oxford OX1 2NP United Kingdom. **Tel** 011 44 1865 59543. **(Subscription address:** Hadrian Books, 122 Bambury Road, Oxford OX2 7BP United Kingdom. **)** ***Continues** BAR International Series (Supplementary), 0143-3059.*
Ind/Abst Curr. Cit.; GeoRef.

LC DA670.B29 B25
DD 936.2/56/005 UK

BEDFORDSHIRE ARCHAEOLOGY. **Added/Corp** Bedfordshire Archaeological Council. (1983)-. Periodical. English. Bedfordshire Archeological CNL, 14 Glebe Avenue, Bedford MK45 1HS United Kingdom. **Tel** 011 44 1525 712778. ***Continues** Bedfordshire Archaeological Journal, 0408-7666.*
Ind/Abst Avery Index Archit. Period. Suppl. Colum. Univ.; BHA : Biblio. Hist. Art.

LC CC5 .B44 **ISSN** 0170-9518
GW

BEITRAEGE ZUR ALLGEMEINEN UND VERGLEICHENDEN ARCHAEOLOGIE. **Added/Corp** Deutsches Archaeologisches Institut. Kommission fuer Allgemeine und Vergleichende Archaeologie. **VFOAT** AVA-Beitraege; A.V.A.-Beitraege; AVA Beitraege; A.V.A. Beitraege. **VAT** Allgemeinen und Vergleichenden Archaeologie Beitraege. (1981)-. German (Spanish; summaries and/or abstracts in English). One time a year. $191.91. Verlag Phillip Von Zabern, Postfach 190930, D-80609 Munich Germany. **Tel** 011 49 89 12151661, FAX 011 49 61 31223710, telex 4187463. **(Subscription address:** Phillip von Zabern Verlag, Nymphenburgerstrasse 84, D 80636 Munich Germany. **Tel** 011 49 89 12151661.**)** ***Continues** Allgemeine und Vergleichende Archaologie Beitrage.*
Ind/Abst BHA : Biblio. Hist. Art.

LC WMLC L 83/5238

AU

BEITRAEGE ZUR MITTELALTERARCHAEOLOGIE IN OESTERREICH / [HERAUSGEGEBER: INSTITUT FUER UR- UND FRUEHGESCHICHTE DER UNIVERSITAET WIEN]. **Added/Corp** Universitat Wien. Institut fuer Ur- und Fruhgeschichte. (1969)-. German. Franz Deuticke Verlagsges MbH, Helferstorferstrasse 4, PF 761, A 1011 Vienna Austria. **Tel** (0222)5331535, FAX (02236)63535240, telex 7PR46 OEBV.

AU

BEITRAEGE ZUR MITTELALTERARCHAOLOGIE IN OESTERREICH. BEIHEFT. **Added/Corp** Osterrreichische Gesellschaft fuer Mittelalterarchaologie. (1986)-. Monographic series. German. Irregular. Price varies per volume.

ISSN 0067-5164
GW

UDC 930.26(430.1-35.65)

●**BEITRAEGE ZUR OBERFALZFORSCHUNG.** **See** History-History of Europe.

GW

BEITRAEGE ZUR UR- UND FRUEHGESCHICHTE DER BEZIRKE ROSTOCK, SCHWERIN UND NEUBRANDENBURG. **Added/Corp** Schwerin. Museum fuer Ur- und Fruehgeschichte. Vol. 1 (1967)-. Monographic series. German. One time a year. Price varies per volume. Deutscher Verlag der Wissenschaften, Taubennstrasste 10, D-10117 Berlin Germany. **Tel** 011 49 30 2291146. **ED** H. Keiling. **Bk Rev**. **Ad Acc**. ctrl circ.
Desc: Monographs the latest archaeological and research findings on the prehistory and early history of the districts of Rostock, Schwerin and Neubrandenburg.

ISSN 0067-5245
DD 572 GW

BEITRAEGE ZUR UR- UND FRUGESCHICHTLICHEN ARCHAOLOGIE DES MITTELMEER-KULTURRAUMES. Vol. 1 (1965)-. Periodical. German. Irregular. Dr. Rudolf Habelt GmbH, Postfach 150104, D-53040 Bonn Germany. **Tel** 011 49 228 232015. **ED** H Hauptmann and Red Schnickel.

GW

BERICHT DER ROEMISCH-GERMANISCHEN KOMMISSION. **Main/Corp** Deutsches Archaeologisches Institut. Roemisch-Germanische Kommission. **Added/Corp** Deutsches Archaeologisches Institut. Roemisch-Germanische Kommission. Vol. 21 (1931)-. Monographic series. German. One time a year. Price varies per volume. Verlag Phillip Von Zabern, Postfach 190930, D-80609 Munich Germany. **Tel** 011 49 89 12151661, FAX 011 49 61 31223710, telex 4187463. cum. index. ctrl circ. ***Continues** Bericht (Deutsches Archaeologisches Institut. Roemisch-Germanische Kommission).*
Desc: Features new reports of different authors, essays, statements and research.
Ind/Abst BHA : Biblio. Hist. Art; Br. Archaeol. Bibliogr.

GW

BERICHT DER STAATLICHEN DENKMALPFLEGE IM SAARLAND. ABTEILUNG BODENDENKMALPFLEGE. **Added/Corp** Saarbruecken. Staatliche Konservatoramt. **VFOAT** Beitraege zur Archaeologie und Kunstgeschichte. (1971)-. German. One time a year. ***Continues in part** Bericht der Staatlichen Denkmalpflege im Saarland.*
Ind/Abst BHA : Biblio. Hist. Art; Numis. Lit.

GW

BERICHT DER STAATLICHEN DENKMALPFLEGE IM SAARLAND. ABTEILUNG KUNSTDENKMALPFLEGE. **Added/Corp** Saarbruecken. Staatliche Konservatoramt. **VFOAT** Beitraege zur Archaeologie und Kunstgeschichte. (1971)-. German. One time a year. ***Continues in part** Bericht der Staatlichen Denkmalpflege im Saarland.*
Ind/Abst BHA : Biblio. Hist. Art.

ISSN 0418-9655
DD 913 GW

BERICHT UEBER DIE AUSGRABUNGEN IN OLYMPIA. **Added/Corp** Deutsches Archaeologisches Institut. Vol. 1 (1936/37)-. Periodical. German. Irregular. Walter de Gruyter Inc., PO Box 303421, D-10728 Berlin Germany. **Tel** 011 49 30 260050, FAX 011 49 30 26005251, telex 184027.

LC GN **ISSN** 0525-5791
DD 571 943 GW

BERICHTE UEBER DIE AUSGRABUNGEN IN HAITHABU. **Added/Corp** Schleswig-Holsteinisches Landesmuseum fuer Vor- und Fruegeschichte in Schleswig. (1969)-. Monographic series. German. Irregular.
Ind/Abst BHA : Biblio. Hist. Art.

LC GN855.I6 B47

IO

BERITA PRASEJARAH. **VFOAT** Bulletin of Prehistory. Vol. 1. (Mar. 1974)-. Bulletin. Multiple languages (English and Indonesian). Irregular. Bidang Prosejarah, Jalan Kimia 12, PO Box 2533, Jakarta Indonesia.

LC CC79.C5 B47 **ISSN** 0344-5089
GW

BERLINER BEITRAEGE ZUR ARCHAOMETRIE. [Berl. Beitr. Archaom.]. **Added/Corp** Staatliche Museen Preussischer Kulturbesitz. (1976)-. Monographic series. German (summaries and/or abstracts in English and French). Irregular. DM38.00. Staatliche Museen Preussischer, Kulturbesitz Stauffenberg 41, D-10785 Berlin Germany. **Tel** 011 49 30 2662605.
Ind/Abst Anthropol. Lit.; Art Archaeol. Tech. Abstr.; BHA : Biblio. Hist. Art.

LC F1636 .B56 **ISSN** 1013-431X
BM

BERMUDA JOURNAL OF ARCHAEOLOGY AND MARITIME HISTORY. **Added/Corp** Bermuda Maritime Museum. Vol. 1 (1989)-. Periodical. English. One time a year. $25.00. Bermuda Maritime Museum, PO Box MA273, Mangrove Bay Bermuda. **Tel** (809)234-1333, FAX (809)234-1735. **ED** J C Arnell. **Bk Rev**. ***Continues** Bermuda Historical Quarterly.*
Desc: Papers on archaeology and maritime history of Bermuda, including underwater archaeology, from 1492 into the 20th Century.

LC DS41 .B4 **ISSN** 0067-6195
DD 913.394 LE
Pr Rev.

BERYTUS (BEIRUT). (BERYTUS; ARCHAEOLOGICAL STUDIES.). [Berytus]. **Added/Corp** American University of Beirut. Museum of Archaeology. Vol. 1 (1934)-(June 1989); (Apr. 13, 1993)-. English (French and German). One time a year. $15.00. American University of Beirut, Archaeology Museum, Beirut Lebanon. **Tel** 011 961 1 8652516, telex AMUNOB 20801 LE. **ED** Helga Seeden and William A. Ward. Index available. cum. index. **Bk Rev**. **Ad Acc**. **Circ:** 500 (ctrl).
Desc: Devoted to historical and archaeological studies on Syria and Lebanon from prehistory to Islamic times.
Ind/Abst Anthropol. Index; Art Archaeol. Tech. Abstr.; BHA : Biblio. Hist. Art; Geogr. Abstr. Human Geogr.; Middle East Abstr. Index; Numis. Lit.; Old Testam. Abstr.

LC BS620.A1 B5 **ISSN** 0006-0895
DD 220.93 US

BIBLICAL ARCHAEOLOGIST, THE. [Biblic. archaeolog.]. **Added/Corp** American Schools of Oriental Research. Vol. 1 (Feb. 1938)-. Periodical. English. Four times a year (Mar., June, Sept., Dec.). $45.00. Scholars Press / Georgia, PO Box 15399, Atlanta GA 30333-0399. **Tel** (404)636-4757, (404)727-2320, FAX (404)727-2348. **ED** Eric M. Meyers. Index available. cum. index (Vols. 36-45, 1973-1982). **Bk Rev**. **Ad Acc**. **Circ:** 7,500. available on microfilm and microfiche from University Microfilms International (UMI). Documents available from UMI Article Clearinghouse.
Desc: Covers news of archaeological discoveries and the results of ongoing historical research from sites in the ancient Near East. The journal also covers articles that illuminate Old and New Testament scriptures and history, interpret the meaning of archaeological finds, and trace the evolution of Western culture and traditions.
Ind/Abst Abstr. Anthropol.; Acad. Search; Anthropol. Index; Art Index; Arts Humanit. Citation Index [Full Cov.]; Christ. Period. Index; EP Collect.; Expand. Acad. Index (1989-); Hist. Source (Jan. 1993-); Homework Help.; Humanit. Index; Humanit. Source; Index Book Rev. Relig.; INFO-SOUTH Abstr.; MasterFile FullTEXT 1000; MasterFile FullTEXT 350; MasterFile FullTEXT 650; MasterFile FullTEXT (Jan. 1993-); Middle East Abstr. Index; MLA Int. Bibl. Books Artic. Mod. Lang. Lit.; New Testam. Abstr.; Newsp. Period. Abstr. (1991-); Numis. Lit.; OCLC; Old Testam. Abstr.; Pub. Lib. FullTEXT; Relig. Index One Period. (1949-); Relig. Theol. Abstr.; Soc. Sci. Cit. Index [Select. Cov.]; Telebase; Abr. Cathol. Period. Lit. Index; Cathol. Period. Lit. Index; Vocat. Search.

LC BS620.A1 B52 **ISSN** 0098-9444
DD 220.9/3/05 US

BIBLICAL ARCHAEOLOGY REVIEW, THE. [Biblic. archaeol. rev.]. **Added/Corp** Biblical Archaeology Society. Vol. 1, No. 1 (Mar. 1975)-. Periodical. English. Six times a year. $27.00. Biblical Archaeology Review, 4710 41st Street Northwest, Washington DC 20016. **(Subscription address:** CDS Agency Hard Copy, PO Box 4966, Des Moines IA 50340. **Tel** (515)247-7569.**)** **ED** Hershel Shanks. **Circ:** 115,000.
Desc: Devoted to the archaeology of the biblical world. Old and New Testament issues are covered by archaeologists and biblical scholars. Covers understandings of biblical history and interpretations of biblical heritage.
Ind/Abst Abstr. Anthropol.; Avery Index Archit. Period. Suppl. Colum. Univ. (1990-); Christ. Period. Index (19??-); Guide Soc. Sci. Relig.; Index Book Rev. Relig.; Middle East Abstr. Index; New Testam. Abstr.; Old Testam. Abstr.; Relig. Index One Period. (1981-); Relig. Theol. Abstr.

UK

BIBLICAL ARCHAEOLOGY REVIEW. **See** Religions and Theology.

LC Z5111 .B47 GN25 **ISSN** 0896-8101
DD 016.301/05 US

BIBLIOGRAPHIC GUIDE TO ANTHROPOLOGY AND ARCHAEOLOGY. [Bibliogr. guide anthropol. archaeol.]. **Added/Corp** G.K. Hall & Company. **VFOAT** Anthropology and Archaeology; Anthropology & Archaeology. (1987)-. English. One time a year. $230.00. GK Hall & Co., 100 Front Street, Riverside NJ 08075. **Tel** (800)257-5755 ext. 2223.
Desc: Contains entries for books, serials, pamphlets, microforms, manuscripts, maps and films on anthropology, archaeology and ethnology cataloged by the Tozzer Library at Harvard University.

LC Z5133.R46 B5 CC79.5 .A5 **ISSN** 0232-4865
DD 016.9301 GW

BIBLIOGRAPHIE ZUR ARCHAO-ZOOLOGIE UND GESCHICHTE DER HAUSTIERE. **See** Archaeology-Abstracting, Bibliographies and Statistics.

Archaeology

ISSN 0732-6440
US

BIBLIOTHECA MESOPOTAMICA.
Added/Corp International Institute for Mesopotamian Area Studies. (1975)-. Monographic series. English. Irregular. Price varies per volume. Undena Publications, PO Box 97, Malibu CA 90265. **Tel** (310)649-2612. **(Subscription address:** Crescent Academic Services, 29528 Madera Avenue, Shafter CA 93263. **Tel** (805)746-5870.) **ED** G. Buccellati. **Circ**: 350.
Desc: Primary sources and interpretive analysis for the study of Mesopotamian civilization from late prehistoric times to the end of the cuneiform tradition.

LC Z3001 .B58 **ISSN 0006-1913**
DD 016.9133 NE

BIBLIOTHECA ORIENTALIS. [Bibl. orient.].
Added/Corp Nederlands Instituut voor het Nabije Oosten. Nederlandsch Archaeologisch-Philologisch Instituut voor het Nabije Oosten. Vol. 1 (April 1943)-. Periodical. Dutch (German and French). Four times a year. $179.85. Nederlands Institution Nabije Oosten, PO Box 9515, 2300 RA Leiden Netherlands. **Tel** 071-27 20 20. **ED** H J A De Meulenaere, M J Mulder, C Nijland, M Stol, E Van Donzel and D J W Meijer. Index available. cum. index. **Bk Rev**. **Circ:** 700 (ctrl).
Desc: Archaeology of the Near East and Assyriology, Hethites, Old Testament, Hebrew and cognate languages: Arabic, Persian, Turkish and Islam.
Ind/Abst Index Book Rev. Relig.; Middle East Abstr. Index; New Testam. Abstr.; Numis. Lit.; Old Testam. Abstr.; Middle East J.

UA

BIBLIOTHEQUE D'ETUDE. **Added/Corp**
Institut Francais d'Archeologie Orientale du Caire. (1908)-. Monographic series. French. Price varies per volume. Institut Francais d'Archeologie Orientale du Caire, 37 Mounira Street, Cairo Rae Egypt. **(Subscription address:** Leila Bookshop, PO Box 31 El Daher, 11271 Cairo Egypt. **Tel** 011 202 3924475, 011 202 3507399.)
Desc: Selected texts from the works of ancient Egyptian literature and illustration of the civilization of the first inhabitants of the Nile Valley.

LC GN814.M4 B6
GW

BODENDENKMALPFLEGE IN MECKLENBURG-VORPOMMERN : JAHRBUCH. **Added/Corp** Museum fuer Ur- und Fruehgeschichte (Schwerin, Germany) Archaeologisches Landesmuseum Mecklenburg-Vorpommern. **VFOAT** Bodendenkmalpflege in Mecklenburg. (1990)-. German. Irregular. Landesamt fuer Bodendenkmalpflege, Schloss Wiligrad, D-19069 Luebstorf Germany. **Continues** Bodendenkmalpflege in Mecklenburg, 0067-9461.
Ind/Abst BHA : Biblio. Hist. Art.

LC F2519 .I57B
BL

BOLETIM DO INSTITUTO DE ARQUEOLOGIA BRASILEIRA. **Main/Corp**
Instituto de Arqueologia Brasileira. (19??)-. Bulletin. Portuguese (English and Spanish). One time a year. Cr$1,200.00 Brazil; $10.00 US. Instituto de Arqueologia Brasileira, Caixa Postal 2892, CEP 20001, Rio de Janeiro Brazil. **ED** Eilana Carvalho and Ondemar Dias Jr. Index available. **Ad Acc**. **Circ:** 500 (ctrl).
Desc: Covers Brazilian prehistoric archaeology, archaic and formative cultures of Rio de Janeiro, Ninas Gerais, Acre and the Amazonas states. Includes methodologies, field reports, theses and essays. Also includes catalogs referents to archaeological exhibitions.
Ind/Abst Ethnoarts Index.

ISSN 0034-0863
SP
UDC 930

BOLETIN ARQUEOLOGICO (TARRAGONA. 1943). [Bol. arqueol. Tarragona. 1943]. **VFOAT** Butlleti Arqueologic (Tarragona. 1979). (1943)-. Multiple languages. One time a year. $10.00. Real Sociedad Arqueologica Tarraconense, Museo Nacional Arqueologic, Tarragona Spain. **ED** Rodolfo Cortes. **Bk Rev**. **Circ:** 1,000 (ctrl). available with illustrations. **Continues** Butlleti Arqueologic (Tarragona. 1927), 0211-4291.
Ind/Abst BHA : Biblio. Hist. Art.

ISSN 0210-8445
SP
UDC 902

BOLETIN AURIENSE. [Bol. auriense]. **VFOAT**
Boletin Avriense. (1971)-. Periodical. Spanish. One time a year. **Continues** Boletin del Museo Arqueologico Provincial de Orense, 0212-3681.
Ind/Abst BHA : Biblio. Hist. Art.

LC F2269 .B73
DD 986.1/01/05 CK

BOLETIN DE ARQUEOLOGIA. Vol. 1, No. 1 (Jan. 1986)-. Periodical. Spanish. Three times a year.
Ind/Abst Anthropol. Lit.

ISSN 0212-5544
SP

BOLETIN DEL MUSEO ARQUEOLOGICO NACIONAL. [Bol. Mus. Arqueol. Nac.]. **Added/Corp**
Museo Arqueologico Nacional (Spain). **VFOAT** Boletin del Museo Arqueologico Nacional, Madrid. Vol. 1, No. 1 (1983)-. Periodical. Spanish. One time a year. 850ptas. Museo Arqueologico Nacional, Serrano 13, Madrid 1 Spain. **Tel** 4312757.
Ind/Abst Anthropol. Lit.; BHA : Biblio. Hist. Art.

LC QH7 .M5922 **ISSN 0326-1484**
AG

BOLETIN DEL MUSEO DE CIENCIAS NATURALES Y ANTROPOLOGICAS JUAN CORNELIO MOYANO. [Bol. Mus. Cienc. Nat. Antropol. "Juan Cornelio Moyano"]. No. 1 (1980)-. Periodical. Spanish. Two times a year. Free. Subsuelo Plaza Independencia, CP 5500, Mendoza Argentina. **ED** Jose Luis Bianchi. Index available. cum. index. **Bk Rev**. **Circ:** 800 (ctrl). **Continues** Revista del Museo de Historia Natural de Mendoza.
Desc: The journal provides several studies never published previously in any form.
Ind/Abst GeoRef.

LC F2319 .B59
DD 987/.01/05 VE

BOLETIN DEL PROGRAMA ARQUEOLOGIA DE RESCATE / CORPOZULIA -UNIVERSIDAD DEL ZULIA, CENTRO DE ESTUDIOS HISTORICOS. Yearly Vol. 1 (Jan./Dec. 1979)-. Periodical. Spanish. Irregular. Programa Arqueologia de Rescate Corpozulia-Lux, Apartado 1153, Maracaibo Venezuela.

SP

BOLETIN DEL SEMINARIO DE ESTUDIOS DE ARTE Y ARQUEOLOGIA.
Added/Corp Universidad de Valladolid. Facultad de Filosofia y Letras. Universidad de Valladolid. Seminario de Estudios de Arte y Arqueologia. **VFOAT** BSAA. Vol. 23 (1957)-. Spanish. Universidad de Valladolid / Filosofia, Facultad de Filosofia y Letras, Valladolid Spain. **Continues** Universidad de Valladolid. Seminario de Estudios de Arte y Arqueologia. Boletin de Trabajos.
Ind/Abst BHA : Biblio. Hist. Art; Numis. Lit.

BO

BOLETIN / SIARB, SOCIEDAD DE INVESTIGACION DEL ARTE RUPESTRE DE BOLIVIA. (1987)-. Spanish. One time a year. $10.00. SIARB, Casilla 3091, La Paz Bolivia.
Ind/Abst Ethnoarts Index.

ISSN 0212-7458
SP
UDC 902

BOLLETI DE LA SOCIETAT ARQUEOLOGICA LULIANA 1978. (1978)-. Periodical. Multiple languages. One time a year.
Ind/Abst BHA : Biblio. Hist. Art.

LC GN818.C3 C46a **ISSN 0577-2168**
DD 945/.26 IT

BOLLETTINO DEL CENTRO CAMUNO DI STUDI PREISTORICI. See The Arts-Art.

IT

BOLLETTINO DELLA SOCIETA PER GLI STUDI STORICI, ARCHEOLOGICI ED ARTISTICI NELLA PROVINCIA DI CUNEO. See History-History of Europe.

ISSN 0922-1433
NE
NLM W1; BO707F

BONES. Vol. 1 91988)-. English. One time a year. $15.00. Department of Anthropo-Osteology, Rijksuniversiteit Utrecht, Jutfdaseweg 7, 3522 HA Utrecht The Netherlands.

LC CC5 .B67 **ISSN 0344-810X**
DD 930.1/05 GW

BOREAS (MUENSTER). (BOREAS : MUENSTERSCHE BEITRAEGE ZUR ARCHAEOLOGIE.). [Boreas]. Vol. 1 (1978)-. German.
Ind/Abst Avery Index Archit. Period. Suppl. Colum. Univ.; BHA : Biblio. Hist. Art; Numis. Lit.

ISSN 0964-7104
UK

BRITISH ARCHAEOLOGICAL BIBLIOGRAPHY. See Archaeology-Abstracting, Bibliographies and Statistics.

LC WMLC 93/2725 **ISSN 0269-1906**
UK
TITLE CHANGE

BRITISH ARCHAEOLOGICAL NEWS.
Added/Corp Council for British Archaeology. Vol. 1, No. 1 (Mar. 1986)-(1994). Periodical. English. Council for British Archaeology, Bowes Morrell House, 111 Walmgate, York YO1 2UA United Kingdom. **Tel** 011 44 1904 671417, FAX 011 44 1904 671384. **ED** Henry Cleere, Peter Marchant. **Bk Rev**. **Ad Acc**. ctrl circ. **Continues** CBA Newsletter. **Continued by** British Archaeology, 1357-4442.
Desc: Publishes current news in British archaeology with a calendar of days where volunteer help is needed.

ISSN 1357-4442
UK

BRITISH ARCHAEOLOGY (YORK).
Added/Corp York Council for British Archaeology. (1995)-. English. Ten times a year. $38.00. Council for British Archaeology, Bowes Morrell House, 111 Walmgate, York YO1 2UA United Kingdom. **Tel** 011 44 1904 671417, FAX 011 44 1904 671384. **Continues** British Archaeological News, 0269-1906.

ISSN 1148-795X
FR
UDC 908(444.1)

BULLETIN ANNUEL DE LA SOCIETE D'ARCHEOLOGIE ET D'HISTOIRE DU TONNEROIS. **VFOAT** Bulletin Annuel de la SAHT; Societe d'Archeologie et d'Histoire du Tonnerois. (1938)-. Bulletin. French. One time a year.
Ind/Abst BHA : Biblio. Hist. Art.

ISSN 0249-9320
FR

BULLETIN ANNUEL / SOCIETE D'ARCHEOLOGIE ET D'HISTOIRE DU PAYS DE LORIENT. **Added/Corp** Societe d'Archeologie et d'Histoire du Pays de Lorient. (198?)-. Bulletin. French. One time a year. Soc Archeol Hist Pays Lorient, Cite Allende, F 56100 Lorient France. **Tel** 011 33 97 337353 OR 655315. **Continues** Conferences et Travaux (Societe Lorientaise d'Archeologie).

ISSN 0221-8321
FR

BULLETIN ARCHEOLOGIQUE DE PROVENCE. **Added/Corp** Centre Archeologique et Historique des Rives de l'Etang de Berre. **VFOAT** B.A.P.; BAP. No 1 (Jan. 1978)-. Bulletin. French. Two times a year.
Ind/Abst BHA : Biblio. Hist. Art.

LC DC2 .F81 **ISSN 0071-8394**
FR
TITLE CHANGE

BULLETIN ARCHEOLOGIQUE DU COMITE DES TRAVAUX HISTORIQUES ET SCIENTIFIQUES. **Added/Corp** France. Comite des Travaux Historiques et Scientifiques. (1885)-(1964); New Ser. (1965)-(19??). Bulletin. French. Bibliotheque Nationale, 58 rue de Richelieu, 75084 Paris Cedex 02 France. **Tel** 011 33 1 47038385. **Continues** Bulletin du Comite des Travaux Historiques et Scientifiques. **Superseded by** Bulletin Archeologique du Comite des Travaux Historiques et Scientifiques. Fasc. A, Antiquites Nationales, 0997-5322 **and** Bulletin Archeologique du Comite des Travaux Historiques et Scientifiques. Fasc. B, Afrique du Nord, 0997-5306.
Ind/Abst BHA : Biblio. Hist. Art (-19??).

LC DC30 .B85 **ISSN 0997-5322**
DD 944/.01/05 FR

BULLETIN ARCHEOLOGIQUE DU COMITE DES TRAVAUX HISTORIQUES ET SCIENTIFIQUES. FASCICULE A, ANITQUITES NATIONALES. [Bull. archeol. Com. trav. hist. sci., Fasc, A Antiq. natl.]. **Added/Corp** France. Comite des Travaux Historiques et Scientifiques. **VFOAT** Antiquites Nationales. (19??)-. Bulletin. French. One time a year. 300.00F. Bibliotheque Nationale, 58 rue de Richelieu, 75084 Paris Cedex 02 France. **Tel** 011 33 1 47038385. **Continues in part** Bulletin Archeologique du Comite des Travaux Historiques et Scientifiques, 0071-8394.
Ind/Abst Anthropol. Lit.; Avery Index Archit. Period. Suppl. Colum. Univ. (19??-199?); Numis. Lit.

LC DT191 .B84 **ISSN 0997-5306**
DD 939/.7/005 FR

BULLETIN ARCHEOLOGIQUE DU COMITE DES TRAVAUX HISTORIQUES ET SCIENTIFIQUES. FASCICULE B, AFRIQUE DU NORD. [Bull. archeol. Com. trav. hist. sci., Fasc, B Afr. Nord]. **VFOAT** Afrique du Nord. (19??)-. Bulletin. French. One time a year. **Continues in part** Bulletin Archeologique du Comites des Travaux Historiques et Scientifiques.
Ind/Abst Avery Index Archit. Period. Suppl. Colum. Univ. (19??-199?).

ISSN 1140-7409
FR

BULLETIN ARCHEOLOGIQUE DU VEXIN FRANCAIS. **Added/Corp** Centre de Recherches Archeologiques du Vexin Francais. (1965)-. Bulletin. French. One time a year. cum. index.
Ind/Abst BHA : Biblio. Hist. Art.

Archaeology

ISSN 0384-6547
DD 930/.1/06271   **CN**
BULLETIN - CANADIAN SOCIETY FOR ARCHAEOLOGY ABROAD, THE.
Main/Corp Canadian Society for Archaeology Abroad. **VFOAT** Le Bulletin - Societe Canadienne d'Archeologie a l'Etranger. (April 1970)-. Bulletin. English (French). Irregular. $4.00. A J Mills, Royal Ontario Museum Egyptian Department, 100 Queens Park, Toronto Ontario M5S 2C6 Canada.

ISSN 0844-3416
DD 935/.005 2 19   **CN**
                                     CCC
Pr Rev
BULLETIN / CANADIAN SOCIETY FOR MESOPOTAMIAN STUDIES.
[Bull. - Can. Soc. Mesop. Stud.]. **Added/Corp** Canadian Society for Mesopotamian Studies. (Oct. 1988)-. Bulletin. English (French and German). Two times a year (May and Sep.). 20.01Can$. CSMS / Canadian Society for Mesopotamian Studies, University of Toronto, RIM Project 4th Floor, 4 Bancroft Avenue, Toronto Ontario M5S 1A1 Canada. **Tel** (416)978-4531, **FAX** (416)978-5294. **ED** Michael Fortin (editor's address: Laval University, History Department, Quebec, Quebec Canada; phone: (418)656-2547). **Bk Rev**, (Qty: 2 / year); **Circ:** 300 (ctrl). **Continues** Bulletin (Society for Mesopotamian Studies), 0822-2533.
    Desc: Publication of lecture transcripts, submitted manuscripts approved by the editorial board, events listings, press cuttings, current research, and society news.

LC WMLC L 83/2748   **ISSN** 0525-1133
                                       FR
BULLETIN D'ARCHEOLOGIE ALGERIENNE.
Added/Corp Algeria. Wizarat Al-Tarbiyah Al-Wataniyah. Algeria. Wizarat Al-Akhbar Wa-Al-Thaqafah. **VFOAT** Majallat Al-Athar Al-Jazairiyah. (1962)-. Bulletin. French (table of contents in Arabic). Imprimerie Officielle Algeria, 7 9 13 Avenue Abdelkader Benbarek, Algier Algeria. **Tel** 011 213 651815, 011 213 651817.
Ind/Abst BHA : Biblio. Hist. Art.

LC DT311 .B84   **ISSN** 0068-4015
                                       MR
BULLETIN D'ARCHEOLOGIE MAROCAINE.
Added/Corp Morocco. Maslahat al-Athar. Service des Antiquites du Maroc. Morocco. Division des Monuments Historiques et des Antiquites. **VFOAT** Nashrah Al-Athariyah Al-Maghribiyah. Vol. 1 (1956)-. Bulletin. French. Institut National des Sciences de l'Archaeologie et du Patrimoine, Avenue John Kennedy, Routes des Zaers, Rabat Souissi Morocco.
Ind/Abst Anthropol. Index; Anthropol. Lit.; BHA : Biblio. Hist. Art; Numis. Lit.

LC DR20 .B85
                                       RM
BULLETIN D'ARCHEOLOGIE SUD-EST EUROPEENNE.
Added/Corp International Association for South Eastern European Studies. Commission d'Archeologie. (19??)-. Bulletin. French. Irregular. Association Internationale d'Etudes du Sud-Est Europeen, Str. IC Frimu, Nr. 9, Bucharest Romania.
Ind/Abst Am. Hist. Life.

LC DC611.P285 C59   **ISSN** 0750-1331
DD 944/.27/005   **FR**
BULLETIN DE LA COMMISSION DEPARTEMENTALE D'HISTOIRE ET D'ARCHEOLOGIE DU PAS-DE-CALAIS.
Added/Corp Commission Departementale d'Histoire et d'Archeologie du Pas-de-Calais. Vol. 11, No. 1 (1982)-. Bulletin. French. One time a year. 130.00F. Commission Departementale d'Historie et d'Archeologie du Pas-de-Calais, Archives Departementales, rue du 19 Mars 1962, 62000 Dainville France. **Tel** 21711090. **ED** B. Ghienne. Index available. cum. index. **Circ:** 400. **Continues** Bulletin de la Commission Departementale des Monuments Historiques du Pas-de-Calais.
Ind/Abst BHA : Biblio. Hist. Art.

ISSN 1145-7295
                                       FR
UDC 06.055(443.72)
                       CODEN 908(443.7)
BULLETIN DE LA SOCIETE ARCHEOLOGIQUE CHAMPENOISE (1954).
(1954)-. Periodical. French. Four times a year. 180.00F (individuals); 220.00F (institutions) Comes with Societe Archaelogique Champenoise membership. Societe Archaelogique Champenoise, 53 rue Simon, 51100 Reims France. **Tel** 011 33 26 852326.
Ind/Abst BHA : Biblio. Hist. Art.

LC CC   **ISSN** 1153-2521
DD 930.1   **FR**
UDC 061.22(445.4)
BULLETIN DE LA SOCIETE ARCHEOLOGIQUE DE TOURAINE.
VFOAT Bulletin Trimestriel de la Societe Archeologique de Touraine. (1871)-. Bulletin. French. One time a year. Societe Archeologique de Touraine, BP 1105, 37011 Tours Cedex France.
Ind/Abst BHA : Biblio. Hist. Art.

LC CB   **ISSN** 1149-6770
DD 909   **FR**
UDC 902.03(445.1)
BULLETIN DE LA SOCIETE ARCHEOLOGIQUE D'EURE-ET-LOIR.
(1984)-. Periodical. French. Four times a year. **Absorbed** Bulletin de la Societe Archeologique d'Eure-et-Loir. Documents (1975), 0223-694X **and** Bulletin de la Societe Archeologique d'Eure-et-Loir. Chroniques (1975), 0223-6966.
Ind/Abst BHA : Biblio. Hist. Art.

LC DC611.F497A2 S8   **ISSN** 0249-6763
                                       FR
BULLETIN DE LA SOCIETE ARCHEOLOGIQUE DU FINISTERE.
Main/Corp Societe Archeologique du Finistere. (1873)-. Bulletin. French. cum. index.
Ind/Abst BHA : Biblio. Hist. Art.

ISSN 0337-579X
                                       FR
UDC 06.055(445.2)
                       CODEN 908(445)
BULLETIN DE LA SOCIETE ARCHEOLOGIQUE ET HISTORIQUE DE L'ORLEANAIS.
VFOAT Bulletin Trimestriel de la Societe Archeologique et Historique de l'Orleanais. (1959)-. Periodical. French. Four times a year.
Ind/Abst BHA : Biblio. Hist. Art.

ISSN 0182-3876
                                       FR
UDC 92
BULLETIN DE LA SOCIETE ARCHEOLOGIQUE ET HISTORIQUE DES HAUTS CANTONS DE L'HERAULT.
(1978)-. Periodical. French. One time a year.
Ind/Abst BHA : Biblio. Hist. Art.

ISSN 0184-7651
                                       FR
UDC 930.26
BULLETIN DE LA SOCIETE ARCHEOLOGIQUE ET HISTORIQUE DU LIMOUSIN.
(1846)-. Periodical. French. One time a year (October). 150.00F France; 175.00F other. Societe Archeologique et Historique Limousin, 54 rue Bourneville, 87000 Limoges France. **Tel** 011 33 55 509760. **Bk Rev**, (Qty: 1). **Circ:** 1,000 (ctrl).
                                       FR
Pr Rev
BULLETIN DE LA SOCIETE ARCHEOLOGIQUE ET HISTORIQUE DU LIMOUSIN.
Main/Corp Societe Archeologique et Historique du Limousin, Limoges. Vol. 1, (1846)-. Bulletin. French. One time a year. $39.37. Societe Archeologique et Historique Limousin, 54 rue Bourneville, 87000 Limoges France. **Tel** 011 33 55 509760. **ED** J. Perrier. Index available. cum. index. **Bk Rev**, (Qty: 1). **Circ:** 1,000.
Ind/Abst BHA : Biblio. Hist. Art.

BULLETIN DE LA SOCIETE ARCHEOLOGIQUE, HISTORIQUE ET ARTISTIQUE, LE VIEUX PAPIER, POUR L'ETUDE DE LA VIE ET DES MRS D'AUTREFOIS.
Added/Corp Vieux Papier (Paris, France). (Apr. 1, 1900)-. Bulletin. French. cum. index.
Ind/Abst BHA : Biblio. Hist. Art.

ISSN 0037-8895
                                       FR
UDC 061.22(447.71)
                      CODEN 902(447.71)
BULLETIN DE LA SOCIETE ARCHEOLOGIQUE HISTORIQUE LITTERAIRE & SCIENTIFIQUE DU GERS.
VFOAT Bulletin de la Societe Archeologique Historique Litteraire et Scientifique du Gers. (1936)-. Periodical. French. Four times a year. Comes with membership to La Societe Archeologique du Gers. Societe Archeologique du Gers, 13 Place Saluste du Bartas, 32000 Auch France. **Tel** 011 33 62 630837. **ED** M. Georges Courtes.
Ind/Abst BHA : Biblio. Hist. Art.

LC DT57 .S6
                                       UA
BULLETIN DE LA SOCIETE D'ARCHEOLOGIE COPTE.
Added/Corp Jamiyat Al-Athar Al-Qibtiyah (Egypt). **VFOAT** Majallat Jamiyat Al-Athar Al-Qibtiyah. (1938)-. Bulletin. French (English, German, Arabic and Italian). **Continues** Bulletin de l'Association des Amis de l'Art Copte.
Ind/Abst BHA : Biblio. Hist. Art.

ISSN 0762-8129
                                       FR
UDC 930.26
BULLETIN DE LA SOCIETE DES FOUILLES ARCHEOLOGIQUES ET DES MONUMENTS HISTORIQUES DE L'YONNE.
[Soc. fouil. archeol. monum. hist. Yonne]. (1984)-. Periodical. French. One time a year.
Ind/Abst BHA : Biblio. Hist. Art.

ISSN 0153-937X
                                       FR
UDC 008
BULLETIN DE LA SOCIETE D'ETUDES SCIENTIFIQUES ET ARCHEOLOGIQUES DE DRAGUIGNAN ET DU VAR.
[Bull. Soc. etud. sci. archeol. Draguignan Var]. (1956)-. Periodical. French. One time a year. **Continues** Bulletin de la Societe d'Etudes Scientifiques et Archeologiques de la Ville de Draguignan, 0991-921X; **Absorbed** Bulletin Mensuel de la Societe d'Etudes Scientifiques et Archeologiques de Draguignan, 1149-4611.
Ind/Abst BHA : Biblio. Hist. Art.

ISSN 1017-849X
                                       SZ
UDC 930.2
                               CODEN 908
BULLETIN DE LA SOCIETE D'HISTOIRE ET D'ARCHEOLOGIE DE GENEVE.
See History-History of Europe.

LC DC   **ISSN** 1153-3277
DD 944   **FR**
UDC 061.22(445.7)
BULLETIN DE LA SOCIETE D'HISTOIRE ET D'ARCHEOLOGIE DE VICHY ET DE SES ENVIRONS.
See History-History of Europe.

ISSN 1154-368X
                                       FR
BULLETIN DE LA SOCIETE HISTORIQUE ET ARCHELOGIQUE DE CORBEIL, DE L'ESSONNE ET DU HUREPOIX.
See History-History of Europe.

LC DC611.L27 S7
                                       FR
BULLETIN DE LA SOCIETE HISTORIQUE ET ARCHEOLOGIQUE DE LANGRES.
See History-History of Europe.

LC DC611.P441 S6   **ISSN** 0037-9425
DD 944/.72/05   **FR**
BULLETIN DE LA SOCIETE HISTORIQUE ET ARCHEOLOGIQUE DU PERIGORD.
See History-History of Europe.

ISSN 0750-6570
                                       FR
UDC 551.44
BULLETIN DE LA SOCIETE MERIDIONALE DE SPELEOLOGIE ET DE PREHISTOIRE.
(BULLETIN DE LA SOCIETE MERIDIONALE DE SPELEOLOGIE ET DE PREHISTOIRE.). (1976)-. Bulletin. French. One time a year.
Ind/Abst Anthropol. Lit.

LC GN700 .S573A
DD 936.4   **FR**
BULLETIN DE LA SOCIETE PREHISTORIQUE FRANCAISE.
Main/Corp Societe Prehistorique Francaise. Vol. 75 (1978)-. Bulletin. French. Irregular. 170. Societe Prehistorique Francaise, 22 rue Saint-Ambroise, Paris LLE CCP 406-44 France. **Formed by the union of** Bulletin. Comptes Rendus des Seances Mensuelles **and** Bulletin. Etudes Ettravaux.
Ind/Abst Anthropol. Index; Anthropol. Lit.; Br. Archaeol. Bibliogr.

ISSN 0776-0086
                                       BE
UDC 55
BULLETIN DE LA SOCIETE ROYALE BELGE D'ETUDES GEOLOGIQUES ET ARCHEOLOGIQUES LES CHERCHEURS DE WALLONIE.
See Earth Sciences-Geology.

                                       FR
BULLETIN DE LA SOCIETE SCIENTIFIQUE HISTORIQUE ET ARCHEOLOGIQUE DE LA CORREZE.
Main/Corp Societe Scientifique, Historique et Archeologique de la Correze. (19??)-. Bulletin. French. One time a year. $28.44. Societe Scientifique Historique et Archeologique de la Correze, 15 rue Dr. Massenat,

Archaeology

19100 Brive Gaillarde France. cum. index. **Bk Rev. Circ:** 1,050. available on microfilm.
Ind/Abst BHA : Biblio. Hist. Art.

BE
BULLETIN DE L'ASSOCIATION SCIENTIFIQUE LIEGEOISE POUR LA RECHERCHE ARCHEOLOGIQUE.
Added/Corp Association Scientifique Liegeoise pour la Recherche Archeologique. (19??)-. Bulletin. French.
Ind/Abst Anthropol. Lit.

ISSN 0776-1260
BE
UDC 930.26
BULLETIN DE L'INSTITUT ARCHEOLOGIQUE LIEGEOIS. [Bull. Inst. archeol. liegeois]. (1853)-. Bulletin. French. One time a year.
Ind/Abst BHA : Biblio. Hist. Art; Numis. Lit.

LC DT57 .F81
DD 932/.005
UA
BULLETIN DE L'INSTITUT FRANCAIS D'ARCHEOLOGIE ORIENTALE. Main/Corp
Institut Francais d'Archeologie Orientale du Caire. Vol. 1 (1901)-. Bulletin. French (English). One time a year. $85.00. Institut Francais d'Archeologie Orientale du Caire, 37 Mounira Street, Cairo Rae Egypt. **(Subscription address:** Leila Bookshop, PO Box 31 El Daher, 11271 Cairo Egypt. **Tel** 011 202 3924475, 011 202 3507399.) cum. index.
Ind/Abst BHA : Biblio. Hist. Art.

BE
BULLETIN DES ARCHIVES VERVIETOISES. See History-History of Europe.

ISSN 0525-1249
FR
BULLETIN DES SOCIETES D'HISTOIRE ET D'ARCHEOLOGIE DE LA MEUSE. See History-History of Europe.

ISSN 0988-9477
FR
UDC 930 (445.51)
BULLETIN DU GROUPE D'HISTOIRE ET D'ARCHEOLOGIE DE BUZANCAIS. See History-History of Europe.

FR
BULLETIN DU MUSEE BASQUE. See History-History of Europe.

LC AM101.B927 A3
HU
BULLETIN DU MUSEE HONGROIS DES BEAUX-ARTS / O.M. SZEPMUVESZETI MUZEUM KOZLEMENYEI. See The Arts-Art.

LC E43 .E27a **ISSN** 0749-0100
DD 974/.006 US
BULLETIN - EASTERN STATES ARCHEOLOGICAL FEDERATION (U.S.). MEETING. (BULLETIN : EASTERN STATES ARCHEOLOGICAL FEDERATION ANNUAL MEETING PROCEEDINGS.). [Bulletin - East. States Archeol. Fed. (U.S.), Meet.]. Main/Corp Eastern States Archeological Federation (U.S.). Meeting. Added/Corp Eastern States Archeological Federation (U.S.). VFOAT Eastern States Archeological Federation Annual Meeting Proceedings. Nov. 5, 6, 7, (1982)-. Bulletin. English. One time a year. $30.00. Eastern States Archaeology Federation, PO Box 386, Bethlehem CT 06751. Tel (203)266-7741. Circ: 500. Separated from Archaeology of Eastern North America, 0360-1021.
Desc: Prehistoric and historic archaeology of the Eastern United States and Canada.

ISSN 0750-1412
FR
UDC 930.26 (441.5)
BULLETIN ET MEMOIRES DE LA SOCIETE ARCHEOLOGIQUE DU DEPARTEMENT D'ILLE-ET-VILAINE. [Bull. mem. Soc. archeol. dep. Ille-et-Vilaine]. VFOAT Memoires de la Societe Archeologique du Departement d'Ille-et- Vilaine. (1861)-. Periodical. French. One time a year.
Ind/Abst BHA : Biblio. Hist. Art.

LC F21 .B84 **ISSN** 0542-1292
DD 974.1/01 US
BULLETIN / MAINE ARCHAEOLOGICAL SOCIETY. [Bull. - Me. Archaeol. Soc.]. Added/Corp Maine Archaeological Society. VFOAT Bulletin of the Maine Archaeological Society; Maine Archeological Society Bulletin; Maine Archeological Society Inc. Bulletin. (19??)-. Bulletin. English. Two times a year (April, Oct.). $15.00. Maine Archaeological Society, PO Box 982, Augusta ME 04330. Tel (207)289-2132. ED Eric Lahti. Bk Rev. Ad Acc. Circ: 350 (ctrl). Continues Maine Archaeological Society.

Desc: Features articles about Northeast prehistory and the early historic period.
Ind/Abst Abstr. Anthropol. (19??-); Anthropol. Lit.; Ethnoarts Index.

ISSN 0585-3214
SW
BULLETIN - MEDELHAVSMUSEET.
Main/Corp Medelhavsmuseet (Stockholm, Sweden). (1961)-. Bulletin. English. One time a year. $20.00. Museum of Mediterranean & Near Eastern Antiquities, Box 5404, 114 84 Stockholm Sweden. **Tel** 011 46 8 7839418, FAX 011 46 8 6607284.
Desc: Mediterranean archaeology.

LC DS714 .S7 **ISSN** 0081-5691
DD 931/.005 SW
BULLETIN - MUSEUM OF FAR EASTERN ANTIQUITIES. (BULLETIN / THE MUSEUM OF FAR EASTERN ANTIQUITIES (OSTASIATISKA MUSEET) STOCKHOLM.). [Bull. - Mus. Far East. Antiq.]. Added/Corp Ostasiatiska Museet. No. 32 (1960)-. Bulletin. English (French and German). One time a year (May). $56.90. Ostasiatiska Museet, Museum of Far Eastern Antiquities, Box 16 381, 103 27 Stockholm Sweden. Tel 011 46 8 6664250, FAX 011 46 8 6112845. ED Jan Wirgin. Circ: 800. Continues Bulletin (Ostasiatiska Samlingarna (Stockholm, Sweden)).
Desc: Paintings, sculpture, ceramics, bronzes, Chinese, Japanese, Indian and Thailand archaeology.
Ind/Abst Anthropol. Index; MLA Int. Bibl. Books Artic. Mod. Lang. Lit.

ISSN 0709-2628
DD 971.3/01 CN
BULLETIN - MUSEUM OF INDIAN ARCHAEOLOGY. UNIVERSITY OF WESTERN ONTARIO. See Museums and Galleries.

LC F121 .B84 **ISSN** 1046-2368
DD 974.7/005 US
CODEN BJNAE9
BULLETIN - NEW YORK STATE ARCHEOLOGICAL ASSOCIATION (1987), THE. (THE BULLETIN : JOURNAL OF THE NEW YORK STATE ARCHAEOLOGICAL ASSOCIATION.). [Bull. - N. Y. State Arch. Assoc.]. Added/Corp New York State Archaeological Association. No. 95 (Fall 1987)-. Bulletin. English. Two times a year. Comes with New York State Archaeological Association membership. New York State Archaeological Association, 2990 Tyler Road, Newark NY 14513. Tel (315)331-4005. ED Charles Hayes III. Circ: 750 (ctrl). Continues Bulletin and Journal of the Archaeology for New York State, 0730-5710.
Desc: Contains technical papers by NYSAA members.
Ind/Abst Am. Hist. Life (1986-1988); Anthropol. Lit.; Ceram. Abstr. (19??-).

ISSN 0306-1612
UK
BULLETIN OF MONUMENTAL BRASS SOCIETY. [Bull. Monum. Brass Soc.]. VFOAT Bulletin - Monumental Brass Society. (1972)-. Periodical. English. Three times a year. Comes with Monumental Brass Society membership. £18.00 (membership). Society of Antiquarries, Burlington House, Picadilly, London W1V 0HS United Kingdom.
Ind/Abst BHA : Biblio. Hist. Art.

ISSN 0003-097X
DD 913 US
BULLETIN OF THE AMERICAN SCHOOLS OF ORIENTAL RESEARCH.
[Bull. Am. Schools Orient. Res.]. **Main/Corp** American Schools of Oriental Research. **VFOAT** BASOR. (1921)-. Bulletin. English. Four times a year (February, May, August, November). $80.00. Scholars Press / Georgia, PO Box 15399, Atlanta GA 30333-0399. **Tel** (404)636-4757, (404)727-2320, FAX (404)727-2348. **ED** Walter E. Rast. **Bk Rev. Ad Acc. Circ:** 2,400. available on microfilm and microfiche from University Microfilms International (UMI). Documents available from The Genuine Article. **Continues** Bulletin of the American School of Oriental Research in Jerusalem, 0276-7732.
Desc: A review of Near-Eastern archaeology for the professional scholar and determined amateur.
Ind/Abst Abstr. Anthropol.; Anthropol. Index; Anthropol. Lit.; Art Index; Arts Humanit. Citation Index [Full Cov.]; Curr. Contents Arts Humanit.; Index Book Rev. Relig.; Linguist. Lang. Behav. Abstr.; Middle East Abstr. Index; New Testam. Abstr.; Numis. Lit.; Old Testam. Abstr.; Relig. Index One Period. (1973-); Relig. Theol. Abstr.; Res. Alert [Full Cov.]; Soc. Plann. Policy Dev. Abstr.; Soc. Sci. Cit. Index [Select. Cov.]; Sociol. Abstr.

LC AS36.A497 A2 **ISSN** 0003-1186
DD 091 US
BULLETIN OF THE AMERICAN SOCIETY OF PAPYROLOGISTS, THE. [Bull. Am. Soc. Papyrol.]. Main/Corp American Society of Papyrologists. Vol. 1 (1964)-. Bulletin. English. Four times a year. $25.00. Scholars Press / Georgia, PO Box 15399, Atlanta GA 30333-0399. Tel (404)636-4757, (404)727-2320, FAX (404)727-2348. ED Gerald M. Browne. Circ: 250.

Documents available from The Genuine Article.
Desc: Exists to provide a medium both for publication of new texts and for the study of the significance of those already published. It also publishes articles from time to time on inscriptions and subjects in the history of the Greek and Roman world.
Ind/Abst Arts Humanit. Citation Index (19??-19??) [Full Cov.]; Curr. Contents Arts Humanit.; Index Book Rev. Relig.; Relig. Index One Period.; Res. Alert [Full Cov.].

LC DS56 .B85
DD 935/.005 JA
BULLETIN OF THE ANCIENT ORIENT MUSEUM. See Museums and Galleries.

ISSN 0266-2442
UK
BULLETIN OF THE ANGLO-ISRAEL ARCHAEOLOGICAL SOCIETY.
Added/Corp Anglo-Israel Archaeological Society (London, England). **VFOAT** Bulletin of the Anglo Israel Archaeological Society. (1982)-. Bulletin. English. One time a year (May). $25.67. Anglo-Israel Archaeological Society, 3 St. Johns Wood Road, London NW8 84B United Kingdom. **Tel** 011 44 171 2861176. **ED** Sharon Gibson. **Bk Rev**, (Qty: 1).
Desc: Contains lectures about archaeological work in Israel given at the society's meetings throughout the previous year.
Ind/Abst Index Book Rev. Relig.; Relig. Index One Period.

LC CC21 .A75
US
BULLETIN OF THE ARCHAEOLOGICAL INSTITUTE OF AMERICA. Main/Corp
Archaeological Institute of America. (Jan. 1883)-. Bulletin. English. One time a year (Jan.). $9.00. Archaeological Institute of America, Boston University, 675 Commonwealth Avenue, Boston MA 02215-1401. **Tel** (617)353-9361, FAX (617)353-6550. **ED** Galina Gorokhoff. **Circ:** 1,000. available on microfilm and microfiche from University Microfilms International (UMI).
Desc: Report on the institute containing all financial, programs, and member analysis information.

LC F96 .A732 **ISSN** 0739-5612
DD 913.746 US
BULLETIN OF THE ARCHAEOLOGICAL SOCIETY OF CONNECTICUT. [Bull. Arch. Soc. Conn.]. Main/Corp Archaeological Society of Connecticut. No. 1 (Jan. 1935)-. Bulletin. English. One time a year (Nov.). $25.00 Comes with Archaeological Society of Connecticut membership. Archaeological Society of Connecticut, 163 Old Main Street, Rocky Hill CT 06067. Tel (203)529-0628. ED Roger W. Moeller. Bk Rev. Circ: 500 (ctrl).
Desc: The archaeology of New England, especially the state of Connecticut.
Ind/Abst Anthropol. Lit.; Ethnoarts Index.

LC F161 .A74 **ISSN** 0003-8067
DD 975.1/01/05 US
BULLETIN OF THE ARCHAEOLOGICAL SOCIETY OF DELAWARE. [Bull. Archeal. Soc. Del.]. Main/Corp Archaeological Society of Delaware. Vol. 1-9 New Series, No. 1 (1933)-. Bulletin. English. Irregular. $8.00 (junior), $10.00 (individuals and institutions), $15.00 (family), $30.00 (contributing), $50.00 (sustaining) Comes with Archaeological Society of Delaware membership. Archaeological Society of Delaware, PO Box 301, Wilmington DE 19899. Tel (302)831-6590. available on microfilm and microfiche from University Microfilms International (UMI).
Desc: This magazine joins amateur and professional archaeologists together in the study and appreciation of archaeology in general and archaeological investigations in Delaware.
Ind/Abst Anthropol. Lit.; Ethnoarts Index.

LC E78.N6 A68 **ISSN** 0196-8319
DD 913.749 974.9* US
CODEN BASJEW
BULLETIN OF THE ARCHAEOLOGICAL SOCIETY OF NEW JERSEY. [Bull. Archaeol. Soc. N. J.]. Main/Corp Archeological Society of New Jersey. VFOAT Bulletin - Archeological Society of New Jersey. No. 1 (July 1948)-. Bulletin. English. One time a year. Free (members). Archaeological Society of New Jersey, Seton Hall University, Humanities Building/Room 226, South Orange NJ 07097. Tel (201)761-9543. ED Charles A. Bello and Herbert C. Kraft. Index available. cum. index. Bk Rev. Circ: 500 (ctrl).
Desc: Information on the Indians of North America.
Ind/Abst Anthropol. Lit.; Ethnoarts Index; GeoRef.

LC DT57 .E65a **ISSN** 0270-210X
DD 932 US
Pr Rev. SUSPENDED
BULLETIN OF THE EGYPTOLOGICAL SEMINAR. [Bull. Egyptol. Semin.]. Main/Corp
Egyptological Seminar of New York. Vol. 1 (1979)-Suspended (1995). Bulletin. English. One time a year (Dec.). $22.00. Brooklyn Museum, 200 Eastern Parkway, Brooklyn NY 11238. Tel (718)638-6909, FAX (718)398-6930. ED Dr. Donald Spanel (editor's address:

Archaeology

The Brooklyn Museum, Brooklyn, NY 11238, phone: (718)638-5000 ext. 211). **Circ:** 200.
Ind/Abst Old Testam. Abstr.

ISSN 1062-4740
DD 930 US
BULLETIN OF THE HISTORY OF ARCHAEOLOGY : BHA. [Bull. hist. archaeol.]. **VFOAT** BHA; Bulletin on the History of Archaeology. Vol. 1, No. 1 (May 1991)-. Bulletin. English. Two times a year (May and November). $5.00. St. Louis Community College, Department of Behavioral Science, 11333 Big Bend, St. Louis MO 63122. **Tel** (314)984-7987, FAX (314)225-7117. **ED** Douglas Givens. **Bk Rev**, (Qty: 7). **Circ:** 500.
Desc: An international journal devoted to all aspects of the history of archaeology. The bulletin serves as a forum of discourse relating to the history of archaeology in the form of short articles, book reviews, archival/collections sources in the history of archaeology, books and journal articles published on the subject of some facet of the history of archaeology, and books suggested for reading by the bulletin's readership.

ISSN 0076-0722
UK
BULLETIN OF THE INSTITUTE OF ARCHAEOLOGY / UNIVERSITY OF LONDON, INSTITUTE OF ARCHAEOLOGY. **Main/Corp** University of London. Institute of Archaeology. **Added/Corp** University of London. Institute of Archaeology. University of London. Institute of Archaeology. Annual Report. **VFOAT** Institute of Archaeology Bulletin. No. 1 (1958)-. Bulletin. English. One time a year. £15.25 England; £15.35 other. University College London / Archaeology, Institute of Archaeology, 31-34 Gordon Square, London WC1H OPY United Kingdom. **Tel** 011 44 171 3879651. **ED** J D Evans. Index available. **Bk Rev**. **Circ:** 750 (ctrl).
Desc: Articles on many aspects of archaeology, prehistoric to Roman; archaeological science, bioarchaeology, computer applications, experimental archaeology and excavation reports.
Ind/Abst Anthropol. Index; Anthropol. Lit.; Br. Archaeol. Bibliogr.; Br. Humanit. Index; Numis. Lit.

LC F66 .M368 **ISSN** 0148-1886
DD 913.744 974.4* US
BULLETIN OF THE MASSACHUSETTS ARCHAEOLOGICAL SOCIETY. **Main/Corp** Massachusetts Archaeological Society. **VFOAT** Massachusetts Archaeological Society Bulletin. Vol. 1 (1939)-. Bulletin. English. Two times a year. $30.00. Massachusetts Archaeological Society, Robbins Museum of Archaeology, Box 700, Middleboro MA 02346. **Tel** (508)947-9005 Wed. only. **ED** Elizabeth Little. Index available. cum. index. **Bk Rev**, (Qty: 6-7). **Ad Acc**, **Adv Mgr:** Tom Lux. **Circ:** 800.
Desc: Site reports, artifact studies, archaeological pieces of broad range, especially concerning Massachusetts.
Ind/Abst Abstr. Anthropol. (19??-); Anthropol. Lit.; Ethnoarts Index.

LC E51 .B84 **ISSN** 0741-5672
DD 973 US
CCC
BULLETIN OF THE SOCIETY FOR AMERICAN ARCHAEOLOGY. [Bull. Soc. Am. Archaeol.]. **Added/Corp** Society for American Archaeology. (1983)-. Bulletin. English. Five times a year. $30.00. Society for American Archaeology, 900 Second Street NE, Suite 12, Washington DC 20002. **Tel** (202)789-8200, FAX (202)789-0284. **(Subscription address:** Society for American Archaeolgy, Department 0123, Washington DC 20073. **Tel** (202)789-8200.**)** **Circ:** 6,000.

ISSN 0953-6191
UK
CEASED
BULLETIN OF THE SUTTON HOO RESEARCH COMMITTEE. [Bull. Sutton Hoo Res. Comm.]. No. 1 (April 1983)-(1993). Bulletin. English. M O H Carver/Research Director Committee, Sutton Hoo Project Centre, Birmingham University Field Archaeology Unit, POB 363, Birmingham B15 2TT United Kingdom.
Ind/Abst Anthropol. Lit.; Br. Archaeol. Bibliogr.

LC F381 .T32 **ISSN** 0082-2930
DD 976.4 US
CODEN BTASDX
BULLETIN OF THE TEXAS ARCHAEOLOGICAL SOCIETY. [Bull. Tex. Archeol. Soc.]. **Main/Corp** Texas Archaeological Society. **Added/Corp** Texas Archaeological Society. Vol. 24 (1953)-. Bulletin. English. One time a year. $25.00 Comes with Texas Archaeological Society Membership. Texas Archaeological Society, Center for Archaeological Research, University of Texas at San Antonio, 6900 North Loop 1604 West, San Antonio TX 78285-0658. **Tel** (210)691-4393. **ED** Jimmy L. Mitchell (editor's address: 926 Toepperwein, Converse, TX 78109). Index available. cum. index. **Bk Rev**. **Circ:** 1,250. **Continues** Bulletin of the Texas Archaeological and Paleontological Society.
Desc: Technical reports of interest to archeologists and anthropologists primarily in Texas, but occasionally other surrounding areas.
Ind/Abst Abstr. Anthropol.; Anthropol. Index; Anthropol. Lit.; Art Archaeol. Tech. Abstr.; Ethnoarts Index; GeoRef.

LC AS9-911 **ISSN** 1149-932X
DD 061 FR
UDC 061.22(444.1)
BULLETIN - SOCIETE ARCHEOLOGIQUE DE SENS. **VFOAT** Bulletin de la Societe Archeologique de Sens (1983). (1983)-. Periodical. French. One time a year. **Continues** Bulletin de Liaison - Societe Archeologique de Sens, 1153-3250.
Ind/Abst BHA : Biblio. Hist. Art.

SZ
BULLETIN / SOCIETE D'EGYPTOLOGIE, GENEVE. **VFOAT** Bulletin de la Societe d'Egyptologie, Geneve; B.S.E.G.; BSEG. No. 1 (May 1979)-. Bulletin. French (English and German). One time a year. Societe d'Egyptologie Geneve, Case Postale 27, CH-1218 Grand Saconnex Geneva, Switzerland.
Ind/Abst BHA : Biblio. Hist. Art.

ISSN 0954-7029
DD 609.4238 UK
BULLETIN - SOMERSET INDUSTRIAL ARCHAEOLOGICAL SOCIETY. (BULLETIN.). [Bull. - Somerset Ind. Archaeol. Soc.]. (1975)-. Bulletin. English. Three times a year. $1.95. Somerset Industrial Archaeological Society, 52 Stoke Road, Taunton Somerset TA1 3EJ United Kingdom. **Tel** 011 44 1823 286957. **ED** D.W. Warren. Index available. **Bk Rev**, (Qty: 2).

ISSN 0020-2177
BE
BULLETIN TRIMESTRIEL DI L'INSTITUT ARCHEOLOGIQUE DU LUXEMBOURG. **Main/Corp** Institut Archeologique du Luxemburg, Arlon, Belgium. (Jan. 5, 1925)-. Bulletin. French. Four times a year. 150F. Institut du Luxembourg, rue des Martyrs 13, B 6700 Arlon Belgium. **Tel** 011 32 63 221236. **Ad Acc**.
Ind/Abst BHA : Biblio. Hist. Art.

LC DG803 .R7
IT
BULLETTINO DELLA COMMISSIONE ARCHEOLOGICA COMUNALE DI ROMA. **Main/Corp** Commissione Archeologica Comunale di Roma. **Added/Corp** Rome (Italy). Museo dell'Impero Romano. Bullettino. Rome (Italy). Commissione Archeologica Municipale. Vol. 1 (Nov. 1872)-. Periodical. Italian (English, French and German). One time a year. L250000. L'Erma di Bretschneider SPA, via Cassiodoro 19, 00193 Rome Italy. **Tel** 011 39 6 6874127, 011 39 6 6874129, FAX 011 39 6 6874129. cum. index.
Ind/Abst Avery Index Archit. Period. Suppl. Colum. Univ. (19??-199?); BHA : Biblio. Hist. Art.; Numis. Lit.

LC BS620.A1 B87 **ISSN** 0007-6260
AT
BURIED HISTORY. (BURIED HISTORY : QUARTERLY JOURNAL OF THE AUSTRALIAN INSTITUTE OF ARCHAEOLOGY.). [Buried hist.]. **Added/Corp** Australian Institute of Archaeology. Vol. 1 (March 1964)-. Academic Scholarly Publication. English. Four times a year. 12.33Aus$. Australian Institute of Archaeology, 174 Collins Street, Melbourne Victoria 3000 Australia. **Tel** 011 61 3 6503477, FAX 011 61 3 6542774, telex 03 650 3477. **ED** Piers T. Crocker. Index available. **Bk Rev**, (Qty: 5). **Circ:** 500 (ctrl).
Desc: Reviews of and reports on ancient Near Eastern and Biblical archaeology.
Ind/Abst Old Testam. Abstr.

ISSN 0870-6425
PO
CADERNOS DE ARQUEOLOGIA (BRAGA, PORTUGAL). (CADERNOS DE ARQUEOLOGIA.). [Cad. arqueol.]. (1981)-. Portuguese. One time a year.
Ind/Abst Anthropol. Lit.

LC CC37 .S3 **ISSN** 0007-9502
DD 930.1/05 SP
CAESARAUGUSTA. (CAESARAUGUSTA : PUBLICACIONES DEL SEMINARIO DE ARQUEOLOGIA Y NUMISMATICA ARAGONESAS.). [Caesaraugusta]. **Added/Corp** Institucion "Fernando el Catolico". Seminario de Arqueologia y Numismatica Aragonesas. Institucion "Fernando el Catolico". (1954)-. Spanish. Irregular. 2500ptas. Inst Fernando El Catolico, Plaza de Espana 2, Zaragoza 50004 Spain. **Tel** 011 34 76 229652, FAX 22.18.42. **Continues** Publicaciones del Seminario de Arqueologia y Numismatica Aragonesas.
Ind/Abst Am. Hist. Life (1957-1970); BHA : Biblio. Hist. Art; Br. Archaeol. Bibliogr. (?-?); Numis. Lit.

LC DC648.6 .C33 **ISSN** 0575-0385
DD 936.4/008 FR
CAHIERS ALSACIENS D'ARCHEOLOGIE, D'ART ET D'HISTOIRE. [Cah. alsac. archeol., art hist.]. **Added/Corp** Societe pour la Conservation des Monuments Historiques d'Alsace. **VFOAT** Anzeiger fur Elsassische Altertumskunde. (1957)-. Periodical. French (German). Societe pour Conservation des Monuments Historiques d'Alsace, 2 Place du Chateau, 67000 Strasbourg France. **Tel** 011 33 88 525000. cum. index.
Ind/Abst BHA : Biblio. Hist. Art.

LC CC3 .C34 **ISSN** 0068-4945
DD 913.05 FR
CAHIERS ARCHEOLOGIQUES. [Cah. archeol.]. Vol. 1 (1945)-. Periodical. French. Four times a year. Editions A et J Picard, 82 rue Bonaparte, 75006 Paris France. **Tel** 011 33 1 43269778. **ED** J. Thirion and T. Velmans.
Desc: Covers the study of archaeology.
Ind/Abst Art Index; Avery Index Archit. Period. Suppl. Colum. Univ. (1990-); BHA : Biblio. Hist. Art; Br. Archaeol. Bibliogr.

ISSN 0007-9693
FR
CAHIERS D'ARCHEOLOGIE ET D'HISTORIE DU BERRY. **Added/Corp** Societe d'Archeologie et d'Histoire du Berry. (Feb. 1965)-. Periodical. French. Four times a year. $50.31. Societe d'Archeologie et d'Histoire du Berry, 8 Place des 4 Piliers, BP 69, 18002 Bourges Cedex France. **Tel** 011 33 48 243340.
Ind/Abst BHA : Biblio. Hist. Art; GeoRef.

LC CC77.U5 C34
DD 930/.1/02804 FR
CAHIERS D'ARCHEOLOGIE SUBAQUATIQUE. No. 1 (1972)-. Periodical. French. Cahiers D'Archeologie, 1637 Av Marechal Lattre Tassig, 83600 Frejus France.
Ind/Abst Br. Archaeol. Bibliogr. (?-?).

LC DS261 .D44a **ISSN** 0765-104X
DD 935/.005 FR
CAHIERS DE LA DAFI. (CAHIERS DE LA DELEGATION ARCHEOLOGIQUE FRANCAISE EN IRAN.). [Cah. DAFI]. **Main/Corp** Delegation Archeologique Francaise en Iran. **Added/Corp** Association Paleorient. (1971)-. French. Irregular. 312.00F US. Association Paleorient, BP 5005, 75222 Paris Cedex 5 France. **Tel** 011 33 1 44203890.
(Subscription address: Editions Faton, Service Paleorient, BP 90, 21803 Quetigny Cedex France. **Tel** 011 33 80 469393.**)**
Ind/Abst Anthropol. Lit.

LC DS79.89.E863 C33
DD 935 FR
CAHIERS DE L'EUPHARATE. (1978)-. Periodical. French. Editions du CNRS, 22 rue Saint Armand, F 75015 Paris France. **Tel** 011 33 1 45075050, telex 200 356 F.

ISSN 0399-1415
FR
CAHIERS LEOPOLD DELISLE. See History-History of Europe.

IT
SUSPENDED
CAHIERS LIGURES DE PREHISTOIRE ET DE PROTOHISTOIRE. See History.

FR
CAHIERS LORRAINS, LES. See History-History of Europe.

LC GN1 .C25 **ISSN** 0272-5452
US
CALIFORNIA ANTHROPOLOGIST. See Anthropology.

LC CC1 .C35 **ISSN** 0959-7743
DD 930.1/05 UK
CCC
CAMBRIDGE ARCHAEOLOGICAL JOURNAL. **Added/Corp** McDonald Institute for Archaeological Research. Vol. 1, No. 1 (Apr. 1991)-. Academic Scholarly Publication. English. Two times a year (April and October). $72.00. Cambridge University Press, The Edinburgh Building, Shaftesbury Road, Cambridge CB2 2RU United Kingdom. **Tel** 011 44 1223 312393, FAX 011 44 1223 315052, telex 851-817256. **(Subscription address:** Cambridge University Press / North America, 110 Midland Avenue, Port Chester NY 10573. **Tel** (800)431-1580, (914)937-9600.**)** **ED** Chris Scarre.
Desc: Covers archaeological research, both theoretical and descriptive. Ranging widely in space and time, it focuses on general topics in archaeology.
Ind/Abst Anthropol. Lit.

Archaeology

LC F1019 .C36   ISSN 0705-2006
DD 971/.01/05   CN
Pr Rev.
CANADIAN JOURNAL OF ARCHAEOLOGY. [Can. j. archaeol.]. **Added/Corp** Canadian Archaeological Association. **VFOAT** Journal Canadien d'Archeologie. No. 1 (1977)-. Periodical. English (French). One time a year (June). 52.02Can$. Canadian Archaeological Association, 3170 Tillicum Road Space 162, Victoria BC V9A 7H7 Canada. **Tel** (604)479-1147, FAX (604)381-3890. **ED** Mima Kapches (editor's telephone: (416)586-5727). Index available. cum. index. **Bk Rev**, (Qty: 5-6). **Circ**: 600 (ctrl). *Continues Canadian Archaeological Association. Bulletin, 0315-761X.*
Desc: Covers Canadian archaeology and contains theoretical/field reports.
Ind/Abst ASTIS Curr. Aware. Bull. (1978-); Anthropol. Lit.; ASTIS Bibliogr. (1978-); Br. Archaeol. Bibliogr. (?-?); Ethnoarts Index.

ISSN 1061-4257
US
CASE STUDIES IN GREAT LAKES ARCHAEOLOGY. (1992)-. Monographic series. English. Two times a year. Price varies per volume. Great Lakes Archaeological Press, Inc., 1659 North Jackson Street, Milwaukee WI 53202.

LC DS62.2 .C34   ISSN 0733-8058
DD 939/.4   US
CATASTROPHISM AND ANCIENT HISTORY. See History.

ISSN 0330-2210
TI
UDC 930.26
CEDAC - CARTHAGE. [CEDAC - Carthage]. **VFOAT** Centre d'Etudes et de Documentation Archeologique de la Conservation de Carthage. (1978)-. Periodical. French. Two times a year.
Ind/Abst BHA : Biblio. Hist. Art.

LC E75 .C4   ISSN 0008-9559
US
CENTRAL STATES ARCHAEOLOGICAL JOURNAL. Added/Corp Central States Archaeological Societies. Central States Archaeological Society. Central States Archaeological Group. Vol. 1 (July 1954)-. Periodical. English. Four times a year. $15.00. Central States Archaeology Society, 2615 East 29th Court, Davenport IA 52803. **Tel** (319)355-1616. Index available. cum. index. **Bk Rev**. **Circ**: 8,000 (ctrl). *Supersedes Illinois State Archaeological Society. Journal.*
Desc: Published by a joint effort of thirteen independent state archaeological societies. Includes photos in color, and articles from archaeologists, museums, and institutions of learning as well as non-professionals.
Ind/Abst Abstr. Anthropol.; Ethnoarts Index.

LC F388 .C46   ISSN 0882-3693
DD 976.4/101/05   US
Pr Rev.
CENTRAL TEXAS ARCHEOLOGIST. (CENTRAL TEXAS ARCHEOLOGIST : JOURNAL OF THE CENTRAL TEXAS ARCHEOLOGICAL SOCIETY.). [Cent. Tex. archeol.]. **Added/Corp** Central Texas Archeological Society. No. 3 (Dec. 1937)-. Monographic series. English. Irregular. Price varies per issue. Central Texas Archaeological Society, 4229 Mitchel Road, Waco TX 76710. **Tel** (817)772-0027. **ED** Albert Redder. **Circ**: 500. *Continues Bulletin of the Central Texas Archeological Society.*
Desc: Archeological studies of the Southwest and particularly Central Texas.
Ind/Abst Anthropol. Lit.

ISSN 0577-3334
US
CERAMICA DE CULTURA MAYA ET AL. Added/Corp Temple University. Dept. of Anthropology. No. 1 (June 1961)-. Periodical. English (Spanish). Irregular. Price varies per volume. Temple University Laboratory of Anthropology, Gladfelter Hall L-5, Philadelphia PA 19122. **Tel** (215)787-1418. **ED** Carol A. Gifford and Muriel Kirkpatrick. Index available. **Circ**: 250.
Desc: Articles on the excavation, documentation, analysis, description, classification, and illustration of pottery from the Maya and other Middle American and New World cultures.
Ind/Abst Anthropol. Lit.; Ethnoarts Index.

LC DR211 .C46
DD 939/.8   RM
CERCETARI ARHEOLOGICE / MUZUEL NATIONAL DE ISTORIE. Added/Corp Muzeul de Istorie al Republicii Socialiste Romania. (1975)-. Periodical. French (Romanian; summaries and/or abstracts in English and German). One time a year. Muzeul de Istorie a Romania, Calea Victoriei Nr. 12, Bucharest Romania. **Tel** 011 40 1 157055, FAX 011 40 1 3113356.
Ind/Abst BHA : Biblio. Hist. Art; Numis. Lit.

BE
CHERCHEURS DE LA WALLONIE: BULLETIN DE LA SOCIETE ROYALE BELGE D'ETUDES GEOLOGIQUES ET ARCHEOLOGIQUE, LES. See Earth Sciences-Geology.

LC DA670.C6 C43   ISSN 0965-2787
DD 936   UK
CHESHIRE PAST : AN ANNUAL REVIEW OF ARCHAEOLOGY IN CHESHIRE. Added/Corp Cheshire (England). County Council. Issue 1 (1992)-. English. Cheshire Past, 11 Wold Court, Hawarden Clwyd CH5 3LN United Kingdom. *Continues Cheshire Archaeological Bulletin.*

LC E77.8 .C5   ISSN 0009-3300
DD 970   US
Pr Rev.
CHESOPIEAN, THE. [Chesopiean]. **Added/Corp** Chesopiean Archaeological Association. Chesopiean Library of Archaeology. Pennsylvania Institute of Anthropology. Vol. 1 (Feb. 1963)-. Periodical. English. Four times a year. $15.00. Institute for Human History, PO Box 648, Gloucester VA 23061. **Tel** (804)642-2851. **ED** Christine W. Dragoo. Index available. cum. index. **Bk Rev**, (Qty: 8-10). **Ad Acc**. **Circ**: 500.
Ind/Abst Abstr. Anthropol.; Am. Hist. Life (1968, 1979-); Anthropol. Lit.; Ethnoarts Index.

US
CHOKE CANYON SERIES. Vol. 1 (1981)-. Monographic series. English. Irregular. Price varies per volume. Center for Archaeological Research, University of Texas at San Antonio, San Antonio TX 78285.

ISSN 0009-6067
BE
CHRONIQUE D'EGYPTE. [Chron. Egypte]. **Added/Corp** Fondation Egyptologique reine Elisabeth. Vol. 1 (Dec. 1925)-. French (English and German). Two times a year. $93.29. Fondation Egyptologique, Reine Elisabeth, Parc du Cinquantenaire 10, B-1040 Brussels Belgium. **Tel** 011 32 2 7339610 Ext. 366. Index available. cum. index. **Bk Rev**. **Ad Acc**. **Circ**: 1,000.
Desc: Egyptology and papyrology.
Ind/Abst BHA : Biblio. Hist. Art; MLA Int. Bibl. Books Artic. Mod. Lang. Lit.

FR
CHRONIQUES DES FOUILLES ET DECOUVERTES ARCHEOLOGIQUES EN GRECE EN. Added/Corp Ecole Francaise d'Athenes. (19??)-. French. One time a year. 375.00F. Diffusion de Boccard, 11 rue de Medicis, 75006 Paris France. **Tel** 011 33 1 43260037.

LC F3069.1.A74 C47   ISSN 0716-1182
DD 983/.1   CL
CHUNGARA. Added/Corp Universidad del Norte (Chile). Sede Arica. Depto. de Antropologia. Universidad de Tarapaca. Depto. de Antropologia. Universidad de Tarapaca. Instituto de Antropologia. **VFOAT** Chungara Arica; Revista Chungara. No. 1/2 (1972/1973)-. Periodical. Spanish. Two times a year. $28.00. Revista Chungara, Universidad de Tarapaca, Department Arqueologia, Casilla Cas 6 D Arica Chile. **Tel** 011 56 42393.

ISSN 0268-425X
UK
Pr Rev.
CIRCAEA : BULLETIN OF THE ASSOCIATION FOR ENVIRONMENTAL ARCHAEOLOGY. Added/Corp Association for Environmental Archaeology. Vol. 1, No. 1 (Jan. 1983)-. Bulletin. English. Two times a year. £12.00 (individuals); £18.00 (institutions). Association for Environmental Archaeology, University Museum, Parks Road, Oxford OX1 3PW United Kingdom. **Tel** 011 44 1865 272983. **ED** Harry Karward and Alan Hall. **Bk Rev**, (Qty: varies). **Circ**: 450.
Desc: Includes material of a controversial nature where important issues in environmental archaeology are involved as well as short articles, reviews and methodological papers.
Ind/Abst Br. Archaeol. Bibliogr.

LC F806 .C63   ISSN 0190-8626
DD 979.1/01   US
COCHISE QUARTERLY, THE. [Cochise q.]. **Added/Corp** Cochise County Historical and Archaeological Society. Vol. 1, No. 1 (Mar. 1971)-. Periodical. English. Four times a year. $20.00 institutions; $15.00 individuals. Cochise County History and Archaeology Society, PO Box 818, Douglas AZ 85608. **Tel** (602)364-5226, (602)364-7501.
Ind/Abst Am. Hist. Life.

ISSN 0821-3801
CN
COLLECTION PALEO-QUEBEC. [Collect. Paleo-Que.]. **VAT** Paleo-Quebec. No. 1 (1974)-. Monographic series. English (French). Irregular. Price varies per volume. Universite du Quebec a Trois-Rivieres, CP 500, Des Forges Trois-Rivieres, Quebec G9A 5H7 Canada. **Tel** (819)376-5085, FAX (819)376-5092. Index available. cum. index. **Ad Acc**. **Circ**: 500.
Desc: The collection is designed to assemble and rapidly disseminate original contributions and monographs in keeping with current research in Quebec (prehistory, paleogeography, paleoecology and archaeology).
Ind/Abst GeoRef.

ISSN 0069-5971
US
COLONIAL WILLIAMSBURG ARCHAEOLOGICAL SERIES. [Coloni. Williamsburg archeol. ser.]. **Added/Corp** Colonial Williamsburg Foundation. No. 1 (1969)-. Monographic series. English. Irregular. Price varies per volume. Colonial Williamsburg Foundation, PO Box C, Williamsburg VA 23187. **Tel** (804)229-1000. **Bk Rev**.

US
COLUMBIA STUDIES IN ARCHAEOLOGY AND ETHNOLOGY. (1943)-. Monographic series. English. Irregular. Price varies per volume. Columbia University Press, 136 South Broadway, Irvington NY 10533. **Tel** (914)591-9111.

LC DB920 .C65
HU
Pr Rev.
COMMUNICATIONES ARCHEOLOGICAE HUNGARIAE. Added/Corp Nepmuvelesi Propaganda Iroda. **VFOAT** Communicationes Archaeologicae Hungariae. (1981)-. Academic Scholarly Publication. Hungarian (summaries and/or abstracts in English, German and Russian). One time a year. $6.00. Magyar Nemzeti Muzeum, PF 364, H-1370 Budapest Hungary. **Tel** 011 36 1 1382662, FAX 011 36 1 1177806. **Bk Rev**, (Qty: 8). **Circ**: 800 (ctrl). available in bound issues from the publisher.
Desc: Strives to encourage archaeologists who deal with the material stockpiled in the storage rooms of museums. Also provides preliminary reports on important excavations in Hungary.

ISSN 0144-0179
UK
CONFERENCE TRANSACTIONS - BRITISH ARCHAEOLOGICAL ASSOCIATION. (CONFERENCE TRANSACTIONS FOR THE YEAR ...). [Conf. trans. - Br. Archaeol. Assoc.]. **Main/Corp** British Archaeological Association. Vol. 1 (1978)-. Monographic series. English. Price varies per volume.
Ind/Abst Archit. Period. Index (1978-).

LC DC30 .S6   ISSN 0069-8881
FR
CONGRES ARCHEOLOGIQUE DE FRANCE. (CONGRES ARCHEOLOGIQUE DE FRANCE : [PROCEEDINGS].). [Congr. archeol. Fr.]. **Added/Corp** Societe Francaise d'Archeologie. (1904)-. Monographic series. French. One time a year. $92.96. Societe Francaise d'Archeologie, Musee Nationale Francaise, Palais de Chaillot, 1 place du Trocadero, F-75116 Paris France. **Bk Rev**. **Ad Acc**. ctrl circ. *Continues Congres Archeologique de France. Seances Generales Tenues a ... en ... par la Societe Francaise pour la Conservation des Monuments Historiques.*
Ind/Abst Art Index; Avery Index Archit. Period. Suppl. Colum. Univ. (19??-199?); BHA : Biblio. Hist. Art.

LC D51   ISSN 1350-5033
DD 930   UK
Pr Rev.
●**CONSERVATION AND MANAGEMENT OF ARCHAEOLOGICAL SITES.** (1993)-. Academic Scholarly Publication. English. Two times a year. $75.00. Taylor & Francis Ltd. / UK, Rankine Road, Basingstoke, Hampshire RG24 8PR United Kingdom. **Tel** 011 44 1256 840366, FAX 011 44 1256 479438, telex 858540. (**Subscription address:** Taylor & Francis Inc., 1900 Frost Road, Suite 101, Bristol PA 19007-1598. **Tel** (215)785-5800, (800)821-8312, FAX (215)785-5515.) **ED** Jeanne Teutonico and Kathryn Gleason.
Desc: Deals with the long-term preservation of worldwide archaeological sites.

US
CONTRACT SERIES. REPORTS IN CONTRACT ARCHAEOLOGY. Added/Corp Southern Illinois University at Edwardsville. **VFOAT** Reports in Contract Archaeology. No. 1 (1977)-. Monographic series. English. Irregular. Price varies per volume. Southern Illinois University / Edwardsville, Edwardsville Board of Trustees, Edwardsville IL 62026-1438. **Tel** (618)692-3190.

Archaeology

CONTRIBUTIONS IN ANTHROPOLOGY (PORTALES, N.M.). See Anthropology.
LC E51 .C2
ISSN 0070-8232
US

ISSN 0068-5933
US
CONTRIBUTIONS OF THE UNIVERSITY OF CALIFORNIA ARCHAEOLOGICAL RESEARCH FACILITY. Main/Corp University of California, Berkeley. Archaeological Research Facility. **Added/Corp** University of California, Berkeley. Archaeological Research Facility. **VFOAT** Contributions of the Archaeological Research Facility of the University of California at Berkeley. No. 1 (Sept. 1965)-. Monographic series. English. Irregular. Price varies per volume. Regents of University of California / UC Department of Anthropology, Berkeley CA 94720. **Tel** (415)642-2212. **ED** John A. Graham. **Ad Acc. Circ:** 400.
Desc: Technical publication series on topics concerning Mesoamerican, California, Great Basin and Old World archaeology, ethnology and scientific methodology.
Ind/Abst Ethnoarts Index.

ISSN 0070-024X
UK
CORNISH ARCHAEOLOGY. [Corn. archaeol.]. **VFOAT** Hendhyscans Kernow. (1962)-. Periodical. Multiple languages. One time a year. $17.11. Royal Institution of Cornwall, 8 Dunheved Road, Saltash PL12 4BW United Kingdom. **Tel** 011 44 172 674763.
Continues Proceedings of the West Cornwall Field Club.
Ind/Abst Anthropol. Lit.; BHA : Biblio. Hist. Art.

ISSN 0589-8021
GW
CORPUS DER MINOISCHEN UND MYKENISCHEN SIEGEL. VFOAT CMS. Vol. 1-. Monographic series. German (English and French). Irregular. Price varies per volume. Gebrueder Mann Verlag, Lindenstrasse 76, D-10969 Berlin Germany. **Tel** 011 49 30 25913589, telex 183723. Index available. **Circ:** 800.
Desc: Minoan and Mycenaean seals.

LC DP302.C55 C8
ISSN 0212-1824
DD 936.6
SP
CUADERNOS DE PREHISTORIA Y ARQUEOLOGIA CASTELLONENSES.
Added/Corp Castellon (Spain : Province). Departamento de Arqueologia. Castellon (Spain : Province). Servicio de Arqueologia. 1 (1974)-. Periodical. Spanish (Catalan).
Ind/Abst Anthropol. Lit.

UK
CUNEIFORM TEXTS FROM NIMRUD.
Added/Corp London. University. Institute of Archaeology. British School of Archaeology in Iraq. Vol.1 (1972)-. Monographic series. English. Irregular. £18.00 (volume one), £18.00 (volume two), £30.00 (volume three) UK; $40.00 (volume one), $40.00 (volume two), $65.00 (volume three) US. British School of Archaeology, 31-34 Gordon Square, London WC1 United Kingdom. **Tel** 011 44 181 6758343. **Circ:** 242.
Desc: Publication of the Akkadian texts found at the site of Nimrud in northern Iraq.

LC DA90 .C99
ISSN 0011-3212
DD 913.362/03/05
UK
CURRENT ARCHAEOLOGY. [Curr. archaeol.]. No. 1 (March 1967)-. Periodical. English. Six times a year. $25.67. Current Archaeology, 9 Nassington Road, London NW3 2TX United Kingdom. **Tel** 011 44 171 4357517. **ED** Andrew Selkirk. Index available. cum. index. **Bk Rev. Ad Acc. Circ:** 6,000 (ctrl).
Desc: Latest news of British archaeology, bridging the gap between the amateur and the professional.
Ind/Abst Art Archaeol. Tech. Abstr.; BHA : Biblio. Hist. Art; Br. Archaeol. Bibliogr.

LC F528 .C87
US
CURRENT RESEARCH IN INDIANA ARCHAEOLOGY AND PREHISTORY : ABSTRACTS OF PAPERS PRESENTED AT THE ANNUAL MEETING OF THE INDIANA HISTORICAL SOCIETY.
Main/Corp Indiana Historical Society. Meeting. (1986)-. English. One time a year. Free on request. University of Indiana, Glenn A. Black Laboratory of Archaeology, 9th & Fess Street, Bloomington IN 47405. **Tel** (812)855-9544.

LC DL621 .C87
ISSN 1102-7355
DD 930.1
SW
● **CURRENT SWEDISH ARCHAEOLOGY.**
Added/Corp Svenska Arkeologiska Samfundet. Vol 1 (1993)-. English. Swedish Archaeological Society, Box 5405, S-11484 Stockholm Sweden. **Tel** 011 46 8 7839000. **Continues** Swedish Archaeology.

LC DR211 .R3
ISSN 0070-251X
RM
DACIA. (DACIA; REVUE D'ARCHEOLOGIE ET D'HISTOIRE ANCIENNE). [Dacia]. **Added/Corp** Academia Republicii Populare Romine. Institutul de Arheologie. Vol. 1 (1924)-. French (English, French, German, Italian and Russian). One time a year. $137.00. (**Subscription address:** Orion Press SRL, SPL Independentei 202-A, Bucharest 6 Romania. **Tel** 011 401 3122425.)
Desc: Contains articles on archaeology, ancient history, and numismatics.
Ind/Abst Anthropol. Index; BHA : Biblio. Hist. Art; Numis. Lit.

ISSN 0494-4445
CH
UDC 001(31)
DALU ZAZHI TEKAN. See History-History of Asia.

LC DS94.5 .D33
ISSN 0176-2354
DD 939/.4/005
GW
DAMASZENER MITTEILUNGEN.
[Damaszen. Mitt.]. **Added/Corp** Deutsches Archaeologisches Instittut. Station Damaskus. (1983)-. Monographic series. English (French and German). Every 2 years. Price varies per volume. Verlag Phillip Von Zabern, Postfach 190930, D-80609 Munich Germany. **Tel** 011 49 89 12151661, FAX 011 49 61 31223710, telex 4187463.
Ind/Abst Anthropol. Lit.; BHA : Biblio. Hist. Art.

ISSN 0954-8874
UK
DEAN ARCHAEOLOGY. Added/Corp Dean Archaeological Group. No. 1 (1988)-. English. One time a year. £4.95. Dean Archaeological Group, 5 Park Court, Bathurst Park Road, Lydney G1S 5HG United Kingdom. **Tel** 011 44 1594 843548. **ED** Alf Webb. **Circ:** 500.
Desc: Archaeology of West Gloucestershire between Severn and Wye.

LC CC1
ISSN 1105-5758
DD 930
GR
UDC 930
DELTION HRISTIANIKES ARHAIOLOGIKES ETAIREIAS. [Delt. Hrist. Arhaiol. Etair.]. (1892)-. Periodical. Multiple languages. Irregular.
Ind/Abst BHA : Biblio. Hist. Art.

ISSN 0070-3788
UK
DERBYSHIRE ARCHAEOLOGICAL JOURNAL, THE. Added/Corp Derbyshire Archaeological Society. Vol. 81 (1961)-. English. One time a year. $20.53. FAO / Derbyshire Archaeological Society / England, 12 Longbow Close Stretton, Berton Trent DE13 OXY United Kingdom. **Tel** 011 44 1283 530218. cum. index. **Continues** Derbyshire Archaeological Society. Journal of the Derbyshire Archaeological and Natural History Society.
Ind/Abst BHA : Biblio. Hist. Art.

LC GN700 .D5
ISSN 0417-4046
DD 949.7 913
CI
DIADORA. Added/Corp Zadar, Dalmatia. Arheoloski Muzej. Vol. 1 (1959)-. Serbo-Croatian (Roman) (summaries and/or abstracts in French, German, Italian and English; table of contents in French and German).
Ind/Abst BHA : Biblio. Hist. Art.

ISSN 1013-7521
SA
DIGGING STICK, THE. Added/Corp South African Archaeological Society. Vol. 1, No. 1 (Apr. 1984)-. Periodical. English. Four times a year. comes with South African Archaeological Bulletin. South African Archaeological Society, PO Box 15700, 8018 Vlaeberg South Africa. **Tel** 011 27 21 243330. **Continues** South African Archaeological Society Newsletter.

ISSN 0184-1068
FR
Pr Rev.
DOCUMENTS D'ARCHEOLOGIE MERIDIONALE. [Doc. archeol. merid.].
Added/Corp Association pour la Diffusion de l'Archeologie Meridionale (France). No. 1 (1978)-. French (English, Spanish and Italian). One time a year. $76.56. Association pour la Diffusion de l'Archeologie Meridionale, 390 Avenue de Perols, F 34970 Lattes France. **Tel** 011 33 67 653167, FAX 011 33 67 225515. **ED** Arcelin Palnice. **Ad Acc.** ctrl ctrl.
Desc: Covers archaeology, Spanish and French protohistory, Roman, and post-Roman history from 6 BC to 6 AD.
Ind/Abst Anthropol. Lit.; Art Archaeol. Tech. Abstr.; BHA : Biblio. Hist. Art.

ISSN 0249-8316
FR
DOCUMENTS D'ARCHEOLOGIE MERIDIONALE. NUMERO SPECIAL, SERIE METHODES ET TECHNIQUES.
Added/Corp Association pour la Diffusion de L'Archeologie Meridionale (France). **VFOAT** Methodes et Techniques; Serie Methodes et Techniques. Vol. 2, (1982)-. Monographic series. French. Irregular. Price varies per volume. Association pour la Diffusion de L'Archeologie Meridion, 390 Avenue de Perols, F 34970 Lattes France. **Tel** 011 33 67 653167. **Continues** Documents d'Archeologie Meridionale. Numero Special.

ISSN 0073-8212
FR
DOCUMENTS, ETUDES ET REPERTOIRES. Main/Corp France. Institut de Recherche et d'Histoire des Textes. (1963)-. Monographic series. French. One time a year. Price varies per volume. Editions du CNRS, 22 rue Saint Armand, F 75015 Paris France. **Tel** 011 33 1 45075050, telex 200 356 F. **Circ:** 1,500. **Continues** France. Institut de Recherche et d'Histoire des Textes. Publication.
Desc: Studies in archaeology and history on North Africa from prehistoric times up to the Arab conquest.

ISSN 0150-0104
FR
UDC 061.7 (442.7/.8)
TITLE CHANGE
DOSSIERS ARCHEOLOGIQUES, HISTORIQUES ET CULTURELS DU NORD ET DU PAS-DE-CALAIS. See History-History of Europe.

FR
DOSSIERS D'ARCHEOLOGIE, LES. No. 139 (June 1989)-. Periodical. French. Ten times a year. $123.58. Editions Faton, BP90, 21803 Quetigny Cedex France. **Tel** 011 33 80 469393, FAX 011 33 80 469350. **Continues** Dossiers, Histoire et Archeologie.
Ind/Abst Repere.

LC DC801.S235 D67
ISSN 0399-6662
DD 936.4
FR
DOSSIERS DU CENTRE REGIONAL ARCHEOLOGIQUE D'ALET, LES.
Added/Corp Societe d'Histoire et d'Archeologie de l'Arrondissement de Saint-Malo. Centre Regional Archeologique d'Alet. **VFOAT** Dossiers du Ce.R.A.A.; Dossiers du CeRAA. No 1 (1973)-. French. One time a year. $41.56. CeRAA / Centre Regional Archeologique d'Alet, rue de Gaspe, BP 60, 35413 St. Malo Cedex France. **Tel** 011 33 1 99826373.
Ind/Abst BHA : Biblio. Hist. Art.

ISSN 0070-7554
US
DUMBARTON OAKS STUDIES.
Added/Corp Dumbarton Oaks. Vol. 1 (1950)-. Monographic series. English. Irregular. Price varies per volume. Dumbarton Oaks Publishing / Maryland, PO Box 4866, Hampden Station, Baltimore MD 21211. **Tel** (410)516-6954.

ISSN 0265-8038
UK
Pr Rev.
DURHAM ARCHAEOLOGICAL JOURNAL. Vol. 1 (1984)-. Periodical. English. One time a year. £6.00 (individuals), £10.00 (institutions). Department of Archaeology / Durham, 46 Saddler Street, Durham United Kingdom. **ED** A F Harding. **Bk Rev. Circ:** 350. **Continues** Transactions of the Architectural and Archaeological Society of Durham and Northumberland, 0066-6203.
Desc: Articles on archaeology and architecture, especially of northeast England.
Ind/Abst Archit. Period. Index; BHA : Biblio. Hist. Art; Br. Archaeol. Bibliogr.; Br. Humanit. Index.

ISSN 0961-7345
UK
EAANNOUNCEMENTS CAMBRIDGE.
[EAANnouncements Camb.]. **VFOAT** East Asian Archaeology Network Anouncements. (1990)-. Periodical. English. Three times a year (Feb., June, Oct). $22.25. East Asian Archaeology Network, St. Johns College, Cambridge CB2 1TP United Kingdom. **Tel** 011 44 1223 333322, FAX 011 44 1223 333503. **ED** Gina L. Barns. **Bk Rev.** (Qty: 5). **Circ:** 250 (ctrl).

LC E78.G3 E2
ISSN 0422-0374
US
EARLY GEORGIA. See History-History of North and South America.

LC AP37 .E22
ISSN 0012-8376
DD 055/.1
IT
EAST AND WEST (ROME, ITALY). See The Arts-Art.

LC DA670.E13 E13
DD 936.2/6
UK
Pr Rev.
EAST ANGLIAN ARCHAEOLOGY.
Added/Corp Suffolk (England). County Planning Dept. Suffolk (England). County Council. Report No. 1 (1975)-. Monographic series. English. Irregular. Price varies per volume. University of East Anglia, Centre for Research in Linguistics, School of Modern Languages, Norwich NR4 7TJ United Kingdom. **Tel** 011 44 1603 592738, FAX 011 44 1603 250599. **ED** J. Glazebrook.
Ind/Abst BHA : Biblio. Hist. Art.

Archaeology

LC DA670.Y59 E23   ISSN 0012-852X
DD 936.2/83   UK
EAST RIDING ARCHAEOLOGIST : A JOURNAL OF THE EAST RIDING ARCHAEOLOGICAL SOCIETY. Vol. 1, Pt. 1 (1968)-. Periodical. English.
Ind/Abst BHA : Biblio. Hist. Art.

ISSN 0012-9356
CN
ECHOS DU MONDE CLASSIQUE. **Added/Corp** Classical Association of Canada. **VFOAT** EMC; E.M.C.; Classical Views. Vol. 26, New Ser. 1, No. 1 (1982)-. Periodical. English (French). Three times a year. 30.00Can$. University of Calgary Press, 2500 University Drive Northwest, Calgary Alberta T2N 1N4 Canada. **Tel** (403)220-7578, FAX (403)282-0085. **ED** J. C. Yardley and Martin Cropp. **Bk Rev. Ad Acc. Circ:** 700 (ctrl). *Continues Echos du Monde Classique.*
Desc: Provides a medium for reports on the activities of Canadian classical archaeologists and articles on archaeological subjects.
Ind/Abst BHA : Biblio. Hist. Art.

ISSN 0952-9748
DD 930.1071041   UK
EDUCATION BULLETIN COUNCIL FOR BRITISH ARCHAEOLOGY. [Educ. bull. Counc. Br. Archeol.]. (1986)-. Periodical. English. Council for British Archaeology, Bowes Morrell House, 11 Walmgate, York YO1 2UA United Kingdom. **Tel** 011 44 1904 671417, FAX 011 44 1904 671384. *Continues Bulletin of Archaeology for Schools, 0263-0079.*
Ind/Abst Museum Abstr.

UK
EGYPTIAN ARCHAEOLOGY : BULLETIN OF THE EGYPT EXPLORATION SOCIETY. **Added/Corp** Egypt Exploration Society. No. 1 (Summer 1991)-. Bulletin. English. Egypt Exploration Society, 3 Doughty Mews, Longon WC1N 2PG United Kingdom. **Tel** 011 44 171 2421880.

ISSN 0013-4023
DD 930   US
EL PASO ARCHAEOLOGY. [El Paso archaeol.]. **Main/Corp** El Paso Archaeological Society. (19??)-. Periodical. English. Twelve times a year. $25.00. El Paso Archaeological Society Inc, PO Box 4345, El Paso TX 79914. **Tel** (915)751-3295. **ED** Tom O'Laughlin. **Ad Acc. Circ:** 225.
Desc: Archaeology studies of the Southwestern United States area.

LC DP44 .A57
DD 930.102   SP
EMPURIES. **Added/Corp** Barcelona (Spain : Province). Diputacion Provincial. Vol. 45-46 (1984)-. Catalan (French, Spanish, Italian, Portuguese and English). Irregular. 4806ptas. Museo de Arqueologia Institut Per, Parc de Montjuic, 08038 Barcelona Spain. **Tel** 011 34 3 4232149 or 4235601. *Continues Ampurias, 0212-0909.*
Ind/Abst Anthropol. Lit.; BHA : Biblio. Hist. Art.

LC N1 .A13   ISSN 0393-5183
DD 720/.917/671   IT
ENVIRONMENTAL DESIGN (ROME, ITALY). See Architecture.

LC CN135 .E65
RU
EPIGRAFIKA VOSTAKA. **Added/Corp** Akademiia Nauk SSSR. Institut Istorii Materialnoi Kultury. Sektor Srednei Azii. Akademiia Nauk SSSR. Institut Arkheologii. Vol. 1 (1947)-. Russian.
Desc: Information on Oriental inscriptions.
Ind/Abst BHA : Biblio. Hist. Art; Numis. Lit.

ISSN 1061-5938
DD 905   US
EPIGRAPHIC SOCIETY OCCASIONAL PAPERS, THE. (THE EPIGRAPHIC SOCIETY OCCASIONAL PAPERS : ESOP). [Epigr. Soc. occas. pap.]. **Added/Corp** Epigraphic Society. **VFOAT** ESOP; Occasional Papers. Vol. 19 (1990)-. English (French, German, Spanish and Portuguese). Irregular. $40.00. The Epigraphic Society, 6625 Bamburgh Drive, San Diego CA 92117. **Tel** (619)571-1344, FAX (619)571-1124. Index available. *Continues Epigraphic Society. Occasional Publications - The Epigraphic Society, 0192-5148.*
Desc: Contains articles and photographs of discoveries and decipherments of ancient inscriptions in current research.

LC CN1 .E6   ISSN 0013-9572
IT
EPIGRAPHICA (FAENZA). (EPIGRAPHICA.). **Added/Corp** Universita di Bologna. Dipartimento di Storia Antica. Centro "Bartolomeo Borghesi.". Vol. 1, (Jan./Mar. 1939)-. Periodical. Italian. One time a year. $90.00. Fratelli Lega Editori, Corso Mazzini 33, 48018 Faenza Ravenna Italy. **Tel** 011 39 546 21060. **ED** Aristide Calderini.

LC CC5 .E73
GW
ERDSTALL, DER. No. 1- 1975-. German. 15.00. Arbeitskreis fur Erdstallforschung, Schorndorfestr 31 8495, Roding Germany.

ISSN 0425-1768
SZ
ERETRIA. Vol. 1 (1968)-. Monographic series. Multiple languages (English, French and German). Irregular. Price varies per volume. Francke Verlag, Neuengasse 43, Postfach 1445, CH-3001 Bern Switzerland. **Tel** 011 41 31 221715, FAX 011 41 31 221723, telex 911822.

LC DS107.4 .E7
DD 956.94/005   IS
ERETZ MAGAZINE. **Added/Corp** Hevrah La-Haganat Ha-Teva. **VFOAT** Eretz. Vol. 1 No. 1 (Autumn 1985)-. Periodical. English (Hebrew). Six times a year. $39.95. Eretz Magazine, 5 Avida, Jerusalem 94268 Israel. **Tel** 011 972 2 248090, 011 972 2 243045, FAX 011 972 2 244153. **(Subscription address:** Eretz Magazine, PO Box 8074, Syracuse NY 13217. **Tel** (315)437-5972.**) ED** Radin Roman. **Ad Acc. Circ:** 12,000.
Desc: Explores Israel's ancient cultures, peoples and landscapes through pages of articles and photography.
Ind/Abst Relig. Theol. Abstr. (19??-).

ISSN 0927-3026
UDC 902   NE
ERFGOED VAN INDUSTRIE EN TECHNIEK. See History-History of Europe.

GW
ERGON TES ARCHAILOGIKES HETAIRIAS. (19??)-. German. One time a year. DM32.00. Wasmuth KG, Hardenbergstrasse 9A, D-10623 Berlin Germany. **Tel** 011 49 30 3131920.

ISSN 0308-3462
UK
Pr Rev.
ESSEX ARCHAEOLOGY AND HISTORY : THE TRANSACTIONS OF THE ESSEX ARCHAEOLOGICAL SOCIETY. See History-History of Europe.

ISSN 0014-0961
UK
ESSEX JOURNAL. See History-History of Europe.

LC F3069.1.S24 E87
AG
ESTUDIOS ARQUEOLOGICOS. **Added/Corp** Museo Arqueologico de Cachi. **VFOAT** Estudios de Arqueologia. (1972)-. Spanish. Museo Arqueologica de Cachi, 4417 Cachi Argentina.

LC WMLC L 83/2119   ISSN 0425-3507
SP
ESTUDIOS DE ARQUEOLOGIA ALAVESA / DIPUTACION FORAL DE ALAVA, CONSEJO DE CULTURA. [Estud. arqueol. alav.]. (1966)-. Spanish. Every 2 years.
Ind/Abst Anthropol. Lit.

LC DP302.M1 E77   ISSN 0213-0246
DD 936.6   SP
ESTUDIOS DE PREHISTORIA Y ARQUEOLOGIA MADRILENAS. [Estud. prehist. arqueol. madr.]. (1982)-. Spanish. One time a year. Delegacion de Cultura del Ayuntamiento de Madrid, Plaza de la Villa 4, Madrid 12 Spain.
Ind/Abst Anthropol. Lit.

LC GN301   ISSN 0871-3332
DD 306   PO
ESTUDIOS REGIONAIS. (VIANA DO CASTELO, PORTUGAL). See Anthropology.

LC E78.C15 E8   ISSN 0071-1799
DD 970.4/94   US
ETHNIC TECHNOLOGY NOTES. See Anthropology.

LC GN700 .E752   ISSN 0012-7477
GW
ETHNOGRAPHISCH-ARCHAOLOGISCHE ZEITSCHRIFT : EAZ. **Added/Corp** Humboldt-Universitaet zu Berlin. Institut fuer Ur- und Fruehgeschichte. Humboldt Universitaet zu Berlin. Institut fuer Voelkerkunde und Deutsche Volkskunde. Humboldt Universitaet zu Berlin. Bereich Ur- und Fruehgeschichte. Humboldt Universitaet zu Berlin. Bereich Ethnographie. **VFOAT** EAZ. Vol. 1, No. 1 (1960)-. Periodical. German (German; summaries and/or abstracts in English and Russian; table of contents in English and Russian). Four times a year. $95.57. Dr. Alfred Huethig Verlag GmbH, Postfach 102869, D-69018 Heidelberg Germany. **Tel** 011 49 6221 489281, FAX 011 49 6221 489279. **(Subscription address:** WEPF Publishing Services GmbH, Auf dem Wolf 4, CH-4018 Basel Switzerland. **Tel** 011 41 61 3115125.**)** *Continues Ethnographisch-Archaologische Forschungen, 0425-4589.*
Ind/Abst Anthropol. Index; Anthropol. Lit.; BHA : Biblio. Hist. Art; Ethnoarts Index.

LC GN1 .E88   ISSN 0014-1844
DD 572.05   SW
NLM W1 ET447   CODEN ESEMBP
ETHNOS. See Anthropology.

ISSN 0373-1928
FR
ETUDES CELTIQUES. See Linguistics.

ISSN 0425-4813
FR
SUSPENDED
ETUDES D'ARCHEOLOGIE CLASSIQUE. **Added/Corp** Universite de Nancy. Faculte des Lettres. Universite de Nancy. Faculte des Lettres et Sciences Humaines. Universite de Nancy II. (1956)-Suspended (Nov. 1994). Monographic series. French. Irregular. Price varies per volume. Presses Universitaires Nancy, 42 44 avenue de la Liberation, BP 3347, 54001 Nancy Cedex France. **Tel** 011 33 83 935830, FAX 011 33 83 935839. **ED** C. Brixhe. **Circ:** 800 (ctrl).

ISSN 0771-5692
BE
UDC 930.26
ETUDES ET DOCUMENTS DU CERCLE ROYAL D'HISTOIRE ET D'ARCHEOLOGIE D'ATH ET DE LA REGION. See History-History of Europe.

ISSN 0777-2173
BE
UDC 930.26
ETUDES ET RECHERCHES ARCHEOLOGIQUES DE L'UNIVERSITE DE LIEGE. [Etud. rech. archeol. Univ. Liege]. **VFOAT** ERAUL. (1982)-. Periodical. Multiple languages. Irregular. Societe Geographique de Liege, Univ Liege, 7 place Vingt Aout, B 4000 Liege Belgium. *Formed by the union of E.R.A.U.L. Etudes et Recherches Archeologiques de l'Universite de Liege. Serie A, 0773-4085; E.R.A.U.L. Etudes et Recherches Archeologiques de l'Universite de Liege. Serie B, 0773-8277; E.R.A.U.L. Etudes et Recherches Archeologiques de l'Universite de Liege. Serie C, 0773-8161; E.R.A.U.L. Etudes et Recherches Archeologiques de l'Universite de Liege. Serie D, 0773-817X and E.R.A.U.L. Etudes et Recherches Archeologiques de l'Universite de Liege. Serie E, 0773-8188.*
Ind/Abst BHA : Biblio. Hist. Art.

ISSN 0079-3566
PL
UDC 930.26
ETUDES ET TRAVAUX - CENTRE D'ARCHEOLOGIE MEDITERRANEENNE DE L'ACADEMIE POLONAISE DES SCIENCES. (ETUDES ET TRAVAUX.). [Etud. Trav. - Cent. Archeol. Mediterran. Acad. Pol. Sci.]. **VFOAT** Studia i Prace. (1966)-. Monographic series. French (English and Italian). Irregular. Price varies per volume. Polska Akademia Nauk / Zaklad Archeologii Srodziemnomorskiej, Palac Kultury i Nauki p. 2105, 00-901 Warsaw Poland. **Tel** 011 48 22 248593, FAX 011 48 22 207651.
Desc: Archaeology of the Mediterranean.
Ind/Abst BHA : Biblio. Hist. Art.

ISSN 1121-1628
IT
EUTOPIA. **Added/Corp** Associazione Culturale Roma Europa. (1992)-. Periodical. Italian (English, French and German). Two times a year. L51100. Edizioni Quasar Severino Togno, via Quattro Novembre 152, 00187 Rome Italy. **Tel** 011 39 6 6789888, 011 39 6 6796522. *Continues Dialoghi di Archeologia, 0392-8535.*

ISSN 0071-3279
SP
EXCAVACIONES ARQUEOLOGICAS EN ESPANA. **Added/Corp** Spain. Servicio Nacilonal de Excavaciones Arqueologicas. (1962)-. Monographic series. Spanish. Irregular. Price varies per volume. Consejo Superior Investigacion Cientificas / CSIC, Vitruvio 8, 28006 Madrid Spain. **Tel** 011 34 1 5612833, FAX 011 34 1 4113077, telex 42182.

LC DS111.A1 H33   ISSN 0334-1607
DD 933/.005   IS
EXCAVATIONS AND SURVEYS IN ISRAEL. [Excav. surv. Isr.]. **Added/Corp** Israel. Agaf Ha-Atikot Veha-Muzeonim. Vol. 1 (1982)-. Monographic series. English (Hebrew). Irregular. Price varies per volume. Israel Antiquities Authority, PO Box 586, Jerusalem 91004 Israel. **Tel** 011 972 2 292607, FAX 011 972 2 292628. **Circ:** 1,000 (ctrl).
Desc: Provides information on archaeological excavations.

Archaeology

EXCAVATIONS OF THE ATHENIAN AGORA: PICTURE BOOK. [Excav. Athen. Agora, Pict. book]. **Added/Corp** American School of Classical Studies at Athens. No. 1 (1958)-. Monographic series. English (French, German and Greek, Modern). Irregular. Price varies per volume. American School of Classical Studies, Institute of Advanced Study, Princeton NJ 08543. **Tel** (609)734-8387, FAX (609)924-0578. **ED** Marian McAllister. **Circ:** 10,000 (ctrl).
  Desc: Results of excavations at the Agora in Athens Greece.
  ISSN 0569-7425
  US

LC GN1 .E9
DD 301.2/05
Pr Rev.
EXPEDITION. [Expedition]. **Added/Corp** University of Pennsylvania. University Museum. Vol. 1 (Fall 1958)-. Periodical. English. Three times a year (March, July, Nov.). $20.00. University Museum, 33rd and Spruce Streets, Philadelphia PA 19104. **Tel** (215)898-4124, FAX (215)898-0657. **ED** Lee Horne. Index available. cum. index. **Circ:** 6,000. available on microfilm and microfiche from University Microfilms International (UMI). Documents available from UMI Article Clearinghouse.
  Continues University Museum Bulletin, 0096-2953.
  Desc: Presents coverage of archaeological and anthropological subjects. Stresses current fieldwork, archaeological studies and ethnographic studies.
  Ind/Abst Amer. Anthropol.; Acad. Search; Anthropol. Lit. (-Vol. 11, 1989); Art Archaeol. Tech. Abstr.; Art Index; Avery Index Archit. Period. Suppl. Colum. Univ. (1988-); Br. Archaeol. Bibliogr.; Ceram. Abstr. (19??-); EP Collect.; Ethnoarts Index; Expand. Acad. Index (1992-); Homework Help.; INFO-SOUTH Abstr.; Mag. Search; MasterFile FullTEXT 1000; MasterFile FullTEXT 350; MasterFile FullTEXT 650; MasterFile FullTEXT (Jan. 1993-); Middle East Abstr. Index; Newsp. Period. Abstr. (1988-); Numis. Lit.; OCLC; Telebase.
  ISSN 0014-4738
  US

LC DF261.D3 E3
  FR
EXPLORATION ARCHEOLOGIQUE DE DELOS FAITE PAR L'ECOLE FRANCAISE D'ATHENES. **Main/Corp** Ecole Francaise d'Athenes. No. 1 (1909)-. Monographic series. French. Irregular. Price varies per volume. Diffusion de Boccard, 11 rue de Medicis, 75006 Paris France. **Tel** 011 33 1 43260037.

LC DK4008 .F37
  PL
FASCICULI ARCHAEOLOGIAE HISTORICAE. No. 1- 1986-. French (Russian, Polish, German and English). Irregular. Polska Akademia Nauk / Zaklad Narodowy im. Ossolinskich, Ossolineum Publishing House of the Polish Academy of Sciences, Ulitsa Rynek 9, 50-106 Wroclaw Poland. **Tel** 011 48 71 38625, FAX 011 48 71 448103, telex 0712771.
  Ind/Abst Am. Hist. Life (1986-).
  ISSN 0860-0007

LC GN700 .I552
  IT
FASTI ARCHAEOLOGICI. **Added/Corp** International Association for Classical Archaeology. (1946)-. English (French, German and Italian). Irregular. L400000 Italy; L450000 other. IRSA Verlag GES MBH, Ruedengasse 6, A 1030 Vienna Austria. **Tel** 011 43 222 7130136, FAX 011 43 222 7130130, telex 5704661.
  Ind/Abst Br. Archaeol. Bibliogr.; Numis. Lit.

  US
●**FEDERAL ARCHAEOLOGY.** (1994)-. English. Four times a year. Free on request. National Park Service, PO Box 37127, Washington DC 20013-7127. **Tel** (202)343-3395. **Continues** Federal Archaeology Report, 1057-1582.
  ISSN 0391-7517
  IT
FELIX RAVENNA. [Felix Ravenna]. **Added/Corp** Universita di Bologna. Istituto di Antichita Ravennati e Bizantine, Ravenna. No. 1 (Jan. 1911)-. Periodical. Italian (English, French, Dutch and Spanish). Two times a year. L34060. Edizioni del Girasole, via P Costa 10, 48100 Ravenna Italy. **Tel** 011 39 544 212830, FAX 011 39 544 38432. **ED** Raffaella Farioli Companati. Index available. cum. index. **Bk Rev. Circ:** 500.
  Desc: Studies on art history and archaeology of Ravenna and its cultural ancient and medieval area.
  Ind/Abst Avery Index Archit. Period. Suppl. Colum. Univ. (19??-199?); BHA : Biblio. Hist. Art.
  ISSN 0015-0576
  NE

UDC 93
FIBULA : DEN HAAG. See History.
  ISSN 0265-9921
  UK
FIELD ARCHAEOLOGIST, THE. [Field archaeol.]. No. 1 (Feb. 1984)-. Periodical. English. Two times a year.

  ISSN 0015-0711
  US
FIELD NOTES - ARKANSAS ARCHAEOLOGICAL SOCIETY. (FIELD NOTES.). [Field notes - Ark. Archeol. Soc.]. **VFOAT** Field Notes of the Arkansas Archaeological Society. No. 1 (1965)-. Periodical. English. Six times a year (Feb., Apr., June, Aug., Oct., Dec.). $25.00 US/ $30.00 US/ $30.00 (institutions and supporting members), $35.00 (contributing members) other. Arkansas Archaeological Survey, PO Box 1249, Fayetteville AR 72702. **Tel** (501)575-3556. **ED** Hester A Davis. Index available (published irregularly). **Bk Rev.** (Qty: 8-10/yr). **Circ:** 875 (ctrl).
  Desc: Information of history and prehistory of Arkansas; information on activities of the Arkansas Archeological Society.
  Ind/Abst Am. Hist. Life.

LC DK445
  US
FINSKT MUSEUM. Vol. 1 (Jan. 1894)-. Finnish (summaries and/or abstracts in German). Suomen Muniaismuistoyhdistys, Nervanderinkatu 13, 00100 Helsinki 10 Finland.
  Ind/Abst Am. Hist. Life (1967-); Anthropol. Lit.; BHA : Biblio. Hist. Art; Numis. Lit.

LC F313 .F56
DD 975.9/01/05
  US
FLORIDA ARCHAEOLOGY. [Fla. archaeol.]. **Added/Corp** Florida Bureau of Archaeological Research. No. 1 (1986)-. Periodical. English. Irregular. Price varies per volume. Florida Historical Association, Gray Building, South Bronough Street, Tallahassee FL 32399. **Tel** (904)487-2299. **ED** James J. Miller.
  Desc: Presents reports of archaeology, anthropology and the history of Florida and the Southeast United States. Informs the public of the activities of the Florida Bureau of Archaeological Research.
  Ind/Abst Anthropol. Lit.

  ISSN 0133-2023
  HU
Pr Rev.
FOLIA ARCHAEOLOGICA BUDAPEST. [Folia archaeol.Bp.]. (1939)-. Academic Scholarly Publication. Multiple languages. One time a year. 450.00ft. Magyar Nemzeti Muzeum, PF 364, H-1370 Budapest Hungary. **Tel** 011 36 1 1382662, FAX 011 36 1 1177806. **ED** Istvan Fodor. Index available. cum. index. **Acid Free. Circ:** 800 (ctrl). available in bound issues from the publisher.
  Desc: Publishes articles on the archaeology and art of Hungary from the emergence of mankind until the end of the 19th century AD. Authors are mainly from the Hungarian National Museum.
  Ind/Abst BHA : Biblio. Hist. Art.

LC DK409 .F6
  PL
FONTES ARCHAEOLOGICI POSNANIENSES. (FONTES ARCHAEOLOGICI POSNANIENSES; ANNALES MUSEI ARCHEOLOGICI POSNANIENSIS.). **Added/Corp** Posen. Muzeum Archeologiczne. Vol. 1 (1950)-. Academic Scholarly Publication. Multiple languages (Polish; summaries and/or abstracts in French). One time a year. Price varies per volume. Muzeum Archeologiczne - Poznan, Ul. Wodna 27, Palac Gorkow, 61-781 Poznan Poland. **Tel** 011 48 61 525306. **Bk Rev.**
  Ind/Abst Anthropol. Index; Anthropol. Lit.; BHA : Biblio. Hist. Art.

LC N3 .F6
  GW
FORSCHUNGEN ZUR KUNSTGESCHICHTE UND CHRISTLICHEN ARCHAOLOGIE. See The Arts-Art.

LC AM101.C6827 A28
DD 069.09
  IT
FORUM IULII. **Main/Corp** Museo Archeologico Nazionale di Cividale del Friuli. (1977)-. Italian. One time a year.
  Ind/Abst BHA : Biblio. Hist. Art.

  FR
FOUILLES DE DELPHES. **Main/Corp** Ecole Francaise d'Athenes. Vol. 1 (1902)-. Monographic series. French. Irregular. Price varies per volume. Diffusion de Boccard, 11 rue de Medicis, 75006 Paris France. **Tel** 011 33 1 43260037.

LC Z5132 .B85
  FR
FRANCIS BULLETIN SIGNALETIQUE. 526, ART ET ARCHEOLOGIE. **Added/Corp** Institut de l'Information Scientifique et Technique (France). Sciences Humaines et Sociales. **VFOAT** Art et Archeologie; Art et Archeologie (Proche-Orient, Asie, Amerique); Art and Archaeology (Near East, Asia, America). Vol. 45, No. 1 (1991)-. Bulletin. French. Four times a year. 300.00F France; 315.00F other. CNRS / Institut d'Information Scientifique et Technique, (Centre National de la Recherche Scientifique), 15 Quai Anatole France, 75700 Paris France. **Tel** 011 33 1 47531515, FAX 011 33 1 45517307, telex 260034. **(Subscription address:** Institut d'Information Scientifique et Technique Diffusion, 2 Allee du Parc de Brabois, 54514 Vandoeuvre Nancy France. **Tel** 011 33 83 504664, FAX 011 33 83 504666, telex 961942.) Index available (free). available on CD-ROM. **Continues** Bulletin Signaletique. 526, Art et Archeologie-Proche-Orient, Asie, Amerique, 0007-5612.

LC DD801.B23 F85
  GW
FUNDBERICHTE AUS BADEN-WURTTEMBERG. **Added/Corp** Landesdenkmalamt Baden-Wurttemberg. (19??)-. German. One time a year. $176.56. E. Schweizerbartische Verlagsbuchhandlung, Johannesstrasse 3A, D-70176 Stuttgart Germany. **Tel** 011 49 711 625001, FAX 011 49 711 625005, telex 723363 SCHB D. **ED** H Schach-Doerges. **Bk Rev. Ad Acc.**
  Desc: Covers prehistoric sciences and archaeology.
  Ind/Abst Anthropol. Lit.; Art Archaeol. Tech. Abstr.; BHA : Biblio. Hist. Art; Br. Archaeol. Bibliogr.

  ISSN 0071-9889
  GW
FUNDBERICHTE AUS HESSEN.
Added/Corp Hesse. Amt fur Bodendenkmalpflege im Regierungsbezirk Darmstadt. Hesse. Amt fur Bodenalterturmer (Regierungsbezirk Kassel) Hesse. Landesamt fur Kulturgeschichtliche Bodenalterturmer (Regierungsbezirk Wiesbaden). Vol. 1 (1961)-. German. Irregular. Dr. Rudolf Habelt GmbH, Postfach 150104, D-53040 Bonn Germany. **Tel** 011 49 228 232015.
  Ind/Abst BHA : Biblio. Hist. Art; Numis. Lit.

LC WMLC L 83/1811
  AU
FUNDBERICHTE AUS OESTERREICH.
Added/Corp Austria. Bundesdenkmalamt. Austria. Bundesdenkmalamt. Mitteilungen. (1933)-. Monographic series. German. Irregular. Price varies per volume. Verlag Ferdinand Berger & Soehne, Wienerstrasse 21-23, A-3580 Horn Austria. **Tel** 011 43 2982 4161232. **Bk Rev.**
  Ind/Abst Art Archaeol. Tech. Abstr.; BHA : Biblio. Hist. Art; Br. Archaeol. Bibliogr.; Numis. Lit.

  ISSN 0723-8630
DD 936.3/005
  GW
FUNDE UND AUSGRABUNGEN IM BEZIRK TRIER. (FUNDE UND AUSGRABUNGEN IM BEZIRK TRIER : AUS DER ARBEIT DES RHEINISCHEN LANDESMUSEUMS TRIER.). [Funde Ausgrab. Bez. Trier]. **Added/Corp** Rheinisches Landesmuseum Trier. (1980)-. Academic Scholarly Publication. German. One time a year. DM11.00. Rheinisches Landesmuseum Trier, Ostallee 44, Bibliothek W-55 Trier Germany. **Tel** 011 0651 48368. **Acid Free. Circ:** 2,000. **Continues in part** Kurtrierisches Jahrbuch, 0452-9081.
  Ind/Abst Anthropol. Lit.

  ISSN 0427-7945
DD 948.94
  DK
FYNSKE MINDER. See History-History of Europe.

  ISSN 0254-8240
LC F2229 .G33
DD 981./01/05
  PE
GACETA ARQUEOLOGICA ANDINA.
[Gac. arqueol. andina]. **Added/Corp** Instituto Andino de Estudios Arqueologicos (Peru). Vol. 1, No. 1 (March 1982)-. Periodical. Spanish. Four times a year. Instituto Andino de Estudios Arqueologicos, Apartado 11279, Lima 14 Peru. **Tel** 674348. **Bk Rev. Ad Acc. Circ:** 2,000 (ctrl).
  Desc: Short articles about Andean archaeology with newest research results from Venezuela, Colombia, Ecuador, Peru, Bolivia, Chile and Argentina.

  FR
GALLIA INFORMATIONS ARCHEOLOGIQUES. French. Editions du CNRS, 22 rue Saint Armand, F 75015 Paris France. **Tel** 011 33 1 45075050, telex 200 356 F.

  ISSN 0072-0100
  FR
GALLIA PREHISTOIRE. SUPPLEMENT.
[Gallia prehist., Suppl.]. 1- 1963-. Monographic series. French. One time a year. Price varies per volume. Editions du CNRS, 22 rue Saint Armand, F 75015 Paris France. **Tel** 011 33 1 45075050, telex 200 356 F. **Circ:** 1,500.
  Desc: Archaeological research in France. Reports on studies and findings.
  Ind/Abst GeoRef.

LC CC9 .G46
  ISSN 0390-2196
  IT
  CODEN GARCDQ
GEO-ARCHEOLOGIA. [Geo-archeol.].
Added/Corp Associazione Geo-Archeologica Italiana. (1973)-. Academic Scholarly Publication. Italian. Two times a year. L4000. Herder Editrice e Libreria SRL, Piazza Montecitorio 117-120, 00186 Rome Italy. **Tel** 011

Archaeology

39 6 679 4628, FAX 011 39 6 678 4751. Documents available from CASDDS.
Ind/Abst Chem. Abstr.; GeoRef.

LC CC77.5 .G46   **ISSN** 0883-6353
DD 930.1   US
     CODEN GEOAEY

GEOARCHAEOLOGY. [Geoarchaeology]. Vol. 1, No. 1 (Jan. 1986)-. Periodical. English. Six times a year. $342.00. John Wiley & Sons, Inc., 605 Third Avenue, New York NY 10158-0012. **Tel** (212)850-6000, (212)850-6645, FAX (212)850-6088, telex 12-7063. **(Subscription address:** John Wiley & Sons / UK, Baffins Lane, Chichester, West Sussex PO19 1UD United Kingdom. **Tel** 011 44 1243 779777, FAX 011 44 243 776128, telex 86290 WIBOOKG.) **ED** Jack Donahue. **Bk Rev. Ad Acc.** available on CD-ROM; available on microfilm and microfiche from University Microfilms International (UMI).
  Desc: Publishes original reports on the environmental settings of archaeological sites, materials analysis of artifacts, and process papers describing new techniques and equipment. It serves as an interface between geology as it relates to the archaeology field. This journal includes book reviews, calendars of events, professional news and a bibliography of recent research in the field.
  Ind/Abst Abstr. Anthropol. (19??-); Anthropol. Lit.; Art Archaeol. Tech. Abstr.; Br. Archaeol. Bibliogr.; Ceram. Abstr. (19??-); Ecol. Abstr. (?-?); Geogr. Abstr. Human Geogr. (?-?); Geol. Abstr.; GeoRef; Soils Fert.

LC DD53 .A33   **ISSN** 0016-8874
     GW

GERMANIA (BERLIN). (GERMANIA.). **Added/Corp** Archaeologisches Institut des Deutschen Reichs. Romisch-Germanische Kommission. Vol. 1 (1917)-. Monographic series. German. Irregular. Price varies per volume. Verlag Phillip Von Zabern, Postfach 190930, D-80609 Munich Germany. **Tel** 011 49 89 12151661, FAX 011 49 61 31223710, telex 4187463. **(Subscription address:** MI Verlags Service GmbH, Justus von Liebig STR 1, D 86899 Landsberg Germany. **Tel** 011 49 8191 125214.) ctrl circ.
  Desc: New reports, essays and statements by different authors.
  Ind/Abst Anthropol. Index; Anthropol. Lit.; BHA : Biblio. Hist. Art; Numis. Lit.

     ISSN 0418-9779
DD 943   GW

GERMANISCHE DENKMALER DER VOLKERWANDERUNGSZEIT. SERIES B. DIE FRANKISCHEN ALTERTUMER DES RHEINLANDES. **Main/Corp** Deutsches Archaologisches Institut. Romisch-Germanische Kommission. **Added/Corp** Deutsches ArchEaologisches Institut. Romisch-Germanische Kommission. Serie B: Die FrEankischen Altertumer des Rheinlandes. Deutsches Archaologisches Institut. Romisch-Germanische Kommission. Frankischen Altertumer des Rheinlandes. **VFOAT** GDB. Serie B.; Frankischen Altertumer des Rheinlandes. Vol. 1 (1958)-. Monographic series. German. Irregular. Price varies per volume. Franz Steiner Verlag GmbH, Postfach 101061, D-70009 Stuttgart Germany. **Tel** 011 49 711 2582372, FAX 011 49 711 2582290, fax 7233636 daz d. **ED** Kurt Bohner. **Ad Acc. Circ:** 650. **Supersedes in part** Deutsches Archaologisches Institut. Romisch-Germanische Kommission. Germanische Denkmaler der Volkerwanderungszeit.
  Desc: Monographs about German monuments from the times of mass migration (4th to 6th centuries B.C.).

     ISSN 0017-050X
     IT

GIORNALE STORICO DELLA LUNIGIANA. **Added/Corp** Istituto Internazionale di Studi Liguri, Bordighera. Sezione Lunense. (Jan./June 1950)-. Periodical. Italian. One time a year. Istituto Internationale Studi Liguri, Museo Bicknell, via Romana 39, 18012 Bordighera Italy. **Tel** 011 39 184 263601. **Bk Rev. Circ:** 1,000 (ctrl).
  Desc: Local medieval and modern history of archaeological and historical/artistical activities in the Eastern Ligurian Riviera.
  Ind/Abst BHA : Biblio. Hist. Art.

     UK

GLASGOW ARCHAEOLOGICAL JOURNAL. **Added/Corp** Glasgow Archaeological Society. Vol. 1 (1969)-. English. One time a year. £10.00. Glasgow Archaeological Society, University of Glasgow, Department of Archaeology, Glasgow G12 8OQ United Kingdom. **Tel** 011 44 41 3398855, FAX 011 44 41 3304808. **ED** A. Morrison. cum. index. **Bk Rev. Circ:** 400. **Continues** Glasgow Archaeological Society. Transactions.
  Desc: Publishes reliable information and responsible views on archaeological work in northern Britain, particularly in western Scotland.
  Ind/Abst Anthropol. Lit.; Br. Archaeol. Bibliogr.

LC DB231 .S27a
     BN

GLASNIK ZEMALJSKOG MUZEJA BOSNE I HERCEGOVINE U SARAJEVU. ARHEOLOGIJA. **Main/Corp** Zemaljski Muzej Bosne i Hercegovine. **VFOAT** Bulletin du Musee de la Republique Socialiste de Bosnie-Herzegovine a Sarajevo. Archeologie. (1967)-. Bulletin. Serbo-Croatian (Roman) (Serbo-Croatian (Cyrillic) and German). One time a year. **Continues** Zemaljski Muzej u Sarajevu. Glasnik Zemaljskog Muzeja u Sarajevu. Arheologija.
  Ind/Abst BHA : Biblio. Hist. Art.

     AU

GRAZER BEITRAEGE. SUPPLEMENTBAND. **Added/Corp** Universitat Graz. Institut fuer Klassische Philologie. (1980)-. Monographic series. German (Greek, Modern and English). One time a year. Price varies per volume. Verlag Ferdinand Berger & Soehne, Wienerstrasse 21-23, A-3580 Horn Austria. **Tel** 011 43 2982 4161232. cum. index. **Bk Rev.** ctrl circ.

     GW

HABELTS DISSERTATIONSDRUCKE. REIHE KLASSISCHE ARCHAOLOGIE. Vol. 1- 1969-. Periodical. German. Irregular. Dr. Rudolf Habelt GmbH, Postfach 150104, D-53040 Bonn Germany. **Tel** 011 49 228 232015.

     SP

HABIS. See Classical Studies.

LC DS111.A1   **ISSN** 0047-1569
DD 933   IS

HADASHOT ARKHEOLOGIYOT. [Hadashot arkeologiyyot]. **Added/Corp** Israel. Agaf Ha-Atikot Veha-Muzeonim. Israel. Agaf Ha-Atikot Veha-Muzeonim. **VFOAT** Archaeological News. (1961)-. Academic Scholarly Publication. Hebrew. Two times a year. $24.00. Israel Antiquities Authority, PO Box 586, Jerusalem 91004 Israel. **Tel** 011 972 2 292607, FAX 011 972 2 292628. **ED** Ayala Sussmann. **Circ:** 1,200. available with illustrations.
  Desc: Summarized initial reports on all excavations and surveys carried out in Israel.

LC DD901.H245 H3   **ISSN** 0173-0886
     GW

HAMMABURG : VOR- U. FRUHGESCHICHTLICHE FORSCHUNGEN AUS DEM NIEDERELBISCHEN RAUM. See History-History of Europe.

     GW

HANDBUCH DER ALTERTUMSWISSENSCHAFT. (1923)-. German. Irregular. Price varies per volume. CH Beck Verlagsbuchhandlung, D-80791 Munich Germany. **Tel** 011 49 89 381891. cum. index. **Continues** Handbuch der Klassischen Altertumswissenschaft.

     GW

HANDBUCH DER ARCHAEOLOGIE. (19??)-. German. CH Beck Verlagsbuchhandlung, D-80791 Munich Germany. **Tel** 011 49 89 381891.

     ISSN 0774-286X
     BE

HANDELINGEN DER MAATSCHAPPIJ VOOR GESCHIEDENIS EN OUDHEIDKUNDE TE GENT. See History-History of Europe.

     ISSN 0890-1678
DD 996   US
Pr Rev.

HAWAIIAN ARCHAEOLOGY. [Hawaii. archaeol.]. **Added/Corp** Society for Hawaiian Archaeology. Vol. 1, No. 1 (1984)-. English. One time a year. $28.00. Society Hawaiian Archaeology, PO Box 23292, Honolulu HI 96823. **ED** Bion Griffin. **Ad Acc. Circ:** 130 (ctrl).
  Desc: A journal to serve as a vehicle for disseminating the results of research in Hawaiian archaeology.
  Ind/Abst Ethnoarts Index.

     ISSN 0174-2086
     GW

HEPHAISTOS (BAD BRAMSTEDT). (HEPHAISTOS.). [Hephaistos]. (1979)-. Periodical. German (French and English). One time a year.
  Ind/Abst Avery Index Archit. Period. Suppl. Colum. Univ.; BHA : Biblio. Hist. Art.

LC DA670.H49 H46   **ISSN** 0440-7342
DD 913.362   UK

HERTFORDSHIRE ARCHAEOLOGY. **Added/Corp** St. Albans Architectural and Archaeological Society. East Hertfordshire Archaeological Society. Vol. 1 (1968)-. English. **Supersedes** East Hertfordshire Archaeological Society. Transactions **and** St. Albans and Hertfordshire Architectural and Archaeological Society. Transactions.
  Ind/Abst BHA : Biblio. Hist. Art.

LC DL121 .H45
     DK

HIKUIN. See History-History of Europe.

LC TS2270 .H57   **ISSN** 0747-8801
DD 688/.42   US

HISTORIC CLAY TOBACCO PIPE STUDIES. [Hist. clay tob. pipe stud.]. (1980)-. English. Irregular. Price varies per volume. Historic Clay Pipe Studies, PO Box 2282, Ponca City OK 74602. **Tel** (405)762-3346. **ED** Byron Sudbury. **Bk Rev. Circ:** 1,000 (ctrl).
  Desc: Historical and scientific studies of clay tobacco pipes from an archaeological perspective. Includes when, where, and how pipes were manufactured and used, and by whom.

LC E11 .S625   **ISSN** 0440-9213
DD 970/.005   US
Pr Rev.

HISTORICAL ARCHAEOLOGY. [Hist. archaeol.]. **Added/Corp** Society for Historical Archaeology. Vol. 1 (1967)-. Periodical. English. Four times a year (Mar., June, Oct., Dec.). $65.00 (institutions); $50.00 (individuals) Comes with membership. Society for Historical Archaeology, PO Box 30446, Tucson AZ 85751. **Tel** (520)886-8006. **ED** Ronald L. Michael. Index available. cum. index. **Bk Rev. Ad Acc. Circ:** 2,000.
  Ind/Abst Abstr. Anthropol. (19??-); Acad. Search; Am. Hist. Life (1973-); Anthropol. Lit.; Art Archaeol. Tech. Abstr.; Br. Archaeol. Bibliogr. (1975-); Ceram. Abstr.; EP Collect.; Hist. Source (July 1993-); Homework Help.; Humanit. Source; INFO-SOUTH Abstr.; Mag. Search; MasterFile FullTEXT 1000; MasterFile FullTEXT 350; MasterFile FullTEXT 650; MasterFile FullTEXT (July 1993-); OCLC; Telebase.

LC DB329 .H57   **ISSN** 0350-6320
     CI

HISTRIA ARCHAEOLOGICA. (HISTRIA ARCHAEOLOGICA : CASOPIS ARHEOLOSKOG MUZEJA ISTRE.). [Histria archaeol.]. **Added/Corp** Arheoloski Muzej Istre. Vol. 1, No. 1 (1970)-. Monographic series. Serbo-Croatian (Roman) (Italian; summaries and/or abstracts in English and German). Price varies per volume.
  Ind/Abst Art Archaeol. Tech. Abstr.; BHA : Biblio. Hist. Art.

LC QE699 .H62   **ISSN** 0959-6836
DD 551.7/93   UK
     CCC
     CODEN HOLOE6
Pr Rev.

HOLOCENE (SEVENOAKS). See Earth Sciences-Geology.

LC GN282 .H64
DD 573.3   BE

HOMINID REMAINS. **Added/Corp** Universite Libre de Bruxelles. Dept. of Anthropology and Human Genetics. Societe Royale Belge d'Anthropologie et de Prehistoire. No. 1 (Dec. 1988)-. English. One time a year. price varies. Universite Libre de Bruxelles, 50 Avenue F D Roosevelt CP 188, 1050 Brussels Belgium. **Tel** 011 32 2 6423611.

LC DS793.H7 H7576
DD 931   CC

HU-NAN KAO KU CHI KAN / HU-NAN SHENG PO WU KUAN PIEN. **VFOAT** Human Archaeology. 1-. Periodical. Chinese. RMBY1.20. Yueh Lu Shu She, Chang-Sha, People's Republic of China.

     ISSN 0735-4576
     US

HYST'RY MYST'RY MAGAZINE. See History.

     AU

I.C. NACHRICHTEN. **Main/Corp** Kanarenistitut. **Added/Corp** Kanarenistitut. Nachrichten. Kanarenistitut. Bulletin des Institutum Canarium. Gesellschaft fuer Interdisziplinare Sahara-Forschung (GISAF). **VFOAT** Bulletin des Institutum Canarium. **VAT** Institutum Canarium. Bulletin. (19??)-. Bulletin. German. Irregular. Institutum Canarium, Postfach 48, A-5400 Hellein Austria.

LC T37 .I13   **ISSN** 0160-1040
DD 609   US
Pr Rev.

IA, THE JOURNAL OF THE SOCIETY FOR INDUSTRIAL ARCHEOLOGY. (IA.). **Added/Corp** Society for Industrial Archeology. **VFOAT** Industrial Archeology. Vol. 1 No. 1 (Summer 1975)-. Periodical. English. Two times a year. $40.00 (institutions), $35.00 (individuals) Comes with Society for Industrial Archaeology membership. Society for Industrial Archeology, National Museum of History, Smithsonian Institute, Room 5014, Washington DC 20560. **Tel** (202)357-2228. **ED** David Starbuck. Index available. cum. index. **Bk Rev. Ad Acc. Circ:** 1,400 (ctrl).
  Ind/Abst Am. Hist. Life (1988-); Avery Index Archit. Period. Suppl. Colum. Univ. (1989-).

LC QE720.5 .I25 ISSN 1042-0940
DD 560 SZ
CCC
CODEN ICHSER

ICHNOS (CHUR, SWITZERLAND). (ICHNOS : AN INTERNATIONAL JOURNAL FOR PLANT AND ANIMAL TRACES.). [Ichnos]. Vol. 1, No. 1 (1990)-. Periodical. English. Four times a year (1 volume). $287.00 (academic institutions), $448.00 (corporate institutions). Harwood Academic Publishers, PO Box 90, Reading RG1 8JL United Kingdom. **Tel** 011 44 1734 560080, FAX 011 44 1734 568211.
Ind/Abst AESIS Q.; Curr. Aware. Biol. Sci., CABS; Ecol. Abstr.; Geogr. Abstr. Phys. Geogr.

LC N5740
DD 709.37 NE

•**ICONOLOGICAL STUDIES IN ROMAN ART.** See The Arts-Art.

ISSN 0893-2271
DD 979 US
Pr Rev.

IDAHO ARCHAEOLOGIST. [Ida. archaeol.]. **Added/Corp** Idaho Archaeological Society. Great Basin Chapter. Idaho Archaeological Society. Vol. 1, No. 1 (1977)-. Periodical. English. Two times a year. $12.00. Idaho Archaeologist, Anthropology Department, 1910 University Drive, Boise ID 83725. **Tel** (208)385-3023. **ED** Mark Plew. Index available. cum. index. **Bk Rev. Circ:** 500.
Ind/Abst Am. Hist. Life (1988-); Anthropol. Lit.

US

INA QUARTERLY, THE. **Added/Corp** Institute of Nautical Archaeology (U.S.). **VFOAT** Institute of Nautical Archaeology Quarterly. Vol. 19, No. 1 (Spring 1992)-. Periodical. English. Four times a year. $25.00. Institute of Nautical Archaeology, PO Drawer HG, College Station TX 77841-5137. **Tel** (409)845-6694, FAX (409)845-6399. ***Continues*** *INA Newsletter (Institute of Nautical Archaeology (U.S.)), 0738-4505.*

LC DS416 .I42 ISSN 0536-7832
DD 913.34/031 II

INDIAN ARCHAEOLOGY. **Main/Corp** India (Republic) Archaeological Survey. (1960/61)-. English. One time a year. Price varies. Government of India / International Archives, International Archives of India, Janpath New Delhi 11 India. **(Subscription address:** Prints India, 11 Darya Ganj, New Delhi 110002 India. **Tel** 011 91 11 3268645, FAX 011 91 11 3275542, telex 31-61087 PRIN-IN.) ***Continues*** *Indian Archaeology, 0536-7832.*

LC WMLC 93/5150 ISSN 0736-265X
DD 973 US

INDIAN-ARTIFACT MAGAZINE. [Indian-artifact mag.]. **VFOAT** Indian Artifact Magazine. Vol. 1, No. 1 (June 1982)-. Periodical. English. Four times a year. $20.00. Indian Artifact Magazine Inc., Road 1, Box 240, Turbotville PA 17772. **Tel** (717)437-3698. **ED** Gary L. Fogelman. Index available. **Bk Rev**, (Qty: 6-10). **Ad Acc, Adv Mgr:** JoAnne Fogelman. **Circ:** 3,900.
Desc: Covers prehistoric American Indian history, including artifacts, lifestyles, customs, legends, and tribes.
Ind/Abst Am. Hist. Life.

LC DS401 .I53 ISSN 0019-686X
II

INDICA. See History-History of Asia.

ISSN 0156-1316
AT

INDO-PACIFIC PREHISTORIC ASSOCIATION BULLETIN. **Main/Corp** Indo-Pacific Prehistory Association. **Added/Corp** Indo-Pacific Prehistory Association. **VFOAT** IPPA Bulletin. Bulletin No. 1 (1978)-. Bulletin. English. One time a year. 22.80Aus$ Australia; 29.70Aus$ other. Anutech Pty. Limited, GPO Box 4, Canberra ACT 2601 Australia. **Tel** 011 61 6 2492479, FAX 011 61 6 2575088. **ED** Peter Bellwood. **Circ:** 300 (ctrl).
Desc: Articles on the prehistory of the peoples of South, Southeast and East Asia and the Pacific Islands.
Ind/Abst Anthropol. Lit.

ISSN 0309-0051
UK

•**INDUSTRIAL ARCHAEOLOGY NEWS : BULLETIN OF THE ASSOCIATION FOR INDUSTRIAL ARCHAEOLOGY.** **Added/Corp** Association for Industrial Archaeology. (Spring 1994)-. Bulletin. English. Four times a year. Association for Industrial Archaeology, Wharfage Ironbridge Telford, Shropshire TF8 7AW United Kingdom. **Tel** 011 44 1952 433522. ***Continues*** *AIA Bulletin, 0309-0051.*
Ind/Abst Museum Abstr.

LC T37 .I53 ISSN 0309-0728
DD 609/.41 UK

INDUSTRIAL ARCHAEOLOGY REVIEW. [Ind. archaeol. rev.]. **Added/Corp** Association for Industrial Archaeology. Vol. 1 (Autumn 1976)-. Periodical. English. Two times a year. $68.45. Association for Industrial Archaeology, Wharfage Ironbridge Telford, Shropshire TF8 7AW United Kingdom. **Tel** 011 44 1952 433522. **ED** Marilyn Palmer and Peter Neaverson. **Bk Rev. Ad Acc. Circ:** 1,000 (ctrl). ***Continues*** *Journal of Industrial Archaeology.*
Desc: Articles on conservation and industrial archaeology, photographs and book reviews.
Ind/Abst Am. Hist. Life (1976-); Archit. Period. Index; Art Archaeol. Tech. Abstr.; Avery Index Archit. Period. Suppl. Colum. Univ. (Autumn 1989-); BHA : Biblio. Hist. Art; Br. Archaeol. Bibliogr.; Br. Humanit. Index; Curr. Cit.; Geogr. Abstr. Phys. Geogr.; Geogr. Abstr. Human Geogr.; Int. Bibliogr. Sociol.; Museum Abstr.

ISSN 0019-7971
UK

INDUSTRIAL ARCHAEOLOGY (TAVISTOCK). (INDUSTRIAL ARCHAEOLOGY.). [Ind. archaeol.]. Vol. 1, (May 1964)-. Periodical. English. Four times a year (Feb., Mar., Aug., Nov.). $41.07. Graphmitre Ltd., 1 West Street, Tavistock, Devon PL19 8DS United Kingdom. **Tel** 011 44 1822 612785, FAX 011 44 1822 612078. **ED** T. D. Bridge. Index available. cum. index. **Bk Rev. Ad Acc. Circ:** 2,000 (ctrl). available on microfilm. ***Continues*** *Journal of Industrial Archaeology.*
Desc: Articles and features on industry and technology world-wide. Also includes news of societies and collectors.
Ind/Abst Am. Hist. Life (1977-198?-); Archit. Period. Index; Avery Index Archit. Period. Suppl. Colum. Univ.; BHA : Biblio. Hist. Art; Br. Archaeol. Bibliogr.; Coal Abstr.; Geogr. Abstr. Human Geogr.; Middle East Abstr. Index.

LC CC13.S66 I53
DD 930.1/05 SP

INFORMACIO ARQUEOLOGICA : BULLETI INFORMATIU DE L'INSTITUT DE PREHISTORIA I ARQUEOLOGIA DE LA DIPUTACIO PROVINCIAL DE BARCELONA. (1978)-. Periodical. Catalan (Spanish). Two times a year. ***Continues*** *Informacion Arqueologica.*
Ind/Abst BHA : Biblio. Hist. Art.

ISSN 1057-2414
DD 913 UK

INTERNATIONAL JOURNAL OF NAUTICAL ARCHAEOLOGY, THE. [Int. j. naut. archaeol.]. **Added/Corp** Nautical Archaeology Society. Vol. 20, No. 1 (Feb. 1991)-. Academic Scholarly Publication. English. Four times a year. $196.79. Academic Press Ltd., A Division of Harcourt Brace & Company Ltd., 24-28 Oval Road, London NW1 7DX United Kingdom. **Tel** 011 44 171 2674466, FAX 011 44 171 4822293, 011 44 171 4854752, telex 25775 ACPRES G. **(Subscription address:** Harcourt Brace & Company, Ltd., Foots Cray High Street, Sidcup Kent DA14 5HP United Kingdom. **Tel** 011 44 181 3003322, FAX 011 44 181 3090807, telex 896 377 ACADEM.) **ED** V. Fenwick. Index available. ***Continues*** *International Journal of Nautical Archaeology and Underwater Exploration, 0305-7445.*
Desc: Covers all aspects of nautical archaeological research. The journal strives to keep readers abreast of the latest explorations, discoveries and technical innovations in the field. Includes studies about ancient ships, harbours, and cargos, whether from excavations or documentary sources. Aimed at the naval architect, historian, and archaeologist.
Ind/Abst BHA : Biblio. Hist. Art.

ISSN 1047-482X
DD 930 UK
NLM W1; IN771FF **CODEN** IJOHEA

INTERNATIONAL JOURNAL OF OSTEOARCHAEOLOGY. (1991)-. Periodical. English. Four times a year (Jan., Apr., July, Oct.). $295.00. John Wiley & Sons Ltd., Baffins Lane, Chichester, West Sussex PO19 1UD United Kingdom. **Tel** 011 44 1243 779777, FAX 011 44 1243 776128 BTG:JWP001, telex 86290 WIBOOKG. **(Subscription address:** John Wiley & Sons, Inc. / Philadelphia, PO Box 7247, Philadelphia PA 19170. **Tel** (212)850-6645, (800)225-5945.) **ED** Ann Stirland and Tony Waldron (editors' address: Institute of Archaeology, 31-34 Gordon Square, Longon WC1H 0PY United Kingdom). available on microfilm and microfiche from University Microfilms International (UMI).
Desc: Provides a forum for the publication of papers dealing with all aspects of the study of human and animal bones from an archaeological context.

FR

INTERNATIONAL NEWSLETTER ON ROCK ART : I.N.O.R.A. **Added/Corp** International Council on Monuments and Sites. International Rock Art Committee. International Union of Prehistoric and Protohistoric Sciences. Commission 9. Association Pour le Rayonnement de l'Art Parietal Europeen. France. Direction du Patrimoine. Sous-Direction de l'Archeologie). **VFOAT** I.N.O.R.A.; INORA. No. 1 (1992)-. Newsletter. English (French). Three times a year. $19.69. CAR Jean Clottes, 11 rue Du Fourcat, 09000 Foix France.

ISSN 0075-0050
GW

INVENTARIA ARCHAEOLOGICA. DENMARK. (1965)-. Monographic series. English. Irregular. Dr. Rudolf Habelt GmbH, Postfach 150104, D-53040 Bonn Germany. **Tel** 011 49 228 232015. **ED** M.E. Marien.
Desc: Complete listing of archaeological items in Denmark.

ISSN 0075-0115
GW

INVENTARIA ARCHAEOLOGICA. JUGOSLAVIJA. (1958)-. Periodical. French. Irregular. Dr. Rudolf Habelt GmbH, Postfach 150104, D-53040 Bonn Germany. **Tel** 011 49 228 232015.

LC N5310 .A3 ISSN 0075-0468
GW

IPEK. (IPEK; JAHRBUCH FUER PRAHISTORISCHE UND ETHNOGRAPHISCHE KUNST.). **VFOAT** Jahrbuch fuer Prahistorische und Ethnographische Kunst. Vol. 1 (1925)-. Monographic series. Multiple languages (German, French, English, Spanish and Italian). Irregular. Price varies per volume. Walter de Gruyter Inc., PO Box 303421, D-10728 Berlin Germany. **Tel** 011 49 30 260050, FAX 011 49 30 26005251, telex 184027. **(Subscription address:** Walter de Gruyter Inc. / North America, 200 Saw Mill River Road, Hawthorne NY 10532. **Tel** (914)747-0110.) **ED** Herbert Kuhn and others.
Ind/Abst Anthropol. Index; BHA : Biblio. Hist. Art; Ethnoarts Index.

LC DS251 .I77 ISSN 0021-0870
DD 955 BE

IRANICA ANTIQUA. [Iran. antiq.]. (1961)-. English (French and German). Irregular. 3200F. Editions Peeters SA, Bondgenotenlaan 153, BP 41, B-3000 Leuven Belgium. **Tel** 011 32 16 235170, FAX 011 32 16 228500, telex 65987 PUL B. **ED** L. Vanden Berghe and A. Tourovets.
Desc: Journal of the seminar for archaeology of the Near-East of the State University of Gent.
Ind/Abst Art Index; Avery Index Archit. Period. Suppl. Colum. Univ.; Numis. Lit.

LC DS78.A2 I7 ISSN 0021-0889
DD 913.35 UK

IRAQ. [Iraq]. **Added/Corp** British School of Archaeology in Iraq. Vol. 1, Pt. 1 (April 1934)-. Periodical. English. One time a year. $55.00. British School of Archaeology, 31-34 Gordon Square, London WC1 United Kingdom. **Tel** 011 44 181 6758343. **ED** J D Hawkins. Index available. cum. index. **Circ:** 700.
Desc: Devoted to studies of history, art, archaeology, religion, economic and social life of Iraq and neighboring countries from earliest times to about 1700 AD.
Ind/Abst Anthropol. Index; Anthropol. Lit.; Art Archaeol. Tech. Abstr.; Avery Index Archit. Period. Suppl. Colum. Univ. (19??-199?); Index Book Rev. Relig.; Middle East Abstr. Index; Relig. Index One Period.

LC DS111.A1 I87 ISSN 0021-2059
DD 933 IS
CODEN IEXJAM
Pr Rev.

ISRAEL EXPLORATION JOURNAL. [Isr. explor. j.]. **Added/Corp** Israel. Agaf ha-Atikot Veha-Muzeonim. Hevrah la-Hakirat Erets-Yisrael ve-Atikoteha. Universitah ha-Ivrit bi-Yerushalayim. Makhon le-Arkheologyah. Vol. 1 (1951)-. Periodical. English (French). Irregular. $48.00. Israel Exploration Society, 5 Avida Street, 91070 Jerusalem Israel. **Tel** 011 972 2 227991. **ED** J. Grienfield. Index available. cum. index. **Bk Rev. Circ:** 2,500 (ctrl). available on microfilm and microfiche from University Microfilms International (UMI). Documents available from The Genuine Article.
Desc: Includes articles on ancient history, Biblical archaeology, preliminary excavation reports, special discoveries and finds.
Ind/Abst Anthropol. Lit.; Art Archaeol. Tech. Abstr.; Arts Humanit. Citation Index [Full Cov.]; BHA : Biblio. Hist. Art; Curr. Contents Arts Humanit.; Curr. Contents Soc. Behav. Sci.; GeoRef; Index Book Rev. Relig.; Index Jew. Period. (19??-199?); Middle East Abstr. Index; New Testam. Abstr.; Numis. Lit.; Old Testam. Abstr.; Relig. Index One Period. (1950/1951-); Relig. Theol. Abstr.; Res. Alert [Full Cov.]; Soc. Sci. Cit. Index [Full Cov.].

LC DS41 .I8 ISSN 0341-9142
GW

ISTANBULER MITTEILUNGEN. (ISTANBULER MITTEILUNGEN / HERAUSGEGEBEN VON DER ABTEILUNG ISTANBUL DES ARCHAEOLOGISCHEN INSTITUTS DES DEUTSCHEN REICHES.). [Istanb. Mitt.]. **Added/Corp** Deutsches Archaeologisches Institut. Abteilung Istanbul. (1933)-. Monographic series. German (English). Irregular. Price varies per volume. Verlag Ernst Wasmuth Tuebingen, Postfach 2728, D-72017 Tuebingen Germany. **Tel** 011 49 7071 33658. **Circ:** 600.
Desc: Essays on Asia Minor and Istanbul, especially about archaeology.
Ind/Abst Avery Index Archit. Period. Suppl. Colum. Univ. (19??-199?); BHA : Biblio. Hist. Art.

ISSN 0323-9535
BU
UDC 930.26
IZVESTIA NA ARHEOLOGICESKIA INSTITUT. [Izv. Arheol. inst.]. **VFOAT** Bulletin de l'Institut d'Archeologie. (1910)-. Academic Scholarly Publication. Multiple languages. Every 3 years. Bulgarska Akademiia na Naukite, 7 Noemvri 1, Sofia Bulgaria.
Ind/Abst BHA : Biblio. Hist. Art.

NE
JAARBERICHT VAN HET VOORAZIATISCH-EGYPTISCH GENOOTSCHAP "EX ORIENTE LUX". ANNUAIRE DE LA SOCIETE ORIENTALE "EX ORIENTE LUX.". See History-History of Asia.

LC GN841 **ISSN** 0252-1881
DD 913 SZ
JAHRBUCH DER SCHWEIZERISCHEN GESELLSCHAFT FUER UR- UND FRUEHGESCHICHTE. (JAHRBUCH DER SCHWEIZERISCHEN GESELLSCHAFT FUER UR- UND FRUEHGESCHICHTE = ANNUAIRE DE LA SOCIETE SUISSE DE PREHISTOIRE ET D'ARCHEOLOGIE = ANNUARIO DELLA SOCIETA SVIZZERA DI PREISTORIA E D'ARCHEOLOGIA.). [Jahrb. Schweiz. Ges. Ur- Fruehgesch.]. **Main/Corp** Schweizerische Gesellschaft fuer Ur- und Fruehgeschichte. **Added/Corp** Schweizerische Gesellschaft fuer Ur- und Fruehgschichte. Annuaire de la Societe Suisse de Prehistoire et d'Archeologie. Schweizerische Gesellschaft fuer Ur- und Fruehgeschichte. Annuario della Societa Svizzera di Preistoria e d'Archeologia. **VFOAT** Annuaire de la Societe Suisse de Prehistoire et d'Archeologie; Annuairo della Societa Svizzera di Preistoria e d'Archeologia. Vol. 53 (1967)-. Academic Scholarly Publication. German (French and Italian). One time a year. Huber & Co Ag, Postfach, CH-8501 Frauenfeld Switzerland. **Tel** 011 41 54 271111. Index available. **Bk Rev.** ***Continues*** *Schweizerische Gesellschaft fuer Urgeschichte. Jahrbuch der Schweizerischen Gesellschaft fuer Urgeschichte, 0373-2169.*
Ind/Abst Anthropol. Index; BHA : Biblio. Hist. Art. ; Numis. Lit.

LC DE2 .D5 **ISSN** 0070-4415
DD 931 GW
JAHRBUCH DES DEUTSCHEN ARCHAOLOGISCHEN INSTITUTS. [Jahrb. Dtsch. Archaolog. Inst.]. **Added/Corp** Deutsches Archaologisches Institut. Vol. 33 (1918)-. Academic Scholarly Publication. German. One time a year. $126.00. Walter de Gruyter Inc., PO Box 303421, D-10728 Berlin Germany. **Tel** 011 49 30 260050, FAX 011 49 30 26005251, telex 184027. cum. index. ***Continues*** *Jahrbuch des Kaiserlich Deutschen Archaologischen Instituts.*
Ind/Abst Art Index; Avery Index Archit. Period. Suppl. Colum. Univ. (19??-199?); BHA : Biblio. Hist. Art; Br. Archaeol. Bibliogr.

ISSN 0078-3579
AU
JAHRESHEFTE DES OESTERREICHISCHEN ARCHAEOLOGISCHEN INSTITUTES IN WIEN. **Main/Corp** Oesterreichisches Archaeologisches Institut (Vienna, Austria). Vol. 1 (1898)-. Monographic series. German. Irregular (2 volumes published per year). Price varies per volume. Rudolf M Rohrer Verlag, Wassergasse 1, A-2500 Baden Vienna Austria. **Tel** 011 43 2252 886000. cum. index. **Circ:** 500. ***Continues*** *Archaeologisch-Epigraphische Mittheilungen aus Osterreich-Ungarn.*
Ind/Abst BHA : Biblio. Hist. Art.

ISSN 0075-2932
GW
JAHRESSCHRIFT FUER MITTELDEUTSCHE VORGESCHICHTE. Vol. 1, (1902)-. Academic Scholarly Publication. German. One time a year. DM140.00. Deutscher Verlag der Wissenchaften, Taubennstrasse 10, D-10117 Berlin Germany. **Tel** 011 49 30 2291146. **ED** H. Behrens. **Bk Rev. Ad Acc.** ctrl circ. ***Continues*** *Halle. Provinzial-Museum Mitteilungen.*
Desc: Articles on the prehistory and early history of the G.D.R. districts of Halle and Magdeburg, which the museum archaeologically deals with. Above all, new finds are shown.
Ind/Abst Anthropol. Index; Anthropol. Lit.; BHA : Biblio. Hist. Art; Br. Archaeol. Bibliogr.; Numis. Lit.

ISSN 1001-0327
DD 930.1 CC
JIANGHAN KAOGU. **VFOAT** Jianghan Archaeology. Vol. 1, No. 1 (1980)-. Academic Scholarly Publication. Chinese. Four times a year. $13.70. **(Subscription address:** China International Book Trading Corporation, PO Box 399, Library Service Department, Beijing 100044 People's Republic of China. **Tel** 011 86 1 8414284, FAX 011 86 1 8412023, telex 22496 CIBTC CN.)

LC E51 .S68 **ISSN** 0037-9174
DD 970.01 FR
JOURNAL DE LA SOCIETE DES AMERICANISTES. [J. soc. am.]. **Main/Corp** Societe des Americanistes de Paris. **Added/Corp** Societe des Americanistes (France). Vol.1-5; New Series Vol. 1 (1903)-. French (English and Spanish). One time a year. $56.87. Societe des Americanistes, Musee l'Homme, 17 Place du Trocadero, 75116 Paris France. **Tel** 011 33 1 47046311. **ED** M. Dominique Michelet. Index available. cum. index. **Bk Rev**, (Qty: 1). **Ad Acc. Circ:** 1,000 (ctrl). available in microform. ***Continues*** *Journal de la Societe des Americanistes de Paris;* ***Absorbed*** *Guyout, Mireille. Bibliographie Americaniste. Archeologie et Prehistoire, Anthropologie et Ethnohistoire.*
Desc: This journal contains research on American societies and cultures.
Ind/Abst Am. Hist. Life (1963-); Anthropol. Lit.; Ethnoarts Index; Hisp. Am. Period. Index, HAPI.

ISSN 0300-953X
FR
JOURNAL DE LA SOCIETE DES OCEANISTES [MICROFILM]. **Added/Corp** Societe des Oceanistes. Musee de l'Homme (Museum National d'Histoire Naurelle). (1945)-. Periodical. French. Two times a year. 300.00F. Societe des Oceanistes, Musee de l'Homme, 75116 Paris France. **Tel** 011 33 1 47046340. **Circ:** 1,100. ***Continues*** *Societe des Oceanistes. Bulletin de la Societe des Oceanistes.*
Ind/Abst Anthropol. Lit.

LC Discard **ISSN** 8756-8071
DD 976 US
JOURNAL / HOUSTON ARCHEOLOGICAL SOCIETY. [J. - Houst. Archeol. Soc.]. **Added/Corp** Houston Archeological Society. No. 72 (April 1982)-. Periodical. English. Three times a year (Apr., Aug., Dec.). $15.00. Houston Archeological Society, PO Box 6751, Houston TX 77265. **Tel** (713)663-2249. **ED** Richard L Gregg. **Bk Rev. Circ:** 260 (ctrl). available on microfiche. ***Continues*** *Houston Archeological Society Newsletter.*
Desc: Covers historic and prehistoric archeology, local and general subjects.
Ind/Abst Anthropol. Lit.

LC E78.A28 J6 **ISSN** 0449-2153
US
JOURNAL OF ALABAMA ARCHAEOLOGY. (1955)-. Academic Scholarly Publication. English. Two times a year. Alabama Archaeological Society, 13075 Moundville Park, Moundville AL 35474. **Tel** (205)371-2266. available on microfilm and microfiche from University Microfilms International (UMI).
Desc: Journal of the Alabama Archaeology Society.
Ind/Abst Abstr. Anthropol.; Am. Hist. Life (1989-); Anthropol. Lit.

LC CC79.E85 J68 **ISSN** 0278-4165
DD 306/.072 US
CCC
Pr Rev.
JOURNAL OF ANTHROPOLOGICAL ARCHAEOLOGY. [J. anthropol. archaeol.]. Vol. 1, No. 1 (March 1982)-. Academic Scholarly Publication. English. Four times a year. $141.00. Academic Press Inc., 6277 Sea Harbor Drive, Orlando FL 32887. **Tel** (800)543-9534, (407)345-4100, FAX (407)352-3445. **ED** Robert Whallon. Documents available from The Genuine Article.
Desc: Devoted to the development of theory and, in a broad sense, methodology for the systematic and rigorous understanding of the organization, operation, and evolution of human societies. The discipline served by the journal is characterized by its goals and approach, not by geographical or temporal bounds.
Ind/Abst Abstr. Anthropol.; Anthropol. Lit.; Arts Humanit. Citation Index [Select. Cov.]; Br. Archaeol. Bibliogr.; Curr. Cit.; Curr. Contents Soc. Behav. Sci.; Geogr. Abstr. Human Geogr. (?-?); Int. Dev. Abstr. (?-?); Res. Alert [Full Cov.]; Soc. Sci. Cit. Index [Full Cov.].

LC CC75 .J68 **ISSN** 1072-5369
DD 930 US
CODEN JAMTEI
•**JOURNAL OF ARCHAEOLOGICAL METHOD AND THEORY.** [J. archaeol. method thoery]. Vol. 1, No. 1 (Mar. 1994)-. Academic Scholarly Publication. English. Four times a year. $115.00. Plenum Press, 233 Spring Street, New York NY 10013-1578. **Tel** (212)620-8000, (800)221-9369, FAX (212)463-0742, (212)807-1047, telex 23/421139. ***Continues*** *Archaeological Method and Theory.*

ISSN 1059-0161
DD 930 US
CODEN JARRE3
•**JOURNAL OF ARCHAEOLOGICAL RESEARCH.** [J. archaeol. res.]. Vol. 1, No. 1 (Mar. 1993)-. English. Four times a year. $125.00. Plenum Press, 233 Spring Street, New York NY 10013-1578. **Tel** (212)620-8000, (800)221-9369, FAX (212)463-0742, (212)807-1047, telex 23/421139.

LC CC1 .J68 **ISSN** 0305-4403
DD 930/.1 UK
CCC
CODEN JASCDU
Pr Rev.
JOURNAL OF ARCHAEOLOGICAL SCIENCE. [J. archaeol. sci.]. Vol. 1 (Mar. 1974)-. Academic Scholarly Publication. English. Six times a year. $504.81. Academic Press Ltd., A Division of Harcourt Brace & Company Ltd., 24-28 Oval Road, London NW1 7DX United Kingdom. **Tel** 011 44 171 2674466, FAX 011 44 171 4822293, 011 44 171 4854752, telex 25775 ACPRES G. **(Subscription address:** Harcourt Brace & Company, Ltd., Foots Cray High Street, Sidcup Kent DA14 5HP United Kingdom. **Tel** 011 44 181 3003322, FAX 011 44 181 3090807, telex 896 377 ACADEM.) **ED** Karl W. Butzer, Susan Limbrey, Kevin J. Edwards and Richard G. Klein. Documents available from The Genuine Article, BIOSIS Document Express.
Desc: This scholarly publication is aimed at archaeologists and scientists with particular interests in advances in the application of scientific techniques and methodologies to all aspects of archaeology. Publishes original research papers, major review articles, and short notes of wide archaeological significance. Also provides an international forum for archaeologists and scientists from a wide variety of scientific backgrounds who share a common interest in using scientific methods to increase the information derived from archaeological research worldwide.
Ind/Abst Abstr. Anthropol.; Anthropol. Index; Anthropol. Lit.; Art Archaeol. Tech. Abstr.; Arts Humanit. Citation Index [Full Cov.]; Avery Index Archit. Period. Suppl. Colum. Univ. (Sept. 1989); Biol. Abstr.; Br. Archaeol. Bibliogr.; Ceram. Abstr.; Curr. Cit.; Curr. Contents Arts Humanit.; Curr. Contents Soc. Behav. Sci.; Ecol. Abstr.; Geogr. Abstr. Phys. Geogr.; Geogr. Abstr. Human Geogr.; Geol. Abstr.; GeoRef; Middle East Abstr. Index; Res. Alert [Full Cov.]; Rev. Agric. Entomol.; Soc. Sci. Cit. Index [Full Cov.]; Soils Fert.

LC DS785.A1 J68
DD 958/.005 PK
JOURNAL OF CENTRAL ASIA. See History-History of Asia.

LC DL121 .J68 **ISSN** 0108-464X
DD 936/.3 DK
JOURNAL OF DANISH ARCHAEOLOGY. [J. Dan. archaeol.]. Vol. 1 (1982)-. English. One time a year (September). Kr200.00, Kr225.00 (single issue). Odense University Press, 55 Campusvej, DK-5230 Odense M Denmark. **Tel** 011 45 7 66157999, FAX 011 45 7 66158126. **ED** Poul Otto Nielsen. Index available. **Bk Rev. Ad Acc.** ctrl circ.
Desc: Archaeological research relevant to the study of North European prehistory and early history. Includes topics from the paleolithic and Renaissance periods. A discussion column offers a forum for debate on theory and methodology. Indexes latest literature from the field.
Ind/Abst Anthropol. Lit.; BHA : Biblio. Hist. Art; Br. Archaeol. Bibliogr.; Geogr. Abstr. Phys. Geogr. (?-?); Geol. Abstr.; GeoRef.

LC DT57 .E332 **ISSN** 0075-4234
UK
JOURNAL OF EGYPTIAN ARCHAEOLOGY, THE. [J. Egypt. archaeol.]. **Added/Corp** Egypt Exploration Fund. Egypt Exploration Society. Vol. 1 (Jan. 1914)-. Academic Scholarly Publication. English (French and German). One time a year. $51.33. Egypt Exploration Society, 3 Doughty Mews, Longon WC1N 2PG United Kingdom. **Tel** 011 44 171 2421880. **ED** M. A. Leahy. cum. index. **Bk Rev. Circ:** 3,000. Documents available from The Genuine Article. ***Continues*** *Archaeological Report (London, England).*
Ind/Abst Art Index; Arts Humanit. Citation Index (19??-19??) [Full Cov.]; Avery Index Archit. Period. Suppl. Colum. Univ. (1990-); Curr. Contents Arts Humanit.; Middle East Abstr. Index; Old Testam. Abstr.; Res. Alert [Full Cov.].

LC CC1 .J69 **ISSN** 0093-4690
DD 930/.1/05 US
Pr Rev.
JOURNAL OF FIELD ARCHAEOLOGY. [J. field archaeol.]. **Added/Corp** Association for Field Archaeology. Vol. 1 (1974)-. Periodical. English. Four times a year. $60.00. Boston University Scholarly Publications, 985 Commonwealth Avenue, Boston MA 02215. **Tel** (617)353-4106. **ED** Creighten Gabel. Index available. cum. index. **Bk Rev. Ad Acc. Circ:** 1,600 (ctrl). available on microfilm and microfiche from University Microfilms International (UMI). Documents available from The Genuine Article.
Desc: Publishes articles that deal with reports of field excavation and survey. Also presents studies of methodological and technical matters, scientific advances

Archaeology

in archaeology, and larger interpretive studies.
Ind/Abst Abstr. Anthropol.; Anthropol. Lit.; Art Archaeol. Tech. Abstr.; Art Index; Arts Humanit. Citation Index [Full Cov.]; Avery Index Archit. Period. Suppl. Colum. Univ. (1989-); BHA : Biblio. Hist. Art; Br. Archaeol. Bibliogr.; Ceram. Abstr. (19??-); Curr. Contents Arts Humanit.; Curr. Contents Soc. Behav. Sci.; Curr. Geogr. Publ. (199?-); Ethnoarts Index; GeoRef; Middle East Abstr. Index; Old Testam. Abstr.; Res. Alert [Full Cov.]; Soc. Sci. Cit. Index [Full Cov.].

ISSN 0268-537X
IE
JOURNAL OF IRISH ARCHAEOLOGY, THE. [J. Ir. archaeol.]. VFOAT JIA. Vol. 1 (1983)-.
Academic Scholarly Publication. English. Irregular (one or two times per year). 7p Ireland; 11p other. The Journal of Irish Archaeology, University College Galway, Department of Archaeology, National Museum of Ireland, Kildare Street Dublin Ireland. **ED** R. O. Floinn. **Bk Rev.**
Continues Irish Archaeological Research Forum.
Ind/Abst Anthropol. Lit.

LC CC77.U5 J68
DD 909/.09824
II
JOURNAL OF MARINE ARCHAEOLOGY.
Added/Corp Society for Marine Archaeology (India). **VFOAT** Marine Archaeology. Vol. 1 (Jan. 1990)-. Periodical. English. One time a year. $20.00. Society of Marine Archaeology, Dona Paula Goa India. **(Subscription address:** Prints India, 11 Darya Ganj, New Delhi 110002 India. **Tel** 011 91 11 3268645, FAX 011 91 11 3275542, telex 31-61087 PRIN-IN.)

LC DE1 .J68 **ISSN** 0253-6625
DD 930/.0982/2 GR
CODEN JMAADI
JOURNAL OF MEDITERRANEAN ANTHROPOLOGY & ARCHAEOLOGY.
See Anthropology.

LC DE1 .J69 **ISSN** 0952-7648
DD 909/.09822 UK
JOURNAL OF MEDITERRANEAN ARCHAEOLOGY. VFOAT JMA. Vol. 1, No. 1 (July 1988)-. Periodical. English. Two times a year (Jan., June). $88.00 institutions. Sheffield Academic Press, Mansion House, 19 Kingfield Road, Sheffield S11 9AS United Kingdom. **Tel** 011 44 114 2554433, FAX 011 44 114 2554626.
Desc: Publishes material dealing with local or regional development, production, interaction, and change in the Mediterranean world, and with the assumptions that can be extrapolated from relevant archaeological data. Deals with broader archaeological and interdisciplinary issues of the circum-Mediterranean region.
Ind/Abst Anthropol. Lit.; Geogr. Abstr. Human Geogr.

LC E78.M65 J68 **ISSN** 0883-9697
DD 974/.01 US
CODEN JMAAEJ
Pr Rev.
JOURNAL OF MIDDLE ATLANTIC ARCHAEOLOGY. [J. Middle Atl. archaeol.]. Vol. 1 (1985)-. Periodical. English. One time a year (November). $20.00 (all except Canada). Archaeological Services, PO Box 386, Bethlehem CT 06751. **Tel** (203)266-7741. **ED** Roger W Moeller. **Bk Rev,** (Qty: 10+). **Circ:** 250.
Desc: Dedicated to the archaeology of the Middle Atlantic region.
Ind/Abst Abstr. Anthropol.; Anthropol. Lit.; Ceram. Abstr. (19??-); Ethnoarts Index.

ISSN 1047-7594
DD 930 US
Pr Rev.
JOURNAL OF ROMAN ARCHAEOLOGY. [J. Roman archaeol.].
Added/Corp University of Michigan. **VFOAT** JRA. Vol. 1 (1988)-. Periodical. English (French, German, Italian and Spanish). One time a year. $65.00. Journal of Roman Archaeology, 1216 Bending Road, Ann Arbor MI 48103. **Tel** (313)662-7132, FAX (313)662-3240. **ED** John H. Humphrey. **Bk Rev. Circ:** 1,050 (ctrl).
Desc: Archaeology and history of the Roman world 700 BC to 700 AD.

ISSN 1063-4304
DD 930 US
Pr Rev.
JOURNAL OF ROMAN ARCHAEOLOGY. SUPPLEMENTARY SERIES. [J. Roman archaeol., Suppl. ser.]. No. 1 (1990)-. Monographic series. English. Irregular. $65.00. Journal of Roman Archaeology, 1216 Bending Road, Ann Arbor MI 48103. **Tel** (313)662-7132, FAX (313)662-3240.
Desc: Archaeology and history of the Roman world 700 BC to 700 AD.

ISSN 0068-1288
UK
JOURNAL OF THE BRITISH ARCHAEOLOGICAL ASSOCIATION. [J. Br. Archaeol. Assoc.]. Main/Corp British Archaeological Association. Vol. 1 (April 1845)-. English. One time a year (Dec.). $17.50 (institutions), $12.50 (individuals). British Archaeology Association, W S Maney & Son Ltd., Hudson Road, Leeds LS9 7PL United Kingdom. **Tel** 011 44 1532 497481, FAX 011 44 1532 2486983. **ED** D. Nartin Henig. Index available. cum. index. **Bk Rev. Circ:** 800 (ctrl).
Desc: Aims to promote the study of archaeology, preserve national antiquities, and encourage research in art and antiquities from Roman to post-medieval periods.
Ind/Abst Art Archaeol. Tech. Abstr.; Avery Index Archit. Period. Suppl. Colum. Univ. (1990-); BHA : Biblio. Hist. Art; Br. Archaeol. Bibliogr.; Br. Humanit. Index; Numis. Lit.

LC DA670.C5 C6 **ISSN** 0309-359X
DD 913.362 UK
JOURNAL OF THE CHESTER ARCHAEOLOGICAL SOCIETY. Main/Corp
Chester Archaeological Society. Vol. 54 (1967)-. English.
Continues Chester and North Wales Architectural, Archaeological, and Historic Society. Journal of the Chester and North Wales Architectural, Archaeological, and Historic Society.
Ind/Abst BHA : Biblio. Hist. Art.

ISSN 0010-8731
IE
JOURNAL OF THE CORK HISTORICAL AND ARCHAEOLOGICAL SOCIETY. See
History-History of Europe.

JOURNAL OF THE COUNTY KILDARE ARCHAEOLOGICAL SOCIETY. Main/Corp
County Kildare Archaeological Society. Vol. 1 (1891)-. Academic Scholarly Publication. English. One time a year. $10.00. County Kildare Archaeological Society, St. Patrick's College, Department of Modern History, Maynooth County, Kildare Ireland. **ED** Raymond Gillespie. Index available (back issues available). **Bk Rev. Ad Acc. Circ:** 600.
Ind/Abst BHA : Biblio. Hist. Art.

LC DA990.L89 J68 **ISSN** 0070-1327
DD 941.8/25/005 IE
JOURNAL OF THE COUNTY LOUTH ARCHAEOLOGICAL AND HISTORICAL SOCIETY. [J. Cty. Louth Archaeol. Hist. Soc.].
Added/Corp County Louth Archaeological and Historical Society. **VFOAT** Co. Louth Archaeological and Historical Journal. (1970)-. English. One time a year. $12.24. County Louth Archaeological & Historical Journal, 5 Oliver Plunkett Park, Dundalk Ireland. **Tel** 011 353 1 4231679. **ED** Noel Ross. **Bk Rev. Circ:** 650 (ctrl).
Continues Journal of the County Louth Archaeological Society.
Ind/Abst BHA : Biblio. Hist. Art.

ISSN 0332-415X
DD 941505 IE
JOURNAL OF THE GALWAY ARCHAEOLOGICAL AND HISTORICAL SOCIETY. See History.

HK
JOURNAL OF THE HONG KONG ARCHAEOLOGICAL SOCIETY. Added/Corp
Hong Kong Archaeological Society. (1968)-. English (Chinese). Irregular. $15.00. Hong Kong Archaeology Society, Hong Kong Museum of History, Block 58, Kowloon Park Hong Kong. **Tel** 011 852 2372335765. **ED** J. R. Crawford. Index available. **Bk Rev. Circ:** 800.

LC E78.I6 I65 **ISSN** 0535-5729
DD 977.7/005 US
JOURNAL OF THE IOWA ARCHEOLOGICAL SOCIETY. Main/Corp
Iowa Archeological Society. Vol. 1 Oct. (1951)-. Academic Scholarly Publication. English. One time a year. $20.00. Iowa Archeological Society, c/o OSA, Eastlawn Building, The University of Iowa, Iowa City IA 52242. **Tel** (319)335-2389, FAX (319)335-2776. **ED** Stephen C Lensink. Index available. cum. index. **Bk Rev,** (Qty: 1). **Circ:** 500. *Formed by the union of* Newsletter - Iowa Archeological Society, 0578-655X.
Desc: Journal publishes scholarly articles on Midwest archaeology and frontier history.
Ind/Abst Anthropol. Lit.; Ethnoarts Index.

LC DA900 .R88 **ISSN** 0035-9106
DD 936.1/5/005 IE
JOURNAL OF THE ROYAL SOCIETY OF ANTIQUARIES OF IRELAND, THE. See
History-History of Europe.

LC CC **ISSN** 0307-1723
DD 930.1 UK
CEASED
JOURNAL OF THE SOMERSET INDUSTRIAL ARCHAEOLOGICAL SOCIETY. Main/Corp Somerset Industrial
Archaeology Society. **VFOAT** SIAS Journal. No. 1 (1975)-(19??). Periodical. English. Somerset Industrial Archaeological Society, 52 Stoke Road, Taunton Somerset TA1 3EJ United Kingdom. **Tel** 011 44 1823 286957.
Ind/Abst Archit. Period. Index (1981-19??).

LC F2136.3 .V57A **ISSN** 0363-1168
DD 972.9/722 VI
JOURNAL OF THE VIRGIN ISLANDS ARCHAEOLOGICAL SOCIETY. Main/Corp
Virgin Islands Archaeological Society. Vol. 1 (1974)-. Periodical. English. Four times a year. $10.00. Virgin Islands Archaeological Society, PO Box 4986, St Thomas Virgin Islands 00801.
Ind/Abst Anthropol. Index; Ethnoarts Index.

LC GN700 .J68 **ISSN** 0892-7537
DD 930.1 US
CCC
JOURNAL OF WORLD PREHISTORY. [J.
world prehist.]. Vol. 1, No. 1 (March 1987)-. Periodical. English. Four times a year. $215.00. Plenum Press, 233 Spring Street, New York NY 10013-1578. **Tel** (212)620-8000, (800)221-9369, FAX (212)463-0742, (212)807-1047, telex 23/421139. **ED** Fred Wendorf and Angela E. Close. available on microfilm and microfiche from University Microfilms International (UMI). Documents available from The Genuine Article.
Ind/Abst Abstr. Anthropol.; Am. Bibliogr. Slavic East Europ. Stud.; Anthropol. Lit.; Arts Humanit. Citation Index [Full Cov.]; Curr. Contents Arts Humanit.; Geogr. Abstr. Human Geogr.; Res. Alert [Full Cov.]; Soc. Sci. Cit. Index [Select. Cov.].

LC CN1 .K3 **ISSN** 0022-7498
GW
CCC
KADMOS. [Kadmos]. Vol. 1 (1962)-. Periodical.
English (French, German, Italian and Spanish). Two times a year. $158.15. Walter de Gruyter Inc., PO Box 303421, D-10728 Berlin Germany. **Tel** 011 49 30 260050, FAX 011 49 30 26005251, telex 184027. cum. index.
Ind/Abst MLA Int. Bibl. Books Artic. Mod. Lang. Lit.; Numis. Lit.

SP
KALATHOS : REVISTA DEL SEMINARIO DE ARQUEOLOGIA Y ETNOLOGIA TUROLENSE, COLEGIO UNIVERSITARIO DE TERUEL. (1981)-.
Periodical. Spanish. Seminario de Arqueologia y Etnologia Turolense, Colegio Universitario de Teruel, Apartado 1, Teruel Spain.
Ind/Abst Anthropol. Lit.

ISSN 0453-2899
CC
KAO KU. VFOAT Kaogu Tongxun; Kaogu;
Archaeology; Arkhelogiia. No. 1 (1955)-. Academic Scholarly Publication. Chinese. Twelve times a year. $158.40. Science Press, 16 Donghuangchenggen North Street, Beijing 100707, People's Republic of China. **Tel** 011 86 1 4019821, 011 86 1 4010642, FAX 011 86 1 4012180, 011 86 1 4019810, telex 210147. **(Subscription address:** China International Book Trading Corporation, PO Box 399, Library Service Department, Beijing 100044 People's Republic of China. **Tel** 011 86 1 8414284, FAX 011 86 1 8412023, telex 22496 CIBTC CN.)
Desc: Contains information on archaeology.

LC DS715 .K35
DD 931 CH
KAO KU HSUEH CHI KAN. VFOAT Papers on
Chinese Archeology. 1 (Nov. 1981)-. Periodical. Chinese (Chinese). NT$3.00. Hsi Hua Shu Tien Pei-Ching Fa Hsing so, Beijing, People's Republic of China.

LC DS715 .K28
DD 931/.005 CC
KAO KU YU WEN WU. VFOAT Kao Ku Yu Wen
Wu Chi Kan; Kaogu Yu Wenwu; Archaeology and Cultural Relics. 1980 Vol. 1-7-. Periodical. Chinese. Six times a year. Science Press, 16 Donghuangchenggen North Street, Beijing 100707, People's Republic of China. **Tel** 011 86 1 4019821, 011 86 1 4010642, FAX 011 86 1 4012180, 011 86 1 4019810, telex 210147.

LC DS715 .K365 **ISSN** 0453-2902
DD 931 CC
CODEN KKHPAO
KAOGU XUEBAO. (KAO KU HSUEH PAO).
[Kaogu xuebao]. **Added/Corp** Chung-kuo ko Hsueh Yuan. Kao ku Yen Chiu So. Chung-kuo She Hui ko Hsueh Yuan. Kao ku Yen Chiu So. **VFOAT** Chinese Journal of Archaeology; Journal of Archaeology; Acta Archaeologia Sinica; Kaogu Xuebao; Kaogu Siuebao. (19??)-. Academic Scholarly Publication. Chinese (summaries and/or abstracts in English). Four times a year. $79.60. Science Press, 16 Donghuangchenggen North Street, Beijing 100707, People's Republic of China. **Tel** 011 86 1 4019821, 011 86 1 4010642, FAX 011 86 1 4012180, 011 86 1 4019810, telex 210147. **(Subscription address:** China International Book Trading Corporation, PO Box 399, Library Service Department, Beijing 100044 People's Republic of China. **Tel** 011 86 1 8414284, FAX 011 86 1 8412023, telex 22496 CIBTC CN.)
Desc: Contains information on archaeology.
Ind/Abst Biol. Abstr. (?-1974); GeoRef.

ISSN 1000-7830
DD 930.1 CC
KAOGU YU WENWU. **VFOAT** Archaeology and Cultural Relics. (19??)-. Periodical. Chinese. Six times a year. $18.20. **(Subscription address:** China International Book Trading Corporation, PO Box 399, Library Service Department, Beijing 100044 People's Republic of China. **Tel** 011 86 1 8414284, FAX 011 86 1 8412023, telex 22496 CIBTC CN.**)**
Desc: Covers archaeology and cultural relics.

LC DT269.C3 K3 ISSN 0453-3429
FR
KARTHAGO. **Added/Corp** Mission Archeologique Francaise en Tunisie. France. Commission des Fouilles et Missions a l'Etranger. Universite de Paris. Centre d'Etudes Archeologiques de la Mediterranee Occidentale. Vol. 1 (1950)-. French (English). One time a year. $61.24. Centre d'Arch Med Paris Sorb, 3 rue Michelet, F 75006 Paris France. **Tel** 011 33 1 43255099. **ED** G. Picard. Index available (free). **Bk Rev**. **Ad Acc**. ctrl circ.
Desc: Archaelogy of North Africa and the Mediterranean world.
Ind/Abst Avery Index Archit. Period. Suppl. Colum. Univ. (19??-199?); BHA : Biblio. Hist. Art; Numis. Lit.

LC DA670.K2 A56 ISSN 0023-0014
DD 914.22/3/03105 UK
KENT ARCHAEOLOGICAL REVIEW. **Added/Corp** Kent Archaeological Research Groups' Council. (1965)-. Periodical. English. Four times a year. Kent Archaeological Society, Barnfield Church Lane, East Peckham, Tonbridge KT TN12 5JJ United Kingdom. **Tel** 011 44 1622 871945.
Ind/Abst BHA : Biblio. Hist. Art.

ISSN 0228-4111
DD 971.3/2601/06 CN
KEWA. (KEWA : NEWSLETTER OF THE LONDON CHAPTER, ONTARIO ARCHAEOLOGICAL SOCIETY.). [Kewa]. **Added/Corp** Ontario Archaeological Society. London Chapter. 77/1 (Mar. 1977)-. Newsletter. English. Eleven times a year. comes with membership. London Chapter of the Ontario Archaeological Society, 17 Western Road, London Ontario N5G 1G5 Canada. **Tel** (519)645-2845.

LC F786 .K58 ISSN 0023-1940
DD 913.791 US
Pr Rev.
KIVA (TUSCON, ARIZ.), THE. (THE KIVA.). [Kiva]. **Added/Corp** Arizona Archaeological and Historical Society. Vol. 1, (May 1935)-. Periodical. English. Four times a year (Jan., Apr., July, Oct.). $50.00. Arizona Archaeological and Historical Society, Arizona State Museum, University of Arizona, Tucson AZ 85716. **Tel** (602)621-4011, FAX (602)621-2976. **ED** Gayle Harrison Hartmann. Index available. cum. index. **Bk Rev**, (Qty: 10). **Ad Acc**, **Adv Mgr Tel** (602)621-4794. **Circ:** 1,300 (ctrl).
Desc: Accepts original research related to the prehistoric and historic archaeology, ethnology, history and ethnohistory of the Southwest United States and Northern Mexico.
Ind/Abst Abstr. Anthropol.; Am. Hist. Life (1963-); Anthropol. Lit.; Ethnoarts Index.

LC DT57 .K68 ISSN 1053-0827
DD 932 US
KMT (SAN FRANCISCO, CALIF.). (KMT : A MODERN JOURNAL OF ANCIENT EGYPT.). [KMT]. Premiere Issue (Spring 1990)-. Periodical. English. Four times a year. $32.00. KMT Communications, 1531 Golden Gate Avenue, San Francisco CA 94115. **Tel** (415)346-9439. **ED** Dennis C. Forbes.
Desc: Concentrates on archaeology of the Middle East, Egypt in particular.

LC DS903 .K583
KO
KO MUNHWA. **Added/Corp** Hanguk Taehak Pangmulgwan Hyophoe. **VFOAT** Korean Antiquity. Vol. 1 (1962)-. Periodical. Korean. Two times a year. $50.00. Korean Association of University Museums, 72-1 Sangsu-Dong/Mapo-gu, Seoul Korea.

LC DS815 .K586 ISSN 0452-2516
DD 952 JA
KODAI. **Added/Corp** Waseda Daigaku. Koko Gakkai. **VFOAT** Journal of the Archaeological Society of Waseda University. (19??)-. Periodical. Japanese. ¥900 (single issue). Archaeological Society of Waseda University, 1-go Nishi Waseda 1-chome Shinjuku-ku, Tokyo-to 160 Japan.

LC DS11 .K65 ISSN 0003-8075
JA
KOKOGAKU ZASSHI. **Added/Corp** Koko Gakkai (Japan) Nihon Koko Gakkai. **VFOAT** Kokogaku Zasshi, or, The Archaeological Journal; Archaeological Journal; Journal of the Archaeological Society; Journal of the Archaeological Society of Nippon. (1910)-. Periodical. Japanese (summaries and/or abstracts in English). Four times a year. $88.00. Archaeological Society of Japan - Nihon Koko Gakkai, c/o Tokyo National Museum, 13-9 Ueno Park, Daito-ku Tokyo 110 Japan. **(Subscription address:** Maruzen Company Ltd., PO Box 5050, Import & Export Department, Tokyo 100 31 Japan. **Tel** 011 81 3 32789224.**)** cum. index. ***Continues** Kokokai.*
Ind/Abst Anthropol. Lit.; Art Archaeol. Tech. Abstr.

LC GN700 .A45 ISSN 0130-2620
RU
●KRATKIE SOOBSHCHENIIA. [Kratk. soobs. - Inst. arheol.]. **Added/Corp** Institut Arkheologii (Rossiiskaia Akademiia Nauk) Roemisch-Germanisches Zentralmuseum Mainz. **VFOAT** Kratkie Soobsenia - O Dokladah i Polevyh Issledovaniah Instituta Arheologii. (1993)-. Periodical. Russian (summaries and/or abstracts in German). Four times a year. **(Subscription address:** East View Publications Inc., 3020 Harbor Lane North, Suite 110, Minneapolis MN 55447. **Tel** (800)477-1005, (612)550-0961, FAX (612)559-2931.**)** ***Continues** Kratkie Soobshcheniia (Institut Arkheologii (Akademiia Nauk SSSR)).*
Ind/Abst BHA : Biblio. Hist. Art.

RU
KRATKIE SOOBSHCHENIIA - AKADEMIIA NAUK SSSR, INSTITUT ARKHEOLOGII. **Main/Corp** Akademiia Nauk SSSR. Institut Arkheologii. (1970)-. Academic Scholarly Publication. Russian. Izdatelstvo Nauka / Akademiia Nauk, (Publishing House of the Russian Academy of Sciences), Leninskii Porspekt 14, 117901 Moscow Russia. **Tel** 011 95 9542153, FAX 011 95 9382144, telex 411964. ***Continues** Kratkie Soobshcheniia o Dokladakh i Polevykh Issledovaniiakh Instituta Arkheologii.*
Ind/Abst Anthropol. Lit.

ISSN 0221-5896
FR
KTEMA. **See** Classical Studies.

GW
KULTURGESCHICHTE DER ANTIKEN WELT. (19??)-. Monographic series. German. Irregular. Price varies per volume. Verlag Phillip Von Zabern, Postfach 190930, D-80609 Munich Germany. **Tel** 011 49 89 12151661, FAX 011 49 61 31223710, telex 4187463.
Desc: Books on the history of civilization in Greece, Rome and Egypt in antiquity.
Ind/Abst Br. Archaeol. Bibliogr. -?.

LC DL271.J8 K85 ISSN 0454-6245
DK
KUML. **Added/Corp** Jysk Arkologisk Selskab. Vol. 1 (1951)-. Academic Scholarly Publication. Danish (summaries and/or abstracts in English and German). One time a year. Aarhus University Press, Aarhus University, Building 170, DK-8000 Aarhus C Denmark. **Tel** 011 45 86 197033, FAX 011 45 86 198433, telex 16600.
Ind/Abst Anthropol. Lit.

LC DP302.L48 L34 ISSN 0212-8985
DD 936.6 SP
LAIETANIA. [Laietania]. **Added/Corp** Museu Municipal de Mataro. Seccio Arqueologica. (1981)-. Periodical. Catalan (French). One time a year. $10.00. Museu Comarcal del Maresme Mataro, Sant Pelegri Bloc Mestres, Mataro Spain. ***Continues** Quaderns de Prehistoria I Arqueologia del Maresme, 0473-6303.*
Desc: Scientific publication of archaeology and history of Maresma.
Ind/Abst Anthropol. Lit.

SP
LAROUCO / GRUPO ARQUEOLOXICO LAROUCO. **Added/Corp** Grupo Arqueoloxico Larouco. (1991)-. Periodical. Gallegan.

LC F1219 .L37 E65 .L383 ISSN 1045-6635
DD 980/.01/05 US
CCC
Pr Rev.
LATIN AMERICAN ANTIQUITY. (LATIN AMERICAN ANTIQUITY : A JOURNAL OF THE SOCIETY FOR AMERICAN ARCHAEOLOGY.). [Latin Am. antiq.]. **Added/Corp** Society for American Archaeology. Vol. 1, No. 1 (Mar. 1990)-. Periodical. English (Spanish). Four times a year. $105.00. Society for American Archaeology, 900 Second Street NE, Suite 12, Washington DC 20002. **Tel** (202)789-8200, FAX (202)789-0284. **(Subscription address:** Society for American Archaology, Department 0123, Washington DC 20073. **Tel** (202)789-8200.**)** **ED** Prudence M. Rice. **Ad Acc**. available on microfilm and microfiche from University Microfilms International (UMI).
Desc: Articles dealing with the archaeology, prehistory, and ethnohistory of Mesoamerica, Central America, South America and culturally related areas.
Ind/Abst Acad. Abstr.; Acad. Search; Anthropol. Lit.; EP Collect.; Geogr. Abstr. Human Geogr.; Hisp. Am. Period. Index, HAPI; Homework Help.; Humanit. Source; MasterFile FullTEXT 1000; MasterFile FullTEXT 350; MasterFile FullTEXT 650; MasterFile FullTEXT (July 1993-); OCLC; Pub. Lib. FullTEXT; Telebase; Vocat. Search.

LC CC13.P67 L4 ISSN 0870-0044
DD 930.1/05 PO
LEBA. **Added/Corp** Portugal. Junta de Investigacoes Cientificas do Ultramar. Seccao de Pre-Historia e Arqueologia. Centro de Pre-Historia e Arqueologia (Instituto de Investigacao Cientifica Tropical). No. 1 (1978)-. Periodical. Portuguese (summaries and/or abstracts in English and French). Irregular. 6500$00. Instituto de Investigacao Cientifica Tropical, Centro de Documentacao e Informacao, rua Jau 47, 1 300 Lisbon Portugal. **Tel** 645321. Index available. **Circ:** 1,000 (ctrl).
Desc: Articles on anthropobiology, physical anthropobiology, human ecology, evolution and growth genetics and physiology of populations.

LC DS56 .L48 ISSN 0075-8914
DD 913.3/9/40305 UK
LEVANT (LONDON). (LEVANT.). [Levant]. **Added/Corp** British School of Archaeology in Jerusalem. British Institute at Amman for Archaeology and History. Vol. 1 (1969)-. Periodical. English. One time a year (Mar. or Apr.). $55.00. British School of Archaeology / United Kingdon, 21 Buccleuch Place, University of Edinburgh, Edinburgh EH8 9LN United Kingdom. **Tel** 011 44 131 6503975, FAX 011 44 131 6503975. **ED** Dr. Kay Praq. **Bk Rev**, (Qty: varies). **Circ:** 700 (ctrl).
Desc: This journal is primarily devoted to the archaeology of Palestine and neighbouring countries.
Ind/Abst Anthropol. Lit.; BHA : Biblio. Hist. Art; Index Book Rev. Relig.; Middle East Abstr. Index; New Testam. Abstr.; Old Testam. Abstr.; Relig. Index One Period. (1979-); Relig. Theol. Abstr.

LC WMLC 91/2754 ISSN 0459-2980
LY
LIBYA ANTIQUA. **Added/Corp** Libya. Idarah al-Ammah lil-Athar wa-al-Matahif wa-al-Mahfuzat. Libya. Maslahat al-Athar. **VFOAT** Libya Al-Qadimah. Vol. 1 (1964)-. English (Arabic, French and Italian). Irregular. L900000. Bardi Editore, Salita de Crescenzi 16, 00186 Rome Italy. **Tel** 011 39 6 6878576. **Bk Rev**. **Ad Acc**. **Circ:** 500 (ctrl).
Ind/Abst Numis. Lit.

ISSN 0459-4371
GW
LIMESFORSCHUNGEN. **Added/Corp** Deutsches Archaologisches Institut. Romisch-Germanische Kommission. Vol. 1 (1959)-. Monographic series. German. Irregular. Price varies per volume. Gebrueder Mann Verlag, Lindenstrasse 76, D-10969 Berlin Germany. **Tel** 011 49 30 25913589, telex 183723. **(Subscription address:** Gebrueder Mann Verlag / KNO, Postfach 800620, Koch, Neff & Oetinger, D-70506 Stuttgart Germany. **Tel** 011 49 711 78992022.**)** **Ad Acc**. **Circ:** 800.
Desc: Studies concerning the organization of the Roman Empire boundaries on the Rhine and Donau rivers.

LC DA670.L69 L57 ISSN 0459-4487
DD 942.5/3/005 UK
LINCOLNSHIRE HISTORY AND ARCHAEOLOGY. **See** History-History of Europe.

UK
LIST OF MEMBERS. **Main/Corp** Royal Archaeological Institute. (1975)-. Periodical. English. Royal Archaeological Institute, Society of Antiquaries, Burlington House, Piccadilly London W1V 0HS United Kingdom. **Tel** 011 44 171 7340193.

ISSN 0197-7261
US
Pr Rev.
LITHIC TECHNOLOGY. [Lithic technol.]. **Added/Corp** University of Texas at San Antonio. Center for Archaeological Research. Vol. 6 (1977)-. Periodical. English. Two times a year. $17.00. University of Tulsa / Anthropology, Department of Anthropology, 600 South College, Tulsa OK 74104. **Tel** (918)631-2348, FAX (918)631-2540. **ED** George H. Odell (editor's phone: (918)631-3082). **Bk Rev**. **Circ:** 350 (ctrl). ***Continues** Newsletter of Lithic Technology.*
Desc: Devoted to archaeological stone tool production and analysis. Its focus is international, and its subjects emcompass all aspects of knowledge concerning stone tools.
Ind/Abst Anthropol. Lit.; Br. Archaeol. Bibliogr.

LC DA677.1 L78 ISSN 0024-5984
DD 913.3/6 UK
LONDON ARCHAEOLOGIST, THE. [Lond. archaeol.]. **Added/Corp** London Archaeologist Association. Vol. 1, (Winter 1968)-. Periodical. English. Four times a year. $15.00. The London Archaeologist, 8 Woodview Crescent Hildenboro, Tonbridge Kent TN11 9HD United Kingdom. **Tel** 011 44 1732 838698. **ED** Clive Orton. Index available. **Bk Rev**, (Qty: varies). **Ad Acc**. **Circ:** 1,750.
Desc: A magazine providing readers with reports on current aspects of the archaeology and allied history of the London region and discussion of recent excavation discoveries. Contains articles by researchers, includes commentary, reviews articles, book reviews, letters, excavation notices, diary of lectures, meetings, and conferences.
Ind/Abst Art Archaeol. Tech. Abstr.; Avery Index Archit. Period. Suppl. Colum. Univ. (Winter 1989-); BHA : Biblio. Hist. Art; Br. Archaeol. Bibliogr.

ISSN 1071-7358
DD 930 US
Pr Rev.
LOUISIANA ARCHAEOLOGY. [La. archaeol.]. **Main/Corp** Louisiana Archaeological Society. No. 1, (1974)-. English. One time a year. Free to members;

Archaeology

$15.00 (regular/libraries), $300.00 (sustaining), $2.00 (associate) membership. Louisiana Archaeological Society, 305 Hickory Street, Springhill LA 71075. **Tel** (318)539-5944. **ED** Robert Neuman. **Bk Rev. Circ:** 300 (ctrl).
Ind/Abst Am. Hist. Life (1983-); Anthropol. Lit.

LC DP44 .L8   **ISSN** 0213-2338
DD 936.6/005   SP
LUCENTUM. [Lucentum]. **Added/Corp** Universidad de Alicante. **VFOAT** Lvcentvm. (1982)-. Spanish (summaries and/or abstracts in English and French). One time a year.
Ind/Abst BHA : Biblio. Hist. Art.

LC DD901.L84 L77a
DD 936.3   GW
LUEBECKER SCHRIFTEN ZUR ARCHAEOLOGIE UND KULTURGESCHICHTE. **Added/Corp** Luebeck (Germany). Amt fuer Vor- und Fruehgeschichte (Bodendenkmalpflege). (1978)-. Monographic series. German. Irregular. Price varies per volume. Dr. Rudolf Habelt GmbH, Postfach 150104, D-53040 Bonn Germany. **Tel** 011 49 228 232015.
Ind/Abst BHA : Biblio. Hist. Art.

ISSN 0350-1639   XN
MACEDONIAE ACTA ARCHAEOLOGICA. **Added/Corp** Arheolosko Drustvo na SR Makedonija. Vol. 1 (1975)-. Macedonian. One time a year.
Ind/Abst BHA : Biblio. Hist. Art.

LC DP44 .M2   **ISSN** 0418-9744
DD 913   GW
MADRIDER MITTEILUNGEN. [Madrid. Mitt.]. **Added/Corp** Deutsches Archaeologisches Institut. Abteilung Madrid. (1960)-. Periodical. German. One time a year. DM198.00. Verlag Phillip Von Zabern, Postfach 190930, D-80609 Munich Germany. **Tel** 011 49 89 12151661, FAX 011 49 61 31223710, telex 4187463. (Subscription address: MI Verlags Service GmbH, Justus von Liebig Strasse 1, D 8169 Landsberg Germany. **Tel** 011 49 8191125214.)
Desc: Essays and articles of different authors concerning archaeology.
Ind/Abst Am. Hist. Life (1967-); Avery Index Archit. Period. Suppl. Colum. Univ. (19??-199?); BHA : Biblio. Hist. Art; Br. Archaeol. Bibliogr.; Numis. Lit.

LC DS815 .A32   JA
MAIZO BUNKAZAI HAKKUTSU CHOSA HOKOKU. **Added/Corp** Japan. Bunkacho. **VFOAT** Reports on Excavations of Buried Cultural Properties. No. 7 (1974)-. Periodical. Japanese (summaries and/or abstracts in English). Maizo Bunkazai Hakkutsu Chosa Hokoku, 2-bam 8-go Hongo 7-chome, Bunkyo-ku 113, Yoshikawa Kobunkan, Tokyo Japan. **Continues** Maizo Bunkazai Hakkutsu Chosa Hokok.

ISSN 1015-2830   IR
MAJOLLAH-'I BASTANSHINASI VA-TARIKH. (1986)-. Academic Scholarly Publication. Persian. Two times a year. £15.00 Middle East; £19.00 Europe and Asia; £23.00 America and Far East. Iran University Press, 85 Park Avenue, PO Box 15875/4748, Tehran Iran. **Tel** 011 98 21 623232, FAX 011 98 21 4661749, telex 213636-8-D5300. **ED** Ahmad H.A. Moojani. available with illustrations.
Desc: Contains articles related to history and archaeology in general and historical topics directly related to Iran.

LC E61 .M25   **ISSN** 8755-6898
DD 970.01   US
MAMMOTH TRUMPET. Vol. 1, No. 1 (Winter 1984)-. Periodical. English. Four times a year. $20.00. Oregon State University / Corvallis, CSFA Weniger 355, Corvallis OR 97331. **Tel** (503)737-3854, (503)737-4595. **ED** Marcella Sorg. **Bk Rev. Circ:** 2,000 (ctrl).
Desc: Reports developments in research about earliest peopling of the Americas for the professional and general reader. Includes interviews, research reports, new references and resources.

ISSN 0959-4272   UK
DD 930.1075
MAN. MUSEUM ARCHAEOLOGISTS NEWS. (MAN.). [MAN, Mus. archaeol. news]. **VFOAT** Museum Archaeologists News. (1985)-. Periodical. English. Two times a year.
Ind/Abst Museum Abstr.

ISSN 1188-5424   CN
DD 971.27/01/05
MANITOBA ARCHAEOLOGICAL JOURNAL. [Manit. archaeol. j.]. **Added/Corp** Manitoba Archaeological Society. Vol. 1, No. 1 (1991)-. Periodical. English. Two times a year (Jan. and July). $20.00 (individuals); $30.00 (institutions). Manitoba Archaeolog Society, Box 1171, Manitoba R3C 2Y4 Canada. **Tel** (204)942-7243. **Continues** Manitoba Archaeological Quarterly, 0705-2669.

LC DS99.M3 M36
DD 939/.4   FR
MARI : ANNALES DES RECHERCHES INTERDISCIPLINAIRES. **VFOAT** MARI; M.A.R.I. (1982)-. Periodical. French (English). Association Diffusion Pense Francaise, 9 rue Anatole de la Forge, 75017 Paris France. **Tel** 011 33 1 42273297.
Ind/Abst Anthropol. Lit.

ISSN 0148-6012
DD 975   US
MARYLAND ARCHEOLOGY. (MARYLAND ARCHEOLOGY : JOURNAL OF THE ARCHAEOLOGICAL SOCIETY OF MARYLAND INC.). [Md. archeol.]. **Added/Corp** Archeological Society of Maryland. Vol. 4, No. 1 (March 1968)-. Periodical. English. Two times a year (Mar. & Sept.). $20.00 Comes with Archeological Society of Maryland membership. Archeological Society of Maryland, 17 East Branch Lane, 1 McGillivray, Baltimore MD 21202. **Tel** (410)727-6417. **ED** Dennis Curry, (editor's address: Office of Archeology, Maryland Historical Trust, 100 Community Place, Crownsville, MD 21032). Index available. cum. index. **Bk Rev. Circ:** 450 (ctrl). **Continues** Journal of the Archaeological Society of Maryland.
Desc: Articles by professionals and vocational archeologists on historic and prehistoric archeology in Maryland.
Ind/Abst Anthropol. Lit.

LC CC1 .P45a   **ISSN** 1048-5325
DD 930.1/05   US
                        CODEN MRPAEQ
MASCA RESEARCH PAPERS IN SCIENCE AND ARCHAEOLOGY. [MASCA res. pap. sci. archaeol.]. **Added/Corp** University of Pennsylvania. Museum Applied Science Center for Archaeology. **VFOAT** Research Papers in Science and Archaeology. **VAT** Museum Applied Science Center for Archaeology Research Papers in Science and Archaeology. Vol. 5 (1988)-. English. One time a year. $20.00. University Museum, 33rd and Spruce Streets, Philadelphia PA 19104. **Tel** (215)898-4124, FAX (215)898-0657. Documents available from CASDDS. **Continues** University of Pennsylvania. Museum Applied Science Center for Archaeology. MASCA Journal, 0198-0106.
Ind/Abst Anthropol. Lit.; Art Archaeol. Tech. Abstr. (1988-); BHA : Biblio. Hist. Art; Ceram. Abstr. (19??-); Chem. Abstr.; GeoRef (1988-).

LC GN796.G3 I57
DD 573.3   GW
MATERIALIEN ZUR VOR- UND FRUHGESCHICHTE VON HESSEN. **Added/Corp** Landesamt fuer Denkmalpflege Hessen. Abteilung fuer Vor- und Fruhgeschichte. Vol. 1 (1976)-. Monographic series. German. Irregular. Price varies per volume. Dr. Rudolf Habelt GmbH, Postfach 150104, D-53040 Bonn Germany. **Tel** 011 49 228 232015.

LC CC135 .M34
DD 702/.8/805   US
MATERIALS ISSUES IN ART AND ARCHAEOLOGY. See The Arts-Art.

ISSN 0130-3740   RU
UDC 930.26
MATERIALY PO ARHEOLOGII EVROPEJSKOGO SEVERO-VOSTOKA. [Mater. arheol. Evr. Sev.-Vost.]. (1962)-. Russian.
Ind/Abst BHA : Biblio. Hist. Art.

ISSN 0458-4767   SW
MEDDELANDEN FRAN LUNDS UNIVERSITETS HISTORISKA MUSEUM. [Medd. Lunds univ. hist. mus.]. **VFOAT** Papers of the Archaeological Institute, University of Lund. (1958)-. Multiple languages. Two times a year.
Ind/Abst Anthropol. Index; Anthropol. Lit.

                              BE
MEDEDELINGEN VAN DE GESCHIED-EN OUDHEIDKUNDIGE KRING VOOR LEUVEN EN OMGEVING. See History-History of Europe.

LC D111 .M46   **ISSN** 0076-6097
DD 913.05   UK
MEDIEVAL ARCHAEOLOGY. See History-History of Europe.

                              UK
MEDIEVAL ARCHAEOLOGY NEWSLETTER : NEWSLETTER OF THE SOCIETY FOR MEDIEVAL ARCHAEOLOGY. **Added/Corp** Society for Medieval Archaeology. No. 1 (Oct. 1989)-. Periodical. English. Four times a year. $42.78. W. S. Maney and Son Ltd., Hudson Road, Leeds LS9 7DL United Kingdom. **Tel** 011 44 1532 497481, FAX 011 44 1532 486983.

LC DC607.1 .S8   **ISSN** 0373-1901
                              FR
MEMOIRES DE LA SOCIETE ARCHEOLOGIQUE DU MIDI DE LA FRANCE. **Main/Corp** Societe Archeologique du Midi de la France. (1832)-. French. cum. index.
Ind/Abst BHA : Biblio. Hist. Art.

ISSN 0240-8260   FR
MEMOIRES DE LA SOCIETE ARCHEOLOGIQUE ET HISTORIQUE DE NANTES ET DE LOIRE-ATLANTIQUE. **Added/Corp** Societe Archeologique et Historique de Nantes et de Loire-Atlantique. **VFOAT** Bulletin de la Societe Archeologique et Historique de Nantes et de Loire-Atlantique. (1978)-. Bulletin. French. One time a year. **Continues** Memoires de la Societe d'Histoire et d'Archeologie de Nantes et de Loire-Atlantique, 0223-8926.
Ind/Abst BHA : Biblio. Hist. Art.

ISSN 0249-664X   FR
UDC 571
MEMOIRES DE LA SOCIETE DES SCIENCES NATURELLES ET ARCHEOLOGIQUES DE LA CREUSE. (1857)-. Monographic series. French. Price varies per volume.
Ind/Abst BHA : Biblio. Hist. Art.

                              FR
MEMOIRES DE LA SOCIETE D'HISTOIRE ET D'ARCHEOLOGIE DE BRETAGNE. **Main/Corp** Societe d'Histoire et d'Archeologie de Bretagne. (1920)-. French. One time a year. cum. index.
Ind/Abst BHA : Biblio. Hist. Art.

LC DC801.C31 S7   FR
MEMOIRES DE LA SOCIETE D'HISTOIRE ET D'ARCHEOLOGIE DE CHALON-SUR-SAONE. **Main/Corp** Societe d'Histoire et d'Archeologie de Chalon-sur-Saone. (1844)-. Periodical. French. cum. index.
Ind/Abst BHA : Biblio. Hist. Art.

ISSN 1148-8093   BE
MEMOIRES DE LA SOCIETE ROYALE D'HISTOIRE ET D'ARCHEOLOGIE DE TOURNAI. **Added/Corp** Societe Royale d'Histoire et d'Archeologie de Tournai. (1980)-. Periodical. French. One time a year.
Ind/Abst BHA : Biblio. Hist. Art.

                              FR
MEMOIRES - FEDERATION DES SOCIETES D'HISTOIRE ET D'ARCHEOLOGIE DE L'AISNE. (MEMOIRES.). [Mem. - Fed. soc. hist. archeol. Aisne]. (1962)-. Periodical. French. One time a year. Archives Dept Federation des Societes Historiques et Arc Heologiques de l'AISNE, 28 rue F Christ, 0200 Laon France. **Tel** 011 33 1 23246149. **Continues** Memoires de la Federation des Societes Savantes du Departement de l'Aisne, 0425-9106.
Ind/Abst BHA : Biblio. Hist. Art.

ISSN 0248-6644   FR
MEMOIRES / SOCIETE D'HISTOIRE ET D'ARCHEOLOGIE DE BEAUNE (COTE-D'OR). **Added/Corp** Societe d'Histoire et d'Archeologie de Beaune (Cote-d'Or). (1960)-. French. One time a year. **Continues** Societe d'Archeologie de Beaune. Memoires.
Ind/Abst BHA : Biblio. Hist. Art.

ISSN 1188-8296   CN
DD 971.4
MEMOIRES VIVES (MONTREAL). (MEMOIRES VIVES : REVUE QUEBECOISE D'ARCHEOLOGIE HISTORIQUE.). [Mem. vives]. **Added/Corp** Groupe PGV Diffusion de l'Archeologie. (1992)-. Periodical. French (summaries and/or abstracts in English). Three times a year. 28.01Can$. Goupe PGV Diffusion Archeologie, 5846 Cartier, Montreal Quebec, H2G 2V2 Canada. **Tel** (514)277-5812, FAX (514)277-5812. **Bk Rev**, (Qty: 3). **Ad Acc**. available on CD-ROM from SDM.

LC CC20- CC51   US
DD 930.106
MEMOIRS OF THE COLORADO ARCHAEOLOGICAL SOCIETY. (1977)-. Periodical. English. Colorado Archaeological Society, 920 Balsam Street, Cortex CO 81321-2608. **Tel** (719)275-9679.

LC E51 .H336 US

MEMOIRS OF THE PEABODY MUSEUM OF ARCHAEOLOGY AND ETHNOLOGY, HARVARD UNIVERSITY. **VFOAT** Memoirs of the Peabody Museum. Vol. 7, Pt. 1 (1937)-. Monographic series. English. Price varies per volume. Peabody Museum of Harvard University, 11 Divinity Avenue, Cambridge MA 02138. **Tel** (617)495-3938. ***Continues*** *Memoirs of the Peabody Museum of American Archaeology and Ethnology, Harvard University.*

ISSN 0259-3548 US

MESOLITHIC MISCELLANY. [Mesolith. misc.]. **Added/Corp** International Union of Prehistoric and Protohistoric Sciences. Mesolithic Commission. Vol. 1, No. 1 (Nov. 1980)-. Periodical. English (French). Two times a year. $4.00. University of Wisconsin / Department of Anthropology, 1180 Observatory Drive, Madison WI 53706. **Tel** (608)262-2575, (608)262-2869. **ED** T. Douglas Price. Index available. **Bk Rev. Circ:** 175.
Desc: Research reports on new archaeology regarding European Mesolithic, 10,000 - 3,000 BC.
Ind/Abst Br. Archaeol. Bibliogr.

ISSN 0391-4135 IT

MESOPOTAMIA. **Added/Corp** Universita di Torino. Facolta di Lettere e Filosofia. Centro Ricerche Archeologiche e Scavi di Torino per il Medio Oriente e l'Asia (Italy). (1966)-. Italian. Irregular. L340000 Italy; 400000 other (latest edition). Le Lettere, Costa San Giorgio 28, 50125 Florence Italy. **Tel** 011 39 55 2342710. **(Subscription address:** Licosa s.p.a., PO Box 552, 50125 Florence Italy. **Tel** 011 39 55 645415.**)** **ED** Giorgio Gullini.
Desc: A journal of the Institute of Archaeology at the University of Torino.
Ind/Abst Anthropol. Lit.; Numis. Lit.

LC F1219 .M748 **ISSN** 0720-5988 GW CCC

MEXICON. **See** History-History of North and South America.

LC WMLC L 83/314 **ISSN** 0543-9728
DD 930 US
CODEN MACGAQ
Pr Rev.

MICHIGAN ARCHAEOLOGIST. [Mich. archaeol.]. **Added/Corp** Michigan Archaeological Society. Vol. 3, No. 1 (Mar. 15, 1957)-. Periodical. English. Four times a year (Mar., June, Sept., Dec.). $30.00. Michigan Archaeological Society, PO Box 359, Saginaw MI 48606. **Tel** (313)629-6739. **ED** Susan Martin and Caven Clark. **Circ:** 400. ***Continues*** *Michigan Archaeological Society. News.*
Desc: Contains articles relating to prehistoric and historic native Americans written by professionals and amateurs in the Great Lakes area. Michigan centered.
Ind/Abst Am. Hist. Life (1990-); Anthropol. Lit.; Ceram. Abstr. (199?-); Ethnoarts Index.

LC DS111.A1 M53 **ISSN** 0334-7311
DD 933/.005 IS

MICHMANIM / MIKHMANIM. **Added/Corp** Muzeon Reuven ve-Idit Hekht. **VFOAT** Mikhmanim. Vol. 1 (May 1985)-. Periodical. Hebrew (summaries and/or abstracts in English; table of contents in Hebrew and English). One time a year. University of Haifa / Hecht Museum, Haifa 31905 Israel. **Tel** 011 972 4 257773, 011 972 4 240577. available with illustrations.

LC E77.8 .M43 **ISSN** 0146-1109
DD 973.926/05 US
CCC

MIDCONTINENTAL JOURNAL OF ARCHAEOLOGY, MCJA. Vol. 1 (Feb. 1976)-. Periodical. English. Two times a year. $28.00 (one-year), $54.00 (two-year) (institutions), $19.00 (one-year), $36.00 (two-year) (individuals) US; $31.00 (one-year), $60.00 (two-year) (institutions), $22.00 (one-year), $42.00 (two-year) other. Kent State University Press / Journals Manager, Kent OH 44242-0001. **Tel** (216)672-7913, FAX (216)672-3104. **ED** David S. Brose. cum. index. **Ad Acc. Circ:** 600. available on microfilm and microfiche from University Microfilms International (UMI).
Desc: Features site reports, new techniques in excavation and analysis, and studies of the ethno-history and ethnography of the area, with relevant illustrations and data. Covers the central regions of the North American continent from the Appalachians to the Great Plains, from the Boreal Forest to the Gulf.
Ind/Abst Am. Hist. Life (1986-); Anthropol. Lit.; Bibliogr. Mission.; Ceram. Abstr. (199?-); Ethnoarts Index.

ISSN 0047-7222 CN

MIDDEN, THE. **Added/Corp** Archaeological Society of British Columbia. Publications Committee. Vol. 2, No. 5 (Dec. 1970)-. Periodical. English. Five times a year (Feb., Apr., June, Oct., Dec.). 14.50Can$ Canada; 17.00Can$ other. Archeological Society of British Columbia, PO Box 520 Station A, Vancouver BC V6C 2N3 Canada. **Tel** (604)873-5958. **ED** Kathryn Bernick. Index available. **Bk Rev. Circ:** 350. ***Continues*** *Archaeological Society of British Columbia. Newsletter of the Archaeological Society of British Columbia., 0380-4798.*
Desc: Archaeology of British Columbia, Canada.
Ind/Abst Abstr. Anthropol.; Ethnoarts Index.

LC CC1 .M56 **ISSN** 0957-7718 UK

MINERVA (LONDON. 1989). (MINERVA.). [Minerva]. **VFOAT** Minerva Magazine. Vol. 1, No. 1 (Jan. 1990)-. Periodical. English. Six times a year (July/Aug. issues combined). $34.23. Aurora Publication Limited, 14 Old Bond Street, London W1X 4JL United Kingdom. **Tel** 011 44 171 4952590, FAX 011 44 171 4911595. ***Absorbed*** *Archaeology Today, 0952-1240.*

LC F608 .M5 **ISSN** 0026-5403
DD 913.776 US

MINNESOTA ARCHAEOLOGIST, THE. [Minn. archaeol.]. **Added/Corp** Minnesota Archaeological Society. (June 1935)-. Periodical. English. Two times a year. $20.00. Minnesota Archaeological Society, Ft Snelling/History Center, St Paul MN 55111. **Tel** (612)644-1386. **ED** Ted Lofstrom. Index available. cum. index. **Bk Rev. Circ:** 300. available on microfilm and microfiche from University Microfilms International (UMI).
Desc: Articles of historic and prehistoric archaeological interest in Minnesota and nearby areas.
Ind/Abst Anthropol. Lit.; BHA : Biblio. Hist. Art; Ethnoarts Index.

US

MINNESOTA PREHISTORIC ARCHAEOLOGY SERIES. **Added/Corp** Minnesota Historical Society. No. 1 (1969)-. Monographic series. English. Irregular. Price varies per volume. Minnesota Historical Society, 345 Kellogg Boulevard West, St. Paul MN 55102. **Tel** (612)297-3243, (800)647-7827, FAX (612)297-3343.

LC E78.M73 M56 **ISSN** 0738-775X US

MISSISSIPPI ARCHAEOLOGY. [Miss. archaeol.]. **Added/Corp** Mississippi. Dept. of Archives and History. Mississippi Archaeological Association. **VFOAT** Newsletter. Vol. 9, No. 5 (May 1974)-. Periodical. English. Two times a year. $10.00 (individuals); $12.00 (institutions). Mississippi Archaeological Association, PO Box 571, Jackson MS 39205. **Tel** (601)359-6863, FAX (601)359-6905. **ED** Patricia Galloway (editor's address: Mississippi Department of Archives and History, PO Box 571, Jackson, MS 39205-0571, (601)359-6863). **Bk Rev.** ctrl circ. ***Continues*** *Newsletter (Mississippi Archaeological Association : 1973).* ***Continued in part by*** *Newsletter from the President's Desk.*
Ind/Abst Abstr. Anthropol.; Anthropol. Lit.

LC F468 .M54 **ISSN** 0743-7641
DD 977.8/01/05 US

MISSOURI ARCHAEOLOGICAL SOCIETY QUARTERLY. [Mo. Archaeol. Soc. q.]. **Added/Corp** Missouri Archaeological Society. **VFOAT** Quarterly; MAS Quarterly. Vol. 1, No. 1 (Jan./March 1984)-. Periodical. English. Four times a year (Mar., June, Sept., Dec.). Comes with membership to Missouri Archaeological Society - $15.00. Missouri Archaeological Society, PO Box 958, 908 Woodson Way, Columbia MO 65205. **Tel** (314)882-3544, FAX (314)882-9410. **ED** Michael J. O'Brien. **Bk Rev**, (Qty: 4-8). **Circ:** 800. available with illustrations. ***Continues*** *News Letter (Missouri Archaeological Society), 0076-955X.*
Desc: Professional and non-professional articles on archaeology in Missouri and the Midwest. Includes book reviews, chapter news, editorial comments, brief bibliographies and milestones.
Ind/Abst Abstr. Anthropol.; Ethnoarts Index.

LC F468 .M55 **ISSN** 0076-9576
DD 977.8/004/97 US

MISSOURI ARCHAEOLOGIST, THE. [Mo. archaeol.]. **Added/Corp** Missouri Archaeological Society. Vol. 1 (Mar. 1935)-. Periodical. English. One time a year. comes with Missouri Archaeological Society membership. Missouri Archaeological Society, PO Box 958, 908 Woodson Way, Columbia MO 65205. **Tel** (314)882-3544, FAX (314)882-9410. **ED** W. Raymond Wood (Editor's Address: Department of Anthropology, 200 Swallow Hall, University of Missouri, Columbia, MO 65211; Editor's telephone: (314)882-4362).
Desc: Publishes articles relevant to Missouri history and prehistory, as well as to Midwest history and prehistory. Publishes manuscript-length articles in a 6-x-9 inch format.
Ind/Abst Anthropol. Lit.

IS

MITEKUFAT HAEVEN. **VFOAT** Journal of the Israel Prehistoric Society. (19??)-. English (French and Hebrew). One time a year. $27.00. Israel Prehistoric Society, PO Box 1502, Jerasulem 91014 Israel.
Ind/Abst Anthropol. Lit.

LC GN2 .B56 **ISSN** 0178-7896
DD 570 GW

MITTEILUNGEN DER BERLINER GESELLSCHAFT FUER ANTHROPOLOGIE, ETHNOLOGIE UND URGESCHICHTE. **See** Anthropology.

ISSN 0342-1287 GW

MITTEILUNGEN DES DEUTSCHEN ARCHAEOLOGISCHEN INSTITUTS, ROEMISCHE ABTEILUNG. [Mitt. Dtsch. Archeol. Inst. Rom. Abt.]. **Main/Corp** Deutsches Archaeologisches Institut. Roemische Abteilung. **VFOAT** Bullettino dell'Istituto Archeologico Germanico, Sezione Romana. (1931)-. Monographic series. German. Price varies per volume. Verlag Phillip Von Zabern, Postfach 190930, D-80609 Munich Germany. **Tel** 011 49 89 12151661, FAX 011 49 61 31223710, telex 4187463. ctrl circ.
Desc: Report of the German Archaeological Institute on various subjects.
Ind/Abst Art Index; Avery Index Archit. Period. Suppl. Colum. Univ. (19??-199?); BHA : Biblio. Hist. Art.

LC DE2 .D44 **ISSN** 0342-1295
DD 949.5 GW

MITTEILUNGEN DES DEUTSCHEN ARCHAEOLOGISCHEN INSTITUTS, ATHENISCHE ABTEILUNG. [Mitt. Dtsch. Archaeolog. Inst., Athen. Abt.]. **Added/Corp** Deutsches Archaeologisches Institut. Athenische Abteilung. German (English, French). One time a year. DM100.00. Gebrueder Mann Verlag, Lindenstrasse 76, D-10969 Berlin Germany. **Tel** 011 49 30 25913589, telex 183723. Index available. **Circ:** 550. ***Continues*** *Mittheilungen des Kaiserlich Deutschen Archaeologischen Instituts, Athensche Abteilung.*
Desc: Scholarly articles on research done in collaboration with the German Archaeological Institute/Athens Branch in the field of classical archaeology.
Ind/Abst Art Index; BHA : Biblio. Hist. Art; Numis. Lit.

LC DE2 .D445
DD 949.5 913 GW

MITTEILUNGEN DES DEUTSCHEN ARCHAEOLOGISCHEN INSTITUTS, ATHENISCHE ABTEILUNG. BEIHEFT. [Mitt. Dtsch. Archaeolog. Inst., Athen. Abt. Beiheft.]. **Main/Corp** Deutsches Archaeologisches Institut. Athenische Abteilung. **Added/Corp** Deutsches Archaeologisches Institut. Athenische Abteilung. **VFOAT** Beiheft. (1971)-. Monographic series. German (English, French). One time a year. Price varies per volume. Gebrueder Mann Verlag, Lindenstrasse 76, D-10969 Berlin Germany. **Tel** 011 49 30 25913589, telex 183723. Index available. **Circ:** 600.
Desc: Contributions to archaeology.

LC DT57 .D48 **ISSN** 0342-1279 GW

MITTEILUNGEN DES DEUTSCHEN ARCHAOLOGISCHEN INSTITUTS. **Main/Corp** Deutsches Archaologisches Institut. Abteilung Kairo. **VFOAT** Mitteilungen. (1930)-. Monographic series. English (French, German and Italian). Irregular. Price varies per volume. Verlag Phillip Von Zabern, Postfach 190930, D-80609 Munich Germany. **Tel** 011 49 89 12151661, FAX 011 49 61 31223710, telex 4187463. ctrl circ.
Desc: Reports of the German Archeological Institute on various subjects.
Ind/Abst Avery Index Archit. Period. Suppl. Colum. Univ. (19??-199?); BHA : Biblio. Hist. Art.

ISSN 1059-8065
DD 973 US

MMAP LOG. (MMAP LOG : THE NEWSLETTER OF THE MARYLAND MARITIME ARCHAEOLOGY PROGRAM.). [MMAP log]. **Added/Corp** Maryland Maritime Archaeology Program. **VAT** Maryland Maritime Archaeology Program Log. Vol. 1, No. 1 (Feb. 1992)-. Newsletter. English. Four times a year. Free. Maryland Maritime Archaeology Program, 100 Community Place, Crownsville MD 21401.

LC QE696 .S94a **ISSN** 0168-6151
DD 551.7/9/05 NE
CCC

MODERN QUATERNARY RESEARCH IN SOUTHEAST ASIA. **See** Paleontology.

LC CC9 .M65
DD 930/.1/05 IT

MONDO ARCHEOLOGICO. No. 1 (Mar. 1976)-. Periodical. Italian. 5.400. C Tedeschi, Via Massaia 98, Firenze 50134 Italy.

ISSN 0077-4093 IT

MONOGRAFIE DI ARCHEOLOGIA LIBICA. (1948)-. Monographic series. Italian. Irregular. Price varies per volume. L'Erma di Bretschneider SPA, via Cassiodoro 19, 00193 Rome Italy. **Tel** 011 39 6 6874127, 011 39 6 6874129, FAX 011 39 6 6874129.

Archaeology

MONOGRAPH SERIES - COLT ARCHAEOLOGICAL INSTITUTE.
ISSN 0588-5132 UK
Main/Corp Colt Archaeological Institute. 1- 1962-). Periodical. English.

MONOGRAPH / UNIVERSITY OF OXFORD, COMMITTEE FOR ARCHAEOLOGY. UK
Added/Corp University of Oxford. Committee for Archaeology. (198?)-. Monographic series. English. Price varies per volume. Oxbow Books Ltd., Park End Place, Oxford OX1 1HN United Kingdom. **Tel** 011 44 1865 241249.
Ind/Abst Curr. Cit.

LC CC
DD 930.1
ISSN 1055-2316 US
MONOGRAPHS IN WORLD ARCHAEOLOGY. [Monogr. world archaeol.]. No. 1 (1991)-. Monographic series. English. Prehistory Press, 1705 Jefferson Street, Madison WI 53711-2109.

ISSN 0077-1384 GW
MONUMENTA AMERICANA. Added/Corp Berlin. Ibero-Amerikanisches Institut. Vol. 1 (1954)-. Monographic series. German (English and Spanish). Irregular. Price varies per volume. DuMont Buchverlag GmbH & Co. KG, Postfach 100468, D-50441 Cologne Germany. **Tel** 011 49 221 20530, **FAX** 011 49 221 2053281. **Circ:** 800.
Desc: Features Ibero-American archaeology.

Pr Rev.
ISSN 0363-7565 US
MONUMENTA ARCHAEOLOGICA (LOS ANGELES). (MONUMENTA ARCHAEOLOGICA.). **Added/Corp** University of California, Los Angeles. Institute of Archaeology. Vol. 1 (1976)-. Monographic series. English. Irregular. Price varies per volume. Institute of Archaeology, University of California, Los Angeles CA 90024. **Tel** (213)825-7411. **ED** Ernestine S. Elster. **Bk Rev. Ad Acc. Circ:** 100 (ctrl).
Desc: Comprehensive reports on archaeological excavations and essays on cultural systems derived from archaeological analyses.

UDC 930.2
ISSN 1148-6023 FR
MONUMENTS ET MEMOIRES PARIS. [Monum. mem. Paris]. (1894)-. Periodical. French. Irregular. 450.00F. Presses Universitaires de France, Department des Revues, 17 Rue Souflot, 75005 Paris France. **Tel** 011 33 1 43267741, telex PUF 600 474 F.
Ind/Abst BHA : Biblio. Hist. Art.

LC DP532 .M86
ISSN 0871-0996 PO
MUNDA : REVISTA DO GRUPO DE ARQUEOLOGIA E ARTE DO CENTRO. Added/Corp Grupo de Arqueologia e Arte do Centro (Portugal). No. 1 (May 1981)-. Periodical. Portuguese. Two times a year.
Ind/Abst BHA : Biblio. Hist. Art.

LC PA3 .M73
DD 480/.05
ISSN 0027-4054 SZ CCC
MUSEUM HELVETICUM. [Mus. helv.]. **Added/Corp** Schweizerische Geisteswissenschaftliche Gesellschaft. Vol. 1 (1944)-. Periodical. German (French, English and Italian). Four times a year. $97.55. Schwabe & Company Ltd., Farnsburgerstrasse 8 PF 254, CH-4132 Muttenz 1 Switzerland. **Tel** 011 41 61 4613001, **FAX** 01 41 61 4612500. **ED** Walter Burkert. **Bk Rev. Ad Acc. Circ:** 700 (ctrl).
Desc: A review of archaeology; deals with all fields of classical archaeology such as history of literature, philosophy, linguistics, ancient history, etc.
Ind/Abst BHA : Biblio. Hist. Art; MLA Int. Bibl. Books Artic. Mod. Lang. Lit.

DD 971.3/201
ISSN 0709-2725 CN
MUSEUM NOTES (LONDON). See Museums and Galleries.

GW
NACHRICHTEN AUS NIEDERSACHSENS URGESCHICHTE. No. 1 (1927)-. Periodical. German. One time a year. Lax Verlagsbuchhandlung, Kreuzstr 21, D-31134 Hildesheim Germany. **Tel** 011 49 5121 134565. **ED** Herbert Jankuhn. **Bk Rev. Circ:** 500. **Continues** Nachrichtenblatt fur Niedersachsens Vorgeschichte.
Ind/Abst Anthropol. Lit.; BHA : Biblio. Hist. Art; Br. Archaeol. Bibliogr.; Numis. Lit.

ISSN 0027-7835 IT
NAPOLI NOBILISSIMA. See The Arts.

UK
NATURAL HISTORY OF EGYPT, THE. See Natural History.

LC F2229 .N37
DD 980.1
ISSN 0077-6297 US
NAWPA PACHA. [Nawpa pacha]. **Added/Corp** Institute of Andean Studies. (1963)-. Monographic series. Multiple languages (Spanish and French). Irregular. $20.00. Institute of Andean Studies, PO Box 9307, Berkeley CA 94709. **Tel** (510)525-7816. **ED** John H. Rowe and Patricia J. Lyon. **Circ:** 500 (ctrl).
Desc: Archaeology of the Andean region and related topics such as history, ethnobotany, ethnography and geography.
Ind/Abst Anthropol. Index; Anthropol. Lit.; Ethnoarts Index; Hisp. Am. Period. Index, HAPI.

LC DS56 .B86
DD 939/.4/005
ISSN 0739-0068 US
NEAR EAST ARCHAEOLOGICAL SOCIETY BULLETIN. [c]. **Added/Corp** Near East Archaeological Society (U.S.). (1975)-. Bulletin. English. Two times a year. $25.00. Near East Archaeological Society, 2313 East 20th Street, Joplin MO 64804. **Tel** (417)623-7573. **ED** Dr. Glenn A. Carnagey, Sr. (editor's address: 4401 Park Glen Road #337, St Louis Park, MN 55416-4769; editor's phone: (612)925-2201). **Bk Rev**, (Qty: 5-10). **Ad Acc, Adv Mgr:** Glenn A. Carnagey, **Tel** (612)925-2201. **Circ:** 350. **Continues** Bulletin Series of the Near East Archaeological Society, 0742-4418.
Desc: Original reports on archaeological excavations and articles relating to biblical research. Evangelical Christian viewpoint.
Ind/Abst Index Book Rev. Relig.; Relig. Index One Period.

DD 938
ISSN 0028-2812 US
NESTOR. See Archaeology-Abstracting, Bibliographies and Statistics.

LC DD491.H245 N4
DD 943/.59
ISSN 0548-2682 GW
NEUE AUSGRABUNGEN UND FORSCHUNGEN IN NIEDERSACHSEN. See History-History of Europe.

LC F36 .N48
DD 974.2/01
ISSN 0077-8346 US
NEW HAMPSHIRE ARCHEOLOGIST, THE. Vol. 1, No. 1 (Nov. 1950)-. Periodical. English. One time a year. $8.00. New Hampshire Archeological Society, 49 College Road, Manchester NH 03102.
Ind/Abst Anthropol. Lit.; Ethnoarts Index.

LC DU416 .N33
DD 993.101/05
Pr Rev.
ISSN 0110-540x NZ
NEW ZEALAND JOURNAL OF ARCHAEOLOGY. Added/Corp New Zealand Archaeological Association. University of Otago. **VFOAT** Journal of Archaeology. (1979)-. Periodical. English. One time a year. $25.00. New Zealand Archaeological Association, Private Bag 92018, Auckland 1 New Zealand. **Tel** 011 64 3 4798751, **FAX** 011 64 3 4741607.
Ind/Abst Anthropol. Lit.

LC E159.5 .N49
DD 973.1
ISSN 0735-1399 US
NEWS JOURNAL - SOCIETY FOR COMMERCIAL ARCHEOLOGY (U.S.). See Architecture.

LC DT57 .A58
ISSN 0402-0731 US
NEWSLETTER - AMERICAN RESEARCH CENTER IN EGYPT. [Newsl. - Am. Res. Cent. Egypt]. **Main/Corp** American Research Center in Egypt. **VFOAT** ARCE Newsletter. (19??)-. Newsletter. English. Four times a year (Feb., May, Sept., Nov.). $25.00. American Research Center in Egypt / NYU, 50 Washington Square South, New York NY 10012. **Tel** (212)998-8890, **FAX** (212)995-4144. **ED** Susan Weeks. **Bk Rev. Circ:** 950 (ctrl).
Desc: Brief articles summarizing research in Egypt. Topics include Egyptology, archaeology, art history, humanities, social sciences, Islamic studies, etc.
Ind/Abst Recent. Publ. Artic.

LC DS101 .A46
DD 950/.072/073
ISSN 0361-6029 US
NEWSLETTER - AMERICAN SCHOOLS OF ORIENTAL RESEARCH. See Education-International Education.

LC CC21 .S617
DD 950/.1/05
ISSN 0036-1275 US
NEWSLETTER AND PROCEEDINGS OF THE S.E.H.A. Main/Corp Society for Early Historic Archaeology. **VAT** Newsletter and Proceedings of the Society for Early Historic Archaeology. (19??)-. Newsletter. English. Irregular. Society for Early Historic Archaeology, 140 Maeser Building, Brigham Young University, Provo UT 84601.

ISSN 0168-7913 NE
NEWSLETTER - DEPARTMENT OF POTTERY TECHNOLOGY, UNIVERSITY OF LEIDEN. (NEWSLETTER / DEPARTMENT OF POTTERY TECHNOLOGY.). [Newsl. - Dep. Pottery Technol. Univ. Leiden]. **Added/Corp** Rijksuniversiteit te Leiden. Dept. of Pottery Technology. 1 (1983)-. Newsletter. English. Institute of Pottery Technology, Archaeological Centre, Reuvensplaats 4, PO Box 9515, 2300 ra Leiden The Netherlands.
Ind/Abst Anthropol. Lit.

LC NX7475
DD 709
ISSN 8755-4593 US
NEWSLETTER, EAST ASIAN ART & ARCHAEOLOGY. See The Arts-Art.

UK
NEWSLETTER / KENT ARCHAEOLOGICAL SOCIETY. Added/Corp Kent Archaeological Society. **VFOAT** Kent Archaeological Society Newsletter. (1982)-. Newsletter. English. Two times a year. Kent Archaeological Society, Barnfield Church Lane, East Peckham, Tonbridge KT TN12 5JJ United Kingdom. **Tel** 011 44 1622 871945. **ED** N.V. Caigeo. **Circ:** 1,250 (ctrl).

DD 930
ISSN 1052-9101 US
NEWSLETTER - MISSISSIPPI ARCHAEOLOGICAL ASSOCIATION (1983). (NEWSLETTER - MISSISSIPPI ARCHAEOLOGICAL ASSOCIATION.). [Newsl. - Miss. Archaeol. Assoc.]. **Added/Corp** Mississippi Archaeological Association. **VFOAT** Mississippi Archaeological Association Newsletter. Vol. 18, No. 1 (Jan. 1983)-. Newsletter. English. Six times a year. comes with membership. Mississippi Archaeological Association, PO Box 571, Jackson MS 39205. **Tel** (601)359-6863, **FAX** (601)359-6905. **Continues** Newsletter From the President's Desk.

LC E78.N74 A73
US
NEWSLETTER / NORTH CAROLINA ARCHAEOLOGICAL SOCIETY. Added/Corp North Carolina Archaeological Society. Vol. 1, No. 1 (Fall 1991)-. Newsletter. English. Four times a year. $25.00 (institutions), $10.00 (individuals). North Carolina Archaeological Society, 109 East Jones Street, Raleigh NC 27601-2807. **Tel** (919)733-7342, **FAX** (919)733-8653. **ED** Mark Mathis. **Continues** News Letter (Archaeological Society of North Carolina).

DD 971.24/01/05
ISSN 0227-7514 CN
NEWSLETTER - SASKATCHEWAN ARCHAEOLOGICAL SOCIETY. [Newsl. - Sask. Archaeol. Soc.]. **Main/Corp** Saskatchewan Archaeological Society. Vol. 1 (Feb. 1980)-. Newsletter. English. Six times a year (Feb., Apr., June, Aug., Oct., Dec.). 26.00Can$. Saskatchewan Archaeological Society, #5 816 1st Avenue North, Saskatoon Saskatchewan S7K 1Y3 Canada. **Tel** (306)664-4124, **FAX** (306)665-1928. **ED** Jim Finnigan. Index available. cum. index. **Circ:** 350. **Supersedes in part** Saskatchewan Archaeology Newsletter, 0581-832X.
Desc: Contains items of current and upcoming interest: Chapter news, seminars, films, meetings, field trips, short archaeological articles and news items on world archaeology.

US
NEWSLETTER / SUFFOLK COUNTY ARCHAEOLOGICAL ASSOCIATION.
Main/Corp Suffolk County Archaeological Association. (19??)-. Newsletter. English. Three times a year. $20.00 (individuals), $50.00 (sustaining), $100.00 (contributing), $200.00 (patron) Comes with Suffolk County Archaeological Association membership. Suffolk County Archaeological Association, PO Drawer 1542, Stony Brook NY 11790. **Tel** (516)929-8725, **FAX** (516)929-6967. **ED** Gaynell Stone, Ph.D. **Bk Rev. Circ:** 300 (ctrl).
Desc: The archaeological and historical news of the Long Island region.

LC DS815 .N512
JA
NIHON KOKOGAKU NEMPO. VFOAT Archaeologia Japonica. (1948)-. Japanese. ¥2000. Waseda Daigaku Kokogaku Kenkyushitsu, 647 Totsukamachi 1 Shinjuku-tu, Tokyo 160 Japan.

LC DA670.N59 N8
ISSN 0142-7962 UK
NORFOLK ARCHAEOLOGY. Added/Corp Norfolk and Norwich Archaeological Society. (19??)-. Periodical. English. Three times a year. $25.67. Norfolk and Norwich Archaeological Society, Garsett House, St. Andrews Hall Place, Norwich NR4 1AT United Kingdom.

Tel 011 44 1683 59913. ***Continues** Norfolk Archaeology, or, Miscellaneous Tracts Relating to the Antiquities of the County of Norfolk.*
Ind/Abst Art Archaeol. Tech. Abstr.; BHA : Biblio. Hist. Art; Br. Archaeol. Bibliogr.; Br. Humanit. Index; Numis. Lit.

LC E43 .N67 **ISSN** 0197-6931
DD 970/.005 US
CODEN NAAREU

NORTH AMERICAN ARCHAEOLOGIST. [North Am. archaeol.]. Vol. 1 (1980)-. Periodical. English. Four times a year. $132.50. Baywood Publishing Company Inc., 26 Austin Avenue, PO Box 337, Amityville NY 11701. **Tel** (516)691-1270, (800)638-7819, FAX (516)691-1770. **ED** Roger W. Moeller. cum. index. **Bk Rev**.
Desc: Concerned with all aspects of American archaeology; spans the entire range of cultural evolution in America from Paleo-Indian studies to industrial archaeology. Theoretical and methodological articles, provided their data base is North America, are also accepted and research based on cultural resource management; work by state and local societies is solicited along with more traditional academic-museum projects.
Ind/Abst Abstr. Anthropol.; Am. Hist. Life (1986-); Anthropol. Lit.; BHA : Biblio. Hist. Art; Br. Archaeol. Bibliogr.

US

NORTH DAKOTA ARCHAEOLOGICAL ASSOCIATION NEWSLETTER. Added/Corp North Dakota Archaeological Association. Vol. 2, No. 3 (Aug. 1981)-. Newsletter. English. Irregular (3 or 4 yearly). comes with membership. North Dakota Archaeological Association, 2002 University Avenue, Grand Forks ND 58203. ***Continues** Notes on North Dakota Archaeology.*

ISSN 0332-0820
DD 913.031419 IE

NORTH MUNSTER ANTIQUARIAN JOURNAL. [North Munst. antiq. j.]. (1936)-. Periodical. English. One time a year. ***Continues** Journal of the North Munster Archaeological Society, 0332-0952.*
Ind/Abst BHA : Biblio. Hist. Art.

LC DL421 .N75 **ISSN** 0029-3652
NO
CCC
CODEN NRACBX

NORWEGIAN ARCHAEOLOGICAL REVIEW. [Norw. archaeol. rev.]. **Added/Corp** Universitetsforlaget. Norsk Arkeologisk Kommisjon. Norske Arkeologmtet. Vol. 1, (1968)-. Periodical. English. Two times a year. $56.00. Scandinavian University Press, PO Box 2959 Toeyen, N 0608 Oslo 6 Norway. **Tel** 011 47 2 2575400, FAX 011 47 2 2575353, telex 71896 UROR N. **(Subscription address:** Scandinavian University Press, 200 Meacham Ave., Elmont NY 11003. **Tel** (516)352-7300, FAX (516)352-7377.**)** **ED** Ericka Engelstad. cum. index. **Bk Rev. Ad Acc. Circ:** 700. Documents available from CASDDS.
Desc: Presents articles of special interest of Scandinavian archaeological research. Concentrates on the European area, but description and discussion of archaeological methodology, and theory based on results from other parts of the world are also accepted.
Ind/Abst Anthropol. Lit.; BHA : Biblio. Hist. Art; Br. Archaeol. Bibliogr.; Chem. Abstr.; Geogr. Abstr. Human Geogr.; GeoRef; Numis. Lit.

BE

NOTAE PRAEHISTORICAE : INFORMATIEBLAD UITGEGEVEN DOOR DE N F W O CONTACTGROEP, PREHISTOIRE. Added/Corp Prehistoire--Groupe de Contact F.N.R.S. (1981)-. Periodical. French (Dutch, German and English). Laboratorium voor Prehistorie, Redingenstraat 16 Bis, B-3000 Louvain Belgium. **Tel** 016 22 69 20.

IT

NOTIZIE DEGLI SCAVI DI ANTICHITA. Main/Corp Accademia Nazionale dei Lincei. (19??)-. Periodical. Italian (English, French, German and Spanish). Irregular. Price varies per volume. Accademia Nazionale dei Lincei, Via Lungara 10 Uff Diff Pubbl., 00165 Rome Italy. **Tel** 011 39 6 6838831. **ED** C.F. Golisano. **Circ:** 800. ***Continues** Reale Accademia Nazionale dei Lincei. Notizie Degli Scabi di Antichita.*
Desc: Publishes preliminary excavation reports made in Italy by domestic or foreign archaeologists.
Ind/Abst BHA : Biblio. Hist. Art; Numis. Lit.

LC Z6205 .N67
RU

•NOVAIA LITERATURA PO SOTSIALNYM I GUMANITARNYM NAUKAM. ISTORIIA, ARKHEOLOGIIA, ETNOLOGIIA / ROSSIISKAIA AKADEMIIA NAUK, INSTITUT NAUCHNOI INFORMATSII PO OBSHCHESTVENNYM NAUKAM. Added/Corp Institut Nauchnoi Informatsii po Obshchestvennym Naukam (Rossiiskaia Akademiia Nauk). **VFOAT** Istoriia, Arkheologiia, Etnologiia. (1993)-. Periodical. Russian (table of contents in English). Twelve times a year. Inion An SSSR, Ulitsa Krasikova D 28/45, Moscow Russia. **Tel** 128.89.71. **(Subscription address:** East View Publications Inc., 3020 Harbor Lane North, Suite 110, Minneapolis MN 55447. **Tel** (800)477-1005, (612)550-0961, FAX (612)559-2931.**)** ***Formed by the union of** Novaia Otechestvennaia Literatura po Obshchestvennym Naukam. Istoriia, Arkheologiia, Etnografiia **and** Novaia Inostrannaia Literatura po Obshchestvennym Naukam: Istoriia, Arkheologiia, Etnografiia.*

ISSN 0130-7754
RU

NUMIZMATIKA I EPIGRAFIKA / AKADEMIIA NAUK SSSR, INSTITUT ARKHEOLOGII. **See** Hobbies-Numismatics.

LC DT13 .N9 **ISSN** 0713-5815
DD 960/.1/05 CN
CODEN NYAKE7
Pr Rev.

NYAME AKUMA. [Nyame akuma]. **Added/Corp** University of Calgary. Dept. of Archaeology. Society of Africanist Archaeologists in America. **VFOAT** Newsletter of African Archaeology; Newsletter of the Society of Africanist Archaeologists in Africa. No. 1 (Oct. 1972)-. Periodical. English (French). Two times a year (June & Dec.). $20.00. Society of Africanist Archaeologists, 427 Grinter Hall, University of Florida, Gainesville FL 32611. **Tel** (904)392-6929. **Bk Rev. Circ:** 300 (ctrl).
Desc: Research reports on current research in African archaeology. Concentrating on prehistoric times and excluding classical of the North Africa.
Ind/Abst Anthropol. Lit.; Ceram. Abstr. (199?-); Ethnoarts Index.

ISSN 0748-7339
DD 974 US

OCCASIONAL PAPER - BOSTON UNIVERSITY. CENTER FOR ARCHAEOLOGICAL STUDIES. (OCCASIONAL PAPER / CENTER FOR ARCHAEOLOGICAL STUDIES, BOSTON UNIVERSITY.). [Occas. pap. - Boston Univ., Cent. Archaeol. Stud.]. #1 (Feb. 1984)-. Monographic series. English. Irregular. Price varies per volume. Center for Archaeological Studies, 232 Bay State Road, Boston University, Boston MA 02215.

ISSN 0473-7482
US
CEASED

OCCASIONAL PAPERS IN ARCHAEOLOGY. Added/Corp Colonial Williamsburg Foundation. **VFOAT** Colonial Williamsburg Occasional Papers in Archaeology. (1973)-Series complete with Vol. 2. Monographic series. English. University Press of Virginia, PO Box 3608, Charlottesville VA 22903. **Tel** (804)924-3469.

UK

OCCASIONAL PUBLICATION (UNIVERSITY OF LONDON. INSTITUTE OF ARCHAEOLOGY). (OCCASIONAL PUBLICATION.). **Added/Corp** University of London. Institute of Archaeology. No. 1 (1977)-. Monographic series. English. Irregular. Price varies per volume. Institute of Archaeology / London, 31-34 Gordon Square, London WC1H 0PY United Kingdom. **Tel** 011 44 171 3879651.

ISSN 0276-8607
DD 974 US

OCCASIONAL PUBLICATIONS IN NORTHEASTERN ANTHROPOLOGY. **See** Anthropology.

ISSN 0272-1856
DD 913 US

OFFICE OF THE STATE ARCHEOLOGIST REPORTS. [Off. State Archeol. rep.]. **Main/Corp** Texas. Office of the State Archeologist. **Added/Corp** Texas. Office of the State Archeologist. Texas Historical Survey Committee. Texas Historical Commission. **VFOAT** Archeological Report. No. 22 (1972)-. Monographic series. English. Price varies per volume. Texas Historical Commission, PO Box 12276 Capitol Station, Austin TX 78711. **Tel** (512)463-6100, FAX (512)463-6095. ***Continues** Archeological Report (Texas Historical Survey Committee), 0563-2404.*

ISSN 0048-153X
DD 977 US

OHIO ARCHAEOLOGIST. [Ohio archaeol.]. **Added/Corp** Archaeological Society of Ohio. Ohio Archaeological Society. Ohio Indian Relic Collectors Society. Vol. 1, (Apr. 1951)-. Periodical. English. Four times a year. $17.50. Archaeological Society of Ohio, 5210 Coonpath Road, Pleasantville OH 43148. **Tel** (800)736-7815. **ED** Robert N. Converse, (editor's address: 199 Converse Dr, Plain City, OH 43064). **Circ:** 2,500 (ctrl). available on microfilm; available on microfiche; available on an online database. ***Continues** Ohio Indian Relic Collectors Society. Bulletin.*
Desc: The publication of articles and photos of archaeological sites and material found for the purpose of promoting a better understanding among students and collectors.
Ind/Abst Abstr. Anthropol.; BHA : Biblio. Hist. Art; Ethnoarts Index.

ISSN 0732-1635
US

OLD WORLD ARCHAEOLOGY NEWSLETTER. [Old world arch. newsl.]. **Added/Corp** Wesleyan University (Middletown, Conn.). Classics Dept. **VFOAT** OWAN. Vol. 1 (Jan. 1977)-. Newsletter. English (German, French and Italian). Three times a year (Jan., Apr., Oct.). $10.00. Wesleyan University Department of Classics, Middletown CT 06459. **Tel** (203)347-9211 ext. 2804, FAX (203)343-3903. **ED** Carla Antonaccio and Clark Maines (editor's phone: (203)347-9411 ext. 3124). **Bk Rev**, (Qty: 2-3). **Ad Acc, Adv Mgr:** D. Sierpinsk, **Tel** (203)347-9411 ext. 2804. **Circ:** 200. available on an online database.

CN

ONTARIO ARCHAEOLOGICAL SOCIETY INDEX TO PUBLICATIONS, THE. Main/Corp Ontario Archaeological Society. **VFOAT** Index to Publications. 1950-1990, Published in 1990-. English. 55.00Can$ (institutions), 34.00Can$ (family), 28.00Can$ (individuals), 400.00Can$ (lifetime membership). Ontario Archaeological Society, 126 Willowdale Avenue, North York Ontario M2N 4Y2 Canada. **Tel** (416)730-0797, FAX (416)730-0797.

ISSN 0078-4672
CN
CODEN ONAREU

ONTARIO ARCHAEOLOGY. No. 1 (April 1954)-. Periodical. English. Two times a year. $55.00 Comes with Ontario Archaeological Society membership. Ontario Archaeological Society, 126 Willowdale Avenue, North York Ontario M2N 4Y2 Canada. **Tel** (416)730-0797, FAX (416)730-0797. **Circ:** 800.
Ind/Abst Am. Hist. Life (1986-); Anthropol. Lit.

LC DR1227 .O65 **ISSN** 0473-0992
CI

OPUSCULA ARCHAEOLOGICA (ZAGREB, CROATIA). (OPUSCULA ARCHAEOLOGICA.). **Added/Corp** SveuciliÈste u Zagrebu. Arheoloski Institut. Sveuciliste u Zagrebu. Odsjek Za Arheologiju. SveuciliÈste u Zagrebu. Arheoloski Zavod. (1956)-. Periodical. Serbo-Croatian (Cyrillic) (summaries and/or abstracts in English and German). Irregular. Arheoloski Zavod Filozofski Fakultet, Djure Salaja 3, PO Box 171, 41001 Zagreb Croatia. **Tel** telex 620 130, 620-133. **Bk Rev. Circ:** 500 (ctrl).

LC DS41 .O73
DD 956/.005 JA

ORIENT. Added/Corp Nihon Orient Gakkai. Vol. 1 (1960)-. Multiple languages (English, French and German). One time a year (July). $50.00. Society for Near East Studies in Japan, 9 Kanda Nishiki-cho 1-chome, Chiyoda-ku Tokyo 101 Japan. **Tel** 011 81 3 32917519. **ED** H. Ogawa, K. Nakamura and Y. Nagata. ctrl circ.
Desc: Islamic studies; history and archaeology of Near East; art of Near East.

ISSN 0069-3367
US

ORIENTAL INSTITUTE PUBLICATIONS. (THE UNIVERSITY OF CHICAGO ORIENTAL INSTITUTE PUBLICATIONS.). **Added/Corp** University of Chicago. Oriental Institute. **VFOAT** Oriental Institute Publications. (19??)-. Monographic series. English. Irregular. Price varies per volume. University of Chicago Oriental Institute, 1155 East 58th Street, Chicago IL 60637. **Tel** (312)702-9508. **ED** Tom Holland and Tom Urban. **Circ:** 750 (ctrl).
Desc: Final definitive reports on archaeological excavations, history, linguistics and other materials discovered in the ancient Near East.

ISSN 0332-088X
DD 941.54193 IE

OTHER CLARE. **See** History-History of Europe.

ISSN 0702-7974
DD 930/.1/06271384 CN

OTTAWA ARCHAEOLOGIST, THE. Vol. 6, No. 1 (Sept. 1976)-. Periodical. English. Irregular. 15.00Can$. Ottawa Chapter of the Ontario Archaeological Society, Archaeological Survey of Canada, Ashton Press Building, Bells Corners, Ottawa Ontario K1A 0M8 Canada. **Tel** (819)994-6117. **ED** Clyde C Kennedy. **Bk Rev. Circ:** 100 (ctrl). ***Continues** Archaic Notes, 0381-8357.*
Desc: Current archaeological activities and research in Eastern Ontario/Ottawa Valley, Ontario and neighboring regions. Notice of meetings, current heritage issues in archaeology, history and related disciplines also covered.

LC CC1 .O9 **ISSN** 0262-5253
DD 930/.05 UK
CCC
CODEN OJARE2

OXFORD JOURNAL OF ARCHAEOLOGY. [Oxf. j. archaeol.]. Vol. 1, No. 1 (Mar. 1982)-. Academic Scholarly Publication. English. Three times a year. $259.00. Basil Blackwell Publishers

Archaeology

Ltd., 108 Cowley Road, Oxford OX4 1JF United Kingdom. **Tel** 011 44 1235 465500, FAX 011 44 1235 465556, telex 837022 OXBOOK G. **(Subscription address:** Blackwell Publishers / UK, 108 Cowley Road, Oxford OX4 1JF United Kingdom. **Tel** 011 44 1865 791100, FAX 011 44 1865 791347.) **ED** John Boardman, Barry Cunliffe and Sheppard Frere. available on microfilm and microfiche from University Microfilms International (UMI).
Desc: Publishes articles and encourages debate on the whole range of European archaeology, from prehistoric to medieval times.
Ind/Abst Anthropol. Lit.; Art Archaeol. Tech. Abstr.; Avery Index Archit. Period. Suppl. Colum. Univ. (1989-); BHA : Biblio. Hist. Art; Br. Archaeol. Bibliogr.; Curr. Cit.; Ecol. Abstr. (?-?); Geogr. Abstr. Human Geogr.; Middle East Abstr. Index; Soc. Plann. Policy Dev. Abstr.

LC DA690.O97 O753
DD 942.57
UK

OXONIENSIA. Added/Corp Oxfordshire Architectural & Historical Society. Oxford Architectural & Historical Society. Vol. 1 (1936)-. Periodical. English. One time a year. $27.37. Oxfordshire Architectural & Historical Society, Ashmolean Museum, Oxford OX1 2PH United Kingdom. **ED** Simon Townley. Index available. **Bk Rev. Circ:** 600 (ctrl).
Desc: A journal dealing with the archaeology, history and architecture of Oxford and Oxfordshire. Includes archaeological reports, historical papers and architectural surveys.
Ind/Abst BHA : Biblio. Hist. Art; Br. Archaeol. Bibliogr.; Br. Humanit. Index; Numis. Lit.

ISSN 0078-740X
US
CEASED

PACIFIC ANTHROPOLOGICAL RECORDS. See Anthropology.

LC E78.C15 P15
DD 917.9/03
ISSN 0552-7252
US

PACIFIC COAST ARCHAEOLOGICAL SOCIETY QUARTERLY. [Pac. Coast Archaeol. Soc. q.]. **Main/Corp** Pacific Coast Archaeological Society. **Added/Corp** Pacific Coast Archaeological Society. Quarterly. Vol. 1 (1965)-. Academic Scholarly Publication. English. Four times a year. $41.00. Pacific Coast Archaeological Society, PO Box 10926, Costa Mesa CA 92627. **Tel** (714)646-1314. **ED** David M Van Horn. Index available. cum. index. **Circ:** 300 (ctrl).
Desc: Scholarly articles on prehistoric and historic archaeology of Orange County, California and its culturally related areas.
Ind/Abst Am. Hist. Life (1986-); Anthropol. Lit.; Calif. Period. Index (19??-); Calif. Period. Microfi. (19??-); Ethnoarts Index.

LC CC75 .P32
ISSN 0257-8727
FR
CODEN PACTBV

PACT : REVUE DU GROUPE EUROPEEN D'ETUDES POUR LES TECHNIQUES PHYSIQUES, CHIMIQUES ET MATHEMATIQUES APPLIQUEES A L'ARCHEOLOGIE. Added/Corp European Study Group on Physical, Chemical, and Mathematical Techniques Applied to Archaeology. Council of Europe. Parliamentary Assembly. **VFOAT** P A C T. (1977)-. Academic Scholarly Publication. French (English, French, German and Italian; summaries and/or abstracts in English and French). One time a year. Price varies per volume. Council of Europe, avenue de l'Europe Palais EU, 67075 Strasbourg Cedex 01 France. **Tel** 011 33 88 412000. **ED** Tony Hackens. **Circ:** 500. Documents available from CASDDS.
Ind/Abst Art Archaeol. Tech. Abstr.; BHA : Biblio. Hist. Art; Chem. Abstr.; Numis. Lit.

ISSN 0393-0149
IT

PADUSA. Added/Corp Centro Polesano di Studi Storici Archeologici ed Etnografici (Rovigo, Italy. (1965)-. Periodical. Italian. Irregular. Price varies per volume. Libraccio Sas Zielo & C, Via del Portello 42, 35129 Padua Italy. **Tel** 011 39 49 8075035.
Ind/Abst BHA : Biblio. Hist. Art.

LC DS378 .P3
ISSN 0078-7868
PK

PAKISTAN ARCHAEOLOGY. Added/Corp Pakistan. Dept. of Archaeology. Pakistan. Dept. of Archaeology & Museums. No. 1 (1964)-. English. Irregular. Price varies per volume. Government Pakistan, Department of Archaeology, 27A Ctrl Union Commerc Shaheed, Millat Road, Karachi 5B Pakistan. **Tel** 011 92 21 441186.
Ind/Abst Anthropol. Lit.

LC CC1 .A45
ISSN 0552-9344
NE
CCC

PALAEOHISTORIA (HAARLEM). (PALAEOHISTORIA.). [Palaeohistoria]. **Added/Corp** Rijksuniversiteit te Groningen. Biologisch-Archeologisch Instituut. (1951)-. English (French and German). Irregular. Fl.220.00. AA Balkema, Box 1675, 3000 BR Rotterdam Netherlands. **Tel** 011 31 10 4145822, FAX 011 31 10

4135947, telex 41605. Documents available from BIOSIS Document Express.
Ind/Abst Anthropol. Lit.; Biol. Abstr.; Middle East Abstr. Index.

ISSN 0148-4737
US

NLM W1 PA361V
Pr Rev.
PALEOPATHOLOGY NEWSLETTER. (Mar. 1973)-. Newsletter. English (French, German and Spanish). Four times a year (March, June, Sept., Dec.). $25.00. Paleopathology Association, 18655 Parkside, Detroit MI 48221. **Tel** (313)864-7944, FAX (313)864-7944. **ED** Eve Cockburn. Index available (five-year index). cum. index. **Bk Rev**, (Qty: 70-80). **Circ:** 600.
Desc: Reports, short articles, annotated bibliography, news of members, queries, ect. in paleopathology.
Ind/Abst Br. Archaeol. Bibliogr.

LC GN855.M628 P35
ISSN 0153-9345
FR
CODEN PALEDX

PALEORIENT. [Paleorient]. **Added/Corp** Association Paleorient. Vol. 1 (1973)-. Periodical. English (French and German). Irregular. Price varies. Editions du CNRS, 22 rue Saint Armand, F 75015 Paris France. **Tel** 011 33 1 45075050, telex 200 356 F. **(Subscription address:** CNRS Editions, 20-22 rue Saint Amand, c/o Mme. Bodet, 75015 Paris France. **Tel** 011 33 1 45331600.) **Circ:** 1,500.
Desc: Multi-disciplinary journal of prehistory and protohistory of Southwest Asia.
Ind/Abst Anthropol. Lit.; Art Archaeol. Tech. Abstr.; GeoRef; Middle East Abstr. Index.

ISSN 0031-0328
UK

Pr Rev.
PALESTINE EXPLORATION QUARTERLY. Added/Corp Palestine Exploration Fund. Palestine Exploration Fund. Quarterly Statement. (Jan./March 1869)-. Periodical. English. Two times a year (May and November). £30.00. Palestine Exploration Fund, 2 Hinde Mews Marylebone Lane, London W1M 5RR United Kingdom. **Tel** 011 44 171 9355379. **ED** G.I. Davies. Index available (published separately). cum. index. **Bk Rev**, (Qty: 20-30). **Circ:** 900 (ctrl).
Desc: Covers history and archaeology of Palestine from ancient times until 1918.
Ind/Abst Abstr. Anthropol. (19??-); Anthropol. Index; Art Index; BHA : Biblio. Hist. Art; Index Book Rev. Relig.; Middle East Abstr. Index; New Testam. Abstr.; Numis. Lit.; Relig. Index One Period.; Relig. Theol. Abstr.

ISSN 0826-9971
CN

DD 069/.9971301
PALISADE POST. (THE PALISADE POST / MUSEUM OF INDIAN ARCHAEOLOGY (LONDON).). **Added/Corp** Museum of Indian Archaeology. Vol. 7, No. 1 (Dec. 1984)-. Periodical. English. Irregular. 6.00Can$. London Museum of Archaeology, 1600 Attawandaron Road, London Ontario N6A 3M6 Canada. **Tel** (519)473-1360.

ISSN 0031-0506
XR

PAMATKY ARCHEOLOGICKE. Added/Corp Archeologicky Ustav (Ceskoslovenska Akademie Ved). (19??)-. Periodical. Czech (summaries and/or abstracts in English, French, German and Russian; table of contents in English, German and Russian). Two times a year. $177.00. Veskoslovenska Akademie Ved, Archeologicky Ustav, Vodick 40, 11229 Prague 1 Czechoslovakia Republic. **(Subscription address:** Kubon & Sagner, ABT Zeitschriftenimport, D 80328 Munich Germany. **Tel** 011 49 89 54218130.) **ED** Josef Poulik and Karla Motykova. Index available. cum. index. **Bk Rev. Ad Acc.** ctrl circ.
Continues Pamatky Archeologicke a Mistopisne.
Desc: Basic studies on evolution in the prehistorical and earlier historical periods, methodical articles of a general character, studies dealing with recent research as well as museum collections.
Ind/Abst Anthropol. Index; Anthropol. Lit.; BHA : Biblio. Hist. Art.

LC DK508.3 .P27
ISSN 0131-2685
UN

PAMATNIKI UKRANI. See History-History of Europe.

ISSN 0965-9315
UK

PAPERS FROM THE INSTITUTE OF ARCHAEOLOGY. [Pap. Inst. Archaeol.]. (1990)-. English. One time a year. $8.55. Institute of Archaeology / London, 31-34 Gordon Square, London WC1H 0PY United Kingdom. **Tel** 011 44 171 3879651.

ISSN 0706-0475
CN

PAPERS IN MANITOBA ARCHAEOLOGY. FINAL REPORT. No. 1 (1976)-. Monographic series. English. Price varies per volume. Department of Tourism Recreation & Cultural Affairs, Historic Resources Branch, 1981 Portage Avenue, Winnpeg Man. R3J 0J9 Canada.

ISSN 0706-0505
CN

PAPERS IN MANITOBA ARCHAEOLOGY. POPULAR SERIES. No. 1 (1976)-. Monographic series. English. Price varies per volume. Manitoba Department of Tourism, Recreation and Cultural Affairs, Historic Resources Branch, 1981 Portage Avenue, Winnpeg Man. R3J 0J9.

LC F1062.9 .P36
ISSN 0706-0491
DD 971.27
CN

PAPERS IN MANITOBA ARCHAEOLOGY. PRELIMINARY REPORT. No. 1 (1976)-. Monographic series. English. Price varies per volume. Department of Tourism, Recreation and Cultural Affairs, 1981 Portage Avenue, Winnipeg Man. R3J 0J9.

ISSN 0587-1719
DD 978
US

PAPERS OF THE ARCHAEOLOGICAL SOCIETY OF NEW MEXICO. [Pap. Archaeol. Soc. N.M.]. **Main/Corp** Archaeological Society of New Mexico. (1968)-. Monographic series. English. One time a year. Price varies per volume. Archaeological Society of New Mexico, PO Box 3485, Albuquerque NM 87110. **ED** Melina S Duran and David T Kirkpatrick. **Circ:** 400.
Absorbed Supplement - Archaeological Society of New Mexico, 0731-9762.
Desc: Presents collected papers on archaeology, ethnology or anthropology of the Southwest, especially of New Mexico, frequently on a single theme and honoring notable scientists.
Ind/Abst Ethnoarts Index.

LC DG12 .B85
ISSN 0068-2462
UK

Pr Rev.
PAPERS OF THE BRITISH SCHOOL AT ROME. See Humanities.

LC F1219 .N475
ISSN 0077-8915
DD 970/.004/97 S
US

PAPERS OF THE NEW WORLD ARCHAEOLOGICAL FOUNDATION. Main/Corp New World Archaeological Foundation. (1959)-. Monographic series. English. Irregular. Price varies per volume. New World Archaeological Foundation, Brigham Young University, Provo UT 84602. **Tel** (801)378-4971.
Ind/Abst Ethnoarts Index.

LC E51 .H337
ISSN 0079-0303
DD 913
US
CODEN HPAEAQ

PAPERS OF THE PEABODY MUSEUM OF ARCHAEOLOGY AND ETHNOLOGY, HARVARD UNIVERSITY. [Pap. Peabody Mus. Archaeol. Ethnol. Harv. Univ.]. **Added/Corp** Peabody Museum of Archaeology and Ethnology. **VFOAT** Peabody Museum Papers. Vol. 49, No. 2 (1954)-. Monographic series. English. Irregular. Price varies per volume. Harvard University Press, 79 Garden Street, Cambridge MA 02138. **Tel** (617)496-1344, (800)448-2242. Documents available from BIOSIS Document Express. *Continues* Papers of the Peabody Museum of American Archaeology and Ethnology, Harvard University.
Ind/Abst Biol. Abstr.; GeoRef.

IT

PAPIRI. Main/Corp Milan. Universita. Istituto di Papirogogia. Vol. 1 (19??)-. Periodical. Italian. Irregular. L85000 (Volume 7). Cisalpino IST Edit Universitar, via Ferrarese 119 2, 40128 Bologna Italy. **Tel** 011 39 51 370337.

NE

PAPYROLOGICA LUGDUNO-BATAVA. Added/Corp Leyden. Rijksuniversiteit. Papyrologisch Istituut. (1941)-. Monographic series. Dutch (French). Irregular. Price varies per volume. E.J. Brill, Postbus 9000, 2300 PA Leiden The Netherlands. **Tel** 011 31 71 312624, FAX 011 31 71 317532, telex 39296 BRILL NL.

LC DA670.S97 S967
UK

●**PAST & PRESENT : THE SUSSEX ARCHAEOLOGICAL SOCIETY NEWSLETTER. Added/Corp** Sussex Archaeological Society. **VFOAT** Past and Present; Sussex Archaeological Society Newsletter. No. 71 (Dec. 1993)-. Newsletter. English. Three times a year. comes with membership. Sussex Archaeological Society, Barbican House, High Street, Lewes BN7 1YE United Kingdom. **Tel** 011 44 171 474379. *Continues* SAS News.

ISSN 0245-8411
FR

PAYS D'ALSACE. See History-History of Europe.

ISSN 0031-3394
FR

PAYS LORRAIN, LE. See History-History of Europe.

Archaeology

LC E78.P4 P5
DD 913.748
ISSN 0031-4358
US
CODEN PEARA8
Pr Rev.

PENNSYLVANIA ARCHAEOLOGIST. [Pa. archaeol.]. **Added/Corp** Society for Pennsylvania Archaeology. (1932)-. Periodical. English. Two times a year. Comes with membership to Society for Pennsylvania Archaeology - $18.00. Society for Pennsylvania Archaeology, PO Box 386, Bethlehem CT 06751. **Tel** (203)266-7741. **ED** Ron Michael. **Bk Rev. Circ:** 800 (ctrl). *Continues* Bulletin of the Society for Pennsylvania Archaeology, 0742-9479.
 Desc: Archaeological excavation, analysis, and interpretation relevant to the cultures of Pennsylvania.
 Ind/Abst Abstr. Anthropol. (19??-); Am. Hist. Life (1970-1971, 1986-); Anthropol. Lit.; Ceram. Abstr. (1970-1971); Ethnoarts Index.

LC DS156.P4 P4
DD 913
ISSN 0418-968X
GW

PERGAMENISCHE FORSCHUNGEN / DEUTSCHES ARCHAEOLOGISCHES INSTITUT. **Added/Corp** Deutsches Archaeologisches Institut. **VFOAT** PF. Vol. 1 (1968)-. Monographic series. German. Irregular. Price varies per volume. Walter de Gruyter Inc., PO Box 303421, D-10728 Berlin Germany. **Tel** 011 49 30 260050, FAX 011 49 30 26005251, telex 184027.

LC DS56 .P47
DD 913.39
NE

PHOENIX. **Added/Corp** Vooraziatisch-Egyptisch Genootschap Ex Oriente Lux. Vol. 1 (1955)-. Periodical. Dutch. Two times a year. $54.81. Ex Oriente Lux, Postbus 9515, 2300 RA Leiden Netherlands. **Tel** 011 31 71 272016. **ED** L M J Zonhoven. **Bk Rev. Circ:** 1,400.

LC GN814.P6 P62
ISSN 0556-0691
PL
SUSPENDED

POMORANIA ANTIQUA. **Added/Corp** Muzeum Archeologiczne (Gdansk, Poland). (196?)-Suspended with Vol. 14 (1990). Academic Scholarly Publication. Polish (summaries and/or abstracts in English). Polska Akademia Nauk / Zaklad Narodowy im. Ossolinskich, Ossolineum Publishing House of the Polish Academy of Sciences, Ulitsa Rynek 9, 50-106 Wroclaw Poland. **Tel** 011 48 71 38625, FAX 011 48 71 448103, telex 0712771. **(Subscription address:** Ars Polona-Ruch, PO Box 1001, Krakowskie Przedmiescie 7, 00-068 Warsaw Poland. **Tel** 011 48 22 261201.) *Continues* Pomerania Antiqua.
 Desc: Material culture from ancient Pomerania.
 Ind/Abst BHA : Biblio. Hist. Art.

LC DR211 .P65
DD 939/.51
RM

PONTICA. **Added/Corp** Muzeul de Arheologie Constanta. **VFOAT** Acta Musei Tomitani. (1968)-. French (German and Romanian; summaries and/or abstracts in English). One time a year. *Supersedes* Pontice.
 Ind/Abst BHA : Biblio. Hist. Art.

LC CC1 .P63
DD 913/.031/05
ISSN 0300-774X
US

POPULAR ARCHAEOLOGY. Vol. 1 (Aug. 1972)-. Periodical. English. Six times a year. $15.95 North America; $17.95 other. Life and Lettres Publishers, PO Box 11256, Alexandria VA 22312. **Bk Rev. Ad Acc. Circ:** 1,500 (ctrl). available on microfilm.
 Ind/Abst Ceram. Abstr.

US

POPULAR ARCHAEOLOGY. TECHNICAL PUBLICATION. **VFOAT** Technical Publication. (1979)-. Monographic series. English. Irregular. Price varies per volume. Life and Lettres Publishers, PO Box 11256, Alexandria VA 22312. **ED** W. Jack Hranicky. **Bk Rev. Ad Acc. Circ:** 1,500 (ctrl). available on microfilm.
 Desc: Worldwide archaeology with a focus on American prehistory and artifacts.

LC DR1371 .P67
XV

POROCILO O RAZISKOVANJU PALEOLITA, NEOLITA IN ENEOLITA V SLOVENIJI / UNIVERZA V LJUBLJANI, ARHEOLOSKI ODDELEK FILOZOSKE FAKULTETE. **Added/Corp** Univerza v Ljubljani. Arheoloski Oddelek. Univerza Edvarda Kardelja v Ljubljani. Arheoloski Oddelek. (1976)-. Slovenian (summaries and/or abstracts in English, German and Slovenian). *Continues* Porocilo o Raziskovanju Neolita in Eneolita v Sloveniji.
 Ind/Abst Anthropol. Lit.

LC DA90 .P67
DD 914.2/03
ISSN 0079-4236
UK

POST-MEDIEVAL ARCHAEOLOGY. [Post-mediev. archaeol.]. **Added/Corp** Society for Post-Medieval Archaeology. Vol. 1 (1967)-. English. Three times a year (publishes in Spring / Newsletter publishes two times per year). $48.00. Society for Post-Medieval Archaeology, 20 Lytton Road, Clarendon Park, Leicester L32 1WJ United Kingdom. **Tel** 011 44 116 2707999. cum. index.
 Ind/Abst Avery Index Archit. Period. Suppl. Colum. Univ. (1989); BHA : Biblio. Hist. Art.

ISSN 0738-8020
US

POTTERY SOUTHWEST. *See* Glass and Ceramics.

ISSN 0458-1520
PL

PRACE I MATERIALY MUZEUM ARCHEOLOGICZNEGO I ETNOGRAFICZNEGO W LODZI. SERIA ARCHEOLOGICZNA. **Main/Corp** Muzeum Archeologiczne i Etnograficzne w Lodzi. No. 1 (1956)-. Monographic series. Polish (summaries and/or abstracts in English). Irregular. Price varies per volume. Muzeum Archeologiczne i Etnograficzne w Lodzi, Pl. Wonosci 14, 91-415 Lodz Poland. **(Subscription address:** Ars Polona-Ruch, PO Box 1001, Krakowskie Przedmiescie 7, 00-068 Warsaw Poland. **Tel** 011 48 22 261201.) **Circ:** 500.
 Ind/Abst Anthropol. Lit.; BHA : Biblio. Hist. Art.

LC DS493 .P68
NP

PRACINA NEPALA : [PURATATTVA VIBHAGAKO MUKHAPATRA]. **Added/Corp** Nepal. Puratattva Vibhaga. **VFOAT** Ancient Nepal. No. 1 (Oct. 1967)-. Periodical. English (Nepali). Four times a year.
 Ind/Abst Avery Index Archit. Period. Suppl. Colum. Univ. (1984, 1986, 1988-1989).

GW

PRAHISTORISCHE BRONZEFUNDE. (19??)-. Monographic series. German. Irregular. Price varies per volume. Franz Steiner Verlag GmbH, Postfach 101061, D-70009 Stuttgart Germany. **Tel** 011 49 711 2582372, FAX 011 49 711 2582290, telex 723636 daz d. **(Subscription address:** Brockhaus Commission, Kreidlerstrasse 9, D-70806 Kornwestheim Germany. **Tel** 011 49 7154 13270.) **ED** Albrecht Jockenhovel, Wolf Kubach.
 Ind/Abst Br. Archaeol. Bibliogr.

ISSN 1105-0969
GR

PRAKTIKA TES EN ATHENAIS ARCHAIOLOGIKES HETAIREIAS. **Added/Corp** Archaiologike Hetaireia. (19??)-. Greek, Modern. One time a year. Athenais Archaiologikes Hetaireias / Athens Archaeology Society, 22 Panepistimiou Street, Athens Greece 10672. **Tel** 011 30 1 3600583.
 Ind/Abst BHA : Biblio. Hist. Art.

LC GN803.A1 P7
BE

PREHISTOIRE EUROPEENNE = EUROPEAN PREHISTORY. **Added/Corp** Universite de Liege. Service de Prehistoire. **VFOAT** European Prehistory; Revue de Prehistoire Europeene. Vol. 1 (Sept. 1992)-. Academic Scholarly Publication. English (French). Irregular. $41.05. University of Liege Service Prehistorie, 7 PL du 20 AOUT, BAT A1, 4000 Leige, Belgium. **Tel** 011 32 41 665341.

LC E77.8 .R42
DD 930
ISSN 1060-0965
US

PREHISTORIC AMERICA. *See* The Arts-Art.

IT

PREISTORIA ALPINA. **Added/Corp** Museo Tridentino di Scienze Naturali. (19??)-. Italian (English, French and German). One time a year. L17040. Museo Tridentino di Scienze Naturali Trento, Via Calepina 14, 38100 Trento Italy. **Tel** 011 39 461 270311. Index available. cum. index. **Circ:** 1,000.
 Desc: Concerned with North Italian prehistory.
 Ind/Abst Anthropol. Lit.

LC NX
DD 700
ISSN 0079-5208
US

PRINCETON MONOGRAPHS IN ART AND ARCHAEOLOGY. *See* The Arts-Art.

SZ

PRO CALIMA : PERIODISCHE PUBLIKATION DER VEREINIGUNG PRO CALIMA. Vol. 1 (Oct. 1980)-. English (summaries and/or abstracts in French and German). Free. Frau Ursula Kubli, Hubel, CH-3038 Kirchlindach Switzerland.
 Ind/Abst Anthropol. Lit.

US

PROCEEDINGS / AMERICAN SOCIETY FOR CONSERVATION ARCHAEOLOGY. **Main/Corp** American Society for Conservation Archaeology. (1976)-. Proceedings. English. One time a year. American Society Conservation Archaeology, 711 Rimrock, Billings MT 59102.
 Ind/Abst Anthropol. Lit.

ISSN 0305-5795
UK
Pr Rev.

PROCEEDINGS - DEVON ARCHAEOLOGICAL SOCIETY. [Proc. - Devon archaeol. soc.]. (1967)-. Academic Scholarly Publication. English. One time a year. £9.00. Devon Archaeological Society, R A M Museum, Queen Street, Exeter EX43RX United Kingdom. **ED** John Allan. **Circ:** 950. Documents available from BLDSC. *Continues* Proceedings - Devon Archaeological Exploration Society.
 Desc: Annual proceedings. Publishes final reports on excavations, topographical studies, artifact studies, and building analysis relating to Devon, England.
 Ind/Abst BHA : Biblio. Hist. Art.

LC DA670.D69 D6
ISSN 0070-7112
UK

PROCEEDINGS - DORSET NATURAL HISTORY AND ARCHAEOLOGICAL SOCIETY. *See* Natural History.

ISSN 1065-1233
US
Pr Rev.

PROCEEDINGS / EASTERN GREAT LAKES AND MIDWEST BIBLICAL SOCIETIES. [Proc. - East. Gt. Lake Biblic. Soc.]. **Main/Corp** Eastern Great Lakes Biblical Society. **Added/Corp** Society of Biblical Literature. Mid-West Region. Vol. 1 (1981)-. Proceedings. English. One time a year (January). $9.00. Canisius College, 2001 Main Street, Buffalo NY 14208. **Tel** (716)888-2822, (716)883-7000, FAX (716)888-2525. **ED** Terrance Callan. **Bk Rev,** (Qty: 2). **Ad Acc, Adv Mgr:** Benjamin Fiore. **Circ:** 100.
 Desc: Journal of biblical studies selected from papers given at the annual meetings of the Eastern Great Lakes and Midwest Biblical Societies.

ISSN 0142-8950
UK

PROCEEDINGS OF THE HAMPSHIRE FIELD CLUB AND ARCHAEOLOGICAL SOCIETY. [Proc. Hamps. Field Club Archaeol. Soc.]. **VFOAT** Proceedings of the Hampshire Field Club. (1958)-. Proceedings. English. One time a year. *Continues* Papers and Proceedings of the Hampshire Field Club and Archaeological Society.
 Ind/Abst Anthropol. Lit.; BHA : Biblio. Hist. Art; Br. Archaeol. Bibliogr.; Numis. Lit. (?-?).

LC CT93
DD 920
ISSN 0035-8991
IE

PROCEEDINGS OF THE ROYAL IRISH ACADEMY. SECTION C. ARCHAEOLOGY, CELTIC STUDIES, HISTORY, LINGUISTICS AND LITERATURE. [Proc. R. Ir. Acad., Section C Archaeol. Celt. stud. hist. linguist. lit.]. **Main/Corp** Royal Irish Academy. Vol. 68 (1969)-. Proceedings. English. Irregular. Price varies. Royal Irish Academy, 19 Dawson Street, Dublin 2 Ireland. **Tel** 011 353 1 762570. **ED** B Young. Index available. cum. index. **Circ:** 600. available with illustrations; available with charts. Documents available from The Genuine Article. *Continues* Royal Irish Academy. Proceedings of the Royal Irish Academy. Section C. Archaeology, Linguistics and Literature.
 Ind/Abst Am. Hist. Life; Anthropol. Index; Arts Humanit. Citation Index (19??-19??) [Full Cov.]; BHA : Biblio. Hist. Art; Res. Alert [Full Cov.].

LC F863 .S63A
DD 979.4/01
ISSN 0897-0947
US

PROCEEDINGS OF THE SOCIETY FOR CALIFORNIA ARCHAEOLOGY. (PROCEEDINGS OF THE SOCIETY FOR CALIFORNIA ARCHAEOLOGY : PAPERS PRESENTED AT THE ANNUAL MEETING OF THE SOCIETY FOR CALIFORNIA ARCHAEOLOGY.). [Proc. Soc. Calif. Archaeol.]. **Main/Corp** Society for California Archaeology. Meeting. Vol. 1 (1988)-. Proceedings. English. One time a year. $10.00. Society for California Archaeology, 1276 Morena Boulevard, San Diego CA 92110.
 Ind/Abst Anthropol. Lit.

ISSN 0262-6004
UK

PROCEEDINGS OF THE SUFFOLK INSTITUTE OF ARCHAEOLOGY AND HISTORY. **Main/Corp** Suffolk Institute of Archaeology and History. Vol. 34 (1977)-. Proceedings. English. One time a year. $25.67. Suffolk Institute of Archaeology and History, Ampners Little Green Thrandest, Suffolk 1P21 4BX United Kingdom. **Tel** 011 44 1362 037983. *Continues* Proceedings of the Suffolk Institute of Archaeology.
 Ind/Abst BHA : Biblio. Hist. Art.

Archaeology

PROCEEDINGS - UNIVERSITY OF BRISTOL SPELAEOLOGICAL SOCIETY. See Earth Sciences-Geophysics.
ISSN 0373-7527
CODEN SPOPBD
UK

PROFILE, THE. Added/Corp Society for Georgia Archaeology. No. 13 (Sept. 1976)-. Periodical. English. Four times a year. $30.00 (institutions), $15.00 (individuals) Comes with Georgia Archaeology membership. Society of Georgia Archaeology, 2909 Chesterfield Way, Conyers GA 30208. **Tel** (404)922-2131. **ED** David Allison. **Circ:** 175 (ctrl). *Continues* Newsletter of the Society for Georgia Archaeology.
US

LC N4 .P76
DD 705
ISSN 0394-0802
IT

PROSPETTIVA. See The Arts-Art.

LC CC1 .P966
IT
SUSPENDED

PROSPEZIONI ARCHEOLOGICHE QUADERNI. Added/Corp Fondazione Lerici. **VFOAT** Quaderni di Prospezioni Archeologiche; Prospezioni Archeologiche/Quaderni. (1990)-(1990). Periodical. English (Italian). One time a year. Fondazione Lerici Prospezioni Archeologiche, Vie V Veneto 108, 00187 Rome Italy. *Continues* Prospezioni Archeologiche, 0079-7022.

LC DC611.P9795 S6
DD 944/.37
ISSN 0399-0508
FR

PROVINS ET SA REGION : BULLETIN DE LA SOCIETE D'HISTOIRE ET D'ARCHEOLOGIE DE PROVINS. Added/Corp Societe d'Histoire et d'Archeologie de l'Arrondissement de Provins. **VFOAT** Bulletin. (19??)-. Bulletin. French. One time a year. Price varies. M Jean-Marie Deforge, 1 rue Max-Michelin, 77160 Provins C C P Paris 6648-04 U Paris France. *Continues* Bulletin de la Societe d'Histoire et d'Archeologie de l'Arrondissement de Provins.
Ind/Abst BHA : Biblio. Hist. Art.

LC DS409 .P7
ISSN 0079-7138
PL

PRZEGLAD ARCHEOLOGICZNY. Added/Corp Polskie Towarzystwo Prehistoryczne. Polskie Towarzystwo Archeologiczne. Instytut Historii Kultury Materialnej (Polska Akademia Nauk). (1919)-. Monographic series. Polish (English and German; summaries and/or abstracts in French; table of contents in French). Irregular. Price varies per volume. Polska Akademia Nauk / Instytut Historii Kultury Materialnej, Al. Solidarnosci 105, 00-140 Warsaw Poland. **(Subscription address:** Ars Polona-Ruch, PO Box 1001, Krakowskie Przedmiescie 7, 00-068 Warsaw Poland. **Tel** 011 48 22 261201.) **Bk Rev. Circ:** 500.
Desc: Material culture in Poland and the rest of Europe.
Ind/Abst Anthropol. Index; Anthropol. Lit.; BHA : Biblio. Hist. Art.

DD 930
ISSN 1075-3737
US

●**PUBLIC ARCHAEOLOGY REVIEW.** (PUBLIC ARCHAEOLOGY REVIEW / CENTER FOR ARCHAEOLOGY IN THE PUBLIC INTEREST.). [Public archaeol. rev.]. **Added/Corp** Center for Archaeology in the Public Interest. Vol. 1, No. 1 (Fall 1993)-. Periodical. English. Irregular. $20.00. Center for Archaeology, 425 University Blvd, Anthropology Department, Indianapolis IN 46202. **Tel** (317)274-1406.

CN

PUBLICATION. Added/Corp Simon Fraser University. Dept. of Archaeology. **VFOAT** Department of Archaeology Publications. (1972)-. Monographic series. English. Irregular. Price varies per volume. Simon Fraser University Department of Archaeology, Burnaby BC V5A 1S6 Canada. **Tel** (604)291-3135.

BE

PUBLICATIONS. Main/Corp Louvain. Universite Catholique. Section d'Archeologie et d'Historie de l'Art. (1970)-. Periodical. Irregular. Universite Catholique de Louvain / Academie Erasme, Grand rue 25 115, B-1348 Louvain La Neuve Belgium. **Tel** 011 32 10 452395. **ED** Tony Hackens. **Bk Rev. Circ:** 3,000 (ctrl).

ISSN 0076-0986
US

PUBLICATIONS. Main/Corp Los Angeles. Southwest Museum. Frederick Webb Hodge Anniversary Publication Fund. Vol. 1 (1937)-. English. Southwest Museum, PO Box 41558, Los Angeles CA 90041. **Tel** (213)221-2164. **ED** Steven A. LeBlanc.
Desc: Occasional publications on topics of interest to scholars of Native American history and prehistory.

DD 973
ISSN 8755-5743
US

PUBLICATIONS IN ARCHAEOLOGY (COLUMBIA, MO.). (PUBLICATIONS IN ARCHAEOLOGY.). [Publ. archaeol.]. No. 1-. Monographic series. English. Irregular. Price varies per volume. American Archaeology Division, Department of Anthropology, Switzer Hall/Room 15, University of Missouri, Columbia MO 65211.

ISSN 0712-4260
CN

PUBLICATIONS IN ARCHAEOLOGY (OTTAWA). (PUBLICATIONS IN ARCHAEOLOGY.). [Publ. archaeol.]. **Main/Corp** National Museum of Man. **VAT** Publications d'Archeologie. Monographic series. English (summaries and/or abstracts in French). Irregular. Price varies per volume. McClelland and Stewart Ltd, 25 Hollinger Road, Toronto Ontario M4B 3G2 Canada.

LC DA670.Y59 T4
DD 942.8/19
ISSN 0082-4232
UK

PUBLICATIONS OF THE THORESBY SOCIETY. Main/Corp Thoresby Society. **Added/Corp** Thoresby Society. (1889)-. Monographic series. English. Irregular. Price varies per volume. Thoresby Society, 23 Clarendon Road, Leeds LS2 9NZ United Kingdom. cum. index.
Ind/Abst Br. Archaeol. Bibliogr.

LC DS498 .P87
DD 954.799
II

PURABHILEKH-PURATATVA : JOURNAL OF THE DIRECTORATE OF ARCHIVES, ARCHAEOLOGY AND MUSEUM, PANAJI-GOA. Added/Corp Goa, Daman and Diu (India). Directorate of Archives, Archaeology, and Museum. **VFOAT** Purabhilekh Puratatva. Vol. 1, No. 1 (July-Dec. 1983)-. Periodical. English (Marathi and Portuguese). Two times a year. Rs25.00. Directorate of Archives Archaeology and Museum, rua de Ourem, Panaji-Goa 403001 India. **ED** P.P. Shirodkar. **Bk Rev. Circ:** 700 (ctrl).
Desc: Covers Indo-Portuguese history in original documents and articles, Portuguese palaeography, Modi (Marathi) documents, church and temple architecture, Goan archaeology, museums and museum objects.

ISSN 0970-2105
II

UDC 571

PURATATTVA NEW DELHI. [Puratattva New Delhi]. (1967)-. Periodical. English. One time a year. Price varies. DK Agencies, A 15 17 Mohan Garden Najaf Road, New Delhi 110059 India. **Tel** 011 91 11 5598899. **(Subscription address:** Prints India, 11 Darya Ganj, New Delhi 110002 India. **Tel** 011 91 11 3268645, FAX 011 91 11 3275542, telex 31-61087 PRIN-IN.)
Desc: Bulletin of the Indian Archaeological Society.
Ind/Abst Anthropol. Lit.

ISSN 0079-8215
SP

PYRENAE. [Pyrenae]. **Added/Corp** Universidad de Barcelona. Instituto de Arqueologia y Prehistoria. (1965)-. Spanish. One time a year. 2000ptas. University of Barcelona / Just Arquelogia, Avenue de Jose Antonio, 585 Barcelona Spain.
Ind/Abst Am. Hist. Life (1966-); BHA : Biblio. Hist. Art.

LC DS111.A1 I812
ISSN 0033-4839
IS

QADMONIOT. (KADMONIYOT.). [Qadmoniot]. Vol. 1, No. 1/2 (1968)-. Periodical. Hebrew. Four times a year. $23.00. Israel Exploration Society, 5 Avida Street, 91070 Jerusalem Israel. **Tel** 011 972 2 227991. **ED** E Stern. Index available. cum. index. **Bk Rev. Circ:** 5,000 (ctrl). available in microform; available on CD-ROM.
Supersedes Yediot (Hevrah Ha-Ivrit Le-Hakirat Erets-Yisrael Ve-Atikoteha).
Desc: Includes articles on ancient history, biblical archaeology, preliminary excavation reports, special discoveries and finds.
Ind/Abst Middle East Abstr. Index; New Testam. Abstr.; Old Testam. Abstr.; Relig. Theol. Abstr.

Pr Rev.
IS

QEDEM MONOGRAPHS OF THE INSTITUTE OF ARCHAEOLOGY. (1975)-. Monographic series. English. Three times a year. Price varies per volume. Israel Exploration Society, 5 Avida Street, 91070 Jerusalem Israel. **Tel** 011 972 2 227991. **Circ:** 1,500.
Desc: Series of monographs on archaeology, biblical archaeology and reports on excavations.

IT

QUADERNI D'ARCHEOLOGIA REGGIANA / SOCIETA REGGIANA D'ARCHEOLOGIA. Added/Corp Societa Reggiana d'Archeologia. (1970)-. Periodical. Italian.
Ind/Abst BHA : Biblio. Hist. Art.

IT

QUADERNI DEI DIALOGHI DI ARCHEOLOGIA. VFOAT Quaderni di Dialoghi di Archeologia. Monographic series. Italian. Price varies per volume. Edizioni Quasar Severino Togno, via Quattro Novembre 152, 00187 Rome Italy. **Tel** 011 39 6 6789888, 011 39 6 6796522.

ISSN 0393-6821
IT

QUADERNI DELL'ISTITUTO DI ARCHEOLOGIA E STORIA ANTICA. Added/Corp Universita "G. D'Annunzio." Istituto di Archeologia e Storia Antica. (1980)-. Periodical. Italian (summaries and/or abstracts in English). One time a year. Price varies. Viella SRL, Via delle Alpi 32, 00198 Rome Italy. **Tel** 011 39 6 8417758.
Ind/Abst BHA : Biblio. Hist. Art.

LC CC
DD 930.1
ISSN 0079-8258
IT

QUADERNI DI ARCHEOLOGIA DELLA LIBIA. Added/Corp Italy. Ministero dell'Africa Italiana. Ufficio Studi. (1950)-. Monographic series. Italian. Price varies per volume. L'Erma di Bretschneider SPA, via Cassiodoro 19, 00193 Rome Italy. **Tel** 011 39 6 6874127, 011 39 6 6874129, FAX 011 39 6 6874129. **Bk Rev. Ad Acc. Circ:** 500.
Ind/Abst BHA : Biblio. Hist. Art.

ISSN 0211-478X
SP

QUADERNS D'ARQUEOLOGIA I HISTORIA DE LA CIUTAT. Added/Corp Seminari d'Investigacio "A. Duran i Sanpere.". No. 18 (1980)-. Periodical. Catalan. *Continues* Cuadernos de Arqueologia e Historia de la Ciudad.
Ind/Abst BHA : Biblio. Hist. Art.

LC F221 .A672
DD 913.755 975.5
ISSN 0003-8202
US

QUARTERLY BULLETIN - ARCHEOLOGICAL SOCIETY OF VIRGINIA. Main/Corp Archeological Society of Virginia. Vol. 1 (Jan./Mar. 1942)-. Bulletin. English. Four times a year. $15.00. Archeological Society of Virginia, PO Box 340, Courtland VA 23837. **ED** Paul Y Inashima (editor's address: 11512 Ialewood Road, Silver Spring MD 20906). cum. index. **Circ:** 800 (ctrl). available on microfiche.
Desc: Virginia prehistoric and historic archeology expressed by description of projects, theoretical analysis, and historic research.
Ind/Abst Am. Hist. Life (1986-); Anthropol. Lit.

LC DS489.1 .Q37
DD 934
CE

QUARTERLY OF THE CULTURAL TRIANGLE. Added/Corp Central Cultural Fund (Sri Lanka). Vol. 1 (Dec. 1983)-. Periodical. English. Four times a year. Central Cultural Fund Office, 212 Bauddhaloka Mawatha, Colombo Sri Lanka.

ISSN 0814-3021
AT

Pr Rev.

QUEENSLAND ARCHAEOLOGICAL RESEARCH. Added/Corp University of Queensland. Dept. of Anthropology and Sociology. **VFOAT** QAR. Vol. 1 (1984)-. English. One time a year. 20.00Aus$ (Australia); 24.50Aus$ (other). University of Queensland / Anthropology and Sociology Department, St. Lucia BC Brisbane Australia. **Tel** 011 61 7 3773111, FAX 011 61 7 3651544, telex 40315. **ED** H J Hall. **Circ:** 250.
Ind/Abst Anthropol. Lit.; APAIS, Aust. Public Aff. Inf. Ser.

LC F3169 .R37
DD 930
Pr Rev.
ISSN 1040-1385
US

RAPA NUI JOURNAL. [Rapa nui j.]. **Added/Corp** Easter Island Foundation. (198?)-. Periodical. English (Spanish and French). Four times a year (Mar., June, Oct., Dec.). $25.00. Rapa Nui Journal, Box 6774, Los Osos CA 93412. **Tel** (805)528-6279, FAX (805)534-9301. **ED** Georgia Lee and Frank Morin. Index available. cum. index. **Bk Rev. (Qty: varies). Ad Acc. Circ:** 500.
Continues Rapa Nui Notes, 0890-2097.
Desc: Covers current Easter Island events and scientific studies.

BU

RAZKOPKI I PROUCHVANIIA. FOUILLES ET RECHERCHES. Main/Corp Naroden Arkheologicheski Muzei. **VFOAT** Fouilles et

Archaeology

Recherches. (1948)-. Periodical. Bulgarian (summaries and/or abstracts in French; table of contents in French).
Ind/Abst Anthropol. Lit.

GW

REALLEXIKON DER ASSYRIOLOGIE UND VORDERASIATISCHEN ARCHEOLOGIE. (19??)-. German. Walter de Gruyter Inc., PO Box 303421, D-10728 Berlin Germany. **Tel** 011 49 30 260050, FAX 011 49 30 26005251, telex 184027.

UK

RECORD SERIES / YORKSHIRE ARCHAEOLOGICAL SOCIETY. Main/Corp Yorkshire Archaeological Society. Vol. 14 (1893)-. Periodical. English. One time a year. $25.67. Yorkshire Archaeological Society, Claremont Clarendon Road, Leeds LS2 9NZ United Kingdom. **Tel** 011 44 1532 457910. **Continues** Record Series.

ISSN 0967-2885
UK

RECORDS OF BUCKINGHAMSHIRE, OR, PAPERS AND NOTES ON THE HISTORY, ANTIQUITIES, AND ARCHITECTURE OF THE COUNTY, TOGETHER WITH THE PROCEEDINGS OF THE ARCHITECTURAL AND ARCHAEOLOGICAL SOCIETY FOR THE COUNTY OF BUCKINGHAM. See Architecture.

ISSN 0521-4785
HU

UDC 902
REGESZETI DOLGOZATOK. VFOAT Dissertationes Archaeologicae. (1958)-. English. One time a year.
Ind/Abst BHA : Biblio. Hist. Art.

ISSN 0894-5217
DD 621 US

REMOTE SENSING NEWSLETTER IN ANTHROPOLOGY AND ARCHAEOLOGY. See Anthropology.

LC DS111.A1 B893a
DD 913/.031/071156944 UK

REPORT AND ACCOUNTS. Main/Corp British School of Archaeology in Jerusalem. (19??)-. English. One time a year. British School of Archaeology / United Kingdom, 21 Buccleuch Place, University of Edinburgh, Edinburgh EH8 9LN United Kingdom. **Tel** 011 44 131 6503975, FAX 011 44 131 6503975. **Circ:** 500 (ctrl).

ISSN 0589-9208
UK

REPORT - COUNCIL FOR BRITISH ARCHAEOLOGY. Main/Corp Council for British Archaeology, London. (1???). Academic Scholarly Publication. English. One time a year. £8.00. Council for British Archaeology, Bowes Morrell House, 111 Walmgate, York YO1 2UA United Kingdom. **Tel** 011 44 1904 671417, FAX 011 44 1904 671384. **ED** R. U. Morris. **Circ:** 2,000. Documents available from Documents on Demand, FAXON Xpress.
Ind/Abst Br. Archaeol. Bibliogr.

US

REPORT OF INVESTIGATIONS / NEW WORLD RESEARCH. Added/Corp New World Research, Inc. (1977)-. Monographic series. English. Four times a year. Price varies per volume. New World Research Inc, PO Box 4246, Ft Walton Beach FL 32549-4246. **Tel** (904)243-5992. **Ad Acc.** ctrl circ.
Desc: Results of archaeological investigation for CRM with emphasis on interpretation of cultural patterns.

US

REPORT - OFFICE OF STATE ARCHAEOLOGIST. Main/Corp Iowa. Office of State Archaeologist. No. 1 (1970)-. Monographic series. English. Irregular. Price varies per volume. University of Iowa / Publications Order Department, Oakdale Hall, Iowa City IA 52242. **Tel** (319)335-4589, FAX (319)335-4039. **Circ:** 500 (ctrl).
Desc: Contains results of archaeological research pertaining to Iowa and the midwestern United States.

LC DS11 .C43 ISSN 0577-3199
DD 913.34 IT

REPORTS AND MEMOIRS. Main/Corp Centro Scavi E Ricerche Archeologiche in Asia Dell'Is. M.E.O. E di Torino. Vol. 1 (1962)-. Monographic series. Italian (Italian). Irregular. Price varies per volume. **Bk Rev.**
Desc: Monographic series on excavations of ISMEO in Afghanistan, Iran and Pakistan.

LC CC ISSN 0330-843X
DD 930.1 TI

REPPAL. Added/Corp Markaz al-Dirasat al-Finiqiyah al-Buniyah wa-al-Athar al-Lubiyah. **VFOAT** Revue des Etudes Pheniciennes-Puniques et des Antiquites Libyques; Majallat al-Dirasat al-Finiqiyah al-Buniyah wa-al-Athar al-Lubiyah. (1985)-. French (Arabic). One time a year.
Ind/Abst BHA : Biblio. Hist. Art.

ISSN 0950-5830
UK

RESCUE NEWS. (1972)-. Periodical. English. Three times a year. £8.00 (schools and individuals), £10.00 (institutions). Rescue British Archaeological Trust, 15A Bull Plain, Hertford Hert SG14 1DX United Kingdom. **Tel** 011 44 1992 553377. **ED** Hedley Swain. **Bk Rev. Ad Acc. Circ:** 1,200.
Desc: Articles , illustrations, and information about British rescue archaeology.

US

RESEARCH MANUSCRIPT SERIES - INSTITUTE OF ARCHEOLOGY AND ANTHROPOLOGY, UNIVERSITY OF SOUTH CAROLINA. Main/Corp University of South Carolina. Institute of Archeology and Anthropology. (19??)-. Monographic series. English. Irregular. Price varies per volume. University of South Carolina / Institute of Archeology & Anthropology, Columbia SC 29208. **Tel** (803)777-8170. **ED** Kenn Pinson. **Circ:** 3,500 (ctrl).
Desc: Disseminates prehistoric and historic news on South Carolina archaeology.

ISSN 0270-5486
US

RESEARCH PAPER - NEVADA ARCHEOLOGICAL SURVEY. [Res. pap. - Nev. Archeol. Surv.]. **Main/Corp** Nevada Archaeological Survey. No. 1-. Monographic series. English. Four times a year. Price varies per volume. University of Nevada Department of Anthropology, Mack S. S. Building, Reno NV 89557. **Tel** (702)784-6704.
Ind/Abst GeoRef.

ISSN 0589-9036
DD 913 UK
CODEN RRCADF

RESEARCH REPORT / COUNCIL FOR BRITISH ARCHAEOLOGY. [Res. rep. - Council for British Archaeology]. **Added/Corp** Council for British Archaeology. **VFOAT** CBA Research Report. (1955)-. Academic Scholarly Publication. English. Irregular. Price varies per volume. Council on British Archaeology, Bowes Morrell House, 111 Walmgate, York YO1 2UA United Kingdom. **Tel** 011 44 1904 671417, FAX 011 44 1904 671384. **ED** Julie Gardiner. **Circ:** 500. Documents available from CASDDS.
Desc: A monograph series on British archaeology.
Ind/Abst Chem. Abstr.

ISSN 0882-2042
DD 975 US
Pr Rev.

RESEARCH SERIES. [Re. ser. - Chicora Found.]. **Added/Corp** Chicora Foundation. **VFOAT** Chicora Foundation Research Series. Monographic series. English. Irregular. Price varies per volume. Chicora Foundation Inc, PO Box 8664, Columbia SC 29202. **Tel** (803)787-6910. **ED** Michael Trinkley. **Circ:** 150 (ctrl).
Desc: Discusses the foundation's archaeological research in South and North Carolina. Prehistoric and historical archaeology topics are included.

ISSN 0160-3086
US

RESEARCH SERIES (UNIVERSITY OF OKLAHOMA. ARCHAEOLOGICAL RESEARCH AND MANAGEMENT CENTER). (RESEARCH SERIES - ARCHAEOLOGICAL RESEARCH AND MANAGEMENT CENTER, UNIVERSITY OF OKLAHOMA.). **Added/Corp** University of Oklahoma. Archaeological Research and Management Center. No. 1 (1978)-. Monographic series. English. Price varies per volume. Archaeological Research and Management Center, University of Oklahoma, 1808 Newton Drive, Norman OK 73069. **Supersedes** Archaeological Site Report, 0078-4478 w (OCoLC)1111960.

UK

RESEARCH VOLUME OF THE SURREY ARCHAEOLOGICAL SOCIETY. Main/Corp Surrey Archaeological Society. No. 1 (1974)-. English.
Ind/Abst BHA : Biblio. Hist. Art.

LC WMLC L 83/6502 ISSN 0565-8802
DD 571 973 US

REVIEW AND ANALYSIS OF ARCHEOLOGY PROGRAM. Main/Corp United States. Office of Archeology and Historic Preservation. **VFOAT** Archeology Program. (1967)-. Periodical. English. National Park Service, PO Box 37127, Washington DC 20013-7127. **Tel** (202)343-3395. **Continues** United States. National Park Service. Division of Archeology. Review of Analysis of the Archeology Programs.

LC CC ISSN 1050-4877
DD 930.1 US

REVIEW OF ARCHAEOLOGY, THE. [Rev. archaeol.]. Vol. 10, No. 1 (Spring 1989)-. Periodical. English. Two times a year. $18.00. Review of Archaeology, Inc., 10 Liberty Street, Salem MA 01970. **Tel** (508)745-1876, FAX (508)745-8303. **ED** Frederick Hadleigh West. Index available (bound in second issue).
Bk Rev. Continues Quarterly Review of Archaeology, 0278-9825.
Desc: Devoted exclusively to the extended comprehensive evaluation of contemporary literature in archaeology and related sciences.

CK

REVISTA DE ANTROPOLOGIA Y ARQUEOLOGIA. See Anthropology.

LC E61 .R46 ISSN 0188-3631
MX

REVISTA DE ARQUEOLOGIA AMERICANA / INSTITUTO PANAMERICANO DE GEOGRAFIA E HISTORIA. Added/Corp Pan American Institute of Geography and History. No. 1 (1990)-. Periodical. Spanish (summaries and/or abstracts in English, French, Portuguese and Spanish). Two times a year. $38.00. Instituto Panamericano de Geographico Historia, APDO 18879 Secretaria General, 11870 Mexico DF Mexico. **Tel** 011 52 5 2775888, 011 52 5 2775791, FAX 011 52 5 2716172. **ED** Oscar Fonseca. **Circ:** 750.
Ind/Abst Anthropol. Lit.; Geogr. Abstr. Phys. Geogr.; Geogr. Abstr. Human Geogr.

LC CC13.S66 R48 ISSN 0212-0062
DD 930 SP

REVISTA DE ARQUEOLOGIA (MADRID, SPAIN). (REVISTA DE ARQUEOLOGIA.). [Rev. arqueol.]. (1980)-. Periodical. Spanish. Twelve times a year. 9000.00ptas. Zugarto Ediciones SA, C O Pablo Aranda 3, 28006 Madrid Spain. **Tel** 011 34 1 41114264.
Ind/Abst BHA : Biblio. Hist. Art.

LC F2519 .R478
DD 981/.01 BL

REVISTA DE ARQUEOLOGIA (RIO DE JANEIRO, BRAZIL). (REVISTA DE ARQUEOLOGIA.). Vol. 1, No. 1 (July/Dec. 1983)-. Periodical. English (French and Portuguese). Two times a year. Institute de Arqueologia Brasileira, Caixa Postal 2892, Rio de Janeiro Brazil. **Bk Rev. Ad Acc. Circ:** 1,000 (ctrl).
Desc: Covers Brazilian prehistoric and historic archaeology. Includes methodologies, field reports, theses, resumes, essays and current researches.
Ind/Abst Anthropol. Lit.

LC F3401 .L56 ISSN 0304-2367
DD 913.85 PE
SUSPENDED

REVISTA DEL MUSEO NACIONAL (LIMA). See Anthropology.

LC BR130 .R5 ISSN 0035-6042
VC

REVISTI DI ARCHEOLOGIA CRISTIANA. (RIVISTA DI ARCHEOLOGIA CRISTIANA, DELLA PONTIFICIA COMISSIONE DI ARCHEOLOGIA SACRA, ROMA.). [Riv. archeol. crist.]. **Added/Corp** Pontificio Istituto di Archeologia Cristiana. Pontificia Commissione di Archeologia Sacra, Rome. Vol. 1 (1924)-. Periodical. Italian (French, Spanish and German). Two times a year. L68130. Pontificio Istituto di Archeologia Cristiana, Via Napoleone 3-1, 00185 Vatican City Rome Italy. **Tel** 011 39 6 4465574, FAX 011 39 6 4469197. cum. index. **Ad Acc.** ctrl circ. **Supersedes** Nuovo Bullettino di Archeologia Cristiana.
Ind/Abst Art Archaeol. Tech. Abstr.; Avery Index Archit. Period. Suppl. Colum. Univ. (19??-199?); Bibliogr. Mission.; BHA : Biblio. Hist. Art; New Testam. Abstr.

LC CC3 .R4 ISSN 0035-0737
FR
CCC

REVUE ARCHEOLOGIQUE. [Rev. archeol.]. Vols. 1-16 (Apr. 1844)-(Sept. 1859)-. Periodical. French. Two times a year. $124.67. Presses Universitaires de France, Department des Revues, 17 Rue Souflot, 75005 Paris France. **Tel** 011 33 1 43267741, telex PUF 600 474 F. **ED** Roland Martin. cum. index. available on microfilm from University Microfilms International (UMI).
Desc: French antiquities and Graeco-Roman archaeology are richly illustrated in this publication. Recent discoveries are documented and discussed, when possible by the discoverer himself.
Ind/Abst Art Index; Avery Index Archit. Period. Suppl. Colum. Univ. (1988-); BHA : Biblio. Hist. Art; Br. Archaeol. Bibliogr.; Numis. Lit.

ISSN 1154-1342
FR

REVUE ARCHEOLOGIQUE DE BORDEAUX. Added/Corp Societe Archeologique de Bordeaux. (1988)-. French. One time a year.

Archaeology

Continues Societe Archeologique de Bordeaux : [Revue].
Ind/Abst BHA : Biblio. Hist. Art.

LC DC30 .R45
DD 936.4/005
ISSN 0035-0745
FR
REVUE ARCHEOLOGIQUE DE L'EST ET DU CENTRE-EST. [Rev. archeol. est cent.-est]. (Jan./March 1950)-. Monographic series. French (summaries and/or abstracts in German). Two times a year (July and Dec.). 175.00F. Editions du CNRS, 22 rue Saint Armand, F 75015 Paris France. **Tel** 011 33 1 45075050, telex 200 356 F. cum. index. **Circ:** 1,500.
Desc: Archaeological discoveries and reports covering a period from origins to 800 A.D. in the eastern and east-central of France.
Ind/Abst Anthropol. Lit.; Avery Index Archit. Period. Suppl. Colum. Univ. (19??-199?); BHA : Biblio. Hist. Art; Br. Archaeol. Bibliogr.; Numis. Lit.

ISSN 0220-7796
FR
UDC 92/99
REVUE ARCHEOLOGIQUE DE L'EST ET DU CENTRE-EST SUPPLEMENT. (1974)-. Monographic series. French. Editions du CNRS, 22 rue Saint Armand, F 75015 Paris France. **Tel** 011 33 1 45075050, telex 200 356 F.
Ind/Abst BHA : Biblio. Hist. Art.

LC DC609.4 .R48
DD 944/.01/05
ISSN 0767-709X
REVUE ARCHEOLOGIQUE DE L'OUEST. [Rev. archeol. Ouest]. **VFOAT** RAO. Vol. 1 (1984)-. Periodical. French.
Ind/Abst Anthropol. Lit.; BHA : Biblio. Hist. Art.

LC DC609.4
DD 944/.01/05
ISSN 1166-8261
REVUE ARCHEOLOGIQUE DE L'OUEST. SUPPLEMENT. **VFOAT** RAO. Supplement. (1984)-. Periodical. French. Irregular.
Ind/Abst BHA : Biblio. Hist. Art.

LC DC801.N24 R48
DD 936.4
ISSN 0557-7705
FR
REVUE ARCHEOLOGIQUE DE NARBONNAISE. [Rev. archeol. Narbonn.]. (1968)-. Monographic series. French. One time a year. Price varies per volume. Editions du CNRS, 22 rue Saint Armand, F 75015 Paris France. **Tel** 011 33 1 45075050, telex 200 356 F. **Circ:** 1,500.
Desc: Covers archaeology in southern France, concentrating on discoveries for the period from the beginning of the Iron Age to 800 A.D.
Ind/Abst Avery Index Archit. Period. Suppl. Colum. Univ. (19??-199?); BHA : Biblio. Hist. Art; Br. Archaeol. Bibliogr.; Numis. Lit.

FR
REVUE ARCHEOLOGIQUE DE NARBONNAISE. SUPPLEMENT. (1969)-. Monographic series. French. Irregular. Price varies per volume. Editions du CNRS, 22 rue Saint Armand, F 75015 Paris France. **Tel** 011 33 1 45075050, telex 200 356 F. (**Subscription address:** CNRS Editions, 20-22 rue Saint Amand, c/o Mme. Bodet, 75015 Paris France. **Tel** 011 33 1 45331600.)
Ind/Abst BHA : Biblio. Hist. Art.

ISSN 0752-5656
FR
CODEN RAPCE2
REVUE ARCHEOLOGIQUE DE PICARDIE. [Rev. archeol. Picardie]. **Added/Corp** Societe des Antiquites Historiques de Picardie (France). (1982)-. Periodical. French. Two times a year. 215.48F France;220.00F other. Societe des Antiquites Historiques de Picardie, 5 rue Henri Daussy, 80000 Amiens France. **Tel** 011 33 22 973345. *Formed by the union of* Cahiers Archeologique de Picardie, 0398-3064 *and* Revue Archeologique de l'Oise, 0752-5648.
Ind/Abst BHA : Biblio. Hist. Art.

LC DC30 .R46
DD 944/.005
ISSN 0220-6617
FR
REVUE ARCHEOLOGIQUE DU CENTRE DE LA FRANCE. Vol. 17, No. 1-2 (Jan./June 1978)-. Periodical. French. Four times a year. $65.61. R.A.C.F., 25 Quai D Orleans, Chateau Tour, 37000 Tours France. **Tel** 011 33 47 667237. *Continues* Revue Archeologique du Centre, 0556-7203.
Ind/Abst BHA : Biblio. Hist. Art.

ISSN 0181-0448
FR
UDC 944.383; 943.44
REVUE D'ALSACE. See History-History of Europe.

ISSN 0294-0965
REVUE D'ARCHEOLOGIE MODERNE ET D'ARCHEOLOGIE GENERALE : RAMAGE. **Added/Corp** Universite de Paris IV: Paris-Sorbonne. Centre d'Archeologie Moderne et Contemporaine. **VFOAT** RAMAGE. (1982)-. Monographic series. French. One time a year. Price varies per volume. Presses de l'Universite de Paris-Sorbonne, 18 rue de la Sorbonne, 75005 Paris France.
Ind/Abst BHA : Biblio. Hist. Art.

ISSN 0399-1237
FR
REVUE D'ARCHEOMETRIE. (REVUE D'ARCHEOMETRIE : BULLETIN DE LIAISON DU GROUPE DES METHODES PHYSIQUES ET CHIMIQUES DE L'ARCHEOLOGIE.). [Rev. archeom.]. (1977)-. Bulletin. French. One time a year. L Langouet, Universite de Rennes, F-35042 Rennes Cedex France.
Ind/Abst Anthropol. Lit.; Art Archaeol. Tech. Abstr.; Numis. Lit.

LC PJ3103 .R4
DD 935/.03/05
ISSN 0373-6032
CCC
REVUE D'ASSYRIOLOGIE ET D'ARCHEOLOGIE ORIENTALE. [Rev. assyriol. archeol. orient.]. (1884)-. Periodical. French. Two times a year. 400.00F France; 465.00 other. Presses Universitaires de France, Department des Revues, 17 Rue Souflot, 75005 Paris France. **Tel** 011 33 1 43267741, telex PUF 600 474 F. **ED** Pierre Amiet and Paul Garelli. cum. index.
Desc: Assyrian and Near-Eastern archaeology are explored and systematically documented by French and other specialists.
Ind/Abst Old Testam. Abstr.

ISSN 0035-1059
FR
REVUE DE COMMINGES. See History-History of Europe.

LC NK3700 .R48
ISSN 0294-202X
FR
REVUE DE LA CERAMIQUE ET DU VERRE, LA. See Glass and Ceramics.

ISSN 1161-7721
FR
REVUE DE LA MANCHE. **Added/Corp** Societe d'Archeologie et d'Histoire de la Manche. Vol. 33, Iss. 131 (July 1991)-. Periodical. French. Four times a year. *Continues* Revue du Departement de la Manche, 0583-8193.

LC CC3 .R44
DD 930/.1
ISSN 0080-2530
BE
REVUE DES ARCHEOLOGUES ET HISTORIENS D'ART DE LOUVAIN. [Rev. Archeol. Hist. Art Louvain]. **Added/Corp** Universite Catholique de Louvain (1835-1969). Institut Superieur d'Archeologie et d'Histoire de l'Art. (1968)-. Periodical. French (English, German and Dutch). One time a year. $95.15. Association Diplomes Historiens Art Archeo, 28 A Avenue Leopold, B 1330 Rixensart Belgium. **Tel** 011 32 10 472579, telex B 59150 OLEFFE. **ED** Tony Hackens, R Van Schoute, P Culot, R Van Halle, G Bernard, S H Mouchaerte, C De Bralkeleer, M L Anuaert-Lany, R Didier, A Denis, A Maystadt, P H Depreay, and E De Corte. **Bk Rev.** ctrl circ. available on diskette.
Desc: Covering archaeology, musicology, museology, and folklore including connected fields like numismatics, manuscripts, sciences in art and archaeology, history of technology and restoration. Dissertation abstracts at length of MA and PhD in our institute.
Ind/Abst Art Archaeol. Tech. Abstr.; Avery Index Archit. Period. Suppl. Colum. Univ. (19??-199?); BHA : Biblio. Hist. Art; Numis. Lit.

FR
REVUE DROMOISE. **Added/Corp** Societe d'Archeologie et de Statistique de la Drome. Vol. 80, No. 399 (Mar. 1976)-. Periodical. French. Four times a year. *Continues* Bulletin d'Archeologie et de Statistique de la Drome.
Ind/Abst BHA : Biblio. Hist. Art.

ISSN 0035-3272
FR
REVUE HISTORIQUE ARDENNAISE. See History-History of Europe.

LC DC801.L665 S6
FR
REVUE HISTORIQUE ET ARCHEOLOGIQUE DU LIBOURNAIS ET DE LA VALLEE DE LA DORDOGNE. **Added/Corp** Societe Historique et Archeologique de Libourne. Vol. 50, No. 183 (1982)-. Periodical. French. Four times a year. Societe Histoire Archeologique, Place Saint Pierre, 60300 Senlis France. **Tel** 011 33 44530080. *Continues* Revue Historique et Archeologique du Libournais.
Ind/Abst BHA : Biblio. Hist. Art.

LC DQ721 .R4
DD 949.4
SZ
REVUE HISTORIQUE VAUDOISE. See History-History of Europe.

GW
RHEINISCHE AUSGRABUNGEN. **Added/Corp** Landschaftsverband Rheinland. Rheinisches Landesmuseum Bonn. Vol. 1 (1968)-. Periodical. German. Irregular. DM198.00. Dr. Rudolf Habelt GmbH, Postfach 150104, D-53040 Bonn Germany. **Tel** 011 49 228 232015.
Ind/Abst Br. Archaeol. Bibliogr.

LC CC
DD 930.1
GW
●RHEINISCHES LANDESMUSEUM BONN. KATALOGE. (1994)-. Monographic series. English. Irregular. Price varies. Rheinland Verlag & Betriebsges, PF 2140 Abtei Brauweiler, D-50250 Pulheim Germany. **Tel** 011 49 2234 80516, FAX 011 49 2234 82503. (**Subscription address:** Rudolf Habelt GmbH, Am Buchenhang 1, 53115 Bonn Germany. **Tel** 011 49 228 232016, FAX 011 49 228 232017.)

ISSN 0080-3235
IT
UDC 930.26
RIVISTA ARCHEOLOGICA DELLA PROVINCIA E ANTICA DIOCESI DI COMO. [Riv. archeol. prov. antica dioc. Como]. **VFOAT** Rivista Archeologica dell'Antica Provincia e Diocesi di Como. (1872)-. Periodical. Italian. One time a year. Price varies per volume. Societa Archeologica Comense, Piazza Medaglie d'Oro 1, 22100 Como Italy.
Ind/Abst BHA : Biblio. Hist. Art.

LC DE2 .I7
IT
RIVISTA DELL'ISTITUTO NAZIONALE D'ARCHEOLOGIA E STORIA DELL'ARTE. **Added/Corp** Istituto Nazionale di Archeologia e Storia dell'Arte (Italy). New Series, Vol. 1 (1952)-. Periodical. Italian. Irregular. Rivista dell'Istituto, via Cassiodoro 19, Rome 00193 Italy. *Continues* R. Instituto d'Archeologie e Storia dell'Arte. Rivista.
Ind/Abst BHA : Biblio. Hist. Art.

LC CC9 .R58
DD 930.1/05
ISSN 0392-0895
IT
RIVISTA DI ARCHEOLOGIA. [Riv. archeol.]. (1977)-. Periodical. Italian (English and German). One time a year. L200.000. Giorgio Bretschneider Editore, Via Crescenzio 43, 00193 Rome Italy. **Tel** 011 39 6 6879361. **Bk Rev. Ad Acc. Circ:** 150.
Ind/Abst Avery Index Archit. Period. Suppl. Colum. Univ. (1988-).

LC GN700 .R58
ISSN 0035-6514
RIVISTA DI SCIENZE PREISTORICHE. **Added/Corp** Istituto Italiano di Preistoria e Protostoria. Vol. 1 (1946)-. Periodical. Italian (English and French; summaries and/or abstracts in French). One time a year. L42920. Rivista di Scienze Presitorich, Via S Egidio 21, 50122 Florence Italy. **Tel** 011 39 55 230765. Index available. cum. index. ctrl circ.
Desc: Presents reviews concerning prehistorical archaeology.
Ind/Abst Anthropol. Index; Anthropol. Lit.; Br. Archaeol. Bibliogr. (?-?).

LC DS81 .R48
DD 939/.44
IT
RIVISTA DI STUDI FENICI. **Added/Corp** Centro di Studio per la Civilta Fenicia e Punica. Vol. 1 (1973)-. Multiple languages (English, French, Italian and Spanish). Two times a year. L120000.00. Herder Editrice e Libreria SRL, Piazza Montecitorio 117-120, 00186 Rome Italy. **Tel** 011 39 6 679 4628, FAX 011 39 6 678 4751. **ED** Enrico Acquaro. **Bk Rev. Circ:** 800.
Desc: Organ of the Instituto per la Civilta Fenicia e Punica, sponsored by the Consiglio Nazionale delle Ricerche.
Ind/Abst Index Book Rev. Relig.; Numis. Lit.

LC DG55.L5 R58
IT
RIVISTA DI STUDI LIGURI. **Added/Corp** Istituto Internazionale di Studi Liguri. Deputazione di Storia Patria per la Liguria. Sezione Ingauna e Intemelia. Bollettino. Vol. 1 (1934)-. Periodical. Italian. Four times a year. Istituto Internationale Studi Liguri, Museo Bicknell, via Romana 39, 18012 Bordighera Italy. **Tel** 011 39 184 263601. cum. index. **Bk Rev. Circ:** 2,000 (ctrl).
Continues Revue d'Etudes Ligures.
Desc: Prehistorical and archaeological discoveries; also studies about prehistory, protohistory, ancient topography, Roman and palaeochristian archaeology.
Ind/Abst Anthropol. Index; Anthropol. Lit.; Numis. Lit.

IT
RIVISTA INGAUNA E INTEMELIA. **Added/Corp** Deputazione di Storia Patria per la Liguria. Sezione Ingauna e Intemelia. Istituto Internazionale di Studi Liguri. Sezione Rivierasche. (1946)-. Italian. Four times a year. Istituto Internationale Studi Liguri, Museo

Archaeology

Bicknell, via Romana 39, 18012 Bordighera Italy. **Tel** 011 39 184 263601. cum. index. **Bk Rev. Circ:** 1,700 (ctrl).
Desc: Local medieval and modern history of archaeological and historical-artistical activities in the Western Ligurian Riviera.
Ind/Abst BHA : Biblio. Hist. Art.

ISSN 0813-0426
AT
Pr Rev.
ROCK ART RESEARCH. (ROCK ART RESEARCH : THE JOURNAL OF THE AUSTRALIAN ROCK ART RESEARCH ASSOCIATION (AURA).). [Rock art res.]. **Added/Corp** Australian Rock Art Research Association. Vol. 1, No. 1 (May 1984)-. Periodical. English (French, Spanish and German). Two times a year (May & Nov.). 26.31Aus$. Australian Rock Art Research, PO Box 216, Caulfield South Victoria, 3162 Australia. **Tel** 011 61 3 5230549. **ED** R. G. Bednarik. **Bk Rev**, (Qty: 4-8). **Ad Acc, Adv Mgr:** R. G. Bednarik. **Circ:** 1,000 (ctrl).
Desc: A scientific journal on prehistoric art and cognitive archaeology.
Ind/Abst Anthropol. Lit.; Art Archaeol. Tech. Abstr.; Ethnoarts Index.

LC DD901.S11 A15
DD 913.43058
GW
SAALBURG-JAHRBUCH. **Added/Corp** Saalburgmuseum (Bad Homburg vor der Haohe, Germany). (1910)-. German. One time a year. DM65.00. Verlag Phillip Von Zabern, Postfach 190930, D-80609 Munich Germany. **Tel** 011 49 89 12151661, FAX 011 49 61 31223710, telex 4187463. **ED** Dietwulf V. Baatz.
Desc: Articles and essays from different authors concerning archaeology.
Ind/Abst BHA : Biblio. Hist. Art; Br. Archaeol. Bibliogr.

LC F869.S22 S36
DD 913.794 979.49
US
SAN DIEGO MUSEUM PAPERS. See Anthropology.

UK
SARMIZEGETUSA MONOGRAPH. (19??)-. Monographic series. English. Irregular. Price varies per volume. British Archaeological Reports, 5 Centremead Osney Mead, Oxford 0X2 0E5 United Kingdom.

ISSN 0899-8922
DD 930
US
CODEN SARTE6
SAS BULLETIN. [SAS bull.]. **Added/Corp** Society for Archaeological Sciences (U.S.). **VAT** Bulletin. Vol. 12, No. 1 (Jan.-Mar. 1989)-. Bulletin. English. Four times a year (Jan., Apr., July, Oct.). $30.00. Society for Archaeological Sciences, Department of Anthropology, University of California, Riverside CA 92521. **Tel** (909)787-5521, FAX (909)787-5409. **ED** Robert Sternberg, (phone: (717)291-4134). cum. index. **Bk Rev**, (Qty: 5). **Ad Acc. Circ:** 500. **Continues** SAS Newsletter, 0739-0637.
Desc: Reports on the activities and scientific applications in archaeology.
Ind/Abst Ceram. Abstr. (199?-).

LC F1071.9 .S27   ISSN 0227-5872
DD 971.24/01/05
CN
SASKATCHEWAN ARCHAEOLOGY. (SASKATCHEWAN ARCHAEOLOGY : THE JOURNAL OF THE SASKATCHEWAN ARCHAEOLOGICAL SOCIETY.). [Sask. archaeol.]. **Added/Corp** Saskatchewan Archaeological Society. Vol. 1, No. 1 (June 1980)-. Periodical. English. One time a year. 26.00Can$. Saskatchewan Archaeology, #5 816 1st Avenue North, Saskatoon Saskatchewan S7K 1Y3 Canada. **Tel** (306)664-4124, FAX (306)665-1928. **ED** Maureen Rollans, Miggs Greene and Peggy McKeand (telephone: (306)975-3863). **Circ:** 600 (ctrl). **Continues in part** Saskatchewan Archaeology Newsletter.
Desc: Different articles from the Archaeological Society of Saskatchewan.
Ind/Abst Anthropol. Lit.; Ethnoarts Index.

ISSN 0231-7915
XR
UDC 930.26
SBORNIK PRACI FILOZOFICKE FAKULTY BRNENSKE UNIVERZITY. RADA ARCHEOLOGICKO-KLASICKA. **VFOAT** Studia Minora Facultatis Philosophicae Universitatis Brunensis. Series Archeologica et Classica. (1956)-. Periodical. Multiple languages. One time a year. Masarykova Universita, A. Novaka 1, 660 88 Brno Czech Republic.
Ind/Abst BHA : Biblio. Hist. Art.

LC QE71   ISSN 0445-3395
DD 557
US
Pr Rev.
SCIENTIFIC PAPERS / ILLINOIS STATE MUSEUM. See History-History of North and South America.

UK
SCOTTISH ARCHAEOLOGICAL FORUM. Vol. 1 (1969)-. Proceedings. English. Irregular. £4.00. Edinburgh University Press Ltd., 22 George Square, Edinburgh EH8 9LF United Kingdom. **Tel** 011 44 131 6506207, FAX 011 44 131 6620053.
Desc: The proceedings of an annual forum on research topics of archaeology in Scotland.
Ind/Abst Br. Archaeol. Bibliogr.

ISSN 0958-2002
UK
SCOTTISH ARCHAEOLOGICAL NEWS. **Added/Corp** Council for Scottish Archaeology. (Autumn 1989)-. Periodical. English. Three times a year. **Continues** Scottish Archaeological Gazette, 0262-978X.
Ind/Abst Museum Abstr.

ISSN 0262-4389
UK
SCOTTISH ARCHAEOLOGICAL REVIEW : SAR. **VFOAT** SAR; S.A.R. (1982)-. Periodical. English. Two times a year. Martinus Nijhoff Publishers, Subsidiary of Kluwer Academic Publishers, Koraalrood 50, 2718 SC Zoetermeer Netherlands. **Tel** 011 31 79 684400.
Ind/Abst Anthropol. Lit.; BHA : Biblio. Hist. Art.

ISSN 0554-8195
PL
SERIA ARCHEOLOGIA / UNIWERSYTET IM. ADAMA MICKIEWICZA W POZNANIU, WYDZIAL FILOZOFICZNO-HISTORYCZNY. **Added/Corp** Uniwersytet im. Adama Mickiewicza w Poznaniu. Wydzial Filozoficzno-Historyczny. **VFOAT** Archeologia; Prace Wydzialu Filozoficzno-Historycznego. Seria Archeologia. (1966)-. Monographic series. Polish (summaries and/or abstracts in English and German; table of contents in German). Irregular. Price varies per volume. Uniwersytet im Adama Mickiewicza / Adam Mickiewicz University Press, Nowowiejskiego 55, 61734 Poznan Poland. **Tel** 011 48 61 527380, FAX 011 48 61 526425. **Continues** Prace Wydzialu Filozoficzno-Historycznego. Seria Archeologia.
Desc: Research and monographs in archaeology by scholars from the university.
Ind/Abst BHA : Biblio. Hist. Art.

LC DP702.S47 S48
DD 946.9/42
PO
SETUBAL ARQUEOLOGICA. **Added/Corp** Museu de Arqueologia e Etnografia do Distrito de Setubal. Vol. 1 (1975)-. Periodical. Portuguese.
Ind/Abst Anthropol. Lit.

LC DS894.49.T6235 S55
JA
SHIMOTSUKE KOKOGAKU. **Added/Corp** Shimotsuke Kokogaku Kenkyukai. (1980)-. Monographic series. Japanese. One time a year. Price varies per volume. Shimotsuke Kokogaku Kenkyukai, c/o Igarashi Toshikatsu, 3-25 Ichijo 3-chome, Utsunomiya-shi Japan. **Tel** 286-34-3694. **ED** Toshikatsu Igarashi. **Circ:** 150.
Desc: A bulletin of The Archaeological Society of Shimotsuke with reports and articles about archaeology in Tochigi prefecture.

UK
SHIRE EGYPTOLOGY. Monographic series. English. Price varies per volume.

ISSN 0559-9628
IT
UDC 903
SIBRIUM. (1953)-. Periodical. Italian. Irregular. L45000 Italy; L50000 other. Centro di Studi Preistorici Archeologici, Musei Civici Villa Mirabello, 21100 Varese Italy. **Tel** 011 39 332 281590.
Ind/Abst Anthropol. Lit.; BHA : Biblio. Hist. Art.

ISSN 0080-9594
PL
SILESIA ANTIQUA. See History-History of Europe.

LC DP802.C5 S57
DD 946.9
PO
SINTRIA. **Added/Corp** Gabinete de Estudos de Arqueologia, Arte e Etnografia. Sintra (Portugal). Camara Municipal. Servicos Culturais. Vol. 1, No. 1/2 (1983)-. Periodical. Portuguese. Conselho Redactorial de Sintria, Museu Regional de Sintra, Praca da Republica, 23 2710 Sintra Portugal.
Ind/Abst BHA : Biblio. Hist. Art.

LC WMLC L 83/1   ISSN 0560-1894
DK
SKALK. [Skalk]. **Added/Corp** Aarhus. Forhistorisk Museum. (1957)-. Danish. Six times a year. $29.23. Tidsskriftet Skalk, Jelshojuaenget 29, D-8270 Hojbjerg Denmark. **Tel** 011 45 86 273711. **ED** Troels Wingender. Index available. cum. index. **Circ:** 45,000.
Desc: Articles on Danish cultural history and archaeology.
Ind/Abst Anthropol. Lit. (?-Vol. 11, 1989); Art Archaeol. Tech. Abstr.; BHA : Biblio. Hist. Art.

LC DD491.S445 S55   ISSN 0520-9250
PL
SLASKIE SPRAWOZDANIA ARCHEOLOGICZNE. **Added/Corp** Breslau. Uniwersytet. Katedra Archeologii Polski. (1958)-. Monographic series. Polish. Irregular. Price varies per volume. Wydawnictwo Uniwersytetu Wroclawskiego, Pl. Uniwersytecki 9-13, 50-137 Wroclaw Poland. **Tel** 011 48 71 441006.
Ind/Abst BHA : Biblio. Hist. Art.

LC D147 .S5   ISSN 0080-9993
PL
SLAVIA ANTIQUA. **Added/Corp** Uniwersytet Warszawski. Katedra Archeologii Pradziejowej i Wczesno,sredniowiecznej. Uniwersytet im. Adama Mickiewicza w Poznaniu. Katedra Archeologii Pradziejowej. Vol. 1 (1948)-. Polish (French and Czech; summaries and/or abstracts in English). One time a year. $22.00. **(Subscription address:** Ars Polona-Ruch, PO Box 1001, Krakowskie Przedmiescie 7, 00-068 Warsaw Poland. **Tel** 011 48 22 261201.)
Ind/Abst Anthropol. Index; BHA : Biblio. Hist. Art; Numis. Lit.

LC DB670 .S5   ISSN 0037-6949
XO
SLOVENSKA ARCHEOLOGIA. **Added/Corp** Slovenska Akademia Vied. Vol. 1 (1953)-. Periodical. Czech (German, Russian and French; summaries and/or abstracts in Russian, English and Multiple languages). Two times a year. Kcs150.00; $48.00 other. Veda, Publishing House of the Slovak Academy of Sciences, Klemensova 19, 814 30 Bratislava Slovakia. **Tel** (7)583-15. **(Subscription address:** Kubon & Sagner, ABT Zeitschriftenimport, D 80328 Munich Germany. **Tel** 011 49 89 54218130.) **ED** Bohuslav Chropovsky. **Bk Rev. Ad Acc. Circ:** 1,000 (ctrl).
Desc: Studies on the problems of Slovakia primeval and adjacent territories, on questions of the entire Carpathian basin and on early Slavic history in general.
Ind/Abst Anthropol. Index; Anthropol. Lit.; BHA : Biblio. Hist. Art; Numis. Lit.

ISSN 0154-0505
FR
UDC 908
SOCIETE HISTORIQUE ET ARCHEOLOGIQUE DE L'ORNE. See History-History of Europe.

US
SOCIETY FOR HISTORICAL ARCHAEOLOGY CONFERENCE UNDERWATER PROCEEDINGS. Proceedings. English. One time a year. $16.75 US; $16.25 other. Society for Historical Archaeology / Arizona, PO Box 30446, Tucson AZ 85751. **Tel** (602)886-8006. **Circ:** 300.
Desc: Underwater archaeology papers presented at the annual conference, addressing method, theory and legislation.

LC T37 .S62   ISSN 0160-1067
DD 609
US
SOCIETY FOR INDUSTRIAL ARCHEOLOGY NEWSLETTER. [Soc. Ind. Archeol. newsl.]. **Added/Corp** Society for Industrial Archeology. **VFOAT** Newsletter; SIA Newsletter. Vol. 1, No. 1 (Jan. 1972)-. Newsletter. English. Four times a year. Membership: $40.00 institutions; $35.00 individuals. Society for Industrial Archeology, National Museum of History, Smithsonian Institute, Room 5014, Washington DC 20560. **Tel** (202)357-2228. **ED** Robert M. Frame. **Bk Rev. Circ:** 1,400 (ctrl).
Ind/Abst Avery Index Archit. Period. Suppl. Colum. Univ. (19??-199?).

ISSN 0081-2056
UK
SOMERSET ARCHAEOLOGY AND NATURAL HISTORY. (SOMERSET ARCHAEOLOGY AND NATURAL HISTORY : THE PROCEEDINGS OF THE SOMERSETSHIRE ARCHAEOLOGICAL AND NATURAL HISTORY SOCIETY FOR ...). [Somerset archaeol. net. hist.]. **Added/Corp** Somersetshire Archaeological and Natural History Society. **VFOAT** Proceedings of the Somerset Archaeology and Natural History Society; Proceedings of the Somersetshire Archaeological and Natural History Society. Vol. 112 (1968)-. Proceedings. English. One time a year. $29.94. Somerset Archaeology and Natural History Society, Taunton Castle, Taunton TA1 4AD United Kingdom. **Tel** 011 44 823 272429. **Continues** Proceedings of the Somersetshire Archaeological and Natural History Society.
Ind/Abst BHA : Biblio. Hist. Art.

UK
SOMERSET LEVELS PAPERS. **Added/Corp** Somerset Levels Project. No. 1 (1975)-. English. One time a year. University of Cambridge / Archaeology, Department of Archaeology, Cambridge CB3 9DR United Kingdom.
Ind/Abst Anthropol. Lit. (?-1990); Br. Archaeol. Bibliogr.

Archaeology

LC NX
DD 700
ISSN 0737-4453
US
SOURCE (NEW YORK, N.Y.). See The Arts-Art.

LC GN865.S5 S68
DD 968
ISSN 0038-1969
SA
CODEN SARBAG
SOUTH AFRICAN ARCHAEOLOGICAL BULLETIN, THE. [S. Afr. archaeol. bull.]. **VFOAT** Suid-Afrikaanse Argeologiese Bulletin. (1945)-. Bulletin. English. Two times a year (June & Dec.). $35.78. South African Archaeological Society, PO Box 15700, 8018 Vlaeberg South Africa. **Tel** 011 27 21 243330. **ED** Dr. J. Deacon. Index available. **Bk Rev. Ad Acc, Adv Mgr:** C. Borr, **Tel** (021)243330 ext. 2086. **Circ:** 1,300 (ctrl).
Desc: Articles on Southern African archaeology and other related fields.
Ind/Abst Am. Hist. Life (1970-); Anthropol. Index; Anthropol. Lit.; Br. Archaeol. Bibliogr. -?; Ethnoarts Index; GeoRef.

LC F653 .S7
DD 978.3/005
ISSN 0276-5543
US
SOUTH DAKOTA ARCHAEOLOGY. (SOUTH DAKOTA ARCHAEOLOGY : THE JOURNAL OF THE SOUTH DAKOTA ARCHAEOLOGICAL SOCIETY.). **Added/Corp** South Dakota Archaeological Society. **VFOAT** Journal of the South Dakota Archaeological Society. (1977)-. Periodical. English. One time a year. $25.00. Archaeological Society of South Dakota, Archaeology Laboratory, 2032 South Grange, Sioux Falls SD 57105. **Tel** (605)336-5493, FAX (605)336-4368. **ED** L Adrien Hannus and Lynette Rossum. **Bk Rev**, (Qty: 1-2). **Circ:** 250 (ctrl).
Desc: Scholarly publication with articles of enduring scientific interest focusing on the archaeology of South Dakota and the surrounding Plains region. Contains items of current interest relating to South Dakota prehistory / history. Contains book reviews, short articles and announcements.
Ind/Abst Anthropol. Lit.; Ethnoarts Index.

LC F211 .S62
DD 975/.01/05
ISSN 0734-578X
US
CODEN SARHE4
Pr Rev.
SOUTHEASTERN ARCHAEOLOGY. [Southeast. archaeol.]. Vol. 1, No. 1 (Summer 1982)-. Periodical. English. Two times a year. Free to members of the Southeastern Archaeological Conference; $50.00 (institutions), $25.00 (individuals) membership. Southeastern Archaeological Conference, University of Mississippi, Department of Sociology, University MS 38677. **ED** Vernon J. Knight. **Bk Rev. Ad Acc. Circ:** 700 (ctrl).
Desc: Contains papers on the prehistoric and historic archaeology of the Southeastern United States and neighboring regions.
Ind/Abst Abstr. Anthropol.; Anthropol. Lit.; Ethnoarts Index.

ISSN 0076-0994
SOUTHWEST MUSEUM PAPERS. **Added/Corp** Southwest Museum (Los Angeles, Calif.). **VFOAT** Papers / Southwest Museum. No. 1 (Apr. 1928)-. English. Southwest Museum, PO Box 41558, Los Angeles CA 90041. **Tel** (213)221-2164. **ED** Steven A. LeBlanc. **Bk Rev. Ad Acc.**
Desc: Publication containing occasional papers focusing on the anthropology and the archaeology of the Americas.

LC F778 .S69
DD 913.788
ISSN 0038-4844
US
SOUTHWESTERN LORE. [Southwest. lore]. **Added/Corp** Colorado Archaeological Society. Southwestern Colorado Archaeological Society. Museum of Western State College. Vol. 1, (June 1935)-. Periodical. English. Four times a year (Seasonally). $25.00. Colorado Archaeological Society, 920 Balsam Street, Cortex CO 81321-2608. **Tel** (719)275-9679. **ED** Marcia J. Tate. Index available (2 diskettes with print programs, $30.00). cum. index. **Bk Rev**, (Qty: 12). **Circ:** 1,000 (ctrl).
Desc: Publication covering historic and prehistoric archaeology of the Rocky Mountain region. Also contains descriptive site reports and related information.
Ind/Abst Am. Hist. Life (1968-1971, 1981-); Anthropol. Lit.; Art Archaeol. Tech. Abstr.; Ethnoarts Index.

ISSN 0145-9031
US
CODEN SPCHDX
Pr Rev.
SPECIAL PUBLICATION - CARNEGIE MUSEUM OF NATURAL HISTORY. See Natural History.

ISSN 0735-5467
US
SPECIAL PUBLICATIONS - MISSOURI ARCHAEOLOGICAL SOCIETY. (SPECIAL PUBLICATIONS.). [Spec. publ. - Mo. Archaeol. Soc.]. **Added/Corp** Missouri Archaeological Society. **VFOAT** Missouri Archaeological Society Special Publications. (19??)-. Monographic series. English. Irregular. Price varies per volume. Missouri Archaeological Society, PO Box 958, 908 Woodson Way, Columbia MO 65205. **Tel** (314)882-3544, FAX (314)882-9410. **ED** W. Raymond Wood. **Circ:** 900.
Desc: Contains monographs on specific aspects of archaeology in Missouri and the Midwest.

LC D1 .S685
ISSN 0038-7487
NE
UDC 930.9
SPIEGEL HISTORIAEL. See History.

ISSN 0137-222X
PL
UDC 72.025
SPOTKANIA Z ZABYTKAMI. (1977)-. Academic Scholarly Publication. Polish. Twelve times a year. Price on request. **(Subscription address:** Ars Polona-Ruch, PO Box 1001, Krakowskie Przedmiescie 7, 00-068 Warsaw Poland. **Tel** 011 48 22 261201.)

LC GN700 .S6
ISSN 0081-3834
PL
SPRAWOZDANIA ARCHEOLOGICZNE. **Added/Corp** Polska Akademia Nauk. Instytut Historii Kultury Materialnej. (1955)-. Academic Scholarly Publication. Polish (summaries and/or abstracts in Russian and English; table of contents in Russian and English). One time a year. Price varies per volume. Polska Akademia Nauk, Oddzial w Krakowie / Instytut Archeologii i Etnologii, Ul. Slawkowska 17, 31-016 Krakow Poland. **Tel** 011 48 12 224853, FAX 011 48 12 222791. **Circ:** 700.
Ind/Abst Anthropol. Index; BHA : Biblio. Hist. Art.

ISSN 0959-2369
DD 069.53
UK
SSCR JOURNAL. [SSCR j.]. **VFOAT** Scottish Society for Conservation & Restoration Journal. (1990)-. Periodical. English. Four times a year. $56.47. Scottish Society for Conservation and Restoration, Overhall, Kirkfieldbank, Lanark, ML11 9TZ United Kingdom. **Tel** 011 44 1555 66291. **Continues** Bulletin - Scottish Society for Conservation & Restoration, 0264-9039.
Desc: Publication that covers conservation of historic and artistic objects. Also contains papers on conservation methods and treatments, reviews of books, and details of symposiums and conferences. Details on Scottish Society for Conservation and Restoration (SSCR) meetings and publications and interviews with members of the conservation profession.
Ind/Abst Museum Abstr.

ISSN 0266-4992
UK
STAFFORDSHIRE ARCHAEOLOGICAL STUDIES. [Staffs. archaeol. stud.]. **VFOAT** Museum Archaeological Society Report. (1984)-. Academic Scholarly Publication . English. **Continues** Report - City of Stoke-on-Trent Museum Archaeological Society.
Ind/Abst Anthropol. Lit.

LC DR311.A1 S7
YU
STARINAR. **Added/Corp** Srpsko Arkheolosko Drustvo, Belgrad. Srpska Akademija Nauka i Umetnosti, Belgrad. Arkheoloski Institut. Vols. 1-12 (1884-1895); New Series 2, Vols. 1-6 (1906-1911); New Series 3, Vols. 1-15 (1922-1940); New Series 4, Vol. 1 (1950)-. Serbo-Croatian (Cyrillic).
Ind/Abst Anthropol. Lit.; BHA : Biblio. Hist. Art.

CI
STARINE. **Added/Corp** Jugoslavenska Akademija Znanosti i Umjetnosti. (1869)-. One time a year. Slovenska Akademija Znanosti i Umjetnosti / Filozofski Institut, Razred ZA Prirodne Znanosti, 41000 Zagreb Croatia.
Ind/Abst BHA : Biblio. Hist. Art.

LC DG59
DD 936
ISSN 0140-654X
US
STONEHENGE VIEWPOINT. [Stonehenge viewp.]. (197?)-. Periodical. English. Six times a year. $16.00 (two-year). Stonehenge Viewpoint, Box 30887, Santa Barbara CA 93105. **Tel** (805)687-9350. **ED** Joan L. Gyr and Donald L. Gyr. Index available. **Circ:** 2,000 (ctrl).
Desc: Publication that covers archaeology, astronomy, geology, meteorology, related arts and sciences.

LC E78.A28 S86
DD 970.00497
US
●**STONES & BONES.** **Added/Corp** Alabama Archaeological Society. **VFOAT** Alabama Archaeological Society Stones & Bones; Stones and Bones. **VAT** Stones and bones. (1994)-. Academic Scholarly Publication. English. Alabama Archaeological Society, 13075 Moundville Park, Moundville AL 35474. **Tel** (205)371-2266. **Continues** Stones & Bones Newsletter.
Desc: Publication of the Alabama Archaeological Society in Moundville, Alabama.

LC BR130
DD 246.08
IT
STUDI DI ANTICHITA CRISTIANA. Monographic series. Italian (French, English, German and Spanish). Price varies per volume. Pontificio Istituto Di Archeologia Cristiana, Via Napoleone 3 I, 00185 Rome Italy. ctrl circ.

ISSN 0081-6140
IT
STUDI DI ARCHITETTURA ANTICA. **Added/Corp** Turin. Politecnico. Istituto di Storia dell'Architettura. Vol. 1, (1966)-. Monographic series. Italian. Irregular. Price varies per volume. L'Erma di Bretschneider SPA, via Cassiodoro 19, 00193 Rome Italy. **Tel** 011 39 6 6874127, 011 39 6 6874129, FAX 011 39 6 6874129. **Circ:** 400.

LC DT56.8 .S78
DD 932/.005
IT
STUDI DI EGITTOLOGIA E DI ANTICHITA PUNICHE. **VFOAT** SEAP. Vol. 1 (1987)-. Periodical. Italian. Irregular. Giardini Editori Stampatori, Via Santa Bibbiana 28, 56127 Pisa Italy. **Tel** 011 39 50 934242.

LC DS99.E25 S86
DD 939/.4
IT
STUDI EBLAITI. **Added/Corp** Missione Archeologica Italiana in Siria. (1979)-. Periodical. Italian (English, French and Italian). Irregular. L40000.00. Herder Editrice e Libreria SRL, Piazza Montecitorio 117-120, 00186 Rome Italy. **Tel** 011 39 6 679 4628, FAX 011 39 6 678 4751. **ED** Paolo Matthiae.
Desc: Archaeology, philology, linguistics and history from excavations at Tell-Mardikh-Ebla in Syria.
Ind/Abst Anthropol. Lit.

LC WMLC L 83/2336
ISSN 0081-6787
PL
STUDIA PALMYRENSKIE. ETUDES PALMYRENIENNES. **Added/Corp** Uniwersytet Warszawski. Wydzia Historyczny. Katedra Archeologii Srodziemnomorskiej. **VFOAT** Etudes Palmyreniennes. Vol. 1 (1966)-. Polish (English and French; summaries and/or abstracts in French). Irregular. **(Subscription address:** Ars Polona-Ruch, PO Box 1001, Krakowskie Przedmiescie 7, 00-068 Warsaw Poland. **Tel** 011 48 22 261201.)

LC GN700 .S78
BU
STUDIA PRAEHISTORICA. **Added/Corp** Arkheologicheski Institut (Bulgarska Akademiia na Naukite). Institut Arkheologii (Akademiia Nauk SSSR). (1978)-. Russian (English, French and German). Irregular. Ban Zentralna Biblioteka, 1 7 Noemvri Str, 1000 Sofia Bulgaria.
Ind/Abst Anthropol. Lit.

LC DT61 .S935
DD 932/.01
ISSN 0340-2215
GW
STUDIEN ZUR ALTAGYPTISCHEN KULTUR. (1974)-. Monographic series. German (English and French). One time a year. DM158.00 (latest edition). Helmut Buske Verlag Hamburg, Postfach 760244, D-22052 Hamburg Germany. **Tel** 011 49 40 2999580, FAX 011 49 40 2993614. **ED** Hartwig Altenmueller and Dietrich Wildung. **Circ:** 400.
Desc: Egyptology.

ISSN 0952-4975
UK
STUDIES IN ANCIENT CHRONOLOGY. See History.

ISSN 0081-7554
US
STUDIES IN ANCIENT ORIENTAL CIVILIZATION. **Added/Corp** University of Chicago. Oriental Institute. No. 1 (1931)-. Monographic series. English. Irregular. Price varies per volume. University of Chicago Oriental Institute, 1155 East 58th Street, Chicago IL 60637. **Tel** (312)702-9508. **ED** Tom Holland and Tom Urban. **Circ:** 1,000 (ctrl).
Desc: General studies in the archaeology and history of the ancient Near East.

LC NX
DD 700
NE
STUDIES IN ASIAN ART AND ARCHAEOLOGY. See The Arts-Art.

LC N8560 .S82
ISSN 0039-3630
UK
CODEN SCONAH
Pr Rev.
STUDIES IN CONSERVATION. See The Arts-Art.

Archaeology

ISSN 0081-8232
SW

STUDIES IN MEDITERRANEAN ARCHAEOLOGY. [Stud. Mediterr. archaeol.]. (1962)-. Monographic series. English (French and German). Irregular. Price varies per volume. Paul Astrom Forlag, William Gibsons Vag II, S 43376 Partille Sweden. **Tel** 011 46 31 956600, FAX 011 46 31 7956710. **ED** Paul Astrom. **Circ:** 1,000 (ctrl).
Desc: Concerned with prehistoric Greek, Roman, Cypriot and Near Eastern archaeological books.
Ind/Abst Art Archaeol. Tech. Abstr.

ISSN 0283-8494
SW

STUDIES IN MEDITERRANEAN ARCHAEOLOGY AND LITERATURE. POCKET-BOOK. (1987)-. Monographic series. Swedish (English and German). Price varies per volume. Paul Astrom Forlag, William Gibsons Vag II, S 43376 Partille Sweden. **Tel** 011 46 31 956600, FAX 011 46 31 7956710. **Continues** Studies in Mediterranean Archaeology. Pocket-Book.

LC E51 .S85
ISSN 0585-7023
US

STUDIES IN PRE-COLUMBIAN ART AND ARCHAEOLOGY. Added/Corp Harvard University. Robert Woods Bliss Collection of Pre-Columbian Art, Washington, D.C. No. 1 (1966)-. Monographic series. English. Irregular. Price varies per volume. Dumbarton Oaks Publishing / Maryland, PO Box 4866, Hampden Station, Baltimore MD 21211. **Tel** (410)516-6954.
Ind/Abst Ethnoarts Index.

LC DS153.3 .S75
DD 939/.4/005
JO

STUDIES IN THE HISTORY AND ARCHAEOLOGY OF JORDAN. Added/Corp Jordan. Dairat al-Athar al-Ammah. (1982).-. Academic Scholarly Publication. English (French and Arabic). Department of Antiquities / Jordan, Hasemite Kingdom of Jordon, PO Box 88, Amman Jordan. **Tel** 011 962 6 644482.
Ind/Abst Anthropol. Lit. (?-1989).

LC E78.O5 S86
ISSN 0706-1226
DD 971.3/01/05
CN

STUDIES IN WEST PATRICIA ARCHAEOLOGY. No. 1 (1978-1979)-. Academic Scholarly Publication. English. One time a year. Ontario Government Bookstore, 880 Bay Street, Toronto Ontario M7A 1N8 Canada.

ISSN 0921-9080
NE

UDC 902
CODEN 949.2

STUDIES OF THE DUTCH ARCHAEOLOGICAL AND HISTORICAL SOCIETY. (1969)-. Monographic series. English. Irregular. Price varies per volume. E.J. Brill, Postbus 9000, 2300 PA Leiden The Netherlands. **Tel** 011 31 71 312624, FAX 011 31 71 317532, telex 39296 BRILL NL.

LC DR211 .S78
DD 913.39/8
RM

STUDII SI CERCETARI DE ISTORIE VECHE SI ARHEOLOGIE. Added/Corp Institutul de Arheologie (Academia de Stiinte Sociale si Politice a Republicii Socialiste Romania). (1974)-. Academic Scholarly Publication. Romanian (summaries and/or abstracts in French and German). Four times a year. DM260.00. **(Subscription address:** Kubon & Sagner, ABT Zeitschriftenimport, D 80328 Munich Germany. **Tel** 011 49 89 54218130.) cum. index. **Continues** Studii Si Cercetari de Istorie Veche.
Ind/Abst Anthropol. Index; BHA : Biblio. Hist. Art; Numis. Lit.

LC GN705 .S54
XO

STUDIJNE ZVESTI ARCHEOLOGICKEHO USTAVU SLOVENSKEJ AKADEMIE VIED. Added/Corp Slovenska Akademia Vied. Archeologicky Ustav. (19??)-. Monographic series. Slovak (summaries and/or abstracts in German and Russian; table of contents in German and Russian). Irregular. Price varies per volume. Veda, Publishing House of the Slovak Academy of Sciences, Klemensova 19, 814 30 Bratislava Slovakia. **Tel** (7)583-15.
Ind/Abst Anthropol. Lit.

ISSN 1257-5631
FR

UDC 908(442.7/.8)

●**SUCELLUS. BERCK-SUR-MER. See** History-History of Europe.

LC DS67 .S76
ISSN 0081-9271
DD 913.35
IQ
CODEN SUMRA9

SUMER (BAGHDAD). (SUMER.). [Sumer]. **Added/Corp** Iraq. Mudiriyat al-Athar al-Quadimah al-Ammah. VFOAT Sumir. Vol. 1 (Jan. 1945)-. Arabic (English, French and German). One time a year. $60.00. Laam Ltd. State Antiquities Organization, PO Box 249A Surbiton, Surrey KT6 5AX United Kingdom. **Tel** 011 44 181 3905818. cum. index.
Ind/Abst Anthropol. Lit.; BHA : Biblio. Hist. Art; GeoRef; Middle East Abstr. Index; Numis. Lit.

LC DK445 .S7
ISSN 0355-1822
FI

SUOMEN MUINAISMUISTOYHDISTYKSEN AIKAKAUSKIRJA = FINSKA FORNMINNESFOERENINGENS TIDSKRIFT. Added/Corp Suomen Muinaismuistoyhdistys. VFOAT Suomen Muinaismuisto-Yhdistyksen Aikakauskirja; Finska Fornminnesforeningens Tidskrift; Zeitschrift der Finnischen Alterthumsgesellschaft. (18??)-. Monographic series. Finnish (English, French, German and Swedish). Price varies per volume. **Continues** Suomen Muinaismuisto-yhtio Aikakauskirja.
Ind/Abst BHA : Biblio. Hist. Art.

LC DK445 .S8
ISSN 0355-1806
DD 930.1
FI

SUOMEN MUSEO. Added/Corp Suomen Muinaismuistoyhdistys. (1894)-. Academic Scholarly Publication. Finnish (summaries and/or abstracts in German). One time a year. Suomen Muinaismuistoyhdistys, Finnish Antiquarian Society, Box 913, FIN-00101 Helsinki 10 Finland. **ED** T Talvio. cum. index.
Ind/Abst Anthropol. Lit.; BHA : Biblio. Hist. Art; Numis. Lit.

UA

SUPPLEMENT AUX ANNALES DU SERVICE DES ANTIQUTES DE L'EQYPTE. Main/Corp Egypt. Maslahat Al-Athar. **Added/Corp** Cairo. Institut Francais d'Archeologie Orientale. No. 1 (1946)-. Periodical. English (French and German). One time a year. Institut Francais d'Archeologie Orientale du Caire, 37 Mounira Street, Cairo Rae Egypt. **(Subscription address:** Leila Bookshop, PO Box 31 El Daher, 11271 Cairo Egypt. **Tel** 011 202 3924475, 011 202 3507399.)

Pr Rev.
UK

SURREY ARCHAEOLOGICAL COLLECTIONS. (SURREY ARCHAEOLOGICAL COLLECTIONS, RELATING TO THE HISTORY AND ANTIQUITIES OF THE COUNTY.). **Main/Corp** Surrey Archaeological Society, Guilford. Vol. 1 (1854)-. Academic Scholarly Publication. English. Irregular. £12.00. Surrey Archaeological, Castle Arch, Guildford Surrey GU1 3SX United Kingdom. cum. index. available on microfiche.
Ind/Abst BHA : Biblio. Hist. Art.

LC DA670.S97 S9
ISSN 0143-8204
UK

SUSSEX ARCHAEOLOGICAL COLLECTIONS. (SUSSEX ARCHAEOLOGICAL COLLECTIONS RELATING TO THE HISTORY AND ANTIQUITIES OF THE COUNTY.). [Sussex archaeol. collect.]. **Added/Corp** Sussex Archaeological Society. Vol. 1 (1848)-. Academic Scholarly Publication. English. One time a year. comes with Sussex Archaeological Society membership. Sussex Archaeological Society, Barbican House, High Street, Lewes BN7 1YE United Kingdom. **Tel** 011 44 171 474379. Index available. cum. index. **Circ:** 1,600 (ctrl).
Desc: Contains articles on the history and archaeology of Sussex.
Ind/Abst Avery Index Archit. Period. Suppl. Colum. Univ. (1988); BHA : Biblio. Hist. Art.

LC GN845.P7 S9
ISSN 0082-044X
PL

SWIATOWIT. Added/Corp Muzeum Archeologiczne im. Er. Majewskiego. Muzeum Prahistoryczne Imienia Erazma Majewskiego. Uniwersytet Warszawski. Katedra Archeologii Pierwotnej i Wczesnosredniowiecznej. Uniwersytet Warszawski. Katedra Archeologii Pradziejowej i Wczesnosredniowiecznej. Uniwersytet Warszawski. Instytut Archeologii. (1889)-. Monographic series. Polish. Irregular. Price varies per volume. Wydawnictwo Uniwersytetu Warszawskiego, Ul. Nowy Swiat 4, 00-497 Warsaw Poland. **Tel** 011 48 22 200381, 011 48 22 6253044. **(Subscription address:** Ars Polona-Ruch, PO Box 1001, Krakowskie Przedmiescie 7, 00-068 Warsaw Poland. **Tel** 011 48 22 261201.) cum. index.
Ind/Abst BHA : Biblio. Hist. Art.

LC DS94.5 .S8
ISSN 0039-7946
DD 913.394
FR

SYRIA. [Syria]. **Added/Corp** France. Haut Commissariat de la Republique Francaise en Syrie et au Liban. Institut Francais d'Archeologie de Beyrouth. Vol. 1 (1920)-. Periodical. French. Two times a year. 450.00F. Librairie Orientaliste Paul Geuthner, 12 rue Vavin, 75006 Paris France. **Tel** 011 33 1 46347130.
Ind/Abst Avery Index Archit. Period. Suppl. Colum. Univ. (19??-199?); BHA : Biblio. Hist. Art; Index Book Rev. Relig.; MLA Int. Bibl. Books Artic. Mod. Lang. Lit.; Numis. Lit.; Relig. Index One Period. (1949-).

LC AP95.C4 T3554
DD 951/.24905/05
CH

TA LU TSA CHIH. See History-History of Asia.

ISSN 0740-0241
US

TAARS NEWS AND NOTES. [TAARS news notes]. **Added/Corp** Toledo Area Aboriginal Research Society, Inc. VFOAT T.A.A.R.S. News and Notes. **VAT** Toledo Area Aboriginal Research Society News and Notes. (19??)-. Periodical. English. Twelve times a year. $12.00. TAARS Department of Anthropology, University of Toledo, Toledo OH 43606. **ED** David M. Stothers. **Bk Rev. Circ:** 100.
Desc: Juried accepted research defining nature of prehistoric cultures that occupied the Western Basin region of Lake Erie, Southeast Michigan, North and Northwest Ohio, Southwest Ontario, Canada, and Northeast Indiana.

LC DS111.A1 T44
ISSN 0334-4355
DD 933
IS
CODEN TEAVEY

TEL AVIV (1974). (TEL AVIV.). [Tel Aviv]. **Added/Corp** Universitat Tel-Aviv. Makhon le-arkheologyah. Makhon le-arkheologyah a. sh. Sonyah u-Marko Nadler. Vol. 1 (1974)-. Academic Scholarly Publication. English. Two times a year. $34.00. Friends of the Archaelogical Institute, Tel Aviv University, PO Box 39040, Ramat Aviv 69978 Israel. **Tel** 11 972 3 6409417, FAX 011 972 3 6407237. **ED** D Ussishkin. **Circ:** 400.
Desc: The journal of the Tel Aviv University Institute of Archaeology. Publishes studies on the history, culture and archaeology of the Ancient Near East.
Ind/Abst Anthropol. Lit.; Art Archaeol. Tech. Abstr.; Middle East Abstr. Index; New Testam. Abstr.; Numis. Lit.; Old Testam. Abstr.; Relig. Theol. Abstr.

LC DA990.L8 T46
DD 936.1/62
IE

TEMPLEMORE : JOURNAL OF THE NORTH WEST ARCHAEOLOGICAL AND HISTORICAL SOCIETY. Added/Corp North West Archaeological and Historical Society. Vol. 1, No. 1 (1985)-. Periodical. English. One time a year. $6.84. North West Archaeological and Historical Society, 1 Summerhill Prehen, Derry Ireland. **Tel** 011 353 1504 454444.

LC F438 .T4
ISSN 0040-3180
DD 913.768
US

TENNESSEE ARCHAEOLOGIST. Added/Corp Tennessee Archaeological Society. Vol. 1 (Dec. 1944)-. Periodical. English. Four times a year. Tennessee Archaeological Society, Route 1 Box 237, Rockford TN 37853.
Ind/Abst Anthropol. Index; Ethnoarts Index.

ISSN 0082-2949
DD 976
US

TEXAS ARCHEOLOGY. [Tex. archeol.]. **Added/Corp** Texas Archeological Society. Midland Archeological Society. Vol. 1, No. 1 (Apr. 1957)-. Newsletter. English. Four times a year (Jan., Apr., July, Oct.). $25.00 Comes with Texas Archeological Society membership. Texas Archeological Society, Center for Archeological Research, University of Texas at San Antonio, 6900 North Loop 1604 West, San Antonio TX 78285-0658. **Tel** (210)691-4393.

ISSN 0563-3087
GW

TEXTE UND KOMMENTARE; EINE ALTERTUMSWISSENSCHAFTLICHE REIHE. Vol. 1 (1963)-. Monographic series. German. Irregular. Price varies per volume. Bayerische Schulbuch Verlag, Hubertusstrasse 4, D-80639 Munich Germany. **Tel** 011 49 89 179120.

UA

TEXTES ARABES ET ETUDES ISLAMIQUES. Main/Corp Cairo. Institut Francais d'Archeologie Orientale. (19??)-. Monographic series. English (French and Arabic). Irregular. Price varies per volume. Institut Francais d'Archeologie Orientale du Caire, 37 Mounira Street, Cairo Rae Egypt. **(Subscription address:** Leila Bookshop, PO Box 31 El Daher, 11271 Cairo Egypt. **Tel** 011 202 3924475, 011 202 3507399.) Index available.

Archaeology

TEXTS FROM EXCAVATIONS. Added/Corp
ISSN 0307-5125 UK
Egypt Exploration Society. (1975)-. Monographic series. English. Irregular. Price varies per volume. Egypt Exploration Society, 3 Doughty Mews, Longon WC1N 2PG United Kingdom. **Tel** 011 44 171 2421880. **ED** W. J. Tait. **Circ**: 250.

THORIKOS. BE
Vol. 1 (1961)-. French. Irregular. Comite des Fouilles Belges, Blandijnberg 2, B9000 Gent Belgium. **Tel** 91-257571.
Desc: Preliminary reports on excavations in Thorikos, miscellaneous information about Greece and guides of the excavations.

THUNDERBIRD (PULLMAN, WASH.), THE.
ISSN 0737-5557 US
(THE THUNDERBIRD.). [Thunderbird]. (19??)-. Periodical. English. Irregular.
Ind/Abst Ethnoarts Index.

TIERRA (SOUTHERN TEXAS ARCHAEOLOGICAL ASSOCIATION), LA.
LC E78.T4 T53
DD 976.4/01/05
ISSN 0163-0695 US
(LA TIERRA.). **Added/Corp** Southern Texas Archaeological Association. Vol. 1, No. 1 (Jan. 1974)-. Periodical. English. Four times a year. $30.00. South Texas Archaeological Association, PO Box 791032, San Antonio TX 78279. **Tel** (210)732-5970. **ED** Evelyn Lewis (editor's telephone: (210)684-9250). Index available ($1.00). cum. index. **Circ**: 500.
Desc: Reports on archaeological sites and artifacts, prehistoric and historic, primarily in south Texas.
Ind/Abst Abstr. Anthropol. (19??-); Anthropol. Lit.; Ethnoarts Index.

TOMBE D'ETA SAITICA A SAQQARA. IT
(1977)-. Monographic series. Italian. Irregular. Price varies per volume. Giardini Editori Stampatori, Via Santa Bibbiana 28, 56127 Pisa Italy. **Tel** 011 39 50 934242.

TRABAJOS DE ARQUEOLOGIA NAVARRA.
DD 936.6 SP
VFOAT Arqueologia Navarra. (1979)-. Monographic series. Spanish. Price varies per volume. Diputacion Foral de Navarra, Ansoleaga 10, Pamplona Spain.
Ind/Abst Anthropol. Lit.

TRABAJOS DE PREHISTORIA (INSTITUTO ESPANOL DE PREHISTORIA).
LC GN835.A1 T7a
DD 936.6
ISSN 0082-5638 SP
CODEN TRPREI
(TRABAJOS DE PREHISTORIA.). [Trab. prehist.]. **Added/Corp** Instituto Espanol de Prehistoria. Universidad Complutense de Madrid. Departamento de Prehistoria. New Series, Vol. 26 (1969)-. Monographic series. Spanish. One time a year. Price varies per volume. Consejo Superior Investigacion Cientificas / CSIC, Vitruvio 8, 28006 Madrid Spain. **Tel** 011 34 1 5612833, FAX 011 34 1 4113077, telex 42182.
Bk Rev. **Continues** Trabajos de Prehistoria (Universidad Complutense de Madrid. Seminario de Historia Primitiva del Hombre).
Desc: Currently accepts articles on Spanish prehistory primarily, while printing research on Latin American prehistory from time to time. Comprises two sections: articles and bibliographic notes.
Ind/Abst Anthropol. Lit.; GeoRef.

TRANSACTIONS - BIRMINGHAM AND WARWICKSHIRE ARCHAEOLOGICAL SOCIETY. UK
Main/Corp Birmingham and Warwickshire Archaeological Society. Vol. 84 (1967)-. Periodical. English. One time a year. £18.00. Birmingham and Warwickshire Archaeological Society, 47 Goldsmith Road, Kings Heath, Birmingham B14 7EH United Kingdom. **Tel** 011 4 21 4464545 ext. 299. **Continues** Birmingham Archaeological Society, Birmingham, Eng. Transactions and Proceedings.
Ind/Abst BHA : Biblio. Hist. Art.

TRANSACTIONS - BRISTOL AND GLOUCESTERSHIRE ARCHAEOLOGICAL SOCIETY.
ISSN 0068-1032 UK
[Trans. Bristol Glouces. Archaeol. Soc.]. **Main/Corp** Bristol and Gloucestershire Archaeological Society. Vol. 1 (1876)-. English. One time a year (March or April). $22.25. Bristol and Gloucestershire Archaeological Society, 22 Beaumont Road, Gloucester GL2 0EJ United Kingdom. **Tel** 011 44 1452 302610. **ED** G. C. Boon, (editor's address: 43 Westbourne Road, Penartu, Cardiff CF6 2HA UK). Index available (Bound in each issue). cum. index. **Bk Rev**, (Qty: 6). **Circ**: 1,000.
Desc: Research articles in archaeology, local history, buildings and antiques of Bristol and Gloucestershire.
Ind/Abst BHA : Biblio. Hist. Art; Br. Archaeol. Bibliogr.; Br. Humanit. Index; Numis. Lit.

TRANSACTIONS - LEICESTERSHIRE ARCHAEOLOGICAL AND HISTORICAL SOCIETY.
ISSN 0140-3990 UK
[Trans. - Leics. Archaeol. Hist. Soc.]. (1955)-. English. One time a year. **Continues** Transactions of the Leicestershire Archaeological Society.
Ind/Abst BHA : Biblio. Hist. Art.

TRANSACTIONS OF THE CUMBERLAND & WESTMORLAND ANTIQUARIAN & ARCHAEOLOGICAL SOCIETY.
ISSN 0309-7986 UK
See History-History of Europe.

TRANSACTIONS OF THE LONDON AND MIDDLESEX ARCHAEOLOGICAL SOCIETY.
LC DA675 .L84
ISSN 0076-0501 UK
Main/Corp London and Middlesex Archaeological Society. **VAT** Transactions of the London & Middlesex Archaeological Society. Vol. 1 (July 1856)-Vol. 7 (1888); New Ser. Vol. 1 (1905)- Vol. 11 (1954); Vol. 18 (1955)-. English. One time a year. $13.00 (institutions); $10.00 (individuals) Comes with membership. London and Middlesex Archaeological Society, Museum of London, London Wall, London EC2 Y5HN United Kingdom. **Tel** 011 44 171 9729111. cum. index. **Absorbed** London & Middlesex Historian, 0459-7486.
Ind/Abst BHA : Biblio. Hist. Art.

TRANSACTIONS OF THE MONUMENTAL BRASS SOCIETY.
ISSN 0143-1250 UK
[Trans. Monum. Brass Soc.]. No. 13 (Jan. 1894)-. Periodical. English. One time a year. comes with membership. Society of Antiquaries, Burlington House, Picadilly, London W1V 0HS United Kingdom. **ED** S.G.H. Freeth. Index available. **Bk Rev**. **Circ**: 650 (ctrl). **Continues** Transactions of the Cambridge University Association of Brass Collectors.
Ind/Abst Art Archaeol. Tech. Abstr.; BHA : Biblio. Hist. Art; Br. Humanit. Index.

TRANSACTIONS OF THE SHROPSHIRE ARCHAEOLOGICAL AND HISTORICAL SOCIETY.
ISSN 0143-5175 UK
Main/Corp Shropshire Archaeological and Historical Society. Vol. 66 (1989)-. Periodical. English. Shropshire Archaeological Society, Westcott Farm, Pontesbury Shropshire SY5 0SQ United Kingdom. **Tel** 011 44 1743 790531. **Continues** Transactions of the Shropshire Archaeological Society.
Ind/Abst BHA : Biblio. Hist. Art.

TRANSACTIONS OF THE WORCESTERSHIRE ARCHAEOLOGICAL SOCIETY.
ISSN 0143-2389 UK
[Trans. Worcs. Archaeol. Soc.]. (1924)-. English. Every 2 years. Comes with Worcestershire Archaeological Society membership; £15.00 (membership). Worcestershire Archaeological Society, 14 Scobell Close Pershore, Worcestershire WR10 1QJ United Kingdom. **Tel** 011 44 1386 554886. available on microfilm from University Microfilms International (UMI). **Continues in part** Reports and Papers - Associated Architectural Societies.
Ind/Abst BHA : Biblio. Hist. Art.

TRANSACTIONS - SOUTH STAFFORDSHIRE ARCHAEOLOGICAL AND HISTORICAL SOCIETY.
LC DA670.S69 L55a
DD 913.362
ISSN 0457-7817 UK
(TRANSACTIONS.). [Trans. - S. Staffords. Archaeol. Hist. Soc.]. **Main/Corp** South Staffordshire Archaeological and Historical Society. Vol. 10 (1968/1969)-. English. One time a year (Nov). $23.96. South Staffordshire Archaeological and Historical Society, 32 Birchwood Road Parkside, Litchfield Staffordshire, WS14 9UW United Kingdom. **Tel** 011 44 1543 252384. **Continues** Lichfield and South Straffordshire Archaeological and Historical Society. Transactions.
Ind/Abst Avery Index Archit. Period. Suppl. Colum. Univ. (19??-199?); BHA : Biblio. Hist. Art.

TRIBUNA D'ARQUEOLOGIA. Added/Corp
LC DP302.C615 T73
DD 936.6 SP
Catalonia (Spain). Servei d'Arqueologia. Catalonia (Spain). Departament d'Ensenyament i Cultura. (19??)-. Periodical. Catalan.
Ind/Abst Anthropol. Lit.

TUNG-PEI KAO KU YU LI SHIH. VFOAT
LC DS782.5 83
DD 951/.8 CC
Memoris of Archaeology and History of Northeast China. 1 (1982)-. Periodical. Chinese. RMBY2.70. Science Press, 16 Donghuangchenggen North Street, Beijing 100707, People's Republic of China. **Tel** 011 86 1 4019821, 011 86 1 4010642, FAX 011 86 1 4012180, 011 86 1 4019810, telex 210147.

U MUT MAYA : AN UNOFFICIAL COLLECTION OF PAPERS, REPORTS, AND READINGS BY ATTENDANTS OF THE ... ADVANCED SEMINAR ON MAYA HIEROGLYPHIC WRITING HELD AT THE UNIVERSITY OF TEXAS AT AUSTIN ... . US
See History-History of North and South America.

ULSTER JOURNAL OF ARCHAEOLOGY.
LC DA990.U45 U4
DD 941.6/005
ISSN 0082-7355
CODEN UJAYAH
[Ulst. j. archaeol.]. **Added/Corp** Ulster Archaeological Society. Vol. 1 (1853)-. Periodical. English. One time a year. $10.27. Ulster Archaeological Society, Queens University, Belfast BT7 INN United Kingdom. **Tel** 011 44 1232 245133. **ED** M. Avery. Index available. cum. index. **Bk Rev**. **Ad Acc**. **Circ**: 600 (ctrl).
Desc: Covers the archaeology of Ulster.
Ind/Abst Am. Hist. Life (1955-1956); Art Archaeol. Tech. Abstr.; BHA : Biblio. Hist. Art; Br. Archaeol. Bibliogr.; GeoRef; Numis. Lit.

UNIVERSITETETS OLDSAKSAMLINGS ARSBERETNING.
LC DL421 .U73a NO
Main/Corp Universitetet i Oslo. Universitetets Oldsaksamling. (1971)-. Norwegian. **Continues in part** Universitetet i Oslo. Universitetets Oldsaksamling.; **Continues** Arbok-Universitetets Oldsaksamling.
Ind/Abst Art Archaeol. Tech. Abstr.

UNIVERSITETETS OLDSAKSAMLINGS TILVEKST.
LC DL21 .O68a NO
Main/Corp Universitetet i Oslo. Universitetets Oldsaksamling. **Added/Corp** Universitetet i Oslo. Universitetets Oldsaksamling. Tilvekst. (1971)-. Norwegian. **Continues in part** Arbok - Universitetets Oldsaksamling.

UNIVERSITY OF GEORGIA LABORATORY OF ARCHAEOLOGY SERIES.
DD 975.8/01
ISSN 0433-5732 US
[Univ. Ga. Lab. Archaeol. ser.]. **Added/Corp** University of Georgia. Laboratory of Archaeology. **VFOAT** Series. Report. No. 1, (19??)-. Monographic series. English. Irregular. Price varies per volume. University of Georgia Department of Anthropology, Baldwin Hall, Athens GA 30602. **Tel** (706)542-3922. **ED** David J. Hally. **Circ**: 150.
Desc: Historical archaeology and prehistoric archaeology of Georgia.

USPEKHI SREDNEAZIATSKOI ARKHEOLOGII. Added/Corp
LC DK855 .U84
ISSN 0136-7455 RU
Institut Arkheologii (Akademiia Nauk SSSR) Nauchnyi Sovet po Problemam Arkheologii Srednei Azii i Kazakhstana (Akademiia Nauk SSSR). (1972)-. Periodical. Russian. Izdatelstvo Nauka St. Petersburg, Mendeleevskaia Liniia 1, 199034 St. Petersburg, B-34 Russia. **Tel** 011 7 812 2182612.

UTAH ARCHAEOLOGY (NEWSLETTER).
LC F828 .U83
DD 979.2/01
ISSN 0500-7860 US
Pr Rev.
(UTAH ARCHAEOLOGY.). [Utah archaeol.]. **Added/Corp** Utah Statewide Archaeology Society. **VFOAT** U.S.A.S. Newsletter; Newsletter; USAS Newsletter. (March 1955)-. English. One time a year. $15.00. Utah Archaeology, Utah Division of State History, 300 Rio Grande, Salt Lake City UT 84101. **Tel** (801)533-3529, FAX (801)533-3503. **ED** Kenin Jones and Bob Kohl (editors' phone: (801)533-3500). **Bk Rev**. ctrl circ.

VALENTIANA. VALENCIENNES.
UDC 908 (442.8)
ISSN 0989-6139 FR
(VALENTIANA.). [Valentiana Valenciennes]. (1988)-. Periodical. French. Two times a year (June and Dec.). 153.55F Europe; 167.00F Europe. Valenciana, Bibliotheque Municipale BP 282, 59300 Valenciennes France. **Tel** 011 33 1 27225700.
Ind/Abst BHA : Biblio. Hist. Art.

ISSN 0079-4376
GW

VEROFFENTLICHUNGEN DES BRANDENBURGISCHEN LANDESMUSEUMS FUER UR- UND FRUEHGESCHICHTE. **Main/Corp** Museum fuer Ur- und Fruhgeschichte Potsdam. **Added/Corp** Museum fuer Ur- und Fruehgeschichte Potsdam. (1992)-. Monographic series. German. Price varies per volume. Deutscher Verlag der Wissenschaften, Taubennstrasse 10, D-10117 Berlin Germany. **Tel** 011 49 30 2291146. **Bk Rev**. **Ad Acc**. ctrl circ. ***Continues*** *Veroffentlichungen des Museums fuer ur- und Fruehgeschichte Potsdam, 0079-4376.*
Desc: Publishes the latest archaeological finds and research findings on the prehistory and early history of the districts of Potsdam, Frankfurt-O and Cottbus, with additional articles from scientific branches.
Ind/Abst Anthropol. Index; Anthropol. Lit.; BHA : Biblio. Hist. Art.

GW

VEROFFENTLICHUNGEN DES ZENTRALINSTITUTS FUER ALTE GESCHICHTE UND ARCHAOLOGIE DER AKADEMIE DER WISSENSCHAFTEN DER DDR. **Added/Corp** Akademie der Wissenschaften der DDR. Zentralinstitut fuer Alte Geschichte und Archaologie. (1973)-. Monographic series. German. Irregular. Price varies per volume. Akademie-Verlag GmbH, Postfach, D-13162 Berlin Germany. **Tel** 011 49 30 47889300, FAX 011 49 30 47889357. **(Subscription address:** VCH Publishers Inc., 303 Northwest 12th Avenue, Journals Department, Deerfield FL 33442. **Tel** (800)367-8249, (305)428-5566.)

GW

VERZEICHNIS DER MITGLIEDER / DEUTSCHES ARCHAOLOGISCHES INSTITUT. **Main/Corp** Deutsches Archaologisches Institut. Periodical. German. One time a year. Deutsches Archaologisches Institut / Berlin, Lindenstrasse 76, 10969 Berlin Germany. **Tel** 030-2591-3589, FAX 030-2591-3565.

LC DB361 .Z2 **ISSN** 0350-7165
CI

VJESNIK ARHEOLOSKOG MUZEJA U ZAGREBU. [Vjesn. Arheol. muz. Zagrebu]. **Added/Corp** Arheoloski Muzej u Zagrebu. (1958)-. Periodical. Serbo-Croatian (Roman) (summaries and/or abstracts in English and German). One time a year. Arheoloski Muzej u Zagrebu, Trg N Zrinskog 19, 41000 Zagreb Croatia. **Bk Rev**. **Circ:** 600. available with illustrations. ***Continues*** *Viestnik Hrvatskoga Arheoloskoga Drustva.*
Ind/Abst BHA : Biblio. Hist. Art.

LC DB401 .S65 **ISSN** 0350-8447
DD 913.031 CI

VJESNIK ZA ARHEOLOGIJU I HISTORIJU DALMATINSKU. (VJESNIK ZA ARHEOLOGIJU I HISTORIJU DALMATINSKU = BULLETIN D'ARCHEOLOGIE ET D'HISTOIRE DALMATE.). [Vjesn. arheol. hist. dalm.]. **Added/Corp** Arheoloski Muzej u Splitu. Arheoloski Muzej u Zadru. **VFOAT** Bulletin d'Archeologie et d'Histoire Dalmate. (1878)-. Bulletin. Serbo-Croatian (Roman) (summaries and/or abstracts in Multiple languages). Irregular. Price varies. Arheoloski Muzej u Split, Zrinsko-Frankopanska 25, PO Box 15, 58000 Split Croatia. **Tel** 011 58 44 685. **ED** E. Marin. **Bk Rev**. **Circ:** 775.
Ind/Abst BHA : Biblio. Hist. Art.

LC DB200 .V97
XR

VYZKUMY V CECHACH. **Added/Corp** Archeologicky Ustav (Ceskoslovenska Akademie Ved). (1969)-. Academic Scholarly Publication. Czech. One time a year. Academia, Publishing House of the Czechoslovak Academy of Sciences, Vodickova 40, PO Box 896, 112 29 Prague 1, Czech Republic. **Tel** 011 42 2 245117. **ED** E. Cujanova. available with illustrations. ***Supersedes*** *Ceskoslovenska Akademie Ved. Archeologicky Ustav. Zachranne Oddeleni. Bulletin Zachranneho Oddeleni.*
Ind/Abst BHA : Biblio. Hist. Art.

LC CC **ISSN** 0231-956X
DD 930.1 XR
UDC 902

VYZKUMY V CECHACH. SUPPLEMENTUM. [Vyzk. Cech., Suppl.]. (1974)-. Academic Scholarly Publication. Multiple languages. Irregular. Academia, Publishing House of the Czechoslovak Academy of Sciences, Vodickova 40, PO Box 896, 112 29 Prague 1, Czech Republic. **Tel** 011 42 2 245117.
Ind/Abst BHA : Biblio. Hist. Art.

LC DS777.55 .K577
DD 931/.005 CC

WEN WU TIEN TI. **VFOAT** Wenwu Tiandi; Cultural Objects. Vol. 1 (1981)-. Periodical. Chinese. Six times a year. RMBY13.20. Wenhua Bu, Minstry of Culture, (Guwenxian Yanjiushi), China Cultural Relics Research Institute, No. 29 Wusi Street, Beijing 100009, People's Republic of China. **Tel** 4015577. **(Subscription address:** China International Book Trading Corporation, PO Box 399, Library Service Department, Beijing 100044 People's Republic of China. **Tel** 011 86 1 8414284, FAX 011 86 1 8412023, telex 22496 CIBTC CN.) **ED** Wu Tiemei. ***Continues*** *Ko Ming Wen Wu.*

LC GN865.W45 W46 **ISSN** 0083-8160
DD 916.6/03 NR

WEST AFRICAN JOURNAL OF ARCHAEOLOGY. (1971)-. Periodical. English. Two times a year. West African Journal of Archaeology, Department of Archaeology, University of Ibadan, Ibadan Nigeria. **Tel** 011 234 302 462550. **ED** B. W. Andah. cum. index. **Bk Rev**. **Ad Acc**. ctrl circ. ***Supersedes*** *West African Archaeological Newsletter.*
Ind/Abst Anthropol. Index (19??-); Anthropol. Lit. (19??-); Br. Archaeol. Bibliogr. (-19??); Ethnoarts Index (19??-).

ISSN 0166-4301
NE
UDC A902

WESTERHEEM. [Westerheem]. (1952)-. Periodical. Dutch. Six times a year. Awn H Schoorl, Postbus 100, 2180 AC Hillegom Netherlands. **Tel** 31 02520-16482.
Ind/Abst BHA : Biblio. Hist. Art (19??-).

ISSN 0739-1080
US

WESTERN PREHISTORIC RESEARCH ARCHEOLOGICAL MONOGRAPH. [West. Prehist. Res. archeol. monogr.]. (19??)-. Monographic series. English. Irregular. Price varies per volume. Western Prehistoric Research, PO Box 1761, Rock Springs WY 82902. **Tel** (307)367-4262. **Bk Rev**. **Circ:** 1,000.
Desc: Covering Northwestern Plains, the Rocky Mountain, and Great Basin Archaeology.

ISSN 0043-5082
PL

WIADOMOSCI ARCHEOLOGICZNE. **Added/Corp** Warsaw. Panstwowe Muzeum Archeologiczne. **VFOAT** Bulletin Archeologique Polonais. Vol. 1 (1873)-. Bulletin. Polish. Two times a year. $20.00. **(Subscription address:** Ars Polona-Ruch, PO Box 1001, Krakowskie Przedmiescie 7, 00-068 Warsaw Poland. **Tel** 011 48 22 261201.) cum. index.
Ind/Abst Anthropol. Index; Anthropol. Lit.; BHA : Biblio. Hist. Art; Br. Archaeol. Bibliogr. (?-?).

LC DA670.W69 W517 **ISSN** 0262-6608
DD 936.2/31 UK

WILTSHIRE ARCHAEOLOGICAL AND NATURAL HISTORY MAGAZINE (1982). (THE WILTSHIRE ARCHAEOLOGICAL AND NATURAL HISTORY MAGAZINE.). **Added/Corp** Wiltshire Archaeological and Natural History Society. Vol. 76 (1981)-. Periodical. English. One time a year. Comes with Wiltshire Archaeological and Natural History Society membership - £24.00. Wiltshire Archaeological and Natural History Society, The Museum, 41 Long Street Devizes, Wiltshire SN10 1NS United Kingdom. **Tel** 011 44 1380 727369. **ED** Kate Fielden. Index available. cum. index. **Bk Rev**. **Circ:** 1,500 (ctrl). ***Formed by the union of Wiltshire Natural History Magazine, 0309-3468 and*** *Wiltshire Archaeological Magazine, 0309-3476.*
Ind/Abst Art Archaeol. Tech. Abstr.; BHA : Biblio. Hist. Art; Br. Archaeol. Bibliogr.; Br. Humanit. Index; Numis. Lit. (?-?).

LC N5325 .A8
GW

WINCKELMANNSPROGRAMM DER ARCHAEOLOGISCHEN GESELLSCHAFT ZU BERLIN. **Main/Corp** Archaeologische Gesellschaft zu Berlin. (1841)-. Periodical. German. Irregular. Walter de Gruyter Inc., PO Box 303421, D-10728 Berlin Germany. **Tel** 011 49 30 260050, FAX 011 49 30 26005251, telex 184027.

LC E78.W8 W8 **ISSN** 0043-6364
DD 977.5/005 US
Pr Rev.

WISCONSIN ARCHEOLOGIST, THE. **Added/Corp** Wisconsin Natural History Society. Archeological Section. Wisconsin Archeological Society. Vol. 1 (Oct. 1901)-. Periodical. English. Four times a year. $30.00. Wisconsin Archeological Society, PO Box 1292, Milwaukee WI 53201. **Tel** (414)229-4273. **ED** David Overstreet. Index available (Vol. 52, No. 4). cum. index. **Bk Rev**, (Qty: varies). **Circ:** 550.
Ind/Abst Am. Hist. Life (1988-); Anthropol. Lit.; Ethnoarts Index.

ISSN 0352-1990
BN
UDC 93

WISSENSCHAFTLICHE MITTEILUNGEN DES BOSNISCH-HERZEGOWINISCHEN LANDESMUSEUMS. HEFT A : ARCHAOLOGIE. [Wiss. Mitt. Bosnisch-Herzeg. Landesmus., A, Archaeol.]. (1971)-. Academic Scholarly Publication. German. Irregular. Zemaljski Muzej Bosne i Hercegovine, Vojvode Putnika 7, Sarajevo Bosnia Hercegovina. **ED** Vlajko Palavestra.
Ind/Abst BHA : Biblio. Hist. Art.

LC CC1 .W6 **ISSN** 0043-8243
DD 905 UK
CCC
CODEN WOAREN
Pr Rev.

WORLD ARCHAEOLOGY. [World archaeol.]. (1969)-. Periodical. English. Three times a year (Feb., Jun., Oct.). $120.00. Routledge, 11 New Fetter Lane, London EC4P 4EE United Kingdom. **Tel** 011 44 171 5839855, FAX 011 44 171 5830701. **(Subscription address:** Kinokuniya Company Ltd., 38-1 Sakuragaoka 5, chome Setagaya-ku, Tokyo 156 Japan. **Tel** FAX 011 03 3439 0136.) **ED** J Oates. **Bk Rev**. **Ad Acc**. **Circ:** 1,100. Documents available from The Genuine Article, UMI Article Clearinghouse.
Desc: A journal of archaeology with a respected international reputation drawing on many of the top archaeologists of our time.
Ind/Abst Abstr. Anthropol.; Acad. Search; Anthropol. Lit.; Art Archaeol. Tech. Abstr.; Arts Humanit. Citation Index [Full Cov.]; Avery Index Archit. Period. Suppl. Colum. Univ. (Feb., Oct. 1990); BHA : Biblio. Hist. Art; Br. Archaeol. Bibliogr.; Br. Humanit. Index; Ceram. Abstr. (199?-); Curr. Cit.; Curr. Contents Arts Humanit.; Curr. Contents Soc. Behav. Sci.; Curr. Geogr. Publ. (199?-); Ecol. Abstr. (?-?); EP Collect.; Ethnoarts Index; Expand. Acad. Index (1989-); Geogr. Abstr. Phys. Geogr.; Geogr. Abstr. Human Geogr.; Homework Help.; Humanit. Index; Humanit. Source; INFO-SOUTH Abstr.; Mag. Search; MasterFile FullTEXT 1000; MasterFile FullTEXT 350; MasterFile FullTEXT 650; MasterFile FullTEXT (July 1993-); Middle East Abstr. Index; Newsp. Period. Abstr. (1991-); OCLC; Res. Alert [Full Cov.]; Soc. Sci. Cit. Index [Full Cov.]; Telebase.

ISSN 0043-9665
US

WYOMING ARCHAEOLOGIST, THE. **Added/Corp** Wyoming Archaeological Society. Vol. 2, No. 4 (May 1959)-. Periodical. English. Two times a year. $15.00 (institutions), $10.00 (associates) US; $19.00 (institutions), $19.00 (associates) other. Wyoming Archaeological Society, 1617 Westridge Terrace, Casper WY 82604. **ED** Bonnie Johnson. **Bk Rev**, (Qty: 3-4). **Circ:** 450. ***Continues*** *Smoke Signal.*
Ind/Abst Am. Hist. Life (1986-); Anthropol. Lit.; Ethnoarts Index.

LC CC **ISSN** 1121-9688
DD 930.1 IT

XENIA ANTIQUA. (1992)-. Periodical. Italian (English). L'Erma di Bretschneider SPA, via Cassiodoro 19, 00193 Rome Italy. **Tel** 011 39 6 6874127, 011 39 6 6874129, FAX 011 39 6 6874129. ***Continues*** *Xenia, 0394-4059.*

ISSN 0084-4276
UK

YORKSHIRE ARCHAEOLOGICAL JOURNAL, THE. **Added/Corp** Yorkshire Archaeological Society. (1893)-. English. One time a year. £15.00 (comes with membership). Yorkshire Archaeological Society, Claremont Clarendon Road, Leeds LS2 9NZ United Kingdom. **Tel** 011 44 1532 457910. **ED** R.M. Butler. Index available. cum. index. **Bk Rev**. **Circ:** 1,500 (ctrl). ***Continues*** *Yorkshire Archaeological and Topographical Journal.*
Ind/Abst BHA : Biblio. Hist. Art; Br. Archaeol. Bibliogr.; Br. Humanit. Index; Numis. Lit.

ISSN 0044-1481
PL

Z OTCHANI WIEKOW. **Added/Corp** Muzeum Archeologiczne w Poznaniu. Polskie Towarzystwo Prehistoryczne. Polskie Towarzystwo Archeologiczne i Numizmatyczne. Polskie Towarzystwo Archeologiczne. Vol. 1 (1926)-. Periodical. Polish (summaries and/or abstracts in English; table of contents in English and French). Four times a year. Price on request. **(Subscription address:** Ars Polona-Ruch, PO Box 1001, Krakowskie Przedmiescie 7, 00-068 Warsaw Poland. **Tel** 011 48 22 261201.) cum. index. ***Absorbed*** *Dawna Kultura.*

ISSN 0560-222X
XN

ZBORNIK - ARHEOLOSKI MUZEJ NA MAKEDONIJA. RECUEIL DES TRAVAUX. **Main/Corp** Skopje, Yugoslavia. Arheoloski Muzej. **Added/Corp** Skopje, Yugoslavia. Arheoloski Muzej. Recueil des Travaux. **VFOAT** Recueil des Travaux. (1956)-. Serbo-Croatian (Cyrillic) (French, German and Macedonian).
Ind/Abst BHA : Biblio. Hist. Art.

LC AM101 .B3824 **ISSN** 0522-8352
YU

ZBORNIK NARODNOG MUZEJA U BEOGRADU. (ZBORNIK NARODNOG MUZEJA.). [Zb. Nar. muz. Beogr.]. **Added/Corp** Narodni Muzej--Beograd. **VFOAT** Zbornik Narodnog Muzeja u Beogradu, Arheologija; Zbornik Narodnog Muzeja u Beogradu, Istorija Umetnosti; Zbornik Narodnog Muzeja u

Archaeology

Beogradu; Recueil du Musee National de Belgrade; Recueil du Musee National. (1964)-. Periodical. Serbo-Croatian (Cyrillic) (summaries and/or abstracts in English, French and German). Prosveta Export Import Agency, PO Box 180, Terazije 16, 1101 Belgrade Yugoslavia. **Tel** 011 862 687441, telex 862-11609. *Continues* Zbornik Radova Narodnog Muzeja (Belgrade, Serbia).
 Ind/Abst Anthropol. Lit.

ISSN 0012-1169
GW
CCC

ZEITSCHRIFT DES DEUTSCHEN PALAESTINA-VEREINS (1953). See History-History of the Near East.

LC PJ1004 .Z4   ISSN 0044-216X
GW

ZEITSCHRIFT FUER AGYPTISCHE SPRACHE UND ALTERTUMSKUNDE.
Added/Corp Deutsche Morgenlandische Gesellschaft. Vol. 1 (July 1863)-. Periodical. German. Two times a year. $160.00. Akademie-Verlag GmbH, Postfach, D-13162 Berlin Germany. **Tel** 011 49 30 47889300, FAX 011 49 30 47889357. **(Subscription address:** VCH Publishers Inc., 303 Northwest 12th Avenue, Journals Department, Deerfield FL 33442. **Tel** (800)367-8249, (305)428-5566.) **ED** E. Blumenthal, E. Hornung. cum. index.
 Desc: Dedicated to the whole field of Egyptology including Demotic, Coptic and Meroitic studies.
 Ind/Abst Arts Humanit. Citation Index [Full Cov.]; BHA : Biblio. Hist. Art.

LC CC5 .Z45   ISSN 0044-233X
DD 930.1/05   GW

ZEITSCHRIFT FUER ARCHAEOLOGIE.
Added/Corp Deutsche Akademie der Wissenschaften zu Berlin. Institut fuer Ur- und Fruehgeschichte. Akademie der Wissenschaften der DDR. Zentralinstitut fuer Alte Geschichte und Archaeologie. **VFOAT** Zeitschrift fuer Archaeologie. (1967)-. Periodical. German. Two times a year. $76.00. Dr. Alfred Huethig Verlag GmbH, Postfach 102869, D-69018 Heidelberg Germany. **Tel** 011 49 6221 489281, FAX 011 49 6221 489279. Documents available from The Genuine Article.
 Ind/Abst Anthropol. Index; Anthropol. Lit.; Arts Humanit. Citation Index (19??-19??) [Full Cov.]; BHA : Biblio. Hist. Art; Curr. Contents Arts Humanit.; Curr. Contents Soc. Behav. Sci.; Res. Alert [Full Cov.].

LC D125 .Z4   ISSN 0340-0824
DD 940.1   GW

ZEITSCHRIFT FUER ARCHAEOLOGIE DES MITTELALTERS. [Z. Archaeol. Mittelalters]. Vol. 1 (1973)-. German. Irregular. DM174.00. Dr. Rudolf Habelt GmbH, Postfach 150104, D-53040 Bonn Germany. **Tel** 011 49 228 232015.
 Ind/Abst Avery Index Archit. Period. Suppl. Colum. Univ. (19??-199?); BHA : Biblio. Hist Art; Br. Archaeol. Bibliogr.

LC PJ3104 .Z5   ISSN 0084-5299
GW
CCC

ZEITSCHRIFT FUER ASSYRIOLOGIE UND VORDERASIATISCHE ARCHAOLOGIE. [Z. Assyriol. vorderasiat. Archaol.]. Vol. 45 (1939)-. Periodical. German (English and French). Two times a year. $170.00. Walter de Gruyter Inc., PO Box 303421, D-10728 Berlin Germany. **Tel** 011 49 30 260050, FAX 011 49 30 26005251, telex 184027. *Continues* Zeitschrift fur Assyriologie und Verwandte Gebiete.
 Ind/Abst Index Book Rev. Relig.; MLA Int. Bibl. Books Artic. mod. Lang. Lit.; Old Testam. Abstr.; Relig. Index One Period.

LC DQ30 .Z4   ISSN 0044-3476
DD 913.494   SZ

ZEITSCHRIFT FUER SCHWEIZERISCHE ARCHAEOLOGIE UND KUNSTGESCHICHTE. **Added/Corp** Zurich. Schweizerisches Landesmuseum. Verband der Schweizerischen Altertumssammlungen. Gesellschaft fuer Schweizerische Kunstgeschichte, Zurich. **VFOAT** Revue Suisse d'Art et d'Archeologia; Rivista Svizzera d'Arte e d'Archeologia. Vol. 1 (1939)-. Periodical. Multiple languages (German and French). Four times a year. $70.72. Karl Schwegier AG, Hoganholzstrasse 71, CH-8050 Zurich Switzerland. **Tel** 011 41 1 3631126. cum. index. **Bk Rev**. **Ad Acc**. **Circ:** 1,200. *Supersedes* Anzeiger fur Schweizerische Altertumskunde.
 Ind/Abst Archit. Period. Index (1979-); Art Archaeol. Tech. Archit.; ARTbibliogr. Mod.; Avery Index Archit. Period. Suppl. Colum. Univ. (19??-199?); BHA : Biblio. Hist. Art; Br. Archaeol. Bibliogr.; Numis. Lit.

LC CC13.S66 Z4   ISSN 0514-7336
SP

ZEPHYRUS. [Zephyrus]. **Added/Corp** Universidad de Salamanca. Seminario de Arqueologia. Vol. 1 (1950)-. Spanish. One time a year. 4000ptas. Ediciones Universidad de Salamanca, Apartado Postal 325, 37080 Salamanca Spain. **Tel** 011 34 23 294598, FAX 011 34 23 263046.
 Ind/Abst Am. Hist. Life (1964-1967); Anthropol. Lit.; Numis. Lit.

LC GN705 .K73   ISSN 0083-4300
DD 930.1   PL

ZESZYTY NAUKOWE UNIWERSYTETU JAGIELLONSKIEGO. PRACE ARCHEOLOGICZNE = ACTA SCIENTIARUM LITTERARUMQUE. SCHEDAE ARCHEOLOGICAE. Main/Corp Uniwersytet Jagiellonski. **Added/Corp** Uniwersytet Jagiellonski. **VFOAT** Prace Archeologiczne; Schedae Archeologicae; Acta Scientiarum Litterarumque. Schedae Archeologicae. (1960)-. Monographic series. Polish (English; summaries and/or abstracts in French, German and Russian; table of contents in French, German and Russian). Irregular. Price varies per volume. Uniwersytet Jagiellonski, Ul. Golebia 24, 31-007 Krakow Poland. **(Subscription address:** Ars Polona-Ruch, PO Box 1001, Krakowskie Przedmiescie 7, 00-068 Warsaw Poland. **Tel** 011 48 22 261201.)
 Ind/Abst Anthropol. Index; BHA : Biblio. Hist. Art.

LC DK511.L162 L37a
LV

ZINATNISKAS ATSKAITES SESIJAS MATERIALI PAR ARHEOLOGU UN ETNOGRAFU PETIJUMU REZULTATIEM. See Anthropology.

ABSTRACTING, BIBLIOGRAPHIES AND STATISTICS

LC Z3656.A2 A6
DD 016.932   NE

ANNUAL EGYPTOLOGICAL BIBLIOGRAPHY. **Added/Corp** International Association of Egyptologists. **VFOAT** Bibliographie Egyptologique Annuelle. Vol. 1 (1947)-. English (French). One time a year. Price varies per volume. E.J. Brill, Postbus 9000, 2300 PA Leiden The Netherlands. **Tel** 011 31 71 312624, FAX 011 31 71 317532, telex 39296 BRILL NL. cum. index.
 Desc: Series covering egyptology.

LC Z5132 .A67   ISSN 0341-8308
GW
CEASED

ARCHAEOLOGISCHE BIBLIOGRAPHIE. (ARCHAEOLOGISCHE BIBLIOGRAPHIE. BEILAGE ZUM JAHRBUCH DES DEUTSCHEN ARCHAEOLOGISCHEN INSTITUTS.). [Archaeol. Bibliogr.]. **Added/Corp** Deutsches Archaeologisches Institut. Jahrbuch. Supplement. (1932)-(1993). German. Walter de Gruyter Inc., PO Box 303421, D-10728 Berlin Germany. **Tel** 011 49 30 260050, FAX 011 49 30 26005251, telex 184027. *Continues* Bibliographie zum Jahrbuch des Deutschen Archaeologischen Instituts.
 Ind/Abst Avery Index Archit. Period. Suppl. Colum. Univ. (19??-199?); Br. Archaeol. Bibliogr. (?-?).

LC AM1 .A7   ISSN 0004-2994
DD 069.05   US
CODEN AATABU

ART AND ARCHAEOLOGY TECHNICAL ABSTRACTS. See The Arts-Abstracting, Bibliographies and Statistics.

LC Z5133.R46 B5 CC79.5 .A5   ISSN 0232-4865
DD 016.9301   GW

BIBLIOGRAPHIE ZUR ARCHAO-ZOOLOGIE UND GESCHICHTE DER HAUSTIERE. [Bibliogr. Archao-Zool. Gesch. Haustiere]. (1971)-. German. Akademie der Wissenschaften Zentinst, Permoserstrasse 15, O-7010 Leipzig Germany.
 Ind/Abst Br. Archaeol. Bibliogr.

ISSN 0964-7104
UK

BRITISH ARCHAEOLOGICAL BIBLIOGRAPHY. Vol. 1, No. 1 (Apr. 1992)-. Abstracting/Indexing Service. English. Two times a year (Apr. & Oct.). £90.00 (individuals); £200.00 (institutions). Council for British Archaeology, Bowes Morrell House, 111 Walmgate, York YO1 2UA United Kingdom. **Tel** 011 44 1904 671471, FAX 011 44 1904 671384. **ED** Cherry Lavell. Index available. **Bk Rev. Circ:** 500. available on microfilm and microfiche. *Continues* British Archaeological Abstracts, 0007-0270.
 Desc: Abstracts of books and articles relating to the archaeology of Great Britain and Ireland, palaeolithic to present. This journal covers some sources cover-to-cover; others are scanned selectively.

ISSN 0028-2812
DD 938   US

NESTOR. [Nestor]. **Added/Corp** University of Wisconsin. Institute for Research in the Humanities. Indiana University. Program in Classical Archaeology. Vol. 1, (Feb. 1957)-. Newsletter. English (French) (monthly except June, July, Aug.). $12.50. Program in Classical Archaeology, Indiana University, 408 North Indiana Avenue, Bloomington IN 47405. **Tel** (812)855-1421. **ED** Karen D. Vitelli. Index available (bound in 9th issues). **Ad Acc. Circ:** 550. available on diskette from University Microfilms International (UMI).
 Desc: A bibliography of material relevant to prehistoric archaeology, Homeric studies, Indo-European linguistics, and related fields, in the Eastern Mediterranean and Southeast Europe.

ARCHITECTURE

ISSN 0144-7726
UK

9H. [9H]. **VFOAT** Nine H; Bartlett Translations. No. 1 (1980)-. Periodical. English. Two times a year. £28.00 (institutions), £15.50 (individuals) UK; £29.50 (institutions), £17.00 (individuals) other. 9H, 3 Holly Hill, London NW3 6QN United Kingdom. *Continues in part* Bartlett Translations.
 Ind/Abst Archit. Period. Index (1980-1982); Avery Index Archit. Period. Suppl. Colum. Univ. (1989-).

LC NA7385 .A2
DD 720/.946   SP
Pr Rev.   TITLE CHANGE

A & V, MONOGRAFIAS DE ARQUITECTURA Y VIVIENDA. **Added/Corp** Sociedad Estatal de Gestion para la Rehabilitacion y Construccion de Viviendas. **VFOAT** A y V; Monografias de Arquitectura y Vivienda. (19??)-(Nov.-Dec. 1994). Periodical. Spanish (summaries and/or abstracts in English; translations available in English). AVISA - Arquitectura Viva SL, Rosario 31, 28005 Madrid Spain. **Tel** 011 34 1 2669900, FAX 011 34 1 3640151. **ED** Luis Fernandez-Galiano. cum. index. **Ad Acc. Circ:** 5,000 (ctrl). *Absorbed* Anuario ..., Arquitectura Espanola, 1133-0082. *Continued by* AV (Madrid, Spain).
 Desc: Each issue revolves around a chosen architect, city or theme. Critical articles and projects described and illustrated in detail.
 Ind/Abst Avery Index Archit. Period. Suppl. Colum. Univ. (No. 21, 1990-).

BE

A+ APLUS. **Added/Corp** Centre d'Information de l'Architecture, de l'Urbanisme et du Design. (19??)-. Periodical. French (Dutch). Six times a year. $104.47. CIAUD ASBL / Centre d'Information de l'Architecture de l' Urbanisme et du Design, Chaussee de Ruisbroek 83, 1190 Brussels Belgium. **Tel** 011 32 2 3322472, FAX 011 32 2 3322208. **Bk Rev. Ad Acc. Circ:** 10,000 (ctrl). *Continues* A+ Magazine.
 Ind/Abst Archit. Period. Index (July/Aug. 1977-).

US

A-E BUSINESS REVIEW. (19??)-. English. Twelve times a year. $138.00 (one-year), $238.00 (two-year). A-E Business Review, PO Box 4808, Cave Creek AZ 85331. **Tel** (602)258-2117, FAX (602)488-0311. **ED** Clarke G. Ross. **Bk Rev**, (Qty: 2-4). **Circ:** 3,000 (ctrl). available on an online database.
 Desc: Management and marketing information for architects and engineers.

LC K1 .E14   ISSN 0090-2411
DD 344/.73/01762   US

A.E. LEGAL NEWSLETTER. (A/E LEGAL NEWSLETTER.). [A.E. leg. newsl.]. **Added/Corp** Victor O. Schinnerer & Company. **VFOAT** Legal Newsletter. (19??)-. Newsletter. English. Ten times a year. $200.00. V O Schinnerer & Company, Two Wisconsin Circle, Chevy Chase MD 20815. **Tel** (301)961-9800, FAX (301)951-5444, telex 261829. **ED** Victor Schinnerrer. (Free). cum. index. **Circ:** 800 (ctrl).

LC HF   ISSN 0732-7943
DD 380.1   US

A/E MARKETING JOURNAL. See Business and Economics-Marketing and Purchasing.

US

"A" MAGAZINE. **Added/Corp** University of California, Los Angeles. School of Architecture and Urban Planning. **VFOAT** A. No. 1 (Summer 1976)-. Periodical. English.
 Ind/Abst Mag. Index (1977-?).

ISSN 1180-0933
DD 724/.6/05   CN
SUSPENDED

A/R/C, ARCHITECTURE, RESEARCH, CRITICISM. [A/R/C, archit. res. crit.]. **VFOAT** Architecture, Research, Criticism. Vol. 1, No. 1 (Spring 1990)-(19??). Periodical. English. Four times a year. 28.01Can$. 15B Sullivan Street, Toronto Ontario M5T 1B8 Canada. **Tel** (416)531-7848.

ISSN 0389-9160
JA

A + U. (KENCHIKU TO TOSHI). [A + U]. **VFOAT** A and U; A.+U.; Architecture and Urbanism (1971)-. Periodical. English (Japanese). Twelve times a year. $350.00. Japan Architect Company Ltd., 31-2 Yushima 2-chome, Bunkyo-ku, Tokyo 113 Japan. **Tel** 011 81 3

3816 2935, 011 81 3 3816 2936, FAX 011 81 3 3816 2937. **(Subscription address:** Maruzen Company Ltd., PO Box 5050, Import & Export Department, Tokyo 100 31 Japan. **Tel** 011 81 3 32789224.**)** Documents available from The Genuine Article.
Ind/Abst Archit. Period. Index (July 1977-); Art Index; Arts Humanit. Citation Index (19??-19??) [Full Cov.]; Avery Index Archit. Period. Suppl. Colum. Univ. (No. 21, 1990-); Res. Alert [Full Cov.]; Soc. Sci. Cit. Index [Select. Cov.].

ISSN 0824-5576
DD 720/.97123/4 CN
A3. (A3 : ART AND ARCHITECTURE.). [A3]. **Added/Corp** A3 Partnership. **VFOAT** Art and Architecture. (1983)-. Periodical. English. Six times a year. $2.00 per issue. A3, 1826-17th Street SW/Suite 1, Calgary Alberta T2T4M2 Canada.

UK
A3 TIMES. **VFOAT** A3times; A 3 Times; A Three Times. (198?)-. Periodical. English. Four times a year.
Ind/Abst Archit. Period. Index (Vol. 5 No. 12, 1989-).

UK
AA EVENTS. (19??)-. English. Thirty-two times a year. £20.00. AA Publications, 34-36 Bedford Square, London WC1B 3ES United Kingdom. **Tel** 011 44 171 6360974, FAX 011 44 171 4368740.

LC NA1.A1 A22 **ISSN** 0261-6823
DD 720/.5 UK
Pr Rev.
AA FILES. (AA FILES : ANNALS OF THE ARCHITECTURAL ASSOCIATION SCHOOL OF ARCHITECTURE.). [AA files]. **Added/Corp** Architectural Association (Great Britain). School of Architecture. **VFOAT** A.A. Files; Files. **VAT** Architectural Association Files. Vol. 1 No. 1 (Winter 1981/1982)-. Periodical. English. Two times a year (July & Dec.). $56.47. AA Publications, 34-36 Bedford Square, London WC1B 3ES United Kingdom. **Tel** 011 44 171 6360974, FAX 011 44 171 4368740. **ED** Mary Wall. Index available. cum. index. **Bk Rev**, (Qty: 6). **Circ:** 2,500 (ctrl). ***Continues** AAQ. Architectural Association Quarterly, 0001-0189.*
Desc: An international centre for the public discussion and the display of the theory and practice of architecture. Based on lectures, symposia and exhibitions.
Ind/Abst Archit. Period. Index (1981/1982-); ARTbibliogr. Mod. (1984-); Avery Index Archit. Period. Suppl. Colum. Univ. (Spring 1990-); BHA : Biblio. Hist. Art; Int. Civil Eng. Abstr.; Soft. Abstr. Eng.

ISSN 0352-1982
XV
AB, ARHITEKTOV BILTIN. (ARHITEKTOV BILTEN.). [AB, Arhit. bilt.]. **VFOAT** Architect's Bulletin; AB. (1970)-. Bulletin. Serbo-Croatian (Roman) (English). Irregular. $40.00. Arhitektov Bilten, Erjavceva 15, 6100 Ljubljana Slovenia. **Tel** 011 38 61221612.

IT
CEASED
ABACUS (MILAN, ITALY). (ABACUS.). Vol. 1, No. 1 (Dec. 1985)-(Dec. 1993). Periodical. Italian (summaries and/or abstracts in English, French and Spanish). Sinopia Ed, Via G. Murat 84, 20159 Milan Italy. **Tel** 011 39 2 688-3641, FAX 011 39 2 668-02971.
Ind/Abst Archit. Period. Index (Dec. 1985-); Avery Index Archit. Period. Suppl. Colum. Univ. (Vol. 6, No. 21 Jan./Mar. 1990-).

ISSN 0966-9647
DD 721 UK
ABC AND D. ARCHITECT BUILDER CONTRACTOR AND DEVELOPER. (ARCHITECT BUILDER, CONTRACTOR AND DEVELOPER.). [ABCD. Archit. build. contract. dev.]. (19??)-. Periodical. English. Twelve times a year. $32.51. Ascent Publishing, Subs Dept, 91/93 High Street, Bromsgrove W0RC B618AF United Kingdom. **Tel** 011 44 1527 836600. **ED** Peter Harris. **Bk Rev. Ad Acc, Adv Mgr:** Nick Rapley. **Circ:** 24,350 (ctrl).

LC NK1700 .A24 **ISSN** 0001-3218
DD 747/.05 IT
ABITARE. **See** Interior Design and Decoration.

IT
ABITARE ANNUAL. **VFOAT** AA. (1986)-. Italian (English). Eleven times a year. $115.00. Editrice Abitare Segesta Spa, Corso Monforte 15, 20122 Milan Italy. **Tel** 011 39 2 76090214, FAX 011 39 2 791904, telex 315302 ABIT I. **ED** Italo Lupi. **Bk Rev. Ad Acc. Circ:** 65,000. available with illustrations.

LC NA1455.F5 A4
FI
ACANTHUS. **Added/Corp** Suomen Rakennustaiteen Museo. (1990)-. English.
Ind/Abst Archit. Period. Index (1990-).

ISSN 0959-1591
UK
ACCESS BY DESIGN. **Added/Corp** Centre for Accessible Environments (London, England). (1990)-. Periodical. English. Three times a year (April, Aug., Dec.). $25.67. Centre on Environment for the Handicapped, 35 Great Smith Street, London SW1P 3BJ United Kingdom. **Tel** 011 44 71 4822247. **ED** Ann Sawyer. Index available (bound in Dec. issue). **Bk Rev**, (Qty: 6). **Ad Acc. Circ:** 800. ***Continues** Design for Special Needs, 0309-3042.*
Desc: Focuses on and promotes good practice in designing buildings that meet the needs of people with disabilities.

ISSN 0704-0083
DD 971.3 CN
ACORN, THE ARCHITECTURAL CONSERVANCY OF ONTARIO R NEWSLETTER. **Main/Corp** Architectural Conservancy of Ontario. **VAT** Architectural Conservancy Ontario Revived Newsletter. (1976)-. Newsletter. English. Three times a year. 20.01Can$. Architectural Conservancy Ontario, 10 Adelaide Street East, 204 Ontario Hert, Toronto Ontario M5C 1J3 Canada. **Tel** (416)367-8075. ***Supersedes** Architectural Conservancy of Ontario. News Letter, 0704-0075.*

UK
SUSPENDED
ACROSS ARCHITECTURE. **Added/Corp** Architectural Association (Great Britain). School of Architecture. **VFOAT** ACAR. (1984)-Suspended (1995). Periodical. English. Across Architecture, 40 Radnor Mews, London W2 2SA United Kingdom. **Tel** 011 44 71 262 1557.

LC NA2103 .A82a
US
ACSA DIRECTORY. **Main/Corp** Association of Collegiate Schools of Architecture. (199?)-. English. Irregular. Association of Collegiate Schools of Architecture, 1735 New York Avenue Northwest, Washington DC 20006. **Tel** (202)785-2324, (800)232-2724. ***Continues** Association of Collegiate Schools of Architecture. ACSA Annual Directory.*

IT
AD / ARCHITECTURAL DIGEST. (19??)-. Italian. Twelve times a year. L72000 Italy; L130000 other. Giorgio Mondadori Intl, Via A Ponti 10, 20143 Milan Italy. **Tel** 011 39 2 891661.

IS
ADRICHALUT YISRAELIT. (19??)-. English (Hebrew). Four times a year. $42.00 Israel; $70.00 US. Adrichalut Yisraelit, PO Box 302, Herziliya B Israel. **ED** Ami Ran. **Circ:** 10,000 (ctrl).

ISSN 1199-4363
DD 720 CN
•ADVANCED BUILDINGS NEWSLETTER. [Adv. build. newsl.]. **Added/Corp** Royal Architectural Institute of Canada. Canada Centre for Mineral and Energy Technology. Canada. Natural Resources Canada. Federal Panel on Energy Research and Development (Canada). **VFOAT** Advanced Buildings. Vol. 1, No. 1 (Jan. 1994)-. Periodical. English. Six times a year. 59.09Can$. Royal Architectural Institute of Canada, 55 Murray Street, Suite 330, Ottawa Ontario K1N 5M3 Canada. **Tel** (613)241-3600.

LC NA7205 .A353
DD 728/.37/0222 US
AFFORDABLE HOMES : QUALITY CUSTOM HOUSE PLANS. (19??)-. Periodical. English. Irregular. Homes for Living, 363 Seventh Avenue, New York NY 10001.

LC NA11 .A45 **ISSN** 1079-9656
DD 720 US
•AIA SEATTLE ARCHITECT, THE. [AIA Seattle archit.]. **Added/Corp** American Institute of Architects. Seattle Chapter. **VFOAT** American Institute of Architects Seattle Architect. Vol. 21, #4 (Jan. 1994)-. Periodical. English. Twelve times a year. American Institute of Architects / Seattle Chapter, 1911 First Avenue, Seattle WA 98101. ***Continues** Seattle Chapter Architect, 0745-2977.*

LC NA11 .A447 **ISSN** 1079-3933
DD 720 US
•AIARCHITECT (WASHINGTON, D.C.). (AIARCHITECT : THE NEWSPAPER OF AMERICA'S COMMUNITY OF ARCHITECTS.). [AIArchitect]. **Main/Corp** American Institute of Architects. **VFOAT** AIA Architect; AIAArchitect. (Oct. 1994)-. Periodical. English. Twelve times a year. $50.00. American Institute of Architects / Washington DC, 1735 New York Avenue Northwest, Washington DC 20006. **Tel** (202)626-7460, FAX (202)626-7587. **ED** Stephanie Stubbs. ***Continues** American Institute of Architects. Memo, 0001-1487.*

LC NK1700 .I5 **ISSN** 0173-8046
DD 720/.5 GW
CCC
AIT. ARCHITEKTUR, INNENARCHITEKTUR, TECHNISCHER AUSBAU. (ARCHITEKTUR, INNENARCHITEKTUR, TECHNISCHER AUSBAU : AIT.). [AIT. Archit., Innenarchit., tech. Ausbau]. **Added/Corp** Bund Deutscher Innenarchitekten. **VFOAT** AIT. (1980)-. Trade Publication. German. Ten times a year. $199.59. Verlagsantalt A Koch GmbH, Postfach 102741, Fasanenweg 18 Leinfelden, D-70023 Stuttgart Germany. **Tel** 011 49 711 75911, FAX 011 49 711 7591266, telex 7255609 DRW. Index available. **Bk Rev. Ad Acc. Circ:** 10,000 (ctrl). ***Continues** Architektur + Wohnwelt, 0340-3912.*
Desc: The official journal of the Association of German Interior Decorators and Architects.
Ind/Abst Archit. Period. Index (Vol. 88 No. 1, 1980-); Avery Index Archit. Period. Suppl. Colum. Univ. (1984-).

ISSN 0951-5380
UK
AJ FOCUS. **VAT** Architects' Journal Focus. Vol. 1, No. 1 (Apr. 1987)-. Trade Publication. English. Twelve times a year. $82.13. EMAP Architecture, 33 39 Bowling Green Lane, London EC1R 0DA United Kingdom. **Tel** 011 44 171 8371212, FAX 011 44 171 2784003. **(Subscription address:** EMAP Business Publishing, 4 Admiral House Cardinal Way, Middlesex HA3 5SQ United Kingdom. **Tel** 011 44 181 8684499.**)**
Ind/Abst Archit. Period. Index (Vol. 1 No. 1 (Apr. 1987-).

SZ
TITLE CHANGE
AKTUELLES BAUEN. **VFOAT** Aktuelles Bauen Baumarkt. (Feb. 20, 1992)-(1993). Periodical. German. Schueck Soehne AG, Bahnhofstrasse 24, CH-8803 Rueschlikon Switzerland. **Tel** 011 41 1 7247766. ***Continues** Schweizer Baumarkt, 0255-699X. **Continued by** Baukader.*

LC NA1465 .B56
SU
AL-BINA. **VFOAT** Albenaa. Vol. 1, No. 1 (Feb./March 1979)-. Periodical. Arabic (English). Six times a year. $48.00. Albenaa, PO Box 522, Riyadh Saudi Arabia.
Ind/Abst Archit. Period. Index (Aug./Sept. 1979-).

US
ALABAMA ARCHITECTURE. English. One time a year. $25.00. Alabama Architect, PO Box 237, Montgomery AL 36101-0237. **Tel** (334)264-3037. **ED** Edward M Brummal. **Bk Rev. Ad Acc. Circ:** 1,800 (ctrl).
Desc: Varied themes regarding architecture in Alabama.

LC NA1465.3 .A4
UA
ALAM AL-BINA. **Added/Corp** Markaz Al-Dirasat Al-Takhtitiyah Wa-al-Mimariyah. **VFOAT** Alam al Bena; World of Construction. (Aug. 1980)-. Periodical. Arabic (English). Twelve times a year. $72.00. Society of Revivinal Architecture and Planning Heritage, 14 El Sobky Street M El Bakry, Heliopolis Cairo Egypt. **Tel** 011 20 2 670843, 011 20 2 670744, 011 20 2670271, FAX 011 20 2 2919341. **ED** Dr. Abdelbaki Jbrahim. Index available. cum. index. **Bk Rev. Ad Acc. Circ:** 5,000 (ctrl).
Desc: The main target of this magazine is to spread architectural and planning concepts among all people and to establish a sort of intellectual contact among all those practicing the profession of building, in order to attain a better future for either those actually practicing it, or generations to come.
Ind/Abst Archit. Period. Index (Aug. 1980-).

NE
CEASED
ALURAMA. (1979)-(Jan. 1993). Dutch. Misset Uitgeverij BV / Doetinchem, Postbus 4, 7000 BA Doetinchem Netherlands. **Tel** 011 31 8340 49911, 011 31 8340 49562, FAX 011 31 8340 43839, 011 31 8340 40515.

LC NC **ISSN** 1062-0966
DD 745 US
Pr Rev.
AMERICAN CENTER FOR DESIGN JOURNAL. [Am. Cent. Des.]. **Added/Corp** American Center for Design. (199?)-. Trade Publication. English. Two times a year. $46.00 US; $52.00 other. American Center for Design, 233 East Ontario St. 500, Chicago IL 60611. **Tel** (312)787-2018. **ED** Rob Dewey. Index available (published separately). cum. index. **Circ:** 4,000. ***Continues** Design Journal (Chicago Ill.).*
Desc: Dedicated to expounding the boundaries of design, for professional designers, educators and students.

ISSN 0276-668X
US
AMERICAN INSTITUTE OF ARCHITECTS MEMBERSHIP DIRECTORY. (MEMBERSHIP DIRECTORY / AMERICAN INSTITUTE OF ARCHITECTS.). [Am. Inst. Archit. membsh. dir.]. **Main/Corp** American Institute of Architects. (1973)-. Directory. English. One time a year. $75.00. American Institute of Architects / Washington DC, 1735 New York Avenue Northwest, Washington DC 20006. **Tel** (202)626-7460, FAX (202)626-7587. ***Continues** AIA Membership Directory.*

ISSN 0066-1392
DD 930 DK
ANALECTA ROMANA INSTITUTI DANICI. **See** Archaeology.

Architecture

ANALECTA ROMANA INSTITUTI DANICI. SUPPLEMENTUM. See Archaeology.
ISSN 0066-1406
DK

ISSN 0214-4727
SP
ANALES DE ARQUITECTURA : REVISTA DEL DEPARTAMENTO DE TEORIA DE LA ARQUITECTURA Y PROYECTOS ARQUITECTONICOS, ESCUELA TECNICA SUPERIOR DE ARQUITECTURA DE VALLADOLID. Added/Corp Escuela Tecnica Superior de Arquitecture (Universidad de Valladolid). Departamento de Teoria de la Arquitecture y Proyectos Arquitectonicos. (1989)-. Spanish. One time a year. Universidad Valladolid Secretariado Publicaciones, Juan Mambrillia 14, 47003 Valladolid Spain. **Tel** 011 34 83 294144, 011 34 82 294499.

IT
ANFIONE ZETO. (1988)-. Periodical. Italian (English). Three times a year. L120000.00 Italy; L240000.00 other. Pagus Edizioni, Via Curtatone 10, 31038 Paese Treviso Italy. **Tel** 011 39 422 950264.
Ind/Abst Avery Index Archit. Period. Suppl. Colum. Univ. (1989-).

LC NA15 .A56
DD 720/.5
IT
ANNALI DI ARCHITETTURA : RIVISTA DEL CENTRO INTERNAZIONALE DI STUDI DI ARCHITETTURA ANDREA PALLADIO. Added/Corp Centro Internazionale di Studi di Architettura "Andrea Palladio" di Vicenza. (1989)-. Periodical. Italian. One time a year. L55000. Elemond Arte SRL, Via Trentacoste 7, 20134 Milan Italy. **Tel** 011 39 2 215631. **(Subscription address:** Courier SAS, via I a de Bosis 25 27, 50145 Florence Italy. **Tel** 011 39 55 300010.) **Continues** Bolletino del Centro Internazionale di Studi di Architettura "Andrea Palladio", 0577-3008.
Ind/Abst Archit. Period. Index (No. 1 1989-); BHA : Biblio. Hist. Art.

ISSN 1181-9057
DD 354.7130085/9
CN
Pr Rev.
ANNUAL ARCHAEOLOGICAL REPORT, ONTARIO. [Annu. archaeol. rep. Ont.]. Added/Corp Ontario Heritage Foundation. **VFOAT** Archaeological Report. (1990)-. English. One time a year. 5.00Can$. Ontario Heritage Foundation, 77 Bloor Street West, Toronto Ontario M7A 2R9 Canada. **Tel** (416)965-9504, FAX (416)965-4315.
Ind/Abst Curr. Cit.

LC NA4411 .A3
DD 351.85/4
ISSN 0738-5870
US
ANNUAL REPORT OF THE ARCHITECT OF THE CAPITOL FOR THE PERIOD ... . Main/Corp United States. Architect of the Capitol. July 1, 1975 through Sept. 30, 1976-. Periodical. English. One time a year. US Architect of the Capitol, Washington DC 20515.
Continues Report of the Architect of the Capitol.

LC TA24.N2 A3
DD 720.07
ISSN 0275-8008
US
ANNUAL REPORT OF THE NEBRASKA STATE BOARD OF EXAMINERS FOR PROFESSIONAL ENGINEERS AND ARCHITECTS. See Engineering.

LC NA875 .A57
DD 720.9861
CK
ANUARIO DE LA ARQUITECTURA EN COLOMBIA. Added/Corp Sociedad Colombiana de Arquitectos. (19??)-. Spanish. Sociedad Columbian de Arquitectos, J Plazas S, Apartado Aereo 27765, Bogota Colombia.
Ind/Abst Avery Index Archit. Period. Suppl. Colum. Univ. (19??-199?).

LC NA705 .A58
DD 720/.973/05
ISSN 1068-4220
US
●**ANY (NEW YORK, N.Y.).** (ANY : ARCHITECTURE NEW YORK.). [Any]. Added/Corp Anyone Corporation. **VFOAT** Architecture New York. (July/Aug. 1993)-. Periodical. English. Six times a year. $50.00. Anyone Corporation, 40 West 25th Street, 10th Floor, New York NY 10010. **Tel** (212)989-2221, FAX (212)989-6630. **ED** Cynthia C. Davidson. **Bk Rev**, (Qty: 2-3). **Photos**. **Pub. Size:** Tabloid. **Circ:** 4,000.
Desc: A journal of architectural theory in tabloid form. Contains essays on new architecture and urbanism.

ISSN 0848-8525
DD 721/.028/8
CN
APT BULLETIN (1986). (APT BULLETIN.). [APT bull.]. Added/Corp Association for Preservation Technology. **VAT** Association for Preservation Technology Bulletin. Vol. 18, No. 4 (1986)-. Bulletin. English. Four times a year. Association for Preservation Technology / Canada, Box 2487 Station D, Ottawa Ontario K1P 5W6 Canada. **Tel** (613)238-1972, FAX (613)238-1839. **Continues** Bulletin - Association for Preservation Technology, 0044-9466.
Ind/Abst Am. Hist. Life (1978-); Archit. Period. Index; Art Archaeol. Tech. Abstr.; Avery Index Archit. Period. Suppl. Colum. Univ. (1986-); Constr. Index; Garden Lit. (1992-).

ISSN 1062-6190
US
APT COMMUNIQUE. Added/Corp Association for Preservation Technology. Association for Preservation Technology International. **VFOAT** Communique. **VAT** Association for Preservation Technology Communique. Vol. 18, No. 1 (Feb. 1989)-. Periodical. English. Six times a year. Association for Preservation Technology, PO Box 2165, Albuquerque NM 81103. **Tel** (505)265-3838.
Continues Communique - Association for Preservation Technology.

TU
ARA-YAYIN DIZISI / OCCASIONAL PAPER SERIES / M.E.T.U. FACULTY OF ARCHITECTURE. O.D.T.U. MIMARLIK FAKULTESI. Added/Corp Orta Dogu Teknik Universitesi. Mimarlik Fakultesi. **VFOAT** Occasional Paper Series; M.E.T.U. Fac. of Arch. Occasional Paper Series. (1978)-. Periodical (Turkish). Middle East Technical University Faculty of Architecture, Ankara Turkey.
Ind/Abst Archit. Period. Index (Feb. 1978-July 1980).

LC NA680 .A67
DD 724.6
IT
ARCA, L'. Vol. 1 (Nov. 1986)-. Periodical. English (Italian). Eleven times a year (monthly). L150000. Arca Edizioni Spa, Via Mose Bianchi 101, 20149 Milan Italy. **Tel** 011 39 2 48014743, FAX 011 39 2 48014829.
Ind/Abst Archit. Period. Index (Vol. 1 No. 1, Nov. 1986-); Avery Index Archit. Period. Suppl. Colum. Univ. (No. 34, Jan. 1990-).

LC NA1 .A733
US
CEASED
ARCADE (SEATTLE, WASH.). (ARCADE.). (March 1981)-(19??). Periodical. English. Arcade / Seattle, PO Box 54, 2318 2nd Avenue, Seattle WA 98121. **Tel** (206)682-5725. **Bk Rev**. **Ad Acc**. **Circ:** 1,400 (ctrl).
Desc: An independent publication for architecture, planning and design. Features on design news, critiques, book reviews, technical information and occasional fiction.

ISSN 0587-3452
GW
ARCH +. (ARCH +.). [Arch +]. Added/Corp Stuttgart. Universitaet. Abteilung fuer Architektur. **VFOAT** Arch Plus. Vol. 1 (Jan. 1968)-. Trade Publication. Swedish (German; summaries and/or abstracts in English). Four times a year (Mar., June, Sept., Dec.). $61.42. ARCH + Verlag-GmbH, Charlottenstrabe 14, D52070 Aachen Germany. **Tel** 011 49 241 508329.
Desc: Aimed toward architects.
Ind/Abst Avery Index Archit. Period. Suppl. Colum. Univ.; Int. Civil Eng. Abstr.

LC DA20 .R86
ISSN 0066-5983
UK
ARCHAEOLOGICAL JOURNAL, THE. See Archaeology.

NE
ARCHIS. Vol. 1 (1986)-. Trade Publication. Dutch. Twelve times a year. Fl273.58. Misset Uitgeverij BV / Doetinchem, Postbus 4, 7000 BA Doetinchem Netherlands. **Tel** 011 31 8340 49911, 011 31 8340 49562, FAX 011 31 8340 43839, 011 31 8340 40515.
Continues Wonen Tabk, 0165-3504.
Ind/Abst Archit. Period. Index (Jan. 1986-); Avery Index Archit. Period. Suppl. Colum. Univ. (Oct. 1989-); BHA : Biblio. Hist. Art.

ISSN 0044-8621
NE
ARCHITECT. (DE ARCHITECT.). [Architect]. (19??)-. Trade Publication. Dutch. Fifteen times a year (monthly with combined July/Aug. and 4 supplements). $263.79. Ten Hagen and Stam BV, Postbus 34, 2501 AG The Hague Netherlands. **Tel** 011 31 70 3045700. **ED** C. Zwinkels and J. Rodermond. Index available. cum. index. **Bk Rev**. **Ad Acc**. **Circ:** 4,500.
Desc: For architects, interior designers and urban-designers, made for Dutch readers but with an international scope.
Ind/Abst Archit. Period. Index (1979-); Avery Index Archit. Period. Suppl. Colum. Univ. (1989-); EMBASE.

ISSN 0003-8407
SA
ARCHITECT AND BUILDER. [Archit. Build.]. **VFOAT** Architect & Builder. (1951)-. Trade Publication. English. Twelve times a year. $82.00. Laurie Wale Pty Ltd., PO Box 4591, Cape Town 8000 South Africa. **Tel** 011 27 21 4618029.
Ind/Abst Archit. Period. Index (Sept./Oct. 1977-); Avery Index Archit. Period. Suppl. Colum. Univ. (July 1989-).

ISSN 0003-8423
US
ARCHITECT AND CONTRACTOR. Periodical. English. Twelve times a year. Architect and Contractor, Box 119, Yountville CA 94599.

LC N1 .A2627
ISSN 0308-8596
UK
TITLE CHANGE
ARCHITECT & SURVEYOR. Added/Corp Incorporated Association of Architects and Surveyors. **VFOAT** Architect and Surveyor. (19??)-(19??). Periodical. English. Association of Building Engineers, Jubilee House, Billing Brook Road, Northampton NN3 4NW United Kingdom. **Tel** 011 44 1604 404121, FAX 011 44 1604 784220. **ED** J. Scott. **Bk Rev**. **Ad Acc**. **Circ:** 5,000 (ctrl). **Continues** A&S, 0308-4930.
Desc: Of interest to architects, surveyors, town planners and those interested in building and construction.
Ind/Abst Archit. Period. Index; Int. Civil Eng. Abstr.; Soft. Abstr. Eng.

ISSN 1034-4101
DD 728.0994
AT
ARCHITECT DESIGNED HOUSES. (ARCHITECT DESIGNED HOUSES.). [Archit. des. houses]. (1990)-. English. One time a year. 13.98Aus$. Architecture Media Australia, 4 Princes Street Third Floor, Port Melbourne Victoria 3207 Australia. **Tel** 011 61 3 6464760, FAX 011 61 3 6464918. **ED** Ian Close. **Ad Acc**, **Adv Mgr:** Carolyn Winton.

LC NA123 .N363
US
ARCHITECT REGISTRATION EXAMINATION. GRAPHIC HANDBOOK / NCARB. Added/Corp National Council of Architectural Registration Boards. **VFOAT** NCARB Architect Registration Examination. Graphic Handbook; Graphic Handbook. (19??)-. English. One time a year. $60.00. National Council Architectural Registration Boards, 1735 NW Avenue/Suite 700, Washington DC 20006. **Tel** (202)659-3996. **Continues in part** NCARB Architect Registration Examination handbook.

LC NA123 .N362
US
CEASED
ARCHITECT REGISTRATION EXAMINATION. MULTIPLE CHOICE HANDBOOK. Added/Corp National Council of Architectural Registration Boards. **VFOAT** NCARB Architect Registration Examination. Multiple Choice Handbook; Multiple Choice Handbook. (19??)-(1993). English. One time a year. $30.00. National Council Architectural Registration Boards, 1735 NW Avenue/Suite 700, Washington DC 20006. **Tel** (202)659-3996.
Continues in part NCARB Architect Registration Examination handbook.

LC NA
DD 720
UDC 72
ISSN 0925-6830
NE
ARCHITECT THEMA, DE. [Archit., Thema]. **VFOAT** Architect Thema. (1980)-. Periodical. Dutch. Four times a year. Comes with De Architect. Ten Hagen and Stam BV, Postbus 34, 2501 AG The Hague Netherlands. **Tel** 011 31 70 3045700.
Ind/Abst Avery Index Archit. Period. Suppl. Colum. Univ. (1990-).

LC NA1 .A34
DD 720/.5
ISSN 0003-8393
AT
ARCHITECT, W.A. : THE OFFICIAL JOURNAL OF THE ROYAL AUSTRALIAN INSTITUTE OF ARCHITECTS, W.A. CHAPTER, THE. Added/Corp Royal Australian Institute of Architects. Western Australian Chapter. **VFOAT** Architect, Western Australia. (19??)-. Trade Publication. English. Four times a year (Mar., June, Sept., Dec.). 18.09Aus$. Royal Australia Institute of Architects, PO Box 191, West Australia Chapter, West Perth WA 6005 Australia. **Tel** 011-61-9-3217114, FAX 011-61-9-3214708. **Bk Rev**, (Qty: 3). **Ad Acc**, **Adv Mgr:** Brian Wart, **Tel** (09)321-1960. **Circ:** 1,200 (ctrl). **Continues** Architect (Perth, W.A.).
Ind/Abst Archit. Period. Index; Avery Index Archit. Period. Suppl. Colum. Univ. (1989-).

LC NA673 .A73
DD 720/.5
PO
ARCHITECTI. Vol. 1, No. 1 (Feb. 1989)-. Periodical. Portuguese (Spanish). Five times a year. $176.40. Editora Triforio Lda, AMarques de Tomar 68-4 Esq, 1000 Lisbon Portugal. **Tel** 011 351 7938451, FAX 011 351 1 7938341. **ED** Luiz Tri Gueiros and Raul Carvalho. Index available. **Ad Acc**. **Circ:** 15,000. available on Slides.
Desc: Each issue presents two contemporary buildings designed by a Portuguese architect and by a Spanish architect, including criticism and drawings, both in Portuguese and Spanish speaking countries.

LC NA1 .I48 **ISSN** 0970-6852
DD 720.6254 II
UDC 72
ARCHITECTS INDIA. [Archit. India]. (1989)-. Trade Publication. English. Six times a year (Jan., Mar., May, July, Sept., Nov.). $20.00. Architects Publishing Corporation of India, 51 Sujata/Ground Floor, Rani Sati Marg, Malad East, Bombay 400 097 India. **Tel** 840 4442 or 8405510, FAX 680 5510. **ED** Santosh Kumar. **Bk Rev. Ad Acc. Circ:** 3,500. ***Continues*** *Architects Trade Journal, 0304-8594.*

LC TH1 .A7 **ISSN** 0003-8466
DD 720.5 UK
CCC
ARCHITECTS' JOURNAL (LONDON). (THE ARCHITECTS' JOURNAL.). [Archit. j.]. **VFOAT** AJ. The Architects' Journal. Vol. 49 (1919)-. Trade Publication. English. One time a week. £59.00 UK; £99.00 other. EMAP Architecture, 33 39 Bowling Green Lane, London EC1R 0DA United Kingdom. **Tel** 011 44 171 8371212, FAX 011 44 171 2784003. **(Subscription address:** EMAP Business Publishing, 4 Admiral House Cardinal Way, Middlesex HA3 5SQ United Kingdom. **Tel** 011 44 181 8684499.**) ED** Colin Davies. Index available. **Bk Rev. Ad Acc. Circ:** 19,000. available on microfilm and microfiche from University Microfilms International (UMI). ***Continues*** *Architects' and Builders' Journal.*
Ind/Abst Anbar Account. Finan. Abstr. [Full Txt.]; Anbar Mark. Distr. Abstr. [Full Txt.]; Anbar Top Manage. Abstr. [Full Txt.]; Archit. Period. Index (1977-); Art Archaeol. Tech. Abstr.; Art Index; Avery Index Archit. Period. Suppl. Colum. Univ. (1990-); Br. Humanit. Index; Curr. Technol. Index; Highw. Res. Abstr.; Int. Build. Serv. Abstr.; Int. Civil Eng. Abstr.; Leadscan; Manage. Bibliogr. Rev.; Oper. Prod. Manage. Abstr. [Full Txt.]; Person. Train. Abstr. [Full Txt.]; Saf. Health Work; Soft. Abstr. Eng.; Surf. Treat. Technol. Abstr.; Women Manage. Rev. [Full Txt.]; World Ceram. Abstr.

LC NA200 .A69 **ISSN** 0044-863X
DD 722 GW
ARCHITECTURA. [Architectura]. Vol. 1 (1971)-. Trade Publication. English (German, French and Italian). Two times a year. DM92.00. Deutscher Kunstverlag, Postfach 190354, D-80603 Munich Germany. **Tel** 011 49 89 1215160. **ED** Wulf Schirmer, Wolfgang Muller-Wiener, and George Hersey. **Bk Rev. Circ:** 500. Documents available from The Genuine Article. ***Continues*** *Zeitschrift fuer Geschichte der Zankunst; Journal of the History of Architecture.*
Desc: History of architecture.
Ind/Abst Archit. Period. Index (1977-); Art Index; ARTbibliogr. Mod.; Arts Humanit. Citation Index (19??-19??) [Full Cov.]; Avery Index Archit. Period. Suppl. Colum. Univ. (1989-); BHA : Biblio. Hist. Art; Res. Alert [Full Cov.].

LC NA1211 .A69 **ISSN** 0106-3030
DK
ARCHITECTURA. Added/Corp Selskabet for Arkitekturhistorie (Denmark). (1979)-. Periodical. Danish. One time a year. Arkitektens Forlag / The Danish Architectural Press, Nyhavn 43, DK-1051 Copenhagen K Denmark. **Tel** 011 45 33 136200, FAX 011 45 33 912770. **ED** E. Hiort. **Circ:** 1,025.
Ind/Abst Archit. Period. Index (1979-); BHA : Biblio. Hist. Art.

ISSN 1071-4634
US
•**ARCHITECTURAL & CONSTRUCTION MEDIA SOURCE. Added/Corp** Standard Rate & Data Service. **VFOAT** Architectural and Construction Media Source. (1994)-. English. $149.00. SRDS / Standard Rate & Data Service, 3004 Glenview Road, Wilmette IL 60091. **Tel** (708)375-5049, (800)851-7737, FAX (708)375-5003. ***Continues*** *SRDS Media & Market Planner. Architectural & Construction Markets, 1064-5500.*

LC NA
DD 720 UK
ARCHITECTURAL ASSOCIATION ANNUAL REVIEW, THE. Main/Corp Architectural Association (Great Britain). **Added/Corp** Architectural Association (Great Britain) Annual Review. (1977)-. English. One time a year. Diplomat Consular Yearbook Ltd., London United Kingdom.
Ind/Abst Archit. Period. Index (1979-1981).

CN
ARCHITECTURAL CONSERVATION TECHNOLOGY SERIES. (19??)-. English. Canada Communication Group Publishers, Order Processing, Ottawa Ontario K1A 0S9 Canada. **Tel** (819)956-4800, (819)956-4802.

LC NA1 .A563 **ISSN** 0003-8504
DD 720/.5 UK
CCC
ARCHITECTURAL DESIGN. (ARCHITECTURAL DESIGN : A.D.). [Archit. des.]. **VFOAT** A.D.; AD. (Jan. 1971)-. Trade Publication. English. Six times a year. $142.00. Academy Editions, 42 Leinster Gardens, London W2 3AN United Kingdom. **Tel** 011 44 171 4022141, FAX 011 44 171 7239540, telex 896928 ACADEM G. **(Subscription address:** VCH Publishers Inc., 303 Northwest 12th Avenue, Journals Department, Deerfield FL 33442. **Tel** (800)367-8249, (305)428-5566.**) ED** Andreas C. Papadakis. **Bk Rev. Ad Acc. Circ:** 12,000 (ctrl). Documents available from The Genuine Article, Documents on Demand. ***Continues*** *A.D. (London, England : 1970), 0003-8504.*
Desc: Articles on architectural theory, practice and criticism. Most issues are guest-edited by critics with contributions from historians and architects.
Ind/Abst Archit. Period. Index (1977-); Art Index; ARTbibliogr. Mod.; Arts Humanit. Citation Index (19??-19??) [Full Cov.]; Avery Index Archit. Period. Suppl. Colum. Univ. (1989-); Curr. Contents Arts Humanit.; Energy Inf. Abstr.; Environ. Abstr.; Leadscan; Res. Alert [Full Cov.]; Soc. Sci. Cit. Index [Select. Cov.].

LC NA7205 .A73 **ISSN** 0747-5179
DD 728.3/7/0223 US
ARCHITECTURAL DESIGNS. [Archit. des.]. Vol. 1, No. 1 (Feb. 1984)-. Periodical. English. Three times a year. $3.95. Woodworker Inc., 274 Riverside Avenue, Westport CT 06880-4823. **Tel** (203)222-1113, FAX (203)221-9255. **Ad Acc. Circ:** 27,000.
Desc: Home plans from twenty-five architects. Readers can order full working blueprints from which to build. Each issue features over 200 plans of varying styles.

LC NA730.C2 A7 **ISSN** 0003-8520
US
ARCHITECTURAL DIGEST (LOS ANGELES, CALIF.). (ARCHITECTURAL DIGEST.). [Archit. dig.]. **VFOAT** Architectural Digest 100; AD 100. Vol. 1 (1925)-. Periodical. English. Twelve times a year. $39.95. Conde Nast Publications / New York, 350 Madison Avenue, New York NY 10017. **Tel** (212)880-8800, (800)777-0700, FAX (212)880-8331. **(Subscription address:** Neodata / Colorado, PO Box 2606, Boulder CO 80322. **) ED** Paige Rense. **Circ:** 600,146. Documents available from The Genuine Article, UMI Article Clearinghouse.
Desc: Magazine of interior design, with columns including special features on art, antiques, and architecture from collectors, gallery owners, and art experts.
Ind/Abst Acad. Abstr. Full Text Elite; Acad. Abstr.; Acad. Ind. [Computer File] (1992-); Acad. Search; Art Index; ARTbibliogr. Mod.; Arts Humanit. Citation Index [Full Cov.]; Avery Index Archit. Period. Suppl. Colum. Univ. (1989-); Curr. Contents Arts Humanit.; EP Collect.; Expand. Acad. Index (1992-); Garden Lit. (1992-); Gen. Period. Index (1985-); Homework Help.; Mag. Artic. Summar. Elite; Mag. Artic. Summar. Select; Mag. Artic. Summar. CD-ROM; Mag. Index Plus (1989-); Mag. Index. Sel. (1986-); Mag. Search; MasterFile FullTEXT 1000; MasterFile FullTEXT 350; MasterFile FullTEXT 650; MasterFile FullTEXT (Jan. 1984-); Newsp. Period. Abstr. (1988-); OCLC; Pub. Lib. FullTEXT; Read. Guide Abstr. Select Ed.; Read. Guide Period. Lit.; Res. Alert [Full Cov.]; Telebase; Mag. Index (1977-); Vocat. Search.

LC N9 .A377 **ISSN** 0743-5517
DD 700 US
ARCHITECTURAL DIGEST. THE ... ART AND ANTIQUES ANNUAL. [Archit. dig., Art antiq. annu.]. **VFOAT** Art and Antiques Annual. Vol. 1, No. 1 (1984)-. English. One time a year. $5.95 US; $8.45 other. Knapp Communications Corporation, 5900 Wilshire Boulevard, Los Angeles CA 90036.

LC TA26 .A7 **ISSN** 0846-8583
DD 338.4/362/000971 CN
ARCHITECTURAL, ENGINEERING, AND SCIENTIFIC SERVICES. [Archit. eng. sci. serv.]. **Added/Corp** Statistics Canada. Retail Trade Section. **VFOAT** Bureaux d'Architectes, d'Ingenieurs-Conseils et de Services Scientifiques. (19??)-. English (French). Irregular. 33.00Can$ Canada; $40.00 US; $47.00 other. Statistics Canada Publications Sales and Services, R.H. Coats Building 6th Floor, Ottawa Ontario K1A 0T6 Canada. **Tel** (613)951-5078, (800)267-6677, FAX (613)951-1584, telex 053-3585.

LC NA972 .A73
DD 720/.9411 UK
ARCHITECTURAL HERITAGE : THE JOURNAL OF THE ARCHITECTURAL HERITAGE SOCIETY OF SCOTLAND. Added/Corp Architectural Heritage Society of Scotland. **VFOAT** Journal of the Architectural Heritage Society of Scotland. (1990)-. English. One time a year. $34.00. Edinburgh University Press Ltd., 22 George Square, Edinburgh EH8 9LF United Kingdom. **Tel** 011 44 131 6506207, FAX 011 44 131 6620053. ***Continues*** *Journal (Architectural Heritage Society of Scotland).*
Ind/Abst Archit. Period. Index (No. 1, 1990-); BHA : Biblio. Hist. Art.

LC NA190 .A72 **ISSN** 0066-622X
DD 720/.9 UK
ARCHITECTURAL HISTORY. [Archit. hist.]. **Added/Corp** Society of Architectural Historians of Great Britain. Vol. 1 (1958)-. English. One time a year (September). $60.00. Society of Architecture Historians of Great Britain, 4 Woodlands Avenue, Finchley, London N3 2NR United Kingdom. **Tel** 011 44 181 3465139. **ED** Peter Draper. cum. index. **Bk Rev. Circ:** 1,100. Documents available from The Genuine Article.
Ind/Abst Archit. Period. Index (1978-); Art Index; ARTbibliogr. Mod.; Arts Humanit. Citation Index (19??-19??) [Full Cov.]; Avery Index Archit. Period. Suppl. Colum. Univ. (1990-); BHA : Biblio. Hist. Art; Br. Archaeol. Bibliogr.; Br. Humanit. Index; Curr. Contents Arts Humanit.; Res. Alert [Full Cov.].

LC Z5941 .A66 NA1 **ISSN** 0570-6483
DD 016.7205 US
ARCHITECTURAL INDEX, THE. (19??)-. English. One time a year (Mar.). $27.00. Architectural Index, PO Box 1168, Boulder CO 80306. **Tel** (303)443-5354, FAX (303)449-3748. **ED** E. J. Bell. Index available. **Circ:** 4,000.
Desc: Comprehensive index to 11 major American architectural magazines.

LC N7327 .A77
DD 709/.599 PH
ARCHITECTURAL JOURNAL. Vol. 2, No. 11 (Mar. 1982)-. Periodical. English. Twelve times a year. Philippine Journalists, Editorial and Business Offices and 20th Street, Port Area Manila Philippines. ***Continues*** *Arts, Designs, Gardens, and Home Interiors Architectural Journal.*

LC TH7700 .A717 **ISSN** 0894-0436
DD 621.32 US
CCC
Pr Rev.
ARCHITECTURAL LIGHTING. [Archit. light.]. Vol. 1, No. 1 (Jan. 1987)-. Periodical. English. Four times a year. $24.00. Miller Freeman Inc., 600 Harrison Street, San Francisco CA 94107. **Tel** (415)905-2337, (415)905-2200, FAX (415)905-2240, telex 278273. **ED** Charles Linn. Index available. cum. index. **Bk Rev. Ad Acc. Circ:** 57,000 (ctrl). available on microfilm from University Microfilms International (UMI).
Desc: Devoted exclusively to lighting in commercial, industrial, institutional, and residential settings. Offered to architects, landscape architects, lighting designers and electrical engineers. Each issue offers an in-depth cover story, case studies, articles on every aspect of interior and exterior electric and daylighting techniques, software reviews, new products and literature, book reviews and an industry calendar.
Ind/Abst Constr. Index (19??-).

ISSN 0141-2191
UK
ARCHITECTURAL MONOGRAPHS. [Archit. monogr.]. (1978)-. Monographic series. English (summaries and/or abstracts in French, German, Italian and Spanish). Irregular. Price varies per volume. Academy Editions, 42 Leinster Gardens, London W2 3AN United Kingdom. **Tel** 011 44 171 4022141, FAX 011 44 171 7239540, telex 896928 ACADEM G. **(Subscription address:** VCH Publishers Inc., 303 Northwest 12th Avenue, Journals Department, Deerfield FL 33442. **Tel** (800)367-8249, (305)428-5566.**) ED** Andreas C. Papadakis. **Bk Rev. Ad Acc. Circ:** 12,000.
Desc: Recent titles include Terry Farrell and John Soane. Forthcoming Richard Rogers and architects and Le Corbusier.
Ind/Abst Archit. Period. Index (1978-).

LC NA1.A1 **ISSN** 1081-2369
DD 720 US
•**ARCHITECTURAL PHOTOFILE.** (ARCHITECTURAL PHOTOFILE [COMPUTER FILE].). [Archit. photofile]. **VFOAT** Architectural Photo File. (1993)-. English. Irregular. Loggia, 1519 24th Street, Detroit MI 48216.

LC NA109.G7 A73 **ISSN** 0262-219X
DD 363.6/9/0941 UK
ARCHITECTURAL PRESERVATION AND NEW DESIGN IN CONSERVATION. [Archit. preserv. new des. conserv.]. **VFOAT** AP; A.P.; Architectural Preservation. Vol. 1 No. 1 (Apr. 1982)-. Periodical. English. Four times a year. $22.22. Architectural Preservation, 214 Panther House, 38 Mount Pleasant, London WC1X 0AP.
Ind/Abst Archit. Period. Index (April 1982-); Avery Index Archit. Period. Suppl. Colum. Univ. (19??-199?).

UK
SUSPENDED
ARCHITECTURAL PSYCHOLOGY NEWSLETTER. Added/Corp Kingston Polytechnic. School of Architecture. Psychology Reseach Unit. Vol. 1 (July 1969)-Suspended (19??). Newsletter. English. Four times a year. Kingston Polytechnic, Kingston Upon Thames, Surrey KT1 2QJ United Kingdom. **Tel** 01 549 6151. **ED** Sue-Ann Lee. **Bk Rev. Circ:** 300.
Desc: Research summaries, articles, reviews, and information on courses, meetings and publications concerning the inter-relationship between people and their physical environment.

LC NA1 .A6 **ISSN** 0003-858X
DD 720/.5 US
CCC
CODEN ACURAV
ARCHITECTURAL RECORD. [Archit. rec.]. **VFOAT** AR. Vol. 1 (July 1891)-. Trade Publication. English. Twelve times a year. $54.00. McGraw Hill Publishing Company, Inc., 1221 Avenue of the Americas,

New York NY 10020. **Tel** (212)512-6410, (800)525-5003, FAX (212)512-6111. **(Subscription address:** Architectural Record, PO Box 564, Hightstown NJ 08520) cum. index. **Ad Acc. Circ:** 65,535. available on microfilm and microfiche from University Microfilms International (UMI); available on an online database from Dow Jones News/Retrieval; NEWSNET; DIALOG; and Lexis-Nexis. Documents available from Article Express International, The Genuine Article, UMI Article Clearinghouse, Documents on Demand. ***Absorbed** American Architect and Architecture; Western Architect and Engineer.*
Desc: Edited for architects and engineers in commercial, institutional, and governmental building.
Ind/Abst Acad. Abstr. Full Text Elite; Acad. Abstr.; Acad. Ind. [Computer File] (1985-); Acad. Search; Archit. Period. Index (1977-); Art Index; ARTbibliogr. Mod.; Arts Humanit. Citation Index [Full Cov.]; Avery Index Archit. Period. Suppl. Colum. Univ. (1990-); Bioeng. Abstr.; Bus. Index (1985-); Concr. Abstr.; Constr. Index; Curr. Cit.; Curr. Contents Arts Humanit.; Ei Page One; Energy Inf. Abstr.; Eng. Index Annu.; Environ. Abstr.; EP Collect.; Expand. Acad. Index (1985-); Gen. BusinessFile (1985-); Gen. Period. Index (1985-); Health Plan. Adminis.; Homework Help.; Hosp. Health Admin. Index; Int. Civil Eng. Abstr.; J. Plan. Lit.; Mag. Artic. Summar. Elite; Mag. Artic. Summar. Select; Mag. Artic. Summar. CD-ROM; Mag. Index Plus (1989-); Mag. Index. Sel. (1986-); Mag. Search; MasterFile FullTEXT 1000; MasterFile FullTEXT 350; MasterFile FullTEXT 650; MasterFile FullTEXT (May 1984-); Newsp. Period. Abstr. (1986-); OCLC; Pub. Lib. FullTEXT; Read. Guide Abstr. Select Ed.; Read. Guide Period. Lit.; Res. Alert [Full Cov.]; Soc. Sci. Cit. Index [Select. Cov.]; Soft. Abstr. Eng.; Stat. Ref. Index; Telebase; Mag. Index (1977-); Trade Ind. Index; Vocat. Search.

LC NA1 .A69 **ISSN** 0003-861X
DD 720/.5 UK
ARCHITECTURAL REVIEW (LONDON).
(THE ARCHITECTURAL REVIEW.). [Archit. rev.]. **VFOAT** AR. Vol. 1 (Nov. 1896)-. Trade Publication. English. Twelve times a year. $150.00. EMAP Architecture, 33 39 Bowling Green Lane, London EC1R 0DA United Kingdom. **Tel** 011 44 171 8371212, FAX 011 44 171 2784003. **(Subscription address:** Fenner Reed & Jackson, PO Box 754, Manhasset NY 11030-0754. **Tel** (516)627-3836, FAX (516)627-1972.) available on microfilm and microfiche from University Microfilms International (UMI). Documents available from The Genuine Article, UMI Article Clearinghouse. ***Absorbed** Details.*
Ind/Abst Archit. Period. Index (1977-); Art Index; ARTbibliogr. Mod.; Arts Humanit. Citation Index [Full Cov.]; Avery Index Archit. Period. Suppl. Colum. Univ. (1990-); BHA : Biblio. Hist. Art; Br. Humanit. Index; Curr. Contents Arts Humanit.; Expand. Acad. Index (1992-); Garden Lit. (1992-); Int. Civil Eng. Abstr.; Leadscan; Newsp. Period. Abstr. (1992-); Res. Alert [Full Cov.]; Soft. Abstr. Eng.; Trade Ind. Index.

LC NA2103 .A73 **ISSN** 0092-7856
DD 720/.7/117 US
TITLE CHANGE
ARCHITECTURAL SCHOOLS IN NORTH AMERICA.
Added/Corp Association of Collegiate Schools of Architecture. (19??)-(19??). Periodical. English. Association of Collegiate Schools of Architecture, 1735 New York Avenue Northwest, Washington DC 20006. **Tel** (202)785-2324, (800)232-2724. ***Continued by** Guide to Architecture Schools.*

LC NA1 .A744 **ISSN** 0003-8628
DD 720.5 AT
CODEN ASRVA4
ARCHITECTURAL SCIENCE REVIEW.
[Archit. sci. rev.]. Vol. 1, (Nov. 1958)-. Periodical. English. Four times a year (Mar., June, Sept., Dec.). 57.55Aus$. Architectural Science Review, Department of Architectural Science, University of Sydney, Sydney New South Wales 2006 Australia. **Tel** 011 61 2 6922191, FAX 011 61 2 6923031, telex 26169. **ED** Emeritus Professor Henry J. Cowan, (phone: 011 62 2 692 2191). Index available. cum. index. **Bk Rev. Ad Acc.** Full Page (B&W) 300.00Aus$. Half Page (B&W) 200.00Aus$. **Circ:** 750. available on microfilm from University Microfilms International (UMI). Documents available from Article Express International.
Desc: The science of architecture, heating, acoustics, lighting, etc.
Ind/Abst Archit. Period. Index (Nov. 1958-); Bioeng. Abstr.; Ei Page One; Eng. Index Annu.; For. Prod. Abstr.; Int. Build. Serv. Abstr.; Int. Civil Eng. Abstr.; Pollut. Abstr. Indexes; Saf. Health Work; Soft. Abstr. Eng.; World Ceram. Abstr.

ISSN 1068-8560
DD 721 US
•ARCHITECTURAL SPECIFIER.
[Archit. specif.]. Vol. 1, No. 1 (Spring 1993)-. Trade Publication. English. Six times a year. $15.00. Century Communications Inc., 6201 Howard Street, Niles IL 60714-3435. **Tel** (708)647-1200, FAX (708)647-7055.

LC NA2542.4 .A7 **ISSN** 0379-8585
DD 720/.1/03 SZ
ARCHITECTURE & COMPORTEMENT.
[Archit. comport.]. **VFOAT** Architecture & Behaviour; Architecture et Comportement; Architecture and Behaviour. Vol. 1, No. 1 (1980)-. Periodical. English (French; summaries and/or abstracts in English and French). Four times a year (Mar., July, Oct., Dec.). $141.39. Architecture and Behaviour, POB 555, 1001 Lausanne Switzerland. **Tel** 011 44 21 6934225, FAX 011 41 21 6176317. **ED** Dr. Kaj Noschis, (phone: 011 41 21 6168238). Index available (Bound in 4th iss.). cum. index. **Bk Rev. Ad Acc. Circ:** 1,000-1,500.
Desc: An interdisciplinary journal, scientific & bilingual, devoted to all aspects of the relations between man and his built environment.
Ind/Abst Archit. Period. Index (1980-); Avery Index Archit. Period. Suppl. Colum. Univ. (1990-); BHA : Biblio. Hist. Art; Geogr. Abstr. Human Geogr.; Int. Dev. Abstr.; Psychol. Abstr. (1980-); Sage Urban Stud. Abstr.

BU
ARCHITECTURE AND SOCIETY = ARKHITEKTURA I OBSHCHESTVO : AS.
VFOAT AS; Arkhitektura i Obshchestvo. (1983)-. Periodical. English (Russian; summaries and/or abstracts in French and Spanish).
Ind/Abst Archit. Period. Index (No. 2, 1984-).

LC NA1 .A775 **ISSN** 0003-8725
DD 720/.5 AT
ARCHITECTURE AUSTRALIA.
[Archit. Aust.]. **Added/Corp** Royal Australian Institute of Architects. (1904)-. Periodical. English. Six times a year. 34.53Aus$. Architecture Media Australia, 4 Princes Street Third Floor, Port Melbourne Victoria 3207 Australia. **Tel** 011 61 3 6464760, FAX 011 61 3 6464918. **Bk Rev. Ad Acc.** ***Continues** Architecture in Australia.*
Desc: Records Australian architecture descriptions, criticisms of buildings, architectural theory, book reviews, letter, and new products.
Ind/Abst APAIS, Aust. Public Aff. Inf. Ser. (1963-); Archit. Period. Index (1977-);; Avery Index Archit. Period. Suppl. Colum. Univ. (1989-); Curr. Cit.; EP Collect.; Homework Help.; MasterFile FullTEXT 1000; MasterFile FullTEXT 350; MasterFile FullTEXT 650; MasterFile FullTEXT; OCLC; Telebase; World Mag. Bank.

LC NA730.C2 A74 **ISSN** 0738-1131
DD 720/.9794 US
ARCHITECTURE CALIFORNIA.
[Archit. Calif.]. **Added/Corp** CCAIA (Organization). (1979)-. Periodical. English. Two times a year (May & Nov.). $34.00. The American Institute of Architects, California Council, 1303 J Street, Suite 200, Sacramento CA 95814. **Tel** (916)448-9082, FAX (916)442-5346. **ED** Lian Hurst Mann, AIA. **Bk Rev. Circ:** 10,000 (ctrl).
Desc: Provides a forum for the exchange of ideas among architects and other disciplines on the issues currently shaping California architecture. It discusses the practice of architecture, as well as the relationship of the profession to the interests of the public.

ISSN 0003-8687
CN
SUSPENDED
ARCHITECTURE CONCEPT.
[Archit. concept]. Vol. 23, No. 271 (Jan./Feb. 1969)-Suspended (19??). Trade Publication. French. Four times a year (Feb., Apr., June, Aug.). 43.27Can$ Canada; $60.00 US; $80.00 other. Editions CR Inc, CP PO Box 1010, Victoriaville G6P 8Y1 Canada. **Tel** (819)752-4243, FAX (819)758-8812. **ED** Marcas Dumont. **Bk Rev. Ad Acc. Circ:** 4,052 (ctrl). ***Continues** Architecture-Batiment-Construction, 0317-6819.*
Desc: Serves the architectural, interior and industrial design, architectural landscaping and other related design services in French Canada.
Ind/Abst Archit. Period. Index (Jan./Feb. 1977-); Avery Index Archit. Period. Suppl. Colum. Univ. (19??-199?); BHA : Biblio. Hist. Art; Can. Period. Index (19??-19??); Repere (1979-1980).

ISSN 0003-8695
BE
ARCHITECTURE D'AUJOURD'HUI, L'.
[Archit. aujourd'hui]. Vol. 1 (1930)-. Periodical. French. Six times a year. $178.91. Groupe Expansion, Le Ponant, 25 rue LeBlanc, 75842 Paris Cedex 15 France. **Tel** 011 33 1 40604115. **(Subscription address:** L'Architecture d'Aujourd Hui, Service Abbonements B 060, 60732 Suite Genev Cedex 9 France.) **ED** Marc Emery. **Bk Rev. Ad Acc. Circ:** 25,791 (ctrl). available on microfilm and microfiche from University Microfilms International (UMI). Documents available from The Genuine Article. ***Absorbed** Architecture.*
Desc: Covers contemporary architecture.
Ind/Abst Archit. Period. Index (1977-); Art Index; Arts Humanit. Citation Index [Full Cov.]; Avery Index Archit. Period. Suppl. Colum. Univ. (1989-); BHA : Biblio. Hist. Art; Curr. Cit.; Curr. Contents Arts Humanit.; Repere (1979-1980); Res. Alert [Full Cov.]; Soc. Sci. Cit. Index [Select. Cov.].

LC NA1504 .A73
II
ARCHITECTURE + DESIGN.
VFOAT Architecture and Design; Architecture Plus Design. Vol. 1, No. 1 (Nov./Dec. 1984)-. Periodical. English. Six times a year. $45.00. Media Transasia, Bombay India. **(Subscription address:** Prints India, 11 Darya Ganj, New Delhi 110002 India. **Tel** 011 91 11 3268645, FAX 011 91 11 3275542, telex 31-61087 PRIN-IN.)
Ind/Abst Archit. Period. Index (Vol. 1 No. 5, July/Aug. 1985-); Avery Index Archit. Period. Suppl. Colum. Univ. (May/June 1989, Nov./Dec. 1989, Jan./Feb 1990-); J. Plan. Lit.

ISSN 1059-4434
DD 720 US
ARCHITECTURE/GEORGIA.
[Archit./Ga.]. **Added/Corp** American Institute of Architects. Georgia Association. **VFOAT** Architecture Georgia. Vol. 1, No. 1 (Oct. 1990)-. English. Four times a year. $15.00. Georgia Association of the American Institute of Architects, 231 Peachtree Street Northeast, Suite B 04, Atlanta GA 30303. **Tel** (404)222-0099, FAX (404)222-9916.

US
SUSPENDED
ARCHITECTURE GEORGIA / GEORGIA ASSOCIATION, AMERICAN INSTITUTE OF ARCHITECTS.
Added/Corp American Institute of Architects. Georgia Association. Vol. 1, No. 1 (Oct. 1990)-Suspended (19??). Periodical. English. Four times a year. Georgia Association of the American Institute of Architects, 231 Peachtree Street Northeast, Suite B 04, Atlanta GA 30303. **Tel** (404)222-0099, FAX (404)222-9916.

LC NA2 .A83 **ISSN** 0294-8567
DD 720/.5 FR
ARCHITECTURE INTERIEURE-C.R.E.E.
(ARCHITECTURE INTERIEURE-CREE.). [Archit. inter. C.R.E.E.]. No. 158 (March 1977)-. Periodical. French. Six times a year. $184.82. Architecture Interieure CREE, 106 BD Malesherbes, 75017 Paris France. **Tel** 011 33 1 47660460. ***Formed by the union of** Architecture Interieure **and** CREE.*
Ind/Abst Archit. Period. Index (1977-); ARTbibliogr. Mod.; Avery Index Archit. Period. Suppl. Colum. Univ. (1990-).

ISSN 0129-5829
SI
ARCHITECTURE JOURNAL.
Added/Corp National University of Singapore. School of Architecture. (1983)-. English.
Ind/Abst Archit. Period. Index (1985-).

LC NA1458 .A73 **ISSN** 0761-7909
DD 720/.9182/2 FR
ARCHITECTURE MEDITERRANEENNE.
French (summaries and/or abstracts in English; table of contents in English). One time a year. $98.43. Robert Khaiat, 43 rue de Forbin, 13002 Marseille France.
Ind/Abst Archit. Period. Index.

LC NA730.M6 A73 **ISSN** 0149-9106
DD 720/.9776 US
Pr Rev.
ARCHITECTURE MINNESOTA.
[Archit. Minn.]. **Added/Corp** Minnesota Society of Architects. American Institute of Architects. Minnesota Society. **VFOAT** AM. Vol. 1 (May/June 1975)-. Periodical. English. Six times a year (Jan., Mar., May, July, Sept., Nov.). $18.00. American Institute of Architects Minnesota, 275 Market Street, Suite 54, Minneapolis MN 55405. **Tel** (612)338-6763, FAX (612)338-7981. **ED** Eric Kudalis. Index available. **Bk Rev,** (Qty: 20). **Ad Acc, Adv Mgr:** J. VanDyne, **Tel** (612)338-6763. **Circ:** 7,000 (ctrl). ***Supersedes** Northwest Architect, 0029-330X.*
Desc: A midwest regional magazine reviewing the design arts including architecture, interior design and urban design.
Ind/Abst Avery Index Archit. Period. Suppl. Colum. Univ. (1990-).

ISSN 0360-6562
US
ARCHITECTURE. NEW ENGLAND.
Vol. 1 (March 1975)-. Periodical. English. Ten times a year. $10.00. New Hampshire Profiles Publishing, PO Box A40, Hanover NH 03755. **Tel** (603)772-5252.

LC NA11 .A75 **ISSN** 0003-8733
DD 720/.5 US
CEASED
ARCHITECTURE NEW JERSEY.
[Archit. N.J.]. **Added/Corp** New Jersey Society of Architects. **VFOAT** New Jersey Architecture. (19??)-(1993). Trade Publication. English. New Jersey Society of Architects, 1000 Route 9, Woodbridge NJ 07095. **Tel** (201)636-5680, FAX (201)636-5681. **Bk Rev. Ad Acc. Circ:** 5,000.
Desc: Advances increased public awareness of the built environment and carries articles and representations of buildings of current interest.
Ind/Abst Avery Index Archit. Period. Suppl. Colum. Univ. (1984-).

ISSN 0113-4566
NZ
CCC
ARCHITECTURE NEW ZEALAND.
[Archit. N.Z.]. **VFOAT** Architecture; ANZ. (Jan./Feb. 1988)-. Trade Publication. English. Twelve times a year. Associated Group Media Ltd, Private Bag 99915, Newmarket, Auckland 1031 New Zealand. **Tel** 11 64 9 3795393, FAX 11 64 9 3089523, telex 79121057. **ED**

Carol Bocknell. **Bk Rev**. **Ad Acc**. **Circ:** 8,500 (ctrl). ***Continues*** *New Zealand Architect, 0110-425X.*
Ind/Abst Archit. Period. Index.

KE
ARCHITECTURE : OFFICIAL JOURNAL OF THE ARCHITECTURAL ASSOCIATION OF KENYA. Added/Corp Architectural Association of Kenya. (198?)-. Periodical. English. Twelve times a year. News Publishers Ltd / Kenya, Norwich Union House/4th Floor, Mama Ngina Street, PO Box 30339, Nairobi Kenya. ***Continues*** *Build Kenya.*

LC NA1 .A7935 **ISSN** 0090-9521
DD 720/.5 US
ARCHITECTURE PLUS. Vol. 1 (Feb. 1973)-. Periodical. English. Twelve times a year. $18.00. Informat Publishing Co., 1345 6th Avenue, New York NY 10019.

ISSN 0250-054X
DD 720.968 SA
ARCHITECTURE SA. [Archit. SA]. **VFOAT** Argitektuur SA; Architecture South Africa. (1978)-. Trade Publication. Multiple languages. Six times a year. $28.63. George Warman Publications Pty, PO Box 704, Cape Town 8000 South Africa. **Tel** 011 27 21 245320, **FAX** 011 27 21 261332, telex 5-21849. **Ad Acc**. **Circ:** 4,100 (ctrl).
Ind/Abst Archit. Period. Index (Mar. 1978-199?); Avery Index Archit. Period. Suppl. Colum. Univ. (May-Aug., Nov.-Dec. 1989, Nov.-Dec. 1990); EP Collect.; Homework Help.; MasterFile FullTEXT 1000; MasterFile FullTEXT 350; MasterFile FullTEXT 650; MasterFile FullTEXT; OCLC; Telebase; World Mag. Bank.

ISSN 0958-6407
UK
Pr Rev.
ARCHITECTURE TODAY. [Archit. today]. (Sept. 1989)-. Periodical. English. Ten times a year (monthly except Aug. & Dec.). $82.13. Architecture Today, 161 Rosenbery Avenue, London EC1R 4QX United Kingdom. **Tel** 011 44 171 4366916, **FAX** 011 44 171 4362958. **ED** Ian Latham and Dr. Mark Swenarton. cum. index. **Bk Rev**, (Qty: 10). **Ad Acc**, **Adv Mgr:** S. Peters. **Circ:** 22,000 (ctrl).
Desc: Aimed at the practising architect; features new and refurbished buildings in Britain and Europe, plus articles of a technical and practical nature.

ISSN 0761-7305
FR
UDC 930.26
ARCHITECTURE VERNACULAIRE, L'. (1981)-. Periodical. French. One time a year.
Ind/Abst BHA : Biblio. Hist. Art.

LC NA1 .A326 **ISSN** 0746-0554
DD 720/.973 US
CCC
ARCHITECTURE (WASHINGTON, D.C.). (ARCHITECTURE : THE AIA JOURNAL.). [Architecture]. **Added/Corp** American Institute of Architects. Vol. 72, No. 7 (July 1983)-. Periodical. English (summaries and/or abstracts in French and Spanish). Twelve times a year. $42.00 US; $49.00 Canada; $65.00 other. Billboard Publications Inc., 1515 Broadway Billboard, New York NY 10036. **Tel** (212)764-7300, **FAX** (305)755-7048, telex WU TWX 710-581-6279. **(Subscription address:** Fulfillment Corporation of America / Marion Ohio, 205 West Center Street, Marion OH 43302. **Tel** (800)669-1002, (614)383-5231.**)** **ED** Donald C Canty. **Circ:** 50,741. available on microfilm and microfiche from University Microfilms International (UMI). Documents available from The Genuine Article, UMI Article Clearinghouse. ***Continues*** *AIA Journal. American Institute of Architects., 0001-1479;* ***Absorbed*** *Architectural Technology, 0740-6142.*
Desc: Edited for architects, specifiers and design professionals responsible for designing and specifying products in today's new building construction, existing rehabilitation and remodeling projects.
Ind/Abst Archit. Period. Index (1983-); Art Index; Arts Humanit. Citation Index [Full Cov.]; Avery Index Archit. Period. Suppl. Colum. Univ. (1990-); Constr. Index; Curr. Cit.; Curr. Contents Arts Humanit.; Hosp. Health Admin. Index; Newsp. Period. Abstr. (1992-); Res. Alert [Full Cov.]; Sage Urban Stud. Abstr (?-?); Soc. Sci. Cit. Index [Select. Cov.]; Urban Aff. Abstr.

ISSN 0308-6747
UK
ARCHITECTURE WEST MIDLANDS. [Archit. West Midl.]. **VFOAT** AWM. Architecture West Midlands. (1970)-. Periodical. English. Six times a year.
Ind/Abst Archit. Period. Index (June 1977-1981).

ISSN 1076-4518
DD 720 US
•**ARCHITECTURESOUTH (NASHVILLE, TENN.).** (ARCHITECTURESOUTH.). [ArchitectureSouth]. **Added/Corp** American Institute of Architects. Gulf States Regional Council. **VFOAT** Architecture South. Vol. 1, No. 1 (Spring 1994)-. Periodical. English. Four times a year. $25.00. Point Communications, 6518 Highway 100, Nashville TN 37205.

LC NA1 .A7937 **ISSN** 1054-4666
DD 720/.5 US
ARCHITECTUS (SAINT PAUL, MINN.). (ARCHITECTUS.). [Architectus]. (Spring/Summer 1991)-. Periodical. English. Irregular (four issues publishes in two double issues). $30.00. Cultura, PO Box 130744, St. Paul MN 55113.

ISSN 0169-4421
NE
UDC 72
Pr Rev.
ARCHITECTUUR, BONWEN. VFOAT AB. (1985)-. Trade Publication. Dutch. Twelve times a year. $222.68. Ten Hagen and Stam BV, Postbus 34, 2501 AG The Hague Netherlands. **Tel** 011 31 70 3045700. **ED** Tom Maas. Index available. cum. index. **Bk Rev**. **Ad Acc**. **Circ:** 5,445.

ISSN 0003-875X
GW
ARCHITEKT (STUTTGART), DER. (DER ARCHITEKT.). [Architekt]. **Added/Corp** Bund Deutscher Architekten. Vol. 1 (1952)-. Trade Publication. German. Twelve times a year. $113.00. Wilhelm Ernst & Sohn, Muehlenstr 33 34 170, D-13187 Berlin Germany. **Tel** 011 49 30 47889200. **(Subscription address:** VCH Publishers Inc., 303 Northwest 12th Avenue, Journals Department, Deerfield FL 33442. **Tel** (800)367-8249, (305)428-5566.**)** Index available. **Bk Rev**. **Ad Acc**. **Circ:** 8,000 (ctrl).
Desc: Covers lean energy, construction, urban renewal, experiments in housing construction, planning and execution problems, and producer information.
Ind/Abst Archit. Period. Index (1977-)(Jan. 1953-); Avery Index Archit. Period. Suppl. Colum. Univ. (1989-); BHA : Biblio. Hist. Art.

ISSN 0066-6262
GR
ARCHITEKTONIKA THEMATA. VFOAT Architecture in Greece. Vol. 1 (1967)-. Trade Publication. Greek, Modern (summaries and/or abstracts in English). One time a year (June). $45.00. Orestis B. Doumanis, PO Box 3545, GR-102 10 Athens Greece. **Tel** 011 30 1 7225930, **FAX** 011 30 1 7213916. **ED** Orestis B. Doumanis. **Bk Rev**. **Ad Acc**. **Circ:** 5,000.
Desc: Concerned with ideas and projects influencing the human environment in Greece, with coverage of major international trends and developments, architectural competitions, student projects and architectural book reviews.
Ind/Abst Archit. Period. Index (1967-); Avery Index Archit. Period. Suppl. Colum. Univ. (19??-199?).

ISSN 0570-6602
AU
ARCHITEKTUR AKTUELL FACH-JOURNAL. VFOAT Architektur Aktuell. (1967)-. Trade Publication. German. Twelve times a year. $88.00. Springer-Verlag Vienna, Sachsenplatz 4 6, PO Box 89, A-1201 Vienna Austria. **Tel** 011 43 1 33024150, **FAX** 011 43 1 330242665. **(Subscription address:** Springer-Verlag New York Inc. / North America, PO Box 2485, Journal Fulfillment, Secaucus NJ 07096. **Tel** (201)348-4033, (800)777-4643, **FAX** (201)348-4505.**)** **Bk Rev**. **Ad Acc**. ctrl circ. available on videocassette.

AU
ARCHITEKTUR & BAUFORUM. (19??)-. German. Six times a year. S540.00. Osterreichischer Wirtschaftsvg, Nikolsdorfer Gasse 7 11, A 1051 Vienna Austria. **Tel** 011 43 1 555585. ***Continues*** *Bauforum.*
Ind/Abst Archit. Period. Index (Vol. 23 No. 137, 1990-).

ISSN 0171-7928
GW
UDC 643
CODEN 728
ARCHITEKTUR & WOHNEN. VFOAT Architektur und Wohnen. (1971)-. Periodical. German. Six times a year. $67.71. Jahreszeiten Verlag GmbH, Postfach 60 12 20, D-22212 Hamburg Germany. **Tel** 011 49 40 27173529, **FAX** 011 49 40 27172079.
Ind/Abst Avery Index Archit. Period. Suppl. Colum. Univ. (Feb. 1990-).

GW
ARCHITEKTUR IN DEUTSCHLAND. (1981)-. German. Every 2 years. Karl Kramer Verlag GmbH & Company, Schulze-Delitzsch-Strasse 15, PF 800650, W 7000 Stuttgart 80 Germany. **Tel** 011 49 711 620893, **FAX** 0711-628955, telex 722203 KKBAUD.

GW
ARCHITEKTUR JAHRBUCH. Added/Corp Deutsches Architekturmuseum. **VFOAT** Architecture Annual. (1992)-. German (summaries and/or abstracts in English). One time a year. $40.00 US; $58.00 Canada; DM58.00 other. Deutsches Architektur-Museum, Direktion, Hedderichstrasse 108-110, D-60596 Frankfurt am Main Germany. **ED** Vittorio Magnago Lampugnani, Annette Becker. ***Continues*** *Jahrbuch fur Architektur, 0720-4590.*
Desc: Forum for the discussion of contemporary architectural concerns.

LC NA2335 .A72 **ISSN** 0341-2784
DD 720/.79 GW
ARCHITEKTUR WETTBEWERBE. [Archt. Wettbew.]. **VFOAT** Architektur + Wettbewerbe; Architektur plus Wettbewerbe. (1939)-. Periodical. German (summaries and/or abstracts in English). Four times a year (Mar., June, Sept., Dec.). $101.03. Karl Kramer Verlag GmbH & Company, Schulze-Delitzsch-Strasse 15, PF 800650, W 7000 Stuttgart 80 Germany. **Tel** 011 49 711 620893, **FAX** 0711-628955, telex 722203 KKBAUD. **Ad Acc**. **Circ:** 4,000 (ctrl).
Desc: Specialized for architects, and planners. Contains information for townplanners, property owners, the local authorities and politicians.
Ind/Abst Archit. Period. Index (1977-); Avery Index Archit. Period. Suppl. Colum. Univ. (1989-).

XR
ARCHITEKTURA. Added/Corp Svaz Ceskych Architektu. Vol. 49, No. 1, (1990)-. Periodical. Czech (summaries and/or abstracts in English, French, German and Russian). Six times a year. Svaz Ceskych Architektura, Letenska 120 5, 110 00 Prague Czech Republic. ***Continues*** *Architektura CSR.*
Ind/Abst Archit. Period. Index (Vol. 49 No. 1, 1990-).

ISSN 0044-8680
XO
ARCHITEKTURA A URBANIZMUS. Added/Corp Slovenska Akademia Vied. Ustav Stavebnictva a Architektury. Vol. 1 (1967)-. Periodical. Slovak (Czech; summaries and/or abstracts in German, English and Russian). Four times a year. $153.15. **(Subscription address:** Kubon & Sagner, ABT Zeitschriftenimport, D 80328 Munich Germany. **Tel** 011 49 89 54218130.**)** **ED** Emanuel Hruska. **Bk Rev**. **Ad Acc**. **Circ:** 1,150 (ctrl).
Desc: Deals with architecture, questions of style, urban reorganization and town planning.
Ind/Abst BHA : Biblio. Hist. Art.

ISSN 0066-6270
HU
UDC 72
ARCHITEKTURA BUDAPEST. [Architektura Bp.]. (1966)-. Monographic series. Hungarian. Irregular. Price varies per volume. Magyar Tudomanyos Akademia Prielle K, u. 19-35, 1117 Budapest Hungary.
Ind/Abst BHA : Biblio. Hist. Art.

ISSN 0003-8822
IT
ARCHITETTO, L'. (1956)-. Italian. Ten times a year. Consiglio Nazionale di Architetti, Via S Maria dell'Anima 10, 00186 Rome Italy. **Tel** 011 39 6 8966009, **FAX** 011 39 6 866414. **ED** Gianni Boeri.
Ind/Abst Archit. Period. Index (Jan./Feb. 1981-July/Aug. 1982).

LC NA4 .A778 **ISSN** 0003-8830
DD 720/.5 IT
ARCHITETTURA, L'. [Architettura]. (May/June 1955)-. Periodical. Italian (English, French, German and Spanish). Twelve times a year. cum. index.
Ind/Abst Archit. Period. Index (May/June 1955-); Art Index; Avery Index Archit. Period. Suppl. Colum. Univ.; BHA : Biblio. Hist. Art.

ISSN 0570-6629
IT
CEASED
ARCHITETTURA; CRONACHE E STORIA, L'. No. 1 (May/June 1955)-(June 1995). Periodical. Italian. Etas SRL, Via Mecenate 89, 20138 Milan Italy. **Tel** 011 39 2 580841.
Ind/Abst Archit. Period. Index (Aug./Sept. 1977-); Art Index; Avery Index Archit. Period. Suppl. Colum. Univ. (1987, 1989/1990-).

IT
ARCHITETTURA INTERSEZIONI. (1995)-. Italian. Two times a year. L24500. Il Cardo Editore SRL, San Polo 2160, 30125 Venice Italy. **Tel** 011 39 41 5240243.

IT
ARCHITETTURA/MATERIALI. VFOAT Architettura/Materiali Cinema; Architettura/Materiali Teatro. Vol. 1 (1978)-. Monographic series. Italian. Price varies per volume. Edizioni Kappa, Via S Benco 14, 00177 Rome Italy. **Tel** 011 39 6 273903.

IT
ARCHITETTURA, STORIA E DOCUMENTI : RIVISTA SEMESTRALE DI STORIA DELL'ARCHITETTURA DEL CENTRO DI STUDI STORICO-ARCHIVISTICI PER LA STORIA DELL'ARTE E DELL'ARCHITETTURA MEDIOEVALE E MODERNA. Added/Corp Centro di Studi Storico-Archivistici per la Storia dell'Arte e dell'Architettura Medioevale e Moderna. **VFOAT** Architettura. (1985)-. Periodical. Italian (summaries and/or abstracts in English). Two times a year. L43600.

Gangemi Editore, via Cavour 255, 00184 Rome Italy. **Tel** 011 39 6 4821661. **ED** Renato Bonelli and Fausto Fusceddu. **Bk Rev**. **Ad Acc**. **Circ:** 900 (ctrl).

LC NA1.A1 A72 **ISSN** 1010-4089
DD 720/.5 SZ

ARCHITHESE (1980). (ARCHITHESE.). [Archithese]. **Added/Corp** Verband Freierwerbender Schweizer Architekten. (Jan./Feb. 1980)-. Periodical. German (French and German). Six times a year. $130.12. Verlag Arthur Niggli AG, Steinackerstrasse 8, CH-8583 Sulgen Switzerland. **Tel** 011 41 72 424666, FAX 011 41 72 423578. Index available in last issue of volume--attached. ***Continues in part*** *Werk-Archithese, 0257-9359.*
Ind/Abst Archit. Period. Index (1980-); ARTbibliogr. Mod. (1985-); Avery Index Archit. Period. Suppl. Colum. Univ. (1990-); BHA : Biblio. Hist. Art.

ISSN 0222-2027
FR

ARCHIVERT. [Archivert]. (Jan./Mar.1979)-. Periodical. French. Four times a year.
Ind/Abst Archit. Period. Index (Jan./Mar. 1979-1981); Avery Index Archit. Period. Suppl. Colum. Univ. (19??-19??).

LC NA4 .A785 **ISSN** 0394-0055
DD 720/.5 IT

AREA (MILAN, ITALY). (AREA.). Vol. 1, No. 1 (Sept. 1981)-. Periodical. English (Italian). Six times a year. L68130. Azzurra Editrice SRL, Via Della Moscova 49, 20121 Milan Italy. **Tel** 011 39 2 29010364, FAX 011 39 2 29002192. **Bk Rev**. **Ad Acc, Adv Mgr:** Givsi Brivio. ctrl circ.
Ind/Abst Avery Index Archit. Period. Suppl. Colum. Univ. (1989-).

ISSN 0570-8869
XV

ARGO / NARODNI MUZEJ V LJUBLJANI. **See** Museums and Galleries.

ISSN 0300-5356
RM
SUSPENDED

ARHITECTURA. [Arhitectura]. (1965)-(19??). Periodical. Romanian (summaries and/or abstracts in English, French, German and Russian). Six times a year. $65.00. **(Subscription address:** Orion Press SRL, SPL Independentei 202-A, Bucharest 6 Romania. **Tel** 011 401 3122425.) ***Continues*** *Arhitectura R.P.R.*
Desc: Covers architectural and building matters.
Ind/Abst Archit. Period. Index (1965-); BHA : Biblio. Hist. Art (?-?).

ISSN 0324-1254
BU

UDC 72+711

ARHITEKTURA. [Arhitektura]. **VFOAT** Architectura. (1954)-. Periodical. Bulgarian. Ten times a year. DM166.00. **(Subscription address:** Kubon & Sagner, ABT Zeitschriftenimport, D 80328 Munich Germany. **Tel** 011 49 89 54218130.)
Ind/Abst BHA : Biblio. Hist. Art.

ISSN 0350-3666
CI

ARHITEKTURA. **Added/Corp** Savez Drulstava Inlzenjera i Tehnilcara FNRJ. Sekcija Arhitekata. Savez Arhitekata Hrvatske. Vol. 1 (1947)-. Periodical. Serbo-Croatian (Roman) (summaries and/or abstracts in English, French, German and Russian). Four times a year. Savez Drustava Arhitekata Hrvatske, Trg Republike 3 1, 41000 Zagreb Croatia. **Tel** 011 38 41 274618, 011 38 41 274796.
Ind/Abst Archit. Period. Index (Vol. 29, No. 155, 1975-).

LC NA6 .A724 **ISSN** 0004-1238
CI

ARHITEKTURA, URBANIZAM. [Arhit. urban.]. **Added/Corp** Savez Arhitekata (Yugoslavia). Savez Arhitekata Jugoslavije. Savez Urbanistickih Drustava Jugoslavije. Urbanisticki Savez Jugoslavije. Savez DruEstava Arhitekata Srbije. Urbanisticki Savez Srbije. Udruzenje Likovnih Umetnika Primenjenih Umetnosti i Dizajnera Srbije. (1960)-. Periodical. Serbo-Croatian (Roman) (summaries and/or abstracts in English). Four times a year. $35.00. Savez Drustava Arhitekata Hrvatske, Trg Republike 3 1, 41000 Zagreb Croatia. **Tel** 011 38 41 274618, 011 38 41 274796. **ED** A. Laslo. Index available. **Bk Rev**. **Ad Acc**. **Circ:** 2,300.
Ind/Abst Archit. Period. Index (Vol. 25, No. 6, 1985-1987); Avery Index Archit. Period. Suppl. Colum. Univ. (19??-19??).

LC NA1 .A75 **ISSN** 1063-1305
DD 720 US

ARIS (PITTSBURGH, PA.). (ARIS : JOURNAL OF THE CARNEGIE MELLON DEPARTMENT OF ARCHITECTURE.). [Aris]. **Added/Corp** Carnegie-Mellon University. Dept. of Architecture. (1992)-. English. One time a year. $20.00. Carnegie Mellon University Press, PO Box 30, Baker Hall, Pittsburgh PA 15213. **Tel** (412)268-6348.

LC NA1 .A794 **ISSN** 0004-1416
US

ARIZONA ARCHITECT. [Ariz. archit.]. Vol. 1 (Sept. 1957)-. Periodical. English. Six times a year. $4.00. Arizona Architect, PO Box 4000A, Tucson AZ 85717. available on microfilm and microfiche from University Microfilms International (UMI).

BW

ARKHITEKTURA I STROITELSTVO BELORUSSII. **Added/Corp** Soiuz Arkhitektorov Belorussii. (1991)-. Periodical. Russian. Six times a year. ***Continues*** *Stroitelstvo i Arkhitektura, 0321-4370.*

LC TH4 .N28 **ISSN** 0235-7259
RU

ARKHITEKTURA I STROITELSTVO ROSSII : AS. **Added/Corp** Gosudarstvennyi Komitet RSFSR po Delam Stroitelstva. Soiuz Arkhitektorov RSFSR. **VFOAT** AS. Vol. 1 (1989)-. Periodical. Russian. Twelve times a year. $79.95. **(Subscription address:** East View Publications Inc., 3020 Harbor Lane North, Suite 110, Minneapolis MN 55447. **Tel** (800)477-1005, (612)550-0961, FAX (612)559-2931.) ***Continues*** *Na Stroikakh Rossii, 0135-0048.*
Desc: Information on architecture, building and city planning.

LC NA6 .B76

UN

ARKHITEKTURA UKRAINY. **Added/Corp** Spilka Arkhitektoriv Ukrainy. Ukraine. Derzhavnyi Komitet v Spravakh Budivnytstva i Arkhitektury. **VFOAT** Architecture of the Ukraine; Architecture in Ukraine. (1991)-. Periodical. Ukrainian (summaries and/or abstracts in English and Russian). Six times a year. $99.95. **(Subscription address:** East View Publications Inc., 3020 Harbor Lane North, Suite 110, Minneapolis MN 55447. **Tel** (800)477-1005, (612)550-0961, FAX (612)559-2931.) ***Continues*** *Stroitelstvo i Arkhitektura (Kiev, Ukraine : 1957), 0321-4346.*
Ind/Abst Archit. Period. Index (No. 1, Jan./Feb. 1991-).

IS

ARKHITEKTURAH = ARCHITECTURE IN ISRAEL. **VFOAT** Architecture in Israel. (19??)-. Hebrew (summaries and/or abstracts in English). Architecture of Israel, PO Box 302, Herzliya B Israel. ***Continues*** *Adrikhalut.*
Desc: An architecture and interior design publication dealing with the unique interpretations of Israelie architects and designers, the meeting point of east and west reality. Contains colored photos and professional articles.
Ind/Abst Archit. Period. Index (1978-1985, 1988-).

LC NA17 .A614 **ISSN** 0320-0841
RU

ARKHITEKTURNOE NASLEDSTVO. [Arhit. nasled.]. **Added/Corp** Institut Istorii i Teorii Arkhitektury (Akademiia Arkhitektury SSR). (1951)-. Russian. **(Subscription address:** East View Publications Inc., 3020 Harbor Lane North, Suite 110, Minneapolis MN 55447. **Tel** (800)477-1005, (612)550-0961, FAX (612)559-2931.)
Ind/Abst Am. Hist. Life (1980-); BHA : Biblio. Hist. Art.

LC NA6 .A77 **ISSN** 0004-198X
DD 720/.5 DK

ARKITEKTEN. [Arkitekten]. **Added/Corp** Danske Arkitekters Landsforbund. Vol. 59 (Jan. 8, 1957)-. Trade Publication. Danish. Eighteen times a year. kr759.00 Scandinavia; kr810.00 other. Arkitektens Forlag / The Danish Architectural Press, Nyhavn 43, DK-1051 Copenhagen K Denmark. **Tel** 011 45 33 136200, FAX 011 45 33 912770. **ED** Kim Dirckinck-Holmfeld. **Bk Rev**. **Ad Acc**. **Circ:** 7,100 (ctrl). ***Formed by the union of*** *Arkitekten; Manedshaefte* ***and*** *Arkitekten; Ugehaefte.*
Desc: The official journal of The Federation of Danish Architects. Articles on professional subjects, projects, and competitions.
Ind/Abst Archit. Period. Index (1977-); Avery Index Archit. Period. Suppl. Colum. Univ. (1989-); BHA : Biblio. Hist. Art.

ISSN 0004-1998
DD 720 NO
CCC

ARKITEKTNYTT. [Arkitektnytt]. **Added/Corp** Norske Arkitekters Landsforbund. (1951)-. Trade Publication. Norwegian. Twenty times a year. $95.93. Byggekunst, Josffinesgt Gate 34, 0351 Olso 3 Norway. **Tel** 47 2 602290, FAX 47 2 695948.
Ind/Abst BHA : Biblio. Hist. Art.

ISSN 0004-2013
DK

ARKITEKTUR DK. [Arkit. DK]. Vol. 16 (1972)-. Periodical. Danish (English, Danish and German). Eight times a year. kr637.00 Scandinavia; kr715.00 other. Arkitektens Forlag / The Danish Architectural Press, Nyhavn 43, DK-1051 Copenhagen K Denmark. **Tel** 011 45 33 136200, FAX 011 45 33 912770. **ED** Kim Dirckinck-Holmfeld. **Ad Acc**. **Circ:** 4,300 (ctrl). ***Continues*** *Arkitektur, 0900-3819.*
Desc: Review on Scandinavian architecture.
Ind/Abst Archit. Period. Index (1977-); Avery Index Archit. Period. Suppl. Colum. Univ. (1989-); BHA : Biblio. Hist. Art.

ISSN 1016-7293
IC

ARKITEKTUR OG SKIPULAG. **Added/Corp** Skipulags Arkitekta- og Verkfristofan. (19??)-. Periodical. Icelandic. Four times a year.
Ind/Abst BHA : Biblio. Hist. Art.

LC NA6.S85 A75 **ISSN** 0004-2021
SW

ARKITEKTUR (STOCKHOLM, SWEDEN : 1959). (ARKITEKTUR.). [Arkitektur]. **Added/Corp** Stockholms Byggnadsforening (Sweden) Svenska Teknologforeningen. Svenska Arkitektforeningen. No. 1 (1959)-. Periodical. Swedish (summaries and/or abstracts in English). Eight times a year. $125.02. Arkitektur, PO Box 1742, S-11187 Stockholm Sweden. **Tel** 011 46 8 6976105, FAX 08-20 52 70. ***Continues in part*** *Arkitektur; Byggmastaren.*
Desc: Covers fields in architecture which have come to play roles in public discussions in recent years.
Ind/Abst Archit. Period. Index (1977-); Avery Index Archit. Period. Suppl. Colum. Univ. (1990-); BHA : Biblio. Hist. Art.

LC NA6 .A793 **ISSN** 0004-2129
DD 720/.94897 FI

ARKKITEHTI. (ARKKITEHTI. FINSK ARKITEKTURTIDSKRIFT. FINNISH ARCHITECTURAL REVIEW.). [Arkkitehti]. **Added/Corp** Suomen Arkkitehtiliitto. **VFOAT** Finsk Arkitekturtidskrift; Finnish Architectural Review; Arkitekten. (1921)-. Periodical. Finnish (Swedish and English; summaries and/or abstracts in French, German and English). Eight times a year. Fmk435.00 Finland; Fmk570.00 other. Suomen Arkkitehtiliitto, Yrjonkatu 11 A, 00120 Helsinki Finland. **Tel** 011 358 0 640801, FAX 011 358 0 604479. **ED** Pentti Kareoja. Index available. **Ad Acc**. **Circ:** 5,000 (ctrl). ***Absorbed*** *Arkitekten, 0782-789X.*
Ind/Abst Archit. Period. Index (1977-);(1929-); Avery Index Archit. Period. Suppl. Colum. Univ. (1989-).

LC NA6.F56 A74 **ISSN** 0066-7676
DD 720/.94897/05 FI

ARKKITEHTUURIKILPAILUJA. (ARKKITEHTUURIKILPAILUJA : ARK.). [Arkkitehtuurikilpailuja]. **Added/Corp** Suomen Arkkitehtiliitto. **VFOAT** Ark; Architectural Competitions in Finland. Vol. 1 (1966)-. Periodical. Finnish (English and Swedish; summaries and/or abstracts in English). Fmk435.00. Suomen Arkkitehtiliitto, Yrjonkatu 11 A, 00120 Helsinki Finland. **Tel** 011 358 0 640801, FAX 011 358 0 604479.
Ind/Abst Archit. Period. Index (1966-); Avery Index Archit. Period. Suppl. Colum. Univ. (19??-199?).

LC WMLC 93/4097 **ISSN** 0716-0852
CL

ARQ. [ARQ]. **Added/Corp** Universidad Catolica de Chile. Escuela de Arquitectura. **VFOAT** Arquitectura. (1980)-. Periodical. Spanish. Three times a year. $58.00 Americas; $68.00 other. Editorial Universitaria SA de Chile, Casilla 10220, Santiago Chile. **Tel** 011 56 2 2325057, FAX 011 56 2 2322571.
Ind/Abst Avery Index Archit. Period. Suppl. Colum. Univ. (1989-).

ISSN 0710-1163
DD 720/.9714 CN

ARQ : ARCHITECTURE/QUEBEC. [ARQ, Archit./Que.]. **Added/Corp** Ordre des Architectes du Quebec. **VFOAT** Architecture/Quebec. Vol. 1, No. 1 (May 1981)-. Periodical. French (English). Six times a year (Feb., Apr., June, Aug., Oct., Dec.). 41.60Can$ (individuals) Canada; 48.00Can$ other; $69.34Can$ (institutions). Groupe Culturel Prefontaine, 1463 rue Prefontaine, Montreal Quebec H1W 2N6 Canada. **Tel** (514)523-6832. **ED** Pierre Boyer-Mercier. **Bk Rev**. **Ad Acc**. **Circ:** 5,000 (ctrl).
Desc: Promotes architecture in Quebec, architects, and the building industry. Covers quality of architectural projects, diverse design fields, and other related topics.
Ind/Abst Avery Index Archit. Period. Suppl. Colum. Univ. (1990-)(1984-); BHA : Biblio. Hist. Art; Repere.

LC NA830 .A75

AG

●ARQUIS : REVISTA DEL CENTRO DE INVESTIGACIONES EN ARQUITECTURA, UNIVERSIDAD DE PALERMO. **Added/Corp** Universidad de Palermo (Palermo, Buenos Aires, Argentina). Centro de Investigaciones en Arquitectura. Editorial CP67. **VFOAT** Arquitectura y Urbanismo. (1994)-. Periodical. Spanish. Four times a year. Universidad de Palermo, Libreria Tecnica CP67 S.A., Florida 683, Local 18, 1375 Buenos Aires, Argentina.

Architecture

LC NA5 .A78
ISSN 0004-2676
PE

ARQUITECTO PERUANO, EL. Vol. 1, No. 1 (Aug. 1937)-. Periodical. Spanish. Six times a year. Arquitecto Peruano, Box 2142, Lima Peru.
Ind/Abst Archit. Period. Index.

MX

ARQUITECTOS DE MEXICO. VFOAT Revista Arquitectos de Mexico. No. 1 (July 1956)-. Periodical. Spanish (English).

UY

ARQUITECTURA. (19??)-. Periodical. Spanish. One time a year. $7.00. Sociedad de Arquitectos, Avenue Rondo 1546, Montivideo 11100 Uruguay. **Tel** 011 598 2 900259.
Ind/Abst Archit. Period. Index (No. 253, 1985-).

LC NA5 .A84
ISSN 1010-3821
DD 720/.5
CU

ARQUITECTURA CUBA. [Arquit. Cuba]. (1960)-. Periodical. Spanish (summaries and/or abstracts in French and English). Irregular. $15.00. Ediciones Cubanas, Obispo 527 Altos ESQ Bernaza, CP 10100 Havana Cuba. **Circ:** 20,000 (ctrl). **Continues** *Arquitectura*.
Desc: Offers information on projects, completed works and technology for the various levels of construction design: planning, city planning and architecture.
Ind/Abst Archit. Period. Index (1960-).

LC NA5 .A795
ISSN 0004-2706
DD 720/.5
SP

ARQUITECTURA (MADRID, 1959). (ARQUITECTURA.). [Arquitectura]. **Added/Corp** Colegio Oficial de Arquitectos de Madrid. No. 1 (1959)-. Periodical. Spanish (English). Four times a year. $113.63. Ediciones Reunidas, O'Donnell 12 Planta Baja, 28009 Madrid Spain. **Tel** 011 31 1 5863300. **ED** E. Sobejano.
Ind/Abst Archit. Period. Index (1977-); Avery Index Archit. Period. Suppl. Colum. Univ. (1990-); BHA : Biblio. Hist. Art.

LC NA5 .A834
ISSN 0004-2684
DD 720/.972
MX

ARQUITECTURA/MEXICO. VFOAT Arquitectura Mexico. No. 21 (Nov. 1946-1982)(1993)-. Periodical. Spanish. Six times a year. $95.00. Arq Editores SA de CV, Boulevard Ma Camacho 184 Piso 11, Mexico 11620 DF Mexico. **Tel** 011 52 5 6266899. available on microfilm from University Microfilms International (UMI). **Continues** *Arquitectura (Mexico City, Mexico)*.
Ind/Abst Archit. Period. Index (May/June 1977-Nov./Dec. 1978).

ISSN 0214-1256
SP
Pr Rev.

ARQUITECTURA VIVA. [Arquit. viva]. (1988)-. Periodical. Spanish (English). Six times a year. 8000ptas Spain; 10000ptas Europe; 14000ptas other. AVISA - Arquitectura Viva SL, Rosario 31, 28005 Madrid Spain. **Tel** 011 34 1 2669900, FAX 011 34 1 3640151. **ED** Luis Fernandez-Galiano. **Bk Rev. Ad Acc. Circ:** 8,000 (ctrl).
Desc: Covers the latest in architecture and other related cultural fields.
Ind/Abst Avery Index Archit. Period. Suppl. Colum. Univ. (Jan. 1990-).

SP
CEASED

ARQUITECTURA Y DECORACION HOSTELERIA. (19??)-(19??). Trade Publication. Spanish. Edidec Sa, C Ferranz 11, 28008 Madrid Spain. **Tel** 011 34 1 5415055. **ED** M. Alonso Sanchez. **Circ:** 14,000.

SP
CEASED

ARQUITECTURA Y DECORACION OFICINAS. (19??)-(19??). Periodical. Spanish. Edidec Sa, C Ferranz 11, 28008 Madrid Spain. **Tel** 011 34 1 5415055. **Circ:** 12,000.

CU

ARQUITECTURA Y URBANISMO. (19??)-. Periodical. Spanish (summaries and/or abstracts in English). Four times a year. Ediciones Cubanas, Obispo 527 Altos ESQ Bernaza, CP 10100 Havana Cuba. **Continues** *Ciencias Technicas. Arquitectura y Urbanismo*, 0254-8461.
Ind/Abst Archit. Period. Index.

LC WMLC 93/4113
CL

ARQUITECTURAS DEL SUR. Added/Corp Universidad del Bio-Bio. Facultad de Arquitectura, Construccion y Diseno. Universidad del Bio-Bio. Departamento de Arquitectura. (1983)-. Periodical. Spanish. Three times a year (triquarterly). $8.00. University del Bio Bio, Collao 1202 Department Arquitectura, Conception, Chile. **Tel** 011 56 41 314364.

LC NA850 .A6
DD 720/.981
BL

ARQUITETURA DO BRASIL : AB. VFOAT AB; A.B. (19??)-. Periodical. English (Portuguese). One time a year. Arquitetura Brasileira, Caixa Postal 1429, 20000 Rio de Janeiro RJ Brasil. **Tel** (021)252-3909. **ED** Vicente B. Gagliardi. **Bk Rev. Ad Acc. Circ:** 3,000.
Continues *AB : Arquitetura Brasileira*.

ISSN 1048-5945
DD 720
US
Pr Rev.

ARRIS (ATLANTA, GA.). (ARRIS : JOURNAL OF THE SOUTHEAST CHAPTER OF THE SOCIETY OF ARCHITECTURAL HISTORIANS.). [Arris]. **Added/Corp** Society of Architectural Historians. Southeast Chapter. Vol. 1 (1989)-. Periodical. English. One time a year (normally in fall). $15.00. Society of Architectural Historians / Southeast Chapter, Georgia Institute of Technology, College of Architecture, Atlanta GA 30332. **Tel** (404)325-2543, (404)894-3395, FAX (404)853-9060. **ED** Rachel McCann (editor's address: School of Architecture PO Drawer AQ Mississippi State University Starkville MS 39762, editor's phone number: (601)325-2202 or (601)325-2543). **Bk Rev**, (Qty: varies).
Circ: 250.

ISSN 0280-2686
SW

ARSBOK / ARKITEKTURMUSEET.
Main/Corp Arkitekturmuseet (Stockholm, Sweden). **VFOAT** Arkitekturmuseets Arsbok. (19??)-. Swedish.
Ind/Abst Archit. Period. Index (1979-); BHA : Biblio. Hist. Art.

LC NC997
ISSN 0267-3991
DD 741.6
UK

ART & DESIGN. See The Arts-Graphic Arts.

SA

ART, DESIGN, ARCHITECTURE : ADA. See The Arts-Art.

LC Z711 .A787
ISSN 1050-2548
US
Pr Rev.

●**ART REFERENCE SERVICES QUARTERLY. See** The Arts-Art.

UK

ARTS & THE ISLAMIC WORLD. See The Arts-Art.

ISSN 0951-0850
UK

ARUP JOURNAL. (THE ARUP JOURNAL.). [Arup j.]. **Added/Corp** Ove Arup & Partners. Ove Arup Partnership. Vol. 1, No. 1 (Mar. 1966)-. Periodical. English. Four times a year (Jan., Apr., July, Oct.). Free on request. Ove Arup Partnership, 13 Fitzroy Street, London W1P 6BQ United Kingdom. **Tel** 011 44 171 6361531. **ED** David J. Brown (editor's phone: 011 44 171 4853828). **Circ:** 1,600 (ctrl).
Ind/Abst Archit. Period. Index (1977-); Avery Index Archit. Period. Suppl. Colum. Univ. (1989-); Int. Civil Eng. Abstr.

TH

ASA. VFOAT Qasa. Vol. 1 (Sept. 1972)-. Periodical. English (Thai and English).

ISSN 0143-3717
UK

ASHLAR. (197?)-. English.
Ind/Abst Archit. Period. Index (Dec. 1989-).

ISSN 0956-4241
DD 526.9
UK

ASI JOURNAL LONDON. (ASI JOURNAL.). [ASI j. Lond.]. **Added/Corp** Architects & Surveyors Institute. (1989)-. Trade Publication. English. Six times a year. Highwood Publications Limited, Premier House, 150 Southampton Row, London WC1B 5AL United Kingdom.

ES

ASIA : ORGANO DE DIVULGACION TECNICA E INFORMACION DE LA ASOCIACION SALVADORENA DE INGENIEROS Y ARQUITECTOS. See Engineering.

LC HD9715.A1 A75
DD 338.4/7624/095
HK

ASIAN ARCHITECT AND CONTRACTOR. Added/Corp International Federation of Asian and Western Pacific Contractors' Associations. (19??)-. Trade Publication. English. Twelve times a year. $65.00. Thomson Press Hong Kong Ltd, 233 Hollywood Road, Room 202 3, Sheung Wan Hong Kong. **Tel** 011 852 28159111, FAX 011 852 28511933, telex 61504 THOMS HX. **ED** Glenn Rogers. **Bk Rev. Ad Acc, Adv Mgr:** Teresa Chan. **Circ:** 17,600 (ctrl). **Absorbed** *Asia Pacific Contractor*.
Desc: This is a news and technical magazine for the Asian building industry.
Ind/Abst Avery Index Archit. Period. Suppl. Colum. Univ. (1989-).

ISSN 0264-8164
HK

ASIAN BUILDING & CONSTRUCTION.
[Asian build. constr.]. **VAT** Asian Building and Construction. (Oct. 1971)-. Periodical. English. Twelve times a year. Far East Trade Press Ltd., BL C 10 F Seaview E, 2 8 Watson, North Point Hong Kong. **Tel** 011 852 25668381, FAX 011 852 25710780, telex 83434.
Continues *Far East Builder*.
Ind/Abst Archit. Period. Index (Nov. 1977-Dec. 1986); Int. Civil Eng. Abstr.

LC NA1 .A86
ISSN 0889-3012
DD 720/.5
US
CCC

ASSEMBLAGE. [Assemblage]. Vol. 1 (Oct 1986)-. Periodical. English. Three times a year. $122.00. Massachusetts Institute of Technology (MIT) Press, 55 Hayward Street, Cambridge MA 02142. **Tel** (617)253-2889, (617)625-8481, FAX (617)258-6779. **ED** K. Michael Hays, Catherine Ingraham, and Alicia Kennedy. available on microfilm from University Microfilms International (UMI).
Desc: Dealing with architectural theory and criticism, it appraises contemporary practice and examines the relationships between culture and design, and between theory and material reality.
Ind/Abst Archit. Period. Index; ARTbibliogr. Mod.; Avery Index Archit. Period. Suppl. Colum. Univ. (June 1988, 1989); BHA : Biblio. Hist. Art; MLA Int. Bibl. Books Artic. Mod. Lang. Lit.

ISSN 0951-8088
UK

ATRIUM (LONDON). (ATRIUM.). [Atrium Lond.]. (1987)-. Periodical. English. Six times a year. £15.00. London BIAT Services / British Institute of Architectural Technicians, 397 City Road, London EC1V 1NE United Kingdom. **Tel** 011 44 171 2782206. **ED** Francesca Berriman. **Bk Rev. Ad Acc. Circ:** 11,600. **Continues** *Architectural Technology (London)*, 0265-2110.
Ind/Abst Archit. Period. Index (June 1987-July 1990).

ISSN 0530-9778
IT

ATTI - COLLEGIO REGIONALE LOMBARDO DEGLI ARCHITETTI.
Main/Corp Collegio Regionale Lombardo Degli Architetti. Periodical. Italian. Corso Venezia 55, 20121 Milan Italy.

LC VG590
ISSN 0373-3475
DD 623.047
IT

ATTI ERASSEGNA TECNICA - SOCIETA DEGLI INGEGNERI E DEGLI ARCHITETTI IN TORINO. See Engineering.

ISSN 0102-8979
BL

UDC 71

AU. ARQUITETURA E URBANISMO. [AU, Arq. urban.]. **VFOAT** Arquitetura e Urbanismo. (1985)-. Periodical. Portuguese. Six times a year. $80.00. Editora Pini Ltda, Rua Anhaia 637, 01130-Bom Retiro-SP Brazil. **Tel** 011 55 2219545, FAX 011 55 2237178.

ISSN 1033-8934
AT

AUGUSTA MELBOURNE. (1989)-. Consumer Publication. English. Four times a year. RMIT, GPO Box 2476V, Melbourne 3001 Australia. **Tel** 011 61 3 6670284. **ED** Peter Brew. **Bk Rev**, (Qty: 6). **Ad Acc, Adv Mgr:** Lallum Fraser. Full Page (B&W) 600.00Aus$. Half Page (B&W) 300.00Aus$. **Circ:** 1,000. Documents available from BLDSC.
Desc: Covers transition in architecture.
Ind/Abst Aust. Educ. Index.

ISSN 0199-1531
US
SUSPENDED

AUSTIN HOMES & GARDENS. See Interior Design and Decoration.

LC NA7385 .A2
DD 720/.946
SP

●**AV. VFOAT** AV Monografias; AV Monographs. Vol. 51-52 (Apr. 1995)-. Periodical. Spanish (English; summaries and/or abstracts in English; translations available in English). AVISA - Arquitectura Viva SL, Rosario 31, 28005 Madrid Spain. **Tel** 011 34 1 2669900, FAX 011 34 1 3640151. **ED** Luis Fernandez-Galiano. cum. index. **Ad Acc. Circ:** 5,000 (ctrl). **Continues** *A & V*, 0213-487X.
Desc: Each issue revolves around a chosen architect, city or theme. Critical articles and projects described and illustrated in detail.
Ind/Abst Avery Index Archit. Period. Suppl. Colum. Univ.

US

AVERY INDEX TO ARCHITECTURAL PERIODICALS / CD-ROM. (19??)-. Abstracting/Indexing Service. English. $450.00, $995.00 CD-ROM, $495.00 CD-ROM Updates. GK Hall & Co., 100 Front Street, Riverside NJ 08075. **Tel** (800)257-5755 ext. 2223.

LC Z5945 .C653 1973 Suppl. NA1.A1 **ISSN** 0196-0008
DD 016.72 US

AVERY INDEX TO ARCHITECTURAL PERIODICALS. SECOND EDITION. REVISED AND ENLARGED. SUPPLEMENT. **See** Architecture-Abstracting, Bibliographies and Statistics.

LC Microfilm (o) 88/453 **ISSN** 0196-0008
US

AVERY INDEX TO ARCHITECTURAL PERIODICALS. SUPPLEMENT [MICROFORM] / COLUMBIA UNIVERSITY. **Added/Corp** Columbia University. Columbia University. Getty Art History Information Program. (1975)-. English. Irregular. GK Hall & Co., 100 Front Street, Riverside NJ 08075. **Tel** (800)257-5755 ext. 2223. ***Continues*** *Avery Library. Avery Index to Architectural Periodicals. Supplement.*

LC NA2340 .A87 **ISSN** 0093-8254
DD 720/.973 US

AWARD WINNING ARCHITECTURE/USA. 1st- Ed.; 1972-. English. Irregular. Artists/USA, Box 11617, Philadelphia PA 19116.

ISSN 1120-5407
IT
UDC 645.63
CODEN 72

BAGNO & CUCINA. ARCHITETTURA & INTERIOR DESIGN. **VFOAT** Bagno e Cucina. Architettura e Interior Design. (1990)-. Periodical. Italian. Four times a year. L25000 Italy; L50000 Europe; L70000 other. Tecniche Nuove SPA, Via Ciro Menotti 14, 20129 Milan Italy. **Tel** 011 39 2 75701, FAX 011 39 2 7570205, telex 334647 TECHS I.

LC NA1309.C15 B37
DD 720/.964/905 SP

BASA : PUBLICACION DEL COLEGIO OFICIAL DE ARQUITECTOS DE CANARIAS. **Added/Corp** Colegio Oficial de Arquitectos de Canarias. No. 1 (Dec. 1983)-. Periodical. Spanish. Two times a year. $65.00. Colegio Oficial Arquitectos de Canarias, Rambla General Franco 123, 38001 Sta Cruz Canarias Spain. **Tel** 011 34 271600.
Ind/Abst Archit. Period. Index (No. 1, Dec. 1983-).

ISSN 0256-2529
AU

BAU, UM. (1979)-. German.
Ind/Abst Archit. Period. Index (Dec. 1981-).

ISSN 0255-3104
SZ
UDC 693.8

BAUEN IN STAHL. [Bau. Stahl]. **VFOAT** Construire en Acier; Costruire in Acciaio. (1???)-. Trade Publication. German. Six times a year. $67.89. Die Presse, Parking 12A Postfach 6, A1015 Vienna Austria. **Tel** 11 43 222 51414, FAX 011 43 222 51414 251, telex 847 114110 or 01 1250 Mocow A.
Desc: Descriptions of modern steel buildings and bridges.

GW

BAUEN MIT HOLZ. **See** Building and Construction.

SZ

BAUERNHAUSER DER SCHWEIZ, DIE. **VFOAT** Les Maisons Rurales de Suisse; La Casa Rurale nella Svizzera. (19??)-. German (French and Italian). Schweizerische Gesellschaft fuer Volkskunde, Augustinergasse 19, CH-4051 Basel Switzerland. **Tel** 011 41 61 2619900. **Circ:** 4,000.

SZ
TITLE CHANGE

BAUKADER : AKTUELLES BAUEN = CONSTRUCTION ACTUELLE. **Added/Corp** Schweizerischer Baukaderverband. **VFOAT** Aktuelles Bauen; Construction Actuelle. (1994)-(1994). Periodical. German (French and Italian). Schueck Soehne AG, Bahnhofstrasse 24, CH-8803 Rueschlikon Switzerland. **Tel** 011 41 1 7247766. ***Continues*** *Aktuelles Bauen (Solothurn, Switzerland : 1992).* ***Absorbed by*** *Schweizer Baublatt.*

ISSN 0005-674X
GW
CCC

BAUMEISTER. [Baumeister]. Vol. 1 (Oct. 1902)-. Trade Publication. German. Twelve times a year. $175.03. Verlag Georg DW Callwey GmbH., Postfach 800409, D-81604 Munich Germany. **Tel** 011 49 89 43600533. **ED** Panthaus Peters. **Bk Rev. Ad Acc. Circ:** 13,723 (ctrl).
Desc: Covers architecture, engineering, construction, and planning of architectural design.
Ind/Abst Archit. Period. Index (1977-); Avery Index Archit. Period. Suppl. Colum. Univ. (1990-).

GW
CODEN BAUTE4

BAUTECHNIK, DIE. 24.- Yearly volume; Oct. 1947-. Academic Scholarly Publication. German. Twelve times a year. DM280.00. VCH Publishers Inc, 220 East 23rd Street, New York NY 10010. **Tel** (212)683-8333, FAX (212)481-0897. **(Subscription address:** VCH Publishers Inc., 303 Northwest 12th Avenue, Journals Department, Deerfield FL 33442. **Tel** (800)367-8249, (305)428-5566.**)** ***Continues*** *Bautechnik, Beton-und Stahlbetonbau, der Stahlbau.*
Ind/Abst Coal Abstr.; EMBASE; Int. Civil Eng. Abstr.; Soft. Abstr. Eng.

ISSN 0005-6847
GW
CCC

BAUVERWALTUNG. [Bauverwaltung]. **Added/Corp** Deutscher Verdingungsausschusses fuer Bauleistungen. Vol. 1 (1952)-. Periodical. German. Twelve times a year. $238.74. Curt R. Vincentz Verlag, Postfach 6247, D-30062 Hannover Germany. **Tel** 011 49 511 990980, FAX 011 49 511 9909899, telex 923846. **ED** Frank Vincentz. Index available. cum. index. **Bk Rev. Ad Acc. Circ:** 2,010 (ctrl).
Desc: Organ of the governmental and local building authorities dealing with their architectural concerns; including typical examples of large public buildings ranging from their project planning up to their completion.
Ind/Abst Energy Res. Abstr. (Sept. 1977-).

LC TH3 .B32 **ISSN** 0005-6855
GW

BAUWELT (BERLIN, GERMANY : WEST : 1952). (BAUWELT.). [Bauwelt]. **VFOAT** Stadtbauwelt. Vol. 43, No. 18 (May 5, 1962)-. Academic Scholarly Publication. German. Forty-eight times a year. $170.62. Bertelsmann Fachzeitschriften GmbH, Carl Bertelsmann Strasse 270, D-33311 Frankfurt Germany. **Tel** 011 49 5241 802199. ***Continues*** *Neue Bauwelt.*
Ind/Abst Archit. Period. Index (1977-); Avery Index Archit. Period. Suppl. Colum. Univ. (1989-); BHA : Biblio. Hist. Art; Coal Abstr.; EMBASE; Energy Res. Abstr. (Apr. 1973-); Int. Civil Eng. Abstr.; Soft. Abstr. Eng.

ISSN 1043-5468
DD 748 US
CEASED

BEAUTIFUL GLASS FOR HOME & OFFICE. **See** Glass and Ceramics.

LC NA7205 .B42 **ISSN** 0278-8810
DD 728.3/7/0223 US

BEAUTIFUL HOME PLANS. English. $7.95. House Plan Headquarters Inc, 48 West 48th Street, New York NY 10036.

LC N1 .B43 **ISSN** 0757-2271
DD 705 FR

BEAUX ARTS MAGAZINE. **See** The Arts-Art.

LC JS6251 **ISSN** 0349-2834
DD 352.0485 SW

BEBYGGELSEHISTORISK TIDSKRIFT. **See** Housing and Urban Development.

ISSN 0310-1452
AT

BELLE (SYDNEY, N.S.W.). (BELLE.). [Belle]. (1972)-. Periodical. English. Six times a year. 62.15Aus$. Australian Consolidated Press Ltd., Private Bag 92615 Symonds St, Auckland New Zealand. **Tel** 011 64 9 3735408, FAX 011 64 9 3022889.

LC NA7205 .B44 **ISSN** 0146-9681
DD 728.3 US

BEST HOME PLANS. English. $0.75 per issue. Archway Press Inc, 19th West 44th Street, New York NY 10036. **Tel** (212)757-5580.

LC NA7205 .D38 **ISSN** 1075-8399
DD 728/.37/0222 US

BEST HOME PLANS DESIGNS. [Best home plans des.]. **VFOAT** Home Plans; Best Home Plan Designs. (199?)-. English. NYT Company Women's Magazines, 110 Fifth Avenue, New York NY 10011. ***Continues*** *Decorating Remodeling. Best Home Plan Designs.*

LC NA7205 .B46
DD 728.3 US

BETTER HOMES AND GARDENS HOME PLAN IDEAS. **VFOAT** Home Plans You Can Buy. (19??)-. Periodical. English. Four times a year. $3.99. Meredith Publications / Special Interest Section, 1716 Locust Street, Des Moines IA 50309. **Tel** (515)284-3000. **ED** Jeffrey Abugel. Index available. **Ad Acc.**
Desc: Feature stories about new homes as well as floor plans and elevations. Blueprints for all the houses shown are available through the magazine.

LC Z5939 .N56a N7420 **ISSN** 0360-2699
DD 016.7 US

BIBLIOGRAPHIC GUIDE TO ART AND ARCHITECTURE. **See** The Arts-Abstracting, Bibliographies and Statistics.

LC NA5 .B55
PO

BINARIO. Portuguese (summaries and/or abstracts in English). $12.00. Praca de Londres 10 R/C-DT, Lisbon Portugal.

LC N NA **ISSN** 1055-6826
DD 702 720 US

BIO-BIBLIOGRAPHIES IN ART AND ARCHITECTURE. **See** The Arts-Abstracting, Bibliographies and Statistics.

LC NA730.M2 B56
DD 720/.92/2741 B US

BIOGRAPHICAL DICTIONARY OF ARCHITECTS IN MAINE, A. **Added/Corp** Maine Historic Preservation Commission. (198?)-. English. Irregular. Free on request. Main Historic Preservation Company, 55 Capitol Street, Station 65, Augusta ME 04333.

LC NA968 .B58 **ISSN** 0268-4926
DD 720/.941/05 UK

BLUEPRINT (LONDON. 1983). (BLUEPRINT.). [Blueprint]. No. 1 (Oct. 1983)-. Periodical. English. Ten times a year (Dec./Jan. and July/Aug. issues combined). $98.00. Wordsearch Ltd., #26 Cramer Street, London W1M 3HE United Kingdom. **Tel** 011 44 171 4867419, FAX 011 44 171 4861451. **(Subscription address:** Wordsearch Ltd. / North America Subscriptions, Subscription Office, PO Box 1584, Birmingham AL 35201-1584. **Tel** (800)633-4931, (205)995-1567 (outside US and Canada), FAX (205)995-1588.**) ED** Deyan Sudjic. cum. index. **Bk Rev**, (Qty: 30 per year). **Ad Acc, Adv Mgr:** R. Leeks, **Tel** 011 44 171 4867419. **Circ:** 9,500.
Desc: Features ideas, photography and articles from around the world in the fields of design and architecture.
Ind/Abst Archit. Period. Index; ARTbibliogr. Mod.; Avery Index Archit. Period. Suppl. Colum. Univ. (1990-).

LC NA705 .B54 **ISSN** 0742-0552
DD 720/.973 US

BLUEPRINTS - NATIONAL BUILDING MUSEUM (U.S.). (BLUEPRINTS / NATIONAL BUILDING MUSEUM.). [Blueprints - Natl. Build. Mus. (U.S.)]. **Added/Corp** National Building Museum (U.S.). Vol. 1, No. 1 (Summer 1981)-. Periodical. English. Irregular. $35.00 (regular), $55.00 (family), $100.00 (sponsor), $250.00 (benefactor), $500.00 (patron) Comes with National Building Museum membership. National Building Museum, 440 G Street Northwest, Pension Building, Washington DC 20001. **Tel** (202)272-2448, FAX (202)272-2564. **ED** Joyce Elliott. **Bk Rev. Circ:** 10,000 (ctrl). ***Continues*** *Blueprints (Committee for a National Museum of the Building Arts).*
Desc: Reports on activities, present, past, and future, in America's built environment.
Ind/Abst Archit. Period. Index (1981-19??); Avery Index Archit. Period. Suppl. Colum. Univ. (19??-199?).

LC NA5826 .A35 **ISSN** 0870-1466
DD 726.509469 PO
CEASED

BOLETIM DA DIRECCAO GERAL DOS EDIFICIOS E MONUMENTOS NACIONAIS. [Bol. Dir.-Geral Edif. Monum. Nac.]. **Added/Corp** Portugal. Direccao Geral dos Edificios e Monumentos Nacionais. Portugal. Ministerio das Obras Publicas. Portugal. Ministerio das Obras Publicas e Comunicacoes. No. 1 (1935)-No. 131. Monographic series. Portuguese. Ministerio das Ubras Publicas, Praca do Comercio, 1100 Lisbon Portugal. **Tel** 832 01 879541, FAX 011 832 1 870101.
Ind/Abst Avery Index Archit. Period. Suppl. Colum. Univ.; BHA : Biblio. Hist. Art.

ISSN 0506-600X
VE

BOLETIN DEL CENTRO DE INVESTIGACIONES HISTORICAS Y ESTETICAS. [Bol. Cent. invest. hist. est,et.]. **Added/Corp** Universidad Central de Venezuela. Centro de Investigaciones Historicas y Esteticas. Universidad Central de Venezuela. Facultad de Arquitectura y Urbanismo. **VFOAT** Boletin. No. 1 (1964)-. Periodical. Spanish (English). Universidad Central de Venezuela / Facultad de Arquitectura y Urbanismo, Biblioteca 106, Caracas Venezuela.
Ind/Abst Am. Hist. Life (1966-1974); Archit. Period. Index (No. 23, Jan. 1978-); BHA : Biblio. Hist. Art.

IT

BOLLETTINO ARCHITETTI. (19??)-. Italian. Six times a year. L95000. Bollettino Architetti, Via Il Prato 27, 50123 Florence Italy. **Tel** 011 39 55 283544.

IT

BOLLETTINO DEL CENTRO DI STUDI PER LA STORIA DELL'ARCHITETTURA. **Added/Corp** Centro de Studi per la Storia dell'Archittura (Italy). No. 7 (1953)-. Monographic series. Italian. One time a year. L'Erma di Bretschneider SPA, via Cassiodoro 19, 00193 Rome Italy. **Tel** 011 39 6 6874127, 011 39 6 6874129, FAX 011 39 6 6874129. ***Continues*** *Bollettino del Centro di Studi di Storia dell'Architettura.*
Ind/Abst BHA : Biblio. Hist. Art.

Architecture

ISSN 0743-0043
US
BRICK IN ARCHITECTURE. [Brick archit.].
Added/Corp Brick Institute of America. Vol. 32, No. 1 (Jan./Feb. 1975)-. Periodical. English (summaries and/or abstracts in Italian and Russian). Five times a year. $9.00. Brick Institute of America, 11490 Commerce Park Drive, Suite 300, Reston VA 22091. **Tel** (703)620-0010. **Continues** Brick and Tile.

LC NA7238.N6 B76   **ISSN 0883-962X**
DD 728   US
BROWNSTONER, THE. [Brownstoner].
Added/Corp Brownstone Revival Committee. (Nov. 1968)-. Periodical. English. Four times a year. $35.00. Brownstone Revival Committee, PO Box 577, New York NY 10113. **Tel** (212)561-2154. **Bk Rev. Ad Acc. Circ:** 1,000 (ctrl).
Desc: Promotes brownstone living in New York area.
Ind/Abst Avery Index Archit. Period. Suppl. Colum. Univ. (1990-).

LC NA7205 .B78   **ISSN 0748-5549**
DD 728.3/7/0222   US
BUDGET-WISE HOUSE PLANS. VFOAT Budget Wise House Plans. English. One time a year. $2.00. House Plan Headquarters Inc, 48 West 48th Street, New York NY 10036.

AG
BUENOS AIRES BIENAL ... ARQUITECTURA. **Added/Corp** Centro de Arte y Comunicacion (Buenos Aires, Argentina). VFOAT Buenos Aires; Bienal Arquitectura; Arquitectura. (19??)-. Periodical. Spanish. Irregular. Centro de Arte y Comunicacion, Viamonte 452, 1053 Buenos Aires, Argentina.

LC TH13.2.C2 C35   **ISSN 0227-0595**
DD 690/.029/471   CN
BUILDCORE INDEX. [Buildcore index]. VFOAT Products and Standards; Product & Standards. **VAT** Products and Standards. (1981)-. Trade Publication. English. Two times a year. 164.30Can$. Daily Communications News, 580 Yorkland Boulevard, North York Ontario M2J 4Z6 Canada. **Tel** (905)494-4990. **ED** S. Kelchek. **Ad Acc. Circ:** 14,000 (ctrl). **Continues** Canadian Construction Product Directory, 0316-6376.
Desc: Sourcing guide to suppliers of construction products, materials, equipment and furniture available in Canada. Includes classification, keyword index and list of trade names. Also includes list of related standards.

LC NA7205 .B85   **ISSN 1079-4891**
DD 728/.37/0223   US
BUILDER'S BEST HOME PLANS. [Build. best home plans]. VFOAT Home Plans. (199?)-. English. Four times a year. Hanley-Wood Inc., 1 Thomas Circle Northwest, Suite 600, Washington DC 20005. **Tel** (202)452-0800, FAX (202)785-1974. **Continues** Builder's Best Home Designs, 1055-3460.

ISSN 0007-3423
UK
BUILDING DESIGN. [Build. des.]. No. 1 (1969)-. Trade Publication. English. One time a week. $178.00. Morgan Grampian, 40 Beresford Street Woolwich, London SE18 6BQ United Kingdom. **Tel** 011 44 181 8557777, FAX 011 44 181 8555548, telex 896238. available on microfilm from University Microfilms International (UMI); available on an online database (file 771/Full-Text) from DIALOG.
Ind/Abst Archit. Period. Index (1970-); Avery Index Archit. Period. Suppl. Colum. Univ. (1989-); Int. Civil Eng. Abstr.; Soft. Abstr. Eng.

LC TH1 .M27   **ISSN 0007-3407**
DD 721/.05   US
    CCC
BUILDING DESIGN & CONSTRUCTION.
[Build. des. constr.]. **VAT** Building Design and Construction. (1970)-. Periodical. English. Twelve times a year. $99.90. Cahners Publishing Company, 249 West 17th Street, New York NY 10011. **Tel** (212)645-0067, FAX (212)242-6987. **(Subscription address:** Cahners Publishing Company / Colorado, Paid Subscription Service Center, PO Box 7610, Highlands Ranch CO 80126-7610. **Tel** (303)470-4466, FAX (303)470-4691.**)** available on microfilm and microfiche from University Microfilms International (UMI); available on an online database (file 648/Full-Text) from DIALOG. **Continues** Building Construction.
Desc: A magazine published for architects, contractors, and engineers involved in the design and construction of nonresidential buildings (commercial, institutional, and industrial). Covers emerging technology, design, market trends, management, law and industrial news.
Ind/Abst Avery Index Archit. Period. Suppl. Colum. Univ. (1984-); Bus. Index (1985-); Concr. Abstr.; Constr. Index; Energy Res. Abstr. (Feb. 1976-); EP Collect.; Gen. BusinessFile (1985-); Gen. Period. Index (1985-); Homework Help.; Int. Civil Eng. Abstr.; Mag. Search; MasterFile FullTEXT 1000; MasterFile FullTEXT 350; MasterFile FullTEXT 650; MasterFile FullTEXT (July 1993-); OCLC; Soft. Abstr. Eng.; Stat. Ref. Index; Telebase; Trade Ind. ASAP [Full Txt.]; Trade Ind. Index (1981-) [Full Txt.]; Vocat. Search.

LC NA7100 .B85   **ISSN 0093-0938**
DD 728.3/7/0222   US
BUILDING IDEAS (DES MOINES).
(BUILDING IDEAS.). VFOAT Building Ideas. (Spring/Summer 1973)-. English. Four times a year. Meredith Corporation, Locust at 17th, Des Moines IA 50309. **Tel** (515)284-3000, FAX (515)284-2568. **ED** Bill Yates. **Ad Acc. Continues** Home Building Ideas.

ISSN 1000-9507
CC
SUSPENDED
BUILDING IN CHINA. See Building and Construction.

US
●**BUILDINGS, LANDMARKS AND HISTORIC SITES.** See History-History of North and South America.

ISSN 0522-7496
BE
BULLETIN DE LA COMMISSION ROYALE DES MONUMENTS ET DES SITES. See The Arts-Art.

BE
BULLETIN DE LA FONDATION JULIEN ET LAURE VANHOVE-VONNECHE. No. 1 (1981)-. Bulletin. French. Fondation Julien et Laure Vanhove-Vonneche, Hotel de Croix, rue J Saintraint, B-5000 Namur Belgium.

ISSN 0757-2859
FR
UDC 658.8
BULLETIN DE L'ACHETEUR, LE. (1982)-. Periodical. French. Eleven times a year. 499.51F (one-year), 802.15F (two-year). Editions de l'Enterprise, 26 rue de Marechal Foch, 67000 Strasbourg France. **Tel** 011 33 88 355147, FAX 011 33 88 251984, telex 889000. **ED** Gerard de Angeli (Editor's telephone: 011 33 88 368529). **Bk Rev**, (Qty: 4). **Circ:** 1500.

ISSN 0241-2977
FR
UDC 72
BULLETIN DE L'OEUVE DE LA CATHEDRALE DE METZ. [Bull. Oeuvre cathedr. Metz]. (1979)-. Bulletin. French. **Continues** Bulletin de l'Association Dite Oeuvre de la Cathedrale de Metz, 0241-2985.
Ind/Abst BHA : Biblio. Hist. Art.

ISSN 0223-5331
FR
BULLETIN D'INFORMATIONS ARCHITECTURALES. Bulletin. French. Twelve times a year. $76.56. Institut Francais Architecture, 6 rue de Tournon, 75006 Paris France. **Tel** 011 33 1 46339036, FAX 46.33.02.11, telex IFA 206765. **Continues** Bulletin d'Information Inter-Etablissements.
Desc: Publishes commentary of recent architectural expositions or those in progress, critiques city planning and landscape, and supplies a calendar for future realizations. Three supplements a year.

ISSN 0950-5644
UK
BULLETIN OF THE SCOTTISH GEORGIAN SOCIETY. [Bull. Scott. Georgian Soc.]. **Main/Corp** Scottish Georgian Society. Vol. 1 (1972)-. Bulletin. English.
Ind/Abst Archit. Period. Index (1974/1975-).

ISSN 0228-0744
CN
DD 720/.971
Pr Rev.
BULLETIN / SOCIETY FOR THE STUDY OF ARCHITECTURE IN CANADA. [Bull. - Soc. Study Archit. Can.]. **Added/Corp** Society for the Study of Architecture in Canada. No. 4/5 (Sept. 1980)-. Bulletin. English (French). Four times a year. comes with membership. Society for the Study of Architecture in Canada, PO Box 2302 Station D, Ottawa Ontario K1P 5W5 Canada. **Tel** (613)237-1066. **Continues** Society for the Study of Architecture in Canada. Nouvelles, 0228-0744.
Ind/Abst Avery Index Archit. Period. Suppl. Colum. Univ. (199?-).

LC NA6 .B78   **ISSN 0007-7518**
    NO
    CCC
BYGGEKUNST. [Byggekunst]. **Added/Corp** Norske Arkitekters Landsforbund. (1919)-. Periodical. Norwegian. Eight times a year. $109.88. Byggekunst, Josffinesgt Gate 34, 0351 Olso 3 Norway. **Tel** 47 2 602290, FAX 47 2 695948. **ED** Ulf Gronvold. **Bk Rev. Ad Acc. Circ:** 5,440 (ctrl).
Desc: Reviews the development of Norwegian and international architecture.
Ind/Abst Archit. Period. Index (1977-); Avery Index Archit. Period. Suppl. Colum. Univ. (1989-); BHA : Biblio. Hist. Art; Int. Civil Eng. Abstr.; Soft. Abstr. Eng.

ISSN 0007-7550
SW
BYGGMAESTAREN. **Added/Corp** Stockholms Byggnadsfoerening. Svenska Arkitektfoereningen. (Jan. 1959)-. Periodical. Swedish. Twelve times a year. Byggfoerlaget, PO Box 5456, S-114 81 Stockholm Sweden. **Tel** 011 46 8 6635100, FAX 011 46 8 6677075, telex 14579 BYGGF S. **Supersedes in part** Byggmaestaren.
Ind/Abst Archit. Period. Index (Mar. 1978-Dec. 1981).

ISSN 0345-1941
SW
UDC 69(051)
BYGGREFERAT. [Byggreferat]. (1971)-. Periodical. Swedish. Six times a year. Kr525.00. Byggdok, Haelsingegatan 47, S 113 31 Stockholm Sweden. **Tel** 011 46 8 340170, FAX 011 46 8 324859. **ED** Olle Malu. Index available. cum. index. **Bk Rev. Ad Acc. Circ:** 1,200. available on an online database from the publisher. Documents available from the publisher. **Formed by the union of** Aktuellt fran Biblioteket **and** Nordisk Artikelindex for Bygg.

ISSN 0109-6249
DK
BYGNINGSARKOLOGISKE STUDIER.
[Bygnin.arkol. stud.]. (1984)-. Periodical. Danish. One time a year.
Ind/Abst BHA : Biblio. Hist. Art.

LC NA855 .C14
BL
C. J. ARQUITETURA. VFOAT Casa & I.E. E Jardim Arquitetura; Casa e Jardim Arquitetura. (19??)-. Periodical. Portuguese. Irregular. 200.00. EFECE, Av Presidente Vargar, 502 - 19O Andar, Rio de Janeiro Brazil.

CL
CA : REVISTA OFICIAL DEL COLEGIO DE ARQUITECTOS DE CHILE. **Added/Corp** Colegio de Arquitectos de Chile. (19??)-. Periodical. Spanish. Two times a year. Colegio de Arquitectos de Chile, Alameda B. O'Higgins 115, Santiago Chile.
Ind/Abst Archit. Period. Index (No. 17, Dec. 1976-); Avery Index Archit. Period. Suppl. Colum. Univ. (1989-).

LC WMLC L 83/321
BL
CADERNOS BRASILEIROS DE ARQUITETURA. (1976)-. Periodical. Portuguese. Three times a year. Projeto Editores Associados Ltda, Avenue Dr. Arnaldo 1947, CEP 01255 Sao Paulo Brazil. **ED** Adail Rodriquez da Motta.

ISSN 0871-8806
PO
UDC 741/744
CADERNOS DE DESIGN. [Cad. des.]. (1992)-. Periodical. Portuguese. Four times a year. $20.67. Centro Portugues de Design, Estrada do Paco do Lumiar, 1699 Lisbon Portugal. **Tel** 011 351 1 7163735.

ISSN 0150-9535
FR
CAHIERS DE LA RECHERCHE ARCHITECTURALE, LES. [Cah. rech. archit.]. **Added/Corp** France. Ministere de la Culture et de l'Environnement. France. Ministere de l'Environnement et du Cadre de Vie. Centre d'Etudes et de Recherches Architecturales (Paris, France). No. 1 (Dec. 1977)-. Periodical. French. Four times a year. 333.00F France; 380.00F other. Editions Parentheses, 72 Cours Julien, 13006 Marseille France. **Tel** 011 33 91 487444, FAX 011 33 91 426806.
Ind/Abst Archit. Period. Index (1977-); BHA : Biblio. Hist. Art.

ISSN 1248-7945
FR
UDC 72
●**CAHIERS DU PATRIMOINE ARCHITECTURAL DE PARIS.** (1993)-. Monographic series. French. Price varies per volume. Service Livres Diffusion, 7 rue de Calais, 75425 Paris Cedex 09 France. **Tel** 011 33 42820662.

ISSN 1040-4317
DD 720   US
CALIFORNIA ARCHITECTURE AND ARCHITECTS. [Calif. archit. archit.]. No. 1-. Monographic series. English. Price varies per volume. Hennessey & Ingalls Inc, 1254 Santa Monica Mall, Santa Monica CA 90401.

LC NA1 .C29   **ISSN 0008-2872**
DD 720.971   CN
    CCC
CANADIAN ARCHITECT, THE. [Can. archit.]. Vol. 1 (Nov./Dec. 1955)-. Periodical. English. Twelve times a year. 68.75Can$. Southham Information & Technical Group Inc, 1450 Don Mills Road, Don Mills Ontario M3B 2X7 Canada. **Tel** (416)445-6641, (800)668-2374, FAX (416)442-2261. available on microfilm and microfiche from University Microfilms International (UMI). **Absorbed** Bulletin. Royal

Architecture

Architectural Institute of Canada, 0319-132X.
Ind/Abst Archit. Period. Index (1955-?, 1977-); Art Index; Avery Index Archit. Period. Suppl. Colum. Univ. (1990-); Can. Period. Index.

ISSN 0008-6878
FR

CARRE BLEU, LE. (1959)-. Periodical. French (translations available in English). Four times a year (Jan., Apr., Sept., Nov.). $52.49. Feuille Internationale d'Arch, 33 rue des Francs Bourgeois, 75004 Paris France. **Tel** 011 33 1 43261084. **ED** Philiffe Fousuey & Andre Schimmerlino.

US

CARTOUCHE. Added/Corp New School of Architecture (San Diego, Calif.) (1986)-. Periodical. English. Three times a year. Free on request. New School of Architecture, 1249 F Street, San Diego CA 92101. **Continues** *Off the Wall (Chula Vista, Calif.)*.
Ind/Abst Avery Index Archit. Period. Suppl. Colum. Univ. (Winter 1990-).

LC NK2063.A1 C37
DD 728/.09469
PO

CASA & DECORACAO. VFOAT Casa e Decoracao. (19??)-. Periodical. Portuguese. Twelve times a year. Lucidus Publicacoes LDA, R Joaquim Antonio Aguiar 45 5, 1000 Lisbon Portugal. **Tel** 011 351 1 3862175.

ISSN 0008-7173
IT

CASA VOGUE. See Interior Design and Decoration.

LC NA4 .C3 **ISSN** 0008-7181
DD 720.5 IT

CASABELLA (MILAN, ITALY, 1965). (CASABELLA.). [Casabella]. (1965)-. Periodical. Italian. Eleven times a year. L144610. **(Subscription address:** Agenzia Italiana Esportazione, Via Manzoni 12, 20089 Rozzano Milan, Italy. **Tel** 011 39 2 57512575.) cum. index. **Continues** *Casabella Continuita*.
Ind/Abst Archit. Period. Index (1977-); Art Index; ARTbibliogr. Mod.; Arts Humanit. Citation Index (19??-19??) [Full Cov.]; Avery Index Archit. Period. Suppl. Colum. Univ. (1987/1990-); BHA : Biblio. Hist. Art.

IT

CASTELLUM. (CASTELLUM : RIVISTA DELL'ISTITUTO ITALIANO DEI CASTELLI.). [Castellum]. **Added/Corp** Istituto Italiano dei Castelli. (1965)-. Periodical. Italian. One time a year. L42000. Istituto Italiano dei Castelli, Via G A Borgese 14, 20154 Milan Italy. **Tel** 011 39 2 347237.
Ind/Abst BHA : Biblio. Hist. Art.

ISSN 0008-7505
SP

CASTILLOS DE ESPANA. Added/Corp Asociacion Espanola de Amigos de los Castillos. (Jan/Feb/Mar 1967)-. Periodical. Spanish. Two times a year. **Continues** *Boletin de la Asociacion Espanola de Amigos de los Castillos, 0210-8429*.
Ind/Abst Am. Hist. Life.

LC NA1118 **ISSN** 0576-8896
IT

CATALOGO BOLAFFI DELL'ARCHITETTURA ITALIANA.
1963/66-. Periodical. Italian. G Bolaffi, Via Cavour 17F, Turin 10123 Italy.

ISSN 0008-7874
US

CATHEDRAL AGE. Added/Corp Protestant Episcopal Foundation, Washington, D.C. Vol. 1 (Apr. 1925)-. Periodical. English. Four times a year. $15.00. Washington National Cathedral, Mount Saint Alban, Washington DC 20016. **Tel** (202)537-6247, FAX (202)364-6600. **ED** Nancy S. Montgomery. **Bk Rev**. **Circ**: 34,500 (ctrl). available on microfilm from University Microfilms International (UMI).
Desc: A publication of the Washington National Cathedral describing ministry, fine arts and architecture of cathedrals around the world.

LC NA705 .C4 **ISSN** 8755-2019
DD 720/.973 US

CENTER (AUSTIN, TEX.). (CENTER.). [Center]. **Added/Corp** University of Texas at Austin. Center for the Study of American Architecture. Vol. 1 (1985)-. Periodical. English. One time a year. $35.00. University of Texas Press, PO Box 7819, Austin TX 78713. **Tel** (512)471-4531, FAX (512)320-0668, telex 776453 UTEXPRES AUS.

ISSN 0942-7023
GW

CENTRUM : JAHRBUCH ARCHITEKTUR UND STADT. VFOAT Jahrbuch Architektur und Stadt. (1992)-. German. Vieweg Publishing, PO Box 5829, D-65048 Wiesbaden Germany. **Tel** 011 49 611 160230, FAX 011 49 611 534430.

ISSN 0838-9330
DD 728/.0971 CN

CENTURY HOME (1988). (CENTURY HOME.). [Century home]. No. 28 (Feb. 1988)-. Periodical. English. Eight times a year. 19.41Can$. Bluestone House Inc., 12 Mill Street South, Port Hope Ontario L1A 2S5 Canada. **Tel** (905)885-2449, FAX (905)885-5355. **Continues** *Canada Century Home, 0821-5774*; **Continues in part** *Re-New, 0845-5341*.
Desc: This magazine includes information both for decorating and restoring features.

IT

CERAMICA PER L'ARCHITETTURA : CA. See Glass and Ceramics.

ISSN 0009-0697
DD 720 XR

CESKOSLOVENSKY ARCHITEKT. Vol. 1 (1955)-. Periodical. Czech. Twenty-six times a year. Association of Architects, Letenska 5, 118 45 Prague 1, Mala Strana Czech Republic. **Tel** (02)539768, telex 122064 SCAR C. **ED** Jiri Horsky. cum. index. **Bk Rev**. **Ad Acc**. **Circ**: 7,500 (ctrl).

US

CHAPTERLETTER. Added/Corp Boston Society of Architects. **VFOAT** Chapter Letter; Chapterletter of the Boston Society of Architects; Chapter Letter of the Boston Society of Architects; BSA Chapter Letter; BSA Chapterletter. (19??)-. Periodical. English. Eleven times a year. $65.00. Boston Society of Architects, 52 Broad Street, Boston MA 02109. **Tel** (617)951-1433 Ext. 221.

ISSN 0323-1437
UDC 643/645 CS

CHATAR. [Chatar]. (1969)-. Periodical. Czech. Twelve times a year. DM79.00. **(Subscription address:** Kubon & Sagner, ABT Zeitschriftenimport, D 80328 Munich Germany. **Tel** 011 49 89 54218130.)
Ind/Abst BHA : Biblio. Hist. Art.

LC NA1540 .C523
DD 722/.11/09 CH

CHIEN CHU LI SHIH YU LI LUN / CHUNG-KUO CHIEN CHU HSUEH HUI CHIEN CHU LI SHIH HSUEH SHU WEI YUAN HUI PIEN. VFOAT Corpus of Architectural History and Theory; Jianzhu Lishi Yu Lilun; Architectural History and Theory; Corpus of Architectural History & Theory. Vol. 1- 1980. Periodical. Chinese (Chinese). NT$1.22. Chiang-Su Sheng, Hsin Hua Shu Tien, Nan-Ching, People's Republic of China.

LC NA1549.8.C49
DD 720/.951/249 CH

CHIEN CHU SHIH (TAIPEI, TAIWAN). (CHIEN CHU SHIH.). **Added/Corp** Chung-hua min kuo Chien chu Shih Kung hui Chuan kuo Lien ho hui. Tai-wan Sheng Chien chu Shih Kung hui. **VFOAT** Chinese Architect; Chung-Hua Min Kuo Chien Chu Shih Tsa Chih. (1975)-. Corporate Report. Chinese (English). Twelve times a year. NT$2,100 Taiwan; $119.00 US. Chinese Architect, 13F-2 51 Sec 2, Keelung Road, Taipei Taiwan. **Tel** 02 3788016, FAX 02 7357471. **ED** Jung-Sheng Ting, Amy Tang, Arwin Lin, Percy Hu, Shiang-Ying Chen, Ching-Sui Hung, and Winnie Yu. cum. index. **Bk Rev**. **Ad Acc**. **Adv Mgr**: Chou Yu Ying. Full Page (B&W) $2,400.00. Half Page (B&W) $1,200.00. **Circ**: 6,500 (ctrl).
Desc: The magazine contains the architectural trends and new projects in Taiwan. Media and communications coverage with the National Union of Architects and its members.
Ind/Abst Archit. Period. Index (19??-19??).

ISSN 0529-1488
IT

CHIESA E QUARTIERE; QUADERNI DI ARCHITETTURA SACRA. VFOAT Quaderni di Chiesa e Quartiere. No. 1- March 1957-. Periodical. Italian (summaries and/or abstracts in English, French and German). Chiesa Quartiere, Via Altabella 2, Bologna Italy.

LC NA2500 .C49 **ISSN** 1198-449X
CN

●**CHORA. Added/Corp** McGill University. History and Theory of Architecture Graduate Program. (1994)-. English. Every 2 years. McGill Queen's University Press, 1020 Pine Avenue West, Montreal Quebec H3A 1A2 Canada. **(Subscription address:** University of Toronto Press, 5201 Dufferin Street, Downsview Ontario M3H 5T8 Canada. **Tel** (416)667-7791.)

ISSN 0268-912X
DD 726.50941 UK

CHURCH BUILDING LIVERPOOL. [Church build. Liverp.] (1984)-. Periodical. English. Two times a year. $41.07. **VFOAT** Magazine of Ecclesiastical Design. Gabriel Communications Ltd, 1st Floor, St. James Building, Oxford M1 8PS United Kingdom. **Tel** 011 44 171 2787321. **ED** Nigel Melnuish (editor's phone: 011 44 61 236 8856).
Ind/Abst Archit. Period. Index (1985-).

LC NB1750 **ISSN** 0262-4966
DD 726 UK

CHURCHSCAPE. (1981)-. Periodical. English. One time a year (Sept.). £2.95. Council for Care of Churches, 83 London Wall, London EC2M 5NA United Kingdom. **Tel** 011 44 171 6380971, FAX 011 44 171 6380184. **ED** Jonathan Goodchild. **Bk Rev**. **Ad Acc**. **Circ**: 1,500. Documents available from BLDSC.

ISSN 0009-6830
FR

CIMAISE. See The Arts-Art.

ISSN 0210-0479
UDC 624 SP

CIMBRA. [Cimbra]. (1964)-. Periodical. Spanish. Ten times a year. $26.64. Cimbra, Adelfas 34, 28007 Madrid Spain. **Tel** 011 34 1 501-4959.

LC NA735.H68 C58 **ISSN** 8755-0415
DD 720 US

CITE (HOUSTON, TEX.). (CITE: A PUBLICATION OF THE RICE DESIGN ALLIANCE.). [Cite]. **Added/Corp** Rice Design Alliance (Houston, Tex.). **VFOAT** Cite at 5. (Aug. 1982)-. Periodical. English. Two times a year. $8.00. Cite: The Architecture and Design Review of Houston / Rice Design Alliance, PO Box 1892, Rice University, Houston TX 77251-1892. **Tel** (713)524-6297, FAX (713)285-5277. **ED** Ann Sieber. **Bk Rev**. **Ad Acc**, **Adv Mgr**: Lynn Kelly, **Tel** (713)524-6297. **Circ**: 6,000 (ctrl).
Desc: Covers architectural, design, and civic issues. Primarily covers the Houston area and its surrounding regions, but with some coverage of national issues.
Ind/Abst Avery Index Archit. Period. Suppl. Colum. Univ. (1990-).

ISSN 1079-4484
DD 307 US

●**CITY (LOS ANGELES, CALIF.).** See Housing and Urban Development.

LC NA9052 .C49A
DD 720/.79 UK

CIVIC TRUST AWARDS. Main/Corp Civic Trust. English. One time a year. Civic Trust / England, 17 Carleton House Terrace, London SW1Y 5AW United Kingdom. **Tel** 01 930 0914. **Continues** *Civic Trust Award*.

ISSN 1076-2922
DD 720 US

●**CLASSICIST (NEW YORK, N.Y.), THE.** (THE CLASSICIST.). [Classicist]. **Added/Corp** New York Academy of Art. Institute for the Study of Classical Architecture. No. 1 (1994/95)-. English. One time a year. $18.00. Transaction Publishers / Rutgers State University, Department 3091 or 3092, New Brunswick NJ 08903. **Tel** (908)932-2280 ext. 105, FAX (908)932-3138.

ISSN 0898-0284
DD 690 US

CLEM LABINE'S TRADITIONAL BUILDING. [Clem Labine's tradit. build.]. **VFOAT** Traditional Building. (1988)-. Periodical. English. Six times a year (Jan., Mar., May, July, Sept., Nov.). $18.00. Historical Trends Corporation, 69A Seventh Avenue, Brooklyn NY 11217. **Tel** (718)636-0788, FAX (718)636-0750. **ED** Clem Labine. **Bk Rev**, (Qty: 18). **Ad Acc**. **Circ**: 15,400 (ctrl).
Desc: Lists and illustrates sources for hard to find historically styled products and both for restoration and new construction.
Ind/Abst Avery Index Archit. Period. Suppl. Colum. Univ. (May/June 1989, Jan./Feb. 1990-); Constr. Index.

ISSN 0930-8555
GW

COLONIA ROMANICA. (COLONIA ROMANICA : JAHRBUCH DES FORDERVEREINS ROMANISCHE KIRCHEN KOELN E.V.). [Colon. Rom.]. Vol. 1 (1986)-. German. One time a year. Forderverein Romanische Kirchen Koln EV, Vorstandssekretariat, c/o Stadtsparkasse Koln, Habsburgerring 2-12, W-5000 Cologne 1 Germany.

LC E162 .H68 **ISSN** 0195-1416
DD 728.3/7/0974 US

COLONIAL HOMES. (19??)-. Periodical. English. Six times a year. $14.97. The Hearst Corporation, 250 West 55th Street, New York NY 10019. **Tel** (212)649-4014, (800)925-0485. **(Subscription address:** CDS Agency Hard Copy, PO Box 4966, Des Moines IA 50340. **Tel** (515)247-7569.) available on microfilm and microfiche from University Microfilms International (UMI). Documents available from UMI Article Clearinghouse. **Continues** *House Beautiful's Colonial Homes, 0164-6214*.
Ind/Abst Avery Index Archit. Period. Suppl. Colum. Univ. (Feb. 1990-); EP Collect.; Garden Lit. (1992-); Gen. Period. Index (1989-); Homework Help.; Mag. Artic. Summar. Elite; Mag. Artic. Summar. Select; Mag. Artic. Summar. CD-ROM; Mag. Index Plus (1989-); Mag. Search; MasterFile FullTEXT 1000; MasterFile FullTEXT

Architecture

350; MasterFile FullTEXT 650; MasterFile FullTEXT (Jan. 1985-June 1989); Newsp. Period. Abstr. (1988-); OCLC; Telebase; Mag. Index (1989-).

IT

COLTELLO DI DELFO. (19??)-. Italian. Four times a year. L40000 Italy; L60000 other. ICMAI, Via Della Vite 27, 00187 Rome Italy. **Tel** 011 39 6 6790369. Index available. cum. index. **Bk Rev**, (Qty: 8). **Ad Acc**.

ISSN 1065-304X
DD 720 US

COLUMBIA DOCUMENTS OF ARCHITECTURE AND THEORY. [Columbia doc. archit. theory]. **Added/Corp** Columbia University. Graduate School of Architecture, Planning, and Preservation. **VFOAT** D. (1992)-. Periodical. English. Two times a year. $50.00. Columbia Documents of Architecture and Theory, Subscription Service, 403 Avery Hall, Columbia University, New York NY 10027. **Tel** (212)854-5885. **ED** Bernard Tschum, Stephen Perrella, Lois Nesbitt, and Tony Wong. **Circ:** 3,000 (ctrl).
 Desc: Information on exhibitions, lectures and conferences taking place at Columbia University's Graduate School of Architecture, Planning and Preservation.

LC NK1700
DD 747 AT

COMFORTABLE LIVING AND QUEENSLAND HOMES. See Interior Design and Decoration.

JA

COMMERCIAL ARCHITECTURE. (19??)-. Periodical. Japanese. Twelve times a year. $347.00. Shoten Kenchikusha, (Shoten Kenchikusha Co. Ltd.), 1-2 Okubo 1 Chome, Shinjukuku Tokyo 160 Japan. **(Subscription address:** Maruzen Company Ltd., PO Box 5050, Import & Export Department, Tokyo 100 31 Japan. **Tel** 011 81 3 32789224.)

ISSN 0319-4558
DD 690/.24/06271 US

COMMUNIQUE - ASSOCIATION FOR PRESERVATION TECHNOLOGY. (COMMUNIQUE - ASSOCIATION POUR LA PRESERVATION ET SES TECHNIQUES.). [Commun. - Assoc. Preserv. Technol.]. **Main/Corp** Association for Preservation Technology. **Added/Corp** Association for Preservation Technology. Vol. 4, No 4 (1975)-. Periodical. English (English). Four times a year. $85.00 (individuals), $115.00 (institutions) Comes with Association for the Preservation of Technology membership. Association for the Preservation of Technology, PO Box 8178, Fredericksburg VA 22404. **Tel** (703)373-1621, FAX (703)373-6050. **Continues** Association for Preservation Technology. Newsletter., 0319-454X.

ISSN 0700-4389
DD 720.9714/281 CN

COMMUNIQUE - SOCIETE D'ARCHITECTURE DE MONTREAL. **Main/Corp** Societe d'Architecture de Montreal. First issue in 1973?. Periodical. French. Societe d'Architecture de Montreal, 1825 Ouest boulevard Dorchester, Montreal Quebec H3H 1R4 Canada. **Supersedes** Societe des Architectes de Montreal. Communique, 0700-4370.

LC NA53 .C64   ISSN 0145-1855
DD 338.7/61/71140973 US

COMMUNITY DESIGN CENTERS : PROFILE. English. One time a year. American Institute of Architects / Washington DC, 1735 New York Avenue Northwest, Washington DC 20006. **Tel** (202)626-7460, FAX (202)626-7587.

LC NA1 .C667
US

COMPETITIONHOTLINE. **VFOAT** Competition Hotline. Vol. 1, No. 1/2 (1991)-. English. Four times a year. Comes with Competition. Competitions, Box 20445, Louisville KY 40250. **Tel** (602)451-3623.

LC NA2340 .C66   ISSN 1058-6539
DD 720/.7973 US

COMPETITIONS (LOUISVILLE, KY.). (COMPETITIONS.). [Competitions]. **Added/Corp** Competition Project, Inc. (Winter 1991)-. Trade Publication. English. Four times a year (Feb., May, Aug., Nov.). $28.00. Competitions, Box 20445, Louisville KY 40250. **Tel** (602)451-3623. **ED** Stanley Collyer. **Bk Rev**, (Qty: 1-2). **Ad Acc**. **Circ:** 2,000 (ctrl).

LC N7 .C62   ISSN 0214-4832
DD 705 SP
SUSPENDED

COMPOSICION ARQUITECTONICA = ART & ARCHITECTURE. **Added/Corp** Fundacion Faustino Orbegozo. Instituto de Arte y Humanidades. **VFOAT** Art and Architecture; Art & Architecture. No. 1 (Oct. 1988)-Suspended with Issue 10 (1993). Periodical. Spanish (Basque and English). Three times a year. Composicion Arquitectonica, PO Box 1342, Sabino Arana 28 10, 48013 Bilbao Spain. **Tel** 011 34 4 441116.
 Ind/Abst Archit. Period. Index (No. 1, Oct. 1988-).

LC NA105   ISSN 0884-7053
DD 363.69 US

CONNECTICUT PRESERVATION. [Conn. preserv.]. **Added/Corp** Connecticut Trust for Historic Preservation. (July 1978)-. Periodical. English. Three times a year. Connecticut Trust for Historic Preservaiton, 940 Whitney Avenue, Hamden CT 06517. **Tel** (203)562-6312.
 Ind/Abst Avery Index Archit. Period. Suppl. Colum. Univ. (1989-).

LC Z7914.B9 C62 Th1   ISSN 0892-2047
DD 016.69 US

CONSTRUCTION INDEX. See Building and Construction-Abstracting, Bibliographies and Statistics.

LC NA673 .C66
DD 724/.6 FR

CONSTRUCTION MODERNE. **Added/Corp** Centre d'Information de l'Industrie Cimentiere (France). (197?)-. Periodical. French. Four times a year. Free on request. Cimbeton, 41 Avenue de Friedland, 75008 Paris France. **Tel** 011 31 43590893. **Continues** Construction Moderne, 0010-6852.
 Ind/Abst Archit. Period. Index (No. 1, 1975-).

AT

●**CONTENT / AUSTRALIA.** (1995)-. English. Two times a year. 57.55Aus$. University of Sidney Department of Architectural Science, Sydney NSW 2006 Australia. **Tel** 011 61 02 3512822.

ISSN 0714-9476
DD 720/.28/8/09714 CN

CONTINUITE. See The Arts-Art.

SW

CONTRACT INTERNATIONAL. (198?)-. Periodical. English (Swedish). $48.09. Contract Council AB, Box 1083, S 269 21 Baestad Sweden. **Tel** 011 46 431 69000. **Continues** Contract (Baestad, Sweden).

US

CONTRACTORS MANAGEMENT JOURNAL. English. Twelve times a year. $197.00. FMI Corporation, 5151 Glenwood Avenue, Raleigh NC 27622. **Tel** 800-877-1364. **ED** David Cheatham. Index available. cum. index. **Circ:** 1,000 (ctrl).

ISSN 1058-9120
US

CONTRIBUTIONS TO THE STUDY OF ART AND ARCHITECTURE. See The Arts-Art.

DD 720   IT

CONTROSPAZIO. (June 1969)-. Periodical. Italian. Six times a year. L40000 Italy; L80000 otherd. Gangemi Editore, via Cavour 255, 00184 Rome Italy. **Tel** 011 39 6 4821661. **Bk Rev**. **Ad Acc**. ctrl circ.

AT

CORPORATE AND OFFICE DESIGN. (19??)-. Periodical. English. Two times a year. 16.44Aus$. Australian Consolidated Press Ltd., Private Bag 92615 Symonds St, Auckland New Zealand. **Tel** 011 64 9 3735408, FAX 011 64 9 3022889.

ISSN 0394-1590
UDC 69 IT

COSTRUIRE IN LATERIZIO. [Costr. laterizio]. (1988)-. Periodical. Italian. Six times a year. L61310. Editoriale PEG Spa, Via Fratelli Bressan 2, 20126 Milan Italy. **Tel** 011 39 2 2579841, FAX 011 39 2 255-2779, telex 323088 PEGMOS I. **ED** Marina Kern. Index available. cum. index. **Bk Rev**. **Ad Acc**. **Circ:** 17,500 (ctrl). **Continues** In Laterizio, 0394-8269.
 Desc: Architectural plans, realizations, art, technology and rules in building with special attention to use of clay structural tiles, bricks and tiles in general. A constant comparison between Italy and other countries.

ISSN 0954-7843
UK

COUNTRY TIMES AND LANDSCAPE. **VFOAT** Country Times. Vol. 1, No. 7 (Nov. 1988)-. Periodical. English. Twelve times a year. £21.00 UK; £26.00 Europe and Ireland; £43.00 (airmail) Middle East; £48.00 (airmail) US, Canada, Africa, India, Australia, New Zealand, and Japan; £26.00 (surface mail) other. Haymarket Publishing Ltd., 12 14 Ansdell Street, London W8 5TR United Kingdom. **Tel** 011 44 171 9380705, 011 44 171 2786686, FAX 011 44 171 9380772. **Formed by the union of** Landscape (London, England), 0951-7669 **and** Country Times (Twickenham, London, England), 0954-2078.
 Desc: Contains articles on country life, landscape protection, and historic buildings.

ISSN 0307-8086
UK

COURTAULD INSTITUTE ILLUSTRATION ARCHIVES. ARCHIVE 4, LATE 18TH & 19TH CENTURY SCULPTURE IN THE BRITISH ISLES. See Library and Information Sciences-Archives and Manuscripts.

ISSN 0011-0728
CI

UDC 71
COVJEK I PROSTOR. **VFOAT** Man and Space; CIP : Covjek i Prostor. (1954)-. Periodical. Serbo-Croatian (Roman). Twelve times a year. $35.00. Savez Drustava Arhitekata Hrvatska, Trg Republike 3 1, 41000 Zagreb Croatia. **Tel** 011 38 41 274618, 011 38 41 274796. **ED** Tomislav Premerl. **Bk Rev**. **Ad Acc**. **Circ:** 3,000.
 Ind/Abst Archit. Period. Index (Sept. 1977-); BHA : Biblio. Hist. Art.

LC NA1 .T37   ISSN 0277-6863
DD 720/.5 US

CRIT. [Crit]. **Added/Corp** American Institute of Architects. Association of Student Chapters. **VFOAT** CRIT/ASJ. (Fall 1977)-. Periodical. English. Two times a year. Available with Institute of Architecture Students membership only. American Institute of Architecture Students, 1735 New York Avenue Northwest, Washington DC 20006. **Tel** (202)785-7272. **ED** Leigh Chatham Hubbard. **Circ:** 15,000. **Continues** Telesis (Washington, D.C.), 0364-6521.
 Desc: Reflects the concerns, goals and design trends of 30,000 future architects. Includes competition and convention announcements, projects, and opinions.
 Ind/Abst Archit. Period. Index (1977-); Avery Index Archit. Period. Suppl. Colum. Univ. (1989-).

AT

CRITIQUES (MELBOURNE, VIC.). (CRITIQUES.). **Added/Corp** University of Melbourne. Dept. of Architecture and Building. (1987)-. Periodical. English. University of Melbourne / Department of Architecture and Building, Parkville Victoria 3052 Australia.

LC NA5 .C7   ISSN 0212-5633
SP

CROQUIS. (EL CROQUIS DE ARQUITECTURE Y DE DISENO.). [Croquis]. (1982)-. Periodical. Spanish (English). Five times a year. $239.70. El Croquis Editorial, Barcelo 15 #5, 28004 Madrid Spain. **Tel** 011 34 1 4452149, FAX 5932192.
 Ind/Abst Archit. Period. Index (Vol. 6, No. 2, 1987-); Avery Index Archit. Period. Suppl. Colum. Univ. (Dec. 1989-).

LC F1219.3.A6 C8   ISSN 0185-5131
DD 722/.91/0972 MX

CUADERNOS DE ARQUITECTURA MESOAMERICANA. No. 1 (Feb. 1984)-. Periodical. Spanish (English). Three times a year. $2.50 single issue. Division de Estudios de Posgrado, Facultad de Arquitectura, Mexico DF Mexico.
 Ind/Abst Anthropol. Lit.; Archit. Period. Index; Ethnoarts Index.

LC NA753 .C8   ISSN 0185-8572
DD 720/.972/05 MX

CUADERNOS DE ARQUITECTURA VIRREINAL. **Added/Corp** Universidad Nacional Autonoma de Mexico. Facultad de Arquitectura. Universidad Nacional Autonoma de Mexico. Facultad de Arquitectura. Division de Estudios de Posgrado. (1984)-. Periodical. Spanish.
 Ind/Abst Archit. Period. Index (No. 10, 1991-); BHA : Biblio. Hist. Art.

UK
CEASED
CURRENT INFORMATION IN THE CONSTRUCTION INDUSTRY. See Building and Construction.

LC NA7208 .C87   ISSN 1055-3479
DD 728/.37/097305 US

CUSTOM HOME. [Cust. home.]. Vol. 1, No. 1 (Feb. 1991)-. Trade Publication. English. Six times a year. $24.00. Hanley-Wood Inc., 1 Thomas Circle Northwest, Suite 600, Washington DC 20005. **Tel** (202)452-0800, FAX (202)785-1974. **(Subscription address:** Custom Home, PO Box 1067, Skokie IL 60076. **Tel** (708)647-9775.)
 Desc: The magazine for the custom home market targeted to builders, architects and interior designers.

FR

D A D ARCHITECTURES. (19??)-. French. Ten times a year. 75.00F (architects), 150.00F other. Soc d'Editions Architecturales, 7 rue de Chaillot, 75116 Paris France. **Tel** 011 33 149520362.

IT

D A : RIVISTA D'ARCHITETTURA. (19??)-. Italian. Four times a year. L35000.00. Editoriale d'Architettura, Via Degli Alpini 5, 67051 Avezzano Italy. **Tel** 011 39 863 34163.

ISSN 1130-3794
SP
SUSPENDED
D'A PALMA DE MALLORCA. [D'a Palma de Mallorca]. (1989)-Suspended (19??). Periodical. Spanish (Catalan). Three times a year. 5500ptas Spain; 7500ptas Europe; 11500ptas other. Collegi d'Arquitectes de Baleares, Calle Portella 14, Palma de Mallorca Spain. **Tel**

339

011 34 971 727759. **(Subscription address:** Editorial Gustavo Gili, Apartado 35 149, 08080 Barcelona Spain. **Tel** 011 34 3 3228161.) **Bk Rev. Ad Acc, Adv Mgr:** Angel Hevia. **Circ:** 2000 (ctrl).

LC NA1.A1 D34 **ISSN** 0721-4235
DD 720/.5 GW
CCC

DAIDALOS. (DAIDALOS : BERLIN ARCHITECTURAL JOURNAL.). [Daidalos]. **VFOAT** Berlin Architectural Journal. (1981)-. Trade Publication. English (German). Four times a year. $134.34. Bertelsmann Fachzeitschriften GmbH, Carl Bertelsmann Strasse 270, D-33311 Frankfurt Germany. **Tel** 011 49 5241 802199. **(Subscription address:** Translibris GmbH, PO Box 301373, D 50783 Cologne Germany. **Tel** 011 49 221 542085, FAX 011 49 221 542086.) **ED** G. Auer, H. Bohringer, U. Conrads, G. Feuerstein, W. Meisenheimer, R Middleton, W. Oechslin and Jan Pieper. Index available. **Ad Acc. Circ:** 2,653 (ctrl).
Desc: Essays and scientific treatises by architecture and art critics, historians and writers. Full-page, color reproductions of mostly unpublished architectural drawings and paintings.
Ind/Abst Archit. Period. Index (1981-); ARTbibliogr. Mod. (1984-); ARTbibliogr. Curr. Titles; Avery Index Archit. Period. Suppl. Colum. Univ. (1989-); BHA : Biblio. Hist. Art.

LC TH4809.G7 D34
DD 728.3/7/0941 UK

DAILY MAIL BOOK OF HOME PLANS. (19??)-. English. One time a year. £1.95. Associated Newspapers Limited, Carmelite House, London ECAY OJA United Kingdom. **Bk Rev. Ad Acc. Circ:** 20,000.
Desc: A comprehensive guide to new housing to build on your own site. Also includes home plans.

LC NA673 .D37 **ISSN** 1145-0835
DD 720/.5 FR

D'ARCHITECTURES : D'A. VFOAT D'A. No. 1 (Dec. 1989)-. French. Twelve times a year. Societe d'Editions Architecturales, 7 rue de Chaillot, 75116 Paris France.
Ind/Abst Archit. Period. Index (Dec. 1989-).

IT

D'ARS. See The Arts-Art.

LC NA1 .D44 **ISSN** 0359-7105
DD 720 FI

DATUTOP, DEPARTMENT OF ARCHITECTURE, TAMPERE UNIVERSITY OF TECHNOLOGY OCCASIONAL PAPERS. (DEPARTMENT OF ARCHITECTURE, TAMPERE UNIVERSITY OF TECHNOLOGY, OCCASIONAL PAPERS : DATUTOP.). [DATUTOP, Dep. Archit., Tamp. Univ. Technol. occas. pap.]. **Added/Corp** Tampereen Teknillinen Korkeakoulu. Arkkitehtuurin Osasto. **VFOAT** DATUTOP; Occasional Papers; DATUTOP Series. (1982)-. Monographic series. English. Irregular. Price varies per volume. Tampere University of Technology / Department of Architecture, PO Box 699, SF-33101 Tampere 10 Finland. **Tel** 358-31-32941, telex 22-313 TTKTR-SF. **ED** Jorma Manty. Index available. cum. index. **Bk Rev. Circ:** 800.
Desc: Discussional papers on theoretical and philosophical issues of architecture and environmental planning and design.
Ind/Abst Archit. Period. Index (No. 4, 1983-).

LC NA3 .B33 **ISSN** 0721-1902
DD 720/.5 GW
CCC

DB. DEUTSCHE BAUZEITUNG (1981). (DB : DEUTSCHE BAUZEITUNG.). [DB, Dtsch. Bauztg.]. **VFOAT** Deutsche Bauzeitung; D.B. (198?)-. Trade Publication. German (English). Twelve times a year. DM119.40 Germany; DM124.80 other. DVA Deutsche Verlagsanstalt, Neckarstrasse 121, D-70190 Stuttgart Germany. **Tel** 011 49 711 26310. **(Subscription address:** Zenit Pressvertrieb GmbH, Postfach 810640, D 70523 Stuttgart Germany. **Tel** 011 49 711 7252191.) **ED** Wilfried Dechau. Index available. cum. index. **Bk Rev. Ad Acc. Circ:** 35,000 (ctrl). ***Continues*** *Deutsche Bauzeitung, 0415-5599.*
Desc: Mainly covers German and international architecture. Also contains information on the engineering and technical details of buildings.
Ind/Abst Archit. Period. Index; Avery Index Archit. Period. Suppl. Colum. Univ. (1989-); Int. Civil Eng. Abstr.; Soft. Abstr. Eng.

ISSN 0011-4782
DD 690 GW

DBZ-DEUTSCHE BAUZEITSCHRIFT. (DEUTSCHE BAUZEITSCHRIFT.). [DBZ-Dtsch. Bauzeitschr.]. **VFOAT** DBZ-Deutsche Bauzeitschrift; DBZ. Vol. 1 (1953)-. Trade Publication. German. Twelve times a year. $167.66. Bertelsmann Fachzeitschriften GmbH, Carl Bertelsmann Strasse 270, D-33311 Frankfurt Germany. **Tel** 011 49 5241 802199. **(Subscription address:** Translibris GmbH, PO Box 301373, D 50783 Cologne Germany. **Tel** 011 49 221 542085, FAX 011 49 221 542086.)
Ind/Abst Archit. Period. Index (1977-); Avery Index Archit. Period. Suppl. Colum. Univ. (1989-).

ISSN 0889-1931
DD 705 US

DEADLINES (HAWLEY, MASS.). (DEADLINES : THE MONTHLY PUBLICATION OF THE DESIGN COMPETITION REGISTRY.). **Added/Corp** Design Competition Registry (Organization). (April 1985)-. Periodical. English. Twelve times a year. $26.00. Design Competition Registry, PO Box 323, Charlemont MA 01339. **Tel** (413)339-4018. **ED** Peter Beck and Ken Berby. **Circ:** 950.

LC NA **ISSN** 0998-5956
DD 720 FR
UDC 719 (44)

DEMEURE HISTORIQUE (PARIS), LA. (LA DEMEURE HISTORIQUE.). (1966)-. Periodical. French. Four times a year. $74.36. Hotel de Nesmond, 57 Quai de la Tournelle, Paris 75005 France. **Tel** 011 33 1 43290286.

ISSN 0291-1191
FR
UDC 659.13

DEMEURES & CHATEAUX. VFOAT Demeures et Chateaux. (1981)-. Periodical. French. Eight times a year (monthly Feb.-March, May-July, Oct.-Dec.). $196.84. Demeures et Chateaux, BP17, 19230 Arnac Pampadour France. **Tel** 011 33 16 55733237. ***Continues*** *Demeures & Chateaux en France, 0180-3905.*

ISSN 0947-031X
GW

●**DENKMALPFLEGE, DIE.** (1994)-. German. Two times a year. DM48.00. Deutscher Kunstverlag, Postfach 190354, D-80603 Munich Germany. **Tel** 011 49 89 1215160. ***Continues*** *Deutsche Kunst und Denkmalpflege.*

LC NA109.G3 D456
DD 720/.28/80943305 GW

DENKMALPFLEGE INFORMATIONEN. AUSGABE D. Added/Corp Bayerisches Landesamt fur Denkmalpflege. (19??)-. Monographic series. German. Price varies per volume. Bayerisches Landesamt fur Denkmalpflege, Hofgraben 4, W-8000 Munich 22 Germany.

LC NA1 .D45 **ISSN** 0011-9261
II
SUSPENDED

DESIGN. [Design]. (Jan. 1957)-?. Academic Scholarly Publication. English. Four times a year. $20.00. 11 Amrita Shergil Marg, New Delhi 110003 India. **Tel** 617981. **ED** S Patwant Singh. **Bk Rev. Ad Acc. Circ:** 2,000 (ctrl). ***Absorbed*** *Indian Builder.*
Desc: Architecture, design, art, ideas and archeological features.
Ind/Abst Anbar Account. Finan. Abstr. [Full Txt.]; Anbar Mark. Distr. Abstr. [Full Txt.]; Anbar Top Manage. Abstr. [Full Txt.]; EMBASE; Manage. Bibliogr. Rev.; Oper. Prod. Manage. Abstr. [Full Txt.]; Person. Train. Abstr. [Full Txt.]; Women Manage. Rev. [Full Txt.].

LC NA2599.9 .D47 **ISSN** 0737-5344
DD 720 US
CCC

DESIGN BOOK REVIEW. (DESIGN BOOK REVIEW : DBR.). [Des. book rev.]. **VFOAT** DBR; D.B.R. (Winter 1983)-. Periodical. English. Four times a year. $101.00. Massachusetts Institute of Technology (MIT) Press, 55 Hayward Street, Cambridge MA 02142. **Tel** (617)253-2889, (617)625-8481, FAX (617)258-6779. **ED** Richard Ingersoll. Index available. **Bk Rev. Ad Acc. Circ:** 20,000. available on microfilm and microfiche from University Microfilms International (UMI).
Desc: Review of books on architecture, design, landscape architecture, and urbanism. DBR features interviews, essays, and symposia on specific themes, post-modern urbanism, the rise of architectural publishing, and other topics.
Ind/Abst ARTbibliogr. Mod. (1985-); Avery Index Archit. Period. Suppl. Colum. Univ. (1989-); BHA : Biblio. Hist. Art; Book Rev. Index; Garden Lit. (1992-); Linguist. Lang. Behav. Abstr.; Soc. Plann. Policy Dev. Abstr.; Sociol. Abstr.

LC TH435 .D37 **ISSN** 1054-3163
DD 692/.5/0973 US

DESIGN COST AND DATA. [Des. cost data]. **VFOAT** Design Cost & Data. Vol. 34, No. 3 and 4 (Mar/Apr. 1990)-. Trade Publication. English. Four times a year. $48.00. Lee Rector, 8175 South Virginia Street, Suite 850 A, Reno NV 89511. **Tel** (702)828-1111, FAX (702)828-1503. **ED** Greg Campbell. **Ad Acc, Adv Mgr:** Rob Rizzi. **Circ:** 12,500 (ctrl). ***Continues*** *Design Cost & Data for Building Design Management, 0739-3946.*
Desc: Guide to and for predetermining project cost of building during early design planning for architects and builders.

ISSN 1120-9720
IT
UDC 72

DESIGN DIFFUSION NEWS. [Des. diffus. news]. (1990)-. Periodical. Multiple languages. Nine times a year. L61310. Design Diffusion SRL, Via Lucano 3, 20135 Milan Italy. **Tel** 011 39 2 5516109.

DK

DESIGN DK. Added/Corp Dansk Design Center. (1991)-. Periodical. English (Danish). Six times a year. $96.82. Danish Design Center, H C Andersens Boulevard 18, DK 1553 Copenhagen Denmark. **Tel** 011 45 33146688, FAX 011 45 33320048. **Bk Rev,** (Qty: 3-4). **Circ:** 6,000 (ctrl). ***Continues*** *Design (Copenhagen, Denmark), 0900-3517.*

LC NA7100 .D39
IT

DESIGN E HABITAT. Vol. 1, No. 1 (Jan./Feb. 1973)-. Periodical. Italian (Italian). 7000.

IT

DESIGN/INTERNATIONAL REVIEW. VFOAT Design International Review; Design. No. 1 (Jan./Feb. 1986)-. Periodical. Italian (English). Six times a year. Design/International Review, Via G Paglia 3, 24100 Bergamo Italy.

ISSN 0747-9360
DD 745 US
CCC

DESIGN ISSUES. [Des. issues]. **Added/Corp** University of Illinois at Chicago. School of Art and Design. Vol. 1, No. 1 (Spring 1984)-. Periodical. English. Three times a year. $84.00. Massachusetts Institute of Technology (MIT) Press, 55 Hayward Street, Cambridge MA 02142. **Tel** (617)253-2889, (617)625-8481, FAX (617)258-6779. **ED** Victor Margolin, Dennis Doordan, Richard Buchanan. **Bk Rev. Ad Acc. Circ:** 500. available on microfilm and microfiche from University Microfilms International (UMI).
Desc: Devoted to the questions of criticism, history and theory as they relate to the professions of design.
Ind/Abst ARTbibliogr. Mod. (1985-); BHA : Biblio. Hist. Art; MLA Int. Bibl. Books Artic. Mod. Lang. Lit.

JA

DESIGN JAPAN. (19??)-. Periodical. English. Two times a year. ¥440.00. Japan Industrial Design Organization, 4th Floor Annex, World Trade Center, Minato-ku Tokyo 105 Japan. **Tel** 011 81 3 3435, 011 81 3 5639. ***Continues*** *Design Quarterly Japan.*

LC NA9000 .D15 **ISSN** 1067-9359
DD 711/.05 US
Pr Rev.

DESIGN METHODS. (DESIGN METHODS : THEORIES, RESEARCH, EDUCATION AND PRACTICE.). [Des. methods]. **Added/Corp** Design Methods Institute. California Polytechnic State University, San Luis Obispo. Vol. 26, No.1 (Jan/Mar. 1992)-. Periodical. English. Four times a year (Mar., June, Sept., Dec.). $33.00. Design Methods Institute, PO Box 3, San Luis Obispo CA 93406. **Tel** (510)642-2658. **ED** Donald P. Grant. Index available (Bound in 4th iss., in Dec.). cum. index. **Bk Rev,** (Qty: 1-5). ***Continues*** *Design Methods and Theories, 0147-1147.*

ISSN 0886-8492
DD 720 US

DESIGN QUARTERLY (ATLANTA, GA.). (DESIGN QUARTERLY.). [Des. q.]. **Added/Corp** Heery & Heery. (19??)-. Periodical. English. Four times a year.
Ind/Abst Archit. Period. Index (Summer 1978-Winter 1983).

LC TS171.A1 D474
DD 745.2/0952 JA
TITLE CHANGE

DESIGN QUARTERLY JAPAN. Added/Corp Nihon Sangyo Dezain Shinkokai. (198?)-(19??). Periodical. English. Japan Industrial Design Organization, 4th Floor Annex, World Trade Center, Minato-ku Tokyo 105 Japan. **Tel** 011 81 3 3435, 011 81 3 5639. ***Continued by*** *Design Japan.*

LC NK1 .E9 **ISSN** 0011-9415
DD 745.05 US
CCC

DESIGN QUARTERLY (MINNEAPOLIS, MINN.). (DESIGN QUARTERLY.). [Des. q.]. **Added/Corp** Walker Art Center. No. 29 (1954)-. Periodical. English. Four times a year. $80.00. Massachusetts Institute of Technology (MIT) Press, 55 Hayward Street, Cambridge MA 02142. **Tel** (617)253-2889, (617)625-8481, FAX (617)258-6779. **ED** Robert Jensen. available on microfilm and microfiche from University Microfilms International (UMI). Documents available from The Genuine Article, Magazine Collection, UMI Article Clearinghouse. ***Continues*** *Everyday Art Quarterly.*
Desc: Developments in architecture, product design, and graphic design.
Ind/Abst Acad. Search; Archit. Period. Index (1968-); Art Archaeol. Tech. Abstr.; Art Index; ARTbibliogr. Mod.; Arts Humanit. Citation Index [Full Cov.]; Avery Index Archit. Period. Suppl. Colum. Univ. (1959-199?); BHA : Biblio.

Architecture

Hist. Art; Curr. Contents Arts Humanit.; EP Collect.; Garden Lit. (1992-); Gen. Period. Index (1985-); Homework Help.; INFO-SOUTH Abstr.; Mag. Index Plus (1989-); Mag. Search; MasterFile FullTEXT 1000; MasterFile FullTEXT 350; MasterFile FullTEXT 650; MasterFile FullTEXT (Jan. 1993-); Newsp. Period. Abstr. (1988-); OCLC; Res. Alert [Full Cov.]; Soc. Sci. Cit. Index [Select. Cov.]; Telebase; Mag. Index (1959-?, 1977-); Vocat. Search.

LC NA2750 .D415   **ISSN** 0277-3538
DD 729/.05   US
DESIGN SOLUTIONS. (DESIGN SOLUTIONS : THE JOURNAL OF THE ARCHITECTURAL WOODWORK INSTITUTE.). [Des. solut.]. Vol. 1, No. 1 (Spring 1981)-. English. Six times a year. $18.00. Architectural Woodwork Institute, 13924 Braddock Road, Centreville VA 22020. **Tel** (703)222-1100, FAX (703)820-7839. **ED** Elaine Ferri. Index available. cum. index. **Bk Rev**. **Ad Acc**. **Circ:** 33,000 (ctrl).
   Desc: Features architectural projects and solutions involving architectural woodwork.
   Ind/Abst Constr. Index.

   ISSN 0950-3676
   UK
DESIGN WEEK. See Interior Design and Decoration.

LC NK1490.A1 D47   **ISSN** 0810-6029
   AT
DESIGN WORLD. [Des. world]. No. 1 (March 1983)-. Trade Publication. English. Three times a year. 54.00Aus$ (airmail) New Zealand and Papua New Guinea; 58.00Aus$ (airmail) Malaysia, Singapore and Fiji; 63.00Aus$ (airmail) Far East; 68.00Aus$ (airmail) US, Canada and Middle East; 46.00Aus$ (surface mail) Australia; 74.00Aus$ (airmail), 50.00Aus$ (surface mail) other. Design World, 11 School Road, Ferny Creek Victoria 3786 Australia. **Tel** (03)755 1149, FAX (03)755 1155. **ED** Colin Wood. **Bk Rev**. **Ad Acc**. **Circ:** 14,000.
   Desc: Journal of design in commerce and industry. Interior, graphic, industrial design; corporate identity and design education.

LC NA7205 .D45
DD 728.3/7/0223   US
DESIGNER HOME PLANS. (198?)-. Periodical. English. Three times a year. Woodworker Inc., 274 Riverside Avenue, Westport CT 06880-4823. **Tel** (203)222-1113, FAX (203)221-9255.

LC WMLC L 83/8689   **ISSN** 0897-6228
DD 728   US
DESIGNERS' COLLECTION HOME PLANS. (DESIGNERS' COLLECTION HOME PLANS / HOMESTYLES SOURCE 1 DESIGNERS' NETWORK.). [Des. collect. home plans]. **Added/Corp** HomeStyles Source 1 Designers' Network. **VFOAT** Home Plans; Designers' Collection. (198?)-. Periodical. English. Four times a year. $15.00. Homestyles Publishing Company, 275 Market Street, Suite 521, Minneapolis MN 55405. **Tel** (612)927-6767, (800)547-5570, FAX (612)927-5149. **ED** Dianne Talmage. **Circ:** 65,000.
   Desc: Designed for people who love houses and are looking for new designs concepts and styles. More than 228 new and award-winning homes designed by America's most prestigious designers appear in each issue.

   JA
DESIGNERS WORKSHOP. Japanese (English). Six times a year. ¥6120.00. Bijutsu Shuppan Sha Ltd., 2-36 Kanda Jinbocho Chiyodaku, Tokyo 101 Japan. **Tel** 011 81 3 3234 2151.

   ISSN 1035-0500
   AU
   CEASED
DESIGNINK. **VFOAT** Design Ink. (1990)-(1993). English. Design Editorial Pty Ltd, A.C.N. 005 763 744, 11 School Road, Ferny Creek Victoria 3786 Australia. **Tel** 011 61 3 7551149, FAX 011 61 3 7551155. **ED** Colin Wood. **Bk Rev**. **Ad Acc**. **Adv Mgr:** P Bernadou, **Tel** 61 3 8169895.
   Desc: Keeps you up to date with a full picture of design activity. Includes newsworthy and topical items of interest such as profiles, exhibitions, previews, reviews, and newly released books.

LC NA2835 .D4   **ISSN** 0011-9571
DD 720   GW
   CCC
DETAIL (MUNCHEN). (DETAIL : ZEITSCHRIFT FUER ARCHITEKTUR & BAUDETAIL & EINRICHTUNG.). [Detail]. (1961)-. Trade Publication. German (English). Six times a year. $139.71. Institute of International Architecture - Doc GmbH, Innere Cramer Klett Str 6, D-90403 Nuernberg Germany. **Tel** 011 49 911 5325178. **Bk Rev**. **Ad Acc**. **Circ:** 13,058 (ctrl).
   Desc: Reviews and explains architectural developments internationally with diagrams and troubleshooting editorials.
   Ind/Abst Archit. Period. Index (1977-); Avery Index Archit. Period. Suppl. Colum. Univ. (1990-).

LC N3 .D43   **ISSN** 0012-0375
DD 709   GW
   TITLE CHANGE
DEUTSCHE KUNST UND DENKMALPFLEGE. [Dtsch. Kunst Denkmalpfl.]. **Added/Corp** Vereinigung der Landesdenkmalpfleger in der Bundesrepublik Deutschland. Vol. 10 (1952)-(1993). Periodical. German. Deutscher Kunstverlag, Postfach 190354, D-80603 Munich Germany. **Tel** 011 49 89 1215160. **ED** Johannes Habich and Hans-Herbert Moller. Index available. cum. index. **Bk Rev**. **Circ:** 700. Documents available from The Genuine Article.
   Supersedes Deutsche Kunst und Denkmalpflege; Kunstpflege. **Continued by** Die Denkmalpflege.
   Desc: Architectural art restoration.
   Ind/Abst Archit. Period. Index (1977-1991); Art Archaeol. Tech. Abstr.; ARTbibliogr. Mod.; Arts Humanit. Citation Index [Full Cov.]; Avery Index Archit. Period. Suppl. Colum. Univ. (1989-); BHA : Biblio. Hist. Art; Curr. Contents Arts Humanit.; Res. Alert [Full Cov.]; Soc. Sci. Cit. Index [Select. Cov.].

   ISSN 0012-1215
   GW
DEUTSCHES ARCHITEKTENBLATT. AUSGABE BADEN-WUERTTEMBERG. (DEUTSCHES ARCHITEKTENBLATT.). [Dtsch. Archit.bl. Ausg. Baden-Wuertt.]. **Added/Corp** Bundesarchitektenkammer (Bundesgemeinschaft der Architektenkammern). (1969)-. Trade Publication. German. Twelve times a year. Forum Verlag GmbH, Julius Hoelderstrasse 4, D-70597 Stuttgart Germany. **Tel** 011 49 711 7257414, FAX 011 49 711 7257411. **Circ:** 73,000.
   Desc: Construction, construction damages collection, construction material, presentation of building objects and urban renewal.
   Ind/Abst Avery Index Archit. Period. Suppl. Colum. Univ. (1989-).

   US
DIRECTORY OF AIA FIRMS IN MASSACHUSETTS, THE. **Added/Corp** Boston Society of Architects. American Institute of Architects. **VFOAT** Architectural Firms in Massachusetts. **VAT** Directory of American Institute of Architects Firms in Massachusetts. (1990)-. Directory. English. Boston Society of Architects, 52 Broad Street, Boston MA 02109. **Tel** (617)951-1433 Ext. 221.

LC NA53 .D48   **ISSN** 0363-4531
DD 720/.5/573   US
DIRECTORY OF ARCHITECTURAL FIRMS. Directory. English. $88.32. American Institute of Architects / Washington DC, 1735 New York Avenue Northwest, Washington DC 20006. **Tel** (202)626-7460, FAX (202)626-7587.

LC Z675.A85 D56   **ISSN** 0811-6253
DD 026/.7/002594   AT
DIRECTORY OF ARTS LIBRARIES AND RESOURCE COLLECTIONS IN AUSTRALIA. See Library and Information Sciences.

   ISSN 0848-8134
DD 690/.087   CN
DIRECTORY OF BARRIER-FREE BUILDING PRODUCTS. [Dir. barrier-free build. prod.]. **VFOAT** Barrier-Free Building Products. (1989/90)-. Trade Publication. English. One time a year. $49.95 per vol. Barrier-Free Design Centre, 2075 Bayview Avenue, Toronto Ontario M4N 3M5 Canada.

LC NA11 .A423   **ISSN** 1054-2000
DD 720/.25/73   US
DIRECTORY OF INSTITUTE/COMPONENT OFFICERS. [Dir. inst. compon. off.]. **Main/Corp** American Institute of Architects. **VFOAT** Directory of Institute Component Officers. Directory. English. American Institute of Architects / Washington DC, 1735 New York Avenue Northwest, Washington DC 20006. **Tel** (202)626-7460, FAX (202)626-7587.

LC NA60.G7 D57
DD 350/.00025/41   UK
DIRECTORY OF OFFICIAL ARCHITECTURE & PLANNING. **VAT** Directory of Official Architecture and Planning. (1974/1975)-. Directory. English. One time a year. George Godwin Ltd, House 4, Catherine Street, London WC2B 5JN United Kingdom. **Continues** Directory of Official Architects & Planners, 0070-5977.

LC TA12 .D493
DD 624/.025778   US
DIRECTORY OF REGISTERED ARCHITECTS, PROFESSIONAL ENGINEERS, LAND SURVEYORS, AND ARCHITECTURAL, ENGINEERING AND LAND SURVEYING CORPORATIONS. Directory. English. One time a year. Missouri Board of Architects, Professional Engineers and Land Surveyors, PO Box 184, Jefferson City MO 65101.

LC NA54.V57 D57   **ISSN** 0732-782X
DD 620/.0025/729722   VI
DIRECTORY OF REGISTERED PROFESSIONAL ARCHITECTS, ENGINEERS, AND LAND SURVEYORS. Directory. English. Virgin Islands Board for Architects, Engineers and Land Surveyors, PO Box 476, St Thomas Virgin Islands 00801.

   ISSN 1121-8770
   IT
DISEGNO DI ARCHITETTURA, IL. (1989)-. Italian. Four times a year. L33390. Edizioni Angelo Guerini e Associatión, Via Amatore Sciesa 7, 20135 Milan Italy. **Tel** 011 39 2 5469589, FAX 011 39 2 55191053.

LC NA7205 D58   **ISSN** 0897-6236
DD 728/.37/0222   US
DISTINGUISHED HOME PLANS. HOMES FOR SLOPING SITES. [Disting. home plans]. (19??)-. Periodical. English. Four times a year. $20.00. Homestyles Publishing Company, 275 Market Street, Suite 521, Minneapolis MN 55405. **Tel** (612)927-6767, (800)547-5570, FAX (612)927-5149. **ED** Dianne Talmage. Index available. **Ad Acc**. **Circ:** 70000.
   Desc: America's most popular home plans magazine. Each issue features over 200 pages of newly designed classic and traditional homes.

LC NA1474 .D6   **ISSN** 0420-0810
DD 720   IT
DOCUMENTI DI ARCHITETTURA ARMENA. **Added/Corp** Politecnico di Milano. Facolta di Architettura. Haykakan SSH Gitutyunneri Akademia. **VFOAT** Documents of Armenian Architecture. (1968)-. Monographic series. English (Italian and Armenian). Irregular. Price varies per volume. Om Edizioni, Corte Zappa D Duro 1602, 20123 Venice Italy. **Tel** 011 39 41 5224225. **Circ:** 3,000 (ctrl).
   Desc: Old and medieval Armenian architecture.

   ISSN 0214-9249
   SP
UDC 72
DOCUMENTOS DE ARQUITECTURA ALMERIA. [Doc. arquit.Almeria]. (1987)-. Periodical. Spanish. Three times a year. $93.22. Colegio Arquitectos Almeria, Calle Martinez Campos 29, 04002 Almeria Spain. **Tel** 011 34 1 231255, 231456.

   PE
DOCUMENTOS DE ARQUITECTURA Y URBANISMO : DAU. **Added/Corp** Instituto de Investigacion de Arquitectura y Urbanismo (Peru). **VFOAT** DAU. Vol. 1, No. 1 (1986)-. Periodical. Spanish. Irregular. Documentos de Arquitectura y Urbanismo, Avenue Jose Prado 557, Dpto. 1002, Lima 18, Peru.

   ISSN 0419-5671
   US
DOCUMENTS OF MODERN ARCHITECTURE. 1- 1961-. English. Universe Publishing-Rizzoli, 300 Park Avenue South 5th Floor, New York NY 10010-5313.

   ISSN 0419-5981
   GW
   CEASED
DOKUMENTE DER MODERNEN ARCHITEKTUR. Vol. 1 (1961)-(19??). German (English and French). Karl Kramer Verlag GmbH & Company, Schulze-Delitzsch-Strasse 15, PF 800650, W 7000 Stuttgart 80 Germany. **Tel** 011 49 711 620893, FAX 0711-628955, telex 722203 KKBAUD. **ED** Karl H. Kramer.

LC N4 .D6   **ISSN** 0012-5377
DD 709   IT
DOMUS. See Interior Design and Decoration.

   ISSN 0394-8315
   IT
UDC 72
Pr Rev.
DOSSIER. L'UFFICIO TECNICO. [Doss., UFF. tec.]. **VFOAT** Ufficio Tecnico. Dossier. (1981)-. Periodical. Italian. Four times a year. L64.000 (individuals); L128.000 (institutions). Maggioli Editore, Casella Postale 290, 47037 Rimini Italy. **Tel** 011 39 541 628666, FAX 011 39 541 742217. **Bk Rev**. **Ad Acc**. **Circ:** 6,100 (ctrl).
   Desc: Covers urbanistic and environmental issues.

   ISSN 0759-9048
   FR
DOSSIERS ET DOCUMENTS - INSTITUT FRANCAIS D'ARCHITECTURE. (DOSSIERS ET DOCUMENTS.). [Doss. doc. - Inst. fr. archit.]. **Added/Corp** Institut Francais d'Architecture. (Feb. 1983)-. Periodical. French. Irregular. Le Monde, Svc des Abonnements, BP 50709 75422 Paris Cedex 09 France. **Tel** 011 33 1 2467223.

Architecture

ISSN 1078-7321
DD 346 US
● **DRAFTING DOCUMENTS FOR CONDOMINIUMS, PUDS, AND GOLF COURSE COMMUNITIES.** (DRAFTING DOCUMENTS FOR CONDOMINIUMS, PUDS, AND GOLF COURSE COMMUNITIES : ALI-ABA COURSE OF STUDY MATERIALS.). [Draft. doc. condom. PUDs golf course communities]. **Added/Corp** American Law Institute-American Bar Association Committee on Continuing Professional Education. **VFOAT** ALI-ABA Course of Study Materials; Drafting Documents for Condominiums. (Mar. 25-27, 1993)-. English. One time a year (2 volume set). $150.00. American Law Institute, 4025 Chestnut Street, Philadelphia PA 19104-3099. **Tel** (215)243-1661, (800)253-6397, FAX (215)243-1664. **Continues** Drafting for Planned Unit Developments, Golf Course Communities, and Condominiums.

ISSN 0140-5039
UK
Pr Rev.
EAR. EDINBURGH ARCHITECTURAL RESEARCH. (EAR). [EAR, Edinb. archit. res.]. **Added/Corp** University of Edinburgh. Dept. of Architecture. **VFOAT** E.A.R.; Edinburgh Architecture Research; Edinburgh Architecture Research. (1973)-. English. One time a year. £10.00. University of Edinburgh / Department of Architecture, 20 Chambers Street, Edinburgh EH1 1JZ United Kingdom. **Tel** 011 44 131 6502332.
Ind/Abst Archit. Period. Index (Vol. 5, 1978-); Avery Index Archit. Period. Suppl. Colum. Univ. (19??-19??); BHA : Biblio. Hist. Art.

US
EARTHWORD. See Environmental Issues-Ecology.

AT
EASY LIVING HOMES. (19??)-. English. Six times a year. 23.70Aus$ Australia; 33.10Aus$ other. Australian Consolidated Press Ltd., Private Bag 92615 Symonds St, Auckland New Zealand. **Tel** 011 64 9 3735408, FAX 011 64 9 3022889.

LC NA7205 .E28   **ISSN 0278-2650**
DD 728.3/7/0223
ECONOMY HOME PLANS FOR TODAY!. **Added/Corp** House Plan Headquarters. (19??)-. Periodical. English. House Plan Headquarters Inc, 48 West 48th Street, New York NY 10036.

LC TH6021 .E65   **ISSN 0531-9293**
US
EDRA; PROCEEDINGS OF THE ANNUAL ENVIRONMENTAL DESIGN RESEARCH ASSOCIATION CONFERENCE. **Main/Corp** Environmental Design Research Association. **Added/Corp** Environmental Design Research Association. Proceedings of the Annual Environmental Design Research Association Conference. **VFOAT** Proceedings of the Annual Environmental Design Research Association Conference. 1st (1969)-. Proceedings. English. One time a year. $45.00 (nonmembers); $35.00 (members). Environmental Design Research Association, PO Box 7146, Edmond OK 73083. **Tel** (405)330-4863.
Ind/Abst Psychol. Abstr. (1979-); PsycLit.

LC NA1 .E5   **ISSN 0013-6751**
DD 720.62747 US
EMPIRE STATE ARCHITECT. [Emp. state archit.]. **Added/Corp** New York State Association of Architects. Vol. 1 (Apr. 1941)-. Periodical. English. Four times a year. $30.00. AIA New York State, 235 Lark Street, Albany NY 12210. **Tel** (518)449-3334.
Desc: Jan/Feb issues include list of members of the association.

LC TA   **ISSN 0969-9988**
DD 624 UK
CCC
Pr Rev.
● **ENGINEERING CONSTRUCTION AND ARCHITECTURAL MANAGEMENT.** See Engineering-Civil Engineering.

ISSN 0013-9017
US
ENTRELINEAS. Vol. 1 (Feb./Mar. 1971)-. Periodical. Spanish (English). Irregular. Free on request. Entrelineas, 3201 Southwest Traffic Way, Kansas City MO 64111. available on microfilm from University Microfilms International (UMI).

LC N1 .A13   **ISSN 0393-5183**
DD 720/.917/671 IT
ENVIRONMENTAL DESIGN (ROME, ITALY). (ENVIRONMENTAL DESIGN : JOURNAL OF THE ISLAMIC ENVIRONMENTAL DESIGN RESEARCH CENTRE.). **Added/Corp** Islamic Environmental Design Research Centre (Genzano di Roma, Italy). **VFOAT** AARP Environmental Design; A.A.R.P. Environmental Design; Journal of the Islamic Environmental Design Research Centre. Vol. 1 (1985)-. Periodical. English (Italian). Two times a year. $65.00. Lavis Marketing, 73 Lime Walk Headington, Oxford OX3 7AD United Kingdom. **Tel** 011 44 865 67575. **ED** Attilio Petruciolli. **Bk Rev.** **Circ:** 450. **Continues** AARP, 0308-5597.
Desc: Art and Archaeology Research Papers Environment Design - covers the territory and town architecture in the Islamic countries.
Ind/Abst Archit. Period. Index (1986-).

ISSN 0014-0481
FR
ESPACES ET SOCIETES. See Housing and Urban Development.

ISSN 1130-0124
SP
ESPACIO, TIEMPO Y FORMA. SERIE 7, HISTORIA DEL ARTE : REVISTA DE LA FACULTAD DE GEOGRAFIA E HISTORIA. See The Arts-Art.

ISSN 1182-5510
DD 720/.9714/05 CN
ESQUISSES (MONTREAL). (ESQUISSES : BULLETIN D'INFORMATION DE L'ORDRE DES ARCHITECTES DU QUEBEC.). [Esquisses]. **Added/Corp** Ordre des Architectes du Quebec. Vol. 1, No 1 (April 1990)-. Bulletin. French. Ten times a year. 40.01Can$. Ordre des Architectes du Quebec, 1825 West Rene Levesque, Montreal Quebec H3H 1R4 Canada. **Tel** (514)937-6168. **Continues** Nouvelles OAQ, 0822-6652.

LC NA   **ISSN 1051-1717**
DD 712 US
EXACT CHANGE. [Exact change]. (1985)-. Periodical. English. One time a year. $35.00. Exact Change, PO Box 544, Cambridge MA 02139. **Tel** (617)269-6227, FAX (617)464-0802.

LC NA1 .E94
DD 720/.5 AT
EXEDRA : THE JOURNAL OF THE SCHOOL OF ARCHITECTURE, DEAKIN UNIVERSITY. **Added/Corp** Deakin University. School of Architecture. (1989)-. Periodical. English. Two times a year. Deakin University Press, Deakin University, Geelong Victoria 3217 Australia. **Tel** 011 61 52 472020. Documents available from CASDDS.
Ind/Abst Chem. Abstr.; Zentralbl. Math. Ihre Grenzgeb.

ISSN 1033-1867
AT
Pr Rev.
FABRICATIONS : THE JOURNAL OF THE SOCIETY OF ARCHITECTURAL HISTORIANS, AUSTRALIA & NEW ZEALAND. **Added/Corp** Society of Architectural Historians, Australia and New Zealand. (Dec. 1989)-. Periodical. English. One time a year. 24.67Aus$. University of Canberra, Sahanz Fed PO Box 1, Belconnen ACT 2616 Australia. **Tel** 011 61 6 2012579. **ED** Desley Luscombe. **Bk Rev.**
Ind/Abst Archit. Period. Index (Dec. 1989-).

LC WMLC 93/318   **ISSN 1045-0483**
DD 720 US
FABRICS & ARCHITECTURE. [Fabr. archit.]. **Added/Corp** Industrial Fabrics Association International. **VFOAT** Fabrics and Architecture; F&A. Vol. 1, No. 1 (Summer 1989)-. Trade Publication. English. Seven times a year. $21.00. Industrial Fabrics Association International, 345 Cedar Street, Suite 800, St Paul MN 55101. **Tel** (612)222-2508, (800)225-4324, FAX (612)222-8215, telex TWX (612)222-7862. **ED** Gene Rebeck. cum. index. **Ad Acc.** **Circ:** 8,000 (ctrl).
Desc: Case histories and other articles to provide architects with designs, ideas and technical information on the applications of fabric products in architecture.

ISSN 1199-1321
DD 363.6/9/09712405 CN
FACADE (REGINA). (FACADE / SASKATCHEWAN ARCHITECTURAL HERITAGE SOCIETY.). [Facade]. **Added/Corp** Saskatchewan Architectural Heritage Society. (1987)-. Periodical. English. Four times a year. free to members. Saskatchewan Agricultural Heritage Society, 2326 College Avenue, Regina, Saskatchewan S4P 1C7 Canada.

LC WMLC 93/315   **ISSN 0258-6800**
SZ
FACES. **Added/Corp** Universite de Geneve. Ecole d'Architecture. (19??)-. Periodical. French. Four times a year. $89.58. Faces / Journal d'Architectures, IAUG, Case Postale 387, CH 1211 Geneva 12 Switzerland. **Tel** 011 41 22 7057148, FAX 011 41 22 3112546. **ED** Giairo Daghini (phone: 011 41 22 7057148). Index available. **Ad Acc, Adv Mgr:** M. Staeho, **Tel** 011 41 22 3290140. ctrl circ.

ISSN 1045-7089
DD 690 US
NLM W1; FA185U
FACILITIES PLANNING NEWS. [Facil. planing news]. **VFOAT** FPN. (198?)-. Trade Publication. English. Twelve times a year. $220.00. Tradeline Inc., PO Box 1568, 115 Orinda Way, Orinda CA 94563. **Tel** (510)254-1744, FAX (510)254-2744. **ED** Mr. Lee Ingalls (phone: (510)254-6386). Index available (Free). cum. index. **Bk Rev**, (Qty: 6-8). **Ad Acc, Adv Mgr:** Todd Stone, **Tel** (510)254-1744. **Circ:** 7,000 (ctrl).
Desc: Provides field data on the planning, design and construction of healthcare facilities, R & D labs, biotech facilities, training facilities, computer centers, office, and other related projects. Management perspectives, design and budgetary issues are analyzed.

LC NA4605 .F33   **ISSN 0014-7001**
DD 726.509 US
FAITH & FORM. [Faith form]. **Added/Corp** Guild for Religious Architecture. **VAT** Faith and Form. Vol. 1 (Jan. 1967)-. Periodical. English. Three times a year (Jan., Jun., Sept.). $26.00. Interfaith Forum on Religion Art and Architecture, 1735 New York Avenue Northwest, Washington DC 20006. **Tel** (617)965-3018, (202)626-7305. (**Subscription address:** Faith & Forum, PO Box 51307, Durham NC 27717.) **ED** Betty H. Meyer. **Bk Rev.** **Ad Acc, Adv Mgr:** Konrad Yoes, **Tel** (206)321-8497. **Circ:** 2,000.
Desc: Devoted to creative solutions to today's challenges in art and architectural designs, renovation, restoration and adaptive use of religious buildings of all faiths.
Ind/Abst Avery Index Archit. Period. Suppl. Colum. Univ. (19??-199?).

ISSN 0229-7094
CN
FIFTH COLUMN. (THE FIFTH COLUMN.). [Fifth column]. **Added/Corp** McGill University. Architectural Undergraduate Society. (1980)-. Periodical. English (French). Two times a year (Apr. and Oct.). 14.40Can$. The Fifth Column, 815 Sherbrooke Street West, Suite G4 McDonald Harrington Building, Montreal Canada H3A 2K6 Canada. **Tel** (514)398-8944. **ED** Richard Klopp and Marlene Druker. **Bk Rev.** **Circ:** 500 (ctrl).
Desc: Forum for discussion of architectural issue.
Ind/Abst Archit. Period. Index (1980-); Avery Index Archit. Period. Suppl. Colum. Univ. (19??-199?).

US
FINE ARTS AND ARCHITECTURE [MICROFORM]. See The Arts.

ISSN 0015-3907
US
FLORIDA ARCHITECT. **Added/Corp** American Institute of Architects. Florida Association. (19??)-. Periodical. English. Six times a year. $18.00. Florida Association of American Institute of Architects, PO Box 10388, Tallahassee FL 32302. **Tel** (904)222-7590. **ED** Diane D Greer. **Bk Rev.** **Ad Acc.** **Circ:** 6,000 (ctrl).
Desc: Specifically concerns new and old architecture in Florida. Also new products news and member news section.

ISSN 1040-0893
DD 720 US
FLORIDA ARCHITECTURE (1966). (FLORIDA ARCHITECTURE.). [Florida archit.]. 1966-. Periodical. English. One time a year. $18.00 US; $23.00 other. Florida Architecture, 3009 Kirk Street, Coconut Grove FL 33133. **Tel** (407)573-4242. **ED** Patricia G Ernst. **Ad Acc.** **Circ:** 41,000. **Continues** Architecture International.
Desc: Luxury publication of architecture, interior design, and landscaping of Florida.

US
FOCUS. **Added/Corp** rchitects, Designers, Planners for Social Responsibility. Los Angeles County Chapter. **VFOAT** ADPSR Focus. (19??)-. English. Four times a year. $30.00. ADPSR, 175 Fifth Avenue, Suite 2210, New York NY 10010. **Tel** (212)924-7893.

ISSN 0015-766X
SW
FORM. See Interior Design and Decoration.

FR
FORMES ET STRUCTURES : ARCHITECTURE, GENIE CIVIL, ENVIRONNEMENT. (1991)-. Periodical. French (English). Four times a year. $196.84. Editions AMP, 9 rue de Trevise, 75009 Paris France. **Tel** 011 33 1 47705001, FAX 011 33 1 48009811. **ED** Simone Tayeb. **Circ:** 5,000.
Desc: Covers architectural projects and realizations in France and abroad. A magazine made by and for architects.
Ind/Abst Archit. Period. Index (199?-).

LC NA6 .F67
NE
FORUM (AMSTERDAM, NETHERLANDS : 1984). (FORUM.). **Added/Corp** Genootschap "Architectura et Amicitia"

Architecture

(Amsterdam, Netherlands). **VFOAT** Forum voor Architectuur en Daarmee Verbonden Kunsten. (1984)-. Periodical. Dutch (English). Four times a year. F63.00 Netherlands; F93.00 other. Forum / Netherlands, Waterlooplein 211, 1011 PB Amsterdam Netherlands. **Tel** 011 31 20 6220188. **Continues** Forum Architectuur. **Ind/Abst** Archit. Period. Index (1985-); Avery Index Archit. Period. Suppl. Colum. Univ. (Mar. 1989, Sept. 1990).

IT

FRAMES ARCHITETTURA DEI SERRAMENTI.
(19??)-. Italian. Nine times a year. L79000 Italy; L112000 other. Faenza Editrice, Via P de Crescenzi 44, 48018 Faenza Italy. **Tel** 011 39 546 663488, FAX 011 39 546 660440, telex 550387. **Continues** Frames. Port & Finestre.

LC NA737.W7 F6785

US

FRANK LLOYD WRIGHT QUARTERLY.
Added/Corp Frank Lloyd Wright Foundation. Vol. 1, No. 1 (Spring 1990)-. Periodical. English. Four times a year (Jan., April, July, Oct.). $40.00. Frank Lloyd Wright Foundation, Taliesin West, Scottsdale AZ 85261. **Tel** (602)860-2700, FAX (602)451-0254. **ED** Dixie Legler. **Bk Rev**, (Qty: 8-10). **Continues** Friends of Taliesin. **Desc:** Stories about Wright's life and work, and a national calendar of events and exhibits. **Ind/Abst** Archit. Period. Index (Spring 1990-).

ISSN 0429-5714

DD 720

GW

FRANKFURTER FORSCHUNGEN ZUR ARCHITEKTURGESCHICHTE. Vol. 1 (1957)-.
German. Irregular. Gebrueder Mann Verlag, Lindenstrasse 76, D-10969 Berlin Germany. **Tel** 011 49 30 25913589, telex 183723. **ED** Wolfram Prinz. **Ad Acc. Circ:** 800. **Desc:** Publishes scientific articles in the field of art history, which cover work done at the University of Frankfurt or in cooperation with the University.

ISSN 0890-9717

DD 720

US

FRIENDS OF KEBYAR. [Friends Kebyar].
VFOAT FOK. (Jan. 1983)-. Periodical. English. Irregular. $35.00. Friends of Kebyar Inc., 7430 Southwest Canyon Drive, Portland OR 97225. **Tel** (503)292-2684. **ED** Jean Eckenfels (editor's address: 5344 South Hyde Park Boulevard, Chicago, IL 60615). **Bk Rev. Circ:** 400. **Desc:** A journal of avant-garde architecture. A network of architects, artists and those interested in the creative and adventurous horizons beyond the main-stream. **Ind/Abst** Avery Index Archit. Period. Suppl. Colum. Univ. (Oct. 1989-).

LC NA109.E9 C68a   ISSN 0252-0842
DD 363.6/9/094

FR

FUTURE FOR OUR PAST / COUNCIL OF EUROPE, A. Main/Corp
Council of Europe. (19??)-. Periodical. English. Council of Europe, avenue de l'Europe Palais EU, 67075 Strasbourg Cedex 01 France. **Tel** 011 33 88 412000. **Ind/Abst** Museum Abstr.

ISSN 0389-0066

JA

GA DOCUMENT. [GA doc.].
VFOAT Global Architecture. (1980)-. Periodical. English (Japanese). Four times a year. Edita Tokyo Co Ltd, 3-12-14 Sendagaya Shibuy-ku, Tokyo Japan. **(Subscription address:** GA International Company Ltd, 594 Broadway 3rd Floor, New York NY 10012. **Tel** (212)274-9683.) **Ind/Abst** Archit. Period. Index (1980-); Art Index; Avery Index Archit. Period. Suppl. Colum. Univ. (1990-).

JA

GA HOUSES. VFOAT
Global Architecture Houses; G.A. Houses. Vol. 1 (1976)-. Periodical. Japanese (English; summaries and/or abstracts in English). **(Subscription address:** Maruzen Company Ltd., PO Box 5050, Import & Export Department, Tokyo 100 31 Japan. **Tel** 011 81 3 32789224.) **Ind/Abst** Archit. Period. Index; Avery Index Archit. Period. Suppl. Colum. Univ. (Mar. 1990-).

LC NA7205 .G35   ISSN 0899-4404
DD 728.3/7/0222

US

GALLERY OF FINE HOME PLANS. [Gallery fine home plans].
English. $9.50. The Garlinghouse Company, PO Box 1717, Middletown CT 06457. **Tel** (203)343-5970, FAX (203)343-5984. **ED** Ed Rothwell. **Bk Rev. Ad Acc.** ctrl circ. **Desc:** Features over 130 home plan designs with hundreds of illustrations. The designs cover a broad range of styles and tastes.

LC WMLC 93/883   ISSN 1069-3084
DD 635

US

GARDEN, DECK & LANDSCAPE PLANNER. [Gard. deck landsc. plan.].
VFOAT Garden, Deck and Landscape Planner; Better Homes and Gardens Garden, Deck & Landscape Planner. (19??)-. English. Four times a year. Meredith Corporation, Locust at 17th, Des Moines IA 50309. **Tel** (515)284-3000, FAX (515)284-2568.

LC WMLC 93/4494

US

GARDEN, DECK & LANDSCAPE PLANNER. VFOAT
Garden, Deck and Landscape Planner; Better Homes and Gardens Garden, Deck & Landscape Planner. (19??)-. English. Four times a year. Meredith Corporation, Locust at 17th, Des Moines IA 50309. **Tel** (515)284-3000, FAX (515)284-2568.

ISSN 0394-1132

IT

GB PROGETTI. (1990)-.
Periodical. English. Eleven times a year. L81750. Editrice Progetti, Viale Stelvio 57, 20159 Milan Italy. **Tel** 011 39 2 66802114. **Continues** Gran Bazaar.

UK

GENIUS OF ARCHITECTURE. (1984)-.
Monographic series. English. Price varies per volume. Unwin Hyman Ltd., 15 17 Broadwick Street, London W1V 1FP United Kingdom. **Tel** 011 44 171 4393126, FAX 011 44 171 7343884. **Continues** Studies in Architecture (George Allen & Unwin).

LC NA966 .G46   ISSN 0963-1070
DD 720/.942/09033

UK

GEORGIAN GROUP JOURNAL, THE.
Added/Corp Georgian Group (London, England). **VFOAT** Group Journal; Report and Journal. (19??)-. Periodical. English. One time a year. $21.66. Georgian Group, 37 Spital Fields Square, London E1 6DY United Kingdom. **Tel** 011 44 71 3771722. **Continues** Georgian Group (London, England). Report and Journal. **Ind/Abst** Archit. Period. Index (1991-); BHA : Biblio. Hist. Art.

LC N6280 .G4   ISSN 0016-920X

US

GESTA (FORT TRYON PARK, N.Y.). See
The Arts-Art.

UK

GLASS & GLAZING. (19??)-.
Periodical. English. Twelve times a year. £30.00 Europe; £42.00 other. EMAP Readerlink, Audit House, 260 Field End Road, Ruislip Middlesex HA9 9LT United Kingdom. **Tel** 011 44 1773 63100, FAX 011 44 1733 87367.

ISSN 0261-0329

UK

GLAZED EXPRESSIONS. [Glaz. expr.]. (1981)-.
Academic Scholarly Publication. English. Two times a year. $40.00 (Tiles and Architectural Ceramics Society membership). Tiles & Architectural Ceramics Society, 3 Browns Rise Buckland Common, Tring Hertfordshire HP23 6NJ United Kingdom. **Tel** 011 44 1494 758687. **(Subscription address:** Tile Heritage Foundation, PO Box 1850, Healdsburg CA 95448. **Tel** (707)431-8453.) **ED** Chris Blanchett. Index available. cum. index. **Bk Rev**, (Qty: 4 or 5). **Circ:** 400. Documents available from BLDSC. **Desc:** Caters to those interested in manufacture, preservation, conservation, history, collection, and use of tiles, terra cotta, and other building ceramics. **Ind/Abst** Avery Index Archit. Period. Suppl. Colum. Univ. (Spring 1989); World Ceram. Abstr.

ISSN 0348-4114

SW

GOTHENBURG STUDIES IN ART & ARCHITECTURE. See The Arts-Art.

ISSN 1047-6997

DD 338

US

GREENLINE GUIDE TO RESIDENTIAL ARCHITECTS. [Greenline guide resid. archit.].
VFOAT Greenline Guide. (1990)-. Periodical. English. One time a year. $34.95. Greenline Marketing Group Inc, 29 East 19th, New York NY 10003. **Tel** (800)733-7441. **ED** Richard O'Neill. **Desc:** Approximately 3,000 US architectural firms that do residential work.

ISSN 1032-867X

DD 728.3709944

AT

GREGORY'S BEST PROJECT & KIT HOMES. [Gregory's best proj. kit homes]. (1989)-.
English. Two times a year. 9.90Aus$ Australia; 19.90NZ$ New Zealand; 17.00Aus$ other. Australian Consolidated Press Ltd., Private Bag 92615 Symonds St, Auckland New Zealand. **Tel** 011 64 9 3735408, FAX 011 64 9 3022889.

ISSN 0383-7335

DD 720/.9716/005

CN

GRIFFIN (HALIFAX). (THE GRIFFIN.). Vol. 1 (Feb./March 1976)-.
Periodical. English. Heritage Trust of Nova Scotia, PO Box 217, Halifax NS B3J 2N3 Canada. **Supersedes** Heritage Trust of Nova Scotia. Newsletter, 0440-713X.

ISSN 0746-3677

US

GSD NEWS (1983). (GSD NEWS.). [GSD news].
Added/Corp Harvard University. Graduate School of Design. **VFOAT** G.S.D. News. **VAT** Graduate School of Design News. Vol. 12, No. 1 (Sept./Oct. 1983)-. Periodical. English. Three times a year. $25.00. Harvard University Graduate School of Design, Gund Hall, 48 Quincy Street, Cambridge MA 02138. **Tel** (617)495-4315. **ED** Debra Edelstein. **Circ:** 10,000 (ctrl). **Continues** Harvard University. Graduate School of Design. HGSD News, 0193-6107. **Desc:** A publication for alumni, students, faculty and other design professionals of Harvard University Graduate School of Design. Articles on school activities and academic programs. **Ind/Abst** Archit. Period. Index; Avery Index Archit. Period. Suppl. Colum. Univ.

US

●GUIDE TO ARCHITECTURE SCHOOLS.
(1994)-. English. Association of Collegiate Schools of Architecture, 1735 New York Avenue Northwest, Washington DC 20006. **Tel** (202)785-2324, (800)232-2724. **Continues** Guide to Architecture Schools in North America.

LC SB469.43.U6 G84   ISSN 0882-4444
DD 712/.07/1173

US

GUIDE TO EDUCATIONAL PROGRAMS IN LANDSCAPE ARCHITECTURE, A.
[Guide educ. programs landsc. archit.]. **Added/Corp** American Society of Landscape Architects. Professional Practice Institute. **VFOAT** Landscape Architecture. (1985)-. English. Every 2 years. American Society of Landscape Architects, 4401 Connecticut Avenue Northwest, 5th Floor, Washington DC 20008. **Tel** (202)686-2752.

ISSN 0740-8102

US

GUIDE TO GRADUATE DEGREE PROGRAMS IN ARCHITECTURAL HISTORY.
[Guide grad. degree programs archit. hist.]. **Added/Corp** Society of Architectural Historians. (1982)-. English. Every 2 years. $6.00. Society of Architectural Historians, 1232 Pine Street, Philadelphia PA 19107. **Tel** (215)735-0224.

LC DA875 .G84
DD 914.11/04558

UK

GUIDE TO OVER 100 PROPERTIES. See History.

US

GUIDELINES LETTER. Vol. 7, No. 4 (Apr. 1978)-.
Periodical. English. Twelve times a year. $56.00. Guidelines / California, PO Box 456, Orinda CA 94563. **Tel** (510)299-1323, (800)634-7779, FAX (510)299-0181. **ED** Fred A. Stitt. **Circ:** 1,100. **Continues** Guidelines Architectural Letter. **Desc:** New directions and techniques in the design professions.

PK

HABITAT PAKISTAN : A JOURNAL OF ARCHITECTURE, PLANNING, ENVIRONMENT, AND THE ARTS IN ASIA.
VFOAT Habitat; HP. Vol. 1 (1986)-. Periodical. English. $25.00/$30.00. Habitat Pakistan, PO Box 12713, Pechs Karachi-2909 Pakistan. **Ind/Abst** Archit. Period. Index (1986-).

LC NA7126 .H3
DD 728/.022/2

IT

HABITATION SPACE. Vol. 1 (1979)-. English
(French, German, Italian and Spanish). Habitation Space International, Milan Italy.

ISSN 0724-6528

UDC 72

GW

HAEUSER. [Haeuser].
VFOAT Houses; Maisons; Casas; Case; Huizen. (197?)-. Periodical. German. Six times a year. $79.22. Gruner und Jahr Ag & Co, Abonnenten Service, D-20080 Hamburg Germany. **Tel** 011 49 40 37030, FAX 011 49 40 37035657. **(Subscription address:** Deutscher Pressevertrieb Buch, POB 101602 Hansa GMBH, D-20010 Hamburg Germany. **Tel** 011 49 40 23711249.) **ED** Horst Rasch. **Bk Rev. Ad Acc. Circ:** 72,000. **Desc:** Covers international housing and agricultural trends.

KO

HANGUK DIJAIN CHONGNAM. Added/Corp
Dijain Sinmunsa (Seoul, Korea). **VFOAT** Korea Design Annual. (1992)-. Korean. Dijhain Sinmunsa, 168-4 Tonggyo-Dong, Mapo-Ku Seol Korea.

Architecture

LC N1 .H34
DD 720/.5
ISSN 0194-3650
US
CCC
CEASED

HARVARD ARCHITECTURE REVIEW, THE. [Harvard archit. rev.]. **Added/Corp** Harvard University. Graduate School of Design. Vol. 1 (Spring 1980)-Vol. 9, (1993). Periodical. English. Rizzoli International Publishing Inc, 300 Park Avenue South, New York NY 10010. **Tel** (212)387-3500, (800)462-2387, **FAX** (212)982-3866. Documents available from The Genuine Article.
Ind/Abst Archit. Period. Index (1980-); Art Index; Arts Humanit. Citation Index (19??-19??) [Full Cov.]; Avery Index Archit. Period. Suppl. Colum. Univ. (19??-199?); BHA : Biblio. Hist. Art; Curr. Contents Arts Humanit.; J. Plan. Lit.; Res. Alert [Full Cov.].

DD 720
ISSN 0191-8311
US
TITLE CHANGE

HAWAII ARCHITECT. [Hawaii archit.]. **Added/Corp** American Institute of Architects. Hawaii Society. (1972)-(19??). Periodical. English. PMP Company Ltd., 1034 Kilani Avenue Suite 108, Wahiawa HI 96786. **Tel** (808)621-8200, **FAX** (808)622-3025. **ED** Peggi Murchison. **Ad Acc. Circ:** 3,500. **Continues** Kaha Kii. **Continued by** Hawaii Pacific Architect.
Desc: Articles and photographs of interest to architects, engineers, interior designers, contractors, and developers; publication of Hawaii Society, American Institute of Architects.

US

HAWAII PACIFIC ARCHITECT. (19??)-. English. Twelve times a year. $24.00. PMP Company Ltd., 1034 Kilani Avenue Suite 108, Wahiawa HI 96786. **Tel** (808)621-8200, **FAX** (808)622-3025. **Continues** Hawaii Architect.

ISSN 0017-9515
NE

UDC 7.02

HEENSCHUT. (1924)-. Periodical. Dutch. Six times a year. F90.00 (includes membership). Heemschut, Niewezijds Kolk 28, 1012 PV Amsterdam Netherlands. **Tel** 31 20 6225292, **FAX** 31 20 0240571. **ED** T. Kamerking. Index available (bound in second issue). **Bk Rev**, (Qty: 30-40). **Ad Acc, Adv Mgr:** A Moolenaak, **Tel** 31 21 5482211. **Circ:** 9,000 (ctrl).
Ind/Abst Archit. Period. Index (Jan. 1979-Dec. 1983).

ISSN 1195-5899
CN

●**HERITAGE CANADA (1993).** (HERITAGE CANADA.). [Herit. Can.]. **Added/Corp** Heritage Canada. **VFOAT** Heritage Canada. Vol. 1, No. 1 (Sept./Oct. 1993)-. Periodical. English (French). Five times a year. 25.00Can$. Heritage Canada, 412 MacLaren, Ottawa Ontario K2P 0M8 Canada. **Tel** (613)237-1066, **FAX** (613)237-5987. **ED** Veronica Vaillancourt. **Bk Rev. Circ:** 3,000. **Continues** Impact, the Voice of the Canadian Heritage Network, 0840-9676.

ISSN 0103-626X
AT

HERITAGE NEWS (CANBERRA, A.C.T.). (HERITAGE NEWS.). **Added/Corp** Australian Heritage Commission. Vol. 11, No. 3 (Nov. 1988)-. Periodical. English. Four times a year. Free on request. Australian Heritage Commission, 53 Blackall Street, Barton ACT 2601 Australia. **Tel** 011 61 6 2712111, **FAX** 011 61 6 2732395. **ED** James Morrison, Australian Heritage Commission, GPO Box 1567, Canberra Australia; Telephone: 11 61 6 2712170. ctrl circ. **Continues** Heritage Newsletter (Canberra, A.C.T.), 0313-6701.

LC HT243.G7 H47
DD 307/.0941/05
ISSN 0261-1988
UK
TITLE CHANGE

HERITAGE OUTLOOK. (HERITAGE OUTLOOK : THE JOURNAL OF THE CIVIC TRUST.). [Herit. outlook]. **Added/Corp** Civic Trust. Vol. 1, No. 1 (Jan./Feb. 1981)-(1993). Periodical. English. Heritage Outlook, 17 Carlton House Terrace, London SW1Y 5AW United Kingdom. **Tel** 011 44 171 9300914, **FAX** 011 44 171 3210180. **ED** Angela Carvill. Index available. cum. index. **Bk Rev. Ad Acc. Circ:** 3,000 (ctrl). **Continues** Civic Trust News. **Continued by** Urban Focus. Journal of Civic Trust, 0967-4764.
Desc: The conservation of both the built and natural environment including urban regeneration, countryside preservation, legislation and the work of local amenity societies.
Ind/Abst Avery Index Archit. Period. Suppl. Colum. Univ.

ISSN 0394-2783
IT
SUSPENDED

HINTERLAND. [Hinterland]. Year 1- Dec. 1977/Jan. 1978-?. Periodical. Italian. Irregular. $17.82. Hinterland, Via Revere 7, 20123 Milan Italy.
Ind/Abst Archit. Period. Index (1977/1978-).

ISSN 1067-4284
US

DD 709

HISTORIANS OF NETHERLANDISH ART NEWSLETTER. See The Arts-Art.

UK

HISTORIC HOUSE. (19??)-. English. Twelve times a year. £40.00. Hall McCartney Ltd, PO Box 21, Unit 7 Campus 5, Hertfordshire SG6 2JF United Kingdom. **Tel** 011 44 1462 675848, **FAX** 011 44 1462 679356.
Ind/Abst Archit. Period. Index (Spring 1985-); Museum Abstr.

DD 973
ISSN 1074-567X
US

HISTORIC HUNTSVILLE QUARTERLY OF LOCAL ARCHITECTURE AND PRESERVATION, THE. [Hist. Huntsv. q. local archit. preserv.]. **Added/Corp** Historic Huntsville Foundation. **VFOAT** Historic Huntsville Quarterly. (19??)-. Periodical. English. Four times a year. $14.00. Historic Huntsville Foundation, PO Box 786, Huntsville AL 35804. **Tel** (205)539-2817. **ED** Elise Stephens. **Circ:** 800 (ctrl).
Desc: Deals with the preservation of architecture.

LC NA106 .P75
DD 363
ISSN 1056-6309
US

HISTORIC PRESERVATION FORUM. See History.

SZ

HOCHPARTERRE. See Engineering-Industrial Engineering.

LC TH4805 .H653
DD 728
ISSN 0194-0627
US

HOME PLAN IDEAS. See Building and Construction.

LC NA7205 .H647
DD 728/.37/0222
ISSN 1040-547X
US

HOME PLANNER. See Building and Construction.

LC NA7100 .H524
DD 728.3
ISSN 0360-2079
US

HOME PLANNING & DESIGN. VAT Home Planning and Design. (19??)-. English. $1.60. Hudson Home Publications, 175 S San Antonio Rd., Los Altos CA 94022. **Tel** (310)937-5486.

LC NA7100 .H525
DD 728.3
ISSN 0364-653X
US

HOME PLANS & PROJECTS. VAT Home Plans and Projects. English. $1.60 single issue. Hudson Home Publications, 175 S San Antonio Rd., Los Altos CA 94022. **Tel** (310)937-5486.

LC NA7205 .H653
DD 728.3/7/0223
ISSN 0899-4374
US
CEASED

HOME PLANS GUIDE. [Home plans guide]. **Added/Corp** Garlinghouse Company. **VFOAT** Garlinghouse Home Plans Guide. (19??)-(Oct. 1995). English. The Garlinghouse Company, PO Box 1717, Middletown CT 06457. **Tel** (203)343-5970, **FAX** (203)343-5984. **ED** Ed Rothwell. **Bk Rev. Ad Acc.** ctrl circ.
Desc: Features home plan designs with illustrations. The designs cover a broad range of styles and tastes.

LC NA7205 .H656
DD 728
ISSN 0899-4366
US
CEASED

HOME PLANS TO BUILD. [Home plans build]. **Added/Corp** Garlinghouse Company. **VFOAT** Home Plans. (19??)-(Jan. 1996). English. Four times a year. $11.80 US; $20.20 Canada, Mexico, and Puerto Rico; $28.80 other. The Garlinghouse Company, PO Box 1717, Middletown CT 06457. **Tel** (203)343-5970, **FAX** (203)343-5984. **ED** Nancy Garlinghouse. **Ad Acc, Adv Mgr:** Jeff Posner, **Tel** (212)686-8042. ctrl circ.
Desc: Features over 130 home plan designs with hundreds of illustrations. The designs cover a broad range of styles and tastes.

LC TH4816 .H654
DD 643/.7/0299
ISSN 1043-8831
US

HOME-TECH REMODELING AND RENOVATION COST ESTIMATOR. See Interior Design and Decoration.

DD 690/.8/05
ISSN 1187-0974
CN

HOMES & COTTAGES. [Homes cottag.]. **VFOAT** Homes and Cottages. (1991)-. Trade Publication. English. Eight times a year. 14.98Can$ Canada; 29.96Can$ other. In-Home Show Ltd, Suite D, 6557 Mississauga Road, Mississauga, Ontario, L5N 1A6 Canada. **Tel** (905)567-1440, **FAX** (905)567-1442. **ED** Janica E. Naisby. **Bk Rev. Ad Acc. Circ:** 54,000. **Continues** The In-Home Show News., 1186-6160.

LC NA7574 .H56
DD 728
ISSN 0364-6548
US

HOMES FOR LEISURE LIVING. English. $1.60 single issue. Hudson Home Publications, 175 S San Antonio Rd., Los Altos CA 94022. **Tel** (310)937-5486.

LC NA7205 .H675
DD 728/.37/0222
ISSN 0897-621X
US

HOMESTYLES HOME PLANS. VFOAT Homestyles. (1986)-. Periodical. English. Four times a year. $17.50. Homestyles Publishing, 275 Market Street, Suite 521, Minneapolis MN 55405. **Tel** (800)547-5570, (612)927-6767. **Continues** Homestyles.
Desc: Newly designed recreational, vacation, starter and retirement homes. The focus is on energy efficient, economical homes and homes for "do-it-yourselfers."

LC NA
DD 720
US

HONOR AWARDS PROGRAM. Main/Corp American Institute of Architects. Seattle Chapter. **Added/Corp** American Institute of Architects. Seattle Chapter. Annual Report. Seattle Architectural Foundation. Annual Report. (1976)-. English.

LC NA2340 .H665
DD 720/.973/05
ISSN 1063-4118
US

HONORS AND AWARDS PROGRAM. [Honors awards prog.]. **Added/Corp** American Institute of Architects. (19??)-. English. Irregular. American Institute of Architects / Washington DC, 1735 New York Avenue Northwest, Washington DC 20006. **Tel** (202)626-7460, **FAX** (202)626-7587.

ISSN 1121-0001
IT

UDC 728.5

HOTEL DOMANI. [Hotel domani]. **VFOAT** Hoteldomani. (1973)-. Periodical. Italian. Twelve times a year. L47690. Tecniche Nuove SPA, Via Ciro Menotti 14, 20129 Milan Italy. **Tel** 011 39 2 75701, **FAX** 011 39 2 7570205, telex 334647 TECHS I.

LC NA7100 .H6
DD 640/.5
ISSN 0018-6406
US
CEASED

HOUSE & GARDEN (NEW YORK). See Interior Design and Decoration.

LC NA7100 .H65
ISSN 0018-6422
US

HOUSE BEAUTIFUL. [House beautiful]. Vol. 1 (Dec. 1896)-. Periodical. English. Twelve times a year. $19.97. The Hearst Corporation, 250 West 55th Street, New York NY 10019. **Tel** (212)649-4014, (800)925-0485. **(Subscription address:** CDS Agency Hard Copy, PO Box 4966, Des Moines IA 50340. **Tel** (515)247-7569.) **Ad Acc.** available on microfilm and microfiche from University Microfilms International (UMI); available on an online database (file 647/Full-Text) from DIALOG. Documents available from UMI Article Clearinghouse, Magazine Collection. **Absorbed** Domestic Science Monthly; Indoors and Out; Modern Homes; American Suburbs and Home and Field.
Desc: Covers travel, food, entertainment, architecture, remodeling, decorating, and gardening features.
Ind/Abst Acad. Abstr. Full Text Elite; Acad. Abstr.; Acad. Search; Access (1980-1988); Avery Index Archit. Period. Suppl. Colum. Univ.; Consum. Index Prod. Eval. Inf. Source; EP Collect.; Garden Lit. (1992-); Gen. Period. Index (1985-); Homework Help.; INFO-SOUTH Abstr.; Mag. Artic. Summar. Elite; Mag. Artic. Summar. Select; Mag. Artic. Summar. CD-ROM; Mag. Index Plus (1989-); Mag. Index. Sel. (1986-); Mag. Search; MasterFile FullTEXT 1000; MasterFile FullTEXT 350; MasterFile FullTEXT 650; MasterFile FullTEXT (Jan. 1984-); Newsp. Period. Abstr. (1988-); OCLC; Pub. Lib. FullTEXT; Read. Guide Period. Lit.; Telebase; Mag. Index (1977-); Vocat. Search; World Mag. Bank.

US

HOUSE BEAUTIFUL'S HOME BUILDING. See Building and Construction.

US

HOUSE BEAUTIFUL'S HOUSES AND PLANS. VFOAT Houses and Plans. (19??)-. English. Five times a year. The Hearst Corporation, 250 West 55th Street, New York NY 10019. **Tel** (212)649-4014, (800)925-0485. **Ad Acc. Continues** Architecture, Domestic.
Desc: Each issue features professional designed homes of major styles. Comes with blueprints and other specifications available for purchase.

LC NA7127 .H832
DD 728.37
US

HOUSE PLAN FAVORITES. English. One time a year. $2.95 single issues. Archway Press Inc., 19 West 44th Street, New York NY 10036. **Tel** (212)757-5580.

Architecture

LC NA7205 .H686
DD 728/.37/0222 US
HOUSE PLANS. VFOAT PB House Plans. **VAT** Professional builder house plans. (19??)-. English. Twelve times a year. $195.95. Cahners Publishing Company, 249 West 17th Street, New York NY 10011. **Tel** (212)645-0067, FAX (212)242-6987. **ED** Ed Fitch.

LC NA7205 .H687 **ISSN** 1049-4634
DD 728/.37/0222 US
HOUSE PLANS FOR BETTER LIVING. [House Plans Better Living]. **Added/Corp** Home Planners, Inc. (19??)-. English. Irregular. Home Planners Inc / Arizona, 3275 West Ina Road, Suite 110, Tucson AZ 85741.

LC NA7328 .H77
DD 728/.0941 UK
HOUSING DESIGN AWARDS. Added/Corp Great Britain. Dept. of the Environment. NHBC (Council : Great Britain) Royal Institute of British Architects. Vol. 1, No. 1 (19??)-. English. Irregular (every 2 years). Building Publishers Ltd, Builder House, London E14 9BR United Kingdom.

IR
HUNAR VA MIMARI. ART AND ARCHITECTURE. VFOAT Art and Architecture.; Hunr o Mamari. (19??)-. Periodical. Persian. Six times a year.
Ind/Abst Archit. Period. Index (Mar./July 1977-Apr./July 1979).

ISSN 0161-1895
US
I.D.E.A.S. INTERIORS, DESIGN, ENVIRONMENT, ARTS, STRUCTURES. See Interior Design and Decoration.

LC D910.5 .I57a
DD 940/.05 NE
IBI BULLETIN. Added/Corp International Castles Institute. **VFOAT** International Castles Institute Bulletin; Bulletin. No. 43 (1985)-. Bulletin. English (French and German). One time a year. $30.83. International Castles Institute, Lange Voorhout 35, 2514 EC Hague Netherlands. **Tel** 011 31 70 3560333. **Continues** International Castles Institute. Bulletin, 1011-1093.
Ind/Abst Archit. Period. Index (No. 46, 1988/1989-); BHA : Biblio. Hist. Art.

ISSN 0844-1901
DD 720/.74 NE
ICAM NEWS. (ICAMNEWS / INTERNATIONAL CONFERENCE OF ARCHITECTURAL MUSEUMS.). [ICAM news]. **Added/Corp** International Confederation of Architectural Museums. **VAT** International Confederation of Architectural Museums News. (Oct./Mar. 1979)-. Periodical. English. Two times a year (June & December). $40.00. Dutch Architectural Institute, Postbus 237, 3000 AE Rotterdam Netherlands. **Tel** 011 31 10 4361155, FAX 011 31 10 436697557. **ED** R. Brouwers (editor's address: Museumpark 25, 3015 CB Rotterdam, Netherlands; telephone: 011 31 10 4401200). ctrl circ. **Continues** ICAM, 0844-1898.
Ind/Abst Archit. Period. Index (Apr./Sept. 1980-).

ISSN 1188-5092
DD 363.6/9/097105 CN
ICOMOS CANADA BULLETIN. [ICOMOS Can. bull.]. **Added/Corp** ICOMOS Canada. **VFOAT** Bulletin ICOMOS Canada. **VAT** International Council of Monuments and Sites Canada Bulletin. (1992)-. Bulletin. English (French). Three times a year. Free to members. ICOMOS Canada, PO Box 737, Station B, Ottawa, Ontario K1P 5R4 Canada. **Continues** Bulletin (ICOMOS Canada)., 1196-233X; **Absorbed** Momentum (Ottawa, Ont.)., 1196-2348.

LC WMLC 93/1891
FR
ICOMOS NEWS. Periodical. French. Three times a year. $32.81. ICOMOS, 75 rue du Temple, 75003 Paris France. **Tel** 011 33 1 42773576. **Continues** ICOMOS / Information (0394-218X).

ISSN 0217-4995
SI
ID. Vol. 9, No. 4 (Aug./Sept. 1991)-. Periodical. English. Six times a year. Metropolitan Publishing, 61A/65A EU Court, Stamford Road, Singapore 0617. **Continues** Interior Digest.

LC NA7205 .I34 **ISSN** 1049-2968
DD 728/.37/0222 US
IDEAL HOME PLANS. [Ideal home plans]. **VFOAT** Home Plans. (19??)-. English. One time a year. $1.95. Archway Press Inc, 19th West 44th Street, New York NY 10036. **Tel** (212)757-5580. ctrl circ.
Desc: Contains perspective renderings and floor plans of single family detached homes.

LC NA730.I3 I45 **ISSN** 0747-6345
DD 720/.25/773 US
ILLINOIS ARCHITECTURE REFERENCE DIRECTORY, THE. VFOAT Architecture Reference Directory. 1984-. Directory. English. One time a year. $20.00. Metropolitan Press Publications Inc., 1165 North Clark Street, 2nd Floor, Chicago IL 60610. **Tel** (312)280-0131. **ED** Christian K Laine. Index available. **Bk Rev. Ad Acc. Circ:** 10,000.
Desc: A comprehensive listing of all arts, architecture, urban planning, preservationist, and landmark organizations in the United States. A special editorial on a small Illinois city and a listing of Illinois architects.

LC NA7205 .I44 **ISSN** 0197-7806
DD 728.3/7/0223 US
ILLUSTRATED HOUSE PLANS. (19??)-. English. Archway Press Inc., 19 West 44th Street, New York NY 10036. **Tel** (212)757-5580.

LC KF480.Z9 I47
DD 346.7301/3 347.30613 US
IMPLEMENTING THE AMERICANS WITH DISABILITIES ACT. See Physically Impaired.

ISSN 0308-8154
UK
IN-HOUSE. [In-house]. (1976)-. Periodical. English. Four times a year.
Ind/Abst Archit. Period. Index (Nov. 1977-Nov. 1981).

LC NA17.Z3 Z314 **ISSN** 1015-0862
DD 720/.96894 ZA
IN SITU (LUSAKA). (IN SITU : JOURNAL OF THE ZAMBIA INSTITUTE OF ARCHITECTS.). [In situ]. **Added/Corp** Zambia Institute of Architects. Surveyors Institute of Zambia. (19??)-. Periodical. English. Four times a year. In Situ, PO Box 721, Lusaka Zambia. Documents available from The Genuine Article.
Ind/Abst Archit. Period. Index (Dec. 1977-Nov. 1984); Avery Index Archit. Period. Suppl. Colum. Univ. (19??-19??); Res. Alert [Full Cov.].

ISSN 0141-0415
UK
IN TRUST. (1975)-. English. Four times a year.
Ind/Abst Archit. Period. Index (No. 6, 1978-).

LC Z5941 .I46 NA25 **ISSN** 0194-1356
DD 016.72 US
INDEX TO ARCHITECTURE SERIES--BIBLIOGRAPHY. No. A1/A29 (June/Dec. 1978)-. Bibliography. English. Two times a year. $30.00. Vance Bibliographies, PO Box 229, Monticello IL 61856. **Tel** (217)762-3821. **ED** Mary Vance. Index available. cum. index. **Circ:** 100.
Desc: Listed by author, title, subject and issue number. January issue covers previous year, July issue covers January-June of current year.

LC NA1 .I46 **ISSN** 0019-4409
II
INDIAN ARCHITECT, THE. [Indian archit.]. (1959)-. Trade Publication. English. Twelve times a year. (**Subscription** address: Prints India, 11 Darya Ganj, New Delhi 110002 India. **Tel** 011 91 11 3268645, FAX 011 91 11 3275542, telex 31-61087 PRIN-IN.) **ED** D. N. Dhar.
Ind/Abst Archit. Period. Index.

LC NA1501 .I59
DD 720/.954/05 II
INDIAN ARCHITECT & BUILDER. VFOAT Indian Architect and Builder. (198?)-. Periodical. English. Twelve times a year. $40.00. Business Press Pvt. Ltd., Bombay India. (**Subscription** address: Prints India, 11 Darya Ganj, New Delhi 110002 India. **Tel** 011 91 11 3268645, FAX 011 91 11 3275542, telex 31-61087 PRIN-IN.)

LC NA730.I6 I5 **ISSN** 0445-8605
DD 720/.5 US
INDIANA ARCHITECT. [Indiana archit.]. **Added/Corp** Indiana Society of Architects. American Institute of Architects. Northern Indiana Chapter. American Institute of Architects. Central Southern Indiana Chapter. American Institute of Architects. Indianapolis Chapter. Vol. 1 (May 1957)-. Periodical. English. Four times a year. $12.50. Image Builders / Rowland Printing Company Inc., PO Box 69, Noblesville IN 46060.
Ind/Abst Avery Index Archit. Period. Suppl. Colum. Univ. (19??-199?).

ISSN 1047-8353
DD 720 US
INFORM (RICHMOND, VA.). (INFORM : ARCHITECTURE, DESIGN, THE ARTS.). [Inform]. **Added/Corp** American Institute of Architects. Virginia Society. Vol. 1, No. 1 (1990)-. Periodical. English. Six times a year (Jan., Mar., May, July, Sept., Nov.). $16.00. Virginia Society of American Institute Architecture, 15 South 5th Street, Richmond VA 23219. **Tel** (804)644-3041, FAX (804)613-4607.

LC NA722 .I54 **ISSN** 0020-1472
DD 720/.977 US
INLAND ARCHITECT. [Inland archit.]. **Added/Corp** Inland Architect Press. Inland Architect Corporation. American Institute of Architects. Chicago Chapter. (1957)-. Periodical. English. Six times a year. $50.00. Inland Architect, PO Box 10394, Chicago IL 60610. **Tel** (312)321-0584, FAX (312)321-9334. **ED** Cynthia E Davidson-Powers. **Bk Rev**, (Qty: 10). **Ad Acc, Adv Mgr:** T.W.Hill. **Circ:** 7,500. available on microfilm and microfiche from University Microfilms International (UMI).
Desc: Professional design magazine with emphasis on the Midwest. Contains articles on building and interior design, furnishings, architects, design firms, preservation, city planning and urbanism.
Ind/Abst Archit. Period. Index (1978-); ARTbibliogr. Mod.; Avery Index Archit. Period. Suppl. Colum. Univ.

ISSN 1068-4328
DD 363 US
INSPIRED (PHILADELPHIA, PA.). (INSPIRED.). [Inspired]. **Added/Corp** Philadelphia Historic Preservation Corporation. (1986)-. Periodical. English. Four times a year. $20.00. Philadelphia Historic Preservation Corp, 1616 Walnut Street, Suite 2310, Philadelphia PA 19103. **Tel** (215)546-1146, FAX (215)546-1180. **ED** Catherine Goulet. Index available (Published separately). cum. index (on request). **Bk Rev. Ad Acc, Adv Mgr:** Maryann Devine. **Circ:** 3,000 (ctrl).
Desc: Publication that provides technical assistance to owners and managers of older houses of worship, and encourages congregations to better repair, maintain and manage their landmark structures. Comprises case studies, technical articles, and articles on architectural styles.

ISSN 1251-9812
FR
●**INTERFOLIO LEVALLOIS-PERRET.** (INTERFOLIO.). (1993)-. Periodical. French. Four times a year. 100.00F France; 150.00F other. L'Exote, 28 rue Rivay, 92300 Levallois France. **Tel** 011 33 1 47309492, FAX 011 33 1 47398010. **ED** Henri Bresler (editor's phone: 011 33 1 42961029).

US
INTERNATIONAL DICTIONARY OF ARCHITECTS AND ARCHITECTURE. (1992)-. English. $250.00. St. James Press, An Imprint of Gale Research Inc., PO Box 33477, Detroit MI 48232-5477. **Tel** (800)345-0392. **ED** Randall Van Vynckt.
Desc: A guide to more than four-hundred fifty masterworks and five-hundred Western architects, from ancient Greece to present.

LC NA2850 .I68
US
INTERNATIONAL INTERIOR DESIGN. (19??)-. Periodical. English. Every 2 years. Abbeville Press, 488 Madison Avenue, New York NY 10022.

UK
CODEN ISSTER
INTERNATIONAL JOURNAL OF SPACE STRUCTURES. Vol. 3, No. 1 (1988)-. Periodical. English. Four times a year. $189.94. Multi Science Publishing Company Ltd., 107 High Street, Brentwood, Essex CM14 4RX United Kingdom. **Tel** 011 44 1277 224632, FAX 011 44 1277 223453, telex 89-8452. **ED** H. Nooshin, Z.S. Makowski. available on microfiche. **Continues** Space Structures, 0266-3511.
Desc: A publication that strives to provide an international forum for the interchange of information on all aspects of analysis, design and construction of space structures.

LC NA1.A1 I54 **ISSN** 1049-6564
DD 720/.5 US
INTERSIGHT (BUFFALO, N.Y.). (INTERSIGHT.). [Intersight]. **Added/Corp** State University of New York at Buffalo. School of Architecture and Planning. (1990)-. Periodical. English. Irregular. $45.00 (instiutions), $45.00 (individuals). Intersight, State University of New York at Buffalo / School of Architecture and Planning, Hayes Hall, Buffalo NY 14214.

ISSN 0769-3710
FR
UDC 645
INTRAMUROS. [Intramuros]. (1985)-. Periodical. French. Six times a year. $80.93. Le Groupe Moniteur, 17 rue d'Uzes, 75002 Paris France. **Tel** 011 33 1 19401330.

ISSN 0021-0439
US
IOWA ARCHITECT. Added/Corp American Institute of Architects. Iowa Chapter. (1953)-. Periodical. English. Four times a year. $15.00. Iowa Architect, 1000 Walnut Street, Suite 101, Des Moines IA 50309. **Tel** (515)244-7502, FAX (515)244-5347. **ED** William Anderson. **Bk Rev**, (Qty: 10-20). **Ad Acc, Adv Mgr:** Kelly Roberson. **Circ:** 4,000 (ctrl).
Desc: Review of Midwest architecture, design, arts and projects.
Ind/Abst Avery Index Archit. Period. Suppl. Colum. Univ. (Winter 1989-).

Architecture

ISSN 0790-8342
IE
IRISH ARCHITECT. VFOAT IA; IA (Dublin). (1987)-. Trade Publication. English. Six times a year. $111.23. Irish Architect, 66 Patrick St., Dublin Ireland. Tel 011 353 1 2800424. *Continues The Riai Bulletin, 0790-2360.*
Ind/Abst Archit. Period. Index (Apr./May 1987-).

SA
ISILILI SAM SISE AFRIKA. Added/Corp Cape Town. University of Cape Town. School of Architecture. Vol. 1 (Oct. 1977)-. Periodical. English. Four times a year. $17.00. University of Cape Town / English Department, Private Bag, Rondebosch 7700 South Africa. Tel 011 27 21 6509111.
Ind/Abst Archit. Period. Index (Oct. 1977-July 1978).

ISSN 1064-6906
DD 728 US
ISLAND HOME. [Isl. home]. VFOAT IH. (199?)-. Periodical. English. Six times a year. $24.00. Pacific Publishing, 1221 Kapiolani Blvd, Penthouse 40, Honolulu HI 96814-3503. Tel (808)593-2800, FAX (808)593-2900. Index available (free). **Circ:** 7,500. *Continues Hawaiian Island Home, 1051-3787.*
Desc: Architecture and design magazine. Features exclusive residences, a dining-out section, art and collectibles, and travel and leisure departments.

LC NK1 .E9 **ISSN** 0361-4492
DD 720/.5 US
ISSUES IN ARCHITECTURE. Added/Corp Walker Art Center. (1975)-. English.

LC N1 .N8784 **ISSN** 0960-8648
ISSUES IN ARCHITECTURE ART AND DESIGN. Added/Corp Polytechnic of East London. School of Architecture, Art and Design. VFOAT Issues. Vol. 1, No. 2 (Winter 1990/91)-. Periodical. English. Two times a year. $32.51. Polytechnic of East London, Holbrook Centre, Holbrook Road, London E13 3EA United Kingdom. Tel 011 44 181 5907722, FAX 011 44 181 8493686. *Continues Issues in the Theory and Practice of Architecture Art, and Design.*
Ind/Abst BHA : Biblio. Hist. Art.

ISSN 0167-9082
UDC 745 NE
TITLE CHANGE
ITEMS. [Items]. (1982)-(1993). Periodical. Dutch. Marcel Vosse, Postbus 15751, 1001 NG Amsterdam Netherlands. Tel 011 31 20 6205171. *Absorbed by Items; Items Vak.*

NE
ITEMS VAK. Dutch. Eight times a year. Fl210.00. Roos Computerworks, Postbus 5841, 3008 AV Rotterdam Netherlands. Tel 011 31 10 4193335. *Absorbed Items, 0167-9082.*

LC TH4 .R8
DD 690.0(5/6) RU
CODEN IVUSEL
IZVESTIIA VYSSHIKH UCHEBNYKH ZAVEDENII. STROITELSTVO. Added/Corp Novosibirskii Inzhenerno-Stroitelnyi Institut im. V.V. Kuibysheva. Soviet Union. Gosudarstvennyi Komitet po Narodnomu Obrazovaniiu. VFOAT Stroitelstvo. (1991)-. Periodical. Russian (table of contents in English). Twelve times a year. (Subscription address: Victor Kamkin, 4956 Boiling Brook Parkway, Rockville MD 20852. Tel (301)881-5973.) *Continues in part Izvestiia Vysshikh Uchebnykh Zavedenii. Stroitelstvo i Arkhitektura (Novosibirsk, R.S.F.S.R. : 1984).*

JA
JA QUARTERLY. (19??)-. English. Four times a year (Mar., June, Sept., Dec.). $227.00. Japan Architect Company Ltd., 31-2 Yushima 2-chome, Bunkyo-ku, Tokyo 113 Japan. Tel 011 81 3 3816 2935, 011 81 3 3816 2936, FAX 011 81 3 3816 2937. ED Yasuhiro Teramatsu. Ad Acc. *Continues Japan Architect, 0448-8512.*

ISSN 0925-7845
NE
JAARBOEK MONUMENTENZORG. Added/Corp Netherlands. Rijksdienst voor de Monumentenzorg. VFOAT Monumentenzorg. (1990)-. Dutch. One time a year.
Ind/Abst BHA : Biblio. Hist. Art.

LC N6879 .J3 **ISSN** 0341-924X
DD 709/.43/55 GW
JAHRBUCH DER RHEINISCHEN DENKMALPFLEGE. See The Arts-Art.

LC N9.3 .J34 **ISSN** 0177-8978
DD 709 GW
CEASED
JAHRBUCH DES ZENTRALINSTITUTS FUER KUNSTGESCHICHTE. See The Arts-Art.

LC TH4805 .A72a **ISSN** 0172-2727
DD 728/.05 GW
JAHRBUCH FUER HAUSFORSCHUNG.
Added/Corp Arbeitskreis fuer Hausforschung (Germany). VFOAT Bericht uber die Tagung des Arbeitskreises fuer Hausforschung. (1976)-. German. One time a year. *Continues Arbeitskreis fuer Hausforschung (Germany). Bericht uber die Tagung des Arbeitskreises fuer Hausforschung e. V.*
Ind/Abst BHA : Biblio. Hist. Art.

LC NA1545 .C452 **ISSN** 0529-1399
DD 720/.951 CC
JIANZHU XUEBAO. (CHIEN CHU HSUEH PAO.). [Jianzhu xuebao]. Added/Corp Chung-Kuo Chien Chu Hsueh Hui. VFOAT Jianzhuxuebao; Jianzhu Xuebao; Architectural Journal. (1954)-. Periodical. Chinese. Twelve times a year. $46.20. (Subscription address: China International Book Trading Corporation, PO Box 399, Library Service Department, Beijing 100044 People's Republic of China. Tel 011 86 1 8414284, FAX 011 86 1 8412023, telex 22496 CIBTC CN.)
Ind/Abst Archit. Period. Index (1973-); Coal Abstr.

ISSN 0870-1504
UDC 72 PO
JORNAL ARQUITECTOS. [J. arquit.]. (1981)-. Periodical. Portuguese. Twelve times a year. $70.00. Assoc Arquitectos Portuguese, Av 24 de Yulho 52 1 Esq, 1200 Lisbon Portugal.

ISSN 0738-0895
DD 720 US
CCC
CODEN JAPRER
Pr Rev.
JOURNAL OF ARCHITECTURAL AND PLANNING RESEARCH. [J. archit. plann. res.]. Vol. 1, No. 1 (June 1984)-. Periodical. English. Four times a year. $111.00. JAPR, PO Box 146413, Chicago IL 60614. (Subscription address: Locke Science Publishing Company Inc, PO Box 5082, Bryan TX 77805.) ED Andrew D Seidel (editor's address: College of Architecture, Texas A&M University, College Station, TX 77843-3137). Documents available from The Genuine Article, Ask*IEEE. *Continues Journal of Architectural Research.*
Desc: Includes articles on theoretical and applied research and their implications for implementation in architecture, urban design and the design professions, planning and public policy.
Ind/Abst Abstr. Anthropol.; Archit. Period. Index; Arts Humanit. Citation Index [Select. Cov.]; Avery Index Archit. Period. Suppl. Colum. Univ. (Autumn 1989-); Crim. Justice Abstr.; Curr. Cit.; Curr. Contents Soc. Behav. Sci.; Ecol. Abstr. (?-?); Educ. Adm. Abstr. (?-?); Ei Page One; Environ. Period. Bibliogr.; Geogr. Abstr. Human Geogr.; Hum. Resour. Abstr. (?-?); INSPEC (June 1984-); Int. Bibliogr. Sociol.; Int. Dev. Abstr.; J. Plan. Lit.; PAIS Int. Print (1991-); Psychol. Abstr. (1984-); PsycINFO; PsycLit; Res. Alert [Full Cov.]; Sage Urban Stud. Abstr; Soc. Plann. Policy Dev. Abstr.; Soc. Sci. Cit. Index [Full Cov.]; Sociol. Abstr.

ISSN 1046-4883
DD 720 US
CCC
Pr Rev.
JOURNAL OF ARCHITECTURAL EDUCATION (WASHINGTON, D.C. : 1984). (JOURNAL OF ARCHITECTURAL EDUCATION.). [J. archit. educ.]. Added/Corp Association of Collegiate Schools of Architecture. VFOAT JAE. Vol. 37, No. 3 & 4 (Spring and Summer 1984)-. Periodical. English. Four times a year. $145.00. Massachusetts Institute of Technology (MIT) Press, 55 Hayward Street, Cambridge MA 02142. Tel (617)253-2889, (617)258-8481, FAX (617)258-6779. ED Diane Ghirardo. *Continues JAE, 0149-2993.*
Desc: Explores theory, history and design concepts in the educational setting.
Ind/Abst Archit. Period. Index; Art Index; Avery Index Archit. Period. Suppl. Colum. Univ. (1990-).

ISSN 1076-0431
US
●**JOURNAL OF ARCHITECTURAL ENGINEERING.** See Engineering-Civil Engineering.

LC NA673 .J68 **ISSN** 0953-220X
DD 724/.6 UK
JOURNAL OF ARCHITECTURAL THEORY AND CRITICISM / UIA.
Added/Corp International Union of Architects. VFOAT UIA Journal of Architectural Theory and Criticism. Vol. 1, No. 1 (1988)-. Periodical. English. Irregular. Academy Editions, 42 Leinster Gardens, London W2 3AN United Kingdom. Tel 011 44 171 4022141, FAX 011 44 171 7239540, telex 896928 ACADEM G. (Subscription address: VCH Publishers Inc., 303 Northwest 12th Avenue, Journals Department, Deerfield FL 33442. Tel (800)367-8249, (305)428-5566.)
Ind/Abst Archit. Period. Index (1988-).

LC NA1 .I48 **ISSN** 0019-4913
DD 720.6254 II
JOURNAL OF THE INDIAN INSTITUTE OF ARCHITECTS. [J. Indian Inst. Archit.]. Added/Corp Indian Institute of Architects. Vol. 1 (April 1934)-. Periodical. English. Six times a year. $9.31. Architects Publishing Corporation of India, 51 Sujata/Ground Floor, Rani Sati Marg, Malad East, Bombay 400 097 India. Tel 840 4442 or 8405510, FAX 680 5510. (Subscription address: Prints India, 11 Darya Ganj, New Delhi 110002 India. Tel 011 91 11 3268645, FAX 011 91 11 3275542, telex 31-61087 PRIN-IN.) ED Santosh Kumar. Bk Rev. Ad Acc. Circ: 4,000.
Desc: This journal is the official organ of the Indian Institute of Architects.
Ind/Abst Archit. Period. Index (1934-); Avery Index Archit. Period. Suppl. Colum. Univ. (19??-199?).

ISSN 0024-6158
UK
JOURNAL OF THE LONDON SOCIETY, THE. See The Arts-Art.

LC NA1 .A327 **ISSN** 0037-9808
DD 720/.9 US
JOURNAL OF THE SOCIETY OF ARCHITECTURAL HISTORIANS. [J. Soc. Archit. Hist.]. **Main/Corp** Society of Architectural Historians. Vol. 5 (1945/1946)-. Academic Scholarly Publication. English. Four times a year (Mar., June, Sept., Dec.). $110.00. Society of Architectural Historians, 1232 Pine Street, Philadelphia PA 19107. Tel (215)735-0224. ED Elisabeth MacDougall. cum. index. Bk Rev. Ad Acc. Circ: 4,000. available on microfilm and microfiche from University Microfilms International (UMI). Documents available from The Genuine Article. *Continues American Society of Architectural Historians. Journal of the American Society of Architectural Historians.*
Desc: Leading scholarly publication in the field. Provides an international forum for those who care about architecture and its related arts.
Ind/Abst Am. Hist. Life (1963-); Am. Bibliogr. Slavic East Europ. Stud.; Archit. Period. Index (1945/1946-); Art Index; ARTbibliogr. Mod.; Arts Humanit. Citation Index [Full Cov.]; Avery Index Archit. Period. Suppl. Colum. Univ. (1990-); BHA : Biblio. Hist. Art; Br. Archaeol. Bibliogr.; Curr. Contents Arts Humanit.; Garden Lit. (1992-); Math. Rev.; Middle East Abstr. Index; Res. Alert [Full Cov.]; Soc. Sci. Cit. Index [Select. Cov.].

ISSN 0264-5157
DD 738.605 UK
Pr Rev.
JOURNAL OF THE TILES & ARCHITECTURAL CERAMICS SOCIETY. [J. Tiles Archit. Ceram. Soc.]. VFOAT Journal of the Tiles and Architectural Ceramics Society. (1982)-. Academic Scholarly Publication. English. Two times a year. comes with membership. Tiles & Architectural Ceramics Society, 3 Browns Rise Buckland Common, Tring Hertfordshire HP23 6NJ United Kingdom. Tel 011 44 1494 758687. ED Chris Blanchett. Circ: 400 (ctrl). Documents available from BLDSC.
Desc: Scholarly papers on history, conservation, and preservation and design of tiles and architectural ceramics.

CC
CODEN TTHPDJ
JOURNAL OF TUNG-CHI UNIVERSITY = [TUNG-CHI TA HSUEH HSUEH PAO (ROMANIZED FORM)]. Added/Corp Tung-Chi ta Hsueh. VFOAT Tongji Daxue Xuebao; Tung-Chi Ta Hsueh Hsueh Pao (Romanized Form). No. 1 (Feb. 1956)-. Periodical. English (Chinese). Four times a year. RMB914.00. Science Press, 16 Donghuangchenggen North Street, Beijing 100707, People's Republic of China. Tel 011 86 1 4019821, 011 86 1 4010642, FAX 011 86 1 4012180, 011 86 1 4019810, telex 210147. ED He Yun-Feng. Documents available from Ask*IEEE.
Desc: Covers architecture, building structure, bridge engineering, geotechnical engineering, engineering geology, environmental engineering, engineering mechanics, heating and ventilation, computer engineering and marine geology.
Ind/Abst INSPEC (1981-).

LC NA12 .R53 **ISSN** 0953-6973
UK
TITLE CHANGE
JOURNAL (ROYAL INSTITUTE OF BRITISH ARCHITECTS : OVERSEAS ED.). (JOURNAL / ROYAL INSTITUTE OF BRITISH ARCHITECTS.). Added/Corp Royal Institute of British Architects. VFOAT RIBA Journal. VAT Royal Institute of British Architects Journal. Vol. 95, No. 11 (Nov. 1987)-(1993). Trade Publication. English. RIBA Companies Ltd., Finsbury Mission, 39 Moreland Street, London EC1V 8BB United Kingdom. Tel 011 44 171 2510791, FAX 011 44 171 6082375. available on microfilm. *Continues Architect (Royal Institute of British Architects : Overseas Ed.), 0950-8902; Absorbed RIBA Interiors, 0950-8910. Continued by RIBA Journal (1993).*

IT
JULIET ART MAGAZINE. See The Arts-Art.

Architecture

KENCHIKU BUNKA. ISSN 0003-8490 JA
VFOAT Architectural Culture. Vol. 1 (1946)-. Periodical. Japanese (English; summaries and/or abstracts in English). Twelve times a year. $334.00. Shokukusha Publ Company Inc, 25 Sakamachi Shinjuku-ku, 16Q Tokyo Japan. **Tel** 011 81 3 3359 3231, FAX 011 81 3 3357 3961.
Ind/Abst Avery Index Archit. Period. Suppl. Colum. Univ. (1990-).

LC NA1555 .K44

KENCHIKU JISSHI SEKKEI REI SHIRYO. JA
Added/Corp SD, Supesu Dezain. No. 1 (1972)-. Periodical. Japanese. Twelve times a year. ¥2400. Kajima Shuppankai, 5-13 Akasaka 6 Minato-ku, Tokyo 107 Japan.

DD 381

●**KITCHEN & BATH SHOWROOM.** ISSN 1082-4766 US
[Kitchen bath showr.]. VFOAT Kitchen and Bath Showroom; Showroom. Vol. 1, No. 1 (Apr./May 1995)-. Periodical. English. Six times a year. $49.95 US; $59.95 Canada; $65.95 other. Hanley-Wood Inc., 1 Thomas Circle Northwest, Suite 600, Washington DC 20005. **Tel** (202)452-0800, FAX (202)785-1974. (**Subscription address:** Kitchen & Bath Showroom Magazine, PO Box 1185, Skokie IL 60076-8185. **Tel** (202)736-3310.)
Desc: A design-oriented magazine for design specialist. Helps showroom dealers develop a more profitable business.

LC NA5586.C7 Z43

KOLNER DOMBLATT. ISSN 0450-6413 GW
(KOLNER DOMBLATT; JAHRBUCH DES ZENTRAL-DOMBAUVEREINS.). [Koln. Dombl.]. (19??)-. Monographic series. Irregular. DM48.00. JP Bachem Verlag GmbH, Ursulaplatz 1, Bachemhaus, W5000 Cologne 1 Germany. **Tel** 011 49 221 1619122, FAX (0221)3771-128. **Bk Rev. Circ:** 4,500.
Ind/Abst Avery Index Archit. Period. Suppl. Colum. Univ. (19??-199?); BHA : Biblio. Hist. Art.

KULTURBAUTEN. ISSN 0233-2337 GW
(1985)-. German. **Formed by the union of** Bauten der Kultur, 0323-5696 **and** Grundlage fur den Neubau und die Rekonstruktion von Kulturbauten, 0138-3744.

LC NX
DD 700

KUNST UND KIRCHE. See The Arts-Art. ISSN 0023-5431 AU

ISSN 0566-263X SZ

●**KUNST+ARCHITEKTUR IN DER SCHWEIZ.** See The Arts-Art.

LC NX
DD 700 SZ

KUNSTDENKMALER DER SCHWEIZ, DIE. See The Arts-Art.

LC WMLC L 83/5250

KURSKATALOG. CIVILINGENJOERS- OCH ARKITEKTLINJER / CHALMERS TEKNISKA HOEGSKOLA = COURSE PROGRAMS. FACULTY OF ENGINEERING / CHALMERS UNIVERSITY OF TECHNOLOGY. See Engineering-Civil Engineering. SW

LC NA6 .K9

KWARTALNIK ARCHITEKTURY I URBANISTYKI. ISSN 0023-5865 PL
[Kwart. archit. urban.]. **Added/Corp** Polska Akademia Nauk. Sekcja Architektury i Urbanistyki. Polska Akademia Nauk. Komitet Architektury i Urbanistyki. VFOAT Quarterly of Architecture and Town Planning. (Jan. 1956)-. Periodical. Polish (Russian; table of contents in English and Russian). Four times a year. $45.00. (**Subscription address:** Ars Polona-Ruch, PO Box 1001, Krakowskie Przedmiescie 7, 00-068 Warsaw Poland. **Tel** 011 48 22 261201.)
Ind/Abst Avery Index Archit. Period. Suppl. Colum. Univ. (19??-199?); BHA : Biblio. Hist. Art.

LC NA1 .L12

L. A. ARCHITECT. ISSN 0885-7377 US
[Los Angeles architect]. **Added/Corp** American Institute of Architects. Los Angeles Chapter. American Institute of Architects. Southern California Chapter. VFOAT LA Architect. VAT Los Angeles Architect. Vol. 1 (Jan. 1975)-. Newsletter. English. Eleven times a year (monthly except Aug.). $20.00. American Institute of Architects / Los Angeles, 3780 Wilshire Boulevard, Suite 900, Los Angeles CA 90010. **Tel** (213)380-4595. **ED** Barbara Goldstein. **Bk Rev. Ad Acc.**
Desc: Contains critiques, columns, news, reports, and events about the American Institute of Architects.
Ind/Abst Avery Index Archit. Period. Suppl. Colum. Univ. (Jan. 1990-).

LANDSCAPE INSTITUTE YEARBOOK AND DIRECTORY. ISSN 0265-4199 UK
Main/Corp Landscape Institute. VFOAT Yearbook and Directory. No. 4 (1987)-. Directory. English. One time a year. £10.00. Landscape Design Truse, 5A West Street, Reigate Surrey RH2 9BL United Kingdom. **Continues** Landscape Institute Yearbook, 0265-4199.

LATENT IMAGE. ISSN 0198-585X US
Vol. 1 (1978)-. Periodical. English. Four times a year. $20.00 US; $24.00 other. Dirsmith Group Inc, 318 Maple Avenue, Highland Park IL 60035.

LC KF902 .L44
DD 343.73/078624 347.30378624

LEGAL HANDBOOK FOR ARCHITECTS, ENGINEERS AND CONTRACTORS. See Law. ISSN 0887-1183 US

LC N5 .L45
DD 705

LEIDS KUNSTHISTORISCH JAARBOEK. See The Arts-Art. ISSN 0169-4855 NE

LEONARDO (KISSING). ISSN 0935-1108 GW
(LEONARDO.). [Leonardo]. (1988)-. Trade Publication. German. Six times a year. DM96.00. Weka Handels GmbH, Berliner Allee 28 B C, D-86167 Ausberg Germany. **Tel** 011 49 821 50410. **Ad Acc.**

LHAT BULLETIN. US
Added/Corp League of Historic American Theatres. (1989)-. Bulletin. English. Six times a year. $75.00 (non-profit organizations); $50.00 (individuals); $195.00 (theatres) Comes with League of Historic American Theatres membership. League of Historic American Theatres, 1511 K Street Northwest, Suite 923, Washington DC 20005. **Tel** (202)783-6966, FAX (202)393-2141. **Bk Rev. Ad Acc. Circ:** 600 (ctrl)
Continues Bulletin (League of Historic American Theatres).
Desc: Contains information on both general and technical news relevant to restoring and operating historic theatres.

LC NA60.S6 C64A

LISTIN DE COLEGIADOS - COLEGIO OFICIAL DE APAREJADORES Y ARQUITECTOS TECNICOS DEL CENTRO DE ESPANA. SP
Main/Corp Colegio Oficial de Aparejadores y Arquitectos Tecnicos del Centro de Espana. Spanish. Colegio Oficial de Aparejadores Y Arquitectos Tecnicos del Centro de Espana, Avda Generalisimo 73, Madrid 10 Spain.

LC NA1208 .L58
DD 720/.948/05

LIVING ARCHITECTURE : SCANDINAVIAN DESIGN. ISSN 0108-4135 DK
No. 1 (1983)-. English (summaries and/or abstracts in Danish). One time a year. Living Architecture, Box 2076, Bredgade 34, DK-1260 Copenhagen Denmark. **Tel** 011 45 33 137613, FAX 011 45 33 326989. **Ad Acc. Circ:** 45,000.
Desc: The latest in Scandinavian architecture and design as well as traditional classics.
Ind/Abst Archit. Period. Index; Avery Index Archit. Period. Suppl. Colum. Univ. (1990).

LC TH4840 .L647
DD 728/.37

LOG HOME LIVING. ISSN 1041-830X US
[Log home living]. Vol. 1, No. 1 (Spring 1989)-. Periodical. English. Six times a year (Feb., Apr., June, Aug., Oct., Dec.). $19.95. Home Buyer Publications Inc, PO Box 220039, Chantilly VA 22022. **Tel** (703)478-0435, (800)826-3893. **ED** Roland Sweet. **Ad Acc. Circ:** 103,000. **Absorbed** Log Homes Annual Buyer's Guide.
Desc: Focuses on families living in log homes and companies producing and building log homes. Seeks to capture the essence of modern log homes.

LC NA4 .L68
DD 720/.5

LOTUS INTERNATIONAL. IT
VFOAT Lotus. Vol. 8 (1974)-. English (Italian). Four times a year. L118820. Arnoldo Mondadori Editore, UFF Cont Abbonamenti, 20090 Segrate MI Italy. **Tel** 011 39 2 75422015, telex 320457 MONDMI I. Documents available from The Genuine Article. **Continues** Lotus.
Ind/Abst Archit. Period. Index (1974/1977-); Art Index; Art Humanit. Citation Index [Full Cov.]; Avery Index Archit. Period. Suppl. Colum. Univ. (1986,1989/1990-); BHA : Biblio. Hist. Art; Curr. Contents Arts Humanit.; Res. Alert [Full Cov.]; Soc. Sci. Cit. Index [Select. Cov.].

DD 720/.28/8

LUCARNE. ISSN 0711-3285 CN
(LA LUCARNE / ASSOCIATION DES PROPRIETAIRES DE MAISONS ANCIENNES DU QUEBEC (APMAQ).). [Lucarne]. **Added/Corp** Association des Proprietaires de Maisons Anciennes du Quebec. Vol. 1, No. 1 (Jan. 1981)-. Newsletter. French (English). Four times a year (Mar., June, Sept, Dec). 9.61Can$. APMAQ - Association Propietaires Maison Anciennes of Quebec, 145-56 Avenue, Lachine Quebec H8T 3B8 Canada. **Tel** (514)634-4246. Index available.
Bk Rev. Circ: 2,000.
Desc: Covers the Quebec Old House Association: travel, books, exchange of information, visits, lectures, conservation and maintenance methods.

UDC 72 ISSN 1101-5462 SW
SUSPENDED

LUND ART PRESS. [Lund art press]. (1990)-(19??). Periodical. Swedish. Four times a year. Kr200.00. Lund Univ School of Architect, Dept of Theoretical, Box 1507, Lund 1 Sweden. **Tel** 011 46 46107610.

LC NA109.B4 M66 ISSN 0770-4984 BE

M & L. MONUMENTEN EN LANDSCHAPPEN. (MONUMENTEN EN LANDSCHAPPEN : M & L.). [M & L, Monum. landsch.]. **Added/Corp** Monumenten Belgium. Rijksdienst voor Monumenten- en Landschapszorg. VFOAT M en L; M & L. (1981)-. Periodical. Dutch. Six times a year. $36.57. Monumenten en Landschappen / M & L, Belliard Straat 18, B-1040 Brussels Belgium. **Tel** 011 32 2 5139920.
Ind/Abst Art Archaeol. Tech. Abstr.; Avery Index Archit. Period. Suppl. Colum. Univ. (1984,1989/1990-).

TU
SUSPENDED

M.E.T.U. JOURNAL OF THE FACULTY OF ARCHITECTURE. **Main/Corp** Orta Dogu Teknik Universitesi (Ankara, Turkey). Mimarlk Fakultesi. VFOAT Journal of the Faculty of Architecture; O.D.T.U. Mimarlk Fakutesi Dergisi. Vol. 1 (Spring 1975)-(19??). Periodical. Multiple languages (English and Turkish). Two times a year. Middle East Technical University, Faculty of Economic and Administrative Sciences, Ankara 06531 Turkey. **Tel** 011 91 41 2101000 ext. 2006.
Ind/Abst Archit. Period. Index (Fall 1977-); Avery Index Archit. Period. Suppl. Colum. Univ. (19??-199?).

LC NA6 .M3 ISSN 0025-0082 HU
DD 720/.5

MAGYAR EPITOMUVESZET (BUDAPEST, 1952). (MAGYAR EPITOMUVESZET.). [M. epitomuv.]. **Added/Corp** Magyar Epitomuveszek Szoevetsege. (1952)-. Periodical. Hungarian. Six times a year. $34.00. (**Subscription address:** Kultura, PO Box 143, H-1300 Budapest 3 Hungary. **Tel** 011 36 1 2500194.)
Ind/Abst Archit. Period. Index (1954-); Avery Index Archit. Period. Suppl. Colum. Univ. (19??-199?); BHA : Biblio. Hist. Art.

LC NA25 .H8 NA109.H9 ISSN 0580-4736 HU

MAGYAR MUEEMLE KVEDELEM. (MAGYAR MUEMLKVEDELEM.). **Added/Corp** Orszagos Muemleki Felueygyeloseg (Hungary). (1949)-. Academic Scholarly Publication. Hungarian (summaries and/or abstracts in German). Akademiai Kiado, Publishing House of the Hungarian Academy of Sciences, Prielle Kornelia u. 19-35, H-1117 Budapest Hungary. **Tel** 011 36 1 1811991, FAX 011 36 1 1811991, telex 22-6228 AKNYO H.
Ind/Abst BHA : Biblio. Hist. Art.

LC NA7286.M435 M34 MQ
DD 728/.097298/205

MAISON MAGAZINE, ANTILLES : M. VFOAT M; Maison Magazine, Martinique; Maison Magazine. French. Twelve times a year. Maison Magazine, 106 Route des Religieuses, 97200 Fort-de-France Martinique.

MY

MAJALAH ARKITEK. **Added/Corp** Pertubuhan Akitek Malaysia. VFOAT Ma. Vol. 1, No. 1 (Jan./Feb. 1989)-. Periodical. English. Six times a year. $50.00. Pusat Binaan Sdn Bhd, PO Box 10855 Tangsi, 50725 Kuala Lumpur, Malaysia. **Tel** 011 60 3 2984136, FAX 011 60 3 2928782. **Continues** Majallah Akitek, 0126-7604.
Ind/Abst Archit. Period. Index (Jan./Feb. 1989-).

LC NA2543.S6 M35 ISSN 0025-1550 US
DD 720
NLM W1 MA59K
SUSPENDED

MAN-ENVIRONMENT SYSTEMS. [Man-environ. syst.]. **Added/Corp** Association for the Study of Man-Environment Relations. VFOAT Man Environment Systems. Vol. 1 (July 1969)-Suspended (1995). Periodical. English. Six times a year. $37.50. Association for the Study of Man-Environment Relations, PO Box 57, Orangeburg NY 10962. **Tel** (914)634-8221. **ED** Aristide H. Esser. **Bk Rev. Ad Acc. Circ:** 600 (ctrl)

Architecture

available on microfilm and microfiche from University Microfilms International (UMI).
Desc: A forum for communications bearing on the interface between research in the behavioral social sciences and the design and management of the sociophysical environment.
Ind/Abst Int. Dev. Abstr. (?-?); Psychol. Abstr. (1972-); PsycINFO; PsycLit; Soc. Plann. Policy Dev. Abstr.; Sociol. Abstr.

ISSN 0228-8222
DD 720/.68 CN
MANUEL DE PRATIQUE DE L'ARCHITECTURE. [Man. prat. archit.]. **Added/Corp** Ordre des Architectes du Quebec. (1980)-. French. Irregular. 40.82Can$. Ordre des Architectes du Quebec, 1825 West Rene Levesque, Montreal Quebec H3H 1R4 Canada. **Tel** (514)937-6168.

LC TH4 .S8645
DD 690 UZ
MASKAN : ARKHITEKTURA I STROITELSTVO UZBEKISTANA, AZERBAIDZHANA, KYRGYZSTANA, TADZHIKISTANA, TURKMENISTANA.
Added/Corp Gosstroi UzSSR. Gosstroi Uzbekistana. **VFOAT** Maskan. No. 9 (1991)-. Periodical. Russian (summaries and/or abstracts in English). Twelve times a year. $109.95. **(Subscription address:** East View Publications Inc., 3020 Harbor Lane North, Suite 110, Minneapolis MN 55447. **Tel** (800)477-1005, (612)550-0961, FAX (612)559-2931.) **Continues** Arkhitektura i Stroitelstvo Uzbekistana, 0039-243X.

IT
MATERIA. Italian. Three times a year. L4400.00. Quarzo s.r.l., via Radici Nord 112, 42014 Castellarano Re Italy. **Tel** 011 39 536 850404.

ISSN 1121-0516
IT
MATERIA : RASSEGNA TECNICA DI MOTIVI D'ARCHITETTURA = AN ARCHITECTURAL REVIEW. (1989)-. Periodical. Italian (English). Three times a year. L30000. Quarzo s.r.l., via Radici Nord 112, 42014 Castellarano Re Italy. **Tel** 011 39 536 850404.

LC N8554 .M38
IT
MATERIALI E STRUTTURE. Added/Corp "Erma" di Bretschneider. (1990)-. Periodical. Italian (English). Three times a year. L85.000 Italy; L100.000 other. L'Erma di Bretschneider SPA, via Cassiodoro 19, 00193 Rome Italy. **Tel** 011 39 6 6874127, 011 39 6 6874129, FAX 011 39 6 6874129. Index available. **Bk Rev. Ad Acc. Circ:** 600 (ctrl).
Desc: Critical review of research technologies and materials in the field of restoration activities.

LC TH435 .M425 **ISSN 0888-6709**
DD 692/.5 US
TITLE CHANGE
MEANS FACILITIES COST DATA. [Means facil. cost data]. **Added/Corp** Means (Firm). **VFOAT** Facilities Cost Data. 1st Ed. (1986)-(1993). English. RS Means Company Inc. / Trade Sales, 100 Construction Plaza, PO Box 800, Kingston MA 02364. **Tel** (617)585-7880, (800)448-8182, FAX (617)585-7466. **Continued by** Means Facilities Construction Cost Data, 1075-0789.

LC SB469 .A632a
US
●**MEMBER ... DIRECTORY. Main/Corp** American Society of Landscape Architects. (1995)-. English. Irregular. American Society of Landscape Architects, 4401 Connecticut Avenue Northwest, 5th Floor, Washington DC 20008. **Tel** (202)686-2752. **Continues** American Society of Landscape Architects ASLA Members' Handbook, 0192-5067.

LC WMLC 91/1568 NA11 .S635
US
MEMBERSHIP DIRECTORY / SOCIETY OF ARCHITECTURAL HISTORIANS.
Main/Corp Society of Architectural Historians. **VFOAT** Society of Architectural Historians Membership Directory. (1990)-. Directory. English. Society of Architectural Historians, 1232 Pine Street, Philadelphia PA 19107. **Tel** (215)735-0224.

ISSN 0001-1487
US
TITLE CHANGE
MEMO - AMERICAN INSTITUTE OF ARCHITECTS (1971). (MEMO - AMERICAN INSTITUTE OF ARCHITECTS.). [Memo - Am. Inst. Archit.]. **Main/Corp** American Institute of Architects. No. 432, (July 1971)-(19??). Periodical. English. American Institute of Architects / Washington DC, 1735 New York Avenue Northwest, Washington DC 20006. **Tel** (202)626-7460, FAX (202)626-7587. **ED** Phillip Schreiner. **Continues** AIA Memo, 0732-2593. **Continued by** AIArchitect.

Ind/Abst Archit. Period. Index (1977-1982); Avery Index Archit. Period. Suppl. Colum. Univ. (1984-199?); Constr. Index (199?-?).

US
MEMO PAD. English. Eleven times a year (monthly with combined July / Aug.). $90.07 (members), $147.34 (nonmembers). Architects Council of New York, 275 Seventh Avenue, New York NY 10001. **Tel** (212)675-5922. Index available in last issue of volume--attached. cum. index.
Desc: Provides useful information to architects practicing in New York City in areas such as: materials and equipment approved for New York City use, local laws and rules, and related agencies' rules and regulations from the Fire Department, Board of Standards and Appeals, Marine and Aviation, and Department of Air Resources.

ISSN 1188-8296
DD 971.4 CN
●**MEMOIRES VIVES MONTREAL.**
(MEMOIRES VIVES.). [Mem. vivesMontr.]. (1992)-. Periodical. French (summaries and/or abstracts in English). Three times a year. 14.50Can$ (individuals), 23.50Can$ (institutions) Canada; 18.00Can$ (individuals), 30.00Can$ (institutions) other. Goupe PGV Diffusion Archeologie, 5846 Cartier, Montreal Quebec, H2G 2V2 Canada. **Tel** (514)277-5812, FAX (514)277-5812. **ED** Francois Grondin. **Ad Acc. Circ:** 1,000.

LC TH1 .M4 **ISSN 0885-5781**
DD 721 US
METAL ARCHITECTURE. [Met. archit.].
(198?)-. Trade Publication. English. Twelve times a year. Free on request. Modern Trade Communications, 7450 North Skokie Boulevard, Skokie IL 60077. **Tel** (708)674-2200, FAX (708)674-3676. **ED** Bob Fittro. **Ad Acc, Adv Mgr:** J.Riester, **Tel** (708)674-2200. **Circ:** 28,000 (ctrl).

ISSN 0893-8490
DD 725 US
METROPOLITAN REVIEW (CHICAGO, ILL.). See Housing and Urban Development.

ISSN 0258-5316
UDC 72 TU
MIMARLIK FAKULTESI DERGISI. [Mimar. fak. derg.]. **VFOAT** Journal of the Faculty of Architecture. (1975)-. Periodical. English. Two times a year.
Ind/Abst BHA : Biblio. Hist. Art.

ISSN 0165-5302
UDC 749 NE
Pr Rev.
MOBILIA (AMSTERDAM). See Interior Design and Decoration-Home Furnishings.

ISSN 0391-3635
IT
MODO DESIGN MAGAZINE. See Interior Design and Decoration.

LC NA1 .M63 **ISSN 0191-4022**
DD 720/.5 US
MODULUS. [Modulus]. **Added/Corp** University of Virginia. School of Architecture. (19??)-. English. One time a year. $24.95. Princeton Architectural Press, 37 East 7th Street, New York NY 10003. **Tel** (212)995-9620. **ED** Patrick E. Deaton. **Bk Rev. Circ:** 2,000.
Desc: Exploring architectural themes in articles contributed by well-known and up and coming architects.
Ind/Abst Archit. Period. Index (1979-); Avery Index Archit. Period. Suppl. Colum. Univ. (19??-199?); BHA : Biblio. Hist. Art.

LC HD4677 .M6G6 **ISSN 0367-4959**
RU
SUSPENDED
MOIA MOSKVA. Added/Corp Moskovskii Gorodskoi Sovet Narodnykh Deputatov. (1990)-Suspended (1993). Periodical. Russian. Four times a year. **(Subscription address:** East View Publications Inc., 3020 Harbor Lane North, Suite 110, Minneapolis MN 55447. **Tel** (800)477-1005, (612)550-0961, FAX (612)559-2931.) **Continues** Gorodskoe Khoziaistvo Moskvy.

ISSN 0998-4194
FR
MONITEUR ARCHITECTURE AMC, LE.
No. 1 (May 1989)-. French. Eleven times a year. 450.00F France; 550.00F other. Publications du Moniteur, 17 rue d'Uzes, 75108 Paris Cedex 02 France. **Tel** 011 33 1 40133030, FAX 011 33 1 40419405 customer service, 40133037 advertising, telex UPRESSE 680876 F. **ED** Elisabeth Allain. **Bk Rev. Ad Acc. Circ:** 15,000 (ctrl). **Continues** AMC, 0336-1675.
Ind/Abst Archit. Period. Index (July/Aug. 1989-); Avery Index Archit. Period. Suppl. Colum. Univ. (1989-).

ISSN 0741-6849
DD 720 US
MONTANA STATE ARCHITECTURAL REVIEW. [Mont. State Archit. rev.]. **Added/Corp** Montana State University (Bozeman). School of Architecture. Vol. 1 (Spring 1983)-. English. One time a year. $4.00. Montana State University / School of Architecture, Bozeman MT 59717. **Tel** (406)994-0211.
Ind/Abst Avery Index Archit. Period. Suppl. Colum. Univ. (1990-).

LC DR913 .M66
AA
MONUMENTET. Added/Corp Instituti i Monumenteve te Kultures (Tirana, Albania). (1971)-. Periodical. Albanian (summaries and/or abstracts in French). Two times a year. **(Subscription address:** Book Distribution Enterprise, Rruga Konferenca e Pezes, Tirana Albania.)
Ind/Abst BHA : Biblio. Hist. Art.

LC DG11 .M6
IT
MONUMENTI ANTICHI. SERIE MISCELLANEA. Added/Corp Accademia Nazionale dei Lincei. Vol. 1 (1971)-. Monographic series. Italian. Irregular. Price varies per volume. Accademia Nazionale dei Lincei, Via Lungara 10 Uff Diff Pubbl., 00165 Rome Italy. **Tel** 011 39 6 6838831. **(Subscription address:** Bardi Editore, Salita de Crescenzi 16, 00186 Rome Italy. **Tel** 011 39 6 68801490.)
Ind/Abst BHA : Biblio. Hist. Art.

LC DG11 .M63
IT
MONUMENTI ANTICHI. SERIE MONOGRAFICA / ACCADEMIA NAZIONALE DEI LINCEI. Added/Corp Accademia Nazionale dei Lincei. **VFOAT** Serie Monografica. Vol. 1 (1979)-. Monographic series. Italian. Irregular. Price varies per volume. Accademia Nazionale dei Lincei, Via Lungara 10 Uff Diff Pubbl., 00165 Rome Italy. **Tel** 011 39 6 6838831. **(Subscription address:** Giorgio Bretschneider Editore, Via Crescienzo 43, 00193 Rome Italy. **Tel** 011 39 6 6879361.) **Supersedes in part** Accademia Nazionale dei Lincei. Monumenti Antichi.
Ind/Abst BHA : Biblio. Hist. Art.

LC N8997 .M64 **ISSN 0242-830X**
FR
MONUMENTS HISTORIQUES (1980).
(MONUMENTS HISTORIQUES.). [Monum. hist.]. **Added/Corp** Caisse Nationale des Monuments Historiques et des Sites (France). No. 107 (1980)-. Periodical. French. Six times a year. $82.03. Caisse Nationale des Monuments Historiques, 62 rue St. Antoine, 75004 Paris France. **Tel** 011 33 1 44612000. **ED** Veronique Hartmann. Index available. cum. index. **Bk Rev. Ad Acc. Circ:** 12,000 (ctrl). Documents available from The Genuine Article. **Continues** Monuments Historiques : MH and Les Monuments Historiques de la France.
Desc: Architectural history of French heritage, restoration, preservation and rehabilitation of urban centers, industrial buildings and protected sites.
Ind/Abst Archit. Period. Index (1971, 1979-); Art Archaeol. Tech. Abstr.; Arts Humanit. Citation Index [Full Cov.]; Avery Index Archit. Period. Suppl. Colum. Univ. (1990-); BHA : Biblio. Hist. Art; Curr. Contents Arts Humanit.; Res. Alert [Full Cov.]; Soc. Sci. Cit. Index [Select. Cov.].

LC NA6400 **ISSN 0540-8539**
DD 725.4 FR
UDC 7.025(443.63)
MONUMENTS HISTORIQUES DE SEINE ET MARNE. [Monum. hist. Seine et Marne]. (1961)-. Monographic series. French.
Ind/Abst BHA : Biblio. Hist. Art.

LC NA6 .A7276 **ISSN 0868-7110**
RU
CODEN MOZHE8
MOSKOVSKII ZHURNAL. Added/Corp Moskovskii Gorodskoi Sovet Narodnykh Deputatov. No. 1 (1991)-. Periodical. Russian. Twelve times a year. $99.95. Redaktsiia Zhurnala, 117218 Moscow V-218, Ulitsa Krzhizhanovskogo D 15, Korp 2 Komn 426 Russia. **(Subscription address:** East View Publications Inc., 3020 Harbor Lane North, Suite 110, Minneapolis MN 55447. **Tel** (800)477-1005, (612)550-0961, FAX (612)559-2931.) **Continues** Arkhitektura i Stroitelstvo Moskvy (1987), 0234-0577.

US
●**MOUNTAIN LIVING. See** Leisure and Recreation.

LC NA6 .M8 **ISSN 0541-2439**
HU
MUEMLEKVEDELEM. Added/Corp Magyar Epitomuveszek Szovetsege. Muemleki Bizottsaga. Tudomanyos Ismeretterjeszto Tarsulat. Muveszeti Orszagos Valasztmany. Orszagos Muemleki Felugyeloseg. Vol. 1 (1957)-. Periodical. Hungarian (English; summaries and/or abstracts in English and French). Four times a year. $16.00. Tancsics M U 1, H 1014 Budapest Hungary. **Tel** 569-722, telex 22-6379.

Architecture

(Subscription address: Kultura, PO Box 143, H-1300 Budapest 3 Hungary. **Tel** 011 36 1 2500194.) **ED** Laszlo Gero. Index available. cum. index. **Bk Rev**. **Ad Acc**. **Circ**: 3,500.
 Desc: Review of the history of architecture and of conservation of historical monuments.
 Ind/Abst Art Archaeol. Tech. Abstr.; BHA : Biblio. Hist. Art; Numis. Lit.

LC NA6.A8 M84

TI

MUJTAMA WA-UMRAN. **VFOAT** Mujtamaa Wa Umran. Vol. 1, No. 1 (Jan./March 1982)-. Periodical. Arabic. $20.00. 5 Nahj Ibn Rashiq, Tunis S B 409 Tunisia.

LC NK1471.F5 M86   **ISSN** 0358-3511

FI

MUOTO / TEOLLISUUSTAITEEN LIITTO ORNAMO. **Added/Corp** Teollisuustaiteen Liitto Ornamo. (1980)-. Periodical. Finnish (summaries and/or abstracts in English and Swedish). Four times a year. Academic Bookstore Akateeminen, Postilokero 23, FIN-00371 Helsinki Finland. **Tel** 011 358 0 12141.

LC N6260 .M83   **ISSN** 0732-2992
DD 709/.17/671   US

CCC

MUQARNAS. [Muqarnas]. **Added/Corp** Aga Khan Program for Islamic Architecture. Vol. 1 (1983)-. Periodical. English. One time a year. $51.50 (latest edition). E.J. Brill, Postbus 9000, 2300 PA Leiden The Netherlands. **Tel** 011 31 71 312624, FAX 011 31 71 317532, telex 39296 BRILL NL. **ED** O. Grabar.
 Ind/Abst Archit. Period. Index (1983-); Avery Index Archit. Period. Suppl. Colum. Univ. (1990-).

FR

MUR VIVANT, LE. (19??)-. Periodical. French. Four times a year. Editions AMP, 9 rue de Trevise, 75009 Paris France. **Tel** 011 33 1 47705001, FAX 011 33 1 48009811.
 Ind/Abst Archit. Period. Index (1977-1990); Avery Index Archit. Period. Suppl. Colum. Univ. (No. 93, 1989-).

LC NA1540 .N36
DD 722/.11/05   CC

NAN FANG CHIEN CHU = NANFANG JIANZHU. **Added/Corp** Chung-Kuo Chien chu Hsueh Hui. Kuang-Tung Fen Hui. **VFOAT** Nanfang Jianzhu. (1981)-. Periodical. Chinese. Four times a year. NT$0.65. Kuang-Tung Sheng Hsin Hua Shu, Tien Kuang-chou Shih, People's Republic of China.

LC N400
DD 708   BN

NASE STARINE. **Added/Corp** Zavod za Zastitu Spomenika Kulture S.R. Bosne i Hercegovine. Zavod za Zastitu Spomenika Kulture Prirodnih Znamenitosti i Rijetkosti Bosne i Hercegovine. (1953)-. Periodical. Serbo-Croatian (Roman) (summaries and/or abstracts in French). One time a year.
 Ind/Abst BHA : Biblio. Hist. Art.

LC NA6830 .N37
DD 725/.822/0973   US

NATIONAL LIST OF HISTORIC THEATRE BUILDINGS. (19??)-. English. One time a year. League of Historic American Theatres, 1511 K Street Northwest, Suite 923, Washington DC 20005. **Tel** (202)783-6966, FAX (202)393-2141.

US

NATIONAL REGISTER BULLETIN. **Added/Corp** United States. National Park Service. Interagency Resource Management Division. National Register of Historic Places. (1985)-. Bulletin. English. Price varies per volume. US Department of the Interior / National Park Service, 1849 C Street NW, Room 3104, Washington DC 20240. **Tel** (202)208-4621, FAX (202)208-7520. **Continues** National Register of Historic Places Bulletin.
 Ind/Abst Avery Index Archit. Period. Suppl. Colum. Univ. (1989-).

ISSN 0266-8068
UK

NATIONAL TRUST. [Natl. Trust]. **Added/Corp** National Trust (Great Britain). No. 17 (Summer 1973)-. Periodical. English. Three times a year. $11.98. National Trust / England, PO Box 39, Bromley Kent BR1 1NH United Kingdom. **Tel** 011 44 181 4641111. **Continues** National Trust News.
 Ind/Abst Archit. Period. Index (Spring 1978-); Avery Index Archit. Period. Suppl. Colum. Univ. (19??-19??).

ISSN 0028-1026
GW
CCC

NATURSTEIN. See Building and Construction.

NE

NATUURSTEEN. Dutch. Fl75.00 Netherlands, Fl120.00 US; Fl90.00 other. Wijlhuizen Uitgeverij BV, Wilhelminasingel 4, 6524 AK Nijmegen, The Netherlands. **Tel** 080-605253, FAX 080-605210.

BE

NEUF; ARCHITECTURES NOUVELLES, MATERIAUX NOUVEAUX. **VFOAT** Architectures Nouvelles, Materiaux Nouveaux. (19??)-. Periodical. French (Dutch). Six times a year. 2250F Belgium; 2850F other. Socorema, rue du Merlo 84 A, 1180 Brussels Belgium. **Tel** 011 32 2 3323421, 011 32 2 376 62 28, 011 32 2 3323421. **Ad Acc**.

ISSN 1079-4603
DD 728   US

●**NEW HAMPSHIRE HOME**. [N.H. home]. **VFOAT** Home; New Hampshire Home Magazine; A.N H home. Vol. 1, Issue 1 (1994)-. Periodical. English. Six times a year. $11.95. Ceres Publications, 801 Islington Street, Suite CC5, Portsmouth NH 03801. **Tel** (603)436-5079.

IE

NEW IRISH ARCHITECTURE. **Added/Corp** Architectural Association. Architecture Association of Ireland. (1986)-. Periodical. English. One time a year. $11.98. Architectural Association of Ireland, 8 Marrion Square, Dublin 2 Ireland. **Tel** 011 353 1 761703.

ISSN 0545-3151
US
SUSPENDED

NEW MEXICO ARCHITECTURE. [N.M. archit.]. **VFOAT** NMA. (196?)-. Periodical. English. Six times a year. $15.00. New Mexico Architecture, Box 935, Santa Fe NM 87504. **Tel** (505)983-6948. **ED** John P Conron. Index available. **Bk Rev**. **Ad Acc**. **Circ**: 3,000. **Continues** New Mexico Architect.
 Desc: Publishes the work of current New Mexico architects, as well as articles devoted to the architectural history of New Mexico.
 Ind/Abst Avery Index Archit. Period. Suppl. Colum. Univ. (1990-).

US

NEW YORK ARCHITECTS. **Added/Corp** American Institute of Architects. New York Chapter. **VFOAT** Directory of Architecture Firms; NYC/AIA Directory of Architecture Firms. (1991)-. English. American Institute of Architects / New York, 457 Madison Avenue, New York NY 10022. **Tel** (212)838-9670.

ISSN 0149-2446
US

NEWS - ASSOCIATION OF COLLEGIATE SCHOOLS OF ARCHITECTURE. [News - Assoc. Coll. Sch. Archit.]. **Main/Corp** Association of Collegiate Schools of Architecture. **VFOAT** ACSA News. (Mar. 1974)-. Periodical. English. Nine times a year (Sept - May). $50.00. Association of Collegiate Schools of Architecture, 1735 New York Avenue Northwest, Washington DC 20006. **Tel** (202)785-2324, (800)232-2724. **ED** Karen L. Eldridge. **Ad Acc**, **Adv Mgr**: John Edwards, **Tel** (202)785-2324. **Circ**: 4,000 (ctrl). **Continues** ACSA Newsletter.
 Ind/Abst Avery Index Archit. Period. Suppl. Colum. Univ. (1984-).

LC E159.5 .N49   **ISSN** 0735-1399
DD 973.1   US

NEWS JOURNAL - SOCIETY FOR COMMERCIAL ARCHEOLOGY (U.S.). (NEWS JOURNAL.). [News j. - Soc. Commer. Archeol. (U.S.)]. **Main/Corp** Society for Commercial Archeology (U.S.). **VFOAT** S.C.A. News Journal; S.C.A.N.; Society for Commercial Archeology News Journal; SCA News Journal; SCAN; SCA Journal. Vol. 1, No. 1 (Sept. 1978)-. Periodical. English. Three times a year. $20.00. Society of Commercial Archaeology, National Museum of American History / Room 5010, Washington DC 20560. **Tel** (202)882-5424. **Bk Rev**. **Ad Acc**. **Circ**: 500. **Continued in part by** Society for Commercial Archeology News, 1069-0492.
 Desc: History and preservation of roadside architecture.

ISSN 0882-7478
US

NEWS LETTER / PRESERVATION LEAGUE OF NEW YORK STATE. **Added/Corp** Preservation League of New York State. **VFOAT** Newsletter. Vol. 1 (1975)-. Periodical. English. Four times a year. Preservation League of New York State, 44 Central Avenue, Albany NY 12206. **Tel** (518)462-5658, FAX (518)462-5684. **ED** Jonathan Walters.
 Ind/Abst Avery Index Archit. Period. Suppl. Colum. Univ. (Spring 1990-).

ISSN 1062-6301
US

NEWS / SOCIETY OF ARCHITECTURAL HISTORIANS, SOUTHERN CALIFORNIA CHAPTER. Periodical. English. Six times a year. SAH/SCC, 4808 Hollywood Boulevard, Hollyhock House, Los Angeles CA 90027. **Continues** Newsletter (Society of Architectural Historians. Southern California Chapter), 8756-4580.

ISSN 0715-4100
DD 721/.06/0711   CN

NEWS, VIEWS AND REVIEWS - ARCHITECTURAL INSTITUTE OF BRITISH COLUMBIA. (NEWS, VIEWS AND REVIEWS.). [News, views rev. - Archit. Inst. B.C.]. **Main/Corp** Architectural Institute of British Columbia. Vol. 1, No. 1 (Jan. 1981)-. Periodical. English. Free to members. Architectural Institute of British Columbia, 970 Richards Street, Vancouver British Columbia V6B 3C1 Canada.

ISSN 0141-559X
UK

NEWSLETTER - CHARLES RENNIE MACKINTOSH SOCIETY. (1973)-. Newsletter. English. Four times a year. Free to members of the Charles Rennie Mackintosh Society. Charles Rennie Mackintosh Society, Queens Cross, 870 Garscube Road, Glasgow G20 7EL United Kingdom. **Tel** 011 44 41 9466600.
 Desc: Strives to foster interest in and conserve the buildings and artifacts designed by Charles Rennie Mackintosh and his associates.
 Ind/Abst Archit. Period. Index (Spring 1975-); Avery Index Archit. Period. Suppl. Colum. Univ. (Spring 1990-); Museum Abstr.

ISSN 0381-0119
DD 720/.9713/7106271371   CN

NEWSLETTER - FRONTENAC HISTORIC FOUNDATION. **Main/Corp** Frontenac Historic Foundation. **VAT** Frontenac Historic Foundation Newsletter. (June 1973)-. Newsletter. English. Four times a year. 18.00Can$. Frontenac Historic Foundation, PO Box 27, Kingston Ontario Canada. **Tel** (613)542-4764. **ED** Paul Banfield. **Bk Rev**. **Circ**: 250 (ctrl).
 Desc: Articles dealing with the preservation/conservation of historic sites, buildings, artifacts; general historical themes relating to the region's architects and architecture.

LC Z682.2.U6 N4
US

NEWSLETTER OF THE ASSOCIATION OF ARCHITECTURE SCHOOL LIBRARIANS / AASL, ASSOCIATION OF ARCHITECTURE SCHOOL LIBRARIANS. **Added/Corp** AASL (Association). (19??)-. Newsletter. English. Irregular. Weigel Library of Architecture and Design, Kansas State University, Manhattan KS 66502. **Continues** AASL Newsletter.

UK

NEWSLETTER OF THE TILES AND ARCHITECTURAL CERAMICS SOCIETY. (1985)-. Newsletter. English. Four times a year. Comes with Society membership - $40.00 (membership). Tiles & Architectural Ceramics Society, 3 Browns Rise Buckland Common, Tring Hertfordshire HP23 6NJ United Kingdom. **Tel** 011 44 1494 758687. **ED** Chris Blanchett. Index available. cum. index. **Bk Rev**, (Qty: varies). **Circ**: 400 (ctrl).
 Desc: Current information on conservation, preservation, exhibitions, and books relevant to tiles and architectural ceramics; includes society information.

LC NA12 .S635
DD 720/.6/041   UK

NEWSLETTER / SOCIETY OF ARCHITECTURAL HISTORIANS OF GREAT BRITAIN. **Added/Corp** Society of Architectural Historians of Great Britain. (19??)-. Newsletter. English. Four times a year. Society of Architectural Historians of Great Britain, 4 Woodlands Avenue Finchley, London N3 2NR United Kingdom. **Tel** 011 44 181 3465139.
 Ind/Abst BHA : Biblio. Hist. Art.

ISSN 0049-1195
US

NEWSLETTER - THE SOCIETY OF ARCHITECTURAL HISTORIANS. [Newsl. - Soc. Archit. Hist.]. **Main/Corp** Society of Architectural Historians. Vol. 1 (Sept. 1957)-. Newsletter. English. Six times a year. $15.00. Society of Architectural Historians, 1232 Pine Street, Philadelphia PA 19107. **Tel** (215)735-0224. **ED** Elisabeth MacDougall. **Bk Rev**. **Ad Acc**. **Circ**: 4,000.
 Desc: Provides an international forum for those who care about architecture and its related arts. Encourages scholarly research in the field and promotes preservation of significant architectural monuments.
 Ind/Abst Avery Index Archit. Period. Suppl. Colum. Univ. (1990-).

Architecture

ISSN 1052-5831
DD 720 US
NEWSLINE - (COLUMBIA UNIVERSITY. GRADUATE SCHOOL OF ARCHITECTURE PLANNING AND PRESERVATION). (NEWSLINE.). [Newsline - (Columbia Univ., Grad. Sch. Archit. Plan. Preserv.)]. **Added/Corp** Columbia University. Graduate School of Architecture Planning and Preservation. **VFOAT** News Line. (19??)-. Periodical. English. Columbia University School of Architecture, Planning and Preservation, 403 Avery Hall, New York NY 10027.
Ind/Abst Avery Index Archit. Period. Suppl. Colum. Univ. (Feb. 1990-).

LC NA1599.N5 N53
NR
NIAJ : A JOURNAL OF THE NIGERIAN INSTITUTE OF ARCHITECTS. Added/Corp Nigerian Institute of Architects. **VFOAT** Journal of the Nigerian Institute of Architects for the Advancement of the Architectural Profession; Nigerian Institute of Architects Journal. (19??)-. Periodical. English. Four times a year. *Continues NIA Journal, 0189-1162.*
Ind/Abst Archit. Period. Index.

BE
TITLE CHANGE
NIEUW NEUF. (19??)-(19??). French (Dutch). Socorema, rue du Merlo 84 A, 1180 Brussels Belgium. **Tel** 011 32 2 3323421, 011 32 2 376 62 28, 011 32 2 3323421. **Bk Rev. Ad Acc. Circ:** 10,000. *Continued by Dynamics.*

ISSN 0385-0870
DD 720 JA
NIKKEI AKITEKUCHUA. [Nikkei akitekuchua]. **VFOAT** Nikkei Architecture. (1976)-. Periodical. Japanese. Twenty-six times a year. Nihon Keizai Shimbun Inc., 9-5 Otemachi 1 Chome, Chiyoda-ku Tokyo 100 Japan. **Tel** 011 81 3 32700251, 011 81 3 52108502 (Nikkei Business Publications Inc.), FAX 011 81 3 52552661, 011 81 3 52108119 (Nikkei Business Publications Inc.). **(Subscription address:** OCS / Overseas Courier Service of America Inc., 5 East 44th Street, New York NY 10017. **Tel** (212)599-4517.**)**

ISSN 0916-9555
JA
NIKKEI SUTOA DEZAIN. See Interior Design and Decoration.

ISSN 1102-5824
SW
UDC 72
NORDISK ARKITEKTURFORSKNING. [Nord. arkit.forsk.]. **VFOAT** Nordic Journal of Architectural Research. (1992)-. Periodical. Swedish (English, Norwegian and Danish). Four times a year. $80.14. Chalmers Tekniska Hegskola, Arkitektur, S 0412 96 Gothenburg Sweden. **Tel** 011 46 31 7722456, telex 2369 CHALBIB S. *Continues Tidskrift for Arkitekturforskning, 0284-2998.*

ISSN 1045-3253
DD 720 US
NORTH CAROLINA ARCHITECTURE. [N. C. archit.]. **Added/Corp** American Institute of Architects. North Carolina Chapter. **VFOAT** NCA. Vol. 35, No. 3 (May/June 1987)-. Trade Publication. English. Six times a year. $30.00. American Institute of Architects / North Carolina, 115 West Morgan Street, Raleigh NC 27601. **Tel** (919)833-6656, FAX (919)833-2015. **ED** John Roth (editor's phone: (919)286-0135). **Ad Acc. Circ:** 3,000 (ctrl). *Continues North Carolina Architect (Raleigh, N.C. : 1978), 0029-2427.*

LC NA1 .N76 **ISSN** 0305-0173
DD 720.5 UK
NORTHERN ARCHITECT. Added/Corp Northern Architectural Association, Newcastle-Upon-Tyne. Royal Institute of British Architects. Northern Region. No. 1 (Nov. 1961)-. Periodical. English. Four times a year. Paul & Goode Publishing Ltd., Clavering House, Newcastle-upon-Tyne NE99 1LR United Kingdom. **ED** Roy Gazzard. **Bk Rev. Ad Acc. Circ:** 2,250.
Ind/Abst Archit. Period. Index (1977-); Avery Index Archit. Period. Suppl. Colum. Univ. (19??-19??).

LC F227 .N69 **ISSN** 0163-1632
DD 975.5/005 US
NOTES ON VIRGINIA. See History-History of North and South America.

ISSN 0773-9796
BE
NOUVELLES DU PATRIMOINE. (1985)-. French. Six times a year. $18.66. Association des Amis de l Unesco, Avenue Gen C de Gaulle 17, 1050 Brussels Belgium. **Tel** 011 32 2 6488006.
Ind/Abst Avery Index Archit. Period. Suppl. Colum. Univ. (Oct. 1989, Feb. 1990).

LC Z5941 .N683 NA2500
RU
NOVOSTI TEKHNICHESKOI LITERATURY. RAZDEL SERIIA III: RAIONNAIA PLANIROVKA I GRADOSTROITELSTVO. STROITELSTVO I ARKHITEKTURA. Added/Corp Moscow. Tsentralnyi Institut Nauchnoi Informatsii po Stroitelstvu i Arkhitekture. Tsentralnaia Nauchne-Tekhnicheskaia Biblioteka po Stroite. (1974)-. Periodical. Multiple languages. Twelve times a year. Tsentralnyi Institut Nauchnoi Informatsii po Stroitelstvu i Arkhitekture, Ul Gorkogo Dom 38, 125047 A-47 Moscow Russia. *Continues Razdel A. Seriia III: Gradostroitelstvo, Zhilye I Obshchestvennye Zdaniia I Sooruzheniia.*

LC Z5853.N14 N68 TA403
RU
NOVOSTI TEKHNICHESKOI LITERATURY. STROITEL'STVO I ARKHITEKTURA. RAZDEL A. SERIIA VII. STROITEL'NYE MATERIALY I IZDELIIA, KHARAKTERISTIKA I PRIMENENIE. See Building and Construction.

LC WMLC 93/1286 **ISSN** 0029-5701
AG
NUESTRA ARQUITECTURA. [Nuestra arquit.]. (1929)-. Periodical. Spanish. Six times a year. Editorial Contempora SRL, Sarmiento 643-5 Piso, 1382 Buenos Aires Argentina. cum. index.
Ind/Abst Archit. Period. Index (1936-).

ISSN 0389-3693
DD 720 JA
OBAYASHI REPOTO. [Obayashi repoto]. (1978)-. Periodical. Japanese. Obayashi Corporation, 75 3-chome Kyobashi, Higashi-ku, Osaka Japan.
Ind/Abst Abstr. J. Earthq. Eng.

LC N1 .O175 **ISSN** 0885-5927
DD 720 US
OCULUS (NEW YORK, N. Y.). (OCULUS.). [Oculus]. **Added/Corp** American Institute of Architects. New York Chapter. (19??)-. Periodical. English. Twelve times a year. American Institute of Architects / New York, 457 Madison Avenue, New York NY 10022. **Tel** (212)838-9670.
Ind/Abst Avery Index Archit. Period. Suppl. Colum. Univ. (Sept. 1990-).

LC N3 .O48 **ISSN** 0029-9626
DD 705 AU
OESTERREICHISCHE ZEITSCHRIFT FUER KUNST UND DENKMALPFLEGE. See The Arts-Art.

US
CEASED
OFFRAMP. Added/Corp Southern California Institute of Architecture. **VFOAT** Off Ramp. (Spring 1988)-(1994). Periodical. English. Offramp, Sci-Arc, 5454 Beethoven Street, Los Angeles CA 90066. **Tel** (410)574-1123. **(Subscription address:** Princeton Architectural Press, 37 East 7th Street, New York NY 10003. **Tel** (212)995-9620.**)**
Ind/Abst Avery Index Archit. Period. Suppl. Colum. Univ. (Spring 1988).

ISSN 1079-3941
US
●**OLD-HOUSE INTERIORS. VFOAT** OHI. (1995)-. Consumer Publication. English. Four times a year. $18.00. Dovetale Publishers, 2 Main Street, Gloucester MA 01930. **Tel** (508)283-3200, (508)281-8803, FAX (508)283-4629. **(Subscription address:** Neodata / Colorado, PO Box 2606, Boulder CO 80322.**) ED** Patrica Poore.
Desc: Celebrates the charm of old houses. Articles cover style ideas, how-to advice, and affordable reproductions for every room.

ISSN 1071-0868
DD 721 US
●**OLD-HOUSE JOURNAL'S HISTORIC HOUSE PLANS, THE. VFOAT** Historic House Plans. Vol. 1, No. 1 (Spring 1994)-. Periodical. English. Every 2 years. $11.95. Dovetale Publishers, 2 Main Street, Gloucester MA 01930. **Tel** (508)283-3200, (508)281-8803, FAX (508)283-4629. **(Subscription address:** Neodata / Colorado, PO Box 2606, Boulder CO 80322.**) ED** Laura Marshall.

LC TJ859 .O43 **ISSN** 0276-3338
DD 621.2/1/0973 US
OLD MILL NEWS. [Old mill news]. **Added/Corp** Society for the Preservation of Old Mills. Vol. 1 No. 1 (Oct. 1972)-. Periodical. Four times a year. $12.50. Society for the Preservation of Old Mills, PO Box 335, Friendville TN 33737. **Tel** (615)567-7757. **ED** Michael J LaForest. Index available. cum. index. **Bk Rev. Ad Acc. Adv Mgr:** Tom Freestone. **Circ:** 1,500 (ctrl).
Desc: Devoted to the preservation and restoration of water-powered gristmills and to the history of milling.
Ind/Abst Avery Index Archit. Period. Suppl. Colum. Univ. (1989-).

LC F6 .O43 **ISSN** 0030-2031
US
SUSPENDED
OLD-TIME NEW ENGLAND. [Old-time New Engl.]. **Added/Corp** Society for the Preservation of New England Antiquities. **VFOAT** Old Time New England. (1920)-(Vol. 71, 1981). Periodical. English. Two times a year. $35.00. Society for Preserving New England Antiques, 141 Cambridge Street, Boston MA 02114. available on microfilm and microfiche from University Microfilms International (UMI). *Continues Society for the Preservation of New England Antiquities. Bulletin of the Society for the Preservation of New England Antiquities.*
Ind/Abst Am. Hist. Life (1966-1981).

LC NX **ISSN** 0030-3305
DD 770 IT
OP CIT. See The Arts-Art.

US
OPEN HOUSE. See Interior Design and Decoration.

ISSN 0168-2601
NE
OPEN HOUSE INTERNATIONAL.
Added/Corp Stichting Architecten Research (Eindhoven, Netherlands). Vol. 7, No. 2 (1982)-. Periodical. English. Four times a year. $128.34. Cardo School of Architecture, Univ of Newcastle Upon Tyne, Newcastle Tyne NE1 3RE United Kingdom. **Tel** 011 44 191 2226008, FAX 011 44 191 2611182. **ED** N. Wilkinson. *Continues Openhouse, 0921-3864.*
Ind/Abst Archit. Period. Index (1982,1983-); Avery Index Archit. Period. Suppl. Colum. Univ. (1984, 1988-).

BE
OPENBAAR KUNSTBEZIT IN VLAANDEREN. See The Arts.

ISSN 0882-7087
DD 720 US
OPUS INCERTUM. VFOAT Inserted Work. Vol. 1-. Periodical. English. Every 2 years. $4.50. University of Texas School of Architecture, Sutton Hall 2.130, Austin TX 78712. **Tel** (512)471-1922. **ED** Patrick Perry. **Circ:** 4,000.
Desc: Journal of student work at University of Texas at Austin School of Architecture, with interviews of noted architecture and planning professionals.

LC NA7205 .O75 **ISSN** 0899-4390
DD 728/.37/0222 US
CEASED
ORIGINAL HOME PLANS. [Orig. home plans]. **Added/Corp** Garlinghouse Company. **VFOAT** Home Plans. (19??)-(Spring 1994). English. The Garlinghouse Company Inc, 34 Industrial Park Place, PO Box 1717, Middletown CT 06457. **Tel** (203)632-1064, FAX (203)632-0712.
Desc: Home plans and related material.

ISSN 0391-7487
IT
TITLE CHANGE
OTTAGONO. (1986)-(19??). Periodical. English. *Merged with Ottagono to form Ottagono (Milan, Italy : 1991).*
Desc: Concerned with industrial design, architecture, and interior decoration.

IT
TITLE CHANGE
OTTAGONO. See Interior Design and Decoration.

US
OWNER BUILT HOME PLANS. English. Two times a year. $3.54 US; $7.74 Canada and Mexico; $12.04 other. The Garlinghouse Company Inc, 34 Industrial Park Place, PO Box 1717, Middletown CT 06457. **Tel** (203)632-1064, FAX (203)632-0712. **Ad Acc. Circ:** 100,000.
Desc: Compilation of Garlinghouse home plans and related material.

LC NX
DD 700 UK
OXFORD STUDIES IN THE HISTORY OF ART AND ARCHITECTURE. See The Arts-Art.

LC DA690.O97 O753
DD 942.57 UK
OXONIENSIA. See Archaeology.

LC NA712 .O9 **ISSN** 0888-7802
DD 720/.973 US
OZ (MANHATTAN, KAN.). (OZ.). [Oz]. **Added/Corp** Kansas State University. College of Architecture and Design. (1979)-. Periodical. English. One time a year. $22.50. Kansas State University / College of Architecture and Design, Seaton Hall, Manhattan KS 66506. **Tel** (913)532-7996. **ED** Sukhwant Jhaj, Kevin Heath, Jim Mitchell. Index available. **Ad Acc. Circ:** 650 (ctrl).

Desc: Dedicated to exploring ideas in architecture through the publication of essays and projects by students and faculty of Kansas State University as well as distinguished practitioners.
Ind/Abst Avery Index Archit. Period. Suppl. Colum. Univ. (1989-).

DD 720 — ISSN 0741-7543 US
PALLADIAN STUDIES IN AMERICA.
[Palladian stud. Am.]. **Added/Corp** Center for Palladian Studies in America (Charlottesville, Va.). (1984)-. English. Irregular. $30.00. University Press of Virginia, PO Box 3608, Charlottesville VA 22903. **Tel** (804)924-3469. **ED** Mario D. Valmarana. **Circ:** 500.
Desc: Essays on buildings in America, influenced in style and design by Palladio.

LC NA4 .P45 — ISSN 0031-0379 IT
PALLADIO.
[Palladio]. Vol. 1 (1937)-Vol. 1 (1951)-. Italian. Two times a year. L57840. Istituto Poligrafico Zecca Stato, Piazza Verdi 10, 00198 Rome Italy. **Tel** 011 39 6 85082307, 011 39 6 85082221.
Ind/Abst Archit. Period. Index (1974/76-); Art Index; Avery Index Archit. Period. Suppl. Colum. Univ. (1988-); BHA : Biblio. Hist. Art.

DD 621.317 — ISSN 0965-4712 UK
PANEL BUILDING.
[Panel build.]. (1991)-. Trade Publication. English. Six times a year. £35.00 UK; £40.00 Europe; £55.00 other. IML Group, Blair House, 184-186 High Street, Tonbridge Kent, TN9 1BQ United Kingdom. **Tel** 011 44 1732 359990, FAX 011 44 1732 770049.

ISSN 0065-681X IT
PAPERS AND MONOGRAPHS - AMERICAN ACADEMY IN ROME.
Main/Corp American Academy in Rome. Vol. 1 (1919)-. Monographic series. English. Irregular. Price varies per volume. Pennsylvania State University Press, 820 North University Drive, Suite 1, University Park PA 16802-1003. **Tel** (814)865-1327, (800)326-9180, FAX (814)863-1408.

ISSN 0031-1731 IT
PARAMETRO. See Housing and Urban Development.

DD 720/.9714/6 — ISSN 0835-6181 CN
PATRIMOINE ESTRIE.
[Patrim. Estrie]. **Added/Corp** Fonds du Patrimoine Estrien. Vol. 1, No 1 (1987)-. Periodical. French (summaries and/or abstracts in English). Four times a year. free. Fonds du Patrimoine Estrien, 92 nord, rue Wellington, Sherbrooke, Quebec J1H 5B8 Canada.

UDC 72 — ISSN 0865-6622 HU
PAVILON.
(1990)-. Hungarian. Four times a year. $25.00. **(Subscription address:** Kultura, PO Box 143, H-1300 Budapest 3 Hungary. **Tel** 011 36 1 2500194.**)**

LC NA730.P4 P46 — ISSN 1062-8649
DD 720/.9748/05 US
PENNSYLVANIA ARCHITECT.
[Pa. archit.]. **Added/Corp** Pennsylvania Society of Architects. Vol. 1, No. 1 (Fall 1984)-. Trade Publication. English. Four times a year. $10.00. Pennsylvania Society Architects, PO Box 5570, Harrisburg PA 17110. **Tel** 9717)236-4055. **ED** John Fatula, A.I.A., (phone: (215)854-9955). **Ad Acc. Circ:** 3,500.(ctrl).
Desc: Intended to highlight the Pennsylvania architects and their projects. Also contains articles relating to architecture.

ISSN 0213-0513 SP
UDC 72
PERIFERIA.
[Periferia]. (1984)-. Periodical. Spanish. Two times a year. 2500ptas. Revista Periferia, Plaza Cristo de Burgos 35, 41003 Seville Spain. **Tel** 011 34 5 4222910. **(Subscription address:** Revista Periferia, C Veronica de la Virgen V, 15, 18005 Granada Spain. **Tel** 011 34 58 522021.**)**
Ind/Abst Archit. Period. Index (June 1984-).

ISSN 0261-3204 UK
PERIOD HOME.
[Period home]. (19??)-. Periodical. English. Six times a year.
Ind/Abst Archit. Period. Index (1980-Aug. 1985).

LC N6 .P4 — ISSN 0553-6707 CI
Pr Rev.
PERISTIL (ZAGREB). See The Arts-Art.

LC NA1 .P46 — ISSN 0079-0958
DD 720 US
PERSPECTA.
[Perspecta]. **Added/Corp** Yale University. School of Architecture. Yale University. School of Design. **VFOAT** Yale Architectural Journal; Yale Papers on Architecture. (1952)-. Periodical. English. One time a year. $30.00. Rizzoli International Publishing Inc, 300 Park Avenue South, New York NY 10010. **Tel** (212)387-3500, (800)462-2387, FAX (212)982-3866. Documents available from The Genuine Article.
Ind/Abst Archit. Period. Index (1952,1980-); Art Index; Arts Humanit. Citation Index (19??-19??) [Full Cov.]; Avery Index Archit. Period. Suppl. Colum. Univ. (1990-); BHA : Biblio. Hist. Art; Res. Alert [Full Cov.].

IT
CEASED
PHALARIS : NUOVA SERIE DEL GIORNALE BIMESTRALE DI ARCHITETTURA DELLA FONDAZIONE A. MASIERI.
Added/Corp Fondazione A. Masieri. **VFOAT** Falaris. No. 1 (Mar./Apr. 1989)-(Jan. 1993). Italian. Arsenale Editrice Srl, Casella Postale 341, 30100 Venice Italy. **Continues** Galleria di Architettura.

ISSN 1071-1651
DD 720 US
Pr Rev.
PHILADELPHIA ARCHITECT.
[Phila. archit.]. **Added/Corp** American Institute of Architects. Philadelphia Chapter. (19??)-. Periodical. English. Twelve times a year. $24.00. Philadelphia Chapter of the American Institute of Architects, 117 South 17th Street, Philadelphia PA 19103. **Tel** (215)569-3186, FAX (215)569-9226. **ED** Peter Dobrin. **Bk Rev**, (Qty: 12). **Ad Acc. Circ:** 2,000.

LC TA1 .P46 — ISSN 0031-7470
DD 624.09914 PH
PHILIPPINE ARCHITECTURE, ENGINEERING, & CONSTRUCTION RECORD.
VAT Philippine Architecture, Engineering, and Construction Record. Periodical. English. Twelve times a year. Jacobs & Sons, PO Box 1899, Manila Philippines.
Ind/Abst Philip. Sci. Technol. Abstr.

ISSN 0295-5725 FR
UDC 725.74
PISCINES, SPAS MAGAZINE.
[Piscines spas mag.]. **VFOAT** Spas, Piscines Magazine. (1985)-. Periodical. French. Four times a year. $62.34. Editions Christian Ledoux Praxys, 68 rue des Bruyeres, 93260 Les Lilas France. **Tel** 011 33 1 48971414. **Continues** Piscines, Spas, Saunas, 0769-6604.

LC NA2542.35 .P53 — ISSN 0731-0455
DD 720 US
CCC
PLACES (CAMBRIDGE, MASS.).
(PLACES.). [Places]. **Added/Corp** University of California, Berkeley. College of Environmental Design. Massachusetts Institute of Technology. School of Architecture and Planning. Vol. No. 1 (Fall 1983)-. Periodical. English. Three times a year. $50.00. Allen Press Inc., 810 East 10th Street, PO Box 1897, Lawrence KS 66044-8897. **Tel** (913)843-1221, (800)627-0629, FAX (913)843-1274. **ED** Donlyn Lyndon. **Ad Acc. Acid Free. Circ:** 2,500. available on microfilm from University Microfilms International (UMI). Documents available from The Genuine Article.
Desc: A forum for observations and opinions on how places are designed, built, used, and maintained. Examines the role of the architects, landscape architects, engineers, urban designers, and planners in the formation of places, and the roles of citizens, politicians, lawyers, and others with influence.
Ind/Abst Archit. Period. Index (1984-); Arts Humanit. Citation Index [Full Cov.]; Avery Index Archit. Period. Suppl. Colum. Univ. (1989-); Garden Lit. (1992-); Geogr. Abstr. Human Geogr. (?-?); Int. Dev. Abstr. (?-?); Res. Alert [Full Cov.].

LC TH119.S66 P57
DD 690/.0968 SA
Pr Rev.
PLANNING.
(198?)-. Periodical. English. Six times a year. $41.75. Avonwold Publishing Company Pty Limited, PO Box 52068, Saxonwold 2132, South Africa. **Tel** 11 27 11 7881610. **Continues** Planning & Building Developments, 0377-2780.
Ind/Abst Archit. Period. Index.

LC NA6.I53 P64
IO
POLA.
1- Sept. 1973-. Indonesian. 100 single issue. Ikatan Mahasiswa Arsitektur Gunadharma ITB, Jl Dipati Ukur 9, Bandung Indonesia.

ISSN 1105-5537 GR
POLYDIASTATO NTIZ'AIN. See Interior Design and Decoration.

UK
PRACTICE : ISSUED TO THE MEMBERS OF THE ROYAL INSTITUTE OF BRITISH ARCHITECTS BY THE PRACTICE DEPARTMENT.
Added/Corp Royal Institute of British Architects. Practice Dept. (19??)-. Periodical. English. Twelve times a year. £25.00. Royal Institute of British Architects, 66 Portland Place, London W1N 4AD United Kingdom. **Tel** 011 44 171 2510791.
Ind/Abst Archit. Period. Index (Apr. 1984-).

ISSN 1059-7239
DD 720 US
PRACTICES (CINCINNATI, OHIO).
(PRACTICES / CSPA.). [Practices]. **Added/Corp** Center for the Study of the Practice of Architecture. **VFOAT** CSPA Practices. (1992)-. Periodical. English. Two times a year. $100.00. CSPA - Center for the Study and Practice of Architecture, University of Cincinnati, Cincinnati OH 45221. **Tel** (513)556-3413, FAX (513)556-3288. **ED** Daniel S. Friedman and Gordon Simmons. **Bk Rev**, (Qty: 1). **Circ:** 1,500.

ISSN 0888-3424
DD 720 US
PRACTICING ARCHITECT.
(PRACTICING ARCHITECT : A PUBLICATION OF THE SOCIETY OF AMERICAN REGISTERED ARCHITECTS.). [Pract. archit.]. **Added/Corp** Society of American Registered Architects. (19??)-. Periodical. English. Four times a year. $15.00. Society of American Registered Architects, 1245 S Highland Avenue, Lombard IL 60148. **Tel** (708)932-4622. **ED** Stanley D Banash. **Bk Rev. Ad Acc. Circ:** 30,000 (ctrl).
Desc: Combines practical information on the business aspects of operating an architectural office or firm, maintaining professional ethics. Includes new product information, and features articles covering the creative aspects of the profession regarding new and existing buildings, as well as government related updates on issues affecting the architectural design field.
Ind/Abst Avery Index Archit. Period. Suppl. Colum. Univ. (19??-199?).

ISSN 0225-0993
DD 720/.6/0714 CN
PRATIQUE PRIVEE, LA.
[Prat. privee]. Vol. 1 (Oct. 1979)-. Periodical. English (French). Irregular. Free. Association des Architectes en Pratique Privee du Quebec, 3634 Aylmer Street, Montreal Quebec H2X 2C2 Canada.

LC NA1 .P67 — ISSN 0883-7279
DD 720/.5 US
CEASED
PRATT JOURNAL OF ARCHITECTURE.
[Pratt j. archit.]. **Added/Corp** Pratt Institute. School of Architecture. **VFOAT** Journal of Architecture. Vol. 1 (1985)-(19??). English. Rizzoli International Publishing Inc, 300 Park Avenue South, New York NY 10010. **Tel** (212)387-3500, (800)462-2387, FAX (212)982-3866. **Circ:** 5,000.
Ind/Abst Archit. Period. Index; Avery Index Archit. Period. Suppl. Colum. Univ. (1988).

LC NA2300.C635 P74 — ISSN 0887-8781
DD 720/.5 US
CEASED
PRECIS (NEW YORK, N.Y.).
(PRECIS / COLUMBIA UNIVERSITY, GRADUATE SCHOOL OF ARCHITECTURE AND PLANNING.). [Precis]. **Added/Corp** Columbia University. Graduate School of Architecture and Planning. Vol. 1 (1979)-(19??). Periodical. English. Rizzoli International Publishing Inc, 300 Park Avenue South, New York NY 10010. **Tel** (212)387-3500, (800)462-2387, FAX (212)982-3866.

LC NA2349 .M52a
DD 724/.6 SP
PREMIO EUROPEO DE ARQUITECTURA PABELLON MIES VAN DER ROHE.
Main/Corp Mies van der Rohe Pavilion Award for European Architecture. **Added/Corp** Mies van der Rohe Foundation. Commission of the European Communities. (1992)-. Spanish. Every 2 years. Editorial Gustavo Gili SA, Rossello 87-89, 08029 Barcelona, Spain.

LC NA1 .P68 — ISSN 0478-1392
DD 363.3/9/0975915 US
PRESERVATION PROGRESS (CHARLESTON).
(PRESERVATION PROGRESS.). Vol. 1 (Dec. 1956)-. Periodical. English. Twelve times a year. $15.00 North America; $25.00 other. Preservation Society of Charleston, Box 521, Charleston SC 29402. **Tel** (803)722-4630. **Ad Acc. Circ:** 1,500 (ctrl).

ISSN 0741-9023
DD 721 US
PRESERVATION TECH NOTES.
[Preserv. tech notes]. **Added/Corp** United States. National Park Service. Preservation Assistance Division. **VFOAT** Tech Notes. PTN-1 (Jan. 1984)-. Monographic series. English. Three times a year. Price varies per volume. National Park Service, PO Box 37127, Washington DC 20013-7127. **Tel** (202)343-3395.
Ind/Abst Avery Index Archit. Period. Suppl. Colum. Univ. (Nov. 1986, June 1989, Sept. 1989).

LC NA53 .A39a — ISSN 0190-8766
DD 720/.25/73 US
PRO FILE: THE OFFICIAL DIRECTORY OF THE AMERICAN INSTITUTE OF ARCHITECTS.
Main/Corp American Institute of Architects. **VFOAT** ProFile. (1983)-. Directory. English. One time a year. $179.00. American Institute of Architects

Architecture

/ Washington DC, 1735 New York Avenue Northwest, Washington DC 20006. **Tel** (202)626-7460, FAX (202)626-7587. **(Subscription address:** American Institute of Architects, 2 Winter Sport Lane, PO Box 60, Williston VT 05495. **Tel** (800)365-2724.**) Continues** *Pro File: Professional File, Architectural Firm, 0190-8766.*

ISSN 0032-9150
CK

PROA. [Proa]. (Aug. 1946)-. Periodical. Spanish. Ten times a year (February through November). $110.00. Lorenzo Forseca, Calle 40 No 19-52, Bogota Colombia. **Tel** 011 57 1 2456447. **ED** Lorenzo Fonseca. Index available. cum. index. **Bk Rev. Ad Acc. Circ:** 4,000 (ctrl).
Desc: Recent architectural development and buildings, articles on architectural history and criticism, defense of our architectural heritage, student and international sections. Emphasis on Colombia.
Ind/Abst Archit. Period. Index (1979-); Avery Index Archit. Period. Suppl. Colum. Univ. (1988-).

LC QA76.9.A73 S9a ISSN 1063-6897
DD 004.2/2 US
PROCEEDINGS. See Computers.

LC NA673 .P76 ISSN 0386-037X
JA
PROCESS, ARCHITECTURE. [Process archit.]. **VFOAT** Architecture. No. 1 (Aug. 1977)-. Periodical. English (Japanese). Ten times a year. $312.00. **(Subscription address:** Maruzen Company Ltd., PO Box 5050, Import & Export Department, Tokyo 100 31 Japan. **Tel** 011 81 3 32789224.**) ED** Bunji Murotani. **Ad Acc. Circ:** 2,000 (ctrl).
Desc: Each issue is devoted to a specific architect, theme or geographic area.
Ind/Abst Archit. Period. Index (1977-); Avery Index Archit. Period. Suppl. Colum. Univ. (1989-).

IT
PROFESSIONE, ARCHITETTO. Added/Corp Ordine degli Architetti di Firenze. **VFOAT** A.P:A. (198?)-. Periodical. Italian. Four times a year. L27250. Alinea Editrice, Via da Palestrina 17-19, Rosso 50144 Florence Italy. **Tel** 011 39 55 333428.

LC NA1 .P7 ISSN 0033-0752
DD 720 US
CCC
CODEN PGRAAM
PROGRESSIVE ARCHITECTURE. [Prog. archit.]. **VFOAT** PA. Vol. 26, No. 10 (Oct. 1945)-. Periodical. English. Twelve times a year. $48.00. Penton Publishing, 1100 Superior Avenue, Cleveland OH 44114-2543. **Tel** (216)696-7000, FAX (216)696-0836. **(Subscription address:** Progressive Architecture, PO Box 724, Mt. Morris IL 61054. **) ED** John Dixon, Tom Fisher, and James Murphy. Index available. **Ad Acc. Circ:** 75,000. available on microfilm and microfiche from University Microfilms International (UMI); available on an online database (file 648/Full-Text) from DIALOG. Documents available from Article Express International, The Genuine Article, UMI Article Clearinghouse.
Continues *Pencil Points (East Stroudsburg, PA. : 1944), 0890-6378.*
Ind/Abst Acad. Search; Appl. Sci. Technol. Index; Archit. Period. Index (1977-); Art Archaeol. Tech. Abstr.; Art Index; ARTbibliogr. Mod.; Arts Humanit. Citation Index [Full Cov.]; Avery Index Archit. Period. Suppl. Colum. Univ. (1990-); Bioeng. Abstr.; Bus. Index (1985-); Concr. Abstr.; Constr. Index; Curr. Cit.; Curr. Contents Arts Humanit.; Ei Page One; Eng. Index Annu.; EP Collect.; Expand. Acad. Index (1992-); Garden Lit. (1992-); Gen. BusinessFile (1985-); Gen. Period. Index (1985-); Health Plan. Adminis.; Homework Help.; Hosp. Health Admin. Index; J. Plan. Lit.; Mag. Search; MasterFile FullTEXT 1000; MasterFile FullTEXT 350; MasterFile FullTEXT 650; MasterFile FullTEXT (July 1993-); Newsp. Period. Abstr. (1992-); OCLC; Res. Alert [Full Cov.]; Soc. Sci. Cit. Index [Select. Cov.]; Telebase; Trade Ind. ASAP [Full Txt.]; Trade Ind. Index [Full Txt.].

ISSN 0265-4644
UK
PROJECTS REVIEW (LONDON, ENGLAND). (PROJECTS REVIEW.). **Added/Corp** Architectural Association (Great Britain). School of Architecture. (1982)-. English. One time a year. £15.00. AA Publications, 34-36 Bedford Square, London WC1B 3ES United Kingdom. **Tel** 011 44 171 6360974, FAX 011 44 171 4368740. ctrl circ. **Continues** *AA Projects Review.*

LC HC186 .P73 ISSN 0101-1766
DD 338.981 BL
PROJETO. [Projeto]. (19??)-. Portuguese. Eleven times a year. $160.00. Arco Editorial LTDA, Rua General Jardim 633-3 Andar, 01223-011 Sao Paulo SP Brazil. **Tel** 011 55 11 259 9688, FAX 011 55 11 259 9688, telex 1180461. **ED** Arlindo Munglioli.
Ind/Abst Archit. Period. Index (1980-).

ISSN 0143-8883
DD 720.9411 UK
PROSPECT (EDINBURGH. 1978). [Prospect Edinb. 1978]. (1978)-. Trade Publication. English. Four times a year. Royal Incorporation of Architects in Scotland, 15 Rutledge Square, Edinburgh EH1 2BE United Kingdom. **Tel** (031)229-7205. **Continues** *Newsletter - Royal Incorporation of Architects in Scotland.*
Ind/Abst Museum Abstr.

LC N8700 .P83 ISSN 1040-211X
DD 711 US
Pr Rev.
PUBLIC ART REVIEW. See The Arts-Art.

LC VM156 .G6
DD 623.8/1 SW
PUBLIC RESEARCH REPORT. VFOAT SSPA Public Research Report. Monographic series. English. Irregular. Price varies per volume. **Continues** *Publication (Marintekniska Institutet (Sweden)), 0280-4255.*

ISSN 0167-6652
NE
PUBLICATIONS DE LA SOCIETE HISTORIQUE ET ARCHEOLOGIQUE DANS LE LIMBOURG. [Publ. Soc. Hist. Archeol. Limbg.]. **Main/Corp** Limburgs Geschied- en Oudheidkundig Genootschap. **Added/Corp** Limburgs Geschied- en Oudheidkundig Genootschap. Jaarboek. (1864)-. Periodical. Multiple languages (Dutch and French). One time a year. Free to members of Societe Historique et Archeologique dans le Limbourg. Societe Historique et Archeologique, Bureau LGOG, PO Box 83, Maastricht 6200 AB Netherlands. **Tel** 011 31 43 212586. cum. index.
Ind/Abst Am. Hist. Life (1964-1984); BHA : Biblio. Hist. Art.

ISSN 1064-4733
US
PUBLICITY DIRECTORY FOR THE DESIGN, ENGINEERING, AND BUILDING INDUSTRIES, THE. See Building and Construction.

LC NA
DD 720 VE
PUNTO. Added/Corp Universidad Central de Venezuela. Facultad de Arquitectura y Urbanismo. Division de Extension Cultural. (1961)-. Periodical. Spanish. Centro de Informacion y Documentacion, Facultad de Arquitectura y Urbanismo, Universidad Central de Venezuela, Apartado Postal 40362, Caracas 1040-A Venezuela. **Bk Rev. Ad Acc. Circ:** 3,000.
Desc: A review of state-of-the-art architecture in Venezuela. Special interest in the production of architecture in other Latin American countries.
Ind/Abst Avery Index Archit. Period. Suppl. Colum. Univ. (19??-199?).

LC WMLC L 83/2804 ISSN 0485-4152
IT
QUADERNI DELL'ISTITUTO DI STORIA DELL'ARCHITETTURA. (QUADERNI DELL'ISTITUTO DI STORIA DELL'ARCHITETTURA / FACOLTA DI ARCHITETTURA, UNIVERSITA DI ROMA.). [Quad. ist. stor. archit.]. **Added/Corp** Universita di Roma. Istituto di Storia dell'Architettura. Universita di Roma. Facolta di Architettura. Series. 1 (1953)-. Italian. Irregular. Bonsignori Editore, Viale del Quattro Venti 47, 00152 Rome Italy. **Tel** 011 39 6 5881496, FAX 011 39 6 5882839.
Ind/Abst BHA : Biblio. Hist. Art.

LC NA4 .G45A
IT
QUADERNO. Main/Corp Genoa. Universita. Istituto di Progettazione Architettonica. (Oct. 1968)-. Italian. 10500 single issue. Edizioni dell'Istituto de Progettazione Architettonica, Universita Degli Studi di Genova, Via Opera Pia Causa 11, Genova 16145 Italy.

LC NA1301 .Q3 ISSN 0211-9595
SP
Pr Rev.
QUADERNS D'ARQUITECTURA I URBANISME. [Quad. arquit. urban.]. **Added/Corp** Collegio Oficial de Arquitectos de Cataluna y Baleares. **VFOAT** Quaderns. (Jan./Feb. 1981)-. Periodical. Catalan (English and Spanish). Four times a year (Jan., Apr., July, Oct.). $102.14. Colegio Arquitectos Cataluna, Place Nova 5, 08002 Barcelona Spain. **Tel** 011 34 3 3015000, FAX 011 34 3 4123964, telex 50873. **ED** Manuel Gause. Index available. **Ad Acc, Adv Mgr:** Ignasi Perez Arnal, **Tel** 301-50-00 Ext. 296. **Circ:** 10,000 (ctrl). **Continues** *Cuadernos de Arquitectura y Urbanismo.*
Desc: Covers national and international architectual projects of current interest.
Ind/Abst Archit. Period. Index (Jan. 1981-); Avery Index Archit. Period. Suppl. Colum. Univ. (July-Dec. 1988, Apr.-Sept 1989, Jan. 1990-); BHA : Biblio. Hist. Art.

LC NA1301 .Q3
SP
QUADERNS D'ARQUITECTURA I URBANISME. Added/Corp Collegi Oficial de Arquitectos de Catalunya y Baleares. (19??)-. Periodical. Catalan (English and Spanish). Four times a year. 640000ptas (Spain); 1150000ptas (North and South America); 850000ptas (Europe except Spain); 1450000ptas (other). Colegio Arquitectos Cataluna, Place Nova 5, 08002 Barcelona Spain. **Tel** 011 34 3 3015000, FAX 011 34 3 4123964, telex 50873. **Ad Acc. Circ:** 8,000.

LC NA9224.C3 Q3
DD 711/.4/09467 SP
QUADERNS D'ARQUITECTURA I URBANISME. EXTRA. Added/Corp Collegi Oficial de Arquitectos de Catalunya y Baleares. (1981)-. Monographic series. Catalan. Irregular. Price varies per volume. Colegio Arquitectos Cataluna, Place Nova 5, 08002 Barcelona Spain. **Tel** 011 34 3 3015000, FAX 011 34 3 4123964, telex 50873.

IT
QUASAR ITALY. Italian. Two times a year (June, Dec.). L27250. Karta Sas, Via Slataper 10, 50134 Florence Italy. **Tel** 011 39 55 496502.
Ind/Abst BHA : Biblio. Hist. Art.

LC VM4 .R36 ISSN 0916-0981
JA
RAN / BULLETIN OF THE KANSAI SOCIETY OF NAVAL ARCHITECTS, JAPAN / KANSAI ZOSEN KYOKAI. Added/Corp Kansai Zosen Kyokai. **VFOAT** Tomozuna; Bulletin of the Kansai Society of Naval Architects, Japan. (1988)-. Periodical. Japanese. Four times a year. $108.09. Kansai Society of Naval Architects, Osaka University, Campus 2 1 Yamada Oka Ste, Shi Osaka 565 Japan. **Tel** 011 81 6 8775111.

ISSN 0393-0203
IT
RASSEGNA (BOLOGNA). (RASSEGNA.). [Rassegna]. (1979)-. Periodical. Italian (English; summaries and/or abstracts in English, French and German). Four times a year. L64720. CIPIA s.r.l., via Stalingrado 97/2, 40128 Bologna Italy. **Tel** 011 39 51 327929, FAX 011 39 51 327877. Index available. cum. index. **Ad Acc.**
Ind/Abst Archit. Period. Index (1979-); Avery Index Archit. Period. Suppl. Colum. Univ.

LC WMLC 93/253 ISSN 0392-8608
IT
RASSEGNA DI ARCHITETTURA E URBANISTICA. [Rass. architet. urban.]. **Added/Corp** Universita di Roma. (1980)-. Periodical. Italian. Two times a year. Edizioni Kappa, Via S Benco 14, 00177 Rome Italy. **Tel** 011 39 6 273903. **Continues** *Rassegna dell'Istituto di Architettura e Urbanistica, 0021-2458.*
Ind/Abst Avery Index Archit. Period. Suppl. Colum. Univ. (1989-); BHA : Biblio. Hist. Art.

US
RE/ALIGNMENT. VFOAT Realignment; Re Alignment. Vol. 1, No. 1 (Nov. 1992)-. Periodical. English. Two times a year. $14.00. Debates / MLA Program Harvard, Graduate School of Design, 48 Quincy Street, Cambridge MA 02138. **Tel** (617)868-5862. **(Subscription address:** Re Alignment, PO Box 380947, Cambridge MA 02238. **)**

ISSN 0213-8948
SP
UDC 72.02
Pr Rev.
RE. REVISTA DE EDIFICACION. [RE, Rev. edif.]. **VFOAT** Revista de Edificacion. (1987)-. Periodical. Spanish. Four times a year. 2200.00ptas. Anuario Filosofico / Edificio de Bibliotecas / Universidad de Navarra, Campus Universitario, 31080 Pamplona Spain. **Tel** 011 34 948 252700 Ext 2490, FAX 011 34 948 173650. **Ad Acc. Circ:** 3,000.

LC NA2 .R33 ISSN 0373-4285
DD 720/.5 FR
RECHERCHE ET ARCHITECTURE. (RECHERCHE & I.E. ET ARCHITECTURE.). [Rech. archit.]. **Added/Corp** Centre Scientifique et Technique du Batiment (France) Centre Scientifique et Technique du Batiment (France) Cahiers. (1970)-. Periodical. French. Four times a year. 55.00F. Centre Scientifique et Technique du Batiment, 84 Avenue Jean Jaures, BP 2, 77421 Marne la Vallee Cedex 2 France. **Tel** 011 31 1 64688436, FAX 011 31 1 64688478.
Ind/Abst Archit. Period. Index (1970-); EMBASE (19??-199?); World Ceram. Abstr.

US
RECORD HOUSES AND APARTMENTS OF THE YEAR. See Interior Design and Decoration.

ISSN 0967-2885
UK
RECORDS OF BUCKINGHAMSHIRE, OR, PAPERS AND NOTES ON THE HISTORY, ANTIQUITIES, AND ARCHITECTURE OF THE COUNTY, TOGETHER WITH THE PROCEEDINGS OF THE ARCHITECTURAL AND ARCHAEOLOGICAL SOCIETY FOR THE COUNTY OF BUCKINGHAM. Added/Corp Architectural and Archaeological Society for the County of

Architecture

Buckingham. Buckinghamshire Archaeological Society. Vol. 1 (1858)-. Proceedings. English. One time a year. $28.23. Bucks Arch Society County Museum, Church Street, Aylesbury Buckinghamshire HP20 2QP United Kingdom. **Tel** 011 44 12 9620984. cum. index.
Ind/Abst BHA : Biblio. Hist. Art.

ISSN 0392-4599
IT

UDC 69+712.3/7
Pr Rev.
RECUPERARE. EDILIZIA DESIGN IMPIANTI.
[Recuper. Edil. Des. Impianti]. (1982)-. Periodical. Italian (summaries and/or abstracts in English and French). Nine times a year. $121.00. Editoriale PEG Spa, Via Fratelli Bressan 2, 20126 Milan Italy. **Tel** 011 39 2 2579841, FAX 011 39 2 255-2779, telex 323088 PEGMOS I. **ED** Marina Kern. Index available. cum. index. **Bk Rev. Ad Acc. Circ:** 10,200 (ctrl).
Desc: Discusses technical, practical problems of building rehabilitation referred to large, medium and small civil, industrial and residential buildings.
Ind/Abst Archit. Period. Index.

US
REDWOOD NEWS. See Forests and Forestry-Lumber and Wood.

LC NA11 .R44
US
REFERENCE BOOK / AIA GEORGIA.
Added/Corp American Institute of Architects. Georgia Association. **VFOAT** AIA Georgia Reference Book. (19??)-. Trade Publication. English. Irregular. Publications Concepts, 1240 Johnson Ferry Place, Suite E-10, Marietta GA 30068. **Continues** Georgia Architect's Handbook.

LC NA12 .I47
DD 720/.6/041
UK
REFERENCE BOOK & LIST OF MEMBERS.
Main/Corp Incorporated Association of Architects and Surveyors. **VFOAT** Reference Book and List of Members. (19??)-. English. Millbank Publications Ltd, 25 Catherine Street, London WC2B 5JW United Kingdom.

US
REFERENCE GUIDE TO HOMEBUILDING ARTICLES.
Added/Corp National Association of Home Builders (U.S.). Library and Information Center. **VFOAT** Reference Guide to Home Building Articles. (1992)-. English. Four times a year. $15.00. National Association of Home Builders, 15th and M Street NW, Washington DC 20005. **Tel** (202)822-0203. **Continues** Homes and Homebuilding, 0441-6856.

US
REFERENCE GUIDE TO HOMEBUILDING ARTICLES.
Added/Corp National Association of Home Builders (U.S.). Library and Information Center. **VFOAT** Reference Guide to Home Building Articles. 4th Quarter (1991)-. English. Four times a year. National Association of Home Builders, 15th and M Street NW, Washington DC 20005. **Tel** (202)822-0203. **Continues** NAHB Library Bulletin.

LC NA2000 .R39
DD 720/.1
ISSN 0739-9448
US
Pr Rev.
REFLECTIONS (CHAMPAIGN, ILL.).
(REFLECTIONS : THE JOURNAL OF THE SCHOOL OF ARCHITECTURE, UNIVERSITY OF ILLINOIS AT URBANA-CHAMPAIGN.). [Reflections]. **Added/Corp** University of Illinois at Urbana-Champaign. School of Architecture. Vol. 1, No. 1 (Fall 1983)-. Periodical. English. One time a year. $18.00. University of Illinois at Urbana-Champaign / School of Architecture, 106 Architecture Building, Champaign IL 61820. **Tel** (217)333-1330, FAX (217)244-2900. **ED** Paul J. Armstrong.
Desc: An architectural journal dedicated to theory and criticism.
Ind/Abst Avery Index Archit. Period. Suppl. Colum. Univ. (Spring 1990).

DD 721
ISSN 1040-1377
US
REGIONALE WEST.
[Reg. west]. Vol. 1, No. 1 (Oct. 1988)-. Periodical. English. Six times a year. $17.95. Regionale West Publications Inc, PO Box 44-1463, 10660 East Bethany Drive, Auora CO 80044-9909. **Tel** (303)751-4752. **ED** Victoria Masterson. **Circ:** 22,000.
Desc: Shows how culture in the west influences architecture and design.

LC NA50
DD 720/.25/7123
ISSN 1182-6606
CN
REGISTER AND FIRM INDEX.
[Regist. firm index - Alta. Assoc. Arch.]. **Main/Corp** Alberta Association of Architects. (1991)-. English. Alberta Association of Architects, 10515 Saskatchewan Drive, Edmonton Alberta T6E 4S1 Canada. **Continues** Alberta Association of Architects. Architects Register., 0842-2966.

LC NA9127
DD 711.09774
US
REPORT - DETROIT. METROPOLITAN AREA REGIONAL PLANNING COMMISSION.
Main/Corp Detroit. Metropolitan Area Regional Planning Commission. Periodical. English. One time a year. Metro Regional Planning Commission, 800 Cadillac Square Building, Detroit MI 48201.

LC NA124.K2 A3
DD 720.69
US
REPORT - KANSAS. STATE REGISTRATION AND EXAMINING BOARD FOR ARCHITECTS.
Main/Corp Kansas. State Registration and Examining Board for Architects. No. 1 (1949/50)-. English. One time a year. Kansas State Registration & Examining Board for Architects, Topeka KS 66620.

UK
RESEARCH AND ADVANCED STUDIES BULLETIN / UNIVERSITY OF STRATHCLYDE, DEPARTMENT OF ARCHITECTURE AND BUILDING SCIENCE. See Building and Construction.

LC NA4590 .B55
DD 726.5
ISSN 0305-2206
UK
RESEARCH BULLETIN - INSTITUTE FOR THE STUDY OF WORSHIP AND RELIGIOUS ARCHITECTURE.
(RESEARCH BULLETIN - INSTITUTE FOR THE STUDY OF WORSHIP AND RELIGIOUS ARCHITECTURE (BIRMINGHAM, ENGLAND).). [Res. bull. - Inst. Study Worsh. Relig. Archit.]. **Main/Corp** Birmingham, Eng. University. Institute for the Study of Worship and Religious Architecture. (1966)-. Bulletin. English. One time a year.
Ind/Abst Archit. Period. Index (1966-19??, 1977-).

LC Z5941 .R47 NA200
DD 016.72/09
UK
RESEARCH REGISTER LIST / THE SOCIETY OF ARCHITECTURAL HISTORIANS OF GREAT BRITAIN.
Added/Corp Society of Architectural Historians of Great Britain. (19??)-. English. Irregular. Society of Architectural Historians of Great Britain, 4 Woodlands Avenue Finchley, London N3 2NR United Kingdom. **Tel** 011 44 181 3465139. **ED** John Archer. **Circ:** 1,100.
Desc: List of research projects in architectural history, not a regular serial publication but an occasional publication issued to members.

LC NA109.I8 R46
DD 363.6/9/0946
IT
RESTAURO.
Added/Corp Edizioni Scientifiche Italiane. **VFOAT** Architettura e Citta Antiche. **VAT** Quaderni di Restauro dei Monumenti e di Urbanistica dei Centri Antiche. (1984)-. Trade Publication. Italian. Four times a year. L102080. Edizioni Scientifiche Italiane, Via Chiatamone 7, 80121 Naples Italy. **Tel** 011 39 81 7645768, 011 39 81 7645443, FAX 011 39 81 7646477.
Ind/Abst Avery Index Archit. Period. Suppl. Colum. Univ. (Sept./Oct. 1987, May-Dec. 1989, May-June 1990); BHA : Biblio. Hist. Art.

LC NA108.A85 R47
DD 720/.28/809758231
US
RESTORATION RESOURCE GUIDE.
Added/Corp Atlanta Preservation Center. (19??)-. English. Irregular. Atlanta Preservation Center, 401 The Flatiron Building, 84 Peachtree Street Northwest, Atlanta GA 30303.

DD 720/.5
ISSN 0705-1913
CN
REVIEW OF ARCHITECTURE AND LANDSCAPE ARCHITECTURE.
Spring 1977-. Periodical. English. Programmes in Architecture, University of Toronto, 230 College Street, Toronto Ontario M5S 1A1 Canada. **Supersedes** After School, 0382-9235.

DD 720
ISSN 0734-3884
US
REVIEW / SOCIETY OF ARCHITECTURAL HISTORIANS, SOUTHERN CALIFORNIA CHAPTER.
[Rev. - Soc. Archit. Hist., South. Calif. Chapter]. **VFOAT** SAH/SCC Review; S.A.H./S.C.C. Review. Vol. 1, No. 1 (Fall 1981)-. Periodical. English. Three times a year. $12.00 membership. **Continues in part** Society of Architectural Historians Southern California Chapter Newsletter. **Continued in part by** Newsletter (Society of Architectural Historians. Southern California Chapter), 8756-4580.
Ind/Abst Archit. Period. Index.

LC NX7 .R463
ISSN 0185-3570
MX
REVISTA DE BELLAS ARTES (MEXICO, D.F.). See The Arts-Art.

ISSN 0102-2571
BL
REVISTA DO PATRIMONIO HISTORICO E ARTISTICO NACIONAL.
(REVISTA DO PATRIMONIO HISTORICO E ARTISTICO NACIONAL / MINISTERIO DA EDUCACAO E SAUDE.). [Rev. Patrim. Hist. Artist. Nac.]. **Added/Corp** Brazil. Diretoria do Patrimonio Historico e Artistico Nacional. Fundacao Nacional Pro-Memoria (Brazil). **VFOAT** Revista do Patrimonio. No. 10 (1946)-. Periodical. Portuguese. Two times a year. **Continues** Revista do Servico do Patrimonio Historico e Artistico Nacional, 0102-2563.
Ind/Abst BHA : Biblio. Hist. Art.

LC TA4 .R5
DD 620.5
ISSN 0035-0028
MX
REVISTA MEXICANA DE INGENIERIA Y ARQUITECTURA : ORGANO DE LA ASSOCIACION DE INGENIEROS Y ARQUITECTOS DE MEXICO. See Engineering.

UK
● ### RIBA JOURNAL.
Added/Corp Royal Institute of British Architects. **VFOAT** Royal Institute of British Architects Journal. Vol. 100, No. 9 (Sept. 1993)-. Periodical. English. Twelve times a year. $130.05. RIBA Companies Ltd., Finsbury Mission, 39 Moreland Street, London EC1V 8B8 United Kingdom. **Tel** 011 44 171 2510791, FAX 011 44 171 6082375. **Continues** Journal (Royal Institute of British Architects : Overseas ed.), 0953-6973.
Ind/Abst Curr. Cit.
Desc: Official journal of the Royal Institute of British Architects..

UK
RIBA MEMBERS.
Main/Corp Royal Institute of British Architects. **VFOAT** RIBA Directory of Members; Building by Design. **VAT** Royal Institute of British Architects Members. English. Royal Institute of British Architects, 66 Portland Place, London W1N 4AD United Kingdom. **Tel** 011 44 171 2510791. **Continues** Directory of RIBA Members, 0269-0829.
Desc: Directory of the Royal Institute of British Architects.

LC NA8205 .A3
ISSN 0080-2964
IT
RICERCHE SULLE DIMORE RURALI IN ITALIA.
Added/Corp Italy. Consiglio Nazionale delle Ricerche. Comitato Nazionale per la Geologia, la Geografia e la Talassografia. Italy. Consiglio Nazionale delle Ricerche. Italy. Centro di Studi per la Geografia Etnologica. (1938)-. Monographic series. Italian. Irregular. Price varies per volume. Casa Editrice Leo S. Olschki, Viuzzo del Pozzetto, Casella Postale 66, 50126 Florence Italy. **Tel** 011 39 55 6530684, FAX 011 39 55 6530214.

LC NA124.F6 A3
DD 720.69
US
ROSTER - FLORIDA STATE BOARD OF ARCHITECTURE.
Main/Corp Florida State Board of Architecture. **VFOAT** Architects Registered in the State of Florida. English.
Desc: Directory of the members of the State Board of Architecture. Provides a listing of member architects.

US
ROSTER OF REGISTERED ARCHITECTS AND ARCHITECTURAL CORPORATIONS AS OF ... / NORTH CAROLINA STATE BOARD OF ARCHITECTURE.
Added/Corp North Carolina Board of Architecture. **VFOAT** North Carolina Roster of Architects; Roster of Registered Architects; A.NC roster of architects. (19??)-. English. North Carolina Board of Architecture, 501 North Blount Street, Raleigh NC 27604-1197. **Continues** Roster of Registered Architects in North Carolina.
Desc: Listing of the registered architects and corporations of North Carolina.

LC NA54.M2 M34A
DD 720/.25/741
US
ROSTER OF REGISTERED ARCHITECTS AND LANDSCAPE ARCHITECTS YEAR ENDING JUNE 30 ... / MAINE STATE BOARD FOR REGISTRATION OF ARCHITECTS AND LANDSCAPE ARCHITECTS.
Main/Corp Maine State Board for Registration of Architects and Landscape Architects. English. One time a year.
Desc: Listing of the registered architects and landscape architects of the state of Maine.

Architecture

LC NA54.T4 R67   **ISSN** 0149-0486
DD 720/.25/764   US
ROSTER OF REGISTERED ARCHITECTS (AUSTIN). (ROSTER OF REGISTERED ARCHITECTS.). [Roster regist. archit.]. English. Texas Board of Architectural Examiners, 202 Richmond Building, 1411 West Avenue, Austin TX 78701.

LC NA11 .M57
DD 720/.25/762   US
ROSTER OF REGISTERED ARCHITECTS / MISSISSIPPI STATE BOARD OF ARCHITECTURE. Main/Corp Mississippi State Board of Architecture. English. One time a year. Mississippi State Board of Architecture, 239 N Lamar Street/Suite 502, Jackson MS 39201-1311. **Continues** Mississippi State Board of Architecture. Annual Report.

LC NA54.S6 S67a
DD 720/.25/757   US
ROSTER : REGISTERED ARCHITECTS, FIRMS, PROFESSIONAL CORPORATIONS, BUSINESS CORPORATIONS, AND PARTNERSHIPS. Added/Corp South Carolina. State Board of Architectural Examiners. (19??)-. English. Architectural Exam, 3710 Landmark Drive/Suite 206, Columbia SC 29204. **Continues** State of South Carolina Roster of Registered Architects, Firms, Corporations, and Partnerships.

LC TA12 .H38A
DD 620/.0025/969   US
ROSTER - STATE BOARD OF REGISTRATION OF PROFESSIONAL ENGINEERS, ARCHITECTS AND LAND SURVEYORS. See Engineering.

LC NA5 .S63A   **ISSN** 0325-1179
    AG
RSCA. [RSCA]. **Main/Corp** Sociedad Central de Arquitectos, Buenos Aires. **VFOAT** Revista. **VAT** Revista - Sociedad Central de Arquitectos. Periodical. Spanish. $4.00. Montevideo 942, Buenos Aires Argentina.

    ISSN 0563-0991
    JA
S D; SPACE DESIGN. VFOAT Space Design; Supesu Dezain. No. 1 (1965)-. Periodical. Japanese (summaries and/or abstracts in English). Twelve times a year. $324.28. Kajima Institute Publishing Company Ltd., 5-13-6-chome Akasaka, 245151006 Tokyo Japan. **Tel** 011 81 3 35822251, FAX 011 81 3 35892928. **ED** Kobun Ito. **Bk Rev**. **Ad Acc**. **Circ:** 30,000.
Desc: Information on eminent works and products of architecture, interior, industrial products, home furnishings and also fine art.
Ind/Abst Archit. Period. Index (1975-19??); Avery Index Archit. Period. Suppl. Colum. Univ. (1990-).

LC NA6 .A7274
    RU
    CODEN SPPAEA
S.-PETERBURGSKAIA PANORAMA.
VFOAT Sankt-Peterburgskaia Panorama; Sankt Peterburgskaia Panorama. (1991)-. Periodical. Russian. Twelve times a year. $89.95. Lenizdat, Fontanka 59, St. Petersburg Russia. **(Subscription address:** East View Publications Inc., 3020 Harbor Lane North, Suite 110, Minneapolis MN 55447. **Tel** (800)477-1005, (612)550-0961, FAX (612)559-2931.) **Continues** Leningradskaia Panorama, 0233-7010.
Ind/Abst Archit. Period. Index.

    SZ
SCHWEIZER BAUBLATT. VFOAT Baukader. (19??)-. Periodical. German. Irregular (104 issues). 420.00F Europe; 495.00F other. Schueck Soehne AG, Bahnhofstrasse 24, CH-8803 Rueschlikon Switzerland. **Tel** 011 41 1 7247766. **Absorbed** Baukader.

    ISSN 0251-0960
    SZ
    CODEN SIARD4
SCHWEIZER INGENIEUR UND ARCHITEKT. See Engineering-Civil Engineering.

LC NA   **ISSN** 1121-9122
DD 720   IT
SCIENCE AND TECHNOLOGY FOR CULTURAL HERITAGE : JOURNAL OF THE "COMITATO NAZIONALE PER LA SCIENZA E LA TECNOLOGIA DEI BENI CULTURALI," CNR. Added/Corp Consiglio Nazionale delle Ricerche (Italy). Comitato Nazionale per la Scienza e la Tecnologia dei beni Culturali (Italy). (1992)-. Periodical. English (summaries and/or abstracts in Italian). Irregular. Giardine Editori e Stampatori in Pisa, via delle Sorgenti 23, 56010 Agnano Pisano, Italy.

LC NA60.G7 S36
DD 720/.25/411   UK
SCOTTISH ARCHITECTS DIRECTORY, THE. Added/Corp Royal Incorporation of Architects in Scotland. (19??)-. Directory. English. £12.00. Royal Incorporation of Architects in Scotland, 15 Rutledge Square, Edinburgh EH1 2BE United Kingdom. **Tel** (031)229-7205. **Ad Acc**. **Circ:** 3,000.

LC NA1 .S53   **ISSN** 1043-0946
DD 016.72/05   US
SEARCH. [Search]. (Jan., Feb., Mar. 1988)-. Periodical. English. Four times a year (Feb. issue is the annual and the other 3 are updates). $99.00. Search Publishing Inc, 102 Brighton Circle, Devon PA 19333. **Tel** (610)889-0535, FAX (610)889-9497. **ED** Don Colangelo. cum. index. **Circ:** 800.
Desc: Index to periodicals read by architects and interior designers. Special features include keyword list, reference to illustrations and listing of full design team.

    ISSN 0715-9781
DD 724.9/105   CN
SECTION A - REVUE D'ARCHITECTURE. (SECTION A : REVUE D'ARCHITECTURE : ARCHITECTURE MAGAZINE.). [Sect. a - rev. archit.]. Vol. 1, No. 1 (Feb./March 1983)-. Periodical. English (French). Six times a year. Section A, Box 909, La Cite, Montreal Quebec H2W 2P5 Canada. **ED** Odile Henault. **Bk Rev**. **Ad Acc**. **Circ:** 5,000.
Desc: An illustrated architecture magazine reaching architects and designers who want the latest design news and serious investigation into the building environment.
Ind/Abst Archit. Period. Index; Avery Index Archit. Period. Suppl. Colum. Univ. (19??-199?).

    ISSN 0848-8266
DD 747/.05   CN
SELECT HOMES & FOOD. RENOVATION IDEAS. [Sel. homes food, Renov. ideas]. **VFOAT** Renovation Ideas. (1989)-. Periodical. English. Four times a year. National Telemedia Council Inc, 120 East Wilson Street, Madison WI 53703. **Tel** (608)257-7712. **Continues** Select Homes (Vancouver, B.C.). Renovation Ideas., 0848-8274.

    ISSN 0009-871X
    US
SEMESTER REVIEW, THE. Added/Corp Clemson Architectural Foundation. Clemson University. College of Architecture. Vol. 9 (Spring 1975)-. Periodical. English. Four times a year. Free on request (to foundation members, Clemson Architecture students and accredited schools of architecture), $6.00 other. Clemson Architectural Foundation, Clemson University, College of Architecture, Clemson SC 29632. **Continues** Semester Review of the Clemson College of Architecture.

LC NA25 .B73 NA21
    PL
SERIA KONFERENCJE. Main/Corp Politechnika Wroclawska. Instytut Architektury i Urbanistyki. **Added/Corp** Politechnika Wroclawska. Instytut Architektury i Urbanistyki. Conferences. **VFOAT** Conferences. No. 1 (1977)-. Monographic series. Polish (summaries and/or abstracts in English and Russian). Price varies per volume. **(Subscription address:** Ars Polona-Ruch, PO Box 1001, Krakowskie Przedmiescie 7, 00-068 Warsaw Poland. **Tel** 011 48 22 261201.)

LC TH4809.N6 S5
DD 728/.0967   NR
SHELTER TROPICS. Vol. 1 (1976)-. English. Nigeria Department of Architecture, University of Nigeria, Enugu Campus, Nsukka Nigeria.

LC NA1 .S58   **ISSN** 0049-0520
DD 720/.5   SI
SIAJ - JOURNAL OF THE SINGAPORE INSTITUTE OF ARCHITECTS. (SIAJ.). [SIAJ - J. Singap. Inst. Archit.]. **Main/Corp** Singapore Institute of Architects. **VAT** Singapore Institute of Architects Journal. (19??)-. Periodical. English. Six times a year. $70.19. Singapore Institute of Architects, 20 Orchard Road #02-00 SMA House, Singapore 0923 Singapore. **Tel** 011 65 3388977, FAX 011 65 3368708, telex 22652. **ED** John Ting. **Bk Rev**. **Ad Acc**. **Circ:** 1,400.
Desc: Published for the architectural and allied professions as well as the public.
Ind/Abst Archit. Period. Index (1967-).

LC NA7205 .S55
DD 728/.37/0222   US
SINGLE FAMILY HOME PLANS. VFOAT Home Plans. (19??)-. Periodical. English. One time a year. $2.00. Archway Press Inc, 219 West 44th Street, New York NY 10036. **Tel** (212)757-5580. **Continues** Illustrated Ranch Homes.
Desc: Featuring renderings and floor plans of popular architect-designed homes for which construction blueprints are available.

    ISSN 0900-0518
DD 720   DK
    CEASED
SKALA. [Skala]. (Apr. 1985)-(1994). Periodical. Danish. Henning Larsens Tegnestue, Vimmelskaftet 49, 1161 Copenhagen K Denmark. **(Subscription address:** Byggecentrum, Dr Neerggaards Vej 15, 2970 Horsholm Denmark. **Tel** 011 45 767373.)
Ind/Abst Archit. Period. Index (Apr. 1985-); Avery Index Archit. Period. Suppl. Colum. Univ. (No. 20, 1990-); BHA : Biblio. Hist. Art.

LC T37 .S62   **ISSN** 0160-1067
DD 609   US
SOCIETY FOR INDUSTRIAL ARCHEOLOGY NEWSLETTER. See Archaeology.

    ISSN 0730-6164
    US
SOURCEBOOK (WASHINGTON, D.C.), THE. (THE SOURCEBOOK : LEARNING BY DESIGN, THE ENVIRONMENTAL EDUCATION PROGRAM OF THE AMERICAN INSTITUTE OF ARCHITECTS.). **VFOAT** Source Book; Learning by Design. No. 1-. English. One time a year. $35.00. American Institute of Architects / Washington DC, 1735 New York Avenue Northwest, Washington DC 20006. **Tel** (202)626-7460, FAX (202)626-7587.

LC N7392 .S63
DD 705   SA
SOUTH AFRICAN JOURNAL OF ART AND ARCHITECTURAL HISTORY = SUID-AFRIKAANSE TYDSKRIF VIR KUNS- EN ARGITEKTUURGESKIEDENIS. See The Arts-Art.

    ISSN 0199-896X
    US
SOUTHERN CALIFORNIA HOME & GARDEN. VAT Southern California Home and Garden. Vol. 1 (April/May 1980)-. Periodical. English. Six times a year. Southern California Home & Garden, PO Box 16478, Los Angeles CA 91615.

LC NA9251 .S68   **ISSN** 0970-0501
DD 711/.0954/05   II
SPACE : JOURNAL OF SCHOOL OF PLANNING AND ARCHITECTURE, NEW DELHI. Added/Corp School of Planning and Architecture (New Delhi, India). Vol. 1, No. 1 (Jan. 1986)-. Periodical. English. Four times a year. $22.00. School of Planning and Architecture, 4 Block B Indraprastha Estate, New Delhi - 110002 India. **Tel** 011 91 11 3317892. **(Subscription address:** Prints India, 11 Darya Ganj, New Delhi 110002 India. **Tel** 011 91 11 3268645, FAX 011 91 11 3275542, telex 31-61087 PRIN-IN.) **ED** Professor B. Misna (editor's phone: 011 91 11 3318054). **Continues** SPA, 0970-0706.
Ind/Abst Archit. Period. Index (Oct. 1986-).

LC NA2765 .S63   **ISSN** 0392-4947
DD 720/.5   IT
SPAZIO E SOCIETA. [Spaz. soc.]. **VFOAT** Espaces et Societes; Space & Society; Space and Society. (1978)-. Periodical. English (Italian). Four times a year. Gangemi, Via Cavour 255, 00184 Rome Italy. **Tel** 011 39 6 4821661. Documents available from The Genuine Article.
Ind/Abst Archit. Period. Index (1984-); Arts Humanit. Citation Index [Full Cov.]; Avery Index Archit. Period. Suppl. Colum. Univ. (1989-); Curr. Contents Arts Humanit.; Res. Alert [Full Cov.].

    UK
SPON'S ARCHITECT'S AND BUILDER'S PRICE BOOK. See Building and Construction.

    ISSN 1064-5500
DD 658   US
SRDS MEDIA & MARKET PLANNER. ARCHITECTURAL & CONSTRUCTION MARKETS. See Building and Construction.

LC DB879.P8 A53
    XR
STALETA PRAHA. Main/Corp Prazske Stredisko Statni Pamatkove Pece a Ochrany Prirody. (1965)-. Czech (summaries and/or abstracts in English, French, German and Russian). Orbis, 46 Vinohradska, 120 41 Prague 2 Czech Republic. **Tel** 011 42 2 257741.
Ind/Abst BHA : Biblio. Hist. Art.

LC NA
DD 720   AU
STEINE SPRECHEN. Added/Corp Verein fuer Denkmal- und Stadtbildpflege. (1962)-. Bulletin. German. Four times a year. Oesterreichische Gesellschaft fuer Denkmal und Ortsbildpflege, Karlsplatz 5, A-1010 Vienna Austria. **Tel** 011 43 1 58796630. **ED** Mario Schwartz. **Bk Rev**. **Circ:** 1,300.

Desc: Covers history and the care of historical gardens, monuments and buildings.
Ind/Abst BHA : Biblio. Hist. Art.

LC NA1510.8.B36 S74

BG

STHAPATYA O NIRMANA. VFOAT Quarterly Sthapattya o Nirman. (1991)-. Periodical. Bengali. Four times a year. Tk20.00. Sampadaka, Sthapatya o Nirmana, 12 Bi 4tha Tala, Ramakrshna Misana Roda, Dhaka 1203 Bangladesh.

ISSN 0390-4253
IT

STORIA ARCHITETTURA. [Stor. archit.]. Vol. 1 (1974)-. Periodical. Italian (summaries and/or abstracts in English and German). One time a year. Bonsignori Editore, Viale dei Quattro Venti 47, 00152 Rome Italy. **Tel** 011 39 6 5881496, FAX 011 39 6 5882839. **Ad Acc.** ctrl circ.
Desc: Monograph about the life and work of architects, history of ancient buildings, and studies of university people.
Ind/Abst Art Archaeol. Tech. Abstr.; Avery Index Archit. Period. Suppl. Colum. Univ. (1987-); BHA : Biblio. Hist. Art.

IT

STRUTTURE AMBIENTALI. Added/Corp Centro Internazionale Ricerche Sulle Strutture Ambientali Pio Manzu. Vol. 1 (1970)-. Italian.
Ind/Abst Archit. Period. Index (Dec. 1976-).

LC N11 .N68 **ISSN** 0078-1444
DD 700/.5 US

STUDENT PUBLICATION OF THE SCHOOL OF DESIGN. [Stud. publ. Sch. Des.]. **Added/Corp** North Carolina State University. School of Design. North Carolina State College. School of Design. Vol. 1 (1951)-. Monographic series. English. Irregular. Price varies per volume. Student Publications / NC State University, Raleigh NC 27607. **Tel** (919)515-2201. cum. index. **Bk Rev. Ad Acc.**
Desc: Covers architecture, urban design, landscape architecture product design, and visual design.
Ind/Abst Archit. Period. Index (1978-); Avery Index Archit. Period. Suppl. Colum. Univ. (19??-199?).

LC NA4 .S853 **ISSN** 0301-6455
DD 720/.5 IT

STUDI E DOCUMENTI DI ARCHITETTURA. [Studi doc. archit.]. **Added/Corp** Universita di Firenze. Istituto di Composizione Architettonica. (1973)-. Monographic series. Italian. Irregular. Price varies per volume. Alinea Editrice, Via da Palestrina 17-19, Rosso 50144 Florence Italy. **Tel** 011 39 55 333428. **(Subscription address:** Courier SAS, via l a de Bosis 25 27, 50145 Florence Italy. **Tel** 011 39 55 300010.) **Supersedes** Quaderni.
Ind/Abst Archit. Period. Index; Avery Index Archit. Period. Suppl. Colum. Univ. (19??-199?); BHA : Biblio. Hist. Art.

LC NA2216.C6 A73a

DK

STUDIEINFORMATION. Main/Corp Kunstakademiet (Denmark). Arkitektskolen. (19??)-. Academic Scholarly Publication. Danish. One time a year. Free. Kunstakademiets Arkitektskole Studiekontoret, Peder Skramsgade 1, 1054 Kebenhavn K Denmark. **Tel** 33 12 38 60. **ED** Ida Pagh. **Circ:** 2,000.

LC NA830 .S86 **ISSN** 0327-9022
DD 720/.5 AG

●**SUMMA+. VFOAT** Summa Mas; Summa Plus; A.Summa del dise%no. (1993)-. Periodical. Spanish. Six times a year. $140.00. Donn SA, Cortejarena 1862 2DO Piso, 1281 Buenos Aires Argentina. **Tel** 011 54 1 214985, 011 54 1 285397, FAX 011 54 1 285398. **ED** Adriana Yrigoyen and Horacio Pozzo. **Ad Acc.** ctrl circ.
Continues Summa (Buenos Aires, Argentina), 0325-4615.
Desc: Presents Latinoamerican architectural examples with commentaries photographs and plans.

LC TH1 .S9 **ISSN** 0744-8872
DD 338.4/769/00979 US

SUN/COAST ARCHITECT/BUILDER. See Building and Construction.

LC NA1996 .S92 **ISSN** 0275-9691
DD 331.2/8172 US

SURVEY OF ARCHITECTURAL DRAFTING & DESIGNERS' SALARIES. VFOAT Architectural Drafting & Designer Salaries Survey. **VAT** Survey of Architectural Drafting and Designers' Salaries. (19??)-. English. One time a year. $98.00. Dietrich Associates Inc, Box 511, Phoenixville PA 19460. **Tel** (610)935-1563.
Desc: Salary data as of November 1st on levels of architectural drafters, levels of designers, and interior designers analyzed by industry groups and by size of firms, and geographic areas. Provides base salary data, bonus/incentive pay, and total compensation.

LC NA1995 .S9 **ISSN** 0739-9944
DD 331.2/8172/0973 US

SURVEY OF ARCHITECTURAL SALARIES. [Surv. archit. salaries]. **VFOAT** Architectural Salaries Survey. (Winter 1978)-. English. One time a year. $210.00. Dietrich Associates Inc, Box 511, Phoenixville PA 19460. **Tel** (610)935-1563.
Desc: Salary data as of November 1st on 9 levels of architects. Data analyzed by industry groups, geographic areas, and size of firms. Includes data on salary ranges, years since degree, salary budgeting, and overtime pay.

ISSN 1059-1486
US

SYNERGETICA JOURNAL : JOURNAL OF APPLIED SYNERGETICS AND DESIGN SCIENCE. [Synergetica j.]. **Added/Corp** Buckminster Fuller Institute. Vol. 1, No. 1 (Winter 1991)-. Periodical. English. Two times a year. Buckminster Fuller Institute, 1743 South La Cienega Boulevard, Los Angeles CA 90035.

ISSN 0843-4352
DD 712/.05 CN

SYNTHESIS (GUELPH). (SYNTHESIS.). [Synthesis]. **Added/Corp** University of Guelph. School of Landscape Architecture. Vol. 1, No. 1 (Mar. 1988)-. Periodical. English. Four times a year. University of Quelph / School of Landscape Architecture, Guelph, Ontario, N1G 2W1 Canada.

IT

T-SPORT. Italian (summaries and/or abstracts in English). Twelve times a year. L90.000 Italy; L160.00 other. Sinopia Ed, Via G. Murat 84, 20159 Milan Italy. **Tel** 011 39 2 688-3641, FAX 011 39 2 668-02971. **Circ:** 79,660.
Desc: Sports facilities, games and recreation, swimming pools, fitness, fittings for municipal services.

ISSN 0317-8854
DD 720/.6/2714 CN

TABLEAU DES MEMBRES - ORDRE DES ARCHITECTES DU QUEBEC. Main/Corp Order of Architects of Quebec. **VFOAT** Membership Roll - Order of Architects of Quebec. 1974-. Periodical. Multiple languages (French and English). One time a year. Order of Architects of Quebec, 1825 Dorchester boulevard West, Montreal Quebec H3H 1R4 Canada. **Tel** (514)933-0242. **Circ:** 5,000 (ctrl).
Supersedes Province of Quebec Association of Architects. Registre, 0317-8846.
Desc: Includes lists of all architects practising in Quebec.

LC WMLC L 83/1792

AT

TECHNICAL AND FURTHER EDUCATION. ARCHITECTURAL AND BUILDING STUDIES. Main/Corp Western Australia. Technical Education Division. **VFOAT** Architectural and Building Studies. (19??)-. Periodical. English. Irregular. Nelson Wadsworth, PO Box 4725, Melbourne Victoria, 3001 Australia. **Tel** 03 329-5199.

LC TH2 .T4 **ISSN** 0373-0719
DD 720/.5 FR

TECHNIQUES ET ARCHITECTURE. [Tech. archit.]. **VFOAT** T A. Vol. 1-34 (Sept./Oct. 1941)-(April 1972) No. 290 (Dec. 1972)-. Periodical. French. Six times a year. $220.91. Altedia Communications, 54 Bis rue Dombasle, 75015 Paris France. **Tel** 011 33 1 45310605, FAX 011 33 1 45315311.
Ind/Abst Archit. Period. Index (1941-1972,1977-);(1941-1972); Avery Index Archit. Period. Suppl. Colum. Univ. (1990-); BHA : Biblio. Hist. Art; Int. Civil Eng. Abstr.; Soft. Abstr. Eng.

LC N8554 .T4 **ISSN** 0146-1214
DD 702/.8 US
 CODEN TECODM

TECHNOLOGY & CONSERVATION. See The Arts-Art.

ISSN 0214-4662
SP

TECNOLGIA Y ARQUITECTURA. (TECNOLOGIA Y ARQUITECTURA = HIRIGINTZA ETA ERAIKINTZARI BURUZKO ALDIZKARIA.). [Tecnol. arquit.]. **Added/Corp** Pais Vasco (Spain). Direccion de Arquitectura. **VFOAT** Hirigintza eta Eraikintzari Buruzko Aldizkaria. (1988)-. Periodical. Spanish (Basque, English and French). Four times a year. $53.30. Ignacio Saez de Ibarra, Samaniego 6, 01008 Vitoria-Gasteiz Spain. **Tel** 011 34 1 45248100.

ISSN 0079-3450
PL

UDC 72

TEKA KOMISJI URBANISTYKI I ARCHITEKTURY. (1967)-. Monographic series. Polish. One time a year. Price varies per volume. Polska Akademia Nauk / Zaklad Narodowy im. Ossolinisckich, Ossolineum Publishing House of the Polish Academy of Sciences, Ulitsa Rynek 9, 50-106 Wroclaw Poland. **Tel** 011 48 71 38625, FAX 011 48 71 448103, telex 0712771.
Desc: Architecture - town planning, fortification, etc.
Ind/Abst BHA : Biblio. Hist. Art.

JA

TELESCOPE. Added/Corp Kenchiku Toshi Wakushoppu. **VFOAT** Teresukopu. (May/June 1988)-. Periodical. English (Japanese). Four times a year. $63.40. Workshop for Architecture and Urbanism, Yk Aoyama Building, 2-4-7 Shibuya, Shibuya-Ku Tokyo 150 Japan. **Tel** 011 81 3 3407 4753.
Desc: Information on architecture, design and city planning.

IT

TEMA (ITALY). (19??)-. Italian. Four times a year. L88000 Italy; L120000 other. Franco Angeli Riviste SRL, Viale Monza 106, 20127 Milan Italy. **Tel** 011 39 2 2827651, 011 39 2 289562, FAX 011 39 2 258004, telex 051-511650.

IT

TERRAZZO. No. 1 (Fall 1988)-. Periodical. English. Two times a year. $25.00. St. Martin's Press, 175 Fifth Avenue, New York NY 10010. **Tel** 1 (800)221-7945, (212)982-3900, FAX (212)777-6359. **ED** Barbara Radice. Index available. **Ad Acc. Circ:** 10,000.

ISSN 1105-3070
GR

TEUCHOS. VFOAT Tefchos, International Review of Architecture, Art, and Design; Architektonike TechnÆe; Design, Art, Architecture; Tefchos; Tefchos Review; Periodiko Teuchos. (1989)-. Periodical. Greek, Modern (English). Four times a year (Seasonally). $80.00. Tefchos CO Publisher, Yorgos Tzirtzilakis, 3 Kolok Street, Athens 105 62 Greece. **Tel** 011 30 1 8211638, 011 30 1 3252695.

LC NA1 .T4 **ISSN** 0040-4179
DD 720.5 US

TEXAS ARCHITECT. [Texas archit.]. **Added/Corp** Texas Society of Architects. (195?)-. Periodical. English. Six times a year (Jan., March, May, July, Sept., Nov.). $21.00. Texas Society of Architects, 1400 Norwood Tower, Austin TX 78701. **Tel** (512)478-7386, FAX (512)478-7402. **ED** Vincent Houser (editor's address: 114 West 7th Street #1400 Austin TX 78701). **Bk Rev,** (Qty: varies). **Ad Acc, Adv Mgr:** Mark Denton. **Circ:** 10,000 (ctrl).
Desc: Edited for architects and building and design professionals. Covers significant building projects in Texas or projects by Texas firms. Contains design trends and business practices.
Ind/Abst ARTbibliogr. Mod.; Avery Index Archit. Period. Suppl. Colum. Univ. (1990-).

LC NK1451 .T45 **ISSN** 0074-1191
DD 705 GR

THEMATA CHOROU + TECHNON. [Themata horou + technon]. **VFOAT** Design and Art in Greece; Themata Chorou Kai Technon; Design in Greece; Design + Art in Greece. (1972)-. Trade Publication. Greek, Modern (English). One time a year (Feb.). $55.00. Orestis B. Doumanis, PO Box 3545, GR-102 10 Athens Greece. **Tel** 011 30 1 7225930, FAX 011 30 1 7213916. **ED** Orestis B. Doumanis. **Bk Rev. Ad Acc, Adv Mgr:** Orestis Doumanis. **Circ:** 5,000. **Continues** Themata Esoterikou Chorou.
Desc: Ideas and projects influencing and shaping the human environment in Greece. Architecture and furnishing of houses, offices and shops, visual and applied arts, industrial and graphic design are also included.
Ind/Abst Archit. Period. Index (1981-); Avery Index Archit. Period. Suppl. Colum. Univ. (19??-199?); BHA : Biblio. Hist. Art.

UK

TIMBER FOR ARCHITECTS. See Forests and Forestry-Lumber and Wood.

LC NA7205 .T63 **ISSN** 1059-5252
DD 728.3/7/0222 US

TODAY'S FAMILY HOME PLANS. [Today's fam. home plans]. **VFOAT** Home Plans. (19??)-. English. One time a year. $3.95. Archway Press Inc., 19 West 44th Street, New York NY 10036. **Tel** (212)757-5580.

LC NA **ISSN** 0389-1720
DD 720 JA

TOHOKU DAIGAKU KENCHIKU GAKUHO. [Tohoku Daigaku kenchiku gakuho]. **VFOAT** Kenchiku Gakuho; Architectural Reports of the Tohoku University. (1952)-. Periodical. Japanese (English). One time a year. Tohoku University, Sendai 980 Japan. **Tel** 0222-27-6200.
Ind/Abst Abstr. J. Earthq. Eng.

LC N17 .T5317

JA

TOKYO KOKURITSU BUNKAZAI KENKYUJO YORAN. Main/Corp Tokyo Kokuritsu Bunkazai Kenkyujo. Japanese. Bunkacho Tokyo Kokuritsu Bunkazai Kenkyujo Hozon Kagakubu, (Department of Conservation Science, Tokyo National

Architecture

Research Institute of Cultural Properties, Agency for Cultural Affairs), Ueno Koen Taitoku Tokyo 110 Japan. **Tel** 03-823-2241, FAX 03-828-2431.

ISSN 0950-2181
UK
TITLE CHANGE

TRADITIONAL HOMES. VFOAT Traditional Garden. (Oct. 1984)-(19??). Periodical. English. EMAP Consumer Magazine, 1st Floor, Stephenson House Brunel C, Milton Keynes MK2 2EW United Kingdom. **Tel** 011 44 171 4379011, FAX 011 44 171 4340656, telex 266400. *Absorbed Period Homes.* **Absorbed by** *Period Living and Traditional Homes, 0958-1987.*
Ind/Abst Archit. Period. Index (Oct. 1984-); Avery Index Archit. Period. Suppl. Colum. Univ. (Jan. 1990-); Child. Lit. Abstr. (19??-).

LC NA500   ISSN 0260-4116
DD 724   UK

TRADITIONAL KENT BUILDINGS. (TRADITIONAL KENT BUILDINGS : STUDIES BY STUDENTS AT THE SCHOOL OF ARCHITECTURE, CANTERBURY COLLEGE OF ART.). [Tradit. Kent build.]. **Added/Corp** Canterbury College of Arts. School of Architecture. Kent (England). County Council. Education Committee. (1980)-. Periodical. English. Irregular. Kent Institute of Art and Design, School of Architecture, New Dover Road, Canterbury United Kingdom. **Tel** 011 44 1227 769371, FAX 011 44 1227 451320. **ED** J. Wade. **Circ:** 1,700. available with illustrations.
Ind/Abst Archit. Period. Index (1980-).

LC NA109.G7 T7   ISSN 0142-5803
DD 720/.28/8   UK

TRANSACTIONS - ASSOCIATION FOR STUDIES IN THE CONSERVATION OF HISTORIC BUILDINGS. (TRANSACTIONS / ASCHB.). [Trans. - Assoc. Stud. Conserv. Hist. Build.]. **Added/Corp** Association for Studies in the Conservation of Historic Buildings (Great Britain). (1973)-. Academic Scholarly Publication. English. One time a year. Price varies. ASCHB Transactions, Hamilton's Kilmersdon, Near Bath Somerset BA3 5TE United Kingdom. **Tel** 011 44 1761 435134. **ED** Stephen Marks. cum. index. **Circ:** 450.
Desc: Publishes reports of meetings, visits and articles on methods of repair, survey techniques, philosophy of conservation, work carried out and historical building methods.
Ind/Abst Archit. Period. Index (1973-); BHA : Biblio. Hist. Art.

LC TA680 .T68
DD 624.1/834   JA

TRANSACTIONS OF THE JAPAN CONCRETE INSTITUTE. See Engineering-Civil Engineering.

LC NA1 .M37a
DD 720./5   UK

TRANSACTIONS OF THE MARTIN CENTRE FOR ARCHITECTURAL & URBAN STUDIES. Main/Corp Martin Centre for Architectural and Urban Studies. Vol. 1 (1976)-. Periodical. English. Two times a year. £16.70. Martin Centre for Architectural and Urban Studies, Woodhead Faulkner, Fitzwilliam House, 32 Trumpington Street, Cambridge CB2 1QY United Kingdom. **Tel** 011 44 1223 66733, FAX 011 44 1223 461428.
Ind/Abst Archit. Period. Index.

ISSN 0035-8967
UK

TRANSACTIONS OF THE ROYAL INSTITUTION OF NAVAL ARCHITECTS. Main/Corp Royal Institution of Naval Architects. Vol. 1 (1960)-. English. One time a year. $188.23. Royal Institution of Naval Architects, 10 Upper Belgrave Street, London SW1X 8BQ United Kingdom. **Tel** 011 44 71 2354622, FAX 011 44 71 245 6959, telex 265844 SINAI G. *Continues* Institution of Naval Architects. Transactions.

ISSN 1148-7194
FR

TRANSFORMATIONS (PARIS). (TRANSFORMATIONS : BULLETIN DE LA SOCIETE FRANCAISE DES ARCHITECTES.). **Added/Corp** Societe Francaise des Architectes. (19??)-. Bulletin. French. Four times a year. Architectes, 140 Av Victor Hugo, Paris 75116 France. **Tel** 011 33 1 45535856.

LC NA1 .T73   ISSN 0157-7344
DD 720/.5   AT
Pr Rev.

TRANSITION. Added/Corp Royal Melbourne Institute of Technology (Australia). Faculty of Architecture and Building. Vol. 1, No. 1 (July 1979)-. Periodical. English. Four times a year. Royal Melbourne Institute of Technology, GPO Box 2476V, Melbourne Victoria 3001 Australia. **Tel** 011 61 3 6603752, FAX 011 61 3 6632891, telex 36406. **ED** Peter Brew. **Bk Rev**, (Qty: varies). **Ad Acc, Adv Mgr:** Callum Fraser, **Tel** 011 61 3 660 2968.

Full Page (B&W) 720.00Aus$. Half Page (B&W) 360.00Aus$. **Circ:** 1,200 (ctrl).
Ind/Abst APAIS, Aust. Public Aff. Inf. Ser. (1988-); Archit. Period. Index (1979-); Avery Index Archit. Period. Suppl. Colum. Univ.

IT

UFFICIOSTILE. Italian (English). Twelve times a year. Propaganda Edit Grafica PEG, Via Fratelli, Bressan 2, 20126 Milan Italy. **Tel** (02)29003009, FAX (02)29003015. **Bk Rev. Ad Acc.** $240,000 (ctrl).
Desc: The international monthly magazine giving information and documentation on the real organization problems of the office work.

ISSN 0276-0398
US

UNDERLINE. (UNDERLINE / UNDERGROUND SPACE CENTER, UNIVERSITY OF MINNESOTA.). 1979. Periodical. English. Four times a year. Underground Space Center, 790 Civil, Mineral Engineering Building, Minneapolis MN 55455. **Tel** (612)376-5341. **ED** Donna Ahrens. **Bk Rev. Ad Acc. Circ:** 1,000 (ctrl).
Desc: Newsletter on events and research in earth-sheltered and underground construction.

LC HD1390.5 .U55   ISSN 0747-7465
DD 333.33/8   US

UNIQUE HOMES. (1973)-. Periodical. English. Six times a year. $30.00. Unique Homes, 801 Second Avenue, New York NY 10017. **Tel** (212)986-5100. (Subscription address: Kable Publishers Aide / Illinois, 308 East Hitt Street, Subscription Department, Mt. Morris IL 61054-1473. **Tel** (815)734-1261.)

LC NX   ISSN 0566-263X
DD 700   SZ
TITLE CHANGE

UNSERE KUNSTDENKMAELER. See The Arts-Art.

SW
Pr Rev.

UTBLICK LANDSKAP. (1984)-. English. Four times a year. Kr430.00. Utblick Landskap, Norrlandsgatan 18 4 TR, S-111 43 Stockholm Sweden. **Tel** 011 46 8 789 8996. **ED** Thomas Andersson, Thorbjourn Andersson, Tove Jonstoin, Randi Mossige-Norheim and Carola Wingren. **Bk Rev. Ad Acc. Circ:** 5,000.
Desc: Presents Scandinavian landscape architecture and photography.
Ind/Abst BHA : Biblio. Hist. Art.

LC NA208 .V47   ISSN 0305-5477
DD 728/.67/05   UK

VERNACULAR ARCHITECTURE. [Vernac. archit.]. **Added/Corp** Vernacular Architecture Group (York, England). Vol. 1/2 (1970-71)-. Periodical. English (French). One time a year. $40.00. Vernacular Architecture Group, 16 Trefor Road Aberystwyth, Dyfed SY23 2EH United Kingdom. **Tel** 011 44 1970 617716. (Subscription address: Vernacular Architecture Group, c/o Carl Lounsbury, PO Box 638, Williamsburg VA 23187. **Tel** (804)220-7650.) **ED** Pauline Fenley. Index available (Free). **Bk Rev. Ad Acc. Circ:** 1,000 (ctrl).
Desc: A study of vernacular buildings and their construction, history, geographical distribution and context, world wide interests but mainly Great Britain and Europe.
Ind/Abst Anthropol. Lit. (19??-); Archit. Period. Index (1970-); Art Archaeol. Tech. Abstr. (19??-); Avery Index Archit. Period. Suppl. Colum. Univ. (19??-199?); BHA : Biblio. Hist. Art (19??-); Br. Archaeol. Bibliogr. (19??-).

ISSN 0267-3088
UK

VERNACULAR BUILDING. (VERNACULAR BUILDING / SCOTTISH VERNACULAR BUILDINGS WORKING GROUP.). [Vernac. build.]. **Added/Corp** Scottish Vernacular Buildings Working Group. (1975)-. English.
Ind/Abst Archit. Period. Index (1978-1980); Avery Index Archit. Period. Suppl. Colum. Univ. (19??-19??).

ISSN 0506-8347
US

VIA (CAMB.). (VIA.). [Via]. **Added/Corp** University of Pennsylvania. Graduate School of Fine Arts. (1968)-. Monographic series. English. Price varies per volume. Rizzoli International Publishing Inc, 300 Park Avenue South, New York NY 10010. **Tel** (212)387-3500, (800)462-2387, FAX (212)982-3866. Documents available from The Genuine Article.
Ind/Abst Arts Humanit. Citation Index (19??-19??) [Full Cov.]; Curr. Contents Arts Humanit. (19??-); Res. Alert (19??-) [Full Cov.].

LC NK2115.5.V53 V52   ISSN 0744-415X
DD 747.213   US

VICTORIAN HOMES. [Vic. homes]. Vol. 1, Issue 1 (Winter 1982)-. Periodical. English. Six times a year. $24.00. Vintage Publications Inc, PO Box 61, Miller Falls MA 01349. **Tel** (413)659-3785, FAX (413)659-3796, (413)659-3113. **ED** Carolyn Flaherty. **Bk Rev. Ad Acc. Circ:** 70,000.
Desc: Victorian decorative arts and lifestyles of the Victorian and Edwardian eras. Provides ideas, inspiration and information on how architecture and designs can be adapted and made relevant to today's living.
Ind/Abst Avery Index Archit. Period. Suppl. Colum. Univ. (1990-); Garden Lit. (1992-).

UK

VICTORIAN SOCIETY ANNUAL, THE. Main/Corp Victorian Society. **Added/Corp** Victorian Society. Annual. (197?)-. Academic Scholarly Publication. English. One time a year. Comes with Victorian Society membership - £36.00 (institutions), £27.00 (individuals). Victorian Society, No. 1 Priory Gardens, Bedford London W4 1TT United Kingdom. **Tel** 011 44 181 9941019. *Continues* Victorian Society. Annual Report - Victorian Society, 0306-588X.
Ind/Abst Archit. Period. Index (1981-); BHA : Biblio. Hist. Art.

ISSN 0049-6316
FR
UDC 72(44)

VIEILLES MAISONS FRANCAISES PARIS. (VIEILLES MAISONS FRANCAISES.). (1959)-. Periodical. French. Four times a year. Vieilles Maisons Francaises, 93 rue de l'Universite, 75007 Paris France. **Tel** 011 33 1 45517896.
Ind/Abst Avery Index Archit. Period. Suppl. Colum. Univ. (Dec. 1989-).

ISSN 0893-9543
DD 710   US

VILLAGE VIEWS. [Village views]. **Added/Corp** Society for the Architecture of the City (New York, N.Y.). Vol. 1, No. 1 (Winter 1984)-. Periodical. English. Four times a year. Village Views, 45 Christopher Street, Suite 2E, New York NY 10014.
Ind/Abst Avery Index Archit. Period. Suppl. Colum. Univ. (1989-).

ISSN 0140-4571
UK

VOLE. Vol. 1 (1977)-. Periodical. English. Twelve times a year. Wheatear Productions Ltd., 20 Fitzroy Square, London United Kingdom.
Ind/Abst Archit. Period. Index (1977-1981).

US

VOLUMEZERO. Added/Corp Rensselaer Polytechnic Institute. School of Architecture. **VFOAT** Volume Zero. (1986)-. English. Irregular (Publishes every 2 or 3 years). $16.00 (latest edition). Volumezero, School of Architecture, Rensselaer Polytechnic Institute, Troy NY 12180. **Tel** (518)276-6460.

ISSN 0005-6529
GW

WERK, BAUEN + WOHNEN (GERMAN ED.). (WERK, BAUEN + WOHNEN.). **VFOAT** Werk, Bauen und Wohnen. Vol. 37, No. 1-2 (Jan./Feb. 1982)-. Trade Publication. German (English and French). Twelve times a year. $68.00. German Language Publications Inc., 560 Sylvan Avenue, Englewood Cliffs NJ 07632. **Tel** (201)871-1010. *Formed by the union of Bauen + Wohnen and Werk, Bauen + Wohnen (Swiss Ed.).*
Ind/Abst Archit. Period. Index (198?-); Art Index; Avery Index Archit. Period. Suppl. Colum. Univ. (1989-); BHA : Biblio. Hist. Art.

LC TH3411 .W46   ISSN 0229-1738
DD 721/.028/8   CN

WHO IS DOING WHAT IN HISTORIC PRESERVATION. VFOAT APT Directory of Members. English. One time a year. Association for Preservation Technology / Canada, Box 2487 Station D, Ottawa Ontario K1P 5W6 Canada. **Tel** (613)238-1972, FAX (613)238-1839.

ISSN 0920-1629
NE
UDC 72 (492)

WIEDERHALL. [Wiederhall]. **VFOAT** Wiederhall Architectural Serial. (1986)-. Periodical. English. Twelve times a year. Wiederhall FDN, 010 Publ Watertonwet 180, 3063 Ha Rotterdam Netherlands.
Desc: Each issue also has a theme title.
Ind/Abst Archit. Period. Index (1986-).

US

WISCONSIN ARCHITECT. Added/Corp State Association of Wisconsin Architects. Wisconsin Architects Association. American Institute of Architects. Wisconsin Chapter. Wisconsin Society of Architects. (1933)-. Trade Publication. English. Six times a year. $30.00. Wisconsin Architect, 321 South Hamilton, Madison WI 53703. **Tel** (608)257-8477. **ED** Cheryl Seurinck. **Ad Acc. Circ:** 3,700 (ctrl).
Desc: Provides the design and construction industry with articles of interest pertaining to recent developments and current issues dealing with design and construction.

ISSN 0888-6822
DD 728   US

WISCONSIN HOME GALLERY MAGAZINE. See Interior Design and Decoration.

LC NA14 .W4   ISSN 0509-9773
GE
CODEN WZAWA9
WISSENSCHAFTLICHE ZEITSCHRIFT.
Main/Corp Weimar. Hochschule fuer Architektur und Bauwesen. (1953)-. Academic Scholarly Publication. German. Six times a year. Hochschule fuer Architektur und Bauwesen, Wilhelm-Bode-Str. 1, 99425 Weimar Germany. Documents available from CASDDS. **Continued in part by** Wissenschaftliche Zeitschrift der Hochschule fuer Architektur und Bauwesen Weimar. Ausgabe A, 0863-0712 **and** Wissenschaftliche Zeitschrift der Hochschule fuer Architektur und Bauwesen Weimar. Ausgabe B, 0863-0720.
Ind/Abst Chem. Abstr. (1953-1985).

ISSN 0863-0712
GW
UDC 72
WISSENSCHAFTLICHE ZEITSCHRIFT DER HOCHSCHULE FUER ARCHITEKTUR UND BAUWESEN. (19??)-.
Periodical. Multiple languages. Eight times a year. DM240.00. Hab Weimar, Coudraystrasse 7, D-99421 Weimar Germany. **Tel** 011 49 3643 581150, FAX 011 49 3643 581156. **Absorbed** Wissenschaftliche Zeitschrift der Hochschule fuer Architektur und Bauwesen Weimar Ausgabe A.
Ind/Abst BHA : Biblio. Hist. Art; Zentralbl. Math. Ihre Grenzgeb.

ISSN 0863-0720
GW
UDC 69
WISSENSCHAFTLICHE ZEITSCHRIFT DER HOCHSCHULE FUER ARCHITEKTUR UND BAUWESEN WEIMAR AUSGABE B. [Wiss. Z. Hochsch. Archit. Bauwes. Weimar, B].
VFOAT Wissenschaftliche Zeitschrift der Hochschule fur Architektur und Bauwesen Weimar. Reihe B. (1985)-. Academic Scholarly Publication. Multiple languages. Six times a year. Documents available from CASDDS. **Continues in part** Wissenschaftliche Zeitschrift der Hochschule fur Architektur und Bauwesen Weimar, 0509-9773.
Ind/Abst BHA : Biblio. Hist. Art; Chem. Abstr.; Zentralbl. Math. Ihre Grenzgeb.

ISSN 0457-3943
GW
CODEN WZMNAS
WISSENSCHAFTLICHE ZEITSCHRIFT DER HOCHSCHULE FUER BAUWESEN LEIPZIG. [Wiss. Z. Hochsch. Bauwes. Leipz.].
Main/Corp Hochschule fuer Bauwesen Leipzig. (1955)-. Academic Scholarly Publication. German. Four times a year. Deutscher Judo Verband, Redaktion Ippon Segewaldweg 40, D-12557 Berlin Germany. **Tel** 011 49 711 210770, telex 051 678. Documents available from BIOSIS Document Express, CASDDS.
Ind/Abst Biol. Abstr.; Chem. Abstr.; Math. Rev.

LC NA6.K67 W64
DD 720/.5   KO
WOLGAN KONCHUK MUNHWA. VFOAT
Konchuk Munhwa; Magazine for Architectural Culture. Periodical. English (Korean). Twelve times a year. W3,500 each issue. Wolgan Konchuk Munhwasa, 18-21 6-kA Ulji-ro Chung-ku, Seoul Korea.

LC NK1174 .W65   ISSN 0735-3421
DD 745.4/442   US
WOMEN IN DESIGN INTERNATIONAL COMPENDIUM. (WOMEN IN DESIGN INTERNATIONAL COMPENDIUM : WIDI.). [Women Des. Int. compend.].
VFOAT Compendium; WIDI; W.I.D.I. Vol. 1 (1982)-. English. One time a year. $15.95. Women in Design International, 1626 Tiburon Boulevard, Tiburon CA 94920.

US
WOOD DESIGN FOCUS. Added/Corp Wood
Products Information Center. Wood Products Center. **VFOAT** Wood Design; Focus. Vol. 1, No. 1 (Spring 1990)-. Periodical. English. Four times a year. $25.00 (one-year), $50.00 (two-year), $75.00 (three-year), $2.00 (single copy) $40.00 (one-year), $4.00 (single copy) other. World Forestry Center, 4033 SW Canyon Rd, Portland OR 97221. **Tel** (503)228-0819, FAX (503)228-3624. **ED** Bob Leichti (editor's address: Forest Research Lab 105, Oregon State University, Corvallis, OR 97331; editor's telephone: (503)737-4212). Index available (published separately). cum. index. **Ad Acc, Adv Mgr:** Jennifer McBlaine, **Tel** (503)228-0819. **Circ:** 1,200.
Desc: Intended for design professionals, educators, researchers, building code officials, and industry through publication of contemporary design, technology practical applications, and discussion of issues related to engineered wood construction.
Ind/Abst Constr. Index (199?-).

LC NA1131 .W66
BE
WOONSTEDE DOOR DE EEUWEN HEEN = MAISONS D'HIER ET D'AUJOURD'HUI, DE. Added/Corp Association Royale des Demeures
Historiques de Belgique. Nederlandse Kastelenstichting. International Council of Monuments and Sites. **VFOAT** Maisons d'Hier et d'Aujourd'hui. (19??)-. Periodical. Dutch (French). Four times a year. $52.80. KVHWB, Vergotestraat 24, B-1200 Brussels Belgium. **Tel** 011 32 2 7350965.
Ind/Abst Avery Index Archit. Period. Suppl. Colum. Univ. (1989-).

ISSN 0956-9758
UK
WORLD ARCHITECTURE (LONDON. 1989). (WORLD ARCHITECTURE.). [World archit.].
Added/Corp International Academy of Architecture. (1989)-. Trade Publication. English. Twelve times a year. $150.00. Cheerman Limited, Halpern House 301, 305 Euston Road, London NW1 3SS United Kingdom. **Tel** 011 44 171 3835757, FAX 011 44 171 3833181. **ED** Martin Pawley. **Photos**. Documents available from BLDSC. **Absorbed** Interiors Quarterly.
Desc: Provides information on contemporary architects and the latest styles in architecture.
Ind/Abst Archit. Period. Index (1989-).

LC NA737.W7 W754   ISSN 1045-7992
DD 720/.92   US
WRIGHT STUDIES. [Wright stud.]. Vol. 1 (1992)-.
Monographic series. English. Irregular. Price varies per volume. Southern Illinois Press, Box 3697, Carbondale IL 62902-3697. **Tel** (618)453-6619, (618)453-2281.

LC DA690.Y6 Y64   ISSN 0309-3743
DD 942.8/43/005   UK
YORK HISTORIAN. Added/Corp Yorkshire
Architectural and York Archaeological Society. Vol. 1 (1976)-. Periodical. English. Every 2 years. Yorkshire Architectural and Archaeological Society, c/o York Archaeological Trust, 1 Pavement, York Y01 2NA United Kingdom. **Tel** 011 44 1904 643211. **ED** Hugh Murray and Alison R Goodall. **Circ:** 500.
Desc: Includes articles, notes and records relevant to the history, architecture and archaeology of the York district.
Ind/Abst BHA : Biblio. Hist. Art; Br. Archaeol. Bibliogr. (?-?).

LC NA7205 .Y68   ISSN 0275-2174
DD 728.3/7/0223   US
YOUR NEW ECONOMY HOME PLANS.
[Your new econ. home plans]. English. One time a year. $1.50. House Plan Headquarters Inc, 48 West 48th Street, New York NY 10036.

LC N8850 .Z35   ISSN 0514-616X
YU
ZBORNIK ZASTITE SPOMENIKA KULTURE. RECUEIL DES TRAVAUX SUR LA PROTECTION DES MONUMENTS HISTORIQUES. See The
Arts-Art.

LC NA1596.6.R5 Z56   ISSN 1016-152X
DD 720/.96891/05   RH
ZED. ZIMBABWE ENVIRONMENT & DESIGN. (ZIMBABWE ENVIRONMENT & DESIGN : ZED.). [ZED, Zimb. environ. des.]. Added/Corp Institute
of Architects of Zimbabwe. Zimbabwe Institute of Regional and Urban Planners. **VFOAT** Zimbabwe Environment and Design; ZED. No. 1 (Apr. 1981)-. Periodical. English. Two times a year.
Ind/Abst Archit. Period. Index (Apr. 1981-); Avery Index Archit. Period. Suppl. Colum. Univ. (19??-19??).

LC NA25 .Z6
RU
ZODCHESTVO. Added/Corp Soiuz Arkhitektorov
SSSR. (1975)-. Russian. Stroiizdat, Ulitsa Shchousseva rm. 60, 103001 Moscow Russia. **Supersedes** Sovetskaia Arkhitektura.

LC NA1 .Z63   ISSN 0394-9249
DD 720/.5   IT
ZODIAC (MILAN, ITALY : 1988). (ZODIAC.).
Vol. 1 (1988)-. Periodical. English. Two times a year. L54500. Editrice Abitare Segesta Spa, Corso Monforte 15, 20122 Milan Italy. **Tel** 011 39 2 76090214, FAX 011 39 2 791904, telex 315302 ABIT I. **(Subscription address:** Slack Inc., 6900 Grove Raod, Thorofare NJ 08086. **Tel** (609)848-1000.) **Continues** Zodiac (Milan, Italy), 0044-4936.
Ind/Abst Archit. Period. Index (1988-).

Architecture —Computer Applications

ABSTRACTING, BIBLIOGRAPHIES AND STATISTICS

LC Z5941 .A69 NA1.A1   ISSN 0266-4380
DD 016.72   UK
API. ARCHITECTURAL PERIODICALS INDEX. (ARCHITECTURAL PERIODICALS INDEX.).
[API. Archit. period. index]. **Added/Corp** Royal Institute of British Architects. Library. British Architectural Library. Sir Banister Fletcher Library. Vol. 1 (1973)-. Abstracting/Indexing Service. English. Four times a year. $325.13. RIBA Companies Ltd., Finsbury Mission, 39 Moreland Street, London EC1V 8B8 United Kingdom. **Tel** 011 44 171 2510791, FAX 011 44 171 6082375. **ED** C Dembsky. cum. index. **Circ:** 1,000. available on an online database from DIALOG. Documents available from BLDSC. **Supersedes** Royal Institute of British Architects. RIBA Library Bulletin; Royal Institute of British Architects. RIBA Annual Review of Periodical Articles, 0557-4013.
Desc: Abstracts of articles from architectural and planning journals from all over the world.

LC NA   ISSN 1357-0536
DD 720   UK
●### ARCHITECTURAL PUBLICATIONS INDEX ON DISC. (1995)-. Abstracting/Indexing
Service. English. Four times a year. £700.00. RIBA Companies Ltd., Finsbury Mission, 39 Moreland Street, London EC1V 8B8 United Kingdom. **Tel** 011 44 171 2510791, FAX 011 44 171 6082375.

LC Z5961.A35 A7   ISSN 1044-8640
DD 016.73   US
ARTS OF AFRICA : AN ANNOTATED BIBLIOGRAPHY, THE. See The
Arts-Abstracting, Bibliographies and Statistics.

LC Z5945 .C653 1973 Suppl. NA1.A1   ISSN 0196-0008
DD 016.72   US
AVERY INDEX TO ARCHITECTURAL PERIODICALS. SECOND EDITION. REVISED AND ENLARGED. SUPPLEMENT. (AVERY INDEX TO
ARCHITECTURAL PERIODICALS. SUPPLEMENT / COLUMBIA UNIVERSITY.). **Added/Corp** Columbia University. Getty Art History Information Program. No. 1 (1975)-. Abstracting/Indexing Service. English (Multiple languages). Irregular. $425.00. GK Hall & Co., 100 Front Street, Riverside NJ 08075. **Tel** (800)257-5755 ext. 2223. **Continues** Avery Library. Avery Index to Architectural Periodicals. Supplement.
Desc: Includes citations to articles in all significant periodicals on architecture, architectural design and history, and encompasses landscape architecture, historic preservation, city planning and interior design.

LC N NA   ISSN 1055-6826
DD 702 720   US
BIO-BIBLIOGRAPHIES IN ART AND ARCHITECTURE. See The Arts-Abstracting,
Bibliographies and Statistics.

COMPUTER APPLICATIONS

ISSN 0277-1659
US
A-E-C AUTOMATION NEWSLETTER.
[A-E-C autom. newsl.]. **VAT** Architects, Engineers, Constructors Automation Newsletter. (1977)-. Newsletter. English. Twelve times a year. $225.00. A-E-C Automation Newsletter, 5920 Roswell Road #B-107336, Atlanta GA 30328-4922. **Tel** (404)565-3282, FAX (404)565-3286. **ED** Carleton R. Howk. **Bk Rev**, (Qty: 12). **Circ:** 5,200.
Desc: Reports describes the analyzes developments in automation for architects, engineers, and constructors. It serves as information source for design-build management. Covers automation methods in computer-aided design (CAD/CAE) and expert systems.

LC NA2728 .A25   ISSN 1079-9680
DD 720   US
Pr Rev.
ACADIA QUARTERLY. [ACADIA q.].
Added/Corp Association Computer-Aided Design in Architecture. Vol. 11, No. 1 (Winter 1992)-. Periodical. English. Four times a year (Mar., June, Sept., Dec.). $80.00. Association Computer Aided Design Architecture, 961 Taylor Street, c/o B. J. Novitski, Eugene OR 97402. **Tel** (503)343-7177, FAX (503)344-4152. **Circ:** 300. **Continues** ACADIA, 0896-0178.

ISSN 0748-660X
US
DD 604
COMPUTERIZED DRAFTING AND DESIGN NEWSLETTER. [Comput. draft. des.
newsl.]. (Jan. 1984)-. Newsletter. English. Four times a year. $20.00. Computer Drafting and Design, 8854 Broadway, San Antonio TX 78217. **Tel** (512)824-2754. **ED** Les Hall. **Bk Rev. Circ:** 1,867 (ctrl)

Architecture —Computer Applications

Desc: Serves the architect, engineer, and educator using computer systems for drafting, and design. Has product and general information, reviews, employment, and useful 'how to' tips.

ISSN 1055-7350
DD 004 US
MACINTOSH CONSTRUCTION FORUM.
See Computers-Microcomputers, Personal Computers.

LC TK174 .M525 ISSN 1057-9567
DD 006.6 US
MICROSTATION MANAGER. [MicroStn. manag.]. (Sept./Oct. 1991)-. Trade Publication. English. Twelve times a year. $60.00. Connectpress, 2530 Camino Entrada, Santa Fe NM 87505. **Tel** (505)473-4242, FAX (505)438-7171. **ED** Susan Smith. **Bk Rev**, **Ad Acc**, **Adv Mgr Tel** (505)471-8822. **Circ:** 20,000 (ctrl).

LC QA76.9.A73 T76a ISSN 1063-6749
DD 04.3/3/05 US
PROCEEDINGS - TRON PROJECT SYMPOSIUM. (PROCEEDINGS / THE ... TRON PROJECT SYMPOSIUM ; SPONSORED BY THE TRON ASSOCIATION.). [Proc. - TRON Proj. Symp.]. **Added/Corp** TRON Association. IEEE Computer Society. Institute of Electrical and Electronics Engineers. (1991)-. Proceedings. English. Irregular. IEEE Computer Society, 10662 Los Vaqueros Circle, PO Box 3014, Los Alamitos CA 90720-1264. **Tel** (714)821-8380, (800)272-6657, FAX (714)821-4641. **Continues** TRON Project Symposium. TRON Project.

THE ARTS

ISSN 1041-3111
DD 700 US
13TH STREET JOURNAL, THE. (THE 13TH STREET JOURNAL.). [13th Str. j.]. **Added/Corp** Boulder Center for the Visual Arts. **VFOAT** Thirteenth Street Journal. (Sept./Oct. 1988)-. Periodical. English. Six times a year. Free (local). Boulder Center for the Visual Arts, 1750-13th Street, Boulder CO 80302. **Tel** (303)443-2122. **ED** Ina Russell. **Bk Rev**. **Ad Acc**. ctrl circ. **Continues** Art Review (Boulder, Colo.), 0896-4971.
Desc: Cultural arts information for Boulder, Colorado and Northern Colorado containing reviews, fiction, and art criticism.

ISSN 0762-3291
FR
303. [303]. **VFOAT** Trois Cent Trois; Revue des Pays de la Loire; Recherches et Creations; Pay de la Loire. (1984)-. Periodical. French. Four times a year. $74.36. 303, Recherches et Creations, Hotel de la Region, Ile Beaulieu, 44047 Nantes Cedex 02 France. **Tel** 011 33 1 40414141.
Ind/Abst BHA : Biblio. Hist. Art.

IT
A & C INTERNATIONAL. (19??)-. Italian. Three times a year (May, Sept., Dec.). L36790. Gangemi Editore, via Cavour 255, 00184 Rome Italy. **Tel** 011 39 6 4821661.

ISSN 0065-0129
US
A.W. MELLON LECTURES IN THE FINE ARTS. **Added/Corp** United States. National Gallery of Art. (1953)-. Monographic series. English. Irregular. Price varies per volume. Princeton University Press, 41 William Street, Princeton NJ 08540. **Tel** (609)258-4900.
Desc: One of the Bollingen Series; covers the fine arts.

ISSN 0212-6117
UDC 7 SP
ABRENTE. [Abrente]. **Added/Corp** Academia de Bellas Artes de Nuestra Señora del Rosario. La Coruña. (1969)-. Spanish. One time a year.
Ind/Abst BHA : Biblio. Hist. Art.

ISSN 0001-3366
IT
ABRUZZO. **Added/Corp** Istituto di Studi Abruzzesi. Roma. Vol. 1 (1963)-. Periodical. Italian. Four times a year (Mar., June, Sept., Dec.). L20.000 Italy; L35.000 other. Edizioni Menabo SRL, via Caduse 64, 66026 Ortona CH Italy. **Tel** 011 39 85 9064999. cum. index.
Ind/Abst BHA : Biblio. Hist. Art.

LC NX7 .A26 ISSN 0567-560X
DD 700/.946 SP
ACADEMIA (REAL ACADEMIA DE BELLAS ARTES DE SAN FERNANDO). (ACADEMIA : BOLETIN DE LA REAL ACADEMIA DE BELLAS ARTES DE SAN FERNANDO.). **Added/Corp** Real Academia de Bellas Artes de San Fernando. (1951)-. Periodical. Spanish. Two times a year. 5000ptas. Real Academia de Bellas Artes de San Fernando, Alcala 13, 28014 Madrid Spain. **Tel** 011 34 1 5221491.

Continues Boletin de la Real Academia de Bellas Artes de San Fernando.
Ind/Abst BHA : Biblio. Hist. Art.

LC AP86 .A27
RM
ACADEMICA : REVISTA DE STIINTA, CULTURA SI ARTA (ACADEMIA ROMANA). **Added/Corp** Academia Romana. (1991)-. Periodical. Romanian (table of contents in French). Twelve times a year. DM133.00. Editura Academia Republicii Socialiste Romania, Calea Victoriei Nr 125, R-79717 Bucuresti Romania. **Tel** telex 10376 PRSFI R. **(Subscription address:** Kubon & Sagner, ABT Zeitschriftenimport, D 80328 Munich Germany. **Tel** 011 49 89 54218130.)

ISSN 0833-451X
DD 700/.971 CN
ACE. ASSOCIATION OF CULTURAL EXECUTIVES. (ACE : THE NEWSLETTER OF THE ASSOCIATION OF CULTURAL EXECUTIVES.). [ACE, Assoc. Cult. Exec.]. **Added/Corp** Association of Cultural Executives. **VFOAT** Cultural Executive Employment Exchange; ACE News and Employment Exchange; ACE News. (Feb. 1986)-. Newsletter. English. Ten times a year. 136.00Can$. Association of Cultural Executives, 1140 Sheppard Avenue West, Unit 7, Toronto Ontario M5S 2R4 Canada. **Tel** (416)633-6663. **Continues** ACE News, 0827-5696.

ISSN 0860-7443
PL
ACTA UNIVERSITATIS LODZIENSIS. FOLIA SCIENTIAE, ARTIUM, ET LITTERARUM. **Added/Corp** Uniwersytet Lodzki. **VFOAT** Folia Scientiae, Artium, et Litterarum. (1990)-. Monographic series. Polish. Irregular. Price varies per volume. Wydawnictwo Uniwersytetu Lodzkiego, Ul. Jaracza 34, Lodz Poland. **Tel** 011 48 42 331671, 011 48 42 336341. **(Subscription address:** Ars Polona-Ruch, PO Box 1001, Krakowskie Przedmiescie 7, 00-068 Warsaw Poland. **Tel** 011 48 22 261201.) **Continues** Acta Universitatis Lodziensis. Folia Scientiarum, Artium, et Librorum, 0208-6115.

ISSN 0815-5992
DD 052 AT
ADELAIDE REVIEW. [Adel. rev.]. No. 1 (1984)-. Newspaper. English. Twelve times a year. 16.44Aus$. Adelaide Review, 1 Dequetteville Terrace, Kent Town SA 5067 Australia. **Tel** 011 61 8 3627699, FAX 011 61 8 3627878. **ED** Christopher Pearson. **Bk Rev**, (Qty: 50). **Ad Acc**; **Adv Mgr**: Phillip Virgo. **Circ:** 40,000 (ctrl).

ISSN 0891-7213
DD 880 US
SUSPENDED
AEGEAN REVIEW. **See** Literature.

LC DS36 .A33
IQ
AFAQ ARABIYAH. **VFOAT** Afaq Arabia. No. 1 (Sept. 1975)-. Periodical. Arabic (English). Six times a year (bimonthly). $84.00 US. Ministry of Cultural Affairs / Iraq, PO Box 4032, Baghdad (Adhamiya) Iraq. **Tel** 011 964 1 4436044, 011 964 1 4435446, FAX 011 964 1 4446780, telex 214135. **ED** Muhsin al-Musawi. Index available. **Bk Rev**. **Circ:** 20,000.
Desc: Concentrates on the arts and humanities.

LC NX587 .A6 ISSN 0001-9933
US
Pr Rev.
AFRICAN ARTS. [Afr. arts]. **Added/Corp** University of California, Los Angeles. African Studies Center. **VFOAT** Arts d'Afrique. Vol. 1 (Autumn 1967)-. Periodical. English (French). Four times a year (Jan., Apr., July, Oct.). $64.00. UCLA African Studies Center, 405 Hilgard Avenue, 10244 Bunche Hall, Los Angeles CA 90024. **Tel** (310)825-3686. **ED** Donald Cosentino, John Povey, and Doran Ross. Index available. cum. index. **Bk Rev**. **Ad Acc**. **Circ:** 6,500. available on microfilm and microfiche from University Microfilms International (UMI). Documents available from The Genuine Article, UMI Article Clearinghouse.
Desc: Covers the arts of Africa, traditional and contemporary.
Ind/Abst Acad. Abstr.; Acad. Ind. [Computer File] (1987-); Acad. Search; Anthropol. Index; Anthropol. Lit.; Art Archaeol. Tech. Abstr.; Art Index; ARTbibliogr. Mod.; ARTbibliogr. Curr. Titles; Arts Humanit. Citation Index [Full Cov.]; Avery Index Archit. Period. Suppl. Colum. Univ. (19??-199?); Curr. Contents Arts Humanit.; EP Collect.; Ethnoarts Index; Expand. Acad. Index (1989-); Hist. Source (July 1990-); Homework Help.; Humanit. Index; Humanit. Source; INFO-SOUTH Abstr.; Mag. Search; Humanit. Source FullTEXT 1000; MasterFile FullTEXT 350; MasterFile FullTEXT 650; MasterFile FullTEXT (July 1990-) [Full Txt.]; MLA Int. Bibl. Books Artic. Mod. Lang. Lit.; Newsp. Period. Abstr. (1991-); OCLC; Pub. Lib. FullTEXT; Res. Alert [Full Cov.]; Soc. Sci. Cit. Index [Select. Cov.]; Telebase.

LC NX
DD 709.9405 AT
Pr Rev.
AGENDA (PARKVILLE). (AGENDA). [Agenda Parkville]. (1988)-. Periodical. English. Five times a year (Mar., May., July, Sept., Nov.). 19.74Aus$. Royal Melbourne Institute of Technology, GPO Box 2476V, Melbourne Victoria 3001 Australia. **Tel** 011 61 3 6603752, FAX 011 61 3 6632891, telex 36406. **ED** Penny Webb. Index available (free upon request). cum. index. **Bk Rev**, (Qty: 5). **Ad Acc**. **Circ:** 2,000.
Desc: Contemporary visual art reviews, books, film reviews, and essays on contemporary cultural theory.

LC NX1 ISSN 8755-500X
DD 705 US
AHA. (AHA! : HISPANIC ARTS NEWS : A PUBLICATION OF THE ASSOCIATION OF HISPANIC ARTS.). [Aha!]. **Added/Corp** Association of Hispanic Arts (New York, N.Y.). **VFOAT** A.H.A.; AHA. (198?)-. Periodical. English (Spanish). Nine times a year (June/July, Aug./Sept. & Dec./Jan. issues combined). $45.00. Association of Hispanic Arts, 173 East 116th Street, 2nd Floor, New York NY 10029. **Tel** (212)860-5445. **ED** Dolores Prida. **Ad Acc**. **Continues** Hispanic Arts (Association of Hispanic Arts (New.York, N.Y.)), 0732-1643.

LC NX8.J3 A34 ISSN 0289-0569
JA
AICHI KYOIKU DAIGAKU KENKYU HOKOKU. SOSAKU HEN. **Added/Corp** Aichi Kyoiku Daigaku. (19??)-. Periodical. Japanese (English). One time a year. Aichi Kyoiku Daigaku, Hirosawa 1 Igaya-cho, Kariya-shi Aichi-ken 448 Japan. cum. index.

LC NX571.P6 A38 ISSN 0208-6220
DD 700/.9438 PL
AKCENT : A. **VFOAT** A. (1980)-. Periodical. Polish. Four times a year. zl.6.00. RSW Prasa-Kriazka-Ruch, Centrala Kolporatzu Prazy i Wydawnictw, Towarowa 28, 00-958 Warsaw Poland. **(Subscription address:** Ars Polona-Ruch, PO Box 1001, Krakowskie Przedmiescie 7, 00-068 Warsaw Poland. **Tel** 011 48 22 261201.)

LC NX573.6.Y42 S584
YE
AL-FUNUN. Vol. 1 (February 1980)-. Periodical. Arabic. Twelve times a year. Muassasat, 14 Uktubar Lil-Tibaah Wa-Al-Nashr Wa-Al-Tawzi Wa-Al-Ilan, Adan Yemen.

LC NX588.A1 S47
UA
AL-SHASHAH AL-SAGHIRAH. No. 1 (Oct. 8, 1979)-. Periodical. Arabic. Twelve times a year. £E0.20 single issue. 28 Shari Sharif Al-Dur Al-Thalith, Al-Qahirah Egypt.

LC PN9 .T47
IQ
AL-THAQAFAH AL-AJNABIYAH. **See** Literature.

LC NX573 .T47
FR
AL-THAQAFAH AL-THAWRIYAH. **VFOAT** El-Thakapha El-Thawria; Thakapha El-Thawria. Vol. 1 (1978)-. Periodical. Arabic. 3 Bis rue de la Reunion, 75020 Paris France.

US
ALABAMA ARTS. **Added/Corp** Alabama State Council on the Arts and Humanities. Vol. 7, No. 1 (Feb. 1987)-. Periodical. English. Two times a year. Free on request. Alabama State Council on the Arts and Humanities, One Dexter Avenue, Montgomery AL 36130. **Tel** (334)242-4076, FAX (334)240-3269. **ED** Sharon Heflin. **Continues** Ala-Arts, 0146-9398.

ISSN 0002-5631
DD 700 850 IT
ALLA BOTTEGA. [Alla bottega]. Vol. 1, No. 1 (Sept./Oct. 1963)-. Periodical. Italian. Six times a year. L50000 Italy; L100000 other. Alla Bottega, via Plinio 38, 20129 Milan Italy. **Tel** 224177. **ED** G. Lucano. Index available. cum. index. **Bk Rev**. **Ad Acc**. **Circ:** 4,050. available with illustrations.
Ind/Abst MLA Int. Bibl. Books Artic. Mod. Lang. Lit.

ISSN 0344-1822
GW
UDC 246/247 :[282 :262.3](430.1-37.28-37.357-37.433.-21)
ALTE UND NEUE KUNST. [Alte neue Kunst]. (1970)-. German. Irregular. **Continues** Alte und Neue Kunst im Erzbistum Paderborn, 0516-8252.
Ind/Abst BHA : Biblio. Hist. Art.

LC AS36 .A474
DD 061/.3 US
AMERICAN ACADEMY AND INSTITUTE OF ARTS AND LETTERS. REPORT OF ACTIVITIES. English. One time a year. $12.00 libraries and book sellers, $15.00 individuals. American Academy and Institute of Arts and Letters, 633 West

The Arts

155th Street, New York NY 10032. **Tel** (212)368-5900, FAX (212)491-4615. *Continues American Academy of Arts and Letters. Report of Activities.*

ISSN 1053-1327
US
AMERICAN FESTIVAL MAGAZINE.
(1992)-. Periodical. English. Twelve times a year. $23.40. William Chase, PO Box 643, Cedarburg WI 53012.

AMERICAN INDIAN NEWS. See Ethnic Interests.

ISSN 0890-412X
DD 700 US
AMERICAN UNIVERSITY STUDIES. SERIES XX, FINE ARTS. [Am. univ. stud., Ser. XX Fine arts]. **VFOAT** American University Studies. Series Twenty, Fine Arts; Fine Arts. (1989)-. Monographic series. English. Irregular. Price varies per volume. Peter Lang Publishing, 62 West 45th Street, 4th Floor, New York NY 10036. **Tel** (212)764-1471, (800)770-5264, FAX (212)302-7574, telex 6973364 PLNY.

RM
AMFITEATRU : REVISTA LITERARA SI ARTISTICA EDITATA DE UNIUNEA ASOCIATIILOR STUDENTILOR COMUNISTI DIN ROMANIA. Added/Corp Uniunea Asociatiilor Studentilor Comunisti din Romania. (1966)-. Periodical. Romanian. Twelve times a year. (**Subscription address:** Rompresfilatelia, PO Box 12 201, Bucharest Romania. **Tel** 011 40 0 10376.) available on microfilm from The Library of Congress Photoduplication Service.
Desc: Contains artistical and literary creations of the students.
Ind/Abst Annu. Bibliogr. Engl. Lang. Lit.

LC Z5935.3 .M87a NX454 ISSN 0898-7300
DD 016.7/009/04 US
ANNUAL BIBLIOGRAPHY OF MODERN ART. See The Arts-Abstracting, Bibliographies and Statistics.

LC NX24.A4 A6a
DD 353.97980085 US
ANNUAL REPORT / ADVISORY COUNCIL ON CULTURAL FACILITIES.
Main/Corp Alaska. Advisory Council on Cultural Facilities. (1980)-. English. Advisory Council on Cultural Facilities, Pouch D, Juneau AK 99811.

LC NX28.R52 N376
DD 354/.689/100854 RH
ANNUAL REPORT AND BALANCE SHEET AND REVENUE AND EXPENDITURE ACCOUNT. Main/Corp National Arts Foundation of Rhodesia. (19??)-. English. One time a year. National Arts Foundation of Zimbabwe, PO Box UA 463 Union Avenue, 95 Manica Road, Harare Zimbabwe. **Tel** 707898, 793343. **ED** T.P. Mahoso and J.T.E. Mapondera. Index available. **Circ:** 600 (ctrl).
Desc: Annual report and statement of accounts of the National Arts Council of Zimbabwe.

LC NX24.A8 A74A
DD 353.97670085/4 US
ANNUAL REPORT / ARKANSAS ARTS COUNCIL. Main/Corp Arkansas Arts Council. English. One time a year. Arkansas Arts Council, Continental Building/Suite 500, Little Rock AR 72201.

LC NX28.A92 A853
DD 338.4/7/700994 AT
ANNUAL REPORT - AUSTRALIA COUNCIL. Main/Corp Australia Council. 1974/75-. English. One time a year. Northside Gardens, 168 Walker Street, North Sydney New South Wales 2060 Australia. **Tel** 011 61 2 9233333, FAX 011 61 2 9227560, telex 26023. **ED** Gwennett Deamer. **Circ:** 3,000 (ctrl).
Supersedes Annual Report - Australian Council for the Arts.

LC NX24.M6 C46A
DD 353.9776 US
ANNUAL REPORT / CENTRAL MINNESOTA ARTS COUNCIL. Main/Corp Central Minnesota Arts Council. English. One time a year. Central Minnesota Arts Council, PO Box 1442, St Cloud MN 56301.

LC NX24.I6 I513 ISSN 0098-2040
DD 353.9/772/00854 US
ANNUAL REPORT - INDIANA ARTS COMMISSION. Main/Corp Indiana Arts Commission. (19??)-. English. One time a year. Indiana Arts, 47 South Pennsylvania, Suite 701, Indianapolis IN 46204. **Tel** (317)632-7894.

LC NX24.M7 M56a ISSN 0360-1099
DD 353.9/762/0085 US
ANNUAL REPORT - MISSISSIPPI ARTS COMMISSION. Main/Corp Mississippi Arts Commission. (19??)-. English. One time a year. Free. Mississippi Arts Commission, 239 North Lamar Street/Ste 207, Jackson MS 39201-1393. **Tel** (601)359-6030, FAX (601)359-6008.

LC NX22 .N314 ISSN 0083-2103
DD 700/.61/73 US
ANNUAL REPORT - NATIONAL ENDOWMENT FOR THE ARTS/NATIONAL COUNCIL ON THE ARTS. (ANNUAL REPORT / NATIONAL ENDOWMENT FOR THE ARTS.). **Main/Corp** National Endowment for the Arts. **Added/Corp** National Council on the Arts. Annual Report. National Endowment for the Arts. Office of Communications. National Endowment for the Arts. National Endowment for the Arts. Office of Public Affairs. National Endowment for the Arts. Public Information Office. **VFOAT** National Endowment for the Arts ... Annual Report. (1967)-. English. One time a year. Free on request. National Endowment for the Arts, 1100 Pennsylvania Avenue Northwest, Washington DC 20506. **Tel** (202)682-5400, (202)682-5435.
Desc: Lists grants and brief description of projects funded, by discipline.

LC NX398 .N38A ISSN 0882-245X
DD 700/.6/073 US
ANNUAL REPORT - NATIONAL FOUNDATION FOR ADVANCEMENT IN THE ARTS (U.S.). (ANNUAL REPORT.). [Annu. rep. - Natl. Found. Adv. Arts (U.S.)]. **Main/Corp** National Foundation for Advancement in the Arts (U.S.). 1st (1981-82)-. English. One time a year. Free. National Foundation for Advancement in the Arts, 3915 Biscayne Boulevard, 2nd Floor, Miami FL 33137. **Tel** (305)573-5490, FAX (305)573-4870. **ED** Suzette Harvey. **Circ:** 2,000 (ctrl).
Desc: Narrative and statistical report of NFAA programs for a 12-month period.

LC J2 ISSN 1187-2454
DD 354.71510085/4 CN
ANNUAL REPORT - NEW BRUNSWICK ARTS BOARD. (RAPPORT ANNUEL / CONSEIL DES ARTS DU NOUVEAU-BRUNSWICK.). [Annu. rep. - N.B. Arts Board]. **Main/Corp** Conseil des Arts du Nouveau-Brunswick. **VFOAT** Annual Report. **VAT** Rapport Annuel - Conseil des Arts du Nouveau-Brunswick. (1991)-. French (English).

ISSN 1187-2454
DD 354.71510085/4 CN
ANNUAL REPORT / NEW BRUNSWICK ARTS BOARD. [Annu. rep. - N.B. Arts Board]. **Main/Corp** New Brunswick Arts Board. **VFOAT** Rapport Annuel. **VAT** Rapport Annuel - Conseil des Aarts du Nouveau-Brunswick. (1991)-. English (French).

LC NX28.C32 S2515 ISSN 0701-6433
DD 354.7124/0854 CN
ANNUAL REPORT - SASKATCHEWAN CENTRE OF THE ARTS. Main/Corp Saskatchewan Centre of the Arts. (1971)-. Corporate Report. English. One time a year. Saskatchewan Centre of the Arts, 200 Lakeshore Drive, Regina Saskatchewan S4P 3V7 Canada. **Tel** (306)584-5050.

LC NX24.T2 T47A ISSN 0091-259X
DD 338.4/7/7009768 US
ANNUAL REPORT - TENNESSEE ARTS COMMISSION. (ANNUAL REPORT.). **Main/Corp** Tennessee Arts Commission. English. One time a year. Tennessee Arts Commission, 222 Capitol Hill Building, Nashville TN 37219.

ISSN 0066-4782
SZ
ANTIKE KUNST. BEIHEFT. See Archaeology.

US
ANTIQUES AND THE ARTS WEEKLY. See Antiques.

LC NX1.A1 A68
GW
APOZITIA. No. 1 (1973/75). Multiple languages (French, German and Romanian). Ion Dimitriu, Siegfriedstrasse 3, W-8000 Munich 40 Germany.

LC NX504 .A7 ISSN 0884-2213
DD 700/.973 US
APPEARANCES. [Appearances]. **Added/Corp** New York State Council on the Arts. (1979)-. Periodical. English. Robert Witz, 165 West 26th Street, New York NY 10001. **Tel** (212)675-3026.

LC NX458 .A18
DD 700/.9/04 GW
AQ. Periodical. English (French and German). Kantstrasse 43, W-6602 Dudweiler Germany.

ISSN 1067-5108
DD 781 US
AQUARIAN WEEKLY, THE. See Music.

ISSN 0712-3310
CN
ARC-EN-CIEL (ROUYN). (L'ARC-EN-CIEL / CONSEIL REGIONAL DE LA CULTURE DE L'ABITIBI-TEMISCAMINGUE.). [Arc-en-ciel]. Vol. 1, No. 1-. Periodical. French. Three times a year. Free to members. Arc-en-Ciel, Conseil de la Culture de l'Abitibi-Temiscamingue, 102 Avenue du Lac, Rouyn Quebec J9X 4N4 Canada. **Tel** (819)764-9511. **ED** Camille Gauthier. **Circ:** 750 (ctrl).

LC AP8 .A68 ISSN 0004-1343
DD 052 IS
ARIEL (ENGLISH EDITION). (ARIEL.). [Ariel]. **Added/Corp** Israel. Misrad Ha-Huts. Mahlakah le-Kishre Tarbut u-Mada. Israel. Misrad Ha-Huts. Mahlakah le-Kishre Tarbut. Israel. Misrad Ha-Huts. Lishkah le-Kishre Tarbut. **VFOAT** Ariel. No. 1 (Jan. 1962)-. Periodical. English (French, German and Spanish). Four times a year. Ariel, 211 E 43rd Street, New York NY 10017. **Tel** (914)878-4100. **ED** Asher Weil. **Bk Rev. Ad Acc. Circ:** 20,000 (ctrl). *Supersedes Cultural Events in Israel.*
Desc: Journal in the field of arts and culture in Israel.
Ind/Abst Index Jew. Period.; Middle East Abstr. Index; MLA Int. Bibl. Books Artic. Mod. Lang. Lit.; Romant. Move.

US
ARIS FUNDING REPORTS. CREATIVE ARTS AND HUMANITIES REPORT. VFOAT Creative Arts and Humanities Report. **VAT** Academic Research Information System Funding Reports. Creative Arts and Humanities Report. Vol. 14, No. 3 (March 17, 1989)-. Periodical. English. Eight times a year. $135.00. Academic Research Information System, 2940 16th Street, Suite 314, San Francisco CA 94103. **Tel** (415)558-8133, FAX (415)558-8135. **ED** Rosemary Topp. Index available (bound in each issue). *Continues ARIS Funding Messenger. Creative Arts and Humanities Report.*
Desc: Provides grant information in the arts & humanities from both federal & private sources.

LC NX456 .A67 ISSN 0737-0407
DD 700/.5 US
ARISTOS. [Aristos]. Vol. 1, No. 1 (July 1982)-. Periodical. English. Six times a year. $30.00 US; $31.00 Canada; $36.00 other. Aristos Foundation, PO Box 1105, Radio City Station, New York NY 10101. **Tel** (212)678-8550. **ED** Louis Torres. Index available. **Bk Rev. Ad Acc.** ctrl circ.
Desc: Dedicated to the preservation and advancement of traditional values in the arts, as well as to objective standards in criticism.
Ind/Abst Am. Humanit. Index.

ISSN 1054-8963
US
ARIZONA EVENTS CALENDAR. (1991)-. English. Four times a year. $35.00. Pacific Publications / California, PO Box 4500, Laguna Beach CA 92652. **Tel** (714)497-7108. *Continues in part Nevada Events Calendar, Arizona Events Calendar.*

US
ARRIBA (COMMITTEE FOR HISPANIC ARTS AND RESEARCH, AUSTIN, TX.). (ARRIBA : ARTS AND ENTERTAINMENT MAGAZINE.). **Added/Corp** Committee for Hispanic Arts and Research (Austin, Tex.). Vol. 1, No. 1 (July 1980)-. English (Spanish and English). Twelve times a year. $10.00. Committee for Hispanic Arts & Research, PO Box 12865, Austin TX 78711.

ISSN 0780-9859
FI
UDC 351
CODEN 82
ARSIS. (1984)-. Periodical. Finnish (summaries and/or abstracts in English). Four times a year. Free. The Arts Council of Finland, Mariankatu 5, PO Box 293, 00171 Helsinki Finland. **Tel** 011 358 0 134171, FAX 011 358 0 624313. **ED** Eija Ristimaki. Index available. cum. index. **Bk Rev. Circ:** 2,500.

LC NX2 .A74 ISSN 0774-1863
DD 700/.5 BE
ART & FACT. [Art fact]. **Added/Corp** Universite de Liege. **VFOAT** Art et Fact. No 1 (1982)-. French. 800F.
Ind/Abst BHA : Biblio. Hist. Art.

ISSN 1188-4282
DD 700/.25/714 CN
●**ART ET CULTURE AU QUEBEC.** (REPERTOIRE DESCRIPTIF. ART ET CULTURE AU QUEBEC.). [Art cult. Que.]. **Added/Corp** Quebec dans le Monde (Association). (1992/1993)-. French. Every 2 years. 44.95Can$. Quebec Dans Le Monde, CP 8503, Sainte-Foy Quebec G1V 4N5 Canada. **Tel** (418)659-5540, FAX (418)659-6143. *Continues Repertoire Descriptif. Le Monde de la Culture au Quebec., 0847-4958.*

The Arts

LC NX2 .A75
DD 700/.5
FR
ART ET POESIE. Added/Corp Societe des Poetes et Artistes de France. (1960)-. Periodical. French. Four times a year. $29.52. Societe Poetes Artistes France, 59 boulevard Raymond Poincare, 55000 Bar le Duc France. **Tel** 011 33 29 450495. *Supersedes France-Poesie.*

CN
ART FOCUS. (19??)-. English. Four times a year (Jan., Apr., July, Oct). 14.40Can$. Fleisher Fine Arts Inc., 15 McMurrich Street, Suite 706, Toronto Ontario M5R 3M6 Canada. **Tel** (416)925-5564. **(Subscription address:** ArtFocus Subscriptions Department, PO Box 1063, Station F, Toronto Ontario M4Y 2T7 Canada. **Tel** (416)925-5564.) *Continues Art Post, 0829-0784.*

LC N1 .A423 ISSN 0004-3184
DD 705 US
SUSPENDED
ART GALLERY, THE. (1957)-Suspended with Vol. 24, No. 1, Fall (1980). Periodical. English. Four times a year. $25.00. Hollycroft Press, PO Box 278, Ivoryton CT 06442.
Ind/Abst ARTbibliogr. Mod. (1984-).

ISSN 1062-8819
US
●**ART IMAGE MAGAZINE.** (1992)-. Periodical. English. Six times a year. $24.00. Selph Image, PO Box 191694, Atlanta GA 30319.

ISSN 0193-6867
US
ART REFERENCE COLLECTION. See The Arts-Abstracting, Bibliographies and Statistics.

IT
ARTE ARGOMENTI. (19??)-. Italian. Four times a year. Cinzia Piccioni, Piazza G Tavani Arquati 103, 00153 Rome Italy.

LC NX533.A1 A774
BL
ARTE EM REVISTA. Added/Corp Centro de Estudos de Arte Contemporanea (Sao Paulo, Brazil). (Jan./Mar.) 1979)-. Periodical. Portuguese. Four times a year. Centro de Estudos de Arte Contemporanea, Kairos Livraria e Editora Ltda, Av Paulista 2650 CEP 01310, Sao Paulo Brazil.

LC N4 .A53 ISSN 0004-3443
IT
Pr Rev.
ARTE LOMBARDA. [Arte lomb.]. **Added/Corp** Universita di Milano. Istituto di Storia Dell'Arte. Vol. 1 (1955)-. Periodical. Italian (English, French and German). Four times a year. L224810. Istituto Storia Arte Lombarda, Piazza Duomo 14, 20122 Milan Italy. **Tel** 011 39 2 878475, FAX 011 39 2 86463412. **ED** Alessandro Rovetta. Index available. cum. index. **Circ:** 800.
Desc: Covers Lombard art, architecture, painting, sculpture repair, and minor arts.
Ind/Abst Art Archaeol. Tech. Abstr.; ARTbibliogr. Mod.; Avery Index Archit. Period. Suppl. Colum. Univ. (1989-); BHA : Biblio. Hist. Art; RILA, Int. Rep. Lit. Art.

ISSN 0345-0015
SW
ARTES. Added/Corp Kungl. Musikaliska Akademien (Stockholm, Sweden) Konstakademien, Stockholm. Svenska Akademien. Vol. 1 (1975)-. Periodical. Swedish. Four times a year. $61.43. Pressdata, Box 3263, 103 65 Stockholm Sweden. **Tel** 011 46 8 7996200.
Ind/Abst BHA : Biblio. Hist. Art.

ISSN 1104-8247
SW
CODEN a7
●**ARTES INTERNATIONAL. VFOAT** Artes. (1994)-. Periodical. English. One time a year. $20.00. Ecco Press, 100 West Broad Street, Hopewell NJ 08525. **Tel** (609)466-4748, FAX (609)466-4706.

LC NX541.A1 A75
DD 700/.987
VE
ARTESANIA Y FOLKLORE DE VENEZUELA. VFOAT Artisanat et Folklore du Venezuela. Year 1, No. 1 (July 1975)-. Periodical. Spanish. Six times a year. Bs80.00 Venezuela; $4.00 US. Apartado 60935 Chacao, Caracas 1060- Venezuela. **Tel** 6619856/6623694, FAX (02) 729118. **ED** Fructuoso Pernia and Ismanda Correa. **Bk Rev. Ad Acc. Circ:** 5,000.
Desc: Reports, information and reviews about topics related to the traditional popular arts of Venezuela and other countries of Latin America.
Ind/Abst Ethnoarts Index.

US
CEASED
ARTIMES. English. Artimes Inc, PO Box 4276, Highland Park NJ 08904. **Tel** (201)819-0990.

LC NX1 .A69 ISSN 0304-8640
DD 700/.5 II
ARTIST (CALCUTTA). (ARTIST.). (19??)-. English. One time a year. Rs50.00. Artist International Publication, 35/8 Kayasthapara Main Road, Calcutta 700078 India. **Tel** 422270. **ED** Ashit Paul. cum. index. **Bk Rev. Ad Acc. Circ:** 5,000 (ctrl).
Desc: Publishes the contents of contemporary graphics and visual arts of India and abroad since 1970. Contemporary literature, experimental writing also published in every issue.

LC NX396.5 .A77
DD 700/.25/751 US
ARTISTS IN EDUCATION DIRECTORY.
Added/Corp Delaware State Arts Council. (19??)-. Directory. English. Irregular (Every 2 or 3 years). Free on request. Delaware State Arts Council, State Office Building, 820 North French Street, Wilmington DE 19801. **Tel** (302)577-3540.

LC NX1 .A72
DD 700/.9/04 FR
ARTITUDES INTERNATIONAL. No. 1- Oct./Nov. 1972-. Periodical. Multiple languages (English and French). $15.00.
Ind/Abst ARTbibliogr. Mod.

LC NX163 .N38
DD 700 US
●**ARTJOB : A PUBLICATION OF THE WESTERN STATES ARTS FEDERATION. Added/Corp** Western States Arts Federation. **VFOAT** Art Job. Vol. 13, Issue #6 (Mar. 26, 1993)-. Periodical. English. Twenty-six times a year (published every other Friday with a break at midsummer and Christmas). $55.00. Western States Arts Federation, 236 Montezuma Avenue, Santa Fe NM 87501. **Tel** (505)988-1166, FAX (505)982-9307. **ED** Kelly Briggs, Meg Hachmann. **Ad Acc. Circ:** 15,000. available on an online database from Artswire. *Continues ARTJOB/Bank, 1070-8901.*
Desc: Employment opportunities listed for the arts fields.

LC NX163 .N38 ISSN 1070-8901
DD 700
TITLE CHANGE
ARTJOB/BANK (SANTA FE, N.M.).
(ARTJOB/BANK : A PUBLICATION OF THE WESTERN STATES ARTS FEDERATION.). [ARTJOB/bank].
Added/Corp Western States Arts Federation. **VFOAT** Art Job Bank; Jobbank; Job Bank. Vol. 13, Issue #1 (Jan. 8, 1993)-Vol. 13, Issue #5 (Mar. 12, 1993). Periodical. English. *Continues Westaf's National Arts Jobbank, 1046-7718.* **Continued by** *ARTJOB.*
Desc: Focuses on job vacancies in the arts.

LC N1 .A6 ISSN 0004-3273
DD 705 US
ARTNEWS. [ARTnews]. **VFOAT** Art News. (Feb. 1923)-. Periodical. English. Ten times a year. $32.95. ARTnews Associates, 48 West 38th Street, 9th Floor, New York NY 10018. **Tel** (212)398-1690, FAX (212)819-0394. **(Subscription address:** Neodata / Colorado, PO Box 2606, Boulder CO 80322.) **ED** Milton Esterow. **Ad Acc. Circ:** 73,000. Documents available from The Genuine Article, UMI Article Clearinghouse, Magazine Collection. *Continues American Art News.*
Desc: Completely illustrated, devoted to all aspects of the fine arts.
Ind/Abst Abr. Read. Guide Period. Lit.; Acad. Abstr. Full Text Elite; Acad. Abstr. Acad. Ind. (Computer File) (1984-); Acad. Search; Am. Bibliogr. Slavic East Europ. Stud.; Archit. Period. Index; Art Archaeol. Tech. Abstr.; Art Index; ARTbibliogr. Mod.; Arts Humanit. Citation Index [Full Cov.]; Avery Index Archit. Period. Suppl. Colum. Univ. (19??-1989?); BHA : Biblio. Hist. Art; Book Rev. Index; Curr. Cit.; Curr. Contents Arts Humanit.; EP Collect.; Expand. Acad. Index (1985-); Gen. Period. Index (1985-); Homework Help.; Humanit. Source; INFO-SOUTH Abstr.; Mag. Artic. Summar. Elite; Mag. Artic. Summar. Select; Mag. Artic. Summar. CD-ROM; Mag. Index Plus (1989-); Mag. Index. Sel. (1986-); Mag. Search; MasterFile FullTEXT 1000; MasterFile FullTEXT 350; MasterFile FullTEXT 650; MasterFile FullTEXT (Jan. 1984-); Middle East Abstr. Index; Newsp. Period. Abstr. (1986-); OCLC; Pub. Lib. FullTEXT; Read. Guide Abstr. Sel. Ed.; Read. Guide Period. Lit.; Res. Alert [Full Cov.]; Telebase; Mag. Index (1977-); Vocat. Search.

LC NX593.A1 A87 ISSN 1171-8536
DD 700/.993/05 NZ
ARTS ADVOCATE. Added/Corp Queen Elizabeth II Arts Council of New Zealand. (Apr. 1992)-. Periodical. English. Three times a year. Free on request. Queen Elizabeth II Arts Council, PO Box 3806, Wellington New Zealand. **Tel** 011 64 4 4730880, FAX 011 64 4 4712865.

ISSN 1171-8536
DD 700.99305 NZ
ARTS ADVOCATE WELLINGTON. (ARTS ADVOCATE.). [Arts advocate Wellingt.]. (1992)-. Periodical. English. Three times a year (Spring, Autumn, and Winter). Free on request. Queen Elizabeth II Arts Council, PO Box 3806, Wellington New Zealand. **Tel** 011 64 4 4730880, FAX 011 64 4 4712865. *Continues Arts Times, 0112-9376.*
Ind/Abst Museum Abstr.

ISSN 0004-3931
US
ARTS AND ACTIVITIES. See Education-Teaching and Curriculum.

ISSN 1047-3297
DD 704 US
CCC
ARTS & CULTURE FUNDING REPORT. [Arts cult. funding rep.]. **Added/Corp** Education Funding Research Council. **VFOAT** Arts and Culture Funding Report. Vol. 1, No. 1 (June 1989)-. Periodical. English. Twelve times a year. $138.00. Education Funding Research Council, 4301 North Fairfax Drive, Suite 875, Arlington VA 22203. **Tel** (703)528-1082.

ISSN 0813-3425
DD 371.3078 AT
SUSPENDED
ARTS AND EDUCATION. See Education.

US
ARTS & HUMANITIES SEARCH. VFOAT A&H Search. (19??)-. English. One time a week. Magnetic Tape: $17,695.00 (academic), $22,130.00 (corporate). Institute for Scientific Information, 3501 Market Street, Philadelphia PA 19104. **Tel** (215)386-0100, (800)523-1850, FAX (215)386-6362, telex 84-5305. **(Subscription address:** Institute for Scientific Information, PO Box 71416, Chicago IL 60694.)
Desc: Online format of the Arts & Humanities Citation Index.

ISSN 0893-4088
DD 700 US
ARTS & LETTERS (DAYTON, TENN.). (ARTS & LETTERS.). [Arts lett.]. **Added/Corp** Bryan College. English Dept. **VFOAT** Arts and Letters. Vol. 1, No. 1 (Jan. 1987)-. Periodical. English. Two times a year. $5.00. Arts & Letters, PO Box 7000, Bryan College, Dayton TN 37321. **Tel** (615)775-2041.

ISSN 0703-8720
DD 001.5/05 CN
ARTS & SCIENCE MONOGRAPHS. (Sept. 1976)-. Periodical. English. Concordia University Bookstores, Loyola Campus, 7141 Sherbrooke Street West, Montreal Quebec H4B 1R6 Canada.

PH
ARTS & SCIENCES JOURNAL. VFOAT Arts and Sciences Journal. 1981-. English. Two times a year. no fixed rate. University Research Center, Mindanao State University, PO Box 5594, 9200 Iligan City Philippines. **Ad Acc. Circ:** 500 (ctrl).

LC N2 .A83 ISSN 0004-3958
DD 709/.5 FR
ARTS ASIATIQUES (PARIS). (ARTS ASIATIQUES.). [Arts asiat.]. **Added/Corp** Ecole Francaise d'Extreme-Orient. Musee Guimet (Paris, France) Musee Cernuschi. Vol. 1 (1954)-. French (English). One time a year. 225.00F. Librairie d'Amerique et Dorien, 11 rue Saint Sulpice, F 75006 Paris France. **Tel** 011 33 1 43268635. **Bk Rev.** *Supersedes Revue des Arts Asiatiques, 0995-7510.*
Ind/Abst Art Index; Avery Index Archit. Period. Suppl. Colum. Univ. (1990-).

ISSN 0706-9731
CN
ARTS B. C. Added/Corp British Columbia Cultural Programme. British Columbia. Cultural Services Branch. **VAT** Arts British Columbia. Vol. 1 (June 1975)-. Periodical. English. Four times a year (Jan., Apr., July, Oct.)-. Free. Minis Tour Recreation Culture Service Branch, Parliament Buildings, Victoria British Columbia V8V 1X4 Canada. **Tel** (604)387-1011 Ext. 263.

ISSN 0843-2260
DD 700/.9713/52 CN
ARTS BEAT (HAMILTON). (ARTS BEAT : THE NEWSLETTER OF THE HAMILTON & REGION ARTS COUNCIL.). [Arts beat]. **Added/Corp** Hamilton and Region Arts Council. **VFOAT** Artsbeat. Vol. 1, No. 1 (Sept. 1987)-. Newsletter. English. Six times a year. Comes with Arts Council Membership. Hamilton & Region Arts Council, 116 King Street, Hamilton Ontario L8P 4V3 Canada. **Tel** (905)529-9485. **ED** Krista Foss. **Ad Acc. Circ:** 1,500. *Continues Art-I-Fact (1981), 0843-2252.*
Desc: Dedicated to fostering a deeper appreciation of the arts in the greater Hamilton area.

ISSN 1202-4732
DD 700.9712305 CN
ARTS BRIDGE. [Arts bridge]. **Added/Corp** Alberta. Arts Branch Alberta. Alberta Community Development. (1992)-. Periodical. English. Alberta Culture & Multiculture, 10158 103rd Street, 3rd Floor, Edmonton Alberta T5J 0X6 Canada. **Tel** (403)427-2031. *Formed by the union of Visual Arts Newsletter, 0709-1206 and Working Title, 1180-3819.*

LC NX588.75 .A77 ISSN 0337-1603
DD 700/.967 FR
ARTS D'AFRIQUE NOIRE. [Arts Afr. noire]. No. 2 (1972)-. Periodical. French. Four times a year. $62.34. Arts d'Afrique Noire, 24 rue de Draguignan, 95400 Arnouville France. **Tel** 011 33 39 872752. **ED** Raoul Lehuard. Index available. **Bk Rev**, (Qty: 4). **Ad Acc, Adv Mgr:** DITO. ctrl circ. ***Continues** Arts d'Afrique.*
Desc: Studies on the art and ethnology of black Africa.
Ind/Abst Anthropol. Lit.; Art Index; Ethnoarts Index.

ISSN 0843-2198
DD 700/.25713/52 CN
ARTS DIRECTORY (HAMILTON). (ARTS DIRECTORY.). [Arts dir.]. **Added/Corp** Hamilton and Region Arts Council. (1987)-. English. Every 3 years. Hamilton and Region Arts Council, 116 King Street West, Hamilton Ontario L8P 4V3 Canada. **Tel** (905)529-9485. ***Continues** Artsovation, 0824-2011.*
Desc: A guide to the arts in the greater Hamilton & Burlington area.

LC NK1160 ISSN 1355-4654
DD 700.7041 UK
ARTS EDUCATION. (ARTS EDUCATION : THE MAGAZINE OF THE NATIONAL FOUNDATION FOR ARTS EDUCATION.). [Arts educ.]. (1991)-. English. Six times a year (Feb., Apr., June, Aug., Oct., Dec.). $56.13. National Foundation for Arts Education, The Spendlove Centre, Enstone Road, Charlbury Oxfordshire OX7 3PQ United Kingdom. **Tel** 011 44 1608 811488, FAX 011 44 1608 811323. **ED** Andrew Warsdale (Telephone; 011 44 0223 333388). **Bk Rev. Ad Acc. Circ:** 1,500 (ctrl). ***Continues** Newsletter - National Foundation for Arts Education.*
Desc: Articles on arts-teaching practices of interest to teachers and artists working in education. Also includes information, comments, and reviews of current trends in the arts.

LC NK1160 .D4 ISSN 1063-2913
DD 700/.7 US
CCC
ARTS EDUCATION POLICY REVIEW. [Arts educ. policy rev.]. **Added/Corp** Music Educators National Conference (U.S.). Vol. 94, No. 1 (Sept./Oct. 1992)-. Periodical. English. Six times a year. $63.00. Heldref Publications, 1319 Eighteenth Street Northwest, Washington DC 20036-1802. **Tel** (202)296-6267, (800)365-9753, FAX (202)296-5149. ***Continues** Design for Arts & Education, 0732-0973.*
Ind/Abst Acad. Abstr.; Acad. Search; Curr. Cit.; EP Collect.; Homework Help.; Humanit. Source; Mag. Artic. Summar. Elite; Mag. Artic. Summar. Select; Mag. Artic. Summar. CD-ROM; Mag. Search; MasterFile FullTEXT 1000; MasterFile FullTEXT 350; MasterFile FullTEXT 650; MasterFile FullTEXT (Sept. 1992-) [Full Txt.]; OCLC; Pub. Lib. FullTEXT; Telebase; Vocat. Search.

ISSN 0999-4084
FR
UDC 62
ARTS ET METIERS MAGAZINE PARIS. [Arts metiers mag.Paris]. (1989)-. Periodical. French. Ten times a year. $64.26. Arts & Metiers Magazine, 9 Bis Avenue D Iena, F 75783 Paris Cedex 16 France. **Tel** 011 33 1 47236164. ***Continues** AM. Ingenieurs Arts et Metiers (Paris), 0980-3459.*

ISSN 1197-432X
DD 700/.71/0711 CN
ARTS IN EDUCATION NEWSLETTER. [Arts educ. newsl.]. **Added/Corp** Arts in Education Council (Vancouver, B.C.). (1992)-. Newsletter. English. Four times a year. comes with British Columbia Arts in Education Membership. British Columbia Arts & Education Council, 837 Davie Street, Vancouver British Columbia, V6Z 1B7 Canada. **Tel** (604)738-2552. ***Continues** Arts in Ed., 0829-0245.*

ISSN 0824-5495
DD 700/.9713/43 CN
ARTS IN GUELPH, THE. [Arts Guelph]. Vol. 1, No. 1 (July 1975)-. Periodical. English. Eleven times a year. Free with membership, 15.00Can$ nonmembers. Guelph Arts Council, 21 King Street, Guelph Ontario N1E 4P5. **ED** H C Stone. **Circ:** 1,600.
Desc: An events calendar and articles on local arts groups and individuals are featured.

ISSN 0004-4032
US
CEASED
ARTS IN VIRGINIA. [Arts Va.]. **VFOAT** AIV, Arts in Virginia. Vol. 1 Fall, (1960)-(19??). Periodical. English. Virginia Museum of Fine Arts, 2800 Grove Avenue, Richmond VA 23221-2466. **Tel** (804)367-0589, FAX (804)367-9393. **ED** George A Cruger. **Circ:** 16,000 (ctrl).
Desc: Aspects of museum collections, Virginia art, architecture, artists, and related topics.
Ind/Abst Art Index; ARTbibliogr. Mod.; ARTbibliogr. Curr. Titles; BHA : Biblio. Hist. Art.

ISSN 0897-859X
US
ARTS INDIANA. [Arts Indiana]. Vol. 9 No. 6 (Sept. 1987)-. Periodical. English. Ten times a year (Sept. - June). $25.00. Arts Indiana, 47 South Pennsylvania, Suite 701, Indianapolis IN 46204. **Tel** (317)632-7894, FAX (317)632-7966. **ED** Hank Nuwer. **Bk Rev**, (Qty: 4-6). **Ad Acc, Adv Mgr:** Kay Ivcevich, **Tel** (317)259-1407. **Circ:** 10,000. ***Continues** Arts Insight, 0738-9787.*
Desc: Covers the arts of all disciplines: theatre, music, architecture, visual art, dance, throughout the state of Indiana. Contains feature stories, critical commentary, reviews, and regular columns.

LC NX2 .A79a
DD 700/.5 FR
ARTS MAGAZINE (PARIS, FRANCE). (ARTS MAGAZINE.). (19??)-. Periodical. French (French). One time a week. 260F. 106 rue de Richelieu, Paris 2E France.
Ind/Abst ARTbibliogr. Mod.; ARTbibliogr. Curr. Titles.

ISSN 0004-4067
US
ARTS MANAGEMENT. [Arts manage.]. Vol. 1 (1962)-. Periodical. English. Five times a year. $20.00. Radius Group Inc, 408 West 57th Street, New York NY 10019. **Tel** (212)245-3850. **ED** Alvin H Reiss. **Bk Rev.** ctrl circ. available on microfilm and microfiche from University Microfilms International (UMI).
Desc: National news service for arts administrators and cultural organizations. News and bibliographies are included.
Ind/Abst Museum Abstr.

US
TITLE CHANGE
ARTS MARKETING POWER. (19??)-(19??). English. Arts Marketing Association, 1033 South Yamhill Street, Suite 203, Portland OR 97205. **Tel** (503)221-0548.

LC NX572 .A75 ISSN 0004-4083
HK
ARTS OF ASIA. [Arts Asia]. Vol. 1, No. 1 (Jan./Feb. 1971)-. Periodical. English. Six times a year. $65.00. Arts of Asia Publications Ltd, 1309 Kowloon Centre, 29-39 Ashley, Kowloon Hong Kong. **Tel** 011 852 23762228, FAX 011 852 23763713. **ED** Tuyet Nguyet. Index available. cum. index. **Bk Rev. Ad Acc. Circ:** 17,500 (ctrl). Documents available from The Genuine Article.
Desc: Intended for educated people and connoisseurs who are interested in works of art and antiques.
Ind/Abst Art Archaeol. Tech. Abstr.; Art Index; ARTbibliogr. Mod.; ARTbibliogr. Curr. Titles; Arts Humanit. Citation Index [Full Cov.]; Avery Index Archit. Period. Suppl. Colum. Univ. (1989-); Curr. Contents Arts Humanit.; Index Islam. Lit.; Res. Alert [Full Cov.].

LC NX2 .A79A
DD 700/.5 FR
ARTS (PARIS, FRANCE). (ARTS.). No. 25 (July 1981)-. Periodical. French (French). One time a week. 240F. ***Continues** Arts Magazine (Paris, France).*

ISSN 0066-8168
US
ARTS PATRONAGE SERIES. Added/Corp Washington International Arts Letter. Vol. 1 (1970)-. Monographic series. English. Irregular. Price varies per volume. Washington International Arts Letter, PO Box 12010, Des Moines IA 50312. **Tel** (800)364-6484. **ED** Nancy A. Fandel. **Bk Rev. Circ:** 10,000.
Desc: Designed to give those in the arts a basis for continued life and growth through the necessary grants and other aids on which they must depend in part.

ISSN 1065-8130
DD 700 US
Pr Rev.
ARTS REACH. [Arts reach]. (1992)-. Periodical. English. Six times a year (Feb., Apr., June, Aug., Oct., Dec.). $97.50. Arts Reach, PO Box 3393, Half Moon Bay CA 94019. **Tel** (415)726-4494, FAX (415)726-3075. **ED** John Zorn. Index available (Bound in all issues). cum. index. **Ad Acc. Circ:** 1,000. ***Continues** Arts Marketing Power.*
Desc: Discusses the latest effective fundraising and marketing techniques in the arts.

ISSN 0004-4091
UK
TITLE CHANGE
ARTS REVIEW (LONDON). (ARTS REVIEW.). [Arts rev.]. Vol. 13, No. 6 (Mar. 1961)-(1993). Periodical. English. Art Review Ltd., 20 Prescott Place, London SW4 6BT United Kingdom. **Tel** 011 44 171 9781000, FAX 011 44 171 9781102. ***Continues** Art News and Review.* ***Continued by** Art Review (London, England : 1993).*
Desc: News and reviews, comprehensive pull-out exhibition guide listings, special arts supplements, and guides to art festivals in Britain.
Ind/Abst ARTbibliogr. Mod.; ARTbibliogr. Curr. Titles.

US
ARTS : THE ARTS IN RELIGIOUS & THEOLOGICAL STUDIES. (19??)-. English. Three times a year. $13.00. United Theological Seminary / New Brighton, 3000 Fifth Street Northwest, New Brighton MN 55112. **Tel** (612)633-4311, FAX (312)633-4315. **ED** Wilson Yates. Index available. **Bk Rev. Circ:** 900.
Desc: Primary purpose is to enhance dialogue between theology, religious studies and the arts.

ISSN 0066-8095
DD 300 AT
ARTS : THE JOURNAL OF THE SYDNEY UNIVERSITY ARTS ASSOCIATION. Added/Corp Sidney University Arts Association. Vol. 1, (1958)-. English. Irregular. Price varies per volume. Sydney University Arts Association, Department of Latin, University of Sydney, Sydney New South Wales 2006 Australia.

LC NX
DD 700 AT
ARTS WEST. (19??)-. English. Six times a year. 61.00Aus$. Troubadour Publications, PO Box 8162, Perth 6849 Australia. **Tel** 011 61 9 3283877, FAX 011 61 9 328389. **ED** Adrian Kenyon. Index available. cum. index. **Bk Rev. Ad Acc, Adv Mgr:** Coby Hagedoca, **Tel** 011 61 9 3283877. **Circ:** 5,000 (ctrl).

LC NX513.A3 M373 ISSN 0704-7916
DD 700/.9715 CN
ARTSATLANTIC. [ArtsAtl.]. **Added/Corp** Confederation Centre Art Gallery and Museum. **VFOAT** Arts Atlantic. Vol. 1 (Fall 1977)-. Periodical. English (French). Three times a year (Feb., June, Oct.). 18.65Can$ Canada; $28.65 US. ArtsAtlantic, 145 Richmond Street, Charlottetn PE1 1J1 Canada. **Tel** (902)628-6111, FAX (902)566-4648. **ED** Joseph Sherman. cum. index. **Bk Rev. Ad Acc, Adv Mgr:** Lori Devine, **Tel** (902)628-6134. **Circ:** 1,600. available in microform from Micromedia Limited.
Desc: Reports on and features Atlantic Canada's fine arts including cinema/video, artisanship, performance, etc. Includes reviews, art news and an activities calendar.
Ind/Abst ARTbibliogr. Curr. Titles; BHA : Biblio. Hist. Art; Can. Index; Can. Period. Index (19??-).

ISSN 1191-4785
DD 700/.97123/05 CN
ARTWALK MAGAZINE. [Artwalk mag.]. Vol. 1, No. 2 (Apr. 1992)-. Periodical. English. Four times a year. $1.00 per issue. G. Linn, Artwalk Magazine, PO Box 86, Lethbridge Alberta T1J 3Y7 Canada. ***Continues** Artwalk (Lethbridge, Alta.)., 1188-1852.*

ISSN 1057-5413
DD 705 US
ARTWORLD HOTLINE. [ArtWorld hotline]. **VFOAT** Art World Hotline. (1991)-. Periodical. English. Twelve times a year. $26.00. ArtNetwork Press, 18757 Wildflower Drive, Penn Valley CA 95949. **Tel** (916)432-7630. **ED** Constance Smith. **Ad Acc, Adv Mgr:** Sarah Meyers. **Circ:** 100 (ctrl).

LC NX110 .A93a ISSN 0097-7276
DD 352/.94/5402573 US
ASSOCIATION OF COLLEGE, UNIVERSITY AND COMMUNITY ARTS ADMINISTRATORS, INC. See Education-School Management and Organization.

LC P99 .A83
DD 302.23/05 IT
Pr Rev.
ATHANOR. See Linguistics.

LC NX4 .A84
IT
ATHENA MEDITERRANEA. Year 10- Nov. 1975-. Periodical. Italian. L5.000. Athena Mediterranea, C C P 6/192 Int, Naples Italy.

LC AS222 .U22
DD 065 IT
ATTI DELL'ACCADEMIA DI SCIENZE, LETTERE E ARTI DI UDINE. Added/Corp Accademia di Scienze, Lettere e Arti di Udine. Series 6, Vol. 5 (1939)-. Italian. One time a year. cum. index. ***Continues** Atti della Accademia di Udine Pel Biennio.*
Ind/Abst BHA : Biblio. Hist. Art.

LC NX24.N3 N34A ISSN 0093-075X
DD 706/.1793 US
AUDIT REPORT - STATE OF NEVADA. NEVADA STATE COUNCIL ON THE ARTS. (NEVADA STATE COUNCIL ON THE ARTS AUDIT REPORT.). **Main/Corp** Nevada. Legislative Counsel Bureau. English. One time a year. Nevada Legislative Counsel Bureau / Carson City, Legislative Building, Carson City NV 89701.

ISSN 1035-3437
AT
AUSCON CLAYTON. (1990)-. Periodical. English. Five times a year. 20.55Aus$. National Center for Australian Studies, Monash University, Clayton Victoria 3168 Australia. **Tel** 011 61 3 9055232, FAX 011 61 3 9055238. **ED** Carol Hinschen.
Desc: Provides a listing of events on Australian themes.

LC NX7 .A88
AG
AUTORES. No. 1 (Oct. 20, 1971)-. Periodical. Spanish. Twenty-four times a year. Guia Practica del Exportador e Importador, Lavalle 1125, P 3 of 8, 1048 Buenos Aires Argentina. **Tel** 011 54 1 358533.

The Arts

LC NX1.A1 A93
NE
●**AVANT GARDE CRITICAL STUDIES.**
VFOAT AvantGarde Critical Studies. (1994)-. English (French and German). Irregular. $69.00. Editions Rodopi BV, Keizersgracht 302-304, 1016 Ex Amsterdam Netherlands. **Tel** 011 31 20 6227507, FAX 011 31 20 380948. **Continues** Avant Garde (Amsterdam, Netherlands), 0921-2515.

ISSN 0394-4719
IT
UDC 7
B.C.A. [B,C,A,]. **VFOAT** Beni Culturali e Ambientali; B.C.A. Beni Culturali e Ambientali. Sicilia. (1980)-. Periodical. Italian. Four times a year.
Ind/Abst BHA : Biblio. Hist. Art.

LC NX1 .B33   ISSN 0091-1488
DD 700/.5   US
BACHY. [Bachy]. Vol. 1 (July 1972)-. Periodical. English. Two times a year. $3.50. Papa Back Paperback, 3017 Santa Monica Boulevard, #164, Santa Monica CA 90404-2535.
Ind/Abst Index Am. Period. Verse.

ISSN 0115-9321
PH
BAGONG PAMANA. See Literature.

ISSN 0733-0308
US
BAMBOO RIDGE. See Literature.

LC NX451.5.B3 B34   ISSN 0525-5708
BL
BARROCO. [Barroco]. **VFOAT** Revista de Ensaio E Pesquisa. 1- 1969-. Portuguese. One time a year. UFMG - Universidade Federal de Minas Gerais / Faculdade Direito, Av Alvares Cabral 211-1206, 30170-000 Belo Horizonte Brazil. **Tel** 011 55 31 2248507.
Ind/Abst MLA Int. Bibl. Books Artic. Mod. Lang. Lit.

ISSN 0005-2841
DD 700   US
BCA NEWS (NEW YORK, N.Y.). (BCA NEWS : A PUBLICATION OF THE BUSINESS COMMITTEE FOR THE ARTS, INC.). [BCA news]. **Added/Corp** Business Committee for the Arts. **VFOAT** B.C.A. News. **VAT** Business Committee for the Arts News. No. 1 (Apr. 1968)-. English. Four times a year (Seasonally). $55.00. Business Committee for the Art, 1775 Broadway, Suite 510, New York NY 10019. **Tel** (212)664-0600, FAX (212)956-5980. **ED** Allison V. Malcolm. **Bk Rev**.

GW
BEITRAEGE ZUR KUNSTGESCHICHTE.
Vol. 1 (1968)-. Monographic series. German. Irregular. Price varies per volume. Walter de Gruyter Inc., PO Box 303421, D-10728 Berlin Germany. **Tel** 011 49 30 260050, FAX 011 49 30 26005251, telex 184027.

LC Z5937 .B5 N1.A1
DD 016.7   GW
BIBLIOGRAPHIE ZUR KUNSTGESCHICHTLICHEN LITERATUR IN OST- UND SUDOSTEUROPAISCHEN ZEITSCHRIFTEN. See The Arts-Abstracting, Bibliographies and Statistics.

LC NX24.W6 W5713
DD 353.9/775/00854   US
TITLE CHANGE
BIENNIAL REPORT - WISCONSIN ARTS BOARD. Main/Corp Wisconsin. Arts Board. (1977)-(197?). English. Wisconsin Arts Board, 131 W Wilson Street/Suite 301, Madison WI 53702. **Circ**: 2,000 (ctrl). **Continued by** Wisconsin Arts Board. Annual Report (1991).
Desc: Description of funding programs and listing of grant recipients.

LC BH8.J3 B53   ISSN 0520-0962
DD 100 700   JA
BIGAKU. See Philosophy.

ISSN 0045-2165
US
BLACK GRAPHICS INTERNATIONAL.
VFOAT A Journal of Revolutionary Literature & Art. Vol. 1 (1971)-. Periodical. English. Black Graphics International, PO Box 732, Detroit MI 48206.

ISSN 0263-2543
DD 791.0941   UK
CEASED
BLITZ LONDON. [BlitzLond.]. (1980)-(19??). Periodical. English. Blitz Magazine, 40-41 Newman Street, London W1P 3PA United Kingdom. **Tel** 011 44 171 4365211, FAX 011 44 171 4365290. **ED** Bonnie Vaughan. **Bk Rev. Ad Acc. Circ**: 60,000.

US
Pr Rev.
BLU R. See Music.

ISSN 1189-3109
DD 700/.9711/3305   CN
BOARDWALK (SURREY). (BOARDWALK.). [Boardwalk]. Vol. 1, No. 1 (Sept./Oct. 1991)-. Periodical. English. Six times a year. Free. Boardwalk, #203-74, 15515-24th Avenue, Surrey British Columbia V4A 2J4 Canada.

LC N3470 .B6
DD 708.6   SP
BOLETIN DE BELLAS ARTES. Added/Corp
Seville. Museo Provincial de Bellas Artes. Academia de Bellas Artes de Santa Isabel de Hungaria, Seville. (1934)-. Periodical. Spanish. One time a year.
Ind/Abst BHA : Biblio. Hist. Art.

LC NX458 .B65   ISSN 0743-3204
DD 700/.9/04   US
BOMB (NEW YORK, N.Y.). (BOMB.). [Bomb]. **Added/Corp** X Motion Picture and Center for New Art Activities (New York, N.Y.) Center for New Art Activities (New York, N.Y.). **VFOAT** Bomb Magazine. Vol. 1, Issue 1 (Spring 1981)-. Periodical. English. Four times a year (Mar., May, Oct., Dec.). $22.00. Bomb Magazine, 594 Broadway, Suite 1002A, New York NY 10012. **Tel** (212)431-3943, FAX (212)431-5880. **ED** Betsy Sussler. **Photos. Ad Acc, Adv Mgr**: M. Monforton, **Tel** (212)431-3943 Ext. 3. **Circ**: 10,000.
Desc: Covers new art, writing, theater and film. Publishes interviews with artists and publishes contemporary fiction and original artwork.
Ind/Abst Am. Humanit. Index; ARTbibliogr. Mod.; Index Am. Period. Verse.

ISSN 0831-2559
DD 700/.97127   CN
BORDER CROSSINGS (WINNIPEG, MAN.). (BORDER CROSSINGS.). [Border crossings]. **Added/Corp** Arts Manitoba. Vol. 4, No. 4 (Fall 1985)-. Periodical. English. Four times a year (Jan., April, July, Oct.). $23.00. Border Crossings, 300-393 Portage Avenue, Winnipeg Manitoba R3B 3H6 Canada. **Tel** (204)942-5778, FAX (204)949-0793. **ED** Robert Enright, Meeka Walsh. Index available. **Bk Rev. Ad Acc. Circ**: 3,200. available on microfiche; available in microform. **Continues** Arts Manitoba, 0702-7427.
Desc: Covers the fine arts, including architecture, dance, photography, painting, sculpture, theatre, music, poetry and fiction, as well as areas where the arts and politics overlap, such as broadcast policy or urban development issues.
Ind/Abst BHA : Biblio. Hist. Art; Can. Index; Can. Period. Index (19??-).

CN
BORDERLINES. (19??)-. English. Four times a year. Bethune College, York University, 4700 Keele Street, North York Ontario M3J 1P3 Canada.
Ind/Abst Can. Period. Index (19??-).

ISSN 1196-6785
DD 700/.9711/2805   CN
TITLE CHANGE
BOULEVARD (VICTORIA. 1992).
(BOULEVARD.). [Boulevard]. **VFOAT** Victoria Boulevard. Vol. 4, Issue 1 (Autumn 1992)-Vol. 4, Issue 4 (Summer 1993). Periodical. English. Bay Publishing Ltd., PO Box 5667, Station B, Victoria British Columbia V8R 6S4 Canada. **Tel** (604)598-8111. **Continues** Boulevard Magazine, 1189-6051. **Merged with** Easy Living's Victoria, 1189-7120 **to form** Victoria Boulevard (1993), 1196-6793.

ISSN 1196-6807
DD 700/.9711/2805   CN
●**BOULEVARD (VICTORIA. 1994).**
(BOULEVARD.). [Boulevard]. **VFOAT** Victoria Boulevard. Vol. 1, Issue 4 (Apr./May 1994)-. Periodical. English. Six times a year. Bay Publishing Ltd., PO Box 5667, Station B, Victoria British Columbia V8R 6S4 Canada. **Tel** (604)598-8111. **Continues** Victoria Boulevard (1993), 1196-6793.

LC NX5 .B7
NE
BRES. (196?)-. Dutch. Irregular. $64.31. Bres BV, Postbus 3296, 1001 AH Amsterdam The Netherlands. **Tel** 011 31 20 6278510.

LC PS1 .B75   ISSN 0161-1577
DD 810.5   US
BRILLIANT CORNERS. (BRILLIANT CORNERS; A MAGAZINE OF THE ART'S.). Vol. 1 (1975)-. Periodical. English. Gleerup Bokforlag, Box 1205, 22105 Lund Sweden.

LC BH1 .B7   ISSN 0007-0904
DD 111   CCC
BRITISH JOURNAL OF AESTHETICS.
(THE BRITISH JOURNAL OF AESTHETICS.). [Br. j. aesthet.]. **Added/Corp** British Society of Aesthetics. Vol. 1 (Nov. 1960)-. Periodical. English. Four times a year. $116.00. Oxford University Press / UK, Walton Street, Oxford OX2 6DP United Kingdom. **Tel** 011 44 1865 56776/7, FAX 011 44 1865 267773, telex 851/837330 OXPRES G. (Subscription address): Oxford University Press / USA, Journals Marketing Department, Oxford University Press, 2001 Evans Road, Cary NC 27513. **Tel** (800)451-7556, (919)677-0977, FAX (919)677-1714.) **ED** T. J. Diffey. Index available. **Bk Rev. Ad Acc. Circ**: 1,200. available on microfilm and microfiche from University Microfilms International (UMI). Documents available from The Genuine Article, UMI Article Clearinghouse.
Desc: Discussions of general philosophical aesthetics and articles on the principles of appraisal which apply in the various arts.
Ind/Abst Abstr. Engl. Stud.; Acad. Search; Annu. Bibliogr. Engl. Lang. Lit.; Art Index; ARTbibliogr. Mod. (1984-); ARTbibliogr. Curr. Titles; Arts Humanit. Citation Index [Full Cov.]; BHA : Biblio. Hist. Art; Br. Humanit. Index; Curr. Cit.; Curr. Contents Arts Humanit.; EP Collect.; Expand. Acad. Index (1989-); Film Lit. Index (1973-1985); Homework Help.; Humanit. Index; Humanit. Source; INFO-SOUTH Abstr.; Linguist. Lang. Behav. Abstr.; MasterFile FullTEXT 1000; MasterFile FullTEXT 350; MasterFile FullTEXT 650; MasterFile FullTEXT (July 1993-); MLA Int. Bibl. Books Artic. Mod. Lang. Lit.; Music Index (-19??); Newsp. Period. Abstr. (1991-); OCLC; Philos. Index; Res. Alert [Full Cov.]; Pollment. Move.; Soc. Plann. Policy Dev. Abstr.; Soc. Sci. Cit. Index [Select. Cov.]; Sociol. Abstr.; Telebase.

LC AS36 .A48516   ISSN 0002-712X
US
BULLETIN - AMERICAN ACADEMY OF ARTS AND SCIENCES. [Bull. - Am. Acad. Arts Sci.]. **Main/Corp** American Academy of Arts and Sciences. Vol. 1 (Jan. 1948)-. Bulletin. English. Eight times a year (Monthly Oct.-May). $12.00. Bulletin of the American Academy of Arts and Sciences, Nortons Woods, 136 Irving Street, Cambridge MA 02138. **Tel** (617)492-8800. **ED** Alexandra Oleson. Index available. **Circ**: 3,500 (ctrl). available on microfilm from University Microfilms International (UMI).
Desc: Reports on meetings and projects of the American Academy of Arts and Sciences.
Ind/Abst Am. Hist. Life.

LC AS242 .B3413   ISSN 0378-0716
BE
BULLETIN DE LA CLASSE DE BEAUX-ARTS ACADEMIE ROYALE DE BELGIQUE. (BULLETIN DE LA CLASSE DE BEAUX-ARTS.). [Bull. classe beaux-arts, Acad. r. Belg.]. **Main/Corp** Academie Royale des Sciences, des Lettres des Beaux-Arts de Belgique. Classe des Beaux-Arts. (1919)-. Bulletin. French. Twelve times a year. Etablissements Emile Bruylant, 67 rue de la Regence, 1000 Brussels Belgium. **Tel** 011 32 2 5129845, FAX 011 32 2 5117202. Index available in last issue of volume--attached. **Circ**: 500 (ctrl). **Continues** Annexe aux Bulletins de la Classe de Beaux-Arts.
Ind/Abst Art Archaeol. Tech. Abstr.; ARTbibliogr. Mod.; BHA : Biblio. Hist. Art.

ISSN 0988-1557
FR
UDC 908 (4.8)
BULLETIN DE LA SOCIETE ARIEGEOISE DES SCIENCES LETTRES ET ARTS. **VFOAT** Bulletin Periodique de la Societe Ariegeoise des Sciences, Lettres & Arts et de la Societe des Etudes du Couserans; Bulletin Annuel - Societe Ariegeoise Sciences Lettres et Arts; Bulletin Periodique de la Societe Ariegeoise des Sciences, Lettres & Arts. (1882)-. Bulletin. French.
Ind/Abst BHA : Biblio. Hist. Art.

ISSN 0373-952x
FR
BULLETIN DE LA SOCIETE D'AGRICULTURE, SCIENCES ET ARTS DE LA SARTHE. **Main/Corp** Societe d'Agriculture, Sciences et Arts de la Sarthe. **VFOAT** Bulletin de la Societe Royale d'Agriculture, Sciences et Arts du Mans. (1833)-. Bulletin. French. cum. index.
Ind/Abst BHA : Biblio. Hist. Art.

US
BULLETIN DE L'INSTITUT ROYAL DU PATRIMOINE ARTISTIQUE. MICROFORM. Added/Corp Institut Royal du Patrimoine Artistique (Brussels, Belgium). (1958)-. Bulletin. French (Dutch and English). One time a year. 625F Belgium; $16.50 US. Institut Royal du Patrimoine Artistique, Pard du Cinquentenaire 1, B-1040 Brussels Belgium. **Tel** 32 2 739 6711, FAX 32 2 739 6868. **Circ**: 1,000 (ctrl).
Desc: Covers art conservation and art history, particularly in Belgium.
Ind/Abst Art Archaeol. Tech. Abstr.; BHA : Biblio. Hist. Art.

LC N3540 .A28   ISSN 0347-7835
DD 709/.4/074087   SW
BULLETIN - NATIONALMUSEUM.
(NATIONALMUSEUM BULLETIN.). [Bull. - Natl.mus.]. **Main/Corp** Nationalmuseum (Sweden). **Added/Corp**

The Arts

Nationalmuseum (Sweden). Bulletin. Vol. 1 (1977)-. Bulletin. English (Swedish).
Ind/Abst BHA : Biblio. Hist. Art.

GW

BUNTE ILLUSTRIERTE MUENCHNER/FRANKFURTER. VFOAT
Bunte Illustrierte. (1963)-. Periodical. German. One time a week (53 per year). $190.00. Burda Verlag GmbH, Postfach 1230, D-77602 Offenburg Germany. **Tel** 011 49 7818401, **FAX** 011 49 781843155. **(Subscription address:** German Language Publications Inc., 153 South Dean Street, Englewood NJ 07631. **Tel** (201)871-1010, (800)457-4443.) **Continues** Bunte Muenchner/Frankfurter Illustrierte.

ISSN 1193-8625
DD 709/.71/05
CN

C MAGAZINE (1992). (C MAGAZINE). [C mag.].
VFOAT C. Issue 34 (Summer 1992)-. Periodical. English (summaries and/or abstracts in French). Four times a year (Mar., June, Sept., Dec.). $25.00 (individuals), $35.00 (institutions). C Magazine, 988 Queen Street West, Toronto Ontario M6J 1H1 Canada. **Tel** (416)539-9495, **FAX** (416)531-7610. **ED** Joyce Mason. Index available. **Bk Rev**, (Qty: varies). **Ad Acc**, **Adv Mgr:** Carol Peaker. **Circ:** 3,000. available on microfilm from Micromedia Limited. **Continues** C (Toronto, Ont. : 1987)., 0838-0392.
Desc: Covers the topics and controversies that surround contemporary art in Canada and abroad.

US

CALIFORNIA ARTS ADVOCATE. (19??)-.
Periodical. English. Irregular (2 to 6 times per year). $50.00. California Confederation of the Arts, 740 O Street, Sacramento CA 95814. **Tel** (916)447-7811, **FAX** (916)447-7891. **ED** Ken Larsen. **Bk Rev**. **Ad Acc**. **Circ:** 1,500. **Continues** Newsletter/California Confederation of the Arts.
Desc: Cultural policy, legislation and appropriation coverage for California's 10,000 nonprofit arts organizations.

LC NX506 .C34 **ISSN** 0161-2492
DD 700/.8996075 US
CCC

CALLALOO. [Callaloo]. No. 1 (Dec. 1976)-.
Periodical. English. Four times a year. $65.00. Johns Hopkins University Press, 2715 North Charles Street, Baltimore MD 21218-4319. **Tel** (410)516-6987, **FAX** (410)516-6968. **ED** Charles H. Rowell. **Bk Rev**. **Ad Acc**. **Circ:** 1,000 (ctrl). available on CD-ROM; available on microfilm and microfiche from University Microfilms International (UMI). Documents available from UMI Article Clearinghouse.
Desc: Publishes original works and critical studies of black writers in the Americas and Africa, including poetry, short stories, plays, folklore, critical essays, cultural studies, interviews, visual art, and annotated bibliographies.
Ind/Abst Abstr. Engl. Stud.; Am. Hist. Life (1986-); Am. Humanit. Index; Book Rev. Index; Child. Lit. Abstr. (19??-); EP Collect.; Expand. Acad. Index (1992-); Homework Help; Index Am. Period. Verse; Lit. Crit. Regist.; Mag. Search; MasterFile FullTEXT 1000; MasterFile FullTEXT 350; MasterFile FullTEXT 650; MasterFile FullTEXT (July 1993-); MLA Int. Bibl. Books Artic. Mod. Lang. Lit.; Newsp. Period. Abstr. (1990-); OCLC; Pub. Lib. FullTEXT; Telebase; Vocat. Search.

UK

CAMBRIDGE GUIDE TO THE ARTS IN BRITAIN. Academic Scholarly Publication. English.
Irregular. Price varies per volume. Cambridge University Press, The Edinburgh Building, Shaftesbury Road, Cambridge CB2 2RU United Kingdom. **Tel** 011 44 1223 312393, **FAX** 011 44 1223 315052, telex 851-817256. **(Subscription address:** Cambridge University Press / North America, 110 Midland Avenue, Port Chester NY 10573. **Tel** (800)431-1580, (914)937-9600.)

ISSN 0008-199X
UK
CCC

CAMBRIDGE QUARTERLY. See Literary and Political Reviews.

ISSN 1190-9862
DD 382 CN

●CANADA'S EXPORT STRATEGY, THE INTERNATIONAL TRADE BUSINESS PLAN. 10, CULTURAL INDUSTRIES. [Can. export strategy int. trade bus. plan, 10 Cult. ind.].
Added/Corp Canada. **VFOAT** Cultural Industries. (1996)-. Government Publication. English. Irregular. **Continues** Canada's International Trade Business Plan. 4, Arts and Cultural Industries, 1200-1120.

ISSN 0826-9726
CN

CANADIAN ART. CATALOGUE OF THE NATIONAL GALLERY OF CANADA.
(19??)-. Catalog. English (French). Every 2 years. 74.95Can$. National Gallery of Canada, Publications Division, 380 Sussex Drive, Ottawa Ontario K1N 9N4 Canada. **Tel** (613)990-0537, **FAX** (613)990-7460.

(Subscription address: University of Chicago Press, 5801 Ellis Avenue, Chicago IL 60637-1496.) **ED** Charles C. Hill and Pierre B. Landry. Index available. cum. index. available with illustrations.
Desc: Comprises works by over 300 artists (from Adamson to Fuller). Covers paintings, sculptures, drawings, prints, decorative art objects, and video works. Entries are illustrated and preceded by concise biographies of the artists.

LC NX562.A1 C36
DD 700/.946 SP

CANELOBRE. No. 1 (Jun. 1984)-. Periodical.
Spanish (Catalan). Three times a year. 1600ptas. Instituto de Cultura Juan Gil-Albert, Avda de la Estacion 6, 03005 Alicante Spain. **Tel** 96.512.12.16. cum. index. **Bk Rev**. **Ad Acc**.

ISSN 1077-8438
DD 700 US

●CANEWS (ARLINGTON, MASS.). See Religions and Theology.

ISSN 0822-918X
DD 700/.29/471384 CN

CAPITAL REGION CREATIVE SERVICES DIRECTORY, THE. [Cap. reg. creat. serv. dir.].
VFOAT Directory. 1983-. Directory. English. One time a year. $15.00 per volume. Local Association of Media Professionals, PO Box 220 Station A, Ottawa Ontario K1P 6C4. **Continues** Creative Services Directory, 0822-9171.

LC NK4001 **ISSN** 1121-6441
DD 738 IT
UDC 738

CASTELLI TERAMO. (CASTELLI.). [Castelli Teramo]. (1989)-. Periodical. Italian. Two times a year. Edizioni Grafiche Italiane, Teramo Italy.
Ind/Abst BHA : Biblio. Hist. Art.

ISSN 0728-5256
DD 016.7929099461 AT

CATALOGUE OF SCRIPTS HELD AT THE SALAMANCA SCRIPT RESOURCE CENTRE. [Cat. scr. held Salamanca Scr. Resour. Cent.]. (1981)-. English. Five times a year (Mar., June, July, Sept., Dec.). 35.00Aus$ (individuals), 45.00Aus$ (institutions) Australia; 60.00Aus$ other. Australian Script Centre, 77 Salamanca Place, Hobart Tasmania 7004 Australia. **Tel** 011 61 2 23675, **FAX** 011 61 2 240245.

ISSN 1185-9318
DD 700/.25/7146 CN

CATALOGUE-REPERTOIRE DES CREATEURS-CONCEPTEURS. [Cat. repert. creat. concept.]. **Main/Corp** Corporation des Metiers d'Art du Quebec en Estrie. (1991)-. French. Every 2 years. Limited free distribution. Corporation des Metiers D'Art du Quebec en Estrie, 17 Nord rue Belvedere, Sherbrooke Quebec J1H 4A7 Canada.

UK

CENCRASTUS. No. 1 (Autumn 1979)-. Periodical.
English (Gaelic (Scots)). Four times a year. Cencrastus, 34 Queen Street, Edinburgh EH2 1JX United Kingdom. **Tel** 011 44 131 2265606. **ED** Raymond J Ross and Thom Nairn. **Bk Rev**. **Ad Acc**. **Circ:** 3,000.
Desc: Scottish and international literature, arts and cultural affairs.
Ind/Abst Annu. Bibliogr. Engl. Lang. Lit.

ISSN 0705-6842
DD 700/.71/071233 CN

CENTRE LETTER (BANFF). (CENTRE LETTER.). No. 1 (Jan. 27, 1978)-. English. Free. Banff Centre, School of Fine Arts, Box 1020, Banff Alberta T0L 0C0 Canada. **Tel** (403)762-6159. **ED** Ena Spalding. **Ad Acc**, **Circ:** 500 (ctrl). **Supersedes** Centre Stage, 0319-4728.
Desc: General corporate information about the Banff Centre, its programs and alumni, and in general, information on the arts and management studies.

US

CHALLENGE II GRANTS. VFOAT Challenge Two Grants; Challenge 2 Grants. 1989-. English. One time a year. National Endowment for the Arts, 1100 Pennsylvania Avenue Northwest, Washington DC 20506. **Tel** (202)682-5400, (202)682-5435.

LC NX583.A1 C4237
DD 700/.951 CC

CHANG-CHIANG WEN I. VFOAT Changjiang Wenyi. (19??)-. Periodical. Chinese. Twelve times a year. $20.65. **(Subscription address:** China International Book Trading Corporation, PO Box 399, Library Service Department, Beijing 100044 People's Republic of China. **Tel** 011 86 1 8414284, **FAX** 011 86 1 8412023, telex 22496 CIBTC CN.) **Continues** Hu-Pei Wen I, 0301-9756.

LC NX551.A1 C46
GR

CHARTES. 1 (July 1982)-. Periodical. Greek, Modern. Six times a year. $22.00. Solomou 16, 148 Athens Greece.

LC NX583.A3 H663
DD 509/.51212 CC

CHI TUNG WEN I = JIDONG WENYI.
VFOAT Jidong Wenyi. (19??)-. Periodical. Chinese. Six times a year. RMBY0.25. Post Office Tang-Shan Shih, Tang-Shan Shih, People's Republic of China.

LC NX511.C45 C44 **ISSN** 1061-8864
DD 700/.9773/1105 US

CHICAGO ARTS & COMMUNICATION.
[Chic. arts commun.]. **Added/Corp** Columbia College (Chicago, Ill.). Journalism Dept. **VFOAT** Chicago Arts and Communication. Vol. 1, No. 1 (June 1991)-. Periodical. English. Columbia College, Journalism Department, 600 South Michigan Avenue, Chicago IL 60605.

LC NX584.6.A1 .C47
KO

CHOSON CHUNGANG ILBO. Jan. 1933-.
Periodical. Korean. Choson Chungang Yonguso, 221 Huksok-dong, Kwanak-ku, Seoul Korea.

LC NX7 .C54 **ISSN** 0210-119X
DD 700/.5 SP

CIMAL. (19??)-. Catalan (Spanish, English and French). Four times a year. $72.80. Ediciones Cimal Internacional, Jofrens 6, 460001 Valencia Spain. **Tel** 011 34 6 3915655. **ED** D. Pascual Lucas Catala.
Ind/Abst ARTbibliogr. Mod. (1984-); BHA : Biblio. Hist. Art.

ISSN 0886-6570
DD 791 US
Pr Rev.

CINEMATOGRAPH. [Cinematograph].
Added/Corp San Francisco Cinematheque (Calif.) Foundation for Art in Cinema. Vol. 1, (1985)-. English. One time a year. $25.00. Cinematograph, 480 Potrero Avenue, San Francisco CA 94110. **Tel** (415)558-8129, **FAX** (415)558-0455. **ED** Albert Kilchesty. **Ad Acc**. **Circ:** 1,800 (ctrl). available on microfilm from University Microfilms International (UMI).
Desc: A journal of film and media criticism, theory and reviews. Contains a listing of articles, photographs, collages, poems, and letters by today's film and video artists.
Ind/Abst Film Lit. Index.

LC DR201 .C56
RM
CEASED

CINTAREA ROMANIEI / REVISTA EDITATA DE CONSILIUL CULTURII SE EDUCATIEI SOCIALISTE. Vol. 1 (Aug. 1980-19??). Periodical. Romanian. **Continues** Indrumatorul Cultural.
Desc: Publishes articles on methodology of activists in the domain of culture.

ISSN 0744-0456
US

CITY PAGES. (198?)-. Periodical. English. One time a week. $39.00. City Pages Inc, PO Box 59183, Minneapolis MN 55459. **Tel** (612)375-1015, **FAX** (612)375-9819. **ED** Steve Perry. **Bk Rev**. **Pub. Size:** Tabloid. **Circ:** 100,000. available with illustrations. **Continues** Sweet Potato, 0199-3712.

LC NX504 .C58 **ISSN** 0740-9311
DD 700/.973/05 US

CLOCKWATCH REVIEW. VFOAT Clock Watch Review. Vol. 1, No. 1 (Summer 1983)-. Periodical. English. Two times a year. $10.00. Clockwatch Review, Illinois Wesleyan University, Bloomington IL 61702. **Tel** (309)556-3352. **ED** James Plath. Index available. cum. index. **Bk Rev**, (Qty: 6-8). **Ad Acc**. **Circ:** 1,500.
Desc: Seeks to present quality work and attract a general and literary/academic audience.
Ind/Abst Am. Humanit. Index; Index Am. Period. Verse.

LC NX7 .C64 **ISSN** 0870-3841
DD 705 PO

COLOQUIO : ARTES. [Coloquio, Artes].
Added/Corp Fundacao Calouste Gulbenkian. Vol. 1, (Feb. 1971)-. Periodical. Portuguese (summaries and/or abstracts in French). Four times a year (Mar., July, Sept., Dec.). $80.00. Nobar Grupo Editorial L DA, Rua da Cruz da Carreira 4B, 1100 Lisbon Portugal. **Tel** 011 351 1 3522490. Documents available from The Genuine Article. **Continues in part** Coloquio (Lisbon, Portugal).
Ind/Abst ARTbibliogr. Mod.; ARTbibliogr. Curr. Titles; Arts Humanit. Citation Index [Full Cov.]; BHA : Biblio. Hist. Art; Curr. Contents Arts Humanit.; Res. Alert [Full Cov.]; Soc. Sci. Cit. Index [Select. Cov.].

ISSN 0900-0925
DD 700 DK
CODEN 70

COLPO DEL BARBARI, IL. [Colpo barbar.].
VFOAT Barbarernes Hug. (1985)-. Periodical. Multiple languages. Two times a year. Il Colpo del Barbari, Milano Hellerup Denmark.
Ind/Abst BHA : Biblio. Hist. Art.

LC NX504 .C63 **ISSN** 1048-8790
DD 700/.9789/61 US
CONCEPTIONS SOUTHWEST. [Concept. southwest]. **Added/Corp** University of New Mexico. Vol. 1 (spring 1978)-. English (Spanish). Two times a year. $8.00 (individuals), $10.00 (institutions). Associated Students of the University of New Mexico, Box 20, Albuquerque NM 87131. ***Continues*** *Thunderbird.*

ISSN 1045-5175
DD 700 US
CONKLIN'S GUIDE. [Conklin's guide]. 1989-. Periodical. English. One time a year. $90.00. Leeward Shore Press, PO Box 939A, Brisbane CA 94005.

LC NX165 .C65 **ISSN** 1052-8164
DD 700/.1/9 US
CONSTRUCTIVE CRITICISM. (CONSTRUCTIVE CRITICISM : A JOURNAL OF CONSTRUCT PSYCHOLOGY AND THE ARTS.). [Constr. crit.]. **Added/Corp** Center for the Study of Construct Psychology and the Arts. Vol. 1, No. 1 (Mar. 1991)-. Periodical. English. Four times a year. $30.00. Center for the Study of Construct Psychology and the Arts, PO Box 162, Gambier OH 43022.

LC PS536.2 .C64 **ISSN** 0270-6687
DD 810/.8/0054 US
CORONA (BOZEMAN). See Literature.

UK
CORPUS RUBENIANUM LUDWIG BURCHARD. **Added/Corp** Nationaal Centrum voor de Plastische Kunsten van de XVIde en XVIIde Eeuw. Pt. 1 (1968)-. Monographic series. English. Irregular. Price varies per volume. Biblios Distribution, Star Road Partridge Green, West Sussex RH13 8LD United Kingdom. **Tel** 011 44 1403 710971.

ISSN 0304-3126
BL
UDC 341.16:001
CODEN NU053
CORREIO DA UNESCO, O. [Corr. Unesco Ed. port.]. (1972)-. Periodical. Portuguese. Twelve times a year. $65.00. Fundacao Getulio Vargas, Praia de Botafogo, 190 6 Andar, 22253-900 Rio de Janeiro RJ Brazil. **Tel** 011 5521 551 0698, FAX 011 5521 551 1596, 011 5521 551 5755. available with illustrations.
Desc: Illustrated articles about arts, education, sciences, communication and culture signed by world-famous specialists.

ISSN 0392-5269
IT
UDC 7
CORSI DI CULTURA SULL'ARTE RAVENNATE E BIZANTINA. [Corsi cult. arte ravenn. biz.]. (1957)-. Periodical. Italian. One time a year. Angelo Longo Editore, Via Paolo Costa 33, CP 431, 48100 Ravenna Italy. **Tel** 011 39 544 217026, FAX 011 39 544 217026. ***Continues*** *Corsi d'Arte Ravennate e Bizantina.*
Ind/Abst BHA : Biblio. Hist. Art.

ISSN 0887-9427
DD 700 US
SUSPENDED
COW IN THE ROAD. [Cow road]. Vol. 1, No. 1 (Winter 1986)-?. Periodical. English. Four times a year. $6.50. Cow in the Road, 455 South 2nd Street, San Jose CA 95113.

ISSN 0820-7909
DD 700/.9713/52 CN
CREATIVE ARTS (HAMILTON). (CREATIVE ARTS.). [Creat. arts]. July 1980-. Periodical. English. Festival of Friends, PO Box 2717, Bloomington IN 47402-2717.

LC NX1 .C63 **ISSN** 0363-292X
DD 700/.5 US
CRIMMER'S. (1976)-. English. One time a year. $3.00 per copy. Crimmer's, 104 East 40th Street, Office 114, New York NY 10016. ***Continues*** *Crimmer's, The Harvard Journal of Pictorial Fiction, 0362-2932.*

LC NX1 .C64 **ISSN** 0093-1896
DD 700/.9 US
CCC
CRITICAL INQUIRY. [Crit. inq.]. (Sept. 1974)-. Periodical. English. Four times a year. $92.00. University of Chicago Press / Journals Division, PO Box 37005, 5720 South Woodlawn, Chicago IL 60637. **Tel** (312)753-3347, FAX (312)753-0811. **ED** W.J.T. Mitchell, Arnold I. Davidson, Elizabeth Helsinger, Francoise Meltzer, Joel Snyder, Harry Harootunian and Lauren Berlant. **Ad Acc. Acid Free.** available on microfilm and microfiche from University Microfilms International (UMI). Documents available from The Genuine Article, UMI Article Clearinghouse.
Desc: Publishes critical thoughts in the arts and humanities. Presents articles by critics, scholars, and artists on a variety of issues central to contemporary criticism and culture.
Ind/Abst Abstr. Engl. Stud.; Acad. Abstr.; Acad. Ind. [Computer File] (1992-); Acad. Search; Am. Hist. Life (1974-); Am. Bibliogr. Slavic East Europ. Stud.; Am. Humanit. Index (1974-); Annu. Bibliogr. Engl. Lang. Lit.; ARTbibliogr. Mod.; Arts Humanit. Citation Index [Full Cov.]; BHA : Biblio. Hist. Art; Child. Lit. Abstr. (19??-); Curr. Cit.; Curr. Contents Arts Humanit.; EP Collect.; Expand. Acad. Index (1989-); Film Lit. Index; Homework Help.; Humanit. Index; Humanit. Source; INFO-SOUTH Abstr.; Linguist. Lang. Behav. Abstr.; Lit. Crit. Regist. (1974-); Mag. Search; MasterFile FullTEXT 1000; MasterFile FullTEXT 350; MasterFile FullTEXT 650; MasterFile FullTEXT (July 1990-); Middle East Abstr. Index; MLA Int. Bibl. Books Artic. Mod. Lang. Lit.; Music Artic. Guide (1974-?); Newsp. Period. Abstr. (1990-); OCLC; Philos. Index; Pub. Lib. FullTEXT; Res. Alert [Full Cov.]; Romant. Move.; Soc. Plann. Policy Dev. Abstr.; Soc. Sci. Cit. Index [Select. Cov.]; Sociol. Abstr.; Telebase.

US
CRITICAL PERSPECTIVES. **VFOAT** Critical Perspectives Series. (19??)-. Monographic series. English. Irregular. Price varies per volume. Three Continents Press, PO Box 38009, Colorado Springs CO 80937. **Tel** (719)579-0977. Documents available from The Genuine Article.
Ind/Abst Arts Humanit. Citation Index (19??-19??) [Full Cov.]; Res. Alert [Full Cov.].

LC AP4 .C887 **ISSN** 0011-1562
DD 820/.5 UK
CCC
CODEN CRQUEF
CRITICAL QUARTERLY, THE. See Literature.

LC AS30.W3 A2 **ISSN** 0011-1589
DD 051 US
CRITICISM (DETROIT). (CRITICISM.). [Criticism]. Vol. 1 (Winter 1959)-. Periodical. English. Four times a year (Jan., Apr., Jul., Oct.). $55.00. Wayne State University Press, 4809 Woodward Avenue, The Leonard N. Simons Building, Detroit MI 48201-1309. **Tel** (313)577-6119, (313)577-6120, FAX (313)577-6131. **ED** Ross Pudaloff. Index available (bound in 4th issue). **Bk Rev. Ad Acc. Circ:** 1,200 (ctrl). available on microfilm and microfiche from University Microfilms International (UMI). Documents available from The Genuine Article, UMI Article Clearinghouse.
Desc: Examines literature and arts of all periods and nations either individually or in their inter-relationships; also the critical theory regarding them.
Ind/Abst Abstr. Engl. Stud.; Acad. Search; Arts Humanit. Citation Index [Full Cov.]; BHA : Biblio. Hist. Art; Book Rev. Index; Curr. Cit.; Curr. Contents Arts Humanit.; EP Collect.; Expand. Acad. Index (1989-); Film Lit. Index (1986-1991); Homework Help.; Humanit. Index; Humanit. Source; INFO-SOUTH Abstr.; Lit. Crit. Regist.; Mag. Search; MasterFile FullTEXT 1000; MasterFile FullTEXT 350; MasterFile FullTEXT 650; MasterFile FullTEXT (July 1993-); Middle East Abstr. Index; MLA Int. Bibl. Books Artic. Mod. Lang. Lit.; Newsp. Period. Abstr. (1991-); OCLC; Res. Alert [Full Cov.]; Romant. Move.; Soc. Sci. Cit. Index [Select. Cov.]; Telebase.

ISSN 0704-6588
DD 051 CN
CROSSCURRENTS (SASKATOON). (CROSSCURRENTS.). No. 1 (Aug. 1975)-. Periodical. English. Twelve times a year. 10.00Can$. Crosscurrents / Canada, Greenwich-Meridian, 516 Avenue K South, Saskatoon Saskatchewan S7M 2E2 Canada. **Tel** (306)244-0679. **ED** Bob Fink. Index available. cum. index. **Bk Rev. Circ:** 1,000.
Desc: Deals with universal themes underlying arts and political events. Also involved with the interdisciplinary nature of reality, but always cites concrete examples.
Ind/Abst Am. Humanit. Index.

LC NX7 .G7a **ISSN** 0210-962X
SP
CUADERNOS DE ARTE DE LA UNIVERSIDAD DE GRANADA. **Added/Corp** Universidad De Granada. Vol. 11, (1974)-. Periodical. Spanish. 650ptas. Universidad de Granada / Hospital, Secretaria de Publicaciones, Hospital Real, Avda del Hospicio S/N, 18001 Granada Spain. ***Continues*** *Cuadernos De Arte y Literatura.*
Ind/Abst BHA : Biblio. Hist. Art.

ISSN 0392-1506
IT
UDC 930.25 (450.323)
CULTURA ATESINA. [Cult. Atesina]. **VFOAT** Kultur des Etschlandes. (1947)-. Periodical. Multiple languages. Three times a week.
Ind/Abst BHA : Biblio. Hist. Art.

LC NX742.C22 L7c
US
CULTURAL AFFAIRS NEWS. **Main/Corp** Los Angeles (Calif.). Cultural Affairs Dept. 1st Quarter (1991)-. English. Four times a year. ***Formed by the union of*** *City Arts News* ***and*** *Folk Arts News.*

LC NX573.A3 K383
DD 954/.6/005 II
CULTURAL DIGEST, THE. Periodical. English. T Fotedar, 72 Narpirstan Srinagar Kashmir, Srinagar 190001 India.

LC NX **ISSN** 1186-9348
DD 700 CN
TITLE CHANGE
CULTURAL EVENTS - NATIONAL LIBRARY OF CANADA. (ANIMATION CULTURELLE.). [Cult. events - Natl. Libr. Can.]. **Main/Corp** Bibliotheque Nationale du Canada. **VFOAT** Cultural Events. (April, 1991)-(1994). Periodical. French (English). Bibliotheque Nationale du Canada, Ottawa. ***Continued by*** *Bibliotheque Nationale du Canada. Programmes Publics, 1202-6654.*

ISSN 0229-0154
DD 700/.25/71384 CN
CULTURAL GUIDE (OTTAWA). (CULTURAL GUIDE ...). **VFOAT** Guide Culturel. 1980-. English (French). $2.50. Cultural Guide, City of Ottawa Recreation Branch, Cultural Section, 111 Sussex Drive, Ottawa Ontario K1N 5A1 Canada. ***Continues*** *Cultural Handbook, 0706-8271.*

LC NX543 .C85 **ISSN** 0954-8963
DD 338.4/77/00941021 UK
CCC
CULTURAL TRENDS. **Added/Corp** Policy Studies Institute. Issue 1 (Jan 1989)-. Periodical. English. Four times a year. $129.00. Carfax Publishing Company, PO Box 25, Abingdon, Oxfordshire OX14 3UE United Kingdom. **Tel** 011 44 1235 555335, FAX 011 44 1235 553559, telex 817484. ***Continues*** *Facts about the Arts.*
Ind/Abst Curr. Cit.; Leis., Rec., Tour. Abstr.; Museum Abstr.

ISSN 0824-3077
DD 700/.92/2 CN
CULTURAMA. [Culturama]. **Added/Corp** Canadian Cultural Programmes L.A.E. Inc. Vol. 101 (Nov. 1982)-. Periodical. English (French). Irregular. Free. Canadian Cultural Programmes, Suite 1401/2 Westmount Square, Westmount Quebec H3Z 2S4 Canada.

LC F1021.2 .C85 **ISSN** 1183-9155
DD 338.4/7306/0971 CN
CEASED
CULTURE SERVICE BULLETIN. **Added/Corp** Statistics Canada. **VFOAT** Culture Bulletin de Service. Vol. 14, No. 4 (1991)-(199?). Bulletin. English (French). Statistics Canada Publications Sales and Services, R.H. Coats Building 6th Floor, Ottawa Ontario K1A 0T6 Canada. **Tel** (613)951-5078, (800)267-6677, FAX (613)951-1584, telex 053-3585. ***Continues*** *Culture Communique, 0822-6016.*

LC NX555.A57 C84
BE
CULTUREEL JAARBOEK STAD ANTWERPEN. (1983)-. Dutch. One time a year.
Ind/Abst BHA : Biblio. Hist. Art.

LC NX1 .C86 **ISSN** 0195-7848
DD 700/.5 US
CUMBERLAND JOURNAL. No. 9 (Winter 1980)-. Periodical. English. Four times a year. $8.00. Cumberland Journal, 161 East Gates Street, Columbus OH 43206-3623. **Tel** (717)255-8443. ***Continues*** *X (Harrisburg, Pa.), 0162-069X.*

LC Q11 .B7 **ISSN** 0011-5266
DD 505 US
CCC
NLM W1 DA229 **CODEN** DAEDAU
Pr Rev.
DAEDALUS (CAMBRIDGE). (DAEDALUS : PROCEEDINGS OF THE AMERICAN ACADEMY OF ARTS AND SCIENCES.). [Daedalus]. **Added/Corp** American Academy of Arts and Sciences. Vol. 86, No. 1 (May 1955)-. Proceedings. English. Four times a year. $45.00. Daedalus, 136 Irving Street, Suite 100, Cambridge MA 02138. **Tel** (617)491-2600, FAX (617)576-5088. available on microfilm and microfiche from University Microfilms International (UMI). Documents available from The Genuine Article, BIOSIS Document Express, Ask*IEEE, UMI Article Clearinghouse, CASDDS, Magazine Collection. ***Continues*** *American Academy of Arts and Sciences. Proceedings of the American Academy of Arts and Sciences, 0199-9818.*
Ind/Abst ABC POL SCI; Abstr. Anthropol.; Acad. Abstr. Full Text Elite; Acad. Abstr.; Acad. Ind. [Computer File] (1984-); Acad. Search; Am. Hist. Life (1963-); Am. Hist. Life Part B (1963-); Am. Bibliogr. Slavic East Europ. Stud.; Annu. Bibliogr. Engl. Lang. Lit.; ARTbibliogr. Mod.; Arts Humanit. Citation Index [Full Cov.]; BHA : Biblio. Hist. Art; Biol. Abstr.; Book Rev. Index; Br. Archaeol. Bibliogr.; Chem. Abstr.; Child. Lit. Abstr. (19??-); Curr. Cit.; Curr. Contents Arts Humanit.; Curr. Contents Soc. Behav. Sci.; Curr. Geogr. Publ. (199?-); EP Collect.; Expand. Acad. Index (1984-); Gen. Period. Index (1985-); Geogr. Abstr. Human Geogr. (?-?); Guide Soc. Sci. Relig.; Health Devices Alerts; Health Plan. Adminis.; High. Educ. Abstr. (1965-19??); Homework Help.; Hosp. Health Admin. Index (Winter 1975-Summer 1989); Hum. Rights Intern. Rep.; Humanit. Index; Humanit. Source; Index Period. Artic. Relat. Law; INFO-SOUTH Abstr.; INIS Atomindex [Micro.]; INSPEC (1968-Winter 1980); Int. Bibliogr. Sociol.; Int. Dev. Abstr. (?-?); Int. Polit. Sci. Abstr.; J. Plan. Lit.; Linguist. Lang. Behav. Abstr.; Mag. Index Plus (1989-); Mag. Search; MasterFile FullTEXT 1000;

The Arts

MasterFile FullTEXT 350; MasterFile FullTEXT 650; MasterFile FullTEXT (July 1990-); Middle East Abstr. Index; MLA Int. Bibl. Books Artic. Mod. Lang. Lit.; Newsp. Period. Abstr. (1988-); OCLC; PAIS Int. Print (1991-); Peace Res. Abstr. J. (1961-1963, 1972); Psychol. Abstr.; PsycINFO; PsycLit; Pub. Lib. FullTEXT; Read. Guide Period. Lit.; Res. Alert [Full Cov.]; Res. High. Educ. Abstr.; Soc. Plann. Policy Dev. Abstr.; Soc. Sci. Cit. Index [Full Cov.]; Soc. Work Abstr. (?-?); Sociol. Abstr.; Telebase; Mag. Index (1977-); U.S. Polit. Sci. Doc.; West. Hist. Q.

ISSN 0969-3505
DD 700.87 UK
DAM GRIMSBY. [DAM Grimsby]. **VFOAT** Disability Arts Magazine. (1992-). Periodical. English. Four times a year. $30.80. Disability Arts Magazine, 10 Woad Lane Great Coates, Grimsby DN37 9NH United Kingdom. **Tel** 011 44 1472 280031, FAX 011 44 1472 280031. *Continues* Disability Arts Magazine, 0961-7485.

ISSN 0011-6807
DD 810 US
DASEIN. See Literature.

LC NX456 .D42 ISSN 0162-7139
DD 700/.9/04 US
DECADE. (Jan. 1979-). Periodical. English. Twelve times a year. $23.40. Excalibur Publications, Room 111/Central Square Bldg., York University, 4700 Keele Street, Downsview Ontario M3J 1P3 Canada. **Tel** (416)736-5238.

LC NX ISSN 0835-0337
DD 700/.5 CN
DEFI-A.C.L. (LE DEFI-A.C.L. : ARTS, CINEMA, LETTRES.). [Defi-A.C.L.]. **VFOAT** Arts, Cinema, Lettres. 6.40Can$. Samir Nasr, Editions le Defi-ACL, CP 1351H, Station H, Montreal Quebec H3H 1N0 Canada. **Tel** (514)768-0570. Index available. **Ad Acc. Circ:** 1,000.

LC NX8.G7 D46
DD 700 GR
DENTRO, TO. (19??-). Periodical. Greek, Modern. Six times a year. Dentro, Diou Eginitou 34, Athens 115 28 Greece. **Tel** 011 30 1 72 45553.

LC AS472.D3 A37
DD 052 BG
●**DHAKA UNIVERSITY STUDIES : JOURNAL OF THE FACULTY OF ARTS, THE. Added/Corp** University of Dhaka. Faculty of Arts. Vol. 48, No. 2, Vol. 49, No. 1 & 2, Vol. 50, No. 1 (Dec. 1991-June 1993). Academic Scholarly Publication. English. Irregular. University of Dhaka / Registrar, Ramna, Dhaka 2 Bangladesh. *Continues* Dhaka University Studies. Part A. **Desc:** Covers the arts, humanities and social science.

LC AP8 .D54 ISSN 0012-2858
DD 378.91 PH
DILIMAN REVIEW, THE. See Social Sciences.

IT
DIPINTI DEL XIX SECOLO. CATALOGO E LISTINO. (19??-). Italian. Twelve times a year. L149880. Finarte Casa d'Arte, Piazzetta Bossi 4, 20121 Milan Italy. **Tel** 011 39 2 877041.

LC Z675.A85 D56 ISSN 0811-6253
DD 026/.7/002594 AT
DIRECTORY OF ARTS LIBRARIES AND RESOURCE COLLECTIONS IN AUSTRALIA. See Library and Information Sciences.

LC NX24.M7 D56 ISSN 0098-4477
DD 700/.6/2762 US
DIRECTORY OF ARTS ORGANIZATIONS IN MISSISSIPPI. (1974/75-). Directory. English. Mississippi Arts Commission, 239 North Lamar Street/Suite 207, Jackson MS 39201-1393. **Tel** (601)359-6030, FAX (601)359-6008.

ISSN 0832-865X
DD 700/.25/71 CN
DIRECTORY OF THE ARTS (OTTAWA). (DIRECTORY OF THE ARTS.). [Dir. arts]. **Added/Corp** Canadian Conference of the Arts. (1987-). Directory. English. One time a year. 26.37Can$. Canadian Conference of the Arts, 189 Laurier Avenue East, Ottawa Ontario K1N 6P1 Canada. **Tel** (613)238-3561, FAX (613)238-4849. **ED** Jocelyne Dubois and Peggy McDonald. cum. index. ctrl circ. *Formed by the union of* Who's Who (Toronto, Ont.), 0383-1116 *and* Who Does What, 0700-2661.

LC NX110 .D58 ISSN 0191-3719
DD 700/.25/753 US
DIRECTORY OF WASHINGTON CREATIVE SERVICES. (1978-). Directory. English. One time a year. Constance A Miller, 1506 19th Street NW, Washington DC 20036.

LC PN1 ISSN 1042-4768
DD 805 US
DIRTY GOAT, THE. [Dirty goat]. (1989-). Periodical. English. Four times a year. $40.00 institutions, $25.00 individuals. Host Publications Inc, 2717 Wooldridge, Austin TX 78703.

LC NX180.S46 D57
DD 302.2 SP
DISCURSO (SEVILLE, SPAIN). See Linguistics.

ISSN 0935-7114
GW
DISSERTATIONEN ZUR KUNSTGESCHICHTE. (19??-). Monographic series. German. Boehlau Verlag GmbH & Cie / Cologne, Theodor Heuss STR 76, D-51149 Cologne Germany. **Tel** 011 49 2203 307021, FAX 011 49 2203 307349.
Ind/Abst BHA : Biblio. Hist. Art.

ISSN 0166-6304
NE
DOCUMENTATIEBLAD WERKGROEP ACHTTIENDE EEUW. Added/Corp Werkgroepe 18e Eeuw (Nijmegen, Netherlands). (Nov. 1968-). Monographic series. Dutch. Irregular. $34.26. APA Holland Universitaits Pers, Postbus 12, 3600 AC Maarssen Netherlands. **Tel** 011 33 30 436166.
Ind/Abst BHA : Biblio. Hist. Art.

LC NX504 .D65 ISSN 1071-8613
DD 700/.973/05 US
DOCUMENTS (NEW YORK, N.Y.). (DOCUMENTS.). [Documents]. (1992-). Periodical. English. Four times a year. $50.00. Documents Magazine Inc, 611 Broadway, Suite 742, New York NY 10012. **Tel** (212)254-4118.

ISSN 0899-5443
DD 810 US
DRUM. See Literature.

LC NX456 .D85 ISSN 1069-8329
DD 700/.9/04 US
DUMB OX, THE. [Dumb ox]. Vol. 1 (Summer 1976)-. Periodical. English. Four times a year. $8.00. J. Hugunin, 629 Quail Drive, Los Angeles CA 90065. **ED** J Hugunin and T Kelley.

US
EARLY DRAMA, ART, AND MUSIC MONOGRAPH SERIES. (1977-). Monographic series. English. Irregular. Price varies per volume. Medieval Institute Publisnations, Western Michigan University, Kalamazoo MI 49008-3851. **Tel** (616)387-8755, FAX (616)387-8750. **ED** Clifford Davidson. **Bk Rev.** ctrl circ.
Desc: Studies of medieval drama, arts, and music; while the focus is usually on drama, some volumes deal with questions of iconography or music in a fairly independent way.
Ind/Abst MLA Int. Bibl. Books Artic. Mod. Lang. Lit.

ISSN 1059-1168
DD 709 US
EARLY DRAMA, ART, AND MUSIC REFERENCE SERIES. [Early drama art music ref. ser.]. (1978-). Monographic series. English. Medieval Institute Publisnations, Western Michigan University, Kalamazoo MI 49008-3851. **Tel** (616)387-8755, FAX (616)387-8750.
Ind/Abst MLA Int. Bibl. Books Artic. Mod. Lang. Lit.

LC NX449 .E37 ISSN 1048-9401
DD 700 US
EARLY DRAMA, ART, AND MUSIC REVIEW, THE. [Early drama art music rev.]. **Added/Corp** Western Michigan University. Medieval Institute. Vol. 12, No. 1 (Fall 1989)-. Periodical. English. Two times a year (May & Nov.). $10.00. Medieval Institute Publisnations, Western Michigan University, Kalamazoo MI 49008-3851. **Tel** (616)387-8755, FAX (616)387-8750. **ED** Clifford Davidson. **Bk Rev. Continues** EDAM Newsletter, 0196-5816.
Ind/Abst MLA Int. Bibl. Books Artic. Mod. Lang. Lit.

US
TITLE CHANGE
EAST COAST ROCKER. See Music.

ISSN 1189-7120
DD 051 CN
TITLE CHANGE
EASY LIVING'S VICTORIA. [Easy living's Vic.]. **VFOAT** Victoria Magazine. (Sept. or Oct. 1992)-(May 1993). Periodical. English. Bay Publishing Ltd., PO Box 5667, Station B, Victoria British Columbia V8R 6S4 Canada. **Tel** (604)598-8111. *Continues* Easy Living's Victoria Magazine, 1187-6379. *Merged with* Boulevard (Victoria, B.C. : 1992), 1196-6785 *to form* Victoria Boulevard (1993), 1196-6793.

ISSN 0227-6402
CN
EDITION SPECIALE - CHASSE-GALERIE. (EDITION SPECIALE.). [Ed. spec. - Chasse-Galerie]. Vol. 1, No. 1-. Periodical. French (summaries and/or abstracts in English). Chasse-Galerie, 204 rue Saint-George, Toronto Ontario M5R 2N5 Canada.

ISSN 0822-8108
DD 700/.97123/3 CN
EDMONTON BULLET, THE. [Edmont. bullet]. Vol. 1, No. 1 (Mar. 25, 1983)-. Periodical. English. $15.00. Edmonton Bullet, 201-1008 105 Street, Edmonton Alberta T5J 1C6 Canada.

LC NX452 .E54 ISSN 0013-2586
DD 700.5 US
EIGHTEENTH-CENTURY STUDIES. [Eighteen.-century stud.]. **Added/Corp** University of California, Davis. Dept. of English. University of California, Davis. University of Southern California. American Society for Eighteenth-Century Studies. **VFOAT** Eighteenth Century Studies. Vol. 1 (Fall 1967)-. Periodical. English (French, Latin and German). Four times a year. $65.00. Johns Hopkins University Press, 2715 North Charles Street, Baltimore MD 21218-4319. **Tel** (410)516-6987, FAX (410)516-6968. **ED** Arthur McGuinness and Robert Hopkins. cum. index. **Bk Rev. Ad Acc. Circ:** 3,000 (ctrl). available on microfilm. Documents available from The Genuine Article, UMI Article Clearinghouse.
Desc: Articles and reviews on Eighteenth Century subjects including English and American literature, other languages and literatures. Classics, drama, history, religion, philosophy, music, science, and political science.
Ind/Abst Abstr. Engl. Stud.; Acad. Search; Am. Hist. Life (1973-); Annu. Bibliogr. Engl. Lang. Lit.; Arts Humanit. Citation Index [Full Cov.]; BHA : Biblio. Hist. Art; Book Rev. Index (1986-); Child. Lit. Abstr. (19??-); Curr. Contents Arts Humanit.; EP Collect.; Expand. Acad. Index (1989-); Homework Help.; Humanit. Index; Humanit. Source; INFO-SOUTH Abstr.; Mag. Search; MasterFile FullTEXT 1000; MasterFile FullTEXT 350; MasterFile FullTEXT 650; MasterFile FullTEXT (July 1993-); MLA Int. Bibl. Books Artic. Mod. Lang. Lit.; Newsp. Period. Abstr. (1991-); OCLC; Res. Alert [Full Cov.]; Romant. Move.; Soc. Sci. Index [Select. Cov.]; Soc. Work Abstr. (?-?); Telebase.

ISSN 0424-8848
DD 704 800 HU
ELET ES IRODALOM. (1957-). Periodical. Hungarian. One time a week. $73.00. **(Subscription address:** Kultura, PO Box 143, H-1300 Budapest 3 Hungary. **Tel** 011 36 1 2500194.)

LC NX1 .E47 ISSN 0276-2374
DD 700/.5 US
CODEN ESAREN
Pr Rev.
EMPIRICAL STUDIES OF THE ARTS. [Empir. stud. arts]. Vol. 1, No. 1 (1983)-. Academic Scholarly Publication. English. Two times a year. $85.50. Baywood Publishing Company Inc., 26 Austin Avenue, PO Box 337, Amityville NY 11701. **Tel** (516)691-1270, (800)638-7819, FAX (516)691-1770. **ED** Colin Martindale.
Desc: For professionals interested in any aspect of art, music or literature.
Ind/Abst Ethnoarts Index; Lang. Lang. Behav. Abstr.; Psychol. Abstr. (1983-); PsycINFO; PsycLit; Soc. Plann. Policy Dev. Abstr.; Sociol. Abstr.

ISSN 0191-0728
US
ENDYMION. (1972-). Periodical. English. One time a year. David M. Katz, 562 West End Avenue / 6A, New York NY 10024. **Tel** (212)864-8263. **ED** L. Stern and D.M. Katz.

LC NX2 .E55
DD 700/.5 FR
ENNEMI, L'. 1 (1980-). Periodical. French. One time a year. 100.00F. 8 rue Garanciere, Paris 6 EME France. **Circ:** 1,200 (ctrl).
Desc: A literary and art review. Has a cosmopolitan vision of modernity with French original texts and numerous translations of authors and original art works of various artists.

ISSN 0228-1244
DD 700/.9711/33 CN
ENNUI. [Ennui]. Vol. 1 (Jan./Feb. 1980)-. Periodical. English. Six times a year. $6.00. Ennui, #4-4196 Main Street, Vancouver British Columbia V5V 3P7 Canada.

ISSN 1057-3720
DD 917 US
ENTERTAINMENT ATLANTA : YOUR HOUR-BY-HOUR GUIDE TO ENTERTAINMENT ATLANTA. See Leisure and Recreation.

US
ENTERTAINMENT INDUSTRY OUTLOOK. (19??-). English. Twelve times a year. $149.00. Cahners Publishing Company, 249 West 17th

The Arts

Street, New York NY 10011. **Tel** (212)645-0067, FAX (212)242-6987. **(Subscription address:** Cahners Economics, PO Box 59, New Town Branch, Boston MA 02258. **Tel** (800)445-0678, (617)630-2124.**)**
Desc: Provides economic analysis and forecasts relevant to decision makers in the entertainment industry.

DD 790   **ISSN** 1048-5112   US   CCC

ENTERTAINMENT MARKETING LETTER. See Business and Economics-Marketing and Purchasing.

LC NX4 .E73
DD 700/.5   IT
ERA, L'. Vol. 1 (Sept./Oct. 1976)-. Periodical. Italian. Six times a year. L2.500. Conto Corrente Ordinario N, 178 Intestato a Salvatore Amodei, c/o Banco di Rome Filiale di Pontedera, Pontedera Italy.

   IT
ERBA D'ARNO. (1980)-. Periodical. Italian. Four times a year. L23850. Aldemaro Toni, Via Castruccio 1, 50054 Fucecchio Italy. **Tel** 011 39 571 242093. **ED** Aldemaro Toni. Index available. cum. index. **Bk Rev**, (Qty: 10-15). **Ad Acc.** ctrl circ.

LC NX7 .E85
DD 700/.9/04   US
ESCANDALAR. Vol. 1 (Feb./Mar. 1978)-. Periodical. Spanish. Four times a year. Escandalar, 40-40 Hampton Street, Elmhurst NY 11373. **ED** O. Armand.
Ind/Abst Hisp. Am. Period. Index, HAPI (19??-).

LC BH6 .E78   **ISSN** 0014-1291   XR   CCC
ESTETIKA. [Estetika]. **Added/Corp** Ceskoslovenska Akademie Ved. Vol. 1 (1964)-. Periodical. Czech (summaries and/or abstracts in French, German, English and Russian). Four times a year. $92.88. **(Subscription address:** Kubon & Sagner, ABT Zeitschriftenimport, D 80328 Munich Germany. **Tel** 011 49 89 54218130.**)**
Desc: Concerned with the theoretical aspects of art, the theory of literature and of music, media, the function and theory of architecture, plastic arts, applied arts, the aesthetics of work, and so on.
Ind/Abst ARTbibliogr. Mod.; BHA : Biblio. Hist. Art; Philos. Index.

   CN
EUROPEAN AND AMERICAN PAINTING, SCULPTURE AND DECORATIVE ARTS. (1987)-. Catalog. English (French). Every 2 years. 130.00Can$ Canada; $130.00 US. National Gallery of Canada, Publications Division, 380 Sussex Drive, Ottawa Ontario K1N 9N4 Canada. **Tel** (613)990-0537, FAX (613)990-7460. **(Subscription address:** University of Chicago Press, 5801 Ellis Avenue, Chicago IL 60637-1496. **) ED** Myron Laskin and Michael Pantazzi. Index available. available with illustrations.
Desc: A projected series documenting works from the National Gallery's European and American collections.

DD 332   **ISSN** 8756-775X   US
EVALUATOR (RIVER FOREST, ILL.). (THE EVALUATOR.). [Evaluator]. Periodical. English. Four times a year. The Evaluator, PO Box 280, River Forest IL 60305. **Tel** (312)848-3340. **ED** Elizabeth Carr. **Bk Rev**. Circ: 1,000 (ctrl).

Pr Rev.   UK
EXETER STUDIES IN AMERICAN AND COMMONWEALTH ARTS. Added/Corp AmCAS. No. 1 (1986)-. Monographic series. English. Irregular. Price varies per volume. University of Exeter, Exeter EX4 4QR United Kingdom. **Tel** 011 44 1392 263066, FAX 011 44 1392 263064. **ED** Richard Maltby. Documents available from BLDSC. **Continues** American Arts Pamphlet.
Desc: Devoted to examining and defining aspects of the arts and cultures of the United States, Commonwealth countries and persons of Commonwealth descent resident in Britain.

LC NX700   **ISSN** 0160-0087
DD 700.79   US
EXPANSION ARTS. VFOAT Expansion Arts Program. (19??)-. English. One time a year. Expansion Arts Program/Schedules, National Endowment for the Arts, 1100 Pennsylvania Avenue NW, Washington DC 20506.

LC NX   **ISSN** 1192-6074
DD 700/.9713/541   CN
EYE WEEKLY. [Eye wkly.]. (Oct. 10, 1991)-. Newspaper. English. One time a week. Free. Toronto Star Newspapers Ltd., 1 Yonge Street, Toronto Ontario M5E 1E6 Canada. **Tel** (416)367-2123, FAX (416)869-4587. available via internet (http://www.interlog.com:80/eye).
Desc: Covers movies, music, theatre and other entertainment events in Toronto.

   ISSN 0214-4514   SP
FAIG ARTS. (1989)-. Periodical. Catalan. Omnium Cultural, Apartat 255, Manresa Spain. **Continues** Faig, 0214-4522.

DD 979   **ISSN** 1058-7667   US
FAIRBANKS ARTS : A PUBLICATION OF THE FAIRBANKS ARTS ASSOCIATION. [Fairbanks arts]. **Added/Corp** Fairbanks Arts Association. Vol. 2, Issue 1 (Sept. Oct. 1991)-. Periodical. English. Six times a year. $15.00. Fairbanks Arts, PO Box 72786, Fairbanks AK 99707. **Continues** Fairbanks Arts Association Magazine.

   ISSN 0264-7060   UK   CEASED
FAN. FEMINIST ARTS NEWS. See Women's Interests.

LC NX574.A1 F37   IR
FASLNAMAH-I HUNAR. Periodical. Persian. Four times a year. Farhangsara-Yi Niyavaran, Khiyaban-I Pasdaran, Tehran Iran.

LC NX735 .N38A   **ISSN** 0363-5902
DD 338.4/7/700973   US
FEDERAL-STATE PARTNERSHIP.
Main/Corp National Endowment for the Arts. English. National Endowment for the Arts, 1100 Pennsylvania Avenue Northwest, Washington DC 20506. **Tel** (202)682-5400, (202)682-5435.

LC N6512.5 V53 .F45   US
Pr Rev.
FELIX. Vol. 1, No. 1 (Spring 1991)-. Periodical. English. One time a year (three issues covering a three year period). $34.00. Standby Program Inc., PO Box 184, Prince Street Station, New York NY 10012. **Tel** (212)219-0951, FAX (212)219-0563. **ED** Kathy High. **Ad Acc.** Circ: 2,500.
Desc: Devoted to fostering critical discussion around questions of concern to the independent video community while providing an arena for video-makers to exchange in written form.

   ISSN 1143-676X   FR
FESTIN, LE. (19??)-. Periodical. French. Four times a year.
Ind/Abst BHA : Biblio. Hist. Art.

LC NX510.P4 F53   **ISSN** 0193-9548
DD 700/.5   CEASED
FIELD OF VISION (PITTSBURGH). (FIELD OF VISION.). **Added/Corp** Pittsburgh Film-Makers Inc. (19??)-. Periodical. English. Pittsburgh Film-Makers Inc, PO Box 7200, Pittsburgh PA 15213.

   IT
FIGURE (SALERNO, ITALY). (FIGURE.). No. 1 (Aug. 1988)-. Periodical. Italian. **Continues** Figure.
Ind/Abst BHA : Biblio. Hist. Art.

   ISSN 0015-1084   BE
FILM EN TELEVISIE EN VIDEO. See Motion Picture.

LC WMLC 93/3101   **ISSN** 1071-1015
DD 709   US   CEASED
FINE ART & ANTIQUES INTERNATIONAL. [Fine art antiq. int.]. **VFOAT** Fine Art & Antiques; Fine and Antiques; A.Fine art and antiques international. (1993)-(Jan. 1994). Periodical. English. Art of California, 1125 Jefferson Street, Napa CA 94559. **Tel** (707)226-1776. **Continues** Art of California, 1045-8913.

   US
FINE ARTS AND ARCHITECTURE [MICROFORM]. Added/Corp NewsBank, Inc. Vol. 9, Card 42 (March 1983)-. Periodical. English. Six times a year. $210.00 libraries; $165.00 high schools and junior high schools; $324.00 commerical subscribers. Newsbank Inc., 58 Pine Street, New Canaan CT 06840. **Tel** (800)243-7694, (800)762-8182, FAX (203)966-6254. **Continues** Newsbank. Fine Arts and Architecture, 0737-4003.

LC NX510.F6 F57   **ISSN** 0162-5616
DD 700/.25/759   US
FLORIDA FOLK ARTS DIRECTORY.
Directory. English. Stephen Foster Center, White Springs FL 32096. **Tel** (904)397-2192. ctrl circ.
Desc: Lists artists, interpreters, scholars, and others related to the folklife field.

   ISSN 0381-9469   CN
FOLIO (SASKATOON). (FOLIO.). Vol. 3 (Jan. 1975)-. Newsletter. English. Six times a year. Membership only. Mendel Art Gallery, PO Box 569, Saskatoon Saskatchewan S7K 3L6 Canada. **Tel** (306)975-7610. **ED** Helen B. Coleman. Circ: 2,500 (ctrl).
Continues Where It's At, 0381-9450.
Desc: Newsletter of the Mendel Art Gallery.
Ind/Abst Graph. Arts Bull. Inst. Pap. Sci. Technol. (Feb. 1989-March 1989, May 1989, Aug. 1989-Dec. 1989).

   US
FOR THE WORKING ARTIST. (19??)-. English. Irregular. $30.00. National Network Artist Placement, 935 West Avenue 37, Los Angeles CA 90065. **Tel** (213)222-4035, FAX (213)222-4035.
Desc: Practical ways of managing one's career in the arts.

DD 700   **ISSN** 0890-2992   US
FOR YOUR INFORMATION (NEW YORK, N. Y.). (FOR YOUR INFORMATION.). [For your inf.]. **Added/Corp** Center for Arts Information. New York (N.Y.). Dept. of Cultural Affairs. New York Foundation for the Arts. **VFOAT** For Your Information : FYI; FYI. Vol. 1, No. 1 (Winter 1985)-. Periodical. English. Four times a year. $50.00. New York Foundation for Arts, 5 Beekham Street, Suite 600, New York NY 10038. **Tel** (212)233-3900, FAX (212)791-1813. **ED** David Green. Index available. cum. index. **Ad Acc, Adv Mgr Tel** (212)366-6900 ext.212. Circ: 25,000 (ctrl). available on an online database.
Desc: Contains information on topics affecting individual artists, companies, and organizations. Includes funding, deadlines, reports, taxes, etc.

LC AS611 .F6   **ISSN** 0015-8054   SA   **CODEN** FHPADE
FORT HARE PAPERS. [Fort Hare pap.]. **Added/Corp** South African Native College, Fort Hare. Vol. 1 (June 1945)-. Periodical. English (Afrikaans). Irregular. R5.00. Fort Hare University Press, Private Bag X1314, Alice Republic of Ciskei, South Africa. **Tel** FAX 0404-32011, telex 250863. **ED** N.J. Prins. available on microfilm from University Microfilms International (UMI). Documents available from BIOSIS Document Express.
Desc: Includes information on the arts, humanities, and economics in South Africa.
Ind/Abst Annu. Bibliogr. Engl. Lang. Lit.; Anthropol. Index; Biol. Abstr. (-1987); MLA Int. Bibl. Books Artic. Mod. Lang. Lit.

   ISSN 0046-4694   IE
Pr Rev.
FORTNIGHT (BELFAST). See Literary and Political Reviews.

DD 700.9941   **ISSN** 0816-6919   AT   CCC
FREMANTLE ARTS REVIEW. [Fremantle arts rev.]. (1986)-. Periodical. English. Twelve times a year. 25.00Au$ (membership Fremantle Arts Centre). Fremantle Arts Centre, PO Box 891, Fremantle WA 6160 Australia. **Tel** 011 61 03 335-8244.
Desc: Examines the arts in Western Australia.

LC NX573.6.I7 F86   UA
FUNUN. VFOAT Funoon. Periodical. Arabic. One time a week. 0.100ID each issue. Kiradat Maryam, Baghdad Iraq.

LC NX8.A7 F83   UA
FUNUN (CAIRO, EGYPT : 1979).
(AL-FUNUN YUSDIRUHA AL-ITTIHAD AL-AMM LI-NIQABAT AL-MIHAN AL-TAMTHILIYAH WA-AL-SINIMAIYAH WA-AL-MUSIQIYAH.). Vol. 1, No. 1 (October 1979)-. Periodical. Arabic. Majallat Al-Funun, 9-11 Shari Urabi, Al-Quahirah United Arab Republic Egypt.

LC NX513.A1F88   **ISSN** 0838-603X
DD 700/.971   CN   CCC
Pr Rev.
FUSE MAGAZINE. [Fuse mag.]. **Added/Corp** Arton's Cultural Affairs Society and Publishing. Vol. 11 No. 4 (Winter 1988)-. Periodical. English. Five times a year (Jan., Mar., May, July, Sept.). 30.42Can$. Fuse Magazine, 401 Richmond Street West, Toronto Ontario M5V 3A8 Canada. **Tel** (416)367-0159, FAX (416)340-8458. Index available (bound in each issue). cum. index. **Bk Rev**, (Qty: 20-30). **Ad Acc, Adv Mgr:** Shawn Venasse, **Tel** (416)340-8026. Circ: 4,000. available on microfilm and microfiche from Micromedia Limited; available on microfiche from University Microfilms International (UMI). **Continues** Fuse, 0226-8086.
Ind/Abst Altern. Press Index (199?-); Can. Period. Index.

The Arts

LC NX1.A1 F87 **ISSN** 0742-8561
DD 700/.5 US
FUSTA, LA. [Fusta]. (Spring 1976)-. Periodical. English (Italian and Spanish). Two times a year. Rutgers University / Department of Italian, 18 Seminary Place, New Brunswick NJ 08903. **Tel** (908)932-7031.
Ind/Abst MLA Int. Bibl. Books Artic. Mod. Lang. Lit.

IT
FUTURISMO-OGGI. **VFOAT** Futurismo Oggi. Periodical. Italian. Twelve times a year. Edizioni Arte Viva, Rome Italy. **ED** Enzo Benedetto.

LC NX525.A1 N83 **ISSN** 0138-8770
DD 700/.97291 CU
GACETA DE CUBA. **Added/Corp** Union de Escritores y Artistas de Cuba. (1986)-. Periodical. Spanish. Twelve times a year. Ediciones Cubanas, Obispo 527 Altos ESQ Bernaza, CP 10100 Havana Cuba. **Continues** Nueva Gaceta (Havana, Cuba).

LC NX7 .G34
DD 700/.5 VE
GALAXIA 71 [I.E. SETENTA Y UNO]. **Added/Corp** Grupo Escritores de Venezuela. Vol. 1, No. 1 (1971)-. Trade Publication. Spanish. Three times a year. $10.00. Grupo Escritores de Venezuela, Apartado de Carreos 4023, Camelitas 101 Caracus Venezuela. **ED** Modesto Vargas Lopez. **Bk Rev**. **Circ**: 5,000 (ctrl). available with illustrations.

LC AP5 .G33 **ISSN** 0713-3545
DD 051 CN
GAMUT (TORONTO). (GAMUT.). [Gamut]. Vol. 1 (Summer 1982)-. Periodical. English. Four times a year. 11.61Can$. Gamut, 238 Davenport Road, Suite 171, Toronto Ontario M5R 1J6 Canada. **Tel** (416)967-9195. **ED** Alfredo Romano and Haygo Demir. **Bk Rev**. **Ad Acc**. **Circ**: 2,500 (ctrl).
Desc: A magazine of the literary, performing and visual arts as well as issues of social concern. Presenting new and established artists in a fresh and provocative format.

 ISSN 8755-0776
DD 700 US
GAZETTE (MIAMI, FLA.), THE. (THE GAZETTE.). [Gazette]. Vol. 4, Issue 11 (July 1981)-. Periodical. English. Twelve times a year. Florida Arts Gazette, Biscayne Executive Plaza, 2895 Biscayne Boulevard, Suite 269, Miami FL 33137. **Continues** Florida Arts Gazette.

LC NX8.J3 G44
DD 705 JA
GEIJUTSU-GAKU. THE ART SCIENCE. **Added/Corp** Nihon Daigaku Geijutsu Gakkai. **VFOAT** Art Science. (19??)-. Japanese. Nihon Daigaku Geijutsugakubu, 2-42 Asahi-gaoka Nerima-ku, Tokyo Japan.

LC NX584.A1 G4423 **ISSN** 0385-5694
 JA
GEIJUTSU NENKAN (OSAKA, JAPAN). (GEIJUTSU NENKAN.). Japanese. One time a year. 3500. Geijutsu Shunjusha, C/O DAI 2 Fujikawa Building, 2F 6-12 Matsuya-Machi, Minami-Ku Osaka=Shi 542 Japan.

 ISSN 1181-6554
DD 700/.971/05 CN
GEIST (VANCOUVER). (GEIST.). [Geist]. **Added/Corp** Geist Foundation. (Oct. 1990)-. Periodical. English. Five times a year. 16.01Can$. Geist Foundation, 1062 Homers Street, Suite 100, Vancouver British Columbia, V6B 2W9 Canada. **Tel** (604)681-9161, FAX (604)681-8250. **ED** Stephen Osborne. **Bk Rev**. **Ad Acc**, **Adv Mgr**: Kevin Barefoot. **Circ**: 13,000 (ctrl). available on microfiche from University Microfilms International (UMI).

LC NX3 .G45
DD 700/.5 GW
GEMEINSAME WEG, DER. Periodical. German. Four times a year. DM15.00. Stiftung Ostedeutscher Kulturrat, Kaiserstr 113, 5300 Bonn Germany.

LC AS30 .G48 **ISSN** 0898-4557
DD 814 US
GETTYSBURG REVIEW (1988). (THE GETTYSBURG REVIEW.). [Gettysbg. rev.]. **Added/Corp** Gettysburg College. **VFOAT** Gettysburg. (Winter 1988)-. Periodical. English. Four times a year (Jan., Apr., July, Oct.). $18.00. The Gettysburg Review, Gettysburg College, Gettysburg PA 17325. **Tel** (717)337-6770, FAX (717)337-6775. **ED** Peter Stitt. Index available in last issue of volume--attached. **Bk Rev**, (Qty: 20). **Ad Acc**. **Adv Mgr**: E. Clarke, **Tel** (717)337-6771. **Circ**: 2,500 (ctrl). **Continues** Gettysburg Review.
Desc: A multidisciplinary journal of art and ideas featuring original poetry, fiction, essays, essay reviews and artwork by well-known and beginning professionals.
Ind/Abst Am. Hist. Life (1988-); Am. Humanit. Index; Index Am. Period. Verse; MLA Int. Bibl. Books Artic. Mod. Lang. Lit.

LC NX573.6.I7 G55
DD 700/.9567 IQ
GILGAMESH. **Added/Corp** Iraq. Wizarat al-Thaqafah Wa-al-Ilam. Vol. 1 (1986)-. Periodical. English. Four times a year. $20.00. Dar Al-Mamun for Translation and Publishing, PO Box 8018, Baghdad Iraq. **Tel** (011 964 1 5383171, telex 212984 MAMUN IK. **ED** Naji Al-Hadithi. **Bk Rev**. **Ad Acc**. **Circ**: 5,000.
Desc: Aimed at introducing modern Iraqi arts to foreign readers. Presents a number of short stories, poems and studies on various aspects of cultural life in Iraq.

LC NX1 .G7
DD 700/.5 II
GRAY BOOK. Vol. 1 (Spring 1972)-. Periodical. English. $4.00. Post Box 39 1, Cuttack India.

 ISSN 0265-0088
 UK
 TITLE CHANGE
GREEN BOOK BATH. [Green bookBath]. (1979)-(19??). Periodical. English. Contemporary Art Publishers Ltd, 2 Sydney Place, Bath BA2 6NF United Kingdom. **Tel** 011 44 1225 332527. **Continued by** Contemporary Art.

 ISSN 0017-4181
DD 040 SP
GRIAL. [Grial]. **Added/Corp** Editorial Galaxia. No. 1 (1963)-. Periodical. Spanish. Four times a year. 4116ptas. Editorial Galaxia, Reconquista 1, Vigo 36201 Spain. **Tel** 011 34 86 432100.
Ind/Abst MLA Int. Bibl. Books Artic. Mod. Lang. Lit.

LC NX552.S27 G76
DD 700/.945/9 IT
GROTTA DELLA VIPERA, LA. **Added/Corp** Gruppo Promozione Culturale (Cagliari, Italy). (19??)-. Periodical. Italian. Four times a year. L20440. Cuec Editrice, via Iz Mirrionis 12, 09123 Cagliari Italy. **Tel** 011 39 70 271573.

 SP
GUADALIMAR. **See** Plastics.

LC NX571.5 .G85 **ISSN** 1133-360X
DD 700/.9182/205 SP
GUIA : ARTE DEL ARCO MEDITERRANEO, EL. **VFOAT** Arte del Arco Mediterraneo. (1988)-. Periodical. Spanish (English, French and Italian). Twelve times a year. $54.50. Guia Edicion, Montcada 21, 08003 Barcelona Spain. **Tel** 011 34 93 2681793, FAX 011 34 93 2681961. Index available. **Bk Rev**. **Ad Acc**. **Circ**: 15,000.
Desc: Marketing and creation of paintings, video, photography and sculpturing.

LC NX765 .S85
DD 700/.68 US
●**GUIDE TO ARTS ADMINISTRATION TRAINING / CENTER FOR ARTS ADMINISTRATION, GRADUATE SCHOOL OF BUSINESS, UNIVERSITY OF WISCONSIN - MADISON, AND ASSOCIATION OF ARTS ADMINISTRATION EDUCATORS.** **Added/Corp** University of Wisconsin--Madison. Center for Arts Administration. Association of Arts Administration Educators (U.S.) American Council for the Arts. (1994)-. Periodical. English. One time a year. $15.95. American Council for the Arts, 1 East 53rd Street, New York NY 10022. **Tel** (212)223-2787 Ext. 242. **Continues** Survey of Arts Administration Training.

LC PN163 .G85 **ISSN** 1055-6087
DD 070.5/2 380.1/457/002573 US
GUIDE TO LITERARY AGENTS & ART/PHOTO REPS. [Guide lit. agents art/photo reps]. **Added/Corp** Writer's Digest Books (Firm). **VFOAT** Guide to Literary Agents and Art/Photo Reps; Literary Agents & Art/Photo Reps; Literary Agents and Art Photo Reps. (1992)-. Periodical. English. One time a year. $21.99. Writer's Digest Books, 1507 Dana Avenue, Cincinnati OH 45207. **Tel** (513)531-2222, (800)289-0963, FAX (513)531-4744.

LC NX24.M3 M3B
DD 353.97440085/4 US
GUIDE TO PROGRAMS & SERVICES. **Main/Corp** Massachusetts Council on the Arts and Humanities. (19??)-. English. One time a year. $0.58. Massachusetts Council on the Arts and Humanities, 1 Ashburton Place, Room 619, Boston MA 02108.

LC NX398 .N37A **ISSN** 0360-3407
DD 338.4/7/700973 US
GUIDE TO PROGRAMS - NATIONAL ENDOWMENT FOR THE ARTS. (GUIDE TO PROGRAMS : ARCHITECTURE+ENVIRONMENTAL ARTS, DANCE, EDUCATION, EXPANSION ARTS, FEDERAL-STATE PARTNERSHIP, LITERATURE, MUSEUMS, MUSIC, PUBLIC MEDIA, SPECIAL PROJECTS, THEATRE, VISUAL ARTS.). **Main/Corp** National Endowment for the Arts. English. One time a year. National Endowment for the Arts, 1100 Pennsylvania Avenue Northwest, Washington DC 20506. **Tel** (202)682-5400, (202)682-5435.

 US
GUIDE TO THE NATIONAL ENDOWMENT FOR THE ARTS. English. One time a year. Free. National Endowment for the Arts, 1100 Pennsylvania Avenue Northwest, Washington DC 20506. **Tel** (202)682-5400, (202)682-5435.
Desc: Explains and describes activities and mission of the arts endowment.

 ISSN 1055-8985
DD 808 US
GUILT & GARDENIAS. **Added/Corp** Society for the Preservation of Vaudeville and Variety Arts. Arts Council of Fayetteville/Cumberland County (Fayetteville, N.C.). **VFOAT** Guilt and Gardenias. Vol. 1, No. 1 (1991)-. Periodical. English. Four times a year. $7.00. Society for the Preservation of Vaudeville and Variety Arts, 301 Hay Street, PO Box 318, Fayetteville NC 28302-0318.

LC NX8.K8 H33
 KO
HAEOE MUNYE. Vol. 1 (1979)-. Periodical. Korean. Hanguk Manhwa Yesul Chingung Won, 31 Tongsung-dong, Chongno-ku, Seoul South Korea.

 ISSN 0776-2976
 BE
UDC 908
HANDELINGEN VAN DE KONINKLIJKE KRING VOOR OUDHEIDKUNDE, LETTEREN EN KUNST VAN MECHELEN. [Handel. K. Kring Oudheidk. Lett. Kunst Mechelen]. (1889)-. Periodical. Dutch. One time a year (May or June). $27.99. Koninklijke Kring Oudheidkunde, Leopoldstraat 35, 2800 Mechelen Belgium. **Tel** 011 32 15 412186.
Ind/Abst BHA : Biblio. Hist. Art.

 ISSN 0776-5533
 BE
UDC 930.26
HANDELINGEN VAN DEN GESCHIED- EN OUDHEIDKUNDIGE KRING VAN KORTRIJK. **VFOAT** Handelingen - Koninklijke Geschied- en Oudheidkundige Kring van Kortrijk. (1908)-. Periodical. Dutch. One time a year. 566.00F Europe; 600.00F other. Stadsarchief, Sint-Walburgastraat 9, 9700 Oudenaarde Belgium. **Tel** 011 32 55 300706.
Ind/Abst BHA : Biblio. Hist. Art.

 ISSN 1059-678X
DD 700 US
HAWAII ARTS MONTHLY : A PUBLICATION OF HAWAII PUBLIC RADIO. [Hawaii arts mon.]. **Added/Corp** Hawaii Public Radio. Vol. 1, No. 1 (Oct. 1991)-. Periodical. English. Twelve times a year. Hawaii Arts Monthly, 738 Kaheka Street, #101, Honolulu HI 96814.

 ISSN 1061-4109
 US
HAWAII'S VOICES. **See** Women's Interests.

LC PN1 .J46a **ISSN** 0792-0393
DD 809 IS
 CEASED
HEBREW UNIVERSITY STUDIES IN LITERATURE AND THE ARTS. **See** Literature.

 NE
HERMENEUS; MAANBLAD VOOR DE ANTIEKE CULTUUR. (Sept. 15, 1928)-. Periodical. Dutch. Six times a year. $65.09. Martinus Nijhoff Publishers, Subsidiary of Kluwer Academic Publishers, Koraalrood 50, 2718 SC Zoetermeer Netherlands. **Tel** 011 31 79 684400.
Ind/Abst BHA : Biblio. Hist. Art.

LC NX7 .H57 **ISSN** 0738-5625
DD 700/.5 US
HISPANIC AMERICAN ARTS. [Hisp. Am. arts]. **VFOAT** Hispanic American Arts. (Jan./Feb. 1974)-. Periodical. Spanish (English). Three times a year (Jan., May, Sept.). $43.00. E Darino /CBA, 222 Park Avenue South 2A, New York NY 10003. **Tel** (212)228-4024. **ED** E. Darino. **Bk Rev**. ctrl circ.
Desc: Covers news related to the arts by or from the Hispanic American artist of today.
Ind/Abst Ethnoarts Index.

LC AS551 .H5 **ISSN** 0073-2788
DD 052 JA
HITOTSUBASHI JOURNAL OF ARTS & SCIENCES. [Hitotsubashi j. arts sci.]. **Added/Corp** Hitotsubashi Daigaku. Hitotsubashi Gakkai. **VFOAT** Hitotsubashi Journal of Arts and Sciences. (Dec. 1960)-. English (French and German). One time a year. Hitotsubashi Daigaku Hitotsubashi Gakkai, (Hitotsubashi University), Hitotsubashi Academy, 2-1 Naka Kunitachishi, Tokyo 186 Japan. **ED** H. Arai. Index

The Arts

available. cum. index. **Circ:** 900. **Continues in part** *Annals of the Hitotsubashi Academy*, 0439-2841.
Ind/Abst MLA Int. Bibl. Books Artic. Mod. Lang. Lit.

ISSN 0437-6668
JA

●**HOLLYWOOD INTERACTIVE ENTERTAINMENT DIRECTORY.** No. 1 (1995)-. Directory. English. One time a year. $53.00. Hollywood Creative Directory, 3000 Olympic Boulevard, Santa Monica CA 90404. **Tel** (310)315-4815, FAX (310)315-4816.

LC DS **ISSN** 0385-6046
DD 950 JA
HOPPO BUNKA KENKYU. [Hoppo bunka kenkyu]. **VFOAT** Bulletin of the Institute for the Study of North Eurasian Cultures, Hokkaido University. (1967)-. Bulletin. Japanese (summaries and/or abstracts in English). One time a year. **Formed by the union of** *Yurashia Bunka Kenkyu*, 0441-0602 **and** *Hoppo Bunka Kenkyu Hokoku*.
Ind/Abst MLA Int. Bibl. Books Artic. Mod. Lang. Lit.

ISSN 1180-5455
CN
HORIZONS (WINNIPEG. 1990). (HORIZONS.). [Horizons]. **Main/Corp** University of Manitoba. Faculty of Arts. Vol. 1, No. 1 (Fall 1990)-. Periodical. English. Two times a year. Limited free distribution. University of Manitoba Faculty of Arts, Fort Garry Manitoba R3T 1R4 Canada.

LC ML82 .H69 **ISSN** 0747-8887
DD 780/.88042 US
CEASED
HOT WIRE. See Women's Interests.

US
HOUSTON ARTS MAGAZINE. Vol. 6, No. 1 (Sept. 1982)-. Periodical. English. Twelve times a year. **Formed by the union of** *Performing Arts* **and** *Tonight!*.

ISSN 1105-0462
GR
UDC 71
HRONIKA AISTHETIKES. **VFOAT** Annales d'Esthetique. (1962)-. Periodical. Multiple languages. One time a year.
Ind/Abst BHA : Biblio. Hist. Art.

LC NX551.A1 C47 **ISSN** 0302-136X
GR
HRONIKO (ATHENAI). (CHRONIKO.). [Hroniko]. Greek, Modern. One time a year. Kallitechniko Pneumatiko Kentro Hora, Xenophontos 7, Athens Greece.

LC NX8.C45 H77
DD 700/.051 CC
HSIEN TAI WEN I LUN TSUNG. Periodical. Chinese. RMBY1.05. Hsin Hua Shu Tien / Shang-Hai Fa Hsing So, Shanghai, People's Republic of China.

LC NX579.A3 S563
DD 700/.9595/7 SI
HSIN CHIA PO WEN I. **VFOAT** Xinjiapo Wenyi; Hsing Chia Po Wen I. First published in Jan. 1976/-. Periodical. Chinese. Irregular. Hsn-Chia-Po Wen I Yen Chiu Hui, 122-B Sime Avenue, Singapore 1438 Singapore.

LC NX583.A3 S564
DD 700/.951/249 CC
HSIN-CHIANG I SHU. **VFOAT** Xinjiang Art. (19??)-. Periodical. Chinese. Six times a year. RMBY0.48. Chung-Kuo Chu Pan Tui Wai Mao I Tsung Kung SSU, PO Box 614, Beijing, People's Republic of China.

ISSN 0205-5295
RU
UDC 7.072
HUDOZESTVENNOE NASLEDIE. [Hudoz. nasled.]. (1975)-. Russian. Irregular.
Ind/Abst BHA : Biblio. Hist. Art.

ISSN 0131-7555
RU
UDC 730+745+75+76
HUDOZNIK. [Hudoznik]. (1958)-. Periodical. Russian. Twelve times a year.
Ind/Abst BHA : Biblio. Hist. Art.

LC AP2 .H886 **ISSN** 0018-702X
DD 805 US
HUDSON REVIEW, THE. See Literary and Political Reviews.

LC NX7 .H83
DD 700/.5 PE
HUESO HUMERO. (April/June 1979)-. Spanish. Irregular. Libreria Studium S A, Francia 1164, Apartado 2139, Lima Peru. **Tel** 011 51 14 326278. **ED** F. Campodonico.
Desc: Journal of arts and letters. Aspires to give a forum to modern Peruvian poetry, with critical donnees of the new movement. Contains essays on the arts.
Ind/Abst Hisp. Am. Period. Index, HAPI.

LC NX584.6.A1 H9
KO
HYONDAE YESUL. **VFOAT** The Modern Art. Vol. 1, No. 1 (1977)-. Periodical. Korean (Korean). W700 single issue.

LC NX8.C45 I15
CH
I HAI TSA CHIH. (April 1977)-. Periodical. Chinese. $12.00. I Hai Tsa Chih, 7th Floor/No 212 Shinn Yih Road/Section 2, Taipei Taiwan.

LC NX588.A1 I23
UA
IBDA. Vol. 1, No. 1 (Jan. 1983)-. Periodical. Arabic. Twelve times a year. £E0.50 single issue. S B 626, 27 Shari Abd Al-Khaliq, Tharwat Al-Qahirah Egypt.

ISSN 1183-6962
CN
CEASED
ICON (TORONTO). (ICON.). [Icon]. **VFOAT** Icon Magazine. Vol. 1, No. 1 (1991)-(19??). Periodical. English. Icon Magazine, 111 Huron Street, Toronto Ontario M5T 2A9 Canada.

LC NX571.P6 I56 **ISSN** 0860-5769
PL
IKONOTHEKA : PRACE INSTYTUTU HISTORII SZTUKI UNIWERSYTETU WARSZAWSKIEGO. **Added/Corp** Uniwersytet Warszawski. Instytut Historii Sztuki. (1990)-. Monographic series. Polish (summaries and/or abstracts in English). Irregular. Price varies per volume. Uniwersytetu Warszawskiego / Instytut Historii Sztuki, Ul. Krakowskie Przedmiescie 26/28, 00-927 Warsaw Poland. **Circ:** 500.
Ind/Abst BHA : Biblio. Hist. Art.

LC DS924.I48 I47
KO
IMSIL MUNHWA. Vol. 1 (1982)-. Periodical. Korean. One time a year. Imsil Munhwawon, 617 Ido-ri Imsil-up Imsil-gun, Chonbuk Korea.

ISSN 0946-0497
GW
●**IN : GERMAN-AMERICAN CULTURAL REVIEW.** **Added/Corp** Inter Nationes. **VFOAT** German-American Cultural Review. (Oct. 6, 1993)-. Periodical. English. Four times a year. Free on request. Inter Nationes EV, Postfach 200749, D-53137 Bonn Germany. **Tel** 11 49 228 880470, FAX 11 49 228 880355, telex 228308. **ED** David Galloway.

ISSN 1060-6734
DD 705 US
IN PROCESS (NEW YORK, N.Y.). (IN PROCESS : THE QUARTERLY NEWSLETTER OF THE PUBLIC ART FUND INC.). [In process]. **Added/Corp** Public Art Fund (New York, N.Y.). (Fall 1991)-. Newsletter. English. Four times a year. Free. Public Art Fund, One East 53rd Street, 11th Floor, New York NY 10022. **Tel** (212)980-4575, FAX (212)980-3610.

US
INDIAN ART MARKET. See Ethnic Interests.

LC NX7 .I49
BL
INEDITOS. (May/June 1976)-. Portuguese. $15.00 single issue. Editora Ineditos, rua Jornalista Jair Silva 291 Apto 103, Belo Horizonte Brazil.

ISSN 0825-8708
DD 700/.9714 CN
Pr Rev.
INTER. [Inter]. (Autumn 1984)-. Periodical. French. Three times a year. LES Editions Intervention, 345 rue du Pont, Quebec G1K 6M4 Canada. **Tel** (418)529-9680, FAX (418)648-9201. **ED** Alain-Martin Richard. **Bk Rev.** **Ad Acc, Adv Mgr:** Frederique Richard. **Circ:** 1200 (ctrl)
Continues *Intervention*, 0705-1972.

LC NX735 .I587
US
INTER-ARTS. GRANTS TO PRESENTING ORGANIZATIONS, SERVICES TO PRESENTING ORGANIZATIONS, SPECIAL TOURING INITIATIVES: APPLICATION GUIDELINES. **Added/Corp** National Endowment for the Arts. **VFOAT** Inter Arts. Grants to Presenting Organizations, Services to Presenting Organizations, Special Touring Initiatives; Grants to Presenting Organizations, Services to Presenting Organizations, Special Touring Initiatives. Fiscal Year (1992)-. English. $10.00. **Continues** *Inter-Arts. Presenting Organizations, Artist Colonies, Services to the Arts*.

ISSN 0890-8338
DD 792 US
INTERCHANGE (ALLIANCE FOR ARTS EDUCATION (U.S.)). (INTERCHANGE.). [Interchange]. **Added/Corp** Alliance for Arts Education (U.S.). (1977)-. English. Four times a year. Free. Alliance for Arts Education, Kennedy Center 5, Education Program, Washington DC 20566. **Tel** (202)254-7190. **Circ:** 10,000.
Desc: Publication that presents recent developments in different arts education programs throughout the United States.

LC NX **ISSN** 1355-6169
DD 700.68 UK
INTERNATIONAL ARTS MANAGER. [Int. arts manag.]. (1988)-. Periodical. English. Twelve times a year. £45.00. International Arts Publishing, 4 Hassam Street, London E1 7QS United Kingdom. **Tel** 011 44 171 2470066, FAX 011 44 171 2476868.

US
INTERSECTION NEWSLETTER. **Added/Corp** Center for Religion and the Arts. (19??)-. Newsletter. English. One time a year. Intersection Newsletter, 766 Valencia, San Francisco CA 94110.

ISSN 1035-3127
AT
ISLAND. See Literature.

IT
ITALIA ARTISTICA, L'. (18??)-. Periodical. Italian. Four times a year. Magalini, via Gramsci 5, 25086 Rezzato BS Italy. **Tel** 011 39 30 2792968.

LC NX552.A1 I78 **ISSN** 0161-4622
DD 700/.945 US
Pr Rev.
ITALIAN CULTURE. [Ital. cult.]. (1979)-. Periodical. English (Italian and French). One time a year. comes with membership. American Association For Italian Studies, Kent State University, Kent OH 44242. **Tel** (216)672-2151. **ED** Douglas Radcliff-Umstead. **Bk Rev.** **Ad Acc. Circ:** 500.
Desc: Examines all aspects of Italian culture including fine arts, literature, history, and politics. All kinds of critical methods are encouraged.
Ind/Abst MLA Int. Bibl. Books Artic. Mod. Lang. Lit.

ISSN 0774-2851
BE
UDC 06
JAARBOEK - ARCA LOVANIENSIS ARTES ATQUE HISTORIAE RESERANS DOCUMENTA. [Jaarb. - Arca Lovan. artes atque hist. reserans doc.]. (1972)-. Monographic series. Dutch. One time a year.
Ind/Abst BHA : Biblio. Hist. Art.

LC WMLC L 83/458 **ISSN** 0931-8313
GW
JAHRBUCH .... **Added/Corp** Manner vom Morgenstern, Heimatbund an Elb- und Wesermundung. **VFOAT** Jahrbuch der Manner vom Morgenstern. (19??)-. German. **Continues** *Jahresbericht der Manner vom Morgenstern*.
Ind/Abst BHA : Biblio. Hist. Art.

LC NX550.A1 J34 **ISSN** 0932-0229
DD 700/.5 GW
JAHRBUCH / BAYERISCHE AKADEMIE DER SCHONEN KUNSTE. [Jahrb. - Bayer. Akad. Schonen Kunste]. **Added/Corp** Bayerische Akademie der Schonen Kunste. Periodical. Vol. 1, No. 1 (1987)-. German. One time a year. CH Beck Verlagsbuchhandlung, D-80791 Munich Germany. **Tel** 011 49 89 381891.

ISSN 0373-9767
GW
CODEN JAWGAP
JAHRBUCH DER AKADEMIE DER WISSENSCHAFTEN IN GOETTINGEN. [Jahrb. akad. wiss. Gëott.]. **Main/Corp** Akademie der Wissenschaften in Goettingen. (1940)-. German. One time a year. Vandenhoeck & Ruprecht, Robert Bosch Breite 6, D-37079 Goettingen Germany. **Tel** 011 49 551

695911, FAX 011 49 551 695917, telex 965226 VAN d. **Continues** *Gesellschaft der Wissenschaften zu Goettingen. Nachrichten von der Gesellschaft der Wissenschaften zu Goettingen. Jahresbericht.*
Ind/Abst BHA : Biblio. Hist. Art.

ISSN 0930-4592
GW

UDC 001.891
JAHRESBERICHT - FRITZ-THYSSEN-STIFTUNG. [Jahresber. - Fritz-Thyssen-Stift.]. (1975)-. Periodical. German. One time a year. Franz Steiner Verlag GmbH, Postfach 101061, D-70009 Stuttgart Germany. **Tel** 011 49 711 2582372, FAX 011 49 711 2582290, telex 723636 daz d. **Continues** *Bericht der Fritz-Thyssen-Stiftung Uber Ihre Tatigkeit, 0532-7288.*
Ind/Abst BHA : Biblio. Hist. Art.

LC ML3505.8 .J44 ISSN 1055-5722
DD 781.65/05 US
JAZZSOUTH (ATLANTA, GA.). See Music.

LC NX26.N4 J14A ISSN 0273-012X
DD 700/.79 US
JDR 3RD FUND REPORT, THE. [JDR 3rd Fund rep.]. **Main/Corp** JDR 3rd Fund. **VAT** John Davison Rockefeller Third Fund Report. 1963/1967-. Periodical. English. One time a year. JDR 3rd Fund, 50 Rockefeller Plaza, New York NY 10020.

ISSN 0278-0178
US
JLAG REVIEW. No. 32-. Periodical. English. Four times a year. $3.00. Joycean Lively Arts Guild, POB 459, East Douglas MA 01516. **Continues** *Joycean Lively Arts Guild Review.*

PO
JORNAL DE LETRAS, ARTES E IDEIAS :
JL. VFOAT JL. Year 1, No. 1 (3-16 March 1981)-. Periodical. Portuguese. Twenty-six times a year. Publicacoes Projornal SA SVC, Assinaturas AV Liberdade 202 2, 1200 Lisbon Portugal. **Tel** 011 351 1 574520, 011 351 1 574593.

LC NX7 .J67
BL
JOSE. No. 1- July 1976-. Periodical. Portuguese (Portuguese). $10.00. Editora Fontana, rua Visconde de Piraja 430 - S503 - Ipanema ZC 37, Rio de Janeiro Brazil.

LC E78.A3 J74
DD 700/.89970798 US
JOURNAL OF ALASKA NATIVE ARTS / INSTITUTE OF ALASKA NATIVE ARTS, INC. Added/Corp Institute of Alaska Native Arts (Alaska). (Sept./Oct. 1984)-. Periodical. English. Four times a year. $25.00. Institute of Alaska Native Arts, PO Box 80583, Fairbanks AK 99708. **Tel** (907)456-7406, FAX (907)451-7268. **Continues** *Newsletter of Native Arts.*
Ind/Abst Ethnoarts Index.

LC NX1 .J67 ISSN 0970-5309
DD 700/.5 II
JOURNAL OF ARTS & IDEAS. [J. arts ideas]. **VFOAT** Journal of Arts and Ideas. (Oct./Dec. 1982)-. Periodical. English. Four times a year (Jan., Apr., July, Oct.). $50.00. Journal of Arts & Ideas / Social Scientists, R-271 Lower Ground Floor, Greater Kailash-I, New Delhi 110048 India. **(Subscription address:** Prints India, 11 Darya Ganj, New Delhi 110002 India. **Tel** 011 91 11 3268665, FAX 011 91 11 3275542, telex 31-61087 PRIN-IN.) **ED** Vivaan Sundaram and Geeta Kapoor. Index available. **Bk Rev. Ad Acc. Circ:** 2,000.
Desc: Aimed at meeting the need for a forum of communication where writers, artists and critics can engage in a dialogue on theoretical and practical aspects of the entire gamut of cultural and literary activities.
Ind/Abst Avery Index Archit. Period. Suppl. Colum. Univ. (19??-199?).

LC NX180.S6 J68 ISSN 0885-2545
DD 338.4/77 NE
CCC
JOURNAL OF CULTURAL ECONOMICS.
[J. cult. econ.]. **Added/Corp** Association for Cultural Economics. Vol. 1, No. 1, June (1977)-. Periodical. English. Four times a year. $248.00. Kluwer Academic Publishers, Postbus 322, 3300 AH Dordrecht The Netherlands. **Tel** 011 31 78 524400, FAX 011 31 78 183273, telex 20083. **ED** William S. Hendon. Index available. cum. index. **Bk Rev. Circ:** 1,100 (ctrl).
Desc: Deals with all areas of the arts and the economics involved in establishing and supporting artistic endeavors.
Ind/Abst Curr. Cit.; Econ. Lit. Index; J. Econ. Lit.; Leis., Rec., Tour. Abstr.; Rural Dev. Abstr.; World Agric. Econ. Rural Sociol. Abstr.

ISSN 1055-8888
US
●**JOURNAL OF INDEPENDENT RESEARCH. See** Education.

LC CB351 .R57A ISSN 0195-8453
DD 909.07 US
UDC 940.1/.2
JOURNAL OF THE ROCKY MOUNTAIN MEDIEVAL AND RENAISSANCE ASSOCIATION. See History.

ISSN 0710-2143
DD 700/.9714 CN
JOURNAL OPTION GLOBALE. [J. option globale]. No. 1 (22 Nov. 1976)-. Periodical. French. Twelve times a year. $5.00. Action Globale, 1249 rue Conseil, Sherbrooke Quebec J1G 1M9 Canada.

LC NX5 .K85 ISSN 0022-7277
BE
K & I.E. EN C. KUNST EN CULTUUR.
VFOAT Kunst en Cultuur. Periodical. Dutch (French). Twelve times a year. 25.00F single issue. Paleis voor Schone Kunster, Koningstraat 10, 1000 Brussels Belgium. **Tel** 02/507 82 31, FAX 02/574 3044. **Bk Rev. Ad Acc.** ctrl circ. **Continues** *Kunst- en Cultuuragenda.*
Ind/Abst MLA Int. Bibl. Books Artic. Mod. Lang. Lit.

LC NX576.A1 K34
II
KALAKSHETRA QUARTERLY. Vol. 1 (Apr. 1978)-. Periodical. English. Four times a year.
Supersedes *Kalakshetra.*
Ind/Abst ARTbibliogr. Mod.

LC NX504 .K34 ISSN 0735-7885
DD 700/.88042 US
Pr Rev.
KALLIOPE. Added/Corp Kalliope Poetry and Fiction Collectives. Florida. Division of Cultural Affairs. Florida. Fine Arts Council. Jacksonville Women's Poetry Collective. Florida Junior College at Jacksonville. Center for the Continuing Education of Women. Vol. 1, No. 1 (Winter 1979)-. Periodical. English. Three times a year (Spring, Fall, Winter). $21.00. Florida Community College at Jacksonville, 3939 Roosevelt Boulevard, Kent E-112, Jacksonville FL 32205. **Tel** (904)381-3511. **ED** Mary Sue Koeppel. Index available. cum. index. **Bk Rev. Circ:** 6-10 per year). **Circ:** 1,100 (ctrl). available on microfilm and microfiche from University Microfilms International (UMI).
Desc: Offers support and encouragement to women in the arts. Promotes the pursuit of excellence in visual and verbal art forms. Provides a medium of communication for women artists.
Ind/Abst Am. Humanit. Index.

LC NX583.A1 K36
DD 700/.951 CC
KANG CHAN WEN I YEN CHIU. VFOAT Kangzhan Wenyiyanjiu. (19??)-. Periodical. Chinese. Four times a year. RMBY0.60. SSU-Chuan Sheng She Hui Ko, Hsueh Yuan Fa Hsing Ko, Cheng-tu, People's Republic of China.

PE
KANTU. No. 1 (June 1986)-. Periodical. Spanish. Six times a year.
Ind/Abst BHA : Biblio. Hist. Art.

LC NX8.K8 K66 ISSN 0454-3114
KO
KONGGAN. VFOAT Space. Vol. 1 (1966)-. Periodical. Korean. Twelve times a year. W12.000. Konggan SA, 219 Wonso-dong, Chongno-ku, Seoul Korea.

NE
KONINKLIJKE VERENIGING VOOR NEDERLANDSE MUZIEKGESCHIEDENIS LIDMAATSCHAP. See Music.

LC NX28.K62 H35615
DD 700/.6/15195 KO
KOREAN CULTURE & ARTS FOUNDATION, THE. Main/Corp Han'guk Munhwa Yesul Chinhungwon. English. The Korean Culture & Arts Foundation, 31 Dong-soong-dong Jong-ro-gu, Seoul Korea.

LC NX584.6.A1 K69
DD 700/.9519/5 KO
KOREANA. Added/Corp International Cultural Society of Korea. Vol. 1, No. 1 (1987)-. Periodical. English. Four times a year (Mar., June, Sept., Dec.). $32.00. Korea Herald, CPO Box 6479, Seoul 100 771 Korea. **(Subscription address:** Korea Herald, PO Box 312, Hartsdale NY 10530. **Tel** (212)582-5205.) **ED** Cook-chin Ahn. **Bk Rev. Ad Acc. Circ:** 150,000 (ctrl).
Desc: Art and culture magazine of Korea. Korea's answer to Smithsonian Magazine.
Ind/Abst Bibliogr. Mission.

LC NX8.T8 K82
TU
KUBBEALT AKADEMI MECMUAS. Vol. 1- Jan. 1972-. Periodical. Turkish. 10.25. Kubbealt Cemiyeti, Yeniciriler Caddesi 81 Carsikapi, Istanbul Turkey.

ISSN 0934-1730
GW
KUENSTLER (MUENCHEN). (KUENSTLER.). [Kuenstler]. (1988)-. Periodical. German. Four times a year (June, July, Sept., Dec.). $164.28. Weltkunst Verlag GmbH, Postfach 190918, 80603 Munich Germany. **Tel** 011 49 89 1269900, FAX 011 49 89 1269911, telex 5216731. **ED** Lothar Romain and Detlef Bluemler. Index available in last issue of volume--attached. **Circ:** 7,000 (ctrl).
Desc: Contemporary artists in all kinds of arts.

LC NX573 .K84
LY
KULL AL-FUNUN. Periodical. Arabic. 1.00. Al-Muassasah Al-Ammah Lil-Sihafah, PO Box 4814, Tarabulus Al-Gharb Libya.

LC DD260.3 .K84 ISSN 0724-343X
DD 943/.005 GW
KULTUR CHRONIK. VFOAT Kulturchurnik. Vol. 1 (1983)-. Periodical. English (German, Russian, French and Spanish). Six times a year. Free on request. Inter Nationes EV, Postfach 200749, D-53137 Bonn Germany. **Tel** 11 49 228 880470, FAX 11 49 228 880355, telex 228308. **ED** Dr. Dieter W. Benecke. **Bk Rev,** (Qty: 20). **Circ:** 50,000 (ctrl).
Desc: Compressed report about the German cultural scene.
Ind/Abst Museum Abstr.

LC HA1911 .A3 NX565.A1
DD 314 TU
KULTUR ISTATISTIKLERI. See The Arts-Abstracting, Bibliographies and Statistics.

LC NX550.6.A1 K84
SZ
KULTUR UND FREIZEIT. Periodical. German. Twelve times a year. Deutscher Judo Verband, Redaktion Ippon Segewaldweg 40, D-12557 Berlin Germany. **Tel** 011 49 711 210770, telex 051 678.

GW
KULTURGESCHICHTE DER ANTIKEN WELT. See Archaeology.

LC NX8.E8 S5
ER
●**KULTUURILEHT.** No. 1 (Feb. 11, 1994)-. Periodical. Estonian. One time a week. **(Subscription address:** Victor Kamkin, 4956 Boiling Brook Parkway, Rockville MD 20852. **Tel** (301)881-5973.) **Continues** *Sirp.*

ISSN 0172-8350
GW
KUNSTSPIEGEL. VFOAT Kunst Spiegel. Periodical. German. Arbeitskreis Kunstspiegel GBR, 8500 Nurnberg Germany.
Ind/Abst BHA : Biblio. Hist. Art.

LC NX180.R45 L43 ISSN 0160-1857
US
LEFT CURVE. [Left curve]. (1974)-. Periodical. English. Three times a year. $35.00. Left Curve, PO Box 472, Oakland CA 94604. **Tel** (510)763-7193. **ED** C. Polony (editor's address: 410 Webster Street, Oakland CA). **Bk Rev. Ad Acc. Adv Mgr:** C. Polony. **Circ:** 1,200. available on microfilm from University Microfilms International (UMI).
Desc: An artist-produced critical journal that addresses the problems of culture forms emerging from the crisis of modernity and that strive to be independent from the control of dominant institutions, and free from the shackles of instrumental rationality.
Ind/Abst Altern. Press Index; ARTbibliogr. Mod.; Left Index.

ISSN 1071-4391
DD 705 US
●**LEONARDO ELECTRONIC ALMANAC.**
(LEONARDO ELECTRONIC ALMANAC [COMPUTER FILE]). [Leon. electron. alm.]. **Added/Corp** International Society for the Arts, Sciences, and Technology. (1993)-. Periodical. English. Twelve times a year. $15.00. Massachusetts Institute of Technology (MIT) Press, 55 Hayward Street, Cambridge MA 02142. **Tel** (617)253-2889, (617)625-8481, FAX (617)258-6779. **ED** Craig Harris.
Desc: Provides current perspectives in the art, science, and technology domains. Provides insights into contemporary activities through columns which feature artists' statements about their own work, and profiles of media in arts facilities.

LC DG451 .L38 ISSN 0393-6457
DD 945.092/05 IT
LETTERA DALL'ITALIA. Added/Corp Istituto della Enciclopedia Italiana. Vol. 1, No. 1 (April 1986)-. Periodical. Italian. Four times a year. Price varies per volume. Istituto Enciclopedia Italiana, Piazza Paganica 4, 00186 Rome Italy. **Tel** 011 39 6 68982464.

The Arts

LC NX533.A1 .L49
BL
LEVIATA. (19??)-. Periodical. Portuguese. Six times a year. Leviata Publicacoes Ltda., Magalhaes Couto 535 202, 20731 Rio de Janeiro RJ Brazil. **Tel** 021 551-9759, FAX 227-5944.

ISSN 0227-227X
DD 792/.09713
CN
Pr Rev.
LIAISON (THEATRE-ACTION). See Theater.

CN
LIASON. (19??)-. French. Five times a year. Liason, CP 358, Succ. A, Ottawa Ontario K1N 8V3 Canada. **Ind/Abst** Can. Period. Index (19??-).

ISSN 0229-7221
DD 700/.9714
CN
LIBRAIRIE ILLUSTREE, LA. [Libr. illus.]. **VFOAT** Librairie. Vol. 1, No. 1 (Nov. 1976)-. Periodical. French (English). $12.00 Canada, $18.00 other. La Librairie Illustree, 81 rue de la Reine, Sorel Quebec J3P 4R6 Canada.

ISSN 0989-6023
FR
LIGEIA. No. 1 (Apr.-June 1988)-. Periodical. French. Four times a year. $62.12. Ligeia / Dossiers de l'Art, BP 327, 75266 Paris Cedex 06 France. **Tel** 011 33 1 40390376. **ED** Lista Srovanni. **Bk Rev**. **Ad Acc**.
Ind/Abst BHA : Biblio. Hist. Art.

US
CEASED
LIMELIGHT. Main/Corp Birmingham Metropolitan Arts Council. (1991)-(199?). Periodical. English. **ED** Ray Martin. **Ad Acc**.

SW
LITTERATUR, TEATER, FILM. Added/Corp Lund. Universitet. Litteraturvetenskapliga Institutionen. (1972)-. Monographic series. Swedish. Irregular. Price varies per volume. Lund University Press, Box 141, S-22100 Lund Sweden. **Tel** 011 46 46 312000, FAX 011 46 46 305338, telex 33345 EDUCATE S.
Desc: Dissertations on the subjects literature, theatre and motion pictures.

LC NX556.A3 L775
ISSN 0207-1258
DD 709.47
LI
LITUANISTIKA V SSSR: ISKUSSTVOVEDENIE. Added/Corp Lietuvos TSR Mokslu Akademija. Visuomenes Mokslu Informacijos Sektorius. **VFOAT** Iskusstvovedenie. No. 1 (1978)-. Periodical. Russian. One time a year. 0.80rub (single issue). Sector of Information of Social Sciences, Institute of Philosophy Sociology and Law, Academy of Sciences of Lithuanian SSR, 232000 Vilnius Lenin Avenue, 3 Vilnius Lithuania.

US
LIVING HISTORY. See History-History of North and South America.

ISSN 0957-8137
DD 709.41
UK
LOCAL ARTS UK. (LOCAL ARTS.). [Local arts UK]. Added/Corp TS Development Association. (1989)-. Periodical. English. Six times a year. Arts Development Association, Arts Centre Vane Terr Darlingt, County Durham DL3 7AX United Kingdom. **Tel** 011 44 1325 465930. **Continues** Arts Centres UK, 0268-8859.
Ind/Abst Br. Educ. Index.

US
LOCAL PROGRAMS. English. One time a year. Free. National Endowment for the Arts, 1100 Pennsylvania Avenue Northwest, Washington DC 20506. **Tel** (202)682-5400, (202)682-5435.
Desc: The purpose of the program is to enhance the quality and availability of the arts by fostering expansion of public support for the arts at the local level.

ISSN 0260-9592
UK
LONDON REVIEW OF BOOKS, THE. See Literary and Political Reviews.

LC NX28.S8 L624
ISSN 0024-6891
DK
LOUISIANA-REVY. [Louisiana rev.]. **Main/Corp** Louisiana (Museum). Vol. 1 (Sept. 1960)-. Periodical. Danish (summaries and/or abstracts in English). Three times a year. Price varies. Munksgaard International Publishers Ltd, PO Box 2148, DK-1016 Copenhagen K Denmark. **Tel** 011 45 33 127030, FAX 011 45 33 129387, telex 19431 MUNKS DK.
Ind/Abst ARTbibliogr. Mod.; ARTbibliogr. Curr. Titles; BHA : Biblio. Hist. Art.

LC NX553.A1 L68
ISSN 0779-5815
BE
●**LOW COUNTRIES : ARTS AND SOCIETY IN FLANDERS AND THE NETHERLANDS, A YEARBOOK, THE.**
Added/Corp Stichting Ons Erfdeel. (1994)-. English. One time a year. $52.07. Stichting Ons Erfdeel VZW, Murissonstraat 260, 8931 Rekkem Belgium. **Tel** 011 32 56 411201, FAX 011 32 56 411707.

LC AP58.B8 L8
US
LUCH. Added/Corp Association of Bulgarian Writers and Artists in Exile. (19??)-. Periodical. Bulgarian (English). Association of the Bulgarian Writers and Artists in Exile, 1823 North Normandie Avenue, Apartment D, Los Angeles CA 90027.

LC NX1 .M42
ISSN 1040-8576
DD 700
US
Pr Rev.
M/E/A/N/I/N/G (NEW YORK, N.Y.).
(M/E/A/N/I/N/G.). [M/e/a/n/i/n/g]. **VFOAT** Meaning. No. 1 (Dec. 1986)-. Periodical. English. Two times a year. $20.00. Mira Schor, 60 Lispenard Street, New York NY 10013. **Tel** (212)431-3697. **ED** Mira Schor and Susan Bee. **Bk Rev**. (Qty: 10). Circ: 1,000 (ctrl).
Desc: Contains theoretical and critical writings by visual artists and critics.
Ind/Abst ARTbibliogr. Mod.

ISSN 0024-886X
UK
MABON. Vol. 1 (Spring 1969)-. Periodical. English. Two times a year. North Wales Association for the Arts, 9-11 Wellfield House Britain. available on microfilm from University Microfilms International (UMI).

LC NX456 .M3
BL
MAC REVISTA. Added/Corp Universidade de Sao Paulo. Museu de Arte Contemporanea. **VFOAT** MAC; Revista do Museu de Arte Contemporanea da Universidade de Sao Paulo. No. 1 (Apr. 1992)-. Periodical. Portuguese. Two times a year. Universidade de Sao Paulo / Museu de Arte Contemporanea, Pavilhao de Bienal 3o Piso, Caixa Postal 22031, 01499 Sao Paulo SP Brazil. **Tel** 011 55 11 5739925. **ED** Ana Mae T.B. Barbosa & Marcelo G.S. Lima. Circ: 1,000.

LC DR701.M13 M33
US
●**MACEDONIA, CURIOSUM MUNDI.**
Added/Corp Macedonian Arts Council. **VFOAT** Macedonia. (1993)-. Periodical. English. Four times a year. $25.00. Macedonian Arts Council, PO Box 905, New York NY 10023. **Tel** (212)799-0009.

LC NX531.A1 M34
DD 700/.982/05
AG
MAGA, LA. Vol. 1, No. 1 (1991)-. Periodical. Spanish. Twenty-four times a year. Taller Escuela Agencia, Ediciones Periodismo x Periodistas, Chile 537, Piso 5o Office 20-21, 1098 Buenos Aires Argentina. **ED** Carlos Ares.

LC NX549.A1 C52
DD 700/.5
FR
MAGAZINE (CENTRE GEORGES POMPIDOU). (LE MAGAZINE / CENTRE NATIONAL D'ART ET DE CULTURE GEORGES POMPIDOU.). Added/Corp Centre Georges Pompidou. No. 51 (May 15-July 15, 1989)-. Periodical. French (English). Six times a year. $20.56. Editions du Centre Pompidou, Service Commerical, 75195 Paris Cedex 04 France. **Tel** 011 33 1 44784288, 011 33 1 44781233, FAX 011 33 1 42725650, telex CNAC GP 212 726. **Continues** CNAC Magazine, 0290-3059.

ISSN 0737-8688
US
MALINI. See Ethnic Interests.

ISSN 0176-1226
GW
CEASED
MANA, MANNHEIMER ANALYTIKA.
(MANNHEIMER-ANALYTIKA / MANNHEIM ANALYTIQUES.). [MANA, Mannh. Anal.]. Added/Corp Universitat Mannheim. Lehrstuhl Romanistik I. **VFOAT** Mannheim Analytiques; Mannheim-Analytika; MANA. (1983)-Series Completed (19??). Monographic series. German (French and English). Universitat de Mannheim, Schloss Sekretaer Romanistik, D-68131 Mannheim 1 Germany. **Tel** 011 49 621 2925666.
Ind/Abst Film Lit. Index (19??-).

GW
MANUSKRIPTE ZUR KUNSTWISSENSCHAFT IN DER WERNERSCHEN VERLAGSGESELLSCHAFT. Added/Corp Wernersche Verlagsgesellschaft. 1984-. Monographic series. German. Price varies per volume.

LC DS778.M3 M3327
DD 700/.1/03
CC
MAO TSE-TUNG WEN I SSU HSIANG YEN CHIU / CHUAN KUO MAO TSE-TUNG WEN I SSU HSIANG YEN CHIU HUI PIEN. (1982)-. Periodical. Chinese. Hsin Hua Shu Tien / Hu-Nan Sheng China, People's Republic of China.

LC N1 .M46
ISSN 0025-2913
II
MARG. [Marg]. Added/Corp Modern Architectural Research Group. Modern Artists and Architects Research Group. **VFOAT** Pathway. Vol.1 (Oct. 1946)-. Periodical. English. Four times a year. $40.00. Marg Publications, Army Navy Building/3rd Floor, 148 Mahatma Gandhi Road, Fort Bombay 400-023 India. **Tel** 011 91 22 242520, FAX 011 91 22 2049522. **(Subscription address**: Prints India, 11 Darya Ganj, New Delhi 110002 India. **Tel** 011 91 11 3268645, FAX 011 91 11 3275542, telex 31-61087 PRIN-IN.) **ED** Pratapaditya Pal. **Ad Acc**. Circ: 1,500 (ctrl).
Desc: Deals with the arts, sculpture, crafts, music, dance and architecture of India and its sister civilizations.
Ind/Abst Art Index; ARTbibliogr. Mod. (1982-); Avery Index Archit. Period. Suppl. Colum. Univ. (1989-); Index Islam. Lit.

ISSN 1019-360X
KE
UDC 009
MASENO JOURNAL OF EDUCATION, ARTS, AND SCIENCE. See Education.

ISSN 0318-3610
DD C810/.8/0054
CN
MATRIX (LENNOXVILLE). (MATRIX.). [Matrix (Lennoxv.)]. Added/Corp Champlain Regional College. Lennoxville Campus. Dept. of English. Vol. 1 (Spring 1975)-. Periodical. English. Three times a year. 17.61Can$. Linda Leith, CP 100St Anne de Bellevue, Quebec H9X 3L4 Canada. **Tel** (514)426-8654, FAX (514)426-8658. **ED** Linda Leith and Kenneth Radu. **Bk Rev**. (Qty: 30-40). **Ad Acc**, **Adv Mgr**: Beryl Parker or Linda Leith. Circ: 2,000. available on microfilm from Micromedia Limited; available on microfiche from Micromedia Limited; available on an online database from Micromedia Limited.
Desc: Includes opinionated articles on film, theatre, photography, art, a substantial review section, plus translations, travel writing, interviews, original fiction and poetry.
Ind/Abst Can. Index; Can. Lit. Index (1985-1986); Can. Period. Index (1989-); Curr. Contents Life Sci.

SZ
●**MAYER.** **VFOAT** Guide Mayer. (1995)-. English (French, German and Italian). One time a year (Feb., or Mar.). 293.00F Europe; 310.00F others. Editions Acatos, Avenue Villamont 17, CH-1005 Lausanne Switzerland. **Tel** 011 41 21 3120652, FAX 011 41 21 3129108. **(Subscription address**: Servedit, 15 rue Victor Cousin, 75005 Paris France. **Tel** 011 33 1 44414930, FAX 011 33 1 43257741.) **Ad Acc**, **Adv Mgr**: Helsaudra Sokolon, **Tel** 011 33 1 44414930. available on CD-ROM. **Continues** International Auction Records.

LC NX4 .M36
ISSN 0393-8190
DD 700/.5
IT
MCM. [MCM]. **VFOAT** Manualita, Creativita, Maestria; Storia delle Cose. No. 1 (Sept. 1985)-. Periodical. Italian. Three times a year. L31340. Maria Cristina Montemayor Edit, Viale A Volta 173, 50131 Florence Italy. **Tel** 011 39 55 579800, 011 39 55 2302457. **Bk Rev**. (Qty: 6-7/yr). **Ad Acc**.

LC NX5 .V58
BE
MEDEDELINGEN VAN DE KONINKLIJKE ACADEMIE VOOR WETENSCHAPPEN, LETTEREN EN SCHONE KUNSTEN VAN BELGIËE, KLASSE DER SCHONE KUNSTEN.
Added/Corp Koninklijke Academie voor Wetenschappen, Letteren en Schone Kunsten van Belgiee. Klasse der Schone Kunsten. Vol. 34 (1972)-. Proceedings. Dutch (English). Irregular. Price varies per volume. Koninklijke Academie voor Wetenschappen, Letteren en Schone Kunsten Van Belgie, Hertogsstraat 1, B-1000 Brussels Belgium. **Tel** 011 32 2 5112623, FAX 011 32 2 5110143. **ED** G. Verbeke. Index available. Circ: 800. **Continues** Mededelingen van de Koninklijke Vlaamse Academie voor Wetenschappen, Letteren en Schone Kunsten van Belgie, Klasse der Schone Kunsten.
Desc: Proceedings of the fine arts section of the Academy, containing articles on fine arts and music.

ISSN 0713-0317
CN
DD 700/.9713
MEDIA FIVE BULLETIN, THE. [Media Five bull.]. Bulletin. English. One time a week. Media Five, 219 Oxford Street West, London Ontario N6H 1S5 Canada. **Continues** Voidstaff Bulletin, 0713-0309.

US
MEDIA INC. Vol. 2, Issue 12 (Dec. 1988)-. Periodical. English. Twelve times a year. Media Index Publishing, PO Box 24365, Seattle WA 98124-0365. **Tel** (206)382-9220. **Continues** Aperture Northwest.

ISSN 0714-4520
DD 700/.9714/22
CN
MEDIATEUR, LE. [Mediateur]. Vol. 1, No. 1 (June 1982)-. Periodical. French. Twelve times a year. Free. available on microfilm from University Microfilms International (UMI).

The Arts

ISSN 1032-254X
AT
DD 994.51063
MELBURNIAN FITZROY. (THE MELBURNIAN.). [Melburnian Fitzroy]. (1987)-. Periodical. English. Eleven times a year (Dec. & Jan. combined). 15.62Aus$. Melburnian, 316 328 Napier St., Fitzroy Victoria, 3065 Australia. **Tel** 011 61 3 4173121. **ED** Phil Pianta. **Bk Rev**, (Qty: 100). **Ad Acc. Circ:** 9,200 (ctrl).
Desc: Designed for people with an interest in the arts, cultural affairs and associated issues.

ISSN 1157-075X
FR
MEMOIRES. See Humanities.

LC AS242 **ISSN** 0378-7923
DD 068.493 BE
UDC 7
MEMOIRES - ACADEMIE ROYALE DE BELGIQUE. CLASSE DES BEAUX-ARTS. COLLECTION IN 8. [Mem. - Acad. r. Belg., Cl. b.-arts, Coll. 8]. **VFOAT** Verhandelingen - Koninklijke Academie van Belgie. Klasse der Schone Kunsten. Verzameling in 8. (1920)-. Periodical. French. Irregular. Librarie Alain Feraton, Chausse de Charleroi 162, B 1060 Brussels Belgium. **Tel** 011 32 2 5386917. **Continues** Memoires - Academie Royale de Belgique. Classe des Sciences Morales et Politiques et de la Classe des Beaux-Arts. Collection in 8, 0770-805X.
Ind/Abst BHA : Biblio. Hist. Art.

ISSN 0249-6747
FR
MEMOIRES DE LA COMMISSION DES ANTIQUITES DU DEPARTEMENT DE LA COTE-D'OR. See Humanities.

ISSN 0369-1896
FR
CODEN MSBTAG
MEMOIRES DE L'ACADEMIE DES SCIENCES, INSCRIPTIONS ET BELLES-LETTRES DE TOULOUSE. See Humanities.

LC AS242 .H2 **ISSN** 0373-7667
BE
CODEN MSAHA9
MEMOIRES ET PUBLICATIONS DE LA SOCIETE DES SCIENCES, DES ARTS ET DES LETTRES DU HAINAUT. [Mem. publ. Soc. sci., arts lett. Hainaut]. **Main/Corp** Societe des Aciences, des Arts et des Lettres du Hainaut. Vol. 1 (1839)-. French. One time a year. Price varies. Societe Science Art et Lettres Hainaud, rue de Nimy 37, 7000 Mons Belguim. **(Subscription address:** L'Oiseau Lire, rue de la Clef 38, 7000 Mons Belguim. **Tel** 011 32 65312873.)
Ind/Abst BHA : Biblio. Hist. Art; Zentralbl. Math. Ihre Grenzgeb.

ISSN 0188-4824
MX
MEMORIA DE PAPEL. Added/Corp Consejo Nacional Para la Cultura y las Artes (Mexico). Vol 1, No. 1 (Apr. 1991)-. Periodical. Spanish. Two times a year.

ISSN 0278-1190
US
SUSPENDED
MENDOCINO REVIEW, THE. See Literature.

ISSN 0844-3637
DD 790/.09713/541 CN
METROPOLIS. (METROPOLIS : TORONTO'S FREE ARTS AND ENTERTAINMENT WEEKLY.). [Metropolis]. (May 19, 1988)-. Periodical. English. One time a week. $30.00. Metropolis Press Inc, 355 Adelaide Street West/2nd Floor, Toronto Ontario M5V 1S2 Canada.

LC NX6 .N6
RU
MIR ISKUSSTV. (1992)-. Periodical. Russian. Twelve times a year. Izdatelstvo Znanie, Novaya Ploshchad 3-4, 101835 Moscow Russia. **Continues** Novoe v Zhizni, Nauke, Tekhnike. Seriia Iskusstvo.

ISSN 0739-0424
US
MISSISSIPPI MUD, THE. VFOAT Mud. (197?)-. Periodical. English. Four times a year. $19.00 (for 4 issues). Mississippi Mud, 1336 SE Marion Street, Portland OR 97202. **Tel** (503)236-9962. **ED** Joel Weinstein. **Ad Acc. Circ:** 1,500 (ctrl).
Desc: Writing and art from the American scene.

ISSN 1013-4239
RM
MITROPOLIA OLTENIEI. [Mitrop. Olten.]. (1???)-. Periodical. Romanian. Six times a year. DM169.00. **(Subscription address:** Kubon & Sagner, ABT Zeitschriftenimport, D 80328 Munich Germany. **Tel** 011 49 89 54218130.)
Ind/Abst BHA : Biblio. Hist. Art.

LC NX584.A3 M595
DD 709.52 JA
MIYAGI-KEN GEIJUTSU NENKAN. Added/Corp Miyagi, Japan (Prefecture). Seikatsu Kankyobu. Kemminka. (1971)-. Japanese. Miyagi-Ken, 8-1 Honcho 3-chome, Sendai 980 Japan.

JA
CEASED
MIZUE : A MONTHLY REVIEW OF THE FINE ARTS. (19??)-(19??). Japanese. **(Subscription address:** Kinokuniya Company Ltd., 38-1 Sakuragaoka 5, chome Setagaya-ku, Tokyo 156 Japan. **Tel** FAX 011 03 3439 0136.)
Ind/Abst BHA : Biblio. Hist. Art (?-?).

ISSN 0026-8739
FR
UDC 646.2
MODES ET TRAVAUX. (1929)-. Periodical. French. Twelve times a year. $53.59. Modes et Travaux, 10 11 13 rue de col Pierre Avia, 75754 Paris Cedex 15 France. **Tel** 011 33 1 46622050.

ISSN 0893-0279
US
MOMA (NEW YORK, N.Y.). (MOMA.). [MoMA]. **Main/Corp** Museum of Modern Art (New York, N.Y.). (19??)-. Periodical. English. Four times a year. comes with membership. Museum of Modern Art, 11 West 53rd Street, New York NY 10019. **Tel** (212)708-9888, FAX (212)708-9889.

ISSN 0895-8246
DD 705 US
MORFOGEN ASSOCIATES NEWS.
[Morfogen Assoc. news]. **Added/Corp** Morfogen Associates. **VFOAT** News; Morfogen Associates Newsletter. Vol. 1, No. 1 (April 1987)-. Periodical. English. Four times a year (Jan., Apr., July, Oct.). $100.00. Morfogen Associates, Elm Road, Box 324, Mt Lakes NJ 07046. **Tel** (201)334-0675, FAX (201)334-7458. **ED** Zachary P. Morfogen.
Desc: Cultural news around the world and upcoming events.

ISSN 1061-8341
US
MORNING (NEW YORK, N.Y.). (MORNING: EXPLORING THE UNDERLYING SUBTLETIES OF ART AND CULTURE.). **Added/Corp** Hunter College. (1992)-. Periodical. English. $8.00. Hunter College / Thomas Hunter Building, Room 214, 695 Park Avenue, New York NY 10021.

ISSN 0707-1248
DD 378.713/541 CN
MULTI-YEAR PLAN - HUMBER COLLEGE OF APPLIED ARTS AND TECHNOLOGY. Main/Corp Humber College of Applied Arts and Technology. **Added/Corp** Ontario Council of Regents for Colleges of Applied Arts and Technology. **VAT** Multi-Year Plan for the Ontario Council of Regents (Rexdale). (1971)-. English. One time a year. Humber College of Applied Arts and Technology / Centre for Women, PO Box 1900, Rexdale Ontario M9W 5L7 Canada.

LC NX584.6.A1 M8
KO
MUNHWA YESUL. VFOAT Korean Culture and Arts; Korean Culture & Arts. Periodical. Korean (Korean). Six times a year. W9,000 Korea; $12.00 US. Hanguk Munhwa Yesul Chinhungwon, 31 Tongsung-dong Chongno-ku, Seoul Korea. **Tel** 762-5231, FAX 742-6058, telex TKACF K29598. **ED** Ki-won Suh. Index available. **Circ:** 2,000 (ctrl).
Desc: The journal gives current information on Korean and overseas culture and arts.

LC NX8.K8 M86
KO
MUNYE CHINHUNG. VFOAT Culture & Arts Promotion. Periodical. Korean. Hanguk Munhwa Yesul Chinhungwon, 31 Tongsung-dong Chongno-ku, Seoul Korea. **Tel** 762-5231, FAX 742-6058, telex TKACF K29598.

LC NX **ISSN** 0158-9571
DD 700 AT
MUSE. ARTS AND ENTERTAINMENT IN CANBERRA. (1980)-. Periodical. English. Eleven times a year (no issue in Jan.). 20.55Aus$. Muse Subscriptions, Ainslie Avenue, Gorman House, Braddon ACT 2601 Australia. **Tel** 011 61 62 476298, FAX 011 61 62 477728. **ED** Helen Musa. **Bk Rev**, (Qty: varies). **Ad Acc. Circ:** 6,000.
Desc: Arts and entertainment magazine.

ISSN 0027-5247
HU
MUVESZETTORTENETI ERTESITO.
[Muvtort. ert.]. **Added/Corp** Magyar Regeszeti, Muveszettorteneti es Eremtani Tarsulat. Vol. 1 (1952)-. Academic Scholarly Publication. Hungarian. Four times a year. $35.00. Akademiai Kiado, Publishing House of the Hungarian Academy of Sciences, Prielle Kornelia u.

19-35, H-1117 Budapest Hungary. **Tel** 011 36 1 1811991, FAX 011 36 1 1811991, telex 22-6228 AKNYO H. **(Subscription address:** Kultura, PO Box 143, H-1300 Budapest 3 Hungary. **Tel** 011 36 1 2500194.) **ED** M. Mojzer. **Bk Rev. Circ:** 700.
Desc: History of the arts.
Ind/Abst Am. Hist. Life; ARTbibliogr. Mod. (1984-); ARTbibliogr. Curr. Titles; Avery Index Archit. Period. Suppl. Colum. Univ. (19??-199?); BHA : Biblio. Hist. Art; Numis. Lit.

ISSN 0027-7835
IT
NAPOLI NOBILISSIMA. (NAPOLI NOBILISSIMA : RIVISTA DI ARTI FIGURATIVE, ARCHEOLOGIA E URBANISTICA.). [Napoli nobl.]. Vol. 1, No. 1 (1961)-. Periodical. Italian. Six times a year. L73580. Societa l'Arte Tipografica, Via S Biagio dei Librai 39, 80138 Naples Italy. **Tel** 011 39 81 5517099.
Ind/Abst BHA : Biblio. Hist. Art.

ISSN 1185-880X
DD 700/.971/05 CN
NARC (KITCHENER). (NARC : NEW ARTIST REVIEW CO-OP.). [Narc]. **VFOAT** New Artist Review Co-op. Issue 1 (Jan. 1991)-. Periodical. English. Four times a year. $1.50. NARC, PO Box 1929, Station C, Kitchener Ontario N2G 4R4 Canada.

ISSN 8756-0925
DD 700 US
NASAA NEWS. [NASAA news]. **Added/Corp** National Assembly of State Arts Agencies (U.S.). **VAT** National Assembly of State Arts Agencies News. (Oct. 1981)-. English. Four times a year (Mar., June, Sept., Dec.). $35.00. National Assembly of State Arts Agencies, 1010 Vermont Avenue, Suite 920, Washington DC 20005. **Tel** (202)347-6352. **ED** Ellen Ehrenreich. **Bk Rev. Continues** National Assembly of State Arts Agencies (U.S.) NASAA Newsletter, 8756-0933.

LC DS35.62 .N37
TU
NASHRAH AL-IKHBARIYAH (RESEARCH CENTRE FOR ISLAMIC HISTORY, ART, AND CULTURE).
(AL-NASHRAH AL-IKHBARIYAH.). (19??)-. Academic Scholarly Publication. Arabic (English and French). Three times a year. PO Box 24, Besiktas Istanbul Turkey. **Tel** 1605988, telex 26484 ISAM TR. **Circ:** 10,000 (ctrl).
Desc: Detailed information about projects, studies, scholarly meetings, exhibition of the Research Centre for Islamic history, art and culture (IRCICA) and news on similar activities of other research institutions dealing with Islamic culture, arts, etc.

LC NX396.6 .N38 **ISSN** 1043-092X
DD 700/.79/73 US
NATIONAL DIRECTORY OF ARTS INTERNSHIPS. [Natl. dir. arts internsh.]. **Added/Corp** California Institute of the Arts. (1985/86)-. Directory. English. One time a year. $54.00. National Network Artist Placement, 935 West Avenue 37, Los Angeles CA 90065. **Tel** (213)222-4035, FAX (213)222-4035.
Desc: Expanded listings of entry opportunities for artists seeking experience in every art form produced in the United States.

LC AS36
DD 061 US
NATIONAL INSTITUTE OF ARTS AND LETTERS, AMERICAN ACADEMY OF ARTS AND LETTERS. VFOAT National Institute of Arts and Letters. Periodical. English. $12.00 libraries and booksellers, $15.00 other. National Institute of Arts and Letters, 633 West 155th Street, New York NY 10032. **Tel** (212)368-5900. **Bk Rev. Ad Acc. Circ:** 700. **Absorbed** American Academy of Arts and Letters.
Desc: Speeches and citations by prominent persons in the arts at annual induction and award ceremony; commemorative tributes to artists, writers and composers by their colleagues.

ISSN 0748-1934
DD 700 US
NC ARTS. [NC arts]. **VFOAT** North Carolina Arts. Vol. 1, No. 1 (Oct. 1984)-. Periodical. English. Irregular. Free. North Carolina Arts Council, Department of Cultural Resources, Raleigh NC 27601-2807. **Tel** (919)733-2111. **ED** Deborah McGill. **Circ:** 33,000 (ctrl).
Desc: Examines issues that shape the arts across the state and report the work of the NC Arts Council.

ISSN 0028-2383
NE
UDC 65.012.6
NEERLANDIA. [Neerlandia]. (1898)-. Periodical. Dutch. Five times a year (Jan., May, July, Sep., Dec.). $47.96. Algemeen Nederlands Verbond, Jan Van Nassaustraat 109, 2596 BS The Hauge Netherlands. **Tel** 001 31 70 3245514, FAX 001 31 70 3246186.

The Arts

LC WMLC L 83/2709 **ISSN** 0077-7862
GW
NEUSSER JAHRBUCH. Added/Corp
Clemens-Sels-Museum. **VFOAT** Neusser Jahrbuch fur Kunst, Kulturgeschichte und Heimatkunde. (19??)-. German. One time a year.
Ind/Abst BHA : Biblio. Hist. Art.

ISSN 0277-6138
US
NEW ARTS REVIEW. (19??)-. Periodical. English. Six times a year. $3.50. Athens Avant-Garde Society, Inc., PO Box 887, Athens GA 30603. **Continues** New Arts.

LC NX503 .N48 **ISSN** 0734-0222
DD 700/.5 US
NEW CRITERION (NEW YORK, N.Y.), THE. (THE NEW CRITERION.). [New criterion]. **Added/Corp** Foundation for Cultural Review (U.S.). Vol. 1, No. 1 Sept. (1982)-. Periodical. English. Ten times a year (monthly except July and Aug.). $36.00. The New Criterion, 850 Seventh Avenue, Room 503, New York NY 10019. **Tel** (212)247-6980, FAX (212)247-3127. **ED** Hilton Kramer. Index available. cum. index. **Bk Rev,** (Qty: 50). **Ad Acc, Adv Mgr:** F. Stern. **Circ:** 6,000. available on microfilm and microfiche from University Microfilms International (UMI).
Desc: Articles on the arts, exhibitions, theater, music, dance, and original poetry.
Ind/Abst Acad. Search; Am. Humanit. Index; Annu. Bibliogr. Engl. Lang. Lit.; Art Index; ARTbibliogr. Mod.; BHA : Biblio. Hist. Art; Curr. Cit.; EP Collect.; Homework Help.; INFO-SOUTH Abstr.; Mag. Search; MasterFile FullTEXT 1000; MasterFile FullTEXT 350; MasterFile FullTEXT 650; MasterFile FullTEXT (July 1993-); MLA Int. Bibl. Books Artic. Mod. Lang. Lit.; OCLC; Telebase.

ISSN 0028-4580
UK
NEW DEPARTURES. No. 1 (Summer 1959)-. Periodical. English. Irregular. $30.00. New Departures, Piedmont Bisley Shroud, Gloucestershire GL6 7BU United Kingdom. **Tel** 011 44 1452 813424. **ED** Michael Horovitz. **Bk Rev. Ad Acc. Circ:** 10,000. **Continues** Departure.
Desc: International anthologies bringing all the arts together, special accents on experimental and performance work and criticism, reviews and diverse visuals.

LC NX1 .N48 **ISSN** 0028-6575
DD 700/.5 US
CCC
NEW RENAISSANCE, THE. [New Renaiss.]. Vol.1 (1968)-. English. Two times a year. $19.50 US; $21.00 Canada; $23.00 other. New Renaissance, 9 Heath Road, Arlington MA 02174. **Tel** (617)646-0118. **ED** Louise T. Reynolds & Patricia Michaud. Index available (Bound in third issue of each volume). **Bk Rev,** (Qty: 2-4). **Circ:** 11,500.
Desc: An international magazine of ideas and opinions, emphasizing literature and the arts. Offers lead articles on current events, fiction, and poetry including bilingual poetry presentations, artwork, essays, reviews, commentary and graphics.
Ind/Abst Abstr. Engl. Stud.; Am. Humanit. Index; Index Am. Period. Verse.

ISSN 0149-1040
US
SUSPENDED
NEW YORK LITERARY FORUM. See Literature.

CN
NEWEST REVIEW, THE. See Literary and Political Reviews.

LC NX1 .N5 **ISSN** 0160-3736
DD 700/.5
NEWORLD. Added/Corp Inner City Cultural Center, Los Angeles. Vol. 1 (Fall 1974)-. Periodical. English. Four times a year. $5.00. Inner City Cultural Center, 1308 South New Hampshire Avenue, Los Angeles CA 90006.

US
CEASED
NEWS - AFFILIATE ARTISTS. Main/Corp Affiliate Artists, Inc. (1979)-(19??)-. Periodical. English. Affiliate Artists Inc, 155 West 68th Street, New York NY 10023. **Tel** (212)874-6021.
Ind/Abst Music Artic. Guide (?-?).

ISSN 0957-9044
UK
DD 700.941
NEWS - NATIONAL CAMPAIGN FOR THE ARTS. (NEWS). [News - Natl. Campaign Arts]. (1986)-. English. Four times a year.
Ind/Abst Museum Abstr.

ISSN 0891-1827
US
DD 708
NEWS - NATIONAL MUSEUM OF WOMEN IN THE ARTS (U.S.). See Women's Interests.

ISSN 0715-3341
CN
DD 700/.097124/4
NEWS WAVE. [News wave]. **VAT** Newswave Vol. 1, No. 1 (Mar. 3, 1980)-. Periodical. English. Twelve times a year. News Wave, PO Box 4497, Regina Saskatchewan S4P 3W7 Canada.

ISSN 0316-8409
CN
DD 700/.6/2701
NEWSLETTER - ASSOCIATION FOR NATIVE DEVELOPMENT IN THE PERFORMING AND VISUAL ARTS. Main/Corp Association for Native Development in the Performing and Visual Arts. Vol. 1 (June 1974)-. Newsletter. English. Six times a year. Free. The Bugle, 27 Carlton Street/Suite 208, Toronto Ontario M5B 1L2 Canada. **Tel** (416)977-2512. **ED** Daniel David Moses. **Bk Rev. Ad Acc. Circ:** 2,500.
Desc: To support and promote native arts and artists.

ISSN 1032-9617
AT
DD 706.94
NEWSLETTER - NATIONAL ASSOCIATION FOR THE VISUAL ARTS. [Newsl. - Natl. Assoc. Visual Arts]. **VFOAT** NAVA. (1988)-. Periodical. English. Four times a year (Mar., June, Sept., Dec.). 27.00Aus$. National Association for Visual Arts, PO Box 60, Potts Pint NSW 2011 Australia. **Tel** 011 61 2 3681900, FAX 011 61 2 3586909. **ED** Barbara Allen. **Ad Acc. Circ:** 3,000. **Continues** Visual Arts Newsletter (Sydney), 1030-326X.
Desc: Articles, staff, organization, arts and industry news.

LC NX8.J3 N54a
JA
NIHON DAIGAKU GEIJUTSUGAKUBU KIYO. Main/Corp Nihon Daigaku. Geijutsu Gakubu. No. 6 (1976)-. Periodical. Multiple languages (Japanese and English). Nihon Daigaku Geijutsugakubu, 2-42 Asahi-gaoka Nerima-ku, Tokyo Japan. **Continues** Nihon Daigaku Geijutsugakubu Gakujutsu Kenkyu.

LC NX584.A1 N5a
JA
NIHON DAIGAKU GEIJUTSUGAKUBU KIYO: SOSAKUHEN. Main/Corp Nihon Daigaku. Geijutsu Gakubu. No. 3 (1978)-. Periodical. Japanese. Nihon Daigaku Geijutsugakubu, 2-42 Asahi-gaoka Nerima-ku, Tokyo Japan.

LC NX28.J3 N515
JA
NIHON GEIJUTSUIN YORAN. Main/Corp Nihon Geijutsuin. Japanese. Nihon Geijutsuin, 1-30 Ueno Koen Taito-ku, Tokyo 110 Japan.

LC DG975.F85 N65 **ISSN** 0029-1080
DD 945/.39 IT
NONCELLO, IL. See History-History of Europe.

ISSN 1188-1321
CN
DD 700/.9715/54
NORD OUEST (SAINT-BASILE). (LE NORD OUEST.). [Nord ouest]. (Jan. 1992)-. Periodical. French. Twelve times a year. 2.95Can$. Les Editions Lavigne, C.P. 373, Saint-Basile New Brunswick, E0L 1H0 Canada.

ISSN 1148-5841
FR
UDC 008(442.7)
NOROIT ARRAS. See Literature.

ISSN 0824-3484
CN
DD 700/.9712
NORTHERN MOSIAC (LLOYDMINSTER). (NORTHERN MOSAIC.). Vol. 1 (Mar. 1981)-. Periodical. English. Four times a year. 5.00Can$ individuals, 7.00Can$ institutions. Thunder Bay Multicultural Association, 17 North Court Street, Thunder Bay Ontario P7A 4T4 Canada. **Tel** (807)345-0551. **ED** John Potestio. **Bk Rev. Ad Acc. Pub. Size:** Tabloid. **Circ:** 2,000.

ISSN 0894-3362
US
DD 700
NORTHERN REVIEW, THE. [North. rev.]. Vol. 1, No. 1 (Spring 1987)-. Periodical. English. Two times a year. $8.00 North America; $15.00 other. University of Wisconsin / Stevens Point Press, Academic Achievement Center, Room 018 LRC, Stevens Point WI 54481. **Tel** (715)346-3528. **ED** Richard Behm. Index available. **Bk Rev. Ad Acc.**
Desc: A general interest journal of essays, articles, interviews, reviews, poetry, fiction, and art.
Ind/Abst Am. Humanit. Index; Can. Index; Ethnoarts Index.

CN
Pr Rev.
NORTHERN REVIEW (WHITEHORSE). (THE NORTHERN REVIEW.). [North. rev.]. **Added/Corp** Northern Review Society. No. 1, (Summer 1988)-. English. Two times a year. 28.81Can$. Yukon College Northern Review, PO Box 2799, Whitehorse Yukon Y1A 5K4 Canada. **Tel** (403)668-8735, FAX (403)668-8828. **ED** Aron Senkpiel, Ken Coates and Judith Kleinfeld. Index available. cum. index (After #10 iss.). **Bk Rev,** (Qty: 30). **Ad Acc, Adv Mgr:** A. Graham. **Circ:** 500. available on microfiche from Micromedia Limited.
Desc: Multidisciplinary journal of the arts and social sciences of the North.

ISSN 0886-7151
US
DD 974
NOTICIAS DEL PUERTO DE MONTEREY. Added/Corp Monterey History and Art Association (Monterey, Calif.). Vol. 1 (Mar. 1957)-. Periodical. English. Four times a year (Mar., June, Sept., Dec.). $10.00. Monterey History & Art Association, 5 Custom House Plaza, Monterey CA 93940. **Tel** (408)372-2608.

LC NX7 .N68
PO
NOVA. Portuguese (Spanish). $80.00 single issue. Av 1 Duque de Loule 70-3O 1, Lisbon Portugal.

LC NX7 .B8
DD 700/.982/11 AG
NUESTRA CIUDAD. Periodical. Spanish. Twelve times a year. $5.000 single issue. Secretaria de Cultura, Avda de Mayo 525, 4 Piso, Buenos Aires Argentina. **Continues** Guia de Cultura.

LC PQ7074.5 .N84 **ISSN** 0898-1140
DD 860.8/098/05 US
CEASED
NUEZ (NEW YORK, N.Y.), LA. See Literature.

LC NX583.A1 N87
DD 700/.951 CH
NUNG TSUN WEN I. VFOAT Nong Cun Wen Yi. Chinese. NT$0.30. Hsin Hua Shu Tien / Chi-Nan, Chi-Nan Shih, People's Republic of China.

LC NX180.S6 O27
RU
OBSHCHIE PROBLEMY KULTURY I KULTURNOGO STROITELSTVA: NAUCHNYI REFERATIVNYI SBORNIK. Added/Corp Informtsentr po Problemam Kultury i Iskusstva (Soviet Union). (19??)-. Periodical. Russian. Three times a year. Gosudarstvennaia Biblioteka, Informatsionnyi Tsentr, Imeni V. I. Lenina, Prospekt Kalinina 3, 121019 Moscow Russia.

LC NX **ISSN** 0472-4682
DD 700 JA
OCHANOMIZU JOSHI DAIGAKU JIMBUN KAGAKU KIYO. Main/Corp Ochanomizu Joshi Daigaku, Tokyo. **Added/Corp** Ochanomizu Joshi Daigaku, Tokyo Jimbun Kagaku Kiyo. **VFOAT** Ochanomizu University Studies in Arts and Culture; Studies in Arts and Culture; Jimbun Kagaku Kiyo. (1952)-. Periodical. Japanese (English; table of contents in English). Two times a year.
Ind/Abst Am. Hist. Life (1955-1969).

LC NX1 .O27 **ISSN** 0162-2870
DD 700/.5 US
CCC
OCTOBER (CAMBRIDGE, MASS.). (OCTOBER.). [October]. **Added/Corp** Institute for Architecture and Urban Studies. (Spring 1976)-. Periodical. English. Four times a year. $95.00. Massachusetts Institute of Technology (MIT) Press, 55 Hayward Street, Cambridge MA 02142. **Tel** (617)253-2889, (617)625-8481, FAX (617)258-6779. **ED** Rosalind Kraus, Annette Michelson, Joan Copjec, Yve-Alain Bois, Benjamin H.D. Buchloh, Hal Foster, Denis Hollier, and John Rajchman. **Ad Acc. Circ:** 1,400. available on microfilm and microfiche from University Microfilms International (UMI). Documents available from The Genuine Article.
Desc: Critical attention on the contemporary arts and their various contexts of interpretation.
Ind/Abst Art Archaeol. Tech. Abstr.; Art Index; ARTbibliogr. Mod. (1981-); Am. Humanit. Index; Citation Index [Full Cov.]; BHA : Biblio. Hist. Art (1981-); Curr. Cit.; Curr. Contents Arts Humanit.; Film Lit. Index; Libr. Lit.; Res. Alert [Full Cov.].

ISSN 0029-862X
SZ
UDC 7
OEIL LAUSANNE, L'. [Oeil Lausanne]. (1955)-. Periodical. French. Ten times a year. $199.90. L'Oeil, Chemin du Closel 5, CP 350, 1020 Renens Switzerland. **Tel** 011 41 21 6350427, FAX 011 41 21 6359646.
Ind/Abst Art Index; ARTbibliogr. Curr. Titles; Repere (1979-).

ISSN 1181-9405
CN
DD 700/.9714/605
OEIL NU. (L'OEIL NU : BULLETIN DU REGROUPEMENT DES ARTISTES DES CANTONS DE L'EST.). [Oeil nu]. **Added/Corp** Regroupement des Artistes des Cantons de l'Est. **VFOAT** Bulletin du Regroupement des Artistes des Cantons de l'Est. 2nd Series, Vol. 1, No 9 (Oct. 1990)-. Bulletin. French. Three times a year. Limited free distribution. Regroupement des Artistes des Cantons de l'Est, 906 Ouest rue King, Sherbrooke Quebec J1R 1S2 Canada. **Continues** Le Bulletin du RACE., 1180-1891.

The Arts

LC NX24.O3 O28 ISSN 0731-3284
DD 353.97710085 US
OHIO ARTS COUNCIL BIENNIAL REPORT. [Ohio Arts Counc. bienn. rep.]. **Main/Corp** Ohio Arts Council. (19??)-. English. Every 2 years. Free on request. Ohio Arts Council, 727 East Main Street, Columbus OH 43205. **Tel** (614)466-2613. *Continues Ohio Arts Council. Annual Report.*

ISSN 0030-1248
US
OHIOANA QUARTERLY. See Literature.

ISSN 1068-8625
DD 781 US
●**ON THE TRACKS.** See Music.

BE
OPENBAAR KUNSTBEZIT IN VLAANDEREN. (19??)-. Consumer Publication. Dutch (English, French and German). Four times a year. $25.38. Openbaar Kunstbezit in Vlaanderen, Kasteelstraat 97, B-8700 Tielt Belgium. **Tel** 011 32 51 424299, FAX 011 32 51 408478. **ED** Rudy Vercruysse. Index available. **Bk Rev. Ad Acc.**
Desc: A presentation of arts and architecture in Belgium.

IT
OPERE D'ARTE CONTEMPORANEA : CATALOGHI E LISTINI. (19??)-. Italian. Irregular. L238440. Finarte Casa d'Arte, Piazzetta Bossi 4, 20121 Milan Italy. **Tel** 011 39 2 877041.

LC NX2 .O6 ISSN 0048-2056
FR
OPUS INTERNATIONAL. [Opus int.]. No. 1 (April 1967)-. Periodical. French (English). Six times a year. $65.61. Opus International SARL, 57 Quai des Grands Augustins, F 75006 Paris France. **Tel** 011 33 1 43290950. **ED** J.L. Chalumeau, Gioxanni Joppolo, G.G. Lemaire, G. Gassiot-Talabot. **Bk Rev. Ad Acc. Circ:** 20,000. available on microfilm from University Microfilms International (UMI).
Ind/Abst ARTbibliogr. Mod.; BHA : Biblio. Hist. Art.

LC NX24.O7 O73a
DD 706/.2795 US
OREGON ARTS COMMISSION: ANNUAL REPORT. Main/Corp Oregon Arts Commission. **Added/Corp** Oregon Arts Commission. Annual Report. (19??)-. English. One time a year. Oregon Arts Commission, 316 Oregon Building, 494 State Street, Salem OR 97301.

ISSN 0474-8158
GW
OSNABRUECKER MITTEILUNGEN. Added/Corp Verein fuer Geschichte und Landeskunde, Osnabrueck. Verein fuer Geschichte und Landeskunde, Osnabrueck. Mitteilungen. (1848)-. Periodical. German.
Ind/Abst BHA : Biblio. Hist. Art.

LC WMLC L 83/2 ISSN 0078-6845
GW
OSTBAIRISCHE GRENZMARKEN. (OSTBAIRISCHE GRENZMARKEN; PASSAUER JAHRBUCH FUER GESCHICHTE, KUNST UND VOLKSKUNDE.) [Ostbair. Grenzmarken]. **Added/Corp** Verein fuer Ostbairische Heimatforschung, Passau. Institut fuer Ostbairische Heimatforschung. **VFOAT** Passauer Jahrbuch fuer Geschichte, Kunst und Volkskunde. (1957)-. German. One time a year. Verein fuer Ostbairische Heimatforschung, Schustergasse 19 21, F 94032 Passau F R Germany. **Tel** 011 49 851 509640. *Supersedes* Ostbairischen Grenzmarken.
Ind/Abst BHA : Biblio. Hist. Art.

ISSN 0819-7288
DD 820.8003 AT
OTIS RUSH. [Otis rush]. (1987)-. Periodical. English. Irregular (1 or 2 per year). $60.00 for 4 issues. SA Publishing Ventures, Box 21, No Adelaide SA, 5006 Australia. **Tel** 11 61 08 2117505, FAX 011 61 08 2117323. **ED** Ken Bolton. **Bk Rev**, (Qty: varies). **Ad Acc. Circ:** 500.
Desc: Covers new writing, new art, reviews and criticism.

ISSN 1069-2215
DD 810 US
Pr Rev.
OWEN WISTER REVIEW. See College and School Publications.

ISSN 1037-1311
DD 700.994 AT
OZ ARTS MAGAZINE. [Oz arts mag.]. (1991)-. Periodical. English. Four times a year. 34.53Aus$. Oz Arts Magazine, Private Mail Bag 5, Wentworth Falls, New South Wales, 2782 Australia. **Tel** 11 61 47 574001, FAX 11 61 47 573797. **ED** Carolyn Skinner. **Bk Rev. Ad Acc. Circ:** 30,000.

LC NX6 .P35
RU
PAMIATNIKI KULTURY. NOVYE OTKRYTIIA. Added/Corp Nauchnyi Sovet po Istorii Mirovoi Kultury (Akademiia Nauk SSSR). **VFOAT** Monuments of Culture New Discoveries. (1974)-. Russian. Irregular. Izdatelstvo Nauka St. Petersburg, Mendeleevskaia Liniia 1, 199034 St. Petersburg, B-34 Russia. **Tel** 011 7 812 2182612.

LC NX556.A1 P34
RU
PAMIATNIKI OTECHESTVA : ALMANAKH VSEROSSIISKOGO OBSHCHESTVA OKHRANY PAMIATNIKOV ISTORII I KULTURY. Added/Corp Vserossiiskoe Obshchestvo Okhrany Pamiatnikov Istorii i Kultury. (1980)-. Periodical. Russian. One time a year. Pamyatniki Otechestva, 103009 Tverskoi bul. 16, 103009 Moscow Russia. **Tel** 7 095 2915584, FAX 7 095 2912424.

II
PANJAB UNIVERSITY RESEARCH BULLETIN. ARTS. Added/Corp Panjab University. **VFOAT** Research Bulletin. Arts; Arts. Vol. 1 (1970)-. Bulletin. English (Hindi and Panjabi). Two times a year. *Continues* Research Bulletin. Arts, 0970-5252.
Ind/Abst MLA Int. Bibl. Books Artic. Mod. Lang. Lit.

LC NX6 .P37
RU
PANORAMA ISKUSSTV. (1977)-. Periodical. Russian. Izdatelstvo Sovetskii Khudozhnik, Ulitsa Cherniakhovskoga 4a, 12319 Moscow Russia.

GR
CEASED
PANTHEON. (19??)-(19??). Greek, Modern. Lambrakis Press SA, 3 Christou Lada, 102 37 Athens Greece. **Tel** 011 30 1 3237283, 011 30 1 3230221. Documents available from The Genuine Article.
Ind/Abst Art Index; ARTbibliogr. Mod.; Arts Humanit. Citation Index (19??-19??) [Full Cov.]; Res. Alert [Full Cov.].

ISSN 0892-3809
DD 051 US
PAPER (NEW YORK, N.Y.). See General Interest-General Interest-North America.

ISSN 0031-1650
IT
PARAGONE. (PARAGONE. ARTE.). [Paragone]. Vol. 1, No. 1 (June 1950)-. Periodical. Italian. Six times a year. Price varies. Licosa Spa, PO Box 552, 50125 Florence Italy. **Tel** 011 39 55 645415. Documents available from The Genuine Article.
Desc: Offers confrontation between works of figurative art, ancient or modern, and the literary arts, in all their manifestations and in all ages. Includes criticism, poetry and fiction.
Ind/Abst Art Index; ARTbibliogr. Mod. (1984-); ARTbibliogr. Curr. Titles; Arts Humanit. Citation Index (19??-19??) [Full Cov.]; Avery Index Archit. Period. Suppl. Colum. Univ. (19??-199?); BHA : Biblio. Hist. Art; Curr. Contents Arts Humanit.; Res. Alert [Full Cov.]; Romant. Move.

LC PN80 .P37 ISSN 0264-8334
DD 700/.1 UK
CCC
PARAGRAPH (MODERN CRITICAL THEORY GROUP). See Literature.

LC NX4 .P36 ISSN 0391-7622
IT
PARMA NELL'ARTE. [Parma arte]. (1969)-. Periodical. Italian. 6.000. Via Cavestro, Parma 14 Italy.
Ind/Abst BHA : Biblio. Hist. Art.

AU
PARNASS. Vol. 1 (Sept./Oct. 1981)-. Periodical. German. Six times a year. Morawa & Company, Wollzeile 11, Postfach 159, 1011 Vienna Austria. **Tel** 011 43 1 51562404.

FR
PAYS DE DINAN, LE. Added/Corp Entente Culturelle du Pays de Dinan. (1981)-. French. One time a year.
Ind/Abst BHA : Biblio. Hist. Art.

ISSN 0776-3689
BE
UDC 908
PAYS GAUMAIS, LE. [Pays gaumais]. (1940)-. Periodical. French. Four times a year.
Ind/Abst BHA : Biblio. Hist. Art.

LC NX7 .P48 ISSN 0031-6652
NQ
PEZ Y LA SERPIENTE, EL. No. 1 (1961)-. Periodical. Spanish. Four times a year. C$41.00. El Pez y la Serpiente, Apartado Postal 192, Managua, Nicaragua. **Tel** FAX 011 505 2 43569, telex 2051-375-2051. **ED** Pablo A. Cuadra. **Bk Rev. Circ:** 1,000.

Desc: Art, history, poetry, and anthropology from the intellectuals in Central America.
Ind/Abst Hisp. Am. Period. Index, HAPI (19??-).

US
PFA NEWSLETTER. See Photography.

ISSN 0711-7515
DD 700/.9711/33 CN
PHAT : PRESENTATION HOUSE ARTS TABLOID. Added/Corp Presentation House. **VFOAT** Presentation House Arts Tabloid; PHAT : Presentatiion House Arts Tabloid. **VAT** Presentation House Arts Tabloid (June 1, 1981). Vol. 1, No. 3 (June 1, 1981)-. Periodical. English. Twelve times a year. 15.00Can$ Canada; $11.00 US. Presentation House, 333 Chesterfield Avenue North, Vancouver British Columbia V7M 3G9 Canada. **Tel** (604)986-1351. **Ad Acc. Circ:** 500 (ctrl). *Continues* Presentation House Arts Tabloid, 0711-7507.
Desc: Summary of theatrical and arts exhibitions being offered at Presentation House.

ISSN 0110-4993
NZ
PILGRIMS. (19??)-. Periodical. English. Three times a year. $24.00. Pilgrims South Press, PO Box 5101, Dunedin New Zealand.

ISSN 1122-1305
IT
PIMPA MILANO. (PIMPA.). (1987)-. Periodical. Italian. Twelve times a year. L24530. Panini, Viale Corassori 24, 41100 Modena Italy. **Tel** 011 39 59 343572.

ISSN 0048-4288
UK
CODEN y
PLANET. Added/Corp Welsh Arts Council. No. 1 (Aug./Sept. 1970)-. Periodical. English. Six times a year (Feb., Apr., June, Aug., Oct., Dec.). $30.00. Freepost, PO Box 44, Aberystwyth Dyfed United Kingdom. **Tel** 011 44 970 611255, FAX 011 44 970 623311. **ED** John Barnie. Index available. **Bk Rev**, (Qty: 60). **Ad Acc Mgr:** Tia Jones, **Tel** 011 44 9790 911996. **Circ:** 1,400.
Desc: Arts, current affairs, and literature from wealthy international aspects.
Ind/Abst Abstr. Engl. Stud.; Annu. Bibliogr. Engl. Lang. Lit.

LC NX1 .P57 ISSN 0048-4474
DD 700/.9/04 US
PLOUGHSHARES. See Literature.

LC NX7 .P6 ISSN 0185-4925
DD 700/.5 MX
CEASED
PLURAL. (PLURAL : REVISTA CULTURAL DE EXCELSIOR). [Plural]. **Added/Corp** Universidad Nacional Autonoma de Mexico. (1971)-(Dec. 1994). Periodical. Spanish. Excelsior Cia Editorial Scl, Paseo Reforma 10, Subscripciones, Mexico 1 df Mexico. **Tel** 011 52 5 7054441, 011 52 5 5669360, FAX 011 52 5 5465218. **Ad Acc. Circ:** 14,000.
Desc: Poetry, stories, essays, art reproduction, interviews, bibliographic commentary, music, literature, society and history.
Ind/Abst Hisp. Am. Period. Index, HAPI; MLA Int. Bibl. Books Artic. Mod. Lang. Lit.

BE
CEASED
PLUS-MOINS-ZERO. REVUE D'ART COMTEMPORAIN. (19??)-No. 84 (1993). French. (monthly except July/Aug.). Plus Moins Zero, 11 Avenue de la Claireau, 1200 Brussels Belgium. **Tel** 011 32 2 7724847. **ED** Rona Stephaine.

LC NX571.P6 P63 ISSN 0208-7243
DD 700/.5 PL
POLISH ART STUDIES. [Pol. art stud.]. **Added/Corp** Instytut Sztuki (Polska Akademia Nauk). (1979)-. Monographic series. English (French). Irregular. Price varies per volume. Polska Akademia Nauk, Instytut Sztuki / Polish Academy of Sciences, Institute of Fine Arts, Ul. Dluga 26/28, 00-950 Warsaw Poland. **Tel** 011 48 22 313271, FAX 011 48 22 313149. (**Subscription address:** Ars Polona-Ruch, PO Box 1001, Krakowskie Przedmiescie 7, 00-068 Warsaw Poland. **Tel** 011 48 22 261201.)
Ind/Abst Am. Hist. Life (1987-); ARTbibliogr. Mod. (1984-); Avery Index Archit. Period. Suppl. Colum. Univ. (19??-199?); BHA : Biblio. Hist. Art.

ISSN 0892-5941
DD 470 US
POMPEIIANA NEWSLETTER. See Linguistics.

The Arts

PRAIRIE ARTS. [Prairie arts]. Vol. 1, No. 1 (Sept./Oct. 1982)-. Periodical. English. Six times a year. $12.00 US; $15.00 other. Leopard's Head Publishing, PO Box 232, Saskatoon Sask S7K 3K4.
ISSN 0821-4891 — CN
DD 700/.97124

PRECIS ANALYTIQUE DES TRAVAUX DE L'ACADEMIE DES SCIENCES, BELLES-LETTRES ET ARTS DE ROUEN. See Humanities.
FR

PRENSA LITERARIA, LA. (197?)-. Periodical. Spanish. One time a week. cum. index. *Absorbed* Prensa Literaria Centroamericana. **Ind/Abst** Am. Hist. Life (1964-1966).
LC NX
DD 700
NQ

●**PRESENTING. Added/Corp** National Endowment for the Arts. **VFOAT** Application Guidelines for Fiscal Year ... . (1996)-. Government Publication. English. Irregular. National Endowment for the Arts, 1100 Pennsylvania Avenue Northwest, Washington DC 20506. **Tel** (202)682-5400, (202)682-5435. *Formed by the union of* Presenting and Commissioning *and* Presenting & Commissioning. Commissioning.
LC NX700
DD 700.79
US

PRESENTING AND COMMISSIONING. Added/Corp National Endowment for the Arts. **VFOAT** Presenting & Commissioning. (1993)-(1995). English. National Endowment for the Arts, 1100 Pennsylvania Avenue Northwest, Washington DC 20506. **Tel** (202)682-5400, (202)682-5435. *Continues* Inter-Arts. *Merged with* Presenting & Commissioning. Commissioning *to form* Presenting.
LC NX735 .P74
DD 700.79
US
TITLE CHANGE

PROBLEMI NA IZKUSTVOTO. Added/Corp Institut za Izkustvoznanie (Bulgarska Akademiia na Naukite). Vol. 1 (1969)-. Periodical. Bulgarian (summaries and/or abstracts in English, French, German and Russian; table of contents in French and Russian). Four times a year. DM138.00. In-T Za Izkustvoznanie Pri Ban, Sofia Bulgaria. **(Subscription address:** Kubon & Sagner, ABT Zeitschriftendienst, D 80328 Munich Germany. **Tel** 011 49 89 54218130.)
Ind/Abst ARTbibliogr. Mod.; ARTbibliogr. Curr. Titles; BHA : Biblio. Hist. Art.
LC NX6 .P75
DD 700/.5
BU

●**PROCEEDINGS OF THE AMERICAN ACADEMY OF ARTS AND LETTERS.**
Main/Corp American Academy of Arts and Letters (1993-). 2nd Ser., No. 44 (1993)-. Proceedings. English. One time a year (Aug.). $15.00. American Academy and Institute of Arts and Letters, 633 West 155th Street, New York NY 10032. **Tel** (212)368-5900, FAX (212)491-4615. **ED** Kathy Talalay. **Circ:** 500 (ctrl). *Continues* American Academy and Institute of Arts and Letters. Proceedings of the American Academy and Institute of Arts and Letters, 0145-8493.
Desc: Speeches and citations given at annual induction and award ceremony and commemorative tributes to members, written by their associates.
US

PROCEEDINGS - STATEN ISLAND INSTITUTE OF ARTS AND SCIENCES. See Science and Technology.
ISSN 0039-0240 — US
DD 505
CODEN PSIAAR
SUSPENDED

PRODUCTION NOTES. (19??)-. English. Five times a year (July, Oct., Dec., Feb., May). $125.00. Exhibitor Relations Co., Inc., 116 North Robertson Boulevard, Suite 606, Los Angeles CA 90048. **Tel** (310)657-2005, FAX (310)657-7283.
US

PROFILE SURVEY - ASSOCIATION OF COLLEGE, UNIVERSITY AND COMMUNITY ART ADMINISTRATORS. (PROFILE SURVEY.). **Main/Corp** Association of College, University and Community Arts Administrators. (19??)-. English. Every 2 years. Association of College, University, and Community Art Administrators, 1112 16th Street NW/#620, Washington DC 20036. **Tel** (202)833-2787. *Continues* Association of College and University Concert Managers (U.S.). Profile Survey.
LC ML27.U5 A849
DD 700/.68
ISSN 0736-9360 — US

PROGRAMME D'AIDE ... DU MINISTERE DES AFFAIRES CULTURELLES. (PROGRAMME D'AIDE ... DU MINISTERE DES AFFAIRES CULTURELLES. CENTRES D'ARTISTES EN ARTS VISUELS.). [Program. aide Minist. aff. cult.]. **Added/Corp** Quebec (Province). Ministere des Affaires Culturelles. **VFOAT** Centres d'Artistes en Arts Visuels. (1989)-. French. Gouvernement du Quebec, Ministere des Affaires Culturelles, Quebec Quebec Canada. *Continues* Soutien aux Organismes Regionaux en Arts Visuels, 1186-6411.
DD 700
ISSN 1186-642X — CN

PROGRAMME D'AIDE ... DU MINISTERE DES AFFAIRES CULTURELLES AIDE AUX ARTISTES PROFESSIONNELS. [Programme aide Minist. aff. cult., Aide artist. prof.]. **Added/Corp** Quebec (Province). Ministere des Affaires Culturelles. **VFOAT** Aide aux Artistes Professionnels. (1990-1991)-. French. *Continues* Programme d'Aide aux Artistes Professionnels., 0839-9484.
DD 700
ISSN 1187-0621 — CN

PROPOSITO : REVISTA DE LITERATURA, ARTE Y CINE, A. Vol. 1, No. 1 (March 1992)-. Periodical. Spanish. Two times a year. Revista a Proposito, Los Caobos Calle 21-M-11, Ponce Puerto Rico 00731.
PR

PROSPETTIVE D'ARTE. [Prospett. arte]. (1975)-. Periodical. Italian. Six times a year. Prospettive d'Arte, Via Gentilino 9/A, 20136 Milan Italy. **Tel** 011 39 2 8322566.
UDC 7
ISSN 0393-0165 — IT

PROTEUS (ALEXANDRIA, VA.). (PROTEUS.). [Proteus]. Vol. 1 (Fall 1972)-. Periodical. English. Irregular. $4.00. Frank Gatling, 1004 North Jefferson Street, Arlington VA 22205. **Tel** (703)534-2961.
Ind/Abst MLA Int. Bibl. Books Artic. Mod. Lang. Lit.
LC NX1 .P77
DD 700/.5
ISSN 0090-2071 — US

PROZAH. See Literature.
LC PJ5038 .P76
IS

PUBLIC CULTURE. (PUBLIC CULTURE : BULLETIN OF THE PROJECT FOR TRANSNATIONAL CULTURAL STUDIES.). [Public cult.]. **Added/Corp** University of Pennsylvania. Project for Transnational Cultural Studies. Vol. 1, No. 1 (Fall 1988)-. Bulletin. English. Three times a year. $75.00. University of Chicago Press / Journals Division, PO Box 37005, 5720 South Woodlawn, Chicago IL 60637. **Tel** (312)753-3347, FAX (312)753-0811. **ED** Carol Breckenridge. **Acid Free.**
Desc: A cultural studies publication for the critical multidisciplinary reader. Concerned with global flows and the cultural sphere, it features essays dealing with the increasing deterritorialization of cultural expressions and the rapid emergence of cosmopolitan forms, such as cinema, television, museums and tourism, in different national settings.
Ind/Abst Arts Humanit. Citation Index [Select. Cov.]; Curr. Cit.; Film Lit. Index (19??-); Int. Bibliogr. Sociol.; Soc. Plann. Policy Dev. Abstr.; Soc. Sci. Cit. Index [Full Cov.].
LC NX180.S6 P8
DD 306.4/7/05
ISSN 0899-2363 — US
CODEN PUCUE7

●**PUBLIC DOMAIN REPORT.** [Public domain rep.]. **Added/Corp** Public Domain Research Corp. Vol. 1 No. 1 (Aug. 1993)-. English. Twelve times a year. $395.00. Voicings Publications, PO Box 3102, Margate NJ 08402. **Tel** (609)822-9401.
DD 346
ISSN 1070-2555 — US

PUBLIC (TORONTO). (PUBLIC.). [Public]. **Added/Corp** Public Access Collective. No. 1, (Winter 1988)-. Periodical. English. Two times a year (Spring & Fall). 30.00Can$ individuals; 60.00Can$ institutions. Public Access Collective, 192 Spadina Avenue, Suite 307 Toronto, Ontario M5T 2C2 Canada. **Tel** (416)868-1161. **ED** Tom Taylor & Marc du Guerre. **Ad Acc. Circ:** 1,500.
Desc: Contains articles on the arts, aesthetics, humanities, and cultural theory.
DD 705
ISSN 0845-4450 — CN

PUBLICATION - AMERICAN ACADEMY AND INSTITUTE OF ARTS AND LETTERS. [Publ. - Am. Acad. Inst. Arts Lett.]. **Main/Corp** American Academy of Institute of Arts and Letters. (1977)-. Monographic series. English. Price varies per volume. American Academy and Institute of Arts and Letters, 633 West 155th Street, New York NY 10032. **Tel** (212)368-5900, FAX (212)491-4615. *Continues* Publication - American Academy of Arts and Letters, 0270-7063.
ISSN 0275-505X — US

PUBLICATIONS. See Archaeology.
BE

QUEBEC EN REVUE(S). (LE QUEBEC EN REVUE(S) : BULLETIN D'INFORMATION DE L'ASSOCIATION DES EDITEURS DE PERIODIQUES CULTURELS QUEBECOIS.). [Que. rev.]. **Added/Corp** Association des Editeurs de Periodiques Culturels Quebecois. Societe de Developpement des Periodiques Culturels Quebecois. No. 1 (Fall 1991)-. Bulletin. French. Irregular. Free. Association des Editeurs de Periodiques Culturels Quebecois, C P 786 Succursale Place d'Armes, Montreal Quebec H2Y 3J2 Canada. **Tel** (514)523-7724. *Continues* Repertoire des Periodiques Culturels Quebecois, 0710-5991.
Desc: List and editorial description of all periodicals that are members of the Association of Publishers of Cultural Periodicals in Quebec; prices and subscription conditions with subscription form.
DD 700/.25/714
ISSN 0711-5598 — CN

QUEEN STREET MAGAZINE. (June 1973)-. Periodical. English. Three times a year. $1.00 each number. Goathair Press, PO Box 251 Station B, Toronto Ontario M5T 2W1.
LC AS720.Q43 L57
DD 700/.9713/541
ISSN 0380-2000 — CN

QUEENSLAND CULTURAL ORGANISATIONS AND MAJOR NATIONAL AND INTERSTATE ORGANISATIONS. Added/Corp Queensland. Division of Cultural Activities. **VFOAT** Queensland Cultural Organisations. (August 1986)-. English. Office of the Director of Cultural Activities for Queensland, PO Box 155, North Quay Queensland 4000 Australia. *Continues* List of Cultural Organisations in Queensland and Major National and State Organisations Outside Queensland.
LC NX
DD 700
AT

RAADSADVIEZEN / RAAD VOOR DE KUNST. [Raadsadviezen - Raad Kunst]. (1992)-. Monographic series. Dutch. Irregular. Price varies per volume. SDU Openbaar Kunstbezit, Postbus 30446, 2500 GK Den Haag Netherlands. **Tel** 011 31 70 3429700. *Continues* Informatiebulletin - Raad Voor de Kunst, 0167-0913.
UDC 7(492)
ISSN 0927-9806 — NE

RACKHAM JOURNAL OF THE ARTS AND HUMANITIES, THE. [Rackham j. arts humanit.]. **Added/Corp** University of Michigan. **VFOAT** RAJAH. (Fall 1980)-Suspended (1995). Periodical. English (French, Spanish and German). One time a year. $4.00. Rajah / University of Michigan, 411 Mason Hall, Ann Arbor MI 48109. **Tel** (313)763-2351. **ED** Catharine Krieps, Thomas Mussio, Mary Lacey, John Cantu, Raymond Lee, Gina Hauskneckt and Julie Burch Mussio. Index available. cum. index. **Ad Acc.** *Continues* Rackham Literary Studies, 0360-7887.
Desc: An interdisciplinary journal that publishes nearly exclusively the work of graduate students at the University of Michigan.
Ind/Abst Abstr. Engl. Stud.; MLA Int. Bibl. Books Artic. Mod. Lang. Lit.
LC PN2 .R25
DD 700/.5
ISSN 0731-4817 — US
SUSPENDED

RADIUS (MENDOCINO, CALIF.). (RADIUS.). Vol. 1, No. 1 (Dec. 1985/Jan. 1986)-. Trade Publication. English. Six times a year. $25.00. California Assembly of Local Arts Agency, 188 The Embarcadero, San Francisco CA 94105. **Tel** (415)979-2345. **ED** Ken Larsen. **Ad Acc. Circ:** 2,000 (ctrl).
Desc: Each issue lists dozens of resources for local arts development, including funding sources, legislation and tax options, publications, conferences, and services.
ISSN 0886-7771 — US

RAGIONI CRITICHE, LE. [Ragioni crit.]. 1-1971-. Periodical. Italian. Four times a year. Ragioni Critiche, L-6000 Piazza Trento 3/D, 95128 Catania Italy. **Ind/Abst** MLA Int. Bibl. Books Artic. Mod. Lang. Lit.; Romant. Move.
LC NX4 .R33
ISSN 0391-4283 — IT

RAJANI PUBLICATIONS U.S.A., INC. (RAJANI PUBLICATIONS U.S.A., INC. : LEADING MALAYALAM LITERARY, ARTS & CULTURAL MONTHLY PUBLISHED IN THE UNITED STATES.). [Rajani Publ. U. S. A. Inc.]. **VFOAT** Rajani Publications USA Inc.; Rajani Magazine. Vol. No. 1, No. 2 (Feb. 1991)-. Periodical. Malayalam. Twelve times a year. Rajani Publications USA Inc., 13461 Lindsay Street, Philadelphia PA 19116. *Continues* Rajani (Philadelphia, Pa.), 1057-6460.
DD 051
ISSN 1057-6835 — US

RAMPIKE (TORONTO). See Literature.
DD C810/.8/0054
ISSN 0711-7647 — CN

LC DK1 .A823   **ISSN** 0033-9857
IT
RASSAGNA SOVIETICA. Added/Corp
Associazione Italiana per i Rapporti Culturali con l'Unione Sovietica. Vol.1 (1950)-. Periodical. Italian. Four times a year. *Continues* Rassegna della Stampa Sovietica.
Ind/Abst BHA : Biblio. Hist. Art.

IT
RASSEGNA DEL CENTRO DI CULTURA E STORIA AMALFITANA. Added/Corp Centro di Cultura e Storia Amalfitana. Vol. 1, No. 1 (1981); New Ser. Vol. 1, No. 1 (1991)-. Periodical. Italian. Two times a year.
Ind/Abst BHA : Biblio. Hist. Art.

ISSN 0394-4808
IT
UDC 681.81   **CODEN** 76
RASSEGNA DI STUDI E NOTIZIE. RACCOLTA DELLE STAMPE A. BERTARELLI. RACCOLTA DI ARTE APPLICATA. MUSEO DEGLI STRUMENTI MUSICALI. (1973)-. Periodical. Italian. One time a year.
Ind/Abst BHA : Biblio. Hist. Art.

ISSN 1054-5212
DD 051   US
RE: ARTS & LETTERS (1989). See Literature.

GW
REALLEXIKON ZUR DEUTSCHEN KUNSTGESCHICHTE. (19??)-. Monographic series. German. Irregular. Price varies per volume. CH Beck Verlagsbuchhandlung, D-80791 Munich Germany. **Tel** 011 49 89 381891.

LC AS36 .A48517   **ISSN** 0065-6844
DD 061/.44/61   US
RECORDS OF THE ACADEMY. [Rec. Acad.]. **Main/Corp** American Academy of Arts and Sciences. (1958/59)-. Directory. English. One time a year. $10.00. Bulletin of the American Academy of Arts and Sciences, Nortons Woods, 136 Irving Street, Cambridge MA 02138. **Tel** (617)492-8800. **ED** Anne E Fisher. **Circ:** 3,500 (ctrl).
Desc: Membership directory and report of the American Academy of Arts and Sciences.

SZ
RECUEIL DES TRAVAUX. Main/Corp Universite de Neuchatel. Faculte des Lettres. Issue No. 1-. French. Irregular. Librairie Droz SA, 11 rue Massot BP 389, CH-1211 Geneva 12 Switzerland. **Tel** 011 41 22 3466666, FAX 011 41 22 472391.
Desc: Covers all subjects of teaching in the faculty of arts.

IT
●**RECUPERO AND CONSERVAZIONE.**
(1995)-. Italian. Six times a year. L40880. Eredi de Lettera Editore, via Bazzini 17, 20131 Milan Italy. **Tel** 011 39 2 2666345.

ISSN 0883-0126
DD 051   US
CEASED
RED BASS. [Red bass]. **Added/Corp** Anti-Media. (19??)-Vol. 6 (19??). Periodical. English. Red Bass, 2425 Burgundy Street, New Orleans LA 70117. **Tel** (504)949-5256. **ED** Jay Murphy. **Bk Rev. Ad Acc. Circ:** 3,000.
Desc: An activist arts magazine that publishes poetry, fiction, reviews, interviews, essays, and visual art that furthers social change and criticism of existing society.
Ind/Abst Altern. Press Index; Am. Humanit. Index; Index Am. Period. Verse.

ISSN 0229-9437
DD 700/.97123/3   CN
RELEASE (CALGARY). (THE RELEASE.). [Release (Calgary)]. Vol. 1, Issue 1 (Fall 1979)-. Periodical. English. Irregular. $1.50 each number. Release / Canada, Suite 929/5th Avenue South West, Calgary Alberta T2P 0N8 Canada.

ISSN 1079-9265
US
●**RELIGION & THE ARTS (CHESTNUT HILL, MASS.).** (RELIGION & THE ARTS.). **VFOAT** Religion and the Arts. (1996)-. English. Three times a year. $60.00. Religion and the Arts, 25 Lawrence Street, Boston College, Chestnut Hill MA 02167. **(Subscription address:** Allen Press, PO Box 1897, Lawrence KS 66044. **Tel** (800)627-0629.)

JA
RENAISSANCE MONOGRAPHS.
Added/Corp Renaissance Institute. (1974)-. Monographic series. English. One time a year. $90.50. **(Subscription address:** Japan Publications Trading Company Ltd., PO Box 5030, Tokyo International, Tokyo 100-31 Japan. **Tel** 011 81 3 3292 3753.)
Ind/Abst MLA Int. Bibl. Books Artic. Mod. Lang. Lit.

ISSN 0393-2931
IT
UDC 902   **CODEN** 7
RENDICONTI DELLA R. ACCADEMIA DI ARCHEOLOGIA LETTERE E BELLE ARTI. (1937)-. Periodical. Italian. One time a year.
Ind/Abst BHA : Biblio. Hist. Art.

ISSN 0761-4241
FR
UDC 7
REPERES (PARIS. 1982). (REPERES CAHIERS D'ART CONTEMPORAIN.). [Reperes Paris, 1982]. **VFOAT** Reperes. Cahiers d'Art Contemporain. (1982)-. Monographic series. French. Irregular. Price varies per volume. Galerie LeLong, 13 rue de Teheran, 75008 Paris France. **Tel** 011 33 1 45631319.

ISSN 0831-9286
DD 700/.9714/13   CN
REPERTOIRE DES ORGANISMES CULTURELS DE L'ABITIBI-TEMISCAMINGUE. [Repert. org. cult. Abitibi-Temiscamingue]. Vol. 1 (1985)-. French. One time a year. 6.00Can$ each volume. Conseil de la Culture de l'Abitibi-Temiscamingue, 102 Avenue de LAC, Rouyn Quebec J9X 4N4 Canada. **Tel** (819)764-9511. **Circ:** 500 (ctrl). *Continues* Repertoire des Intervenants Culturels de l'Abitibi-Temiscamingue, 0820-6147.

ISSN 1183-6598
DD 700   CN
REPERTOIRE DES RESSOURCES CULTURELLES DES ILES-DE-LA-MADELEINE. [Repert. ressour. cult. Iles-de-la-Madeleine]. **Added/Corp** Arrimage (Corporation). (1991)-. French. Limited free distribution. Arrimage, CP 339, Cap Aux Meules, Iles-de-la-Madeline Quebec G0B 1B0 Canada.

ISSN 0712-6530
DD 700/.7/1171233   CN
REPERTOIRE (UNIVERSITY OF CALGARY. FACULTY OF FINE ARTS).
(REPERTOIRE / THE UNIVERSITY OF CALGARY, THE FACULTY OF FINE ARTS.). [Repert. - Univ. Calg., Fac. Fine Arts]. No. 1 (Summer 1980)-. English. One time a year. Free. Faculty of Fine Arts, The University of Calgary, 2500 University Drive NW, Calgary Alberta T2N 1N4 Canada.

UK
REPORT AND TRANSACTIONS - THE DEVONSHIRE ASSOCIATION FOR THE ADVANCEMENT OF SCIENCE, LITERATURE AND ART. Main/Corp
Devonshire Association for the Advancement of Science, Literature and Art. **Added/Corp** Devonshire Association for the Advancement of Science, Literature and Art. Transactions. Vol. 1 (1866)-. English. Devonshire Association, 7 Cathedral Close, Exeter EX1 1EZ United Kingdom. **Tel** 011 44 139274727. cum. index.
Ind/Abst BHA : Biblio. Hist. Art.

UK
REPORT - ARTS COUNCIL OF GREAT BRITAIN. Main/Corp Arts Council of Great Britain. 1st- 1945/46-. Periodical. English. One time a year. Arts Council of Great Britain, 105 Piccadilly, London W1V 0AU United Kingdom. **Tel** 011 44 171 6299495.

ISSN 8755-3864
DD 700   US
SUSPENDED
RESEARCH CENTER FOR THE ARTS AND HUMANITIES REVIEW. (RESEARCH CENTER FOR THE ARTS AND HUMANITIES REVIEW : RCAH REVIEW.). [Res. Cent. Arts Humanit. rev.]. **Added/Corp** University of Texas at San Antonio. Research Center for the Arts and Humanities. **VFOAT** RCAH Review; R.C.A.H. Review. Vol. 5, No. 4 (Oct. 1982)-Suspended No. 6 (1983). Periodical. English. Four times a year. $6.00. The University of Texas at San Antonio, Research Center for the Arts and Humanities, San Antonio TX 78285. *Continues* Research Center for the Arts Review.
Ind/Abst Hisp. Am. Period. Index, HAPI (19??)-.

LC NX7 .R44   **ISSN** 0034-5865
DD 705   US
RESUMEN (MIAMI). (RESUMEN.). Vol. 1 (June/July 1966)-. Periodical. Spanish. Six times a year. Free. W Alcover, 613 SW 4th Street, Miami FL 33130.

US
REVIEW : LATIN AMERICAN LITERATURE AND ARTS. Added/Corp
Americas Society. **VFOAT** Latin American Literature and Arts. Vol. 37 (Jan./June 1987)-. Periodical. English (Spanish; translations available in Spanish). Two times a year. $25.00. The Americas Society, 680 Park Avenue, New York NY 10021. **Tel** (212)249-8950, FAX (212)248-5868. **(Subscription address:** Americas Society, Subscription Department, PO Box 3000, Denville NJ 07834. **Tel** 800-783-4903, (201)627-2427, FAX (201)627-5872.) **ED** Daniel Shapiro. **Bk Rev,** (Qty: 20-25 per year). **Ad Acc, Adv Mgr:** Daniel Shapiro, **Tel** (212)249-8950. **Circ:** 5,000 (ctrl). available on an online database, CD-ROM, magnetic tape, and microfilm. *Continues* Review (Center for Inter-American Relations : 1985), 0890-5762.
Desc: Publishes selections of fiction, poetry, and nonfiction in English translation. Articles and other information on arts.
Ind/Abst Hisp. Am. Period. Index, HAPI (19??)-.

LC P87 .C584   **ISSN** 0102-0897
DD 001.51/05   BL
REVISTA COMUNICACOES E ARTES.
See Communications.

ISSN 0104-0111
BL
REVISTA DE CIENCIAS HUMANAS : REVISTA DA UFPR. See Humanities.

LC NX7 .R464
DD 700/.5   BL
REVISTA DO CENTRO DE ARTES E LETRAS / UNIVERSIDADE FEDERAL DE SANTA MARIA, CENTRO DE ARTES E LETRAS. Vol. 1, No. 1 (Jan./June 1979)-. Periodical. Portuguese. Two times a year. Centro de Artes e Letras, Universidade Federal de Santa Maria, 97.100 Santa Maria RS Brazil.

LC AP63 .R87   **ISSN** 0864-1315
DD 709/.7291   CU
REVOLUCION Y CULTURA (HAVANA, CUBA : 1984). (REVOLUCION Y CULTURA.). No. 1 (Jan. 1984)-. Periodical. Spanish. Six times a year. $35.00. Ediciones Cubanas, Obispo 527 Altos ESQ Bernaza, CP 10100 Havana Cuba. **(Subscription address:** The Center for Cuban Studies, 124 West 23nd Street, New York NY 10011. **Tel** (212)242-0559.) *Continues* Revolucion y Cultura.

ISSN 0035-1342
FR
UDC 061.22
REVUE DE L'AVRANCHIN ET DU PAYS DE GRANVILLE. [Rev. Avranchin et pays Granville]. (1886)-. Periodical. French. Four times a year. 16.00F. Societe d'Archeologie del Litterature Sciences et Arts d'Avranches Mortain et Granville, 26 rue d'Auditoire, Avranches France. **Ad Acc.** available with charts; available with illustrations. *Continues* Revue Trimestrielle de la Societe d'Archeologie de Litterature Sciences et Arts d'Avranches et de Mortain, 1158-2693.
Ind/Abst BHA : Biblio. Hist. Art.

LC NX588.75 .R48   **ISSN** 1157-4127
DD 700/.89/96   FR
REVUE NOIRE. VFOAT Noire. No. 1 (Spring 1991)-. Periodical. French (English). Four times a year (Mar., June, Sept., Dec.). $118.11. Revue Noire, 8 rue Cels, 75014 Paris France. **Tel** 011 33 1 43209200, 43202814, FAX 011 33 1 43229260. **ED** Jean Loup Pivin. Index available. **Bk Rev,** (Qty: 4). **Ad Acc. Circ:** 6,000.

ISSN 0711-1258
DD 700/.9715   CN
REZO. [Rezo]. Dec. 1, 1981-. Periodical. French. REzo, Suite #14 885 rue Main, Moncton New Brunswick E1C 1G5 Canada.

ISSN 0894-3737
DD 050   US
SUSPENDED
RICOCHET (NEW YORK, N.Y.).
(RICOCHET.). [Ricochet (N.Y. N.Y.)]. (1987)-?. Periodical. English. Four times a year. $16.00. Transfer Publications Inc, 12 West 29th Street, New York NY 10001. **Tel** (212)213-4677. **ED** William Joyce McTighe. **Circ:** 60,000.
Desc: Presents the cultural spectrum of one city with a focus on art and fashion. Covers the visual and performing arts, architecture and design, and literature.

ISSN 0035-5739
IT
RIVISTA ABRUZZESE. [Riv. abruzz.]. Vol. 1, No. 1 (1947)-. Periodical. Italian. Four times a year. L27250. Rivisat Abruzzese, via C Fagiani 37, 66034 Lanciano CH Italy. **Tel** 011 39 872 49445.
Ind/Abst BHA : Biblio. Hist. Art; MLA Int. Bibl. Books Artic. Mod. Lang. Lit.

LC NX165 .R58
DD 700/.1/9   IT
RIVISTA DI PSICOLOGIA DELL'ARTE.
Vol. 1, No. 1 (Dec. 1979)-. Periodical. Italian (English). One time a year. L13630. Lombardo Sergio, Jartrakar Via Dei Pianellari 20, 00186 Rome Italy. **Tel** 011 39 6 6867824. Index available. cum. index. **Bk Rev. Ad Acc. Circ:** 2,000.
Desc: Empirical studies in the fields of aesthetics and contemporary arts (fine arts, music, literature), psychological and psychoanalytic theories of art.
Ind/Abst Psychol. Abstr.; PsycINFO (1983-); PsycLit.

LC T1 .S64
DD 050 UK
RSA JOURNAL. **Main/Corp** Royal Society of Arts (Great Britain). **VFOAT** RSA, The Royal Society for the Encouragement of Arts, Manufactures, and Commerce Journal. **VAT** Royal Society of Arts Journal. Vol. 136, No. 5377 (Dec. 1987)-. Periodical. English. Ten times a year. $119.79. Royal Society of the Arts, 8 John Adam Street, London WC2N 6EZ United Kingdom. **Tel** 011 44 171 9305115, FAX 011 44 171 8395805, telex 892351. **ED** Sarah Curtis. Index available. **Bk Rev. Ad Acc. Circ:** 15,400. ***Continues*** *Journal of the Royal Society of Arts, 0035-9114.*
Desc: Active in five main areas: the arts, manufactures and commerce, design, education and the environment.
Ind/Abst Archit. Period. Index; Avery Index Archit. Period. Suppl. Colum. Univ. (Mar. 1990-); BHA : Biblio. Hist. Art; Br. Humanit. Index; Curr. Cit.; Geogr. Abstr. Human Geogr.; World Ceram. Abstr.

ISSN 0822-2908
DD 700/.9714/45 CN
Pr Rev.
SABORD, LE. [Sabord]. Vol. 1, No 1 (Oct./Nov. 1983)-. Periodical. French. Three times a year (Jan., Apr., and Oct.). 28.08Can$ (institutions), 20.51Can$ (individuals) Canada; 35.00Can$ other. Le Sabord, CP 1925, Trois-Rivieres G9A 5M6 Canada. **Tel** (819)375-6223, FAX (819)372-4632. Index available. **Ad Acc, Adv Mgr:** L.A. Gervais. **Circ:** 1,800 (ctrl).
Desc: Dedicated particularly to the arts of Quebec. The basic articles cover novels, poems, photos and designs.

LC AS36.C17 A3 **ISSN** 0097-8051
DD 051 US
SUSPENDED
SAN JOSE STUDIES. [San Jose stud.]. **Added/Corp** San Jose State University. Vol. 1 (Feb. 1975)-Suspended with Vol. 21 (1995). Academic Scholarly Publication. English. Three times a year. $18.00. San Jose Studies, San Jose State University, San Jose CA 95192. **Tel** (408)924-4476. **ED** Fauneil J. Rinn. Index available. **Circ:** 500. available on microfilm from University Microfilms International (UMI).
Desc: Journal of general and scholarly interest featuring critical, creative, and informative writing in the arts, businesses, humanities, social sciences, and sciences; also includes poetry and fiction.
Ind/Abst Am. Hist. Life (1975-); Am. Humanit. Index; Annu. Bibliogr. Engl. Lang. Lit.; ARTbibliogr. Mod. (1984-); Child. Lit. Abstr. (19??-); MLA Int. Bibl. Books Artic. Mod. Lang. Lit.; Romant. Move.; Soc. Plann. Policy Dev. Abstr.; Sociol. Abstr.; Women Stud. Abstr.

ISSN 1064-6116
US
SCENE ENTERTAINMENT WEEKLY. **VFOAT** Cleveland Scene; Scene. (1970)-. Periodical. English. One time a week. $25.00. Scene Entertainment Weekly, 1375 Euclid Avenue, #312, Cleveland OH 44115. **Tel** (216)241-7550, FAX (216)241-6275. **ED** Mark Holan and Judy Black. **Ad Acc.** ctrl circ.

IT
SCHIFANOIA : NOTIZIE DELL'ISTITUTO DI STUDI RINASCIMENTALI DI FERRARA. **Added/Corp** Istituto di Studi Rinascimentali (Ferrara, Italy). (1986)-. Italian (English and French). Two times a year. L54500. Panini, Viale Corassori 24, 41100 Modena Italy. **Tel** 011 39 59 343572.
Ind/Abst BHA : Biblio. Hist. Art.

LC Z5961.G4 D4 **ISSN** 0080-7176
DD 016.7 GW
SCHRIFTTUM ZUR DEUTSCHEN KUNST. **See** The Arts-Abstracting, Bibliographies and Statistics.

LC DA750 .S368 **ISSN** 1350-7508
DD 941.206 UK
Pr Rev.
•**SCOTLANDS.** (1994)-. Academic Scholarly Publication. English. Two times a year. £35.00 UK and Europe; $65.00 US; £38.00 other. Edinburgh University Press Ltd., 22 George Square, Edinburgh EH8 9LF United Kingdom. **Tel** 011 44 131 6506207, FAX 011 44 131 6620053. **ED** Christopher MacLachlan. **Ad Acc, Adv Mgr:** Kathryn MacLean. **Circ:** 500.
Desc: Articles and essays on the Scottish arts: literature, history, music, art, film and television.

LC AS222.S593 A35
DD 700/.5 IT
SEDUTA INAUGURALE - SOCIETA NAZIONALE DI SCIENZE, LETTERE E ARTI IN NAPOLI. **Main/Corp** Societa Nazionale di Scienze, Lettere e Arti in Napoli. (19??)-. Italian. Societe Nazionale di Scienze Lettere e Arti in Napoli, Via Mezzocannone 8, Naples Italy.

ISSN 0391-3910
IT
UDC 7
SEGNO PESCARA. (SEGNO.). [Segno Pescara]. (1976)-. Periodical. Italian. Thirteen times a year (10 regular issues plus 3 supplements). L40880. Umberto Sala Editore, C So Manthone 57, 65100 Pescara Italy. **Tel** 011 39 85 61712, FAX 011 39 85 4510229. **Bk Rev. Ad Acc.**

LC AS552.S44 A27
JA
SEIJO BUNGEI. **See** Societies and Clubs.

LC NX1 .S44 **ISSN** 1072-4478
DD 700/.5 US
•**SEVEN ARTS (PHILADELPHIA, PA.).** (SEVEN ARTS : THE PHILADELPHIA CULTURAL REVIEW.). **Added/Corp** WHYY (Television Station : Philadelphia, Pa.) WHYY (Radio Station : Philadelphia, Pa.). (Oct. 1993)-. Periodical. English. Twelve times a year. $15.00. Philadelphia Cultural Review, 260 South Broad Street, 3rd Floor, Philadelphia PA 19102. **Tel** (215)735-6900, FAX (215)735-7247. **ED** Virginia Moles, Judith West, Lou Harry, Sarah Jordan. **Bk Rev. Ad Acc, Adv Mgr:** BK Hedler. **Circ:** 135,000 (ctrl). ***Continues*** *Applause (Philadelphia, Pa.), 1072-480X.*
Desc: Delaware Valley's magazine for arts and culture. Contains insightful articles exploring the foremost personalities and organizations in the cultural scene, inside hints on upcoming performances and activities, and more.

ISSN 0895-8351
DD 700 US
CEASED
SHIFT (SAN FRANCISCO, CALIF.). (SHIFT.). [Shift]. No. 1 (1987)-(Jan. 1994). Periodical. English. Artspace Publications, 123 South Park, San Francisco CA 94103. **Tel** (415)626-9100, FAX (415)431-6612.

LC NX576.8.B3 S53
DD 700/.5 BG
SHILPAKALA. Vol. 1 (1978)-. Periodical. English. One time a year. TK50.00. University Press Limited / Bangladesh, 114 Motijheel Commercial Area, Post Box 88, Dacca-2 Bangladesh.

LC NX8.C45 N55
DD 700/.951/75 CC
SHUO FANG. **VFOAT** Shuofang. No. 82 (Apr. 1980)-. Periodical. Chinese. Twelve times a year. $18.85. Science Press, 16 Donghuangchenggen North Street, Beijing 100707, People's Republic of China. **Tel** 011 86 1 4019821, 011 86 1 4010642, FAX 011 86 1 4012180, 011 86 1 4019810, telex 210147. **(Subscription address:** China International Book Trading Corporation, PO Box 399, Library Service Department, Beijing 100044 People's Republic of China. **Tel** 011 86 1 8414284, FAX 011 86 1 8412023, telex 22496 CIBTC CN.) ***Continues*** *Ning-Hsia Wen I.*
Desc: Includes various literary forms describing specific customs and practices of China, especially Ning Xia.

LC N1 .S54 **ISSN** 0161-715X
DD 700/.5 US
SIBYL-CHILD. Vol. 1 (Winter 1975)-. Periodical. English. Three times a year. $16.00. Sibyl-Child, 12618 Billington Road, Silver Spring MD 20904.

US
SIGMA ALPHA IOTA : ZETA CHAPTER, INDIANAPOLIS ALUMNAE, PATRONESS CLUB. **Main/Corp** Sigma Alpha Iota. Zeta Chapter (Jordan College of Fine Arts). (1979)-. English. One time a year. Sigma Alpha Iota / Jordan College of Fine Arts, Butler University, Indianapolis IN 46208. ***Continues*** *Sigma Alpha Iota. Zeta Chapter (Jordan College of Music). Sigma Alpha Iota.*

LC NX7 .S56 **ISSN** 0035-0451
CL
SIGNOS. **Added/Corp** Cuba. Departamento de Expresion de los Pueblos. Vol. 1, No. 1 (Nov. 1969)-. Spanish. Two times a year. $33.00 the Americas; $35.00 other. Ediciones Universitarias de Valparaiso, Casilla 1415, Valparaiso Chile. **Tel** 011 56 31 252900. **Circ:** 10,000 (ctrl).
Desc: Concerned with the original forms of signs, letters, musical notes and drawings.

LC NX7 .S54
DD 700/.5 PY
SIGNOS. No. 1-. Periodical. Spanish. Estado Unidos 1120, Asuncion Paraguay.

LC NX576.8.B3 S56
BG
SILPAKALA : BAMLADESA SILPAKALA EKADEMIRA SHANMASIKA MUKHAPATRA. Vol. 1, No. 1 (Grishma 1384 May/June 1977)-. Bengali (Bengali). Two times a year.

LC NX8.E8 S5
ER
TITLE CHANGE
SIRP. **VFOAT** Kultuurileht Sirp. No. 1 (Jan. 4, 1991)-(Feb. 1994). Periodical. Estonian. **(Subscription address:** Victor Kamkin, 4956 Boiling Brook Parkway, Rockville MD 20852. **Tel** (301)881-5973.) ***Continues*** *Reede.* ***Continued by*** *Kultuurileht.*

LC NX1 .S53 **ISSN** 0747-9409
DD 700/.5 US
SITES (NEW YORK, N.Y.). (SITES.). [Sites]. (1979)-. Periodical. English. One time a year. $20.00. Lumen Books, 446 West 20th Street, New York NY 10011. **Tel** (212)989-7914. **(Subscription address:** Consortium Book Sales and Distribution, 1045 Westgate Drive, St. Paul MN 55114. **Tel** (612)221-9035, FAX (800)283-3572.) **ED** Dennis L. Dollens. **Bk Rev. Ad Acc. Circ:** 3,000.
Desc: Contains essays, interviews, new projects and gallery reviews.
Ind/Abst Avery Index Archit. Period. Suppl. Colum. Univ. (19??-199?).

LC NX542 .S57 **ISSN** 0737-7002
DD 700/.947 US
SLAVIC AND EAST EUROPEAN ARTS. [Slav. East Eur. arts]. **Added/Corp** Slavic Cultural Center (Port Jefferson, N.Y.) State University of New York at Stony Brook. Dept. of Germanic and Slavic. Vol. 1, No. 1 (Spring 1982)-. Periodical. English. Two times a year. $14.00. State University of New York / German & Slavic, Department of Germanic & Slavic Languages, Stony Brook NY 11794. **Tel** (516)632-7360.
Ind/Abst Am. Bibliogr. Slavic East Europ. Stud.; BHA : Biblio. Hist. Art.

LC NX1 .S65 **ISSN** 0093-0776
DD 705 US
SOMETHING ELSE YEARBOOK. 1974-. English. $3.95. Something Else Yearbook, PO Box 26, West Glover VT 05875.

ISSN 0706-7410
DD 700/.9714 CN
SONECRAN. No. 1-18 (Dec. 1978)-. Periodical. French. Twenty-six times a year. $17.00 (individuals), $25.00 (institutions) Canada; $30.00 other. Sonecran, CP 309 Bureau Outremont, Montreal Quebec H2V 4N1.

HK
SONIC REVIEW. (19??)-. Chinese. Twelve times a year. HK$570.00. Intl Art Prom Ctr, 907 Block A, Watsons Estate, 2-8 Watson Road, North Point Hong Kong. **Tel** 011 852 28060028, FAX 011 852 28060530.

LC N3350 .A6535 **ISSN** 0132-1501
RU
SOOBSHCHENIIA GOSUDARSTVENNOGO ERMITAZHA. **Main/Corp** Gosudarstvennyi Ermitazh (Soviet Union). **Added/Corp** Gosudarstvennyi Ermitazh (Russia). **VFOAT** Bulletin du Musee de l'Ermitage; Reports of the Hermitage Museum. (1940)-. Bulletin. Russian (summaries and/or abstracts in English; table of contents in English and French).
Ind/Abst BHA : Biblio. Hist. Art.

LC NX1 .S67 **ISSN** 0149-6824
DD 700/.5 US
SOUTH SHORE. [South shore]. (1977)-. Periodical. English. Three times a year. $5.00. Avery Color Studios, Box 95, Autrain MI 49806.

LC F207.3 .S67 **ISSN** 8756-5544
DD 975/.0025 US
SOUTHEAST CREATIVE DIRECTORY, THE. **VFOAT** South East Creative Directory. (19??)-. Directory. English. Southeast Creative Directory, 382 Golfview Road NW, Atlanta GA 30309.

LC AS30 .S658 **ISSN** 0038-4496
DD 061 US
Pr Rev.
SOUTHERN QUARTERLY, THE. [South. q.]. **Added/Corp** University of Southern Mississippi. Vol. 1 (Oct. 1962)-. Periodical. English. Four times a year. $30.00. University of South Mississippi, Box 5078 Southern Station, Hattiesburg MS 39406-5078. **Tel** (601)266-4370, FAX (601)266-5800. **ED** Stephen Flinn Young. Index available (in Summer issue). **Bk Rev,** (Qty: 50). **Ad Acc. Circ:** 1,000. available on microfilm.
Desc: Includes essays, critiques of literature, art, music, and dance in the South. Contains book reviews, performance reviews, annual bibliography of visual arts and portfolios of art.
Ind/Abst Abstr. Engl. Stud.; Am. Hist. Life (1962-); Am. Humanit. Index; Annu. Bibliogr. Engl. Lang. Lit.; Film Lit. Index; GeoRef; Index Book Rev. Humanit.; Lit. Crit. Regist.; MLA Int. Bibl. Books Artic. Mod. Lang. Lit.; Recent. Publ. Artic.; Romant. Move.; Soc. Plann. Policy Dev. Abstr.; Soc. Welf. Soc. Plan./Policy Soc. Dev.; Sociol. Abstr.; West. Hist. Q.; Writ. Am. Hist.

LC NX508.6 .S68 **ISSN** 0895-6049
DD 700/.978 US
DEAD
SOUTHWEST PROFILE. [Southwest profile]. (197?)-(Aug. 1993). Periodical. English. Ten times a year. $25.00. Whitney Publishing Company Inc, PO Box 1380, Taos NM 87571. **Tel** (505)984-1773. **(Subscription address:** Whitney Publishing Company, PO Box 1236, Sante Fe NM 87504. **Tel** (505)984-1773.) **ED** Stephen M Parks. **Bk Rev. Ad Acc. Circ:** 20,000. ***Continues*** *Santa Fe Profile.*
Desc: Views the arts in New Mexico and Arizona, and modern art that transcends the region.

The Arts

UDC 82
ISSN 0394-4816
IT
CODEN 7.72
SPAZIO UMANO, LO. (1981)-. Periodical. Multiple languages. Four times a year. L50000. Editoriale Spazio Umano, Via S Michele del Carso 6, 20144 Milan Italy. **Tel** 011 39 2 4981012.

DD 700
ISSN 0747-7775
US
SPECTRA (STONY BROOK, N.Y.). (SPECTRA.). [Spectra]. **Main/Corp** State University of New York at Stony Brook. Center for Contemporary Arts and Letters. Vol. 1 (Nov. 1974)-. Periodical. English. Four times a year.
Ind/Abst BHA : Biblio. Hist. Art.

LC GV1 .S56
DD 793.2
ISSN 0038-738X
IT
SPETTACOLO, LO. (Jan./Mar. 1951)-. Periodical. Italian (summaries and/or abstracts in English and French). Four times a year. L32700. Societa Italiana Degli Autori, Viale Della Letteratura 30, 00144 Rome Italy. **Tel** 011 39 6 5990630, FAX 011 39 6 5923351. **Ad Acc. Circ:** 2,000.
Desc: Economic and social survey of entertainments and cultural and artistic activities.
Ind/Abst Film Lit. Index (19??-); Leis., Rec., Tour. Abstr.

DD 700/.9714/281
ISSN 0225-9044
CN
SPIRALE (MONTREAL). (SPIRALE.). [Spirale (Montr.)]. (Sept. 1979)-. Periodical. French. Nine times a year. 32.01Can$. Spirale, 426 Sherbrooke East / 2nd Floor, Montreal Quebec H2L 1J6 Canada. **Tel** (514)982-3725.
Ind/Abst Can. Period. Index (19??-); Repere.

US
STATE AND REGIONAL PROGRAM/ NATIONAL ENDOWMENT FOR THE ARTS, OFFICE FOR PUBLIC PARTNERSHIP. **Added/Corp** National Endowment for the Arts. Office for Public Partnership. (1992)-. English. Every 2 years. Nancy Hanks Center, 1100 Pennsylvania Avenue NW, Washington DC 20506. **Tel** (202)682-5400.

IT
STATE OF ART. (19??)-. Italian. Three times a year. Free on request. State of Art, Cas Postale 1747, 16100 Genoa Italy. **Tel** 011 39 10 303595.

DD 384
ISSN 1190-9870
CN
●**STRATEGIE D'EXPORTATION DU CANADA, PLAN DE PROMOTION DU COMMERCE EXTERIEUR. 10, INDUSTRIES CULTURELLES.** [Strateg. export. Can. plan promot. commerc. exter., 10 Ind. cult.]. **Added/Corp** Canada. **VFOAT** Industries Culturelles. (1996)-. Government Publication. French. Irregular.
Continues Plan de Promotion du Commerce Exterieur du Canada. 4, Arts et Culture, 1200-1139.

LC NX1 .S84
DD 700
ISSN 0148-1029
US
Pr Rev.
STUDIES IN ICONOGRAPHY. [Stud. iconogr.]. Vol. 1 (1975)-. English. One time a year. $35.00. Medieval Institute Publishing, Western Michigan University, Kalamazoo MI 49008. **Tel** (616)387-8755. **ED** Anthony Gully. **Bk Rev. Circ:** 480 (ctrl) Documents available from The Genuine Article.
Desc: The journal is interdisciplinary in nature. Articles focus on problems of iconography in critical studies of art and literature. All periods are covered.
Ind/Abst Annu. Bibliogr. Engl. Lang. Lit.; ARTbibliogr. Mod.; Arts Humanit. Citation Index; Avery Index Archit. Period. Suppl. Colum. Univ. (19??-199?); BHA : Biblio. Hist. Art; Curr. Contents Arts Humanit.; Res. Alert.

LC NX501.5 .S78
DD 700/.98
ISSN 0730-9139
US
Pr Rev.
STUDIES IN LATIN AMERICAN POPULAR CULTURE. [Stud. Lat. Am. pop. cult.]. Vol. 1 (1982)-. English. One time a year (June). $55.00. University of Arizona, College of Humanities, 345 Modern Languages Building, Tucson AZ 85721-0067. **Tel** (602)621-1044, FAX (602)621-5594. **ED** Charles M. Tatum and Harold E. Hinds, Jr. **Bk Rev**, (Qty: 10). **Ad Acc. Circ:** 500 (ctrl) Documents available from The Genuine Article.
Desc: Covers Latin American popular culture; film, T.V., radio, comic books, photonovels, newspapers, etc.
Ind/Abst Acad. Abstr.; Acad. Search; Am. Hist. Life (1986-); Arts Humanit. Citation Index [Full Cov.]; Chicano Index; Curr. Contents Arts Humanit.; EP Collect.; Hisp. Am. Period. Index, HAPI; Homework Help.; Mag. Artic. Summar. Elite; Mag. Artic. Summar. Select; Mag. Artic. Summar. CD-ROM; MasterFile FullTEXT 1000; MasterFile FullTEXT 350; MasterFile FullTEXT 650; MasterFile FullTEXT (Jan. 1994-) [Full Txt.]; MLA Int. Bibl. Books Artic. Mod. Lang. Lit.; OCLC; Pub. Lib. FullTEXT; Res. Alert [Full Cov.]; Soc. Sci. Source; Telebase.

LC NX1 .S86
DD 700/.5
ISSN 0364-457X
US
STUDIO ONE. Spring 1976-. Periodical. English. Two times a year. College of St Benedict, Oden House, Box 1340, St Joseph MN 56374.

DD 700/.9714/27105
ISSN 1181-8514
CN
SUCCES (LAVAL). (SUCCES : LE MAGAZINE DES ARTS DE LAVAL). [Succes]. **Added/Corp** Laval (Quebec). Service des Arts. Vol. 1, No 1 (Oct./Nov./Dec. 1990)-. Periodical. French. Four times a year. Limited Free Distribution. Laval Service des Arts, 1395 Ouest boulevard de la Concorde, Laval Quebec H7N 5W1 Canada.

DD 700
ISSN 1187-063X
CN
SUPPORT FOR PROFESSIONAL ARTISTS. [Supp. prof. artists]. **Added/Corp** Quebec (Province). Ministere des Affaires Culturelles. **VFOAT** Programme d'Aide ... du Ministere des Affaires Culturelles, Support for Professional Artists. (1990/1991)-. English. Ministere Affaires Culturelles, 225 Grande Allee Est, Quebec Quebec G1R 5G5 Canada. *Continues* Support Program for Professional Artists., 0844-6962.

LC NX
DD 700/.5
ISSN 1188-2492
CN
SURFACES (MONTREAL). (SURFACES.). [Surfaces]. **Added/Corp** Universite de Montreal. Departement de Litterature Comparee. Vol. 1 (Dec. 1991)-. English (French). Irregular. University of Montreal / Departement de Litterature Comparee, CP 6128, Succursale A, Montreal Quebec H3C 3J7 Canada. available via Internet (gopher.umontreal.ca 7070).

DD 052
ISSN 1032-2892
AT
SYDNEY REVIEW (1988). (THE SYDNEY REVIEW.). [Syd. rev. 1988]. (1988)-. Periodical. English. Twelve times a year. 19.74Aus$. Sydney Review, 199 Crown Street, Darlinghurst NSW 2010 Australia. **Tel** 011 61 2 3312389, FAX 011 61 2 3315980. **ED** Michael Vanstone. **Bk Rev**, (Qty: 40). **Ad Acc. Circ:** 30,000.

GW
TABULATUR, DIE. Vol. 1 (1965)-. Periodical. German. Irregular. Broude Brothers Limited, 141 White Oaks Road, Williamstown MA 01267. **Tel** (413)458-8132, (800)525-8559.

FI
TAITEEN KESKUSTOIMIKUNNAN KASIKIRJOJA. (1989)-. Multiple languages. Irregular. The Arts Council of Finland, Mariankatu 5, PO Box 293, 00171 Helsinki Finland. **Tel** 011 358 0 134171, FAX 011 358 0 624313.

LC NX28.F5 T34a
FI
TAITEEN KESKUSTOIMIKUNNAN TIEDOTUSLEHTI. **Main/Corp** Finland. Taiteen Keskustoimikunta. (1984)-. Finnish (Swedish). Four times a year. Free. The Arts Council of Finland, Mariankatu 5, PO Box 293, 00171 Helsinki Finland. **Tel** 011 358 0 134171, FAX 011 358 0 624313. **ED** Eija Ristimaki. cum. index. **Bk Rev. Ad Acc. Circ:** 2,500.
Desc: Articles, reviews and news on Finnish cultural life, the arts, and on international cultural affairs.

DD 700
ISSN 1183-8728
CN
TALK B.A.C. [Talk B.A.C.]. **Added/Corp** Brampton Arts Council. **VAT** Talk Brampton Arts Council. Vol. 1, Issue 1 (Feb. 1991)-. Periodical. English. Twelve times a year. Free on request. Brampton Arts Council, 24 A Alexander Street, Brampton Ontario L6V 1H6 Canada.

CN
SUSPENDED
TALKING STICK. (19??)-Suspended (1995). Periodical. English. Four times a year. 20.00Can$ Canada; 25.00Can$ other. Circle Vision Arts Corporation, 2114 College Avenue, Regina Saskatchewan S4P 1C5 Canada. **Tel** (306)780-9242, FAX (306)780-9443. **ED** Debra Piapot. **Ad Acc. Circ:** 5,000.
Desc: Aboriginal multidisciplinary arts periodical. Dedicated to the artistic life of Canada's native peoples.

LC NX576.A3 T3573
CE
TARAKAI. 1 (August 1981)-. Periodical. Tamil (Tamil). Twelve times a year.

ISSN 0792-5891
US
TARBUT (NEW YORK, N.Y. : 1989). (TARBUT.). (Jan./April 1989)-. Newsletter. English. Four times a year. Free. Israeli Consulate in New York, Department of Cultural Affairs, 800 Second Avenue, New York NY 10017. **Tel** (212)351-5242. **ED** Eliza de Sola Mendes. **Bk Rev. Circ:** 10,000.
Desc: Covers Israeli cultural events in the USA with book reviews and special sections.

LC NX645 .T37
DD 700
LI
TARYBU LIETUVOS VISUOMENES MOKSLAI. MENOTYRA. **Added/Corp** Lietuvos TSR Mokslu Akademija. Visuomenes Mokslu Informacijos Sektorius. **VFOAT** Menotyra; Iskusstvovedenie; Obshchestvennye Nauki v Litovskoi SSR. Iskusstvovedenie. (19??)-. Lithuanian. Mintis / Idea, Z Sierakausko 15, Vilnius 2600 Lithuania. **Tel** 011 7 3702 632943.

LC NX1 .T44
DD 700/.5
ISSN 0262-4524
UK
CEASED
TEMENOS. (TEMENOS.). [Temenos]. 1 (1981)-(1993). Periodical. English. Lindisfarne Press, PO Box 778, 195 Main Street, Great Barrington MA 01230. **Tel** (413)232-4377. **ED** Kathleen Raine. **Bk Rev. Circ:** 2,000.

ISSN 1016-0809
SZ
TEMPORALE. **VFOAT** Rivista d'Arte di Cultura. Vol. 1, No. 1 (1983)-. Periodical. Italian (French and German). Four times a year.
Ind/Abst BHA : Biblio. Hist. Art.

DD 790.2/079/714
ISSN 1182-4948
CN
THEATRE, DANSE, MUSIQUE, ARTS MULTIDISCIPLINAIRES ET MULTIMEDIAS. **Added/Corp** Quebec (Province). Ministere des Affaires Culturelles. (1991)-. French. *Formed by the union of* Theatre (Quebec (Province). Ministere des Affaires Culturelles)., 0839-9492; Musique (Quebec (Province). Ministere des Affaires Culturelles)., 0839-9476 *and* Arts Multidisciplinaires., 0839-945X.

LC AS615 .N315
DD 082
ISSN 0040-5817
SA
THEORIA (PIETERMARITZBURG). *See* Humanities.

US
THICKET. **Added/Corp** Texas. University at Austin. Graduate School. Vol. 1, Issue 1 (1976)-. Periodical. English. Three times a year. $7.50. Thicket, PO Box 387, J Yearwood, Woodville TX 75979. **Tel** (713)283-2516.

ISSN 0741-5958
US
THIRD RAIL (LOS ANGELES, CALIF.). *See* Literature.

DD 810
ISSN 0275-1410
US
THREEPENNY REVIEW, THE. *See* Literature.

UDC 311.3
ISSN 0788-0278
FI
CODEN 7.0
TILASTOTIETOA TAITEESTA. **VFOAT** Facts About the Arts. (1990)-. Multiple languages. The Arts Council of Finland, Mariankatu 5, PO Box 293, 00171 Helsinki Finland. **Tel** 011 358 0 134171, FAX 011 358 0 624313.

DD 705
ISSN 0712-7391
CN
TRAFICS. [Trafics]. **VAT** Trafics Magazine. No. 1 (Winter 82)-. Periodical. French (English). Four times a year. $20.00. Trafics, CP 472 Succursale N, Montreal Quebec H2X 3N3 Canada.

ISSN 0967-3962
UK
TRAINING MATTERS. (1991)-. English.
Ind/Abst Museum Abstr.

DD 700/.9714
CN
TRAJECTOIRES. Vol. 1 (May 1979)-. Periodical. French. Irregular. $10.00 Canada; $20.00 other. Editions du Cap, 16 rue Beaufort, Dollard-Des-Ormeaux Quebec H9A 2M6 Canada.

ISSN 0742-034X
US
TRENDS (SCOTTSDALE, ARIZ.). (TRENDS.). Vol. 1, No. 1 (Nov. 1982)-. Periodical. English. Ten times a year. $18.00. Dandick Publishing Company, PO Box 8508, Scottsdale AZ 85252. **Tel** (602)948-1799. **ED** Penny Johnson. **Ad Acc.** ctrl circ.

LC AP8 .T75
DD 052
ISSN 0041-3135
II
TRIVENI (GUNTUR). (TRIVENI; JOURNAL OF INDIAN RENAISSANCE.). [Triveni]. (1928)-. Periodical. English. Four times a year. $22.00. Triveni Publishers, Masulipatam India. (Subscription address: Prints India, 11 Darya Ganj, New Delhi 110002 India. **Tel** 011 91 11 3268645, FAX 011 91 11 3275542, telex 31-61087 PRIN-IN.) *Continues* Triveni Quarterly.
Ind/Abst MLA Int. Bibl. Books Artic. Mod. Lang. Lit.

The Arts

LC WMLC 93/1299
DD 974
ISSN 0896-2022
US
TURTLE QUARTERLY. See Ethnic Interests.

ISSN 0788-5318
FI
UDC 7
CODEN 351/354
TYOPAPEREITA - TAITEEN KESKUSTOIMIKUNTA. (1990)-. Monographic series. Multiple languages. Irregular. Price varies per volume. The Arts Council of Finland, Mariankatu 5, PO Box 293, 00171 Helsinki Finland. **Tel** 011 358 0 134171, FAX 011 358 0 624313.

CN
UJ ELET. (19??)-. Periodical. Hungarian. UJ ELET, PO Box 31, Mt Brydges Ontario N0L 1W0 Canada.
Desc: Reviews for theatre, music, art, and cinema.

ISSN 1183-1839
DD 700/.9713/585
CN
UMBRELLA (BELLEVILLE). (THE UMBRELLA.). [Umbrella]. **Added/Corp** Quinte Arts Council. Vol. 1, No. 1 (Mar./Apr. 1991)-. Periodical. English. Four times a year. Limited free distribution. Quinte Arts Council, PO Box 225, Belleville Ontario K8N 5A2 Canada.

LC NX578.6.V55 V35
VM
VAN HOA NGHE THUAT. Added/Corp Nong Quoc Chan. (19??)-. Periodical. Vietnamese. Twelve times a year. $10.00. Xunhasaba Exports and Imports, 7 Nguyen Thi Minh Khai Str, Dit 1 Ho Chi Minh City Vietnam. **Tel** 011 84 8 294893, telex 278 XUNHASABA.

ISSN 1185-0310
DD 700/.9711/3305
CN
CEASED
VANCOUVER STEP (1991). (THE VANCOUVER STEP.). [Vanc. step]. **VFOAT** Step Magazine. (Nov. 15, 1990/Jan. 15, 1991)-(June 1993). Periodical. English. Sidestep Media, 1265 West 7th, Avenue, Vancouver British Columbia V6H 1B7 Canada.
Continues Step (Vancouver, B.C.), 1185-0302.

TU
VARLIK. See Literature.

SP
VEINTIUNO. (19??)-. Periodical. Spanish. Four times a year. $35.52. Fundacion Canovas del Castillo, Marques de la Ensenada 16, 28004 Madrid Spain. **Tel** 011 34 1 319 5908.

ISSN 1196-6793
DD 700/.9711/2805
TITLE CHANGE
VICTORIA BOULEVARD (1993). (VICTORIA BOULEVARD.). [Vic. blvd.]. Vol. 1, Issue 1 (Oct./Nov. 1993)-Vol. 1, Issue 3 (Feb./Mar. 1994). Periodical. English. Bay Publishing Ltd., PO Box 5667, Station B, Victoria British Columbia V8R 6S4 Canada. **Tel** (604)598-7171. **Formed by the union of** Easy Living's Victoria, 1189-7120 **and** Boulevard (Victoria, B.C. : 1992), 1196-6785. **Continued by** Boulevard (Victoria, B.C. : 1994), 1196-6807.

LC NX456 .V48
BL
VIDA DAS ARTES. Vol. 1 (June 1975)-. Portuguese. $50.00. Industrias Graficas Libra, rua Visconde de Carandai 19, Jardim Botanico, Rio de Janeiro Brazil.

LC NX2 .V53
DD 700/.5
ISSN 0042-5435
CN
VIE DES ARTS. [Vie arts]. (Jan./Feb. 1956)-. Periodical. French (French). Four times a year. 19.20Can$. Vie Des Arts, CP70 Succursale Longueuil, Longueuil Quebec J4K 4Y3 Canada. **Tel** (514)923-9381, FAX (514)923-0864, telex 055-62172. **Bk Rev. Ad Acc.** ctrl circ.
Desc: Arts in Canada and all over the world, in the past, the present and in the future. Main exhibits all over the world.
Ind/Abst ARTbibliogr. Mod.; ARTbibliogr. Curr. Titles; BHA : Biblio. Hist. Art; Can. Period. Index; Repere (1983-).

LC BL1 .V57
DD 291.3/05
ISSN 0169-5606
NE
CCC
CEASED
VISIBLE RELIGION / INSTITUTE OF RELIGIOUS INCONOGRAPHY, STATE UNIVERSITY GRONINGEN. See Religions and Theology.

ISSN 0042-692X
PH
VISION. Added/Corp Manila. University of Santo Tomas. College of Architecture and Fine Arts. (19??)-. Periodical. English. Two times a year. $19.00. University of Santo Tomas / Espana Street, College of Architecture and Fine Arts, Sampaloc Manila Phillipines. **Tel** 011 63 2 7313101.

LC NX512.2 .V58
DD 700/.89
ISSN 0736-7686
US
VISIONS (KINGSTON, N.Y.). (VISIONS.). [Visions]. Vol. 1, No. 1 (Spring 1982)-. Periodical. English. Four times a year. Kingston Artists Group Inc, Road 1 Box 485 Route 28A, West Hurley NY 12491-9801.

US
TITLE CHANGE
VISUAL ARTS. ORGANIZATIONS / NATIONAL ENDOWMENT FOR THE ARTS. Added/Corp National Endowment for the Arts. (1989)-(1993). English. National Endowment for the Arts, 1100 Pennsylvania Avenue Northwest, Washington DC 20506. **Tel** (202)682-5400, (202)682-5435. **Continues** Visual Arts. Grants to Organizations. **Continued by** Visual Arts. Visual Artists Organizations, Visual Artists Public Projects, Special Projects.

ISSN 0042-7683
BE
VLAANDEREN. (1952)-. Periodical. Dutch (English, French and German). Six times a year. $37.31. Christelijk Vlaams Kunstenaarsverbond, Lindenlaan 18, B-8700 Tielt Belgium. **Tel** 011 32 51 402122. **ED** R. Declerck. Index available. **Bk Rev. Ad Acc. Circ:** 6,650.
Ind/Abst BHA : Biblio. Hist. Art (19??-).

ISSN 1188-5017
CN
VOIR (QUEBEC). (VOIR.). [Voir]. **VFOAT** Voir Quebec. Vol. 1, No 1 (Mar. 1992)-. Periodical. French. One time a week. Limited free distribution. Communications Voir, 4126 Saint Denis Street, Suite 302 Montreal, PQ H2W 2M5 Canada. **Tel** (514)848-0777, FAX (514)848-0360.

LC NX456 .V66
DD 700/.971/05
ISSN 1198-5682
CN
VOLUTE (MONTREAL). (VOLUTE : CONCORDIA FINE ARTS MAGAZINE.). [Volute]. **Added/Corp** Concordia University. Concordia Art History Undergraduate Student Association. Concordia University. Art History Dept. (1991)-. Periodical. English (summaries and/or abstracts in French). One time a year (Sept.). 18.00Can$ (institutions); 13.00Can$ (individuals). Concordia University/Art History Department, 1455 de Maisonneuve West, Montral Que H3G 1M8 Canada. **Tel** (514)848-7424, FAX (514)848-8327. **ED** Martin Kapustianyk.

LC BH41 .V592
RU
VOPROSY ISTORII I TEORII ESTETIKI.
Added/Corp Moskovskii Gosudarstvennyi Universitet Im. M. V. Lomonosova. Kafedra Estetiki. Vol. 10 (1977)-. Periodical. Russian. Izdatelstvo Moskovskogo Universiteta, K-9 Ulitsa Gertsena 5/7, 103009 Moscow Russia. **Tel** (301)881-5973. **Continues** Voprosy Teorii i Istorii Estetiki.

SP
VOZ DE LA CULTURA, LA. (19??)-. Spanish. Twelve times a year. 3.000ptas Spain; 6.000ptas North America; 4.500ptas other. Editorial el Paisaje / Aranguren, La Penorra 8-2, 48850 Aranguren Spain. **Tel** (94) 639 07 74. **ED** Agustin Garcia Alonso. **Bk Rev. Ad Acc. Circ:** 2,000 (ctrl).

SP
WAD-AL-HAYARA. Added/Corp Guadalajara, Spain (Province). Diputacion Provincial. Institucion Provincial de Cultura "Marques de Santillana". No. 1 (1974)-. Periodical. Spanish. One time a year.
Ind/Abst BHA : Biblio. Hist. Art.

LC NX8.C45 W35
DD 709
CC
WAI KUO WEN I SSU CHAO / CHUNG-KUO SHE HUI KO HSUEH YUAN CHING PAO YEN CHIU SO PIEN I. Vol. 1 (May 1982)-. Periodical. Chinese. RMBY1.20. Hsin Hua Shu Tien / Shang-Hai Fa Hsing So, Shanghai, People's Republic of China.

LC N11 .W23
DD 706.273
ISSN 1045-4349
US
WALPOLE SOCIETY NOTE BOOK, THE.
[Walpole Soc. note book]. **Main/Corp** Walpole Society (U.S.). (1936)-. English. Irregular.
Ind/Abst BHA : Biblio. Hist. Art.

LC PN56.W3 W34
DD 700
ISSN 1046-6967
US
Pr Rev.
WAR, LITERATURE, AND THE ARTS. See Literature.

ISSN 0315-2871
DD 700/.971
CN
WARPATH (OTTAWA). (WARPATH.). Vol. 1 (1974)-. Periodical. English. Four times a year. $3.00. Warpath Magazine, PO Box 2501 Station D, Ottawa Ontario K1P 5Y3 Canada.

ISSN 0163-903X
US
WASHINGTON REVIEW. Added/Corp Friends of the Washington Review of the Arts. Vol. 3, No. 1 (Spring 1977)-. Periodical. English. Six times a year. $15.00. Washington Review, PO Box 50132, Washington DC 20091-0132. **Tel** (202)638-0515. **ED** Mary Swift. **Bk Rev,** (Qty: 9). **Ad Acc. Circ:** 2,000. available on microfilm. **Continues** Washington Review of the Arts.
Desc: Journal of arts and literature including poetry, fiction, book and art reviews, essays on the arts, and original art work. Emphasis on arts of Washington D.C., with one special issue on a single topic each year.
Ind/Abst Am. Humanit. Index.

US
WCA NATIONAL UPDATE. Main/Corp Women's Caucus for Art. **VFOAT** National Update. Vol. 1, No. 2 (Summer 1990)-. Periodical. English. Four times a year (Seasonally). $75.00 one-year membership. Womens Caucus of Art, Moore College of Art, 1920 Race Street, Philadelphia PA 19103-1178. **Tel** (215)845-0922, FAX (215)854-0915. **ED** Jackie MacLelland (phone: (214)222-2177). **Bk Rev. Ad Acc. Circ:** 4,000. **Continues** Women's Caucus for Art. National Update, 1052-4959.
Desc: Multi-disciplinary organization for women in the visual arts.

LC NX8.C45 W434
DD 700/.5
CC
WEN HUI YUEH KAN = ENCOUNTER MONTHLY. VFOAT Wen Hui; Encounter Monthly; Wenhui Yuekan. No. 1 (June 1980)-. Periodical. Chinese. Twelve times a year. RMBY8.2. Chung-Kuo Kuo Chi Tu Shu Mao I Tsung Kung SSU, PO Box 2820, Beijing, People's Republic of China. **ED** Mei Duo. **Bk Rev. Ad Acc. Circ:** 150,000 (ctrl).
Desc: Comprehensive articles especially on reportage, biography, fiction, poetry, prose, music, dance, film and fine arts, etc.

LC NX8.C45 .W447
DD 700/.1/005
CC
WEN I LI LUN YEN CHIU. VFOAT Wenyi Yanjiu; Wen I Li Yen Chiu Chi Kan; Theoretical Studies of Literature and Art. Periodical. Chinese. Four times a year. $4.86. Science Press, 16 Donghuangchenggen North Street, Beijing 100707, People's Republic of China. **Tel** 011 86 1 4019821, 011 86 1 4010642, FAX 011 86 1 4012180, 011 86 1 4019810, telex 210147.

ISSN 0083-8039
GW
WERKE DER KUNST IN HEIDELBERG : EINE SCHRIFTENREIHE IM AUFTRAG DER JOSEPHINE UND EDVARD VON PORTHEIM-STIFTUNG FUR WISSENSCHAFT UND KUNST. Added/Corp Josephine und Edvard von Portheim-Stiftung fur Wissenschaft und Kunst. (1964)-. Monographic series. German. Irregular. Price varies per volume. Springer-Verlag GmbH & Company KG, Heidelberger Platz 3, D-14197 Berlin Germany. **Tel** 011 49 30 8207223, FAX 011 49 30 8214091, telex 183 319 SPBLN D. (**Subscription address:** Springer-Verlag New York Inc. / North America, PO Box 19386 Books, Newark NJ 07195. **Tel** (201)348-4033.)

ISSN 0508-6191
US
WESTWIND (LOS ANGELES, CALIF.).
(WESTWIND.). **Added/Corp** California. University. University at Los Angeles. Associated Students. Communications Board. California. University. University at Los Angeles. Associated Students. Board of Comminications. (Spring 1957)-. Periodical. English. Three times a year. $10.00. University of California Los Angeles / Kerckhoff, 112 Kerckhoff Hall, Los Angeles CA 90024. **Tel** (310)825-2787. **ED** Erik Bucy. **Ad Acc. Circ:** 3,000. **Supersedes** Chimera.
Desc: Features the poetry, prose, music, fine art, photography and graphic designs of UCLA students. Interviews and essays on the arts are also published.

DD 700/.25/73 2 19
US
WHOLE ARTS DIRECTORY. (1987)-. Directory. English. Midmarch Arts Press, 300 Riverside Drive, New York NY 10025. **Tel** (212)666-6990. **ED** Cynthia Navavetta. Index available. cum. index.

ISSN 1055-1719
DD 051
US
WINDOW ON THE ARTS, LITERATURE, AND SOCIETY, THE. [Window arts lit. soc.]. **VFOAT** Window. Vol. 1, No. 1 (Jan. 1991)-. Periodical. English. Twelve times a year. $12.00. The Window, PO Box 300128, Minneapolis MN 55403-0128.

LC CB3 .W64
KO
WOLGAN TONGSO MUNHWA. = MONTHLY EAST AND WEST. See History.

LC HQ1591 .W64 ISSN 0957-4042
UK
CCC

WOMEN. See Women's Interests.

LC N6512 .W587 ISSN 0149-7081
DD 704/.042/0973 US
TITLE CHANGE

WOMEN ARTISTS NEWS. [Women artists news]. **Added/Corp** Midmarch Associates. (197?)-(1994). Periodical. English. Midmarch Arts Press, 300 Riverside Drive, New York NY 10025. **Tel** (212)666-6990. **Bk Rev**, (Qty: 40-50). **Ad Acc. Circ:** 5,000. ***Continues*** *Women Artists Newsletter, 0361-9117.* ***Continued by*** *Women Artists News Book Review.*
Desc: Focus on women in the arts; exhibition reviews, book reviews, opportunities, general interest and information relevant to arts: academic, museums, etc.
Ind/Abst Art Index; ARTbibliogr. Mod.; ARTbibliogr. Curr. Titles; BHA : Biblio. Hist. Art; RILA, Int. Rep. Lit. Art.

LC NX180.F4 W6585
DD 700/.1/03 US

WOMEN'S MUSIC PLUS. See Women's Interests.

LC NX1 .W64 ISSN 0266-6286
DD 700/.5 UK
CCC

WORD & IMAGE (LONDON. 1985). (WORD & IMAGE.). [Word image]. **VFOAT** Word and Image. Vol. 1, No. 1 (Jan./March 1985)-. Periodical. English. Four times a year. $260.00. Taylor & Francis Ltd. / UK, Rankine Road, Basingstoke, Hampshire RG24 8PR United Kingdom. **Tel** 011 44 1256 840366, FAX 011 44 1256 479438, telex 858540. **(Subscription address:** Taylor & Francis Inc., 1900 Frost Road, Suite 101, Bristol PA 19007-1598. **Tel** (215)785-5800, (800)821-8312, FAX (215)785-5515.) **ED** John Dixon Hunt. available on microfilm from University Microfilms International (UMI). Documents available from The Genuine Article.
Desc: Recent interdisciplinary work has established the study of the encounters, dialogues and mutual collaboration (or hostility) between verbal and visual languages as one of the prime new areas of humanistic criticism. Provides a forum for articles that focus exclusively on this special study of the relations between words and images.
Ind/Abst Am. Hist. Life (1985-); Annu. Bibliogr. Engl. Lang. Lit.; ARTbibliogr. Mod.; Arts Humanit. Citation Index [Full Cov.]; BHA : Biblio. Hist. Art; Curr. Contents Arts Humanit.; MLA Int. Bibl. Books Artic. Mod. Lang. Lit.; Res. Alert [Full Cov.]; RILA, Int. Rep. Lit. Art (1985-1989); Romant. Move.; Soc. Plann. Policy Dev. Abstr.

LC NX ISSN 0886-2060
DD 700 US

WORKS AND DAYS. [Works days]. No. 1 (1979)-. Periodical. English. Two times a year. $25.00. Works & Days, Indiana University of Pennsylvania, English Department, 110B Leonard Hall, Indiana PA 15705. **Tel** (412)357-6486, FAX (412)357-3056. **ED** David B. Downing. Index available. cum. index. **Bk Rev**, (Qty: 4). **Ad Acc. Circ:** 400 (ctrl).
Desc: Publishes essays and reviews which explore the relations between the arts and their socio-historical and socio-cultural contents.
Ind/Abst Am. Humanit. Index; MLA Int. Bibl. Books Artic. Mod. Lang. Lit.

UK

WRITERS' & ARTISTS' YEARBOOK. **VFOAT** Writers' and Artists' Yearbook. (1984)-. English. One time a year. £9.99. Adam and Charles Black, 35 Bedford Row, London WC1R 4JH United Kingdom. **Tel** 011 44 171 2420946, FAX 011 44 171 4805014, telex 32524 ACBLAC. ***Continues*** *International Writers' & Artists' Yearbook.*
Desc: Handbook and directory for writers, artists, publishers, photographers, designers and composers.

ISSN 0824-2178
DD C810/.8/0054 CN

X-IT. See Literature.

LC NX584.6.A1 Y43
KO

YECHONG PAEKSO. Korean. Hanguk Yesul Munhwa Tanche Chong, Yonhaphoe 110 Insa-dong, Chongno-ku, Seoul Korea. ctrl circ.

LC NX584.6.A1 Y484
KO

YESUL KWA PIPYONG. 1st Vol. (1984). Periodical. Korean. Four times a year. W3,000 each issue. Soul Sinmunsa, 31 1-ka Taepyong-no, Chung-ku, Seoul South Korea.

LC NX584.6.A1 Y49
KO

YESUL PYONGNON (HANGUK YESUL PYONGNONGA HYOBUIHOE). (YESUL PYONGNON.). **VFOAT** Art Review. 1st Vol. (Dec. 1981)-. Periodical. Korean. W2.000. Hanguk Yesul Pyongnonga Hyobuihoe, 1-133 Tonhsung-dong Korea.

LC N3 .Z55 ISSN 0044-2135
DD 705 GW
CCC

ZEITSCHRIFT DES DEUTSCHER VEREINS FUER KUNSTWISSENSCHAFT (1963). (ZEITSCHRIFT DES DEUTSCHEN VEREINS FUER KUNSTWISSENSCHAFT.). [Z. Dtsch. Ver. Kunstwiss.]. **Added/Corp** Deutscher Verein fur Kunstwissenschaft. Vol. 17 (1963)-. Periodical. German. Three times a year. DM40.00. Deutscher Verlag fur Kunstwissenschaft, Lindenstr 76, W-1000 Berlin 61 Germany. **Tel** 30/2591 3865, telex 183723. Index available. **Circ:** 1,500. Documents available from The Genuine Article. ***Continues*** *Zeitschrift fur Kunstwissenschaft, 0721-958X.*
Desc: Official publication of the West German Society of the Arts; contributions to German arts.
Ind/Abst Art Index; ARTbibliogr. Mod.; Arts Humanit. Citation Index [Full Cov.]; Avery Index Archit. Period. Suppl. Colum. Univ. (19??-199?); BHA : Biblio. Hist. Art; Res. Alert [Full Cov.]; Romant. Move.; Soc. Sci. Cit. Index [Select. Cov.].

ABSTRACTING, BIBLIOGRAPHIES AND STATISTICS

LC DR91 .B86 ISSN 0205-3799
DD 949.7703 BU

ABSTRACTS OF BULGARIAN SCIENTIFIC LITERATURE. CULTURE.
Added/Corp Bulgarska Akademiia na Naukite. T Sentur za Nauchna Informatsiia. **VFOAT** Culture. Vol. 32 No. 1 (1989)-. Periodical. English. Four times a year. Bulgarian Academy of Sciences, 1 rue 15 Noemvri, 1040 Sofia Bulgaria. **Tel** 011 359 2 803127. ***Continues*** *Bulletin d'Analyses de la Litterature Scientifique Bulgare. Culture, 0204-983X.*

LC AM141
DD 016.7516 US

ABSTRACTS OF PAPERS PRESENTED AT THE ... ANNUAL MEETING ... .
Main/Corp American Institute for Conservation of Historic and Artistic Works. **VFOAT** AIC Abstracts. (19??)-. English. One time a year. AIC and FAIC, 1400 16th Street NW/Suite 340, Washington DC 20036. **Tel** (202)232-6636. Index available. cum. index. ctrl circ.

ISSN 0065-6968
US
NLM N 40 A512

AMERICAN ART DIRECTORY. [Am. art dir.]. **Added/Corp** R.R. Bowker Company. American Federation of Arts. Vol. 38 (1952)-. Directory. English. One time a year. $199.95. R.R. Bowker, A Reed Reference Publishing Company, Part of Reed International PLC, PO Box 31, 121 Chanlon Drive, New Providence NJ 07974. **Tel** (908)464-6800, (800)521-8110, FAX (908)665-6688, telex 138-755. ***Continues*** *American Art Annual.*
Desc: Access to over 7,000 art institutions across the United States and Canada, as well as overseas. Entries are indexed geographically and by institution, personnel and subject.

LC Z5935.3 .M87a NX454 ISSN 0898-7300
DD 016.7/009/04 US

ANNUAL BIBLIOGRAPHY OF MODERN ART. [Annu. bib. mod. art]. **Main/Corp** Museum of Modern Art (New York, N.Y.). Library. **VFOAT** Bibliography of Modern Art. (1986)-. Bibliography. English. One time a year (Nov.). Price varies. GK Hall & Co., 100 Front Street, Riverside NJ 08075. **Tel** (800)257-5755 ext. 2223.

ISSN 0157-4043
AT

ARLIS/ANZ NEWS. [Arlis, ANZ news]. **Added/Corp** Art Libraries Society/Australia and New Zealand. **VFOAT** A.R.L.I.S./A.N.Z. News; Art Libraries Society/Australia and New Zealand News; Arlis Anz News. No. 1 (1977)-. Periodical. English. Four times a year (June, Sept., Nov., Dec.). $20.00 (individuals), $40.00 (institutions). Arlis/Anz Treasurer, 511 Station Street, North Carlton Victoria 3054 Australia. **Tel** 011 61 3 685 0264. **ED** Barbara Cameron. **Bk Rev. Circ:** 130 (ctrl).
Desc: Articles on Australian art libraries, documentations of arts, books, and events.
Ind/Abst Aust. Educ. Index (199?-); Aust. Libr. Inf. Sci. Abstr. (1989-).

LC AM1 .A7 ISSN 0004-2994
DD 069.05 US
CODEN AATABU

ART AND ARCHAEOLOGY TECHNICAL ABSTRACTS. [Art archaeol. tech. abstr.]. **Added/Corp** New York University. Institute of Fine Arts. International Institute for Conservation of Historic and Artistic Works. Vol. 6 (1966)-. Abstracting/Indexing Service. English. Two times a year. $125.00. Getty Conservation Institute, 4503 Glencoe Avenue, Marina del Rey CA 90292. **Tel** (310)822-2299, FAX (310)821-9409. **ED** Jessica Brown. Index available in last issue of volume--attached. **Circ:** 4,500 (ctrl). ***Continues*** *I.I.C. Abstracts.*
Desc: A collection of summaries of world literature concerning methods of conservation, documentation, preservation, and technical analysis of works of fine and applied art and archaeology. Materials considered include - stone, glass, lacquer, amber, metals, textiles, paper, wood, paintings, ceramics, hair, feathers, bone, ivory, and synthetic materials.
Ind/Abst AESIS Q.; Ethnoarts Index; For. Prod. Abstr.; Museum Abstr.; Text. Technol. Dig.; World Surf. Coat. Abstr.

LC Z5937 .A78 ISSN 0004-3222
DD 016.7 US
NLM Z 5937 A784
Pr Rev.

ART INDEX. [Art index]. Vol. 1 (Jan. 1929/Sept. 1932)-. Abstracting/Indexing Service. English. Four times a year (plus a permananent annual cloth-bound cumulation). $1495.00 CD-ROM; Print edition sold on the service basis. H W Wilson Company, 950 University Avenue, Bronx NY 10452. **Tel** (800)367-6770, (718)588-8400 ext. 2245, FAX (718)681-1511, telex 4990003 HWILSON. **ED** Delli Bertrun. Index available. cum. index. ctrl circ. available on CD-ROM from WILSONDISC; available on magnetic tape from WILSONTAPE; available on an online database from BRS; and WILSONLINE; available on diskette from WILSONSEARCH. Documents available from BLDSC, The UnCover Company.
Desc: Offers a single-alphabet, subject-author index of over 200 domestic and foreign periodicals, selected yearbooks, and museum bulletins.

LC N8670 .A69 ISSN 1073-6611
DD 700 US

•ART PRICE INDEX INTERNATIONAL. [Art price index int.]. **VFOAT** Art Price Index. (1993)-. English. One time a year. $175.00. Sound View Press, 170 Boston Post Road, Madison CT 06443. **Tel** (203)458-3544, (203)245-2246.

ISSN 0193-6867
US

ART REFERENCE COLLECTION. [Art ref. collect.]. (1980)-. Monographic series. English. Irregular. Price varies per volume. Greenwood Press Inc., PO Box 5007, Westport CT 06881-5007. **Tel** (203)226-3571, FAX (203)222-1502.
Desc: The series is devoted to providing indexes, bibliographies, and other reference materials for scholars, students, and librarians in the visual and the fine arts.

LC N8670 .A66
DD 707/.5 UK

ART SALES INDEX (WEYBRIDGE, SURREY : 1985). (THE ART SALES INDEX.). (1984)-. English. One time a year. $174.00. Apollo Book, 5 Schoolhouse Lane, PO Box 3839, Poughkeepsie NY 12603-4907. **Tel** (914)473-6560. **ED** Richard Hislop. **Bk Rev. Ad Acc.** available on microfilm. ***Continues*** *Annual Art Sales Index (Art Sales Index Ltd. : 1979), 0143-0688.*
Desc: Over 66,000 international auction sale results for 25,000 artists. Prices in US dollars, pounds and original currency of sale.

LC Z5937 .A793 ISSN 0307-9961
DD 016.7 UK

ARTBIBLIOGRAPHIES. CURRENT TITLES. [Artbibliogr. curr. titles]. **VFOAT** Art Bibliographies. Current Titles; Art Bibliographies -- Current Titles; ACT. Vol. 1 (Sept. 1972)-. Abstracting/Indexing Service. English. Six times a year (Feb., Apr., June, Aug., Oct., Dec.). £200.00. CLIO Press, 35 A Great Clarendon Street, Oxford OX2 6AT United Kingdom. **Tel** 011 44 1865 331350, FAX 011 44 1865 790358, telex 83130. **ED** Robert Neville.
Desc: Reproduces the table of contents for journals in art and design. Also lists table of contents for annuals, museum bulletins and other publications issued at irregular intervals.

LC Z5935 .L64 ISSN 0300-466X
DD 016.709/04 UK

ARTBIBLIOGRAPHIES MODERN. [Artbibliogr. mod.]. **VFOAT** Art Bibliographies Modern. Vol. 1 (1969)-. Abstracting/Indexing Service. English (French and German). Two times a year. Price varies. ABC Clio Inc, PO Box 1911, 130 Cremona, Santa Barbara CA 93116. **Tel** (805)968-1911, (800)422-2546, FAX (805)685-9685. **ED** Tony Sloggett. Index available. cum. index. **Circ:** 1,000. available on an online database (file no. 56) from DIALOG; available on CD-ROM (as ARTbibliographies Modern on Disc). Documents available from SWETS. ***Continues*** *LOMA; Literature on Modern Art, 0090-7235.*
Desc: Abstracts, provided for major books, dissertation, articles, and exhibition catalogues. Annotations for other material and for visual material in brief.

LC Z5939 .A83 N5300 ISSN 0294-135X
DD 016.7/074 FR

ARTRACES. BULLETIN. **VFOAT** Art Traces. Bulletin. No. 1 (Oct. 1983)-. Bulletin. French (English). Six times a year. 1 rue de Lille, F-75007 Paris France.

ISSN 1060-9202
DD 016 US
ARTS & HUMANITIES CITATION INDEX (COMPACT DISC ED.). (ARTS & HUMANITIES CITATION INDEX [COMPUTER FILE].). [Arts humanit. cit. index]. **Added/Corp** Institute for Scientific Information. **VFOAT** Arts and Humanities Citation Index. (1980/1989)-. English. Three times a year. $5330.00 US. Institute for Scientific Information, 3501 Market Street, Philadelphia PA 19104. **Tel** (215)386-0100, (800)523-1850, FAX (215)386-6362, telex 84-5305.

LC AI3 .A63 **ISSN** 0162-8445
DD 016.05 US
ARTS & HUMANITIES CITATION INDEX (PRINT ED.). (ARTS & HUMANITIES CITATION INDEX.). [Arts humanit. cit. index]. **VAT** Arts and Humanities Citation Index. (1976)-. Abstracting/Indexing Service. English. Two times a year. $5330.00 (print); $5665.00 (CD-ROM); $7275.00 (combination print and CD-ROM). Institute for Scientific Information, 3501 Market Street, Philadelphia PA 19104. **Tel** (215)386-0100, (800)523-1850, FAX (215)386-6362, telex 84-5305. **(Subscription address:** Institute for Scientific Information, PO Box 71416, Chicago IL 60694. **)** available on magnetic tape and an online database (as Arts & Humanities Search); available on CD-ROM from Institute for Scientific Information; available on an online database (File no.439) from DIALOG; and BRS.
Desc: Covers journals from the full range of arts and humanities disciplines.

LC Z5961.A35 A7 **ISSN** 1044-8640
DD 016.73 US
ARTS OF AFRICA : AN ANNOTATED BIBLIOGRAPHY, THE. [Arts Afr.]. **Added/Corp** African Studies Association. Vol. 1 (1986 and 1987)-. English. Every 2 years. $7.95. African Studies Association Press, Credit Union Building, Emory University, Atlanta GA 30322. **Tel** (404)329-6410.

LC Z999 .H334a
DD 017.3 GW
AUKTION. **Main/Corp** Hartung & Karl. Vol. 1 (1972)-. Catalog. German. Two times a year. DM50.00 Germany; $40.00 (airmail) US. Hartung & Hartung, Karolinenplatz 5A, D-80333 Munich Germany. **Tel** (089)284034. **ED** Karl Hartung and Felix Hartung. **Circ:** 4,000.
Desc: Auction catalogues containing bibliographical descriptions of valuable old books, manuscripts, autograph letters and graphic arts.

LC Z5939 .N56a N7420 **ISSN** 0360-2699
DD 016.7 US
BIBLIOGRAPHIC GUIDE TO ART AND ARCHITECTURE. **Main/Corp** New York Public Library. Art and Architecture Division. **Added/Corp** New York Public Library. Art and Architecture Division. Dictionary Catalog of the Art and Architecture Division. (1975)-. English. One time a year (Feb.). $200.00. Macmillan Publishing Company / New Jersey, 100 Front Street, Box 500, Riverside NJ 08075-7500. **Tel** (800)257-5755, (609)461-6500, FAX (609)461-7070. ***Continues*** *New York Public Library. Art and Architecture Division. Dictionary Catalog of the Art and Architecture Division. Supplement* ***and*** *Art and Architecture Book Guide.*

LC Z5931 .B47 N5300
DD 016.7 GW
CEASED
BIBLIOGRAPHIE BILDENDE KUNST. **Added/Corp** Saechsische Landesbibliothek. (19??)-(1993). German. Sachsische Landesbibliothek, Marienallee 12, Dresden 806 Germany. **Tel** 011 49 351 52677, telex 2-368. **ED** Hans-Joachim Kunz. Index available. cum. index. **Circ:** 280 (ctrl).

LC Z5937 .B5 N1.A1
DD 016.7 GW
BIBLIOGRAPHIE ZUR KUNSTGESCHICHTLICHEN LITERATUR IN OST- UND SUDOSTEUROPAISCHEN ZEITSCHRIFTEN. Vol. 1 (1974)-. Multiple languages. One time a year. DM35.00. Zentralinstitut fuer Kunstgeschichte, Meiserstrasse 10, W-8 Munich 2 Germany. ***Supersedes*** *Bibliographie zur Kuustgeschichtlichen Literatur in Slawischen Zeitschriften.*

LC Z5940 .B5 N7141 **ISSN** 0252-9556
DD 016.7 SZ
BIBLIOGRAPHIE ZUR SCHWEIZER KUNST, BIBLIOGRAPHIE ZUR DENKMALPFLEGE / BIBLIOGRAPHIE DE L'ART SUISSE, BIBLIOGRAPHIE DE LA CONSERVATION DES BIENS CULTURELS / ETH, EIDGENOESSISCHE TECHNISCHE HOCHSCHULE ZUERICH, INSTITUT FUER DENKMALPFLEGE. **Added/Corp** Eidgenoessische Technische Hochschule Zuerich. Institut fuer Denkmalpflege. **VFOAT** Bibliographie zur Denkmalpflege; Bibliographie de la Conservation des Biens Culturels; Bibliographie de l'Art Suisse, Bibliographie de la Conservation des Biens Culturels; Bibliographie de l'Art Suisse, Bibliographie de la Conservation; Biens Culturels. (1985/1986)-. German (French and Italian). One time a year. 45.00F. Institut fuer Denkmalpflege, Eth-Zentrum, CH-8092 Zurich Switzerland. **Tel** 011 41 1 6322284. Index available. **Circ:** 500. ***Continues*** *Bibliographie zur Schweizerischen Kunst und Denkmalpflege.*

LC Z5937 .B53 N7510 **ISSN** 1150-1588
DD 016.7 FR
Pr Rev.
BIBLIOGRAPHY OF THE HISTORY OF ART : BHA = BIBLIOGRAPHIE D'HISTOIRE DE L'ART. **Added/Corp** Institut de l'Information Scientifique et Technique (France) Getty Art History Information Program. Comite International d'Histoire de l'Art. Comite Francais d'Histoire de l'Art. College Art Association of America. Art Libraries Society of North America. **VFOAT** BHA; Bibliographie d'Histoire de l'Art. Vol. 1/1 (1991)-. Abstracting/Indexing Service. English (French). Four times a year. 1959.00F France; 2285.00F other. CNRS / Institut d'Information Scientifique et Technique, (Centre National de la Recherche Scientifique), 15 Quai Anatole France, 75700 Paris France. **Tel** 011 33 1 47531515, FAX 011 33 1 45517307, telex 260034. **(Subscription address:** Institut d'Information Scientifique et Technique Diffusion, 2 Allee du Parc de Brabois, 54514 Vandoeuvre Nancy France. **Tel** 011 33 83 504664, FAX 011 33 83 504666, telex 961942.**)** **ED** Michael Rinehart. Index available (published quarterly). cum. index. **Circ:** 1,000. ***Formed by the union of*** *Repertoire International de la Litterature de l'Art, 0145-5982* ***and*** *Repertoire d'Art et d'Archeologie, 0080-0953.*
Desc: BHA surveys the current literature of Western art from late antiquity (4th century A.D.) to the present, including the complete artistic production of the European and New World successors to the Greco-Roman world and those peoples and cultures related to them. Contemporary art is selectively covered to include critical and theoretical publications concerning art up to the present. Citations from publications in related disciplines, e.g., music, history, and literature, are incorporated insofar as they pertain to the study of the visual arts and material culture.

LC N NA **ISSN** 1055-6826
DD 702 720 US
BIO-BIBLIOGRAPHIES IN ART AND ARCHITECTURE. **VFOAT** Bio Bibliographies in Art and Architecture. (1991)-. Periodical. English. Greenwood Press Inc., PO Box 5007, Westport CT 06881-5007. **Tel** (203)226-3571, FAX (203)222-1502.

LC Z999 .H322A **ISSN** 0093-1047
DD 016.9173/03 US
COLLECTORS' AUCTION (BALTIMORE). (COLLECTORS' AUCTION.). **Main/Corp** Harris Auction Galleries. English. Irregular. $25.00. Harris Auction Galleries, 873-875 North Howard Street, Baltimore MD 21201. **Tel** (410)728-7040. **ED** Christopher Bready. **Circ:** 1,000 (ctrl).
Desc: Listings include 19th and 20th century photographica, rare books, fine art, graphics and Civil War material.

ISSN 0163-3155
DD 700 US
CURRENT CONTENTS. ARTS & HUMANITIES. [Curr. contents, Arts humanit.]. **Added/Corp** Institute for Scientific Information. **VFOAT** Arts & Humanities. **VAT** Current Contents. Arts and Humanities. Vol. 1, No. 1 (Jan. 1, 1979)-. Abstracting/Indexing Service. English. Twenty-six times a year. $530.00. Institute for Scientific Information, 3501 Market Street, Philadelphia PA 19104. **Tel** (215)386-0100, (800)523-1850, FAX (215)386-6362, telex 84-5305. **(Subscription address:** Institute for Scientific Information, PO Box 71416, Chicago IL 60694. **)** available on magnetic tape and an online database (as Current Contents Search); available on an online database from BRS. Documents available from The Genuine Article.
Desc: Presents the tables of contents from arts and humanities journals.
Ind/Abst Arts Humanit. Citation Index [Full Cov.]; Curr. Contents Arts Humanit.; Res. Alert [Full Cov.]; Soc. Sci. Cit. Index [Select. Cov.].

LC NX600.D3 D34 **ISSN** 0084-9537
DD 700/.9/04 US
Pr Rev.
DADA SURREALISM. [Dada surreal.]. **Added/Corp** Association for the Study of Dada and Surrealism. No. 1 (1971)-. English. One time a year. $15.00. University of Iowa Comparative Literature, 425 English Philosophy Building, Iowa City IA 52242. **Tel** (319)335-0330, FAX (319)335-2535. **ED** Ruedi Kuenzli, (319)335-0324. **Ad Acc. Circ:** 1,000.
Desc: Contains critical essays, documents, and bibliographies in the field of Dada and Surrealism in art and literature. Each issue is organized around a specific topic.
Ind/Abst Am. Humanit. Index; ARTbibliogr. Mod.; BHA : Biblio. Hist. Art; MLA Int. Bibl. Books Artic. Mod. Lang. Lit.; RILA, Int. Rep. Lit. Art; Romant. Move.

LC NK1160 .D45 **ISSN** 0953-0681
DD 016.7454 UK
DESIGN & APPLIED ARTS INDEX. **VFOAT** Design and Applied Arts Index; DAAI. Vol. 1, Pt. 1 (1987)-. English. Two times a year. $325.13. Design Documentation, Woodlands, Stonecross, Mayfield, East Sussex TN20 6EJ United Kingdom. **Tel** 011 44 1435 873763, FAX 011 44 1435 873759.
Desc: An international index to current design and design-related journals covering over 250 titles.

LC N51 .D57 **ISSN** 0897-3989
DD 707/.1/173 US
DIRECTORY OF ART AND DESIGN FACULTIES IN COLLEGES AND UNIVERSITIES, U.S. AND CANADA. [Dir. art des. fac. coll. univ. U. S. Can.]. **VAT** Directory of Art and Design Faculties in Colleges and Universities, United States and Canada. 1st Edition (1986-1988)-. Directory. English. One time a year. $55.00. College Music Society / CMS Publications, 202 West Spruce Street, Missoula MT 59802. **Tel** (406)728-2002, (800)729-0235, FAX (406)721-9419. **ED** Robby D. Gunstream. Index available. **Circ:** 500. available on labels.
Desc: Lists institutions in alphabetical order within each state or province. Lists teachers by specializations. Contains an international alphabetical listing, an index to graduate degrees in art and design, and an alphabetical listing of institutions.

LC N5310.7 .T74 **ISSN** 0893-0120
DD 709/.01/1 US
ETHNOARTS INDEX. [Ethnoarts index]. **VFOAT** EAI. Vol. 5, No. 1 (Jan./Mar. 1987)-. Abstracting/Indexing Service. English. Four times a year. $60.00. Data Arts, PO Box 30789, Seattle WA 98103. **Tel** (206)783-9580. **ED** Eugene C. Burt. cum. index (five year). **Bk Rev**, (Qty: 10-12). **Ad Acc. Circ:** 100 (ctrl). available on diskette (for microcomputers). ***Continues*** *Tribal Arts Review, 0748-0024.*
Desc: Covering recent literature on the visual arts of the indigenous peoples of Africa, Oceania, and the Americas.

LC Z119 .G869 **ISSN** 1064-9638
DD 686 US
GRAPHIC ARTS BULLETIN OF THE INSTITUTE OF PAPER SCIENCE AND TECHNOLOGY. [Graph. arts bull. Inst. Pap. Sci. Technol.]. **Added/Corp** Institute of Paper Science and Technology. **VFOAT** Graphic Arts Bulletin; GABIPST. Vol. 39, No. 1 (Jan. 1992)-. Bulletin. English. Twelve times a year. $270.00. Institute of Paper Science and Technology, 500 10th Street Northwest, Atlanta GA 30318. **Tel** (404)853-9500, FAX (404)853-9510. ***Continues*** *Graphic Arts Literature Abstracts, 0090-8207.*

LC N4390 .I52
DD 016.7/074 UK
INDEX TO ART EXHIBITION CATALOGUES ON MICROFICHE. **Added/Corp** Chadwyck-Healey Ltd. Somerset House (Teaneck, N.J.). (1976)-. English. Two times a year. £185.00 UK; $340.00 other. Chadwyck-Healey Limited, The Quorum Barnwell Road, Cambridge CB5 8SW United Kingdom. **Tel** 011 44 1223 215512, FAX 011 44 1223 215513, telex 9312102281 CH G. Index available. cum. index. available on microfiche.
Desc: Subject index to the 45,000 exhibition catalogs in the collection of the Arts Library.

LC Z5937 .C55 SUPPL N1.A1 **ISSN** 0099-0965
DD 016.7 US
INDEX TO ART PERIODICALS. SUPPLEMENT. **Main/Corp** Chicago. Art Institute. Ryerson Library. English (Multiple languages). Irregular. GK Hall & Co., 100 Front Street, Riverside NJ 08075. **Tel** (800)257-5755 ext. 2223.

UK
INTERNATIONAL DICTIONARY OF ART AND ARTISTS. (19??)-. English. $300.00. St. James Press, An Imprint of Gale Research Inc., PO Box 33477, Detroit MI 48232-5477. **Tel** (800)345-0392. **ED** James Vinson.
Desc: Biography, bibliography and criticism on five-hundred masterworks and five-hundred leading artists of Western art from the thirteenth century to the present are found in this important two-volume reference source.

LC Z5937 .N56 N7425.55
DD 016.7 RU
IZOBRAZITEL'NOE ISKUSSTVO; BIBLIOGRAFICHESKAIA INFORMATSIIA. **Added/Corp** Soviet Union. Ministerstvo Kultury. Informtsentr po Problemam Kultury i Iskusstva (Soviet Union) Vsesoiuznaia Gosudarstvennaia Biblioteka Inostrannoi Literatury (Soviet Union). **VFOAT** Izobrazitel'noe Iskusstvo. (Jan./Feb. 1979)-. Russian.

Three times a year. $30.30. **(Subscription address:** Victor Kamkin, 4956 Boiling Brook Parkway, Rockville MD 20852. **Tel** (301)881-5973.**) Continues** Novosti Nauchnoi Literatury: Izobrazitelnoe Iskusstvo.

LC HA1911 .A3 NX565.A1
DD 314
TU
KULTUR ISTATISTIKLERI. VFOAT Cultural Statistics. English (Turkish). One time a year.

LC N1 .N6347 **ISSN** 0891-3498
DD 750 US
NEWS FROM RILA. [News RILA]. **Added/Corp** J. Paul Getty Center for the History of Art and the Humanities. **VFOAT** News from R.I.L.A. Issue No. 1 (Feb. 1983)-. Abstracting/Indexing Service. English. One time a year. free on request. RILA, J. Paul Getty Trust, Clark Art Institute, Williamstown MA 01267. **Tel** (413)458-8260, FAX (413)458-8503. cum. index. **Circ**: 1,000.
Desc: An abstracting and indexing service for current publications in the history of art. It covers Western art from Late Antiquity (4th century) to the present.

LC PN2304 .P47 **ISSN** 0838-4452
DD 791/.0971/021 CN
CEASED
PERFORMING ARTS. Added/Corp Statistics Canada. Education, Culture and Tourism Division. **VFOAT** Arts d'Interpretation; Culture Statistics; Statistiques de la Culture. (198?)-(1993). English (French). Statistics Canada Publications Sales and Services, R.H. Coats Building 6th floor, Ottawa Ontario K1A 0T6 Canada. **Tel** (613)951-5078, (800)267-6677, FAX (613)951-1584, telex 053-3585.
Desc: Presents data on Canada's professional, non-profit performing arts companies.

LC Z
DD 011 US
PERFORMING ARTS BIOGRAPHY MASTER INDEX. 2nd Ed. (1981)-. Abstracting/Indexing Service. English. Irregular. $175.00. Gale Research Inc., 835 Penobscot Building, 645 Griswold Street, Detroit MI 48226. **Tel** (800)877-GALE, (313)961-2242, FAX (313)961-6083, (800)414-5043, telex TWX 810-221-7086. **ED** Barbara McNeil and Miranda Herbert. **Continues** Theatre, Film, and Television Biographies Master Index.
Desc: Contains more than 260,000 citations to biographical articles and sketches appearing in 100 sources.

LC N2 .R37 **ISSN** 0035-077X
DD 705 BE
REVUE BELGE D'ARCHEOLOGIE ET D'HISTOIRE DE L'ART. [Rev. belge archeol. hist. art]. **Added/Corp** Academie Royale d'Archeologie de Belgique. Fondation Universitaire de Belgique. **VFOAT** Belgisch Tijdschrift voor Oudheidkunde en Kunstgeschiedenis. Vol. 1 No. (Jan. 1931)-. Bibliography. French (Dutch and English). One time a year (Jan.). 1556.60F. Academie Royale d'Archeologie de Belgique, 10 Jubelpark, 1040 Brussels Belgium. **Tel** 011 32 2 3434049. **Bk Rev**. **Circ**: 350. **Formed by the union of** Academie Royale d'Archeologie de Belgique. Bulletin **and** Academie Royale d'Archeologie de Belgique. Annales.
Desc: General news and bibliography in arts and museums in Belgium.
Ind/Abst Art Index; ARTbibliogr. Mod.; Avery Index Archit. Period. Suppl. Colum. Univ. (19??-199?); BHA : Biblio. Hist. Art; Numis. Lit.

LC Z5961.G4 D4 **ISSN** 0080-7176
DD 016.7 GW
SCHRIFTTUM ZUR DEUTSCHEN KUNST. (SCHRIFTTUM ZUR DEUTSCHEN KUNST.). **Added/Corp** Germanisches Nationalmuseum NEurnberg. Bibliothek. Deutscher Verein fuer Kunstwissenschaft. (1933)-. German. Irregular. Deutscher Verlag Kunstwissenschaft, Lindenstrasse 76, D-10969 Berlin Germany. **Tel** 011 49 30 25913864, 25913865. **Circ**: 450.
Desc: Bibliography of the literature of the arts in German-speaking countries from the early Middle Ages to the beginning of the 20th Century.

LC N6536 .W5 **ISSN** 0000-0191
DD 709/.22 US
CCC
NLM N 40 W628
WHO'S WHO IN AMERICAN ART. [Who's who Am. art]. **Added/Corp** American Federation of Arts. Vol. 1 (1937)-. English. Every 2 years. $201.92. R.R. Bowker, A Reed Reference Publishing Company, Part of Reed International PLC, PO Box 31, 121 Chanlon Drive, New Providence NJ 07974. **Tel** (908)464-6800, (800)521-8110, FAX (908)665-6688, telex 138-755. Index available. available on magnetic tape and an online database. **Continues in part** American Art Annual.
Desc: Over 11,800 entries, the guide's concise listings detail entrants' date and place of birth, education and training, commissions, exhibitions, professional positions, and awards (all dated by year); museums holding their work; books and articles by and about them; the media they work in; and their dealer or representative and mailing address.

ART

DD 709/.714 **ISSN** 0714-6906
CN
10.5155.20 : ART CONTEMPORAIN. [10,5155,20: art contemp.]. **VFOAT** Art Contemporain. 1 No. (Autumn 1982)-. Periodical. French. Four times a year. $3.00 per no. 10.5155.20 a/s Editions Alternatives, CP 608, Sherbrooke Quebec J1H 5K5 Canada.

LC IN PROCESS BH151 .S59 **ISSN** 1065-3112
DD 111 US
●**1650-1850 (NEW YORK, N.Y.). See** Philosophy.

LC NX
DD 700 US
●**A-C JOURNAL.** (1996)-. Government Publication. English. Two times a year. Michigan Council for Arts and Cultural Affairs, 1200 16th Avenue, Suite 1180, Detroit MI 48226. **Tel** (313)256-3731, FAX (313)256-3781. **ED** Jan Fedewa. **Circ**: 12,000.

AT
A + T. VFOAT Art and Text; A A and T; Art & Text. No. 36 (May 1990)-. Periodical. English. Three times a year (Jan., May, Sept.). 32.88Au$. Art & Text, PO Box 259, Paddington New South Wales 2021 Australia. **Tel** 011 61 2 3850735, FAX 011 61 2 3850706. **ED** Paul Foss. **Bk Rev**. **Ad Acc**. **Circ**: 3,500 (ctrl). **Continues** Art & Text.
Desc: Critical discussion of contemporary visual arts in an international context.
Ind/Abst BHA : Biblio. Hist. Art.

DD 720/.97123/4 **ISSN** 0824-5576
CN
A3. See Architecture.

LC N6886.A15 A6 **ISSN** 0515-0612
DD 709/.43/55 GW
AACHENER KUNSTBLATTER (DUMONT BUCHVERLAG). (AACHENER KUNSTBLATTER.). [Aachen. Kunstbl.]. **Added/Corp** Museumsverein Aachen. (19??)-. Periodical. German. One time a year. DM140.00. **(Subscription address:** VVA Bertelsmann Distributors GmbH, Postfach 7600, D-33310 Guetersloh Germany. **Tel** 011 49 5241 803294.)
Ind/Abst ARTbibliogr. Mod.; Avery Index Archit. Period. Suppl. Colum. Univ. (19??-199?); BHA : Biblio. Hist. Art.

ISSN 0567-4999
GW
ABHANDLUNGEN ZUR KUNST-, MUSIK- UND LITERATURWISSENSCHAFT. [Abh. Kunst-, Musik- Literaturwiss.]. Vol. 1 (1957)-. Monographic series. German (English). Irregular. Price varies per volume. Bouvier GmbH & Co. KG ABT Verlag, Am HOF 28, D-53113 Bonn Germany. **Tel** 011 49 228 7290141, FAX 011 49 228 7290179.
Desc: A serial with reference to art, music and literature.
Ind/Abst MLA Int. Bibl. Books Artic. Mod. Lang. Lit.

UK
ACCORDIA RESEARCH PAPERS : THE JOURNAL OF THE ACCORDIA RESEARCH CENTRE. Added/Corp Accordia Research Centre. **VFOAT** ARP; Journal of the Accordia Research Centre. Vol. 1 (1990)-. English. One time a year (Dec.). $59.89. University of London Mediterranean Studies, Mile End Road, Queen Mary & King William Field, London E1 4NS United Kingdom. **Tel** 011 44 181 5306406.
Ind/Abst BHA : Biblio. Hist. Art.

LC N1.A1 A25 **ISSN** 0065-0900
DD 709 IT
ACTA AD ARCHAEOLOGIAM ET ARTIUM HISTORIAM PERTINENTIA. [Acta archaeol. artium hist. pertinen.]. **Added/Corp** Det Norske institutt i Roma. (1962)-. Monographic series. English (French, German and Italian). Irregular. Price varies per volume. Giorgio Bretschneider Editore, Via Crescenzio 43, 00193 Rome Italy. **Tel** 011 39 6 6879361. Index available. **Ad Acc**. **Circ**: 300 (ctrl).
Ind/Abst Avery Index Archit. Period. Suppl. Colum. Univ. (19??-199?); BHA : Biblio. Hist. Art.

LC N6 .A25 **ISSN** 0001-5830
HU
CCC
ACTA HISTORIAE ARTIUM ACADEMIAE SCIENTARIUM HUNGARICAE. (ACTA HISTORIAE ARTIUM.). [Acta hist. artium Acad. Sci. Hung.]. **Added/Corp** Magyar Tudomanyos Akademia. Vol. 1 (1953)-. Academic Scholarly Publication. English (French, German, Italian and Russian). Four times a year. $128.00. Akademiai Kiado, Publishing House of the Hungarian Academy of Sciences, Prielle Kornelia u. 19-35, H-1117 Budapest Hungary. **Tel** 011 36 1 1811991, FAX 011 36 1 1811991, telex 22-6228 AKNYO H. **ED** Rozsa Gyorgy. Index available. Documents available from The Genuine Article.

The Arts —Art

Desc: Presents papers on history of art extending from the Middle Ages to contemporary art. Includes critical analyses of Hungarian and international research publications in the appropriate field.
Ind/Abst Am. Hist. Life (1985-); Art Archaeol. Tech. Abstr.; ARTbibliogr. Mod. (1984-); ARTbibliogr. Curr. Titles; Arts Humanit. Citation Index [Full Cov.]; Avery Index Archit. Period. Suppl. Colum. Univ. (19??-199?); BHA : Biblio. Hist. Art.

ISSN 0293-9789
FR
UDC 373 (084.12)
ACTUALITE DES ARTS PLASTIQUES. [Actual. arts plast.]. **VFOAT** Collection Actualite des Arts Plastiques. (1970)-. French. Three times a year. $94.05. Centre National Documentation Pedagogique, 21 Square St. Charles, BP 7, 75012 Paris France. **Tel** 011 33 1 40020333, 011 33 1 46349425.

ISSN 0393-8522
IT
UDC 8.01
AESTHETICA. PRE-PRINT. [Aesthetica, Pre-print]. **VFOAT** Aesthetica. Preprint. (1983)-. Monographic series. Italian. Irregular. Price varies per volume.
Ind/Abst BHA : Biblio. Hist. Art.

ISSN 0989-0165
FR
UDC 7.071
AFFICHE PARIS. (AFFICHE.). (1981)-. Periodical. French.
Ind/Abst BHA : Biblio. Hist. Art.

LC DT251 .A45
DD 930 TI
AFRICA (TUNIS). See Archaeology.

ISSN 1060-3247
DD 069 US
AIC NEWS : NEWSLETTER OF THE AMERICAN INSTITUTE FOR CONSERVATION OF HISTORIC AND ARTISTIC WORKS. [AIC news - Am. Inst. Conserv. Hist. Artist. Works]. **Added/Corp** American Institute for Conservation of Historic and Artistic Works. **VAT** American Institute for Conservation News. Vol. 16, No. 6 (Nov. 1991)-. Newsletter. English. Six times a year. $160.00 Comes with American Institute for the Conservation of Historic and Artistic Works membership. American Institute of Conservation / AIC, 1717 K Street Northwest, Suite 301, Washington DC 20006. **Tel** (202)452-9545. **Continues** AIC Newsletter (American Institute for Conservation of Historic and Artistic Works), 0887-705X.
Ind/Abst Museum Abstr.

SZ
CEASED
AICARC. Added/Corp International Association of Art Critics. Vol. 10, No. 18 (1983)-(1993). English. Archives and Documentation Centers for Modern and Contemporary Art, Swiss Inst Art Research POB, CH8024 Zurich Switzerland. **Tel** 41 1 2512486. **Continues** AICARC Bulletin.

ISSN 0347-4240
SW
TITLE CHANGE
AICARC BULLETIN. Added/Corp International Association of Art Critics. No. 1 (1974)-(19??). Bulletin. Multiple languages (English and French). Archives and Documentation Centers for Modern and Contemporary Art, Swiss Inst Art Research POB, CH8024 Zurich Switzerland. **Tel** 41 1 2512486. **Continued by** AICARC.
Ind/Abst BHA : Biblio. Hist. Art (-19??).

LC NC915.A35 A38 **ISSN** 1040-8509
DD 751.4/94/05 US
AIRBRUSH ACTION. [Air Brush Action]. **VFOAT** Air Brush Action. (1985)- Vol. 9 No. 3 (Sept/Oct. 1993)-Vol. 9 No. 4 (Nov/Dec 1993)-. Trade Publication. English. Six times a year. $21.95. Airbrush Action, PO Box 2052, Lakewood NJ 08701. **Tel** (908)364-2111, FAX (908)367-5908. **ED** Cliff Sheqlitz. **Ad Acc**.
Desc: Focuses on illustration, T-shirt art, textile art, fine art, signcraft, muralin and more. "How-tos", featured artists and new products, and tips. For art students and enthusiasts.

ISSN 0394-9427
IT
UDC 908
ALBA POMPEIA. [Alba Pompeia]. (1908)-. Periodical. Italian. Two times a year.
Ind/Abst BHA : Biblio. Hist. Art.

LC NX456 .A46
SP
ALBUM (MADRID, SPAIN). (ALBUM.). **VFOAT** Album Letras-Artes; Album Letras y Artes; Album-Letras y Artes; Album Letras y Artes. **VAT** Album Letras Artes; Album Letras y Artes. No. 1 (Dec/Jan. 1986)-. Periodical. Spanish. Four times a year. 85.00ptas Span; 150.00ptas

The Arts —Art

other. Letras y Artessa, Juan Alvarez Mendizabal 58, 28008 Madrid Spain. **Tel** 011 34 1 2489027. Index available. **Ad Acc. Circ:** 25,000 (ctrl).

ISSN 0391-724X
IT

UDC 061.7
ALMA ROMA. [Alma Roma]. (1960)-. Periodical. Italian. Three times a year.
Ind/Abst BHA : Biblio. Hist. Art.

ISSN 0569-1346
IT

UDC 93
ALTAMURA. (1954)-. Periodical. Italian. Irregular.
Ind/Abst BHA : Biblio. Hist. Art.

LC N650 .A45a
DD 700/.5
AMAM NEWS. **Main/Corp** Allen Memorial Art Museum. **VFOAT** Allen Memorial Art Museum News. (19??)-. Newsletter. English. Three times a year. Allen Memorial Art Museum, Oberlin College, Oberlin OH 44074. **Tel** (216)775-8665, FAX (216)775-8799. **ED** Anne F. Moore and Leslie Miller.

ISSN 0065-6968
US

NLM N 40 A512
AMERICAN ART DIRECTORY. See The Arts-Abstracting, Bibliographies and Statistics.

LC N6505 .A618
DD 709/.73
ISSN 0002-7359
US
AMERICAN ART JOURNAL, THE. [Am. art j.]. **Added/Corp** Kennedy Galleries. Vol. 1 (Spring 1969)-. Periodical. English. Two times a year (Jan., Apr., July, and Oct.). $35.00. Kennedy Galleries Inc., 730 Fifth Avenue, 2nd Floor, New York NY 10019. **Tel** (212)541-9600, FAX (212)333-7451. **ED** Jane Van Norman Turano. Index available. cum. index. **Bk Rev. Circ:** 1,400 (ctrl). available on microfilm and microfiche from University Microfilms International (UMI). Documents available from The Genuine Article.
Desc: Published as a non-commercial forum for the presentation of important new American art scholarship. Aimed at public and private collectors, institutions and students.
Ind/Abst Am. Hist. Life (1970-); Art Archaeol. Tech. Abstr.; Art Index; ARTbibliogr. Mod.; ARTbibliogr. Curr. Titles; Arts Humanit. Citation Index (19??-19??) [Full Cov.]; Avery Index Archit. Period. Suppl. Colum. Univ. (1989-); BHA : Biblio. Hist. Art; Curr. Contents Arts Humanit.; Res. Alert [Full Cov.]; Romant. Move.

LC N6505 .S56
DD 709/.73
ISSN 1073-9300
US
Pr Rev.
AMERICAN ART / NATIONAL MUSEUM OF AMERICAN ART, SMITHSONIAN INSTITUTION. See Museums and Galleries.

LC N6505 .A619
DD 709/.73
ISSN 0092-1327
US
AMERICAN ART REVIEW. [Am. art rev.]. Vol. 1 (Sept./Oct. 1973)-. Periodical. English. Six times a year. $21.00. American Art Review, PO Box 480500, Kansas City MO 54148. **Tel** (913)451-8801. available on microfilm from University Microfilms International (UMI).
Ind/Abst Art Index; Avery Index Archit. Period. Suppl. Colum. Univ. (19??-199?); Bibliogr. Mission. (1973-); BHA : Biblio. Hist. Art; Mag. Index Plus (1989-); Mag. Index (1977-?).

ISSN 1066-4076
US
DD 618
AMERICAN ART THERAPY ASSOCIATION NEWSLETTER. See Medical Sciences-Psychiatry.

LC N1 .A243
DD 707
ISSN 0002-7375
US
CCC
AMERICAN ARTIST. Vol. 1 (April 1937)-. Periodical. English. Twelve times a year. $26.95. Billboard Publications Inc., 1515 Broadway Billboard, New York NY 10036. **Tel** (212)764-7300, FAX (305)755-7048, telex WU TWX 710-581-6279. **ED** M. Stephen Doherty. available on microfilm and microfiche from University Microfilms International (UMI). Documents available from UMI Article Clearinghouse, Magazine Collection.
Desc: Read by artists in both fine and commercial fields, art teachers, art students, amateurs and all those interested in a down-to-earth discussion of art. Profiles of contemporary figurative American painters, illustrators and sculptors describe technical approach and professional insights. How-to articles and service features for the professional.
Ind/Abst Acad. Abstr. Full Text Elite; Acad. Abstr.; Acad. Ind. [Computer File] (1984-); Acad. Search; Annu. Bibliogr. Engl. Lang. Lit.; Art Index; ARTbibliogr. Mod.; ARTbibliogr. Curr. Titles; Book Rev. Index; Curr. Cit.; EP Collect.; Expand. Acad. Index (1985-); Gen. Period. Index (1985-); Guide Soc. Sci. Relig.; Homework Help.; INFO-SOUTH Index; Mag. Artic. Summar. Elite; Mag. Artic. Summar. Select; Mag. Artic. Summar. CD-ROM; Mag. Express (1988-) [Full Txt.]; Mag. Index Plus (1989-); Mag. Index Sel. Microfiche (1990-) [Full Txt.]; Mag. Index Sel. (1986-); Mag. Search; MasterFile FullTEXT 1000; MasterFile FullTEXT 350; MasterFile FullTEXT 650; MasterFile FullTEXT (Jan. 1984-); Newsp. Period. Abstr. (1988-); OCLC; Pub. Lib. FullTEXT; Read. Guide Abstr. Select Ed.; Read. Guide Period. Lit.; Resource/One Ondisc; Telebase; Mag. Index (1977-); TOM Gen. Index (1985-) [Full Txt.]; Vocat. Search.

LC N328 .A44
DD 707/.073
ISSN 0146-9606
US
AMERICAN ARTIST DIRECTORY OF ART SCHOOLS AND WORKSHOPS. [Am. artist dir. art sch. workshops]. **VFOAT** American Artist Art School Directory. **VAT** American Artist Directory of Art Schools and Workshops. (1977)-. Directory. English. One time a year. $3.50. Billboard Publications Inc., 1515 Broadway Billboard, New York NY 10036. **Tel** (212)764-7300, FAX (305)755-7048, telex WU TWX 710-581-6279. **Ad Acc. Circ:** 163,000. **Continues** American Artist Art School Directory, 0002-7375.

LC N6512 .A5857
DD 709/.2/2 B
ISSN 0276-5691
US
AMERICAN ARTISTS OF RENOWN. (1982)-. English. Every 2 years. $35.00. Wilson Publishing Company, PO Box 10998 No 450, Austin TX 78766.

LC AP2 .A44
DD 051
ISSN 0569-7344
US
SUSPENDED
AMERICAN REVIEW OF ART AND SCIENCE. (Nov. 1957)-. Periodical. English. Four times a year. $5.00. Pescara Enterprises, 300 West 49th Street, New York NY 10019.

LC N16 .M5
DD 706.272
ISSN 0185-1276
MX
ANALES DEL INSTITUTO DE INVESTIGACIONES ESTETICAS. [An. Inst. Invest. Estet.]. **Main/Corp** Universidad Nacional Autonoma de Mexico. Instituto de Investigaciones Esteticas. Vol. 1 No. 1 (1937)-. Periodical. Spanish. One time a year. $20.00. Universidad Nacional Autonoma de Mexico / Anales de Instituto de Investigaciones Esteticas, Torre 1 de Humanidades Piso 6, 04510 Mexico City DF Mexico. **Tel** 011 52 5 5484117. **ED** Lic Xavier Moyssen. **Bk Rev. Circ:** 2,000 (ctrl).
Desc: Prehispanic, colonial history, contemporary art, modern art, literature, architecture, dance, cinema and folklore, etc.
Ind/Abst Am. Hist. Life (1965-1972); BHA : Biblio. Hist. Art; Ethnoarts Index; Hisp. Am. Period. Index, HAPI; Indice Hist. Esp. (1965-1972).

ISSN 0266-6057
UK
SUSPENDED
AND. JOURNAL OF ART AND ART EDUCATION. (19??)-Suspended (1995). English. Four times a year. £4.50 UK; £6.50 other Europe; £10.00 other. AND Journal of Art and Art Education, 10 Back Church Lane, London E1 1LX United Kingdom. **Tel** 011 44 171 7397380. **ED** J.Boswell-Jones and I.Saray. Index available. **Bk Rev,** (Qty: 4). **Circ:** 2,000.
Desc: Covers a wide spectrum of issue-based visual arts. Voluntarily produced by practicing artists; includes an education section which raises current approaches within art and design education.

ISSN 0771-2723
BE
ANNALES D'HISTOIRE DE L'ART ET D'ARCHEOLOGIE. (ANNALES D'HISTOIRE DE L'ART ET D'ARCHEOLOGIE: PUBLICATION ANNUELLE DE LA SECTION D'HISTOIRE DE L'ART ET D'ARCHEOLOGIE DE L'UNIVERSITE LIBRE DE BRUXELLES.). [Ann. hist. art, archeol.]. **Added/Corp** Universite Libre de Bruxelles. Section d'Histoire de l'Art et d'Archeologie. **VFOAT** Annales distoire de l'Art & d'Archeologie. (1979)-. French.
Ind/Abst BHA : Biblio. Hist. Art.

LC N6911 .A64
DD 709/.45
ISSN 0394-1744
IT
ANNALI / FONDAZIONE DI STUDI DI STORIA DELL'ARTE ROBERTO LONGHI, FIRENZE. **Added/Corp** Fondazione Roberto Longhi. (1984)-. Periodical. Italian.
Ind/Abst BHA : Biblio. Hist. Art.

FR
ANNUAIRE DE L'ART INTERNATIONAL. (1969)-. Periodical. French. One time a year (Nov.). $109.36. Sermadiras Publicite SA, 11 rue Arsene Houssaye, 75008 Paris France. **Tel** 011 33 1 47665121 Mlle Botter. **ED** Max Fourny and Patrick Sermadiras. **Continues** Annuaire International des Galeries d'Art.

LC N8670 .A59
DD 707/.5
FR
ANNUAIRE DES COTES INTERNATIONAL / INTERNATIONAL ART PRICE ANNUAL. **VFOAT** International Art Price Annual; ADEC. (1988-). English (French). One time a year (Mar.). $185.00. ADEC Production, BP 114, 06802 Cagnes Cedex France. **Tel** 011 33 92 049364.

LC N8640 .A55
DD 707/.5
FR
TITLE CHANGE
ANNUAIRE INTERNATIONAL DES VENTES. (1963)-(19??). French (English). Editions Acatos, Avenue Villamont 17, CH-1005 Lausanne Switzerland. **Tel** 011 41 21 3120652, FAX 011 41 21 3129108. **ED** E. Mayer. **Bk Rev. Ad Acc. Circ:** 5,000. **Continued by** Le Livre International des Ventes.

LC NE2825 .O8
US
ANNUAL CATALOGUE OF ART CALENDARS ... . **Main/Corp** Osborne Company. English.

LC NB212 .N35B
DD 730/.973/07401471
ISSN 0098-4817
US
ANNUAL EXHIBITION - NATIONAL SCULPTURE SOCIETY. **Main/Corp** National Sculpture Society, New York. Academic Scholarly Publication. English. One time a year. $25.00. National Sculpture Society, 1177 Avenue of the Americas, 15th Floor, New York NY 10036. **Tel** (212)764-5645, FAX (212)545-0779. **ED** Jean Henery. **Circ:** 2,000.
Desc: Catalog of retrospective 100 years of figurative sculpture with scholarly articles.

LC N5055.R52 A56
DD 759.94/074
UK
ANNUAL EXHIBITION OF OLD MASTER PAINTINGS. (19??)-. English. One time a year. Richard Green, 44 Dover Street, London W1X 4JZ United Kingdom.

ISSN 0318-4978
DD 759.11
CN
ANNUAL EXHIBITION OF THE CANADIAN SOCIETY OF PAINTERS IN WATER COLOUR. **Main/Corp** Canadian Society of Painters in Water Colour. (1926)-. Periodical. English. Two times a year. $30.00. Canadian Society of Painters in Water Colours, 1140 Shephard Avenue West, Unit 7, North York ON M3K 2A2 Canada. **Tel** (416)638-1983, FAX (416)630-8349. **Bk Rev. Ad Acc. Circ:** 350 (ctrl).

US
●**ANNUAL REPORT : REPORT FOR ... / NORTH CAROLINA MUSEUM OF ART.** **Main/Corp** North Carolina Museum of Art. (1993)-. English. North Carolina Museum of Art, 2110 Blue Ridge Boulevard, Raleigh NC 27607. **Tel** (919)833-1935. **Separated from** Preview (Raleigh, N.C.).

ISSN 0083-5161
CN
ANNUAL REPORT - VANCOUVER ART GALLERY. **Main/Corp** Vancouver Art Gallery. (1971)-. Periodical. English. Vancouver Art Gallery, 1145 West Georgia Street, Vancouver BC V6E 3H2. **Supersedes** Vancouver Art Gallery Association Annual Report, 0315-4424.

LC ND1928 .O43a
DD 759.2/05
ISSN 0958-8825
UK
CEASED
ANNUAL VOLUME / THE OLD WATER-COLOUR SOCIETY'S CLUB. **Main/Corp** Old Water-Colour Society (London, England). Club. No. 1 (1923)-(19??). English. Old Water-Colour Society's Club, 48 Hopton Street, London SE1 9JH United Kingdom. **Tel** 011 44 181 9287521, FAX 011 44 181 9282820. **ED** David Brown. **Bk Rev. Ad Acc. Circ:** 1,000 (ctrl).
Desc: Articles on watercolorists, past and present, illustrated with colour and black and white reproductions.
Ind/Abst ARTbibliogr. Mod.; BHA : Biblio. Hist. Art.

ISSN 0826-4376
DD 704.9/4997/80074011233
CN
ANNUAL WILD WEST SHOW. [Annu. wild west show]. **Main/Corp** Alberta College of Art. Gallery. **VFOAT** Wild West Show. (1982)-. English. One time a year. Alberta College of Art Gallery S A I T Campus, 1301 16th Avenue North West, Calgary Alberta Canada.

IT
ANNUARIO DEL RESTAURO O DEI BENI CULTURALI / CON IL PATROCINIO DEL MINISTERO PER I BENI CCULTURALI E AMBIENTALI. **Added/Corp** Italy. Ministero per I Beni Culturali E Ambientali. (1991)-. Italian.

ISSN 0003-5645
IT

Pr Rev.

ANTICHITA VIVA. [Antich. viva]. Vol.1 (Jan. 1962)-. Periodical. Italian (English; summaries and/or abstracts in English). Six times a year. L88560. Casa Editrice Edam SRL, Via Pier Capponi 24, 50132 Firenze Italy. **Tel** 011 39 55 576974, FAX 011 39 55 680493. **ED** Pietro Milone. Index available. cum. index. **Bk Rev**, (Qty: 8). **Ad Acc. Circ:** 1,500 (ctrl).
Desc: Covers art history.
Ind/Abst Art Archaeol. Tech. Abstr.; ARTbibliogr. Mod.; ARTbibliogr. Curr. Titles; Avery Index Archit. Period. Suppl. Colum. Univ. (1989-); BHA : Biblio. Hist. Art.

LC NK1125 .A25 **ISSN** 0003-5653
DD 745/.05 NE

ANTIEK. [Antiek]. Vol. 1 (June/July 1966)-. Periodical. Dutch. Ten times a year (monthly except July and Sept.). $83.07. Waanders Uitgevers, Postbus 1129, 8001 BC Zwolle Netherlands. **Tel** 011 31 38 658628, FAX 038-655989. **ED** J. Bottema. Index available. **Bk Rev. Ad Acc. Circ:** 6,000.
Desc: Leading magazine on arts and antiques in the Netherlands. Covers art nouveau and art deco.
Ind/Abst Art Archaeol. Tech. Abstr.; ARTbibliogr. Mod.; ARTbibliogr. Curr. Titles; BHA : Biblio. Hist. Art.

LC N5320 .A55 **ISSN** 0003-5688
DD 709/.01 SZ

ANTIKE KUNST. **See** Archaeology.

ISSN 0518-018X
GW

ANTIKE PLASTIK. **Added/Corp** Deutsches Archaologisches Institut. (1962)-. Periodical. German (English). Irregular. DM233.00. Gebrueder Mann Verlag, Lindenstrasse 76, D-10969 Berlin Germany. **Tel** 011 49 30 25913589, telex 183723. Index available. cum. index. **Circ:** 1,000.
Desc: Monuments of Greek and Roman sculptures from the beginnings of Greek sculpture in the 7th century before Christ to the end of antiquity; statues, reliefs, busts and small artifacts are featured.

LC N1.A1 A57 **ISSN** 0394-0136
IT

ANTOLOGIA DI BELLE ARTI. [Antol. belle arti]. (March 1977)-. Periodical. English (French and Italian). One time a year. L80000 Italy; L100000 other. Umberto Allemandi, Via Mancini 8, 10131 Turin Italy. **Tel** 11 39 11 8193133, FAX 11 39 11 8193090, telex 224149.
Ind/Abst ARTbibliogr. Mod.; BHA : Biblio. Hist. Art.

LC N16 .A6513
AG

ANUARIO - ACADEMIA NACIONAL DE BELLAS ARTES. **Main/Corp** Academia Nacional de Bellas Artes, Buenos Aires. (1973)-. Spanish. One time a year. Academia Nacional de Bellas Artes, Sanchez de Bustamante 2663, 1425 Buenos Aires Argentina. **Tel** 011 54 1 8022469.

LC N9.7 .C36a
SP

ANUARIO DEL ARTE ESPANOL. (1973)-. Spanish. One time a year. Iberico Europea de Ediciones SA, Serrano 44, 1 Madrid Spain.

LC DD1 .A61 **ISSN** 0341-8383
GW

ANZEIGER DES GERMANISCHEN NATIONALMUSEUMS. [Anz. Ger. Nationalmus.]. **Main/Corp** Germanisches Nationalmuseum Nuernberg. (1886)-. German. One time a year. DM65.00. Germanisches Nationalmuseum Nuernberg, Postfach 119580, 90105 Nuernberg Germany. **Tel** 011 49 911 13310, FAX 011 49 611 1331200. Index available. **Circ:** 600. Documents available from BLDSC. ***Supersedes in part*** *Germanisches Nationalmuseum Nuernberg. Anzeiger fuer Kunde der Deutschen Vorzeit.*
Ind/Abst BHA : Biblio. Hist. Art.

LC N1 .A255 **ISSN** 0003-6536
DD 705 UK

APOLLO (LONDON. 1925). (APOLLO.). [Apollo]. Vol. 1 (Jan. 1925)-. Periodical. English. Twelve times a year. $125.00. Apollo Magazine Ltd., 29 Chesham Place, London SW1X 8HB United Kingdom. **Tel** 011 44 171 2351998, FAX 011 44 171 2351689, telex 919034. **ED** Robin Simon. Index available. **Bk Rev. Ad Acc. Circ:** 10,000 (ctrl). available on microfilm and microfiche from University Microfilms International (UMI). Documents available from The Genuine Article.
Desc: Covers painting, sculpture, architecture and decorative arts from Ancient Greece to the 20th Century. Also includes news on exhibitions, auctions and book reviews.
Ind/Abst Annu. Bibliogr. Engl. Lang. Lit.; Archit. Period. Index (Feb 1978-); Art Archaeol. Tech. Abstr.; Art Index; ARTbibliogr. Mod.; Arts Humanit. Citation Index [Full Cov.]; Avery Index Archit. Period. Suppl. Colum. Univ. (1990-); BHA : Biblio. Hist. Art; Book Rev. Index; Br. Humanit. Index; Curr. Cit.; Curr. Contents Arts Humanit.; Res. Alert [Full Cov.]; Romant. Move.

LC WMLC 91/1116
IC

ARBOK LISTASAFNS ISLANDS. **Added/Corp** Listasafn Islands. **VFOAT** Yearbook of the National Gallery of Iceland. (1988)-. Icelandic. One time a year.
Ind/Abst BHA : Biblio. Hist. Art.

LC GR1 .A59 **ISSN** 0066-6513
AU

ARCHIV FUER VOLKERKUNDE. **See** Anthropology.

LC N6841 .A9
FR

ARCHIVES DE L'ART FRANCAIS. **Added/Corp** Societe de l'Histoire de l'Art Francais (Paris, France). (1907)-. French. Irregular. Librarie des Arts et Metiers, BP 23, 28210 Nogent le Roi France. **Tel** 011 33 37514429, FAX 011 33 37514851. Index available. cum. index. **Bk Rev. Ad Acc.** ctrl circ. ***Continues*** *Nouvelles Archives de l'Art Francais.*
Desc: Studies on French arts and artists from XVth to XXth Century made by museum curators.
Ind/Abst ARTbibliogr. Mod.; BHA : Biblio. Hist. Art.

LC N7260 .A68 **ISSN** 0066-6637
DD 705/.5 US

ARCHIVES OF ASIAN ART. [Arch. Asian art]. **Added/Corp** Asia Society. Vol. 20 (1966-1967)-. English. One time a year (Oct.). $36.50. The Asia Society Archives, 725 Park Avenue, Department of Gallery, New York NY 10021. **Tel** (212)288-6400 Ext.231, FAX (212)517-8315, telex 224953 ASIA UR. **ED** Richard Barnhart. **Circ:** 600. Documents available from The Genuine Article. ***Continues*** *Archives of the Chinese Art Society of America.*
Desc: Articles written by established and emerging scholars, containing research, as well as an annotated, illustrated review of the major accessions of Asian art made by North American museums.
Ind/Abst Art Index; Arts Humanit. Citation Index (19??-19??) [Full Cov.]; Avery Index Archit. Period. Suppl. Colum. Univ.; Curr. Contents Arts Humanit.; Res. Alert [Full Cov.].

IT

ARCHIVI. **Added/Corp** Centro Camuno di Studi Preistorici. No. 3 (1972)-. Monographic series. Italian (English and French). Irregular. Price varies per volume. Centro Canuno di Studi Preistoici, via Marconi 7, 25044 Capo di Ponte Brescia Italy. **Tel** 011 39 364-42091, FAX 011 39 364-42572, telex 301504 ARCHEO I. **ED** Emmanuel Anati. **Circ:** 4,500 (ctrl). ***Continues*** *Archivi di Arte Preistorica.*
Desc: Monographs on prehistoric and primitive art; methodology of research.
Ind/Abst Am. Hist. Life (1955-1956).

ISSN 0211-5808
SP

ARCHIVO DE ARTE VALENCIANO; PUBLICACION DE LA REAL ACADEMIA DE BELLAS ARTES DE SAN CARLOS. **Added/Corp** Real Academia de Bellas Artes de San Carlos de Valencia. Vol. 1 (Mar. 31, 1915)-. Spanish. One time a year.
Ind/Abst Am. Hist. Life (1963-1965); BHA : Biblio. Hist. Art.

LC N7 .A68 **ISSN** 0004-0428
SP

ARCHIVO ESPANOL DE ARTE. [Arch. esp. arte]. **Added/Corp** Instituto Diego Velazquez. Vol. 14, No. 40 (July/Aug. 1940)-. Periodical. Spanish. Four times a year (Jan., Apr., July, Oct.). $117.85. Puvill Libros SA, Boters 10 Y Paja 29, 08002 Barcelona Spain. **Tel** 011 34 3 3181848. Index Available, published separately, free-automatically sent. cum. index. **Bk Rev.** Documents available from The Genuine Article. ***Continues in part*** *Archivo Espanol de Arte y Arqueologia.*
Desc: Journal devoted to Spanish and Latin American art and art from Western Europe held in Spain. Includes a bibliography of recent Spanish art and abstracts of articles. Also lists Spanish art for sale or auction.
Ind/Abst Am. Hist. Life (1962-1972); Art Index; ARTbibliogr. Mod. (1984-); Arts Humanit. Citation Index [Full Cov.]; Avery Index Archit. Period. Suppl. Colum. Univ. (1989-); BHA : Biblio. Hist. Art; Curr. Contents Arts Humanit.; Indice Hist. Esp.; Res. Alert [Full Cov.].

IT

ARCHIVUM ARCIS. **Added/Corp** Museo Nazionale di Castel Sant'Angelo. (1987)-. Italian.
Ind/Abst BHA : Biblio. Hist. Art.

ISSN 0570-8869
XV

ARGO / NARODNI MUZEJ V LJUBLJANI. **See** Museums and Galleries.

ISSN 0044-5711
SW

ARIS. [Aris]. **Added/Corp** Konsthistoriska Institutionen i Lund. Lunds Universitet. Institutionen for Konstvetenskap. Vol. 1 (1969)-. Monographic series. English (Swedish, German and French). Irregular. Price varies per volume. Lund University Press, Box 141, S-22100 Lund Sweden. **Tel** 011 46 46 312000, FAX 011 46 46 305338, telex 33345 EDUCATE S. **ED** Sven Sandstrom.
Desc: Collection of studies in the areas of modern art and art life; studies of environment and experiencing of art and environment.
Ind/Abst Avery Index Archit. Period. Suppl. Colum. Univ. (19??-199?); BHA : Biblio. Hist. Art.

LC N7161 .A79
TU

ARKEOLOJI-SANAT TARIHI DERGISI. (1982)-. Turkish (German and English). One time a year. Ege Universitesi / Edibiyat, Edebiyat Fakultesi, Cografya Bolumu, Bornova Izmir Turkey. **Tel** 9-51-180110.

LC Z675.A85 A777 **ISSN** 0743-040X
DD 026.7 US

ARLIS/NA UPDATE. **See** Library and Information Sciences.

ISSN 0571-1304
HU

ARRABONA. **Added/Corp** Gyor, Hungary. Xantus Janos Muzeum. (1959)-. Hungarian (summaries and/or abstracts in English, French, German and Russian). One time a year.
Ind/Abst BHA : Biblio. Hist. Art; Numis. Lit.

LC N6 .A77 **ISSN** 0044-9008
XO

ARS. [Ars]. **Added/Corp** Slovenska Akademia Vied. (1967)-. Periodical. Slovak (summaries and/or abstracts in English and Russian; table of contents in English, French, German and Russian). Two times a year. $22.00. Veda, Publishing House of the Slovak Academy of Sciences, Klemensova 19, 814 30 Bratislava Slovakia. **Tel** (7)583-15. **ED** Jan Dekan.
Ind/Abst Avery Index Archit. Period. Suppl. Colum. Univ.; BHA : Biblio. Hist. Art.

LC N6812 .A78 **ISSN** 0133-1531
HU

ARS HUNGARICA. [Ars Hung.]. **Added/Corp** Magyar Tudomanyos Akademia. Muveszettorteneti Kutato Csoport. (1973)-. Periodical. English (German and Italian; summaries and/or abstracts in English, German and Italian). Two times a year. $16.00. **(Subscription address:** Kultura, PO Box 143, H-1300 Budapest 3 Hungary. **Tel** 011 36 1 2500194.)
Ind/Abst ARTbibliogr. Mod.; Avery Index Archit. Period. Suppl. Colum. Univ. (19??-199?); BHA : Biblio. Hist. Art.

ISSN 0571-1371
DD 709.5 US

ARS ORIENTALIS. (ARS ORIENTALIS; THE ARTS OF ISLAM AND THE EAST.). [Ars orient.]. **Added/Corp** University of Michigan. Center for Chinese Studies. Freer Gallery of Art University of Michigan. Dept. of the History of Art. **VFOAT** Arts of Islam and the East. Vol. 1 (1954)-. English (French and German). One time a year. $40.00. University of Michigan Department of the History of Art, Tappan Hall, Ann Arbor MI 48109-1357. **Tel** (313)747-3329. **ED** Candace Morton and Elisabeth Thoburn. **Bk Rev.** ctrl circ. ***Continues*** *Ars Islamica.*
Ind/Abst Art Index; Avery Index Archit. Period. Suppl. Colum. Univ. (1989-).

ISSN 0349-6236
SW

ARSBOK FOR STATENS KONSTMUSEER. **Added/Corp** Nationalmuseum (Sweden). (1979)-. Monographic series. Swedish. Price varies per volume. Raben and Sjogren, Stockholm Sweden. ***Continues*** *Arsbok for Svenska Statens Konstsamlingar.*
Ind/Abst ARTbibliogr. Mod.

LC NX282 .A76 **ISSN** 1040-7812
DD 707 US

ART & ACADEME. [Art acad.]. **VFOAT** Art and Academe. (1988)-. Periodical. English. Two times a year (Spring and Fall). $16.00. Visual Art Press, 209 East 23rd Street, Humanities and Science, New York NY 10010. **Tel** (212)679-7350.

LC N6505 .A55 **ISSN** 0195-8208
DD 705 US

ART & ANTIQUES (NEW YORK, N.Y. : 1984). (ART & ANTIQUES.). [Art antiq.]. **VFOAT** Art and Antiques. (Mar. 1984)-. Periodical. English. Eleven times a year. $35.00. Billian Publishing Inc., 2100 Powers Ferry Road, Atlanta GA 30339. **Tel** (404)955-5656, FAX (404)952-0669. **(Subscription address:** CDS Special Interest Division, PO Box 4966, Des Moines IA 50340-0167.) **ED** Robert Kenner. **Bk Rev. Ad Acc. Circ:** 60,000. available on microfilm and microfiche from University Microfilms International (UMI). ***Continues*** *Art & Antiques, 0195-8208.*
Desc: Covers fine and decorative arts, from painting, sculpture and architecture to photography, furniture and design. Features on museums, galleries, auction houses and antique shops.
Ind/Abst Access (1981-); Am. Hist. Life (1979-88); Art Index; ARTbibliogr. Mod.; Avery Index Archit. Period. Suppl. Colum. Univ. (1990-); BHA : Biblio. Hist. Art; Curr. Cit.

The Arts — Art

ART AND AUSTRALIA. [Art Aust.]. Vol. 1, No. 1 (May 1963)-. Periodical. English. Four times a year. 44.39Aus$. Art & Australia, Box 480, Roseville NSW 2069 Australia. **Tel** 011 61 2 4171723, FAX (02)498 2775. **ED** Leon Paroissien. Index available. **Bk Rev. Ad Acc. Circ:** 11,600.
 Desc: Art scene in Australia and overseas; associated subjects of architecture, photography, textiles, etc., and all aspects of fine arts included.
 Ind/Abst APAIS, Aust. Public Aff. Inf. Ser. (1964-); ARTbibliogr. Mod.; ARTbibliogr. Curr. Titles; BHA : Biblio. Hist. Art; EP Collect.; Homework Help.; MasterFile FullTEXT 1000; MasterFile FullTEXT 350; MasterFile FullTEXT 650; MasterFile FullTEXT (Jan. 1994-); Telebase; World Mag. Bank.

ISSN 0004-301X
AT

LC N2 .A45
DD 705
ISSN 0004-3168
FR

ART & DECORATION. Vol. 1 (Jan. 1897)-. Periodical. French. Eight times a year. $51.40. Editions Charles Massin & Cie, 16 18 rue de l'Amiral Mouchez, 75686 Paris Cedex 14 France. **Tel** 011 33 1 45654848. cum. index. **Absorbed** Art Decoratif; Architecte; Echos d'Art and Decor d'Aujourd'hui.
 Ind/Abst Repere (1979-1980).

DD 707.10411
ISSN 0269-7858
UK
CEASED

ART AND DESIGN NEWSLETTER. [Art des. newsl.]. (1985)-(19??). Periodical. English. Philip Allan Publishers Ltd., Market Place, Deddington, Oxfordshire OX15 0SE United Kingdom. **Tel** 011 44 1869 338652, FAX 011 44 1869 338803.

DD 705
ISSN 8756-7695
US

ART & OXYGEN. [Art oxyg.]. VFOAT Art and Oxygen. (Fall 1984)-. Periodical. English. Four times a year. $10.00 US; $15.00 Canada. Art & Oxygen, 623 Broadway, New York NY 10012.

LC NX456 .A68
DD 700/.9/04
II

ART AND POETRY TODAY. VFOAT Art & Poetry Today. (1978)-. Periodical. English. Four times a year. $25.00. Samkaleen Parkashan, 2762 Rajguru Marg, New Delhi 110055 India. **Tel** 523520. (Subscription address: Prints India, 11 Darya Ganj, New Delhi 110002 India. **Tel** 011 91 11 3268645, FAX 011 91 11 3275542, telex 31-61087 PRIN-IN.) **ED** Krishan Khullar. Index available. **Bk Rev. Ad Acc. Circ:** 1,100 (ctrl). **Continues** Criteria (New Delhi, India).
 Desc: World poetry, art, book reviews, criteria: illustrated, whole magazine printed on art. Plus paper articles about world poetry and art.

ISSN 0727-1182
AT
TITLE CHANGE

ART & TEXT. VFOAT Art and Text; A & T; A and T. (1981)-(19??). Periodical. English. Art & Text, PO Box 259, Paddington New South Wales 2021 Australia. **Tel** 011 61 2 3850735, FAX 011 61 2 3850706. **ED** Paul Foss. **Bk Rev. Ad Acc. Circ:** 5,000. **Continued by** A & T.
 Desc: Art theory and practice.
 Ind/Abst ARTbibliogr. Mod.; BHA : Biblio. Hist. Art (?-19??).

LC N1 .A386
DD 705
II

ART AND THE ARTIST. **Added/Corp** Academy of Fine Arts (Calcutta, India). (July 1962)-. English. Academy of Fine Arts, 14-2 Old China Bazaar Street, 1 Calcutta India.

LC N8600 .A73
DD 332.6/78
ISSN 0161-1232
US

ART-ANTIQUES INVESTMENT REPORT, THE. (THE ART/ANTIQUES INVESTMENT REPORT.). Vol. 1 (Jan. 5, 1976)-. Periodical. English. Twenty-six times a year. $125.00. Wall Street Reports Publishing Corporation, 99 Wall Street/22nd Floor, New York NY 10005. **Tel** (212)747-9500, FAX (212)668-9842.

LC N8670 .A677
DD 750/.75
ISSN 1046-4999
US

ART AT AUCTION IN AMERICA. [Art auction Am.]. (1989)-. English. One time a year. $35.00. Krex Press, 10169 New Hampshire Avenue, Silver Springs MD 20903. **Tel** (301)445-6009. **ED** Ernest R. Beyard. **Bk Rev. Ad Acc.**
 Desc: An American art price guide.

GW

ART AUREA. (1989)-. Periodical. English (German). Four times a year. $62.33. Ebner Verlag GmbH & Co KG, Postfach 3060, D-89020 ULM Donau Germany. **Tel** 011 49 731 152031.

ISSN 1352-0733
UK

●**ART BOOK : INTERNATIONAL PUBLISHING REVIEW, THE.** VFOAT International Publishing Review. Vol. 1, No. 1 (Winter 1994)-. Periodical. English. Four times a year. $42.78. International Publishing Review Ltd., Park Business Centre, F25 Kilburn Park, London NW6 5LF United Kingdom. **Tel** 011 44 171 6258084, FAX 011 44 171 3724801.

LC N11 .C4
DD 705
ISSN 0004-3079
US

ART BULLETIN (NEW YORK, N.Y.), THE. (THE ART BULLETIN.). [Art bull.]. **Added/Corp** College Art Association of America. Vol. 2 (Sept. 1919)-. Bulletin. English. Four times a year. Comes with College Art Association of America membership - $145.00. College Art Association of America, 275 Seventh Avenue, New York NY 10001. **Tel** (212)691-1051, FAX (212)627-2381. cum. index. available on microfilm and microfiche from University Microfilms International (UMI). Documents available from The Genuine Article, UMI Article Clearinghouse. **Continues** Bulletin of the College Art Association of America, 0272-8192.
 Ind/Abst Acad. Abstr.; Acad. Ind. [Computer File] (1987-); Acad. Search; Archit. Period. Index (1977-); Art Archaeol. Tech. Abstr.; Art Index; ARTbibliogr. Mod.; ARTbibliogr. Curr. Titles; Arts Humanit. Citation Index [Full Cov.]; Avery Index Archit. Period. Suppl. Colum. Univ. (1990-); BHA : Biblio. Hist. Art; Book Rev. Index; Br. Archaeol. Abstr.; Curr. Contents Arts Humanit.; EP Collect.; Expand. Acad. Index (1987-); Homework Help.; Humanit. Index; Humanit. Source; INFO-SOUTH Abstr.; Mag. Search; MasterFile FullTEXT 1000; MasterFile FullTEXT 350; MasterFile FullTEXT 650; MasterFile FullTEXT (July 1990-); Middle East Abstr. Index; Newsp. Period. Abstr. (1990-); OCLC; Pub. Lib. FullTEXT [Full Cov.]; Res. Alert [Full Cov.]; Romant. Move.; Telebase.

LC N3948 .A26a
DD 709/.945
ISSN 0066-7935
AT

ART BULLETIN OF VICTORIA. [Art bull. Vic.]. **Main/Corp** Victoria, Australia. National Gallery, Melbourne. Council of Trustees. (1969)-. Bulletin. English. One time a year. 12.00Aus$. National Gallery of Victoria, 180 St. Kilda Road, Melbourne Victoria 3004 Australia. **Tel** 011 61 3 96180222, FAX 011 61 3 96144337, telex AA 151258. **ED** Sonia Dean. **Circ:** 1,500. **Continues** National Gallery of Victoria. Annual Bulletin of the National Gallery of Victoria.
 Desc: A scholarly journal on the visual and decorative arts.
 Ind/Abst APAIS, Aust. Public Aff. Inf. Ser. (1980-); ARTbibliogr. Curr. Titles; Avery Index Archit. Period. Suppl. Colum. Univ. (19??-199?); BHA : Biblio. Hist. Art.

LC N1 .A414
DD 706/.8/8
ISSN 0273-5652
US
CCC

ART BUSINESS NEWS. [Art bus. news] Vol. 7, Issue 7 (Nov.-Dec. 1980)-. Trade Publication. English. Twelve times a year. $43.00. Advanstar Communications Inc., 131 West First Street, Duluth MN 55802. **Tel** (218)723-9477, (800)346-0085, FAX (218)723-9437. **ED** Jo Yanow Schwartz. **Bk Rev. Ad Acc. Circ:** 27,989 (ctrl). **Continues** Art Dealer & Framer, 0091-9780.
 Desc: News of the art/framing industry; business management, new products and art industry trends.

DD 705
ISSN 0893-3901
US
Pr Rev.

ART CALENDAR (GREAT FALLS, VA.). (ART CALENDAR.). [Art cal.]. (1986)-. Trade Publication. English. Twelve times a year. $45.00. Art Calendar, PO Box 199, Upper Fairmount MD 21867. **Tel** (410)651-9150, FAX (410)651-5313. **ED** Carolyn Blakeslee. Index available (in August, $15.00). cum. index. **Bk Rev. Ad Acc.** available on an online database.
 Desc: The magazine for visual artists and the definitive source of listings nationwide.

US

ART CATALOGUES. (19??)-. English. One time a year. Free. Art Catalogues, PO Box 650, Springville CA 93265. **Tel** (800)835-4404.

DD 709
ISSN 0195-4148
US

ART CRITICISM. [Art crit.]. **Added/Corp** State University of New York at Stony Brook. Dept. of Art. Vol. 1, No. 1 (Spring 1979)-. Periodical. English. Two times a year. $20.00. State University of New York at Stony Brook, Fine Arts Center 4290, Department of Art, Sony Brook NY 11794. **Tel** (516)632-7250. **ED** Donald Kuspit. **Bk Rev.** Documents available from The Genuine Article.
 Ind/Abst ARTbibliogr. Mod.; Arts Humanit. Citation Index [Full Cov.]; BHA : Biblio. Hist. Art; Res. Alert [Full Cov.].

ISSN 0571-1509
FR

ART DE BASSE-NORMANDIE. No. 1 (1956)-. Periodical. French. Four times a year.
 Ind/Abst BHA : Biblio. Hist. Art.

SA

ART, DESIGN, ARCHITECTURE : ADA. VFOAT Architecture, Design, Art; ADA; ADA Magazine. No. 1 First Quarter (1986)-. Periodical. English. Two times a year. $35.78. ADA Magazine, PO Box 16093, 8018 Vlaeberg South Africa. **Tel** 011 27 21 4619937, FAX 011 27 21 4619937. **ED** Jennifer Sorrell. **Bk Rev**, (Qty: 4). **Ad Acc, Adv Mgr:** Nico Dekker, **Tel** 02 462 2018. **Circ:** 10,000.
 Ind/Abst Avery Index Archit. Period. Suppl. Colum. Univ. (1989-).

US

ART DIRECTORS' INDEX, THE. VFOAT Art Directors' Index to Photographers, Film & Media Production. (19??)-. English. W W Norton & Company Inc., 500 Fifth Avenue, New York NY 10110. **Tel** (800)233-4830.

LC Z5937 .A19 Z674.2
DD 026/.7
ISSN 0730-7187
US
Pr Rev.

ART DOCUMENTATION. See Library and Information Sciences.

LC N4 .A37
DD 705
ISSN 0394-0179
IT

ART E DOSSIER. [Art doss.]. No. 1 (Apr. 1986)-. Periodical. Italian. Eleven times a year. L44960. Giunti Gruppo Editore, Via Bolognese 165, 50139 Florence Italy. **Tel** 011 39 55 6679267, 011 39 55 6679257, FAX 011 39 55 268312, telex 571438. **ED** Valerio Eletti. **Bk Rev. Ad Acc. Circ:** 35,000.
 Desc: Magazine containing a monograph concerning either peculiar art periods or specific artists.
 Ind/Abst Avery Index Archit. Period. Suppl. Colum. Univ. (June-Aug. 1989).

LC N81 .A86
DD 707
ISSN 0004-3125
US

ART EDUCATION (RESTON). (ART EDUCATION.). [Art educ.]. **Added/Corp** National Art Education Association. Vol. 1 (Jan./Feb. 1948)-. Periodical. English. Six times a year (Jan., Mar., May, Jul., Sept., Nov.). $50.00. National Art Education Association, 1916 Association Drive, Reston VA 22091-1590. **Tel** (703)860-8000, FAX (703)860-2960. **ED** Jerome Hausman. cum. index. **Bk Rev. Ad Acc. Circ:** 15,902 (ctrl). available on microfilm and microfiche from University Microfilms International (UMI).
 Desc: Contains distinctive articles on current directions, problems and exemplary approaches in visual art education at all instructional levels. Articles may focus on the art curriculum, teaching strategies, innovative programs, or a special area of the curriculum such as studio, art criticism, or art history. Includes four full-color reproductions of works of art, with commentary and lesson plan suggestions for use at both elementary and secondary levels.
 Ind/Abst Acad. Search; Contents Pages Educ.; Curr. Cit.; Curr. Index J. Educ.; Educ. Index; EP Collect.; Homework Help.; Humanit. Source; INFO-SOUTH Abstr.; Mag. Search; MasterFile FullTEXT 1000; MasterFile FullTEXT 350; MasterFile FullTEXT 650; MasterFile FullTEXT (July 1993-) [Full Txt.]; OCLC; Telebase.

DD 707
ISSN 0708-5354
CN

ART EDUCATION (SASKATOON). (ART EDUCATION.). [Art educ.]. **Added/Corp** Saskatchewan Society for Education Through Art. (Jan. 1979)-. Periodical. English. Two times a year. comes with membership. Saskatchewan Society for Education through Art, 132 510 Cynthia Street, Saskatoon Saskatchewan S7K 7K7 Canada. **Tel** (306)975-0829. **Circ:** 200 (ctrl). **Continues** Discovery through Art, 0315-9027.
 Ind/Abst Can. Educ. Index.

ISSN 0764-9673
FR

ART ET ARCHEOLOGIE EN RHONE ALPES. **Added/Corp** Association les Amis du Chateau des Allymes et de Rene de Lucinge. VFOAT Cahiers Rene de Lucinge. No 2 (1986)-. French (summaries and/or abstracts in English). One time a year. **Continues** Art et Archeologie dans l'Ain et Rhone-Alpes, 0766-1150.
 Ind/Abst BHA : Biblio. Hist. Art.

FR

ART ET METIERS DU LIVRE. See Publishing-Books and Bookmaking.

ISSN 0293-4906
FR

UDC 7.01

ART ET THERAPIE. See Education-Special Education and Rehabilitation.

ISSN 0843-9184
DD 708.11/6225 CN
ART GALLERY OF NOVA SCOTIA JOURNAL. See Museums and Galleries.

LC N3 .A77 ISSN 0173-2781
DD 705 GW
ART (HAMBURG). (ART.). [Art]. (Oct. 1979)-. Periodical. German. Twelve times a year. $90.00. Gruner und Jahr Ag & Co, Abonnenten Service, D-20080 Hamburg Germany. **Tel** 011 49 40 37030, FAX 011 49 40 37035657. **(Subscription address:** German Language Publications Inc., 153 South Dean Street, Englewood NJ 07631. **Tel** (201)871-1010, (800)457-4443.**)**
Ind/Abst ARTbibliogr. Mod.; BHA : Biblio. Hist. Art.

LC N7304 .A75a
DD 709/.54/074095456 II
ART HERITAGE : CATALOG. **Main/Corp** Art Heritage (Gallery). (198?)-. Catalog. English. One time a year. Rs60.00 India; £5.00 UK; $10.00. Art Heritage, Triveni Kala Sangam 205 Tansen Marg, New Delhi 110001 India. **Tel** 389470. **ED** Roshan Alkazi. Index available. **Circ:** 1,000 (ctrl). ***Continues*** *Art Heritage, Catalogue.*

LC N7480 .A77 ISSN 0141-6790
DD 709 UK
CCC
ART HISTORY. [Art hist.]. Vol. 1 (Mar. 1978)-. Academic Scholarly Publication. English. Four times a year. $169.00. Basil Blackwell Publishers Ltd., 108 Cowley Road, Oxford 0X4 1JF United Kingdom. **Tel** 011 44 1235 465500, FAX 011 44 1235 465556, telex 837022 OXBOOK G. **(Subscription address:** Blackwell Publishers / UK, 108 Cowley Road, Oxford OX4 1JF United Kingdom. **Tel** 011 44 1865 791100, FAX 011 44 1865 791347.**)** **ED** J Onions. **Bk Rev. Ad Acc. Circ:** 1,500. available on microfilm and microfiche from University Microfilms International (UMI). Documents available from The Genuine Article, UMI Article Clearinghouse.
Desc: Contributes to the development of art as a major field of intellectual activity, and which encompasses other disciplines.
Ind/Abst Acad. Search; Am. Hist. Life (1980-); Archit. Period. Index (1978-); Art Index; ARTbibliogr. Mod.; ARTbibliogr. Curr. Titles; Arts Humanit. Citation Index [Full Cov.]; Avery Index Archit. Period. Suppl. Colum. Univ. (1990-); BHA : Biblio. Hist. Art; Br. Humanit. Index; Curr. Cit.; Curr. Contents Arts Humanit.; EP Collect.; Expand. Acad. Index (1989-); Hist. Source (July 1993-); Homework Help.; Humanit. Index; Humanit. Source; INFO-SOUTH Abstr.; Mag. Search; MasterFile FullTEXT 1000; MasterFile FullTEXT 350; MasterFile FullTEXT 650; MasterFile FullTEXT (July 1993-); Newsp. Period. Abstr. (1991-); OCLC; Res. Alert [Full Cov.]; Romant. Move.; Telebase.

ISSN 0831-2133
DD 759.11 CN
ART IMPRESSIONS. [Art impress.]. (Aug. 1985)-. Periodical. English. Five times a year (Feb., May, July, Aug., Nov.). 16.84Can$. Branta Publishing, 22 Keele Street South, King City L0G 1K0 Canada. **Tel** (416)833-2737, FAX (416)833-3763.
Desc: A national magazine aimed at antique lovers and collectors. Diverse articles focus on providing factual information to seasoned and beginner collectors. Interesting reports on "Around the Shows" and "Around the Shops" with extensive pictorial coverage and prices that keep the reader informed on "the state of the Market."

LC N1 .A43 ISSN 0004-3214
DD 705 US
ART IN AMERICA (1939). (ART IN AMERICA.). [Art Am.]. Vol. 27, No. 3 (July 1939)-. Periodical. English. Twelve times a year. $39.95. Brant Publishing, 575 Broadway, New York NY 10012. **Tel** (212)941-2800. **(Subscription address:** CDS / SIFD Agency Control, 1901 Bell Avenue, Des Moines IA 50315. **Tel** (515)246-6812.**)** **ED** E. Baker. Index available. cum. index. **Bk Rev. Ad Acc. Circ:** 68,300. available on microfilm and microfiche from University Microfilms International (UMI); available in microform. Documents available from The Genuine Article, UMI Article Clearinghouse, Magazine Collection. ***Continues*** *Art in America and Elsewhere.*
Desc: Presents a wide range of information, criticism and analysis covering the entire field of the visual arts - contemporary American art, old and modern masters, sculpture, architecture, photography, oriental and primitive arts, crafts, and the decorative arts.
Ind/Abst Acad. Abstr. Full Text Elite; Acad. Abstr.; Acad. Ind. [Computer File] (1984-); Acad. Search; Am. Hist. Life (1963-); Art Archaeol. Tech. Abstr.; Art Index; ARTbibliogr. Mod.; Arts Humanit. Citation Index [Full Cov.]; Avery Index Archit. Period. Suppl. Colum. Univ. (1987/1990-); BHA : Biblio. Hist. Art; Book Rev. Digest; Book Rev. Index; Curr. Cit.; Curr. Contents Arts Humanit.; EP Collect.; Expand. Acad. Index (1985-); Film Lit. Index; Gen. Period. Index (1985-); Homework Help.; Humanit. Index; Humanit. Source; INFO-SOUTH Abstr.; Mag. Artic. Summar. Elite; Mag. Artic. Summar. Select; Mag. Artic. Summar. CD-ROM; Mag. Index Plus (1989-); Mag. Index. Sel. (1986-); Mag. Search; MasterFile FullTEXT 1000; MasterFile FullTEXT 350; MasterFile FullTEXT 650; MasterFile FullTEXT (Jan. 1984-); Newsp. Period. Abstr. (1988-); OCLC; Pub. Lib. FullTEXT; Read. Guide Abstr. Select Ed.; Read. Guide Period. Lit.; Res. Alert [Full Cov.]; Romant. Move.; Soc. Sci. Cit. Index [Select. Cov.]; Telebase; Mag. Index (1977-); Vocat. Search.

ISSN 0736-7619
US
ART IN AMERICA. ANNUAL GUIDE TO GALLERIES, MUSEUMS, ARTISTS. See Museums and Galleries.

LC Z5937 .A78 ISSN 0004-3222
DD 016.7 US
NLM Z 5937 A784
Pr Rev.
ART INDEX. See The Arts-Abstracting, Bibliographies and Statistics.

ISSN 0194-9071
DD 705 US
ART INSIGHT. (AI. ART INSIGHT.). [Art insight]. **VFOAT** Art Insight. (19??)-. Periodical. English. Six times a year. ***Continues*** *Southwestern Art, 0038-4739.*

US
ART INSTITUTE OF CHICAGO NEWS & EVENTS, THE. **Added/Corp** Art Institute of Chicago. **VFOAT** Art Institute of Chicago News and Events; News & Events. (Sept./Oct. 1987)-. Periodical. English. Six times a year. comes with membership. Art Institute of Chicago, 111 South Michigan Avenue, Chicago IL 60603. **Tel** (312)443-3600, (312)443-3536, FAX (312)443-0849. **ED** Diane Planer Lovejoy. **Circ:** 110,000. ***Continues*** *Mosaic (Chicago, Ill.), 0891-2009.*

LC N8680 .A77 ISSN 0090-9211
DD 381/.45/7 US
ART INVESTMENT REPORT, THE. Periodical. English. Twenty-six times a year. $275.00. Wall Street Reports Publishing Corporation, 99 Wall Street/22nd Floor, New York NY 10005. **Tel** (212)747-9500, FAX (212)668-9842.

ISSN 1046-8471
DD 700 US
ART ISSUES. [Art issues]. (198?)-. Periodical. English. Six times a year. $25.00. Art Issues, 8721 Santa Monica Boulevard, Suite 6, Los Angeles CA 90069. **Tel** (213)876-4508, FAX (213)876-5061. **ED** Gary Kornblau. **Bk Rev,** (Qty: 1-2). **Ad Acc. Circ:** 9,000 (ctrl).
Desc: Critical writings on visual art and culture.

LC N81 .A887 ISSN 0004-3249
DD 705 US
ART JOURNAL (NEW YORK. 1960). (ART JOURNAL.). [Art j.]. **Added/Corp** College Art Association of America. Vol. 20 (Fall 1960)-. Periodical. English. Four times a year. $45.00. College Art Association of America, 275 Seventh Avenue, New York NY 10001. **Tel** (212)691-1051, FAX (212)627-2381. **Bk Rev. Ad Acc, Adv Mgr:** R. Ramirez. **Circ:** 8,500. available on microfilm and microfiche from University Microfilms International (UMI). Documents available from The Genuine Article, UMI Article Clearinghouse. ***Continues*** *College Art Journal.*
Desc: Devoted to methodological, critical, and aesthetic issues in the arts of the 19th and 20th centuries. Each issue addresses a specific theme in art and art history.
Ind/Abst Acad. Abstr.; Acad. Ind. [Computer File] (1987-); Acad. Search; Annu. Bibliogr. Engl. Lang. Lit.; Archit. Period. Index; Art Archaeol. Tech. Abstr.; Art Index; ARTbibliogr. Mod.; Arts Humanit. Citation Index [Full Cov.]; Avery Index Archit. Period. Suppl. Colum. Univ. (19??-199?); BHA : Biblio. Hist. Art; Book Rev. Index; Curr. Cit.; Curr. Contents Arts Humanit.; EP Collect.; Expand. Acad. Index (1987-); Homework Help.; Humanit. Index; Humanit. Source; INFO-SOUTH Abstr.; Mag. Search; MasterFile FullTEXT 1000; MasterFile FullTEXT 350; MasterFile FullTEXT 650; MasterFile FullTEXT (July 1990-); Middle East Abstr. Index; Newsp. Period. Abstr. (1990-); OCLC; Pub. Lib. FullTEXT; Res. Alert [Full Cov.]; Romant. Move.; Soc. Sci. Cit. Index [Select. Cov.]; Telebase.

LC Z675.A85 A78 ISSN 0307-4722
DD 026/.7 UK
ART LIBRARIES JOURNAL. See Library and Information Sciences.

ISSN 8756-0895
US
ART/LIFE. [Art/life]. **VFOAT** Art Life. (198?)-. Periodical. English. Eleven times a year (publishes monthly except Jan.). $450.00. Art Life Limited Edition, PO Box 23020, Ventura CA 93002.

ISSN 1066-4173
US
ART MATERIALS TODAY. (1993)-. Periodical. English. Six times a year. $49.00. F&W Publications, 1507 Dana Avenue, Cincinnati OH 45207. **Tel** (513)531-2222, FAX (513)531-1843. **(Subscription address:** CDS Agency Hard Copy, PO Box 4966, Des Moines IA 50340. **Tel** (515)247-7569.**)**
Desc: The new magazine for art materials retailers - each issue comes with reviews of issues and products affecting the art materials business. Also included is a special section on new products as well as detailed information on how to market products to art materials buyers.

LC N1 .A57 ISSN 0142-6702
DD 705 UK
ART MONTHLY. [Art mon.]. No. 1 (Oct. 1976)-. Periodical. English. Ten times a year (monthly with Dec./Jan. & July/Aug. issues combined). $90.70. Art Monthly, 26 Charing Cross Road, Suite 17, London WC2H 0DG United Kingdom. **Tel** 011 44 171 5804168, 011 44 171 2400389, FAX 011 44 171 2400389. **ED** Patricia Bickers (editor's address: 66 Wigmore Street, London W1H 0HQ UK). Index available. cum. index. **Bk Rev. Ad Acc. Circ:** 4,000.
Desc: For those involved in contemporary visual arts. Features include in-depth exhibition, book, video, film and performance reviews, artists' books, salesroom reports, correspondence, art notes and art law.
Ind/Abst ARTbibliogr. Mod.; BHA : Biblio. Hist. Art; Br. Humanit. Index.

ISSN 1033-40253
AT
ART MONTHLY AUSTRALIA. **VFOAT** Art Monthly. No. 18 (March 1989)-. Periodical. English. Twelve times a year. 28.78Aus$. Anu Arts Centre, GPO Box 4, Art Mthly Sub, Davie Canberra Act 2601 Australia. **Tel** 011 61 62 480321, FAX 011 61 62 478935. ***Continues*** *Australian and International Art Monthly, 0819-5838.*

US
ART MUSCLE. Vol. 1, Issue 1 (Sept./Nov. 1986)-. English. Six times a year (Feb., Apr., June, Aug., Oct., Dec.). $12.00. Art Muscle Milwaukee Inc., PO Box 93219, Milwaukee WI 53203. **Tel** (414)672-8485, FAX (414)672-8485. **ED** Debra Brehmer, (editor's address: 901 West National Avenue, Milwaukee, WI 53204, phone: (414)672-8485). Index available ($3.00). **Bk Rev. Ad Acc, Adv Mgr:** Angel French. **Circ:** 17,000 (ctrl).
Desc: Provides insight into the ideas and issues that inspire artistic creation. It is for and about art and culture, with special emphasis on Wisconsin artists.

LC N1 .A725 ISSN 0274-7073
DD 709 US
ART NEW ENGLAND. [Art New Engl.]. Vol. 1, No. 1 (Dec. 1979)-. Periodical. English. Six times a year. $24.00 (individuals); $44.00 (institutions). Art New England, 425 Washington Street, Brighton MA 02135. **Tel** (617)782-3008, (617)782-4184, FAX (617)782-4218. **(Subscription address:** Art New England, PO Box 3000, Denville NJ 07834-9946. **)** **ED** Carla Munsat. **Bk Rev,** (Qty: 10). **Ad Acc, Adv Mgr:** C. Errett, **Tel** (617)782-3008. **Circ:** 28,000 (ctrl).
Desc: Concerns native New England artists, architects, designers and craftsmen and their work.

LC N7406 .A74 ISSN 0110-1102
DD 709/.931 NZ
ART NEW ZEALAND. [Art N. Z.]. (Aug./Sept. 1976)-. Periodical. English. Four times a year. $35.00 New Zealand; $65.00 other. Art Magazine Press Ltd, PO Box 10249, Auckland 4 New Zealand. **Tel** 011 64 9 6301328. **ED** William Dart. **Bk Rev. Ad Acc. Circ:** 4,000.
Desc: Covers all aspects of the arts from painting and sculpture through to film and intermedia.
Ind/Abst ARTbibliogr. Mod.; ARTbibliogr. Curr. Titles; BHA : Biblio. Hist. Art.

LC N1 ISSN 0960-6556
IT
ART NEWSPAPER. [Art newspaper]. (1990). Newspaper. Italian. Twelve times a year. $48.00. Umberto Allemandi & Co Publ, Via Mancini 8, 10131 Turin Italy. **Tel** 011 39 11 882556. **Bk Rev,** (Qty: 100/yr). **Ad Acc, Adv Mgr:** L. Comoy. **Circ:** 30,000. ***Absorbed*** *Journal of Art (New York, N.Y. : 1989).*
Ind/Abst Museum Abstr.

CK
ART NEXUS. No. 1 (May 1991)-. Periodical. Spanish (English; translations available in English). Four times a year. $32.00. Arte en Colombia, Apartado Aereo 90193, Bogota Colombia. **Tel** 011 57 1 4136374. **(Subscription address:** Art Nexus, 8877 Collins Ave, Surfside FL 33154. **Tel** (305)868-9583.**)** ***Continues*** *Arte en Colombia (Edicion International), 0120-713X.*
Ind/Abst ARTbibliogr. Curr. Titles; BHA : Biblio. Hist. Art.

US
ART OF ANTIQUITY. **Added/Corp** Boston. Museum of Fine Arts. Dept. of Classical Art. (19??)-. Monographic series. English. Irregular. Price varies per volume. Museum of Fine Arts / Boston, 465 Huntington Avenue, Boston MA 02115. **Tel** (617)267-9300.

LC WMLC 93/3101 ISSN 1045-8913
DD 709 US
TITLE CHANGE
ART OF CALIFORNIA. [Art Calif.]. **VFOAT** Art of California Magazine. Vol. 1, No. 1 (Oct./Nov. 1988)-(1993). Periodical. English. Art of California, 1125 Jefferson Street, Napa CA 94559. **Tel** (707)226-1776. ***Continues*** *Fine Art & Antiques International, 1071-1015.* ***Continued by*** *Fine Art & Antiques International, 1071-1015.*

The Arts —Art

Desc: Covers art and artists in California from 1850 to the present.
Ind/Abst BHA : Biblio. Hist. Art (?-?).

ISSN 1047-4994
DD 700 US

ART OF THE WEST. [Art West] Vol. 1, No. 1 (1987)-. Periodical. English. Six times a year (Jan., Mar., May, July, Sept., Nov.). $21.00. Art of the West, 15612 Highway 7, Suite 235, Minnetonka MN 55345. **Tel** (612)935-5850, FAX (612)935-6546. **ED** Vicki Stavig. Index available. cum. index. **Ad Acc, Adv Mgr:** Tim Tierrey. **Circ:** 15,000.
Desc: Native american art, mountain men art, and "cowboy" art, from the old wild west days to the working cowboy of today.

ISSN 1062-9459
US

ART ON SCREEN. **Added/Corp** Program for Art on Film (New York, N.Y.). (1992)-. Periodical. English. Three times a year. Free. Art on Screen, 980 Madison Avenue, New York NY 10021.

ISSN 1062-9467
US

ART ON SCREEN CLOSE-UPS.
Added/Corp Program for Art on Film (New York, N.Y.). **VFOAT** Art on Screen Close Ups. (1992)-. Periodical. English. Three times a year. $5.00 (single issue). Art on Screen, 980 Madison Avenue, New York NY 10021.

LC NX506 .A77 ISSN 0278-1441
Pr Rev. US

ART PAPERS. [Art pap.] Vol. 5, No. 1 (Jan/Feb. 1981)-. Periodical. English. Six times a year (Jan., Mar., May, July, Sept., Nov.). $25.00. Atlanta Art Papers, PO Box 77348, Atlanta GA 30357. **Tel** (404)588-1837, FAX (404)588-1836. **ED** Glenn Harper. Index available. cum. index. **Bk Rev,** (Qty: 8). **Ad Acc, Adv Mgr:** Ashley Wisner, **Tel** (404)588-1837. **Circ:** 4,000. available on microfiche from Bell & Howell; available on microfilm and microfiche from University Microfilms International (UMI). **Formed by the union of** Contemporary Art/Southeast, 0147-6297 **and** Atlanta Art Papers, 0271-2083.
Desc: Perspectives on artists and their contemporary art. Keeps up with current ideas, new art, and emerging artists in articles, reviews, news and interviews.
Ind/Abst ARTbibliogr. Mod. (1985-).

LC NX2 .A78 ISSN 0245-5676
DD 700/.5 FR

ART PRESS (PARIS, FRANCE : 1981).
(ART PRESS.). (Feb. 1980)-. Periodical. French. Twelve times a year. $179.36. Art Press, 2 rue Saint Simon, 75007 Paris France. **Tel** 011 33 1 45441200, FAX 011 33 1 42221236, telex 205 866 F. **ED** Jean Yves Jovannais. Index available. **Bk Rev. Ad Acc, Adv Mgr:** Amy Pinel. ctrl circ. **Continues** Art Press International.
Desc: Contemporary art magazine, includes elaborate studies and dossiers on art, literature and spectacles; information on the present cultural situation in France and in the world.
Ind/Abst ARTbibliogr. Mod. (1984-); BHA : Biblio. Hist. Art.

LC N8670 .A69 ISSN 1073-6611
DD 700 US

•ART PRICE INDEX INTERNATIONAL. See The Arts-Abstracting, Bibliographies and Statistics.

ISSN 1036-2045
AT

ART READING MATERIAL. **VFOAT** ARM. Art Reading Material. (1991)-. Periodical. English. Four times a year. Comes with Institute of Contemporary Arts membership. Institute of Contemporary Arts, GPO Box P1221, Perth WA 6000 Australia. **Tel** 011 61 9 2276144.

LC Z711 .A787 ISSN 1050-2548
Pr Rev. US

•ART REFERENCE SERVICES QUARTERLY. (ART REFERENCE SERVICES QUARTERLY : ARSQ.). **VFOAT** ARSQ. Vol. 1, No. 1 (1993)-. Periodical. English. Four times a year. $75.00. The Haworth Press Inc., 10 Alice Street, Binghamton NY 13904-1580. **Tel** (607)722-5857, (800)3-HAWORTH, FAX (607)722-1424. **ED** Edward H. Teague (editor's address: Architecture and Fine Arts Library, 201 Fine Arts Building A, Gainesville, FL 32611). **Bk Rev. Ad Acc. Acid Free.** available on microfiche. Documents available from Haworth Document Delivery Service.
Desc: Provides practical and theoretical articles about a wide range of reference issues, with focus on the service needs associated with architecture and the visual arts, broadly defined to include architecture, interior design, landscape architecture, urban planning, art history, archaeology, photography, and studio arts.
Ind/Abst Inf. Sci. Abstr.; Left Index; Libr. Inf. Sci. Abstr.; Sage Urban Stud. Abstr (?-?).

LC N1 .A77 UK

•ART REVIEW : THE ESSENTIAL MONTHLY GUIDE. (1993)-. Periodical. English. Twelve times a year. £64.00 US, Canada and Mexico;
£57.00 Europe; £29.50 UK. Art Review Ltd., 20 Prescott Place, London SW4 6BT United Kingdom. **Tel** 011 44 171 9781000, FAX 011 44 171 9781102. **Continues** Arts Review (London, England), 0004-4091.
Ind/Abst ARTbibliogr. Mod.

LC N8670 .A66 ISSN
DD 707/.5 UK

ART SALES INDEX (WEYBRIDGE, SURREY : 1985). See The Arts-Abstracting, Bibliographies and Statistics.

ISSN 0276-5659
US

ART SCAPE. (ART SCAPE / MIDLAND ART COUNCIL.). **Added/Corp** Midland Art Council. (19??)-. Periodical. English. Four times a year. Free membership, $5.00 other. Midland Art Council, 1801 West St. Andrews Street, Midland MI 48640.

LC N330.A1 A7 US

ART SCHOOL DIRECTORY (WASHINGTON (D.C.)). (ART SCHOOL DIRECTORY.). **Added/Corp** American Federation of Arts. Vol. 1 (1939/40)-. Directory. English. One time a year. $2.50. Billboard Publications Inc., 1515 Broadway Billboard, New York NY 10036. **Tel** (212)764-7300, FAX (305)755-7048, telex WU TWX 710-581-6279.

NE

ART SCHOOL MAGAZINE. (19??)-. Dutch. Six times a year. F45.00 Netherlands; F90.00 other. Art School Bilthoven BV, PB 350, 3720 AJ Bilthoven Netherlands. **Tel** 011 31 30 252255, FAX 31 30 286224. **ED** Anton Kriegsman. Index available. **Bk Rev. Ad Acc. Continues** Tedenen en Schilderen.
Desc: Aimed at free-time artists.

ISSN 0741-496X
US

ART-TALK. **VFOAT** Art Talk. Vol. 3, No. 1 (Oct. 1983)-. Periodical. English. Nine times a year. $18.00. Art Talk Inc., PO Box 8508, Scottsdale AZ 85252. **Tel** (602)948-1799, FAX (602)994-9284. **ED** Thom Romeo. **Bk Rev. Ad Acc. Circ:** 38,000 (ctrl). **Continues** Arizona Art-Talk.
Desc: Fine art with an emphasis on current news and events.

ISSN 0742-1656
US
NLM W1; AR9482
Pr Rev.

ART THERAPY : JOURNAL OF THE AMERICAN ART THERAPY ASSOCIATION. See Medical Sciences-Psychiatry.

ISSN 0891-9070
DD 700 US

ART TIMES (SAUGERTIES, N.Y.). (ART TIMES.). (1984)-. Periodical. English. Eleven times a year (Jan./Feb. issue combined). $15.00. Art Times/Cultural & Creative, PO Box 730, Mount Marion NY 12456. **Tel** (914)246-5170. **ED** Raymond J. Steiner, (phone: (914)246-6944). **Bk Rev,** (Qty: 10). **Ad Acc, Adv Mgr:** Cornelia, **Tel** (914)246-6944. **Circ:** 15,000.
Desc: A literary journal which publishes essays on music, dance, theatre, visual arts, film, art book reviews, short stories and poetry. Also a resource for the Arts in the Hudson Valley Region of New York State. Calendar is an extensive listing of cultural events in the region as well as exhibits at the major museums in New York City, Washington DC and Boston. Includes an opportunities section for artists.

LC N5310.7 .A78
DD 709/.01/105 SZ

ART TRIBAL. **Added/Corp** Musee Barbier-Muller. Association des Amis. **VFOAT** Bulletin (Musee Barbier-Mueller). (1978)-. Bulletin. English (French). Two times a year (Spring & Autumn). $70.00 Switzerland, $80.00 other Comes with Association des Amis du Musee Barbier-Mueller membership. Association des Amis du Musee Barbier-Mueller, 10 rue Calvin, CH-1204 Geneva Switzerland. **Tel** 011 41 22 7864646. ctrl circ.
Ind/Abst Anthropol. Lit.; Ethnoarts Index.

ISSN 0925-1332
UDC 659.12 NE

ART VIEW VIANEN. [Art viewVianen]. (1990)-. Periodical. Dutch. Six times a year. F126.76. Art View, Postbus 1346, 1300 BH Almere Netherlands. **Tel** 011 31 3240 60680.

LC N6512 .A758 ISSN 0272-2097
DD 709/.73 US

ART VOICES (WEST PALM BEACH, FLA.). (ART VOICES.). Vol. 4, No. 1 (Jan./Feb. 1981)-. Periodical. English. Six times a year. $21.00. Art Voices Publishing Company, Commerce Building/Suite 313-314, 324 Datura Street, West Palm Beach FL 33401. **Formed by the union of** Art Voices South, 0147-8761 **and** Artcraft Magazine, 0195-8755.
Ind/Abst ARTbibliogr. Mod.

IT
Pr Rev.

ART WORLD. (19??)-. Italian. Twelve times a year. L45.00 Italy; L50.00 other. Art World Media, Via Tevlie 1, 20136 Milan Italy. **Tel** 02/8379857, FAX 02/58308190. **ED** Marco Lupis di Santa Margherita. **Ad Acc. Circ:** 22,000.
Desc: Lists both national and international art shows, art fairs, art events and auctions.

ISSN 0194-1070
US
SUSPENDED

ART/WORLD (NEW YORK. 1976). (ART/WORLD.). [Art/world]. **VFOAT** Art World. Vol. 1 (Oct. 9, 1976)-Suspended (19??). Periodical. English. Twelve times a year. $20.00 US; $30.00 other. Art/World, 55 Wheatley Road, Glen Head NY 11545. **Tel** (212)626-0914, (212)427-2897. **ED** Theodora W Hooton, Brice Duff Hooton. **Bk Rev. Ad Acc. Circ:** 26,000.
Desc: Reviews on current exhibitions including an international section. Gallery and museum guide, tastemakers (a photograph section of prominent people in the art world).

LC N8 .A73 ISSN 0004-3354
RM

ARTA (BUCURESTI). (ARTA.). [Arta]. **Added/Corp** Uniunea Artistilor Plastici din R.S. Romania. Vol. 15, No. 8 (1968)-. Periodical. Romanian (summaries and/or abstracts in French; table of contents in Russian). Twelve times a year. $86.00. **(Subscription address:** Orion Press SRL, SPL Independentei 202-A, Bucharest 6 Romania. **Tel** 011 401 3122425.) **Continues** Arta Plastica.
Desc: Review of information in fine arts.
Ind/Abst ARTbibliogr. Mod.; BHA : Biblio. Hist. Art.

LC Z5937 .A793 ISSN 0307-9961
DD 016.7 UK

ARTBIBLIOGRAPHIES. CURRENT TITLES. See The Arts-Abstracting, Bibliographies and Statistics.

LC Z5935 .L64 ISSN 0300-466X
DD 016.709/04 UK

ARTBIBLIOGRAPHIES MODERN. See The Arts-Abstracting, Bibliographies and Statistics.

LC N8.A34 A75
DD 705 SA

ARTE, DE. **Added/Corp** University of South Africa. Dept. of History of Art and Fine Arts. (19??)-. Afrikaans (English). Two times a year. $4.84. University of South Africa, PO Box 392, Pretoria 0001 South Africa. **Tel** 011 27 12 4293111, FAX 011 27 12 4293221. **ED** Marion Arnold. **Bk Rev. Ad Acc. Circ:** 800 (ctrl).
Desc: Covers academic art both historical and critical. South African art research is emphasized.
Ind/Abst ARTbibliogr. Mod.

IT

ARTE A BOLOGNA : BOLLETTINO DEI MUSEI CIVICI D'ARTE ANTICA. See Museums and Galleries.

AG

ARTE AL DIA : REVISTA QUINCENAL DE INFORMACIONES DEL MERCADO DE ARTE Y ANTIGUEDADES. (1980)-. Spanish (English). Four times a year. $60.00. Diego Costa Peuser, Bolivar 1542, 1141 Buenos Aires Argentina. **Tel** (541)26-7329, FAX (541)26-7329. **Circ:** 10,000.

LC N7810 .A8 ISSN 0004-3400
DD 704.9/482/05 IT
Pr Rev.

ARTE CRISTIANA. [Arte crist.]. **Added/Corp** Scuola Beato Anglico (Milan, Italy) Societa Amici dell' Arte Cristiana (Milan, Italy) Amici dell' Arte Cristiana (Milan, Italy). Vol.1 (Jan. 1913)-. Periodical. Italian (English). Six times a year. L68130. Scuola Beato Angelico, Viale S Gimignano 19, 20146 Milan Italy. **Tel** 011 39 2 48302854, 011 39 2 48302857. Index available. cum. index. **Bk Rev. Ad Acc. Circ:** 1000 (ctrl).
Desc: Historical studies and contemporary issues.
Ind/Abst Art Archaeol. Tech. Abstr.; ARTbibliogr. Mod. (1985-); Avery Index Archit. Period. Suppl. Colum. Univ. (1989-); BHA : Biblio. Hist. Art.

LC N6911 .A758 ISSN 1121-0524
DD 709/.45/05 IT

ARTE DOCUMENTO. **Added/Corp** Universita di Udine. Cattedra di Storia dell'Arte Moderna I. Centro per la Promozione e lo Sviluppo del Corso di Laurea in Storia e Tutela dei Beni Cultuali. (1988)-. Periodical. Italian. One time a year (Apr.). L90000 (Italy); L120000 (other). Elemond Arte SRL, Via Trentacoste 7, 20134 Milan Italy. **Tel** 011 39 2 215631.
Ind/Abst BHA : Biblio. Hist. Art.

LC N55.S7 A78
DD 702/.5/46 SP

ARTE ESPANOL. (1976)-. Spanish. One time a year. Ediciones L Revista la Piz, c/o Grauina 10, 28004 Madrid Spain. **Tel** 011 34 1 91 2222971. **Bk Rev. Ad**

Acc. Circ: 5,000.
Desc: Annual of Spanish arts (in general, architecture, photography, picture, esculture, etc.). With all the addresses and dates of the expositions, prices of art, and antique dealers.

LC N6758 .A78 **ISSN** 0771-761X
DD 700/.94 BE
CEASED

ARTE FACTUM (ANTWERPEN). (ARTEFACTUM.). [Arte Factum]. **VFOAT** Arte Factum. No. 1 (Dec. 1983)-(Jan. 1995). Periodical. French (English, Dutch and German). Artefactum, Amerikalei 125, B 2000 Antwerpen Belgium. **Tel** 011 32 3 2382089, FAX 011 32 3 2374079. **ED** Anne Schraenen. Index available. **Bk Rev. Ad Acc, Adv Mgr:** D. E. Deyrie. **Circ:** 7,500.
Desc: Information about contemporary art. Lists of recent catalogues, translations on German, French, English, Dutch, and agenda of exhibitions.
Ind/Abst ARTbibliogr. Mod.; BHA : Biblio. Hist. Art.

LC N7 .A7453
DD 705 BL
ARTE HOJE. July (1977)-. Periodical. Portuguese. Twelve times a year. Cr$325. Rio Grafica E Editora, rua Itapiru 1209, 20 000 Rio de Janeiro Brazil.

LC N6480 .A8
DD 700/.5 IT
ARTE IN. Vol. 1, No. 1 (July 1988)-. Periodical. Italian. Six times a year. L32700. Associazione Arte In, via Dell Atomo 6, 30175 Venice Marghera Italy. **Tel** 011 39 41 937830. **Bk Rev**, (Qty: 15). **Ad Acc, Adv Mgr:** Matteo Altilia, **Tel** 011 39 02 26144639. **Circ:** 20,000 (ctrl).

LC N6919.F7 A76
DD 709/.45/39 IT
ARTE IN FRIULI, ARTE A TRIESTE. (19??)-. Periodical. Italian.
Ind/Abst BHA : Biblio. Hist. Art.

LC N5950 .A78 **ISSN** 0393-7267
DD 709/.02 IT
ARTE MEDIEVALE. (1983)-. English (French, German and Italian). Two times a year. L170310. Viella SRL, Via delle Alpi 32, 00198 Rome Italy. **Tel** 011 39 6 8417758. **ED** Angiola Maria Romanini. **Bk Rev. Circ:** 500 (ctrl).
Desc: Aims to provide the state of research on specific questions in areas of medieval art.
Ind/Abst Art Archaeol. Tech. Abstr.; Avery Index Archit. Period. Suppl. Colum. Univ. (1990-); BHA : Biblio. Hist. Art.

ISSN 0390-1319
IT
UDC 75
Pr Rev.
ARTE NAIVE. [Arte naive]. (1974)-. Periodical. Italian. Two times a year. L12260. Arte Naive - AGE, Via Casorati 29, 42100 Reggio Emilia Italy. **Tel** 011 39 522 921276. **ED** Va Casorati. **Bk Rev. Ad Acc. Circ:** 1000.

LC N7262 .A77
IT
ARTE ORIENTALE IN ITALIA. Added/Corp Museo Nazionale d'Arte Orientale (Italy). (1971)-. Italian. Irregular. Museo Nazionale d'Arte Orientale, Via Merulana 248, Rome 00185 Italy.

LC N6921 .A6 **ISSN** 0392-5234
IT
ARTE VENETA : RIVISTA DI STORIA DELL'ARTE. [Arte veneta]. Vol. 1 (1947)-. Italian (summaries and/or abstracts in English). One time a year. $147.42 US and Canada; L140000.00 other. Elemond Arte SRL, Via Trentacoste 7, 20134 Milan Italy. **Tel** 011 39 2 215631. **ED** Rodolfo Pallucchini. **Ad Acc. Circ:** 7,000.
Desc: History of Venetian arts, artists, painters, and architects from the years 1200 to 1800.
Ind/Abst ARTbibliogr. Mod.; Avery Index Archit. Period. Suppl. Colum. Univ. (1988); BHA : Biblio. Hist. Art.

ISSN 1181-8441
DD 708.11/4281/05 CN
ARTEFACT (MONTREAL). See Museums and Galleries.

LC N7108 .A6894 **ISSN** 0211-5271
DD 709/.46/05 SP
ARTEGUIA. [Artequia]. (19??)-. Spanish. Six times a year. $57.74. Fernando Fernandez, Luna 28, 28004 Madrid Spain. **Tel** 011 34 1 5321982.
Ind/Abst BHA : Biblio. Hist. Art.

LC N7 .A768 **ISSN** 0300-4953
DD 700/.972 MX
ARTES DE MEXICO. [Artes Mex.]. **Added/Corp** Universidad Nacional Autonoma de Mexico. Frente Nacional de Artes Plasticas (Mexico). No. 1 (Oct./Nov. 1953)-No. 201/202-New Series No. 1 (1988)-. Periodical. Spanish (English). Six times a year (Jan., Mar., May, July, Sept., Nov.). $150.00. Artes de Mexico del Mundo SA, Plaza Rio de Janiero 52, 06700 Mexico DF Mexico. **Tel** 011 52 5 5255905, 011 52 5 5254036, FAX 011 52 5 5255925.
Desc: Devoted to the range of Mexican art; an encyclopedia of past and present Mexican art.
Ind/Abst ARTbibliogr. Mod.; BHA : Biblio. Hist. Art; Hisp. Am. Period. Index, HAPI (19??-).

ISSN 0871-9276
PO
UDC 73/76
ARTES PLASTICAS LISBOA. [Artes plast.Lisb.]. (1990)-. Periodical. Portuguese. Twelve times a year.
Ind/Abst BHA : Biblio. Hist. Art.

LC N6555 .A75
DD 709/.72 MX
ARTES PLASTICAS : REVISTA DE LA ESCUELA NACIONAL DE ARTES PLASTICAS, UNIVERSIDAD NACIONAL AUTONOMA DE MEXICO. Added/Corp Escuela Nacional de Artes Plasticas (Mexico). (19??)-. Periodical. Spanish. Four times a year.
Ind/Abst BHA : Biblio. Hist. Art.

LC N6612 .A77
PR
ARTES VISUALES. Periodical. Spanish. $10.00. Box 5718 Pta De Tierra, San Juan 00906 Puerto Rico.

ISSN 0278-3827
US
ARTEXTREME. [Artextreme]. **VAT** Art Extreme. 1 (Fall/Winter 1981-82)-. Periodical. English. Two times a year. $5.00. Waisnis, RFD 3 Route 32, Richmond NH 03470.

ISSN 0312-6765
DD 354.9400854 AT
ARTFORCE. [Artforce]. (1975)-. Periodical. English. Four times a year. Free on request. Australia Council, PO Box 788, Strawberry Hills, New South Wales 2012 Australia. **Tel** 02 9509000, FAX 02 9509111.

LC N1 .A814
US
ARTFORUM INTERNATIONAL. VFOAT Art Forum International; Artforum; Artforum International. Vol. 20, No. 9 (May 1982)-. Periodical. English. Ten times a year (monthly except July and Aug.). $66.00. Artforum, 65 Blecker Street, New York NY 10012. **Tel** (212)475-4000, FAX (212)529-1257. **(Subscription address:** Artforum, PO Box 3000, Department AF, Denville NJ 07834-9950. **)** **ED** Ida Pancelli. **Bk Rev. Ad Acc. Circ:** 30,000. ***Continues** Artforum, 0004-3532.*
Desc: A critical journal for contemporary culture worldwide. Contains design and color illustrations.

LC N8 .A75 **ISSN** 0004-3648
DD 705 SZ
ARTIBUS ASIAE. [Artibus Asiae]. **Added/Corp** New York University. Institute of Fine Arts. Vol. 1 (1926)-. Periodical. English (French and German). Four times a year (Jan., Apr., July, Oct.). $100.00. Museum Rietberg Zurich, Gablerstrasse 15, CH-8002 Zurich Switzerland. **Tel** 011 41 1 2024528, FAX 011 41 1 2025201. **ED** Alexander C. Soper. Index available. cum. index. **Bk Rev. Ad Acc. Circ:** 1,200. Documents available from The Genuine Article.
Desc: Asian art and archaeology for scholars and connoisseurs.
Ind/Abst Art Archaeol. Tech. Abstr.; Art Index; ARTbibliogr. Mod.; ARTbibliogr. Curr. Titles; Arts Humanit. Citation Index [Full Cov.]; Avery Index Archit. Period. Suppl. Colum. Univ. (1988/89-1990-); Curr. Contents Arts Humanit.; Index Islam. Lit.; Res. Alert [Full Cov.].

SZ
ARTIBUS ASIAE. SUPPLEMENTUM. Vol. 1 (1937)-. Monographic series. English (German). Irregular. Price varies per volume. Museum Rietberg Zurich, Gablerstrasse 15, CH-8002 Zurich Switzerland. **Tel** 011 41 1 2024528, FAX 011 41 1 2025201. **ED** Alexander C Soper. cum. index. **Bk Rev. Ad Acc. Circ:** 1,200.
Desc: A series of full-length books dealing with kindred subjects: Asian art and archaeology, architecture, Chinese, Japanese, Indian painting and sculpture etc., religion and any branch of Asian studies.
Ind/Abst Art Index.

LC NX1.A1 A77 **ISSN** 0391-9064
DD 705 AU
ARTIBUS ET HISTORIAE. [Artibus hist.]. **Added/Corp** IRSA (Organization). No. 1 (1980)-. Periodical. English (French, German and Italian). Two times a year. $139.00. IRSA Verlag GES MBH, Ruedengasse 6, A 1030 Vienna Austria. **Tel** 011 43 222 7130136, FAX 011 43 222 7130130, telex 5704661. **ED** Jozef Grabski, 0222-713-01-36 (phone). **Ad Acc. Circ:** 1,000.
Desc: Articles on topics in art history by international scholars; coverage of the current trends in the field.
Ind/Abst Am. Hist. Life (1989-); ARTbibliogr. Mod. (1985-); Avery Index Archit. Period. Suppl. Colum. Univ. (19??-199?); BHA : Biblio. Hist. Art.

ISSN 0847-3277
DD 709.712/3/05 CN
ARTICHOKE (CALGARY). (ARTICHOKE.). [Artichoke]. (Fall 1989)-. Periodical. English. Three times a year (Jan., June., Sept.). 25.00Can$. Artichoke Publishing, 901 Jervis Street, Suite 210, Vancouver British Columbia, V6E 2B6 Canada. **Tel** (604)683-1941, FAX (604)684-8799. **Bk Rev**, (Qty: 8). **Ad Acc. Circ:** 1,000.
Desc: A visual arts magazine focusing on western Canada and Alberta in particular.

AG
Pr Rev.
ARTINF. VFOAT Arte Informa. Vol. 9, No. 50/51 (Jan./Feb./March/April 1985)-. Periodical. Spanish. Three times a year (Apr., July, Oct.). $200.00. ARTINF, Las Heras 3807, 1425 Burenos Aires Argentina. **Tel** 011 51 1 8046129, FAX 011 54 1 8017280. **ED** Silvia de Ambrosini. Index available. cum. index. **Bk Rev. Ad Acc, Adv Mgr:** Ines Katzenstein, **Tel** 322 3215 / 804-6129. **Circ:** 2,000 (ctrl). ***Continues** Arte Informa.*
Desc: Includes important artistic manifestations in Argentina; has photography, theater, and music sections.
Ind/Abst Ethnoarts Index.

ISSN 0393-747X
IT
UDC 7(450.55)
TITLE CHANGE
ARTINUMBRIA. [Artinumbria]. (1984)-(19??). Periodical. Italian. Grafiche Benucci Srl, Via Volta, 06087 Pte S Giovanni PG Italy. **Tel** 011 39 75 39441.
***Continued by** Titolo.*

SZ
ARTIS AUSSTELLUNGSKALENDAR. (19??)-. Periodical. German. Six times a year. Comes with Artis : Zeitschrift fuer Neue Kunst. Hallwag AG, Nordring 4, CH-3001 Bern Switzerland. **Tel** 011 41 31 3323131, FAX 011 41 31 414133, telex 912661 HAWA CH. ***Separated from** Artis.*

ISSN 0004-3842
GW
TITLE CHANGE
ARTIS (KONSTANZ). (ARTIS.). [Artis]. (1966)-(Feb. 1994). Periodical. German. Hallwag AG, Nordring 4, CH-3001 Bern Switzerland. **Tel** 011 41 31 3323131, FAX 011 41 31 414133, telex 912661 HAWA CH. **ED** Peter Vetsch. Index available. cum. index. **Bk Rev. Ad Acc. Circ:** 10,000. ***Continues** Speculum Artis.* ***Split into** Artis and Artis Ausstellungskalendar.*
Desc: Covers modern and contemporary paintings. Contains an exhibition/fairs calendar together with news, art-political questions, news about auctions, fairs and the art trade.
Ind/Abst ARTbibliogr. Mod. (1984-); BHA : Biblio. Hist. Art.

SZ
ARTIS : ZEITSCHRIFT FUER NEUE KUNST. (19??)-. Periodical. German. Six times a year. $70.69. Hallwag AG, Nordring 4, CH-3001 Bern Switzerland. **Tel** 011 41 31 3323131, FAX 011 41 31 414133, telex 912661 HAWA CH. ***Separated from** Artis.*

LC N1 .A815 **ISSN** 0004-3877
UK
ARTIST (LONDON. 1931). (THE ARTIST.). [Artist]. (1931)-. Periodical. English. Twelve times a year. $50.00. Artist Publishing Company Ltd., Caxton House, 63-65 High Street, Tenterden Kent TN30 6BD United Kingdom. **Tel** 011 44 15806 3315, FAX 011 44 15806 5411. **ED** Sally Bulgin. Index available. **Bk Rev. Ad Acc, Adv Mgr:** P. Hunter. **Circ:** 18,000. available on microfilm and microfiche from University Microfilms International (UMI). ***Formed by the union of** Art & Artists (Brevet Publishing Limited), 0004-3001.*
Desc: Aspects of fine arts with emphasis on instruction in painting and drawing (all media) by UK's most distinguished practicing painters, plus technical information, materials, exhibitions, etc.
Ind/Abst Art Index; ARTbibliogr. Mod.

LC N6921.T93 A77
DD 709/.45/505 IT
ARTISTA (FLORENCE, ITALY). (ARTISTA.). (1989)-. Periodical. Italian. One time a year (June). L80000 (Italy); L100000 (other). Le Lettere, Costa San Giorgio 28, 50125 Florence Italy. **Tel** 011 39 55 2342710. **(Subscription address:** Licosa s.p.a., PO Box 552, 50125 Florence Italy. **Tel** 011 39 55 645415.**)**
Ind/Abst BHA : Biblio. Hist. Art.

UK
ARTISTS AND ILLUSTRATORS. (19??)-. English. Twelve times a year. £22.20 UK; £27.00 other. Artists & Illustrators Ltd, 4 Brandon Road, London N7 9TP United Kingdom. **Tel** 011 44 171 6092177.

LC N11 .A8413 **ISSN** 0161-6692
DD 706/.273 US
ARTISTS EQUITY NEWS. Periodical. English. Artists Equity Association, 3726 Albemarle Street NW, Washington DC 20016. ***Continues** Artists Equity Association. National Newsletter.*

LC N7430 .A734 ISSN 0741-3351
DD 702/.8 US
ARTIST'S MAGAZINE, THE. [Artist's mag.]. Vol. 1, No. 1 (Jan. 1984)-. Periodical. English. Twelve times a year. $24.00. F&W Publications, 1507 Dana Avenue, Cincinnati OH 45207. **Tel** (513)531-2222, FAX (513)531-1843. **(Subscription address:** CDS Agency Hard Copy, PO Box 4966, Des Moines IA 50340. **Tel** (515)247-7569.) **ED** Mike Ward. Index available. **Bk Rev. Ad Acc. Circ:** 200,841. available on microfilm from University Microfilms International (UMI).
Desc: Colorful how-to magazine for artists, featuring step-by-step art instruction and advice on how and where to exhibit and sell artwork.
Ind/Abst Index Inf. (June 1989-).

ISSN 1053-4156
DD 709 US
ARTISTS RESOURCE GUIDE TO NEW ENGLAND, THE. (ARTISTS RESOURCE GUIDE TO NEW ENGLAND.). [Artists resour. guide N. Engl.]. **Added/Corp** Artists Foundation. Pate Poste. **VFOAT** Artists Resource Guide to New England Galleries, Grants, and Services. (1988)-. English. Artists Foundation, 100 Boylston Street, Boston MA 02116. ***Formed by the union of** Money Business: Grants and Awards for Creative Artists, 0161-5866 **and** Artists Guide to New England Galleries.*

LC NX180.T4 D57
DD 700/.1/0502573 US
ARTISTS USING SCIENCE AND TECHNOLOGY DIRECTORY. Added/Corp Ylem (Organization). (199?)-. Directory. English. YLEM, Artists Using Science and Technology, PO Box 749, Orinda CA 94563. ***Continues** Directory of Artists Using Science and Technology.*

LC N6 .A79 ISSN 0239-202X
PL
ARTIUM QUAESTIONES. Added/Corp Uniwersytet im. Adama Mickiewicza w Poznaniu. Uniwersytet im. Adama Mickiewicza w Poznaniu. Instytut Historii Sztuki. 1- (1979)-. Periodical. English (French and Polish). $65.00. **(Subscription address:** Ars Polona-Ruch, PO Box 1001, Krakowskie Przedmiescie 7, 00-068 Warsaw Poland. **Tel** 011 48 22 261201.)

LC N ISSN 1059-7263
DD 702-709 US
●**ARTLANTA.** (ARTLANTA : THE MAGAZINE OF ATLANTA'S WHO'S WHO IN ART.). **VFOAT** Art Atlanta. (1993)-. Periodical. English. Six times a year. $48.00. Selph Image, PO Box 191694, Atlanta GA 30319.

LC N726 .C763
US
ARTLETTER. Main/Corp Crocker Art Museum. **VFOAT** Art Letter; Crocker Art Museum Calendar; Calendar. Vol. 1, No. 1 (July/Aug. 1991)-. English. Six times a year. ***Continues** Calendar.*

ISSN 0727-1239
DD 705 AT
CCC
ARTLINK. [Artlink]. (1981)-. Periodical. English. Four times a year (Mar., June, Sept., Dec.). 90.44Aus$. Artlink, 363 Espanade, Henley Beach SA 5022 Australia. **Tel** 011 61 8 356 8511, FAX 011 61 8 235 1280. **ED** Stepanie Britton. Index available. cum. index. **Bk Rev. Ad Acc, Adv Mgr:** S. Britton. **Circ:** 3,000 (ctrl).
Ind/Abst EP Collect.; Homework Help.; MasterFile FullTEXT 1000; MasterFile FullTEXT 350; MasterFile FullTEXT 650; MasterFile FullTEXT; OCLC; Telebase; World Mag. Bank.

AT
ARTLOOK. Vol. 1, (Feb. 1975)-. Periodical. English. Twelve times a year. Artlook, Stirling Street, PO Box 8268, Perth 6000 Western Australia. **Tel** 011 61 9 3289188.

ISSN 1060-3662
DD 708 US
ARTNEWS INTERNATIONAL DIRECTORY OF CORPORATE ART COLLECTIONS. [ARTnews int. dir. corp. art collect.]. **Added/Corp** International Art Alliance. **VFOAT** Art News International Directory of Corporate Art Collections; International Directory of Corporate Art Collections. (1988)-. Directory. English. Every 2 years. $109.95. ARTnews Associates, 48 West 38th Street, 9th Floor, New York NY 10018. **Tel** (212)398-1690, FAX (212)819-0394. **ED** Shirley Feiff Howarth. Index available. ***Continues** ARTnews Directory of Corporate Art Collections, 0895-4658.*
Desc: A single source of corporate art buying and investment knowledge. Lists over 1,000 corporate art collections in the US and abroad. Completely cross-indexed.

LC N1 .A839 ISSN 0145-7241
DD 338.4/7/7 US
ARTNEWSLETTER, THE. [ARTnewsl.]. **VFOAT** Art Newsletter. Vol. 1, (Sept. 2, 1975)-. Newsletter. English. Twenty-four times a year. $249.00. ARTnews Associates, 48 West 38th Street, 9th Floor, New York NY 10018. **Tel** (212)398-1690, FAX (212)819-0394. **ED** Milton Esterow. **Bk Rev. Circ:** 2,000. available on microfilm from University Microfilms International (UMI).
Desc: Coverage includes art auctions in US and overseas. Analyses of price attribution, controversies, art legislation, private sales, interviews with dealers, collectors and curators.

LC N1 .A776 ISSN 0739-8646
DD 700 US
CEASED
ARTPAPER. [Artpaper]. **Added/Corp** Visual Arts Information Service (Minneapolis, Minn.). **VFOAT** Art Paper. (1982)-(Oct. 1993). Periodical. English. Visual Arts Information Service, 2402 University Avenue West, Suite 206, St. Paul MN 55114. **Tel** (612)645-5542, FAX (612)644-3643. **ED** Lane Relyea. **Bk Rev. Ad Acc. Circ:** 3,000 (ctrl). available on microfilm.
Desc: An alternative journal on art and culture which contains the nation's most comprehensive listing of grants and competitions for visual artists.

LC N81 .A8885 ISSN 0518-8172
DD 707/.073 US
ARTS AND ACTIVITIES YEARBOOK. [Arts act. yearb.]. **VFOAT** Living Art Ideas. No. 1 (1960)-. English. One time a year. Arts and Activities Yearbook, 591 Camino de la Reina/Suite 200, San Diego CA 92108.

UK
ARTS & THE ISLAMIC WORLD. [Arts Islam. world]. **VFOAT** Arts and the Islamic World. Vol. 1, No. 1 (Winter 1982/1983)-. English. Four times a year. $60.00 (surface mail); $75.00 (airmail). Arts & the Islamic World, 144 146 Kings Cross Road, London WC1X 9DH United Kingdom. **Tel** 011 44 171 8338275, FAX 011 44 171 2784797. **ED** Jalal Uddin Ahmed. **Bk Rev. Ad Acc.**
Desc: Dedicated to all aspects of Islamic art, architecture and crafts.
Ind/Abst ARTbibliogr. Mod.; Avery Index Archit. Period. Suppl. Colum. Univ. (Summer 1990-); Ethnoarts Index.

ISSN 0220-2220
FR
UDC 92
ARTS DE L'OUEST. (1976)-. Periodical. French.
Ind/Abst BHA : Biblio. Hist. Art.

ISSN 0889-2172
DD 707 US
SUSPENDED
ARTS EDUCATION REVIEW OF BOOKS, THE. [Art educ. rev. books]. Vol. 1, No. 1 (Winter 1985)-Suspended with Vol. 5. Periodical. English. Three times a year. $20.00 US; $23.00 other. The Arts Education Review of Books, 340 Hopkins Hall, Columbus OH 43210. Index available. **Bk Rev. Ad Acc. Circ:** 200.

US
CEASED
ARTS MAGAZINE. INTERNATIONAL DIRECTORY OF EXHIBITION CATALOGUES. VFOAT International Directory of Exhibition Catalogues; Arts Magazine International Directory of Exhibition Catalogues. (1991/1992)-(1993). Directory. English. Arts Magazine, 561 Broadway, New York NY 10012.

ISSN 0740-9214
DD 708 US
ARTS QUARTERLY (NEW ORLEANS, LA. 1978). **See** Museums and Galleries.

ISSN 1064-6620
US
ARTSOURCE (RENAISSANCE, CALIF.). (ARTSOURCE.). **VFOAT** Art Source; Art Source Quarterly; ArtSource Quarterly. (1992)-. Periodical. English. Four times a year. $19.00. Art Network, 13284 Rices Crossing Road, Suite #3, PO Box 369, Renaissance CA 95962. **Tel** (916)692-1355, FAX (916)692-1370. **ED** Constance Franklin-Smith. **Bk Rev,** (Qty: 3). **Ad Acc, Adv Mgr:** Sarah Meyers. **Circ:** 3,000 (ctrl).
Desc: Provides information that will assist fine artists in marketing and producing top quality work.

US
ARTSPACE. (19??)-. English. Four times a year (Jan., Apr., July, Oct.). Free. Ohio Arts Council, 727 East Main Street, Columbus OH 43205. **Tel** (614)466-2613.

LC NX508.6 .A77 ISSN 0193-6956
DD 700/.978 US
CEASED
ARTSPACE. Added/Corp Artspace, Inc. Vol. 1 (Fall 1976)-Vol. 17, No. 162 (June 1993). Periodical. English. ARTSPACE, 5657 Wilshire Blvd, Suite 340, Los Angeles CA 90036. **Tel** (213)1433, FAX (213)931-1435. **(Subscription address:** Artspace, Department ARS, PO Box 3000, Denville NJ 07834-9818.) **ED** William Peterson. **Bk Rev,** (Qty: 1/yr). **Ad Acc, Adv Mgr:** R Heller. **Circ:** 15,000.
Desc: Feature articles on the contemporary visual arts in the Southwestern U.S. and California in full color.
Ind/Abst Access (1979-); ARTbibliogr. Mod.; ARTbibliogr. Curr. Titles.

ISSN 1065-1543
DD 709 US
ARTSPEAK (NEW YORK, N.Y.). (ARTSPEAK.). [Artspeak]. **VFOAT** Art Speak. Vol. 1, No. 1 (Dec. 6, 1979)-. English. Nine times a year. $30.00. Art Liaison Inc., 245 8th Avenue, Suite 285, New York NY 10011. **Tel** (212)924-6531. **ED** Margot Palmer Poroner. Index available. cum. index. **Bk Rev,** (Qty: 5). **Ad Acc.** available on an online database from Internet.
Desc: News and information on art and reviews.

ISSN 0146-2342
US
ARTVIEW. Periodical. English. Three times a year. $5.00. Artview, Federation of Staten Island Artists and Craftsmen, PO Box 202, Staten Island NY 10314.

ISSN 0004-4121
DD 705 US
ARTWEEK (CASTRO VALLEY, CALIF.). (ARTWEEK.). [Artweek]. **VFOAT** Art Week; West Coast Art News. Vol. 1, No. 1 (Jan. 3, 1970)-. Trade Publication. English. Twelve times a year. $34.00. Artweek, 2149 Paragon Drive, Suite 100, San Jose CA 95131. **Tel** (408)441-7065. **ED** Bruce Nixon. available on microfilm and microfiche from University Microfilms International (UMI).
Desc: Coverage of West Coast art. Reviews painting, sculpture, photography; with gallery guide, classified ads, photography and performance schedules, events listings, and competition listings. Also art-related news and reports of appointments, acquisitions and grants.
Ind/Abst Art Index; ARTbibliogr. Mod.; ARTbibliogr. Curr. Titles.

ISSN 1033-0216
DD 705 AT
ARTWORK MAGAZINE. [Artwork mag.]. (1988)-. Periodical. English. Four times a year. Comes with Community Arts Network membership. SA Community Arts Network, 278 Halifax Street, Adelaide SA 5000 Australia. **Tel** 011 61 8 2324343.
Ind/Abst Museum Abstr.

US
ARTWORLD. (19??)-. Periodical. English. Four times a year. $48.00 (institutions), $32.00 (individuals). Latin American Art Magazine, PO Box 9888, 7824 East Lewis Street, Scottsdale AZ 85257. **Tel** (602)947-8422, FAX (602)947-8947. ***Continues** Latin American Art.*

LC N6750 .A77 ISSN 1062-8312
DD 709/.4/05 US
Pr Rev.
ARTWORLD EUROPE. [Artworld Eur.]. **Added/Corp** Humanities Exchange, Inc. **VFOAT** Art World Europe; Artworld Europe. (Fall 1990)-. Periodical. English. Six times a year (Jan., Mar., May, July, Sept., Nov.). $59.00. The Humanities Exchange, PO Box 1608, Largo FL 34294. **Tel** (813)581-7328, FAX (813)585-6398. **ED** Shirley R. Howarth. Index available. cum. index. **Bk Rev,** (Qty: 10). **Circ:** 2,000. available on diskette (each back issue available from publisher).
Desc: Provides information on European museums, art exhibitions, art fairs and other art events and news.

ISSN 0394-0624
IT
UDC 7
ARX. [Arx]. (1979)-. Periodical. German. Two times a year.
Ind/Abst BHA : Biblio. Hist. Art.

JA
ASAHI GURAFU. VFOAT Asahi Graph. (1923)-. Periodical. Japanese. One time a week. $424.00. **(Subscription address:** Japan Publications Trading Company Ltd., PO Box 5030, Tokyo International, Tokyo 100-31 Japan. **Tel** 011 81 3 3292 3753.)

LC N7358 .A85
JA
ASAHI GYARARI NENKAN. VFOAT Asahi Gallery Annual. 1978-. Periodical. Japanese. ¥3000. Kabushiki Kaisha Sampo Janaru, 10-17 Hamamatsucho 1 Minato-ku, Tokyo 105 Japan. ***Continues** Asahi Geijutsu Nenkan.*

ISSN 0518-8520
GW
UDC 908.430.1-35.61
ASCHEFFENBURGER JAHRBUCH FUER GESCHICHTE, LANDESKUNDE UND KUNST DES UNTERMAINGEBIETES. [Aschaffenbg. Jahrb. Gesch., Landeskd. Kunst Untermaingeb.]. **VFOAT** Aschaffenburger Jahrbuch. (1952)-. Periodical. German. Irregular.
Ind/Abst BHA : Biblio. Hist. Art.

LC N7262 .A877 ISSN 0894-234X
DD 709/.5 US
CCC
Pr Rev. TITLE CHANGE
ASIAN ART. [Asian art]. **Added/Corp** Arthur M. Sackler Gallery (Smithsonian Institution). Vol. 1, No. 1 (Fall/Winter 1988)-(1993). Periodical. English. Oxford University Press / New York, 200 Madison Avenue, New

The Arts — Art

York NY 10016. **Tel** (212)679-7300, (919)677-0977, (800)451-7556, (800)445-9714, FAX (919)677-1303. **ED** Karen Sagstetter. **Ad Acc.** available on microfilm from University Microfilms International (UMI). Documents available from The Genuine Article. *Continued by Asian Art & Culture, 1352-2744.*
Desc: Each issue contains articles on painting, sculpture, decorative arts, ceramics, textiles, photography, architecture, and folk traditions from ancient times to the present.
Ind/Abst Curr. Contents Arts Humanit.; Res. Alert [Full Cov.].

LC N7262 .A877   ISSN 1352-2744
Pr Rev.   US

●**ASIAN ART & CULTURE. Added/Corp** Arthur M. Sackler Gallery (Smithsonian Institution). **VFOAT** Asian Art and Culture. Vol. 7, No. 1 (Winter 1994)-. Periodical. English. Three times a year. $90.00. Oxford University Press / New York, 200 Madison Avenue, New York NY 10016. **Tel** (212)679-7300, (919)677-0977, (800)451-7556, (800)445-9714, FAX (919)677-1303. **(Subscription address:** Oxford University Press / USA, Journals Marketing Department, Oxford University Press, 2001 Evans Road, Cary NC 27513. **Tel** (800)451-7556, (919)677-0977, FAX (919)677-1714.**)** *Continues Asian Art, 0894-234X.*

HK

ASIAN ART NEWS. (19??)-. English. Six times a year. $38.00 Canada; $28.00 US; $60.00 other. Asian Art News, Suite 2A Glenealy Mansion, 7 Glenealy Central Hong Kong. **Tel** 011 852 25223443, FAX 011 852 25215268. **ED** Ian Findley-Brown. **Bk Rev**, (Qty: various). **Ad Acc, Adv Mgr:** Amy Schrier. **Circ:** 10,000.
Desc: Focuses on issues surrounding contemporary art in Asia.

ISSN 0333-6476
UDC 7.03   IS

ASSAPH. SECTION B. STUDIES IN ART HISTORY. [Assaph, Sect. B, Stud. art hist.]. (1980)-. Periodical. English. One time a year. Tel Aviv University / Visual & Performing Arts, Faculty of Visual & Performing Arts, Ramat Aviv, 69978 Tel Aviv Israel. **Tel** 011 972 3 420612.
Ind/Abst BHA : Biblio. Hist. Art.

ISSN 0224-0718
UDC 92   FR

ASSOCIATION LEONARD-DE-VINCI. **VFOAT** Leonard-de-Vinci Etudes et Recherches; Bulletin de l'Association Leonard-de-Vinci (1983). (1974)-. Bulletin. French. One time a year. L'Association Leonard-de-Vinci, Amboise France. *Continues Bulletin de l'Association Leonard-de-Vinci, 0571-5903.*
Ind/Abst BHA : Biblio. Hist. Art.

GW

ASSOCIATION OF HISTORIANS OF AMERICAN ART NEWSLETTER. Main/Corp Association of Historians of American Art. **VFOAT** Newsletter; AHAA Newsletter. (19??)-. Newsletter. English. Two times a year. $5.00. Stony Brook Foundation / AHAA, 830 Fireplace Road, Polock Krasner House, East Hampton NY 11937. **Tel** (516)324-4929, FAX (516)324-8768. **ED** Helen A. Harrison. **Circ:** 500 (ctrl). *Continues Association of Historians of American Art. A.H.A.A. Newsletter.*
Desc: Provides information concerning current exhibitions, catalogs, and in-progress studies in American art. Also publishes scholarly queries.

ISSN 1065-1101
DD 708   US

AT THE MUSEUM. See Museums and Galleries.

ISSN 0789-9343
FI

ATENEUM HELSINKI. (ATENEUM.). VFOAT Finnish National Gallery Bulletin. (1992)-. Bulletin. Multiple languages. One time a year.
Ind/Abst BHA : Biblio. Hist. Art.

LC N1 .A92   ISSN 0732-1619
DD 705   US

ATHANOR (TALLAHASSEE, FLA.). (ATHANOR.). [Athanor]. **Added/Corp** Florida State University. Art History Students' Organization. (1981)-. English. One time a year. $5.00. Florida State University Fine Arts, 250 Fab Gallery, Tallahassee FL 32306. **Tel** (904)644-6836. **ED** Francois Bucher, Allys Palladino-Craig. Index available. **Circ:** 300 (ctrl).
Desc: Graduate students' essays on topics of art history and humanities.
Ind/Abst BHA : Biblio. Hist. Art.

LC DS111.A1 A82   ISSN 0792-8424
DD 950   IS

ATIQOT. Added/Corp Israel. Rashut Ha-Atikot. **VFOAT** Atikot. Vol. 20 (1991)-. Israel Antiquities Authority Scholarly Publication. English (Hebrew). Israel Antiquities Authority, PO Box 586, Jerusalem 91004 Israel. **Tel** 011 972 2 292607, FAX 011 972 2 292628. **ED** Ayala Sussmann.

Circ: 1,500. *Formed by the union of* Atiqot. English Series, 0066-488X *and* Atikot. Sidrah Ivrit, 0067-0138.
Ind/Abst BHA : Biblio. Hist. Art; Numis. Lit.

ISSN 0267-484X
UK

ATLAS (LONDON, ENGLAND : 1985). (ATLAS.). No. 1 (1985)-. Periodical. English (French and German). Irregular. Atlas / London, 16 Talfourd Road, London SE15 5NY United Kingdom. **Tel** 011 44 171 7013689. **ED** Jake Tilson. **Ad Acc. Circ:** 2,500.
Desc: A multiple art form.
Ind/Abst Peace Res. Abstr. J. (1985-1986).

LC N8.J28 A87
JA

ATORIE = ATELIER. VFOAT Atelier. (1924)-. Periodical. Japanese. Twelve times a year. $308.50. Atoriesha, c/o Shinichi Building, 8, Yotsuya 2, Shinjuku-ku, Tokyo 160. **(Subscription address:** Japan Publications Trading Company Ltd., PO Box 5030, Tokyo International, Tokyo 100-31 Japan. **Tel** 011 81 3 3292 3753.**)**

LC N4 .A88   ISSN 0394-7157
IT

ATTI E MEMORIE / ACCADEMIA CLEMENTINA. Added/Corp Accademia Clementina. (19??)-. Italian.
Ind/Abst BHA : Biblio. Hist. Art.

LC DG402 .S65
IT

ATTI E MEMORIE DELLA SOCIETA TIBURTINA DI STORIA E D'ARTE. See History-History of Europe.

LC N6505 .A9   ISSN 0144-3690
UK

AUCTION PRICES OF AMERICAN ARTISTS. (1978)-. English. Every 2 years. $40.00. Art Sales Index Ltd, 1 Thames Road, Weybridge Surrey KT1 38JG United Kingdom. **Tel** 011 44 1932 856426, FAX 011 44 1932 842482.

US

AUCTIONEER, THE. Added/Corp Phillips, Son & Neale, Firm, New York. (19??)-. Trade Publication. English. Three times a year. $300.00. Phillips, 406 East 79th Street, Catalog Department, New York NY 10021. **Tel** (212)570-4830.
Desc: Auction catalogues, including Americana, art nouveau, art deco, American and European paintings, books and manuscripts, and jewelry.

ISSN 0004-8062
DD 850   IT

AUREA PARMA. See Literature.

LC PT1856.Z5 A9
GW

AURORA (WUERZBURG). See Literature.

ISSN 0935-7157
UDC 069   GW

AUS HESSISCHEN MUSEEN. [Aus hess. Mus.]. (1975)-. Periodical. German. Irregular.
Ind/Abst BHA : Biblio. Hist. Art.

ISSN 1032-1942
DD 707.05   AT

AUSTRALIAN ART EDUCATION. [Aust. art educ.]. **Added/Corp** Australian Institute of Art Education. (1988)-. Periodical. English. Three times a year (May, Aug., Dec.). 32.88Aus$. Australian Institute of Art Education, Thornlie Snir High School, Ovens Road, Thornlie WA 6108 Australia. **Tel** 011 61 9 4592544. **(Subscription address:** Australian Institute of Art Education, Springwood High School, C. Hales, Logan Queensland 4127 Australia. **Tel** 011 61 7 2087277.**)** *Continues Journal of the Institute of Art Education, 0729-5995.*
Ind/Abst APAIS, Aust. Public Aff. Inf. Ser. (19??-); Aust. Educ. Index; Curr. Index J. Educ.

ISSN 0813-8095
DD 700.2394   AT

AUSTRALIAN ARTIST. [Aust. artist]. (1984)-. Periodical. English. Twelve times a year. 40.69Aus$. Australian Artist, PO Box 978, Chatswood NSW 2067 Australia. **Tel** 61 2 4196333.
Ind/Abst EP Collect.; Homework Help.; MasterFile FullTEXT 1000; MasterFile FullTEXT 350; MasterFile FullTEXT 650; MasterFile FullTEXT (Sept. 1994-); Telebase; World Mag. Bank.

LC N7400 .A816   ISSN 0314-6464
DD 705   AT
Pr Rev.

AUSTRALIAN JOURNAL OF ART. (AUSTRALIAN JOURNAL OF ART / ART ASSOCIATION OF AUSTRALIA.). [Aust. j. art]. **Added/Corp** Art Association of Australia. (1978)-. Periodical. English. One time a year (May). 45.00Aus$ Comes with Art Association of Australia membership. Art Association of Australia, Art History Department, La Trobe University, Bundoora Victoria 3083 Australia. **Tel** 011 61 3 4792354. **ED** Helen Grace (editor's address: Faculty of Visual & Performing

Arts, University of Western Sydney - Nepean, PO Box 10, Kingswood, New South Wales, 2767 Australia; e-mail # h.grace@hepean.uws.edu.av.). **Bk Rev**, (Qty: 3-4). **Ad Acc, Adv Mgr:** Helen Grace. **Circ:** 500 (ctrl).
Desc: Publishes original papers on all areas/periods of art history, theory, and criticism. Papers accepted from overseas authors.
Ind/Abst APAIS, Aust. Public Aff. Inf. Ser. (1984-); ARTbibliogr. Mod.; BHA : Biblio. Hist. Art.

LC WMLC 93/1742   ISSN 1041-6994
DD 909   US

AVISTA FORUM. [AVISTA forum]. **Added/Corp** Association Villard de Honnecourt for the Interdisciplinary Study of Medieval Technology, Science and Art. **VFOAT** Forum. (1986)-. Periodical. English. Two times a year (Feb/Mar. and Oct/Nov.). $15.00 one-year for students and retirees; $20.00 (individuals); $25.00 (institutions). University of Oregon Department of Art History, Eugene OR 97403. **Tel** (503)346-3675. **ED** Michael Davis (phone: (413)538-2200). **Circ:** 200 (ctrl).
Desc: A semi-annual journal containing articles, notes and queries section, reviews of sciences, new articles, and information on conferences related to art and technology and art and science.
Ind/Abst BHA : Biblio. Hist. Art.

ISSN 0829-982X
DD 971.3/541   CN

AZURE (TORONTO). See Interior Design and Decoration.

LC N7310.8.B25 B35
DD 709/.549/2   BG

BANGLADESH LALIT KALA. Added/Corp Dacca Museum. Vol. 1 (Jan. 1975)-. English (English). Two times a year. $15.00. Dacca Museum, Director, GPO Box 355, Dacca 2 Bangladesh.

ISSN 0210-0274
UDC 7   SP

BATIK. [Batik]. (1973)-. Periodical. Spanish. Four times a year. $70.00. Batik, Rambla de Prat 6 Principal 1, 08012 Barcelona Spain. **Tel** 011 31 3 2174520, FAX 011 31 3 2174520. **ED** Manuek Rufi-Gibert.
Ind/Abst BHA : Biblio. Hist. Art.

ISSN 0710-0744
DD 707   CN

BCATA JOURNAL FOR ART TEACHERS (1979). (BCATA JOURNAL FOR ART TEACHERS.). [BCATA j. art teach]. **Added/Corp** British Columbia Art Teachers' Association. **VFOAT** Journal. **VAT** Journal - British Columbia Art Teachers' Association (1979); British Columbia Art Teachers' Association Journal for Art Teachers (1979). Vol. 19, No. 3 (Apr. 1979)-. Periodical. English. Irregular. 29.61Can$. British Columbia Teachers Federation, 100-550 West 6th Avenue, Vancouver British Columbia V5Z 4P2 Canada. **Tel** (604)871-2283, (800)663-9163, FAX (604)871-2294, (604)871-2290. *Continues British Columbia Art Teachers' Association. Journal, 0708-9430.*

BE

BEAUX ARTS. (19??)-. Periodical. Dutch (French).
Ind/Abst BHA : Biblio. Hist. Art.

LC N1 .B43   ISSN 0757-2271
DD 705   FR

BEAUX ARTS MAGAZINE. [Beaux arts mag.]. **VFOAT** Beaux Arts; Magazine Beaux Arts; Beaux-Arts Magazine. (19??)-. Periodical. French. Eleven times a year (monthly except combined July and Aug.). $97.76. Beaux Arts Magazine, 9 rue Gaillard, 75018 Paris France. **Tel** 011 33 1 49251717, FAX 011 33 1 49251721. **ED** Guy Boyer, Elisabeth Leibovici Louis Gaillenmin. Index available. **Bk Rev. Ad Acc. Circ:** 72,000 (ctrl).
Desc: Current exhibitions and current events in painting and architecture; extensive calendar of exhibitions in Europe.
Ind/Abst ARTbibliogr. Mod.; BHA : Biblio. Hist. Art.

ISSN 0067-5121
GW

BEITRREAGE ZUR KUNST DES CHRISTLICHEN OSTENS. Vol. 1 (1964)-. Monographic series. German. Irregular. Price varies per volume. Verlag Aurel Bongers KG, Postfach 100264, D-45602 Recklinghausen Germany. **Tel** 011 49 2361 41101, 011 49 2361 41102.

LC N   ISSN 0253-1666
DD 702   PO

BELAS-ARTES. [Belas-artes]. **Added/Corp** Academia Nacional de Belas Artes, Lisbon. **VFOAT** Belas Artes. 2nd Ser., No. 1 (1948)-. Periodical. Portuguese.

The Arts —Art

cum. index. **Continues** Academia Nacional de Belas Artes, Lisbon. Boletim.
Ind/Abst BHA : Biblio. Hist. Art.

AT

BENALLA ART GALLERY NEWSLETTER. (1991)-. Newsletter. English. Irregular. 8.0Aus$ single; 12.00Aus$ family Comes with Benalla Art Gallery membership. Benalla Art Gallery, PO Box 320, Benalla Victoria 3672 Australia. **Tel** 057 623027.

GW

BERICHT DER STAATLICHEN DENKMALPFLEGE IM SAARLAND. ABTEILUNG BODENDENKMALPFLEGE. See Archaeology.

GW

BERICHT DER STAATLICHEN DENKMALPFLEGE IM SAARLAND. ABTEILUNG KUNSTDENKMALPFLEGE. See Archaeology.

ISSN 1010-559X
GW

BERNER KUNSTMITTEILUNGEN.
Added/Corp Kunstmuseum Bern. Kunstmuseum Bern. Verein der Freunde. Kunsthalle Bern. Bernische Kunstgesellschaft. 123/124 (Jan./Feb. 1971)-. Periodical. German. Five times a year. Free on request. Kunstmuseum Bern, Hodlerstrasse 12, CH-3011 Bern Switzerland. **Tel** 011 41 31 3110944, FAX 011 41 31 3117263. **Continues** Mitteilungen (Kunstmuseum (Bern, Switzerland)), 0405-5888.
Ind/Abst ARTbibliogr. Mod. (1985-); BHA : Biblio. Hist. Art.

LC N8.J28 B46   ISSN 0287-2226
JA

BESSATSU BIJUTSU TECHO. VFOAT Quarterly Art Magazine, Bessatsu Bijutsu Techo. (19??)-. Periodical. Japanese. Irregular. ¥980 (per issue). Bijutsu Shuppan Sha Ltd., 2-36 Kanda Jinbocho Chiyodaku, Tokyo 101 Japan. **Tel** 011 81 3 3234 2151.

LC Z5939 .N56a N7420   ISSN 0360-2699
DD 016.7   US

BIBLIOGRAPHIC GUIDE TO ART AND ARCHITECTURE. See The Arts-Abstracting, Bibliographies and Statistics.

LC Z5931 .B47 N5300
DD 016.7
GW
CEASED

BIBLIOGRAPHIE BILDENDE KUNST. See The Arts-Abstracting, Bibliographies and Statistics.

LC Z5940 .B5 N7141   ISSN 0252-9556
DD 016.7   SZ

BIBLIOGRAPHIE ZUR SCHWEIZER KUNST, BIBLIOGRAPHIE ZUR DENKMALPFLEGE / BIBLIOGRAPHIE DE L'ART SUISSE, BIBLIOGRAPHIE DE LA CONSERVATION DES BIENS CULTURELS / ETH, EIDGENOESSISCHE TECHNISCHE HOCHSCHULE ZUERICH, INSTITUT FUER DENKMALPFLEGE. See The Arts-Abstracting, Bibliographies and Statistics.

LC Z5937 .B53 N7510   ISSN 1150-1588
DD 016.7   FR
Pr Rev.

BIBLIOGRAPHY OF THE HISTORY OF ART : BHA = BIBLIOGRAPHIE D'HISTOIRE DE L'ART. See The Arts-Abstracting, Bibliographies and Statistics.

LC DG975.V85 B53   ISSN 0392-2545
IT

BIBLIOTECA E SOCIETA : RIVISTA DEL CONSORZIO PER LA GESTIONE DELLE BIBLIOTECHE COMUNALE DEGLI ARDENTI E PROVINCIALE "ANSELMO ANSELMI" DI VITERBO. Added/Corp Consorzio per la Gestione delle Biblioteche Comunale Degli Ardenti e Provinciale "Anselmo Anselmi". (19??)-. Periodical. Italian. Two times a year. L14000. Consorzio Gestione Biblioteche, Vle Trento Palazzo Garbini, 01100 Viterbo Italy. **Tel** 011 39 761 228162.
Ind/Abst BHA : Biblio. Hist. Art.

IT

BIENNALE DI VENEZIA : CATALOGO, LA. Main/Corp Biennal di Venezia. 1.- 1895-. Italian.

US

BIENNIAL REPORT / SANTA BARBARA MUSEUM OF ART. See Museums and Galleries.

ISSN 0021-907X
JA

BIJUTSU KENKYU. THE JOURNAL OF ART STUDIES. Added/Corp Tokyo. Institute of Art Research. **VFOAT** Journal of Art Studies. No. 1 (Jan. 1932)-. Periodical. Multiple languages (Japanese and English). Four times a year. $74.50. **(Subscription address:** Japan Publications Trading Company Ltd., PO Box 5030, Tokyo International, Tokyo 100-31 Japan. **Tel** 011 81 3 3292 3753.) cum. index.
Ind/Abst BHA : Biblio. Hist. Art.

ISSN 0021-907X
DD 709   JA

BIJUTSU SHI. Added/Corp Bijutsushi Gakkai. Bijutsushi Gakkai. Journal. **VFOAT** Journal of the Japanese Art History Society. Vol. 1 (1950)-. Periodical. Japanese. Two times a year. $93.50. **(Subscription address:** Japan Publications Trading Company Ltd., PO Box 5030, Tokyo International, Tokyo 100-31 Japan. **Tel** 011 81 3 3292 3753.)

LC NX8.J3 B53   ISSN 0287-2218
JA

BIJUTSU TECHO. (1948)-. Periodical. Japanese. Twelve times a year. $318.00. **(Subscription address:** Japan Publications Trading Company Ltd., PO Box 5030, Tokyo International, Tokyo 100-31 Japan. **Tel** 011 81 3 3292 3753.) **ED** Yoichi Kimura. **Circ:** 60,000.
Desc: Basic knowledge about design and living-design information is introduced.

LC NX   ISSN 0387-2688
DD 709   JA

BIJUTSUSHIGAKU (SENDAI. 1978).
[Bijutsushigaku Sendai. 1978]. **VFOAT** Art History (Sendai. 1978). (1978)-. Periodical. Japanese (summaries and/or abstracts in English).
Ind/Abst BHA : Biblio. Hist. Art.

ISSN 0006-3967
PL

BIULETYN HISTORII SZTUKI. [Biul. hist. sztuki]. **Added/Corp** Panstwowy Instytut Sztuki (Poland) Stowarzyszenie Historykow Sztuki. Vol. 12 (1950)-. Periodical. Polish (summaries and/or abstracts in French). Four times a year. $64.00. **(Subscription address:** Ars Polona-Ruch, PO Box 1001, Krakowskie Przedmiescie 7, 00-068 Warsaw Poland. **Tel** 011 48 22 261201.) **Continues** Biuletyn Historii Sztuki I Kultury.
Ind/Abst Am. Hist. Life (1984-); ARTbibliogr. Mod.; ARTbibliogr. Curr. Titles; BHA : Biblio. Hist. Art.

LC PS M NX
DD 810 780 700   US

●**BLACK DOG MAGAZINE. See** Literature.

LC N3 .B562
GW

BLAETTER + BILDER. VAT Blaetter und Bilder. Vol. 1 (1962)-. Periodical. German. Irregular. Blatter und Bilder, Hofweg 12, D-97209 Veitshocheim Germany. **Continues** Blaetter & Bilder.

LC DB681 .B5   ISSN 0006-4459
DD 943.65   AU

BLAETTER FUER HEIMATKUNDE ... .
See History-History of Europe.

NE

BLIND (AMSTERDAM, NETHERLANDS).
(BLIND.). Vol. 1, No. 1 (Winter 1988/89)-. Four times a year. $20.00 Europe; $30.00 outside Europe. The Blind Trust, Prinsengracht 218, 1016 HD Amsterdam Netherlands. **Tel** 011 31 20 258146, FAX 011 31 20 238892. **ED** Gerald van der Kaap, Peter Klasmorst and Paul Groot. **Bk Rev. Ad Acc. Circ:** 1,500 (ctrl). **Continues** Zien.

ISSN 0211-8483
SP
UDC 7

BOLETIN DE ARTE MALAGA. [Bol. arteMalaga]. **Added/Corp** Universidad de Malaga. Departamento de Historia del Arte. (1980)-. Periodical. Spanish. One time a year.
Ind/Abst BHA : Biblio. Hist. Art.

LC N7 .B64   ISSN 0211-3171
DD 709   SP

BOLETIN DEL MUSEO E INSTITUTO CAMON AZNAR. [Bol. Mus. Inst. "Camon Aznar"]. 1 (1980)-. Periodical. Spanish. $50.00. Museu e Instituto de Humanidades Camon Aznar, Espoz y Mina 23, Zaragoza Spain.
Ind/Abst ARTbibliogr. Mod.

SP

BOLETIN DEL SEMINARIO DE ESTUDIOS DE ARTE Y ARQUEOLOGIA. See Archaeology.

LC N8554 .C43a
MX

BOLETIN INFORMATIVO - CEDOCLA.
Main/Corp Cedocla. 1 (1972)-. Bulletin. Spanish. Cedocla, Antiguo Convento de Churubusco, Mexico Mexico.

LC DG670 .B64   ISSN 0394-1027
DD 708.5/31/05   IT

BOLLETTINO (CIVICI MUSEI VENEZIANI D'ARTE E DI STORIA). See Museums and Galleries.

LC N4 .B6   ISSN 0391-9854
IT

BOLLETTINO D'ARTE. (BOLLETTINO D'ARTE / MINISTERO DELLA EDUCAZIONE NAZIONALE, DIREZIONE GENERALE DELLE ANTICHITA E BELLE ARTE.). [Boll. arte]. **Added/Corp** Italy. Direzione Generale per le Antichita e Belle Arti. Italy. Ministero per i Beni Culturali e Ambientali. Vol. 25, No. 1 (1931)-. Periodical. Italian. Four times a year. L176940. Istituto Poligrafico Zecca Stato, Piazza Verdi 10, 00198 Rome Italy. **Tel** 011 39 6 85082307, 011 39 6 85082221. cum. index. **Continues** Bollettino d'Arte del Ministero della Educazione Nazionale.
Ind/Abst Art Archaeol. Tech. Abstr.; Art Index; ARTbibliogr. Mod.; Avery Index Archit. Period. Suppl. Colum. Univ. (1989/1990-); BHA : Biblio. Hist. Art.

LC N4 .B63
DD 705

BOLLETTINO D'ARTE. SUPPLEMENTO / MINISTERO PER I BENI CULTURALI E AMBIENTALI, UFFICIO CENTRALE PER I BENI AMBIENTALI, ARCHITETTONICI, ARCHEOLOGICI, ARTISTICI E STORICI. Added/Corp Italy. Ufficio Centrale per i Beni Ambientali, Architettonici, Archeologici, Artistici e Storici. Vol. 1 (1982)-. Periodical. Italian. Four times a year. L260000 Italy; L300000 other. Istituto Poligrafico Zecca Stato, Piazza Verdi 10, 00198 Rome Italy. **Tel** 011 39 6 85082307, 011 39 6 85082221.
Ind/Abst Bibliogr. Mission.

LC GN818.C3 C46a   ISSN 0577-2168
DD 945/.26   IT

BOLLETTINO DEL CENTRO CAMUNO DI STUDI PREISTORICI. Main/Corp Centro Camuno di Studi Preistoici. **VFOAT** BCSP. Vol. 1 (1964)-. Monographic series. English (French, German and Italian). Irregular. Price varies per volume. Centro Canuno di Studi Preistoici, via Marconi 7, 25044 Capo di Ponte Brescia Italy. **Tel** 011 39 364-42091, FAX 011 39 364-42572, telex 301504 ARCHEO I. **ED** Emmanuel Anati. **Circ:** 4,300 (ctrl).
Desc: World journal of prehistoric and primitive art. Special interest in rock paintings and engravings, tribal religions, mythology, ethnology and archaeology.
Ind/Abst Anthropol. Index; Anthropol. Lit.; Ethnoarts Index.

IT

BOLLETTINO DELLA SOCIETA PER GLI STUDI STORICI, ARCHEOLOGICI ED ARTISTICI NELLA PROVINCIA DI CUNEO. See History-History of Europe.

ISSN 0394-4727
IT
UDC 7(091)

BOLLETTINO DELLA UNIONE STORIA ED ARTE. [Boll. Unione stor. arte]. (1957)-. Periodical. Italian. Four times a year. **Continues** Unione Storia ed Arte per l'Educazione e la Cultura del Popolo, 0394-5588.
Ind/Abst BHA : Biblio. Hist. Art.

ISSN 0578-9850
IT
UDC 93(450.62)

BOLLETTINO DELL'ISTITUTO DI STORIA E DI ARTE DEL LAZIO MERIDIONALE. See History.

LC N15 .I8   ISSN 0391-8211
IT

BOLLETTINO DELL'ISTITUTO STORICO ARTISTICO ORVIETANO.
Main/Corp Istituto Storico Artistico Orvietano.
Added/Corp Istituto Storico Artistico Orvietano. (1945)-. Academic Scholarly Publication. Italian. Irregular. Free on request. Istituto Storico Artistico Orvietano, Piazza Febei 1, 05018 Orvieto Italy. **Bk Rev. Ad Acc. Circ:** 1,000 (ctrl).
Desc: Publishes articles on the art history of Orvieto.
Ind/Abst BHA : Biblio. Hist. Art.

LC N2940 .V39A   ISSN 1018-4317
VC

BOLLETTINO - MONUMENTI, MUSEI E GALLERIE PONTIFICIE. See Museums and Galleries.

LC N1 .B65a
II

BOMBAY ART SOCIETY'S ART JOURNAL. Added/Corp Bombay Art Society. **VFOAT** Art Journal. Vol. 1, No. 1 (Oct. 1971)-. Periodical.

The Arts — Art

English. Four times a year. Bombay Art Society, Jehangir Art Gallery, 16-B Mahatma Gandhi Road, Bombay 400 001 India.

DD 709
ISSN 0520-5700
SW
BONNIERS SMA KONSTBOCKER. (1962)-. Periodical. Swedish. Bonniers Sma Konstbocker, Box 3159, Stockholm 103 63 Sweden.

LC Z700.9 .B66
DD 025.7
ISSN 0887-8978
US
BOOK & PAPER GROUP ANNUAL, THE. [Book Rap. Group annu.]. **Added/Corp** American Institute for Conservation of Historic and Artistic Works. Book and Paper Group. **VFOAT** Book and Paper Group Annual. Vol. 2 (1983)-. English. One time a year (Apr.). $33.00. American Institute Conservation, 1717 K Street Northwest, Suite 301, Washington DC 20006. **Tel** (202)542-9545, **FAX** (202)542-9328.
  Desc: Papers on conservation of works of art on paper, books, library and archival materials.

IT
●**BOTTEGA DEL RESTAURO, LA.** (1995)-. Periodical. Italian. Ten times a year. L37470. Incontri Editoriale SRL, Vicolo delle Coppelle 61, 00186 Rome Italy. **Tel** 011 39 6 3725070.

DD 741
ISSN 1065-7363
US
BREAKING IN (ATLANTA, GA.). (BREAKING IN.). [Break.]. (1992)-. Periodical. English. Twelve times a year. $65.00. Breaking In, PO Box 89147, Atlanta GA 30312.

LC Z1035.A1 B714
DD 028.1 028.1/05
ISSN 0382-8565
CN
BRICK. See Literary and Political Reviews.

UK
BRITISH ART DIRECTORS ANNUAL. (19??)-. English. One time a year. $47.19 Maryland; $44.95 other. **(Subscription address:** RC Publications, 3200 Tower Oaks Boulevard, Rockville MD 20852-9789. **Tel** (800)222-2654, (301)770-2900, FAX (301)984-3203.)

DD 730
ISSN 0884-8815
US
BROOKGREEN JOURNAL. [Brookgreen j.]. **Added/Corp** Brookgreen Gardens. Vol. 15, No. 2 (1985)-. Periodical. English. Four times a year. $7.50. Brookgreen Gardens, Route 1 Box 3, US Highway 17 South, Murrells Inlet SC 29576. **Tel** (803)237-4218. **Bk Rev. Circ:** 2,500 (ctrl). **Continues** Brookgreen Bulletin, 8755-5018.
  Desc: Covers American figurative sculpture; native and exotic plants of the Southeast; native animals of the Southeast; and history of South Carolina.
  Ind/Abst Garden Lit. (1992-).

LC N6868.5.E9 B68
ISSN 0300-2039
GW
BRUCKE-ARCHIV. [Brucke-Arch.]. **Main/Corp** Brucke-Museum. German. Irregular. DM24.00. Brucke Museum, Bussardsteig 9, 1000 Berlin 33 Germany. **Tel** 030-831 20 2G. **ED** M M Moeller.
  Ind/Abst BHA : Biblio. Hist. Art.

LC N3 .P3
DD 705
GW
BRUCKMANNS PANTHEON. **Added/Corp** F. Bruckmann KG. **VFOAT** Pantheon. Vol. 38, No. 3 (July/Sept. 1980)-. English (German; summaries and/or abstracts in English and French). One time a year. DM98.00. F. Bruckmann KG, Postfach 200353, D-80003 Munich Germany. **Tel** 011 49 89 125701, FAX 011 49 89 1257269, telex 5-23739 BRUKG D. **Ad Acc. Circ:** 1,500. **Continues** Pantheon.
  Ind/Abst ARTbibliogr. Curr. Titles; BHA : Biblio. Hist. Art.

ISSN 0720-0056
GW
BRUCKMANNS PANTHEON. [Bruckmanns Pantheon]. (1980)-. Periodical. Multiple languages. Four times a year. DM98.00. F. Bruckmann KG, Postfach 200353, D-80003 Munich Germany. **Tel** 011 49 89 125701, FAX 011 49 89 1257269, telex 5-23739 BRUKG D. **Continues** Pantheon, 0031-0999.

UDC 70
LC N8193.A1 B84
ISSN 0004-2889
JA
BUKKYO GEIJUTSU. **Added/Corp** Bukkyo Geijutsu Gakkai (Japan). **VFOAT** Ars Buddhica; Buddhist Art. (1948)-. Periodical. Japanese. Six times a year. $245.00. Manichi Shinbunsha, Tokyo Honsha, 1-1 Hitotsubashi 1, Chiyoda-Ku Tokyo-to 100 Japan. **(Subscription address:** Japan Publications Trading Company Ltd., PO Box 5030, Tokyo International, Tokyo 100-31 Japan. **Tel** 011 81 3 3292 3753.)
  Ind/Abst Art Archaeol. Tech. Abstr.

LC N650 .A3
DD 700/.5
US
BULLETIN / ALLEN MEMORIAL ART MUSEUM. **Added/Corp** Allen Memorial Art Museum. **VFOAT** Allen Memorial Art Museum Bulletin. Vol. 7, No. 1 (Fall 1949)-. Bulletin. English. Two times a year. $15.00 per issue. Allen Memorial Art Museum, Oberlin College, Oberlin OH 44074. **Tel** (216)775-8665, FAX (216)775-8799. **ED** Marjorie Wieseman (Editor's telephone: (216)775-8624). Index available ($1.00). **Circ:** 550. available on microfilm from University Microfilms International (UMI); available with illustrations. **Continues** Bulletin of the Allen Memorial Art Museum, Oberlin, Ohio, 0002-5739.
  Ind/Abst Art Index.

ISSN 0983-3943
FR
BULLETIN - AMIS DE GUSTAVE COURBET. **VFOAT** Les Amis de Gustave Courbet. (1947)-. Bulletin. French. Two times a year. $26.25. Amis de G Courbet, 32 rue du Seult, 25290 Ornans France. **Tel** 011 33 81 622330. **ED** J. J. Ferwin. Index available. cum. index. **Bk Rev. Ad Acc. Circ:** 600.
  Ind/Abst BHA : Biblio. Hist. Art.

US
BULLETIN / DALLAS MUSEUM OF ART. **Added/Corp** Dallas Museum of Art Bulletin. (Fall 1983)-. Bulletin. English. Four times a year. **Continues** Dallas Museum of Fine Arts. Bulletin.
  Ind/Abst BHA : Biblio. Hist. Art.

US
BULLETIN - DAYTON ART INSTITUTE. **Main/Corp** Dayton Art Institute. Bulletin. English. Irregular. Dayton Art Institute, 456 Belmonte Park North, Dayton OH 45405. **Tel** (513)223-5277, FAX (513)223-3140. **ED** Marianne Lorenz. **Circ:** 3,500 (ctrl).
  Ind/Abst ARTbibliogr. Mod.

ISSN 0522-7496
BE
BULLETIN DE LA COMMISSION ROYALE DES MONUMENTS ET DES SITES. [Bull. comm. r. monum. sites]. **Main/Corp** Belgium. Commission Royale des Monuments et des Sites. **VFOAT** Bulletin van de Koninklijke Commissie voor Monumenten en Landschappen. (1949)-. Bulletin. French (Dutch). Price varies. Commission Royale des Monuments et des Sites, rue Joseph II 30, 1040 Brussels Belgium. **Supersedes** Belgium. Commission Royales d'Art et d'Archeologie. Bulletin, 0777-7035.
  Ind/Abst Avery Index Archit. Period. Suppl. Colum. Univ. (19??-199?); BHA : Biblio. Hist. Art; Br. Archaeol. Bibliogr.

BULLETIN DE LA SOCIETE ARCHEOLOGIQUE, HISTORIQUE ET ARTISTIQUE, LE VIEUX PAPIER, POUR L'ETUDE DE LA VIE ET DES MRS D'AUTREFOIS. See Archaeology.

LC N6841 .A92
DD 709/.44
ISSN 0301-4126
FR
BULLETIN DE LA SOCIETE DE L'HISTOIRE DE L'ART FRANCAIS. [Bull. Soc. hist. art fr.]. **Main/Corp** Societe de l'Histoire de l'Art Francais (Paris, France). **Added/Corp** Centre National de la Recherche Scientifique (France). Vol. 1-4 (1875-1878)-(1907)-. Bulletin. One time a year (Nov.). 200.00F Comes with membership. Societe de l'Histoire de l'Art Francais, 107 rue de Rivoli, 75001 Paris France. Index available. cum. index.
  Ind/Abst ARTbibliogr. Mod.; Avery Index Archit. Period. Suppl. Colum. Univ. (1988-); BHA : Biblio. Hist. Art.

ISSN 0521-7032
FR
BULLETIN DES MUSEES ET MONUMENTS LYONNAIS. See Museums and Galleries.

LC AM101.B927 A3
HU
BULLETIN DU MUSEE HONGROIS DES BEAUX-ARTS / O.M. SZEPMUVESZETI MUZEUM KOZLEMENYEI. **Main/Corp** Szepmuveszeti Muzeum (Hungary). **Added/Corp** Szepmuveszeti Muzeum Kozlemenyei. **VFOAT** O.M. Szepmuveszeti Muzeum Kozlemenyei. No. 1 (May 1947)-. Bulletin. French (Hungarian). Two times a year. Musee Hongrois des Beaux-Arts, Hungary. **Tel** 011 36 1 429759, FAX 011 36 1 1228298. **Circ:** 1,400 (ctrl).
  Desc: Classic archaeology, European art history, egyptology, chiefly thirteenth to the twentieth century.
  Ind/Abst ARTbibliogr. Mod. (1984-); BHA : Biblio. Hist. Art.

ISSN 0540-7575
FR
BULLETIN DU MUSEE INGRES. **Added/Corp** Societe des Amis du Musee Ingres. (1956)-. Bulletin. French. One time a year (Jan.). $34.99. Societe Amis du Musee Ingres, 7 rue E Pouirllon, 82000 Montauban France. **Tel** 011 33 63 662688.
  Desc: The life and works of painter Dominique Ingres and E. A. Bourdelle and their students.
  Ind/Abst BHA : Biblio. Hist. Art.

ISSN 0521-713X
FR
BULLETIN HISTORIQUE ET ARTISTIQUE DU CALAISIS. See History-History of Europe.

LC N13 .B7
ISSN 0085-1892
BE
BULLETIN (INSTITUT ROYAL DU PATRIMOINE ARTISTIQUE (BRUXELLES)). (BULLETIN / INSTITUT ROYAL DU PATRIMOINE ARTISTIQUE, KONINKLIJK INSTITUUT VOOR HET KUNSTPATRIMONIUM.). [Bull. Inst. r. patrim. artist.]. Vol. 1 (1958)-. Bulletin. French (Dutch and English). Irregular. 625.00F. Patrimoine Musees Royaux d'Art et d'Histoire, Parc du Cinquantenaire 10, 1040 Brussels Belgium. **Tel** 011 32 2 7417211. **Circ:** 1,000 (ctrl). available on microfilm.
  Desc: Art conservation and art history, particularly in Belgium.
  Ind/Abst BHA : Biblio. Hist. Art.

ISSN 0705-3029
CN
BULLETIN - INTERNATIONAL ASSOCIATION FOR MOBILIZATION OF CREATIVITY. **Main/Corp** International Association for Mobilization of Creativity. **VFOAT** I. A. M. C. Bulletin. **VAT** International Association for Mobilization of Creativity Bulletin; Bulletin. Association Internationale pour la Mobilisation de la Creativite. Vol. 1 (Jan. 1978)-. Bulletin. English (French). Six times a year. Price varies per volume. International Association for Mobilization of Creativity, Box 123, Montreal Quebec H3X 3T3 Canada.

UK
BULLETIN - INTERNATIONAL INSTITUTE FOR CONSERVATION OF HISTORIC AND ARTISTIC WORKS. **Added/Corp** International Institute for Conservation of Historic and Artistic Works. **VFOAT** IIC Bulletin; I.I.C. Bulletin. Vol. 1, No. 1/2 (March 1976)-. Bulletin. English. Irregular. £50.00 (associates); £76.00 (fellow); £100.00 (supporting) Comes with International Institute for Conservation of Historic and Artistic Works membership. International Institute for Conservation of Historic and Artistic Works / England, 6 Buckingham Street, London WC2N 6BA United Kingdom. **Tel** 011 44 171 8395975, FAX 011 44 171 9761564. **Formed by the union of** IIC News, 0536-1737 **and** Appointments Vacant Bulletin.
  Ind/Abst Museum Abstr.

LC N7241 .J78
CI
BULLETIN - JUGOSLAVENSKA ADAKEMIJA ZNANOSTI I UMJETNOSTI, RAZRED ZA LIKOVNE UMJETNOSTI. **Main/Corp** Jugoslavenska Akademija Znanosti I Umjetnosti. Razred Za Likovne Umjetnosti. (19??)-. Bulletin. Serbo-Croatian (Roman) (summaries and/or abstracts in English, French, German and Italian).
  Ind/Abst Avery Index Archit. Period. Suppl. Colum. Univ. (19??-199?); BHA : Biblio. Hist. Art.

LC N610 .A4
DD 708
ISSN 0026-1521
US
BULLETIN - METROPOLITAN MUSEUM OF ART. See Museums and Galleries.

LC N2 .B95
ISSN 0007-473X
FR
BULLETIN MONUMENTAL. [Bull. monum.]. **Added/Corp** Societe Francaise d'Archeologie. Bulletin Monumental ou, Collection de Memoires et de Renseignements. Societe Francaise d'Archeologie. Bulletin Monumental; ou, Recueil de Documents et de Memoires Relatifs aux Differentes Branches de l'Archeologie. Societe Francaise d'Archeologie. **VFOAT** Bulletin Monumental, ou, Collection de Memoires et de Renseignements. (1834)-. Bulletin. French. Four times a year. $92.96. Soc Fran Archeol-Mus Ntl Franc Trocdr, Pal de Chaillot, 1 de Tracadero, 75116 Paris France. **Tel** 33-1-44053910. **ED** Alain Erlande-Brandenburg. cum. index. **Bk Rev**, (Qty: 4 per year). Documents available from The Genuine Article.
  Ind/Abst Art Index; Arts Humanit. Citation Index [Full Cov.]; Avery Index Archit. Period. Suppl. Colum. Univ. (1990-); BHA : Biblio. Hist. Art; Curr. Contents Arts Humanit.; Res. Alert [Full Cov.]; Soc. Sci. Cit. Index [Select. Cov.].

LC N6823 .B85
DD 708/.37/2
XR
BULLETIN MORAVSKE GALERIE V BRNE / MG. See Museums and Galleries.

LC N1830 .A3
ISSN 0027-3856
BE
BULLETIN - MUSEES ROYAUX DES BEAUX-ARTS DE BELGIQUE. See Museums and Galleries.

The Arts —Art

LC N715.R2 A25   **ISSN** 0029-2567
US
SUSPENDED
BULLETIN - NORTH CAROLINA MUSEUM OF ART. See Museums and Galleries.

ISSN 0110-4888
NZ
BULLETIN OF NEW ZEALAND ART HISTORY. [Bull. N.Z. art hist.]. (1972)-. Bulletin. English.
Ind/Abst BHA : Biblio. Hist. Art.

LC N552 .A3   **ISSN** 0009-8841
DD 069   US
CEASED
BULLETIN OF THE CLEVELAND MUSEUM OF ART, THE. See Museums and Galleries.

LC N560 .A42   **ISSN** 0011-9636
US
BULLETIN OF THE DETROIT INSTITUTE OF ARTS. See Museums and Galleries.

ISSN 0862-8912
XR
BULLETIN OF THE NATIONAL GALLERY IN PRAGUE. See Museums and Galleries.

LC N685 .A45   **ISSN** 0031-7314
DD 708/.148/11   US
BULLETIN - PHILADELPHIA MUSEUM OF ART. See Museums and Galleries.

LC N559.D3 A25   **ISSN** 0883-9239
DD 708   US
BULLETIN / THE DAYTON ART INSTITUTE. [Bull. - Dayt. Art Inst.]. **Main/Corp** Dayton Art Institute. **VFOAT** Dayton Art Institute Bulletin. (193?)-. Bulletin. English. One time a year. Dayton Art Institute, 456 Belmonte Park North, Dayton OH 45405. **Tel** (513)223-5277, **FAX** (513)223-3140. Circ: 4,000 (ctrl).
Ind/Abst ARTbibliogr. Mod.; BHA : Biblio. Hist. Art.

LC N582.M26 J2   **ISSN** 1041-9063
DD 069   US
BULLETIN / THE J. PAUL GETTY TRUST. [Bull. - J. Paul Getty Trust]. **Main/Corp** J. Paul Getty Trust. **VFOAT** J. Paul Getty Trust Bulletin. Vol. 1, No. 1 (Fall 1986)-. Bulletin. English. Three times a year. Free on request. J. Paul Getty Trust, Department 1875, Century Park East, Los Angeles CA 90067. **Tel** (213)277-9188.
Ind/Abst Avery Index Archit. Period. Suppl. Colum. Univ. (Winter 1990-); Museum Abstr.

LC N729 .A33   **ISSN** 0009-7691
DD 708/.178/66   US
BULLETIN - THE ST. LOUIS ART MUSEUM. See Museums and Galleries.

LC N513 .A2   **ISSN** 0076-8391
DD 708.174/35   US
BULLETIN - UNIVERSITY OF MICHIGAN. MUSEUM OF ART. See Museums and Galleries.

LC N2460 .A3   **ISSN** 0165-9510
NE
BULLETIN VAN HET RYKSMUSEUM. (BULLETIN VAN HET RIJKSMUSEUM.). [Bull. REyksmus.]. **Main/Corp** Rijksmuseum (Netherlands). (1953)-. Bulletin. Dutch (summaries and/or abstracts in English). Four times a year. $35.56. Total Mail Service BV, Energieweg 41B, 2382 NC Zoeterwoude Netherlands. **Tel** 011 31 71 419193. **ED** W. Halsema Kubes and J.F. Heisbroek. **Bk Rev**. Circ: 4,000.
Desc: Articles on objects the museum owns: paintings, sculpture, applied arts, graphic arts and also articles on objects illustrating the history of the Netherlands.
Ind/Abst Art Index; ARTbibliogr. Mod.; Avery Index Archit. Period. Suppl. Colum. Univ. (19??-199?); BHA : Biblio. Hist. Art.

LC N716.V45 A18   **ISSN** 0363-3519
DD 708   US
TITLE CHANGE
BULLETIN - VIRGINIA MUSEUM OF FINE ARTS. See Museums and Galleries.

RM
BURIDAVA / MUZEUL JUDETEAN VILCEA. See Museums and Galleries.

LC N1 .B95   **ISSN** 0007-6287
DD 705   UK
BURLINGTON MAGAZINE. (THE BURLINGTON MAGAZINE.). [Burlington mag.]. Vol. 90 (Jan. 1948)-. Academic Scholarly Publication. English (Italian). Twelve times a year. $381.00. Burlington Magazine Publications Ltd., 14-16 Dukes Road, London WC1H 9AD United Kingdom. **Tel** 011 44 171 3881228, **FAX** 011 44 171 3881229. **ED** Caroline Elam, Richard Shone and Duncan Bull. Index available. cum. index. **Bk Rev**. **Ad Acc**. available on microfilm and microfiche from University Microfilms International (UMI). Documents available from The Genuine Article. **Continues** Burlington Magazine for Connoisseurs, 0951-0788.
Desc: Leading international magazine for the fine and decorative arts. Scholarly articles, book and exhibition reviews, exhibition catalogues and other supplements. Contains a monthly calendar of events worldwide.
Ind/Abst Annu. Bibliogr. Engl. Lang. Lit.; Archit. Period. Index (1977-); Art Archaeol. Tech. Abstr.; Art Index; ARTbibliogr. Mod.; ARTbibliogr. Curr. Titles; Arts Humanit. Citation Index [Full Cov.]; Avery Index Archit. Period. Suppl. Colum. Univ. (1990-); BHA : Biblio. Hist. Art; Book Rev. Index; Br. Humanit. Index; Curr. Contents Arts Humanit.; Res. Alert [Full Cov.]; Romant. Move.; Soc. Sci. Cit. Index [Select. Cov.].

LC E98.A7 B85   **ISSN** 0095-3083
DD 380.1/45/745   US
BUYERS GUIDE TO INDIAN ART. (1974)-.
Consumer Publication. English. One time a year. Buyers Guide To Indian Art Publishing Company, Box 7, McIntosh NM 87032.

ISSN 0890-5908
DD 709   US
Pr Rev.
CAC NEWS - CHICAGO ARTISTS' COALITION. (CAC NEWS.). [CAC news - Chic. Artists' Coalit.]. **Added/Corp** Chicago Artists' Coalition. **VFOAT** Chicago Artists' Coalition News. **VAT** Chicago Artists' Coalition News - Chicago Artists' Coalition. Vol. 10, No. 10 (Oct. 1984)-. Periodical. English. Eleven times a year. $30.00. Chicago Artists Coalition, 11 East Hubbard Street, 7th Floor, Chicago IL 60611. **Tel** (312)670-2060, **FAX** (312)670-2521. **ED** Jeff Abell. **Bk Rev**, (Qty: 5). **Ad Acc**. Circ: 3,000 (ctrl) **Continues** CAC Newsletter (Chicago, Ill.).

ISSN 0765-9326
FR
UDC 7(4)"18/19"
CAHIER DES ARTS ET DES ARTISTES.
[Cah. arts artist.]. (1984)-. Periodical. French. One time a year.
Ind/Abst BHA : Biblio. Hist. Art.

LC N6841 .S35a
DD 702/.8/8   FR
CAHIER - LA SAUVEGARDE DE L'ART FRANCAIS. **Main/Corp** Sauvegarde de l'Art Francais (Association). (1979)-. Periodical. French. Sauvegarde de l'Art Francais, 82 rue Bonaparte, 75006 Paris France.
Ind/Abst BHA : Biblio. Hist. Art.

LC N6999.M34 C33
DD 709/.2/4   SZ
CAHIER MALEVITCH. **VFOAT** Malevitch. (1983)-. Periodical. French. Editions l'Age d'Homme / Switzerland, Case Postale 67, CH-1211 Geneva 25 Switzerland. **Tel** 011 41 21 220095.

LC DC648.6 .C33   **ISSN** 0575-0385
DD 936.4/008   FR
CAHIERS ALSACIENS D'ARCHEOLOGIE, D'ART ET D'HISTOIRE. See Archaeology.

ISSN 0769-1912
FR
UDC 75
CAHIERS DE LA PEINTURE, LES. (1973)-.
Periodical. French. Twenty-four times a year.
Ind/Abst BHA : Biblio. Hist. Art.

ISSN 1140-7530
FR
CAHIERS DE SAINT-MICHEL DE CUXA, LES. [Cah. St. Michel Cuxa]. **Added/Corp** Centre Permanent de Recherches et d'Etudes Preromanes et Romanes. Association Culturelle de Cuxo. No. 1 (April 1970)-. Periodical. French. One time a year (July). 180.00F. Association Culturelle de Cuxa, Abbaye Saint Michel du Cuxa, Codalet 66500 Prades France. **Tel** 011 33 68 671139.
Ind/Abst Avery Index Archit. Period. Suppl. Colum. Univ. (1990-); BHA : Biblio. Hist. Art.

LC NK2 .C3
FR
CAHIERS DES ARTS ET TECHNIQUES D'AFRIQUE DU NORD. **Added/Corp** Morocco.
Service des Metiers et Arts Marocains. Societe Tunisienne de Diffusion. No. 1 (1952)-. Periodical. French. Cahiers des Artes et Techniques d'Afrique du Nord, 1 Avenue Habib Thameur, Tunis Tunisia.

LC N6490 .C213
DD 709/.04   FR
CAHIERS D'HISTOIRE DE L'ART CONTEMPORAIN. DOCUMENTS. Vol. 1 (1972)-. French. Three times a year. 20.00F. Musee d'Art et d'Industrie, Centro de Documentation et d'Etudes d'Histoire, 2 place Louis Comte 42, Saint-Etienne France.

FR
CAHIERS DU DESSIN FRANCAIS. No. 1 (1985)-. Monographic series. French. Irregular. $25.00. Ars Libri Ltd, 560 Harrison Avenue, Boston MA 02118. **Tel** (617)357-5212.

LC N6490 .P27a   **ISSN** 0181-1525
DD 709/.04   FR
CAHIERS DU MUSEE NATIONAL D'ART MODERNE. See Museums and Galleries.

US
CALENDAR. **Main/Corp** National Museum of African Art (U.S.). (Spring 1991)-. Periodical. English. Four times a year. Smithsonian Institution / African Art, National Museum of African Art, 950 Independence Avenue SW, Washington DC 20560. **Continues** Calendar of Exhibitions and Programs.

LC N11
US
CALENDAR OF REGULAR MEETINGS OF THE ART ORGANIZATIONS IN NEW YORK CITY ... . **Main/Corp** Fine Arts Federation of New York. Periodical. English.

ISSN 0890-8850
DD 700   US
CALENDAR / UNIVERSITY ART MUSEUM BERKELEY. See Museums and Galleries.

LC N716.V45 A18   **ISSN** 1084-676X
DD 708   US
CALENDAR - VIRGINIA MUSEUM OF FINE ARTS. See Museums and Galleries.

ISSN 0068-5909
US
CALIFORNIA STUDIES IN THE HISTORY OF ART. Monographic series. English. Irregular. Price varies per volume. University of California Press, 2120 Berkeley Way, Berkeley CA 94720. **Tel** (510)642-4191, (510)642-3907, **FAX** (510)642-9917. **ED** W. J. McClung.
Desc: Various titles in all fields of art and art history.

LC NX513   **ISSN** 0384-1588
DD 709/.71   US
CANADIAN ART INVESTOR'S GUIDE, THE. [Can. art investor's guide]. (March 1975)-. Periodical. English. 20.00Can$. Art Consulting and Information Services, PO Box 2006, 340 Laurier Avenue West, Ottawa Ontario K1P 5K3 Canada.

LC N6540 .C33   **ISSN** 0229-8961
DD 709/.71/0750971   CN
CANADIAN ART SALES INDEX ..., THE.
[Can. art sales index]. (1980)-. English. One time a year (Nov.). 50.00Can$. Westbridge Publications Ltd, 1683 Chestnut Street, Vancouver BC V6J 4M6 Canada. **Tel** (604)734-4944, **FAX** (604)731-4576. **ED** Anthony R. Westbridge. Index available. **Ad Acc**. Circ: 2,000.
Desc: Reference guide to prices of Canadian paintings, watercolours, prints and sculpture sold at auction each year in Canada and the United Kingdom.

ISSN 0825-3854
DD 709/71/05   CN
CANADIAN ART (TORONTO, 1984).
(CANADIAN ART.). [Can. art]. Vol. 1, No. 1 (Fall 1984)-. Periodical. English. Four times a year. 19.20Can$. Canadian Art, 6 Church Street, 2nd Floor, Toronto Ontario M5E 1M1 Canada. **Tel** (416)368-8854, **FAX** (416)594-3575. **ED** Jocelyn Lawrence. **Ad Acc**. Circ: 20,000. available in microform. **Continues** Artscanada, 0004-4113; Artmagazine, 0318-6644.
Desc: Magazine about the visual arts in Canada. Information for the gallery-goer, art collector, artist and general reader. Each issue contains news, profiles and feature articles on a wide range of topics, from historical to contemporary art, from the practical to the political, all in a format that shows art and artists.
Ind/Abst ARTbibliogr. Mod.; BHA : Biblio. Hist. Art; Can. Index; Can. Period. Index (19??-).

LC N6545 .C25   **ISSN** 0316-6015
DD 709/.2/2   CN
CANADIAN ARTISTS IN EXHIBITION.
(CANADIAN ARTISTS IN EXHIBITION. ARTISTES CANADIENS: EXPOSITIONS.). **Added/Corp** Roundstone Council for the Arts. **VFOAT** Artistes Canadiens : Expositions. (1973)-. English (French). One time a year. $16.95. Roundstone Council for the Arts, PO Box 6471 Station A, Toronto Ontario M5W 1X3 Canada.

The Arts —Art

DD 707/.1/071
ISSN 0706-8107
CN
CANADIAN REVIEW OF ART EDUCATION, RESEARCH AND ISSUES. [Can. rev. art educ. res. issues]. **Added/Corp** Canadian Society for Education Through Art. **VFOAT** Canadian Review of Art Education Research; Revue Canadienne de Recherche en Education Artistique; Revue Canadienne d'Education Artistique, Recherche et Questions d'Actualite Artistique. Vol. 4 (Winter 1977)-. Academic Scholarly Publication. English (summaries and/or abstracts in French). Two times a year (one or two issues per year). Comes with Canadian Society for Education Through Art membership; 65.00Can$ (membership). Canadian Society for Education Through Art, 1487 Parish Lane, Oakville Ontario L6M 2Z6 Canada. **Tel** (905)847-0975. **ED** N. Webb. **Bk Rev**. **Circ**: 600 (ctrl). **Formed by the union of** Investigart, 0318-9961 **and** Canadian Society for Education through Art. Research, 0384-1839.
Desc: Presents reviews and reports on speculative or empirical matters of a scholarly nature in art education.
Ind/Abst Curr. Index J. Educ.

LC F3401 .C35
ISSN 0576-7423
DD 985/.06/05 056
PE
CARETAS : ILUSTRACION PERUANA.
Vol. 1, No. 1 (Sept. 1950)-. Periodical. Spanish. Fifty-one times per year. $500.00. Marketing Directo SA, Apartado 303, Lima 18 Peru. **Tel** 011 51 14 465378, 011 51 14 468220, FAX 011 51 14 478424.

LC N6530.N7 C73a
ISSN 0732-3530
DD 709/.747/074
US
CATALOG OF NEW YORK STATE VISUAL ARTISTS SELECTED FOR THE CREATIVE ARTISTS PUBLIC SERVICE PROGRAM, A. **Main/Corp** Creative Artists Public Service Program. **Added/Corp** Gallery Association of New York State. **VFOAT** C.A.P.S. ..., Graphic Artists, Painters, Photographers, Sculptors; Photographers, Sculptors, Painters, Printmakers; Painters, Sculptors, Photographers, Graphic Artist; CAPS ..., Graphic Artists, Painters, Photographers, Sculptors; (1972/1973)-. Catalog. English. One time a year. Creative Artists Public Service Program, 250 West 57th Street, Room 1424, New York NY 10107.

IE
CATALOG OF ... - SOTHEBY'S IN IRELAND. **Main/Corp** Sotheby's in Ireland. Catalog. English. Irregular.

LC N7525 .C38
IT
CATALOGHI D'ARTE: INDICI ANALITICI. **Added/Corp** Centro Di. **VFOAT** Art Catalogues: Analytical Indexes. (19??)-. Multiple languages (English and Italian). Two times a year. Centro di, Piazza de Mozzi 1r, 50125 Florence Italy.

ISSN 0531-9811
IT
CATALOGHI DI MOSTRE. **Main/Corp** Fondazione Giorgio Cini, Venice. Centro di Cultura e Civilita. Istituto di Storia dell'Arte. Vol. 1 (1955)-. Monographic series. Italian. Irregular. Price varies per volume. Biblioteca Apostolica Vaticana, Citta del Vaticano, 00120 Vatican City. **Tel** 011 396 6 69885051.

LC N8610 .C37
IT
CATALOGO INTERNAZIONALE BOLAFFI D'ARTE ANTICA E DI ANTIQUARIATO. No. 1 (1973)-. Catalog. Italian. L10000. Bolaffi Mondadori, Via Cavour 17, 10123 Turin Italy.

FR
CATALOGUE DES TRAVAUX DE JEAN DUBUFFET. (19??)-. French. Irregular. Les Editions de Minuit, 7 rue Bernard-Palissy, 75006 Paris France. **Tel** 011 33 1 44393920, FAX 011 33 1 45448236.

ISSN 0715-5956
DD 705
CN
CBAC NEWS. [CBAC news]. **Added/Corp** Council for Business and the Arts in Canada. **VAT** Council for Business and the Arts in Canada News. Vol. 1, No. 1 (Nov. 1975)-. Periodical. English. Four times a year (Mar., June, Sept., Dec.). 12.71Can$. Council for Business and the Arts in Canada, PO Box 7, Suite 1507/The Simpson Tower, 401 Bay Street, Toronto Ontario M5H 2Y4 Canada. **Tel** (416)869-3016, FAX (416)869-0435. **ED** Eileen Love. **Circ**: 1,000.

LC N330.W3 C457
US
CENTER ... RECORD OF ACTIVITIES AND RESEARCH REPORTS / NATIONAL GALLERY OF ART, CENTER FOR ADVANCED STUDY IN THE VISUAL ARTS. **Main/Corp** Center for Advanced Study in the Visual Arts (U.S.). **Added/Corp** National Gallery of Art (U.S.). **VFOAT** Center. (1992)-. English. National Gallery of Art, 6th Street Constitution Avenue Northwest, Washington DC 20565. **Tel** (202)789-2681. **(Subscription address:** National Gallery of Art, 2000 B Club Drive, Landover MD 20785. **Tel** (202)737-4215, (301)322-5900.) **Continues** Center for Advanced Study in the Visual Arts (U.S.). Center ... Research Reports and Record of Activities.

ISSN 0820-781X
DD 700/.9714
CN
CHAMBRE BLANCHE. (LA CHAMBRE BLANCHE : BULLETIN.). [Chamb. blanche]. (1978)-. Bulletin. French (English; summaries and/or abstracts in English). Irregular. 15.00Can$. La Chambre Blanche, 549 East boulevard Charest, Quebec Quebec G1K 3J2 Canada. **Tel** (418)529-2715. **Ad Acc**. **Circ**: 350 (ctrl).
Desc: Bulletin on the activities of the gallery. Texts by artists and art historians, plus photographs of works of art.

LC NX
ISSN 1380-7811
DD 700
NE
UDC 82.07+7
●**CHIASMA AMSTERDAM.** (CHIASMA). [Chiasma Amst.]. **VFOAT** Chiasma (Atlanta). (1995)-. Monographic series. English. Irregular. Editions Rodopi BV, Keizersgracht 302-304, 1016 Ex Amsterdam Netherlands. **Tel** 011 31 20 6227507, FAX 011 31 20 380948.

IT
CHIESE DI ROMA ILLUSTRATE, LE.
Monographic series. Italian. Price varies per volume.

IT
CHRISTIES CATALOGO GENERALE ASTE DI ROMA. Italian. Irregular. Christies Int SA, P Lancellotti, Pizza Navona 114, 00186 Rome Italy. **Tel** 011 39 6 6872787.

LC N8610 .C48
ISSN 0266-1217
DD 707/.4
UK
CHRISTIE'S INTERNATIONAL MAGAZINE. [Christie's int. mag.]. **Added/Corp** Christie, Manson & Woods. (1984)-. Periodical. English. Seven times a year. $50.00. Christie's Publications, 21-24 44th Avenue, Long Island NY 11101. **Tel** (800)395-6300, (718)784-1480, FAX (800)395-5600, (718)786-0941.
Desc: Articles that preview the most important and interesting items being offered in Christie's salesroom around the world. Provides information about special events and exhibitions, house sales, charity auctions, lectures and fine arts programs. Contains a calendar of all of Christie's upcoming sales.

ISSN 0246-1331
UDC 726
FR
CHRONIQUES D'ART SACRE. (1985)-. Periodical. French. Four times a year. $52.49. Cahiers du Livre & du Disque, 42 Avenue des Platanes, BP 203, 37172 Chambray l'Tours France. **Tel** 011 33 47 282068. **Continues** Espace (Paris. 1978), 0180-7013.
Ind/Abst BHA : Biblio. Hist. Art.

LC NB1750
ISSN 0262-4966
DD 726
UK
CHURCHSCAPE. See Architecture.

ISSN 0831-3091
DD 331.3/4/09714
CN
TITLE CHANGE
CIEL VARIABLE :LE MANIFESTE DU TEMPS. [Ciel var.]. **Added/Corp** Vox Populi (Organisation) Collectif des Jeunes Sans-Emploi de St-Louis-du-Parc. **VFOAT** Manifeste du Temps. Vol. 1, No 1, June (1986)-(19??). Periodical. French. Les Productions Ciel Variable, 4060 boulevard St. Laurent #301, Montreal Quebec H2W 1Y9 Canada. **Tel** (514)849-0508, FAX (514)284-6775. cum. index. **Ad Acc**. **Circ**: 1,000. **Continued by** C V Photo.

ISSN 0009-6830
FR
CIMAISE. [Cimaise]. (1953)-. Periodical. French (English, German and Spanish). Six times a year. $88.00. CIMAISE, 3 rue Maurice Loewry, 75014 Paris France. **Tel** 011 33 1 43271540. **(Subscription address:** Cimaise, Subscription Office, PO Box 1831, Birmingham AL 35201-1831. **Tel** (800)633-4931, (205)995-1567 (outside US and Canada, FAX (205)995-1588.) cum. index. **Bk Rev**. **Ad Acc**. **Circ**: 15,000 (ctrl) Documents available from The Genuine Article.
Desc: Present day art and architecture.
Ind/Abst Art Index; ARTbibliogr. Mod. (1984-); ARTbibliogr. Curr. Titles; Arts Humanit. Citation Index [Full Cov.]; BHA : Biblio. Hist. Art; Curr. Contents Arts Humanit.; Repere (1979-1980); Res. Alert [Full Cov.].

ISSN 0263-9475
UK
CIRCA (BELFAST, NORTHERN IRELAND). (CIRCA). **Added/Corp** Artists Collective of N. Ireland. (198?)-. Periodical. English. Four times a year. $34.23. Circa Art Magazine, Donegall Pass, Belfast BT7 1DR United Kingdom. **Tel** 011 44 232 230375. **ED** Tanya Kiang. Index available. **Bk Rev**, (Qty: 4-6). **Ad Acc**. **Circ**: 1,500.
Desc: Contemporary visual culture in Ireland. Encourages debate and discussion on issues relating to art in society and reports contemporary developments with news and reviews.
Ind/Abst ARTbibliogr. Mod.; BHA : Biblio. Hist. Art; Film Lit. Index (19??-).

ISSN 0069-4355
DD 700 945
IT
CIVILTA VENEZIANA. FONTI E TESTI. SER.1: FONTI E DOCUMENTI PER LA STORIA DELL'ARTE VENETA. **Added/Corp** Fondazione "Giorgio Cini." Centro di Cultura e Civilta. Istituto di Storia dell'arte. Vol. 1 (1959)-. Periodical. Italian. Irregular. Casa Editrice Leo S. Olschki, Viuzzo del Pozzetto, Casella Postale 66, 50126 Florence Italy. **Tel** 011 39 55 6530684, FAX 011 39 55 6530214.

ISSN 1072-6764
DD 759
US
●**CLASSICAL REALISM JOURNAL.** [Class. realism j.]. **Added/Corp** American Society of Classical Realism. (1993)-. Periodical. English. Four times a year. $12.00. American Society of Classical Realism, 1313 5th Street Southeast, Suite 126D, Minneapolis MN 55414. **Tel** (612)379-3908. **Continues** Classical Realism Quarterly.

US
CLIPPER CREATIVE ART SERVICE. (19??)-. English. Twelve times a year. $430.20 US; $444.00 Canada. Dynamic Graphics Inc., 6000 North Forest Park Drive, Peoria IL 61614. **Tel** (800)255-8800, FAX (309)688-5873. **(Subscription address:** Dynamic Graphics Inc., PO Box 1901, Peoria IL 61656. **Tel** (309)688-8800, 800-255-8800.)

US
COATES ART REVIEW: IMPRESSIONISM. CD-ROM. English. $84.95. Quanta Press, Inc., 1313 Fifth Street Southeast, Suite 208C, Minneapolis MN 55414. **Tel** (612)379-3956, FAX (612)623-4570.
Desc: Over 600 VGA and Super VGA images of Impressionist artworks and the artists. Impressionism on CD-ROM covers the name of work, media, date, size, and the location of the work. Available in DOS and MAC formats.

IT
COLLANA DI SAGGI E TESTI. SEZIONE SESTA, STORIA DELL'ARTE. Vol. 1, (1980)-. Monographic series. Italian (French and English). Irregular. Price varies per volume. Congedo Editore Via Marche, 24 73013 Galatina Leece Italy.

CN
COLLAPSE. (19??)-. English. One time a year. 30.00Can$. **(Subscription address:** Collapse, 127626th Avenue West, Vancouver British Columbia V6H 2A9 Canada. **Tel** (604)733-2003.)

ISSN 1196-4812
DD 707/.5/0971
CN
●**COLLECTIBLES CANADA.** [Collect. Can.]. (1993)-. Periodical. English. Seven times a year. 11.20Can$. Trajan Publishing Corporation, 103 Lakeshore RE, Suite 202, Saint Catherine Ontario, L2N 2T6 Canada. **Tel** (905)646-7744, FAX (905)646-0995. **Continues** Insight on Collectables (1987)., 0836-5873.

FR
COLLECTION SEPTIEME ART 7 ART.
(19??)-. French. Irregular. Editions du CERF, 29 Boulevard Latour Maubourg, 75340 Paris Cedex 07 France. **Tel** 011 33 1 44181212.

ISSN 1046-2252
DD 708
US
Pr Rev.
COLLECTIONS (COLUMBIA, S.C.). See Museums and Galleries.

LC CJ201 .C64
ISSN 0885-2995
US
COLLECTORS' JOURNAL OF ANCIENT ART. [Collect. j. anc. art]. **Added/Corp** Joel L. Malter & Co. Vol. 1, No. 1 (Jan./March 1979)-. Periodical. English. Four times a year. $10.00 US and Canada; $15.00 other. Numismatic Fine Arts Inc, 16661 Ventura Boulevard, Encino CA 91316. **Continues** Journal of Numismatic Fine Arts.

ISSN 0394-2961
UDC 7
IT
COLLOQUI DEL SODALIZIO. [Colloq. Sodalizio]. (1952)-. Periodical. Italian. Every 2 years.
Ind/Abst BHA : Biblio. Hist. Art.

ISSN 0892-6328
US
COLUMBUS ART. **Added/Corp** Columbus Art League (Columbus (Ohio). (1979)-. Periodical. English. Six times a year. $5.00. Columbus Art, 700 Evening Street, Worthington OH 43085. **Tel** (614)292-7183.

The Arts —Art

ISSN 0586-6391
IT
COMMENTARI; RIVISTA DI CRITICA E STORIA DELL'ARTE. [Commentari]. Vol. 1 (Jan. 1950)-. Periodical. Italian. De Luca Editore SRL, Via di S Anna 16, 00186 Rome Italy.
Ind/Abst BHA : Biblio. Hist. Art.

LC N7 .C63
DD 709/.46
SP
COMUN. Added/Corp Fundacion Faustino Orbegozo. Instituto de Arte y Humanidades. (19??)-. Periodical. Basque (Spanish; summaries and/or abstracts in English). Irregular. 1.400. Fundacion Faustino Orbegozo, Instituto de Arte y Humanidades, Spain.
Ind/Abst Archit. Period. Index.

LC N4 .C66
IT
COMUNICAZIONE. Vol. 1 (Sept./Dec. 1975)-. Periodical. Italian. Three times a year. L3.000. 112 Via Palazzuolo, 50 123 Firenze Italy.

LC N2 .C62
ISSN 0395-5907
FR
CONNAISSANCE DES ARTS, PLAISIR DE FRANCE. (CONNAISSANCE DES ARTS.). [Connaiss. arts Plaisir Fr.]. **Added/Corp** Societe Francaise de Promotion Artistique. **VFOAT** C.A.; Connaissance des Arts. Plaisir de France; CA. No. 2 (1952)-. Periodical. French (summaries and/or abstracts in English). Twelve times a year. $95.00. Connaissance des Arts, 25 rue de Ponthieu, 75008 Paris France. **Tel** 011 33 1 43596200, FAX 011 33 1 42564335. **(Subscription address:** Connaissance des Arts, 851 Madison Avenue, New York NY 10021. **Tel** (212)772-6855.) **ED** Philip Jodidio. **Bk Rev. Ad Acc. Circ:** 47,118 (ctrl). Documents available from The Genuine Article. **Continues** Connaisseur; **Absorbed** Plaisir de France (Paris, France : 1945), 0153-8055.
Desc: Publishes articles about antiques, paintings, sculpture, architecture, decoration and the art market.
Ind/Abst Archit. Period. Index (1977-); Art Archaeol. Tech. Abstr.; Art Index; ARTbibliogr. Mod. Arts Humanit. Citation Index [Full Cov.]; Avery Index Archit. Period. Suppl. Colum. Univ. (1990-); BHA : Biblio. Hist. Art; Curr. Contents Arts Humanit.; Res. Alert [Full Cov.]; Romant. Move.; Soc. Sci. Cit. Index [Select. Cov.].

LC N354.C62 C65
DD 700/.7/12746
US
CONNECTICUT ASSESSMENT OF EDUCATIONAL PROGRESS. ART AND MUSIC. / PREPARED FOR CONNECTICUT STATE DEPARTMENT OF EDUCATION, BUREAU OF RESEARCH, PLANNING, AND EVALUATION; PREPARED BY NATIONAL EVALUATION SYSTEMS, INC. See Education-Tests and Measurements.

ISSN 0765-5428
FR
CONSERVATION RESTAURATION. [Conserv. restaur.]. **Added/Corp** FNAROA (Organization). (1984)-. Periodical. French. Two times a year. FNROA, 53 rue de la Tombe Issoire, 75014 Paris France. **Tel** 011 33 1 47611340.

ISSN 1157-688X
FR
UDC 745
CONSERVATION RESTAURATION DES BIENS CULTURELS PARIS. (CONSERVATION RESTAURATION DES BIENS CULTURELS.). **Added/Corp** Association des Restaurateurs d'Art et d'Archeologie de Formation Universitaire (France). (19??)-. Periodical. French. One time a year. 100.00F (members), 150.00F (nonmembers) EEC countries; 120.00F (members), 170.00F (nonmembers) other. Revue CRBC / ARAAFU, 17 rue de Tolbiac, 75013 Paris France. **Circ:** 1,000.

US
CONSERVATION : THE GCI NEWSLETTER. Added/Corp Getty Conservation Institute. **VFOAT** GCI Newsletter. Vol. 6, No. 1 (Fall 1991)-. Newsletter. English. Three times a year. Getty Conservation Institute, 4503 Glencoe Avenue, Marina del Rey CA 90292. **Tel** (310)822-2299, FAX (310)821-9409. **Continues** Getty Conservation Institute Newsletter, 0898-4808.

ISSN 0958-1847
UK
CONSERVATION UPDATE : NEWSLETTER OF THE CONSERVATION UNIT, MUSEUMS & GALLERIES COMMISSION. Main/Corp Great Britain. Museums and Galleries Commission. Conservation Unit. (Autumn 1989)-. Newsletter. English.
Ind/Abst Museum Abstr.

LC N8554 .C66
ISSN 0140-0096
DD 702/.8
UK
CONSERVATOR (LONDON). (THE CONSERVATOR.). [Conservator]. **Added/Corp** International Institute for Conservation of Historic and Artistic Works. United Kingdom Group. (1977)-. Periodical. English. Six times a year. £60.00 institutions; £52.00 students. UK Institute for Conservation / Westminster, Bridge Road, 6 Whitehorse Mews, London SE1 7QD United Kingdom. **Tel** 011 44 71 6203371.
Ind/Abst Art Archaeol. Tech. Abstr.; Br. Archaeol. Bibliogr.; Museum Abstr.

LC ND212.A1 I4
ISSN 0069-9365
DD 759.13
US
CONTEMPORARY AMERICAN PAINTING AND SCULPTURE. Main/Corp Illinois. University at Urbana-Champaign. College of Fine and Applied Arts. (1967)-. English. Irregular. Harper Collins Publishers, Keystone Industrial Park, Scranton PA 18512. **Tel** (800)242-7737, (800)233-4727, FAX (800)822-4090. **Continues** Exhibition of Contemporary American Painting and Sculpture.

UK
CONTEMPORARY ART. (19??)-. English. Four times a year. $36.00 individuals; $42.00 institutions. Contemporary Art Publishers Ltd, 2 Sydney Place, Bath BA2 6NF United Kingdom. **Tel** 011 44 1225 332527. **Continues** Green Book Bath, 0265-0088.

ISSN 0714-9476
DD 720/.28/8/09714
CN
CONTINUITE. [Continuite]. **Added/Corp** Conseil des Monuments et Sites du Quebec. Fondation Canadienne pour la Protection du Patrimoine. No. 17 (Autumn 1982)-. Periodical. French. Four times a year. 23.94Can$. Editions Continuite Inc, 82 Grande Alle Ouest, Quebec Quebec G1R 2G6 Canada. **Tel** (418)647-4525. **ED** Marc Oesjardins. Index available. cum. Rev. **Bk Rev. Ad Acc. Circ:** 6,000. **Continues** Bulletin (Conseil des Monuments et Sites du Quebec), 0226-1286.
Desc: Presents Quebec's history of art, architecture, heritage and urbanism in relation with today's environment and preoccupations. Informs on techniques of restoration and conservation.
Ind/Abst Art Archaeol. Tech. Abstr.; Repere.

ISSN 1058-9120
US
CONTRIBUTIONS TO THE STUDY OF ART AND ARCHITECTURE. (1992)-. Monographic series. English. Price varies per volume. Greenwood Press Inc., PO Box 5007, Westport CT 06881-5007. **Tel** (203)226-3571, FAX (203)222-1502.

UK
CONTROL MAGAZINE. No. 1 (July 1965)-. Periodical. English. Irregular. $40.00. Control Magazine, 5 London Mews, Paddington London W2 1HY United Kingdom. **Tel** 262-3032. **ED** Stephen Willats. **Circ:** 750.
Desc: Works and texts by artists on the social and process basis of their art practice.
Ind/Abst ARTbibliogr. Mod.; ARTbibliogr. Curr. Titles.

IT
CONVERTER & CARTOTECNICA. [Converter Cartotec.]. **VFOAT** Converter e Cartotecnica. (1968)-. Periodical. Multiple languages. Six times a year. Ciessegi Editrice, Via Pietro Colletta 28, 20135 Milan Italy.

ISSN 8755-2582
DD 708
US
SUSPENDED
CORPORATE ARTNEWS. [Corp. artnews]. **VFOAT** Corporate Art News. Vol. 1, No. 1 (May/June 1984)-(19??). Periodical. English. Six times a year. $95.00. ARTnews Associates, 48 West 38th Street, 9th Floor, New York NY 10018. **Tel** (212)398-1690, FAX (212)819-0394.

LC NK4640.C6 I7
IT
CORPUS VASORUM ANTIQUORUM. ITALIA. See Glass and Ceramics.

LC N6250 .C67
DD 709/.02
IT
SUSPENDED
CORSO DI CULTURA SULL'ARTE RAVENNATE E BIZANTINA : [CONFERENZE]. Added/Corp Universita Bologna. Istituto di Antichita Ravennati e Bizantine, Ravenna. (1978)-Suspended with Vol. 40 (1993). Periodical. Italian (French and Italian). One time a year. Angelo Longo Editore, Via Paolo Costa 33, CP 431, 48100 Ravenna Italy. **Tel** 011 39 544 217026, FAX 011 39 544 217026. **Continues** Corsi di Cultura Sull'Arte Ravennate e Bizantina. Corsi di Cultura Sull'Arte Ravennate e Bizantina.
Ind/Abst Avery Index Archit. Period. Suppl. Colum. Univ. (1987).

ISSN 0399-6921
FR
COURRIER DES METIERS D'ART, LE. Added/Corp Societe d'Encouragement aux Metiers d'Art (France). (19??)-. Periodical. French. Four times a year.
Ind/Abst BHA : Biblio. Hist. Art.

LC N6.5 .C7
ISSN 0105-0583
DK
CRAS. (1973)-. Periodical. Danish. Four times a year. kr220.00. Silkeborg Kunstmuseums Forlag, Gudenavaj 7 9, DK 8600 Silkeborg Denmark. **Tel** 011 45 86 825388.
Ind/Abst ARTbibliogr. Mod.; BHA : Biblio. Hist. Art.

ISSN 0011-1511
IT
CRITICA D'ARTE. [Crit. arte]. (1935)-. Periodical. Italian. Four times a year. L57910. Edifir Edizioni Firenze Srl, via Fiume 8, 50123 Florence Italy. **Tel** 011 39 55 289478.
Ind/Abst ARTbibliogr. Mod. (1985-); Avery Index Archit. Period. Suppl. Colum. Univ. (19??-199?); BHA : Biblio. Hist. Art (1985-).

SP
CUADERNOS DE ARTE E ICONOGRAFIA / FUNDACION UNIVERSITARIA ESPANOLA, SEMINARIO DE ARTE MARQUES DE LOZOYA. Added/Corp Fundacion Universitaria Espanola. Seminario de Arte "Marques de Lozoya.". Vol. 1, No. 1 (1988)-. Periodical. Spanish. Two times a year. 4120ptas Spain; 4500ptas other. Pedro Alcantarilla, C Conchas 1, 28013 Madrid Spain. **Tel** 011 34 1 2482630.

ISSN 0070-1688
AG
UDC 7 (091)
CUADERNOS DE HISTORIA DEL ARTE. [Cuad. hist. arte]. (1961)-. Academic Scholarly Publication. Spanish. Irregular. Universidad Nacional de Cuyo Facultad de Filosofia y Letras, Centro Universitario, Parque General San Martin, 5500 Mendoza Argentina. **Bk Rev.** available on CD-ROM.
Ind/Abst BHA : Biblio. Hist. Art.

ISSN 0011-2798
IT
CULTURA NEL MONDO, LA. See Literature.

US
CURRENTS. (19??)-. Newsletter. English. Four times a year. $35.00 (Comes with membership). Historical Association of Southern Florida, 101 West Flagler Street, Miami FL 33130. **Tel** (305)375-1492, FAX (305)375-1609. **Circ:** 5,300 (ctrl).
Desc: Covers museum programs, exhibitions and events in South Florida.

ISSN 1057-3577
US
DD 705
CYANOSIS (SANTA ROSA, CALIF.). (CYANOSIS : JOURNAL OF ART AND WRITING.). [Cyanosis]. Issue 1 (1991)-. Periodical. English. $8.50. Cyanosis, 318 Mendocino Avenue, Suite 30, Santa Rosa CA 95404.

ISSN 0394-5219
IT
DAI CIVICI MUSEI D'ARTE E DI STORIA DI BRESCIA. STUDI E NOTIZIE. See Museums and Galleries.

IT
D'ARS. (1???)-. Periodical. Italian. Four times a year. L100000. D'ars, Via Santagnese 3, 20123 Milan Italy. **Tel** 011 39 2 860290, FAX 011 39 2 865997. **ED** M. C. Spasciani. **Ad Acc. Circ:** 5,000.
Desc: Analysis of the general situation in the visual arts field of today.
Ind/Abst ARTbibliogr. Mod.; BHA : Biblio. Hist. Art.

ISSN 0211-0768
SP
UDC 7
D'ART. [D'Art]. **VFOAT** Revista del Departamento de Historia del Arte. (1972)-. Periodical. Multiple languages. Irregular.
Ind/Abst BHA : Biblio. Hist. Art.

LC N8610 .P6
ISSN 0011-7358
DD 381/.457/005
US
DECOR (ST. LOUIS). (DECOR.). [Decor]. **VFOAT** Decor for ... Vol. 86, No. 1 (Dec. 1965)-. Trade Publication. English. Twelve times a year. Commerce Publishing Company, 408 Olive Street, St Louis MO 63102. **Tel** (314)421-5445. **Continues** Picture and Gift Journal, 1043-8327.

ISSN 0947-031X
GW
●**DENKMALPFLEGE, DIE. See** Architecture.

LC N9000.B3 D46
GW
DENKMALPFLEGE IN BADEN-WURTTEMBERG. Added/Corp Landesdenkmalamt Baden-Wurttemberg. (1972)-. Periodical. German. Four times a year. Landesdenkmalamt Baden-Wuerttemberg, Moerikestr 12, 70178 Stuttgart Germany.
Ind/Abst Art Archaeol. Tech. Abstr.; BHA : Biblio. Hist. Art.

KO
SUSPENDED
DESIGN JOURNAL. (19??)-No. 47 (1992). Korean. Twelve times a year. Art Center Inc, 70-9 Art Center Building, Kalwol-Dong, Yongsan-ku Seoul Korea. **Tel** 011 82 02 718 0455.

LC N3 .D43 ISSN 0012-0375
DD 709 GW
TITLE CHANGE
DEUTSCHE KUNST UND DENKMALPFLEGE. See Architecture.

ISSN 0279-568X
US
DIALOGUE (MUNROE FALLS, OHIO). (DIALOGUE: ARTS IN THE MIDWEST.). **Added/Corp** Akron Art Institute. Ohio Foundation on the Arts. University of Akron. University Galleries. (Sept./Oct. 1978)-. Periodical. English. Six times a year. $20.00. Dialogue Inc, PO Box 2572, Columbus OH 43216-2572. **Tel** (614)621-3704, FAX (614)621-2448. **ED** Lorrie N. Dirkse. **Ad Acc, Adv Mgr:** Tiffany Komasara. **Circ:** 15,000 (ctrl) available on microfilm from University Microfilms International (UMI).
Desc: Devoted to covering the arts in Ohio, Indiana, Illinois, Kentucky. Provides readers with features on artists, cooperative projects, alternative spaces, censorship issues, and economic realities; critical reviews of exhibitions, film/video screenings, and performances; news; and calendar & call for entry listings.
Ind/Abst ARTbibliogr. Mod.; Int. Polit. Sci. Abstr.

ISSN 1058-9775
DD 741 US
DIMENSION X. [Dimens. X]. Vol. 1 (1992)-. Periodical. English. Four times a year. Karl Art Publishing, 1307 Azur Place, Hewlett Harbor NY 11557.

ISSN 0305-7380
UK
DIRECTORY / ART LIBRARIES SOCIETY. Main/Corp Art Libraries Society. (1986)-. Directory. English. £45.00 (institutions membership), £16.00 (individuals membership), £30.00 (enhanced membership), £21.00 (student, retired or unwaged enhanced membership), £7.00 (student, retired or unwaged basic membership) UK and Ireland. ARLIS UK & Ireland, The Art Libraries Society of the United Kingdom and Ireland, 18 College Road Bromsgrove, Worcestershire B60 2NE United Kingdom. **Tel** 011 44 1527 579298. **ED** Philip Pacey. **Continues** Art Libraries Society. Directory of Members, 0305-7380.
Desc: Offers an unparalleled perspective on art librianship worldwide. Frequently includes conference papers of the IFLA Section of Art Libraries.

LC N328.N37
DD 707/.1/173 US
DIRECTORY / NATIONAL ASSOCIATION OF SCHOOLS OF ART AND DESIGN.
Main/Corp National Association of Schools of Art and Design (U.S.). (1982)-. Directory. English. One time a year (Aug.). $11.00. National Association of Schools of Art/Design - NASAD, 11250 Roger Bacon Drive, Suite 21, Reston VA 22090. **Tel** (703)437-0700. **Continues** National Association of Schools of Art (U.S.). Membership Directory.
Desc: This directory lists accredited institutions and major degree programs. Includes addresses, telephone numbers, and art/design executives for all members.

LC N51 .D57 ISSN 0897-3989
DD 707/.1/173 US
DIRECTORY OF ART AND DESIGN FACULTIES IN COLLEGES AND UNIVERSITIES, U.S. AND CANADA. See The Arts-Abstracting, Bibliographies and Statistics.

ISSN 1067-8506
DD 702 US
TITLE CHANGE
DIRECTORY OF ARTISTS USING SCIENCE AND TECHNOLOGY. [Dir. artists using sci. technol.]. **Added/Corp** Ylem (Organization). (1991)-(199?). Directory. English. YLEM, Artists Using Science and Technology, PO Box 749, Orinda CA 94563.
Continues Artists Using Science and Technology Directory. **Continued by** Artists Using Science and Technology Directory (Orinda, Calif. : 1992).

LC N8630 .D57 ISSN 1053-2854
DD 380.1/457/0294 US
DIRECTORY OF FINE ART REPRESENTATIVES & CORPORATIONS COLLECTING ART. [Dir. fine art represent. corp. collect. art]. **Added/Corp** Directors Guild Publishers. **VFOAT** Fine Art Representatives & Corporations Collecting Art; Fine Art Representatives and Corporations Collecting Art; Fine Art Representatives. 2nd Ed.(1990)-. Directory. English. ArtNetwork Press, 18757 Wildflower Drive, Penn Valley CA 95949. **Tel** (916)432-7630.
Continues Directory of Fine Art Representatives & Corporate Art Consultants, 1042-2242.

LC N50 .D57 ISSN 0196-8475
DD 709/.2/2 US
DIRECTORY OF HISTORIANS OF LATIN AMERICAN ART. [Dir. hist. Lat. Am. art]. **Added/Corp** University of Texas at San Antonio. Research Center for the Arts. (1979)-. Directory. English. Irregular. University of Texas at San Antonio, Research Center for Arts and Humanities, San Antonio TX 78285. **Tel** (512)691-4358.

LC N6530.I4 D57 ISSN 0277-0164
DD 702/.5/773 US
DIRECTORY OF ILLINOIS VISUAL ARTISTS. Added/Corp Illinois Arts Council. (19??)-. Directory. English. $2.00. Illinois Arts Council, 100 West Randolph/Suite 10-500, Chicago IL 60601-3220.

LC N8554 .A53b ISSN 1074-7885
DD 701/.8 US
DIRECTORY / THE AMERICAN INSTITUTE FOR CONSERVATION OF HISTORIC AND ARTISTIC WORKS. [Dir. - Am. Inst. Conserv. Hist. Artist. Works]. **Main/Corp** American Institute for Conservation of Historic and Artistic Works. **VFOAT** A.I.C. Directory. (1982)-. Directory. English. One time a year. $58.00. American Institute Conservation, 1717 K Street Northwest, Suite 301, Washington DC 20006. **Tel** (202)452-9545, FAX (202)542-9328. **Continues** American Institute for Conservation of Historic and Artistic Works. AIC Directory.
Desc: Resource for conservators, museum and arts professionals, students, and others who need to make contact with the conservation field. Contains listings of members by name, specialty, and geographic region. Includes other listings such as training programs, funding agencies, and conservation organizations worldwide.

US
DISCOVERING ART HISTORY. (19??)-. English. Irregular. $29.95. Davis Publications Inc, 50 Portland Street, Worcester MA 01608. **Tel** (617)754-7201, (800)533-2847, FAX (508)753-3834.

ISSN 0710-9350
CN
DD 700/.9714
DOCUMENTS DE PRESSE MENSUELS : ARTS PLASTIQUES. [Doc. presse mens., Arts plast.]. **Added/Corp** Quebec (Province). Ministere des Affaires Culturelles. Direction des Communications. **VFOAT** Arts Plastiques. (1976)-. Periodical. French (summaries and/or abstracts in English). Ministere des Affaires Culturelles, Direction des Communications, Montreal Quebec H3C 3R4 Canada.

LC N6 .D66 ISSN 0209-147X
DD 705 PL
DOM. (1982)-. Periodical. Polish. Six times a year. Price on request. Wydawn, Arkady, 00-010 Warszawa Ul, Sienkiewicza 14 Poland. **(Subscription address:** Ars Polona-Ruch, PO Box 1001, Krakowskie Przedmiescie 7, 00-068 Warsaw Poland. **Tel** 011 48 22 261201.)

LC ND1059.M47 A4A
JA
DORITSU MIGISHI KOTARO BIJUTSUKAN HO. Main/Corp Hokkaidoritsu Migishi Kotaro Bijutsukan. (Dec. 12, 197?)-. Japanese. Hokkaidoritsu Migishi Kotaro Bijutsukan, Kita 2-jo Nishi 15-chome, Chuo-ku 060, Sapporo Japan. **Tel** (011)644-8901, FAX (011)646-8902. **Circ:** 1,600 (ctrl)
Desc: Annual report and essays.

FR
DOSSIER DE L'ART. 1 (April/May 1991)-. Periodical. French. Six times a year. SFBD/Archeologia, 25 rue Berbisey, 2100 Dijon France.

ISSN 0012-5709
FR
CODEN DOLIA8
DOUBLE LIAISON. See Paints and Painting.

ISSN 0191-6963
DD 741 US
DRAWING (NEW YORK, N.Y. 1979). (DRAWING.). [Drawing]. **Added/Corp** Drawing Society. Vol. 1, (May/June 1979)-. Academic Scholarly Publication. English. Six times a year (Jan., Mar., May, July, Sept., Nov.,), $50.00 (one-year) membership, US; $62.50 (one-year) membership, other. The Drawing Society, 15 Penn Plaza, Box 66, New York NY 10001-2050. **Tel** (212)563-4822, FAX (212)563-4829. **ED** Pat Hurley and Paul Cummings. **Bk Rev**. **Ad Acc, Adv Mgr:** Dianne Turner. **Circ:** 1,200.
Desc: Scholarly essays on drawings of all periods and cultures. Includes exhibition announcements, international auction reviews, museum acquisitions and gallery listings.
Ind/Abst Art Index; ARTbibliogr. Mod. (1984-); ARTbibliogr. Curr. Titles; Avery Index Archit. Period. Suppl. Colum. Univ. (19??-199?); BHA : Biblio. Hist. Art.

ISSN 0323-4088
GW
DRESDENER KUNSTBLATTER. (DRESDENER KUNSTBLATTER : ZWEIMONATSSCHRIFT DER STAATLICHEN KUNSTSAMMLUNG DRESDEN.). [Dresd. Kunstbl.]. **Added/Corp** Staatliche Kunstsammlungen Dresden. (1960)-. Periodical. German. Six times a year. Staatliche Kunstsammlungen, Georg Treu Platz Albertino, O 8012 Dresden F R Germany. **Continues** Dresdener Galerieblatter.
Ind/Abst BHA : Biblio. Hist. Art.

LC N6918 .D7
DD 709/.45 IT
DS (ROME, ITALY). (DS / CENTRO DI SARRO.). **Added/Corp** Centro Di Sarro. **VFOAT** Arte Nuova in Italia. (1982)-. Italian. One time a year. Centro di Sarro, Il Ventaglio Via Cagliari 42, 00198 Rome Italy.

LC DF503 .D84 ISSN 0070-7546
DD 709.495 US
DUMBARTON OAKS PAPERS. [Dumbarton Oaks pap.]. **Added/Corp** Dumbarton Oaks. Dumbarton Oaks. Center for Byzantine Studies. No. 1 (1941)-. English (German, Italian and French). One time a year. Dumbarton Oaks Publishing / Maryland, PO Box 4866, Hampden Station, Baltimore MD 21211. **Tel** (410)516-6954. **ED** Robert Thomson. Index available. cum. index. **Circ:** 800 (ctrl).
Desc: Articles concerning late classical, early medieval, and Byzantine civilization in the fields of art, architecture, history, theology, literature, and law.
Ind/Abst Am. Bibliogr. Slavic East Europ. Stud.; Avery Index Archit. Period. Suppl. Colum. Univ. (19??-199?); BHA : Biblio. Hist. Art; Numis. Lit.

LC AP37 .E22 ISSN 0012-8376
DD 055/.1 IT
EAST AND WEST (ROME, ITALY). (EAST AND WEST.). [East west]. **Added/Corp** Istituto Italiano per il Medio ed Estremo Oriente. Year 1 (Apr. 1950)-. Periodical. English. Four times a year. L25000.00 Volume 42. Herder Editrice e Libreria SRL, Piazza Montecitorio 117-120, 00186 Rome Italy. **Tel** 011 39 6 679 4628, FAX 011 39 6 678 4751. cum. index.
Desc: Oriental art and archaeology; covers the excavations of the Instituto Italiano per il Medio ed Estremo Oriente in Afghanistan, Iran and Pakistan.
Ind/Abst Am. Hist. Life (1955-1980); Numis. Lit.

LC N7260 .E27 ISSN 0269-8404
DD 709/.5/05 UK
EASTERN ART REPORT : FORTNIGHTLY SURVEY OF THE ARTS OF THE MIDDLE EAST, SOUTH ASIA, CHINA & JAPAN. Added/Corp Centre for Near East, Asia, and Africa Research. (Mar. 1989)-. Periodical. English. Six times a year. $75.00. NEAR / Eastern Art Publishing, Acre House 69, 76 Long Acre, Covenant Garden London WC2E 9AS United Kingdom. **Tel** 011 44 81 392 1122. Each issue contains an index to its own contents (no volume index)--loose.
Desc: Features include interviews, reviews of exhibitions and art auctions, articles, news and comment, worldwide listings of art events and a monthly index of back issues.

IT
ECO D ARTE MODERNA. Italian. IL Candelaio, Via Fra Angelico 3R, 50121 Florence Italy.

LC NX7 .E34
BL
EDICOES CADERNOS CULTURAIS. (19??)-. Portuguese. Irregular. $10.00. Universidade Federal de Pernambuco, Cidade Universitaria 5000 Recife, Brazil.

LC Z5939 .E33 NK1125 ISSN 0277-8394
DD 707/.4/017311 US
EDITIONS CATALOG. [Ed. cat.]. **Added/Corp** Circle Fine Art Corporation. (1981)-. Catalog. English. One time a year. $15.00. Circle Fine Art Corporation, 875 North Michigan Avenue/Suite 3160, Chicago IL 60611. **Tel** (312)943-0664.

LC CR1 .E42 ISSN 0885-968X
DD 929.8/2 US
EMBLEMATICA. See Literature.

ISSN 0822-7683
DD 702/.9/4714281 CN
ENCAN - FRASER BROS. LTD. (ENCAN = AUCTION.). [Encan - Fraser Brothers Ltd.]. **Main/Corp** Fraser Bros. Ltd. **VFOAT** Auction. **VAT** Auction

The Arts — Art

(Montreal). (March 1978)-. English (French). Fraser Brothers Ltd, 4950 Savane Street, Montreal Quebec H4P 1T7 Canada. **Continues** *Auction Sale, 0822-7675.*

FR

ENSEMBLE D'AQUARELLES ET DE DESSINS DE MAITRES SUISSES ET FRANCAIS DU XIXE ET DU XXE SIECLE, UN. **Main/Corp** Galerie Paul Vallotton. (19??)-. French. One time a year.

ISSN 1040-6611
DD 246 US

ENVIRONMENT & ART LETTER. See Religions and Theology-Protestantism.

LC N72.P74 E68
AG

EOS : REVISTA ARGENTINA DE ARTE Y PSICOANALISIS. Added/Corp Fundacion Banco Credito Argentino. Vol. 1 (July 1991)-. Periodical. Spanish (English, French and Italian). One time a year. $30.00. Fundacion Banco Credito Argentino, 11 de Septiembre 1990, 1428 Buenos Aires Argentina. **Tel** 011 54 1 7883819.

LC N7668.H6 E68 ISSN 1044-0224
DD 704.9/432 US

EQUINE IMAGES. [Equine images]. (Aug. 1986)-. Periodical. English. Four times a year. $29.95. Heartland Communications Group Inc., PO Box 916 1003 Central Ave, Fort Dodge IA 50501. **Tel** (800)247-2000, (515)955-1600, FAX (515)955-6636.

ISSN 0899-4005
US

EROTIC ART BY LIVING ARTISTS. (1992)-. English. Every 2 years. $14.95. ArtNetwork Press, 18757 Wildflower Drive, Penn Valley CA 95949. **Tel** (916)432-7630.

ISSN 0821-9222
DD 730/.9714 CN

ESPACE (MONTREAL). (ESPACE.). [Espace]. **Added/Corp** Conseil de la Sculpture du Quebec. Vol. 1, No. 1 (1982)-. Periodical. French. Four times a year (Mar., June, Sept., Dec.). 25.29Can$. ESPACE, 4888 St. Denis, Montreal Quebec H2J 2L6 Canada. **Tel** (514)844-9858. **ED** S. Fisette. **Ad Acc, Adv Mgr:** Y. O'Reilly. **Circ:** 1,500 (ctrl).
Ind/Abst Archit. Period. Index; BHA : Biblio. Hist. Art; Can. Period. Index (19??-); Repere (1992-).

ISSN 1130-0124
SP

ESPACIO, TIEMPO Y FORMA. SERIE 7, HISTORIA DEL ARTE : REVISTA DE LA FACULTAD DE GEOGRAFIA E HISTORIA. Added/Corp Universidad Nacional de Educacion a Distancia. Facultad de Geografia e Historia. **VFOAT** Historia del Arte. (1989)-. Spanish. One time a year. Libreria Marcial Pons, Tamayo y Baus 7, 28004 Madrid Spain. **Tel** 011 34 1 3194254.
Ind/Abst BHA : Biblio. Hist. Art.

ISSN 0831-859X
DD 709.714/281 CN

ESSE. [Esse]. **Added/Corp** Etudiant-e-s en Histoire de l'Art de l'UQAM. **VFOAT** Revue en Art des Etudiants de l'Uqam; Esse : Brevue en Art des Etudiants de l'Uqam. No. 1 (1984)-. Periodical. French. Three times a year. 17.61Can$. Esse Un Groupe de and En Art, DP 2105, Succ Delorimier, Montreal Quebec H2H 2R8 Canada. **Tel** (514)524-1049. Index available. cum. index. **Ad Acc**. **Circ:** 400. **Continues** *Art Contemporain.*
Desc: Critical review of the Quebec and Montreal world of art.

ISSN 0998-8041
FR

ESTAMPILLE, L'OBJET D'ART, L'. VFOAT Estampille/l'Objet d'Art; L'Objet d'Art. (March 1989)-. Periodical. French. Eleven times a year. $124.67. Editions Faton, BP90, 21803 Quetigny Cedex France. **Tel** 011 33 80 469393, FAX 011 33 80 469350. **Formed by the union of** *Estampille, 0184-7724* **and** *Objet d'Art.*
Ind/Abst BHA : Biblio. Hist. Art.

ISSN 0835-7641
DD 709.714/281 CN

ETC (MONTREAL). (ETC MONTREAL.). [Etc]. **Added/Corp** Association des Galeries d'Art Contemporain de Montreal. (Fall 1987)-. Periodical. French. Four times a year. 48.00Can$ Canada (individuals); 28.00Can$ Canada (individuals); 34.00Can$ US (individuals); 34.00Can$ other (individuals). ETC Montreal, 1435 de Bleury, Suite 806, Montreal Quebec H3A 2H7 Canada. **Tel** (514)848-1125, FAX (514)848-0071. **ED** Isabelle Lelarge. cum. index. **Ad Acc, Adv Mgr:** Annie Molin Vasseur, **Tel** (514)842-4319. **Circ:** 2,500 (ctrl). **Continues** *Etc. (Montreal, Quebec), 0835-7641.*
Desc: Offers an alternative to the treatment of information on contemporary art and art critic. Every quarterly, the theme accounts for the role and the stakes of art and society. Interviews with artists and theoricians,

coverage of exhibits, and columns all refer to the understanding of the post-modernism era.
Ind/Abst Repere (Winter 1988-Dec.1990).

LC N5310.7 .T74 ISSN 0893-0120
DD 709/.01/1 US

ETHNOARTS INDEX. See The Arts-Abstracting, Bibliographies and Statistics.

LC DG223.A1 E8 ISSN 1080-1960
DD 937 US

●**ETRUSCAN STUDIES : JOURNAL OF THE ETRUSCAN FOUNDATION. See** History-History of Europe.

ISSN 0240-3994
FR

UDC 92
ETUDES DROMOISES. (1979)-. Periodical. French. Four times a year.
Ind/Abst BHA : Biblio. Hist. Art.

LC N6512 .E885 ISSN 1056-1579
DD 709/.73/074013 US
CEASED

EXHIBITION DIRECTORY. See Museums and Galleries.

ISSN 0928-4109
NE

UDC 616.3
EXKIES 'S-GRAVENHAGE. (EXKIES.). [Exkies 's-Gravenhage]. (1982)-. Trade Publication. Dutch. Eight times a year. $63.38. Samsom Bedrijfsinformatie BV, Postbus 4, 2400 MA Alphen Rij Netherlands. **Tel** 011 31 1720 66633.

ISSN 1063-1321
US

●**EXPOSE: THE VISUAL ARTS MAGAZINE.** (1993)-. Periodical. English. Four times a year. $7.00. Expose, 1323 Scrub Oak, Boulder CO 80303.

LC N6490 .F28 ISSN 0071-3783
DD 709.04 US

FAMOUS ARTISTS ANNUAL. Added/Corp Famous Artists Schools (Westport, Conn.). Vol. 1 (1969)-. English. Kampmann & Company, 226 West 26 Street/8th Floor, New York NY 10001.

LC NX504 .F38 ISSN 0146-5848
DD 700/.973 US

FAULT, THE. (1971)-. Periodical. English. Two times a year. $5.00. Fault, 33513 6th Street, Union City CA 94587.

LC N1 .F43 ISSN 0430-3091
DD 708/.144/61 US

FENWAY COURT. [Fenway court]. **Added/Corp** Isabella Stewart Gardner Museum. Isabella Stewart Gardner Museum. Annual Report. Vol. 1 (Oct. 1966)-. English. One time a year. Isabella Stewart Gardner Museum, 2 Palace Road, Boston MA 02115. **Tel** (617)566-1401.
Ind/Abst Avery Index Archit. Period. Suppl. Colum. Univ.; BHA : Biblio. Hist. Art.

LC N25 .F5 ISSN 0071-481X
DD 709 SW

FIGURA. Added/Corp Uppsala. Universitet. Konsthistoriska Institutionen. (1951)-. Monographic series. English (French, German and Swedish). Irregular. Price varies per volume. Almqvist & Wiksell International, PO Box 4627, S-11691 Stockholm Sweden. **Tel** 011 46 8 6408800.

LC N6503 .F56 ISSN 1057-8269
DD 702/.5/73 US

FINE ART INDEX (NORTH AMERICAN ED.), THE. (THE FINE ART INDEX.). [Fine art index]. (1992)-. English. One time a year. $85.95. International Art Reference, 159 West Burton Place, Chicago IL 60610. **Tel** (312)335-8219.
Desc: Modern, Canadian and American art.

LC N400 ISSN 0848-726X
DD 708.11/384/0294 CN
TITLE CHANGE

FINE ART PUBLICATIONS - NATIONAL GALLERY OF CANADA. See Museums and Galleries.

LC N1.A1 F523 ISSN 0394-1493
DD 700 IT

FLASH ART (INTERNATIONAL EDITION). (FLASH ART.). [Flash art]. **VFOAT** Flash Art International. (1980)-. Periodical. English. Six times a year. L40000. Giancarlo Politi Distribution, Casella Postale 36, 06032 Borgo Trevi PG Italy. **Tel** 011 39 742 780548, FAX 0742 78269. **ED** Giancarlo Politi. **Bk Rev**. **Ad Acc**. **Circ:** 50,000 (ctrl). **Continues in part** *Flash Art, 0015-3524.*
Desc: A publication on the modern art around the world.
Ind/Abst Art Index; ARTbibliogr. Curr. Titles.

LC N1 .F73 ISSN 0731-2636
US

FLUE. (FLUE / FRANKLIN FURNACE.). **Added/Corp** Franklin Furnace (Archive). 1st Edition (Sept. 1980)-. Newsletter. English. Irregular. Price varies. Franklin Furnace, 112 Franklin Street, New York NY 10013. **Tel** (212)925-4671. **ED** Martha Wilson and Harley Spiller. **Bk Rev**. **Circ:** 1,500 (ctrl).
Desc: A newsletter that present articles on exhibition and performance arts. Includes segment on artists and book archives.

ISSN 0214-9400
SP

UDC 008
FMR ED. ESPANOLA. VFOAT Franco Maria Ricci (Ed. Espanola). (1989)-. Periodical. Spanish (English). Six times a year. SA Ebrisa, Gran Via de Carlos III, 58 60A, Barcelona 08028 Spain. **Tel** 011 34 3 3399204.

LC N4 .F58 ISSN 0393-0033
DD 705 IT

FMR (ED. ITALIANA). (FMR.). [FMR]. **Added/Corp** Franco Maria Ricci (Firm). **VFOAT** F.M.R. No. 1 (March 1982)-. Periodical. Italian. Six times a year. L114000. Franco Maria Ricci, via Montecuccoli 32, 20147 Milan Italy. **Tel** 011 39 2 48301524. **ED** Franeo Naria Ricci.
Ind/Abst ARTbibliogr. Mod.

LC N4 .F583 ISSN 0747-6388
DD 705 US

FMR (ENGLISH ED.). (FMR : THE MAGAZINE OF FRANCO MARIA RICCI.). **Added/Corp** Franco Maria Ricci (Firm). **VFOAT** F.M.R. VAT Franco Maria Ricci (English Ed.). No. 1 (June 1984)-. Periodical. English (Italian, French and German). Six times a year. $114.00. FMR Magazines, 3502 48th Avenue, Long Island City NY 11101. **Tel** (212)794-0080, (800)367-2010. (Subscription address: Franco Maria Ricci, via Montecuccoli 32, 20147 Milan Italy. **Tel** 011 39 2 48301524.) **Ad Acc**. **Circ:** 115,000.
Desc: Journal of works of art from antiquity to the present. Photographic essays accompany texts written by scholars and experts. Fresco sequences are reproduced and illuminated codices examined miniature-by-miniature along with exploration of gardens, monuments, and villas. Also covers significant exhibitions and art events in USA and Europe.
Ind/Abst Avery Index Archit. Period. Suppl. Colum. Univ. (Feb. 1990-).

LC N6 .F6 ISSN 0071-6723
DD 705 PL

FOLIA HISTORIAE ARTIUM. [Fol. hist. artium]. **Added/Corp** Polska Akademia Nauk. Komisja Teorii i Historii Sztuki. Vol. 1 (1964)-. Academic Scholarly Publication. Polish (summaries and/or abstracts in French). One time a year. Price varies per volume. Polska Akademia Nauk, Oddzial w Krakowie / Komisja Teorii i Historii Sztuki, Ul. Slawkowska 17, 31-016 Krakow Poland. **Tel** 011 48 12 224853, FAX 011 48 12 222791. **(Subscription address:** Ars Polona-Ruch, PO Box 1001, Krakowskie Przedmiescie 7, 00-068 Warsaw Poland. **Tel** 011 48 22 261201.**)**
Desc: Covers European and occasionally Eastern art historically and contemporarily.
Ind/Abst Am. Hist. Life (1990-); ARTbibliogr. Mod.; ARTbibliogr. Curr. Titles; Avery Index Archit. Period. Suppl. Colum. Univ. (1988-); BHA : Biblio. Hist. Art.

LC NK
DD 745 US

●**FOLK ART ILLUSTRATED.** (1996)-. English. Six times a year (Jan., Mar., May, July, Sept., Nov.). $24.95. Folk Art Illustrated, PO Box 906, Marietta OH 45750. **Tel** (800)355-2781.

ISSN 1083-0308
US

●**FOREHEAD MAGAZINE. See** Clothing Industry and Fashion.

LC N1 .F66 ISSN 0532-1697
UK

FORM (CAMBRIDGE, ENGLAND). (FORM.). (1966)-. Periodical. English. Four times a year.
Ind/Abst ARTbibliogr. Mod.; Graph. Arts Bull. Inst. Pap. Sci. Technol. (Feb. 1989, May 1989-July 1989, Sept. 1989-Dec. 1989).

CK

FORMA Y COLOR COLOMBIA. (1991)-. Spanish. **Continues** *Directorio, Arte y Artistas de Colombia.*

ISSN 0190-678X
US

FORMAT (ST. CHARLES). (FORMAT.). [Format]. (1978)-. Periodical. English. Four times a year. Format, 405 South 7th Street, St Charles IL 60174. **Tel** (312)584-0187. **ED** C.L. Morrison. **Bk Rev**. **Ad Acc**.

The Arts —Art

Circ: 700.
Desc: Concerns the survival of contemporary artists and the art they produce.
GW

FORSCHUNGEN ZUR KUNSTGESCHICHTE UND CHRISTLICHEN ARCHAOLOGIE. German. Irregular. Franz Steiner Verlag GmbH, Postfach 101061, D-70009 Stuttgart Germany. **Tel** 011 49 711 2582372, FAX 011 49 711 2582290, telex 723636 daz d. **ED** R Hamann-McLean and O Fecol.
Desc: Monograph series dedicated to art history, especially early Christian art.

LC N3 .F6   ISSN 0532-2189
GW

FORSCHUNGEN ZUR KUNSTGESCHICHTE UND CHRISTLICHEN ARCHAOLOGIE. [Forsch. Kunstgesch. christl. Archaol.]. Vol. 1 (1952)-. Monographic series. German. Irregular. Price varies per volume. Franz Steiner Verlag GmbH, Postfach 101061, D-70009 Stuttgart Germany. **Tel** 011 49 711 2582372, FAX 011 49 711 2582290, telex 723636 daz d.
Desc: Monographic series covering art and Christian antiquities.
Ind/Abst Avery Index Archit. Period. Suppl. Colum. Univ.

LC N7101 .F7   ISSN 0213-1706
DD 709/.46   SP
SUSPENDED

FRAGMENTOS (MADRID). (FRAGMENTOS.). [Fragmentos]. **Added/Corp** Spain. Ministerio de Cultura. No. 1 (1984)-(March 1991). Periodical. Spanish. Ministerio de Cultura Publ, Calle Plaza del Rey 1, 28004 Madrid Spain. **Tel** 011 34 1 5325089.
Ind/Abst BHA : Biblio. Hist. Art.

LC Z5132 .B85   ISSN 1157-3767
FR

FRANCIS BULLETIN SIGNALETIQUE. 526, ART ET ARCHEOLOGIE. See Archaeology.

LC PN771 .F73   ISSN 0738-9299
DD 808.8/0005   FR
Pr Rev.

FRANK. See Literary and Political Reviews.
GW

FRANKFURTER FORSCHUNGEN ZUR KUNST. Vol. 6, (1977)-. Monographic series. German. Irregular. Price varies per volume. Gebrueder Mann Verlag, Lindenstrasse 76, D-10969 Berlin Germany. **Tel** 011 49 30 25913589, telex 183723. **(Subscription address:** Gebrueder Mann Verlag / KNO, Postfach 800620, Koch, Neff & Oetinger, D-70506 Stuttgart Germany. **Tel** 011 49 711 78992022.) Index available. **Circ:** 800 (ctrl). **Continues** Frankfurter Forschungen zur Architekturgeschichte.
Desc: Publishes scientific articles in the field of art history which cover work done at the University of Frankfurt or in co-operation with the University.
US

FREE FOOD FOR THOUGHT. Issue No. 1 (Mar. 1992)-. Periodical. English. Twelve times a year.

LC NX8.A7 F84
UK

FUNOON ARABIAH. VFOAT Funoon Arabiah. (1981)-. Periodical. Arabic. Four times a year. $7.00. Pan Middle East Graphics and Publishing UK Ltd, Achilles House, London W3 0RX United Kingdom.
AG

GACETA DE LAS ARTES. Added/Corp Asociacion Argentina de Anticuarios y Galerias de Arte. Vol. 1 (Oct. 1968)-. Periodical. Spanish. Twelve times a year.

LC N7101 .G24   ISSN 1130-2747
DD 709/.46/05   SP

GALERIA ANTIQUARIA. VFOAT Antiquaria. (1989)-. Periodical. Spanish. Twelve times a year. 12000ptas. Ediciones Antiquaria, C Nunex de Balboa 118 3C, 28006 Madrid Spain. **Tel** 011 34 1 5637004. **Formed by the union of** Antiquaria (Madrid, Spain), 0212-8810; Galeria (Madrid, Spain), 1130-2755.

ISSN 0228-3778
DD 708.11/4   CN

GALERIE JOLLIET. See Museums and Galleries.
FR

GALERIES MAGAZINE (INTERNATIONAL EDITION). See Museums and Galleries.

ISSN 0838-1658
DD 704/.042   CN

GALLERIE (NORTH VANCOUVER, B.C.). (GALLERIE.). [Gallerie]. Vol. 1, No. 1 (June 1, 1988)-. Periodical. English. Four times a year. 18.00Can$ (institutions), 16.95Can$ (individuals). Gallerie Publications, 2901 Panorama Drive, North Vancouver British Columbia V7G 2A4 Canada. **Tel** (604)929-8706. **ED** Caffyn Kelley. **Circ:** 2,500.
Desc: Women artists from across North America discuss their work and ideas.
Ind/Abst BHA : Biblio. Hist. Art.

ISSN 0826-1121
DD 708.11/23/4   CN

GALLERY (LETHBRIDGE). See Museums and Galleries.

ISSN 1058-9112
DD 810   US

GATHERING OF THE TRIBES, A. See Literature.

LC N8610 .H67
FR

GAZETTE DE L'HOTEL DROUOT, LA. Added/Corp Hotel Drouot. (1891)-. Periodical. French. Forty-six times a year (Published on Fridays). $170.60. Gazette de l'Hotel Drouot, 10 rue du Faubourg Montmartre, 75441 Paris Cedex 09 France. **Tel** 011 33 1 47709300. Index available. cum. index. **Bk Rev. Ad Acc.** ctrl circ.

LC N2 .G3   ISSN 0016-5530
FR

GAZETTE DES BEAUX-ARTS. [Gaz. b.-arts]. **VAT** Gazette des Beaux Arts. (1859)-. Periodical. French. Ten times a year (publishes monthly with May/June and July/Aug. issues combined). 1371.21F (surface mail); 1721.21F (airmail). Gazette des Beaux Arts, Imprimerie Louis Jean, 05002 Gap Cedex France. **Tel** 011 33 9 2535086. cum. index. Documents available from The Genuine Article.
Ind/Abst Art Index; ARTbibliogr. Mod.; Arts Humanit. Citation Index (19??-19??) [Full Cov.]; Avery Index Archit. Period. Suppl. Colum. Univ. (1990-); BHA : Biblio. Hist. Art; Curr. Contents Arts Humanit.; Res. Alert [Full Cov.].
IT
SUSPENDED

GAZZETTA DELLE ARTI. (19??)-Suspended with Vol. 24. Italian. International Art Co. Srl, Via Manin 50, 30174 Venice Mestre Italy. **Tel** 011 39 41 937830.

LC NX440 .G44
JA

GEIJUTSU SHINCHO. (1950)-. Periodical. English. Twelve times a year. $287.00. **(Subscription address:** Japan Publications Trading Company Ltd., PO Box 5030, Tokyo International, Tokyo 100-31 Japan. **Tel** 011 81 3 3292 3753.) **Bk Rev. Ad Acc.**
Desc: Covers various forms of art, including painting, carvings, and more.

ISSN 0072-0585
FR

GENAVA. [Genava]. **Added/Corp** Geneva (Switzerland). Musee d'art et d'Histoire. Bibliotheque Publique et Universitaire de Geneve. Societe des Amis du Musee de Geneve. Geneva (Canton) Commission pour la Conservation des Monuments et la Protection des Sites. (1923)-. French. One time a year (Dec.). $61.27. Musee d'Art et d'Histoire, Case Postale 516, 1211 Geneva 3 Switzerland. **Tel** 011 41 22 7290011. **Continues** Ville de Geneve Bulletin du Musee d'Art d'Histoire.
Ind/Abst Anthropol. Index; Avery Index Archit. Period. Suppl. Colum. Univ. (19??-199?); BHA : Biblio. Hist. Art.

LC N9 .G4
DD 705   BE

GENTSE BIJDRAGEN TOT DE KUNSTGESCHIEDENIS EN OUDHEIDKUNDE. Added/Corp Rijksuniversiteit te Gent. Sectie Kunstgeschiedenis en Oudheidkunde. **VFOAT** Gentse Bijdragen. 27 (1988)-. Periodical. Dutch (English, French and German; summaries and/or abstracts in English and German). Irregular. Price varies per volume. Editions Peeters SA, Bondgenotenlaan 153, BP 41, B-3000 Leuven Belgium. **Tel** 011 32 16 235170, FAX 011 32 16 228500, telex 65987 PUL B. **Continues** Gentse Bijdragen tot de Kunstgeschiedenis, 0772-7151.
Ind/Abst Avery Index Archit. Period. Suppl. Colum. Univ. (1988).

LC Z675.A85 G47   ISSN 0178-9775
DD 027   GW

GESAMTKATALOG DER DUSSELDORFER KULTURINSTITUTE (GDK) [MICROFORM]. See Library and Information Sciences.

LC N6280 .G4   ISSN 0016-920X
US

GESTA (FORT TRYON PARK, N.Y.). (GESTA.). [Gesta]. **Added/Corp** International Center of Medieval Art. International Center of Romanesque Art. Vol. 1 (1964)-. Periodical. English (French, German and Italian). Two times a year (June, Nov.). $50.00 (institutions); $35.00 (individuals) US; $40.00 (individuals) other; $100.00 (contributing). International Center of Medieval Art, The Cloisters, Fort Tryon Park, New York NY 10040. **Tel** (212)928-1146. **ED** Lucy Freeman Sandler, (editor's address: Department of Fine Arts,, 308 Main Building Washington Square, New York, NY 10003 phone: (212)928-1146). **Circ:** 1,000 (ctrl). Documents available from The Genuine Article.
Desc: Articles perta ning to history of medieval art.
Ind/Abst Art Archaeol. Tech. Abstr.; Art Index; Arts Humanit. Citation Index [Full Cov.]; Avery Index Archit. Period. Suppl. Colum. Univ. (1989-); BHA : Biblio. Hist. Art; Br. Archaeol. Bibliogr.; Index Book Rev. Relig.; Relig. Index One Period.; Res. Alert [Full Cov.].

ISSN 0342-104X
GW

GIESSENER BEITRAEGE ZUR KUNSTGESCHICHTE. [Giess. Beitr. Kunstgesch.]. (1970)-. Monographic series. German. Price varies per volume. Wilhelm Schmitz Verlag, Postfach 21108, Pestalozzstr 3, D 35394 Giessen Germany. **Tel** 011 49 641 491919.
Ind/Abst Avery Index Archit. Period. Suppl. Colum. Univ.; BHA : Biblio. Hist. Art.

ISSN 1070-7808
DD 973   US

●**GILCREASE JOURNAL.** [Gilcrease j.]. **Added/Corp** Thomas Gilcrease Museum Association. **VFOAT** Spectacle of the West. Vol. 1, No. 1 (Spring 1993)-. Periodical. English. Two times a year. $25.00. Thomas Gilcrease Museum Association, 1400 Gilcrease Museum Road, Tulsa OK 74127. **Tel** (918)596-2700, FAX (918)592-2248. **ED** Carol Haralson. **Continues** Gilcrease Magazine of American History and Art, 0730-5036.
Ind/Abst Am. Hist. Life.

LC N6911 .G55   ISSN 0394-0543
DD 705   IT

GIORNALE DELL'ARTE (TURIN, ITALY). (IL GIORNALE DELL'ARTE.). [G. arte]. Vol. 1, No. 1 (1983)-. Periodical. Italian. Eleven times a year (Jul/Aug combined). L88000. Umberto Allemandi, Via Mancini 8, 10131 Turin Italy. **Tel** 11 39 11 8193133, FAX 11 39 11 8193090, telex 224149. **Bk Rev. Ad Acc. Adv Mgr:** Patrizia Sbodio. **Circ:** 25,000 (ctrl).
Ind/Abst ARTbibliogr. Mod.

LC DG441 .G43
DD 306.4/0945/05   IT

GIORNI CANTATI (ROME, ITALY). (I GIORNI CANTATI.). **Added/Corp** Cooperativa il Manifesto Anni 80. (198?)-. Periodical. Italian. Four times a year. L20440. Risonanze Srl, Via C Beltrami 23, 00154 Rome Italy. **Tel** 011 39 6 5742711. **ED** Angelo Ruggieri. Index available. cum. index. **Circ:** 2,000. available on diskette.

LC N7249.C7 G63   ISSN 0350-2589
DD 702/.8/8   CI

GODISNJAK ZASTITE SPOMENIKA KULTURE HRVATSKE. Added/Corp RepubliEcki Zavod za Zastitu Spomenika Kulture Zagreb. (1975)-. Periodical. Serbo-Croatian (Roman) (summaries and/or abstracts in English and French). One time a year.
Ind/Abst BHA : Biblio. Hist. Art.

ISSN 0348-4114
SW

GOTHENBURG STUDIES IN ART & ARCHITECTURE. (1978)-. Monographic series. English. Irregular. Price varies per volume. Scandinavian University Press, PO Box 2959 Toeyen, N 0608 Oslo 6 Norway. **Tel** 011 47 2 2575400, FAX 011 47 2 2575353, telex 71896 UROR N. **(Subscription address:** Scandinavian University Press, 200 Meacham Ave., Elmont NY 11003. **Tel** (516)352-7300, FAX (516)352-7377.)

LC N7 .G6   ISSN 0017-2715
SP
Pr Rev.

GOYA. [Goya]. **Added/Corp** Fundacion Lazaro Galdiano. No. 1 (July/Aug. 1954)-. Periodical. Spanish. Six times a year. Price varies. Goya Revista de Arte, Calle Serrano 122, 28006 Madrid Spain. **Tel** 011 34 1 56 35535. **ED** Carlos Saguar Quer. Index available. **Bk Rev. Ad Acc. Circ:** 2,500 (ctrl). Documents available from The Genuine Article.
Desc: Art history, schedule of current art shows and bibliography.
Ind/Abst Am. Hist. Life (1966-1969); Art Index; ARTbibliogr. Mod. (1984-); ARTbibliogr. Curr. Titles; Arts Humanit. Citation Index [Full Cov.]; Avery Index Archit. Period. Suppl. Colum. Univ.; BHA : Biblio. Hist. Art; Curr. Contents Arts Humanit.; Res. Alert [Full Cov.]; Soc. Sci. Cit. Index [Select. Cov.].

LC DR381.V6 G7   ISSN 0434-300X
YU

GRAA ZA PROUCAVANJE SPOMENIKA KULTURE VOJVODINE. Added/Corp Zavod za Zastitu i Naucno Proucavanje Spomenika Kulture Automne Pokrajine Vojvodine. **VFOAT** Materials for the Study of the Cultural Monuments of Vojvodina. (1957)-. Serbo-Croatian (Cyrillic) (summaries and/or abstracts in English; table of contents in English). One time a year.
Ind/Abst BHA : Biblio. Hist. Art.

ISSN 0836-0421
DD 700/.5   CN

GRAMMATEION (TORONTO). (THE GRAMMATEION : THE ST. MICHAEL'S COLLEGE JOURNAL OF THE ARTS.). [Grammateion]. **Added/Corp**

The Arts —Art

University of St. Michael's College. (1975)-. English. $3.50 per issue. St. Michael's College Student Union, 81 St. Mary Street, Box 1, Toronto Ontario M5S 1J4, Canada. **Tel** (416)926-7268.

US

GRAPHIS NUDES. (19??)-. English. Graphis Press Corporation NY, 141 Lexington Avenue, New York NY 10016. **Tel** (212)532-9387.

SP
CEASED

GRECA. (1976)-(Oct. 1993). Spanish. Axel Springer Publicaciones, Pedro Teixeira 8 Planta 8, 28020 Madrid Spain. **Tel** 011 34 1 5560048.

ISSN 0224-0475
FR

UDC 92
GROUPE D'ETUDE DES MONUMENTS ET OEUVRES D'ART DU BEAUVAISIS. **VFOAT** Dossier du G.E.M.O.B. (1975)-. Periodical. French.
Ind/Abst BHA : Biblio. Hist. Art.

ISSN 1011-9094
CH

GUGONG XUESHU JIKAN. **VFOAT** National Palace Museum Research Quarterly. (1983)-. Periodical. Chinese. Four times a year (Jan., Apr., July, Oct.). $50.00 Hong Kong; $54.00 other. National Palace Museum, Wai-Shuang-Hsi Shih-Lin, Taipei Taiwan. **Tel** 011 886 2 8821230, FAX 011 886 2 8821440. **ED** Chang Peter (phone: 001 886 2 8814633). **Bk Rev. Circ:** 1,000 (ctrl). **Continues** Gugong Jikan, 0454-675X.

LC N55.S7 G84
DD 702/.5/46
SP
GUIA DE ARTE (BARCELONA, SPAIN). (GUIA DE ARTE.). 1/82-. Spanish (summaries and/or abstracts in English). One time a year.

ISSN 0997-2676
FR

UDC 64.01(44)
GUIDE DU CADEAU ET DES ARTS DE LA TABLE. (1984)-. French. One time a year. 260.00F. Pierre Johanet et Ses Fils, 7 Avenue Franklin Roosevelt, 75008 Paris France. **Tel** 1 43 59 08 89, FAX 1 42 25 59 47, telex 649712. Index available. cum. index. **Ad Acc. Continues** Guide du Specialiste en Articles de Cadeau (1980), 0752-9295.

PK
HABITAT PAKISTAN : A JOURNAL OF ARCHITECTURE, PLANNING, ENVIRONMENT, AND THE ARTS IN ASIA. See Architecture.

LC ND1055 .H26
JA
HACHIJUKAI TEN. Added/Corp Nichido Garo. **VFOAT** Hachijukai Ten Zuroku. (19??)-. Periodical. Japanese. Nichido Garo, 4-12 Ginza 7 Chuo-ku, Tokyo Japan.

LC L
DD 370
US
HANDBOOK / NATIONAL ASSOCIATION OF SCHOOLS OF ART AND DESIGN. See Education.

LC N9.88.K H36
KO
HAN'GUK MISUL YON'GAM. **VFOAT** Korea Art Annual. (19??)-. Korean (Korean). W15,000. Hanguk Misul Yongam S A, 228 Pyong-dong Chongno-ku, Seoul Korea.

ISSN 1181-943X
DD 709/.71/0904
CN
CEASED
HARBOUR MAGAZINE ON ART AND EVERYDAY LIFE. [Harbour mag. art everyday life]. **VFOAT** Harbour Magazine; Harbour. Vol. 1, No. 1 (Summer 1990)-Vol. 3 No. 1 (19??). Periodical. English. Harbour Art Text, 4001 rue Berri, Suite 101, Montreal Quebec H2L 4H2 Canada. **Tel** (514)849-2842.

LC N1 .H37
DD 708.144/4/05
ISSN 1065-6448
US
HARVARD UNIVERSITY ART MUSEUMS BULLETIN. See Museums and Galleries.

LC N526 .H37c
DD 708.144/4/05
ISSN 1065-819X
US
HARVARD UNIVERSITY ART MUSEUMS REVIEW. See Museums and Galleries.

LC HQ1101 .H43
DD 305.4/05
ISSN 0146-3411
US
HERESIES. See Women's Interests.

ISSN 0544-4225
HU
UDC 069
HERMAN OTTO MUZEUM EVKONYVE, A. See Museums and Galleries.

LC NX655 .H47
ISSN 0930-6897
DD 700
GW
HERMENEIA = ERMENEIA. Added/Corp Hermeneia, Vereinigung zur Foerderung der Ostkirchlichen Kunst. **VFOAT** Zeitschrift fuer Ostkirchliche Kunst; Ermeneia. (Apr. 1985)-. Periodical. German. Four times a year. DM70.68 Germany; DM78.00 other. Typos Verlag, Gruener Weg 40A, D 44791 Bochum Germany. **Tel** 011 49 234 501932. (**Subscription address:** Kolk Werbung Druck, Eschenweg 2, D 45699 Herten Germany. **Tel** 011 49 2366 36075.)
Ind/Abst BHA : Biblio. Hist. Art.

ISSN 0899-9856
DD 709
US
HERMENEUTICS OF ART. [Hermeneut. art]. English. One time a year. Peter Lang Publishing, 62 West 45th Street, 4th Floor, New York NY 10036. **Tel** (212)764-1471, (800)770-5574, FAX (212)302-7574, telex 6973364 PLNY.

ISSN 1070-0544
DD 741
US
●**HERO ILLUSTRATED.** [Hero illus.]. Vol. 1, No. 1 (July 1993)-. Periodical. English. Twelve times a year. $24.95. Sendai Publications, 1920 Highland Avenue, Suite 222, Lombard IL 60148. **Tel** (708)916-7222.

ISSN 0712-5879
DD 706/.07123
CN
HIGHLIGHTS (CALGARY. 1978). (HIGHLIGHTS.). [Highlights]. Vol 3, No. 3 (Autumn 1978)-. Periodical. English. Four times a year. Free. Alberta Society of Artists, Alberta College of Art, Suite 5531/1301-16th Avenue, Calgary Alberta T2M 0L4 Canada. **Continues** Highlights Newsletter, 0384-1162.

ISSN 0384-1162
DD 709/.7123
CN
HIGHLIGHTS NEWSLETTER. New Series, Vol. 1 (July/Aug. 1975)-. Newsletter. English. Alberta Society of Artists, Alberta College of Art, Suite 5531/1301-16th Avenue, Calgary Alberta T2M 0L4 Canada. **Supersedes** Highlights, 0384-1154.

LC N7480 .H57
ISSN 0992-2059
DD 709
FR
Pr Rev.
HISTOIRE DE L'ART (PARIS, 1988). (HISTOIRE DE L'ART : BULLETIN D'INFORMATION DE L'INSTITUT NATIONAL D'HISTOIRE DE L'ART.). [Hist. art]. **Added/Corp** Institut National d'Histoire de l'Art (France) Association des Professeurs d'Archeologie et d'Histoire de l'Art des Universites (France). No. 1/2 (June 1988)-. Bulletin. French (English). Three times a year (May, Oct., Dec.). $72.18. Histoire de l'Art-APAHAU, 3 rue Michelet, F 75006 Paris France. **Tel** 011 33 1 40469390. **ED** Francoise Levaillant. Index available (Dec.). **Ad Acc, Adv Mgr:** Loire Natalie. **Circ:** 1,100 (ctrl).
Desc: Review of research and information on history of art and archaeology; open to young researchers to advertise their work.
Ind/Abst Avery Index Archit. Period. Suppl. Colum. Univ. (Oct. 1990-); BHA : Biblio. Hist. Art.

ISSN 1067-4284
DD 709
US
HISTORIANS OF NETHERLANDISH ART NEWSLETTER. [Hist. Neth. Art newsl.]. **Added/Corp** Historians of Netherlandish Art. (1983)-. Newsletter. English. Two times a year. $100.00 (institutions), $20.00 (individuals) Comes with membership to Historians of Netherlandish Art. Historians of Netherlandish Art, 23 S. Adelaide Ave., Highland Park NJ 08904. **Tel** (908)937-8394, FAX (908)937-8394. **ED** Kristin Lohse Belkin. **Photos. Ad Acc.** ctrl circ. available with illustrations.
Desc: Dedicated to the study of Netherlandish, German and Franco-Flemish art and architecture, 1350-1750. Includes notices and reviews of exhibitions, new acquisitions and other museum news, conferences, recent publications, research in progress, and members' activities.

LC N6488.J3 S263B
JA
HOKKAIDORITSU KINDAI BIJUTSUKAN NENPO. Main/Corp Hokkaidoritsu Kindai Bijutsukan. **VFOAT** Hokkaido Museum of Modern Art. Japanese. One time a year. Hokkaidoritsu Kindai Bijutsukan, Kita Ichijo Nishi 17-chome Chuo-ku, Sapporo-shi Japan.

ISSN 0288-4356
DD 738
JA
HONOO GEIJUTSU. [Honoo geijutsu]. **VFOAT** Yakimono Purasu Arufa. (1982)-. Periodical. Japanese. Four times a year. $181.00. (**Subscription address:** Japan Publications Trading Company Ltd., PO Box 5030, Tokyo International, Tokyo 100-31 Japan. **Tel** 011 81 3 3292 3753.)

LC N7350 .H69
JA
CODEN HKAGDY
HOZON KAGAKU. Added/Corp Tokyo Kokuritsu Bunkazai Kenkyujo. **VFOAT** Science for Conservation. (1964)-. Academic Scholarly Publication. Japanese (English; summaries and/or abstracts in English). One time a year. Free. Bunkacho Tokyo Kokuritsu Bunkazai Kenkyujo Hozon Kagakubu, (Department of Conservation Science, Tokyo National Research Institute of Cultural Properties, Agency for Cultural Affairs), Ueno Koen Taitoku Tokyo 110 Japan. **Tel** 03-823-2241, FAX 03-828-2431. **ED** Hisao Mabuchi and Karoku Miwa. ctrl circ. Documents available from CASDDS.
Ind/Abst Art Archaeol. Tech. Abstr.; Chem. Abstr.

IR
HUNAR VA MIMARI. ART AND ARCHITECTURE. See Architecture.

LC Z733.S24 Q
ISSN 0018-7895
DD 027.4794/93
US
Pr Rev.
HUNTINGTON LIBRARY QUARTERLY, THE. See Library and Information Sciences.

ISSN 0018-8093
DD 839.8
DK
HVEDEKORN. See Literature-Poetry.

LC N7365 .H96
KO
HYONDAE MISUL CHODAEJON. Added/Corp Kungnip Hyondae Misulgwan. **VFOAT** Contemporary Art Festival. (19??)-. English (Korean). Koryo Sojok Chusik Hoesa, 62-7 1-ka Malli-dong Chung-ku, Seoul Korea.

CC
I YUAN TO YING. **VFOAT** Gems from Chinese Fine Arts. (19??)-. Periodical. Chinese. Irregular. $36.00. China National Publishing Import & Export Corporation, 16 Gongti E Rd., Chaoyang Dist., Beijing 100704, People's Republic of China. **Tel** 011 8601 50630169, 5066688, FAX 011 8601 5063101, 5063010, telex 22313. **Bk Rev. Ad Acc.** ctrl circ.
Desc: Introducing Chinese traditional painting of essence.

ISSN 0256-3517
MC
UDC 7
IAB. [IAB]. **VFOAT** International Art Bulletin. (1964)-. Bulletin. Multiple languages. Four times a year.
Ind/Abst BHA : Biblio. Hist. Art.

LC N6540 .C34A
DD 702/.8
CN
ICC. Main/Corp Canadian Conservation Institute. (1976)-. Periodical. French. Canadian Conservation Institute, 1030 Innes Road, Ottawa Ontario K1A 0C8 Canada. **Tel** (613)998-3721.

LC N7957 .I26
ISSN 0106-1348
SW
ICO. Added/Corp Sweden. Riksantikvarieambetet. **VFOAT** Iconographisk Post; Nordic Review of Iconography. (1970)-. Periodical. Swedish (Danish, Norwegian and English; summaries and/or abstracts in English). Four times a year (Mar., June, Sept., Dec.). $33.66. Riksantikvarieambetet, Box 5405, S-114 Stockholm 84 Sweden. **Tel** 011 46 8 783-9062, FAX 011 46 8 660-7284. **ED** Ingalill Pegelow, Mereth Lindgren, and Lennart Karlsson. Index available (Published separately). cum. index. **Bk Rev. Circ:** 900.
Desc: Information on iconography, Christian art and symbolism.
Ind/Abst BHA : Biblio. Hist. Art.

LC WMLC 93/1891
IT
ICOMOS/INFORMATION. See Architecture.

NE
ICONOGRAPHY OF RELIGIONS. SECTION 22 : ISLAM. See Religions and Theology-Islam.

LC N5740
DD 709.37
NE
●**ICONOLOGICAL STUDIES IN ROMAN ART.** (1994)-. Academic Scholarly Publication. English. Irregular. J C Gieben Uitgeverij, Nieuwe Herengracht 35, 1011 Rm Amsterdam The Netherlands. **Tel** 011 33 20 6275170.

CN
IDEAS AND DEBATES : A JOURNAL OF ART WRITING. See Literature.

The Arts — Art

LC N8.J28 I3   **ISSN 0389-0902**
  JA
IDEMITSU BIJUTSUKAN KANPO.
Added/Corp Idemitsu Bijutsukan. **VFOAT** Idemitsu Museum of Arts Bulletin. (19??)-. Directory. Japanese. Idemitsu Bijutsukan, 1-1 Marunouchi, 3 Chiyoda-ku Tokyo Japan.

  RU
IDISHE GAS, DI. See Literature.

LC N8554 .I34   **ISSN 8756-7172**
DD 364.1/62   US
IFAR REPORTS. [IFAR rep.]. **Added/Corp** International Foundation for Art Research. **VAT** International Foundation for Art Research Reports. Vol. 6, No. 1 (Jan./Feb. 1985)-. Periodical. English. Ten times a year. Free to members of the International Foundation for Art Research, 46 East 70th Street, New York NY 10021. **Tel** (212)879-1780, FAX (212)734-4174. **ED** Constance Lowenthal. Index available. cum. index. **Circ:** 1,200.
Formed by the union of Stolen Art Alert, 0197-0208 and Art Research News, 0884-2892.
Desc: Publication contains listings of stolen and missing art with articles on art theft and recovery, art law, cultural property and art authentication.

DD 069/.53/06071   **ISSN 0843-6657**
  CN
IICCG BULLETIN. [IICCG bull.]. **Added/Corp** International Institute for Conservation of Historic and Artistic Works. Canadian Group. **VFOAT** Bulletin de l'IICGC. **VAT** International Institute for Conservation of Historic and Artistic Works, Canadian Group Bulletin. Vol. 15, No. 1 (Mar. 1990)-. Bulletin. English (French). Four times a year. International Institute for Conservation of Historic and Artistic Works / Canada, Canadian Group, PO Box 9195, Ottawa Ontario K1G 3T9 Canada. **Tel** (613)998-3721. **Continues** International Institute for Conservation of Historic and Artistic Works. Canadian Group. Newsletter - International Institute for Conservation, Canadian Group., 0318-6199.

LC N2 .O28   **ISSN 0183-3014**
DD 705   FR
IL, L'. [il]. No. 1 (Jan. 15 1955)-. Periodical. French. Twelve times a year. $90.00. Oeil Rev d'Art, 10 rue Guichard, 75016 Paris France. cum. index.
Ind/Abst Art Index; ARTbibliogr. Mod.; Avery Index Archit. Period. Suppl. Colum. Univ. (19??-199?).

LC N6911 .I36
DD 708.5   IT
ILLUSTRAZIONE ITALIANA (MILAN, ITALY : 1974). See Museums and Galleries.

  ISSN 0129-704X
  SI
IMAGE. See Religions and Theology.

DD 709   **ISSN 0838-2239**
  CN
  TITLE CHANGE
IMPOSTURE (MONTREAL). (IMPOSTURE.). [Imposture]. (Winter 1988)-(1995). Periodical. French. Revue Post, 3550 Jeanne Mance App. 2207, Montreal Quebec, H2X 3P7 Canada. **Tel** (514)287-7487.
Continued by Revue Post.

LC NX504 .I5   **ISSN 0091-6994**
DD 700/.973   US
IN (IOWA CITY). (IN.). [In]. Vol. 1 (Summer 1973)-. Periodical. English. Four times a year. $4.00. Penology Publications, Inc., PO Box 368, Iowa City IA 52240.

LC N4390 .I52
DD 016.7/074   UK
INDEX TO ART EXHIBITION CATALOGUES ON MICROFICHE. See The Arts-Abstracting, Bibliographies and Statistics.

LC Z5937 .C55 SUPPL N1.A1   **ISSN 0099-0965**
DD 016.7   US
INDEX TO ART PERIODICALS. SUPPLEMENT. See The Arts-Abstracting, Bibliographies and Statistics.

LC N8580 .I53   **ISSN 0893-0139**
DD 705   US
INDEX TO REPRODUCTIONS IN ART PERIODICALS : IRAP. [Ind. reprod. art period.]. **VFOAT** IRAP. Vol. 1, No. 1 (Jan/Mar. 1987)-. Abstracting/Indexing Service. English. Four times a year. $50.00. Data Arts, PO Box 30789, Seattle WA 98103. **Tel** (206)783-9580. **ED** Eugene C. Burt. cum. index. **Ad Acc**.
Desc: Indexing of illustrations in common art periodicals. Indexes by artist, title, media and subject.

DD 708   **ISSN 0892-6409**
  US
INDIAN MARKET. See Ethnic Interests.

LC N518.B4 A28   **ISSN 0161-1003**
DD 708/.172/255   US
INDIANA UNIVERSITY ART MUSEUM BULLETIN. See Museums and Galleries.

DD 702   **ISSN 1063-4835**
  US
INFORMART (CASPER, WYO.).
(INFORMART : THE LIMITED EDITION PRINT PRICE JOURNAL.). [InformArt]. (1989)-. Periodical. English. Four times a year. $21.00. Westtown Publishing Company Inc, 1727 East 2nd Street, Casper WY 82601. **Tel** (307)237-1659.

DD 709/.713/68   **ISSN 0705-6907**
  CN
INPRINT (PETERBOROUGH). (INPRINT.). Vol. 1 (June 1977)-. Periodical. English. Six times a year. Free to members. Artspace, 190 Hunter Street West, Peterborough Ontario K9H 2L2 Canada.

DD 615   **ISSN 0264-7141**
  UK
INSCAPE LONDON. See Medical Sciences-Psychiatry.

  ISSN 0159-9135
  AT
INTERACTA. See Education-Teaching and Curriculum.

LC NX1 .I57   **ISSN 0277-8017**
DD 700/.5
INTERMUSE. Vol. 1, No. 1-. Periodical. English. Frederick I Kaplan, 1412 Roxburgh, East Lansing MI 48823.

LC HD9791.A1 I58   **ISSN 0742-7387**
DD 702/.8   US
  CEASED
INTERNATIONAL ART MATERIAL DIRECTORY AND BUYERS' GUIDE. [Int. art mater. dir. buy. guide]. **VFOAT** Art Material Trade News International Directory. (1983)-(1995). Consumer Publication. English. Argus Business, 6151 Powers Ferry Road Northwest, Atlanta GA 30339. **Tel** (404)995-2500, FAX (404)995-0400. **Continues** International Art Material Directory & Buyers Guide, 0742-7387.

  ISSN 0074-1922
  US
INTERNATIONAL AUCTION RECORDS.
Vol. 1 (1967)-. English. One time a year. $184.00. Editions Publisol / New York, 235 East 85th Street, PO Box 339, Gracie Station, New York NY 10028. **Tel** (212)289-3981. **ED** E. Mayer. **Bk Rev**. **Ad Acc**. **Circ:** 6,000.
Desc: An international guide of prices obtained at auctions for paintings, drawings, engravings, watercolors and sculpture.

  UK
INTERNATIONAL DICTIONARY OF ART AND ARTISTS. See The Arts-Abstracting, Bibliographies and Statistics.

LC N5198 .I58   **ISSN 1057-2023**
DD 707/.5   US
INTERNATIONAL FINE ART COLLECTOR. [Int. Fine Art Collect.]. **VFOAT** Fine Art Collector. (1990)-. Periodical. English (summaries and/or abstracts in French and German). Four times a year. $29.95. International Fine Art Collector Magazine, 100 South Sunrise Way, #466, Palm Springs CA 92263. **Tel** (619)327-7616, FAX (619)778-1815. **Circ:** 5,000.

  FR
INTERNATIONAL NEWSLETTER ON ROCK ART : I.N.O.R.A. See Archaeology.

  ISSN 1060-6084
  US
INTERNATIONAL QUARTERLY (TALLAHASS., FLA.). See Literature.

LC NX164.N4 B5   **ISSN 1045-0920**
DD 700/.89/96073   US
INTERNATIONAL REVIEW OF AFRICAN AMERICAN ART, THE. [Int. rev. Afr. Am. art]. **Added/Corp** Museum of African American Art (Santa Monica, Calif.). **VFOAT** African American Art. Vol. 6, No. 1 (1984)-. Periodical. English. Four times a year (Jan., April, July, Oct.). $36.00. University Museum / Virginia, Hampton University, Hampton VA 23668-0101. **Tel** (804) 727-5308, FAX (804) 727-5084. **ED** Juliette Bowles. Index available. cum. index. **Bk Rev**. **Circ:** 4,000. Documents available from The Genuine Article, UMI Article Clearinghouse. **Continues** Black art, 0145-8116.
Desc: Examines the visual culture of African-descended people in the Americas.
Ind/Abst ARTbibliogr. Mod.; Arts Humanit. Citation Index (19??-19??) [Full Cov.]; Curr. Contents Arts Humanit.; Ethnoarts Index; Expand. Acad. Index (1992-); Newsp. Period. Abstr. (1991-); Res. Alert [Full Cov.].

LC N50 .I6   **ISSN 0539-1849**
  GW
INTERNATIONALES KUNST-ADRESSBUCH. **VFOAT** International Directory of Arts; Annuaire International des Beaux-Arts; Annuario Internazionale delle Belle Arti; Anuario Internacional de las Artes. (1952/53)-. German (English, French and Italian). Every 2 years. $225.00. K.G. Saur Verlag KG, A Reed Reference Publishing Company, Part of Reed International PLC, Ortlerstrasse 8, D-81373 Munich Germany. **Tel** 011 49 89 769020, FAX 011 49 89 76902150, telex 5212067-SAUR-D. **Absorbed** Deutsches Kunst Adressbuch.
Desc: Comprehensive guide to art sources and markets in 137 countries. Contains over 150,000 names and addresses of art restorers, publishers, libraries, art dealers and galleries, museums, associations and more.

DD 709/.01/1   **ISSN 0824-0639**
  CN
  CEASED
INUIT ART ENTHUSIASTS NEWSLETTER, THE. [Inuit Art Enthus. newsl.]. (1983)-(19??). Newsletter. English. Inuit Art Enthusiasts, 8734 119 Street, Edmonton Alberta T6G 1W8 Canada. **Tel** (403)432-4409. **ED** Evelyn Blakeman. **Bk Rev**. **Circ:** 250 (ctrl). **Continues** Newsletter (Inuit Art Enthusiasts, Edmonton), 0824-0620.
Desc: Features news, information, announcements, reviews, and photos related to Inuit art and Arctic communities. Lists exhibitions, auctions, conferences, tours, publications, and articles.
Ind/Abst Ethnoarts Index.

DD 704/.0397   **ISSN 0831-6708**
Pr Rev.
INUIT ART QUARTERLY. [Inuit art q.]. **Added/Corp** Inuit Art Foundation. **VFOAT** Inuit Art. Vol. 1, No. 1 (Spring 1986)-. Periodical. English. Four times a year (Feb., May, Aug., Nov.). 25.00Can$. Inuit Art Foundation, 2081 Merivale Road, Nepean K2G 1G9 Canada. **Tel** (613)224-8189, FAX (613)224-2907. **ED** Marybelle Mitchell. Index available. cum. index. **Bk Rev**. **Ad Acc**. **Adv Mgr:** S. Green. **Circ:** 3,816 (ctrl).
Desc: Devoted to the art of the Canadian Inuit. Contains features, interviews, reviews, and news.
Ind/Abst Ethnoarts Index.

LC WMLC 91/3014 N7380 .S95   **ISSN 0897-8573**
DD 709   US
IOWA STUDIES IN AFRICAN ART. [Iowa stud. Afr. art]. **Main/Conf** Symposium on African Art. **Added/Corp** University of Iowa. School of Art and Art History. Vol. 1 (1984)-. Periodical. English. Irregular. University of Iowa School of Art and Art History, Iowa City IO 52242. **Tel** (319)335-1784, (503)686-4414.
Ind/Abst Anthropol. Lit.; Ethnoarts Index.

LC N6782 .G63   **ISSN 0791-3540**
  IE
IRISH ARTS REVIEW YEARBOOK.
Added/Corp GPA (Firm). **VFOAT** Irish Arts Review. Vol. 8 (1992)-. English. One time a year. Irish Arts Review, PO Box 3500, Dublin 4 Ireland. **Tel** 011 353 1 2808461.
Continues GPA Irish Arts Review Yearbook, 0791-038X.
Ind/Abst BHA : Biblio. Hist. Art.

  US
  SUSPENDED
ISSUE (NEW YORK, N.Y. : 1984). (ISSUE : A JOURNAL FOR ARTISTS.). No. 1-?. Periodical. English. Three times a year. $12.00 three issues individual, $18.00 three issues institutions. PO Box 122, Prince Street Station, New York NY 10012.

  ISSN 0167-9082
  NE
UDC 745
  TITLE CHANGE
ITEMS. See Architecture.

  NE
ITEMS VAK. See Architecture.

  ISSN 0737-9447
  US
IWAA NEWS. [IWAA news]. **Added/Corp** International Women Artists Archive. **VFOAT** I.W.A.A. NEWS. **VAT** International Women Artists Archive News. Vol. 1, No. 1 (Jan./Feb. 1983)-. Periodical. English. One time a year. $10.00 institutions; $4.00 individuals. International Women Artists Archive, PO Box 600, Hadley MA 01035. **Tel** (413)634-5096.

LC Z5937 .N56 N7425.55
DD 016.7   RU
IZOBRAZITEL'NOE ISKUSSTVO; BIBLIOGRAFICHESKAIA INFORMATSIIA. See The Arts-Abstracting, Bibliographies and Statistics.

LC PN9 .I9   **ISSN 0021-3381**
DD 891.8   BN
IZRAZ. See Literature.

LC N8554 .J68   **ISSN 0381-0402**
DD 702/.8/8   CN
Pr Rev.
J. IIC-CG : JOURNAL OF THE INTERNATIONAL INSTITUTE FOR CONSERVATION, CANADIAN GROUP.
[J. Intl. Inst. Conserv., Can. Group]. **Added/Corp**

International Institute for Conservation of Historic and Artistic Works. Canadian Group. **VFOAT** Journal of the International Institute for Conservation, Canadian Group. **VAT** J. IIC.CG. Journal of the International Institute for Conservation. Canadian Group. Vol. 2, No. 1 (Autumn 1976)-. Periodical. English (French). One time a year. 75.00Can$. International Institute for Conservation of Historic Artistic Works, Canadian Group, PO Box 9195, Ottawa Ontario K1G 3T9 Canada. **Tel** (613)998-3721. **ED** Charlie Costain. **Bk Rev**. **Circ:** 550. ***Continues*** *International Institute for Conservation of Historic and Artistic Works. Canadian Group. Bulletin, 0318-6202.*
Desc: Conservation, restoration and preservation of cultural property; examination, treatment, storage and display of historic and artistic works of art.
Ind/Abst Art Archaeol. Tech. Abstr.

LC N582.M25 A25 **ISSN** 0362-1979
DD 708/.194/93 US
J. PAUL GETTY MUSEUM JOURNAL, THE. See Museums and Galleries.

NE
JAARBOEK - GESCHIEDKUNDIGE VERENIGING DIE HAGHE. **Main/Corp** Geschiedkundige Vereniging Die Haghe. (1970)-. Dutch. One time a year. Geschiedkundige Ver Die Haghe, Suezkade 166, 2517 CE The Hague Netherlands. **Tel** 011 31 70 3636727. ***Continues*** *Vereniging Die Haghe. Jaarboek.*
Ind/Abst BHA : Biblio. Hist. Art.

ISSN 0771-839X
BE
JAARBOEK / STAD BRUGGE, STEDELIJKE MUSEA. See Museums and Galleries.

BE
JAARBOEK VAN HET KONINKLIJK MUSEUM VOOR SCHONE KUNSTEN. **Main/Corp** Koninklijk Museum voor Schone Kunsten (Belgium). (19??)-. Periodical. Dutch. One time a year. 300F. Koninklijk Museum voor Schone Kunsten, Plaatsnijdersstraat 2, 2000 Antwerp Belgium. **Tel** 32 3 2387809, telex 32 3 2480810. **Circ:** 1,200. ***Continues*** *Antwerp. Musee Royale des Beaux-Arts. Annuaire.*
Desc: Covers contributions to Flemish and Belgian art between the 15th and 20th centuries. Covers mainly the paintings of the Old Masters.
Ind/Abst BHA : Biblio. Hist. Art.

ISSN 0448-1216
CI
JADRANSKI ZBORNIK. **Added/Corp** Povijesno Drustvo Istre. Povijesno Drustvo Rijeke. Povijesno Drustvo Hrvatske. Pedruznica u Rijeci. Povijesno Drustvo Hrvatske. Podruznica u Puli. (1956)-. Serbo-Croatian (Roman) (German and Italian; summaries and/or abstracts in English, French, German and Italian). Izdavacko Poduzece Otokar Kersovani, Rijeka-Pula Croatia.
Ind/Abst BHA : Biblio. Hist. Art.

LC N3 .J16 **ISSN** 0075-2207
GW
JAHRBUCH DER BERLINER MUSEEN. [Jahrb. Berl. Museen]. **Added/Corp** Staatliche Museen Preussischer Kulturbesitz. Vol. 1 (1959)-. German (English and French). One time a year. DM195.00. Gebrueder Mann Verlag, Lindenstrasse 76, D-10969 Berlin Germany. **Tel** 011 49 30 25913589, telex 183723. **(Subscription address:** Gebrueder Mann Verlag / KNO, Postfach 800620, Koch, Neff & Oetinger, D-70506 Stuttgart Germany. **Tel** 011 49 711 78992022.**)** Index available. cum. index. **Circ:** 700. Documents available from The Genuine Article. ***Continues*** *Jahrbuch der Preussischen Kunstsammlungen.*
Desc: Art, paintings and sculpture.
Ind/Abst Art Archaeol. Tech. Abstr.; Art Index; ARTbibliogr. Mod.; Arts Humanit. Citation Index [Full Cov.]; Avery Index Archit. Period. Suppl. Colum. Univ. (1989-); BHA : Biblio. Hist. Art; Curr. Contents Arts Humanit.; Res. Alert [Full Cov.].

AU
JAHRBUCH DER KUNSTHISTORISCHEN SAMMLUNGEN IN WIEN. **Added/Corp** Kunsthistorisches Museum Wien. (1921)-. German. One time a year. $51.29. Verlag Anton Schroll and Company, Spengergasse 39, A-1051 Vienna 1 Austria. **Tel** 011 43 1 5445641, FAX 011 43 1 5445641. ***Continues*** *Jahrbuch der Kunsthistorischen Sammlungen des Allerhochsten Kaiserhauses.*
Ind/Abst Art Index; ARTbibliogr. Mod.; BHA : Biblio. Hist. Art; Numis. Lit.

LC N6879 .J3 **ISSN** 0341-924X
DD 709/.43/55 GW
JAHRBUCH DER RHEINISCHEN DENKMALPFLEGE. [Jahrb. rhein. Denkmalpfl.]. Vol. 21 (1957)-. Periodical. German. One time a year. Dr. Rudolf Habelt GmbH, Postfach 150104, D-53040 Bonn Germany. **Tel** 011 49 228 232015. ***Continues*** *Jahrbuch der Rheinischen Denkmalpflege in Nord-Rheinland.*
Ind/Abst Art Archaeol. Tech. Abstr.; BHA : Biblio. Hist. Art.

ISSN 0419-733X
GW
JAHRBUCH DER STAATLICHEN KUNSTSAMMLUNGEN DRESDEN. [Jahrb. Staatl. Kunstsamml. Dresd.]. **Main/Corp** Staatliche Kunstsammlungen Dresden. (1976/1977)-. German. One time a year (Jan.). Staat Kunstsammlungen, Postfach 120450, D-01006 Dresden Germany. **Tel** 011 49 3514953056. ***Continues*** *Staatliche Kunstsammlungen Dresden. Beitrage und Berichte der Staatlichen Kunstsammlungen Dresden, 0419-733X.*
Ind/Abst Avery Index Archit. Period. Suppl. Colum. Univ. (1986).

LC N6886.B27 J3 **ISSN** 0067-284X
GW
JAHRBUCH DER STAATLICHEN KUNSTSAMMLUNGEN IN BADEN-WUERTTEMBERG. [Jahrb. Staatl. Kunstsamml. Baden-WÉurttemb.]. **Main/Corp** Staatliche Kunstsammlung in Baden-Wuerttemberg. **Added/Corp** Baden-Wuerttemberg (Germany). Kultusministerium. Vol. 1 (1964)-. German. One time a year (Nov.). DM60.00. Deutscher Kunstverlag, Postfach 190354, D-80603 Munich Germany. **Tel** 011 49 89 1215160. **(Subscription address:** Deutscher Kuntsverlag Kno, PF-800620 Koch Neff & Oetinger, D-70506 Stuttgart Germany. **Tel** 011 49 711 78602347.**)**
Ind/Abst Art Archaeol. Tech. Abstr.; Avery Index Archit. Period. Suppl. Colum. Univ. (19??-199?); BHA : Biblio. Hist. Art.

LC N9 .J175 **ISSN** 0723-7871
DD 705 GW
JAHRBUCH DES MUSEUMS FUER KUNST UND GEWERBE HAMBURG. [Jahrb. Mus. Kunst Gewerbe Hambg.]. **Added/Corp** Museum fuer Kunst und Gewerbe Hamburg. Vol. 1 (1982)-. Monographic series. German. Irregular. Price varies per volume. Wasmuth KG, Hardenbergstrasse 9A, D-10623 Berlin Germany. **Tel** 011 49 30 3131920. ***Continues in part*** *Jahrbuch der Hamburger Kunstsammlungen, 0075-2274.*
Ind/Abst ARTbibliogr. Mod.; Avery Index Archit. Period. Suppl. Colum. Univ. (19??-199?); BHA : Biblio. Hist. Art.

LC N **ISSN** 0379-0819
DD 702 AU
JAHRBUCH DES OBEROSTERREICHISCHEN MUSEALVEREINES. BERICHTE. [Jahrb. Oberosterr. Musealver., Ber.]. (19??)-. Periodical. German.
Ind/Abst BHA : Biblio. Hist. Art.

LC N9.3 .J34 **ISSN** 0177-8978
DD 709 GW
CEASED
JAHRBUCH DES ZENTRALINSTITUTS FUER KUNSTGESCHICHTE. [Jahrb. Zent. Kunstgesch.]. **Added/Corp** Zentralinstitut fuer Kunstgeschichte in Munchen. (1985)-Completed Series (Vol. 5 6, 19??). Monographic series. German. Wasmuth KG, Hardenbergstrasse 9A, D-10623 Berlin Germany. **Tel** 011 49 30 3131920.
Ind/Abst BHA : Biblio. Hist. Art.

LC N3 .J14 **ISSN** 0258-9524
DD 705 GW
UDC 7.072 (494)
JAHRBUCH / SCHWEIZERISCHES INSTITUT FUER KUNSTWISSENSCHAFT. [Jahrb. - Schweiz. Inst. Kunstwiss.]. **Added/Corp** Schweizerisches Institut fur Kunstwissenschaft. (1970)-. German. Prestel Verlag, Mandlstrasse 26, D-80802 Munich Germany. **Tel** 011 49 89 3817090, FAX 011 49 89 38170935, telex 5216366.
Ind/Abst BHA : Biblio. Hist. Art.

LC N2405.5 .A29a **ISSN** 0176-9030
DD 708.3/55 GW
JAHRESBERICHT / VON DER HEYDT-MUSEUM KUNST- UND MUSEUMSVEREIN. See Museums and Galleries.

ISSN 1013-6916
SZ
JAHRESBERICHT - ZURCHER KUNSTGESELLSCHAFT. [Jahresber. - Zur. Kunstges.]. **VFOAT** Zurcher Kunstgesellschaft Jahresbericht.... (1885)-. Periodical. German. One time a year.
Ind/Abst BHA : Biblio. Hist. Art.

LC N7415 .J68 **ISSN** 0792-0660
DD 704/.03924 IS
JEWISH ART (JERUSALEM. 1986). (JEWISH ART.). [Jew. art]. **Added/Corp** Universitah ha-Ivrit bi-Yerushalayim. Merkaz le-Omanut Yehudit. Vol. 12-13 (1987)-. English. One time a year. Center for Jewish Art, Terra Sancta Building, PO Box 4262. **Tel** 011 972 2 586605. **(Subscription address:** Hebrew Publishing Company, PO Box 157, Rockaway NJ 11693**)** Documents available from The Genuine Article.
Continues *Journal of Jewish Art, 0160-208X.*
Ind/Abst Art Index; Arts Humanit. Citation Index [Full Cov.]; Avery Index Archit. Period. Suppl. Colum. Univ.; BHA : Biblio. Hist. Art; Curr. Contents Arts Humanit.; Res. Alert [Full Cov.].

LC N742.S5 A28
DD 708.159/61 US
JOHN & MABLE RINGLING MUSEUM OF ART : NEWSLETTER. See Museums and Galleries.

ISSN 0823-5023
DD 702/.9/471 CN
JOHNSON'S INDEX TO CANADIAN ART AUCTIONS: PUBLICATION. [Johnson's index Can. art auctions]. **Added/Corp** Johnson's Index to Canadian Art Auctions (Firm). No. 1 (Jan./Mar. 1983)-. Periodical. English. $22.00. Johnson's Index to Canadian Art Auctions, Holstein Ontario N0G 2A0 Canada.

LC N6947 .J66 **ISSN** 0168-9193
NE
JONG HOLLAND. Vol. 1 No. 1 (Feb. 1985)-. Dutch. Four times a year. $65.09. Stichting Jong Holland, PO Box 6642, 3002 AP Rotterdam Netherlands. **Tel** 011 31 10 4254122. **ED** Patricia van Ulzen. Index Bound in First Issue. cum. index. **Bk Rev**, (Qty: 8). **Ad Acc. Circ:** 2,000 (ctrl).
Desc: Focus on modern art from its early beginnings in the nineteenth centry right up to the present, providing readers with insights into the background of the particular art.
Ind/Abst BHA : Biblio. Hist. Art.

LC N11.A735 A15 **ISSN** 0003-9853
DD 709/.73 US
JOURNAL - ARCHIVES OF AMERICAN ART. (ARCHIVES OF AMERICAN ART JOURNAL.). [J. - Arch. Am. Art]. **Added/Corp** Archives of American Art. Vol. 9 No. 4 (197?)-. Periodical. English. Four times a year. $35.00. Archives of American Art, 1285 Avenue of the Americas, 2nd Floor, New York NY 10019. **Tel** (212)399-5030, FAX (212)399-6890. **ED** Garnett McCoy. Index available (back issues, $10.00). **Bk Rev**. Documents available from The Genuine Article. ***Continues*** *Journal (Archives of American Art), 0003-9853.*
Desc: Topics on American artists and their work; collecting activities in the different area centers, and archives information.
Ind/Abst Am. Hist. Life (1985-); Art Index; ARTbibliogr. Mod.; Arts Humanit. Citation Index (19??-19??) [Full Cov.]; BHA : Biblio. Hist. Art; Curr. Contents Arts Humanit.; Res. Alert [Full Cov.].

ISSN 1191-9868
DD 708.11/3541 CN
●**JOURNAL - ART GALLERY OF ONTARIO.** See Museums and Galleries.

ISSN 1196-4081
DD 707 CN
JOURNAL - CANADIAN SOCIETY FOR EDUCATION THROUGH ART. (THE JOURNAL / CANADIAN SOCIETY FOR EDUCATION THROUGH ART / LE JOURNAL / SOCIETE CANADIENNE D'EDUCATION PAR L'ART.). [J. - Can. Soc. Educ. through Art]. **Added/Corp** Canadian Society for Education Through Art. **VFOAT** CSEA Journal. Vol. 19, No. 2 (Dec. 1988)-. Periodical. English (summaries and/or abstracts in French). Two times a year. $55.00. Canadian Society for Education Through Art, 1487 Parish Lane, Oakville Ontario L6M 2Z6 Canada. **Tel** (905)847-0975. ***Continues*** *CSEA Journal, 1196-4073.*

LC N576.H6 A26 **ISSN** 0360-4756
DD 708/.9969/31 US
JOURNAL - HONOLULU ACADEMY OF ARTS. (HONOLULU ACADEMY OF ARTS JOURNAL.). [J. - Honolulu Acad. Arts]. **Main/Corp** Honolulu Academy of Arts. **VFOAT** Journal. Vol. 1 (1974)-. Monographic series. English. Irregular. Price varies per volume. Academy Shop / Honolulu Academy of Arts, 900 South Beretania Street, Honolulu HI 96814. **Tel** (808)538-3693, (808)523-1493, FAX (808)521-6591. **ED** Nancy Kwok.
Desc: Scholarly essays on Japanese paintings in Honolulu Academy of Arts collection.
Ind/Abst ARTbibliogr. Mod.; BHA : Biblio. Hist. Art.

LC N1 .J6 **ISSN** 0021-8529
US
JOURNAL OF AESTHETICS AND ART CRITICISM, THE. [J. aesthet. art crit.]. **Added/Corp** American Society for Aesthetics. Vol. 1 (Spring 1941)-. Academic Scholarly Publication. English. Four times a year. $56.00 (one-year), $110.00 (two-year), $163.00 (three-year), institution. University of Wisconsin Press, Journal Division, 114 North Murray Street, Madison WI 53715. **Tel** (608)262-4952, FAX (608)262-8909. **ED** Donald W. Crawford. Index available. cum. index. **Bk Rev**. **Ad Acc. Circ:** 3,000 (ctrl). available on microfilm and microfiche from University Microfilms International (UMI). Documents available from The Genuine Article, UMI Article Clearinghouse.
Desc: To promote study research, discussion and

publication in aesthetics. The term 'aesthetics' is broadly interpreted, and contributors are primarily academics from the fields of literature, art, music, or philosophy.
Ind/Abst Abstr. Engl. Stud.; Acad. Abstr.; Acad. Ind. [Computer File] (1987-); Acad. Search; Am. Bibliogr. Slavic East Europ. Stud.; Annu. Bibliogr. Engl. Lang. Lit.; Art Index; ARTbibliogr. Mod.; Arts Humanit. Citation Index [Full Cov.]; Avery Index Archit. Period. Suppl. Colum. Univ. (19??-199?); BHA : Biblio. Hist. Art; Book Rev. Digest; Book Rev. Index; Curr. Contents Arts Humanit.; EP Collect.; Expand. Acad. Index (1987-); Film Lit. Index; Homework Help.; Humanit. Index; Humanit. Source; INFO-SOUTH Abstr.; Lit. Crit. Regist.; Mag. Search; MasterFile FullTEXT 1000; MasterFile FullTEXT 350; MasterFile FullTEXT 650; MasterFile FullTEXT (Jan. 1990-); MLA Int. Bibl. Books Artic. Mod. Lang. Lit.; Music Index; Newsp. Period. Abstr. (1991-); OCLC; Philos. Index; Pub. Lib. FullTEXT; Res. Alert [Full Cov.]; Soc. Sci. Cit. Index [Select. Cov.]; Telebase.

LC N81 .J68 **ISSN** 0260-9991
DD 707 UK
CCC

JOURNAL OF ART & DESIGN EDUCATION. **Added/Corp** National Society for Art Education (Great Britain) National Society for Education in Art and Design (Great Britain). **VFOAT** Journal of Art and Design Education. Vol. 1 No. 1 (1982)-. Academic Scholarly Publication. English. Three times a year. $359.00. Basil Blackwell Publishers Ltd., 108 Cowley Road, Oxford 0X4 1JF United Kingdom. **Tel** 011 44 1235 465500, FAX 011 44 1235 465556, telex 837022 OXBOOK G. **(Subscription address:** Blackwell Publishers / UK, 108 Cowley Road, Oxford OX4 1JF United Kingdom. **Tel** 011 44 1865 791100, FAX 011 44 1865 791347.**)** available on microfiche. Documents available from The Genuine Article.
Ind/Abst ARTbibliogr. Mod. (1984-); Arts Humanit. Citation Index [Full Cov.]; Br. Educ. Index; Curr. Cit.; Curr. Contents Arts Humanit.; Curr. Index J. Educ. (March 1990); Educ. Technol. Abstr.; Res. Alert [Full Cov.]; School Organ. Manage. Abstr.; Soc. Sci. Cit. Index [Select. Cov.]; Sociol. Educ. Abstr.; Stud. Women Abstr.; Tech. Educ. Train. Abstr.

LC N6540 .J67 **ISSN** 0315-4297
DD 700/.971 CN

JOURNAL OF CANADIAN ART HISTORY. [J. Can. art hist.]. **VFOAT** Annales d'Historie de l'Art Canadien. Vol. 1 (Spring 1974)-. Academic Scholarly Publication. English (French). Two times a year. 30.00Can$. Concordia University / Canada, VA Building 432, 1455 de Maisonneuve boulevard West, Montreal Quebec H3G 1M8 Canada. **Tel** (514)848-4699. **ED** Sandra Paikowsky. Index available (bound in 2nd issue). **Bk Rev. Circ:** 800 (ctrl). available in microform; available with illustrations. Documents available from The Genuine Article.
Desc: Devoted to the publication of scholarly articles on the history of Canadian art, architecture, photography and the decorative arts. Manuscripts are published in English or French in the form of illustrated articles, short notes and "Sources and Documents."
Ind/Abst Archit. Period. Index (1977/1978-); Art Index; ARTbibliogr. Mod.; Arts Humanit. Citation Index (19??-19??) [Full Cov.]; Avery Index Archit. Period. Suppl. Colum. Univ. (19??-199?); BHA : Biblio. Hist. Art; Can. Index; Can. Period. Index (19??-); Curr. Contents Arts Humanit.; Repere (1983-); Res. Alert [Full Cov.].

LC PN851 .J68 **ISSN** 0252-8169
DD 809/.005 II
CCC

JOURNAL OF COMPARATIVE LITERATURE & AESTHETICS. See Literature.

LC N6480 .J68 **ISSN** 0897-2400
DD 709 US

JOURNAL OF CONTEMPORARY ART. [J. contemp. art]. Vol. 1, No. 1 (Spring 1988)-. Periodical. English. Two times a year. $14.00. Journal of Contemporary Art, PO Box 1472, New York NY 10023. **Tel** (212)799-1436, FAX (212)873-0401. **ED** Klaus Ottman. Index available. cum. index. **Ad Acc. Circ:** 3,000 (ctrl).
Ind/Abst BHA : Biblio. Hist. Art.

LC BH1 .J14 **ISSN** 0318-8558
DD 701/.17 CN

JOURNAL OF EXPERIMENTAL AESTHETICS. **Added/Corp** Aesthetic Research Centre of Canada. **VFOAT** J.E.A., Journal of Experimental Aesthetics. Vol. 1 (May 1977)-. Periodical. English. Irregular (4 issues). Aesthetics Research Center Publishing, PO Box 3044, Vancouver British Columbia V6B 3X5 Canada.

LC PN2 .J585
DD 808.8 II

JOURNAL OF LITERATURE AND AESTHETICS. See Literature.

ISSN 0740-1833
US
Pr Rev.

JOURNAL OF MULTI-CULTURAL AND CROSS-CULTURAL RESEARCH IN ART EDUCATION. [J. multi-cult. cross-cult. res. art educ.]. **Added/Corp** United States Society for Education Through Art. Vol. 1, No. 1 (Fall 1983)-. Periodical. English. One time a year (June or July). $20.00. USSEA / United States Society for Education Through Art, Ohio State University, 128 North Oval Mall, 340 Hopkins Hall, Columbus OH 43210-1363. **Tel** (614)292-3555, FAX (614)292-4401. **ED** Dr. Ron Neperud (editor's address: 7231 Humanities Building, 455 North Park Street, Madison, WI 53706; phone: (608)262-3282). Each issue contains an index to its own contents (no volume index)--loose. **Ad Acc. Circ:** 500.
Desc: Contains articles concerning multiculturalism and comparative research in art education within the United States.
Ind/Abst Curr. Index J. Educ.

ISSN 0956-2834
UK

JOURNAL OF PHILOSOPHY AND THE VISUAL ARTS. See Philosophy.

ISSN 1057-0292
DD 700 US

JOURNAL OF SOCIAL THEORY IN ART EDUCATION, THE. [J. soc. theory art educ.]. **Added/Corp** Caucus on Social Theory & Art Education (U.S.) National Art Education Association. **VFOAT** JSTAE. (198?)-. Periodical. English. One time a year (Apr.). $20.00. Caucus on Social Theory and Art Education, 3200 Wendimere Lane, Billings MT 59102. **Tel** (406)256-6536. ***Continues*** *Bulletin of the Caucus on Social Theory and Art Education.*
Ind/Abst Curr. Index J. Educ.

ISSN 0197-1360
US
CODEN JAICDE
Pr Rev.

JOURNAL OF THE AMERICAN INSTITUTE FOR CONSERVATION. [J. Am. Inst. Conserv.]. **Main/Corp** American Institute for Conservation of Historic and Artistic Works. **VFOAT** JAIC. Vol. 16, No. 2, (Feb. 1977)-. Academic Scholarly Publication. English. Three times a year. $68.00. American Institute Conservation, 1717 K Street Northwest, Suite 301, Washington DC 20006. **Tel** (202)542-9545, FAX (202)542-9328. **ED** Elisabeth West Fitz Hugh. **Bk Rev. Ad Acc. Circ:** 2,500 (ctrl). Documents available from CASDDS. ***Continues*** *Bulletin of the American Institute for Conservation of Historic and Artistic Works, 0146-1257.*
Desc: The foremost periodical on conservation in the United States; contains articles on current issues and technical procedures. Paper on conservation of architectural materials, archaeological objects, books and paper, ethnographic materials, paintings, photographic materials, sculpture, and wooden artifacts. Keep up-to-date materials on new developments.
Ind/Abst Art Archaeol. Tech. Abstr.; BHA : Biblio. Hist. Art; Chem. Abstr. (1977, 1980, 1981-);; Museum Abstr.

ISSN 0882-8504
DD 704 US

JOURNAL OF THE ARTISTS' CHOICE MUSEUM, THE. (THE JOURNAL OF THE ARTISTS' CHOICE MUSEUM : ACM.). [J. Artists' Choice Mus.]. **VFOAT** ACM; ACM Journal. (198?)-. Periodical. English. Two times a year. $10.00. The Artists Choice Museum, PO Box 8008 JAF, New York NY 10116-8008. ***Continues*** *ACM Newsletter.*

ISSN 0897-0521
DD 700 US
CEASED

JOURNAL OF THE FANTASTIC IN THE ARTS. See Literature-Science Fiction, Fantasy and Horror.

LC N17 .I6 **ISSN** 0970-6070
DD 706.254 II

JOURNAL OF THE INDIAN SOCIETY OF ORIENTAL ART. [J. Indian Soc. Orient. Art]. **Main/Corp** Indian Society of Oriental Art. Vol. 1 (1933)-. English. One time a year. $60.00. Indian Society of Oriental Art, 15 Park Street, 5th Floor, Calcutta 16 India. **(Subscription address:** Prints India, 11 Darya Ganj, New Delhi 110002 India. **Tel** 011 91 11 3268645, FAX 011 91 11 3275542, telex 31-61087 PRIN-IN.**)** **ED** Krishna Deva and Gopen Roy. **Bk Rev. Circ:** 225 (ctrl).
Desc: Covers the traditional art of the Orient, and the society's history.
Ind/Abst Art Archaeol. Tech. Abstr.; Avery Index Archit. Period. Suppl. Colum. Univ. (19??-199?).

ISSN 0024-6158
UK

JOURNAL OF THE LONDON SOCIETY, THE. **Added/Corp** London Society. No. 1 (Oct. 1913)-. Periodical. English. Two times a year. $20.53. London Society, 4th Floor, Senate House Malet Street, London WC1E 7HU United Kingdom. **Tel** 011 44 171 5805537. available on microfilm from University Microfilms International (UMI).
Ind/Abst Archit. Period. Index (Oct. 1978-).

LC N520 .A25 **ISSN** 1041-2433
DD 708.144/61 US
SUSPENDED

JOURNAL OF THE MUSEUM OF FINE ARTS, BOSTON. See Museums and Galleries.

ISSN 0842-8417
DD 707/.10713 CN

JOURNAL OF THE ONTARIO SOCIETY FOR EDUCATION THROUGH ART. [J. Ont. Soc. Educ. Art]. **Added/Corp** Ontario Society for Education Through Art. Vol. 17 (1988)-. English. 7.21Can$. Ontario Society for Education Through Art, 150 Water Street South, Kitchener Ontario N2G 1Z5 Canada. ***Continues*** *OSEA Journal, 0380-6340.*

ISSN 0315-940X
CN

JOURNAL - UNIVERSITIES ART ASSOCIATION OF CANADA. **Main/Corp** Universities Art Association of Canada. Vol. 1, (Apr. 1972)-. Periodical. English (French). Two times a year. Free to members; 150.00Can$ institutional membership; 50.00Can$ associate membership. Hughes & Company Management Services, PO Box 5863, Station B, Victoria British Columbia V8R 6S8 Canada. **Tel** (604)480-1026.

IT

JULIET ART MAGAZINE. (19??)-. Italian (English and French). Six times a year. L45000.00 Italy; L80000.00 other. Juliet Art Magazine, PO Box 986, 34100 Trieste Italy. **Tel** 011 39 40 313425, FAX 011 39 40 947833. **Ad Acc. Circ:** 5,000.
Desc: Covers contemporary art-design, architecture and dance.

ISSN 1077-8411
DD 051 US

●**JUXTAPOZ (SAN FRANCISCO, CALIF.).** (JUXTAPOZ.). [Juxtapoz]. Vol. 1, No. 1 (Winter 1994)-. Periodical. English. Four times a year. $14.50. High Speed Productions Inc., PO Box 884570, San Francisco CA 94188. **Tel** (415)822-3083, FAX (415)822-8359. **ED** Robert Williams. **Bk Rev. Ad Acc, Adv Mgr:** Eben Sterling.
Desc: Presents a gallery of underground artists who influence much of the graphics, fashion and new art we see today. Full color layouts by cartoonists, painters, sculptors and photographers are featured along with interviews, rare portfolios, sketches and reviews.

LC N7355 .K34A
JA

KAGAWA DAIGAKU KYOIKUGAKUBU KENKYU HOKOKU : GEIJUTSU SAKUHIN SHU. **Main/Corp** Kagawa Daigaku. Kyoikugakubu. No. 1- ; 1978-. Japanese. 1-1 Saiwaicho (760), Takamatsu Japan.
Ind/Abst Crop Physiol. Abstr.; Nutr. Abstr. Rev., Ser. B, Live Feeds and Feed.; Ornamental Hort.; Plant Breed. Abstr.; Plant Grow. Reg. Abstr.; Rice Abstr.

LC N7301 .K385
DD 709/.54 II

KALAVRITT = KALAVRTTA. **VFOAT** Kalavrtta. (Jan. 1980)-. Periodical. English (Hindi). Four times a year. Rs100.00 India; Rs500.00 other. 2 TA 8 Jawahar Nagar, Jaipur 302 004 India. **Tel** 45729. **ED** Kalavritt Sumahendra. cum. index. **Bk Rev. Ad Acc, Adv Mgr:** Virendra Patni, **Tel** 316628. Full Page (B&W) Rs6000.00. Half Page (B&W) Rs3000.00. **Circ:** 1,500 (ctrl).
Desc: Publishes articles on art and crafts, contemporary and ancient reviews of camps, seminars, exhibitions and books. Monographic series on art and architecture.

LC N2265 .A57 **ISSN** 0588-3431
DD 069 GW

KATALOGE. **Main/Corp** Cologne Wallraf-Richartz-Museum. Vol. 1 (1964)-. Periodical. German. DuMont Buchverlag GmbH & Co. KG, Postfach 100468, D-50441 Cologne Germany. **Tel** 011 49 221 20530, FAX 011 49 221 2053281.

LC NX8.J3 M85a
JA

KENKYU KIYO - MUSASHINO BIJUTSU DAIGAKU. **Main/Corp** Musashino Bijutsu Daigaku. **Added/Corp** Musashino Bijutsu Daigaku. Bulletin of the Musashino Art University. **VFOAT** Bulletin of the Musashino Art University. (1963)-. Bulletin. Japanese (summaries and/or abstracts in English). Irregular. Free. Musashino Art University, 1-736 Ogawamachi, Kodaira-shi, Tokyo 187 Japan. **Tel** 011 81 3 423415011, FAX 011 81 3 423451404. **Circ:** 1,500 (ctrl).
Ind/Abst BHA : Biblio. Hist. Art.

LC N6537.K44 K44 **ISSN** 0163-1861
DD 741/.092/4 US

KENT COLLECTOR, THE. No. 1 (1974)-. Periodical. English. Three times a year. $15.00. Kent Collector, SUNY Plattsburgh Art Museum, Plattsburgh NY

The Arts — Art

12901. **Tel** (518)564-2813, FAX (518)564-7827. **ED** Evelyn Heins. Index available. cum. index. **Bk Rev. Ad Acc, Adv Mgr:** Evelyn Heins. **Circ:** 225.
Desc: Devoted to the life and work of Rockwell Kent.

IT
KERMES : ARTE E TECNICA DEL RESTAURO. Vol. 1, No. 1 (Jan./April 1988)-. Periodical. Italian. Three times a year. L80.000. Nardini Editore SRL, V del Salviatino 1, 50016 Fiesole Fi Italy. **Tel** 011 39 55 598923.
Ind/Abst BHA : Biblio. Hist. Art.

LC N9.6 .K48
RU
KHRONIKA KHUDOZHESTVENNOI ZHIZNI. (19??)-. Russian. Izdatelstvo Sovetskii Khudozhnik, Ulitsa Cherniakhovskoga 4a, 12319 Moscow Russia.

LC N8554 .K5
RU
KHUDOZHESTVENNOE NASLEDIE: KHRANENIE, ISSLEDOVANIE, RESTAVRATSIIA. Added/Corp Vsesoiuznaia Tsentralnaia Nauchno-Issledovatelskaia Laboratoriia Po Konservatsii i Restavratsii Muzeinykh Khudozhestvennykh Tsennostei. (1975)-. Periodical. Russian (summaries and/or abstracts in English). Izdatel'stvo Iskusstvo, Vorotnikovskii Pereulok 11, 103009 Moscow Russia. **Supersedes** Moscow. Vsesoiuznaia Tsentralnaia Nauchno-Issledovatelskaia Laboratoriia Po Konservatsii i Restavratsii Muzeinykh Khudozhestvennykh Tsennostei. Soobshcheniia.

LC N6 .K53
RU
KHUDOZHNIK. Added/Corp Soiuz Khudozhnikov RSFSR. (19??)-. Periodical. Russian. Twelve times a year. $139.95. **(Subscription address:** East View Publications Inc., 3020 Harbor Lane North, Suite 110, Minneapolis MN 55447. **Tel** (800)477-1005, (612)550-0961, FAX (612)559-2931.)
Ind/Abst ARTbibliogr. Mod.

ISSN 0892-8991
US
KIDSART NEWS. See Children and Youth Interests.

LC PK6401 .K54
IR
KILK. See Literature.

LC N7109.P25 K6   **ISSN** 0214-7955
DD 709/.46/6   **SP**
KOBIE. BELLAS ARTES. Added/Corp Vizcaya (Spain). Diputacion Foral. **VFOAT** Bellas Artes; Serie Bellas Artes; KOBIE. Serie Bellas Artes. (19??)-. Periodical. Spanish (summaries and/or abstracts in Basque, English and French). One time a year.
Continues KOBIE. Arte Ederrak.
Ind/Abst BHA : Biblio. Hist. Art.

LC N8.J28 K6   **ISSN** 0454-112X
DD 705   **JA**
KOBIJUTSU. VFOAT Quarterly Review of the Fine Arts; Quarterly Review of Fine Arts. (1963)-. Periodical. Japanese (table of contents in English). Four times a year. $177.50. **(Subscription address:** Japan Publications Trading Company Ltd., PO Box 5030, Tokyo International, Tokyo 100-31 Japan. **Tel** 011 81 3 3292 3753.)

LC DS820.8 .K62   **ISSN** 0368-6272
CODEN KNKAAF   **JA**
KOBUNKAZAI NO KAGAKU. [Kobunkazai no kagaku]. **Added/Corp** Kobunkazai Kagaku Kenkyukai. **VFOAT** Scientific Papers on Japanese Antiques and Art Crafts. (Jan. 1951)-. Periodical. Japanese (summaries and/or abstracts in English). Kobunkazai Kagaku Kenkyukai, Tokyo Japan. Documents available from CASDDS.
Ind/Abst Chem. Abstr.

LC NK1073.6 .K64
KO
KOGO MISUL. Added/Corp Hanguk Misul Sahakhoe. **VFOAT** Art and Archaeology. (1960)-. Periodical. Korean. Irregular. Hanguk Misul Sahakhoe, San 8 Hannam-dong, Yongsan-ku, Seoul South Korea.

LC N8 .K8   **ISSN** 0023-2785
JA
KOKKA. Vol. 1 No. 1 (Oct. 1889)-. Periodical. Japanese (English). Twelve times a year. $748.00. **(Subscription address:** Maruzen Company Ltd., PO Box 5050, Import & Export Department, Tokyo 100 31 Japan. **Tel** 011 81 3 32789224.) cum. index.

LC N6750 .K64
DD 709   **JA**
KOKURITSU SEIYO BIJUTSUKAN NEMPO : BULLETIN ANNUEL DU MUSEE NATIONAL D'ART OCCIDENTAL. See Museums and Galleries.

LC AM51.C64 M87   **ISSN** 0933-257X
DD 069/.97094355   **GW**
KOLNER MUSEUMS-BULLETIN. See Museums and Galleries.

LC ND1055 .K66
JA
KONNICHI NO NIHONGA: YAMATANE BIJUTSUKAN SHO TEN. Added/Corp Yamatane Bijutsukan. **VFOAT** Contemporary Japanese-Style Painting. (1971)-. Periodical. Japanese. Every 2 years. Yamatane, 30 Nohonbash, Chuo-ku Tokyo Japan.

LC N8 .K83   **ISSN** 0023-3609
SW
CCC
KONSTHISTORISK TIDSKRIFT. [Konsthist. tidskr.]. **VFOAT** Art Review. (Feb. 1932)-. Multiple languages (English and Swedish). Four times a year. $91.00. Scandinavian University Press, PO Box 2959 Toeyen, N 0608 Oslo 6 Norway. **Tel** 011 47 2 2575400, FAX 011 47 2 2575353, telex 71896 UROR N. **(Subscription address:** Scandinavian University Press, 200 Meacham Ave., Elmont NY 11003. **Tel** (516)352-7300, FAX (516)352-7377.) **ED** Patrik Reutersward. **Bk Rev. Circ:** 800. Documents available from The Genuine Article.
Desc: Published by the Society of Art History, Stockholm. The articles are written in English and the Scandinavian languages.
Ind/Abst Art Index; ARTbibliogr. Mod.; ARTbibliogr. Curr. Titles; Arts Humanit. Citation Index [Full Cov.]; Avery Index Archit. Period. Suppl. Colum. Univ. (1989-); BHA : Biblio. Hist. Art; Curr. Contents Arts Humanit.; Res. Alert [Full Cov.]; Romant. Move.

ISSN 0347-4453
SW
UDC 70
KONSTPERSPEKTIV. [Konstperspektiv]. (1975)-. Periodical. Swedish. Four times a year. Sveriges Konstfoereningars Riksfoerbund, PO Box 00065, S 216 10 Malmoe Sweden. **ED** Uno Kampmark. available on audiocassette.
Ind/Abst BHA : Biblio. Hist. Art.

LC NK7 .P6   **ISSN** 1230-6142
DD 745.05   **PL**
KONTEKSTY : POLSKA SZTUKA LUDOWA : ANTROPOLOGIA KULTURY, ETNOGRAFIA, SZTUKA. Added/Corp Instytut Sztuki (Polska Akademia Nauk). (1990)-. Periodical. Polish (summaries and/or abstracts in English). Four times a year. $44.00. Polska Akademia Nauk, Instytut Sztuki / Polish Academy of Sciences, Institute of Fine Arts, Ul. Dluga 26/28, 00-950 Warsaw Poland. **Tel** 011 48 22 313271, FAX 011 48 22 313149. **ED** Aleksander Jackowski and Zbigniew Benedyktowicz. Index available. **Bk Rev. Continues** Polska Sztuka Ludowa, 0032-3721.

LC N567 .A15   **ISSN** 0887-9222
DD 708.174/27   **US**
KRESGE ART MUSEUM BULLETIN. See Museums and Galleries.

ISSN 0340-7403
GW
KRITISCHE BERICHTE. (KRITISCHE BERICHTE : MITTEILUNGSORGAN DES ULMER VEREINS VERBAND FUER KUNST- UND KULTURWISSENSCHAFTEN.). [Krit. Ber.]. **Added/Corp** Ulmer Verein fuer Kunstwissenschaft. Ulmer Verein, Verband fuer Kunst- und Kulturwissenschaften. (1973)-. Periodical. German.
Ind/Abst Avery Index Archit. Period. Suppl. Colum. Univ. (1989-); BHA : Biblio. Hist. Art.

LC N5 .V74a   **ISSN** 0166-0381
NE
KRONIEK VAN HET REMBRANDTHUIS, DE. [Kron. Rembrandthuis]. 23rd Volume (1969)-. Periodical. Dutch. Two times a year. $25.00. Het Rembrandthuis, Jodenbreestraat 4-6, 1011 NK Amsterdam Netherlands. **Tel** 011 31 20 6249486.
Continues Kroniek van de Vriendenkring van het Rembrandthuis.
Ind/Abst Avery Index Archit. Period. Suppl. Colum. Univ. (19??-199?); BHA : Biblio. Hist. Art.

LC N7340 .K814
DD 700/.951   **CH**
KU KUNG HSUEH SHU CHI KAN / KUO LI KU KUNG PO WU YUN PIEN CHI. Added/Corp Kuo Li Ku Kung Po Wu Yuan. **VFOAT** National Palace Museum Research Quarterly; National Palace Museum Quarterly, Second Series. Vol. 1 (Autumn 1983)-. Periodical. Chinese. Four times a year. $45.00. National Palace Museum, Wai-Shuang-Hsi Shih-Lin, Taipei Taiwan. **Tel** 011 886 2 8821230, FAX 011 886 2 8821440. **ED** Fung Ming-chu. Index available. **Circ:** 1,000. **Continues** Ku Kung Chi Kan.

LC N8.C5 K8
DD 709/.51   **CH**
KU KUNG WEN WU YUEH KAN = THE NATIONAL PALACE MUSEUM MONTHLY OF CHINESE ART. Added/Corp Kuo Li Ku Kung Po Wu Yuan. **VFOAT** Ku Kung Wen Wu; The National Palace Museum Monthly of Chinese Art; National Palace Museum Monthly of Chinese Art. Vol. 1 (April 1983)-. Periodical. Chinese (English and Japanese). Twelve times a year. $133.00. National Palace Museum, Wai-Shuang-Hsi Shih-Lin, Taipei Taiwan. **Tel** 011 886 2 8821230, FAX 011 886 2 8821440. **ED** Chang Yueh-yun. Index available. cum. index. **Circ:** 10,000.

LC ND1040 .K777
DD 759.951   **CH**
KUANG-TUNG HUA YUAN CHI KAN. **Added/Corp** Kuang-Tung Hua Yuan. Sheng Huo, Tu Shu, Hsin Chih San Lien Shu Tien. Hsiang-Kang Fen Tien. (1982)-. Periodical. Chinese. NT$2.20. Joint Publishing Company, Hong Kong Branch, 9 Queen Victoria Street, Hong Kong. **Tel** 011 852 25230105. **Bk Rev. Circ:** 1,000 (ctrl).
Desc: Articles and mainly pictures of different kinds of painting. A brief account on Chinese artists.

GW
KUENSTLERGILDE; EIN MITTEILUNGSBLATT FUER UNSERE MITGLIEDER, DIE. (19??)-. Dutch. Four times a year. Kuenstlergilde ev Hofenmarkt 2, W-7300 Esslingen Germany. **Tel** 07111359129. **ED** Samuel Beer. **Bk Rev. Circ:** 1,600 (ctrl).

ISSN 0902-8099
DD 700   **DK**
KUNST & KOMMUNIKATION DANSK UDG. (KUNST & KOMMUNIKATION.). [Kunst & kommun.Dan. udg.]. **VFOAT** Kunst og Kommunikation. (1987)-. Periodical. Danish.
Ind/Abst BHA : Biblio. Hist. Art.

ISSN 0924-5251
NE
KUNST & MUSEUMJOURNAAL (DUTCH EDITION). (KUNST & MUSEUMJOURNAAL.). **VFOAT** Kunst en Museumjournaal. (1989)-. Periodical. Dutch. Six times a year. F51.00 Netherlands; F94.00 other. PVO Abonnementenservices, Postbus 77, 5126 ZH Gilze Netherlands. **Tel** 011 31 1615 7450. **ED** Philip Peters. Index available. **Ad Acc. Circ:** 4,600 (ctrl). **Formed by the union of** Museumjournaal **and** Dutch Art + Architecture Today.
Desc: Publication on the modern art in the Netherlands and elsewhere. Contains theory, commentaries, reviews, discussions and portraits.

LC N6948 .K78   **ISSN** 0924-526X
DD 700/.9/04   **NE**
KUNST & MUSEUMJOURNAAL (ENGLISH EDITION). (KUNST & MUSEUMJOURNAAL.). **Added/Corp** Netherlands. Rijksdienst Beeldende Kunst. **VFOAT** Kunst en Museumjournaal. Vol. 1 (1989)-. Periodical. English. Six times a year. F51.00 Netherlands; F94.00 other. PVO Abonnementenservices, Postbus 77, 5126 ZH Gilze Netherlands. **Tel** 011 31 1615 7450. **ED** Philip Peters. Index available. **Ad Acc. Circ:** 3,000 (ctrl). **Formed by the union of** Museumjournaal **and** Dutch Art + Architecture Today, 0169-3123.
Desc: Publication on modern art in the Netherlands and elsewhere. Contains theory, commentaries, reviews, discussions, and portraits.
Ind/Abst Art Index; BHA : Biblio. Hist. Art.

SZ
KUNST BULLETIN. (19??)-. Bulletin. German. Twelve times a year. 31.20F Switzerland; 46.00F other. Zuerichsee Zeitschriftenverlag, Seestrasse 86, CH-8712 Staefa Switzerland. **Tel** 011 41 1 9285611.
Ind/Abst BHA : Biblio. Hist. Art.

LC N8610 .K86
NE
KUNST- EN ANTIEKVEILING. (1979)-. Dutch. One time a year (Nov.). Fl115.00. Waanders Uitgevers, Postbus 1129, 8001 BC Zwolle Netherlands. **Tel** 011 31 38 658628, FAX 038-655989.

LC N8846.N4 K86   **ISSN** 0921-4755
NE
KUNST EN BELEID IN NEDERLAND. (1985)-. Dutch. One time a year. Boekmanstichting Amsterdam Uitgeverij en Boekhandel Van Gennep BV, Spuistraat 283, 1012 VR Amsterdam The Netherlands.

LC N6875 .K8   **ISSN** 0452-8514
GW
KUNST IN HESSEN UND AM MITTELRHEIN. [Kunst Hess. Mittelrhein]. **VFOAT** Schriften der Hessischen Mussen. (1962)-. Periodical. German. 21.90. Hessisches Landesmuseum Darmst, Friedensplatz 1, D-64283 Darmstadt Germany. **Tel** 011 49 61515434. **Bk Rev. Ad**

The Arts —Art

Acc. ctrl circ.
Ind/Abst ARTbibliogr. Mod.; Avery Index Archit. Period. Suppl. Colum. Univ. (1987-); BHA : Biblio. Hist. Art.

LC N8 .K9 **ISSN** 0023-5415
NO

KUNST OG KULTUR. [Kunst kult.]. Vol. 1 (1910)-. Periodical. Norwegian. Four times a year. $98.00. Scandinavian University Press, PO Box 2959 Toeyen, N 0608 Oslo 6 Norway. **Tel** 011 47 2 2575400, FAX 011 47 2 2575353, telex 71896 UROR N. **(Subscription address:** Scandinavian University Press, 200 Meacham Ave., Elmont NY 11003. **Tel** (516)352-7300, FAX (516)352-7377.**) ED** Tone Skedsmo and Oscar Thue. Index available. cum. index. **Bk Rev. Ad Acc. Circ:** 1,700.
Desc: The main Norwegian journal for pictorial art, architecture and handicrafts.
Ind/Abst ARTbibliogr. Mod.; ARTbibliogr. Curr. Titles; BHA : Biblio. Hist. Art.

LC NX **ISSN** 0075-725X
DD 700 GW

KUNST UND ALTERTUM AM RHEIN. No. 1- 1956-. Monographic series. German. Irregular. Price varies per volume. Dr. Rudolf Habelt GmbH, Postfach 150104, D-53040 Bonn Germany. **Tel** 011 49 228 232015.

LC NX **ISSN** 0023-5431
DD 700 AU

KUNST UND KIRCHE. (KUNST UND KIRCHE.). [Kunst Kirche]. **Added/Corp** Evangelischer Kirchbautag. Arbeitsausschuss. Diozesan-Kunstverein Linz. (Feb. 1971)-. Periodical. German (summaries and/or abstracts in English). Four times a year. $67.42. Veritas Landesverlag, Hafenstrasse 1-3, A 4020 Linz Austria. **Tel** 011 43 732 7616223, FAX 011 43 732 7616239. **Bk Rev. Ad Acc. Circ:** 4,000 (ctrl). ***Formed by the union of*** *Christliche Kunstblatter **and** Kunst und Kirche (Darmstadt, Germany : 1957).*
Desc: Gives information on modern art, religion and architecture and their respective interdependence.
Ind/Abst Archit. Period. Index (1971-); ARTbibliogr. Mod.; ARTbibliogr. Curr. Titles; Avery Index Archit. Period. Suppl. Colum. Univ. (1989-).

LC N3 .S58 **ISSN** 0023-544X
DD 700/.5 GW
CEASED

KUNST UND LITERATUR. (KUNSTHISTORISCHES INSTITUT, FLORENCE -MITTEILUNGEN.). [Kunst Lit.]. **Added/Corp** Gesellschaft fur Deutsch-Sowjetische Freundschaft. **VFOAT** Kunst und Literatur. Vol. 1 (1953)-(19??). Periodical. German. Deutscher Judo Verband, Redaktion Ippon Segewaldweg 40, D-12557 Berlin Germany. **Tel** 011 49 711 210770, telex 051 678. cum. index.
Ind/Abst ARTbibliogr. Mod.; ARTbibliogr. Curr. Titles; MLA Int. Bibl. Books Artic. Mod. Lang. Lit.; Music Index (-19??); Romant. Move.

LC NX **ISSN** 0931-7112
DD 700 GW
UDC 372.873/77

KUNST + UNTERRICHT (1985). [Kunst + Unterr. 1985]. **VFOAT** Kunst und Unterricht (1985). (1985)-. Periodical. German. Eleven times a year (10 regular issues and one annual). $101.18. Erhard Friedrich Verlag, Postfach 100150, D-30917 Seelze Germany. **Tel** 011 49 511 4000452. ***Continues*** *K + U. Kunst + Unterricht, 0170-6225; Zeitschrift feur Kunstpadagogik, 0340-6180.*

LC N7068 .N585 N7061 .K86
DD 709 NO
TITLE CHANGE

KUNSTAARBOK = ART YEARBOOK, NORWAY. Added/Corp Kunstnernes Informasjonskontor. **VFOAT** Art Yearbook, Norway; Norsk Kunstaarbok; Norwegian Art Yearbook. (1992)-(1994). Norwegian (English). Scandinavian University Press, PO Box 2959 Toeyen, N 0608 Oslo 6 Norway. **Tel** 011 47 2 2575400, FAX 011 47 2 2575353, telex 71896 UROR N. **(Subscription address:** Scandinavian University Press, 200 Meacham Ave., Elmont NY 11003. **Tel** (516)352-7300, FAX (516)352-7377.**) ED** Olga Schmedling, Elisabeth Tetens Jahn, Rigmor Hovland, Terje Roalkvam, Oystein Ustvedt, Line Waelgaard. ***Continued by*** *Norsk Kunstaarbok.*
Desc: As an overview of contemporary Norwegian art, the serial covers visual arts, applied art, photography and a review of important exhibitions in Norway. Features many illustrations.

ISSN 0566-263X
SZ

•KUNST+ARCHITEKTUR IN DER SCHWEIZ. (KUNST+ARCHITEKTUR IN DER SCHWEIZ = ART+ARCHITECTURE EN SUISSE = ARTE+ARCHITETTURA IN SVIZZERA.). **Added/Corp** Gesellschaft fuer Schweizerische Kunstgeschichte. **VFOAT** Kunst + Architektur in der Schweiz; Kunst und Architektur in der Schweiz; Arte ed Architettura in Svizzera; Art et Architecture en Suisse; Art+Architecture en Suisse; Arte+Architettura in Svizzera. (1994)-. Periodical. German (French and Italian). Four times a year. GSK / Switzerland, Pavillonweg 2, Postfach 3001, Bern Switzerland. ***Continues*** *Unsere Kunstdenkmaeler, 0566-263x.*

LC N8640 .D64 N8650.D58
AU

KUNSTAUKTION. Main/Corp Dorotheum. Kunstabteilung. (19??)-. German. Dorotheum, Dorotheergasse 17, Vienna 1 Austria.

LC N5.K86 **ISSN** 0165-1129
DD 700 NE

KUNSTBEELD. VFOAT Kunst Beeld. (19??)-. Dutch. Irregular. $100.19. Bohn Stafleu van Loghum BV, Postbus 246, 3990 GA Houten Netherlands. **Tel** 011 31 3403 95782. **(Subscription address:** Intermedia BV, Postbus 4, 2400 MA Alphen AD Rijn Netherlands. **Tel** 011 31 1720 66481.)

LC N3 .K92 **ISSN** 0023-5474
GW
CCC

KUNSTCHRONIK. [Kunstchronik]. **Added/Corp** Zentralinstitut fuer Kunstgeschichte in Muenchen. Verband Deutscher Kunsthistoriker. Vol. 1 (1948)-. Periodical. German. Twelve times a year. $82.91. Verlag Hans Carl GmbH & Company KG, Andernacher Strasse 33A, D-90411 Nuernberg Germany. **Tel** 011 49 911 9528531, FAX 011 49 911 9528547. cum. index. **Circ:** 2,600.
Ind/Abst Art Archaeol. Tech. Abstr.; Avery Index Archit. Period. Suppl. Colum. Univ. (1989-); BHA : Biblio. Hist. Art.

LC NX
DD 700 SZ

KUNSTDENKMALER DER SCHWEIZ, DIE. Vol. 1 (1927)-. Monographic series. Multiple languages (French and German). Irregular. Price varies per volume. Birkhaeuser Verlag Ag, Klosterberg 23, PO Box 133, CH-4010 Basel Switzerland. **Tel** 011 41 61 2717400, FAX 011 41 61 2717666, telex 963475 birk ch.

LC N6480 .K86 **ISSN** 0177-3674
DD 709/.04/005 GW

KUNSTFORUM INTERNATIONAL. [Kunstforum int.]. **Added/Corp** Kunstforum International (Firm). **VFOAT** Kunstforum. (March/April 1973)-. Periodical. German. Irregular. DM184.00. Verlag Kunstforum International, Postfach 1147, D-53805 Ruppichteroth Germany.
Ind/Abst ARTbibliogr. Mod.; BHA : Biblio. Hist. Art.

LC NX **ISSN** 0023-5504
DD 700 GW

KUNSTHANDEL, DER. Volume 1 (1909)-. Trade Publication. German. Twelve times a year. DM201.00 Germany; DM223.00 other. Dr. Alfred Huethig Verlag GmbH, Postfach 102869, D-69018 Heidelberg Germany. **Tel** 011 49 6221 489281, FAX 011 49 6221 489279. **(Subscription address:** WEPF Publishing Services GmbH, Auf dem Wolf 4, CH-4018 Basel Switzerland. **Tel** 011 41 61 3115125.**) ED** Edwin Kuntz. **Bk Rev. Ad Acc. Circ:** 6,100. ***Absorbed*** *Bildereinrahmer und Vergolder.*
Desc: International specialized organ for art publishing companies and for the industries of frame materials, frames and mirrors.
Ind/Abst BHA : Biblio. Hist. Art.

LC NX **ISSN** 1015-0129
DD 700 AU

KUNSTHISTORIKER. [Kunsthistoriker]. (1984)-. Periodical. German. Two times a year. Minerva Wissenschaftl Buchhdlg 485, A-1011 Vienna Austria. **Tel** 011 43 222 5330238.

LC N386.G7 A3 **ISSN** 1010-3856
DD 709 AU

KUNSTHISTORISCHES JAHRBUCH GRAZ. [Kunsthist. Jahrbuch Graz]. **Added/Corp** Universitaet Graz. Institut fuer Kunstgeschichte. (1978)-. German. One time a year. Akademische Druck & Verlagsanstalt, Schoenaugasse 6, Postfach 598, A 8010 Graz Austria. **Tel** 011 43 316 813460. **ED** Gerhard H Franz. ***Continues*** *Universitaet Graz. Kunsthistorisches Institut. Jahrbuch des Kunsthistorischen Institutes der Universitaet Graz.*
Ind/Abst ARTbibliogr. Mod.; Avery Index Archit. Period. Suppl. Colum. Univ. (19??-199?); BHA : Biblio. Hist. Art.

LC N6836.L5 K8 **ISSN** 0454-6601
DD 705 AU

KUNSTJAHRBUCH DER STADT LINZ. [Kunstjahrb. Stadt Linz]. **Added/Corp** Stadtmuseum Linz. Linz (Austria). Kulturverwaltung. (1???)-. German. One time a year. Verlag Anton Schroll and Company, Spengergasse 39, A-1051 Vienna 1 Austria. **Tel** 011 43 1 5445641, FAX 011 43 1 5445641. **ED** G Wacha. **Bk Rev.**
Ind/Abst BHA : Biblio. Hist. Art.

LC NX **ISSN** 0343-0456
DD 700 GW

KUNSTMAGAZIN. [Kunstmagazin]. Vol. 17, No. 1 (1977)-. Periodical. German (English). Four times a year. ***Continues*** *Magazin Kunst.*
Ind/Abst ARTbibliogr. Mod.

LC N8670 .K8 **ISSN** 0174-3511
DD 704.95 GW

KUNSTPREISJAHRBUCH. VFOAT Kunstpreis Jahrbuch. No. 35A (1980)-. German (English and French). Two times a year. DM168.00 Germany; DM172.00 other. Weltkunst Verlag GmbH, Postfach 190918, 80603 Munich Germany. **Tel** 011 49 89 1269900, FAX 011 49 89 12699011, telex 5216731. Index available. **Ad Acc. Circ:** 10,000. ***Continues*** *Art-Price Annual (Munich, Germany : 1971).*

LC N3 .K94 **ISSN** 0172-7265
GW

KUNSTREPORT. (Fall 1973)-. Periodical. German. Four times a year. DM21.00. Deutscher Kunstlerband, 15 Kurfurstendamm 65, Berlin 1 Germany. ***Absorbed*** *Deutscher Kuenstlerbund. Ausstellung.*

NE

KUNSTSCHRIFT SDU OPENBAAR KUNSTBEZIT. Added/Corp SDU/Openbaar Kunstbezit (Amsterdam, Netherlands). **VFOAT** Kunstschrift SDU; SDU Openbaar Kunstbezit. (1989)-. Periodical. Dutch. Six times a year. SDU Uitgeverij, Postbus 20014, Christoffel Plantijnstraat, 2500 EA Den Haag Netherlands. **Tel** 011 31 70 3789911. ***Continues*** *Kunstschrift Openbaar Kunstbezit.*

LC N8640 .D64 N8650.D58
AU

KUNSTVERSTEIGERUNG. Main/Corp Dorotheum. Kunstabteilung. German. Dorotheum, Dorotheergasse 17, Vienna 1 Austria.

LC NX
DD 700 GW

KUNSTWISSENSCHAFTLICHE STUDIEN. No. 1 (1929)-. Monographic series. German. Irregular. Price varies per volume. Deutscher Kunstverlag, Postfach 190354, D-80603 Munich Germany. **Tel** 011 49 89 1215160.
Desc: History of art.

LC NX
DD 700 NE

KUNTSBEELD. Dutch. Samsom Bedrijfsinformatie BV, Postbus 4, 2400 MA Alphen Rij Netherlands. **Tel** 011 31 1720 66633.

LC N7 .L3 **ISSN** 1130-5762
DD 700/.5 SP

LABORATORIO DE ARTE : REVISTA DEL DEPARTAMENTO DE HISTORIA DEL ARTE. Added/Corp Universidad de Sevilla. Departamento de Historia del Arte. No. 1 (1988)-. Spanish (summaries and/or abstracts in English). One time a year. Universidad de Sevilla / Secretariado de Publicaciones, Valparaiso 5, 41013 Seville Spain. **Tel** 011 34 5 4231958, 011 34 5 4235976.
Ind/Abst BHA : Biblio. Hist. Art.

LC N6916 .L3 **ISSN** 0393-0807
DD 709/.45 IT

LABYRINTHOS. [Labyrinthos]. (Jan.-Dec. 1982)-. Periodical. English (Italian). Two times a year. L102190. Le Lettere, Costa San Giorgio 28, 50125 Florence Italy. **Tel** 011 39 55 2342710. **(Subscription address:** Licosa s.p.a., PO Box 552, 50125 Florence Italy. **Tel** 011 39 55 645415.**) Bk Rev. Ad Acc. Circ:** 1,500.
Desc: This historical review has been conceived primarily to provide a philological study and critical interpretation of arts and aesthetics from the Middle Ages through the 19th Century.
Ind/Abst Avery Index Archit. Period. Suppl. Colum. Univ. (19??-199?); BHA : Biblio. Hist. Art.

LC N8 .L3 **ISSN** 0458-6506
II

LALIT KALA. Added/Corp Lalit Kala Akademi. No. 1/2 (Apr. 1955/Mar. 1956)-. English. One time a year. $15.00. Lalit Kala Akademi, Rabindra Bhavan, New Delhi 1 India. **(Subscription address:** Prints India, 11 Darya Ganj, New Delhi 110002 India. **Tel** 011 91 11 3268645, FAX 011 91 11 3275542, telex 31-61087 PRIN-IN.)

LC N1 .L3 **ISSN** 0023-7396
II

LALIT KALA CONTEMPORARY. Added/Corp Lalit Kala Akademi. No. 1 (June 1962)-. Periodical. English. One time a year. $1.86. Lalit Kala Akademi, Rabindra Bhavan, New Delhi 1 India. **(Subscription address:** Prints India, 11 Darya Ganj, New Delhi 110002 India. **Tel** 011 91 11 3268645, FAX 011 91 11 3275542, telex 31-61087 PRIN-IN.)

LC NX **ISSN** 0212-1700
DD 700 SP

LAPIZ : REVISTA MENSUAL DE ARTE. Spanish (English). Twelve times a year. $88.82. Ediciones Ele SA, Garvina 10 Ste 1, 28004 Madrid Spain. **Tel** 011 34 1 5222972, FAX 011 91 5224707. Index available. cum. index. **Bk Rev. Ad Acc.** ctrl circ.
Desc: Concerned with the status of the various arts in contemporary culture. Includes essays on general subjects in modern aesthetics and interviews and reviews on today's artistic development.

ISSN 0889-4566
DD 791 US
LATEST COMPOSITE FEATURE RELEASE SCHEDULE. [Latest compos. feature release sched.]. (19??)-. English. Twelve times a year. $140.00. Exhibitor Relations Co., Inc., 116 North Robertson Boulevard, Suite 606, Los Angeles CA 90048. **Tel** (310)657-2005, FAX (310)657-7283.

LC N6502 .L37 **ISSN** 1042-9808
DD 709/.8/05 US
TITLE CHANGE
LATIN AMERICAN ART. [Lat. Am. art]. Vol. 1, No. 1 (Spring 1989)-(19??). Periodical. English. Latin American Art Magazine, PO Box 9888, 7824 East Lewis Street, Scottsdale AZ 85257. **Tel** (602)947-8422, FAX (602)947-8947. **ED** Juliana Murphy Campbell. ***Continued by** Artworld.*
Ind/Abst BHA : Biblio. Hist. Art; Hisp. Am. Period. Index, HAPI.

LC N6995.L3 L35 **ISSN** 0362-7047
DD 702 US
LATVJU MAKSLA. **Added/Corp** American Latvian Association in the United States. Latviesu Instituts. (May 1975)-. Latvian. Irregular. American Latvian Association, Box 4578, Rockville MD 20849.

LC NX
DD 700 SP
LECTURAS DE HISTORIA DEL ARTE. **Added/Corp** EPHIALTE, Instituto de Estudios Conograficos. No. 1 (1989)-. Periodical. Spanish (Portuguese). Every 2 years. $30.18. Instituto Ephialte, Apartado 721, Vitoria Gasteiz Spain. **Tel** 011 34 45 161501, FAX 011 34 45 161505. **Circ:** 1,000 (ctrl).
Desc: Contains articles about the history of art.

LC NX **ISSN** 0024-0257
DD 708.2 UK
LEEDS ARTS CALENDAR. [Leeds arts cal.]. **Added/Corp** Leeds (England). Libraries and Arts Committee. Leeds (England). Leisure Services Committee. Leeds (England). Amenities Committee. Leeds Art Collections Fund. No. 1 (1947)-. Periodical. English. Two times a year. Leeds Arts Collections Fund, Temple Newsam House, Leeds 15, Yorkshire United Kingdom. **ED** Anthony Wells-Cole. **Ad Acc. Circ:** 475. available on microfilm from University Microfilms International (UMI); available with illustrations.
Ind/Abst Archit. Period. Index (1977-1983); ARTbibliogr. Mod. (1980-).

LC N5 .L45 **ISSN** 0169-4855
DD 705 NE
LEIDS KUNSTHISTORISCH JAARBOEK. [Leids kunsthist. jaarb.]. **Added/Corp** Rijksuniversiteit te Leiden. Kunsthistorisch Instituut. Stichting Leids Kunsthistorisch Jaarboek. **VFOAT** LKJ; L.K.J. Vol. 1 (1982)-. Monographic series. Dutch (English and German). Irregular. Price varies per volume. Uitgeversgroep Combo, Postbus 1, NE 3740 AA Baarn Netherlands. **Tel** 011 31 215482411.
Ind/Abst BHA : Biblio. Hist. Art.

LC N6490 .L42 **ISSN** 0024-094X
DD 705 UK
CCC
CODEN LEONDP
LEONARDO (OXFORD). (LEONARDO.). [Leonardo]. **Added/Corp** International Society for the Arts, Sciences, and Technology. Vol. 1, No. 1 (Jan. 1968)-. Periodical. English (French; summaries and/or abstracts in French). Six times a year. $320.00. Massachusetts Institute of Technology (MIT) Press, 55 Hayward Street, Cambridge MA 02142. **Tel** (617)253-2889, (617)625-8481, FAX (617)258-6779. **ED** Roger Malina. available on microfilm and microfiche from University Microfilms International (UMI); and Microfilms International Marketing Corp. Documents available from The Genuine Article, Ask*IEEE. ***Continues** Leonardo Music Journal, 0961-1215.*
Desc: For artists and others interested in the contemporary arts and music. Features articles written by artists about their own work, discussions of new concepts, materials and techniques, and subjects of general artistic interest. Focuses on the visual arts and addresses media, music, kinetic, performance, language, environmental and conceptual arts, especially as they relate to the visual arts.
Ind/Abst Abstr. Hum. Comput. Interact.; Art Archaeol. Tech. Abstr.; Art Index; ARTbibliogr. Mod.; Arts Humanit. Citation Index [Full Cov.]; Avery Index Archit. Period. Suppl. Colum. Univ. (1989); BHA : Biblio. Hist. Art; Curr. Cit.; Curr. Contents Arts Humanit.; HILITES; INSPEC (1987-); Math. Rev.; Res. Alert [Full Cov.]; RILM Abstr.; Romant. Move.

LC N8602 .L46 **ISSN** 0747-6566
DD 707/.5/0973 US
LEONARD'S ANNUAL PRICE INDEX OF ART AUCTIONS. Vol. 2 (1981/82 Auction Season)-. English. One time a year. $245.00. Auction Index Inc, 30 Valentine Park, Newton MA 02165. **Tel** (617)964-2876, FAX (617)969-9912. ***Continues** Leonard's Annual Index of Art Auctions, 0733-5342.*

LC BV652.95 **ISSN** 0891-3927
DD 254 US
LET THE PEOPLE WORSHIP. See Religions and Theology.

LC Z5961.R9 V823 N6981
RU
LETOPIS IZOIZDANII. **Added/Corp** Gosudarstvennyi Komitet Soveta Ministrov SSSR po Delam Izdatelstv, Poligrafii i Knizhnoi Torgovli. Gosudarstvennyi Komitet SSSR po Delam Izdatelstv, Poligrafii i Knizhnoi Torgovli. Vsesoiuznaia Knizhnaia Palata. (1976)-. Periodical. Russian. Twelve times a year. $145.95. Izdatelstvo Kniga, 50 Gorky Ulitsa, 125047 Moscow Russia. **(Subscription address:** East View Publications Inc., 3020 Harbor Lane North, Suite 110, Minneapolis MN 55447. **Tel** (800)477-1005, (612)550-0961, FAX (612)559-2931.) ***Continues** Letopis Pecatnykh Proizvedenii Izobrazitelnogo Iskusstva.*

LC DG655.6 .M54a **ISSN** 0390-1009
DD 945/.21 IT
LIBRI E DOCUMENTI, ARCHIVIO STORICO CIVICO E BIBLIOTECA TRIVULZIANA. See History.

LC NX **ISSN** 0202-3253
DD 700 RU
UDC 7.072
LIETUVOS TSR AUKSTUJU MOKYKLU MOKSLO DARBAI: MENOTYRA. [Liet. TSR aukst. mokyklu mokslo darb., Menot.]. (1967)-. Lithuanian. Irregular. Mintis / Ideа, Z Sierakausko 15, Vilnius 2600 Lithuania. **Tel** 011 7 3702 632943.
Ind/Abst BHA : Biblio. Hist. Art.

LC NX **ISSN** 0161-4223
DD 700 US
LIGHTWORKS. (1975)-. Periodical. English. Irregular. $25.00, $5.00 (sample issue). Lightworks Magazine Inc, PO Box 1202, Birmingham MI 48012-1202. **Tel** (313)626-8026. **ED** Charlton Burch and Gary S. Vasilash. **Bk Rev. Circ:** 2,000 (ctrl).
Desc: Explores and challenges traditional notions of art. Presents art, de facto, in addition to histories of the avant-garde. A brochure describing back issues is available.

LC NX **ISSN** 0733-8503
DD 700 US
LINK (CLEVELAND, OHIO). (LINK : THE CLEVELAND INSTITUTE OF ART NEWSLETTER.). **Added/Corp** Cleveland Institute of Art. Vol. 1 (1966)-. Newsletter. English. Three times a year. Cleveland Institute of Art, 11141 East Boulevard University Circle, Cleveland OH 44106.

LC PN4 .L46 **ISSN** 0024-4627
DD 830 GW
LITERAT, DER. See Literature.

LC NX **ISSN** 0141-335X
DD 700 UK
LITERATURE OF ART, THE. **VAT** Lit. Art. (1978)-. English. Twelve times a year. $12.00. Art Book Company, 18 Endell Street United Kingdom.

LC NX **ISSN** 1154-5445
DD 700 SZ
UDC 73/75
LIVRE INTERNATIONAL DES VENTES PARIS, LE. [Livre int. ventes Paris]. (1990)-. French. One time a year (Feb.). $264.02. Editions Acatos, Avenue Villamont 17, CH-1005 Lausanne Switzerland. **Tel** 011 41 21 3120652, FAX 011 41 21 3129108. **(Subscription address:** Servedit, 15 rue Victor Cousin, 75005 Paris France. **Tel** 011 33 1 44414930, FAX 011 33 1 43257741.) ***Continues** Annuaire International des Ventes (Paris), 1154-5437.*

LC N582.L7 A32 **ISSN** 0197-5021
DD 708.194/94 US
LOS ANGELES COUNTY MUSEUM OF ART REPORT. See Museums and Galleries.

LC NX511.C65 L67
DD 700 US
LOST AND FOUND TIMES. No. 1 (Aug. 1975)-. Periodical. English. Two times a year. $20.00. Luna Bisonte Productions, 137 Leland Avenue, Columbus OH 43214. **ED** John Bennett. **Ad Acc. Circ:** 350.
Desc: Covers avante-garde literature and art.

ISSN 1192-7097
DD 709/.714/1605 CN
•**LUBIE (CHICOUTIMI).** (LUBIE : LE JOURNAL CULTUREL.). [Lubie]. **VFOAT** LUBIE. Vol. 1, No. 1 (May/June 1993)-. Periodical. French. Twelve times a year. 37.40Can$. LUBIE, 397 rue Racine Est, Chicoutimi Quebec G7H 1S8 Canada. **Tel** (418)698-1454.

LC N8610 .L9
DD 707/.5 UK
LYLE OFFICIAL ARTS REVIEW, THE. 1 (1975)-. English. One time a year. $29.01. Lyle Publications, Glenmayne Galashiels Selkirkshire, Scotland United Kingdom. **Tel** 011 44 8962005.

ISSN 0704-6189
DD 707/.1/07127 CN
M A A E BULLETIN. **Main/Corp** Manitoba Association for Art Education. **VAT** Manitoba Association for Art Education Bulletin. No. 1 (Jan. 1977)-. Bulletin. English. Three times a year. 12.01Can$. Manitoba Association for Art Education, 4A 220 Hugo Street North, Winnipeg Manitoba R3M 2N3 Canada. **(Subscription address:** Manitoba Teachers Society, 191 Harcourt Street, Winnipeg Manitoba R3J 3H2, Canada. **Tel** (204)888-7961 ext. 221.) ***Supersedes** Manitoba Association for Art Education. MAAE Newsletter., 0315-6982.*

ISSN 0229-7477
DD 707 CN
M.A.A.E. JOURNAL. [M.A.A.E. j.]. **Added/Corp** Manitoba Association for Art Education. Manitoba Teachers' Society. **VAT** Manitoba Association for Art Education Journal. Vol. 1, No. 1 (Winter 1980)-. Periodical. English. Three times a year. 15.00Can$. Manitoba Teachers Society, 191 Harcourt Street, Winnipeg Manitoba R3J 3H2 Canada. **Tel** (204)888-7961 ext.254, FAX (204)831-0877.

LC NA9335 **ISSN** 0192-2491
DD 725.94 US
M B NEWS. **Main/Corp** Monument Builders of North America. **VAT** Monument Builders News. Vol. 34 (Jan. 1977)-. Trade Publication. English. Twelve times a year. $45.00. Monument Builders of North America, 1740 Ridge Avenue, Evanston IL 60201. **Tel** (708)869-2031. ***Continues** Monument Builder News.*

LC NX **ISSN** 0819-9000
DD 700 AT
M.O.C.A. BULLETIN. **VFOAT** Museum of Contemporary Art Bulletin. (1987)-. Bulletin. English. Twelve times a year. 36.00Aus$ Australia; 48.00Aus$ other. Museum of Contemporary Art / Australia, 8 Petrie Terrace, Brisbane Queensland 4000 Australia. **Tel** 011 61 7 3683228, FAX 011 61 7 3683224. **ED** J. Baker. **Bk Rev. Ad Acc, Adv Mgr:** E. Camp. **Circ:** 400.

ISSN 0821-2422
DD 706/.0715 CN
MAA NEWS. (MAA NEWS / MARITIME ART ASSOCIATION.). [MAA news]. **Main/Corp** Maritime Art Association. (197?)-. Periodical. English. Maritime Art Association, 12 Plymouth Road, Dartmouth Nova Scotia B2X 1X5 Canada.

ISSN 0824-6297
DD 707/.4/0971244 CN
MACKENZIE OUTREACH. [Mackenzie outreach]. **Main/Corp** Norman Mackenzie Art Gallery. (1982)-. English. One time a year. Norman MacKenzie Art Gallery, 3475 Albert Street, Regina Saskatchewan S4S 6X6 Canada. **Tel** (306)522-4242, FAX (306)569-8191. ***Continues** Norman MacKenzie Art Gallery. Community Programme, 0707-770X.*

LC NE892.C2 N38a **ISSN** 0228-7749
DD 769.971/074/011384 CN
MADE IN CANADA. ARTISTS IN BOOKS. (MADE IN CANADA.). [Made Can., Artists books]. **Main/Corp** National Library of Canada. **VFOAT** Artists in Books. (1981)-. English (French). National Library of Canada, 395 Wellington Street, Ottawa Ontario K1A 0N4 Canada. **Tel** (819)995-7969, (819)994-6881, FAX (819)991-0291. available on audiocassette; available in braille; available in large print.
Desc: Covers artists' illustrated books.

ISSN 0844-1707
DD 709/.714 CN
MAGAZIN'ART (WESTMOUNT). (MAGAZIN' ART.). [Magazin'art]. (1988)-. Periodical. French (summaries and/or abstracts in English). Four times a year (Mar., June, Sept., Dec.). 30.42Can$. Editart International Ltee, CP 4066 Succ West-Mont, Westmont Quebec H3Z 2X3 Canada. **Tel** (514)931-3098. **ED** Jacques Latulippe (editor's phone: (514)668-9552). **Ad Acc. Circ:** 7,000 (ctrl). Documents available.

LC N400
DD 708 HU
MAGYAR NEMZETI GALERIA EVKONYVE. **Main/Corp** Magyar Nemziti Galeria. **VFOAT** Annales de la Galerie Nationale Hongroise. No. 1- 1970-. Periodical. Multiple languages (French and Hungarian). Magyar Nemzeti Galeria Evkonyve, PO Box 149, 1389 Budapest Hungary. ***Continues** Magyar Nemzeti Galeria Kozlemenyei, 0524-8671.*
Ind/Abst BHA : Biblio. Hist. Art.

LC N8554 .M89 **ISSN** 0866-4013
HU
MAGYAR RESTAURALAS. **Added/Corp** Kozponti Muzeumi Igazgatosag (Hungary). **VFOAT** Restauralas. Vol. 1 (1991)-. Periodical. Hungarian. Kozponti Muzeumi Igazgatosag, Muzeumi Informacios Kozpont, H-1050, Budapest PF 58 Hungary. ***Continues** Muzeumi Mutargyvedelem.*

LC DD801.B49 M3
DD 943/.33
ISSN 0076-2725
GW
MAINFRANKISCHES JAHRBUCH FUER GESCHICHTE UND KUNST. [Mainfrank. Jahrb. Gesch. Kunst]. **Added/Corp** Freunde Mainfrankischer Kunst und Geschichte. (1949)-. German. One time a year. cum. index. **Supersedes** *Archiv des Historischen Vereins fur Unterfranken und Aschaffenburg.*
Ind/Abst BHA : Biblio. Hist. Art.

LC DD901.M2 M25
ISSN 0076-2792
GW
MAINZER ZEITSCHRIFT. [Mainzer Z.]. Vol. 1 (1906)-. Periodical. German. Irregular. Mainzer Altertumsverein, Rheimallee 3 6, D-55116 Mainz Germany. **Tel** 011 49 6131 122660. **Supersedes** *Mainzer Altertumsverein. Zeitschrift.*
Ind/Abst BHA : Biblio. Hist. Art.

LC AS587.A1 R58a
SU
MAJALLAT KULLIYAT AL-ADAB, JAMIAT AL-MALIK SAUD. **Added/Corp** Jamiat al-Malik Saud. Kulliyat al-Adab. **VFOAT** Journal of the College of Arts, King Saud University. (1982)-. Periodical. Arabic (English). Two times a year. $10.00. cum. index. **Continues** *Jamiat al-Riyad. Kulliyat al-Adab. Majallat Kulliyat al-Adab.*
Ind/Abst MLA Int. Bibl. Books Artic. Mod. Lang. Lit.

LC NB1 .S37
DD 730
ISSN 1079-8811
US
●MAQUETTE (WASHINGTON, D.C.). (MAQUETTE.). [Maquette]. **Added/Corp** International Sculpture Center. (Jan. 1993)-. Periodical. English. Ten times a year. $55.00 comes with membership. International Sculpture Center / Washington, DC, 1050 17th Street, Suite 250, Washington DC 20036. **Tel** (202)785-1144, **FAX** (202)785-0810. **Continues** *Sculpture Maquette.*

LC N9 .M3
DD 705
ISSN 0342-121X
GW
MARBURGER JAHRBUCH FUER KUNSTWISSENSCHAFT. [Marbg. Jahrb. Kunstwiss.]. **Added/Corp** Philipps-Universitat Marburg. Kunstgeschichtliches Seminar. Vol. 1 (1924)-. Monographic series. German. One time a year. ice varies per Volume. Verlag des Kunstgeschichtlich, 3550 Marburg/Lahn Ernst-von-Hulsen-Haushau, D35037 Marburg Lahn Germany. **Tel** 011 49 642 283600. **ED** Richard Hamann and others.
Ind/Abst ARTbibliogr. Mod.; Avery Index Archit. Period. Suppl. Colum. Univ. (19??-199?); BHA : Biblio. Hist. Art.

LC E159.5 .M28
DD 973/.005
ISSN 0277-8726
US
MARKERS. (MARKERS : THE ANNUAL JOURNAL OF THE ASSOCIATION FOR GRAVESTONE STUDIES.). [Markers]. **Added/Corp** Association for Gravestone Studies. Vol 1 (1979/80 Ed.)-. Monographic series. English. One time a year. $32.50. Association for Gravestone Studies / AGS Publications, 30 Elm Street, Worcester MA 01609. **Tel** (508)831-7753. **ED** Theodore Chase. Index available. **Circ:** 500-1,000.
Desc: A scholarly journal, featuring articles on carvers of gravestones, art and symbols, and procedures recommended for the documentation of data and preservation.
Ind/Abst Am. Hist. Life (1979-); MLA Int. Bibl. Books Artic. Mod. Lang. Lit.

LC M
DD 780
UDC 78
ISSN 0985-3286
FR
MARSYAS PARIS. (MARSYAS. REVUE TRIMESTRIELLE DE PEDAGOGIE MUSICALE ET CHOREOGRAPHIQUE). [Marsyas Paris]. (1987)-. Periodical. French. Four times a year. $68.55. Paris Institute Pedagogie Musicale & Chor, 211 Avenue Jean Jaures, 75019 Paris France. **Tel** 011 33 1 42412454, **FAX** 011 33 1 42412510.

LC CC135 .M34
DD 702/.8/805
US
MATERIALS ISSUES IN ART AND ARCHAEOLOGY. **Added/Corp** Materials Research Society. (1988)-. Periodical. English. Every 2 years. $57.00 (members), $65.00 (nonmembers) US; $73.00 (nonmembers) other. Materials Research Society, 9800 McKnight Road, Suite 327, Pittsburgh PA 15237-6006. **Tel** (412)367-3003, **FAX** (412)367-4373.

DD 704/.042/097105
ISSN 1182-6169
CN
MATRIART (TORONTO). (MATRIART.). [Matriart]. **Added/Corp** Women's Art Resource Centre. (Spring 1990)-. Periodical. English. Four times a year. 24.01Can$. Women's Art Resource Centre, 80 Spadina Avenue, Suite 506, Toronto Ontario M5V 2J3 Canada. **Tel** (416)861-0074, **FAX** (416)861-1441. **ED** Linda Abrahams (editor's phone: (416)861-1920). **Bk Rev. Ad Acc.**
Desc: A Canadian feminist art journal; covers contemporary women's art and cultural production.

DD 741
ISSN 1058-7055
US
MC SQUARED (PISCATAWAY, N.J.). (MC SQUARED.). Vol. 1, No. 1 (July 1991)-. Periodical. English. Four times a year. POSRO Inc., PO Box 261, Piscataway NJ 08855.

LC N9 .C6
ISSN 0085-3208
DK
MEDDELELSER FRA NY CARLSBERG GLYPTOTEK. [Medd. Ny Carlsberg Glyptotek]. **Main/Corp** Ny Carlsberg Glyptotek. (1944)-. Danish. One time a year.
Ind/Abst BHA : Biblio. Hist. Art.

LC N1925 .A55
ISSN 0085-7262
DK
MEDDELELSER FRA THORVALDSENS MUSEUM. [Medd. Thorvaldsens Mus.]. **Added/Corp** Thorvaldsens Museum. **VFOAT** Thorvaldsen Museum Bulletin; Bulletin. (1929)-. Bulletin. Danish (summaries and/or abstracts in English, French, German and Norwegian).
Ind/Abst BHA : Biblio. Hist. Art.

LC NX
DD 770
ISSN 0106-469X
DK
MEDDELELSER OM KONSERVERING. [Medd. konserv.]. **Main/Corp** International Institute for Conservation of Historic and Artistic Works. Nordisk Konservatorforbund. Vol. 1 (1965)-. Danish (Swedish and Norwegian; summaries and/or abstracts in English and German).
Ind/Abst BHA : Biblio. Hist. Art.

LC DJ1 .N26
ISSN 0169-6572
NE
MEDEDELINGEN VAN HET NEDERLANDS INSTITUUT TE ROME. [Meded. Ned. Inst. Rome]. Vol. 36 (1974)-. Dutch (English, French, German and Italian). Irregular. Price varies. Van Gorcum & Company BV, PO Box 43, NL 9400 AA Assen Netherlands. **Tel** 011 31 5920 46846, **FAX** 011 31 5920 72064. **Continues** *Mededelingen van het Nederlandsch Historisch Instituut te Rome.*
Ind/Abst BHA : Biblio. Hist. Art.

LC BH8.C4 M43
DD 111/.85
CC
MEI HSUEH / CHUNG-KUO SHE HUI KO HSUEH YUAN CHE HSUEH YEN CHIU SO MEI HSUEH YEN CHIU SHIH, SHANG-HAI WEN I CHU PAN SHE WEN I LI LUN PIEN CHI SHIH HO PIEN. **VFOAT** Mei Xue. Vol. 1 (Nov. 1979)-. Periodical. Chinese. RMBY1.70. Hsin Hua Shu Tien / Shang-Hai Fa Hsing So, Shanghai, People's Republic of China.

LC N7340 .M44
CC
MEI SHU. **VFOAT** Meishu; Fine Arts. (March 1976)-. Chinese. Twelve times a year. $83.20. **(Subscription address:** China International Book Trading Corporation, PO Box 399, Library Service Department, Beijing 100044 People's Republic of China. **Tel** 011 86 1 8414284, **FAX** 011 86 1 8412023, telex 22496 CIBTC CN.**)**

LC N8.C5 M413
HK
MEI SHU CHIA. = ARTIST. **VFOAT** Artist. (April 1978)-. Periodical. Chinese. Six times a year. Artist Publishing Co., 2F, Hong Kong Diamond Exchange Building, 8-10 Duddell Street, Hong Kong Hong Kong.

LC N8.C5 M425
DD 700
CC
MEI SHU SHIH LUN TSUNG KAN. **Added/Corp** Chung-Kuo i Shu Yen Chiu Yuan. Mei Shu Yen Chiu So. **VFOAT** Mei Shu Shi Lun. Vol. 1 (Aug. 1981)-. Periodical. Chinese. Four times a year. $28.70 (surface mail), $52.00 (airmail). **(Subscription address:** China International Book Trading Corporation, PO Box 399, Library Service Department, Beijing 100044 People's Republic of China. **Tel** 011 86 1 8414284, **FAX** 011 86 1 8412023, telex 22496 CIBTC CN.**)**

LC N8.C5 M426
DD 705
CC
MEI SHU TSUNG HENG / CHUNG-KUO MEI SHU CHIA HSIEH HUI CHIANG-SU FEN HUI PIEN. **Added/Corp** Chung-kuo Mei Shu Chia Hsieh Hui. Chiang-su Fen Hui. Vol. 1 (Jan. 1982)-. Periodical. Chinese. Chin Ling Shu Hua She, Nan-Ching, People's Republic of China.

LC N8.C5 M45
DD 705
CC
MEI SHU YEN CHIU. **Added/Corp** Chung Yang Mei Shu Hsueh Yuan (China). **VFOAT** Mei Shu Yan Jiu; Meishuyanjiu. (19??)-. Periodical. Chinese. Four times a year. $15.30. **(Subscription address:** China International Book Trading Corporation, PO Box 399, Library Service Department, Beijing 100044 People's Republic of China. **Tel** 011 86 1 8414284, **FAX** 011 86 1 8412023, telex 22496 CIBTC CN.**)**
Desc: Contains art research.

DD 700/.9714
ISSN 0835-4588
CN
MEMO'ART. (MEMO'ART : BULLETIN D'INFORMATION DE LA DIRECTION DES SERVICES AUX ARTISTES.). [Memo'art]. Vol. 1, No. 1 (1987)-. Bulletin. French. Ministere Affaires Culturelles, 225 Grande Allee Est, Quebec Quebec G1R 5G5 Canada.

LC NX
DD 770
ISSN 0188-1744
MX
MEMORIA. **Added/Corp** Museo Nacional de Arte (Mexico). No. 1 (1989)-. Periodical. Spanish. Two times a year.
Ind/Abst BHA : Biblio. Hist. Art.

LC N6535.N5 M47
DD 709/.747/1
ISSN 0279-4977
US
METROPOLIS (NEW YORK, N.Y.). (METROPOLIS.). [Metropolis]. Vol. 1, No. 1 (July 1981)-. Periodical. English. Ten times a year. $28.00. Bellerophon Publications Inc., 177 East 87th Street, New York NY 10128. **Tel** (212)722-5515, (212)722-5050. **(Subscription address:** Metropolis, PO Box 5052, Vandalia OH 45377-5052. **Tel** (800)344-3046.**)**
Ind/Abst Access (1992-); ARTbibliogr. Mod.; Avery Index Archit. Period. Suppl. Colum. Univ. (1990-); Curr. Cit.

LC N610 .A725
DD 708.1471
ISSN 0077-8958
US
METROPOLITAN MUSEUM JOURNAL. **See** Museums and Galleries.

LC NX
DD 770
ISSN 0185-4569
MX
MEXICO EN EL ARTE (MEXICO CITY, MEXICO). (MEXICO EN EL ARTE.). **Added/Corp** Instituto Nacional de Bellas Artes (Mexico). New Series, 1 (Summer 1983)-. Periodical. Spanish. Inba Direccion de Literatura, San Juan de Letran No 2, 3er Piso Torre, Latinoamericana, Mexico 1 DF Mexico.
Ind/Abst BHA : Biblio. Hist. Art; Hisp. Am. Period. Index, HAPI.

DD C840/.8
ISSN 0705-0437
CN
MILLE PLUMES. (Winter 1978)-. Periodical. French. Four times a year. Mille Plumes, CP 693 Succursale N, Montreal Quebec H2X 3N4 Canada.

LC NX
DD 770
ISSN 0076-910X
US
MINNEAPOLIS INSTITUTE OF ARTS BULLETIN, THE. [Minneap. Inst. Arts bull.]. **Main/Corp** Minneapolis Institute of Arts. **Added/Corp** Minneapolis Society of Fine Arts. Vol. 44, No. 5 (Sept. 1955)-. Bulletin. English. Irregular. Price varies. Minneapolis Institute of Arts, 2400 3rd Avenue South, Minneapolis MN 55404. **Tel** (612)870-3175. **ED** Sandra Lipschultz and Elisabeth Sovik. Index available. **Circ:** 15,000 (ctrl). available on microfilm and microfiche from University Microfilms International (UMI). **Continues** *Minneapolis Institute of Arts. Bulletin.*
Ind/Abst Art Index; ARTbibliogr. Mod.; BHA : Biblio. Hist. Art.

LC NX
DD 770
ISSN 1060-3107
US
MINNESOTA ARTS DIRECTORY. **Added/Corp** St. Paul Art Collective (Minneapolis, Minn.). (1991)-. Directory. English. **Continues** *Minnesota Regional Arts Directory.*

LC NX512.2 .M55
DD 700/.973
ISSN 0148-1037
US
SUSPENDED
MINORITY VOICES. **See** Ethnic Interests.

LC WMLC L 83/5315
DD 708
ISSN 0540-3391
HU
MISKOLCI HERMAN OTTO MUZEUM KOZLEMENYEI, A. **See** Museums and Galleries.

LC N8.K6 6M580
KO
MISUL SEGYE. **VFOAT** Art World. First issue Oct. 1984-. Periodical. Korean (Korean). Twelve times a year. W3,300. Kyongin Misulgwan, 30-1 Kwanhun-dong Chongno-ku, Seoul Korea.

LC N14
AU
MITTEILUNGEN DER GESELLSCHAFT FUER VERGLEICHENDE KUNSTFORSCHUNG IN WIEN. (Sept. 1948)-. Periodical. German. Three times a year.
Ind/Abst ARTbibliogr. Mod.; BHA : Biblio. Hist. Art.

LC N25 .V45a
DD 709/.436
ISSN 0083-615X
AU
MITTEILUNGEN DER OESTERREICHISCHEN GALERIE. [Mitt. oesterr. Galerie]. **Main/Corp** Oesterreichische Galerie. **Added/Corp** Austria. Bundesministerium fuer Wissenschaft und Forschung. Vol. 1 No. 1 (1957)-. German. One time a year.
Ind/Abst BHA : Biblio. Hist. Art.

The Arts — Art

LC NX
DD 770
ISSN 0342-1201
IT
MITTEILUNGEN DES KUNSTHISTORISCHES INSTITUTES FLORENZ. [Mitt. Kunsthist. Inst. Florenz]. **Main/Corp** Kunsthistorisches Institut in Florenz. Vol. 1 (1908)-. Periodical. German (Italian and English). Irregular. DM197.50. Kunsthistorisches Institute, Via Giuseppe, Giusti 44, 50122 Florence Italy. **Tel** 011 39 55 2479161. Index available. **Circ:** 800 (ctrl). Documents available from The Genuine Article.
Desc: Italian art.
Ind/Abst Art Index; Arts Humanit. Citation Index [Full Cov.]; Avery Index Archit. Period. Suppl. Colum. Univ. (19??-199?); BHA : Biblio. Hist. Art; Curr. Contents Arts Humanit.; Res. Alert [Full Cov.].

LC NX
DD 700
CN
●**MIX ARTIST RUN CULTURE. Added/Corp** Canadian Association of Non-profit Artist Centres. **VFOAT** National Parallelogramme. (Sept. 1995)-. Periodical. English (French). Four times a year (Mar., June, Sept., Dec.). 20.01Can$. Parallelogramme Artist Run Culture, 401 Richmond Street West, Suite 446, Toronto Ontario M5V 3A8 Canada. **Tel** (416)506-1012, FAX (416)340-8458. **ED** Lynne Fernie and Monika Gagnon. Index available. **Ad Acc**, **Adv Mgr:** AnneMarie Beneteau, **Tel** (416)869-3854. **Circ:** 5,000. available on microfilm. **Continues** Parallelogramme, 0703-8712.
Desc: Informs and stimulates its readership with coverage of the programming, events and issues of Canadian new art. Articles in French and English concentrate on current issues of interest to a Canadian and foreign readership of artists, curators, educators, art administrators and individuals curious about the arts. Includes articles on aesthetics, politics, theory and funding, with special inserts.
Ind/Abst ARTbibliogr. Mod.; BHA : Biblio. Hist. Art.

LC N40 .M63
DD 709/.2/2
ISSN 1052-1712
US
CEASED
MODERN ARTS CRITICISM. [Mod. arts crit.]. **Added/Corp** Gale Research Inc. **VFOAT** MAC. Vol. 1 (1991)-Vol. 4 (19??). English. Gale Research Inc., 835 Penobscot Building, 645 Griswold Street, Detroit MI 48226. **Tel** (800)877-GALE, (313)961-2242, FAX (313)961-6083, (800)414-5043, telex TWX 810-221-7086. **ED** Lawrence Trudeau.
Desc: Presents biographical background and excerpted critical assessments of important visual artists from the late 19th century to the present.

DD 759
ISSN 0738-0429
US
MODERN MASTERS SERIES. [Mod. masters ser.]. **VFOAT** Abbeville Modern Masters. Vol. 1 (1983)-. Monographic series. English. Irregular. Price varies per volume. Abbeville Press Inc, 80 Twelfth Avenue, Building 424, Edison NJ 08837. **Tel** (212)888-1969, FAX (212)644-5085, telex 428141.

LC N6480 .M63
DD 705
ISSN 0953-6698
UK
MODERN PAINTERS (LONDON, ENGLAND). (MODERN PAINTERS.). [Mod. paint.]. Vol. 1, No. 1 (Spring 1988)-. Periodical. English. Four times a year. $50.00. Central Books Ltd., 99 Wallis Road, London E9 5LN United Kingdom. **Tel** 011 44 181 9864854, FAX 011 44 181 5335821. **ED** Peter Fuller and Karen Wright. **Bk Rev**. **Ad Acc**. **Circ:** 15,000.
Desc: Articles on contemporary visual arts, architecture and aesthetics.
Ind/Abst BHA : Biblio. Hist. Art; EP Collect.; Homework Help.; MasterFile FullTEXT 1000; MasterFile FullTEXT 350; MasterFile FullTEXT 650; MasterFile FullTEXT; OCLC; Telebase; World Mag. Bank.

LC NX
DD 700
UK
CEASED
MODERN SCOTTISH PAINTERS. (19??)-(19??). Monographic series. English. Edinburgh University Press Ltd., 22 George Square, Edinburgh EH8 9LF United Kingdom. **Tel** 011 44 131 6506207, FAX 011 44 131 6620053.

LC NA5 .M6
BL
SUSPENDED
MODULO. (Mar. 1955)- Suspended (1989). Periodical. Portuguese (English and German). Modulo Arte e Kultura, Rua Conde de Lages 25, 20241 Rio de Janeiro Brazil. **Tel** 011 55 21 2311844, FAX 011 55 21 2226445.
Ind/Abst Archit. Period. Index.

LC DR913 .M66
AA
MONUMENTET. See Architecture.

LC DG11 .M6
IT
MONUMENTI ANTICHI. SERIE MISCELLANEA. See Architecture.

LC DG11 .M63
IT
MONUMENTI ANTICHI. SERIE MONOGRAFICA / ACCADEMIA NAZIONALE DEI LINCEI. See Architecture.

LC NA6400
DD 725.4
UDC 7.025(443.63)
ISSN 0540-8539
FR
MONUMENTS HISTORIQUES DE SEINE ET MARNE. See Architecture.

LC DB901 .S93
ISSN 0563-0525
HU
MORA FERENC MUZEUM EVKONYVE, A. See Museums and Galleries.

LC NA6 .A7276
ISSN 0868-7110
RU
CODEN MOZHE8
MOSKOVSKII ZHURNAL. See Architecture.

LC N9 .M8
ISSN 0077-1899
GW
MUNCHNER JAHRBUCH DER BILDENDEN KUNST. [Munch. jahrb. bild. kunst]. **Added/Corp** Bayerischer Verein der Kunstfreunde (Museumsverein) Kunstwissenschaftliche Gesellschaft in Munchen. Staatliche Kunstsammlungen, Munchen. Zentralinstitut fuer Kunstgeschichte in Munchen. (1906)-. Periodical. German. One time a year. Prestel Verlag, Mandlstrasse 26, D-80802 Munich Germany. **Tel** 011 49 89 38170001, FAX 011 49 89 38170935, telex 5216366. **ED** Saskia Durian Ress and Kourad Renger. cum. index.
Desc: Essays on art, listing of new acquisitions. The yearbook of the state museums in Munich.
Ind/Abst Art Index; ARTbibliogr. Mod.; BHA : Biblio. Hist. Art.

LC DP532 .M86
ISSN 0871-0996
PO
MUNDA : REVISTA DO GRUPO DE ARQUEOLOGIA E ARTE DO CENTRO. See Archaeology.

LC N7 .M75
DD 705
ISSN 0870-6190
PO
MUNDO DA ARTE. [Mundo arte]. (1981)-. Periodical. Portuguese (Spanish). Twelve times a year. 1200$00.
Ind/Abst Avery Index Archit. Period. Suppl. Colum. Univ. (19??-199?).

LC N3 .M93
DD 704.9/482/05
ISSN 0027-299X
GW
MUNSTER (MUNCHEN), DAS. (DAS MUNSTER.). [Munster]. Vol. 1 (July/Aug. 1947)-. Periodical. German (Multiple languages). Four times a year (Feb., May, Aug., Nov.). $50.83. Verlag Schnell & Steiner, Postfach 100928, D-93009 Regensburg Germany. **Tel** 011/49/941/787850, FAX 011/49/941/7878516. Index available (published separately); cum. index. **Bk Rev**, (Qty: 20). **Ad Acc**. **Circ:** 1,700 (ctrl).
Ind/Abst Archit. Period. Index (1960,1977-)(1960-); ARTbibliogr. Mod.; Avery Index Archit. Period. Suppl. Colum. Univ. (1990-); BHA : Biblio. Hist. Art.

LC NX
DD 700
US
MURAL CONSERVANCY OF LOS ANGELES JOURNAL. (19??)-. English. Four times a year (Seasonally). $25.00. Los Angeles Mural Conservancy, PO Box 86244, Los Angeles CA 90086. **ED** Bill Lasarow (editor's phone: (213)481-1186). **Circ:** 1,500. **Continues** Los Angeles Mural Conservancy Journal.

LC N584.M5 A3
DD 708.178/29
ISSN 0077-2194
US
MUSE (COLUMBIA). See Museums and Galleries.

LC N400
DD 708
UDC 069
ISSN 0767-7243
FR
MUSEE CONDE. See Museums and Galleries.

LC DG975.F38 A8a
ISSN 0391-4399
IT
MUSEI FERRARESI. See Museums and Galleries.

LC N714.P7 R495
DD 750
ISSN 0027-4097
US
SUSPENDED
MUSEUM NOTES (PROVIDENCE, R.I.). (MUSEUM NOTES.). [Mus. notes]. **Main/Corp** Rhode Island School of Design. Museum of Art. Vol. 1 (Jan. 1943)-Vol. 78 (1991). Periodical. English. One time a year (Oct.). $7.50. Rhode Island School of Design, 2 College Street, Providence RI 02903. **Tel** (401)454-6542. **ED** Judith A. Singesen. **Circ:** 6,600. **Continues** Rhode Island School of Design. Museum of Art. Bulletin of the Museum of Art.
Desc: A bulletin describing important new acquisitions, exhibitions, lectures, loans and other activities for the past year.
Ind/Abst Art Index; ARTbibliogr. Mod.; BHA : Biblio. Hist. Art.

LC N81 .C45
ISSN 0069-3235
US
MUSEUM STUDIES (CHICAGO, ILL.). (MUSEUM STUDIES.). [Mus. stud.]. **Added/Corp** Art Institute of Chicago. **VFOAT** Art Institute of Chicago Museum Studies. Vol. 1 (1966)-. Periodical. English. Two times a year. $32.00. Art Institute of Chicago, 111 South Michigan Avenue, Chicago IL 60603. **Tel** (312)443-3600, (312)443-3536, FAX (312)443-0849. **ED** Michael Sittenfeld (Editor's Phone: (312)443-4963). **Circ:** 1,400. Documents available from The Genuine Article.
Ind/Abst Am. Hist. Life (1988-); Art Index; ARTbibliogr. Mod.; Arts Humanit. Citation Index (19??-19??) [Full Cov.]; Avery Index Archit. Period. Suppl. Colum. Univ.; BHA : Biblio. Hist. Art; Curr. Contents Arts Humanit.; Res. Alert [Full Cov.]; RILA, Int. Rep. Lit. Art.

LC M
DD 780
ISSN 0892-2721
US
MUSIC OF THE SPHERES. See New Age Publications.

LC N6 .M89
RU
MUZEI. (1980)-. Russian (summaries and/or abstracts in English). 3.60rub. Izdatelstvo Sovetskii Khudozhnik, Ulitsa Cherniakhovskoga 4a, 12319 Moscow Russia.

LC NX
DD 700
UK
NACF MAGAZINE. Main/Corp National Art-Collections Fund (Great Britain). **VAT** National Art-Collections Fund Magazine. No. 26 (Christmas 1984)-. Periodical. English. Three times a year. comes with membership. National Art Collections Fund, 20 John Islip Street, London SW1P 4JX United Kingdom. **Tel** 011 44 171 8210404, FAX 011 44 171 6307715. **Continues** NACF News.

LC NX
DD 770
ISSN 0160-6395
US
NAEA NEWS. Added/Corp National Art Education Association. **VAT** National Art Education Association News. Vol. 13 (Sept. 1970)-. Newspaper. English. Six times a year. Included with subscription to Art Education ($50.00). National Art Education Association, 1916 Association Drive, Reston VA 22091-1590. **Tel** (703)860-8000, FAX (703)860-2960. **Bk Rev**. **Continues** National Art Education Association. Newsletter.
Desc: A newspaper reporting events and activities of the association and the state/province news that affects the profession as a whole. Includes reports of art education developments and activities such as lifelong learning, public policy, minority concerns, etc.

LC N400
DD 708
BN
NASE STARINE. See Architecture.

LC N12 .N3
DD 707/.9
UK
NATIONAL ART-COLLECTIONS FUND REVIEW. Main/Corp National Art-Collections Fund (Great Britain). **VFOAT** Review. (1983)-. English. One time a year. £2.95. National Art Collections Fund, 20 John Islip Street, London SW1P 4JX United Kingdom. **Tel** 011 44 171 8210404, FAX 011 44 171 6307715. **Continues** Annual Report / National Art Collections Fund (Great Britain).
Ind/Abst BHA : Biblio. Hist. Art.

LC N6536 .N36
DD 709/.2/273
ISSN 1043-9900
US
NATIONAL ARTIST SURVEY. [Natl. artist surv.]. (198?)-. English. F&W Publications, 1507 Dana Avenue, Cincinnati OH 45207. **Tel** (513)531-2222, FAX (513)531-1843. (**Subscription address:** CDS Agency Hard Copy, PO Box 4966, Des Moines IA 50340. **Tel** (515)247-7569.)

LC ND1630 .L66a
DD 751.6/2
ISSN 0140-7430
UK
NATIONAL GALLERY TECHNICAL BULLETIN. [Natl. Gallery tech. bull.]. **Main/Corp** Great Britain. National Gallery. (1977)-. Bulletin. English. One time a year (January). $37.50. National Gallery Publications, 5/6 Pall Mall East, London SW1Y 5BA United Kingdom. **Tel** 011 44 171 8398544, FAX 011 44 171 9300108. **Bk Rev**.
Desc: Of direct interest to conservators, art historians and conservation scientists in museums and in the academic world, the Bulletin also includes articles on museological subjects such as lighting and climate control of relevance to managers, architects and designers of exhibition and gallery rooms.
Ind/Abst Art Archaeol. Tech. Abstr.; BHA : Biblio. Hist. Art.

LC NX
DD 700
ISSN 0736-7341
US
NATIONAL NETWORK DIRECTORY. (NATIONAL NETWORK DIRECTORY / WOMEN'S CAUCUS FOR ART.). [Natl. netw. dir.]. **Main/Corp**

Women's Caucus for Art. (Fall 1982)-. Directory. English. WCA National Business Office, 1301 East Monte Vista Road, Phoenix AZ 85006.

LC NX28.G72 N3716 **ISSN** 0142-3487
DD 700/.941 UK
NATIONAL TRUST STUDIES. [Natl. Trust stud.]. **Added/Corp** National Trust (Great Britain). (19??)-. Periodical. English. Irregular. $32.50. Rowman & Littlefield Publishing Inc., 8705 Bollman Place, Savage MD 20763. **Tel** (301)306-0400. **(Subscription address:** University Press of America Inc., 4720 Boston Way, Suite A, Lanham MD 20706. **Tel** (800)462-6420, (301)459-3366.**)** ***Continues** National Trust Yearbook.*
Ind/Abst Archit. Period. Index (1979-); Avery Index Archit. Period. Suppl. Colum. Univ. (19??-199?); BHA : Biblio. Hist. Art; Br. Archaeol. Bibliogr.

LC N25 .G65
RU
NAUCHNYE SOOBSHCHENIIA (MOSCOW, R.S.R.S.R.). (NAUCHNYE SOOBSHCHENIIA.). **Added/Corp** Gosudarstvennyi Muzei Iskusstva Narodov Vostoka. (19??)-. Academic Scholarly Publication. Russian. Izdatelstvo Nauka / Akademiia Nauk, (Publishing House of the Russian Academy of Sciences), Leninskii Porspekt 14, 117901 Moscow Russia. **Tel** 011 95 9542153, FAX 011 95 9382144, telex 411964. ***Continues** Gosudarstvennyi Muzei Iskusstva Narodov Vostoka. Soobshcheniia.*
Ind/Abst Coal Abstr.

LC N5 .N4 **ISSN** 0169-6726
DD 705 NE
NEDERLANDS KUNSTHISTORISCH JAARBOEK. (NEDERLANDS KUNSTHISTORISCH JAARBOEK. NETHERLANDS YEARBOOK FOR HISTORY OF ART.). [Ned. kunsthist. jaarb.]. **VFOAT** Netherlands Yearbook for History of Art. (1947)-. Dutch (summaries and/or abstracts in English). One time a year. Fl.195.00. Waanders Uitgevers, Postbus 1129, 8001 BC Zwolle Netherlands. **Tel** 011 31 38 658628, FAX 038-655989. **ED** Victor Schmidt, Jan de Jong, Dulcia Meyers, Frits Scholten, Herman Rodenburg, Reindert Falkenburg. **Circ:** 600.
Ind/Abst Art Index; ARTbibliogr. Mod.; BHA : Biblio. Hist. Art.

LC N6425.N4 N47
DD 709/.03/4105 IT
SUSPENDED
NEOCLASSICO : SEMESTRALE DI ARTI E CULTURA. **Added/Corp** Archivio Europeo del Neoclassico (Trieste, Italy). (1992)-Suspended (1994). Periodical. Italian. Four times a year. L30660. Marsilio Editori, Marittima Fabbricato 205, 30135 Venice Italy. **Tel** 011 39 41 5227822.

LC NX
DD 770 US
NETWORK NEWS. **Main/Corp** Conservation Information Network. (1987)-. Periodical. English. Four times a year.
Ind/Abst Museum Abstr.

LC N3 **ISSN** 0941-6501
DD 700 GW
UDC 73/76
NEUE BILDENDE KUNST. [Neue bild. Kunst]. (1991)-. Consumer Publication. German. Six times a year. $64.48. Neue Bildende Kunst Red GmbH, D-10371 Berlin Germany. **Tel** 011 49 30 2085103. **ED** Matthias Fluegge. **Bk Rev**. Full Page (B&W) $1200.00. Full Page (Color) $1650.00. **Circ:** 7,000. available with illustrations; available with charts. ***Continues** Bildende Kunst (Dresden), 0006-2391.*
Desc: Devoted to contemporary art. Provides reports, criticism, essays, interviews, news and reviews.
Ind/Abst BHA : Biblio. Hist. Art.

LC NX **ISSN** 0176-7062
DD 700 GW
UDC 7.036.7(430.1-37.6-21)
NEUE KUNST IN MUENCHEN. [Neue Kunst Munch.]. (1980)-. Periodical. German. Irregular. Neue Kunst in Munchen, Maximilianstrasse 43, W-8000 Munich 22 Germany. **Tel** 011 49 89 297729.
Ind/Abst BHA : Biblio. Hist. Art.

ISSN 0886-8115
DD 701 US
NEW ART EXAMINER. [New art exam.]. Vol. 12, No. 10 (Summer 1985)-. Periodical. English. Ten times a year. $35.00. New Art Examiner, 1255 South Wabash, 4th Floor, Chicago IL 60605. **Tel** (312)786-0200, FAX (312)786-1565. **ED** Ann Wiens. **Bk Rev**, (Qty: 6 /yr). **Ad Acc, Adv Mgr:** Art Stone. **Circ:** 5,000. ***Formed by the union of** New Art Examiner (Midwest Edition), 8755-108X **and** New Art Examiner (East Coast Edition).*
Desc: The purpose is to examine the definition and transmission of culture in society through the visual arts while being committed to providing an open forum for diverse viewpoints free of the constraints of the market system.
Ind/Abst Art Index; ARTbibliogr. Mod.; ARTbibliogr. Curr. Titles; Avery Index Archit. Period. Suppl. Colum. Univ. (1990-); BHA : Biblio. Hist. Art; Curr. Cit.

LC WMLC L 83/5729 **ISSN** 0145-8388
DD 810 US
NEW LAUREL REVIEW. **See** Literature.

LC NX504 .N45 **ISSN** 0737-5387
DD 700/.5 US
NEW OBSERVATIONS. (1981)-. Periodical. English (French, German, Italian and Spanish). Six times a year. $22.00. New Observations, 611 Broadway, Suite 701, New York NY 10012. **Tel** (212)677-8561. **ED** Diane Karp. Index available ($3.00). cum. index. **Circ:** 1,200.
Desc: Publishes the art and writing of international artists on topics that reach beyond the parameters of the New York art scene.

ISSN 0893-6005
DD 111 US
Pr Rev.
NEW STUDIES IN AESTHETICS. [New stud. aesthet.]. Vol. 1 (1987)-. Monographic series. English. Irregular. Price varies per volume. Peter Lang Publishing, 62 West 45th Street, 4th Floor, New York NY 10036. **Tel** (212)764-1471, (800)770-5264, FAX (212)302-7574, telex 6973364 PLNY. **ED** Robert Ginsberg.
Desc: Explores the philosophy of art as well as the philosophy of life.

LC NX705.5.U62 N75 **ISSN** 8755-7347
DD 700/.79 US
NEW YORK CITY ARTS FUNDING GUIDE. 1982-. English. Every 2 years. $10.00. Center for Arts Information, 1285 Avenue of the Americas/3rd Floor, New York NY 10019.

LC NX **ISSN** 0743-3522
DD 700 US
NEWS / ART DECO SOCIETY OF NEW YORK. [News - Art Deco Soc. N.Y.]. **Added/Corp** Art Deco Society of New York. **VFOAT** Art Deco News. (198?)-. Periodical. English. Irregular. $35.00 (includes membership and membership bulletin). Art Deco Society of New York, 145 Hudson Street, 7th Floor, New York NY 10013. **Tel** (212)925-4946.

LC NX
DD 700 US
NEWS FROM CHRISTIE'S. **Main/Corp** Christie, Manson & Woods International Inc. (19??)-. Periodical. English. Nine times a year. $15.00. Christie's Catalogues, Catalog Subscription Department, 2124 44th Avenue, Long Island City NY 11101. **Tel** (718)784-1480.

LC N1 .N6347 **ISSN** 0891-3498
DD 750 US
NEWS FROM RILA. **See** The Arts-Abstracting, Bibliographies and Statistics.

LC NX **ISSN** 0703-8704
DD 708/.113 CN
NEWSART (TORONTO). **See** Museums and Galleries.

ISSN 0045-5369
DD 707/.1071 CN
CEASED
NEWSLETTER / CANADIAN SOCIETY FOR EDUCATION THROUGH ART. [Newsl. - Can. Soc. Educ. Art]. **VFOAT** Newsletter of the Canadian Society for Education through Art; CSEA Newsletter; Bulletin de la Societe Canadienne d'Education par l'Art. **VAT** Canadian Society for Education through Art Newsletter. (195?)-(1993). Newsletter. English (French). Canadian Society for Education Through Art, 1487 Parish Lane, Oakville Ontario L6M 2Z6 Canada. **Tel** (905)847-0975.
Desc: Contains items that report on the activities of the Canadian Society for Education through Art, as well as its affiliates across Canada.

LC N400
DD 708 US
NEWSLETTER - DIXON GALLERY AND GARDENS. **See** Museums and Galleries.

LC NX7475 **ISSN** 8755-4593
DD 709 US
NEWSLETTER, EAST ASIAN ART & ARCHAEOLOGY. [Newsl. East Asian art archaeol.]. **Added/Corp** University of Michigan. East Asian Program. **VFOAT** Newsletter, East Asian Art and Archaeology; Newsletter, EAAA; Newsletter, E.A.A.A.; East Asian Art & Archaeology; East Asian Art and Archaeology. (19??)-. Newsletter. English. Three times a year (Jan., May, Sept.). $12.00. Newsletter East Asian Art & Archaeology, University of Michigan, Department of Art History, Tappan Hall, Ann Arbor MI 48109-1357. **Tel** (313)764-5555, FAX (313)747-4121. **ED** Jonathan Reynolds. **Bk Rev. Ad Acc, Adv Mgr:** W. Holden, **Tel** (313)936-2539. **Circ:** 350.
Desc: Information regarding exhibitions, lectures, symposiums, research news, grants, jobs, and publications of East Asian art and archaeology.

ISSN 0228-3484
DD 704/.0397 CN
NEWSLETTER - THE INNUIT GALLERY OF ESKIMO ART. [Newsl. - Innuit Gallery Eskimo Art]. **Main/Corp** Innuit Gallery of Eskimo Art. Jan. 1977-. Newsletter. English. Free. Innuit Gallery of Eskimo Art, 30 Avenue Road, Toronto Ontario M5R 2G2 Canada. ctrl circ.
Ind/Abst Ethnoarts Index.

LC N400 **ISSN** 0733-463X
DD 708 US
NEWSLETTER / TRAVELING EXHIBITION INFORMATION SERVICE. **See** Museums and Galleries.

LC N8554 .W47 **ISSN** 1052-0066
DD 702/.8/8 US
NEWSLETTER - WESTERN ASSOCIATION FOR ART CONSERVATION. (WAAC NEWSLETTER.). [Newsl. - West. Assoc. Art Conserv.]. **Added/Corp** Western Association for Art Conservation. **VFOAT** WAAC Newsletter. **VAT** Western Association for Art Conservation Newsletter. Vol. 9, no. 3 (Sept. 1987)-. Newsletter. English. Three times a year. $25.00. Western Association for Art Conservation, c/o Chris Staurodis, 1272 North Flores Street, Los Angeles CA 90069-2904. **Tel** (213)654-8748, FAX (213)656-3220. **ED** Carolyn Tallent. cum. index. **Bk Rev. Acid Free. Circ:** 420. ***Continues** Western Association for Art Conservation : [Newsletter], 1054-4860.*
Desc: Publishes information for art conservators and others who care for art and cultural material.

LC N8.J28 N53
JA
NICHI-FUTSU BIJUTSU GAKKAI KAIHO. **Added/Corp** Nichi-Futsu Bijutsu Gakkai. **VFOAT** Bulletin de la Societe Franco-Japonaise d'Art et d'Archeologie. No. 1 (July 1981)-. Bulletin. French (Japanese). Nichi-Futsu Bijutsu Gakkai, c/o Nichi-Futsu Kaikan, 2-3 Kanda Surugadai Chiyoda-ku, Tokyo-to 101 Japan. **Tel** 03-291-1141.
Ind/Abst BHA : Biblio. Hist. Art.

LC N3 .N5 **ISSN** 0078-0537
GW
NIEDERDEUTSCHE BEITRAEGE ZUR KUNSTGESCHICHTE. [Niederdtsch. Beitr. Kunstgesch.]. (1961)-. Periodical. German. One time a year. DM65.00. Deutscher Kunstverlag, Postfach 190354, D-80603 Munich Germany. **Tel** 011 49 89 1215160. **(Subscription address:** Deutscher Kunstverlag, PF 800620 Koch Neff & Oetinger, D 70506 Stuttgart Germany. **) ED** Hans Werner Grohn.
Desc: History of art.
Ind/Abst ARTbibliogr. Mod.; Avery Index Archit. Period. Suppl. Colum. Univ. (19??-199?); BHA : Biblio. Hist. Art.

LC NX
DD 700 GW
NIEDERSAECHSISCHE DENKMALPFLEGE. **Added/Corp** Hanover. Niedersaechsisches Landesverwaltungsamt. (1954)-. Periodical. German.
Ind/Abst BHA : Biblio. Hist. Art.

LC NX **ISSN** 0549-401X
DD 700 JA
NIHON NO BIJUTSU. No. 1 (1966)-. Periodical. Japanese. Twelve times a year. $321.00. **(Subscription address:** Maruzen Company Ltd., PO Box 5050, Import & Export Department, Tokyo 100 31 Japan. **Tel** 011 81 3 32789224.**)**

LC NX
DD 708/.113 GW
NIKE. **VFOAT** New Art in Europe. Vol. 3, No. 1 (Dec. 1985 Jan./Feb. 1986)-. Periodical. German (English and French). Five times a year (Mar., May, July, Oct., Dec.). $353.12. Edition & Verlag Gerhard Goetz, Klenzestr 40, D-80455 Munich Germany. **Tel** 011 49 89 2603376, FAX 011 49 89 268139. ***Continues** Neue Kunst in Europa, 0175-0038.*

ISSN 0914-7829
DD 700 JA
NIKKEI ATO. [Nikkei ato]. **VFOAT** Nikkei Art. (1988)-. Trade Publication. Japanese. Twelve times a year. ¥17500. Nihon Keizai Shimbun Inc., 9-5 Otemachi 1 Chome, Chiyoda-ku Tokyo 100 Japan. **Tel** 011 81 3 32700251, 011 81 3 52108502 (Nikkei Business Publications Inc.), FAX 011 81 3 52552661, 011 81 3 52108119 (Nikkei Business Publications Inc.). **Circ:** 16,000. available with illustrations.
Desc: Art market information for collectors and investors, including appraisals for paintings, sculptures, prints, etc.

LC N6450 .N53 **ISSN** 0097-5184
DD 909.81/05 US
NINETEENTH CENTURY. [Ninet. century]. **Added/Corp** Victorian Society in America. **VFOAT** 19C; 19 Century. Vol. 1 (Jan. 1975)-. Periodical. English. Four times a year. Comes with membership. Victorian Society in America, East Washington Square, 219 South 6th Street, Philadelphia PA 19106. **Tel** (215)627-4252.

The Arts —Art

available on microfilm and microfiche from University Microfilms International (UMI). **Absorbed in part by** Classic America.
Ind/Abst Am. Hist. Life (1979-1981); Archit. Period. Index (Winter 1977-1984); Art Index; Avery Index Archit. Period. Suppl. Colum. Univ.; Garden Lit. (1992-).

LC N7355 .N57A

JA
NITTEN SAKUHIN SHU. Main/Corp Nitten. Japanese. One time a year. ¥3000. Nitten, 8-5 Sendagi 3 Bunkyo-ku, Tokyo-to 113 Japan.

ISSN 1075-7163
DD 709 US
●**NKA (BROOKLYN, N.Y.).** (NKA : JOURNAL OF CONTEMPORARY AFRICAN ART.). [NKA]. Issue 1 (Fall/Winter 1994)-. Periodical. English. Two times a year. $34.00. NKA Publications, 247 Carlton Avenue, Brooklyn NY 11205.

ISSN 1183-1138
DD 709.714/05 CN
NOIR D'ENCRE. [Noir encre]. Vol. 1, No 1 (Feb., Mar., Apr., May 1991)-. Periodical. French. Three times a year (Feb., June, Oct). 12.00Can$ (individuals), 20.00Can$ (institutions), Canada; $20.00 (individuals), $30.00 (institutions), other. Editions d Noir d Encre, 185 Christopher Colomb East, Quebec Quebec G1K 3S6 Canada. **Tel** (418)529-2715, FAX (418)529-0048.

LC NX549.A1 N65 ISSN 0765-121X
DD 700/.944 FR
NOISE (PARIS, FRANCE). (NOISE.). **Added/Corp** Maeght Editeur. (1985)-. Periodical. French. Four times a year. 560.00F other; 800.00F other. Maeght Editeur, 12 rue Saint Merri, 75004 Paris France. **Tel** 011 33 1 42784344.

LC N7101.N598 ISSN 0213-2214
DD 709/.46/2605 SP
NORBA-ARTE. [Norba, Arte]. **Added/Corp** Universidad de Extremadura (Caceres, Spain). Departamento de Historia del Arte. **VAT** Norba Arte. No. 5(1984)-. Periodical. Spanish. One time a year. University Extremadura Service Publishers / Quien Edita, Donoso Cortes 11, 10003 Caceres Spain. **Tel** 011 34 927 247650. **(Subscription address:** l'Estaquirot S A, Nuestra Senora dell Coll 53, 08023 Barcelona Spain. **Tel** 011 34 3 2850327.) **Continues in part** Norba, 0211-0636.

LC DD491.S622 N6 ISSN 0078-1037
GW
NORDELBINGEN. [Nordelbingen]. **Added/Corp** Gesellschaft fuer Schleswig-Holsteinische Geschichte. (1923)-. German. One time a year. Westholsteinische Verlagsanstalt Boyens und Co., Am Wulf-Isebrandplatz, Postfach 1880, D-25738 Heidelberg Germany. **Tel** 011 49 481 68860. cum. index.
Ind/Abst BHA : Biblio. Hist. Art; MLA Int. Bibl. Books Artic. Mod. Lang. Lit.

LC N7068 .N585 ISSN 0803-6160
NO
●**NORSK KUNSTARBOK = YEARBOOK OF NORWEGIAN ART. Added/Corp** Kunstnernes Informasjonskontor. **VFOAT** Yearbook of Norwegian Art. (1994)-. English. One time a year. $63.00. Scandinavian University Press, PO Box 2959 Toeyen, N 0608 Oslo 6 Norway. **Tel** 011 47 2 2575400, FAX 011 47 2 2575353, telex 71896 UROR N. **Continues** Kunstarbok.

LC PN ISSN 0804-8452
DD 791.43 NO
●**NORSK MEDIETIDSSKRIFT TEKST.** (NORSK MEDIETIDSSKRIFT). [Nor. medietidsskr. Tekst]. (1994)-. Periodical. Multiple languages. Two times a year. Novus Press, PO Box 748 Sentrum, N-0106 Oslo Norway. **Tel** 011 47 22 717450, FAX 011 47 22 718107.

LC N7008 .N69 ISSN 0105-1512
DD 709/.48 DK
NORTH. [North]. No. 1-. Multiple languages (Danish, English and Swedish). $24.00.
Ind/Abst ARTbibliogr. Mod.; BHA : Biblio. Hist. Art.

ISSN 0105-984X
DD 700 DK
NORTH-DEBAT. [North-debat]. **VFOAT** Ny North-Debat. (1978)-. Periodical. Danish.
Ind/Abst BHA : Biblio. Hist. Art.

LC NX ISSN 0105-2624
DD 700 DK
NORTH-INFORMATION. [North-inf.]. (1976)-. Monographic series. Multiple languages. Irregular.
Ind/Abst BHA : Biblio. Hist. Art.

ISSN 0749-6400
DD 705 US
NORTH LIGHT. [North light]. Periodical. English. Twelve times a year. $19.50. Fletcher Arts Services, 32 Berwick Court, Fairfield CT 06430. **Continues** Art Talent.

ISSN 0706-0955
DD 700/.9713/1 CN
CEASED
NORTHWARD JOURNAL. [Northward j.]. No. 13 (Feb. 1979)-(19??). Periodical. English (French; summaries and/or abstracts in North American Indian). Northward Journal, 439 Wellington Street West/3rd Floor, Toronto Ontario M5V 1E7 Canada. **Tel** (416)599-8770. **ED** Robert Stacey. **Bk Rev. Ad Acc.** ctrl circ. available on microfiche. **Continues** Boreal (English and French Ed.), 0315-8144.
Desc: Devoted to documenting, in words and pictures, the role of the North. Contains original writing by northern authors; portfolios of drawings by northern artists; and reviews of art exhibitions and books. Sponsored by the Art Libraries Society of North America.
Ind/Abst Can. Index.

LC N380 .N58 ISSN 0391-4364
IT
SUSPENDED
NOTIZIE DA PALAZZO ALBANI. [Not. Palazzo Albani]. **Added/Corp** Universita di Urbino. Istituto di Storia dell'Arte. (1972)-No. 2 (1992). Periodical. Italian. Two times a year. Argalia Editore, via San Donato, 61029 Urbino Italy. **Tel** 011 39 722 328733. **(Subscription address:** Casalini Libri, via Benedetto da Maiano 3, 50014 Fiesole Italy. **Tel** 011 55 599941.)
Ind/Abst Art Archaeol. Tech. Abstr.; Avery Index Archit. Period. Suppl. Colum. Univ. (1988/1989-); BHA : Biblio. Hist. Art.

LC Z5937 .N55 N1.A1
RU
NOVAIA SOVETSKAIA I INOSTRANNAIA LITERATURA PO ISKUSSTVU: OBSHCHIE VOPROSY ISKUSSTVA, ESTETIKA. Added/Corp Informtsentr po Problemam Kultury i Iskusstva (Soviet Union) Vsesoiuznaia Gosudarstvennaia Biblioteka Inostrannoi Literatury (Soviet Union). (19??)-. Periodical. Russian (Multiple languages). Twelve times a year. Gosudarstvennaia Biblioteka, Informatsionnyi Tsentr, Imeni V. I. Lenina, Prospekt Kalinina 3, 121019 Moscow Russia.

LC NX
DD 700 SP
NUEVO ESTILO. (1977)-. Spanish. Twelve times a year. $81.27. Axel Springer Publicaciones, Pedro Teixeira 8 Planta 8, 28020 Madrid Spain. **Tel** 011 34 1 5560048.

ISSN 0550-3604
DD 704 FR
NUIT DES TEMPS. (INTRODUCTION A LA NUIT DES TEMPS.). **Added/Corp** Zodiac. **VFOAT** Collection la Nuit des Temps; Glossaire. (1965)-. Periodical. French. Irregular. Zodiaqve, Abbaye de la Pierre-qui-Vire, 89630 St. Leger Vauban France. **Tel** 011 33 86 322123, FAX 011 33 86 322233. **ED** Jose Surchamp.

ISSN 0822-644X
DD 709/.71 CN
NUMERO (MONTREAL). (NUMERO.). [Numero]. Vol. 1, No. 1-. French. Four times a year. $75.00 per vol. Revue Numero, 4593 rue Fabre, Montreal Quebec H2S 3V7 Canada.

LC N8670 .N48
DD 109/.931 NZ
NZ ART AUCTION RECORDS. VFOAT Newrick's NZ Art Auction Records. (1972)-. English. Every 2 years. $12.95. Newrick Associates Ltd, PO Box 820, Wellington New Zealand.

LC NX
DD 700 BE
CEASED
+-O I.E. PLUS MOINS ZERO. VFOAT Plus Moins Zero. (19??)-No. 84 (1993). French. 15 rue Saint Jean, B-1050 Brussels Belgium.

ISSN 0832-5618
DD 707/.10713 CN
O.S.E.A. NEWSLETTER. [O.S.E.A. newsl.]. **Added/Corp** Ontario Society for Education Through Art. **VAT** Ontario Society for Education Through Art Newsletter. (Sept. 1985)-. Newsletter. English. Co-Ordinator of OSEA Publications, 150 Water Street South, Kitchener Ontario N2G 1Z5 Canada. **Continues** Newsletter (Ontario Society for Education Through Art)., 0824-6211.

LC AP4 .O32 ISSN 0029-7852
BU
OBZOR. See Literature.

LC NX
DD 700 RU
OBZORNAIA INFORMATSIIA: RESTAVRATSIIA, ISSLEDOVANIE I KHRANENIE MUZEINYKH KHUDOZHESTVENNYKH TSENNOSTEI. **See** Museums and Galleries.

LC Z ISSN 0730-7160
DD 020 US
OCCASIONAL PAPERS - ART LIBRARIES SOCIETY OF NORTH AMERICA. See Library and Information Sciences.

LC N400 ISSN 0893-0589
DD 708 US
OCCASIONAL PAPERS - BOWDOIN COLLEGE. MUSEUM OF ART. See Museums and Galleries.

LC NX ISSN 0071-9382
DD 700 US
OCCASIONAL PAPERS - FREER GALLERY OF ART. Main/Corp Freer Gallery of Art. (1947)-. Monographic series. English. Irregular. Price varies per volume. Smithsonian Institution, 1100 Jefferson Drive Southwest, Washington DC 20560. **Tel** (202)357-2605.
Desc: A series of publications dealing with art history related to the collections of the Freer Gallery of Art.

LC NX ISSN 0923-0033
DD 700 NE
OCULI. (1987)-. Monographic series. English. Irregular. Price varies per volume. John Benjamins BV, Amsteldijk 44, PO Box 75577, 1070 AN Amsterdam Netherlands. **Tel** 011 31 20 6738156, FAX 011 31 20 739773. **(Subscription address:** John Benjamins North America, PO Box 27519, Philadelphia PA 19118-0519. **Tel** (215)836-1200, FAX (215)836-1204.) **ED** Bert W. Meijer, Eric Jan Sluijter and Evert van Uitert.
Desc: Focuses on the art of the Low Countries, corresponding to what are now the Netherlands and Belgium. The series is not limited to a specific period, but ranges from the beginnings of the Netherlandish arts in the 14th and 15th centuries to the present.

LC NX
DD 700 FR
OEIL REVUE D'ART. English. Ten times a year. 440.74F French; 550.00F other. Oeil Revue de l'Art, 10 rue Guichard, 75016 Paris France. **Tel** 011 33 1 45258560. Documents available from The Genuine Article.
Ind/Abst Arts Humanit. Citation Index [Full Cov.]; Res. Alert [Full Cov.].

LC N3 .O48 ISSN 0029-9626
DD 705 AU
OESTERREICHISCHE ZEITSCHRIFT FUER KUNST UND DENKMALPFLEGE. [ËOsterr. Z. Kunst Denkmalpfl.]. **Added/Corp** Austria. Bundesdenkmalamt. Institut fuer Oesterreichische Kunstforschung (Austria). Issue 1 (1952)-. Periodical. German. Five times a year. $49.07. Verlag Anton Schroll and Company, Spengergasse 39, A-1051 Vienna 1 Austria. **Tel** 011 43 1 5445641, FAX 011 43 1 5445641. cum. index. **Continues** Oesterreichische Zeitschrift fuer Denkmalpflege.
Ind/Abst Am. Hist. Life (1977-1978); Archit. Period. Index (1975,1979-); Art Archaeol. Tech. Abstr.; ARTbibliogr. Mod.; Avery Index Archit. Period. Suppl. Colum. Univ. (1988,1990-); BHA : Biblio. Hist. Art.

ISSN 0228-9474
DD 706/.07123 CN
OFFICERS / ALBERTA SOCIETY OF ARTISTS. [Off. - Alta. Soc. Artists]. **Main/Corp** Alberta Society of Artists. (1970)-. English. One time a year. Free to members. Alberta Society of Artists, Alberta College of Art, Suite 5531/1301-16th Avenue, Calgary Alberta T2M 0L4 Canada.

LC N8.H4 O38
IS
OLAM HO-OMANUT. VFOAT World of Art. Vol. 1 (Oct./Nov. 1977)-. Periodical. Hebrew. Two times a year. $30.00. World of Art Inc., 190 Ben Yehuda Street, Tel Aviv 63471 Israel. **Tel** 011 972 3 5237115.

LC NX ISSN 0030-2651
DD 700 BE
ONS ERFDEEL. See Music.

LC NX ISSN 0030-3305
DD 770 IT
OP CIT. (1964)-. Periodical. Italian. Three times a year (Jan., May & Sept.). L13630. OP Cit, Via Vincenzo Padula 2, 80123 Naples Italy. **Tel** 011 39 81 7690783. **Bk Rev.** (Qty: 15). **Ad Acc; Adv Mgr:** Renato De Fusco. ctrl circ.
Ind/Abst ARTbibliogr. Mod.; ARTbibliogr. Curr. Titles.

LC WMLC L 83/4594 N6921.F7 O63
IT
OPD RESTAURO : QUADERNI DELL OPIFICIO DELLE PIETRE DURE E LABORATORI DI RESTAURO DI FIRENZE / MINISTERO PER I BENI CULTURALI E AMBIENTALI, OPIFICIO DELLE PIETRE DURE E LABORATORI DI RESTAURO DI FIRENZE. Added/Corp Opificio delle Pietre Dure. **VFOAT** Restauro; Opificio delle Pietre Dure Restauro. (1986)-. Italian. One time a year.

L80000.00 Italy; L120000.00 other. Opus Libri Srl, Via della Torretta 16, 50137 Florence Italy. **Tel** 011 39 55 660833.
Ind/Abst Avery Index Archit. Period. Suppl. Colum. Univ. (1989); BHA : Biblio. Hist. Art.

LC N8 .O75 **ISSN** 0030-5278
DD 709.5 UK
ORIENTAL ART. [Orient. art]. (1948)-. Periodical. English. Four times a year (Mar., June, Sept., Nov.). $64.00. Oriental Art Magazine Ltd, Flat 3 9 Rutland Gate, London SW7 1BH United Kingdom. **Tel** 011 44 171 5844109, FAX 011 44 171 8238772. **ED** Ann Butler. Index available. cum. index. **Bk Rev**, (Qty: 12). **Ad Acc**, **Adv Mgr:** P. Law, **Tel** (071)586 4109. **Circ:** 3,000. Documents available from The Genuine Article.
Desc: Articles, museum exhibitions, book reviews and art market reports on oriental art.
Ind/Abst Art Archaeol. Tech. Abstr.; Art Index; ARTbibliogr. Mod.; ARTbibliogr. Curr. Titles; Arts Humanit. Citation Index [Full Cov.]; Avery Index Archit. Period. Suppl. Colum. Univ. (1989-); BHA : Biblio. Hist. Art; Curr. Contents Arts Humanit.; Index Islam. Lit.; Res. Alert [Full Cov.].

LC DS501 .O73 **ISSN** 0030-5448
DD 950/.01 HK
ORIENTATIONS (HONG KONG). (ORIENTATIONS.). [Orientations]. (Jan. 1970)-. Periodical. English. Twelve times a year. $99.00. Orientations, 14th Floor, 200 Lockhart Road, Hong Kong Hong Kong. **Tel** 011 852 25111368, FAX 011 852 5074620, telex 62107 IPLPM HX. **ED** Elizabeth Knight. cum. index. **Bk Rev. Ad Acc. Circ:** 12,000.
Desc: Magazine dedicated to Asian art. Authoritative articles on painting, calligraphy, bronzes, ceramics, decorative arts and crafts with quality colour reproduction on luxury art paper.
Ind/Abst ARTbibliogr. Mod.

LC NX556.A1 O75
DD 700/.945/05 IT
ORIGINI (REGGIO EMILIA, ITALY). (ORIGINI.). No. 1 (Nov. 1986)-. Periodical. Italian. Three times a year. L10210. Gall la Scaletta, V S Matteo 25, 42020 S Polo re Italy. **Tel** 011 39 522 873654.
Ind/Abst Anthropol. Lit.

LC WMLC 93/1746
DD 700 IT
SUSPENDED
OSSERVATORIO DELLE ARTI. Added/Corp Accademia Carrara. (1988)- Suspended No.2 (1991). Periodical. Italian. Two times a year. Pier Luigi Lubrina Editore, V Le Vittorio Emuanuele 19, 24100 Bergamo Italy. **Tel** 011 39 35 223050.
Ind/Abst BHA : Biblio. Hist. Art.

LC NX **ISSN** 0078-3633
DD 700 AU
OSTERREICHISCHES JAHRBUCH FUER EXLIBRIS UND GEBRAUCHSGRAPHIK. Added/Corp Osterreichische Exlibris Gesellschaft. Jahresgabe. Osterreichische Exlibris Gesellschaft. Jahrbuch. Osterreichische Exlibris Gesellschaft. Publikation. Osterreichische Exlibris Gesellschaft. (1903)-. Periodical. German. Every 2 years. cum. index.
Ind/Abst BHA : Biblio. Hist. Art.

LC DJ1 .O9 **ISSN** 0030-672X
DD 949.2/005 NE
OUD HOLLAND. [Oud-Holland]. Vol. 1 (1883)-. Periodical. Dutch (English, French and German). Four times a year. $95.93. Drukkerij Nauta BV, Postbus 1, 7200 AA Zutphen Netherlands. **Tel** 011 31 5750 13614. cum. index. Documents available from The Genuine Article.
Ind/Abst Art Index; ARTbibliogr. Mod.; ARTbibliogr. Curr. Titles; Arts Humanit. Citation Index [Full Cov.]; Avery Index Archit. Period. Suppl. Colum. Univ. (1989-); BHA : Biblio. Hist. Art; Res. Alert [Full Cov.].

LC WMLC 93/1885 **ISSN** 1184-2288
DD 708.11/2334 CN
OUTLOOK - EDMONTON ART GALLERY. See Museums and Galleries.

LC N1 .O96 **ISSN** 0142-6540
DD 700 UK
CCC
OXFORD ART JOURNAL. [Oxf. art j.]. Vol. 1 (Oct. 1978)-. Periodical. English. Two times a year. $80.00. Oxford University Press / UK, Walton Street, Oxford OX2 6DP United Kingdom. **Tel** 011 44 1865 56767, FAX 011 44 1865 267773, telex 851/837330 OXPRES G. **(Subscription address:** Oxford University Press / USA, Journals Marketing Department, Oxford University Press, 2001 Evans Road, Cary NC 27513. **Tel** (800)451-7556, (919)677-0977, FAX (919)677-1714.**) ED** Annie E. Coombes, Tamar Garb, Andrew Hemingway, Fred Orton, Deborah Philips and Richard Wrigley. **Bk Rev. Ad Acc. Circ:** 350. available on microfilm and microfiche from University Microfilms International (UMI). Documents available from The Genuine Article.
Desc: New research in the visual arts, drawing from a wide spectrum of academic disciplines. Modern languages, history and cultural studies feature prominently.
Ind/Abst Am. Hist. Life (1987-); Art Index; ARTbibliogr. Mod. (1982-); Arts Humanit. Citation Index [Full Cov.]; Avery Index Archit. Period. Suppl. Colum. Univ. (1990-); BHA : Biblio. Hist. Art; Br. Humanit. Index; Curr. Cit.; Curr. Contents Arts Humanit.; Res. Alert [Full Cov.]; Romant. Move.

LC NX
DD 770 UK
OXFORD HISTORY OF ENGLISH ART. VFOAT English Art. (19??)-. English. Irregular. Oxford University Press / UK, Walton Street, Oxford OX2 6DP United Kingdom. **Tel** 011 44 1865 56767, FAX 011 44 1865 267773, telex 851/837330 OXPRES G. **(Subscription address:** Oxford University Press / USA, Journals Marketing Department, Oxford University Press, 2001 Evans Road, Cary NC 27513. **Tel** (800)451-7556, (919)677-0977, FAX (919)677-1714.**)**

LC NX
DD 700 UK
OXFORD STUDIES IN THE HISTORY OF ART AND ARCHITECTURE. (1971)-. Monographic series. English. Irregular. Price varies per volume. Oxford University Press / UK, Walton Street, Oxford OX2 6DP United Kingdom. **Tel** 011 44 1865 56767, FAX 011 44 1865 267773, telex 851/837330 OXPRES G.

LC N7410 .P33
DD 700/.99 US
Pr Rev.
PACIFIC ARTS. No. 1 & 2 (Jan./July 1990)-. Periodical. English. Two times a year. $40.00. Pacific Arts Association, 900 South Beretania Street, Honolulu HI 96814. **Tel** (808)848-4120. **ED** Dr. Roger Rose and Dr. Philip Dary (editor's address: Bishop Museum, 1525 Berniee Street, Honolulu HI 96817-0916; editor's phone: (808)847-3511 ext. 120). **Bk Rev. Circ:** 350.
Desc: Scholarly and general articles on all aspects of Oceanic Art.

LC N8640.C49 C49a **ISSN** 0737-4291
DD 750/.74/014461 US
PAINTING ANNUAL. Main/Corp Child's Gallery. (19??)-. English. One time a year. $5.00. Child's Gallery, 169 Newbury Street, Boston MA 02116.

LC NX **ISSN** 0276-1971
DD 700 US
PALETTE TALK. Added/Corp M. Grumbacher Inc. (19??)-. Periodical. English. Three times a year. $9.95. Koh I Noor Inc., 100 North Street, Bloomsbury NJ 08804. **Tel** (800)631-7646, (908)479-4124. **(Subscription address:** M. Grumbacher Inc., 460 Finchdene Square, Scarborough Ontario M1X 1C4 Canada. **) Circ:** 70,000 (ctrl).
Desc: Feature articles by fine artists sharing painting tips in oils, acrylics, watercolors, pastels. Answers readers' questions on color mixing and painting problems.

LC N8 .P25 **ISSN** 0031-0352
DD 705 SW
PALETTEN. [Paletten]. **Added/Corp** Goteborgs Konstnarsklubb. (1940)-. Periodical. Swedish. Four times a year (Mar., June, Sept., Dec.). $44.88. Paletten, Karl Gustavsgatabn 10 C, S-411 25 Goteborg Sweden. **Tel** 011 46 31 118739, FAX 011 46 31 117785. **ED** Elizabeth Pethrus. cum. index. **Bk Rev. Ad Acc. Circ:** 3,000.
Desc: All about art, recent and historical. Written by journalists, authors and artists.
Ind/Abst ARTbibliogr. Mod.; ARTbibliogr. Curr. Titles; BHA : Biblio. Hist. Art.

ISSN 0318-7020
DD 709/.714 CN
PARACHUTE. [Parachute]. 1, (Oct. 1975)-. Periodical. English (French). Four times a year. 37.40Can$. Parachute, CP 70 Succursale Longueuil, Longueuil Quebec J4K 4Y3 Canada. **Tel** (514)842-9805, FAX (514)287-7146. **ED** Chnatal Pontbriand. Index available (published separately). **Bk Rev. Ad Acc. Circ:** 4,500 (ctrl).
Desc: In-depth articles (essays and interviews) on the practice and theory of international contemporary art with a historical and critical perspective. Includes book and exhibition reviews by writers from Canada, U.S.A. and Europe.
Ind/Abst ARTbibliogr. Mod.; BHA : Biblio. Hist. Art; Can. Index; Can. Period. Index (19??-); Repere (1983-).

LC N908 **ISSN** 0703-8712
DD 708/.11/05 CN
TITLE CHANGE
PARALLELOGRAMME (VANCOUVER). See Museums and Galleries.

LC NX **ISSN** 1012-0211
DD 700 GR
PARATERETES : PERIODIKE EKDOSE LOGOU KAI TECHNES, O. See Literature.

LC NX **ISSN** 0256-0917
DD 770 SZ
PARKETT. No. 1 (1984)-. Periodical. German (English). Four times a year (Feb., June, Sept., Nov.). $75.00. Parkett Verlag AG, Quellenstrasse 27, CH-8031 Zurich Switzerland. **Tel** 011 44 1 2718140. **(Subscription address:** Parkett Publishers, 636 Broadway, 12th Floor, New York NY 10012. **Tel** (212)673-2660, FAX (212)673-2887.**)**
Desc: Devoted to collaborations with artists from America and Europe, in which specially commissioned texts by critics explore and contextualize each artist's current practice. Also includes articles on all aspects of the international artworld.
Ind/Abst ARTbibliogr. Mod.; ARTbibliogr. Curr. Titles; BHA : Biblio. Hist. Art.

LC NX **ISSN** 0773-9532
DD 700 BE
PART DE L'IL, LA. [Part 'il]. (1985)-. Periodical. French (Multiple languages and English). One time a year (Mar.). $62.16. Part de l Oeil, 144 rue du Midi, 1000 Brussels Belgium. **Tel** 11 32 2 5141841, FAX 011 32 2 5141841.
Ind/Abst BHA : Biblio. Hist. Art.

LC NX7 .P35
DD 700/.5 SP
SUSPENDED
PASEANTE, EL. No. 1 (Winter 1985)-Suspended (19??). Periodical. Spanish. Irregular. Ediciones Siruela, Plaza Manuel Becerra 15, Madrid 28028 Spain. **Tel** 011 34 1 3555720.

LC NX **ISSN** 0475-9516
DD 700 FR
PAYS DE BOURGOGNE. No. 1 (1953)-. Periodical. French. Four times a year. 120.00F. Pays de Bourgogne, 11 Boulevard Marachel Leclerc, 21240 Talant France.
Ind/Abst BHA : Biblio. Hist. Art.

LC NX
DD 700 FR
PEINTURES CAHIERS THEORIQUES. Periodical. French. Irregular. $21.00. Louis Cane, 184 rue St. Maur, F-75010 Paris France.

LC NX **ISSN** 0553-4755
DD 700 UK
PELICAN HISTORY OF ART, THE. (1953)-. Monographic series. English. Irregular. Price varies per volume. Viking Penguin Inc., 120 Woodbine Street, Bergenfield NJ 07621-3524. **Tel** (800)331-4624, (201)387-0600.

ISSN 0833-9414
DD 707/.10711 CN
PEN AND INK. (PEN AND INK : NEWSLETTER OF THE B.C. ART TEACHERS' ASSOCIATION.). [Pen ink]. **Added/Corp** British Columbia Art Teachers' Association. Vol. 1 (1985)-. Newsletter. English. Irregular. 37.00Can$. British Columbia Art Teachers' Association, 105-2235 Burrard Street, Vancouver British Columbia V6J 3H9 Canada. **Tel** (604)731-8121. ***Continues** BCATA Newsletter, 0833-8256.*

LC TS1262 .P46 **ISSN** 1045-1188
DD 681/.6 US
PEN WORLD. See Hobbies.

LC NX **ISSN** 1059-3829
DD 700 US
PENNSYLVANIA ART EDUCATOR, THE. Added/Corp Pennsylvania Art Education Association. (1991)-. Periodical. English. West Chester University / Harvey Green Library, West Chester PA 19383.

LC N6 .P4 **ISSN** 0553-6707
CI
Pr Rev.
PERISTIL (ZAGREB). (PERISTIL.). [Peristil]. **Added/Corp** Povijesno Drustvo Hrvatske. Drustvo Historicara Umjetnosti Hrvatske. Drustvo Povjesnicara Umjetnosti SR Hrvatske. (1954)-. Bulletin. Serbo-Croatian (Roman) (summaries and/or abstracts in English, German and Italian). One time a year. Price varies. Drustvo Povejesnicara Umjetnosti SR Hrvtske, Gajeva 2b, 41000 Zagreb Croatia. **Tel** 041 423 962. **ED** Professor Radovan Ivancevic. **Bk Rev.** ctrl circ. available on photocopies (for requested articles).
Desc: Contains articles concerning art history, architecture, and arts & crafts.
Ind/Abst Art Archaeol. Tech. Abstr.; Avery Index Archit. Period. Suppl. Colum. Univ. (19??-199?); BHA : Biblio. Hist. Art.

LC N857.8 .A55 **ISSN** 0748-559X
DD 704.9/42/09730740153 US
PERMANENT COLLECTION ILLUSTRATED CHECKLIST. See Museums and Galleries.

LC N400
DD 708 FR
PETIT JOURNAL DES GRANDES EXPOSITIONS, LE. Added/Corp Reunion des Musees Nationaux (France). (April/Sept. 1970)-. Periodical. French. One time a year. $36.09. Centre Distribution Reunion Musee Nationale, 1 31 Allee Du 12 Fev 1934, 77186 Noisiel France. **Tel** 11 33 1 60060314.
Ind/Abst Avery Index Archit. Period. Suppl. Colum. Univ. (1989).

The Arts — Art

LC Z990 .P5   ISSN 0031-7969
GW
CCC
PHILOBIBLON. [Philobiblon]. **Added/Corp** Maximilian-Gesellschaft. Vol. 1 (Feb. 1957)-. Trade Publication. German. Four times a year. DM96.00 Germany; DM114.50 other. Dr. Ernst Hauswedell & Co. Verlag, Rosenbergstrasse 113, D-70193 Stuttgart Germany. **Tel** 011 49 711 638265. Index available (bound in Dec. issue).
  Ind/Abst BHA : Biblio. Hist. Art; MLA Int. Bibl. Books Artic. Mod. Lang. Lit.

LC N5300 .P53   ISSN 0193-8061
DD 709   US
PHOEBUS. [Phoebus]. **Added/Corp** Arizona State University. Art History Faculty. (1978)-. Periodical. English. One time a year (Jan.). $12.00. Arizona State University / Art History, College of Fine Arts, Tempe AZ 85281. **Tel** (602)965-7227. **ED** Ju-Hsi Chou and Anthony Gully. **Bk Rev**. **Circ**: 300 (ctrl).
  Desc: Art historical essays and book reviews on art-related topics.
  Ind/Abst BHA : Biblio. Hist. Art; Romant. Move.

LC NX
DD 700   US
PICKER ART GALLERY JOURNAL, THE. See Museums and Galleries.

LC NX   ISSN 0748-4577
DD 700   US
PINTURA, LA. (LA PINTURA : AMERICAN ROCK ART RESEARCH ASSOCIATION NEWSLETTER.). [Pintura]. **Added/Corp** American Rock Art Research Association. (19??)-. Newsletter. English. Irregular. ARARA, PO Box 1539, El Toro CA 92630.
  Ind/Abst Ethnoarts Index.

LC NX   ISSN 0295-1630
DD 708   FR
PLEINE MARGE. No. 1 (May 1985)-. Periodical. French. One time a year. 1200F. Editions Peeters SA, Bondgenotenlaan 153, BP 41, B-3000 Leuven Belgium. **Tel** 011 32 16 235170, FAX 011 32 16 228500, telex 65987 PUL B. **ED** J. Chenieux. **Ad Acc**.

LC NX
DD 700   MX
POLIESTER : PINTURA Y NO PINTURA. (1992)-. Periodical. Spanish (English). Four times a year. $40.00. Mireles Cemaj, Av. Michoacan 139, Col. Condesa 06140, Mexico D.F. **Tel** 011 52 5 2114044 or, 011 52 5 2114039, FAX 011 52 5 2565681.

LC N719 .P67   ISSN 8755-2035
DD 708   US
PORTICUS. [Porticus]. **Added/Corp** University of Rochester. Memorial Art Gallery. Vol. 1 (1978)-. Academic Scholarly Publication. English. Irregular. University of Rochester / Memorial Art Gallery, 500 University Avenue, Rochester NY 14607. **Tel** (716)473-7720, FAX (716)473-6266.
  Ind/Abst BHA : Biblio. Hist. Art.

DD 025.17/73   ISSN 0229-9712
CN
POSITIVE (LONDON). See Library and Information Sciences.

LC NX440   ISSN 0079-466X
DD 709   PL
UDC 7/09/
PRACE KOMISJI HISTORII SZTUKI. POZNANSKIE TOWARZYSTWO PRZYJACIO NAUK. [Pr. Kom. Hist. Szt., Pozn. Tow. Przyj. Nauk]. (1922)-. Periodical. Polish. Irregular. Price varies per volume. Poznanskie Towarzystwo Przyjaciol Nauk, Ul. Mielzynskiego 27-29, 61-725 Poznan Poland. **Tel** 011 48 61 527441. **(Subscription address:** Ars Polona-Ruch, PO Box 1001, Krakowskie Przedmiescie 7, 00-068 Warsaw Poland. **Tel** 011 48 22 261201.**)**

LC NX   ISSN 0032-6925
DD 700   IT
PRATO STORIA E ARTE. Added/Corp Azienda Autonoma di Turismo di Prato. (19??)-. Periodical. Italian. Two times a year.
  Ind/Abst BHA : Biblio. Hist. Art.

LC E77.8 .R42   ISSN 1060-0965
DD 930   US
PREHISTORIC AMERICA. [Prehist. Am.]. **Added/Corp** Society for the Documentation of Prehistoric America. **VFOAT** Prehistoric American. Vol. 24, No. 1 (1990)-. Periodical. English. Four times a year. $15.00. Genuine Indian Relic Society Inc, 8117 Preston Road, LB 16, Dallas TX 75225. **Continues** Prehistoric Artifacts of North America, 0892-2195.

LC NC673 .P74A
DD 741.9/074   SP
PREMI INTERNACIONAL DIBUIX JOAN MIRO. CATALEG. Main/Corp Premi Internacional Dibuix Joan Miro. Secretariat. Multiple languages (Catalan, Italian, Portuguese and Spanish). Secretariat del Premi Internacional de Dibuix Joan Miro, Barcelona Spain.

LC TT   ISSN 0032-7697
DD 745.5   GW
UDC 339.37 :688.78/.9
PRESENT BAMBERG. See The Arts-Crafts and Decorative Arts.

LC N400   ISSN 0892-2896
DD 708   US
PREVIEW. See Museums and Galleries.

LC N400
DD 708   US
PREVIEWS / INDIANAPOLIS MUSEUM OF ART. See Museums and Galleries.

LC NX   ISSN 0079-5208
DD 700   US
PRINCETON MONOGRAPHS IN ART AND ARCHEOLOGY. (19??)-. Monographic series. English. Irregular. Price varies per volume. Princeton University Press, 41 William Street, Princeton NJ 08540. **Tel** (609)258-4900.

LC NX
DD 700   US
PRIZE-WINNING ART. (1966)-. English. One time a year. Allied Publications Inc. / Palm Beach, PO Drawer 189, Palm Beach FL 33480. **Tel** (305)833-4593. **ED** Margaret Harold. **Continues** Award Winning Art.

LC ND195 ND196
DD 759.06   US
PRIZE-WINNING PAINTINGS. (1962)-. English. One time a year. Allied Publications Inc. / Palm Beach, PO Drawer 189, Palm Beach FL 33480. **Tel** (305)833-4593. **ED** Margaret Harold. **Continues** Prize-Winning Oil Paintings.

LC N5015 .A49
DD 706/.273   US
PROGRAM CATALOGUE. Main/Corp American Federation of Arts. (1973)-. English. One time a year. American Federation of Arts, 41 East 65th Street, New York NY 10021. **Tel** (212)988-7708. **Continues** American Federation of Arts Circulating Exhibition Yearbook.

LC N6 .P7   ISSN 0033-0957
DD 705   PL
PROJEKT. (April/June 1956)-. Periodical. Polish (summaries and/or abstracts in English, French and Russian). Six times a year. Price on request. **(Subscription address:** Ars Polona-Ruch, PO Box 1001, Krakowskie Przedmiescie 7, 00-068 Warsaw Poland. **Tel** 011 48 22 261201.**)**
  Ind/Abst Archit. Period. Index; ARTbibliogr. Mod.; Avery Index Archit. Period. Suppl. Colum. Univ. (1989-); BHA : Biblio. Hist. Art.

LC N4 .P76   ISSN 0394-0802
DD 705   IT
PROSPETTIVA. [Prospettiva]. No. 1 (April 1975)-. Periodical. Italian (English). Four times a year (Jan., Apr., July, Oct.). L80000. Centro Di, via Dei Renai 20R, 50125 Florence Italy. **Tel** 011 39 55 2342666, FAX 011 39 55 2342667. **ED** Mauro Cristofani. Index available. **Bk Rev**. **Circ**: 1,300. Documents available from The Genuine Article.
  Desc: Archaeology and art (Medieval, Renaissance, Baroque to Twentieth Century).
  Ind/Abst Art Archaeol. Tech. Abstr.; ARTbibliogr. Mod.; Arts Humanit. Citation Index [Full Cov.]; Avery Index Archit. Period. Suppl. Colum. Univ. (1988/89-); BHA : Biblio. Hist. Art; Res. Alert [Full Cov.].

DD 701   ISSN 0896-7938
US
CEASED
PSYCHOANALYTIC PERSPECTIVES ON ART : PPA. [Psychoanal. perspect. art]. **VFOAT** PPA. Vol. 1 (1985)-Series Complete Vol. 3 (19??). English. Analytic Press, 365 Broadway, Hillsdale NJ 07642. **Tel** (201)666-4110, FAX (201)666-2394. **ED** Mary Mathews Gedo.
  Ind/Abst ARTbibliogr. Mod.; BHA : Biblio. Hist. Art.

LC N7475   ISSN 1062-5089
DD 701.18   US
PUBLIC ART ISSUES. (1992)-. Newsletter. English. Four times a year. $15.45. Public Art Fund, One East 53rd Street, 11th Floor, New York NY 10022. **Tel** (212)980-4575, FAX (212)980-3610. **Circ**: 2,000. **Continues** Issues.
  Desc: Covers issues relevant to the field of public art.

LC N8700 .P83   ISSN 1040-211X
DD 711   US
Pr Rev.
PUBLIC ART REVIEW. [Public art rev.]. Vol. 1, No. 1 (Winter/Spring 1989)-. Periodical. English. Two times a year (Apr. and Oct.). $15.00. Forecast, 2324 University Avenue West, St. Paul MN 55114. **Tel** (612)641-1128, FAX (612)641-0028. **ED** Jack Becker. Index available. **Bk Rev**, (Qty: 2-4). **Ad Acc**. **Circ**: 5,000.
  Desc: Devoted to the field of public art. Each issue provides opinion, analysis, criticism and discussion about the nature and trends in public art.

LC N400   ISSN 1200-3026
DD 708.11/384/0294   CN
●**PUBLICATIONS - NATIONAL GALLERY OF CANADA.** See Museums and Galleries.

LC N716.V45 A2
DD 708.1   US
PUBLICATIONS - VIRGINIA MUSEUM OF FINE ARTS, RICHMOND. See Museums and Galleries.

LC N4 .M44A   ISSN 0391-3813
DD 705   IT
QUADERNI DELL ISTITUTO DI STORIA DELL ARTE MEDIEVALE E MODERNA, FACOLTA DI LETTERE E FILOSOFIA, UNIVERSITA DI MESSINA. (QUADERNI DELLISTITUTO DI STORIA DELLARTE MEDIEVALE E MODERNA, UNIVERSITA DI MESSINA.). [Quad. Ist. stor. arte mediev. mod., Fac. lett. filos., Univ. Messina]. **Main/Corp** Messina. Universita. Istituto di Storia Dellarte Medioevale e Moderna. Vol. 1975-. Italian. Ed de Luca, V de Sant Anna 16, 00186 Rome Italy.
  Ind/Abst BHA : Biblio. Hist. Art.

LC CC   ISSN 0079-8258
DD 930.1   IT
QUADERNI DI ARCHEOLOGIA DELLA LIBIA. See Archaeology.

LC NX
DD 700   IT
QUADERNI DI BRERA (MILANO, 1974-). **Added/Corp** Biblioteca Nazionale Braidense. 1 (1974)-. Monographic series. Italian. Irregular. Price varies per volume. Edizioni il Polifilo, Via Borgonuovo 2, 20121 Milan Italy. **Tel** 011 39 2 6551549.

LC NX
DD 700   IT
QUADERNI DI PALAZZO VENEZIA. **Added/Corp** Italy. Soprintendenza per i beni Artistici e Storici di Roma. Museo di Palazzo Venezia (Rome, Italy). (1981)-. Periodical. Italian.
  Ind/Abst BHA : Biblio. Hist. Art.

LC N1 .R17   ISSN 0315-9906
DD 705   CN
RACAR. (RACAR, REVUE D'ART CANADIENNE. CANADIAN ART REVIEW.). [RACAR]. **Added/Corp** Society for the Promotion of Art History Publications in Canada. Universities Art Association of Canada. **VFOAT** Revue d'Art Canadienne; Canadian Art Review. Vol. 1 (1974)-. English (French). Two times a year (Spring & Fall). 16.01Can$. Hughes & Company Management Services, PO Box 5863, Station B, Victoria British Columbia V8R 6S8 Canada. **Tel** (604)480-1026. **ED** Luis de Moura and Clifford M. Brown. **Circ**: 700. Documents available from The Genuine Article.
  Ind/Abst Am. Hist. Life (1989-); Art Index; ARTbibliogr. Mod.; Arts Humanit. Citation Index (19??-19??) [Full Cov.]; Avery Index Archit. Period. Suppl. Colum. Univ. (19??-); BHA : Biblio. Hist. Art; Can. Period. Index (19??-); Curr. Contents Arts Humanit.; Res. Alert [Full Cov.].

LC ND623.L5 R3
DD 759.5   IT
RACCOLTA VINCIANA. **Added/Corp** Castello Sforzesco. Ente "Raccolta Vinciana". (1929)-. Periodical. Italian. **Continues** Raccolta Vinciana from l'Archivio Storico del Comune di Milano.
  Ind/Abst BHA : Biblio. Hist. Art.

LC N4 .R29
DD 705   IT
RASSEGNA D'ARTE. (19??)-. Periodical. Italian. 2000. G Alparone, Viale Cavalleggeri Aosta 77, Naples 80124 Italy.

LC NX   ISSN 0161-5114
DD 700   US
SUSPENDED
RE-VIEW (NEW YORK). (RE-VIEW.). [Re-view]. **VFOAT** Re-View Magazine. Vol. 1 (Oct. 1977)-. Periodical. English. Irregular. $8.00. Ambrose Arts Foundation, 85 Mercer Street, New York NY 10012. **Tel** (212)431-7238. **ED** Vered Lieb. **Ad Acc**. **Circ**: 2,000.
  Desc: Artist produced magazine with original art and a full page reproduction of art. The main interest is contemporary paintings.

LC NX   ISSN 0739-196X
DD 700   US
CEASED
REAL LIFE MAGAZINE. No. 1 (March 1979)-No. 24 (1995). Periodical. English. Real Life Magazine, 24700 McBean Parkway, California Institute of Arts, Valencia CA 91355. **Tel** (213)857-0441. **ED** T. Lawson and S. Morgan. Index available. cum. index. **Bk Rev**. **Circ**: 1,500.
  Ind/Abst ARTbibliogr. Mod.; BHA : Biblio. Hist. Art.

The Arts — Art

LC N7101 .R43   **ISSN** 0486-0993
SP
REALES SITIOS. [R. sitios]. **Added/Corp** Patrimonio Nacional. Vol. 1, No. 1 (July 1964)-. Periodical. Spanish. Three times a year. $27.50 Spain; $55.00 others. Reales Sitios, Palacio Real C Bailen S N, 28071 Madrid Spain. **Tel** 011 34 1 2487404.
Ind/Abst Avery Index Archit. Period. Suppl. Colum. Univ. (1990-); BHA : Biblio. Hist. Art.

ISSN 1054-3465
DD 700   US
REFLEX (SEATTLE, WASH.). (REFLEX.). [Reflex]. **Added/Corp** Nine One One (Gallery) 911 Media Arts Center. Vol. 1, No. 1 (Jan./Feb. 1987)-. Newspaper. English. Six times a year. $23.00. Xelfer, Reflex Magazine, 105 South Main, Suite 204, Seattle WA 98104. **Tel** (206) 682-7688, (800)833-6388. **ED** Elizabeth Bryant. **Bk Rev.** (Qty: 4-6). **Ad Acc, Adv Mgr:** Judy Kitzman, **Tel** (206)522-6865. **Circ:** 8,000 (ctrl).
Desc: Exclusively devoted to visual arts in the Northwest region. Each issue contains reviews and previews, provocative features, news and analysis of arts issues, and a comprehensive regional calendar of exhibitions and events.

LC N582.L25 A35   **ISSN** 0733-866X
DD 708.181/65   US
REGISTER OF THE SPENCER MUSEUM OF ART, THE. See Museums and Galleries.

LC PN6099
DD 808.81   US
Pr Rev.
RENEGADE (BLOOMFIELD HILLS). See Literature.

LC NX
DD 700   FR
REPERES. No. 1 (1982)-. Monographic series. French. Seven times a year. Price varies per volume. Galerie LeLong, 13 rue de Teheran, 75008 Paris France. **Tel** 011 33 1 45631319. **Continues** Derriere le Miroir.

ISSN 1186-1231
DD 700/.25/71425   CN
REPERTOIRE DES ARTISTES ET DES ARTISANS DE SAINT-EUSTACHE. [Repert. artist. artis. St.-Eustachea]. **Main/Corp** Societe de Developpement Culturel de Saint-Eustache. (1990/91)-. French. Limited free distribution. Societe de Developpement Culturel de Saint-Eustache, 235 rue Saint-Eustache, Saint-Eustache Quebec J7R 2L8 Canada.

ISSN 0226-1391
DD 709/.7123   CN
REPORT - VISUAL ARTS (EDMONTON). (REPORT - VISUAL ARTS.). [Rep. - Vis. Arts (Edmonton)]. **Main/Corp** Alberta. Visual Arts. (1978)-. Monographic series. English. Price varies per volume. Visual Arts Branch, 10158-103 Street, Edmonton Alberta T5J 0X6 Canada.

LC CC   **ISSN** 0330-843X
DD 930.1   TI
REPPAL. See Archaeology.

LC ND1630   **ISSN** 0933-4017
DD 751.6   GW
UDC 7.025.4
RESTAURO MUENCHEN. [Restauro Munch.]. (1988)-. Periodical. German. Four times a year. $142.40. Verlag Georg DW Callwey GmbH., Postfach 800409, D-81604 Munich Germany. **Tel** 011 49 89 43600533.
Continues Maltechnik, Restauro, 0342-3719.

LC N8555 .R47
RU
RESTAVRATSIIA, ISSLEDOVANIE I KHRANENIE MUZEINYKH KHUDOZHESTVENNYKH TSENNOSTEI. **Added/Corp** Informtsentr po Problemam Kultury i Iskusstva (Soviet Union) Soviet Union. Ministerstvo Kultury. (19??)-. Russian.

LC NX7 .R463   **ISSN** 0185-3570
MX
REVISTA DE BELLAS ARTES (MEXICO, D.F.). (REVISTA DE BELLAS ARTES.). [Rev. bellas artes]. **Added/Corp** Instituto Nacional de Bellas Artes y Literatura. Instituto Nacional de Bellas Artes (Mexico). No. 1 (Jan./Feb. 1965)-. Periodical. Spanish. Six times a year. Instituto Nacional de Bellas Artes / Mexico, Reforma y Gandhi, Mexico 5 DF Mexico. **Continues** Cuadernos de Bellas Artes.
Ind/Abst Am. Hist. Life (1962-1963, 1966-1970); Hisp. Am. Period. Index, HAPI; MLA Int. Bibl. Books Artic. Mod. Lang. Lit.

LC NX
DD 700   AG
REVISTA DE ESTETICA. No. 1 (1983)-. Periodical. Spanish. Three times a year. $30.00 US. Cayc Elpidio Gonzalez 4070, 1407 Buenos Aires Argentina. **Tel** FAX 54-1-566-3867, telex ACMAR 17105. **ED** Jorge Glusberg. Index available. cum. index. **Circ:** 8,000 (ctrl).

Desc: Dedicated to different topics concerning art in the whole meaning of the work, e.g. authors, books, techniques and aesthetic works, criticism, and everything about arts throughout the times.

LC N7.R43
DD 705   BL
REVISTA DO MASP. See Museums and Galleries.

LC N2 .R37   **ISSN** 0035-077X
DD 705   BE
REVUE BELGE D'ARCHEOLOGIE ET D'HISTOIRE DE L'ART. See The Arts-Abstracting, Bibliographies and Statistics.

LC NX   **ISSN** 0399-0184
DD 700   FR
UDC 055(444)
REVUE DE LA SAINTONGE ET DE L'AUNIS. [Rev. Saintonge Aunis]. (1975)-. Periodical. French. One time a year.
Ind/Abst BHA : Biblio. Hist. Art.

LC NX
DD 700   FR
REVUE DE LA SOCIETE D'HISTOIRE ET D'ART DE LA BRIE ET DU PAYS DE MEAUX. See History-History of Europe.

LC NX   **ISSN** 0035-1326
DD 770   FR
REVUE DE L'ART. [Rev. art]. No. 1/2 (1968)-. Periodical. French (summaries and/or abstracts in English and German). Four times a year. 415.00F France; 495.00F other. Editions du CNRS, 22 rue Saint Armand, F 75015 Paris France. **Tel** 011 33 1 45075050, telex 200 356 F. (**Subscription address:** Centrale des Revues, 11 rue Gossin, 92543 Montrouge Cedex France. **Tel** 011 33 1 46565266.) **ED** A. Chastel and D. Ternois. **Ad Acc.** Documents available from The Genuine Article.
Continues Art de France.
Desc: Reflection and criticism on interpretations roused by art and its history, as well as works and their creators throughout time and civilization.
Ind/Abst Art Archaeol. Tech. Abstr.; Art Index; ARTbibliogr. Mod.; Arts Humanit. Citation Index; Avery Index Archit. Period. Suppl. Colum. Univ. (1989-); BHA : Biblio. Hist. Art; Curr. Contents Arts Humanit.; Res. Alert; Romant. Move.

LC NX   **ISSN** 0295-5849
DD 700   FR
UDC 666
REVUE DES INDUSTRIES D'ART. VFOAT Revue des Industries d'art et de la Table; Offrir(1966). (1966)-. Periodical. French. Eleven times a year. $118.11. Pierre Johanet & Fils Editeurs SA, 7 Avenue Franklin Roosevelt, 75008 Paris France. **Tel** 33 1 43590887, FAX 33 1 42255947, telex 649712 F.

LC NX   **ISSN** 0035-2608
DD 700   FR
REVUE DU LOUVRE ET DES MUSEES DE FRANCE, LA. See Museums and Galleries.

LC NX
DD 700   CN
●**REVUE POST.** (1995)-. English. Three times a year. 24.01Can$. Revue Post, 3550 Jeanne Mance App. 2207, Montreal Quebec, H2X 3P7 Canada. **Tel** (514)287-7487.
Continues Imposture.

LC WMLC L 83/2560   **ISSN** 0080-262X
DD 700   RM
REVUE ROUMAINE D'HISTOIRE DE L'ART. SERIE BEAUX-ARTS. **Added/Corp** Academia de Stiinte Sociale si Politice a Republicii Socialiste Romania. **VFOAT** Serie Beaux-Arts. Vol. 7, (1970)-. Romanian (Russian, English, French, German and Spanish). Four times a year. $105.00. (**Subscription address:** Orion Press SRL, SPL Independentei 202-A, Bucharest 6 Romania. **Tel** 011 401 3122425.)
Supersedes in part Revue Roumaine de l'Histoire de l'Art.
Desc: Publishes studies on history of the fine arts.
Ind/Abst ARTbibliogr. Mod. (1984-); Avery Index Archit. Period. Suppl. Colum. Univ. (19??-199?); BHA : Biblio. Hist. Art; Numis. Lit.

LC WMLC L 83/2561
RM
REVUE ROUMAINE D'HISTOIRE DE L'ART. SERIE THEATRE, MUSIQUE, CINEMA. **Added/Corp** Academia de Stiinte Sociale si Politice a Republicii Socialiste Romania. **VFOAT** Serie Theatre, Musique, Cinema. Vol. 7, (1970)-. Romanian (English, French, German, Spanish and Russian). One time a year. $105.00. (**Subscription address:** Orion Press SRL, SPL Independentei 202-A, Bucharest 6 Romania. **Tel** 011 401 3122425.) **Supersedes in part** Revue Roumaine d'Histoire de l'Art.
Desc: Studies on theatre, music, and cinematography.

LC NK2 .R13
DD 380.1/45/730094   FR
RIA INTERNATIONAL, REVUE DES INDUSTRIES D'ART EXPORT. (19??)-. Periodical. French (English). Six times a year. 180.00F. Pierre Johanet & Fils Editeurs SA, 7 Avenue Franklin Roosevelt, 75008 Paris France. **Tel** 33 1 43590887, FAX 33 1 42255947, telex 649712 F. **ED P** Johanet. Index available. **Bk Rev. Ad Acc. Continues** RIA, Revue des Industries d'Art Export.

LC N380 .R52   **ISSN** 0392-7202
DD 709   IT
RICERCHE DI STORIA DELL'ARTE. [Ric. stor. arte]. No. 1 (1976)-. Periodical. Italian. Three times a year. L57230. Nuova Italia Scientifica, Via Sardegna 50, 00187 Rome Italy. **Tel** 011 39 6 4870745. Documents available from The Genuine Article.
Ind/Abst Archit. Period. Index (1976-); Art Archaeol. Tech. Abstr.; ARTbibliogr. Mod.; Arts Humanit. Citation Index [Full Cov.]; BHA : Biblio. Hist. Art; Res. Alert [Full Cov.].

LC NX
DD 770   IT
RICERCHE SUL SEI-SETTECENTO IN PUGLIA. **Added/Corp** Universita di Bari. (1979)-. Italian.
Ind/Abst BHA : Biblio. Hist. Art.

LC ML26 .I71965   **ISSN** 0360-8727
DD 780/.08   US
RIDIM/RCMI NEWSLETTER. See Music.

LC PS501 .R57   **ISSN** 0149-8851
DD 810/.8   US
Pr Rev.
RIVER STYX. See Literature.

LC NX
DD 770   IT
SUSPENDED
RIVISTA D'ARTE. Vol. 2, No. 1 (Jan. 1904)- Suspended (1996). Periodical. Italian. Price varies per volume. Casa Editrice Leo S. Olschki, Viuzzo del Pozzetto, Casella Postale 66, 50126 Florence Italy. **Tel** 011 39 55 6530684, FAX 011 39 55 6530214.
Continues Miscellanea d'Arte.
Ind/Abst Am. Hist. Life (1986-); BHA : Biblio. Hist. Art.

LC N9.6 .R58   **ISSN** 0080-3472
PL
ROCZNIK HISTORII SZTUKI. [Rocz. hist. sztuki]. **Added/Corp** Polska Akademia Nauk. Komitet Historii i Teorii Sztuki. Polska Akademia Nauk. Komitet Nauk o Sztuce. Vol. 1 (1956)-. Monographic series. Polish. Irregular. Price varies per volume. (**Subscription address:** Ars Polona-Ruch, PO Box 1001, Krakowskie Przedmiescie 7, 00-068 Warsaw Poland. **Tel** 011 48 22 261201.)
Ind/Abst ARTbibliogr. Mod.; Avery Index Archit. Period. Suppl. Colum. Univ. (19??-199?); BHA : Biblio. Hist. Art.

LC NX   **ISSN** 0557-2231
DD 770   PL
ROCZNIKI SZTUKI SLASKIEJ. **Added/Corp** Breslau. Muzeum Slaskie. (1959)-. Polish (summaries and/or abstracts in French). Every 2 years.
Ind/Abst BHA : Biblio. Hist. Art.

LC NX
DD 770   IT
ROMAGNA ARTE E STORIA. (198?)-. Periodical. Italian. Three times a year. L34060. Editrice Romagna Arte Storia, CP 1139, DI GF Fellini & Co, 47037 Rimini 3 Italy. **Tel** 011 39 541 384988.
Ind/Abst BHA : Biblio. Hist. Art.

LC N6911.A1 R6   **ISSN** 0342-2046
DD 709.45   GW
ROMISCHES JAHRBUCH DER BIBLIOTHECA HERTZIANA. **Added/Corp** Bibliotheca Hertziana, Max-Planck-Institut. Vol. 25 (1989)-. Monographic series. German (English, Italian and French). Irregular. Price varies per volume. Verlag Ernst Wasmuth Tuebingen, Postfach 2728, D-72017 Tuebingen Germany. **Tel** 011 49 7071 33658. cum. index. **Circ:** 400. **Continues** Romisches Jahrbuch fuer Kunstgeschichte.
Desc: Art history in Rome, Italy and a collection of specialists.

LC TR   **ISSN** 0883-735X
DD 770   US
SUSPENDED
ROTKIN REVIEW, THE. See Photography.

LC NX   **ISSN** 0084-2982
DD 700   PL
UDC 7
ROZPRAWY KOMISJI HISTORII SZTUKI. [Rozpr. Kom. Hist. Szt.]. (1957)-. Monographic series. Polish. Irregular. Price varies per volume. Wroclawskie Towarzystwo Naukowe, Ul. Parkowa 13, 50-616 Wroclaw Poland. **Tel** 011 48 71 444061, 011 48 71 484061.

The Arts —Art

Desc: Monographs in art history, including Polish painting, sculpture, etc.
Ind/Abst BHA : Biblio. Hist. Art.

LC N400
DD 708 SP
RS (CENTRO DE ARTE REINA SOFIA). (RS : REVISTA TRIMESTRAL DEL CENTRO DE ARTE REINA SOFIA). No. 1 (1989)-. Periodical. Spanish. Four times a year. 2000ptas. Centro de Arte Reina Sofia, 52 TI4675062, 28012 Madrid Spain.
Desc: Museum exhibitions, actuality in art, museums and artists and other exhibitions in Spain and around the world.

LC NX
DD 700 ISSN 1065-9374 US
●**RUSSIAN AND EAST EUROPEAN STUDIES IN AESTHETICS AND THE PHILOSOPHY OF CULTURE.** (1993)-. Monographic series. English. Price varies per volume. Peter Lang Publishing, 62 West 45th Street, 4th Floor, New York NY 10036. **Tel** (212)764-1471, (800)770-5264, FAX (212)302-7574, telex 6973364 PLNY.

LC PR1170
DD 821.91408 ISSN 1352-0997 UK
●**RUSTIC RUB.** See Literature-Poetry.

LC N1 .R87 ISSN 0194-049X
DD 705
Pr Rev.
RUTGERS ART REVIEW, THE. [Rutgers art rev.]. **Added/Corp** Rutgers University. Graduate Program in Art History. Vol. 1 (Jan. 1980)-. Academic Scholarly Publication. English. One time a year. $14.00. Rutgers Art Review, Rutgers University, Voorhees Hall, New Brunswick NJ 08901. **Tel** (908)932-7041. **ED** Caroline Goeser. Index available. cum. index. **Ad Acc. Circ:** 400.
Desc: Publishes scholarly work by graduate students in art history from both national and international universities. Each issue features an interview with a prominent art historian.
Ind/Abst Am. Hist. Life; ARTbibliogr. Mod.; Avery Index Archit. Period. Suppl. Colum. Univ. (1988-1989); BHA : Biblio. Hist. Art.

LC 704.9482 ISSN 0741-9163
DD NX655 US
SACRED ART JOURNAL. [Sacred art j.]. **Added/Corp** St. John of Damascus Association of Orthodox Iconographers, Iconologists, and Architects. (April 1981)-. Periodical. English. Four times a year. $35.00. Sacred Art Journal, Route 711 North, PO Box 638, Ligonier PA 15658-0638. **Tel** (412)238-3677, FAX (412)238-2102. **ED** George Gaha and Paul D Garrett. **Bk Rev. Ad Acc. Circ:** 500 (ctrl).
Desc: Art and architecture of the Eastern Orthodox Church, iconography painting technique, theology of icons, and nature of historical iconography.

LC N4 .S2 ISSN 0392-713X IT
SAGGI E MEMORIE DI STORIA DELL'ARTE. [Sag. mem. stor. arte]. **Added/Corp** Instituto di Storia dell'Arte (Fondazione "Giorgio Cini"). (1957)-. Italian. One time a year. L250000. Casa Editrice Leo S. Olschki, Viuzzo del Pozzetto, Casella Postale 66, 50126 Florence Italy. **Tel** 011 39 55 6530684, FAX 011 39 55 6530214.
Ind/Abst BHA : Biblio. Hist. Art.

LC DP1 .S3 ISSN 0210-9980 SP
SAITABI. See History-History of Europe.

LC NB198 .S2A
DD 735/.23/007404361 FR
SALON DE LA JEUNE SCULPTURE. CATALOGUE. Main/Corp Salon de la Jeune Sculpture. **VFOAT** Jeune Sculpture; JS. (19??)-. French.

LC DS485.T8 S26 II
SAMATALA. 1st Year, 1st Issue (Apr. 1983)-. Periodical. Bengali (Bengali). 2.50. Abala Prakashani Yogendranagar Agartala, Tipura India.

LC NX ISSN 0391-7819
DD 700 IT
SANTO, IL. See Religions and Theology.

LC N7249.S4 S26 ISSN 0409-008X YU
SAOPSTENJA - REPUBLICKI ZAVOD ZA ZASTITU SPOMENIKA KULTURE SR SRBIJE. (SAOPSTENJA / REPUBLICKI ZAVOD ZA ZASTITU SPOMENIKA KULTURE / COMMUNICATIONS ; INSTITUT POUR LA PROTECTION DES MONUMENTS HISTORIQUES DE LA R.P. DE SERBIE.). [Saopst. - Repub. zavod zast. spomenika kult. SR Srb.]. **Main/Corp** Republiccki Zavod za Zastitu Spomenika Kulture. **Added/Corp** Republicki Zavod za Zastitu Spomenika Kulture. **VFOAT** Saopstenja Republickog Zavoda za Zastitu Spomenika Kulture SR Srbije; Communications. (19??)-. Periodical. Serbo-Croatian (Cyrillic) (summaries and/or abstracts in French). One time a year. Price varies. Repub Zavod Zastitu Spomenika, Bozidara Adzieje 11, 11000 Belgrad Yugoslavia. **Tel** 011 451 692. **Continues** Belgrad. Zavod za Zastitu i Naucno Proucavanje Spomenika Kulture NR Srbije Saopstenja Zavoda za Zastitu i Naucno Proucavanje Spomenika Kulture NR Srbije.
Ind/Abst BHA : Biblio. Hist. Art.

LC F1601 .S26 ISSN 0036-5068
DD 972.9/005 JM
SAVACOU. [Savacou]. **Added/Corp** Caribbean Artists Movement. (June 1970)-. Periodical. English. Irregular. Savacou Publications, PO Box 170, Mona Kingston 7 Jamaica. **ED** E.K. Brathwaite. **Bk Rev. Ad Acc. Circ:** 2,000.
Desc: Covers Caribbean artist movement.
Ind/Abst MLA Int. Bibl. Books Artic. Mod. Lang. Lit.

LC GT500 ISSN 1072-8384
DD 391 US
●**SAVAGE (AGOURA HILLS, CALIF.).** (SAVAGE.). [Savage]. **VFOAT** Tattoo Savage. No. 1 (Jan. 1994)-. Consumer Publication. English. Four times a year. $13.95. Paisano Publications Inc., 28210 Dorothy Drive, PO Box 1050, Agoura Hills CA 91301. **Tel** (818)889-8740, FAX (818)889-4726. **Ad Acc.** available with illustrations.

LC NX440 ISSN 0231-5025
DD 709 XR
UDC 72 + 730 + 74 + 75 + 76
SBORNIK PRACI FILOZOFICKE FAKULTY BRNENSKE UNIVERZITY. RADA UMENOVEDNA. [Sb. pr. filoz. pak. brnen. univ., Rada umenoved.]. **VFOAT** Studia Minora Facultatis Philosophicae Universitatis Brunensis. Series Historiae Artium. (1957)-. Proceedings. Multiple languages. One time a year. Price varies. Univerzita J E Purkyne, Janackovo Nam 2A, Brno Czech Republic. **Bk Rev.**
Desc: Features articles on the theory and history of the arts.
Ind/Abst BHA : Biblio. Hist. Art.

LC N1 .A3845 ISSN 1060-832X
DD 705 US
SCHOLASTIC ART. (SCHOLASTIC ART / PUBLISHED IN COOPERATION WITH THE NATIONAL GALLERY OF ART.). [Scholast. art]. **Added/Corp** National Gallery of Art (U.S.). Vol. 22, No. 4 (Feb. 1992)-. Trade Publication. English. Irregular. $31.80. Scholastic Inc., 2931 East McCarty Street, PO Box 3710, Jefferson City MO 65102-9957. **Tel** (314)636-5271, (800)631-1586. available on microfilm and microfiche from University Microfilms International (UMI). **Continues** Art and Man, 0004-3052.

LC N81 .S4 ISSN 0036-6463
DD 372 US
Pr Rev.
SCHOOL ARTS. [Sch. arts]. Vol. 35, No. 1 (Sept. 1935)-. Trade Publication. English. Nine times a year (September to May). $24.50. Davis Publications Inc., 50 Portland Street, Worcester MA 01608. **Tel** (617)754-7201, (800)533-2847, FAX (508)753-3834. **ED** Kent Anderson. cum. index. **Bk Rev. Ad Acc. Circ:** 23,000 (ctrl). available on micro-opaque from Microcard Editions; available on microform from University Microfilms International (UMI); available on an online database (file 648/Full-Text) from DIALOG. Documents available from UMI Article Clearinghouse. **Continues** School Arts Magazine.
Desc: An art teaching resource for teachers of grades kindergarten through 12, including peer-written articles, clip-card lesson plans, and safety points.
Ind/Abst Acad. Search; Access (1980-1987); Book Rev. Index; Bus. Index (1981-?); Curr. Index J. Educ.; Educ. Index; EP Collect.; Expand. Acad. Index (1992-); Gen. Period. Index (1985-); Homework Help.; Humanit. Source; INFO-SOUTH Abstr.; Mag. Artic. Summar. Elite; Mag. Artic. Summar. Select; Mag. Artic. Summar. CD-ROM; Mag. Index Plus (1989-); Mag. Index Sel. Microfiche (1986-) [Full Txt.]; Mag. Index. Sel. (1986-); Mag. Search; MasterFile FullTEXT 1000; MasterFile FullTEXT 350; MasterFile FullTEXT 650; MasterFile FullTEXT; Mid. Search; Newsp. Period. Abstr. (1988-); OCLC; Prim. Search; Pub. Lib. FullTEXT; Read. Guide Period. Lit.; Telebase; Mag. Index (1977-); TOM Gen. Index (1985-) [Full Txt.].

LC DD901.F75 F67 ISSN 0342-2038 GW
SCHRIFTEN DES HISTORISCHEN MUSEUMS FRANKFURT AM MAIN. Added/Corp Historisches Museum Frankfurt am Main. (19??)-. German.
Ind/Abst BHA : Biblio. Hist. Art.

LC NX ISSN 1016-2879
DD 700 SZ
UDC 007(494)
SCHWEIZER KUNST. [Schweiz. Kunst.]. **VFOAT** Art Suisse; Arte Svizzera. (1972)-. Periodical. Multiple languages. Irregular.
Ind/Abst BHA : Biblio. Hist. Art.

LC NA ISSN 1121-9122
DD 720 IT
SCIENCE AND TECHNOLOGY FOR CULTURAL HERITAGE : JOURNAL OF THE "COMITATO NAZIONALE PER LA SCIENZA E LA TECNOLOGIA DEI BENI CULTURALI," CNR. See Architecture.

LC NX
DD 700 FR
SCIENCE ET TECHNOLOGIE DE LA CONSERVATION ET DE LA RESTAURATION DES OEUVRES D'ART ET DU PATRIMOINE. See Museums and Galleries.

LC N2 .S3
DD 700/1 FR
SCIENCES DE L'ART = SCIENTIFIC AESTHETICS. Added/Corp Institut d'Esthetique et des Sciences de l'Art. **VFOAT** Scientific Aesthetics. Vol. 1 (1964)-. Periodical. French. Two times a year. Institut Esthetique des Sciences Art, 11 rue de Lille, Paris 7E France.

LC NX ISSN 0036-911X
DD 700 UK
SUSPENDED
SCOTTISH ART REVIEW. Added/Corp Glasgow Art Gallery and Museums Association. Glasgow Art Gallery and Museums Association. Art Review. Vol. 1 (Jan. 1946)-(19??). Periodical. English. Glasgow Art Gallery Museum Association, Kelvingrove, Glasgow G38AG United Kingdom. available on microfilm and microfiche from University Microfilms International (UMI).
Ind/Abst Br. Humanit. Index.

LC NB1 .N29 ISSN 0747-5284
DD 730/.5 US
SCULPTURE REVIEW. [Sculpt. rev.]. Vol. 31, No. 4 (1983)-. Periodical. English. Four times a year. $19.00. National Sculpture Society, 1177 Avenue of the Americas, 15th Floor, New York NY 10036. **Tel** (212)764-5645, FAX (212)545-0779. **ED** Fritz Cleary and Theodora Morgan. **Bk Rev. Ad Acc. Circ:** 5,000. available on microfilm and microfiche from University Microfilms International (UMI). Documents available from The Genuine Article.
Desc: Presents contemporary and historical representational American sculpture. About 40 fine reproductions, color tip-ins, news of sculpture and technical information and book reviews are in each issue.
Ind/Abst Art Index; Arts Humanit. Citation Index [Full Cov.]; BHA : Biblio. Hist. Art; Book Rev. Index; Curr. Contents Arts Humanit.; Res. Alert [Full Cov.].

ISSN 0889-728X
DD 730 US
SCULPTURE (WASHINGTON, D.C.). (SCULPTURE.). [Sculpture]. **Added/Corp** International Sculpture Center. Vol. 6, No. 2, (Mar./Apr. 1987)-. Periodical. English. Six times a year. $39.00. International Sculpture Center / Washington, DC, 1050 17th Street, Suite 250, Washington DC 20036. **Tel** (202)785-1144, FAX (202)785-0810. **ED** Suzanne Ramljak. Index available. **Ad Acc, Adv Mgr:** H. Singer, **Tel** (212)343-0202. **Circ:** 20,000. **Continues** International Sculpture, 0887-5472.
Desc: Covers news and issues related to contemporary sculpture.
Ind/Abst Art Archaeol. Tech. Abstr. (April 1987-); BHA : Biblio. Hist. Art.

LC N4390 .S43 ISSN 0272-0620
DD 707/.4/014 US
SEASONS IN ART. [Seas. art]. **Added/Corp** Pennsylvania Academy of the Fine Arts. Women's Committee. 1st Ed. (1978/1979)-. English. One time a year. $5.50. Seasons in Art, Department C, Peale House, 1811 Chestnut Street, Philadelphia PA 19103.

LC N400
DD 708 US
SEATTLE ART MUSEUM. See Museums and Galleries.

LC TR ISSN 1059-2490
DD 770 US
SECOND IMAGE. See Photography.

LC NX ISSN 0487-3491
DD 700 SP
SEMINARIO DE ARTE ARAGONES. [Semin. arte aragon.]. **Added/Corp** Institucion "Fernando el Catolico". Vol. 1 (1945)-. Spanish. Irregular. Consejo Superior Investigacion Cientificas / CSIC, Vitruvio 8, 28006 Madrid Spain. **Tel** 011 34 1 5612833, FAX 011 34 1 4113077, telex 42182.
Ind/Abst Avery Index Archit. Period. Suppl. Colum. Univ. (1988-1989); BHA : Biblio. Hist. Art.

LC N2 .S47
DD 705
FR
SUSPENDED
SERMENT DES HORACES : REVUE D'ART INTERNATIONALE, LE. VFOAT International Art Review. No. 1 (Winter 1989)-. Periodical. English (French). Two times a year. $48.76 France; $55.99 other. Serment des Horaces, 16 rue Saint Gilles, 75003 Paris France. **Tel** 011 33 1 42728420.

LC PL2603.H735　　　　　　　　　　　ISSN 0257-5639
DD 709/.2/251132　　　　　　　　　　　　　　　CC
SHANG-HAI I SHU CHIA. VFOAT Shanghai Artists. Vol. 1 (1987)-. Periodical. Chinese. Six times a year. Chung-Kuo Kuo Chi Tu Shu Mao I Tsung Kung SSU, PO Box 2820, Beijing, People's Republic of China. *Continues* Hsin Chu Tso.

LC N7347.S48 S5
DD 709/.51132　　　　　　　　　　　　　　　CC
SHANG-HAI MEI SHU NIEN KAN / SHANG-HAI MEI SHU NIEN KAN PIEN CHI TSU PIEN. Added/Corp Chung-kuo Mei Shu Chia Hsieh Hui. Shang-hai Fen Hui. (1981)-. Chinese. One time a year. RMBY3.40. Hsin Hua Shu Tien / Shang-Hai Fa Hsing So, Shanghai, People's Republic of China.

LC N8.C5 S44
DD 705　　　　　　　　　　　　　　　　　　CC
SHIH CHIEH MEI SHU. VFOAT Shijiemeishu. (19??)-. Periodical. Chinese. Four times a year. $14.16. Science Press, 16 Donghuangchenggen North Street, Beijing 100707, People's Republic of China. **Tel** 011 86 1 4019821, 011 86 1 4010642, FAX 011 86 1 4012180, 011 86 1 4019810, telex 210147. **(Subscription address:** China International Book Trading Corporation, PO Box 399, Library Service Department, Beijing 100044 People's Republic of China. **Tel** 011 86 1 8414284, FAX 011 86 1 8412023, telex 22496 CIBTC CN.)

LC ND1055 .S427
JA
SHIKI NO ATORIE. (19??)-. Periodical. Japanese. Four times a year. ¥2100 single issue with supplement. Atoriesha, c/o Shinichi Building, 8 Yotsuya 2 Shinjuku-ku, Tokyo-to 160 Japan.

LC N3750.N36 S56
JA
SHOSOIN NEMPO. Added/Corp Shosoin Jimusho (Japan). Annual Report of Office of the Shosoin Treasure House. VFOAT Annual Report of Office of Shosoin Treasure House. (1979)-. Japanese. One time a year. Shosoin Jimusho, 129 Zoshicho, Nara Japan.

LC NX
DD 700　　　　　　　　　　　　　　　　　　CC
SHUFA. VFOAT Chinese Calligraphy. (19??)-. Chinese. Six times a year. $39.56 (airmail). **(Subscription address:** China International Book Trading Corporation, PO Box 399, Library Service Department, Beijing 100044 People's Republic of China. **Tel** 011 86 1 8414284, FAX 011 86 1 8412023, telex 22496 CIBTC CN.)

LC N7001.S56　　　　　　　　　　　　　ISSN 0782-7423
DD 700　　　　　　　　　　　　　　　　　　FI
SIKSI : THE NORDIC ART REVIEW. Added/Corp Nordiskt Konstcentrum. Vol. 1 (1986)-. Periodical. Norwegian (English). Four times a year (Mar., June, Sept., Dec.). $51.17. Siksi / Pohjoismainen Taidekeskus, Nordiskt Konstcentrum, Sveaborg, SF 00190 Helsinki Finland. **Tel** 011 358 0 668143, FAX 011 358 0 668594. **ED** Grethe Grathwol. Index available. **Bk Rev. Ad Acc. Circ:** 2,000 (ctrl).
 Desc: Nordic art magazine which deals primarily with contemporary Nordic art, aims to put it in artistic and philosophical context.
 Ind/Abst ARTbibliogr. Mod.; BHA : Biblio. Hist. Art.

LC N5 S55　　　　　　　　　　　　　　　ISSN 0037-5411
　　　　　　　　　　　　　　　　　　　　　　NE
SIMIOLUS. [Simiolus]. Vol. 1 (1966-67)-. Academic Scholarly Publication. Dutch (English and German). Four times a year. $109.63. Simiolus, Kromme Nieuwgracht 29, NL 3512 HD Utrecht The Netherlands. **Tel** 011 31 30 536526, FAX 011 31 30 516987. **ED** Peter Hecht. Index available. cum. index. **Bk Rev. Ad Acc. Circ:** 850 (ctrl). Documents available from The Genuine Article.
 Desc: Scholarly contributions to the history of Western European art, emphasis on studies in iconology and art theory; mainly Dutch and Flemish material is discussed.
 Ind/Abst Art Index; ARTbibliogr. Mod.; ARTbibliogr. Curr. Titles; Arts Humanit. Citation Index (19??-19??) [Full Cov.]; BHA : Biblio. Hist. Art; Curr. Contents Arts Humanit.; Res. Alert [Full Cov.].

LC N6.S56　　　　　　　　　　　　　　　ISSN 0049-0601
DD 705　　　　　　　　　　　　　　　　　　XV
SINTEZA. (197?)-. Periodical. Slovenian (English, German and Serbo-Croatian (Roman)). Four times a year. $40.00. Sinteza / Arts Magazine, Erjavceve 15/1, 61000 Ljublijana Slovenia. **ED** Stane Bernik. **Bk Rev**, (Qty: 6000). **Ad Acc. Circ:** 6000 (ctrl). *Formed by the union of* Arhitekt *and* Likovna Revija.

Ind/Abst Archit. Period. Index (1965-); BHA : Biblio. Hist. Art.

LC WMLC L 83/7667
GW
SITZUNGSBERICHTE / KUNSTGESCHICHTLICHE GESELLSCHAFT ZU BERLIN. Main/Corp Kunstgeschichtliche Gesellschaft zu Berlin. (19??)-. German. One time a year.
 Ind/Abst BHA : Biblio. Hist. Art.

LC NX513　　　　　　　　　　　　　　　ISSN 0821-2287
DD 709.713/541/025　　　　　　　　　　　　CN
SLATE (TORONTO). *See* Museums and Galleries.

LC NX
DD 700　　　　　　　　　　　　　　　　　　US
SOCIAL HISTORY OF MODERN ART, A. (1987)-. Monographic series. English. Irregular. Price varies per volume. University of Chicago Press / Book Department, 11030 South Langley Avenue, Chicago IL 60628. **Tel** (800)621-2736, (312)568-1550, FAX (312)753-0811, telex 23933.

LC NX　　　　　　　　　　　　　　　　　ISSN 0767-9203
DD 700　　　　　　　　　　　　　　　　　　FR
UDC 347.471.6(446.1)
SOCIETE D'EMULATION DE LA VENDEE (1971). [Soc. emul. Vendee 1971]. (1971)-. French. One time a year. *Continues* Vendee 2000, 0994-8236.
 Ind/Abst BHA : Biblio. Hist. Art.

LC NX　　　　　　　　　　　　　　　　　ISSN 0255-9773
DD 700　　　　　　　　　　　　　　　　　　SZ
UDC 7
SOFTART PRESS. [Softart press]. (1??)-. Periodical. French. Four times a year. Soft Art Press, No 9 Case Postale 858, CH-1001 Lausanne Switzerland.
 Ind/Abst BHA : Biblio. Hist. Art.

LC N8.K6 S66
KO
SON MISUL. VFOAT Sun Art Magazine. (1979)-. Periodical. Korean. Four times a year. Son Misul, 184 Insa-dong, Chongno-ku, Seoul South Korea.

LC N8640 .A7
DD 702.1/6　　　　　　　　　　　　　　　UK
SOTHEBY'S ART AT AUCTION. Main/Corp Sotheby's (Firm). **Added/Corp** Conran Octopus Limited. VFOAT Sotheby's. (1986/87)-. Periodical. English. $75.00 North America; $85.00 other. Sotheby's Subscriptions, PO Box 5111, Norwalk CT 06856. **Tel** (800)444-3709, (203)847-0465. *Continues* Art at Auction, 0084-6783.

LC N8640.S63 S67a
DD 707/.4　　　　　　　　　　　　　　　UK
SOTHERBY'S PREVIEW. Main/Corp Sotheby's (Firm). No. 66 (Oct./Nov. 1986)-. Periodical. English. Six times a year. *Continues* Sotheby's International Preview, 0144-8277.

LC ML1 .S8193　　　　　　　　　　　　　ISSN 0362-3955
DD 700/.5　　　　　　　　　　　　　　　　US
SOUND IMAGE. 1975- No. 1-. Periodical. English. Two times a year. $20.00. Sound Image Inc, County Road, Deerfield MA 01002.

LC NX　　　　　　　　　　　　　　　　　ISSN 0737-4453
DD 700　　　　　　　　　　　　　　　　　　US
SOURCE (NEW YORK, N.Y.). (SOURCE : NOTES IN THE HISTORY OF ART.). [Source]. Vol. 1, No. 1 (Fall 1981)-. Academic Scholarly Publication. English. Four times a year (Jan., Apr., Aug., Oct.). $25.00. Ars Bevis Foundation Inc, 1 East 87th Street, Suite 7 8-A, New York NY 10128. **Tel** (212)369-1667, FAX (212)360-6494. **ED** Laurie Schneider. **Circ:** 1,000. Documents available from The Genuine Article.
 Desc: Short articles on art and archaeology from antiquity to the present.
 Ind/Abst ARTbibliogr. Mod. (1981-); Arts Humanit. Citation Index [Full Cov.]; Avery Index Archit. Period. Suppl. Colum. Univ. (1990-); BHA : Biblio. Hist. Art; Curr. Contents Arts Humanit.; Res. Alert [Full Cov.]; RILA, Int. Rep. Lit. Art.

LC N
DD 702　　　　　　　　　　　　　　　　　　UK
●**SOURCES.** (1994)-. English. One time a year. Fine Arts Trade Guild, 16-18 Empress Place, London SW6 1TT United Kingdom. **Tel** 011 44 171 3816616, FAX 011 44 171 3812596. **ED** Vanessa Giles. **Circ:** 1,700 (ctrl).

LC N7392 .S63
DD 705　　　　　　　　　　　　　　　　　　SA
SOUTH AFRICAN JOURNAL OF ART AND ARCHITECTURAL HISTORY = SUID-AFRIKAANSE TYDSKRIF VIR KUNS- EN ARGITEKTUURGESKIEDENIS. Added/Corp South African Association of Art Historians. VFOAT Art and Architectural History; Kuns- en Argitektuurgeskiedenis; Suid-Afrikaanse Tydskrif vir Kuns- en Argitektuurgeskiedenis; SAJHEW; S. Afr. J. Art Archit. Hist. Vol. 1, No. 1 (Feb. 1990)-. Periodical. English (Afrikaans). Four times a year. $35.78. UNISA, PO Box 392, NJ Coetzee TVW11 47, Pretoria 0001 South Africa. **Tel** 011 27 12 4296212. *Continues in part* South African Journal of Cultural and Art History.
 Ind/Abst BHA : Biblio. Hist. Art.

LC N1 .S72　　　　　　　　　　　　　　　ISSN 1043-5158
DD 705　　　　　　　　　　　　　　　　　　US
SOUTHEASTERN COLLEGE ART CONFERENCE REVIEW. [Southeast. Coll. Art Conf. rev.]. **Added/Corp** Southeastern College Art Conference. VFOAT SECAC Review. Vol. 6, No. 1 (Fall 1973)-. Periodical. English. One time a year. SECAC Subscriptions, PO Box 508, Chapel Hill NC 27514. **Tel** (919)929-0547. *Continues in part* Southeastern College Art Review and Newsletter, 0584-4118.
 Ind/Abst BHA : Biblio. Hist. Art.

LC NX
DD 700　　　　　　　　　　　　　　　　　　US
SOUTHEASTERN FRONT. *See* Literature.

LC NX　　　　　　　　　　　　　　　　　ISSN 0749-5528
DD 700　　　　　　　　　　　　　　　　　　US
SOUTHERN CALIFORNIA WOMEN'S CAUCUS FOR ART. (SOUTHERN CALIFORNIA WOMEN'S CAUCUS FOR ART : NEWSLETTER.). **Added/Corp** Southern California Women's Caucus for Art. VFOAT WCA; W.C.A.; Southern California WCA; Southern California W.C.A. (19??)-. Newsletter. English. The Caucus, PO Box 1707, Santa Monica CA 90406.

LC N6525 .S58　　　　　　　　　　　　　ISSN 0192-4214
DD 705　　　　　　　　　　　　　　　　　　US
SOUTHWEST ART. [Southwest art]. VFOAT Southwest Art Magazine. Vol. 3, No. 1 (Summer 1973)-. Periodical. English. Twelve times a year. $32.00. Southwest Art, 5444 Westheimer, Suite 1440, Houston TX 77056. **Tel** (713)850-0990, FAX (713)850-1314. **(Subscription address:** Neodata / Colorado, PO Box 2606, Boulder CO 80322.) Index available (bound in issue). *Continues* Southwest Art Gallery Magazine, 0091-8830; *Absorbed* Western Art Digest, 0883-8992.
 Ind/Abst Access (1975-); Art Index; ARTbibliogr. Mod. (1984-); ARTbibliogr. Curr. Titles; West. Hist. Q.

LC N6525 .S6　　　　　　　　　　　　　ISSN 0038-4739
DD 705　　　　　　　　　　　　　　　　　　US
TITLE CHANGE
SOUTHWESTERN ART. [Southwest. art]. (1966-)(19??-). Periodical. English. available on microfilm and microfiche from University Microfilms International (UMI). *Continued by* Al. Art Insight, 0194-9071.
 Ind/Abst Am. Hist. Life (1973-1978).

LC DK1 .S5465　　　　　　　　　　　　　ISSN 0134-4315
DD 839.07　　　　　　　　　　　　　　　　RU
TITLE CHANGE
SOVETIS HEYMLAND. *See* Literature.

LC NX　　　　　　　　　　　　　　　　　ISSN 0256-260X
DD 700　　　　　　　　　　　　　　　　　　RU
UDC 7
SOVETSKAA GRAFIKA. [Sov. graf.]. (1???)-. Periodical. Russian. One time a year.
 Ind/Abst BHA : Biblio. Hist. Art.

LC NB688 .S622
RU
SOVETSKAIA SKULPTURA. (1974)-. Periodical. Russian. 1.92rub. Izdatelstvo Sovetskii Khudozhnik, Ulitsa Cherniakhovskogo 4a, 12319 Moscow Russia.

LC N6988 .S653
RU
SOVETSKOE DEKORATIVNOE ISKUSSTVO. (1974)-. Periodical. Russian. One time a year. Izdatelstvo Sovetskii Khudozhnik, Ulitsa Cherniakhovskogo 4a, 12319 Moscow Russia.
 Ind/Abst BHA : Biblio. Hist. Art.

LC N380 .S68
RU
SOVETSKOE ISKUSSTVOZNANIE. Added/Corp Izdatelstvo "Sovetskii Khudozhnik.". (1973)-. Russian (summaries and/or abstracts in English). **(Subscription address:** East View Publications Inc., 3020 Harbor Lane North, Suite 110, Minneapolis MN 55447. **Tel** (800)477-1005, (612)550-0961, FAX (612)559-2931.)
 Ind/Abst BHA : Biblio. Hist. Art.

LC TA1 .C39417
DD 620/.007/1142134　　　　　　　　　　UK
SPANNER. Added/Corp City and Guilds College Union. (1974)-. English. Irregular. £12.00 (3 issues). Spanner, 14 Hopton Road, Hereford HR1 1BE United Kingdom. **Tel** 011 44 1432 277857. **ED** Allen Fisher. **Bk Rev**, (Qty: varies). *Absorbed* Guilds' Engineer.
 Desc: Working series of papers with original art and poetry matter and reviews. Often centers on one artist per issue.

LC NX ISSN 0225-9044
DD 700 CN
SPIRALE (MONTREAL). (SPIRALE.). [Spirale]. (Sept. 1979)-. Periodical. French. Six times a year. 37.20Can$ (one-year), 51.15Can$ (two-year) institutions; 26.04Can$ (one-year), 41.85Can$ (two-year) individuals, Canada; 32.55Can$ (one-year), 46.50Can$ (two-year) individuals, other. Spirale, 426 Sherbrooke East / 2nd Floor, Montreal Quebec H2L 1J6 Canada. **Tel** (514)982-3725.

LC NX ISSN 0947-5427
DD 700 GW
●**SPRINGER HEFTE FUER GEGENWARTSKUNST.** (1995)-. German. Six times a year. DM90.00. Springer-Verlag GmbH & Company KG, Heidelberger Platz 3, D-14197 Berlin Germany. **Tel** 011 49 30 8207223, FAX 011 49 30 8214091, telex 183 319 SPBLN D. **(Subscription address:** Springer-Verlag New York Inc. / North America, PO Box 2485, Journal Fulfillment, Secaucus NJ 07096. **Tel** (201)348-4033, (800)777-4643, FAX (201)348-4505.**)**

LC AP2 ISSN 0896-8276
DD 051 US
ST. PAUL'S FAMILY MAGAZINE. See Literature.

LC NX ISSN 0585-0118
DD 700 GW
STAEDEL-JAHRBUCH. Added/Corp Staedelsches Kunstinstitut. **VAT** Staedel Jahrbuch. (1921)-. German. Every 2 years. DM110.00. Prestel Verlag, Mandlstrasse 26, D-80802 Munich Germany. **Tel** 011 49 89 3817090, FAX 011 49 89 38170935, telex 5216366.
Ind/Abst BHA : Biblio. Hist. Art.

LC N781 .A3 ISSN 1081-4825
DD 708.194/73/06 US
●**STANFORD UNIVERSITY MUSEUM OF ART JOURNAL. See** Museums and Galleries.

LC N8836.C2 S732
US
STATE OF THE ARTS : A PUBLICATION OF THE CALIFORNIA ARTS COUNCIL. Added/Corp California Arts Council. Vol. 1, No. 1 (Spring 1992)-. English. ***Continues*** *California Arts Council.; News.*

LC AP86 .S8
RM
STEAUA. See Literary and Political Reviews.

LC NX
DD 700 US
STEPPING OUT ARTS MAGAZINE. No. 27 (1988)-. Periodical. English. Two times a year (Jan., & Aug.). $7.00. Steppin Out Art Buyers Magazine, 510 Southwest 3rd Avenue, Suite 1, Portland OR 97204. **Tel** (503)241-2787, FAX (503)241-2789. **ED** James Bach. **Ad Acc, Adv Mgr:** J. R. Reimann. **Circ:** 50,000. ***Continues*** *Stepping Out Magazine (Portland, Or. : 1984).*
Desc: Features articles on artists as well as visual art for sale from galleries or private parties.

LC NX ISSN 0491-0850
DD 700 SW
STOCKHOLM STUDIES IN HISTORY OF ART. (1956)-. Monographic series. Multiple languages (English, German and Swedish). Irregular. Price varies per volume. Scandinavian University Press, PO Box 2959 Toeyen, N 0608 Oslo 6 Norway. **Tel** 011 47 2 2575400, FAX 011 47 2 2575353, telex 71896 UROR N. **(Subscription address:** Scandinavian University Press, 200 Meacham Ave., Elmont NY 11003. **Tel** (516)352-7300, FAX (516)352-7377.**)**

LC NB1 .M8 ISSN 0160-7243
DD 338.4/7/7315490973 US
STONE IN AMERICA. Added/Corp American Monument Association. (19??)-. Trade Publication. English. Twelve times a year. $30.00. American Monument Association, 933 High Street / Suite 220, Worthington OH 43085-4046. **Tel** (614)885-2713. **ED** Robert Moon. **Ad Acc. Circ:** 2,200. ***Continues*** *Monumental News-Review.*
Desc: A trade magazine for the monument retailers in the US and other countries.

LC N4 .S84 ISSN 0392-4513
IT
STORIA DELLARTE. [Stor. arte]. (1969)-. Periodical. Italian (English and German). Irregular. L95380. La Nuova Italia Editrice Spa, Via Ernesto Codignola, 50018 Scandicci Florence Italy. **Tel** 011 39 55 75901, FAX 011 39 55 7590208. cum. index. **Circ:** 1,200. Documents available from The Genuine Article.
Ind/Abst ARTbibliogr. Mod.; Arts Humanit. Citation Index [Full Cov.]; Avery Index Archit. Period. Suppl. Colum. Univ. (1989-); BHA : Biblio. Hist. Art; Res. Alert [Full Cov.].

LC PG3199 .S77 ISSN 0747-7287
DD 891 US
STRELEC (JERSEY CITY, N.J.). See Literature.

ISSN 0081-6027
DD 705 CN
STRUCTURIST, THE. [Structurist]. No. 1 (1961)-. Periodical. English. Every 2 years (Oct.). 48.00Can$. University of Saskatchewan, PO Box 378, Saskatoon Saskatchewan S7N 0W0 Canada. **Tel** (306)966-4198, (306)652-9740. **ED** Eli Bornstein. Index available. cum. index. **Bk Rev. Circ:** 1,500. available on microfilm and microfiche from University Microfilms International (UMI).
Desc: Ideas and processes of creation in art and their relationships to nature and society. These issues explore problems and the future of art.
Ind/Abst Am. Humanit. Index (-199?); Art Index; ARTbibliogr. Mod.; Avery Index Archit. Period. Suppl. Colum. Univ. (19??-199?); BHA : Biblio. Hist. Art.

LC NX ISSN 0392-1727
DD 700 IT
STUDI BITONTINI. Added/Corp Centro Ricerche di Storia e Arte Bitontina. **VFOAT** Studibitontini. (19??)-. Periodical. Italian. Three times a year.
Ind/Abst BHA : Biblio. Hist. Art.

LC N6911 .S77
DD 709/.45/05 IT
STUDI DI STORIA DELL'ARTE. (1990)-. Periodical. Italian (English). One time a year. L68130. Ediart, Via XXV Aprile 1A, 06059 Todi PG Italy. **Tel** 011 39 75 8942411.
Ind/Abst BHA : Biblio. Hist. Art.

LC NX
DD 700 IT
STUDI DI STORIA DELLE ARTI. Added/Corp Universita di Genova. Istituto di Storia dell'Arte. (1977)-. Italian. One time a year.
Ind/Abst BHA : Biblio. Hist. Art.

LC N61 ISSN 0081-7104
DD 701 PL
STUDIA Z HISTORII SZTUKI. Added/Corp Warsaw. Pantswowy Instytut Sztuki. (19??)-. Monographic series. Polish. Irregular. Price varies per volume. Polska Akademia Nauk, Instytut Sztuki / Polish Academy of Sciences, Institute of Fine Arts, Ul. Dluga 26/28, 00-950 Warsaw Poland. **Tel** 011 48 22 313271, FAX 011 48 22 313149.
Ind/Abst BHA : Biblio. Hist. Art.

LC N6.5 .S78 ISSN 0039-3452
DD 705 SW
STUDIEKAMRATEN. [Studiekamraten]. **Added/Corp** Arbetarnas Bildningsforbund. Bibliotekstjanst. (19??)-. Periodical. Swedish. Six times a year. Kr170.10. Bibliotekstjanst AB, Box 200, S-221 00 Lund Sweden. **Tel** 011 46 46 180000. cum. index.
Ind/Abst MLA Int. Bibl. Books Artic. Mod. Lang. Lit.

LC NX
DD 700 GE
STUDIEN ZUR KUNSTGESCHICHTE. German. Georg Olms Verlag AG Weidmann, Hagentorwall 6 7, D-31134 Hildesheim Germany. **Tel** 011 49 5121 15010, FAX 011 49 5121 150150, telex 927454 OLMS D.

LC N81 .S84 ISSN 0039-3541
DD 707 US
STUDIES IN ART EDUCATION. [Stud. art ed.]. **Added/Corp** National Art Education Association. Vol. 1 (Fall 1959)-. Academic Scholarly Publication. English. Four times a year (Jan., Apr., Jul., Oct.). $25.00. National Art Education Association, 1916 Association Drive, Reston VA 22091-1590. **Tel** (703)860-8000, FAX (703)860-2960. **ED** Georgia Collins. cum. index. **Bk Rev. Circ:** 5,100. available on microfilm and microfiche from University Microfilms International (UMI).
Desc: A journal of research in visual art education, consisting of scholarly papers which deal in-depth with a topic of historical, empirical, or philosophical issues in art education.
Ind/Abst Acad. Search; ARTbibliogr. Mod.; ARTbibliogr. Curr. Titles; Contents Pages Educ.; Curr. Cit.; Curr. Index J. Educ.; Educ. Index; EP Collect.; Homework Help.; Humanit. Source; INFO-SOUTH Abstr.; Mag. Search; MasterFile FullTEXT 1000; MasterFile FullTEXT 350; MasterFile FullTEXT 650; MasterFile FullTEXT (July 1993-); OCLC; Spec. Educ. Needs Abstr.; Telebase.

LC N380 .M54A ISSN 0146-5244
DD 709 US
STUDIES IN ART HISTORY PRESENTED AT THE MIDDLE ATLANTIC SYMPOSIUM IN THE HISTORY OF ART. Main/Conf Middle Atlantic Symposium in the History of Art. Vol. 1 (1971/73)-. English. University of Maryland / Annual Report of the President, College Park MD 20742.

LC NX
DD 700 NE
STUDIES IN ASIAN ART AND ARCHAEOLOGY. (199?)-. English. E.J. Brill, Postbus 9000, 2300 PA Leiden The Netherlands. **Tel** 011 31 71 312624, FAX 011 31 71 317532, telex 39296 BRILL NL. ***Continues*** *Studies in South Asian Culture, 0169-9865.*

LC NX
DD 700 US
STUDIES IN BRITISH ART. Added/Corp Paul Mellon Centre for Studies in British Art, London. Paul Mellon Foundation for British Art. (19??)-. Monographic series. English. Irregular. Price varies per volume. Yale University Press, PO Box 209040, New Haven CT 06520. **Tel** (203)432-0940, (800)987-7323, FAX (203)432-0948.

LC N8560 .S82 ISSN 0039-3630
UK
CODEN SCONAH
Pr Rev.
STUDIES IN CONSERVATION. [Stud. conserv.]. **VFOAT** Etudes de Conservation. Vol. 1 (Oct. 1952)-. Periodical. English (French). Four times a year (Feb., May, Aug., Nov.). $60.00. International Institute for Conservation, 6 Buckingham Street, London WC2N 6BA United Kingdom. **Tel** 011 44 171 8395975, FAX 011 44 171 9761564. **ED** David Bomford, Ann Moncrieff, David Scott, Velson Horie. Index available. cum. index. **Bk Rev. Ad Acc. Circ:** 5,000. Documents available from CASDDS.
Desc: Original work and reviews on advances in conservation and restoration of historic and artistic works, covering both practical and scientific aspects.
Ind/Abst AESIS Q.; Anthropol. Lit.; Art Archaeol. Tech. Abstr.; Art Index; Avery Index Archit. Period. Suppl. Colum. Univ. (19??-199?); Biodeter. Abstr. (1991-); Br. Archaeol. Bibliogr.; Chem. Abstr.; Curr. Cit.; Museum Abstr.; Numis. Lit.; World Surf. Coat. Abstr.

LC N6512 .S79 ISSN 1058-997X
DD 709/.73/0904 US
STUDIES IN MODERN ART. [Stud. mod. art]. **Added/Corp** Museum of Modern Art (New York, N.Y.). (1991)-. English. One time a year (Nov.). $24.90. Museum of Modern Art, 11 West 53rd Street, New York NY 10019. **Tel** (212)708-9888, FAX (212)708-9889. **ED** John Elaerfield. **Circ:** 2000.
Desc: A publication from the Research and Scholarly Publications Program at The Museum of Modern Art New York, devoted to discussion of the arts of this century, focusing on the Museum's own collections and archival material.
Ind/Abst BHA : Biblio. Hist. Art.

LC E51 .S85 ISSN 0585-7023
US
STUDIES IN PRE-COLUMBIAN ART AND ARCHAEOLOGY. See Archaeology.

LC N6370
DD 709.024 US
STUDIES IN RENAISSANCE ART HISTORY. (1984)-. Monographic series. English. Irregular. Price varies per volume. University Microfilms International, 300 North Zeeb Road, Ann Arbor MI 48106-1346. **Tel** (313)761-4700, (800)521-0600 Exts. 2490, 2491, FAX (313)973-1540.

LC N386.U5 S78 ISSN 0091-7338
DD 709 US
STUDIES IN THE HISTORY OF ART. [Stud. hist. art]. **Added/Corp** National Gallery of Art (U.S.). (1972)-. Monographic series. English. Irregular. Price varies per volume. University Press of New England, 23 South Main Street, Hanover NH 03755. **Tel** (800)421-1561, (603)643-7110, FAX (603)643-1540. Documents available from The Genuine Article. ***Supersedes in part*** *Report and Studies in the History of Art, 0080-1240.*
Desc: Early volumes elaborate on the holdings of the National Gallery. Later volumes concentrate on specific artistic themes.
Ind/Abst Art Archaeol. Tech. Abstr.; Art Index; ARTbibliogr. Mod.; Arts Humanit. Citation Index [Full Cov.]; Avery Index Archit. Period. Suppl. Colum. Univ. (19??-199?); BHA : Biblio. Hist. Art; Curr. Contents Arts Humanit.; Res. Alert [Full Cov.].

LC NX ISSN 0886-0424
DD 709 US
STUDIES IN THE HISTORY OF ART (WILLIAMSTOWN, MASS.). (STUDIES IN THE HISTORY OF ART.). [Stud. hist. art]. **Added/Corp** Williams College. Museum of Art. (197?)-. Monographic series. English. Irregular. Price varies per volume.
Ind/Abst BHA : Biblio. Hist. Art.

LC N8 .S86 ISSN 0039-3983
RM
STUDII SI CERCETARI DE ISTORIA ARTEI. SERIA ARTA PLASTICA. (STUDII SI CERCETARI DE ISTORIA ARTEI. SERIA ARTA PLASTICA / ACADEMIA DE STIINTE SOCIALE SI POLITICE A REPUBLICII SOCIALISTE ROMANIA.). [Stud. cercet. ist. artei, Ser. arta plast.]. **Added/Corp** Institutul de Istoria Artei (Academia de Stiinte Sociale si Politice a Republicii Socialiste Romania) Academia de Stiinte Sociale si Politice a Republicii Socialiste Romania. Academia Republicii Socialiste Romania. **VFOAT** Seria Arta Plastica. Vol. 11 (1964)-. Romanian. One time a year. DM210.00. Editura Academia Republicii Socialiste

Romania, Calea Victoriei Nr 125, R-79717 Bucuresti Romania. **Tel** telex 10376 PRSFI R. **(Subscription address:** Kubon & Sagner, ABT Zeitschriftenimport, D 80328 Munich Germany. **Tel** 011 49 89 54218130.) ***Continues in part*** *Studii si Cercetari de Istoria Artei.*
Desc: Publishes articles and studies in the field of the fine arts.
Ind/Abst BHA : Biblio. Hist. Art; Numis. Lit.

ISSN 1185-3476
DD 709/.7127 CN
STUDIO FILE. [Stud. file]. **Added/Corp** Canadian Artists' Representation Manitoba. Vol. 1, No. 1 (Jan. 1991)-. Periodical. English. Irregular. Canadian Artists' Representation, 221-100 Arthur Street, Winnipeg Manitoba R3B 1H3 Canada. ***Continues*** *Arterra., 0828-3699.*

LC NC348 .S935
DD 741.951 CC
SU MIAO. **VFOAT** Su Miao Tsung Kan. (1981)-. Chinese.

LC NX
DD 700 SP
SUMMA ARTIS, HISTORIA GENERAL DEL ARTE. (1931)-. Spanish. Irregular. Espasa-Calpe SA, Apartado 547, Madrid 28049S Spain. **Tel** 011 34 1 3589689. **ED** F.G. Gutierrez.

LC NX **ISSN** 0039-6168
DD 700 UK
SURREALIST TRANSFORMA(C)TION. **VFOAT** Surrealist Transformation. (196?)-. Periodical. English (French). Irregular (2-3 issues per year). £1.50 (per issue). British Surrealist Group, Tranformacion Peeks Harpford, Sidmouth Devon EX10 0NH United Kingdom. **ED** John Lyle. **Circ:** 1,000. available with illustrations.

LC N55.S9 S95
DD 702/.5/494 SZ
SWISS ART GUIDE. (19??)-. English (French and German). One time a year. Swiss Art Guide, Postfach CH-8034, Zurich Switzerland.

LC DS94.5 .S8 **ISSN** 0039-7946
DD 913.394 FR
SYRIA. **See** Archaeology.

LC N6 .S87 **ISSN** 0324-8232
PL
SZTUKA. [Sztuka]. Vol. 1 (1974)-. Periodical. Polish (summaries and/or abstracts in English and Russian). Twelve times a year. Price on request. **(Subscription address:** Ars Polona-Ruch, PO Box 1001, Krakowskie Przedmiescie 7, 00-068 Warsaw Poland. **Tel** 011 48 22 261201.) ***Continues*** *Przeglad Artystyczny.*
Ind/Abst ARTbibliogr. Mod.; ARTbibliogr. Curr. Titles; BHA : Biblio. Hist. Art.

LC NX **ISSN** 0860-3464
DD 700 PL
UDC 7.067.2
SZTUKA DLA DZIECKA. [Szt. Dziec.]. (1986)-. Periodical. Polish. Six times a year. Price on request. **(Subscription address:** Ars Polona-Ruch, PO Box 1001, Krakowskie Przedmiescie 7, 00-068 Warsaw Poland. **Tel** 011 48 22 261201.)

LC NX **ISSN** 0166-4492
DD 700 NE
TABLEAU (UTRECHT). (TABLEAU.). [Tableau]. (Oct./Nov. 1978)-. Periodical. Dutch (English; summaries and/or abstracts in English). Six times a year. $52.00 US; $100.00 other. Tableau BV, Grote Haven 1, 2851 BM Haastrecht Netherlands. **Tel** 011 31 1821 1216.
Ind/Abst BHA : Biblio. Hist. Art.

LC N400 **ISSN** 0841-8012
DD 708.11/274 CN
TABLEAU (WINNEPEG, MAN.). **See** Museums and Galleries.

LC N8 .T33 **ISSN** 0039-8977
DD 700 FI
TAIDE. [Taide]. **Added/Corp** Suomen Taiteilijaseura. (1960)-. Finnish (English). Six times a year. Fmk235.00 Finland; Fmk275.00 Scandinavia; Fmk315.00 other. Artists Association of Finland, Ainonkatu 3, 00100 Helsinki 10 Finland. **ED** Carolus Enckell and Jaakko Lintinen. Index available. cum. index. **Bk Rev. Ad Acc. Circ:** 7,586 (ctrl). ***Continues*** *Suomen Taide.*
Ind/Abst ARTbibliogr. Mod.; BHA : Biblio. Hist. Art.

LC N5303 .T3 **ISSN** 0355-1938
FI
TAIDEHISTORIALLISIA TUTKIMUKSIA. (TAIDEHISTORIALLISIA TUTKIMUKSIA. KONSTHISTORISKA STUDIER.). [Taidehist. tutk.]. **Added/Corp** Taidehistorian Seura. **VFOAT** Konsthistoriska Studier. (1974)-. Periodical. Finnish (Swedish). One time a year. Academic Bookstore Akateeminen, Postilokero 23, FIN-00371 Helsinki Finland. **Tel** 011 358 0 12141.
Ind/Abst Am. Hist. Life (1982-); ARTbibliogr. Mod. (1984-); BHA : Biblio. Hist. Art.

LC NX **ISSN** 1351-3737
DD 700 UK
TATE. (19??)-. Academic Scholarly Publication. English. Three times a year. $29.00. Wordsearch Ltd., #26 Cramer Street, London W1M 3HE United Kingdom. **Tel** 011 44 171 4867419, FAX 011 44 171 4861451. **(Subscription address:** Wordsearch Ltd. / North America Subscriptions, Subscription Office, PO Box 1584, Birmingham AL 35201-1584. **Tel** (800)633-4931, (205)995-1567 (outside US and Canada), FAX (205)995-1588.) **ED** Tim Marlow. **Bk Rev. Ad Acc.**

LC WMLC L 83/1793
AT
TECHNICAL AND FURTHER EDUCATION. ART, DESIGN AND FASHION. **Main/Corp** Western Australia. Technical Education Division. **VFOAT** Art, Design and Fashion. (19??)-. Periodical. English. Irregular. Nelson Wadsworth, PO Box 4725, Melbourne Victoria, 3001 Australia. **Tel** 03 329-5199.

LC N8554 .T4 **ISSN** 0146-1214
DD 702/.8 US
CODEN TECODM
TECHNOLOGY & CONSERVATION. [Technol. conserv.]. **VAT** Technology and Conservation. (Spring 1976)-. Academic Scholarly Publication. English. Four times a year. $25.00. Technology Organization Inc, One Emerson Place, Boston MA 02114. **Tel** (617)227-8581. **ED** S E Schur. **Bk Rev. Ad Acc. Circ:** 15,500 (ctrl). Documents available from CASDDS.
Desc: Devoted to the analysis, preservation, restoration, rehabilitation, protection, and documentation of art, architecture, and antiquities. Provides art, architectural, and archeological conservators, etc.
Ind/Abst Archit. Period. Index (1976-); Art Archaeol. Tech. Abstr.; Art Index; Avery Index Archit. Period. Suppl. Colum. Univ. (19??-199?); Chem. Abstr.; Constr. Index; Inf. Sci. Abstr. (?-?).

LC NX **ISSN** 1186-611X
DD 700/.835 CN
TEEN ARTS CONNECTION/TORONTO. **See** Children and Youth Interests.

LC NX
DD 700 IT
Pr Rev.
TEMA CELESTE. (Nov. 1983)-. Periodical. Italian (English). Five times a year. L27250. Tema Celeste, Via Rovani 11, 20123 Milan Italy. **Tel** 011 39 2 4813734, FAX 011 39 2 4690305. Index available. cum. index. **Bk Rev**, (Qty: varies). **Ad Acc**, **Adv Mgr Tel** 011 39 2 4813734. **Circ:** 8,000 (ctrl).
Desc: Reviews of exhibitions in Europe and the US. Articles and text on and by artists and galleries.
Ind/Abst BHA : Biblio. Hist. Art.

LC NX
DD 700 IC
TENINGUR. **See** Literature.

LC N3128 .A35 **ISSN** 0802-7323
DD 709/.04/50744823 NO
TERSKEL. **Added/Corp** Museet for Samtidskunst (Norway). **VFOAT** Threshold. (1990)-. Periodical. English (Norwegian). Museet for Samtidskunst, Bankplassen 4, Postboks 8191, Dep. 0034 Oslo Norway.
Ind/Abst BHA : Biblio. Hist. Art.

LC N6490 .T47
IT
TERZOOCCHIO. **VFOAT** Terzo Occhio. Vol. 1 (Jan. 1975)-. Periodical. Italian (English, French, Italian and Spanish). Four times a year. L17040. Edizioni Bora, Via Jacopo di Paolo 42, 40128 Bologna Italy. **Tel** 011 39 51 356133, FAX 011 39 51 374394. **ED** Angelo Mazzei. Index available. cum. index. **Bk Rev**, (Qty: 20). **Ad Acc. Circ:** 10,000 (ctrl).

LC NK1451 .T45 **ISSN** 0074-1191
DD 705 GR
THEMATA CHOROU + TECHNON. **See** Architecture.

LC NX596.3.A1 T5 **ISSN** 0952-8822
UK
CCC
THIRD TEXT. [Third text]. No. 1 (Autumn 1987)-. Periodical. English. Four times a year. £42.00. Carfax Publishing Company, PO Box 25, Abingdon, Oxfordshire OX14 3UE United Kingdom. **Tel** 011 44 1235 555335, FAX 011 44 1235 553559, telex 817484. ***Continues*** *Black Phoenix, 0141-9080.*
Desc: Third World perspectives on contemporary art & culture.
Ind/Abst BHA : Biblio. Hist. Art.

ISSN 1074-455X
DD 738 US
TITLE CHANGE
TILE WORLD. [Tile world]. (198?)-(199?). Periodical. English. Business News Publishing Company, 755 West Big Beaver Road, Suite 1000, Troy MI 48084. **Tel** (810)362-3700, FAX (810)362-0317, telex 230295. **(Subscription address:** Tradelink Publications, PO Box 960, Pearl River NY 10965.) ***Continued by*** *Tile Design & Installation, 1077-6974.*

LC N6480 .T58 **ISSN** 1120-5539
IT
TITOLO : RIVISTA SCIENTIFICO-CULTURALE D'ARTE CONTEMPORANEA. (1990)-. Periodical. Italian. Three times a year. L20440. Grafiche Benucci Srl, Via Volta, 06087 Pte S Giovanni PG Italy. **Tel** 011 39 75 39441. ***Continues*** *Artinumbria, 0393-747X.*

LC ND1042 .T6
DD 759.951 CC
TO YUN. (1981)-. Periodical. Chinese. RMBY2.00. Hsin Hua Shu Tien / Shang-Hai Fa Hsing So, Shanghai, People's Republic of China.

LC DA100 .A72 **ISSN** 0951-001X
DD 941 UK
TRANSACTIONS OF THE ANCIENT MONUMENTS SOCIETY. [Trans. Anc. Monum. Soc.]. **Main/Corp** Ancient Monuments Society. (1924)-. English. One time a year. £12.00. Ancient Monument Society, Saint Anns Vestry, 2 Church Ent, London EC4V 5HB United Kingdom. **Tel** 011 44 171 2363934, FAX 011 44 171 3293677. **ED** Gwyn Meirion-Jones. **Bk Rev. Circ:** 2,300 (ctrl). Documents available from The Genuine Article.
Desc: Founded in 1924, the study and conservation of ancient monuments, historical buildings and fine old craftsmanship.
Ind/Abst Archit. Period. Index (1971-)(1953-); Arts Humanit. Citation Index (19??-19??) [Full Cov.]; Avery Index Archit. Period. Suppl. Colum. Univ. (1990-); BHA : Biblio. Hist. Art; Br. Archaeol. Bibliogr.; Br. Humanit. Index; Curr. Contents Arts Humanit.; Res. Alert [Full Cov.].

LC NX
DD 700 FR
SUSPENDED
TRAVAUX DE L'INSTITUT D'ART PREHISTORIQUE. **Main/Corp** Universite de Toulouse-Le Mirail. Institut d'Art Prehistorique. Vol. 1 (1958)-Suspended (1992). French. One time a year. 90.00F. Universite de Toulouse--Le Mirail, 56 rue du Taur, 31000 Toulouse France. **Tel** 011 33 61 225831, FAX 011 33 61 218420.

LC N6851.L8 U54a **ISSN** 0181-4400
DD 709/.44/5823 FR
TRAVAUX DE L'INSTITUT D'HISTOIRE DE L'ART DE LYON. **Added/Corp** Universite de Lyon II. Institut d'Histoire de l'Art. Centre National de la Recherche Scientifique. Equipe de Recherche Associee (E.R.A. 445). (19??)-. French.
Ind/Abst BHA : Biblio. Hist. Art.

LC NX **ISSN** 0336-9730
DD 700 FR
CEASED
TRAVERSES. **Added/Corp** Centre de Creation Industrielle. (Sept. 1975)-No. 8 (Dec. 1993). Monographic series. French. Editions du Centre Pompidou, Service Commerical, 75191 Paris Cedex 04 France. **Tel** 011 33 1 44784288, 011 33 1 44781233, FAX 011 33 1 42725650, telex CNAC GP 212 726. **ED** Hugette Le Bot.
Desc: Each issue proposes researches about a theme, in connection with the contemporary life and reflection.
Ind/Abst BHA : Biblio. Hist. Art.

LC NX
DD 700 FR
TRIBAL ARTS SALES CATALOGUE. (19??)-. French. Etudes Loudner, 45 rue Lafayette, 75009 Paris France.

LC NX **ISSN** 0396-6356
DD 700 FR
UDC 64
TROUVAILLES (PARIS. 1976). [Trouvailles Paris, 1976]. (1976)-. Periodical. French. Ten times a year. $66.71. Equimag Trouvailles, Domaine de Javercy, 28300 Coltainville France. **Tel** 011 33 1 37319898.

LC ND497.T8 T87 **ISSN** 0260-597X
DD 760/.092/4 UK
CCC
CEASED
TURNER STUDIES. [Turner stud.]. **Added/Corp** Tate Gallery. Vol. 1, No. 1 (1980)-Vol. 11, No. 2 (1993). Periodical. English. Carfax Publishing Company, PO Box 25, Abingdon, Oxfordshire OX14 3UE United Kingdom. **Tel** 011 44 1235 555335, FAX 011 44 1235 553559, telex 817484. **ED** Eric Shanes. **Bk Rev.** available on microfiche.
Desc: An international journal that publishes research into all aspects of the artist's work, life and times.
Ind/Abst ARTbibliogr. Mod. (1984-); BHA : Biblio. Hist. Art (?-?).

The Arts —Art

LC NX
DD 700
ISSN 0041-4565
RU

TVORCHESTVO. [Tvorchestvo]. **Added/Corp** Soiuz Khudozhnikov SSSR. Soiuz Sovetskikh Khudozhnikov i Skulpturov. (1934)-. Periodical. Russian. Twelve times a year. $99.95. Izdatelstvo Sovetskii Khudozhnik, Ulitsa Cherniakhovskoga 4a, 12319 Moscow Russia. **(Subscription address:** East View Publications Inc., 3020 Harbor Lane North, Suite 110, Minneapolis MN 55447. **Tel** (800)477-1005, (612)550-0961, FAX (612)559-2931.) Index available. **Bk Rev**
Ind/Abst ARTbibliogr. Mod.; ARTbibliogr. Curr. Titles; BHA : Biblio. Hist. Art; Numis. Lit.

LC NX
DD 700
GW

TWO THOUSAND TWENTY-NINE : 2029.
VFOAT 2029. English. Irregular. $44.00 (six issues). Peter S Forsten 2029 Magazine, Poolstrasse 7, D-20355 Hamburg Germany. **Tel** 011 49 40 352734.

LC N6505 .U17
DD 709/.73/05
ISSN 0899-1782
US

U.S. ART. [U. S. art]. **VFOAT** US Art. **VAT** United States Art. Vol. 1, No. 1 July/Aug. (1988)-. Periodical. English. Nine times a year (except Feb., June, and Aug.). $29.25. MSP Communication, 220 South 6th Street, Suite 500, Minneapolis MN 55402. **Tel** (612)339-7571, FAX (612)339-5806. **ED** Paul Froiland. **Continues** Midwest Art (Minneapolis, Minn.), 0744-6217.

LC NX
DD 700
ISSN 0734-8401
US

U TURN. Vol. 1 (Fall 1982)-. Periodical. English. One time a year. James Hugunin, 2171 West Giddings Street, Suite 2, Chicago IL 60625. ctrl circ.

LC TS540
DD 681.11
UDC 681.11 :7.074
ISSN 0942-2366
GW

UHREN (1992). [Uhren 1992]. (1992)-. Periodical. German. Six times a year. DM132.00. Verlag Georg DW Callwey GmbH., Postfach 800409, D-81604 Munich Germany. **Tel** 011 49 89 43600533. **Continues** Alte Uhren und Moderne Zeitmessung, 0932-2655.

LC NX
DD 700
NE

UITGAVE VAN DE VERENIGING REMBRANDT. **Added/Corp** Vereniging Rembrandt. **VFOAT** Vereniging Rembrandt, Nationaal Fonds Kunstbehoud. Vol. 1, No. 1 (1991)-. Periodical. Dutch. Two times a year.
Ind/Abst BHA : Biblio. Hist. Art.

LC DB975.K6 U37
ISSN 0133-5332
HU

UJ FORRAS. See Literature.

LC N7350 .U38
JA

UKIYOE GEIJUTSU. **Added/Corp** Nihon Ukiyoe Kyokai. **VFOAT** Ukiyo-E Art; A Journal of the Japan Ukiyo-E Society. (19??)-. Japanese (English). Four times a year. $166.50. **(Subscription address:** Japan Publications Trading Company Ltd., PO Box 5030, Tokyo International, Tokyo 100-31 Japan. **Tel** 011 81 3 3292 3753.)

DD 741
ISSN 1062-9122
US

ULTRA HAWK. [Ultra hawk]. **VFOAT** UltraHawk. (Apr. 1992)-. Periodical. English. Six times a year. $9.00. DMS Enterprises, 245 8th Avenue Suite 281, New York NY 10011.

LC NX
DD 700
UDC 70
ISSN 0160-0699
US

UMBRELLA (GLENDALE). (UMBRELLA.). (Jan. 1978)-. Periodical. English. Irregular. $25.00. Umbrella Associates, PO Box 3640, Santa Monica CA 90403. **Tel** (310)399-1146, FAX (310)399-5070. **ED** Judith A. Hoffberg. **Bk Rev**, (Qty: 200). **Ad Acc**, **Adv Mgr:** Judith Hoffberg, **Tel** (310)399-1146. **Circ:** 1,000. **Desc:** Features news and reviews of artists' publications including artists' books, periodicals, audiocassettes, videos, postcards, and xerography.
Ind/Abst ARTbibliogr. Mod.

LC N6 .U45
ISSN 0049-5123
XR

UMENI. (UMENI : CASOPIS KABINETU THEORII A DEJIN UMENI CESKOSLOVENSKE AKADEMIE VED.). [Umeni]. **Added/Corp** Ceskoslovenska Akademie Ved. Kabinet Theorie a Dejin Umeni. Ustav Teorie a Dejin Umeni CSAV v Praze. Vol. 1 (1953)-. Periodical. Czech (summaries and/or abstracts in Russian, English, German and French). Six times a year. $297.85. **(Subscription address:** Kubon & Sagner, ABT Zeitschriftenimport, D 80328 Munich Germany. **Tel** 011 49 89 54218130.) **Desc:** Devoted especially to Bohemian and Central European art, old as well as contemporary. Contains detailed photographs and illustrated articles, which deal with architecture, painting, sculpture, folk and religious arts, and more.

Ind/Abst Art Archaeol. Tech. Abstr.; ARTbibliogr. Mod.; ARTbibliogr. Curr. Titles; Avery Index Archit. Period. Suppl. Colum. Univ. (1989-); BHA : Biblio. Hist. Art.

LC NX
DD 700
US

UNIT PICTURE COLLECTIONS AND ART PRINTS. **Main/Corp** Florida. General Extension Division. English.

LC NX7 .U54
ISSN 0341-0102
GW

UNIVERSITAS. (1962)-. Periodical. Spanish. Four times a year. DM108.00. Wissenschaftliche Verlagsgesellschaft mbH, Postfach 101061, D-70009 Stuttgart Germany. **Tel** 011 49 711 258260, FAX 011 49 711 2582290, telex 723636 DAZ D.

LC NX
DD 700
US

UNIVERSITY PRINTS CATALOG.
Main/Corp University Prints, Boston. Catalog. English. Two times a year. University Prints, 21 East Street, Winchester MA 01890. **Tel** (617)729-8006. **ED** W E Teel.

LC NX
DD 700
ISSN 0566-263X
SZ
TITLE CHANGE

UNSERE KUNSTDENKMAELER. (UNSERE KUNSTDENKMAELER = NOS MONUMENTS D'ART ET D'HISTOIRE.). [Unsere Kunstdenkmaeler]. **Added/Corp** Gesellschaft fuer Schweizerische Kunstgeschichte. **VFOAT** Nostri Monumentia Storici; Nos Monuments d'Art et d'Histoire. (1950)-(1993). Periodical. German (French). **Continued by** Kunst+Archetektur in der Schweiz.
Ind/Abst Archit. Period. Index (1953, Nov. 1977-1993); Avery Index Archit. Period. Suppl. Colum. Univ. (Vol. 40 No. 1, 1989-1993); BHA : Biblio. Hist. Art.

LC PS
DD 810
ISSN 1078-6686
US

●**URBANUS (1994).** See Literature-Poetry.

LC PN500
DD 808
ISSN 1066-3932
US
TITLE CHANGE

URBANUS, RAIZIRR. See Literature.

LC NX
DD 700
AG

URIZEN. No. 1 (Sept. 1977)-. Periodical. Spanish. Roberto J. Carrera, Cuenca 43 Depto 6, Buenos Aires Argentina. **ED** J. Ramos Lopez and Jose Carrer.

LC N6921.V5 V36
DD 709/.45/3105
IT

VENEZIA ARTI : BOLLETTINO DEL DIPARTIMENTO DI STORIA E CRITICA DELLE ARTI DELL'UNIVERSITA DI VENEZIA. **Added/Corp** Universita degli Studi di Venezia. Dipartimento di Storia e Critica delle Arti. **VFOAT** VA. (1987)-. Italian. One time a year. L81750. Viella SRL, Via delle Alpi 32, 00198 Rome Italy. **Tel** 011 39 6 8417758.
Ind/Abst Avery Index Archit. Period. Suppl. Colum. Univ. (1989-); BHA : Biblio. Hist. Art (19??-).

LC N6916 .V464 N6921.V5 V4
IT

VENEZIA CINQUECENTO. Vol. 1, No. 1 (1991)-. Periodical. Italian. Two times a year. L90000 (Italy); L110000 (other). Bulzoni Editore Srl, Via dei Liburni 14, 00185 Rome Italy. **Tel** 011 39 6 4455207, FAX 011 39 6 4450355.
Ind/Abst BHA : Biblio. Hist. Art.

LC NX
DD 700
SW

VENTE AUX ENCHERES PUBLIQUES TABLEAUX MODERNES ... . See Museums and Galleries.

DD 707/.471428
ISSN 0849-0465
CN

VENTES AUX ENCHERES PUBLIQUES.
Main/Corp Hotel des Encans de Montreal. **VFOAT** Vente aux Encheres Publiques; Hotel des Encans de Montreal. (November 1986)-. Periodical. French. Twelve times a year. 100.00Can$. Hotel des Encans de Montreal, 2825 Bates Street, Montreal Quebec H3S 1B3 Canada. **Tel** (514)344-4081, FAX (514)344-4125. **Ad Acc**.
Desc: Covers antiques and Canadian and international art.

LC PN
DD 800
ISSN 0730-9708
US

VERANO, UN. See Literature.

LC AS221.M3
DD 065
ISSN 1120-3226
IT

VERONA ILLUSTRATA : RIVISTA DEL MUSEO DI CASTELVECCHIO. **Added/Corp** Museo di Castelvecchio (Verona, Italy). No. 1 (1988)-. Italian. One time a year.
Ind/Abst BHA : Biblio. Hist. Art.

LC HQ1060
DD 305.2/6/05
ISSN 0228-2623
CN

VIEIL ART, LE. See Senior Citizens.

DD 080
ISSN 0163-9706
US

VIEW (OAKLAND). (VIEW.). [View]. Vol. 1, No. 1 (Apr. 1978)-. Periodical. English. Six times a year. $30.00 North America; $35.00 other. Crown Point Publishers, 657 Howard Street, San Francisco CA 94105. **Tel** (415)974-6273. **ED** Constance Lewallen. **Circ:** 1,000.
Desc: Each issue consists of an interview with an individual artist.
Ind/Abst BHA : Biblio. Hist. Art (19??-).

LC NX24.O3 O3
DD 338.4/7/009771
ISSN 0361-2678
US

VIEWPOINT (COLUMBUS). (VIEWPOINT.). **Added/Corp** Ohio Arts Council. (19??)-. Periodical. English. Four times a year. Ohio Arts Council, 50 West Broad Street, Columbus OH 43215. **Continues** OAC Newsletter.

LC N6480 .V57
DD 704.9/428/05
ISSN 1071-5266
US

VISIONAIRE (NEW YORK, N.Y.). (VISIONAIRE.). [Visionaire]. No. 1 (Spring 1991)-. Periodical. English. Four times a year (Apri., July, Oct., Dec.). $125.00 (US); $200.00 (other). Visionaire Publishing, 58 Watts Street, Rear Building, New York NY 10013. **Tel** (212) 274-8959, FAX (212) 343-2595. **ED** Stephen Gian, James Kaliardos, Cecilia Dean. **Circ:** 2,000 (ctrl).

LC NX1 .B37a
DD 700/.5
ISSN 0278-7660
US

VISTAS (MERION, PA.). (VISTAS.). [Vistas]. **Added/Corp** Barnes Foundation. Art Dept. Vol. 1, No. 1 (Spring-Summer 1979)-. Periodical. English. Two times a year. $12.00 (current volume). VOLN Press, PO Box 93, Merion Station PA 19066. **Tel** (610)667-3067. **ED** Ellen Homsey. Index available. **Circ:** 1,000 (ctrl) **Continues** Journal of the Art Department.
Desc: Articles on art and education based on objectivity; black and white illustrations.

LC NX
DD 700
US

VISUAL ARTS. FELLOWSHIPS. **VFOAT** Fellowships Visual Arts. (1989/90)-. English. Every 2 years. Visual Arts Programs / Fellowships, Room 729/National Endowment for the Arts, Nancy Hanks Center, 1100 Pennsylvania Avenue NW, Washington DC 20506. **Continues** Visual Artists Fellowships.

DD 702/.5/713
ISSN 0380-5743
CN

VISUAL ARTS HANDBOOK. **Added/Corp** Visual Arts Ontario. Ontario Arts Council. Canada Council. (1975)-. English. Visual Arts Ontario, 439 Wellington Street / 2nd Floor, Toronto Ontario M5V 1E7 Canada. **Tel** (416)362-2546.

LC NX513
DD 709/.716
ISSN 0704-0512
CN

VISUAL ARTS NEWS. **Added/Corp** Visual Arts Nova Scotia. (Nov. 1976)-. Periodical. English. Four times a year. 12.50Can$. Visual Arts Nova Scotia, 1809 Barrington Street, Suite 901, Halifax Nova Scotia B3J 3K8 Canada. **Tel** (902)423-4694, FAX (902)422-0881. **ED** Gil McElroy (Editor's telephone: (902)423-3156). **Bk Rev**, (Qty: 1-2). **Ad Acc**. **Circ:** 600. **Absorbed** Visual Arts Nova Scotia Presents - Halifax/Dartmouth Artists Supplement.
Desc: Published as a forum for artists, art critics, and concerned individuals through which news, views and reviews can be expressed.

LC N81 .R49
DD 707/.2
Pr Rev.
ISSN 0736-0770
US

VISUAL ARTS RESEARCH. [Vis. arts res.]. No. 16 (Fall 1982)-. Periodical. English. Two times a year (April and November). $27.00. University of Illinois / Art and Design, 119 Art & Design, 408 East Peabody, Champaign IL 61820. **Tel** (217)333-8952, FAX (217)244-7688. **ED** Nancy Gardener. **Bk Rev**, (Qty: 1-2). **Circ:** 500. **Continues** Review of Research in Visual Arts Education, 0160-3221.
Desc: Provides a forum for the issues that shape our understanding of artistic perception. Serves as an outlet for critical analysis of theoretical and empirical research of the visual arts.
Ind/Abst BHA : Biblio. Hist. Art; Curr. Index J. Educ.; Educ. Index (1992-); Psychol. Abstr. (1984-); PsycINFO; PsycLit.

LC N347 .V57o
US

●**VISUAL ARTS. VISUAL ARTISTS ORGANIZATIONS, VISUAL ARTISTS PUBLIC PROJECTS, SPECIAL PROJECTS.** **Added/Corp** National Endowment for the Arts. **VFOAT** Visual Artists Organizations, Visual Artists Public Projects, Special Projects. (1994)-. English. National Endowment for the Arts, 1100 Pennsylvania

Avenue Northwest, Washington DC 20506. **Tel** (202)682-5400, (202)682-5435. **Continues** Visual Arts. Organizations.

LC N1 .V56   **ISSN** 0360-4225
DD 705   US
VISUAL DIALOG. [Vis. dialog]. Vol. 1 (Sept./Nov. 1975)-. Periodical. English. Four times a year. $10.00. R Loach, PO Box 1438, Los Altos CA 94022.

LC N3998 .V57   **ISSN** 0197-3762
DD 025.177   US
   CCC
   CODEN VRVRDZ
VISUAL RESOURCES. (VISUAL RESOURCES : VR.). [Vis. resour.]. **VFOAT** VR. Vol. 1, No. 1 (Spring 1980)-. Periodical. English. Irregular. $186.00 (academic institutions), $291.00 (corporate institutions). Gordon & Breach Science Publishers, Inc., PO Box 786, Cooper Station, New York NY 10276. **Tel** (212)206-8900, FAX (212)645-2459. **ED** Helene E. Roberts and Christine L. Sundt. Index available. cum. index. **Bk Rev. Ad Acc.** Documents available from Ask*IEEE.
Desc: Current and comprehensive information on visual formats reprographic technology and related topics.
Ind/Abst ARTbibliogr. Mod. (1981-); BHA : Biblio. Hist. Art (19??-); INSPEC (1980-); Libr. Inf. Sci. Abstr. (19??-).

LC N72.P5 I57   **ISSN** 1046-9001
DD 778.9/7   US
VISUAL RESOURCES ASSOCIATION BULLETIN. [Vis. Resour. Assoc. bull.]. **Added/Corp** Visual Resources Association. **VFOAT** Bulletin. Vol. 16, No. 1 (Spring 1989)-. Bulletin. English. Four times a year. $75.00 institutions; $55.00 (North America), $70.00 (other) individuals. Visual Resources Association, University of Virginia, Fiske Kimball Fine Arts, Charlottesville VA 22903. **Tel** (804)924-6604, FAX (804)982-2678. **ED** Joy Blouin (editor's phone: University of Michigan, Department of Art History, 20A Tappan Hall, Ann Arbor, MI 48109-1357; phone: (313)763-6114). Index available (published separately): **Ad Acc. Circ:** 775. **Continues** International Bulletin for Photographic Documentation of the Visual Arts, 0197-8020.
Desc: Professional journal of the Visual Resources Association. Focuses on issues relating to collections of visual materials for use by students and scholars. Contains information of interest to professionals who work with visual collections (slides, photographs, etc.). Publishes news of upcoming conferences and workshops as well as articles about the management of visual collections (such as cataloging and technical information).

LC N12 .W3   **ISSN** 0141-0016
DD 709/.41/05   UK
VOLUME OF THE WALPOLE SOCIETY, THE. [Vol. Walpole Soc.]. Vol. 5 (1915/16 and 1916/17)-. English. Every 2 years. British Museum, Walpole Society, Department of Prints & Drawings, London WC1B 3DG United Kingdom. **Tel** 011 44 171 3630735. **Continues** Annual Volume of the Walpole Society.
Ind/Abst BHA : Biblio. Hist. Art.

LC PS   **ISSN** 1052-8814
DD 808   US
VOX MAGAZINE (NEW YORK, N.Y. 1990). See Literature.

LC N6995.W5 V94
   BW
VYIAULENCHAE MASTATSTVA BELARUSI. (19??)-. Periodical. Byelorussian. 1.31rub. Belarus, Prospekt Masherova 11, 220600 Minsk Byelarus. **Tel** 0172 23-77-34, FAX 0172 20-91-25, telex 252964.

LC NX
DD 700   XR
VYTVARNA VYCHOVA. Added/Corp Univerzita Palackeho v Olomouci. (19??)-. Czech. Three times a year. DM122.00. (Subscription address: Kubon & Sagner, ABT Zeitschriftenimport, D 80328 Munich Germany. **Tel** 011 49 89 54218130.)

LC NX   **ISSN** 0139-7214
DD 700   XO
UDC 7.072
VYTVARNY ZIVOT. [Vytv. ziv.]. (1956)-. Periodical. Slovak. Six times a year. DM134.00. (Subscription address: Kubon & Sagner, ABT Zeitschriftenimport, D 80328 Munich Germany. **Tel** 011 49 89 54218130.)
Ind/Abst BHA : Biblio. Hist. Art.

LC N8555
DD 702.88   US
WAAC MEMBERSHIP DIRECTORY.
Main/Corp Western Association for Art Conservation. (19??)-. Directory. English. One time a year. (Comes with Western Association for Art Conservation membership). Western Association for Art Conservation, c/o Chris Staurodis, 1272 North Flores Street, Los Angeles CA 90069-2904. **Tel** (213)654-8748, FAX (213)656-3220. **ED** Carolyn Tallent.

LC N6879 .W2   **ISSN** 0083-7105
   GW
Pr Rev.
WALLRAF-RICHARTZ-JAHRBUCH.
[Wallraf-Richartz-Jahrb.]. **Added/Corp** Wallraf-Richartz-Museum. Freunde. Museum Ludwig. Freunde. Freunde des Wallraf-Richartz-Museums und Museums Ludwig. Vol. 14 (1952)-. German. One time a year. DM128.00. DuMont Buchverlag GmbH & Co. KG, Postfach 100468, D-50441 Cologne Germany. **Tel** 011 49 221 20530, FAX 011 49 221 2053281. **(Subscription address:** BDK Buecherdienst GmbH, Postfach 900120, D 51111 Cologne Germany. **Tel** 011 49 2203 10020.)
Continues Westdeutsches Jahrbuch fur Kunstgeschichte.
Desc: Articles with many color photographs regarding current art issues, especially in Europe.
Ind/Abst Art Index (19??-); Avery Index Archit. Period. Suppl. Colum. Univ. (19??-199?); BHA : Biblio. Hist. Art (19??-).

LC N5220 .W4363   **ISSN** 1044-8683
DD 708.152/6/05   US
WALTERS (BALTIMORE, MD.), THE. (THE WALTERS.). [Walters]. **Main/Corp** Walters Art Gallery (Baltimore, Md.). **VFOAT** Walters Art Gallery Bulletin. Vol. 42, No. 1 (Jan. 1989)-. Bulletin. English. Ten times a year (monthly with combined June, July, and Aug.). $12.00. Walters Art Gallery, 600 North Charles Street, Baltimore MD 21201. **Tel** (410)547-9000 ext. 278. **ED** Nini Sarmiento. **Circ:** 10,000. **Continues** Walters Art Gallery (Baltimore, Md.).
Desc: Research on the arts, exhibition discussions, programs and calendar.

LC NX
DD 700   US
WATERCOLOR : AN AMERICAN ARTIST PUBLICATION. (1986)-. Periodical. English. Three times a year. $19.95. American Artists, PO Box 1944, 1 Color Court, Marion OH 43306. **Tel** (212)536-5178.

LC NK   **ISSN** 0043-261X
DD 745.13   GW
WELTKUNST, DIE. [Weltkunst]. **VFOAT** World-Art Review; Beaux-Arts du Monde. (1931)-. Periodical. German. Twenty-four times a year. DM250.00. Weltkunst Verlag GmbH, Postfach 190918, 80603 Munich Germany. **Tel** 011 49 89 1269900, FAX 011 49 89 1269011, telex 5216731. **ED** J. Kleidt. Index available. **Bk Rev. Ad Acc. Circ:** 15,000. **Continues** Kunstauktion; **Absorbed** Kunst und Antiquitaeten.
Desc: International art and antiques market. Historical aspects of art and the works of art.
Ind/Abst Art Archaeol. Tech. Abstr.; ARTbibliogr. Mod.; BHA : Biblio. Hist. Art.

   ISSN 0043-3357
   US
WEST ART. (WESTART.). (19??)-. Periodical. English. Twenty-four times a year. $15.00. West Art Publishers, PO Box 6868, Auburn CA 95604. **Tel** (916)885-0969.
Ind/Abst Calif. Period. Index (19??-).

   ISSN 1191-3371
DD 707/.5/0971   CN
WESTBRIDGE ART MARKET REPORT. [Westbridge art market rep.]. **VFOAT** Art Market Report. Vol. 18, No. 1 (Mar. 1992)-. Periodical. English. Ten times a year. 43.21Can$. Westbridge Publications Ltd, 1683 Chestnut Street, Vancouver BC V6J 4M6 Canada. **Tel** (604)734-4944, FAX (604)731-4576. **ED** Anthony R. Westbridge. **Bk Rev. Ad Acc. Circ:** 500. **Continues** Fine Art & Auction Review., 0833-0891.

LC NX   **ISSN** 0705-310X
DD 381/.45/7451025712   CN
WESTERN CANADIAN ANTIQUE & ART DEALERS YEARBOOK. See Antiques.

LC ML3930   **ISSN** 0318-1065
DD 780   CN
UDC 78
WHETSTONE (LETHBRIDGE). See Literature.

LC N1 .W49   **ISSN** 0190-9835
Pr Rev.
WHITEWALLS (CHICAGO, ILL.). See Literature.

LC N618 .W45   **ISSN** 0511-8824
DD 708/.147/1   US
WHITNEY REVIEW. See Museums and Galleries.

LC N6536 .W5   **ISSN** 0000-0191
DD 709/.22   US
   CCC
NLM N 40 W628
WHO'S WHO IN AMERICAN ART. See The Arts-Abstracting, Bibliographies and Statistics.

LC N9 .W5   **ISSN** 0083-9981
   AU
WIENER JAHRBUCH FUER KUNSTGESCHICHTE. [Wien. Jahrb. Kunstgesch.]. **Added/Corp** Institut fuer Kunstforschung (Austria). Vol. 1 (1921/1922)-. Monographic series. German. Irregular. Price varies per volume. Boehlau Verlag GmbH & Co KG, Sachsenplatz 4 6 PF 87, A 1201 Vienna Austria. **Tel** 011 43 222 3302427. **(Subscription address:** Vereinsbuchhandlung und Verlag der Wissenschaftlichen Buchhdlg, Sachsenplatz 4 6, Postfach 88, A 1201 Vienna Austria. **Tel** 011 43 1 3302433.) **Supersedes** Jahrbuch des Kunsthistorischen Institutes, 0258-5588.
Ind/Abst ARTbibliogr. Mod.; Avery Index Archit. Period. Suppl. Colum. Univ. (19??-199?); BHA : Biblio. Hist. Art.

LC N7660 .W45   **ISSN** 1084-7855
DD 704.9/432/05   US
●**WILDLIFE ART.** [Wildl. art]. Vol. 14, No. 5 (Sept./Oct. 1995)-. Periodical. English. Six times a year. $32.95 (one-year), $60.95 (two-year). Pothole Publications, 4725 Highway 7, PO Box 16246, St. Louis Park MN 55416. **Tel** (800)221-6547, (612)927-9056, FAX (612)441-1349. **Continues** Wildlife Art News, 0746-9640.
Desc: Original art, sculpture, prints, art trends, decoys, stamp news, calendar of events, print prices and articles on new and established international wildlife artists.

LC N7660 .W45   **ISSN** 0746-9640
DD 704.9/432/05   US
   TITLE CHANGE
WILDLIFE ART NEWS. [Wildl. art news]. (1982)-(1995). Periodical. English. Pothole Publications, 4725 Highway 7, PO Box 16246, St. Louis Park MN 55416. **Tel** (800)221-6547, (612)927-9056, FAX (612)441-1349. **ED** Robert J. Koenke. Index available. **Bk Rev. Ad Acc. Circ:** 40,000. **Continued by** Wildlife Art, 1084-7855.
Desc: Original art, sculpture, prints, art trends, decoys, stamp news, calendar of events, print prices and articles on new and established international wildlife artists.

LC N7560   **ISSN** 0827-2409
DD 704.9/432   CN
WILDLIFE COLLECTABLES JOURNAL, THE. See Environmental Issues-Conservation and Natural Resources.

LC N5325 .A8
   GW
WINCKELMANNSPROGRAMM DER ARCHAEOLOGISCHEN GESELLSCHAFT ZU BERLIN. See Archaeology.

LC AP2   **ISSN** 0888-0832
DD 051   US
WINDHAM PHOENIX. See Literature.

LC PS55   **ISSN** 0822-2363
DD 810/.8/09283   CN
WINDSCRIPT. See Literature.

LC N9 .W52   **ISSN** 0084-0416
DD 708 709   US
   CCC
WINTERTHUR PORTFOLIO. [Winterthur portf.]. **Added/Corp** Henry Francis du Pont Winterthur Museum. Vol. 1 (1964)-. English. Three times a year. $83.00. University of Chicago Press / Journals Division, PO Box 37005, 5720 South Woodlawn, Chicago IL 60637. **Tel** (312)753-3347, FAX (312)753-0811. **ED** Catherine E. Hutchins. **Acid Free.** available on microfilm and microfiche from University Microfilms International (UMI). Documents available from The Genuine Article.
Desc: Devoted to publishing articles on the arts and artifacts of America and the historical context within which they developed.
Ind/Abst Am. Hist. Life (1964-); Archit. Period. Index (1964-); Art Index; ARTbibliogr. Mod.; ARTbibliogr. Curr. Titles; Arts Humanit. Citation Index [Full Cov.]; Avery Index Archit. Period. Suppl. Colum. Univ. (1989-); BHA : Biblio. Hist. Art; Curr. Contents Arts Humanit.; MLA Int. Bibl. Books Artic. Mod. Lang. Lit.; Res. Alert [Full Cov.]; Soc. Plann. Policy Dev. Abstr.; Soc. Sci. Cit. Index [Select. Cov.]; Sociol. Abstr.

LC PS580 .W57   **ISSN** 0147-0868
DD 811.5/408   US
WITTENBERG REVIEW OF LITERATURE & ART. See Literature-Poetry.

LC N72.F45 W64   **ISSN** 0270-7993
DD 704/.042/05   US
Pr Rev.
WOMAN'S ART JOURNAL. [Woman's art j.]. Vol. 1 (Spring/Summer 1980)-. Periodical. English. Two times a year (May & Nov.). $25.00. Womans Art Journal, 1711 Harris Road, Laverock PA 19118. **Tel** (215)233-0639. **ED** Elsa Honig Fine. Index available (Vol. 13, No. 2). cum. index. **Bk Rev, (Qty: 34). Ad Acc. Circ:** 2200. available on microfilm and microfiche from University Microfilms International (UMI). Documents available from The Genuine Article.
Desc: Devoted exclusively to women and issues related to women in all areas of the visual arts. Articles range in subject matter from antiquity to the present.

The Arts — Art

Ind/Abst Art Index; ARTbibliogr. Mod.; Arts Humanit. Citation Index [Full Cov.]; BHA : Biblio. Hist. Art; Curr. Cit.; Res. Alert [Full Cov.].

LC N6512 .W587   **ISSN** 0149-7081
     US

● **WOMEN ARTISTS NEWS BOOK REVIEW.** See Women's Interests.

LC NX
DD 700   US
WOMEN IN THE ARTS BULLETIN.
Added/Corp Women in the Arts Foundation, Inc. Vol. 5 (Oct. 1977)-. Bulletin. English. Four times a year. $15.00. Women in the Arts Foundation, 1175 York Avenue, New York NY 10021. **Tel** (212)751-1915. **ED** Jacqueline Skiles. **Bk Rev. Ad Acc. Circ:** 300. **Continues** Women in the Arts Foundation, Inc. WIA Newsletter.
Desc: Professional issues and problems of women visual artists and efforts to overcome discrimination against women artists.

LC N858.N36 A3   **ISSN** 1058-7217
DD 709   US
WOMEN IN THE ARTS / THE NATIONAL MUSEUM OF WOMEN IN THE ARTS.
[Women arts]. **Added/Corp** National Museum of Women in the Arts (U.S.). Vol. 8, No. 4 (Winter 1991)-. Periodical. English. Four times a year. National Museum of Women in the Arts, 1250 New York Avenue NW, Washington DC 20005. **Tel** (202)783-5000, FAX (202)393-3235. **Continues** News (National Museum of Women in the Arts (U.S.)), 0891-1827.

LC NX
DD 700   UK
WOMEN'S ART MAGAZINE. Added/Corp
Women Artists Slide Library (London, England). **VFOAT** Women's Art. No. 36 (Sept./Oct. 1990)-. Periodical. English. Six times a year. $90.70. Women Artists Slide Library, Fulham Palace, Bishops Avenue, London SW6 6EA United Kingdom. **Tel** 011 44 171 7317618, FAX 011 44 171 3841110. **ED** Sally Townsend. **Bk Rev. Ad Acc. Circ:** 10,000. **Continues** Women Artists Slide Library Journal.
Ind/Abst BHA : Biblio. Hist. Art.

LC NX
DD 700   AT
WOMENS ART REGISTER BULLETIN.
See Women's Interests.

LC NX   **ISSN** 1058-0409
DD 700   US
WORKS OF ART (CHICAGO, ILL.).
(WORKS OF ART.). (1991)-. Periodical. English. $9.95. Dewayne E Pullum, 7649 Champlain Avenue, Chicago IL 60619-2514.

LC ND47 .W6   **ISSN** 0084-1498
DD 759.085   NE
WORLD COLLECTORS ANNUARY. Vol. 1 (1946/1949)-. English. One time a year (Nov.). Price varies. World Collectors, PO Box 263, 2270 AG Voorburg The Netherlands. **Tel** 011 31 1720 75523. **(Subscription address:** IBD Limited, 24 Hudson Street, Kinderhook NY 12106. **Tel** (518)758-1411.**) ED** A. M. E. van Voorthuijsen and H. E. van der Lande. Index available. cum. index. **Ad Acc. Circ:** 400.
Desc: Reports of auction results of the International Art Market. Features essential data on exhibitions and literature.

     ISSN 0084-3415
DD 709   US
YALE PUBLICATIONS IN THE HISTORY OF ART. [Yale publ. hist. art]. **Added/Corp** Yale University. **VFOAT** Publications in the History of Art. (1939)-. Monographic series. English. Irregular. Price varies per volume. Yale University Press, PO Box 209040, New Haven CT 06520. **Tel** (203)432-0940, (800)987-7323, FAX (203)432-0948. **Continues** Yale Historical Publications. History of Art, 0897-7380.

LC ND1040 .Y54
DD 759.951   CH
YING CHUN HUA. (1979)-. Periodical. Chinese. Four times a year. Tianjin People's Fine Art Publishers, 150 Machang Dao, Heping Qu, Tianjin 300050, People's Republic of China.

LC N380 .Z33   **ISSN** 0352-6844
     YU
ZBORNIK MATICE SRPSKE ZA LIKOVNE UMETNOSTI / MATICA SRPSKA, ODELJENJE ZA LIKOVNE UMETNOSTI. Added/Corp Matica Srpska (Novi Sad, Serbia). Odeljenje za Likovne Umetnosti. **VFOAT** Recherches sur l'art. (19??)-. Serbo-Croatian (Cyrillic) (Serbo-Croatian (Roman), English and Russian) summaries and/or abstracts in English, French and German).
Ind/Abst BHA : Biblio. Hist. Art.

LC NX
DD 700   XV
ZBORNIK ZA UMETNOSTNO ZGODOVINO. ARCHIVES D'HISTOIRE DE L'ART. See History-History of Europe.

LC N8850 .Z35   **ISSN** 0514-616X
     YU
ZBORNIK ZASTITE SPOMENIKA KULTURE. RECUEIL DES TRAVAUX SUR LA PROTECTION DES MONUMENTS HISTORIQUES. Added/Corp
Belgrad. Savezni Institut za Zastitu Spomenika Kulture. **VFOAT** Recueil des Travaux sur la Protection des Monuments Historiques. (1950)-. Serbo-Croatian (Cyrillic) (French). One time a year. cum. index.
Ind/Abst BHA : Biblio. Hist. Art.

LC N9 .J195   **ISSN** 0044-2186
     GW
ZEITSCHRIFT FUER ASTHETIK UND ALLGEMEINE KUNSTWISSENSCHAFT (BONN, GERMANY). (ZEITSCHRIFT FUER ASTHETIK UND ALLGEMEINE KUNSTWISSENSCHAFT.). Vol. 11 (1966)-. German (English). Irregular. Price varies. Bouvier Gmbh & Co. KG ABT Verlag, Am HOF 28, D-53113 Bonn Germany. **Tel** 011 49 228 7290141, FAX 011 49 228 7290179. **ED** H. Lutzeler. cum. index. **Bk Rev. Continues** Jahrbuch fuer Asthetik und Allgemeine Kunstwissenschaft.
Desc: Philosophy of art aesthetics.
Ind/Abst ARTbibliogr. Mod. (1984-); BHA : Biblio. Hist. Art; Romant. Move.

LC N3 .Z53   **ISSN** 0044-2992
DD 705   GW
     CCC
ZEITSCHRIFT FUER KUNSTGESCHICHTE. [Z. kunstgesch.]. Vol. 1 (June 1932)-. Periodical. German (English, French and Italian). Four times a year. DM180.00 Germany; DM192.00 others. Deutscher Kunstverlag, Postfach 190354, D-80603 Munich Germany. **Tel** 011 49 89 1215160. **ED** Georg Kauffmann. Index available. **Bk Rev. Circ:** 1,000. Documents available from The Genuine Article. **Formed by the union of** Repertorium fuer Kunstwissenschaft; Zeitschrift fuer Bildende Kunst **and** Jahrbuch fuer Kunstwissenschaft.
Desc: History of art.
Ind/Abst Am. Hist. Life (1987-); Art Index; ARTbibliogr. Mod. (1984-); Arts Humanit. Citation Index [Full Cov.]; Avery Index Archit. Period. Suppl. Colum. Univ. (1988-); BHA : Biblio. Hist. Art; Curr. Contents Arts Humanit.; Res. Alert [Full Cov.]; Romant. Move.

LC N8554 .Z44   **ISSN** 0931-7198
     GW
ZEITSCHRIFT FUER KUNSTTECHNOLOGIE UND KONSERVIERUNG. [z. Kunsttechnol. Konserv.]. **Added/Corp** Deutscher Restauratorenverband. **VFOAT** Kunsttechnologie und Konservierung. Vol. 1, No. 1 (1987)-. Periodical. German (English and French). Two times a year (April & October). DM102.00. Wernersche Verlagsgesellschaft GmbH, Liebfrauenring 17, D-67547 Worms Germany. **Tel** 011 49 6241 43574. **(Subscription address:** Brockhaus Commission, Kreidlerstrasse 9, D-70806 Kornwestheim Germany. **Tel** 011 49 7154 13270.**)**

LC NX   **ISSN** 0083-4424
DD 700   PL
UDC 7.0
ZESZYTY NAUKOWE UNIWERSYTETU JAGIELLONSKIEGO. PRACE Z HISTORII SZTUKI. [Zesz. Nauk. Uniw. Jagiell., Pr. Hist. Szt.]. **VFOAT** Universitas Iagellonica. Acta Scientiarum Litterarumque. Schedae ad Artis Historiam Pertinentes. (1962)-. Monographic series. Polish. Irregular. Price varies per volume. **(Subscription address:** Ars Polona-Ruch, PO Box 1001, Krakowskie Przedmiescie 7, 00-068 Warsaw Poland. **Tel** 011 48 22 261201.**)**

LC N5950 .Z6   **ISSN** 0514-7867
     YU
ZOGRAF : CASOPIS ZA SREDNJOVEKOVNU UMETNOST.
Added/Corp Galerija Fresaku u Beogradu. **VFOAT** Zographe. Vol. 1 (1966)-. Serbo-Croatian (Cyrillic) (summaries and/or abstracts in French).
Ind/Abst BHA : Biblio. Hist. Art.

LC PS561 .Z98   **ISSN** 8756-5633
DD 810.8/0979/05   US
ZYZZYVA. See Literature.

COMPUTER APPLICATIONS

LC N380 .C663   **ISSN** 1048-6798
DD 702/.85   SZ
     CCC
     CODEN CHIAEF
COMPUTERS AND THE HISTORY OF ART. [Comput. hist. art]. **Added/Corp** CHArt (Organization). Vol. 1, Pt. 1 (1990)-. Periodical. English. Two times a year. $55.00 (per volume). Harwood Academic Publishers, PO Box 90, Reading RG1 8JL United Kingdom. **Tel** 011 44 1734 560080, FAX 011 44 1734 568211. **ED** William Vaughan. **Continues** CHArt Newsletter, 7081-239X.
Desc: Aims to provide a forum for the discussion of new developments in the application of computers to the history of art. Includes research articles about new methodologies as well as review articles looking at how installations have developed.
Ind/Abst BHA : Biblio. Hist. Art.

     ISSN 1191-9795
DD 709.1   CN
IMAGES DU FUTUR. [Images futur]. **Added/Corp**
Cite des Arts et des Nouvelles Technologies de Montreal. (1988)-. Periodical. English (French). Irregular. 10.00Can$. Cite des Arts et des Nouvelles Technologies de Montreal, 15 West rue de la Commune, Montreal, Quebec H2Y 2C6 Canada.

     ISSN 0748-2043
DD 702   US
SMALL COMPUTERS IN THE ARTS NEWS. (SMALL COMPUTERS IN THE ARTS NEWS : SCAN). [Small comput. arts news]. **VFOAT** SCAN; S.C.A.N. (198?)-. Periodical. English. Three times a year. $15.00. SCAN, Box 1954, Philadelphia PA 19105. **Tel** (215)923-3299. **ED** Dick Moberg and Julie Shay. cum. index. **Bk Rev. Ad Acc. Circ:** 200.
Desc: Contains articles, reviews, network news, events, publications, openings, courses of instruction, and other information related to the use of computers and new technology in the arts.

CRAFTS AND DECORATIVE ARTS

     ISSN 0276-9069
     US
1001 CRAFT IDEAS. VFOAT One Thousand and One Craft Ideas. (Sept. 1981)-. Periodical. English. Six times a year. $13.30. Family Media Inc., 3 Park Avenue, New York NY 10016. **Tel** (212)340-9200.

LC NX   **ISSN** 0892-3582
DD 700   US
A.S.A. ARTISAN. Added/Corp American Society of Artists. **VFOAT** ASA Artisan. **VAT** American Society of Artists Artisan. (1983)-. Periodical. English. Four times a year. American Society of Artists Inc, PO Box 1326, Palatine IL 60078. **Tel** (312)751-2500. ctrl circ. **Continues** A.S.A. Bulletin.
Desc: Contains information for and about artist/craftsmen membership.

     ISSN 0883-668X
DD 751   US
AIRBRUSH TECHNIQUES. [Airbrush tech.]. (1985)-. Periodical. English. Six times a year. $20.00. Charter Publishing Inc, PO Box 2255, Portland OR 97208.

     ISSN 0834-910X
DD 745.5/06/07123   CN
ALBERTA CRAFT MAGAZINE. [Alta. craft mag.]. **Added/Corp** Alberta Craft Council. (Jan./Feb. 1987)-. Periodical. English. Six times a year. 10.00Can$. Alberta Craft Council, 509 10136-100 Street, Edmonton Alberta T5J 0P1 Canada. **Tel** (403)428-1654. **ED** R.M. Hoffman. **Ad Acc. Circ:** 1,200 (ctrl). **Continues** Alberta Craft (1985), 0833-8248.

LC NX
DD 700   US
ALPHABET : THE JOURNAL OF THE FRIENDS OF CALLIGRAPHY. Added/Corp
Friends of Calligraphy (San Francisco, Calif.). **VFOAT** Journal of the Friends of Calligraphy. Vol. 15, No. 1 (Fall 1989)-. Periodical. English. Three times a year. $30.00 comes with membership to Friends of Calligraphy. Friends of Calligraphy Inc, PO Box 5194, San Francisco CA 94101. **Tel** (415)524-8329. **ED** Jane Brenner (Editor's Telephone: (510)652-3035). **Bk Rev.** (Qty: 3). **Circ:** 700 (ctrl). **Continues** Journal of the Friends of Calligraphy.

LC NX
DD 700   GW
ALTES HANDWERK. Added/Corp
Schweizerische Gesellschaft fuer Volkskunde. Abteilung Film. (1972)-. Monographic series. German (French and Italian). Irregular. Price varies per volume. Deutsche Gesellschaft fuer Volkskunde e.V., Friedlaender Weg 2,

D-37085 Goettingen Germany. **Tel** 044 49 551 399489, 395352. **ED** Paul Hugger. **Circ:** 1,000. ***Continues*** *Sterbendes Handwerk.*
Desc: A series on Swiss handicrafts.

LC TT900.C4 D42 **ISSN** 1044-4904
DD 745.594/12/05 US
AMERICAN COUNTRY CHRISTMAS. [Am. ctry. Christmas]. (1989)-. English. One time a year. Oxmoor House, PO Box 1862, Birmingham AL 35201. **Tel** (205)877-6000. ***Continues*** *Creative Ideas for Christmas, 0883-9085.*

LC NK1 .C73 **ISSN** 0194-8008
DD 745/.0973 US
AMERICAN CRAFT. [Am. craft]. **Added/Corp** American Craft Council. Vol. 39 No. 3 (June/July 1979)-. Consumer Publication. English. Six times a year. $50.00. American Craft Council, 72 Spring Street, 6th Floor, New York NY 10012. **Tel** (212)274-0630, (800)562-1973, FAX (212)274-0650. **(Subscription address:** American Craft Council, Membership Department AC, PO Box 3000, Denville NJ 07834. **) ED** Lois Moran. **Bk Rev. Ad Acc. Circ:** 40,000. available on microfilm and microfiche from University Microfilms International (UMI); available on CD-ROM from University Microfilms International (UMI); available with illustrations. Documents available from UMI Article Clearinghouse, FAXON Xpress, The UnCover Company, BLDSC. ***Continues*** *Craft Horizons with Craft World, 0164-9191.*
Ind/Abst Acad. Abstr. Full Text Elite; Acad. Abstr.; Acad. Search; Art Index; ARTbibliogr. Mod.; Avery Index Archit. Period. Suppl. Colum. Univ. (1988-); Book Rev. Index; Ceram. Abstr.; EP Collect.; Gen. Period. Index (1985-); Homework Help.; Mag. Artic. Summar. Elite; Mag. Artic. Summar. Select; Mag. Artic. Summar. CD-ROM; Mag. Index Plus (1989-); Mag. Index. Sel. (1986-); Mag. Search; MasterFile FullTEXT 1000; MasterFile FullTEXT 350; MasterFile FullTEXT 650; MasterFile FullTEXT (Jan. 1984-); Med. Rev. Dig.; Newsp. Period. Abstr. (1988-); OCLC; Pub. Lib. FullTEXT; Read. Guide Abstr. Select Ed.; Read. Guide Period. Lit.; Telebase; Mag. Index (1979-); Vocat. Search.

LC TT1 .A46 **ISSN** 0147-5169
DD 745.5 US
AMERICAN HOME'S BEST PROJECTS. Vol. 1 (1977)-. Periodical. English. $1.50 per issue. American Home Publishing Co., 641 Lexington Avenue, New York NY 10022.

LC NX **ISSN** 0192-9968
DD 700 US
AMERICAN INDIAN ART MAGAZINE. [Am. Indian art mag.]. Vol. 2, No. 3 (Summer 1977)-. Periodical. English. Four times a year. $20.00. American Indian Art Magazine, 7314 East Osborn Drive, Scottsdale AZ 85251. **Tel** (602)994-5445, FAX (602)945-9533. **ED** Roanne P. Goldfein. Index available. cum. index. **Bk Rev. Ad Acc. Circ:** 17,500. ***Continues*** *American Indian Art, 0362-2630.*
Desc: Features American Indian painting, beadwork, carving, textiles, basketry, ceramics, jewelry, book and exhibition reviews, museum and gallery announcements.
Ind/Abst Am. Hist. Life (1977-); Anthropol. Lit. (?-Vol. 11, 1989); Art Index; ARTbibliogr. Mod.; Ethnoarts Index; West. Hist. Q.

LC E98.A7 A45 **ISSN** 0362-9767
DD 745 US
AMERICAN INDIAN ARTIFACT PRICE GUIDE. **VFOAT** American Indian Artifact Catalog & Price Guide. (19??)-. English. $5.00. American Indian Artifact Catalog Company, PO Box 1005, Watsonville CA 95076.
Ind/Abst Ethnoarts Index.

LC NK **ISSN** 1064-1718
DD 745 US
●**AMERICA'S BEST QUILTING PROJECTS.** **See** Home Economics-Sewing and Needlework.

LC WMLC L 83/9329
GW
ANNA : BURDA KNITTING & NEEDLECRAFTS. (19??)-. Trade Publication. English. Twelve times a year. $40.00. Burda Verlag GmbH, Postfach 1230, D-77602 Offenburg Germany. **Tel** 011 49 7818401, FAX 011 49 781843155.

ISSN 1184-0307
DD 745.5/029/4713 CN
ANNUAL CRAFT FAIRS IN ONTARIO. [Annu. craft fairs Ont.]. **Added/Corp** Ontario Crafts Council. Craft Resource Centre. (1990)-. English. Ontario Crafts Council, 35 McCaul Street, Chalmers Building, Toronto Ontario M5T 1V7 Canada. **Tel** (416)977-3551, FAX (416)977-3551. ***Continues*** *Shows List, 0714-6655.*

ISSN 1189-4555
DD 381/.457455/025713 CN
ANNUAL CRAFT SHOWS IN ONTARIO. [Annu. craft shows Ont.]. **Added/Corp** Ontario Crafts Council. Craft Resource Centre. **VFOAT** Craft Shows in Ontario. (1992)-. English. Craft Resource Centre, Ontario Crafts Council, Chalmers Building, 35 McCaul Street, Toronto Ontario M5T 1V7 Canada. ***Continues*** *Craft Shows in Ontario., 1184-2628.*

LC TT6.U6 O535a **ISSN** 0273-3838
DD 745/.0973 US
ANNUAL TRADITIONAL CRAFT DAYS. BOOKLET. **Main/Corp** Madison County Historical Society (N.Y.). (19??)-. English. One time a year. Madison County Historical Society, 435 Main Street, PO Box 415, Oneida NY 13421. **Tel** (315)363-4136.

LC WMLC L 83/5286 **ISSN** 0405-4474
DD 600 NO
ARBOK. **Main/Corp** Vestlandske kunstindustrimuseum. (19??)-. Periodical. Norwegian. A.S. John Griegs Boktrykkeri, Mohlenspribsk 3, Bergen Norway. **Tel** (05)32 51 08. cum. index.
Desc: Covers arts and crafts, handicrafts, decorative arts and design.

LC N6873 .B29 **ISSN** 0341-8480
DD 709 GW
ARS BAVARICA. [Ars Bavarica]. (1973)-. Periodical. German. Kunstbuchverlag M Weber, Metzstrasse 5, 8000 Munich 80 Germany.
Ind/Abst Avery Index Archit. Period. Suppl. Colum. Univ. (1989-); BHA : Biblio. Hist. Art.

LC NK9 .A69 **ISSN** 0133-6673
HU
ARS DECORATIVA. **Added/Corp** Iparmuveszeti Museum (Hungary) Hopp Ferenc Kelet-Azsiai Muveszeti Muzeum (Hungary). **VFOAT** Iparmuveszet. (1973)-. Bulletin. Multiple languages (English, French and German). Irregular. Iparmuveszeti Museum / Hopp Ferenc Kelet-Azsiai Muveszeti Muzeum, Ulloi ut 33-37, 1091 Budapest 9 Hungary. **Tel** 011 36 1 2175222, FAX 011 36 1 2175838. **(Subscription address:** Kultura, PO Box 143, H-1300 Budapest 3 Hungary. **Tel** 011 36 1 2500194.**) Circ:** 1,000. ***Supersedes*** *Iparmuveszeti Muzeum es a Hopp Ferenc Keletazsiai Muveszeti Muzeum Evkonyve.*
Ind/Abst BHA : Biblio. Hist. Art.

LC NK
DD 745 UK
ART & CRAFT DESIGN TECHNOLOGY. (19??)-. English. Twelve times a year. £31.00. Scholastic Publishing, Westfield Road, Southam Leamington Spa, Warwickshire CV33 0JH United Kingdom. **Tel** 011 44 1926 813910, FAX 011 44 1926 883331, telex 312138 SPLSG. ***Continues*** *Art & Craft.*

LC NK
DD 745 US
TITLE CHANGE
ART & CRAFTS CATALYST. (1992)-(199?). English. Art and Crafts Catalyst, PO Box 433, South Whitley IN 46787. **Tel** (219)344-1174. **ED** Ann Porter. **Bk Rev. Ad Acc.** ctrl circ. ***Absorbed*** *National Calendar of Open Competitive Art Exhibitions.* ***Merged into*** *SAC News Monthly.*
Desc: Provides entry information for amateur/professional artist and crafts-persons, who actively exhibit and sell their creations at shows and festivals nationwide.

ISSN 0711-1312
DD 707/.0715 CN
ART LINE. [Art line]. **VFOAT** Artline. Vol. 7, No. 1 (Apr. 1980)-. Periodical. English. Three times a year. Free. New Brunswick Teachers' Association, PO Box 752, Fredericton New Brunswick E3B 5R6 Canada. **Tel** (506)452-8921. ctrl circ. ***Continues*** *Pipeline (New Brunswick Teachers' Association. Art Education Council).*

ISSN 0892-1202
DD 745 US
ART LOVERS' ART & CRAFT FAIR BULLETIN. [Art lovers' art craft fair bull.]. **Added/Corp** American Society of Artists. **VFOAT** Art Lovers' Art and Craft Fair Bulletin. (197?)-. Bulletin. English. Four times a year. $8.50. American Society of Artists Inc, PO Box 1326, Palatine IL 60078. **Tel** (312)751-2500. ctrl circ.

ISSN 0254-1572
DD 745.50987 VE
ARTESANIA Y FOLKLORE DE VENEZUELA. (ARTESANIA Y FOLKLORE DE VENEZUELA : REVISTA BIMESTRAL AL SERVICIO DEL SECTOR ARTESANAL DE CORPOINDUSTRIA Y FEDEINDUSTRIA.). [Artes. folk. Venez.]. **VFOAT** Revista Bimestral al Servicio del Sector Artesanal de Corpoindustria y Fedeindustria. (1975)-. Periodical. Spanish. Six times a year. Artesania y Folklore de Venezuela, Apartado 60935 Chacao, Caracas 1060 Venezuela. **Tel** 011 2 662 36 94, FAX 011 81 86 28 57. **Photos.**
Desc: Articles cover the arts, crafts, and music of Venezuela with emphasis on the folklore and culture they represent. Articles cover both current artisans and the history of Venezuela's artistic traditions.

LC 745
DD NK EC
ARTESANIAS DE AMERICA. **VFOAT** Revista del CIDAP. No. 12 (Dec. 1982)-. Spanish (Portuguese and English). Three times a year. $10.00. CIDAP, Hermano Miguel 3-23, Apartado 557, Cuenca Ecuador. Index available. **Bk Rev. Circ:** 1,500. ***Continues*** *Boletin de Informacion del Centro Interamericano de Artesanias y Artes Populares.*
Ind/Abst Ethnoarts Index.

LC NK
DD 745 US
ARTS AND CRAFTS MAGAZINE. (19??)-. English. Four times a year. $20.00. Arts and Crafts Magazine, Box 3592, Station E, Trenton NJ 08629. **Tel** (609)585-2546.
Desc: Devoted to mission and design, furniture and decorative arts.

LC WMLC 93/4512 **ISSN** 1074-4568
DD 745 US
TITLE CHANGE
ARTS & CRAFTS QUARTERLY MAGAZINE. [Arts crafts q. mag.]. **VFOAT** Arts and Crafts Quarterly Magazine; Arts and Crafts Quarterly; Arts & Crafts Quarterly. (199?)-(1994). Periodical. English. (Feb., May, Aug., Nov.). Arts & Crafts Quarterly, 9 South Main Street, Lambertville NJ 08530. **Tel** (609)397-4104, FAX (609)397-9377. **ED** Michelle Roemer Schoen. **Bk Rev**, (Qty: 6). **Ad Acc. Circ:** 6,000. ***Continues*** *Arts & Crafts Quarterly.* ***Continued by*** *Style 1900, 1080-451X.*

ISSN 1067-1463
DD 381 US
CCC
CEASED
ARTS & CRAFTS RETAILER. [Arts crafts retail.]. **VFOAT** Arts and Crafts Retailer. Vol. 1, No. 1 (Jan./Feb. 1993)-(Nov. 1993). Trade Publication. English. Argus Business, 6151 Powers Ferry Road Northwest, Atlanta GA 30339. **Tel** (404)995-2500, FAX (404)995-0400. ***Continues*** *Art Material Trade News, 0004-3265.*

ISSN 0883-5810
DD 746 US
ATHA. (ATHA : NEWSLETTER OF THE ASSOCIATION OF TRADITIONAL HOOKING ARTISTS.). [ATHA]. **Added/Corp** Association of Traditional Hooking Artists. (198?)-. Newsletter. English. Six times a year. $10.00. Association of Traditional Hooking Artists, 1315 Bell Road, Niles MI 49120.

LC 745
DD NK US
ATHENAEUM ANNOTATIONS. **Added/Corp** Philadelphia. Athenaeum. Vol. 1, (Spring 1976)-. Periodical. English. Irregular. Comes with Athenaeum of Philadelphia membership. Athenaeum of Philadelphia, 219 South Sixth Street, Philadelphia PA 19106. **Tel** (215)925-2688.

ISSN 0715-5093
DD 745.5/06/07182 CN
ATUAGATSANGA / LABRADOR CRAFT PRODUCERS ASSOCIATION. [Atuagatsanga - Labrador Craft Producers Association]. **Main/Corp** Labrador Craft Producers Association. **VAT** Labrador Craft Producers Association (Inuktitut Edition). Periodical. Eskimo. Four times a year. $2.00 (Comes with membership). Labrador Craft Producers Association, PO Box 489, Happy Valley Newfoundland A0P 1E0 Canada. **Tel** (709)896-3081.

LC NK
DD 745 AT
CEASED
AUSTRALIAN DECORATING CRAFTS. (19??)-(Sept. 1995). Periodical. English. Federal Publishing Co Pty Ltd., PO Box 199, 180 Bourke Road, Alexandria New South Wales 2015 Australia. **Tel** 011 61 2 3539992, FAX 011 61 2 66923059935. **(Subscription address:** Federal Publishing Co. Pty Ltd., PO Box 199, Alexandria NSW 2015 Australia. **Tel** 011 61 2 3530666.**)**

LC 745
DD NK US
BASKET BITS. (1989)-. English. Four times a year. $14.00. Jim Rutherford, Box 8, Loudonville OH 44842. **Tel** (419)994-3256. **Bk Rev. Ad Acc.** ctrl circ.

LC TT879.B3 B37 **ISSN** 0897-3458
DD 746.41/2/05 US
BASKETMAKER (WESTLAND, MICH.). (BASKETMAKER.). [Basketmaker]. **VFOAT** Basketmaker Magazine. (1988)-. Periodical. English. Four times a year. $16.00. MKS Publications Inc, PO Box 340, Westland MI 48185. **ED** Sue Kurginski. **Bk Rev. Ad Acc. Circ:** 4,000. ***Continues*** *Basketmaker Quarterly, 0892-5356.*
Desc: A magazine of interest to designers, weavers and collectors of basketry.

ISSN 1072-4931
DD 745 US
●**BEAD & BUTTON.** [Bead button]. **VFOAT** Bead and Button. (Feb. 1994)-. Periodical. English. Six times a year. $19.95. Conterie Press Inc, PO Box 1020, Norwalk

CT 06856. **Tel** (203)857-5355. **(Subscription address:** Neodata / Colorado, P.O. Box 2606, Boulder CO 80322. **)**

LC 745.5 **ISSN** 0278-7415
DD TT US
BETTER HOMES AND GARDENS CREATIVE IDEAS. **VFOAT** Creative Ideas. (19??)-. Periodical. English. Six times a year. Meredith Corporation, Locust at 17th, Des Moines IA 50309. **Tel** (515)284-3000, FAX (515)284-2568.

LC TT1 .O5 **ISSN** 0090-6468
DD 684/.08/05 US
BETTER WAYS TO DO IT. [Better ways to do it]. (19??)-. English. One time a year. $1.00. The Hearst Corporation, 250 West 55th Street, New York NY 10019. **Tel** (212)649-4014, (800)925-0485. ***Continues*** *1033 Better Ways To Do It.*

LC Z5956.F6 B53 NK805 **ISSN** 1046-9931
DD 016.745/0973 US
BIBLIOGRAPHY OF AMERICAN FOLK ART. (BIBLIOGRAPHY OF AMERICAN FOLK ART FOR THE YEAR ...). [Bibliogr. Am. folk art]. **Added/Corp** Museum of American Folk Art. (1987)-. Bibliography. English. One time a year. Museum of American Folk Art, 61 West 62nd Street, New York NY 10023-7015. **Tel** (212)977-7170, FAX (212)977-8134.

LC 745.5 **ISSN** 0397-7102
DD TT FR
BULLETIN MENSUEL D'INFORMATION DU CENTRE DE CREATION INDUSTRIELLE. **Added/Corp** Centre de Creation Industrielle. (19??)-. Bulletin. French. Ten times a year. 97.94F France; 96.15F other. Editions du Centre Pompidou, Service Commerical, 75191 Paris Cedex 04 France. **Tel** 011 33 1 44784288, 011 33 1 44781233, FAX 011 33 1 42725650, telex CNAC GP 212 726.

LC NK5750 .B83 **ISSN** 0261-7080
DD 736/.24/05 US
BULLETIN OF THE FRIENDS OF JADE, THE. [Bull. Friends Jade]. **Added/Corp** Friends of Jade (Great Britain). Vol. 1, No. 1 (Fall 1980)-. Bulletin. English. Irregular (published approximately ever 18 to 20 months). $35.00. Friends of Jade, 5004 Ensign Street, San Diego CA 92117. **Tel** (619)281-1032. **ED** Robert L. Frey. Index available. cum. index. **Bk Rev. Circ:** 200 (ctrl).
Desc: Articles and illustrations on all facets of jade, covering world sources, ancient and modern carving methods and reports on worldwide jade auction markets.

ISSN 1182-5561
DD 746.1/4 CN
BULLETIN - ONTARIO HANDWEAVERS AND SPINNERS. (BULLETIN.). [Bull. - Ont. Handweavers Spinners]. **Added/Corp** Ontario Handweavers and Spinners. **VFOAT** Magazine of the Ontario Handweavers & Spinners. Vol. 33, No. 2 (summer 1990)-. Bulletin. English. Four times a year. I Coles, 17 Whitman Street, Willowdale Ontario M2M 3H7 Canada. ***Continues*** *Ontario Handweavers and Spinners Bulletin., 0227-6445.*

LC TT12 .A45a **ISSN** 0272-6246
DD 745/.029/473 US
BUYERS BOOK OF AMERICAN CRAFTS, THE. [Buy. book Am. crafts]. **Main/Corp** American Craft Enterprises. (1979)-. English. One time a year. American Craft Enterprises Industries, Box 10, New Paltz NY 12561.

ISSN 1042-6280
DD 745 US
CA CRAFT CONNECTION, THE. [CA craft connect.]. **VFOAT** CA Craft Connection Newspaper. **VAT** California Craft Connection Newspaper; California Craft Connection. Vol. 1, Issue 1 (Feb. 1989)-. Trade Publication. English. Six times a year. $16.50. Craftmaster Enterprises, PO Box 39429, Downey CA 90239. **Tel** (310)869-5882. **ED** E. S. Matz. Index available. **Bk Rev. Ad Acc. Circ:** 6,000. ***Continues*** *Crafty Doings Newspaper, 0895-5794.*
Desc: Trade newspaper for professional crafts people.

LC Z43.A1 C34 **ISSN** 0145-1731
DD 745.6/1/05 US
CALLIGRAFREE CRIBE. (19??)-. Periodical. English. Six times a year. $12.00. Calligrafree Cribe, 43 Ankara Avenue, Brookville OH 45309. ***Continues*** *Calligrafree, 0099-0221.*

ISSN 0749-954X
DD 745 US
CALLIGRAPH. (CALLIGRAPH / SOCIETY FOR CALLIGRAPHY.). [Calligraph]. Periodical. English. Three times a year. $24.00. Society for Calligraphy, PO Box 64174, Los Angeles CA 90064. **Tel** (310)457-2968. **ED** Donna Lee. **Bk Rev. Circ:** 1,200.
Desc: Contains articles about letterforms, pens, inks, papers, the history of letters, interviews with well-known calligraphers; a schedule of coming activities and reports on Speaker Program Meetings and Workshops.

LC Z43.A1 C35 **ISSN** 0895-7819
DD 745.6/1/05 US
TITLE CHANGE
CALLIGRAPHY REVIEW (NORMAN, OKLA.). (CALLIGRAPHY REVIEW.). [Callig. rev.]. **VFOAT** Calligraphy. Vol. 5, No. 1 (Fall 1987)-(199?). Periodical. English. Calligraphy Review Inc, 1624 24th Avenue Southwest, Norman OK 73072. **Tel** (405)364-8794, FAX (405)364-8914. **ED** Karyn L. Gilman. Index available (bound in 4th issue.). cum. index. **Bk Rev**, (Qty: 6-8). **Ad Acc. Circ:** 5,400. ***Continues*** *Calligraphy Idea Exchange, 0737-318X.* ***Continued by*** *Letters Arts Review.*
Desc: A colorful publication dedicated to the art of the fine hand lettering - both contemporary and historical.

ISSN 0740-0780
DD 731 US
CARROUSEL ART. (1978)-. Periodical. English. Four times a year. $25.00. Cameo Productions, PO Box 992, Garden Grove CA 92642. **Tel** (714)895-6203. **ED** Sondra L. Evans. **Bk Rev. Ad Acc. Circ:** 1,200 (ctrl).
Desc: A publication (back issues available) chronicling the carousel industry in the United States between 1867 and 1930. Presents photos of wooden, antique figures, with articles on carvers and manufacturers.

LC NK **ISSN** 0009-0190
DD 745 US
CERAMIC ARTS & CRAFTS. **See** Glass and Ceramics.

ISSN 1065-2299
DD 746 US
CHART CONNECTION, THE. [Chart connect.]. No. 1 (Sept./Oct. 1992)-. Periodical. English. Six times a year. $16.00. Craft Source, 7509 7th Place SW, Seattle WA 98106.

ISSN 0889-8189
DD 745 US
CHINA PAINTER, THE. [China paint.]. **Added/Corp** World Organization of China Painters. (19??)-. Periodical. English. Six times a year. $25.00. China Painter, 2641 N W 10th St, Oklahoma City OK 73107. **Tel** (405)521-1234, FAX (405)521-1265.

LC WMLC 91/3380 **ISSN** 1047-0328
DD 745 US
CEASED
CHRISTMAS (BIRMINGHAM, ALA.). (CHRISTMAS : YEAR-ROUND NEEDLEWORK & CRAFT IDEAS.). [Christmas]. Vol. 1, No. 1 (1990)-(19??). Periodical. English. Oxmoor House, PO Box 1862, Birmingham AL 35201. **Tel** (205)877-6000. **(Subscription address:** Palm Coast Data, PO Box 420163, Agency Department, Palm Coast FL 32142. **Tel** (904)445-4662 ext. 669, (800)829-5475.**)**

LC TT900.C4 C467 **ISSN** 0748-8106
DD 745.5 US
CHRISTMAS IDEAS. (1975)-. English. Meredith Corporation, Locust at 17th, Des Moines IA 50309. **Tel** (515)284-3000, FAX (515)284-2568.

LC TT900.C4 C475 **ISSN** 0883-9077
DD 745.594/1 US
CHRISTMAS IS COMING! (HARDCOVER). (CHRISTMAS IS COMING!.). [Christmas coming]. (1985)-. English. One time a year (Oct.). $24.20. Oxmoor House, PO Box 1862, Birmingham AL 35201. **Tel** (205)877-6000. **ED** Linda Martin Stewart.
Desc: Christmas publication offering holiday projects for children and parents. Complete with full-color patterns and instructions as well as recipes for children.

LC TT900.C4 C487 **ISSN** 0747-7791
DD 745.594/1 US
CHRISTMAS WITH SOUTHERN LIVING. (19??)-. English. One time a year. $28.20. Oxmoor House, PO Box 1862, Birmingham AL 35201. **Tel** (205)877-6000. **ED** Kathleen English.
Desc: Offers ideas for unique holiday decorations, plus ideas for gift-giving and festive party planning.

ISSN 0529-6463
DD 709 HK
CHUNG-KUO SHU-HUA. CHINESE PAINTING AND CALLIGRAPHY. **VFOAT** Chinese Painting and Calligraphy. (July 1961)-. Periodical. Chinese (English). Peoples Fine Arts Publishing House, 32 Beizongbu Hutong, Beijing, People's Republic of China. **Tel** 55.5260, FAX 55.3405, telex 5019. **Bk Rev. Circ:** 10,000.
Desc: Covers calligraphy, seal cutting and some works of traditional Chinese painting including some introductory articles. Appeals to both professional and amateur artists.

LC WMLC 93/927 **ISSN** 8755-2655
DD 745 US
CLOTH DOLL, THE. [Cloth doll]. (July 1982)-. Periodical. English. Four times a year. $15.95. The Cloth Doll, Box 2167, Lake Oswego OR 97035. **Tel** (503)244-3539. **ED** Leta Bergman. **Bk Rev. Ad Acc. Circ:** 5,000.
Desc: News, information, and techniques for cloth doll making and designing. Regular columns features helpful hints, supply sources, and several free patterns in every issue.
Ind/Abst Index Inf. (1984-).

LC NK **ISSN** 1071-8036
DD 745 US
COUNTRY COLLECTIBLES. (19??)-. English. Four times a year. $14.97. Harris Publications, 1115 Broadway, 8th Floor, New York NY 10010. **Tel** (212)807-7100.

LC TT1 .C715 **ISSN** 0731-5376
DD 745.5/05 US
COUNTRY CRAFTS. [Ctry. crafts]. (19??)-. Periodical. English. One time a year. $3.50. Meredith Publications / Special Interest Section, 1716 Locust Street, Des Moines IA 50309. **Tel** (515)284-3000.

LC TT23 .C673 **ISSN** 1047-4625
DD 745/.0973/05 US
COUNTRY FOLK ART MAGAZINE. [Ctry. folk art mag.]. Vol. 1, No. 1 (Winter 1988)-. Periodical. English. Twelve times a year. $29.99. Long Publications, 8393 East Holly Road, Holly MI 48442. **Tel** (313)634-9675, FAX (313)634-0301.

ISSN 1053-2277
DD 745 US
COUNTRY GALLERY. [Ctry. gallery]. Vol. 1, No. 1 (Summer 1991)-. Periodical. English. Four times a year. $12.00. Country Gallery, PO Box 210, Honaker VA 24260-0210.

LC NK **ISSN** 0745-3116
DD 745 US
TITLE CHANGE
COUNTRY HANDCRAFTS. [Ctry. handcr.]. (1982)-(1994). Periodical. English. Reiman Publications, 5400 South 60th Street, Greendale WI 53129. **Tel** (414)423-0100 Ext. 421, FAX (414)423-1143. **ED** Jill Nickerson. **Circ:** 500,000. available on microfilm from University Microfilms International (UMI). ***Continued by*** *Crafting Traditions, 1082-1376.*
Desc: Country-oriented and original craft patterns. Over thirty full-size, full-color patterns in each issue.

LC TT23 .J36 **ISSN** 0272-7889
DD 745/.05 US
COUNTRY SAMPLER: NORTH AMERICAN FOLK ART. Vol. 1 (1979)-. English. Jo Sonja's Folk Art Studio, PO Box 744, Redlands CA 92373.

LC WMLC 91/3165 **ISSN** 1058-3769
DD 694 US
COUNTRY WOOD PROJECTS. [Ctry. wood proj.]. (1988)-. Periodical. English. Four times a year. $17.97. Harris Publications, 1115 Broadway, 8th Floor, New York NY 10010. **Tel** (212)807-7100.

ISSN 1030-9713
DD 745.505 AT
CRAFT & DECORATING. [Craft decor.]. (1988)-. Periodical. English. Six times a year. 20.55Aus$. Tracy Marsh Publishing Pty. Ltd., 97 Rose Street, Chippendale New South Wales, 2008 Australia. **Tel** 011 61 2 3180488, FAX 011 61 2 3193731.

LC NK **ISSN** 0814-6586
DD 745 AT
CRAFT ARTS. Issue 1 (Oct./Dec. 1984)-. Periodical. English. Four times a year. 32.88Aus$. Craft Art PTY Limited, PO Box 363, Neutral Bay Junction, Sydney NSW 2089 Australia. **Tel** (02)908 4797, FAX (02)953 1576. **ED** Ken Lockwood. **Circ:** 15,000.
Ind/Abst EP Collect.; Homework Help.; MasterFile FullTEXT 1000; MasterFile FullTEXT 350; MasterFile FullTEXT 650; MasterFile FullTEXT (Sept. 1994-); Telebase; World Mag. Bank.

LC NK1 .C7 **ISSN** 1067-8328
DD 745 US
CRAFT CONNECTION. (CRAFT CONNECTION : A MIDWEST PUBLICATION OF THE MINNESOTA CRAFTS COUNCIL.). [Craft connect.]. **Added/Corp** Minnesota Crafts Council. Vol. 1, No. 1 (Spring 1975)-. Periodical. English. Four times a year. $20.00. Minnesota Crafts Council, 528 Hennepine Avenue South, Minneapolis MN 55403. **Tel** (612)333-7789. **ED** Elizabeth Barnard. **Bk Rev. Ad Acc, Adv Mgr:** Jim Schiller. **Circ:** 800 (ctrl).
Desc: Includes articles on crafts, events, and personalities in the upper midwest. Also includes calendar of shows, fairs, and exhibits.

LC NC **ISSN** 1193-3208
DD 745.50607182 CN
CRAFT CONNECTION. (THE CRAFT CONNECTION.). [Craft connect.]. (1991)-. Periodical. English. Four times a year. Comes with Labrador Craft Producers Association membership. LCPA, PO Box 489, Station B Happy Val, Labrador A0P 1E0 Canada. **Tel** (709)896-3081, FAX (709)896-0700. ***Continues*** *Newsletter - Labrador Craft Producers Association, 0715-5077.*

ISSN 0823-2148
DD 745.5/09711 CN
CRAFT CONTACTS (1983). (CRAFT CONTACTS.). [Craft contacts]. **Added/Corp** Craftsmen's Association of British Columbia. Circle Craft (Association). (March 1983)-. Periodical. English. Twelve times a year. $37.00. Craftsmen's Association of British Columbia, 1411 Cartwright Street, Granville Island British Columbia V6H 3R7 Canada. **Bk Rev**. **Ad Acc**. ctrl circ. ***Continues*** *Circle Craft, CABC, 0821-1868.*

LC NK
DD 745 US
CRAFT DIGEST. (19??)-. English. Twelve times a year. $30.00. Craft Digest, PO Box 155, New Britian CT 06050. **Tel** (203)225-8875. **ED** Joseph Mehan. **Bk Rev**, (Qty: 30-40). **Ad Acc, Adv Mgr:** Harry Langenheim, **Tel** (203)489-4723. **Circ:** 3,500 (ctrl).

ISSN 0228-7498
DD 745.5/097124 CN
CRAFT FACTOR. (THE CRAFT FACTOR : A QUARTERLY PUBLICATION OF THE SASKATCHEWAN CRAFT COUNCIL.). [Craft factor]. **Added/Corp** Saskatchewan Craft Council. Vol. 2, No. 1 (Mar. 1977)-. Periodical. English. Three times a year. 9.61Can$. Saskatchewan Craft Council, 813 Broadway Avenue, Saskatoon Saskatchewan S7N 1B5 Canada. **Tel** (306)653-3616. **ED** Sandra Flood. **Bk Rev**. **Ad Acc**. **Circ:** 700. ***Continues*** *Saskatchewan Craft Council News, 0228-748X.*
Desc: Devoted to all aspects of professional craft development as it relates to Saskatchewan and where applicable in Canada, US and worldwide. Official journal of Saskatchewan Craft Council.

LC NK
DD 745 AT
•**CRAFT FORUM.** (1995)-. English. Six times a year. 23.02Aus$. Crafty Publications, PO Box 18178, Collins Street East, Melbourne VIC 8003 Australia. **Tel** 011 61 3 94196993.

LC NK ISSN 0953-931X
DD 745 UK
CRAFT HISTORY. [Craft hist.]. Vol. 1 (Oct. 1988)-. Periodical. English. Four times a year. Combined Arts, 52 Broughton Street Glsy 8, Edinburgh EH1 3SA United Kingdom.

ISSN 1044-4009
DD 745 US
CRAFT INTERNATIONAL. (CRAFT INTERNATIONAL : CI.). [Craft int.]. **Added/Corp** Craft and Folk Art Museum. World Crafts Foundation. **VFOAT** CI; C.I. (198?)-. Periodical. English. Four times a year. Craft International, Administrative Director, 24 Spring Street, New York NY 10012.
Ind/Abst Art Index; ARTbibliogr. Mod. (1985-).

LC NK ISSN 0199-5200
DD 745 US
CRAFT RANGE. (1978)-. Periodical. English. Six times a year. $12.00. Craft Range Magazine, PO Box 61505, Denver CO 80206. **Tel** (303)986-4891. **ED** Blu Wagner. **Bk Rev**. **Ad Acc**. **Circ:** 10,000 (ctrl).
Desc: Articles, interviews, shows, reviews, calendar of events and opportunities in craft and design.

ISSN 0712-2659
DD 745.5/07/1171551 CN
CRAFT SCHOOL. (CRAFT SCHOOL = ECOLE D'ARTISANAT.). [Craft sch.]. **Added/Corp** New Brunswick Craft School. **VFOAT** Ecole d'Artisanat. No. 1 (1981)-. Periodical. English (French). New Brunswick Craft School, PO Box 6000, Fredericton New Brunswick E3B 5H1 Canada.

LC NK ISSN 0882-7486
DD 745 US
CRAFT SHOW DIGEST. (1984)-. Periodical. English. Two times a year. $12.00. Craft Show Digest, PO Box 3275, Falls Church VA 22043. **Tel** (703)532-3111. **ED** Allena Wood. **Bk Rev**. **Ad Acc**. **Circ:** 12,000 (ctrl).
Desc: Current listings of craft shows, craft shops, classifieds, reference and compilation of information in marketing crafts. Media between promoters and crafters nationally.

ISSN 1059-8766
DD 745 US
CRAFT SUPPLY MAGAZINE. [Craft supply mag.]. **VFOAT** Craft Supply. (1991)-. Trade Publication. English. Four times a year. $30.00. Hobby Publications Inc., 225 Gordons Corner Road, Box 420, Manalapan NJ 07726. **Tel** (908)446-4900. ***Continues*** *Craft Supply Report, 1056-0343.*

ISSN 0158-7048
DD 746.509945 AT
TITLE CHANGE
CRAFT VICTORIA. [Craft Vic.]. (1976)-(1993). Periodical. English. (monthly with combined Jan./Feb. and Nov./Dec.). Crafts Council of Victoria, 114 Gertrudest, Fitzroy 3065 Australia. **Tel** 011 61 3 4173111, FAX 011 61 3 4197295. ***Continues*** *Victorian Craft News.* ***Continued by*** *Craft Victoria Newsletter, 1320-4858.*
Desc: Seeks to develop the quality and diversity of craft exhibitions in Australia through the exhibition program and collaboration with other organizations.

LC NC ISSN 1320-4858
DD 745.5099405 AT
•**CRAFT VICTORIA NEWSLETTER.** [Craft Vic. newsl.]. (1993)-. Periodical. English. Six times a year (March, May, June, Aug., Oct., Dec.). 32.88Aus$. Crafts Council of Victoria, 114 Gertrudest, Fitzroy 3065 Australia. **Tel** 011 61 3 4173111, FAX 011 61 3 4197295. ***Continues*** *Craft Victoria, 0158-7048.*

LC NK1135 ISSN 1082-1376
DD 745 US
•**CRAFTING TRADITIONS.** [Crafting tradit.]. Vol. 13, No. 5 (May/June 1995)-. Periodical. English. Six times a year. Reiman Publications, 5400 South 60th Street, Greendale WI 53129. **Tel** (414)423-0100 Ext. 421, FAX (414)423-1143. ***Continues*** *Country Handcrafts, 0745-3116.*

ISSN 0319-7832
DD 745.5/06/2713 CN
CRAFTNEWS (TORONTO). (CRAFTNEWS.). [CraftNews]. **Added/Corp** Ontario Crafts Council. (Jan. 1976)-. Periodical. English. Eight times a year. 40.00Can$ Canada; 45.00Can$ other (includes Ontario Craft and membership to Ontario Crafts Council). Ontario Crafts Council, 35 McCaul Street, Chalmers Building, Toronto Ontario M5T 1V7 Canada. **Tel** (416)977-3551, FAX (416)977-3551. **ED** Anne McPherson. **Bk Rev**. **Ad Acc, Adv Mgr:** Susan Browne, **Tel** (416)886-6640. **Circ:** 4,000. ***Continues in part*** *Craft Ontario, 0315-7075.*
Desc: For serious hobbyists and professional craftsmen. Covers opportunities, significant events, education, show reviews, and book reviews. Contains monthly calendar.
Ind/Abst Can. Index.

LC NK
DD 745 SZ
CRAFTS COUNCIL. (19??)-. English (French and German). Four times a year. 60.00F. Crafts Council Switzerland, Case Postale 898, CH-2501 Bienne Switzerland. **Tel** 011 41 32 516369.

LC TT1 .C73 ISSN 0306-610X
DD 745.5/05 UK
CCC
CRAFTS (CRAFTS ADVISORY COMMITTEE). (CRAFTS.). [Crafts]. **Added/Corp** Crafts Council (Great Britain) Crafts Advisory Committee. (Mar. 1973)-. Trade Publication. English. Six times a year (Jan., Mar., May, July, Sept., Nov.). $78.00. Crafts Council, 44A Pentonville Road, Islington London N19BY United Kingdom. **Tel** 011 44 171 2787700, FAX 011 44 171 8376891. **ED** Geraldine Rudge. **Bk Rev**. **Ad Acc**. **Circ:** 15,000. available on microfilm and microfiche from University Microfilms International (UMI).
Desc: Contemporary British crafts set in an international and historical context.
Ind/Abst Art Index; ARTbibliogr. Mod.

LC TT855 .C68 ISSN 0146-6607
DD 745.5/05 US
CRAFTS 'N THINGS. [Crafts things]. **VFOAT** Crafts and Things. (19??)-. Periodical. English. Ten times a year. $16.97. Clapper Communications, 2400 Devon, Suite 375, Des Plaines IL 60018. **Tel** (800)272-3871, (708)635-5800. **(Subscription address:** Clapper Communications, 2400 Devon, Suite 375, Des Plaines IL 60018. **)** **ED** Nancy Tosh. Index available. cum. index. **Bk Rev**. **Ad Acc**. **Circ:** 365,000. available on microfilm and microfiche from University Microfilms International (UMI). Documents available from UMI Article Clearinghouse, Magazine Collection. ***Absorbed*** *Creative Crafts & Miniatures., 0734-0176.*
Desc: The craft magazine that assists with large color photos, step-by-step instructions and full-size patterns.
Ind/Abst EP Collect.; Gen. Period. Index (1986-); Homework Help.; Mag. Artic. Summar. Elite; Mag. Artic. Summar. Select; Mag. Artic. Summar. CD-ROM; Mag. Index Plus (1989-); Mag. Search; MasterFile FullTEXT 1000; MasterFile FullTEXT 350; MasterFile FullTEXT 650; MasterFile FullTEXT (July 1989-); Newsp. Period. Abstr. (1988-); OCLC; Pub. Lib. FullTEXT; Telebase; Mag. Index; Vocat. Search.

LC TT1 .C735 ISSN 0148-9127
DD 746 US
CRAFTS (PEORIA, ILL.). (CRAFTS.). [Crafts]. **VFOAT** Crafts Magazine. Vol. 1, No. 1 (May 1978)-. Periodical. English. Twelve times a year. $19.98. PJS Publications Inc., News Plaza, PO Box 1790, Peoria IL 61656. **Tel** (309)682-6626, FAX (309)682-7394. **(Subscription address:** CDS / SIFD Agency Control, 1901 Bell Avenue, Des Moines IA 50315. **Tel** (515)246-6812.**)** **ED** Judy Brossart. **Bk Rev**. **Ad Acc**. **Circ:** 330,000.

ISSN 0833-8337
DD 746/.05 CN
CRAFTS PLUS. [Crafts plus]. (Nov./Dec. 1985)-. Periodical. English. Eight times a year. 17.56Can$. Camar Publications Ltd., 130 Spy Court, Markham Ontario L3R 5H6 Canada. **Tel** (416)475-8440, FAX (416)475-9246. available on microfilm and microfiche from Micromedia Limited.
Ind/Abst Can. Index.

ISSN 1053-2013
DD 680 US
CRAFTS RELATED NEWSLETTERS, PERIODICALS, AND PUBLICATIONS ETC. [Craft relat. newsl. period. publ. etc.]. **VFOAT** Craft Related Newsletters. Vol. 1:1 (1990)-. Newsletter. English. Every 2 years. $7.50 North America; $12.50 other. Prosperity & Profits Unlimited, PO Box 416, Denver CO 80201-0416. **Tel** (303)575-5676. **ED** A.C. Doyle. **Circ:** 1,500.
Desc: A how-to source for information, pamphlets and brochures on crafts.

ISSN 0160-7650
DD 658 US
CRAFTS REPORT, THE. [Crafts rep.]. Vol. 1, (April 1975)-. Trade Publication. English. Twelve times a year. $29.00. Crafts Report Publishing Company Inc, 300 Water Street, Wilmington DE 19801. **Tel** (302)656-2209, FAX (302)656-4894. **ED** Marilyn Stevens. Index available. **Bk Rev**, (Qty: 30). **Ad Acc, Adv Mgr:** Maryann Parker. **Circ:** 23,000. available on microfilm and microfiche from University Microfilms International (UMI). ***Absorbed*** *Working Craftsman, 0149-0206.*
Desc: Trade journal for the professional crafts industry.
Ind/Abst AGRICOLA; ARTbibliogr. Mod. (-1987).

LC WMLC L 83/5653 ISSN 0891-0588
DD 745 US
CRAFTWORKS FOR THE HOME. [Craftworks home]. **VFOAT** Craftworks; Craft Works for the Home. Vol. 1, No. 1 (Sept. 1985)-. Periodical. English. Twelve times a year. $30.00. All American Crafts Inc., 243 Newton Sparta Road, Newton NJ 07860. **Tel** (201)383-8080, telex 844380. **(Subscription address:** Kable Publishers Aide / Illinois, 308 East Hitt Street, Subscription Department, Mt. Morris IL 61054-1473. **Tel** (815)734-1261.**)**

ISSN 1193-1140
DD 746.9/2/0971405 CN
CREATEURS QUEBECOIS. [Creat. que.]. **Added/Corp** Association pour la Promotion des Designers de Mode du Quebec. (Autumn/Winter 1991/1992)-. Periodical. English (French). Two times a year. Limited free distribution. Association pour la Promotion des Designers de Mode au Quebec, 33 Prince Street, Montreal Quebec H3C 2M7 Canada. ***Continues*** *Revenge (Montreal, Quebec)., 1193-1132.*

ISSN 1193-1140
DD 746.9/2/0971405 CN
CREATEURS QUEBECOIS. [Creat. que.]. **Added/Corp** Association pour la Promotion des Designers de Mode du Quebec. (Autumn/Winter 1991/1992)-. Periodical. French (English). Two times a year. Limited free distribution. Association pour la Promotion des Designers de Mode au Quebec, 33 Prince Street, Montreal Quebec H3C 2M7 Canada. ***Continues*** *Revenge (Montreal, Quebec)., 1193-1132.*

LC NK ISSN 0741-6504
DD 745 US
CREATIVE OHIO. **Added/Corp** Ohio Arts & Crafts Guild. (197?)-. Periodical. English. Six times a year. $20.00. Ohio Arts & Crafts Guild, PO Box 3080, Lexington OH 44904. **Tel** (419)884-9622. **Bk Rev**. **Ad Acc**. ctrl circ.
Desc: Contains information, show evaluations, profiles of artists and craftspeople, marketing and technical tips, classified ads, show schedule updates, book reviews, educational opportunities, photo gallery, suppliers, advertisements and much more.

ISSN 1072-3943
DD 646 US
•**CREATIVE RETIREMENT.** [Creat. retire.]. (1994)-. Periodical. English. Four times a year. $11.80. Vacation Publications Inc, 1502 Augusta Drive, Suite 415, Houston TX 77057. **Tel** (713)974-6903, FAX (713)974-0445.

ISSN 1056-3377
DD 745 US
CROES LETTER, THE. [The Croes lett.]. Vol. 1, No. 1 (Aug. 1991)-. Periodical. English. Twelve times a year. $60.00. Keith J Croes, PO Box 269, Mt Royal NJ 08061-0269.

ISSN 1056-7542
DD 746 US
CROSS STITCH! MAGAZINE. (CROSS STITCH MAGAZINE.). [Cross stitch mag.]. No. 1 (Oct.Nov. 1990)-. Periodical. English. Six times a year. $12.95. Needlecraft Shop, 23 Old Pecan Road, Big Sandy TX 75755. **Tel** (903)636-4011 ext 211, FAX (903)636-2288. **ED** Carolyn Christmas. **Circ:** 130,000 (ctrl).
Desc: Cross-stitch designs, charts and needlecraft designs.

ISSN 1048-3969
DD 746 US
CROSS-STITCH QUICK & EASY. [Cross-stitch quick easy]. **VFOAT** Cross-Stitch Quick and Easy; Cross Stitch Quick and Easy; Cross Stitch Quick & Easy; Quick & Easy; Quick and Easy. Vol. 2, No. 4 (Apr./May 1990)-. Periodical. English. Six times a year.

The Arts —Crafts and Decorative Arts

$19.97. Cross Quick, 4118 Lakeside Drive, Richmond CA 94806. **Tel** (510)223-3144. **Continues** Cross Quick, 0899-5613.

DD 709.04   **ISSN** 0969-1189 UK
CV GUIDE TO THE ARTS. [CV guide arts].
(?988)-. English. One time a year (Sept.). $51.33. CV Publications, Waters EDN, Broom Water West, Teddington TW11 9QH United Kingdom. **Tel** 011 44 181 9772122.

LC NK   **ISSN** 0954-1608
DD 745   UK
               TITLE CHANGE
CV : JOURNAL OF ART AND CRAFTS.
VFOAT CV Journal of Art and Crafts. Vol. 1, No. 1 (Nov. 1988)-(199?). English. Process Communication Ltd, 10 Barley Mow Passage, Chiswick London W4 4PH United Kingdom. **Continued by** CV Guide to the Arts, 0969-1189.

DD 747   **ISSN** 1064-3095 US
DECORATING DIGEST CRAFT AND HOME PROJECTS. [Decor. dig. craft home proj.].
VFOAT Decorating Digest Craft and Home Projects. (19??)-. Periodical. English. Six times a year. $24.00. Hochman Associates, 950 Third Avenue, 16th Floor, New York NY 10022. **Tel** (212)371-4932. **(Subscription address:** CDS Agency Hard Copy, PO Box 4966, Des Moines IA 50340. **Tel** (515)247-7569.) **Continues** Decorating Digest, 0889-2210.

DD 745   **ISSN** 0893-1097 US
DECORATIVE ARTIST'S WORKBOOK.
[Decor. artist. workb.]. (1987)-. Periodical. English. Six times a year. $19.00. F&W Publications, 1507 Dana Avenue, Cincinnati OH 45207. **Tel** (513)531-2222, FAX (513)531-1843. **(Subscription address:** CDS Agency Hard Copy, PO Box 4966, Des Moines IA 50340. **Tel** (515)247-7569.) **ED** Sandra Carpenter. available on microfilm from University Microfilms International (UMI). **Continues** Artists' Workbook.
    Desc: Practical, how-to-magazine for decorative artists, featuring projects to decorate the home. Each issue includes step-by-step worksheets for decorative painting on wood, porcelain, fabric and other surfaces. Also includes marketing tips, shoppers' guide, news of shows, seminars and fairs, and pull-out patterns and designs.
    Ind/Abst Index Inf.

DD 745   **ISSN** 1067-0068 US
               TITLE CHANGE
DECORATIVE ARTS PAINTING. [Decor. arts paint.].
Vol. 8, No. 2 (Mar./Apr. 1993)-(199?). Periodical. English. Clapper Communications, 2400 Devon, Suite 375, Des Plaines IL 60018. **Tel** (800)272-3871, (708)635-5800. **(Subscription address:** CDS Agency Hard Copy, PO Box 4966, Des Moines IA 50340. **Tel** (515)247-7569.) **Continues** Decorative Arts Digest, 0888-076X. **Continued by** Painting (Des Plaines, Ill.), 1079-6819.

DD 745   **ISSN** 0884-4011 US
DECORATIVE ARTS SOCIETY NEWSLETTER, THE. [Decor. Arts Soc. newsl.].
Added/Corp Decorative Arts Society (Society of Architectural Historians). Vol. 4, No. 4 (Dec. 1978)-. Newsletter. English. Four times a year (Mar., June, Sept., Dec.). $30.00 (institutions), $25.00 (individuals). Decorative Arts Society / New York, 333 East 69th Street, Apt. 8E, New York NY 10021. **Tel** (212)860-6963. **Bk Rev. Circ:** 300 (ctrl). **Continues** Decorative Arts Newsletter, 0740-5634.
    Desc: Provides a forum for those interested in American and European decorative arts of all periods and encourages research in the field.
    Ind/Abst BHA : Biblio. Hist. Art.

LC NK1160 .H533   **ISSN** 0277-1160
DD 745.05   US
DECORATOR (GLENS FALLS, N.Y.), THE. (THE DECORATOR.). [Decorator]. **Added/Corp**
Historical Society of Early American Decoration. Esther Stevens Brazer Guild. Vol. 1 (Oct 1946)-. Periodical. English. Two times a year. $5.00. Historical Society of Early American Decoration Inc, c/o New York Historical Association, PO Box 800, Cooperstown NY 13326.

LC NK7 .D4   **ISSN** 0130-3031 RU
DEKORATIVNOE ISKUSSTVO / UCHREDITELI SKH SSSR. **Added/Corp**
Soiuz Khudozhnikov SSSR. **VFOAT** DI; Zhurnal Dekorativnoe Iskusstvo. (1991)-. Periodical. Russian (English). Twelve times a year. $103.95. **(Subscription address:** East View Publications Inc, 3020 Harbor Lane North, Suite 110, Minneapolis MN 55447. **Tel** (800)477-1005, (612)550-0961, FAX (612)559-2931.) **Continues** Dekorativnoe Iskusstvo SSSR.

LC NK1160 .D39   **ISSN** 0304-033X IT
DESIGN (BERGAMO). (DESIGN.). Mar./May
1973-. Periodical. Italian (Italian). 6.000.

LC NK1457.A1 D47   **ISSN** 0108-0695
DD 745.2/0948   DK
DESIGN FROM SCANDINAVIA. [Des. Scand.].
(19??)-. English (French, German and Swedish). One time a year. kr83.00 Europe; kr100.00 other. World Pictures APS, 8 Martinsvej, 1926 Frederiksberg C Denmark. **Tel** 011 45 35 370044, FAX 011 45 35 370481. **ED** Kirsten Bjerregaard. Index available. cum. index. **Ad Acc. Circ:** 50,000. **Continues** Design from Denmark.
    Desc: Covers Scandinavian design in furniture, textiles, lighting, and selected applied arts.

DD 745   **ISSN** 0747-4997 US
DIRECTORY AND LISTING OF PAINTINGS AS SHOWN IN THE MAGAZINE "ANTIQUES", A. (1968)-.
Directory. English. One time a year. $3.00. Paul J. Fredyma, 999 Lyme Road, Hanover NH 03755. **Tel** (603)643-4276. **ED** Paul J. Fredyma.
    Desc: Soft cover, facsimile print, 20-25 pages listing oil paintings and artists in Antiques Magazine for the years 1968-1984.

LC TT163 .D57
DD 607/.741   US
DIRECTORY OF MAINE INDUSTRIAL EDUCATION TEACHERS. 1980-81-. Directory.
English. One time a year. Bureau of Vocational Education, State House Station #23, Augusta ME 04333. Index available. **Continues** Directory of Maine Industrial Arts and Trade & Industry Teachers.

LC E98.A7 I46a
DD 745/.08997   US
DIRECTORY OF MEMBERS AND BUYERS GUIDE / INDIAN ARTS & CRAFTS ASSOCIATION. **Main/Corp** Indian
Arts & Crafts Association (U.S.). (1985/86)-. Directory. English. Indian Arts and Crafts Association, 4215 Lead SE, Albuquerque NM 87108. **Tel** (505)265-9149. **Continues** Directory of Members.

LC TT1 .D57   **ISSN** 0278-7474
DD 670   US
DO-IT-YOURSELF PROJECTS. **VFOAT** Do It
Yourself Projects. (19??)-. English. Four times a year. $14.00. Meredith Corporation, Locust at 17th, Des Moines IA 50309. **Tel** (515)284-3000, FAX (515)284-2568.

LC TT175 .D58   **ISSN** 0363-7972
DD 745.59/22   US
DOLL CASTLE NEWS. (19??)-. Periodical.
English. Six times a year (Jan., Mar., May, July, Sept., Nov.). $16.95. Doll Castle News, PO Box 247, Washington NJ 07882. **ED** Edwina L Mueller. **Bk Rev. Ad Acc. Circ:** 12,000.
    Desc: Of interest to the general collector of dolls and miniatures. Also covers dollmaking.

DD 745   **ISSN** 0746-9624 US
DOLL CRAFTER. Vol. 1, No. 1 (Sept.-Oct. 1983)-.
Periodical. English. Twelve times a year. $35.60. Scott Publications, 30595 West Eight Mile Road, Livonia MI 48152. **Tel** (313)477-6650, (800)458-8237, FAX (810)477-6795.
    Desc: Aimed at those who create and collect dolls. This is a how-to-do-it magazine with doll show dates, tips, hints, business updates, etc.
    Ind/Abst Index Inf. (April 1990-).

DD 745   **ISSN** 1050-4796 US
               CEASED
DOLL DESIGNS. [Doll des.]. **VFOAT** Women's
Circle Doll Designs. (198?)-(19??). Consumer Publication. English. House of White Birches, 306 East Parr Road, Berne IN 46711. **Tel** (219)589-8741, FAX (219)589-8093. **ED** Cary Raesner. **Bk Rev. Ad Acc, Adv Mgr:** Everett Knapp, **Tel** (800)226-0148. **Circ:** 24,150.

LC 747
DD NK1700   IT
●DOMUS DOSSIER. (1993)-. Periodical. Italian. One
time a year. $31.00 Europe; $39.00 other; $180.00 combined subscription with Domus. Editoriale Domus, via Achille Grandi 5-7, 20089 Rozzano Milan Italy. **Tel** 011 39 2 82472276, FAX 011 39 2 8255033.

LC TT180
DD 745.51   NE
DUTCH & FLEMISH ETCHINGS, ENGRAVINGS AND WOODCUTS. (1995)-.
Monographic series. English. Two times a year. Price varies per volume. Koninklijke Van Poll, Postbus 19, 4700 AA Roosendaal Netherlands. **Tel** 011 31 1650 34950. **(Subscription address:** IBD Limited, 24 Hudson Street, Kinderhook NY 12106. **Tel** (518)758-1411.) **ED** Thomas Beek. **Circ:** 600 (ctrl).
    Desc: Focuses on the history of art in the period between 1450 and 1700.

LC NK805 .E26   **ISSN** 1042-1785
DD 745.1/0973/075   US
EAGLES (NEW MARKET, FREDERICK COUNTY, MD.). (EAGLES.). Vol. 1, No. 1 (Jan.
1988)-. Periodical. English. Twelve times a year. Eagles Americana Review, Box 277, New Market MD 21774. **Tel** (301)865-5021.

LC NK8800   **ISSN** 1083-1940
DD 746   US
EASY-DOES-IT NEEDLEWORK & CRAFTS. See Home Economics-Sewing and
Needlework.

DD 709.04   **ISSN** 0818-8734 AT
EYELINE. [Eyeline]. (1987)-. Periodical. English. Four
times a year. 24.67Aus$. Queensland Artworkers Alliance, 497 Adelaide Street, Bisbane Queensland 4000 Australia. **Tel** 011 61 7 8322230, FAX 011 61 7 8322231. **ED** Sarah Follent. **Bk Rev**, (Qty: 3-4). **Ad Acc, Adv Mgr:** D. Beattie, **Tel** 011 61 7 8322225. **Circ:** 2,000 (ctrl).
    Desc: Covers contemporary visual arts and craft of the East Coast of Australia.

DD 680   **ISSN** 1051-6921 US
FASHION & CRAFTS (PALM COAST, FLA.). (FASHION & CRAFTS.). [Fash. crafts]. **VFOAT**
Fashion and Crafts. No. 1 (Oct. 1990)-. Periodical. English. Six times a year. $14.85. Bonnier Magazines & Books Ltd, 4984 Palm Coast Parkway Northwest, Suite 6, Palm Coast FL 32137.

LC NK
DD 745   US
FINE CRAFTS IN PENNSYLVANIA : A SIGHTSEERS AND SHOPPERS GUIDE.
Main/Corp Pennsylvania Council on the Arts. Interagency Crafts Committee. (1980)-. English. One time a year.

LC TT154 .F54   **ISSN** 0277-979X
DD 745.592/8/05   US
FINESCALE MODELER. [FineScale model.].
VFOAT Fine Scale Modeler. Vol. 1, No. 1 (Fall 1982)-. Periodical. English. Nine times a year. $26.95. Kalmbach Publishing Company, 21027 Crossroads Circle, PO Box 1612, Waukesha WI 53187. **Tel** (414)796-8776 ext. 411, FAX (414)796-0126. **ED** Bob Hayden. Index available. **Bk Rev. Ad Acc. Circ:** 77,144.
    Desc: Information on constructing realistic and accurate models; includes new project ideas and tips and techniques for model aircraft, military vehicles, ships, cars, spacecraft, historical figures and dioramas.
    Ind/Abst Index Inf.

LC NK
DD 745   US
●FOLK & TRADITIONAL ARTS. **Added/Corp**
National Endowment for the Arts. **VFOAT** Folk and Traditional Arts. (1994)-. Academic Scholarly Publication. English. Every 2 years. National Endowment for the Arts, 1100 Pennsylvania Avenue Northwest, Washington DC 20506. **Tel** (202)682-5400, (202)682-5435.

LC NK   **ISSN** 0738-8357
DD 745   US
FOLK ART FINDER. (Mar./Apr. 1980)-.
Periodical. English. Four times a year (Jan., Apr., July, Oct.). $14.00. Gallery Press, 117 North Main Street, Essex CT 06426. **Tel** (203)767-0313. **ED** Florence Laffal. Index available. **Bk Rev**, (Qty: varies). **Ad Acc.**
    Desc: The aim of the newsletter is to foster an exchange of information among artists, collectors, galleries, and museums in the field of contemporary folk art. Includes exhibitions, book reviews, commentary and features new artists.

DD 745   **ISSN** 1043-5026 US
FOLK ART MESSENGER. [Folk art
messenger]. **Added/Corp** Folk Art Society of America. Vol. 1, No. 1 (Fall 1987)-. Periodical. English. Four times a year. $25.00. Folk Art Society of America, PO Box 17041, Richmond VA 23226. **Tel** (804)355-6709. **ED** Ann Oppenhimer. Index available. cum. index. **Bk Rev**, (Qty: 4). **Circ:** 1,000.
    Desc: Published by Folk Art Society of America, which discovers, studies, promotes, preserves, exhibits, and documents folk art, folk artists, and folk art environments.

LC TT1 .J36   **ISSN** 0271-3098
DD 745/.05   US
FOLK ART SAMPLER. Vol. 1 (1978)-. English.
One time a year. Jo Sonja's Folk Art Studio, PO Box 744, Redlands CA 92373.

LC NX511.B6 R47   **ISSN** 1052-9195
DD 700/.25/74461   US
FOLK ARTS NETWORK'S FOLK DIRECTORY, THE. [Folk Arts Netw. folk dir.].
Added/Corp Folk Arts Network (Mass.). **VFOAT** Folk

Directory. (1988)-. Directory. English. Every 2 years. $5.00. Folk Arts Network Inc, PO Box 867, Cambridge MA 02238. ***Continues*** *Annual Folk Arts Network Resource Guide, 1052-9691.*

LC TT180
DD 745.51 NE
GERMAN ENGRAVINGS ETCHINGS AND WOODCUTS. (19??)-. English. Two times a year. Price varies per volume. Koninklijke Van Poll, Postbus 19, 4700 AA Roosendaal Netherlands. **Tel** 011 31 1650 34950. **(Subscription address:** IBD Limited, 24 Hudson Street, Kinderhook NY 12106. **Tel** (518)758-1411.) **ED** Thomas Beek. **Circ:** 600 (ctrl).
Desc: Focuses on the history of art in the period between 1450 and 1700.

LC NK
DD 745 US
GIFT BASKET IDEA NEWSLETTER. (19??)-. Newsletter. English. One time a year (Jan.). $5.00. Prosperity & Profits Unlimited, PO Box 416, Denver CO 80201-0416. **Tel** (303)575-5676. **ED** A. C. Doyle. **Circ:** under 2,400. available on audiocassette.
Desc: Ideas on gift baskets and gift basket business.

LC HD9999.G49 G54 **ISSN** 0016-9889
DD 381/.4567/05 US
CCC
GIFTS & DECORATIVE ACCESSORIES. See Gifts, Toys.

LC TT157 .W62 **ISSN** 0092-3850
DD 745.5/05 US
GIFTS YOU CAN MAKE FOR CHRISTMAS. (WOMAN'S DAY GIFTS YOU CAN MAKE FOR CHRISTMAS.). **VFOAT** Gifts You Can Make for Christmas. (19??)-. English. Irregular. $0.95. Sunset Publishing Corporation, 80 Willow Road, Menlo Park CA 94025. **Tel** (415)321-3600, (800)777-0117.

LC NK **ISSN** 0162-2765
DD 745 US
GOODFELLOW REVIEW OF CRAFTS, THE. (19??)-. Periodical. English. Irregular. Goodfellow Catalog of Wonderful Things, PO Box 4520, Berkeley CA 94704. **Tel** (510)845-7645. available on microfilm and microfiche from University Microfilms International (UMI).
Ind/Abst Ceram. Abstr.

LC TT **ISSN** 1036-5915
DD 745.5 AT
GREETINGS AND GIFTS. See Gifts, Toys.

LC TT12 .G84 **ISSN** 0097-7012
DD 338.4/7/745502573 US
GUIDE TO THE CRAFT WORLD. VFOAT Artisan Crafts Guide to the Craft World. 1st- Ed.; 1974-. English. One time a year. $10.00. O & E Enterprises, Star Route 4 Gobbler's Mountain, Reed Spring MO 65737.

LC NK1127 .G87 **ISSN** 0885-3975
DD 745 US
GUILD (NEW YORK, N.Y.). (THE GUILD.). [Guild]. (1986)-. English. One time a year. $42.50. Kraus Sikes Inc, 228 State Street, Madison WI 53703. **Tel** (212)242-3730. Index available. **Bk Rev. Ad Acc. Circ:** 19,000 (ctrl).

ISSN 0897-5345
DD 790 US
H.A.N.D.S. ON GUIDE. (HANDS ON GUIDE.). [H. A .N .D. S. guide]. **VFOAT** HANDS on Guide. **VAT** Hobbies, Arts, Needlework, Designing, Shows On Guide. Vol. 1, No. 2 (Mar. 1988)-. Trade Publication. English. Eleven times a year (monthly with Dec./Jan. combined). $28.00. Hands on Guide, 255 Cranston Crest, Escondido CA 92025. **Tel** (619)747-8206, FAX (619)747-8206. **ED** Christel Luther. **Ad Acc. Circ:** 2,000.
Desc: Art and craft shows, fairs, festivals, boutiques, bazaars and many other events for California and ten other western states. Detailed information for vendors and shoppers, as well as listings for guilds, clubs and associations.

ISSN 1057-8382
DD 745 US
HALLMARK GALLERIES MAGAZINE. [Hallmark Galleries Mag.]. **VFOAT** Galleries Magazine; Hallmark Galleries. Vol. 1, No. 1 (1992)-. Periodical. English. Two times a year. Hallmark Galleries, PO Box 750009, Petaluma CA 94975.

ISSN 0703-7864
DD 745.5/09713 CN
HAND-MADE. No. 1 (Spring 1977)-. Periodical. English. Four times a year. $3.00. Standing Oak, PO Box 78, Pakenham Ontario K0A 2X0.

LC NK
DD 745 AT
HANDCRAFT & HOME. (19??)-. Periodical. English. Six times a year. 27.00Aus$ Australia; 39.00Aus$ New Zealand and Papua New Guinea; 45.00Aus$ US, Canada, Europe, Africa; 42.00Aus$ Singapore, Malaysia, Indonesia, Hong Kong, China, Japan, India. Federal Publishing Co Pty Ltd., PO Box 199, 180 Bourke Road, Alexandria New South Wales 2015 Australia. **Tel** 011 61 2 3539992, FAX 011 61 2 66923059935. **(Subscription address:** Federal Publishing Co. Pty Ltd., PO Box 199, Alexandria NSW 2015 Australia. **Tel** 011 61 2 3530666.)

ISSN 1072-0529
DD 745 US
•**HANDCRAFT ILLUSTRATED.** [Handcr. illus.]. (1993)-. Periodical. English. Six times a year. $24.95. Natural Health Limited Partners, PO Box 569, Brookline Village MA 02147. **Tel** (617)232-1000, FAX (617)232-1572. **(Subscription address:** Neodata / Colorado, PO Box 2606, Boulder CO 80322. **)** Index available. cum. index. **Circ:** 60,000.

LC TT
DD 745.5 AT
HANDMADE. (19??)-. Periodical. English. Six times a year. 29.35Aus$. Australian Consolidated Press Ltd., Private Bag 92615 Symonds St, Auckland New Zealand. **Tel** 011 64 9 3735408, FAX 011 64 9 3022889.

LC NK955 .H44
GR
HELLENIKE LAIKE TECHNE. Added/Corp Ethnikos Organismos Hellenikes Cheirotechnias. **VFOAT** Hellenic Popular Art. Vol. 1 (1970)-. Periodical. Greek, Modern. Four times a year. $3.00. Ethnikos Organismos Hellenikes Cheirotechnias, 9 Mitropoleos Street, T T 118 Athens Greece.

LC TT1 .H58 **ISSN** 0278-7490
DD 745.5/05 US
HOLIDAY CRAFTS. (19??)-. Periodical. English. One time a year. $3.50. Meredith Publications / Special Interest Section, 1716 Locust Street, Des Moines IA 50309. **Tel** (515)284-3000.

DD 745.594/12 US
HOLIDAY CRAFTS & GRANNY SQUARES. VFOAT Holiday Crafts and Granny Squares. (Sept. 1990)-. English. $2.95 (per issue). Diamandis Communications, Inc., 1633 Broadway, New York NY 10019.

LC TT12 .I45 **ISSN** 0095-5337
DD 745.5/025/773 US
ILLINOIS HANDCRAFTS DIRECTORY. (1973)-. Directory. English. One time a year. Illinois Handcraft Directory, PO Box 157, Bondville IL 61815.

ISSN 1180-9558
DD 745.6/197/05 CN
ILLUMINATIONS (VANCOUVER). (ILLUMINATIONS : JOURNAL OF THE WESTCOAST CALLIGRAPHY SOCIETY.). [Illuminations]. **Added/Corp** Westcoast Calligraphy Society. **VFOAT** Journal of the Westcoast Calligraphy Society. Issue #54 (Nov. 1989)-. Periodical. English. Westcoast Calligraphy Society, PO Box 48390 Bentall Center, Vancouver British Columbia V7X 1A2 Canada. **Tel** (604)669-3198. ***Continues*** *Newsletter (Westcoast Calligraphy Society)., 0834-3993.*

LC NC975.A1 I5 **ISSN** 0073-5477
DD 741.64058 US
TITLE CHANGE
ILLUSTRATORS. Added/Corp Society of Illustrators (New York, N.Y.). (1959)-(19??). English. Watson Guptill Publications, PO Box 2014, Lakewood NJ 08701. **Tel** (800)451-1741, (908)363-5679, FAX (908)363-0338. ***Continued by*** *Society of Illustrators.*

LC Z271.3.M37 I54 **ISSN** 0894-0479
DD 686.3/6 US
INK & GALL. [Ink gall]. **VFOAT** Ink and Gall. Vol. 1, No. 1 (June 1987)-. Trade Publication. English. Two times a year. $35.00. Ink & Gall, PO Box 1469, Taos NM 87571. **Tel** (505)586-1607. **ED** Polly Fox. **Bk Rev. Ad Acc. Circ:** 1,000.
Desc: Devoted to the art of marbling. Offers opportunity for marblers, collectors, and learning centers the world over to communicate with each other. Promotes copyright protection for artists' original works and education for beginning marblers. The journal is also a lobby for appreciation of marbling as fine art as well as a long-respected craft.
Ind/Abst Abstr. Bull. Inst. Pap. Sci. Tech.

ISSN 0898-1094
DD 700 US
INTERNATIONAL DIRECTORY OF RESOURCES FOR ARTISANS, THE. [Int. dir. resour. artis.]. (1988/89)-. Directory. English. Every 2 years. $59.95 North America; $75.00 other. The Crafts Center, 1001 Connecticut Avenue NW/Suite 925, Washington DC 20036. **Tel** (202)728-9603. **ED** Caroline C Ramsay and Sheila A Mooney. Index available. **Bk Rev. Ad Acc. Circ:** 7,000. available on diskette.
Desc: Provides a listing of 7,000 national and international organizations which provide training and technical assistance in organization, management, production, and marketing, as well as credit, materials, and equipment for artisans and crafts groups.

LC NK
DD 745 RU
ISKUSSTVO UDMURTII : SBORNIK STATEI. Added/Corp Udmurtskii Nauchno-Issledovatelskii Institut Istorii, Ekonomiki, Literatury Iazyka. (1975)-. Periodical. Russian. Udmurdskii Institut Istorii, Ekonomiki, Literatury, Sovetskaya 14, 426020 Izhevsk, Udmurt A.R. Russia.

LC 745.61 **ISSN** 0021-3039
DD Z43 US
ITALIMUSE ITALIC NEWS. VFOAT Italic News. No. 1- Fall 1969-. Periodical. English. Irregular. Italimuse Inc, Route 3 Box 90, Colfax WI 54730. **Tel** (715)962-3085. **ED** Fred Eager. available on microfilm from University Microfilms International (UMI).
Desc: The art of producing elegant handwriting-calligraph; aimed at kindergarten through junior high.

LC 745.61
DD Z43 US
JOURNAL FOR THE CALLIGRAPHIC ARTS. Added/Corp Center for the Calligraphic Arts (Wichita, Kan.). (19??)-. Periodical. English. Six times a year. $22.00. Center for the Calligraphic Arts, PO Box 8005, Wichita KS 67208. **Tel** (316)683-1076. **ED** M. Jane Van Milligen. **Bk Rev. Ad Acc, Adv Mgr:** James Michae. **Circ:** 2,200 (ctrl).
Desc: Research articles on calligraphy or the related arts.

LC NK1 .J68 **ISSN** 0888-7314
DD 700/.5 US
JOURNAL OF DECORATIVE AND PROPAGANDA ARTS, THE. [J. decor. propag. arts]. **Added/Corp** Wolfson Foundation of Decorative and Propaganda Arts. **VFOAT** DAPA. Vol. 1 (Spring 1986)-. Periodical. English. One time a year. $25.00 (institutions), $19.00 (individuals). Wolfson Foundation, 2399 Northeast, Second Avenue, Miami FL 33137. **Tel** (305)573-9170.
Desc: A forum for scholars to explore decorative and propaganda arts.
Ind/Abst Am. Bibliogr. Slavic East Europ. Stud.; ARTbibliogr. Mod.; Avery Index Archit. Period. Suppl. Colum. Univ. (1990); BHA : Biblio. Hist. Art.

LC N6520 .J67 **ISSN** 0098-9266
DD 709/.75 US
JOURNAL OF EARLY SOUTHERN DECORATIVE ARTS. [J. early south. decor. arts]. **Added/Corp** Museum of Early Southern Decorative Arts. Vol. 1 (May 1975)-. Periodical. English. Two times a year (May, Nov.). $65.10. Museum of Early Southern Decorative Arts, PO Box 10310, Winston Salem NC 27108-0310. **Tel** (910)721-7360, FAX (910)721-7367. **ED** Cornelia Wright (phone:(910)721-7365). Index available. cum. index. **Bk Rev**, (Qty: occasional). **Circ:** 1,200 (ctrl).
Desc: Informs members of new discoveries and recent scholarships on such subjects as furniture, silver, ceramics, needlework, paintings, the craftsmen themselves and the conditions under which they worked.
Ind/Abst Am. Hist. Life (1988-); BHA : Biblio. Hist. Art.

LC NK **ISSN** 0260-9568
DD 745 UK
JOURNAL OF THE DECORATIVE ARTS SOCIETY 1890-1940. (THE JOURNAL OF THE DECORATIVE ARTS SOCIETY.). [J. Decor. Arts Soc. 1890-1940]. **Added/Corp** Decorative Arts Society 1890-1940. (1978)-. Bulletin. English. One time a year. comes with membership. Decorative Arts Society / UK, 47 Coombe Crescent Bury Pulborough, West Sussex RH20 1PE United Kingdom. **Tel** 011 44 0798 831734. cum. index. **Ad Acc. Circ:** 600 (ctrl). ***Continues*** *Bulletin of the Decorative Arts Society 1890-1940.*
Ind/Abst Archit. Period. Index (1981-); ARTbibliogr. Mod. (1985-); BHA : Biblio. Hist. Art.

LC Z43.A1 S64a **ISSN** 0037-9743
DD 652/.1 UK
JOURNAL OF THE SOCIETY FOR ITALIC HANDWRITING, THE. Main/Corp Society for Italic Handwriting. No. 32 (Autumn 1962)-. Periodical. English. Four times a year. £12.00. Society for Italic Handwriting, Timbertrack, 53 Sea Avenue, Rustington, West Sussex BN16 2DN United Kingdom. **ED** B Wolpe and F P Greenwood. **Bk Rev. Ad Acc. Circ:** 1,250 (ctrl). ***Continues*** *Bulletin of the Society for Italic Handwriting.*
Desc: Practice, teaching, history and theory of italic handwriting.

LC AS122 .W653 **ISSN** 0084-0254
UK
JOURNAL OF THE WILLIAM MORRIS SOCIETY, THE. [J. William Morris Soc.]. **Added/Corp** William Morris Society. **VFOAT** Journal. Vol. 1, No. 1 (Winter 1961)-. Periodical. English. Two times a year. £25.00 (institutions); £20.00 (individuals) Comes with William Morris Society membership. William Morris Society, Kelmscott House, 26 Upper Mall, Hammersmith, London W6 9TA United Kingdom. **Tel** 011 44 181 7413735. **ED** Peter Faulkner. Index available. cum.

The Arts —Crafts and Decorative Arts

index. **Bk Rev**. **Ad Acc**. **Circ:** 2,500 (ctrl).
Ind/Abst Abstr. Engl. Stud.; Annu. Bibliogr. Engl. Lang. Lit.; MLA Int. Bibl. Books Artic. Mod. Lang. Lit.

LC NK1160 .K55

KO

KKUMIM. **VFOAT** Ggumim. Vol. 1 (Jan./Feb. 1977)-. Periodical. Korean (summaries and/or abstracts in English). W6.500.

LC NX
DD 700

AU

K+R KERAMISCHE RUNDSCHAU KLIMA + RAUM. (19??)-. German. Twelve times a year. S990.00. Verlag Lorenz, Ebendorferstrasse 10, A-1010 Vienna Austria. **Tel** 011 43 222 426695, **FAX** 011 43 222 438693.

LC NK925 .K8

GW

KUNSTHANDWERK & DESIGN. **VFOAT** Kunsthandwerk und Design. (Jan./Feb. 1992)-. Periodical. German. Six times a year. $88.28. Verlagsgesellschaft Ritterbach, Postfach 1820, D-50208 Frechen Germany. **Tel** 011 49 2234 18660. **Continues** Kunst + Handwerk, 0454-6539.

LC TT
DD 745.5

ISSN 0731-9959
US

LADY'S CIRCLE 1,001 CHRISTMAS IDEAS. **VFOAT** Lady's Circle One Thousand and One Christmas Ideas. (1981)-. English. One time a year. $1.95. Lopez Publications Inc., 152 Madison Avenue, Suite 905 & 906, New York NY 10016. **Tel** (212)689-3933. Each issue contains an index to its own contents (no volume index)--loose.

LC NK
DD 745

ISSN 0731-9983
US

LADY'S CIRCLE HOME MAKING CRAFT IDEAS. **VFOAT** Craft Ideas. (19??)-. Periodical. English. One time a year. $1.95. Lopez Publications Inc., 152 Madison Avenue, Suite 905 & 906, New York NY 10016. **Tel** (212)689-3933.

LC TT
DD 745.5

ISSN 0738-2936

LAPEL PIN POTPOURRI. See Home Economics-Sewing and Needlework.

DD 745

ISSN 1082-4480
US

●**LEATHER CRAFTERS & SADDLERS JOURNAL.** **VFOAT** Leather Crafters and Saddlers Journal. Vol. 5, No. 2 (Mar./Apr. 1995)-. Periodical. English. Six times a year. $24.00. W R Reis, 331 Annette Court, Rhinelander WI 54501. **Tel** (715)362-5393. **Continues** Leather Crafters Journal, 1056-4225.

DD 745

ISSN 1056-4225
US
TITLE CHANGE

LEATHER CRAFTERS JOURNAL, THE. [Leather crafters j.]. Vol. 1, No. 1 (Jan./Feb. 1991)-(1995). Periodical. English. W R Reis, 331 Annette Court, Rhinelander WI 54501. **Tel** (715)362-5393. **Continued by** Leather Crafters & Saddlers Journal, 1082-4480.

DD 746

ISSN 0890-6386
US

LEISURE ARTS. [Leis. arts]. Vol. 1, No. 1 (Nov./Dec. 1986)-. Periodical. English. Six times a year. $16.00. Leisure Arts, PO Box 5595, Little Rock AR 72215. **Tel** (501)868-8800 ext. 338. **(Subscription address:** Palm Coast Data, PO Box 420163, Agency Department, Palm Coast FL 32142. **Tel** (904)445-4662 ext. 669, (800)829-5475.**)**

LC NK
DD 746

UK

LEISURE PAINTER AND CRAFTSMAN. (1967)-. English. Twelve times a year. £21.50 UK; $49.00 US; 59.00Can$ Canada; 34.00p Southern Ireland; £25.00 other. Artist Publishing Company Ltd., Caxton House, 63-65 High Street, Tenterden Kent TN30 6BD United Kingdom. **Tel** 011 44 15806 3315, **FAX** 011 44 15806 5411. **ED** Irene Briers. Index available. **Bk Rev**. **Ad Acc**, **Adv Mgr:** P. Hunter. **Circ:** 23,000.

LC Z43.A1 C35
DD 745.6/1/05

ISSN 1076-7339
US

●**LETTER ARTS REVIEW.** [Lett. arts rev.]. (1994)-. Periodical. English. Four times a year. $42.00. Calligraphy Review Inc, 1624 24th Avenue Southwest, Norman OK 73072. **Tel** (405)364-8794, **FAX** (405)364-8914. **Continues** Calligraphy Review (Norman, Okla.), 0895-7819.

LC NK
DD 745

US

LUMINARY : THE NEWSLETTER OF THE MUSEUM OF EARLY SOUTHERN DECORATIVE ARTS, THE. **Added/Corp** Museum of Early Southern Decorative Arts. Vol. 1, No. 1 (Winter 1980)-. Newsletter. English. Two times a year. Comes with membership. Museum of Early Southern Decorative Arts, PO Box 10310, Winston Salem NC 27108-0310. **Tel** (910)721-7360, **FAX** (910)721-7367.

ISSN 1049-3700
US

MACHINE KNITTERS SOURCE, THE. [Mach. knitt. source]. Vol. 6, Issue 35 (March/April 1990)-. Periodical. English. Six times a year. $23.95. Machine Knitters Source, PO Box 1527, 17627 Vashon Highway Southwest, Vashon WA 98070-1527. **Tel** (206)463-6100. **Continues** WKMG, 1049-166X.
Ind/Abst Index Inf.

LC TX631
DD 641

ISSN 0889-4884
US

MAILBOX NEWS. See Home Economics.

LC MT
DD 780/.7/9713541

ISSN 0712-6263
CN

MARIPOSA FOLK FESTIVAL. See Music.

LC NK8800
DD 746

ISSN 1072-8295
US

●**MCCALL'S QUILTING. See** Home Economics-Sewing and Needlework.

LC NK6400 .M43
DD 739/.05

ISSN 0270-1146
US

METALSMITH. [Metalsmith]. **Added/Corp** Society of North American Goldsmiths. (Fall 1980)-. Trade Publication. English. Four times a year. $26.00. Society of North American Goldsmiths, 5009 Londonderry Drive, Tampa FL 33647. **Tel** (813)977-5326, **FAX** (813)977-8462. **ED** Frank Lewis, 2755 North Murray Avenue, Milwaukee, WI 53211; Telephone: (414)332-6375; Fax: (414)332-6837. Index available (every 2 years). **Bk Rev**, (Qty: 4). **Ad Acc**. **Circ:** 4,400 (ctrl). **Continues** Goldsmiths Journal, 0197-0127.
Desc: Concerned with fostering, encouraging and teaching the art of metalsmithing and jewelry.
Ind/Abst Art Index.

DD 745

ISSN 1073-7618
US

MICHAELS ARTS & CRAFTS. [Michaels arts & crafts]. **VFOAT** Arts and Crafts; Michaels Arts and Crafts; Michaels Arts and Crafts Magazine; Michaels Arts & Crafts Magazine. (19??)-. Periodical. English. Six times a year. $15.95. Summit Group, 1227 West Magnolia, Garden Level, Fort Worth TX 76104. **Tel** (800)856-8060, (817)921-9300.

LC TT178 .M56
DD 745.592/8

ISSN 0732-3697
US

MINIATURE PATTERNS & PRODUCTS MAGAZINE. **VFOAT** Miniature Patterns and Products Magazine. Vol. 1 (1983)-. Periodical. English. Six times a year. Jean Dickey Publications, PO Box 406, Westmont IL 60559.

LC TT
DD 688

ISSN 0896-7288
US
CEASED

MINIATURES SHOWCASE. See Hobbies.

LC NK1073.6.A1 M58

ISSN 0540-4568
KO

MISUL CHARYO. **Added/Corp** Kungnip Pangmulgwan (Korea) Kungnip Chungang Pangmulgwan (Korea). **VFOAT** National Museum of Korea Art Magazine. Vol. 1 (1960)-. Periodical. Korean (table of contents in English). Two times a year. National Museum of Korea Department of Fine Arts, 1 Sejong-no, Chongno-gu, Seoul 110 050 South Korea.
Ind/Abst Energy Res. Abstr. (Sept. 1980-).

KO

MISUL KONGYE = ART & CRAFTS. **VFOAT** Art and Crafts; Ato wa Kuraeputu; Art & Crafts; Wolgan atu & Kuraeputu; Atu & Kuraeputu. (March 1992)-. Periodical. Korean. Twelve times a year. Dijain Hausu, 186-210 2-Ka Changchung-Dong, Chung-Ku, Seoul 100-392 Korea. **Continues** Wolgan Dijain + Kongye.

LC NK976.U5 N3
DD 745/.0947/71

ISSN 0130-6936
UN

NARODNA TVORCHIST TA ETNOGRAFIIA. [Nar. tvorc. etnogr.]. **Added/Corp** Ukraine. Ministerstvo Kultury. Instytut Mystetstvoznavstva, Folkloru ta Etnohrafii (Akademiia Nauk Ukrainskoi RSR) Instytut Mystetstvoznavstva, Folkloru ta Etnohrafii im. M.T. Rylskoho. (1957)-. Periodical. Ukrainian. Six times a year. $79.95. Nardona Tvorchist ta Etnografii, Kirova 4, 252001 MCP Kiev-1 Ukraine. **Tel** 011 7 44 2285873. **(Subscription address:** East View Publications Inc., 3020 Harbor Lane North, Suite 110, Minneapolis MN 55447. **Tel** (612)550-0961, **FAX** (612)559-2931.**)** **ED** Kostiuk Oleksandr Hzyhozovych. Index available. **Bk Rev**. **Circ:** 6,000.
Ind/Abst Anthropol. Index; BHA : Biblio. Hist. Art; MLA Int. Bibl. Books Artic. Mod. Lang. Lit.

LC TT740
DD 746.4
Pr Rev.

US

NEEDLE ARTS. See Home Economics-Sewing and Needlework.

LC NK
DD 745

UK

NEWSLETTER / DECORATIVE ARTS SOCIETY 1890-1940. **Main/Corp** Decorative Arts Society 1890-1940. (19??)-. Newsletter. English. Decorative Arts Society / UK, 47 Coombe Crescent Bury Pulborough, West Sussex RH20 1PE United Kingdom. **Tel** 011 44 0798 831734.

DD 706/.2/7123

ISSN 0704-0296
CN

NEWSLETTER - VISUAL ARTS & CRAFTS COMMUNICATION COUNCIL OF ALBERTA. **Main/Corp** Visual Arts and Crafts Communication Council of Alberta. (March 1977)-. Newsletter. English. Free. Visual Arts and Crafts Communication Council of Alberta, University of Alberta, Department of Art and Design, Edmonton Alberta T6G 2C9 Canada. ctrl circ.

DD 745/.06/271351

ISSN 0703-6825
CN

NIAGARA GUILD OF CRAFTS. Mar. 1968-. Periodical. English. Irregular. Niagara Guild of Crafts, R.R. #3 Lakeshore Road, Niagara-on-the-Lake, Ontario L0S 1S0 Canada.

LC NK
DD 745
Pr Rev.

US

NOTES ON AMERICA'S FOLK ART ENVIRONMENTS. (19??)-. English. $25.00 US; $29.00 other. Saving and Preserving Arts and Cultural Environments, 1804 North Van Ness, Los Angeles CA 90028. **Tel** (310)463-1629. Index available. cum. index. **Bk Rev**. **Circ:** 750 (ctrl).
Desc: Notes and information on America's contemporary folk art environments. Includes news, reviews, and preservation information.

DD 745.5/09716

ISSN 1193-011X
CN

NOVA SCOTIA CRAFT NEWS. [N.S. craft news]. **Added/Corp** Nova Scotia Designer Crafts Council. **VFOAT** NSDCC Newsletter. (Spring 1992)-. Periodical. English. Four times a year. Nova Scotia Designer Crafts Council, PO Box 3355, South Halifax Nova Scotia B3J 3J1 Canada. **Continues** Newsletter (Nova Scotia Designer Crafts Council)., 0834-3829.

LC TT178 .N88
DD 745.592/8/05

ISSN 0164-3290
US

NUTSHELL NEWS. [Nutshell news]. (19??)-. Periodical. English. Twelve times a year (monthly). $34.95. Kalmbach Publishing Company, 21027 Crossroads Circle, PO Box 1612, Waukesha WI 53187. **Tel** (414)796-8776 ext. 411, **FAX** (414)796-0126. **ED** Sybil Harp. **Bk Rev**. **Ad Acc**. **Circ:** 34,622.
Desc: News and innovations in the world of miniatures. Shares aspects of the hobby from constructing miniatures to becoming a more knowledgeable collector.

LC NK
DD 745
UDC 745:502

ISSN 0929-5844
NE

●**O2 MAGAZINE.** [O2 mag.]. (1993)-. Periodical. Dutch. Three times a year. $41.11. Vereninging 02 Nederland, Postbus 519, 3000 AM Rotterdam Netherlands. **Tel** 011 010 265099.

LC NK
DD 745

ISSN 8756-047X
US

OCCASIONAL PAPERS ON ANTIQUITIES. See Antiques.

LC NK
DD 745

US

OLD FASHIONED PATCHWORK. (19??)-. English. Four times a year. $8.97. Harris Publications, 1115 Broadway, 8th Floor, New York NY 10010. **Tel** (212)807-7100.

LC WMLC L 83/2620
DD 746

ISSN 1050-9518
US

OLD-TIME CROCHET. **Added/Corp** House of White Birches. **VFOAT** Old Time Crochet. Vol. 11, No. 3 (Fall 1989)-. English. Four times a year. $11.97. House of White Birches, 306 East Parr Road, Berne IN 46711. **Tel** (219)589-8741, **FAX** (219)589-8093. **(Subscription address:** Palm Coast Data, PO Box 420163, Agency Department, Palm Coast FL 32142. **Tel** (904)445-4662 ext. 669, (800)829-5475.**)** **ED** Marion Kelly & Anne Morgan Jackson. **Circ:** 73,500. **Continues** Old-Time Crochet Patterns & Designs, 0195-2013.
Desc: Includes authentic, collectible crochet patterns from the late 1800s to 1950, including vintage doilies, edgings, tablecloths and apparel accents.

ISSN 0229-1320
DD 745.5/09713 CN
Pr Rev.
ONTARIO CRAFT. [Ont. craft]. **Added/Corp** Ontario Crafts Council. Vol. 6, No. 1 (Spring 1981)-. Trade Publication. English. Four times a year (Mar., June, Sept., Dec.). 23.00Can$. Ontario Crafts Council, 35 McCaul Street, Chalmers Building, Toronto Ontario M5T 1V7 Canada. **Tel** (416)977-3551, FAX (416)977-3551. **ED** Anne McPherson. **Photos**. **Ad Acc**, **Adv Mgr:** Susan Browne, **Tel** (416)886-6640. **Circ:** 4,000. available on microfiche. ***Continues*** *Craftsman., 0319-7840.*
Desc: Provides coverage of the contemporary craft movement. It is of particular interest to craftsmen, artists, teachers and students.
Ind/Abst Can. Index; Can. Period. Index.

ISSN 1181-9790
DD 745.5/09714/05 CN
OPTIMA (MONTREAL). (OPTIMA : REVUE TRIMESTRIELLE DU CONSEIL DES METIERS D'ART DU QUEBEC.). [Optima]. **Added/Corp** Conseil des Metiers d'Art. **VFOAT** OptiMA. Vol. 1, No 1 (Dec. 1990)-. Periodical. French. Four times a year. Free for members. Conseil des Metiers d'Art, Bureau 219, Est rue Jean-Talon, Montreal Quebec H2R 1V5 Canada.

LC T129 .O83
DD 745.2/071045 IT
OSSERVATORIO ISFOL. **VFOAT** Osservatorio. **VAT** Osservatorio Istituto per lo Sviluppo della Formazione Professionaledei Lavoratori. Periodical. Italian. Six times a year. ISFOL, Via Bartolomeo Eustachio 8, 00161 Rome Italy. ***Continues*** *Osservatorio sul Mercato del Lavoro e delle Professioni, 0391-3775.*

LC WMLC 93/1600 ISSN 1079-6819
DD 745 US
●**PAINTING (DES PLAINES, ILL.).** (PAINTING.). [Painting]. Vol. 10, No. 1 (Feb. 1995)-. Periodical. English. Six times a year. $19.95. Clapper Communications, 2400 Devon, Suite 375, Des Plaines IL 60018. **Tel** (800)272-3871, (708)635-5800. ***Continues*** *Decorative Arts Painting, 1067-0068.*

LC TT ISSN 0268-5620
DD 746.46 UK
PATCHWORK & QUILTING. **See** Home Economics-Sewing and Needlework.

ISSN 1034-0580
DD 705 AT
Pr Rev.
PERIPHERY LISMORE. (PERIPHERY.). [Peripher.Lismore]. (1989)-. Periodical. English. Four times a year (Feb., May, Aug., Nov.). 12.33Aus$. Periphery Inc., 10 Kallaroo Road, Riverview NSW 2066 Australia. **Tel** 011 61 66 882163. **ED** Geoff Levitus (editor's address: 18 Dunois Street Longvevills NSW 2066 Australia, editor's phone number: 011 61 2 4271229). **Bk Rev**, (Qty: 1 or 2). **Ad Acc. Circ:** 3,000 (ctrl).
Desc: Regional art and crafts journal with a regular focus on indigenous art and craft, reviews, profiles, discussion of regionalism on a wide scale.

LC NK ISSN 1052-9977
DD 749 US
PICTURE FRAMING MAGAZINE. **See** Hobbies.

LC TT740 .P54 ISSN 1067-2249
DD 746.4/05 US
●**PIECEWORK (LOVELAND, COLO.).** (PIECEWORK.). [Piecework]. **VFOAT** Piece Work. Vol. 1, No. 1 (Mar./Apr. 1993)-. Periodical. English. Six times a year. $24.00. Interweave Press, 201 East 4th Street, Loveland CO 80537. **Tel** (303)669-7672, FAX (303)667-8317.
Desc: Promotes historic and ethnic handwork by offering articles and projects in knitting, quilting and other crafts.

ISSN 1080-384X
DD 746 US
●**PLASTIC CANVAS CRAFTS.** [Plast. canvas crafts]. (Aug. 1994)-. Periodical. English. Six times a year. $14.97. House of White Birches, 306 East Parr Road, Berne IN 46711. **Tel** (219)589-8741, FAX (219)589-8093. ***Continues*** *Plastic Canvas and More.*

ISSN 1045-1854
DD 746 US
PLASTIC CANVAS! MAGAZINE. **VFOAT** Plastic Canvas. No. 1 (Mar./Apr. 1989)-. Periodical. English. Six times a year. $12.95. Needlecraft Shop, 23 Old Pecan Road, Big Sandy TX 75755. **Tel** (903)636-4011 ext 211, FAX (903)636-2288.

ISSN 1072-6373
DD 745 US
PLASTIC CANVAS WORLD. [Plast. canvas world]. (1991)-. Periodical. English. Six times a year. $14.97. House of White Birches, 306 East Parr Road, Berne IN 46711. **Tel** (219)589-8741, FAX (219)589-8093. **(Subscription address:** Palm Coast Data, PO Box 420163, Agency Department, Palm Coast FL 32142. **Tel** (904)445-4662 ext. 669, (800)829-5475.) **ED** Marjorie Pearl. **Circ:** 69,649.
Desc: Provides plastic canvas projects from top designers for home, holidays, family and friends with full-color photos and easy-to-follow patterns.

LC NK ISSN 1045-3806
DD 745 US
PLASTICS CANVAS CORNER. [Plast. canvas corner]. **VFOAT** Plastic Canvas. 1989-. Periodical. English. Six times a year. $19.97. Leisure Arts, PO Box 5595, Little Rock AR 72215. **Tel** (501)868-8800 ext. 338.

LC NK ISSN 0144-2937
DD 745 UK
POPULAR CRAFTS. (19??)-. Periodical. English. Twelve times a year. $49.00. Argus Specialist Publications, Argus House, Boundary Way / Hemel, Hempstead Herts HP27ST United Kingdom. **Tel** 011 44 181 6671033, FAX 011 44 181 6889573, telex 948669 TOPJNL G.
Desc: Aimed at craft and hobby enthusiasts - a practical magazine including projects and color features, patterns, and diagrams along with end-result photographs.

LC NK
DD 745 UK
POPULAR CRAFTS PROJECTS. Periodical. English. Four times a year. Argus Specialist Publications, Argus House, Boundary Way / Hemel, Hempstead Herts HP27ST United Kingdom. **Tel** 011 44 181 6671033, FAX 011 44 181 6889573, telex 948669 TOPJNL G.
Desc: Each issue concentrates on a single topic, and includes correlating projects.

ISSN 0969-6946
DD 746.46 UK
●**POPULAR PATCHWORK.** [Pop. patchw.]. (1993)-. Periodical. English. Six times a year. Argus Specialist Publications, Argus House, Boundary Way / Hemel, Hempstead Herts HP27ST United Kingdom. **Tel** 011 44 181 6671033, FAX 011 44 181 6889573, telex 948669 TOPJNL G.
Desc: Offers information on tools and equipment along with patterns and projects for patchworkers and quilters.

ISSN 0703-7171
DD 745/.09713/5 CN
PRE-CONFEDERATION TIMES. Vol. 1 (Jan./June 1977)-. Periodical. English. Two times a year. Free. Pre-Confederation Furniture, 1700 Dundas Street East, London Ontario N5W 3C9 Canada.

LC TT ISSN 0032-7697
DD 745.5 GW
UDC 339.37 :688.78/.9
PRESENT BAMBERG. (1961)-. Trade Publication. Multiple languages. Twelve times a year. $79.63. Meisenbach GmbH, Postfach 2069, D-96011 Bamberg Germany. **Tel** 011 49 951 861135, FAX 011 49 951 861161. **ED** Christing Dicker. **Ad Acc.** Full Page (B&W) DM3415.00. Full Page (Color) DM5596.00.

LC HD2346.U5 P76 ISSN 0147-5304
DD 658.89/7455/0973 US
PROFITABLE CRAFT MERCHANDISING. [Profitab. craft merch.]. **VFOAT** PCM. (19??)-. Periodical. English. Twelve times a year. $30.00. PJS Publications Inc., News Plaza, PO Box 1790, Peoria IL 61656. **Tel** (309)682-6626, FAX (309)682-7394. **(Subscription address:** PCM, PO Box 1790, Peoria IL 61656. **)**

LC NK8647 .P76 ISSN 0147-5274
DD 745.1 US
PROSIT. Periodical. English. Four times a year. Stein Collectors International, PO Box 16326, St. Paul MN.

LC Discard ISSN 0277-349X
US
QUALITY CRAFTS MARKET, THE. **Added/Corp** National Information Center for Crafts Management and Marketing (U.S.). Vol. 4, No. 5 (May 1978)-. Periodical. English. Four times a year. $24.00. Quality Crafts Market, 521 Fifth Avenue, Suite 1700, New York NY 10017. ***Continues*** *Craft Market News.*

ISSN 1048-5341
DD 746 US
QUICK & EASY PLASTIC CANVAS. [Quick easy plast. canvas]. **VFOAT** Quick and Easy Plastic Canvas. No. 1 (Aug./Sept. 1989)-. Periodical. English. Six times a year. $12.95. Needlecraft Shop, 23 Old Pecan Road, Big Sandy TX 75755. **Tel** (903)636-4011 ext 211, FAX (903)636-2288. **ED** Carolyn Christmas. **Circ:** 160,000 (ctrl).
Desc: A variety of smaller/easier plastic canvas projects.

ISSN 1059-0684
DD 746 US
QUILT (NEW YORK, N.Y.). (QUILT.). [Quilt]. (1978)-. Periodical. English. Four times a year. $12.97. Harris Publications, 1115 Broadway, 8th Floor, New York NY 10010. **Tel** (212)807-7100.

LC WMLC 93/99 ISSN 1043-8009
DD 623.8201 US
RADIO CONTROL BOAT MODELER. [Radio control boat model.]. **VFOAT** Boat Modeler; R/C Boat Modeler. Vol. 2, No. 3 (Summer 1988)-. Periodical. English. Seven times a year. $20.00. Air Age Publishing, 251 Danbury Road, Wilton CT 06897. **Tel** (203)834-2900, FAX (203)762-9803. **(Subscription address:** Radio Control Boat Modeler, PO Box 433, Mount Morris IL 61054. **Tel** (800)877-5160.) ***Continues*** *American Boat Modeler, 0890-0078.*
Desc: Dedicated to the radio control boat modeling enthusiast. Covers various facets of the hobby including offshore racers, ships, yachts, and sport boats. Feature articles and columns present technical and general information on building electric and gas R/C boats. Modifications, modeling equipment, R/C electronics, major competition events, modeling personalities, and products. "How to" articles and in-depth product evaluations, and many beginner articles are included.

LC TT154.5 .R32 ISSN 0090-9157
DD 338.4/7/6881 US
RADIO CONTROL PRODUCTS DIRECTORY. [Radio control prod. dir.]. **VFOAT** RC Products Directory. 1973-. Directory. English. One time a year. $2.25. Potomac Aviation Publications, 733-15th Street NW, Washington DC 20005.

LC NK480.G6 A3
SW
RAOHSSKA KONSTSLAOJDMUSEETS AARSBOK. **Added/Corp** Roahsska Konstslaojdmuseet (Goteborg, Sweden). **VFOAT** Aarsbok. (1964)-. Periodical. Swedish (summaries and/or abstracts in English). Every 3 years. ***Continues*** *Rohsska konstslojdmuseets Aarstryck.*
Ind/Abst BHA : Biblio. Hist. Art.

LC NK ISSN 0955-1182
DD 745 UK
RAW VISION. [Raw vis.]. **Added/Corp** Outsider Archive. No. 1, (Spring 1989)-. Periodical. English (French). Three times a year. $42.50. Raw Vision, 42 Llanvanor Road, London NW2 2AP United Kingdom. **Tel** 011 44 1923 856644, FAX 011 44 1923 859897. **ED** John Maizels. **Bk Rev**, (Qty: 12). **Ad Acc. Circ:** 5,000.

LC NK ISSN 0996-5912
DD 745 FR
UDC 747
REFERENCES DESIGN MALAKOFF. (REFERENCES DESIGN.). (1989)-. Periodical. French (summaries and/or abstracts in English). One time a year. 90.00F. Mad-Cap Publications, 10 rue Caron, 92240 Malakoff France. **Tel** FAX 011 33 1 46577432. Index available. **Ad Acc.** ***Continues*** *Les Carnets du Design.*

LC U311 .R46
DD 745.59/282/05 US
REPLICA WRAP-UP, THE. **Added/Corp** IPMS Space Park. (19??)-. Periodical. English. Six times a year. $3.00. International Plastic Modelers Society, Box 7704, Long Beach CA 90807. **Tel** (213)427-8001.

LC N8 .R6 ISSN 0035-8215
II
ROOPA-LEKHA. **Added/Corp** Fine Arts & Crafts Syndicate (Delhi, India) All-India Fine Arts & Crafts Society. No. 1 (Jan. 1929)-Vol. 4, Serial No. 13-Vol. 1, Serial No. 1 (July 1939)-. English. One time a year. All India Fine Arts and Crafts Society, Rafi Marg, New Delhi 1 India.

LC TT850 .R82 ISSN 1045-4373
DD 746.7/4/05 US
RUG HOOKING. [Rug hook.]. **VFOAT** R.U.G Hooking. Vol. 1, No. 1 (May/June 1989)-. Periodical. English. Five times a year (Jan., Mar., June, Sep., Nov.). $27.95. Stackpole Magazines, 500 Vaughn Street, Harrisburg PA 17110. **Tel** (717)234-5041, (800)732-3669, FAX (717)234-1359. **ED** MacDonald Kennedy (editor's address: 500 Vaughn Street, Harrisburg PA 17110). Index available. cum. index. **Bk Rev**, (Qty: 3). **Ad Acc**, **Adv Mgr:** Diana Marcum, **Tel** (717)238-6401. **Circ:** 10,500.
Desc: For craft enthusiasts who are rediscovering the folk art of traditional rug hooking.

LC NK
DD 745 US
●**SAC NEWS MONTHLY.** (199?)-. Newspaper. English. Twelve times a year. $24.00. SAC News Monthly, PO Box 159, Bogalusa LA 70429. **Tel** (800)825-3722, FAX (504)732-3744. **ED** Wayne Smith. **Bk Rev. Ad Acc**, **Adv Mgr Tel** (800)825-3722. **Circ:** 3,000 (ctrl). ***Absorbed*** *Art & Crafts Catalyst;* ***Continues*** *National Arts & Crafts Network.*
Desc: A newspaper that lists thousands of art and craft shows nationwide.

LC WMLC 91/724 ISSN 1061-6756
DD 746 US
CEASED
SAMPLER & ANTIQUE NEEDLEWORK QUARTERLY. [Sampl. antiq. needlework q.]. **VFOAT** Sampler and Antique Needlework Quarterly. Vol. 1 (1991)-Vol. 12 (Nov. 1993). Periodical. English. Symbol of Excellence Publishing, 405 Riverhills Business Park, Birmingham AL 35242. **Tel** (205)995-8860.

LC NK
US
SANTA CLAUS. VFOAT Better Homes and Gardens Santa Claus. (1991)-. Periodical. English. One time a year. $4.95. Meredith Publications / Special Interest Section, 1716 Locust Street, Des Moines IA 50309. **Tel** (515)284-3000.

ISSN 0748-8378
DD 363 US
SUSPENDED
SAVING AND PRESERVING ARTS AND CULTURAL ENVIRONMENTS. (SAVING AND PRESERVING ARTS AND CULTURAL ENVIRONMENTS : SPACES [MAGAZINE].). [Sav. Preserv. Arts Cult. Environ.]. **Added/Corp** Saving and Preserving Arts and Cultural Environments (Organization : U.S.). **VFOAT** SPACES; S.P.A.C.E.S. Vol. 1, No. 1 (1982)-Suspended (19??). Newsletter. English. Three times a year. Free to members of the Saving and Preserving Arts and Cultural Environments. Saving and Preserving Arts and Cultural Environments, 1804 North Van Ness, Los Angeles CA 90028. **Tel** (310)463-1629. **ED** Seymour Rosen. **Bk Rev. Ad Acc. Circ:** 1,500 (ctrl).
Desc: Documentation of folk art environments and publication of research, honoring those in the field.

LC NK
DD 745 US
SCENTERPIECE UPDATE. English. One time a year. $5.00 North America; $8.00 other. Prosperity & Profits Unlimited, PO Box 416, Denver CO 80201-0416. **Tel** (303)575-5676. **ED** A.C. Doyle. **Circ:** 1,500.
Desc: Recipes for scented centerpieces (potpourri).

LC NK8800 **ISSN** 1051-1032
DD 746 US
SCREEN PLAY (DALLAS, TEX.). See The Arts-Graphic Arts.

LC NK
DD 745 FR
SERIE ICONOGRAPHIQUE. (19??)-. Monographic series. French. Irregular. Institut Natl de la Jeunesse, Val Flory rue Paul Leplat, 78160 Marly Le Roi France. **Tel** 011 33 1 39584911.

ISSN 1062-9696
DD 745 US
SHOPNOTES (DES MOINES, IOWA). (SHOPNOTES.). [Shopnotes]. Issue 1 (Jan. 1992)-. Periodical. English. Six times a year. $19.95. Woodsmith Publishing, 2200 Grand Avenue, Des Moines IA 50312. **Tel** (515)282-7000, (800)333-5075, FAX (515)282-6741. **(Subscription address:** SIFD Agency Control, 1901 Bell Avenue, Des Moines IA 50312. **Tel** (515)246-6812.**)**

LC NK3634.A2 S568
DD 745.619951 CC
SHU FA. VFOAT Shufa. (1977)-. Periodical. Chinese. Six times a year. $30.12. **(Subscription address:** China International Book Trading Corporation, PO Box 399, Library Service Department, Beijing 100044 People's Republic of China. **Tel** 011 86 1 8414284, FAX 011 86 1 8412023, telex 22496 CIBTC CN.**) ED** Zhou Zhigao, Fang Chuanxin, Gao Shixiong, Wang Zhuanghong, and Pan Dexi. **Bk Rev. Circ:** 300,000.
Desc: Introduces outstanding ancient and contemporary Chinese rubbings, calligraphies, seal-engravings and achievements of theoretical research.

LC NK3634.A2 S572
DD 745.6/19951 CC
SHU FA TSUNG KAN / WEN WU PIEN CHI WEI YUAN HUI PIEN. Added/Corp Wen Wu Pien Chi Wei Yuan Hui. Vol. 1, (Feb. 1981)-. Periodical. Chinese. RMBY2.50. Hsin Hua Shu Tien, Beijing, People's Republic of China. **Tel** 011 89 1 551253.

LC NK3634.A2 S58
HK
CEASED
SHU PU. Vol. 1 (July 1974)-(19??). Periodical. Chinese. Shu Pu, 507 S Stoneman Avenue, Alhambra CA 91801. **Tel** (818)282-0387.

LC NK3634.A2 S585
DD 745.6/19951/05 CC
SHU YU HUA. (19??)-. Periodical. Chinese. Six times a year. RMBY0.43. Shanghai Calligraphy and Painting Publishers, 83 Kangping Road, Shanghai 200030, People's Republic of China. **Tel** 4334156.

LC TT848 .S53 **ISSN** 0049-0423
DD 746.1/05 US
SHUTTLE, SPINDLE & DYEPOT. [Shuttle spindle dye.]. **Added/Corp** Handweavers Guild of America. **VAT** Shuttle, Spindle and Dyepot. (Dec. 1969)-. Periodical. English. Four times a year. $30.00 (one-year), $58.00 (two-year) US; $35.00 (one-year), $68.00 (two-year) other. Handweavers Guild of America, 2402 University Avenue, Suite 702, St. Paul MN 55114. **Tel** (612)646-0802, FAX (612)646-0806. **ED** Sandra Bowles. **Bk Rev. Ad Acc. Adv Mgr:** Teri Goddard, **Tel** (404)495-7702. **Circ:** 15,000 (ctrl). available on microfilm and microfiche from University Microfilms International (UMI).
Desc: Features include how-to articles, interviews, historical aspects and new techniques in fiber arts and handweaving fields. Provides a calendar of events for fiber shows and exhibitions and includes stories on museum collections and well-known people in the fiber arts field. Comes with Handweavers Guild of America membership.
Ind/Abst AGRICOLA; Art Archaeol. Tech. Abstr.; Art Index; Index Inf.

LC NK7143.A1 S5
DD 739.2/3/742 UK
SILVER AUCTION RECORDS. (19??)-. English. One time a year. $75.00. Hilmarton Manor Press, Wiltshire SN11 8SB United Kingdom. **ED** H. Baile de Laperriere.

LC NK
DD 745 US
SOCIETY OF ILLUSTRATORS. (19??)-. English. One time a year. Price varies. Watson Guptill Publications, PO Box 2014, Lakewood NJ 08701. **Tel** (800)451-1741, (908)363-5679, FAX (908)363-0338. ***Continues** Illustrators.*

LC NK
DD 745 US
SOURCE DIRECTORY : NATIVE AMERICAN OWNED AND OPERATED ARTS AND CRAFTS BUSINESSES. Main/Corp United States. Indian Arts and Crafts Board. **Added/Corp** United States. Indian Arts and Crafts Board. **VFOAT** Native American Owned and Operated Arts and Crafts Businesses. (1979)-. Directory. English. Every 2 years. Indian Arts and Crafts Board, Room 4004/US Department of the Interior, Washington DC 20240.

ISSN 0898-3550
DD 745 US
TITLE CHANGE
SOUTHERN CALIFORNIA WOODWORKER, THE. [South. Calif. woodwork.]. (1988)-(1993). Periodical. English. Southern California Woodworker, PO Box 66751, Los Angeles CA 90066. **Tel** (310)398-5931. **ED** Ron Goldman. **Bk Rev. Ad Acc. Circ:** 8,000. ***Continued by** Woodworker West, 1080-0042.*

LC ND1457.K6 S69
KO
SOYE. VFOAT Wolgan Soye. (19??)-. Periodical. Korean. Six times a year. Wolgan Soye, 138-1 Kongpyong-Dong, Chong-ku, Seoul South Korea.

LC NK3700 **ISSN** 0341-0676
DD 738 GW
UDC 666
SPRECHSAAL (1976). See Glass and Ceramics.

ISSN 0228-7846
DD 745/.09714 CN
ST-LAURENT. (LE ST-LAURENT : BULLETIN DE LA SOCIETE DES ARTS TRADITIONNELS DU ST-LAURENT.). [St-Laurent]. **Added/Corp** Societe des Arts Traditionnels du St-Laurent. **VAT** Saint-Laurent. (1977)-. Bulletin. French. Six times a year. Free. Le St-Laurent, Bureau 205, 8440 St. Laurent, Montreal Quebec H2P 2M5 Canada.

LC NK1 .S78 **ISSN** 1069-8825
DD 745/.05 US
Pr Rev.
•STUDIES IN THE DECORATIVE ARTS. (STUDIES IN THE DECORATIVE ARTS.). [Stud. decor. arts]. **Added/Corp** Bard Graduate Center for Studies in the Decorative Arts. **VFOAT** Decorative Arts. Vol. 1, No. 1 (Fall 1993)-. Periodical. English. Two times a year (Sept., & Mar.). $30.00. Bard Graduate Center, 18 West 86th Street, New York NY 10024. **Tel** (212)875-0595, FAX (212)875-0597. **(Subscription address:** The Bard Graduate Center, PO Box 3000, Denville NJ 07834. **) ED** Sarah B. Sherrill. **Bk Rev**, (Qty: 10-20). **Circ:** 500.
Desc: A forum for the exposition of new research and interpretation in the field. Addresses the decorative arts as documents of material culture and also from the view point of connoisseurship studies.
Ind/Abst BHA : Biblio. Hist. Art.

LC WMLC 93/4512 **ISSN** 1080-451X
DD 745 US
•STYLE 1900. [Style 1900]. **VFOAT** Style Nineteen Hundred. Vol. 7, No. 4 (1995)-. Periodical. English. Four times a year. $25.00. Style 1900, 17 South Main Street, Lambertville NJ 08530. **Tel** (609)397-4104. ***Continues** Arts & Crafts Quarterly Magazine, 1074-4568.*

LC ML35 **ISSN** 1182-6630
DD 780/.7/971318 CN
SUMMERFOLK MUSIC & CRAFTS FESTIVAL. See Music.

ISSN 1081-6542
DD 745 US
SUNSHINE ARTIST. [Sunshine artist]. (19??)-. Periodical. English. Twelve times a year. $29.95. Sunshine Artists U.S.A. Inc., 2600 Temple Drive, Winter Park FL 32789. **Tel** (407)539-1399, FAX (407)539-1499. **ED** Kristine Petterson. **Ad Acc. Circ:** 15,000. ***Continues** Sunshine Artists, U.S.A., 0199-9370.*
Desc: Comprehensive listings of arts and craft shows throughout the United States.

LC TT **ISSN** 0199-9370
DD 745.5 US
TITLE CHANGE
SUNSHINE ARTISTS, U.S.A. VAT Sunshine Artists, United States of America. (1972)-(19??). Periodical. English. Sunshine Artists U.S.A. Inc., 2600 Temple Drive, Winter Park FL 32789. **Tel** (407)539-1399, FAX (407)539-1499. **ED** Kristine Petterson (editor's address: 422 West Fairbanks Avenue, Winter Park, FL 32789, phone: (407)539-3939). **Ad Acc. Circ:** 15,000. ***Continued by** Sunshine Artist, 1081-6542.*
Desc: A magazine for readers wanting to earn their livings through arts and crafts. Contains a list of shows throughout the USA.

ISSN 0824-6254
DD 745.5/05 CN
SUPERMAGAZINE D'ARTISANAT LES MOUSTARTS. Vol. 1 (1981)-. Periodical. French. 12.50Can$. Supermagazine, 9128 Pascal-Gagnon, Bureau 212, St-Leonard PQ H1P 1Z4 Canada. **Tel** (514)955-0305, FAX (514)321-9550. **ED** Roger Chakot. **Bk Rev. Ad Acc. Circ:** 20,000.
Desc: Handicraft magazine with information and details.

LC TT **ISSN** 0355-7421
DD 745.5 FI
Pr Rev.
TAITO. Added/Corp Kasi- Ja Taideteollisuusliitto. (1991)-. Periodical. Finnish (summaries and/or abstracts in Swedish). Six times a year. Fmk271.00 Scandinavia; Fmk319.00 Europe; Fmk355.00 other. Finnish Crafts and Arts Organization, POB 186, Kalevankatu 61, 00181 Helsinki Finland. **Tel** 011 358 0 906949766, 011 358 0 906940012, 011 358 0 906940023, FAX 011 358 0 90 6940067. **ED** Pirkko Toivanen. **Bk Rev. Ad Acc. Circ:** 12,000 (ctrl). ***Continues** Kotiteollisuus, 0355-7421.*
Desc: Arts and crafts magazine.

LC ND1457.J32 T67a
DD 745.61 JA
TANSHOKUBAN NITTEN SHOSHU. Main/Corp Nitten. (19??)-. Japanese. Nitten, 8-5 Sendagi 3 Bunkyo-ku, Tokyo-to 113 Japan.

LC TT **ISSN** 0210-3761
DD 745.5 SP
UDC 747
TG. TAPICERIAS GANCEDO. [TG, Tapicerias Gancedo]. **VFOAT** TG. Revista de las Artes Decorativas. (1969)-. Periodical. Spanish. Four times a year.
Ind/Abst BHA : Biblio. Hist. Art.

LC TT **ISSN** 0199-4514
DD 745.5 US
TOLE WORLD. (1977)-. Periodical. English. Six times a year. $17.97. EGW Publishing Company, 1041 Shary Circle, Concord CA 94518. **Tel** (510)671-9852, (800)777-1164, FAX (510)671-0692. **(Subscription address:** Neodata / Colorado, PO Box 2606, Boulder CO 80322. **) ED** Barbara Campbell. **Bk Rev. Ad Acc. Circ:** 35,000.
Ind/Abst Index Inf.

LC TT753 .T73 **ISSN** 1059-2466
DD 746/.05 US
CEASED
TREASURES IN NEEDLEWORK. See Home Economics-Sewing and Needlework.

ISSN 0826-2918
DD 700/.971 CN
TROUBADOUR : BULLETIN BIMESTRIEL. [Troubadour]. **Added/Corp** Canadian Folk Arts Council. **VFOAT** Bulletin Troubadour; Troubadour Newsletter; Directory of Heritage Arts Festivals in Canada; Repertoire des Festivals de l'Heritage Culturel au Canada. **VAT** Bulletin Trimestriel - Conseil Canadien des Arts Populaires. (1983)-. Bulletin. French. Six times a year. 7.00Can$. Canadian Folk Arts Council / Toronto, 263 Adelaide Street West/5th Floor, Toronto Ontario M5H 1Y2 Canada. **Tel** (416)977-8311.

LC NK8 .U4 **ISSN** 0139-5815
XR
UMENI REMESLA. (UMENI A REMESLA : U&R.). [Umeni remesla]. **Added/Corp** Ustredi Lidove Umelecke Vyroby v Praze. **VFOAT** U&R; U & R; U a R. (1959)-. Periodical. Czech (summaries and/or abstracts in English, German and Russian; table of contents in English and French). Four times a year. DM92.00. **(Subscription address:** Kubon & Sagner, ABT Zeitschriftenimport, D 80328 Munich Germany. **Tel** 011 49 89 54218130.**) Circ:** 7,250 (ctrl).
Desc: Covers architecture, handicraft, decorative arts, sculpture, visual arts, design, glass, jewelry, museums, folk art, ethnography, tapestry, furniture, fashion, art education, ceramics, housing culture, and care of historic treasures.
Ind/Abst Am. Hist. Life (1971-1983); ARTbibliogr. Mod.; BHA : Biblio. Hist. Art.

LC HD2346.I5 H3
II

VARSHIKA RIPORTA - HAINDIKRAPHTSA ENNDA HAINDALUMSA EKSAPORTASA KARPORESANA APHA INDIYA. Main/Corp
Handicrafts and Handlooms Exports Corporation of India. **VFOAT** HHEC Annual Report; Handicrafts and Handlooms Exports Corporation of India Ltd. Annual Report; Annual Report. (1972/)-. Hindi (English). Lok Kalyan Bhavan, 11-A Rouse Avenue Lane, New Delhi 1 India. **Continues** *Varshika Sucana.*

DD 746.92   **ISSN** 1188-0511 CN

VERTIGO. [Vertigo]. Vol. 1, No 1 (1991)-. Periodical. French. Four times a year. 4.25Can$ per issue. Editions Vertigo, 33 rue Prince, Montreal Quebec H3C 2M7 Canada.

LC TT
DD 745.5
UDC 7
ISSN 0134-8450 RU

VOPROSY OTECESTVENNOGO I ZARUBEZNOGO ISKUSSTVA. (1975)-.
Russian. Irregular.
Ind/Abst BHA : Biblio. Hist. Art.

LC NK   **ISSN** 1065-3317
DD 745   US

WALLPAPER REPRODUCTION NEWS.
(19??)-. Periodical. English. Four times a year. $30.00. Wallpaper Reproduction News Associates, PO Box 187, Lee MA 01238. **Tel** (413)243-3489. **ED** Robert M. Kelly. Index available (published separately). **Bk Rev**, (Qty: 4). **Desc:** Aimed at professionals in the field of wallpaper reproduction: designers, museum curators, screenprinters and installers.

LC TT560 .W414   **ISSN** 1073-0680
DD 746.9/2/05   CEASED

WEARABLE CRAFTS. [Wearable crafts]. (Apr. 1993)-(June/July 1995). Periodical. English. House of White Birches, 306 East Parr Road, Berne IN 46711. **Tel** (219)589-8741, FAX (219)589-8093. (**Subscription address:** Palm Coast Data, PO Box 420163, Agency Department, Palm Coast FL 32142. **Tel** (904)445-4662 ext. 669, (800)829-5475.) **ED** Beth Schwartz Wheeler. **Circ:** 81,345. **Continues** *Wearable Wonders, 1057-7556.* **Desc:** Contains designer artwear projects in clothing, jewelry, and accessories.

LC TT180   **ISSN** 0886-3407
DD 745.51   US

WILDFOWL CARVING AND COLLECTING. VFOAT Wildfowl Carving & Collecting. (198?)-. Periodical. English. Four times a year. $29.95. Wildfowl Carving & Collecting, 500 Vaughn Street, Harrisburg PA 17110. **Tel** (717)234-5091, FAX (717)234-1359. **ED** Cathy Lee Hart. Index available (bound in Spring issue). cum. index. **Bk Rev**, (Qty: 3/year). **Ad Acc**, **Adv Mgr:** Diana Marcum. **Circ:** 14,500. **Desc:** Reference instruction for carvers and collectors of wooden wildfowl sculpture.

LC TT   **ISSN** 0509-089X
DD 745.5   US

WOMEN'S CIRCLE. See Home Economics-Sewing and Needlework.

LC TT   **ISSN** 0745-0575
DD 745.5   US   CEASED

WOMEN'S HOUSEHOLD CROCHET. See Home Economics-Sewing and Needlework.

LC TH5601   **ISSN** 1058-3815
DD 694   TITLE CHANGE

WOOD PROJECTS (NEW YORK, N.Y. 1991). See Building and Construction-Carpentry and Woodwork.

LC NK   **ISSN** 1080-0042
DD 745   US

●WOODWORKER WEST. See Building and Construction-Carpentry and Woodwork.

LC TT697 .W67   **ISSN** 0162-9123
DD 745   US

WORKBASKET AND HOME ARTS MAGAZINE, THE. [Workbasket home arts mag.]. VFOAT Workbasket. (19??)-. Periodical. English. Six times a year. $14.95. KC Publishing Inc., 700 West 47th Street, Suite 310, Kansas City MO 64112. **Tel** (816)531-5730, (800)444-0801. (**Subscription address:** CDS Agency Hard Copy, PO Box 4966, Des Moines IA 50340. **Tel** (515)247-7569.) **ED** Roma Jean Rice. Index available. **Bk Rev**. **Ad Acc**. **Circ:** 1,200,000. available on microfilm from University Microfilms International (UMI). Documents available from UMI Article Clearinghouse. **Continues** *Workbasket.* **Desc:** Covers knitting, crocheting, tatting designs and instructions, craft projects, recipes and gardening for the homemaker.

Ind/Abst EP Collect.; Homework Help.; MasterFile FullTEXT 1000; MasterFile FullTEXT 350; MasterFile FullTEXT 650; MasterFile FullTEXT (July 1994-) [Full Txt.]; Newsp. Period. Abstr. (1988-); OCLC; Pub. Lib. FullTEXT; Telebase; Mag. Index (1978-May 1984).

LC TT   **ISSN** 0730-7640
DD 745.5   US

YARNCRAFT. See Home Economics-Sewing and Needlework.

GRAPHIC ARTS

LC NE
DD 760   US

●3-D DESIGN. (Sept. 1995)-. English. Twelve times a year. $49.95. Miller Freeman Inc., 600 Harrison Street, San Francisco CA 94107. **Tel** (415)905-2337, (415)905-2200, FAX (415)905-2240, telex 278273.

DD 741   **ISSN** 1065-1276 US

3-DIMENSIONAL ILLUSTRATORS AWARDS ANNUAL. (3-DIMENSIONAL ILLUSTRATORS AWARDS ANNUAL : THE BEST IN 3-D ADVERTISING AND PUBLISHING WORLDWIDE.). [3 dimens. illus. awards annu.]. VFOAT Three-Dimensional Illustrators Awards Annual. (1992)-. English. Rockport Publishers Inc, 5 Smith Street, PO Box 396, Rockport MA 01966.

DD 760   **ISSN** 1058-9503 US

3D ARTIST. [3D artist]. VFOAT Three D Artist. Issue #1 (Dec. 1991)-. Periodical. English. Irregular (8 or 10 issues per year). Price varies. Columbine, Inc., PO Box 4787, Santa Fe NM 87502-4787. **Tel** (505)982-3532. **Desc:** Information on creating 3-D art and animation on Amiga, Macintosh, and PC computers; for home and professional users.

LC NC997.A1 A359   **ISSN** 0191-4278
DD 760   US

ADIX. Vol. 1, No. 1 (May 1979)-. Periodical. English. Twelve times a year. $10.00. Sophist Communications Inc, One Union Square, Suite 508, New York NY 10003. **Tel** (212)691-8989.

LC NC998.5.A1 A33   **ISSN** 0887-4514
DD 741.6/0973/074019494   US   CEASED

ADLA. [ADLA]. Added/Corp Art Directors Club of Los Angeles. VAT Art Directors Club of Los Angeles. (1986)-Vol. 6. English. Madison Square Press, 10 East 23rd Street, New York NY 10010. **Tel** (212)505-0950, (800)451-1741, FAX (212)979-2207. **Continues** *Art Directors Club of Los Angeles.*

LC NC997.A1 A3   **ISSN** 0736-5322
DD 741.6   US

AIGA JOURNAL OF GRAPHIC DESIGN.
[AIGA j. graph des.]. **Added/Corp** American Institute of Graphic Arts. **VFOAT** A.I.G.A. Journal of Graphic Design; Journal of Graphic Design; AIGA Journal; A.I.G.A. Journal. **VAT** American Institute of Graphic Arts Journal of Graphic Design. No. 1 (June 1982)-. Trade Publication. English. Four times a year. $21.50. American Institue of Graphic Arts, 1059 3rd Avenue, New York NY 10021. **Tel** (212)752-0813, FAX (212)755-6749. **ED** Steven Heller. **Bk Rev**. **Ad Acc**, **Adv Mgr:** Michelle Kalvert. **Circ:** 9,000 (ctrl). **Continues** *Journal of the American Institute of Graphic Arts, 0065-8820.* **Desc:** A journal of graphic design history, criticism, reviews and professional practice.

LC NC998.5.A1 A44   **ISSN** 0278-8128
DD 741.6/0973   US   TITLE CHANGE

AMERICAN ILLUSTRATION SHOWCASE. [Am. illus. showc.]. VFOAT American Showcase Illustration. (19??)-(199?). Trade Publication. English. American Showcase, 915 Broadway, 14th Floor, New York NY 10010. **Tel** (212)673-6600, FAX (212)673-9795, telex 880356 AMSHOW P. **ED** Ira Shapiro. **Bk Rev**. **Ad Acc**. **Circ:** 34,550 (ctrl). **Continues in part** *American Showcase, 0742-6100.* **Continued by** *American Showcase. Illustration.* **Desc:** Contains the latest work from America's commercial illustrators and graphic designers.

LC NC1300 .A53   **ISSN** 1071-8745
DD 741.5/0973/05   US

●AMERICAN JOURNAL OF ANTHROPOMORPHICS, THE. VFOAT AJA. (1993)-. Periodical. English. Four times a year. $35.00. Med Systems Company, PO Box 580009, Flushing NY 11358-0009.

LC NC998.5.A1 A44
DD 741.6/0973   US

AMERICAN SHOWCASE. ILLUSTRATION. VFOAT Illustration; American Showcase Illustration. (199?)-. Trade Publication. English. One time a year (March). $85.00. American Showcase, 915 Broadway, 14th Floor, New York NY 10010. **Tel** (212)673-6600, FAX (212)673-9795, telex 880356 AMSHOW P. **Bk Rev**. **Ad Acc**. **Circ:** 34,550 (ctrl). **Continues** *American Illustration Showcase, 0278-8128.* **Desc:** Contains the latest work from America's commercial illustrators and graphic designers.

DD 741.67   US

ANDY AWARDS ANNUAL, THE. Added/Corp Advertising Club of New York. VFOAT Andy Awards. (198?)-. Periodical. English. The Advertising Club of New York, 235 Park Ave. S., New York NY 10003-1405. **Tel** (212)533-1570. **Continues** *Andy Awards, 0270-2525.*

LC NC997.A1   **ISSN** 0971-4705
DD 741.6/0971/05   CN

APPLIED ARTS MAGAZINE. (1992)-. English. Five times a year. 64.00Can$. Applied Arts, 885 Don Mills Road Suite 324, Don Mills Ontario M3C 1V9 Canada. **Tel** (905)510-0909. **Ad Acc**, **Adv Mgr:** Brian Patterson. **Continues** *Applied Arts Quarterly, 0829-9242.*

DD 741.6/0971   **ISSN** 0829-9242 CN   TITLE CHANGE

APPLIED ARTS QUARTERLY (TORONTO, ONT.). (APPLIED ARTS QUARTERLY.). [Appl. arts q.]. VFOAT Applied Arts. Vol. 1, No. 1 (Spring 1986)-. Periodical. English. Applied Arts, 885 Don Mills Road Suite 324, Don Mills Ontario M3C 1V9 Canada. **Tel** (905)510-0909. **Continued by** *Applied Arts Magazine.*
Ind/Abst Can. Period. Index (1989-).

LC NC997   **ISSN** 0882-4932
DD 741.6   US   TITLE CHANGE

ARIZONA PORTFOLIO, THE. (19??)-(Jan. 1995). Periodical. English. Arizona Portfolio, 7041 East Orange Blossom Lane, Scottsdale AZ 85253. **Tel** (602)252-2332, FAX (602)941-5561. **Ad Acc**. ctrl circ. **Continued by** *Southwest Creative Sourcebook.*

LC NC997   **ISSN** 0267-3991
DD 741.6   UK

ART & DESIGN. VFOAT Art and Design; A;D; AD. Vol. 1, No. 1 (Feb. 1985)-. Trade Publication. English. Six times a year. $135.00. Academy Editions, 42 Leinster Gardens, London W2 3AN United Kingdom. **Tel** 011 44 171 4022141, FAX 011 44 171 7239540, telex 896928 ACADEM G. (**Subscription address:** VCH Publishers Inc., 303 Northwest 12th Avenue, Journals Department, Deerfield FL 33442. **Tel** (800)367-8249, (305)428-5566.) **ED** Andreas C. Papdakis. **Bk Rev**. **Ad Acc**. **Circ:** 12,000. **Desc:** Extensively illustrated articles, features and interviews presenting all aspects of the visual arts. **Ind/Abst** Archit. Period. Index; ARTbibliogr. Mod.

DD 760   **ISSN** 1055-2286 US   CODEN ADENEI

ART & DESIGN NEWS. [Art des. news]. VFOAT Art and Design News. Vol. 13, No. 1 (Jan./Feb. 1991)-. Trade Publication. English. Six times a year (Jan., Mar., May., July, Sept., Nov.). $15.00. Boyd Publishing Co., Inc., 5783 Park Plaza Court, Indianapolis IN 46220. **Tel** (317)849-6110. **ED** Rebecca Tapley. Index available. **Bk Rev**. **Ad Acc**, **Adv Mgr:** Jeanne Pulliam. **Circ:** 47,000 (ctrl). **Continues** *Art Product News, 0163-7460.* **Desc:** Product information for graphic arts and computer art field.

LC NC997.A1 A684   **ISSN** 0004-3109
DD 741.6/05   US   CCC

ART DIRECTION. [Art dir.]. Added/Corp National Association of Art Directors (U.S.). (1956)-. Trade Publication. English. Twelve times a year. $29.97 (one-year), $55.97 (two-year), $82.49 (three-year) US; $46.50 (one-year), $87.00 (two-year), $128.50 (three-year) surface mail other; $91.50 (one-year), $177.00 (two-year), $261.00 (three-year) airmail other. Advertising Trade Publishers Inc, 10 East 39th Street, New York NY 10016. **Tel** (212)889-6500. **ED** Dan Barron. **Circ:** 10,500. available on microfilm from University Microfilms International (UMI). **Continues** *Art Director & Studio News.* **Desc:** Current visual advertising art, design photography, typography.
Ind/Abst Art Index; ARTbibliogr. Mod.; Book Rev. Index; GATFWORLD (1984); Infobank (Jan. 1979-); Mark. Advert. Ref. Serv.

LC Z244.6.L35 A75
DD 338.4/7/68620258   AG

ARTES GRAFICAS. See Printing Industry.

LC NX   **ISSN** 1075-0894
DD 700   US

●ARTIST'S AND GRAPHIC DESIGNER'S MARKET. See Occupations and Careers.

The Arts —Graphic Arts

LC N8600 .A746
DD 706/.8/8
ISSN 1075-0894
US
●**ARTIST'S & GRAPHIC DESIGNER'S MARKET.** (ARTIST'S & GRAPHIC DESIGNER'S MARKET : WHERE & HOW TO SELL YOUR ILLUSTRATION, FINE ART, GRAPHIC DESIGN & CARTOONS.). [Artist's graph. des. mark.]. **VFOAT** Artist's and Graphic Designer's Market. (1995)-. English. One time a year. $27.49. Writer's Digest Books, 1507 Dana Avenue, Cincinnati OH 45207. **Tel** (513)531-2222, (800)289-0963, FAX (513)531-4744. **Continues** Artist's Market, 0161-0546; **Absorbed in part** Guide to Literary Agents & Art/Photo Reps, 1055-6087.
Desc: Lists buyers of art. Includes geographic indexes to help artists tap their local markets. Articles and interviews with professionals.

DD 760
ISSN 0269-4697
UK
ARTIST'S AND ILLUSTRATOR'S MAGAZINE. [Artist's illus. mag.]. (1986)-. Consumer Publication. English. Twelve times a year. $46.21. The Artists and Illustrators Magazine Ltd., The Fitzpatrick Building, 188-194 York Way, London N7 9QR United Kingdom. **Tel** 011 44 171 6092177, FAX 011 44 171 7004985. **ED** Rada Petrovic. Index available. cum. index. **Bk Rev.** (Qty: 120). **Ad Acc. Adv Mgr:** Paul Harris, **Tel** 071 609 2177. **Circ.:** 35,000.
Desc: Information on techniques artists, materials, exhibitions, seminars, workshops, and events. For amateur and semi-professional artists.

LC N8600 .A76
DD 380.1/45/702573
ISSN 0161-0546
US
TITLE CHANGE
ARTIST'S MARKET (1979). (ARTIST'S MARKET.). (1979)-(1994). English. Writer's Digest Books, 1507 Dana Avenue, Cincinnati OH 45207. **Tel** (513)531-2222, (800)289-0963, FAX (513)531-4744. **ED** Laurie Miller. Index available (free). **Bk Rev. Ad Acc. Supersedes in part** Art & Crafts Market, 0147-2461. **Continued by** Artist's & Graphic Designer's Market, 1075-0894.
Desc: Lists buyers of all types of art. Includes geographic indexes to help artists tap their local markets. Articles and interviews with successful professionals give artists the tips they need to succeed.

LC NE
DD 760
ISSN 0040-1366
FR
ARTS ET TECHNIQUES GRAPHIQUES. Periodical. French. Six times a year. **Absorbed in part** Terre d'Images.

DD 741
ISSN 1080-3491
US
●**ASPIRING CARTOONIST, THE.** (1993)-. Periodical. English. Three times a year. Yendie Boox, PO Box 18679, Indianapolis IN 46218.

LC Z999 .H334a
DD 017.3
GW
AUKTION. See The Arts-Abstracting, Bibliographies and Statistics.

DD 745
ISSN 1060-4030
US
BA PAPYRUS. (BA PAPYRUS : A NEWSLETTER FOR THE AFRICAN GREETING CARD COLLECTIVE.). [Ba pap.]. **Added/Corp** African Greeting Card Collective. **VFOAT** Soul Papers. (1991)-. Newsletter. English. Irregular. (2-4 issues per year). $10.00 (institutions), $5.00 (individuals). African Greeting Card Collective, PO Box 90485, Washington DC 20090-0485. **Tel** (202)269-0064. **ED** Aziza Gibson-Hunter. **Ad Acc.**
Desc: Covers African American greeting cards for gift manufacturers and retailers.

LC E839.5 .B45
DD 320.973/0207
ISSN 0737-9498
US
BEST EDITORIAL CARTOONS OF THE YEAR. 2nd (1974)-. English. One time a year. $17.20. Pelican Publishing Company, PO Box 3110, Gretna LA 70054. **Tel** (504)368-1175, (800)843-1724, FAX (504)368-1195. **ED** Charles Brooks. **Continues** Best Editorial Cartoons, 0091-2220.
Desc: A compendium of cartoonists' views on national and international issues.

LC NC975 .B47
DD 741.6/0973
US
BEST IN COVERS & POSTERS, THE. **VFOAT** Best in Covers and Posters. 2nd Ed. (1977)-. Trade Publication. English. Every 2 years. $27.50. RC Publications Inc., 3200 Tower Oaks Boulevard, Rockville MD 20852. **Tel** (800)222-2654, (301)770-2900, FAX (301)984-3203. **Formed by the union of** Best in Covers and Best in Posters.

LC NC998.5.A1 B47
DD 745.4/4973
ISSN 0360-8271
US
BEST IN ENVIRONMENTAL GRAPHICS, THE. (1975)-. Trade Publication. English. Every 2 years. $17.50. RC Publications Inc., 3200 Tower Oaks Boulevard, Rockville MD 20852. **Tel** (800)222-2654, (301)770-2900, FAX (301)984-3203.

LC NE
DD 760
IT
BIENNALE INTERNAZIONALE DELLA GRAFICA D'ARTE. **Added/Corp** Unione Fiorentina. (19??)-. Italian. Every 2 years. Unione Fiorentina, Italy.
Ind/Abst BHA : Biblio. Hist. Art.

LC Z475 .B56
DD 338.8/2616862/02573
ISSN 1065-8521
US
●**BLUE BOOK OF PRINTING AND GRAPHIC ARTS BUYERS (NATIONAL ED.).** See Printing Industry.

LC NC997.A1 B63
DD 741.6
ISSN 1062-7774
US
BOARD REPORT FOR GRAPHIC ARTISTS. [Board rep. graph. artists]. **Added/Corp** American Professional Graphic Artists. **VFOAT** Board Report. (July 1980)-. Periodical. English. Twelve times a year. $96.00. Board Report Publishing Company, PO Box 4416, Circulation Department, Denver CO 80204. **Tel** (303)839-9058, FAX (303)839-1272. **ED** Drew Miller. ctrl circ. **Continues** Board Report from APGA.

LC NC998.6.G7 D47
DD 741.6/0941
UK
BRITISH DESIGN & ART DIRECTION : D & AD. **Added/Corp** Designers and Art Directors Association of London. **VFOAT** D and AD; British Design and Art Direction; D & AD; Design and Art Direction. (19??)-. English. One time a year. $107.81. Internos Books, 18 Colville Road, London W3 8BL United Kingdom. **Tel** 011 44 181 9920008, FAX 011 44 181 9928313. **Continues** British Design and Art Direction.

DD 659
ISSN 0894-8186
US
CAMERON'S READYART BULLETIN. [Cameron's readyArt bull.]. **VFOAT** Cameron's Ready Art Bulletin. (19??)-. Bulletin. English. Twelve times a year. $95.00. Cameron's Publications, 5325 Sheridan Drive, PO Box 1160, Williamsville NY 14221-9160. **Tel** (716)833-4369, FAX (716)834-4159. **ED** Nina L. Cameron. ctrl circ.
Desc: Art work for restaurants and hotels.

DD 790.13/2
ISSN 0705-2197
CN
CANADIAN GRAPHIC COLLECTOR. No. 1 (Jan./Feb. 1978)-. Periodical. English. 7.50Can$. Dark Horse Grafix, 320 Kennedy Street, Winnipeg Manitoba R3B 2M6 Canada.

DD 769/.05
ISSN 0824-6904
CN
SUSPENDED
CANADIAN PRINT & PORTFOLIO. [Can. print. portf.]. **VFOAT** Print & Portfolio. Vol. 1, No. 1 (1984)-Suspended. Periodical. English. Four times a year. $10.00. Canadian Print & Portfolio, 3152 Dundas Street West, Toronto Ontario M6P 2A1 Canada.

DD 769/.9/7195
ISSN 0319-0463
CN
CAPE DORSET PRINTS. **VFOAT** Cape Dorset Estampes. 1972-. Multiple languages (English and French). One time a year. Canadian Arctic Producers Ltd, PO Box 4130 Station E, Ottawa Ontario K1S 5B2 Canada. **Supersedes** Cape Dorset, 0319-0455.

LC NC1300 .C35
DD 741.5/0973
ISSN 0008-7068
US
CARTOONIST PROFILES. No. 1 (Winter 1969)-. Periodical. English. Four times a year. $35.00. Cartoonist Profiles, PO Box 325, Fairfield CT 06430. **Tel** (203)227-2542, FAX (203)336-5381. available on microfilm and microfiche from University Microfilms International (UMI).
Desc: Magazine in which currently-syndicated top comic artists detail how they reached their goals.

DD 741
ISSN 1061-849X
US
CHAMPION OF KATARA (SEATTLE, WASH.), THE. (THE CHAMPION OF KATARA.). [Champion Katara]. No. 1 (Jan. 1992)-. English. Four times a year. $7.50. MU Press, 5014-D Roosevelt Way NE, Seattle WA 98105. **Continues** Champion of Katara, 1061-849X.

DD 741
ISSN 1056-3709
US
CHILD'S PLAY (WHEELING, W. VA.). (CHILD'S PLAY.). [Child's play]. (1991)-. Periodical. English. Twelve times a year. $3.00 (single issue). Innovation Publishing, 3622 Jacob Street, Wheeling WV 26003.

LC NE1183.3 .C597
DD 769.951
CH
CHUNG-KUO PAN HUA NIEN CHIEN / CHUNG-KUO PAN HUA NIEN CHIEN PIEN CHI WEI YUAN HUI PIEN. (1982)-. Chinese. One time a year. NT$4.65. Liao-Ning Sheng Hsin Hua Shu Tien, Shen-Yang, People's Republic of China.

LC HE6187 .C65
DD 769.56/075
IT
COLLEZIONISTA FRANCOBOLLI, IL. (19??)-. Periodical. Italian. Twenty-four times a year. L44290. Alberto Bolaffi SRL, via Cavour 17F, 10123 Turin Italy. **Tel** 011 39 11 5571655. **Continues** Collezionista.

LC NE3000 .C64
DD 760
ISSN 0748-4399
US
COLOR XEROX ANNUAL. [Color Xerox annu.]. (19??)-. English. One time a year. $45.00. Barbara Cushman, PO Box 26082, San Francisco CA 94126.

ISSN 1062-6964
COMIC ART STUDIES. (COMIC ART STUDIES : A NEWSLETTER FROM THE RUSSEL B. NYE POPULAR CULTURE COLLECTION.). [Comic art stud.]. **Added/Corp** Russel B. Nye Popular Culture Collection (Michigan State University). No. 47 (May 2, 1992)-. Newsletter. English. Four times a year. Free. Michigan State University Libraries, International Library, East Lansing MI 48824. **Continues** Comic Art Collection, 0192-5881.

LC NC997.A1 C2
DD 741.6/05
ISSN 0010-3519
US
COMMUNICATION ARTS. [Commun. arts]. **VFOAT** Communication Arts Magazine; CA, Communication Arts Magazine. Vol. 11, No. 2 (1969)-. Trade Publication. English. Eight times a year. $53.00. Communication Arts, 410 Sherman Avenue, Palo Alto CA 94303-0807. **Tel** (415)326-6040, FAX (415)326-1648. **(Subscription address:** Communication Arts, Subscription Department, PO Box 10300, Palo Alto CA 94303-9979.) **ED** Patrick Coyne. **Ad Acc. Circ:** 54,348. Documents available from UMI Article Clearinghouse. **Continues** CA Magazine (Palo Alto, Calif.), 0884-0008.
Desc: Professional journal for designers, art directors, design firms illustrators, advertising agencies, photographers, students, and everyone involved in visual communication.
Ind/Abst Abstr. Bull. Inst. Pap. Sci. Tech.; Acad. Ind. [Computer File] (1992-); Acad. Search; Art Index; ARTbibliogr. Mod.; EP Collect.; Expand. Acad. Index (1992-); Graph. Arts Bull. Inst. Pap. Sci. Technol. (May 1989-); Homework Help.; Humanit. Source; INFO-SOUTH Abstr.; Mag. Search; MasterFile FullTEXT 1000; MasterFile FullTEXT 350; MasterFile FullTEXT 650; MasterFile FullTEXT (July 1993-); Newsp. Period. Abstr. (1989-); OCLC; Telebase; Trade Ind. Index.

LC TS1088 .C57
DD 676/.28/029473
US
COMPETITIVE GRADE FINDER FOR THE PAPER AND GRAPHIC ARTS INDUSTRIES, THE. See Paper and Pulp Industry.

LC NE771.4 .C66
DD 769.952
JA
CONTEMPORARY JAPANESE PRINTS. (1983)-. English. Irregular. Kodansha International, 114 5th Avenue, New York NY 10011. **Tel** (212)727-6460.

LC TR706 .C67
DD 770/.25/73
ISSN 0742-9975
US
CORPORATE SHOWCASE. See Photography.

LC NE1 .C7
DD 760/.5
ISSN 0275-7516
US
COUNTERPROOF. **Added/Corp** Print Club (Philadelphia, Pa.). Vol. 1, No. 1 (Fall 1978)-. Periodical. English. Four times a year. $1.00. The Print Club, 1614 Latimer Street, Philadelphia PA 19103.

LC NE
DD 760
UK
CREATIVE HANDBOOK, THE. (19??)-. English. One time a year (Jan.). $186.00. Reed Information Services Ltd., Windsor Court, East Grinstead House, East Grinstead RH19 1BR United Kingdom. **Tel** 011 44 1342 326972, FAX 011 44 1342 335977, telex 95127 INFSER G. **Ad Acc. Circ:** 10,000 (ctrl).
Desc: A creative directory for all involved in advertising, design and the communication industry.

LC NC997
DD 741.6
ISSN 0726-3589
AT
CREATIVE SOURCE AUSTRALIA. **VFOAT** Wizards of Oz. 2nd Book (1982)-. Monographic series. English. One time a year. Price varies per volume. Armadillo Publishers Pty Ltd., 205-207 Scotchmer Street/Fitzroy, North Melbourne Victoria 3068 Australia. **Tel** 011 61 03 489-9559, FAX 011 61 03 489-5576. **ED** David Lyons and Elaine Howell. **Ad Acc. Circ:** 3,500. **Continues** Art Directors Guide to Photographers in Australia.
Desc: Pictorial reference book of creative work in Australia. Contains photography, illustration, design, SFX food, styling, etc.

LC NC998.6.G7 X993
DD 741.6
UK
●**CREATIVE TECHNOLOGY.** (Sept. 1994)-. English. Twelve times a year. $102.67. Haymarket Publishing Ltd., 12 14 Ansdell Street, London W8 5TR

The Arts —Graphic Arts

United Kingdom. **Tel** 011 44 171 9380705, 011 44 171 2786686, FAX 011 44 171 9380772. **Continues** *XYZ Design & Technology.*

DD 741.5   **ISSN** 1183-8159
CN
CROC CLASSIQUE. [Croc class.]. No 1 (1991)-. Periodical. French. Four times a year. 3.95Can$ per number. Croc Classique, 5800 rue Monkland, Montreal Quebec H4A 1G1 Canada.

LC Z119 .D35
DK
DANSK GRAFIA. See Printing Industry.

DD 741   **ISSN** 1060-684X
US
DARK SHADOWS (WHEELING, W. VA.). (DARK SHADOWS). [Dark shad.]. (1992)-. English. Six times a year. $42.00 (12 issues). Innovative Corp., 3622 Jacob Street, Wheeling WV 26003.

DD 741   **ISSN** 1059-0773
US
CEASED
DEATHLOK. [Deathlok]. (July 1991)-(199?). Periodical. English. Twelve times a year. $21.00 US; $26.00 via Canada. Deathlok, 387 Park Avenue South, New York NY 10016.

LC N6941.D45   **ISSN** 0923-9790
NE
DELINEAVIT ET SCULPSIT. **Added/Corp** Rijksuniversiteit te Leiden. Prentenkabinet. Vrienden. No. 1 (Aug. 1989)-. Periodical. Dutch. Two times a year. $50.00. Delineavit et Sculpsit, Rapenburg 65, 2311 GJ Leiden Netherlands. **Tel** 011 31 71 272790. Index available. cum. index.
Ind/Abst BHA : Biblio. Hist. Art.

LC NK1160 .D45   **ISSN** 0953-0681
DD 016.7454   UK
DESIGN & APPLIED ARTS INDEX. See The Arts-Abstracting, Bibliographies and Statistics.

LC NK1403 .D46   **ISSN** 0278-1522
DD 745.4/4973   US
DESIGN ARTS (NEW YORK, N.Y.). (DESIGN ARTS). [Des. arts]. **Added/Corp** Cooper Union for the Advancement of Science and Art. National Endowment for the Arts. Vol. 1, No. 1 (Aug. 1980)-. Periodical. English. Cooper Union for the Advancement of Science and Art, 41 Cooper Square, New York NY 10003.

LC NK1490.A1 D48   **ISSN** 1033-4467
AT
DESIGN DOWN UNDER. **Added/Corp** Design Down Under (Firm). (1989)-. English. Every 2 years. 102.77Aus$. Foliograph Books, 3 Ward Street, North Sydney New South Wales 2060 Australia. **Tel** 011 61 02 5651028.

LC NE   **ISSN** 1320-3088
DD 760   AT
●**DESIGN GRAPHICS.** **Added/Corp** Australian Graphic Design Association. **VFOAT** Analogue & Digital Design Graphics. (Oct. 1993)-. Periodical. English. Six times a year. 49.00Aus$ Australia; 75.00Aus$ US and Canada; 85.00Can$ elsewhere. Design Editorial Pty Ltd, A.C.N. 005 763 744, 11 School Road, Ferny Creek Victoria 3786 Australia. **Tel** 011 61 3 7551149, FAX 011 61 3 7551155.

LC NK1160 .D44
SZ
TITLE CHANGE
DESIGN INDEX ... FOR THE CORPORATE MANAGER, THE. **VFOAT** Design Index. (1991)-Vol. 6 (199?). English (French and German). Rotovision SA, Route Suisse 9, CH1295 Mies Switzerland. **Tel** 011 41 22 7553055, FAX 011 41 22 7554072, telex 419246. **(Subscription address:** Keng Seng Enterprises Inc., 4030 rue St Ambroise, Suite 227, Montreal Quebec H4C 2C7 Canada. **Tel** (514)393-3971, FAX (514)898-1922.**) Continues** *Designer's Index.* **Continued by** *Graphic Designer's Index.*

LC TA   **ISSN** 1066-7504
DD 620   US
CCC
CEASED
DESIGN TECHNOLOGIES. See Engineering-Industrial Engineering.

LC NE
DD 760   UK
TITLE CHANGE
DESIGN TECHNOLOGY TEACHING. Vol. 22, No. 1 (Spring 1990)-(1995). Academic Scholarly Publication. English. Trentham Books Limited, Westview House, 734 London Road, Oakhill Stoke on Trent, Staffordshire ST4 5NP United Kingdom. **Tel** 011 44 1782 745567, FAX 011 44 1782 745553. **Bk Rev**. **Ad Acc**, **Adv Mgr Tel** 0222 360839. **Circ:** 4,500. **Continues** *Studies in Design Education Craft & Technology.* **Continued by** *Journal of Design and Technology.*
Desc: Focuses on developments in the field of design and technology education ranging from art to applied science and technology. Includes selection of important researches and studies in design education.

LC NC997
DD 741.6   GW
DESIGNERS DIGEST MAGAZINE. **VFOAT** Designers Digest. No. 1 (Jan./Feb./March 1990)-. Periodical. German. Four times a year. Verlag Design und Technik GmbH, Schultestrasse 27, Postfach 7 17 44, Munich 71 Germany. **Tel** 089 1917045, FAX 089 7918883. **ED** Klaus Tiedge. **Bk Rev**. **Ad Acc**. **Circ:** 25,000. **Continues** *Grafik Design + Technik, 0930-9675.*

LC Z244.6.M6 D57
MX
DIRECTORIO DE LA INDUSTRIA DE LAS ARTES GRAFICAS. See Printing Industry.

LC N328.N37
DD 707/.1/173   US
DIRECTORY / NATIONAL ASSOCIATION OF SCHOOLS OF ART AND DESIGN. See The Arts-Art.

LC N51 .D57   **ISSN** 0897-3989
DD 707/.1/173   US
DIRECTORY OF ART AND DESIGN FACULTIES IN COLLEGES AND UNIVERSITIES, U.S. AND CANADA. See The Arts-Abstracting, Bibliographies and Statistics.

DD 741   **ISSN** 1044-7172
US
DOCTOR STRANGE, SORCERER SUPREME. [Dr. Strange sorcerer supreme]. **VFOAT** Doctor Strange. No. 1 (Nov. 1988)-. Periodical. English. Irregular. $17.95. Marvel Entertainment Group Inc., 387 Park Avenue South, New York NY 10016. **Tel** (212)576-8595, FAX (212)576-9289.

LC 745   **ISSN** 0197-470X
DD 760   US
DURBIN DATA SHEETS. **Main/Corp** Durbin Associates. (19??)-. English. One time a year (includes annual two-volume set and monthly updates). $395.00. Durbin Associates, 3711 Southwood Drive, Easton PA 18042. **Tel** (610)252-6331. **Continues** *Seybold Data Sheets.*
Desc: Includes information on process cameras, scanners, desktop publishing, image setters, and other pre-press graphic arts equipment.

DD 760   **ISSN** 0889-0528
US
EDITOR'S CHOICE CLIP ART QUARTERLY. [Ed. choice clip art q.]. **VFOAT** Editor's Choice. (198?)-. Periodical. English. Six times a year. $276.06 New York; $258.00 other. Roberts Publishing Incorporated, 500 South Salina Street, 6th Floor, Syracuse NY 13202. **Tel** (800)962-1353, FAX (315)472-5258. **ED** Mary DeSantis, 500 S Salina St, Syracuse, NY 13202 (phone# (315)472-4555). **Circ:** 150.
Desc: Contains graphics and illustrations designed for the editors of in-house and employee publications. Contains graphics and illustrations on a variety of subjects such as employee relations, special seasonal events, wellness, publication standing heads, business and industry graphics.

DD 760   **ISSN** 1045-3717
US
EMIGRE (BERKELEY, CALIF.). (EMIGRE). [Emigre]. (1984)-. Trade Publication. English. Four times a year (Feb., May, Aug., Nov.). $28.00 US; $35.00 Canada; $58.00 other. Emigre Graphics, 4475 D Street, Sacramento CA 95819. **Tel** (415)845-4344, FAX (415)451-4351. **ED** Rudy Vanderlans. **Ad Acc**. **Circ:** 7000 (ctrl).

LC NE   **ISSN** 0741-7160
DD 760   US
EXPORT GRAFICAS USA. [Export graf. USA]. **VFOAT** Export Graficas U.S.A.; Export Graficas. Trade Publication. Spanish. One time a year. $30.00 US; $50.00 other. Graphics Arts Trade Journal International Inc, 1680 Southwest Bayshore Boulevard, Port St. Lucie FL 34984. **Tel** (407)879-6666. **Bk Rev**. **Ad Acc**. **Circ:** 12,000 (ctrl). **Continues in part** *Export Grafics USA, 0147-409X.*
Desc: Technical articles pertaining to trends and new developments within the printing, packaging and converting industries worldwide, in addition to international news, new products section, and sources of supplies section for management, technical and sales personnel.

LC Z119 .E88   **ISSN** 0344-2039
DD 686   GW
CCC
TITLE CHANGE
EXPORT POLYGRAPH INTERNATIONAL. [Export polygr. int.]. **VFOAT** Export Polygraph; EPI. No. 14 (1958)-(199?). Periodical. English (summaries and/or abstracts in French and Spanish). Polygraph Verlag GmbH, Schaumainkai 85, D-60596 Frankfurt Germany. **Tel** 011 49 69 6300860, FAX 011 49 69 6316302. **ED** Ulrike Schulz. Index available (free). **Bk Rev**. **Ad Acc**. **Continues** *Export-Polygraph.* **Continued by** *Polygraph International, 0943-0083.*
Desc: Export magazine for the printing industry. Links graphic arts industries on five continents, bridging the gap between suppliers and the printing industry.
Ind/Abst GATFWORLD (1979) ; Graph. Arts Bull. Inst. Pap. Sci. Technol. (Aug. 1989, Oct. 1989); Print. Abstr.

DD 760/.0971   **ISSN** 1183-9163
CN
EXTENSION (TORONTO). (EXTENSION.). [Extension]. **Added/Corp** Print and Drawing Council of Canada. Vol. 1, No. 1 (Summer 1991)-. Periodical. English. Four times a year. Print and Drawing Council of Canada, c/o Extension, Suite 503, 80 Spadina Avenue, Toronto Ontario M5V 2J3 Canada. **Continues** *Index (Print and Drawing Council of Canada), 1187-077X.*

LC NE   **ISSN** 0960-779X
DD 760   UK
EYE : THE INTERNATIONAL REVIEW OF GRAPHIC DESIGN. **VFOAT** Eye. (1990)-. Trade Publication. English (French and German). Four times a year. $86.00. EMAP Architecture, 33 39 Bowling Green Lane, London EC1R 0DA United Kingdom. **Tel** 011 44 171 8371212, FAX 011 44 171 2784003. **(Subscription address:** Eye / North America Subscriptions, Subscription Office, PO Box 830409, Birmingham AL 35283-0409. **Tel** (800)633-4931, FAX (205)995-1588.**) ED** Rick Poynor. **Bk Rev**. **Ad Acc**. **Circ:** 7,000.
Desc: An international review of graphic design which looks at the ideas that shape the industry.

DD 741   **ISSN** 1040-757X
US
FANTASY FRONTIERS. [Fantasy front.]. (1986)-. Periodical. English. Four times a year. $2.25 (per issue). Robert Tomlinson, PO Box 555, Ely NV 89301.

LC NE
DD 760   GW
FIX UND FOXI. (19??)-. German. One time a week. $100.00. **(Subscription address:** German Language Publications Inc., 153 South Dean Street, Englewood NJ 07631. **Tel** (201)871-1010, (800)457-4443.**)**

DD 741   **ISSN** 1057-2910
US
FLARE ADVENTURES. [Flare adventures]. Vol. 1 (Feb. 1992)-. Periodical. English. Twelve times a year. $6.00. Heroic Publishing Inc., 6433 California Avenue, Long Beach CA 90895.

DD 741   **ISSN** 1054-0997
US
FLARE FIRST EDITION. [Flare first ed.]. **VFOAT** Flare. Vol. 1, No. 1 (June 1991)-. Periodical. English. Six times a year. $21.00. Innovative Corp., 3622 Jacob Street, Wheeling WV 26003.

LC NC   **ISSN** 1055-3142
DD 741   US
FLASH (LOS ANGELES/WEST). (FLASH.). [Flash]. (1990)-. Periodical. English. Six times a year. Flash Report Publishers, 212 West Superior, Suite 656, Chicago IL 60610. **Tel** (312)944-5115. **Continues in part** *Chicago/Midwest Flash, 0882-1925.*

DD 741   **ISSN** 0892-7960
US
FRENCH ICE. [French ice]. Vol. 1 (1987)-. Periodical. English (translations available in French). Six times a year. $10.00. Renegade Press, 2705 E 7th Street, Long Beach CA 90804-4708. **Tel** (310)433-4874.

DD 741   **ISSN** 1059-082X
US
FURKINDRED (SEATTLE, WASH.). (FURKINDRED.). [Furkindred]. No. 1 (Mar. 199?)-. Periodical. English. Two times a year. $30.00. MU Press, 5014-D Roosevelt Way NE, Seattle WA 98105.

LC Z120.G69 A3   **ISSN** 0094-4211
DD 331.88/11/6862   US
G.A.I.U. HANDBOOK OF WAGES, HOURS AND FRINGE BENEFITS. See Business and Economics-Labor.

LC Z119 .G37   **ISSN** 1048-0293
DD 686.2/2   US
GATFWORLD (PITTSBURGH, PA.). See Printing Industry.

LC NE85 .G67   **ISSN** 0160-6298
DD 769/.12   US
GORDON'S PRINT PRICE ANNUAL. [Gordon's print price annu.]. **Added/Corp** Martin Gordon Inc. (1978)-. Directory. English. One time a year (April). $371.00. Gordons Art Reference, 1840 8th Street South, Naples FL 33940. **Tel** (914)434-6842, FAX (914)434-6969. **ED** Marty Gordon. **Bk Rev**, (Qty: 4). **Ad Acc**. **Circ:** 1,000. available on CD-ROM.
Desc: Reference for dealers of fine prints, museums, and serious collectors.

The Arts —Graphic Arts

LC NE
DD 760
IT
GRAFICA (SALERNO, ITALY). (GRAFICA.).
Added/Corp Associazione Italiana Creativi Comunicazione Visiva. No. 1 (Feb. 1985)-. Periodical. Italian. Two times a year. L34060. Edizioni 10-17, via A Sabatini 9, 84100 Salerno Italy. **Tel** 011 39 89 241336.

LC Z278 **ISSN** 0773-591X
DD 070.5
BE
GRAFISCH NIEUWS. See Publishing.

LC NE
DD 760
SW
GRAFISKT FORUM. Added/Corp Svenska Boktryckareforeningen. Vol. 40 (1935)-. Trade Publication. Swedish. Twelve times a year. Kr250.00. Grafiskt Forum, Blasieholmsgatan 4A, Box 16383, Stockholm 16 Sweden. **ED** Gunnar Svensson. Index available. **Bk Rev. Ad Acc. Circ:** 6,000 (ctrl).
Continues Svenska Boktryckareforeningens Meddelanden.
Desc: Trade magazine for the graphic arts industry in Sweden.
Ind/Abst Print. Abstr.

LC NC999 .D57
DD 741.6/025/73
US
GRAPHIC ARTISTS GUILD'S DIRECTORY OF ILLUSTRATION.
Added/Corp Graphic Artists Guild (U.S.). (1988)-. Directory. English. One time a year. $39.95. Graphic Artists Guild, 11 West 20th Street, 8th Floor, New York NY 10011-3704. **Tel** (212)463-7730, FAX (212)463-8779. **(Subscription address:** RC Publications, 3200 Tower Oaks Boulevard, Rockville MD 20852-9789. **Tel** (800)222-2654, (301)770-2900, FAX (301)984-3203.)
Continues Directory (Graphic Artists Guild (U.S.)), 0733-9216.
Desc: A collection from contemporary prominent illustrators. Covers new trends, new styles, and commercial artists. Indexed to locate subjects from nature, portraits, products, romance, science, sports, etc.

LC Z244.6.U5 P74 **ISSN** 1044-7970
DD 686.2/2616862/02574
US
GRAPHIC ARTS BLUE BOOK (DELAWARE VALLEY-OHIO ED.). See Printing Industry.

LC Z475 .P8N **ISSN** 1044-8527
DD 338.8/2616862/025747
US
GRAPHIC ARTS BLUE BOOK (METROPOLITAN NEW YORK-NEW JERSEY ED.). See Printing Industry.

LC Z475 .G76 **ISSN** 1044-8535
DD 686.2/025/77
US
GRAPHIC ARTS BLUE BOOK (MIDWESTERN ED.). See Printing Industry.

LC Z475 .P78 **ISSN** 1044-646X
DD 381/.45002025/74
US
GRAPHIC ARTS BLUE BOOK (NORTHEASTERN ED.). See Printing Industry.

LC Z475 .P79 **ISSN** 1044-7989
DD 381/.45002/02575
US
GRAPHIC ARTS BLUE BOOK (SOUTHEASTERN ED.). See Printing Industry.

LC Z475 .P8W **ISSN** 1046-8005
DD 381/.45002/02575
US
GRAPHIC ARTS BLUE BOOK (WEST COAST ED.). See Printing Industry.

LC Z119 .G869 **ISSN** 1064-9638
DD 686
US
GRAPHIC ARTS BULLETIN OF THE INSTITUTE OF PAPER SCIENCE AND TECHNOLOGY. See The Arts-Abstracting, Bibliographies and Statistics.

LC Z243.F5 G72 **ISSN** 0359-2464
FI
GRAPHIC ARTS IN FINLAND. See Printing Industry.

LC HD9980 **ISSN** 0705-7571
DD 338.4/7/68620971
CN
GRAPHIC ARTS MARKET IN CANADA (1978). See Printing Industry.

LC HD9980 **ISSN** 1047-9325
DD 655
CCC
CODEN GAMOE4
GRAPHIC ARTS MONTHLY (1987). See Printing Industry.

LC Z116 **ISSN** 0274-5976
DD 686
US
CCC
CEASED
GRAPHIC ARTS PRODUCT NEWS (CHICAGO). See Printing Industry.

LC HD9999 **ISSN** 0380-917X
DD 338.4/7/68620971
CN
GRAPHIC ARTS PURCHASE PREFERENCE STUDY. See Printing Industry.

LC NE
DD 760
US
GRAPHIC ARTS TECHNICAL FOUNDATION : GATF. Added/Corp Graphic Arts Technical Foundation. **VFOAT** GATF. (19??)-. Periodical. English. Ten times a year. $40.00 US; $50.00 other. Graphic Arts Technical Foundation, 4615 Forbes Avenue, Pittsburgh PA 15213. **Tel** (412)621-6941, FAX (412)621-3049, telex 9103509221.
Desc: The foundation's research, educational, technical services, and technical information programs embrace many graphic arts processes and applications.

LC Z244.6.U5 G7 **ISSN** 0072-5498
DD 686.2/025773
US
GRAPHIC ARTS TRADE DIRECTORY & REGISTER. See Printing Industry.

LC NC998.6.G7 G7
DD 741.6/5/0942
UK
GRAPHIC DESIGN BRITAIN. (1970)-. English. One time a year. Watson Guptill Publications, PO Box 2014, Lakewood NJ 08701. **Tel** (800)451-1741, (908)363-5679, FAX (908)363-0338. **ED** F. Lambert.

LC NC998.6.J3 G7
DD 741.6/0952
JA
SUSPENDED
GRAPHIC DESIGN IN JAPAN / JAPAN GRAPHIC DESIGNERS ASSOCIATION.
Added/Corp Japan Graphic Designers Association. Vol. 1 (1982)-Suspended Vol. 8 (1988). English. Irregular. $80.00. The Putnam Publishing Group, 390 Murray Hill Parkway East, Rutherford NJ 07073. **Tel** (800)631-8571.

LC NC998.5.A1 G67
DD 741.6/0973
US
CODEN GDUSE9
GRAPHIC DESIGN, USA. Vol. 18, No. 7 (July 1983)-. Periodical. English. Twelve times a year. $60.00. Graphic Design USA, 1556 Third Avenue, Suite 405, New York NY 10128. **Tel** (212)534-5500, FAX (212)534-4415. **ED** Gordon D. Kaye (editor's phone: (212)534-5515. Index available. **Bk Rev. Ad Acc. Circ:** 30,000 (ctrl).
Continues Graphics Design, USA.
Desc: A collection of exhibitions of selected works.

LC NC998.5.A1 A37
DD 741.6.0973/074
US
GRAPHIC DESIGN USA (NEW YORK, N.Y. : 1986). (GRAPHIC DESIGN U.S.). **Added/Corp** American Institute of Graphic Arts. **VFOAT** Annual of the American Institute of Graphic Arts. (1986)-. English. One time a year. Price varies per volume. Waston-Gruptill Publications Inc, PO Box 2014, Lakewood NJ 08701. **Tel** 800 451-1741 or, (908)363-5679. **ED** Steven Heller. **Circ:** 13,000.
Continues AIGA Graphic Design USA, 0275-9470.
Desc: Showcase of the institute's competitive exhibitions.

LC NE
DD 760
SZ
GRAPHIC DESIGNER'S INDEX. VFOAT Design Index. (19??)-. English (French and German). One time a year. Rotovision SA, Route Suisse 9, CH1295 Mies Switzerland. **Tel** 011 41 22 7553055, FAX 011 41 22 7554072, telex 419246. **(Subscription address:** Keng Seng Enterprises Inc., 4030 rue St. Ambroise, Suite 227, Montreal Quebec H4C 2C7 Canada. **Tel** (514)393-3971, FAX (514)898-1922.) **Continues** Design Index for the Corporate Manager.

LC Z116 **ISSN** 0227-2806
DD 686.2/05
CN
GRAPHIC MONTHLY, THE. See Printing Industry.

LC NE **ISSN** 1047-7004
DD 760
US
GRAPHICS DESIGN JOURNAL, THE. (1990)-. Periodical. English. Four times a year. $32.00. Owens-Laing Publications Ltd, 903-5th Avenue, No 102, Kirkland WA 98033.

ISSN 0821-5588
DD 741.5/971/05
CN
GRAPHICS EXCHANGE. (GRAPHICS EXCHANGE / CANADIAN UNIVERSITY PRESS.). [Graph. exch.]. **Added/Corp** Canadian University Press. No. 1 (Sept. 3, 1982)-. Periodical. English. Eight times a year. 26.80Can$. Graphic Exchange, 65090 358 Danforth Avenue, Toronto, Ontario, M4K 3Z2 Canada. **Tel** (416)961-0941.

LC NE **ISSN** 1350-0937
DD 760
UK
●**GRAPHICS INTERNATIONAL.** Issue 16 (Aug./Sept. 1993)-. Trade Publication. English. Six times a year. $84.70. Creative Magazines Ltd., 35 Britannia Row, London N1 8QH United Kingdom. **Tel** 011 44 171 2261739, FAX 011 44 171 2261540. **Continues** Hot Graphics International, 0962-7308.

LC NE
DD 760
US
GRAPHICS MASTER. (1974)-. English. Irregular (every three or four years). $74.50 professional edition; $54.50 student edition. Dean Lem Associates Inc., PO Box 959, Kihei HI 96753-0959. **Tel** (808)874-5461, (800)562-2562, FAX (808)875-1404. **ED** Carol Lem. Index available.
Desc: Technical manual and reference guide for prepress graphic arts production.

LC Z119 .G914
DD 760/.05
IT
GRAPHICS WORLD. See Printing Industry.

ISSN 0142-8853
DD 741.6
UK
GRAPHICS WORLD. [Graph. world]. No. 1 (Jan. 1977)-. Trade Publication. English. Six times a year. $89.84. Datateam Publishing Ltd., Datateam House Tovil Hill, Maidstone Kent ME15 6QS United Kingdom. **Tel** 011 44 1622 687031, FAX 011 44 1622 757646.

LC N8 .G73 **ISSN** 0017-3452
DD 705
SZ
GRAPHIS. [Graphis]. **Added/Corp** Verband Schweizerischer Graphiker. Vol. 1, No. 1/2 (Sept./Oct. 1944)-. Periodical. English (German and French). Six times a year. $89.00. Graphis Press Corporation NY, 141 Lexington Avenue, New York NY 10016. **Tel** (212)532-9387. **ED** H B Martin Pedersen. Index available. cum. index. **Bk Rev. Ad Acc. Circ:** 16,500 (ctrl). Copies available from The Genuine Article, UMI Article Clearinghouse.
Desc: Offers a rich array of information about the international graphic design scene on some 100 pages carrying about 300 illustrations.
Ind/Abst Acad. Ind. [Computer File] (1992-); Art Index; ARTbibliogr. Mod.; Arts Humanit. Citation Index [Full Cov.]; BHA : Biblio. Hist. Art; Curr. Contents Arts Humanit.; Expand. Acad. Index (1992-); Film Lit. Index; GATFWORLD (1979); Newsp. Period. Abstr. (1992-); Res. Alert [Full Cov.]; Trade Ind. Index.

LC HF5719 .G72
SZ
GRAPHIS ANNUAL REPORTS. VFOAT International Yearbook of Annual Reports. Vol. 1 (1988)-. Trade Publication. English (German and French). One time a year. $75.00. Graphis Press Corporation / Zurich, Dufourstrasse 107, CH-8008 Zurich Switzerland. **Tel** 011 41 1 3838211, FAX 011 41 1 3831643, telex 845/57222.

LC NC997
DD 741.6
SZ
GRAPHIS DESIGN. (1989)-. English (French and German). One time a year. $69.00. Graphis Press Corporation / Zurich, Dufourstrasse 107, CH-8008 Zurich Switzerland. **Tel** 011 41 1 3838211, FAX 011 41 1 3831643, telex 845/57222. **Continues** Graphis Design Annual.

LC NC997
DD 741.6
SZ
GRAPHIS DIAGRAM. Vol. 1 (1988)-. English (French and German). Graphis Press Corporation / Zurich, Dufourstrasse 107, CH-8008 Zurich Switzerland. **Tel** 011 41 1 3838211, FAX 011 41 1 3831643, telex 845/57222.

LC NC1002.L47 G7
DD 741.6
SZ
GRAPHIS LETTERHEAD. (1991)-. Trade Publication. English (French and German). Every 2 years. $69.00. Graphis Press Corporation NY, 141 Lexington Avenue, New York NY 10016. **Tel** (212)532-9387.

LC NC1002.L63 G7
DD 741.6
SZ
GRAPHIS LOGO. (1991)-. Trade Publication. English (French and German). Every 2 years. $50.00 Logo 1; $60.00 Logo 2. Graphis Press Corporation NY, 141 Lexington Avenue, New York NY 10016. **Tel** (212)532-9387.

LC HF5828 .P27
DD 741.6
SZ
GRAPHIS PACKAGING. (19??)-. Periodical. English (French and German). Irregular (Publishes every 4 to 5 years). $75.00 (latest volume). Graphis Press Corporation NY, 141 Lexington Avenue, New York NY 10016. **Tel** (212)532-9387. **(Subscription address:** Watson Guptill Publications, PO Box 2014, Lakewood NJ 08101.) **Continues** Packaging.

LC NC1800 .G7
DD 769/.5
SZ
GRAPHIS POSTERS. VFOAT Graphis Poster. (1973)-. Multiple languages (English, French and German). One time a year. $69.95. Graphis Press

Corporation / Zurich, Dufourstrasse 107, CH-8008 Zurich Switzerland. **Tel** 011 41 1 3838211, FAX 011 41 1 3831643, telex 845/57222. **(Subscription address:** Watson Guptill Publications, PO Box 2014, Lakewood NJ 08101. **) ED** B. Martin Pedersen (editor's address: 141 Lexington Avenue, New York, NY 10016, phone: (212)532-9387). **Circ:** 12,000.

LC NE1 .G73
DD 760/.5 GW
GRAPHISCHE KUNST. (1973)-. German. Two times a year (Apr., Nov.). $47.60. Edition Curt Visel, Weberstrasse 36, Postfach 1636, W-8940 Memmingen Germany. **Tel** 011 49 8331 2853, FAX 011 49 8331 490364. **ED** Curt Visel. cum. index. **Bk Rev**. **Circ:** 1,000 (ctrl).
Desc: Graphic art and artists in the 20th Century, especially in the classical disciplines such as woodcut, etching, lithography and drawing.
Ind/Abst ARTbibliogr. Mod. (1984-).

LC NE **ISSN** 0314-6685
DD 760 AT
GRAPHIX PRAHRAN. [Graphix Prahran]. (1975)-. Periodical. English. Eleven times a year. 41.11Aus$. Peter Isaacson Publications, 46-50 Porter Street, Prahran Victoria, 3181 Australia. **Tel** 011 61 3 2457777, FAX 011 61 3 2457606. ***Continues*** *Graphic Arts (Prahran), 0310-5792.*

LC Z1008 .G98 **ISSN** 0072-9094
GW
GUTENBERG-JAHRBUCH. See Printing Industry.

ISSN 1188-3693
DD 769.56/3/097105 CN
HERITAGE POST. [Herit. post]. **Added/Corp** CRB Foundation. Canada Post Corporation. **VFOAT** Courrier du Patrimoine. (1990)-. Periodical. English (French). Free on request. National Philatelic Centre, Canada Postal Corporation, Station 1, Antigonish Nova Scotia B2G 2R8 Canada. **Tel** (902)863-6550, (800)565-4362, FAX (902)863-6796.

LC HD9999
DD 338.4768 GW
HIGH QUALITY : HQ. See Printing Industry.

LC NE3000 .I17 **ISSN** 0741-2940
DD 760 US
I.S.C.A. QUARTERLY, THE. Added/Corp International Society of Copier Artists. **VFOAT** ISCA Quarterly. **VAT** International Society of Copier Artists Quarterly. (19??)-. Periodical. English. Four times a year (Apr., June, Sept., Dec.). $90.00. The International Society of Copier Artists, 800 West End Avenue, New York NY 10025. **Tel** (212)662-5533. **ED** Louise Neaderland. **Bk Rev**, (Qty: 2-3). **Circ:** 150 (ctrl).
Desc: The original xerographic prints and artists bookworks contributed by the artist members.

LC NC997.A1 A34 **ISSN** 0019-1299
JA
IDEA. VFOAT Idea. (1953)-. Periodical. Japanese (summaries and/or abstracts in English). Six times a year. $349.58. Seibundo Shinkosha Publishing Company, 1-5-5 Kanda Nishikicho, Chiyoda-ku Tokyo 101 Japan. **Tel** 011 81 3 3292 1221, FAX 011 81 3 3292 1220. **(Subscription address:** Nippon IPS Co. Ltd., 11 6 3 Chome Iidabashi, Chiyodaku Tokyo 102 Japan. **) ED** Seibundo Shinkosha. **Bk Rev**. **Ad Acc**. **Circ:** 30,000.
Desc: Art direction, print ads, photography, illustration, typography, packaging, posters exhibit design, etc.
Ind/Abst ARTbibliogr. Mod.

ISSN 0899-3483
DD 741 US
CCC
IDENTITY (CINCINNATI, OHIO). (IDENTITY.). [Identity]. Vol. 1, No. 1 (Summer 1988)-. Periodical. English. Six times a year. $24.00. Signs of the Times Publishing Company, 407 Gilbert Avenue, Cincinnati OH 45202. **Tel** (513)421-2050, (800)925-1110, FAX (513)421-5144. **ED** Bill Dorsey. **Ad Acc**. **Circ:** 10,500 (ctrl).
Desc: Focuses on signage and corporate graphics programs from the perspective of developers, architects, franchisers, retailers, graphics designers and major sign buyers.

LC NC960 .I42 **ISSN** 0019-2457
GW
ILLUSTRATION 63. I.E. DREIUNDSECHZIG. (April 1964)-. Periodical. German. Three times a year (Apr., July, Nov.). $141.24. Edition Curt Visel, Weberstrasse 36, Postfach 1636, W-8940 Memmingen Germany. **Tel** 011 49 8331 2853, FAX 011 49 8331 490364. **ED** Curt Visel. Index available. cum. index. **Bk Rev**. **Circ:** 700 (ctrl).
Desc: Exclusively dedicated to book illustration, especially of the 20th Century. Each issue contains four original graphics as separates.
Ind/Abst ARTbibliogr. Mod.

LC NC991 .I4
DD 741.6/0952 JA
ILLUSTRATION IN JAPAN (TOKYO, JAPAN). (ILLUSTRATION IN JAPAN.). **Added/Corp** Kodansha Intanashonaru Kabushiki Kaisha. Vol. 1 (1981)-. English (Japanese). One time a year. $52.00. Kodansha International, 114 5th Avenue, New York NY 10011. **Tel** (212)727-6460.

LC NE
DD 760 US
ILLUSTRATION INDEX. (1957)-. Monographic series. English. Irregular. Price varies per volume. VOYA Scarecrow, 4720 Boston Way, Lanham MD 20706. **Tel** (800)462-6420 ext. 7132.

LC NC997.A1 I62a **ISSN** 0019-2465
DD 741.6/05 US
ILLUSTRATOR, THE. [Illustrator]. **Added/Corp** Art Instruction Schools (Minneapolis, Minn.). (1978)-. English. Two times a year (Apr., Oct.). $8.00. Art Instruction Schools, 500 South 4th Street, Minneapolis MN 55415. **Tel** (612)339-6656. **ED** Don L. Jardine. **Bk Rev**. **Ad Acc**. **Circ:** 35,000 (ctrl). ***Continues*** *Illustrator (Minneapolis, Minn. : 1942).*
Desc: Covers all areas of art including drawing, painting, design, lettering and cartooning. Features America's top artists. Every issue is in full-color.

LC NC976.B6 I58
DD 741.6/0981 BL
ILUSTRADORES DO BRASIL. (1982)-. Portuguese. One time a year. Conceito Editora Technica Ltd, Avenue Nova Cantareira 229-S/16-A, CEP 02331 Sao Paulo SP Brazil.

ISSN 1046-6614
DD 769 US
IMAGE FILE. [Image file]. **Added/Corp** Curt Teich Postcard Collection (Lake County Museum). (1989)-. Periodical. English. Four times a year. $30.00 institutions; $20.00 individuals. Curt Teich Postcard Archives- Lake County Museum, 27277 Forest Preserve Drive, Wauconda IL 60084. **Tel** (708)526-8638, FAX (708)526-1545. **ED** Christine Pyle. Index available. cum. index. **Bk Rev**, (Qty: 2). **Circ:** 1,300 (ctrl). ***Continues*** *Postcard Journal, 0743-7617.*

ISSN 0313-3907
DD 760.5 AT
IMPRINT. [Imprint]. (1966)-. Periodical. English. Four times a year. Comes with membership. Print Council of Australia, 1st Floor 459 Swanston St., Melbourne Victoria, 3000 Australia. **Tel** 011 61 3 6392463. **ED** Di Waite. **Bk Rev**. **Ad Acc**. **Circ:** 1,000.

LC NE505 .I48 **ISSN** 0277-7061
DD 769.973 US
IMPRINT (NEW YORK, N.Y. : 1976). (IMPRINT : JOURNAL OF THE AMERICAN HISTORICAL PRINT COLLECTORS SOCIETY.). [Imprint]. **Added/Corp** American Historical Print Collectors Society. Vol. 1, No. 1 (Feb. 1976)-. English. Two times a year. American Historical Print Collectors Society, 915 Sherwood Drive, Lake Bluff IL 60044. **ED** Rona Schneider. **Bk Rev**. **Circ:** 475 (ctrl).
Desc: Devoted solely to scholarly and popular articles on American Graphic Arts prior to 1900. Includes original prints used for book illustrations as topics for articles.
Ind/Abst Am. Hist. Life (1984-); BHA : Biblio. Hist. Art.

LC Z116 **ISSN** 0883-6973
DD 686 US
CCC
IN HOUSE GRAPHICS. See Printing Industry.

LC NC1300 .I586 **ISSN** 1054-8548
DD 741 US
IN TOON. [In toon]. **VFOAT** In Tune. (19??)-. Periodical. English. Four times a year. $18.00. In Toon, PO Box 487, White Plains NY 10603. **Tel** (914)993-6218, FAX (914)993-6218. **ED** Bruce Sheinhaus. **Bk Rev**. **Ad Acc**. **Circ:** 5,000.
Desc: Devoted to the collecting of animation art. Contains interviews, previews of new art, retrospectives, and more.

LC PN6700 **ISSN** 1071-9156
DD 741.5 US
•**INKS (COLUMBUS, OHIO).** (INKS : CARTOON AND COMIC ART STUDIES.). (1994)-. Periodical. English. Three times a year (Feb., May, Nov.). $40.00. Ohio State University Press, 1070 Carmack Road, Columbus OH 43210. **Tel** (614)292-6930, (614)292-1407, FAX (614)292-2065. **ED** Lucy Shelton Caswell (Cartoon, Graphic and Photographic Arts Research Library, Ohio State University).
Desc: Covers cartoons, their development, the role they have played in society, the values and opinions they represent, and the techniques and artistry they embody.

LC NE **ISSN** 1074-9349
DD 760 US
•**INTERNATIONAL DESIGN REVIEW.** (INTERNATIONAL DESIGN REVIEW [COMPUTER FILE].). (1994)-. English. Two times a year. $155.00. Penrose Press, PO Box 470925, San Francisco CA 94147. **Tel** (415)567-4157.

LC N1 .N8784 **ISSN** 0960-8648
UK
ISSUES IN ARCHITECTURE ART AND DESIGN. See Architecture.

LC NE
DD 760 JA
JAPAN GRAPHIC ARTS. See Printing Industry.

ISSN 1055-4815
DD 741 US
JASON AND THE ARGONAUTS. Vol. 1, No. 1 (1991)-. Periodical. English. Twelve times a year. $2.50 (single issue, U.S.), $3.25 (single issue, Canada). Tome Press, G21B South Main Street, Plymouth MI 48170.

LC NE
DD 760 UK
•**JOURNAL OF DESIGN AND TECHNOLOGY EDUCATION.** (1995)-. English. Three times a year. $59.89. Trentham Books Limited, Westview House, 734 London Road, Oakhill Stoke on Trent, Staffordshire ST4 5NP United Kingdom. **Tel** 011 44 1782 745567, FAX 011 44 1782 745553. ***Continues*** *Design and Technology Teaching;* ***Absorbed*** *Primary Data.*

LC NE **ISSN** 1062-7979
DD 760 US
•**JOURNAL OF GRAPHOLOGICAL ARTS & SCIENCES. Added/Corp** American Academy of Graphological Arts & Sciences. **VFOAT** Journal of Graphological Arts and Sciences. (1993)-. Periodical. English. $7.50 US; $8.50 other. American Academy of Graphological Arts, PO Box 55697, Sherman Oaks CA 91413.

ISSN 0820-8832
DD 741.5/971 CN
JOURNEY (KITCHENER). (JOURNEY.). [Journey]. Vol. No. 1 (March 1983)-. Periodical. English. Six times a year. $1.60 per no. US and Canada. Aardvark-Vanaheim, PO Box 1674, Station C, Kitchener Ontario N2G 4R2.

LC NE **ISSN** 0741-1766
DD 760 US
KAITE, EL. (EL KAITE : A BI-MONTHLY NEWSLETTER OF CONCILIO DE ARTE POPULAR.). (March/Apr. 1983)-. Newsletter. English (English). Six times a year. $10.00. Self-Help Graphics & Art Inc, 3802 Brooklyn Avenue, Los Angeles CA 90063.

ISSN 1057-2929
DD 741 US
LADY ARCANE. [Lady arcane]. (1992)-. Periodical. English. Four times a year. $12.00. Heroic Publishing Inc., 6433 California Avenue, Long Beach CA 90895.

LC Z244.6.L35 L37
SP
LATINGRAFICA. See Printing Industry.

ISSN 1059-3187
DD 769 US
CEASED
LAWRENCE'S DEALER PRINT PRICES. [Lawrence's deal. print prices]. **VFOAT** Dealer Print Prices. (1992)-(1994). Periodical. English. Gordons Art Reference, 1840 8th Street South, Naples FL 33940. **Tel** (914)434-6842, FAX (914)434-6969.

LC NE85 .L46 **ISSN** 1064-0452
DD 760/.075 US
LEONARD'S ANNUAL PRICE INDEX OF PRINTS, POSTERS & PHOTOGRAPHS. See Photography.

ISSN 0712-6700
DD 760/.6/0714 CN
L'ESTAMPE, DE. (DE L'ESTAMPE : BULLETIN D'INFORMATION DU CONSEIL DE LA GRAVURE DU QUEBEC.). **Added/Corp** Conseil de la Gravure du Quebec. Vol. 1, No. 1 (April 1982)-. Bulletin. French. One time a year. 50.00Can$ (membership, Conseil Quebecois de l'Estampe). Conseil Quebecois de l'Estampe, 811 rue Ontario Est, Montreal Quebec H2L 1P1 Canada. **Tel** (514)525-2621.

LC PN6700 .L53
DD 741.5/05 CC
LIEN HUAN HUA LUN TSUNG = LIAN HUAN HUA LUN CONG. VFOAT Lian Huan Hua Lun Cong. (1980)-. Periodical. Chinese. Four times a year. RMBY0.42. Hsin Hua Shu Tien Pei-Ching Fa Hsing So, Beijing, People's Repulic of China. **Tel** 55.5260. **ED** Yu Ming-chuang. **Circ:** 2,000.
Desc: Covers Chinese classic and modern arts, painting, sculpture, architecture, industrial art, folk art, calligraphy, seal engraving, photography and art theories, etc.

LC Z257 .L56 **ISSN** 0024-3744
DD 769.5 IT
LINEAGRAFICA. VFOAT Linea Grafica. (198?)-. Periodical. Italian (English). Six times a year. L78350. Azzurra Editrice SRL, Via Della Moscova 49, 20121 Milan Italy. **Tel** 011 39 2 29010364, FAX 011 39 2 29002192.

Bk Rev. **Ad Acc**, **Adv Mgr:** Brivio Givsi. ctrl circ. ***Continues*** *Nuova Linea Grafica.*
Desc: Cultural and technical themes on graphics, computer graphics, printing, photography, packaging.

LC Z119 .M35 **ISSN** 0479-480X
HU

MAGYAR GRAFIKA. **See** Printing Industry.

LC DS820.8 .M36 **ISSN** 1051-8177
DD 952/.005 US

MANGAJIN (ATLANTA, GA.). (MANGAJIN.). [Mangajin]. Vol. 1, No. 1 (June 1990)-. Periodical. English. Ten times a year (every 5 weeks). $39.95. Mangajin, Inc, PO Box 7119, Marietta GA 30065. **Tel** (404)590-0091. **ED** Vaughan Simmons (editor's address: 200 N. Cobb Parkway, Ste. 421, Marietta, GA. 30062; phone (404)590-0092). **Bk Rev**, (Qty: 2). **Ad Acc**, **Adv Mgr:** Greg Tenhover, **Tel** (404)590-0270. **Circ:** 30,000.
Desc: Teaches by illustration and translation the Japanese language and culture.

LC NC1 .M3 **ISSN** 0025-5025
DD 741 US

MASTER DRAWINGS. [Master draw.]. Vol. 1 (Spring 1963)-. Periodical. English. Four times a year. $45.00 US; $50.00 other. Master Drawings Association Inc, 29 East 36th Street, New York NY 10016. **Tel** (212)685-0008, FAX (212)685-4740. **ED** Anne Marie Logayi. Index available. cum. index. **Bk Rev**. **Ad Acc**. **Circ:** 1,250. Documents available from The Genuine Article.
Desc: Compilation of old master drawings with written discussion.
Ind/Abst Archit. Period. Index; Art Archaeol. Tech. Abstr.; Art Index; ARTbibliogr. Mod. (1984-); Arts Humanit. Citation Index [Full Cov.]; BHA : Biblio. Hist. Art; Curr. Contents Arts Humanit.; Res. Alert [Full Cov.]; Romant. Move.

LC NE30 .A54 **ISSN** 1067-8980
DD 769/.49973 US

MEMBER DIRECTORY - AMERICAN HISTORICAL PRINT COLLECTORS SOCIETY. (MEMBER DIRECTORY / AMERICAN HISTORICAL PRINT COLLECTORS SOCIETY, INC.). [Memb. dir. - Am. Hist. Print Collect. Soc.]. **Main/Corp** American Historical Print Collectors Society. (1990/1991)-. Directory. English. American Historical Print Collectors Society, 915 Sherwood Drive, Lake Bluff IL 60044. ***Continues*** *American Historical Print Collectors Society. Membership Directory, 1049-1716.*

LC NE **ISSN** 0737-6928
DD 760 US

MIKE BRUNO'S WHAT'S NEW(S) IN GRAPHIC COMMUNICATIONS. [Mike Bruno's what's news graph. commun.]. **VFOAT** What's New(s) in Graphic Communications. (19??)-. Periodical. English. Six times a year. $50.00. Michael H. Bruno, 6281 Timberlake Drive, H-6, Sarasota FL 34243. **Tel** (813)751-4838.
Ind/Abst Abstr. Bull. Inst. Pap. Sci. Tech.; Print. Abstr.

ISSN 1062-838X
DD 741 US

MURKY AT BEST. [Murky best]. Vol. 1, No. 1 (May/June 1992)-. Periodical. English. Six times a year. Bamburak Designs Publications, PO Box 22, Bound Brook NJ 08805-0022.

LC TT867 .N38 **ISSN** 0747-5527
DD 760 US

NATIONAL STAMPAGRAPHIC. Issue 1 (Oct. 1982)-. Periodical. English. Four times a year (Jan., Apr., July, Oct.). $18.00. National Stampagraphic, 1952 Everett Street, North Valley Stream NY 11580. **Tel** (516)285-5587, FAX (516)285-0742. **ED** Melody Hope and Franklin Stein. Index available. cum. index. **Bk Rev**, (Qty: 2-3). **Ad Acc**. **Circ:** 5,000.
Desc: Devoted to art rubberstampers and filled with reviews of products, publications and videos, profiles of stamp artists, exchanges and contests.

LC NC991 .A66
JA

NENKAN NIHON NO IRASUTORESHON. **Added/Corp** Daiichi Shuppan SentÂa. **VFOAT** Illustration in Japan. (1972)-. Japanese. One time a year. ¥12,000. Kodansha Ltd / Japan, 12-21 Otowa 2-chome, 112 Bunkyo-ku, Tokyo Japan. **Tel** 03 5395 3517, FAX 03 9466200, telex 22570. **Bk Rev**. **Ad Acc**. ***Continues*** *Annual of Illustration.*
Desc: Gathers examples of illustration in Japan, and is an up-to date volume available on Japanese illustrative style.

ISSN 0913-3429
DD 741.6 JA

NIKKEI DEZAIN. [Nikkei dezain]. **VFOAT** Nikkei Design. (1987)-. Periodical. Japanese. Twelve times a year. $342.00. Nihon Keizai Shimbun Inc., 9-5 Otemachi 1 Chome, Chiyoda-ku Tokyo 100 Japan. **Tel** 011 81 3 32700251, 011 81 3 52108502 (Nikkei Business Publications Inc.), FAX 011 81 3 52552661, 011 81 3 52108119 (Nikkei Business Publications Inc.). **(Subscription address:** OCS / Overseas Courier Service of America Inc., 5 East 44th Street, New York NY 10017. **Tel** (212)599-4517.**)** **ED** Akiko Moriyama.

FR

NINETY. No. 1 (1990)-. Periodical. French (English). Five times a year. 650.00F. Ninety, 28 Avenue Jean Jaures, 94220 Charenton France. **ED** Catherine Flohic. **Bk Rev**. **Circ:** 1,000. ***Continues*** *Eighty.*
Desc: Monography of two contemporary painters in each publication.
Ind/Abst BHA : Biblio. Hist. Art.

LC NE **ISSN** 0029-4926
DD 760 BE

NOUVELLES GRAPHIQUES. [Nouv. graph.]. (1950)-. Trade Publication. Dutch (French). Twenty-two times a year. $73.93. Keesing Uitgevers, Keesinglaan 2 20, 2100 Antwerp Deurne, Belgium. **Tel** 011 32 3 3243890, FAX 011 32 3 324 3898, telex 32507. **ED** Alain Vermeire, Vitgevery Keesing. **Ad Acc**. **Circ:** 7,000.
Desc: News and evolutions in the graphic industry.
Ind/Abst Print. Abstr.

LC NC997.A1 G4 **ISSN** 0302-9794
DD 741.6/05 GW
CCC

NOVUM GEBRAUCHSGRAPHIK. [Nov. Gebrauchsgraph.]. **VFOAT** Novum. (1972)-. Periodical. English (French, German and Spanish). Twelve times a year. $139.00. F. Bruckmann KG, Postfach 200353, D-80003 Munich Germany. **Tel** 011 49 89 125701, FAX 011 49 89 1257269, telex 5-23739 BRUKG D. **(Subscription address:** Novum Gebrauchsgraphik / North American Subscriptions, Subscription Office, PO Box 830409, Birmingham AL 35283-0409. **Tel** (800)633-4931, (205)995-1567, FAX (205)995-1588.**)** **ED** Brigitta Nitsch. Index available. **Bk Rev**. **Ad Acc**. **Circ:** 12,000 (ctrl). ***Continues*** *Gebrauchsgraphik, 0016-5743.*
Desc: International journal for communications design for advertising and marketing experts, commercial artists, designers, photographers, and managers.
Ind/Abst Art Index; ARTbibliogr. Mod.; BHA : Biblio. Hist. Art.

LC NE885 .O36 **ISSN** 0747-8178
DD 769/.12 US

OFFICIAL PRICE GUIDE TO COLLECTOR PRINTS, THE. **See** Hobbies.

LC NC975 .O45 **ISSN** 0736-9824
DD 741.6/025/771 US

OHIO REGIONAL ART DIRECTORY, THE. 1983-. Directory. English. One time a year. Ohio Regional Art Directory, 1861 West 25th, Cleveland OH 44113.

LC NC999 .O45 **ISSN** 1067-5957
DD 741.6/025/771 US

OHIO'S OFFICIAL SOURCEBOOK. (OHIO'S OFFICIAL SOURCEBOOK : THE COMPLETE ADVERTISING AND GRAPHIC REFERENCE BOOK.). [Ohio's off. sourceb.]. **VFOAT** Official Sourcebook; Ohio's Sourcebook. No. 2 (1992)-. English. $45.00. Black Book Marketing Group, 10 Astor Place, 6th Floor, New York NY 10003. **Tel** (212)539-9800, FAX (212)539-9801. ***Continues*** *Ohio Sourcebook, 1054-2361.*

LC NE1 .O63 **ISSN** 0891-7604
DD 760.5 US

OLD PRINT SHOP PORTFOLIO, THE. [Old Print Shop portf.]. **Main/Corp** Old Print Shop (New York, N.Y.). **VFOAT** Old Print Shop Portfolio. Vol. 1 (Sept. 1941)-. Periodical. English. Twelve times a year. Old Print Shop, 150 Lexington Avenue at 30th Street, New York NY 10016.

ISSN 1061-4060
DD 760 US

OLSON'S BOOK OF LIBRARY CLIP ART. [Olson's book libr. clip art]. **Added/Corp** Chris Olson & Associates. **VFOAT** Book of Library Clip Art. (1992)-. Periodical. English. $45.00 US; $49.50 other. Chris Olson & Associates, 857 Twin Harbor Drive, Arnold MD 21012. **Tel** (410)647-6708, FAX (410)647-0415. available on diskette.

LC NE **ISSN** 0147-4693
DD 760 US

ON THE LINE MAGAZINE. **VFOAT** On the Line. Vol. 1 (Winter 1977)-. Periodical. English. Four times a year. $8.00. K A Murray, 152 East 22nd Street, New York NY 10010.

LC NE1183.A1 P35
DD 769.951 CC

PAN HUA I SHU = BAN HUA YI SHU. **VFOAT** Ban Hua Yi Shu. (19??)-. Periodical. Chinese. Hsin Hua Shu Tien / Shang-Hai Fa Hsing So, Shanghai, People's Republic of China.

ISSN 0828-9247
DD 791.43/3 CN

PEGBAR. **Added/Corp** Vancouver Society of Independent Animators. No. 1 (1984)-. Periodical. English. Irregular. $20.00. Vancouver Society of Independent Animators, PO Box 3014, Vancouver British Columbia V6B 3X5 Canada. **Tel** (604)681-7261. **ED** Linda Wilson. **Bk Rev**. **Ad Acc**. **Circ:** 2,000.
Desc: Animation art magazine featuring articles, original art, hand painted-silk screen covers.

LC Z119 **ISSN** 0943-0083
DD 686 GW

POLYGRAPH INTERNATIONAL (1992). (POLYGRAPH INTERNATIONAL.). [Polygr. int.]. (1992)-. Periodical. English (summaries and/or abstracts in French and Spanish). Six times a year (Jan., Mar., May, Jul., Sept., Nov.). DM102.00. Polygraph Verlag GmbH, Schaumainkai 85, D-60596 Frankfurt Germany. **Tel** 011 49 69 6300860, FAX 011 49 69 6313502. ***Continues*** *Export Polygraph International, 0344-2039.*

ISSN 0897-4020
DD 769 US

POSTCARD CLASSICS. [Postc. class.]. **Added/Corp** Deltiologists of America. No. 1 (Jan./Feb. 1988)-. Periodical. English. Six times a year. $10.00 one-year; $28.00 three-year, (Korean Postcard Collector's Newsletter; $15.00 US; $28.00 other, for Deltiologists of America. Deltiologists of America, PO Box 8, Norwood PA 19074. **Tel** (610)485-8572. **ED** James Lewis Lowe. **Bk Rev**, (Qty: 2). **Ad Acc**. **Circ:** 1,200 or 200 (Korean). ***Continues*** *Deltiology.*
Desc: Newsletter featuring interesting articles about postcards and postcard collecting, check lists of important sets and series, adverts by collectors and dealers who have cards wanted or for sale, a list of postcard sources, regular mail auction sales for buying and selling cards, information about local postcard clubs, details about the latest reference books published by the society and more.

LC Z116 **ISSN** 8750-2224
DD 686 US

PREPRESS BULLETIN, THE. **See** Printing Industry.

LC NE
DD 760 US

PRINT : AMERICA'S REGIONAL DESIGN ANNUAL. (19??)-. English. One time a year. $35.00. RC Publications Inc., 3200 Tower Oaks Boulevard, Rockville MD 20852. **Tel** (800)222-2654, (301)770-2900, FAX (301)984-3203.

LC NE **ISSN** 0273-9550
DD 760 US

PRINT & GRAPHICS. **See** Printing Industry.

LC NE1 .P69 **ISSN** 0032-8537
DD 769/.075 US

PRINT COLLECTOR'S NEWSLETTER, THE. [Print collect. newsl.]. Vol. 1 (Mar./Apr. 1970)-. Newsletter. English. Six times a year. $60.00. Print Collectors Newsletter, 119 East 79th Street, New York NY 10021. **Tel** (212)988-5959, FAX (212)988-6107. **ED** Jacqueline Brody. Index available. cum. index. **Bk Rev**, (Qty: 20). **Ad Acc**, **Adv Mgr:** F. Hirsch. **Circ:** 5,000.
Desc: Newsletter covering prints and photographs in scholarly articles, interviews, book reviews, news and notes. Includes reviews of recent prints published and listings of recent auction prices.
Ind/Abst Art Index; ARTbibliogr. Mod. (1984-); ARTbibliogr. Curr. Titles; Avery Index Archit. Period. Suppl. Colum. Univ. (19??-199?); BHA : Biblio. Hist. Art.

LC NE **ISSN** 0048-5314
DD 760 US

PRINT-EQUIP NEWS. (PRINT EQUIP NEWS.). (19??)-. Trade Publication. English. Twelve times a year. $24.00. PEN Publications Inc, 215 Allen Avenue, PO Box 5540, Glendale CA 91221-5540. **Tel** (818)954-9495, FAX (818)954-0452. **ED** Paul B. Kissel. **Ad Acc**, **Adv Mgr:** Jeff Jotras, **Tel** (818)954-9495. **Circ:** 25,000 (ctrl).
Desc: Published for management, supervisory personnel and buyers of graphic arts equipment, supplies and services.

LC Z119 .P8985 **ISSN** 0032-8510
DD 070.5/068 US

PRINT (NEW YORK). (PRINT : AMERICA'S GRAPHIC DESIGN MAGAZINE.). [Print]. Vol. 1, No. 1 (June 1940)-. Trade Publication. English. Six times a year (includes Print : America's Regional Design Annual). $57.00. RC Publications Inc., 3200 Tower Oaks Boulevard, Rockville MD 20852. **Tel** (800)222-2654, (301)770-2900, FAX (301)984-3203. **ED** Martin Fox. **Bk Rev**. **Ad Acc**. **Circ:** 50,000. available on microfilm and microfiche from University Microfilms International (UMI). Documents available from UMI Article Clearinghouse. ***Absorbed*** *Printing Art; Print Collectors' Quarterly.*
Desc: Graphic design reporting on new techniques, trends and the people who make up the visual communication industry. Directed to design professionals - shows what is happening in advertising, graphic design, corporate identity, television, film, computer-aided design, illustration and photography, typographic design, annual reports, magazine design, packaging, and environmental graphics.
Ind/Abst Acad. Search; Art Index; ARTbibliogr. Mod.; BHA : Biblio. Hist. Art; Curr. Cit.; EP Collect.; Expand. Acad. Index (1992-); Film Lit. Index; Graph. Arts Bull. Inst. Pap. Sci. Technol. (April 1989, June 1989, Sept. 1989); Homework Help.; Mag. Search; MasterFile FullTEXT

1000; MasterFile FullTEXT 350; MasterFile FullTEXT 650; MasterFile FullTEXT (July 1993-); Newsp. Period. Abstr. (1992-); OCLC; Print. Abstr.; Telebase.

LC NE65 .P75 **ISSN** 1058-2339
DD 769/.12 US
PRINT PRICE INDEX. [Print price index]. **VFOAT** PPI. (1992)-. English. $149.00. Sound View Press, 170 Boston Post Road, Madison CT 06443. **Tel** (203)458-3544, (203)245-2246.

LC Z475 .P677 **ISSN** 0741-1979
DD 070.5/025/73 US
PRINTING AND GRAPHIC ARTS BUYERS : PGAB. **See** Printing Industry.

LC NE491 .P77 **ISSN** 0734-2721
DD 769.92/2 US
PRINTWORLD DIRECTORY OF CONTEMPORARY PRINTS AND PRICES. [Printworld dir. contemp. prints prices]. **VFOAT** Printworld Directory. 1st Ed. (1982)-. Directory. English. Every 2 years. $259.95. Printworld International Inc., PO Box 1957, West Chester PA 19380. **Tel** (800)788-9101, (610)431-6654. **ED** Selma L Smith. **Ad Acc. Circ:** 20,000 (ctrl).
Desc: Complete reference research manual of limited edition fine art, prints with full documentation photos, prices, comprehensive artists, biography publisher galleries, institutional, corporate, and private collectors.

LC NE
DD 760 US
•**PRO TOONER.** (March 1995)-. Trade Publication. English. Twelve times a year (monthly). $50.00. Pro Tooner, PO Box 2270, Daly City CA 94017-2270. **ED** Joyce-Ann Miller. **Ad Acc. Circ:** 200. Documents available from Magazine Collection.
Desc: A trade journal for professional cartoonists and gagwriters.

ISSN 0082-2299
DD 760 US
CODEN TAPRAV
Pr Rev.
PROCEEDINGS - TAGA. (PROCEEDINGS - TECHNICAL ASSOCIATION OF THE GRAPHIC ARTS.). [Proc. - TAGA]. **Main/Corp** Technical Association of the Graphic Arts. **Added/Corp** Technical Association of the Graphic Arts. TAGA Proceedings. **VFOAT** TAGA Proceedings. **VAT** Proceedings - Technical Association of the Graphic Arts. (1963)-. Academic Scholarly Publication. English. One time a year. $70.00 North America; $95.00 other. Technical Association of the Graphic Arts, Rochester Institute of Technology, PO Box 0887 Arts, Rochester NY 14623-0887. **Tel** (716)272-0557, FAX (716)475-2250. **ED** Michael H. Bruno. Index available. cum. index. **Circ:** 1,500. available on microfilm from University Microfilms International (UMI). Documents available from CASDDS. ***Continues*** *Proceedings of the Annual Meeting - Technical Association of the Graphic Arts, Inc, 0277-5026.*
Desc: Technical papers presented at annual conference describing research and developments in the graphic arts field industry.
Ind/Abst Abstr. Bull. Inst. Pap. Sci. Tech.; Chem. Abstr. (1963-1982); Curr. Cit.; Print. Abstr.

LC NE
DD 760 US
PRODUCTIVITY AND TRAINING REPORT. Added/Corp Graphic Arts Technical Foundation. **VFOAT** GATF Productivity & Training Report. No. 27 (June/July 1981)-. Periodical. English. Graphic Arts Technical Foundation, 4615 Forbes Avenue, Pittsburgh PA 15213. **Tel** (412)621-6941, FAX (412)621-3049, telex 9103509221. **ED** D. Mulvihill. ***Continues*** *Education Report (Graphic Arts Technical Foundation).*

LC NC975 .P83 **ISSN** 0885-6370
DD 741.65/0973 US
PUBLICATION DESIGN ANNUAL. (THE ... PUBLICATION DESIGN ANNUAL.). [Publ. des. annu.]. **Added/Corp** Society of Publication Designers (U.S.). (1982)-. Trade Publication. English. One time a year. $45.00. Madison Square Press, 10 East 23rd Street, New York NY 10010. **Tel** (212)505-0950, (800)451-1741, FAX (212)979-2207. **(Subscription address:** RC Publications, 3200 Tower Oaks Boulevard, Rockville MD 20852-9789. **Tel** (800)222-2654, (301)770-2900, FAX (301)984-3203.**)** ***Continues*** *Publication Design.*
Desc: Examples of the year's editorial designs from publications in consumer, trade and corporate magazines, newspapers, annual reports, and other publications in magazine form.

LC NE
DD 760 US
PUBLIQUE ARTE. [COMPUTER FILE]. (19??)-. English. $104.95. Quanta Press, Inc., 1313 Fifth Street Southeast, Suite 208C, Minneapolis MN 55414. **Tel** (612)379-3956, FAX (612)623-4570.
Desc: Public domain clip art images in .PCX (PC Paintbrush) format. A convenient viewing program is provided along with a special ZIP section for bulletin board users. Available in DOS and MAC formats.

LC AP2 .P96 **ISSN** 1054-3686
DD 760 US
PUSH (NEW YORK, N.Y.). (PUSH!). [Push!]. (Mar. 1991)-. Periodical. English. Four times a year. Leon Lecash Publishing, 284 5th Avenue, New York NY 10001. **ED** Leon Lecash. **Ad Acc.**

ISSN 1184-1508
DD 741.6/94/075 CN
SADDLE & STRIKER (1990). (SADDLE & STRIKER / TRANS-CANADA MATCHCOVER CLUB.). [Saddle strik.]. **Added/Corp** Trans-Canada Matchcover Club. **VFOAT** Saddle and Striker. No. 139 (Dec. 1990)-. Periodical. English. Four times a year. Free to members. Trans-Canada Matchcover Club, 46 Chiltin Drive, Stoney Creek Ontario L8J 1N2 Canada. ***Continues*** *Newsletter (Trans-Canada Matchcover Club)., 0849-3170.*

LC NE508 .S6 **ISSN** 0163-4577
DD 769/.973/07401471 US
SAGA NATIONAL PRINT EXHIBITION. Main/Corp Society of American Graphic Artists. **VFOAT** National Print Exhibition. **VAT** Society of American Graphic Artists Print Exhibition. English. Society of American Graphic Artists, 663 Fifth Avenue, New York NY 10022. ***Continues*** *SAGA Annual Print Exhibition.*

ISSN 0319-5465
DD 769/.9719/4 CN
SANAVIK COOPERATIVE BAKER LAKE PRINTS. Main/Corp Sanavik Cooperative. **VFOAT** Sanavik Cooperative Baker Lake Estampes. 1974-. Multiple languages (Eskimo, English and French). One time a year. Canadian Arctic Producers Ltd., C.P. 4130 Succursale E, Ottawa K1S 5B2. ***Supersedes*** *Baker Lake Prints, 0319-5473.*

LC NK8800 **ISSN** 1051-1032
DD 746 US
SCREEN PLAY (DALLAS, TEX.). (SCREEN PLAY.). [Screen play]. **VFOAT** Screenplay. (198?)-. Trade Publication. English. Twelve times a year (Jan. issue is Annual Buyer's Guide). $36.00. Signs of the Times Publishing Company, 407 Gilbert Avenue, Cincinnati OH 45202. **Tel** (513)421-2050, (800)925-1110, FAX (513)421-5144.
Desc: Trade publication for garment graphics production.

LC NK1160 .S96a
US
TITLE CHANGE
SDA NEWS. Main/Corp Surface Design Association (U.S.). **VFOAT** Surface Design Association News. (19??)-Vol. 7, No. 4 (Fall 1994). Periodical. English. Surface Design Association, PO Box 20799, Oakland CA 94620. **Tel** (510)841-2008, FAX (707)829-3285. **ED** Patricia Malarcher (editor's address: 93 Ivy Lane, Englewood, NJ 07631, phone: (201)568-1084). ***Continues*** *Surface Design Association (U.S.) Newsletter.* ***Continued by*** *Surface Design Association (U.S.). Surface Newsletter.*
Desc: Provides leadership in the fields of art and design by stimulating, promoting, and improving the professional opportunities and education.

LC NE
DD 760 US
SEALS OF THE U.S. GOVERNMENT. [COMPUTER FILE]. (19??)-. English. $49.95. Quanta Press, Inc., 1313 Fifth Street Southeast, Suite 208C, Minneapolis MN 55414. **Tel** (612)379-3956, FAX (612)623-4570. available in print.
Desc: Contains 588 identifying seals and logos of the U.S. Federal Government. Resource for Government contractors. Available in DOS and MAC formats.

LC TS1262 **ISSN** 0834-9304
DD 681/.6 CN
SECOND IMPRESSIONS. **See** Printing Industry.

LC NE70 .S55 **ISSN** 0743-7609
DD 769/.029/4753 US
SHOWCASE. (SHOWCASE / OLD PRINT GALLERY.). **Added/Corp** Old Print Gallery (Washington, D.C.). Vol. 2, No. 1 (Jan. 1975)-. English. The Old Print Gallery Inc, 1220 31st Street NW, Washington DC 20007. ***Continues*** *Catalog (Old Print Gallery (Washington, D.C.)), 0748-1640.*

LC HF5841 .S54 **ISSN** 0270-4757
DD 338.4/765913 US
SIGNCRAFT. [Signcraft]. **VFOAT** Sign Craft; Signcraft Magazine; Sign Craft Magazine. Vol. 1, No. 1 (1980)-. Trade Publication. English. Six times a year (Jan., Mar., May, July, Sept., Nov.). $25.00. Signcraft Magazine, PO Box 06031, Ft Myers FL 33906. **Tel** (813)939-4644, FAX (813)939-0607. **ED** Tom McIltrot. Index available. cum. index. **Ad Acc. Circ:** 20,000.
Desc: The magazine for the sign artist and commercial sign shop. Includes features on sales, pricing and design.

LC NE **ISSN** 0274-774X
DD 760 US
SOUTHERN GRAPHICS. [South. graph.]. (1976)-. Periodical. English. Twelve times a year. $15.00. Coast Publishing Inc, 1680 Southwest Bayshore Boulevard, Port St Lucie FL 34984. **Tel** (407)879-6666, FAX (407)879-7388. **ED** Kenneth Moran. **Bk Rev. Ad Acc. Circ:** 16,000. ***Formed by the union of*** *Graphics, 0192-7256* ***and*** *Southern Printer, 0164-4378.*
Desc: Information and news pertaining to graphic arts industry in 14 states from Texas to Washington DC and the South through Florida and the Caribbean.
Ind/Abst Abstr. Bull. Inst. Pap. Sci. Tech.; GATFWORLD (1984); Graph. Arts Bull. Inst. Pap. Sci. Technol. (June 1989-Sept. 1989, Nov. 1989).

LC NE
DD 760 US
•**SOUTHWEST CREATIVE SOURCEBOOK.** (1995)-. English. Arizona Portfolio, 7041 East Orange Blossom Lane, Scottsdale AZ 85253. **Tel** (602)252-2332, FAX (602)941-5561. ***Continues*** *Arizona Portfolio.*

ISSN 1064-2218
DD 741 US
SPARKPLUG (LONG BEACH, CALIF.). (SPARKPLUG.). [Sparkplug]. (Mar. 1993)-. Periodical. English. Six times a year. Heroic Publishing, 6433 California Avenue, Long Beach CA 90805.

LC HE6187 .S769
DD 769.56/075 UK
STAMPS (PETERBOROUGH, CAMBRIDGESHIRE). (STAMPS.). (1986)-. Periodical. English. Twelve times a year. Stamps and Foreign Stamps, Competition House, Farndon Road, Market Harborough, Leicestershire LE16 9NR United Kingdom. ***Continues*** *Stamps and Foreign Stamps.*

ISSN 1081-1362
DD 741 US
•**STAR WARS GALAXY MAGAZINE.** [Star wars galaxy mag.]. (Fall 1994)-. Periodical. English. Four times a year. $13.97. Topps Company, 1 Whitehall Street, New York NY 10004. **Tel** (212)376-0300.

ISSN 0886-7682
DD 760 US
CODEN SSGRE3
STEP-BY-STEP GRAPHICS. [Step-by-step graph.]. **Added/Corp** Dynamic Graphics Educational Foundation (Peoria, Ill.). **VFOAT** Step by Step Graphics. Vol. 1, No. 1 (Nov./Dec. 1985)-. Trade Publication. English. Six times a year. $42.00. Dynamic Graphics Inc., 6000 North Forest Park Drive, Peoria IL 61614. **Tel** (800)255-8800, FAX (309)688-5873. **(Subscription address:** Dynamic Graphics Inc., PO Box 1901, Peoria IL 61656. **Tel** (309)688-8800, 800-255-8800.**) ED** Nancy Aldrich-Rvenzel. Index available. cum. index. **Bk Rev. Ad Acc. Circ:** 45,000.
Ind/Abst Abstr. Bull. Inst. Pap. Sci. Tech.; Acad. Search; EP Collect.; Graph. Arts Bull. Inst. Pap. Sci. Technol. (May 1989, Sept. 1989, Nov. 1989); Homework Help.; INFO-SOUTH Abstr.; Mag. Search; MasterFile FullTEXT 1000; MasterFile FullTEXT 350; MasterFile FullTEXT 650; MasterFile FullTEXT (July 1993-); OCLC; Telebase.

LC NC997 **ISSN** 1202-0249
DD 741.6 CN
STUDIO (REXDALE). (STUDIO.). [Studio]. Vol. 11, No. 1 (Jan./Feb. 1992)-. Periodical. English. Seven times a year. 40.00Can$. Roger Murray and Associates, 124 Galaxy Boulevard, Toronto Ontario M9W 4Y6 Canada. **Tel** (416)675-1997. **ED** Barbara J. Murray. **Bk Rev. Circ:** 10,000. ***Continues*** *The Studio Magazine., 0715-6626.*
Desc: Designed to inspire and inform graphic designers, illustrators, photographers and creative graphic arts personnel, computer and A/V production personnel. Presents ideas, artistic and photographic portfolios, new product releases and news and events relating to the advertising and professional design community.

LC NK1160 .S96a
US
•**SURFACE NEWSLETTER. Main/Corp** Surface Design Association (U.S.). **VFOAT** Surface Design Association News; Surface SDA Newsletter; SDA News. Vol. 8, No. 1 (Winter 1994)-. Newsletter. English. Four times a year (Feb., May, Aug., Nov.). $45.00 comes with membership. Surface Design Association, PO Box 20799, Oakland CA 94620. **Tel** (510)841-2008, FAX (707)829-3285. **ED** Patricia Malarcher (editor's address: 93 Ivy Lane, Englewood, NJ 07631, phone: (201)568-1084). ***Continues*** *Surface Design Association (U.S.) SDA News.*
Desc: Provides leadership in the fields of art and design by stimulating, promoting, and improving the professional opportunities and education.

LC NE2250 .T35 **ISSN** 0276-3397
DD 763/.05 US
TAMARIND PAPERS, THE. (THE TAMARIND PAPERS: TTP.). [Tamarind pap.]. **Added/Corp** Tamarind Institute. **VFOAT** TTP; T.T.P. Vol. 2, No. 1 (Autumn 1978)-. Periodical. English. Irregular (Publishes every eighteen months). $48.00. University of New Mexico Press, 1720 Lomas Boulevard Northeast, Albuquerque NM 87131. **Tel** (505)277-2346, FAX (505)277-9270. **ED** Clinton Adams. Index available. **Bk Rev. Ad Acc. Circ:** 540 (ctrl). ***Continues*** *Tamarind Technical Papers, 0740-1019.*

The Arts — Graphic Arts

Desc: Technical, critical and historical studies on the art of the lithograph.
Ind/Abst BHA : Biblio. Hist. Art.

ISSN 0895-6529
DD 760 US
T&E NEWS. (T & E NEWS / TECHNICAL AND EDUCATION CENTER OF THE GRAPHIC ARTS.). [T&E news]. **Added/Corp** Rochester Institute of Technology. Technical and Education Center of the Graphic Arts. **VFOAT** T and E News. **VAT** Technical and Education News. Vol. 14, No. 5 (Sept. 1986)-. Periodical. English. Irregular. Free on request. Rochester Institute of Technology, Technical and Education Center, PO Box 9887, Rochester NY 14623-0887. **Tel** (716)475-2737, FAX (716)475-7052. **Continues** T & E Center Newsletter (Rochester, N.Y. : 1985), 0895-6642.
Ind/Abst Abstr. Bull. Inst. Paper Chem. (1986-); Print. Abstr. (1986-).

LC NE
DD 760 ISSN 0738-9507
CN
TECHNOLOGY WATCH FOR THE GRAPHIC ARTS AND INFORMATION INDUSTRIES. [Technol. watch graph. arts inf. ind.]. **Added/Corp** Policy Studies Corporation. **VFOAT** Technology Watch. (19??)-. Periodical. English. Twelve times a year. 295.00Can$. Evans Research Corporation, 2005 Sheppard Avenue East, 4th Floor, Willowdale Ontario M2J 5B1 Canada. **Tel** (416)498-6664, (416)497-9562, FAX (416)498-7275. **ED** Henry B. Freedman. **Ad Acc. Circ:** 600 (ctrl).

LC NK1160 .T45
SP
TEMES DE DISSENY. No. 1 (Oct. 1986)-. Periodical. Catalan. Irregular. 2800ptas (Spain); 4000ptas (other). Escola Disseny, Val Major 11, 08021 Barcelona Spain. **(Subscription address:** Gustavo Gili, Rosello 87 89, 08029 Barcelona Spain. **Tel** 011 34 3 3228161.)

ISSN 1058-5303
DD 740 US
THE POINT (HANCOCK, MICH.), TO. (TO THE POINT : THE NEWSLETTER FOR THE COLORED PENCIL SOCIETY OF AMERICA.) **Added/Corp** Colored Pencil Society of America. Vol. 1, No. 1 (Nov. 1990)-. Newsletter. English. Three times a year. Colored Pencil Society of America, 204 Harris Street, Hancock MI 49930.

ISSN 1191-0909
DD 741.5 CN
TINY WAILS. [Tiny wails]. No. 1 (Dec. 1991)-. Periodical. English. $1.00. B Luhtala, 163 Beechwood Avenue, Victoria British Columbia V8S 3W4 Canada.

LC HE6185.U5 T74 ISSN 0041-1175
DD 769.56/7/0973 US
TRANSIT POSTMARK COLLECTOR. [Transit postmark collect.]. **Added/Corp** Mobile Post Office Society. (19??)-. Periodical. English. Six times a year. Warren F Kimball Jr, RFD 1 Box 91, Contoocook NH 03229. **Continues** H.P.O. Notes.

ISSN 1056-2931
DD 741 US
TUNDRA SKETCHBOOK SERIES, THE. [Tundra sketchb. ser.]. (1991)-. Monographic series. English. Six times a year. Tundra Publishing Ltd., 320 Riverside Drive, Northampton MA 01060.

LC NE
DD 760 SZ
TYPOGRAFISCHE MONATSBLAETTER = REVUE SUISSE DE L'IMPRIMERIE.
Added/Corp Schweizerischer Typographenbund. Gewerkschaft Druck und Papier fur Foerderung der Berufsbildung (Switzerland). **VFOAT** Typografische Monatsblaetter; Revue Suisse de l'Imprimerie; Swiss Typographic Monthly Magazine; TM SGM; TM; RSI; Schweizer Grafische Mitteilungen; SGM. (1???)-. Periodical. German (English and French). Six times a year. $127.24. Zollikofer AG, Fuerstenlandstr 122, CH-9001 St. Gallen Switzerland. **Tel** 011 41 71 297777, FAX 011 41 71 257487, telex 77537. **Bk Rev. Ad Acc. Circ:** 4,000. **Continues** Schweizer Reklame und Schweizer Graphische Mitteilungen; **Absorbed** Typografische Monatsblaetter (Zurich, Switzerland).
Ind/Abst Print. Abstr.

LC HE6185.U6 U62 ISSN 0276-7244
DD 769.56/6/0973 US
UNITED STATES POSTAL CARD CATALOG. [U. S. post. card cat.]. **Added/Corp** United Postal Stationery Society. (19??)-. Catalog. English. Irregular. United Postal Stationery Society, Central Office, PO Box 48, Redlands CA 92373.

LC NE
DD 760 IT
SUSPENDED
UOVO DI COLOMBO. (19??)-(1991). Italian. Four times a year. L40.000 Italy; L50.000 other. L'Atelier, Via Vitt Veneto 91/95, 41100 Modena Italy. **Tel** 011 39 59 219917, FAX 011 39 59 236210.
Desc: A publication of advices, news, and opinions for all the people who use the Apple Macintosh computer in graphic and press.

ISSN 1186-1258
DD 741.5 CN
VESTIBULLES (MONTREAL).
(VESTIBULLES.). [Vestibulles]. **Added/Corp** College du Vieux Montreal. **VFOAT** Vestibule. Vol. 1, No 1 (1990)-. Periodical. French. Two times a year. Limited free distribution. College du Vieux Montreal, CP 1444, Succursale C, Montreal Quebec H2X 3M8 Canada.

LC NC997
DD 741.6 US
VOLK "CLIP BOOK". (19??)-. English. Twelve times a year. $253.93. Dynamic Graphics Inc., 6000 North Forest Park Drive, Peoria IL 61614. **Tel** (800)255-8800, FAX (309)688-5873. **(Subscription address:** Dynamic Graphics RSA Pty Ltd., PO Box 589, Kraaifontein 7569 South Africa. **Tel** 011 27 21 988 1694.)

ISSN 1062-3248
DD 741 US
WARLOCK AND THE INFINITY WATCH.
Vol. 1, No. 1 (Feb. 1992)-. Periodical. English. Twelve times a year. $21.00. Marvel Entertainment Group Inc., 387 Park Avenue South, New York NY 10016. **Tel** (212)576-8595, FAX (212)576-9289. **(Subscription address:** Marvel Direct Marketing Corporation, PO Box 1979, Danbury CT 06813. **Tel** (203)792-4700.)

LC NC45 .W5
DD 741 SZ
WHO'S WHO IN GRAPHIC ART. See Biographies.

LC NC1300 .W5 ISSN 0892-9807
DD 741 US
WITTYWORLD. [WittyWorld]. **VFOAT** Witty World. (Summer 1987)-. Trade Publication. English. Four times a year. $19.95. WittyWorld Publications, PO Box 1458, North Wales PA 19454. **Tel** (215)699-2626, FAX (215)699-0627. **ED** Joseph George Szabo. **Bk Rev**, (Qty: 4 or more). **Ad Acc, Adv Mgr:** Joseph George Szabo. **Circ:** 5,000.
Desc: International cartoon magazine covering all genres of cartoon art.

LC NE
DD 760 US
WORKBOOK (LOS ANGELES, CALIF.).
(THE WORKBOOK.). (198?)-. Directory. English. Four times a year (Published in 4 vol. set). $80.00. Scott and Daughters Publishing, 940 North Highland Avenue, Los Angeles CA 90038. **Tel** (213)856-0008.
Desc: Directory for advertising and design professionals.

LC NC998.5.A1 W67 ISSN 1065-6103
DD 741.6/0973/05 US
WORKBOOK'S SINGLE IMAGE. [Workb. single image.]. **VFOAT** Single Image. Vol. 1, No. 1 (1990)-. English. Three times a year (Apr., Sept., Nov.). $45.00. Scott and Daughters Publishing, 940 North Highland Avenue, Los Angeles CA 90038. **Tel** (213)856-0008.
Desc: Strives to bridge the gap between commercial and fine art.

LC HD9980
DD 338.476 UK
WORLD EXCELLENCE IN CORRUGATED GRAPHICS. English. One time a year. £45.00. Brunton Business Pub Ltd., Thruston Down House, Thruston Down, Hampshire SP11 8PR United Kingdom. **Tel** 011 44 1264 889533, FAX 011 44 1264 889622, telex 859562.

LC NC998.6.G7 X993
DD 741.6 UK
TITLE CHANGE
XYZ DESIGN & DIRECTION. **VFOAT** XYZ Design and Direction; XYZ. (1993)-(1994). English. Haymarket Publishing Ltd., 12 14 Ansdell Street, London W8 5TR United Kingdom. **Tel** 011 44 171 9380705, 011 44 171 2786686, FAX 011 44 171 9380772. **Continues** XYZ Direction. **Continued by** Creative Technology.

PERFORMING ARTS

LC PN1970 .P66 ISSN 0275-9195
DD 791.5/3/05 US
A PROPOS - AMERICAN CENTER OF UNIMA. (A PROPOS.). **Added/Corp** American Center of Unima. (19??)-. Periodical. English. Two times a year (Apr. & Sept.). $25.00. UNIMA USA / American Center Union International de la Marionnette, c/o Vincent Anthony SS, 1404 Spring Street Northwest, Atlanta GA 30309. **Tel** (404)266-5953. available on microfilm from University Microfilms International (UMI).

LC PN1560
DD 790.2 US
ACUCAA BULLETIN. **Main/Corp** Association of College, University and Community Arts Administrators. **VFOAT** Bulletin. Vol. 17, No. 5 (June 1974)-. Bulletin. English. Ten times a year. Association of Performing Arts Presenters, 1112 16th Street Northwest, Suite 620, Washington DC 20036. **Tel** (202)833-2787, FAX (202)833-1543. **ED** Gayle Stamler. **Bk Rev. Circ:** 1,700 (ctrl). **Continues** ACUCM Bulletin.
Desc: Publication to members of professional associations serving performing arts presenters nationwide. Regular features include columns on management, advocacy, and government issues relating to the arts.

LC PN2990.S83 M87
SU
AL-MUSIQA WA-AL-MASRAH. **Added/Corp** Mahad al-Musiqa Wa-al-Masrah (Khartoum, Sudan). (19??)-. Periodical. Arabic. Mahad Al-Musiqa Wa-Al-Masrah Al-Khartum, SB 8039, Al-Imarat, Al-Khartum Saudi Arabia.

LC PN2003 .A43
DD 792/.05 BE
ALTERNATIVES THEATREALES. (197?)-. Periodical. French. Four times a year. $59.70. Alternatives Theatreales, 13 rue des Poissonniers Bte 15, 1000 Brussels Belgium. **Tel** 011 32 2 5117858.

ISSN 0882-4487
DD 790 US
AMERICAN INDIAN REGISTRY FOR THE PERFORMING ARTS, THE. [Am. Indian Regist. Perform. Arts]. **Added/Corp** American Indian Registry for the Performing Arts. **VFOAT** Newsletter. Vol. 1, No. 1 (Summer 1984)-. Newsletter. English. Twelve times a year. American Indian Registry for the Performing Arts, 3330 Barham Boulevard, Suite 208, Los Angeles CA 90068.

LC PN2289 .A67 ISSN 0882-4495
DD 790.2/08997 US
AMERICAN INDIAN TALENT DIRECTORY. [Am. Indian talent dir.]. **Added/Corp** American Indian Registry for the Performing Arts. (1984)-. Directory. English. American Indian Registry for the Performing Arts, 3330 Barham Boulevard, Suite 208, Los Angeles CA 90068.

ISSN 0830-8586
DD 790.2/025/71 CN
SUSPENDED
AMI (MISSISSAUGA, ONT.). (AMI : THE ENTERTAINMENT INDUSTRY GUIDE.). (1981)-Suspended (1992). Periodical. English (French). Two times a year. 47.45Can$ Canada; 53.15Can$ other. AMI Publishing, PO Box 35, 20 Wellington St. East, Aurora Ontario, L4G 3H1 Canada. **Tel** (905)841-5200. **ED** Ron Garant. **Ad Acc. Circ:** 2,500 (ctrl).
Desc: Contains listings of products and services involved in media and communications production of audio, video, computer graphics, music film and audio visual.

LC PN1560
DD 790.2 IT
ANIMAZIONE ED ESPRESSIONE. TEMPO SERENO. (19??)-. Italian. Six times a year. L40880. Editrice Scuola Spa, Via L Cadorna 11, 25186 Brescia Italy. **Tel** 011 39 30 2993246.

ISSN 0229-3153
DD 338.4/77902/0971 CN
ANNUAL CBAC SURVEY OF PERFORMING ARTS ORGANIZATIONS.
(ANNUAL CBAC SURVEY OF PERFORMING ARTS ORGANISATIONS : THEATRE, DANCE, MUSIC & OPERA / PREPARED BY THE COUNCIL FOR BUSINESS AND THE ARTS IN CANADA (CBAC).). [Annu. CBAC surv. perform. arts organz.]. **Added/Corp** Council for Business and the Arts in Canada. **VFOAT** CBAC Survey. **VAT** Annual Council for Business and the Arts in Canada Survey of Performing Arts Organisations; Council for Business and the Arts in Canada Survey. (Dec. 1980)-. English. One time a year. 51.40Can$. Council for Business and the Arts in Canada, PO Box 7, Suite 1507/The Simpson Tower, 401 Bay Street, Toronto Ontario M5H 2Y4 Canada. **Tel** (416)869-3016, FAX (416)869-0435. **ED** Sarah Iley. ctrl circ. **Continues** Council for Business and the Arts in Canada. Annual CBAC Survey of Selected Performing Arts Organizations., 0227-3756.

LC PN1573.C2 A5212 ISSN 0226-0816
DD 354.71230085/4 CN
ANNUAL REPORT - THE ALBERTA FOUNDATION FOR THE PERFORMING ARTS. [Annu. rep. - Alta. Found. Perform. Arts]. **Main/Corp** Alberta Foundation for the Performing Arts. 1979-. English. One time a year. Alberta Foundation for the Performing Arts, Suite 911 Financial Building, 10621 100th Avenue, Edmonton Alberta T5J 0B3 Canada.

LC PN1560
DD 790.2 UK
ARC NEWS LETTER. **Added/Corp** American Reference Centre for the Study of British Performing Arts (London, England). **VFOAT** A.R.C. News Letter. **VAT** American Reference Centre News Letter. (197?)-. Periodical. English. Six times a year. American Reference Centre for the Study of British Performing Arts, PO Box 491, London W2 2YN United Kingdom.

ISSN 0896-0364
DD 791 US
TITLE CHANGE
ARIZONA FILM, THEATRE & TELEVISION : AFT & T. [Ariz. film theatre telev.]. **VFOAT** Arizona Film, Theatre and Television; AFT & T; AFT&T. (19??)-(19??). Periodical. English. Arizona Production Association, 3900 East Camelback Suite 200, Suite 200, Phoenix AZ 85018. **Tel** (602)345-6464, FAX (602)957-4828. **ED** Laurie Fagan and Shannon O'Bryan. ***Continued by*** *On the Arizona Set.*

LC N1 .A647 ISSN 0197-7903 US
NLM W1; AR94775
ART HAZARDS NEWS. [Art hazards news]. **Added/Corp** Center for Occupational Hazards (New York, N.Y.). **VFOAT** Art Hazards Newsletter. Vol. 1 (Oct. 1978)-. Periodical. English. Five times a year. $24.00. Center for Safety in the Arts, 5 Beekman Street/Suite 1030, New York NY 10038. **Tel** (212)227-6220, FAX (212)233-3846. **ED** Michael McCann. Index available in last issue of volume--attached. cum. index. **Circ:** 3,000.
Desc: Covers new hazards, precautions, legislation and government regulations, lawsuits and coming events on visual and performing arts.
Ind/Abst Art Archaeol. Tech. Abstr.

ISSN 0882-8571
DD 705 US
ARTS CALENDAR QUARTERLY, THE. [Arts cal. q.]. Vol. 1, No. 1 (Fall 1984/Winter 1985)-. Periodical. English. Four times a year. $28.00 (individuals), $45.00 (institutions), basic service, $75.00 (institutions), full service Comes with Arts Calendar membership. The Arts Calendar Inc., 600 West 58th Street, Suite 9217, New York NY 10019. **Tel** (212)496-2787.

ISSN 0823-9746
DD 331.12/417902/0971 CN
ARTSBOARD (TORONTO). (ARTSBOARD.). [Artsboard]. **Added/Corp** Professional Association of Canadian Theatres. Vol. 1, No. 1 (Oct. 1984)-. Periodical. English. Twelve times a year. 16.01Can$. PACT Communications Centre, 64 Charles Street East, Toronto Ontario M4Y 1T1 Canada. **Tel** (416)968-3033, FAX (416)968-3035. **ED** Tracy Sigurdson. **Circ:** 600.
Desc: Employment opportunities, project grants and new programs in the performing arts.

LC PN1560 ISSN 0730-9023
DD 790.2 US
ARTSEARCH. [Artsearch]. **Added/Corp** Theatre Communications Group. **VFOAT** Art Search. (1981)-. Periodical. English. Twenty-three times a year. $75.00. Theatre Communications Group, 355 Lexington Avenue, New York NY 10017. **Tel** (212)697-5230, FAX (212)983-4847. **Ad Acc. Circ:** 3,000.
Desc: A job listing service for employment in the arts. Lists an average 250 positions in all art related fields. Categories include: admission, artistic, production, education (university), and career development (development and apprenticeships). Jobs range from entry level to upper management.

LC PN2620 .A18
DD 790.2/0944 FR
AS, ANNUAIRE DU SPECTACLE. VFOAT Annuaire du Spectacle. **VAT** Annuaire Spectacle, Annuaire du Spectacle. 1956-. French. One time a year. 60F single issue. ***Continues*** *Annuaire du Spectacle, Theatre, Cinema, Musique, Radio, Television.*

LC ML1 .A834 ISSN 0044-9202
DD 780/.95 US
CCC
Pr Rev.
ASIAN MUSIC. See Music.

LC PN1560
DD 790.2 US
AUDITION NEWS. (19??)-. English. Twelve times a year. $24.95. Chicago Entertainment Company, 6272 W North Avenue, Chicago IL 60639. **Tel** (312) 637-4695. **ED** Gary Conway. **Ad Acc.**

LC PN1560
DD 790.2 AT
Pr Rev.
AUSTRALIAN ITI NEWS. (19??)-. English. Eight times a year. 20.55Aus$. Australian Center of the International Theatre, 8A/245 Chalmers Street, Redfern 2016 Australia. **Tel** 011 61 02 319 0718, FAX 011 61 02 698 3557. ***Continues*** *ITI International News Round Up.*
Desc: List of performing arts events, conferences, workshops, training programs, festivals, scholarships and awards overseas and in Australia. Also, provides information on movements by performing arts professionals.

LC PN1561 .B335
US
●**BACK STAGE WEST.** (July 1993)-. Periodical. English. One time a week. $69.00. Billboard Publications Inc., 1515 Broadway Billboard, New York NY 10036. **Tel** (212)764-7300, FAX (305)755-7048, telex WU TWX 710-581-6279.

LC GV1787 .B278
DD 792.8/05 IT
BALLETTO OGGI. See Dance.

LC ML19 .A5 ISSN 0361-221X
DD 785/.06/7108 US
BATON TWIRLING RULES AND REGULATIONS. Main/Corp Amateur Athletic Union of the United States. **VFOAT** AAU Official Handbook Baton Twirling. (19??)-. English. Amateur Athletic Union / AAU, 3400 West 86th Street, PO Box 68207, Indianapolis IN 46268. **Tel** (317)872-2900, FAX (317)875-0548.

LC PN1590.F47 B47 ISSN 0882-4193
DD 790.2/025/73 US
BEST FESTIVALS OF NORTH AMERICA. Added/Corp Spivack, Carol, 1934- Weinstock, Richard A., 1939-. 1st Ed. (March 1984)-. English. Irregular. Printwheel Press, 2674 East Main Street / Suite C-124, Ventura CA 93003. **Tel** (805)643-0965. **ED** Carol Spivack and Richard A. Weinstock. Index available. **Bk Rev.**
Desc: A guide to performing arts festivals in North America: classical music, dance, theater, jazz, film, folk, ethnic, and children's. Includes seating, stage facilities, ticket prices, nearby sights and lodging.

ISSN 1053-6671
DD 791 US
BEST OF THE SUPERSTARS, THE. (THE BEST OF THE SUPERSTARS : THE YEAR IN SEX.). (1991)-. English. $9.95 US; $11.95 Canada. P J Powers, 601 South Tyler Drive, Sarasota FL 34236.

ISSN 1062-3825
DD 790 US
BLACK TALENT NEWS. (BLACK TALENT NEWS : THE NEWSLETTER FOR CREATIVE BLACK TALENT.). [Black talent news]. (1991)-. Newsletter. English. Ten times a year (July/Aug. and Dec./Jan. combined). $21.00. Love Child Publishing, PO Box 7374, Culver City CA 90233. **Tel** (310)642-7658.

ISSN 0714-6981
DD 790.2/09713/541 CN
BRAVO (TORONTO). (BRAVO.). [Bravo]. **Added/Corp** Massey Hall (Toronto, Ont.). Roy Thompson Hall. Vol. 1 No. 1 (Sept. 1982)-. Periodical. English. Six times a year. Free to libraries. National Theatre Publications, 30 St. Claire, Suite 805, Toronto Ontario M4V 3A1 Canada. **Tel** (416)926-7595.

LC PN1560 ISSN 0759-6898
DD 790.2 FR
BREF (PARIS). (BREF.). (1983)-. French.
Ind/Abst Film Lit. Index (19??-).

LC PN1560
DD 790.2 UK
BRITISH PERFORMING ARTS NEWS LETTER. Added/Corp American Reference Centre for the Study of British Performing Arts (London, England). **VFOAT** British Performing Arts Newsletter. Vol. 2, Issue no. 1 (Sept. 1980)-. Periodical. English. Six times a year. American Reference Centre for the Study of British Performing Arts, PO Box 491, London W2 2YN United Kingdom. ***Continues*** *News Letter (American Reference Centre for the Study of British Performing Arts (London, England)).*

LC PN1560 ISSN 0951-5208
DD 790.2 UK
BRITISH PERFORMING ARTS YEARBOOK. (1988)-. Periodical. English. One time a year. $35.25 UK; $37.97 other. Rhinegold Publishing Ltd., 241 Shaftesbury Avenue, London WC2H 8EH United Kingdom. **Tel** 011 44 171 2405749, FAX 011 44 171 5287991, telex 264675 GILDED. **ED** Sheena Barbour. **Ad Acc.**
Desc: A complete guide to venues, performers, arts centres, festivals, supporting organisations, and services, for arts professionals.

LC PN1560 ISSN 0319-664X
DD 790.2 CN
BULLETIN - CANADIAN TALENT LIBRARY. See Library and Information Sciences.

LC PN2289 .C35
DD 790.2 US
CALVACADE OF ACTS & ATTRACTIONS. VFOAT Cavalcade of Acts and Attractions. (19??)-. English. One time a year (Dec.). $60.00. Amusement Business, PO Box 24970, Nashville TN 37202. **Tel** (615)321-4250, FAX (615)327-1575. **ED** Leslie Shaver and Rusty Terry. **Bk Rev. Ad Acc. Circ:** 7,000 (ctrl). ***Continues*** *Cavalcade and Directory of Acts & Attractions.*
Desc: Features more than 5,500 listings of acts and shows performing in the U.S., Canada and many foreign countries. Listings include musical performing artists - from rock to classical to country - plus rodeos, carnivals, circuses, fireworks firms, and comedians along with names of booking agents and management contacts.

LC PN2016.N32 A3 ISSN 0746-2328
DD 790.2/0973 US
CAMPUS ACTIVITIES PROGRAMMING. [Campus act. program.]. **Added/Corp** National Association for Campus Activities (U.S.). **VFOAT** Programming. Vol. 16, No. 3 (Sept. 1983)-. Periodical. English. Nine times a year. $20.00 (one-year); $190.00 (regional), $380.00 (national) Comes with National Association for Campus Activities membership. National Association for Campus Activities, 13 Harbison Way, PO Box 6828, Columbia SC 29260. **Tel** (803)782-7121. **ED** Preston McLaurin, Heidi Mohn and Mary Anne Banich. **Bk Rev. Ad Acc. Circ:** 6,500 (ctrl). available on microfilm from University Microfilms International (UMI). ***Continues*** *Student Activities Programming, 0098-1664.*
Desc: Educational articles, news, reports, evaluations and advertising related to student activities at colleges and universities and the entertainers who play the college market.
Ind/Abst Curr. Index J. Educ. (March 1990); High. Educ. Abstr. (1983-).

ISSN 1042-3281
DD 791 US
CANALES (NEW YORK, N.Y.). (CANALES.). [Canales]. (19??)-. Periodical. Spanish (English). Twelve times a year. $20.00. Canales Publ, 215 West 92nd Street/#8E, New York NY 10025. **Tel** (212)724-8805. **ED** Fernando Campos.

LC PN1560
DD 790.2 IT
CELEBRIANO. Vol. 1 (Jan. 1971)-. Periodical. Italian. Six times a year. 48000L Italy; 57000L other. Edizioni Carrara, Via da Calepio 4, 24100 Bergamo Italy. **Tel** 011 39 35 243618.

LC PN1587.K4 C46 ISSN 0748-6464
DD 790.2/05 US
CENTER (LOUISVILLE, KY.), THE. (THE CENTER : KENTUCKY CENTER FOR THE ARTS MAGAZINE.). **Added/Corp** Kentucky Center for the Arts. **VFOAT** Kentucky Center for the Arts Magazine. Vol. 2, No. 6 (Aug. 1984)-. English. Ten times a year (monthly except June and July). $32.00. Kentucky Premiere Inc., 118 Bauer Avenue, Louisville KY 40207. ***Continues*** *Kentucky Premiere Magazine.*
Ind/Abst Hum. Rights Intern. Rep.

LC PN1993.5.U6 C38 ISSN 1058-9252
DD 384/.8/0977 US
TITLE CHANGE
CENTRAL CITIES SIGHT AND SOUND. [Cent. cities sight sound]. **VFOAT** Sight and Sound; Central Cities Sight & Sound. Vol. 1, No. 1 (Nov./Dec. 1991)-(1995). Periodical. English. Central Cities Communications, 1343 Bruck Street, Columbus OH 43206. ***Formed by the union of*** *Central Cities Connector, 1054-8270* ***and*** *Zooming In Magazine.* ***Merged with*** *Southwest Sight and Sound* ***to form*** *Central Cities, Southwest Sight and Sound, 1085-1623.*

LC PN1993.5.U6 C38 ISSN 1085-1623
DD 384/.8/0977 US
●**CENTRAL CITIES, SOUTHWEST SIGHT AND SOUND.** [Cent. cities, Southwest sight sound]. **VFOAT** Sight and Sound; Central Cities, Southwest Sight & Sound. Vol. 4, No. 5 (May/June 1995)-. Periodical. English. Six times a year. Central Cities, Southwest Sight & Sound, Columbus OH. ***Formed by the union of*** *Central Cities Sight and Sound, 1058-9252* ***and*** *Southwest Sight and Sound.*

LC PL2253 .C65 ISSN 0193-7774
DD 782.81/0951 US
Pr Rev.
CHINOPERL PAPERS. [CHINOPERL pap.]. **Main/Conf** Conference on Chinese Oral and Performing Literature. **Added/Corp** Cornell University. China-Japan Program. **VFOAT** Chung-Kuo Yen Chang Wen I Yen Chiu Hui Lun Chi. **VAT** Chinese Oral and Performing Literature Papers. No. 6 (1976)-. Monographic series. English (Chinese). Irregular. Price varies per volume. CHINOPERL Papers, 110 Music Building, University of Pittsburgh, Pittsburgh PA 15260. **ED** Harold Shadick, Samuel Cheung, and Lindy Li Mark. **Circ:** 300. ***Continues*** *CHINOPERL News.*
Desc: Contains articles dealing primarily with oral Chinese literature (popular story telling, opera, ceremonial chanting, folksong) and various genres of Chinese verse and prose.

ISSN 0711-6179
DD 790.2/025/71423 CN
CIRCUL'ART. (CIRCUL'ART : [REPERTOIRE].). [Circul'art]. **Added/Corp** Circul'Art. (1980)-. French. One time a year. Circul'Art, 185 du Palais, Saint-Jerome Quebec J7Z 1X6 Canada.

LC PN2285 .C58 ISSN 0749-064X
DD 791/.092/2 B US
CONTEMPORARY THEATRE, FILM, AND TELEVISION. [Contemp. theatre film telev.]. **Added/Corp** Gale Research Company. **VFOAT** C.T.F.T.; CTFT. Vol. 1 (1984)-. English. Irregular. $125.00. Gale Research Inc., 835 Penobscot Building, 645 Griswold Street, Detroit MI 48226. **Tel** (800)877-GALE, (313)961-2242, FAX (313)961-6083, (800)414-5043,

The Arts — Performing Arts

telex TWX 810-221-7086. **ED** Emily J. McMurray. *Continues* Who's Who in the Theater.
Desc: Complete biographical and career information on currently popular individuals active in theatre, film, and television, including performers, directors, writers, producers, designers, managers, choreographers, technicians, composers, executives, dancers, and critics. Gives complete career credits, not just highlights, for work in theatre, film, and television, plus details on writings, recordings, awards, and memberships.

LC PN1993 .C675   **ISSN** 1030-4312
DD 791.43/0994/05   AT
    CCC

CONTINUUM (MT. LAWLEY, W.A.). See Motion Picture.

LC PN1560   **ISSN** 0163-3821
DD 790.2   US

CONTRIBUTIONS IN DRAMA AND THEATRE STUDIES. See Theater.

    ISSN 0818-7339
DD 784.4944   AT
Pr Rev.
CORNSTALK GAZETTE. [Cornstalk gaz.]. (1985)-. Periodical. English. Eleven times a year (Dec./Jan. combined). 20.55Aus$. Folk Federation NSW Inc, Box A182, Sydney New South Wales 2000 Australia. **Tel** 02 8185780. **ED** Constance Ellwood. **Bk Rev**. **Ad Acc**. **Circ:** 480 (ctrl). *Continues* Newsletter - New South Wales Folk Federation, 0811-9457.
Desc: Voluntary and non-profit magazine that covers folk and folklore information, whats on record and where, books, and performance reviews.

    ISSN 1188-0163
DD 790   CN
COTTAGER (VICTORIA BEACH. MANITOBA ED.). (THE COTTAGER.). [Cottager]. Vol. 1, No. 1 (Spring/Summer 1992)-. Periodical. English. Two times a year. $2.00 per issue. The Cottager, PO Box 40, Victoria Beach Manitoba R0E 2C0 Canada.

LC PN2277.C4 C54   **ISSN** 0363-745X
DD 790.2/025/77311   US
CU DIRECTORY. **Main/Corp** Chicago Unlimited, Inc. **Added/Corp** Chicago Unlimited, inc. Directory. **VAT** Chicago Unlimited Directory. (19??)-. Directory. English. Two times a year. $30.00. Chicago Unlimited Inc, 619 North Wabash/2nd Floor, Chicago IL 60611-2713. *Continues* Chicago Directory.

LC PN1560
DD 790.2   US
    TITLE CHANGE
CURRENT COMEDY FOR SPEAKERS. **Added/Corp** Comedy Center. **VFOAT** Current Comedy. (1989)-(19??). Periodical. English. Comedy Center, 300 Water Street, Wilmington DE 19801. **Tel** (302)656-2209. *Continues* Orben's Current Comedy. **Merged into** American Speaker.

    ISSN 0732-0299
DD 790.2   US
DALLAS OBSERVER. (Oct. 2, 1980)-. Periodical. English. One time a week. $60.00. Dallas Observer, PO Box 190289, Dallas TX 75219. **Tel** (214)637-2072. **ED** Bob Walton. **Bk Rev**. **Ad Acc**. **Circ:** 70,000 (ctrl).
Desc: An arts and entertainment publication.

    ISSN 0707-5510
DD 790/.09714   CN
DEMARCHE, LA. Vol. 1 (April 1978)-. Periodical. French. Irregular. Conseil Regional De Loisirs Centre Du Quebec, 2-445 rue Lindsay, Drummondville Quebec J2B 1G9.

    ISSN 0702-8830
DD 792/.05   CN
DERIVE URBAINE, LA. No. 1- 1976-. French. One time a year. $2.00 per no. Groupe De Planification Des Derives Urbaines, CP 1443 Succursale B, Hull Quebec J8X 3Y3 Canada. **Supersedes** Exil, 0315-4165.

LC WMLC 93/5126   **ISSN** 0932-3724
    GW
●**DESIGN REPORT / RAT FUER FORMGEBUNG.** **Added/Corp** Rat fuer Formgebung (Germany). (1993)-. Periodical. German. Twelve times a year. $101.79. Macup Verlag GmbH, Grosse Elbstrasse 277, D-22767 Hamburg Germany. **Tel** 011 49 40 3910901. (**Subscription address:** IA Inter ABO Betreuungs GmbH, Postfach 103245, D-20022 Hamburg Germany. **Tel** 011 49 30 68834451, 011 49 30 6884453.)

    ISSN 1058-711X
DD 790   US
DIAMOND DUDS. [Diam. duds]. Vol. 1, No. 1 (June 1991). Periodical. English. Six times a year. $20.00. Pearl Publications Group, PO Box 10153, Silver Springs MD 20904-0153.

LC PN1560   **ISSN** 0736-7759
DD 790.2   US
DIRECTORY OF FREE PROGRAMS, PERFORMING TALENT AND ATTRACTIONS, THE. (19??)-. English. One time a year. $75.00. Shelly Marketing Services, 525 Murdock Drive, Greenfield Park Quebec J4V 1G8 Canada. **Tel** (514)678-5774. **ED** Robert D. Shelley and Eileen Shelley. Index available. **Bk Rev**.
Desc: A unique directory providing names, addresses, telephone numbers and descriptive information about sources of free entertainment, free speakers, free programs, free promotions and attractions available to groups, organizations, and businesses.

LC ML5 .M9475
DD 781.64/0943/05   GW
DISCO-MAGAZIN. See Music.

LC L
DD 371.3   UK
DRAMA IN EDUCATION. **VFOAT** Annual Survey. Vol. 1 (1972)-. Periodical. English. One time a year. Longman Group Ltd., Fourth Avenue, Longman House, Harlow Essex CM19 5SR United Kingdom. **Tel** 011 44 1279 429655, FAX 011 44 1279 431067, telex 81259.

LC PN1560   **ISSN** 0012-5989
DD 790.2   US
DRAMATICS. **Added/Corp** International Thespian Society. National Thespian Dramatic Honor Society for High Schools (U.S.) National Thespian Society (U.S.) Educational Theatre Association (U.S.). **VFOAT** Dramatics. P. Curtain Edition; Dramatics Magazine. Vol. 16, No. 1 (Oct. 1944)-. Periodical. English. Nine times a year. September through May. Educational Theatre Association, 3368 Central Parkway, Cincinnati OH 45225. **Tel** (513)559-1996. *Continues* High School Thespian. **Absorbed in part by** Dramatics' Curtain.

    ISSN 0380-5123
DD 790/.097123/3   CN
EDMONTON CULTURE VULTURE, THE. **VFOAT** Culture Vulture. Vol. 1 (Sept. 1975)-. Periodical. English. Twelve times a year. Culture Vulture Publishing Ltd, Alberta T6G 2C5 Canada.

LC ML5 .E57   **ISSN** 0013-8231
DD 793.3105   UK
ENGLISH DANCE AND SONG. [Engl. dance song]. **Added/Corp** English Folk Dance and Song Society. **VFOAT** English Dance & Song. Vol. 1 (Sept. 1936)-. Periodical. English. Four times a year. £30.00 UK; £35.00 other. English Folk Dance and Song Society, Cecil Sharp House, 2 Regents Park Road, London NW1 7AY United Kingdom. **Tel** 011 44 171 4852206. **ED** Dave Arthur. **Bk Rev**. **Ad Acc**. **Circ:** 8,000 (ctrl). available on microfilm and microfiche from University Microfilms International (UMI). *Continues* E.F.D.S. News.
Desc: All aspects of English folk dance, song, and music plus related aspects of popular culture.
Ind/Abst Anthropol. Index; MLA Int. Bibl. Books Artic. Mod. Lang. Lit.; Music Index (-19??); RILM Abstr.

LC PN1560
DD 790.2   US
ENSEMBLE. (1987)-. English. Four times a year. $30.00. Corporeal Studio Ltd, One Hudson Street, New York NY 10013. **Tel** (212)619-0152. (**Subscription address:** Plenum Press Subscription Department, PO Box 730, Canal Street, Station NY 10013-1578. **Tel** (212)620-8000, (212)620-8466.) **ED** J.R. Moore. **Bk Rev**. **Ad Acc**. **Circ:** 12,500 (ctrl).
Desc: Focuses on a variety of arts including mimes, clowns, juggling, ventriloquism and comedy.

LC HD4801   **ISSN** 1055-1131
DD 331   US
ENTERTAINMENT EMPLOYMENT NETWORK. See Business and Economics-Labor.

LC HD4801   **ISSN** 1055-114X
DD 331   US
ENTERTAINMENT EMPLOYMENT WEEKLY. See Business and Economics-Labor.

LC PN2289 .E57   **ISSN** 0271-8014
DD 381/.457902/029479493   US
ENTERTAINMENT INDUSTRY DIRECTORY, THE. **Added/Corp** Star Maker Informative Listing Enterprises. (19??)-. Directory. English. One time a year. $11.95. Star Maker Informative Listing Enterprises, 6255 Sunset Boulevard, Hollywood CA 90028.

LC KF4290.A152 E57   **ISSN** 0739-1897
DD 343.73/0787902 347.303787902   US
ENTERTAINMENT, PUBLISHING AND THE ARTS HANDBOOK. [Entertain., publ. arts handb.]. **Added/Corp** Clark Boardman Company. (1983)-. English. One time a year. $79.50. Clark Boardman Callaghan, 155 Pfingsten Road, Deerfield IL 60015. **Tel** (800)323-8067. *Continues* Entertainment Law Journal (Entertainment Law Journal Association).

LC PN1993 .E59   **ISSN** 1049-0434
DD 791.4/05   US
ENTERTAINMENT WEEKLY. [Entertain. wkly.]. **VFOAT** Entertainment. No. 1 (Feb. 16 1990)-. Periodical. English. One time a week. $51.48. Time Inc. / New York, Time & Life Building, Rockefeller Center, New York NY 10020. (**Subscription address:** Time Customer Service, PO Box 60050, Tampa FL 33609. **Tel** (800)541-9955.) **ED** Jason McManus; James W. Seymour (managing editor). **Photos**. **Ad Acc**, **Adv Mgr:** Michael J. Kelly. available on microfilm and microfiche from University Microfilms International (UMI); available on an online database (files 647,746/Full-Text) from DIALOG.
Desc: Gives insight into the entertainment world. Features movies, T.V., video, music, and books.
Ind/Abst Acad. Abstr.; Book Rev. Index; EP Collect.; Homework Help.; Mag. Artic. Summar. Elite; Mag. Artic. Summar. Select; Mag. Artic. Summar. CD-ROM; Mag. Search; MasterFile FullTEXT 1000; MasterFile FullTEXT 350; MasterFile FullTEXT 650; MasterFile FullTEXT (Mar. 1992-); OCLC; Pub. Lib. FullTEXT; Telebase; World Mag. Bank.

LC PN2306.S77 .F36   **ISSN** 0046-3256
    CN
FANFARES. See Literature.

    ISSN 1062-3906
DD 791   US
FEMME FATALES OF THE FILMS. **VFOAT** Femme Fatales. Vol. 1, No. 1 (Summer 1992)-. Periodical. English. Four times a year. $21.00. Frederick S. Clarke, 7240 West Roosevelt Road, Forest Park IL 60130.

LC Z5784.M9 F45   **ISSN** 0093-6758
DD 791.43/01/6   US
FILM LITERATURE INDEX. See Motion Picture-Abstracting, Bibliographies and Statistics.

LC PN1560
DD 790.2   IT
FIRENZE SPETTACOLO. (1995)-. Italian. Eleven times a year (monthly except Aug.). L20440. Nuova ed Florence Press, Via Fabroni 9, 50134 Florence Italy. **Tel** 011 39 55 461572.

LC N1 .F73   **ISSN** 0731-2636
    US
FLUE. See The Arts-Art.

LC ML27.U5 N3676   **ISSN** 8756-8667
DD 788/.5/05   US
FLUTIST QUARTERLY, THE. See Music.

LC PN1560
DD 790.2   US
FOOTNOTES*. (197?)-. Catalog. English. Four times a year. Randolph Associates Inc, 1300 Arch Street, Philadelphia PA 19107. **Tel** (215)567-6662. **ED** Randolph Swartz. **Circ:** 150,000 (ctrl).
Desc: Catalogue of performing arts books.

LC PN1560   **ISSN** 1058-8191
DD 790.2   US
FRESH TRACKS. **VFOAT** Fresh Tracks Entertainment Publication. (1991)-. Periodical. English. Twelve times a year. $30.00. Partners in Entertainment, Sears Tower, PO Box 06555, Chicago IL 60606.

LC PN1560   **ISSN** 0885-0747
DD 790.2   US
FRONT ROW. **VFOAT** Front Row Magazine. Vol. 4, No. 1 (Sept. 1985)-. Periodical. English. Eleven times a year. Northwest Cultural Information Associates, PO Box 11438, Eugene OR 97440. *Continues* On State (Eugene, OR.).

LC PN1560   **ISSN** 0017-0232
DD 790.2   IT
UDC 792
GIORNALE DELLO SPETTACOLO. [G. Spett.]. (1945)-. Periodical. Italian. One time a week. L54500. GEA SRL, Via di Villa Patrizi 10, 00161 Rome Italy. **Tel** 011 39 6 88473265.

    ISSN 0704-7371
DD 790/.09713/83   CN
GLOUCESTER GUIDE. [Glos. guide]. **VAT** Monthly Gloucester Guide. May 1976-. Periodical. English (French). Free. Wynnmur Publications, PO Box 709, Orleans Ontario K0A 2V0.

    ISSN 0896-8802
DD 791   US
    CEASED
GOREZONE (NEW YORK, N.Y.). (GOREZONE.). [GoreZone]. **VFOAT** Gore Zone. (May 1988)-No. 26 (1993). Periodical. English. Starlog Press Inc., 475 Park Avenue South, New York NY 10016. **Tel** (212)689-2830, FAX (212)889-7933.

LC PN2289 .H34   **ISSN** 0898-7955
DD 791/.02573   US
HANDEL'S NATIONAL DIRECTORY FOR THE PERFORMING ARTS. [Handel's natl. dir. perform. arts]. **VFOAT** National Directory for the

The Arts —Performing Arts

Performing Arts. 4th Ed. (1988)-. Directory. English. Irregular. $250.00 (latest edition). R.R. Bowker, A Reed Reference Publishing Company, Part of Reed International PLC, PO Box 31, 121 Chanlon Drive, New Providence NJ 07974. **Tel** (908)464-6800, (800)521-8110, FAX (908)665-6688, telex 138-755. *Formed by the union of National Directory for the Performing Arts and Civic Centers, 0092-0738 and National Directory for the Performing Arts/Educational.*

LC PN1569.K6 H36
KO

HANGUK YONYE. **Added/Corp** Hanguk Yonye Hyophoe. Vol. 1 (1979)-. Periodical. Korean. Four times a year. Hanguk Yonye Hyophoe, 110 Insa-dong, Chongno-ku, Seoul South Korea.

LC NX600.P47 H53 **ISSN** 0160-9769
DD 790.2 US
SUSPENDED

HIGH PERFORMANCE (LOS ANGELES). (HIGH PERFORMANCE.). [High perform.]. Vol. 1 (Feb. 1978)- Suspended (1995). Periodical. English. Four times a year (Mar., June, Sept., Dec.). $26.00 (institutions), $22.00 (individuals) US; $28.00 Canada and Mexico; $58.00 (airmail). High Performance, 1641 18th Street, Santa Monica CA 90404-3807. **Tel** (310)315-9383, FAX (213)315-9383. **ED** Steven Durland. Index available. **Bk Rev**, **Ad Acc**, **Circ:** 5,000. available on microfilm and microfiche from University Microfilms International (UMI).
Desc: A magazine devoted to progressive thinking in the arts, spotlighting performance and multimedia from around the world.
Ind/Abst Art Index; ARTbibliogr. Mod.; ARTbibliogr. Curr. Titles; BHA : Biblio. Hist. Art; Curr. Cit.

ISSN 0226-272X
DD 790/.09713/5 CN

HIGHLIGHTS (MISSISSAUGA). (HIGHLIGHTS.). [Highlights]. **VAT** Highlights Entertainment Magazine. Apr. 1980-. Periodical. English. Twelve times a year. $1.50 per no. Highlights Entertainment Magazine, Suite 4 2395 Cawthra Road, Mississauga Ontario L5A 2W8 Canada.

LC PN2277.L59 H65 **ISSN** 1075-6531
DD 790.2/025794/94 US

HOLLYWOOD AGENTS/MANAGERS DIRECTORY. [Hollywood agent/manag. dir.]. **VFOAT** Hollywood Agents and Managers Directory; Hollywood Agents & Managers Directory; A.Hollywood Creative Directory, 3000 Olympic Boulevard, Santa Monica CA 90404. **Tel** (310)315-4815, FAX (310)315-4816. *Continues Hollywood Agents Directory.*

LC PN2005 .H97
DD 792/.05 IT

HYSTRIO. See Theater.

LC PN1560 **ISSN** 0112-9341
DD 790.2 NZ

ILLUSIONS. See Motion Picture.

LC P92.I7 I52
DD 790.2/05 II

INDIAN JOURNAL OF COMMUNICATION ARTS. No. 1 (Sept. 1975)-. Periodical. English. Twelve times a year. Hem Publishers, C-123 Greater Kailash, New Delhi 110048 India. **(Subscription address:** Prints India, 11 Darya Ganj, New Delhi 110002 India. **Tel** 011 91 11 3268645, FAX 011 91 11 3275542, telex 31-61087 PRIN-IN.**)**
Ind/Abst Commun. Abstr. (?-?).

LC PN1561 .I57 **ISSN** 1069-2029
DD 791 US

INSIDE ARTS. [Inside arts]. **Added/Corp** Association of Performing Arts Presenters. Vol. 2, No. 1 (March 1990)-. Trade Publication. English. Six times a year. $36.00. Association of Performing Arts Presenters, 1112 16th Street Northwest, Suite 620, Washington DC 20036. **Tel** (202)833-2787, FAX (202)833-1543. **ED** Gayle Stamler. **Bk Rev**, (Qty: 6-8). **Ad Acc, Adv Mgr:** Kim Kerker, **Tel** (202)833-2787. **Circ:** 2,500. *Continues Inside Performance, 1050-7973.*
Desc: News about the association and its members.

ISSN 1186-7477
DD 700 CN

INSIDE ENTERTAINMENT. [Inside entertain.]. **VFOAT** In Side Entertainment. Vol. 1, No. 1 (Jan. 24/Feb. 6, 1991)-. Periodical. English. Twenty-six times a year. $26.00 per year. Inside Entertainment, 210-645 Fort Street, Victoria British Columbia V8W 1G2 Canada.

LC PN2000
DD 792 AU

JACOBEAN DRAMA STUDIES. See Theater.

LC PN2000 .P47 **ISSN** 1063-2921
DD 790.2/0973 US

JOURNAL OF ARTS MANAGEMENT, LAW, AND SOCIETY. [J. arts manag. law, soc.]. **Added/Corp** Helen Dwight Reid Educational Foundation. **VFOAT** Arts Management, Law, and Society. (1992)-. Periodical. English. Four times a year. $92.00. Heldref Publications, 1319 Eighteenth Street Northwest, Washington DC 20036-1802. **Tel** (202)296-6267, (800)365-9753, FAX (202)296-5149. *Continues Journal of Arts Management and Law, 0733-5113.*
Ind/Abst Acad. Search; EP Collect.; Homework Help.; MasterFile FullTEXT 1000; MasterFile FullTEXT 350; MasterFile FullTEXT 650; MasterFile FullTEXT (July 1994-) [Full Txt.]; OCLC; Soc. Sci. Cit. Index [Select. Cov.]; Telebase.

LC MT820.J68
DD 780 US
CEASED

JOURNAL OF RESEARCH IN SINGING AND APPLIED VOCAL PEDAGOGY. See Music.

LC PN1569.K6 K33
KO

KAEKSOK. Vol. 1 (1984)-. Periodical. Korean. Twelve times a year. W36000. Chusik Hoesa Yeum, 24-3 1-ka Chungmuro Chung-ku, Seoul Korea. **Tel** 753 4263 7. **ED** Soung Tai Kim. **Circ:** 30,000.

LC PN2000 **ISSN** 1073-7103
DD 792 US

●LIMON JOURNAL. See Dance.

LC PN1560 .L55 **ISSN** 0377-0982
DD 790.2/0954 II

LIPIKA. Vol. 1 (Feb. 1972)-. Periodical. English. Four times a year. RS20.00. Lipika, F-20 Nizamuddin West, New Delhi 13 India.

ISSN 0962-4856
DD 780.78 UK

LIVE/PRO LIGHT & SOUND. [Live! St. Albans]. (1991)-. Trade Publication. English. Twelve times a year. $128.34. Mountain Lion Production Ltd, 35 High Street Sandridge, St. Albans Hertfordshire AL4 9DD United Kingdom. **Tel** 011 44 1727 842888, FAX 011 44 1727 844417. **ED** Jerry Gilbert. **Ad Acc, Adv Mgr:** Jay Green, **Tel** 011 44 1727 821861. **Circ:** 14,500 (ctrl).
Desc: Trade magazine for the live performance industry covering lighting, equipment, and reviews.

ISSN 0158-099X
DD 790.20994 AT

LOWDOWN (1982). [Lowdown 1982]. (1982)-. Trade Publication. English. Seven times a year (Jan., Mar., May, July, Sept., Nov. and 1 issue directions). 42.76Aus$. Carclew Youth Performing Arts Center, 11 Jeffcott Street, Center/Assites, N Adelaide SA 5006 Australia. **Tel** 011 61 8 2675111. **ED** Belinda MacQueen. **Bk Rev**, (Qty: 24). **Ad Acc, Adv Mgr:** Polly O'Neil, **Tel** 08 2675111. **Circ:** 1,500 (ctrl). *Continues AYPAA Lowdown, 0812-2911.*
Desc: For those interested or involved in Australian Youth Arts. Features articles on trends and developments in organizations, festivals and education. Also includes information on the politics and new works of Australian artists.

LC L **ISSN** 0726-9072
DD 370 AT

MASK (BLACKBURN). See Education-Teaching and Curriculum.

ISSN 1061-0316
DD 791 US

MEDIA AND FILM. [Media film]. Vol. 1, No. 1 (Feb. 1992)-. Periodical. English. Twelve times a year. $75.00. Gig Publishing Group, 110-64 Queens Boulevard, Suite 288, Forest Hills NY 11375.

LC RC **ISSN** 0885-1158
DD 616 CCC
NLM W1; ME416RU **CODEN** MPPAEC
Pr Rev

MEDICAL PROBLEMS OF PERFORMING ARTISTS. See Industrial Health and Safety.

LC PN2587 .M43 **ISSN** 0143-3784
DD 792/.0942/0902 UK

MEDIEVAL ENGLISH THEATRE. See Theater.

ISSN 0886-8719
DD 791 US

MIDNIGHT MARQUEE. [Midnight marquee]. **VFOAT** MidMar. (19??)-. Periodical. English. $3.25. Richard Svehla, 4000 Glenarm Avenue, Baltimore MD 21206.
Ind/Abst Film Lit. Index.

ISSN 1081-2555
DD 791 US

MOVIE ADVERTISING COLLECTOR. [Movie Advert. Collect.]. **VFOAT** A.M.A.C. (Feb. 1990)-. Periodical. English. Six times a year. $10.00. Movie Advertising Collector, PO Box 28587, Philadelphia PA 19149.

LC ML12 .M88 **ISSN** 0735-7788
DD 780/.25 US

MUSICAL AMERICA. INTERNATIONAL DIRECTORY OF THE PERFORMING ARTS. See Music.

LC PN1560 **ISSN** 1037-700X
DD 790.2 AT

NADIE AUSTRALIA JOURNAL, THE. **VFOAT** National Association for Drama in Education Journal. (1987)-. Periodical. English. Two times a year. Visual & Performing Arts Unit, Studies Directorate, PO Box 33, North Quay Queensland 4002 Australia. **Tel** 011 61 7 2370424. *Continues NADIE Journal, 0159-6659.*

ISSN 0836-0197
DD 790/.05 CN

NETWORK (TORONTO. 1987). (NETWORK : CANADA'S ENTERTAINMENT MAGAZINE.). [Network]. (Spring 1987)-. Periodical. English. Six times a year. 11.22Can$. Control Media Communication, 287 Macpherson Avenue, Toronto Ontario M4V 1A4 Canada. **Tel** (416)928-2909, FAX (416)966-1181. **ED** Maureen Littlejohn. **Ad Acc, Adv Mgr:** H.Wolfe. **Circ:** 149,400 (ctrl).

LC GV1580.N48 **ISSN** 1040-8908
DD 792 US
CEASED

NEW DANCE REVIEW, THE. See Dance.

LC PN2000 .N443 **ISSN** 1050-9720
DD 792/.05 US
Pr Rev

NEW ENGLAND THEATRE JOURNAL. See Theater.

ISSN 0712-2772
DD 792.8/06/071 CN

NOTATION (ENGLISH EDITION). (NOTATION / THEATRE-BALLET CANADIEN = THEATRE BALLET OF CANADA.). [Notation]. **Added/Corp** Theatre Ballet of Canada. Vol. 1, No. 1 (Dec. 1980)-. Periodical. English. Four times a year. Free. Notation / Theatre Ballet of Canada, PO Box 366 Station A, Ottawa Ontario K1N 8V3 Canada.

LC Z6935 .N68 PN1584
RU

NOVAIA SOVETSKAIA I INOSTRANNAIA LITERATURA PO ISKUSSTVU: TANETS, TSIRK, ESTRADA. **Added/Corp** Informtsentr po Problemam Kultury i Iskusstva (Soviet Union) Vsesoiuznaia Gosudarstvennaia Biblioteka Inostrannoi Literatury (Soviet Union). (19??)-. Periodical. Russian. (Multiple languages). Twelve times a year. Gosudarstvennaia Biblioteka, Informatsionnyi Tsentr, Imeni V. I. Lenina, Prospekt Kalinina 3, 121019 Moscow Russia.

ISSN 0229-5296
DD 790/.09715/23 CN

NOW (RIVERVIEW). (NOW : PEOPLE BELIEVE IN NOW.). [Now]. **VFOAT** Now Weekly Magazine. **VAT** Now Weekly. (1977)-. Periodical. English. One time a week. Now / Riverview, 230 Downey Avenue, Riverview New Brunswick E1B 1W7 Canada. *Continues Show Biz.*

LC PN1560 **ISSN** 0163-2132
DD 790.2 US

ON STAGE (WASHINGTON). (ON STAGE.). **Added/Corp** American Theatre Association. (19??)-. Periodical. English. Four times a year. $30.00 (includes membership), $15.00 (student membership). On Stage, PO Box 4040, Fullerton CA 92634.

LC PN1560
DD 790.2 US

ON THE ARIZONA SET. (19??)-. English. Twelve times a year. $48.00. Arizona Production Association, 3900 East Camelback Suite 200, Suite 200, Phoenix AZ 85018. **Tel** (602)345-6464, FAX (602)957-4828. *Continues Arizona Film Theatre & Television.*

ISSN 1056-103X
DD 791 US

OUT IN VIDEO. [Out video]. (1991)-. Periodical. English. Four times a year. $10.00. Persona Press, Box 14022, San Francisco CA 94114.

ISSN 1067-2222
DD 790 US

P FORM. (P FORM : PERFORMANCE ART MAGAZINE.). [P form]. **VFOAT** Performance Art Magazine; P-Form. (1986)-. Periodical. English. Four times a year (Feb., May, Aug., Nov.). $20.00. Randolph Street Gallery, 756 North Milwaukee, Chicago IL 60622. **Tel** (312)666-7737, FAX (312)666-8986. **ED** Ken Thompson. Index available. cum. index. **Bk Rev**, (Qty: 20). **Ad Acc, Adv Mgr:** Ken. **Circ:** 1,700.
Desc: Multi-disciplinary experimental arts journal profiling performance, video, installation and electronic/media arts and general cultural and arts issues.

ISSN 1075-3133
DD 791 US
PAGEANTRY (ALTAMONTE SPRINGS, FLA.). (PAGEANTRY : THE MAGAZINE FOR THE PAGEANT INDUSTRY.). [Pageantry]. **Added/Corp** Pageantry, Talent & Entertainment Services, Inc. World Pageant Association. **VFOAT** Pageantry Magazine. (June 1980)-. Trade Publication. English. Four times a year (published within the seasons). $16.00. Pageantry Magazine, 1855 West State Road 434, Suite 254, Longwood FL 32750. **Tel** (407)260-2262, FAX (407)260-5131. **ED** Brian Chambers. Index available. cum. index. **Bk Rev**, (Qty: 4). **Ad Acc**, **Adv Mgr:** C. Dunn. **Circ:** 100,000.
Desc: For pageant, talent, modeling participants, and for directors, judges, teachers, and coaches. Gives information regarding events, prizes, scholarships awards, career goals, success stories by noted famous people, and inspirational stories to achieve. Fashion, grooming, fitness, photography, modeling and achievement are what Pageantry offers.

ISSN 0705-9213
DD 790/.09714/2 CN
PANORAMA (HULL). (PANORAMA.). **VAT** Revue Panorama. Vol. 1 (July/Aug. 1977)-. Periodical. French. Free. Les Editions Segala, 75 boulevard St. Raymond, Hull Quebec J8Y 1S4 Canada.

LC PN1993.5.U6 ISSN 1064-7236
DD 384/.83/097305 US
PAUL KAGAN'S BOX OFFICE CHAMPIONS. ACTORS/ACTRESSES. **See** Motion Picture-Abstracting, Bibliographies and Statistics.

LC PN1560
DD 790.2 US
PERFORMANCE. (19??)-. English. Four times a year. $12.00. Bill Communications Inc., 355 Park Avenue South, New York NY 10010-1789. **Tel** (800)360-5200, (212)592-6200, FAX (212)592-6209.

LC PN1560 .P47 ISSN 0006-1883
DD 790/.05 US
PERFORMANCE. Vol. 1 (Dec. 1971)-. Periodical. English. Six times a year. $9.00. Performance, 249 West 13th Street, New York NY 10011. available on microfilm from University Microfilms International (UMI).

ISSN 0882-9314
DD 790 US
Pr Rev.
PERFORMANCE (FORT WORTH, TEX.). (PERFORMANCE.). [Performance]. (19??)-. Periodical. English. Fifty-one times per year (weekly except New Year's). $189.00. Performance Magazine Texas, 1101 University Drive, Suite 108, Ft Worth TX 76107. **Tel** (817)338-9444, FAX (817)877-4273. **ED** Carol Noel. **Ad Acc**, **Adv Mgr:** Diana Augustine. **Circ:** 20,000. ***Continues** Performance Newspaper, 0746-9772.*
Desc: A business magazine for the live entertainment concert touring industry.

ISSN 0229-7965
DD 790.2/09713/541 CN
PERFORMANCE (TORONTO). (PERFORMANCE.). [Performance]. (May/June 1978)-. Periodical. English. Four times a year. 8.00Can$. National Theatre Publications, 30 St. Claire, Suite 805, Toronto Ontario M4V 3A1 Canada. **Tel** (416)926-7595. ***Continued in part by** National Ballet Magazine (Toronto, Ont.); Canadian Opera Company Magazine, 0844-384X.*

LC PN2304 .P47 ISSN 0838-4452
DD 791/.0971/021 CN
CEASED
PERFORMING ARTS. **See** The Arts-Abstracting, Bibliographies and Statistics.

LC PN1582.C3 P47 ISSN 1185-3433
DD 790.2/0971 CN
Pr Rev.
PERFORMING ARTS & ENTERTAINMENT IN CANADA. [Perform. arts entertain. Can.]. **VFOAT** Performing Arts and Entertainment in Canada. **VAT** Performing Arts and Entertainment in Canada. Vol. 26, No. 3 (Spring 1991)-. Periodical. English. Four times a year (Mar., June, Sept., Dec.). 6.40Can$. Performing Arts and Entertainment in Canada, 104 Glenrose Avenue, Toronto Ontario M4T 1K8 Canada. **Tel** (416)484-4534, FAX (416)484-6214. **ED** Karen Bell. **Ad Acc**, **Adv Mgr:** G.Hencz. **Circ:** 45,000. available on microfilm and microfiche from University Microfilms International (UMI). Documents available from The Genuine Article, UMI Article Clearinghouse, Magazine Collection. ***Continues** Performing Arts in Canada, 0031-5230.*
Desc: Covers news and information in the areas of arts, entertainment, and personalities.
Ind/Abst Acad. Abstr.; Acad. Search; Arts Humanit. Citation Index [Full Cov.]; Can. Index; Curr. Contents Arts Humanit.; EP Collect.; Gen. Period. Index (1991-); Homework Help.; Humanit. Source; Mag. Index Plus (1991-); MasterFile FullTEXT 1000; MasterFile FullTEXT 350; MasterFile FullTEXT 650; MasterFile FullTEXT (Jan. 1992-); Newsp. Period. Abstr. (1988-); OCLC; Pub. Lib. FullTEXT; Res. Alert [Full Cov.]; Telebase; Mag. Index; TOM Gen. Index (1991-) [Full Txt.].

LC Z
DD 011 US
PERFORMING ARTS BIOGRAPHY MASTER INDEX. **See** The Arts-Abstracting, Bibliographies and Statistics.

LC PN1580 .P43 ISSN 1074-2840
DD 790.2/023/73 US
•PERFORMING ARTS CAREER DIRECTORY. [Perform. arts career dir.]. **Added/Corp** Gale Research Inc. **VFOAT** Performing Arts. 1st Ed. (1994)-. Directory. English. $34.00 (hardcover), $17.95 (softcover). Gale Research Inc., 835 Penobscot Building, 645 Griswold Street, Detroit MI 48226. **Tel** (800)877-GALE, (313)961-2242, FAX (313)961-6083, (800)414-5043, telex TWX 810-221-7086.
Desc: Allows readers to know what life as a performer is really like.

LC PN1560 ISSN 0739-1161
DD 790.2 US
PERFORMING ARTS FORUM. [Perform. arts forum]. **Added/Corp** International Society of Performing Arts Administrators. Vol. 1, No. 1 (Jan./Feb. 1976)-. Periodical. English. Ten times a year. $30.00. International Society of Performing Arts Administrators, 2920 Fuller Avenue Northeast, Suite 205, Grand Rapids MI 49505. **Tel** (616)364-3000, FAX (616)364-9010. **ED** Michael C. Hardy. **Ad Acc. Circ:** 750 (ctrl). ***Continues** International Society of Performing Arts Administrator. Bulletin - International Society of Performing Arts Administrators, 0099-0582.*

LC PN1560 ISSN 0730-9031
DD 790.2 US
PERFORMING ARTS IDEABOOKS. [Perform. arts ideabook]. **Added/Corp** Theatre Communication Group. **VFOAT** Performing Arts Idea Book; TCG Performing Arts Ideabook. (1982)-. Monographic series. English. Price varies per volume. Theatre Communications Group, 355 Lexington Avenue, New York NY 10017. **Tel** (212)697-5230, FAX (212)983-4847.

LC PN1561 .P47 ISSN 0735-8393
DD 790.2/05 US
CCC
PERFORMING ARTS JOURNAL. [Perform. arts j.]. (Spring 1976)-. Periodical. English. Three times a year (Jan., May, & Sept.). $46.00. Johns Hopkins University Press, 2715 North Charles Street, Baltimore MD 21218-4319. **Tel** (410)516-6987, FAX (410)516-6968. **(Subscription address:** John Hopkins University Press, Journals Publishing Division, PO Box 19966, Baltimore MD 21211. **Tel** (410)516-6987, (800)548-1784, FAX (410)516-6968.**)** **Bk Rev. Ad Acc. Circ:** 4,000. available on microfilm and microfiche from University Microfilms International (UMI). Documents available from The Genuine Article, UMI Article Clearinghouse.
Desc: International critique of the performing arts covering plays, productions, essays, dance, opera and related topics. Includes playscripts.
Ind/Abst Acad. Search; Am. Humanit. Index (19??-199?); Arts Humanit. Citation Index [Full Cov.]; Book Rev. Index; Curr. Contents Arts Humanit.; EP Collect.; Expand. Acad. Index (1989-); Homework Help.; Humanit. Index; Humanit. Source; INFO-SOUTH Abstr.; Mag. Search; MasterFile FullTEXT 1000; MasterFile FullTEXT 350; MasterFile FullTEXT 650; MasterFile FullTEXT (July 1993-); MLA Int. Bibl. Books Artic. Mod. Lang. Lit.; Newsp. Period. Abstr. (1991-); OCLC; Res. Alert [Full Cov.]; Telebase.

LC PN1560 ISSN 0031-5222
DD 790.2 US
CEASED
PERFORMING ARTS (LOS ANGELES EDITION). (PERFORMING ARTS.). [Perform. arts]. Vol. 1 (Nov. 1967)-(19??). Periodical. English. Performing Arts Network, 2999 Overland Avenue/201, Los Angeles CA 90064-4243. **Tel** (310)839-8000. **ED** Herbert Glass. **Bk Rev. Ad Acc. Circ:** 825,000 (ctrl).
Desc: In-theatre magazines for California and Texas including program material and general editorial matter.
Ind/Abst Music Artic. Guide (?-?).

LC PN1560
DD 790.2 US
PERFORMING ARTS (NEWSBANK, INC.). (PERFORMING ARTS [MICROFORM].). Vol. 9, Card 61 (March 1983)-. Periodical. English. Twelve times a year. ***Continues** Newsbank. Performing Arts, 0737-3996.*

LC Z6935 .P46 ISSN 0360-3814
DD 016.7902/08 US
PERFORMING ARTS RESOURCES. [Perform. arts resour.]. **Added/Corp** Theatre Library Association. (1974)-. Academic Scholarly Publication. English. Irregular. Theatre Library Association, 111 Amsterdam Avenue, New York NY 10023. **Tel** (212)870-1670. **ED** B. Cohen-Stratyner (editor's address: 265 Riverside Drive, New York, NY 10025). **Circ:** 500 (ctrl).
Desc: Designed to gather and disseminate scholarly articles dealing with the location of resource materials relating to theatre, film, television and radio. Includes listings and descriptions, and previously unpublished monographs of original source material.
Ind/Abst MLA Int. Bibl. Books Artic. Mod. Lang. Lit.

LC PN1560 ISSN 1068-8153
DD 790.2 US
•PERFORMING ARTS STUDIES. (1993)-. Monographic series. English. Price varies per volume. Harwood Academic Publishers / New York, PO Box 786, Cooper Station, New York NY 10276. **Tel** (212)206-8900, (201)643-7500. **ED** Janice Rieman.
Desc: Provides resource books of both a practical and philosophical nature for teachers and students of the performing arts.

LC PN1560
DD 790.2 FR
PLATEAUX. (19??)-. French. Four times a year. 60.00F France; 70.00F other. Plateaux, 21 Bis rue Victor Masse, 75009 Paris France. **Tel** 011 33 1 42858811, FAX 011 33 1 45264721. **ED** M. Morange and J. Shuman. **Ad Acc. Circ:** 3,.000.
Desc: A professional journal for performers and those involved in the performing arts. Published by the French performers.

LC PN1560 ISSN 0048-4415
DD 790.2 CN
PLAYBOARD. **Added/Corp** Playhouse Theatre Company, Vancouver, B.C. Vancouver Opera. Vol. 1 (Oct. 1966)-. English. Twelve times a year. 12.00Can$. Arch-Way Publishers, 7560 Lawrence Drive, Burnaby BC V5A 1T6 Canada. **Tel** (604)420-6115, FAX (604)420-6115. **ED** Ralph Westbrook. **Ad Acc. Circ:** 50,000.
Desc: Advancement of the professional and performing arts, live theatre, musical concerts, operas, and special events.

LC PN1560 ISSN 0924-2937
DD 790.2 NE
PODIUMKUNSTEN. **Added/Corp** Netherlands. Centraal Bureau voor de Statistiek. Hoofdafdeling Sociaal-Culturele Statistieken. **VFOAT** Performing Arts. (1989)-. Dutch (summaries and/or abstracts in English). One time a year. Centraal Bureau voor de Statistiek, AFD ALG Zaken, Postbus 959, 2270 AZ Voorburg Netherlands. **Tel** 011 31 70 3373800, FAX 011 31 70 0387429, telex 32692 CBS NL. ***Formed by the union of** Muziek en Theater **and** Uitgaan.*

ISSN 1188-195X
DD 791.45 CN
POSTECRAN. [PostEcran]. **Added/Corp** Association Nationale des Telespectateurs et Telespectatrices. **VFOAT** Post-Ecran. Vol. 1, No 1 (Nov. 1991)-. Periodical. French. Twelve times a year. Limited free distribution. Association Nationale des Telespectateurs et Telespectatrices, 4005 rue Bellechasse, Montreal Quebec H1X 1J6 Canada.

LC PN1560
DD 790.2 US
PROFILE SURVEY - ASSOCIATION OF PERFORMING ARTS PRESENTERS. (19??)-. English. $325.00 US; $345.00 Canada; $390.00 other. Association of Performing Arts Presenters, 1112 16th Street Northwest, Suite 620, Washington DC 20036. **Tel** (202)833-2787, FAX (202)833-1543.

LC PN1970 .P85 ISSN 0033-443X
DD 791.53 US
PUPPETRY JOURNAL, THE. **Added/Corp** Puppeteers of America. Vol. 1 (1949)-. Periodical. English. Four times a year (March, June, Sept., Dec.). $30.00. Puppeteers of America, 5 Cricklewood Path, Pasadena CA 91107. **Tel** (818)797-5748. **ED** George Latshaw. **Bk Rev. Ad Acc. Circ:** 2,000 (ctrl). available on microfilm and microfiche from University Microfilms International (UMI).

LC PN3203 ISSN 1070-3624
DD 791.62 US
•PUPPETRY YEARBOOK, THE. [Puppetry yearb.]. Vol. 1 (1995)-. English. One time a year. $49.95. Edwin Mellen Press, 415 Ridge Street, PO Box 450, Lewiston NY 14092. **Tel** (716)754-2266, (716)754-2788, FAX (716)754-4056. **ED** James Fisher.
Desc: Explores the history of the art of puppetry.

ISSN 0828-6140
DD 790.2/09714 CN
QUI FAIT QUOI. [Qui fait quoi]. Vol. 1, No. 1 (Jan. 1984)-. Periodical. French. Eleven times a year (Dec/Jan issues combined). 120.05Can$. Qui Fait Quoi, 1276 Amherst, Montreal Quebec H2L 3K8 Canada. **Tel** (514)842-5333, FAX (514)842-6717.

LC Z1035.A1 W45 ISSN 1061-6861
DD 028 US
RAPPORT (LOS ANGELES, CALIF.). (RAPPORT : WEST COAST REVIEW OF BOOKS, ART & ENTERTAINMENT.). [Rapport]. **VFOAT** Rapport Magazine. Vol. 16, No. 3 (Oct./Nov. 1991)-. Periodical.

The Arts —Performing Arts

English. Six times a year (Jan., Mar., May, July, Sept., Nov.). $11.97. Rapport Publishing Company Inc., 5265 Fountain Avenue, Upper Terrace, Los Angeles CA 90029. **Tel** (213)660-0433. **ED** D. David Dreis. **Bk Rev**, (Qty: 60). **Ad Acc, Adv Mgr:** Glen Kenyon. **Circ:** 60,000. *Continues West Coast Review Bf Books, 0095-3555.* **Desc:** Book & CD reviews, feature articles, artist, profiles, entertainment oriented consumer magazine. **Ind/Abst** Book Rev. Index.

ISSN 0820-8425
DD 790.2/025/714
CN

REPERTOIRE DES MEMBRES DE L'UNION DES ARTISTES.
[Repert. memb. union artistes]. **Main/Corp** Union des Artistes. (1982)-. French. One time a year. 20.01Can$. Union de Artistes, 1290 rue St. Denis, Montreal Quebec H2X 3J7 Canada. **Tel** (514)288-6682. **Circ:** 7,400 (ctrl) *Continues Union des Artistes. Repertoire, 0710-443X.*

LC PN1560
DD 790.2
US

RESOURCE DIRECTORY. PRESENTERS OF PERFORMING ARTS.
VFOAT Presenters of Performing Arts. (1981)-. Directory. English. Arts Midwest, 528 Hennepin Avenue, Suite 310, Minneapolis MN 55403. **Tel** (612)341-0755.

LC PN2273.G73 R39   **ISSN** 0738-3681
DD 790.2/025/77
US

RESOURCE DIRECTORY. TOURING PERFORMING COMPANIES.
(RESOURCE DIRECTORY. TOURING PERFORMING COMPANIES / GREAT LAKES ARTS ALLIANCE.). **Added/Corp** Great Lakes Arts Alliance. (1983)-. Directory. English. Arts Midwest, 528 Hennepin Avenue, Suite 310, Minneapolis MN 55403. **Tel** (612)341-0755.

ISSN 1198-2837
DD 791.43/05
CN

●**REVERSE SHOT.** [Reverse shot]. **Added/Corp** Pacific Cinematheque. Vol. 1, No. 1 (Jan. 1994)-. Periodical. English. Three times a year. 15.00Can$. Pacific Cinematheque, 200-1131 Howe Street, Vancouver, British Columbia, V6Z 2L7 Canada.

ISSN 0319-7131
DD 790.2/09714/281
CN

RIDEAU. Vol. 1 (Sept. 1975)-. Periodical. French. Irregular. Rideau, Bureau 300 1454 rue De La Montagne, Montreal Quebec H3G 1Z6 Canada.

ISSN 1186-8368
DD 790.2
CN
CEASED

RIVE CULTURELLE. [Rive cult.]. Vol. 1, No 1 (June 1991)-(199?). Periodical. French. Rive Culturelle, 865 rue St-Jean #5, Longueuil Quebec J4H 2Y9.

LC PN1560   **ISSN** 1060-6858
DD 790.2
US

SAN FRANCISCO PERFORMING ARTS LIBRARY AND MUSEUM SERIES.
Added/Corp San Francisco Performing Arts Library and Museum. (1992)-. Monographic series. English. Price varies per volume. San Francisco Performing Arts Library and Museum Journal, 399 Grove Street, San Francisco CA 94102. **Tel** (415)255-4800. *Continues San Francisco Performing Arts Library and Museum Journal, 1047-4110.*

LC N17 .S2   **ISSN** 0036-4339
II

SANGEET NATAK. **Added/Corp** Sangeet Natak Akademi. (1965)-. Periodical. English. Four times a year. $15.00. Sangeet Natak Akademi, Rabindra Bhaven/Feroze Shah Road, New Delhi 110001 India. **Tel** 387246. **(Subscription address:** Prints India, 11 Darya Ganj, New Delhi 110002 India. **Tel** 011 91 11 3268645, FAX 011 91 11 3275542, telex 31-61087 PRIN-IN.) **ED** Abhijit Chatterjee. **Bk Rev. Circ:** 750. **Desc:** A journal of Indian music, dance and theatre. **Ind/Abst** RILM Abstr.

ISSN 1079-6851
DD 791
US

●**SCENARIO (NEW YORK, N.Y.).** (SCENARIO : THE MAGAZINE OF SCREENWRITING ART.). [Scenar.]. Vol. 1, No. 1 (Winter 1995)-. Periodical. English. Four times a year. $59.95. RC Publications Inc., 3200 Tower Oaks Boulevard, Rockville MD 20852. **Tel** (800)222-2654, (301)770-2900, FAX (301)984-3203.

LC PN1993.5.U65 S37   **ISSN** 0890-5266
US
TITLE CHANGE

SCREEN ACTOR HOLLYWOOD. See Motion Picture.

LC ML136   **ISSN** 0826-5216
DD 780/.25/713541
CN

SEE THE MUSIC. See Music.

LC PR3091 .B77   **ISSN** 0748-2558
DD 792.9/5/05
US
Pr Rev.

SHAKESPEARE BULLETIN. See Theater.

LC PN1560
DD 790.2
AT
CEASED

SHOWCAST. (19??)-(19??). Directory. English. Showcast Publications, Suite 4 No. 5 Alexander Street, Crows Nest 2065 New South Wales Australia. **Tel** 011 61 2 4382144. Index available. **Ad Acc. Desc:** Performers casting directory.

ISSN 1188-0007
DD 791.43
CN

SILENCE -- ON TOURNE (MONTREAL). (SILENCE -- ON TOURNE.). [Silence tourne]. (Sept. 1991)-. Periodical. French. Twelve times a year. Free. Silence ... On Tourne, Bureau A, 12147 boulevard St-Germain, Montreal Quebec H4J 2A4 Canada.

ISSN 1054-8491
DD 791
US
CEASED

SIMPSONS ILLUSTRATED. [Simpsons illus.]. Vol. 1, No. 1 (Spring 1991)-(Summer 1993). Periodical. English. Simpson's Illustrated, PO Box 10195, Des Moines IA 50340.

LC ML28.B815 C767   **ISSN** 8756-8861
DD 780/.5
US

SOCIETY NEWS (BROOMALL, PA.). See Music.

LC M   **ISSN** 0191-9504
DD 780
US

SOUNDINGS NORTHWEST. See Music.

LC PN2001 .S68
SA
Pr Rev.

SOUTH AFRICAN THEATRE JOURNAL : SATJ.
See Theater.

LC PN1993.5.U6 C38   **ISSN** 1082-8435
DD 384/.8/0977
US
TITLE CHANGE

SOUTHWEST SIGHT AND SOUND. [Southwest sight sound]. (1995)-(1995). Periodical. English. Falcon Enterprises, Columbus OH. *Merged with Central Cities Sight and Sound, 1058-9252 to form Central Cities, Southwest Sight and Sound, 1085-1623.*

LC PN1560   **ISSN** 0584-522X
DD 790.2
RU

SOVETSKAIA ESTRADA I TSIRK. **Added/Corp** Russia (1923-U.S.S.R.) Ministerstvo Kultury. (19??)-. Periodical. Russian. Twelve times a year. $79.95.

LC PN1560   **ISSN** 0309-0183
DD 790.2
UK

SPOTLIGHT. ACTORS. [Spotlight. Actors]. (1927)-. Directory. English. One time a year. $94.66. Spotlight / London, 7 Leicester Place, London WC2H 7BP United Kingdom. **Tel** 011 44 171 4377631, FAX 011 44 171 4375881. **ED** Christine Barry. **Ad Acc. Desc:** Casting directory containing information pertinent to actors.

LC PN2597 .S67   **ISSN** 0308-9827
DD 792/.09713/02541
UK

SPOTLIGHT. ACTRESSES. [Spotlight. Actresses]. (1927)-. Directory. English. One time a year. $94.66. Spotlight / London, 7 Leicester Place, London WC2H 7BP United Kingdom. **Tel** 011 44 171 4377631, FAX 011 44 171 4375881. **ED** Christine Barry. **Ad Acc.** ctrl circ. available on CD-ROM from the publisher. **Desc:** Casting directory containing information pertinent to actresses.

LC PN1560   **ISSN** 0010-7344
DD 790.2
UK

SPOTLIGHT CONTACTS. **VFOAT** Contacts. No. 23 (1956)-. Periodical. English. One time a year. $15.41. Spotlight / London, 7 Leicester Place, London WC2H 7BP United Kingdom. **Tel** 011 44 171 4377631, FAX 011 44 171 4375881. **ED** Christine Barry. **Ad Acc.** ctrl circ.

ISSN 0821-4778
DD 792.7
CN

SPOTLIGHT (VANCOUVER). (SPOTLIGHT.). [Spotlight]. (1981)-. Periodical. English. Six times a year. $10.00. Access Communications, PO Box 69805 Station K, Vancouver British Columbia V5K 4Y7 Canada.

LC PN2277.W2 S66   **ISSN** 0095-7461
DD 790.2/025/753
US

SPOTS. 1974/75-. English. One time a year. $2.00. Gambit, PO Box 1122, Rockville MD 20850.

ISSN 1033-3975
DD 790.209945
AT
CEASED

STAGES MELBOURNE. (STAGES.). [Stages'Melb.]. (1989)-(May/June 1995). Periodical. English. Victorian Arts Centre, 100 Street Kilda Road, Melbourne Victoria 3004 Australia. **Tel** 011 61 3 6848484. **Circ:** 5,000. *Continues Victorian Arts Centre Magazine, 0811-5478.*

LC GV1580 .D247
DD 791/.025
US

STERN'S PERFORMING ARTS DIRECTORY.
See Dance.

ISSN 1040-3167
DD 791
US

STORYBOARD (ANAHEIM HILLS, CALIF.).
(STORYBOARD.). (198?)-. Periodical. English. Six times a year. $24.97. Storyboard Magazine Group, 2512 Artesia Boulevard, Redona Beach CA 90278. **Tel** (213)376-8788.

LC PN2306.S77 S767B   **ISSN** 0085-6770
DD 792/.09713/23
CN

STRAFFORD FESTIVAL. (STRATFORD FESTIVAL : [PROGRAM].). **Main/Corp** Stratford Festival (Ont.). (1957)-. English. One time a year. 10.00Can$. Stratford Shakespearean Festival Foundation of Canada, PO Box 520, Stratford Ontario M5A 6V2 Canada. **Tel** (519)271-4040, (905)364-8355. **Ad Acc. Circ:** 20,000. *Supersedes Stratford Festival. Annual Festival of Drama and Annual Festival of Music., 0319-7190.*

ISSN 1065-397X
DD 790
US

STROKE & DAGGER. [Stroke dagger]. **VFOAT** Stroke and Dagger. Vol. 1, No. 1 (1992)-. Periodical. English. Six times a year. $18.00. Freman Publications, 9800 Topanga Canyon Boulevard, Suite 145, Chatsworth CA 91311.

LC PN1560
DD 790.2
RU

STSENICHESKAIA TEKHNIKA I TEKHNOLOGIIA.
Added/Corp Gosudarstvennyi Institut po Proektirovaniiu Teatralno-Zrelishchnykh Predpriiatii. Moscow. Publichnaia Biblioteka. Informatsionnyi Tsentr po Problemam Kultury i Iskusstva. (1963)-. Periodical. Russian (Russian; table of contents in English and German). Six times a year. $28.40. **(Subscription address:** Victor Kamkin, 4956 Boiling Brook Parkway, Rockville MD 20852. **Tel** (301)881-5973.)

LC PN1609.R6 S8   **ISSN** 0039-3991
RM

STUDII SI CERCETARI DE ISTORIA ARTEI. SERIA TEATRU, MUZICA, CINEMATOGRAFIE.
[Stud. cercet. ist. artei, Ser. teatru muz. cinematogo]. **Added/Corp** Academia Republicii Populare Romine. Academia Republicii Socialiste Romania. Academia de Stiinte Sociale Si Politice a Republicii Socialiste Romania. **VFOAT** Seria Teatru, Muzica, Cinematografie; Etudes et Recherches d'Histoire de l'Art. Serie Theatre, Musique, Cinema. Vol. 11 (1964)-. Romanian. One time a year. $45.00. Editura Academia Republicii Socialiste Romania, Calea Victoriei Nr 125, R-79717 Bucuresti Romania. **Tel** telex 10376 PRSFI R. **(Subscription address:** Rompresfilatelia, PO Box 12 201, Bucharest Romania. **Tel** 011 40 0 10376.) *Supersedes in part Studi si Cercetari de Istoria Artei.* **Desc:** Publishes studies on Romanian theater, cinema and music, as well as on the aesthetic arts. **Ind/Abst** RILM Abstr.

LC PN1560 .P48A
SA

SUKOVS-NUUS. **Main/Corp** Performing Arts Council, O.F.S. **VFOAT** PACOFS News. Multiple languages (Afrikaans and English). Performing Arts Council OFS, PO Box 1292, Bloemfontein South Africa.

ISSN 1070-7522
DD 791
US

TAFRIJA (TUCKER, GA.). (TAFRIJA.). [Tafrija]. **VFOAT** Tafrija Magazine. (19??)-. Periodical. English. Twelve times a year. $18.00. Tafrija, 1841 Montreal Avenue, Suite 207, Tucker GA 30084. **Tel** (404)938-0267, FAX (404)938-0436. **Bk Rev. Ad Acc. Circ:** 70,000 (ctrl). available on microfilm.

ISSN 1181-6090
DD 791/.0922715
CN

TALENT CATALOGUE / ACTRA ATLANTIC CANADA.
[Talent cat. - ACTRA Atl. Can.]. **Added/Corp** Alliance of Canadian Cinema, Television and Radio Artists. Atlantic Canada. Canadian Actors' Equity Association. **VFOAT** ACTRA Atlantic Canada Talent Catalogue. **VAT** Talent Catalogue - Alliance of Canadian Cinema, Television and Radio Artists, Atlantic Canada. 2nd Ed. (1991)-. English. Every 2 years. Actra Atlantic Canada, 5510 Spring Garden Road, Halifax Nova Scotia B3J 1G5 Canada. *Continues Atlantic Cinema, Television, Radio Artists Talent Catalog, 1184-7565.*

LC PN1566.M87   **ISSN** 0905-3026
DD 790.205
DK

TEATER-ET. **Added/Corp** Musik & Teater (Institution). **VFOAT** Teater Et; ITT Arbog. (1989)-. Periodical. Danish. Four times a year. Musik og Teater, 191 DK-1006 Kbenhaven. *Formed by the union of Teater (Copenhagen, Denmark), 0902-1957 and Teater i Danmark, 0106-7672.*

The Arts —Performing Arts

LC PN2724 .T337
RU
TEATRALNO-KONTSERTNAIA MOSKVA. (19??)-. Periodical. Russian. One time a week. Izdatelstvo Reklama / Russia, Sytinskii Per 2, Moscow Russia.

LC PN441 **ISSN** 1046-2937
DD 809 US
CODEN TPQUEI
TEXT AND PERFORMANCE QUARTERLY. See Literature.

LC PN2004 .T57 **ISSN** 0723-1172
DD 792/.0943 GW
THEATERZEITSCHRIFT. See Theater.

LC PN2275.C3 T47 **ISSN** 0737-0172
DD 790.2/09794/6 US
THEATRE DIRECTORY OF THE SAN FRANCISCO BAY AREA. See Theater.

ISSN 0892-0796
DD 792 US
THEATRE JOBLIST. [Theatre joblist].
Added/Corp Association for Theatre in Higher Education (U.S.). **VFOAT** Theatre Job List. Vol. 1 No. 1 (Jan 1987)-. Periodical. English. Eleven times a year (monthly except Aug.). $45.00. Theatre Service, PO Box 15282, Evansville IN 47716. **Tel** (812)474-0549. **ED** Patricia Angotti. **Ad Acc.** **Circ:** 500 (ctrl).
Desc: Vacancy listing service specifically designed to meet the needs of educational theatre programs. In addition, theatre employers with job openings or career development opportunities in children's, professional, and community theatres have a billboard for advertising positions to the largest population of trained and qualified job seekers.

LC PN1560
DD 790.2 US
TIPPS DIRECTORY OF TALENT, INFORMATION, PROPS, PLACES, SERVICES FOR ADVERTISING, FILM AND THEATRE. **VFOAT** Directory of Talent, Information, Props, Services for Advertising, Film and Theatre. (1985)-. English. One time a year. $35.00 (latest edition). Harbin Communications Group, 7420 FDR Station, New York NY 10150. **Tel** (212)319-9085.

LC PN2002 .M5 **ISSN** 0040-9170
NE
TONEEL TEATRAAL. See Theater.

LC PN1560
DD 790.2 CN
TOURPLUS. (19??)-. Periodical. English. Four times a year. Free on request. Canada Council Touring Office, PO Box 1047, Ottawa Ontario K1P 5V8 Canada. **Circ:** 3,500.
Desc: Aimed at establishing a dialogue between people interested in the dissemination of the performing arts in Canada.

LC PN1970 .U543
FR
UNIMA INFORMATIONS. **Main/Corp** Union Internationale des Marionnettes. (19??)-. Czech (English, French, German, Russian and Spanish). One time a year. Union Internationale de la Marionnette, BP 249, 08103 Charleville-Mezieres France.

LC PN1997.A1 V49
DD 791.46/75/05 SP
VIRIDIANA. **Added/Corp** Fundacion Viridiana. Siglo Vientiuno Editores. **VFOAT** Revista Viridiana. (1991)-. Periodical. Spanish. Four times a year. $62.18. Fundacion Viridiana, Almirante 15 1 Derecha, 28004 Madrid Spain. **Tel** 011 34 1 5326794.

ISSN 0824-8214
DD 790.2/09714/281 CN
VIVA VIRUS. [Viva virus]. Vol. 6, No. 7 (Sept. 83)-. Periodical. French. Irregular. $2.50 each number. Viva Virus, CP 217 Succursale E, Montreal Quebec H2T 3A7 Canada. **Continues** Virus (Montreal, Quebec), 0704-8475.

ISSN 0960-300X
DD 791 UK
VOX LONDON. [Vox Lond.]. (1990)-. Periodical. English. Twelve times a year. $93.00. IPC Magazines Ltd., Perrymount Road, Haywards Heath, West Sussex RH16 3DH United Kingdom. **Tel** 011 44 1444 440421, **FAX** 011 44 1444 445599.
Ind/Abst EP Collect.; Homework Help.; MasterFile FullTEXT 1000; MasterFile FullTEXT 350; MasterFile FullTEXT 650; MasterFile FullTEXT; Telebase; World Mag. Bank.

ISSN 1185-345X
DD 790/.09713/58 CN
WHAT'S HAPPENING MAGAZINE (BELLEVILLE. 1991). [WHAT'S HAPPENING MAGAZINE.]. [What's happen. mag.]. **VFOAT** What's Happening. (Mar/Apr 1991)-. Periodical. English. Six times a year. $15.00. Susan K Bailey Enterprises Ltd., 6A North Front Street, PO Box 307, Belleville Ontario K8N 5A5 Canada. **Continues** In Touch With What's Happening., 0845-7611.

ISSN 1187-1350
DD 790/.09713/8405 CN
WHERE OTTAWA-HULL. [Where Ott.-Hull]. Vol. 33, No. 10 (Oct. 1990)-. Periodical. English (French). Twelve times a year. 22.41Can$. Capital Publishers, 400 Cumberland Street, Ottawa Ontario K1N 8X3 Canada. **Tel** (613)241-7888. **ED** Marc Choma. **Continues** What's On (1980)., 0043-468X.

LC PN1560
DD 790.2 US
WORDSTUFF. (19??)-. Newsletter. English. Four times a year. Free on request. Frederick Douglass Creative Arts Center Inc., 270 West 96th Street, New York NY 10025. **Tel** (212)864-3375.
Desc: Newsletter for African-American creative arts, including writing, acting, radio production, etc.

ISSN 1038-6963
DD 796.4705 AT
WORLD ACROBATICS. [World acrobat.].
Added/Corp Association of Acrobats. (1976)-. Trade Publication. English. Twelve times a year. $36.00. Association of Acrobats, 10 Minkara Road, Unit 84, Bayview New South Wales 2104 Australia. **Tel** 011 61 991851. **ED** Ralph Samuels. **Bk Rev.** **Ad Acc.**
Desc: Coverage of all forms of acrobatics for stages and circus.

LC GV1787 .W67
DD 792.8/05 UK
WORLD BALLET AND DANCE. See Dance.

LC HE8700 .W67 **ISSN** 1051-2896
DD 791 US
WORLD SCREEN NEWS. [World screen news]. (19??)-. Trade Publication. English. Six times a year. $30.00. World Screen News Inc., 1123 Broadway Suite 901, New York NY 10010. **Tel** (212)924-7620.
Desc: Publication for program buyers at stations, networks, and cable and satellite facilities around the world.

ISSN 0897-4721
DD 791 US
WOW! (NEW YORK, N.Y. 1987). (WOW!). [WOW!]. Vol. 1, No. 1 (Oct. 1987)-. Periodical. English. Six times a year. $17.95. Wandsworth Publishing, PO Box 304, Brookfield CT 06804. **Tel** (203)775-0190. **(Subscription address:** Kable Publishers Aide / Illinois, 308 East Hitt Street, Subscription Department, Mt. Morris IL 61054-1473. **Tel** (815)734-1261.) **Absorbed** Hot.

LC ML37.G7 B745a **ISSN** 0309-8044
DD 791/.079 UK
YEAR BOOK - BRITISH FEDERATION OF MUSIC FESTIVALS. **Main/Corp** British Federation of Music Festivals. (19??)-. English. One time a year. £10.50. British Federation of Music Festivals, 198 Park Lane / Festivals House, Macclesfield SK11 6UD United Kingdom. **Tel** 011 44 1625 28297. **Ad Acc.** **Circ:** 2,000 (ctrl).
Desc: Handbook of amateur competitive festivals.

LC Z6935 .Z73 PN2720 **ISSN** 0207-9739
RU
ZRELISHCHNYE ISKUSSTVA. **Added/Corp** Gosudarstvennaia Biblioteka SSSR Imeni V. I. Lenina. (1983)-. Russian. Three times a year. 0.50rub (single issue). Gosudarstvennaia Biblioteka, Informatsionnyi Tsentr, Imeni V. I. Lenina, Prospekt Kalinina 3, 121019 Moscow Russia.

ASTROLOGY

ISSN 0002-7529
DD 133 US
AMERICAN ASTROLOGY. [Am. astrol.]. (1953)-. Periodical. English. Twelve times a year. $18.98. Starlog Press Inc., 475 Park Avenue South, New York NY 10016. **Tel** (212)689-2830, **FAX** (212)889-7933. **(Subscription address:** Kable Publishers Aide / Illinois, 308 East Hitt Street, Subscription Department, Mt. Morris IL 61054-1473. **Tel** (815)734-1261.) **ED** Ken Irving and Lee Chapman. **Bk Rev.** **Ad Acc.** **Circ:** 225,000. available on microfilm from University Microfilms International (UMI). **Continues** American Astrology Magazine.

LC BF1651 .A544 **ISSN** 1053-0584
DD 133.5/05 US
ASPECTS (ENCINO, CALIF.). (ASPECTS : A QUARTERLY ASTROLOGICAL MAGAZINE.). [Aspects]. (1975)-. Periodical. English. Four times a year. $25.00 US; $30.00 Canada. Aquarius Workshops Inc, PO Box 556, Encino CA 91426.

LC BF1651 **ISSN** 0392-226X
DD 133.5 IT
UDC 133.52
ASTRA MILANO. [AstraMilano]. (1977)-. Periodical. Italian. Twelve times a year. $85.00. RCS Rizzoli Periodici, Via A Rizzoli 2, 20132 Milan Italy. **Tel** 011 39 2 27200720. **(Subscription address:** Speedimpex USA, Inc., 35 02 48th Avenue, Long Island City NY 11101. **Tel** (718)392-7477.)

LC BF1651
DD 133.5 IT
ASTRAGALO. (19??)-. Italian. Edizioni L Arciere SRL, Via Rome 8, 12100 Cuneo Italy.

LC BF1651 **ISSN** 1065-7584
DD 133.5 US
ASTRO AGENTS. (1992)-. Periodical. English. Four times a year. $30.00. Astro Caster, PO Box 1702, Pacific Palisades CA 90272. **(Subscription address:** Event Horizon Press, Box 867, Desert Hot Springs CA 92240. **Tel** (619)329-3950.) **Ad Acc, Adv Mgr:** Taaffe O'Connell. **Circ:** 20,000.
Desc: This publication provides a breakdown of Hollywood agents including their addresses, telephone numbers, and astrological signs.

LC BF1651 .A545 **ISSN** 0748-1659
DD 133.5 US
ASTRO-CARTO-GRAPHY. **VFOAT** Astro Carto Graphy; Astro Cartography. (19??)-. English. Irregular. Astro-Carto-Graphy, PO Box 959, El Cerrito CA 94530.

LC BF1651 **ISSN** 1065-7533
DD 133.5 US
ASTRO CASTER. (1992)-. Periodical. English. Three times a year. $27.00. Astro Caster, PO Box 1702, Pacific Palisades CA 90272. **(Subscription address:** Event Horizon Press, Box 867, Desert Hot Springs CA 92240. **Tel** (619)329-3950.) **Ad Acc, Adv Mgr:** Taaffe O'Connell. **Circ:** 20,000.
Desc: This publication provides a listing of casting directors in Hollywood with studio information, show assignments, and astrological signs.

LC BF1651 **ISSN** 0743-4227
DD 133.5 US
ASTRO-NEWS (BATON ROUGE, LA.). (ASTRO-NEWS.). **VFOAT** Astro News. (Nov. 1983)-. Periodical. English. Six times a year. $10.00 US; $15.00 other. Astro News, 5821 Cyrus Street, Baton Rouge LA 70805. **Tel** (504)355-7282. **ED** Edna Lewis Rowland. **Bk Rev.** **Circ:** 300 (ctrl).
Desc: Astrological study of cycles in relation to behavioral sciences such as psychology. Book reviews on astrology and feminism are included.

LC BF1651 **ISSN** 1074-6196
DD 133.5 US
●**ASTRO SIGNS DIGEST.** [AStro signs dig.]. Vol. 1, No. 1 (Apr. 1994)-. Consumer Publication. English. Six times a year. $1.99 (single issue). JMT Publications, Inc., 350 Theodore Fremd Avenue, Rye NY 10580. **Tel** (914)967-1565, **FAX** (914)967-1565. **Circ:** 100,000.

LC BF1651 .A67 **ISSN** 0004-6140
DD 133.505 II
ASTROLOGICAL MAGAZINE, THE. (1895)-. Periodical. English. Twelve times a year. $77.01. Raman Publications, 28 Nehru Circle Seshadripuram, Bangalore 560020 Mysore India. **Tel** 011 91 3348646, 011 91 369229. **ED** Dr. B. V. Raman (Editor in Chief), Gayatri Devi Vasudev (Associate Editor). **Bk Rev.** **Ad Acc, Adv Mgr:** B. Niranjan Babu. **Circ:** 25,000 (ctrl).
Desc: Contains thought-provoking articles on different aspects of astrology and allied subjects, with coverage of Indian astrology and popular features.

LC BF1651 .A68 **ISSN** 0044-9784
DD 133.505 US
ASTROLOGICAL REVIEW, THE.
Added/Corp Astrologers' Guild of America. Astrologers' Guild (U.S.). Research Committee. Astrologers' Guild (U.S.). Feb. 1929)-. Periodical. English. Twelve times a year. 32.88Aus$. Dengar Publications, PO Box 172, Fivedock NSW 2046 Australia. **Tel** 011 6 1 2 7137784. **ED** Raymond H. Webb. **Bk Rev.** **Ad Acc.** ctrl circ.
Desc: For astrologers, by astrologers.

LC BF1651 **ISSN** 0587-5641
DD 133.5 FR
UDC 133.52
ASTROLOGUE PARIS, L'. (L'ASTROLOGUE.). (1968)-. Periodical. French. Four times a year. Editions Traditionnelles, 11 Quai St. Michel, F 75005 Paris France. **Tel** 011 33 1 43540332.

ISSN 0885-7148
DD 133 US
ASTROLOGY & PARAPSYCHOLOGY TODAY. [Astrol. parapsychol. today]. **VFOAT** Astrology and Parapsychology Today; Astrology & Parapsychology; Astrology and Parapsychology; A.P.T.; APT. (1986)-. Periodical. English. Six times a year. Astrology & Parapsychology Today, 75 Alto Drive, Oak View CA 93022.

Astrology

LC BF1651 **ISSN** 0363-4310
DD 133.5 US
ASTROLOGY ANNUAL CALENDAR EPHEMERIS, THE. (19??)-. English. One time a year. $1.95 single issue. Symbols & Signs, PO Box 4536, North Hollywood CA 91607.

LC BF1651 .A737 **ISSN** 0363-4140
DD 133.5/05 US
ASTROLOGY ANNUAL REFERENCE BOOK, THE. Added/Corp American Federation of Astrologers. (19??)-. English. One time a year. $4.95 single issue. Symbols & Signs, PO Box 4536, North Hollywood CA 91607.

ISSN 0004-6191
DD 133 US
ASTROLOGY GUIDE. [Astrol. guide]. (1937)-. Periodical. English. Six times a year. Available on newstand only. Sterling Macfadden, 233 Park Avenue South, New York NY 10003. **Tel** (212)979-4800.

LC BF1651 .E85 **ISSN** 0195-0851
DD 133.5/4/05 US
ASTROLOGY (NEW YORK). (ASTROLOGY.). **VFOAT** Astrology, Your Daily Horoscope. (195?)-. Periodical. English. Twelve times a year. $24.00. Hachette Magazines Inc., 1633 Broadway, New York NY 10019. **Tel** (212)767-6000. **(Subscription address:** Neodata / Colorado, PO Box 2606, Boulder CO 80322. **)** available on microfilm and microfiche from University Microfilms International (UMI). **Continues** Your Everyday Horoscope and Astrology.

LC BF1651
DD 133.5 UK
ASTROLOGY QUARTERLY. (1926)-. Academic Scholarly Publication. English. Four times a year. £18.00. Astrological Lodge of London, BM Astrolodge, London WC1N 3XX United Kingdom. **Tel** 011 44 171 8374410. **Bk Rev**, (Qty: 4). **Ad Acc**, **Adv Mgr:** Nicholas Campion. **Circ:** 400.

LC BF1651 **ISSN** 0146-3365
DD 133.5 US
CAO TIMES. Main/Corp Congress of Astrological Organizations. **VAT** Congress of Astrological Organizations Times. (1975)-. Periodical. English. Four times a year. $26.00 North America; $32.00 other. Al H. Morrison, Box 75 Old Chelsea Station, New York NY 10113-0075. **ED** Al H. Morrison. **Bk Rev**. **Ad Acc**. **Circ:** 1,000 (ctrl).
Desc: Deals with astrology.

LC BF1621 .C63 **ISSN** 1066-4920
DD 133.5/05 US
CONSIDERATIONS (MOUNT KISCO, NY). (CONSIDERATIONS.). [Considerations]. (1983)-. Periodical. English. Four times a year. $30.00 US. Considerations, Inc, PO Box 655, Mount Kisco NY 10549.

LC BF1651 .C65 **ISSN** 0260-8790
DD 133.5/05 UK
CORRELATION. Added/Corp Astrological Association (Great Britain). (19??)-. Periodical. English. Two times a year. Astrological Association, West Court, Bramshott Court, Bramshott NR Liphook Hampshire United Kingdom. **ED** Simon Best. Index available. **Bk Rev**. **Circ:** 500 (ctrl).

LC BF1651 **ISSN** 0148-5369
DD 133.5 US
DAILY PLANET ALMANAC, THE. (19??)-. English. One time a year. $2.95. And/Or Press, PO Box 2246, Berkeley CA 94702.

LC BF1651 **ISSN** 1080-1421
DD 133.5 US
DELL HOROSCOPE. (199?)-. Periodical. English. Twelve times a year. Dell Publishing Company Inc., 1540 Broadway, 9th Floor, New York NY 10036-4021. **Tel** (212)782-8532, **FAX** (212)782-8338. **Continues** Horoscope, 0018-5116.

ISSN 0710-510X
DD 133.5/05 CN
FRATERNITY NEWS - FRATERNITY FOR CANADIAN ASTROLOGERS. (THE FRATERNITY NEWS.). [Fratern. news - Fratern. Can. Astrol.]. **Added/Corp** Fraternity for Canadian Astrologers. Vol. 2, Issue No. 1 (Winter 1979)-. Periodical. English (summaries and/or abstracts in French). Four times a year. Free. Fraternity for Canadian Astrologers / British Columbia, 13155-24th Avenue, Surrey British Columbia V4A 2G2 Canada. **Tel** (416)466-2258. **ED** Donna Van Toen, Randy Pond. **Bk Rev**. **Ad Acc**. **Circ:** 500 (ctrl). **Continues** Fraternity Newsletter.
Desc: Journal geared to intermediate level astrology students and professional astrologers.

LC BF1651 **ISSN** 0960-670X
DD 133.5 UK
TITLE CHANGE
GEMINI (HERSTMONCEUX, EAST SUSSEX). (GEMINI : NEWSLETTER OF THE ROYAL GREENWICH OBSERVATORY.). **Added/Corp** Royal Greenwich Observatory. No. 1 (May 1982)-(1993). Newsletter. English. Royal Greenwich Observatory, Madingley Road, Cambridge CB3 0HA United Kingdom. **Tel** 011 44 1223 374000, **FAX** 011 44 1223 374700, telex 83159. **ED** K.P. Tritton. **Circ:** 1,200. **Continues** RGO Information Bulletin. **Merged with** Ukirt Newsletter **to form** Spectrum.

LC BF1717.5 .H67 **ISSN** 1049-6858
DD 133.5/6/05 US
HORARY PRACTITIONER, THE. (THE HORARY PRACTITIONER : A QUARTERLY JOURNAL OF TRADITIONAL HORARY ASTROLOGY.). [Horary pract.]. (Apr./May 1989)-. Periodical. English. Four times a year. $20.00 US; $24.00 Canada. Justus and Associates, 1420 Northwest Gilman, Suite 2154, Issaquah WA 98027-5327.

ISSN 1182-6304
DD 133.5/4/05 CN
HOROSCOPE (ANDRE MAURICE). (HOROSCOPE.). [Horoscope]. (1991)-. French. 12.95Can$ per volume. Edimag, Bureau 2, 1880 Est rue Ste-Catherine, Montreal Quebec H2K 2H5 Canada.

LC BF1651 **ISSN** 8750-3042
DD 133.5 US
HOROSCOPE GUIDE. (19??)-. Periodical. English. Twelve times a year. $14.00. Quinn Publishing Company, PO Box 988, Department 2, Ft Washington PA 19034. **Tel** (215)628-0924.

LC BF1651 **ISSN** 0018-5116
DD 133.5 US
TITLE CHANGE
HOROSCOPE (NEW YORK). (HOROSCOPE : A PERSONAL DAILY GUIDE FOR EVERYONE.). (19??)-(199?). Periodical. English. Dell Publishing Company Inc., 1540 Broadway, 9th Floor, New York NY 10036-4021. **Tel** (212)782-8532, **FAX** (212)782-8338. available on microfilm from University Microfilms International (UMI). **Continued by** Dell Horoscope, 1080-1421.

ISSN 1182-6312
DD 133.5/4/05 CN
HOROSCOPE (VERONIQUE CHARPENTIER). (HOROSCOPE.). [Horoscope]. (1991)-. French. 12.95Can$ per volume. Edimag, Bureau 2, 1880 Est rue Ste-Catherine, Montreal Quebec H2K 2H5 Canada.

LC BF1651 .I59 **ISSN** 0095-0378
DD 133.5/025 US
INTERNATIONAL ASTROLOGICAL REGISTER. Added/Corp Fresno Astrology Book Center. (19??)-. English. One time a year. Fresno Astrology Book Center, 2306 East McKinley Avenue, Fresno CA 93703.

LC BF1409 .I57 **ISSN** 0273-3749
DD 133/.025 US
INTERNATIONAL DIRECTORY OF ASTROLOGERS & PSYCHICS, THE. [Int. dir. astrol. psych.]. **VAT** International Directory of Astrologers and Psychics. (19??)-. Directory. English. $14.98. Car/Lo Publications, PO Box 7078, Myrtle Beach SC 29577.

LC QC811 .I85 **ISSN** 0202-7275
RU
ITOGI NAUKI I TEKHNIKI. SERIIA GEOMAGNETIZM I VYSOKIE SLOI ATMOSFERY. Added/Corp Vsesoiuznyi Institut Nauchnoi i Tekhnicheskoi Informatsii (Soviet Union). **VFOAT** Seriia Geomagnetizm i Vysokie Sloi Atmosfery; Geomagnetizm i Vysokie Sloi Atmosfery; Itogi Nauki i Tekhniki. Geomagnetizm i Vysokie Sloi Atmosfery. (1980)-. Monographic series. Russian. Price varies per volume. VINITI - Vsesoyuznyi Institut Nauchno-Tekhnicheskoi Informatsii, All-Union Scientific and Technical Information Institute, Baltiiskaia ulitsa 14, 125219 Moscow Russia. **Tel** 011 7 95 2384600, **FAX** 011 7 95 9430060, telex 411160. **Continues** Itogi Nauki i Tekhniki. Geomagnetizm i Vysokie Sloi Atmosfery.

LC BF1404
DD 133 SZ
JAHRBUCH DER ESOTERIK. See Parapsychology and Occultism.

LC BF1651 .J67 **ISSN** 0882-4517
DD 133.5/05 US
JOURNAL OF RESEARCH OF THE AMERICAN FEDERATION OF ASTROLOGERS. [J. res. Am. Fed. Astrol.]. **Added/Corp** American Federation of Astrologers. **VFOAT** Journal of Research. Vol. 1, No. 1 (Aug. 1982)-. Periodical. English. Two times a year. American Federation of Astrologers Inc, PO Box 22040, Tempe AZ 85282. **Tel** (602)838-1751. **ED** Richard Nolle. **Circ:** 200 (ctrl).
Desc: A journal of serious astrological research, with an emphasis on controlled statistical experimentation. Distributed free to members of the American Federation of Astrologers Research Section.

LC BF1651 .J93
II
JYOTISHA-KALPA. VFOAT Jyotish-Kalpa. Periodical. Multiple languages (Hindi and English). 10.00. Bharatiga Jyotir Vijyan Parishad, 78 Ashta Bhuji Durga Marg Aminabad Road, 4 Lucknow India.

LC BF1404 **ISSN** 0278-8101
DD 133.5 US
KOSMOS (TORRANCE, CALIF.). (KOSMOS.). [Kosmos]. **Added/Corp** International Society for Astrological Research. (19??)-. Academic Scholarly Publication. English. Four times a year. $30.00. International Society of Astrological Research, PO Box 38613, Los Angeles CA 90038. **Tel** (818)333-8702, **FAX** (213)461-3417. Index available. cum. index. **Bk Rev**. **Circ:** 500 (ctrl). Documents available from CASDDS.
Desc: Information on astrology.
Ind/Abst Chem. Abstr.

LC WMLC 91/3232 **ISSN** 1061-7507
DD 133 US
LLEWELLYN'S DAILY PLANETARY GUIDE & ASTROLOGER'S DATEBOOK. [Llewellyn's dly. planet. guide astrol. dateb.]. **VFOAT** Llewellyn's Daily Planetary Guide and Astrologer's Datebook; Daily Planetary Guide. (19??)-. English. $6.95. **Continues** Llewellyn's ... Daily Planetary Guide, 0743-6408.

LC BF1404 **ISSN** 0199-7165
DD 133.5 US
MIDNIGHT HOROSCOPE. (19??)-. Periodical. English. Four times a year. $6.00. Globe International, PO Box 11, Rouse Point NY 12979. **Tel** (514)849-7733, **FAX** (514)849-8330.

ISSN 1079-1345
DD 133 US
MOUNTAIN ASTROLOGER, THE. [Mt. astrol.]. (19??)-. Periodical. English. Nine times a year. $30.00. Mountain Astrologer, PO Box 17275, Boulder CO 80308. **Tel** (303)444-9578.

ISSN 0848-3787
DD 133.5/05 CN
PREDICTIONS ASTROLOGIQUES. [Pred. astrol.]. (1989)-. Periodical. French. Irregular. Les Productions Discoblet, 1677 est Avenue Mont-Royal, Montreal, Quebec H2J 1Z6 Canada.

ISSN 0846-068X
DD 133.5/05 CN
PREDICTIONS (JOJO SAVARD). (PREDICTIONS.). [Predictions]. (1991)-. Periodical. French. 17.00F. Edimag, Bureau 2, 1880 Est rue Ste-Catherine, Montreal Quebec H2K 2H5 Canada.

ISSN 0848-0826
DD 133.5/05 CN
PREVISIONS (MONTREAL). (PREVISIONS.). [Previsions]. **VFOAT** Previsions ... au Fil des Sstres. (1990)-. French. Irregular. 13.95Can$. Editions Quebecor, 4435 Boul. des Grandes Praiies, Montreal Quebec H1R 3N4 Canada.

LC BF1651 .A523 **ISSN** 1067-1439
DD 133.5/05 US
TODAY'S ASTROLOGER. [Today's astrol.]. **Added/Corp** American Federation of Astrologers. **VFOAT** American Federation of Astrologers Bulletin; AFA Bulletin Today's Astrologer. (199?)-. Bulletin. English. Twelve times a year. $35.00. American Federation of Astrologers, Inc., 6535 South Rural Road, PO Box 22040, Tempe AZ 85285. **Tel** (602)838-1751, **FAX** (602)838-8293. **ED** Kris Brandt Riske. **Bk Rev**. **Circ:** 4,200. (ctrl). available with charts. **Continues** Bulletin (American Federation of Astrologers), 0735-4797.
Desc: Includes articles, data information, new and activity calendars regarding members of the astrology federation.

LC R733 .U72 **ISSN** 0132-1900
RU
URANIIA / URANIA. See New Age Publications.

ISSN 0820-8891
DD 133.5/4/05 CN
VOTRE HOROSCOPE (MONTREAL. 1982). (VOTRE HOROSCOPE.). [Votre horosc.]. (198?)-. French. One time a year. Presses Select, 1555 Ouest rue de Louvain, Montreal Quebec H4N 1G6 Canada. **Continues** Horoscope, 0316-0459.

ISSN 0711-1231
DD 133.5/4/05 CN
YOUR DAILY CYCLE GUIDE (MONTHLY ED.). (YOUR DAILY CYCLE GUIDE : UNIVERSAL SOLAR CYCLES CHART.). [Your dly. cycle guide]. **VAT** Universal Solar Cycles Chart. (1971)-. Periodical. English. Twelve times a year. $22.00. Solar Cycles Foundation, MPO Box 2099-SC, Vancouver BC V6B 3T2.

Astronomy

ASTRONOMY

LC QB
DD 520   AT
A.A.O. NEWSLETTER. Added/Corp
Anglo-Australian Observatory. **VFOAT** AAO Newsletter. (19??)-. Newsletter. English. Four times a year. Free on request. Anglo-Australian Observatory, PO Box 296, Epping NSW 2121 Australia. **Tel** 011 61 2 3724800.

LC QB
DD 520   **ISSN** 0197-2979
    US
    CODEN AACID5
AAVSO CIRCULAR. [AAVSO circ.]. **Main/Corp** American Association of Variable Star Observers. **Added/Corp** American Association of Variable Star Observers. Circular. **VAT** American Association of Variable Star Observers Circular. No. 1 (Nov. 1970)-. Periodical. English. Twelve times a year. $40.00. American Association of Variable Star Observers / AAVSO, 25 Birch Street, Cambridge MA 02138. **Tel** (617)354-0484, FAX (617)354-0665. **ED** Charles Scovil and John Bortle. **Circ:** 300 (ctrl). Documents available from Ask*IEEE. **Supersedes** American Association of Variable Star Observers. Circular.
 Desc: Preliminary observations of some eruptive and other interesting variables.
 Ind/Abst INSPEC (May 1981-).

DD 523   **ISSN** 0892-4244
    US
    CODEN AMONET
AAVSO MONOGRAPH. (AAVSO MONOGRAPH / AMERICAN ASSOCIATION OF VARIABLE STAR OBSERVERS.). [AAVSO monogr.]. **Added/Corp** American Association of Variable Star Observers. **VAT** American Association of Variable Star Observers Monograph. Vol. 1 (1985)-. Monographic series. English. Irregular. Price varies per volume. American Association of Variable Star Observers / AAVSO, 25 Birch Street, Cambridge MA 02138. **Tel** (617)354-0484, FAX (617)354-0665. **Circ:** 500 (ctrl). Documents available from Ask*IEEE. **Continues** AAVSO Report, 0097-5265.
 Ind/Abst INSPEC (1985-).

LC QB
DD 520   **ISSN** 0934-4438
    GW
    CODEN AGESEK
ABSTRACT SERIES - ASTRONOMISCHE GESELLSCHAFT. (ABSTRACT SERIES / ASTRONOMISCHE GESELLSCHAFT.). [Abstr. ser. - Astron. Ges.]. **Added/Corp** Astronomische Gesellschaft (Germany). (1988)-. English (German). Irregular. DM5.00. H.U. Keller Planetarium Stuttgart, Neckarstrasse 47, D-7000 Stuttgart 1 Germany.
 Ind/Abst INSPEC.

LC QB
DD 520   **ISSN** 0001-5237
    PL
    CODEN AASWAM
ACTA ASTRONOMICA. [Acta astron.]. **Added/Corp** Polska Akademia Nauk. Komitet Astronomii. Vol. 6 (1956)-. Periodical. Multiple languages (English, French, German, Polish and Russian). Four times a year. $80.00. (**Subscription address:** Ars Polona-Ruch, PO Box 1001, Krakowskie Przedmiescie 7, 00-068 Warsaw Poland. **Tel** 011 48 22 261201.) Documents available from Ask*IEEE, CASDDS. **Formed by the union of** Acta Astronomica. Serie A; Acta Astronomica. Serie B **and** Acta Astronomica. Serie C.
 Ind/Abst Chem. Abstr.; INSPEC (1969-); Int. Aerosp. Abstr. (1991-); Sci. Cit. Index.

LC QB460 .A44   **ISSN** 0146-4043
DD 523.01/05   US
ALBRIGHT JOURNAL, THE. Vol. 1 (Jan. 30, 1974)-. Periodical. English. Irregular. Grey Castle Press, Pocket Knife Square, Lakeville CT 06039.

DD 520/.5   **ISSN** 0226-7160
    CN
ALMAGESTE. (L'ALMAGESTE.). [Almageste]. **Added/Corp** Centre Amateur de Recherche Astronomique du Quebec. Vol. 1 (July 1979)-. Periodical. French. Centre Amateur de Recherche Astronomique du Quebec, c/o Centre de Loisirs, 301 rue Racine, Loretteville Quebec G2B 1E7 Canada.

DD 520/.5   **ISSN** 0384-7691
    CN
ALMANACH-GRAPHIQUE - CENTRE DE QUEBEC, SOCIETE ROYALE D'ASTRONOMIE DU CANADA. Main/Corp Societe Royale d'Astronomie du Canada. Centre de Quebec. **Added/Corp** Quebec (Province). Ministere des Terres et Forets. Universite Laval. Departement de Physique. (1973)-. Periodical. French. One time a year. Centre de Quebec de la S R A, CP 9396, Quebec Quebec G1V 4B5 Canada. **Supersedes** Almanach Astronomica, 0384-7683.

LC QB
DD 520   US
●**AMERICAN ASTRONOMICAL SOCIETY CD-ROM SERIES [COMPUTER FILE], THE. Added/Corp** American Astronomical Society. **VFOAT** AAS CD-ROM Series; Astrophysics on Disc. (1993)-. English. Irregular. American Astronomical Society, 2000 Florida Avenue Northwest, Suite 300, Washington DC 20009.

LC QB88 .A67a
DD 522/.2994   AT
ANGLO-AUSTRALIAN OBSERVATORY : REPORT OF THE ANGLO-AUSTRALIAN TELESCOPE BOARD. Main/Corp Anglo-Australian Telescope Board. (1988)-. English. Irregular. Australian Government Publishing Service, GPO Box 84, Canberra ACT 2601 Australia. **Tel** 011 61 6 2954411, FAX 011 61 6 2954455. **Continues** Anglo-Australian Telescope Board. Anglo-Australian Telescope, 0728-6554.

LC QB1   **ISSN** 0825-9984
DD 520/.5   CN
    TITLE CHANGE
ANNUAIRE ASTRONOMIQUE (MONTREAL). (ANNUAIRE ASTRONOMIQUE.). [Annu. astron.]. **Added/Corp** Societe d'Astronomie de Montreal. Vol. 20 (1985)-(1994). French. Societe d'Astronomie de Montreal, CP 206, Station 5 Michel, Montreal Quebec H2A 3L9 Canada. **Tel** (514)728-4422. **ED** Patrice Gerin-Roze. **Circ:** 1,000. **Continues** Annuaire Astronomique de l'Amateur, 0318-4420. **Continued by** Observer le Ciel, 1196-7390.
 Desc: Handbook for amateur astronomers.

LC QB4   **ISSN** 0895-5123
DD 522   US
ANNUAL REPORT OF THE FIVE COLLEGE RADIO ASTRONOMY OBSERVATORY. [Annu. rep. Five Coll. Radio Astron. Obs.]. **Main/Corp** Five College Radio Astronomy Observatory (New Salem, Mass.). (19??)-. Academic Scholarly Publication. English. One time a year. Five College Radio Astronomy Observatory, 619 Lederle Graduate Research Center, University of Massachusetts, Amherst MA 01003.

LC QB1 .A2884   **ISSN** 0066-4146
DD 520   US
    CODEN ARAAAJ
Pr Rev.
ANNUAL REVIEW OF ASTRONOMY AND ASTROPHYSICS. [Annu. rev. astron. astrophys.]. Vol. 1 (1963)-. English. One time a year (September). $65.00. Annual Reviews Inc., 4139 El Camino Way, PO Box 10139, Palo Alto CA 94303-0139. **Tel** (415)493-4400, (800)523-8635, FAX (415)855-9815. **ED** Geoffrey Burbidge. Index available. cum. index. ctrl circ. available on microfilm and microfiche from University Microfilms International (UMI). Documents available from The Genuine Article, Ask*IEEE, CASDDS.
 Desc: Reviews the current research literature in astronomy and astrophysics; written by acknowledged experts in the field.
 Ind/Abst Astron. Astrophys. Abstr.; Chem. Abstr.; Curr. Contents Phys. Chem. Earth Sci.; Energy Res. Abstr.; Index Sci. Rev. [Full Cov.]; INSPEC Res. Alert [Full Cov.]; Sci. Cit. Index; SCISEARCH.

LC QE1 .A674   **ISSN** 0084-6597
DD 550/.5   US
    CODEN AREPCI
Pr Rev.
ANNUAL REVIEW OF EARTH AND PLANETARY SCIENCES. See Earth Sciences.

LC QB
DD 520   CN
ANNUAL SCIENTIFIC MEETING ... / CANADIAN ASTRONOMICAL SOCIETY. Main/Corp Canadian Astronomical Society. **Added/Corp** David Dunlap Observatory. (19??)-. Academic Scholarly Publication. English. One time a year. David Dunlap Observatory / University of Toronto, PO Box 360, Richmond Hill Ontario L4C 4Y6 Canada.

LC QB
DD 520   IT
●**ANNUARIO DELLA SPECOLA CIDNEA "ANGELO FERRETTI TORRICELLI" PER L'ANNO ... . Added/Corp** Specola Cidnea "Angelo Ferretti Torricelli". **VFOAT** Specola Cidnea Almanac. (1994)-. Italian (English). One time a year. Comune di Brescia, Assessorato alla Cultura, Civici Musei di Scienze, Brescia Italy.

LC QB9 .I5   **ISSN** 0174-254X
DD 523.8   GW
APPARENT PLACES OF FUNDAMENTAL STARS. [Apparent places fundam. stars]. **Added/Corp** Great Britain. Admiralty. Astronomisches Rechen-Institut, Heidelberg. International Astronomical Union. Great Britain. Nautical Almanac Office. **VFOAT** Scheinbare Orter der Fundamentalsterne. (1941)-. English. One time a year. $66.01. G. Braun Verlag, Postfach 1709, D-76006 Karlsruhe Germany. **Tel** 011 49 721 165392.

LC GN799.A8 A72   **ISSN** 0142-7253
DD 520/.9/01   UK
    CCC
    CODEN ARHADN
Pr Rev.
ARCHAEOASTRONOMY. See Archaeology.

LC E59.A8 A684   **ISSN** 1062-189X
DD 930   US
ARCHAEOASTRONOMY & EHNOASTRONOMY NEWS. (ARCHAEOASTRONOMY & ETHNOASTRONOMY NEWS : THE QUARTERLY BULLETIN OF THE CENTER FOR ARCHAEOASTRONOMY.). [Archaeoastron. ethnoastron. news]. **Added/Corp** University of Maryland, College Park. Center for Archaeoastronomy. **VFOAT** Archaeoastronomy and Ethnoastronomy News; A and E News; A & E News. (Sept. 1991)-. Bulletin. English. Four times a year. $60.00 (institutions), $36.00 (individuals) (Comes with Archaeoastronomy (College Park)). The Center for Archaeoastronomy, PO Box X, College Park MD 20740. **Tel** (301)864-6637.

LC E59.A8 A68   **ISSN** 0190-9940
DD 520/.93   US
ARCHAEOASTRONOMY (COLLEGE PARK). See Archaeology.

    ISSN 0843-8978
DD 520/.6/0714   CN
ASTRO-NOTES (MONTREAL). (ASTRO-NOTES : BULLETIN D'INFORMATION, SOCIETE D'ASTRONOMIE DE MONTREAL.). [Astro-notes]. **Added/Corp** Societe d'Astronomie de Montreal. **VFOAT** Astronotes. (1989)-. Periodical. French. Four times a year. free to members. Societe d'Astronomie de Montreal, CP 206, Succursale St. Michael, Montreal H2A 3L9 Canada. **Continues** Bulletin (Societe d'Astronomie de Montreal)., 0848-029X.

LC QB   **ISSN** 1056-9650
DD 520   US
ASTRO-WEATHER (PACIFIC TIME ED.). (ASTRO-WEATHER.). **VFOAT** Astro Weather. (1992)-. English. $8.95. TMA Publishing, PO Box 1342, Morton Grove IL 60053.

LC QB460 .A85   **ISSN** 0324-1459
    BU
    CODEN ASISDL
ASTROFIZICHESKIE ISSLEDOVANIIA. [Astrofiz. issled.]. **Added/Corp** Bulgarska Akademiia na Naukite. **VFOAT** Astrophysical Investigations. Vol. 1 (1975)-. Academic Scholarly Publication. Russian (summaries and/or abstracts in English). Irregular. 2.00lv single issue. Izdatelstvo na Bulgarskata Akademiia na Naukite, 6 Rouski Boulevard, Sofia Bulgaria. **Tel** FAX 011 359 2 801341, telex 22267 HEMKIK. **ED** N. Nikolov. **Circ:** 800. Documents available from CASDDS. **Supersedes** Izvestiia na Sektsiia po Astronomia, 0525-0897.
 Ind/Abst Chem. Abstr. (1975-1977); Int. Aerosp. Abstr.

LC QB460 .A862   **ISSN** 0190-2709
DD 523.01   US
    CCC
    CODEN BSACDC
ASTROFIZICHESKIE ISSLEDOVANIIA. (BULLETIN OF THE SPECIAL ASTROPHYSICAL OBSERVATORY-NORTH CAUCASUS.). [Bull. Spec. Astrophys. Obs.-North Caucasus]. **Added/Corp** Spetsialnaia astrofizicheskaia observatoriia (Akademiia nauk SSSR). (19??)-. Bulletin. English (Russian). Irregular. $230.00. Vertex International, 7205 Hart Lane, Suite 1012, Austin TX 78731. **Tel** (512)345-9944. Documents available from Ask*IEEE.
 Ind/Abst INSPEC (1978-).

LC QB461   **ISSN** 0571-7132
DD 523.01   AI
    CODEN ASTKBG
ASTROFIZIKA. (ASTROFIZIKA.). [Astrofiz.]. **Added/Corp** Haykakan SSR Gitutyunneri Akademia. **VFOAT** Astrafizika. (1965)-. Periodical. Russian (summaries and/or abstracts in English; table of contents in English). Six times a year. $109.95. (**Subscription address:** East View Publications Inc., 3020 Harbor Lane North, Suite 110, Minneapolis MN 55447. **Tel** (800)477-1005, (612)550-0961, FAX (612)559-2931.) Documents available from Ask*IEEE, CASDDS.
 Desc: Information on astrophysics.
 Ind/Abst Astron. Astrophys. Abstr.; Chem. Abstr.; INSPEC (1968-); Int. Aerosp. Abstr.; Math. Rev.

LC QB121 .A77   **ISSN** 0094-1417
DD 522/.622/05   US
ASTROGRAPH (ARLINGTON), THE. (THE ASTROGRAPH.). [Astrograph]. (19??)-. Periodical. English. Six times a year. $12.00. Astrograph, PO Box 2283 Eads Station, Arlington VA 22202. **Tel** (703)830-2229. **ED** Robert Price. **Bk Rev. Ad Acc. Circ:**

Astronomy

1,000 (ctrl).
Desc: Specialized publication dealing with astrophotography.

LC QB
DD 520   IT

ASTRONOMIA, L'. No. 1 (Nov./Dec. 1979)-.
Periodical. Italian. Six times a year. Comes with Unione Astrofili Italiani membership. Biroma, Via San Pio X 108, 35015 Galliera Pd Italy. **Tel** 011 39 49 9422177.

LC QB8.U6 A77   ISSN 0737-6421
DD 528   US
    CODEN ASALET

ASTRONOMICAL ALMANAC, THE. (THE ASTRONOMICAL ALMANAC FOR THE YEAR ...).
[Astron. alm.]. **Added/Corp** United States Naval Observatory. Nautical Almanac Office. Great Britain. Nautical Almanac Office. Science and Engineering Research Council (Great Britain) Science Research Council (Great Britain). **VFOAT** Astronomical Almanac. (1981)-. Government Publication. English. One time a year. $40.00. Superintendent of Documents, US Government Printing Office, Washington DC 20402. **Tel** (202)275-3328, FAX (202)786-2377. Documents available from Ask*IEEE. **Formed by the union of** *American Ephemeris and Nautical Almanac, 0065-8189* **and** *Astronomical Ephemeris for the Year ...* .
Ind/Abst INSPEC (1986).

LC QB1 .A2963   ISSN 1055-6796
DD 520/.5   US
    CCC
    CODEN AATREG

ASTRONOMICAL AND ASTROPHYSICAL TRANSACTIONS.
(ASTRONOMICAL AND ASTROPHYSICAL TRANSACTIONS : THE JOURNAL OF THE SOVIET ASTRONOMICAL SOCIETY.). [Astron. astrophys. trans.]. **Added/Corp** Soviet Astronomical Society. Vol. 1, Issue 1 (1991)-. Periodical. English. Four times a year. $676.00 (academic institutions), $1,056.00 (corporate institutions). Gordon & Breach Science Publishers, Inc., PO Box 786, Cooper Station, New York NY 10276. **Tel** (212)206-8900, FAX (212)645-2459. **(Subscription address:** Gordon & Breach Science Publishers / US, 820 Town Center Drive, Langhorne PA 19047. **Tel** (215)750-2642.) Documents available from Ask*IEEE.
Ind/Abst INSPEC (1992-).

    ISSN 1051-6174
    US

ASTRONOMICAL CALENDAR. [Astron. cal.].
Added/Corp Furman University. Dept. of Physics. Astronomical League. (1974)-. English. One time a year (current year edition published in Oct. of the prior year). $16.00. Astronomical Workshop, Furman University, Greenville SC 29613. **Tel** (803)294-2208, FAX (803)294-3523. **ED** Guy Ottewell. **Circ:** 20,000.

LC QB   ISSN 1080-7926
DD 520   US

ASTRONOMICAL DATA ANALYSIS SOFTWARE AND SYSTEMS. (199?)-.
English. Irregular. Astronomical Society of the Pacific, 390 Ashton Avenue, San Francisco CA 94112. **Tel** (415)337-1100, FAX (415)337-5205.

    ISSN 0888-8353
    US

ASTRONOMICAL DATA CENTER BULLETIN. [Astron. Data Cent. bull.]. **Added/Corp**
Astronomical Data Center (U.S.) National Space Science Data Center. World Data Center A for Rockets and Satellites. Vol. 1, No. 1 (July 1980)-. Bulletin. English. Astronomical Data Center, NASA Goddard Space Flight Center, Greenbelt MD 20771.
Ind/Abst Astron. Astrophys. Abstr.

LC QB1 .A299
DD 523.2/021/2   SA

ASTRONOMICAL HANDBOOK FOR SOUTHERN AFRICA. **Added/Corp**
Astronomical Society of Southern Africa. (1972)-. English. Astronomical Society of South Africa, PO Box 841, Cape Town 8000 South Africa. **Continues** *Handbook (Astronomical Society of Southern Africa).*

LC QB   ISSN 0374-2466
DD 520   JA
    CODEN TGEPAC

ASTRONOMICAL HERALD. (TENMON GEPPO). [Astron. her.]. **Added/Corp** Nihon Tenmon Gakkai. **VFOAT** Astronomical Herald. (1908)-. Periodical. Japanese. Twelve times a year. $125.50. Nihon Tenmon Gakkai, (Astronomical Soc. of Japan), Tokyo Tenmondai, 21-1 Osawa 2 Chome, Mitakashi Tokyo 181 Japan. **(Subscription address:** Japan Publications Trading Company Ltd., PO Box 5030, Tokyo Internatioanl, Tokyo 100-31 Japan. **Tel** 011 81 3 3292 3753.) Documents available from Ask*IEEE, CASDDS.
Ind/Abst Chem. Abstr.; Energy Res. Abstr. (June 1972-); INSPEC (Feb. 1970-1991); Int. Aerosp. Abstr.

LC QB1 .A3   ISSN 0004-6256
    US
    CCC
    CODEN ANJOAA

ASTRONOMICAL JOURNAL (NEW YORK), THE. (THE ASTRONOMICAL JOURNAL.).
[Astron. j.]. **Added/Corp** American Institute of Physics. American Astronomical Society. Vol. 1 (Nov. 1849)-. Periodical. English. Twelve times a year. $300.00. American Institute of Physics, 500 Sunnyside Boulevard, Woodbury NY 11797-2999. **Tel** (516)576-2270, (800)344-6902, FAX (516)349-9704, telex 960983. cum. index. available on microfilm. Documents available from The Genuine Article, Ask*IEEE, CASDDS. **Superseded in part by** *Bulletin - American Astronomical Society, 0002-7537.*
Ind/Abst Astron. Astrophys. Abstr.; Chem. Abstr.; Curr. Contents Phys. Chem. Earth Sci.; Curr. Phys. Index; Energy Res. Abstr.; Gen. Sci. Index; INIS Atomindex [Micro.]; INSPEC (1968-); Int. Aerosp. Abstr. (1991-); Math. Rev.; Res. Alert [Full Cov.]; Sci. Cit. Index; SCISEARCH; SPIN (1970-).

LC QB3 .U6   ISSN 0097-7055
    US

ASTRONOMICAL PAPERS.
(ASTRONOMICAL PAPERS PREPARED FOR THE USE OF THE AMERICAN EPHEMERIS AND NAUTICAL ALMANAC.). **Added/Corp** United States. Navy Dept. Bureau of Navigation. United States Naval Observatory. Nautical Almanac Office. Vol. 1 (1882)-. English. Irregular. US Naval Observatory, 345H & Massachusetts Avenue N2, Washington DC 20390.

LC QB9 .U55   ISSN 0083-2421
DD 525/.5   US

ASTRONOMICAL PHENOMENA.
(ASTRONOMICAL PHENOMENA FOR THE YEAR.). [Astron. phenom.]. **Added/Corp** United States Naval Observatory. Nautical Almanac Office. Great Britain. Nautical Almanac Office. (1951)-. English. One time a year. Government Printing Office / Washington, Washington DC 20402. **Tel** (202)783-3238.

LC QB   ISSN 1050-3390
DD 520   US

ASTRONOMICAL SOCIETY OF THE PACIFIC CONFERENCE SERIES. [Astron. Soc. Pac. conf. ser.]. **Added/Corp** Astronomical Society of the Pacific. (1988)-. Monographic series. English. Four times a year. $40.00. Astronomical Society of the Pacific, 390 Ashton Avenue, San Francisco CA 94112. **Tel** (415)337-1100, FAX (415)337-5205.

LC QB4.9.A8 A88   ISSN 0067-0006
DD 523   AT

ASTRONOMICAL YEARBOOK.
Added/Corp Astronomical Society of Victoria. (19??)-. English. Irregular. $12.00. Astronomical Society of Victoria, GPO Box 1059J, Melbourne Victoria, 3001 Australia.

LC QB1 .A466   ISSN 0373-191X
    RU
    CODEN ASTZAQ

ASTRONOMICESKIJ CIRKULJAR, IZDAVAEMYJ BJURO ASTRONOMICESKIH SOOBSCENIJ AKADEMII NAUK SSSR.
(ASTRONOMICESKII TSIRKULIAR.). [Astron. cirk., izd. Bjuro astron. soobsc. Akad. nauk SSSR]. **Added/Corp** Akademiia Nauk SSSR. Biuro Astronomicheskikh Soobshchenii. No. 1 (1940)-. Periodical. Russian. Irregular. cum. index.
Ind/Abst Astron. Astrophys.; Energy Res. Abstr.

LC QB1 .A467   ISSN 0320-930X
    RU
    CCC
    CODEN ASVEA7

ASTRONOMICESKIJ VESTNIK.
(ASTRONOMICHESKII VESTNIK.). [Astron. vestn.]. **Added/Corp** Vsesoiuznoe Astronomo-Geodezicheskoe Obshchestvo. Vol. 1 (1967)-. Academic Scholarly Publication. Russian. Six times a year. $134.00. Izdatelstvo Nauka / Akademiia Nauk, (Publishing House of the Russian Academy of Sciences), Leninskii Porspekt 14, 117901 Moscow Russia. **Tel** 011 95 9542153, FAX 011 95 9382144, telex 411964. **(Subscription address:** East View Publications Inc., 3020 Harbor Lane North, Suite 110, Minneapolis MN 55447. **Tel** (800)477-1005, (612)550-0961, FAX (612)559-2931.) Documents available from Ask*IEEE, CASDDS. **Continues** *Vsesoiuznoe Astronomo-Geodezicheskoe Obshchestvo. Biulleten.*
Ind/Abst Astron. Astrophys. Abstr.; Chem. Abstr.; Energy Res. Abstr.; GeoRef; INSPEC (Oct.-Dec. 1969-); Int. Aerosp. Abstr. (1991-).

LC QB1 .A46
    RU
    CODEN ASEZEN

●ASTRONOMICHESKII EZHEGODNIK NA ... GOD. **Added/Corp** Institut Teoreticheskoi Astronomii (Rossiiskaia Akademiia Nauk). (1994)-. Russian. **Continues** *Astronomicheskii Ezhegodnik SSSR, 0373-3343.*

LC QB1 .A46   ISSN 0373-3343
    RU
    TITLE CHANGE

ASTRONOMICHESKII EZHEGODNIK SSSR. **Added/Corp** Gosudarstvennyi Vychislitelnyi Institut (Leningrad, R.S.F.S.R.) Akademiia Nauk SSSR. Astronomicheskii Institut. Institut Teoretickeskoi Astronomii (Akademiia Nauk SSSR). Vol. 1 (1922)-(199?). Russian. Izdatelstvo Nauka / Akademiia Nauk, (Publishing House of the Russian Academy of Sciences), Leninskii Porspekt 14, 117901 Moscow Russia. **Tel** 011 95 9542153, FAX 011 95 9382144, telex 411964. **Continued by** *Astronomicheskii Ezhegodnik na ... g.*

LC QB   ISSN 0004-6299
DD 520   RU
    CCC
    CODEN ASZHA2

ASTRONOMICHESKII ZHURNAL.
Added/Corp Akademiia Nauk SSSR. **VFOAT** Russian Astronomical Journal. (1928)-. Academic Scholarly Publication. Russian. Six times a year. $300.00. Izdatelstvo Nauka / Akademiia Nauk, (Publishing House of the Russian Academy of Sciences), Leninskii Porspekt 14, 117901 Moscow Russia. **Tel** 011 95 9542153, FAX 011 95 9382144, telex 411964. **(Subscription address:** East View Publications Inc., 3020 Harbor Lane North, Suite 110, Minneapolis MN 55447. **Tel** (800)477-1005, (612)550-0961, FAX (612)559-2931.) Documents available from The Genuine Article, Ask*IEEE, CASDDS. **Continues** *Russkii Astronomicheskii Zhurnal.*
Ind/Abst Astron. Astrophys. Abstr.; Chem. Abstr.; Curr. Contents Phys. Chem. Earth Sci.; Energy Res. Abstr. (Nov. 1980-); INSPEC (1968-); Int. Aerosp. Abstr. (1991-); Math. Rev.; Res. Alert [Full Cov.]; Sci. Cit. Index; SCISEARCH; Zentralbl. Math. Ihre Grenzgeb.

LC QB
DD 520   FR

ASTRONOMIE MAGAZINE, L'. **Added/Corp** Societe Astronomique de France. (1991)-. Periodical. French. Twelve times a year (11 monthly bulletins & annual brochure Ephemerides Astronomiques). $109.36. Societe Astronomique de France, 3 rue Beethoven, 75016 Paris France. **Tel** 011 33 1 42241374. **ED** Monique Gros. Index available (published separately). **Bk Rev**, (Qty: 10). **Ad Acc. Continues** *Astronomie (Societe Astronomique de France : 1950).*

DD 520   CN

ASTRONOMIE-QUEBEC. **Added/Corp** Association des Groupes d'Astronomes Amateurs. Vol. 1, No 1 (May/Jun 1991)-. Periodical. French. Six times a year. 22.47Can$. Editions Astronomiques, 4545 Avenue Pierre de Coubertin, Montreal Quebec H1V 3R2 Canada. **Tel** (514)252-3038, FAX (514)251-8038. **ED** Jean-Pierre Urbain. **Bk Rev**, (Qty: 10). **Ad Acc. Circ:** 2,500. **Continues** *Le Quebec Astronomique., 0318-0492.*
Ind/Abst Repere (1991-).

LC QB1 .A77   ISSN 0004-6337
    GW
    CCC
    CODEN ASNAAN

Pr Rev.

ASTRONOMISCHE NACHRICHTEN.
[Astron. nachr.]. **Added/Corp** Astronomische Gesellschaft (Germany) Deutsche Akademie der Wissenschaften zu Berlin. Vol. 1, No 1 (1823)-. Periodical. German (English). Six times a year. $425.00. Akademie-Verlag GmbH, Postfach, D-13162 Berlin Germany. **Tel** 011 49 30 47889300, FAX 011 49 30 47889357. **(Subscription address:** VCH Publishers Inc., 303 Northwest 12th Avenue, Journals Department, Deerfield FL 33442. **Tel** (800)367-8249, (305)428-5566.) cum. index. Documents available from The Genuine Article, Ask*IEEE, CASDDS.
Ind/Abst Astron. Astrophys. Abstr.; Chem. Abstr.; Curr. Contents Phys. Chem. Earth Sci.; Ei Page One; Energy Res. Abstr.; INSPEC (1976-); Int. Aerosp. Abstr. (1991-); Math. Rev.; Res. Alert [Full Cov.]; Sci. Cit. Index; SCISEARCH; Soc. Sci. Cit. Index [Select. Cov.]; Zentralbl. Math. Ihre Grenzgeb.

LC WMLC L 82/283   ISSN 0004-6345
    DK
    CODEN ANTKBF

ASTRONOMISK TIDSSKRIFT. [Astron. tidsskr.]. **Added/Corp** Astronomisk Selskab, Copenhagen. Norsk Astronomisk Selskab, Oslo. Svenska Astronomiska Sallskapet, Stockholm. Vol. 1 (1968)-. Periodical. Danish. Four times a year. kr267.52. Arnold Busck Internationale AS, Kobmagergade 49, PO Box 2180, 1150 Copenhagen K Denmark. **Tel** 011 45 33 122453. Documents available from Ask*IEEE. **Supersedes** *Nordisk Astronomisk Tidsskrift.*
Ind/Abst Astron. Astrophys. Abstr.; Energy Res. Abstr. (Feb. 1973-); INSPEC (1974-).

LC Z5153 .A862   ISSN 0067-0022
DD 016.52   GW
    CCC

ASTRONOMY AND ASTROPHYSICS ABSTRACTS. See Astronomy-Abstracting, Bibliographies and Statistics.

LC QB1 .A83 **ISSN** 0004-6361
DD 520/.5 GW
CCC
CODEN AAEJAF

Pr Rev.

ASTRONOMY AND ASTROPHYSICS (BERLIN). (ASTRONOMY AND ASTROPHYSICS.). [Astron. astrophys.]. **Added/Corp** European Southern Observatory. Vol. 1 (Jan. 1969)-. Periodical. English (French and German). Thirty-six times a year. $2697.00. Springer-Verlag GmbH & Company KG, Heidelberger Platz 3, D-14197 Berlin Germany. **Tel** 011 49 30 8207223, FAX 011 49 30 8214091, telex 183 319 SPBLN D. **(Subscription address:** Springer-Verlag New York Inc. / North America, PO Box 2485, Journal Fulfillment, Secaucus NJ 07096. **Tel** (201)348-4033, (800)777-4643, FAX (201)348-4505.**) ED** J Lequeux and M Grewing. available on microfilm and microfiche from University Microfilms International (UMI). Documents available from The Genuine Article, Ask*IEEE, CASDDS. ***Absorbed*** *Arkiv for Astronomi, 0004-2048; Bulletin of the Astronomical Institutes of Czechoslovakia, 0004-6248;* ***Formed by the union of*** *Annales d'Astrophysique, 0365-0499; Bulletin of the Astronomical Institutes of the Netherlands, 0365-8910; Bulletin Astronomique, 0245-9787; Journal des Observateurs, 0368-3389* ***and*** *Zeitschrift fuer Astrophysik, 0372-8331.*
Desc: Presents papers on all aspects of astronomy and astrophysics- theoretical, observational, and instrumental- regardless of the techniques employed- optical, radio, particles, space vehicles, numerical analysis, etc.
Ind/Abst Astron. Astrophys. Abstr. (May 1970-); Chem. Abstr.; Coal Abstr. (May 1970-); Curr. Cit.; Curr. Contents Phys. Chem. Earth Sci.; Ei Page One; Energy Res. Abstr.; INSPEC (May 1970-); Int. Aerosp. Abstr. (1991-); Math. Rev.; Phys. Briefs; Res. Alert [Full Cov.]; Sci. Cit. Index; SCISEARCH; Zentralbl. Math. Ihre Grenzgeb. (May 1970-).

LC Z5153 .A87 QB1 **ISSN** 0147-4669
DD 016.52 US

ASTRONOMY AND ASTROPHYSICS MONTHLY INDEX. Added/Corp Olivetree Associates. (Jan. 1976)-. Periodical. English. Twelve times a year. $322.00. Olivetree Associates, PO Box 236, Sierra Madre CA 91025. **ED** Helen Zollars Knudsen. **Circ:** 100 (ctrl). available on magnetic tape; available via Internet.
Desc: Provides coverage of articles appearing in the most frequently cited scientific journals of value to the professional astronomer and the research staff. Conference proceedings and their ordering information are included as they become available.

LC QB1.A8645 **ISSN** 0935-4956
DD 520 GW
CCC
CODEN AASREB

ASTRONOMY AND ASTROPHYSICS REVIEW, THE. [Astron. astrophys. rev.]. Vol. 1 No. 1 (Apr 1989)-. Periodical. English. Four times a year. $271.00. Springer-Verlag GmbH & Company KG, Heidelberger Platz 3, D-14197 Berlin Germany. **Tel** 011 49 30 8207223, FAX 011 49 30 8214091, telex 183 319 SPBLN D. **(Subscription address:** Springer-Verlag New York Inc. / North America, PO Box 2485, Journal Fulfillment, Secaucus NJ 07096. **Tel** (201)348-4033, (800)777-4643, FAX (201)348-4505.**) ED** L. Woltjer. available on microfilm and microfiche from University Microfilms International (UMI). Documents available from The Genuine Article, Ask*IEEE.
Desc: Provides important reviews that present a reasonably complete and well-balanced survey of the world literature and allows authors to represent an appropriate cross-section of the astronomical community.
Ind/Abst Curr. Contents Phys. Chem. Earth Sci.; Ei Page One; INSPEC (1989-); Int. Aerosp. Abstr. (1991-); Res. Alert [Select. Cov.]; SCISEARCH.

LC QB1 .A832 **ISSN** 0365-0138
DD 520/.5 FR
CCC
CODEN AAESB9

Pr Rev.

ASTRONOMY & ASTROPHYSICS. SUPPLEMENT SERIES. [Astron. astrophys. Suppl. ser.]. **Added/Corp** Sterrewacht Leiden. European Southern Observatory. **VFOAT** Astronomy and Astrophysics. Supplement Series. **VAT** Astronomy and Astrophysics. Supplement Series. Vol. 1 (Jan. 1970)-. Academic Scholarly Publication. English (French and German). Eighteen times a year. $984.25. Les Editions de Physique, 7 Avenue du Hoggar, Z.I. de Courtaboeuf - BP 112, 91944 les Ulis Cedex A France. **Tel** 011 33 1 69187575, FAX 011 33 1 69288491, telex EDITPHY 692321F. **ED** F. Praderie and M. Grewing. Index available. cum. index. **Bk Rev. Ad Acc. Circ:** 800. Documents available from Article Express International, The Genuine Article, Ask*IEEE, CASDDS.
Desc: Includes observation data and original articles.
Ind/Abst Astron. Astrophys. Abstr. (19??-); Chem. Abstr. (19??-); Curr. Contents Phys. Chem. Earth Sci. (19??-); Energy Res. Abstr. (19??-); Eng. Index Annu. (19??-) [Select. Cov.]; INSPEC (1972-); Int. Aerosp. Abstr. (1991-); Math. Rev. (19??-); Res. Alert (19??-) [Full Cov.]; Sci. Cit. Index (19??-); SCISEARCH (19??-).

LC QB1 .S764 **ISSN** 1063-7737
DD 520/.5 US
CCC
CODEN ALETEO

●**ASTRONOMY LETTERS.** [Astron. lett.]. **Added/Corp** American Institute of Physics. Consultants Bureau. Vol. 19, No. 1 (Jan.-Feb. 1993)-. Periodical. English (translations available in Russian). Six times a year. $935.00. American Institute of Physics, 500 Sunnyside Boulevard, Woodbury NY 11797-2999. **Tel** (516)576-2270, (800)344-6902, FAX (516)349-9704, telex 960983. Index available (bound in last issue). ***Continues*** *Soviet Astronomy Letters, 0360-0327.*
Ind/Abst Sci. Cit. Index.

LC QB1 .A7998 **ISSN** 0091-6358
DD 520/.5 US
CODEN ASTRD5

ASTRONOMY (MILWAUKEE). (ASTRONOMY.). [Astronomy]. Vol. 1 (Aug. 1973)-. Periodical. English. Twelve times a year (monthly). $29.95. Kalmbach Publishing Company, 21027 Crossroads Circle, PO Box 1612, Waukesha WI 53187. **Tel** (414)796-8776 ext. 411, FAX (414)796-0126. **ED** Richard Berry. **Bk Rev. Ad Acc. Circ:** 160,000. available on microfilm and microfiche from University Microfilms International (UMI); available on CD-ROM from University Microfilms International (UMI). Documents available from UMI Article Clearinghouse, Ask*IEEE, Magazine Collection, BLDSC, FAXON Xpress, The UnCover Company, SWETS.
Desc: Includes star and planet chart, tips on telescope observing, and techniques for taking astrophotographs.
Ind/Abst Acad. Abstr. Full Text Elite; Acad. Abstr.; Acad. Ind. [Computer File] (1984-); Acad. Search; Book Rev. Index; Ei Page One; EP Collect.; Expand. Acad. Index (1984-); Gen. Period. Index (1985-); Gen. Sci. Index; Gen. Sci. Source; GeoRef; Homework Help.; INFO-SOUTH Abstr.; INSPEC (April 1976-); Int. Aerosp. Abstr. (1983-); Mag. Artic. Summar. Elite; Mag. Artic. Summar. Select; Mag. Artic. Summar. CD-ROM; Mag. Express (1986-) [Full Txt.]; Mag. Index Plus (1989-); Mag. Index. Sel. (1986-); Mag. Search; MasterFile FullTEXT 1000; MasterFile FullTEXT 350; MasterFile FullTEXT 650; MasterFile FullTEXT (July 1984-) [Full Txt.]; Mid. Search; Newsp. Period. Abstr. (1986-); OCLC; Pub. Lib. FullTEXT; Read. Guide Abstr. Select Ed.; Read. Guide Period. Lit.; Resource/One Ondisc; Telebase; Mag. Index (1977-); Vocat. Search.

LC QB **ISSN** 0951-9726
DD 520 UK
CODEN ASNOEZ

ASTRONOMY NOW. [Astron. now]. Vol. 1 (1987)-. Periodical. English. Twelve times a year. £23.00 UK; £30.00 EEC countries; £43.00 Europe excpet EEC and UK North Africa; £48.00 other. Hall Park Publications Ltd., 32 34 Simpson Road, Bletchley, Milton Keynes MK1 1BA United Kingdom. **Tel** 011 44 1908 377559, FAX 011 44 1908 366744. **ED** Steven Young. **Bk Rev**, (Qty: 12). **Ad Acc, Adv Mgr:** Helen Holmes. **Circ:** 25,000. Documents available from Ask*IEEE.
Ind/Abst Ei Page One; INSPEC (Jan. 1988-).

LC QB63 .A79 **ISSN** 1077-5153
DD 520 US

●**ASTRONOMY PRESENTS OBSERVER'S GUIDE.** [Astron. presents obs. guide]. **VFOAT** Observer's Guide. (1995)-. English. Irregular. $4.95. Kalmbach Publishing Company, 21027 Crossroads Circle, PO Box 1612, Waukesha WI 53187. **Tel** (414)796-8776 ext. 411, FAX (414)796-0126.

LC QB1 .A4713 **ISSN** 1063-7729
DD 520 US
CCC
CODEN ATROES

●**ASTRONOMY REPORTS.** [Astro. rep.]. **Added/Corp** American Institute of Physics. **VFOAT** Astronomy. Vol. 37, No. 1 (Jan./Feb. 1993)-. Periodical. English (translations available in Russian). Six times a year. $1410.00. American Institute of Physics, 500 Sunnyside Boulevard, Woodbury NY 11797-2999. **Tel** (516)576-2270, (800)344-6902, FAX (516)349-9704, telex 960983. Index available (bound in last issue). Documents available from Ask*IEEE. ***Continues*** *Soviet Astronomy, 0038-5301.*
Ind/Abst Curr. Phys. Index; Energy Res. Abstr.; INSPEC; Int. Aerosp. Abstr.; Math. Rev.; SPIN.

LC QB **ISSN** 0861-265X
DD 520 BU
UDC 523.9

ASTROPHYSICAL INVESTIGATIONS. [Astrophys. Investig.]. **VFOAT** Astrofiziceski Izsledvanija. (1991)-. Periodical. Multiple languages. One time a year. Bulgarian Academy of Sciences Department of Astronomy, 71 Lenin Boulevard, 1784 Sofia Bulgaria. ***Continues*** *Astrofiziceskie Issledovanija (Sofija), 0324-1459.*

LC QB1 .A9 **ISSN** 0004-637X
DD 523.05 US
CCC
CODEN ASJOAB

Pr Rev.

ASTROPHYSICAL JOURNAL, THE. [Astrophys. j.]. **Added/Corp** American Astronomical Society. University of Chicago. Vol. 1 (Jan. 1895)-. Periodical. English. Twenty-four times a year. $800.00. University of Chicago Press / Journals Division, PO Box 37005, 5720 South Woodlawn, Chicago IL 60637. **Tel** (312)753-3347, FAX (312)753-0811. **ED** Helmut A. Abt (Managing editor) and A. Dalgarno (Letters editor). cum. index. **Acid Free.** available on microfilm and microfiche from University Microfilms International (UMI). Documents available from The Genuine Article, Ask*IEEE, CASDDS. ***Supersedes*** *Astronomy and Astro-Physics (Goodsell Observatory).*
Desc: Research journal devoted to developments, discoveries, and theories in astronomy and astrophysics. Also presents recent work on magnetic fields, x-rays, and interstellar matter.
Ind/Abst Astron. Astrophys. Abstr. (1968-); Chem. Abstr.; Chem. Titles (1968-); Curr. Cit.; Curr. Contents Phys. Chem. Earth Sci.; Energy Res. Abstr. (1968-); INIS Atomindex [Micro.]; INSPEC (1968-); Int. Aerosp. Abstr. (1991-); Math. Rev. (?-199?); Res. Alert [Full Cov.]; Sci. Cit. Index; SCISEARCH; SPIN (1970-).

LC QB1 .A88 **ISSN** 0067-0049
DD 523.05 US
CCC
CODEN APJSA2

Pr Rev.

ASTROPHYSICAL JOURNAL. SUPPLEMENT SERIES, THE. [Astrophys. j., suppl. ser.]. **Added/Corp** American Astronomical Society. Vol. 1 (March 1954)-. Academic Scholarly Publication. English. Twelve times a year. $180.00 US; $192.60 Canada, including GST; $180.00 other (paper or microfiche). University of Chicago Press / Journals Division, PO Box 37005, 5720 South Woodlawn, Chicago IL 60637. **Tel** (312)753-3347, FAX (312)753-0811. **ED** Helmut A. Abt. Index available. **Acid Free.** available on microfiche. Documents available from The Genuine Article, Ask*IEEE, CASDDS.
Desc: Published in conjunction with The Astrophysical Journal. Designed to bring substantial, extensive support to the material found in the journal. Contains many of the most frequently cited papers in astronomical literature.
Ind/Abst Astron. Astrophys. Abstr.; Chem. Abstr.; Chem. Titles; Curr. Contents Phys. Chem. Earth Sci.; Energy Res. Abstr.; INSPEC (May 1980-); Int. Aerosp. Abstr. (1991-); Math. Rev.; Res. Alert [Full Cov.]; Sci. Cit. Index; SCISEARCH; SPIN (1973-).

LC QB460 .A87 **ISSN** 0888-6512
DD 523.01 US
CCC
CODEN ALECE7

Pr Rev.

ASTROPHYSICAL LETTERS AND COMMUNICATIONS. [Astrophys. lett. commun.]. **VFOAT** Astrophysical Letters and Communications. Vol. 26, No. 1/2 (1987)-. Periodical. English. Six times a year. Gordon & Breach Science Publishers, PO Box 90, Reading, Berkshire RG1 8JL United Kingdom. **Tel** 011 44 1734 560080, FAX 011 44 1734 568211. **(Subscription address:** Gordon & Breach Science Publishers / US, 820 Town Center Drive, Langhorne PA 19047. **Tel** (215)750-2642.**) ED** G. Palumbo. Index available. **Bk Rev. Ad Acc.** Documents available from The Genuine Article, Ask*IEEE. ***Continues*** *Astrophysical Letters, 0004-6388.*
Desc: Covers research in modern astronomy and astrophysics, observational, theoretical and instrumental. Focuses on related areas of physics, such as plasma physics and elementary particle physics.
Ind/Abst Astron. Astrophys. Abstr.; Curr. Contents Phys. Chem. Earth Sci.; INIS Atomindex [Micro.]; INSPEC (1987-); Res. Alert [Full Cov.]; Sci. Cit. Index.

LC QB461 .A77 **ISSN** 0571-7256
DD 523 US
CCC
CODEN ATPYAA

ASTROPHYSICS. [Astrophysics]. **Added/Corp** Consultants Bureau. Vol. 1 (Jan./Mar. 1965)-. Periodical. English (Russian). Four times a year. $975.00. Consultants Bureau, A Division of Plenum Publishing Corporation, 233 Spring Street, New York NY 10013. **Tel** (212)620-8000, (212)620-8466, FAX (212)463-0742, telex 23/421139. **ED** L. V. Mirzoyan. Index available. available on microfilm and microfiche from University Microfilms International (UMI). Documents available from Ask*IEEE, CASDDS.
Ind/Abst Appl. Mech. Rev.; Chem. Abstr.; INSPEC (1968-); Int. Aerosp. Abstr.; Math. Rev.; Life Sci. Collect.

ISSN 1071-703X
DD 523 UK

●**ASTROPHYSICS AND SPACE PHYSICS REVIEWS.** [Astrophys. space phys. rev.]. (1994)-. Academic Scholarly Publication. English. Irregular. Harwood Academic Publishers, PO Box 90, Reading RG1 8JL United Kingdom. **Tel** 011 44 1734 560080, FAX 011 44 1734 568211. ***Continues*** *Soviet Scientific Reviews. Section E, Astrophysics and Space Physics Reviews, 0143-0432.*
Ind/Abst Chem. Abstr.; INSPEC; Int. Aerosp. Abstr.

Astronomy

LC QB460 .A876 ISSN 0004-640X
DD 500.5/05 NE
 CCC
 CODEN APSSBE
Pr Rev.
ASTROPHYSICS AND SPACE SCIENCE.
[Astrophys. space sci.]. Vol. 1, No. 1 (Jan. 1968)-. Periodical. English. Twenty-four times a year (12 vols.). $3470.00. Kluwer Academic Publishers, Postbus 322, 3300 AH Dordrecht The Netherlands. **Tel** 011 31 78 524400, FAX 011 31 78 183273, telex 20083. **ED** John Dyson and Jurgen Rahe. cum. index. **Bk Rev. Ad Acc. Acid Free. Circ:** 700. available on microfilm and microfiche from University Microfilms International (UMI). Documents available from The Genuine Article, Ask*IEEE, CASDDS. *Absorbed Cosmic Electrodynamics, 0010-9509; Space Science Instrumentation, 0377-7936.*
 Desc: Contains original contributions from the entire domain of astrophysics and allied fields of cosmochemistry, dynamics, etc. Covers stellar, galactic and extragalactic - excluding the sun.
 Ind/Abst Astron. Astrophys. Abstr. (1968-); Chem. Abstr.; Curr. Cit.; Curr. Contents Phys. Chem. Earth Sci.; Energy Res. Abstr.; INSPEC (1968-); Int. Aerosp. Abstr. (1991-); Math. Rev.; Meteorol. Geoastrophys. Abstr.; Nucl. Sci. Abstr.; Res. Alert [Full Cov.]; Sci. Cit. Index; SCISEARCH; Zentralbl. Math. Ihre Grenzgeb. (1968-).

LC QB ISSN 0067-0057
DD 520 NE
 CODEN ASSLAD
ASTROPHYSICS AND SPACE SCIENCE LIBRARY. [Astrophys. space sci. libr.]. Vol. 1 (1965)-. Monographic series. English. Irregular. Price varies per volume. Kluwer Academic Publishers, Postbus 322, 3300 AH Dordrecht The Netherlands. **Tel** 011 31 78 524400, FAX 011 31 78 183273, telex 20083. Documents available from Ask*IEEE, CASDDS.
 Ind/Abst Chem. Abstr.; Curr. Cit.; Energy Res. Abstr. (April 1973-); GeoRef; INSPEC; Math. Rev.

LC QB
DD 520 NE
Pr Rev.
ASTRUIM. (19??)-. Dutch. Six times a year. Fl25.00. NJRS, PO Box 38, 5340 AA OSS Netherlands. **Tel** 011 31 8894 19929. **ED** G. Keyzers. **Ad Acc.** ctrl circ.

LC QB
DD 520 AT
ATNF NEWSLETTER. Added/Corp Commonwealth Scientific and Industrial Research Organization (Australia). Division of Radiophysics. **VFOAT** Australia Telescope National Facility Newsletter. (19??)-. Newsletter. English. CSIRO Publications, PO Box 89, 314 Albert Street, East Melborne Victoria 3002 Australia. **Tel** 011 61 3 4187333, 4187217, FAX 011 61 3 4190459, telex AA 30236. *Continues AT Newsletter.*

LC QB4.9.A8 A94 ISSN 0814-5628
DD 520/.5 AT
 CODEN AJOAE3
AUSTRALIAN JOURNAL OF ASTRONOMY. Vol. 1, No. 1 (April 1985)-. Periodical. English. Three times a year. 9.86Aus$. Astral Press, PO Box 107, Wembley Western Australia 6014 Australia.
 Ind/Abst Astron. Astrophys. Abstr.

LC QB1.B34
DD 520 LI
BALTIC ASTRONOMY. (1992)-. Periodical. English. Four times a year. $48.00. Institute of Theoretical Physics and Astronomy, Dir Z. Rudzikas, K Pozelos 54, Vilnius 2600 Lithuania. **Tel** 011 3702 613440, FAX 011 3702 224694, telex 261135. **ED** V. Straizys. Index available. cum. index. **Ad Acc.**

LC QB1.B34 ISSN 0405-5497
DD 520 GW
BAV RUNDBRIEF: MITTEILUNGSBLATT DER BERLINER ARBEITSGEMEINSCHAFT F. VERAENDERLICHE STERNE E. V. VFOAT Mitteilungsblatt der Berliner Arbeitsgemeinschaft F. Veranderliche Sterne E.V. **VAT** Berliner Arbeitsgemeinschaft fuer Veranderliche Sterne. (1952)-. Periodical. German. Four times a year.
 Ind/Abst Astron. Astrophys. Abstr.

LC QB
DD 520 SZ
BBSAG BULLETIN. Added/Corp Bedeckungsveranderliche Beobachter Schweizerischer Astronomischer Gesellschaft. No. 1 (Feb. 5, 1972)-. Bulletin. English. Six times a year.
 Ind/Abst Astron. Astrophys. Abstr.

LC QB475.A1 C65a ISSN 0812-339X
 AT
BIENNIAL REPORT / CSIRO, DIVISION OF RADIOPHYSICS. Main/Corp Commonwealth Scientific and Industrial Research Organization (Australia). Division of Radiophysics. (July 1981 to June 1983)-. English. Every 2 years. CSIRO Publications, PO Box 89, 314 Albert Street, East Melborne Victoria 3002 Australia. **Tel** 011 61 3 4187333, 4187217, FAX 011 61 3 4190459, telex AA 30236.

LC QB
DD 520 US
BIMONTHLY SUMMARY / MULTIPLE MIRROR TELESCOPE OBSERVATORY, SMITHSONIAN ASTROPHYSICAL OBSERVATORY, AND STEWARD OBSERVATORY, UNIVERSITY OF ARIZONA. Added/Corp Multiple Mirror Telescope Observatory. (1989)-. Periodical. English. Six times a year. Smithsonian Astrophysical Obersvatory and Steward Observatory, University of Arizona, Tuscon AZ 85721. *Continues Monthly Summary (Multiple Mirror Telescope Observatory), 1052-0260.*

LC QB1 .A1512 ISSN 0258-7327
 GS
BIULETENI - ABASTUMNIS ASTROPIZIKURI OBSERVATORIA. MTA QANOBILI. (BIULETENI / ABSTUMNIS ASTROPIZIKURI OBSERVATORIA = BIULLETEN / ABSTUMANSKAIA ASTROFIZICHESKAIA OBSERVATORIIA = BULLETIN / ABASTUMANI ASTROPHYSICAL OBSERVATORY.). [Biul. - Abastumnis astropiz. obs., Mta Qanobili]. **Added/Corp** Abastumnis Astropizikuri Observatoria. **VFOAT** Biulleten; Bulletin. (1937)-. Monographic series. Georgian (English and Russian). Irregular. Price varies per volume.
 Desc: Information on astronomy and astrophysics.
 Ind/Abst Int. Aerosp. Abstr.

LC QB475.A1 L37a LV
BIULLETEN RADIOASTROFIZICHESKOI OBSERVATORII AKADEMII NAUK LATVIISKOI. Main/Corp Radioastrofizikas Observatorija (Latvijas PSR Zinatnu Akademija). (1973)-. Academic Scholarly Publication. Russian (English; summaries and/or abstracts in English and Latvian). Two times a year. Zinatne / Science Publishing House, Turgeneva Iela 19, Riga Latvia 1530. **Tel** 3712 212 797. **ED** Arturs Balklavs. ctrl circ.
 Desc: Solar astronomy, solar - terrestrial physics, red giant stars with peculiarities of the chemical composition, usage of the observation instruments.

LC QB4 .S822 ISSN 0321-4885
DD 522.1 TA
BJULLETEN INSTITUTA ASTROFIZIKI. (BIULLETENI INSTITUTI ASTROFIZIKA.). [Bjull. Inst. astrofiz.]. **Added/Corp** Instituti Astrofizika (Akademiiai Fanhoi RSS Tojikiston). **VFOAT** Biulleten Instituta Astrofiziki; Biulleten Instituta Astrofiziki Akademii Nauk Tadzhikskoi SSR. No. 24 (1958)-. Periodical. Russian (summaries and/or abstracts in English). *Continues Biulleten Stalinabadskoi Astronomicheskoi Observatorii, 0568-6865.*
 Desc: Information on astrophysics.
 Ind/Abst Energy Res. Abstr. (Jan. 1972-); Int. Aerosp. Abstr.

LC QB1 .B65
DD 520/.5 CL
BOLETIN / ASOCIACION CHILENA DE ASTRONOMIA Y ASTRONAUTICA. Added/Corp Asociacion Chilena de Astronomia y Astronautica. (19??)-. Bulletin. Spanish. Twelve times a year. Asociacion Chilena de Astronomia y Astronautica, Casilla 3904 Santiago, Chile.

LC QB4.M195 M36a ISSN 0373-7101
 SP
BOLETIN ASTRONOMICO DEL OBSERVATORIO DE MADRID. [Bol. Astron. Obs. Madrid]. **Main/Corp** Observatorio Astronomico de Madrid. Vol. 1 (1932)-. Periodical. Spanish (English). One time a year. 150ptas Spain; 300ptas other. Observatorio de Madrid, Observatorio Astronomico Nacional, Alfonso XII 3, 28014 Madrid Spain. **Tel** (91)2270107, telex 49880 OANME. Index available. **Circ:** 400 (ctrl).
 Desc: Publishes mainly results of observations technical reports.
 Ind/Abst Astron. Astrophys. Abstr.

LC QB4.O15 O2a
DD 522.1 EC
BOLETIN ASTRONOMICO. SERIE B. Main/Corp Observatorio Astronomico de Quito. No. 1 (1967)-. Spanish. Observatorio Astronomico de Quito, Apartado 165, Quito Ecuador.
 Desc: Information on astronomy.

LC QB1 .I44a ISSN 0303-7584
DD 520/.5 MX
 CODEN BITOD5
BOLETIN DEL INSTITUTO DE TONANTZINTLA. [Bol. Inst. Tonantzintla]. **Main/Corp** Instituto Nacional de Astrofisica, Optica y Electronica (Mexico). Vol 1 (Dec 1973)-. Academic Scholarly Publication. English (summaries and/or abstracts in Spanish). Instituto de Tonantzintla, Apartados Postales Nos 216 Y 51, Puebla Mexico. Documents available from Ask*IEEE, CASDDS. *Continues in part Boletin de los Observatorios Tonantzintla y Tacubaya, 0082-4879.*
 Ind/Abst Chem. Abstr.; INSPEC (Dec. 1973-).

LC QB1 .O19 ISSN 0302-2277
 AG
BOLETIN - OBSERVATORIO ASTRONOMICO MUNICIPAL DE ROSARIO. (BOLETIN.). [Bol. - Obs. Astron. Munic. Rosario]. **Main/Corp** Observatorio Astronomico Municipal de Rosario. (19??)-. Spanish (summaries and/or abstracts in English). Parque Urquiza, Rosario Argentina.
 Ind/Abst Numis. Lit. (?-?).

LC QB ISSN 0264-4185
DD 520 UK
 CODEN BAACDM
BRITISH ASTRONOMICAL ASSOCIATION CIRCULAR. [Circ. - Br. Astron. Assoc.]. **Main/Corp** British Astronomical Association. **Added/Corp** British Astronomical Association. Circular. No. 1 (March 1923)-. Periodical. English. Ten times a year. $17.60. British Astronomical Association, Burlington House, Piccadilly, London 9AG United Kingdom. **Tel** 011 44 171 7344145. Documents available from Ask*IEEE.
 Ind/Abst Astron. Astrophys. Abstr.; INSPEC (April 1981-).

LC QB ISSN 0002-7537
DD 520 US
 CODEN AASBAR
BULLETIN - AMERICAN ASTRONOMICAL SOCIETY. See Astronomy-Abstracting, Bibliographies and Statistics.

LC QB1 .B428
DD 520/.5 YU
BULLETIN ASTRONOMIQUE DE BELGRADE. Added/Corp Astronomska Opservatorija u Beogradu. Univerzitet u Beogradu. Institute of Astronomy. (1992)-. English (French; summaries and/or abstracts in Serbo-Croatian (Cyrillic)). Irregular. Astronomical Observatory, Volgina 7, 11050 Beograd Yugoslavia. *Formed by the union of Bulletin de l'Observatoire Astronomique de Beograd, 0373-3734 and Publications of the Department of Astronomy, 0350-3283.*

LC QB
DD 520 FR
BULLETIN DE L'ASSOCIATION FRANCAISE D'OBSERVATEURS D'ETOILES VARIABLES. Main/Corp Association Francaise d'Observateurs d'Etoiles Variables. Vol. 1 (1932)-. Bulletin. French. *Supersedes Bulletin de l'Oberservatoire de Lyon.*
 Ind/Abst Astron. Astrophys. Abstr.

LC QB
DD 520 FR
BULLETIN D'INFORMATION - CENTRE DE DONNEES STELLAIRES. Main/Corp Centre de Donnees Stellaires. No. 13 (July 1971)-. Bulletin. English (French). Two times a year. Free. Observatoire de Strasbourg, Centre de Donnes Stollaires, 11 rue de l'Universite, 67000 Strasbourg France. **Tel** 011 33 1 88358216, FAX 011 33 1 88250160, telex 890506 STAROBSF. **ED** Michel Creze. cum. index. **Circ:** 600. Documents available from Ask*IEEE. *Continues Information Bulletin (Centre de Donnees Stellaires).*
 Ind/Abst Astron. Astrophys. Abstr.; INSPEC (March 1982-).

LC QB1 .C273a ISSN 0242-6536
DD 523.8/05 FR
 CODEN BICSDY
BULLETIN D'INFORMATION DU CENTRE DE DONNEES STELLAIRES. [Bull. inf. - Cent. donnees stellaires]. **Added/Corp** Centre de Donnees Stellaires. No. 13 (1977)-. Bulletin. English (French). Observatoire de Strasbourg, Centre de Donnes Stollaires, 11 rue de l'Universite, 67000 Strasbourg France. **Tel** 011 33 1 88358216, FAX 011 33 1 88250160, telex 890506 STAROBSF. Documents available from Ask*IEEE. *Continues Bulletin d'Information (Centre de Donnees Stellaires).*
 Ind/Abst INSPEC (March 1982-).

 ISSN 0382-9804
DD 520/.5 CN
BULLETIN DU CENTRE DE QUEBEC DE LA S R A C. Main/Corp Societe Royale d'Astronomie du Canada. Centre de Quebec. (1967)-. Bulletin. French. Two times a year. 4.00Can$ Canada; 4.10Can$ US. Centre Quebec de la SRAC, CP 9396, Sainte-Foy Quebec G1V 4B5 Canada.

LC QB1 .B45a ISSN 0304-9523
DD 520/.5 II
 CODEN BANID3
Pr Rev.
BULLETIN OF THE ASTRONOMICAL SOCIETY OF INDIA. [Bull. Astron. Soc. India]. **Main/Corp** Bharatiya Jyotir Vijyan Parishad. Vol. 1 (June 1973)-. Bulletin. English. Four times a year. $30.00. Dr R

K Kochhar, Indian Institute of Astrophysics, Bangalore 560034 India. **Tel** 530672, telex 0845-2763 11AB IN. **(Subscription address:** Prints India, 11 Darya Ganj, New Delhi 110002 India. **Tel** 011 91 11 3268645, FAX 011 91 11 3275542, telex 31-61087 PRIN-IN.) **ED** S.K. Trehan, R.K. Kochhar. Index available. **Bk Rev. Ad Acc. Circ:** 600 (ctrl). Documents available from Ask*IEEE, CASDDS.
Desc: Includes review articles, research papers and reports from Indian astronomical centers, with book reviews.
Ind/Abst Astron. Astrophys. Abstr.; Chem. Abstr.; INSPEC (March 1977-); Int. Aerosp. Abstr. (1991-).

ISSN 1187-1571
DD 520/.6/071 CN
BULLETIN - ROYAL ASTRONOMICAL SOCIETY OF CANADA. (BULLETIN / ROYAL ASTRONOMICAL SOCIETY OF CANADA = LA SOCIETE ROYALE D'ASTRONOMIE DU CANADA.). [Bull. - R. Astron. Soc. Can.]. **Added/Corp** Royal Astronomical Society of Canada. **VFOAT** S.A.S.C. Bulletin; Bulletin S.R.A.C. Vol. 1, No. 1 (Feb. 1991)-. Bulletin. English (summaries and/or abstracts in French). Six times a year. Free to subscribers of the Journal of the Royal Astronomical Society of Canada. Royal Astronomical Society of Canada, 136 Dupont Street, Toronto Ontario M5R 1V2 Canada. **Tel** (416)924-7973, FAX (416)924-7973. ***Continues*** *Newsletter (Royal Astronomical Society of Canada)., 0846-8877;* ***Absorbed*** *Royal Astronomical Society of Canada. Annual Report., 0846-2682.*

LC QB **ISSN** 0516-9518
DD 520 US
CODEN BAAODO
BULLETIN - THE AMERICAN ASSOCIATION OF VARIABLE STAR OBSERVERS. **Main/Corp** American Association of Variable Star Observers. No. 1 (Jan. 1954)-. Bulletin. English. One time a year. Free. American Association of Variable Star Observers, 187 Concord Avenue, Cambridge MA 02138. **Tel** (617)354-0484, FAX (617)354-0665. **ED** Janet Akyuz Mattei. **Circ:** 1,300 (ctrl). Documents available from Ask*IEEE.
Desc: Predicted dates of maximum and minimum of long period variable stars.
Ind/Abst Astron. Astrophys. Abstr.; INSPEC (1981-).

ISSN 0705-9108
DD 520/.92/4 CN
BULLISIANA. [Bullisiana]. No. 1 (Summer 1981)-. Periodical. English (French). Irregular. Free. Bullisiana, PO Box 1473/Station B, Hull Quebec J8X 3Y3 Canada. **Tel** (613)232-0884. **ED** E.L. Zilberbogen-Chapdelaine. Index available. cum. index. **Bk Rev. Ad Acc.** ctrl circ.
Desc: Studies on Ismael Boulliau.

LC QB528 .P3
DD 523.75 FR
CARTES SYNOPTIQUES DE LA CHROMOSPHERE SOLAIRE ET CATALOGUES DES FILAMENTS ET DES CENTRES D'ACTIVITE. **Added/Corp** Observatoire de Paris. Section d'Astrophysique, a Meudon. (1962)-. Periodical. French. Every 2 years. DASPO, 1 place Jules Janssen, F-92195 Meudon Principal Cedex France. **Tel** 011 33 1 45077797, FAX 011 33 1 45077469, telex 270 912 OBSASTR. **ED** B. Leroy, M.J. Martres, G. Zlicaric. ctrl circ. ***Continues*** *Cartes Synoptiques de la Chromosphere Solaire et Catalogue des Filaments de la Couche Superieure.*

ISSN 0715-4747
DD 520/.6/071 CN
CASSIOPEIA (VICTORIA). (CASSIOPEIA.). [Cassiopeia]. **Added/Corp** Canadian Astronomical Society. (1973)-. Periodical. English (French). Four times a year. Free. Cassiopeia, Department of Physics and Astronomy, University of Victoria, PO Box 1700, Victoria British Columbia V8W 2Y2 Canada. **Tel** (604)721-7740, (604)721-7715, telex 049-7222. **ED** Colin D. Scarfe. Index available. cum. index. **Bk Rev. Circ:** 400 (ctrl).
Desc: Includes meeting reports, information from society executive, job vacancy notices, contributions from members, etc.

LC QB351 .C4 **ISSN** 0923-2958
DD 521/.05 NE
CCC
CODEN CLMCAV
Pr Rev.
CELESTIAL MECHANICS AND DYNAMICAL ASTRONOMY. [Celest. mech. dyn. astron.]. **VFOAT** Celestial Mechanics & Dynamical Astronomy. Vol. 46, No. 1 (1989)-. Periodical. English (French). Twelve times a year. $1099.00. Kluwer Academic Publishers, Postbus 322, 3300 AH Dordrecht The Netherlands. **Tel** 011 31 78 524400, FAX 011 31 78 183273, telex 20083. **ED** Jacques Henrard, Michele Moons. **Acid Free.** available on microfilm and microfiche from University Microfilms International (UMI). Documents available from Ask*IEEE. ***Continues*** *Celestial Mechanics, 0008-8714.*
Desc: An international journal of space dynamics that is concerned with the broadest range of dynamical astronomy and its applications, as well as with peripheral fields.
Ind/Abst Appl. Mech. Rev.; Astron. Astrophys. Abstr.; Curr. Contents Phys. Chem. Earth Sci.; INSPEC (1989-); Int. Aerosp. Abstr.; Math. Rev.; Phys. Briefs; Refer. Z.; Sci. Cit. Index (19??-19??).

LC QB1 .H24a **ISSN** 0253-3065
DD 520/.5 KO
CODEN CHACDE
CEN MUN HAGHOI JI. (CHONMUN HAKHOE CHI. THE JOURNAL OF THE KOREAN ASTRONOMICAL SOCIETY.). [Cen mun haghoi ji]. **Main/Corp** Hanguk Chonmun Hakhoe. **Added/Corp** Hanguk Chonmun Hakhoe. Journal. **VFOAT** Journal of the Korean Astronomical Society. (1967)-. Academic Scholarly Publication. Korean (English and Korean). Documents available from CASDDS.
Ind/Abst Astron. Astrophys. Abstr.; Chem. Abstr.

LC QB1 .C35 **ISSN** 0275-1062
DD 520./.5 UK
CCC
CODEN CASGEY
CHINESE ASTRONOMY AND ASTROPHYSICS. [Chin. astron. astrophys.]. **VFOAT** Chinese Astronomy & Astrophysics. Vol. 5, No. 1 (1981)-. Periodical. English. Four times a year. $926.00. Pergamon Press, An Imprint of Elsevier Science Ltd., The Boulevard, Langford Lane, Kidlington, Oxford OX5 1GB United Kingdom. **Tel** 011 44 1865 843000, 011 44 1865 843699, FAX 011 44 1865 843010. **(Subscription address:** Elsevier Science Ltd. / Oxford Fulfillment Centre, PO Box 800, Kidlington OX5 1DX United Kingdom. **Tel** 011 44 865 843355.) **ED** Wang Shouguan. available on microfilm and microfiche from University Microfilms International (UMI); available on an online database from Elsevier Electronic Subscriptions (EES). Documents available from Ask*IEEE. ***Continues*** *Chinese Astronomy, 0146-6364.*
Ind/Abst Astron. Astrophys. Abstr.; INSPEC (March 1985-); Int. Aerosp. Abstr. (19??-19??); Math. Rev.

LC QB **ISSN** 0373-9139
DD 520 FR
UDC 52
CIEL ET ESPACE REVUE. (CIEL ET ESPACE.). [Ciel espace Rev.]. (1970)-. Periodical. French. Six times a year. $107.83. Assn Francaise d'Astronomie, 17 rue Emile Deutsch Meurthe, 75014 Paris France. **Tel** 011 33 1 45898144. **(Subscription address:** Ciel et Espace, 99 rue d'Amsterdam, 75008 Paris France. **Tel** 011 33 1 42806855.) Documents available from Ask*IEEE. ***Continues*** *Ciel et Fusees, 0150-052X.*
Ind/Abst INSPEC (1982-).

LC QB1 .C5 **ISSN** 0009-6709
BE
CODEN CIELAV
CIEL ET TERRE. [Ciel terre]. **Added/Corp** Societe Belge d'Astronomie. Societe Belge d'Astronomie, Meteorologie et de Physique du Globe. (March 1, 1880-Feb. 15, 1881)-. Periodical. French. Six times a year. $74.62. Societe Royale Belge d'Astronomie, Meteorologie et de Physique du Globe, Ave Circulaire 3, 1180 Brussels Belgium. **Tel** 011 32 2 3730253 ext. 579. **ED** J. Sauval. Index available. **Bk Rev. Ad Acc. Circ:** 1,200 (ctrl). Documents available from Ask*IEEE. ***Absorbed*** *Bulletin de la Societe Belge d'Astronomie.*
Desc: Concerned with popularisation of astronomy, meteorology, geophysics and space research.
Ind/Abst Astron. Astrophys. Abstr.; GeoRef; INSPEC (May/June 1970-); Int. Aerosp. Abstr.; Life Sci. Collect.

LC QB **ISSN** 0081-0304
DD 523 US
CODEN IANUAB
CIRCULAR - CENTRAL BUREAU FOR ASTRONOMICAL TELEGRAMS, INTERNATIONAL ASTRONOMICAL UNION. [Circ. - Cent. Bur. Astron. Telegr. Int. Astron. Union]. **Main/Corp** International Astronomical Union. Central Bureau for Astronomical Telegrams. **Added/Corp** Smithsonian Astrophysical Observatory. (19??)-. Periodical. English. Irregular. $180.00. Central Bureau for Astronomical Telegrams, Smith Astrophysical Observatory, 60 Garden Street, Cambridge MA 02138. **Tel** (617)495-7244, (617)495-7440, (617)495-7444. **ED** Brian G. Marsden and D.W.E. Green. **Circ:** 750. available on an online database. Documents available from Ask*IEEE.
Desc: Postcard notices giving information about astronomical phenomena requiring prompt dissemination. The great majority of information tends to concern comets and unusual minor planets.
Ind/Abst INSPEC (Feb. 1974-).

LC QB4 .S747a **ISSN** 0376-7884
DD 523/.005 SA
CIRCULARS - SOUTH AFRICAN ASTRONOMICAL OBSERVATORY. **Main/Corp** South African Astronomical Observatory. No. 1 (1973)-. English. One time a year. Free on request. South African Astronomical Observatory, PO Box 9, Observatory CP7635 South Africa. **Tel** 011 27 21 7612112. **Circ:** 500 (ctrl). ***Continues*** *Circulars (Republic Observatory, Johannesburg).*
Desc: Contains papers, often of a tabular nature, which seem more suited to in-house publications.

LC QB461 .C66 **ISSN** 0146-2970
DD 523.01/05 US
CCC
CODEN COASD9COASB7
COMMENTS ON ASTROPHYSICS. [Comments astrophys.]. Vol. 6, No. 4 (1976)-. Academic Scholarly Publication. English. Six times a year (1 volume). $425.00 (academic institutions), $662.00 (corporate institutions). Gordon & Breach Science Publishers, Inc., PO Box 786, Cooper Station, New York NY 10276. **Tel** (212)206-8900, FAX (212)645-2459. **ED** B.F. Burke. **Bk Rev. Ad Acc.** Documents available from Ask*IEEE, CASDDS. ***Continues*** *Comments on Astrophysics and Space Physics;* ***Absorbed*** *Earth and Extraterrestrial Sciences, 0070-7902.*
Ind/Abst Astron. Astrophys. Abstr.; Chem. Abstr.; Energy Res. Abstr. (May 1977-); INIS Atomindex [Micro.]; INSPEC (1976-); Int. Aerosp. Abstr.

LC Q **ISSN** 1012-070X
DD 500 TU
COMMUNICATIONS DE LA FACULTE DES SCIENCES DE L'UNIVERSITE D'ANKARA. SERIES A2, A3, PHYSICS, ENGINEERING PHYSICS AND ASTRONOMY. **See** Physics.

LC Q46 .C7
DD 500.2 FR
CODEN CRAMED
•**COMPTES RENDUS DE L'ACADEMIE DES SCIENCES. SERIE II, MECANIQUE, PHYSIQUE, CHIMIE, ASTRONOMIE.** **See** Physics.

LC QB **ISSN** 0278-5021
DD 520 US
CONSTELLATION (MIDDLE ATLANTIC PLANETARIUM SOCIETY). (CONSTELLATION.). **Added/Corp** Middle Atlantic Planetarium Society. (19??)-. Periodical. English. Four times a year. Constellation, 44 Wyoming Drive, Huntington Station NY 11746.

LC QB1 I43 **ISSN** 0537-7560
BE
CONTRIBUTION - INSTITUT D'ASTRONOMIE ET DE GEOPHYSIQUE GEORGES LEMAITRE. MEDEDELINGEN VAN HET ASTRONOMISCH INSTITUUT VAN DE KATHOLIEKE UNIVERSITEIT LEUVEN. **Main/Corp** Institut d'Astronomie et de Geophysique Georges Lemaitre. **Added/Corp** Astronomisch Instituut van de Katholieke Universitet, Leuven. Mededelingen. Louvain. Universite Catholique. Centre de Physique Nucleaire. **VFOAT** Mededelingen van het Astronomisch Instituut van de Katholieke Universiteit Leuven. No. 3 (1967)-. Monographic series. French (summaries and/or abstracts in English). Irregular. Price varies per volume. ***Continues*** *Communication - Institut d'Astronomie et de Geophysique Georges Lemaitre.*

LC QC801 .K613 **ISSN** 0010-9525
DD 523.01 US
CCC
NLM W1 CO932 **CODEN** CSCRA7
COSMIC RESEARCH. **See** Earth Sciences-Geophysics.

LC BL300 .C65 **ISSN** 0269-8773
DD 291.2/4/05 UK
COSMOS (EDINBURGH). **See** Religions and Theology.

LC QB470.A1 C75 **ISSN** 1018-9009
DD 522/.68 US
CRYOGENIC OPTICAL SYSTEMS AND INSTRUMENTS. (CRYOGENIC OPTICAL SYSTEMS AND INSTRUMENTS / COOPERATING ORGANIZATIONS, OPTICAL SCIENCES CENTER/UNIVERSITY OF ARIZONA, INSTITUTE OF OPTICS/UNIVERSITY OF ROCHESTER.). [Cryog. opt. syst. instrum.]. **Added/Corp** University of Arizona. Optical Sciences Center. University of Rochester. Institute of Optics. Society of Photo-Optical Instrumentation Engineers. (Aug. 23-24, 1984)-. Academic Scholarly Publication. English. Every 2 years. International Society for Optical Engineering, PO Box 10, Bellingham WA 98227-0010. **Tel** (360)676-3290, FAX (360)647-1445, telex 46-7053.

LC QB1 .C95 **ISSN** 0732-4421
DD 520/.5 UK
CURRENT TOPICS IN CHINESE SCIENCE. SECTION E, ASTRONOMY. [Curr. top. Chin. sci., Sect. E, Astron.]. **VFOAT** Astronomy. Vol. 1 (1982)-. English. One time a year. Gordon & Breach Science Publishers, PO Box 90,

Astronomy

Reading, Berkshire RG1 8JL United Kingdom. **Tel** 011 44 1734 560080, FAX 011 44 1734 568211.
Ind/Abst Astron. Astrophys. Abstr.

LC QB33.C85 D38
DD 522/.197291   CU
DATOS ASTRONOMICOS PARA CUBA = INSTITUTO DE GEOFISICA Y ASTRONOMIA. **Added/Corp** Instituto de Geofisica y Astronomia (Academia de Ciencias de Cuba). (19??)-. Spanish. Irregular. Instituto de Geofisica y Astronomia, Calle 212, No. 2906, ent. 29 y 31, Zona Postal Mariano 16, Havana, Cuba.

ISSN 0713-5904
DD 522/.19713547   CN
DAVID DUNLAP DOINGS, THE. **Added/Corp** David Dunlap Observatory. **VFOAT** Doings - David Dunlap Observatory. (1968)-. Periodical. English. Free. David Dunlap Observatory / University of Toronto, PO Box 360, Richmond Hill Ontario L4C 4Y6 Canada. **Circ**: 200 (ctrl).

ISSN 1041-5440
DD 520   US
DIO (BALTIMORE, MD.). (DIO & THE JOURNAL FOR HYSTERICAL ASTRONOMY.). [Dio]. **VFOAT** Dio and the Journal for Hysterical Astronomy; Journal for Hysterical Astronomy; DIO. Vol. 1, No. 1 (1991)-. Periodical. English. Three times a year. Dennis Rollins, PO Box 19935, Baltimore MD 21211-0935.

LC QE1 .E12   **ISSN** 0012-821X
DD 550./5   NE
   CCC
   CODEN EPSLA2
Pr Rev.
EARTH AND PLANETARY SCIENCE LETTERS. See Earth Sciences-Geology.

LC QB581 .M65   **ISSN** 0167-9295
DD 523.2   NE
   CCC
   CODEN EMPLD3
Pr Rev.
EARTH, MOON, AND PLANETS. [Earth, moon, planets]. Vol. 30, No. 1 (Feb. 1984)-. Academic Scholarly Publication. English. Twelve times a year. $1166.00. Kluwer Academic Publishers, Postbus 322, 3300 AH Dordrecht The Netherlands. **Tel** 011 31 78 524400, FAX 011 31 78 183273, telex 20083. **ED** A.G.W. Cameron, Z. Kopal, V. Vanysek. **Bk Rev**. **Ad Acc**. Acid Free. **Circ**: 550. available on microfilm and microfiche from University Microfilms International (UMI). Documents available from The Genuine Article, Ask*IEEE, CASDDS. **Continues** Moon and the Planets, 0165-0807.
Desc: An interdisciplinary medium for the publication of original investigations of all aspects of planetary studies - including those of the earth as a celestial body - with an emphasis on results obtained by spacecraft and remote sensing, alongside those obtained by more traditional methods of astronomical research.
Ind/Abst Astron. Astrophys. Abstr. (Feb. 1984-); Chem. Abstr. (1984-); Curr. Contents Phys. Chem. Earth Sci.; Geogr. Abstr. Phys. Geogr. (Feb. 1984-); Geol. Abstr. (1984-); GeoRef; INSPEC (Feb. 1984-); Int. Aerosp. Abstr.; Meteorol. Geoastrophys. Abstr. (199?-); Res. Alert [Full Cov.]; Sci. Cit. Index; SCISEARCH; Zentralbl. Math. Ihre Grenzgeb. (1984-).

LC QB
DD 520   US
ELECTRONIC JOURNAL OF THE ASTRONOMICAL SOCIETY OF THE ATLANTIC [ELECTRONIC JOURNAL], THE. **Added/Corp** Astronomical Society of the Atlantic. **VFOAT** EJASA. (1991)-. Periodical. English. Twelve times a year.

LC QB495 .E82
DD 500.5   DK
ESA FLGEFORSKNING. **Added/Corp** Denmark. Forskningssekretariatet. **VFOAT** E.S.A. Flgeforskning. (19??)-. Danish. Forskningssekretariatet, Holmens Kanal 7, DK-1060 Copenhagen K Denmark. **Tel** (01)114300.

LC QB
DD 520   SP
ESA IUE NEWSLETTER. **Added/Corp** ESA IUE Observatory. **VFOAT** E.S.A. I.U.E. Newsletter. **VAT** European Space Agency International Ultraviolet Explorer Newsletter. No. 7 (July 1980)-. Newsletter. English. Four times a year. Free. The Esa Iue Observatory, Villafranca Satellite Tracking Station, Apartado 54065, Madrid Spain. **Tel** 1-401 96 61, telex 42555 VILS E. **ED** C. Lloyd. **Circ**: 1,200. **Continues** IUE ESA Newsletter.
Desc: Contains reports on spacecraft status, instrument calibration and data reduction to keep the community abreast of developments within the IUE project.

ISSN 1065-3597
LC QB
DD 520   US
EUVE (BERKELEY, CALIF.). (EUVE [COMPUTER FILE] : INFORMAL ELECTRONIC NEWSLETTER FOR THE EUVE SCIENCE PAYLOAD.). [EUVE]. **Added/Corp** Center for EUV Astrophysics, University of California, Berkeley. EUVE Observatory. **VFOAT** EUVE Electronic Newsletter; Extreme Ultraviolet Explorer. Vol. 1, No. 1 (July 8, 1991)-. Periodical. English. Twelve times a year. Free. Center for EUV Astrophysics, University of California, 2150 Kittredge Street, Berkeley CA 94720. **ED** Brett Stroozas. available via Internet (http://www.cea.berkeley.edu).
Desc: Provides information on ultraviolet astronomy.

ISSN 1075-6485
DD 520   US
●EUVE SCIENCE BULLETIN. (EUVE SCIENCE BULLETIN : NEWSLETTER OF THE EXTREME ULTRAVIOLET EXPLORER.). [EUVE sci. bull.]. **Added/Corp** Center for EUV Astrophysics. Extreme Ultraviolet Explorer Guest Observer Program. **VFOAT** Science Bulletin. **VAT** Extreme Ultraviolet Explorer science bulletin. (Jan. 1994)-. Periodical. English. Four times a year. Free. Center for EUV Astrophysics, University of California, 2150 Kittredge Street, Berkeley CA 94720. **Continues** EUVE Technical Bulletin, 1065-3589.

LC QB84.5 .E97   **ISSN** 0922-6435
DD 522   NE
   CCC
   CODEN EXASER
Pr Rev.
EXPERIMENTAL ASTRONOMY. [Exp. astron.]. Vol. 1, No. 1 (1989)-. Periodical. English. Four times a year. $234.00. Kluwer Academic Publishers, Postbus 322, 3300 AH Dordrecht The Netherlands. **Tel** 011 31 78 524400, FAX 011 31 78 183273, telex 20083. **ED** J. Beckers, T. deGraauw, S. Holt, R. Schilizzi, V. Schonfelder, R. Hanisch, Webster Cash, Jr. **Ad Acc**. Acid Free. **Circ**: 60. available on microfilm and microfiche from University Microfilms International (UMI). Documents available from Ask*IEEE.
Desc: Publishes short and long research articles, research letters and reviews on advances in astronomical detection techniques in instruments and in techniques of data analysis and image-processing.
Ind/Abst INSPEC (1989-); Int. Aerosp. Abstr.

LC QB474 .E98   **ISSN** 1069-7497
DD 523   US
●EXTREME ULTRAVIOLET EXPLORER SCIENCE ARCHIVE, THE. (THE EXTREME ULTRAVIOLET EXPLORER SCIENCE ARCHIVE [COMPUTER FILE].). [Extrem. utrav. explor. sci. arch.]. **Added/Corp** Center for EUV Astrophysics. Goddard Space Flight Center. (1993)-. Periodical. English. Irregular. Center for EUV Astrophysics, University of California, 2150 Kittredge Street, Berkeley CA 94720.

LC QB   **ISSN** 0146-7662
DD 520   US
EYEPIECE. **Added/Corp** Amateur Astronomers Association. Observing Group. (19??)-. Periodical. English. Twelve times a year. $32.00 US; $40.00 other. Amateur Astronomers Association Inc, 1010 Park Avenue, New York NY 10028. **Tel** (212)525-2922. **ED** Jack Dittrick. **Circ**: 600 (ctrl).
Desc: News and features pertaining to astronomy in New York City area.

ISSN 0827-1356
DD 520/.5   CN
FEUILLETS DU NATURALISTE, ASTRONOMIE, LES. [Feuill. nat. astron.]. **Added/Corp** Cercles des Jeunes Naturalistes. (1970)-. Monographic series. French. Irregular. 0.50Can$. Cercles des Jeunes Naturalistes, 4101 rue Sherbrooke Est, Montreal, Quebec H1X 2B2 Canada. **Tel** (514)452-3023.
Desc: Addresses topics in science and astronomy with special emphasis for young people.

LC QB   **ISSN** 1154-2675
DD 520   FR
UDC 527
FLASH ESPACE TOULOUSE. (FLASH ESPACE.). (198?)-. Periodical. French. Twelve times a year. Free on request. Centre de Documentation du Centre Spatial de Toulouse, 18 Av Edouard Belin, 31055 Toulouse Cedex France. **Tel** 011 33 61 273825.

LC QC801 .F86   **ISSN** 0094-5846
DD 539.7/223   US
   CCC
   CODEN FNCPAXFNCPA
FUNDAMENTALS OF COSMIC PHYSICS. [Fundam. cosm. phys.]. Vol. 1 (Jan. 1974)-. Periodical. English. $847.00 (academic institutions); $1321.00 (corporate institutions). Gordon & Breach Science Publishers, Inc., PO Box 786, Cooper Station, New York NY 10276. **Tel** (212)206-8900, FAX (212)645-2459. **ED** V. M. Canuto. **Bk Rev**. **Ad Acc**. Documents available from Ask*IEEE, CASDDS.
Ind/Abst Astron. Astrophys. Abstr.; Chem. Abstr. (1974-1986); INSPEC (1978-); Int. Aerosp. Abstr.

LC QC811 .G383   **ISSN** 0016-7932
DD 538/.7/05   US
   CCC
   CODEN GMARAX
GEOMAGNETISM AND AERONOMY. See Physics-Magnetism.

LC QC809.F5 G46   **ISSN** 0309-1929
DD 551   US
   CCC
   CODEN GAFDD3
Pr Rev.
GEOPHYSICAL AND ASTROPHYSICAL FLUID DYNAMICS. See Earth Sciences-Geophysics.

LC QB33.I8 G56   **ISSN** 0390-1106
   IT
GIORNALE DI ASTRONOMIA : PUBBLICAZIONE DELLA SOCIETA ASTRONOMICA ITALIANA. [G. astron.]. **Added/Corp** Societa Astronomica Italiana. (1975)-. Periodical. Italian. Four times a year. L32000. Societa Astronomica Italiana / Florence, Largo E Fermi 5, 50125 Florence Italy. **Tel** 011 39 55 2752270.

LC Q   **ISSN** 0147-1821
DD 500   CCC
GRADUATE PROGRAMS IN PHYSICS, ASTRONOMY AND RELATED FIELDS. See Physics.

LC QB1 .G7   **ISSN** 0195-3982
DD 520.5   US
GRIFFITH OBSERVER, THE. **Added/Corp** Griffith Observatory. Vol. 1 (Feb. 1937)-. Periodical. English. Twelve times a year. $15.00. Griffith Observatory, 2800 East Observatory Road, Los Angeles CA 90027. **Tel** (213)664-1181, FAX (213)663-4323. **ED** EC Krupp. Index available. cum. index. **Bk Rev**. **Circ**: 3,000.
Desc: Contains astronomy and science-related articles.

ISSN 1061-8252
DD 522   US
GRO NEWSLETTER. (GRO NEWSLETTER / NASA GODDARD SPACE FLIGHT CENTER.). [GRO newsl.]. **Added/Corp** Gamma-Ray Observatory. Science Support Center. Vol. 1, No. 1 (Jan. 1991)-. Periodical. English. Four times a year. free. Goddard Space Flight Center NASA, Code 513, Greenbelt MD 20771. **Tel** (301)286-8956.

LC QB43.2 .H35   **ISSN** 0141-0326
DD 520   **CODEN** HAAGDW
HANDBOOK OF ASTRONOMY, ASTROPHYSICS, AND GEOPHYSICS. [Handb. astron. astrophys. geophys.]. Vol. 1 (1978)-. Academic Scholarly Publication. English. Irregular. Price varies per volume. Gordon & Breach Science Publishers, Inc., PO Box 786, Cooper Station, New York NY 10276. **Tel** (212)206-8900, FAX (212)645-2459. Documents available from CASDDS.
Ind/Abst Chem. Abstr. (1978).

LC QB1 .b75   **ISSN** 0068-130X
   UK
HANDBOOK OF THE BRITISH ASTRONOMICAL ASSOCIATION, THE. **Main/Corp** British Astronomical Association, London. (1922)-. English. One time a year (Oct.). $17.52. British Astronomical Association, Burlington House, Piccadilly, London 9AG United Kingdom. **Tel** 011 44 171 7344145. **Ad Acc**. **Circ**: 4,500 (ctrl). Documents available from Ask*IEEE.
Desc: Comprehensive details of astronomical events to occur during the year.
Ind/Abst INSPEC.

LC QB4 .Z9 aQB528
DD 520 S 523.7/4   SZ
HELIOGRAPHIC MAPS OF THE PHOTOSPHERE. (19??)-. English. Schulthess Polygraphischer Verlag, Zwingliplatz 2, CH-8022 Zurich Switzerland. **Tel** 011 41 1 2519336.

LC QB1 .I3   **ISSN** 0019-1035
DD 520   US
   CCC
   CODEN ICRSA5
Pr Rev.
ICARUS (NEW YORK, N.Y. 1962). (ICARUS.). [Icarus]. **Added/Corp** American Astronomical Society. Division for Planetary Sciences. Vol. 1 (May 1962)-. Academic Scholarly Publication. English. Twelve times a year. $1242.00 US and Canada; $1398.00 other. Academic Press Inc, 6277 Sea Harbor Drive, Orlando FL 32887. **Tel** (800)543-9534, (407)345-4100, FAX (407)352-3445. **ED** Joseph A. Burns. Documents available from The Genuine Article, Ask*IEEE, UMI Article Clearinghouse, CASDDS.
Desc: Devoted to the publication of original contributions in the field of solar system studies. The journal reports the results of new research - observational, experimental, or theoretical - concerning the astronomy, geology, meteorology, physics, chemistry, biology, and other scientific aspects of the solar or extrasolar systems.
Ind/Abst Astron. Astrophys. Abstr.; Chem. Abstr.; Curr. Cit.; Curr. Contents Phys. Chem. Earth Sci.; Energy Res. Abstr.; GeoRef; INIS Atomindex [Micro.]; INSPEC

Astronomy

(1968-); Int. Aerosp. Abstr.; Math. Rev.; Meteorol. Geoastrophys. Abstr.; Newsp. Period. Abstr. (1989-); Res. Alert [Full Cov.]; Sci. Cit. Index; SCISEARCH.

LC QB82.J32 M54a
DD 522.1 JA
IDO KANSOKUJO JIGYO HOKOKU.
Main/Corp Ido Kansokujo (Mizusawa-Shi, Japan). (19??)-. Japanese. Ido Kansokujo, 2-12 Hoshigaoka, Mizusa Japan.

LC QB82.J32 M54b JA
IDO KANSUKOJO GAIYO. INTERNATIONAL LATITUDE OBSERVATORY OF MIZUSAWA.
Main/Corp Ido Kansokujo (Mizusawa-shi, Japan). **VFOAT** International Latitude Observatory of Mizusawa. (19??)-. Japanese. Ido Kansokujo, 2-12 Hoshigaoka, Mizusa Japan.

LC QB1   **ISSN** 1048-6127
DD 525   US
IERS BULLETIN--A. [IERS bull., A]. **Added/Corp** International Earth Rotation Service. (1988-). Periodical. English. One time a week. International Earth Rotation Service, US Naval Observatory, Department of the Navy, Washington DC 20392-5100. **Tel** (202)653-0066. **Continues** NEOS Earth Orientation Bulletin.

LC QB4.R43 I54
DD 528/.54 II
INDIAN ASTRONOMICAL EPHEMERIS, THE. **Added/Corp** India. Regional Meteorological Centre, Calcutta. India. Meteorological Dept. (1979)-. English. One time a year. Price varies. Controller of Publications / Civil Lines, Government of India, Civil Lines, New Delhi 110054 India. **Tel** 011 91 3015984, telex 3166415. **(Subscription address:** Prints India, 11 Darya Ganj, New Delhi 110002 India. **Tel** 011 91 11 3268645, FAX 011 91 11 3275542, telex 31-61087 PRIN-IN.) **Supersedes** Indian Ephemeris and Nautical Almanac.

LC QC801 .I42 **ISSN** 0367-8393
DD 523.01/05 II
  CODEN IJRSAK
Pr Rev.
INDIAN JOURNAL OF RADIO & SPACE PHYSICS. [Indian j. radio space phys.]. **Added/Corp** Council of Scientific & Industrial Research (India) Indian National Science Academy. **VAT** Indian Journal of Radio and Space Physics. Vol. 1 (Mar. 1972)-. Periodical. English. Six times a year. $100.00. Council of Scientific & Industrial Research, Publications & Information Director, Hillside Road, New Delhi 110012 India. **Tel** FAX 011 91 11 5731353. **(Subscription address:** Prints India, 11 Darya Ganj, New Delhi 110002 India. **Tel** 011 91 11 3268645, FAX 011 91 11 3275542, telex 31-61087 PRIN-IN.) Documents available from The Genuine Article, Ask*IEEE, CASDDS.
Ind/Abst Astron. Astrophys. Abstr.; Curr. Cit.; Curr. Contents Phys. Chem. Earth Sci.; INPSEC (March 1972-); Int. Aerosp. Abstr.; Res. Alert [Select. Cov.]; SCISEARCH.

LC QB1 .I625a **ISSN** 0538-4753
DD 520/.5 NE
INFORMATION BULLETIN / INTERNATIONAL ASTRONOMICAL UNION. **Main/Corp** International Astronomical Union. No. 1 (June 1959)-. Bulletin. English. Two times a year. **Continues** Circular (International Astronomical Union).
Ind/Abst Int. Aerosp. Abstr.

LC QB **ISSN** 0538-4761
DD 500 HU
  CODEN IBVSDL
Pr Rev.
INFORMATION BULLETIN ON VARIABLE STARS. No. 1 (Oct. 4, 1961)-. Bulletin. English. Irregular. $50.00. Konkoly Observatory, Box 67, 1525 Budapest Hungary. **Tel** 36 1 1754122, FAX 36 1 2754 668, telex 61 227460 Konobh. Index available. cum. index. **Circ:** 400. Documents available from Ask*IEEE.
Ind/Abst Astron. Astrophys. Abstr.; INSPEC (March 1981-).

  ISSN 0736-6922
DD 523 US
  CODEN ICOQDL
Pr Rev.
INTERNATIONAL COMET QUARTERLY, THE. [Int. comet q.]. **Added/Corp** Appalachian State University. Physics Dept. **VFOAT** IQC. Vol. 1 (Jan. 1979)-. Periodical. English. Five times a year. $31.00. Smithsonian Institutions, Astrophysical Observatory, 60 Garden Street, Cambridge MA 02138. **Tel** (617)495-7440, FAX (710)320-6842. **ED** Daniel W.E. Green. Index available. **Bk Rev**. **Ad Acc**. **Circ:** 300 (ctrl). Documents available from Ask*IEEE. **Supersedes** Comet Quarterly.
  Desc: Non-profit journal devoted to the study of comets. Includes tabulated observations, recent news and research articles, review papers, ephemerides, illustrations.
Ind/Abst Astron. Astrophys. Abstr.; INSPEC (Jan. 1979-).

LC QB1 .I644
DD 520/.6/01 FR
INTERNATIONAL DIRECTORY OF ASTRONOMICAL ASSOCIATIONS AND SOCIETIES : I.D.A.A.S. = REPERTOIRE INTERNATIONAL D'ASSOCIATIONS ET DE SOCIETES ASTRONOMIQUES.
Added/Corp Centre de Donnees Stellaires. Centre de Donnees de Strasbourg. **VFOAT** IDAAS; I.D.A.A.S.; Repertoire International d'Associations et de Societes Astronomiques. (1986)-. Academic Scholarly Publication. English. Irregular. Observatoire Astronomique de Strasbourg, 11 rue de l'Universite, 6700 Strasbourg France. **Tel** 011 33 88 358218, FAX 011 33 88 350160, telex 890 506 STAROBS F. **Continues** International Directory of Amateur Astronomical Societies.

  ISSN 0893-3618
DD 523 US
INTERNATIONAL HALLEY WATCH.
(INTERNATIONAL HALLEY WATCH : IHW]. [Int. Halley Watch]. **Added/Corp** Jet Propulsion Laboratory (U.S.). **VFOAT** IHW; IHW Newsletter; International Halley Watch Newsletter. No. 1 (Aug. 1, 1982)-. Periodical. English. Jet Propulsion Laboratory, 4800 Oak Grove Drive / MS264-786, Pasadena CA 91103. **Tel** (818)354-5090.
Ind/Abst Astron. Astrophys. Abstr.

LC QB460 .I579 **ISSN** 0218-2718
DD 523.01/05 SI
INTERNATIONAL JOURNAL OF MODERN PHYSICS. D, GRAVITATION, ASTROPHYSICS, COSMOLOGY. **VFOAT** Gravitation, Astrophysics, Cosmology. Vol. 1, No. 1 (1992)-. Periodical. English. Six times a year. $259.00. World Scientific Publishing Company, PO Box 128, Farrer Road, Singapore 9128 Singapore. **Tel** 011 65 3825663, FAX 011 65 3825919, telex RS 28561 WSPC. **(Subscription address:** World Scientific Publishing Company, Inc., 1060 Main Street, Suite 1 B, River Edge NJ 07661. **Tel** (800)227-7562, (201)487-9655.) **ED** Fang Li Zhi and Abhay Ashtekar.
  Desc: Features reviews and research papers on theoretical, observational and experimental findings in the fields of gravitation astrophysics and cosmology. Covers topics such as general relativity, quantum gravity, gravitational experiments, quantum cosmology, observational cosmology, particle cosmology, large scale structure, high energy astrophysics, compact objects, cosmic particles and radiation.

LC Q **ISSN** 0074-9931
DD 500 US
  CODEN IMTPA8
INTERSCIENCE MONOGRAPHS AND TEXTS IN PHYSICS AND ASTRONOMY.
See Physics.

LC QB
DD 520 US
IONOSPHERIC STATION INFORMATION BULLETIN. **Added/Corp** International Union of Radio Science. Ionospheric Network Advisory Group. World Data Center A for Solar-Terrestrial Physics. (19??)-. Bulletin. English. Two times a year. Free. National Oceanic and Atmospheric Administration NOAA/SEL, 325 Broadway, R/E/SE, Boulder CO 80303-3328. **Tel** (303)497-3171, FAX (303)497-7392.

LC QB
DD 520 US
IPAC NEWSLETTER. **Added/Corp** California Institute of Technology. Infrared Processing and Analysis Center. **VAT** Infrared Processing and Analysis Center Newsletter. Vol. 1, No. 1 (Dec. 1985)-. Academic Scholarly Publication. English. Irregular. California Institute of Technology, Engineering, and Science, 315 South Hill Avenue, Pasadena CA 91125. **Tel** (818)395-6327.

LC QB1 .I753 **ISSN** 0021-1052
  UK
  CODEN IRAJAW
IRISH ASTRONOMICAL JOURNAL, THE.
[Ir. astron. j.]. **Added/Corp** Irish Astronomical Society. Vol. 1 (March 1950)-. Periodical. English. Two times a year. $45.00. Armagh Observatory, College Hill, Armagh BT61 9DG United Kingdom. **Tel** 011 44 1861 522928, FAX 011 44 1861 527174, telex 94082559. **ED** M. De Groot. Index available. **Bk Rev**. **Ad Acc**. **Circ:** 600. Documents available from Ask*IEEE.
  Desc: This journal is a general review of astronomical knowledge and related subjects of interest to both the general reader or amateur and the specialist.
Ind/Abst Astron. Astrophys. Abstr.; INSPEC (March-June 1969-); Int. Aerosp. Abstr.

  ISSN 1047-0220
DD 522 US
IRTF NEWS. [IRTF news]. **Added/Corp** NASA Infrared Telescope Facility. **VAT** Infrared Telescope Facility news. (Oct. 1986)-. Periodical. English. Four times a year. NASA Infrared Telescope Facility / Institute for Astronomy, 2680 Woodlawn Drive, Honolulu HI 96822.

LC QB
DD 520 UK
ISO/IRAS NEWSLETTER. **Added/Corp** Rutherford Appleton Laboratory. **VFOAT** ISO IRAS Newsletter. **VAT** Infrared Space Observatory/Infrared Astronomical Satellite Newsletter. Vol. 2, No. 1 (Apr. 1991)-. Newsletter. English. Documents available from Ask*IEEE. **Continues** IRAS (UK) Newsletter.
Ind/Abst INSPEC (April 1991-).

LC QB520 .L37a
  LV
  CODEN ISKZD4
ISSLEDOVANIE SOLNTSA I KRASNYKH ZVEZD. **Main/Corp** Radiostrofizikas Observatorija (Latvijas PSR Zimantu Akademija). **Added/Corp** Radioastrofizikas Observatorija (Latvijas PSR Zinatnu Akademija). Saules un Sarkano Zvaigznu Petisana. **VFOAT** Saules Un Sarkano Zvaigznu Petisana; Investigations of the Sun and Red Stars. (1974)-. Russian (summaries and/or abstracts in English and Latvian). Zinatne / Science Publishing House, Turgeneva iela 19, Riga Latvia 1530. **Tel** 3712 212 797.
  Desc: Emphasis on red giants.
Ind/Abst Astron. Astrophys. Abstr.

LC QB1 .A887 **ISSN** 1015-5295
DD 520 TU
  CODEN IUFDEU
ISTANBUL UNIVERSITESI, FEN FAKULTESI ASTRONOMI VE FIZIK DERGISI. (ASTRONOMI VE FIZIK DERGISI.). [Istanb. Univ. Fen Fak. astron. fiz. derg.]. **Added/Corp** Istanbul Universitesi. Fen Fakultesi. **VFOAT** Istanbul Universitesi, Fen Fakultesi, Astronomi ve Fizik Dergisi; Journal of Astronomy and Physics. (1989)-. Periodical. English (summaries and/or abstracts in Turkish). Documents available from Ask*IEEE, CASDDS. **Continues** Reviews of Faculty of Science, University of Istanbul. Serie C, 0253-2638.
Ind/Abst Chem. Abstr.; INSPEC (1989-); Int. Aerosp. Abstr.

LC QB1 .A17642
  RU
IZVESTIIA KRYMSKOI ASTROFIZICHESKOI OBSERVATORII.
Added/Corp Krymskaia Astrofizicheskaia Observatoriia. (19??)-. Periodical. Russian. Nauka, 103717 GSP K-62, Podsosenskii Per 21, Moscow Russia. **Tel** 296-472. **Continues** Izvestiia Ordena Trudovogo Krasnogo Znameni Krymskoi Astrofizicheskoi Observatorii.

LC QB1 .I982 **ISSN** 0190-2717
DD 520/.5 US
  CODEN BCAOD4
IZVESTIIA ORDENA TRUDOVOGO ASTROFIZICH ESKOI OBSERVATORII.
(BULLETIN OF THE CRIMEAN ASTROPHYSICAL OBSERVATORY.). [Bull. Crime. Astrophys. Obs.]. **Added/Corp** Krymskaia astrofizicheskaia observatoriia. (1979)-. Bulletin. English. Irregular. $180.00 per volume. Allerton Press Inc., 150 Fifth Avenue, New York NY 10011. **Tel** (212)924-3950, FAX (212)463-9684, telex 427441 ALPRES. Documents available from Ask*IEEE.
Ind/Abst INSPEC (1979-).

LC QC1 .W43a
DD 530/.05 GW
  TITLE CHANGE
JAHRESBERICHT / MAX-PLANCK-INSTITUT FUER PHYSIK UND ASTROPHYSIK, WERNER-HEISENBERG-INSTITUT FUER PHYSIK. See Physics.

LC QB
DD 520 UK
JCMT-UKIRT NEWSLETTER, THE.
Added/Corp Royal Observatory, Edinburgh. Joint Astronomy Centre (Hilo, Hawaii) Royal Observatory, Edinburgh. JCMT Section. Royal Observatory, Edinburgh. UKIRT Section. **VAT** James Clerk Maxwell Telescope-United Kingdom Infrared Telescope Newsletter. No. 1 (Mar. 1991)-. Newsletter. English. Two times a year. Free. Royal Observatory, Blackford Hill, Edinburgh EH9 3HJ United Kingdom. **Tel** 011 44 131 6688100, FAX 011 44 131 6688264, telex 72383 ROEDIN-G. **ED** E.B. Thompson. **Formed by the union of** Proto Star, 0267-1247 **and** U.K.I.R.T. Newsletter, 0143-0599.

Astronomy

LC QB15 .J68 ISSN 0021-8286
DD 520/.9 UK
  CCC
  CODEN JHSAA2
Pr Rev.
JOURNAL FOR THE HISTORY OF ASTRONOMY. [J. hist. astron.]. **VFOAT** History of Astronomy. Vol. 1, No. 1 (Feb. 1970)-. Academic Scholarly Publication. English. Four times a year (plus supplement Archaeoastronomy published in May). $124.00. Science History Publications Ltd., 16 Rutherford Road, Cambridge CB2 2HH United Kingdom. **Tel** 011 44 1223 565532, FAX 011 44 1223 565532. **ED** M. A. Hoskin (Editor's address: Churchill College, Cambridge, England CB3 0DS; telephone: 011 44 223 840284). Index available. cum. index. **Bk Rev. Ad Acc. Circ:** 700. available with illustrations. Documents available from Ask*IEEE.
 Desc: Research articles on history of astronomy and allied topics.
 Ind/Abst Am. Hist. Life; Astron. Astrophys. Abstr.; INSPEC (Feb. 1970-); Math. Rev.; Middle East Abstr. Index.

LC QB ISSN 1080-6423
DD 520 US
JOURNAL - NATIONAL COUNCIL FOR GEOCOSMIC RESEARCH. (JOURNAL / NCGR.). **VFOAT** NCGR Journal. (1972)-. English (German, French and Spanish). Two times a year. $35.00 (includes membership in the National Council for Geocosmic Research, Inc.). National Council for Geocosmic Research, Box 34487, San Diego CA 92103-0802. **Tel** (619)297-9203. **ED** Maria Kay Simms. **Bk Rev. Ad Acc. Circ:** 2,200 (ctrl).
 Desc: Scholarly articles and research reports on correspondences between earth and cosmos.

LC QB460 .J68 ISSN 0250-6335
DD 523.01/05 II
  CODEN JASRD7
Pr Rev.
JOURNAL OF ASTROPHYSICS AND ASTRONOMY. [J. astrophys. astron.]. **Added/Corp** Indian Academy of Sciences. Vol. 1, No. 1 (Sept. 1980)-. Academic Scholarly Publication. English. Four times a year. $75.00. Indian Academy of Sciences Circulation, PO Box 8005, Department of Sadashivanagar, Bangalore 560 080 India. **Tel** 011 91 812 342546, 342310, telex 0845-2178 ACAD IN. **(Subscription address:** Prints India, 11 Darya Ganj, New Delhi 110002 India. **Tel** 011 91 11 3268645, FAX 011 91 11 3275542, telex 31-61087 PRIN-IN.) **ED** J C Bhattacharyya. cum. index. **Circ:** 500 (ctrl). Documents available from The Genuine Article, Ask*IEEE, CASDDS.
 Desc: Devoted to research on all aspects of astrophysics and astronomy, theoretical and observational, from laboratory astrophysics and instrumentation to quasars and cosmology.
 Ind/Abst Astron. Astrophys. Abstr.; Chem. Abstr.; Curr. Contents Phys. Chem. Earth Sci.; INSPEC (Sept. 1980-); Int. Aerosp. Abstr.; Res. Alert [Full Cov.]; Sci. Cit. Index; SCISEARCH.

LC QB835 .A455 ISSN 0271-9053
DD 523.8/44/05 US
  CODEN JAAODA
JOURNAL OF THE AMERICAN ASSOCIATION OF VARIABLE STAR OBSERVERS, THE. [J. Am. Assoc. Var. Star Obs.]. **Added/Corp** American Association of Variable Star Observers. Vol. 1, No. 1 (Spring 1972)-. Periodical. English. Two times a year (April, September). $40.00. American Association of Variable Star Observers / AAVSO, 25 Birch Street, Cambridge MA 02138. **Tel** (617)354-0484, FAX (617)354-0665. **ED** Charles Whitney. Index available in last issue of volume--attached. cum. index. **Bk Rev. Circ:** 1,500 (ctrl). Documents available from Ask*IEEE.
 Desc: Contains scientific papers on variable star research presented at meetings and additional papers submitted to the journal. Also contains reports of the AAVSO committees, reports of the AAVSO director, treasurer's reports, table of AAVSO observers' totals and letters to the editor.
 Ind/Abst Astron. Astrophys. Abstr.; INSPEC (1980-); Int. Aerosp. Abstr.

LC QB1 .B75 ISSN 0007-0297
DD 520/.5 UK
  CODEN JBAAA6
JOURNAL OF THE BRITISH ASTRONOMICAL ASSOCIATION. [J. Br. Astron. Assoc.]. **Added/Corp** British Astronomical Association. Vol. 1 (Oct. 1890)-. Periodical. English. Six times a year. $54.00. British Astronomical Association, Burlington House, Piccadilly, London 9AG United Kingdom. **Tel** 011 44 171 7344145. **ED** J. Mitton. cum. index. **Bk Rev. Ad Acc. Circ:** 3,500. Documents available from Ask*IEEE.
 Desc: Includes meeting reports and papers submitted by members on various aspects of astronomy.
 Ind/Abst Astron. Astrophys. Abstr.; Energy Res. Abstr. (Jan. 1971-); INSPEC (1968-); Int. Aerosp. Abstr.

LC QB1 .R485 ISSN 0035-872X
DD 520.6271 CN
  CODEN JRASA2
Pr Rev.
JOURNAL OF THE ROYAL ASTRONOMICAL SOCIETY OF CANADA, THE. [J. R. Astron. Soc. Can.]. **Main/Corp** Royal Astronomical Society of Canada. Vol. 1 (Jan./Feb. 1907)-. Periodical. English. Six times a year (Feb., Apr., June, Aug., Oct., Dec.). 82.00Can$. Royal Astronomical Society of Canada, 136 Dupont Street, Toronto Ontario M5R 1V2 Canada. **Tel** (416)924-7973, FAX (416)924-7973. **ED** Jeremy B. Tatum. Index available in last issue of volume--attached. cum. index. **Bk Rev. Circ:** 3,500 (ctrl). available on microfilm and microfiche from University Microfilms International (UMI). Documents available from The Genuine Article, Ask*IEEE, CASDDS. **Supersedes** Royal Astronomical Society of Canada. Transactions.
 Desc: The journal contains articles of interest to both amateur and professional astronomers, educators and the general reader.
 Ind/Abst Astron. Astrophys. Abstr.; Chem. Abstr.; Curr. Contents Phys. Chem. Earth Sci.; Energy Res. Abstr.; INIS Atomindex [Micro.]; INSPEC (1968-); Int. Aerosp. Abstr.; Res. Alert [Select. Cov.]; Romant. Move.; SCISEARCH.

LC QB461 .K52 ISSN 0233-7665
  UN
  CODEN KFNTEZ
KINEMATIKA I FIZIKA NEBESNYH TEL. (KINEMATIKA I FIZIKA NEBESNYKH TEL.). [Kinemat. fiz. nebesnyh tel]. **Added/Corp** Akademiia Nauk Ukrainskoi RSR. Viddilennia Fizyky i Astronomii. Vol. 1 (1985)-. Academic Scholarly Publication. Russian (Russian; summaries and/or abstracts in English). Six times a year. $119.95. Izdatelstvo Naukova Dumka / Ukrainian Academy of Sciences, Yu. A. Khramov, Dir., Ul. Repina 3, 252 601 Kiev Ukraine. **Tel** 011 7 44 4303441, 011 7 44 2254182, telex 131376. **(Subscription address:** East View Publications Inc., 3020 Harbor Lane North, Suite 110, Minneapolis MN 55447. **Tel** (800)477-1005, (612)550-0961, FAX (612)559-2931.) Documents available from Ask*IEEE, CASDDS. **Formed by the union of** Astrometriia i Astrofizika, 0582-3198; Vraschenie i Prilivnye Deformatsii Zemli; Problemy Kosmicheskoj Fiziki, 0555-2796; Vestnik I'Vovskogo Universiteta. Seriia Astronomicheskaia Astronomiia Solnechnoi Sistemy **and** Astronomiia Solnechnoi Sistemy.
 Ind/Abst Astron. Astrophys. Abstr.; Chem. Abstr. (1985-); GeoRef; INSPEC (Jan./Feb. 1985-); Int. Aerosp. Abstr.; Math. Rev.

LC QB460 .K56 ISSN 0884-5913
DD 523.01
  CCC
  CODEN KPCBEU
KINEMATIKA I FIZIKA NEBESNYKH TEL. (KINEMATICS AND PHYSICS OF CELESTIAL BODIES.). [Kinemat. phys. celest. bodies]. Vol. 1, No. 1 (1985)-. Periodical. English (translations available in Russian). Six times a year. $820.00. Allerton Press Inc., 150 Fifth Avenue, New York NY 10011. **Tel** (212)924-3950, FAX (212)463-9643, telex 427441 ALPRES. Documents available from Ask*IEEE.
 Ind/Abst INSPEC (1987-).

LC QB ISSN 0343-5725
DD 520 GW
KLEINHEUBACHER BERICHTE. [Kleinheub. Ber.]. **Added/Corp** Germany (West). Fernmeldetechnisches Zentralamt. (19??)-. German. One time a year. $36.85. Deutsche Bundespost Telekom, Postfach 100003, Forsch & Tech Urs1, D-64276 Darmstadt Germany.
 Ind/Abst Int. Aerosp. Abstr.

LC QB1 .K63 ISSN 0915-6321
  JA
  CODEN KTENE2
KOKURITSU TENMONDAI HO = REPORT OF THE NATIONAL ASTRONOMICAL OBSERVATORY OF JAPAN. **Added/Corp** Kokuritsu Tenmondai (Japan). **VFOAT** Report of the National Astronomical Observatory of Japan. (1990)-. Periodical. Japanese (summaries and/or abstracts in English). One time a year. National Astronomical Observatory / Tokyo, 21-2 Osawa 2 chome, Mitakashi Tokyo 181 Japan. **Tel** FAX 011 81 3 413690.

LC QB717
DD 523.6 RU
KOMETNYI TSIRKULIAR. **Added/Corp** Gruppa po Issledovaniiu Komet v MGSS (Soviet Union) Kyivskyi Derzhavnyi Universytet im. T.H. Shevchenka. Gruppa po Issledovaniiu Komet i Asteroidov Astroseva i MGK AN SSSR. Vol. 7 (Feb. 1964)-. Periodical. Russian. Irregular. **Continues** Biulleten (Komitet Po Mezhdunarodnomu Godo Spokoinogo Solntsa (Soviet Union).
 Ind/Abst Astron. Astrophys. Abstr.

LC QB717 ISSN 0568-6199
DD 523.6 TA
  CODEN KMMTB8
KOMETY I METEORY. [Komety meteory].
 Added/Corp Akademiiai Fanhoi RSS Tojikiston. Akademiia Nauk SSSR. Astronomicheskii Sovet. (196?)-. Russian. Irregular. **Continues** Biuleten Komisii Po Kometam i Meteoram Astronomicheskogo Soveta an SSSR.
 Ind/Abst Astron. Astrophys. Abstr.; Int. Aerosp. Abstr.

LC Q224.3.I5 P87a
  IO
LAPORAN TAHUNAN PUSAT DOKUMENTASI ILMIAH NASIONAL.
 Main/Corp Pusat Dokumentasi Ilmiah Nasional (Indonesia). (19??)-. Indonesian. One time a year. Pusat Dokumentasi Ilmiah Nasl, PO Box 3065 JKT, Djakarta 10002 Indonesia. **Tel** (021)583465, telex 62875 IA. **Bk Rev. Ad Acc. Circ:** 1,000.
 Desc: Report of the national scientific documentation center, Indonesian Institute of Sciences.

LC QB601 .L83 ISSN 0889-9622
DD 523.4/9 US
LOCAL PLANET VISIBILITY REPORT.
 Added/Corp Astronomical Data Service. (19??)-. Statistical Publication. English. One time a year. $15.00. Astronomical Data Service, 3922 Leisure Lane, Colorado Springs CO 80917. **Tel** (719)597-4068.
 Desc: Contains local visibility information for Mars, Mercury, Venus, Jupiter and Saturn.

  ISSN 1054-0059
DD 522 US
LOWELL OBSERVER (FLAGSTAFF, ARIZ.). (THE LOWELL OBSERVER.). [Lowell obs.].
 Added/Corp Lowell Observatory. (1988)-. Periodical. English. Four times a year. Lowell Observatory, 1400 West Mars Hill Road, Flagstaff AZ 86001. **Tel** (802)774-3358.

LC WMLC 93/4372 ISSN 0891-4664
DD 520 US
  CODEN LPIBE3
LUNAR & PLANETARY INFORMATION BULLETIN. [Lunar planet. inf. bull.]. **Added/Corp** Lunar and Planetary Institute. **VFOAT** Lunar and Planetary Information Bulletin; LPIB. (1978)-. Bulletin. English. Lunar and Planetary Institute, 3600 Bay Area Boulevard, Houston TX 77058. **Tel** (713)486-2172. Documents available from Ask*IEEE.
 Ind/Abst GeoRef; INSPEC (1985-); Int. Aerosp. Abstr.

LC QB ISSN 0748-9781
DD 520 US
LUNAR SAMPLE NEWSLETTER. [Lunar sample newsl.]. **Added/Corp** United States. Planetary Materials Branch. (19??)-. Newsletter. English. Douglas P Blanchard, Planetary Materials Branch/SN 2 Nasa/JSC, Houston TX 77058.

LC QB1 .M18
  NE
MACRO. **Added/Corp** Stichting Macro. (19??)-. Periodical. Dutch. Twelve times a year. Haarlem Postbus 281, Haarlem Netherlands.

LC QB600
DD 523.43 US
MARS UNDERGROUND NEWS.
 Added/Corp Planetary Society. (19??)-. Periodical. English. Four times a year. $15.00. The Planetary Society, 65 North Catalina Avenue, Pasadena CA 91107. **Tel** (818)793-5100, telex 757511. **ED** Charlene Anderson. **Circ:** 16,000.
 Desc: Articles and information on Mars from scientists all around the world including from Russia.

LC QB ISSN 0102-4914
DD 520 BL
MATHEMATICAL AND DYNAMICAL ASTRONOMY SERIES. [Math. dyn. astron. ser.]. **Added/Corp** Universidade de Sao Paulo. Instituto Astronomico e Geofisico. Vol. 1 (1979)-. Monographic series. English. Price varies per volume.
 Ind/Abst Math. Rev.; Zentralbl. Math. Ihre Grenzgeb.

LC QB1 .A2852 ISSN 1061-9038
DD 520/.607 US
MEMBERSHIP DIRECTORY - AMERICAN ASTRONOMICAL SOCIETY (1984). (MEMBERSHIP DIRECTORY / AMERICAN ASTRONOMICAL SOCIETY.). [Membersh. dir. - Am. Astron. Soc.]. **Main/Corp** American Astronomical Society. **Added/Corp** American Astronomical Society. Electronic Mail Directory. **VFOAT** Membership Directory of the American Astronomical Society. (1984)-. Directory. English. One time a year. $20.00. American Astronomical Society, 2000 Florida Avenue Northwest, Suite 300, Washington DC 20009. **Continues** American Astronomical Society. Directory of the American Astronomical Society.

LC QB ISSN 0970-5295
DD 520 II
CODEN MASIDD

MEMOIRS OF THE ASTRONOMICAL SOCIETY OF INDIA. [Mem. Astron. Soc. India]. **Added/Corp** Astronomical Society of India. Vol. 1 (Sept. 1979)-. Periodical. English. Free to subscribers of the Bulletin. Astronomical Society of India, Indian Institute of Astrophysics, Bangalore 56 00 34 India. Documents available from Ask*IEEE.
Ind/Abst Astron. Astrophys. Abstr.; INSPEC (Sept. 1979-).

LC QB82.S842 .M36a
DD 522/.1946/41 SP

MEMORIA / OBSERVATORIO ASTRONOMICO NACIONAL. **Main/Corp** Observatorio Astronomico de Madrid. (19??)-. Periodical. Spanish. Observatorio Astronomico Nacional, Alfonso XII, 3 Madrid 28014 Spain.

LC QB ISSN 0037-8720
DD 520 IT
CODEN MSATAB

MEMORIE DELLA SOCIETA ASTRONOMICA ITALIANA. [Mem. Soc. astron. ital.]. **Main/Corp** Societa Astronomica Italiana. Vol. 1 (1872)-. Periodical. Italian (Italian). Four times a year. $105.00. Societa Astronomica Italiana / Florence, Largo E Fermi 5, 50125 Florence Italy. **Tel** 011 39 55 2752270. **(Subscription address:** Vaghi Periodicals, Via Teodosio 18, 20131 Milan Italy. **Tel** 011 39 2 2665377.) cum. index. Documents available from Ask*IEEE, CASDDS.
Ind/Abst Astron. Astrophys. Abstr.; Chem. Abstr.; INSPEC (1968-); Int. Aerosp. Abstr.; Math. Rev.

LC QB1 .M43 ISSN 0047-6773
DD 520.5 US
CODEN MRCYAT

MERCURY (SAN FRANCISCO). (MERCURY / ASTRONOMICAL SOCIETY OF THE PACIFIC.). [Mercury]. **Added/Corp** Astronomical Society of the Pacific. Vol. 1, No. 1 (Jan./Feb. 1972)-. Periodical. English. Six times a year. $35.00. Astronomical Society of the Pacific, 390 Ashton Avenue, San Francisco CA 94112. **Tel** (415)337-1100, FAX (415)337-5205. **ED** Andrew Fraknoi. **Bk Rev**. **Ad Acc**. **Circ:** 7,000. available on microfilm and microfiche from University Microfilms International (UMI). Documents available from Ask*IEEE, UMI Article Clearinghouse. ***Continues*** *Leaflet (Astronomical Society of the Pacific), 0004-6272.*
Desc: Non-technical articles on recent developments in astronomy and space science, in literatures, bibliographies, news items, articles on history and education in astronomy.
Ind/Abst Acad. Search; Astron. Astrophys. Abstr.; Curr. Index J. Educ.; EP Collect.; Gen. Sci. Index; Gen. Sci. Source; Homework Help.; INFO-SOUTH Abstr.; INSPEC (Sept./Oct. 1977-); Int. Aerosp. Abstr.; Mag. Search; MasterFile FullTEXT 1000; MasterFile FullTEXT 350; MasterFile FullTEXT 650; MasterFile FullTEXT (July 1993-); Newsp. Period. Abstr. (1991-); OCLC; Telebase.

LC QB717 ISSN 0146-9959
DD 523.5 US

METEOR NEWS. **Added/Corp** Astro-Gator Astronomy Club. (1970)-. Periodical. English. Four times a year. $6.00. Meteor News, Route 3 Box 1062, Callahan FL 32011. **Tel** (904)879-2646. **ED** Karl Simmons and Wanda Simmons. Index available. cum. index. **Bk Rev**, (Qty: 5). **Ad Acc**. **Circ:** 350 (ctrl).
Desc: The latest news on meteorites, meteor showers, meteorite craters and current research in these areas.

LC QB755 .A4 ISSN 0369-2507
RU
CODEN MTTKAI

METEORITIKA. [Meteoritika]. **Added/Corp** Akademiia Nauk SSSR. Komitet po Meteoritam. (1941)-. Academic Scholarly Publication. Russian (summaries and/or abstracts in English). Documents available from CASDDS.
Ind/Abst Chem. Abstr.; GeoRef; Int. Aerosp. Abstr.

LC QB741 .M444
RU

METEORNYE ISSLEDOVANIIA. **Added/Corp** Akademiia Nauk SSSR. Mezhduvedomstvennyi Geofizicheskii Komitet. **VFOAT** Meteor Investigations. No. 4 (1977)-. Periodical. Russian (summaries and/or abstracts in English). ***Continues*** *Issledovaniia Meteorov.*
Ind/Abst Int. Aerosp. Abstr.

ISSN 1052-8091
DD 523 US

MINOR PLANET BULLETIN, THE. [Minor planet bull.]. **Added/Corp** Association of Lunar and Planetary Observers. Minor Planets Section. **VFOAT** MPB. (1973)-. Bulletin. English. Four times a year (Mar., June, Sept., Dec.). $9.00. Minor Planet Bulletin, 10385 East Observatory Drive, Tucson AZ 85747. **Tel** (602)762-5504. **ED** Richard Binzel. **Circ:** 180 (ctrl).
Desc: Bulletin of the Minor Planet Section of the Association of Lunar and Planetary Observers.
Ind/Abst Astron. Astrophys. Abstr.

LC QB740 ISSN 0736-6884
DD 523.5 US
CODEN MPCIB2

MINOR PLANET CIRCULARS/MINOR PLANETS AND COMETS. [Minor planet circ./minor planets comets]. **Added/Corp** Minor Planet Center (Cambridge, Mass.). **VFOAT** Minor Planet Circulars; Minor Planets and Comets; MPC; M.P.C. (June 1979)-. English. Irregular. Minor Planet Center, Smithsonian Astrophysical Observatory, 60 Garden Street, Cambridge MA 01238. **Tel** (617)495-7440. Documents available from Ask*IEEE. ***Continues*** *M.P.C.*
Ind/Abst Astron. Astrophys. Abstr.; INSPEC (June 1979-).

LC QB1 .A66 ISSN 0374-1958
GW
CODEN MASGC6

MITTEILUNGEN DER ASTRONOMISCHEN GESELLSCHAFT. [Mitt. Astron. Ges.]. **Added/Corp** Astronomische Gesellschaft (Germany). (1949)-. German (English). Irregular (two or three issues per year). Dr. Karl Schaifer's Landesstern, Koenigstuhl, D-69117 Heidelberg Germany. **Tel** 06221-10036, telex 461 153. **Circ:** 1,200. Documents available from Ask*IEEE.
Desc: Publishes the annual reports of the German-speaking countries and the proceedings of all meetings of the Astronomische Gesellschaft.
Ind/Abst Astron. Astrophys. Abstr.; Energy Res. Abstr. (June 1972-); INSPEC (1976-); Int. Aerosp. Abstr.

LC QB1 .M64 ISSN 0091-1046
DD 520/.5 US

MODERN ASTRONOMY (BUFFALO). (MODERN ASTRONOMY.). Vol. 3 (Jan./Mar. 1972)-. Periodical. English. Six times a year. $3.00. Modern Astronomy, 18 Fairhaven Drive, Buffalo NY 14225. ***Continues*** *Amateur Astronomer.*

LC QC676 .M63
UK

MODERN RADIO SCIENCE. **Added/Corp** International Union of Radio Science. (1988)-. English. Every 2 years. Oxford University Press / UK, Walton Street, Oxford OX2 6DP United Kingdom. **Tel** 011 44 1865 56767, FAX 011 44 1865 267773, telex 851/837330 OXPRES G.

LC QB ISSN 0141-1128
DD 520 US

MONOGRAPHS ON ASTRONOMICAL SUBJECTS. (197?)-. Monographic series. English. Irregular. Price varies per volume. Oxford University Press / UK, Walton Street, Oxford OX2 6DP United Kingdom. **Tel** 011 44 1865 56767, FAX 011 44 1865 267773, telex 851/837330 OXPRES G. **(Subscription address:** Oxford University Press / USA, Journals Marketing Department, Oxford University Press, 2001 Evans Road, Cary NC 27513. **Tel** (800)451-7556, (919)677-0977, FAX (919)677-1714.) **ED** A.J. Meadows. Documents available from Ask*IEEE.
Ind/Abst INSPEC.

LC QB ISSN 0024-8266
DD 520 SA
CODEN MASAAK

MONTHLY NOTES OF THE ASTRONOMICAL SOCIETY OF SOUTHERN AFRICA. [Mon. notes Astron. Soc. South. Afr.]. **Main/Corp** Astronomical Society of Southern Africa. **VFOAT** MNASSA. Monthly Notes of the Astronomical Society of Southern Africa. Vol. 1 (May 1940)-. Periodical. English. Six times a year. $22.00. South African Astronomical Observatory, PO Box 9, Observatory CP7635 South Africa. **Tel** 011 27 21 7612112. **ED** J. Churms, I.S. Glass. Index available. cum. index. **Bk Rev**. **Ad Acc**. **Circ:** 650. Documents available from Ask*IEEE.
Ind/Abst Astron. Astrophys. Abstr.; INSPEC (1968-); Int. Aerosp. Abstr.

LC QB1 .R7 ISSN 0035-8711
UK
CCC
CODEN MNRAA4

Pr Rev.

MONTHLY NOTICES OF THE ROYAL ASTRONOMICAL SOCIETY. [Mon. not. R. Astron. Soc.]. **Added/Corp** Royal Astronomical Society. **VFOAT** Monthly Notices; Monthly Notices of the R.A.S. Vol. 2, No. 1 (Jan. 14, 1831)-. Academic Scholarly Publication. English (summaries and/or abstracts in Russian). Twenty-four times a year. $2350.00. Blackwell Scientific Publications Ltd, Marston Book Services, PO Box 88, Oxford OX2 ONE United Kingdom. **Tel** 011 44 1865 206206, FAX 011 44 1865 206219, telex 837 515 MARDIS G. **ED** R. J. Tayler. Index available (bound in last issue). **Circ:** 1,550. available on microfilm and microfiche from University Microfilms International (UMI). Documents available from The Genuine Article, Ask*IEEE, CASDDS. ***Continues*** *Monthly Notices of the Astronomical Society of London.*
Desc: Covers research papers in positional and dynamical astronomy, astrophysics, radio astronomy, cosmology, space research and the design of astronomical instruments.
Ind/Abst Astron. Astrophys. Abstr.; Chem. Abstr.; Curr. Cit.; Curr. Contents Phys. Chem. Earth Sci.; GeoRef; INSPEC (1968-); Int. Aerosp. Abstr.; Math. Rev.; Res. Alert [Full Cov.]; Sci. Cit. Index; SCISEARCH; Soc. Sci. Cit. Index [Select. Cov.]; Stat. Theory Method Abstr. (1959-1963); Zentralbl. Math. Ihre Grenzgeb.

ISSN 1044-7059
DD 520 US

NATIONAL AMATEUR ASTRONOMY NEWS. [Natl. amat. astron. news]. Vol. 1, No. 1, (July 1989)-. Periodical. English. Twelve times a year. $18.00. Scott Publishing Company / Texas, Route 14, Box 394-A, Tyler TX 75707.

LC QB1 .A39 ISSN 0148-9992
DD 520/.5 US

NEWS LETTER OF THE ASTRONOMICAL SOCIETY OF NEW YORK. **Main/Corp** Astronomical Society of New York. Vol. 1 (Aug. 1976)-. Periodical. English. Dudley Observatory, 100 Fuller Road, Albany NY 12205.
Ind/Abst Astron. Astrophys. Abstr.

LC QB
DD 520 US

NEWSLETTER OF LABORATORY SPECTROSCOPY FOR PLANETARY SCIENCES. **Added/Corp** United States. Ames Research Center, Moffett Field, California. Vol. 1 (Nov. 1976)-. Newsletter. English. Two times a year. Free. NASA - Ames Research Center, Moffett Field CA 94035.

ISSN 0894-5985
DD 522 US

NRAO NEWSLETTER. [NRAO newsl.]. **Added/Corp** National Radio Astronomy Observatory (U.S.). **VAT** National Radio Astronomy Observatory Newsletter. (1981)-. Newsletter. English. Six times a year.
Ind/Abst Int. Aerosp. Abstr.

LC QB
DD 520 US

NTIS ALERT. ASTRONOMY & ASTROPHYSICS. **Added/Corp** United States. National Technical Information Service. (19??)-. Periodical. English. Twenty-four times a year. $140.00 US; $195.00 other. National Technical Information Service - NTIS, Room 2027S, 5285 Port Royal Road, Springfield VA 22161. **Tel** (703)487-4630, (703)487-4660, (703)487-4650, FAX (703)321-8547, telex 89-9405.

LC QB1 .O2 ISSN 0029-7704
DD 520/.5 UK
CODEN OBSEAR

Pr Rev.

OBSERVATORY, THE. [Observatory]. Vol. 1, No. 1 (April 1877)-. Academic Scholarly Publication. English. Six times a year (Feb., Apr., June, Aug., Oct., Dec.). $42.00. Rutherford Appleton Lab / Space, Astrophysics Division, Oxfordshire OX11 0QX United Kingdom. **Tel** 011 44 1235 21900, FAX 011 44 1235 445848, telex 83159 G. **ED** D. J. Stickland, C. R. Jenkins, M. G. Watson, I. D. Howarth. Index available. cum. index. **Bk Rev**. **Ad Acc**. **Circ:** 3,300 (ctrl). Documents available from The Genuine Article, Ask*IEEE, CASDDS.
Desc: RAS specialist discussion meeting, papers, and book reviews, all concerned with astrophysics and astronomy.
Ind/Abst Astron. Astrophys. Abstr.; Chem. Abstr.; Curr. Cit.; Curr. Contents Phys. Chem. Earth Sci.; INSPEC (1968-); Int. Aerosp. Abstr.; Res. Alert [Full Cov.]; Sci. Cit. Index; SCISEARCH.

LC QB1 ISSN 1196-7390
DD 520/.5 CN

●**OBSERVER LE CIEL.** [Obs. ciel]. (1995)-. French. Irregular. Editions Astronomiques, 4545 Avenue Pierre de Coubertin, Montreal Quebec H1V 3R2 Canada. **Tel** (514)252-3038, FAX (514)251-8038. ***Continues*** *Annuaire Astronomique (Montreal, Quebec), 0825-9984.*

LC QB9 .R7 ISSN 0080-4193
DD 523/.002/02 CN

OBSERVER'S HANDBOOK, THE. **Added/Corp** Royal Astronomical Society of Canada. (1911)-. Periodical. English. One time a year (current edition year published in Nov. of the prior year). 16.95Can$. Royal Astronomical Society of Canada, 136 Dupont Street, Toronto Ontario M5R 1V2 Canada. **Tel** (416)924-7973, FAX (416)924-7973. **ED** Dr. Roy L. Bishop. **Circ:** 15,000. ***Continues*** *Canadian Astronomical Handbook, 0316-5914.*
Desc: The standard North American reference for data on the sky. The material in the Handbook is of interest to professional astronomers and other scientists, amateur astronomers, teachers at all levels, students, science writers, campers, scout and guide leaders, as well as interested general readers. An integral part of many astronomy courses at the secondary and university levels.

LC QB
DD 520 US
OBSERVING SUMMARY. **Main/Corp** National Radio Astronomy Observatory (U.S.). (19??)-. Periodical. English. Irregular. National Radio Astronomy Observatory, 520 Edgemont Road, Charlottesville VA 22903. **Tel** (804)296-0211, FAX (804)296-0278.

LC QB **ISSN** 0737-6766
DD 523 US
OCCULTATION NEWSLETTER. [Occult. newsl.]. **Added/Corp** International Occultation Timing Association. (19??)-. Newsletter. English. Four times a year (Mar., June, Sept., Dec.). $25.00. International Occultation Timing Association, 2760 Southwest Jewell, Topeka KS 66611-1614. **Tel** (913)232-3693. **Circ:** 300 (ctrl).
Ind/Abst Astron. Astrophys. Abstr.

LC QB46 .O3a **ISSN** 0163-0946
DD 520/.5 US
ODYSSEY (PETERBOROUGH, N.H.). **See** Children and Youth Interests.

LC QB **ISSN** 0030-557X
DD 520 SZ
ORION. [Orion]. Vol. 14, No. 1-115, (Oct. 1943)-. Periodical. German (French). Six times a year (Feb., Mar., June, Aug., Oct., Dec.). $61.29. Schweizerische Astronomische, Chemin du Marais Long 10, CH-1217 Meyrin Switzerland. **Tel** 011 41 22 7823228, FAX 011 41 22 7823211. **Ad Acc. Circ:** 4,000 (ctrl).
Ind/Abst Energy Res. Abstr. (May 1974-).

LC QB **ISSN** 1146-545X
DD 520 FR
UDC 011
PASCAL. E 48, ENVIRONNEMENT COSMIQUE TERRESTRE, ASTRONOMIE ET GEOLOGIE EXTRATERRESTRE. **VFOAT** PASCAL. E 48, Terrestrial Cosmic Environment, Astronomy and Extraterrestrial Geology; PASCAL. E Quarante-huit, Environnement Cosmique Terrestre, Astronomie et Geologie Extraterrestre. (1990)-. Periodical. Multiple languages. Eleven times a year. 1240.00F France; 1320.00F other. CNRS / Institut d'Information Scientifique et Technique, (Centre National de la Recherche Scientifique), 15 Quai Anatole France, 75700 Paris France. **Tel** 011 33 1 47531515, FAX 011 33 1 45517307, telex 260034. ***Continues*** *Pascal Explore. E 48, Environnement Cosmique Terrestre, Astronomie et Geologie Extraterrestre, 0761-2109.*

LC QB835 .P4 **ISSN** 0373-7683
DD 523.8 RU
PEREMENNYE ZVEZDY. [Perem. zvezdy]. **Added/Corp** Gorkovskoe Astronomo-Geodezicheskoe Obshchestvo. Akademiia Nauk SSSR. Astronomicheskii Sovet. **VFOAT** Variable Stars. Vol. 1, No. 1, (May 1928)-. Academic Scholarly Publication. Russian (English and German; summaries and/or abstracts in English). Izdatelstvo Nauka / Akademiia Nauk, (Publishing House of the Russian Academy of Sciences), Leninskii Porspekt 14, 117901 Moscow Russia. **Tel** 011 95 9542153, FAX 011 95 9382144, telex 411964.
Ind/Abst Astron. Astrophys. Abstr.

LC QB835 .P42
RU
PEREMENNYE ZVEZDY. PRILOZHENIE. **Added/Corp** Akademiia Nauk SSSR. Astronomicheskii Sovet. **VFOAT** Variable Stars. Supplement. (1971)-. Academic Scholarly Publication. Russian. Izdatelstvo Nauka / Akademiia Nauk, (Publishing House of the Russian Academy of Sciences), Leninskii Porspekt 14, 117901 Moscow Russia. **Tel** 011 95 9542153, FAX 011 95 9382144, telex 411964.
Ind/Abst Astron. Astrophys. Abstr.

LC QB1 .P44 **ISSN** 0320-0108
RU
CCC
CODEN PAZHDA
PISMA V ASTRONOMICESKIJ ZURNAL. (PISMA V ASTRONOMICHESKII ZHURNAL.). [Pisma Astron. z.]. **Added/Corp** Akademiia Nauk SSSR. (1975)-. Academic Scholarly Publication. Russian (summaries and/or abstracts in English). Twelve times a year. $387.20. Izdatelstvo Nauka / Akademiia Nauk, (Publishing House of the Russian Academy of Sciences), Leninskii Porspekt 14, 117901 Moscow Russia. **Tel** 011 95 9542153, FAX 011 95 9382144, telex 411964. **(Subscription address:** East View Publications Inc., 3020 Harbor Lane North, Suite 110, Minneapolis MN 55447. **Tel** (800)477-1005, (612)550-0961, FAX (612)559-2931.**)** Documents available from Ask*IEEE, CASDDS.
Ind/Abst Astron. Astrophys. Abstr.; Chem. Abstr.; GeoRef; INSPEC (1975-); Int. Aerosp. Abstr.

LC QB1 .P46 **ISSN** 0090-3213
DD 523/.0074 US
PLANETARIAN, THE. [Planetarian]. **Added/Corp** International Society of Planetarium Educators. (1972)-. Periodical. English. Four times a year. $24.00. International Planetarium Society, Fleischmann 272 University of Nevada, Reno NV 89557. **Tel** (702)784-4812. **ED** John Mosley. Index available. cum. index. **Bk Rev**, (Qty: 8). **Ad Acc. Circ:** 600. available on microfilm from University Microfilms International (UMI).
Desc: Intended to serve as an avenue of communication for International Planetarium Society members, and others interested in planetariums and astronomy education.

LC QC801 .P5 **ISSN** 0032-0633
DD 523.01 UK
CCC
CODEN PLSSAE
Pr Rev.
PLANETARY AND SPACE SCIENCE. [Planet. space sci.]. Vol. 1 (Jan. 1959)-. Periodical. English. Twelve times a year. $1718.00. Pergamon Press, An Imprint of Elsevier Science Ltd., The Boulevard, Langford Lane, Kidlington, Oxford OX5 1GB United Kingdom. **Tel** 011 44 1865 843000, 011 44 1865 843699, FAX 011 44 1865 843010. **(Subscription address:** Elsevier Science Ltd. / Oxford Fulfillment Centre, PO Box 800, Kidlington OX5 1DX United Kingdom. **Tel** 011 44 865 843355.**)** **ED** David Bates. cum. index. available on microfilm from Pergamon Press; available on microfilm and microfiche from University Microfilms International (UMI); available on an online database from Elsevier Electronic Subscriptions (EES). Documents available from The Genuine Article, Ask*IEEE, CASDDS.
Ind/Abst Chem. Abstr.; Curr. Cit.; Curr. Contents Phys. Chem. Earth Sci.; Environ. Period. Bibliogr. (?-?); GeoRef; INSPEC (1968-); Int. Aerosp. Abstr.; Meteorol. Geoastrophys. Abstr.; Pollut. Abstr. Indexes; Res. Alert [Full Cov.]; Sci. Cit. Index; SCISEARCH; Soc. Sci. Cit. Index [Select. Cov.].

ISSN 0882-5408
DD 523 US
PLANETARY ENCOUNTER. [Planet. encount.]. Vol. 1, No. 1 (Sept. 1985)-. Periodical. English. Twelve times a year. $30.00. Randall M. Schuller, PO Box 98, Sewell NJ 08080-0098. **Tel** (609)478-6396.

LC QB600 .P54 **ISSN** 0736-3680
DD 523.4/05 US
PLANETARY REPORT, THE. [Planet. rep.]. **Added/Corp** Planetary Society. Vol. 1, No. 1 (Dec. 1980/Jan. 1981)-. Periodical. English. Six times a year. $25.00 (one-year), $45.00 (two-year) US; $50.00 (two-year) Canada; $35.00 (one-year), $65.00 (two-year) other. The Planetary Society, 65 North Catalina Avenue, Pasadena CA 91107. **Tel** (818)793-5100, telex 757511. **ED** Charlene M. Anderson, James D. Burke, Donna Stevens, Karl Stall. Index available. cum. index. **Bk Rev**, (Qty: 6). **Circ:** 100,000.
Desc: We cover planetary exploration and the search for extraterrestrial intelligence, with articles written by the people actually doing the research.
Ind/Abst Int. Aerosp. Abstr.

LC QB1 .P835 **ISSN** 0032-5414
DD 520/.5 PL
CODEN PYAIAJ
POSTEPY ASTRONOMII. [Postepy astron.]. **Added/Corp** Polskie Towarzystwo Astronomiczne. Polska Akademia Nauk. Komitet Astronomii. (1953)-. Periodical. Polish (summaries and/or abstracts in English and Russian). Four times a year. $24.00. **(Subscription address:** Ars Polona-Ruch, PO Box 1001, Krakowskie Przedmiescie 7, 00-068 Warsaw Poland. **Tel** 011 48 22 261201.**)** Documents available from Ask*IEEE, CASDDS.
Ind/Abst Astron. Astrophys. Abstr.; Chem. Abstr.; INSPEC (1968-); Int. Aerosp. Abstr.

LC QB1.A37 A33 **ISSN** 0066-9997
DD 520/.5 AT
CODEN AAUPBC
Pr Rev. **TITLE CHANGE**
PROCEEDINGS - ASTRONOMICAL SOCIETY OF AUSTRALIA. [Proc. - Astron. Soc. Aust.]. **Main/Corp** Astronomical Society of Australia. (Jan. 1967)-(1994). Proceedings. English. CSIRO Publications, PO Box 89, 314 Albert Street, East Melborne Victoria 3002 Australia. **Tel** 011 61 3 4187333, 4187217, FAX 011 61 3 4190459, telex AA 30236. **ED** Ravi Sood. Index available. **Bk Rev. Circ:** 600 (ctrl). Documents available from The Genuine Article, Ask*IEEE, CASDDS. ***Continued by*** *Astronomical Society of Australia Publications, 1323-3580.*
Desc: Covers galactic and extragalactic astronomy (optical, UV, IR, radio, x-ray, gravitation), theoretical astrophysics and astronomical instrumentation.
Ind/Abst Astron. Astrophys. Abstr.; Chem. Abstr.; Curr. Contents Phys. Chem. Earth Sci.; INSPEC (1968-); Int. Aerosp. Abstr. (1991-); Res. Alert [Full Cov.]; Sci. Cit. Index; SCISEARCH.

LC QB600
DD 523.4 US
PROCEEDINGS OF LUNAR AND PLANETARY SCIENCE. **Added/Corp** Lunar and Planetary Institute. Vol. 21 (1991)-. Proceedings. English. Lunar and Planetary Institute, 3600 Bay Area Boulevard, Houston TX 77058. **Tel** (713)486-2172. ***Continues*** *Lunar and Planetary Science Conference. Proceedings of the ... Lunar and Planetary Science Conference, 0270-9511.*
Desc: Mostly papers presented at the Lunar and Planetary Science Conferences.
Ind/Abst Sci. Cit. Index.

LC QB755.5.A6 N56a **ISSN** 0914-5621
DD 523.5/1/0989 JA
CODEN PNMEES
PROCEEDINGS OF THE NIPR SYMPOSIUM ON ANTARCTIC METEORITES. **Added/Corp** Kokuritsu Kyokuchi Kenkyujo. No. 1 (Mar. 1988)-. Academic Scholarly Publication. English. One time a year. National Institute of Polar Research, 9-10 Kaga 1-Chome, Itabashi-ku Tokyo 173 Japan. **Tel** 011 81 3 9624711, FAX 011 81 3 9622529. **ED** Hoshiai Takao. **Bk Rev. Circ:** 900 (ctrl). Documents available from CASDDS. ***Continues*** *Symposium on Antarctic Meteorites. Proceedings of the ... Symposium on Antarctic Meteorites.*
Ind/Abst Chem. Abstr.; GeoRef.

LC QB755 .A75 **ISSN** 0570-9652
US
CODEN AZMPAA
PUBLICATION - ARIZONA STATE UNIVERSITY. CENTER FOR METEORITE STUDIES. (PUBLICATION - CENTER FOR METEORITE STUDIES, ARIZONA STATE UNIVERSITY, TEMPE.). [Publ. - Ariz. State Univ., Cent. Meteor. Stud.]. **Added/Corp** Arizona State University. Center for Meteorite Studies. No. 1 (1962)-. Monographic series. English. Price varies per volume. Arizona State University / Center for Meteorite Studies, Tempe AZ 85281.
Ind/Abst GeoRef.

LC QB **ISSN** 0989-6228
DD 520 FR
PUBLICATION DE L'OBSERVATOIRE ASTRONOMIQUE DE STRASBOURG. SERIE ASTRONOMIE ET SCIENCES HUMAINES. [Publ. Obs. astron. Strasbg.. Ser. astron. sci. hum.]. **Added/Corp** Observatoire de Strasbourg. **VFOAT** Serie Astronomie et Sciences Humaines; Astronomie et Sciences Humaines. (1988)-. Periodical. French (English). Two times a year. Observatoire Astronomique de Strasbourg, 11 rue de l'Universite, 6700 Strasbourg France. **Tel** 011 33 88 358218, FAX 011 33 88 350160, telex 890 506 STAROBS F. **ED** C. Jaschek, P. Erny.

LC QB1.A37 A33 **ISSN** 1323-3580
AT
CODEN PASAFO
•**PUBLICATIONS / ASTRONOMICAL SOCIETY OF AUSTRALIA.** **Main/Corp** Astronomical Society of Australia. **VFOAT** Publications of the Astronomical Society of Australia. Vol. 12, No. 1 (April 1995)-. Periodical. English. Three times a year. 90.00Aus$. CSIRO Publications, PO Box 89, 314 Albert Street, East Melborne Victoria 3002 Australia. **Tel** 011 61 3 4187333, 4187217, FAX 011 61 3 4190459, telex AA 30236. ***Continues*** *Astronomical Society of Australia. Proceedings - Astronomical Society of Australia, 0066-9997.*
Desc: Covers galactic and extragalactic astronomy (optical, UV, IR, radio, x-ray, gravitation), theoretical astrophysics and astronomical instrumentation.
Ind/Abst Chem. Abstr. (1995-).

LC QB1 .N5 **ISSN** 0004-6264
DD 520 JA
CODEN PASJAC
Pr Rev.
PUBLICATIONS OF THE ASTRONOMICAL SOCIETY OF JAPAN. [Publ. Astron. Soc. Jpn.]. **Main/Corp** Nihon Temmon Gakkai. **VFOAT** Nihon Tenmon Gakkai Obun Kenkyu Hokoku. Vol. 1 (1949)-. Periodical. English. Six times a year. $275.00. Nihon Tenmon Gakkai, (Astronomical Soc. of Japan), Tokyo Tenmondai, 21-1 Osawa 2 Chome, Mitakashi Tokyo 181 Japan. **(Subscription address:** Maruzen Company Ltd., PO Box 5050, Import & Export Department, Tokyo 100 31 Japan. **Tel** 011 81 3 32789224.**)** Documents available from The Genuine Article, Ask*IEEE, CASDDS.
Desc: Devoted to original papers in all fields of astronomy and astrophysics including theoretical and observational categories.
Ind/Abst Astron. Astrophys. Abstr.; Chem. Abstr.; Curr. Contents Phys. Chem. Earth Sci.; Energy Res. Abstr.; INSPEC (1968-); Int. Aerosp. Abstr. (1983-); Res. Alert [Full Cov.]; Sci. Cit. Index; SCISEARCH.

LC QB1 .A4 **ISSN** 0004-6280
US
CODEN PASPAU
Pr Rev.
PUBLICATIONS OF THE ASTRONOMICAL SOCIETY OF THE PACIFIC. [Publ. Astron. Soc. Pac.]. **Main/Corp** Astronomical Society of the Pacific. Vol. 1, No. 1 (Feb. 1889)-. English. Twelve times a year. $175.00 US and possessions; $190.00 (surface mail) other. Astronomical Society of the Pacific, 390 Ashton Avenue, San Francisco CA 94112. **Tel** (415)337-1100, FAX (415)337-5205. **ED** D. H. McNamara. Index available. cum. index. **Circ:** 2,500. available on microfilm and microfiche from University Microfilms International (UMI). Documents available from The Genuine Article, Ask*IEEE, CASDDS.
Desc: A refereed journal of research reports and review

papers in astronomy and astrophysics.
Ind/Abst Astron. Astrophys. Abstr. (1968-); Chem. Abstr.; Curr. Cit.; Curr. Contents Phys. Chem. Earth Sci.; Energy Res. Abstr.; INSPEC (1968-); Int. Aerosp. Abstr. (1991-); Res. Alert [Full Cov.]; Sci. Cit. Index; SCISEARCH.

LC QB
DD 520 SA
PUBLICATIONS OF THE DEPARTMENT OF ASTRONOMY OF THE UNIVERSITY OF CAPE TOWN. **Added/Corp** University of Cape Town. Dept. of Astronomy. No. 1 (1981)-. Monographic series. English. Price varies per volume. University of Cape Town, Private Bag, Rondebosch 7700 Cape Town South Africa.

LC QB4 .V74 **ISSN** 0160-2519
US
CODEN PLMVDU
PUBLICATIONS OF THE LEANDER MCCORMICK OBSERVATORY OF THE UNIVERSITY OF VIRGINIA. [Publ. Leander McCormick Obs. Univ. Va.]. **Main/Corp** Leander McCormick Observatory. **Added/Corp** University of Virginia. Leander McCormick Observatory. Vol. 1 (1883)-. Monographic series. English.
Ind/Abst Int. Aerosp. Abstr.

LC QB4.K68 P83 **ISSN** 0915-3640
DD 520 JA
CODEN PNAJEH
PUBLICATIONS OF THE NATIONAL ASTRONOMICAL OBSERVATORY OF JAPAN. [Publ. Natl. Astron. Obs. Jpn.]. **Added/Corp** Kokuritsu Tenmondai (Japan). **VFOAT** Kokuritsu Tenmondai Obun Hokoku. Vol. 1 No. 1 (1989)-. English. National Astronomical Observatory / Tokyo, 21-2 Osawa 2 chome, Mitakashi Tokyo 181 Japan. **Tel** FAX 011 81 3 413690. **Circ:** 1,050. Documents available from Ask*IEEE. ***Formed by the union of*** *Annals of the Tokyo Astronomical Observatory, 0082-4704; Publications of the International Latitude Observatory of Mizusawa* ***and*** *Tokyo Astronomical Bulletin, 0082-4690.*
Ind/Abst INSPEC (1989-); Int. Aerosp. Abstr.

LC QB299.5.U6 N38a **ISSN** 0747-6698
DD 526.3/05 US
PUBLICATIONS OF THE NATIONAL GEODETIC SURVEY. [Publ. Natl. Geod. Surv.]. **Main/Corp** National Geodetic Survey (U.S.). **Added/Corp** United States. National Ocean Service. Office of Charting and Geodetic Services. (198?)-. English. One time a year. National Geodetic Survey, NOAA-NOS, N/CG17X2, Rockville MD 20852. **Tel** (301)443-8316. available on microfiche (Vols. for (1985-) distributed to depository libraries).

LC QB
DD 520 US
PUBLICATIONS OF THE UNITED STATES NAVAL OBSERVATORY [MICROFORM]. **Added/Corp** United States Naval Observatory. (1900)-. Government Publication. English. Irregular. US Naval Observatory, 345H & Massachusetts Avenue N2, Washington DC 20390. ***Continues*** *Astronomical, Magnetic and Meteorological Observations Made During the Year ... at the United States Naval Observatory.*

LC QB835 .R63a **ISSN** 0111-736X
DD 523.8/44/05 NZ
Pr Rev.
PUBLICATIONS OF VARIABLE STAR SECTION, ROYAL ASTRONOMICAL SOCIETY OF NEW ZEALAND. **Main/Corp** Royal Astronomical Society of New Zealand. Variable Star Section. No. 1 (1973)-. English. Irregular (1 or 2 issues per year). $26.51. Astronomical Research Ltd., PO Box 3093 Greerton, Tauranga New Zealand. **Tel** 011 64 75 410216. **ED** F.M. Bateson. Index available. cum. index. **Bk Rev. Ad Acc, Adv Mgr:** Audrey Walsh. **Circ:** 250. ***Continues*** *Circular (Royal Astronomical Society of New Zealand. Variable Star Section).*
Ind/Abst Astron. Astrophys. Abstr.

LC QB **ISSN** 0035-8738
DD 520 UK
CCC
CODEN QJRAAK
QUARTERLY JOURNAL OF THE ROYAL ASTRONOMICAL SOCIETY, THE. [Q. j. R. Astron. Soc.]. **Main/Corp** Royal Astronomical Society. **VFOAT** Quarterly Journal of the RAS. Vol. 1 (Sept. 1960)-. Academic Scholarly Publication. English. Four times a year. $155.00. Blackwell Scientific Publications Ltd, Marston Book Services, PO Box 88, Oxford OX2 ONE United Kingdom. **Tel** 011 44 1865 206206, FAX 011 44 1865 206219, telex 837 515 MARDIS G. **ED** G. Cole. Index available (bound in last issue). **Ad Acc. Circ:** 3,250. available on microfilm and microfiche from University Microfilms International (UMI). Documents available from The Genuine Article, Ask*IEEE, CASDDS. ***Supersedes*** *Royal Astronomical Society. Occasional Notes.* ***Continued in part by*** *Royal Greenwich Observatory. Royal Greenwich Observatory Report, 0308-3322.*
Desc: Carries articles, conference reports, review papers and RAS domestic news. Covers geophysics and astronomy, plus reports from the world's observatories.
Ind/Abst Astron. Astrophys. Abstr.; Chem. Abstr.; Curr. Contents Phys. Chem. Earth Sci.; GeoRef; INSPEC (1968-); Int. Aerosp. Abstr. (19??-19??); Res. Alert [Full Cov.]; Sci. Cit. Index; SCISEARCH; Soc. Sci. Cit. Index [Select. Cov.].

LC QB468
DD 522.682 BE
•**RADIO SCIENCE BULLETIN, THE.** **Added/Corp** International Union of Radio Science. No. 271 (Dec. 1994)-. Bulletin. English. Four times a year. International Union of Radio Science, 41 St. Pietersnieuwstraat, B-9000 Gent Belgium. **Tel** 011 32 9 2643320. ***Continues*** *Radioscientist & Bulletin, 0779-9993.*

LC QB468 **ISSN** 0779-9993
DD 522.682 BE
TITLE CHANGE
RADIOSCIENTIST & BULLETIN, THE. **Added/Corp** International Union of Radio Science. **VFOAT** Radioscientist and Bulletin. Vol. 5, No. 1 (Mar. 1994)-(1994). Periodical. English (French). URSI Secretariat University of Ghent, Sint Pietersnieuwstraat 41, B 9000 Gent Belgium. **Tel** 011 32 92643320, FAX 011 32 92643593. ***Formed by the union of*** *International Union of Radio Science. Information Bulletin - International Union of Radio Science* ***and*** *Radioscientist, 1170-5833.* ***Continued by*** *Radio Science Bulletin.*

LC QB
DD 520 UK
RAPHAEL'S ASTRONOMICAL EPHEMERIS OF THE PLANETS' PLACES. (1???)-. English. One time a year. W Foulsham & Company Ltd, Yeovil Road, Slough SL1 4JH United Kingdom.

LC QB209 .B79b **ISSN** 0068-4236
DD 529/.05 FR
RAPPORT ANNUEL - BUREAU INTERNATIONAL DE L'HEURE. [Rapp. annu. - Bur. int. heure]. **Main/Corp** Bureau International de l'Heure, Paris. **Added/Corp** International Council of Scientific Unions. Federation of Astronomical and Geophysical Services. (1967)-. English (French). Bureau International de l'Heure, 61 Avenue de l'Observatoire, Paris France. ***Continues in part*** *Bulletin Horaire du Bureau International de l'Heure (B.I.H.). Serie J.*

LC QB1 .I43517
DD 520/.72044 FR
RAPPORT D'ACTIVITE / INSTITUT NATIONAL DES SCIENCES DE L'UNIVERS. **Main/Corp** Institut National des Sciences de l'Univers (France). (1984/1985)-. French. Institut National des Sciences de l'Univers, 77 Avenue Denfert-Rochereau, 75014 Paris France. ***Continues*** *Institut National d'Astronomie et de Geophysique (France). Rapport d'Activite de l'Institut National d'Astronomie et de Geophysique.*

ISSN 0847-5865
DD 520/.971/05 CN
RECHERCHE ASTRONOMIQUE. (LA RECHERCHE ASTRONOMIQUE.). [Rech. astron.]. **Added/Corp** Societe Pour la Recherche Astronomique. (1990)-. Periodical. French. Four times a year. Societe pour la Recherche Astronomique, 74 Dufferin, Laval, Quebec H7L 2K2 Canada.

LC QB1 .R35 **ISSN** 0486-2236
RU
REFERATIVNYI ZHURNAL. 51, ASTRONOMIIA. **Added/Corp** Vsesoiuznyi Institut Nauchnoi i Tekhnicheskoi Informatsii (Soviet Union). **VFOAT** Astronomiia. (1963)-. Abstracting/Indexing Service. Russian. Twelve times a year. VINITI - Vsesoyuznyi Institut Nauchno-Tekhnicheskoi Informatsii, All-Union Scientific and Technical Information Institute, Baltiiskaia ulitsa 14, 125219 Moscow Russia. **Tel** 011 7 95 2384600, FAX 011 7 95 9430060, telex 411160. **(Subscription address:** Victor Kamkin, 4956 Boiling Brook Parkway, Rockville MD 20852. **Tel** (301)881-5973.**)** ***Supersedes in part*** *Referativnyi Zhurnal. Astronomiia I Geodeziia, 0486-2244.*

LC QB
DD 520 RU
REFERATIVNYI ZHURNAL: ISSLEDOVANIE KOSMICHESKOGO PROSTRANSTVA. **Added/Corp** Akademiia Nauk SSSR. Institut Nauchnoi Informatsii. (1964)-. Periodical. Russian. Twelve times a year. VINITI - Vsesoyuznyi Institut Nauchno-Tekhnicheskoi Informatsii, All-Union Scientific and Technical Information Institute, Baltiiskaia ulitsa 14, 125219 Moscow Russia. **Tel** 011 7 95 2384600, FAX 011 7 95 9430060, telex 411160. **(Subscription address:** Victor Kamkin, 4956 Boiling Brook Parkway, Rockville MD 20852. **Tel** (301)881-5973.**)**

LC QB461 .O8 **ISSN** 0078-6780
DD 523.01 NO
CODEN OTARAY
REPORT - INSTITUTE OF THEORETICAL ASTROPHYSICS. (REPORT / INSTITUTE OF THEORETICAL ASTROPHYSICS, BLINDERN, OSLO.). [Rep. - Inst. heor. astrophysics]. **Added/Corp** Universitetet i Oslo. Institutt for Teoretisk Astrofysikk. No. 1 (1952)-. Monographic series. English. Documents available from CASDDS.
Ind/Abst Chem. Abstr.

ISSN 0732-7935
DD 523 US
CODEN JILRAP
REPORT (JOINT INSTITUTE FOR LABORATORY ASTROPHYSICS). (REPORT / JOINT INSTITUTE FOR LABORATORY ASTROPHYSICS.). [Rep. - Jt. Inst. Lab. Astrophys.]. **VFOAT** JILA Report. Academic Scholarly Publication. English. University of Colorado Joint Institute for Laboratory Astrophysics, Boulder CO 80309. **Tel** (303)492-7801. Documents available from CASDDS.
Desc: Bibliographies and evaluated compilations of data on electron and photon collisions with atoms and ions and low-energy heavy particle collisions.
Ind/Abst Chem. Abstr. (1962-1981).

LC QB495 .E93a
DD 500.5/07204 FR
REPORT ON THE ACTIVITIES OF SPACE SCIENCE DEPARTMENT IN ... . **Main/Corp** European Space Agency. Space Science Dept. (19??)-. English. ESA Estec, c/o De Zwaan, PO Box 299, 2200 AB Noordwijk Netherlands. **Tel** 011 31 1719 83405, FAX 011 31 1719 17408.

LC QB82.G72 H8743a **ISSN** 0308-3322
DD 522/.19/4225 UK
REPORT - ROYAL GREENWICH OBSERVATORY. (THE ROYAL GREENWICH OBSERVATORY REPORT.). [Rep. - R. Greenwich Obs.]. **Main/Corp** Royal Greenwich Observatory. **Added/Corp** Science Research Council (Great Britain) Royal Greenwich Observatory. Report. (1974)-. English. One time a year. Royal Greenwich Observatory, Madingley Road, Cambridge CB3 0HA United Kingdom. **Tel** 011 44 1223 374000, FAX 011 44 1223 374700, telex 83159. **Bk Rev. Ad Acc. Circ:** 4,000 (ctrl). ***Continues in part*** *Quarterly Journal of the Royal Astronomical Society, 0035-8738.*

LC QB **ISSN** 0915-0021
DD 520 JA
REPRINT / NATIONAL ASTRONOMICAL OBSERVATORY. **Added/Corp** Kokuritsu Tenmondai (Japan). (1989)-. Monographic series. English. Irregular. National Astronomical Observatory / Tokyo, 21-2 Osawa 2 chome, Mitakashi Tokyo 181 Japan. **Tel** FAX 011 81 3 413690. ***Continues*** *Reprints (Tokyo Tenmondai), 0082-4712.*

LC QB1 .R37
DD 520/.5 GW
CODEN RMASEP
REVIEWS IN MODERN ASTRONOMY. **Added/Corp** Astronomische Gesellschaft (Germany). (1988)-. English. One time a year. Price varies per volume. Springer-Verlag GmbH & Company KG, Heidelberger Platz 3, D-14197 Berlin Germany. **Tel** 011 49 30 8207223, FAX 011 49 30 8214091, telex 183 319 SPBLN D. **(Subscription address:** Springer-Verlag New York Inc. / North America, PO Box 2485, Journal Fulfillment, Secaucus NJ 07096. **Tel** (201)348-4033, (800)777-4643, FAX (201)348-4505.**)** Documents available from CASDDS.
Ind/Abst Astron. Astrophys. Abstr.; Chem. Abstr.

LC WMLC L 83/1935 **ISSN** 0374-4272
AG
REVISTA ASTRONOMICA. **Added/Corp** Asociacion Argentina Amigos de la Astronomia. Vol. 1 (1929)-. Periodical. Spanish. Four times a year. Asociacion Argentina de los Amigos de la Astronomia, Correo Central, Casilla 369, 1000 Buenos Aires Argentina. **Tel** 54 1 883366. **Bk Rev. Ad Acc.**
Ind/Abst Astron. Astrophys. Abstr.

LC QB1 .R38 **ISSN** 0185-1101
DD 520/.5 MX
CODEN RMAAD4
Pr Rev.
REVISTA MEXICANA DE ASTRONOMIA Y ASTROFISICA. [Rev. mex. astron. astrofis.]. **Added/Corp** Universidad Nacional Autonoma de Mexico. Instituto de Astronomia. Vol. 1 (April 1974)-. Academic Scholarly Publication. English (summaries and/or abstracts in Spanish). Two times a year. Instituto de Astronomia, Universidad Nacional Autonoma de Mexico, Apartado 70-264, Mexico 20 Mexico. **Tel** 011 52 5 5485305, 011 52 5 5485306, FAX 011 52 5 5483712. **ED** Silvia Torres-Peimbert, Paris Pismis, Elizabeth Themsel. Index available. **Circ:** 1,500 (ctrl). Documents available from The Genuine Article, Ask*IEEE, CASDDS. ***Continues in part*** *Boletin de los Observatorios de Tonantzintla y Tacubaya, 0082-4879.*

Desc: Covers high level research in the field.
Ind/Abst Astron. Astrophys. Abstr.; Chem. Abstr.; Curr. Contents Phys. Chem. Earth Sci.; INSPEC (April 1974-); Int. Aerosp. Abstr.; Math. Rev.; Res. Alert [Full Cov.]; Sci. Cit. Index; SCISEARCH.

LC QB1 **ISSN** 1405-2059
DD 520 MX
CODEN RMAAF6

●REVISTA MEXICANA DE ASTRONOMIA Y ASTROFISICA. SERIE DE CONFERENCIAS. **Added/Corp** Universidad Nacional Autonoma de Mexico. Instituto de Astronomia. **VFOAT** Serie de Conferencias. Vol. 1 (1995)-. Monographic series. English (summaries and/or abstracts in Spanish). Two times a year. Universidad Nacional Autonoma de Mexico Instituto de Astronomia, Apdo. Postal 70-264, 04510 Mexico DF Mexico. **Tel** FAX (525)616-0653. ***Continues*** *Revista Mexicana de Astronomia y Astrofisica, 0185-1101.*
Ind/Abst Chem. Abstr. (1995-).

LC QB **ISSN** 1220-5168
DD 520 RM
UDC 52

●ROMANIAN ASTRONOMICAL JOURNAL. [Rom. Astron. J.]. (1992)-. Periodical. English. Two times a year. $138.00. **(Subscription address:** Orion Press SRL, SPL Independentei 202-A, Bucharest 6 Romania. **Tel** 011 401 3122425.**)**

LC QB
DD 520 NZ
Pr Rev.

ROYAL ASTRONOMICAL SOCIETY OF NEW ZEALAND VARIABLE STAR MONTHLY CIRCULARS M. (19??)-. English. Twelve times a year. 18.00NZ$ New Zealand; 23.80NZ$ other. Astronomical Research Ltd., PO Box 3093 Greerton, Tauranga New Zealand. **Tel** 011 64 75 410216. **ED** F.M. Bateson. **Bk Rev**. **Ad Acc**, **Adv Mgr:** Audrey Walsh. **Circ:** 120.

LC Q77 .S34 **ISSN** 0388-5607
DD 530/.05 JA
CODEN SRTAD9

SCIENCE REPORTS OF THE TOHOKU UNIVERSITY. EIGHTH SERIES. PHYSICS AND ASTRONOMY, THE. **See** Physics.

LC QB
DD 520 IT

SCIENZA E STORIA. **Added/Corp** Centro Internazionale A. Beltrame di Storia Dello Spazio e del Tempo. **VFOAT** Bollettino del Centro Internazionale di Storia Dello Spazio e del Tempo. (1988)-. Periodical. Italian (French). Two times a year. L47690. International Center Storia Spazio Tempo, via Roma 100, 25020 Brugine Italy. **Tel** 011 39 49 5806768, FAX 011 39 49 5806048. ***Continues*** *Bollettino del Centro Internazionale A. Beltrame di Storia Dello Spazio e del Tempo.*

LC QB
DD 520 US

SELECTED ASTRONOMICAL CATALOGS [COMPUTER FILE]. **Added/Corp** Astronomical Data Center (U.S.) National Space Science Data Center. (19??)-. English. Irregular. Goddard Space Flight Center NASA, Code 513, Greenbelt MD 20771. **Tel** (301)286-8956.

ISSN 1055-6435
DD 520 US

SERC NEWSLETTER, THE. (THE SERC NEWSLETTER / NASA / UNIVERSITY OF ARIZONA, SPACE ENGINEERING RESEARCH CENTER.). [SERC newsl.]. **Added/Corp** Space Engineering Research Center (Tucson, Ariz.). **VAT** Space Engineering Research Center Newsletter. (1990)-. Periodical. English. Irregular. Space Engineering Research Center, University of Arizona, 4717 East Fort Lowell Road, Tucson AZ 85712.

LC BD511 .S45 **ISSN** 0266-8599
DD 291.2/4/05 UK
TITLE CHANGE

SHADOW : THE NEWSLETTER OF THE TRADITIONAL COSMOLOGICAL SOCIETY. **Added/Corp** Traditional Cosmology Society. Vol. 1, No. 1 (June 1984)-Vol. 10 (1993). Newsletter. English. Two times a year. $11.00, $6.00 (student membership). James P Hardie Treasurer, Traditional Cosmology Society, School of Scottish Studies, University of Edinburgh, 27 George Square, Edinburgh EH8 9LD United Kingdom. ***Absorbed by*** *Cosmos (Edinburgh, Scotland), 0269-8773.*

LC QB4.S5 S53
DD 523/.005 CC

SHANG-HAI TIEN WEN TAI NIEN KAN / ANNALS OF THE SHANGHAI OBSERVATORY, ACADEMIA SINICA / CHUNG-KUO KO HSUEH YUAN. **Added/Corp** Chung-kuo ko Hsueh Yuan. Shang-hai Tien Wen Tai. **VFOAT** Annals of the Shanghai Observatory, Academia Sinica; Annals of Shanghai Observatory; Chung-kuo Ko Hsueh Yuan Shang-Hai Tien Wen Tai Nien Kan. Vol. 1 (1979)-. Periodical. Chinese (summaries and/or abstracts in English). One time a year. NT$2.20. Hsin Hua Shu Tien / Shang-Hai Fa Hsing So, Shanghai, People's Republic of China. ***Continues*** *Tien Wen Nien Kan.*

ISSN 1062-1555
DD 520 US

SIRIUS ASTRONOMER. (SIRIUS ASTRONOMER : NEWSLETTER OF THE ORANGE COUNTY ASTRONOMERS.). [Sirius astron.]. **Added/Corp** Orange County Astronomers. (19??)-. Periodical. English. One time a year. free to members. Sirius Astronomer, 2195 Raleigh Avenue, Costa Mesa CA 92627.

LC QB **ISSN** 1035-932X
DD 520 AT

SKY & SPACE. **VFOAT** Sky and Space. Vol. 5, No. 6 (Nov./Dec. 1992)-. Periodical. English. Six times a year (Jan., March, May, July, Sept., Nov.). 24.67Aus$. Sky and Space, 80 Ebley Street, Bondi Junction NSW 2022 Australia. **Tel** 011 61 2 3693344, FAX 011 61 2 3693366. **ED** Jonathan Nally. Index available. cum. index. **Bk Rev**, (Qty: 6). **Ad Acc**, **Adv Mgr:** L. Romble. **Circ:** 17,000-18,000. ***Continues*** *Southern Astronomy, 1030-0015.*
Desc: Coverage of all aspects of astronomy and space exploration with specific emphasis on Australian scientific endeavosr.

LC QB1 .S536 **ISSN** 0037-6604
DD 520.5 US
CCC
CODEN SKTEA3

SKY AND TELESCOPE. [Sky telesc.]. **Added/Corp** Harvard College Observatory. **VFOAT** Sky & Telescope. Vol. 1 (Nov. 1941)-. Periodical. English. Twelve times a year. $33.00. Sky Publishing Corporation, 49 Bay State Road, Cambridge MA 02138. **Tel** (617)864-7360, FAX (617)864-6117. **(Subscription address:** Sky Publishing Corporation, PO Box 9111, Belmont MA 02178. **)** **ED** Leif J. Robinson. Index available. cum. index. **Bk Rev**. **Ad Acc**. **Circ:** 98,000. available on microfilm and microfiche from University Microfilms International (UMI). Documents available from Ask*IEEE, UMI Article Clearinghouse. ***Formed by the union of*** *Sky, 0361-8242* ***and*** *Telescope (Cambridge).*
Desc: An amateur astronomy magazine with feature articles on new developments in the science, plus departments on books, observing, equipment, computer software, sky predictions, etc.
Ind/Abst Acad. Abstr. Full Text Elite; Acad. Abstr.; Acad. Ind. [Computer File] (1984-); Acad. Search; Astron. Astrophys. Abstr.; Book Rev. Index; Energy Res. Abstr.; EP Collect.; Expand. Acad. Index (1984-); Gen. Period. Index (1985-); Gen. Sci. Index; GeoRef; Homework Help.; Index Inf.; INFO-SOUTH Abstr.; INSPEC (Jan. 1970-); Int. Aerosp. Abstr.; Mag. Artic. Summar. Elite; Mag. Artic. Summar. Select; Mag. Artic. Summar. CD-ROM; Mag. Index Plus (1989-); Mag. Index. Sel. (1986-); Mag. Search; MasterFile FullTEXT 1000; MasterFile FullTEXT 350; MasterFile FullTEXT 650; MasterFile FullTEXT (Feb. 1984-) [Full Txt.]; Newsp. Period. Abstr. (1986-); OCLC; Pub. Lib. FullTEXT; Read. Guide Abstr. Select Ed.; Read. Guide Period. Lit.; Sci. Cit. Index (19??-19??); Telebase; Mag. Index (1977-); Vocat. Search.

LC QB **ISSN** 0733-6314
DD 520 US

SKY CALENDAR. (SKY CALENDAR.). **Added/Corp** Abrams Planetarium. (1968)-. English. Twelve times a year. $7.50. Abrams Planetarium, Michigan State University, East Lansing MI 48824. **Tel** (517)355-4676. **ED** Robert C. Victor. **Bk Rev**. **Ad Acc**. **Circ:** 7,000.
Desc: Diagrams illustrating easily observable events in the sky. Recommended for skywatchers of all ages.

ISSN 0889-9614
DD 527 US

SKYWATCHER'S ALMANAC. **Added/Corp** Astronomical Data Service. (19??)-. English. One time a year (Oct.). $18.00. Astronomical Data Service, 3922 Leisure Lane, Colorado Springs CO 80917. **Tel** (719)597-4068. **ED** R. L. Mansfield. ctrl circ.
Desc: An almanac for astronomy educators which includes sun and moon rise/set times custom-computed for purchasers geographical location.

LC QB **ISSN** 0271-8480
DD 520 US

SOLAR BULLETIN (RAMSEY). (SOLAR BULLETIN.). [Sol. bull.]. **Added/Corp** American Association of Variable Star Observers. Solar Division. (19??)-. Bulletin. English. Twelve times a year. $40.00. American Association of Variable Star Observers / AAVSO, 25 Birch Street, Cambridge MA 02138. **Tel** (617)354-0484, FAX (617)354-0665. **ED** Peter O. Taylor. **Circ:** 500 (ctrl).
Desc: Notes on solar activity, daily American and international sunspot numbers, and sudden ionospheric disturbance data.

LC QB521 .S6 **ISSN** 0038-0938
DD 523.7/05 NE
CCC
CODEN SLPHAX
Pr Rev.

SOLAR PHYSICS. [Sol. phys.]. Vol. 1 (Jan. 1967)-. Periodical. English. Fourteen times a year. $2192.00. Kluwer Academic Publishers, Postbus 322, 3300 AH Dordrecht The Netherlands. **Tel** 011 31 78 524400, FAX 011 31 78 183273, telex 20083. **ED** C. De Jager, Z. Sveska, and R.F. Howard. cum. index. **Bk Rev**. **Ad Acc**. **Acid Free**. **Circ:** 750. available on microfilm and microfiche from University Microfilms International (UMI). Documents available from The Genuine Article, Ask*IEEE, CASDDS.
Desc: The basic concern of this periodical is the fundamental study of the sun. This publication treats all aspects of solar physics, ranging from the sun's history and evolution, the internal structure of the sun, the outer corona and the solar wind that exists in interplanetary space.
Ind/Abst Astron. Astrophys. Abstr. (1968-); Chem. Abstr. (1968); Curr. Contents Phys. Chem. Earth Sci.; GeoRef; INSPEC (1968-); Int. Aerosp. Abstr.; Meteorol. Geoastrophys. Abstr. (1968-); Res. Alert [Full Cov.]; Sci. Cit. Index; SCISEARCH.

LC QB501 .S64 **ISSN** 0038-0946
US
CCC
CODEN SSYRAL

SOLAR SYSTEM RESEARCH. [Sol. syst. res.]. **Added/Corp** Consultants Bureau. Vol. 1 (Jan/Mar 1967)-. Periodical. English (Russian). Six times a year. $1075.00. MAIK Nauka / Interperiodica, Ulitsa Profsoyuznaia 90, Moscow 117864 Russia. **ED** M. Ya Marov. Index available. available on microfilm and microfiche from University Microfilms International (UMI). Documents available from Article Express International, Ask*IEEE, CASDDS.
Ind/Abst Chem. Abstr.; Ei Page One; Energy Res. Abstr.; Eng. Index Annu.; GeoRef; INSPEC (Jan./March 1972-); Int. Aerosp. Abstr.; Pollut. Abstr. Indexes.

LC QC801 .S863 **ISSN** 0386-5444
DD 551.5/145/05 JA
CODEN SERJD3

SOLAR TERRESTRIAL ENVIRONMENTAL RESEARCH IN JAPAN. [Sol. terr. environ. res. Jpn.]. **Added/Corp** Tokyo Daigaku. Uchu Koku Kenkyujo. Taiyo Chikyu Kankyo Kagaku Semmon Iinkai. Vol. 1 (Dec. 1977)-. Periodical. English. One time a year. Uchu Kagaku Kenkyujo, (Institute of Space and Astronautical Science), 1-1 Yoshinodai 3 chome, Sagamiharashi Kanagawaken 229 Japan. Documents available from Ask*IEEE. ***Continues*** *Report of Ionosphere and Space Research in Japan, 0034-4672.*
Ind/Abst Energy Res. Abstr. (Nov. 1978-); INSPEC (Dec. 1977-); Int. Aerosp. Abstr.

LC QB4 .P985 **ISSN** 0552-5829
RU
CODEN SODAA7

SOLNECHNYE DANNYE. [Soln. dannye]. **Added/Corp** Glavnaia Astronomicheskaia Observatoriia (Soviet Union) Akademiia Nauk SSSR. Komissiia Po Issledovaniiu Solntsa. Akademiia Nauk SSSR. Astronomicheskii Sovet. (1954)-. Periodical. Russian (summaries and/or abstracts in English; table of contents in English). Twelve times a year. Izdatelstvo Nauka St. Petersburg, Mendeleevskaia Liniia 1, 199034 St. Petersburg, B-34 Russia. **Tel** 011 7 812 2182612.
Ind/Abst Astron. Astrophys. Abstr.; GeoRef.

LC QB4 .B995 **ISSN** 0370-8691
AI
CODEN SBOAA5

SOOBSCENIJA BJURAKANSKOJ OBSERVATORII. (SOOBSHCHENIIA BIURAKANSKOI OBSERVATORII. BYURAKANI ASTGHADITARANI HAGHORDUMNER.). [Soobsc. Bjurakanskoj obs.]. **Main/Corp** Byurakani Astghaditaran. **VFOAT** Byurakani Astghaditarani Haghordumner. Vol. 1 (1946)-. Periodical. Russian.
Ind/Abst Int. Aerosp. Abstr.

LC QB1 .R788 **ISSN** 0049-1640
DD 520.6294 NZ
CCC

SOUTHERN STARS. **Added/Corp** Royal Astronomical Society of New Zealand. New Zealand Astronomical Society. Vol. 1 (Nov. 1934)-. Periodical. English. Four times a year. $35.82. Royal Astronomical Society of New Zealand, PO Box 3181, Wellington New Zealand. **Tel** 011 64 4 4728167. **ED** Dr. Edwin Budding. Index available. cum. index. **Bk Rev**, (Qty: 128). **Ad Acc**. **Circ:** 500.
Desc: This publication consists of various wide-ranging records of different reported astronomical activities in the country of New Zealand. These diverse reports include information regarding observational activities and research activities. Also included are more general astronomical subjects.
Ind/Abst Astron. Astrophys. Abstr.

LC QB1 .A8252 ISSN 0038-5301
DD 520 US
CCC
CODEN SAAJAN
TITLE CHANGE

SOVIET ASTRONOMY. [Soviet astron.]. **Added/Corp** American Institute of Physics. Vol. 17 (1973/1974)-(1993). Periodical. English (Russian). American Institute of Physics, 500 Sunnyside Boulevard, Woodbury NY 11797-2999. **Tel** (516)576-2270, (800)344-6902, FAX (516)349-9704, telex 960983. Documents available from Ask*IEEE. ***Continues*** *Soviet Astronomy. AJ, 0278-3495.* ***Continued by*** *Astronomy Reports.*
Ind/Abst Curr. Phys. Index; INSPEC (1974-); Int. Aerosp. Abstr.; Math. Rev.; SPIN (1974-); Zentralbl. Math. Ihre Grenzgeb.

LC QB460 .S67 ISSN 0143-0432
DD 523.01 SZ
CCC
CODEN SSRVDZ

SOVIET SCIENTIFIC REVIEWS. SECTION E, ASTROPHYSICS AND SPACE PHYSICS REVIEWS. [Sov. sci. rev., E, Astrophys. space phys. rev.]. **VFOAT** Astrophysics and Space Physics Reviews. Vol. 1 (1981)-. Academic Scholarly Publication. English (translations available in Russian). One time a year. $441.00 (academic institutions), $688.00 (corporate institutions). Harwood Academic Publishers, PO Box 90, Reading RG1 8JL United Kingdom. **Tel** 011 44 1734 560080, FAX 011 44 1734 568211. **ED** R. A. Syunyaev. Documents available from Ask*IEEE, CASDDS.
Ind/Abst Chem. Abstr.; INSPEC; Int. Aerosp. Abstr. (1984-).

LC QB1 .S7647 ISSN 0204-9104
DD 500.5/05 BU
CODEN SRBUDD

SPACE RESEARCH IN BULGARIA. [Space res. Bulg.]. **Added/Corp** Bulgarska Akademiia na Naukite. **VFOAT** Kosmichni Izsledvaniya v Bulgariia. Vol. 1 (1978)-. Academic Scholarly Publication. English (summaries and/or abstracts in Russian). Irregular. Bulgarska Akademiia na Naukite, 7 Noemvri 1, Sofia Bulgaria. **(Subscription address:** Hemus Foreign Trade Organization, 1B Raiko Daskalov Sq Books, 1000 Sofia Bulgaria. **Tel** 011 359 2 882544, 011 359 2 801575.**) ED** K. Serafimov. **Bk Rev. Ad Acc. Circ:** 700 (ctrl). Documents available from CASDDS.
Desc: Covers space research in Bulgaria.
Ind/Abst Chem. Abstr. (1978-1980); Geol. Abstr.; Int. Aerosp. Abstr.

LC QB1 .S77 ISSN 0038-6308
DD 500.5/05 NE
CCC
CODEN SPSRA4
Pr Rev.

SPACE SCIENCE REVIEWS. [Space sci. rev.]. Vol. 1 (June 1962)-. Periodical. English (Dutch, French, German and Russian). Irregular (Sixteen issues per year). $1285.00. Kluwer Academic Publishers, Postbus 322, 3300 AH Dordrecht The Netherlands. **Tel** 011 31 78 524400, FAX 011 31 78 183273, telex 20083. **ED** C. de Jager, S.I. Akasofu, and S. Rasool. **Bk Rev. Ad Acc. Acid Free. Circ:** 800. available on microfilm and microfiche from University Microfilms International (UMI). Documents available from The Genuine Article, Ask*IEEE, CASDDS.
Desc: Scientific research by means of rockets, rocket-propelled vehicles, stratospheric balloons, and at observatories on the earth and moon.
Ind/Abst Acoust. Abstr. (1968-); Astron. Astrophys. Abstr.; Chem. Abstr. (1968); Curr. Contents Phys. Chem. Earth Sci.; Index Sci. Rev. [Full Cov.]; INSPEC (1968-); Int. Aerosp. Abstr.; Meteorol. Geoastrophys. Abstr.; Res. Alert [Full Cov.]; Sci. Cit. Index; SCISEARCH.

LC QB ISSN 0195-4253
DD 520 US

SPACE SCIENCE TEXT SERIES. (19??)-. Monographic series. English. Irregular. Price varies per volume. John Wiley & Sons, Inc., 605 Third Avenue, New York NY 10158-0012. **Tel** (212)850-6000, (212)850-6645, FAX (212)850-6088, telex 12-7063. **(Subscription address:** John Wiley & Sons / UK, Baffins Lane, Chichester, West Sussex PO19 1UD United Kingdom. **Tel** 011 44 1243 779777, FAX 011 44 243 776128, telex 86290 WIBOOKG.)

LC QB
DD 520 UK

SPACE TELESCOPE SCIENCE INSTITUTE SYMPOSIUM SERIES. **Added/Corp** Space Telescope Science Institute (U.S.). (1986)-. Monographic series. English. Irregular. Price varies per volume. Cambridge University Press, The Edinburgh Building, Shaftesbury Road, Cambridge CB2 2RU United Kingdom. **Tel** 011 44 1223 312393, FAX 011 44 1223 315052, telex 851-817256. **(Subscription address:** Cambridge University Press / North America, 110 Midland Avenue, Port Chester NY 10573. **Tel** (800)431-1580, (914)937-9600.)

ISSN 0889-6054
DD 520 US
SUSPENDED

SPACE TODAY. [Space today]. **VFOAT** Space Today Magazine. Vol. 1, No. 1 (Aug. 1986)-Suspended. Periodical. English. Twelve times a year. $34.95 US and Canada; $50.00 other. Arcsoft Publishers, PO Box 132, Woodsboro MD 21798. **Tel** (301)845-8856. **ED** Anthony R Curtis. Index available. **Bk Rev. Ad Acc.**
Desc: This journal covers space from earth to the edge of the Universe.

LC QB
DD 520 UK

•**SPECTRUM : NEWSLETTER OF THE ROYAL OBSERVATORIES.** **Added/Corp** Royal Greenwich Observatory. Royal Observatory, Edinburgh. Royal Greenwich Observatory. Isaac Newton Group of Telescopes (Santa Cruz de La Palma, Canary Islands) Royal Observatory, Edinburgh. Joint Astronomy Centre (Hilo, Hawaii). (1994)-. Newsletter. English. Four times a year. Free on request. Royal Greenwich Observatory, Madingley Road, Cambridge CB3 0HA United Kingdom. **Tel** 011 44 1223 374000, FAX 011 44 1223 374700, telex 83159. ***Formed by the union of*** *Gemini (Herstmonceux, England)* ***and*** *Ukirt Newsletter (1993).*

DD 528.2 UK

STAR ALMANAC FOR LAND SURVEYORS / PREPARED BY H. M. NAUTICAL ALMANAC OFFICE, THE. **Added/Corp** Great Britain. Nautical Almanac Office. (19??)-. English. One time a year (May). £5.50. Her Majesty's Stationery Office, 51 Nine Elms Lane, London SW8 5DR United Kingdom. **Tel** 011 44 171 8738459, 011 44 171 8738499, FAX 011 44 171 8738499, 011 44 171 8738456, telex 297138. **(Subscription address:** Her Majesty's Stationery Office, PO Box 276, Public Centre, London SW8 5DT United Kingdom. **Tel** 011 44 171 8738499, 011 44 171 8738456.)

LC QB ISSN 0164-5994
DD 520 US

STAR & SKY. [Star sky]. **VAT** Star and Sky. Vol. 1 (Jan. 1979)-. Periodical. English. Twelve times a year. $15.00 US; $18.00 Canada. Star and Sky Magazine, 44 Church Lane, Westport CT 06880.
Ind/Abst Int. Aerosp. Abstr.

LC WMLC 93/4793 ISSN 0889-3098
DD 520 US
Pr Rev.

STAR DATE (AUSTIN, TEX.). (STAR DATE : THE ASTRONOMY NEWS REPORT.). [Star date]. **Added/Corp** McDonald Observatory. Public Information Office. Vol. 14, No. 5 (May 1986)-. Periodical. English. Six times a year (Jan., Mar., May, July, Sept., Nov.). $15.00. Star Date, 2609 University Avenue, Room 3118, Austin TX 78712. **Tel** (512)471-5285, (512)471-7756, FAX (512)471-5060. **ED** David Portree (editor's phone: (512)475-6763). **Bk Rev**, (Qty: 12). **Ad Acc, Adv Mgr:** Susanne Harm, **Tel** (512)475-6760. **Circ:** 13,000 (ctrl). available on an online database from Internet. ***Continues*** *McDonald Observatory News, 0745-1997.*
Desc: Each issue contains jargon-free articles, astronomy news, and photographs of celestial objects. Contains a calendar of upcoming celestial events, as well as star maps. The calendar and maps provide tips on how to best observe stars and planets.

LC QB600
DD 523.8 US

STARGAZING NOTES FOR ... : A POPULAR LEVEL MONTHLY MAGAZINE FROM THE U.S. NAVAL OBSERVATORY. **Added/Corp** United States Naval Observatory. (1984)-. Government Publication. English. Twelve times a year. US Naval Observatory, 345H & Massachusetts Avenue N2, Washington DC 20390. ***Continues*** *Notes for Stargazers.*

LC QB ISSN 0039-1255
DD 520 GW
CODEN STNEA2

STERNE, DIE. [Sterne]. Vol. 1, (1921)-. Academic Scholarly Publication. German. Six times a year. $48.00. Johann Ambrosius Barth, Prager Strasse 16 B, D-04103 Leipzig Germany. **Tel** 011 49 341 9781570, FAX 011 49 341 9781575. **(Subscription address:** Huethig Publishing Inc., 29 Macintosh Drive, Oxford CT 06478. **Tel** (203)881-2647.) Documents available from CASDDS. ***Absorbed*** *Sirius.*
Ind/Abst Astron. Astrophys. Abstr.; Chem. Abstr.; Energy Res. Abstr.

LC QB1 .S854 ISSN 0039-1263
GW
CCC
CODEN STUWAN

STERNE UND WELTRAUM. [Sterne Weltraum]. (1962)-. Periodical. German. Twelve times a year. $120.00. Verlag Sterne und Weltraum, Portiastrasse 10, D-81545 Munich Germany. **Tel** 011 49 89 646947, telex 461789. **ED** H.J. Staude. Index available. **Bk Rev. Ad Acc. Circ:** 12,500 (ctrl). Documents available from CASDDS.
Desc: Reports and original articles on professional and amateur astronomy, history of astronomy, space science and astronomy at school.
Ind/Abst Astron. Astrophys. Abstr.; Chem. Abstr.; Energy Res. Abstr.; Int. Aerosp. Abstr.

LC QB1 .S86
DD 520/.5 NE

STERRENGIDS. **Added/Corp** Stichting De Koepel. Nederlandse Vereniging voor Weer- en Sterrenkunde. (19??)-. Dutch. One time a year (Sept.). Wolters Noordhoff BV, Postbus 567, 9700 AN Groningen Netherlands. **Tel** 011 31 50 226886, FAX 011 31 50 264866. **Ad Acc. Circ:** 6,500.
Desc: Yearbook describes what you see in the heavens for a particular year: planets, moon and comets.

LC DG59 ISSN 0140-654X
DD 936 US

STONEHENGE VIEWPOINT. See Archaeology.

LC QB1 .S88 ISSN 0039-2502
US

STROLLING ASTRONOMER, THE. [Stroll. astron.]. **Added/Corp** Association of Lunar and Planetary Observers (U.S.). **VFOAT** Journal of the Association of Lunar and Planetary Observers. Vol. 1, No. 1 (Mar. 1, 1947)-. Periodical. English. Four times a year (Jan., Apr., July, Nov.). $16.00 (4 issues) North America; $20.00 (4 issues) other; $26.00 (8 issues) North America; $33.00 (8 issues) other. Association of Lunar and Planetary Observers, PO Box 143, Heber Springs AR 72543. **Tel** (501)362-7624. **ED** John F. Westfall (editor's address: PO Box 16131, San Francisco, CA 94116). **Bk Rev. Ad Acc. Circ:** 700 (ctrl). Documents available from Ask*IEEE.
Ind/Abst Astron. Astrophys. Abstr.; INSPEC (1982-); Int. Aerosp. Abstr. (1991-).

LC QB ISSN 0074-1809
DD 520 NE
CODEN IASYAE

SYMPOSIUM - INTERNATIONAL ASTRONOMICAL UNION. [Symp. - Int. Astron. Union]. **Main/Corp** International Astronomical Union. No. 1 (1953)-. Academic Scholarly Publication. English. Irregular. Price varies per volume. Kluwer Academic Publishers, Postbus 322, 3300 AH Dordrecht The Netherlands. **Tel** 011 31 78 524400, FAX 011 31 78 183273, telex 20083. **(Subscription address:** Kluwer Academic Publishers / US Subscriptions, PO Box 253, Accord Station, Hingham MA 02018. **Tel** (617)871-6600.) Documents available from Ask*IEEE, CASDDS.
Ind/Abst Chem. Abstr.; Curr. Cit.; GeoRef; INSPEC.

LC QB ISSN 0736-6965
DD 520 US
CODEN TNPEDI

TECHNICAL NEWS - PERKIN-ELMER CORPORATION. (TECHNICAL NEWS.). [Tech. news - Perkin-Elmer Corp.]. **Added/Corp** Perkin-Elmer Corporation. (19??)-. Academic Scholarly Publication. English. Four times a year. Editorial Office Optical Group, 100 Wooster Heights, Danbury CT 06810. Documents available from Ask*IEEE, CASDDS.
Ind/Abst Alum. Ind. Abstr.; Chem. Abstr.; INSPEC (June 1982-); Met. Abstr.

LC QB1 .T46
JA

TENKAI. THE HEAVENS. **Added/Corp** Toa Temmongakkai. **VFOAT** Heavens. (19??)-. Periodical. Japanese. Twelve times a year. ¥2500. Toa Temmongakkai, c/o Yamamoto Temmondai, Otsu Japan.

LC QB461 .T54 ISSN 0253-2379
DD 523.01 CC
CODEN TWXUDX

TIANTI WULI XUEBAO. (TIEN TI WU LI HSUEH PAO.). [Tianti wuli xuebao]. **Added/Corp** Pei-ching Tien Wen Hsueh Hui. Chung-kuo Tien Wen Hsueh Hui. **VFOAT** Acta Astrophysica Sinica. Vol. 1 (1981)-. Academic Scholarly Publication. Chinese (summaries and/or abstracts in English). Four times a year. $39.08. **(Subscription address:** China International Book Trading Corporation, PO Box 399, Library Service Department, Beijing 100044 People's Republic of China. **Tel** 011 86 1 8414284, FAX 011 86 1 8412023, telex 22496 CIBTC CN.) Documents available from Ask*IEEE, CASDDS.
Desc: Contains information on astrophysics.
Ind/Abst Astron. Astrophys. Abstr.; Chem. Abstr.; Ei Page One; Energy Res. Abstr. (Oct. 1982-); INSPEC (April 1984-); Math. Rev.; SPIN (1982-).

LC QB1 .T54 ISSN 0001-5245
DD 520/.5 CC
CODEN TIWHAO

TIEN WEN HSUEH PAO. [Tien wen hsueh pao]. **Added/Corp** Chung-kuo Tien Wen Hsueh Hui. **VFOAT** Acta Astronomica Sinica. (Aug. 1953)-. Academic Scholarly Publication. Chinese (summaries and/or abstracts in English). Four times a year. $44.90. Science Press, 16 Donghuangchenggen North Street, Beijing 100707, People's Republic of China. **Tel** 011 86 1 4019821, 011 86 1 4010642, FAX 011 86 1 4012180, 011 86 1 4019810, telex 210147. **(Subscription address:**

Astronomy

China International Book Trading Corporation, PO Box 399, Library Service Department, Beijing 100044 People's Republic of China. **Tel** 011 86 1 8414284, FAX 011 86 1 8412023, telex 22496 CIBTC CN.) cum. index. available on microfilm from University Microfilms International (UMI). Documents available from Ask*IEEE.
Ind/Abst Astron. Astrophys. Abstr.; Curr. Phys. Index; Energy Res. Abstr. (June 1971-); INSPEC (1974-); Int. Aerosp. Abstr.; Math. Rev.; SPIN (1982-).

LC QB
DD 520   CC
CODEN TWTHD8

T'IEN WEN T'UNG HSUN = ASTRONOMICAL CIRCULAR. Main/Corp
Tzu-Chin Shan T'ien Wen T'ai, Nanking. **Added/Corp** Chung-kuo T'ien Wen Hsueh Hui. **VFOAT** Astronomical Circular. No. 1 (April 1978)-. Periodical. Chinese (English). Documents available from Ask*IEEE.
Ind/Abst Astron. Astrophys. Abstr.; INSPEC (May 1979-).

LC Q
DD 500   RM

TOPICS IN ASTROPHYSICS, ASTRONOMY AND SPACE SCIENCES.
Added/Corp Centrul de Astronomie si Stiinte Spatiale (Romania). **VFOAT** Cercetari de Astrofizica Astronomie si Stiinte Spatiale. (1985)-. Periodical. English. Irregular. The Central Institute of Physics / Centre for Astronomy and Space Sciences, Cutitul de Argint 5, 75 212 Bucharest, Romania.

LC QB   **ISSN** 0251-107X
DD 520   UK

TRANSACTIONS OF THE INTERNATIONAL ASTRONOMICAL UNION. [Trans. Int. Astron. Union]. Main/Corp
International Astronomical Union. **Added/Corp** International Council of Scientific Unions. International Research Council. Vol. 1 (May 2nd to May 10th, 1922)-. Monographic series. English. Irregular. Price varies per volume. Kluwer Academic Publishers, Postbus 322, 3300 AH Dordrecht The Netherlands. **Tel** 011 31 78 524400, FAX 011 31 78 183273, telex 20083. **(Subscription address:** Kluwer Academic Publishers / US Subscriptions, PO Box 253, Accord Station, Hingham MA 02018. **Tel** (617)871-6600.) Documents available from Ask*IEEE.
Ind/Abst INSPEC.

LC QB   **ISSN** 0131-3940
DD 520   RU
CODEN TRAIBF

TRUDY ASTROFIZICESKOGO INSTITUTA. (TRUDY ASTROFIZICHESKOGO INSTITUTA.). [Tr. Astrofiz. inst.]. Added/Corp
Astrofizicheskii Institut (Qazaq SSR Gylym Aademiiasy). (1961)-. Academic Scholarly Publication. Russian (summaries and/or abstracts in English; table of contents in English). Price varies per volume. Documents available from CASDDS.
Ind/Abst Chem. Abstr. (1961-1978); Energy Res. Abstr.; Math. Rev.; Zentralbl. Math. Ihre Grenzgeb.

LC QB   **ISSN** 0201-6745
DD 520   RU

TRUDY ASTRONOMICHESKOI OBSERVATORII (LENINGRAD, R.S.F.S.R.). (TRUDY ASTRONOMICHESKOI OBSERVATORII.). Added/Corp
Leningradskii Gosudarstvennyi Universitet Imeni A.A. Zhdanova. Astronomicheskaia Observatoriia. **VFOAT** Publications of the Leningrad University Astronomical Observatory; Transactions of the Astronomical Observatory. Vol. 13, (1949)-. Russian (summaries and/or abstracts in English). Irregular. St. Petersburg State University / Izdatelstvo Leningradskogo Universiteta, Universitetskaia Nab 7/9, 199034 St. Petersburg Russia. **Tel** 011 7 812 2189788, FAX 011 7 812 2185152, telex 121481. **Continues** Trudy Astronomicheskoi Observatorii Leningradskogo Gosudarstvennogouniversiteta.

LC QB1   **ISSN** 0371-6791
DD 520.(5/6)   RU
  CEASED

TRUDY GOSUDARSTVENNOGO ASTRONOMICHESKOGO INSTITUTA IM. P.K. SHTERNBERGA. [Tr. Gos. astron. inst. im. P.K. Shternberga]. Added/Corp
Gosudarstvennyi Astronomicheskii Institut im. P.K. Shternberga. Moskovskii Gosudarstvennyi Universitet im. M.V. Lomonosova. **VFOAT** Publications of the Sternberg State Astronomical Institute. (1933)-(1995). Academic Scholarly Publication. Russian (English, French and German). Moskovskii Universitet / Gosudarstvennyi Astronomicheskii Institut im. P.K. Shternberga, Universitetskii Prospekt 13, Moscow V-234 Russia. **Continues** Trudy Gosudarstvennogo Astrofizicheskogo Instituta.
Ind/Abst Math. Rev.

LC QB495 .U273   **ISSN** 0285-2853
  JA

UCHU KAGAKU KENKYUJO HOKOKU. TOKUSHU. Added/Corp
Uchu Kagaku Kenkyujo (Japan). No. 1 (Nov. 1981)-. Japanese. Irregular. Uchu Kagaku Kenkyujo, (Institute of Space and Astronautical Science), 1-1 Yoshinodai 3 chome, Sagamiharashi Kanagawaken 229 Japan.

LC QB500.266.J3 U24a
  JA

UCHU KAGAKU KENKYUJO NENJI YORAN. Main/Corp
Uchu Kagaku Kenkyujo (Japan). (1983)-. Japanese. One time a year. Uchu Kagaku Kenkyujo, (Institute of Space and Astronautical Science), 1-1 Yoshinodai 3 chome, Sagamiharashi Kanagawaken 229 Japan. **Continues** Uchu Kagaku Kenkyujo (Japan). Uchu Kagaku Kenkyujo Yoran.

LC QB4 .W34   **ISSN** 0097-0336
DD 520/.5   US

UNITED STATES NAVAL OBSERVATORY CIRCULAR. [U. S. Nav. Obs. circ.]. Added/Corp
United States Naval Observatory. **VFOAT** Circular. No. 1 (July 18, 1949)-. Monographic series. English. Irregular. Price varies per volume. US Naval Observatory, 345H & Massachusetts Avenue N2, Washington DC 20390. cum. index.

  ISSN 0890-6866
DD 520

UNIVERSE IN THE CLASSROOM, THE.
(THE UNIVERSE IN THE CLASSROOM : A NEWSLETTER ON TEACHING ASTRONOMY.). [Universe classr.]. **Added/Corp** American Astronomical Society. Astronomical Society of the Pacific. Canadian Astronomical Society. **VFOAT** Teachers' Newsletter. (Winter 1984)-. Newsletter. English. Irregular (3 or 4 times per year). Free on request. Astronomical Society of the Pacific, 390 Ashton Avenue, San Francisco CA 94112. **Tel** (415)337-1100, FAX (415)337-5205. **ED** Andrew F. Fraknoi. **Circ**: 35,000 (ctrl).
Desc: Newsletter on teaching astronomy in grades 3-12.

  ISSN 0082-3546
DD 520   US

UNIVERSITY OF TEXAS MONOGRAPHS IN ASTRONOMY. [Univ. Tex. monogr. astron.].
Added/Corp University of Texas at Austin. Dept. of Astronomy. University of Texas at Austin. **VFOAT** Monographs in Astronomy. (1964)-. Monographic series. English. Irregular. University of Texas Press, PO Box 7819, Austin TX 78713. **Tel** (512)471-4531, FAX (512)320-0668, telex 776453 UTEXPRES AUS.

LC QB1 .S5523
  EC

UNIVERSO, EL. Added/Corp
Sociedad Astronomica de Mexico. (19??)-. Periodical. Spanish. One time a week. $23.21. El Universo, PO Box 531, Guayaquil Ecuador.
Ind/Abst Int. Dev. Abstr.

LC QB1 .U7   **ISSN** 0042-0794
  PL

URANIA. [Urania]. Added/Corp
Polskie Towarzystwo Miosnikow Astronomii. (19??)-. Periodical. Polish. Twelve times a year. $48.00. **(Subscription address:** Ars Polona-Ruch, PO Box 1001, Krakowskie Przedmiescie 7, 00-068 Warsaw Poland. **Tel** 011 48 22 261201.) **Continues** Uranja.
Ind/Abst GeoRef.

LC QB   **ISSN** 0083-5293
DD 520   VC

VATICAN OBSERVATORY PUBLICATIONS. [Vatican Obs. publ.].
Added/Corp Specola Vaticana. (1970)-. Monographic series. English (Italian). Irregular. Price varies per volume. Specola Vaticana / Vatican Observatory, 00120 Vatican City / Rome, State of the Vatican City. **Tel** 011 39 6 6983411, FAX 011 39 6 6984671, telex 2020 VATOBS VA.
Ind/Abst Int. Aerosp. Abstr.

LC QB   **ISSN** 0321-3927
DD 520   UN

VESTNIK KIEVSKOGO UNIVERSITETA. ASTRONOMIIA. Added/Corp
Kyivskyi Derzhavnyi Universytet im. T.H. Shevchenka. Ukraine. Ministerstvo Vyshchoi i Serednoi Spetsialnoi Osvity. **VFOAT** Astronomiia. Vol. 19 (1977)-. Russian. One time a year. Izdatelstvo Moskovskogo Universiteta, K-9 Ulitsa Gertsena 5/7, 103009 Moscow Russia. **Tel** (301)881-5973. **Continues** Visnyk Kyivskoho Universytetu. Seriia Astonomii, 0321-3927.
Ind/Abst Astron. Astrophys. Abstr.

LC Q   **ISSN** 0579-9392
DD 500   RU
  CCC
CODEN VMUFAO

VESTNIK MOSKOVSKOGO UNIVERSITETA. SERIIA III, FIZIKA, ASTRONOMIIA. See Physics.

LC QA
DD 510   RU

VESTNIK SANKT-PETERBURGSKOGO UNIVERSITETA. SERIIA 1, MATEMATIKA, MEKHANIKA, ASTRONOMIIA. See Mathematics.

LC QB1 .V56   **ISSN** 0083-6656
DD 520/.5   UK
  CCC
CODEN VASTA6VASTA

VISTAS IN ASTRONOMY. [Vistas astron.].
Added/Corp International Astronomical Union. International Union of the History and Philosophy of Science. Vol. 1 (1955)-. Academic Scholarly Publication. English. Four times a year. $493.00. Pergamon Press, An Imprint of Elsevier Science Ltd., The Boulevard, Langford Lane, Kidlington, Oxford OX5 1GB United Kingdom. **Tel** 011 44 1865 843000, 011 44 1865 843699, FAX 011 44 1865 843010. **(Subscription address:** Elsevier Science Ltd. / Oxford Fulfillment Centre, PO Box 800, Kidlington OX5 1DX United Kingdom. **Tel** 011 44 865 843355.) **ED** Peter Beer, A. Roy, and R. White. available on microfilm and microfiche from University Microfilms International (UMI); available on an online database from Elsevier Electronic Subscriptions (EES). Documents available from Ask*IEEE, CASDDS. **Absorbed** Astronomy Quarterly, 0364-9229.
Ind/Abst Astron. Astrophys. Abstr.; Chem. Abstr.; GeoRef; INSPEC (1975-); Int. Aerosp. Abstr.; Math. Rev.

LC QB600 .W34
  JA

WAKUSEI KAGAKU. Added/Corp
Nihon Wakusei Kagaku Rengo. **VFOAT** Planetary Sciences; Planetary Science. Vol. 1, No. 1 (1979)-. Periodical. Japanese (summaries and/or abstracts in English). ¥300 single issue. Nihon Wakusei Kagaku Rengo, c/o Tokyo Daigaku Rigakubu, Chikyu Butsurigaku Kyoshitsu, Bunkyo-ku Tokyo Japan.

LC QB1 .Y4   **ISSN** 0084-3660
DD 523.058   US
  CEASED

YEARBOOK OF ASTRONOMY.
(1962)-(1993). English. W W Norton & Company Inc., 500 Fifth Avenue, New York NY 10110. **Tel** (800)233-4830. **ED** EP Swenson.
Desc: Information for the amateur astronomer, with articles on topical astronomical events and research.

LC QB1 .Z47   **ISSN** 0044-3948
  RU

ZEMLJA I VSELENNAJA. (ZEMLIA I VSELENNAIA.). [Zemlja vselennaja]. Added/Corp
Akademiia Nauk SSSR. Sektsiia Fiziko-Teknicheskikh i Matematicheskikh Nauk. Vsesoiuznoe Astronomo-Geodezicheskoe Obshchestvo. Vol. 1, (Jan./Feb. 1965)-. Academic Scholarly Publication. Russian. Six times a year. $134.00. Izdatelstvo Nauka / Akademiia Nauk, (Publishing House of the Russian Academy of Sciences), Leninskii Porspekt 14, 117901 Moscow Russia. **Tel** 011 95 9542153, FAX 011 95 9382144, telex 411964. **(Subscription address:** East View Publications Inc., 3020 Harbor Lane North, Suite 110, Minneapolis MN 55447. **Tel** (800)477-1005, (612)550-0961, FAX (612)559-2931.) Index available.
Ind/Abst GeoRef; Int. Aerosp. Abstr. (1984-).

LC QB
DD 520   NE

ZENIT. Vol. 1 (Jan. 1974)-. Periodical. Dutch. Eleven times a year. Fl.115.00. Stichting De Koepel, Zonnenburg 2, 3512 Utrecht Netherlands. **Tel** 011 31 30 311360. **Supersedes** Hemel en Dampkring, 0018-0289 **and** Macro.
Ind/Abst EMBASE.

LC QB980 .A27   **ISSN** 0137-2386
  PL

ZESZYTY NAUKOWE UNIWERSYTETU JAGIELLONSKIEGO. ACTA COSMOLOGICA. (ACTA COSMOLOGICA.).
[Zesz. Nauk. Uniw. Jagiell., Acta Cosmol.]. **Added/Corp** Uniwersytet Jagiellonski. Vol. 1 (1972)-. English (English). One time a year. Panstwowe Wydawnictwo Naukowe / PWN, (Polish Scientific Publishers PWN Ltd.), Ul. Miodowa 10, PO Box 391, 00-251 Warsaw Poland. **Tel** 011 48 22 212728, FAX 011 48 22 267163.
Ind/Abst Astron. Astrophys. Abstr.; Energy Res. Abstr. (Sept. 1980-).

LC Q   **ISSN** 0254-5896
DD 500   CC

ZHONGGUO KEXUE. A, SHUXUE, WULIXUE, TIANWENXUE, JISHUKEXUE.
See Mathematics.

Astronomy

LC QB
DD 520
Pr Rev
ISSN 0135-129X
LV

ZVAIGZNOTA DEBESS. Added/Corp Radioastrofizikas Observatorijas. (Fall 1958)-. Periodical. Latvian (English and Russian). Four times a year. $16.00. Radioastrofizical Observatory of the Latvian Academy of Sciences, Turgeneva iela 19, 1524 Riga Latvia. **Tel** 3712 226796, **FAX** 3712 228784. **ED** Dr. A. Balklavs. Index available. cum. index. **Bk Rev**. **Ad Acc. Circ:** 2,000-4,000.
 Desc: Illustrated popular scientific quarterly containing information on astronomy, physics and mathematics.
 Ind/Abst Astron. Astrophys. Abstr.; Numis. Lit.

ABSTRACTING, BIBLIOGRAPHIES AND STATISTICS

LC Z5153 .A862
DD 016.52
ISSN 0067-0022
GW
CCC

ASTRONOMY AND ASTROPHYSICS ABSTRACTS. [Astron. astrophys. abstr.]. **Added/Corp** Astronomisches Rechen-Institut, Heidelberg. International Astronomical Union. Vol. 1 (1969)-. Abstracting/Indexing Service. English. Two times a year. Price varies. Springer-Verlag GmbH & Company KG, Heidelberger Platz 3, D-14197 Berlin Germany. **Tel** 011 49 30 8207223, **FAX** 011 49 30 8214091, telex 183 319 SPBLN D. **(Subscription address:** Springer-Verlag New York Inc. / North America, PO Box 2485, Journal Fulfillment, Secaucus NJ 07096. **Tel** (201)348-4033, (800)777-4643, **FAX** (201)348-4505.) **ED** S. Bohme, G. Burkhardt, U. Esser, W. Fricke, H. Hefele, I. Heinrich, W. Hofmann, D. Krahn, V.R. Matas, L.D. Schmadel, R. Wielen, G. Zech. cum. index. Documents available from Ask*IEEE. **Continues** Astronomischer Jahresbericht.
 Ind/Abst Energy Res. Abstr. (Feb. 1982-); INSPEC.

LC QB
DD 520
ISSN 0002-7537
US
CODEN AASBAR

BULLETIN - AMERICAN ASTRONOMICAL SOCIETY. [Bull. - Am. Astron. Soc.]. **Main/Corp** American Astronomical Society. **Added/Corp** American Institute of Physics. **VFOAT** Bulletin of the American Astronomical Society. Vol. 1 (1969)-. Bulletin. English. Four times a year. $50.00. American Institute of Physics, 500 Sunnyside Boulevard, Woodbury NY 11797-2999. **Tel** (516)576-2270, (800)344-6902, **FAX** (516)349-9704, telex 960983. **ED** Peter B. Boyce. **Circ:** 1,900 (ctrl). available on microfilm; available in microform. Documents available from Ask*IEEE. **Supersedes in part** Astronomical Journal, 0004-6256.
 Desc: Abstracts of papers presented at society meetings, reports of observatories, additional reports and notices of interest to the Astronomical Society.
 Ind/Abst INIS Atomindex [Micro.]; INSPEC (1969-).

LC Z5153 .B85
DD 016.52
ISSN 0240-849X
FR

BULLETIN SIGNALETIQUE. 120, GEOPHYSIQUE EXTERNE, ASTRONOMIE ET ASTROPHYSIQUE. **Added/Corp** Informascience (Centre National de la Recherche Scientifique) CNRS - PASCAL (Center). **VFOAT** Geophysique Externe, Astronomie et Astrophysique. Vol. 42, No. 1 (1981)-. Bulletin. French. Twelve times a year. 775.00F. Service des Abonnements du CDSH, 54 Bd Raspail, 75270 Paris Cedex 06 France. **Tel** 45 48 10 18, telex MSH 203 104F. **Continues** Bulletin Signaletique. 120, Astronomie, Physique Spatiale, Geophysique.

COMPUTER APPLICATIONS

LC QB127.4 .C33
DD 522./63
ISSN 1074-875X
US

●**CCD ASTRONOMY.** (1994)-. Consumer Publication. English. Four times a year. $22.00. Sky Publishing Corporation, 49 Bay State Road, Cambridge MA 02138. **Tel** (617)864-7360, **FAX** (617)864-6117. **(Subscription address:** Sky Publishing Corporation, PO Box 9111, Belmont MA 02178.) **ED** Laurence A. Marschall. **Circ:** 7,500. Documents available from UMI Article Clearinghouse.
 Desc: Focuses on electronic imaging in astronomy.
 Ind/Abst Acad. Search; EP Collect.; Homework Help.; MasterFile FullTEXT 1000; MasterFile FullTEXT 350; MasterFile FullTEXT 650; MasterFile FullTEXT (July 1994-) [Full Txt.]; OCLC; Pub. Lib. FullTEXT; Telebase; Vocat. Search.

DD 005
ISSN 1061-8236
US

COSMIC UPDATE. (COSMIC UPDATE : A PUBLICATION OF COSMIC, NASA'S COMPUTER SOFTWARE MANAGEMENT AND INFORMATION CENTER.). [COSMIC update]. **Added/Corp** Computer Software Management and Information Center. (1988)-. Periodical. English. Four times a year. COSMIC/The University of Georgia, 112 Barrow Hall, Athens GA 30602. **Tel** (706)542-3265, **FAX** (706)542-4807.

DD 522
ISSN 1051-676X
US

IRAF NEWSLETTER. [IRAF newsl.]. **Added/Corp** National Optical Astronomy Observatories (U.S.). **VAT** Image Reduction and Analysis Facility Newsletter. No. 1 (June 1986)-. Periodical. English. Three times a year. Central Computer Services, National Optical Astronomy Observatories, PO Box 26732, Tuscon AZ 85726.

BEAUTY AND COSMETICS

LC TT955
DD 646.7
US

ACUPOLL REPORTS - HEALTH & BEAUTY AIDS & HOUSEHOLD PRODUCTS. See Consumer Education and Protection.

DD 051
ISSN 0883-5349
US

ALLURE (NEW YORK, N.Y. 1985). (ALLURE.). [Allure]. Vol. 1, No. 2 (Nov. 1985)-. Periodical. English. Twelve times a year. $15.00. Conde Nast Publications / New York, 350 Madison Avenue, New York NY 10017. **Tel** (212)880-8800, (800)777-0700, **FAX** (212)880-8331. **(Subscription address:** Neodata / Colorado, PO Box 2606, Boulder CO 80322.) **ED** Linda Wells. **Ad Acc, Adv Mgr:** Lauren Michaels.
 Desc: Covers all aspects of beauty. Reports on the news, analyzes the trends and reveals the facts about cosmetics, fragrance, skin and health care.

LC TT500 .A34
DD 391/.005
ISSN 0148-9135
US

AMBIANCE. See Clothing Industry and Fashion.

LC TT950 .A5
DD 646.7/242/05
ISSN 0741-5737
US
CCC

AMERICAN SALON : OFFICIAL PUBLICATION OF THE NHCA. [Am. salon]. **Added/Corp** National Hairdressers and Cosmetologists Association. Vol. 107, No. 1, (Jan. 1984)-. Trade Publication. English. Twelve times a year. $24.00. Advanstar Communications Inc., 131 West First Street, Duluth MN 55802. **Tel** (218)723-9477, (800)346-0085, **FAX** (218)723-9437. **ED** Jody Byrne. **Ad Acc. Circ:** 122,053 (ctrl). **Continues** American Hairdresser Salon Owner, 0095-1404.
 Ind/Abst EP Collect.; Homework Help.; MasterFile FullTEXT 1000; MasterFile FullTEXT 350; MasterFile FullTEXT 650; MasterFile FullTEXT (Jan. 1995-); OCLC; Telebase.

LC HD9999.B25 G74
DD 338.4/76885/029473
ISSN 1044-8705
US

AMERICAN SALON'S GREEN BOOK. [Am. salon's green book]. **VFOAT** Green Book. (198?)-. Trade Publication. English. One time a year (Jan.). $80.00. Advanstar Communications Inc., 131 West First Street, Duluth MN 55802. **Tel** (218)723-9477, (800)346-0085, **FAX** (218)723-9437. **(Subscription address:** Advanstar Marketing Service / Ohio, 7500 Old Oak Road, Cleveland OH 44130. **Tel** 800 598-6008, (216)891-2631.) **Continues** Green Book, 0160-1563.

LC TT950 .S67A
DD 353.97570082/43
US

ANNUAL REPORT FOR THE YEAR ENDING JUNE 30 ... / SOUTH CAROLINA, STATE BOARD OF COSMETIC ART EXAMINERS. Main/Corp South Carolina. State Board of Cosmetic Art Examiners. English. One time a year. State Board of Cosmetic Art Examiners, 3710 Landmark Drive/Suite 205, Columbia SC 29204.

DD 646.7/245/05
ISSN 8750-0477
CN
CEASED

ART & STYLE INTERNATIONAL. [Art. style int.]. Vol. 9, No. 2 (April/Summer 1984)-(Jan. 1993). Periodical. English (French). Art & Style International, PO Box 8890, Sainte-Foy Quebec G1V 4N7 Canada. **Tel** (418)651-3347. **ED** Guy Roberge. **Circ:** 18,000. **Continues** CBC, Coiffur, Beaute Charme, 0381-9175.
 Desc: Hairstyle magazine, gives latest fashion from all over the world.

LC TT955
DD 646.7242
US

AUDIT OF THE SENATE BUILDING BEAUTY SHOP FOR THE FISCAL YEAR ENDED ... . (1978/79)-. Government Publication. English. One time a year. US General Accounting Office / District of Columbia, 441 G Street Northwest, Room 4528, Washington DC 20548. **Tel** (202)275-2812.

DD 646.72
ISSN 0726-2566
AT
CEASED

AUSTRALIAN BEAUTY COUNTER. [Aust. beauty count.]. **VFOAT** Beauty Counter. (1981)-(Nov. 1993). Periodical. English. Reed Business Publishing Pty Ltd. / Australia, PO Box 5487, W Chatswood New South Wales 2057, Australia. **Tel** 011 61 2 3125222, **FAX** 011 61 2 4197533. **ED** Kerry Eastman. Index available. cum. index. **Ad Acc. Circ:** 8,500 (ctrl).
 Desc: Provides information to assist sales people in increasing their skills and knowledge.

DD 646.720994
ISSN 0156-9821
AT

AUSTRALIAN BEAUTY THERAPIST. [Aust. beauty ther.]. (1979)-. Periodical. English. Four times a year (Mar., June, Sept., Nov.). 49.34Aus$. Australian Beauty Therapist, PO Box 568, Milsons Point, 2061 Australia. **Tel** 11 61 2 9550455, **FAX** 11 61 2 9543443. **ED** Ginger Sims.
 Desc: Professional, technical and educational articles, new treatments, information and product news. Australian and international beauty news and updates plus articles by industry experts.

DD 646
ISSN 0886-8751
US
SUSPENDED

BEAUTY CLASSIC. VFOAT Beauty Classic Magazine. (198?)-Suspended (19??). Periodical. English. Four times a year. $10.00 US; $12.00 Canada. Beauty Classic, PO Box 6069, Tulsa OK 74148. **Ad Acc. Circ:** 27,000 (ctrl).

LC TT950
DD 646.72
ISSN 0960-3751
UK

BEAUTY COUNTER LONDON. [Beauty count. Lond.]. (1985)-. Trade Publication. English. Twelve times a year. £56.00 UK; £66.00 other. Benn Publications Ltd., Sovereign Way, Tonbridge TN9 1RW United Kingdom. **Tel** 011 44 1732 364422, **FAX** 011 44 1732 361534, telex 95132 BENTON G. **ED** Aileen Scoular. **Bk Rev,** (Qty: varies). **Ad Acc, Adv Mgr:** Liz Barnes, **Tel** 44 71 334 7334. **Circ:** 14,000 (ctrl). available on an online database from DIALOG. **Continues** Beauty Counter and Perfumery & Toiletries Buyer, 0263-6085.
 Ind/Abst PROMT [Full Txt.].

DD 646
ISSN 1052-4169
US

BEAUTY EDUCATION. [Beauty educ.]. Vol. 42, No. 9 (Sept. 1990)-. Trade Publication. English. Twelve times a year. Milady Publishing Corporation, 220 White Plains Road, 4th Floor, Tarrytown NY 10591. **Tel** (212)881-3000. **(Subscription address:** Beauty Education, 3 Columbia Circle Drive, Box 12519, Albany NY 12212. **Tel** (800)998-7498 ext. 3356.) **Continues** National Beauty School Journal, 0027-8769.
 Ind/Abst Mag. Search.

LC TT950
DD 646.72
UDC 665.58
ISSN 0944-0364
GW

BEAUTY-FORUM KARLSRUHE. [Beauty-Forum Karlsr.]. (1992)-. Periodical. German. Twelve times a year. $70.62. G. Braun Verlag, Postfach 1709, D-76006 Karlsruhe Germany. **Tel** 011 49 721 165392. **Formed by the union of** Cosmetic-Forum, 0938-8176 **and** Beauty (Gronau), 0932-7398.

LC TT950 HD28
DD 646.7 658
ISSN 1078-1781
US

BEAUTY INC. : FOR BEAUTY DISTRIBUTION PROFESSIONALS. [Beauty Inc.]. **Added/Corp** Beauty and Barber Supply Institute (New Jersey). **VFOAT** Beauty Inc. for Beauty Distribution Professionals. Vol. 1, No. 1 (May/June 1994)-. Trade Publication. English. Six times a year. Free. Beauty & Barber Supply Institute, Inc., 271 U.S. Highway 46, Suite F209, Fairfield NJ 07004-2415. **Tel** (201)808-7444, **FAX** (201)808-9099. **ED** Denise M. Rucci. **Circ:** 5,000 (ctrl).
 Desc: Concerned with beauty supply technology, trends, etc.

LC TT950
DD 646.72
ISSN 0405-1203
US

BEAUTY TRADE. Trade Publication. English. Four times a year. $11.00. Calvin News Service, 15 Columbus Circle Gulf Western, New York NY 10023. **Tel** (212)757-7589.

DD 646
ISSN 1062-3035
US

BEAUTYFACTS (NEW YORK, N.Y.). (BEAUTYFACTS ... DIRECTORY.). [BeautyFacts]. **Added/Corp** Cosmetic World (Firm). **VFOAT** Beauty

Beauty and Cosmetics

Facts. (1992)-. Directory. English. One time a year. $75.00. Cosmetic World Inc, 530 Fifth Avenue, 4th Floor, New York NY 10036. **Tel** (212)840-8800.

ISSN 1064-8844
DD 646 US
BEST OF HAIRDO IDEAS, THE. VFOAT
Hairdo Ideas ... Best. (1992)-. Periodical. English. Two times a year. $3.50 (single issue). Harris Publications, 1115 Broadway, 8th Floor, New York NY 10010. **Tel** (212)807-7100.

LC TT953.M6 M56a
DD 351.82/43 US
BIENNIAL REPORT OF EXAMINING AND LICENSING BOARDS. Main/Corp Minnesota.
Board of Barber Examiners. (19??)-. English. Every 2 years. Board of Barber Examiners / Minnesota, 500 Metro Square Building, St. Paul MN 55101.

ISSN 0707-4395
DD 613/.05
BIOESTHETIQUE.
Vol. 1 (Jan. 1979)-. Periodical. French. Twelve times a year. $1.50 per no. Editions du CRCM, Revue Bioesthetique, 800 rue Berri, Vieux Montreal Quebec H2Y 2E7 Canada.

LC WMLC 91/2943 ISSN 1058-0999
DD 646 US
BLACK HAIR CARE.
[Black hair care]. (19??)-. Periodical. English. Six times a year. $14.42. Harris Publications, 1115 Broadway, 8th Floor, New York NY 10010. **Tel** (212)807-7100.

LC TT950
DD 646.72 US
BLACK PASSION : INTERNATIONAL HAIR MAGAZINE.
English. Two times a year. $54.00. Intra-American Beauty Network, PO Box 629, 14 Commerce Drive, North Branford CT 06471.
Desc: Covers black hair styles for men and women.

LC TT950 ISSN 0765-9261
DD 646.72 FR
BULLETIN D'ESTHETIQUE DERMATOLOGIQUE ET COSMETOLOGIE.
(1984)-. French. Ten times a year. $174.69. Editions de l'Interligne, 47 rue de Charonne, 75011 Paris France. **Tel** 011 33 1 48068466.

ISSN 0955-7105
DD 338.476685 UK
BUYERS' GUIDE FOR COSMETICS & TOILETRIES MANUFACTURERS SUPPLIERS.
[Buy. guide cosmet. toilet. manuf. suppliers]. VFOAT Buyers' Guide for Cosmetics and Toiletries Manufacturers and Suppliers. (1987)-. English. One time a year.
Ind/Abst PROMT.

LC TT950 ISSN 0008-3720
DD 646.72 CN
CANADIAN HAIRDRESSER.
(1953)-. Trade Publication. English (French). Six times a year. 31.81Can$. Canadian Hairdresser, 131 Bloor Street West, Suite 200, Toronto Ontario M5S 1R1 Canada. **Tel** (416)923-1111. **ED** Gregory Robins. **Bk Rev**. **Ad Acc**. **Circ:** 11,000.
Desc: Covers skin care, hairdressing (with photos), techniques of hairstyling, aesthetics, new hair/skin care products, massages, tanning parlors, fashion, cosmetics, beauty aids and salon design and equipment.

LC TT950
DD 646.72 US
CATEGORY REPORT - HEALTH & BEAUTY AIDS. CRH.
See Consumer Education and Protection.

ISSN 1058-3009
DD 646 US
CELEBRITY HAIRSTYLES PRESENTS MAKEOVER GUIDE.
[Celebr. hairstyles presents makeover guide]. VFOAT Celebrity Hairstyles Makeover guide; Makeover Guide. (198?)-. Periodical. English. Six times a year. Harris Publications, 1115 Broadway, 8th Floor, New York NY 10010. **Tel** (212)807-7100.

LC GT500 ISSN 0823-7794
DD 391/.005 CN
C'EST MOI!.
See Clothing Industry and Fashion.

ISSN 0711-0340
DD 391/.005 CN
CLIN D'OEIL (VILLE MONT-ROYAL).
(CLIN D'OEIL.). [Clin oeil]. No. 1 (Sept. 1980)-. Periodical. French. Twelve times a year. 23.48Can$. Publications Quebecor le Nordais, 5800 rue St. Denis Bar 605, Montreal Quebec H2S 3L5 Canada. **Tel** (514)272-7079, FAX (514)270-7079.
Ind/Abst Repere (1989-1990).

DD 646.7/242/09714
COIFFBEC.
[Coiffbec]. Vol. 1, No. 1 (June 1977)-. Periodical. French. Twelve times a year. $5.00. Journal Coiffbec, 100 Succursale Ahuntsic, Montreal Quebec H3L 3NZ Canada.

LC TT950
DD 646.72 NE
COIFFURE.
(19??)-. Dutch. Twelve times a year. Hofstad Vakpers BV, Postbus 119, 2700 AC Zoetermeer Netherlands. **Tel** 011 31 079 711811.

LC TT950 .C65
DD 646.7/242/05 FR
COIFFURE DE PARIS, LA.
(19??)-. Periodical. French. Ten times a year (monthly with combined July and Aug.). 295.00F France; 60.00Can$ Canada; 2030F Luxembourg; 80.00F Switzerland; 5984ptas Spain; 1730F Belgium; L69000 Italy; $48.00 US. SEMP - Societe d'Editions Modernes Parisienne, 38 rue Jean Mermoz, 75008 Paris France. **Tel** 011 33 1 42669236, FAX 011 33 1 42666064, telex 650016. Index available. cum. index. **Bk Rev**. **Ad Acc**. ctrl circ.
Desc: Technical hairdressing demonstrations, outfits, posters, new haircare products. Includes articles concerning management, resale, various trends, interviews, agenda, ads, inquiries, etc.

LC TT950
DD 646.72
COIFFURE DE PARIS ARTS & COIFFURE.
(19??)-. English (summaries and/or abstracts in English, Spanish, Dutch, German and Japanese). Eleven times a year. $67.00. Vance Publishing Corporation, 400 Knightsbridge Parkway, Lincolnshire IL 60069. **Tel** (800)255-5113, (708)634-2600.

ISSN 0226-1383
DD 646.7/242/05 CN
COIFFURE DU CANADA.
Vol. 1 (Nov. 1979)-. Periodical. English. Four times a year. $12.00 per no. Coiffure du Canada, 2 Wincrest Drive, Scarborough Ontario M1P 4J4 Canada.

LC TT950 ISSN 1161-899X
DD 646.72 FR
UDC 687.5
COIFFURE ET STYLES PARIS.
(COIFFURE ET STYLES.). (1991)-. Periodical. French. Eleven times a year (publishes monthly with July/Aug. issues combined). $120.30. SEID, 17 R Notre Dame des Victoires, 75002 Paris France. **Tel** 011 33 1 42615324. **Continues** Le Coiffeur de France (Paris), 0750-3563; **Absorbed** L Officiel de la Coiffure et de la Beaute, 0750-3490.

LC TT950
DD 646.72 UK
COIFFURE Q : INTERNATIONAL HAIR MAGAZINE.
(19??)-. English. Four times a year. $75.00. Image Media International Inc., 4054 Del Rey Avenue, Suite 203, Marina Del Rey CA 90292. **Tel** (310)821-1244, (800)362-7071, FAX (310)827-7035. **ED** Helen Moy. **Circ:** 100,000 (ctrl).
Desc: Covers women's hair styles.

ISSN 1069-1448
DD 668 US
COSMETIC BENCH REFERENCE.
[Cosmet. bench ref.]. (19??)-. Periodical. English. Every 2 years (every two years). $95.00. Allured Publishing Corporation, 362 South Schmale Road, Carol Stream IL 60188-2787. **Tel** (708)653-2155, FAX (708)653-2192.

LC TT950 ISSN 0275-4681
DD 646.72 US
CCC
COSMETIC INSIDER'S REPORT.
Vol. 1, No. 1 (Mar. 2, 1981)-. Trade Publication. English. Twenty-four times a year. $189.00. Advanstar Communications Inc., 131 West First Street, Duluth MN 55802. **Tel** (218)723-9477, (800)346-0085, FAX (218)723-9437. available on an online database from DATA-STAR; and (files 16,636/Full-Text) DIALOG.
Ind/Abst PROMT; PTS Newsl. Database [Full Txt.].

LC TT950
DD 646.72 IT
CODEN COSNDG
COSMETIC NEWS : CN. VFOAT CN.
(19??)-. Academic Scholarly Publication. Italian. Six times a year. L40880. Sepem SRL, Via G Livraghi 9, 20126 Milan Italy. **Tel** 011 39 2 27001110, FAX 011 39 2 27000652. **ED** Ra Bruna Benfenati. **Bk Rev**, (Qty: 6-12). **Ad Acc, Adv Mgr:** Franco Mattei. **Circ:** 3,000 (ctrl). Documents available from CASDDS.
Desc: Publishes articles about cosmetology, dermatology, cosmetological chemistry and more.
Ind/Abst Chem. Abstr.

LC TT950
DD 646.72 FR
CEASED
COSMETIC RESEARCH.
(19??)-(19??). Periodical. English (French). Cosmetic Research International, 10 rue Louis Philippe, 92200 Neuilly France.

Tel 011 33 1 46242467.
Desc: Information about new products including photos, major claims, listing of ingredients, etc.

ISSN 0887-6541
DD 668 US
CCC
NLM W1; CO927 CODEN CSTSEV
COSMETIC SCIENCE AND TECHNOLOGY SERIES.
[Cosmet. sci. technol. ser.]. Vol. 1 (1984)-. Monographic series. English. Price varies per volume. Marcel Dekker Inc., 270 Madison Avenue, New York NY 10016. **Tel** (212)696-9000, (800)228-1160, FAX (212)685-4540, telex 421419. **(Subscription address:** Marcel Dekker Inc., PO Box 5017, Monticello NY 12701. **Tel** (800)228-1160.**)** Documents available from CASDDS.
Desc: Each volume presents information on some aspect of cosmetics and the cosmetics industry, from preservation to clinical safety.
Ind/Abst Chem. Abstr.

LC TT950 ISSN 0589-8447
DD 646.72 US
COSMETIC WORLD.
(196?)-. Trade Publication. English. One time a week. $175.00. Cosmetic World Inc, 530 Fifth Avenue, 4th Floor, New York NY 10036. **Tel** (212)840-8800. **ED** John G. Ledes. **Bk Rev**. **Ad Acc**. **Circ:** 3,900.

LC TP983 .A2215 ISSN 0305-0319
DD 338.4/7/668505 UK
CODEN CSWNAR
COSMETIC WORLD NEWS.
[Cosmet. world news]. (June 1974)-. Periodical. English. Six times a year. $156.00. Cosmetic World News, 130 Wigmore Street, London W1H 0AT United Kingdom. **Tel** 011 44 181 4866757, FAX 011 44 181 4875436. **ED** M.A. Murray-Pearce. **Bk Rev**. **Ad Acc**. **Circ:** 6,000. available on microfilm from University Microfilms International (UMI); available on an online database (file 648/Full-Text) from DIALOG.
Desc: The international news magazine of the perfumery, cosmetics and toiletries industry.
Ind/Abst BioBusiness; Trade Ind. ASAP [Full Txt.]; Trade Ind. Index [Full Txt.].

LC TT950 ISSN 1150-1677
DD 646.72 FR
UDC 687.5
Pr Rev.
COSMETICA DISTRIBUTION LEVALLOIS-PERRET.
(COSMETICA DISTRIBUTION.). (1990)-. Periodical. French. Twelve times a year. $72.18. CEP Communications Groupe LSA, 6 rue Marius Aufan, 92300 Levallois Perret France. **Tel** 011 33 1 47 582000, FAX 011 33 1 47 586070. **ED** Marie-Laure Prost. **Ad Acc**. **Circ:** 12,500.
Desc: Covers current events (new products and people); product family studies; performances (marketing, merchandising); foreign market studies; and reviews of the British, American, and German press.

LC TT950 ISSN 0817-637X
DD 646.72 AT
CODEN CTAUEH
Pr Rev.
COSMETICS AEROSOLS & TOILETRIES IN AUSTRALIA.
[Cosmet. aerosols toilet. Aust.]. (1986)-. English. Five times a year. 60.00Aus$. Manor Enterprises PTY Limited, PO Box 2684, North Parramatta 2151 NSW Australia. **Tel** 011 61 2 6306435, FAX 011 61 2 6831741. **Circ:** 2,700.
Ind/Abst BioBusiness (1990-).

LC TP983 .A222 ISSN 0361-4387
DD 668/.5/05 US
CCC
NLM W1 CO93K CODEN CTOIDGACPFB5
COSMETICS AND TOILETRIES.
[Cosmet. toiletries]. VAT Cosmetics & Toiletries. Vol. 91 (Jan. 1976)-. Trade Publication. English (Spanish and Italian). Twelve times a year. $72.00 US; $100.00 Canada; $142.00 other. Allured Publishing Corporation, 362 South Schmale Road, Carol Stream IL 60188-2787. **Tel** (708)653-2155, FAX (708)653-2192. **ED** Fred Miller. Index available (bound in Jan. issue). **Bk Rev**. **Ad Acc**. **Circ:** 3,200. available on microfilm and microfiche from University Microfilms International (UMI); available on an online database (file 648/Full-Text) from DIALOG. Documents available from BIOSIS Document Express, CASDDS. **Supersedes in part** Cosmetics and Perfumery, 0090-6581.
Desc: Deals with new materials/developments in formulation techniques, quality control, safety and efficacy in cosmetics and toiletries. For all research and development chemists in this industry.
Ind/Abst Appl. Sci. Technol. Index (-1990); Art Archaeol. Tech. Abstr.; BioBusiness (1989-); Biol. Abstr. (1987-); Chem. Abstr.; Curr. Biotechnol.; Curr. Cit.; EMBASE; Int. Pharm. Abstr.; Life Sci. Collect.; Predicasts; Trade Ind. ASAP [Full Txt.]; Trade Ind. Index [Full Txt.].

Beauty and Cosmetics

LC TT950
DD 646.72
IT
CODEN CTEIEZ
Pr Rev.
COSMETICS & TOILETRIES. VFOAT
Cosmetics and Toiletries. (1980)-. Academic Scholarly Publication. Italian. Six times a year. L75000 Italy; L100000 other. Cosmeo Srl, Viale Legioni Romane 55, 20147 Milan Italy. **Tel** 011 39 2 416337, FAX 011 39 2 48300981. Index available. cum. index. **Bk Rev. Ad Acc. Circ:** 18,000 (ctrl). Documents available from CASDDS.
Ind/Abst Chem. Abstr. (1985); F&S Index Plus Text, Int. [Select. Cov.]; Infomat Int. Bus.; PROMT.

LC TT950
DD 646.72
JA
COSMETICS & TOILETRIES & HOUSEHOLD PRODUCTS MARKETING NEWS IN JAPAN. (19??)-. English. Twelve times a year. $825.00. Pacific Research Consulting, 18 2 Shikahama 4 Chome, Adachi Ku Tokyo 123 Japan. **Tel** 011 81 3 3899 9953. available on an online database (files 16,570,636/Full-Text) from DIALOG. **Continues** Cosmetic Toiletry & Miscellaneous Household Marketing News in Japan.
Ind/Abst Mark. Advert. Ref. Serv. [Full Txt.]; PROMT [Full Txt.]; PTS Newsl. Database [Full Txt.].

LC TT950
DD 646.72
UK
COSMETICS AND TOILETRIES MANUFACTURERS AND SUPPLIERS.
English. Six times a year. £42.00 UK and Northern Ireland; $110.00 other. Morgan Grampian, 40 Beresford Street Woolwich, London SE18 6BQ United Kingdom. **Tel** 011 44 181 8557777, FAX 011 44 181 8555548, telex 896238. available on an online database (files 16,570/Full-Text) from DIALOG.

LC TT950
DD 646.72
ISSN 0315-1301
CN
CODEN COSMEE
COSMETICS (DON MILLS). (COSMETICS.).
(1972)-. Periodical. English (French). Six times a year. 34.41Can$. MacLean Hunter Ltd. Business Publishers / Canada, Box 9100, Station A, Toronto Ontario M5W 1A5 Canada. **Tel** (416)596-5000, , FAX (416)596-5552. **(Subscription address:** Indas Customer Service, 35 Riviera Drive, Building 17, Markham Ontario L3R 8N4 Canada. **Tel** (905)946-0406.) **Ad Acc.** ctrl circ. available on microfilm and microfiche from University Microfilms International (UMI).
Ind/Abst BioBusiness (1988-).

DD 338.4/7/668502571
ISSN 0316-9871
CN
COSMETICS HANDBOOK. 1972-. Periodical. English. One time a year. Maclean Hunter Canada / Montreal, 1001 bvd. de Maisonneuve W., Montreal Quebec H3A 3E1 Canada. **Tel** (514)845-5141, FAX (514)845-4302, telex 055-60604. **Supersedes** Cosmeticians' Handbook, 0316-9863.

LC TT950
DD 646.72
UK
CODEN COSIDZ
COSMETICS INTERNATIONAL. (198?)-.
Periodical. English. Twenty-two times a year (biweekly except Aug. & Dec.). $495.00. Cosmetics Communications Ltd., 335 Linen Hall, London W1R 5TB United Kingdom. **Tel** 011 44 181 4341530, FAX 011 44 181 4370915, telex 262433 3441. **(Subscription address:** Stonehart Subscription Services, Hainault Road Little Heath, Bromford RM6 5NP United Kingdom. **Tel** 011 44 181 5977335.) **ED** Liz Jones. Index available. **Ad Acc. Circ:** 10,000 (ctrl). available on an online database from Lexis-Nexis; and (file 648[Full/Text]) DIALOG.
Desc: Covers emerging market trends, company profiles, latest news and mergers and acquisitions within the cosmetics industry.
Ind/Abst F&S Index Plus Text, Int. [Select. Cov.]; Infomat Int. Bus.; PROMT; Trade Ind. ASAP [Full Txt.]; Trade Ind. Index [Full Txt.].

LC TP
DD 668.55
ISSN 1358-3387
UK
●**COSMETICS INTERNATIONAL.**
COSMETIC PRODUCTS REPORT. (1994)-.
Periodical. English. Twelve times a year. $395.00. Cosmetics Communications Ltd., 335 Linen Hall, W1R 5TB United Kingdom. **Tel** 011 44 181 4341530, FAX 011 44 181 4370915, telex 262433 3441. **Continues** Cosmetics International. New Products Review.
Desc: Presents international new product launches. Segmentation by product sector (fragrances, makeup, skincare, bodycare, haircare, and suncare for men). Records new product concepts, innovations in packaging and marketing techniques.

LC TP
DD 668.55
UK
TITLE CHANGE
COSMETICS INTERNATIONAL. NEW PRODUCTS REVIEW. (19??)-. English. Cosmetics Communications Ltd., 335 Linen Hall, London W1R 5TB United Kingdom. **Tel** 011 44 181 4341530, FAX 011 44 181 4370915, telex 262433 3441. **ED** Liz Jones. Index available. **Ad Acc. Circ:** 10,000 (ctrl). **Continued by** Cosmetics International Cosmetic Products Report, 1358-3387.
Desc: Presents international new product launches and records new product concepts, innovations in packaging and marketing techniques.

LC TP
DD 668.55
UDC 668.5
ISSN 0980-0875
FR
COSMETIQUE NEWS PARIS. (COSMETIQUE NEWS.). [Cosmet. news Paris]. (1986)-. Periodical. French. Twenty-four times a year. $251.53. Aguesseau Communication Presse, 175 177 rue d'Aguesseau, 92100 Boulogne France. **Tel** 011 33 1 46041212.

LC AP2 .H4
DD 051
ISSN 0010-9541
US
COSMOPOLITAN (1952). See Women's Interests.

LC AP
DD 051
UDC 05
ISSN 0923-6872
NE
COSMOPOLITAN AMSTERDAM. See Women's Interests.

LC AP2
DD 052
ISSN 0310-2076
AT
COSMOPOLITAN AUSTRALIAN EDITION. See Women's Interests.

LC TT950
DD 646.72
UK
COSMOPOLITAN. (ENGLAND EDITION). See General Interest-General Interest-Europe.

LC TT950
DD 646.72
ISSN 1161-2258
FR
COSMOPOLITAN (PARIS). See General Interest-General Interest-Europe.

LC TT950
DD 646.72
NLM W1 C94K
ISSN 0090-0591
US
CODEN CTFJA5
CTFA COSMETIC JOURNAL. Main/Corp
Cosmetic, Toiletry and Fragrance Association. **VAT**
Cosmetic, Toiletry and Fragrance Association Cosmetic Journal. Vol. 3 (1971)-. Periodical. English. Four times a year. Cosmetic Toiletry and Fragrance Association, PO Box 471, Annapolis Junction MD 20701. **Tel** (301)953-2614. Documents available from BIOSIS Document Express. **Continues** Toilet Goods Association. TGA Cosmetic Journal.
Ind/Abst Biol. Abstr. (-1981); Int. Pharm. Abstr.

LC TP983 .A2225
DD 668./5/02234
ISSN 1058-4080
US
CTFA ... INTERNATIONAL BUYERS' GUIDE. [CTFA int. buyers' guide]. **Added/Corp**
Cosmetic, Toiletry and Fragrance Association. **VFOAT**
CTFA International Buyers' Guide; Cosmetic, Toiletry and Fragrance Association International Buyers' Guide; International Buyers' Guide. (1991)-. Consumer Publication. English. Cosmetic Toiletry and Fragrance Association, PO Box 471, Annapolis Junction MD 20701. **Tel** (301)953-2614.

LC TT950
DD 646.72
ISSN 0274-8851
US
CUTTER, THE. (19??)-. Trade Publication. English. Twelve times a year. $48.00. Cutter Magazine, PO Box 240, Denver CO 80201. **Tel** (303)893-2211. **ED** Dan McAlpine. Index available. **Circ:** 20,000.
Desc: Business publication for salon owners. Taxes, small business, financial, trade information and business practices are covered in-depth.

DD 646/.34/05
ISSN 0706-6449
CN
DAZZLE. (Sept. 1978)-. Periodical. English. Four times a year. $6.00. Dazzle, 11-415 West Cordova Street, Vancouver British Columbia V6B 1EB Canada.

DD 338
ISSN 1075-055X
US
DERMASCOPE (DALLAS, TEX.).
(DERMASCOPE.). [Dermascope]. **Added/Corp**
Aestheticians International Association. **VFOAT**
Dermascope Magazine. (19??)-. Trade Publication. English. Six times a year. $35.00. Dermascope, 4447 McKinney Avenue, Dallas TX 75205. **Tel** (800)285-5277, (214)526-0752.

LC TP1177
DD 668.54
FR
DICTIONARY OF PERFUMES. English.
Irregular. $25.00 per copy. Beauty Fashion Inc, 530 5th Avenue, New York NY 10036. **Tel** (212)840-8800.

LC TT950
DD 646.72
FR
DICTIONARY OF SKIN CARE PRODUCTS. (19??)-. Periodical. English. Irregular. $25.00. Edition Sermadiras. **(Subscription address:** Beauty Fashion Inc., 530 5th Avenue, 4th Floor, New York NY 10036. **Tel** (212)840-8800.)

DD 646
ISSN 1073-290X
US
●**DR. HAIR COSMETOLOGY NEWS JOURNAL.** [Dr. Hair cosmetol. news j.]. **VFOAT**
Doctor Hair Cosmetology News Journal; Dr. Hair; Doctor Hair; Cosmetology News Journal. (1994)-. Newsletter. English. Six times a year. $24.95. Dr. Hair Cosmetology News Journal, 12777 Jones Road, Suite 425, Houston TX 77070. **Tel** (713)897-9171, FAX (713)370-8887. **ED** Michael Tucker. available with illustrations.
Desc: A forum for student as well as professional cosmetologists.

LC RS1 .D63
DD 615.105/6
NLM W1 DR514
ISSN 0012-6527
CCC
CODEN DCINAQ
DRUG & COSMETIC INDUSTRY. See Pharmacy and Pharmacology.

LC TT950
DD 646.72
NE
DW : DROGISTEN WEEKBLAD. (19??)-. Dutch. Irregular (48 issues). Fl75.00 (latest issue). Van Der Weij Periodieken BV, Postbus 285, 1200 AG Hilversum Netherlands. **Tel** 011 31 35 49741.

LC TT950
DD 646.72
NE
ELEGANCE. See Women's Interests.

LC TT950
DD 646.72
HK
ELEGANCE. Chinese. Twelve times a year. $93.00. ZYC Holding Ltd, 661 Kings Road, Cheung King Building, Quarry Bay Hong Kong. **(Subscription address:** Evergreen Publ & Stationery, 760 West Garvey Avenue, Monterey Park CA 91754. **Tel** (818)281-3622.)

LC TT950
DD 646.72
NE
ELLE. See Women's Interests.

LC TT500
DD 391
AT
ELLE (AUSTRALIAN EDITION). See Women's Interests.

LC TT950
DD 646.72
UDC 391 & B79
ISSN 1120-4397
IT
ELLE ED. ITALIANA. See Women's Interests.

LC TT500 .E44
DD 391/.2/05
ISSN 0935-462X
GW
ELLE (MUNICH, GERMANY). See Women's Interests.

LC TT500 .E44
DD 391/.2/05
ISSN 0888-0808
US
ELLE (NEW YORK, N.Y.). See Women's Interests.

DD 054/.1
ISSN 0843-6363
CN
ELLE QUEBEC. [Elle Que.]. **VFOAT** Belle et Bien Dans sa Peau. No 1 (Sept. 1989)-. Periodical. French. Twelve times a year. 22.41Can$. Les Editions Telemedia, 2001 rue University Bureau 900, Montreal Quebec H3A 2A6 Canada. **Tel** (514)875-1974. **(Subscription address:** Abonnement Quebec, 25 Boulevard Taschereau, Bureau 201, Greenfield PK Quebec J4V 3P1 Canada. **Tel** (514)875-4444.)
Ind/Abst Repere (Jan. 1991-).

LC TP670
DD 665
ISSN 0014-0902
IT
CODEN EDAGAH
ESSENZE E DERIVATI AGRUMARI.
[Essenze deriv. agrum.]. **Added/Corp** Stazione Sperimentale Per L'industria Delle Essenze e dei Derivati Agrumari. (1953)-. Academic Scholarly Publication. Italian. Four times a year. L51100. Stazione Sperimentale, Corso Cittorio Emanuele, 89100 Reggio Calabria Italy. **Tel** 0965/24315-6. **ED** Angelo Di Giacomo. **Bk Rev. Ad Acc. Circ:** 500. available in microform. Documents available from CASDDS. **Continues** Stazione Sperimentale per L'industria Delle Essenze e dei Derivati Dagi Argrumi. Bolletttino Ufficiale della Stazione Sperimentale per L'industria delle Essenze e dei Derivati Dagli Agrumi.
Desc: Essential oils and citrus products.
Ind/Abst AGRICOLA; Chem. Abstr.; Food Sci. Technol. Abstr.; Life Sci. Collect.

LC TP1177 **ISSN** 1142-2599
DD 668.4 FR
CEASED
ESTHETICA (PARIS, 1989). (ESTHETICA : LE MAGAZINE DE LA BEAUTE SUR MESURE.). (1989)-(199?). French. Editions Mega Medias, 58 rue St. Georges, 75009 Paris France. **Tel** 011 33 1 42855100.

LC TT950
DD 646.72 FR
CEASED
ESTHETICA PROFESSIONNEL. (1989)-(19??). French. Editions Mega Medias, 58 rue St. Georges, 75009 Paris France. **Tel** 011 33 1 42855100.

LC TT950
DD 646.72 NE
ESTHETICIENNE. Dutch. Twelve times a year. Koggeschip Vakbladen BV, Postbus 1198, 1000 BD Amsterdam Netherlands. **Tel** 011 31 20 6916666.

ISSN 0957-1515
DD 338.476685 UK
EUROPEAN COSMETIC MARKETS. [Eur. cosmet. mark.]. (1983)-. Periodical. English. Twelve times a year. $1112.28. Nicholas Hall & Company, 35 Alexandra Street, Southend-on-Sea, Essex SS1 1BW United Kingdom. **Tel** 011 44 1702 433422, FAX 011 44 1702 430787. **ED** A. Wilkinson. Index available. **Ad Acc. Circ:** 5,000. available on an online database from DIALOG; and Predicasts, Inc.
Desc: Covering the European cosmetics and toiletries industry; analysis of the five major European markets and US company profiles, country reviews, product news, industry news and views, and special features.
Ind/Abst Mark. Advert. Ref. Serv. [Full Txt.]; PROMT [Full Txt.]; PTS Newsl. Database [Full Txt.]; Trade Ind. ASAP [Full Txt.]; Trade Ind. Index [Full Txt.].

ISSN 1064-7953
DD 051 US
FACE (MALIBU, CALIF.). (FACE.). [Face]. Vol. 1, No. 2 (Jan/Feb 1993)-. Periodical. English. Five times a year. $39.00 US; $44.00 Canada; $75.00 other. Transpacific Media Incorporated, 23715 West Malibu Road, Suite 390, Malibu CA 90265. **Tel** (310)456-0790, FAX (310)456-3724. **ED** Shi Kagy (editor's addres: P.O. Box 4260, Mailbu, CA 90264-4260, phone: (310)589-2600 ext. 111). **Bk Rev**, (Qty: 18). **Ad Acc, Adv Mgr:** Shi Kagy, **Tel** (310)589-2600 ext. 111. **Circ:** 25,000.
Desc: Beauty and fashion magazine for the Asian woman.

LC TT500 **ISSN** 0228-829X
DD 391/.005 CN
FASHION IMAGES. See Clothing Industry and Fashion.

LC TP1177 **ISSN** 0279-1110
DD 668.54 US
CCC
FDC REPORTS. TOILETRIES, FRAGRANCES AND SKIN CARE. VFOAT Rose Sheet. Vol. 1, No. 1 (May 5, 1980)-. Government Publication. English. One time a week. $580.00. FDC Reports Inc., 5550 Friendship Boulevard, Suite 1, Chevy Chase MD 20815. **Tel** (301)657-9830. ***Continues in part*** *FDC Reports. Drugs and Cosmetics, 0162-7945.*
Desc: Provides specialized coverage of regulatory, legislative, scientific, financial and legal news. Gives marketing information, line extensions, and promotions.
Ind/Abst PROMT (19??-); Trade Ind. Index (19??-).

LC TT500 .G46 **ISSN** 0017-0747
DD 687.082 US
GLAMOUR. See Clothing Industry and Fashion.

LC TT500 **ISSN** 0990-6479
DD 391 FR
UDC 087.2-055.2
TITLE CHANGE
GLAMOUR PARIS. See Women's Interests.

LC TT950 .T49a
DD 353.97640082/43 US
GOVERNOR'S REPORT FOR THE PERIOD ... / TEXAS COSMETOLOGY COMMISSION. Main/Corp Texas Cosmetology Commission. (197?)-. English. One time a year. Texas Cosmetology Commission, PO Box 26700, Austin TX 78755-0700.

ISSN 0897-3903
DD 646 US
HAIR & BEAUTY NEWS. [Hair beauty news]. **VFOAT** Hair and Beauty News. (1988)-. Periodical. English. Twelve times a year. $29.00. Hair & Beauty News, 1300 Cummins Road, Des Moines IA 50315.

ISSN 1058-2983
DD 646 US
HAIR CUT AND STYLE. [Hair cut style]. **VFOAT** Hair Cut & Style. (1991)-. Periodical. English. Four times a year. $2.95 (U.S., single issue) $3.50 (Canada, single issue). Harris Publications, 1115 Broadway, 8th Floor, New York NY 10010. **Tel** (212)807-7100.

LC TT950
DD 646.72 US
HAIR DESIGN. (19??)-. English. Two times a year. $15.00. Hair Design, 19458 San Juan Drive, Detroit MI 48221. **Tel** (313)862-2970. **ED** Billy Cason. **Ad Acc.**

LC HD2321 **ISSN** 0887-803X
DD 338 US
HAIR INTERNATIONAL NEWS. Periodical. English. Six times a year. $24.00. Hair International, 1318 Starbrook Drive, Charlotte NC 23210. **Tel** (704)552-6233. **Ad Acc. Circ:** 2,500 (ctrl).

LC TT950 **ISSN** 0143-7968
DD 646.72 UK
HAIR (LONDON). (HAIR.). **VFOAT** Hair, Incorporating Hair & Good Looks. (19??)-. Periodical. English. Six times a year. $25.75. IPC Magazines Ltd., Perrymount Road, Haywards Heath, West Sussex RH16 3DH United Kingdom. **Tel** 011 44 1444 440421, FAX 011 44 1444 445599.

ISSN 1058-0980
DD 646 US
HAIRDO IDEAS. [Hairdo ideas]. (19??)-. Periodical. English. Six times a year. $17.77. Harris Publications, 1115 Broadway, 8th Floor, New York NY 10010. **Tel** (212)807-7100.

ISSN 0143-6910
DD 646.72405 UK
HAIRDRESSERS JOURNAL INTERNATIONAL. [Hairdr. j. int.]. **VFOAT** Hairdressers' Journal (1976). (1976)-. Trade Publication. English. One time a week. $105.00. Reed Business Publishing / West Sussex, England, Perrymount Road, Haywards Heath, West Sussex RH16 3DH United Kingdom. **Tel** 011 44 1444 441212, FAX 011 44 1444 445447. ***Continues*** *Hairdressers' Journal (1949), 0017-6761.*

LC TT950 **ISSN** 0277-0334
DD 646.724 US
Pr Rev.
HOW TO DOUBLE YOUR INCOME. (1981)-. Periodical. English. Twelve times a year. $49.50. How to Double Your Income, 6031 North 7th Street, Phoenix AZ 85013. **Tel** (602)266-5637. **ED** Ken Lange. **Bk Rev. Circ:** 2,000 (ctrl).
Desc: Edited for hairstylists, with reports on new perm and color techniques from publications worldwide; includes advertising and business techniques.

LC TP1101 **ISSN** 0019-607X
DD 668.54 II
CODEN IPERAS
INDIAN PERFUMER. (INDIAN PERFUMER = BHARATIYA GANDHIKA.). [Indian perfum.]. **Added/Corp** Essential Oil Association of India. **VFOAT** Bharatiya Gandhika. (1957)-. Periodical. English. Four times a year (Mar., June, Sept., Dec.). $80.00. Essential Oil Association of India, H B T I Campus, Dua Complex 24, Veer Savarkar Block, New Delhi 110 092 India. **Tel** 011 91 11 3162434, FAX 011 91 11 2204284. **ED** Dr. S.N. Sobti (editor's address: 610 Sectror A, Vasant Kunj, New Delhi 110070). Index available ($20.00). cum. index. **Ad Acc. Circ:** 750. Documents available from CASDDS.
Ind/Abst Agric. Eng. Abstr. (1991-); Agrofor. Abstr. (1991-); Biocont. News Inf. (1991-); Biodeter. Abstr. (19??-19??); Chem. Abstr.; Crop Physiol. Abstr.; Curr. Cit.; For. Prod. Abstr. (19??-19??); For. Abstr.; Hortic. Abstr.; Index Vet.; Irr. Drain. Abstr.; NAPRALERT; Nutr. Abstr. Rev., Ser. A, Hum. Exp.; Ornamental Hort. (19??-19??); Plant Breed. Abstr.; Plant Genet. Resour. Abstr.; Plant Grow. Reg. Abstr.; Postharvest News Inf.; Rev. Agric. Entomol.; Rev. Med. Vet. Entomol.; Rev. Med. Vet. Mycology; Rev. Plant Pathol.; Seed Abstr.; Soils Fert.; Weed Abstr.

LC HQ1219 .I57
DD 305.4/079 US
INTERNATIONAL DIRECTORY OF PAGEANTS. Added/Corp World Pageants, Inc. (1988)-. English. One time a year. $55.00. World Pageants Inc., 18761 West Dixie Highway, Suite 284, North Miami Beach FL 33180. **Tel** (305)933-2993.

LC TP1101
DD 668.54 UK
NLM W1; IN7655E
INTERNATIONAL JOURNAL OF AROMATHERAPY. Vol. 1, No. 1 (Feb. 1988)-. Periodical. English. Four times a year (Feb., May, Aug., Nov.). $30.80. Aromatherapy Publications, 65 Church Street, Home East Sussex BN3 2BD United Kingdom. **Tel** 011 44 127 3772479.

LC TP983 .A233 **ISSN** 0142-5463
DD 668/.55/05 UK
CCC
NLM W1 IN766F **CODEN** IJCMDW
Pr Rev.
INTERNATIONAL JOURNAL OF COSMETIC SCIENCE. [Int. j. cosmet. sci.]. **Added/Corp** Society of Cosmetic Scientists (Great Britain). Societe Francaise de Cosmetologie. (Feb. 1979)-. Academic Scholarly Publication. English (French). Six times a year. $319.00. Chapman & Hall, 2-6 Boundary Row, London SE1 8HN United Kingdom. **Tel** 011 44 171 8650066, FAX 011 44 171 5229623, telex 290164 CHAPMA G. **ED** J. M. Blakeway. Index available. **Bk Rev. Ad Acc. Circ:** 2,000. available on microfilm and microfiche from University Microfilms International (UMI). Documents available from BIOSIS Document Express, CASDDS, ADONIS. ***Separated from*** *Journal of the Society of Cosmetic Chemists, 0037-9832.*
Desc: Presents current scientific research, both pure and applied, in cosmetics, toiletries, perfumery and allied fields. Specific subject areas include: human and animal testing of skin, hair and oral products; physical chemistry and technology of emulsion of dispersed systems; theory application of surface-active agents; aerosol technology; new developments in olfactive research and selected aspects of analytical chemistry.
Ind/Abst ADONIS; Biol. Abstr.; Chem. Abstr.; Curr. Biotechnol.; Curr. Cit.; EMBASE [Select. Cov.]; Int. Pharm. Abstr.; PESTDOC; Sci. Cit. Index (19??-19??); SCISEARCH.

LC TT950 **ISSN** 0887-9788
DD 646.72 US
IOWA STYLE. Added/Corp National Hairdressers and Cosmetologists Association of Iowa. (198?)-. Periodical. English. Six times a year. $4.00 (members), $6.50 (nonmembers). National Hairdressers and Cosmetologists Association of Iowa, 315 Eddy Place, Maquoketa IA 52060. ***Continues*** *Iowa Coiffeur News.*

LC TP670 **ISSN** 0003-021X
DD 665 US
CCC
CODEN JJASDH
Pr Rev.
JOURNAL OF THE AMERICAN OIL CHEMISTS' SOCIETY. (JAOCS, JOURNAL OF THE AMERICAN OIL CHEMISTS' SOCIETY.). [J. Am. Oil Chem. Soc.]. **Added/Corp** American Oil Chemists' Society. **VFOAT** Journal of the American Oil Chemists' Society. Vol. 57 (Jan. 1980)-. Academic Scholarly Publication. English. Twelve times a year. $195.00. American Oil Chemists Society, PO Box 3489, Champaign IL 61826-3489. **Tel** (217)359-2344, FAX (217)351-8091, telex 4938651 AOCS UI. **ED** Thomas Applewhite. Index available. cum. index. **Circ:** 5,000. available on microfilm and microfiche from University Microfilms International (UMI). Documents available from Article Express International, The Genuine Article, BIOSIS Document Express, CASDDS. ***Continues*** *Journal of the American Oil Chemists' Society, 0003-021X.*
Desc: Fats and oil technology including about 20 papers per month.
Ind/Abst Abstr. Bull. Inst. Pap. Sci. Tech.; AGRICOLA [Select. Cov.]; Agrofor. Abstr.; Anal. Abstr.; Appl. Sci. Technol. Index; AQUAREF; Art Archaeol. Tech. Abstr.; BioBusiness; Biodeter. Abstr. (19??-19??); Bioeng. Abstr.; Biol. Abstr.; Chem Inform; Chem. Abstr.; Chem. Titles; Coal Abstr.; Crop Physiol. Abstr.; Curr. Biotechnol.; Curr. Cit.; Dairy Sci. Abstr.; Ei Page One; EMBASE; Energy Res. Abstr.; Eng. Index Annu.; Field Crop Abstr.; Food Sci. Technol. Abstr.; For. Abstr.; Grass. Forage Abstr.; Hortic. Abstr.; INIS Atomindex [Micro.]; Leadscan; Maize Abstr.; Mass Spect. Bull.; NAPRALERT; Nutr. Abstr. Rev., Ser. B, Live Feeds and Feed.; Nutr. Abstr. Rev., Ser. A, Hum. Exp.; Life Sci. Collect.; PESTDOC; Plant Breed. Abstr.; Plant Genet. Resour. Abstr.; Plant Grow. Reg. Abstr.; Postharvest News Inf.; Potato Abstr.; Proc. Chem. Eng.; Ref. Upd. Deluxe Ed.; Res. Alert [Full Cov.]; Rev. Med. Vet. Mycology; Rev. Plant Pathol.; Rice Abstr.; Sci. Cit. Index; SCISEARCH; Seed Abstr.; Soyabean Abstr.; Sug. Indus. Abstr.; Surf. Treat. Technol. Abstr.; Text. Technol. Dig.; Theor. Chem. Eng.; World Surf. Coat. Abstr.; World Text. Abstr.

LC TP983.A1 S6 **ISSN** 0037-9832
DD 668 US
CCC
NLM W1 JO954T **CODEN** JSCCA5
Pr Rev.
JOURNAL OF THE SOCIETY OF COSMETIC CHEMISTS. [J. Soc. Cosmet. Chem.]. **Added/Corp** Society of Cosmetic Chemists (U.S.). Vol. 1, No. 1 (July 1947)-. Periodical. English. Six times a year. $110.00. Society of Cosmetic Chemists, 120 Wall Street, Suite 2400, New York NY 10005. **Tel** (212)668-1500. **ED** Frank Girard. (bound in last issue). cum. index. **Bk Rev. Ad Acc. Circ:** 4,200. Documents available from The Genuine Article, BIOSIS Document Express, CASDDS. ***Continued in part by*** *International Journal of Cosmetic Science, 0142-5463.*
Desc: Scientific research/cosmetic science.
Ind/Abst Biol. Abstr.; Chem. Abstr.; Curr. Cit.; Curr. Contents Life Sci.; EMBASE; Int. Pharm. Abstr.; NAPRALERT; Res. Alert [Full Cov.]; Saf. Health Work; Sci. Cit. Index; SCISEARCH.

LC TT955 **ISSN** 0165-2192
DD 646.72 NE
UDC 665.5
KOSMETIEK. [Kosmetiek]. (1972)-. Periodical. Dutch. Eleven times a year (monthly with July/Aug. combined). Fl70.75. Nassauplein Publikaties, Postbus 765, 2270 AT Voorburg Netherlands. **Tel** 011 31 70 3368195.

Beauty and Cosmetics

LC TT955
DD 646.72
GW
KOSMETIK INTERNATIONAL. Vol. 26, No. 287 (July 1976)-. Periodical. German. Twelve times a year. $105.94. Tessner Verlag, Schulstrasse 12, Postfach 2280, 7570 Baden-Baden Germany. **Tel** 011 49 7221 65027, FAX 011 49 7221 61859. **Bk Rev. Ad Acc. Circ:** 22,000 (ctrl). *Continues Kosmetikerinnen-Fachzeitung.*
Desc: Professional journal for aestheticians, beauticians, perfumery and toiletry-branch.

DD 746
ISSN 8755-4313
US
LC & YOU. [LC you]. **VFOAT** L.C. and You; LC and You. **VAT** Lori Chapman and You. Vol. 1, No. 1 (198?)-. Periodical. English. Four times a year. $9.00. Lori Chapman and Company, 260 South Beverly Drive/Suite 303, Beverly Hills CA 90212. **Tel** (310)278-6733. **ED** Lori Chapman, Shirley Mask, Winona Johnson and Gwen Roland. **Bk Rev. Ad Acc. Circ:** 10,000.
Desc: Covers fashion and beauty.

LC TP
DD 660
UDC 646.4
ISSN 0024-936X
GW
MADAME. (1952)-. Periodical. German. Twelve times a year. $101.33. Magazinpresse Verlag GmbH, Postfach 201441, D-80014 Munich Germany. **Tel** 011 49 89 55135180.

LC AP2 .M2334
DD 051
ISSN 0024-9394
US
MADEMOISELLE (NEW YORK, N.Y. 1935). See General Interest-General Interest-North America.

LC TT950
DD 646.72
ISSN 1352-755X
UK
●**MARIE CLAIRE HEALTH AND BEAUTY.** [Marie Claire health beauty]. (1994)-. Consumer Publication. English. Twelve times a year. IPC Magazines Ltd., Perrymount Road, Haywards Heath, West Sussex RH16 3DH United Kingdom. **Tel** 011 44 1444 440421, FAX 011 44 1444 445599.

LC TT500 .M2
DD 051
ISSN 0024-8908
US
CODEN MCCAEQ
MCCALL'S. See Women's Interests.

LC TP983.A6 S65a
DD 668/.55/06073
ISSN 0730-7756
US
MEMBERSHIP DIRECTORY / SOCIETY OF COSMETIC CHEMISTS. Main/Corp Society of Cosmetic Chemists (U.S.). (19??)-. Directory. English. Irregular. Society of Cosmetic Chemists, 120 Wall Street, Suite 2400, New York NY 10005. **Tel** (212)668-1500.

LC TT950 .M55
DD 646.724
KO
MIYONG SAENGHWAL. Vol. 1 (1984)-. Periodical. Korean. Twelve times a year. W3,000 each issue. Chusik Hoesa Yowon, 511 Socho-dong Kangnam-ku, Seoul 135 Korea.

LC AP
DD 051
FR
MODELE MAGAZINE. French. Twelve times a year. 285.00F (one-year), 520.00F (two-year) France; 340.00F (one-year), 640.00 (two-year) other. Editions Lariviere Naryse Menn, 15 17 Quai de l Oise Sec. Abonn., 75166 Paris Cedex 19 France. **Tel** 011 33 1 40342207, FAX 011 33 1 40358441, telex 211678.

LC RL76.A1 M6
DD 646.7/2/05
ISSN 0148-4001
US
CCC
MODERN SALON. [Mod. salon]. Vol. 63, No. 8 (Aug. 1977)-. Periodical. English. Twelve times a year. $20.00. Vance Publishing Corporation, 400 Knightsbridge Parkway, Lincolnshire IL 60069. **Tel** (708)255-5113, (708)634-2600. available on microfilm and microfiche from University Microfilms International (UMI). *Continues Modern Beauty Shop.*

LC TP1101
DD 668.54
NLM W1 FO404 v.12 suppl. etc.
ISSN 0276-704X
UK
MONOGRAPHS ON FRAGRANCE RAW MATERIALS. [Monogr. fragr. raw mater.]. **VFOAT** Fragrance Raw Materials Monographs. (Dec. 1974)-. Monographic series. English. Price varies per volume. Pergamon Press, An Imprint of Elsevier Science Ltd., The Boulevard, Langford Lane, Kidlington, Oxford OX5 1GB United Kingdom. **Tel** 011 44 1865 843000, 011 44 1865 843699, FAX 011 44 1865 843010. **ED** D L J Opdyke.

LC WMLC L 83/4536
US
N.H.C.A. BULLETIN / NATIONAL HAIRDRESSERS & COSMETOLOGISTS' ASSOCIATION, INC. Main/Corp National Hairdressers and Cosmetologists Association. **VFOAT** NHCA Bulletin. English. Twelve times a year. National Hairdressers and Cosmetologists Association of Iowa, 315 Eddy Place, Maquoketa IA 52060.

DD 646
US
Pr Rev.
NAILPRO (VAN NUYS, CALIF.). (NAILPRO). [Nailpro]. (Feb. 1990)-. Trade Publication. English. Twelve times a year. $31.00. Creative Age Publications, 7628 Densmore Avenue, Van Nuys CA 91406. **Tel** (800)624-4196. **ED** Barbara Feiner.
Desc: Covers the technical, business and management aspects of the nail-care industry, with emphasis on how to effectively build a nail salon business.

LC TT950
DD 646.72
UDC 391
ISSN 1021-8513
SA
●**NEW SALON.** (1993)-. Periodical. English. Irregular. Rs100.00. New Salon Publishing, PO Box 1707, Fourways 2005 South Africa. **Tel** 011 27 11 78936189, 011 27 11 4654275, FAX 011 27 11 7893589, telex 08255549336. **ED** Minx W. Olivier. **Ad Acc, Adv Mgr:** Robert Nel and Karen Staats.

LC RS
DD 615.1
UDC 615.1
ISSN 0927-0574
NE
NIEUWE DROGIST. See Pharmacy and Pharmacology.

LC TP983 .A29
DD 661.8
JA
NIHON KOSHOHIN KAGAKUKAI SHI. **VFOAT** Journal of Japanese Cosmetic Science Society; Koshohin Kagakukai Shi. (1977)-. Academic Scholarly Publication. Japanese (summaries and/or abstracts in English). Nihon Koshohin Kagalilao, c/o Nihon Mohatsu Kagaku Kyokai, 22-2 Yoyogi, 1 Shibuya-ku Tokyo Japan. Documents available from CASDDS.
Ind/Abst Chem. Abstr.

DD 646
ISSN 1043-9641
FR
NOUVELLES ESTHETIQUES (AMERICAN ED.), LES. (LES NOUVELLES ESTHETIQUES.). [Nouv. esthet.]. (198?)-. Trade Publication. English. Twelve times a year. $45.00. Nouvelles Esthetiques, 7 Ave Stephane Mallarme, 75017 Paris France. **Tel** 011 33 1 43800647, FAX 011 33 1 43808363. (**Subscription address:** Nouvelles Esthetiques Inc, 306 Alcazar Avenue, Suite 204, Coral Gables FL 33134. **Tel** (800)775-3072, (305)443-2322.)

LC TT950
DD 646.72
FR
NOUVELLES ESTHETIQUES (FRENCH ED.), LES. (LES NOUVELLES ESTHETIQUES.). (198?)-. Trade Publication. French. Eleven times a year. 410.00F. Nouvelles Esthetiques, 7 Ave Stephane Mallarme, 75017 Paris France. **Tel** 011 33 1 43800647, FAX 011 33 1 43808363. **ED** H. Pierantoni. **Bk Rev. Ad Acc.**
Desc: Trade magazine for beauty therapists.

LC TT950
DD 646.72
FR
NOUVELLES ESTHETIQUES (ITALIAN ED.), LES. (NOUVELLES ESTHETIQUES.). (198?)-. Trade Publication. Multiple languages. Six times a year. 60.00F single copy, France; 390.00F US. Nouvelles Esthetiques, 7 Ave Stephane Mallarme, 75017 Paris France. **Tel** 011 33 1 43800647, FAX 011 33 1 43808363. **Circ:** 14,000.

LC TT950
DD 646.72
AU
OESTERREICHISCHE FRISEUR. (19??)-. Periodical. German. Twelve times a year. $50.19. Der Osterriche Friseur, Mollardgasse 1, A-1060 Vienna Austria. **Tel** 011 43 1 5870420. **ED** Lui Vehzely. **Ad Acc. Circ:** 5,300.
Desc: Articles, hair fashion, dates, presentation and description of new products, photographs, and information on competitions and events.

LC RS
DD 615.1/0212
ISSN 0823-7492
CN
PAGIDEX. See Pharmacy and Pharmacology.

LC TP1101
DD 668.54
AU
PARFUMERIE, DIE. Added/Corp Osterreichischer Parfumeriefachhandel. (19??)-. Periodical. German. Twelve times a year. Osterreich Wirtschaftsverlag, Nibelungenfergasse 7-11, A-1501 Vienna Austria. **Tel** 0222/55-55-85.

LC TP983 .A37
DD 661.8
ISSN 0031-1952
GW
CCC
CODEN PAKOAL
PARFUMERIE UND KOSMETIK. [Parfum. Kosmet.]. **Added/Corp** Verband der Korperpflegemittel-Industrie. Vol. 14, No. 13 (1938)-. Trade Publication. German. Twelve times a year. $200.00. Dr. Alfred Huethig Verlag GmbH, Postfach 102869, D-69018 Heidelberg Germany. **Tel** 011 49 6221 489251, FAX 011 49 6221 489279. (**Subscription address:** Huethig Publishing Inc., 29 Macintosh Drive, Oxford CT 06478. **Tel** (203)881-2647.) **ED** Gustav A. Nowak and Anneliese Matyssek. Index available. **Bk Rev. Ad Acc. Circ:** 4,200. Documents available from CASDDS. *Continues Deutsche Parfumerie-Zeitung.*
Desc: International journal for scientific and technical fundamentals of the perfumery and cosmetics industry.
Ind/Abst Chem. Abstr.; Curr. Cit.; EMBASE; Infomat Int. Bus.; Int. Pharm. Abstr.; Life Sci. Collect.; PESTDOC.

LC TP983 .P23
DD 668/.5/0944
ISSN 0337-3029
FR
CCC
CODEN PCARDV
PARFUMS, COSMETIQUES, AROMES. [Parfums, cosmet., aromes]. (Jan./Feb. 1975)-. Periodical. French. Six times a year. 778.65F France; 875.00F other. Societe d Expansion Technique et Economique, 5 rue de Seze, 75009 Paris France. **Tel** 011 33 16 44945060, telex 650 896 F. Documents available from CASDDS. *Continues Parfums, Cosmetiques, Savons de France, 0031-1960.*
Ind/Abst Anal. Abstr.; Chem. Abstr.; Chem. Bus. Bull.; Chem. Bus. NewsBase (1985-); Chem. Bus. Update; Curr. Cit.; F&S Index Plus Text, Int. [Select. Cov.]; PROMT.

LC TP1101
DD 668.54
SP
PELUQUERIAS. Trade Publication. Spanish (English, French and Italian). Eleven times a year (not published in August). 6507ptas Spain; $69.00 other. Peluquerias, Alcolea 43, 08014 Barcelona Spain. **Tel** 011 34 3 3394907, FAX 011 34 3 4111994. **ED** Juan Prat. **Ad Acc. Circ:** 30,000.
Desc: Album of hairstyles, technicals of how-to styles, fashion hair reports from New York, London, Paris, and information of interest to hairdressers and salon owners.

LC TP983 .A425
DD 668/.54/05
ISSN 0272-2666
US
CCC
CODEN PEFLDI
PERFUMER & FLAVORIST. [Perfum. flavor.]. **VAT** Perfumer and Flavorist. Vol. 5, No. 1 (Feb./March 1980)-. Trade Publication. English. Six times a year. $110.00. Allured Publishing Corporation, 362 South Schmale Road, Carol Stream IL 60188-2787. **Tel** (708)653-2155, FAX (708)653-2192. **ED** Stanley E. Allured. Index available (bound in Jan. issue). **Ad Acc. Circ:** 1,700. available on microfilm and microfiche from University Microfilms International (UMI). Documents available from BIOSIS Document Express. *Continues Perfumer & Flavorist International, 0361-8587.*
Desc: Technical and commercial news of essential oils, chemicals and spices used in flavor and fragrance industry.
Ind/Abst AGRICOLA; Biol. Abstr.; Chemorecept. Abstr.; Curr. Cit.; Food Sci. Technol. Abstr.; Foods Adlibra; Int. Pharm. Abstr.; Life Sci. Collect.

DD 615
ISSN 1049-9156
US
CCC
CODEN PLPREY
PHARMACEUTICAL PROCESSING. See Pharmacy and Pharmacology.

DD 646.7/05
ISSN 0704-7908
CN
PRESTIGE BEAUTE. Vol. 1 (Winter 1977/78)-. Periodical. French. Four times a year. $2.00 per number. Productions Prestige, Prestige Beaute, CP 240 Succursale K, Montreal Quebec H1N 3L1 Canada.

DD 646.7/24
ISSN 0714-850X
CN
PREUVES (MONTREAL). (PREUVES). [Preuves]. Vol. 1, No. 1 (1982)-. Periodical. French. Six times a year. Les Editions Dachel Inc, Bureau 2-342 East, rue Sherbrooke, Montreal Quebec H2X 1E6 Canada.
Ind/Abst Romant. Move.

LC RA778
DD 646.7/042
ISSN 0889-9495
US
RADIANCE. [Radiance]. Vol. 1, No. 1 (Fall 1984)-. Periodical. English. Four times a year (Mar., June, Sept., Dec.). $20.00. Radiance Magazine, PO Box 30246, Oakland CA 94604. **Tel** (510)482-0680, (510)482-0680. **ED** Alice Ansfield and Catherine Taylor. **Bk Rev**, (Qty: 8-10). **Ad Acc. Circ:** 40,000.
Desc: Directed at large women, this magazine strives to be a source of support, information and inspiration. Each issue features articles on health, media, fashion, politics and more.

LC TT953.F6 A3
DD 646.7061759
US
REPORT - FLORIDA. STATE BOARD OF BEAUTY CULTURE. Main/Corp Florida. State Board of Beauty Culture. Government Publication. English. Irregular. Florida State Board of Cosmetology, Tallahassee FL 32301. **Tel** (904)488-5702.

LC AP
DD 051
MX
REVISTA TU. See Women's Interests.

Beauty and Cosmetics

LC TP670
DD 665
ISSN 0392-0445
IT
CODEN RIEPD7

RIVISTA ITALIANA EPPOS. (RIVISTA ITALIANA EPPOS: PUBBLICAZIONE TECNICO-SCIENTIFICA.). [Riv. ital. EPPOS]. **VFOAT** EPPOS; Rivista Italiana E.P.P.O.S.: EPPOS : Rivista Italiana. **VAT** Rivista Italiana Essenze, Profumi, Piante Officinali, Aromi, Saponi, Cosmetici, Aerosol. (1980)-. Academic Scholarly Publication. Italian (English, French, German and Spanish). L150000 (4 issues). Cooperativa CDA Srl, Via Volta 12, 20060 Cassina Pecchi Italy. **Tel** 011 39 2 9522360. (**Subscription address:** Fructamine SPA, via Capitani di Mozzo, 24030 Mozzo BG Italy. **Tel** 011 39 35 468511.) Documents available from CASDDS. Continues Rivista Italiana, Essenze, Profumi, Piante Officinali, Aromi, Saponi, Cosmetici, Aerosols, 0391-4658.
Ind/Abst Chem. Abstr.; Hortic. Abstr.; Int. Pharm. Abstr.

LC TT950
DD 646.7
ISSN 1197-1495
CN

●**SALON MAGAZINE.** [Salon mag.]. (1993)-. Periodical. English. Six times a year. 22.73Can$. Salon Communications Inc, 146 Parliament Street, Toronto Ontario M5A 2Z1 Canada. **Tel** (416)869-3131, FAX (416)869-3008. **ED** Alison Wood. **Bk Rev**. **Ad Acc**. **Circ**: 27,000 (ctrl).

LC TT950
DD 646.7
ISSN 1044-8616
US

SALON NEWS MAGAZINE. **VFOAT** Salon News. (1991)-. Periodical. English. Four times a year. $2.95. Salon News, 1431 Washington Boulevard, Suite 2411, Detroit MI 48226.

LC TT950
DD 646.7
ISSN 0743-6394
US

SALON TODAY. [Salon today]. Vol. 1, No. 1 (1983)-. Trade Publication. English. Six times a year. $42.00. Vance Publishing Corporation, 400 Knightsbridge Parkway, Lincolnshire IL 60069. **Tel** (800)255-5113, (708)634-2600. Index available ($5.00 extra).

LC TT950
DD 646.7
US

●**SALONOVATIONS.** (1994)-. English. Twelve times a year. $19.95. Milady Publishing Corporation, 220 White Plains Road, 4th Floor, Tarrytown NY 10591. **Tel** (212)881-3000.

LC RA778.A1 S44
DD 613/.04244
ISSN 0149-0699
US

SELF (NEW YORK). See Women's Interests.

LC TT950
DD 646.7
US

SHOPTALK. **VFOAT** Shop Talk. Vol. 1, No. 1 (Spring 1982)-. Trade Publication. English. Eight times a year. $42.00. ShopTalk Publications Inc, 8825 South Greenwood Avenue, Chicago IL 60619. **Tel** (312)978-6400.
Ind/Abst MasterFile FullTEXT (Jan. 1993-).

DD 391
ISSN 1071-7684
US

●**SKIN & INK.** [Skin ink]. **VFOAT** Skin and Ink. (1993)-. Periodical. English. Six times a year. $19.95. LFP Inc, 8484 Wilshire Boulevard, Suite 900, Beverly Hills CA 90210. **Tel** (213)651-5400.

DD 668
ISSN 0091-1372
US
CODEN SCCSC8
Pr Rev.

SOAP, COSMETICS, CHEMICAL SPECIALTIES. [Soap cosmet. chem. spec.]. **Added/Corp** Chemical Specialties Manufacturers Association. **VFOAT** Soap/Cosmetics/Chemical Specialties. Vol. 47, No. 7 (July 1971)-. Academic Scholarly Publication. English. Twelve times a year. $60.00. PTN Publishing Company, 445 Broad Hollow Road, Melville NY 11747. **Tel** (516)845-2700, FAX (516)845-7109. **ED** Janet Donohue. **Ad Acc**. **Circ**: 14,000 (ctrl). available on microfilm and microfiche from University Microfilms International (UMI); available on an online database (file 648/Full-Text) from DIALOG. Documents available from The Genuine Article, CASDDS, Documents on Demand. Continues Soap & Chemical Specialties, 0037-7481.
Desc: Covers product and process developments, personnel news in soap and detergent, cosmetics and toiletries and household products industries.
Ind/Abst BioBusiness (1989-); Bus. ASAP (1990-) [Full Txt.]; Bus. Index (1985-); Chem. Abstr.; Chem. Ind. Notes; Curr. Cit.; Curr. Contents Eng. Comput. Technol.; EMBASE; Energy Inf. Abstr.; Environ. Abstr.; EP Collect.; F&S Index Plus Text, Int. [Select. Cov.]; Gen. BusinessFile (1985-); Gen. Period. Index (1985-); Homework Help.; Int. Packag. Abstr.; Mag. Search; MasterFile FullTEXT 1000; MasterFile FullTEXT 350; MasterFile FullTEXT 650; MasterFile FullTEXT (July 1993-); OCLC; PROMT; Res. Alert [Select. Cov.]; Telebase; Trade Ind. ASAP [Full Txt.]; Trade Ind. Index [Full Txt.]; Vocat. Search.

DD 646
ISSN 1042-5276
US

SOPHISTICATE'S BLACK HAIR STYLES AND CARE GUIDE. **VFOAT** Black Hair Styles and Care Guide. (198?)-. Periodical. English. Six times a year. $19.00. Associated Publishing Inc, 1165 North Clark Street, Suite 607, Chicago IL 60610. **Tel** (312)266-8680.

LC TT950
DD 646.7
US

SOPHISTICATE'S HAIRSTYLE GUIDE/1,001 IDEAS. (19??)-. Periodical. English. Six times a year. $17.65. Associated Publications Incorporated / Illinois, 1165 North Clark Street/Suite 607, Chicago IL 60610. **Tel** (312)266-8680.

DD 646.72
ISSN 0036-0759
SA

SOUTH AFRICAN HAIRDRESSING AND BEAUTY CULTURE. [S. Afr. Hairdressing Beauty Cult.]. (1946)-. Trade Publication. English. Twelve times a year. $27.43. George Warman Publications Pty, PO Box 704, Cape Town 8000 South Africa. **Tel** 011 27 21 245320, FAX 011 27 21 261332, telex 5-21849. **Ad Acc**. **Circ**: 2,200 (ctrl).

LC TP1101
DD 668.54
NLM W1 S54
ISSN 0037-749X
UK
CODEN SSPCD2

SPC. SOAP, PERFUMERY, AND COSMETICS. [SPC. soap, perfum., cosmet.]. Vol. 48, No. 3 (Mar. 1975)-. Trade Publication. English. Twelve times a year. $232.72. Wilmington Publishing Ltd., PO Box 200, Field End Road, Ruislip Middlesex HA4 0SY United Kingdom. **Tel** 011 44 181 8413970, FAX 011 44 181 8419676. available on an online database (file 648/Full-Text) from DIALOG. Continues Soap, Perfumery & Cosmetics.
Ind/Abst BioBusiness (1988-); Chem. Bus. Bull. (19??-); Chem. Bus. NewsBase (1985-); Chem. Bus. Update (19??-); Curr. Cit.; EP Collect.; F&S Index Plus Text, Int. (19??-) [Select. Cov.]; Homework Help.; Int. Packag. Abstr.; Int. Pharm. Abstr. (19??-); MasterFile FullTEXT 1000; MasterFile FullTEXT 350; MasterFile FullTEXT 650 (July 1994-); PROMT (19??-); Telebase; Trade Ind. ASAP (19??-) [Full Txt.]; Trade Ind. Index (19??-) [Full Txt.]; Vocat. Search.

LC TT950
DD 646.72
UDC 06
ISSN 0920-7783
NE

STICHTING & VERENIGING. [Sticht. ver.]. (1987)-. Periodical. Dutch. Six times a year. $82.22. Libresso BV, Postbus 878, 7400 GA Deventer Netherlands. **Tel** 011 31 5700 47421.

LC TT950
DD 646.72
ISSN 1044-8608
US

STYLES MAGAZINE. **VFOAT** Styles. (1991)-. Periodical. English. Four times a year. Salon News, 1431 Washington Boulevard, Suite 2411, Detroit MI 48226.

LC TT950
DD 646.72
GW

STYLISTE, LE. (19??)-. French. Two times a year. DM180.00. Mode Information Heinz Kramer, POB 1180, D-51491 Overath Germany. **Tel** 011 49 2206 60070.

LC TT950
DD 646.72
UDC 668.5
ISSN 0751-5774
FR

SUFFRAGES. (Suffrages). (1963)-. Periodical. French. Irregular (6 issues). 245.00F France; 275.00F other. SEMP - Societe d'Editions Modernes Parisienne, 38 rue Jean Mermoz, 75008 Paris France. **Tel** 011 33 1 42669236, FAX 011 33 1 42666064, telex 650016.

DD 646
ISSN 1042-3036
US

TAN MAGAZINE. [Tan mag.]. **VFOAT** Tan. Jan./Feb. 1989-. Periodical. English. Six times a year. $12.00 US; $17.00 other. Tan Magazine, 3131 Page Avenue, Jackson MI 49203. **Tel** (517)784-1772. **ED** Karen France Unruh. **Ad Acc**.
Desc: Especially for customers of tanning salons, this magazine covers health, nutrition, body wraps, spas, travel and tanning indoors and outdoors.

DD 646
ISSN 1062-2748
US

TODAY'S BEAUTY TRENDS. (TODAY'S BEAUTY TRENDS : HAIR, FASHION, PROFILES, EVENTS.). [Today's beauty trends]. **VFOAT** TBT. (1992)-. Periodical. English. Twelve times a year. $2.00. Myra Nicholas, PO Box 18867, Washington DC 20036-8867.

LC HD9970.5.T65 T64
DD 380.1/456685/029473
ISSN 0273-4540
US

TOILETRY AND BEAUTY AIDS MARKET. Vol. 1 (1978)-. Trade Publication. English. One time a year. IMS America Ltd, Butler Pike & Maple Avenue, Ambler PA 19002.

LC TT950
DD 646.72
UDC 687.53
ISSN 0178-9805
GW

TOP HAIR. [Top hair]. (1985)-. Periodical. German. Twenty-four times a year. $144.63. Magazinpresse Verlag GmbH, Postfach 201441, D-80014 Munich Germany. **Tel** 011 49 89 55135180. Formed by the union of DFZ. Deutsche Friseur-Zeitung, 0724-9799 and FH. Friseurhandwerk, Friseurspiegel, 0016-1454.

DD 391/.005
ISSN 0821-7955
CN

TORONTO LIFE FASHION. [Tor. life fash.]. Fall Ed. (1979)-. Periodical. English. Seven times a year. 9.61Can$. Toronto Life, 59 Front Street East, Toronto Ontario M5E 1B3 Canada. **Tel** (416)364-3333, FAX (416)861-1169. Continues Toronto Life Fashion Magazine, 0705-2715.
Ind/Abst Can. Index (?-?).

LC TP110
DD 668.54
ISSN 0939-0448
GW
CCC

TW DERMATOLOGIE : ARZTLICHE KOSMETOLOGIE. **VFOAT** Arztliche Kosmetologie. (1990)-. Trade Publication. German (summaries and/or abstracts in English; table of contents in English). Six times a year. $68.32. G. Braun Verlag, Postfach 1709, D-76006 Karlsruhe Germany. **Tel** 011 49 721 165392. Continues Arztliche Kosmetologie, 0340-5702.

LC TT950
DD 646.72
FR
CEASED

USA NEWS CATEGORY A; MAKE-UP FACE TREATMENT. (19??)-(1995). English (French). Cosmetic Research International, 10 rue Louis Philippe, 92200 Neuilly France. **Tel** 011 33 1 46242467.
Desc: Information about new products along with photos, major claims, listing of ingredients, etc.

LC TT950
DD 646.72
FR
CEASED

USA NEWS CATEGORY C, FRAGRANCES AND MENS LINES. (19??)-(1995). English (French). Cosmetic Research International, 10 rue Louis Philippe, 92200 Neuilly France. **Tel** 011 33 1 46242467.
Desc: Information about new products including photos, major claims, listing of ingredients, etc.

LC TT500 .V714
DD 646/.34/05
ISSN 0042-8027
IT

VOGUE. See Women's Interests.

LC TT500
DD 646/.34/05
UK

VOGUE. (BRITISH EDITION). See Women's Interests.

LC TT500
DD 646/.34/05
UDC 391:687
ISSN 0176-6104
GW

VOGUE MUENCHEN. See Women's Interests.

LC TT500 .V7
DD 646/.34/05
ISSN 0042-8000
US

VOGUE (NEW YORK). See Women's Interests.

LC TT500 .V716
DD 391/.2/05
FR

VOGUE PARIS. See Women's Interests.

LC RA778.A1 V6
DD 613
ISSN 0042-8965
FR

VOTRE BEAUTE, VOTRE SANTE. (19??)-. Periodical. French. Ten times a year. $45.00. SEMP - Societe d'Editions Modernes Parisienne, 38 rue Jean Mermoz, 75008 Paris France. **Tel** 011 33 1 42669236, FAX 011 33 1 42666064, telex 650016. Continues Votre Beaute.

DD 646.7/242/05
ISSN 0705-3037
CN

YOU (VANCOUVER). (YOU.). Vol. 1 (Dec. 1977)-. Periodical. English. Twelve times a year. 12.00Can$ Canada; 15.00Can$ US; 18.00Can$ other. You Magazine, 1658 Robson Street, Vancouver British Columbia V6G 1C7 Canada.

BICYCLES AND CYCLING

ISSN 1074-4983
DD 388 US
AMERICAN BICYCLIST MAGAZINE. [Am. bicycl. mag.]. (199?)-. Periodical. English. Twelve times a year. Cycling Press Inc, 80 8th Avenue, Suite 305, New York NY 10011. **Tel** (212)206-7230, FAX (212)633-0079. ***Continues*** *American Bicyclist and Motorcyclist, 0002-7677.*

LC WMLC L 83/9179
US
AMERICAN BIG TWIN DEALER. (Fall 1990)-. Trade Publication. English. Six times a year. Advanstar Communications, Inc (Santa Ana), 201 Sandpointe Avenue, Suite 600, Santa Ana CA 92705. **Tel** (714) 513-8400, FAX (714) 513-8414. **ED** Robin Hartfiel. **Ad Acc. Circ:** 5,000 (ctrl).

LC GV **ISSN** 8750-5827
DD 796 US
TITLE CHANGE
AMERICAN BMXER (MEMBERSHIP EDITION). (AMERICAN BMXER.). [Am. BMXer, Membersh. ed.]. **Added/Corp** American Bicycle Association. (198?)-(1994). Periodical. English. American Bicycle Association, PO Box 718, Chandler AZ 85224. ***Continues*** *ABA Action.* ***Continued by*** *BMXer, 1081-4108.*

ISSN 8756-5358
DD 796 US
AMERICAN BMXER (NEWSSTAND EDITION). (AMERICAN BMXER.). (1984)-. Periodical. English. Twelve times a year. $20.00 US; $25.00 other. Competition Publications, Box 718, Chandler AZ 85244. ***Continues*** *Bicycles and Dirt Magazine, 8750-426X.*

LC GV1040 .N67a
DD 796.6/09756 US
ANNUAL REPORT, BICYCLE ADVISORY COMMITTEE. **Main/Corp** North Carolina. Dept. of Transportation. Bicycle Advisory Committee. (1975)-. English. One time a year. North Carolina Department of Transportation and Highway Safety, PO Box 25201, Raleigh NC 27611.

LC GV1040
DD 796.60994 AT
AUSTRALIAN CYCLIST. [Aust. cycl.]. (1989)-. English. Six times a year (Feb., Apr., June, Aug., Oct., Dec.). 20.00Aus$ Australia; 30.00Aus$ Asia and Oceania; 40.00Aus$ other. Bicycle Federation of Australia, PO Box 869, Artarmon New South Wales 2064 Australia. **Tel** 011 61 2 4195419, FAX 011 61 2 4151913. **ED** Neil Irvine. **Bk Rev**, (Qty: 6). **Ad Acc, Adv Mgr:** David Turner, **Tel** 02 913 1266. **Circ:** 20,000 (ctrl). available in braille (floppy disk) from the publisher. ***Continues*** *Push On, 0157-0994.*
Desc: Focuses on cycling for transport and recreation with product reviews, advocacy, travel, bicycle road tests, and environmental perspective.
Ind/Abst SPORT Discus.

ISSN 1072-1061
DD 380 US
BDS (CULVER CITY, CALIF.). (BDS.). [BDS]. (199?)-. Periodical. English. Twelve times a year. Miramar Publishing Company, 6133 Bristol Parkway, PO Box 3640, Culver City CA 90231. **Tel** (800)543-4116, (310)337-9717. ***Continues*** *Bicycle Dealer Showcase, 0361-381X.*

LC GV1040
DD 796.6 IT
BICICLETTA. Italian. Bicicletta, Via Della Maratona 66, 00184 Rome Italy.

LC HE5614.3.I8 I57C
DD 312/.4/409777 US
BICYCLE ACCIDENT STATISTICS. **See** Sports and Games-Abstracting, Bibliographies and Statistics.

ISSN 0272-8516
US
BICYCLE BLUE BOOK. BICYCLE SPECIFICATION GUIDE. **VFOAT** Bicycle Specification Guide; United States Bicycle Specification Guide. (1981)-. English. Four times a year. $9.95 per issue. Bicycle Blue Book, PO Box 1555, Palo Alto CA 94302.

LC GV1040 **ISSN** 0272-8524
DD 796.6 US
BICYCLE BLUE BOOK. UNITED STATES BICYCLE TRADE INDEX. **VFOAT** United States Bicycle Trade Index. (1981)-. English. Two times a year. $4.95 per issue. Bicycle Blue Book, PO Box 1555, Palo Alto CA 94302.

LC GV1040 **ISSN** 0745-8126
DD 796.6 US
BICYCLE BUSINESS JOURNAL. [Bicycl. bus. j.]. (198?)-. Trade Publication. English. Twelve times a year. $22.00. Quinn Publications, 1904 Wenneca Street, Ft Worth TX 76102. **Tel** (817)870-0341, FAX (817)332-1619. **ED** Rix Quinn. Index available. **Ad Acc. Circ:** 10,000. ***Continues*** *Bicycle Journal, 0006-2065.*
Desc: News of interest to bicycle dealers.

LC HD9999.B43 U64 **ISSN** 0361-381X
DD 380.1/45/62922720973 US
TITLE CHANGE
BICYCLE DEALER SHOWCASE. **VFOAT** BDS. (19??)-(199?). Periodical. English. Miramar Publishing Company, 6133 Bristol Parkway, PO Box 3640, Culver City CA 90231. **Tel** (800)543-4116, (310)337-9717. **ED** Molly Ingram-Trudeau and Patti Fletcher. **Circ:** 10,661. ***Continued by*** *BDS, 1072-1061.*
Desc: Provides bicycle dealers with practical product and business information.
Ind/Abst SportSearch (May 1987-).

LC GV1040 **ISSN** 0193-8177
DD 796.6 US
BICYCLE FORUM. **Added/Corp** Bicycle Federation. No. 1 (Spring 1978)-. Periodical. English. Four times a year (Feb., May, Aug., Nov.). $19.95. Bicycle Federation of America, 1506 21st Street Northwest, Suite 200, Washington DC 20036. **Tel** (202)463-6622, FAX (202)463-6625. **ED** John Williams. **Bk Rev. Ad Acc. Circ:** 1,000.
Desc: This journal covers bicycle advocacy, cyclist training, bikeway planning and gives encouragement.

LC GV1040 .B48 **ISSN** 0889-289X
DD 796.6/05 US
BICYCLE GUIDE. [Bicycle guide]. (1984)-. Periodical. English. Twelve times a year. $19.94. Petersen Publishing Company, 6420 Wilshire Boulevard, Los Angeles CA 90048. **Tel** (213)782-2485, FAX (213)782-2526. **(Subscription address:** Neodata / Colorado, PO Box 2606, Boulder CO 80322. **) ED** Ted Costantino. **Ad Acc. Circ:** 150,000. ***Continues*** *Bicycle Rider, 0895-075X.*
Desc: Covers all aspects of the sport - racing, training, travel, equipment and technique, personalities, and profiles. Each issue explores "how it works" and "how to do it" in order to aid the reader. Contains equipment reviews, fashion previews, technical tips and fitness features.
Ind/Abst SPORT Discus.

ISSN 0950-0669
DD 629.227205 UK
BICYCLE MAGAZINE. [Bicycle mag.]. **VFOAT** Bicycle. (1982)-. Periodical. English. Thirteen times a year. $82.13. Bicycle, Norhtern Shell Bldg, PO Box 381, Millharbour London, E14 9TW United Kingdom. **Tel** 011 44 171 9875090.

LC GV1040 **ISSN** 0742-8308
DD 796.6 US
BICYCLE PAPER, THE. (19??). Periodical. English. Ten times a year. $12.00. Clark McCall Communications, 1535 11th Avenue, Suite 302, Seattle WA 98122. **Tel** (206)323-3301.

LC Z7514.C9 L8 GV1040 **ISSN** 0193-8584
DD 016.7966 US
BICYCLE RESOURCE GUIDE. (1978)-. English. Silers Printing Company, Denver CO. ***Continues*** *Bicycle Bibliography, 0098-1230.*

LC GV1040 **ISSN** 0743-5495
DD 796.6 US
BICYCLE SPORT. Periodical. English. Twelve times a year. $16.50 US; $21.50 Canada. Bicycle Sport, PO Box 315, Mount Morris IL 61054.

LC TE301 .B525 **ISSN** 0275-6390
DD 625.7 US
BICYCLE TRANSPORTATION. (BICYCLE TRANSPORTATION : A REPORT OF THE BICYCLE TRANSPORTATION COMMITTEE, URBAN TRANSPORTATION DIVISION OF THE AMERICAN SOCIETY OF CIVIL ENGINEERS.). **Added/Corp** American Society of Civil Engineers. Bicycle Transportation Committee. (19??)-. English. American Society of Civil Engineers / ASCE, 345 East 47th Street, New York NY 10017-2398. **Tel** (212)705-7179, FAX (212)705-7300, telex 422847 ASCE UI.

LC GV1040 **ISSN** 1065-1802
DD 796.6 US
BICYCLE TRAVELER, THE. (1992)-. Periodical. English. Twelve times a year. $65.00. PKD Publishing Co., 540 Frontage Road, Suite 3140, Northfield IL 60093.

LC GV1045 .A46 **ISSN** 0747-0371
DD 796.6/0973 US
BICYCLE USA. [Bicycle USA]. **Added/Corp** League of American Wheelmen. **VFOAT** Bicycle U.S.A. Vol. 20, No. 1 (Jan. 1984)-. Periodical. English. Eight times a year. $19.00. League of American Wheelmen Inc., 190 West Ostend Street, Suite 120, Baltimore MD 21230. **Tel** (410)439-3399, FAX (410)539-3496. **ED** John Tighe. **Bk Rev. Ad Acc, Adv Mgr:** D. Jones. **Circ:** 23,000 (ctrl). ***Continues*** *American Wheelmen, 0199-2139.*
Desc: Cycling magazine written for and by bicyclists, with the a ride calendar and cycling news from around the globe.
Ind/Abst SPORT Discus.

LC GV1040 **ISSN** 0746-9454
DD 796.6 US
BICYCLES TODAY. **Added/Corp** National Bicycle League. (19??)-. Periodical. English. Twelve times a year. Free on request. National Bicycle League, PO Box 729, 211 Bradenton Ave, Dublin OH 43017. **Tel** (614)766-1625. **ED** Jill L. Geiger. **Circ:** 20,000.
Ind/Abst SportSearch (May 1987-).

LC GV1040 .B5 **ISSN** 0006-2073
DD 796.6 US
CCC
BICYCLING. [Bicycling]. **VFOAT** Bicycling Magazine; Bicycling Plus Mountain Bike. (Dec. 1968)-. Periodical. English. Eleven times a year. $19.97. Rodale Press Inc., 400 South 10th Street, Emmaus PA 18098. **Tel** (610)967-5171, (800)666-2503, FAX (610)967-8964, telex 847338. **(Subscription address:** CDS Agency Hard Copy, PO Box 4966, Des Moines IA 50340. **Tel** (515)247-7569.**) ED** James C. McCullagh and Ed Pauelka. Index available ($1.00). **Bk Rev. Ad Acc. Circ:** 250,000. available on microfilm and microfiche from University Microfilms International (UMI); available on an online database (file 647/Full-Text) from DIALOG. Documents available from UMI Article Clearinghouse, Magazine Collection. ***Continues*** *American Cycling;* ***Absorbed*** *Bike World* ***and*** *Mountain Bike.*
Desc: Magazine for bicycling enthusiasts featuring product reviews, riding techniques, touring routes, fitness schedules, racing reports and bicycle repair.
Ind/Abst Acad. Abstr. Full Text Elite; Acad. Abstr.; Acad. Ind. [Computer File] (1984-1988); Acad. Search; Access (1976-1988); Consum. Index Prod. Eval. Inf. Source; EP Collect.; Expand. Acad. Index (1984-1988); Gen. Period. Index (1985-); Health Ref. Cent. (1987-) [Full Txt.] [Select. Cov.]; Health Source Plus; Health Source; Homework Help.; Index Inf. (1990-); Mag. Artic. Summar. Elite; Mag. Artic. Summar. Select; Mag. Artic. Summar. CD-ROM; Mag. ASAP Plus [Full Txt.]; Mag. ASAP Sel. [Full Txt.]; Mag. Index Plus (1989-); Mag. Index. Sel. (1986-); Mag. Search; MasterFile FullTEXT 1000; MasterFile FullTEXT 350; MasterFile FullTEXT 650; MasterFile FullTEXT (Feb. 1984-) [Full Txt.]; Mid. Search; Newsp. Period. Abstr. (1988-); OCLC; Phys. Educ. Index; Pub. Lib. FullTEXT; Read. Guide Abstr. Select Ed.; Read. Guide Period. Lit.; SPORT Discus; SportSearch (May 1987-); Telebase; Mag. Index (1977-); Vocat. Search; World Mag. Bank.

ISSN 1034-8085
DD 796.6099405 AT
BICYCLING AUSTRALIA. [Bicycl. Aust.]. (1990)-. English. Six times a year. 41.07Aus$. Lake Wangary Publishing Co. Ltd., PO Box 2058, Port Lincoln SA 5606 Australia. **Tel** 011 61 86 854388, FAX 011 61 86 854323. **ED** Phil Latz. **Ad Acc. Circ:** 10,000.
Ind/Abst SPORT Discus.

LC GV1040 **ISSN** 1072-4869
DD 796.6 US
●**BIKE MAGAZINE.** [Bike mag.]. **VFOAT** Bike. Vol. 1, No. 1 (Mar. 1994)-. Consumer Publication. English. Nine times a year. $17.95. Surfer Publications Inc., PO Box 1028, Dana Point CA 92629. **Tel** (714)496-5922, (800)289-0636, FAX (714)496-7849. **ED** Steve Casimiro.
Desc: Covers mountain biking.

LC GV1040 **ISSN** 1064-492X
DD 796.6 US
BIKE (MIDDLETOWN, R.I.), THE. (BIKE.). (1992)-. Periodical. English. Six times a year. $26.00. NGU Publishing, Inc., Suite 1A, 747 Aquidneck Avenue, Middletown RI 02840.

LC GV1040 **ISSN** 0195-0320
DD 796.6 US
BMX PLUS. (197?)-. Periodical. English. Twelve times a year. $18.98. Hi-Torque Publications, 25233 Anza Drive, Valencia CA 91380. **Tel** (805)295-1910, FAX (805)295-1278. **ED** Karl Rothe. **Ad Acc. Circ:** 102,000. Documents available from UMI Article Clearinghouse.
Desc: Reports on the stars, styles and how-to's of this ever-changing, fast-paced sport with race coverage, bike tests, new product evaluations, personality profiles, and previews.
Ind/Abst EP Collect.; Homework Help.; Mag. Artic. Summar. Elite; Mag. Artic. Summar. Select; Mag. Artic. Summar. CD-ROM; Mag. Search; MasterFile FullTEXT 1000; MasterFile FullTEXT 350; MasterFile FullTEXT 650; MasterFile FullTEXT (July 1989-); Newsp. Period. Abstr. (1992-); OCLC; Telebase.

LC GV **ISSN** 1081-4108
DD 796 US
●**BMXER (PHOENIX, ARIZ.).** (BMXER : THE OFFICIAL PUBLICATION OF THE AMERICAN BICYCLE ASSOCIATION.). [BMXer]. **Added/Corp** American Bicycle Association. Vol. 17, No. 1 (Jan./Feb. 1995)-. Periodical. English. Twelve times a year. $26.00. American Bicycle Association, PO Box 718, Chandler AZ 85224. ***Continues*** *American BMXer (Membership Edition), 8750-5827.*

Bicycles and Cycling

DD 796.6/09714/27
ISSN 0705-0623
CN
BULLETIN - LE MONDE BICYCLETTE.
Main/Corp Citizens on Cycles (Association). (1976)-. Bulletin. English (French). Free to members, $2.00 students and unemployed. Citizen on Cycles, Suite 314/5550 du Parc Avenue, Montreal Quebec H2V 4H1 Canada.

LC HD9999.B4 N48a
DD 331.7
NE
CBS RIJWIEL- EN MOTORRIJWIELINDUSTRIE. Added/Corp
Netherlands. Centraal Bureau voor de Statistiek. Hoofdafdeling Statistieken van Industrie en Bouwnijverheid. **VFOAT** C.B.S. Rijwiel- en Motorrijwielindustrie; Bicycle- and Motorbicycle Industry. (19??)-. Dutch (summaries and/or abstracts in English). One time a year. Fl13.30. Staatsuitgeverij, Christoffel Plantijnstraat 1, 2515 TZ'S Gravenhage Netherlands. **Tel** 070/78-95-70. **Continues** Produktiestatistieken, Rijwiel- en Motorrijwielindustrie.

LC GV1040
DD 796.6
ISSN 0142-890X
UK
Pr Rev.
CLASSIC BIKE.
(19??)-. English. Twelve times a year. $97.54. EMAP National Publications Ltd, Farndon Road, Market Harborough, Leicestershire, LE16 9NR United Kingdom. **Tel** 011 44 116 2555161. (**Subscription address:** Alan Wells International, Memberline House Farndon Road, Leicestershire LE16 9NR United Kingdom. **Tel** 011 44 1858 410510.) **ED** John Pearson. **Ad Acc.**

DD 388
ISSN 1061-6519
US
CROSSWORDS (WALNUT CREEK, CALIF.).
(CROSSWORDS : THE JOURNAL OF MULTI-PURPOSE, MULTI-TERRAIN BICYCLES.). [Crosswords]. **VFOAT** Cross Words. (1991)-. Periodical. English. Four times a year. $3.00. PO Box 3207, Walnut Creek CA 94598. Crosswords, PO Box 3207, Walnut Creek CA 94598.

LC GV1040
DD 796.6
UK
●**CT & C.** (1995)-. English. Six times a year. $25.67. Cyclists Touring Club, 69 Meadrow, Godalming Surrey GU7 3HS United Kingdom. **Tel** 011 44 148 687217, FAX 011 44 148 426994. **Continues** Cycletouring and Campaigning.

DD 796.75
ISSN 0274-7502
US
CYCLE NEWS EAST.
(19??)-. Periodical. English. One time a week. Cycle News Inc, PO Box 498, Long Beach CA 90801. **Tel** (310)427-7433, FAX (310)427-6685. **ED** Jack Mangus. **Bk Rev. Ad Acc. Circ:** 70,000.
Desc: Edited exclusively for motorcycle enthusiasts, covering all aspects of motorcycle sport and recreation.

LC GV1040
DD 796.6
UK
TITLE CHANGE
CYCLE TOURING & CAMPAIGNING. Added/Corp
Cyclists' Touring Club. **VFOAT** Cycle Touring and Campaigning. (Dec. 1988-Jan. 1989)-(1995). Periodical. English. Cyclists Touring Club, 69 Meadrow, Godalming Surrey GU7 3HS United Kingdom. **Tel** 011 44 148 687217, FAX 011 44 148 426994. **ED** Tim Hughes. Index available. cum. index. **Bk Rev. Ad Acc, Adv Mgr:** L. Warburton. **Circ:** 33,500 (ctrl). **Continues** Cycletouring. **Continued by** CT & C.
Desc: Contains information on touring, campaigning, news and features.

LC GV1040
DD 796.6
UK
CYCLE TRADER.
(19??)-. Periodical. English. Nine times a year. £33.00 UK; £44.00 (surface), £73.00 (airmail) other. Turret Group, 177 Hagden Lane, Watford Hertfordshire WD1 8LN United Kingdom. **Tel** 011 44 1923 228577, FAX 011 44 1923 221346.

DD 796
ISSN 0888-739X
US
CYCLEBRATIONS.
(CYCLEBRATIONS / A PUBLICATION OF THE MINNESOTA COALITION OF BICYCLISTS.). [Cyclebrations]. **Added/Corp** Minnesota Coalition of Bicyclists. (Nov./Dec. 1982)-. Periodical. English. Four times a year. Free. Minnesota Coalition of Bicyclists, Minneapolis MN.

LC GV1040
DD 796.6
UK
CYCLING GUIDE.
(1986)-. English. Tantivy Press, 136-148 Tooley Street, London SE1 2TT United Kingdom. **Continues** International Cycling Guide.

DD 796.6/09713
ISSN 0838-9543
CN
CYCLING IN ONTARIO.
(CYCLING IN ONTARIO : HANDBOOK OF THE ONTARIO CYCLING ASSOCIATION.). [Cycl. Ont.]. **Added/Corp** Ontario Cycling Association. (1982)-. English. Ontario Cycling Association, 1220 Sheppard Avenue East, Willowdale Ontario M2K 2X1 Canada. **Tel** (416)495-4141, FAX (416)495-4310.

DD 629
ISSN 1049-8990
US
CYCLING SCIENCE. [Cycl. sci.].
(1989)-. Periodical. English. Four times a year (Mar., June, Sept., Dec.). $24.97. Penner Publishing, 580 Greenwich Court, East Windsor NJ 08520. **Tel** (609)443-0038, FAX (609)443-4471. (**Subscription address:** Cycling Science, PO Box 926, Circulation Department, Heightstown NJ 08520.) **ED** Edmund R. Burke. **Bk Rev. Ad Acc, Adv Mgr:** Mel Katz, **Tel** (609)443-9202. **Circ:** 25,000.
Desc: Covers bicycling technology from training and equipment to aerodynamics and physiology.
Ind/Abst Phys. Educ. Index (1989-); SPORT Discus.

LC GV1040
DD 796.6
ISSN 0274-4813
US
CYCLING U.S.A. Added/Corp
United States Cycling Federation. **VAT** Cycling United States of America. Vol. 1 (Apr. 1980)-. Periodical. English. Twelve times a year. $15.00. US Cycling Federation, 1750 East Boulder Street, Colorado Springs CO 80909. **Tel** (719)578-4581. **ED** Nancy Moore, (editor's phone: (719)578-4581). **Bk Rev,** (Qty: 1-2). **Ad Acc, Adv Mgr:** Mary Ellen Davis. **Circ:** 37,000.
Desc: The official publication of the US Cycling Federation. It publishes articles and information pertinent to bicycle racing.
Ind/Abst SportSearch (May 1987-).

DD 796.605
ISSN 0951-5852
UK
CYCLING WEEKLY. [Cycl. wkly.].
(1986)-. Periodical. English. One time a week. $136.24 (airmail) US and Canada; £75.15 (airmail) Middle East, Africa, Mexico, South America, South Asia; £92.65 (airmail) Rest of Africa, South America and South Asia; £82.59 (airmail) Far East, Australia, New Zealand and Pacific Ocean Islands; £122.64 (regular delivery) US and Canada; £52.95 (regular delivery) UK; £56.75 (regular delivery) other. IPC Magazines Ltd., Perrymount Road, Haywards Heath, West Sussex RH16 3DH United Kingdom. **Tel** 011 44 1444 440421, FAX 011 44 1444 445599. **Continues** Cycling (London. 1964), 0011-4316; **Absorbed** Cyclist Monthly, 0263-5550.
Ind/Abst SPORT Discus.

LC GV1040
DD 796.6
ISSN 0143-0238
UK
CYCLING WORLD. [Cycling world].
(1979)-. Periodical. English. Eleven times a year (Dec./Jan. issues combined). $51.33. Stone Leisure Limited, Andrew House, 2A Granville Road, Sidcup Kent DA14 4BN United Kingdom. **Tel** 011 44 181 3026150, FAX 011 44 181 3002315. **Bk Rev,** (Qty: 4). **Ad Acc, Adv Mgr Tel** 011 41 332 874731. ctrl circ.

LC GV1040 .C9
DD 796.6/05
ISSN 0887-5944
US
CYCLIST (TORRANCE, CALIF.).
(CYCLIST.). (1984)-. Periodical. English. Twelve times a year. $15.97 US, $23.97 Canada. Cyclist, Box 907, Farmingdale NY 11737-0001.

DD 796.6/09714
ISSN 0835-2208
CN
CYCLISTE QUEBECOIS.
(LE CYCLISTE QUEBECOIS : JOURNAL OFFICIEL DE LA FEDERATION QUEBECOISE DES SPORTS CYCLISTES.). [Cycl. qu,e.]. **Added/Corp** Federation Quebecoise des Sports Cyclistes. **VFOAT** Cyclisme Quebecois. (1985)-. Periodical. French. Four times a year. Federation Quebecoise des Sports Cyclistes, 4545 Avenue Pierre de Coubertin, CP 1000 Succursale M, Montreal Quebec H1V 3R2 Canada.

DD 796.6/09714
ISSN 0383-9664
CN
CYCLO NOUVELLES.
Vol. 1 (Nov. 1973)-. Periodical. French. Irregular. Federation Quebecoise de Cyclotourisme, 1415 Est rue Jarry, Montreal Quebec H2E 2Z7 Canada.

LC GV1040
DD 796.6
FR
CYCLOTOURISME ORGANE OFFICIEL DE LA FEDERATION FRANCAISE DE CYCLOTOURISME.
French. Ten times a year. 244.86F France; 250.00F other. Fedn Francaise Cyclotourisme, 8 rue Jean Marie Jego, 75013 Paris France. **Tel** 011 33 1 45803021, FAX 011 33 1 45880241. **Ad Acc. Circ:** 10,000 (ctrl).
Desc: Internal publication of the FFCT, written by its members.

DD 796.6
ISSN 1185-8788
DYNAMO (VANCOUVER). (THE DYNAMO.).
[Dynamo]. (Mar. 1991)-. Periodical. English. $25.00 (Comes with membership to Vancouver Bicycle Club). Vancouver Bicycle Club, 206-2017 17th Avenue, Burnaby BC V3n 1K5.

LC GV1040 .F32
DD 796.6
BE
FABULOUS WORLD OF CYCLING, THE.
(19??)-. English. One time a year. Winning International Europe, 22 rue de la Concorde, 1050 Brussels Belgium. **Tel** 011 32 2 5139510.

LC GV1040
DD 796.6
US
GUIDE FOR THE DEVELOPMENT OF BICYCLE FACILITIES. Added/Corp
American Association of State Highway and Transportation Officials. American Association of State Highway and Transportation Officials. Task Force on Geometric Design. (19??)-. English. American Association of State Highway and Transportation Officials, 444 North Capital Street, Suite 249, Washington DC 20001. **Tel** (202)624-5800.

LC TL410 .J57
DD 629.227
ISSN 0387-7396
JA
JITENSHA GIJUTSU JOHO. Added/Corp
Jitensha Sangyo Shinko Kyokai (Japan). (19??)-. Periodical. Japanese. Four times a year. ¥6000. Jitensha Sangyo Shinko Kyokai 9-3, Akasaka 1-chome Minato-ku, Tokyo-to 107 Japan.

DD 798
ISSN 1061-7140
US
MILES TO GO.
(MILES TO GO: A DISTANCE RIDING MAGAZINE.). [Miles go]. Vol. 1, Issue 1 (May 1992)-. Periodical. English. Six times a year. $18.00. Carol Clark, PO Box 364, Jupiter FL 33468-0364.

LC GV1040
DD 796.6
UDC 79
ISSN 0397-569X
FR
CEASED
MIROIR DU CYCLISME (1960). [Miroir cycl. 1960].
(1960)-(1995). Periodical. French. Edn Vaillant, Miroir, Sprint, 146 rue Faubourg Poissonniere, 75010 Paris France. **Tel** 011 33 1 42819103.

DD 796.6/09714/27
ISSN 0823-5570
CN
MONDE A BICYCLETTE, LE.
Vol. 8, No. 2 (1983)-. Periodical. French (English). Four times a year. $10.00. Le Monde a Bicyclette, C P 1242 Station la Cite, Montreal Quebec H2W 2R3 Canada. **Tel** (514)844-2713. **ED** Robert Silverman and Susan Gray. **Bk Rev. Ad Acc. Circ:** 18,000. available on diskette. **Continues** Vers und Ville Nouvelle, 0713-3227.
Desc: Articles about urban bicycling, urban transport, ecology, and alternative medicine.

LC GV1040
DD 796.6
IT
MONDE CYCLISTE.
Italian. Ghedini, Via della Signora 6, Milan 20122 Italy.
Ind/Abst SPORT Discus.

LC GV1040
DD 796.6
UDC 79
FR
MOTO REVUE.
French. Forty-eight times a year. 570.00F (one-year), 1,035.00F (two-year) France; 887.00F other. Editions Lariviere Naryse Menn, 15 17 Quai de l Oise Sec. Abonn., 75166 Paris Cedex 19 France. **Tel** 011 33 1 40342207, FAX 011 33 1 40358441, telex 214678.

LC WMLC 91/279
DD 796
ISSN 0897-5213
US
MOUNTAIN BIKE. [Mt. bike]. VFOAT
Mountain Bike Magazine. Vol. 6, No. 1 (Feb. 1990)-. Periodical. English. Eleven times a year. $19.97 US; $28.99 other. Rodale Press Inc., 400 South 10th Street, Emmaus PA 18098. **Tel** (610)967-5171, (800)666-2503, FAX (610)967-8964, telex 847338. (**Subscription address:** CDS Agency Hard Copy, PO Box 4966, Des Moines IA 50340. **Tel** (515)247-7569.) **Continues** Mountain Bike, 0897-5213.
Ind/Abst EP Collect.; Homework Help.; MasterFile FullTEXT 1000; MasterFile FullTEXT 350; MasterFile FullTEXT 650; MasterFile FullTEXT (Jan. 1995-); OCLC; Telebase.

LC GV1040
DD 796.6
ISSN 0895-8467
US
MOUNTAIN BIKE ACTION. [Mt. bike action]. VFOAT
Mountain Bike. Vol. 1, No. 1 (Oct. 1986)-. Periodical. English. Twelve times a year. $19.98. Hi-Torque Publications, 25233 Anza Drive, Valencia CA 91380. **Tel** (805)295-1910, FAX (805)295-1278.

LC GV1040
DD 796.6
ISSN 1062-7111
US
MOUNTAIN BIKE ACTION PARTS AND ACCESSORIES GUIDE. VFOAT
Parts and Accessories Guide. (1992)-. English. $3.50 (single issue). Hi-Torque Publications, 25233 Anza Drive, Valencia CA 91380. **Tel** (805)295-1910, FAX (805)295-1278.

LC WMLC 93/3539
DD 388
ISSN 1075-8798
US
●### MOUNTAIN BIKE ACTION TRAVEL & TRAIL GUIDE. [Mt. bike action travel trail guide].
VFOAT Mountain Bike Action Travel and Trail Guide;

Bicycles and Cycling

Travel & Rail Guide. (Fall 1993)-. English. Hi-Torque Publications, 25233 Anza Drive, Valencia CA 91380. **Tel** (805)295-1910, FAX (805)295-1278. **Continues** Mountain Bike Action America's Greatest Trails, 1062-7103.

DD 796   **ISSN** 1062-2918 US
MOUNTAIN BIKING (1992). (MOUNTAIN BIKING.). [Mt. biking]. (19??)-. Periodical. English. Twelve times a year. $31.95. Challenge Publications Inc., 7950 Deering Avenue, Canoga Park CA 91304. **Tel** (818)887-0550. **Continues** Mountain & City Biking, 1046-4875.

DD 796   **ISSN** 1077-0372 US
●**MTB (LOS ANGELES, CALIF.).** (MTB.). [MTB]. Issue 1 (Oct. 1994)-. Periodical. English. Twelve times a year. $19.94. Petersen Publishing Company, 6420 Wilshire Boulevard, Los Angeles CA 90048. **Tel** (213)782-2485, FAX (213)782-2526. **(Subscription address:** Neodata / Colorado, PO Box 2606, Boulder CO 80322. **) ED** Terry Masaoka (Managing Editor). Index available. **Ad Acc, Adv Mgr:** Valerie Baldwin, **Tel** (213)782-2000.
Desc: Contains information on mountain bikes.

DD 796   **ISSN** 0893-4606 US
ON ONE WHEEL. (ON ONE WHEEL : OFFICIAL PUBLICATION OF THE UNICYCLING SOCIETY OF AMERICA.). [On one wheel]. **Added/Corp** Unicycling Society of America. (19??)-. Periodical. English. Four times a year. $15.00 Comes with Unicycling Society of America membership. Unicycling Society of America Inc., PO Box 40534, Redford MI 48240. **Tel** (419)422-8959. **ED** Carol Brichford. **Bk Rev. Ad Acc. Circ:** 350 (ctrl).
Desc: Publishes articles concerning unicycles and unicyclists. Also includes information on related circus arts.

DD 796   **ISSN** 1079-6304 US
OUT YOUR BACKDOOR. [Out your backdoor]. **VFOAT** OYB. No. 1 (July 1990)-. Periodical. English. Four times a year. Out Your Backdoor, 4686 Meridian Road, Williamstown MI 48895.

LC GV1040
DD 796.6   **ISSN** 0146-2652 US CEASED
POPULAR CYCLING. (19??)-(19??). Periodical. English. Argus Publishers Corporation, 12100 Wilshire Boulevard, Suite 250, Los Angeles CA 90025. **Tel** (310)820-3601, FAX (310)207-9388.

LC GV1040
DD 796.6 US
PRO BIKE DIRECTORY. Added/Corp Bicycle Federation. (1980)-. Directory. English. Bicycle Federation of America, 1506 21st Street Northwest, Suite 200, Washington DC 20036. **Tel** (202)463-6622, FAX (202)463-6625.

DD 796   **ISSN** 1064-2765 US
PRO BIKE NEWS. [Pro bike news]. **Added/Corp** Bicycle Federation. Bicycle Federation of America. Vol. 1, No. 1 (May 1981)-. Periodical. English. Twelve times a year. $30.00. Bicycle Federation of America, 1506 21st Street Northwest, Suite 200, Washington DC 20036. **Tel** (202)463-6622, FAX (202)463-6625. **ED** Andy Clarke. **Bk Rev,** (Qty: 7). **Circ:** 700 (ctrl).

LC GV1040
DD 796.6 US
PROCEEDINGS. Added/Corp Metropolitan Association of Urban Designers and Environmental Planners. **VFOAT** Planning, Design and Implementation of Bicycle and Pedestrian Facilities. (19??)-. Proceedings. English. One time a year. MAUDEP, Box 722 Church Street Station, New York NY 10008.

LC WMLC 93/5257   **ISSN** 1080-2428
DD 388 US
●**QUICK THROTTLE.** [Quick throttle]. No. 1 (May 1995)-. Consumer Publication. English. Six times a year. $16.50. Paisano Publications Inc., 28210 Dorothy Drive, PO Box 1050, Agoura Hills CA 91301. **Tel** (818)889-8740, FAX (818)889-4726. **Ad Acc.** available with illustrations.

DD 796   **ISSN** 1078-0084 US
RIDE BMX. [Ride BMX]. (19??)-. Periodical. English. Six times a year. $12.00. Snap Magazines, 1317 North San Fernando Boulevard, Suite 231, Burbank CA 91504. **Tel** (818)846-5475.

LC GV1040
DD 796.6 GW
●**ROLLER.** (1994)-. Consumer Publication. English. One time a year. DM4.00. Vereinigte Motor-Verlage GmbH und Co. KG, Leuschnerstrasse 1, 70162 Stuttgart Germany. **Tel** 011 49 711 1821226, FAX 011 49 711 1821349. **ED** Friedhelm Fiedler. **Ad Acc, Adv Mgr:** Claus Schlosser. Full Page (B&W) DM6400.00. Full Page (Color) DM11200.00. **Circ:** 90,000.

LC GV1040
DD 796.6 US
SOUTH CAROLINA BICYCLE DRIVER'S HANDBOOK. Added/Corp South Carolina. Department of Highways and Public Transportation. **VFOAT** Bicycle Driver's Handbook. (1978)-. English. South Carolina Department of Highways and Public Transportation, Box 191, Columbia SC 29202.

LC WMLC 93/1583   **ISSN** 1065-7649
DD 796 US
●**SPORT RIDER.** [Sport rider]. Issue 1 (Apr. 1993)-. Periodical. English. Six times a year. $13.95. Petersen Publishing Company, 6420 Wilshire Boulevard, Los Angeles CA 90048. **Tel** (213)782-2485, FAX (213)782-2526. **(Subscription address:** Neodata / Colorado, PO Box 2606, Boulder CO 80322. **)**
Desc: Focuses on high-performance street sport bikes. Each issue features track tests and comparisons of bikes. Offers tips and techniques for getting the most performance without compromising safety.

LC WMLC 91/1294   **ISSN** 1060-8419
DD 629 US
SPORTBIKE (NEW YORK, N.Y.). (SPORTBIKE / BY THE EDITORS OF CYCLE MAGAZINE.). [Sportbike]. (1991)-. English. Cycle Magazine, PO Box 56406, Boulder CO 80322-6406.

LC GV1040
DD 796.6 US
●**TANDEM MAGAZINE.** (1994)-. Consumer Publication. English. Four times a year. $12.95 (one-year), $24.95 (two-year). Petzold Publishing, 26895 Petzold Road, Eugene OR 97402. **Tel** (503)485-5262, FAX (503)341-0788. **ED** Greg Shepherd. **Ad Acc. Circ:** 30,000. available with illustrations.
Desc: Concerned with various aspects of tandem cycling; provides information on equipment and travel.

LC GV1040
DD 796.6 US
TEXAS BICYCLIST. English. Eleven times a year. $30.00. Stephen Roulac, 3600 Jeanetta Drive, Suite 1604, Houston TX 77063. **Tel** (713)782-1661, FAX (713)782-7666. **ED** Kim Grob. **Bk Rev. Ad Acc. Circ:** 50,000 (ctrl).
Desc: Contains bicycling tips, touring, and addresses the Texas cycling experience.

LC GV1040
DD 796.6 US
TRAFFIC SAFETY FACTS. PEDALCYCLISTS. Added/Corp United States. National Highway Traffic Safety Administration. **VFOAT** Pedalcyclists. (1992)-. English. US Department of Transportation / National Highway Traffic Safety Administration, 400 7th Street SW, Washington DC 20590.

DD 796   **ISSN** 1063-9349 US
ULTRA CYCLING. (ULTRA CYCLING : THE VOICE OF UMCA AND RAAM.). [Ultra cycl.]. **Added/Corp** Ultra Marathon Cycling Association. Race Across America. **VFOAT** Ultracycling. Vol. 1, No. 1 (1992)-. Periodical. English. Four times a year. $30.00 (membership). UMCA, Ultra Marathon Cycling Association, 2761 North Marengo Avenue, Altadena CA 91001.

DD 796   **ISSN** 0161-1798 US
VELO-NEWS. [Velo-news]. (19??)-. Periodical. English. Eighteen times a year. $37.97. Inside Communications Inc., 1830 North 55th Street, Boulder CO 80301. **Tel** (303)440-0601, FAX (303)444-6788. **ED** John Wilcockson. Index available. **Bk Rev. Ad Acc. Circ:** 47,000. available on microfilm.
Desc: News and features about US and international bicycle racing.
Ind/Abst SPORT Discus; SportSearch (May 1987-).

LC WMLC 94/4309   **ISSN** 1073-581X
DD 629 US
●**VQ (AGOURA HILLS, CALIF.).** (VQ.). [VQ]. **VFOAT** V-Twin Quarterly. No. 1 (Apr. 1994)-. Consumer Publication. English. Four times a year. $44.95. Paisano Publications Inc., 28210 Dorothy Drive, PO Box 1050, Agoura Hills CA 91301. **Tel** (818)889-8740, FAX (818)889-4726. **Ad Acc.**

LC GV1040 .W45   **ISSN** 0195-7023
DD 796.6/05 US
WHEELMEN, THE. (19??)-. Periodical. English. Two times a year. $7.50. Mrs M Fuehrer, 1708 School House Lane, Ambler PA 19002.

LC GV1049 .W52   **ISSN** 1055-7830
DD 796.6/2/05 US
WINNING. (WINNING : BICYCLING ILLUSTRATED.). [Winning]. **VFOAT** Winning, Bicycle Racing Illustrated; Winning, Bicycle Illustrated. No. 85 (Oct. 1990)-. Periodical. English. Eleven times a year. $23.95. Winning Magazine, PO Box 21570, Lehigh Valley PA 18002. **Continues** Winning, Bicycle Racing Illustrated, 1051-9572.
Ind/Abst SPORT Discus.

BIOGRAPHIES

LC CT   **ISSN** 0196-0652
DD 920 US
ABIRA DIGEST. Main/Corp American Biographical Institute Research Association. **VAT** American Biographical Institute Research Association Digest. (1980)-. Periodical. English. Irregular (three to four issues per year). Free to members, $7.50 other. Bulletin of the Menninger Clinic, PO Box 829, Topeka KS 66601. **Tel** (913)273-7500 Ext. 5850, FAX (913)273-8625. **ED** J M Evans and L M Kellander. **Bk Rev. Ad Acc. Circ:** 1,550 (ctrl). **Continues** Newsletter - American Biographical Institute Research Association.
Desc: Covers poetry, essays, announcements and advertisements by its members.

LC CT1920 .A37   **ISSN** 0261-1570 UK
AFRICA WHO'S WHO. 1st Ed. (1981)-. English. £125.00. Africa Journal Ltd, Kirkman House, 54A Tottenham Court Road, London W1P 0BT United Kingdom. **Tel** 011 44 171 6379341, telex 8952670. **ED** Raph Uwechue. **Circ:** 16,000. **Continues in part** Africa Year Book and Who's Who, 0141-3341.
Desc: More than 10,000 biographies of prominent Africans from all walks of life.

LC PR3532 .A15   **ISSN** 0884-5816
DD 828/.609 US
AGE OF JOHNSON, THE. See Literature.

LC ML3486.P8 A4
DD 780/.42/097295
ALBUM DE ORO. Vol. 1, No. 1 (1983)-. Periodical. Spanish. Four times a year. Angel L. Marquez Publications, PO Box 691, Madison Square Station, New York NY 10010. **ED** Angel L. Marquez. **Ad Acc. Circ:** 15,500.
Desc: Biography of well known composers and singers from Latin America, internationally known in the hispanic community.

LC CT104 .B56   **ISSN** 1040-127X
DD 920.02 US
NLM Z 5301; B613
ALMANAC OF FAMOUS PEOPLE.
Added/Corp Gale Research Inc. 4th Ed. (1989)-. English. One time a year. $99.00. Gale Research Inc., 835 Penobscot Building, 645 Griswold Street, Detroit MI 48226. **Tel** (800)877-GALE, (313)961-2242, FAX (313)961-6083, (800)414-5043, telex TWX 810-221-7086. **ED** Beverly Baer, Neil. E. Walker. Index available. **Bk Rev.** available on diskette; available on magnetic tape; available on an online database from Mead Data Central; and (File GALBIO in the PEOPLE, ENTERTAINMENT, and SPORTS Libraries) NEXIS. **Continues** Biography Almanac, 0738-0097.
Desc: Source of information on famous and infamous people from all time periods. Over 27,000 famous individuals and groups are included in two volumes. Entries provide the subject's best known name, complete name, nickname, name of group, dates and places of birth and death, nationality, and occupation or best known activity.

LC CT220 .A58   **ISSN** 0196-3465
DD 920/.073 US
AMERICA'S OUTSTANDING NAMES AND FACES. (1977/78)-. English. One time a year. Maine Bonding Ins, PO Box 539, Building 2, Bedford NH 03102.

LC PR6039.O32 Z55
DD 828/.9/1209 UK
AMON HEN. See Literature.

LC BX3901 .A53
DD 255.1 BE
ANALECTA PRAEMONSTRATENSIA.
See Religions and Theology.

LC PC4001   **ISSN** 0569-9878
DD 460 SP
ANALES CERVANTINOS. See Linguistics.

LC CT1383 .A55
DD 920/.0494 SZ
ANNUAIRE SUISSE DU MONDE ET DES AFFAIRES. VFOAT Wer Ist Wer in der Schweiz; Swiss Biographical Index of Prominent Persons; Annuario Svizzero del Mondo e Degli Affari. (1972/1973)-. Multiple languages (English, French, German and Italian). Every 2 years. 200.00F. International Registry of Who's Who SA, 23 Chemin du Levant, CH-1005 Lausanne Switzerland. **Tel** 011 41 21 200924. **Bk Rev. Ad Acc. Circ:** 5,000.
Desc: Presents information on people important to the Swiss and Liechtenstein economy. A person may be listed by virtue of his position, or the market position of his company. Others have distinguished themselves by outstanding achievements and performance in their own fields.

LC CT120 .A56 ISSN 0278-1573
DD 920/.02 B US
NLM CT 100 A615
CEASED
ANNUAL OBITUARY, THE. [Annu. obit.]. 1st Ed. (1980)-(1993). English. Gale Research Inc., 835 Penobscot Building, 645 Griswold Street, Detroit MI 48226. **Tel** (800)877-GALE, (313)961-2242, FAX (313)961-6083, (800)414-5043, telex TWX 810-221-7086. **ED** Roland Turner.

LC CT
DD 920 GW
AURORA-BUCHREIHE. Added/Corp Eichendorff-Gesellschaft. (1974)-. Monographic series. German. Irregular. Price varies per volume. Jan Thorbecke Verlag GmbH and Company, Karlstrasse 10, Postfach 546, D-72482 Sigmaringen Germany. **Tel** 011 49 7571 728100, FAX 011 49 7571 728280, telex 732534. **ED** Wolfgang Fruhwald, Franz Heiduk, Helmut Koopmann, Peter Horst Neumann. **Circ:** 1,000.
Desc: Monographs on life and work of Joseph von Eichendorff and the romantic period.

LC Z5304.A8 A93 PN452 ISSN 0741-8655
DD 016.809 US
AUTHOR BIOGRAPHIES MASTER INDEX. **See** Biographies-Abstracting, Bibliographies and Statistics.

LC CT25 .A89 ISSN 0898-9575
DD 920/.005 US
AUTO/BIOGRAPHY STUDIES. (AUTO/BIOGRAPHY STUDIES : A/B.). [Auto/biogr. stud.]. **Added/Corp** Joyce and Elizabeth Hall Center for the Humanities. Autobiography Society. **VFOAT** Auto Biography Studies; Autobiography Studies; A/B. (1985)-. Periodical. English. Two times a year (June, Dec.). $15.00 (individuals); $30.00 (institutions) Comes with Autobiography Society Membership. Autobiography Society, University of Kansas, Center for Humanities, Lawrence KS 66045. **Tel** (913)864-4798.
Ind/Abst MLA Int. Bibl. Books Artic. Mod. Lang. Lit.

LC GV865.A1 B385
DD 796.357/092/2 B US
BASEBALL'S FORGOTTEN HEROES. Vol. 1 (July 1984)-. English. $4.95. Stevens Enterprises, 95 Allen Street Box 187, Netcong NJ 07857. **Tel** (201)347-3067. **ED** Frank Stevens. **Bk Rev. Ad Acc.**
Desc: Pictures and biographies of baseball players who are not in the Baseball Hall of Fame.

LC Z5301 CT120 ISSN 0742-2318
DD 012 US
BIO-BASE. (BIO-BASE [MICROFORM].). [Bio-base]. **Added/Corp** Gale Research Company. (1978)-. English. One time a year. $230.00. Gale Research Inc., 835 Penobscot Building, 645 Griswold Street, Detroit MI 48226. **Tel** (800)877-GALE, (313)961-2242, FAX (313)961-6083, (800)414-5043, telex TWX 810-221-7086. **ED** Barbara McNeil. available on magnetic tape; available on diskette; available on an online database (File 287) from DIALOG.
Desc: Furnishes about 5.25 million citations. Each citation provides the subject's full name (as given in the source indexed), birth and/or death dates, and a code indicating the source of biographical data.

LC JC345
DD 929.82 US
BIOGRAPHIC REGISTER, THE. Main/Corp United States. Dept. of State. **Added/Corp** United States. Foreign Service. United States. International Cooperation Administration. United States. Foreign Agricultural Service. United States Information Agency. (1956)-. Government Publication. English. One time a year. Superintendent of Documents, US Government Printing Office, Washington DC 20402. **Tel** (202)275-3328, FAX (202)786-2377. ***Continues*** *Department of State Biographic Register.*

LC JC345
DD 929.82 US
BIOGRAPHICAL DIRECTORY. Main/Corp American Political Science Association. 5th Ed. (1968)-. Directory. English. Irregular (published every 10-15 years). $18.50 members; $23.50 nonmembers. American Political Science Association, 1527 New Hampshire Avenue Northwest, Washington DC 20036. **Tel** (202)483-2512, FAX (202)483-2657. **ED** Samuel C. Patterson and Catherine Rudder. **Bk Rev. Ad Acc. Circ:** 12,000. ***Continues*** *American Political Science Association. Biographical Directory of the American Political Science Association.*

LC Q141 .N2 ISSN 0077-2933
DD 509.2 US
CCC
NLM Q 141 N277B CODEN BMNSAC
BIOGRAPHICAL MEMOIRS. [Biogr. mem.]. **Main/Corp** National Academy of Sciences (U.S.). (1877)-. Monographic series. English. Irregular. Price varies per volume. National Academy Press, PO Box 285, Washington DC 20055. **Tel** (800)624-6242, (202)334-3313, FAX (202)334-2451. Documents available from CASDDS.
Ind/Abst Chem. Abstr.; GeoRef.

LC Q73 .I77413 ISSN 0376-6632
DD 509/.22 II
BIOGRAPHICAL MEMOIRS OF FELLOWS OF THE INDIAN NATIONAL SCIENCE ACADEMY. Main/Corp Indian National Science Academy. (19??)-. English. Rs20.00. Indian National Science Academy, 1 Bahadur Shah Zafar Marg, New Delhi 110 002 India. ***Continues*** *National Institute of Sciences of India. Biographical Memoirs of Fellows.*

LC Q41 ISSN 0080-4606
DD 500 UK
NLM Q 141 R888B
BIOGRAPHICAL MEMOIRS OF FELLOWS OF THE ROYAL SOCIETY. Main/Corp Royal Society of London. (1955)-. English. One time a year. $173.00. Royal Society, 6 Carlton House Terrace, London SW1Y 5AG United Kingdom. **Tel** 011 44 171 8395561, FAX 011 44 171 9761837, telex 917876 ROYAL G. cum. index. **Circ:** 1,450. ***Continues*** *Royal Society of London. Obituary Notices of Fellows.*
Desc: Detailed obituaries of eminent scientists.

LC CT1163 .A2
BE
CEASED
BIOGRAPHIE NATIONALE. Main/Corp Academie Royale des Sciences, des Lettres et des Beaux-Arts de Belgique. (1866)-Series Completed Vol. 44 (1995). Monographic series. French. Etablissements Emile Bruylant, 67 rue de la Regence, 1000 Brussels Belgium. **Tel** 011 32 2 5129845, FAX 011 32 2 5117202.

LC JC345
DD 929.82 BE
BIOGRAPHIE NATIONALE. SUPPLEMENT : PUBLIEE PAR L'ACADEMIE ROYALE DES SCIENCES, DES LETTRES ET DES BEAUX-ARTS DE BELGIQUE. French. Etablissements Emile Bruylant, 67 rue de la Regence, 1000 Brussels Belgium. **Tel** 011 32 2 5129845, FAX 011 32 2 5117202.

ISSN 0380-0830
DD 920/.0714 CN
BIOGRAPHIES CANADIENNES-FRANCAISES. VFOAT Who's Who in Quebec. 1st Ed.; 1920-. French. One time a year. 49.95Can$. Biographies Canadiennes-Francaises, 200 rue de Gaspe, Ile des Soeurs, Montreal Quebec H3E 1E6 Canada. **Tel** (514)651-9548. **Circ:** 5,000.
Desc: Biographies of prominent people of the Province of Quebec.

LC CT
DD 920 GW
BIOGRAPHY & SOCIETY. (19??)-. Newsletter. English. Free to members of the Research Committee of Biography and Society. Uni Dortmund Eco & Soc Scs, Str 50 Ch Grote, D-44227 Dortmund Germany. **Tel** 011 49 231 7553182.

ISSN 1075-3451
DD 920 US
•**BIOGRAPHY AND SOURCE STUDIES.** [Biogr. source stud.]. (1994)-. Academic Scholarly Publication. English. One time a year. $140.00. AMS Press Inc., 56 East 13th Street, New York NY 10003. **Tel** (212)777-4700, FAX (212)995-5413, telex 710 581 2302.

LC CT100 .B54 ISSN 0162-4962
DD 920/.005 US
CODEN BGPYE2
BIOGRAPHY (HONOLULU). (BIOGRAPHY.). [Biography]. **Added/Corp** University of Hawaii at Manoa. Biographical Research Center. Vol. 1 (Winter 1978)-. Periodical. English. Four times a year (Jan., Apr., July, Oct.). $32.00. University of Hawaii Press, 2840 Kolowalu Street, Honolulu HI 96822. **Tel** (808)956-8833, (808)948-8697, FAX (808)988-6052. **ED** George Simson. **Bk Rev. Ad Acc. Circ:** 400. available on microfilm and microfiche from University Microfilms International (UMI). Documents available from The Genuine Article.
Desc: Forum for all well-considered biographical scholarship. Its aim is to stimulate the critical judgment of life-writing by presenting new information, definitions, interpretations, and evaluations.
Ind/Abst Am. Hist. Life (1978-); ARTbibliogr. Mod. (1984-); Arts Humanit. Citation Index [Full Cov.]; Book Rev. Index; Curr. Contents Arts Humanit.; Guide Soc. Sci. Relig.; Int. Bibliogr. Sociol.; Linguist. Lang. Behav. Abstr.; Lit. Crit. Regist.; MLA Int. Bibl. Books Artic. Mod. Lang. Lit.; Res. Alert [Full Cov.]; Soc. Plann. Policy Dev. Abstr.; Soc. Sci. Cit. Index [Select. Cov.]; Sociol. Abstr.

LC CT ISSN 1043-9374
DD 920 US
BIOGRAPHY REVIEW. (1992)-. Periodical. English. Four times a year. $2.00 single issue. Darrel Dahlhaus, PO Box 406, Beverly MA 01915.

LC CT107 .B54 ISSN 1058-2347
DD 920/.009/04 US
Pr Rev.
BIOGRAPHY TODAY. (BIOGRAPHY TODAY: PROFILES OF PEOPLE OF INTEREST TO YOUNG READERS.). [Biogr. today]. Vol. 1, Issue 1 (Jan. 1992)-. Periodical. English. Three times a year (Jan., Apr., Sept.). $46.00. Omnigraphics Inc., 2500 Penobscot Building, 25th Floor, Detroit MI 48226. **Tel** (313)961-1340, (800)234-1340, FAX (313)961-1383. **ED** Laurie L. Harris. Index available. cum. index. **Circ:** 2,000.
Desc: Contains biographies written for young readers. Profiles famous people such as musicians, public figures, and actors covering such topics as birth, youth, first jobs, career highlights, marriage and family. Each ends with a list of further reading and addresses.
Ind/Abst EP Collect.; Homework Help.; MasterFile FullTEXT 1000; MasterFile FullTEXT 350; MasterFile FullTEXT 650; MasterFile FullTEXT (July 1994-); Mid. Search; OCLC; Prim. Search; Pub. Lib. FullTEXT; Telebase.

LC CT21 .B49 ISSN 0933-5315
DD 809/.93592/0005 GW
BIOS : ZEITSCHRIFT FUER BIOGRAPHIEFORSCHUNG UND ORAL HISTORY. (1988)-. Periodical. German. Two times a year. DM66.00. Leske Verlag & Budrich GmbH, Postfach 300551, D-51334 Leverkusen Germany. **Tel** 011 49 21712079, FAX 011 49 217141209.
Ind/Abst Am. Hist. Life (1990-).

LC DA690.B6 B5
DD 942.4/96/0025 UK
BIRMINGHAM POST & MAIL YEAR BOOK AND WHO'S WHO, THE. Added/Corp Birmingham Post & Mail Ltd. **VFOAT** Birmingham Post and Mail Year Book and Who's Who; Birmingham Post & Mail Yearbook and Who's Who; Year Book and Who's Who. 37th (1985/86)-. English. One time a year. £18.90. Kingslea Press Ltd., 137 Newhall Street, Birmingham B3 1SF United Kingdom. **Tel** 011 44 121 2368112, FAX 011 44 121 2001480. **ED** Catherine Coley. Index available. **Ad Acc, Adv Mgr:** Lorraine Watton. **Circ:** 1,500. Documents available from FAXON Xpress, BLDSC. ***Continues*** *Birmingham Post Year Book and Who's Who.*
Desc: Guide of the city of Birmingham's organizations, businesses, and professions.

LC CT
DD 920 UK
BLACK COUNTRY YEAR BOOK AND WHO'S WHO. English. One time a year. £21.70 UK; £25.40 other. Kingslea Press Ltd., 137 Newhall Street, Birmingham B3 1SF United Kingdom. **Tel** 011 44 121 2368112, FAX 011 44 121 2001480.
Desc: Important sources of information on the area's organizations and personalities including local authorities, educational information, and social and cultural activities.

ISSN 0886-7348
DD 810 US
Pr Rev.
BOISE STATE UNIVERSITY WESTERN WRITERS SERIES. [Boise State Univ. west. writ. ser.]. **Added/Corp** Boise State University. **VFOAT** Western Writers Series; BSU Western Writers Series. (1974)-. Monographic series. English. Five times a year. Price varies per volume. Boise State University English Department, 1910 University Drive, Boise ID 83725. **Tel** (208)385-3584, FAX (208)385-4373. **ED** James H. Maguire. **Circ:** 500. ***Continues*** *Boise State College Western Writers Series.*
Desc: Publishes 50-page booklets that are critical and biographical introductions to the lives and works of western American writers.
Ind/Abst MLA Int. Bibl. Books Artic. Mod. Lang. Lit.

LC MT140 ISSN 8755-5832
DD 785 US
BOOMBAH HERALD. **See** Music.

LC CT ISSN 0743-9628
DD 920 US
BORGO BIOVIEWS. [Borgo bioviews]. (1981)-. Monographic series. English. Irregular. Price varies per volume. Borgo Press, PO Box 2845, San Bernardino CA 92406. **Tel** (714)884-5813, (714)885-1161, FAX (714)888-4942.
Desc: Biographies and autobiographies of the prominent men and women of our time.

ISSN 0838-5459
DD 010/.6/0714 CN
BULLETIN - ASSOCIATION QUEBECOISE POUR L'ETUDE DE L'IMPRIME. (LE BULLETIN / ASSOCIATION QUEBECOISE POUR L'ETUDE DE L'IMPRIME.). [Bull. - Assoc. que. etude impr.]. **Added/Corp** Association Quebecoise pour l'Etude de l'Imprime. **VFOAT** Bulletin de l'AQEI. No. 1, (1988)-. Bulletin. French. Two times a year (Mar., Oct.). $25.00 (individuals), $60.00 (institutions) Comes with Association Quebecoise pour l Etude de l Imprime Membership. Association Quebec pour L'Etude Imprime, CP 92, Sherbrooke Quebec J1H 5H5 Canada. **Tel** (819)569-4355, FAX (819)821-7238. **ED** Jacques

Michon (phone: (819)821-7267). **Ad Acc. Circ:** 300 (ctrl).
Desc: Containing information on the history of publishing and book trade and literary reception.

LC PQ2605.L2 Z878 **ISSN** 0037-9506
DD 848/.9/1209 FR
BULLETIN DE LA SOCIETE PAUL CLAUDEL. See Literature.

LC PR4329 .B38
UK
BURNS CHRONICLE. Added/Corp Burns
Federation. (Aug. 1991)-. Periodical. English. Four times a year. £8.00 UK; £9.32 other. Burns Federation, Dick Institute, Elmbank Avenue, Kilmarnock United Kingdom. **Tel** 011 44 563 26401. **ED** Peter Westwood. **Ad Acc. Circ:** 800. ***Continues*** *Burns Chronicle and Club Directory, 0307-8957.*
Desc: Articles on the life and works of Burns; includes Scottish studies, lists of affiliated clubs, reports on their activities and federation activities.

LC HF5500.3.G7 B87 **ISSN** 0308-0390
DD 658.4/2/0922 B UK
BUSINESS WHO'S WHO, THE. [Bus. who's who].
1972-. English. Irregular. £15.00. Leviathan House, PO Box 978, Edison NJ 08817.

LC CT
DD 920 FR
Pr Rev.
CAHIERS HENRI BOSCO. (1981)-. French.
One time a year (June). 120.00F. L'Amitie Henri Bosco, Palais Aurore, 33BD Tzarewitch, 06000 Nice France. **Tel** 011 33 93 375555. **ED** M. Claude Girault. Index available. cum. index. **Circ:** 500. ***Continues*** *Cahiers de l'Amitie Henri Bosco, 0753-4590.*
Desc: Critical articles and works on Henri Bosco and French literature.

LC CT **ISSN** 0084-8239
DD 920 FR
CAHIERS PAUL-LOUIS COURIER.
Added/Corp Societe des Amis de Paul-Louis Courier. (1968)-. French. Two times a year (July, Dec.). $32.81. Ste des Amis de PL Courier, MME Quilici 18 rue d Arsonval, F44600 Saint Nazaire France. **Tel** 011 33 47 202266. **Bk Rev. Ad Acc. Circ:** 300 (ctrl).
Desc: Covers the life and work of Paul Louis Courier in honoring his memory.

ISSN 0068-8134
DD 338.1/7/6502571 CN
CANADA'S WHO'S WHO OF THE POULTRY INDUSTRY. 1st Edition (1955)-.
Trade Publication. English (French). One time a year (June). 8.00Can$. Farm Papers Ltd, 9547 152nd Street, Suite 105A, Surrey BC V3R 5Y5 Canada. **Tel** (604)585-3131, FAX (604)585-1504. **ED** A. Greaves. **Bk Rev. Ad Acc. Circ:** 7,000 (ctrl).
Desc: A listing by province of government, university, hatchery, egg and poultry plants, feed manufacturers, drug companies, industry associations and marketing boards for the Canadian poultry industry.

LC PR **ISSN** 0711-2173
DD 828/.91209 CN
CANADIAN C.S. LEWIS JOURNAL, THE. See Literature.

ISSN 0068-9963
DD 920/.071 CN
CCC
NLM F 1033 C212
CANADIAN WHO'S WHO, THE. Vol. 1
(1910)-. Periodical. English (French). One time a year. $160.00. University of Toronto Press, 5201 Dufferin Street, Downsview Ontario M3H 5T8 Canada. **Tel** (416)667-7781, (416)667-7810, FAX (416)667-7881. **ED** Kieran Simpson. ***Absorbed*** *Who's What in the Canadian Who's Who, 1981?, 0315-7679.*
Desc: Provides biographical information on influential Canadians. Entries give date and place of birth, education, family details, career information, memberships, creative works, honors, and awards together with full addresses.

LC PQ6337 .A26 **ISSN** 0277-6995
DD 863/.3 US
Pr Rev.
CERVANTES (GAINESVILLE, FLA.).
(CERVANTES : BULLETIN OF THE CERVANTES SOCIETY OF AMERICA.). [Cervantes]. **Added/Corp** Cervantes Society of America. Vol. 1, No. 1/2 (Fall 1981)-. Bulletin. English (Spanish). Two times a year. Comes with Cervantes Society of America membership. Cervantes Society of America, Department of Modern Languages, Denison University, Granville OH 43023. **Tel** (614)587-6228, FAX (614)587-6417. **ED** Michael McGaha (editor's address: Pomona College, Claremont CA 91711-6333; editor's phone: (909)621-8555). **Bk Rev**, (Qty: 450). **Circ:** 435.
Desc: Publishes scholarly articles on Cervantes' life and works, reviews, and notes of interest to 'Cervantistas'.
Ind/Abst MLA Int. Bibl. Books Artic. Mod. Lang. Lit.

LC PR4453.C4 Z584 **ISSN** 0317-0500
DD 828/.912/09 828/.912/09 CN
CHESTERTON REVIEW, THE. See Literature.

LC CT203 .C5C48 **ISSN** 0578-0705
DD 920 CH
CHUAN CHI WEN HSUEH. VFOAT
Biographical Literature. Vol. 1, No. 1 (June 1962)-. Periodical. Chinese. Twelve times a year. $82.00 California; $86.00 other. Biographical Literature, PO Box 1 36, Taipei Taiwan ROC. **(Subscription address:** Evergreen Publ & Stationery, 760 West Garvey Avenue, Monterey Park CA 91754. **Tel** (818)281-3622.) cum. index.

LC PL2303 .C444
DD 895.1/08/005 CC
CHUANG TSO (KUEI-YANG SHIH, CHINA). (CHUANG TSO.). VFOAT Chuangzuo.
1981-. Periodical. Chinese. RMBY1.20. Kuei-Chou Sheng Hsin Hua Shu Tien Kuei-Yang Shih, Kuei-Yang, People's Republic of China.

LC PQ2605.L2 Z6224 **ISSN** 0090-1237
DD 848/.9/1209 US
CLAUDEL STUDIES. See Literature.

LC CT
DD 920 US
COLIN WILSON STUDIES. (19??)-. English.
Irregular. Price varies per volume. Borgo Press, PO Box 2845, San Bernardino CA 92406. **Tel** (714)884-5813, (714)885-1161, FAX (714)888-4942. **ED** Colin Stanley.
Desc: This new series provides original and reprint essays on the wellknown British novelist, philosopher, and criminal psychologist.

LC CT226 .C64 **ISSN** 0882-004X
DD 920/.0788 US
COLORADO WHO'S WHO. [Colo. who's who].
1984-. English. Every 2 years. TY Publishing Ltd., PO Box 3734, Littleton CO 80161-3734.

LC E663 .C64 **ISSN** 0741-4161
DD 920/.073 US
COMMUNITY LEADERS OF AMERICA (1981). (COMMUNITY LEADERS OF AMERICA.).
11th Ed. (1981)-. English. One time a year. $49.50. Bulletin of the Menninger Clinic, PO Box 829, Topeka KS 66601. **Tel** (913)273-7500 Ext. 5850, FAX (913)273-8625. **ED** J M Evans. ctrl circ. ***Continues*** *Community Leaders and Noteworthy Americans, 0094-5587.*

LC PR6005.O4 Z5812 **ISSN** 0010-6356
DD 813 US
CONRADIANA. [Conradiana]. Vol. 1 (Summer 1968)-.
Periodical. English. Three times a year (Jan., May, Sept.). $33.00. Texas Tech University Press, Administrative Education Room 43, West Basement, Lubbock TX 79409-1037. **Tel** (800)832-4042, (806)742-2982. **ED** David Leon Higdon. **Bk Rev. Ad Acc. Circ:** 650 (ctrl). available on microfilm and microfiche from University Microfilms International (UMI). Documents available from The Genuine Article.
Desc: Studies of the life and works of Joseph Conrad and his period.
Ind/Abst Abstr. Engl. Stud.; Am. Humanit. Index; Annu. Bibliogr. Engl. Lang. Lit.; Arts Humanit. Citation Index [Full Cov.]; Curr. Contents Arts Humanit.; Lit. Crit. Regist.; MLA Int. Bibl. Books Artic. Mod. Lang. Lit.; Res. Alert [Full Cov.].

LC Z1224 .C6 **ISSN** 0010-7468
DD 928.1 US
CONTEMPORARY AUTHORS.
(CONTEMPORARY AUTHORS; A BIO-BIBLIOGRAPHICAL GUIDE TO CURRENT WRITERS IN FICTION, GENERAL NONFICTION, POETRY, JOURNALISM, DRAMA, MOTION PICTURES, TELEVISION AND OTHER FIELDS.). [Contemp. authors]. **Added/Corp** Gale Research Company. Vol. 1 (1962)-. Periodical. English. Irregular. $119.00. Gale Research Inc., 835 Penobscot Building, 645 Griswold Street, Detroit MI 48226. **Tel** (800)877-GALE, (313)961-2242, FAX (313)961-6083, (800)414-5043, telex TWX 810-221-7086. **ED** Donna Olendorf. cum. index. available on CD-ROM.
Desc: Biographical, career, personal, and publication information on more than 96,000 authors including modern novelists, poets, playwrights, scriptwriters, journalists, television correspondents, sports figures, religious leaders, and other writers.

LC PN453 .C63 **ISSN** 0748-0636
DD 809 US
CONTEMPORARY AUTHORS AUTOBIOGRAPHY SERIES. Added/Corp
Gale Research Company. **VFOAT** Contemporary Authors. Vol. 1 (1984)-. English. Irregular. $119.00. Gale Research Inc., 835 Penobscot Building, 645 Griswold Street, Detroit MI 48226. **Tel** (800)877-GALE, (313)961-2242, FAX (313)961-6083, (800)414-5043, telex TWX 810-221-7086. **ED** Joyce Nakamura.
Desc: First-person details on fiction and nonfiction writers in all genres. Reference material includes bibliographies for each author, plus a Cumulative Index to personal and place names, titles of books, and similar items mentioned in the autobiographical essays.

LC HG4057 .A15646 **ISSN** 1058-2908
DD 338.7/4/02573 US
CCC
CORPORATE YELLOW BOOK.
(CORPORATE YELLOW BOOK : WHO'S WHO AT THE LEADING LISTED U.S. COMPANIES.). [Corp. yellow book]. Vol. 8, No. 1 (Winter 1992)-. Directory. English. Four times a year. $250.00. Leadership Directories, Inc., 104 Fifth Avenue, Second Floor, New York NY 10011. **Tel** (212)627-4140, FAX (212)645-0931. **ED** Laura Gibbons. Index available (published in each issue). **Acid Free.** available on CD-ROM from Chadwyck-Healey, Inc. ***Continues*** *Corporate 1000 Yellow Book, 1049-7943.*
Desc: Provides the names, titles, addresses, telephone and facsimile numbers of over 45,000 executives who manage and direct public and privately held U.S. corporations. Includes business descriptions, product lines and annual revenues.

LC DA690.C75 C59
DD 914.24/8 UK
COVENTRY EVENING TELEGRAPH YEAR BOOK AND WHO'S WHO. (19??)-.
English. One time a year. £14.60 UK; £17.65 other. Kingslea Press Ltd., 137 Newhall Street, Birmingham B3 1SF United Kingdom. **Tel** 011 44 121 2368112, FAX 011 44 121 2001480.
Desc: Coventry City's organizations and personalities; including local authorities, educational information, social and cultural activities.

LC CT100 .C8 **ISSN** 0011-3344
DD 920 US
NLM CT 120 C976
CURRENT BIOGRAPHY. [Curr. biogr.].
Added/Corp H.W. Wilson Company. Vol. 1 (1940)-. Periodical. English. Eleven times a year. $60.00 US and Canada; $70.00 other. H W Wilson Company, 950 University Avenue, Bronx NY 10452. **Tel** (800)367-6770, (718)588-8400 ext. 2245, FAX (718)681-1511, telex 4990003 HWILSON. Documents available from UMI Article Clearinghouse.
Desc: Features the artists, politicians, business people, journalists, actors, authors, sports figures, scientists and others that make today's headlines and tomorrow's history. Provides profiles of men and women about whom timely and reliable information is in demand but often hard to find.
Ind/Abst Acad. Abstr.; Acad. Ind. [Computer File] (1984-); Acad. Search; EP Collect.; Expand. Acad. Index (1984-); Gen. Period. Index (1985-); Homework Help.; Humanit. Source; Index Period. Artic. Relat. Law; INFO-SOUTH Abstr.; Infobank (Jan. 1969-); Libr. Lit.; Mag. Index Plus (1989-); Mag. Index. Sel. (1986-); Mag. Search; MasterFile FullTEXT 1000; MasterFile FullTEXT 350; MasterFile FullTEXT 650; MasterFile FullTEXT (July 1990-); Mid. Search; Newsp. Period. Abstr. (1990-); OCLC; Pub. Lib. FullTEXT; Res. Alert; Telebase; Mag. Index (1977-);; TOM Gen. Index (1985-).

LC CT100 .C8 **ISSN** 0084-9499
DD 920/.009/04 US
NLM CT 120 C9761
CURRENT BIOGRAPHY YEARBOOK.
[Curr. biogr. yearb.]. **Added/Corp** H.W. Wilson Company. (1955)-. English. One time a year. $60.00 US and Canada; $70.00 other. H W Wilson Company, 950 University Avenue, Bronx NY 10452. **Tel** (800)367-6770, (718)588-8400 ext. 2245, FAX (718)681-1511, telex 4990003 HWILSON. Index available in last issue of volume--attached. cum. index. ***Continues*** *Current Biography (Annual).*
Desc: Provides profiles of figures whose achievements are so recent that reliable biographical information is difficult to find.
Ind/Abst Biogr. Index.

LC CT770 .D43
DD 920.041 UK
DEBRETT'S PEOPLE OF TODAY.
(PEOPLE OF TODAY.). **Added/Corp** Debrett's Peerage Limited. **VFOAT** Debrett's People of Today. (1991)-. Directory. English. One time a year (March). £97.50. Debrett's Peerage Ltd, 73-77 Britannia Road, London SW6 2JY United Kingdom. **Tel** 011 44 171 7366524, FAX 011 44 171 7317768. **ED** Jonathan Parker. **Ad Acc.** ctrl circ. ***Continues*** *Debrett's Distinguished People of Today.*
Desc: Information on Britain's most notable and successful people.

LC CS42 .D4 **ISSN** 0418-4904
DD 929 US
DEEP SOUTH GENEALOGICAL QUARTERLY. See Genealogy and Heraldry.

LC DD232.5 .D386
DD 943/.08/08 GW
DEUTSCHE ANNALEN. 1.- Year; 1972-.
German. Druffel-Verlag Starnberger, W 8131 Leoni Am Germany.

Biographies

LC F1005 .D49
DD 920/.071
NLM F 1005 D554
ISSN 0070-4717
CN
DICTIONARY OF CANADIAN BIOGRAPHY.
Vol. 1 (1700)-. Monographic series. English. Irregular. Price varies per volume. University of Toronto Press, 5201 Dufferin Street, Downsview Ontario M3H 5T8 Canada. **Tel** (416)667-7781, (416)667-7810, FAX (416)667-7881.

LC CT
DD 920
UK
DICTIONARY OF INTERNATIONAL BIOGRAPHY.
Added/Corp International Biographical Centre. 21st Ed. (1990/91)-. English. International Biographical Centre, c/o Biblio Distribution Centre, 4720 Boston Way, Lanham MD 20706. **Tel** telex 81584. **Continues in part** Dictionary of International Biography and International Youth in Achievement.

LC PS221 .D5
DD 810/.9 B
ISSN 0731-7867
US
DICTIONARY OF LITERARY BIOGRAPHY YEARBOOK.
[Dict. lit. biogr. yearb.]. **Added/Corp** Gale Research Company. (1980)-. English. One time a year. $120.00. Gale Research Inc., 835 Penobscot Building, 645 Griswold Street, Detroit MI 48226. **Tel** (800)877-GALE, (313)961-2242, FAX (313)961-6083, (800)414-5043, telex TWX 810-221-7086. **ED** James W. Hipp.
Desc: Focuses on a specific literary movement or period, so that the entire series encompasses all who have contributed to literature in America, England, and elsewhere.

LC CT
DD 920
US
DICTIONARY OF SCIENTIFIC BIOGRAPHY.
Added/Corp American Council of Learned Societies. Vol. 1, (1970)-. English. Irregular. $92.00. Macmillan Publishing Company / New Jersey, 100 Front Street, Box 500, Riverside NJ 08075-7500. **Tel** (800)257-5755, (609)461-6500, FAX (609)461-7070.

LC F1005 .D52
ISSN 0420-0446
CN
DICTIONNAIRE BIOGRAPHIQUE DU CANADA.
Vol. 1 (1966)-. Monographic series. French. Irregular. Price varies per volume. Presses de l'Universite Laval, CP 2447 Avenue de la Medicine, Saint Foy Quebec G1K 7P4 Canada. **Tel** (418)656-5106, (418)656-2590.

LC CT
DD 920
ISSN 0415-8091
FR
DICTIONNAIRE DE BIOGRAPHIE FRANCAISE.
French. Six times a year. 248.00F. Letouzey et Ane, 87 boulevard Raspail, 75006 Paris France. **Tel** 011 33 1 45488014.
Desc: Biographies of French people from the Gaule period to the present.

LC CT
DD 920
ISSN 0315-0801
CN
DINOSAURIAN WHO'S-WHO.
No. 1- 1971-. Periodical. English. Richard L Coulton, Bentley Alberta T0C 0J0 Canada.

LC K7051
DD 341.7
ISSN 0417-5131
UK
DIPLOMATIC PRESS DIRECTORY OF THE REPUBLIC OF CYPRUS INCLUDING TRADE INDEX AND BIOGRAPHICAL SECTION. See Political Science-International Relations.

LC CT220 .D573
DD 920/.073
ISSN 0742-3349
US
DIRECTORY OF DISTINGUISHED AMERICANS, THE.
[Dir. disting. Am.]. Directory. English. 205 West Martin Street, PO Box 226, Raleigh NC 27602.

LC CT
DD 920
ISSN 0749-940X
US
DUST (BIG COVE TANNERY, PA.).
(DUST.). No. 1 (Jan. 1985). Periodical. English. Irregular (nominal quarterly). $6.00. The Camel Press, HC 80 Box 160, Big Cove Tannery PA 17212. **Tel** (717)204-3033. **ED** James Hedges. **Circ:** 500.
Desc: Journal of autobiography.

LC JQ3194 .E45
DD 351/.2/09660097541
FR
ELITES AFRICAINES, LES. (19??)-.
Monographic series. French. Irregular. Price varies per volume. IC Publications Ediafric, 10 rue Vineuse, 75116 Paris France. **Tel** 011 33 1 44308100. **Bk Rev**.
Desc: Complete biographies of 1,500 politicians, diplomats, and economists of the Ivory Coast, Senegal, Cameroon and Gabon.

LC TJ163.45 .I58
DD 621.042/092 B
UK
ENERGY & NUCLEAR SCIENCES INTERNATIONAL WHO'S WHO.
Added/Corp Longman (Firm). **VFOAT** Energy and Nuclear Sciences International Who's Who. 2nd Ed. (1987)-. English. $396.00. Longman Group Ltd., Fourth Avenue, Longman House, Harlow Essex CM19 5SR United Kingdom. **Tel** 011 44 1279 429655, FAX 011 44 1279 431067, telex 81259. **(Subscription address:** Gale Research Co., 835 Penobscot Building, Detroit MI 48226. **Tel** (800)347-4253). **Continues** International Who's Who in Energy and Nuclear Sciences, 0952-1100.
Desc: Provides personal, career, and professional data on more than 3,000 energy and nuclear scientists and engineers.

LC CT1353 .E86
SP
ESPANOLES, LOS. (19??)-. Periodical. Spanish. One time a week.

LC PS3529.N5 Z4583
DD 812/.52
Pr Rev.
ISSN 1040-9483
US
EUGENE O'NEILL REVIEW, THE.
[Eugene O'Neill rev.]. **Added/Corp** Eugene O'Neill Society. Suffolk University. Vol. 13, No. 1 (Spring 1989)-. Periodical. English. Two times a year (Spring and Fall). $10.00 US and Canada; $15.00 other; $20.00 membership. Suffolk University / English, Department of English, Boston MA 02114. **Tel** (617)573-8272. **ED** Frederick W Wilkins. Index available. **Bk Rev. Ad Acc. Circ:** 450 (ctrl). **Continues** Eugene O'Neill Newsletter, 0733-0456.
Desc: Essays on O'Neill's life, work and times plus book and performance reviews, photos, news, notes and queries and records of the Eugene O'Neill Society and activity around the world.
Ind/Abst MLA Int. Bibl. Books Artic. Mod. Lang. Lit.

LC JN15 .W47
DD 341.24/2/025
BE
EURO WHO'S WHO: WHO'S WHO IN THE EUROPEAN COMMUNITIES AND IN THE OTHER EUROPEAN ORGANIZATIONS.
VFOAT European Who's Who. (1992)-. English (French and German). **Continues** Who's Who, European Communities and Other European Organizations.

LC CT759 .E93
DD 920.04/03 B
NLM CT 120; W631
BE
EUROPEAN BIOGRAPHICAL DIRECTORY.
8th Ed. (1989-1990)-. English. Irregular. $369.62. Dawson UK Ltd, Cannon House, Folkestone Kent CT19 5EE United Kingdom. **Tel** 011 44 1303 850101, FAX 011 44 1303 850440, telex 96392. **Continues** Who's Who in Europe.

LC PR6045.A97 Z4583
DD 823
Pr Rev.
ISSN 1058-8272
US
EVELYN WAUGH NEWSLETTER AND STUDIES.
[Evelyn Waugh newsl. stud.]. Vol. 24, No. 1 (Spring 1990)-. Newsletter. English. Three times a year. $8.00. Nassau Community College English Department, State University of New York, Garden City NY 11530. **Tel** (516)222-7187. **ED** Dr. Paul A. Doyle (Editor's telephone: (516)572-7792). **Bk Rev**, (Qty: 3-4). **Ad Acc. Circ:** 220.
Continues Evelyn Waugh Newsletter, 0014-3693.
Desc: Research, biographical and bibliographical articles and reviews relating to the life and writings of English satirist and novelist Evelyn Waugh.
Ind/Abst MLA Int. Bibl. Books Artic. Mod. Lang. Lit.

LC CT
DD 920
NE
FACSIMILES OF EARLY BIOGRAPHIES.
(19??)-. Monographic series. English (German, French and Dutch). Irregular. Price varies per volume. Uitgeverij Frits Knuf B V, PO Box 720, 4116 ZJ Buuren Netherlands. **Tel** 011 31 03449-1255, FAX 011 31 03449-2617.

LC PS3511.A86 Z7832126
DD 813/.52
ISSN 0733-6357
US
FAULKNER NEWSLETTER AND YOKNAPATAWPHA REVIEW, THE.
[Faulkner newsl. Yoknapatawpha rev.]. **VFOAT** Faulkner Newsletter; Faulkner Newsletter and Yoknapatawpha Review. Vol. 1, No. 1 (Jan./March 1981)-. Newsletter. English. Four times a year. $12.50. Yoknapatawpha Press, PO Box 248, Oxford MS 38655. **Tel** (601)234-0909. **ED** William Boozer. Index available. **Bk Rev**, (Qty: 6). **Ad Acc, Adv Mgr:** D. Wells. **Circ:** 500.
Desc: Newsletter about the life and work of William Faulkner.

LC CS597.B7 G45
DD 929/.1/07204457
UDC 929.5/.6(44)
ISSN 0223-7237
FR
GENEALOGIES BOURBONNAISES ET DU CENTRE / CERCLE GENEALOGIQUE ET HERALDIQUE DU BOURBONNAIS.
See Genealogy and Heraldry.

LC Z6001 .G425 G67
DD 910/.92/2
US
GEOGRAPHERS : BIOBIBLIOGRAPHICAL STUDIES. See Geography.

LC PT2046 .G73
DD 831/.6
ISSN 0734-3329
US
GOETHE YEARBOOK.
(GOETHE YEARBOOK : PUBLICATIONS OF THE GOETHE SOCIETY OF NORTH AMERICA). [Goethe yearb.]. **Added/Corp** Goethe Society of North America. Vol. 1 (1982)-. Monographic series. English (German). Irregular. $56.95. Camden House, Drawer 2025, Columbia SC 29202. **Tel** (803)736-9455. **(Subscription address:** Camden House Inc., PO Box 4836 Hampden Station, Baltimore MD 21211. **Tel** (410)516-6950, (800)723-9455.) **ED** Thomas Saine. **Bk Rev. Circ:** 300.
Desc: Literary criticism and book reviews on Goethe and the Goethe period.
Ind/Abst MLA Int. Bibl. Books Artic. Mod. Lang. Lit.

LC JC345
DD 929.82
AT
GOVERNMENT WHO'S WHO OF AUSTRALIA. (19??)-.
English. Three times a year. 242.54Aus$. Riddell Information Services Pty Limited, PO Box 3942, Sydney New South Wales 2001 Australia. **Tel** 11 61 23682100, FAX 11 61 23682150, telex 126736.
Continues Business Who's Who Guide to Government.

LC JC345
DD 929.82
US
GREAT LIVES OBSERVED. (19??)-.
Monographic series. English. Irregular. Price varies per volume. Prentice-Hall Law and Business, 270 Sylvan Avenue, Englewood Cliffs NJ 07632. **Tel** (800)223-0231, (201)894-8538, FAX (201)894-8666.

LC PT2328 .H43
ISSN 0073-1692
GW
HEINE-JAHRBUCH. See Literature.

LC F1059.5.G9 H57
DD 971.3/43005
ISSN 0709-5562
CN
HISTORIC GUELPH. See History-History of North and South America.

LC CT1840 .H64
KO
HONGBO INMUL YONGAM. 1983-. Korean.
W35.000. Toso Chulpan Ilsim Sasoham, 5160-Ho Chungang Ucheguk, Seoul Korea.

LC PR4809.H15 H64a
DD 821/.9/12
ISSN 0305-926X
UK
HOUSMAN SOCIETY JOURNAL. See Literature.

LC E185.96
DD 920.0481
NO
HVEM ER HVEM?. (1912)-. Norwegian. Irregular (every four years).
Kr495.00. Olaf Norliss Bokhandel, c/o Universitetsgt 24, Oslo 1 Norway. **Tel** 011 47 2 429135, FAX 011 47 2 111022, telex 79265.

LC Z5301 .M37a CT104
DD 920/.073
ISSN 1080-1154
US
●INDEX TO MARQUIS WHO'S WHO PUBLICATIONS.
[Index Marquis Who's Who publ.]. **Added/Corp** Marquis Who's Who, Inc. (1994)-. Bibliography. English. One time a year (Mar.). $95.00. Marquis Who's Who, A Reed Reference Publishing Company, Part of Reed International PLC, 121 Chanlon Road, New Providence NJ 07974. **Tel** (908)464-6800, (800)521-8110, FAX (908)665-6688, telex 138 755. Index available. **Continues** Marquis Who's Who Index to Who's Who Books, 0884-7118.
Desc: Index to biographies listed in the latest editions of most Marquis Who's Who publications.

LC CT1506 .I53
ISSN 0073-6244
II
INDIA WHO'S WHO. (1969)-.
English. One time a year (October). $95.00. Infa Publications, Parliament Street Jeevandeep, New Delhi 110001 India. **Tel** 011 91 11 3733330. **ED** Inder Jit and Poonam Kaushish. Index available. cum. index. **Bk Rev**, (Qty: 5000). **Ad Acc. Circ:** 5000. available on diskette.
Desc: Contains biographical information about 4,000 of India's personalities who, by virtue of their position and achievement, have proved to be of significant value in their perspective fields.

LC HF3810.J33 J84
DD 380.12/025/598
IO
INDONESIA BUYER'S GUIDE & WHO'S WHO.
VFOAT Indonesia Buyer's Guide and Who's Who; Indonesia Buyer's Guide and Who's Who in Indonesia; I.B.G. and Who's Who in Indonesia; Indonesia Buyer's Guide & Who's Who in Indonesia. (1984)-. English (Indonesian). One time a year. Rp30.000. CV Taro Trade and Industries Publishing and Printing, Sangga Buana Building/Room 204, 44 Jl Senen Raya, PO Box 3472, Jakarta Indonesia. **Continues** JSMBG & Who's Who in Indonesia.

LC Z1010 .I57 ISSN 0143-8263
DD 808 B UK

INTERNATIONAL AUTHORS AND WRITERS WHO'S WHO, THE. [Int. authors writ. who's who]. 7th Ed. (1976)-. Monographic series. English. Every 2 years. Price varies per volume. International Biographical Center, 3 Regal Lane Soham, Ely Cambridge CB7 5BA United Kingdom. **Tel** 011 44 171 353721091, FAX 011 44 171 353721839, telex 81584. **Bk Rev. Circ:** 10,000. ***Continues*** *Author's & Writer's Who's Who;* ***Absorbed*** *International Who's Who in Poetry, 0539-1342.* ***Continued in part by*** *International Who's Who in Poetry and poet's encyclopaedia.*
Desc: Lists biographies of contemporary writers, poets, journalists, critics, editors, etc., from all over the world.

LC HD69.C6 I593 ISSN 0749-2685
DD 001/.025 US

INTERNATIONAL REGISTRY OF ORGANIZATION DEVELOPMENT PROFESSIONALS AND ORGANIZATION DEVELOPMENT HANDBOOK, THE. **Added/Corp** Organization Development Institute. (19??)-. English. One time a year. comes with Organization Develpment Institute Membership. The Organization Development Institute, 11234 Walnut Ridge Road, Chesterland OH 44026. **Tel** (216)461-4333. **ED** Donald W. Cole. **Circ:** 700. ***Continues*** *International Registry of Organization Development Professionals.*
Desc: List credentials of registered organization development professionals plus information on organization development, academic programs, code of ethics, and other organizations.

LC CT120 .I5 ISSN 0074-9613
DD 920.01 UK
CCC

NLM CT 120 I613

INTERNATIONAL WHO'S WHO, THE. **Added/Corp** Europa Publications Limited. 1st Ed. (1935)-. English. One time a year. $280.00. Europa Publications Ltd., 18 Bedford Square, London WC1B 3JN United Kingdom. **Tel** 011 44 171 5808236, telex 21540 EUROPA G. **(Subscription address:** Gale Research Co., 835 Penobscot Building, Detroit MI 48226. **Tel** (800)347-4253.) **ED** Richard Fitzwilliams.
Desc: Provides biographical information on individuals in international affairs, government, diplomacy, the liberal professions, all branches of the arts, and sports. Each entry gives the person's date and place of birth, nationality, education, etc.

LC DS32.6 .I57
DD 950/.07/2 HK

INTERNATIONAL WHO'S WHO IN ASIAN STUDIES. **Added/Corp** Asian Research Service. (1976)-. English. One time a year. $30.00 US. Asian Research Service, Sub Department, GPO Box 2232, Hong Kong Hong Kong. **Tel** 011 852 25707227, FAX 011 852 25128050, telex 63899 CONPA HX. **ED** Nelson Leung. **Circ:** 2,000.
Desc: Provides full biographical information of scholars in Asian and Oriental studies.

LC HV27 .I57 ISSN 0306-3488
DD 361/.0025 UK

INTERNATIONAL WHO'S WHO IN COMMUNITY SERVICE. (1973/74)-. English. Eddison Press, 2 Greycoat Place, London SW1P 1SB United Kingdom. ***Absorbed*** *Directory of Public Affairs; Repertoire d'Affaires Publiques; Who's Who in Public Affairs; Dictionnaire Biographique de Service Publique; Who's Who in Sussex.*

LC TA12 .I575
DD 620/.0092/2 B UK

INTERNATIONAL WHO'S WHO IN ENGINEERING. (1984)-. English. varies. Melrose Press Ltd., 3 Regal Lane Soham, Ely Cambridgeshire, CB7 5BA United Kingdom. **Tel** 011 44 135 3721091, FAX 011 44 135 3721839, telex 81584.

LC ML106.G7 W4 ISSN 0307-2894
DD 780/.92/2 [B] UK

INTERNATIONAL WHO'S WHO IN MUSIC AND MUSICIANS' DIRECTORY. 7th Ed. (1975)-. Directory. English. Irregular (Published every 2 to 3 years). $165.00 (latest edition). Melrose Press Ltd., 3 Regal Lane Soham, Ely Cambridgeshire, CB7 5BA United Kingdom. **Tel** 011 44 135 3721091, FAX 011 44 135 3721839, telex 81584. **(Subscription address:** Taylor & Francis Inc., 1900 Frost Road, Suite 101, Bristol PA 19007-1598. **Tel** (215)785-5800, (800)821-8312, FAX (215)785-5515.) **Bk Rev. Circ:** 5,000. ***Continues*** *Who's Who in Music and Musicians' International Directory.*
Desc: Biographical entries on contemporary musicians, composers, singers, critics and conductors throughout the world. Additional material includes data on orchestras, musical organizations, competitions, music libraries, colleges and other educational establishments.

LC CT1860 .I57
DD 920/.0009174927 UK

INTERNATIONAL WHO'S WHO OF THE ARAB WORLD, THE. **VFOAT** Who's Who of the Arab World. 1st Ed. (1978-79)-. English. International Who's Who of the Arab World Ltd, 184 Hammersmith Road, London W6 7DJ United Kingdom.

LC JA51 .I57 ISSN 0074-9621
DD 305.8 US

INTERNATIONAL YEAR BOOK AND STATESMEN'S WHO'S WHO, THE. (1953)-. English. One time a year. $325.00. Taylor & Francis Ltd. / UK, Rankine Road, Basingstoke, Hampshire RG24 8PR United Kingdom. **Tel** 011 44 1256 840366, FAX 011 44 1256 479438, telex 858540. **(Subscription address:** Taylor & Francis Inc., 1900 Frost Road, Suite 101, Bristol PA 19007-1598. **Tel** (215)785-5800, (800)821-8312, FAX (215)785-5515.)
Desc: Over 10,000 biographies and addresses of leaders in government, commerce, and other fields. Directory of national, international, and regional organizations; surveys of national governments, legal systems, population, financial, commercial and industrial statistics, etc.

LC E184.I6 I65 ISSN 0742-6771
DD 920/.00929162 US

IRISH AMERICAN WHO'S WHO, THE. [Ir. Am. who's who]. **VFOAT** Irish-American Who's Who. English. Irregular. $60.00. Irish American Who's Who, PO Box 735, Pearl River NY 10965. **Tel** (212)350-4557. **ED** John Concannon and Frank Cull. **Circ:** 50,000.
Desc: Contains more than 2,000 biographies plus the Gaelic Hall of Fame and the Gallery of Irish American Presidents.

LC CT
DD 920 JA

JINJI KOSHINROKU. (1903)-. Periodical. Japanese. Every 2 years. $1230.00. Jinji Koshinjo, 2-1-2-chome Marunouchi, Chiyoda-ku Tokyo Japan. **Tel** (03)287-2351. **(Subscription address:** Japan Publications Trading Company Ltd., PO Box 5030, Tokyo International, Tokyo 100-31 Japan. **Tel** 011 81 3 3292 3753.) **ED** Shigeo Takenouchi. **Circ:** 15,000.
Desc: Biographies on chief staff-members of public and business organizations and other significant figures in Japan.

LC PR2248 .A2 ISSN 0738-9655
DD 821/.3 US

JOHN DONNE JOURNAL. **See** Literary and Political Reviews.

LC PR6005.O4 Z754 ISSN 0162-413X
DD 823/.914 US

JOSEPH CONRAD TODAY. Vol. 1 (Oct. 1975)-. Periodical. English. Three times a year. $15.00 (institutions), $12.00 (individuals) US; $18.00 (institutions), $15.00 (individuals) other. Joseph Conrad Society America, Drexel University, Philadelphia PA 19104. **Tel** (215)895-2446, FAX (215)895-4999. **ED** R. Brebach. **Bk Rev. Ad Acc. Circ:** 200.
Desc: Programs, reports, abstracts of Conrad Society, reports and abstracts of other Conrad meetings, publications, research and issues related to Conrad and his works.
Ind/Abst Annu. Bibliogr. Engl. Lang. Lit.

LC B128.C8 J68
DD 299/.512/05 HK

JOURNAL OF CONFUCIUS, THE GRAND MASTER OF ALL AGES, THE. **VFOAT** Confucius; Wan Shih Shih Piao; Confucio, Mestre da Sabedoria; Confucio, Maestro de la Sabiduria. Vol. 1 (Oct. 1982)-. English. One time a year. Clic Ltd, Capital Commercial Building, 4th Floor, 26 Leighton Road, Causeway Bay Hong Kong.

LC CS1 .O7
DD 929.1/05 US

•**JOURNAL / ORANGE COUNTY CALIFORNIA GENEALOGICAL SOCIETY.** **See** Genealogy and Heraldry.

LC CT1836 .K63
DD 920.05 JA

KOKUSAI JINJI KOSHINROKU : ZENKOKUHEN. (1970)-. Periodical. Japanese. ¥60000. Kokusai Jinji Koshinjo, 4-6 Ginza 7-chome Chuo-ku 104, Tokyo Japan.

LC DL144 .K7 ISSN 0900-1476
DK

NLM CT 1263 K89

KRAKS BLA BOG. (1910)-. Danish. One time a year. kr40.00. Kraks Forlag As, Virumgaardsvej 21, DK-2830 Virum Denmark. **Tel** 45 83 45 83, FAX 45 83 10 11. cum. index.
Desc: Contains 8,300 biographies of who's who in Denmark.

LC DB2045 .L4
DD 943.7/1/005 GW

LEBENSBILDER ZUR GESCHICHTE DER BOHMISCHEN LANDER. **Added/Corp** Collegium Carolinum (Munich, Germany). Tagung. (1974)-. German. Irregular. DM28.00. R Oldenbourg Verlag, Postfach 801360, D-81613 Munich Germany. **Tel** 011 49 89 450190, FAX 011 49 89 45019305. **ED** Ferdinand Seibt. **Circ:** 1,000 (ctrl).

LC HF3564.5 .L4
GW

LEITENDE MANNER UND FRAUER DER WIRTSCHAFT. (Aug. 27, 1979)-. German. Verlag Hoppenstedt & Company, Postfach 100139, D-64201 Darmstadt Germany. **Tel** 011 49 6151 380436, 011 49 6151 380361. ***Continues*** *Leitende Manner der Wirtschaft.*

ISSN 0824-4529
DD 971.3/26/00922 CN

LONDON'S WHO & WHY MAGAZINE. [Lond. who why mag.]. **VFOAT** Who & Why. Summer 1983-. Periodical. English. Twelve times a year. $10.00. London's Who & Why Magazine, 148 York Street, London Ontario N6A 1A9 Canada. ***Continues*** *London's Popular Guide to Who's Who and Why, 0824-4537.*

LC PS1329 .M3 ISSN 0025-3499
DD 817.44 US

MARK TWAIN JOURNAL (1954). (MARK TWAIN JOURNAL.). [Mark Twain j.]. Vol. 9, No. 4 (Summer, 1954)-. Periodical. English. Two times a year (Spring & Fall). $18.00. Mark Twain Journal, English Department, Charleston College, Charleston SC 29424. **Tel** (803)723-0487. **ED** Thomas A. Tenney. cum. index (1936-1983). **Circ:** 800. available on microfilm and microfiche from University Microfilms International (UMI). Documents available from The Genuine Article. ***Continues*** *Mark Twain Quarterly.*
Desc: Emphasis is on factual treatment of Twain's life and works, drawing on contemporary sources such as letters, interviews, and photographs.
Ind/Abst Abstr. Engl. Stud.; Am. Humanit. Index; Annu. Bibliogr. Engl. Lang. Lit.; Arts Humanit. Citation Index [Full Cov.]; Curr. Contents Arts Humanit.; Lit. Crit. Regist.; MLA Int. Bibl. Books Artic. Mod. Lang. Lit.; Res. Alert [Full Cov.].

LC Z5301 .M37a CT104 ISSN 0884-7118
DD 920/.073 US
TITLE CHANGE

MARQUIS WHO'S WHO INDEX TO WHO'S WHO BOOKS. [Marquis Who's Who index Who's Who books]. **Added/Corp** Marquis Who's Who, Inc. **VFOAT** Index to Who's Who Books. (1985)-(1993). English. Marquis Who's Who, A Reed Reference Publishing Company, Part of Reed International PLC, 121 Chanlon Road, New Providence NJ 07974. **Tel** (908)464-6800, (800)521-8110, FAX (908)665-6688, telex 138 755. ***Continues*** *Marquis Who's Who, Inc. Marquis Who's Who Publications Index to all Books, 0148-3528.* ***Continued by*** *Index to Marquis Who's Who Publications.*

LC R134 .I57
DD 610/.92/2 B UK
NLM W 22.1; I64

MEDICAL SCIENCES INTERNATIONAL WHO'S WHO. **Added/Corp** Gale Research Company. 3rd Ed. (1987)-. English. One time a year (March). $585.00. Longman Group Ltd., Fourth Avenue, Longman House, Harlow Essex CM19 5SR United Kingdom. **Tel** 011 44 1279 429655, FAX 011 44 1279 431067, telex 81259. **(Subscription address:** Gale Research Co., 835 Penobscot Building, Detroit MI 48226. **Tel** (800)347-4253.) ***Continues*** *International Medical Who's Who.*
Desc: Provides biographical information on nearly 8,000 senior biomedical scientists and their researchers working in more than 90 countries worldwide. Conveniently arranged by scientist's last name, entries provide complete contact details as well as information on degrees, work experience, present position, employers, directorships held, national appointments and memberships and more.

LC D115 .M4 ISSN 0198-9405
DD 920/.009/02 US
Pr Rev.

MEDIEVAL PROSOPOGRAPHY. [Mediev. prosopogr.]. Vol. 1, No. 1 (Spring 1980)-. Periodical. English (German and French). Two times a year. $20.00. Medieval Institute Publiscations, Western Michigan University, Kalamazoo MI 49008-3851. **Tel** (616)387-8755, FAX (616)387-8750. **ED** Candance Porath. Index available. cum. index. **Bk Rev. Ad Acc. Circ:** 250.
Desc: Covers any subject pertaining to life in the medieval period, such as warfare, family structure, business, agriculture, land transfer, government, religion and law.
Ind/Abst Annu. Bibliogr. Engl. Lang. Lit.

Biographies

LC PS2386 .A14
ISSN 0193-8991
US
Pr Rev.
MELVILLE SOCIETY EXTRACTS. [Melville Soc. extr.]. **Main/Corp** Melville Society. **Added/Corp** Melville Society. **VFOAT** Extracts. No. 34 (May 1978)-. Periodical. English. Four times a year (Feb., May, Sept., Nov.). $10.00. Melville Society Extracts, Salisbury State University, Treasurer John Wenke, Salisbury MD 21801. **Tel** (410)543-6445. **ED** John Bryant. Index available (Every 6 years). cum. index. **Bk Rev**, (Qty: 4). **Circ:** 800 (ctrl). **Continues** Extracts - Melville Society, 0193-7626.
Desc: Life, times and writings of the American author Herman Melville (1819-1891).
Ind/Abst Abstr. Engl. Stud.; Am. Humanit. Index; Lit. Crit. Regist.; MLA Int. Bibl. Books Artic. Mod. Lang. Lit.

LC CT120 .M43
DD 920/.009/04
NLM CT 120 M534
ISSN 0306-3666
UK
MEN OF ACHIEVEMENT. Vol. 1 (1974)-. English. Two times a year. $199.00. Melrose Press Ltd., 3 Regal Lane Soham, Ely Cambridgeshire, CB7 5BA United Kingdom. **Tel** 011 44 135 3721091, FAX 011 44 135 3721839, telex 81584. **(Subscription address:** Taylor & Francis Inc., 1900 Frost Road, Suite 101, Bristol PA 19007-1598. **Tel** (215)785-5800, (800)821-8312, FAX (215)785-5515.**) Bk Rev. Circ:** 4,000.
Desc: Biographical entries of contemporary male figures from all over the world.

LC PR3579 .M48
DD 821/.4
ISSN 0026-4326
US
CCC
MILTON QUARTERLY. See Literary and Political Reviews.

LC PS3521.E735 Z783
DD 813/.54
Pr Rev.
ISSN 0196-2604
US
CEASED
MOODY STREET IRREGULARS. See Literature.

LC PG3476.N3 Z94
DD 813/.54
ISSN 0894-7120
US
NABOKOVIAN, THE. [Nabokovian]. **Added/Corp** Vladimir Nabokov Society. No. 13 (Fall 1984)-. Periodical. English. Two times a year. $14.00. Slavic Languages & Literatures, University of Kansas, Lawrence KS 66045. **Tel** (913)864-3313. cum. index. **Continues** Vladimir Nabokov Research Newsletter, 0886-4993.
Desc: Devoted to the life and writings of Vladimir Nabokov. Publishes the annual Nabokov bibliography; news of Nabokov studies around the world; abstracts of articles, books, and dissertations; annotations to Nabokov's works; special features, including previously unpublished interviews and other writings; photographs and illustrations; special bibliographies; notes and queries.
Ind/Abst Am. Bibliogr. Slavic East Europ. Stud.; Annu. Bibliogr. Engl. Lang. Lit.; MLA Int. Bibl. Books Artic. Mod. Lang. Lit.

LC CT
DD 920
ISSN 0737-397X
US
NAMES IN THE NEWS. (NAMES IN THE NEWS [MICROFORM].). [Names news]. **Added/Corp** NewsBank, Inc. Vol. 5, Card 1 (Aug. 1982)-. Periodical. English. Twelve times a year. $329.60 high schools and junior high schools; $595.34 institutions. Newsbank Inc., 58 Pine Street, New Canaan CT 06840. **Tel** (800)243-7694, (800)762-8182, FAX (203)966-6254. **Continues** NewsBank. Names in the News.

LC CT103 .N3
DD 920.02
US
NATIONAL REGISTER OF PROMINENT AMERICANS AND INTERNATIONAL NOTABLES. Monographic series. English. Irregular. Price varies per volume. National Register of Prominent Americans, Drawer 100, Nokomis FL 33555. available on microfilm from University Microfilms International (UMI).

LC CT
DD 920
GW
NEUE DEUTSCHE BIOGRAPHIE. German. Irregular. DM178.00. Duncker und Humblot Verlag, Postfach 410329, D-12113 Berlin Germany. **Tel** 011 49 30 79000612, 011 49 30 79000613.

LC CT120 .N45
DD 920/.009/04
ISSN 0161-2433
US
NEW YORK TIMES BIOGRAPHICAL SERVICE, THE. Vol. 5, No. 12 (Dec. 1974)-. Periodical. English. Twelve times a year. $85.00. University Microfilms International, 300 North Zeeb Road, Ann Arbor MI 48106-1346. **Tel** (313)761-4700, (800)521-0600 Exts. 2490, 2491, FAX (313)973-1540. ctrl circ. **Continues** New York Times Biographical Edition.
Ind/Abst Biogr. Index.

LC HC621 .N4
DD 338
ISSN 0071-9571
NZ
NEW ZEALAND BUSINESS WHO'S WHO, THE. (1935)-. Directory. English. One time a year (Mar.). $220.63. NZ Financial Press Ltd., PO Box 1881, Auckland New Zealand. **Tel** 011 64 9 3071287, FAX 011 64 9 3732634. **ED** Peter Clark. **Bk Rev. Ad Acc. Circ:** 7,000. available on diskette.
Desc: Nationwide business directory containing over 16,150 listings. Information includes company profiles, indexes of directors, products and services, brands, agencies, company ownership and many more.

LC PS1029.A3 Z74
ISSN 0028-9396
US
NEWSBOY. See Literature.

LC CT120 .C663
DD 920/.009/04
ISSN 0899-0417
US
NEWSMAKERS (DETROIT, MICH.). (NEWSMAKERS.). [Newsmakers]. **Added/Corp** Gale Research Inc. Issue 2 (1988)-. Periodical. English. Four times a year. $95.00. Gale Research Inc., 835 Penobscot Building, 645 Griswold Street, Detroit MI 48226. **Tel** (800)877-GALE, (313)961-2242, FAX (313)961-6083, (800)414-5043, telex TWX 810-221-7086. **ED** Louise Mooney. available on magnetic tape; available on diskette; available on an online database (File GALBIO in the PEOPLE, ENTERTAINMENT, AND SPORTS Libraries) from NEXIS. **Continues** Contemporary Newsmakers, 0883-1564.
Desc: Provides biographical profiles of the people making today's headlines. A hardbound cumulation provides a reference source on 200 newsmakers of the year. Other features include: clearly labeled data sections, sidelights, photographs, and sources for additional information.

LC CT
DD 920
FR
NOUVEAU DICTIONNAIRE DES BIOGRAPHIES FRANCAISES ET ETRANGERES. Vol. 1 (1961)-. French. Irregular. Labarre de Railicourt, 5 Square Charles Dickens, F-75016 Paris France.

LC DE7
DD 909
ISSN 1047-3068
US
OLD NEWS (MARIETTA, PA.). See History.

LC AP65 .O7
PO
OPCAO. Vol. 1 (April 29, 1976)-. Periodical. Portuguese. Sociedade de Publicacoes Lda, rua Artur Paiva 38, Lisbon Portugal.

LC E747 .A683 1956
DD 920.073
US
OPPORTUNITY STILL KNOCKS : FREEDOM'S LIVING PROOF OF THE OPPORTUNITIES IN OUR AMERICAN WAY OF LIFE / HORATIO ALGER AWARDS COMMITTEE OF THE AMERICAN SCHOOLS AND COLLEGES ASSOCIATION. Added/Corp American Schools and Colleges Association. Horatio Alger Awards Committee. (1956)-. English. One time a year. Horatio Alger Society, c/o Robert E. Kasper, 585 Street Andrews Drive, Media PA 19063.

LC CT3260 .O75
DD 920.72
US
SUSPENDED
OUTSTANDING YOUNG WOMEN OF AMERICA. See Women's Interests.

LC DT515.9 .O9 O97
DD 966.9/2
NR
OYO STATE YEAR BOOK AND WHO'S WHO. See History-History of Africa.

LC HG8704.5.A4 P33
DD 368/.9/5491
PK
PAKISTAN INSURANCE SURVEY & WHO'S WHO. 1975-. English. $2.00. Bankinsurance News, 4 Amil Street, Karachi 1 Pakistan.

LC CT1230 .P34
ISSN 0137-3234
PL
PAMIETNIKARSTWO POLSKIE. [Pam. pol.]. **Added/Corp** Polska Akademia Nauk. Komitet Badan Socjologicznych. Towarzystwo Przyjacio Pamietnikarstwa. Centrum Pamietnikarstwa Polskiego. (July/Sept. 1971)-. Polish. Four times a year. **(Subscription address:** Ars Polona-Ruch, PO Box 1001, Krakowskie Przedmiescie 7, 00-068 Warsaw Poland. **Tel** 011 48 22 261201.)
Ind/Abst Am. Hist. Life (1954-1956).

LC CT
DD 920
US
PAPERS OF THOMAS A. EDISON. (19??)-. Monographic series. English. Irregular. Price varies per volume. Johns Hopkins University Press, 2715 North Charles Street, Baltimore MD 21218-4319. **Tel** (410)516-6987, FAX (410)516-6968.

LC CS
DD 929
BE
PARCHEMIN, LE. See Genealogy and Heraldry.

DD 920
ISSN 1062-2713
US
PEOPLE IN THE NEWS. [People news]. 1st Ed. (1991)-. English. Macmillan Publishing Company / New York, 866 3rd Avenue, New York NY 10022. **Tel** (212)702-2000, (800)257-5755.

LC F2175 .P4
DD 920/.0729
ISSN 0553-7150
JM
PERSONALITIES CARIBBEAN. (1965)-. English. Every 2 years. Personalities Ltd, PO Box 269, Kingston Jamaica WI. **Continues** Personalities in the Caribbean.

LC CT
DD 920
US
PERSONALITIES OF AMERICA. Added/Corp American Biographical Institute. 1st Edition (1981)-. English. Irregular (Published every one to three times). $75.00. American Biographical Institute, 5126 Bur Oak Circle, PO Box 31226, Raleigh NC 27622. **Tel** (919)781-8710. **ED** J. M. Evans. **Circ:** 3,500 (ctrl). **Continues** Personalities of the South.
Desc: Presents biographical reference volumes on distinguished personalities; regional, national and international in scope.

LC CT1310 .P4
DD 920.048
ISSN 0031-5699
SW
PERSONHISTORISK TIDSKRIFT. [Personhist. tidskr.]. **Added/Corp** Personhistoriska Samfundet (Stockholm, Sweden). (1899)-. Periodical. Swedish. Irregular (1-4 issues). Svenskt Biografiskt Lexinon, Box 34106, 10026 Stockholm Sweden. **Tel** 00947-8-549616. **Bk Rev. Circ:** 800 (ctrl).
Desc: The journal concentrates on publishing articles concerning biographical history, but Swedish genealogy and heraldry is also of interest.
Ind/Abst Am. Hist. Life (1954-); MLA Int. Bibl. Books Artic. Mod. Lang. Lit.

LC F659.P6 P53
DD 929/.1/072078329
UDC 929.5(783)
ISSN 0737-7975
US
PIERRE-FORT - PIERRE GENEALOGICAL SOCIETY, THE. See Genealogy and Heraldry.

DD 540
ISSN 1047-8329
US
CCC
PROFILES, PATHWAYS, AND DREAMS. (PROFILES, PATHWAYS, AND DREAMS : AUTOBIOGRAPHIES OF EMINENT CHEMISTS.). [Profiles pathw. dreams]. **Added/Corp** American Chemical Society. (1990)-. Monographic series. English. Irregular. Price varies per volume. American Chemical Society, 1155 Sixteenth Street Northwest, Washington DC 20036. **Tel** (800)333-9511, (800)227-5558, (614)447-3776, FAX (202)447-3671. **ED** Jeffrey I. Seeman.
Desc: Each contributor describes his research over the range of his career. Illustrates how all disciplines of organic chemistry have progressed over the years.

LC CT1200 .P7
DD 920
ISSN 0555-4608
RU
CEASED
PROMETEI. (1966)-Series Completed (19??). Monographic series. Russian. Izdatelstvo Molodaia Gvardiia, Novodmitrovskaya Ulitsa 5A, 125015 Moscow Russia. **Tel** 011 95 285 1935. **(Subscription address:** East View Publications Inc., 3020 Harbor Lane North, Suite 110, Minneapolis MN 55447. **Tel** (800)477-1005, (612)550-0961, FAX (612)559-2931.**)**

LC PT2046 .E7
ISSN 0959-3683
UK
PUBLICATIONS OF THE ENGLISH GOETHE SOCIETY. See Literature.

LC CS1 .O7
DD 929.1/05
ISSN 0030-4263
US
TITLE CHANGE
QUARTERLY - ORANGE COUNTY CALIFORNIA GENEALOGICAL SOCIETY. See Genealogy and Heraldry.

LC CT214 .Q47
DD 920/.073
ISSN 0148-9844
US
QUEST WHO'S WHO. VFOAT Quest's Who's Who, Distinguished Citizens of North America; Who's Who, Distinguished Citizens of North America. English. Who's Who Honorary Society, Processing Center, Blairsville GA 30512.

LC F3351.L253
DD 984
BO
QUIEN ES QUIEN EN LA PAZ. (1990)-. Spanish.

LC HD278 .R43
DD 333.33/092/2 B
ISSN 0737-3600
US
REAL ESTATE REVIEW'S WHO'S WHO IN REAL ESTATE. VFOAT Who's Who in Real Estate. (1983)-. English. One time a year. Warren

Gorham & Lamont Inc., Park Square Building, 31 St. James Avenue, Boston MA 02116-4112. **Tel** (617)423-2020, (800)950-1207, FAX (617)423-2026.

LC CT
DD 920 CC
REN WU. **VFOAT** Biographies, Reminiscences. (19??)-. Chinese. Six times a year. $15.00 (surface mail). (**Subscription address:** China International Book Trading Corporation, PO Box 399, Library Service Department, Beijing 100044 People's Republic of China. **Tel** 011 86 1 8414284, FAX 011 86 1 8412023, telex 22496 CIBTC CN.)

LC CT **ISSN** 0080-2670
DD 920 GW
RHEINISCHE LEBENSBILDER. **Added/Corp** Gesellschaft fuer Rheinische Geschichtskunde. Vol. 1 (1961)-. Monographic series. German. Irregular. Price varies per volume. Dr. Rudolf Habelt GmbH, Postfach 150104, D-53040 Bonn Germany. **Tel** 011 49 228 232015.

LC CT
DD 920 GW
RICHARD STRAUSS JAHRBUCH. **See** Music.

ISSN 1062-6999
DD 813 US
Pr Rev.
ROBERT FROST REVIEW, THE. [Robert Frost rev.]. **Added/Corp** Robert Frost Society. **VFOAT** RFR. (Fall 1991)-. Periodical. English. One time a year. $15.00. Winthrop University, Department of English, Rock Hill SC 29733. **Tel** (707)938-8314, FAX (707)996-1738. **ED** Dr. Earl J. Wilcox. **Bk Rev**, (Qty: 2-3). **Ad Acc**, **Adv Mgr:** Jeff Glassen, **Tel** (803)323-4566. **Circ:** 350.
Desc: Promotes the study of the life and poetry of Robert Frost. The review contains essays, news items and book reviews that relate to Robert Frost.

LC PS3519.E27 R66 **ISSN** 0300-7936
DD 811/.52 US
Pr Rev.
ROBINSON JEFFERS NEWSLETTER. **See** Literary and Political Reviews.

LC ML410.S4 R55 **ISSN** 0557-1634
GE
SAMMELBANDE DER ROBERT-SCHUMANN-GESELLSCHAFT. **See** Music.

LC CT
DD 920 GW
SAMMLUNG PROFILE. 1983-. Monographic series. German. Price varies per volume. Bouvier GmbH & Co. KG ABT Verlag, Am HOF 28, D-53113 Bonn Germany. **Tel** 011 49 228 7290141, FAX 011 49 228 7290179.

LC PS3503.E4488 Z848 **ISSN** 0735-1550
DD 813/.52 US
Pr Rev.
SAUL BELLOW JOURNAL. [Saul Bellow j.]. Vol. 1, No. 2 (Spring/Summer 1982)-. Periodical. English. Two times a year (Winter and Summer). $28.00. Saul Bellow Journal, 6533 Post Oak Drive, C/O L. Goldman, West Bloomfield MI 48322. **Tel** (313)855-4324, FAX (313)557-6636. **ED** Liela Goldman and Gloria Cronin. **Bk Rev**. **Ad Acc**. ***Continues** Saul Bellow Newsletter.*
Desc: Critical and biographical articles on the works of Saul Bellow as well as book reviews.
Ind/Abst Abstr. Engl. Stud. (1982-); Lit. Crit. Regist.; MLA Int. Bibl. Books Artic. Mod. Lang. Lit.

LC PT2045 .G5
GW
SCHRIFTEN DER GOETHE-GESELLSCHAFT. **See** Literature.

LC PR5366 .A15 **ISSN** 0741-5842
DD 822/.912 US
CCC
SHAW. **See** Literary and Political Reviews.

LC JC345
DD 929.82 US
SIBLEY'S HARVARD GRADUATES. **Added/Corp** Massachusetts Historical Society. Vol. 4 (1690-1700)-. Monographic series. English. Irregular. Price varies per volume. Massachusetts Historical Society, 1154 Boylston Street, Boston MA 02215. **Tel** (617)536-1608. **ED** Conrad E. Wright. **Circ:** 250. ***Continues** Biographical Sketches of Graduates of Harvard University in Cambridge, Mass.*
Desc: Biographical sketches of those who attended Harvard College.

ISSN 0810-5200
DD 784.500924 AT
SINATRA INTERNATIONAL. [Sinatra int.]. (1982)-. Periodical. English. Four times a year. 20.55Aus$. International Sinatra Society, #11 Leicester, North Balwyn VIC 3104 Australia. **Tel** 011 61 03 8577765. **ED** G. Hawkins. **Circ:** 180 (ctrl). ***Continues** Newsletter - International Sinatra Society, 0810-5219.*

ISSN 1071-3905
DD 012 US
SOCIAL REGISTER. [Soc. regist.]. **VFOAT** S.R.; SR. Vol. 91 (1977)-. English. Two times a year. $105.00. Social Register Association, 381 Park Avenue South, New York NY 10805. **Tel** (212)685-2634. **Circ:** 14,000 (ctrl). ***Formed by the union of** Social Register, New York; Social Register, Washington; Social Register, Philadelphia; Social Register, Baltimore; Social Register, Boston; Social Register, St. Louis; Social Register, Pittsburgh; Social Register, Cleveland; Social Register, San Francisco; Social Register, Chicago; Social Register, Buffalo **and** Social Register, Cincinnati & Dayton.*

LC PN451 .S6 **ISSN** 0276-816X
DD 028.52/0922 920 B US
SOMETHING ABOUT THE AUTHOR. [Something author]. **Added/Corp** Gale Research Company. Vol. 1 (1971)-. Periodical. English. Irregular. $85.00 per volume. Gale Research Inc., 835 Penobscot Building, 645 Griswold Street, Detroit MI 48226. **Tel** (800)877-GALE, (313)961-2242, FAX (313)961-6083, (800)414-5043, telex TWX 810-221-7086. **ED** Diane Telgen. cum. index.
Desc: Ongoing reference series that deals with the lives and works of authors and illustrators of children's books. Covers over 7,000 authors and illustrators. The focus is on contemporary figures while providing information on major children's authors and illustrators of the past. Entries include personal and career data, literary sidelights, complete bibliographies, critical comments, etc.

LC DK290 .S66
DD 920/.047 US
SOVIET BIOGRAPHICAL SERVICE. Vol. 1, No. 1 (Jan. 1985)-. English. Four times a year (Jan., Apr., June, Sept.). $100.00. J. L. Scherer, 4900 18th Avenue South, Minneapolis MN 55417. **Tel** (612)722-2947. **Ad Acc.**
Desc: Provides biographies of the political, intellectual and cultural leaders of countries and republics of the former Soviet Union and analyses of current events pertaining to the former Soviet Union.

LC JQ674 .H67a
DD 354.5125/002 B HK
STAFF BIOGRAPHIES, HONG KONG GOVERNMENT / COMPILED IN THE GOVERNMENT SECRETARIAT / HSIANG-KANG CHENG FU KUNG WU YUAN CHIEN CHIEH / PU CHENG SSU SHU PIEN. **Main/Corp** Hong Kong. Government Secretariat. **VFOAT** Hsiang-Kang Cheng fu Kung wu uan Chien Chieh; Hong Kong Government Staff Biographies. (19??)-. Government Publication. English (Chinese). Every 2 years. Hong Kong Government Information Service, Beaconsfield House, 4 Queens Road, Hong Kong Hong Kong. **Tel** 011 852 284288014, 011 852 259881947, FAX 011 852 28459078, 011 852 25987482, telex 61190 HKGIS. ***Continues** Hong Kong. Colonial Secretariat. Staff Biographies, Hong Kong Government.*

LC JC345
DD 929.82 US
STALSBY WILSON'S WHO'S WHO IN FERTILIZER AND AG CHEMCIAL SUPPLY. (19??)-. English. One time a year. $75.00. Stalsby Wilson Associates, PO Box 19976, Houston TX 77224. **Tel** (713)496-1734, FAX (713)531-7229, telex 401428 SWPRESS. ***Continues** Stalsby Wilson's Who's Who in Fertilizer Supply.*

LC JC345
DD 929.82 US
STALSBY WILSON'S WHO'S WHO IN FERTILIZER AND AG-CHEMICAL SUPPLY. English. One time a year. $75.00. Stalsby Wilson Associates, PO Box 19976, Houston TX 77224. **Tel** (713)496-1734, FAX (713)531-7229, telex 401428 SWPRESS.

LC CT120 .S696 **ISSN** 1060-9997
DD 920/.02 US
STAR GUIDE. [Star guide]. (1988/1989)-. English. One time a year (July). $14.90. Axiom Information Resources, PO Box 8015, Ann Arbor MI 48107. **Tel** (313)761-4842, FAX (313)761-3276. Index available. cum. index. **Bk Rev**. **Circ:** 10,000. ***Continues** Celebrity Directory.*
Desc: A guide of over 3,200 addresses of major stars in movies, TV, music, sports, politics, literature and other famous people.

LC PS3537.T3234 Z88 **ISSN** 0039-100X
DD 813/.5/2 US
CEASED
STEINBECK QUARTERLY. [Steinbeck q.]. Vol. 2, No. 3 (Fall 1969)-(Dec. 1993). English. Steinbeck Society, English Department, Ball State University, Muncie IN 47306. **Tel** (317)285-5688. **ED** Tetsumaro Hayashi. Index available. cum. index. **Bk Rev**. **Ad Acc**. **Circ:** 600 (ctrl). available on microfilm and microfiche from University Microfilms International (UMI). Documents available from The Genuine Article. ***Continues** Steinbeck Newsletter.*
Desc: Devoted to criticism of John Steinbeck, Nobel Prize novelist, and his literature. Publishes both critical and biographical essays, bibliographical checklists, etc.
Ind/Abst Am. Humanit. Index; Annu. Bibliogr. Engl. Lang. Lit.; Arts Humanit. Citation Index [Full Cov.]; Curr. Contents Arts Humanit.; Lit. Crit. Regist.; MLA Int. Bibl. Books Artic. Mod. Lang. Lit.; Res. Alert [Full Cov.].

LC WMLC L 83/8512 **ISSN** 0585-4997
IT
STUDI SUL BOCCACCIO. [Studi Boccaccio]. **Added/Corp** Ente Nazionale Giovanni Boccaccio. (1963)-. Italian. Every 2 years. L100000 Italy; L120000 other. Le Lettere, Costa San Giorgio 28, 50125 Florence Italy. **Tel** 011 39 55 2342710.
Desc: Contains original articles on Boccaccio's life and works, critical essays, a bibliography and convention notices.
Ind/Abst MLA Int. Bibl. Books Artic. Mod. Lang. Lit.

LC PR4229 .S7 **ISSN** 0095-4489
DD 821/.8 US
STUDIES IN BROWNING AND HIS CIRCLE. [Stud. Browning his circ.]. Vol. 1 Spring (1973)-. English. One time a year. $17.50. Armstrong Browning Library, Baylor University, PO Box 407, Waco TX 76798. **Tel** (817)755-3566. Index available. cum. index. **Bk Rev**. **Circ:** 400 (ctrl). ***Supersedes** Browning Newsletter, 0007-2532.*
Desc: A journal of criticism, history, and bibliography of Robert Browning and Elizabeth Barrett Browning.
Ind/Abst Abstr. Engl. Stud. (1980-); Am. Humanit. Index; Annu. Bibliogr. Engl. Lang. Lit.; Lit. Crit. Regist.; MLA Int. Bibl. Books Artic. Mod. Lang. Lit.

ISSN 1054-514X
DD 920 US
T.E. NOTES. (T.E. NOTES : A T.E. LAWRENCE NEWSLETTER.). [T.E. notes]. **VFOAT** T E Notes. (1990)-. Newsletter. English. Ten times a year (monthly except July and Aug.). $25.00. T.E. Notes, 653 Park Street, Honesdale PA 18431-1421. **Tel** (717)253-6706, FAX (717)253-6786. **ED** Denis W. McDonnell and Janet Riesman. **Bk Rev**, (Qty: 10-20). **Circ:** 200.
Desc: Dedicated to the research into the life and legend of T.E. Lawrence, Lawrence of Arabia. Includes articles by Lawrencian biographers and scholars, reviews of other publications and news on Lawrencian events.

LC E757.2 .T47A **ISSN** 0161-8423
DD 973.91/1/0924 US
THEODORE ROOSEVELT ASSOCIATION JOURNAL. [Theodore Roosevelt Assoc. j.]. **Main/Corp** Theodore Roosevelt Association. Vol. 1 (Winter/Spring 1975)-. Periodical. English. Four times a year. $30.00. Theodore Roosevelt Association, PO Box 720, Oyster Bay NY 11771. **Tel** (516)922-1221. **ED** John A Gable. **Bk Rev**. **Ad Acc**. **Circ:** 1,500 (ctrl). available on microfiche (from Meckler). ***Continues** Theodore Roosevelt Association Newsletter.*
Desc: Theodore Roosevelt - his life, his times, his interests, his family, including current generations.
Ind/Abst Am. Hist. Life (1989-).

LC PS3053 .A23 **ISSN** 0040-6406
US
Pr Rev.
THOREAU SOCIETY BULLETIN, THE. **See** Literature.

LC AP2.T63 **ISSN** 1064-9654
DD 051 US
TOWN AND COUNTRY MAGAZINE PERSONAL NAME INDEX. **VFOAT** Town & Country Magazine Personal Name Index.; Personal Name Index. (1992)-. English. $59.00. Waltman Associates, 1111 3rd Avenue South, #460, Minneapolis MN 55404.

LC ND497.T8 T87 **ISSN** 0260-597X
DD 760/.092/4 UK
CCC
CEASED
TURNER STUDIES. **See** The Arts-Art.

ISSN 0564-559X
DD 823 US
TWAYNE'S ENGLISH AUTHOR SERIES. [Twayne's Engl. author ser.]. **VFOAT** Twayne's English Author Series; English Authors Series; English Author Series; TEAS. (1964)-. Monographic series. English. Irregular. Price varies per volume. Macmillan Publishing Company / New Jersey, 100 Front Street, Box 500, Riverside NJ 08075-7500. **Tel** (800)257-5755, (609)461-6500, FAX (609)461-7070. **ED** Lewis DeSimone.
Desc: Bio-critical studies of individual authors of the British Isles.
Ind/Abst MLA Int. Bibl. Books Artic. Mod. Lang. Lit.

LC AS911.A2 U56 **ISSN** 0738-176X
DD 920/.073 US
UNITED STATES ACHIEVEMENT ACADEMY NATIONAL AWARDS. [U.S. Achiev. Acad. natl. awards]. **Added/Corp** United States Achievement Academy. **VFOAT** National Awards. (1981)-. English. United States Achievement Academy, 2570 Palumbo Drive, Lexington KY 40509.

Biographies

LC CT120 .V14
DD 920/.0025/73
ISSN 1043-0261
US
V.I.P. ADDRESS BOOK. [V.I.P. address book]. **VFOAT** VIP Address Book. **VAT** Very Important Person Address Book. (1988/1989)-. English. One time a year (Every two years). $80.95. Associated Media Companies Ltd., 1212 Porta Ballena, Alameda CA 94501. **Tel** (510)814-8255. **ED** J. M. Wiggins.
 Desc: A book listing addresses of more than 20,000 of the famous, influential, and powerful people from around the world.

LC CT
DD 920
UK
VACHER'S BIOGRAPHICAL GUIDE ... . (1988)-. English. One time a year. $119.79. Vacher's Publications, 113 High Street Berkhamsted, Hertfordshire HP4 2DJ United Kingdom. **Tel** 011 44 1442 876135, FAX 011 44 1442 870148. **ED** Robbie Gibb (editor's address: BBC Political Research Unit, 4 Millbank, London SW1P 3JQ UK; phone: 011 44 71 9736037). **Circ:** 1,200. available on microfilm and microfiche from University Microfilms International (UMI).
 Desc: Biographies surrounding the House of Lords, House of Commons, MPs, and the top home and overseas civil servants.

LC F221 .V91
ISSN 0042-6636
US
UDC 975.5
VIRGINIA MAGAZINE OF HISTORY AND BIOGRAPHY, THE. See History-History of North and South America.

LC TL139 .W37
DD 338.4/762922220922 B
ISSN 0147-9822
US
WARD'S WHO'S WHO AMONG U.S. MOTOR VEHICLE MANUFACTURERS. Added/Corp Ward's Communications Inc. **VFOAT** Ward's Who's Who. **VAT** Ward's Who's Who Among United States Motor Vehicle Manufacturers. (1977)-. English. Irregular. $29.79. Ward's Communications Inc., 3000 Town Center, Suite 2750, Southfield MI 48075. **Tel** (810)357-0800.

LC CT1836 .W32
JA
WATAKUSHI NO RIREKISHO. Added/Corp Nihon Keizai Shimbunsha. Nihon Keizai Shimbun, Tokyo. Vol. 1 (1957)-. Periodical. Japanese. Nihon Keizai Shimbun Inc., 9-5 Otemachi 1 Chome, Chiyoda-ku Tokyo 100 Japan. **Tel** 011 81 3 32700251, 011 81 3 52108502 (Nikkei Business Publications Inc.), FAX 011 81 3 52552661, 011 81 3 52108119 (Nikkei Business Publications Inc.).

LC DD85 .W3
DD 920.043
GW
WER IST WER?. Vol. 11, (Aug. 1950)-. German. One time a year (Oct.). $276.36. Verlag Max Schmidt-Roemhild, Verlag & Druckhaus, D-23547 Luebeck Germany. **Tel** 011 49 451 703101, telex 26536. Index available. **Bk Rev. Continues** Degeners Wer Ist's?.

LC JQ533 .A335
DD 328.54/82/0922 B
II
WHO IS WHO. Main/Corp Tamil Nadu (India). Legislature. Legislative Council. English. Every 2 years. Rs5.00. India Legislature Tamil Nadu Legislative Council, Madras India. **Tel** 22109. **Circ:** 250 (ctrl).
 Desc: Covers the biographical sketches of the members of the Tamil Nadu Legislative Council.

LC CT2220 .W47
DD 920/.06762
KE
WHO IS WHO IN KENYA. 1982-1983-. English. Africa Book Services Ltd, Quran House, Mfangano Street, PO Box 45245, Nairobi Kenya.

LC CT
DD 920
UK
WHO WAS WHO, A COMPANION TO WHO'S WHO, CONTAINING THE BIOGRAPHIES OF THOSE WHO DIED. Vol. 1, (1897/1916)-. English. Irregular.

LC E176 .W64
DD 920.073
ISSN 0146-8081
US
CCC
NLM E 176 W6281
WHO WAS WHO IN AMERICA. [Who was who Am.]. **VFOAT** Who Was Who in America with World Notables. (1896)-. English. Irregular. $767.50 (twelve-volume set). Marquis Who's Who, A Reed Reference Publishing Company, Part of Reed International PLC, 121 Chanlon Road, New Providence NJ 07974. **Tel** (908)464-6800, (800)521-8110, FAX (908)665-6688, telex 138 755. cum. index ($42.50).
 Desc: Profiles American figures, from the first Jamestown settlers to recently deceased celebrities.

LC CT
DD 920
US
TITLE CHANGE
WHO'S WHAT IN FLORIDA GOVERNMENT. Added/Corp Florida Chamber of Commerce. (19??)-(19??). English. Florida Chamber of Commerce, PO Box 11309, Tallahassee FL 32302. **Tel** 800/940-3034, FAX (904)425-1260. **ED** Gary Cliett (editor's phone: (904)425-1242). **Circ:** 8,000. **Continued by** Pocket Guide to Florida Government.
 Desc: Lists Florida's legislators with their pictures, along with Florida's congressmen, governor, Supreme Court justices, members of the Cabinet and the departments they manage.

LC CT
DD 920
UK
WHO'S WHO. English. A & C Black Publishers Ltd, Howard Road, Eaton Socon, Huntingdon CBS PE193EZ United Kingdom. **Tel** 011 44 1480 212666, FAX 011 44 1480 405014, telex 32524.

LC CT
DD 920
US
●**WHO'S WHO AMONG AFRICAN AMERICANS.** See Ethnic Interests.

LC LA2311 .M4
DD 373.1/8/02573
US
WHO'S WHO AMONG AMERICAN HIGH SCHOOL STUDENTS. (1971/72)-. English. One time a year. $23.95. Educational Communications Inc, 721 North McKinley, Lake Forest IL 60045. **Tel** (312)564-2020. **Continues** Merit's Who's Who Among American High School Students.

LC KF266 .W5
DD 349.73/025 B 347.30025 B
ISSN 0278-6478
US
WHO'S WHO AMONG AMERICAN LAW STUDENTS. See Law.

LC E184.06 W47
DD 920/.009295073/05
ISSN 1075-7104
US
●**WHO'S WHO AMONG ASIAN AMERICANS.** See Ethnic Interests.

LC E185.96 .W52
DD 920/.073
ISSN 0362-5753
US
TITLE CHANGE
WHO'S WHO AMONG BLACK AMERICANS. See Ethnic Interests.

LC F870.N4 W48
DD 305.4/8896073/0794 B
ISSN 0734-5720
US
WHO'S WHO AMONG BLACK WOMEN IN CALIFORNIA. [Who's who black women Calif.]. 1st Ed. (1981-1982)-. English. One time a year. Who's Who Among Black Women in California, 314 East Hillcrest Blvd., Suite 1, Inglewood CA 90301.

LC E184.S75 W53 E184.S75 W36
DD 920/.009268
ISSN 1052-7354
US
NLM E 184; S75
WHO'S WHO AMONG HISPANIC AMERICANS. See Ethnic Interests.

LC LA2311 .W42
DD 378.1/98/.025
US
WHO'S WHO AMONG STUDENTS IN AMERICAN JUNIOR COLLEGES. (1967)-. English. One time a year. $39.95. Randall Publishing, 3200 Rice Mine Road, Tuscaloosa AL 35403. **Tel** (800)777-3748, (205)349-2990.

LC L901 .W49
DD 373.0973
US
WHO'S WHO AMONG STUDENTS IN AMERICAN UNIVERSITIES AND COLLEGES. (1957)-. English. One time a year. $39.95. Who's Who Among Students, PO Box 2029, Tuscaloosa AL 35401. **Tel** (800)633-5953. **Continues** Official Who's Who Among Students in American Universities and Colleges.

LC Z282 .A42A
DD 070.5/025/73
ISSN 0191-8184
US
WHO'S WHO AT THE ABA. Main/Corp American Booksellers Association. **VAT** Who's Who at the American Booksellers Association. 1979-. English. One time a year. Knowledge Industry Publications Inc, 701 Westchester Avenue, White Plains NY 10604. **Tel** (914)328-9157, (800)800-5474, FAX (914)328-9093.

LC HD251 .N339318
DD 333.3/3
ISSN 0148-3773
US
WHO'S WHO (CHICAGO). (WHO'S WHO - NATIONAL ASSOCIATION OF REALTORS). Main/Corp National Association of Realtors. English. One time a year. $25.00. National Association of Realtors, 430 North Michigan Avenue, Chicago IL 60611. **Tel** (312)329-8494, (800)874-6500.

LC E184.M5 W52
DD 350/.26/0973
ISSN 0738-4637
US
SUSPENDED
WHO'S WHO, CHICANO OFFICEHOLDERS. VFOAT Chicano Officeholders. (19??)-Suspended. English. Irregular. $28.95. Who's Who Chicano Officeholders, PO Box 2271, Silver City NM 88062-2271. **Tel** (505)538-6229. **ED** Arthur D. Martinez. **Bk Rev. Ad Acc. Circ:** 1,000. **Continues** Who's Who, Chicano Office Holders, 0738-4637.
 Desc: Lists names, addresses, telephone numbers of over 5,000 Chicano elected and appointed officeholders.

LC DS1.A47347 A25
DD 341.7/67
JA
WHO'S WHO FOR ACCU, A. Main/Corp Asian Cultural Centre for UNESCO. **VFOAT** Who's Who for A.C.C.U. (1979)-. English. Asian Cultural Centre for UNESCO, 6 Fukuromachi, Shinjukuku Tokyo 162 Japan. **Tel** 03 2694435, FAX 03 2694510.

LC E176 .W642
DD 920.073
ISSN 0083-9396
US
CCC
NLM E 176 W628
WHO'S WHO IN AMERICA. [Who's who Am.]. Vol. 1 (1899/1900)-. English. One time a year. $450.00. Marquis Who's Who, A Reed Reference Publishing Company, Part of Reed International PLC, 121 Chanlon Road, New Providence NJ 07974. **Tel** (908)464-6800, (800)521-8110, FAX (908)665-6688, telex 138 755. **ED** Frederick M. Marks. available on magnetic tape, an online database, and CD-ROM. **Absorbed** Who's Who in America Professional Geographic Index.
 Desc: Personal and career information on American leaders and achievers.
 Ind/Abst Curr. Lit. Fam. Plan. (19??-199?).

LC E176 .W64232
DD 920.073
ISSN 1049-8540
US
WHO'S WHO IN AMERICA (JUNIOR & SENIOR HIGH SCHOOL VERSION). (WHO'S WHO IN AMERICA.). [Who's who Am.]. (1991)-. English. Who's Who in America, 3002 Glenview Road, Wilmette IL 60091.

LC LA2311 .W47
DD 370/.92/2
ISSN 1046-7203
CCC
WHO'S WHO IN AMERICAN EDUCATION (OWINGS MILLS, MD.). (WHO'S WHO IN AMERICAN EDUCATION.). [Who's who Am. educ.]. Added/Corp National Reference Institute (U.S.). (1989)-. English. Every 2 years. $150.00. Marquis Who's Who, A Reed Reference Publishing Company, Part of Reed International PLC, 121 Chanlon Road, New Providence NJ 07974. **Tel** (908)464-6800, (800)521-8110, FAX (908)665-6688, telex 138 755. available on magnetic tape and CD-ROM; available on an online database.
 Desc: Provides information on achievers in the field of education.

LC KF372 .W48
DD 340/.092/2 B
ISSN 0162-7880
US
CCC
WHO'S WHO IN AMERICAN LAW. See Law.

LC HV7911.A1 W55
DD 363.2/092/2 B
ISSN 0277-3511
US
WHO'S WHO IN AMERICAN LAW ENFORCEMENT. Added/Corp American Law Enforcement Officers Association. (1980)-. Periodical. English. Every 3 years. $45.00. American Law Enforcement Officers Association, 110 NE 125th Street, North Miami FL 33161. **Tel** (305)891-1700. **ED** Donna Shepherd. **Circ:** 5,000. **Continues** Who's Who in Law Enforcement and American Government, 0148-3382.
 Desc: Biography of law enforcement and security officers that are submitted by the 21,000 chiefs and sheriffs in the United States.

LC E176 .W6424
DD 320/.0922
ISSN 0000-0205
US
CCC
WHO'S WHO IN AMERICAN POLITICS. [Who's who Am. polit.]. 1st Ed. (1968)-. Directory. English. Every 2 years. $256.75. R.R. Bowker, A Reed Reference Publishing Company, Part of Reed International PLC, PO Box 31, 121 Chanlon Drive, New Providence NJ 07974. **Tel** (908)464-6800, (800)521-8110, FAX (908)665-6688, telex 138-755. **ED** P. A. Theis and E. L. Henshaw. available on magnetic tape and an online database.
 Desc: Desktop guide to American political decision-makers at all levels from the President to local town council. Over 24,000 entries.

LC TX907 .L283
DD 647/.9573
ISSN 0743-6122
US
WHO'S WHO IN AMERICA'S RESTAURANTS. [Who's who Am. restaur.]. National 1985 Ed.-. Directory. English. One time a year. $14.95. Who's Who in Restaurants Inc, 1841 Broadway, New York NY 10023. **Tel** (212)581-0360. **ED** Sheldon Landwehr. **Circ:** 100,000. **Continues** Who's Who in America's Restaurants. New York and Eastern States,

Biographies

0735-1801.
Desc: Guide to America's restaurants. Hundreds of geographically-arranged illustrated profiles, plus a compilation of thousands of selected listings.

LC CT
DD 920 UK
WHO'S WHO IN ASIAN AND AUSTRALASIAN POLITICS. 1st Ed. (1991)-.
English. Bowker Saur Ltd., A Reed Reference Publishing Company, Part of Reed International PLC, 59-60 Grosvenor Street, London WIX 9DA United Kingdom. **Tel** 011 44 171 4935841, FAX 011 44 171 4991590.

LC HD2425 .A573 **ISSN** 0360-7038
DD 060 US
NLM HD 2425 A512w
WHO'S WHO IN ASSOCIATION MANAGEMENT.
(WHO'S WHO IN ASSOCIATION MANAGEMENT / ASAE.). **Main/Corp** American Society of Association Executives. **VFOAT** Membership Directory; ASAE Who's Who in Association Management. (195?)-. English. One time a year. $105.25. American Society of Association of Executives, 1575 Eye Street Northwest, Washington DC 20005. **Tel** (202)626-2722, FAX (202)842-1109. **Continues** American Trade Association Executives. Who's Who in Association Management.

LC GV697.A1 W523 **ISSN** 1044-9906
DD 796.071/173 US
Pr Rev.
WHO'S WHO IN ATHLETICS IN AMERICAN COLLEGES AND UNIVERSITIES.
[Who's who athl. Am. coll. univ.]. (1990)-. English. Every 2 years. $75.00. Athletic Press of America, 8268 Streamwood Drive, Baltimore MD 21208. **Tel** (410)922-8115, FAX (410)922-4903. **ED** Dr. Gladson. Index available (bound in June issue).

LC GV697.A1 W526 **ISSN** 1049-9229
DD 796./092/22 US
WHO'S WHO IN ATHLETICS IN AMERICAN HIGH SCHOOLS. (1991)-.
English. Every 2 years. $75.00 (single issue). Athletic Press of America, 8268 Streamwood Drive, Baltimore MD 21208. **Tel** (410)922-8115, FAX (410)922-4903.

LC CT **ISSN** 1049-9237
DD 920 US
WHO'S WHO IN ATHLETICS IN AMERICAN JUNIOR COLLEGES. (1992)-.
English. Every 2 years. $75.00 (single issue). Athletic Press of America, 8268 Streamwood Drive, Baltimore MD 21208. **Tel** (410)922-8115, FAX (410)922-4903.

LC CT
DD 920 UK
CEASED
WHO'S WHO IN AUSTRALASIA AND THE FAR EAST.
Added/Corp International Biographical Centre. (1989)-(19??). English. Taylor & Francis Ltd. / UK, Rankine Road, Basingstoke, Hampshire RG24 8PR United Kingdom. **Tel** 011 44 1256 840366, FAX 011 44 1256 479438, telex 858540. **(Subscription address:** Taylor & Francis Inc., 1900 Frost Road, Suite 101, Bristol PA 19007-1598. **Tel** (215)785-5800, (800)821-8312, FAX (215)785-5515.)

LC CT
DD 920 AT
WHO'S WHO IN AUSTRALIA. (1927)-.
English. Every 3 years. $125.00. Herald & Weekly Times, 44-74 Flinders Street, Melbourne 3000 Australia. **Tel** 03 63-0211. **(Subscription address:** International Publications Service, A Division of Taylor & Francis, 1900 Frost Road, Suite 101, Bristol PA 19007-1598. **Tel** (800)821-8312.) **ED** W.J. Draper. **Circ:** 12,000 (ctrl). **Continues** Who's Who in the Commonwealth of Australia.
Desc: Biographies of men and women who have achieved distinction in all fields. Lists of ministers of the various governments published every three years.

LC CT
DD 920 IT
WHO'S WHO IN AUSTRIA. (19??)-.
Monographic series. English. Irregular (published approximately every 2 to 3 years). Price varies per volume. Whos Who in Italy Srl, CP 61, 20091 Bresso Milan Italy. **Tel** 011 39 2 6100237. **(Subscription address:** Ballen Booksellers International Inc., 125 Ricefield Lane, Hauppage NY 11788. **)**

LC HF5500.3.U54 W53 **ISSN** 0277-5336
DD 658.4/0092/2 B US
WHO'S WHO IN BLACK CORPORATE AMERICA.
[Who's who black corp. Am.]. (1981)-. Directory. English. One time a year. Who's Who in Black Corporate America, 1629 K Street NW, Suite 596, Washington DC 20006.

LC HC252.5.A2 W48 **ISSN** 1068-2260
DD 338.7/092/241 US
WHO'S WHO IN BUSINESS AND INDUSTRY IN THE UK. [Who's who bus. ind. UK].
VFOAT Who's Who in Industry. **VAT** Who's Who in Business and Industry in the United Kingdom. 1st Ed. (1991)-. English. $250.00. St. James Press, An Imprint of Gale Research Inc., PO Box 33477, Detroit MI 48232-5477. **Tel** (800)345-0392. **ED** Juliet Margetts.
Desc: Provides biographies of the 10,000 most important people in British industry, including managers, executives and directors of Britain's top 1,000 companies as well as those involved in distribution, advertising, consulting, civil service, trade associations, unions, journalism and academic pursuits.

LC F860 .W628 **ISSN** 0511-8948
DD 979 US
WHO'S WHO IN CALIFORNIA (1956).
(WHO'S WHO IN CALIFORNIA.). **Added/Corp** Who's Who Historical Society (Calif.). (1956)-. English. One time a year (Jan.). $205.00. Barrett Publishing Inc., 2533 North Carson Street, Suite 1147, Carson City NV 89706. **Tel** (702)882-0412, FAX (702)883-2384. **ED** Edna L. Barrett. **Circ:** 1,000 (ctrl). **Continues** Who's Who in Los Angeles County.
Desc: A biographical reference series listing Californians of achievement in the arts, science, medicine, religion, law and government.

ISSN 0227-3411
DD 338/.092/2 CN
WHO'S WHO IN CANADIAN BUSINESS.
[Who's who Can. bus.]. **VFOAT** Who's Who of Canadian Business. 1st Ed. (1980/81)-. English. One time a year. 147.62Can$. Who's Who Publications, 777 Bay Street, 5th Floor, Toronto ONT M5W 1A7 Canada. **Tel** (416)596-5100. **ED** Kimberly Biggar. **Absorbed** Who's Who in Canadian Finance, 0707-6305.

LC PR9189.6 .W47 **ISSN** 0715-9366
DD 809/.8971 CN
Pr Rev.
WHO'S WHO IN CANADIAN LITERATURE. See Literature.

LC RZ21 .W46 **ISSN** 0147-8265
DD 615/.534/0922 B US
NLM WB 22.1 W626
SUSPENDED
WHO'S WHO IN CHIROPRACTIC, INTERNATIONAL. 1st- Ed. (1976/78)-?.
English. Irregular. $55.00. WWIC International Publishers, Box 2615, Littleton CO 80161. **Tel** (303)333-1581.

LC HF5548.2 .W4634
DD 001.6/4/02541 UK
WHO'S WHO IN COMPUTING. English.
Whos Who in Computing, 80 East Street, Surrey KT17 1HF United Kingdom. **Tel** (416)271-1601.

LC HD9696.A3 U645 **ISSN** 0883-7317
DD 621.381/092/2 US
WHO'S WHO IN CONSUMER ELECTRONICS. [Who's who consum. electron.].
Premiere Ed.-. English. Two times a year. $100.00. Martin Porter Associates, 76 Court Street, Suite 44, Brooklyn NY 11201.

LC CT586 .W47
DD 920/.07286 CR
WHO'S WHO IN COSTA RICA. VFOAT
Lubeck & Lubeck's Who's Who in Costa Rica. English (Spanish). $75.00. Lubeck and Lubeck, PO Box 1264, San Jose Costa Rica.

LC TA1542 .W48 **ISSN** 0161-3669
DD 621.36/75/02573 US
WHO'S WHO IN DISPLAY HOLOGRAPHY. 1978-79-.
English. One time a year. $14.00. Museum of Holography, 11 Mercer Street, New York NY 10013.

LC QH35 .W47 **ISSN** 0091-3154
DD 574.5/092/2B US
NLM WA 22 AA1 W6
WHO'S WHO IN ECOLOGY.
English. Special Reports, Inc., 8 West 40th Street, New York NY 10018.

SZ
●WHO'S WHO IN EUROPEAN INSTITUTIONS AND ENTERPRISES.
(1993)-. English. Whos Who in Italy Srl, CP61, 20091 Bresso Milan Italy. **Tel** 011 39 2 6100237. **Continues** Who's Who in European Institutions, Organizations, and Enterprises.

LC CT
DD 920 AT
WHO'S WHO IN FEDERAL GOVERNMENT DIRECTORY. Directory.
English. Eleven times a year (not published in January). 155.00Au$. Commerce Management Services, PO Box E162 Queen Victoria, Terrace ACT 2600 Australia. **Tel** 011 61 6 2951961, FAX 011 61 6 2590170.

LC HD3861.U6 W48 **ISSN** 0882-0260
DD 338.7/4/02573 US
WHO'S WHO IN FEDERAL GOVERNMENT PRIME CONTRACTORS.
[Who's who fed. gov. prime contract.]. **Added/Corp** Business Research Services (Oak Brook, Ill.). (1985)-. Directory. English. One time a year. $195.00. Business Research Services Inc, 4201 Connecticutt Avenue, Suite 610, Washington DC 20008. **Tel** (800)845-8420, (202)364-6473.
Desc: Lists more than 4,000 purchasing agents within prime government contractors; includes small business firms and minority firms doing business with the federal government.

LC HF3023.A2 W5 **ISSN** 0083-9523
DD 338/.00922 B US
CCC
WHO'S WHO IN FINANCE AND INDUSTRY. 17th Ed. (1973)-.
English. Every 2 years. $249.95. Marquis Who's Who, A Reed Reference Publishing Company, Part of Reed International PLC, 121 Chanlon Road, New Providence NJ 07974. **Tel** (908)464-6800, (800)521-8110, FAX (908)665-6688, telex 138 755. available on magnetic tape and CD-ROM. **Continues** World Who's Who in Finance and Industry, 0190-5058.
Desc: Profiles principal decision-makers from the fields of banking, insurance, transportation, government regulatory agencies, major corporations and many other financial areas.

LC SB404.U5 W45 **ISSN** 0511-8964
DD 635.9/025/73 US
WHO'S WHO IN FLORICULTURE. English.
One time a year. Free to members, $50.00 other. Society of American Florists, 901 North Washington Street, Alexandria VA 22314.

LC CT229 .W5 **ISSN** 0094-7784
DD 920/.0759B US
WHO'S WHO IN FLORIDA. 1st- Ed.; 1973/74-.
English. Scott Baker, 110 Dantzler Ct/5, Lexington KY 40353.

LC DC705.A1 W46 **ISSN** 0083-9531
DD 920.044 FR
WHO'S WHO IN FRANCE. VFOAT
Who's Who in Paris; Qui Est Qui en France. 1st Ed. (1953)-. French. One time a year. $495.12. Editions Jacques Lafitte, 38 rue de Constantinople, 75008 Paris France. **Tel** 011 33 1 45220505. **Ad Acc. Circ:** 12,000 (ctrl).
Desc: Biographic dictionary of prominent people living in France.

LC F869.F8 W47 **ISSN** 0364-7196
DD 920/.0794/82 US
WHO'S WHO IN FRESNO. (1975/76)-.
English. J P Livingston, 4905 North West Avenue/Suite 108, Fresno CA 93705.

LC CT230 .W47 **ISSN** 0093-1233
DD 920/.0758 US
WHO'S WHO IN GEORGIA. 1st- Ed.; 1973-.
English. United States Public Relations Service, Atlanta GA 30333.

LC NC45 .W5
DD 741 SZ
WHO'S WHO IN GRAPHIC ART. English
(French and German). De Clivo Press, PO Box 8600, Dubendorf Zurich Switzerland. **Tel** (01)820-1224. **ED** W Amstutz.

LC HF5549.2.U5 W49 **ISSN** 1047-3130
DD 658 US
WHO'S WHO IN HR. [Who's who HR].
Added/Corp Society for Human Resource Management (U.S.). **VAT** Who's Who in Human Resources. (1990)-. English. Free to members. Society for Human Resource Management, 606 North Washington Street, Alexandria VA 22314. **Tel** (703)548-3440, FAX (703)836-0367, telex 6503902491.

LC CT1503 .W48
DD 920/.054 II
WHO'S WHO IN INDIA (BOMBAY, INDIA).
(WHO'S WHO IN INDIA.). (1985)-. English. One time a year. $13.96. Business Press Private Ltd, Maker Tower E/18th Floor, Cuffe Pd, Bombay 400 005 India. **Tel** 211752 or 217944.

LC T12.5.I5 W48
DD 920 II
WHO'S WHO IN INDIAN ENGINEERING & INDUSTRY. Periodical. English.

LC E77.8 .W47 **ISSN** 0747-7538
DD 730/.08997 US
WHO'S WHO IN INDIAN RELICS.
[Who's who Indian relics]. No. 1 (1960)-. English. Irregular (every four years). $30.00 per copy. Ben W Thompson, 1757 West Adams, Kirkwood MO 63122. **Tel** (314)822-2409. **ED** Ben W Thompson. **Bk Rev. Circ:** 5,000 (ctrl).

LC CT
DD 920 II
WHO'S WHO IN INDIAN SCIENCE. English.
Irregular. $15.00 (latest edition). Kothari Publications, Jute House, 12 India Exchange, Calcutta 700 001 India. **Tel** 20-9563. **ED** H. Kothari. **Ad Acc. Circ:** 2,000.

Biographies

Desc: Lists biodata of Indian scientists with subject classifications and addresses. Includes brief details about science organizations in India.

LC HG8523 .W5   **ISSN** 0083-9574
DD 368.058
WHO'S WHO IN INSURANCE. See Insurance.

LC SB419.25 .A87A   **ISSN** 0733-2440
DD 712/.06/073
WHO'S WHO IN INTERIOR LANDSCAPING. Main/Corp Associated Landscape Contractors of America. Interior Landscape Division. English. One time a year. ALCA/ILD Publications, 1750 Old Meadow road, McLean VA 22102.

LC CT1880 .W46
DD 920.055   GW
WHO'S WHO IN IRAN. Added/Corp Iran Research Group. 1st Ed. (Feb. 1990)-. English.

LC F1407 .W52   **ISSN** 1068-7696
DD 351   US
●WHO'S WHO IN LATIN AMERICA (NEW YORK, N.Y.). (WHO'S WHO IN LATIN AMERICA : GOVERNMENT, POLITICS, BANKING & INDUSTRY.). [Who's who Lat. Am.] 3rd Ed. (1993)-. English. $95.00. Norman Ross Publishing Inc., 330 West 58th Street, Suite 214, New York NY 10019. **Tel** (800)648-8850, (212)765-8200. **Continues** Who is Who, Government, Politics, Banking and Industry in Latin America.

LC DS80.75 .W5   **ISSN** 0083-9612
     LE
NLM DS 80.75 W628
WHO'S WHO IN LEBANON. 1st. Edition (1963/1964)-. French (English). Every 2 years (published every other year). $140.00. Publitec Publications, PO Box 5936, Beirut Lebanon. **Tel** 011 495401. (Subscription address: Gale Research Inc., 835 Penobscot Building, Detroit MI 48226. **Tel** (800)347-4253.) **ED** Charles G. Gedeon.
Desc: Contains approximately 1,000 biographical sketches and a general survey of the country. Provides information on the country's government, industry, banking, tourism, diplomatic representation, etc. Also covers the geography and history of the country.

LC CT1566 .W47   **ISSN** 0217-1910
DD 920/.0595 B   MY
WHO'S WHO IN MALAYSIA & SINGAPORE (PETALING JAYA, SELANGOR). (WHO'S WHO IN MALAYSIA & SINGAPORE.). VFOAT Who's Who in Malaysia and Singapore; Who's Who in Malaysia; Who's Who in Singapore. (1983/84)-. English. Who's Who Publications Sdn Bhd Utama, Petaling Jaya, Selangor Malaysia. **Continues** Who's Who in Malaysia ... & Profiles of Singapore.

LC CT
DD 920   GW
WHO'S WHO IN MEDICINE. (19??)-. English. Who's Who Intl Red Series, Bottroper Str 20, Postfach 103244, W4300 Essen 1 Germany.

LC ML13 .W5   **ISSN** 0191-264X
DD 780/.92/2 B   US
WHO'S WHO IN MUSIC (TUSCALOOSA). (WHO'S WHO IN MUSIC.). (197?)-. English. One time a year. Randall Publishing, 3200 Rice Mine Road, Tuscaloosa AL 35403. **Tel** (800)777-3748, (205)349-2990. **Continues** Who's Who Among Music Students in American High Schools, 0362-3750.

LC GV939.A1 W53   **ISSN** 0094-954X
DD 796.33/2/0922B   US
WHO'S WHO IN NATIONAL ATHLETICS HIGH SCHOOL FOOTBALL. (1974)-. English. One time a year. Josep Communications, Inc., PO Box 1286, Denver CO 80201. **Continues** Who's Who in National High School Football, 0091-6935.

LC DU402 .W5
DD 920.0931   NZ
WHO'S WHO IN NEW ZEALAND. (1908)-. English. Irregular (every 3 to 4 years). $89.95. Reed Publishing New Zealand Limited, Private Bag, Birkenhead New Zealand. **Tel** 011 64 9 4806039. **ED** G.H. Scholefield.

LC CT252 .W48   **ISSN** 0093-4178
DD 920/.0756   US
WHO'S WHO IN NORTH CAROLINA. 1st-Ed.; 1973-. English. $25.00. Scott Baker, 110 Dantzler Ct/5, Lexington KY 40503.

LC CT253 .W48   **ISSN** 0742-6038
DD 920/.0784   US
WHO'S WHO IN NORTH DAKOTA. 1st Ed. (1984)-. English. Every 3 years. Dakota West Enterprise Inc, 303 Northwest 1st Street, Mandan ND 58554.

LC TN695 .W48   **ISSN** 0361-6304
DD 671.3/7/02573   US
WHO'S WHO IN P/M. VAT Who's Who in Powder/Metallurgy. English. One time a year. $50.00 US; $60.00 other. American Powder Metallurgy Institute, 105 College Road East, Princeton NJ 08540. **Tel** (609)452-7700, FAX (609)987-8523. **Ad Acc.** ctrl circ. **Supersedes** American Powder Metallurgy Institute. Membership Directory and Yearbook.
Desc: Vols. for 1975-76 are the membership directories of the American Powder Metallurgy Institute and its parent group, the Metal Powder Industries Federation.

LC HD9580.A1 W48   **ISSN** 0742-020X
DD 388.5   US
WHO'S WHO IN PIPELINING. [Who's who pipelining]. 1983-. English. One time a year. $32.50. Universal News Inc, PO Box 55225, Houston TX 77255. **Tel** (713)468-2626, FAX (713)465-2224. **Separated from** Pipeline Digest, 0197-1506.
Desc: Directory of pipeline operating companies and pipeline contractors and subcontractors, including name, address, phone number and key personnel.

LC CT1230 .W46
DD 920/.0438   SZ
NLM CT 1230; W628
WHO'S WHO IN POLAND (ZURICH, SWITZERLAND). (WHO'S WHO IN POLAND / EDITED BY INTERPRESS PUBLISHERS, WARSAW.). **Added/Corp** Wydawnictwo Interpress. 1st Ed. (1982)-. Directory. English. Irregular. Who's Who in Italy SRL, CP 61, 20091 Bresso Milan Italy. **Tel** 011 39 2 6100237.

LC SB950 .N3   **ISSN** 0272-4219
DD 628.9/6/06073   US
WHO'S WHO IN PROFESSIONAL PEST CONTROL. **Added/Corp** National Pest Control Association. (19??)-. English. One time a year. $50.00. National Pest Control Association, 8100 Oak Street, PO Box 37, Dunn Loring VA 22027. **Tel** (703)573-8330, FAX (703)573-4116. **Continues** National Pest Control Association. Roster of Members.

LC BL2530.U6 W48   **ISSN** 0160-3728
DD 200/.92/2 B   US
WHO'S WHO IN RELIGION. See Religions and Theology.

LC HF3163.R5 W48   **ISSN** 0198-6953
DD 338.4/7/00025755451   US
WHO'S WHO IN RICHMOND BUSINESS. **Added/Corp** Metropolitan Richmond Chamber of Commerce (Richmond, Va.). (19??)-. English. $10.00 members, $20.00 nonmembers. NAPCOA, PO Box 369 Terminal Annex, Los Angeles CA 90051.

LC HG8059.B8 W5
DD 368/.81/002573   US
WHO'S WHO IN RISK MANAGEMENT. See Insurance.

LC CT1890 .W47
DD 920/.053/8   SU
NLM CT 1890 W628
WHO'S WHO IN SAUDI ARABIA. 1976/77-. English. $45.00. Residential Centre 312, PO Box 5455, Jeddah Saudi Arabia.

LC CT1253 .W47
DD 920/.048   GW
NLM CT 1243; W628
WHO'S WHO IN SCANDINAVIA. 1st Ed. (1981)-. English. Two times a year. Who's Who in Italy SRL, CP 61, 20091 Bresso Milan Italy. **Tel** 011 39 2 6100237.

LC Q141 .W576   **ISSN** 1063-5599
DD 509.2/2   US
     CCC
NLM Q 141; W6275
●WHO'S WHO IN SCIENCE AND ENGINEERING. See Science and Technology.

LC CT759
DD 920.04   UK
WHO'S WHO IN SCOTLAND. 1st. Ed. (1986)-. English. One time a year. $54.76. Carrick Media, 2 7 Galt House, 31 Bank Street, Irvine KA12 OLL United Kingdom. **Tel** 011 44 1294 311322, FAX 011 44 1294 311322.

LC CT1570 .W47
DD 920/.05957   SI
WHO'S WHO IN SINGAPORE. 1981/82-. English. One time a year. $50.00. City Who's Who Pte Ltd, Suite 1306/Shaw Towers, Beach Road, Singapore 0718 Singapore.

LC Z673 .S82727   **ISSN** 0278-842X
DD 026/.00025/7   US
WHO'S WHO IN SPECIAL LIBRARIES. [Who's who spec. libr.]. **Added/Corp** Special Libraries Association. (1981)-. English. One time a year (published in Oct.). $65.00. Special Libraries Association, 1700 18th Street Northwest, Washington DC 20009. **Tel** (202)234-4700, FAX (202)265-9317. **Ad Acc. Circ:** 12,000.
Desc: Provides a complete alphabetical listing of members, addresses, telephone numbers, chapter and division affiliations. Also includes business and finance, information technology, and library management, among others.

LC HD9624.S723 U68   **ISSN** 0742-6321
DD 338.7/67485/02573   US
WHO'S WHO IN STAINED GLASS. 1983-. English. One time a year. $9.95. Carl Hungness Publications, PO Box 24308, Speedway IN 46224. **Tel** (317)244-4792.

LC HD9513 .W5   **ISSN** 0511-9049
DD 672   US
WHO'S WHO IN STEEL AND METALS. 1st (1964)-. Periodical. English.

LC DQ52 .W5   **ISSN** 0083-9736
DD 920.0494   SZ
WHO'S WHO IN SWITZERLAND INCLUDING THE PRINCIPALITY OF LIECHTENSTEIN. VFOAT Who's Who in Switzerland. (1950/1951)-. English. Every 2 years. 185.00F. Les Editions Nagel SA, 5 rue de l'Orangerie, 1211 Geneva 7 Switzerland. **Tel** 011 41 22 7341730.

LC CT262 .W45   **ISSN** 0094-6680
DD 920/.0764   US
WHO'S WHO IN TEXAS. 1st- Ed.; 1973/74-. English. United States Public Relations Service, Atlanta GA 30333.

LC DS570.5 .W55
DD 920/.0593   TH
WHO'S WHO IN THAILAND. (May 1973)-. Periodical. English. Twelve times a year. $6.92. International Publishing and Marketing Company, B O A C Building/5th Floor, Rajaprasong Corner, Bangkok Thailand.

LC D198.3 .W5   **ISSN** 0083-9752
DD 920/.009174927 B   LE
NLM D 198.3 W628
WHO'S WHO IN THE ARAB WORLD. 1st Ed. (1965/1966)-. Monographic series. English. Irregular. $280.00. Gale Research Inc., 835 Penobscot Building, 645 Griswold Street, Detroit MI 48226. **Tel** (800)877-GALE, (313)961-2242, FAX (313)961-6083, (800)414-5043, telex TWX 810-221-7086. **ED** Charles G. Gedeon.
Desc: A biographical dictionary, a regional and historical survey, and a geographical directory. Provides 6,000 biographical sketches of outstanding persons in 20 Arab countries. Many fields are represented, from government to religion. Contains a historical outline of the development of the Arab world. This general survey covers the diverse racial groups, their languages, ancient cultures, and religions. Also includes details and analyses on the twenty Arab countries, excluding Lebanon.

LC PN   **ISSN** 0722-916X
DD 800   GW
WHO'S WHO IN THE ARTS AND LITERATURE. See Literature.

LC HD9999.C93 U64
DD 338.7/66/85502573   US
WHO'S WHO IN THE COSMETIC INDUSTRY. **Added/Corp** Cosmetic, Toiletry and Fragrance Association. Cosmetic, Toiletry and Fragrance Association. Membership Directory. VFOAT Membership Directory. (19??)-. Periodical. English. One time a year. $75.00. Cosmetic Toiletry and Fragrance Association, PO Box 471, Annapolis Junction MD 20701. **Tel** (301)953-2614.

LC E176 .W643   **ISSN** 0083-9760
DD 920.07   US
     CCC
WHO'S WHO IN THE EAST. VFOAT Who's Who in the East and Eastern Canada; Who's Who in the East, United States of America and Canada. Vol. 1 (1943)-. English. Every 2 years. $275.00. Marquis Who's Who, A Reed Reference Publishing Company, Part of Reed International PLC, 121 Chanlon Road, New Providence NJ 07974. **Tel** (908)464-6800, (800)521-8110, FAX (908)665-6688, telex 138 755. available on magnetic tape and CD-ROM.
Desc: Information on 29,000 prominent men and women principally known in the eastern US and Canada.
Ind/Abst Curr. Lit. Fam. Plan. (19??-199?).

LC CT
DD 920   UK
WHO'S WHO IN THE EMERGENCY & RESCUE SERVICES. Directory. English. One time a year. £15.00 UK; $29.00 US. Lincoln Publications, 28 Centre Point House, St. Giles Street, London WC2H 8LW United Kingdom. **Tel** 011 44 171 2405562, FAX 011 44 171 4972811. **ED** Derek V Tofts. **Bk Rev. Ad Acc. Circ:** 2,000.
Desc: Directory for all the UK Emergency and Rescue Services. The contents includes a Directory of Public Fire Brigades, Ambulance Service, Police, Civil Defence, giving the names of Chief Officers, Headquarters address, areas covered, equipment and vehicles statistics, etc.

Biographies

LC HD6820.6 .A48
DD 331.88/025/5951 MY
WHO'S WHO IN THE LABOUR MOVEMENT. (1974/75)-. English. $3.00. A Ragunatan, 1 5/15E Jalan Chantek Petaling Java, Kuala Lumpur Malaysia.

LC E176 .W644 **ISSN** 0083-9787
DD 920.07 US
NLM E 176 W6287
WHO'S WHO IN THE MIDWEST. 1st Ed. (1949)-. English. Every 2 years. $249.95. Marquis Who's Who, A Reed Reference Publishing Company, Part of Reed International PLC, 121 Chanlon Road, New Providence NJ 07974. **Tel** (908)464-6800, (800)521-8110, FAX (908)665-6688, telex 138 755. available on magnetic tape and CD-ROM. **Continues** Who's Who in the Central States.
 Desc: Biographies of prominent men and women living in Illinois, Indiana, Iowa, Kansas, Missouri, Minnesota, Michigan, Nebraska, North Dakota, Ohio, South Dakota, Wisconsin and in Canada--Manitoba, and Western Ontario.

LC PN1998.A2 W624 **ISSN** 0278-6516
DD 791.43/023/02573 US
WHO'S WHO IN THE MOTION PICTURE INDUSTRY. [Who's who motion pict. ind.]. 1st Ed. (1981)-. English. One time a year. $23.95. Packard Publishing, PO Box 2187, Beverly Hills CA 90213. **Tel** (213)854-0276. **ED** Rodman W. Gregg. Index available. **Bk Rev. Ad Acc. Circ:** 4,500 (ctrl).
 Desc: A directory of motion picture producers, writers, directors, and cinematographers. Also includes executives of the studios and major production companies. Also includes individual film and television credits.

LC CT **ISSN** 1065-8459
DD 363 US
●**WHO'S WHO IN THE PEACE CORPS.** [Who's who Peace Corps]. (1993)-. English. Reference Press International, PO Box 4126, Greenwich CT 06830.

LC N8551.U6 W56 **ISSN** 0147-2119
DD 338.4/7/7497 US
WHO'S WHO IN THE PICTURE FRAMING INDUSTRY. English. One time a year. $7.50 each issue, (free annual dues for PPFA members). Professional Picture Framers, 5633 South Laburnum Avenue, Richmond VA 23231. **Tel** (804)226-0430. **ED** Katherine R Jeschke. **Ad Acc.** ctrl circ.
 Desc: Membership directory providing names, addresses, and telephone numbers of all PPFA retail, Guild, and supplier members.

LC HG4907 .W54 **ISSN** 0090-418X
DD 332.6/2/0257 US
CEASED
WHO'S WHO IN THE SECURITIES INDUSTRY. Added/Corp Securities Industry Association. (1972)-(1993). English. Economist Publishing Company, 12 East Grand Avenue, Chicago IL 60611. **Supersedes in part** Economist I.B.A. Convention Editions.

LC E176 .W645 **ISSN** 0083-9809
DD 920.O73 US
NLM E 176 W6289 1967
WHO'S WHO IN THE SOUTH AND SOUTHWEST. 1st Ed. (1947)-. English. Every 2 years (Aug.). $229.95. Marquis Who's Who, A Reed Reference Publishing Company, Part of Reed International PLC, 121 Chanlon Road, New Providence NJ 07974. **Tel** (908)464-6800, (800)521-8110, FAX (908)665-6688, telex 138 755. available on magnetic tape and CD-ROM.
 Desc: Biographies of prominent people living in the south and southwest sections of the US, including Puerto Rico, the Virgin Islands and Mexico.

LC CT
DD 920 UK
WHO'S WHO IN THE WATER INDUSTRY. YEARBOOK. See Water Resources.

LC E176 .W646 **ISSN** 0896-7709
DD 920/.078 US
NLM E 176 W6293
WHO'S WHO IN THE WEST (1971). (WHO'S WHO IN THE WEST.). [Who's who West]. 12th Ed. (1971)-. English. Every 2 years. $249.95. Marquis Who's Who, A Reed Reference Publishing Company, Part of Reed International PLC, 121 Chanlon Road, New Providence NJ 07974. **Tel** (908)464-6800, (800)521-8110, FAX (908)665-6688, telex 138 755. available on magnetic tape and CD-ROM. **Continues** Who's Who in the West (and Western Canada), 0897-0629.
 Desc: Biographies of prominent men and women living in Alaska, Arizona, California, Colorado, Hawaii, Idaho, Montana, Nevada, New Mexico, Oregon, Utah, Washington and Wyoming. Also in Canada: Alberta, British Columbia, and Saskatchewan provinces.

LC CT120 .W5 **ISSN** 0083-9825
DD 920.02 US
CCC
NLM CT 120 W635
WHO'S WHO IN THE WORLD. 1st Ed. (1972)-. English. Every 2 years. $329.95. Marquis Who's Who, A Reed Reference Publishing Company, Part of Reed International PLC, 121 Chanlon Road, New Providence NJ 07974. **Tel** (908)464-6800, (800)521-8110, FAX (908)665-6688, telex 138 755. available on magnetic tape and CD-ROM.
 Desc: International biographical reference directory which provides more than 35,000 individual biographies - from leaders in government to the chiefs of the world's major corporations.

LC HD9133 .W48 **ISSN** 0734-208X
DD 381/.45664153/02573 US
WHO'S WHO IN TOBACCO / CONFECTIONERY DISTRIBUTION. VFOAT Tobacco Journal Supplier Directory. (March 1982)-. English. One time a year. BMT Publications Inc, Seven Penn Plaza, New York NY 10001. **Tel** (800)223-9638, (212)594-4120.
 Desc: Information on the tobacco, candy, and confectionery industries and the stationery trade.

LC F2119 .W47
DD 920/.0729/83 TR
WHO'S WHO IN TRINIDAD AND TOBAGO. (1966)-. English. Who's Who in Trinidad and Tobago, PO Box 906, Trinidad West Indies.

LC E747 .W65
DD 973.273 US
WHO'S WHO IN UNITED STATES POLITICS AND AMERICAN POLITICAL ALMANAC. VFOAT American Political Almanac; Who's Who in U.S. Politics. Periodical. English. **ED** R Nowinson.

LC F193 **ISSN** 0732-5673
DD 920/.0753 US
NLM F 193; W629
WHO'S WHO IN WASHINGTON. [Who's who Washington]. 1st Ed. (1983-84)-. English. One time a year. $79.95. Tiber Reference Press, 4340 East-West Highway, Bethesda MD 20814.

LC CT267 .W48 **ISSN** 0742-8510
DD 920/.0754 US
WHO'S WHO IN WEST VIRGINIA (CLARKSBURG, W. VA.). (WHO'S WHO IN WEST VIRGINIA.). [Who's who W. Va.]. 1983-84-. English. Who's Who Historical Society / West Virginia, 102 South Fourth Street, Clarksburg WV 26301.

LC HD9579.C3 W48
DD 338.7/661804/025 US
WHO'S WHO IN WORLD PETROCHEMICAL & PLASTICS. (1990)-. English. Who's Who Information Services, 17 South Brian Hollow Lane, Suite 401, Houston TX 77027. **Continues** Who's Who in World Petrochemicals, 8755-3414.

LC PS129 .W47 **ISSN** 1049-8621
DD 810.9 B US
WHO'S WHO IN WRITERS, EDITORS & POETS, UNITED STATES & CANADA. [Who's who writ. ed. poets U. S. Can.]. VFOAT Who's Who in Writers, Editors & Poets. 3rd Ed. (1989/1990)-. English. Every 2 years. $99.00. December Press, Box 302, Highland Park IL 60035. **Tel** (708)940-4122. **ED** Curt Johnson. **Continues** Who's Who in U.S. Writers, Editors & Poets, 0885-4521.

LC CT360 .W46
DD 920/.07292 JM
WHO'S WHO, JAMAICA. (19??)-. English. 14 Half Way Tree Road, Kingston 5 Jamaica.

LC DA28 .W6 **ISSN** 0083-937X
DD 942.0099 UK
CCC
NLM CT 773 W6282
WHO'S WHO (LONDON. 1849). (WHO'S WHO.). [Who's who]. (1849)-. English. One time a year. $185.00. St. Martin's Press, 175 Fifth Avenue, New York NY 10010. **Tel** (800)221-7945, (212)982-3900, FAX (212)777-6359. **Bk Rev. Ad Acc. Absorbed** Men and Women of the Time.
 Desc: Biographies, compiled by each individual of 29,000 living people of influence and interest in every field. Each entry contains personal details, career, and address.

LC GV884.A1 W48 **ISSN** 1040-7464
DD 796.323/092/2 US
WHO'S WHO OF AMERICAN HIGH SCHOOL BASKETBALL COACHES. [Who's who Am. high sch. basketb. coach.]. 1st Ed. (1988/89)-. English. Every 2 years. $25.00. Gunther Publishing Company, 10207 Heather Hill, Houston TX 77086.

LC E176 .W647 **ISSN** 0083-9841
DD 920.72/0973 US
CCC
NLM E176 W628
WHO'S WHO OF AMERICAN WOMEN. [Who's who Am. women]. 6th Ed. (1971)-. English. Every 2 years. $225.00. Marquis Who's Who, A Reed Reference Publishing Company, Part of Reed International PLC, 121 Chanlon Road, New Providence NJ 07974. **Tel** (908)464-6800, (800)521-8110, FAX (908)665-6688, telex 138 755. available on magnetic tape and CD-ROM. **Continues** Who's Who of American Women and Women of Canada, 0270-2800.
 Desc: Includes biographies of prominent accomplished women across a wide range of disciplines and professions - government, business, the arts, medicine, religion, etc.

LC CT
DD 920 AT
WHO'S WHO OF AUSTRALIAN WRITERS. (19??)-. Directory. English. Irregular. $80.00. D. W. Thorpe, A Reed Reference Publishing Company, A Subsidiary of Reed International Books Australia, 18 Salmon Street, Port Melbourne Victoria 3207 Australia. **Tel** 011 61 3 6451511, FAX 011 61 3 6453981, telex 39476.
 Desc: Offers information on living Australian writers and editors of fiction, nonfiction, poetry, plays, textbooks, and radio and TV scripts.

ISSN 0748-0601
DD 305 US
WHO'S WHO OF CALIFORNIA EXECUTIVE WOMEN. [Who's who Calif. exec. women]. **Added/Corp** International Woman Center. First Ed. (1983-1984)-. English. One time a year. $75.00. International Womens Center, PO Box 417, Davenport CA 95017-0417. ctrl circ.

LC CT3270 .W46 **ISSN** 0823-5015
DD 920.72/0971 CN
WHO'S WHO OF CANADIAN WOMEN. [Who's who Can. women]. (1984)-. English. One time a year. 136.45Can$. Who's Who Publications, 777 Bay Street, 5th Floor, Toronto ONT M5W 1A7 Canada. **Tel** (416)596-5100.

LC CT213 .W48 **ISSN** 0895-965X
DD 920/.073 US
WHO'S WHO OF EMERGING LEADERS IN AMERICA. [Who's who emerg. lead. Am.]. **Added/Corp** Marquis Who's Who, Inc. 1st Edition (1987-1988)-. English. Irregular. $229.00. Marquis Who's Who, A Reed Reference Publishing Company, Part of Reed International PLC, 121 Chanlon Road, New Providence NJ 07974. **Tel** (908)464-6800, (800)521-8110, FAX (908)665-6688, telex 138 755. available on magnetic tape and CD-ROM.
 Desc: Profiles "super achievers" who influence all levels of society, from medicine and business to law and religion.

LC DT752 .S5
SA
WHO'S WHO OF SOUTHERN AFRICA. (1907)-. Directory. English. One time a year. R290.00. Who's Who of Southern Africa, PO Box 81284 Parkhurst, Johannesburg 2120 South Africa. **Tel** 011 27 11 8802406, 8802407, FAX 011 27 11 802366. **(Subscription address:** International Publications Service, A Division of Taylor & Francis, 1900 Frost Road, Suite 101, Bristol PA 19007-1598. **Tel** (800)821-8312.) **Absorbed** Who's Who of the Federation of Rhodesia and Nyasaland, also Portuguese East Africa, 1959 **and** Central and East African Who's Who.
 Desc: Comprehensive sourcebook to influential persons of Southern Africa. Covers business, community, and opinion leaders of Botswana, Lesotho, Malawi, Mauritius, Namibia, Swaziland, and Zimbabwe.

LC CT **ISSN** 1059-5392
DD 920 US
WHO'S WHO OF THE ASIAN PACIFIC RIM. (1992)-. English. One time a year. $175.00. Barons Who's Who, 412 North Coast Highway, Suite B-110, Laguna Beach CA 92651. **Tel** (714)497-8615.

LC CT220 .W55 **ISSN** 1061-4044
DD 920.073 US
●**WHO'S WHO REGISTRY (PLATINUM ED.), THE.** (THE WHO'S WHO REGISTRY.). [Who's who regist.]. VFOAT Who's Who Worldwide Registry. (1993)-. English. Every 3 years. $697.00. Who's Who Worldwide Registry, Inc., 1983 Marcus Avenue, Suite C120, Lake Success NY 11042.

LC CT1567.S27 W48
MY
WHO'S WHO, SARAWAK. VFOAT Who's Who in Sarawak. 82/83-. English. Sarawak Publishing House, PO Box 2957, Kuching Sarawak Malaysia.

ISSN 1056-6708
DD 338 US
WHO'S WHO WORLDWIDE REGISTRY. [Who's who worldw. regist.]. (1990)-. English. One time a year. $697.00. Who's Who Worldwide Registry, Inc., 1983 Marcus Avenue, Suite C120, Lake Success NY 11042.
Desc: A reference source of accomplished individuals and their career positions.

LC HQ1123 .W65
DD 920.72 UK
WORLD WHO'S WHO OF WOMEN, THE. **Added/Corp** International Biographical Centre. Vol. 1 (1973)-. English. Every 2 years. $175.00. Melrose Press Ltd., 3 Regal Lane Soham, Ely Cambridgeshire, CB7 5BA United Kingdom. **Tel** 011 44 135 3721091, FAX 011 44 135 3721839, telex 81584. **(Subscription address:** Taylor & Francis Inc., 1900 Frost Road, Suite 101, Bristol PA 19007-1598. **Tel** (215)785-5800, (800)821-8312, FAX (215)785-5515.) **ED** J. S. Thomson. ***Continues*** *Two Thousand Women of Achievement.*
Desc: Offers illustrated biographical information of the world's women.

LC CT
DD 920 UK
WORLD WHO'S WHO OF WOMEN IN EDUCATION, THE. **Added/Corp** International Biographical Centre. **VFOAT** Women in Education. (1978)-. English. Irregular. Melrose Press Ltd., 3 Regal Lane Soham, Ely Cambridgeshire, CB7 5BA United Kingdom. **Tel** 011 44 135 3721091, FAX 011 44 135 3721839, telex 81584. **(Subscription address:** Taylor & Francis Inc., 1900 Frost Road, Suite 101, Bristol PA 19007-1598. **Tel** (215)785-5800, (800)821-8312, FAX (215)785-5515.)

LC PS1 .W73 ISSN 0084-2699
DD 808 UK
WRITERS DIRECTORY, THE. **See** Literature.

ABSTRACTING, BIBLIOGRAPHIES AND STATISTICS

LC Z5304.A8 A93 PN452 ISSN 0741-8655
DD 016.809 US
AUTHOR BIOGRAPHIES MASTER INDEX. [Author biogr. master index]. **Added/Corp** Gale Research Company. 1st Ed. (1977/1978)-. English. Irregular. $260.00. Gale Research Inc., 835 Penobscot Building, 645 Griswold Street, Detroit MI 48226. **Tel** (800)877-GALE, (313)961-2242, FAX (313)961-6083, (800)414-5043, telex TWX 810-221-7086. **ED** Barbara McNeil. available on magnetic tape; available on diskette.
Desc: Covering all eras and countries, this reference indexes biographies of major literary figures plus those of minor authors about whom it is often difficult to find information.

LC JC345 ISSN 0730-1316
DD 929.82 US
NLM Z 5301 B614
BIOGRAPHY AND GENEALOGY MASTER INDEX. [Biogr. geneal. master index]. **Added/Corp** Gale Research Company. 2nd Ed. (1980)-. English. One time a year. $295.00. Gale Research Inc., 835 Penobscot Building, 645 Griswold Street, Detroit MI 48226. **Tel** (800)877-GALE, (313)961-2242, FAX (313)961-6083, (800)414-5043, telex TWX 810-221-7086. **ED** Barbara McNeil. available on magnetic tape; available on diskette; available on microfiche (as Bio-Base); available on CD-ROM; available on an online database (File 287,288) from DIALOG. ***Continues*** *Biographical Dictionaries Master Index.*
Desc: Reference for locating biographical information on notable people in all fields, living or dead.

US
BIOGRAPHY AND GENEALOGY MASTER INDEX. SUPPLEMENT. **Added/Corp** Gale Research Company. **VFOAT** Supplement. (1981/1982)-. English. One time a year. Gale Research Inc., 835 Penobscot Building, 645 Griswold Street, Detroit MI 48226. **Tel** (800)877-GALE, (313)961-2242, FAX (313)961-6083, (800)414-5043, telex TWX 810-221-7086. **ED** Barbara McNeil. ***Continues*** *Biographical Dictionaries Master Index. Supplement.*
Desc: Adds more than one million citations to biographical sketches appearing in new editions and volumes of titles indexed in the base set, and indexes new titles recently published.

LC CT ISSN 0006-3053
DD 920 US
NLM Z 5301 B615
Pr Rev.
BIOGRAPHY INDEX. [Biogr. index]. **Added/Corp** H.W. Wilson Company. (Jan. 1946/June 1947)-. Abstracting/Indexing Service. English. Four times a year (plus annual and biannual cumulations). $125.00 US and Canada; $135.00 other. H W Wilson Company, 950 University Avenue, Bronx NY 10452. **Tel** (800)367-6770, (718)588-8400 ext. 2245, FAX (718)681-1511, telex 4990003 HWILSON. **ED** Charles Cornell. Index available. cum. index. ctrl circ. available on CD-ROM from WILSONDISC; available on magnetic tape from WILSONTAPE; available on an online database from BRS; and WILSONLINE; available on diskette from WILSONSEARCH.
Desc: Includes information about people from every field and age. Sources include periodicals indexed by H W Wilson and current books.

LC Z5301 ISSN 1063-3286
DD 920 US
BIOGRAPHY INDEX (CD-ROM ED.). (BIOGRAPHY INDEX [COMPUTER FILE].). [Biogr. index]. **VFOAT** Wilsondisc Biography Index. (198?)-. English. Four times a year. $1,095.00. H W Wilson Company, 950 University Avenue, Bronx NY 10452. **Tel** (800)367-6770, (718)588-8400 ext. 2245, FAX (718)681-1511, telex 4990003 HWILSON. **ED** Charles Cornell. Index available. cum. index. ctrl circ. available on magnetic tape from WILSONTAPE; available in print; available on diskette from WILSONSEARCH; available on an online database from WILSONLINE.
Desc: Index to biographical material in periodicals, current books of individual and collective biography, obituaries, including those of national interest in the "New York Times" and biographical passages in nonbiographical books. Portraits noted when they appeared with indexed material.

LC JC345
DD 929.82 IT
DIZIONARIO BIOGRAFICO DEGLI ITALIANI. INDICE. **Added/Corp** Istituto della Enciclopedia Italiana, Rome. Vol. 1 (1973)-. Periodical. Italian. One time a year. L162000. Instituto Enciclopedia Italiana, PZA Enciclopedia Italiana 4, 00186 Rome Italy. **Tel** 011 39 6 68982464.

LC CT
DD 920 US
ST. JAMES GUIDE TO BIOGRAPHY. (1992)-. English. $130.00. St. James Press, An Imprint of Gale Research Inc., PO Box 33477, Detroit MI 48232-5477. **Tel** (800)345-0392. **ED** Paul E. Schellinger.
Desc: Provides complete bibliographical information on the biographies of more than 700 figures from world history...from Alexander the Great to Marilyn Monroe...Napoleon to Henry James...Julius Caeser to Corazon Aquino.

BIOLOGY

ISSN 0084-8824
DD 574 US
ABSTRACTS OF PAPERS PRESENTED AT ... MEETINGS - LABORATORY OF QUNATITATIVE BIOLOGY. **Main/Corp** Cold Spring Harbor, New York. Laboratory of Quantitative Biology. (1969)-. Periodical. English. Irregular. Price varies. Cold Spring Harbor Laboratory, 10 Skyline Drive, Plainview NY 11803. **Tel** (516)349-1930, (800)843-4388, FAX (516)349-1946.
Desc: Abstracts of papers presented at meetings at Cold Spring Harbor Laboratory.

LC Q
DD 500 BL
ACTA AMAZONICA. SUPLEMENTO. **Added/Corp** Brazil. Instituto Nacional de Pesquisas da Amazonia. (19??)-. Monographic series. Portuguese. Price varies per volume. Instituto Nacional Pesquisas Amazonia, Departemento de Documentacao e Informacao, Al Cosme Ferreira, 1756 Aleixo, Manaus 69 083 Amazonas Brasil. **Tel** 011 55 92 6423377, FAX 011 55 92 2360255, telex 0922269.
Ind/Abst Hortic. Abstr.; Rev. Med. Vet. Mycology; Seed Abstr.

LC Q ISSN 0350-5901
DD 500 YU
NLM W1 AC757 CODEN ABMEDG
ACTA BIOLOGIAE ET MEDICINAE EXPERIMENTALIS. [Acta biol. med. exp.]. **Added/Corp** Society for Biology and Experimental Medicine SAP Kosovo. Society of Sciences and Arts of SAP Kosovo. Division of Natural Sciences. Vol. 1 (1976)-. Periodical. English. Two times a year. Documents available from BIOSIS Document Express, CASDDS.
Ind/Abst Biol. Abstr.; Chem. Abstr.

LC Q
DD 500 CC
ACTA BIOLOGIAE EXPERIMENTALIS SINICA. (1???)-. Chinese. Four times a year. $34.80. Institute of Experimental Biology, Academia Sinica, Beijing People's Republic of China. **(Subscription address:** China International Book Trading Corporation, PO Box 399, Library Service Department, Beijing 100044 People's Republic of China. **Tel** 011 86 1 8414284, FAX 011 86 1 8412023, telex 22496 CIBTC CN.) **ED** Chuang Hsiao-Hui. **Circ:** 3,000. Documents available from BIOSIS Document Express.
Desc: Original papers, short communications and short reviews of experimental biology.
Ind/Abst AgBiotech News Inf.; Anim. Breed. Abstr.; Biol. Abstr.; Crop Physiol. Abstr.; Field Crop Abstr.; Grass. Forage Abstr.; Index Med.; Maize Abstr.; Plant Breed. Abstr.; Plant Genet. Resour. Abstr.; Plant Grow. Reg. Abstr.; Rev. Agric. Entomol.; Rev. Med. Vet. Mycology; Rev. Plant Pathol.; Rice Abstr.; Soyabean Abstr.

LC QH301
DD 574 PL
ACTA BIOLOGICA. **Added/Corp** Gdanskie Towarzystwo Naukowe. No. 1 (1976)-. Periodical. Polish. Irregular. Price varies per volume. **(Subscription address:** Ars Polona-Ruch, PO Box 1001, Krakowskie Przedmiescie 7, 00-068 Warsaw Poland. **Tel** 011 48 22 261201.) ***Supersedes*** *Acta Biologica et Medica, 0065-1087.*

LC QH301 .A323 ISSN 0236-5383
DD 574/.05 HU
CCC
NLM W1; AC7631D CODEN ABHUE6
ACTA BIOLOGICA HUNGARICA. [Acta biol. Hung.]. **Added/Corp** Magyar Tudomanyos Akademia. **VFOAT** Acta Biologica. Vol. 34, No. 1 (1983)-. Academic Scholarly Publication. English. Four times a year. $92.00. Akademiai Kiado, Publishing House of the Hungarian Academy of Sciences, Prielle Kornelia u. 19-35, H-1117 Budapest Hungary. **Tel** 011 36 1 1811991, FAX 011 36 1 1811991, telex 22-6228 AKNYO H. **ED** Janos Salanki (editor's address: Acta Biologica, H-8237 Tihany Hungary). cum. index. Documents available from The Genuine Article, BIOSIS Document Express, CASDDS. ***Continues*** *Acta Biologica Academiae Scientiarum Hungaricae.*
Desc: Provides a forum for original research in the field of experimental biology. It covers cytology, morphology, embryology, genetics, endocrinology, radiation biology, cellular level of biological regulation, ethology and environmental biology with emphasis on toxicology.
Ind/Abst Anim. Breed. Abstr.; Biol. Abstr. (1983-); Chem. Abstr. (1983-); Curr. Cit.; Curr. Contents Agric. Biol. Environ. Sci.; Curr. Ref. Fish Res.; Ecol. Abstr. (?-?); EMBASE (1983-); Field Crop Abstr.; Health Plan. Adminis.; Helminthol. Abstr.; Hortic. Abstr.; Index Med.; Index Vet.; Maize Abstr.; Nutr. Abstr. Rev., Ser. A, Hum. Exp.; Life Sci. Collect.; Poult. Abstr.; Res. Alert [Full Cov.]; Rev. Agric. Entomol.; Rev. Med. Vet. Entomol.; Sci. Cit. Index; SCISEARCH; Weed Abstr.

LC QH301 .A3236 ISSN 0301-2123
DD 574/.05 BL
NLM W1 AC7631K CODEN ACBPAW
ACTA BIOLOGICA PARANAENSE. [Acta biol. parana.]. **Added/Corp** Universidade Federal do Parana. Setor de Ciencias Biologicas. Universidade Federal do Parana. Instituto de Biologia. Vol. 1 (1972)-. Academic Scholarly Publication. Portuguese (summaries and/or abstracts in English and French; table of contents in English). Four times a year. Cr$25.00. Universidade Federal Parana / Bibliotec Centrale, Caixa Postal 441, 80001 Curitiba Parana Brazil. **Tel** 011 55 41 25 27022, 011 55 41 25 7244. Documents available from BIOSIS Document Express, CASDDS. ***Continues in part*** *Biologia; Zoologia; Botanica.*
Ind/Abst Biol. Abstr. (1973-1977); Chem. Abstr.; GeoRef.

LC WMLC 93/583
DD 574 PL
CODEN ABSIEP
ACTA BIOLOGICA SILESIANA. **Added/Corp** Uniwersytet Slaski w Katowicach. (1985)-. Periodical. Polish (English; summaries and/or abstracts in English and Russian; table of contents in Russian). Irregular. Wydawnictwo Uniwersytet Slaskiego, Ul. Bankowa 12B, 40-007 Katowice Poland. **Tel** 011 48 32 596915, FAX 011 48 32 599605, telex 0315584 USKPL. **(Subscription address:** Ars Polona-Ruch, PO Box 1001, Krakowskie Przedmiescie 7, 00-068 Warsaw Poland. **Tel** 011 48 22 261201.) ***Continues*** *Acta Biologica (Katowice), 0208-6336.*
Ind/Abst Plant Breed. Abstr.; Plant Grow. Reg. Abstr.

LC QH7 .S94 ISSN 0563-0592
HU
CODEN AUSGAC
ACTA BIOLOGICA (SZEGED. 1955). (ACTA BIOLOGICA.). [Acta biol.]. **Added/Corp** Szegedi Tudomanyegyetem. Termeszettudomanyi Kar. Jozsef Attila Tudomanyegyetem. Termeszettudomanyi Kar. New Series Vol. 1, No. 1-4 (1955)-. Periodical. English (German). Four times a year. **(Subscription address:** Kultura, PO Box 143, H-1300 Budapest 3 Hungary. **Tel** 011 36 1 2500194.) Documents available from BIOSIS Document Express, CASDDS. ***Continues*** *Annales Biologicae Universitatum Hungaricae. Pars Szegediensis, 0404-4591.*
Ind/Abst Biol. Abstr.; Chem. Abstr.

LC QH7 .A523 ISSN 0001-5326
DD 574/.05 VE
CODEN ABVEAO
ACTA BIOLOGICA VENEZUELICA. **See** Natural History.

LC QH301 **ISSN** 0001-5342
DD 574.05 NE
CCC
NLM W1 AC765 **CODEN** ABIOAN
Pr Rev.
ACTA BIOTHEORETICA. [Acta biotheor.]. Vol. 1 (1935)-. Periodical. English (German and French). Four times a year. $232.00. Kluwer Academic Publishers, Postbus 322, 3300 AH Dordrecht The Netherlands. **Tel** 011 31 78 524400, FAX 011 31 78 183273, telex 20083. **ED** P. Dullemeijer, U. van der Heiden, D. Ludwig, J. Demongeot. available on microfilm and microfiche from University Microfilms International (UMI). Documents available from The Genuine Article, BIOSIS Document Express, CASDDS. ***Absorbed*** *Geschriften van de Prof. Dr. van der Hoeven Stichting voor Theoretische Biologie van Dier end Mensch, Verbonden aan de Universiteit te Leiden. Series C, Bibliographia Biotheoretica, 0920-2684.*
Desc: Devoted to the promotion of theoretical biology and publishes papers on all aspects of the subject, including the philosophy of biology and biomathematics. The emphasis of the papers published is on the methodology of biological theory formation in mathematical and verbal form, as well as on the historical origins of and philosophical presuppositions underlying biological theories and concepts. Short notes on interesting new theoretical ideas and book reviews are also published. With their clear statement of biological assumptions, justification for their translation into mathematical form, careful discussion of the mathematical treatment, and their explanation of the relationship between theory and empirical data, the papers published in this journal form an unrivalled source of clear, unambiguous statements of theoretical biology.
Ind/Abst Anim. Breed. Abstr.; Biol. Abstr.; Chem. Abstr. (1935-1982); CSA Neuro. Abstr. (?-?); Curr. Aware. Biol. Sci., CABS; Curr. Cit.; Curr. Contents Agric. Biol. Environ. Sci.; EMBASE; Health Plan. Adminis.; Hortic. Abstr.; Index Med.; Ornamental Hort. (1991-); Ref. Upd. Deluxe Ed.; Res. Alert [Full Cov.]; Sci. Cit. Index; SCISEARCH.

LC R **ISSN** 0567-7734
DD 610 JA
NLM W1 AC835 **CODEN** AMBNAS
ACTA MEDICA ET BIOLOGICA. See Medical Sciences.

LC QP351 .A43 **ISSN** 0065-1400
DD 612.805/6 PL
NLM W1 AC8655 **CODEN** ANEXAC
ACTA NEUROBIOLOGIAE EXPERIMENTALIS. See Medical Sciences-Neurology.

LC QH301 **ISSN** 0001-7124
DD 574 XR
NLM W1 AC954F **CODEN** ACBIBC
ACTA UNIVERSITATIS CAROLINAE. BIOLOGICA. [Acta Univ. Carol., Biol.]. **Main/Corp** Universita Karlova. **Added/Corp** Universita Karlova. **VFOAT** Biologica. (1958)-. Periodical. English (Czech, French and German). Six times a year. $120.00. Carolinum Press, Ovochny TRH 5, 11636 Prague 1 Czech Republic. **Tel** 011 42 2 228441. **ED** J. Zahradnik. **Circ:** 650. available with charts; available with illustrations. Documents available from BIOSIS Document Express. ***Supersedes*** *Universitas Carolina. Biologica;* ***Supersedes in part*** *Acta Universitatis Carolinae.*
Desc: Presents information and research in plant anatomy.
Ind/Abst Anim. Breed. Abstr.; Biol. Abstr.; Dairy Sci. Abstr.; Fish Rev.; Hortic. Abstr.; Leis., Rec., Tour. Abstr.; Microbiol. Abstr. Sect. C; Life Sci. Collect.; Protozoolog. Abstr.; Rural Dev. Abstr.; Vitis Vitic. Enol. Abstr.; Wildl. Rev.; World Agric. Econ. Rural Sociol. Abstr.

LC QH301 **ISSN** 0753-3918
DD 574 FR
UDC 331.88:615
ACTUALITES BIOLOGIQUES. (19??)-. Periodical. French. Ten times a year. 700.00F. Centre National Biologistes, 80 Avenue du Maine, 75014 Paris France. **Tel** 011 33 43229770, FAX 011 33 43217312.
Desc: For the professionals and administrators of biological analysis laboratories.

LC QH301
DD 574 SI
ADVANCED SERIES ON COMPLEX SYSTEMS. Vol. 1 (1986)-. Monographic series. English. World Scientific Publishing Company, PO Box 128, Farrer Road, Singapore 9128 Singapore. **Tel** 011 65 3825663, FAX 011 65 3825919, telex RS 28561 WSPC.
Ind/Abst Math. Rev.; Zentralbl. Math. Ihre Grenzgeb.

LC QH543 .A38 **ISSN** 0942-5225
DD 574.522 GW
CODEN ADVBEX
ADVANCES IN BIOCLIMATOLOGY. [Adv. bioclimatol.]. **VFOAT** Bioclimatology. (1992)-. Monographic series. English. Springer-Verlag GmbH & Company KG, Heidelberger Platz 3, D-14197 Berlin Germany. **Tel** 011 49 30 8207223, FAX 011 49 30 8214091, telex 183 319 SPBLN D. **(Subscription address:** Springer-Verlag New York Inc. / North America, PO Box 19386 Books, Newark NJ 07195. **Tel** (201)348-4033.**)**
Ind/Abst Bibliogr. Agric.

LC QH301 .A3276
DD 574/.05 II
NLM W1; AD44H
ADVANCES IN BIOLOGICAL RESEARCH. Vol. 1, No. 1 (1983)-. Periodical. English. Two times a year. $60.00. **(Subscription address:** Prints India, 11 Darya Ganj, New Delhi 110002 India. **Tel** 011 91 11 3268645, FAX 011 91 11 3275542, telex 31-61087 PRIN-IN.**)**

LC QH301 **ISSN** 0970-0315
DD 574 II
NLM W1; AD449L
ADVANCES IN BIOSCIENCES. Added/Corp Society of Biosciences (India). Vol. 1, No. 1 (Dec. 1982)-. Periodical. English. Two times a year. $20.00. Hira Lal Charitable Trust, Muzaffarnagar India. **(Subscription address:** Prints India, 11 Darya Ganj, New Delhi 110002 India. **Tel** 011 91 11 3268645, FAX 011 91 11 3275542, telex 31-61087 PRIN-IN.**)**
Ind/Abst Curr. Cit.

LC R857.B54 A38 **ISSN** 1061-8945
DD 574/.028 UK
NLM W1; AD449LG **CODEN** ABIOER
ADVANCES IN BIOSENSORS. [Adv. biosens.]. Vol. 1 (1991)-. English. Irregular. $90.25. JAI Press Inc., 55 Old Post Road, Suite 2, PO Box 1678, Greenwich CT 06836-1678. **Tel** (203)661-7602, FAX (203)661-0792. **ED** A.P.F. Turner. Documents available from BIOSIS Document Express.
Desc: Combines the interdisciplinary skills of biologists, physicists, chemists, and engineers to provide solutions to analytical problems. Presents a compendium of research papers, in which authorities in the field of biosensors provide an overview of their laboratory's contribution summarizing the primary research as it has appeared in the journal and conference literature, and reflecting on their findings.
Ind/Abst Biol. Abstr. (1991-).

LC R **ISSN** 0065-2598
DD 610 US
CCC
NLM W1 AD559 **CODEN** AEMBAP
ADVANCES IN EXPERIMENTAL MEDICINE AND BIOLOGY. See Medical Sciences-Experimental Medicine.

LC QH447 .A38 QH447 .A383 **ISSN** 1067-5701
DD 574.87/322 US
NLM W1; AD616
ADVANCES IN GENOME BIOLOGY. [Adv. genome biol.]. Vol. 1 (1992)-. Monographic series. English. $90.25. JAI Press Inc., 55 Old Post Road, Suite 2, PO Box 1678, Greenwich CT 06836-1678. **Tel** (203)661-7602, FAX (203)661-0792. **ED** Ram S. Verma.

LC QH653
DD 574.19/167/05 UK
NLM W1; AD661 **CODEN** ALTBEB
ADVANCES IN LOW-TEMPERATURE BIOLOGY. VFOAT Low-Temperature Biology. Vol. 1 (1992)-. Periodical. English. $90.25. JAI Press Inc., 55 Old Post Road, Suite 2, PO Box 1678, Greenwich CT 06836-1678. **Tel** (203)661-7602, FAX (203)661-0792. **ED** Peter Steponkus.

LC QD461 .A3 **ISSN** 1054-0954
DD 541.2/2/0724 US
CODEN AMMOEM
ADVANCES IN MOLECULAR MODELING. [Adv. mol. model.]. **VFOAT** Molecular Modeling. Vol. 1 (1988)-. Monographic series. English. Irregular. $90.25. JAI Press Inc., 55 Old Post Road, Suite 2, PO Box 1678, Greenwich CT 06836-1678. **Tel** (203)661-7602, FAX (203)661-0792. Documents available from CASDDS.
Ind/Abst Chem. Abstr.

LC QH652.A1 A65 **ISSN** 0065-3292
US
CCC
NLM W1 AD82 **CODEN** ARDBA3
CEASED
ADVANCES IN RADIATION BIOLOGY. [Adv. radiat. biol.]. Vol. 1 (1964)-Series complete with Vol. 28 (1994). Academic Scholarly Publication. English. Irregular. Price varies per volume. Academic Press Inc., 6277 Sea Harbor Drive, Orlando FL 32887. **Tel** (800)543-9534, (407)345-4100, FAX (407)352-3445. **ED** Leroy G. Augenstein, Ronald Mason, Henry Quastler. Documents available from The Genuine Article, CASDDS.
Ind/Abst Chem. Abstr. (1964-1984); Curr. Cit.; Energy Res. Abstr.; Index Sci. Rev. [Full Cov.]; Res. Alert [Full Cov.]; Sci. Cit. Index; SCISEARCH.

LC RC1120 .A38
DD 616.9/80214/05 US
NLM W1; AD858R **CODEN** ASPBE6
ADVANCES IN SPACE BIOLOGY AND MEDICINE. Vol. 1 (1991)-. Periodical. English. One time a year. $90.25. JAI Press Inc., 55 Old Post Road, Suite 2, PO Box 1678, Greenwich CT 06836-1678. **Tel** (203)661-7602, FAX (203)661-0792. **ED** Sjoerd Bonting.

LC QH301 **ISSN** 0065-3446
DD 574 UK
CCC
NLM W3 AD244 **CODEN** AVBIB9
CEASED
ADVANCES IN THE BIOSCIENCES. [Adv. biosci.]. No. 1 (1969)-(1994). English. Pergamon Press, An Imprint of Elsevier Science Ltd., The Boulevard, Langford Lane, Kidlington, Oxford OX5 1GB United Kingdom. **Tel** 011 44 1865 843000, 011 44 1865 843699, FAX 011 44 1865 843010. **ED** A J Colborne. available on microfilm and microfiche from University Microfilms International (UMI). Documents available from BIOSIS Document Express, CASDDS. ***Continued in part by*** *New Developments in Biosciences, 0935-1906.*
Desc: Developments and directions in biological research are outlined and offer scientists insight into the subjects, methods and results of work being done by research teams.
Ind/Abst AGRICOLA; Biol. Abstr.; Chem. Abstr.; Curr. Aware. Biol. Sci., CABS; EMBASE; Energy Res. Abstr. (June 1975-); Health Saf. Sci. Abstr.; Health Plan. Adminis.; Nematol. Abstr.; Life Sci. Collect.; SCISEARCH; Toxicol. Abstr.

LC QH301 **ISSN** 1072-0618
DD 574 SZ
•ADVANCES IN VASCULAR BIOLOGY. (1994)-. Monographic series. English. Price varies per volume. Harwood Academic Publishers, PO Box 90, Reading RG1 8JL United Kingdom. **Tel** 011 44 1734 560080, FAX 011 44 1734 568211.

LC QH301 **ISSN** 0393-5965
DD 574 IE
UDC 579
AEROBIOLOGIA. [Aerobiologia]. (1985)-. Periodical. English. Four times a year. 134p Ireland; $186.00 US. Elsevier Science Ireland Ltd., Bay 15, Shannon Industrial Estate, Co Clare Ireland. **Tel** 011 353 61 471944. **ED** Dr. Paolo Mandrioli (Editor's address: Instituto FISBAT-CNR, via Gobetti 101, 1-40129 Bologna Italy. Editor's fax: 011 39 51 6399647). Index available. **Bk Rev.** available on an online database from Elsevier Electronic Subscriptions (EES).
Desc: Publishes research papers and review articles in the interdisciplinary fields of aerobiology and of biosphere/atmosphere interaction. Covers aeromycology, airborne microbiology, aeropalynology, climatology, biometeorology, biological pollution and biological input to global change.

ISSN 0894-1106
DD 574 US
NLM W1; AF629F
AFRRI REPORTS. [AFRRI rep.]. **VAT** Armed Forces Radiobiology Research Institute Reports. Periodical. English. Four times a year. Armed Forces Radiobiology Research Institute, Defense Nuclear Agency, Washington DC 20814-5145. available on microfiche (Vols. for (Jan./ March 1985) distributed to depository libraries).

LC S **ISSN** 1079-9060
DD 630 US
•AGRIBIOSCAN (PHOENIX, ARIZ.). See Agriculture.

LC QH **ISSN** 0304-8802
DD 574 CL
CODEN AGSUDR
AGRO SUR. See Agriculture.

LC QH301 .H36 **ISSN** 0002-2918
DD 574 AI
NLM W1 BI7676 **CODEN** BZARAZ
AJASTAN KENSABANAKAN ANDES. (HAYASTANI KENSABAHAKAN HANDES = BIOLOGICHESKII ZHURNAL ARMENII.). [Ajastan kensabanakan andes]. **Added/Corp** Haykakan SSR Gitutyunneri Akademia. Haykakan SSH Gitutyunneri Akademia. **VFOAT** Biologicheskii Zhurnal Armenii. Vol. 19 (Jan. 1966)-. Academic Scholarly Publication. Armenian (Russian; summaries and/or abstracts in English; table of contents in English). Twelve times a year. Akademiia Nauk Armianskoi / Armenian Academy of Sciences, Prospekt Marshala Bagramyana 24, 375019 Yerevan Armenia. **Tel** 011 7 8 524580, telex 243344. **(Subscription address:** Victor Kamkin, 4956 Boiling Brook Parkway, Rockville MD 20852. **Tel** (301)881-5973.**)** Documents available from BIOSIS Document Express, CASDDS. ***Continues*** *Teghekagir. Biologiakan Gityunner.*
Ind/Abst AGRICOLA; Biol. Abstr.; Chem. Abstr.; GeoRef; Nematol. Abstr.; Life Sci. Collect.; Plant Breed. Abstr.; Poult. Abstr.; Protozoolog. Abstr.; Seed Abstr.

LC QH1 .A275 **ISSN** 0002-7685
DD 574.07 US
Pr Rev.
AMERICAN BIOLOGY TEACHER, THE. [Am. biol. teach.]. **Added/Corp** National Association of Biology Teachers. **VFOAT** Biology Teacher. Vol. 1 (Oct. 1938)-. Academic Scholarly Publication. English. Eight times a year (monthly except Jun., Jul., Aug. with Nov./Dec. issue combined). $60.00. National Association of Biology Teachers, 11250 Roger Bacon Drive #19, Reston VA 22090. **Tel** (703)471-1134. **ED** Randy Moore and Michelle Robbins. (bound in Nov. issue). cum. index.

Bk Rev. Ad Acc. Circ: 10,000 (ctrl). available on microfilm and microfiche from University Microfilms International (UMI). Documents available from The Genuine Article, UMI Article Clearinghouse, Documents on Demand.
Desc: A nationally recognized journal that features teaching ideas and concepts, reviews and an overview of biology today.
Ind/Abst Acad. Ind. [Computer File] (1992-); Acad. Search; AGRICOLA [Select. Cov.]; Biol. Dig.; Contents Pages Educ.; Curr. Aware. Biol. Sci., CABS; Curr. Cit.; Curr. Contents Agric. Biol. Environ. Sci.; Curr. Index J. Educ.; Curr. Ref. Fish Res.; Ecology Abstr.; Educ. Index; Energy Inf. Abstr.; Environ. Abstr.; EP Collect.; Expand. Acad. Index (1989-); Gen. Sci. Index; Gen. Sci. Source; Homework Help.; INFO-SOUTH Abstr.; Int. Aerosp. Abstr.; Mag. Search; MasterFile FullTEXT 1000; MasterFile FullTEXT 350; MasterFile FullTEXT 650; MasterFile FullTEXT (July 1993-); Med. Rev. Dig.; Newsp. Period. Abstr. (1991-); OCLC; Life Sci. Collect.; Protozoolog. Abstr.; Res. Alert [Select. Cov.]; SCISEARCH; Soc. Sci. Cit. Index [Select. Cov.]; Telebase.

LC QP1 .A49 **ISSN** 1042-0533
DD 612/.005 US
CCC
NLM W1; AM456J **CODEN** AJHUES
AMERICAN JOURNAL OF HUMAN BIOLOGY. (AMERICAN JOURNAL OF HUMAN BIOLOGY : THE OFFICIAL JOURNAL OF THE HUMAN BIOLOGY COUNCIL.). [Am. j. human biol.]. **Added/Corp** Human Biology Council. Alan R. Liss, Inc. (1989)-. Periodical. English. Six times a year. $432.00. John Wiley & Sons, Inc., 605 Third Avenue, New York NY 10158-0012. **Tel** (212)850-6000, (212)850-6645, FAX (212)850-6088, telex 12-7063. **(Subscription address:** John Wiley & Sons / UK, Baffins Lane, Chichester, West Sussex PO19 1UD United Kingdom. **Tel** 011 44 1243 779777, FAX 011 44 243 776128, telex 86290 WIBOOKG.) **ED** Robert M. Malina, Gaston Beunen, and Leslie S. Lieberman. Documents available from The Genuine Article, BIOSIS Document Express.
Desc: Provides an international forum for the publication of studies furthering the body of knowledge relating to human population biology.
Ind/Abst Anthropol. Lit.; Biol. Abstr.; Curr. Cit.; Curr. Contents Life Sci.; Curr. Contents Soc. Behav. Sci.; Nutr. Res. Newsl.; Popul. Index; Res. Alert [Full Cov.]; Soc. Sci. Cit. Index [Full Cov.]; Trop. Dis. Bull.

LC Q184 .A54 **ISSN** 0044-7749
DD 502/.8 US
NLM W1 AM533K **CODEN** ALBYBL
Pr Rev.
AMERICAN LABORATORY (FAIRFIELD). See Chemistry and Chemicals.

LC QH1 .A35 **ISSN** 0003-0031
DD 508 US
CODEN AMNAAF
Pr Rev.
AMERICAN MIDLAND NATURALIST, THE. See Natural History.

LC QR47 **ISSN** 1075-9964
DD 616.01 UK
NLM W1; AN103M
Pr Rev.
•**ANAEROBE (LONDON, ENGLAND).** (ANAEROBE.). (1995)-. Academic Scholarly Publication. English. Six times a year. $308.01. Academic Press Ltd., A Division of Harcourt Brace & Company Ltd., 24-28 Oval Road, London NW1 7DX United Kingdom. **Tel** 011 44 171 2674466, FAX 011 44 171 4822293, 011 44 171 4854752, telex 25775 ACPRES G. **(Subscription address:** Harcourt Brace & Company, Ltd., Foots Cray High Street, Sidcup Kent DA14 5HP United Kingdom. **Tel** 011 44 181 3003322, FAX 011 44 181 3090807, telex 896 377 ACADEM.)

LC QH301 **ISSN** 0041-9133
DD 574 RM
ANALELE STIINTIFICE ALE UNIVERSITATII "AL. I. CUZA" DIN IASI. SERIE NOUA. SECTIUNEA IIA, BIOLOGIE. **Added/Corp** Universitatea "Al. I. Cuza" din Iasi. (1977)-. Romanian (summaries and/or abstracts in English and French). One time a year. DM164.00. **(Subscription address:** Kubon & Sagner, ABT Zeitschriftenimport, D 80328 Munich Germany. **Tel** 011 49 89 54218130.) Documents available from CASDDS. ***Continues in part** Analele Stiintifice ale Universitatii "Al. I. Cuza" din Iasi. Sectiunea II, Biologie, Geologie, Geografie, 0250-2895.*
Ind/Abst Chem. Abstr.

LC QH301 .B743b **ISSN** 0378-8989
DD 574/.05 RM
CODEN AUBBDH
ANALELE UNIVERSITATII BUCURESTI : BIOLOGIE. [An. Univ. Bucur., Biol.]. **Main/Corp** Universitatea Din Bucuresti. **VFOAT** Biologie. Vol. 26 (1977)-. Academic Scholarly Publication. English (French, German and Romanian). One time a year. DM164.00. **(Subscription address:** Kubon & Sagner, ABT Zeitschriftenimport, D 80328 Munich Germany. **Tel** 011 49 89 54218130.) Documents available from BIOSIS Document Express, CASDDS. ***Continues in part** Universitatea din Bucuresti. Analele Universitatii Bucuresti. Stiintele Naturii, 0254-8887.*
Ind/Abst Biol. Abstr.; Chem. Abstr.

LC QH301
DD 574 SP
ANALES DE BIOLOGIA. **Added/Corp** Universidad de Murcia. Facultad de Biologia. Vol. 1 (1984)-. Monographic series. Spanish. Universidad de Murcia, Apartado 4021, 30380 Murcia Spain. **Tel** 011 34 68 363013, 011 34 68 363014.
Ind/Abst Biocont. News Inf.; Crop Physiol. Abstr.; Field Crop Abstr.; Rev. Agric. Entomol.; Rev. Med. Vet. Entomol.; Rice Abstr.; Weed Abstr.; Wheat Barley Trit. Abstr.

LC QH540 .A525 **ISSN** 0213-4004
DD 574/.5/05 SP
CODEN ABSAEZ
ANALES DE BIOLOGIA. SECCION BIOLOGIA AMBIENTAL. See Environmental Issues-Ecology.

LC QH301 **ISSN** 0567-5911
DD 574 BO
NLM W1; AN1487H
ANALES DE LA ACADEMIA NACIONAL DE CIENCIAS. CUADERNO 2 : SERIE CIENCIAS DE LA NATURALEZA. **Added/Corp** Academia Nacional de Ciencias de Bolivia. **VFOAT** Publicacion - Academia Nacional de Ciencias de Bolivia. No. 1 (1961)-. Periodical. Spanish (summaries and/or abstracts in English).

LC QH301 **ISSN** 0365-1932
DD 574.05 MX
NLM W1 ES669P **CODEN** AENBAU
ANALES DE LA ESCUELA NACIONAL DE CIENCIAS BIOLOGICAS (MEXICO). (ANALES DE LA ESCUELA NACIONAL DE CIENCIAS BIOLOGICAS.). [An. Esc. Nac. Cienc. Biol.]. **Main/Corp** Mexico (City). Instituto Politecnico Nacional. Escuela Nacional de Ciencias Biologicas. Vol. 1; Oct./Dec. 1938-. Periodical. Spanish (summaries and/or abstracts in English and German). Four times a year. $25.00. Escuela Nacional de Ciencias Biologicas IPN, Depto de Publicaciones, Carpio y Plan de Ayala, Apartado Postal 42-186, 11340 Mexico DF Mexico. **ED** Martha Eugenia Perez V. **Circ:** 1,000 (ctrl).
Desc: Deals with subjects of zoology, botany, morphology, ecology and any biological technology such as fishing, reproduction, cultivation (crop), etc.
Ind/Abst GeoRef; Life Sci. Collect.; Vitis Vitic. Enol. Abstr.

LC QH301 **ISSN** 1121-1431
DD 574 IT
NLM W1; AN228EF
ANIMAL BIOLOGY. **Added/Corp** "Halocynthia" Association. Vol. 1, No. 1 (1992)-. Periodical. English. Three times a year. L130000.00. Halocynthia, Via Archirafi 18, I 90123 Palermo Italy. **Tel** 011 39 91 6161603. ***Continues** Acta Embryologiae et Morphologiae Experimentalis ("Halocynthia" Association), 0391-9706.*

LC QL1 .A4739 **ISSN** 0255-0105
DD 574/.05 AU
CODEN ANMBEO
ANNALEN DES NATURHISTORISCHEN MUSEUMS IN WIEN. SERIE B, FUER BOTANIK UND ZOOLOGIE. [Ann. Nat.hist. Mus. Wien, Ser. B. Bot. Zool.]. **VFOAT** Fur Botanik und Zoologie. Vol. 84 (1980)-. German. One time a year. Naturhistorisches Museum in Wien, Burgring 7, Vienna 1 Austria. **Tel** (043)0222934541254. Documents available from BIOSIS Document Express. ***Continues in part** Annalen des Naturhistorischen Museums in Wien, 0083-6133.*
Ind/Abst Biocont. News Inf.; Biol. Abstr. (1984-); Fish Rev. (Jan. 1989-July 1992); Life Sci. Collect.; Wildl. Rev. (Jan. 1989-July 1992).

LC QH301 **ISSN** 0066-1988
DD 574 FI
ANNALES ACADEMIAE SCIENTIARUM FENNICAE. SERIES A4: BIOLOGICA. [Ann. Acad. Sci. Fenn., Ser. A4]. **Added/Corp** Suomalainen Tiedeakatemia. Vol. 52 (1961)-. Monographic series. English. Irregular. Price varies per volume. Academic Bookstore Akateeminen, Postilokero 23, FIN-00371 Helsinki Finland. **Tel** 011 358 0 12141. ***Continues** Suomalaisen Tiedeakatemian Toimituksia, Sarja A4 : Biologica.*
Ind/Abst Energy Res. Abstr.

LC QH301 **ISSN** 0253-6390
DD 574 MG
NLM W1 AN345N
ANNALES DE L'UNIVERSITE DE MADAGASCAR. BIOLOGIE, CLINIQUE, SANTE PUBLIQUE. [Ann. Univ. Madag., Biol.-clin.-sante publique]. **Added/Corp** Universite de Madagascar. **VFOAT** Biologie, Clinique, Sante Publique. (1978)-. French. Irregular. ***Continues** Annales de l'Universite de Madagascar. Medecine et Biologie.*

LC QH3 .A62 **ISSN** 0003-4339
DD 574/.05 FR
CCC
CODEN ASNBAQ
Pr Rev.
ANNALES DES SCIENCES NATURELLES. ZOOLOGIE ET BIOLOGIE ANIMALE. See Zoology.

LC QH301 .A477 **ISSN** 1142-2998
DD 574/.05 FR
CODEN ASUBEV
ANNALES SCIENTIFIQUES DE L'UNIVERSITE DE FRANCHE-COMTE. BIOLOGIE-ECOLOGIE. (ANNALES SCIENTIFIQUES DE L'UNIVERSITE DE FRANCHE-COMTE, BESANCON. BIOLOGIE-ECOLOGIE.). [Ann. sci. Univ. Franche-Comte. Biol.-Ecol.]. **Added/Corp** Universite de Franche-Comte. Institut des Sciences Naturelles. **VFOAT** Biologie-Ecologie; Biologie Ecologie. (1989)-. French (summaries and/or abstracts in English). One time a year. Free. Instit des Sciences Naturelles, Place Leclere, Besancon France. ***Formed by the union of** Annales Scientifiques de l'Universite de Besancon. Biologie Vegetale, 0249-7654 **and** Annales Scientifiques de l'Universite de Besancon. Biologie Animale, 0249-7255.*

LC QH301.L8 A2 **ISSN** 0066-2232
DD 547/.05 PL
NLM W1 AN47L **CODEN** AUCBAJ
ANNALES UNIVERSITATIS MARIAE CURIE-SKLODOWSKA. SECTIO C. BIOLOGIA. [Ann. univ. Mariae Curie-Sklodowska, Sect. C.]. **Main/Corp** Uniwersytet Marii Curie-Sklodowskiej. **VFOAT** Roczniki Uniwersytetu Marii Curie-Sklodowskiej w Lublinie. Dzial C. Nauki Biologiczne. Vol. 1 (1946)-. Academic Scholarly Publication. English (Polish and Russian; summaries and/or abstracts in English, French and German). One time a year. Price varies per volume. Uniwersytet Marii Curie-Sklodowskiej, Biuro Wydawnictwo, Pl. Marii Curie-Sklodowskiej 5, 20-031 Lublin Poland. **Tel** 011 48 81 375304, FAX 011 48 81 336699, telex 0643223. Index available. **Circ:** 950 (ctrl). Documents available from CASDDS.
Ind/Abst Chem. Abstr.; Ecol. Abstr. (?-?); Field Crop Abstr.; For. Prod. Abstr.; For. Abstr.; GeoRef; Grass. Forage Abstr.; Hortic. Abstr.; Life Sci. Collect.; Plant Breed. Abstr.

LC QH301 **ISSN** 0082-6871
DD 574 IT
ANNALI DELLA FACOLTA DI SCIENZE AGRARIE DELLA UNIVERSITA DEGLI STUDI DI TORINO. See Agriculture.

LC QH301 .A48 **ISSN** 0003-4746
DD 574.6/05 UK
NLM W1 AN56P **CODEN** AABIAV
Pr Rev.
ANNALS OF APPLIED BIOLOGY. [Ann. appl. biol.]. **Added/Corp** Association of Applied Biologists. Association of Economic Biologists. Vol. 1 (1914/15)-. Periodical. English. Six times a year. $390.00. Association of Applied Biologists, Institute of Horticultural Research, Wellesbourne, Warwick CV35 9EF United Kingdom. **Tel** 011 44 1789 470382, FAX 011 44 1789 470234. Index available. cum. index. **Bk Rev. Ad Acc. Circ:** 1,500 (ctrl). Documents available from The Genuine Article, BIOSIS Document Express, CASDDS.
Ind/Abst AgBiotech News Inf.; AGRICOLA [Select. Cov.]; Agrofor. Abstr. (1991-); BioBusiness; Biocont. News Inf. (19??-19??); Biodeter. Abstr. (19??-19??); Biol. Agric. Index; Biol. Abstr.; Chem. Abstr.; Crop Physiol. Abstr.; Curr. Aware. Biol. Sci., CABS; Curr. Biotechnol.; Curr. Cit.; Curr. Contents Agric. Biol. Environ. Sci.; Ecol. Abstr.; Ecology Abstr.; EMBASE; Entomol. Abstr.; Field Crop Abstr.; Food Sci. Technol. Abstr.; For. Prod. Abstr. (19??-19??); For. Abstr.; Grass. Forage Abstr.; Health Plan. Adminis.; Hortic. Abstr.; Index Med.; Index Vet.; Irr. Drain. Abstr.; Maize Abstr.; Microbiol. Abstr. Sect. A; Microbiol. Abstr. Sect. C; Nematol. Abstr.; Nutr. Abstr. Rev., Ser. A, Hum. Exp.; Ornamental Hort.; Life Sci. Collect.; PESTDOC; Plant Breed. Abstr.; Plant Genet. Resour. Abstr.; Plant Grow. Reg. Abstr.; Postharvest News Inf.; Potato Abstr.; Protozoolog. Abstr.; Res. Alert [Full Cov.]; Rev. Agric. Entomol.; Rev. Med. Vet. Mycology; Rev. Plant Pathol.; Rice Abstr.; Sci. Cit. Index; SCISEARCH; Seed Abstr.; Soils Fert.; Sorghum Mill. Abstr.; Soyabean Abstr.; Stat. Theory Method Abstr. (1959-1963); Vet. Bull.; Virol. AIDS Abstr.; Vitis Vitic. Enol. Abstr.; Weed Abstr.; Wheat Barley Trit. Abstr.; Wildl. Rev.

LC QH301 **ISSN** 0970-0153
DD 574 II
NLM W1; AN563 **CODEN** ANBIEO
ANNALS OF BIOLOGY (LUDHIANA). (ANNALS OF BIOLOGY.). [Ann. biol.]. (1985)-. Academic Scholarly Publication. English. Two times a year. $75.00. Bio-Publishers, 1298 Krishna Nagar, Ludhiana-141 004 India. **(Subscription address:** Prints India, 11 Darya

Ganj, New Delhi 110002 India. **Tel** 011 91 11 3268645, FAX 011 91 11 3275542, telex 31-61087 PRIN-IN.) Documents available from CASDDS.
Ind/Abst Agrindex; Biocont. News Inf.; Chem. Abstr. (1985-); Crop Physiol. Abstr.; Curr. Cit.; Ecol. Abstr.; Entomol. Abstr.; Field Crop Abstr.; Irr. Drain. Abstr.; Maize Abstr.; Nematol. Abstr.; Plant Breed. Abstr.; Plant Grow. Reg. Abstr.; Postharvest News Inf.; Potato Abstr.; Rev. Agric. Entomol.; Rev. Plant Pathol.; Seed Abstr.; Soils Fert.; Wheat Barley Trit. Abstr.

LC QP34.5 .A55 **ISSN** 0301-4460
DD 612/.005 UK
CCC
NLM W1 AN593 **CODEN** AHUBBJ
Pr Rev.
ANNALS OF HUMAN BIOLOGY. [Ann. hum. biol.]. Jan. (1974)-. Academic Scholarly Publication. English. Six times a year. $410.00. Taylor & Francis Ltd. / UK, Rankine Road, Basingstoke, Hampshire RG24 8PR United Kingdom. **Tel** 011 44 1256 840366, FAX 011 44 1256 479438, telex 858540. **(Subscription address:** Taylor & Francis Inc., 1900 Frost Road, Suite 101, Bristol PA 19007-1598. **Tel** (215)785-5800, (800)821-8312, FAX (215)785-5515.) **ED** J M Tanner (editor's address: Institute of Child Health, 30 Guilford Street/Room 115, London, WC1N 1EH United Kingdom), K J Collins (editor's address: University College and Middlesex School of Medicine, St Pancras Hospital, St Pancras Way, London NW 1 OPE United Kingdom) G A Harrison (editor's address: University of Oxford, Department of Biological Anthropology, OX2 6QS United Kingdom). available on microfilm from University Microfilms International (UMI). Documents available from The Genuine Article, BIOSIS Document Express, CASDDS.
Desc: An international journal for the publication of papers concerning research into human population biology, reporting investigations on the nature, development and causes of human variation, embracing the disciplines of human genetics, auxology, environmental physiology, ecology, epidemiology and ageing.
Ind/Abst Anthropol. Index; Anthropol. Lit.; Biol. Abstr.; Chem. Abstr.; Curr. Cit.; Curr. Contents Life Sci.; Dairy Sci. Abstr.; Dev. Med. Child Neurol.; EMBASE; Ergon. Abstr.; Geogr. Abstr. Human Geogr.; Health Plan. Adminis.; Index Med.; Int. Dev. Abstr.; Nutr. Abstr. Rev., Ser. B, Live Feeds and Feed.; Nutr. Abstr. Rev., Ser. A, Hum. Exp.; Nutr. Res. Newsl.; Life Sci. Collect.; Phys. Med. Biol. (19??-19??); Popul. Index; Protozoolog. Abstr.; Res. Alert [Full Cov.]; Sci. Cit. Index; SCISEARCH; Soc. Sci. Cit. Index [Select. Cov.]; SportSearch; Trop. Dis. Bull.

LC QH301 **ISSN** 0003-5017
DD 574 SZ
CCC
NLM W1 AN645 **CODEN** ANBLAT
Pr Rev.
ANNEE BIOLOGIQUE, L'. [Annee biol.]. **Added/Corp** Federation Francaise des Societes de Science Naturelles. Federation des Societes de Science Naturelles. Vol. 1 (1895)-. Periodical. French (table of contents in English). Four times a year. $229.22. Masson Editeur, BP 22, 41354 Vineuil Cedex France. **Tel** 011 33 54 504612, FAX 011 33 54 504611. Documents available from The Genuine Article, BIOSIS Document Express, CASDDS.
Ind/Abst AGRICOLA; Anim. Breed. Abstr.; Biol. Abstr.; Chem. Abstr.; Curr. Contents Agric. Biol. Environ. Sci.; Curr. Ref. Fish Res.; EMBASE; Field Crop Abstr.; GeoRef; Grass. Forage Abstr.; Life Sci. Collect.; Protozoolog. Abstr.; Res. Alert [Select. Cov.]; Rev. Agric. Entomol.; Soils Fert.

LC R
DD 610 US
ANNUAL PROGRESS REPORT / WALTER REED ARMY INSTITUTE OF RESEARCH. **See** Medical Sciences.

LC QH105.N7 B56A **ISSN** 0364-9512
DD 574.92/9747/74 US
ANNUAL REPORT - BIOLOGICAL FIELD STATION, COOPERSTOWN, NEW YORK. **Main/Corp** Biological Field Station, Cooperstown, N.Y. (19??)-. English. One time a year. Canadian Association of Law Libraries, PO Box 1570, 190 Railway Station, Kingston Ontario, K7L 5C8 Canada. **Tel** (613)531-9338, FAX (613)531-0626, telex 0527284.

LC QH301
DD 574 US
ANNUAL REPORT / COLD SPRING HARBOR LABORATORY. **Main/Corp** Cold Spring Harbor Laboratory. (1970)-. English. One time a year. Cold Spring Harbor Laboratory, 10 Skyline Drive, Plainview NY 11803. **Tel** (516)349-1930, (800)843-4388, FAX (516)349-1946. ctrl circ. ***Continues*** *Cold Spring Harbor Laboratory Quantitative Biology. Annual Report.*

LC QH197 .C64a **ISSN** 0158-7404
DD 574.6/0994 AT
ANNUAL REPORT / INSTITUTE OF BIOLOGICAL RESOURCES. **See** Environmental Issues-Conservation and Natural Resources.

LC QH96.A1 K47
DD 574.92/9/624072 SJ
ANNUAL REPORT - UNIVERSITY OF KHARTOUM, HYDROBIOLOGICAL RESEARCH UNIT. **Main/Corp** Jamiat al-Khartum. Hydrobiological Research Unit. (1972)-. English. University of Khartoum Hydrobiological Research Unit, PO Box 321, Khartoum Sudan. ***Continues*** *University of Khartoum. Hydrobiological Research Unit. Annual Report - University of Khartoum, Hydrobiological Research Unit.*

LC QH301 .R85 **ISSN** 0080-4967
DD 574.05 US
NLM W3 AN68B
ANNUAL RESEARCH CONFERENCES OF THE BUREAU OF BIOLOGICAL RESEARCH. **Main/Corp** Rutgers University. Bureau of Biological Research. (1960)-. Monographic series. English. One time a year. Price varies per volume. Rutgers University Press, PO Box 4869, Distribution Center, Baltimore MD 21211. **Tel** (301)338-6947. ***Continues*** *Annual Conferences on Protein Metabolism, 0097-0956.*

LC QH90.A1 **ISSN** 0889-5775
DD 574.92 US
AQUASPHERE (1985). (AQUASPHERE.). **Added/Corp** New England Aquarium Corporation. (1985)-. Monographic series. English. One time a year. $2.50. New England Aquarium Corporation, Central Wharf, Bostan MA 02110. **Tel** (617)742-8830. ***Continues*** *Aquasphere, 0196-0199.*

LC QH301 .A493 **ISSN** 0003-9136
DD 574.92/05 GW
CCC
CODEN AHYBA4
Pr Rev.
ARCHIV FUER HYDROBIOLOGIE. [Arch. Hydrobiol.]. **Added/Corp** International Association of Theoretical and Applied Limnology. Vol. 12 (1918)-. Academic Scholarly Publication. English (German). Twelve times a year. $1123.85. E. Schweizerbartische Verlagsbuchhandlung, Johannesstrasse 3A, D-70176 Stuttgart Germany. **Tel** 011 49 711 625001, FAX 011 49 711 625005, telex 723363 SCHB D. **ED** H J Elster and H C W Ohle. **Bk Rev.** **Ad Acc.** Documents available from The Genuine Article, BIOSIS Document Express, CASDDS, Documents on Demand. ***Continues*** *Archiv fuer Hydrobiologie und Planktonkunde.*
Desc: Limnology, ecology, fisheries, water supply, water hygiene, water chemistry.
Ind/Abst AGRICOLA; Anim. Behav. Abstr.; Aquat. Sci. Fish. Abstr. [CD-ROM Ed.]; Biodeter. Abstr. (19??-19??); Biol. Abstr.; Chem. Abstr.; Curr. Cit.; Curr. Contents Agric. Biol. Environ. Sci.; Curr. Ref. Fish Res.; Ecol. Abstr. (?-?); EMBASE; Energy Inf. Abstr.; Energy Res. Abstr. (June 1974-); Entomol. Abstr.; Environ. Abstr.; Fish Rev.; Food Sci. Technol. Abstr.; Fresh. Aqua. Contents Tables; GeoRef; Irr. Drain. Abstr.; Microbiol. Abstr. Sect. C; Nutr. Abstr. Rev., Ser. B, Live Feeds and Feed.; Life Sci. Collect.; Pollut. Abstr. Indexes; Protozoolog. Abstr.; Res. Alert [Full Cov.]; Rev. Med. Vet. Entomol.; Sci. Cit. Index; SCISEARCH; Sel. Water Resour. Abstr.; Soc. Sci. Cit. Index [Select. Cov.]; Soils Fert.; Weed Abstr.; Wildl. Rev.

LC QK564 .A5 **ISSN** 0342-1120
GW
CCC
ARCHIV FUER HYDROBIOLOGIE. SUPPLEMENTBAND, ALGOLOGICAL STUDIES. (ALGOLOGICAL STUDIES.). [Arch. Hydrobiol., Suppl.bd., Algol. stud.]. **Added/Corp** Algologicka Laborator (Ceskoslovenska Akademie Ved). Vol. 1 (1970)-. Monographic series. Multiple languages (German and English). Ten times a year. Price varies per volume. E. Schweizerbartische Verlagsbuchhandlung, Johannesstrasse 3A, D-70176 Stuttgart Germany. **Tel** 011 49 711 625001, FAX 011 49 711 625005, telex 723363 SCHB D. **ED** Oldrich Lhotsky. **Bk Rev.** **Ad Acc.**
Desc: Contains information on algology/hydrobiology.
Ind/Abst Curr. Cit.; Life Sci. Collect.

LC QH301 **ISSN** 0003-9829
DD 574 IT
NLM W1 AR41 **CODEN** AIBLAS
Pr Rev.
ARCHIVES ITALIENNES DE BIOLOGIE. [Arch. ital. biol.]. Vol. 1 (1882)-. Periodical. Italian (English). Four times a year. L129440. Universita Degli Studi di Pisa Rettorato, L Pacinotti 43, 56100 Pisa Italy. **ED** Ottavio Pompeiano. Index available. cum. index. **Bk Rev.** Documents available from The Genuine Article, BIOSIS Document Express, CASDDS.
Ind/Abst Biol. Abstr.; Chem. Abstr. (1882-1982); CSA Neuro. Abstr.; Curr. Cit.; Curr. Contents Life Sci.; Curr. Ref. Fish Res.; EMBASE; Index Med.; Int. Aerosp. Abstr.; Nutr. Abstr. Rev., Ser. B, Live Feeds and Feed.; Nutr. Abstr. Rev., Ser. A, Hum. Exp.; Life Sci. Collect.; Protozoolog. Abstr.; Psychol. Abstr. (1930-); PsycINFO; PsycLit; Res. Alert [Full Cov.]; Sci. Cit. Index; SCISEARCH.

LC QP82.2.A4 L54a **ISSN** 0250-5037
DD 574.1/9135 PE
NLM W1 AR657C **CODEN** ABANDHARANDH
ARCHIVOS DE BIOLOGIA ANDINA. [Arch. biol. andina]. **Added/Corp** Universidad Nacional Mayor de San Marcos. Instituto de Biologia Andina. Centro de Investigacion. Vol. 7 (Jan./June 1977)-. Academic Scholarly Publication. Spanish (English). Irregular. $8.00. Instituto de Biologia Andina, Box 5073, Lima Peru. Documents available from CASDDS. ***Continues*** *Archivos del Instituto de Biologia Andina.*
Ind/Abst Anthropol. Index; Chem. Abstr. (1977-1979); Rev. Med. Vet. Mycology; Rev. Plant Pathol.

LC QH301 **ISSN** 0004-0533
DD 574 CL
NLM W1 AR657J **CODEN** ABMXA2
Pr Rev. **TITLE CHANGE**
ARCHIVOS DE BIOLOGIA Y MEDICINA EXPERIMENTALES. [Arch. biol. med. exp.]. **Added/Corp** Sociedad de Biologia de Santiago. Vol. 1 (March 1964)-(19??). Academic Scholarly Publication. Spanish (English; summaries and/or abstracts in English; table of contents in English). Sociedad de Biologia de Chile, Casilla 16164, Santiago 9 Chile. **Tel** 2713891, FAX (562)496729. **ED** Tito Ureta Aravena. Index available. cum. index. **Bk Rev.** **Ad Acc.** **Circ:** 1,000. available on microfilm and microfiche from University Microfilms International (UMI). Documents available from BIOSIS Document Express, CASDDS. ***Continued by*** *Biological Research.*
Desc: Original articles, book and journal reviews, review articles, documents, symposium papers, meeting abstracts, and letters.
Ind/Abst Biol. Abstr.; Chem. Abstr.; Crop Physiol. Abstr.; EMBASE; Health Plan. Adminis.; Hortic. Abstr.; Sci. Cit. Index (19??-19??); SCISEARCH.

ISSN 0316-9707
DD 574.9719/2 CN
ARCTIC GAS. BIOLOGICAL REPORT SERIES. (BIOLOGICAL REPORT SERIES.). Vol. 1 (1973)-. Monographic series. English. Price varies per volume. Canadian Arctic Gas Study Ltd., 1270 Galgary Houst, 550 Sixth Avenue, South West Calgary Alta T2P 0S4 Canada.

LC QH301 .A75 **ISSN** 0365-0979
DD 574/.05 BL
CODEN ABTTAP
Pr Rev.
ARQUIVOS DE BIOLOGIA E TECNOLOGIA. [Arq. biol. tecnol.]. **Added/Corp** Instituto de Tecnologia do Parana. Instituto de Biologia e Pesquisas Tecnologicas (Parana, Brazil : State). Vol. 1 (1946)-. Periodical. Portuguese (English, French, German and Spanish; summaries and/or abstracts in English). Four times a year (Mar., June, Sept., Dec.). $55.00. Instituto de Tecnologia do Parana, Caixa Postal 1357, 80030 Curitiba Parana Brasil. **Tel** (041)252 6211, FAX (041)2534279, telex 415321. **ED** Fridolim Schlogel. **Circ:** 500 (ctrl). Documents available from The Genuine Article, CASDDS.
Ind/Abst AgBiotech News Inf.; AGRICOLA; Biocont. News Inf. (1991-); Biodeter. Abstr. (19??-19??); Chem. Abstr.; Crop Physiol. Abstr.; Curr. Biotechnol.; Curr. Cit.; Curr. Contents Agric. Biol. Environ. Sci.; EMBASE; Field Crop Abstr.; Grass. Forage Abstr.; Index Vet.; Maize Abstr.; Nutr. Abstr. Rev., Ser. B, Live Feeds and Feed.; Nutr. Abstr. Rev., Ser. A, Hum. Exp.; Ornamental Hort.; Plant Breed. Abstr.; Poult. Abstr.; Res. Alert [Select. Cov.]; Rev. Agric. Entomol.; Rev. Med. Vet. Entomol.; Rice Abstr.; SCISEARCH; Seed Abstr.; Small Anim. Abstr. Bibliogr.; Soils Fert.; Soyabean Abstr.; Sug. Indus. Abstr.; Vet. Bull.

LC NOT IN LC **ISSN** 0020-3653
DD 630 BL
NLM W1 AR921KI **CODEN** AIBOA3
ARQUIVOS DO INSTITUTO BIOLOGICO (SAO PAULO). (ARQUIVOS DO INSTITUTO BIOLOGICO.). [Arq. Inst. Biol.]. **Added/Corp** Instituto Biologico de Sao Paulo. Vol. 9 (1938)-. Academic Scholarly Publication. Portuguese (English; summaries and/or abstracts in English). Two times a year. $40.00. Instituto Biologico, Consel Rodrigues Alves 1252, 04014 002 Sao Paulo Brazil. **Tel** 011 55 11 5729822. **ED** Maria Mercia Barradas. Each issue contains an index to its own contents (no volume index)--loose. cum. index. Documents available from CASDDS. ***Continues*** *Archivos do Instituto Biologico.*
Ind/Abst Chem. Abstr.; Dairy Sci. Abstr.; EMBASE; Field Crop Abstr.; For. Prod. Abstr. (1991-); Grass. Forage Abstr.; Helminthol. Abstr. (1991-); Hortic. Abstr.; Nutr. Abstr. Rev., Ser. B, Live Feeds and Feed.; Life Sci. Collect.; Pig News Inf.; Plant Breed. Abstr.; Poult. Abstr.; Protozoolog. Abstr.; Rev. Agric. Entomol.; Rev. Med. Vet. Entomol.; Rev. Med. Vet. Mycology; Rev. Plant Pathol.; Soils Fert.; Weed Abstr.

LC QH324.2 .A74 **ISSN** 1064-5462
DD 574/.01/13 US
CCC
NLM W1; AR955TM **CODEN** ARLIEY
●**ARTIFICIAL LIFE.** [Artif. life]. Vol. 1, No. 1/2 (Fall 1993/Winter 1994)-. Periodical. English. Four times a year. $140.00. Massachusetts Institute of Technology

(MIT) Press, 55 Hayward Street, Cambridge MA 02142. **Tel** (617)253-2889, (617)625-8481, FAX (617)258-6779. **ED** Christopher G. Langton.
Desc: Forum for the dissemination of scientific research in the field of artificial life. Spans biological organization, including studies of the origin of life, self-assembly, growth and development, evolutionary and ecological dynamics, animal and robot behavior, social organization, and cultural evolution.

ISSN 0001-2386
DD 574 US
Pr Rev.
ASB BULLETIN, THE. [ASB bull.]. **Main/Corp** Association of Southeastern Biologists. **VAT** Association of Southeastern Biologists Bulletin. Vol. 1 (Mar. 1954)-. Bulletin. English. Four times a year (Jan., Apr., July, Oct.). $20.00 (one-year); $50.00 (three-year) Comes with Association of Southeastern Biologists membership. Association Southeastern Biologists, Towson State University, Department of Biology, Baltimore MD 21204. **Tel** (615)576-8123, FAX (615)576-9939. **ED** Frank J. Schwartz, (editor's address: Institute of Marine Sciences, University of North Carolina, 3431 Avendell Street, Morehead City, NC 28557, phone: (919-726-6841). **Bk Rev**, (Qty: 8-10). **Ad Acc. Circ:** 1,200. available on microfilm and microfiche from University Microfilms International (UMI).
Desc: Contains the program of the annual meeting and abstracts of papers presented, news of science and scientists in the Southeast, a record of Association affairs, and features special articles of regional or timely interest.

LC QH301 **ISSN** 0117-3375
DD 574 PH
Pr Rev.
ASIA LIFE SCIENCES. Vol. 1, 1 & 2 (Jan.-Dec. 1992)-. Academic Scholarly Publication. English. Two times a year. $40.00. University of Philippines / Los Banos, D 206 Biological Sciences Building, Laguna 4031 Philippines. **ED** Willian Sm. Gruezo. **Circ:** 1,000.

LC QH301 **ISSN** 0265-1491
DD 574 UK
ASPECTS OF APPLIED BIOLOGY.
Added/Corp Association of Applied Biologists. (1982)-. Monographic series. English. Irregular. Price varies per volume. Association of Applied Biologists, Institute of Horticultural Research, Wellesbourne, Warwick CV35 9EF United Kingdom. **Tel** 011 44 1789 470382, FAX 011 44 1789 470234.
Ind/Abst AgBiotech News Inf.; AGRICOLA [Select. Cov.]; Agric. Eng. Abstr. (1991-); Agrofor. Abstr. (1991-); Biocont. News Inf. (19??-19??); Biodeter. Abstr.; Cot. Trop. Fibr. Abstr. Bibliogr.; Crop Physiol. Abstr.; Curr. Cit.; Field Crop Abstr.; Food Sci. Technol. Abstr.; For. Abstr.; Grass. Forage Abstr.; Hortic. Abstr.; Irr. Drain. Abstr.; Maize Abstr.; Nematol. Abstr.; Nutr. Abstr. Rev., Ser. B, Live Feeds and Feed.; Nutr. Abstr. Rev., Ser. A, Hum. Exp.; Ornamental Hort.; Plant Breed. Abstr.; Plant Grow. Reg. Abstr.; Postharvest News Inf.; Potato Abstr.; Rev. Agric. Entomol.; Rev. Med. Vet. Entomol.; Rev. Plant Pathol.; Seed Abstr.; Soils Fert.; Soyabean Abstr.; Weed Abstr.; Wheat Barley Trit. Abstr.

ISSN 0894-9026
DD 574 US
NLM W1; AT75T **CODEN** AQNEEP
ATCC QUARTERLY NEWSLETTER.
[ATCC q. newsl.]. **Added/Corp** American Type Culture Collection. **VAT** American Type Culture Collection Quarterly Newsletter. Vol. 6, No. 1 (Jan. 1986)-. Newsletter. English. Four times a year. Free. American Type Culture Collection, 12301 Parklawn Drive, Rockville MD 20852. **Tel** (301)881-2600, FAX (301)231-5826, telex 898-055. **ED** Harold D. Hatt. **Circ:** 25,000 (ctrl). Documents available from Documents on Demand. ***Continues** Quarterly Newsletter (American Type Culture Collection), 0743-4758.*
Desc: Contains news, items and feature articles on microbiology. Describes ATCC's new strains and publications.
Ind/Abst AGRICOLA [Select. Cov.]; Environ. Abstr. (1986-?).

LC QH301
DD 574 UK
NLM W1 AT561K
ATLAS OF MOLECULAR STRUCTURES IN BIOLOGY. (1973)-. English. Irregular. £50.00. Oxford University Press / UK, Walton Street, Oxford OX2 6DP United Kingdom. **Tel** 011 44 1865 56767, FAX 011 44 1865 267773, telex 851/837330 OXPRES G. **ED** D. C. Phillips and F. M. Richards.

LC QH301 **ISSN** 0365-0294
DD 574 IT
CODEN AAMBAV
ATTI DELLA ACCODEMIA PELORITANA DEI PERICOLANTI, CLASSE DI SCIENCE MEDICO-BIOLOGICHE. [Atti Accad. Pelorit. Pericol., Cl. Sci. Med.-Biol.]. (19??)-. Academic Scholarly Publication. Italian. Irregular. Accademia Peloritana dei Pericolanti, Messina Italy. Documents available from CASDDS. ***Continues** Atti Della Reale Accademia Peloritana, Classe di Scienceiisiche, Mathematiche e Biologiche, 0365-5520.*
Ind/Abst Chem. Abstr. (1943-1976/77).

ISSN 0913-4549
DD 630 JA
BAIOMASU HENKAN KEIKAKU KENKYU HOKOKU. [Baiomasu Henkan Keikaku kenkyu hokoku]. **VFOAT** Research Report of Biomass Conversion Program. (1986)-. Periodical. Multiple languages. Six times a year. Norin Suisansho Norin Suisan Gijutsu Kaigi Jimukyoku, (Agriculture Forestry & Fisheries Research Council Ministry of Agriculture Forestry & Fisheries), 2-1 Kasumigaseki 1 Chome, Chiyodaku Tokyo 100 Japan. Documents available from CASDDS.
Ind/Abst Chem. Abstr.

LC QH301 **ISSN** 0198-0068
DD 574 US
CCC
NLM W3 BA19 **CODEN** BANRDU
BANBURY REPORT. [Banbury rep.]. (1978)-. Academic Scholarly Publication. English. Irregular. Price varies per volume. Cold Spring Harbor Laboratory, 10 Skyline Drive, Plainview NY 11803. **Tel** (516)349-1930, (800)843-4388, FAX (516)349-1946. Documents available from BIOSIS Document Express, CASDDS.
Desc: A series in biological risk assessment and genetics.
Ind/Abst Biol. Abstr.; Chem. Abstr.

LC RA407 .B32 **ISSN** 1045-5523
DD 610/.72 US
BASIC AND CLINICAL BIOSTATISTICS.
See Biology-Abstracting, Bibliographies and Statistics.

LC QH301 **ISSN** 0090-5542
DD 574 US
CCC
NLM W3 BA255 **CODEN** BLFSBY
BASIC LIFE SCIENCES. [Basic life sci.]. Vol. 1 (1973)-. Monographic series. English. Irregular. Price varies per volume. Plenum Press, 233 Spring Street, New York NY 10013-1578. **Tel** (212)620-8000, (800)221-9369, FAX (212)463-0742, (212)807-1047, telex 23/421139. Documents available from BIOSIS Document Express, CASDDS.
Desc: Consists of the proceedings of international Latin American symposia.
Ind/Abst Biol. Abstr.; Chem. Abstr.; Curr. Cit.; Energy Res. Abstr. (Dec. 1975-); Health Plan. Adminis.; Index Med.; INIS Atomindex [Micro.]; Life Sci. Collect.; PESTDOC.

ISSN 0067-4672
DD 616 GW
BAYER SYMPOSIUM. [Bayer symp.]. Vol. 1 (1968)-. Monographic series. English. Irregular. Price varies per volume. Springer-Verlag New York Inc., 175 Fifth Avenue, New York NY 10010. **Tel** (212)460-1500 ext 256, FAX (212)533-3503, telex 232 235 SPB UR. **(Subscription address:** Springer-Verlag New York Inc. / North America, PO Box 2485, Journal Fulfillment, Secaucus NJ 07096. **Tel** (201)348-4033, (800)777-4643, FAX (201)348-4505.**)**

LC QP360 .B425 **ISSN** 0140-525X
DD 152/.05 US
CCC
NLM W1 BE129K **CODEN** BBSCDH
Pr Rev.
BEHAVIORAL AND BRAIN SCIENCES, THE. See Psychology.

LC BF671 .B4 **ISSN** 0005-7959
DD 151.305 NE
CCC
NLM W1 BE1342 **CODEN** BEHAA8
Pr Rev.
BEHAVIOUR. [Behaviour]. Vol. 1 (1947)-. Periodical. English. Eight times a year (2 double issues each). $323.00. E.J. Brill, Postbus 9000, 2300 PA Leiden The Netherlands. **Tel** 011 31 71 312624, FAX 011 31 71 317532, telex 39296 BRILL NL. **ED** J. P. Kruijt. **Circ:** 1,300. Documents available from The Genuine Article, BIOSIS Document Express, CASDDS.
Desc: Publishes contributions to the biological analysis of the causation, ontogenetic development, function and evolution of behavior. Open primarily to reports of original research, but theoretical and other papers are accepted if they promote the experimental study of the subject. Physiological, genetic and ecological aspects are also considered.
Ind/Abst Anim. Behav. Abstr.; Anim. Breed. Abstr.; Biol. Abstr.; Chem. Abstr.; Curr. Aware. Biol. Sci., CABS; Curr. Cit.; Curr. Contents Agric. Biol. Environ. Sci.; Curr. Contents Life Sci.; Ecol. Abstr.; Ecology Abstr.; Entomol. Abstr.; Fish Rev.; Geogr. Abstr. Phys. Geogr.; Index Vet.; MLA Int. Bibl. Books Artic. Mod. Lang. Lit.; Life Sci. Collect.; Poult. Abstr.; Psychol. Abstr. (1950-); PsycINFO; PsycLit; Ref. Upd. Deluxe Ed.; Res. Alert [Full Cov.]; Rev. Med. Vet. Entomol.; Sci. Cit. Index; SCISEARCH; Soc. Sci. Cit. Index [Select. Cov.]; Wildl. Rev.

LC QH301 **ISSN** 0092-5616
DD 574 US
NLM W1 BE515
BENCHMARK PAPERS IN BIOLOGICAL CONCEPTS. [Benchmark pap. biol. concept]. Vol. 1 (1973)-. Monographic series. English. Irregular. Price varies per volume. Academic Press Inc., 6277 Sea Harbor Drive, Orlando FL 32887. **Tel** (800)543-9534, (407)345-4100, FAX (407)352-3445.

LC QH301 **ISSN** 0362-3157
DD 574 US
NLM W1 BE517S **CODEN** BPSBDA
BENCHMARK PAPERS IN SYSTEMATIC AND EVOLUTIONARY BIOLOGY. Vol. 1 (1975)-. Monographic series. English. Irregular. Price varies per volume. Academic Press Inc., 6277 Sea Harbor Drive, Orlando FL 32887. **Tel** (800)543-9534, (407)345-4100, FAX (407)352-3445. Documents available from BIOSIS Document Express.
Ind/Abst Biol. Abstr.

LC QH301 **ISSN** 0930-8148
DD 574 GW
UDC 50/59
BERICHTE DER BIOLOGISCHEN ANSTALT HELGOLAND. (1986)-. Monographic series. Multiple languages. Irregular. Price varies per volume. Biologische Anstalt Helgoland, Notkestr 31, D-22607 Hamburg Germany. **Tel** 011 49 40 89693160, telex 274977 BAH D.
Ind/Abst Aquat. Sci. Fish. Abstr. [CD-ROM Ed.].

LC QH301
DD 574 UK
BIA BULLETIN. Bulletin. English. £50.00. Bio Industry Association, 1 Queens Gate, London SW1H 9BT United Kingdom. **Tel** 071 222 2809, FAX 071 222 8876. **Bk Rev. Ad Acc. Circ:** 350 (ctrl). ***Continues** AABB Newsletter.*
Desc: Information on biotechnology.

LC QH301 **ISSN** 0920-8356
DD 574 NE
UDC 57.084(048)
BIBLIOTIPS / VAKGROEP PROEFDIERKUNDE. [Bibliotips - Vakgr. Proefdierkd.]. (1985)-. Periodical. Dutch. Six times a year. $35.00. Prex, PO Box 80166, 3508 TD Utrecht Netherlands. **Tel** 011 31 30 533158.

LC QH301 **ISSN** 0952-0384
DD 574 UK
BIO-ELECTRONICS & BIOSENSORS.
[Bio-electron. biosens.]. **VFOAT** Bio-Electronics and Biosensors. (1988)-. Periodical. English. Six times a year. £105.00. SUBIS, Mansion House 19 Kingfield Road, Sheffield S11 9AS United Kingdom. **Tel** 011 44 114 2554433, FAX 011 44 114 255 4626. **Bk Rev. Ad Acc.** ***Continues** Bio-Electronics, 0268-1633.*
Desc: Current awareness service for researchers and clinicians.

ISSN 0319-3446
DD 574/.06/2714281 CN
BIO-NOUVELLES. Vol. 1 (Jan. 1973)-. Periodical. French. Irregular. Societe De Biologie De Montreal Inc., 230 Est. boulevard Henri -Bourassa, Montreal Quebec H3L 1B8 Canada.

LC QH301 **ISSN** 0970-0889
DD 574 II
BIO-SCIENCE RESEARCH BULLETIN.
(1985)-. Bulletin. English. Two times a year. Rs80.00 India; $16.00 North America; £10.00 UK. Dr A K Sharma, PO Box 38, Modinagar 201204 India. **ED** Ajay Kumar Sharma. **Bk Rev. Ad Acc. Circ:** 100 (ctrl).
Ind/Abst Nematol. Abstr.

LC QH301 .C87 **ISSN** 0303-2647
DD 574/.05 IE
CCC
NLM W1 BI918K **CODEN** BSYMBO
Pr Rev.
BIO SYSTEMS. (BIOSYSTEMS.). [Bio syst.]. Vol. 5, No. 1 (1974)-. Academic Scholarly Publication. English. Nine times a year (3 vols.). $768.00. Elsevier Science Ireland Ltd., Bay 15, Shannon Industrial Estate, Co Clare Ireland. **Tel** 011 353 61 471944. **ED** Alan W. Schwartz, Michael Conrad, and Lynn Margulis. Index available. available on microfilm and microfiche from University Microfilms International (UMI); available on an online database from Elsevier Electronic Subscriptions (EES). Documents available from The Genuine Article, BIOSIS Document Express, CASDDS. ***Continues** Currents in Modern Biology, 0011-4014.*
Desc: Publishes articles that contribute to understanding the origins, evolution, dynamics, assembly and control of biological systems.
Ind/Abst Biol. Abstr.; Chem. Abstr.; Curr. Cit.; Curr. Contents Life Sci.; EMBASE; Fish Rev. (Jan. 1989-July 1992); Health Plan. Adminis.; Index Med.; Int. Aerosp. Abstr.; Nutr. Abstr. Rev., Ser. B, Live Feeds and Feed.; Ref. Upd. Deluxe Ed.; Res. Alert [Full Cov.]; Sci. Cit. Index; SCISEARCH; Wildl. Rev. (Jan. 1989-July 1992).

LC QH650 ISSN 0304-4173
DD 574.19127 NE
CCC

BIOCHIMICA ET BIOPHYSICA ACTA (BR) - REVIEWS ON BIOENERGETICS. (REVIEWS ON BIOENERGETICS.). [Biochim. biophys. acta (BR)]. Vol. BR 1 (1973)-. Academic Scholarly Publication. English. Three times a year (one volume). Fl401.00. Elsevier Science Publishers BV, PO Box 211, 1000 AE Amsterdam Netherlands. **Tel** 011 31 20 4853641, 011 31 20 4853642, FAX 011 31 20 4853598. **ED** P Borst, P Cohen, K van Dam, L L M van Deenen, E P Dennedy, G K Radda, and E C Slater. available on microfilm from University Microfilms International (UMI).
Ind/Abst EMBASE; PESTDOC (?-?).

LC SB ISSN 0143-1404
DD 574/630 UK

BIOCONTROL NEWS AND INFORMATION. [Biocontrol news info.]. **Added/Corp** Commonwealth Agricultural Bureaux. Commonwealth Institute of Biological Control. Vol. 1, No. 1 (Mar. 1980)-. Abstracting/Indexing Service. English. Four times a year. $250.00. CAB International Centre, Wallingford, Oxfordshire OX10 8DE United Kingdom. **Tel** 011 44 1491 832111, FAX 011 44 1491 833508, telex 847964 COMAGG G. **ED** J. R. Metcalfe, D. J. Girling BSc, MSc, MiBiol. **Ad Acc.** available on magnetic tape and CD-ROM; available on an online database from Tsukuba Daigaku; CAN/OLE; STN International; JICST; DATA-STAR; DIMDI; ESA-IRS; CISTI; BRS; and DIALOG. Documents available from BLDSC.
Desc: Published to meet the information needs of biocontrol researchers, pest control centres, aid programs and chemical company researchers and executives.
Ind/Abst Biocont. News Inf. (19??-19??); For. Prod. Abstr.; For. Abstr.; Hortic. Abstr.; Rev. Agric. Entomol.; Weed Abstr.

LC QH301 ISSN 0970-373X
DD 574 II
UDC 57

BIODIGEST DEHRA DUN. **VFOAT** Illustrated Biodigest. (1987)-. Periodical. English. Six times a year. $35.00. **(Subscription address:** Prints India, 11 Darya Ganj, New Delhi 110002 India. **Tel** 011 91 11 3268645, FAX 011 91 11 3275542, telex 31-61087 PRIN-IN.)

ISSN 1195-311X
DD 574/.05 CN

•**BIODIVERSITE MONDIALE, LA.** [Biodivers. mond.]. **Added/Corp** Musee Canadien de la Nature. Vol. 3, No. 1 (1993)-. Periodical. French. Four times a year. 50.00Can$ institutions; 25.00Can$ individuals. Canadian Museum of Nature, PO Box 3443, Station D, Ottawa Ontario K1P 6P4 Canada. **Tel** (613)990-6595, FAX (613)990-0318. **ED** Don E. McAllister. **Bk Rev**, (Qty: 40). **Ad Acc, Adv Mgr:** D. Arnold. **Circ:** 350. ***Continues*** *Bulletin Canadien de la Biodiversite., 1183-3378.*
Desc: Examines biodiversity, the variety of life as expressed in animals, plants, and ecosystems, and the conservation efforts aimed to protect it.

LC QP517.B53 B5 ISSN 0302-4598
SZ
CCC

BIOELECTROCHEMISTRY AND BIOENERGETICS. See Chemistry and Chemicals-Electrochemistry.

LC R725.55 ISSN 0926-261X
DD 291.5 NE
NLM W1; BI663X

BIOETHICS YEARBOOK. See Ethics.

LC QH301 .S6715
DD 574 FR

•**BIOGEOGRAPHICA : COMPTE-RENDU DES SEANCES DE LA SOCIETE DE BIOGEOGRAPHIE.** **Added/Corp** Societe de Biogeographie. **VFOAT** Compte-Rendu des Seances de la Societe de Biogeographie. Vol. 69, No. 1 (1993)-. Periodical. French. Four times a year. Societe de Biogeographie, 45 Bis rue de Buffon, 75005 Paris France. ***Continues*** *Societe de Biogeographie. Compte Rendu des Seances de la Societe de Biogeographie, 0037-9018.*

LC QH301
DD 574 GW

BIOINFORMATION MANAGER. (19??)-. English. Free (Europe); DM120.00 other. Raucon Bioinformatics & Consulting GmbH, PO Box 1069, W-6912 Dielheim Germany. **ED** Dr Norbert Rau. **Bk Rev**. **Ad Acc. Circ:** 6,000 (ctrl).
Desc: Informs managers in the healthcare, biotechnology and environmental businesses of new information resources such as market reports, books, and conferences.

LC QH ISSN 0006-3088
DD 574 XO
NLM W1 BI672 CODEN BLOAAO
Pr Rev.

BIOLOGIA. [Biologia]. **Added/Corp** Slovenska Akademia Vied. (1953)-. Academic Scholarly Publication. Slovak (summaries and/or abstracts in English, French, German and Russian; table of contents in German and Russian). Six times a year. $173.00. **(Subscription address:** Kubon & Sagner, ABT Zeitschriftenimport, D 80328 Munich Germany. **Tel** 011 49 89 54218130.) Documents available from The Genuine Article, BIOSIS Document Express, CASDDS. ***Continues*** *Biologicky Sbornik.*
Ind/Abst AgBiotech News Inf.; Anim. Breed. Abstr.; Biocont. News Inf. (19??-19??); Biodeter. Abstr. (19??-19??); Biol. Abstr.; Chem. Abstr.; Crop Physiol. Abstr.; CSA Neuro. Abstr. (?-?); Curr. Cit.; Curr. Contents Agric. Biol. Environ. Sci.; Ecology Abstr.; EMBASE; Fish Rev. (19??-199?); For. Abstr.; GeoRef; Helminthol. Abstr. (1991-); Index Vet.; Maize Abstr.; Microbiol. Abstr. Sect. A; Microbiol. Abstr. Sect. C; Nematol. Abstr.; Ornamental Hort. (19??-19??); Life Sci. Collect.; Plant Breed. Abstr.; Plant Genet. Resour. Abstr.; Plant Grow. Reg. Abstr.; Potato Abstr.; Protozoolog. Abstr.; Res. Alert [Select. Cov.]; Rev. Med. Vet. Entomol.; Rev. Med. Vet. Mycology; Rev. Plant Pathol.; Saf. Health Work; Seed Abstr.; Soyabean Abstr.; Wildl. Rev. (19??-199?).

LC QH301 .B367 ISSN 0133-3844
DD 574 HU
NLM W1 BI671NL CODEN BIOLD5

BIOLOGIA (BUDAPEST). (BIOLOGIA.). [Biologia]. (1974)-. Periodical. Hungarian (summaries and/or abstracts in English). Two times a year. **(Subscription address:** Kultura, PO Box 143, H-1300 Budapest 3 Hungary. **Tel** 011 36 1 2500194.) **ED** Gy Csaba. **Bk Rev. Circ:** 1,200. Documents available from BIOSIS Document Express, CASDDS. ***Continues*** *Biologiai Koezlemenyek, 0006-3142.*
Ind/Abst Biol. Abstr.; Chem. Abstr.; Irr. Drain. Abstr.; Nutr. Abstr. Rev., Ser. A, Hum. Exp.; Plant Breed. Abstr.; SCISEARCH; Soils Fert.; Weed Abstr.

ISSN 0750-7321
DD 574 FR
CODEN BGAHA8

BIOLOGIA GALLO-HELLENICA. [Biol. gallo-hell.]. **Added/Corp** Groupe Franco-Hellenique de Recherches Biologiques. Station Biologique Franco-Hellenique de Keramou. Vol. 1 (1967/1968)-. Periodical. French (German; summaries and/or abstracts in English, German, French and Greek, Modern). Irregular. 200.00F. Universite Paul Sabatier, 118 Route de Narbonne, 31062 Toulouse Cedex France. **Tel** 011 33 61 556942.
Ind/Abst GeoRef.

LC QH301 .B365 ISSN 0006-3096
DD 574.05 PK
CCC
CODEN BILGA6

BIOLOGIA (LAHORE). (BIOLOGIA.). [Biologia]. **Added/Corp** Biological Society of Pakistan. Vol. 1, No. 1 (June 1955)-. Academic Scholarly Publication. English. Two times a year. $60.00. Principal Government College - Lahre, Biological Society of Pakistan, Lahore Pakistan. **ED** M. Saleem. **Bk Rev**. Documents available from BIOSIS Document Express, CASDDS.
Desc: Subjects related to genetics, biochemistry, taxonomy, anatomy, cell biology and physiology.
Ind/Abst Biocont. News Inf.; Biol. Abstr.; Chem. Abstr.; Field Crop Abstr.; GeoRef; Microbiol. Abstr. Sect. A; Microbiol. Abstr. Sect. C; Plant Breed. Abstr.; Rev. Plant Pathol.

LC Q4 .T618 ISSN 0208-4449
DD 574 PL

BIOLOGIA (POZNAN, POLAND). (BIOLOGIA.). Periodical. Polish (summaries and/or abstracts in English and German). Panstwowe Wydawnictwo Naukowe / PWN, (Polish Scientific Publishers PWN Ltd.), Ul. Miodowa 10, PO Box 391, 00-251 Warsaw Poland. **Tel** 011 48 22 312738, FAX 011 48 22 267163.

LC QH301 ISSN 1216-6626
DD 574 HU
UDC 372.857

•**BIOLOGIA TANITASA SZEGED, A.** [Biol. tan. Szeged]. (1993)-. Periodical. Hungarian. Six times a year. $17.50. **(Subscription address:** Kultura, PO Box 143, H-1300 Budapest 3 Hungary. **Tel** 011 36 1 2500194.)

LC QH301 .B37 ISSN 0006-3169
DD 570.5 US
NLM Z 5321 B615 CODEN BIABA4

BIOLOGICAL ABSTRACTS. See Biology-Abstracting, Bibliographies and Statistics.

LC Z5321 .B672 QH301 ISSN 0192-6985
DD 016.574 US
NLM Z 5321 B618 CODEN BARRDG

BIOLOGICAL ABSTRACTS / RRM. See Biology-Abstracting, Bibliographies and Statistics.

LC QH301 ISSN 1058-4137
DD 574 US

BIOLOGICAL ABSTRACTS / RRM ON COMPACT DISC. See Biology-Abstracting, Bibliographies and Statistics.

LC QH301
DD 574 US

BIOLOGICAL ABSTRACTS. SEMIANNUAL CUMULATIVE INDEX. See Biology-Abstracting, Bibliographies and Statistics.

LC QH301 ISSN 1077-1034
DD 574 US

•**BIOLOGICAL ANALYSIS AND IMAGING METHODS.** (1995)-. Periodical. English. Four times a year. $365.00. Marcel Dekker Inc., 270 Madison Avenue, New York NY 10016. **Tel** (212)696-9000, (800)228-1160, FAX (212)685-4540, telex 421419. ***Continues*** *Journal of Trace and Microprobe Techniques, 0733-4680.*

LC QH301 .B38 ISSN 0006-3185
DD 574 US
NLM W1 BI739 CODEN BIBUBX
Pr Rev.

BIOLOGICAL BULLETIN (LANCASTER), THE. (THE BIOLOGICAL BULLETIN.). [Biol. bull.]. **Added/Corp** Marine Biological Laboratory (Woods Hole, Mass.) Marine Biological Laboratory (Woods Hole, Mass.). Annual Report 1907/08-1952. Vol. 1 (Oct. 1899)-. Bulletin. English. Six times a year. $190.00. Marine Biological Laboratory, MBL Street, Woods Hole MA 02543. **Tel** (508)548-3705 ext. 402, FAX (508)457-1924. **ED** Michael J. Greenberg. cum. index. **Circ:** 2,300. available on microfilm and microfiche from University Microfilms International (UMI). Documents available from The Genuine Article, BIOSIS Document Express, UMI Article Clearinghouse, CASDDS. ***Supersedes*** *Zoological Bulletin, 0898-1051.*
Desc: Accepts original research reports of general interest to biologists.
Ind/Abst Acad. Search; AGRICOLA; Anim. Breed. Abstr.; Aquat. Sci. Fish. Abstr. [CD-ROM Ed.]; Biol. Agric. Index; Biol. Abstr.; Chem. Abstr.; Crop Physiol. Abstr.; Curr. Aware. Biol. Sci., CABS; Curr. Cit.; Curr. Contents Agric. Biol. Environ. Sci.; Curr. Contents Life Sci.; Curr. Ref. Fish Res.; Ecol. Abstr.; EP Collect.; Expand. Acad. Index (1989-); Gen. Sci. Index; Gen. Sci. Source; Geogr. Abstr. Phys. Geogr.; GeoRef; Helminthol. Abstr.; Homework Help.; Index Med.; INFO-SOUTH Abstr.; Mag. Search; Mar. Sci. Contents Tables; MasterFile FullTEXT 1000; MasterFile FullTEXT 350; MasterFile FullTEXT 650; MasterFile FullTEXT (July 1993-); Newsp. Period. Abstr. (1991-); Nutr. Abstr. Rev., Ser. B, Live Feeds and Feed.; Nutr. Abstr. Rev., Ser. A, Hum. Exp.; OCLC; Life Sci. Collect.; Plant Grow. Reg. Abstr.; Protozoolog. Abstr.; Ref. Upd. Deluxe Ed.; Res. Alert [Full Cov.]; Rev. Med. Vet. Entomol.; Sci. Cit. Index; SCISEARCH; Telebase.

LC QH301 ISSN 0254-2900
DD 574 II
NLM W1 BI733F CODEN BBUIDB

BIOLOGICAL BULLETIN OF INDIA. [Biol. bull. India]. **Added/Corp** Biological Society of India. (1979)-. Bulletin. English. Three times a year. $40.00. Biological Society of India, Bhagalpur India. **(Subscription address:** Prints India, 11 Darya Ganj, New Delhi 110002 India. **Tel** 011 91 11 3268645, FAX 011 91 11 3275542, telex 31-61087 PRIN-IN.)

LC QH301
DD 574 PL

BIOLOGICAL BULLETIN OF POZNAN. (19??)-. Monographic series. English (French and German). One time a year. Price varies per volume. Poznanskie Towarzystwo Przyjaciol Nauk, Ul. Mielzynskiego 27-29, 61-725 Poznan Poland. **Tel** 011 48 61 527441. **(Subscription address:** Ars Polona-Ruch, PO Box 1001, Krakowskie Przedmiescie 7, 00-068 Warsaw Poland. **Tel** 011 48 22 261201.) ***Continues*** *Bulletin de la Societe des Amis des Sciences et des Lettres de Poznan. Serie D. Sciences Biologiques, 0079-4570.*

LC QH301 ISSN 0740-4492
DD 574 US

BIOLOGICAL EXTINCTION. **Added/Corp** SSBE (Society : U.S.). Vol. 1, No. 1 (Spring 1982)-. Periodical. English. Four times a year. $28.00. Social Study Biological Extinction, PO Box 92109, San Diego CA 92109.

LC QH1 .L632a ISSN 0024-4066
DD 574/.05 UK
CCC
CODEN BJLSBG

BIOLOGICAL JOURNAL OF THE LINNEAN SOCIETY. [Biol. j. Linn. Soc.]. **Main/Corp** Linnean Society of London. Vol. 1 (April 1969)-. Academic Scholarly Publication. English. Twelve times a year. $855.60. Academic Press Ltd., A Division of Harcourt Brace & Company Ltd., 24-28 Oval Road, London NW1 7DX United Kingdom. **Tel** 011 44 171 2674466, FAX 011 44 171 4822293, 011 44 171 4854752, telex 25775 ACPRES G. **(Subscription address:** Harcourt Brace & Company, Ltd., Foots Cray High Street, Sidcup Kent DA14 5HP United Kingdom. **Tel** 011 44 181 3003322, FAX 011 44 181 3090807, telex 896 377 ACADEM.) **ED** D. R. Lees. **Bk Rev**. Documents available from The Genuine Article, BIOSIS Document Express. ***Supersedes*** *Linnean Society of London. Proceedings.* ***Continued in part by*** *Linnean Society of London. Linnean.*

Desc: Primarily concerned with the processes of organic evolution, although papers are also published in general fields of theoretical, genetic and population biology and ecology.
Ind/Abst AgBiotech News Inf.; AGRICOLA [Select. Cov.]; Anim. Behav. Abstr.; Anim. Breed. Abstr.; Aquat. Sci. Fish. Abstr. [CD-ROM Ed.]; Biocont. News Inf. (19??-19??); Biol. Abstr.; Curr. Aware. Biol. Sci., CABS; Curr. Cit.; Curr. Contents Agric. Biol. Environ. Sci.; Curr. Ref. Fish Res.; Ecol. Abstr.; Ecology Abstr.; Entomol. Abstr.; Field Crop Abstr.; Fish Rev.; For. Prod. Abstr.; For. Abstr.; Genet. Abstr.; Geogr. Abstr. Phys. Geogr.; Geogr. Abstr. Human Geogr. (?-?); Geol. Abstr.; GeoRef; Grass. Forage Abstr.; Helminthol. Abstr. (1991-); Hortic. Abstr.; Index Vet.; Key Word Index Wildl. Res.; NAPRALERT; Nematol. Abstr.; Nutr. Abstr. Rev., Ser. B, Live Feeds and Feed.; Nutr. Abstr. Rev., Ser. A, Hum. Exp.; Ornamental Hort. (1991-); Life Sci. Collect.; Plant Breed. Abstr.; Plant Genet. Resour. Abstr.; Potato Abstr.; Protozoolog. Abstr.; Res. Alert [Full Cov.]; Rev. Agric. Entomol.; Rev. Med. Vet. Entomol.; Rev. Med. Vet. Mycology; Rev. Plant Pathol.; Rice Abstr.; Sci. Cit. Index; SCISEARCH; Soils Fert.; Weed Abstr.; Wildl. Rev.

LC QH301
DD 574 US
CODEN BMASEJ

BIOLOGICAL MACROMOLECULES AND ASSEMBLIES. Vol. 1 (1984)-. Monographic series. English. John Wiley & Sons, Inc., 605 Third Avenue, New York NY 10158-0012. **Tel** (212)850-6000, (212)850-6645, FAX (212)850-6088, telex 12-7063. **(Subscription address:** John Wiley & Sons / UK, Baffins Lane, Chichester, West Sussex PO19 1UD United Kingdom. **Tel** 011 44 1243 779777, FAX 011 44 243 776128, telex 86290 WIBOOKG.**)** Documents available from CASDDS.
Ind/Abst Chem. Abstr.

LC QH601 .B515 **ISSN** 0748-8653
DD 574 US
CCC
NLM W1; BI751L **CODEN** BIMBEY

BIOLOGICAL MEMBRANES (NEW YORK, N.Y. : 1985). (BIOLOGICAL MEMBRANES.). [Biol. membr.]. Vol. 1, No. 1 (Jan. 1985)-. Periodical. English (summaries and/or abstracts in Russian). Twelve times a year. $1560.00 (academic institutions), $2433.00 (corporate institutions). Harwood Academic Publishers / New York, PO Box 786, Cooper Station, New York NY 10276. **Tel** (212)206-8900, (201)643-7500. **(Subscription address:** Harwood Academic Publishers, PO Box 786, Cooper Station, New York NY 10276. **Tel** (201)643-7500.**)**

LC QH301 **ISSN** 0379-8097
DD 574 II
NLM W1 BI751P **CODEN** BMEMDK

BIOLOGICAL MEMOIRS. [Biol. mem.]. Vol. 1 (Dec. 1976)-. Academic Scholarly Publication. English. Three times a year. $45.00. Impex India, 2118 Ansari Road, New Delhi 110002 India. **Tel** 278034. **(Subscription address:** Prints India, 11 Darya Ganj, New Delhi 110002 India. **Tel** 011 91 11 3268645, FAX 011 91 11 3275542, telex 31-61087 PRIN-IN.**) ED** D C Bhardwaj. **Bk Rev. Ad Acc.** Documents available from BIOSIS Document Express, CASDDS.
Desc: Accommodates articles on all aspects of biological sciences.
Ind/Abst Biol. Abstr.; Chem. Abstr.

LC QH301 **ISSN** 0078-3986
DD 574 US
CODEN OBSBBJ
Pr Rev.

BIOLOGICAL NOTES (COLUMBUS). (BIOLOGICAL NOTES.). [Biol. notes (Columbus)]. **Main/Corp** Ohio Biological Survey. **Added/Corp** Ohio State University. Ohio Cooperative Fishery Unit. (1964)-. Monographic series. English. Irregular. Price varies per volume. Ohio Biological Survey, Ohio State University, College of Biological Sciences, 484 West 12th Avenue, 105 Bioscience, Columbus OH 43210. **Tel** (614)292-9645. **ED** Veda M Cafazzo. **Bk Rev. Ad Acc. Circ:** 1,200 (ctrl). Documents available from BIOSIS Document Express.
Desc: Scientific and technical studies of Ohio's flora, fauna, and environment.
Ind/Abst Biol. Abstr.; GeoRef.

LC QH1 .A258 **ISSN** 0568-8604
DD 574/.05 US
Pr Rev.

BIOLOGICAL PAPERS OF THE UNIVERSITY OF ALASKA. [Biol. pap. Univ. Alsk.]. **Main/Corp** University of Alaska (System). **Added/Corp** University of Alaska (College) University of Alaska (System). (1955)-. Monographic series. English. Irregular. Price varies per volume. Institute of Arctic Biology, University of Alaska, Fairbanks AK 99775. **Tel** (907)474-7655, (907)474-6676. **Ad Acc.** ***Continues** Biological Papers of the University of Alaska, 0568-8604.*
Desc: Forum for original research works in all disciplines of circumpolar arctic or arctic life sciences.
Ind/Abst ASTIS Curr. Aware. Bull. (1978-); AGRICOLA [Select. Cov.]; ASTIS Bibliogr. (1978-); Fish Rev.; Key Word Index Wildl. Res.; Wildl. Rev.

LC QH301 **ISSN** 0301-0511
DD 574 NE
CCC
NLM W1 BI754P **CODEN** BLPYAX
Pr Rev.

BIOLOGICAL PSYCHOLOGY. See Psychology.

LC QH301 **ISSN** 0271-9355
DD 574 US
CODEN BRDEDQ

BIOLOGICAL REGULATION AND DEVELOPMENT. [Biol. regul. dev.]. Vol. 1 (1979)-. Academic Scholarly Publication. English. Irregular. Price varies per volume. Plenum Press, 233 Spring Street, New York NY 10013-1578. **Tel** (212)620-8000, (800)221-9369, FAX (212)463-0742, (212)807-1047, telex 23/421139. Documents available from CASDDS.
Ind/Abst Chem. Abstr.

ISSN 0895-1926
DD 574 US
CODEN BRUSEI
TITLE CHANGE

BIOLOGICAL REPORT (WASHINGTON, D.C.). (BIOLOGICAL REPORT.). [Biol. rep.]. **Added/Corp** U.S. Fish and Wildlife Service. (1984)-(19??). Monographic series. English. Department of the Interior Fish and Wildlife Service, C Street Between Eighteenth and Nineteenth Streets Northwest, Washington DC 20240. **Tel** (202)343-3171. Documents available from BIOSIS Document Express, CASDDS. ***Continues** U.S. Fish and Wildlife Service. Office of Biological Services. FWS/OBS, 0197-6087. **Superseded by** Biological Science Report, 1081-292X.*
Ind/Abst Biol. Abstr. (1985-); Chem. Abstr. (-1984); Ecol. Abstr. (?-1984); Ecology Abstr.; Fish Rev. (19??-199?); Geogr. Abstr. Phys. Geogr.; Geogr. Abstr. Human Geogr.; GeoRef; Leis., Rec., Tour. Abstr.; Wildl. Rev. (19??-199?).

LC QH301 **ISSN** 0716-9760
DD 574 CL
NLM W1; BI754PD

BIOLOGICAL RESEARCH. **Added/Corp** Sociedad de Biologia de Chile. Vol. 25, No. 1 (1992)-. Periodical. English. Four times a year. $100.00. Society of Biology Chile, Maria Luisa Santander 0363, Santiago 9 Chile. **Tel** 56 2 2093503, FAX 56 2 2258427. ***Continues** Archivos de Biologia y Medicina Experimentales, 0004-0533.*
Ind/Abst Curr. Cit.; Index Med. (1992-).

LC QH301 **ISSN** 0959-6321
DD 574 UK

BIOLOGICAL RESEARCH IN NORWICH. [Biol. res. Norwich]. English. Two times a year. Free. University of East Anglia School of Biological Sciences, Norwich NR4 7TJ United Kingdom.
Ind/Abst Abstr. BioCommer.; Rev. Plant Pathol.

LC QH301 .J97a
FI

BIOLOGICAL RESEARCH REPORTS FROM THE UNIVERSITY OF JYVAESKYLAE. **Added/Corp** Jyvaeskylaen Yliopisto. (1975)-. Periodical. English (summaries and/or abstracts in Finnish). Jyvaeskylae University Library, SF-40100, Jyvaeskylae Finland. **Tel** 011 358 941 292453. **ED** Jukka Sarkka. **Circ:** 400 (ctrl).
Desc: Contains academic dissertation and other major research.
Ind/Abst Ecology Abstr.

LC QH301 .C243 **ISSN** 0006-3231
DD 574./05 UK
CCC
NLM W1 BI756 **CODEN** BRCPAH
Pr Rev.

BIOLOGICAL REVIEWS OF THE CAMBRIDGE PHILOSOPHICAL SOCIETY. [Biol. rev. Camb. Philos. Soc.]. **Added/Corp** Cambridge Philosophical Society. **VFOAT** Biological Reviews. Vol. 10, No. 1 (Jan. 1935)-. Academic Scholarly Publication. English (French and German). Four times a year (February, May, August and November). $148.00. Cambridge University Press, The Edinburgh Building, Shaftesbury Road, Cambridge CB2 2RU United Kingdom. **Tel** 011 44 1223 312393, FAX 011 44 1223 315052, telex 851-817256. **(Subscription address:** Cambridge University Press / North America, 110 Midland Avenue, Port Chester NY 10573. **Tel** (800)431-1580, (914)937-9600.**) ED** J. T. Fitzsimons. cum. index. available on microfilm and microfiche from University Microfilms International (UMI). Documents available from The Genuine Article, BIOSIS Document Express, UMI Article Clearinghouse, CASDDS. ***Continues** Biological Reviews and Biological Proceedings of the Cambridge Philosophical Society, 0301-7699.*
Desc: Covers the entire range of the biological sciences. Presents three to four review articles per issue. Although scholarly and with extensive bibliographies, the articles are aimed at non-specialist biologists as well as researchers in the field. Reviews serve as extensive introductions to a particular field, to outline the state of the art, and to draw attention to gaps in knowledge.
Ind/Abst Acad. Search; AgBiotech News Inf.; AGRICOLA [Select. Cov.]; Anim. Breed. Abstr.; Biol. Agric. Index; Biol. Abstr.; Chem. Abstr.; Crop Physiol. Abstr.; Curr. Aware. Biol. Sci., CABS; Curr. Cit.; Curr. Contents Agric. Biol. Environ. Sci.; Curr. Contents Life Sci.; Dairy Sci. Abstr.; Ecol. Abstr.; Ecology Abstr.; EMBASE; EP Collect.; Field Crop Abstr.; Fish Rev.; Gen. Sci. Index; Gen. Sci. Source; Geogr. Abstr. Phys. Geogr.; GeoRef; Grass. Forage Abstr.; Homework Help.; Hortic. Abstr.; Index Med.; Index Vet.; INFO-SOUTH Abstr.; Mag. Search; Mar. Sci. Contents Tables; MasterFile FullTEXT 1000; MasterFile FullTEXT 350; MasterFile FullTEXT 650; MasterFile FullTEXT (Jan. 1994-); Newsp. Period. Abstr. (1991-); OCLC; Life Sci. Collect.; Plant Breed. Abstr.; Poult. Abstr.; Protozoolog. Abstr.; Ref. Upd. Deluxe Ed.; Res. Alert [Full Cov.]; Rev. Agric. Entomol.; Rev. Plant Pathol.; Sci. Cit. Index; SCISEARCH; Seed Abstr.; Soc. Sci. Cit. Index [Select. Cov.]; Soils Fert.; SportSearch; Telebase; Vet. Bull.; Weed Abstr.; Wheat Barley Trit. Abstr.; Wildl. Rev.

LC QH527 .J64 **ISSN** 0929-1016
DD 574.1 NE
NLM W1; BI671QT **CODEN** BRHREI

•**BIOLOGICAL RHYTHM RESEARCH.** **Added/Corp** European Society for Chronobiology. (1994)-. Periodical. English. Four times a year. $398.08. Swets & Zeitlinger BV, Heereweg 347B PO Box 825, 2160 SZ Lisse Netherlands. **Tel** 011 31 2521 35111, FAX 011 31 2521 15888, telex 41325. **(Subscription address:** Swets Publishing Service, PO Box 825, 2160 SZ Lisse, The Netherlands. **Tel** 011 31 2521 35111.**)** ***Continues** Journal of Interdisciplinary Cycle Research, 0022-1945.*
Ind/Abst Chem. Abstr.; Curr. Cit.

LC QH301 **ISSN** 1081-292X
DD 574 US
Pr Rev.

•**BIOLOGICAL SCIENCE REPORT.** [Biol. sci. rep.]. **Added/Corp** United States. National Biological Service. (April 1995)-. Government Publication. English. Irregular. US National Biological Service, Information Transfer Center, 1201 Oak Ridge Drive, Suite 200, Ft. Collins CO 80525-5589. **Tel** (970)226-9401, FAX (970)226-9455. available on an online database. ***Supersedes** US Fish and Wildlife Service Biological Report, 0895-1926.*
Desc: Publishes original scientific research, reviews, inventories, and reports.

ISSN 0953-5365
DD 574.05 UK

BIOLOGICAL SCIENCES REVIEW. [Biol. sci. rev.]. (1988)-. Periodical. English. Five times a year. $58.19. Philip Allan Publishers Ltd., Market Place, Deddington, Oxfordshire OX15 0SE United Kingdom. **Tel** 011 44 1869 338652, FAX 011 44 1869 338803.

LC QH301
DD 574 UK

BIOLOGICAL STRUCTURE AND FUNCTION. No. 1 (1972)-. Academic Scholarly Publication. English. Irregular. Cambridge University Press, The Edinburgh Building, Shaftesbury Road, Cambridge CB2 2RU United Kingdom. **Tel** 011 44 1223 312393, FAX 011 44 1223 315052, telex 851-817256.

ISSN 0892-4473
DD 574 UK

BIOLOGICAL TECHNIQUES SERIES. [Biol. tech. ser.]. (1978)-. Monographic series. English. Price varies per volume. Academic Press Ltd., A Division of Harcourt Brace & Company Ltd., 24-28 Oval Road, London NW1 7DX United Kingdom. **Tel** 011 44 171 2674466, FAX 011 44 171 4822293, 011 44 171 4854752, telex 25775 ACPRES G. Documents available from Ask*IEEE.
Ind/Abst INSPEC.

ISSN 1045-1056
DD 614 UK
CCC
NLM W1; BI762 **CODEN** BILSEC

BIOLOGICALS. [Biol.]. (1990)-. Academic Scholarly Publication. English. Four times a year. $251.55. Academic Press Ltd., A Division of Harcourt Brace & Company Ltd., 24-28 Oval Road, London NW1 7DX United Kingdom. **Tel** 011 44 171 2674466, FAX 011 44 171 4822293, 011 44 171 4854752, telex 25775 ACPRES G. **(Subscription address:** Harcourt Brace & Company, Ltd., Foots Cray High Street, Sidcup Kent DA14 5HP United Kingdom. **Tel** 011 44 181 3003322, FAX 011 44 181 3090807, telex 896 377 ACADEM.**) ED** F. Horaud, P. D. Minor and J. F. Obijeski. **Bk Rev.** Documents available from The Genuine Article, BIOSIS Document Express, CASDDS. ***Continues** Journal of Biological Standardization, 0092-1157.*
Desc: Publishes a broad range of reports relevant to the development, preparation, and quality control of biologicals used in human and veterinary medicine. Provides a forum for news and debate on all aspects of biological preparation, standardization, and regulatory requirements. Reports on biologicals derived from new technologies and other contemporary approaches are especially encouraged. Original research reports, short papers and review articles dealing with topics of current interest are welcomed. Comments and letters to the editor, book reviews, meeting and patent/license reports, and information on regulatory and other new publications

are promptly published.
Ind/Abst AgBiotech News Inf.; AGRICOLA [Select. Cov.]; Biol. Abstr.; Chem. Abstr.; Curr. Cit.; Curr. Contents Life Sci.; EMBASE; Health Plan. Adminis.; Index Med.; Index Vet.; Life Sci. Collect.; PESTDOC; Res. Alert [Full Cov.]; Sci. Cit. Index; SCISEARCH; Vet. Bull.; Trop. Dis. Bull.

LC QH601 .B514 **ISSN** 0233-4755
DD 574.872 RU
CCC
CODEN BIMEE9
BIOLOGICHESKIE MEMBRANY. [Biol. membr.]. **Added/Corp** Akademiia Nauk SSSR. No. 1 (1984)-. Academic Scholarly Publication. Russian (summaries and/or abstracts in English; table of contents in English and Russian). Six times a year. $270.00. Izdatelstvo Nauka / Akademiia Nauk, (Publishing House of the Russian Academy of Sciences), Leninskii Porspekt 14, 117901 Moscow Russia. **Tel** 011 95 9542153, FAX 011 95 9382144, telex 411964. **(Subscription address:** East View Publications Inc., 3020 Harbor Lane North, Suite 110, Minneapolis MN 55447. **Tel** (800)477-1005, (612)550-0961, FAX (612)559-2931.) Documents available from The Genuine Article, CASDDS.
Ind/Abst Chem. Abstr. (1984-); Curr. Contents Life Sci.; Res. Alert [Full Cov.]; Rev. Med. Vet. Mycology; Sci. Cit. Index; SCISEARCH.

LC QH
DD 574 RU
BIOLOGICHESKIE RESURSY I PRIRODNYE USLOVIIA MONGOLSKOI NARODNOI RESPUBLIKI = BUGD NAIRAMDAKH MONGOL ARD ULSYN BAIGALIIN BAIALAG. **See** Natural History.

LC QH **ISSN** 0002-2969
DD 574 AI
BIOLOGICHESKII ZHURNAL ARMENII. **Added/Corp** Haykakan SSR Gitowtyownneri Akademia. Haykakan SSR Gitowtyownneri Akademia. Izvestiia -Biologicheskie i Selskokhoziaistvennye Nauki. Haykakan SSR Gitowtyownneri Akademia. Izvestiia -Biologicheskie Nauki. (1948)-. Periodical. Russian (summaries and/or abstracts in Armenian and English). Twelve times a year.
Ind/Abst Biocont. News Inf. (1991-); Biodeter. Abstr. (1991-); Dairy Sci. Abstr.; Field Crop Abstr.; For. Abstr.; Helminthol. Abstr. (1991-); Hortic. Abstr.; Index Vet.; Maize Abstr.; Nutr. Abstr. Rev., Ser. B, Live Feeds and Feed.; Nutr. Abstr. Rev., Ser. A, Hum. Exp.; Plant Breed. Abstr.; Plant Genet. Resour. Abstr.; Poult. Abstr.; Protozoolog. Abstr.; Rev. Agric. Entomol.; Rev. Med. Vet. Entomol.; Rev. Plant Pathol.; Soils Fert.; Vet. Bull.; Weed Abstr.; Wheat Barley Trit. Abstr.

LC QH301 .B3964 **ISSN** 0366-0486
XR
NLM W1 BI778 **CODEN** BILIAC
BIOLOGICKE LISTY. [Biol. listy]. **Added/Corp** Ceskoslovenska Akademie Ved. (1913)-. Academic Scholarly Publication. Czech (Slovak and English; summaries and/or abstracts in English). Four times a year. $181.17. **(Subscription address:** Kubon & Sagner, ABT Zeitschriftenimport, D 80328 Munich Germany. **Tel** 011 49 89 54218130.) **ED** S. Zadrazil. **Bk Rev.** Documents available from BIOSIS Document Express, CASDDS.
Desc: Papers and reviews dealing with general biology and all branches of modern experimental biology, discussions on analogous subjects, and reports on Czechoslovak biology.
Ind/Abst Anim. Breed. Abstr.; Biol. Abstr.; Chem. Abstr.

LC QH7 .B47 **ISSN** 0037-6930
DD 574 XO
CODEN BLGPAT
BIOLOGICKE PRACE (V BRATISLAVA). (BIOLOGICKE PRACE.). [Biol. pr.]. **Added/Corp** Slovenska Akademia Vied. Sekcia Biologickych a Lekarskych Vied. Vol. 1 (1955)-. Periodical. Slovak (summaries and/or abstracts in English, German and Russian). Vydavatelstvo Obzor, 593 34 Bratislava, Cs Armady 35, Bratislava Slovakia. Documents available from BIOSIS Document Express.
Ind/Abst Biocont. News Inf.; Biol. Abstr.; Field Crop Abstr.; Grass. Forage Abstr.; Soils Fert.

LC QH1 .B5 **ISSN** 0366-0567
DD 574.05 BL
NLM W1 BI781 **CODEN** BIOGAL
SUSPENDED
BIOLOGICO, O. [Biologico]. **Added/Corp** Instituto Biologico de Sao Paulo. **VAT** O Biologico. Vol. 1 (Jan. 1935)- Suspended Vol. 55 (1989). Academic Scholarly Publication. Portuguese (summaries and/or abstracts in English). One time a year. Instituto Biologico, Consel Rodrigues Alves 1252, 04014 Sao Paulo Brazil. **Tel** 011 55 11 5729822. **ED** Maria Mercia Barradas. **Bk Rev. Ad Acc. Circ:** 2,000. available on microfilm from University Microfilms International (UMI). Documents available from CASDDS.
Desc: Research on plant and animal parasitology and pathology.
Ind/Abst AGRICOLA; Chem. Abstr.; Field Crop Abstr.; Grass. Forage Abstr.; Hortic. Abstr.; Index Vet.; Maize Abstr.; Nematol. Abstr.; Life Sci. Collect.; PESTDOC; Plant Breed. Abstr.; Poult. Abstr.; Protozoolog. Abstr.; Rev. Agric. Entomol.; Rev. Med. Vet. Entomol.; Rev. Med. Vet. Mycology; Rev. Plant Pathol.; Rice Abstr.; Soyabean Abstr.; Vet. Bull.; Weed Abstr.; Wheat Barley Trit. Abstr.

LC QH **ISSN** 0936-6903
DD 574 GW
UDC 50/59
BIOLOGIE HEUTE. [Biol. heute]. (1989)-. Periodical. German. Twelve times a year. DM48.00. Wissenschaftliche Verlagsgesellschaft mbH, Postfach 101061, D-70009 Stuttgart Germany. **Tel** 011 49 711 258200, FAX 011 49 711 2582290, telex 723636 DAZ D. **ED** Verband Deutscher Biologen.

ISSN 0045-205X
DD 574 GW
CCC
NLM W1; BI7964 **CODEN** BLUZAR
BIOLOGIE IN UNSERER ZEIT. [Biol. unserer zeit]. (Feb. 1971)-. Academic Scholarly Publication. German. Six times a year. $75.00. VCH Gesellschaft GmbH, Postfach 101161, D-69451 Weinheim Germany. **Tel** 011 49 6201 606459, FAX 011 49 6201 606184. **(Subscription address:** VCH Publishers Inc., 303 Northwest 12th Avenue, Journals Department, Deerfield FL 33442. **Tel** (800)367-8249, (305)428-5566.) Documents available from CASDDS.
Ind/Abst Chem. Abstr.; EMBASE; Energy Res. Abstr. (Feb. 1974-); Key Word Index Wildl. Res.

LC QH **ISSN** 0006-3274
DD 574 GW
BIOLOGIEUNTERRICHT, DER. [Biologieunterricht]. Vol. 13, No. 1 (March 1977)-. Periodical. German. Four times a year. Bouvier GmbH & Co. KG ABT Verlag, Am HOF 28, D-53113 Bonn Germany. **Tel** 011 49 228 7290141, FAX 011 49 228 7290179.
Ind/Abst Energy Res. Abstr. (March 1982-).

LC QH
DD 574 RU
BIOLOGIIA V SHKOLE. (1957)-. Periodical. Russian. Eight times a year. $79.95. **(Subscription address:** East View Publications Inc., 3020 Harbor Lane North, Suite 110, Minneapolis MN 55447. **Tel** (800)477-1005, (612)550-0961, FAX (612)559-2931.) ***Supersedes*** *Estestvozhanie V Shkole.*

LC QH96.A1 B57
RU
CODEN BVIBAX
BIOLOGIIA VNUTRENNIKH VOD. **Added/Corp** Institut Biologii Vnutrennikh Vod. Nauchnyi Sovet po Problemam Gidrobiologii, Ikhtiologii i Ispolzovaniia Biologicheskikh Resursov Vodoemov. No. 1 (1967)-. Academic Scholarly Publication. Russian. Institut Biologii Vnutrennikh Vod, Russia. Documents available from CASDDS.
Ind/Abst Chem. Abstr.; Nematol. Abstr.

LC QH
DD 574 LI
BIOLOGIJA. **VFOAT** Biologiia. (1961)-. Periodical. Lithuanian (summaries and/or abstracts in Russian and English; table of contents in English and Russian).
Ind/Abst Biocont. News Inf.

LC QH301 .L52
DD 574.05/6 LI
●**BIOLOGIJA = BIOLOGY = BIOLOGIIA.** **Added/Corp** Lietuvos Mokslu Akademija. Lietuvos Aukstosios Mokyklos. **VFOAT** Biology; Biologiia. (1993)-. Periodical. English (Russian; summaries and/or abstracts in Lithuanian). Four times a year. Leidykla Academia, A. Gostauto 12, 2600 Vilnius Lithuania. ***Continues*** *Eksperimentine Biologija, 0235-7232.*

LC QL605 **ISSN** 0006-3282
DD 597 GW
BIOLOGISCHE ABHANDLUNGEN. No. 1 (1952)-. Monographic series. German (summaries and/or abstracts in English and French). Irregular. Price varies per volume. Biologie Verlag, Schlossallee 10A, D-65388 Schlangenbad Germany. **ED** H Bruns. Index available. **Bk Rev. Ad Acc.** ctrl circ. Documents available from BIOSIS Document Express. ***Supersedes*** *Ornithologische Abhandlungen.*
Ind/Abst Biol. Abstr.

LC QH301 **ISSN** 0006-3304
DD 574 GW
CCC
NLM W1 BI818 **CODEN** BIZNAT
Pr Rev.
BIOLOGISCHES ZENTRALBLATT. [Biol. Zentralbl.]. Vol. 37 (1917)-. Academic Scholarly Publication. English. Four times a year. $199.00. Gustav Fischer Verlag Jena, Postfach 100537, D-07705 Jena Germany. **Tel** 011 49 3641 626444, FAX 011 49 3641 626500. **(Subscription address:** VCH Publishers Inc., 303 Northwest 12th Avenue, Journals Department, Deerfield FL 33442. **Tel** (800)367-8249, (305)428-5566.) available on microfilm and microfiche from University Microfilms International (UMI). Documents available from The Genuine Article, BIOSIS Document Express, CASDDS. ***Continues*** *Biologisches Centralblatt.*
Desc: An international journal of cell biology, genetics, evolution and theoretical biology.
Ind/Abst AgBiotech News Inf.; Anim. Breed. Abstr.; Biol. Abstr.; Chem. Abstr.; Crop Physiol. Abstr.; Curr. Cit.; Curr. Contents Agric. Biol. Environ. Sci.; Curr. Ref. Fish Res.; Ecol. Abstr.; Field Crop Abstr.; Fish Rev.; Genet. Abstr.; Maize Abstr.; Ornamental Hort.; Life Sci. Collect.; Plant Breed. Abstr.; Plant Genet. Resour. Abstr.; Plant Grow. Reg. Abstr.; Res. Alert [Full Cov.]; Rev. Agric. Entomol.; Rev. Plant Pathol.; Sci. Cit. Index; SCISEARCH; Seed Abstr.; Soc. Sci. Cit. Index [Select. Cov.]; Weed Abstr.; Wheat Barley Trit. Abstr.

LC QH132.G73 B56
DK
BIOLOGISKE MILJUNDERSGELSER I NORDGRNLAND. Danish (summaries and/or abstracts in Eskimo).

LC QH1 .I43 **ISSN** 0006-3347
DD 574/.023 UK
CCC
NLM W1; BI834E **CODEN** BLGTB8
BIOLOGIST (LONDON). (BIOLOGIST.). [Biologist]. **Added/Corp** Institute of Biology. Vol. 16, No. 1 (Feb. 1969)-. Periodical. English. Five times a year (Feb., Apr., June, Sept., Nov.). $56.00. Institute of Biology, 20 Queensberry Place, London SW7 2DZ United Kingdom. **Tel** 011 44 171 5818333, FAX 011 44 171 8239409. **ED** R. Dilo. **Bk Rev. Ad Acc. Circ:** 15,000 (ctrl). Documents available from CASDDS, Documents on Demand. ***Continues*** *Institute of Biology Journal.*
Desc: Provides regular overviews on biology, with articles on agriculture, biomedicine, environment and education; includes news and comment on all spheres of biology and its practice.
Ind/Abst Chem. Abstr. (1985-); Curr. Aware. Biol. Sci., CABS; Curr. Cit.; Curr. Ref. Fish Res.; Ecol. Abstr. (?-?); Environ. Abstr.; Fish Rev.; For. Abstr.; Geogr. Abstr. Human Geogr. (?-?); Helminthol. Abstr.; Index Vet.; Nutr. Abstr. Rev., Ser. B, Live Feeds and Feed.; Nutr. Abstr. Rev., Ser. A, Hum. Exp.; Plant Breed. Abstr.; Protozoolog. Abstr.; Vet. Bull.; Wildl. Rev.

LC QH301 **ISSN** 1157-1209
DD 574 FR
UDC 61
BIOLOGISTE ET PRATICIEN PARIS. (1970)-. Periodical. French. Four times a year. $56.87. Biologiste et Praticien, BP 213 16, 75765 Paris Cedex 16 France. **Tel** 011 33 1 47556859, FAX 011 33 1 45658363.

ISSN 0840-8548
DD 574./05 CN
BIOLOGUE (WATERLOO). (BIOLOGUE.). [Biologue]. **Added/Corp** University of Waterloo. Dept. of Biology. No. 1 (Fall 1988)-. Periodical. English. One time a year. 2.99Can$. University of Waterloo Department of Biology, Waterloo Ontario N2L 3G1 Canada. **Tel** (519)885-1211 ext. 6435, FAX (519)746-0614. **ED** Norm Scott and Dale Weber. **Bk Rev. Ad Acc. Circ:** 500 (ctrl). Documents available from Documents on Demand.
Desc: Contains articles primarily of interest to teachers of biology.
Ind/Abst Environ. Abstr.

LC QH301 .B43 **ISSN** 0791-7945
DD 574 IE
●**BIOLOGY AND ENVIRONMENT : PROCEEDINGS OF THE ROYAL IRISH ACADEMY.** **Added/Corp** Royal Irish Academy. Vol. 93B, No. 1 (Mar. 1993)-. Proceedings. English. Three times a year. Royal Irish Academy, 19 Dawson Street, Dublin 2 Ireland. **Tel** 011 353 1 762570. ***Continues*** *Royal Irish Academy. Proceedings of the Royal Irish Academy, Section B. Biological, Geological and Chemical Science, 0035-8983.*

LC QH331 .B47 **ISSN** 0169-3867
DD 574/.01 NE
CCC
NLM W1; BI852D **CODEN** BIOPEI
Pr Rev.
BIOLOGY & PHILOSOPHY. [Biol. philos.]. **VFOAT** Biology and Philosophy. Vol. 1, No. 1 (1986)-. Periodical. English. Four times a year. $252.00. Kluwer Academic Publishers, Postbus 322, 3300 AH Dordrecht The Netherlands. **Tel** 011 31 78 524400, FAX 011 31 78 183273, telex 20083. **ED** Michael Ruse. Index available. **Bk Rev. Ad Acc. Circ:** 900. available on microfilm and microfiche from University Microfilms International (UMI). Documents available from The Genuine Article, BIOSIS Document Express.
Desc: Covers the philosophical foundations of biology and the philosophical and conceptual implications of biological work. It offers both biologists and philosophers a useful vehicle for publication and a reasonable centralized locus for following the interactions between their disparate disciplines. The journal subscribes to no specific school of biology, nor of philosophy. Each issue carries one or more discussions or comparative reviews, permitting the in-depth study of important works and topics.
Ind/Abst Biol. Abstr. (1986-); Curr. Aware. Biol. Sci., CABS; Curr. Cit.; Curr. Contents Soc. Behav. Sci.; Ecol. Abstr.; Fish Rev. (Jan. 1989-July 1992); Philos. Index; Ref. Upd. Deluxe Ed.; Res. Alert [Full Cov.]; Soc. Sci. Cit. Index [Full Cov.]; Wildl. Rev. (Jan. 1989-July 1992).

LC QH301
DD 574 US
BIOLOGY BULLETIN. **Added/Corp** Cornell University. Division of Biological Sciences. (Oct. 1974)-. Bulletin. English. Six times a year. $820.00 US; $960.00 other. Plenum Press, 233 Spring Street, New York NY 10013-1578. **Tel** (212)620-8000, (800)221-9369, FAX (212)463-0742, (212)807-1047, telex 23/421139.

LC QH301 .A346b ISSN 1062-3590
DD 574/.05 US
CCC
NLM W1; IZ7313 CODEN BRASEK
BIOLOGY BULLETIN OF THE RUSSIAN ACADEMY OF SCIENCES. [Biol. bull. Russ. Acad. Sci.]. **Added/Corp** Rossiiskaia Akademiia Nauk. Consultants Bureau. Vol. 19, No. 1 (Jan./Feb. 1992)-. Bulletin. English (translations available in Russian). Six times a year. $940.00 US; $1105.00 other. Consultants Bureau, A Division of Plenum Publishing Corporation, 233 Spring Street, New York NY 10013. **Tel** (212)620-8000, (212)620-8466, FAX (212)463-0742, telex 23/421139. Documents available from CASDDS. ***Continues*** *Akademiia Nauk SSSR. Izvestiia Akademii Nauk SSSR. Seriia Biologicheskaia. English.* ***and*** *Biology Bulletin of the Academy of Sciences of the USSR, 0098-2164.*
Ind/Abst Chem. Abstr.; Curr. Cit.

LC QH301 .B44 ISSN 0095-2958
DD 574/.08 US
BIOLOGY DIGEST. **See** Biology-Abstracting, Bibliographies and Statistics.

LC QH301 .A34
DD 574/.05 US
BIOLOGY (GUILFORD, CONN.). (BIOLOGY.). (198?)-. Periodical. English. One time a year. $12.95. Dushkin Publishing Group Inc., Sluice Dock, Guilford CT 06437. **Tel** (203)453-4351, (800)243-6532, FAX (203)453-6000. ***Continues*** *Readings in Biology, 0090-4384.*

LC QH301 .B445 ISSN 0253-2069
DD 574/.05 FR
CODEN BYILDJ
BIOLOGY INTERNATIONAL. [Biol. int.]. No. 1 (June/July 1980)-. Academic Scholarly Publication. English (French). Two times a year. $40.00. International Union of Biological Sciences, 51 boulevard de Montmorency, 75016 Paris France. **Tel** 011 33 1 4525009, FAX 011 33 1 42889431, telex 630553 F. **ED** Talal Younes. cum. index. **Bk Rev. Ad Acc. Circ:** 2,000 (ctrl). Documents available from CASDDS.
Ind/Abst Chem. Abstr. (1980-1982); For. Abstr.; Plant Breed. Abstr.; Seed Abstr.

LC QH301 .B462
DD 574 FR
BIOLOGY INTERNATIONAL. SPECIAL ISSUES : THE NEWS MAGAZINE OF THE INTERNATIONAL UNION OF BIOLOGICAL SCIENCES (IUBS). No. 1-. English. Two times a year. $25.00. International Union of Biological Sciences, 51 boulevard de Montmorency, 75016 Paris France. **Tel** 011 33 1 4525009, FAX 011 33 1 42889431, telex 630553 F. **ED** T Younes. **Bk Rev. Ad Acc. Circ:** 1,000-1,500 (ctrl).
Desc: Special issues deal with a wide range of subjects within the realm of biologial sciences.

LC QH301 ISSN 0520-1969
XV
NLM W1 BI852R CODEN BIVEAG
BIOLOSKI VESTNIK. [Biol. vestn.]. Vol. 1 (1952)-. Slovenian (German and English). One time a year. Documents available from BIOSIS Document Express.
Ind/Abst Biocont. News Inf.; Biol. Abstr.; For. Abstr.; Grass. Forage Abstr.; Plant Grow. Reg. Abstr.; Rev. Med. Vet. Entomol.; Rev. Plant Pathol.; Soils Fert.

LC QA QH301 ISSN 0067-8821
DD 510 574 GW
NLM W1 BI852T CODEN BMATBJ
BIOMATHEMATICS (BERLIN). (BIOMATHEMATICS.). [Biomathematics]. **VFOAT** Biomathematics Texts. (1970)-. Monographic series. English. Irregular. Price varies per volume. Springer-Verlag GmbH & Company KG, Heidelberger Platz 3, D-14197 Berlin Germany. **Tel** 011 49 30 8207223, FAX 011 49 30 8214091, telex 183 319 SPBLN D. **(Subscription address:** Springer-Verlag New York Inc. / North America, PO Box 2485, Journal Fulfillment, Secaucus NJ 07096. **Tel** (201)348-4033, (800)777-4643, FAX (201)348-4505.**)** **ED** S.A. Levin. Documents available from BIOSIS Document Express.
Desc: Contains articles on population genetics, biological time, ecological problems, and canonical analysis.
Ind/Abst Biol. Abstr.; Index Vet.; Math. Rev.; Rev. Agric. Entomol.; Rev. Med. Vet. Entomol.; Zentralbl. Math. Ihre Grenzgeb.

LC QR1 .M624 ISSN 0961-088X
DD 576/.05 UK
CCC
NLM W1; BI854R CODEN BILEE4
Pr Rev.
BIOMEDICAL LETTERS. **See** Medical Sciences.

LC QH301
DD 574 GW
BIOMEMBRANES. (19??)-. English. Irregular. VCH Gesellschaft GmbH, Postfach 101161, D-69451 Weinheim Germany. **Tel** 011 49 6201 606459, FAX 011 49 6201 606184. **(Subscription address:** VCH Publishers Inc., 303 Northwest 12th Avenue, Journals Department, Deerfield FL 33442. **Tel** (800)367-8249, (305)428-5566.**)**

LC QH301 ISSN 1018-6255
DD 574 SZ
NLM W1; BI858S CODEN BMTHED
BIOMETHODS (BASEL). (BIOMETHODS.). [Biomethods]. (1987)-. Monographic series. English. Price varies per volume. Birkhaeuser Verlag Ag, Klosterberg 23, PO Box 133, CH-4010 Basel Switzerland. **Tel** 011 41 61 2717400, FAX 011 41 61 2717666, telex 963475 birk ch.
Ind/Abst Curr. Cit.

LC QH301 ISSN 8750-0434
US
BIOMETRIC BULLETIN (WASHINGTON, D.C.). (BIOMETRIC BULLETIN.). [Biom. bull.]. **Added/Corp** Biometric Society. Vol. 1, No. 1 (May 1984)-. Bulletin. English. Twelve times a year. $10.00. International Biometric Society, 808 17th Street Northwest, Suite 200, Washington DC 20006. **Tel** (202)223-9669, FAX (202)223-9569.

LC QH ISSN 0006-341X
DD 574 US
CCC
NLM W1 BI859 CODEN BIOMB6
Pr Rev.
BIOMETRICS. [Biometrics]. **Added/Corp** Biometric Society. American Statistical Association. Biometrics Section. Vol. 3 (March 1947)-. Periodical. English (French and German). Four times a year. $100.00. International Biometric Society, 808 17th Street Northwest, Suite 200, Washington DC 20006. **Tel** (202)223-9669, FAX (202)223-9569. **ED** K. Hinkelmann. Index available. cum. index. **Bk Rev. Ad Acc. Circ:** 7,500 (ctrl). available on microfilm and microfiche from University Microfilms International (UMI). Documents available from The Genuine Article, Ask*IEEE. ***Continues*** *Biometrics Bulletin, 0099-4987.*
Desc: A scientific journal which emphasizes the role of mathematics in use of mathematical and statistical methods in pure and applied biological sciences by describing developments in these methods and their applications in a form readily assimilable by experimental scientists.
Ind/Abst Anim. Breed. Abstr.; Biol. Agric. Index; Biostatistica; CompuMath Cit. Index [Full Cov.]; Comput. Rev.; Curr. Aware. Biol. Sci., CABS; Curr. Cit.; Curr. Contents Agric. Biol. Environ. Sci.; Curr. Contents Life Sci.; Curr. Index Stat.; Dairy Sci. Abstr.; Ecol. Abstr.; EMBASE; Energy Res. Abstr.; Fish Rev.; Food Sci. Technol. Abstr.; For. Prod. Abstr.; For. Abstr.; Geogr. Abstr. Phys. Geogr.; Health Plan. Adminis.; Hortic. Abstr.; Index Med.; Index Vet.; INIS Atomindex [Micro.]; INSPEC (June 1982-1985); Int. Aerosp. Abstr.; Int. Dev. Abstr. (?-?); Key Word Index Wildl. Res.; Math. Rev.; Life Sci. Collect.; Pig News Inf.; Plant Breed. Abstr.; Popul. Index (?-?); Poult. Abstr.; Protozoolog. Abstr.; Qual. Control Appl. Stat.; Ref. Upd. Deluxe Ed.; Res. Alert [Full Cov.]; Rev. Med. Vet. Entomol.; Rev. Plant Pathol.; Risk Abstr. (19??-19??); Sci. Cit. Index; SCISEARCH; Soc. Sci. Cit. Index [Select. Cov.]; Soils Fert.; Stat. Theory Method Abstr. (1959-1963, 1966-1984, 1986-1987); Vet. Bull.; Wheat Barley Trit. Abstr.; Wildl. Rev.; Zentralbl. Math. Ihre Grenzgeb.

LC R858.A1 E2 ISSN 0934-9235
DD 610./1/5195 GW
NLM W1; BI859R
TITLE CHANGE
BIOMETRIE UND INFORMATIK IN MEDIZIN UND BIOLOGIE. **See** Medical Sciences.

LC QH301 .B5 ISSN 0006-3444
UK
NLM W1 BI861 CODEN BIOKAX
Pr Rev.
BIOMETRIKA. [Biometrika]. **Added/Corp** University College, London. Biometric Laboratory. Vol. 1, Pt. 1 (Oct. 1901)-. Periodical. English (French, German and Italian). Four times a year (Mar., June, Sept., Dec.). $124.00. Biometrika, University College London, Gower Street, London WCIE 6BT United Kingdom. **Tel** 011 44 171 3807192, FAX 011 44 171 3834703. cum. index. available on microfilm and microfiche from University Microfilms International (UMI). Documents available from The Genuine Article, BIOSIS Document Express, Ask*IEEE, CASDDS.
Ind/Abst Anim. Breed. Abstr.; Biol. Agric. Index; Biol. Abstr.; Biostatistica (19??-); Chem. Abstr.; CompuMath Cit. Index [Full Cov.]; Curr. Aware. Biol. Sci., CABS; Curr. Cit.; Curr. Contents Agric. Biol. Environ. Sci.; Curr. Contents Life Sci.; Curr. Contents Phys. Chem. Earth Sci.; Curr. Index Stat.; Dairy Sci. Abstr.; EMBASE; Fish Rev. (Jan. 1989-July 1992); GeoRef; Hortic. Abstr.; INSPEC (April 1977-1986); Int. Aerosp. Abstr.; Math. Rev.; Life Sci. Collect.; Plant Breed. Abstr.; Protozoolog. Abstr.; Qual. Control Appl. Stat.; Res. Alert [Full Cov.]; Saf. Health Work; Sci. Cit. Index; SCISEARCH; Soc. Sci. Cit. Index [Select. Cov.]; Stat. Theory Method Abstr. (1959-1963, 1966-1984, 1986-1987); Wildl. Rev. (Jan. 1989-July 1992); Zentralbl. Math. Ihre Grenzgeb.

LC QH301 .B52
DD 574/.05 II
NLM W1 BI863W
BIONATURE. **Added/Corp** Bhopal University. Dept. of Genetics. Society of Bionaturalists (India). Vol. 1, No. 1 & 2 (Feb.-Aug. 1981)-. Periodical. English. Two times a year. $30.00. Bhopal University, School of Biological Science, Department of Genetics, Society of Bionaturalists, Bhopal India. **(Subscription address:** Prints India, 11 Darya Ganj, New Delhi 110002 India. **Tel** 011 91 11 3268645, FAX 011 91 11 3275542, telex 31-61087 PRIN-IN.**)**

ISSN 1065-612X
DD 660 US
BIOPEOPLE (SAN MATEO, CALIF.). (BIOPEOPLE.). [BioPeople]. **VFOAT** Bio People. No. 1 (Fall 1992)-. Periodical. English. Four times a year (Jan., Apr., July, Oct.). $28.00. BioVenture Publishing Inc., 32 West 25th Avenue, Suite 203, San Mateo CA 94403-2236. **Tel** (415)574-7128, FAX (415)574-8319. **ED** Cynthia Robbins-Roth Ph.D. **Ad Acc, Adv Mgr:** Bill Stanley, **Tel** (408)732-2555. **Circ:** 4,000 (ctrl).
Desc: This magazine is for reaching the decision makers of the biotechnology industry. Takes an intimate look at the people who create and support the growing biotech industry. The central piece of each issue is the list of the people in the sector targeted for that issue, based on a survey of the industry's top executives.

ISSN 0523-6827
DD 574 US
BIOPOLYMERS SYMPOSIA. No. 1- 1964-. Monographic series. English. Price varies per volume. Interscience Publishers, 605 3rd Avenue, New York NY 10016.

LC QH301 ISSN 0940-5542
DD 574 GW
NLM W1; BI880
BIOPRACTICE : INTERNATIONAL JOURNAL OF APPLIED BIOLOGY, BIOTECHNOLOGY, AND BIONICS. (1992)-. Periodical. English. Four times a year.

ISSN 1064-251X
DD 574 US
BIOPROBES (EUGENE, OR.). (BIOPROBES.). [Bioprobes]. **Added/Corp** Molecular Probes, Inc. (1985)-. Newsletter. English. Three times a year. Free on request. Molecular Probes, Inc., PO Box 22010, Eugene OR 97402-0414. **Tel** (503)465-8300, FAX (503)344-6504. **ED** Iain Johnson. **Ad Acc. Circ:** 40,000 (ctrl).
Desc: Contains technical information on research products.

ISSN 0891-978X
DD 574 US
NLM W1; BI893
BIORHEOLOGY. SUPPLEMENT. (BIORHEOLOGY. SUPPLEMENT : THE OFFICIAL JOURNAL OF INTERNATIONAL SOCIETY OF BIORHEOLOGY.). [Biorhealogy. Supp.]. **Added/Corp** International Society of Biorheology. (1984)-. Monographic series. English. Irregular. Price varies per volume. Pergamon Press, An Imprint of Elsevier Science Ltd., The Boulevard, Langford Lane, Kidlington, Oxford OX5 1GB United Kingdom. **Tel** 011 44 1865 843000, 011 44 1865 843699, FAX 011 44 1865 843010.

LC QH301 ISSN 0005-3155
DD 574 US
NLM W1 BI902R CODEN BIOSAN
BIOS (MADISON, N.J.). **See** Biology-Abstracting, Bibliographies and Statistics.

LC QH
DD 574 UK
Pr Rev.
●**BIOSAFETY.** (1995)-. Academic Scholarly Publication. English. Irregular. £34.00. Science Reviews Ltd., 18 Oaklands Gate, Northwood Middlesex HA6 3AA United Kingdom. **Tel** 011 44 1923 823586, FAX 011 44 1923 823586.

ISSN 0090-3337
DD 574 US
TITLE CHANGE
BIOSCENE. [BioScene]. **Added/Corp** BioSciences Information Service of Biological Abstracts. **VFOAT** Bio Scene; BIOSIS Newsletter. (1971)-(199?). Newsletter. English. BioSciences Information Service, Biological Abstracts / BIOSIS, 2100 Arch Street, Philadelphia PA 19103. **Tel** (800)523-4806, (215)587-4847, FAX

(215)587-2016, telex 831739. **Circ:** 5,000. ***Absorbed*** *ZooScene.* ***Merged with*** *Biosearch, 1041-8946* ***to form*** *BIOSIS Evolution, 1081-8669.*
Desc: A newsletter reporting items of interest to users of all BIOSIS products, including Biological Abstracts, Biological Abstracts/RRM, BIOSIS Previews, Zoological Record, and others.

LC QH1 .A277 **ISSN** 0006-3568
DD 574/.05 US
CCC
NLM W1 BI913 **CODEN** BISNAS
Pr Rev.
BIOSCIENCE. [Bioscience]. **Added/Corp** American Institute of Biological Sciences. Vol. 14, No. 1 (Jan. 1964)-. Periodical. English. Eleven times a year (monthly with July/Aug. combined). $165.00. American Institute of Biological Sciences, 730 11th Street Northwest, Washington DC 20001-4521. **Tel** (202)628-1500, FAX (202)628-1509, telex 209061 AIBS UR. **(Subscription address:** Bioscience/ Outside US Subscriptions, Subscription Office, PO Box 1831, Birmingham AL 35201-1831. **Tel** (800)633-4931, (205)995-1567 (outside US and Canada), FAX (205)995-1588.**)** **ED** Julie Ann Miller. Index available (bound in Dec. issue). cum. index. **Bk Rev. Ad Acc. Circ:** 12,400. available on microfilm and microfiche from University Microfilms International (UMI); available on an online database (file 647/Full-Text) from DIALOG. Documents available from The Genuine Article, BIOSIS Document Express, UMI Article Clearinghouse, CASDDS, Documents on Demand. ***Continues*** *A.I.B.S. Bulletin, 0096-7645.*
Desc: A source of information about the many areas of today's biology. Provides biologists with a view of areas beyond their specialties and of biology's impact on society.
Ind/Abst Abstr. Bull. Inst. Pap. Sci. Tech.; Abstr. BioCommer.; Acad. Abstr. Full Text Elite; Acad. Abstr.; Acad. Ind. [Computer File] (1984-); Acad. Search; AGRICOLA [Select. Cov.]; Agrofor. Abstr. (1991-); Anim. Breed. Abstr.; Biocont. News Inf.; Biol. Agric. Index; Biol. Abstr.; Biol. Dig.; Book Rev. Index; Chem. Abstr. (?-1988); Crop Physiol. Abstr.; CSA Neuro. Abstr. (?-?); Curr. Aware. Biol. Sci., CABS; Curr. Biotechnol.; Curr. Cit.; Curr. Contents Agric. Biol. Environ. Sci.; Curr. Index J. Educ.; Curr. Ref. Fish Res.; Dairy Sci. Abstr.; Ecology Abstr.; EMBASE; Energy Res. Abstr.; Entomol. Abstr.; Environ. Abstr.; Environ. Period. Bibliogr.; EP Collect.; Expand. Acad. Index (1984-); Fish Rev.; For. Abstr.; Garden Lit. (1992-); Gen. Period. Index (1985-); Gen. Sci. Index; Gen. Sci. Source; GeoRef; Grass. Forage Abstr.; Health Plan. Adminis.; Health Ref. Cent. (1987-) [Select. Cov.]; Homework Help.; Hortic. Abstr.; INFO-SOUTH Abstr.; INIS Atomindex [Micro.]; Int. Aerosp. Abstr.; Key Word Index Wildl. Res.; Mag. Artic. Summar. Elite; Mag. Artic. Summar. Select; Mag. Artic. Summar. CD-ROM; Mag. ASAP Plus [Full Txt.]; Mag. ASAP Sel. [Full Txt.]; Mag. Express (1988-) [Full Txt.]; Mag. Index Plus (1989-); Mag. Index. Sel. (1986-); Mag. Search; MasterFile FullTEXT 1000; MasterFile FullTEXT 350; MasterFile FullTEXT 650; MasterFile FullTEXT (Jan. 1984-); Nematol. Abstr.; Newsp. Period. Abstr. (1988-); OCLC; Life Sci. Collect.; Plant Breed. Abstr.; Plant Genet. Resour. Abstr.; Pollut. Abstr. Indexes; Protozoolog. Abstr.; Pub. Lib. FullTEXT; Read. Guide Abstr. Select Ed.; Read. Guide Period. Lit.; Res. Alert [Full Cov.]; Resource/One Ondisc; Rev. Agric. Entomol.; Rev. Med. Vet. Entomol.; Rev. Med. Vet. Mycology; Rev. Plant Pathol.; Rice Abstr.; Sci. Cit. Index; SCISEARCH; Soc. Sci. Cit. Index [Select. Cov.]; Soils Fert.; Telebase; Mag. Index (1977-); Vocat. Search; Wheat Barley Trit. Abstr.; Wildl. Rev.; World Agric. Econ. Rural Sociol. Abstr.

ISSN 1081-8669
DD 574 US
CODEN BIEVEK
•**BIOSIS EVOLUTIONS.** [BIOSIS evol.].
Added/Corp BioSciences Information Service of Biological Abstracts. **VFOAT** Evolutions. Vol. 1, No. 1 (1994)-. Periodical. English. Four times a year. Free on request. BioSciences Information Service, Biological Abstracts / BIOSIS, 2100 Arch Street, Philadelphia PA 19103. **Tel** (800)523-4806, (215)587-4847, FAX (215)587-2016, telex 831739. ***Formed by the union of*** *BioScene, 0090-3337* ***and*** *Biosearch, 1041-8946.*

LC Z695.1.B5 B56 **ISSN** 0898-2414
DD 574 US
TITLE CHANGE
BIOSIS PREVIEWS SEARCH GUIDE.
[BIOSIS previews search guide]. **Added/Corp** BioSciences Information Service of Biological Abstracts. **VAT** Biosciences Information Service of Biological Abstracts Previews Search Guide. (1987)-(199?). English. BioSciences Information Service, Biological Abstracts / BIOSIS, 2100 Arch Street, Philadelphia PA 19103. **Tel** (800)523-4806, (215)587-4847, FAX (215)587-2016, telex 831739. ***Continues*** *Search Guide (BIOSIS Previews Edition), 0898-2422.* ***Continued by*** *BIOSIS Search Guide.*
Desc: Contains information that aids in the development of effective search strategies for the BIOSIS Previews database and its CD-ROM counterpart.

LC QH301
DD 574 US
BIOSIS PREVIEWS [ONLINE DATABASE]. **See** Biology-Abstracting, Bibliographies and Statistics.

LC Z699.5.B53 B56
DD 574 US
•**BIOSIS SEARCH GUIDE. Added/Corp** BioSciences Information Service of Biological Abstracts. **VFOAT** BioSciences Information Service of Biological Abstracts Search Guide; Search Guide. (1995)-. English. Every 2 years. $115.00. BioSciences Information Service, Biological Abstracts / BIOSIS, 2100 Arch Street, Philadelphia PA 19103. **Tel** (800)523-4806, (215)587-4847, FAX (215)587-2016, telex 831739. ***Continues*** *BIOSIS Previews Search Guide, 0898-2414.*
Desc: Contains information that aids in the development of effective search strategies for the BIOSIS Previews database and its CD-ROM counterpart.

LC QH301
DD 574 US
•**BIOSIS SERIAL SOURCES.** (1995)-. Academic Scholarly Publication. English. One time a year. $75.00. BioSciences Information Service, Biological Abstracts / BIOSIS, 2100 Arch Street, Philadelphia PA 19103. **Tel** (800)523-4806, (215)587-4847, FAX (215)587-2016, telex 831739. ***Continues*** *Serial Sources for the Biosis Previews Database.*

LC QH301
DD 574 UK
BIOSOCIAL SOCIETY SERIES. (1988)-. Monographic series. English. Price varies per volume.

LC QH301 **ISSN** 0197-7571
DD 574 US
CODEN BIDID9
BIOSOURCES DIGEST. [Biosources dig.]. Vol. 1 (Jan. 1979)-. Academic Scholarly Publication. English. Four times a year. $45.00. Neus Inc, PO Box 99219, San Diego CA 92109. Documents available from CASDDS.
Ind/Abst Chem. Abstr.; EMBASE.

LC QH323.5 .B5627 **ISSN** 1041-7648
DD 574/.01/519505 US
NLM ZWA 950; B616
BIOSTATISTICA (DAVENPORT, IOWA). **See** Biology-Abstracting, Bibliographies and Statistics.

LC QH301
DD 574 GW
BIOTEC WURZBURG. (BIOTECH : FACHMAGAZIN FUER BIOTECHNOLOGIE.). [BioTec Wurzbg.]. (1989)-. Periodical. German. Six times a year. $46.06. Vogel Verlag, Postfach 6740, D-97064 Wuerzburg Germany. **Tel** 011 49 931 4182145, 011 49 931 4182483, FAX 011 49 931 4182670, telex 841 680131. **Bk Rev. Ad Acc. Circ:** 10,000 (ctrl).

LC QH301 **ISSN** 0740-1221
DD 574 US
BIOTECH MARKET NEWS & STRATEGIES. VFOAT Biotech Market News and Strategies. Vol. 2, No. 9 (Sept. 1983)-. Periodical. English. Twelve times a year. $322.00. Biotech Market News Strategies, PO Box 11155, Fort Lauderdale FL 33339. **Tel** (305)785-2854. ***Continues*** *Biotechnology Marketing Strategies.*

LC QH301
DD 574 NE
Pr Rev.
BIOTECHNOLOGIE. (19??)-. Dutch. Six times a year. Fl99.50 Netherlands; Fl100.00 (surface mail), Fl225.00 (airmail) other. Stam Tijdschriften B V, Postbus 235, 2280 AE Rijswijk Netherlands. **Tel** 011 31 70 3988100, FAX 011 31 70 3988276, telex 33702 STAM NL. **ED** E Kisman. **Bk Rev. Ad Acc. Circ:** 2,042.

LC QH301
DD 574 SP
BIOTECNOLOGIA. Spanish. Twelve times a year. $185.00 institutions; $235.00 corporations. Globotech Inc, Apartado 20147, 28080 Madrid Spain. **Tel** 011 34 1 6502038, FAX 011 34 1 6507887.

LC QH301 **ISSN** 0921-299X
DD 574 NE
CCC
NLM W1; BI919MN **CODEN** BTHREW
BIOTHERAPY (DORDRECHT).
(BIOTHERAPY.). [Biotherapy]. Vol. 1, No. 1 (1988)-. Academic Scholarly Publication. English. Four times a year. $303.00. Kluwer Academic Publishers, Postbus 322, 3300 AH Dordrecht The Netherlands. **Tel** 011 31 78 524400, FAX 011 31 78 183273, telex 20083. **ED** Huub Schellekens. available on microfilm and microfiche from University Microfilms International (UMI). Documents available from The Genuine Article, BIOSIS Document Express, CASDDS.
Desc: Papers published in this journal draw together all research devoted to the use of biological agents in the treatment of disease. Covers molecular biology, protein chemistry, cell biology, immunology, animal models, pharmacology, toxicology, clinical trials and regulatory affairs.
Ind/Abst Biol. Abstr. (1991-); Chem. Abstr.; Curr. Aware. Biol. Sci., CABS; Curr. Cit.; Curr. Contents Life Sci.; EMBASE; Health Plan. Adminis.; Immunol. Abstr.; Index Med.; PESTDOC; Ref. Upd. Deluxe Ed.; Res. Alert [Full Cov.]; Sci. Cit. Index; SCISEARCH.

LC QH107 .B56 **ISSN** 0185-0326
DD 574.972/05 MX
CODEN BIOTDT
CEASED
BIOTICA. (BIOTICA : PUBLICACION DEL INSTITUTO DE INVESTIGACIONES SOBRE RECURSOS BIOTICOS A.C.). [Biotica]. **Added/Corp** Instituto de Investigaciones Sobre Recursos Bioticos (Mexico) Instituto Nacional de Investigaciones Sobre Recursos Bioticos (Mexico). Vol. 2, No. 1 (May 1977)-Vol. 13. Academic Scholarly Publication. Spanish (summaries and/or abstracts in English). Instituto de Investigaciones Sobre Recursos Bioticos, Apartado Postal 63, Xalapa Ver Mexico. **Tel** 281-8-69-10, telex 015542 INRBME. **ED** L Cendreros, A Gomez Pompa, M A Ramos, V Rico Gray, A Zavala Hurtado, B Ludlow Wiechers, and B Gomez Varela. Index available. cum. index. **Circ:** 1,000. Documents available from BIOSIS Document Express, CASDDS. ***Continues*** *Publicacion del Instituto de Investigaciones Sobre Recursos Bioticos.*
Desc: Official journal that contains scientific and technological articles related to the management, use, conservation and knowledge of biotic resources in Mexico.
Ind/Abst Biodeter. Abstr. (1991-); Biol. Abstr.; Chem. Abstr.; For. Prod. Abstr. (19??-19??); Hortic. Abstr.; Sug. Indus. Abstr.

LC QH301 **ISSN** 0125-975X
DD 574 IO
BIOTROP SPECIAL PUBLICATION.
VFOAT B.I.O.T.R.O.P. Special Publication. **VAT** Regional Center for Tropical Biology Special Publication. Monographic series. English. Price varies per volume. Southeast Asian Regional Center for Tropical Biology, POB 17, Jalan Raya Tajur, 6 Bogor Indonesia.
Ind/Abst Agrofor. Abstr.; Biocont. News Inf. (1991-); Field Crop Abstr.; For. Abstr.; Grass. Forage Abstr.; Hortic. Abstr.; Potato Abstr.; Rev. Agric. Entomol.; Rice Abstr.; Seed Abstr.; Weed Abstr.; Wheat Barley Trit. Abstr.

LC QH1 .B54 **ISSN** 0006-3606
DD 574.909/3 570 US
CODEN BTROAZ
Pr Rev.
BIOTROPICA. [Biotropica]. **Added/Corp** Association for Tropical Biology. Vol. 1 (June 1969)-. Periodical. English. Four times a year. $95.00. Association for Tropical Biology / New Orleans, Department of Biology, Tulane University, New Orleans LA 70118. **Tel** (504)865-5191, FAX (504)862-8706. **(Subscription address:** Biotropica, PO Box 1897, Lawrence KS 66044-8897. **)** cum. index. **Acid Free.** available on microfilm and microfiche from University Microfilms International (UMI). Documents available from The Genuine Article, BIOSIS Document Express, CASDDS. ***Supersedes*** *Bulletin. Association for Tropical Biology.*
Desc: Publishes original research in the broad area of tropical biology, including the ecology and management of diverse tropical ecosystems and the evolution, behavior, population biology, and systematics of tropical organisms. Articles report studies carried out in all tropical areas of the world.
Ind/Abst AGRICOLA [Select. Cov.]; Agrofor. Abstr. (19??-19??); Anim. Behav. Abstr.; Biocont. News Inf. (19??-19??); Biol. Abstr.; Chem. Abstr.; Chemorecept. Abstr.; Curr. Aware. Biol. Sci., CABS; Curr. Cit.; Curr. Contents Agric. Biol. Environ. Sci.; Ecol. Abstr.; Ecology Abstr.; EMBASE; Entomol. Abstr.; Fish Rev. (19??-199?); For. Prod. Abstr. (19??-19??); For. Abstr.; Geogr. Abstr. Phys. Geogr.; Geogr. Abstr. Human Geogr.; Hortic. Abstr.; Int. Dev. Abstr.; Irr. Drain. Abstr.; Key Word Index Wildl. Res.; Life Sci. Collect.; Plant Breed. Abstr.; Protozoolog. Abstr.; Res. Alert [Full Cov.]; Rev. Agric. Entomol.; Rev. Med. Vet. Entomol.; Sci. Cit. Index; SCISEARCH; Seed Abstr.; Soils Fert.; Wildl. Rev.

LC QH301 **ISSN** 0250-507X
DD 574 II
CODEN BIOVDZ
BIOVIGYANAM. [Biovigyanam]. **Added/Corp** Maharashtra Association for the Cultivation of Science. Vol. 1 (1975)-. Periodical. English. Two times a year. $25.00. Maharashtra Association for the Cultivation of Science, Poona India. **(Subscription address:** Prints India, 11 Darya Ganj, New Delhi 110002 India. **Tel** 011 91 11 3268645, FAX 011 91 11 3275542, telex 31-61087 PRIN-IN.**)** Documents available from BIOSIS Document Express, CASDDS.
Ind/Abst Biol. Abstr.; Chem. Abstr.; Crop Physiol. Abstr.; Field Crop Abstr.; For. Abstr.; GeoRef; Hortic. Abstr.; Indian Geosci. Abstr.; Maize Abstr.; Plant Breed. Abstr.; Rev. Plant Pathol.; Sorghum Mill. Abstr.; Weed Abstr.; Wheat Barley Trit. Abstr.

LC QH301 **ISSN** 0365-9615
DD 574 RU
CCC
NLM W1 BI99 **CODEN** BEBMAE
BJULLETEN EKSPERIMENTALNOJ BIOLOGII I MEDICINY. (BIULLETEN EKSPERIMENTALNOI BIOLOGII I MEDITSINY.). [Bjull. eksp. biol. med.]. **Added/Corp** Akademiia Meditsinskikh Nauk SSSR. (1936)-. Academic Scholarly Publication. Russian (Russian; summaries and/or abstracts in English). Twelve times a year. $299.95. **(Subscription**

Biology

address: East View Publications Inc., 3020 Harbor Lane North, Suite 110, Minneapolis MN 55447. **Tel** (800)477-1005, (612)550-0961, FAX (612)559-2931.) Documents available from BIOSIS Document Express, CASDDS.
Ind/Abst Biol. Abstr.; Calcium Calcif. Tissue Abstr.; Chem. Abstr.; CSA Neuro. Abstr.; EMBASE; Index Med.; Int. Aerosp. Abstr.; PESTDOC; Virol. AIDS Abstr.

LC Q60 .M82   ISSN 0027-1403
DD 506   RU
    CODEN BYMOAB
BJULLETEN MOSKOVSKOGO OBSCESTVA ISPYTATELEJ PRIRODY. OTDEL BIOLOGICESKIJ. (BIULLETEN MOSKOVSKOGO OBSHCHESTVA ISPYTATELEI PRIRODY. OTDEL BIOLOGICHESKII.). [Bjull. Mosk. obsc. ispyt. prir., Otd. biol.]. **Main/Corp** Moskovskoe Obshchestvo Ispytatelei Prirody. **VFOAT** Bulletin de la Societe des Naturalistes de Moscou. Section Biologique. Vol. 31 (1917)-. Academic Scholarly Publication. French (Russian). Six times a year. $69.95. **(Subscription address:** East View Publications Inc., 3020 Harbor Lane North, Suite 110, Minneapolis MN 55447. **Tel** (800)477-1005, (612)550-0961, FAX (612)559-2931.) Documents available from BIOSIS Document Express. **Continues** Bulletin de la Societe Imperiale des Naturalistes de Moscou.
Ind/Abst Anim. Breed. Abstr.; Biol. Abstr.; EMBASE; GeoRef; Nematol. Abstr.; Plant Breed. Abstr.; Plant Genet. Resour. Abstr.; Protozoolog. Abstr.; Rev. Med. Vet. Entomol.; Seed Abstr.

LC QD71   ISSN 0269-3879
DD 543   UK
    CCC
NLM W1; BI854C   CODEN BICHE2
BMC. BIOMEDICAL CHROMATOGRAPHY. See Chemistry and Chemicals-Analytical Chemistry.

LC R21 .M57   ISSN 0067-9666
    MX
NLM W1 BO229G   CODEN BEMBA2
Pr Rev.
BOLETIN DE ESTUDIOS MEDICOS Y BIOLOGICOS. See Medical Sciences-Experimental Medicine.

LC QH301
DD 574   SP
BOLETIN DE LA SOCIEDAD ESPANOLA DE ANTROPOLOGIA BIOLOGICA. See Anthropology.

LC QH301 .S59   ISSN 0037-8771
    IT
NLM W1 BO474   CODEN BSIBAC
BOLLETTINO DELLA SOCIETA ITALIANA DI BIOLOGIA SPERIMENTALE. [Boll. Soc. ital. biol. sper.]. **Main/Corp** Societa Italiana di Biologia Sperimentale. **VFOAT** Bollettino. Vol. 2, No. 1 (Jan. 1927)-. Academic Scholarly Publication. Italian (English). Twelve times a year. L200000. Casa Editrice Libraria Idelson Gnocchi, Via Alcide De Gasperi 55, 80133 Naples Italy. **Tel** 011 39 81 5524733, FAX 011 39 81 5518295. **ED** P. Defranciscis. Documents available from BIOSIS Document Express, CASDDS. **Continues** Societa di Biologia Sperimentale. Bolletino della Societa di Biologia Sperimentale.
Ind/Abst Anim. Breed. Abstr.; Biol. Abstr.; Chem. Abstr.; Curr. Cit.; Dairy Sci. Abstr.; EMBASE; Health Plan. Adminis.; Index Med.; Index Vet.; Maize Abstr.; Nutr. Abstr. Rev., Ser. B, Live Feeds and Feed.; Nutr. Abstr. Rev., Ser. A, Hum. Exp.; Life Sci. Collect.; PESTDOC; Poult. Abstr.; Rev. Med. Vet. Mycology; Seed Abstr.; Soyabean Abstr.; SportSearch; Vet. Bull.

LC R   ISSN 0100-879X
DD 610   BL
    CCC
NLM W1 BR189N   CODEN BJMRDK
Pr Rev.
BRAZILIAN JOURNAL OF MEDICAL AND BIOLOGICAL RESEARCH. See Medical Sciences-Experimental Medicine.

LC QH315 .B586A   ISSN 0737-7460
DD 574.07/1   US
BSCS JOURNAL, THE. [BSCS j.]. **VFOAT** B.S.C.S. Journal. Vol. 2, No. 4 (Nov. 1979)-. Periodical. English. Four times a year. Biological Sciences Curriculum Study, PO Box 930, Boulder CO 80306. **Continues** Biological Sciences Curriculum Study Journal, 0162-3613.

LC QH301   ISSN 0007-7682
DD 574   RU
    TITLE CHANGE
BULLETEN' MOSKOVSKOGO OBSESTVA ISPYTATELEJ PRIRODY. NOVAA SERIA. OTDEL BIOLOGICESKIJ. [Bull. Mosk. obs. ispyt. prir.,

Nov. ser., Otd. biol.]. **VFOAT** Bulletin of Moscow Society of Naturalists, Biological Series. (1829)-(19??). Russian. **Continued by** Biulleten Moskovskogo Obshchestva Ispytatelei Prirody Otdel Geologicheskii, 0366-1318.
Ind/Abst Biodeter. Abstr.

DD 639.3/0971   ISSN 0840-5417
    CN
BULLETIN - AQUACULTURE ASSOCIATION OF CANADA. (BULLETIN.). [Bull. - Aquac. Assoc. Can.]. **Added/Corp** Association Aquacole du Canada. Edition 86-1 (1986)-. Bulletin. French (English). Four times a year (Mar., June, Sept., Dec.). $40.00 (one-year); $50.00 (individuals), $85.00 (institutions) Comes with Aquaculture Association of Canada membership. Aquaculture Association of Canada, PO Box 1987, Saint Andrews New Brunswick E0G 2X0 Canada. **Tel** (506)529-8854, FAX (506)529-4274.
Desc: This features articles on aquaculture science.

LC RS189 .I46a
DD 610/.28   SZ
    CODEN BAIBDP
BULLETIN D'INFORMATION - ASSOCIATION INTERNATIONALE DE STANDARDISATION BIOLOGIQUE. NEWSLETTER - INTERNATIONAL ASSOCIATION OF BIOLOGICAL STANDARDIZATION. **Main/Corp** International Association of Biological Standardization. **Added/Corp** International Association of Biological Standardization. Newsletter. **VFOAT** Newsletter - International Association of Biological Standardization. No. 15, Jan. (1973)-. Bulletin. English (French). International Association of Biological Standardization, 1211 Geneva 4 Switzerland.

LC QH301 .B79   ISSN 0303-9137
DD 574/.05   BE
    CODEN BNBBAA
BULLETIN - INSTITUT ROYAL DES SCIENCES NATURELLES DE BELGIQUE. BIOLOGIE. [Bull. - Inst. r. sci. nat. Belg., Biol.]. **Main/Corp** Institut Royal des Sciences Naturelles de Belgique. **Added/Corp** Institut Royal des Sciences Naturelles de Belgique. **VFOAT** Biologie; Bulletin de l'Institut Royal des Sciences Naturelles de Belgique. P.Biologie; Bulletin van het Koninklijk Belgisch Instituut voor Natuurwetenschappen. Biologie. Vol. 48 (1972)-. Bulletin. French (English). Irregular. Price varies per volume. Institut Royal des Sciences Naturelles de Belgique, rue Vautier 29, 1040 Brussels Belgium. **Tel** 011 32 2 6482123, FAX 011 32 2 6464433. **ED** Karel Wouters. **Circ:** 850. Documents available from BIOSIS Document Express. **Continues in part** Institut Royal des Sciences Naturelles de Belgique. Bulletin - Institut Royal des Sciences Naturelles de Belgique.
Desc: Scientific papers on vertebrate and invertebrate zoology, systematics and ecology.
Ind/Abst Biol. Abstr.; GeoRef.

LC QH323 .M85   ISSN 0097-0883
DD 574   US
NLM W1 BU748P
BULLETIN - MOUNT DESERT ISLAND BIOLOGICAL LABORATORY (1934). (BULLETIN OF THE MOUNT DESERT ISLAND BIOLOGICAL LABORATORY.). [Bull. - Mt. Desert Isl. Biol. Lab.]. **Main/Corp** Mount Desert Island Biological Laboratory. **VFOAT** Bulletin. (19??)-. Bulletin. English. One time a year (Apr.). $10.00. Mount Desert Island Biological Laboratory, Salsbury Cove ME 04672. **Tel** (207)288-3605. Index available in last issue of volume--attached. cum. index. ctrl circ. **Continues** Mount Desert Island Biological Laboratory. Annual Announcement and Report, 0276-301X.
Ind/Abst Life Sci. Collect.

LC R850   ISSN 0007-4888
DD 619.05   US
    CCC
NLM W1 BU772   CODEN BEXBAN
BULLETIN OF EXPERIMENTAL BIOLOGY AND MEDICINE. See Medical Sciences-Experimental Medicine.

LC QH505.A1 B8   ISSN 0092-8240
DD 574/.01/51   US
    CCC
NLM W1 BU801M   CODEN BMTBAP
Pr Rev.
BULLETIN OF MATHEMATICAL BIOLOGY. [Bull. math. biol.]. **Added/Corp** Society for Mathematical Biology. Vol. 35 (1973)-. Bulletin. English. Six times a year. $700.00. Pergamon Press, An Imprint of Elsevier Science Ltd., The Boulevard, Langford Lane, Kidlington, Oxford OX5 1GB United Kingdom. **Tel** 011 44 1865 843000, 011 44 1865 843699, FAX 011 44 1865 843010. **(Subscription address:** Elsevier Science Ltd. / Oxford Fulfillment Centre, PO Box 800, Kidlington OX5 1DX United Kingdom. **Tel** 011 44 865 843355.) **ED** Lee A. Segal. available on microfilm and microfiche from University Microfilms International (UMI). Documents available from The Genuine Article, BIOSIS Document Express, Ask*IEEE, CASDDS. **Continues** Bulletin of Mathematical Biophysics, 0007-4985.

Ind/Abst Acoust. Abstr.; AgBiotech News Inf.; AGRICOLA; Biocont. News Inf.; Biol. Abstr.; Biostatistica; Chem. Abstr.; CompuMath Cit. Index [Full Cov.]; Curr. Cit.; Curr. Contents Life Sci.; Ecology Abstr.; EMBASE; Energy Res. Abstr. (May 1974-); For. Abstr.; Health Plan. Adminis.; Index Med.; INIS Atomindex [Micro.]; INSPEC (Feb. 1974-1985); Int. Aerosp. Abstr.; Math. Rev.; Oper. Res./Manage. Sci.; Life Sci. Collect.; Plant Breed. Abstr.; Res. Alert [Full Cov.]; Rev. Med. Vet. Entomol.; Sci. Cit. Index; SCISEARCH; Stat. Theory Method Abstr. (1984); Wildl. Rev.; Zentralbl. Math. Ihre Grenzgeb.

LC QH105.O3 A3   ISSN 0078-3994
DD 570   US
    CODEN BOBNAJ
Pr Rev.
BULLETIN OF THE OHIO BIOLOGICAL SURVEY. (BULLETIN / OHIO BIOLOGICAL SURVEY.). [Bull. Ohio Biol. Surv.]. **Added/Corp** Ohio Biological Survey. **VFOAT** Bulletin of the Ohio Biological Survey; Ohio Biological Survey Bulletin Series. (1913)-. Bulletin. English. Irregular. Price varies per volume. Ohio Biological Survey, Ohio State University, College of Biological Sciences, 484 West 12th Avenue, 105 Bioscience, Columbus OH 43210. **Tel** (614)292-9645. **ED** Veda Marie Cafazzo. **Bk Rev. Ad Acc. Circ:** 1,200 (ctrl). Documents available from BIOSIS Document Express. **Continues** Bulletin of the Ohio Biological Survey, 0078-3994.
Desc: Scientific and technological monographs by Ohio authors or authors whose subject matter involves the Ohio biota and environment.
Ind/Abst Biol. Abstr.; Fish Rev.; GeoRef; Life Sci. Collect.; Wildl. Rev.

LC QH301 .P6   ISSN 0239-751X
DD 574.05/6   PL
BULLETIN OF THE POLISH ACADEMY OF SCIENCES. BIOLOGY. (BULLETIN OF THE POLISH ACADEMY OF SCIENCES. BIOLOGICAL SCIENCES.). [Bull. Pol. Acad. Sci., Biol.]. **Added/Corp** Polska Akademia Nauk. **VFOAT** Biological Sciences. Vol. 32, No. 9/10 (1984)-. Bulletin. English (French, German and Russian). Four times a year. $100.00. **(Subscription address:** Ars Polona-Ruch, PO Box 1001, Krakowskie Przedmiescie 7, 00-068 Warsaw Poland. **Tel** 011 48 22 261201.) Documents available from BIOSIS Document Express, CASDDS. **Continues** Bulletin of the Polish Academy of Sciences. Biology, 0239-751X.
Ind/Abst Biol. Abstr. (1984-); Chem. Abstr. (1984-); Crop Physiol. Abstr.; EMBASE; Field Crop Abstr.; Fish Rev. (Jan. 1989-July 1992); Food Sci. Technol. Abstr.; For. Abstr.; GeoRef (1984-); Hortic. Abstr.; Index Vet.; Ornamental Hort. (1991-); Life Sci. Collect.; Plant Breed. Abstr.; Plant Grow. Reg. Abstr.; Postharvest News Inf.; Potato Abstr.; Seed Abstr.; Wildl. Rev. (Jan. 1989-July 1992).

LC QH301   ISSN 0952-8245
DD 574   UK
Pr Rev.
BULLETIN - OVERSEAS DEVELOPMENT NATURAL RESOURCES INSTITUTE. See Agriculture.

LC QH301   ISSN 0922-7911
DD 574   NE
BULLETIN - ROYAL TROPICAL INSTITUTE. [Bull. - R. Trop. Inst.]. **VFOAT** Bulletins of the Royal Tropical Institute. (1988)-. Monographic series. English (French). Four times a year. Price varies per volume. Koninklijk Instituut voor de Tropen, Mauritskade 63, 1092 AD Amsterdam Netherlands. **Tel** 011 31 20 5688272, FAX 011 31 20 5688286. **Ad Acc. Continues** Bulletin - Department of Agriculture Research of the Royal Tropical Institute, 0370-1670.
Ind/Abst Rural Dev. Abstr.; Sorghum Mill. Abstr.

LC QH301
DD 574   FR
BULLETIN SEMENCES. Bulletin. French. Four times a year. FNAMS, 74 rue Jean Jacques Rousseau, 75001 Paris France. **Tel** 011 33 1 42336713.

LC QH301
DD 574   FR
BULLETIN SIGNALETIQUE SCIENCES BIOLOGIQUES ET BIOMEDICALES SECTION 931. Bulletin. English (French). Irregular. Institut de l'Information Scientique et Technique (INIST), 2 Allee du Parc de Brabois, 54514 Vandoeuvre Nancy Cedex France. **Tel** 011 33 83 504600, FAX 011 33 83 504650.

LC QH301   ISSN 0732-9393
DD 574   US
BULLETIN - SOCIETY OF WETLAND SCIENTISTS (U.S.). (BULLETIN / SOCIETY OF WETLAND SCIENTISTS.). [Bull. - Soc. Wetland Sci. (U. S.)]. **Added/Corp** Society of Wetland Scientists (U.S.). **VFOAT** Wetlands Bulletin. (198?)-. Bulletin. English. Three times a year. $50.00. Society of Wetland Scientists, Box 1897, Lawrence KS 66044. **Tel** (913)843-1235, FAX (913)843-1274. **ED** Lyndon C Lee. **Bk Rev. Ad Acc.**

Circ: 900.
Desc: Events, activities, book reviews and other news of interest to wetland scientists.

LC QH301 **ISSN** 0007-7356
DD 574 HU
BUVAR. [Buvar]. **Added/Corp** Tudomanyos Ismeretterjeszto Tarsulat. Tudomanyos Ismeretterjeszto Vallalat. (1960)-. Periodical. Hungarian. Twelve times a year. $32.00. Lapkiado Vallalat, Lenin Korut 9-11, 1073 Budapest 7 Hungary. **Tel** 011 36 1 222408. **(Subscription address:** Kultura, PO Box 143, H-1300 Budapest 3 Hungary. **Tel** 011 36 1 2500194.**) ED** Gyorgy Lanyi. **Bk Rev. Ad Acc. Circ:** 20,000. available with charts; available with illustrations.
Ind/Abst Bibliogr. Agric.

LC QH301
DD 574 FR
CAHIER TECHNIQUE DU BIOLOGISTE, LE. (19??)-. French. Four times a year (Jan., Apr., July, Oct.). 350.00F France; 450.00F other. Centre National Biologistes, 80 Avenue du Maine, 75014 Paris France. **Tel** 011 33 43229770, FAX 011 33 43217312.
Desc: Information about medical prescriptions.

ISSN 0703-0967
DD 574/.05 CN
CAHIERS DE BIOLOGIE (OTTAWA. 1973). (CAHIERS DE BIOLOGIE.). No. 1-. Periodical. French (French and English).

LC QH301
DD 574 FR
CAHIERS DE CANCEROLOGIE. BIOLOGIE CLINIQUE THERAPEUTIQUE. **See** Medical Sciences-Cancer and Neoplastic Syndromes.

LC QH301 **ISSN** 0957-0330
DD 574 UK
CODEN CSBIED
CAMBRIDGE STUDIES IN BIOTECHNOLOGY. [Camb. stud. biotechnol.]. (1985)-. Monographic series. English. Cambridge University Press, 32 East 57th Street, New York NY 10022.
Ind/Abst Biol. Abstr. (1985-); Curr. Cit.

LC QH301 **ISSN** 0263-9424
DD 574/.0151 UK
NLM W1 CA4539M **CODEN** CSMBDC
CAMBRIDGE STUDIES IN MATHEMATICAL BIOLOGY. [Camb. stud. math. biol.]. (1980)-. Monographic series. English. Irregular. Price varies per volume. Cambridge University Press, The Edinburgh Building, Shaftesbury Road, Cambridge CB2 2RU United Kingdom. **Tel** 011 44 1223 312393, FAX 011 44 1223 315052, telex 851-817256. **(Subscription address:** Cambridge University Press / North America, 110 Midland Avenue, Port Chester NY 10573. **Tel** (800)431-1580, (914)937-9600.**)** Documents available from BIOSIS Document Express.
Desc: Series covering biology, mathematics and biometry.
Ind/Abst Biol. Abstr.; Math. Rev.; Zentralbl. Math. Ihre Grenzgeb.

LC QH301
DD 574 UK
CAMBRIDGE STUDIES IN MODERN BIOLOGY. (1980)-. Monographic series. English. Irregular. Price varies per volume. Cambridge University Press, The Edinburgh Building, Shaftesbury Road, Cambridge CB2 2RU United Kingdom. **Tel** 011 44 1223 312393, FAX 011 44 1223 315052, telex 851-817256. **(Subscription address:** Cambridge University Press / North America, 110 Midland Avenue, Port Chester NY 10573. **Tel** (800)431-1580, (914)937-9600.**)**

LC QH301 **ISSN** 0148-9739
DD 574 US
NLM W1 CA874T **CODEN** CABRDF
CAROLINA BIOLOGY READERS. [Carol. biol. readers]. **Added/Corp** Carolina Biological Supply Company. (19??)-. Monographic series. English. Carolina Biological Supply Company, 2700 York Road, Burlington NC 27215. **Tel** (919)584-0381, FAX (919)584-0381, telex 574354. ***Continues*** *Oxford Biology Readers.*

ISSN 0045-5865
DD 574 US
CAROLINA TIPS. [Carol. tips]. **Added/Corp** Carolina Biological Supply Company. Vol. 1 (1938)-. Periodical. English. Four times a year. Free on request. Carolina Biological Supply Co, 2700 York Road, Burlington NC 27215. **Tel** (919)584-0381, FAX (919)584-3399, telex 574-354. **ED** Barbara Kuyper. **Circ:** 125,000 (ctrl).
Desc: Articles for science teachers.

LC QH **ISSN** 0323-0627
DD 574 XR
CODEN CASNAH
CASOPIS SLEZSKEHO MUZEA. SERIE A, VEDY PRIRODNI. [Cas. Slez. muz., Ser. A, Vedy prir.]. **Added/Corp** Slezske Muzeum v Opave. **VFOAT** Vedy Prirodni. (1977)-. Periodical. Czech (German and English; summaries and/or abstracts in Russian). Three times a year. **(Subscription address:** Artia Pegas Press Ltd., Palac Metro Narodni Trida 25, 11210 Prague 1 Czech Republic. **Tel** 011 42 2 24196265, 011 42 2 24196266.**)** Documents available from BIOSIS Document Express. ***Continues*** *Casopis Slezskeho Muzea. Series A, Scientiae Naturales.*
Ind/Abst Biol. Abstr. (-1979); Crop Physiol. Abstr.; For. Abstr.; GeoRef; Hortic. Abstr.; Ornamental Hort. (1991-); Seed Abstr.

ISSN 0164-5609
DD 574 US
NLM W1; CB15
CBE VIEWS. [CBE views]. **Added/Corp** Council of Biology Editors. **VAT** Council of Biology Editors Views. Vol. 1, No. 1 (Feb. 1978)-. Periodical. English. Six times a year (Feb., Apr., June, Aug., Oct., Dec.). $38.00. Council of Biology Editors, 1 Illinois Center, 111 East Wacker Drive, Chciago IL 60601. **Tel** (312)616-0800, FAX (312)616-0223. **ED** Gisella Pollock. **Bk Rev,** (Qty: 6-10). **Ad Acc. Circ:** 1,200 (ctrl). Documents available from Documents on Demand.
Desc: Serves as a vehicle for publication of original articles and for the exchange of information and ideas among professionals concerned with publishing in the life sciences.
Ind/Abst Energy Inf. Abstr.; Environ. Abstr.

LC QH **ISSN** 0069-2379
DD 574 CE
NLM W1 CE939G **CODEN** CYJBA2
CEYLON JOURNAL OF SCIENCE. BIOLOGICAL SCIENCES. [Ceylon j. sci., Biol. sci.]. **Added/Corp** University of Sri Lanka, Peradeniya Campus. University of Ceylon, Colombo. University of Ceylon, Peradeniya. Vol. 1 (Dec. 1957)-. Periodical. English. Two times a year. Sales Centre / University Peradeniya, PO Box 35, Peradeniya Sri Lanka. **Tel** 011 94 8 88678. Documents available from BIOSIS Document Express. ***Formed by the union of*** *Ceylon Journal of Science. Section A: Botany, 0366-8460; Ceylon Journal of Science. Section B: Zoology, 0366-8479* ***and*** *Ceylon Journal of Science. Section C: Fisheries.*
Ind/Abst Biodeter. Abstr. (1991-); Biol. Abstr. (-1986); For. Abstr.; GeoRef; Life Sci. Collect.; Protozoolog. Abstr.; Rev. Med. Vet. Entomol.

ISSN 0714-9956
DD 574/.06/071 CN
CFBS NEWSLETTER / CANADIAN FEDERATION OF BIOLOGICAL SOCIETIES. [CFBS newsl.]. **VFOAT** Bulletin de Nouvelles de la FC-SB. **VAT** Canadian Federation of Biological Societies Newsletter; Bulletin de la Federation Canadienne des Societes de Biologie. No. 1-. Newsletter. English (French). Two times a year. Canadian Federation of Biological Sciences, 360 Booth Street, Ottawa Ontario K1R 7K4 Canada. ***Continues*** *Bulletin de la Federation Canadienne, 0068-8681.*

LC QP501.C43 **ISSN** 1074-5521
DD 574.19/2/05 US
NLM W1; CH359
•**CHEMISTRY & BIOLOGY.** **Added/Corp** Current Biology Ltd. Current Science Group. **VFOAT** Chemistry and Biology. (1994)-. Periodical. English. Twelve times a year. $535.00. Current Science, 20 North 3rd Street, Philadelphia PA 19106. **Tel** (215)574-2266, (800)552-5866, FAX (215)574-2270.

LC QP501
DD 574.19/2/ US
CHEMISTRY AND BIOLOGY OF MINERALIZED TISSUES : PROCEEDINGS OF THE SECOND INTERNATIONAL CONFERENCE ON THE CHEMISTRY AND BIOLOGY OF MINERALIZED TISSUES, THE. **See** Chemistry and Chemicals.

ISSN 0742-0528
DD 574 UK
CCC
NLM W1; CH972T **CODEN** CHBIE4
Pr Rev.
CHRONOBIOLOGY INTERNATIONAL. [Chronobiol. int.]. **Added/Corp** International Society for Chronobiology. Vol. 1, No. 1 (1984)-. Academic Scholarly Publication. English. Six times a year. $350.00. Lippincott - Raven Publishers, 227 East Washington Square, Philadelphia PA 19106. **Tel** (215)238-4200, (800)777-2295, FAX (215)238-4227. **ED** A. Reinberg and M. Smolensky. available on microfilm and microfiche from University Microfilms International (UMI). Documents available from The Genuine Article, CASDDS.
Desc: A multidisciplinary journal encompassing biological-rhythm investigations of periodicity in all life forms.
Ind/Abst Anim. Breed. Abstr.; Chem. Abstr. (1984-); CSA Neuro. Abstr. (1985-?); Curr. Aware. Biol. Sci., CABS; Curr. Cit.; Curr. Contents Life Sci.; Ergon. Abstr. (Vol. 1 No. 1, 1984-); Health Plan. Adminis.; Helminthol. Abstr.; Index Med. (Vol. 1, No. 1, 1984-); Index Vet.; Protozoolog. Abstr.; Psychol. Abstr. (1984-); PsycINFO; PsycLit; Res. Alert [Select. Cov.]; Rev. Med. Vet. Entomol.; Sci. Cit. Index; SCISEARCH; Soc. Sci. Cit. Index [Select. Cov.]; Vet. Bull.

LC QH301 **ISSN** 0009-6768
DD 574 EC
CODEN CINQAN
CIENCIA Y NATURALEZA. [Cienc. nat.]. **Added/Corp** Universidad Central del Ecuador. Instituto de Ciencias Naturales. Vol. 1 (June 1957)-. Periodical. Spanish. One time a year. Free on request. Universidad Central / Ecuador, Instituto de Ciencias Naturales, POB 633, Quito Canje Ecuador. Documents available from BIOSIS Document Express. ***Supersedes*** *Universidad Central del Ecuador. Instituto de Ciencias Naturales. Boletin del Instituto de Ciencias Naturales.*
Ind/Abst Biol. Abstr.; Field Crop Abstr.; GeoRef; Grass. Forage Abstr.

LC QH301 **ISSN** 0138-7154
DD 574/.05 CU
CODEN CIBIDA
CIENCIAS BIOLOGICAS. [Cienc. biol.]. No. 1-. Periodical. Spanish (summaries and/or abstracts in English). Academia de Ciencias de Cuba, Industria No 452, La Habana 2 Cuba. Documents available from BIOSIS Document Express.
Ind/Abst Biol. Abstr.; Life Sci. Collect.; Plant Breed. Abstr.

LC QH83 .C49 **ISSN** 0748-3007
DD 574 US
UDC 57.06:59 **CCC**
CODEN CLADEC
Pr Rev.
CLADISTICS. (CLADISTICS : THE INTERNATIONAL JOURNAL OF THE WILLI HENNIG SOCIETY.). [Cladistics]. Vol. 1, No. 1 (Winter 1985)-. Academic Scholarly Publication. English. Four times a year. $188.23. Academic Press Ltd., A Division of Harcourt Brace & Company Ltd., 24-28 Oval Road, London NW1 7DX United Kingdom. **Tel** 011 44 171 2674466, FAX 011 44 171 4822293, 011 44 171 4854752, telex 25775 ACPRES G. **(Subscription address:** Harcourt Brace & Company, Ltd., Foots Cray High Street, Sidcup Kent DA14 5HP United Kingdom. **Tel** 011 44 181 3003322, FAX 011 44 181 3090807, telex 896 377 ACADEM.**) ED** R T Schuh and J G West. **Bk Rev. Ad Acc. Circ:** 425. Documents available from The Genuine Article, BIOSIS Document Express.
Desc: Provides tools for systematists that often challenge existing ideas and theories regarding evolution and taxonomy. Covers theory, method, the philosophical aspects of systematics, and the role of systematic and evolutionary studies in the investigation of biogeographical and other general biological phenomena.
Ind/Abst AGRICOLA [Select. Cov.]; Biol. Abstr. (1985-); Curr. Cit.; Curr. Contents Agric. Biol. Environ. Sci.; Ecol. Abstr.; Geol. Abstr.; Plant Breed. Abstr.; Res. Alert [Full Cov.]; Sci. Cit. Index; SCISEARCH.

LC QH301 **ISSN** 0962-8827
DD 574 UK
CCC
NLM W1; CL6928 **CODEN** CDYSEJ
CLINICAL DYSMORPHOLOGY. **Added/Corp** UK Dysmorphology Club. Vol. 1, No. 1 (Jan. 1992)-. Periodical. English. Four times a year. $278.00. Chapman & Hall, 2-6 Boundary Row, London SE1 8HN United Kingdom. **Tel** 011 44 171 8650066, FAX 011 44 171 5229623, telex 290164 CHAPMA G. **ED** Michael Baraitser, Dian Donnai, Robin Winter. Documents available from ADONIS.
Desc: Devoted to publishing reports of multiple congenital anomaly syndromes and original studies and review articles on the aetiology, clinical delineation, genetic mapping, and molecular embryology of birth defects. Publishes succinct case reports, with particular emphasis on previously undescribed conditions, rare findings and ethnic differences in existing syndromes, foetal abnormalities and cytogenetic aberrations that might give clues to the localization of developmental genes.
Ind/Abst ADONIS; Index Med.

LC QH301 **ISSN** 0392-1905
DD 574 IT
NLM W3 C162HP **CODEN** CESYDD
CLINICAL ENZYMOLOGY SYMPOSIA. [Clin. enzymol. symp.]. (1977)-. Academic Scholarly Publication. English. **ED** A Brulina and L Galzigna. Documents available from CASDDS.
Ind/Abst Chem. Abstr.

ISSN 0270-1847
DD 574 US
CCC
NLM W1 CO133C **CODEN** CHMSDK
COLD SPRING HARBOR MONOGRAPH SERIES. [Cold Spring Harbor monogr. ser.]. **Added/Corp** Cold Spring Harbor Laboratory. **VFOAT** Monograph. 9A (1979)-. Academic Scholarly Publication. English. Irregular. Price varies per volume. Cold Spring Harbor Laboratory, 10 Skyline Drive, Plainview NY 11803. **Tel** (516)349-1930, (800)843-4388, FAX (516)349-1946. Documents available from BIOSIS Document Express, CASDDS.
Desc: A series in various areas of molecular biology,

cancer, genetics, etc.
Ind/Abst Biol. Abstr.; Chem. Abstr.; Curr. Cit.; Life Sci. Collect.

LC QH301 .C6 ISSN 0091-7451
DD 574/.05 US
  CCC
NLM W3 C162R CODEN CSHSAZ
COLD SPRING HARBOR SYMPOSIA ON QUANTITATIVE BIOLOGY. (COLD SPRING HARBOR SYMPOSIA ON QUANTITATIVE BIOLOGY : PROCEEDINGS.). [Cold Spring Harbor symp. quant. biol.]. **Added/Corp** Long Island Biological Association (N.Y.) Biological Laboratory (Cold Spring Harbor, N.Y.) Cold Spring Harbor Laboratory. **VFOAT** Symposia on Quantitative Biology; Quantitative Biology. Vol. 1 (1933)-. Academic Scholarly Publication. English. One time a year. $95.00 (paperback), $210.00 (cloth). Cold Spring Harbor Laboratory, 10 Skyline Drive, Plainview NY 11803. **Tel** (516)349-1930, (800)843-4388, FAX (516)349-1946. Index available. **Circ:** 3,000. Documents available from The Genuine Article, BIOSIS Document Express, CASDDS. **Continues** Annual Report : Cold Spring Harbor, New York. Laboratory of Quantitative Biology.
Ind/Abst AGRICOLA [Select. Cov.]; Anim. Breed. Abstr.; Biol. Agric. Index; Biol. Abstr.; Chem. Abstr.; Curr. Aware. Biol. Sci., CABS; Curr. Contents Life Sci.; EMBASE; Energy Res. Abstr.; Health Plan. Adminis.; Index Med.; INIS Atomindex [Micro.]; Life Sci. Collect.; Ref. Upd. Basic Ed.; Ref. Upd. Deluxe Ed.; Res. Alert [Full Cov.]; Sci. Cit. Index; SCISEARCH.

LC QH ISSN 0588-2206
DD 574 FR
COLLECTION "LES GRANDS PROBLEMES DE LA BIOLOGIE". (1966)-. Monographic series. French. Irregular. Price varies per volume. Masson Editeur, BP 22, 41354 Vineuil Cedex France. **Tel** 011 33 54 504612, FAX 011 33 54 504611.

LC QH301 ISSN 0078-1053
DD 574 CN
  CODEN CNORE2
COLLECTION NORDICANA. [Collect. Nord.]. **Added/Corp** Universite Laval. Centre d'Etudes Nordiques. No. 30 (1970)-. Monographic series. French (English; summaries and/or abstracts in English). Irregular. Price varies per volume. University of Laval, Centre Etudes Nordiques, BP 2208, Laval Quebec G1K 7P4 Canada. **Tel** (418)656-3340. **ED** Ivan Grenier. **Circ:** 1,000. **Continues** Travaux Divers (Universite Laval. Centre d'Etudes Nordiques)., 0079-8339.
Desc: Publishes works on Nordic research.

LC QH301 ISSN 0069-6285
DD 574 US
COLUMBIA BIOLOGICAL SERIES.
Monographic series. English. Irregular. Price varies per volume. Columbia University Press, 136 South Broadway, Irvington NY 10533. **Tel** (914)591-9111. **Continues** Columbia University Biological Series.

LC QH301 .C655 ISSN 0894-8550
DD 574/.01 UK
  CCC
NLM W1; CO375NF CODEN CTBIEK
COMMENTS ON THEORETICAL BIOLOGY. (COMMENTS ON MODERN BIOLOGY. PART C, COMMENTS ON THEORETICAL BIOLOGY.). [Comments theor. biol.]. Vol. 1, No. 1 (Dec. 1988)-. Periodical. English. Six times a year (1 volume). $339.00 (academic institutions), $529.00 (corporate institutions). Gordon & Breach Science Publishers, PO Box 90, Reading, Berkshire RG1 8JL United Kingdom. **Tel** 011 44 1734 560080, FAX 011 44 1734 568211.

LC QH301
DD 574 US
COMPACT CAMBRIDGE LIFE SCIENCES COLLECTION [COMPUTER FILE]. See Science and Technology.

LC Q2 .A26 ISSN 0764-4469
DD 574/.05 FR
  CCC
NLM W1; CO454T; 8503078 CODEN CRASEV
Pr Rev.
COMPTES RENDUS DE L'ACADEMIE DES SCIENCES. SERIE III, SCIENCES DE LA VIE. [C. r. Acad. sci., Ser. 3, Sci. vie]. **Added/Corp** Academie des Sciences (France). **VFOAT** Sciences de la Vie. Vol. 298 No. 1 (Jan. 7, 1984)-. Academic Scholarly Publication. French (summaries and/or abstracts in English). Twelve times a year. $885.82. Gauthier-Villars, 15 rue Gossin, 92543 Montrouge Cedex France. **Tel** 33 1 40 92 65 00, FAX 33 1 40 92 65 97. (**Subscription address:** Centrale des Revues, 11 rue Gossin, 92543 Montrouge Cedex France. **Tel** 011 33 1 46565266.) Documents available from The Genuine Article, CASDDS. **Continues** Comptes Rendus des Seances de l'Academie des Sciences. Serie III, Sciences de la Vie, 0249-6313.
Ind/Abst AgBiotech News Inf.; Anim. Breed. Abstr.; Biocont. News Inf. (19??-19??); Biodeter. Abstr.; Chem. Abstr. (1984-); Crop Physiol. Abstr.; Curr. Aware. Biol. Sci., CABS; Curr. Cit.; Curr. Contents Agric. Biol. Environ. Sci.; Curr. Contents Life Sci.; Curr. Ref. Fish Res.; Dairy Sci. Abstr.; Ecol. Abstr.; EMBASE; Field Crop Abstr.; Geogr. Abstr. Phys. Geogr.; Geol. Abstr.; Grass. Forage Abstr.; Health Plan. Adminis.; Helminthol. Abstr. (19??-19??); Index Med. (1984-); Index Vet.; Maize Abstr.; Nematol. Abstr.; Nutr. Abstr. Rev., Ser. B, Live Feeds and Feed.; Ornamental Hort. (19??-19??); Life Sci. Collect.; PESTDOC; Pig News Inf.; Plant Breed. Abstr.; Plant Genet. Resour. Abstr.; Plant Grow. Reg. Abstr.; Potato Abstr.; Poult. Abstr.; Protozoolog. Abstr.; Res. Alert; Rev. Med. Vet. Entomol.; Rev. Med. Vet. Mycology; Rev. Plant Pathol.; Rice Abstr.; Sci. Cit. Index; SCISEARCH; Sorghum Mill. Abstr.; Soyabean Abstr.; Vet. Bull.; Wildl. Rev.; Zentralbl. Math. Ihre Grenzgeb.

LC QH301 ISSN 0037-9026
DD 574 FR
  CCC
  CODEN CRSBAW
COMPTES RENDUS DES SEANCES DE LA SOCIETE DE BIOLOGIE ET DES SES FILIALES. [C. r. seances soc. biol. fil.]. **Main/Corp** Societe de Biologie, (Paris, France). (1940)-. Academic Scholarly Publication. French. Six times a year. $228.78. Masson Editeur, BP 22, 41354 Vineuil Cedex France. **Tel** 011 33 54 504612, FAX 011 33 54 504611. Documents available from The Genuine Article, BIOSIS Document Express, CASDDS. **Continues** Comptes Rendus des Seances et Memoires de la Societe de Biologie et des ses Filiales et Associees.
Ind/Abst AGRICOLA; Aquat. Sci. Fish. Abstr. [CD-ROM Ed.]; Biol. Abstr.; Chem. Abstr.; Crop Physiol. Abstr.; Curr. Cit.; Curr. Contents Life Sci.; EMBASE; For. Prod. Abstr. (1991-); For. Abstr.; Health Plan. Adminis.; Hortic. Abstr.; Index Med.; Index Vet.; Nutr. Abstr. Rev., Ser. B, Live Feeds and Feed.; Ornamental Hort.; Life Sci. Collect.; PESTDOC; Plant Breed. Abstr.; Plant Grow. Reg. Abstr.; Protozoolog. Abstr.; Res. Alert [Full Cov.]; Rev. Med. Vet. Entomol.; Rice Abstr.; Sci. Cit. Index; SCISEARCH; Soyabean Abstr.; Vet. Bull.; Wildl. Rev.

LC QH301 ISSN 0326-1956
DD 574 AG
NLM W1; CO427VG CODEN COBIEJ
Pr Rev.
COMUNICACIONES BIOLOGICAS.
[Comun. biol.]. Vol.1, No.1 (August 1982)-. Academic Scholarly Publication. English (summaries and/or abstracts in Spanish). Four times a year. $40.00. Instituto Biologia Celular, Facultad de Medicina, Buenos Aires 1121 Argentina. **Tel** 011 54 1 8245070. **ED** Amanda Pellegrino de Iraldi and Analia Nessi de Avimon. Index available. **Circ:** 300 (ctrl). Documents available from CASDDS.
Desc: Includes short communications, review articles, full length papers, and technical notes.
Ind/Abst Chem. Abstr.; EMBASE.

LC QH301 ISSN 0871-1755
DD 574 PO
COMUNICACOES DO INSTITUTO DE INVESTIGACAO CIENTIFICA TROPICAL, SERIE DE CIENCIAS BIOLOGICAS.
(19??)-. Monographic series. Portuguese. Irregular. Price varies per volume. Instituto de Investigacao Cientifica Tropical, Centro de Documentacao e Informacao, rua Jau 47, 1 300 Lisbon Portugal. **Tel** 645321. **Circ:** 1,000 (ctrl).

LC QH302 .Q4
DD 574.072 CN
CONTRIBUTIONS DE LA STATION BIOLOGIQUE DU ST-LAURENT A TROIS-PISTOLES, P. Q., CANADA.
Main/Corp Station Biologique du St-Laurent. No. 1 (1933)-. Monographic series. English. Irregular. Price varies per volume. Universite Laval, Quebec G1K 7P4 Canada.

LC QH301 .C675 ISSN 0160-5313
DD 574/.05 US
  CODEN CBGMDW
Pr Rev.
CONTRIBUTIONS IN BIOLOGY AND GEOLOGY. [Contrib. biol. geol.]. **Added/Corp** Milwaukee Public Museum. No. 1 (1974)-. Monographic series. English. Irregular. Price varies per volume. Milwaukee Public Museum, 800 West Wells Street, Milwaukee WI 53233. **Tel** (414)278-2702. **ED** Rodney Watkins. **Circ:** 500. Documents available from BIOSIS Document Express.
Desc: Research, systematics and natural history published approximately seven times per year. Emphasis is on paleontology and herpetology but not limited to these subjects.
Ind/Abst Biol. Abstr.; Fish Rev. (19??-199?); GeoRef; Wildl. Rev.

LC QH95.8 .C67 ISSN 0278-324X
DD 574.909/42 US
  CODEN CRENDZ
CORAL REEF NEWSLETTER. See Earth Sciences-Oceanography.

LC RC321 .C73 ISSN 0892-0915
DD 599 US
  CCC
NLM W1; CR216ZD CODEN CCNBE8
CRITICAL REVIEWS IN NEUROBIOLOGY. See Medical Sciences-Neurology.

LC QH301 ISSN 0143-2044
DD 574
  CCC
  CODEN CRLED9
Pr Rev.
CRYO LETTERS. [Cryo-Letters]. Vol. 1 (Oct. 1979)-. Academic Scholarly Publication. English. Six times a year (Feb., April, June, Aug., Oct., Dec.). $180.00. Cryoletters, 7 Wooton Way, Cambridge CB3 9LX United Kingdom. **Tel** 011 44 1223 68315, FAX 011 44 1223 420502. **ED** Felix Franks. Index available (Bound in December issue). **Bk Rev,** (Qty: 6). **Ad Acc. Circ:** 250 (ctrl). Documents available from The Genuine Article, BIOSIS Document Express, CASDDS.
Desc: Low temperature sciences, technology, physics chemistry, biology, medicine and agriculture.
Ind/Abst AgBiotech News Inf.; AGRICOLA [Select. Cov.]; Anim. Breed. Abstr.; Biol. Abstr.; Chem. Abstr.; Curr. Aware. Biol. Sci., CABS; Curr. Cit.; Curr. Contents Life Sci.; Dairy Sci. Abstr.; Field Crop Abstr.; Hortic. Abstr.; Ornamental Hort. (1991-); Pig News Inf.; Plant Breed. Abstr.; Plant Genet. Resour. Abstr.; Potato Abstr.; Res. Alert [Full Cov.]; Rev. Agric. Entomol.; Sci. Cit. Index; SCISEARCH; Sug. Indus. Abstr.

LC QH301 ISSN 0181-1568
DD 574 FR
  CODEN CRALD9
Pr Rev.
CRYPTOGAMIE. ALGOLOGIE. [Cryptogam., Algol.]. **Added/Corp** Laboratoire de Cryptogamie (Museum National d'Histoire Naturelle). **VFOAT** Algologie. Vol.1, No. 1 (1980)-. Academic Scholarly Publication. French (English, German, Spanish and Italian). Four times a year. $83.11. Cryptogamie, 12 rue de Buffon, 75005 Paris France. **Tel** 33 1 40793184. **ED** Françoise Ardre. **Bk Rev,** (Qty: 4). **Circ:** 400 (ctrl). Documents available from The Genuine Article, BIOSIS Document Express, CASDDS. **Continues** Revue Algologique, 0035-0702.
Desc: Covers algology: systematics, biology, ecology, and physiology.
Ind/Abst Aquat. Sci. Fish. Abstr. [CD-ROM Ed.]; Biol. Abstr.; Chem. Abstr.; Curr. Contents Agric. Biol. Environ. Sci.; Ecol. Abstr.; Geogr. Abstr. Phys. Geogr.; GeoRef; Mar. Sci. Contents Tables; Life Sci. Collect.; Res. Alert [Select. Cov.]; SCISEARCH.

LC QH301 .I475 ISSN 0733-4443
DD 016.574 UK
CURRENT AWARENESS IN BIOLOGICAL SCIENCES. See Biology-Abstracting, Bibliographies and Statistics.

LC QH301 .C85 ISSN 0960-9822
DD 574/.05 UK
  CCC
NLM W1; CU69L CODEN CUBLE2
Pr Rev.
CURRENT BIOLOGY. (CURRENT BIOLOGY : CB.). [Curr. biol.]. **VFOAT** CB. Vol. 1, No. 1 (Feb. 1991)-. Academic Scholarly Publication. English. Twelve times a year. $393.00. Current Science / England, Middlesex House, 34-42 Cleveland Street, London W1P 6LB United Kingdom. **Tel** 011 44 171 5808393, 011 44 171 3230323, FAX 011 44 171 5805646. (**Subscription address:** Current Science, 20 North 3rd Street, Philadelphia PA 19106. **Tel** (800)552-5866.) **Ad Acc.** ctrl circ. Documents available from CASDDS.
Desc: Directed toward researchers, educators and students of biology. Presents review articles from an area of concentration covering an entire year's literature with annotated references.
Ind/Abst AgBiotech News Inf.; Anim. Breed. Abstr.; Chem. Abstr.; Curr. Aware. Biol. Sci., CABS; Curr. Cit.; Index Med.; Plant Breed. Abstr.; Plant Genet. Resour. Abstr.; Ref. Upd. Deluxe Ed.; Soc. Sci. Cit. Index [Select. Cov.].

LC Z5321 .C87 QH301 ISSN 0011-3409
DD 016.574 US
NLM ZW 1 C959
CURRENT CONTENTS. LIFE SCIENCES.
See Biology-Abstracting, Bibliographies and Statistics.

LC QP351 .C885 ISSN 0959-4388
DD 591.1/88 UK
  CCC
NLM W1; CU799GFQ CODEN COPUEN
CURRENT OPINION IN NEUROBIOLOGY. See Medical Sciences-Neurology.

LC QH506 .C86 ISSN 0959-440X
DD 574.8/8/05 UK
CCC
NLM W1; CU799GI CODEN COSBEF

CURRENT OPINION IN STRUCTURAL BIOLOGY. [Curr. opin. struct. biol.]. **VFOAT** Structural Biology. Vol. 1, No. 1 (Feb. 1991)-. Academic Scholarly Publication. English. Six times a year. $548.50. Current Science / England, Middlesex House, 34-42 Cleveland Street, London W1P 6LB United Kingdom. **Tel** 011 44 171 5808393, 011 44 171 3230323, FAX 011 44 171 5805646. **(Subscription address:** Current Science, 20 North 3rd Street, Philadelphia PA 19106. **Tel** (800)552-5866.**) ED** W. A. Hendrickson and Sir Aaron Klug. **Ad Acc.** ctrl circ. available on diskette. Documents available from CASDDS.
Desc: Directed towards researchers, educators and students of structural biology. Presents review articles from an area of concentration covering an entire year's literature with annotated references. Each issue features a bibliography of the current world literature published during the previous year.
Ind/Abst Chem. Abstr.; Curr. Aware. Biol. Sci., CABS; Curr. Cit.; Index Med.; Ref. Upd. Deluxe Ed.

LC QH
DD 574 US
Pr Rev.

CURRENT PROTOCOLS IN MOLECULAR BIOLOGY. (19??)-. English. Four times a year. $440.00. John Wiley & Sons, Inc., 605 Third Avenue, New York NY 10158-0012. **Tel** (212)850-6000, (212)850-6645, FAX (212)850-6088, telex 12-7063. **(Subscription address:** John Wiley & Sons / UK, Baffins Lane, Chichester, West Sussex PO19 1UD United Kingdom. **Tel** 011 44 1243 779777, FAX 011 44 243 776128, telex 86290 WIBOOKG.**) ED** Brent Ausubel. Index available. cum. index. ctrl circ.

LC QH320.G7 C87 ISSN 0267-1956
DD 574/.072041 UK
NLM QH 320.G7; C976

CURRENT RESEARCH IN BRITAIN. BIOLOGICAL SCIENCES. (CURRENT RESEARCH IN BRITAIN. BIOLOGICAL SCIENCES : CRB.). [Curr. res. Br., Biol. sci.]. **Added/Corp** British Library. Lending Division. British Library. Document Supply Centre. **VFOAT** CRB. Biological Sciences; Biological Sciences. 1st Edition (1985)-. Monographic series. English. Irregular (4 volumes). Price varies. Longman Group Ltd., Fourth Avenue, Longman House, Harlow Essex CM19 5SR United Kingdom. **Tel** 011 44 1279 429655, FAX 011 44 1279 431067, telex 81259. **(Subscription address:** Southport Brook Distribution Ltd., 12-14 Slaidburn Cres Southport, Merseyside PR9 9TF United Kingdom. **Tel** 011 44 1704 26881.**)** available on an online database from Orbit Search Service. Documents available from BLDSC. ***Continues in part*** *Research in British Universities, Polytechnics and Colleges.*

LC QH301 .C86 ISSN 0732-4413
DD 574/.05 US
CODEN CDBID9

CURRENT TOPICS IN CHINESE SCIENCE. SECTION D, BIOLOGY. [Curr. top. Chin. sci., Sect. D, Biol.]. **VFOAT** Biology. Vol. 1 (1982)-. English. One time a year. Gordon & Breach Science Publishers, Inc., PO Box 786, Cooper Station, New York NY 10276. **Tel** (212)206-8900, FAX (212)645-2459. Documents available from BIOSIS Document Express.
Ind/Abst Biol. Abstr. (-1982).

LC QH
DD 574 UK

•CYTOKINE AND GROWTH FACTOR REVIEWS. (1995)-. English. Four times a year. $334.00. Pergamon Press, An Imprint of Elsevier Science Ltd., The Boulevard, Langford Lane, Kidlington, Oxford OX5 1GB United Kingdom. **Tel** 011 44 1865 843000, 011 44 1865 843699, FAX 011 44 1865 843010. **(Subscription address:** Elsevier Science Ltd. / Oxford Fulfillment Centre, PO Box 800, Kidlington OX5 1DX United Kingdom. **Tel** 011 44 865 843355.**)** available on an online database from Elsevier Electronic Subscriptions (EES). ***Continues*** *Progress in Growth Factor Research.*

LC QK600
DD 589.2 UK

DESCRIPTIONS OF FUNGI & BACTERIA. (19??)-. Academic Scholarly Publication. English. Two times a year. $84.00 (one-year), $159.60 (two-year). CAB International Centre, Wallingford, Oxfordshire OX10 8DE United Kingdom. **Tel** 011 44 1491 832111, FAX 011 44 1491 833508, telex 847964 COMAGG G.

ISSN 0012-1606
DD 574 US
CCC
NLM W1 DE997Q CODEN DEBIAO
Pr Rev.

DEVELOPMENTAL BIOLOGY. [Dev. biol.]. **Added/Corp** Society for Developmental Biology. Vol. 1 (April 1959)-. Academic Scholarly Publication. English. Sixteen times a year. $2036.00. Academic Press Inc., 6277 Sea Harbor Drive, Orlando FL 32887. **Tel** (800)543-9534, (407)345-4100, FAX (407)352-3445. **ED** Peter J. Bryant. Documents available from The Genuine Article, BIOSIS Document Express, CASDDS.
Desc: Publishes original analytical research on mechanisms of development, differentiation, growth, regeneration, and tissue repair in plants and animals at the molecular, cellular, and genetic levels.
Ind/Abst Acad. Search; AgBiotech News Inf.; AGRICOLA [Select. Cov.]; Anim. Breed. Abstr.; Biol. Agric. Index; Biol. Abstr.; Calcium Calcif. Tissue Abstr.; Chem. Abstr.; Chemorecept. Abstr.; Crop Physiol. Abstr.; CSA Neuro. Abstr.; Curr. Aware. Biol. Sci., CABS; Curr. Cit.; Curr. Contents Life Sci.; Curr. Ref. Fish Res.; Dairy Sci. Abstr.; EMBASE; Energy Res. Abstr.; Entomol. Abstr.; EP Collect.; Fish Rev.; Gen. Sci. Index (1992-); Gen. Sci. Source; Genet. Abstr.; Health Plan. Adminis.; Helminthol. Abstr. (1991-); Homework Help.; Hortic. Abstr.; Immunol. Abstr.; Index Med.; INFO-SOUTH Abstr.; INIS Atomindex [Micro.]; Int. Aerosp. Abstr.; Mag. Search; Maize Abstr.; MasterFile FullTEXT 1000; MasterFile FullTEXT 350; MasterFile FullTEXT 650; MasterFile FullTEXT (July 1994-); Microbiol. Abstr. Sect. C; Nematol. Abstr.; Nucl. Acids Abstr.; Nutr. Abstr. Rev., Ser. B, Live Feeds and Feed.; Nutr. Abstr. Rev., Ser. A, Hum. Exp.; OCLC; Oncog. Growth Factors Abstr.; Life Sci. Collect.; Pig News Inf.; Plant Breed. Abstr.; Poult. Abstr.; Protozoolog. Abstr.; Ref. Upd. Basic Ed.; Ref. Upd. Deluxe Ed.; Res. Alert [Full Cov.]; Rev. Agric. Entomol.; Rev. Med. Vet. Entomol.; Sci. Cit. Index; SCISEARCH; Telebase.

LC QH ISSN 0166-0861
DD 574 NE
NLM W1 DE997VK CODEN DBBID6

DEVELOPMENTS IN BIOENERGETICS AND BIOMEMBRANES. Vol. 1 (1977)-. Monographic series. English. Irregular. Price varies per volume. Elsevier Science Publishers BV, PO Box 211, 1000 AE Amsterdam Netherlands. **Tel** 011 31 20 4853641, 011 31 20 4853642, FAX 011 31 20 4853598. Documents available from CASDDS.
Desc: Series covering biological transport and membranes.
Ind/Abst Chem. Abstr.

LC RS189 .D45 ISSN 0301-5149
DD 660/.6 SZ
CCC
NLM W3 DE615E CODEN DVBSA3

DEVELOPMENTS IN BIOLOGICAL STANDARDIZATION. (DEVELOPMENTS IN BIOLOGICAL STANDARDIZATION / EDITED BY THE INTERNATIONAL ASSOCIATION OF BIOLOGICAL STANDARDIZATION.). [Dev. biol. stand.]. **Added/Corp** International Union of Microbiological Societies. International Association of Biological Standardization. **VFOAT** Biological Standardization. Vol. 23, (1974)-. Monographic series. English (French). Two times a year. 220.00F (approx. per volume). S. Karger AG, Allschwilerstrasse 10, PO Box, CH-4009 Basel Switzerland. **Tel** 011 41 61 3061111, FAX 011 41 61 3061234, telex CH 962 652. Documents available from BIOSIS Document Express, CASDDS. ***Formed by the union of*** *Progress in Immunobiological Standardization, 0079-6344* ***and*** *Symposia Series in Immunobiological Standardization, 0082-0768.*
Desc: The International Association of Biological Standardization organizes international meetings towards confronting the numerous practical problems involved in standardization, and as a means of uniting researchers with manufacturers, public health authorities, and government officials. Books in this series, which record these meetings, are respected as definitive references to current work on international biological standards, biological reference preparations, and biological reference reagents.
Ind/Abst AGRICOLA [Select. Cov.]; Biol. Abstr.; Chem. Abstr. (?-1986); Curr. Cit.; Ei Page One; EMBASE; Index Med.; Index Vet.; Life Sci. Collect.; Ref. Upd. Deluxe Ed.; Vet. Bull.

LC QH5 ISSN 1169-0356
DD 570 FR
UDC 57

DIMANCHES BIOLOGIQUES DE LARIBOISIERE ... . **Added/Corp** Association des Pharmaciens Directeurs de Laboratoires d'Analyses Biologiques (France). (?960)-. Monographic series. French. One time a year. Price varies per volume. Documents available from CASDDS.
Ind/Abst Chem. Abstr.

LC QH
DD 574 US

DOCUMENTS ON BIOLOGY. 1- 1970-. English. Irregular. Gordon & Breach Science Publishers, Inc., PO Box 786, Cooper Station, New York NY 10276. **Tel** (212)206-8900, FAX (212)645-2459.

LC QH
DD 574 TU

DOGA BILIM DERGISI. SERI A2, BIYOLOJI. Vol. 8 (1984)-. Turkish (summaries and/or abstracts in English). $10.00 (overseas). Tubitak, Ataturk Bulvari, No: 221, 06100 Kavaklidere Ankara Turkey. ***Continues*** *Doga Bilim Dergisi. Seri A.*
Ind/Abst Dairy Sci. Abstr.

LC QH ISSN 1010-7576
DD 574 TU
CODEN DBSEEC

DOGA. TURK BIYOLOJI DERGISI = DOGA. TURKISH JOURNAL OF BIOLOGY. [Doga, Turk biyol. derg.]. **Added/Corp** Turkiye Bilimsel ve Teknik Arastrma Kurumu. **VFOAT** Turk Biyoloji Dergisi; Turkish Journal of Biology; Biyoloji Serisi; Biology Series; Doga. Turkish Journal of Biology; Doga. Biyoloji Serisi; Doga. Biology Series. Vol 1., No. 1 (Dec. 1976)-. Academic Scholarly Publication. English (Turkish and German). Four times a year. $100.00. Tubitak, Ataturk Bulvari, No: 221, 06100 Kavaklidere Ankara Turkey. **(Subscription address:** Tubitak, Bilimsel Dergiler, Yazi Isleri Mudurlugu, PO Box 5, Kizilay 06420 Ankara Turkey. **Tel** 011 90 312 4685300 ext. 1122, 011 90 312 4270493, FAX 011 90 312 4271336.**) ED** Ahmet Noyan. **Circ:** 700. Documents available from CASDDS. ***Continues*** *Doga Bilim Dergisi. Seri A2, Biyoloji, 1010-0909.*
Desc: Covers genetics, microbiology, cytology, physiology and environmental ecology.
Ind/Abst Biol. Abstr.; Chem. Abstr. (1986-); Field Crop Abstr.; Hortic. Abstr.; Seed Abstr.

ISSN 0012-4966
DD 570 US
CCC
CODEN DKBSAS

DOKLADY. BIOLOGICAL SCIENCES. [Dokl., Biol. sci.]. **Main/Corp** Akademiia Nauk SSSR. **Added/Corp** Consultants Bureau. Consultants Bureau Enterprises. **VFOAT** Biological Sciences. (Jan./June 1964)-. Periodical. English (Russian). Six times a year. $1085.00. MAIK Nauka / Interperiodica, Ulitsa Profsoyuznaia 90, Moscow 117864 Russia. **(Subscription address:** Plenum Press Subscription Department, PO Box 730, Canal Street, Station NY 10013-1578. **Tel** (212)620-8000, (212)620-8466.**) ED** A.A. Baev. Index available. available on microfilm and microfiche from University Microfilms International (UMI). ***Continues in part*** *Akademiia Nauk SSSR. Doklady. Biological Sciences Sections, 0886-7534.*
Ind/Abst AgBiotech News Inf.; AGRICOLA (1984); Bibliogr. Agric.; Biocont. News Inf.; Biodeter. Abstr.; Biol. Abstr. (1974-); Coal Abstr.; Crop Physiol. Abstr.; Dairy Sci. Abstr.; EMBASE; Energy Res. Abstr.; Fish Rev.; For. Abstr.; Helminthol. Abstr.; Hortic. Abstr.; Index Vet.; INIS Atomindex [Micro.]; NAPRALERT; Nutr. Abstr. Rev., Ser. B, Live Feeds and Feed.; Plant Breed. Abstr.; Potato Abstr.; Protozoolog. Abstr.; Rev. Agric. Entomol.; Rev. Med. Vet. Entomol.; Rev. Plant Pathol.; Small Anim. Abstr. Bibliogr.; Soils Fert.; Soyabean Abstr.; Weed Abstr.; Wheat Barley Trit. Abstr.; Wildl. Rev.

LC QH540 ISSN 1012-1692
DD 574.5 VE

ECOTROPICOS : REVISTA DE LA SOCIEDAD VENEZOLANA DE ECOLOGIA. **See** Environmental Issues-Ecology.

LC QH301 .E37
ER
CODEN EATBEC

EESTI TEADUSTE AKADEEMIA TOIMETISED. BIOLOOGIA. **Added/Corp** Eesti Teaduste Akadeemia. **VFOAT** Bioloogia; Biologiia; Biology; Izvestiia Akademii nauk Estonii. Biologiia; Proceedings of the Estonian Academy of Sciences. Biology. (1990)-. Academic Scholarly Publication. English (Estonian, French, German and Russian). Four times a year. $132.95. Kirjastus Perioodika, Pk 107, Parnu Mnt 8, Tallinn EE0090 Estonia. **Tel** 011 372 2 441365, FAX 011 372 2 442484. **(Subscription address:** East View Publications Inc., 3020 Harbor Lane North, Suite 110, Minneapolis MN 55447. **Tel** (800)477-1005, (612)550-0961, FAX (612)559-2931.**)** Documents available from BIOSIS Document Express, CASDDS. ***Continues*** *Eesti NSV Teaduste Akadeemia Toimetised. Bioloogia, 0013-2144.*
Ind/Abst Anim. Breed. Abstr.; Biocont. News Inf. (1991-); Biol. Abstr. (1990-); Chem. Abstr.; Crop Physiol. Abstr.; Field Crop Abstr.; Plant Breed. Abstr.; Plant Grow. Reg. Abstr.; Potato Abstr.; Rev. Agric. Entomol.; Wheat Barley Trit. Abstr.

LC QH301 ISSN 0724-6706
DD 574 US
CCC
NLM W1; EI507

EINSTEIN QUARTERLY, THE. (THE EINSTEIN QUARTERLY JOURNAL OF BIOLOGY AND MEDICINE.). [Einstein q.]. **Added/Corp** Albert Einstein College of Medicine. **VFOAT** Einstein Quarterly. Vol. 1, No. 1 (April 1982)-. Academic Scholarly Publication. English. Four times a year. $104.00. Springer-Verlag New York Inc., 175 Fifth Avenue, New York NY 10010. **Tel** (212)460-1500 ext 256, FAX (212)533-3503, telex 232 235 SPB UR. **(Subscription address:** Springer-Verlag New York Inc. / North America, PO Box 2485, Journal Fulfillment, Secaucus NJ 07096. **Tel** (201)348-4033, (800)777-4643, FAX (201)348-4505.**) ED** L Rosenthal and S Douros. available in microform from University Microfilms International (UMI). Documents available from CASDDS.
Desc: Presents investigations into disciplines at the interface of medicine and the social sciences -

medico-legal and technical studies, epidemiology and public policy, and the history of medicine - in addition to basic scientific research and clinical investigations.
Ind/Abst Chem. Abstr.; Curr. Cit.

LC QH506 .E46 **ISSN** 0261-4189
DD 574.8/8/05 UK
CCC
NLM W1 EM369D **CODEN** EMJODG
Pr Rev.

EMBO JOURNAL, THE. [EMBO j.]. **Added/Corp** European Molecular Biology Organization. **VFOAT** E.M.B.O. Journal. **VAT** European Molecular Biology Organization Journal. Vol. 1, No. 1 (1982)-. Academic Scholarly Publication. English. Twenty-four times a year. $825.00. Oxford University Press / UK, Walton Street, Oxford OX2 6DP United Kingdom. **Tel** 011 44 1865 56767, FAX 011 44 1865 267773, telex 851/837330 OXPRES G. **(Subscription address:** Oxford University Press / USA, Journals Marketing Department, Oxford University Press, 2001 Evans Road, Cary NC 27513. **Tel** (800)451-7556, (919)677-0977, FAX (919)677-1714.**) ED** M. Birnstiel and J. Tooze. available on microfilm and microfiche from University Microfilms International (UMI). Documents available from The Genuine Article, BIOSIS Document Express, CASDDS.
Desc: Covers genetics, gene structure, replication and expression, cell biology, virology, macromolecular structure, molecular genetics, immunology, neurobiology, plant molecular biology, etc.
Ind/Abst AgBiotech News Inf.; AGRICOLA [Select. Cov.]; Anim. Breed. Abstr.; Biol. Agric. Index; Biol. Abstr.; Biotechnol. Res. Abstr.; Chem. Abstr.; Chem. Titles; Crop Physiol. Abstr.; CSA Neuro. Abstr.; Curr. Aware. Biol. Sci., CABS; Curr. Biotechnol.; Curr. Cit.; Curr. Contents Life Sci.; Curr. Ref. Fish Res.; Dairy Sci. Abstr.; EMBASE; Entomol. Abstr.; For. Abstr.; Genet. Abstr.; Health Plan. Adminis.; Helminthol. Abstr. (19??-19??); Hortic. Abstr.; Hum. Genome Abstr.; Immunol. Abstr.; Index Med. (1982-); Index Vet.; Maize Abstr.; Microbiol. Abstr. Sect. B; Microbiol. Abstr. Sect. C; Nematol. Abstr.; Nucl. Acids Abstr.; Oncog. Growth Factors Abstr.; Ornamental Hort. (1991-); Life Sci. Collect.; PESTDOC; Plant Breed. Abstr.; Plant Genet. Resour. Abstr.; Plant Grow. Reg. Abstr.; Postharvest News Inf.; Potato Abstr.; Poult. Abstr.; Protozoolog. Abstr.; Ref. Upd. Basic Ed.; Ref. Upd. Deluxe Ed.; Res. Alert [Full Cov.]; Rev. Agric. Entomol.; Rev. Med. Vet. Entomol.; Rev. Med. Vet. Mycology; Rev. Plant Pathol.; Rice Abstr.; Sci. Cit. Index; SCISEARCH; Soils Fert.; Soyabean Abstr.; Vet. Bull.; Trop. Dis. Bull.; Virol. AIDS Abstr.; Weed Abstr.; Wheat Barley Trit. Abstr.

LC QH301
DD 574 US

EMERGENCY BIOLOGICS LOCATIONS ... WASHINGTON STATE / DEPARTMENT OF HEALTH, DIVISION OF HEALTH INFORMATION, COMMUNICABLE DISEASE EPIDEMIOLOGY SECTION. **Added/Corp** Washington (State). Division of Health Information. Communicable Disease Epidemiology Section. (1991)-. English. ***Continues*** *Emergency Biologics Listing ... Washington State.*

LC QH301
DD 574 US

ENCYCLOPEDIA OF BIOETHICS. (19??)-. English. Prentice Hall Simon & Schuster, PO Box 11071, Des Moines IA 50336. **Tel** (800)947-7700, (515)284-6751.

LC QH301 **ISSN** 0957-3518
DD 574 UK

ENDOTHELIUM. (19??)-. English. Twenty-four times a year. £110.00. SUBIS, Mansion House 19 Kingfield Road, Sheffield S11 9AS United Kingdom. **Tel** 011 44 114 2554433, FAX 011 44 114 255 4626. **Bk Rev. Ad Acc.** available on diskette.
Desc: Current awareness service for researchers in clinical and life sciences.

LC QH301 .E58 **ISSN** 0970-0420
DD 574/.05 II
UDC 614.7
CODEN ENECEV

ENVIRONMENT & ECOLOGY. [Environ. ecol.]. **VFOAT** Environment and Ecology. (1983)-. Periodical. English. Four times a year. $100.00. Prof Qrt, No H-2 Ground Floor, Kalyani 741235 West Bengal India. **(Subscription address:** Prints India, 11 Darya Ganj, New Delhi 110002 India. **Tel** 011 91 11 3268645, FAX 011 91 11 3275542, telex 31-61087 PRIN-IN.) available on CD-ROM. Documents available from CASDDS.
Ind/Abst AgBiotech News Inf.; AGRICOLA; Agrofor. Abstr. (1991-); Biocont. News Inf. (1991-); Biodeter. Abstr. (1991-); Chem. Abstr. (1986-); Cot. Trop. Fibr. Abstr. Bibliogr.; Crop Physiol. Abstr.; CSA Neuro. Abstr. (?-?); Curr. Cit.; Dairy Sci. Abstr.; Ecol. Abstr.; Entomol. Abstr.; Environ. Period. Bibliogr.; Field Crop Abstr.; Fluid Abstr., Civil Eng.; Fluid Abstr. Proc. Eng.; FLUIDEX (199?-); Food Sci. Technol. Abstr.; Geogr. Abstr. Phys. Geogr.; Grass. Forage Abstr.; Health Saf. Sci. Abstr.; Helminthol. Abstr. (19??-19??); Hortic. Abstr.; Int. Dev. Abstr.; Irr. Drain. Abstr.; Maize Abstr.; Microbiol. Abstr. Sect. C; Nematol. Abstr.; Nutr. Abstr. Rev., Ser. B, Live Feeds and Feed.; Ornamental Hort.; Plant Breed. Abstr.; Plant Grow. Reg. Abstr.; Pollut. Abstr. Indexes; Potato Abstr.; Protozoolog. Abstr.; Rev. Agric. Entomol.; Rev. Med. Vet. Entomol.; Rev. Plant Pathol.; Rice Abstr.; Seed Abstr.; Soils Fert.; Sorghum Mill. Abstr.; Soyabean Abstr.; Toxicol. Abstr. (19??-); Wheat Barley Trit. Abstr.

LC QH301 **ISSN** 0094-7237
DD 574 US
CODEN EVBLBS

ENVIRONMENTAL BIOLOGY. (ENVIRONMENTAL BIOLOGY; REPORT.). Vol. 1; Aug. 1972-. Monographic series. English. Irregular. Price varies per volume. Cornell University / Entomology & Limology Department, Ithaca NY 14850. **Tel** (407)255-2080. Documents available from BIOSIS Document Express.
Ind/Abst Biol. Abstr.

LC QH301
DD 574 UZ

ESH LENINCHI : UZBEKISTON LKSM MARKAZII KOMITETINING ORGANI. **Added/Corp** Uzbekiston LKSM. Markazii Komiteti. (1925)-. Newspaper. Uzbek. Irregular (208 issues). **(Subscription address:** East View Publications Inc., 3020 Harbor Lane North, Suite 110, Minneapolis MN 55447. **Tel** (800)477-1005, (612)550-0961, FAX (612)559-2931.**)**

LC QH301
DD 574 US

ESSENTIAL MOLECULAR BIOLOGY. (1991)-. Monographic series. English. Irregular. Price varies per volume. Oxford University Press / UK, Walton Street, Oxford OX2 6DP United Kingdom. **Tel** 011 44 1865 56767, FAX 011 44 1865 267773, telex 851/837330 OXPRES G. **(Subscription address:** Oxford University Press / USA, Journals Marketing Department, Oxford University Press, 2001 Evans Road, Cary NC 27513. **Tel** (800)451-7556, (919)677-0977, FAX (919)677-1714.**) ED** T.A. Brown. available with illustrations.

LC QH301
DD 574 FR
NLM W1; EU576L **CODEN** EROBE4

EUROBIOLOGISTE, L'. **Added/Corp** Centre National des Biologistes (France). (1989)-. Periodical. French (summaries and/or abstracts in English). Six times a year (Feb., Apr., June, Aug., Oct., Dec.). $153.10. Centre National Biologistes, 80 Avenue du Maine, 75014 Paris France. **Tel** 011 33 43229770, FAX 011 33 43217312. ***Continues*** *Le Biologiste (Paris), 0981-6003.*

LC QH301 **ISSN** 0777-0553
DD 574 BE
NLM W1; EU612F **CODEN** EABIEB
TITLE CHANGE

EUROPEAN ARCHIVES OF BIOLOGY. [Eur. arch. biol.]. Vol. 100 (1989)-(19??). Academic Scholarly Publication. English (French). Vaillant Carmanne SA, Zeven Puttensraat 20, 3690 Zutendaal, Belgium. **Tel** 011 31 1122 3361. **(Subscription address:** Swets Publishing Service, PO Box 825, 2160 SZ Lisse, The Netherlands. **Tel** 011 31 2521 35111.) Documents available from BIOSIS Document Express, CASDDS. ***Continues*** *Archives of Biology, 0773-6185.* ***Merged into*** *European Journal of Morphology, 0924-3860.*
Ind/Abst Anim. Breed. Abstr.; Biol. Abstr.; Chem. Abstr.; Curr. Contents Agric. Biol. Environ. Sci.; Fish Rev. (Jan. 1989-July 1992); SCISEARCH; Wildl. Rev. (Jan. 1989-July 1992).

LC QH84.8 .R47 **ISSN** 1164-5563
DD 574.909/4/8 FR
CCC
CODEN EJSBE2

•**EUROPEAN JOURNAL OF SOIL BIOLOGY.** **See** Agriculture-Crop Production and Soils.

LC QK564
DD 589.3 US

EXPERIMENTAL PHYCOLOGY. (1991)-. Monographic series. English. Irregular. Price varies per volume. Springer-Verlag New York Inc., 175 Fifth Avenue, New York NY 10010. **Tel** (212)460-1500 ext 256, FAX (212)533-3503, telex 232 235 SPB UR. **(Subscription address:** Springer-Verlag New York Inc. / North America, PO Box 2485, Journal Fulfillment, Secaucus NJ 07096. **Tel** (201)348-4033, (800)777-4643, FAX (201)348-4505.**)**
Desc: The articles in these volumes are centered on major themes of current interest to algologists and cell biologists.

LC QH301 .F33 **ISSN** 0892-6638
DD 574/.0724 US
CCC
NLM W1; FA9618 **CODEN** FAJOEC
Pr Rev.

FASEB JOURNAL, THE. (THE FASEB JOURNAL : OFFICIAL PUBLICATION OF THE FEDERATION OF AMERICAN SOCIETIES FOR EXPERIMENTAL BIOLOGY.). [FASEB j.]. **Added/Corp** Federation of American Societies for Experimental Biology. **VFOAT** FJ. **VAT** Federation of American Societies for Experimental Biology Journal. Vol. 1, No. 1 (July 1987)-. Academic Scholarly Publication. English. Fifteen times a year. $310.00. Federation of American Societies for Experimental Biology, Room L-2310, 9650 Rockville Pike, Bethesda MD 20814-3998. **Tel** (301)530-7027. **ED** William J Whelan. Index available. **Bk Rev. Ad Acc. Circ:** 24,000. available on microfilm and microfiche from University Microfilms International (UMI). Documents available from The Genuine Article, BIOSIS Document Express, CASDDS. ***Continues*** *Federation Proceedings / Federation of American Societies for Experimental Biology, 0014-9446.*
Desc: Publishes brief, definitive, and essentially final research communications of broad interest that are considered to warrant prompt publication, and state-of-the-art reviews, drawn, as far as possible, from the topics of the FASEB symposia.
Ind/Abst AgBiotech News Inf.; AGRICOLA [Select. Cov.]; Anim. Breed. Abstr.; Biol. Agric. Index; Biol. Abstr. (1987-); Biol. Dig.; Chem. Abstr.; Chem. Titles; CSA Neuro. Abstr. (?-?); Curr. Aware. Biol. Sci., CABS; Curr. Cit.; Curr. Contents Life Sci.; Dairy Sci. Abstr.; EMBASE; Energy Res. Abstr.; Field Crop Abstr.; Food Sci. Technol. Abstr.; Health Plan. Adminis.; Helminthol. Abstr. (1991-); Hortic. Abstr.; Immunol. Abstr.; Index Med. (1987-); Index Vet.; INIS Atomindex [Micro.]; Int. Aerosp. Abstr.; Maize Abstr.; Nutr. Abstr. Rev., Ser. B, Live Feeds and Feed.; Nutr. Abstr. Rev., Ser. A, Hum. Exp.; Nutr. Res. Newsl.; Oncog. Growth Factors Abstr.; Life Sci. Collect.; PESTDOC; Poult. Abstr.; Protozoolog. Abstr.; Ref. Upd. Basic Ed.; Ref. Upd. Deluxe Ed.; Res. Alert [Full Cov.]; Rev. Med. Vet. Entomol.; Rev. Med. Vet. Mycology; Risk Abstr.; Sci. Cit. Index; SCISEARCH; Seed Abstr.; Soc. Sci. Cit. Index [Select. Cov.]; Vet. Bull.; Trop. Dis. Bull.; Weed Abstr.

LC QH301 **ISSN** 0428-2779
DD 574 FR
NLM W1 FE852 **CODEN** FBIOAA

FEUILLETS DE BIOLOGIE. [Feuill. biol.]. **VFOAT** Repertoire Medical Pratique. Serie Biologie. Vol. 1 (June 1960)-. Academic Scholarly Publication. French. Six times a year (Jan., Mar., May, July, Sept., Nov.). $162.81. Editions Orion, 9 Avenue du Bel Air, 95870 Bezons France. **Tel** 011 33 1 39472260. Index available. cum. index. **Ad Acc. Circ:** 4,000 (ctrl). Documents available from BIOSIS Document Express, CASDDS.
Desc: News and reviews are reserved to directors of biological laboratories, hospitals or private.
Ind/Abst Biol. Abstr.; Chem. Abstr.; EMBASE; Energy Res. Abstr. (April 1982-).

ISSN 0701-9033
DD 574.9714 CN
UDC 57

FICHIER BIOLOGIQUE. Vol. 1 (Nov. 1977)-. Periodical. French. Twelve times a year. Free. Service Information Nature Module de Biologie et de Biochimie, Universite de Quebec a Trois-Rivieres, CP 599, Trois-Rivieres Quebec G9A 5H7 Canada.

LC QH345 .F473 **ISSN** 0533-1153
UN

FIZIOLOGICHESKI AKTIVNYE VESHCHESTVA. **Added/Corp** Akademiia Nauk URSR, Kiev. Instytut Organichnoi Khimii. (1966)-. Russian. Documents available from CASDDS.
Ind/Abst Chem. Abstr.

LC QH301 **ISSN** 0985-2662
DD 574 FR
CCC

FLASH ETAT-UNIS. (19??)-. Academic Scholarly Publication. French. Eleven times a year. $374.00. Editions Scientifique Elsevier, 141 rue de Javel, 75747 Paris Cedex 15 France. **Tel** 011 33 1 45589067, FAX 011 33 1 45589424. **(Subscription address:** Editions Scientifiques Elsevier / for North America, PO Box 7247-7576, Philadelphia PA 19170-7576. **)**

LC QH301 **ISSN** 0985-2654
DD 574 FR
CCC

FLASH JAPON. (19??)-. Academic Scholarly Publication. French. Eleven times a year. $374.00. Editions Scientifique Elsevier, 141 rue de Javel, 75747 Paris Cedex 15 France. **Tel** 011 33 1 45589067, FAX 011 33 1 45589424. **(Subscription address:** Editions Scientifiques Elsevier / for North America, PO Box 7247-7576, Philadelphia PA 19170-7576. **)**

LC QH301 **ISSN** 0095-0157
DD 574 US
CODEN FMPUA4

FLORIDA MARINE RESEARCH PUBLICATIONS. [Fla. mar. res. publ.]. **Added/Corp** Florida. Marine Research Laboratory. No. 1 (1973)-. Monographic series. English. Price varies per volume. Department of Natural Resources / Florida, Marine Research Laboratory, St Petersburg FL 33731. **Tel** (813)896-8626. Documents available from BIOSIS Document Express. ***Supersedes*** *Professional Papers Series - Florida Department of Natural Resources. Marine Research Laboratory, 0160-4473; Special Scientific Report; Technical Series (Florida. Dept. of Natural Resources), 0149-4015; Educational Series, 0094-2693; Leaflet Series* ***and*** *Salt Water Fisheries Leaflet Series.*
Ind/Abst Aquat. Sci. Fish. Abstr. [CD-ROM Ed.]; Biol. Abstr.; Fish Rev. (Jan. 1989-July 1992); GeoRef; Ocean. Abstr.; Life Sci. Collect.; Wildl. Rev. (Jan. 1989-July 1992).

LC QH1 .F66 **ISSN** 0098-8251
DD 574/.08 US
FOCUS : BIOLOGY. **VFOAT** Biology. (1975)-. English. One time a year. Dushkin Publishing Group Inc., Sluice Dock, Guilford CT 06437. **Tel** (203)453-4351, (800)243-6532, FAX (203)453-6000. **ED** John W. Crane.
Desc: Collection of public press articles covering current issues in biology. Includes topic guide and complete index.

LC QH301 R **ISSN** 1350-4975
DD 574 610 UK
NLM ZW1; F652
•**FOCUS ON BRITISH BIOLOGICAL AND MEDICAL SCIENCES RESEARCH.**
Added/Corp British Library. Document Supply Centre. (1994)-. Bibliography. English. Twelve times a year. £26.00 UK; £31.00 other. British Library / Document Supply Centre, Boston Spa, Wetherby West Yorkshire LS23 7BQ United Kingdom. **Tel** 011 44 1937 546060, FAX 011 44 1937 546333, telex 557381. **(Subscription address:** Turpin Distribution Services Limited, Blackhorse Road, Letchworth, Hertfordshire SH6 1HN United Kingdom. **Tel** 011 44 1462 672555, FAX 011 44 1462 480947.**)** Index available. **Ad Acc.** Documents available from BLDSC.

LC QH301 **ISSN** 0533-1242
DD 574 US
NLM W1 FO1002R
Pr Rev.
FOCUS (ROCKVILLE). (FOCUS.). **VFOAT** Digest - National Center for Health Services Research and Development. No. 1- Feb. 1969-. Periodical. English. Four times a year. Free. Life Technologies Inc, 8400 Helgerman Court, PO Box 6009, Gaithersburg MD 20877. **Tel** (800)828-6686. **ED** Nancy L Sasavage. Index available. cum. index. **Circ:** 50,000 (ctrl).
Desc: Techniques in the life sciences.

LC QH301 .F6 **ISSN** 0015-5500
DD 574.05/6 XR
CCC
NLM W1 FO1279 **CODEN** FOBLAN
Pr Rev.
FOLIA BIOLOGICA. [Folia biol.]. **Added/Corp** Ceskoslovenska Akademie Ved. Vol. 1 (1955)-. Academic Scholarly Publication. Czech (English and Russian; summaries and/or abstracts in German). Six times a year. $196.79. Academic Press Ltd., A Division of Harcourt Brace & Company Ltd., 24-28 Oval Road, London NW1 7DX United Kingdom. **Tel** 011 44 171 2674466, FAX 011 44 171 4822293, 011 44 171 4854752, telex 25775 ACPRES G. **(Subscription address:** Harcourt Brace & Company, Ltd., Foots Cray High Street, Sidcup Kent DA14 5HP United Kingdom. **Tel** 011 44 181 3003322, FAX 011 44 181 3090807, telex 896 377 ACADEM.**) ED** J. Riman and L. Hlozanek. Index Available, published separately, free-automatically sent. Documents available from The Genuine Article, BIOSIS Document Express, CASDDS. ***Supersedes in part** Ceskoslovenska Biologie, 0411-6038.*
Desc: Presents experimental papers, preliminary reports, and occasional review articles in the areas of molecular, cellular, and developmental genetics. Also covers cytology, immunology, and radiobiology.
Ind/Abst Biol. Abstr.; Chem. Abstr.; CSA Neuro. Abstr. (?-?); Curr. Aware. Biol. Sci., CABS; Curr. Cit.; Curr. Ref. Fish Res.; EMBASE; Health Plan. Adminis.; Index Med.; Nutr. Abstr. Rev., Ser. B, Live Feeds and Feed.; Plant Breed. Abstr.; Poult. Abstr.; Res. Alert [Full Cov.]; Saf. Health Work; Sci. Cit. Index; SCISEARCH; Vet. Bull.

LC QL799 .F6 **ISSN** 0015-5659
DD 591.4 PL
NLM W1 FO255 **CODEN** FOMOAJ
FOLIA MORPHOLOGICA. **See** Zoology.

LC QH545.W3 F67 **ISSN** 0130-5824
DD 574.5 RU
CODEN FKKVD5
FORMIROVANIE I KONTROL KACESTVA POVERHNOSTNYH VOD. (FORMIROVANIE I KONTROL KASHESTVA POVERKHNOSTNYKH VOD.). [Form. kontrol kac. poverhn. vod]. **Added/Corp** Instytut Hidrobiolohii (Akademiia Nauk Ukrainskoi RSR) Vsesoiuznyi Nauchno-Issledovatelskii Institut po Okhrane Vod. (1975)-. Academic Scholarly Publication. Russian. Izdatelstvo Naukova Dumka / Ukrainian Academy of Sciences, Yu. A. Khramov, Dir., Ul. Repina 3, 252 601 Kiev Ukraine. **Tel** 011 7 44 4303441, 011 7 44 2254182, telex 131376. Documents available from CASDDS.
Ind/Abst Chem. Abstr. (-1976).

LC LF2402 .A24
DD 378.1/553/0943375 GW
FORSCHUNGSBERICHT DER UNIVERSITAET AUGSBURG. **Main/Corp** Universitat Augsburg. (1989)-. German. Every 3 years.

LC QH301 **ISSN** 0015-9298
DD 574 XN
CODEN FRBAAB
FRAGMENTA BALCANICA - MUSEI MACEDONICI SCIENTARIUM NATURALIUM. (FRAGMENTA BALCANICA.). [Fragm. balc. - Mus. Maced. Sci. Nat.]. Vol. 1 (1954)-. Monographic series. Serbo-Croatian (Cyrillic). Price varies per volume. Documents available from BIOSIS Document Express.
Ind/Abst AGRICOLA; Biol. Abstr.; Life Sci. Collect.; Wheat Barley Trit. Abstr.

LC QH96.A1 F73 **ISSN** 0046-5070
DD 574.92/9/05 UK
CCC
CODEN FWBLAB
Pr Rev.
FRESHWATER BIOLOGY. [Freshw. biol.]. **Added/Corp** Freshwater Biological Association. Vol. 1 (March 1971)-. Academic Scholarly Publication. English. Six times a year. $965.00. Blackwell Scientific Publications Ltd, Marston Book Services, PO Box 88, Oxford OX2 ONE United Kingdom. **Tel** 011 44 1865 206206, FAX 011 44 1865 206219, telex 837 515 MARDIS G. **ED** C. R. Townsend and A. G. Hildrew. Index available. **Bk Rev. Ad Acc. Circ:** 1,000. available on microfilm and microfiche from University Microfilms International (UMI). Documents available from The Genuine Article, BIOSIS Document Express, CASDDS.
Desc: Covers all aspects of the ecology of lakes and rivers.
Ind/Abst Abstr. Bull. Inst. Pap. Sci. Tech.; AGRICOLA; AQUAREF; Aquat. Sci. Fish. Abstr. [CD-ROM Ed.]; Biol. Agric. Index; Biol. Abstr.; Chem. Abstr.; Coal Abstr.; Curr. Cit.; Curr. Contents Agric. Biol. Environ. Sci.; Curr. Ref. Fish Res.; Ecol. Abstr.; Ecology Abstr.; EMBASE; Energy Res. Abstr. (June 1974-); Entomol. Abstr.; Environ. Period. Bibliogr.; Fish Rev.; For. Abstr.; Fresh. Aqua. Contents Tables; Geogr. Abstr. Phys. Geogr.; Geogr. Abstr. Human Geogr.; Geol. Abstr.; Helminthol. Abstr.; Microbiol. Abstr. Sect. C; Life Sci. Collect.; Pollut. Abstr. Indexes; Protozoolog. Abstr.; Res. Alert [Full Cov.]; Rev. Med. Vet. Entomol.; Rev. Med. Vet. Mycology; Rev. Plant Pathol.; Sci. Cit. Index; SCISEARCH; Weed Abstr.; Wildl. Rev.

LC QH96.A1 F733 **ISSN** 0961-4664
DD 574.92/9/05 UK
CODEN FRFOE9
FRESHWATER FORUM. **Added/Corp** Freshwater Biological Association. (1991)-. Periodical. English. Three times a year (Mar., July, Nov.). $102.67. Ferry House, Far Sawrey, Ambleside, Cumbria LA22 0LP United Kingdom. **Tel** 011 44 161 539 442468, FAX 011 44 161 539 446914. ***Continues** Freshwater Biological Association. Annual Report - Freshwater Biological Association, 0374-7646.*

LC QH301
DD 574 US
FUNDAMENTALS OF MEDICAL CELL BIOLOGY. Periodical. English. $90.25. JAI Press Inc., 55 Old Post Road, Suite 2, PO Box 1678, Greenwich CT 06836-1678. **Tel** (203)661-7602, FAX (203)661-0792. **ED** E. Edward Bittar.

LC R97.7.K6 K37 **ISSN** 0377-9483
KO
NLM W1 KA89K **CODEN** KTUNAA
GATORRIG DAIHAG UIHAG-BU RONMUN-JIB. **See** Medical Sciences.

LC QH **ISSN** 0386-4766
DD 574 JA
CODEN SAIBD8
GEKKAN SAIBO. (GEKKAN SAIBO = THE CELL.). [Gekkan saibo]. **VFOAT** Saibo; Cell. (1969)-. Periodical. Japanese. Twelve times a year. $345.00. Nyu Saiensusha Co. Ltd., 1-3-25 Sendagaya, Shibuga-ku, Tokyo 151 Japan. **Tel** 011 81 3 54748500, FAX 011 81 3 54748900. Documents available from CASDDS.
Ind/Abst Chem. Abstr.

LC QH301 .G425 **ISSN** 0251-1223
DD 574/.05 II
CODEN GBOSBU
GEOBIOS (JODHPUR). (GEOBIOS.). [Geobios]. **Added/Corp** University of Jodhpur. Vol. 1 (Jan. 1974)-. English. Six times a year. $50.00. Geobios International, PO Box 14, Botany Department, Jodhpur 342 001 India. **Tel** 011 91 41428. **(Subscription address:** Prints India, 11 Darya Ganj, New Delhi 110002 India. **Tel** 011 91 11 3268645, FAX 011 91 11 3275542, telex 31-61087 PRIN-IN.**) ED** David N Sen (editor's address: PO Box 14, Botany Department, University of Jodhpur, Jodhpur 342 001 India). Index available. cum. index. **Bk Rev. Circ:** 500 (ctrl). Documents available from The Genuine Article, BIOSIS Document Express, CASDDS.
Desc: Publications of research papers on life sciences with ecological bias.
Ind/Abst Biodeter. Abstr.; Biol. Abstr.; Chem. Abstr.; Curr. Cit.; Curr. Contents Phys. Chem. Earth Sci.; EMBASE; Field Crop Abstr.; Geol. Abstr.; Nutr. Abstr. Rev., Ser. B, Live Feeds and Feed.; Nutr. Abstr. Rev., Ser. A, Hum. Exp.; Plant Breed. Abstr.; Res. Alert [Select. Cov.]; Rev. Med. Vet. Mycology; SCISEARCH; Seed Abstr.; Wheat Barley Trit. Abstr.

LC QH301 .G427
DD 574/.05 II
GEOBIOS NEW REPORTS. **Added/Corp** University of Jodhpur. Vol. 1, No. 1 (1982)-. Academic Scholarly Publication. English. Two times a year. $60.00. Geobios International, PO Box 14, Botany Department, Jodhpur 342 001 India. **Tel** 011 91 41428. **(Subscription address:** Prints India, 11 Darya Ganj, New Delhi 110002 India. **Tel** 011 91 11 3268645, FAX 011 91 11 3275542, telex 31-61087 PRIN-IN.**) ED** David N Sen. Index available. **Bk Rev. Circ:** 300 (ctrl). Documents available from BIOSIS Document Express.
Desc: Reports new species of plants and animals.
Ind/Abst Biodeter. Abstr. (1991-); Biol. Abstr.; EMBASE; Helminthol. Abstr.; Rev. Med. Vet. Mycology; Rev. Plant Pathol.; Seed Abstr.; Sorghum Mill. Abstr.

LC QH77.C2 C33 **ISSN** 1195-3101
DD 574/.05 CN
CCC
•**GLOBAL BIODIVERSITY.** (GLOBAL BIODIVERSITY / CANADIAN MUSEUM OF NATURE.). [Glob. biodivers.]. **Added/Corp** Canadian Museum of Nature. Vol. 3, No. 1 (Summer 1993)-. Periodical. English. Four times a year. 50.00Can$. Canadian Museum of Nature, PO Box 3443, Station D, Ottawa Ontario K1P 6P4 Canada. **Tel** (613)990-6595, FAX (613)990-0318. ***Continues** Canadian Biodiversity, 1183-3254.*

LC QH344 .G59 **ISSN** 0886-6236
DD 574.5/222 US
CCC
CODEN GBCYEP
GLOBAL BIOGEOCHEMICAL CYCLES. [Glob. biogeochem. cycles]. **Added/Corp** American Geophysical Union. Vol. 1, No. 1 (March 1987)-. Periodical. English. Four times a year. $270.00. American Geophysical Union, 2000 Florida Avenue Northwest, Washington DC 20009. **Tel** (202)462-6903, (800)966-2481, FAX (202)328-0566. Documents available from BIOSIS Document Express, CASDDS.
Desc: Covers biogeochemical cycles.
Ind/Abst AGRICOLA [Select. Cov.]; Biol. Abstr. (1989-); Chem. Abstr.; Curr. Cit.; Ecol. Abstr.; Geogr. Abstr. Phys. Geogr.; GeoRef; Rice Abstr.; Sci. Cit. Index; Soils Fert.

LC QH301 **ISSN** 1354-1013
DD 574 UK
CCC
Pr Rev.
•**GLOBAL CHANGE BIOLOGY.** (1995)-. Academic Scholarly Publication. English. Six times a year. $225.00 US and Canada; £128.00 Europe; £140.00 other. Blackwell Scientific Publications Ltd, Marston Book Services, PO Box 88, Oxford OX2 ONE United Kingdom. **Tel** 011 44 1865 206206, FAX 011 44 1865 206219, telex 837 515 MARDIS G. Documents available from BLDSC.

LC QH301 .S765
DD 574.05 BU
GODISHNIK NA SOFIISKIIA UNIVERSITET "SV. KLIMENT OKHRIDSKI," BIOLOGICHESKI FAKULTET / ANNUAIRE DE L'UNIVERSITE DE SOFIA "ST. KLIMENT OHRIDSKI," FACULTE DE BIOLOGIE.
Added/Corp Sofiiski Universitet "Sv. Kliment Okhridski." Biologicheski Fakultet. **VFOAT** Annuaire de l'Universite de Sofia "St. Kliment Ohridski," Faculte de Biologie. (19??)-. Periodical. Bulgarian (English and German; summaries and/or abstracts in English). Izdatelstvo na Bulgarskata Akademiia na Naukite, 6 Rouski Boulevard, Sofia Bulgaria. **Tel** FAX 011 359 2 801341, telex 22267 HEMKIK. ***Continues** Godishnik na Sofiiskiia Universitet "Kliment Okhridski," Biologicheski Fakultet.*

LC QH511.A1 G7 **ISSN** 1041-1232
DD 574.3/05 US
NLM W1; GR919CD **CODEN** GDAGE9
Pr Rev.
GROWTH, DEVELOPMENT, AND AGING. (GROWTH, DEVELOPMENT, AND AGING : GDA.). [Growth dev. aging]. **VFOAT** GDA; Growth, Development & Aging. Vol. 52, No. 1 (Spring 1988)-. Academic Scholarly Publication. English. Four times a year. $90.00. Growth Publishing Company Inc., PO Box 42, Bar Harbor ME 04609-0042. **Tel** (207)288-3533, FAX (207)288-5079. **ED** David E. Harrison (editor's address: Jackson Laboratory, 600 Main Street, Bar Harbor, ME 04609; telephone: (207)288-3371 ext. 1296). Index available. **Bk Rev**, (Qty: 0-1). **Acid Free. Circ:** 650. available on microfilm and microfiche from University Microfilms International (UMI); available with charts; available with illustrations. Documents available from The Genuine Article, BIOSIS Document Express, CASDDS. ***Continues** Growth (1937), 0017-4793.*
Desc: Emphasizes basic biology of growth, development and aging, by approaches including mathematics, genetics, biochemistry, and anatomy.
Ind/Abst Abstr. Anthropol. (19??-); AgBiotech News Inf.; AGRICOLA; Anim. Breed. Abstr.; Biol. Agric. Index; Biol. Abstr. (1988-); Chem. Abstr.; Curr. Aware. Biol. Sci., CABS; Curr. Contents Life Sci.; Dairy Sci. Abstr.; EMBASE; Index Med. (1988-); INIS Atomindex [Micro.]; Nutr. Abstr. Rev., Ser. B, Live Feeds and Feed.; Nutr. Abstr. Rev., Ser. A, Hum. Exp.; Nutr. Res. Newsl.; Pig News Inf. (1988-); Poult. Abstr.; Res. Alert [Full Cov.]; Sci. Cit. Index; SCISEARCH.

DD 574 ISSN 0897-7194 SZ CCC
NLM W1; GR919CDH CODEN GRFAEC
GROWTH FACTORS (CHUR, SWITZERLAND). (GROWTH FACTORS.). [Growth factors]. Vol. 1, No. 1 (1988)-. Periodical. English. Eight times a year. $287.00 (academic institutions), $448.00 (corporate institutions). Harwood Academic Publishers, PO Box 90, Reading RG1 8JL United Kingdom. **Tel** 011 44 1734 560080, FAX 011 44 1734 568211. **ED** Antony Burgess.
Ind/Abst CSA Neuro. Abstr. (?-?); Curr. Aware. Biol. Sci., CABS; Curr. Cit.; EMBASE; Index Med.; Oncog. Growth Factors Abstr.; Ref. Upd. Deluxe Ed.; Sci. Cit. Index.

LC QH301 .N57 **ISSN** 0253-6501
DD 574.05 KO
CODEN HSKNDP
HANGUG SAINHWAR GWAHAG NYENGUNWEN RONCON. (NONCHONG.). [Hangug sainhwar gwahag nyengunwen roncon]. **Added/Corp** Ihwa Yoja Taehakkyo. Hanguk Saenghwal Kwahak Yonguwon. **VFOAT** Hanguk Saenghwal Kwahak Yonguwon Nonchong; Journal of Korean Research Institute for Better Living. (1968)-. Academic Scholarly Publication. English (Korean). Two times a year. Documents available from CASDDS.
Ind/Abst Chem. Abstr.

LC QH301 **ISSN** 0073-0467
DD 574 US
UDC 57
HARVARD BOOKS IN BIOLOGY. No. 1-1959-. Monographic series. English. Irregular. Price varies per volume. Harvard University Press, 79 Garden Street, Cambridge MA 02138. **Tel** (617)496-1344, (800)448-2242.

LC QH301 .H56A **ISSN** 0367-5912
DD 574.05 JA
UDC 581.9(520-15); 591.9(520-15)
CODEN HIRKAC
HIROSHIMA DAIGAKU SEIBUTSU GAKKAI SHI. **Main/Corp** Hiroshima Daigaku Seibutsu Gakkai. **VFOAT** Bulletin of the Biological Society of Hiroshima University; Seibutsugakkaishi. (1949)-. Academic Scholarly Publication. Japanese (English). One time a year. ¥1500 Japan; $10.00 US. Hiroshima Daigaku Seibutsu Gakkai, c/o Hiroshima Daigaku Rigakubu, Higashi Sendacho, Hiroshima 730 Japan. **Tel** 082-241-1221. **ED** Haruto Nomiya. **Ad Acc. Circ:** 350. Documents available from CASDDS.
Desc: Publishes papers in botany, zoology and science education. Most papers dealing with plants and animals in western Japan.
Ind/Abst Chem. Abstr.

LC S18 .H57 **ISSN** 0387-7647
DD 630.5 JA
CODEN HDSKDJ
HIROSHIMA DAIGAKU SEIBUTSU SEISAN GAKUBU KIYO. [Hiroshima Daigaku Seibutsu Seisangakubu kiyo]. **Added/Corp** Hiroshima Daigaku. Seibutsu Seisan Gakubu. **VFOAT** Journal of the Faculty of Applied Biological Science, Hiroshima University. (1979)-. Academic Scholarly Publication. English (Japanese). Two times a year. Hiroshima University Faculty of Applied Biological Science, Saijo Higashi-Hiroshima Japan. Documents available from BIOSIS Document Express, CASDDS. ***Continues*** *Hiroshima Daigaku. Sui-Chikusan Gakubu. Hiroshima Daigaku Sui-Chikusan Gakubu Kiyo, 0440-8756.*
Ind/Abst Biol. Abstr.; Chem. Abstr.; Food Sci. Technol. Abstr.; Nutr. Abstr. Rev., Ser. B, Live Feeds and Feed.; Life Sci. Collect.; Poult. Abstr.; Rev. Agric. Entomol.; SEA Abstr.

LC QE701 .H55 **ISSN** 0891-2963
DD 560/.5 UK
CCC
CODEN HIBIEW
HISTORICAL BIOLOGY. See Paleontology.

LC QC7 .H69 **ISSN** 0890-9997
DD 509 US
CCC
NLM W1; HI799H **CODEN** HSPSEW
Pr Rev.
HISTORICAL STUDIES IN THE PHYSICAL AND BIOLOGICAL SCIENCES. See Physics.

LC QH305 .P82 **ISSN** 0391-9714
DD 570/.9 UK
CCC
NLM W1 PU1EH **CODEN** HPLSDO
Pr Rev.
HISTORY AND PHILOSOPHY OF THE LIFE SCIENCES. [Hist. philos. life sci.]. **Added/Corp** Stazione Zoologica di Napoli. Vol. 1, No. 1 (1979)-. English (French and German). Three times a year. $160.00. Taylor & Francis Ltd. / UK, Rankine Road, Basingstoke, Hampshire RG24 8PR United Kingdom. **Tel** 011 44 1256 840366, FAX 011 44 1256 479438, telex 858540. **(Subscription address:** Taylor & Francis Inc., 1900 Frost Road, Suite 101, Bristol PA 19007-1598. **Tel** (215)785-5800, (800)821-8312, FAX (215)785-5515.**) ED** M. D. Grmek (editor's address: 10 rue de Savoie, 75006 Paris France). available on microfilm and microfiche from University Microfilms International (UMI). Documents available from The Genuine Article, BIOSIS Document Express. ***Continues in part*** *Pubblicazioni Della Stazione Zoologica di Napoli, 0039-081X;* ***Absorbed*** *Episteme (Milan, Italy), 0013-9637.*
Desc: An international journal devoted to the historical development of the life sciences and of their social and epistemological implications. It also covers the broader philosophical concerns of biology and medicine. The main interest of the journal is modern western scientific thought, although it also includes any period in history of the life sciences, and any cultural area.
Ind/Abst AGRICOLA; Am. Hist. Life (1983-); Arts Humanit. Citation Index [Select. Cov.]; Biol. Abstr.; Curr. Contents Soc. Behav. Sci.; Index Med.; Philos. Index; Res. Alert [Full Cov.]; Soc. Sci. Cit. Index [Full Cov.].

ISSN 0228-9296
DD 574.92/07/2071533 CN
HML NEWS. [HML news]. **Main/Corp** Huntsman Marine Laboratory. No. 8 (June 1980)-. Periodical. English. Huntsman Marine Laboratory, Brandy Cove Road, Sainte Andrews New Brunswick E0G 2X0 Canada. ***Continues*** *Huntsman Marine Laboratory. Newsletter, 0226-6512.*

LC QH301 .H58A **ISSN** 0018-3393
DD 574.05 JA
UDC 577.1; 577.3
CODEN HKDSBF
HOKKAIDO KYOIKU DAIGAKU KIYO. DAI 2-BU. [Hokkaido Kyoiku Daigaku kiyo. dai 2-bu; B Seibutsugaku-, chigaku-, nogaku-hen]. **Main/Corp** Hokkaido Kyoiku Daigaku. **VFOAT** Journal of Hokkaido University of Education. Multiple languages (English and Japanese). Hokkaido Kyoiku Daigaku, Nishi 13-chome Minami 24-jo Chuo-ku, Sapporo 064 Japan. Documents available from BIOSIS Document Express.
Ind/Abst AGRICOLA; Biol. Abstr.; GeoRef.

LC QH301
DD 574 II
HORNBILL. **Added/Corp** Bombay Natural History Society. No. 1 (Jan./Mar. 1977)-. Periodical. English. Four times a year. $25.67. Hornbill House, Shahid Bhagat Singh Road, Bombay 400 023 India. **(Subscription address:** Prints India, 11 Darya Ganj, New Delhi 110002 India. **Tel** 011 91 11 3268645, FAX 011 91 11 3275542, telex 31-61087 PRIN-IN.**) ED** Ajay Varadachary, Isaac Kehimkar, Sunioy Mongi. **Bk Rev.** **Ad Acc. Circ:** 3500 (ctrl). ***Supersedes*** *Hornbill Newsletter, 0441-2370.*
Ind/Abst Key Word Index Wildl. Res.

LC QH301 **ISSN** 0441-747X
DD 574 JA
UDC 572; 57
NLM W1 HO69FG **CODEN** HSKEAT
HOSHASEN SEIBUTSU KENKYU. **VFOAT** Radiation Biology Research Communication. Vol. 1 (March 1966)-. Academic Scholarly Publication. Multiple languages. Hoshasen Seibutsu Kenkyukai Jimukyoku, Kyoto Daigaku Igakubu, Hoshano Kiso Igaku Kyoshitsu Nai, Yoshida Konoe-Cho, Sakyo-KU Kyoto-Shi 606. Documents available from CASDDS.
Ind/Abst Chem. Abstr.

LC QR185.8.H93 H85 **ISSN** 0956-960X
DD 616.07/9 US
CCC
NLM W1; HU44NL **CODEN** HANHEX
Pr Rev.
HUMAN ANTIBODIES AND HYBRIDOMAS. [Hum. antib. hybrid.]. Vol. 1, No. 1 (Jan. 1990)-. Periodical. English. Four times a year. $235.00. Forefront Publishing USA, 24 Glen Hill Road, Wilton CT 06897. **Tel** (203)221-9949, FAX (203)834-0940. Index available (bound in Nov. issue). **Ad Acc, Adv Mgr:** M. Rawlins. available on microfilm and microfiche from University Microfilms International (UMI); available on CD-ROM from MEDLINE; available on an online database from MEDLINE.
Desc: Brings together all aspects of human hybridomas and antibody technology under a single, cohesive theme, including fundamental research, applied science and clinical applications.
Ind/Abst Biol. Abstr. (1992-); Curr. Cit.; EMBASE; Index Med. (1990-).

LC GN1 .H8 **ISSN** 0018-7143
DD 570.5 US
NLM W1 HU444U **CODEN** HUBIAA
Pr Rev.
HUMAN BIOLOGY. [Hum. biol.]. **Added/Corp** Human Biology Council. Vol. 1 (Jan. 1929)-. Academic Scholarly Publication. English. Six times a year (Feb., Apr., June, Aug., Oct., Dec.). $128.00. Wayne State University Press, 4809 Woodward Avenue, The Leonard N. Simons Building, Detroit MI 48201-1309. **Tel** (313)577-6119, (313)577-6120, FAX (313)577-6131. **ED** Francis E. Johnston. Index available in last issue of volume--attached. cum. index. **Bk Rev.** **Circ:** 1,600 (ctrl). available on microfilm and microfiche from University Microfilms International (UMI). Documents available from The Genuine Article, BIOSIS Document Express, UMI Article Clearinghouse, CASDDS.
Desc: The focus is human genetics in the broadest sense. Included under this rubric are population genetics, evolutionary and genetic demography, quantitative genetics, genetics epidemiology, behavioral genetics, molecular genetics, and growth and physiology parameters focusing on genetic/environmental interactions.
Ind/Abst Abstr. Anthropol.; Acad. Ind. [Computer File] (1992-); Acad. Search; Annals Behav. Med.; Anthropol. Lit.; Biol. Agric. Index; Biol. Abstr.; Biol. Dig.; Biostatistica (19??-19??); Chem. Abstr.; Chicano Index; Curr. Aware. Biol. Sci., CABS; Curr. Cit.; Curr. Contents Life Sci.; Curr. Titles Dent.; Dairy Sci. Abstr.; Dev. Med. Child Neurol.; EMBASE; Energy Res. Abstr.; EP Collect.; Expand. Acad. Index (1989-); Gen. Sci. Index; Gen. Sci. Source; Health Plan. Adminis.; Homework Help.; Index Med.; INFO-SOUTH Abstr.; INIS Atomindex [Micro.]; Mag. Search; MasterFile FullTEXT 1000; MasterFile FullTEXT 350; MasterFile FullTEXT 650; MasterFile FullTEXT (July 1993-); Middle East Abstr. Index; Multicult. Educ. Abstr.; Newsp. Period. Abstr. (1991-); Nutr. Abstr. Rev., Ser. B, Live Feeds and Feed.; Nutr. Abstr. Rev., Ser. A, Hum. Exp.; OCLC; Life Sci. Collect.; Popul. Index; Protozoolog. Abstr.; Psychol. Abstr.; Res. Alert [Full Cov.]; Sci. Cit. Index; SCISEARCH; Soc. Plann. Policy Dev. Abstr.; Soc. Sci. Cit. Index [Select. Cov.]; Sociol. Abstr.; SportSearch; Stat. Theory Method Abstr. (1959-1963); Telebase.

LC GN537 **ISSN** 0739-2036
DD 572 US
HUMAN ETHOLOGY NEWSLETTER. See Anthropology.

LC GN281 .H8474 **ISSN** 0393-9375
DD 573.2/05 IT
NLM W1; HU446L
Pr Rev.
HUMAN EVOLUTION. See Anthropology.

LC QH90 .H9 **ISSN** 0018-8158
NE
CCC
CODEN HYDRB8HYDKB8
Pr Rev.
HYDROBIOLOGIA. [Hydrobiologia]. Vol. 1, No. 1 (Aug. 15, 1948)-. Academic Scholarly Publication. English. Irregular (75 issues per year). $5982.00. Kluwer Academic Publishers, Postbus 322, 3300 AH Dordrecht The Netherlands. **Tel** 011 31 78 524400, FAX 011 31 78 183273, telex 20083. **ED** H. J. Dumont. cum. index. **Bk Rev.** **Ad Acc. Circ:** 800. available on microfilm and microfiche from University Microfilms International (UMI). Documents available from The Genuine Article, BIOSIS Document Express, CASDDS, Documents on Demand.
Desc: Papers on ecology, physiology, biogeography, methodology and taxonomy are published. Also applied (technological) papers are published, provided they are of general interest and not solely technical in nature.
Ind/Abst AGRICOLA; Anim. Breed. Abstr.; Appl. Sci. Technol. Index; AQUAREF; Biocont. News Inf.; Biol. Abstr.; Chem. Abstr.; Coal Abstr.; Curr. Aware. Biol. Sci., CABS; Curr. Cit.; Curr. Contents Agric. Biol. Environ. Sci.; Curr. Ref. Fish Res.; Ecol. Abstr.; Ecology Abstr.; EMBASE; Energy Res. Abstr.; Entomol. Abstr.; Environ. Abstr.; Environ. Period. Bibliogr.; Fish Rev.; Food Sci. Technol. Abstr.; For. Prod. Abstr.; Fresh. Aqua. Contents Tables; Geogr. Abstr. Phys. Geogr.; Geogr. Abstr. Human Geogr.; GeoRef; Health Saf. Sci. Abstr.; Helminthol. Abstr. (19??-19??); Index Vet.; Int. Dev. Abstr.; Irr. Drain. Abstr.; Leadscan; Microbiol. Abstr. Sect. C; Nematol. Abstr.; Nutr. Abstr. Rev., Ser. B, Live Feeds and Feed.; Nutr. Abstr. Rev., Ser. A, Hum. Exp.; Ocean. Abstr.; Life Sci. Collect.; Pollut. Abstr. Indexes; Protozoolog. Abstr.; Res. Alert [Full Cov.]; Rev. Agric. Entomol.; Rev. Med. Vet. Entomol.; Rev. Med. Vet. Mycology; Rev. Plant Pathol.; Risk Abstr.; Sci. Cit. Index; SCISEARCH; Soc. Sci. Cit. Index [Select. Cov.]; Soils Fert.; Vet. Bull.; Weed Abstr.; Wildl. Rev.

LC QH91.A1 G513 **ISSN** 0018-8166
DD 574.92/05 US
CCC
CODEN HYBJA
HYDROBIOLOGICAL JOURNAL. [Hydrobiol. j.]. **Added/Corp** American Fisheries Society. Scripta Technica, Inc. **VFOAT** Gidrobiologicheskii Zhurnal. Vol. 5 (1969)-. Academic Scholarly Publication. English (translations available in Russian). Seven times a year. $1192.00. Scripta Technica, A Subsidiary of John Wiley & Sons Inc., 7961 Eastern Avenue, Silver Spring MD 20910. **Tel** (301)588-0484, FAX (301)588-5278. **(Subscription address:** John Wiley & Sons, Inc. / Philadelphia, PO Box 7247, Philadelphia PA 19170. **Tel** (212)850-6645, (800)225-5945.**) ED** Robert J. Behnke. **Ad Acc. Circ:** 325. available on microfilm and microfiche from University Microfilms International (UMI). Documents available from BIOSIS Document Express.
Desc: Original work and reviews on physiology, biochemistry, ecology, and conservation of freshwater fish, invertebrates, vascular plants, and plankton, as well as biological effects of pollution of inland waters.
Ind/Abst Anim. Breed. Abstr.; AQUAREF; Aquat. Sci. Fish. Abstr. [CD-ROM Ed.]; Biol. Abstr. (-1977); Can. Environ.; Coal Abstr.; Curr. Cit.; Ecol. Abstr.; Ecology Abstr.; Ei Page One; EMBASE; Energy Res. Abstr. (Aug. 1977-); Fish Rev. (Jan. 1989-July 1992); Fresh. Aqua. Contents Tables; Geogr. Abstr. Phys. Geogr.; Geogr.

Abstr. Human Geogr.; Geol. Abstr.; GeoRef; Helminthol. Abstr. (19??-19??); INIS Atomindex [Micro.]; Nematol. Abstr.; Nutr. Abstr. Rev., Ser. B, Live Feeds and Feed.; Life Sci. Collect.; Protozoolog. Abstr.; Rev. Agric. Entomol.; Rev. Med. Vet. Entomol.; Rev. Med. Vet. Mycology; Sel. Water Resour. Abstr.; Weed Abstr.; Wildl. Rev. (Jan. 1989-July 1992).

LC QH301 **ISSN** 0961-2661
DD 574 FR
CODEN ICSSEE

ICSU PRESS SYMPOSIUM SERIES. (ICSU PRESS SYMPOSIUM SERIES.). [ICSU Press symp. ser.]. No. 1 (1984)-. Monographic series. English. Irregular. Price varies per volume. ICSU, 51 BD de Montmorency, 75016 Paris France. Documents available from BIOSIS Document Express.
Ind/Abst Biol. Abstr.

LC R **ISSN** 0019-1604
DD 610 JA

IGAKU TO SEIBUTSUGAKU. See Medical Sciences.

ISSN 0073-4748
DD 574 US
NLM W1 IL237 **CODEN** ILBMA4

ILLINOIS BIOLOGICAL MONOGRAPHS. [Ill. biol. monogr.]. **Added/Corp** University of Illinois at Urbana-Champaign. Vol. 1 (Nov. 1914)-. Monographic series. English. Irregular. Price varies per volume. University of Illinois Press, 1325 South Oak Street, Champaign IL 61820. **Tel** (217)333-0950, FAX (217)244-8082. available on microfilm from University Microfilms International (UMI). Documents available from BIOSIS Document Express.
Ind/Abst Biol. Abstr.; Life Sci. Collect.

LC R
DD 610 SP

IM; INFORMATICA EN MEDICINA Y BIOLOGIA. See Medical Sciences.

LC QA **ISSN** 0265-0746
DD 510 UK
CCC
NLM W1; IM4572 **CODEN** IJMBEG
Pr Rev.

IMA JOURNAL OF MATHEMATICS APPLIED IN MEDICINE AND BIOLOGY. See Mathematics.

LC QH301 **ISSN** 0923-2532
DD 574 FR
UDC 612.017 **CCC**
Pr Rev.

IMMUNO ANALYSE & BIOLOGIE SPECIALISEE. **VFOAT** Immuno Analyse et Biologie Specialisee. (1989)-. Academic Scholarly Publication. French. Six times a year. $240.00. Editions Scientifique Elsevier, 141 rue de Javel, 75747 Paris Cedex 15 France. **Tel** 011 33 1 45589067, FAX 011 33 1 45589424. **(Subscription address:** Editions Scientifiques Elsevier / for North America, PO Box 7247-7576, Philadelphia PA 19170-7576. **)** available on microfilm and microfiche from University Microfilms International (UMI); available on an online database from Elsevier Electronic Subscriptions (EES). ***Continues** Trait d'Union.*
Ind/Abst EMBASE.

LC QH301 **ISSN** 0994-9895
DD 574 FR
NLM W1; IM484F
SUSPENDED

IMMUNOCLONES. **Added/Corp** European Centre of Documentation on Immunoclones. (199?)-Suspended with Vol. 5 (199?). Periodical. English. Twelve times a year. 1,200.00F. CERDIC, 2229 Route Cretes, 06560 Valbonne France. **Tel** 011 33 92 942288, FAX 011 33 92 653058. Index available. **Ad Acc.** available on diskette.
Desc: Description of new immunoclones recently entered in the Immunoclone Database (ICDB).

LC QH301 .I44 **ISSN** 0302-7554
DD 574/.05 II
CODEN INBID9

INDIAN BIOLOGIST. [Indian biol.]. **Added/Corp** Indian Association of Biological Sciences. (19??)-. Academic Scholarly Publication. English. Two times a year. $22.00. Indian Association of Biological Sciences, c/o Life Science Centre, University of Calcutta, 35 Ballygunge Circular Road, Calcutta 19 India. **(Subscription address:** Prints India, 11 Darya Ganj, New Delhi 110002 India. **Tel** 011 91 11 3268645, FAX 011 91 11 3275542, telex 31-61087 PRIN-IN.**)** Documents available from CASDDS.
Ind/Abst AgBiotech News Inf.; Chem. Abstr.; EMBASE; Plant Breed. Abstr.; Plant Grow. Reg. Abstr.

LC QH301 .I445 **ISSN** 0970-2091
DD 574/.05 II
NLM W1; IN206NU **CODEN** IJAPEW

INDIAN JOURNAL OF APPLIED AND PURE BIOLOGY. [Indian j. appl. pure biol.]. Vol. 1, No. 1 (Jan. 1986)-. Periodical. English. Two times a year. $80.00. Shaukat Saeed Khan, Bhopal India. **(Subscription address:** Prints India, 11 Darya Ganj, New Delhi 110002 India. **Tel** 011 91 11 3268645, FAX 011 91 11 3275542, telex 31-61087 PRIN-IN.**)** Documents available from CASDDS.
Ind/Abst Agrofor. Abstr. (1991-); Biodeter. Abstr. (1991-); Chem. Abstr. (1986-1988); Field Crop Abstr.; For. Prod. Abstr. (1991-); For. Abstr.; Plant Genet. Resour. Abstr.; Postharvest News Inf.; Rev. Agric. Entomol.; Rev. Plant Pathol.; Seed Abstr.; Sorghum Mill. Abstr.; Weed Abstr.

LC QH301 .I45 **ISSN** 0019-5189
DD 574/.05 II
NLM W1 IN208P **CODEN** IJEBA6

INDIAN JOURNAL OF EXPERIMENTAL BIOLOGY. [Indian j. exp. biol.]. **Added/Corp** Council of Scientific & Industrial Research (India) Indian National Science Academy. Vol. 1 (Jan. 1963)-. Academic Scholarly Publication. English. Twelve times a year. $200.00. Council of Scientific & Industrial Research, Publications & Information Director, Hillside Road, New Delhi 110012 India. **Tel** FAX 011 91 11 5731353. **(Subscription address:** Prints India, 11 Darya Ganj, New Delhi 110002 India. **Tel** 011 91 11 3268645, FAX 011 91 11 3275542, telex 31-61087 PRIN-IN.**) ED** S.P. Ambasta and B.S. Jangi. **Bk Rev. Ad Acc. Circ:** 1,000. Documents available from BIOSIS Document Express, CASDDS. ***Continues in part** Journal of Scientific & Industrial Research, 0368-4229 **and** Annals of Biochemistry and Experimental Medicine.*
Desc: Devoted to the publication of research communications in the fields of experimental botany, zoology, microbiology, pharmacology, nutrition, etc.
Ind/Abst AgBiotech News Inf.; AGRICOLA; Agrofor. Abstr. (1991-); Anal. Abstr.; Anim. Breed. Abstr.; Biocont. News Inf. (1991-); Biodeter. Abstr.; Biol. Abstr.; Chem. Abstr.; Crop Physiol. Abstr.; CSA Neuro. Abstr.; Curr. Biotechnol.; Curr. Cit.; Curr. Ref. Fish Res.; Dairy Sci. Abstr.; Ei Page One; EMBASE [Select. Cov.]; Entomol. Abstr.; Field Crop Abstr.; Fish Rev.; Food Sci. Technol. Abstr.; Grass. Forage Abstr.; Helminthol. Abstr. (19??-19??); Hortic. Abstr.; Immunol. Abstr.; Index Med.; Irr. Drain. Abstr.; NAPRALERT; Nutr. Abstr. Rev., Ser. B, Live Feeds and Feed.; Nutr. Abstr. Rev., Ser. A, Hum. Exp.; Life Sci. Collect.; PESTDOC; Pig News Inf.; Plant Breed. Abstr.; Plant Genet. Resour. Abstr.; Plant Grow. Reg. Abstr.; Postharvest News Inf.; Potato Abstr.; Poult. Abstr.; Protozoolog. Abstr.; Rev. Agric. Entomol.; Rev. Med. Vet. Entomol.; Rev. Med. Vet. Mycology; Rev. Plant Pathol.; Rice Abstr.; SCISEARCH; Seed Abstr.; Small Anim. Abstr. Bibliogr.; Soils Fert.; Sorghum Mill. Abstr.; Soyabean Abstr.; Trop. Dis. Bull.; Weed Abstr.; Wildl. Rev.

LC QH301 .I454 **ISSN** 0253-4436
DD 574/.05 II
NLM W1 IN2754J **CODEN** IRLSEG

INDIAN REVIEW OF LIFE SCIENCES. [Indian rev. life sci.]. **Added/Corp** University of Jodhpur. Dept. of Botany. Vol. 1 (1981)-. Academic Scholarly Publication. English. One time a year. $50.00. University of Jodhpur / Department of Botany, Jodhpur India. **(Subscription address:** Prints India, 11 Darya Ganj, New Delhi 110002 India. **Tel** 011 91 11 3268645, FAX 011 91 11 3275542, telex 31-61087 PRIN-IN.**) ED** David N Sen. Index available. **Bk Rev. Ad Acc. Circ:** 700 (ctrl). Documents available from BIOSIS Document Express, CASDDS.
Ind/Abst Anim. Breed. Abstr.; Biocont. News Inf. (1991-); Biol. Abstr.; Chem. Abstr.; Crop Physiol. Abstr.; EMBASE; Field Crop Abstr.; Grass. Forage Abstr.; Helminthol. Abstr.; Maize Abstr.; Plant Breed. Abstr.; Rev. Agric. Entomol.; Rice Abstr.; Seed Abstr.; Sorghum Mill. Abstr.; Weed Abstr.; Wheat Barley Trit. Abstr.

LC QH301 **ISSN** 0270-5443
DD 574 US

INFORMATIVE CIRCULAR - OHIO BIOLOGICAL SURVEY. [Inf. circ. - Ohio Biol. Surv.]. **Main/Corp** Ohio Biological Survey. No. 1 (1962)-. Monographic series. English. Irregular. Price varies per volume. Ohio State University Press, 1070 Carmack Road, Columbus OH 43210. **Tel** (614)292-6930, (614)292-1407, FAX (614)292-2065.
Ind/Abst GeoRef; Rev. Med. Vet. Mycology; Rev. Plant Pathol.

LC QH301
DD 574 FI

INTERNATIONAL AEROBIOLOGY NEWSLETTER. **Added/Corp** International Association for Aerobiology. No. 1 (Oct. 1975)-. Newsletter. English. Irregular. International Association of Aerobiology, Swedish Museum Natural History, S-104 05 Stockholm 50 Sweden. **Tel** 44 0 905 748066, FAX 44 0 905 748667. **ED** Dr. Jean Emberlin (editor's address: Pollen Research Unit, Worcester College of HE, Worcester, UR6 8UE UK). **Bk Rev**, (Qty: 5). **Ad Acc, Adv Mgr:** Dr. Jean Emberlin. **Acid Free. Circ:** 950 (ctrl). ***Continues** IBP Aerobiology Newsletter.*
Desc: Contents includes conference reports, details of upcoming meetings, research news, news about the members, discussion of documents, book reviews, and other recent publications.

LC QH301 **ISSN** 0253-7206
DD 574 II
NLM W1 IN71P **CODEN** IBMOEX

INTERNATIONAL BIOSCIENCE MONOGRAPH. [Int. biosci. monogr.]. **VFOAT** International Bioscience Monographs; International Bioscience Monograph. Vol. 1 (1974)-. Monographic series. English. One time a year. Price varies per volume. International Bio-Science Publishers, Hissar India. **(Subscription address:** Prints India, 11 Darya Ganj, New Delhi 110002 India. **Tel** 011 91 11 3268645, FAX 011 91 11 3275542, telex 31-61087 PRIN-IN.**)** Documents available from BIOSIS Document Express.
Ind/Abst Biol. Abstr. (1985-); Microbiol. Abstr. Sect. A; Microbiol. Abstr. Sect. C.

LC QH301 **ISSN** 0971-1716
DD 574 II
UDC 674

INTERNATIONAL BIOSCIENCE SERIES. [Int. Biosci. Ser.]. (1975)-. Periodical. English. One time a year. Price varies. **(Subscription address:** Prints India, 11 Darya Ganj, New Delhi 110002 India. **Tel** 011 91 11 3268645, FAX 011 91 11 3275542, telex 31-61087 PRIN-IN.**)**

LC BF1 .I44 **ISSN** 1044-811X
DD 610/.5 US
CCC
NLM W1; IN76559 **CODEN** IJMREU
Pr Rev.

INTERNATIONAL JOURNAL OF BIOSOCIAL AND MEDICAL RESEARCH. See Sociology.

LC R **ISSN** 0940-5437
DD 610 GW
CCC
NLM W1; IN766DIH **CODEN** ICLREA

INTERNATIONAL JOURNAL OF CLINICAL AND LABORATORY RESEARCH. **VFOAT** International Journal of Clinical and Laboratory Research. Vol. 21, No. 2 (1991)-. Periodical. English. Four times a year. $299.00. Springer-Verlag GmbH & Company KG, Heidelberger Platz 3, D-14197 Berlin Germany. **Tel** 011 49 30 8207223, FAX 011 49 30 8214091, telex 183 319 SPBLN D. **(Subscription address:** Springer-Verlag New York Inc. / North America, PO Box 2485, Journal Fulfillment, Secaucus NJ 07096. **Tel** (201)348-4033, (800)777-4643, FAX (201)348-4505.**)** Documents available from The Genuine Article. ***Continues** Ricerca in Clinica e in Laboratorio, 0390-5748.*
Desc: Publishes reports of clinical and experimental work concerned with the following fields: clinical chemistry, hematology, immunology, molecular biology and oncology.
Ind/Abst Curr. Aware. Biol. Sci., CABS; Curr. Cit.; Curr. Contents Life Sci.; Index Med. (1991-); Res. Alert [Full Cov.]; Sci. Cit. Index; SCISEARCH.

LC R **ISSN** 1081-3829
DD 610 US

•**INTERNATIONAL JOURNAL OF MEDICAL AND BIOLOGICAL FRONTIERS.** See Medical Sciences.

LC QH652 .I55 **ISSN** 0955-3002
DD 574.191 UK
CCC
NLM W1; IN778F **CODEN** IJRBE7
Pr Rev.

INTERNATIONAL JOURNAL OF RADIATION BIOLOGY. See Physics-Light, Optics, Radiation.

LC Q **ISSN** 0010-2164
DD 502 US
NLM W1 IN805L **CODEN** ILBYA6

INTERNATIONAL LABORATORY. EUROPEAN ED. See Chemistry and Chemicals.

LC RC341 .I5 **ISSN** 0074-7742
DD 612.8082 US
CCC
NLM W1 IN834 **CODEN** IRNEAE

INTERNATIONAL REVIEW OF NEUROBIOLOGY. [Int. rev. neurobiol.]. Vol. 1 (1959)-. Academic Scholarly Publication. English. Irregular. Price varies per volume. Academic Press Inc., 6277 Sea Harbor Drive, Orlando FL 32887. **Tel** (800)543-9534, (407)345-4100, FAX (407)352-3445. **ED** Carl C. Pfeiffer. **Bk Rev. Ad Acc.** Documents available from The Genuine Article, BIOSIS Document Express, CASDDS.
Ind/Abst Biol. Abstr.; Chem. Abstr.; Curr. Aware. Biol. Sci., CABS; Curr. Cit.; EMBASE; Energy Res. Abstr. (Aug. 1982-); Index Med.; Index Sci. Rev. [Full Cov.]; Res. Alert [Full Cov.]; SCISEARCH.

ISSN 0261-4952
DD 016.59204805 UK
CCC

INVERTEBRATE NEUROBIOLOGY. [Invertebr. neurobiol.]. (1982)-. English. Twelve times a year. $179.67. SUBIS, Mansion House 19 Kingfield Road, Sheffield S11 9AS United Kingdom. **Tel** 011 44 114 2554433, FAX 011 44 114 255 4626.

ISSN 0836-3838
DD 574/.09714 CN

INVIVO. (INVIVO : BULLETIN DE L'ASSOCIATION DES BIOLOGISTES DU QUEBEC.). [Invivo]. **Added/Corp** Association des Biologistes du Quebec. **VFOAT** In Vivo. Vol. 6, No. 1 (March 1986)-. Bulletin. French. Irregular. 20.01Can$. Association des Biologistes du Quebec, 1208 rue Beaubien East #102, Montreal Quebec H2S 1T7 Canada. **Tel** (514)279-7115. Index available. **Bk Rev. Ad Acc. Circ:** 500. ***Continues*** *Bulletin d'Information (Association des Biologistes du Quebec).*

ISSN 0790-1747
DD 620.8 IE

IRISH BIOTECH NEWS. [Ir. biotech news]. (1983)-. Periodical. English. Four times a year. Free. BioResearch Ireland, EOLAS, Glasnevin Dublin 9 Ireland. **ED** Jim Ryan and Grainne Walshe. **Bk Rev. Ad Acc.** ctrl circ.
Desc: Reports on the current activities in the Irish and European biotechnology industry. It also covers activities of the European Community biotechnology programs.
Ind/Abst Abstr. BioCommer.; Chem. Bus. Bull.; Chem. Bus. NewsBase (1990-); Chem. Bus. Update.

LC QH301 ISSN 1010-8408
DD 574 SZ
NLM W1; IS6673L CODEN IBIOED

ISSUES IN BIOMEDICINE. [Issues biomed.]. Vol. 13 (1990)-. Academic Scholarly Publication. English. One time a year. 180.00F (approx. per volume). S. Karger AG, Allschwilerstrasse 10, PO Box, CH-4009 Basel Switzerland. **Tel** 011 41 61 3061111, FAX 011 41 61 3061234, telex CH 962 652. **ED** H. Stolte, R.K.H. Kinne, P.H. Bach. Documents available from BIOSIS Document Express, CASDDS. ***Continues*** *Experimental Biology and Medicine, 0071-3384.*
Desc: Recognizing the need for accurate clinical interpretation of advances at the basic level, topics presented in this series are characterized by controversies and conflicting views. All contributions are carefully and critically reviewed by acknowledged authorities in the field, known for their ability to organize areas of confusion into clear lines of evidence and clinical recommendations.
Ind/Abst Biol. Abstr.; Chem. Abstr.; Ref. Upd. Deluxe Ed.

LC QH305 .I88
RU
NLM W1 IS917F

ISTORIKO-BIOLOGICHESKIE ISSLEDOVANIIA. **Added/Corp** Institut Istorii Estestvoznaniia i Tekhniki (Akademiia Nauk SSSR). Vol. 6, (1978)-. Academic Scholarly Publication. Russian (summaries and/or abstracts in English). Izdatelstvo Nauka / Akademiia Nauk, (Publishing House of the Russian Academy of Sciences), Leninskii Porspekt 14, 117901 Moscow Russia. **Tel** 011 95 9542153, FAX 011 95 9382144, telex 411964. ***Continues*** *Iz Istorii Biologii.*

LC QH301 .A346a
DD 574.05 RU

ITOGI NAUCHNYKH RABOT ZA ... GOD. **Added/Corp** Institut Biologii Razvitiia (Akademiia Nauk SSSR) Institut Biologii Razvitiia Im. N.K. Koltsova. (1967/68)-. Russian. One time a year. Izdatelstvo Nauka / Akademiia Nauk, (Publishing House of the Russian Academy of Sciences), Leninskii Porspekt 14, 117901 Moscow Russia. **Tel** 011 95 9542153, FAX 011 95 9382144, telex 411964.

LC QH301 .I98 ISSN 0321-1665
DD 574.05/6 GS

IZVESTIIA AKADEMII NAUK GRUZII. SERIIA BIOLOGICHESKAIA. **Added/Corp** Sakartvelos Mecnierebata Akademia. **VFOAT** Seriia Biologicheskaia; Biological Series; Proceedings of the Academy of Sciences of Georgia. Biological Series. (199?)-. Periodical. Russian (Georgian; summaries and/or abstracts in English). Six times a year. $99.95. **(Subscription address:** East View Publications Inc., 3020 Harbor Lane North, Suite 110, Minneapolis MN 55447. **Tel** (800)477-1005, (612)550-0961, FAX (612)559-2931.**)** Documents available from CASDDS. ***Continues*** *Izvestiia Akademii Nauk Gruzinskoi SSR. Seriia Biologicheskaia.*
Ind/Abst Chem. Abstr.

LC QH301 .A33632 ISSN 0002-3183
KZ
NLM W1 IZ652KB

IZVESTIIA AKADEMII NAUK KAZAKHSKOI SSR. SERIIA BIOLOGICHESKAIA. **Added/Corp** Qazaq SSR Ghylym Akademiiasy. **VFOAT** Seriia Biologicheskaia; Qazaq SSR Ghylym Akademiiasynyng Khabarlary. Seriia Biologicheskaia. No. 2 (1966)-. Periodical. Russian (summaries and/or abstracts in Kazakh). Six times a year. $148.00. Izdatelstvo Gylym / Science Publishing House, Ulitsa Pushkina 111-113, 480100 Alma-Ata Kazakhstan. **Tel** 011 7 3272 611877. **(Subscription address:** Victor Kamkin, 4956 Boiling Brook Parkway, Rockville MD 20852. **Tel** (301)881-5973.**)** ***Continues*** *Izvestiia Akademii Nauk Kazakhskoi SSR. Seriia Biologicheskikh Nauk.*
Ind/Abst Crop Physiol. Abstr.; Helminthol. Abstr. (1991-); Index Vet.; Protozoolog. Abstr.; Vet. Bull.

LC Q
DD 500 KG
CODEN INRNE3

IZVESTIIA AKADEMII NAUK RESPUBLIKI KYRGYZSTAN. KHIMIKO-TEKHNOLOGICHESKIE I BIOLOGICHESKIE NAUKI = KYRGYZ RESPUBLIKASY ILIMDER AKADEMIIASYNYN KABARLARY. KHIMIIA-TEKHNOLOGIIA ZHANA BIOLOGIIA ILIMDERI. See Chemistry and Chemicals-Chemical Technology.

LC SB13 .A57
DD 630.5 TA
CODEN IATBEM

IZVESTIIA AKADEMII NAUK RESPUBLIKI TADZHIKISTAN. OTDELENIE BIOLOGICHESKIKH NAUK. **Added/Corp** Akademiiai Ilmhoi Jumhurii Tojikiston. Shubai Ilmhoi Haetshinosi. **VFOAT** Otdelenie Biologicheskikh Nauk; Shubai Ilhoi Haetshinosi; Akhboroti Akademiiai Ilmhoi Jumhurii Tojikiston. Shubai Ilmhoi Haetshinosi; Izvestiia AN Respubliki Tadzhikistan, Otdelenie Biologicheskikh Nauk. (199?)-. Bulletin. Russian (summaries and/or abstracts in Tajik; table of contents in Tajik). Four times a year. Akademiiai Ilmhoi Jumhurii Tojikiston, Shubai Ilmhoi Haetshinosi, Tajikstan. ***Continues*** *Izvestiia Akademii Nauk Tadzhikskoi SSR. Otdelenie Biologicheskikh Nauk.*
Ind/Abst Chem. Abstr.

LC AS262 .A6245
DD 067 RU
NLM W1; IZ6515 CODEN IRABEC

IZVESTIIA AKADEMII NAUK. SERIIA BIOLOGICHESKAIA. **Added/Corp** Rossiiskaia Akademiia Nauk. **VFOAT** Seriia Biologicheskaia; Series Biological; Izvestiia Rossiiskoi Akademii Nauk. Seriia Biologicheskaia; Proceedings Russian Academy of Sciences. Series Biological. No. 2 (Mar./Apr. 1992)-. Academic Scholarly Publication. Russian (summaries and/or abstracts in English; table of contents in English). Six times a year. $202.00. Izdatelstvo Nauka / Akademiia Nauk, (Publishing House of the Russian Academy of Sciences), Leninskii Porspekt 14, 117901 Moscow Russia. **Tel** 011 95 9542153, FAX 011 95 9382144, telex 411964. **(Subscription address:** East View Publications Inc., 3020 Harbor Lane North, Suite 110, Minneapolis MN 55447. **Tel** (800)477-1005, (612)550-0961, FAX (612)559-2931.**)** Documents available from CASDDS. ***Continues*** *Isvestiia Akademii Nauk SSSR. Seriia Biologicheskaia, 0002-3329.*
Ind/Abst Chem. Abstr.; Crop Physiol. Abstr.; Field Crop Abstr.; For. Abstr.; Index Med.; Index Vet.; Protozoolog. Abstr.; Rev. Med. Vet. Mycology; Rev. Plant Pathol.; Weed Abstr.

LC QH301 .A332a
DD 574.05 MV
CODEN IAMNEN

IZVESTIIA AKADEMII NAUK SSR MOLDOVA. BIOLOGICHESKIE I KHIMICHESKIE NAUKI. **Added/Corp** Akademiia de Shtiintse a RSS Moldova. **VFOAT** Biologicheskie i Khimicheskie Nauki; Stiinte Biologice si Chimice; Buletinul Academiei de Stiinte a R.S.S. Moldova. Stiinte Biologice si Chimice. (1990)-. Periodical. Russian (summaries and/or abstracts in English and Moldavian; table of contents in English and Moldavian). Six times a year. Documents available from CASDDS. ***Continues*** *Izvestiia Akademii Nauk Moldavskoi SSR. Biologicheskie i Khimicheskie Nauki.*
Ind/Abst Chem. Abstr.; Postharvest News Inf.; Rev. Plant Pathol.; Seed Abstr.

LC QH301 ISSN 0002-3329
DD 574 RU

IZVESTIIA AKADEMII NAUK SSSR. SERIIA BIOLOGICHESKAIA. **Main/Corp** Akademiia Nauk SSSR. **VFOAT** Proceedings of the USSR Academy of Sciences. (1939)-. Academic Scholarly Publication. Russian (summaries and/or abstracts in English, French and German). Six times a year. Izdatelstvo Nauka / Akademiia Nauk, (Publishing House of the Russian Academy of Sciences), Leninskii Porspekt 14, 117901 Moscow Russia. **Tel** 011 95 9542153, FAX 011 95 9382144, telex 411964. **(Subscription address:** Victor Kamkin, 4956 Boiling Brook Parkway, Rockville MD 20852. **Tel** (301)881-5973.**)** Index available. Documents available from The Genuine Article. ***Continues*** *Izvestiia Akademii Nauk SSSR. Otdelenie Matematicheskikh i Estestvennykh Nauk. Seriia Biologicheskaia.*
Ind/Abst Biocont. News Inf.; Ocean. Abstr.; Res. Alert [Full Cov.]; Sci. Cit. Index; SCISEARCH.

LC QH301 ISSN 0132-6112
DD 574 AJ
NLM W1 IZ652B CODEN IABLAQ

IZVESTIIA AKADEMIIA NAUK AZERBAIDZHANSKOI SSR. SERIIA BIOLOGICHESKIKH NAUK. [Izv. Akad. Nauk Az. SSR. Ser. Biol. Nauk]. **Main/Corp** Azarbaijan SSR Elmlar Akademiiasy. **Added/Corp** Azarbaijan SSR Elmlar Akademiiasy. Izvestiia. Seriia Biologicheskikh i Meditsinskikh Nauk 1960-64 Azarbaijan SSR Elmlar Akademiiasy. Izvestiia. Seriia Biologicheskikh i sel Skokhoziaistvennykh Nauk 1958-59. (1958)-. Russian. Six times a year. Izdatelstvo Elm, Ul. Narimonova 37, 370073 Baku Azerbaijan. Documents available from BIOSIS Document Express, CASDDS.
Ind/Abst Anim. Breed. Abstr.; Biocont. News Inf.; Biol. Abstr.; Chem. Abstr.; Field Crop Abstr.; Grass. Forage Abstr.; Helminthol. Abstr.; Index Vet.; Nematol. Abstr.; Nutr. Abstr. Rev., Ser. B, Live Feeds and Feed.; Plant Breed. Abstr.; Protozoolog. Abstr.; Rev. Med. Vet. Entomol.; Soils Fert.; Vet. Bull.

LC QH301 ISSN 0321-1746
DD 574 TK
NLM W1 IZ652V CODEN ITUBAK
TITLE CHANGE

IZVESTIIA AKADEMIIA NAUK TURKMENSKOI SSR. SERIIA BIOLOGICHESKIKH NAUK. [Izv. Akad. nauk Turkm. SSR, ser. biol. nauk]. **Main/Corp** Turkmenistan SSR Ylymlar Akademiiasy. **VFOAT** Proceedings of the Academy of Sciences of the Turkmen SSR. (1960)-(19??). Academic Scholarly Publication. Russian (summaries and/or abstracts in English). **(Subscription address:** East View Publications Inc., 3020 Harbor Lane North, Suite 110, Minneapolis MN 55447. **Tel** (800)477-1005, (612)550-0961, FAX (612)559-2931.**)** Documents available from BIOSIS Document Express, CASDDS. ***Supersedes in part*** *Turkmenistan SSR Ylymlar Akademiiasy. Izvestiia.* ***Continued by*** *Turkmenistan Ylymlar Akademiiasynyng Khabarlary. Biologik Ylymlaryng Seriiasy.*
Ind/Abst AGRICOLA; Biocont. News Inf.; Biol. Abstr.; Chem. Abstr.; Cot. Trop. Fibr. Abstr. Bibliogr.; EMBASE; For. Abstr.; Helminthol. Abstr. (1991-); Index Vet.; Maize Abstr.; Nematol. Abstr.; Life Sci. Collect.; Postharvest News Inf.; Protozoolog. Abstr.; Rev. Med. Vet. Entomol.; Seed Abstr.

LC QH301 ISSN 0568-6547
DD 574 RU

IZVESTIIA SIBIRSKOGO OTDELENIIA AKADEMII NAUK SSSR. SERIIA BIOLOGICHESKIKH NAUK. **Main/Corp** Akademiia Nauk SSSR. Sibirskoe Otdelenie. **Added/Corp** Akademiia Nauk SSSR. Sibirskoe Otdelenie. Izvestiia. Seriia Biologo-Meditsinskikh Nauk. (1963)-. Periodical. Russian (summaries and/or abstracts in English). Three times a year. **(Subscription address:** Victor Kamkin, 4956 Boiling Brook Parkway, Rockville MD 20852. **Tel** (301)881-5973.**)** ***Supersedes in part*** *Akademiia Nauk SSSR. Sibirskoe Otdelenie. Izvestiia.*
Ind/Abst Biocont. News Inf.; Crop Physiol. Abstr.; For. Abstr.; Index Vet.; Maize Abstr.; Plant Breed. Abstr.; Potato Abstr.; Rice Abstr.; Soils Fert.

LC S ISSN 0521-2804
DD 630 GW
UDC 632
CODEN 632(066.055.5)(430.1-2.1-2.29)

JAHRESBERICHT - BIOLOGISCHE BUNDESANSTALT FUER LAND- UND FORSTWIRTWIRTSCHAFT IN BERLIN UND BRAUNSCHWEIG. **VFOAT** Jahresbericht der Biologischen Bundesanstalt fuer Land- und Forstwirtschaft in Braunschweig. (19??)-. German. One time a year.
Ind/Abst Nematol. Abstr.

LC QH652.A1 ISSN 0721-930X
DD 574.19/15/05 GW
UDC 574.2/.4
NLM W1 GE763D

JAHRESBERICHT - GESELLSCHAFT FUER STRAHLEN- UND UMWELTFORSCHUNG MHB MUENCHEN. (JAHRESBERICHT.). (1979)-. German (summaries and/or abstracts in English). One time a year. Free. Gesellschaft fur Strahlen- und Unweltforschung, Ingolstadter Landstr 1, 8042 Neuherberg Germany. **Tel** 089-3187-0, FAX 089-3187-3322, telex 898947-STRAL. **Bk Rev. Circ:** 2,500. ***Continues*** *Jahresbericht, Kurzfassung (Gesellschaft fur Strahlen- und Unweltforschung), 0721-930X.*

LC QH301
DD 574 JA
NLM W1; JA869
JAPAN BIOINDUSTRY LETTERS.
Added/Corp Baioindasutori Kyokai. (1984)-. Periodical. English. Four times a year. Free. Bioindustry Development Center, 10-5 Shimbashi 5-Chome, Minato Tokyo 105 Japan. **Tel** 011 81 3 3433, 011 81 3 3545.
Ind/Abst Abstr. BioCommer.

LC R ISSN 0021-5112
DD 610 JA
NLM W1 JA975 CODEN JJMCAQ
Pr Rev.
JAPANESE JOURNAL OF MEDICAL SCIENCE & BIOLOGY. See Medical Sciences.

LC QH301
DD 574 JA
CODEN JISYDG
JIBP SYNTHESIS. [JIBP synth.]. **Main/Corp** International Biological Programme. Japanese National Committee. (19??)-. Academic Scholarly Publication. English. Irregular. Price varies per volume. Japanese International Biological Program, Tokyo Japan. Documents available from CASDDS.
Ind/Abst Chem. Abstr.

LC QP517.M67 J68 ISSN 0952-3499
DD 574.8/8 UK
CCC
NLM W1; JO7739 CODEN JMORE4
JMR. JOURNAL OF MOLECULAR RECOGNITION. (JOURNAL OF MOLECULAR RECOGNITION.). [JMR, J. mol. recognit.]. **VFOAT** JMR; Molecular Recognition. Vol. 1, No. 1 (Feb. 1988)-. Academic Scholarly Publication. English. Six times a year. $465.00. John Wiley & Sons Ltd., Baffins Lane, Chichester, West Sussex PO19 1UD United Kingdom. **Tel** 011 44 1243 779777, FAX 011 44 1243 776128 BTG:JWP001, telex 86290 WIBOOKG. **(Subscription address:** John Wiley & Sons, Inc. / Philadelphia, PO Box 7247, Philadelphia PA 19170. **Tel** (212)850-6645, (800)225-5945.) **ED** Irwin Chaiken and Michael Waring. Index available. **Bk Rev. Ad Acc.** available on microfilm and microfiche from University Microfilms International (UMI). Documents available from CASDDS.
Desc: Devoted to research on the basic principles, characterization and application of specific molecular interactions in chemistry, biology, biotechnology and medicine.
Ind/Abst Chem. Abstr.; Curr. Aware. Biol. Sci., CABS; Curr. Cit.; Index Med.

LC QH301 ISSN 0100-7319
DD 574 BL
NLM W1; JO982R CODEN JLBSD2
JORNAL SUL-AMERICANO DE BIOCIENCIAS. [J. sul-am. biocienc.]. **VFOAT** South American Journal of Bio-Sciences; JSAB. (1980)-. Academic Scholarly Publication. Portuguese (summaries and/or abstracts in English). $20.00. Documents available from BIOSIS Document Express. ***Continues*** *Jornal Sul-Americano de Medicina.*
Ind/Abst Biol. Abstr. (-1982); EMBASE.

LC K10 .O833 ISSN 1145-0762
DD 340.05 FR
NLM W1; JO478S
JOURNAL INTERNATIONAL DE BIOETHIQUE. **Added/Corp** Milazzo Group. ISENB. **VFOAT** International Journal of Bioethics. Vol. 1, No. 1 (March 1990)-. Periodical. English (French). Four times a year. 809.00F. Editions Alexandre Lacassagne, 162 Avenue Lacassagne, 69424 Lyon Cedex 03 France. **Tel** 011 33 72 334040. **(Subscription address:** Diffusion Eska, 27 rue Dunois, 75013 Paris France. **Tel** 011 33 1 44068042.)

LC SH151 .J87 ISSN 0733-2076
DD 636.3/005 US
CCC
CODEN JAQSDY
Pr Rev.
JOURNAL OF AQUARICULTURE & AQUATIC SCIENCES. [J. aquaric. aquat. sci.]. **VFOAT** Journal of Aquariculture and Aquatic Sciences. Vol. 3, No. 1 (1982)-. Academic Scholarly Publication. English. Irregular. $137.50 (libraries), $68.75 (individuals), $165.00 (other). The Written Word, 7601 East Forest Lake Drive, Parkville MO 64152. **Tel** (816)842-5936. **ED** John Farrell Kuhns. Index available. **Bk Rev. Ad Acc. Circ:** 1,000. available on an online database from Compuserve Inc. Documents available from BIOSIS Document Express, CASDDS, BLDSC. ***Continues*** *Journal of Aquariculture, 0197-5420.*
Desc: Peer-reviewed research pertaining to aquarium science, aquaculture, mariculture, marine biology, fishery science, general aquatic sciences and ichthyology.
Ind/Abst Aquat. Sci. Fish. Abstr. [CD-ROM Ed.]; Biol. Abstr.; Chem. Abstr. (1982-1983); Ecol. Abstr. (?-?); Fish Rev.; Fresh. Aqua. Contents Tables; Helminthol. Abstr. (1991-); Index Vet.; Mar. Sci. Contents Tables.

LC QH301 ISSN 0970-5732
DD 574 II
CODEN JBCOES
JOURNAL OF BIOLOGICAL CONTROL. [J. biol. control]. **Added/Corp** Indian Society for Biocontrol Advancement. (1987)-. Periodical. English. Two times a year. $15.00. **(Subscription address:** Prints India, 11 Darya Ganj, New Delhi 110002 India. **Tel** 011 91 11 3268645, FAX 011 91 11 3275542, telex 31-61087 PRIN-IN.) Documents available from BIOSIS Document Express.
Ind/Abst Biol. Abstr.; Potato Abstr.; Seed Abstr.

LC QH301 ISSN 0958-7608
DD 574 UK
CODEN JBCUEC
Pr Rev.
JOURNAL OF BIOLOGICAL CURATION. See Museums and Galleries.

LC QH315 .J66 ISSN 0021-9266
DD 574/.07/1 UK
CCC
CODEN JBIEAO
Pr Rev.
JOURNAL OF BIOLOGICAL EDUCATION. [J. biol. educ.]. **Added/Corp** Institute of Biology. (1967)-. Periodical. English. Four times a year (Mar., June, Sept., Dec.). $109.00. Institute of Biology, 20 Queensberry Place, London SW7 2DZ United Kingdom. **Tel** 011 44 171 5818333, FAX 011 44 171 8239409. **ED** John A. Barker. Index available. **Bk Rev. Ad Acc. Circ:** 2,300 (ctrl). Documents available from The Genuine Article, BIOSIS Document Express, CASDDS, Documents on Demand.
Desc: For biology teachers in schools, colleges and universities, this journal gives practical advice on field and laboratory teaching as well as articles on education research and curriculum developments. Book and educational aid reviews featured, biology 'update' articles have proved popular.
Ind/Abst Acad. Search; Biol. Abstr.; Br. Educ. Index; Chem. Abstr.; CSA Neuro. Abstr. (?-?); Curr. Cit.; Curr. Contents Agric. Biol. Environ. Sci.; Curr. Index J. Educ.; Dairy Sci. Abstr.; Ecol. Abstr.; Ecology Abstr.; Educ. Index; Educ. Technol. Abstr.; Environ. Abstr.; EP Collect.; Gen. Sci. Source; Homework Help.; INFO-SOUTH Abstr.; Leis., Rec., Tour. Abstr.; Mag. Search; MasterFile FullTEXT 1000; MasterFile FullTEXT 350; MasterFile FullTEXT 650; MasterFile FullTEXT (July 1993-); Med. Rev. Dig.; Nematol. Abstr.; OCLC; Life Sci. Collect.; Res. Alert [Select. Cov.]; Rev. Agric. Entomol.; Rev. Med. Vet. Entomol.; Rural Dev. Abstr.; SCISEARCH; Soc. Sci. Cit. Index [Select. Cov.]; Tech. Educ. Train. Abstr.; Telebase; World Agric. Econ. Rural Sociol. Abstr.

LC TR1 .B5 ISSN 0274-497X
DD 574/.028 US
NLM W1 JO564D CODEN JBPHD3
JOURNAL OF BIOLOGICAL PHOTOGRAPHY. [J. biol. photogr.]. **Added/Corp** Biological Photographic Association. **VFOAT** Biological Photography. Vol. 48, No. 1 (Jan. 1980)-. Periodical. English. Four times a year. $65.00. Biological Photographic Association, 1819 Peachtree Street Northeast, Suite 712, Atlanta GA 30309. **Tel** (404)351-6300, FAX (404)351-3348. **ED** Joe Ogrodnick. Index available. **Bk Rev. Circ:** 1,500 (ctrl). available on microfilm and microfiche from University Microfilms International (UMI). Documents available from BIOSIS Document Express. ***Continues*** *Journal of the Biological Photographic Association, 0006-3215.*
Desc: Biological and technical photographic articles.
Ind/Abst Biol. Abstr.; Curr. Cit.; Index Med.; Index Vet.; INIS Atomindex [Micro.].

LC QH301 ISSN 0393-974X
DD 574 IT
CCC
NLM W1; JO564EJ CODEN JBRAER
Pr Rev.
JOURNAL OF BIOLOGICAL REGULATORS AND HOMEOSTATIC AGENTS. [J. biol. regul. homeost. agents]. Vol. 1, No. 1 (Jan./Mar. 1987)-. Periodical. English. Four times a year. L190000. Wichtig Editore, Via Friuli 72 74, 20135 Milan Italy. **Tel** 011 39 2 55195443. **(Subscription address:** Wichtig Editore, Subscription Office, PO Box 830350, Birmingham AL 35283-0350. **Tel** (800)633-4931, (205)995-1567 (outside US and Canada), FAX (205)995-1588.) **ED** G. B. Rossi and F. Dianzani. Index available in last issue of volume--attached. cum. index. **Ad Acc. Circ:** 7,000. Documents available from The Genuine Article, BIOSIS Document Express.
Desc: Provides a forum for interdisciplinary basic and clinical research on the broad range of biological agents, especially those capable of modulating normal or abnormal cell response. Reports include current news and future developments about substances or drugs which could be responsible for cellular regulation of differentiation.
Ind/Abst Biol. Abstr. (1989-); Curr. Cit.; Curr. Contents Life Sci.; EMBASE; Health Plan. Adminis.; Index Med. (1987-); PESTDOC; Ref. Upd. Deluxe Ed.; Res. Alert [Full Cov.]; SCISEARCH.

LC QH527 .J63 ISSN 0748-7304
DD 574.1/882/05 US
NLM W1; JO564EN CODEN JBRHEE
JOURNAL OF BIOLOGICAL RHYTHMS. [J. biol. rhythms]. **VFOAT** JBR. Vol. 1, No. 1 (1986)-. Periodical. English. Four times a year (March, June, Sept., Dec.). $178.00. SAGE Periodical Press, 2455 Teller Road, Thousand Oaks CA 91320. **Tel** (805)499-0721, FAX (805)499-0871, telex 100799. **ED** Fred Turek. available on microfilm and microfiche from University Microfilms International (UMI). Documents available from The Genuine Article, BIOSIS Document Express.
Desc: Contains information on empirical investigations into all aspects of biological rhythmicity. Studies use genetic, biochemical, physiological, behavioral, and modeling approaches.
Ind/Abst AGRICOLA [Select. Cov.]; Anim. Behav. Abstr.; Biol. Abstr. (1986-); CSA Neuro. Abstr.; Curr. Aware. Biol. Sci., CABS; Curr. Cit.; Curr. Contents Life Sci.; EP Collect.; Ergon. Abstr.; Homework Help.; Index Med.; MasterFile FullTEXT 1000; MasterFile FullTEXT 350; MasterFile FullTEXT 650; MasterFile FullTEXT (Jan. 1995-); Nutr. Abstr. Rev., Ser. A, Hum. Exp.; OCLC; Psychol. Abstr. (1986-); PsycINFO (1990-); PsycLit; Ref. Upd. Deluxe Ed.; Res. Alert [Full Cov.]; Rev. Agric. Entomol.; Sci. Cit. Index; SCISEARCH; Telebase.

LC QH1 .B594 ISSN 0021-9282
DD 508 II
NLM W1 JO564F CODEN JBSBAV
JOURNAL OF BIOLOGICAL SCIENCES, THE. [J. biol. sci.]. **Added/Corp** Bombay Biological Association. Vol. 1 (June 1958)-. Academic Scholarly Publication. English. Two times a year. Journal of Biological Sciences, Department of Biology, R. J. College, Ghatkopar Bombay 400086 India. Documents available from BIOSIS Document Express, CASDDS.
Ind/Abst Biol. Abstr.; Chem. Abstr.; Life Sci. Collect.

LC QH301 ISSN 1010-3910
DD 574/.05 IQ
NLM W1; JO564FJ CODEN JBSREF
JOURNAL OF BIOLOGICAL SCIENCES RESEARCH. [J. biol. sci. res.]. **VFOAT** JBSR; J.B.S.; Majallat Buhuth Ulum Al-Hayah; J.B.S.R.; JBS. Vol. 14, No. 2 (July 1983)-. Academic Scholarly Publication. Arabic (English). Three times a year. 20.00ID Iraq; $66.00 other. Editorial Committee / Biological Research Center, Jadiriya, PO Box 2371, Baghdad Iraq. **Tel** 7763250, telex 2187 BATHILMI IK. **ED** Azwar N Khalaf, Walid T Aljumaily. **Circ:** 800 (ctrl). Documents available from CASDDS. ***Continues*** *Journal of Biological Sciences (Markaz Buhuth Ulum Al-Hayah (Baghdad, Iraq)).*
Desc: The journal aims at the publication of research and studies on various fields of biology science especially in relation to animal science, cell biology, hydrology, microbiology, environmental pollution, medicinal plants and plant ecology and taxonomy.
Ind/Abst Chem. Abstr. (1983-); CSA Neuro. Abstr. (?-?); Dairy Sci. Abstr.; Ecology Abstr.; Fish Rev.; Helminthol. Abstr.; Index Vet.; Microbiol. Abstr. Sect. A; Microbiol. Abstr. Sect. C; Nematol. Abstr.; Life Sci. Collect.; Protozoolog. Abstr.; Rev. Med. Vet. Entomol.; Vet. Bull.; Wildl. Rev.

LC QH301 ISSN 0218-3390
DD 574 SI
•JOURNAL OF BIOLOGICAL SYSTEMS. **VFOAT** JBS. Vol. 1, No. 1 (Mar. 1993)-. Periodical. English. Four times a year. $90.00 individuals, $195.00 institutions. World Scientific Publishing Company, PO Box 128, Farrer Road, Singapore 9128 Singapore. **Tel** 011 65 3825663, FAX 011 65 3825919, telex RS 28561 WSPC. **(Subscription address:** World Scientific Publishing Company, Inc., 1060 Main Street, Suite 1 B, River Edge NJ 07661. **Tel** (800)227-7562, (201)487-9655.) **ED** R.V. Jean and P.M. Auger. **Bk Rev.**
Desc: Covers topics such as general systems theory, interdisciplinary approaches in biology and medicine, environmental studies, evolutionary biology, medical systems, numerical simulations and computations, and epistemology.

LC QH ISSN 0250-5991
DD 574 II
NLM W1 JO567N CODEN JOBSDN
Pr Rev.
JOURNAL OF BIOSCIENCES. [J. biosci.]. **Added/Corp** Indian Academy of Sciences. Vol. 1, No. 1 (Mar. 1979)-. Academic Scholarly Publication. English. Four times a year. Comes in combination of Current Science and Indian Academy of Science Option 1. Indian Academy of Sciences Circulation, PO Box 8005, Department of Sadashivanagar, Bangalore 560 080 India. **Tel** 011 91 812 342546, 342310, telex 0845-2178 ACAD IN. **(Subscription address:** Prints India, 11 Darya Ganj, New Delhi 110002 India. **Tel** 011 91 11 3268645, FAX 011 91 11 3275542, telex 31-61087 PRIN-IN.) **ED** G. Padmanaban. Index available. **Circ:** 500. Documents available from The Genuine Article, BIOSIS Document Express, CASDDS, Documents on Demand. ***Continues*** *Proceedings, Experimental Biology Section;* ***Absorbed*** *Proceedings. Plant Sciences., 0253-410x* ***and*** *Proceedings. Animal Sciences., 0253-4113.*
Desc: Devoted to research in biochemistry, biophysics, genetics, molecular biology, immunology, endocrinology,

nutrition, microbiology, clinical sciences.
Ind/Abst AgBiotech News Inf.; Anim. Breed. Abstr.; Biol. Abstr. (1985-); Chem. Abstr.; Crop Physiol. Abstr.; CSA Neuro. Abstr. (?-?); Curr. Aware. Biol. Sci., CABS; Curr. Biotechnol.; Curr. Cit.; Curr. Contents Agric. Biol. Environ. Sci.; Curr. Contents Life Sci.; Dairy Sci. Abstr.; EMBASE [Select. Cov.]; Energy Res. Abstr. (Dec. 1979-); Environ. Abstr.; Genet. Abstr.; Helminthol. Abstr. (19??-19??); Microbiol. Abstr. Sect. B (19??-19??); Microbiol. Abstr. Sect. C; Oncog. Growth Factors Abstr.; Life Sci. Collect.; Plant Breed. Abstr.; Plant Grow. Reg. Abstr.; Protozoolog. Abstr.; Res. Alert [Full Cov.]; Sci. Cit. Index; SCISEARCH; Wheat Barley Trit. Abstr.

ISSN 1079-5383
DD 574 US
NLM W1; JO574F
•JOURNAL OF CAPILLARY ELECTROPHORESIS. **VFOAT** J. cap. elec. Vol. 1, Issue 1 (July/Aug. 1994)-. Periodical. English. Six times a year. $350.00 (institutions), $175.00 (individuals). International Scientific Communications Inc, PO Box 870, 30 Controls Drive, Shelton CT 06484-0870. **Tel** (203)926-9300, FAX (203)926-9310, telex 964292. **ED** Norberto A. Guzman.

ISSN 0843-6150
DD 594/.5/05 US
CODEN JCEBE6
SUSPENDED
JOURNAL OF CEPHALOPOD BIOLOGY. [J. cephalop. biol.]. Vol. 1, No. 1 (Summer 1989)-Vol. 2, No. 2 (199?). Periodical. English. Two times a year. $80.00. Journal of Cephalopod Biology, 209A Snyder Hall, University of Hi Manoa, Honolulu HI 96822. **Tel** (808)956-6307, FAX (808)956-5339. **ED** Dr. J.M. Arnold. **Bk Rev**, (Qty: 2-5). **Ad Acc. Circ:** 100 (ctrl).

LC BD241 **ISSN** 0176-4268
DD 510 US
CCC
Pr Rev.
JOURNAL OF CLASSIFICATION. **See** Mathematics.

ISSN 1066-5277
DD 570 US
NLM W1; JO595KK **CODEN** JCOBEM
•JOURNAL OF COMPUTATIONAL BIOLOGY. [J. comput. biol.]. (1993)-. Periodical. English. Four times a year. $200.00. Mary Ann Liebert Inc., 2 Madison Avenue, Larchmont NY 10538. **Tel** (914)834-3100, (800)M-LIEBERT, FAX (212)289-4697.

ISSN 8755-5093
DD 574 SZ
CCC
NLM W1; JO644BN **CODEN** ENINEG
JOURNAL OF ENZYME INHIBITION. [J. enzym. inhib.]. **VFOAT** Enzyme Inhibition. Vol. 1, No. 1 (Oct. 1985)-. Academic Scholarly Publication. English. Four times a year. $457.00 (academic institutions), $714.00 (corporate institutions). Harwood Academic Publishers, PO Box 90, Reading RG1 8JL United Kingdom. **Tel** 011 44 1734 560080, FAX 011 44 1734 568211. **ED** H. J. Smith. **Bk Rev. Ad Acc.** Documents available from The Genuine Article, CASDDS.
Ind/Abst Chem. Abstr. (1985-); Curr. Aware. Biol. Sci., CABS; Curr. Cit.; Curr. Contents Life Sci.; EMBASE; Index Med. (1985-); PESTDOC; Res. Alert [Full Cov.]; Sci. Cit. Index.

LC QH90.A1 J68 **ISSN** 0970-3594
DD 574.92/05 II
CODEN JOHYE4
JOURNAL OF HYDROBIOLOGY. [J. hydrobiol.]. **Added/Corp** Association of Environmental Scientists. Vol. 1, Nos. 1 and 2 (1985)-. Periodical. English. Two times a year. $50.00. Association of Environmental Scientists, Ujjain India. **(Subscription address:** Prints India, 11 Darya Ganj, New Delhi 110002 India. **Tel** 011 91 11 3268645, FAX 011 91 11 3275542, telex 31-61087 PRIN-IN.**)**

ISSN 0883-1378
DD 574 US
NLM W1; JO707F **CODEN** JIDBE9
JOURNAL OF INFERENTIAL AND DEDUCTIVE BIOLOGY. **VFOAT** JIDB. Vol. 1, No. 1 (1985)-. Academic Scholarly Publication. English. Six times a year. $188.00 (institutions), $79.00 (individuals). Danielli Associates Inc, 185 Highlands Street, Worcester MA 01609. **Tel** (617)752-2591. **ED** Roger Jean and Aletandro Engel. Index available (bound in last issue). **Bk Rev. Ad Acc.** Documents available from CASDDS.
Desc: The application of inferential methods to all fields of biology. Includes both theory and experimental tests.
Ind/Abst Chem. Abstr. (1985-).

LC QP185 .R47 **ISSN** 0741-5400
DD 599/.01/13 US
CCC
NLM W1; J0745H **CODEN** JLBIE7
Pr Rev.
JOURNAL OF LEUKOCYTE BIOLOGY. [J. leukoc. biol.]. **Added/Corp** Reticuloendothelial Society. Federation of American Societies for Experimental Biology. Society for Leukocyte Biology. Vol. 35, No. 1 (Jan. 1984)-. Academic Scholarly Publication. English. Twelve times a year (plus supplement). $696.00. Federation of American Societies for Experimental Biology, Room L-2310, 9650 Rockville Park, Bethesda MD 20814-3998. **Tel** (301)530-7027. **ED** Carleton C. Stewart. Documents available from The Genuine Article, BIOSIS Document Express, CASDDS. ***Continues*** *Reticuloendothelial Society. Res. Journal of the Reticuloendothelial Society, 0033-6890.*
Desc: Presents manuscripts of original investigations on the orgins, including developmental biology and functions, of granulocytes, lymphocytes, and mononuclear phagocytes; their mechanisms of inter-cellular communication; and the ways effector molecules recognize and destroy infectious organisms, foreign tissue, or neoplastic cells.
Ind/Abst Biol. Abstr.; Chem. Abstr. (1984-); Chemorecept. Abstr.; Curr. Aware. Biol. Sci., CABS; Curr. Cit.; Curr. Contents Life Sci.; EMBASE; Immunol. Abstr.; Index Med.; Index Vet.; INIS Atomindex [Micro.]; NAPRALERT; Oncog. Growth Factors Abstr.; Life Sci. Collect.; Pig News Inf.; Poult. Abstr.; Protozoolog. Abstr.; Ref. Upd. Basic Ed.; Ref. Upd. Deluxe Ed.; Res. Alert [Full Cov.]; Rev. Med. Vet. Mycology; Sci. Cit. Index; SCISEARCH; Small Anim. Abstr. Bibliogr.; Soc. Sci. Cit. Index [Select. Cov.]; Vet. Bull.; Virol. AIDS Abstr.

LC QH323.5 .J67 **ISSN** 0303-6812
DD 574/.01/51 AU
CCC
NLM W1 JO748SE **CODEN** JMBLAJ
Pr Rev.
JOURNAL OF MATHEMATICAL BIOLOGY. [J. math. biol.]. Vol. 1 (1974)-. Periodical. English. Eight times a year. $909.00. Springer-Verlag GmbH & Company KG, Heidelberger Platz 3, D-14197 Berlin Germany. **Tel** 011 49 30 8207223, FAX 011 49 30 8214091, telex 183 319 SPBLN D. **(Subscription address:** Springer-Verlag New York Inc. / North America, PO Box 2485, Journal Fulfillment, Secaucus NJ 07096. **Tel** (201)348-4033, (800)777-4643, FAX (201)348-4505.**)** **ED** W alt, K P Hadeler, U an der Heiden, S A Levin, H T Banks, O Diekmann, J Gani, F C Hoppensteadt, D Ludwig, J D Murray, T Nagylaki, S Sawyer, and L A Segel. available on microfilm and microfiche from University Microfilms International (UMI). Documents available from The Genuine Article, Ask*IEEE, Documents on Demand.
Desc: Publishes papers in which mathematics is used to better understand biological phenomena. Also publishes mathematical papers inspired by biological research and papers which yield new experimental data bearing on mathematical models.
Ind/Abst Biocont. News Inf.; Biostatistica; CompuMath Cit. Index [Full Cov.]; CSA Neuro. Abstr. (?-?); Curr. Cit.; Curr. Contents Life Sci.; Ecology Abstr.; EMBASE; Energy Inf. Abstr.; Energy Res. Abstr. (Oct. 1977-); Environ. Abstr.; Helminthol. Abstr. (1991-); Index Med.; INSPEC (1977-); Math. Rev.; Life Sci. Collect.; Plant Breed. Abstr.; Plant Grow. Reg. Abstr.; Protozoolog. Abstr.; Res. Alert [Full Cov.]; Rev. Med. Vet. Entomol.; Sci. Cit. Index; SCISEARCH; Stat. Theory Method Abstr. (1976-1977, 1979-1981, 1983, 1986-1987); Wildl. Rev.; Zentralbl. Math. Ihre Grenzgeb.

LC QH301 **ISSN** 0022-2836
DD 574.8/8/05 UK
CCC
NLM W1 JO773 **CODEN** JMOBAK
Pr Rev.
JOURNAL OF MOLECULAR BIOLOGY. [J. mol. biol.]. Vol. 1 (Apr. 1959)-. Academic Scholarly Publication. English. Fifty times a year. $3405.30. Academic Press Ltd., A Division of Harcourt Brace & Company Ltd., 24-28 Oval Road, London NW1 7DX United Kingdom. **Tel** 011 44 171 2674466, FAX 011 44 171 4822293, 011 44 171 4854752, telex 25775 ACPRES G. **(Subscription address:** Harcourt Brace & Company, Ltd., Foots Cray High Street, Sidcup Kent DA14 5HP United Kingdom. **Tel** 011 44 181 3003322, FAX 011 44 181 3090807, telex 896 377 ACADEM.**)** **ED** P. Wright. Documents available from The Genuine Article, BIOSIS Document Express, CASDDS.
Desc: Provides coverage of the field of molecular biology. Emphasis is given to those areas of cell biology in which the molecular approach is presently achieving substantial results.
Ind/Abst AgBiotech News Inf.; AGRICOLA [Select. Cov.]; Anim. Breed. Abstr.; Biocont. News Inf.; Biol. Agric. Index; Biol. Abstr.; Biostatistica; Chem. Abstr.; Chem. Titles; Crop Physiol. Abstr.; CSA Neuro. Abstr. (?-?); Curr. Aware. Biol. Sci., CABS; Curr. Cit.; Curr. Contents Life Sci.; Dairy Sci. Abstr.; EMBASE; Field Crop Abstr.; Fish Rev. (Jan. 1989-July 1992); Food Sci. Technol. Abstr.; Genet. Abstr.; Grass. Forage Abstr.; Hortic. Abstr.; Immunol. Abstr.; Index Med.; Int. Aerosp. Abstr.; Maize Abstr.; Microbiol. Abstr. Sect. B; Microbiol. Abstr. Sect. C; Nematol. Abstr.; Nucl. Acids Abstr.; Life Sci. Collect.; PESTDOC; Pig News Inf.; Plant Breed. Abstr.; Poult. Abstr.; Protozoolog. Abstr.; Ref. Upd. Basic Ed.; Ref. Upd. Deluxe Ed.; Res. Alert [Full Cov.]; Rev. Agric. Entomol.; Rev. Med. Vet. Entomol.; Rev. Plant Pathol.; Sci. Cit. Index; SCISEARCH; Seed Abstr.; Soyabean Abstr.; Trop. Dis. Bull.; Wildl. Rev. (Jan. 1989-July 1992).

ISSN 0898-9249
DD 574 US
JOURNAL OF MORPHOLOGY. SUPPLEMENT. [J. morph. Suppl.]. Supplement 1 (1987)-. Monographic series. English. Irregular. John Wiley & Sons, Inc., 605 Third Avenue, New York NY 10158-0012. **Tel** (212)850-6000, (212)850-6645, FAX (212)850-6088, telex 12-7063. **(Subscription address:** John Wiley & Sons / UK, Baffins Lane, Chichester, West Sussex PO19 1UD United Kingdom. **Tel** 011 44 1243 779777, FAX 011 44 243 776128, telex 86290 WIBOOKG.**)**
Ind/Abst AGRICOLA [Select. Cov.].

LC QP351 .J55 **ISSN** 0022-3034
DD 612/.8/05 US
CCC
NLM W1 JO784 **CODEN** JNEUBZ
Pr Rev.
JOURNAL OF NEUROBIOLOGY. **See** Medical Sciences-Neurology.

LC R850.A1 J68 **ISSN** 1043-609X
DD 610/.72073 US
CCC
NLM W1; JO795HJ **CODEN** JNREEL
JOURNAL OF NIH RESEARCH, THE. (THE JOURNAL OF NIH RESEARCH : LIFE SCIENCES RESEARCH AND NEWS ABOUT THE NATIONAL INSTITUTES OF HEALTH AND THE ALCOHOL, DRUG ABUSE, AND MENTAL HEALTH ADMINISTRATION.). [J. NIH res.]. **VFOAT** NIH Research. **VAT** Journal of National Institutes of Health Research. Vol. 1, No. 1 (May/June 1989)-. Trade Publication. English. Twelve times a year. $129.00. Journal of NIH Research, 1444 I Street Northwest, Suite 1000, Washington DC 20005. **Tel** (202)785-5333, FAX (202)872-7738. **ED** Deborah Barnes. **Ad Acc. Circ:** 28,000.
Desc: News and research that provides perspective on developments of broad interest to life scientists worldwide, with a special emphasis on biomedical research funded by the United States National Institutes of Health. Includes research review articles, commentaries and viewpoints, legal discussion, techniques updates, clinical trials summaries, and new funding sources.
Ind/Abst BioBusiness (1990-); Curr. Cit.

LC QH **ISSN** 0921-2728
DD 570 NE
CCC
CODEN JOUPE8
Pr Rev.
JOURNAL OF PALEOLIMNOLOGY. [J. paleolimnol.]. Vol. 1, No. 1 (July 1988)-. Periodical. English. Six times a year. $483.00. Kluwer Academic Publishers, Postbus 322, 3300 AH Dordrecht The Netherlands. **Tel** 011 31 78 524400, FAX 011 31 78 183273, telex 20083. **ED** John P Smol. **Ad Acc. Acid Free. Circ:** 100. available on microfilm and microfiche from University Microfilms International (UMI). Documents available from BIOSIS Document Express.
Desc: The aim of the journal is to provide a vehicle for the rapid dissemination of original scientific work dealing with the reconstruction of lake histories. The journal continues to be a major repository for papers dealing with climatic change, as well as other pressing topics, such as global environmental change, lake acidification, eutrophication, long-term monitoring, and other aspects of lake ontongeny.
Ind/Abst Biol. Abstr. (1989-); Curr. Aware. Biol. Sci., CABS; Curr. Cit.; Ecol. Abstr.; Ecology Abstr.; Geogr. Abstr. Phys. Geogr. (1989-); Geol. Abstr. (1989-); Meteorol. Geoastrophys. Abstr. (199?-).

LC QH515 .J68 **ISSN** 1011-1344
DD 574.19/152 SZ
CCC
NLM W1; JO832BH **CODEN** JPPBEG
Pr Rev.
JOURNAL OF PHOTOCHEMISTRY AND PHOTOBIOLOGY. B, BIOLOGY. [J. photochem. photobiol., B Biol.]. **Added/Corp** European Society for Photobiology. **VFOAT** Biology. Vol. 1, No. 1 (Sept. 1987)-. Academic Scholarly Publication. English. Fifteen times a year (5 vols.). $1660.00. Elsevier Sequoia SA, PO Box 564, CH-1001 Lausanne 1 Switzerland. **Tel** 011 41 21 3207381, FAX 011 41 21 3235444. **ED** G. Jori. **Ad Acc, Adv Mgr:** W. van Cattenburch (Amsterdam). available on microfilm and microfiche from University Microfilms International (UMI); available on an online database from Elsevier Electronic Subscriptions (EES). Documents available from The Genuine Article, BIOSIS Document Express, Ask*IEEE, CASDDS. ***Continues in part*** *Journal of Photochemistry, 0047-2670.*
Desc: The journal provides a forum for the publication of papers relating to the various aspects of photobiology and means for communications in this multidisciplinary field.
Ind/Abst Biol. Abstr.; Chem. Abstr.; Crop Physiol. Abstr.; Curr. Aware. Biol. Sci., CABS; Curr. Cit.; Curr. Contents Life Sci.; Field Crop Abstr.; Index Med.; INSPEC; Met. Abstr.; Microbiol. Abstr. Sect. C; Phys. Briefs; Polymer Contents; Res. Alert [Full Cov.]; Sci. Cit. Index; SCISEARCH.

LC QH301 .J74 ISSN 0970-1990
DD 574/.05 II
CODEN JRAAEK

JOURNAL OF RECENT ADVANCES IN APPLIED SCIENCES. [J. recent adv. appl. sci.]. **VFOAT** JRAAS. Vol. 1, No. 1 (Jan. 1986)-. Periodical. English. Two times a year. $200.00. Evoker Research Perfecting Company, Lucknow India. **(Subscription address:** Prints India, 11 Darya Ganj, New Delhi 110002 India. **Tel** 011 91 11 3268645, FAX 011 91 11 3275542, telex 31-61087 PRIN-IN.) Documents available from CASDDS.
Ind/Abst Chem. Abstr.

LC QD541 .J8 ISSN 0095-9782
DD 541/.34/05 US
CCC
NLM W1 JO901D CODEN JSLCAG
Pr Rev.

JOURNAL OF SOLUTION CHEMISTRY. **See** Chemistry and Chemicals-Physical and Theoretical Chemistry.

ISSN 1047-8477
DD 574 US
CCC
NLM W1; JO904UT CODEN JSBIEM

JOURNAL OF STRUCTURAL BIOLOGY. [J. struct. biol.]. Vol. 103, No. 1 (March 1990)-. Academic Scholarly Publication. English. Six times a year. $376.00. Academic Press Inc., 6277 Sea Harbor Drive, Orlando FL 32887. **Tel** (800)543-9534, (407)345-4100, FAX (407)352-3445. **ED** Ueli Aebi and Robert M. Glaeser. Documents available from The Genuine Article, BIOSIS Document Express, CASDDS. ***Continues*** *Journal of Ultrastructure and Molecular Structure Research, 0889-1605.*
Desc: Publishes papers dealing with the structural analysis of biological matter at all levels of organization by means of light and electron microscopy, X-ray diffraction and nuclear magnetic resonance.
Ind/Abst Abstr. Bull. Inst. Pap. Sci. Tech.; AGRICOLA [Select. Cov.]; Anim. Breed. Abstr.; Biol. Abstr. (1991-); Chem. Abstr. (1990-); Crop Physiol. Abstr.; Curr. Aware. Biol. Sci., CABS; Curr. Cit.; Curr. Contents Life Sci.; Dairy Sci. Abstr.; EMBASE; Field Crop Abstr.; Fish Rev. (Jan. 1989-July 1992); Hortic. Abstr.; Index Med. (1990-); Ref. Upd. Basic Ed.; Ref. Upd. Deluxe Ed.; Res. Alert [Full Cov.]; Rev. Med. Vet. Entomol.; Rev. Plant Pathol.; Sci. Cit. Index; SCISEARCH; Seed Abstr.; Trop. Dis. Bull.; Wildl. Rev. (Jan. 1989-July 1992).

LC QH305 .J64 ISSN 0022-5010
DD 574/.09 NE
CCC
NLM W1 JO928L CODEN JHBIA9
Pr Rev.

JOURNAL OF THE HISTORY OF BIOLOGY. [J. hist. biol.]. Vol. 1 (Spring 1968)-. Periodical. English. Three times a year. $242.00. Kluwer Academic Publishers, Postbus 322, 3300 AH Dordrecht The Netherlands. **Tel** 011 31 78 524400, FAX 011 31 78 183273, telex 20083. **ED** Everett Mendelsohn and Shirley Roe. Index available. cum. index. **Bk Rev. Ad Acc. Acid Free. Circ:** 1,100. available on microfilm and microfiche from University Microfilms International (UMI). Documents available from The Genuine Article, BIOSIS Document Express.
Desc: Devoted to the history of the biological sciences, with interest in philosophical and social issues confronting biology. Particular attention is paid to developments during the nineteenth and twentieth centuries.
Ind/Abst Am. Hist. Life (1968-); Biol. Agric. Index; Biol. Abstr.; Curr. Aware. Biol. Sci., CABS; Curr. Contents Agric. Biol. Environ. Sci.; GeoRef; Plant Breed. Abstr. (1968-); Protozoolog. Abstr.; Res. Alert [Full Cov.]; Sci. Cit. Index; SCISEARCH.

LC Q ISSN 0368-2684
DD 500 II
CODEN JISCAF

JOURNAL OF THE INDIAN INSTITUTE OF SCIENCE. SECTION C: BIOLOGICAL SCIENCES. **Main/Corp** Indian Institute of Science, Bangalore. Vol. 59, No. 4 (Apr. 1977)-. Periodical. English. Six times a year. **(Subscription address:** Prints India, 11 Darya Ganj, New Delhi 110002 India. **Tel** 011 91 11 3268645, FAX 011 91 11 3275542, telex 31-61087 PRIN-IN.) Documents available from BIOSIS Document Express. ***Continues in part*** *Indian Institute of Science, Bangalore. Journal of the Indian Institute of Science.*
Ind/Abst Biol. Abstr.; NAPRALERT.

LC QH301 .J75 ISSN 0022-5193
DD 574.05 UK
CCC
NLM W1 JO966C CODEN JTBIAP
Pr Rev.

JOURNAL OF THEORETICAL BIOLOGY. [J. theor. biol.]. Vol. 1 (Jan. 1961)-. Academic Scholarly Publication. English. Twenty-four times a year. $2352.91. Academic Press Ltd., A Division of Harcourt Brace & Company Ltd., 24-28 Oval Road, London NW1 7DX United Kingdom. **Tel** 011 44 171 2674466, FAX 011 44 171 4822293, 011 44 171 4854752, telex 25775 ACPRES G. **(Subscription address:** Harcourt Brace & Company, Ltd., Foots Cray High Street, Sidcup Kent DA14 5HP United Kingdom. **Tel** 011 44 181 3003322, FAX 011 44 181 3090807, telex 896 377 ACADEM.) **ED** S. A. Kauffman and L. Wolpert. cum. index. Documents available from The Genuine Article, BIOSIS Document Express, CASDDS.
Desc: A forum for theoretical papers that give insight into biological processes. Covers topics of interest to biologists in many areas of research. Experimental material bearing on theory is acceptable. Comment on theoretical issues or on papers published in the journal is welcomed in the form of letters to the editors.
Ind/Abst Abstr. Anthropol.; AgBiotech News Inf.; AGRICOLA [Select. Cov.]; Biocont. News Inf. (1991-); Biodeter. Abstr. (1991-); Biol. Abstr.; Biostatistica; Chem. Abstr.; Crop Physiol. Abstr.; CSA Neuro. Abstr. (?-?); Curr. Cit.; Curr. Contents Life Sci.; Dairy Sci. Abstr.; Ecology Abstr.; EMBASE; Entomol. Abstr.; Field Crop Abstr.; Fish Rev.; For. Abstr.; Genet. Abstr.; Helminthol. Abstr. (19??-19??); Index Med.; Int. Aerosp. Abstr.; Key Word Index Wildl. Res.; Math. Rev. (?-199?); Nutr. Abstr. Rev., Ser. B, Live Feeds and Feed.; Oncog. Growth Factors Abstr.; Life Sci. Collect.; Plant Breed. Abstr.; Protozoolog. Abstr.; Ref. Upd. Basic Ed.; Ref. Upd. Deluxe Ed.; Res. Alert [Full Cov.]; Rev. Agric. Entomol.; Rev. Med. Vet. Entomol.; Sci. Cit. Index; SCISEARCH; Seed Abstr.; Soc. Sci. Cit. Index [Select. Cov.]; Sorghum Mill. Abstr.; Stat. Theory Method Abstr. (1967, 1970-1978); Weed Abstr.; Wildl. Rev.

LC R ISSN 0946-672X
DD 610 GW
NLM W1; JO966KDR CODEN JTEDET
Pr Rev.

•**JOURNAL OF TRACE ELEMENTS IN MEDICINE AND BIOLOGY.** **See** Medical Sciences.

LC QH91.75.A1 K34
DD 574.92 JA
UDC 574.5

KAICHU KOEN JOHO. **VFOAT** Marine Parks Journal. Japanese. Kaichu Koen Senta, c/o Toranomon Denku Building, 8-1 Toranomon 2-chome Minato-ku, Tokyo Japan.

LC QH ISSN 0931-380X
DD 574 GW
UDC 635 :631.147

KALENDER FUER DEN BIOGARTEN. [Kal. Biogart.]. (1986)-. German. One time a year. DM12.80. Pala-Verlag AM Eichwald 24, W-6117 Schaafheim Germany. **Tel** 0049/6073, FAX 88119, telex 80017. **ED** Dettmer Gruenefeld. **Bk Rev. Ad Acc. Circ:** 15,000.
Desc: Presents information on biological gardening.

LC QH301 .K25 ISSN 0115-0553
DD 574/.05 PH
CCC
CODEN KPJBAR

KALIKASAN, THE PHILIPPINE JOURNAL OF BIOLOGY. (KALIKASAN.). [Kalikasan, Philipp. j. biol.]. Vol. 1 (1972)-. Academic Scholarly Publication. English. Three times a year. P30.00 (institutions). University of Philippines at Los Banos, PO Box 361, 3720 Laguna Philippines. **Tel** 987181. Documents available from BIOSIS Document Express, CASDDS.
Ind/Abst Biol. Abstr.; Chem. Abstr.; Index Philip. Period. (-199?); Life Sci. Collect.; Philip. Sci. Technol. Abstr.

LC QH301 .K27
DD 74/.05 CC

KAO YUAN SHENG WU HSUEH CHI KAN. **Added/Corp** Chung-kuo k'o Hsueh Yuan. Hsi-pei kao Yuan Sheng wu yen Chiu so. **VFOAT** Acta Biological Plateau Sinica. Vol. 1, (May 1982)-. Periodical. Chinese (summaries and/or abstracts in English).
Ind/Abst Fish Rev. (Jan. 1989-July 1992); Wildl. Rev. (Jan. 1989-July 1992).

LC QH301 .K44 ISSN 0250-8257
DD 574/.05 KE

KENYA JOURNAL OF SCIENCES. SERIES B, BIOLOGICAL SCIENCES. **Added/Corp** Kenya National Academy of Sciences. **VFOAT** Biological Sciences. Vol. 7, No. 1 (1986)-. Periodical. English. Two times a year. PO Box 39450, Nairobi Kenya. **Tel** 721138. ***Continues*** *Kenya Journal of Science and Technology. Series B, Biological Sciences, 0250-8257.*

LC QH301 ISSN 0356-861X
DD 574 FI
Pr Rev.

KEVO NOTES. **Added/Corp** Lapin Tutkimusasema Kevo. (1975)-. Bulletin. English. Price varies per volume. University of Turku, Kevo Subarctic Research Institute, SF 20500 Turku Finland. **Tel** 011 358 21 6335913, FAX 011 44 358 21 3336363. **Circ:** 200 (ctrl).
Ind/Abst Ecol. Abstr.

LC QH301 .J34
DD 574 JA

KISO SEIBUTSUGAKU KENKYUJO NENPO. **Added/Corp** Kiso Seibutsugaku Kenkyujo (Japan). No. 1 (1982)-. Japanese. Okazaki Kokuritsu Kyodo Kenkyu Kiko Kiso Seibutsugaku Kenkyujo, Naka 38 Aza Saigo Myodaiji-machi, Okazaki-shi 444 Japan.

LC QH7 .D4 ISSN 0366-3612
DD 508 DK
CODEN BSVSAQ

KONGELIGE DANSKE VIDENSKABERNES SELSKAB. BIOLOGISKE SKRIFTER. (BIOLOGISKE SKRIFTER.). [K. Dan. vidensk. selsk., Biol. skr.]. **Added/Corp** Kongelige Danske Videnskabernes Selskab. (1939)-. Monographic series. Danish (English and German). Price varies per volume. Munksgaard International Publishers Ltd, PO Box 2148, DK-1016 Copenhagen K Denmark. **Tel** 011 45 33 127030, FAX 011 45 33 129387, telex 19431 MUNKS DK. Documents available from BIOSIS Document Express. ***Formed by the union of*** *Historisk og Filosofisk Afdeling* ***and*** *Naturvidenskabelig og Mathematisk Afdeling.*
Ind/Abst AGRICOLA [Select. Cov.]; Biol. Abstr.; GeoRef; Life Sci. Collect.

LC QH301 .K67 ISSN 0023-4249
DD 574.05/6 PL

KOSMOS (WARSAW, POLAND). (KOSMOS.). **Added/Corp** Polskie Towarzystwo Przyrodnikow Im. Kopernika. (1983)-. Periodical. Polish. Four times a year. $68.00. **(Subscription address:** Ars Polona-Ruch, PO Box 1001, Krakowskie Przedmiescie 7, 00-068 Warsaw Poland. **Tel** 011 48 22 261201.) Documents available from CASDDS. ***Continues*** *Kosmos. Seria A: Biologia, 0023-4249.*
Ind/Abst Chem. Abstr.

LC QH352 .K67 ISSN 0386-4561
DD 574 JA

KOTAIGUN SEITAI GAKKAI KAIHO. **See** Population Studies.

LC QH301
DD 574 JA

KYOTO FURITSU DAIGAKU GAKUJUTSU HOKOKU. RIGAKU, SEIKATSU KAGAKU. SCIENTIFIC REPORTS OF THE KYOTO PREFECTURAL UNIVERSITY. NATURAL SCIENCE AND LIVING SCIENCE. SER. A: NATURAL SCIENCE. A-KEIRETSU: RIGAKU. **Main/Corp** Kyoto Furitsu Daigaku. **Added/Corp** Kyoto Furitsu Daigaku. Scientific Reports of the Kyoto Prefectural University. Natural Science and Living Science. Ser. A: Natural Science. **VFOAT** Scientific Reports of the Kyoto Prefectural University. Natural Science and Living Science. No. 22 (1971)-. Academic Scholarly Publication. Japanese (English). Kyoto Prefectural University / Faculty of Agriculture, Library, Shimogamo Kyoto 606 Japan. ***Continues*** *Kyoto Furitsu Daigaku. Kyoto Furitsu Daigaku Gakujutsu Hokoku. Rigaku, Seikatsu Kagaku, Fukushigaku. A-Keiretsu: Rigaku.*
Ind/Abst Agric. Eng. Abstr.; For. Abstr.; Plant Breed. Abstr.

LC QH301 ISSN 0775-602X
DD 574 BE
UDC 542.2

LAB PRODUCTS INTERNATIONAL. BRUSSELS. (1987)-. Trade Publication. English. Eight times a year. Free to qualified readers; $70.00 US. Pan European Publishing Company, rue Verte 216, 1210 Brussels 21 Belgium. **Tel** 011 32 2 2420611. **ED** Bas Van Oosterhout. **Ad Acc. Circ:** 50,000 (ctrl).
Desc: Reports on new instruments and technologies used in individual and research laboratories.
Ind/Abst Abstr. BioCommer.

LC QD241 ISSN 1120-8376
DD 547 IT
UDC 542.1

LABORATORIO 2000. **See** Chemistry and Chemicals-Organic Chemistry.

LC QD ISSN 0924-4433
DD 540 NE
UDC 542
Pr Rev.

LABORATORIUM PRAKTIJK. [Lab. prakt.]. (1987)-. Periodical. Dutch. Twelve times a year. $68.18. Ten Hagen and Stam BV, Postbus 34, 2501 AG The Hague Netherlands. **Tel** 011 31 70 3045700. Index available. **Bk Rev. Ad Acc. Circ:** 5,095. ***Absorbed*** *LAB/ABC (Zoetermeer), 0168-7417.*

LC QH ISSN 0266-7169
DD 574 UK
CODEN LANEEY

LABORATORY NEWS. (19??)-. Periodical. English. Twelve times a year. $256.68. EMAP Readerlink, Audit House, 260 Field End Road, Ruislip Middlesex HA4 9LT United Kingdom. **Tel** 011 44 1773 63100, FAX 011

44 1733 87367. **ED** Alex Crawford. **Bk Rev**, (Qty: 20). **Ad Acc**, **Adv Mgr**: Ian Sprange, **Tel** 011 44 81 688 7788. **Circ:** 16,500 (ctrl). Documents available from BLDSC. **Absorbed** Laboratory Practice, 0023-6853.
 Ind/Abst Abstr. BioCommer.; Chem. Hazards Ind.; Lab. Hazards Bull.; Mass Spect. Bull.; Rev. Plant Pathol.

LC QH301 .L38A
IO
LAPORAN TAHUNAN. Main/Corp Lembaga
Biologi Nasional. Indonesian. One time a year.

LC QH	ISSN 0303-4283
DD 574	GW
UDC 574.2/.4	
NLM W1 LE305	

LEBEN UND UMWELT. Vol. 11, No. 3 (March
1974)-. Periodical. German. Six times a year. DM30.00. Biologie Verlag, Schlossallee 10A, D-65388 Schlangenbad Germany. Index available. **Bk Rev**.
 Desc: Protection of environment and bioprotection of life forms, human, animal and plant.

LC QH	ISSN 0723-8878
DD 574	US
NLM W3 LE32	CODEN LBBBD5

LECTINS, BIOLOGY, BIOCHEMISTRY, CLINICAL BIOCHEMISTRY. (LECTINS,
BIOLOGY, BIOCHEMISTRY, CLINICAL BIOCHEMISTRY : PROCEEDINGS OF THE ... LECTIN MEETING.). [Lectins, biol., biochem., clin. biochem.]. **VFOAT** Lectins. Vol. 1 (1981)-. Academic Scholarly Publication. English. Irregular. Sigma Chemical Co., 3500 Dekalb, St. Louis MO 63118. **Tel** (314)771-5765. Documents available from BIOSIS Document Express, CASDDS.
 Ind/Abst Biol. Abstr. (1986-); Chem. Abstr.; Curr. Cit.

LC QH	ISSN 0341-633X
DD 574	GW
	CCC
NLM W1 LE334	CODEN LNBMAH

LECTURE NOTES IN BIOMATHEMATICS. [Lect. notes biomath.]. Vol 1
(1974)-. Monographic series. English. Irregular. Springer-Verlag GmbH & Company KG, Heidelberger Platz 3, D-14197 Berlin Germany. **Tel** 011 49 30 8207223, **FAX** 011 49 30 8214091, telex 183 319 SPBLN D. (**Subscription address:** Springer-Verlag New York Inc. / North America, PO Box 2485, Journal Fulfillment, Secaucus NJ 07096. **Tel** (201)348-4033, (800)777-4643, **FAX** (201)348-4505.) **ED** S.A. Levin. available on microfilm. Documents available from Ask*IEEE, CASDDS.
 Desc: Topics include evolutionary dynamics of genetic diversity, and mathematical ecology.
 Ind/Abst Chem. Abstr.; Curr. Cit.; INSPEC; Math. Rev.; Zentralbl. Math. Ihre Grenzgeb.

LC QA	ISSN 0075-8523
DD 510	US
	CCC
NLM W3 LE33	CODEN LMLSAA

LECTURES ON MATHEMATICS IN THE LIFE SCIENCES. See Mathematics.

LC QH301
DD 574
LI
LIETUVOS TSR AUKSTUJU MOKYKLU MOKSLO DARBAI: BIOLOGIJA. VFOAT
Biologija; Nauchnye Trudy Vysshikh Uchebnykh ZavedeniEi LitovskoEi SSR B.Biologiia. (1961)-. Lithuanian (Russian). Mintis / Idea, Z Sierakausko 15, Vilnius 2600 Lithuania. **Tel** 011 7 3702 632943.
 Ind/Abst Crop Physiol. Abstr.; Field Crop Abstr.; For. Abstr.; Plant Breed. Abstr.; Plant Grow. Reg. Abstr.; Potato Abstr.; Soils Fert.

	ISSN 1056-0866
DD 502	US

LIFE SCIENCE LAB PRODUCTS. [Life sci.
lab products]. (1988)-. Periodical. English. Six times a year. $42.00 US; $50.00 North America; $80.00 other. Life Science Lab Products, Knolls Publishing Group Inc, 240 Cedar Knolls Road, Suite 220, Cedar Knolls NJ 07927. **Tel** 201-285-0855, **FAX** 201-285-1472. **ED** Alfred Saint-Jacques and Nancy Salerno Davis. Index available. **Bk Rev**. **Ad Acc**. **Circ:** 39,000 (ctrl).
 Desc: Articles on life science in industry, universities, hospitals, government, pharmaceuticals, biotechnology, and research centers internationally. It presents the latest in new products, services and technologies to the life sciences researcher.
 Ind/Abst Abstr. BioCommer. (-199?).

LC QH1 .L632a
UK
LINNEAN : NEWSLETTER AND PROCEEDINGS OF THE LINNEAN SOCIETY OF LONDON, THE. Main/Corp
Linnean Society of London. Vol. 1, No. 1 (Jan. 1984)-. Newsletter. English. Three times a year (Jan., Mar., Aug.). Linnean Society of London, Burlington House, Piccadilly, London W1V 0LQ United Kingdom. **Tel** 011 44 171 4344479, **FAX** 011 44 171 2879364. **Continues in part** Linnean Society of London. Biological Journal of the Linnean Society, 0024-4066; **Continues** Linnean Society of London. Linnean Newsletter.

LC QH301	ISSN 0024-4090
DD 574	BE
	CODEN LBRBAE

LINNEANA BELGICA. [Linn. belg.]. Vol. 1,
(March 1958)-. Periodical. French (English and Dutch). Four times a year (Mar., June, Sept., Dec.). $72.76. R. Leestmans, 45 Leuvensestraat, D-1800 Vilvoorde Belgium. **Tel** 011 32 22 510541. **ED** Leestmans R. Index available. **Bk Rev**, (Qty: 10). Documents available from BIOSIS Document Express.
 Ind/Abst Biol. Abstr.; Entomol. Abstr.; Life Sci. Collect. (1985-).

LC QH301	ISSN 0308-6739
DD 574	UK

LIST OF MEMBERS / FRESHWATER BIOLOGICAL ASSOCIATION. Main/Corp
Freshwater Biological Association. (1979)-. English. Freshwater Biological Association, Ferryhouse, Ambleside Cumbria LA22 O1P United Kingdom. **Tel** 011 44 15394 42468, **FAX** 011 44 15394 46914, telex 94070416 WIND G.

LC QH301	ISSN 0251-981X
DD 574	FR

MAB TECHNICAL NOTES. [MAB tech. notes].
VAT Programme on Man and Biosphere Technical Notes. (1975)-. Monographic series. English. Irregular. Price varies per volume.
 Ind/Abst Agrofor. Abstr.; GeoRef; Life Sci. Collect.

LC S	ISSN 0126-8643
DD 630	MY
	CODEN MABIDU

Pr Rev.
MALAYSIAN APPLIED BIOLOGY. See
Agriculture.

LC BF1 .M28	ISSN 0025-1615
DD 150/.5	II

MANAB MON. See Psychology.

LC QH	ISSN 0543-0119
DD 574	GW

MATERIAUX ET ORGANISMES. VFOAT
Materials and Organisms; Materiaux et Organismes. (1965)-. Periodical. Multiple languages (English and German; summaries and/or abstracts in English, French, Spanish and German). Four times a year. DM380.00. Duncker und Humblot Verlag, Postfach 410329, D-12113 Berlin Germany. **Tel** 011 49 30 79000612, 011 49 30 79000613. **ED** M. Gersondel and W. Kerner. **Bk Rev**. **Circ:** 250. Documents available from The Genuine Article.
 Ind/Abst AgBiotech News Inf.; Biocont. News Inf. (1991-); Biodeter. Abstr. (19??-19??); Curr. Aware. Biol. Sci., CABS; For. Prod. Abstr. (19??-19??); For. Abstr.; Microbiol. Abstr. Sect. A; Microbiol. Abstr. Sect. C; Res. Alert [Full Cov.]; Rev. Agric. Entomol.; Rev. Plant Pathol.; SCISEARCH; Wheat Barley Trit. Abstr.

LC QH324 .M27	ISSN 0025-5564
DD 574/.01/51	US
	CCC
NLM W1 MA959N	CODEN MABIAR

Pr Rev.
MATHEMATICAL BIOSCIENCES. [Math.
biosci.]. Vol. 1 (March 1967)-. Academic Scholarly Publication. English. Sixteen times a year. $1558.00. Elsevier Science Publishing Company Inc, Madison Square Station, PO Box 882, New York NY 10159-0882. **Tel** (212)633-3950, **FAX** (212)633-3990. **ED** John A Jacquez. **Bk Rev**. **Ad Acc**. **Circ:** 650. available on microfilm and microfiche from University Microfilms International (UMI); available on an online database from Elsevier Electronic Subscriptions (EES). Documents available from Article Express International, The Genuine Article, BIOSIS Document Express, Ask*IEEE, CASDDS.
 Desc: Publishes research and expository papers on the formulation, analysis and solution of mathematical models in the biosciences.
 Ind/Abst Abstr. Anthropol.; AGRICOLA; Anim. Breed. Abstr.; Bioeng. Abstr.; Biol. Abstr.; Biostatistica; Chem. Abstr.; CompuMath Cit. Index [Full Cov.]; CSA Neuro. Abstr. (?-?); Curr. Aware. Biol. Sci., CABS; Curr. Cit.; Curr. Contents Life Sci.; Ecology Abstr.; Ei Page One; EMBASE; Energy Res. Abstr.; Eng. Index Annu.; Fish Rev.; Index Med. (1989-); INSPEC (1968-); Int. Aerosp. Abstr.; Math. Rev.; Life Sci. Collect.; Plant Breed. Abstr.; Pollut. Abstr. Indexes; Protozoolog. Abstr.; Ref. Upd. Deluxe Ed.; Res. Alert [Full Cov.]; Sci. Cit. Index; SCISEARCH; Soc. Sci. Cit. Index [Select. Cov.]; Stat. Theory Method Abstr. (1979-1981); Wildl. Rev.; Zentralbl. Math. Ihre Grenzgeb.

LC QP552.C6 M38	ISSN 0945-053X
DD 591.1/85	GW
NLM W1; MA975	CODEN MTBOEC

●MATRIX BIOLOGY : JOURNAL OF THE INTERNATIONAL SOCIETY FOR MATRIX BIOLOGY. Added/Corp International
Society for Matrix Biology. Vol. 14, No. 1 (Jan. 1994)-. Academic Scholarly Publication. English. Nine times a year. $598.00. Gustav Fischer Verlag Stuttgart, Postfach 720143, D-70577 Stuttgart Germany. **Tel** 011 49 711 458030, **FAX** 011 49 711 4580334, telex 2627-7111488. Documents available from CASDDS. **Continues** Matrix (Stuttgart, Germany), 0934-8832.
 Ind/Abst Chem. Abstr.; Curr. Cit.; Index Med. (1994-).

LC QH301	ISSN 0275-8679
DD 574	US
NLM W1 MB999	CODEN MLBID5

MBL LECTURES IN BIOLOGY. [MBL lect.
biol.]. **Added/Corp** Marine Biological Laboratory (Woods Hole, Mass.). **VFOAT** M.B.L. Lectures in Biology. **VAT** Marine Biological Laboratory Lectures in Biology. Vol. 1 (1980)-. Monographic series. English. Alan R Liss, Inc., 41 East 11th Street, New York NY 10003. Documents available from CASDDS.
 Ind/Abst Chem. Abstr.; Curr. Cit.

LC QH607 .C45	ISSN 0925-4773
	IE
	CCC
NLM W1; ME106AG	CODEN MEDVE6

Pr Rev.
MECHANISMS OF DEVELOPMENT.
VFOAT MOD. Vol. 33, No. 1 (Dec. 1990)-. Academic Scholarly Publication. English. Fifteen times a year (5 volumes). $1571.00. Elsevier Science Ireland Ltd., Bay 15, Shannon Industrial Estate, Co Clare Ireland. **Tel** 011 353 61 471944. available on microfilm and microfiche from University Microfilms International (UMI); available on an online database from Elsevier Electronic Subscriptions (EES). Documents available from The Genuine Article, BIOSIS Document Express, CASDDS. **Continues** Cell Differentiation and Development, 0922-3371.
 Ind/Abst Biol. Abstr.; Chem. Abstr.; Curr. Aware. Biol. Sci., CABS; Curr. Cit.; Curr. Contents Life Sci.; EMBASE; Index Med.; Ref. Upd. Deluxe Ed.; Res. Alert [Full Cov.]; Sci. Cit. Index; SCISEARCH.

LC QH132.G73 M43	ISSN 0106-1054
DD 574.998/2	DK
NLM W1 GR541	

MEDDELELSER OM GRNLAND. BIOSCIENCE. [Medd. Grnl., Biosci.]. Added/Corp
Denmark. Kommissionen for Videnskabelige Undersgelser i Grnland. **VFOAT** Greenland Bioscience. (1979)-. Monographic series. English (French and German). Irregular. Price varies per volume. Arnold Busck International AS, Kobmagergade 49, PO Box 81, 1150 Copenhagen K Denmark. **Tel** 011 45 33 122453. **ED** Gert Steen Mogensen and Hopner Petersen. **Bk Rev**. **Ad Acc**. **Circ:** 800. **Continues in part** Meddelelser om Grnland, 0025-6676.
 Desc: Papers, monographs and thematic volumes presenting results of studies in, or related to Greenland within any field of bioscience.
 Ind/Abst Crop Physiol. Abstr.; Ecol. Abstr. (?-?); For. Abstr.; GeoRef; Life Sci. Collect.; Rev. Plant Pathol.; Seed Abstr.

LC QH301 .M37	ISSN 0302-0800
DD 574.05	BE
NLM W1; ME132F	CODEN MBENDX

MEDECINE, BIOLOGIE, ENVIRONNEMENT. See Medical Sciences.

LC R	ISSN 0767-0974
DD 610	FR
NLM W1; ME148UV	CODEN MSMSE4

Pr Rev.
MEDECINE SCIENCES : M/S. See Medical
Sciences.

LC R	
DD 610	BE

MEDICINE BIOLOGIE ENVIRONMENT.
See Medical Sciences.

LC R	ISSN 0204-6725
DD 610	BU
	CODEN MBIID4

MEDIKO-BIOLOGICESKAJA INFORMACIJA. See Medical Sciences.

LC R	ISSN 0323-9802
DD 610	BU
NLM W1 ME7884	CODEN MBLPA3

MEDIKO-BIOLOGICNI PROBLEMI. See
Medical Sciences.

LC R	
DD 610	US

MEDLARS. See Medical Sciences.

LC QH	
DD 574	US

MEMBERSHIP DIRECTORY. Main/Corp
Association for Tropical Biology. (1991)-. Directory. English. Association for Tropical Biology / New Orleans, Department of Biology, Tulane University, New Orleans LA 70118. **Tel** (504)865-5191, **FAX** (504)862-8706.

ISSN 0161-2883
DD 574 US
NLM W1 ME8935 CODEN MEMPDW

MEMBRANE PROTEINS (NEW YORK, N.Y.). (MEMBRANE PROTEINS.). [Membr. proteins]. Vol. 1 (1977)-. Academic Scholarly Publication. English. Irregular. Price varies per volume. Marcel Dekker Inc., 270 Madison Avenue, New York NY 10016. **Tel** (212)696-9000, (800)228-1160, FAX (212)685-4540, telex 421419. **(Subscription address:** Marcel Dekker Inc., PO Box 5017, Monticello NY 12701. **Tel** (800)228-1160.) **Bk Rev**. Documents available from CASDDS.
Desc: Designed to provide a forum for the publication of significant advances and definite synthesis being on the physics, chemistry and biology of membranes.
Ind/Abst Chem. Abstr.; Life Sci. Collect.

LC QH89 .M45 ISSN 0184-0266
DD 551.4/47 FR
CODEN MBIODM

MEMOIRES DE BIOSPEOLOGIE. [Mem. biospeol.]. (1978)-. Monographic series. French (English, Spanish, German and Italian). Irregular. $60.00. Laboratoire Souterrain du CNRS, Societe de Biospeologie, Moulis 09200 Saint-Girons France. **Tel** 011 33 61 663126. **ED** Christian Juberthie. cum. index. **Bk Rev**. **Ad Acc**. **Circ:** 250. Documents available from BIOSIS Document Express. ***Continues*** *Serie Documents (Laboratoire Souterrain du C.N.R.S.).*
Ind/Abst Biol. Abstr.

LC QH
DD 574 JA
NLM W1 ME895R

MEMOIRS OF NATIONAL INSTITUTE OF POLAR RESEARCH. SERIES E : BIOLOGY AND MEDICAL SCIENCE. **Added/Corp** Kokuritsu Kyokuchi Kenkyujo. **VFOAT** Biology and Medical Science. No. 32 (Mar. 1976)-. Periodical. English. Kokuritsu Kyokuchi Kenkyujo, (National Inst. of Polar Research), 9-10 Kaga 1 Chome, Itabashiku Tokyo 173 Japan. ***Continues*** *JARE Scientific Reports. Series E: Biology.*

LC QH301 .K89A ISSN 0454-7802
DD 574/.05 JA
CODEN MFKBBJ

MEMOIRS OF THE FACULTY OF SCIENCE, KYOTO UNIVERSITY. SERIES OF BIOLOGY. [Mem. Fac. Sci., Kyoto Univ., Ser. biol.]. **Main/Corp** Kyoto Daigaku. Rigakubu. Vol. 1 (Oct. 1967)-. Periodical. English (French, German and Russian). Two times a year. Available on an exchange basis. Kyoto University / Faculty of Science, Yoshida Honmachi Sakyo Ku, Kyotoshi Kyotofu 606 Japan. **Tel** (075)751-2111, telex 5422693 LIBKYU J. **ED** M Tasumi. **Circ:** 800 (ctrl). Documents available from BIOSIS Document Express. ***Supersedes in part*** *Memoirs of the College of Science, University of Kyoto: Series B.*
Ind/Abst Biol. Abstr.

LC QH ISSN 0702-0007
DD 574 CN
CODEN OPBIDL

MEMORIAL UNIVERSITY OF NEWFOUNDLAND OCCASIONAL PAPERS IN BIOLOGY. (OCCASIONAL PAPERS IN BIOLOGY / MEMORIAL UNIVERSITY OF NEWFOUNDLAND.). [Mem. Univ. Nfld. occas. pap. biol.]. **Added/Corp** Memorial University of Newfoundland. No. 1 (1978)-. Monographic series. English. Irregular. Price varies per volume. Memorial University, Department of Biology, St. John's Newfoundland A1B 3X9 Canada. **Tel** (709)737-8141. **ED** G. F. Bennett. Index available. cum. index. Documents available from BIOSIS Document Express.
Ind/Abst Biol. Abstr.

ISSN 1064-3745
DD 574 US
CCC
NLM W1; ME9616J CODEN MMBIED

METHODS IN MOLECULAR BIOLOGY (CLIFTON, N.J.). (METHODS IN MOLECULAR BIOLOGY.). [Methods mol. biol.]. (1984)-. Monographic series. English. Irregular. Price varies per volume. Humana Press Inc., 999 Riverview Drive, Suite 208, Totawa NJ 07512. **Tel** (201)256-1699, FAX (201)256-8341.
Ind/Abst Chem. Abstr.; Index Med.

ISSN 1073-9688
DD 574 US
NLM W1; MI297R CODEN MROCER

•MICROCIRCULATION (NEW YORK, N.Y. 1994). (MICROCIRCULATION : THE OFFICIAL JOURNAL OF THE MICROCIRCULATORY SOCIETY, INC.). [Microcirc.]. **Added/Corp** Microcirculatory Society. Vol. 1, No. 1 (Apr. 1994)-. Periodical. English. Four times a year. $210.00. Chapman & Hall, 2-6 Boundary Row, London SE1 8HN United Kingdom. **Tel** 011 44 171 8650066, FAX 011 44 171 5229623, telex 290164 CHAPMA G. **(Subscription address:** International Thompson Publisher Services Ltd, Subscriptions Department North Way Andover, Hampshire SP10 5BE United Kingdom. **Tel** 011 44 171 8650066.)

LC WMLC 90/0575 ISSN 0540-0163
LV
NLM W1 MI416 CODEN MSBBAU

MIKROELEMENTY V SSSR : BIULLETEN VSESOIUZNOI KOORDINATSONNOI KOMISSII PO MIKROELEMENTAM / AKADEMIIA NAUK LATVIISKOI SSR, INSTITUT BIOLOGII. **Added/Corp** Riga. Akademiia Nauk Latviiskoi, Institut Biologii. No. 1 (1961)-. Russian. Documents available from CASDDS.
Ind/Abst Chem. Abstr.; Crop Physiol. Abstr.; Maize Abstr.; Plant Breed. Abstr.; Soils Fert.; Wheat Barley Trit. Abstr.

LC QH ISSN 0026-3699
DD 574 NE
UDC 681.2

MIKRONIEK. [Mikroniek]. (1968)-. Periodical. Dutch. Six times a year. $90.44. NVFT, Postbus 80-004, 3508 TA Utrecht Netherlands. **Tel** 011 31 30 531710, 011 31 30 531639.

LC QH301 .T344 ISSN 0496-764X
DD 574.05/6 US

MISCELLANEOUS PUBLICATION - TALL TIMBERS RESEARCH STATION. **Main/Corp** Tallahassee. Tall Timbers Research Station. No. 1 (1961)-. Monographic series. English. Irregular. Price varies per volume. Tall Timbers Research Station, Route 1 Box 678, Tallahassee FL 32312. **Tel** (904)893-4153. available on microfilm from University Microfilms International (UMI).

ISSN 1065-3074
DD 574 US
CCC
NLM W1; MO194UK

•MOLECULAR AND CELLULAR DIFFERENTIATION. [Mol. cell. differ.]. Vol. 1, Issue 1 (1993)-. Periodical. English. Four times a year. $237.00. CRC Press Inc., 2000 Corporate Boulevard Northwest, Boca Raton FL 33431. **Tel** (407)994-0555, (800)272-7737, FAX (407)998-9784, (800)374-3401, telex 568689. **(Subscription address:** CRC Press Inc. / New York, PO Box 750, Pearl River NY 10965. **)** **ED** Paul B. Fisher.
Desc: Concerns with biochemical, cellular, and molecular changes associated with and controlling differentiation in both normal and tumor cells.

LC QH506 .M6617 ISSN 0737-4038
DD 574.87/328/05 US
CCC
NLM W1; MO195R CODEN MBEVEO
Pr Rev.

MOLECULAR BIOLOGY AND EVOLUTION. [Mol. biol. evol.]. **Added/Corp** Molecular Biology and Evolution Society. American Society of Naturalists. Society for the Study of Evolution. **VFOAT** MBE; M.B.E. Vol. 1, No. 1 (Dec. 1983)-. Academic Scholarly Publication. English. Ten times a year. $335.00. University of Chicago Press / Journals Division, PO Box 37005, 5720 South Woodlawn, Chicago IL 60637. **Tel** (312)753-3347, FAX (312)753-0811. **ED** Walter Fitch. **Acid Free. Circ:** 950. available on microfilm and microfiche from University Microfilms International (UMI). Documents available from The Genuine Article, BIOSIS Document Express, CASDDS.
Desc: Fills the need for communication between molecular biologists and evolutionary biologists. Publishes papers that critically examine the evolutionary significance of macromolecules - mechanisms of mutational change, processes of developmental control, mechanisms of natural selection, maintenance of genetic polymorphism, phylogenetic relationships of organisms, and theories.
Ind/Abst Abstr. Anthropol. (19??-); AgBiotech News Inf.; Anim. Breed. Abstr.; Biol. Abstr. (1984-); Chem. Abstr.; Chem. Titles (1985-); Curr. Aware. Biol. Sci., CABS; Curr. Cit.; Curr. Contents Life Sci.; Curr. Ref. Fish Res.; EMBASE; Fish Rev.; Index Med. (1983-); Life Sci. Collect.; Plant Breed. Abstr.; Protozoolog. Abstr.; Ref. Upd. Basic Ed.; Ref. Upd. Deluxe Ed.; Res. Alert [Full Cov.]; Rev. Med. Vet. Entomol.; Rice Abstr.; Sci. Cit. Index; SCISEARCH; Wildl. Rev.

LC QH ISSN 0077-0221
DD 574 US
NLM W1 MO195T CODEN MBBBAD

MOLECULAR BIOLOGY, BIOCHEMISTRY, AND BIOPHYSICS. [Mol. biol. biochem. biophys.]. **VFOAT** Molekularbiologie, Biochemie und Biophysik. Vol. 1 (1967)-. Monographic series. English. Irregular. Price varies per volume. Springer-Verlag New York Inc., 175 Fifth Avenue, New York NY 10010. **Tel** (212)460-1500 ext 256, FAX (212)533-3503, telex 232 235 SPB UR. **(Subscription address:** Springer-Verlag New York Inc. / North America, PO Box 19386 Books, Newark NJ 07195. **Tel** (201)348-4033.) **ED** G. F. Springer and H. G. Wittmann. Documents available from BIOSIS Document Express, CASDDS.
Desc: Covers topics from the frontiers of molecular biology, biochemistry and biophysics.
Ind/Abst AGRICOLA [Select. Cov.]; Biol. Abstr.; Chem. Abstr.

LC QH506 .M672 ISSN 0026-8933
US
CCC
NLM W1 MO195N CODEN MOLBBJ

MOLECULAR BIOLOGY (NEW YORK). (MOLECULAR BIOLOGY.). [Mol. biol.]. **Added/Corp** Consultants Bureau. Vol. 1 (Jan./Feb. 1967)-. Periodical. English (Russian). Twelve times a year. $1495.00. Consultants Bureau, A Division of Plenum Publishing Corporation, 233 Spring Street, New York NY 10013. **Tel** (212)620-8000, (212)620-8466, FAX (212)463-0742, telex 23/421139. **ED** A. D. Mirzabekov. available on microfilm and microfiche from University Microfilms International (UMI). Documents available from The Genuine Article, BIOSIS Document Express, CASDDS.
Ind/Abst AGRICOLA [Select. Cov.]; Biol. Abstr. (?-1984); Chem. Abstr.; Curr. Cit.; Curr. Contents Life Sci.; EMBASE; Genet. Abstr.; Index Vet.; Nucl. Acids Abstr.; Life Sci. Collect.; Plant Breed. Abstr.; Res. Alert [Full Cov.]; Rev. Agric. Entomol.; Rev. Plant Pathol.; Sci. Cit. Index; SCISEARCH; Soils Fert.

LC QH506 .M664 ISSN 0301-4851
DD 574.8/8/05 NE
CCC
NLM W1 MO196D CODEN MLBRBU
Pr Rev.

MOLECULAR BIOLOGY REPORTS. [Mol. biol. rep.]. Vol. 1 (June 1973)-. Periodical. English. Four times a year. $284.00. Kluwer Academic Publishers, Postbus 322, 3300 AH Dordrecht The Netherlands. **Tel** 011 31 78 524400, FAX 011 31 78 183273, telex 20083. **ED** H. Bloemendal. **Bk Rev**. **Ad Acc**. **Circ:** 400. available on microfilm and microfiche from University Microfilms International (UMI). Documents available from The Genuine Article, BIOSIS Document Express, CASDDS.
Desc: Open to original papers that contribute to the further development and better understanding of DNA replication; DNA transcription; protein biosynthesis on a molecular level; and related subjects.
Ind/Abst AgBiotech News Inf.; AGRICOLA [Select. Cov.]; Biol. Abstr.; Chem. Abstr.; Curr. Aware. Biol. Sci., CABS; Curr. Cit.; Curr. Contents Life Sci.; Index Med.; Life Sci. Collect.; PESTDOC; Plant Breed. Abstr.; Protozoolog. Abstr.; Ref. Upd. Deluxe Ed.; Res. Alert [Full Cov.]; Sci. Cit. Index; SCISEARCH.

LC RC271.I45 M65 ISSN 0952-8172
DD 616.99/406/005 US
CCC
NLM W1; MO196DC CODEN MOLBEM
CEASED

MOLECULAR BIOTHERAPY. [Mol. biother.]. Vol. 1 (1988)-(Jan. 1993). Periodical. English. Butterworth Heinemann / Woburn, MA, 225 Wildwood Avenue, Unit B, Woburn MA 01801. **Tel** (800)366-2665, FAX (617)928-2620, telex 880052. **ED** Robert K Oldham (editor's address: Biological Therapy Institute, Franklin, TN). Index available in last issue of volume--attached. **Bk Rev**. **Ad Acc**. available on microfilm and microfiche from University Microfilms International (UMI). Documents available from The Genuine Article, BIOSIS Document Express.
Desc: Gathers and presents preclinical and clinical results in biotherapy to practicing physicians. Includes findings from international researchers in medical laboratories and biotechnology companies.
Ind/Abst Biol. Abstr. (1989-); Curr. Aware. Biol. Sci., CABS; Curr. Contents Life Sci.; Health Plan. Adminis.; Immunol. Abstr.; Index Med. (1988-); PESTDOC; Ref. Upd. Deluxe Ed.; Res. Alert [Full Cov.]; Sci. Cit. Index; SCISEARCH.

LC QP356.2 .B73 ISSN 0169-328X
DD 599/.0188 NE
CCC
NLM W1; BR116G CODEN MBREE4
Pr Rev.

MOLECULAR BRAIN RESEARCH. **See** Medical Sciences-Neurology.

ISSN 0899-1987
DD 616 US
CCC
NLM W1; MO196DF CODEN MOCAE8
Pr Rev.

MOLECULAR CARCINOGENESIS. [Mol. carcinog.]. (1988)-. Academic Scholarly Publication. English. Twelve times a year. $684.00. John Wiley & Sons, Inc., 605 Third Avenue, New York NY 10158-0012. **Tel** (212)850-6000, (212)850-6645, FAX (212)850-6088, telex 12-7063. **(Subscription address:** John Wiley & Sons / UK, Baffins Lane, Chichester, West Sussex PO19 1UD United Kingdom. **Tel** 011 44 1243 779777, FAX 011 44 243 776128, telex 86290 WIBOOKG.) **ED** Thomas J. Slaga. Documents available from The Genuine Article, BIOSIS Document Express, CASDDS, ADONIS.
Desc: Devoted to the study of the molecular aspects of mechanisms involved in chemical, physical, and viral (biological) carcinogenesis.
Ind/Abst ADONIS; Biol. Abstr. (1988-); Chem. Abstr.; Curr. Aware. Biol. Sci., CABS; Curr. Cit.; Curr. Contents

Biology

Life Sci.; EMBASE; Genet. Abstr.; Health Plan. Adminis.; Index Med. (Vol. 1, No. 1, 1988-); Nucl. Acids Abstr.; Oncog. Growth Factors Abstr.; Ref. Upd. Deluxe Ed.; Res. Alert [Full Cov.]; Rev. Med. Vet. Mycology; Sci. Cit. Index; SCISEARCH.

LC QH   **ISSN** 1076-1551
DD 574   US
  CCC
NLM W1; MO196MH

●**MOLECULAR MEDICINE (CAMBRIDGE, MASS.).** See Medical Sciences.

LC QH506 .M678   **ISSN** 0375-9415
DD 612.015   UN
NLM W1 MO198B   **CODEN** MLKBAQ
MOLEKULIARNAIA BIOLOGIIA. [Mol. biol.]. **Added/Corp** Akademiia Nauk Ukrainskoi RSR. Instytut Biokhimii im. O.V. Palladina. Akademiia Nauk URSR. Institut Molekuliarnoi Biologii i Genetiki. (1964)-. Monographic series. Russian. Six times a year. Price varies per volume. Izdatelstvo Naukova Dumka / Ukrainian Academy of Sciences, Yu. A. Khramov, Dir., Ul. Repina 3, 252 601 Kiev Ukraine. **Tel** 011 7 44 4303441, 011 7 44 2254182, telex 131376. Documents available from CASDDS.
Ind/Abst Chem. Abstr. (-1984); Life Sci. Collect.; Potato Abstr.

LC QH506 .M68   **ISSN** 0026-8984
DD 612.015   RU
  CCC
NLM W1; MO198   **CODEN** MOBIBO
MOLEKULJARNAJA BIOLOGIJA (MOSKVA). (MOLEKULIARNAIA BIOLOGIIA. MOLECULAR BIOLOGY.). [Mol. biol.]. **Added/Corp** Akademiia Nauk SSSR. **VFOAT** Molecular Biology. Vol. 1, No. 1 (Jan./Feb. 1967)-. Academic Scholarly Publication. Russian (summaries and/or abstracts in English; table of contents in English). Six times a year. $129.20. Izdatelstvo Nauka / Akademiia Nauk, (Publishing House of the Russian Academy of Sciences), Leninskii Porspekt 14, 117901 Moscow Russia. **Tel** 011 95 9542153, FAX 011 95 9382144, telex 411964. **(Subscription address:** East View Publications Inc., 3020 Harbor Lane North, Suite 110, Minneapolis MN 55447. **Tel** (800)477-1005, (612)550-0961, FAX (612)559-2931.**)** Index available in last issue of volume--attached. Documents available from BIOSIS Document Express, CASDDS.
Desc: Information on molecular biology, and cytogenetics.
Ind/Abst AGRICOLA; Biol. Abstr.; Chem. Abstr.; EMBASE; Index Med.; Nucl. Acids Abstr.; PESTDOC; Plant Breed. Abstr.

LC QH301 .M75   **ISSN** 0077-0639
  NE
NLM W1 MO56R   **CODEN** MOBIAN
MONOGRAPHIAE BIOLOGICAE. [Monogr. biol.]. Vol. 5, Dec. 18, (1957)-. Monographic series. English (French and German). Irregular. Price varies per volume. Kluwer Academic Publishers, Postbus 322, 3300 AH Dordrecht The Netherlands. **Tel** 011 31 78 524400, FAX 011 31 78 183273, telex 20083. Documents available from BIOSIS Document Express, CASDDS.
Continues Physiologia Comparata et Oecologia, 0369-8637.
Ind/Abst AGRICOLA; Biol. Abstr.; Chem. Abstr.; Curr. Cit.; Fish Rev.; GeoRef; Life Sci. Collect.; Wildl. Rev.

LC QH   **ISSN** 0077-0825
DD 574   SZ
  CCC
NLM W1 MO567L
MONOGRAPHS IN DEVELOPMENTAL BIOLOGY. [Monogr. dev. biol.]. Vol. 1 (1969)-. Monographic series. English. One time a year. 180.00F (approx. per volume). S. Karger AG, Allschwilerstrasse 10, PO Box, CH-4009 Basel Switzerland. **Tel** 011 41 61 3061111, FAX 011 41 61 3061234, telex CH 962 652. **ED** K. Burki. Documents available from BIOSIS Document Express.
Desc: Individual monographs in this series cover the full spectrum of developmental biology from the biochemical, biophysical, and ultrastructural approach, to the analysis of more complex developmental processes at the organismic level. Studies are based on the latest methodologies and on an exhaustive review of available literature.
Ind/Abst Biol. Abstr.; Index Med.; Ref. Upd. Deluxe Ed.

LC QH   **ISSN** 0077-0930
DD 574   US
NLM W1 MO568L   **CODEN** MPOBA6
MONOGRAPHS IN POPULATION BIOLOGY. [Monogr. pop. biol.]. No. 1 (1967)-. Monographic series. English. Irregular. Price varies per volume. Princeton University Press, 41 William Street, Princeton NJ 08540. **Tel** (609)258-4900. Documents available from BIOSIS Document Express.
Ind/Abst Biol. Abstr.; Energy Res. Abstr. (Aug. 1982-).

LC BF   **ISSN** 0270-0131
DD 150   US
UDC 57.024
NLM W1 MO568P
MONOGRAPHS IN PSYCHOBIOLOGY AND DISEASE. See Psychology.

LC QH491   **ISSN** 0368-9727
DD 574.332   UN
NLM W1 MO914K   **CODEN** MFRGAY
MORFOGENEZ I REGENERATSIIA. [Morfog. regener.]. **Added/Corp** Ukraine. Ministerstvo Okhorony Zdorovia. (19??)-. Monographic series. Russian. Documents available from CASDDS.
Ind/Abst Chem. Abstr. (-1973).

LC QH301 .M565   **ISSN** 0096-3925
DD 574/.05   US
  CCC
NLM W1 MO931N   **CODEN** MUBBDD
MOSCOW UNIVERSITY BIOLOGICAL SCIENCES BULLETIN. [Moscow Univ. biol. sci. bull.]. **Main/Corp** Moskovskiĭ gosudarstvennyĭ universitet im. M.V. Lomonosova. Vol. 29 (1974)-. Bulletin. English (Russian). Four times a year. $795.00. Allerton Press Inc., 150 Fifth Avenue, New York NY 10011. **Tel** (212)924-3950, FAX (212)463-9684, telex 427441 ALPRES. Documents available from BIOSIS Document Express, CASDDS.
Ind/Abst AgBiotech News Inf.; AGRICOLA [Select. Cov.]; Anim. Breed. Abstr.; Biodeter. Abstr. (1991-); Biol. Abstr. (-1983); Chem. Abstr.; Crop Physiol. Abstr.; CSA Neuro. Abstr. (?-?); EMBASE; Field Crop Abstr.; Fish Rev.; For. Prod. Abstr. (1991-); Irr. Drain. Abstr.; Key Word Index Wildl. Res.; Maize Abstr.; Microbiol. Abstr. Sect. C; Plant Breed. Abstr.; Plant Grow. Reg. Abstr.; Rev. Agric. Entomol.; Rev. Plant Pathol.; Rice Abstr.; Wheat Barley Trit. Abstr.; Wildl. Rev.

LC QH301   **ISSN** 0818-8238
DD 574   AT
Pr Rev.
MULGA RESEARCH CENTRE JOURNAL. See Environmental Issues-Ecology.

LC QH460   **ISSN** 0921-8777
DD 575.292   NE
  CCC
  CODEN MUREAV
Pr Rev.
MUTATION RESEARCH. DNA REPAIR. [Mutat. res., DNA repair]. **VFOAT** DNA Repair. Mutation Research. Deoxyribonucleic Acid Repair. Vol. 217, No. 2 (Mar. 1989)-. Academic Scholarly Publication. English. Nine times a year (2 volumes). $858.00. Elsevier Science Publishers BV, PO Box 211, 1000 AE Amsterdam Netherlands. **Tel** 011 31 20 4853641, 011 31 20 4853642, FAX 011 31 20 4853598. available on an online database from Elsevier Electronic Subscriptions (EES). Documents available from ADONIS. **Continues** Mutation Research. DNA Repair Reports, 0167-8817.
Ind/Abst ADONIS; Curr. Aware. Biol. Sci.; CABS; EMBASE; Ref. Upd. Basic Ed.; Ref. Upd. Deluxe Ed.

LC QH460
DD 575.292   NE
  CODEN MUREAV
MUTATION RESEARCH. FUNDAMENTAL AND MOLECULAR MECHANISMS OF MUTAGENESIS. **VFOAT** Fundamental and Molecular Mechanisms of Mutagenesis. Vol. 197, No. 1 (Jan. 1988)-. Academic Scholarly Publication. English. Twelve times a year. Elsevier Science Publishers BV, PO Box 211, 1000 AE Amsterdam Netherlands. **Tel** 011 31 20 4853641, 011 31 20 4853642, FAX 011 31 20 4853598. available on an online database from Elsevier Electronic Subscriptions (EES). **Continues** Mutation Research, 0027-5107.
Ind/Abst Anim. Breed. Abstr.; Curr. Aware. Biol. Sci., CABS; Ref. Upd. Basic Ed.; Ref. Upd. Deluxe Ed.; Rev. Agric. Entomol.; Rev. Med. Vet. Entomol.; Rev. Med. Vet. Mycology.

LC QH301   **ISSN** 0258-1213
DD 574   US
  CODEN NALSDJ
Pr Rev.
NATO ASI SERIES. SERIES A, LIFE SCIENCES. [NATO ASI ser., Ser. A, Life sci.]. **Added/Corp** North Atlantic Treaty Organization. Scientific Affairs Division. **VFOAT** Life Sciences. **VAT** North Atlantic Treaty Organization Advanced Science Institutes Series. Series A, Life Sciences. Vol. 70 (1984)-. Monographic series. English. Irregular. price varies. Springer-Verlag GmbH & Company KG, Heidelberger Platz 3, D-14197 Berlin Germany. **Tel** 011 49 30 8207223, FAX 011 49 30 8214091, telex 183 319 SPBLN D. **(Subscription address:** Springer-Verlag New York Inc. / North America, PO Box 2485, Journal Fulfillment, Secaucus NJ 07096. **Tel** (201)348-4033, (800)777-4643, FAX (201)348-4505.**)** available on an online database. Documents available from BIOSIS Document Express, CASDDS. **Continues** NATO Advanced Science Institutes Series. Series A, Life Sciences.
Ind/Abst Biol. Abstr. (1985-); Chem. Abstr.; Curr. Cit.; Nematol. Abstr.; Nutr. Abstr. Rev., Ser. A, Hum. Exp.

LC QH301 .N3482
  BL
NLM W1; NA799K
NATURA. Periodical. English (Portuguese). Instituto de Biologia da UFBA, rua Barao de Geremoabo-Ondina 40.000, Salvador Brazil.

LC RB113 .N37   **ISSN** 1078-8956
DD 610/.5   US
  CCC
NLM W1; NA812M
Pr Rev.
●**NATURE MEDICINE.** See Medical Sciences.

  ISSN 1072-8368
DD 574   US
  CCC
NLM W1; NA839P   **CODEN** NSBIEW
●**NATURE STRUCTURAL BIOLOGY.** [Nat. struct. biol.]. **VFOAT** Structural Biology; SB. Vol. 1, No. 1 (Jan. 1994)-. Periodical. English. Twelve times a year. $495.00. Nature Publishing Company, 65 Bleecker Street, 12th Floor, New York NY 10012. **Tel** (212)477-9600, (800)524-0328, FAX (212)477-8020.
Ind/Abst Index Med.

LC QH   **ISSN** 0273-5709
DD 574   US
NATURESCAPE. [NatureScape]. **VAT** Nature Scape. (Jan./Feb. 1980)-. Periodical. English. Six times a year. Naturescape, PO Box 965, Arlington Heights IL 60006.

LC QH301 .R79   **ISSN** 0470-4606
  RU
NLM W1 NA958P   **CODEN** BINKBT
NAUCHNYE DOKLADY VYSSHEI SHKOLY. BIOLOGICHESKIE NAUKI. [Nauchn. dokl. vyss. sk., biol. nauki]. **Main/Corp** Soviet Union. Ministerstvo Vysshego Obrazovani I A. **Added/Corp** Soviet Union. Ministerstvo Vysshego i Srednego Spetsialnogo Obrazovaniia. Soviet Union. Gosudarstvennyi Komitet SSSR po Narodnomu Obrazovaniiu. **VFOAT** Biologicheskie Nauki. Vol. 1 (1958)-. Academic Scholarly Publication. Russian (table of contents in English). Twelve times a year. $179.95. Izdatelstvo Vysshaia Shkola, Neglinnaya Ulitsa, Dom 29-14, GSP-4, Moscow 101430 Russia. **(Subscription address:** East View Publications Inc., 3020 Harbor Lane North, Suite 110, Minneapolis MN 55447. **Tel** (800)477-1005, (612)550-0961, FAX (612)559-2931.**)** Documents available from CASDDS.
Ind/Abst AgBiotech News Inf.; AGRICOLA; Biocont. News Inf.; Chem. Abstr.; Crop Physiol. Abstr.; Field Crop Abstr.; For. Abstr.; Hortic. Abstr.; Irr. Drain. Abstr.; Maize Abstr.; Nematol. Abstr.; Nutr. Abstr. Rev., Ser. B, Live Feeds and Feed.; Nutr. Abstr. Rev., Ser. A, Hum. Exp.; Plant Breed. Abstr.; Plant Genet. Resour. Abstr.; Plant Grow. Reg. Abstr.; Potato Abstr.; Protozoolog. Abstr.; Rev. Agric. Entomol.; Rev. Med. Vet. Entomol.; Rev. Plant Pathol.; Seed Abstr.; Soils Fert.; Wheat Barley Trit. Abstr.

LC QP351 .N4273
DD 591.1/88   HU
NLM W1; NE323KB   **CODEN** NROBEZ
●**NEUROBIOLOGY.** See Medical Sciences-Neurology.

LC RC321 .N38
DD 616.8   UK
NEUROBIOLOGY AND PSYCHIATRY. See Medical Sciences-Psychiatry.

LC QL750 .C653   **ISSN** 1074-7427
DD 616   US
  CCC
NLM W1; BE129N
●**NEUROBIOLOGY OF LEARNING AND MEMORY.** See Medical Sciences-Neurology.

LC RC346   **ISSN** 0736-4563
DD 616.8   US
  CCC
NLM W1 NE337B   **CODEN** NEUND9
NEUROLOGY AND NEUROBIOLOGY. See Medical Sciences-Neurology.

LC QP356.2 .N48   **ISSN** 0896-6273
DD 591.1/88/05   US
NLM W1; NE337GC   **CODEN** NERNET
●**NEURON (CAMBRIDGE, MASS.).** See Medical Sciences-Neurology.

LC QH301   **ISSN** 0935-1906
DD 574   GW
NLM W3; NE865   **CODEN** NDBIET
NEW DEVELOPMENT IN BIOSCIENCES. [New dev. biosci.]. **Added/Corp** Schering A.G. (1985)-. Monographic series. English. Irregular. Price varies per volume. Walter de Gruyter Inc., PO Box 303421, D-10728 Berlin Germany. **Tel** 011 49 30 260050, FAX 011 49 30 26005251, telex 184027. **Separated from** Advances in the Biosciences, 0065-3446.
Ind/Abst AGRICOLA.

Biology

LC QH315 .N475   **ISSN** 0077-8877
DD 574/.07/1   FR
NLM W1 NE513C
NEW TRENDS IN BIOLOGY TEACHING.
VFOAT Tendances Nouvelles de l'Enseignement de la Biologie. Vol. 1 (1966)-. English (French; summaries and/or abstracts in Spanish). Irregular. UNIPUB, 4611-F Assembly Drive, Lanham MD 20706-4391. **Tel** (800)274-4888, FAX (301)459-0056, telex 28787 GATT CH.

LC QH83   **ISSN** 0147-7889
DD 069   US
NEWSLETTER - ASSOCIATION OF SYSTEMATICS COLLECTIONS. See
Museums and Galleries.

LC QH   **ISSN** 0250-4294
DD 574   US
NEWSLETTER - IFLA. SECTION OF BIOLOGICAL AND MEDICAL SCIENCES LIBRARIES. See
Library and Information Sciences.

LC QH   **ISSN** 0288-8262
DD 574   JA
NLM W1; NI1426SAM   **CODEN** NKIZDR
NIHON KAIMEN IGAKKAI ZASSHI = JOURNAL OF JAPANESE MEDICAL SOCIETY FOR BIOLOGICAL INTERFACE.
[Nihon Kaimen Igakkai zasshi]. **Added/Corp** Nihon Kaimen Igakkai. **VFOAT** Journal of Japanese Medical Society for Biological Interface. (1977)-. Academic Scholarly Publication. Japanese (English). Two times a year. Nihon Kaimen Igakkai, (Japanese Medical Soc. for Biological Interface), Nihon Daigaku Igakubu Dai, 1 Naikagaku Kyoshitsu, 30-1 Oyaguchi Kamicho, Itabashiku Tokyo 173, Japan. Documents available from CASDDS. *Continues* Igaku to Kaimen Kassei.
Ind/Abst Chem. Abstr.

LC QH   **ISSN** 0181-3684
DD 574   FR
UDC 57
   CODEN 59
NOUVEAU BIOLOGISTE, LE. (1977)-.
Periodical. French. Ten times a year. $120.30. Union des Biologistes, 4 rue Pasquier, 75008 Paris France. **Tel** 011 33 1 42651597. **Bk Rev**. **Ad Acc**. **Circ**: 6,000.

LC Z5320 .N6
   RU
NLM ZW 1 N946
NOVYE KNIGI ZA RUBEZHOM: SERIIA V. BIOLOGIIA, MEDITSINA, SELSKOE KHOZIAISTVO.
(1957)-. Periodical. Russian. Twelve times a year. $145.00. (**Subscription address:** Victor Kamkin, 4956 Boiling Brook Parkway, Rockville MD 20852. **Tel** (301)881-5973.) *Supersedes in part* Novye Knigi Za Rubezhom.

LC R
DD 610   US
NLM ZW1; M48935
NTIS ALERT. MEDICINE & BIOLOGY. See
Medical Sciences.

LC RA773   **ISSN** 0167-4587
DD 613.2
NLM W3 NU776   **CODEN** NUSYD8
Pr Rev.
NUTRICIA SYMPOSIUM. (NUTRICIA
SYMPOSIUM : PROCEEDII .GS.]. [Nutr. Symp.]. (1964)-. Proceedings. English. Irregular. Price varies per volume. Kluwer Academic Publishers / Massachusetts, PO Box 358, Accord Station, Hingham MA 02018. **Tel** (617)871-6600. (**Subscription address:** Kluwer Academic Publishers / Netherlands, PO Box 322, 3300 AH Dordrecht Netherlands. **Tel** 011 31 78 392392, FAX 011 31 78 546474.) Documents available from CASDDS.
Ind/Abst Chem. Abstr. (1964-1978).

   ISSN 0749-2421
DD 574   US
Pr Rev.
OCCASIONAL PAPERS (UNIVERSITY OF NEW MEXICO. MUSEUM OF SOUTHWESTERN BIOLOGY).
(OCCASIONAL PAPERS / THE MUSEUM OF SOUTHWESTERN BIOLOGY]. [Occas. pap. - Mus. Southwest. Biol.]. **Added/Corp** University of New Mexico. Museum of Southwestern Biology. No. 1 (June 17, 1983)-. Monographic series. English. Irregular. Price varies per volume. University of New Mexico - Museum, Department of Biology, Albuquerque NM 87131. **Tel** (505)277-8601 Ext 3700. **ED** James S. Findley, Terry L. Yates, Norman J. Scott, Rayann E. Robino, Robert Miles Sullivan. **Circ**: 1,500.
Desc: This is a peer-reviewed series in the general area of ecology and evolutionary biology. Emphasis is on southwestern studies although any regional, laboratory, or theoretical investigations are considered.

LC QH90
DD 574.92   UK
OCCASIONAL PUBLICATION / FRESHWATER BIOLOGICAL ASSOCIATION.
Added/Corp Freshwater Biological Association. (1976)-. Monographic series. English. Price varies per volume.

LC QH
DD 574   CN
ODOURS AND VOC. (19??)-.
English. $300.00. Centre Recherche Biopro, CP 6079 Centre-Ville, Montreal Quebec H3C 3A7 Canada. **Tel** (514)340-4276.

LC QH491 .O57   **ISSN** 0475-1450
DD 574.3   RU
NLM W1 ON864   **CODEN** ONGZAC
ONTOGENEZ. [Ontogenez]. Added/Corp
Akademiia Nauk SSSR. **VFOAT** Ontogenesis. (1970)-. Academic Scholarly Publication. Russian (summaries and/or abstracts in English; table of contents in English). Six times a year. $465.00. Izdatelstvo Nauka / Akademiia Nauk, (Publishing House of the Russian Academy of Sciences), Leninskii Porspekt 14, 117901 Moscow Russia. **Tel** 011 95 9542153, FAX 011 95 9382144, telex 411964. (**Subscription address:** East View Publications Inc., 3020 Harbor Lane North, Suite 110, Minneapolis MN 55447. **Tel** (800)477-1005, (612)550-0961, FAX (612)559-2931.) Documents available from BIOSIS Document Express, CASDDS.
Ind/Abst AGRICOLA; Biol. Abstr.; Chem. Abstr.; CSA Neuro. Abstr. (?-?); EMBASE; Index Med.; Life Sci. Collect.

LC QH301   **ISSN** 0992-5945
DD 574   FR
UDC 57   CCC
Pr Rev.
OPTION/BIO PARIS. (OPTION/BIO.). [Option/bio
Paris]. (1989)-. Academic Scholarly Publication. French. Twenty-two times a year. $189.00. Editions Scientifique Elsevier, 141 rue de Javel, 75747 Paris Cedex 15 France. **Tel** 011 33 1 45589067, FAX 011 33 1 45589424. (**Subscription address:** Editions Scientifiques Elsevier / for North America, PO Box 7247-7576, Philadelphia PA 19170-7576.) **ED** F. Mauriat. **Ad Acc**. **Ad Acc. Circ:** 7,000. available on microfilm and microfiche from University Microfilms International (UMI); available on an online database from Elsevier Electronic Subscriptions (EES).
Desc: Reports day-to-day news, and scientific information in the medical and biological areas, includes information on diagnostic approaches and technical viewpoints.

LC QH325 .S68   **ISSN** 0169-6149
DD 575/.005   NE
   CCC
NLM W1; OR687N   **CODEN** OLEBEMOGLFAU
Pr Rev.
ORIGINS OF LIFE AND EVOLUTION OF THE BIOSPHERE.
(ORIGINS OF LIFE AND EVOLUTION OF THE BIOSPHERE : THE JOURNAL OF THE INTERNATIONAL SOCIETY FOR THE STUDY OF THE ORIGIN OF LIFE.). [Orig. life evol. biosph.]. **Added/Corp** International Society for the Study of the Origin of Life. **VFOAT** Origins of Life. Vol. 15, No. 1 (1984)-. Academic Scholarly Publication. English. Six times a year. $482.00. Kluwer Academic Publishers, Postbus 322, 3300 AH Dordrecht The Netherlands. **Tel** 011 31 78 524400, FAX 011 31 78 183273, telex 20083. **ED** James P. Ferris. **Acid Free**. available on microfilm and microfiche from University Microfilms International (UMI). Documents available from The Genuine Article, BIOSIS Document Express, Ask*IEEE, CASDDS.
Continues Origins of Life, 0302-1688.
Desc: The main interests revolve around experimental and theoretical studies: evolution of planetary atmospheres, prebiotic chemistry, biochemical evolution, and precambrian studies, to name a few.
Ind/Abst Astron. Astrophys. Abstr. (1985-); Biol. Abstr.; Chem. Abstr. (1985-); Curr. Aware. Biol. Sci., CABS; Curr. Cit.; Curr. Contents Life Sci.; Environ. Period. Bibliogr. (1984-?); GeoRef; Index Med. (1984-); INSPEC (1990-); Int. Aerosp. Abstr.; Refer. Z. (1990-); Ref. Upd. Deluxe Ed.; Res. Alert [Full Cov.]; Sci. Cit. Index; SCISEARCH.

LC QH301   **ISSN** 0958-6601
DD 574   UK
Pr Rev.
OXFORD MONOGRAPHS ON BIOGEOGRAPHY.
[Oxf. monogr. biogeogr.]. No. 1 (1981)-. Monographic series. English. Irregular. Price varies per volume. Oxford University Press / UK, Walton Street, Oxford OX2 6DP United Kingdom. **Tel** 011 44 1865 56767, FAX 011 44 1865 267773, telex 851/837330 OXPRES G. (**Subscription address:** Oxford University Press / USA, Journals Marketing Department, Oxford University Press, 2001 Evans Road, Cary NC 27513. **Tel** (800)451-7556, (919)677-0977, FAX (919)677-1714.) **ED** Editoral Board.
Ind/Abst Fish Rev. (Jan. 1989-July 1992); GeoRef; Wildl. Rev. (Jan. 1989-July 1992).

LC QH359 .O93   **ISSN** 0265-072X
DD 575/.005   UK
NLM W1; OX621TK   **CODEN** OSEBE3
OXFORD SURVEYS IN EVOLUTIONARY BIOLOGY.
[Oxf. surv. evol. biol.]. Vol. 1 (1984)-. Monographic series. English. One time a year. $85.00. Oxford University Press / New York, 200 Madison Avenue, New York NY 10016. **Tel** (212)679-7300, (919)677-0977, (800)451-7556, (800)445-9714, FAX (919)677-1303. **ED** R. Dawkins and M. Ridley. Documents available from BIOSIS Document Express.
Ind/Abst Anim. Breed. Abstr.; Biol. Abstr. (1985-); Curr. Cit.; Fish Rev. (Jan. 1989-July 1992); Rev. Med. Vet. Entomol.; Wildl. Rev. (Jan. 1989-July 1992).

LC QE701 .P17   **ISSN** 0094-8373
DD 560/.5   US
   CCC
   CODEN PALBBM
Pr Rev.
PALEOBIOLOGY. See Paleontology.

LC QH301   **ISSN** 0369-8114
DD 574   FR
   CCC
NLM W1 PA95   **CODEN** PTBIAN
Pr Rev.
PATHOLOGIE ET BIOLOGIE (PARIS).
See Medical Sciences-Pathology.

LC QH301   **ISSN** 0553-4992
DD 574   FR
UDC 57
PENN AR BED BREST. (1953)-. Academic
Scholarly Publication. French. Irregular. SEPND, Boite Postale 32, 29276 Brest Cedex France.
Ind/Abst Ocean. Abstr.

LC QH301 .B47   **ISSN** 0031-5362
DD 574.05   CI
NLM W1 PE791L   **CODEN** PDBIADDBIAD
Pr Rev.
PERIODICUM BIOLOGORUM. [Period. biol.].
Added/Corp Hrvatsko Prirodoslovno Drustvo. Bioloska Sekcija. Vol. 72 (1970)-. Academic Scholarly Publication. English. Irregular. Hrvatsko Prirodoslovno Drustvo, Ilica 16/III, Zagreb 41000 Croatia. **Tel** 011 38 41 425288. (**Subscription address:** Jugoslovenska Knjiga, PO Box 36, YU 11001 Belgrade Yugoslovia. **Tel** 011 38 11 621055, FAX 011 38 11 325970.) **ED** Vlatko Silobrcic. **Bk Rev**. **Ad Acc**. **Circ**: 800 (ctrl). Documents available from The Genuine Article, BIOSIS Document Express, CASDDS. *Continues* Bioloski Glasnik.
Desc: Provides scientific and conference papers in the news, forum discussions on science, book reviews, obituaries, and more.
Ind/Abst Biol. Abstr.; Chem. Abstr.; Crop Physiol. Abstr.; Curr. Cit.; EMBASE; Fish Rev. (Jan. 1989-July 1992); Helminthol. Abstr.; Index Vet.; Life Sci. Collect.; Pig News Inf.; Protozoolog. Abstr.; Res. Alert [Full Cov.]; Rev. Med. Vet. Entomol.; Rev. Med. Vet. Mycology; Sci. Cit. Index; SCISEARCH; Vet. Bull.; Wildl. Rev. (Jan. 1989-July 1992).

LC QH301 .P44   **ISSN** 0031-5982
DD 574/.05   US
   CCC
NLM W1 PE871   **CODEN** PBMEA8
Pr Rev.
PERSPECTIVES IN BIOLOGY AND MEDICINE.
[Perspect. biol. med.]. **Added/Corp** University of Chicago. Division of the Biological Sciences. Vol. 1 (Autumn 1957)-. Academic Scholarly Publication. English. Four times a year. $65.00. University of Chicago Press / Journals Division, PO Box 37005, 5720 South Woodlawn, Chicago IL 60637. **Tel** (312)753-3347, FAX (312)753-0811. **ED** Richard Landau. **Ad Acc**. **Acid Free**. available on microfilm and microfiche from University Microfilms International (UMI). Documents available from The Genuine Article, BIOSIS Document Express, UMI Article Clearinghouse, CASDDS, Documents on Demand.
Desc: Initiated to communicate new ideas and to stimulate original thought in the biological and medical sciences. Not a journal of research reports, it publishes articles on a broad range of subjects with an emphasis on essays in which medicine and basic biology are interrelated, and biomedical science is integrated with the humanities and the social sciences.
Ind/Abst Biol. Agric. Index; Biol. Abstr.; Biol. Dig.; Chem. Abstr.; Curr. Aware. Biol. Sci., CABS; Curr. Cit.; Curr. Contents Life Sci.; Dent. Abstr. (-199?); EMBASE; Energy Inf. Abstr.; Energy Res. Abstr.; Environ. Abstr.; Expand. Acad. Index (1992-); Fish Rev.; Helminthol. Abstr. (1991-); Index Med.; Newsp. Period. Abstr. (1992-); Nutr. Abstr. Rev., Ser. A, Hum. Exp.; Life Sci. Collect.; Protozoolog. Abstr.; Psychol. Abstr. (1966-); PsycINFO (?-?); PsycLit; Ref. Upd. Basic Ed.; Ref. Upd. Deluxe Ed.; Res. Alert [Full Cov.]; Sci. Cit. Index; SCISEARCH; Soc. Plann. Policy Dev. Abstr.; Soc. Sci. Cit. Index [Select. Cov.]; Sociol. Abstr.; Wildl. Rev.

ISSN 1064-0517
DD 591 US
CCC
NLM W1; PE872CS CODEN PDENED
PERSPECTIVES ON DEVELOPMENTAL NEUROBIOLOGY. [Perspect. dev. neurobiol.]. Vol. 1, No. 1 (Sept. 1992)-. Periodical. English. Four times a year. $180.00 (academic institutions), $280.00 (corporate institutions). Gordon & Breach Science Publishers, Inc., PO Box 786, Cooper Station, New York NY 10276. **Tel** (212)206-8900, FAX (212)645-2459. ***Continues*** *Comments on Modern Biology. Part D. Comments on Developmental Neurobiology, 0896-5099.*
Desc: Publishes critical reviews on recent progress in developmental neurobiology, from embryogenesis through aging. Each issue focuses on a single topic.
Ind/Abst Index Med.

LC RS
DD 615.1 SZ
PHARMACEUTICALS & BIOLOGICALS. See Pharmacy and Pharmacology.

LC QH301 ISSN 0080-4622
DD 574 UK
CCC
PHILOSOPHICAL TRANSACTIONS. BIOLOGICAL SCIENCES. **Added/Corp** Royal Society (Great Britain). **VFOAT** Biological Sciences. (1990)-. Periodical. English. Twelve times a year. $1073.00. Royal Society, 6 Carlton House Terrace, London SW1Y 5AG United Kingdom. **Tel** 011 44 171 8395561, FAX 011 44 171 9761837, telex 917876 ROYAL G. ***Continues*** *Philosophical Transactions of the Royal Society of London Series B, Biological Sciences.*
Ind/Abst Curr. Biotechnol.; GeoRef; Index Med.

LC QK564 .S63 ISSN 1322-0829
DD 589 AT
CCC
•**PHYCOLOGICAL RESEARCH.** **Added/Corp** Nihon Sorui Gakkai. (Mar. 1995)-. Academic Scholarly Publication. English. Four times a year. 206.00Aus$. Blackwell Scientific Publications Australia, 54 University Street, PO Box 378, Carlton Victoria 3053 Australia. **Tel** 011 61 3 3470300, FAX 011 61 3 3475001, telex 10716421. ***Continues*** *Sorui, 0038-1578.*

LC G575 .P62
DD 919.8 NO
Pr Rev.
POLAR RESEARCH. See Earth Sciences.

ISSN 0272-6335
DD 599/.09192 US
NLM W1 PO31R CODEN PBIMDF
POLYMERS IN BIOLOGY AND MEDICINE. [Polm. biol. med.]. Vol. 1 (1980)-. Academic Scholarly Publication. English. Price varies per volume. John Wiley & Sons, Inc., 605 Third Avenue, New York NY 10158-0012. **Tel** (212)850-6000, (212)850-6645, FAX (212)850-6088, telex 12-7063. **(Subscription address:** John Wiley & Sons / UK, Baffins Lane, Chichester, West Sussex PO19 1UD United Kingdom. **Tel** 011 44 1243 779777, FAX 011 44 243 776128, telex 86290 WIBOOKG.) Documents available from CASDDS.
Ind/Abst Chem. Abstr.

LC QH ISSN 0177-8382
DD 574 GW
UDC 57
PRAXIS DER NATURWISSENSCHAFTEN BIOLOGIE. [Prax. Nat.wiss., Biol.]. (1980)-. Periodical. German. Twelve times a year. $117.30. Aulis Verlag Deubner & Company, Antwerpenerstrasse 6 12, 50672 Cologne Germany. **Tel** 011 49 221 518051, FAX 011 49 221 518443. ***Continues*** *Praxis der Naturwissenschaften. Biologie im Unterricht der Schulen, 0341-8510.*

LC QH
DD 574 RU
PREPRINT (MURMANSKII MORSKOI. BIOLOGICHESKII INSTITUT). (PREPRINT / AKADEMIIA NAUK SSSR, ORDENA LENINA KOLSKII FILIAL IM. S.M. KIROVA, MURMANSKII MORSKOI BIOLOGICHESKII INSTITUT.). **Added/Corp** Murmanskii Morskoi Biologicheskii Institut. (1988)-. Monographic series. Russian. Irregular. Price varies per volume.

LC QH
DD 574 IT
PROBLEMI DI BIOETICA. Italian. Six times a year. L60000. Ist It Bioetica, Catt Antropolo, Via Del Proconsolo 12, 50122 Florence Italy. **Tel** 011 39 55 298065.

LC QH327 .P7 ISSN 0555-2788
RU
NLM W1 PR58K CODEN PKBBA7
PROBLEMY KOSMICESKOJ BIOLOGII. (PROBLEMY KOSMICHESKOI BIOLOGII.). [Probl. kosm. biol.]. **Added/Corp** Akademiia Nauk SSSR. Otdelenie Fiziologii. Akademiia Nauk SSSR. Otdelenie Biologicheskikh Nauk. Vol. 1 (1962)-. Academic Scholarly Publication. Russian (summaries and/or abstracts in English). Price varies per volume. Izdatelstvo Nauka / Akademiia Nauk, (Publishing House of the Russian Academy of Sciences), Leninskii Porspekt 14, 117901 Moscow Russia. **Tel** 011 95 9542153, FAX 011 95 9382144, telex 411964. **ED** N.M. Sisakian. Each issue contains an index to its own contents (no volume index)--loose. Documents available from BIOSIS Document Express, CASDDS.
Ind/Abst Biol. Abstr. (?-1974); Chem. Abstr.; Index Med.; Int. Aerosp. Abstr.

LC QH324.9.C7 K75
DD 574.191/67 UN
CODEN PKRIEA
PROBLEMY KRIOBIOLOGII. **Added/Corp** Akademiia Nauk SSSR. Otdelenie Fiziologii. Akademiia Nauk Ukrainskoi RSR. Otdelenie Biokhimii, Fiziologii i Teoreticheskoi Meditsiny. **VFOAT** Problems of Cryobiology. (1991)-. Academic Scholarly Publication. Russian (summaries and/or abstracts in English; table of contents in English). Four times a year. **(Subscription address:** Victor Kamkin, 4956 Boiling Brook Parkway, Rockville MD 20852. **Tel** (301)881-5973.) Documents available from BIOSIS Document Express, CASDDS. ***Continues*** *Kriobiologiia, 0233-7673.*
Ind/Abst Biol. Abstr. (1991-); Chem. Abstr.

LC QH301 .P7415 ISSN 0962-8452
DD 574/.05 UK
Pr Rev.
PROCEEDINGS. BIOLOGICAL SCIENCES / THE ROYAL SOCIETY. **Main/Corp** Royal Society (Great Britain). **Added/Corp** Royal Society (Great Britain). **VFOAT** Biological Sciences; Proceedings of the Royal Society of London. Series B. (July 1990)-. Proceedings. English. Twelve times a year. $490.00. Royal Society, 6 Carlton House Terrace, London SW1Y 5AG United Kingdom. **Tel** 011 44 171 8395561, FAX 011 44 171 9761837, telex 917876 ROYAL G. ***Continues*** *Royal Society (Great Britain). Proceedings of the Royal Society of London. Series B. Biological Sciences, 0080-4649.*
Desc: Publishes papers by world-renowned scientists, covering all aspects of the biological sciences.
Ind/Abst Curr. Cit.; Index Med.

LC QH
DD 574 CN
PROCEEDINGS (CANADIAN FEDERATION OF BIOLOGICAL SOCIETIES : 1982). (PROCEEDINGS = RESULTATS DES COMMUNICATIONS.). **Added/Corp** Canadian Federation of Biological Societies. **VFOAT** Resultats des Communications. 25th (1982)-. Proceedings. English. One time a year (June). 9.61Can$. Can Fed Biological Sciences, 575 King Edward Avenue, Ottawa Ontario K1N 7N5 Canada. **Tel** (613)234-9555. ***Continues*** *Programme and Proceedings of the Annual Meeting.*

LC QH652 .T75
DD 574.19 US
PROCEEDINGS OF THE ... ANNUAL TRI-SERVICE CONFERENCE ON THE BIOLOGICAL EFFECTS OF MICROWAVE RADIATION. See Physics-Light, Optics, Radiation.

ISSN 1038-2232
DD 574.192 AT
PROCEEDINGS OF THE AUSTRALIAN SOCIETY FOR BIOCHEMISTRY AND MOLECULAR BIOLOGY. [Proc. Aust. Soc. Biochem. Mol. Biol.]. **Added/Corp** Australian Society for Biochemistry and Molecular Biology. **VFOAT** Proceedings ... Annual Conference - Australian Society for Biochemistry and Molecular Biology. (1991)-. Proceedings. English. One time a year (Sept.). 44.00Aus$. Australian Society for Biochemistry and Molecular Biology, PO Box 2331, Kent Town South Australia 5071 Australia. **Tel** 011 61 8 3620009. **(Subscription address:** DA Information Services Pty., 648 Whitehorse Road, Mitcham 3132 Victoria Australia. **Tel** 011 61 3 8734411.) ***Continues*** *Proceedings of the Australian Biochemical Society, 0067-1703.*

LC QH1 .B4 ISSN 0006-324X
DD 574.062753 US
NLM W1 B1759H CODEN PBSWAO
Pr Rev.
PROCEEDINGS OF THE BIOLOGICAL SOCIETY OF WASHINGTON. [Proc. Biol. Soc. Wash.]. **Main/Corp** Biological Society of Washington. **Added/Corp** Smithsonian Institution. Vol. 1 (Nov. 19, 1880/May 26, 1882)-. Monographic series. English. Four times a year (Mar., June, Sept., Dec.). $40.00. Biological Society of Washington, Room E503B, Smithsonian Natural History, Washington DC 20560. **Tel** (202)357-4990. **(Subscription address:** Proceedings of the Biological Society of Washington, PO Box 1897, Lawrence KS 66044-8897.) **ED** Brian Kensley. cum. index. **Circ:** 1,000 (ctrl). Documents available from The Genuine Article, BIOSIS Document Express.
Desc: A journal of international scope for publication of papers bearing on systematics in the biological sciences (both botany and zoology, including paleontology).
Ind/Abst AGRICOLA [Select. Cov.]; Biol. Abstr.; Curr. Aware. Biol. Sci., CABS; Curr. Cit.; Curr. Contents Agric. Biol. Environ. Sci.; Curr. Ref. Fish Res.; Fish Rev.; Geol. Abstr.; GeoRef; Helminthol. Abstr.; Nematol. Abstr.; Life Sci. Collect.; Res. Alert [Full Cov.]; Rev. Agric. Entomol.; Rev. Med. Vet. Entomol.; Sci. Cit. Index; SCISEARCH; Wildl. Rev.

LC QH301 .N3a ISSN 0073-6600
DD 574/.05 II
NLM W1 PR585WG CODEN PIBSBB
PROCEEDINGS OF THE INDIAN NATIONAL SCIENCE ACADEMY. PART B, BIOLOGICAL SCIENCES. [Proc. Indian Natl. Sci. Acad., Part B]. **Main/Corp** Indian National Science Academy. **VFOAT** Biological Sciences. Vol. 36, No. 1 (Feb. 1970)-. Academic Scholarly Publication. English. Six times a year. $50.00. Indian National Science Academy, 1 Bahadur Shah Zafar Marg, New Delhi 110 002 India. **(Subscription address:** Prints India, 11 Darya Ganj, New Delhi 110002 India. **Tel** 011 91 11 3268645, FAX 011 91 11 3275542, telex 31-61087 PRIN-IN.) Documents available from BIOSIS Document Express, CASDDS. ***Continues*** *National Institute of Sciences of India. Proceedings of the National Institute of Sciences of India. Part B, Biological Sciences.*
Ind/Abst AgBiotech News Inf.; AGRICOLA; Agrofor. Abstr. (1991-); Biocont. News Inf.; Biodeter. Abstr. (19??-19??); Biol. Abstr.; Ceram. Abstr.; Chem. Abstr.; Crop Physiol. Abstr.; Curr. Cit.; EMBASE; Field Crop Abstr.; For. Abstr.; GeoRef; Grass. Forage Abstr.; Helminthol. Abstr. (1991-); Index Vet.; Irr. Drain. Abstr.; Maize Abstr.; NAPRALERT; Nutr. Abstr. Rev., Ser. A, Hum. Exp.; Plant Breed. Abstr.; Plant Genet. Resour. Abstr.; Plant Grow. Reg. Abstr.; Postharvest News Inf.; Rev. Agric. Entomol.; Rev. Med. Vet. Entomol.; Rev. Med. Vet. Mycology; Rev. Plant Pathol.; Rice Abstr.; Seed Abstr.; Soils Fert.; Sorghum Mill. Abstr.; Soyabean Abstr.; Weed Abstr.; Wheat Barley Trit. Abstr.

LC QH331 ISSN 0379-1718
DD 574.015/195 RM
NLM W3 IN1241C
PROCEEDINGS OF THE INTERNATIONAL BIOMETRIC CONFERENCE. **Added/Corp** Biometric Society. Academia Republicii Socialiste Romania. 8th (1974)-. Proceedings. English.
Ind/Abst Biostatistica (19??-19??).

LC QH301 .N52a ISSN 0386-2208
DD 505 JA
NLM W1 PR5853 CODEN PJABDW
PROCEEDINGS OF THE JAPAN ACADEMY. SERIES B: PHYSICAL AND BIOLOGICAL SCIENCES. [Proc. Jpn. Acad. Ser. B]. **Main/Corp** Nihon Gakushiin. **VFOAT** Physical and Biological Sciences. Vol. 53 (April 1977)-. Academic Scholarly Publication. English. Twelve times a year. Nihon Gakushiin, (Japan Academy), 7-32 Ueno Koen Taitoku, Tokyo 110 Japan. **(Subscription address:** Maruzen Company Ltd., PO Box 5050, Import & Export Department, Tokyo 100 31 Japan. **Tel** 011 81 3 32789224.) Documents available from The Genuine Article, BIOSIS Document Express, Ask*IEEE, CASDDS. ***Continues in part*** *Proceedings of the Japan Academy, 0021-4280.*
Ind/Abst AGRICOLA; Biol. Abstr.; Chem. Abstr.; Curr. Biotechnol.; Curr. Cit.; EMBASE; Fish Rev. (Jan. 1989-July 1992); GeoRef; INSPEC (April 1977-); Math. Rev. (?-199?); NAPRALERT; Life Sci. Collect.; Res. Alert [Full Cov.]; Rev. Plant Pathol.; Sci. Cit. Index; SCISEARCH; Wildl. Rev. (Jan. 1989-July 1992).

LC Q57 .P762 ISSN 0924-8323
NE
CODEN PKNSEK
Pr Rev.
PROCEEDINGS OF THE KONINKLIJKE NEDERLANDSE AKADEMIE VAN WETENSCHAPPEN (1990). (PROCEEDINGS OF THE KONINKLIJKE NEDERLANDSE AKADEMIE VAN WETENSCHAPPEN. BIOLOGICAL, CHEMICAL, GEOLOGICAL, PHYSICAL, AND MEDICAL SCIENCES.). [Proc. K. Ned. Akad. Wet.]. **Added/Corp** Koninklijke Nederlandse Akademie van Wetenschappen. **VFOAT** Biological, Chemical, Geological, Physical and Medical Sciences; Proceedings of the Royal Netherlands Academy of Arts and Sciences. Vol. 93 No. 1 (Mar. 26, 1990)-. Academic Scholarly Publication. English (French and German). Four times a year. Fl283.00. Elsevier Science Publishers BV, PO Box 211, 1000 AE Amsterdam Netherlands. **Tel** 011 31 20 4853641, 011 31 20 4853642, FAX 011 31 20 4853598. Documents available from The Genuine Article, BIOSIS Document Express, Ask*IEEE, CASDDS. ***Formed by the union of*** *Proceedings of the Koninklijke Nederlandse Akademie van Wetenschappen. Series B, Palaeontology, Geology, Physics, Chemistry, Anthropology, 0920-2250* ***and*** *Proceedings of the Koninklijke Nederlandse Akademie van Wetenschappen. Series C, Biological and Medical Sciences, 0023-3374.*
Ind/Abst Biol. Abstr. (1991-); Chem. Abstr.; Curr. Contents Agric. Biol. Environ. Sci.; Curr. Contents Phys. Chem. Earth Sci.; GeoRef; INSPEC (1990-); Leadscan; Math. Rev.; Res. Alert [Full Cov.]; Sci. Cit. Index; SCISEARCH.

LC Q41 .E213 **ISSN** 0269-7270
DD 574/.05 UK
NLM W1 PR587PS **CODEN** PRSSDPPREBA3
Pr Rev. **CEASED**

PROCEEDINGS OF THE ROYAL SOCIETY OF EDINBURGH. SECTION B, BIOLOGICAL SCIENCES. (PROCEEDINGS. SECTION B, BIOLOGICAL SCIENCES.). [Proc. R. Soc. Edinb., Sect. B Biol. sci.]. **Added/Corp** Royal Society of Edinburgh. **VFOAT** Biological Sciences; Proceedings of the Royal Society of Edinburgh. Section B. Vol. 76, Pts. 1/3 (1978)-(1994). Academic Scholarly Publication. English. Royal Society of Edinburgh, 22 24 George Street, Edinburgh EH2 2PQ United Kingdom. **Tel** 011 44 131 2256057, FAX 011 44 131 2206889. **ED** R. Watling. Index available. cum. index. **Circ:** 1,200. Documents available from The Genuine Article, BIOSIS Document Express, CASDDS. ***Continues*** *Proceedings. Section B, Natural Environment, 0308-2113.*
Desc: Publishes proceedings of symposia on all topics in the biological sciences; interpreted in the broadest sense.
Ind/Abst Biol. Abstr.; Chem. Abstr.; Curr. Aware. Biol. Sci., CABS; Curr. Cit.; Curr. Contents Agric. Biol. Environ. Sci.; EMBASE; GeoRef; Life Sci. Collect.; Res. Alert [Full Cov.]; Sci. Cit. Index (19??-19??); SCISEARCH; Soc. Sci. Cit. Index [Select. Cov.].

LC QP1 .S8 **ISSN** 0037-9727
DD 616.07/05 US
CCC
NLM W1 PR5865 **CODEN** PSEBAA
Pr Rev.

PROCEEDINGS OF THE SOCIETY FOR EXPERIMENTAL BIOLOGY AND MEDICINE. **See** Medical Sciences-Experimental Medicine.

LC QH301
DD 574 US

PROFESSIONAL PAPERS SERIES (BIOLOGY). **Main/Corp** Nicholls State University. No. 1, (April 1978)-. Monographic series. English. Irregular. Price varies per volume. Nicholls State University, Thibodaux LA 70301.

ISSN 0361-7742
DD 610 US
CCC
NLM W1 PR668E **CODEN** PCBRD2

PROGRESS IN CLINICAL AND BIOLOGICAL RESEARCH. [Prog. clin. biol. res.]. (1975)-. Monographic series. English. Irregular. Price varies per volume. John Wiley & Sons Inc / New Jersey, 1 Wiley Drive, Somerset NJ 08875. **Tel** (800)225-5945, (908)469-4400. **(Subscription address:** John Wiley & Sons / UK, Baffins Lane, Chichester, West Sussex PO19 1UD United Kingdom. **Tel** 011 44 1243 779777, FAX 011 44 243 776128, telex 86290 WIBOOKG.**)** **ED** George Brewer, Nathan Back, Vincent Eijsvoogel, Robert Grover, Kirt Hirschhorn, Seymour Kety, Sidney Udenfriend, and Jonathan Uhr. Documents available from BIOSIS Document Express, CASDDS.
Desc: Includes proceedings and notes on meetings, conferences and symposiums concerning clinical and biological research.
Ind/Abst Biol. Abstr.; Chem. Abstr.; Curr. Cit.; EMBASE; Energy Res. Abstr. (March 1982-); Helminthol. Abstr. (1991-); Hortic. Abstr.; Index Med.; Nutr. Abstr. Rev., Ser. A, Hum. Exp.; Life Sci. Collect.; Ref. Upd. Basic Ed.; Ref. Upd. Deluxe Ed.; Rev. Plant Pathol.; SportSearch; Weed Abstr.

LC QP552.G76 P76 **ISSN** 0955-2235
DD 574.87/6 US
CCC
NLM W1; PR668WK **CODEN** PGFREH
TITLE CHANGE

PROGRESS IN GROWTH FACTOR RESEARCH. [Prog. growth factor res.]. (1989)-(Jan. 1996). Academic Scholarly Publication. English. Pergamon Press, An Imprint of Elsevier Science Ltd., The Boulevard, Langford Lane, Kidlington, Oxford OX5 1GB United Kingdom. **Tel** 011 44 1865 843000, 011 44 1865 843699, FAX 011 44 1865 843010. **(Subscription address:** Elsevier Science Ltd. / Oxford Fulfillment Centre, PO Box 800, Kidlington OX5 1DX United Kingdom. **Tel** 011 44 865 843355.**)** **ED** John Heath. Documents available from BIOSIS Document Express, CASDDS. ***Continued by*** *Cytokine and Growth Factor Reviews.*
Desc: Features reviews of research and applications on growth factors and related regulatory peptides. Includes the structure and function of their receptors and signalling oncogenes, signal transduction pathways and effector systems, and regulation of gene expression.
Ind/Abst Biol. Abstr.; Chem. Abstr.; Curr. Aware. Biol. Sci., CABS; Curr. Cit.; Index Med. (1989-); Oncog. Growth Factors Abstr.

ISSN 0884-6790
DD 616 US
NLM W1; PR6703 **CODEN** PLBIE5

PROGRESS IN LEUKOCYTE BIOLOGY. [Prog. leukoc. biol.]. (1985)-. Academic Scholarly Publication. English. Price varies per volume. Wiley Liss, 605 3rd Avenue, New York NY 10158. **Tel** (212)850-8800, (212)850-6645. Documents available from BIOSIS Document Express, CASDDS.
Ind/Abst Biol. Abstr. (1985-); Chem. Abstr. (1985-).

LC QH506 .P76 **ISSN** 0079-6484
DD 574.8 US
NLM W1 PR6719F **CODEN** PMSBA4

PROGRESS IN MOLECULAR AND SUBCELLULAR BIOLOGY. [Prog. molec. subcell. biol.]. Vol. 1 (1969)-. Monographic series. English. Irregular. Price varies per volume. Springer-Verlag New York Inc., 175 Fifth Avenue, New York NY 10010. **Tel** (212)460-1500 ext 256, FAX (212)533-3503, telex 232 235 SPB UR. **(Subscription address:** Springer-Verlag New York Inc. / North America, PO Box 2485, Journal Fulfillment, Secaucus NJ 07096. **Tel** (201)348-4033, (800)777-4643, FAX (201)348-4505.**)** Documents available from BIOSIS Document Express, CASDDS.
Desc: Contains articles on molecular and subcellular biology.
Ind/Abst AGRICOLA [Select. Cov.]; Biol. Abstr.; Chem. Abstr.; Index Med.; Life Sci. Collect.

LC QP356 .P73 **ISSN** 0301-0082
DD 612/.8/05 UK
CCC
NLM W1 PR672K **CODEN** PGNBA5PNNEA
Pr Rev.

PROGRESS IN NEUROBIOLOGY. **See** Medical Sciences-Neurology.

ISSN 0079-6603
DD 547 US
CCC
NLM W1 PR675I **CODEN** PNMBAF

PROGRESS IN NUCLEIC ACID RESEARCH AND MOLECULAR BIOLOGY. [Prog. nucleic acid res. mol. biol.]. Vol. 3 (1964)-. Monographic series. English. Irregular. Price varies per volume. Academic Press Inc., 6277 Sea Harbor Drive, Orlando FL 32887. **Tel** (800)543-9534, (407)345-4100, FAX (407)352-3445. **ED** J. N. Davidson and W. E. Cohn. Documents available from The Genuine Article, BIOSIS Document Express, CASDDS. ***Continues*** *Progress in Nucleic Acid Research, 0091-4886.*
Desc: Information on nucleic acids research and molecular biology.
Ind/Abst AgBiotech News Inf.; AGRICOLA [Select. Cov.]; Biol. Abstr.; Chem. Abstr.; Curr. Aware. Biol. Sci., CABS; Curr. Cit.; Index Med.; Index Sci. Rev. [Full Cov.]; Maize Abstr.; Plant Breed. Abstr.; Res. Alert [Full Cov.]; Sci. Cit. Index; SCISEARCH; Seed Abstr.; Wheat Barley Trit. Abstr.

LC QH471 **ISSN** 0254-105X
DD 574.16 SZ
CCC
NLM W1; PR681BD **CODEN** PRBMEP

PROGRESS IN REPRODUCTIVE BIOLOGY AND MEDICINE. [Prog. reprod. biol. med.]. Vol. 9 (1983)-. Academic Scholarly Publication. English. One time a year. 200.00F (approx. per volume). S. Karger AG, Allschwilerstrasse 10, PO Box, CH-4009 Basel Switzerland. **Tel** 011 41 61 3061111, FAX 011 41 61 3061234, telex CH 962 652. **ED** M. L'Hermite. Documents available from BIOSIS Document Express, CASDDS. ***Continues*** *Progress in Reproductive Biology, 0304-4262.*
Desc: The importance of human reproduction and the stress placed on research into its mechanisms and implications have stimulated the development of an extremely individualized field of research and technology. This series supports that field through the publication of volumes, each of which is a source book of data and concepts centered on a specific topic serving to summarize the collected work of international experts.
Ind/Abst Biol. Abstr.; Chem. Abstr. (1983-); Ref. Upd. Deluxe Ed.

ISSN 0069-0023
DD 591.971 CN
NLM W2 DC2 W6P **CODEN** CWPNBL

PROGRESS NOTES - CANADIAN WILDLIFE SERVICE. (PROGRESS NOTES - CANADIAN WILDLIFE SERVICE. CAHIERS DE BIOLOGIE.). [Prog. notes - Can. Wildl. Serv.]. **Main/Corp** Canada Wildlife Service. **VFOAT** Cahiers de Biologie. No. 1 (1967)-. Monographic series. English (English and French). Irregular. Price varies per volume. Canadian Wildlife Service Publications, Environment Canada, Ottawa Ontario K1A 0E7 Canada. **Tel** (819)997-1095, FAX (819)997-0547. Index available. **Circ:** 1,200 (ctrl). Documents available from BIOSIS Document Express.
Desc: These notes contain interim data of more extensive studies, the complete results of which are often reported at a later date.
Ind/Abst ASTIS Curr. Aware. Bull. (1978-); ASTIS Bibliogr. (1978-); Biol. Abstr.; Key Word Index Wildl. Res.; Wildl. Rev.

LC QH301 .P77
DD 574/.05 IQ

PROSPECTS OF IRAQ BIOLOGY. **VFOAT** Dirasat an Al-Ahya fi Al-Iraq. Multiple languages (Arabic and English).

LC QH301 .P794
DD 574.05 GW

PUBLIKATIONEN ZU WISSENSCHAFTLICHEN FILMEN. SEKTION BIOLOGIE. **Added/Corp** Institut fuer den Wissenschaftlichen Film (Goettingen, Germany). (1963)-. Academic Scholarly Publication. German (summaries and/or abstracts in English and French). Irregular. Institut fuer den Wissenschaftlichen Film / Gem. GmbH, Gottingen, Nonnenstieg 72, D-37075 Gottingen Germany. **Tel** 011 49 551 50240, FAX 011 49 551 5024400, telex 96691. **(Subscription address:** Institut fuer den Wissenschaftlichen Film, PO Box 2351, 37013 Gottingen Germany. **)** Index available. **Circ:** 400. available in bound issues.

LC QH90.A1 C58a
DD 574.92 IT

QUADERNI DELLA CIVICA STAZIONE IDROBIOLOGICA DI MILANO. **Main/Corp** Civica Stazione Idrobiologica di Milano. (May 1970)-. Italian (summaries and/or abstracts in English). Civica Stazione Idrobiologica di Milano, via le Gadio 2, Milan 20121 Italy.
Ind/Abst Life Sci. Collect. (1985-).

LC QH301 .Q3 **ISSN** 0033-5770
US
CCC
NLM W1 QU458 **CODEN** QRBIAK
Pr Rev.

QUARTERLY REVIEW OF BIOLOGY, THE. [Q. rev. biol.]. **Added/Corp** American Institute of Biological Sciences. American Society of Naturalists. State University of New York at Stony Brook. Vol. 1, No. 1 (Jan. 1926)-. Periodical. English. Four times a year. $111.00. University of Chicago Press / Journals Division, PO Box 37005, 5720 South Woodlawn, Chicago IL 60637. **Tel** (312)753-3347, FAX (312)753-0811. **ED** Frank C Erk, George C Williams. Index available. cum. index. **Bk Rev.** **Ad Acc.** **Acid Free.** **Circ:** 3,200. available on microfilm and microfiche from University Microfilms International (UMI). Documents available from The Genuine Article, BIOSIS Document Express, UMI Article Clearinghouse, CASDDS.
Desc: Review articles and book reviews spanning the entire scope of the life sciences.
Ind/Abst Abstr. Anthropol.; Abstr. Res. Pastor. Care Couns.; Acad. Abstr.; Acad. Ind. [Computer File] (1989-); Acad. Search; AGRICOLA; Biocont. News Inf.; Biol. Agric. Index; Biol. Abstr.; Biol. Dig.; Book Rev. Index; Chem. Abstr.; Curr. Aware. Biol. Sci., CABS; Curr. Cit.; Curr. Contents Agric. Biol. Environ. Sci.; Curr. Ref. Fish Res.; Ecol. Abstr.; Ecology Abstr.; Energy Res. Abstr.; EP Collect.; Expand. Acad. Index (1989-); Fish Rev.; Gen. Sci. Index; Gen. Sci. Source; GeoRef; Homework Help.; Index Med.; Index Sci. Rev. [Full Cov.]; INFO-SOUTH Abstr.; Int. Aerosp. Abstr.; Key Word Index Wildl. Res.; Mag. Search; MasterFile FullTEXT 1000; MasterFile FullTEXT 350; MasterFile FullTEXT 650; MasterFile FullTEXT (July 1990-); Newsp. Period. Abstr. (1991-); Nutr. Abstr. Rev., Ser. B, Live Feeds and Feed.; Nutr. Res. Newsl.; OCLC; Life Sci. Collect.; Res. Alert [Full Cov.]; Rev. Agric. Entomol.; Rev. Med. Vet. Entomol.; Sci. Cit. Index; SCISEARCH; Telebase; Wildl. Rev.

LC QH301 .F67a
DD 574/.05 FR

RAPPORT NATIONAL DE CONJONCTURE SCIENTIFIQUE: SCIENCES DE LA VIE. **Main/Corp** France. Centre National de la Recherche Scientifique. Comite National de la Recherche Scientifique. (19??)-. French. CNRS / Institut d'Information Scientifique et Technique, (Centre National de la Recherche Scientifique), 15 Quai Anatole France, 75700 Paris France. **Tel** 011 33 1 47531515, FAX 011 33 1 45517307, telex 260034.

LC QH652.A1 R43 **ISSN** 0131-355X
DD 574.191 RU
NLM ZWN 610 R332 **CODEN** RZRBDD

REFERATIVNYJ ZURNAL - VSESOJUZNYJ INSTITUT NAUCNOJ I TEHNICESKOJ INFORMACII. 70. RADIACIONNAJA BIOLOGIJA. (REFERATIVNYI ZHURNAL : RADIATSIONNAIA BIOLOGIIA.). [Ref. z. - Vses. inst. naucn. teh. inf., 70, Radiac. biol.]. **Added/Corp** Vsesoiuznyi Institut Nauchnoi i Tekhnicheskoi Informatsii (Soviet Union). **VFOAT** Radiatsionnaia Biologiia. (1973)-. Abstracting/Indexing Service. Russian. Twelve times a year. $199.95. VINITI - Vsesoyuznyi Institut Nauchno-Tekhnicheskoi Informatsii, All-Union Scientific and Technical Information Institute, Baltiiskaia ulitsa 14, 125219 Moscow Russia. **Tel** 011 7 95 2384600, FAX 011 7 95 9430060, telex 411160. **(Subscription address:** East View Publications Inc., 3020 Harbor Lane North, Suite 110, Minneapolis MN 55447. **Tel** (800)477-1005, (612)550-0961, FAX (612)559-2931.**)** Index available. **Circ:** 450 (ctrl). Documents available from CASDDS.
Ind/Abst Chem. Abstr. (1975-1986).

LC QE **ISSN** 0392-9531
DD 551 IT
NLM W1; RE198S **CODEN** RIAMED
RENDICONTI - ISTITUTO LOMBARDO, ACCADEMIA DI SCIENZE E LETTERE, B, SCIENZE CHEMICHE E FISICHE, GEOLOGICHE, BIOLOGICHE E MEDICHE. **See** Earth Sciences-Geology.

LC Q180.N4 N478a
DD 338.99306 NZ
REPORT OF THE MINISTRY OF RESEARCH, SCIENCE AND TECHNOLOGY FOR THE ... MONTHS ENDED 30 JUNE ... . **Main/Corp** New Zealand. Ministry of Research, Science and Technology. English.

ISSN 0885-8306
DD 574 US
CODEN RSBKDD
REPORTS OF THE STATE BIOLOGICAL SURVEY OF KANSAS. [Rep. State Biol. Surv. Kans.]. **Main/Corp** State Biological Survey of Kansas. Monographic series. English. Irregular. Price varies per volume. Kansas Biological Survey, 2041 Constant Avenue, West Campus, Lawrence KS 66047-2906. **Tel** (913)864-4777. **ED** Ralph E Brooks. Index available. cum. index. **Circ:** 150. Documents available from BIOSIS Document Express.
Ind/Abst Biol. Abstr.

LC Q
DD 500 US
RESEARCH IN PROGRESS. PHYSICS, CHEMISTRY, BIOLOGICAL SCIENCES, MATHEMATICS, ENGINEERING SCIENCES, METALLURGY AND MATERIALS SCIENCE, GEOSCIENCES, ELECTRONICS, EUROPEAN RESEARCH PROGRAM / U.S. ARMY RESEARCH OFFICE. **See** Physics.

LC QH9.5 .R48
DD 508.05 RU
RESURSY BIOSFERY. **Added/Corp** International Biological Programme. Sovetskii Natsionalnyi Komitet po Provedeniiu Mezhdunarodnoi Biologicheskoi Programme. **VFOAT** Resources of the Biosphere. Vol. 1 (1975)-. Russian (summaries and/or abstracts in English). Izdatelstvo Nauka St. Petersburg, Mendeleevskaia Liniia 1, 199034 St. Petersburg, B-34 Russia. **Tel** 011 7 812 2182612.

LC QH301 .R427
DD 574/.05 CU
REVISTA BIOLOGIA / UNIVERSIDAD DE LA HABANA. **Added/Corp** Universidad de La Habana. Facultad de Biologia. **VFOAT** Biologia. Vol. 1 No. 1 (1987)-. Periodical. Spanish. Three times a year.
Ind/Abst Biocont. News Inf.; Biodeter. Abstr.; Hortic. Abstr.; Rev. Med. Vet. Mycology; Weed Abstr.

LC QH301 .R43 **ISSN** 0034-7108
DD 574.05 BL
NLM W1 RE307 **CODEN** RBBIAL
REVISTA BRASILEIRA DE BIOLOGIA. [Rev. Bras. biol.]. **Added/Corp** Academia Brasileira de Ciencias. Sociedade de Biologia do Brasil. Vol. 1 (April 1941)-. Periodical. English (French, German, Italian, Portuguese and Spanish). Four times a year (Mar., June, Sept., Dec.). $100.00. Academia Brasileira de Ciencia, CAIXA Postal 229, 20001 Rio de Janeiro RJ Brazil. Documents available from BIOSIS Document Express, CASDDS.
Ind/Abst Biocont. News Inf.; Biol. Abstr.; Chem. Abstr.; Crop Physiol. Abstr.; Ecology Abstr.; For. Prod. Abstr. (1991-); For. Abstr.; GeoRef; Helminthol. Abstr. (19??-19??); Hortic. Abstr.; Index Med.; Index Dent. Lit.; Life Sci. Collect.; Plant Breed. Abstr.; Protozoolog. Abstr.; Rev. Agric. Entomol.; Rev. Med. Vet. Entomol.; Seed Abstr.; Soils Fert.; Weed Abstr.

LC QH301.C42 **ISSN** 0253-5688
DD 574/.05 CU
NLM W1; RE346U **CODEN** RCCBEG
REVISTA CENIC. (REVISTA CENIC. CIENCIAS BIOLOGICAS.). [Rev. CENIC, Cienc. biol.]. **Added/Corp** Centro Nacional de Investigaciones Cientificas (Cuba). **VFOAT** Ciencias Biologicas. Vol. 17 No. 1 (1986)-. Periodical. Spanish (summaries and/or abstracts in English). Four times a year. $22.50. Ediciones Cubanas, Obispo 527 Altos ESQ Bernaza, CP 10100 Havana Cuba. **ED** Esteban Perez Fernanadez. **Bk Rev. Ad Acc. Circ:** 850. available with charts. Documents available from BIOSIS Document Express, CASDDS. ***Continues*** *Revista de Ciencias Biologicas (Havana, Cuba), 0258-6002.*
Desc: Publishes national and international articles in the area of biological sciences. Covers biotechnology, bioengineering, environmental pollution and pharmacology.
Ind/Abst Biol. Abstr. (1986-1990); Chem. Abstr.

LC QH305.2.U8 R48 **ISSN** 0304-971X
DD 574.09 UY
CODEN RBURDA
REVISTA DE BIOLOGIA DEL URUGUAY. [Rev. biol. Urug.]. Vol. 1 (July 1973)-. Periodical. Spanish. Two times a year. $4.00. Universidad de la Republica de Uruguay / Medicina, Facultad de Medicina, General Flores 2125, Montevideo Uruguay. Documents available from BIOSIS Document Express.
Ind/Abst AGRICOLA; Biol. Abstr.

LC QH301 .R439 **ISSN** 0034-7736
PO
NLM W1 RE3734 **CODEN** RVBIAP
REVISTA DE BIOLOGIA (LISBOA). (REVISTA DE BIOLOGIA.). [Rev. biol.]. Vol. 1 (1956)-. Academic Scholarly Publication. Portuguese (English, French, German and Spanish). Irregular. Price varies. Museu Laboratorio e Jardim Botanico, Rua da Escola Politecnica 58, 1294 Lisbon Codex Portugal. **Tel** 601997. **ED** F. M. Catarino. Index available. **Circ:** 150 (ctrl). available on microfilm from University Microfilms International (UMI). Documents available from CASDDS.
Desc: International biological sciences.
Ind/Abst Chem. Abstr.; Field Crop Abstr.; Grass. Forage Abstr.; Key Word Index Wildl. Res.; Life Sci. Collect.; Seed Abstr.; Sug. Indus. Abstr.

LC QH301 **ISSN** 0398-4346
DD 574 FR
Pr Rev.
REVUE ARACHNOLOGIQUE. [Rev. arachnol.]. (June 1977)-. Periodical. French. Irregular. $37.32. Jean Claude Ledoux, 43 rue Paul Bert, 30390 Aramon France. **ED** J.C. Ledoux.
Ind/Abst Life Sci. Collect.

LC QH96.A1 F7 **ISSN** 0240-8783
DD 574.92/9 FR
CODEN RHTRDD
REVUE D'HYDROBIOLOGIE TROPICALE. [Rev. hydrobiol. trop.]. **Added/Corp** O.R.S.T.O.M. (Agency : France). Vol. 14, No. 1 (1981)-. Periodical. French (English and Spanish; summaries and/or abstracts in French, English and Spanish; table of contents in French and English). Four times a year. 250.00F France; 295.00F other. Orstom Editions, 72 route d'Aulnay, F-93143 Bondy Cedex France. **Tel** 011 33 1 48025500. **ED** J. Lemoalle (editor's address: Avenue Agropolis, BP 5045, 34032 Montpellier Cedex France). cum. index. available with charts; available with illustrations. Documents available from BIOSIS Document Express. ***Continues*** *Cahiers O.R.S.T.O.M. Serie Hydrobiologie.*
Desc: International journal with original or theoretical studies concerning continental fresh or brackish waters in the intertropical area.
Ind/Abst Aquat. Sci. Fish. Abstr. [CD-ROM Ed.]; Biol. Abstr.; Ecol. Abstr. (?-?); Energy Res. Abstr. (1981-); Fresh. Aqua. Contents Tables; Geogr. Abstr. Phys. Geogr. (?-?); GeoRef; Helminthol. Abstr. (1991-); Mar. Sci. Contents Tables; Rev. Med. Vet. Entomol.

LC QH301 .R446 **ISSN** 0035-6050
DD 574/.05 IT
NLM W1 RI383 **CODEN** RBILAV
Pr Rev. **SUSPENDED**
RIVISTA DI BIOLOGIA. [Riv. biol.]. **VFOAT** Biology Forum. Vol. 1 (Jan./Feb. 1919)-Suspended (1994). Periodical. English (Italian). Four times a year (Apr., June, Aug., Dec.). $60.00 (individuals), $120.00 (institutions), other; L90000.00 (individuals) Italy; L45000.00 (institutions) other. Edizioni Anicia, Via S Francesco A Ripa 62, 00153 Rome Italy. **Tel** 011 39 6 5894742. **ED** G. Sermonti. Index available. **Bk Rev. Ad Acc. Circ:** 500. Documents available from The Genuine Article, BIOSIS Document Express, CASDDS.
Desc: Theoretical basis of biology and new developments therein.
Ind/Abst AGRICOLA; Biol. Abstr.; Chem. Abstr.; Curr. Contents Agric. Biol. Environ. Sci.; Curr. Ref. Fish Res.; EMBASE; Environ. Period. Bibliogr. (?-?); Index Med.; Life Sci. Collect.; Res. Alert [Select. Cov.].

LC QH301 **ISSN** 0391-1551
DD 574 IT
NLM W1 RI386 **CODEN** RBNPD3
RIVISTA DI BIOLOGIA NORMALE E PATOLOGICA. [Riv. biol. norm. patol.]. **Added/Corp** Centro Universitario di Ricerca sui Tumori. (1975)-. Academic Scholarly Publication. Italian (English and Italian). Six times a year. L10000.00. Universita degli Studi di Messina, Centro Universitario di Ricerca sui Tumori, Via G. Venezian, Messina 98100 Italy. **ED** Camelo Cavallaro. **Bk Rev. Circ:** 300. Documents available from BIOSIS Document Express, CASDDS.
Ind/Abst Biol. Abstr. (-1983); Chem. Abstr.; EMBASE; Trop. Dis. Bull.

LC QH **ISSN** 0393-1137
DD 574 IT
NLM W1; RI766
RIVISTA ITALIANA DI BIOLOGIA E MEDICINA. [Riv. ital. biol. med.]. (Jan./March 1981)-. Periodical. Italian (summaries and/or abstracts in English and French). Four times a year. L155000. Edizioni Minerva Medica, Corso Bramante 83-85, 10126 Turin Italy. **Tel** 011 39 11 678282, FAX 011 39 11 674502. **ED** P.A. Vertova.
Ind/Abst EMBASE [Select. Cov.].

LC QL951 .S68 **ISSN** 1062-3604
DD 573.4105 US
CCC
NLM W1; ON868
RUSSIAN JOURNAL OF DEVELOPMENTAL BIOLOGY. **Added/Corp** Consultants Bureau. (1992)-. Academic Scholarly Publication. English (translations available in Russian). Six times a year. $1045.00. Consultants Bureau, A Division of Plenum Publishing Corporation, 233 Spring Street, New York NY 10013. **Tel** (212)620-8000, (212)620-8466, FAX (212)463-0742, telex 23/421139. Documents available from CASDDS. ***Continues*** *Soviet Journal of Developmental Biology, 0049-173X.*
Ind/Abst Chem. Abstr.; GeoRef; Life Sci. Collect.

LC Q4 .R9B **ISSN** 0286-9640
DD 505 JA
CODEN BCSRDZ
RYUKYU DAIGAKU RIGAKUBU KIYO. **See** Earth Sciences-Oceanography.

LC QH301 .I98 **ISSN** 0321-1665
DD 574.05/6 GS
NLM W1 IZ652G **CODEN** IGSBDO
TITLE CHANGE
SAKARTVELOS SSR MECNIEREBATA AKADEMIIS MACNE. BIOLOGIIS SERIA. (IZVESTIIA AKADEMII NAUK GRUZINSKOI SSR. SERIIA BIOLOGICHESKAIA.). [Sakartv. SSR mecnierebata Akad. macne. Biol. ser.]. **VFOAT** Proceedings of the Academy of Sciences of the Georgian SSR. Biological Series. Vol. 1, No. 1 (1975)-(199?). Academic Scholarly Publication. Russian (summaries and/or abstracts in English and Georgian). Documents available from BIOSIS Document Express, CASDDS. ***Continued by*** *Izvestiia Akademiia Nauk Gruzii. Seriia Biologicheskaia.*

LC QH301 **ISSN** 0231-7753
DD 574 XR
NLM W1 SB65
SBORNIK PEDAGOGICKE FAKULTY UNIVERZITY KARLOVY. BIOLOGIE. [Sb. pedagog. Fak. Univ. Karlovy, Biol.]. **Added/Corp** Univerzita Karlova. Pedagogicka Fakulta. **VFOAT** Biologie. (1969)-. Monographic series. Czech (summaries and/or abstracts in English and Russian). Irregular. Price varies per volume. Charles University / Univerzita Karlova, Ovocnytrh 5, 116 36 Prague 1 Czech Republic. **Tel** 228441.

CC
•SCIENCE IN CHINA. SERIES C, LIFE SCIENCES. (1995)-. English. Six times a year. $240.00. Science Press, 16 Donghuangchenggen North Street, Beijing 100707, People's Republic of China. **Tel** 011 86 1 4019821, 011 86 1 4010642, FAX 011 86 1 4012180, 011 86 1 4019810, telex 210147. ***Separated from*** *Science in China, Series B. Chemistry, Life Sciences, and Earth Sciences.*

LC QH301 .S335 **ISSN** 0098-5600
DD 574/.05 US
CODEN SBJODP
SCIENCE OF BIOLOGY JOURNAL. [Sci. biol. j.]. Vol. 1 (May 1975)-. Academic Scholarly Publication. English. Twelve times a year. $12.00. Science of Biology Journal, PO Box 3512, Terminal Island CA 90731. Documents available from CASDDS.
Ind/Abst Chem. Abstr.

LC QH301 .N53 **ISSN** 0371-2672
DD 574/05 JA
CODEN SRNBAD
SCIENCE REPORTS OF NIIGATA UNIVERSITY. SERIES D (BIOLOGY). [Sci. rep. Niigata Univ., Ser. D]. **Main/Corp** Niigata Daigaku. Rigakubu. **VFOAT** Niigata Daigaku Rigakubu Kenkyu Hokoku. (Seibutsugaku). (1964)-. Academic Scholarly Publication. English. One time a year. Niigata University / Science, Faculty of Science, 8050 Igarashi Nino-cho, Niigata-shi 950-21 Japan. Documents available from BIOSIS Document Express, CASDDS. ***Supersedes in part*** *Journal of the Faculty of Science, Niigata University. Series 2: Biology, Geology and Mineralogy.*
Ind/Abst Biol. Abstr.; Chem. Abstr. (1964-1982); GeoRef.

LC Q
DD 500 JA
CODEN SYUBAT
SCIENCE REPORTS OF THE YOKOHAMA NATIONAL UNIVERSITY. SECTION II: BIOLOGY AND GEOLOGY. **Added/Corp** Yokohama Kokuritsu Daigaku. Kyoiku Gakubu. **VFOAT** Biology and Geology; Yokohama Kokuritsu Daigaku Rika Kiyo. Dai 2-rui. Seibutsugaku Chigaku. No. 27 (Nov. 1980)-. Periodical. English (Japanese). One time a year. Tohoku Daigaku Rigakubu, (Faculty of Science Tohoku University), Aoba Aramaki Sendaishi, Miyagiken 980 Japan. Documents available from BIOSIS Document Express. ***Continues*** *Yokohama*

Biology

Kokuritsu Daigaku. Kyoiku Gakubu. Science Reports of the Yokohama National University. Section II: Biological and Geological Sciences.
Ind/Abst Biol. Abstr.; Plant Breed. Abstr.

LC QH302 .S4
DD 574.05
US

SCIENTIFIC AMERICAN RESOURCE LIBRARY. (READINGS IN THE LIFE SCIENCES.). Vol. 1 (1969)-. English. Irregular. $66.00. W H Freeman & Company Publishers, 41 Madison Avenue, New York NY 10010.

LC BJ
DD 170
US
SUSPENDED

SCIENTIFIC INTEGRITY. (19??)-(19??). English. Four times a year. $6.00 members, $8.00 nonmembers. National Association of Biology Teachers, 11250 Roger Bacon Drive #19, Reston VA 22090. **Tel** (703)471-1134. **ED** William Mayer and Michelle Robbins. ctrl circ.
Desc: Reviews the creationism/evolution debate, bioethics, and other issues in bioeducation.

LC QH90
DD 574.92
ISSN 0367-1887
UK
CODEN FBSPAT

SCIENTIFIC PUBLICATION - FRESHWATER BIOLOGICAL ASSOCIATION. [Sci. publ. Freshw. Biol. Assoc.]. **Main/Corp** Freshwater Biological Association. No. 1 (1939)-. Monographic series. English. Irregular. Price varies per volume. Freshwater Biological Association, Ferryhouse, Ambleside Cumbria LA22 O1P United Kingdom. **Tel** 011 44 15394 42468, FAX 011 44 15394 46914, telex 94070416 WIND G. **ED** D.W. Sutcliffe and J.M. Elliott. **Ad Acc.** Documents available from BIOSIS Document Express.
Desc: Keys to freshwater organisms and handbooks of methods for aquatic sciences.
Ind/Abst Biol. Abstr.; Life Sci. Collect.; Rev. Med. Vet. Entomol.

LC QH
DD 574
ISSN 0231-5777
XR

SCRIPTA FACULTATIS SCIENTIARUM NATURALIUM UNIVERSITATIS PURKYNIANAE BRUNENSIS. BIOLOGIA. [Scr. Fac. sci. nat. Univ. Purkyn. Brun., Biol.]. **Main/Corp** Universita J. E. Purkyne. Prirodovedecka Fakulta. VFOAT Biologia. Vol. 1, No. 1 (1971)-. Periodical. Czech (English, German and Russian). Four times a year. Universita J E Purkyne V, Brno Czech Republic. *Supersedes in part* Universita J. E. Purkyne. Prirodovedecka Fakulta. Folia.
Ind/Abst Math. Rev.

LC QH650
DD 574.191
NLM W1 SE249N
ISSN 0582-4052
JA
CODEN SEBUAL

SEIBUTSU BUTSURI. See Physics.

LC QH6301 .S34
DD 574
ISSN 0045-2033
JA
CODEN SBTKAQ

SEIBUTSU KAGAKU / NIHON SEIBUTSU KAGAKUSHA KYOKAI HENSHU. **Added/Corp** Nihon Seibutsu Kagakusha Kyokai. VFOAT Biological Science. (1949)-. Academic Scholarly Publication. Japanese. Four times a year. $86.00. Iwanami Shoten Publishers, 2-5-5 Hitotsubashi, Chiyoda-ku, Tokyo 101-02 Japan. **Tel** 011 81 3 32654111, FAX 011 81 3 32218998, 011 81 3 32399618, telex 39495. Documents available from CASDDS.
Ind/Abst Chem. Abstr.

LC QH323.J32 S447
JA

SEIBUTSU KAGAKU SOGO KENKYU KIKO KISO SEIBUTSUGAKU KENKYUJO YORAN. **Main/Corp** Kiso Seibutsugaku Kenkyujo (Japan). (1977)-. Japanese. Seibutsu Kagaku Sogo Kenkyo Kiko Kiso Seibutsugako, Aza Saigo, Myodaijicho 444 Okazaki Japan.

LC QH323.J32 S446
JA

SEIBUTSU KAGAKU SOGO KENKYU KIKO YORAN. **Main/Corp** Seibutsu Kagaku Sogo Kenkyu Kiko (Japan). 1977-. Japanese. Seibutsu Kagaku Sogo Kenkyo Kiko Seibutsugako, Aza Saigo, Myodaijicho 444 Okazaki Japan.

LC QH
DD 574
NLM W1 SE2499
JA
CODEN SKCHAT

SEIBUTSU KANKYO CHOSETSU. **Added/Corp** Nihon Seibutsu Kankyo Chosetsu Gakkai. VFOAT Environment Control in Biology. Vol. 12, No. 1 (March 1974)-. Periodical. Japanese. Four times a year. $139.50. Nihon Seibutsu kankyo Chosetsu Gakkai, (Japanese Society of Environment Control in Biology), Tokyo Noko Daigaku Daigakuin Rengo Nogaku Kenkyuka, 5-8, Saiwaicho 3 chome, Fuchushi, Tokyoto 183 Japan. (**Subscription address:** Japan Publications Trading Company Ltd., PO Box 5030, Tokyo International, Tokyo 100-31 Japan. **Tel** 011 81 3 3292 3753.) Documents available from CASDDS.
Ind/Abst Chem. Abstr.; Rice Abstr.

LC QH305 .S37
DD 574.05
ISSN 0386-9539
JA

SEIBUTSUGAKUSHI KENKYU = JAPANESE JOURNAL OF THE HISTORY OF BIOLOGY. **Added/Corp** Nihon Kagakushi Gakkai. Seibutsugaku Bunkakai. VFOAT Japanese Journal of the History of Biology. (19??)-. Periodical. Japanese. Two times a year. ¥1000 single issue. Nihon Kagakushi Gakkai Seibutsugaku Bunkakai, c/o Mizoguchi Hajime Shato Nakazato 50, 7-6 Nakazato 1 Kita-ku Tokyo-to Japan.

LC QH
DD 574
ISSN 0080-8539
JA
CODEN SEZIA3

SEIKEN ZIHO. [Seiken ziho]. **Added/Corp** Kihara Seibutsugaki Kenkyujo. No. 1 (1942)-. Periodical. Japanese (English). One time a year. ¥1000. Yokohama City University, Kihara Institute for Biological Research, 122-20 Mutsukawa 3-chome, Minami-ku, Yokohama-shi, Kanagawa-ken 232 Japan. Documents available from BIOSIS Document Express.
Ind/Abst Biol. Abstr.

LC QH
DD 574
ISSN 0913-0322
JA

SEIRIGAKU KENKYUJO GIJUTSUKA HOKOKU. [Seirigaku Kenkyujo Gijutsuka hokoku]. VFOAT Annual Report of the Technical Division of National Institute for Physiological Sciences. (1986)-. Periodical. Japanese. One time a year. Okazaki Kokuritsu Kyodo Kenkyu Kiko Seirigaku Kenkyujo, (National Inst. for Physiological Sciences Okazaki National Research Institutes), 38 Saigo Naka Myodaiji, Okazakishi Aichiken 444, Japan. Documents available from CASDDS.
Continues in part Seirigaku Gijutsu Kenkyukai Hokoku, 0285-3299.
Ind/Abst Chem. Abstr.

LC QH
DD 574
ISSN 0910-3627
JA
CODEN SEBOE7

SEITAI BOGYO = HOST DEFENSE. [Seitai bogyo]. VFOAT Host Defense. (1984)-. Academic Scholarly Publication. Japanese. Two times a year. Raifu Saiensu Shuppan K K, Masuda Bldg, Kyobashi 2-5-10, Chuo-ku, Tokyo-to 104 Japan. Documents available from CASDDS.
Ind/Abst Chem. Abstr.

LC Q
DD 500
NLM W1 SE26
ISSN 0370-9531
JA
CODEN SEKAA6

SEITAI NO KAGAKU. [Seitai no kagaku]. (1950)-. Periodical. Japanese (summaries and/or abstracts in English). Six times a year. ¥12960.00. Igaku Shoin Ltd., 5-24-3 Hongo Bunkyo-ku, Tokyo 113 Japan. **Tel** 011 81 3 38175670. **ED** Takao Tsubaki and Naobumi Ando. Index available. cum. index. **Ad Acc.** Circ: 1,500. Documents available from CASDDS.
Desc: Current concepts of physiology, biochemistry, and cytology.
Ind/Abst Chem. Abstr.; Curr. Biotechnol.

LC S13 .S436
DD 630.5
ISSN 0131-6397
RU
CODEN SSBLAO
CEASED

SELSKOHOZJAJSTVENNAJA BIOLOGIJA. (SELSKOKHOZIAISTVENNAIA BIOLOGIIA / VSESOIUZNAIA ORDENA LENINA AKADEMIIA SELSKOKHOZIAISTVENNYKH NAUK IMENI V.I. LENINA.). [Selskokhoz. biol.]. **Added/Corp** Vsesoiuznaia Ordena Lenina Akademiia Selskokhoziaistvennykh Nauk Imeni V.I. Lenina. Vol. 1 (1966)-(19??)-. Periodical. Russian (summaries and/or abstracts in English). (**Subscription address:** Victor Kamkin, 4956 Boiling Brook Parkway, Rockville MD 20852. **Tel** (301)881-5973.) Documents available from BIOSIS Document Express, CASDDS.
Ind/Abst AGRICOLA; Biol. Abstr.; Chem. Abstr.; Crop Physiol. Abstr. (?-?); Index Vet.; Maize Abstr.; Nematol. Abstr.; Nutr. Abstr. Rev., Ser. B, Live Feeds and Feed.; Plant Breed. Abstr.; Plant Genet. Resour. Abstr.; Plant Grow. Reg. Abstr.; Potato Abstr.; Poult. Abstr.; Protozoolog. Abstr.; Rev. Plant Pathol. (?-?); Soyabean Abstr.; Vet. Bull.

LC QH
DD 574
NLM W1 SO8539
ISSN 0309-6831
UK
CODEN SEBSDI

SEMINAR SERIES (SOCIETY FOR EXPERIMENTAL BIOLOGY (GREAT BRITAIN)). (SEMINAR SERIES / SOCIETY FOR EXPERIMENTAL BIOLOGY.). [Semin. ser. - Soc. Exp. Biol.]. **Added/Corp** Society for Experimental Biology (Great Britain). VFOAT Society for Experimental Biology Seminar Series. (1976)-. Academic Scholarly Publication. English. Irregular. Price varies per volume. Cambridge University Press, The Edinburgh Building, Shaftesbury Road, Cambridge CB2 2RU United Kingdom. **Tel** 011 44 1223 312393, FAX 011 44 1223 315052, telex 851-817256. (**Subscription address:** Cambridge University Press / North America, 110 Midland Avenue, Port Chester NY 10573. **Tel** (800)431-1580, (914)937-9600.) Documents available from BIOSIS Document Express, CASDDS.
Ind/Abst AGRICOLA [Select. Cov.]; Biol. Abstr.; Chem. Abstr.; CSA Neuro. Abstr. (?-?); Curr. Cit.

LC QH491 .S45
ISSN 1044-5781
US
CCC

NLM W1; SE487ML
TITLE CHANGE

SEMINARS IN DEVELOPMENTAL BIOLOGY. [Semin. dev. biol.]. (1990)-(1995). Academic Scholarly Publication. English. Academic Press Ltd., A Division of Harcourt Brace & Company Ltd., 24-28 Oval Road, London NW1 7DX United Kingdom. **Tel** 011 44 171 2674466, FAX 011 44 171 4822293, 011 44 171 4854752, telex 25775 ACPRES G. (**Subscription address:** Harcourt Brace & Company, Ltd., Foots Cray High Street, Sidcup Kent DA14 5HP United Kingdom. **Tel** 011 44 181 3003322, FAX 011 44 181 3090807, telex 896 377 ACADEM.) *Merged into* Seminars in Cell Biology.
Ind/Abst Curr. Cit.

LC QH301 .S772A
DD 547/.05
ISSN 0377-5232
KO
CODEN SNBAAO

SEOUL NATIONAL UNIVERSITY FACULTY PAPERS : BIOLOGY AND AGRICULTURE SERIES. [Seoul Natl. Univ. fac. pap., Biol. agric. ser.]. **Main/Corp** Soul Taehakkyo. (1971)-. Academic Scholarly Publication. English. One time a year. National University, Biology and Agriculture Series, Seoul 151 Korea. Documents available from CASDDS. *Continues* Seoul University Journal: Biology and Agriculture Series.
Ind/Abst Chem. Abstr.

LC Z5321 .B68a QH301
DD 016.574/05
NLM Z 5321; B615A
ISSN 1044-4297
US
CODEN SSBDE4
TITLE CHANGE

SERIAL SOURCES OF THE BIOSIS PREVIEWS DATABASE. [Ser. sources BIOSIS previews database]. **Main/Corp** BIOSIS. **Added/Corp** BioSciences Information Service of Biological Abstracts. (1989)-(1995). Academic Scholarly Publication. English. BioSciences Information Service, Biological Abstracts / BIOSIS, 2100 Arch Street, Philadelphia PA 19103. **Tel** (800)523-4806, (215)587-4847, FAX (215)587-2016, telex 831739. Documents available from CASDDS. *Continues* BioSciences Information Service of Biological Abstracts. Serial Sources for the BIOSIS Data Base, 0162-2048. *Continued by* BIOSIS Serial Sources.
Desc: Covers the serials indexed in BIOSIS Previews and all products derived there from.
Ind/Abst Chem. Abstr. (1990-).

LC G845 .I56
ISSN 0073-9871
CL
CODEN IACSCK
Pr Rev.

SERIE CIENTIFICA. INSTITUTO ANTARTICO CHILENO. See Earth Sciences.

LC QH301
DD 574
CC

SHENG WU FANG CHIH TUNG PAO. VFOAT Shengwu Fangzhi Tongbao; Biological Prevention Bulletin. Bulletin. Chinese. Four times a year. $9.44. Chinese Academy of Agriculture, Biological Prevention Research Center, Beijing, People's Republic of China. (**Subscription address:** China International Book Trading Corporation, PO Box 399, Library Service Department, Beijing 100044 People's Republic of China. **Tel** 011 86 1 8414284, FAX 011 86 1 8412023, telex 22496 CIBTC CN.)

LC QH301 .S477
DD 574/.05
ISSN 0006-3193
CC

SHENG WU HSUEH TUNG PAO. **Added/Corp** Chung-Kuo Tung Wu Hsueh Hui. Chung-Kuo chih Wu Hsueh Hui. VFOAT Shengwuxue Tongbao; Bulletin of Biology. (1952)-. Bulletin. Chinese. Twelve times a year. $25.80. Science Press, 16 Donghuangchenggen North Street, Beijing 100707, People's Republic of China. **Tel** 011 86 1 4019821, 011 86 1 4010642, FAX 011 86 1 4012180, 011 86 1 4019810, telex 210147. (**Subscription address:** China International Book Trading Corporation, PO Box 399, Library Service Department, Beijing 100044 People's Republic of China. **Tel** 011 86 1 8414284, FAX 011 86 1 8412023, telex 22496 CIBTC CN.)

DD 632.96
ISSN 1000-1034
CC

SHENGWU FANGZHI TONGBAO. VFOAT Chinese Journal of Biological Control. (1985)-. Periodical. Chinese. Four times a year. $8.20. Institute of Biological Control, 30 Bai Shi Chiao Road, Beijing, People's Republic of China. **Tel** 011 86 1 8314433. (**Subscription address:** China International Book Trading Corporation, PO Box 399, Library Service Department, Beijing 100044 People's Republic of China. **Tel** 011 86 1 8414284, FAX

011 86 1 8412023, telex 22496 CIBTC CN.)
Ind/Abst Agrofor. Abstr.; Biocont. News Inf.; Cot. Trop. Fibr. Abstr. Bibliogr.; Hortic. Abstr.; Potato Abstr.; Rev. Plant Pathol.; Soyabean Abstr.

LC QA **ISSN** 1001-9626
DD 510 CC
SHENGWU SHUXUE XUEBAO. See Mathematics.

LC QH **ISSN** 0001-5334
DD 574 CC
NLM W1 SH302W **CODEN** SYSWAE
SHIH YEN SHENG WU HSUEH PAO.
VFOAT Acta Experimentali Biologica Sinica; Acta Experimentali-Biologica Sinica; Acta Biologiae Experimentalis Sinica. (1954)-. Periodical. Chinese (summaries and/or abstracts in English, French, German and Russian; table of contents in English). Four times a year. $30.70. **(Subscription address:** China International Book Trading Corporation, PO Box 399, Library Service Department, Beijing 100044 People's Republic of China. **Tel** 011 86 1 8414284, FAX 011 86 1 8412023, telex 22496 CIBTC CN.) ***Continues*** *Chung-kuo Shih yen Sheng wu Hsueh tsa Chih.*
Desc: Contains information on experimental biology.
Ind/Abst Index Med.; NAPRALERT.

LC AS182 .H4 **ISSN** 0371-0165
DD 063 GW
CODEN SHWMAL
SITZUNGSBERICHTE DER HEIDELBERGER AKADEMIE DER WISSENSCHAFTEN, MATHEMATISCH-NATURWISSENSCHAFTLICHE KLASSE. **See** Mathematics.

AU
•**SITZUNGSBERICHTE UND ANZEIGER. ABTEILUNG 1, BIOLOGISCHE WISSENSCHAFTEN UND ERDWISSENSCHAFTEN.** **Added/Corp** Oesterreichische Akademie der Wissenschaften. Mathematisch-Naturwissenschaftliche Klasse. (1994)-. Periodical. German (summaries and/or abstracts in English). Springer-Verlag GmbH & Company KG, Heidelberger Platz 3, D-14197 Berlin Germany. **Tel** 011 49 30 8207223, FAX 011 49 30 8214091, telex 183 319 SPBLN D. ***Formed by the union of*** *Sitzungsberichte. Abt. 1, Biologische Wissenschaften und Erdwissenschaften, 0723-791X* ***and*** *Anzeiger (Oesterreichische Akademie der Wissenschaften. Mathematisch-Naturwissenschaftliche Klasse), 0376-1606.*

LC QH301 **ISSN** 0885-5951
DD 574 SZ
CCC
SOVIET BIOLOGICAL RESEARCH ABSTRACTS. (1991)-. Periodical. English. Irregular (4 issues per volume). $52.00 institution. Harwood Academic Publishers, PO Box 90, Reading RG1 8JL United Kingdom. **Tel** 011 44 1734 560080, FAX 011 44 1734 568211.

LC QH301 .S784 **ISSN** 0888-4803
DD 574/.05 SZ
CCC
NLM W1; SO996WEE **CODEN** SRFREP
SOVIET SCIENTIFIC REVIEWS. SECTION F, PHYSIOLOGY AND GENERAL BIOLOGY REVIEWS. [Sov. sci. rev., F Physiol. gen. biol. rev.]. **VFOAT** Physiology and General Biology Reviews. Vol. 1 (1987)-. English (translations available in Russian). One time a year. $321.00 (academic institutions), $501.00 (corporate institutions). Harwood Academic Publishers, PO Box 90, Reading RG1 8JL United Kingdom. **Tel** 011 44 1734 560080, FAX 011 44 1734 568211.

ISSN 0196-2361
DD 551 US
SPECIAL REPORT (STATE UNIVERSITY OF NEW YORK AT STONY BROOK. MARINE SCIENCES RESEARCH CENTER). (SPECIAL REPORT - MARINE SCIENCES RESEARCH CENTER, STATE UNIVERSITY OF NEW YORK.). [Spec. rep. - State Univ. N.Y. Stony Brook, Mar. Sci. Res. Cent.]. **Main/Corp** State University of New York at Stony Brook. Marine Sciences Research Center. 1-. Monographic series. English. Irregular. Price varies per volume. Marine Sciences Research Center, State University of New York, Stony Brook NY 11794. **Tel** (516)632-8700.
Ind/Abst GeoRef.

LC QD71 **ISSN** 0712-4813
DD 543/.0858/05 NE
CCC
CODEN SPIJDZ
Pr Rev.
SPECTROSCOPY (OTTAWA, ONT.). See Physics-Light, Optics, Radiation.

LC QE770 **ISSN** 0952-7451
DD 565/.33 UK
Pr Rev.
STEREO-ATLAS OF OSTRACOD SHELLS. See Zoology.

LC QH301
DD 574 RU
STRUKTURA I BIOSINTEZ BELKOV.
Added/Corp Institut Belka (Nauchnyi Tsentr Biologicheskikh Issledovanii). **VFOAT** Seriia Struktura i Biosintez Belkov. (1987)-. Periodical. Russian. Mezhdunarodnyi Tsentr Nauchnoi I Tekhicheskoi Informatsii, Ulitsa Kuusinena 21B, 125252 Moscow Russia.

LC QH301 **ISSN** 0392-0542
DD 574 IT
CODEN STSBDL
STUDI TRENTINI DI SCIENZE NATURALI. ACTA BIOLOGICA. [Studi trentini sci. nat., Acta biol.]. **Added/Corp** Museo Tridentino di Scienze Naturali. **VFOAT** Acta Biologica. Vol. 54 (1977)-. Academic Scholarly Publication. Italian (summaries and/or abstracts in English, French and German). One time a year. L17040. Museo Tridentino di Scienze Naturali Trento, Via Calepina 14, 38100 Trento Italy. **Tel** 011 39 461 270311. Index available. **Circ:** 1,000 (ctrl). Documents available from CASDDS. ***Continues in part*** *Studi Trentini di Scienze Naturali.*
Desc: Covers zoology, entomology, arachnology, mammals, ornithology, limnology, sociobiology.
Ind/Abst Chem. Abstr. (1977-1982).

LC QH301 .C576 **ISSN** 0039-3398
DD 574.05 RM
CODEN SUBBA8
Pr Rev.
STUDIA UNIVERSITATIS BABES-BOLYAI. BIOLOGIA. [Stud. Univ. Babes-Bolyai, Ser. Biol.]. **Main/Corp** Universitatea Babes-Bolai. (1975)-. Academic Scholarly Publication. English (Romanian; summaries and/or abstracts in French, German and Russian). Two times a year. DM230.00. Biblioteca Centrala Universitara, Str. Clinicilor Nr. 2, 3400 Cluj Napoca Romania. **Tel** 95 117092, FAX 95 117633. **(Subscription address:** Kubon & Sagner, ABT Zeitschriftenimport, D 80328 Munich Germany. **Tel** 011 49 89 54218130.) **Ad Acc. Circ:** 325. Documents available from BIOSIS Document Express, CASDDS. ***Continues*** *Studia Universitatis Babes-Bolyai. Series Biologia, 0039-3398.*
Ind/Abst Biol. Abstr.; Chem. Abstr.; EMBASE.

LC unc **ISSN** 0197-9922
US
STUDIES IN AVIAN BIOLOGY. [Stud. avian biol.]. **Added/Corp** Cooper Ornithological Society. No. 1 (1978)-. Monographic series. English. Irregular. Price varies per volume. Cooper Ornithological Society, 439 Calle San Pablo, Camarillo CA 93010. **Tel** (805)388-9944. ***Supersedes*** *Pacific Coast Avifauna, 0161-2913.*
Ind/Abst Fish Rev.; Wildl. Rev.

ISSN 0334-5114
DD 574 US
CODEN SYMBER
Pr Rev.
SYMBIOSIS (PHILADELPHIA, PA.). (SYMBIOSIS.). [Symbiosis]. Vol. 1, No. 1 (July 1985)-. Academic Scholarly Publication. English. Six times a year (Two volumes per year with six issues each). $295.00. Balaban Publishers, PO Box 2039, 76120 Rehovot Israel. **Tel** 011 972 8 476216, FAX 011 972 8 467632. **Circ:** 300. Documents available from The Genuine Article, BIOSIS Document Express, CASDDS.
Ind/Abst AgBiotech News Inf.; AGRICOLA [Select. Cov.]; Biocont. News Inf. (1991-); Biol. Abstr. (1985-); Chem. Abstr. (1985-); Crop Physiol. Abstr.; Curr. Aware. Biol. Sci., CABS; Curr. Cit.; Curr. Contents Agric. Biol. Environ. Sci.; Ecology Abstr.; Field Crop Abstr.; For. Abstr.; Grass. Forage Abstr.; Maize Abstr.; Microbiol. Abstr. Sect. B; Plant Grow. Reg. Abstr.; Res. Alert [Full Cov.]; Rev. Agric. Entomol.; Rev. Plant Pathol.; Rice Abstr.; Sci. Cit. Index; SCISEARCH; Soils Fert.; Sorghum Mill. Abstr.; Soyabean Abstr.; Weed Abstr.; Wheat Barley Trit. Abstr.

LC QH **ISSN** 0537-9032
DD 574 UK
NLM W3 IN105 **CODEN** SYIBA3
SYMPOSIA OF THE INSTITUTE OF BIOLOGY. [Symp. Inst. Biol.]. **Added/Corp** Institute of Biology. (19??)-. Academic Scholarly Publication. English. Irregular. Price varies per volume. Institute of Biology, 20 Queensberry Place, London SW7 2DZ United Kingdom. **Tel** 011 44 171 5818333, FAX 011 44 171 8239409. Documents available from CASDDS.
Ind/Abst Chem. Abstr. (?-1979).

LC QH301 **ISSN** 0081-1386
DD 574 UK
NLM W1 SY432K **CODEN** SSEBA9
SYMPOSIA OF THE SOCIETY FOR EXPERIMENTAL BIOLOGY. [Symp. Soc. Exp. Biol.]. **Main/Corp** Society for Experimental Biology (Great Britain). **VFOAT** S.E.B. Symposia. No. 1 (1947)-. English. One time a year. £48.00 (1991 edition) UK; $85.00 (1991 edition) US. Company of Biologists / Department of Zoology, Downing Street, Cambridge CB2 3EJ United Kingdom. **Tel** 011 44 1223 311789, FAX 011 44 1223 423353. Documents available from BIOSIS Document Express, CASDDS.
Desc: Each publication is a collection of articles on a specific aspect of modern experimental biology.
Ind/Abst AGRICOLA; Art Archaeol. Tech. Abstr.; Biol. Abstr.; Chem. Abstr.; Curr. Cit.; Index Med.; Life Sci. Collect.

ISSN 0583-9009
DD 574 US
CCC
CODEN SBSYAT
... SYMPOSIUM OF THE SOCIETY FOR DEVELOPMENTAL BIOLOGY, THE. [Symp. Soc. Develop. Biol.]. **Main/Corp** Society for Developmental Biology. Symposium. 32nd (1973)-. Academic Scholarly Publication. English. Irregular. Price varies per volume. Wiley Liss, 605 3rd Avenue, New York NY 10158. **Tel** (212)850-8800, (212)850-6645. **(Subscription address:** John Wiley & Sons, Inc. / Philadelphia, PO Box 7247, Philadelphia PA 19170. **Tel** (212)850-6645, (800)225-5945.) Documents available from BIOSIS Document Express, CASDDS. ***Continues*** *Society for Developmental Biology. Symposium. Symposium, 0583-9009.*
Ind/Abst Biol. Abstr.; Chem. Abstr.

LC QH83 .S9 **ISSN** 1063-5157
DD 572/.01/2 US
NLM W1; SY6955 **CODEN** SYBIER
SYSTEMATIC BIOLOGY. [Syst. biol.]. **Added/Corp** Society of Systematic Biologists. Vol. 41, No. 1 (Mar. 1992)-. Academic Scholarly Publication. English. Four times a year (Mar., Jun., Sept., Dec.). $60.00. Society of Systematic Biologists, National Museum of Natural History, Washington DC 20560. **Tel** (202)357-2560, FAX (202)357-1932. Index available (bound in Dec. issue). **Acid Free.** Documents available from The Genuine Article, BIOSIS Document Express, CASDDS. ***Continues*** *Systematic Zoology, 0039-7989.*
Desc: The object of this Society is the advancement of the science of systematic biology in all its aspects of theory, principles, methodology, and practice, for both living and fossil organisms, with emphasis areas of common interest to all taxonomists regardless of individual specialization.
Ind/Abst Biol. Agric. Index; Biol. Abstr.; Chem. Abstr.; Curr. Aware. Biol. Sci., CABS; Curr. Cit.; Curr. Contents Agric. Biol. Environ. Sci.; GeoRef; Nucl. Sci. Abstr.; Life Sci. Collect.; Res. Alert [Full Cov.]; Sci. Cit. Index; Soc. Sci. Cit. Index [Select. Cov.].

LC GF **ISSN** 1019-1224
DD 572 VM
UDC 57
TAP CHI SINH HOC. VFOAT Journal of Biology; Biologiceskij Zurnal. (1983)-. Periodical. Vietnamese. ***Continues*** *Tap Chi Sinh Vat Hoc, 0251-0995.*
Ind/Abst Biodeter. Abstr.

LC QH301 **ISSN** 0766-5725
DD 574 FR
CCC
NLM W1; TE160 **CODEN** TEBIEY
TECHN. BIOL. - 1985. (TECHNIQUE & BIOLOGIE.). **VFOAT** Technique et Biologie; TB. Vol. 11 No. 62 (Feb. 1985)-. Academic Scholarly Publication. French. Six times a year. $109.36. Societe Francaise d'Editions Medicales, 22 rue du Chateau des Rentiers, 75013 Paris France. **Tel** 011 33 1 45835054, FAX 011 33 1 45831354. **Ad Acc. Circ:** 6,000. Documents available from CASDDS. ***Continues*** *Technicien Biologiste, 0337-9965.*
Ind/Abst Chem. Abstr. (-1988).

LC QH301 **ISSN** 0277-6553
DD 574 US
CODEN TPSKDV
TECHNICAL PUBLICATIONS OF THE STATE BIOLOGICAL SURVEY OF KANSAS. [Tech. publ. State Biol. Surv. Kans.]. **Main/Corp** Kansas. State Biological Survey. Monographic series. English. Price varies per volume. State Biological Survey of Kansas, 2045 Avenue A, Campus West, Lawrence KS 66044. Documents available from BIOSIS Document Express.
Ind/Abst Biol. Abstr.

LC QH345 .T44 **ISSN** 0082-2523
DD 574.1/9/028 US
NLM W1 TE197E **CODEN** TBBMAL
TECHNIQUES OF BIOCHEMICAL AND BIOPHYSICAL MORPHOLOGY. [Tech. biochem. biophys. morphol.]. Vol. 1 (1972)-. Monographic series. English. Irregular. Price varies per volume. John Wiley & Sons, Inc., 605 Third Avenue, New York NY 10158-0012. **Tel** (212)850-6000, (212)850-6645, FAX (212)850-6088, telex 12-7063. **(Subscription address:** John Wiley & Sons / UK, Baffins Lane, Chichester, West Sussex PO19 1UD United Kingdom. **Tel** 011 44 1243 779777, FAX 011 44 243 776128, telex 86290 WIBOOKG.) **ED** D Glick and R M Rosenbaum. Each issue contains an index to its own contents (no volume

index)--loose. Documents available from BIOSIS Document Express, CASDDS.
Ind/Abst Biol. Abstr.; Chem. Abstr.

LC QH301 **ISSN** 0275-0120
DD 574 US
CCC
CODEN TBGBDG
Pr Rev.
TOPICS IN GEOBIOLOGY. [Top. geobiol.]. Vol. 1 (1980)-. Monographic series. English. Irregular. Price varies per volume. Plenum Press, 233 Spring Street, New York NY 10013-1578. **Tel** (212)620-8000, (800)221-9369, FAX (212)463-0742, (212)807-1047, telex 23/421139. **ED** Francis G. Stehli and D.S. Jones. Documents available from CASDDS.
Ind/Abst AGRICOLA [Select. Cov.]; Chem. Abstr. (1980-1983).

LC QH **ISSN** 0265-4377
DD 574 UK
CCC
NLM W1; TO54BF **CODEN** TMSBEI
TOPICS IN MOLECULAR AND STRUCTURAL BIOLOGY. [Topics mol. struct. biol.]. (1981)-. Monographic series. English. Irregular. Price varies per volume. Macmillan Distribution Ltd., Houndsmill Basingstoke, Hampshire RG21 2XS United Kingdom. **Tel** 011 44 1256 29242, FAX 011 44 1256 842084.

LC QH84.5 T845 **ISSN** 0795-0101
DD 574.92/9 NR
CODEN TFRBEW
TROPICAL FRESHWATER BIOLOGY. Vol. 1, No. 1 (Nov. 1988)-. Academic Scholarly Publication. English. Two times a year. $25.00. Idodo Umeh Publishers Ltd., 52 Ewah Road, PO Box 3441, Bennin City Nigeria. **Tel** 234 52 244404, telex 41303-IDOMEH-NG. **ED** Dr. Anthony E. Ogbeibu. Full Page (B&W) $500.00. **Circ:** 200 (ctrl).

LC QH301 .A362 **ISSN** 0568-5575
DD 574.05 RU
TRUDY. **Main/Corp** Akademiia Nauk SSSR. Iakutskii Filial. Institut Biologii. Vol. 1 (1955)-. Periodical. Russian. Izdatelstvo Nauka St. Petersburg, Mendeleevskaia Liniia 1, 199034 St. Petersburg, B-34 Russia. **Tel** 011 7 812 2182612.

ISSN 0568-5656
DD 574 RU
CODEN TBVVAC
TRUDY - AKADEMIA NAUK SSSR, INSTITUT BIOLOGII VNUTRENNIH VOD. (TRUDY - AKADEMIIA NAUK SSSR, INSTITUT BIOLOGII VNUTRENNIKH VOD.). [Tr. - Akad. nauk SSSR Inst. biol. vnutr. vod]. **Main/Corp** Institut Biologii Vnutrennikh Vod (Akademiia Nauk SSR). No. 6 (1963)-. Monographic series. Russian (table of contents in English). Price varies per volume. Izdatelstvo Nauka St. Petersburg, Mendeleevskaia Liniia 1, 199034 St. Petersburg, B-34 Russia. **Tel** 011 7 812 2182612. Documents available from CASDDS. ***Continues*** *Trudy Instituta Biologii Vodokhranilishch.*
Desc: Emphasis on freshwater biology.
Ind/Abst AGRICOLA; Chem. Abstr.; GeoRef; Life Sci. Collect.

LC QH197 .T8 **ISSN** 0041-3860
NZ
CCC
CODEN TUATAY
CEASED
TUATARA. (TUATARA : JOURNAL OF THE BIOLOGICAL SOCIETY, VICTORIA UNIVERSITY.). [Tuatara]. (Sept. 1947)-(1993). Periodical. English. Victoria University Info Publ Section, PO Box 600, Wellington New Zealand. **Tel** 011 64 4 4721000. cum. index. Documents available from BIOSIS Document Express.
Ind/Abst AGRICOLA; Biol. Abstr.; Fish Rev. (Jan. 1989-July 1992); Life Sci. Collect.; Wildl. Rev. (Jan. 1989-July 1992).

LC RA773
DD 613 TU
TURK HIJIYEN VE DENEYSEL BIYOLOJI DERGISI = TURKISH BULLETIN OF HYGIENE AND EXPERIMENTAL BIOLOGY. **See** Public Health and Safety.

LC S13 .A573
DD 630.5 TK
TURKMENISTAN YLYMLAR AKADEMIIASYNYNG KHABARLARY. BIOLOGIK YLYMLARYNG SERIIASY. **Added/Corp** Turkmenistan Ylymlar Akademiiasy. **VFOAT** Biologik Ylymlaryng Seriiasy; Seriia Biologicheskikh Nauk.; Series of Biological Sciences; Izvestiia Akademii nauk Turkmenistana. Seriia Biologicheskikh nauk; Proceedings of the Academy of Sciences of the Turkmenistan. Series of Biological Sciences. (199?)-. Periodical. Russian (summaries and/or abstracts in English). Six times a year. Izdatelstvo Ylym, Ulitsa Engelsa 6, 744000 Ashkhabad Turkmenistan. **Tel** 3632 9 04 84. ***Continues*** *Izvestiia Akademii Nauk Turkmenskoi SSR. Seriia Biologicheskikh Nauk, 0321-1746.*
Ind/Abst Hortic. Abstr.

LC QH324.5 .T8 **ISSN** 0096-3895
DD 574.078 US
NLM W1 TU985 **CODEN** TUNEAK
TURTOX NEWS. [Turtox news]. Vol. 1 (1923)-. Periodical. English. Twelve times a year. Crowell Collier, 8200 South Hayne Avenue, Chicago IL 60620. Documents available from BIOSIS Document Express, CASDDS.
Ind/Abst Biol. Abstr.; Chem. Abstr.

ISSN 0082-6979
FI
NLM W1 TU978 **CODEN** ATYBAK
TURUN YLIOPISTON JULKAISUJA. SARJA A 2, BIOLOGICA. GEOGRAPHICA. GEOLOGICA. (TURUN YLIOPISTON JULKAISUJA. SARJA A II, BIOLOGICA-GEOGRAPHICA-GEOLOGICA.). [Turun yliop. julk., Sar. A 2]. **Added/Corp** Turun Yliopisto. **VFOAT** Annales Universitatis Turkuensis. Series A II, Biologica-Geographica-Geologica. 45 (1970)-. Monographic series. English (German). Price varies per volume. Documents available from BIOSIS Document Express. ***Continues*** *Turun Yliopiston Julkaisuja. Sarja A II, Biologia-Geographica.*
Ind/Abst Biol. Abstr.; Geogr. Abstr. Phys. Geogr.; GeoRef.

LC RM862.7 .U47 **ISSN** 0301-5629
DD 616.07/54 US
CCC
NLM W1 UL751 **CODEN** USMBA3
Pr Rev.
ULTRASOUND IN MEDICINE & BIOLOGY. **See** Medical Sciences-Radiology.

LC QH1 .W38 **ISSN** 0083-7571
DD 574.082 US
UNIVERSITY OF WASHINGTON PUBLICATIONS IN BIOLOGY. **Added/Corp** University of Washington. Vol. 1, No. 1 (Aug. 1932)-. Periodical. English. Irregular. Price varies per volume. University of Washington Press Business Department, PO Box 50096, Seattle WA 98145-0096. **Tel** (206)543-8870.

ISSN 0317-3348
DD 574 CN
UNIVERSITY OF WATERLOO BIOLOGY SERIES. **Added/Corp** University of Waterloo. Dept. of Biology. No. 1 (1971)-. Monographic series. English. Irregular. Price varies per volume. University of Waterloo Department of Biology, Waterloo Ontario N2L 3G1 Canada. **Tel** (519)885-1211 ext. 6435, FAX (519)746-0614.

LC QP601 .U56 **ISSN** 1062-0370
DD 574 US
USB MOLECULAR BIOLOGY REAGENTS/PROTOCOLS. [USB mol. biol. reag./protoc.]. **Main/Corp** United States Biochemical Corporation. **VFOAT** USB Molecular Biology Reagents Protocols; Molecular Biology Reagents Protocols; Molecular Biology Reagents/Protocols. **VAT** United States Biochemical Molecular Biology Reagents/Protocols. (19??)-. English. United States Biochemical Corporation, PO Box 22400, Cleveland OH 44122. ***Continues*** *United States Biochemical Corporation. Enzymes & Reagents for Molecular Biology.*

LC QH506 .U83 **ISSN** 0205-0625
DD 574.1 BU
CODEN UMBIEX
USPEHI NA MOLEKULARNATA BIOLOGIA. (USPEKHI NA MOLEKULIARNATA BIOLOGIIA.). [Usp. mol. biol.]. **Added/Corp** Bulgarska Akademiia na Naukite. **VFOAT** Advances in Molecular Biology. (1983)-. Academic Scholarly Publication. Bulgarian (table of contents in English and Russian). Bulgarska Akademiia na Naukite, 7 Noemvri 1, Sofia Bulgaria. Documents available from CASDDS.
Ind/Abst Chem. Abstr. (1983-).

LC QH301 .U7 **ISSN** 0042-1324
DD 574 RU
NLM W1 US912 **CODEN** USBIA3
USPEKHI SOVREMENNOI BIOLOGII. [Uspekhi sovrem. biol.]. **Added/Corp** Akademiia Nauk SSSR. Vol. 1, (1932)-. Academic Scholarly Publication. Russian. Six times a year. $143.75. Izdatelstvo Nauka / Akademiia Nauk, (Publishing House of the Russian Academy of Sciences), Leninskii Porspekt 14, 117901 Moscow Russia. **Tel** 011 95 9542153, FAX 011 95 9382144, telex 411964. **(Subscription address:** East View Publications Inc., 3020 Harbor Lane North, Suite 110, Minneapolis MN 55447. **Tel** (800)477-1005, (612)550-0961, FAX (612)559-2931.**)** **Bk Rev.** Documents available from BIOSIS Document Express, CASDDS.
Ind/Abst AGRICOLA; Anim. Breed. Abstr.; Biol. Abstr. (1978-1988); Chem. Abstr.; CSA Neuro. Abstr. (?-?); Index Dent. Lit.; Index Vet.; Int. Aerosp. Abstr.; Plant Breed. Abstr.; Plant Genet. Resour. Abstr.; Vet. Bull.; Weed Abstr.

LC QH301.A3652 A2 **ISSN** 0042-1685
DD 570 UZ
NLM W1 UZ93 **CODEN** UZBZAZ
UZBEKSKII BIOLOGICHESKII ZHURNAL. [Uzb. biol. z.]. **Added/Corp** Uzbekiston SSR Fanlar Akademiiasi. **VFOAT** Uzbekiston Biologiia Zhurnali. (1958)-. Academic Scholarly Publication. Russian (summaries and/or abstracts in Uzbek; table of contents in Uzbek). Six times a year. $99.95. Akademiia Nauk Uzbekskoi, Ulitsa Gogolya 70, K 105, 700000 Tashkent Uzbekistan. **(Subscription address:** East View Publications Inc., 3020 Harbor Lane North, Suite 110, Minneapolis MN 55447. **Tel** (800)477-1005, (612)550-0961, FAX (612)559-2931.**)** Documents available from BIOSIS Document Express, CASDDS.
Ind/Abst AGRICOLA; Biocont. News Inf. (1991-); Biol. Abstr.; Chem. Abstr.; Cot. Trop. Fibr. Abstr. Bibliogr.; Crop Physiol. Abstr.; Field Crop Abstr.; For. Abstr.; GeoRef; Helminthol. Abstr. (19??-19??); Hortic. Abstr.; Index Vet.; Int. Aerosp. Abstr.; Nematol. Abstr.; Life Sci. Collect.; Plant Breed. Abstr.; Plant Genet. Resour. Abstr.; Plant Grow. Reg. Abstr.; Protozoolog. Abstr.; Rev. Agric. Entomol.; Rev. Med. Vet. Entomol.; Rice Abstr.; Seed Abstr.; Soils Fert.; Weed Abstr.

LC QH301 .M567a **ISSN** 0137-0952
DD 574.05/6 RU
NLM W1 VE839D **CODEN** VMUBDF
VESTNIK MOSKOVSKOGO UNIVERSITETA. SERIA 16. BIOLOGIA. (VESTNIK MOSKOVSKOGO UNIVERSITETA. SERIIA XVI : BIOLOGIIA.). [Vestn. Moskovskogo univ., Ser. XVI, Biologia]. **Main/Corp** Moskovskii Gosudarstvennyi Universitet Im. M.V. Lomonosova. **VFOAT** Biologiia. **VAT** Vestnik Moskovskogo Universiteta. Seriia Shestnadtsat Biologiia. (Jan./Mar. 1977)-. Academic Scholarly Publication. Russian (summaries and/or abstracts in English; table of contents in English). Four times a year. $49.95. Izdatelstvo Moskovskogo Universiteta, K-9 Ulitsa Gertsena 5/7, 103009 Moscow Russia. **Tel** (301)881-5973. **(Subscription address:** East View Publications Inc., 3020 Harbor Lane North, Suite 110, Minneapolis MN 55447. **Tel** (800)477-1005, (612)550-0961, FAX (612)559-2931.**)** Documents available from BIOSIS Document Express, CASDDS. ***Continues in part*** *Moskovskii Gosudarstvennyi Universitet Im. M.V. Lomonosova. Vestnik. Seriia VI: Biologiia, Pochvovedenie, 0579-9422.*
Ind/Abst AGRICOLA; Biol. Abstr.; Chem. Abstr.; CSA Neuro. Abstr. (?-?); Life Sci. Collect.; Plant Breed. Abstr.

LC QH
DD 574 RU
CODEN VSUBEO
VESTNIK SANKT-PETERBURGSKOGO UNIVERSITETA. SERIIA 3, BIOLOGIIA. **Added/Corp** Sankt-Peterburgskii Universitet. **VFOAT** Biologiia; Vestnik SPbGU. Ser. 3. (1992)-. Periodical. Russian (summaries and/or abstracts in English). Four times a year. $66.00. St. Petersburg State University / Izdatelstvo Leningradskogo Universiteta, Universitetskaia Nab 7/9, 199034 St. Petersburg Russia. **Tel** 011 7 812 2189788, FAX 011 7 812 2185152, telex 121481. ***Continues*** *Vestnik Leningradskogo Universiteta. Seriia 3, Biologiia, 0321-186X.*

LC QH301 **ISSN** 0166-6053
DD 630 NE
UDC 631
VRUCHTBARE AARDE. [Vruchtbare aarde]. (1943)-. Periodical. Dutch. Six times a year. Fl46.00. St Mens Op Weg, Weteringschans 76 I, 1017 XR Amsterdam Netherlands. ***Absorbed*** *Duizendblad (Driebergen), 0166-5456.*

ISSN 0899-7241
DD 570 US
NLM W1; WA603H
WASHINGTON INSIGHT. [Wash. insight]. (1988)-. Periodical. English. Four times a year. $85.00. Washington Insight, 11000 Waycroft Way, North Bethesda MD 20852. **Tel** (301) 881-6720. **ED** Georgia J Persinor.

LC QH1 .W39 **ISSN** 0043-0927
DD 570 US
CODEN WMJBA2
WASMANN JOURNAL OF BIOLOGY, THE. [Wasmann j. biol.]. **Added/Corp** University of San Francisco. **VFOAT** Journal of Biology. Vol. 8, No. 1 (1950)-. Periodical. English. One time a year. $6.50. University of San Francisco, Circulation Manager, San Francisco CA 94117. **Tel** (415)666-6381. **ED** R. James Brown. ctrl circ. Documents available from BIOSIS Document Express. ***Continues*** *Wasmann Collector, 0096-7823.*
Desc: Contributions may deal with any field of academic biology.
Ind/Abst AGRICOLA [Select. Cov.]; Biol. Abstr.; Biol. Dig.; Ecol. Abstr.; Fish Rev.; Geogr. Abstr. Phys. Geogr.; Life Sci. Collect.; Rev. Med. Vet. Entomol.; Wildl. Rev.

Biology—Abstracting, Bibliographies and Statistics

LC QH75.A1 W47
DD 333.91/8/0973
ISSN 0277-5212
US
CODEN WETLEU
Pr Rev.
WETLANDS (WILMINGTON, N.C.). See Environmental Issues-Conservation and Natural Resources.

LC R11 .Y25
DD 610.5
ISSN 0044-0086
US
CCC
NLM W1 YA454
CODEN YJBMAU
Pr Rev.
YALE JOURNAL OF BIOLOGY AND MEDICINE, THE. See Medical Sciences.

LC QH
DD 574
UZ
YASHLIK. (19??)-. Russian. Twelve times a year. $109.95. **(Subscription address:** East View Publications Inc., 3020 Harbor Lane North, Suite 110, Minneapolis MN 55447. **Tel** (800)477-1005, (612)550-0961, FAX (612)559-2931.**)**

LC QH7 .Z36
DD 508.05/6
ISSN 0352-1788
YU
ZBORNIK RADOVA PRIRODNO-MATEMATICKOG FAKULTETA. SERIJA ZA BIOLOGIJU. **Added/Corp** Univerzitet u Novom Sadu. Prirodno-Matematicki Fakultet. **VFOAT** Biology Series; Serija Za Biologiju; Review of Research. Biology Series. Vol. 11 (1981)-. Periodical. Serbo-Croatian (Cyrillic) (summaries and/or abstracts in English). Prirodno-Matematickog Fakultet U Novom Sadu, Ul Dr Ilije Djuricica 4, 21000 Novi Sad Yugoslavia. **Continues in part** Univerzitet u Novom Sadu. Prirodno-Matematicki Fakultet. Zbornik Radova, 0350-140X.

LC QL700 .Z4
DD 599
ISSN 0044-3468
GW
CCC
NLM W1 ZE587
CODEN ZSAEA7
Pr Rev.
ZEITSCHRIFT FUER SAUGETIERKUNDE. See Zoology.

LC QH301 .Z38
DD 574/.05
ISSN 0939-5075
GW
CCC
NLM W1; ZE4957
Pr Rev.
ZEITSCHRIFT FUR NATURFORSCHUNG. (ZEITSCHRIFT FUER NATURFORSCHUNG. C, A JOURNAL OF BIOSCIENCES.). [Z. Nat. forsch., C J. biosic.]. **Added/Corp** Max-Planck-Gesellschaft zur Foerderung der Wissenschaften. **VFOAT** Journal of Biosciences; Zeitschrift fur Naturforschung. Section C, A Journal of Biosciences; Zeitschrift fur Naturforschung. Sektion C, A European Journal of Biosciences. Vol. 41, No. 1/2 (Jan./Feb. 1986)-. Academic Scholarly Publication. English (German). Six times a year. DM645.00 Germany; DM665.00 other. Verlag der Zeitschrift fuer Naturforschung Tubingen, PO Box 2645, D-72016 Tuebingen Germany. **Tel** 011 49 7071 31555, FAX 07032/75465. **ED** H Hausen, A Hager, P Karlson, K Hahlbrock, W Hasselbach, F Kaudewitz, J Klein, J St Schell and N Amreim. Index available. **Ad Acc. Circ:** 1,000 (ctrl). Documents available from The Genuine Article, BIOSIS Document Express, CASDDS. **Continues** Zeitschrift fur Naturforschung. Section C, Biosciences, 0341-0382.
Desc: Original papers, letters, and general reviews.
Ind/Abst AGRICOLA; Biol. Abstr.; Chem. Abstr.; Curr. Aware. Biol. Sci., CABS; Curr. Contents Life Sci.; EMBASE; Helminthol. Abstr.; NAPRALERT; Life Sci. Collect.; PESTDOC; Ref. Upd. Deluxe Ed.; Res. Alert [Full Cov.]; Rev. Med. Vet. Entomol.; Sci. Cit. Index; SCISEARCH.

LC QH301
DD 574
UDC 502.5
ISSN 0138-0923
PL
ZESZYTY NAUKOWE AKADEMII GORNICZO-HUTNICZEJ IM. STANISAWA STASZICA. SOZOLOGIA I SOZOTECHNIKA. [Zesz. Nauk. Akad. Gor.-Hut. im. Stanisawa Staszica, Sozol. Sozotech.]. **VFOAT** Scientific Bulletins of University of Mining and Metallurgy. Sozology and Sozotechnics; Zeszyty Naukowe. Sozologia i Sozotechnika. (1974)-. Multiple languages. Irregular. Price varies per volume. Wydawnictwo AGH / Wydawnictwo Akademia Gorniczo-Hutnicza im. S. Staszica, Al. Mickiewicza 30, 30-059 Krakow Poland. **Tel** 011 48 12 338100, FAX 011 48 12 3311014. **ED** Z. Kleczek.
Ind/Abst Curr. Cit.

LC QH301 .U57a
DD 574/.05
ISSN 0867-3357
PL
●**ZESZYTY NAUKOWE. BIOLOGIA.** **Added/Corp** Uniwersytet Gdanski. **VFOAT** Biologia. (1993)-. Periodical. Polish (summaries and/or abstracts in English). **Continues** Zeszyty Naukowe Wydziau Biologii, Geografii i Oceanologii. Biologia, 0208-4961.

LC QH
DD 574
ISSN 0239-5061
PL
CODEN STWBD7
ZESZYTY NAUKOWE WYZSZEJ SZKOLY PEDAGOGICZNEJ W BYDGOSZCZY. STUDIA TECHNICZNE. [Zesz. nauk. Wyz. Szk. Pedagog. Bydg., Stud. tech.]. **Added/Corp** Wyzsza Szkola Pedagogiczna w Bydgoszczy. **VFOAT** Studia Biologiczne. (1980)-. Academic Scholarly Publication. Polish. Wydawnictwo Uczelniane WSP w Bydgoszczy, Bydgoszcz Poland. Documents available from CASDDS. **Continues** Zeszty Naukowe (Wyzsza Szkola Pedagogiczna w Bydgoszczy). Studia Technicze.
Ind/Abst Chem. Abstr.

LC QH
DD 574
ISSN 0044-4596
RU
CCC
NLM W1 ZH4225
CODEN ZOBIAU
Pr Rev.
ZURNAL OBSCEJ BIOLOGI. (ZHURNAL OBSHCHEI BIOLOGII.). [Z. obsc. biol.]. **Added/Corp** Akademiia Nauk SSSR. **VFOAT** Journal of General Biology. Vol. 1, (1940)-. Academic Scholarly Publication. Russian (summaries and/or abstracts in English; table of contents in English). Six times a year. $223.75. Izdatelstvo Nauka / Akademiia Nauk, (Publishing House of the Russian Academy of Sciences), Leninskii Porspekt 14, 117901 Moscow Russia. **Tel** 011 95 9542153, FAX 011 95 9382144, telex 411964. **(Subscription address:** East View Publications Inc., 3020 Harbor Lane North, Suite 110, Minneapolis MN 55447. **Tel** (800)477-1005, (612)550-0961, FAX (612)559-2931.**)** Index available. Documents available from The Genuine Article, BIOSIS Document Express, CASDDS. **Continues** Biologicheskii Zhurnal.
Ind/Abst Biocont. News Inf.; Biol. Abstr.; Chem. Abstr.; Curr. Contents Agric. Biol. Environ. Sci.; Ecol. Abstr. (?-?); EMBASE; GeoRef; Index Med.; Int. Aerosp. Abstr.; Life Sci. Collect.; Plant Grow. Reg. Abstr.; Res. Alert [Full Cov.]; Rev. Agric. Entomol.; Rev. Med. Vet. Entomol.; Sci. Cit. Index; SCISEARCH; Sel. Water Resour. Abstr.; Trop. Dis. Bull.

ABSTRACTING, BIBLIOGRAPHIES AND STATISTICS

LC TP248.13 .A27
DD 661.8
ISSN 0263-6778
UK
CCC
NLM Z 7914.B33; A164
ABSTRACTS IN BIOCOMMERCE. (ABSTRACTS IN BIOCOMMERCE ®). [Abstr. biocommer.]. **VFOAT** ABC; A.B.C. Vol. 1, No. 1 (Aug. 9, 1982)-. Abstracting/Indexing Service. English. Twenty-four times a year. $878.00. Biocommerce Data Ltd., 95 High Street, Slough Berkshire SL1 1DH United Kingdom. **Tel** 011 44 1753 511777, FAX 011 44 1753 512239. **ED** A Crafts-Lighty. Index available. cum. index. **Ad Acc. Circ:** 500 (ctrl). available on an online database (File CELL) from DATA-STAR; and (File 286) DIALOG; available on diskette (as PC-ABC) from the publisher.
Desc: A business news monitoring service summarizing important events in the biotechnology industry worldwide. A comprehensive system indexing articles in major newsletters, magazines and newspapers. Some additional US and UK newspapers that are not individually mentioned are monitored.

LC QK600 .A22
DD 589/.2/08
ISSN 0001-3617
NLM ZQW 180 A164
CODEN ABMYA5
ABSTRACTS OF MYCOLOGY. **Added/Corp** BioSciences Information Service of Biological Abstracts. Vol. 1 Jan. (1967)-. Abstracting/Indexing Service. English. Twelve times a year. $265.00. BioSciences Information Service, Biological Abstracts / BIOSIS, 2100 Arch Street, Philadelphia PA 19103. **Tel** (800)523-4806, (215)587-4847, FAX (215)587-2016, telex 831739. cum. index.
Desc: Current awareness journal containing abstracts and content summaries, including U.S. patents, of research studies involving fungi, lichens and fungicides, in biochemistry, cytology, genetics, microbiology, pathology and systematics.

LC QR
DD 576
CN
ABSTRACTS OF THE CANADIAN SOCIETY OF MICROBIOLOGY. (19??)-. Abstracting/Indexing Service. English. One time a year.
Ind/Abst PESTDOC.

DD 576
ISSN 1060-2011
CCC
NLM W1; AM767
CODEN AGMME8
ABSTRACTS OF THE ... GENERAL MEETING OF THE AMERICAN SOCIETY FOR MICROBIOLOGY. [Abstr. Gen. Meet. Am. Soc. Microbiol.]. **Main/Corp** American Society for Microbiology. General Meeting. (1991)-. English. One time a year (Apr.). $80.00. American Society for Microbiology / DC, 1325 Massachusetts Avenue Northwest, Washington DC 20005-4171. **Tel** (202)737-3600, FAX (202)737-0367. **Continues** American Society for Microbiology. Meeting. Abstracts of the Annual Meeting of the American Society for Microbiology, 0094-8519.
Desc: Contain abstracts of presentations at ASM's general meeting.
Ind/Abst INIS Atomindex [Micro.]; PESTDOC.

LC S494.5.B563 A36
DD 630
ISSN 0954-9897
UK
AGBIOTECH NEWS AND INFORMATION. See Agriculture-Abstracting, Bibliographies and Statistics.

LC S494.5.B563 A363
DD 660
ISSN 1063-1151
US
●**AGRICULTURAL & ENVIRONMENTAL BIOTECHNOLOGY ABSTRACTS.** See Agriculture-Abstracting, Bibliographies and Statistics.

LC QK564
DD 589.3
ISSN 0094-6362
US
NLM Z 5356.A6 A394
ALGAE ABSTRACTS. **Added/Corp** Water Resources Scientific Information Center. Vol. 1 (1969)-. Monographic series. English. Irregular. Price varies per volume. Plenum Press, 233 Spring Street, New York NY 10013-1578. **Tel** (212)620-8000, (800)221-9369, FAX (212)463-0742, (212)807-1047, telex 23/421139. **ED** Editorial Board. Each issue contains an index to its own contents (no volume index)--loose.

LC QK
DD 581
ISSN 0570-2496
JA
ANNUAL INDEX OF THE REPORTS ON PLANT CHEMISTRY. (1961)-. English. Irregular. Hirokawa Publishing Company, 27-14 Hongo 3 Bunkyo-ku, Tokyo 113 Japan. **ED** Tatsuo Kariyone.
Desc: Short abstracts of the current works on plant chemistry, picked out from the chemical journals of the world.

LC TP248.27.M37 M37
DD 660/.6
ISSN 1054-2027
US
NLM ZQT 34; A797
ASFA MARINE BIOTECHNOLOGY ABSTRACTS. [ASFA mar. biotechnol. abstr.]. **VFOAT** Marine Biotechnology Abstracts. **VAT** Aquatic Sciences and Fisheries Abstracts Marine Biotechnology Abstracts. Vol. 2, No. 1 (March 1990)-. Abstracting/Indexing Service. English. Four times a year (plus an annual index). $315.00. Cambridge Scientific Abstracts, 7200 Wisconsin Avenue #601, Bethesda MD 20814-4823. **Tel** (301)961-6750, (800)843-7751, FAX (301)961-6720. **ED** Darrell Stover and Jonathan Sears. Index available. cum. index. **Bk Rev** available on magnetic tape, an online database, and CD-ROM from Cambridge Scientific Abstracts; available via Internet (to the current year's abstracts and five-year backfiles) from Cambridge Scientific Abstracts. **Continues** Marine Biotechnology Abstracts, 1043-8971.
Desc: With information drawn from the prestigious Aquatic Sciences and Fisheries Abstracts Series, this publication examines applications for biotechnology in aquaculture, pharmacotherapy and environmental management. Topics range from isolation, sequencing, and synthesis of nucleic acids and proteins to bioremediation techniques for marine pollution control.

LC RA407 .B32
DD 610/.72
ISSN 1045-5523
US
BASIC AND CLINICAL BIOSTATISTICS. [Basic clin. biostat.]. (1990)-. Periodical. English. Irregular. $25.50 (per copy). Appleton & Lange, (A Subsidiary of Simon & Schuster), Four Stamford Plaza, 107 Elm Street, Stamford CT 06902-3851. **Tel** (203)406-4500, (800)451-3794.

LC QH471
DD 574.16
ISSN 0006-1565
UK
CCC
NLM ZWQ 205 B582
TITLE CHANGE
BIBLIOGRAPHY OF REPRODUCTION. (BIBLIOGRAPHY OF REPRODUCTION : A CLASSIFIED MONTHLY LIST OF REFERENCES COMPILED FROM THE RESEARCH LITERATURE.). [Bibliogr. reprod.]. **Added/Corp** Reproduction Research Information Service Ltd. Society for the Study of Fertility. Society for the Study of Reproduction. Australian Society for Reproductive Biology. Blair Bell Research Society. Vol. 1 (Jan. 1963)-(1994). Bibliography. English. Oxford University Press / UK, Walton Street, Oxford OX2 6DP United Kingdom. **Tel** 011 44 1865 56767, FAX 011 44 1865 267773, telex 851/837330 OXPRES G. **ED** David Cole. Index available. **Bk Rev. Ad Acc. Circ:** 900 (ctrl). **Merged with** Oxford Reviews of Reproductive Biology, 0260-0854 **to form** Human Reproduction Update, 1355-4786.
Desc: Classified title list of the world's research literature on human and animal reproduction.
Ind/Abst Anim. Breed. Abstr.; Dairy Sci. Abstr.; Index Vet.; Popul. Index; Vet. Bull.

LC Z5185.B53 B54 QR82.A35 **ISSN** 0285-7006
DD 016.5899/2 JA
UDC 579.873.13
BIFIDUS, FLORES ET FRUCTUS. Vol. 1, No. 1 (June 1981)-. Periodical. English (English). Four times a year. $50.00. Business Center for Academic Societies Japan, Hon-Komagome 5-16-9, Bunkyo-ku, Tokyo 113 Japan. **Tel** 011 81 3 5814 5811, FAX 011 81 3 5814 5822. **ED** Tomotari Mitsuoka. **Circ:** 500 (ctrl).
Desc: Bibliography of bifidbacteria and microflola.

LC QD **ISSN** 1065-7509
DD 540 US
UDC 54
•**BIOCHEMISTRY & BIOPHYSICS CITATION INDEX.** (BIOCHEMISTRY & BIOPHYSICS CITATION INDEX [COMPUTER FILE] : A CD-ROM DATABASE WITH ABSTRACTS.). **Added/Corp** Institute for Scientific Information. **VFOAT** Biochemistry & Biophysics; Biochemistry and Biophysics; Biochemistry and Biophysics Citation Index. (1993)-. Academic Scholarly Publication. English. Six times a year. $1950.00. Institute for Scientific Information, 3501 Market Street, Philadelphia PA 19104. **Tel** (215)386-0100, (800)523-1850, FAX (215)386-6362, telex 84-5305. **(Subscription address:** Institute for Scientific Information, PO Box 71416, Chicago IL 60694. **)**
Desc: Covers the current literature on cellular chemistry, molecular microbiology, bioenergetics, biotechnology, food and medicinal chemistry, plant molecular biology, thermobiology, photosynthesis, and clinical chemistry.

LC TP HB **ISSN** 1354-280X
DD 660 330 UK
•**BIOCOMMERCE FINANCIAL ABSTRACTS.** (1994)-. Abstracting/Indexing Service. English. Two times a month. £195.00. Biocommerce Data Ltd., 95 High Street, Slough Berkshire SL1 1DH United Kingdom. **Tel** 011 44 1753 511777, FAX 011 44 1753 512239. **ED** A. Crafts-Lighty. available on an online database (File no.286) from Knight-Ridder Information, Inc.; and DATA-STAR.
Desc: Covers articles on the financial aspects of biotechnology company development.

LC R **ISSN** 1068-5693
DD 610 US
•**BIOENGINEERING ABSTRACTS (1993).** (BIOENGINEERING ABSTRACTS.). [BioEng. abstr.]. **Added/Corp** Cambridge Scientific Abstracts, Inc. Engineering Information Inc. Vol. 20, No. 1 (1993)-. Abstracting/Indexing Service. English. Twelve times a year. $625.00. Cambridge Scientific Abstracts, 7200 Wisconsin Avenue, #601, Bethesda MD 20814-4823. **Tel** (301)961-6750, (800)843-7751, FAX (301)961-6720. available via Internet (to the current year's abstracts and five-year backfiles) from Cambridge Scientific Abstracts. ***Continues** Engineering Index Bioengineering and Biotechnology Abstracts, 1041-2913.*
Desc: International scope of bioengineering and biomedical engineering literature.

LC QH301 .B37 **ISSN** 0006-3169
DD 570.5 US
NLM Z 5321 B615 **CODEN** BIABA4
BIOLOGICAL ABSTRACTS. [Biol. abstr.]. **Added/Corp** BioSciences Information Service of Biological Abstracts. Union of American Biological Societies. Vol. 1 (Dec. 1926)-. Abstracting/Indexing Service. English. Twenty-four times a year. $5730.00. BioSciences Information Service, Biological Abstracts / BIOSIS, 2100 Arch Street, Philadelphia PA 19103. **Tel** (800)523-4806, (215)587-4847, FAX (215)587-2016, telex 831739. cum. index. available in microform (BIOSIS Previews and five-year collective indexes); available on magnetic tape; available on CD-ROM (Biological Abstracts on Compact Disc) from BIOSIS; available on an online database from STN International; European Space Agency; (File nos. 5 & 55) DIALOG; DATA-STAR; DIMDI; CISTI; BRS; and (as BIOSIS Previews). ***Formed by the union of** Abstracts of Bacteriology, 0096-5340 **and** Botanical Abstracts, 0096-526X.*
Desc: Provides abstracts of current published research from the biological and biomedical journal literature. Serial Sources for the BIOSIS Previews Database contains a complete list of publications included in Biological Abstracts and Biological Abstracts/RRM; it is available from BIOSIS.
Ind/Abst Anim. Breed. Abstr.; Index Vet.; Popul. Index; Rev. Med. Vet. Mycology; Rev. Plant Pathol.; Vet. Bull.; Weed Abstr.

LC QH301 **ISSN** 1058-4129
DD 574 US
BIOLOGICAL ABSTRACTS ON COMPACT DISC [COMPUTER FILE]. [Biol. abstr. on compact disc]. **Added/Corp** BioSciences Information Service of Biological Abstracts. **VFOAT** BIOSIS [Computer File]; BA on CD [Computer File]. (Jan./Mar. 1990)-. Abstracting/Indexing Service. English. Four times a year. $11,140.00 US and Canada; $12,170.00 other. BioSciences Information Service, Biological Abstracts / BIOSIS, 2100 Arch Street, Philadelphia PA 19103. **Tel** (800)523-4806, (215)587-4847, FAX (215)587-2016, telex 831739. available in print (Biological Abstracts) from BIOSIS; available on an online database (as BIOSIS Previews).
Desc: Alerts researchers to biological and medical research findings, biological techniques and discoveries of new organisms.

LC Z5321 .B672 QH301 **ISSN** 0192-6985
DD 016.574 US
NLM Z 5321 B618 **CODEN** BARRDG
BIOLOGICAL ABSTRACTS / RRM. [Biol. abstr./RRM]. **Added/Corp** BioSciences Information Service of Biological Abstracts. **VAT** Biological Abstracts, Reports, Reviews, Meetings; Biological Abstracts RRM. Vol. 18, (Jan. 1980)-. Abstracting/Indexing Service. English. Twelve times a year. $2900.00. BioSciences Information Service, Biological Abstracts / BIOSIS, 2100 Arch Street, Philadelphia PA 19103. **Tel** (800)523-4806, (215)587-4847, FAX (215)587-2016, telex 831739. Index available. cum. index. **Bk Rev.** available in microform (Five year collective indexes Vol 18-27 (1980-84)); available on CD-ROM (Biological Abstracts/RRM on Compact Disc [Computer File]); available on an online database from STN International; European Space Agency; (Files nos. 5 & 55) DIALOG; DATA-STAR; DIMDI; CISTI; BRS; and (as BIOSIS Previews). ***Continues** Bioresearch Index, 0006-3541.*
Desc: A printed reference publication providing indexed and classified bibliographic entries for research reports, reviews, U.S. patents, and books in biology and biomedicine, also offers unique international meeting coverage.

LC QH301 **ISSN** 1058-4137
DD 574 US
BIOLOGICAL ABSTRACTS / RRM ON COMPACT DISC. (BIOLOGICAL ABSTRACTS / RRM ON COMPACT DISC [COMPUTER FILE] / BIOSIS.). [Biol. abstr./RRM on compact disc]. **Added/Corp** BioSciences Information Service of Biological Abstracts. **VFOAT** Biological Abstracts RRM on Compact Disc; BA RRM on Compact Disc; BA RRM on CD; BA/RRM on Compact Disc; BA/RRM on CD. **VAT** Biological Abstracts, Reports, Reviews, Meetings on Compact Disc. (Mar. 1991)-. Periodical. English. Four times a year. $5680.00. BioSciences Information Service, Biological Abstracts / BIOSIS, 2100 Arch Street, Philadelphia PA 19103. **Tel** (800)523-4806, (215)587-4847, FAX (215)587-2016, telex 831739. available in print (Biological Abstracts/RRM) from BIOSIS; available on an online database (as BIOSIS Previews).
Desc: Provides easy access to critical life science studies published in sources other than journal.

LC QH301
DD 574 US
BIOLOGICAL ABSTRACTS. SEMIANNUAL CUMULATIVE INDEX. **Added/Corp** Biological Abstracts, inc. **VFOAT** Semiannual Cumulative Index. (19??)-. Periodical. English. Two times a year. $2480.00. BioSciences Information Service, Biological Abstracts / BIOSIS, 2100 Arch Street, Philadelphia PA 19103. **Tel** (800)523-4806, (215)587-4847, FAX (215)587-2016, telex 831739.

LC Z5073 .A46 **ISSN** 0006-3177
DD 016.63/05 US
NLM ZS 419 A278
Pr Rev.
BIOLOGICAL & AGRICULTURAL INDEX. [Biol. agric. index]. **Added/Corp** H.W. Wilson Company. **VAT** Biological and Agricultural Index. Vol. 19 (1964)-. Abstracting/Indexing Service. English. Eleven times a year (monthly except Aug.). $1495.00 CD-ROM; Print edition sold on the service basis. H W Wilson Company, 950 University Avenue, Bronx NY 10452. **Tel** (800)367-6770, (718)588-8400 ext. 2245, FAX (718)681-1511, telex 4990003 HWILSON. **ED** Syed Shah. Index available. cum. index. ctrl circ. available on CD-ROM from WILSONDISC; available on magnetic tape from WILSONTAPE; available on diskette from WILSONSEARCH; available on an online database from BRS; and WILSONLINE. ***Continues** Agricultural Index, 0196-5883.*
Desc: Offers comprehensive and accurate information available on the entire range of sciences related to biology and agriculture. Provides easy access to the fundamental research underlying key current topics. Coverage encompasses the core literature in the field.

LC Z5073
DD 574 630 US
BIOLOGICAL & AGRICULTURAL INDEX [COMPUTER FILE]. **Added/Corp** H.W. Wilson Company. **VFOAT** Biological and Agricultural Index. (198?)-. Periodical. English. Twelve times a year. $1495.00. H W Wilson Company, 950 University Avenue, Bronx NY 10452. **Tel** (800)367-6770, (718)588-8400 ext. 2245, FAX (718)681-1511, telex 4990003 HWILSON. available in print.
Desc: Provides access to important and current information in the biological sciences, agriculture, and related areas.

LC QH301 .B44 **ISSN** 0095-2958
DD 574/.08 US
BIOLOGY DIGEST. [Biol. dig.]. Vol. 1 (Sept. 1974)-. Abstracting/Indexing Service. English. Nine times a year. $129.00. Plexus Publishing Inc., 143 Old Marlton Pike, Medford NJ 08055. **Tel** (609)654-6500, FAX (609)654-4309. **ED** Mary Suzanne Hogan. Index available. cum. index. **Bk Rev. Ad Acc. Circ:** 1,900. available on microfilm and microfiche from University Microfilms International (UMI).
Desc: Life sciences research and news is being generated at a tremendous rate. Captures this stream of information, organizes it, indexes it, and presents it in digest form. Periodicals and books are used as source material for the lengthy digests, and over 4,000 digests appear in each volume.

LC QH301 **ISSN** 0006-3436
DD 574 BE
CEASED
BIOMETRIE-PRAXIMETRIE. **Added/Corp** Societe Adolfe Quetelet. Vol. 1 (1960)-Vol. 34 No. 3-4 (19??). Periodical. Dutch (English, French and German). Societe Adolphe Quetelet, Station de Phytopatholgie de l'Etab., Chemin de Livoux, B 5030 Gembloux Belgium. **Tel** 011 32 81 611660, FAX 011 32 81 613511. **Bk Rev. Circ:** 400.
Desc: Devoted to the mathematical and statistical aspects of biology.
Ind/Abst Curr. Index Stat.; Stat. Theory Method Abstr. (1961-1963, 1966-1968, 1970, 1983-1984, 1986-1987).

LC QH301 **ISSN** 0005-3155
DD 574 US
NLM W1 BI902R **CODEN** BIOSAN
BIOS (MADISON, N.J.). (BIOS.). **Added/Corp** Beta Beta Beta Biological Fraternity. Beta Beta Beta Biological Society. Vol. 1 (March 1930)-. Periodical. English. Four times a year (Mar., May, Sept., Dec.). $15.00. Beta Biological Society, Box 670, Madison NJ 07940. **Tel** (201)377-8407. **ED** James J. Nagle. Index available. **Bk Rev. Ad Acc. Acid Free. Circ:** 10,500. available on microfilm from University Microfilms International (UMI). Documents available from BIOSIS Document Express, CASDDS.
Desc: Publishes undergraduate research papers, reviews of current biology texts, review articles by professional biologists, editorials, event calendars, and news of the Beta Biological Society.
Ind/Abst Biol. Abstr. (1989-); Biol. Dig.; Chem. Abstr.; Curr. Aware. Biol. Sci., CABS; Zool. Rec.

LC QH301
DD 574 US
BIOSIS PREVIEWS [ONLINE DATABASE]. (19??)-. English. BioSciences Information Service, Biological Abstracts / BIOSIS, 2100 Arch Street, Philadelphia PA 19103. **Tel** (800)523-4806, (215)587-4847, FAX (215)587-2016, telex 831739. available in print (as Biological Abstracts and Biological Abstracts/RRM) from BIOSIS; available on CD-ROM from BIOSIS; available on magnetic tape.
Desc: Online version of Biological Abstracts and Biological Abstracts/RRM.

LC QH323.5 .B5627 **ISSN** 1041-7648
DD 574/.01/519505 US
NLM ZWA 950; B616
BIOSTATISTICA (DAVENPORT, IOWA). (BIOSTATISTICA.). Vol. 1, No. 1 (Jan./Mar. 1990)-. Abstracting/Indexing Service. English. Four times a year. $99.00. Executive Sciences Institute, 1005 Mississippi Avenue, PO Box 4318, Davenport IA 52808-4318. **Tel** (319)324-4463, FAX (319)322-3725. **(Subscription address:** Executive Sciences Institute, PO Box 4318, Davenport IA 52808. **Tel** (319)324-4463.**) ED** Bruce Brocka. Index available. **Bk Rev.**
Desc: Covers epidemiology, mathematical biology, modeling and of biological systems.

LC TP248
DD 660.6 UK
NLM Z 7914.B33; D484
•**BIOTECHNOLOGY ABSTRACTS.** **VFOAT** Derwent Biotechnology Abstracts. (1993)-. Abstracting/Indexing Service. English. Twenty-six times a year. $1750.00. Derwent Publications Ltd., Derwent House 14, Great Queen Street, London WC2B 5DF United Kingdom. **Tel** 011 44 171 3442800, FAX 011 44 171 3442899. ***Continues** Derwent Biotechnology Abstracts, 0262-5318.*
Desc: Covers aspects of biotechnology from genetic manipulation through biochemical engineering and fermentation to downstream processing.

LC TP248.2 .B57 **ISSN** 0733-5709
DD 660/.6 US
NLM ZQW 25; B616
CEASED
BIOTECHNOLOGY RESEARCH ABSTRACTS. [Biotechnol. res. abstr.]. **Added/Corp** Cambridge Scientific Abstracts, Inc. Vol. 1, No. 1 (Jan. 1984)-(19??). Abstracting/Indexing Service. English. Cambridge Scientific Abstracts, 7200 Wisconsin Avenue, #601, Bethesda MD 20814-4823. **Tel** (301)961-6750, (800)843-7751, FAX (301)961-6720. **ED** Darrell Stover. Index available. cum. index. **Bk Rev.** available on magnetic tape; available on CD-ROM; available on an online database. ***Continued in part by** Medical & Pharmaceutical Biotechnology Abstracts, 1063-1178 **and** Agricultural & Environmental Biotechnology Abstracts, 1063-1151.*
Desc: Covers genetic engineering, cloning vectors, gene manipulation, transfer, and expression; patents issued in the US, products and applications of biotechnology, and

much more. Provides important information for scientists in wide-ranging fields for specialists concerned with pollution and environment and for academic, governmental, and industrial information specialists.

LC QP551 **ISSN** 8756-7512
DD 574.87/328/05 US
UDC 577.113(048.3)
NLM ZQU 58; N964

TITLE CHANGE

CAMBRIDGE SCIENTIFIC BIOCHEMISTRY ABSTRACTS: PART 2 NUCLEIC ACIDS. [Camb. Sci. biochem. abstr., 2, Nucleic acids]. **VFOAT** Nucleic Acids. Vol. 15, No. 1 (Jan. 1985)-(19??). Academic Scholarly Publication. English. Cambridge Scientific Abstracts, 7200 Wisconsin Avenue, #601, Bethesda MD 20814-4823. **Tel** (301)961-6750, (800)843-7751, FAX (301)961-6720. **ED** David Cheyney. Index available. cum. index. available on magnetic tape; available on CD-ROM; available on an online database. ***Continues** Biochemistry Abstracts. Part 2: Nucleic Acids, 0143-3318.* ***Continued by** Nucleic Acids Abstracts, 1070-2466.*
Desc: Resource for scientists who need to keep up with the latest perspectives in molecular biology. Summarizes significant papers relevant to physical, chemical, or biological aspects of nucleic acids and nucleoproteins. Nucleosides and methods manuals are also covered. Contains detailed perspectives on every facet of RNA, DNA and Enzymes.

LC QP455 .C48 **ISSN** 0300-1261
DD 016.5911/826 US
NLM ZWL 102 C517

CHEMORECEPTION ABSTRACTS. [Chemorecept. abstr.]. **Added/Corp** Information Retrieval Limited. Cambridge Scientific Abstracts, Inc. Vol. 1 (Jan. 1973)-. Abstracting/Indexing Service. English. Four times a year (plus annual index). $435.00. Cambridge Scientific Abstracts, 7200 Wisconsin Avenue, #601, Bethesda MD 20814-4823. **Tel** (301)961-6750, (800)843-7751, FAX (301)961-6720. **ED** Graciela Duran-Troise. Index available. cum. index (Annual). **Bk Rev.** available on magnetic tape; available on an online database from STN International; DIALOG; and BRS; available on CD-ROM from Compact Cambridge; available via Internet (to the current year's abstracts and five-year backfiles) from Cambridge Scientific Abstracts. Documents available from BLDSC.
Desc: Covers multi-disciplinary sciences of taste, smell, and related phenomena, including animal behavior studies, odor pollution, flavor and aroma studies of food and perfumery.

LC QD415.A1 C48 **ISSN** 1045-2680
DD 574.19/2/05 US
CCC
NLM W1; CH41GR **CODEN** CMBIE5

CHEMTRACTS. BIOCHEMISTRY AND MOLECULAR BIOLOGY. [Chemtracts, Biochem. mol. biol.]. **VFOAT** Biochemistry and Molecular Biology. Vol. 1, No. 1 (Jan./Feb. 1990)-. Academic Scholarly Publication. English. Four times a year. $280.00. Data Trace Publishing Group, PO Box 1239, Brooklandville MD 21022. **Tel** (410)494-4994, (800)342-0454, FAX (410)494-0515. **(Subscription address:** Data Trace Chemistry Publishers, Inc., PO Box 1239, Brooklandville MD 21022. **Tel** (410)494-4994, FAX (410)494-0515.**)** Documents available from CASDDS.
Desc: Quick reporting of the most important current articles by internationally recognized authorities on site-directed mutagenesis, physical studies on enzymes, RNA as an enzyme, enzyme inhibition, hormones, etc.
Ind/Abst Chem. Abstr. (1990-).

LC Z5180 .C87 **ISSN** 0964-8712
DD 016.576 UK
NLM ZQW 4; C976

CURRENT ADVANCES IN APPLIED MICROBIOLOGY & BIOTECHNOLOGY. **VFOAT** Current Advances in Applied Microbiology and Biotechnology. Vol. 9, No. 1 (Jan. 1992)-. Abstracting/Indexing Service. English. Twelve times a year. $961.00. Elsevier Geo Abstracts, An Imprint of Elsevier Science Ltd., The Boulevard, Langford Lane, Kidlington, Oxford OX5 1GB United Kingdom. **Tel** 011 44 1865 843000, 011 44 1865 843699, FAX 011 44 1865 843010. **(Subscription address:** Elsevier Science Ltd. / Oxford Fulfillment Centre, PO Box 800, Kidlington OX5 1DX United Kingdom. **Tel** 011 44 865 843355.**) ED** Harry Smith. available on microfilm and microfiche from University Microfilms International (UMI); available on an online database from Elsevier Electronic Subscriptions (EES); and BRS. Documents available from BLDSC, UMI Article Clearinghouse. ***Continues** Current Advances in Microbiology, 0741-1669.*
Desc: A current literature searching service which is fast, comprehensive, economical and easy to use. It enables pure and applied scientists to keep abreast of the ever increasing literature being published in their subject area, by providing a subject categorized listing of titles, authors, bibliographic details and authors' addresses. A few major subject areas covered include: culture selection and improvement; microbial biotechnology; diseases and parasites; and plant pathology.

LC Z5322.C3 C87 QH573 **ISSN** 0741-1626
DD 016.57487 UK
NLM Z 5322.C3; C976

CURRENT ADVANCES IN CELL AND DEVELOPMENTAL BIOLOGY. [Curr. adv. cell dev. biol.]. **VFOAT** Current Advances in Cell and Developmental Biology. Vol. 1, No. 1 (Jan. 1984)-. Abstracting/Indexing Service. English. Twelve times a year (1 volume). $1093.00. Elsevier Geo Abstracts, An Imprint of Elsevier Science Ltd., The Boulevard, Langford Lane, Kidlington, Oxford OX5 1GB United Kingdom. **Tel** 011 44 1865 843000, 011 44 1865 843699, FAX 011 44 1865 843010. **(Subscription address:** Elsevier Science Ltd. / Oxford Fulfillment Centre, PO Box 800, Kidlington OX5 1DX United Kingdom. **Tel** 011 44 865 843355.**) ED** Harry Smith (editor's address: Department of Botany, University of Leicester, University Road, Leicester LW1 7QQ UK) and Peter N Campbell (editor's address: Department of Biochemistry, University College, London WC1E 6BT UK). **Circ:** 1,200. available on microfilm and microfiche from University Microfilms International (UMI); available on an online database from Elsevier Electronic Subscriptions (EES); and BRS. Documents available from BLDSC, UMI Article Clearinghouse. ***Continues in part** Current Awareness in Biological Sciences.*
Desc: Provides titles of cell and developmental biology papers published throughout the world classified into 77 major areas. Full bibliographical citations and reprint addresses are included.

LC Z5322.G4 C88 QH426 **ISSN** 0741-1642
DD 016.5751 UK
NLM Z 5322.G4; C9762

CURRENT ADVANCES IN GENETICS & MOLECULAR BIOLOGY. [Curr. adv. genet. mol. biol.]. **VFOAT** Current Advances in Genetics and Molecular Biology. Vol. 1, No. 1 (Jan. 1984)-. Abstracting/Indexing Service. English. Twelve times a year. $1269.00. Elsevier Geo Abstracts, An Imprint of Elsevier Science Ltd., The Boulevard, Langford Lane, Kidlington, Oxford OX5 1GB United Kingdom. **Tel** 011 44 1865 843000, 011 44 1865 843699, FAX 011 44 1865 843010. **(Subscription address:** Elsevier Science Ltd. / Oxford Fulfillment Centre, PO Box 800, Kidlington OX5 1DX United Kingdom. **Tel** 011 44 865 843355.**) ED** Harry Smith (editor's address: Department of Botany, University of Leicester, University Road, Leicester LE1 7QQ UK) and Peter N Campbell (editor's address: Department of Biochemistry, University College, London WC1E 6BT UK). **Circ:** 1,200. available on microfilm and microfiche from University Microfilms International (UMI); available on an online database from Elsevier Electronic Subscriptions (EES); and BRS. Documents available from BLDSC, UMI Article Clearinghouse. ***Continues** Current Advances in Genetics, 0360-8360.*
Desc: Gives listings of titles of genetical papers published throughout the world classified into 75 main areas; provides a comprehensive listing of review articles.

LC Z5353 .C86 **ISSN** 0306-4484
DD 016.58 UK
CODEN CAPSCJ

CURRENT ADVANCES IN PLANT SCIENCE. [Curr. adv. plant sci.]. Vol. 1 (July 1972)-. Abstracting/Indexing Service. English. Twelve times a year. $1357.00. Elsevier Geo Abstracts, An Imprint of Elsevier Science Ltd., The Boulevard, Langford Lane, Kidlington, Oxford OX5 1GB United Kingdom. **Tel** 011 44 1865 843000, 011 44 1865 843699, FAX 011 44 1865 843010. **(Subscription address:** Elsevier Science Ltd. / Oxford Fulfillment Centre, PO Box 800, Kidlington OX5 1DX United Kingdom. **Tel** 011 44 865 843355.**) ED** Harry Smith (editor's address: (Department of Botany, University of Leicester, University Road, Leicester LE1 7QQ UK) and Peter N Campbell (Department of Biochemistry, University College, London WC1E 6BT UK). available on microfilm and microfiche from University Microfilms International (UMI); available on diskette; available on an online database from Elsevier Electronic Subscriptions (EES); and BRS. Documents available from BLDSC, The UnCover Company, UMI Article Clearinghouse.
Desc: Biological journals covering all aspects of plant science are scanned to provide a subject-categorized listing of titles, authors, bibliographic details and authors' addresses. Titles are presented under 47 subject headings with full cross-referencing.

LC Z5524.B54 C87 QH345 **ISSN** 0965-0504
DD 016.57419/2 UK
NLM ZQU 4; C976

CURRENT ADVANCES IN PROTEIN BIOCHEMISTRY. Vol. 9, No. 1 (Jan. 1992)-. Abstracting/Indexing Service. English. Twelve times a year. $920.00. Elsevier Geo Abstracts, An Imprint of Elsevier Science Ltd., The Boulevard, Langford Lane, Kidlington, Oxford OX5 1GB United Kingdom. **Tel** 011 44 1865 843000, 011 44 1865 843699, FAX 011 44 1865 843010. **(Subscription address:** Elsevier Science Ltd. / Oxford Fulfillment Centre, PO Box 800, Kidlington OX5 1DX United Kingdom. **Tel** 011 44 865 843355.**) ED** Harry Smith. available on microfilm and microfiche from University Microfilms International (UMI); available on an online database from Elsevier Electronic Subscriptions (EES); and BRS. Documents available from BLDSC, UMI Article Clearinghouse. ***Continues** Current Advances in Biochemistry, 0741-1618.*
Desc: A few major subject areas include: purification and analysis, primary structures, enzyme inhibitors, nuclear proteins, and membrane proteins.

LC Z5524.B54 **ISSN** 0965-0504
DD 574.192 UK

CURRENT ADVANCES IN PROTEIN CHEMISTRY. **VFOAT** CABS. Vol. 9, No. 1 (Jan. 1992)-. Abstracting/Indexing Service. English. Twelve times a year. Pergamon Press, An Imprint of Elsevier Science Ltd., The Boulevard, Langford Lane, Kidlington, Oxford OX5 1GB United Kingdom. **Tel** 011 44 1865 843000, 011 44 1865 843699, FAX 011 44 1865 843010. ***Continues** Current Advances in Biochemistry, 0741-1618.*

LC QH301 .I475 **ISSN** 0733-4443
DD 016.574 UK

CURRENT AWARENESS IN BIOLOGICAL SCIENCES. (CURRENT AWARENESS IN BIOLOGICAL SCIENCES : CABS.). [Curr. aware. biol. sci.]. **VFOAT** CABS; C.A.B.S. Vol. 100, No. 1 (Mar. 1983)-. Abstracting/Indexing Service. English. Twelve times a year (144 issues). $5610.00 The Americas; £3765.00 other. Elsevier Geo Abstracts, An Imprint of Elsevier Science Ltd., The Boulevard, Langford Lane, Kidlington, Oxford OX5 1GB United Kingdom. **Tel** 011 44 1865 843000, 011 44 1865 843699, FAX 011 44 1865 843010. **(Subscription address:** Elsevier Science Ltd. / Oxford Fulfillment Centre, PO Box 800, Kidlington OX5 1DX United Kingdom. **Tel** 011 44 865 843355.**) ED** H. Smith and P. N. Campbell. **Circ:** 1,000. available in microform; available on an online database from Elsevier Electronic Subscriptions (EES); and BRS. Documents available from BLDSC, UMI Article Clearinghouse. ***Continues** International Abstracts of Biological Sciences, 0020-5818.* ***Continued in part by** Current Advances in Neuroscience; Current Advances in Cell & Developmental Biology, 0741-1626.*
Desc: Comprehensive update of the world's biological literature classified into over 1,600 sections and providing full bibliographic references to the original articles.

LC TP248.2 .C87 **ISSN** 0960-5037
DD 660.6/05 UK
NLM ZQU 4; C7964 **CODEN** CUBIER

CURRENT BIOTECHNOLOGY. **Added/Corp** Royal Society of Chemistry (Great Britain). Vol. 9, Issue 1 (Jan. 1991)-. Abstracting/Indexing Service. English. Twelve times a year. $879.00. Royal Society of Chemistry, Thomas Graham House, Science Park, Cambridge CB4 4WF United Kingdom. **Tel** 011 44 1223 420066, FAX 011 44 1223 423623, telex 818293 ROYAL. **(Subscription address:** Royal Society of Chemistry, Turpin Distribution Services Ltd., Blackhorse Road, Letchworth, Hertfordshire SG6 1HN United Kingdom. **Tel** 011 44 1462 672555, FAX 011 44 1462 480947.**)** Index available. **Ad Acc.** available on an online database from CAN/OLE; ESA-IRS; DIALOG; and DATA-STAR. Documents available from BLDSC. ***Continues** Current Biotechnology Abstracts, 0264-3391.*
Desc: A current awareness periodical which reports on the latest scientific, technical and commercial advances in the field of biotechnology- the development of biological systems to create useful products. It covers the production and use of biological, inorganic, organic chemicals for the agricultural, food, pharmaceutical and other industries and biotechnology in energy production and waste treatment.

LC Z5071 .C86 **ISSN** 0090-0508
DD 016.63 US
NLM Z 5071 C976 **CODEN** CABEA

CURRENT CONTENTS. AGRICULTURE, BIOLOGY, & ENVIRONMENTAL SCIENCES. **See** Agriculture-Abstracting, Bibliographies and Statistics.

LC Z5071 **ISSN** 1073-1245
DD 016 US

•CURRENT CONTENTS. AGRICULTURE, BIOLOGY & ENVIRONMENTAL SCIENCES (CD-ROM VERSION). **See** Agriculture-Abstracting, Bibliographies and Statistics.

LC Z5321 .C87 QH301 **ISSN** 0011-3409
DD 016.574 US
NLM ZW 1 C959

CURRENT CONTENTS. LIFE SCIENCES. [Curr. contents. Life sci.]. **Added/Corp** Institute for Scientific Information. Vol. 10 (1967)-. Abstracting/Indexing Service. English. One time a week. $488.00. Institute for Scientific Information, 3501 Market Street, Philadelphia PA 19104. **Tel** (215)386-0100, (800)523-1850, FAX (215)386-6362, telex 84-5305. **(Subscription address:** Institute for Scientific Information, PO Box 71416, Chicago IL 60694. **) Ad Acc. Circ:** 340,000. available on diskette; available on magnetic tape and an online database (as Current Contents Search); available on CD-ROM; available on an online database from BRS. Documents available from The Genuine Article. ***Continues** Current Contents. Your Weekly Guide to the Chemical, Pharmaco-Medical & Life Sciences, 0272-1503.*
Desc: Listing of tables of contents from over 1,200 journals in the life sciences.
Ind/Abst Abstr. Bull. Inst. Pap. Sci. Tech.; Curr. Contents

Life Sci.; Res. Alert [Full Cov.]; Sci. Cit. Index; SCISEARCH; Soc. Sci. Cit. Index [Full Cov.]; Trop. Dis. Bull.

LC Z5071 **ISSN** 1062-3167
DD 016 US
CURRENT CONTENTS ON DISKETTE. AGRICULTURE, BIOLOGY & ENVIRONMENTAL SCIENCES. See Agriculture-Abstracting, Bibliographies and Statistics.

LC Z5071 **ISSN** 1062-3124
DD 016 US
CURRENT CONTENTS ON DISKETTE WITH ABSTRACTS. AGRICULTURE, BIOLOGY & ENVIRONMENTAL SCIENCES. See Agriculture-Abstracting, Bibliographies and Statistics.

LC TP248.13 .D47 **ISSN** 0262-5318
DD 660.6/05 UK
NLM Z 7914.B33; D484
TITLE CHANGE
DERWENT BIOTECHNOLOGY ABSTRACTS. [Derwent biotechnol. abstr.]. Vol. 1, No. 1 (July 15, 1982)-(Mar. 1993). Abstracting/Indexing Service. English. Derwent Publications Ltd., Derwent House 14, Great Queen Street, London WC2B 5DF United Kingdom. **Tel** 011 44 171 3442800, FAX 011 44 171 3442899. Index available. ctrl circ. ***Continued by*** *Biotechnology Abstracts.*
Desc: Covers all aspects of biotechnology from genetic manipulation through biochemical engineering and fermentation to downstream processing. Papers dealing exclusively with the application of the products of biotechnological processes in nonindustrial fields, methods of nonindustrial waste disposal when unrelated to the processing of industrial waste and when no economically valuable product is formed, or brewing and the preparation of established fermented foods and feedstuffs are not included.

ISSN 0367-1089
DD 016.612 NE
CCC
NLM ZW 1 E955
EXCERPTA MEDICA. SECTION 2A. PHYSIOLOGY. (EXCERPTA MEDICA. SECTION 2. PHYSIOLOGY.). [Excerpta Med., Section 2a, Physiol.]. **VFOAT** Physiology. **VAT** Excerpta Medica. Section Two-A. Physiology. Vol. 22 (1969)-. Abstracting/Indexing Service. English. Thirty times a year (3 vols.). Fl.3267.00. Excerpta Medica Publishing Group, PO Box 548, 1000 AM Amsterdam Netherlands. **Tel** 011 31 20 5803243, FAX 011 31 20 5803222. **(Subscription address:** Excerpta Medica Journals, PO Box 85, Limerick Ireland. **Tel** 011 353 61 471944.) available on microfilm from University Microfilms International (UMI); available on CD-ROM; available on an online database from BRS. Documents available from CASDDS. ***Continues*** *Excerpta Medica. Section 2A. Physiology, 0367-1089.*
Desc: Covers all aspects of mammalian physiology and the physiology of lower animals of interest to medical science.
Ind/Abst Chem. Abstr. (1969-).

LC Z5320
DD 016.57 NE
NLM ZW 1; E9571 **CODEN** MBVMA
EXCERPTA MEDICA. SECTION 4. MICROBIOLOGY, BACTERIOLOGY, MYCOLOGY, PARASITOLOGY, AND VIROLOGY. See Medical Sciences-Abstracting, Bibliographies and Statistics.

LC Z5320 **ISSN** 0300-5372
DD 016.57 NE
CCC
NLM ZW 1 E978I **CODEN** CLBIDV
EXCERPTA MEDICA. SECTION 29. CLINICAL BIOCHEMISTRY. **VFOAT** Clinical Biochemistry. Vol. 27 (1973)-. Abstracting/Indexing Service. English. Forty times a year (4 volumes). $2317.00. Excerpta Medica Publishing Group, PO Box 548, 1000 AM Amsterdam Netherlands. **Tel** 011 31 20 5803243, FAX 011 31 20 5803222. **(Subscription address:** Excerpta Medica Journals, PO Box 85, Limerick Ireland. **Tel** 011 353 61 471944.) available on CD-ROM; available on an online database from BRS. Documents available from CASDDS. ***Continues*** *Excerpta Medica. Section 29. Biochemistry, 0014-4339.*
Desc: Contains information on clinical chemistry and biochemistry.
Ind/Abst Chem. Abstr.

LC QH431 .G432 **ISSN** 0016-674X
DD 575.1/08 US
NLM Z 5322.G4 G328
GENETICS ABSTRACTS. [Genet. abstr.]. **Added/Corp** Cambridge Scientific Abstracts, Inc. Information Retrieval Limited. Vol. 1, No. 1 (Nov. 1968)-. Abstracting/Indexing Service. English. Twelve times a year (includes annual index). $995.00. Cambridge Scientific Abstracts, 7200 Wisconsin Avenue, #601, Bethesda MD 20814-4823. **Tel** (301)961-6750, (800)843-7751, FAX (301)961-6720. **ED** David Cheyney. Index available. cum. index. **Bk Rev.** available on magnetic tape; available on an online database; available on CD-ROM; available via Internet (to the current year's abstracts and five-year backfiles) from Cambridge Scientific Abstracts.
Desc: All aspects of molecular, chromosomal, extra-chromosomal, viral, bacterial, fungal, algal, plant, animal, and human genetics, as well as medical genetics and genetic engineering.
Ind/Abst Anim. Breed. Abstr.; Weed Abstr.

ISSN 1045-4470
DD 573 US
NLM Z 5322.H8; H918
HUMAN GENOME ABSTRACTS. [Hum. genome abstr.]. **Added/Corp** Cambridge Scientific Abstracts, Inc. Vol. 1, No. 1 (Feb. 1990)-. Abstracting/Indexing Service. English. Six times a year (plus annual index). $325.00. Cambridge Scientific Abstracts, 7200 Wisconsin Avenue, #601, Bethesda MD 20814-4823. **Tel** (301)961-6750, (800)843-7751, FAX (301)961-6720. **ED** David Cheyney. available on magnetic tape; available on an online database; available on CD-ROM; available via Internet (to the current year's abstracts and five-year backfiles) from Cambridge Scientific Abstracts.
Desc: Emphasizes the integration of basic and applied research in human and comparative analysis. In-depth coverage includes: methodology of nucleic acid sequencing, cloning vectors, gene cloning, and sequencing results for all major systems of the human body; Also gene therapy, RFLP mapping, medical genetics, genetic screening, genetic counseling, oncogene research and more.

ISSN 1063-1178
DD 615 US
•MEDICAL & PHARMACEUTICAL BIOTECHNOLOGY ABSTRACTS. [Med. pharm. biotechnol. abstr.]. **Added/Corp** Cambridge Scientific Abstracts, Inc. **VFOAT** Medical and Pharmaceutical Biotechnology Abstracts. Vol. 1, No. 1 (1993)-. Abstracting/Indexing Service. English. Six times a year. $325.00. Cambridge Scientific Abstracts, 7200 Wisconsin Avenue, #601, Bethesda MD 20814-4823. **Tel** (301)961-6750, (800)843-7751, FAX (301)961-6720. available on magnetic tape, an online database, and CD-ROM; available via Internet (to the current year's abstracts and five-year backfiles) from Cambridge Scientific Abstracts. ***Continues in part*** *Biotechnology Research Abstracts, 0733-5709.*
Desc: New applications for biotechnology in medicine and phamacology, human health, and the diagnosis and treatment of disease are highlighted in this journal. Topics include: genetic engineering and gene therapy - drug development and drug delivery systems - vaccines, blood factors, and products - antisense technology, and many other key areas.

LC QR53 .I532 **ISSN** 0300-838X
DD 660/.62/05 US
NLM ZQW 4 M625Z
MICROBIOLOGY ABSTRACTS. SECTION A, INDUSTRIAL & APPLIED MICROBIOLOGY. [Microbiol. abstr., Sect. A]. **Added/Corp** Cambridge Scientific Abstracts, Inc. Information Retrieval Limited. **VFOAT** Microbiology Abstracts. Section A, Industrial and Applied Microbiology; Industrial and Applied Microbiology; Industrial & Applied Microbiology. **VAT** Microbiology Abstracts. Section A: Industrial and Applied Microbiology. Vol. 7 (Jan. 1972)-. Abstracting/Indexing Service. English. Twelve times a year (includes annual index). $925.00. Cambridge Scientific Abstracts, 7200 Wisconsin Avenue, #601, Bethesda MD 20814-4823. **Tel** (301)961-6750, (800)843-7751, FAX (301)961-6720. **ED** Darrell Stover. Index available. cum. index. available on magnetic tape; available on an online database; available on CD-ROM; available via Internet (to current year's abstracts and five-year backfile) from Cambridge Scientific Abstracts. ***Continues*** *Microbiology Abstracts. Section A. Industrial Microbiology, 0544-0130.*
Desc: Significant findings and practical applications in agricultural, food and beverage, chemical, and pharmaceutical industries are assembled. Specific aspects addressed in each issue include: pharmaceutical, food and beverage, agricultural, environmental aspects and methodology and research. Contains patents registered in the United States included with listings under the subject index for easy access.

LC QR1 .M62 **ISSN** 0300-8398
DD 576/.05 US
NLM ZQW 4 M626
MICROBIOLOGY ABSTRACTS. SECTION B, BACTERIOLOGY. [Microbiol. abstr., Sect. B.]. **Added/Corp** Information Retrieval Limited. Cambridge Scientific Abstracts, Inc. **VFOAT** Microbiology Abstracts. Section B, Bacteriology Abstracts; Bacteriology. Vol. 7, No. 1 (Jan. 1972)-. Abstracting/Indexing Service. English. Twelve times a year (includes annual index). $995.00. Cambridge Scientific Abstracts, 7200 Wisconsin Avenue, #601, Bethesda MD 20814-4823. **Tel** (301)961-6750, (800)843-7751, FAX (301)961-6720. **ED** Darrell Stover. Index available. cum. index. available on magnetic tape; available on an online database; available on CD-ROM; available via Internet (to current year's abstracts and five-year backfile) from Cambridge Scientific Abstracts. ***Continues*** *Microbiology Abstracts. Section B: General Microbiology and Bacteriology, 0544-0149.*
Desc: Each issue covers: methods; taxonomy; cell properties; genetics; antibiotics and other antimicrobials; toxins; immunology; medical, veterinary, and invertebrate bacteriology; plant diseases; ecological aspects, and much more.

LC QK564 .M5 **ISSN** 0301-2328
DD 589/.08 US
NLM ZQW 4 M626A
MICROBIOLOGY ABSTRACTS. SECTION C, ALGOLOGY, MYCOLOGY & PROTOZOOLOGY. [Microbiol. abstr., Sect. C]. **Added/Corp** Information Retrieval Limited. Cambridge Scientific Abstracts, Inc. **VFOAT** Microbiology Abstracts. Section C, Algology, Mycology, and Protozoology; Algology, Mycology and Protozoology; Algology, Mycology & Protozoology. **VAT** Microbiology Abstracts. Section C: Algology, Mycology, and Protozoology. Vol. 1 (Jan. 1972)-. Abstracting/Indexing Service. English. Twelve times a year (includes annual index). $885.00. Cambridge Scientific Abstracts, 7200 Wisconsin Avenue, #601, Bethesda MD 20814-4823. **Tel** (301)961-6750, (800)843-7751, FAX (301)961-6720. **ED** Darrell Stover. Index available. cum. index. available on an online database; available on magnetic tape; available on CD-ROM; available via Internet (to current year's abstracts and five-year backfile) from Cambridge Scientific Abstracts.
Desc: Covers research on algae, fungi, protozoa, and lichens, including reproduction, growth, life cycles, biochemistry, genetics, infection and immunity in humans, other animals and plants.

LC SB998.N4 **ISSN** 0957-6797
DD 595.1 016.59 UK
NLM ZQX 200; H479B **CODEN** NEABEA
NEMATOLOGICAL ABSTRACTS. [Nematol. abstr.]. **Added/Corp** C.A.B. International. Information Services. C.A.B. International. Bureau of Crop Protection. C.A.B. International. Institute of Parasitology. Vol. 59, No. 1 (March 1990)-. Abstracting/Indexing Service. English. Four times a year. $235.00. CAB International Centre, Wallingford, Oxfordshire OX10 8DE United Kingdom. **Tel** 011 44 1491 832111, FAX 011 44 1491 833508, telex 847964 COMAGG G. **ED** S. F. Siddiqi, BSc. **Circ:** 1,000. available on magnetic tape and CD-ROM; available on an online database from Tsukuba Daigaku; CAN/OLE; STN International; JICST; DATA-STAR; DIMDI; ESA-IRS; CISTI; BRS; and DIALOG. ***Continues*** *Helminthological Abstracts. Series B, Plant Nematology, 0300-8320.*
Desc: Covers the world literature on nematodes parasitic in or on plants, free-living nematodes, nematodes parasitic in insects or other anthropods.

LC Z5320 **ISSN** 1070-2466
DD 16.574 US
NLM ZQU 58; N964
•NUCLEIC ACIDS ABSTRACTS (1994). (NUCLEIC ACIDS ABSTRACTS.). **Added/Corp** Cambridge Scientific Abstracts, inc. (1994)-. Abstracting/Indexing Service. English. Twelve times a year. $845.00. Cambridge Scientific Abstracts, 7200 Wisconsin Avenue, #601, Bethesda MD 20814-4823. **Tel** (301)961-6750, (800)843-7751, FAX (301)961-6720. available via Internet (to the current year's abstracts and five-year backfiles) from Cambridge Scientific Abstracts. ***Continues*** *Cambridge Scientific Biochemistry Abstracts, Part 2: Nucleic Acids, 8756-7512.*
Desc: Resource for scientists who need to keep up with the latest perspectives in molecular biology. Summarizes significant papers relevant to physical, chemical, or biological aspects of nucleic acids and nucleoproteins, nucleosides and methods manuals. Includes detailed perspectives on every facet of RNA, DNA and Enzymes.

LC Z5354.P5 P47 QK882
DD 016.5811/3342 NE
UDC 016:581.132
PHOTOSYNTHESIS BIBLIOGRAPHY. Vol. 1 (1966/70)-. Bibliography. English. Irregular. SPB Academic Publishing, PO Box 97747, 2509 GC The Hague Netherlands. **Tel** 011 31 70 3280616, 011 31 70 3250616. **ED** Z Sestak and J Catsky. cum. index. **Circ:** 300.

LC QH505 .P47 **ISSN** 0031-9155
DD 574.191 UK
CCC
NLM W1 PH844 **CODEN** PHMBA7
Pr Rev.
PHYSICS IN MEDICINE & BIOLOGY. [Phys. med. biol.]. **Added/Corp** Hospital Physicists' Association. Canadian Association of Physics. Medical and Biological Physics Division. International Organization for Medical Physics. Institute of Physics (Great Britain) American Institute of Physics. Deutsche Gesellschaft fËur Medizinische Physik. American Association of Physicists in Medicine. **VFOAT** Physics in Medicine and Biology. Vol. 1 (July 1956)-. Abstracting/Indexing Service. English (French and German; summaries and/or abstracts in German and French). Twelve times a year. $1080.00. Institute of Physics, Techno House, Redcliffe Way, Bristol BS1 6NX United Kingdom. **Tel** 011 44 117 9297481, FAX 011 44 117 9294318, telex 449149 INSTP G. **(Subscription**

address: American Institute of Physics, Publishing Sales, 500 Sunnyside Blvd., Woodbury NY 11797. **Tel** (516)576-2200.) **ED** B L Diffey. Index available (bound in last issue). available on microfiche. Documents available from The Genuine Article, BIOSIS Document Express, Ask*IEEE, CASDDS, ADONIS.
Desc: An international journal for all physicists concerned with the applications of theoretical and practical physics to medicine, physiology and biology. Contains regular book reviews, and comprehensive listing of forthcoming events.
Ind/Abst Acoust. Abstr.; ADONIS; Biol. Abstr.; Chem. Abstr.; CSA Neuro. Abstr. (?-?); Curr. Aware. Biol. Sci., CABS; Curr. Cit.; Curr. Contents Life Sci.; Ei Page One; EMBASE; Index Med.; INSPEC (1968-); Int. Aerosp. Abstr.; Phys. Med. Biol. (19??-19??); Res. Alert [Full Cov.]; Sci. Cit. Index; SCISEARCH.

ISSN 0966-0100
DD 581.1505 UK
PLANT GENETIC RESOURCES ABSTRACTS. [Plant genet. resour. abstr.]. (1992)-. Abstracting/Indexing Service. English. Four times a year. $232.72. CAB International Centre, Wallingford, Oxfordshire OX10 8DE United Kingdom. **Tel** 011 44 1491 832111, FAX 011 44 1491 833508, telex 847964 COMAGG G. available on magnetic tape and CD-ROM; available on an online database from Tsukuba Daigaku; CAN/OLE; STN International; JICST; DATA-STAR; DIMDI; ESA-IRS; BRS; and DIALOG.

LC QH92
DD 574.9 RU
REFERATIVNYI ZHURNAL. GEOGRAFIIA. D, BIOGEOGRAFIIA.
Added/Corp Institut Nauchnoi Informatsii (Akademiia Nauk SSSR). (19??)-. Abstracting/Indexing Service. Russian. Twelve times a year. VINITI - Vsesoyuznyi Institut Nauchno-Tekhnicheskoi Informatsii, All-Union Scientific and Technical Information Institute, Baltiiskaia ulitsa 14, 125219 Moscow Russia. **Tel** 011 7 95 2384600, FAX 011 7 95 9430060, telex 411160. **(Subscription address:** Mezhdunarodnaya Kniga, Dimitrova ulitsa 39, 113095 Moscow Russia. **)**
Ind/Abst Bibliogr. Carto.; Chem. Abstr.

LC QH7 .A5433 **ISSN** 0034-2300
DD 508.05 RU
NLM Z 5321 R332 **CODEN** RZBLAS
REFERATIVNYJ ZURNAL - VSESOJUZNYJ INSTITUT NAUCNOJ I TEHNICESKOJ INFORMACII. BIOLOGIJA. (REFERATIVNYI ZHURNAL. BIOLOGIIA.). **Added/Corp** Institut Nauchnoi Informatsii (Akademiia nauk SSSR) Vsesoiuznyi Institut Nauchnoi i Tekhnicheskoi Informatsii (Soviet Union). **VFOAT** Biologiia. (1954)-. Periodical. Russian. Twelve times a year. VINITI - Vsesoyuznyi Institut Nauchno-Tekhnicheskoi Informatsii, All-Union Scientific and Technical Information Institute, Baltiiskaia ulitsa 14, 125219 Moscow Russia. **Tel** 011 7 95 2384600, FAX 011 7 95 9430060, telex 411160. Index available. **Circ:** 2,930. Documents available from CASDDS. ***Absorbed in part** Referativnyi Zhurnal. Obshchie Voprosy Patologii.*
Ind/Abst Chem. Abstr. (-1972).

LC SB599 .R4 **ISSN** 0034-6438
DD 632 UK
REVIEW OF PLANT PATHOLOGY. [Rev. plant pathol.]. **Added/Corp** C.A.B. International. Information Services. Commonwealth Mycological Institute (Great Britain). (Jan. 1970)-. Abstracting/Indexing Service. English. Twelve times a year. $680.00. CAB International Centre, Wallingford, Oxfordshire OX10 8DE United Kingdom. **Tel** 011 44 1491 832111, FAX 011 44 1491 833508, telex 847964 COMAGG G. **ED** J. R. Brunt. Index available. cum. index. **Circ:** 2,000. available on magnetic tape and CD-ROM; available on an online database from Tsukuba Daigaku; CAN/OLE; STN International; JICST; DATA-STAR; DIMDI; ESA-IRS; CISTI; BRS; DIALOG; and CAB Abstracts Database. Documents available from The UnCover Company. ***Continues** Review of Applied Mycology.*
Desc: Covers all aspects of plant pathology, including fungal, bacterial and viral diseases, other non-parasitic factors, and their control.
Ind/Abst Hortic. Abstr.; Nematol. Abstr.; Life Sci. Collect.; Trop. Dis. Bull.

LC HA1651 .A334 HA1634.S4 S47
DD 314 CI
ROENI U SR SRBIJI. (1970)-(1976). Serbo-Croatian (Roman). 80.00 Din. Republicki Zavod za Statistiku, Central Bureau of Statistics of the Republic of Croatia, Ilica 3, Zagreb Croatia. **Tel** 011 385 41 45 44 22, FAX 011 385 41 42 94 13, 011 385 41 42 37 11, telex 21130 DZSTAT RH.

LC Z5351
DD 016.581 NE
CEASED
WATER-IN-PLANTS BIBLIOGRAPHY.
VFOAT Water in Plants Bibliography. (1975)- Series complete (19??). English. SPB Academic Publishing, PO Box 97747, 2509 GC The Hague Netherlands. **Tel** 011 31 70 3280616, 011 31 70 3250616. Each issue contains an index to its own contents (no volume index)--loose.

BIOENGINEERING

LC QD415
DD 574.192 US
ABC DETAILS. (19??)-. English. Six times a year. Free to members. Association of Biotechnology Companies, 1220 L Street NW/Suite 615, Washington DC 20005.
Ind/Abst Abstr. BioCommer.

LC TP248.13 .A27 **ISSN** 0263-6778
DD 661.8 UK
CCC
NLM Z 7914.B33; A164
ABSTRACTS IN BIOCOMMERCE. See Biology-Abstracting, Bibliographies and Statistics.

LC TA164 .A35 **ISSN** 0138-4988
DD 574/.05 GW
CCC
NLM W1 AC764M **CODEN** ACBTDD
Pr Rev.
ACTA BIOTECHNOLOGICA. [Acta biotechnol.]. **Added/Corp** Akademie der Wissenschaften der DDR. Institut fuer Technische Chemie. Institut fuer Technische Mikrobiologie (Germany) Institut fuer Enzymologie und Technische Mikrobiologie (Germany). Vol. 1, No. 1 (1981)-. Academic Scholarly Publication. English (German and Russian). Four times a year. $340.00. Akademie-Verlag GmbH, Postfach, D-13162 Berlin Germany. **Tel** 011 49 30 47889300, FAX 011 49 30 47889357. **(Subscription address:** VCH Publishers Inc., 303 Northwest 12th Avenue, Journals Department, Deerfield FL 33442. **Tel** (800)367-8249, (305)428-5566.**)** **ED** M. Ringpfeil and G. Vetterlein. Index available. **Bk Rev. Ad Acc. Circ:** 450 (ctrl). available on an online database. Documents available from The Genuine Article, BIOSIS Document Express, CASDDS.
Desc: Publishes original papers, short communications, reports and reviews from the whole field of biotechnology.
Ind/Abst AgBiotech News Inf.; BioBusiness; Biocont. News Inf. (1991-); Biol. Abstr.; Biotechnol. Res. Abstr.; Chem. Abstr.; Coal Abstr.; Curr. Aware. Biol. Sci., CABS; Curr. Biotechnol.; Curr. Cit.; Curr. Contents Agric. Biol. Environ. Sci.; Dairy Sci. Abstr.; EMBASE; Food Sci. Technol. Abstr.; Index Vet.; Microbiol. Abstr. Sect. B; Microbiol. Abstr. Sect. A; Microbiol. Abstr. Sect. C; PESTDOC; Pig News Inf.; Plant Breed. Abstr.; Res. Alert [Full Cov.]; Rev. Plant Pathol.; Sci. Cit. Index; SCISEARCH; Sug. Indus. Abstr.; Vet. Bull.; Virol. AIDS Abstr.; Weed Abstr.; Wheat Barley Trit. Abstr.

LC TP248.13
DD 661.8 UK
ADONIS [COMPUTER FILE]. (19??)-. Abstracting/Indexing Service. English. One time a week. Fl32000.00. ADONIS BV, PO Box 17005, 1001 JA Amsterdam Netherlands. **Tel** 011 31 20 6262629.
Desc: Journals are primarily from biomedical disciplines.

LC TP248.3 .A38 **ISSN** 0724-6145
DD 660/.63/05 GW
CCC
NLM W1 AD436N **CODEN** ABEBDZ
ADVANCES IN BIOCHEMICAL ENGINEERING/BIOTECHNOLOGY. [Adv. biochem. eng. biotechnol.]. Vol. 26 (1983)-. Academic Scholarly Publication. English. Irregular. Price varies per volume. Springer-Verlag GmbH & Company KG, Heidelberger Platz 3, D-14197 Berlin Germany. **Tel** 011 49 30 8207223, FAX 011 49 30 8214091, telex 183 319 SPBLN D. **(Subscription address:** Springer-Verlag New York Inc. / North America, PO Box 2485, Journal Fulfillment, Secaucus NJ 07096. **Tel** (201)348-4033, (800)777-4643, FAX (201)348-4505.**)** Documents available from Article Express International, BIOSIS Document Express, CASDDS. ***Continues** Advances in Biochemical Engineering, 0065-2210.*
Ind/Abst AGRICOLA [Select. Cov.]; Biodeter. Abstr.; Bioeng. Abstr.; Biol. Abstr. (1986-); Chem. Abstr. (1983-); Curr. Cit.; Ei Page One; Eng. Index Annu.; Index Med. (1983-); Life Sci. Collect.; PESTDOC.

LC R856.A1 A29 **ISSN** 0360-9960
DD 610/.28 US
CCC
NLM W1 AD437L **CODEN** ADBIDL
ADVANCES IN BIOENGINEERING. [Adv. bioeng.]. **Added/Corp** American Society of Mechanical Engineers. (197?)-. English. One time a year (published in Dec.). $90.00 nonmember, $72.00 member. American Society of Mechanical Engineers, 22 Law Drive, Fairfield NJ 07007. **Tel** (201)882-1167, (212)705-7722 (editorial). Documents available from Article Express International, BIOSIS Document Express, CASDDS.
Desc: Covers biomedical engineering and bioengineering.
Ind/Abst Bioeng. Abstr.; Biol. Abstr.; Chem. Abstr.; Ei Page One; Eng. Index Annu.

LC QH501 **ISSN** 0272-3840
DD 574.12 UK
CCC
NLM W3 AD23 **CODEN** ABIODQ
Pr Rev.
ADVANCES IN BIOMATERIALS. [Adv. biomater.]. Vol. 1 (1980)-. Academic Scholarly Publication. English. Irregular. Price varies per volume. John Wiley & Sons Ltd., Baffins Lane, Chichester, West Sussex PO19 1UD United Kingdom. **Tel** 011 44 1243 779777, FAX 011 44 1243 776128 BTG:JWP001, telex 86290 WIBOOKG. **ED** George D. Winter, Jenny Upton. Documents available from Article Express International, BIOSIS Document Express, CASDDS.
Ind/Abst Biol. Abstr.; Chem. Abstr.; Eng. Index Annu.

LC TP248.3 .A385 **ISSN** 0736-2293
DD 660/.6/05 US
CCC
NLM W1 AD449M **CODEN** ABIPDT
ADVANCES IN BIOTECHNOLOGICAL PROCESSES. [Adv. biotechnol. process.]. Vol. 1 (1983)-. Academic Scholarly Publication. English. Irregular. Price varies per volume. John Wiley & Sons, Inc., 605 Third Avenue, New York NY 10158-0012. **Tel** (212)850-6000, (212)850-6645, FAX (212)850-6088, telex 12-7063. **(Subscription address:** John Wiley & Sons, Inc. / Philadelphia, PO Box 7247, Philadelphia PA 19170. **Tel** (212)850-6645, (800)225-5945.**)** **ED** Avshalom Mizrahi and Antonius L. van Wezel. Documents available from Article Express International, BIOSIS Document Express, CASDDS.
Desc: Covers biochemical engineering, biochemistry and microbiology.
Ind/Abst AGRICOLA [Select. Cov.]; BioBusiness; Biol. Abstr.; Chem. Abstr. (1983-); Eng. Index Annu.; Health Plan. Adminis.; Immunol. Abstr.; Microbiol. Abstr. Sect. A; Life Sci. Collect.; PESTDOC.

LC R856 QC501
DD 610.28 537 US
Pr Rev.
•**ADVANCES IN ELECTROMAGNETIC FIELDS IN LIVING SYSTEMS.** (1994)-. Monographic series. English. Irregular. Price varies. Plenum Press, 233 Spring Street, New York NY 10013-1578. **Tel** (212)620-8000, (800)221-9369, FAX (212)463-0742, (212)807-1047, telex 23/421139. **ED** James C. Lin.
Desc: Covers electromagnetic fields in biology and medicine.

LC QH
DD 574 UK
ADVANCES IN GENE TECHNOLOGY. (1990)-. Periodical. English. Irregular. $90.25. JAI Press Inc., 55 Old Post Road, Suite 2, PO Box 1678, Greenwich CT 06836-1678. **Tel** (203)661-7602, FAX (203)661-0792.

LC RS400 .A424 **ISSN** 1067-5698
DD 615/.19/005 US
NLM W1; AD679PT **CODEN** ADCHEO
ADVANCES IN MEDICINAL CHEMISTRY. [Adv. med. chem.]. Vol. 1 (1992)-. English. Irregular. $90.25. JAI Press Inc., 55 Old Post Road, Suite 2, PO Box 1678, Greenwich CT 06836-1678. **Tel** (203)661-7602, FAX (203)661-0792. **ED** Bruce Maryanoff and Cynthia Maryanoff.
Desc: Presents first hand accounts of industrial and academic reserach projects in medicinal chemistry. Representation of the organic chemical facets of drug discovery and development.

LC S494.5.B563 A36 **ISSN** 0954-9897
DD 630 UK
AGBIOTECH NEWS AND INFORMATION. See Agriculture-Abstracting, Bibliographies and Statistics.

LC S **ISSN** 1066-0569
DD 630 US
AGBIOTECH STOCK LETTER. [AgBiotech stock lett.]. (198?)-. Periodical. English. Twelve times a year. $165.00. Agbiotech Investors, PO Box 40460, Berkeley CA 94704.
Ind/Abst Abstr. BioCommer.

LC S494.5.B563 A363 **ISSN** 1063-1151
DD 660 US
•**AGRICULTURAL & ENVIRONMENTAL BIOTECHNOLOGY ABSTRACTS.** See Agriculture-Abstracting, Bibliographies and Statistics.

LC TP368 **ISSN** 1120-6012
DD 664 IT
CODEN AIHTEI
AGRO-INDUSTRY HI-TECH. See Agriculture.

ISSN 0749-3223
DD 574 US
NLM W1; AM281V **CODEN** ABLAEY
Pr Rev.
AMERICAN BIOTECHNOLOGY LABORATORY. [Am. biotechnol. lab.]. **VFOAT** American Biotechnology Laborarory. News Edition; ABL. (Dec. 1983)-. Academic Scholarly Publication. English. Eight times a year. $145.00. International Science

Communications Inc, PO Box 870, 30 Controls Drive, Shelton CT 06430. **Tel** (203)926-9300. **ED** Brian Howard. **Circ:** 73,000. Documents available from The Genuine Article, CASDDS.
Ind/Abst Abstr. BioCommer. (-199?); AGRICOLA [Select. Cov.]; BioBusiness; Biotechnol. Res. Abstr.; Chem. Abstr. (1983-); Curr. Aware. Biol. Sci., CABS; Curr. Biotechnol.; Curr. Cit.; Curr. Contents Agric. Biol. Environ. Sci.; Life Sci. Collect.; Protozoolog. Abstr.; Res. Alert [Full Cov.]; SCISEARCH.

LC SF140.B54 A55 **ISSN** 1049-5398
DD 636 US
CCC
NLM W1; AN228EJ **CODEN** ANBTEN
ANIMAL BIOTECHNOLOGY. See Veterinary Sciences.

LC R856.A1 A55 **ISSN** 0090-6964
DD 610/.28 US
CCC
NLM W1 AN564 **CODEN** ABMECF
Pr Rev.
ANNALS OF BIOMEDICAL ENGINEERING. [Ann. biomed. eng.]. **Added/Corp** Biomedical Engineering Society. **VFOAT** Biomedical Engineering. Vol. 1 (Sept. 1972)-. Academic Scholarly Publication. English. Six times a year. $450.00. Blackwell Scientific Publishers, 238 Main Street, Cambridge MA 02142. **Tel** (617)547-7110, (800)835-6770, FAX (617)547-0789. **ED** Hun H. Sun. Index available (bound in Dec. issue). available on microfilm and microfiche from University Microfilms International (UMI). Documents available from Article Express International, The Genuine Article, BIOSIS Document Express, Ask*IEEE. ***Absorbed*** *Journal of Bioengineering, 0145-3068.*
Desc: Publishes reports of original research on the application of sound engineering theory or practice to significant biomedical questions and problems.
Ind/Abst Appl. Mech. Rev.; Biol. Abstr.; Ceram. Abstr.; CSA Neuro. Abstr.; Curr. Aware. Biol. Sci., CABS; Curr. Cit.; Curr. Contents Life Sci.; Ei Page One; EMBASE; Energy Res. Abstr. (April 1974-); Eng. Index Annu.; Health Plan. Adminis.; Index Med.; INIS Atomindex [Micro.]; INSPEC (Dec. 1974-); Int. Aerosp. Abstr.; Life Sci. Collect.; Phys. Med. Biol. (19??-19??); Res. Alert [Full Cov.]; Sci. Cit. Index; SCISEARCH.

LC RD701 **ISSN** 0263-2535
DD 617.307 UK
NLM W1; AN76WF
ANNUAL REPORT OF THE OXFORD ORTHOPAEDIC ENGINEERING CENTRE. See Medical Sciences-Orthopedics.

LC TP248.3 .J68
DD 660/.63/05 US
NLM W1 AP5196D **CODEN** ABIBDL
Pr Rev. **TITLE CHANGE**
APPLIED BIOCHEMISTRY AND BIOTECHNOLOGY. See Biology-Biological Chemistry.

LC QR53 .E87 **ISSN** 0175-7598
DD 660/.62/05 GW
CCC
NLM W1; AP528B **CODEN** AMBIDG
Pr Rev.
APPLIED MICROBIOLOGY AND BIOTECHNOLOGY. See Biology-Microbiology.

LC QH **ISSN** 0734-5151
DD 574 US
ARIES' BIOTECHNOLOGY CHEMONOMIES REPORT. [Aries' biotechnol. chemon. rep.]. **Added/Corp** Economics of Technologies. **VFOAT** Biotechnology Chemonomics Report; Biotechnology Chemonomics. Vol. 1, No. 1 (Sept. 1982)-. Periodical. English. Twelve times a year. $290.00. Economics of Technologies, PO Box 6558, 49 East 41st Street, New York NY 10163. **Tel** (718)429-3132. **ED** Robert S. Aries, Sigm Xi.
Desc: Deals with economic comments on the basic trends, marketing, costs and effects of technology and technical transfer with or without patents of the chemical process industries, particularly biotechnology.

LC QD415
DD 574 US
ARIS FUNDING REPORT. (19??)-. English. Irregular (published every six weeks). $225.00. Academic Research Information System, 2940 16th Street, Suite 314, San Francisco CA 94103. **Tel** (415)558-8133, FAX (415)558-8135. **ED** Betty L. Traynor. available on diskette.
Desc: Provides grant information in the biomedical sciences from both federal and private sources.

LC R856.A1 B56 **ISSN** 1073-1199
DD 610.28 US
CCC
NLM W1; AR955G
●**ARTIFICIAL CELLS, BLOOD SUBSTITUTES, AND IMMOBILIZATION BIOTECHNOLOGY.** (1994)-. Periodical. English. Six times a year. $850.00. Marcel Dekker Inc., 270 Madison Avenue, New York NY 10016. **Tel** (212)696-9000, (800)228-1160, FAX (212)685-4540, telex 421419. **(Subscription address:** Marcel Dekker Inc., PO Box 5017, Monticello NY 12701. **Tel** (800)228-1160.) ***Continues*** *Biomaterials, Artificial Cells, and Immobilization Biotechnology, 1055-7172.*
Ind/Abst Curr. Cit.; Index Med.

LC TP248.27.M37 M37 **ISSN** 1054-2027
DD 660/.6 US
NLM ZQT 34; A797
ASFA MARINE BIOTECHNOLOGY ABSTRACTS. See Biology-Abstracting, Bibliographies and Statistics.

ISSN 0887-3127
DD 605 US
ASIAN MEDICAL & BIOTECHNOLOGY NEWS. [Asian med. biotechnol. news]. **VFOAT** Asian Medical & Biotechnology News. (1985)-. Periodical. English. Six times a year. $65.00. Asian Medical & Biotechnology, PO Box 1182, Ames IA 50010. **Tel** (515)296-9919.

LC TP248.27.M37 **ISSN** 1036-7128
DD 660/.6 AT
NLM W1; AU237 **CODEN** AUBIE5
Pr Rev.
AUSTRALASIAN BIOTECHNOLOGY. [Australas. biotechnol.]. **Added/Corp** Australian Biotechnology Association. Vol. 1, No. 1 (Aug. 1991)-. Periodical. English. Six times a year. 72.00Aus$ (Australia); 96.00Aus$ (other). Australian Biotechnology Association Ltd, PO Box 4, Gardenvale 3185 Australia. **Tel** 011 61 3 5968879, FAX 011 61 3 5968874. **ED** M. J. Playne. **Bk Rev**, (Qty: 10). **Ad Acc, Adv Mgr:** Gary Dolder. **Circ:** 1,000. ***Formed by the union of*** *ABA Bulletin* ***and*** *Australian Journal of Biotechnology.*
Desc: Reports on the activities of biobusiness in Australia and New Zealand; on the commercialization of new products and processes; on political, government and regulatory decisions affecting the performance of biobusinesses and on export opportunities.
Ind/Abst Abstr. BioCommer. (199?-); BioBusiness (1992-); Curr. Aware. Biol. Sci., CABS; Curr. Cit.; Food Sci. Technol. Abstr.; Soc. Sci. Cit. Index [Select. Cov.].

LC QH650 **ISSN** 0158-9938
DD 530 AT
NLM W1 AU335H **CODEN** AUPMDI
Pr Rev.
AUSTRALASIAN PHYSICAL & ENGINEERING SCIENCES IN MEDICINE. (AUSTRALASIAN PHYSICAL & ENGINEERING SCIENCES IN MEDICINE.). [Australas. phys. eng. sci. med.]. **Added/Corp** Australasian College of Physical Scientists in Medicine. Australasian Association of Physical Sciences in Medicine. **VFOAT** Australasian Physical and Engineering Sciences in Medicine. New Series, Vol. 3, No. 1, Serial No. 86 (Jan/Feb 1980)-. Academic Scholarly Publication. English. Four times a year (Mar., Jun., Sept., Dec.). 65.78Aus$. Australasian Physical & Engineering Sciences in Medicine, Centre for Medical and Health Physics, Queensland University of Technology, GPO Box 2434 Queensland 4001 Australia. **Tel** 011 61 7 38642591, FAX 011 61 7 38641521, telex AA 89764. **ED** Dr. Tim van Doorn. Index available (volume index bound in last issue). **Bk Rev. Ad Acc. Circ:** 500. Documents available from Article Express International, BIOSIS Document Express, Ask*IEEE, CASDDS. ***Continues*** *Australasian Physical Sciences in Medicine, 0157-9738.*
Desc: Application of the physical sciences and engineering to medical and clinical problems. Back issues available.
Ind/Abst Biol. Abstr. (1985-); Chem. Abstr.; Comput. Inf. Syst. Abstr. J. [Full Cov.]; Curr. Cit.; Elect. Comm. Abstr.; Eng. Index Annu.; Health Plan. Adminis.; Index Med. (1983-); INSPEC (Jan.-Feb. 1980-); Mater. Sci. Eng. Abstr.; Phys. Med. Biol. (19??-19??); Pollut. Abstr. Indexes; Solid State Supercond. Abstr.

LC TP248 **ISSN** 1032-8068
DD 660.6 AT
SUSPENDED
AUSTRALIAN AND NEW ZEALAND BIOTECHNOLOGY DIRECTORY. VFOAT Australian and New Zealand Biotechnology Directory. (1989)-Suspended (1993). Directory. English. Three times a year. 70.00Aus$. Australian Biotechnology Association Ltd, PO Box 4, Gardenvale 3185 Australia. **Tel** 011 61 3 5968879, FAX 011 61 3 5968874. **ED** Michael Deves. **Ad Acc. Circ:** 1,000.
Desc: A directory of Australian and New Zealand Biotechnology companies.

LC R858.A1 A9 **ISSN** 0095-0963
DD 610/.28/54 US
CCC
NLM W1 AU873P **CODEN** AUMDC9
AUTOMEDICA (NEW YORK). (AUTOMEDICA.). [Automedica]. Vol. 1 (Jan. 1974)-. Periodical. English. Irregular (publishes four issues per volume). $988.00 university and hospital libraries, $1542.00 other. Gordon & Breach Science Publishers, Inc., PO Box 786, Cooper Station, New York NY 10276. **Tel** (212)206-8900, FAX (212)645-2459. **(Subscription address:** Gordon & Breach Science Publishers / England, PO Box 90 Reading, Berkshire RG1 8JL United Kingdom. **Tel** 011 44 734 560080.) Documents available from Article Express International, BIOSIS Document Express, Ask*IEEE.
Desc: A multi-national publication for automation in the medical sciences.
Ind/Abst Biol. Abstr. (?-1984); Comput. Rev.; Curr. Cit.; Ei Page One; Energy Res. Abstr. (May 1974-); Eng. Index Annu.; INSPEC (1974-).

LC TP248.13 .B35
DD 661.8 JA
BAIO-INDASUTORI. VFOAT Baioindastori; Bioindustry; Bio-Industry. Vol. 1 No. 1, (1984)-. Periodical. Japanese. Twelve times a year. $823.50. Shi Emu Shi, (CMC Co. Ltd.), Miyako Biru, 5-4 Uchikanda 1 Chome, Chiyodaku Tokyo 101 Japan. **(Subscription address:** Japan Publications Trading Company Ltd., PO Box 5030, Tokyo International, Tokyo 100-31 Japan. **Tel** 011 81 3 3292 3753.)

LC TP248
DD 660.6 US
●**BBSRC BUSINESS. Main/Corp** Biotechnology and Biological Sciences Research Council. (1994)-. Newsletter. English. Four times a year. Biotechnology and Biological Sciences Research Council, Polaris House, North Star Avenue, Swindon SN2 1UH United Kingdom. **Tel** 011 44 1793 413200, FAX 011 44 1793 413201. **ED** Dr. Monica Winstanley. **Circ:** 5,000 (ctrl).

LC TP248
DD 660.6 CN
BC BIOTECHNOLOGY ALLIANCE BIOFAX. (19??)-. English. Twenty-four times a year. Free to members; 200.00Can$ (corporate membership). Biotechnology Alliance, Suite 800, 4710 Kingsway, Burnaby British Columbia V5H 4M2 Canada.
Ind/Abst Abstr. BioCommer.

LC TP248
DD 660.6 UK
BIA NEWSLETTER. (19??)-. Newsletter. English. Twelve times a year. Free to members; membership rates available on application. BioIndustry Association, 1 Queen Anne's Gate, London SW1H 9BT United Kingdom.
Ind/Abst Abstr. BioCommer.

ISSN 1073-7464
DD 332 US
SUSPENDED
●**BIG INC.** (BIG INC. : BIOTECH INVESTMENT NEWSLETTER.). [BIG Inc]. **Added/Corp** Biotechnology Investors Group. (Sept. 1993)-Suspended (Mar. 1995). Periodical. English. Twelve times a year. $495.00. Biotechnology Investors Group, 29 Broadway 9th Floor, New York NY 10006. **Tel** (800)224-4462.

LC TP248 **ISSN** 0291-2430
DD 660.6 FR
CCC
BIO : LA LETTRE DES BIOTECHNOLOGIES. (1992)-. Periodical. French. Eighteen times a year. $546.80. A Jour, 11 rue du Marche St. Honore, 75001 Paris France. **Tel** 011 33 1 44553849. **ED** P. Dacquin.

LC R857.M3 B48 **ISSN** 0959-2989
DD 610/.28 US
CCC
NLM W1; BI854X **CODEN** BMENEO
BIO-MEDICAL MATERIALS AND ENGINEERING. [Bio-med. mater. eng.]. **VFOAT** Biomedical Materials and Engineering. Vol. 1, No. 1 (1990)-. Academic Scholarly Publication. English. Six times a year. $507.03. Pergamon Press, An Imprint of Elsevier Science Ltd., The Boulevard, Langford Lane, Kidlington, Oxford OX5 1GB United Kingdom. **Tel** 011 44 1865 843000, 011 44 1865 843699, FAX 011 44 1865 843010. **(Subscription address:** Elsevier Science Ltd. / Oxford Fulfillment Centre, PO Box 800, Kidlington OX5 1DX United Kingdom. **Tel** 011 44 865 843355.) **ED** T. Yokobori. available on microfilm and microfiche from University Microfilms International (UMI); available on an online database from Elsevier Electronic Subscriptions (EES). Documents available from The Genuine Article, CASDDS.
Desc: Interdisciplinary journal that publishes original research papers, review articles and brief notes on materials and engineering for biological and medical systems.
Ind/Abst Alum. Ind. Abstr.; Chem. Abstr.; Eng. Mater. Abstr.; Met. Abstr.; Res. Alert [Full Cov.].

LC TP248 **ISSN** 0292-8418
DD 660.6 FR
NLM W1; BI91WP **CODEN** BIOSER
BIO-SCIENCES. [Bio-sciences]. **VFOAT** Biosciences. No. 1 (Jan./Feb. 1982)-. Academic Scholarly Publication. French (summaries and/or abstracts in English). Six times a year. 380.00F (one-year), 650.00F (two-year) France; 450.00F (one-year), 750.00F (two-year) other. Biosciences, BP 19, 78117 Chateaufort France. **Tel** 011 33 1 39565210. Documents available from CASDDS.
Ind/Abst Chem. Abstr.; Curr. Biotechnol.; Energy Res. Abstr. (Feb. 1983-).

LC TP248.3 .B557 ISSN 0733-222X
DD 660/.6/05 US
CCC
CODEN BTCHDA
Pr Rev.

BIO/TECHNOLOGY (NEW YORK, N.Y. 1983). (BIO/TECHNOLOGY.). [Bio/technology]. **Added/Corp** Nature Publishing Company. **VFOAT** Biotechnology; Bio Technology. Vol. 1, No. 1 (March 1983)-. Academic Scholarly Publication. English (Japanese). Twelve times a year (plus annual Buyer's Guide). $398.00. Nature Publishing Company, 65 Bleecker Street, 12th Floor, New York NY 10012. **Tel** (212)477-9600, (800)524-0328, FAX (212)477-8020. **(Subscription address:** Bio Technology, PO Box 1721, Riverton NJ 08077. **Tel** (800)524-0328.**)** **ED** Douglas K. McCormick Biauy, Jennifer van Brunt, and Arthur Klavsner. Index available. cum. index. **Bk Rev. Ad Acc. Circ:** 20,000 (ctrl). available on microfilm and microfiche from University Microfilms International (UMI); available on an online database (file 16/Full-Text) from DIALOG. Documents available from The Genuine Article, BIOSIS Document Express, CASDDS.
Desc: International journal with original research papers specifically-designed for biotechnologists. It also contains news, features, evaluations and original research by top experts.
Ind/Abst Abstr. Bull. Inst. Pap. Sci. Tech.; AgBiotech News Inf.; AGRICOLA [Select. Cov.]; Anim. Breed. Abstr.; Biodeter. Abstr. (19??-19??); Biol. Abstr.; Biotechnol. Res. Abstr.; Chem. Abstr. (1983-); Chem. Ind. Notes; CSA Neuro. Abstr. (?-?); Curr. Aware. Biol. Sci., CABS; Curr. Biotechnol.; Curr. Cit.; Dairy Sci. Abstr.; EMBASE; Energy Res. Abstr. (March 1983-); F&S Index Plus Text, Int. [Select. Cov.]; Field Crop Abstr.; Food Sci. Technol. Abstr.; Foods Adlibra; For. Abstr.; Genet. Abstr.; Immunol. Abstr.; Index Vet.; INIS Atomindex [Micro.]; Maize Abstr.; Microbiol. Abstr. Sect. B; Microbiol. Abstr. Sect. A; Microbiol. Abstr. Sect. C; Nutr. Abstr. Rev., Ser. A, Hum. Exp.; Life Sci. Collect. (1985-); PESTDOC; Plant Breed. Abstr.; Plant Grow. Reg. Abstr.; Potato Abstr.; Poult. Abstr.; PROMT [Full Txt.]; Protozoolog. Abstr.; Res. Alert [Full Cov.]; Rev. Agric. Entomol.; Rev. Med. Vet. Entomol.; Rev. Plant Pathol.; Rice Abstr.; Sci. Cit. Index; SCISEARCH; Soc. Sci. Cit. Index [Select. Cov.]; Soyabean Abstr.; Weed Abstr.; Wheat Barley Trit. Abstr.

LC TP248 ISSN 0267-4254
DD 660.6 UK

BIOBULLETIN. (BIOBULLETIN : THE NEWSLETTER OF SERC'S BIOTECHNOLOGY DIRECTORATE.). [Biobulletin]. **Added/Corp** Science and Engineering Research Council (Great Britain). Biotechnology Directorate. (1984)-. Periodical. English. Two times a year. Free. Science and Engineering Research Council, Biotechnology Directorate, Polaris House, North Star Avenue, Swindon SN2 1ET United Kingdom.
Ind/Abst Abstr. BioCommer.; Curr. Biotechnol.

LC TP248
DD 660.6 US

BIOCENTURY : THE BERNSTEIN REPORT ON BIOBUSINESS. (19??)-. English. One time a week (50 issues). $735.00. BioCentury Publications Inc., PO Box 3415, Redwood City CA 94064. **Tel** (415)347-1043.
Ind/Abst Abstr. BioCommer.

LC TP HB ISSN 1354-280X
DD 660 330 UK

•**BIOCOMMERCE FINANCIAL ABSTRACTS.** **See** Biology-Abstracting, Bibliographies and Statistics.

LC R856 ISSN 0208-5216
DD 610.28 PL
NLM W1 BI662M

BIOCYBERNETICS AND BIOMEDICAL ENGINEERING. **Added/Corp** Instytut Biocybernetyki i Inzynierii Biomedycznej (Polska Akademia Nauk). Polish Academy of Sciences, Institute of Biocybernetics and Biomedical Engineering. Vol. 1, No. 1/2 (1981)-. Monographic series. English (summaries and/or abstracts in Polish). Irregular. Price varies per volume. Panstwowe Wydawnictwo Naukowe / PWN, (Polish Scientific Publishers PWN Ltd.), Ul. Miodowa 10, PO Box 391, 00-251 Warsaw Poland. **Tel** 011 48 22 312738, FAX 011 48 22 267163. **(Subscription address:** Ars Polona-Ruch, PO Box 1001, Krakowskie Przedmiescie 7, 00-068 Warsaw Poland. **Tel** 011 48 22 261201.**)** **ED** Maciej Nalecz.
Desc: Papers on biocybernetics and biomedical engineering.

LC R ISSN 1068-5693
DD 610 US

•**BIOENGINEERING ABSTRACTS (1993).** **See** Biology-Abstracting, Bibliographies and Statistics.

LC TP248.13 .B54 ISSN 0178-2029
DD 660/.6 GW
CCC
NLM W1; BI663ND CODEN BENGEQ
CEASED

BIOENGINEERING (GRAFELFING, GERMANY). (BIOENGINEERING.). [Bioengineering]. **VFOAT** Bio Engineering. (198?)-Issue 6 (1994). Academic Scholarly Publication. German. Resch Media Mail Verlag GmbH, Postfach 1260, D-82166 Graefelfing Germany. **Tel** 011 49 89 8580710. Documents available from The Genuine Article, CASDDS.
Ind/Abst Chem. Abstr. (1986-); Curr. Biotechnol.; Curr. Cit.; Food Sci. Technol. Abstr.; Res. Alert [Full Cov.].

ISSN 0275-4207
DD 574 US
NLM W1; BI663NM
CEASED

BIOENGINEERING NEWS. [BioEng. news]. (1980)-(March 1993). Periodical. English. Deborah Mysiewicz Publishers, PO Box 2009, Oak Harbor WA 98277. **Tel** (415)689-2972. **ED** Thomas Mysiewicz. Index available. cum. index. **Bk Rev.** available on microfiche.
Desc: Biotech newsletter package. Includes World Biotech Company Directory and World Biolicensing and Patent Report. Original reporting on commercial, legal and regulatory affairs in Bioengineering News. World Biotechnology Company Directory describes over 1,000 firms.
Ind/Abst AGRICOLA [Select. Cov.].

ISSN 0951-5291
DD 610.28 UK

BIOENGINEERING NOW. [Bioeng. now]. (1987)-. English. Six times a year (Feb., Apr., June, Aug., Oct., Dec.). $179.67. Sarratt Information Services, 68 Saint Andrew's Road, Henley-on-Thames, Oxfordshire RG9 1JE United Kingdom. **Tel** 011 44 181 4224384. **ED** Brandl Graham Kay. Index available (Published separately). **Circ:** 50.
Desc: This publication is a bibliographic listing of world wide articles published on bioengineering, biomaterials and conference listing.

LC TP248.13 .B545 ISSN 0294-3506
DD 660/.6/05 FR
CCC
NLM W1; BI665KE CODEN BIOFEM
Pr Rev.

BIOFUTUR. [Biofutur]. (1982)-. Academic Scholarly Publication. French (English). Eleven times a year. $195.00. Editions Scientifique Elsevier, 141 rue de Javel, 75747 Paris Cedex 15 France. **Tel** 011 33 1 45589067, FAX 011 33 1 45589424. **(Subscription address:** Editions Scientifiques Elsevier / for North America, PO Box 7247-7576, Philadelphia PA 19170-7576. **)** available on microfilm and microfiche from University Microfilms International (UMI); available on an online database from Elsevier Electronic Subscriptions (EES). Documents available from The Genuine Article. ***Absorbed** Biofutur. Technoscope, 0992-4221.*
Ind/Abst AgBiotech News Inf.; Biodeter. Abstr. (1991-); Curr. Aware. Biol. Sci., CABS; Curr. Biotechnol.; Curr. Cit.; Curr. Contents Agric. Biol. Environ. Sci.; Dairy Sci. Abstr.; EMBASE; For. Abstr.; Helminthol. Abstr. (1991-); Hortic. Abstr.; Index Vet.; Infomat Int. Bus.; Maize Abstr.; Methods Organ. Synth.; Nematol. Abstr.; Nutr. Abstr. Rev., Ser. B, Live Feeds and Feed.; PESTDOC; Plant Breed. Abstr.; Plant Genet. Resour. Abstr.; Potato Abstr.; Protozoolog. Abstr.; Res. Alert [Full Cov.]; Rev. Agric. Entomol.; Rev. Plant Pathol.; SCISEARCH; Soc. Sci. Cit. Index [Select. Cov.]; Weed Abstr.; World Agric. Econ. Rural Sociol. Abstr.

LC TP248
DD 660.6 SP

BIOINGENIERIA Y CLINICA. (19??)-. Spanish. Four times a year. Puntex SA, Via Laietana 30 4 F, 08003 Barcelona Spain. **Tel** 011 34 3 2680444.

ISSN 0886-7461
DD 660 US
NLM W1; BI667JK

BIOINVENTION. [BioInvention]. **VFOAT** Bio Invention. Vol. 5, No. 1 (Jan. 1986)-. Periodical. English. Twelve times a year. $425.00. Biosource, Inc., PO Box 550, Howell NJ 07731. **Tel** (908)905-5728, FAX (908)905-5847. **ED** Thomas J. Puskar. available in bound issues. ***Continues** Biotechnology Patent Digest, 0730-1057.*
Ind/Abst Abstr. BioCommer. (-199?).

ISSN 1056-9138
DD 574 US
CODEN BENUEY

BIOLOGICAL EFFECTS OF NONIONIZING ELECTROMAGNETIC RADIATION DIGEST UPDATE (PHILADELPHIA, PA.). (BIOLOGICAL EFFECTS OF NONIONIZING ELECTROMAGNETIC RADIATION DIGEST UPDATE.). **Added/Corp** Information Ventures, Inc. **VFOAT** BENER Digest Update. Vol. 1, No. 1 (June 1991)-. Periodical. English. Four times a year. $315.00. Information Ventures Inc., 1500 Locust Street, Suite 3216, Philadelphia PA 19102. **Tel** (215)732-9083, FAX (215)732-3754. **ED** Robert Goldberg. Index available (bound in all issues). available on CD-ROM from Info Ventures.
Desc: Documents and critically reviews current research on the biological and health effects of nonionizing electromagnetic radiation.

ISSN 1052-9306
DD 610 UK
CCC
NLM W1; BI671QL CODEN BIMSEH
Pr Rev. TITLE CHANGE

BIOLOGICAL MASS SPECTROMETRY. [Biolo. mass. spectrom.]. (1991)-(199?). Academic Scholarly Publication. English. John Wiley & Sons Ltd., Baffins Lane, Chichester, West Sussex PO19 1UD United Kingdom. **Tel** 011 44 1243 779777, FAX 011 44 1243 776128 BTG:JWP001, telex 86290 WIBOOKG. **ED** Richard Caprioli. Index available. **Bk Rev. Ad Acc. Circ:** 700. available on microfilm and microfiche from University Microfilms International (UMI). Documents available from Article Express International, The Genuine Article, BIOSIS Document Express, CASDDS, Documents on Demand, ADONIS. ***Continues** Biomedical & Environmental Mass Spectrometry, 0887-6134.* ***Continued by** Journal of Mass Spectrometry, 1076-5174.*
Desc: This journal's original papers are devoted to the use of mass spectrometry in the qualitative or quantitative study of compounds in the biological, environmental and medical fields. New techniques and instrumentation, as well as applications in a wide range of disciplines, are also explored.
Ind/Abst ADONIS; Anal. Abstr.; Biol. Abstr.; Chem. Abstr. (1991-); Curr. Aware. Biol. Sci., CABS; Curr. Chem. React.; Curr. Cit.; Curr. Contents Life Sci.; Ei Page One; EMBASE; Eng. Index Annu.; Environ. Abstr.; Environ. Period. Bibliogr. (?-?); Index Chem.; Mass Spect. Bull. (?-?); Life Sci. Collect.; Pollut. Abstr. Indexes; Ref. Upd. Deluxe Ed.; Res. Alert [Full Cov.]; Sci. Cit. Index; SCISEARCH; Weed Abstr.

LC TP ISSN 0968-5685
DD 660 UK
CCC
Pr Rev.

•**BIOLOGICAL PRODUCTS.** Vol. 1 (1994)-. Academic Scholarly Publication. English. Four times a year. $209.00. Butterworth Heinemann Publishers, Linacre House Jordan Hill, Oxford OX2 8DP United Kingdom. **Tel** 011 44 1865 310366, FAX 011 44 1865 310898. **(Subscription address:** Elsevier Science Ltd. / Oxford Fulfillment Centre, PO Box 800, Kidlington OX5 1DX United Kingdom. **Tel** 011 44 865 843355.**)** **ED** Board. available in microform from University Microfilms International (UMI).

LC QP901 ISSN 0869-4842
DD 612.015 RU
NLM W1; BI852RG

BIOMATERIAL-LIVING SYSTEM INTERACTIONS. **VFOAT** Biomaterial Living System Interactions. (199?)-. Periodical. English. Four times a year. $139.95. **(Subscription address:** East View Publications Inc., 3020 Harbor Lane North, Suite 110, Minneapolis MN 55447. **Tel** (800)477-1005, (612)550-0961, FAX (612)559-2931.**)**

LC R857.M3 B568 ISSN 0142-9612
DD 610/.28/05 UK
CCC
NLM W1 BI852RJ CODEN BIMADU
Pr Rev.

BIOMATERIALS. [Biomaterials]. Vol. 1, No. 1 (Jan. 1980)-. Academic Scholarly Publication. English. Twenty-four times a year. $1431.00. Butterworth Heinemann Publishers, Linacre House Jordan Hill, Oxford OX2 8DP United Kingdom. **Tel** 011 44 1865 310366, FAX 011 44 1865 310898. **(Subscription address:** Elsevier Science Ltd. / Oxford Fulfillment Centre, PO Box 800, Kidlington OX5 1DX United Kingdom. **Tel** 011 44 865 843355.**)** **ED** G.W. Hastings, N.A. Peppas, R.S. Langer. Index available. **Ad Acc.** available on microfilm and microfiche from University Microfilms International (UMI); available on an online database from Elsevier Electronic Subscriptions (EES). Documents available from Article Express International, The Genuine Article, BIOSIS Document Express, Ask*IEEE, CASDDS. ***Absorbed** Clinical Materials.*
Desc: Includes papers that study both synthetic and naturally occurring materials. It was established to bring together the work of specialists in many different disciplines and fully reflects on the diversity and rapid growth of this challenging subject. Covers the structure, properties, interactions and functions of biomaterials as well as their clinical applications.
Ind/Abst BioBusiness; Biol. Abstr.; Ceram. Abstr.; Chem. Abstr.; Curr. Aware. Biol. Sci., CABS; Curr. Biotechnol.; Curr. Cit.; Curr. Contents Life Sci.; Curr. Technol. Index; Curr. Titles Dent.; EMBASE; Eng. Index Annu.; Health Plan. Adminis.; Index Med. (-1980); INSPEC (Jan. 1980-); Polymer Contents; Ref. Upd. Deluxe Ed.; Res. Alert [Full Cov.]; Sci. Cit. Index; SCISEARCH.

LC QD415 ISSN 1076-6286
DD 574.192 US
Pr Rev.

•**BIOMATERIALS SCIENCE AND ENGINEERING.** (1994)-. Periodical. English. Four times a year. $168.00. Mary Ann Liebert Inc., 2 Madison

Biology —Bioengineering

Avenue, Larchmont NY 10538. **Tel** (914)834-3100, (800)M-LIEBERT, FAX (212)289-4697. **ED** ChoKyun Rha and Anthony J. Sinskey.
  Desc: Presents information on applications and utilizations of biomaterials in biochemical, biophysical, medical, industrial, food, and environmental processes.

LC R ISSN 0778-4910
DD 610 BE
UDC 167(4)
CODEN CE
BIOMEDICAL & HEALTH RESEARCH.
[Biomed. health res.]. **VFOAT** Biomedical and Health Research; Newsletter Biomedical & Health Research. (1990)-. Periodical. Multiple languages. Four times a year. Free. Commission of the European Communities, DG XII-E-4, Medical Research Division, rue de la Loi 200, B-1049 Brussels Belgium. **Tel** FAX 011 32 2 2955365. **ED** Manuel Hallen.
  Desc: Provides news and information on biomedical research. Also announces recent publications and conferences in the field.

LC R856 .M4513 ISSN 0006-3398
DD 610/.28 US
CCC
NLM W1 BI854I CODEN BIOEAF
BIOMEDICAL ENGINEERING.
[Biomed. eng.]. **Added/Corp** Consultants Bureau. Vol. 1 (Jan. 1967)-. Academic Scholarly Publication. English (Russian). Six times a year. $1025.00. Consultants Bureau, A Division of Plenum Publishing Corporation, 233 Spring Street, New York NY 10013. **Tel** (212)620-8000, (212)620-8466, FAX (212)463-0742, telex 23/421139. **ED** V. A. Viktorov. available on microfilm and microfiche from University Microfilms International (UMI). Documents available from Article Express International, BIOSIS Document Express, Ask*IEEE, CASDDS.
  Desc: Covers recent advances in the growing field of biomedical technology, instrumentation, and administration.
  Ind/Abst Bioeng. Abstr.; Biol. Abstr. (?-1984); Chem. Abstr.; Ei Page One; EMBASE; Energy Res. Abstr. (May 1974-); Eng. Index Annu.; Health Plan. Adminis.; INIS Atomindex [Micro.]; INSPEC (Jan.-Feb. 1972-).

LC R ISSN 0194-2778
DD 610 US
CCC
NLM W1 BI854IH
BIOMEDICAL ENGINEERING AND COMPUTATION SERIES.
[Biomed. eng. comput. ser.]. Vol. 1 (1979)-. Monographic series. English. Irregular. Price varies per volume. Harwood Academic Publishers / New York, PO Box 786, Cooper Station, New York NY 10276. **Tel** (212)206-8900, (201)643-7500.
  Desc: Contains information on biomedical engineering.

LC R856 ISSN 0190-0951
DD 610.28 US
BIOMEDICAL ENGINEERING AND HEALTH SYSTEMS.
(19??)-. Monographic series. English. Irregular. Price varies per volume. John Wiley & Sons Inc / New Jersey, 1 Wiley Drive, Somerset NJ 08875. **Tel** (800)225-5945, (908)469-4400. **ED** John H. Milsum.
  Ind/Abst Math. Rev.

LC R856 ISSN 1062-5488
DD 610.28 US
BIOMEDICAL ENGINEERING CITATION INDEX.
(BIOMEDICAL ENGINEERING CITATION INDEX [COMPUTER FILE] : A CD-ROM DATABASE WITH ABSTRACTS.). **Added/Corp** Institute for Scientific Information. **VFOAT** Biomedical Engineering. (1992)-. English. Six times a year. $2,250.00. Institute for Scientific Information, 3501 Market Street, Philadelphia PA 19104. **Tel** (215)386-0100, (800)523-1850, FAX (215)386-6362, telex 84-5305. (**Subscription address:** Institute for Scientific Information, PO Box 71416, Chicago IL 60694.)
  Desc: Current literature on medical imaging, biomaterials, biomechanics, biorheology, and physiology as applied to the design of biomedical equipment and materials.

LC R856 ISSN 0730-8027
DD 610.28 US
CODEN BLTRDZ
BIOMEDICAL LABORATORY TECHNICAL REPORT.
[Biomed. Lab. tech. rep.]. **Added/Corp** United States. Army. Biomedical Laboratory. (19??)-. Academic Scholarly Publication. English. Price varies per volume. US Army Medical Research and Development Command, Biomedical Laboratory, Aberdeen Proving Ground MD 21010. Documents available from CASDDS.
  Ind/Abst Chem. Abstr.

LC Z ISSN 1064-699X
DD 026 US
BIOMEDICAL LIBRARY ACQUISITIONS BULLETIN.
See Library and Information Sciences.

ISSN 1064-4180
DD 338 US
Pr Rev.
BIOMEDICAL MARKET NEWSLETTER.
[Biomed. mark. newsl.]. Vol. 1, No. 1 (Sept. 1991)-. Newsletter. English. Twelve times a year. $795.00. Biomedical Market Newsletter, 3237 Idaho Place, Costa Mesa CA 92626. **Tel** (714)434-9500, (800)875-8181, FAX (714)434-9755. Index available ($65.00). available on an online database from Compuserve Inc.; and (files 16,636/Full-Text) DIALOG.
  Ind/Abst PROMT [Full Txt.]; PTS Newsl. Database [Full Txt.].

LC R856 ISSN 0955-7717
DD 610.28 UK
CCC
NLM W1; BI854V CODEN BMATEM
BIOMEDICAL MATERIALS. (198?)-.
Periodical. English. Twelve times a year. $474.00. Elsevier Advanced Technology, An Imprint of Elsevier Science Ltd., The Boulevard, Langford Lane, Kidlington, Oxford OX5 1GB United Kingdom. **Tel** 011 44 1865 843000, 011 44 1865 843699, FAX 011 44 1865 843010. (**Subscription address:** Elsevier Science Ltd. / Oxford Fulfillment Centre, PO Box 800, Kidlington OX5 1DX United Kingdom. **Tel** 011 44 1865 843355.) **ED** R. Juniper, P. Read. available on microfilm from University Microfilms International (UMI); available on an online database from Elsevier Electronic Subscriptions (EES); (file 636/Full-Text) DIALOG; and DATA-STAR. Documents available from BLDSC. **Continues** Biomedical Polymers.
  Desc: International newsletter covering all significant aspects and applications of biomedical polymer technology.
  Ind/Abst PTS Newsl. Database [Full Txt.].

ISSN 0192-1266
DD 610 US
CCC
BIOMEDICAL PRODUCTS. [Biomed. prod.].
(19??)-. Periodical. English. Twelve times a year. $30.00 US, Canada and Mexico; $42.00 (surface mail), $93.00 (airmail) other. Cahners Publishing Company, 249 West 17th Street, New York NY 10011. **Tel** (212)645-0067, FAX (212)242-6987. (**Subscription address:** Gordon Publications, Inc., Paid Circulation Department, 301 Gibralter Drive, Box 650, Morris Plains NJ 07950-0650. **Tel** (201)292-5100 ext. 351, FAX (201)898-9281.)
  Desc: Reaches directors, principle investigators, biochemists, chemists, medical researchers, microbiologists, professors and medical school teachers in the life science/biotech research laboratories of universities, medical institutions, pharmaceutical companies, industry, and biotechnology and research centers.

LC R856 ISSN 0970-938X
DD 610.28 II
NLM W1; BI8564 CODEN BIRSE8
BIOMEDICAL RESEARCH. [Biomed. res.].
Vol. 1 (Jan. 1990)-. Newsletter. English. Two times a year. $60.00. Scientific Publishers, PO Box 91, Ratanada Road, Jodhpur 342011 India. (**Subscription address:** Prints India, 11 Darya Ganj, New Delhi 110002 India. **Tel** 011 91 11 3268645, FAX 011 91 11 3275542, telex 31-61087 PRIN-IN.) Documents available from BIOSIS Document Express.
  Ind/Abst Biol. Abstr. (1991-); EMBASE [Select. Cov.].

LC R856 ISSN 0388-6107
DD 610.28 JA
NLM W1 BI856C CODEN BRESD5
Pr Rev.
BIOMEDICAL RESEARCH (TOKYO).
(BIOMEDICAL RESEARCH.). [Biomed. res.]. **Added/Corp** Biomedical Research Foundation (Japan). Vol. 1, No. 1 (Feb. 1980)-. Academic Scholarly Publication. English. Six times a year. $234.00. Baiomedikaru Risachi Fandeshon, 4-1 Nishishinjuku 2 Chome, Shinjukuku Tokyo 163 Japan. (**Subscription address:** Maruzen Company Ltd., PO Box 5050, Import & Export Department, Tokyo 100 31 Japan. **Tel** 011 81 3 32789224.) Documents available from The Genuine Article, BIOSIS Document Express, CASDDS.
  Desc: Publishes original research articles and reviews of high quality in the fields of experimental and medical biology, encouraging interdisciplinary discussion of topics in these fields.
  Ind/Abst Biol. Abstr.; Chem. Abstr.; Chem. Titles; CSA Neuro. Abstr. (?-?); Curr. Aware. Biol. Sci., CABS; Curr. Cit.; Curr. Contents Life Sci.; Dairy Sci. Abstr.; EMBASE; Life Sci. Collect.; Protozoolog. Abstr.; Res. Alert [Full Cov.]; Sci. Cit. Index; SCISEARCH.

LC R856
DD 610.28 BU
NLM W1; BI856GGG
BIOMEDICAL REVIEWS. Vol. 1 (1992)-.
Periodical. English. DM86.00. (**Subscription address:** Kubon & Sagner, ABT Zeitschriftenimport, D 80328 Munich Germany. **Tel** 011 49 89 54218130.)

LC R856 US
DD 610.28
BIOMEDICAL SCIENCES PROCEEDINGS.
(19??)-. Academic Scholarly Publication. English. One time a year. $42.50. Instrument Society of America, 67 Alexander Drive, Research Triangle NC 27709. **Tel** (919)549-8411, FAX (919)549-8288, telex 802 540. **Continues** Biomedical Sciences Instrumentation, 0067-8856.
  Desc: Proceedings of the jointly-sponsored ISA Biomedical Sciences Division/Rocky Mountain Bioengineering Symposium/Engineering in Medicine and Science Group of IEEE Conference.

LC R856 ISSN 1352-7673
DD 610.28 UK
●**BIOMEDICAL SCIENTIST.** (1994)-. English. Twelve times a year. $77.01. IBMS Professional Services, 12 Coldbath Square, London EC1R 5HL United Kingdom. **Tel** 011 44 171 6368192, FAX 011 44 171 4364946. **Continues** IMLS Gazette, 0267-2928.
  Ind/Abst Curr. Cit.

ISSN 1073-1210
DD 610 US
NLM W1; BI856U
TITLE CHANGE
BIOMEDICAL TECHNOLOGY MANAGEMENT.
[Biomed. technol. manag.]. **VFOAT** Technology. (Jan.-Feb. 1994)-(1995). Trade Publication. English. Second Source Publications Inc., 10 Risho Avenue, East Providence RI 02914. **Tel** (401)434-1050. **Continues** Second Source Biomedical, 1053-6868. **Continued by** Healthcare Technology Management.

LC R856 ISSN 0753-3322
DD 610.28 FR
CCC
NLM W1 BI857J CODEN BIPHEX
Pr Rev.
BIOMEDICINE & PHARMACOTHERAPY. See Pharmacy and Pharmacology.

LC R856.A1 B58 ISSN 0013-5585
DD 610.28 GW
CCC
NLM W1 BI858 CODEN BMZTA7
Pr Rev.
BIOMEDIZINISCHE TECHNIK.
(BIOMEDIZINISCHE TECHNIK. BIOMEDICAL ENGINEERING.). [Biomed. Tech.]. **Added/Corp** Deutsche Gesellschaft fuer Biomedizinische Technik. **VFOAT** Biomedical Engineering. Vol. 16 (Feb. 1971)-. Academic Scholarly Publication. German (English and German; summaries and/or abstracts in English and German). Ten times a year. $469.80. Fachverlag Schiele & Schoen, Postfach 610280, D-10924 Berlin Germany. **Tel** 011 49 30 25375223. Documents available from Article Express International, The Genuine Article, Ask*IEEE, CASDDS. **Continues** Elektromedizin.
  Ind/Abst Chem. Abstr.; Curr. Cit.; Curr. Contents Clin. Med.; EMBASE; Energy Res. Abstr. (July 1974-); Eng. Index Annu.; Health Plan. Adminis.; Index Med.; INSPEC (Feb. 1971-); Life Sci. Collect.; Protozoolog. Abstr.; Res. Alert [Full Cov.]; Saf. Health Work; Sci. Cit. Index; SCISEARCH; Soc. Sci. Cit. Index [Select. Cov.].

ISSN 1059-0153
DD 500 US
CCC
NLM W1; BI862G CODEN BIMIEL
BIOMIMETICS (NEW YORK, N.Y.).
(BIOMIMETICS.). [Biomimetics]. Vol. 1 No. 1 (Mar. 1992)-. Academic Scholarly Publication. English. Four times a year. $145.00. Plenum Press, 233 Spring Street, New York NY 10013-1578. **Tel** (212)620-8000, (800)221-9369, FAX (212)463-0742, (212)807-1047, telex 23/421139. **ED** J.F. Vincent. **Bk Rev**. Documents available from CASDDS.
  Desc: Publishes research papers and short notes on mechanical and chemical analysis of structural biological materials leading to an understanding of their performance; development and production of materials based on direct copying of nature; analysis of the mechanical performance of materials produced using biotechnical processes; novel applications of biomimetic materials; improvements in the design of current organisms based on mechanical analysis of their structure; and analysis of the optimization criteria used in natural materials and structures.
  Ind/Abst Chem. Abstr.

LC TP248.3 .B5585 ISSN 0883-0878
DD 660/.63 US
BIOPROCESS ENGINEERING. Added/Corp
Bioprocess Engineering Society International. **VFOAT** Bio-Process Engineering. **VAT** BioProcess Engineering (Tampa, Fla.). Vol. 1, No. 1 (1984)-. Periodical. English. Twelve times a year. Bioprocess Engineering, 324 Monroe A, Dunedin FL 33528-5740. Documents available from The Genuine Article.
  Ind/Abst Curr. Contents Agric. Biol. Environ. Sci.; PESTDOC; Res. Alert [Full Cov.]; SCISEARCH.

LC TP248 **ISSN** 0178-515X
DD 660.63 GW
CCC
NLM W1; BI88P **CODEN** BIENEU
Pr Rev.
BIOPROCESS ENGINEERING (BERLIN, WEST). (BIOPROCESS ENGINEERING.). [Bioprocess eng.]. Vol. 1, No. 1 (1986)-. Academic Scholarly Publication. English. Twelve times a year. $1174.00. Springer-Verlag GmbH & Company KG, Heidelberger Platz 3, D-14197 Berlin Germany. **Tel** 011 49 30 8207223, FAX 011 49 30 8214091, telex 183 319 SPBLN D. **(Subscription address:** Springer-Verlag New York Inc. / North America, PO Box 2485, Journal Fulfillment, Secaucus NJ 07096. **Tel** (201)348-4033, (800)777-4643, FAX (201)348-4505.**)** **ED** H Brauer. available on microfilm and microfiche from University Microfilms International (UMI). Documents available from BIOSIS Document Express, CASDDS, ADONIS.
Desc: Concerned with all technical and economical aspects of the processes in which natural or derived biological substances are the basic material.
Ind/Abst Abstr. BioCommer.; ADONIS; AGRICOLA [Select. Cov.]; Biodeter. Abstr.; Biol. Abstr. (1989-); Chem. Abstr. (1986); Curr. Aware. Biol. Sci., CABS; Curr. Cit.; Ei Page One; EMBASE.

ISSN 0888-7470
DD 660 US
CCC
NLM W1; BI88U **CODEN** BPTEEP
BIOPROCESS TECHNOLOGY. [Bioprocess technol.]. Vol. 1 (1986)-. Monographic series. English. Irregular. Price varies per volume. Marcel Dekker Inc., 270 Madison Avenue, New York NY 10016. **Tel** (212)696-9000, (800)228-1160, FAX (212)685-4540, telex 421419. **(Subscription address:** Marcel Dekker Inc., PO Box 5017, Monticello NY 12701. **Tel** (800)228-1160.**)** Documents available from CASDDS.
Desc: Covers topics in biotechnology such as anaerobic fermentation, yeast strain selections and sensors in bioprocess control.
Ind/Abst Chem. Abstr.; Curr. Cit.

LC TP248 **ISSN** 0269-7572
DD 660.6 UK
CODEN BRECEQ
TITLE CHANGE
BIORECOVERY (BERKHAMSTED). (BIORECOVERY.). [Biorecovery]. Vol. 1, No. 1 (1988)-(19??). Periodical. English. (four issues per volume). AB Academic Publishers, PO Box 42 Bicester, Oxfordshire OX6 7NW United Kingdom. **Tel** 011 44 1869 320949, FAX 011 44 1869 320949. **ED** Robert Edyvean. Documents available from The Genuine Article, BIOSIS Document Express, CASDDS, Documents on Demand. ***Merged into*** *International Journal of Resource and Environmental Biotechnology.*
Desc: Covers the use of living organisms and their products in extraction recovery of minerals, oils, and other materials.
Ind/Abst Biodeter. Abstr. (1991-); Biol. Abstr. (1989-); Chem. Abstr.; Curr. Biotechnol.; Curr. Cit.; Energy Inf. Abstr.; Environ. Abstr.; Environ. Period. Bibliogr.; Res. Alert [Full Cov.].

LC HD9999.B44 B56 **ISSN** 0887-6207
DD 338.7/6208/025 US
NLM QT 22.1; B615
BIOSCAN. [BioScan]. **VAT** Bio Scan. Vol. 1 (1987)-. English. Six times a year. $975.00. Oryx Press, 4041 North Central Avenue #700, Phoenix AZ 85012-3397. **Tel** (800)279-6799, (602)265-2651, FAX (602)265-6250, (800)279-4663, (800)279-6799. **(Subscription address:** Eurospan Ltd., 3 Henrietta Street Covent Garden, London WC2E 8LU United Kingdom. **Tel** 011 44 181 2400856, FAX 011 44 181 3790609.**)** available in Loose-leaf; available on diskette; available on an online database.
Desc: An information service covering 550 US companies and 365 foreign companies involved in product research and development. Reports on industry leaders and identifies new and emerging companies. Information includes product development, business strategy, investments, parent company and percentage owned, financial information, research and development activities, history and new facility information.

LC QH301 .B56 **ISSN** 0916-8451
DD 574.05/6 JA
CCC
NLM W1; BI91H **CODEN** BBBIEJ
BIOSCIENCE, BIOTECHNOLOGY, AND BIOCHEMISTRY. **Added/Corp** Nihon Nogei Kagakkai. Vol. 56, No. 1 (Jan. 1992)-. Periodical. English. Twelve times a year. $350.00. **(Subscription address:** Japan Publications Trading Company Ltd., PO Box 5030, Tokyo International, Tokyo 100-31 Japan. **Tel** 011 81 3 3292 3753.**)** Documents available from The Genuine Article, Documents on Demand. ***Continues*** *Agricultural and Biological Chemistry, 0002-1369.*
Ind/Abst Biol. Agric. Index; Curr. Aware. Biol. Sci., CABS; Curr. Contents Agric. Biol. Environ. Sci.; Curr. Contents Life Sci.; Environ. Abstr.; Food Sci. Technol. Abstr.; Foods Adlibra; Ref. Upd. Deluxe Ed.; Res. Alert [Full Cov.]; Sci. Cit. Index; Soc. Sci. Cit. Index [Select. Cov.].

LC R857.B54 B56 **ISSN** 0956-5663
DD 610.28 UK
CCC
NLM W1; BI1915R **CODEN** BBIOE4
Pr Rev.
BIOSENSORS & BIOELECTRONICS. [Biosens. bioelectron.]. **VFOAT** Biosensors and Bioelectronics. Vol. 5, No. 1 (1990)-. Academic Scholarly Publication. English. Twelve times a year. $563.00. Elsevier Advanced Technology, An Imprint of Elsevier Science Ltd., The Boulevard, Langford Lane, Kidlington, Oxford OX5 1GB United Kingdom. **Tel** 011 44 1865 843000, 011 44 1865 843699, FAX 011 44 1865 843010. **(Subscription address:** Elsevier Science Ltd. / Oxford Fulfillment Centre, PO Box 800, Kidlington OX5 1DX United Kingdom. **Tel** 011 44 865 843355.**)** available on microfilm and microfiche from University Microfilms International (UMI); available on an online database from Elsevier Electronic Subscriptions (EES). Documents available from Article Express International, The Genuine Article, BIOSIS Document Express, Ask*IEEE, CASDDS, ADONIS. ***Continues*** *Biosensors, 0265-928X.*
Ind/Abst Abstr. BioCommer.; ADONIS; AGRICOLA [Select. Cov.]; Biol. Abstr. (1991-); Chem. Abstr. (1990-); Curr. Aware. Biol. Sci., CABS; Curr. Cit.; Curr. Contents Agric. Biol. Environ. Sci.; EMBASE; Eng. Index Annu.; Health Plan. Adminis.; Index Med. (1990-); INSPEC (1990-); PESTDOC; Res. Alert [Full Cov.]; Sci. Cit. Index; SCISEARCH.

LC TP248.25.S47 B56 **ISSN** 0923-179X
DD 661.8 NE
CCC
NLM W1; BI915W **CODEN** BISPE4
Pr Rev.
BIOSEPARATION. Vol. 1, No. 1 (May 1990)-. Periodical. English. Six times a year. $470.72. Kluwer Academic Publishers, Postbus 322, 3300 AH Dordrecht The Netherlands. **Tel** 011 31 78 524400, FAX 011 31 78 183273, telex 20083. **ED** Tony Atkinson. **Acid Free.** available on microfilm and microfiche from University Microfilms International (UMI). Documents available from The Genuine Article, CASDDS.
Desc: Publishes papers on all aspects of separation science applicable or potentially applicable to commercial scale biotechnological processes.
Ind/Abst Chem. Abstr.; Curr. Aware. Biol. Sci., CABS; Curr. Cit.; Food Sci. Technol. Abstr.; Res. Alert [Full Cov.].

LC TP950 **ISSN** 0393-9146
DD 661.8 IT
CODEN BBRCED
Pr Rev.
BIOTEC : RIVISTA BIMESTRALE DI BIOTECNOLOGIA. [Biotec]. Vol. 1, No. 1 (1986)-. Monographic series. Italian (English). Six times a year. L70000.00. Clas International, Via Pace 8, 25122 Brescia Italy. **Tel** 011 39 30 3772712. **Bk Rev**, (Qty: 15-20/yr). **Ad Acc, Adv Mgr:** Michele Francaviglia. **Circ:** 4000. Documents available from BIOSIS Document Express, CASDDS.
Desc: Biotechnology applied to different fields of medicine.
Ind/Abst AGRICOLA [Select. Cov.]; Biol. Abstr. (1988-); Chem. Abstr.; Ei Page One.

ISSN 0899-5702
DD 338 US
CCC
BIOTECH BUSINESS. [Biotech bus.]. (Jan. 1988)-. Periodical. English. Twelve times a year. $150.00. Worldwide Videotex, PO Box 3273, Boynton Beach FL 33424-3273. **Tel** (407)738-2276, FAX (407)738-2275. **ED** Mark Wright. **Bk Rev**, (Qty: 12). available on an online database from DATA-STAR; (file 636/Full-Text) DIALOG; and NEWSNET.
Desc: Provides news and information on biotechnology products and companies.
Ind/Abst PTS Newsl. Database [Full Txt.].

LC TP248.13 .B5583 **ISSN** 1067-1196
DD 660/.6/05 US
CCC
NLM W1; BI918KRF
TITLE CHANGE
BIOTECH DAILY. [Biotech dly.]. Vol. 1, No. 1 (Aug. 11, 1992)-(199?). Periodical. English. King Publishing Group, 627 National Press Building, Washington DC 20045. **Tel** (202)638-4260, FAX (202)662-9744. ***Continues*** *Genetic Engineering Letter, 0276-1882.* ***Merged with*** *Pharmaceutical Daily, 1071-5096* ***to form*** *Pharmaceutical & Biotech Daily, 1074-8636.*
Ind/Abst Abstr. BioCommer.

LC HG **ISSN** 0891-3161
DD 332 US
BIOTECH INVESTOR. [BioTech investor]. **VFOAT** Bio Tech Investor. (1987)-. Periodical. English. Twelve times a year. $495.00. Casdin Associates, World Financial Center, Oppenhei Tower/8th Floor, New York NY 10281. **Tel** (212)397-4400, FAX (212)397-4402. **ED** David Webber. Index available.
Desc: Provides commentary on the market for biotech stocks as well as in-depth analysis of the biotech companies and research into issues of concern to the biotechnology community

LC TP **ISSN** 0953-2226
DD 660 UK
CCC
NLM ZQT 34; B61578
BIOTECH KNOWLEDGE SOURCES. (BIOTECH KNOWLEDGE SOURCES : BKS.). [Biotech. knowl. sources]. **Added/Corp** British Library. Biotechnology Information Service. BioCommerce Data Ltd. **VFOAT** BKS. (1987)-. Abstracting/Indexing Service. English. Twelve times a year. $315.00. Biocommerce Data Ltd., 95 High Street, Slough Berkshire SL1 1DH United Kingdom. **Tel** 011 44 1753 511777, FAX 011 44 1753 512239. **ED** A. Crafts-Lighty. Index available. cum. index. **Bk Rev. Ad Acc, Adv Mgr:** A. Crafts-Lighty, **Tel** 011 44 1753 511777. **Circ:** 200 (ctrl).
Desc: An alerting service listing new books, market surveys and other publications on biotechnology and forthcoming conferences and courses worldwide. Includes reviews of new information products and case studies of services.

LC TP248
DD 660.6 UK
NLM W1; BI918KT
BIOTECH NEWS. (198?)-. Academic Scholarly Publication. English. Twelve times a year. $154.87. Springfield Information Services / Petersborough, PO Box 31, Cross Street Court, Peterborough PE1 1SD United Kingdom. **Tel** 011 44 1733 267272, FAX 011 44 1733 267272. **ED** John Franks. Documents available from CASDDS.
Ind/Abst Abstr. BioCommer.; Chem. Abstr.

ISSN 0898-2813
DD 610 US
BIOTECH PATENT NEWS. [Biotech pat. news]. (1987)-. Periodical. English. Twelve times a year. $95.00. Biotech Patent News, PO Box 4482, Metuchen NJ 08840. **Tel** (908)549-1356, FAX (908)549-1356. **ED** Richard S. Parr. **Ad Acc, Adv Mgr:** Alicia Parr. **Circ:** 180. available on an online database (files 16,636/Full-Text) from DIALOG; and (dialog-predicasts).
Desc: Newsletter exclusively devoted to worldwide patent, licensing and litigation information relating to biotechnology.
Ind/Abst Abstr. BioCommer.; PROMT [Full Txt.]; PTS Newsl. Database [Full Txt.].

ISSN 1069-4773
DD 630 US
•**BIOTECH REPORTER.** [Biotech report.]. Vol. 10, No. 6 (May 1993)-. Periodical. English. Twelve times a year. $185.00. Freiberg Publishing, Box 7, Cedar Falls IA 50613-0007. **Tel** (319)277-3599. ***Continues*** *Agbiotechnology News, 0899-3998.*

LC QH613 .B56 **ISSN** 1052-0295
DD 574.8/212 US
CCC
NLM W1; BI918KV **CODEN** BIHIEU
BIOTECHNIC & HISTOCHEMISTRY. (BIOTECHNIC & HISTOCHEMISTRY : OFFICIAL PUBLICATION OF THE BIOLOGICAL STAIN COMMISSION.). [Biotech. histochem.]. **Added/Corp** Biological Stain Commission. **VFOAT** Biotechnic and Histochemistry. Vol. 1, No. 1 (1991)-. Academic Scholarly Publication. English. Six times a year. $109.00 (institutions) $64.00 (individuals) US; $94.00 (individuals), $139.00 (institutions) other. Williams & Wilkins Company, 428 East Preston Street, Baltimore MD 21202-3993. **Tel** (410)528-4000, (800)638-6423, FAX (410)528-8596, telex 87669. **(Subscription address:** Williams & Wilkins, PO Box 64380, Baltimore MD 21264. **Tel** 800 638-6423.**)** Documents available from , The Genuine Article, BIOSIS Document Express, CASDDS, , Quick Copies. ***Continues*** *Stain Technology, 0038-9153.*
Desc: Covers the new materials, apparatus, and methods involved in preparation of biological specimens for pathologists, histologists, and histochemists.
Ind/Abst Abstr. Bull. Inst. Paper Chem.; Abstr. Bull. Inst. Pap. Sci. Tech.; AGRICOLA [Select. Cov.]; Biocont. News Inf. (1991-); Biol. Abstr. (1991-); Chem. Abstr.; Curr. Aware. Biol. Sci., CABS; Curr. Cit.; Curr. Contents Life Sci.; EMBASE; GeoRef; Health Plan. Adminis.; Index Med. (1991-); Int. Aerosp. Abstr.; Life Sci. Collect.; Potato Abstr.; Protozoolog. Abstr.; Ref. Upd. Basic Ed.; Ref. Upd. Deluxe Ed.; Res. Alert [Full Cov.]; Rev. Plant Pathol.; Sci. Cit. Index; SCISEARCH; Soc. Sci. Cit. Index [Select. Cov.]; Weed Abstr.

LC TP248 **ISSN** 0736-6205
DD 660.6 US
CCC
NLM W1 BI918L **CODEN** BTNQDO
Pr Rev.
BIOTECHNIQUES. [BioTechniques]. **VFOAT** Bio Techniques. Vol. 1, No. 1 (March/April 1983)-. Periodical. English. Twelve times a year. $105.00. Eaton Publishing Company, 154 East Central Street, Natick MA 01760. **Tel** (508)655-8282, FAX (508)655-9910. **ED** James Ellingbol. cum. index. **Ad Acc. Circ:** 50,000 (ctrl). Documents available from The Genuine Article, CASDDS. ***Absorbed*** *Biochromatography, 0888-4404.*
Desc: Contains research reports and review articles concerning new laboratory techniques, methods and products of interest to scientists engaged in genetic engineering and general laboratory.
Ind/Abst Abstr. BioCommer.; AgBiotech News Inf.; AGRICOLA [Select. Cov.]; Anal. Abstr.; Anim. Breed.

Abstr.; Biol. Abstr.; Biotechnol. Res. Abstr.; Chem. Abstr. (1983-); Curr. Aware. Biol. Sci., CABS; Curr. Biotechnol.; Curr. Cit.; Curr. Contents Life Sci.; EMBASE; Field Crop Abstr.; Food Sci. Technol. Abstr.; Genet. Abstr.; Health Plan. Adminis.; Index Med.; Nucl. Acids Abstr.; Life Sci. Collect.; PESTDOC; Plant Breed. Abstr.; Ref. Upd. Basic Ed.; Ref. Upd. Deluxe Ed.; Res. Alert [Full Cov.]; Rev. Plant Pathol.; Sci. Cit. Index; SCISEARCH; Wheat Barley Trit. Abstr.

LC TP248
DD 660.6 UK
NLM Z 7914.B33; D484
•**BIOTECHNOLOGY ABSTRACTS. See** Biology-Abstracting, Bibliographies and Statistics.

LC TP248.2 .B55 **ISSN** 0734-9750
DD 660/.6/05 UK
CCC
NLM W1; BI918MF **CODEN** BIADDD
Pr Rev.
BIOTECHNOLOGY ADVANCES.
[Biotechnol. adv.]. Vol. 1, No. 1 (1983)-. Academic Scholarly Publication. English. Four times a year. $495.00. Pergamon Press, An Imprint of Elsevier Science Ltd., The Boulevard, Langford Lane, Kidlington, Oxford OX5 1GB United Kingdom. **Tel** 011 44 1865 843000, 011 44 1865 843699, FAX 011 44 1865 843010. **(Subscription address:** Elsevier Science Ltd. / Oxford Fulfillment Centre, PO Box 800, Kidlington OX5 1DX United Kingdom. **Tel** 011 44 865 843355.**) ED** Murray Moo Young. available on microfilm and microfiche from University Microfilms International (UMI); available on an online database from Elsevier Electronic Subscriptions (EES). Documents available from Article Express International, The Genuine Article, CASDDS, ADONIS.
Desc: Devoted to all areas of biotechnology including aspects of its disciplinary underpinnings in biology, chemistry and engineering. Provides reviews of advances in this field for students, researchers, managers, government and academia.
Ind/Abst ADONIS; AgBiotech News Inf.; AGRICOLA [Select. Cov.]; BioBusiness; Biodeter. Abstr. (19??-19??); Biostatistica; Chem. Abstr. (1983-); Curr. Aware. Biol. Sci., CABS; Curr. Biotechnol.; Curr. Cit.; Curr. Contents Agric. Biol. Environ. Sci.; Eng. Index Annu.; For. Prod. Abstr.; Index Sci. Rev. [Full Cov.]; Maize Abstr.; Nutr. Abstr. Rev., Ser. B, Live Feeds and Feed.; Oper. Res./Manage. Sci.; Life Sci. Collect. (1985-); PESTDOC; Plant Breed. Abstr.; Plant Genet. Resour. Abstr.; Postharvest News Inf.; Res. Alert [Full Cov.]; Sci. Cit. Index; SCISEARCH; Weed Abstr.

LC QP501 .J66 **ISSN** 0885-4513
DD 660/.6 US
CCC
NLM W1; BI918MJ **CODEN** BABIEC
Pr Rev.
BIOTECHNOLOGY AND APPLIED BIOCHEMISTRY. [Biotechnol. appl. biochem.]. **Added/Corp** International Union of Biochemistry. Vol. 8, No. 1 (Feb. 1986)-. Academic Scholarly Publication. English. Six times a year (including an annual subject index). $204.00. Portland Press Ltd., PO Box 32 Commerce Way, Colchester CO2 8HP Essex United Kingdom. **Tel** 011 44 1206 796351, FAX 011 44 1206 799331, telex 987275 BIOSOC G. **ED** P. N. Campbell. Documents available from The Genuine Article, BIOSIS Document Express, CASDDS. ***Continues** Journal of Applied Biochemistry, 0161-7354.*
Desc: A journal devoted to biochemistry and molecular biology, and the role they play in the development of biotechnology. Results of fundamental studies directly related to the design of new biotechnology, the improvement of existing biochemical processes, and the preparation, utilization, conversion, or application of biological materials are emphasized.
Ind/Abst Abstr. Bull. Inst. Pap. Sci. Tech.; AgBiotech News Inf.; AGRICOLA [Select. Cov.]; BioBusiness; Biodeter. Abstr.; Biol. Abstr. (1986-); Chem. Abstr. (1986-); Coal Abstr. (1986-); Curr. Aware. Biol. Sci., CABS; Curr. Biotechnol.; Curr. Cit.; Curr. Contents Agric. Biol. Environ. Sci.; Curr. Contents Life Sci.; EMBASE (1986-); Energy Res. Abstr. (1986-); Food Sci. Technol. Abstr.; Foods Adlibra; Genet. Abstr.; Health Plan. Adminis.; Immunol. Abstr.; Index Med. (1986-); Microbiol. Abstr. Sect. B (19??-19??); Microbiol. Abstr. Sect. A; Microbiol. Abstr. Sect. C; Life Sci. Collect. (1986-); PESTDOC; Protozoolog. Abstr.; Res. Alert [Full Cov.]; Rev. Agric. Entomol.; Rev. Med. Vet. Entomol.; Rev. Med. Vet. Mycology; Sci. Cit. Index; SCISEARCH.

LC QH324 .B5 **ISSN** 0006-3592
DD 574 US
CCC
NLM W1 BI918N **CODEN** BIBIAU
Pr Rev.
BIOTECHNOLOGY AND BIOENGINEERING. [Biotechnol. bioeng.]. **VFOAT** Biotechnology & Bioengineering. Vol. 4 (March 1962)-. Academic Scholarly Publication. English. Twenty-four times a year. $1944.00. John Wiley & Sons, Inc., 605 Third Avenue, New York NY 10158-0012. **Tel** (212)850-6000, (212)850-6645, FAX (212)850-6088, telex 12-7063. **(Subscription address:** John Wiley & Sons / UK, Baffins Lane, Chichester, West Sussex PO19 1UD United Kingdom. **Tel** 011 44 1243 779777, FAX 011 44 243 776128, telex 86290 WIBOOKG.**) ED** Eleftherios T. Papoutsakes. available on microfilm and microfiche from University Microfilms International (UMI). Documents available from Article Express International, The Genuine Article, BIOSIS Document Express, CASDDS, ADONIS. ***Continues** Journal of Biochemical and Microbiological Technology and Engineering.*
Desc: An international forum for original research on all aspects of biochemical and microbial technology, this journal's purview encompasses a wide range of disciplines. Included among the topics covered are insights into biotechnology in energy production and conservation, computer applications in fermentation technology and single-cell protein from renewable and nonrenewable sources.
Ind/Abst Abstr. Bull. Inst. Pap. Sci. Tech.; ADONIS; AgBiotech News Inf.; AGRICOLA [Select. Cov.]; Agric. Eng. Abstr. (1991-); AQUAREF; BioBusiness; Biodeter. Abstr. (19??-19??); Bioeng. Abstr.; Biol. Agric. Index; Biol. Abstr.; Biotechnol. Res. Abstr.; Chem. Abstr.; Chem. Titles; Coal Abstr.; Comput. Inf. Syst. Abstr. J. [Full Cov.]; Crop Physiol. Abstr.; Curr. Aware. Biol. Sci., CABS; Curr. Biotechnol.; Curr. Cit.; Curr. Contents Agric. Biol. Environ. Sci.; Curr. Contents Life Sci.; Dairy Sci. Abstr.; Ei Page One; Elect. Comm. Abstr.; EMBASE; Energy Res. Abstr.; Eng. Index Annu.; Environ. Eng. Abstr.; Food Sci. Technol. Abstr.; Foods Adlibra; For. Prod. Abstr. (1991-); For. Abstr.; Gas Abstr.; Health Plan. Adminis.; Hortic. Abstr.; INIS Atomindex [Micro.]; Int. Aerosp. Abstr.; Mater. Sci. Eng. Abstr.; Mech. Eng. Abstr.; Microbiol. Abstr. Sect. B; Microbiol. Abstr. Sect. A; Microbiol. Abstr. Sect. C; Nutr. Abstr. Rev., Ser. B, Live Feeds and Feed.; Life Sci. Collect.; PESTDOC; Plant Grow. Reg. Abstr.; Pollut. Abstr. Indexes; Proc. Chem. Eng.; Ref. Upd. Deluxe Ed.; Res. Alert [Full Cov.]; Rev. Agric. Entomol.; Rev. Med. Vet. Mycology; Rice Abstr.; Sci. Cit. Index; SCISEARCH; Solid State Supercond. Abstr.; Soyabean Abstr.; Sug. Indus. Abstr.; Theor. Chem. Eng.; Weed Abstr.

LC TP248 **ISSN** 0572-6565
DD 574.28 US
NLM W3 BI617 **CODEN** BIBSBR
BIOTECHNOLOGY AND BIOENGINEERING SYMPOSIUM.
[Biotechnol. bioeng. symp.]. No. 1 (1969)-. English. One time a year. Price varies per volume. John Wiley & Sons, Inc., 605 Third Avenue, New York NY 10158-0012. **Tel** (212)850-6000, (212)850-6645, FAX (212)850-6088, telex 12-7063. **(Subscription address:** John Wiley & Sons / UK, Baffins Lane, Chichester, West Sussex PO19 1UD United Kingdom. **Tel** 011 44 1243 779777, FAX 011 44 243 776128, telex 86290 WIBOOKG.**)** Documents available from Article Express International, BIOSIS Document Express, CASDDS.
Ind/Abst BioBusiness; Bioeng. Abstr.; Biol. Abstr.; Chem. Abstr.; Coal Abstr.; Curr. Biotechnol.; Curr. Contents Agric. Biol. Environ. Sci.; Curr. Contents Life Sci.; Dairy Sci. Abstr.; Ei Page One; EMBASE; Energy Res. Abstr. (Aug. 1977-); Eng. Index Annu.; Food Sci. Technol. Abstr.; INIS Atomindex [Micro.]; Nutr. Abstr. Rev., Ser. B, Live Feeds and Feed.; Nutr. Abstr. Rev., Ser. A, Hum. Exp.; Life Sci. Collect.; Proc. Chem. Eng.; Theor. Chem. Eng.

LC TP248
DD 660.6 BU
BIOTECHNOLOGY AND BIOTECHNOLOGICAL EQUIPMENT.
(19??)-. English (Bulgarian). Four times a year. $120.00. Diagnosis Press Ltd., 125 Tsarigradsko Boulevard, Bl 2520, Sofia 1113 Bulgaria. **Tel** 011 359 2 705176. Documents available from The Genuine Article.
Ind/Abst Res. Alert.

LC TP248
DD 660.6 NE
BIOTECHNOLOGY AND DEVELOPMENT MONITOR. Added/Corp Netherlands. Directoraat-Generaal Internationale Samenwerking. Universiteit van Amsterdam. **VFOAT** Monitor. No. 1 (Sept. 1989)-. Periodical. English. Documents available from The Genuine Article.
Ind/Abst Abstr. BioCommer.; Plant Genet. Resour. Abstr.; Res. Alert [Full Cov.].

LC TP248.13 .B56 **ISSN** 0264-8725
DD 660/.6/05 UK
CCC
NLM W1; BI918Q **CODEN** BGERES
BIOTECHNOLOGY & GENETIC ENGINEERING REVIEWS. [Biotechnol. genet. eng. rev.]. **VFOAT** Biotechnology and Genetic Engineering Reviews. Vol. 1 (1984)-. Academic Scholarly Publication. English. One time a year. $162.57. Intercept Ltd., PO Box 716, Andover Hampshire SP10 1YG United Kingdom. **Tel** 011 44 1264 334748, FAX 011 44 1264 334058, telex 41103 PEPSOS G. Index available. Documents available from The Genuine Article, CASDDS.
Desc: Articles covering developments in industrial, agricultural and medical applications of biotechnology (wide sense) with particular emphasis on the genetic manipulation of the organisms concerned.
Ind/Abst AGRICOLA [Select. Cov.]; BioBusiness (Vol. 1, 1984-); Chem. Abstr. (1984-); Curr. Biotechnol.; Curr. Cit.; Health Plan. Adminis.; Index Med. (Vol. 1, 1984-);; Index Sci. Rev. [Full Cov.]; PESTDOC; Potato Abstr.; Res. Alert [Full Cov.]; SCISEARCH.

LC TP248 **ISSN** 0261-6904
DD 660.6 UK
TITLE CHANGE
BIOTECHNOLOGY BULLETIN. [Biotechnol. bull.]. (1982)-(1995). Bulletin. English. Legal Studies and Services Publishing Ltd., IBC/37-41 Mortimer Street, Mortimer House, London W1N 7RJ United Kingdom. **Tel** 011 44 171 6374383, FAX 011 44 171 9362303. **(Subscription address:** IBC Subscription Services, IBC House, Vickers Drive, Weybridge, Surrey KT13 OXS United Kingdom. **Tel** 011 44 1932 354020.**) ED** John Elkington. ***Merged into** Biotechnology Business News.*
Ind/Abst Abstr. BioCommer.; AGRICOLA [Select. Cov.]; Chem. Bus. Bull.; Chem. Bus. NewsBase (1989-); Chem. Bus. Update; Curr. Biotechnol.

LC TP248
DD 660.6 UK
BIOTECHNOLOGY BUSINESS NEWS.
(199?)-. Newsletter. English. Twenty-four times a year. $795.71. Financial Times Magazines, Greystoke Place, Fetter Lane, London EC4A 1ND United Kingdom. **Tel** 011 44 171 8316577. available on an online database (files 16,636/Full-Text) from DIALOG. ***Absorbed** Biotechnology Bulletin.*
Ind/Abst PROMT [Full Txt.]; PTS Newsl. Database [Full Txt.].

LC TP248 **ISSN** 0965-9595
DD 660.6 UK
BIOTECHNOLOGY BUSINESS NEWS.
[Biotechnol. bus. news]. (1991)-. Newsletter. English. Twenty-six times a year. £390.00 UK; £414.00 other. Financial Times Magazines, Greystoke Place, Fetter Lane, London EC4A 1ND United Kingdom. **Tel** 011 44 171 8316577.
Ind/Abst Abstr. BioCommer.

ISSN 0892-7987
DD 338 US
BIOTECHNOLOGY BUSINESS REPORT. [Biotechnol. bus. rep.]. (1986)-. Periodical. English. Twelve times a year. Quest Ventures, PO Box 146671, Chicago IL 60614-6671.
Desc: Written for business professionals interested in the commercial development of genetic engineering and technology. News and editorial articles by industry experts address joint ventures, new products, marketing strategies and patent positions in biotech.

LC TP248.13 .B58 **ISSN** 1057-607X
DD 016 US
BIOTECHNOLOGY CITATION INDEX.
(BIOTECHNOLOGY CITATION INDEX [COMPUTER FILE].). [Biotechnol. cit. index]. **Added/Corp** Institute for Scientific Information. (Jul/Aug 1991)-. English. Irregular. $1969.00. Institute for Scientific Information, 3501 Market Street, Philadelphia PA 19104. **Tel** (215)386-0100, (800)523-1850, FAX (215)386-6362, telex 84-5305. **(Subscription address:** Institute for Scientific Information, PO Box 71416, Chicago IL 60694. **)**
Desc: Covers current literature on antiviral and anticancer therapy, molecular and clinical genetics, and molecular microbiology.

LC TP248.13 .B5755 **ISSN** 1055-2162
DD 660/.6/05 US
NLM W1; BI918PH **CODEN** BCUPE6
BIOTECHNOLOGY, CURRENT PROGRESS. [Biotechnol. curr. prog.]. **VFOAT** Biotechnology. Vol. 1 (1991)-. Periodical. English. Irregular. $68.00. Technomic Publishing Company, Inc., 851 New Holland Avenue, Box 3535, Lancaster PA 17604. **Tel** (717)291-5609, (800)233-9936, FAX (717)295-4538. Documents available from BIOSIS Document Express.
Ind/Abst Biol. Abstr. (1991-).

LC TP248.3 .I56 **ISSN** 1059-7352
DD 660/.6/025 US
CCC
NLM QT 22.1; B616b
BIOTECHNOLOGY DIRECTORY (NEW YORK, N.Y.), THE. (THE BIOTECHNOLOGY DIRECTORY.). [Biotechnol. dir.]. (1985)-. Directory. English. One time a year (Jan.). $275.00. Stockton Press, 345 Park Avenue South, 10th Floor, New York NY 10010. **Tel** (800)221-2123, (212)689-9200. **ED** J. Coombs. Index available (bound in Dec. issue). ***Continues** International Biotechnology Directory, 0265-3877.*
Desc: Contains information on biotechnology industries, biochemical engineering and bionics.

LC TP248.13 .B576 **ISSN** 0955-6621
US
NLM W1; BI918LDK
CEASED
BIOTECHNOLOGY EDUCATION.
[Biotechnol. educ.]. (1989)-Vol. 3, No. 4. Periodical. English. Helix Publishing, 1 Howard Court, 94-96 Blackheath Hill, Greenwich, London SE10 8AF United Kingdom. **ED** Paul Wymer. Documents available from The Genuine Article.
Desc: Provides an enabling resource to teachers of biology, biochemistry and allied subjects who wish to introduce aspects of biotechnology into their existing courses. Articles give details of simple, tried and tested

class experiments to illustrate practical applications.
Ind/Abst AgBiotech News Inf.; Curr. Aware. Biol. Sci., CABS; Curr. Index J. Educ.; Res. Alert [Full Cov.].

LC TP248.13 .J353 **ISSN** 0935-1043
DD 660/.6 GW
NLM W1; JA168

BIOTECHNOLOGY FOCUS. [Biotechnol. focus]. (1988)-. English (translations available in German). Irregular. John Wiley & Sons, Inc., 605 Third Avenue, New York NY 10158-0012. **Tel** (212)850-6000, (212)850-6645, FAX (212)850-6088, telex 12-7063.

LC QD415 **ISSN** 0938-5584
DD 574.192 GW
UDC 57.08

BIOTECHNOLOGY (FRANKFURT 1991). **VFOAT** Biotechnology : Apparatus, Plant, and Equipment. (1991)-. Periodical. English. Twelve times a year. $244.00. Royal Society of Chemistry, Thomas Graham House, Science Park, Cambridge CB4 4WF United Kingdom. **Tel** 011 44 1223 420066, FAX 011 44 1223 423623, telex 818293 ROYAL. **(Subscription address:** Royal Society of Chemistry, Turpin Distribution Services Ltd., Blackhorse Road, Letchworth, Hertfordshire SG6 1HN United Kingdom. **Tel** 011 44 1462 672555, FAX 011 44 1462 480947.**)**
Desc: Contains abstracts on the practical methods and hardware used by biotechnologists, with emphasis on environmental and safety aspects, downstream processing, microbiological corrosion and the control, design and construction of biochemical reactors.

ISSN 1052-6153
DD 660 US
NLM W1; BI918PQ **CODEN** BHANE3

BIOTECHNOLOGY HANDBOOKS. [Biotechnol. handb.]. Vol. 1 (1987)-. Monographic series. English. Irregular. Price varies per volume. Plenum Press, 233 Spring Street, New York NY 10013-1578. **Tel** (212)620-8000, (800)221-9369, FAX (212)463-0742, (212)807-1047, telex 23/421139. **ED** Tony Atkinson and Roger F. Sherwood.
Ind/Abst AGRICOLA [Select. Cov.]; Curr. Cit.

LC TP248 **ISSN** 0934-943X
DD 660 US
CCC

BIOTECHNOLOGY IN AGRICULTURE AND FORESTRY. [Biotechnol. agricult. for.]. (1986)-. Monographic series. English. Irregular. Price varies per volume. Birkhaeuser Boston Books, Springer Verlag, POB 19386, Newark NJ 07195. **Tel** (201)348-4033. **ED** Y.P.S. Bajaj.
Ind/Abst Curr. Cit.

ISSN 0891-9283
DD 620 US
CEASED

BIOTECHNOLOGY IN JAPAN NEWSSERVICE. [Biotechnol. Jpn. newsserv.]. **Added/Corp** Japan Pacific Associates. **VFOAT** Biotechnology in Japan. (198?)-(Dec. 1993). Periodical. English. Japan Pacific Association, 467 Hamilton Avenue/Suite 2, Palo Alto CA 94301. **Tel** (415)322-8441, FAX (415)322-8454. **ED** Yoriko Kishimoto. ctrl circ.
Desc: Covers biotechnology trends and developments in Japan for biotechnology, technical, or business managers.
Ind/Abst Abstr. BioCommer.; Curr. Biotechnol.; Curr. Cit.

LC TP248
DD 660.6 US

BIOTECHNOLOGY IN JAPAN YEARBOOK. **Added/Corp** Nikkei Biotechnology. Japan Pacific Associates. (1990/1991)-. English. Japan Pacific Association, 467 Hamilton Avenue/Suite 2, Palo Alto CA 94301. **Tel** (415)322-8441, FAX (415)322-8454.

LC TP248 **ISSN** 0277-9773
DD 660.6 US

BIOTECHNOLOGY INVESTMENT OPPORTUNITIES. [Biotechnol. investm. oppor.]. **VFOAT** Biotechnology. (Sept. 1981)-. Periodical. English. Twelve times a year. $195.00 US; $220.00 other. High Tech Publishing Company, 10 Ridge Road, PO Box 1923, Brattleboro VT 05301. **Tel** (802)254-3539. available on an online database from NEWSNET; DIALOG; DATA-STAR; and BRS.
Ind/Abst PTS Newsl. Database [Full Txt.].

LC KF3827.G4 A132 **ISSN** 0730-031X
DD 344.73/095 347.30495 US
NLM W1; BI918R **CODEN** BLREEL

BIOTECHNOLOGY LAW REPORT. **See** Law.

LC QR53 .B536 **ISSN** 0141-5492
DD 660/.6/05 UK
UDC 663.15 CCC
NLM W1 BI918T **CODEN** BILED3
Pr Rev.

BIOTECHNOLOGY LETTERS. [Biotechnol. lett.]. Vol. 1 (1979)-. Academic Scholarly Publication. English. Twelve times a year. $590.00. Chapman & Hall, 2-6 Boundary Row, London SE1 8HN United Kingdom. **Tel** 011 44 171 8650066, FAX 011 44 171 5229623, telex 290164 CHAPMA G. **(Subscription address:** International Thomson Publishing Services Ltd., North Way Andover, Hampshire SP10 5BE United Kingdom. **Tel** 011 44 1264 332424.**)** **ED** J. D. Bulock. **Ad Acc. Circ:** 1,000. Documents available from The Genuine Article, BIOSIS Document Express, CASDDS, Documents on Demand.
Desc: Short original communications of new work in any topic relevant to the practical applications of biological reactions including process and reactor design.
Ind/Abst AgBiotech News Inf.; AGRICOLA [Select. Cov.]; BioBusiness; Biocont. News Inf. (19??-19??); Biodeter. Abstr. (19??-19??); Biol. Abstr.; Biotechnol. Res. Abstr.; Chem. Abstr.; Chem. Titles; Curr. Aware. Biol. Sci., CABS; Curr. Biotechnol.; Curr. Cit.; Curr. Contents Agric. Biol. Environ. Sci.; Curr. Contents Life Sci.; Dairy Sci. Abstr.; EMBASE; Energy Inf. Abstr.; Environ. Abstr.; Food Sci. Technol. Abstr.; Foods Adlibra; For. Prod. Abstr. (1991-); For. Abstr.; Genet. Abstr.; Health Saf. Sci. Abstr.; Hortic. Abstr.; Immunol. Abstr.; Maize Abstr.; Microbiol. Abstr. Sect. B; Microbiol. Abstr. Sect. A; Microbiol. Abstr. Sect. C; Nutr. Abstr. Rev., Ser. A, Hum. Exp.; Life Sci. Collect.; PESTDOC; Plant Genet. Resour. Abstr.; Plant Grow. Reg. Abstr.; Pollut. Abstr. Indexes; Ref. Upd. Deluxe Ed.; Res. Alert [Full Cov.]; Rev. Agric. Entomol.; Rev. Med. Vet. Entomol.; Sci. Cit. Index; SCISEARCH; Soyabean Abstr.; Sug. Indus. Abstr.; Weed Abstr.

LC TP248 **ISSN** 0930-8938
DD 660.6 GW
NLM W1; BI18LF **CODEN** BIMOE5

BIOTECHNOLOGY MONOGRAPHS. [Biotechnol. monogr.]. Vol. 1 (1985)-. Academic Scholarly Publication. English. Irregular. Price varies per volume. Springer-Verlag GmbH & Company KG, Heidelberger Platz 3, D-14197 Berlin Germany. **Tel** 011 49 30 8207223, FAX 011 49 30 8214091, telex 183 319 SPBLN D. **(Subscription address:** Springer-Verlag New York Inc. / North America, PO Box 2485, Journal Fulfillment, Secaucus NJ 07096. **Tel** (201)348-4033, (800)777-4643, FAX (201)348-4505.**)** **ED** S. Aiba, L.T. Fan, A. Fiechter, J. Klein, K. Schuegerl. Documents available from BIOSIS Document Express, CASDDS.
Desc: Series covering all aspects of biotechnology including biomedical engineering.
Ind/Abst Biol. Abstr. (1985-); Chem. Abstr. (1985-).

LC TP248 **ISSN** 0738-4076
DD 660.6 US

BIOTECHNOLOGY MONTHLY UPDATE. [Biotechnol. mon. update]. **Added/Corp** G. V. Olsen Associates. **VFOAT** Biotechnology. (19??)-. English. Twelve times a year. $150.00 US; $175.00 other. G V Olsen Associates, 123 Picketts Ridge Road, West Redding CT 06896. **Tel** (203)938-4188, FAX (203)938-4186. **ED** Gustav V. Olsen. **Circ:** 75.

LC TP248 **ISSN** 0275-7559
DD 660.6 US

BIOTECHNOLOGY (NEW YORK, N.Y. : 1983). (BIOTECHNOLOGY.). [Biotechnology]. (1987)-. Periodical. English. Six times a year. $78.00. Bio/Technology, Subscription Department, PO Box 316, Martinsville NJ 08836. **Tel** (212)477-9600. **ED** Douglas McCormich. **Bk Rev. Ad Acc. Circ:** 15,000.
Desc: Industrial biology, news research products and techniques from start to full scale processes profiles on films and personalities.
Ind/Abst Abstr. BioCommer.; BioBusiness; For. Prod. Abstr.; Genet. Abstr.; Maize Abstr.; Ornamental Hort.; Plant Breed. Abstr.; Plant Grow. Reg. Abstr.; Potato Abstr.; Ref. Upd. Deluxe Ed.; Rice Abstr.

ISSN 0273-3226
DD 660 US
CCC
NLM W1; BI918TG **CODEN** BINWEY

BIOTECHNOLOGY NEWS. [Biotechnol. news]. Vol. 1, No. 1 (Jan. 1, 1981)-. Periodical. English. Thirty times a year. $538.00. CTB International Publishing Inc., PO Box 218, Maplewood NJ 07040. **Tel** (201)379-7749, FAX (201)379-1158. **ED** Christopher Brogna. Index available (2/yr). cum. index. **Bk Rev. Ad Acc.**
Desc: Covers genetic engineering, enzymes, diagnostics, fermentation, monoclonals, applied molecular biology, tissue culture, plant biotechnology and microbial technology.
Ind/Abst Abstr. BioCommer.; AGRICOLA [Select. Cov.]; Chem. Bus. Bull.; Chem. Bus. NewsBase (1989-); Chem. Bus. Update; Chem. Ind. Notes; Curr. Biotechnol.

LC TP248
DD 660.6 US

BIOTECHNOLOGY NEWSWATCH. Vol. 7, No. 23 Dec. 7, (1987)-. Newsletter. English. Twenty-four times a year. $875.00. McGraw Hill Publishing Company, Inc., 1221 Avenue of the Americas, New York NY 10020. **Tel** (212)512-6410, (800)525-5003, FAX (212)512-6111. **(Subscription address:** McGraw Hill Management Information Center, 1221 Avenue of the Americas, 36th Floor, New York NY 10020. **Tel** (800)223-6180, (212)512-6410.**)** available on an online database from Dow Jones News/Retrieval; NEWSNET; Lexis-Nexis; and (file 624/Full-Text) DIALOG. ***Continues McGraw-Hill's Biotechnology Newswatch, 0275-3685.***
Ind/Abst AGRICOLA [Select. Cov.]; Chem. Bus. Bull.; Chem. Bus. NewsBase (1989-); Chem. Bus. Update; Curr. Biotechnol.; Trade Ind. Index.

LC TP248.13 .B578 **ISSN** 8756-7938
DD 660/.6/05 US
CCC
NLM W1; BI918V **CODEN** BIPRET
Pr Rev.

BIOTECHNOLOGY PROGRESS. [Biotechnol. prog.]. **Added/Corp** American Institute of Chemical Engineers. American Institute of Chemical Engineers. Food, Pharmaceutical, and Bioengineering Division. American Chemical Society. **VFOAT** BiotechnologyProgress. Vol. 1, No. 1 (March 1985)-. Academic Scholarly Publication. English. Six times a year. $416.00. American Chemical Society, 1155 Sixteenth Street Northwest, Washington DC 20036. **Tel** (800)333-9511, (800)227-5558, (614)447-3776, FAX (202)447-3671. **(Subscription address:** American Chemical Society / Ohio, Department L 0011, Columbus OH 43268-0011.**)** **ED** Jerome S. Schultz. **Acid Free.** available on microfilm and microfiche from University Microfilms International (UMI). Documents available from Article Express International, The Genuine Article, BIOSIS Document Express, CASDDS, Documents on Demand.
Desc: Focuses on the application of fundamental chemical and engineering principles to biological phenomena and to processor product design.
Ind/Abst Abstr. BioCommer.; AGRICOLA [Select. Cov.]; Appl. Sci. Technol. Index (1991-); BioBusiness; Biodeter. Abstr. (19??-19??); Biol. Abstr. (1985-); Biotechnol. Res. Abstr.; Chem. Abstr. (1985-); Coal Abstr.; Curr. Aware. Biol. Sci., CABS; Curr. Cit.; Curr. Contents Agric. Biol. Environ. Sci.; Eng. Index Annu.; Environ. Abstr.; Food Sci. Technol. Abstr.; Foods Adlibra; Gas Abstr.; Microbiol. Abstr. Sect. B; PESTDOC; Ref. Upd. Deluxe Ed.; Res. Alert [Full Cov.]; Rice Abstr.; SCISEARCH; Sug. Indus. Abstr.

LC TP248.2 .B57 **ISSN** 0733-5709
DD 660/.6 US
NLM ZQW 25; B616
CEASED

BIOTECHNOLOGY RESEARCH ABSTRACTS. **See** Biology-Abstracting, Bibliographies and Statistics.

LC AZ **ISSN** 0749-0372
DD 001 US
NLM W1; BI918Y **CODEN** BSOFEO
TITLE CHANGE

BIOTECHNOLOGY SOFTWARE. [Biotechnol. softw.]. **VFOAT** Biotechnology Software Report; BSR. Vol. 1, No. 1 (Sept./Oct. 1984)-(1994). Periodical. English. Mary Ann Liebert Inc., 2 Madison Avenue, Larchmont NY 10538. **Tel** (914)834-3100, (800)M-LIEBERT, FAX (212)289-4697. **ED** Kevin Ahern, Indira Rajagopal. ***Continued by Biotechnology Software Journal, 1077-4890.***
Desc: Interface between computers and the researcher who is not a computer scientist. Prevents the duplication of effort that exists when a new computer application is designed that has already been devised in another laboratory.

LC TP248 **ISSN** 0951-208X
DD 660.6 UK
CCC
NLM W1; BI9184 **CODEN** BTECE6
Pr Rev.

BIOTECHNOLOGY TECHNIQUES. [Biotechnol. tech.]. Vol. 1, No. 1 (Mar. 1987)-. Periodical. English. Twelve times a year. $474.00. Chapman & Hall, 2-6 Boundary Row, London SE1 8HN United Kingdom. **Tel** 011 44 171 8650066, FAX 011 44 171 5229623, telex 290164 CHAPMA G. **(Subscription address:** International Thomson Publishing Services Ltd., North Way Andover, Hampshire SP10 5BE United Kingdom. **Tel** 011 44 1264 332424.**)** **ED** Colin Ratledge. Index available. **Bk Rev. Ad Acc. Circ:** 600. available on microfilm from University Microfilms International (UMI). Documents available from The Genuine Article, BIOSIS Document Express, CASDDS, Documents on Demand.
Desc: Provides working accounts of innovative and improved procedures that have been demonstrated experimentally.
Ind/Abst AgBiotech News Inf.; AGRICOLA [Select. Cov.]; Anal. Abstr.; BioBusiness; Biodeter. Abstr. (19??-19??); Biol. Abstr. (1987-); Chem. Abstr.; Curr. Aware. Biol. Sci., CABS; Curr. Biotechnol.; Curr. Cit.; Curr. Contents Agric. Biol. Environ. Sci.; Dairy Sci. Abstr.; Environ. Abstr.; Field Crop Abstr.; For. Prod. Abstr. (1991-); Immunol. Abstr.; Microbiol. Abstr. Sect. B; Microbiol. Abstr. Sect. A; Microbiol. Abstr. Sect. C; Nutr. Abstr. Rev., Ser. B, Live Feeds and Feed.; PESTDOC; Res. Alert [Full Cov.]; Rice Abstr.; Weed Abstr.

LC RM666.R37 B56 **ISSN** 0898-2848
DD 610/.28 US
CCC
NLM W1; BI9185 **CODEN** BITHEJ
Pr Rev. **CEASED**

BIOTECHNOLOGY THERAPEUTICS. [Biotechnol. ther.]. Vol. 1, No. 1 (1989)-Vol. 5 (April 1994). Periodical. English. Marcel Dekker Inc., 270 Madison Avenue, New York NY 10016. **Tel** (212)696-9000, (800)228-1160, FAX (212)685-4540, telex 421419. **(Subscription address:** Marcel Dekker Inc., PO Box 5017, Monticello NY 12701. **Tel** (800)228-1160.**)** **ED** Steven Gillis, Arthur Ammann and Susanna

Cunningham-Rundles. **Ad Acc.** ctrl circ. Documents available from The Genuine Article, ADONIS.
Desc: This journal is devoted solely to presenting results of preclinical and clinical trials throughout all phases of biotechnologically produced therapeutic agents. Emphasizes the utility of a broad array of rapidly emerging products from molecular biology for potential and actual medicine practice. This journal features original contributions by both researchers and clinicians comprising basic and applied research articles, review articles, short reports, conference papers, and symposia as topical volumes. It details these agents' success in the treatment of the entire range of diseases, including infections, malignancies, immunological disease, hematologic disorders, and others.
Ind/Abst ADONIS; Curr. Aware. Biol. Sci., CABS; Curr. Cit.; EMBASE; Index Med.; Ref. Upd. Deluxe Ed.; Res. Alert [Full Cov.].

LC TP248 **ISSN** 1061-3471
DD 660.6 US
BIOTECHNOLOGY WEEK. (1992)-. Periodical. English. Twenty-four times a year. Cahners Publishing Company, 249 West 17th Street, New York NY 10011. **Tel** (212)645-0067, FAX (212)242-6987. **(Subscription address:** Cahners Publishing Company / Colorado, Paid Subscription Service Center, PO Box 7610, Highlands Ranch CO 80126-7610. **Tel** (303)470-4466, FAX (303)470-4691.) Documents available from The Genuine Article.
Ind/Abst Res. Alert [Full Cov.].

LC TP248 **ISSN** 0864-4551
DD 660.6 CU
NLM W1; BI918LB
Pr Rev.
BIOTECNOLOGIA APLICADA : REVISTA DE LA SOCIEDAD IBEROLATINOAMERICANA PARA INVESTIGACIONES SOBRE INTERFERON Y BIOTECNOLOGIA EN SALUD. **Added/Corp** Sociedad Iberolatinoamericana para Investigaciones sobre Interferon y Biotecnologia en Salud. Vol. 7, No. 1 (1990)-. Periodical. English (Spanish). Three times a year (April, Aug., Dec.). $60.00. Palacio de las Convenciones, PO Box 6072, 6 Habana Cuba. **ED** Ileana Filgueiras (21-8854). Index available (Published in April). cum. index. **Ad Acc, Adv Mgr:** Alfredo Delgado, **Tel** 21-8854. **Circ:** 3,000 (ctrl). Documents available from CASDDS. ***Continues*** *Interferon y Biotecnologia, 0258-9222.*
Desc: This journal is the vehicle of communication among Latin American specialists in the fields of biotechnology and its applications. This journal publishes original articles and reviews.
Ind/Abst Chem. Abstr.; EMBASE [Select. Cov.]; Rev. Med. Vet. Entomol.; Soils Fert.

LC TP248 **ISSN** 0234-2758
DD 660.6 RU
CODEN BTKNEZ
BIOTEHNOLOGIA (MOSKVA). (BIOTEKHNOLOGIIA.). [Biotehnologia]. (1985)-. Academic Scholarly Publication. Russian (table of contents in English). Six times a year. $119.95. **(Subscription address:** East View Publications Inc., 3020 Harbor Lane North, Suite 110, Minneapolis MN 55447. **Tel** (800)477-1005, (612)550-0961, FAX (612)559-2931.) Documents available from BIOSIS Document Express, CASDDS.
Ind/Abst BioBusiness; Biocont. News Inf.; Biodeter. Abstr.; Biol. Abstr.; Chem. Abstr. (1985-); Curr. Biotechnol.; Hortic. Abstr.; Index Vet.; PESTDOC; Postharvest News Inf.; Potato Abstr.; Rev. Med. Vet. Entomol.

LC TP248.19.S65 B56 **ISSN** 0890-734X
DD 660/.6/0947 US
CCC
NLM W1; SO996C **CODEN** SOVBE2
TITLE CHANGE
BIOTEKHNOLOGIIA. (SOVIET BIOTECHNOLOGY.). [Soviet biotechnol.]. **VFOAT** Biotekhnologiya. No. 1 (1986)-(1993). Periodical. English (translations available in Russian). Allerton Press Inc., 150 Fifth Avenue, New York NY 10011. **Tel** (212)924-3950, FAX (212)463-9684, telex 427441 ALPRES. ***Continued by*** *Russian Biotechnology.*
Ind/Abst AGRICOLA [Select. Cov.]; Biocont. News Inf. (1991-); Biodeter. Abstr. (1991-); Dairy Sci. Abstr.; For. Prod. Abstr. (1991-); Hortic. Abstr.; Microbiol. Abstr. Sect. A; Nutr. Abstr. Rev., Ser. B, Live Feeds and Feed.; Nutr. Abstr. Rev., Ser. A, Hum. Exp.; Rev. Agric. Entomol.; Rev. Med. Vet. Entomol.; Rev. Plant Pathol.; Soils Fert.; Sug. Indus. Abstr.; Wheat Barley Trit. Abstr.

LC TP248.13 .B585
DD 661.8 BU
BIOTEKHNOLOGIIA & BIOTEKHNIKA : IZDANIE NA NATSIONALNIIA SUVET PO BIOTEKHNOLOGIIA KUM DURZHAVNIIA KOMITET ZA IZSLEDVANIIA I TEKHNOLOGII. **Added/Corp** Natsionalen Suvet po Biotekhnologiia Kum Durzhavniia Komitet za Izsledvaniia i Tekhnologii (Bulgaria). **VFOAT** Biotekhnologiia i Biotekhnika; Biotechnology and Bioindustry; Biotechnology & Bioindustry; Journal of Biotechnology and Bioindustry. (19??)-. Periodical. Bulgarian (English; summaries and/or abstracts in Russian). Two times a year. DM75.00. **(Subscription address:** Kubon & Sagner, ABT Zeitschriftenimport, D 80328 Munich Germany. **Tel** 011 49 89 54218130.) Documents available from CASDDS.
Ind/Abst Chem. Abstr.

ISSN 0892-1903
DD 338 US
CCC
NLM W1; BI192G **CODEN** BIVIEW
BIOVENTURE VIEW. [BioVenture view]. **VFOAT** Bio Venture View. (1986)-. Newsletter. English. Eleven times a year (Aug./Sept. issues combined). $550.00. BioVenture Publishing Inc., 32 West 25th Avenue, Suite 203, San Mateo CA 94403-2236. **Tel** (415)574-7128, FAX (415)574-8319. **ED** Dr. Cynthia Robbins Roth. **Ad Acc, Adv Mgr:** Bill Stanley, **Tel** (408)732-2555. **Circ:** 850 (ctrl). available on an online database from Compuserve Inc.
Desc: Biotechnology newsletter that circulates nationally and internationally by and to company directors, corporate executives, venture capitalists, analysts and major industry investors.
Ind/Abst Abstr. BioCommer.; AGRICOLA [Select. Cov.]; Trade Ind. Index.

LC TP248
DD 660.6 US
BMES BULLETIN. (1976)-. Bulletin. English. Four times a year. Biomedical Engineering Society, PO Box 2399, Culver City CA 90231. **Tel** (310)618-9322.

LC TP248 **ISSN** 0255-7924
DD 660.6 CR
BOLETIN DE BIOTECNOLOGIA : ORGANO DE DIFUSION DEL COMITE PERMANENTE DE BIOTECNOLOGIA DE LA ASOCIACION INTERCIENCIA. **Added/Corp** Consejo Nacional de Investigaciones Cientificas y Tecnologicas (Costa Rica) Asociacion Interciencia. Comite Permanente de Biotecnologia. (198?)-. Periodical. Spanish (English). Two times a year. **ED** Editorial Board.
Ind/Abst Trop. Dis. Bull.

LC RC **ISSN** 0967-4845
DD 616 UK
CCC
NLM W1; BR508 **CODEN** BJMSEO
•**BRITISH JOURNAL OF BIOMEDICAL SCIENCE.** **See** Medical Sciences.

ISSN 1040-9416
DD 620 US
BT CATALYST. [BT catal.]. **Added/Corp** North Carolina Biotechnology Center. **VAT** Biotechnology Catalyst. Vol. 1 No. 1 (Nov. 1987)-. Periodical. English. Twelve times a year. Free. North Carolina Biotechnology Center, PO Box 13547, Research Triangle Park NC 27709-3547. available on an online database (file 636/Full-Text) from DIALOG.
Ind/Abst Abstr. BioCommer.; PTS Newsl. Database [Full Txt.].

ISSN 1188-455X
DD 620.8 CN
CANADIAN BIOTECH NEWS. [Can. biotech news]. Vol. 1, No. 1 (Jan. 15, 1992)-. Periodical. English. Twenty-six times a year. 360.15Can$. Canadian Biotech News Service, 340 Richmond Road, Ottawa Ontario K2A 0E8 Canada. **Tel** (613)726-0115, FAX (613)726-7344. **ED** Peter Winter (editor's address: 20 Stone Park Lane, Nepean, Ontario K2H 9P4 Canada). Index available (published separately). cum. index. **Bk Rev**, (Qty: 50). **Ad Acc, Adv Mgr:** Carole Cheetham. **Circ:** 3,000. available on microfilm; available on microfiche. ***Continues*** *New Biotech Busine$$ Canada., 0838-5777.*
Desc: Progress and prospects of the Canadian biotech industry. Details on companies, products, and emerging research and development.
Ind/Abst Abstr. BioCommer.

ISSN 0884-7479
DD 610 US
CODEN CBUBE2
CAS BIOTECH UPDATES. BIOSENSORS. **Added/Corp** American Chemical Society. Chemical Abstracts Service. **VFOAT** Biosensors. **VAT** Chemical Abstracts Service Biotech Updates. Biosensors. (198?)-. Periodical. English. Twenty-six times a year. $220.00. Chemical Abstracts Service, (Subsidiary of The American Chemical Society), 2540 Olentangy River Road, PO Box 3012, Columbus OH 43210-0012. **Tel** (614)447-3731, (800)753-4227, FAX (614)447-3751. **(Subscription address:** Chemical Abstracts Service, Customer Service Department, PO Box 3012, Columbus OH 43210. **Tel** (800)848-6538, (614)447-3600.)
Desc: Provides information on the use of immobilized enzymes, immunological components, and cell fractions or whole cells for biochemical analysis, body fluid monitoring, and diagnostics. Coverage includes electrodes, thermistors, transistors and light-detection-type biosensors in the detection and determination of sample components.

ISSN 1040-709X
DD 574 US
CODEN CUCCEE
CAS BIOTECH UPDATES. CELL & TISSUE CULTURE. [CAS biotech updates, Cell tissue cult.]. **Added/Corp** American Chemical Society. Chemical Abstracts Service. **VFOAT** CAS Biotech Updates. Cell and Tissue Culture; Cell & Tissue Culture; Cell and Tissue Culture. **VAT** Chemical Abstracts Service Biotech Updates. Cell & Tissue Culture. (Jan. 9, 1989)-. English. Twenty-six times a year. $220.00. Chemical Abstracts Service, (Subsidiary of The American Chemical Society), 2540 Olentangy River Road, PO Box 3012, Columbus OH 43210-0012. **Tel** (614)447-3731, (800)753-4227, FAX (614)447-3751. **(Subscription address:** Chemical Abstracts Service, Customer Service Department, PO Box 3012, Columbus OH 43210. **Tel** (800)848-6538, (614)447-3600.)

ISSN 0884-7452
DD 574 US
CODEN CBEBEO
CAS BIOTECH UPDATES. ENVIRONMENTAL BIOTECHNOLOGY. [CAS biotech updates, Environ. biotechnol.]. **Added/Corp** American Chemical Society. Chemical Abstracts Service. **VFOAT** Environmental Biotechnology. **VAT** Chemical Abstract Service Biotech Updates Environmental Biotechnology. (Jan. 13, 1986)-. Periodical. English. Twenty-six times a year. $220.00. Chemical Abstracts Service, (Subsidiary of The American Chemical Society), 2540 Olentangy River Road, PO Box 3012, Columbus OH 43210-0012. **Tel** (614)447-3731, (800)753-4227, FAX (614)447-3751. **(Subscription address:** Chemical Abstracts Service, Customer Service Department, PO Box 3012, Columbus OH 43210. **Tel** (800)848-6538, (614)447-3600.)

ISSN 1040-7081
DD 660 US
CODEN CUEBEL
CAS BIOTECH UPDATES. ENZYMES IN BIOTECHNOLOGY. [CAS biotech updates, Enzym. biotechnol.]. **Added/Corp** American Chemical Society. Chemical Abstracts Service. **VFOAT** Enzymes in Biotechnology. **VAT** Chemical Abstracts Service Biotech Updates. Enzymes in Biotechnology. (Jan. 9, 1989)-. English. Twenty-six times a year. $220.00. Chemical Abstracts Service, (Subsidiary of The American Chemical Society), 2540 Olentangy River Road, PO Box 3012, Columbus OH 43210-0012. **Tel** (614)447-3731, (800)753-4227, FAX (614)447-3751. **(Subscription address:** Chemical Abstracts Service, Customer Service Department, PO Box 3012, Columbus OH 43210. **Tel** (800)848-6538, (614)447-3600.)

LC QD415
DD 574.192 CI
NLM W1; CH239 **CODEN** CBEQEZ
Pr Rev.
CHEMICAL AND BIOCHEMICAL ENGINEERING QUARTERLY. **See** Engineering-Chemical Engineering.

LC QD415 **ISSN** 0277-4038
DD 574.192 UK
NLM WI CH248F
CHEMICAL ENGINEERING ASPECTS OF BIOMEDICINE RESEARCH STUDIES SERIES. **See** Engineering-Chemical Engineering.

LC QD415 **ISSN** 0722-6764
DD 543 GW
NLM W1; CL122E **CODEN** CCLBEW
CHEMIE IN LABOR UND BIOTECHNIK : CLB. **See** Chemistry and Chemicals-Analytical Chemistry.

LC QD415 **ISSN** 0392-839X
DD 574.192 IT
CODEN CHOGDS
CHIMICA OGGI. **See** Biology-Biological Chemistry.

LC TP248.13 .C48 **ISSN** 1042-749X
DD 660/.6 US
CCC
NLM W1; CH761
CHINESE JOURNAL OF BIOTECHNOLOGY. [Chin. j. biotechnol.]. Vol. 4, No. 1 (1989)-. Periodical. English (translations available in Chinese). Four times a year. $460.00. Allerton Press Inc., 150 Fifth Avenue, New York NY 10011. **Tel** (212)924-3950, FAX (212)463-9684, telex 427441 ALPRES.
Ind/Abst AgBiotech News Inf.; Field Crop Abstr.; Health Plan. Adminis.; Index Med. (1988-); Irr. Drain. Abstr.; Plant Breed. Abstr.; Plant Grow. Reg. Abstr.; Potato Abstr.; Rice Abstr.; Soils Fert.; Wheat Barley Trit. Abstr.

LC R856 **ISSN** 0386-8109
DD 610.28 JA
NLM W1; CH872 **CODEN** CHRYDT
CHIRYOGAKU. (CHIRYOGAKU = BIOMEDICINE & THERAPEUTICS.). [Chiryogaku]. **VFOAT** Biomedicine & Therapeutics; Biomedicine and Therapeutics. Vol. 1, No. 1 (1978)-. Periodical. Japanese. Twelve times a year.

Raifu Saiensu Shuppan K K, Masuda Bldg, Kyobashi 2-5-10, Chuo-ku, Tokyo-to 104 Japan. Documents available from CASDDS.
Ind/Abst Chem. Abstr.

ISSN 0715-4828
DD 610/.28/09715 CN
CIRCUIT (FREDERICTON). (CIRCUIT / PROGRAMME DE GENIE MEDICAL DES HOPITAUX DU N.-B. / NEW BRUNSWICK HOSPITALS MEDICAL ENGINEERING PROGRAM.). [Circuit]. **Added/Corp** New Brunswick Hospitals Medical Engineering Program. Vol. 1 (1982)-. Periodical. English (French). Six times a year. Free. Circuit, c/o Institute of Biomedical Engineering, University of New Brunswick, PO Box 4400, Fredericton New Brunswick E3B 5A3 Canada. **Tel** (506)453-4966. **ED** Virginia Patterson. **Circ:** 175. ***Formed by the union of*** *New Brunswick Hospitals Medical Engineering Program. Newsletter, 0383-0586* ***and*** *New Brunswick Hospitals Medical Engineering Program. Circulaire, 0383-0594.*

ISSN 1046-3305
DD 620 US
NLM W1; CL668W
Pr Rev. **CEASED**
CLINICAL BIOTECHNOLOGY. [Clin. biotechnol.]. Vol. 1, No. 1 (Nov./Dec. 1989)-(19??). Periodical. English. Mary Ann Liebert Inc., 2 Madison Avenue, Larchmont NY 10538. **Tel** (914)834-3100, (800)M-LIEBERT, FAX (212)289-4697. Documents available from The Genuine Article.
Desc: Focuses on those aspects of biotechnology research which have a strong nexus with the clinical sciences, especially for understanding the pathological state and for diagnosis, prognosis, and therapy.
Ind/Abst Res. Alert [Full Cov.].

LC R856 **ISSN** 0277-0393
DD 610.28 US
NLM W1; CL696CJ
Pr Rev.
CLINICAL ENGINEERING INFORMATION SERVICE. [Clin. eng. inf. serv.]. **VFOAT** CEIS. Vol. 1, No. 1 (Jan./Feb. 1977)-. Periodical. English. Six times a year. $110.00. Scientific Enterprises Inc, 5104 Randolph Road, North Little Rock AR 72116. **Tel** (501)771-1775, FAX (501)771-1775. **ED** David Simmons. Index Available published separately, bound from publisher, free-automatically sent. cum. index.
Desc: A resource to administrators, hospital engineers, clinical/biomedical engineers, and biomedical equipment technicians in management and technology. Topics such as use of computers, safety, helpful suggestions, technical discussions and maintenance management and FDA recalls are covered.
Ind/Abst Health Devices Alerts; Hosp. Health Admin. Index (1983-1987).

LC R856 **ISSN** 0730-7578
DD 610.28 US
NLM W1 CL715N
Pr Rev.
CLINICAL INSTRUMENT SYSTEMS : CIS. [Clin. instrum. syst.]. **VFOAT** CIS; C.I.S. Vol. 1, No. 1 (Aug. 1980)-. Periodical. English. Ten times a year. $225.00. Clinical Instrument Systems, 447 Glenbrook Road, Stamford CT 06906. **Tel** (203)329-9220, FAX (203)327-3462. **ED** Nelson L. Alpert. Index available. cum. index.
Desc: A technical information resource providing laboratory personnel and pathologists with information on instrumentation in fields of clinical chemistry, RIA, hematology, microbiology and blood banking.

LC R856
DD 610.28 UK
COMLINE NEWS SERVICE. (19??)-. English. Twelve times a year. $855.60. MicroInfo Ltd., PO Box 3, Omega Park, Alton Hampshire GU34 2PG United Kingdom. **Tel** 011 44 1420 86848, FAX 011 44 1420 89889, telex 858431 MINFO G. ***Absorbed*** *Machine Tool Industry* ***and*** *Factory Automation.*
Ind/Abst Abstr. BioCommer.

LC Q **ISSN** 1012-0718
DD 500 TU
CODEN CSUEES
COMMUNICATIONS DE LA FACULTE DES SCIENCES DE L'UNIVERSITE D'ANKARA. SERIES C, BIOLOGY AND GEOLOGICAL ENGINEERING. (COMMUNICATIONS. SERIES C, BIOLOGY AND GEOLOGICAL ENGINEERING = COMMUNICATIONS DE LA FACULTE DES SCIENCES DE L'UNIVERSITE D'ANKARA.). [Commun. Fac. sci. Univ. Ank., S,er. C biol. geol. eng.]. **Added/Corp** Ankara Universitesi. Fen Fakultesi. **VFOAT** Biology and Geological Engineering; Communications de la Faculte des Sciences de l'Universite d'Ankara. Vol. 4, No. 1/2 (1986)-. Periodical. English. Two times a year. Faculty of Sciences, University of Ankara 06 100, Ankara Turkey. **Tel** (4)212-6720. **ED** Timur Dogu. ***Formed by the union of*** *Communications de la Faculte des Sciences de l'Universite d'Ankara. Serie C, Biologie, 0256-7865* ***and*** *Communications de la Faculte des Sciences de l'Universite d'Ankara. Serie Cb1s, Geologie, 0253-1216.*

LC TP248 **ISSN** 0737-4674
DD 660.6 US
NLM W3 CO978NM
CONSENSUS DEVELOPMENT CONFERENCE SUMMARIES. [Consens. dev. conf. summ.]. **Added/Corp** National Institutes of Health (U.S.). Vol. 3 (1980)-. English. One time a year. Free on request. US Department of Health and Human Services National Institutes of Health, 9000 Rockville Pike, Bethesda MD 20892. **Tel** (301)496-9291, FAX (301)496-2443. ***Continues*** *National Institutes of Health Consensus Development Conference Summaries, 0195-6213.*
Ind/Abst Abstr. Clin. Care Guidel.; Health Plan. Adminis.

LC R856 **ISSN** 0734-1407
DD 610.28 US
NLM W1 C559
CRC HANDBOOK OF CLINICAL ENGINEERING. [CRC handb. clin. eng.]. **VFOAT** Handbook of Clinical Engineering; C.R.C. Handbook of Clinical Engineering. **VAT** Chemical Rubber Company Handbook of Clinical Engineering. Vol. 1 (1980)-. English. Irregular. Price varies per volume. CRC Press Inc., 2000 Corporate Boulevard Northwest, Boca Raton FL 33431. **Tel** (407)994-0555, (800)272-7737, FAX (407)998-9784, (800)374-3401, telex 568689. Each issue contains an index to its own contents (no volume index)--loose.

LC R856
DD 610.28 US
●**CRISP : BIOMEDICAL RESEARCH INFORMATION ON CD-ROM.** (1994)-. Government Publication. English. Four times a year. $87.00 US; $108.75 other. Superintendent of Documents, US Government Printing Office, Washington DC 20402. **Tel** (202)275-3328, FAX (202)786-2377.
Desc: Covers information on projects and administration of biomedical research.

LC R856.A1 C5 **ISSN** 0278-940X
DD 610/.28/05 US
CCC
NLM W1 CR216W **CODEN** CRBEDR
CRITICAL REVIEWS IN BIOMEDICAL ENGINEERING. [Crit. rev. biomed. eng.]. **VFOAT** C.R.C. Critical Reviews in Biomedical Engineering; CRC Critical Reviews in Biomedical Engineering. **VAT** Chemical Rubber Company Critical Reviews in Biomedical Engineering. Vol. 7, Issue 1 (1981)-. Academic Scholarly Publication. English. Six times a year. $405.00. Begell House Inc., 79 Madison Avenue, New York NY 10016-7892. **Tel** (212)725-1999, FAX (212)213-8368. **(Subscription address:** Begell House Inc., PO Box 1109, Pearl River NY 10965. **Tel** (212)725-1999.**)** **ED** John R. Bourne. Index available (free). Documents available from Article Express International, The Genuine Article, BIOSIS Document Express, Ask*IEEE. ***Continues*** *Critical Reviews in Bioengineering, 0731-6984.*
Desc: Provides critical evaluations of current research and development.
Ind/Abst Biol. Abstr.; Curr. Aware. Biol. Sci., CABS; Curr. Cit.; Curr. Contents Life Sci.; EMBASE; Energy Res. Abstr. (1981-); Eng. Index Annu.; Health Plan. Adminis.; Index Med.; Index Sci. Rev. [Full Cov.]; INSPEC (1983-); Life Sci. Collect.; Res. Alert [Full Cov.]; Sci. Cit. Index; SCISEARCH; SportSearch.

LC TP248.13 .C74 **ISSN** 0738-8551
DD 660/.6 US
CCC
NLM W1; CR216ZB **CODEN** CRBTE5
Pr Rev.
CRITICAL REVIEWS IN BIOTECHNOLOGY. [Crit. rev. biotechnol.]. **Added/Corp** Chemical Rubber Company. **VFOAT** C.R.C. Critical Reviews in Biotechnology; CRC Critical Reviews in Biotechnology. **VAT** Chemical Rubber Company Critical Reviews in Biotechnology. Vol. 1, Issue 1 (1983)-. Academic Scholarly Publication. English. Four times a year. $300.00. CRC Press Inc., 2000 Corporate Boulevard Northwest, Boca Raton FL 33431. **Tel** (407)994-0555, (800)272-7737, FAX (407)998-9784, (800)374-3401, telex 568689. **(Subscription address:** CRC Press Inc. / New York, PO Box 750, Pearl River NY 10965. **)** **ED** Graham G. Stewart, Inge Russell. Documents available from Article Express International, The Genuine Article, CASDDS.
Desc: Provides a forum for critical evaluation of current and recent publications and for state-of-the-art reports from various geographic areas around the world.
Ind/Abst AgBiotech News Inf.; AGRICOLA [Select. Cov.]; Biocont. News Inf. (19??-19??); Biodeter. Abstr. (1991-); Biotechnol. Res. Abstr.; Chem. Abstr. (1983-); Crop Physiol. Abstr.; Curr. Aware. Biol. Sci., CABS; Curr. Biotechnol.; Curr. Cit.; Curr. Contents Agric. Biol. Environ. Sci.; Eng. Index Annu. [Select. Cov.]; Field Crop Abstr.; Food Sci. Technol. Abstr.; Health Plan. Adminis.; Index Med. (Vol. 6, No. 1, 1987-); Index Sci. Rev. [Full Cov.]; Maize Abstr.; Life Sci. Collect.; PESTDOC; Ref. Upd. Deluxe Ed.; Res. Alert [Full Cov.]; Rev. Plant Pathol.; Sci. Cit. Index; SCISEARCH.

LC Z5180 .C87 **ISSN** 0964-8712
DD 016.576 UK
NLM ZQW 4; C976
CURRENT ADVANCES IN APPLIED MICROBIOLOGY & BIOTECHNOLOGY. **See** Biology-Abstracting, Bibliographies and Statistics.

LC TP248 **ISSN** 0735-956X
DD 660.6 US
CURRENT AWARENESS IN BIOTECHNOLOGY. [Curr. aware. biotech.]. (Dec. 1981)-. English. Irregular. Bernard Wolnak and Associates, 360 North Michigan Avenue/Suite 706, Chicago IL 60601. **Tel** (312)782-4926. **ED** Bernard Wolnak. ctrl circ.
Desc: Presents a realistic perspective and a critical evaluation of the many and varied developments in biotechnology that can have an impact in the commercial world.

LC TP248.2 .C87 **ISSN** 0960-5037
DD 660.6/05 UK
NLM ZQU 4; C7964 **CODEN** CUBIER
CURRENT BIOTECHNOLOGY. **See** Biology-Abstracting, Bibliographies and Statistics.

LC TP248.13 .C87 **ISSN** 0958-1669
DD 660/.6 UK
CCC
NLM W1; CU799GBL **CODEN** CUOBE3
CURRENT OPINION IN BIOTECHNOLOGY. Vol. 1, No. 1 (Oct. 1990)-. Academic Scholarly Publication. English. Six times a year. $693.50. Current Science / England, Middlesex House, 34-42 Cleveland Street, London W1P 6LB United Kingdom. **Tel** 011 44 171 5808393, 011 44 171 3230323, FAX 011 44 171 5805646. **(Subscription address:** Current Science, 20 North 3rd Street, Philadelphia PA 19106. **Tel** (800)552-5866.**)** Documents available from The Genuine Article, BIOSIS Document Express, CASDDS.
Desc: Directed toward researchers and educators in biotechnology. Presents review articles from an area of concentration covering an entire year's literature with annotated references. Each issue features evaluations and complete listing of key references and patents.
Ind/Abst AgBiotech News Inf.; Biol. Abstr. (1992-); Chem. Abstr. (1990-); Curr. Aware. Biol. Sci., CABS; Curr. Cit.; Plant Breed. Abstr.; Ref. Upd. Deluxe Ed.; Res. Alert [Full Cov.].

LC SB621 **ISSN** 0924-1949
DD 581.2 NE
CODEN CPBAE2
Pr Rev.
CURRENT PLANT SCIENCE AND BIOTECHNOLOGY IN AGRICULTURE. **See** Agriculture-Crop Production and Soils.

LC R856 **ISSN** 0167-7209
DD 610.28 NE
NLM W1 CU8093L **CODEN** CRBID5
CURRENT REVIEWS IN BIOMEDICINE. [Curr. rev. biomed.]. (1981)-. Academic Scholarly Publication. English. Irregular. Price varies per volume. Elsevier Science Publishers BV, PO Box 211, 1000 AE Amsterdam Netherlands. **Tel** 011 31 20 4853641, 011 31 20 4853642, FAX 011 31 20 4853598. Documents available from CASDDS.
Ind/Abst Chem. Abstr.

LC QH573 **ISSN** 0920-9069
DD 574.87 NE
CCC
NLM W1; CY88 **CODEN** CYTOER
Pr Rev.
CYTOTECHNOLOGY (DORDRECHT). **See** Biology-Cytology.

LC QD415 **ISSN** 0731-4027
DD 574.192 US
NLM W1; DJ66
TITLE CHANGE
D-J-M ENZYME REPORT. [D-J-M enzym. rep.]. **VFOAT** D J M Enzyme Report. Vol. 1, No. 1 (Mar. 1982)-(19??). Periodical. English. Deborah Mysiewicz Publishers, PO Box 2009, Oak Harbor WA 98277. **Tel** (415)689-2972. **ED** Thomas Mysiewicz. **Bk Rev.** available on microfiche. ***Merged into*** *Bioengineering News, 0275-4207.*
Desc: Covers commercial enzymology, including developments in engineered and immobilized enzymes. Includes patents and patent applications.

LC TP248 **ISSN** 0934-3792
DD 660.6 GW
NLM W1; DE111AL **CODEN** DBCOEU
DECHEMA BIOTECHNOLOGY CONFERENCES. **Added/Corp** Dechema. **VFOAT** DECHEMA Biotechnology Conferences Series. Vol. 1 (1987)-. Monographic series. English. One time a year. VCH Gesellschaft GmbH, Postfach 101161, D-69451 Weinheim Germany. **Tel** 011 49 6201 606459, FAX 011 49 6201 606184. **(Subscription address:** VCH Publishers Inc., 303 Northwest 12th Avenue, Journals

Biology — Bioengineering

Department, Deerfield FL 33442. **Tel** (800)367-8249, (305)428-5566.) Documents available from CASDDS. **Ind/Abst** Chem. Abstr.

LC TP248
DD 660.6
CODEN DEIGDM JA
DENSHI IGAKU = MEDICAL ELECTRONICS. [Denshi igaku]. **Added/Corp** Denpa Jikkensha. **VFOAT** Medical Electronics. (1966)-. Academic Scholarly Publication. Japanese. Denpa Jikkensha, 15-4 Shimouma 6-chome, Setagaya-ku Tokyo 154 Japan. Documents available from CASDDS.
Ind/Abst Chem. Abstr.

LC TP248.13 .D47 **ISSN** 0262-5318
DD 660.6/05 UK
NLM Z 7914.B33; D484
TITLE CHANGE
DERWENT BIOTECHNOLOGY ABSTRACTS. **See** Biology-Abstracting, Bibliographies and Statistics.

LC TP155
DD 660 FR
●DICTIONNAIRE PERMANENT: BIOETHIQUE ET BIOTECHNOLOGIES. (1995)-. English. Editions Legislatives et Admin, 80 82 Avenue de la Marne, 92546 Montrouge Cedex France. **Tel** 011 33 1 40926868, FAX 011 33 1 46560015, telex 632 855 F. **ED** Daniel Vigneau.
Desc: Articles are concerned with legal issues in bioethics and biotechnology.

LC TP248 **ISSN** 1060-4200
DD 660 US
DIRECTORY OF PLANT BIOTECHNOLOGY COMPANIES IN USA. **See** Biology-Botany.

LC Z6663.N85 **ISSN** 1065-707X
DD 660 US
NLM W1; EN98K
TITLE CHANGE
ENTREZ (BETHESDA, MD.). (ENTREZ. SEQUENCES [COMPUTER FILE].). [Entrez, Seq.]. **Added/Corp** National Center for Biotechnology Information (U.S.). **VFOAT** Sequences. (1992)-(1994). Government Publication. English. US Department of Health and Human Services, 200 Independence Avenue Southwest, Washington DC 20201. (**Subscription address:** Superintendent of Documents, US Government Printing Office, Washington DC 20402.) *Merged with Entrez. References, 1072-3072 to form Entrez Document Retrieval System, 1078-7712.*

LC QP625.N89 **ISSN** 1078-7712
DD 016 US
●ENTREZ DOCUMENT RETRIEVAL SYSTEM. (ENTREZ DOCUMENT RETRIEVAL SYSTEM [COMPUTER FILE].). [Entrez doc. retr. syst.]. **Added/Corp** National Center for Biotechnology Information (U.S.). **VFOAT** Entrez. (Oct. 1994)-. English. Six times a year. US Department of Health and Human Services, 200 Independence Avenue Southwest, Washington DC 20201. (**Subscription address:** Superintendent of Documents, US Government Printing Office, Washington DC 20402.) *Formed by the union of Entrez. Sequences, 1065-707X; Entrez. References, 1072-3072.*

LC TP248.E5 E565 **ISSN** 0141-0229
DD 660/.6/05 UK
CCC
NLM W1 EN986P **CODEN** EMTED2
ENZYME AND MICROBIAL TECHNOLOGY. [Enzyme microb. technol.]. Vol. 1 (Jan. 1979)-. Academic Scholarly Publication. English. Sixteen times a year. $1100.00. Butterworth Heinemann / Woburn MA, 225 Wildwood Avenue, Unit B, Woburn MA 01801. **Tel** (800)366-2665, FAX (617)928-2620, telex 880052. (**Subscription address:** Elsevier Science Inc. / New York Books, 655 Avenue of the Americas, New York NY 10010. **Tel** (212)633-3650.) available on microfilm and microfiche from University Microfilms International (UMI). Documents available from Article Express International, The Genuine Article, BIOSIS Document Express, CASDDS, ADONIS.
Ind/Abst ADONIS; Biocont. News Inf.; Bioeng. Abstr.; Biol. Abstr.; Chem. Abstr.; Curr. Aware. Biol. Sci.; CABS; Curr. Biotechnol.; Curr. Cit.; Curr. Contents Agric. Biol. Environ. Sci.; Curr. Contents Life Sci.; Ei Page One; EMBASE; Eng. Index Annu.; Food Sci. Technol. Abstr.; Foods Adlibra; For. Prod. Abstr.; Life Sci. Collect.; PESTDOC; Ref. Upd. Deluxe Ed.; Res. Alert; Rev. Plant Pathol.; Sci. Cit. Index; SCISEARCH; Sug. Indus. Abstr.

LC TP248.E5 E57 **ISSN** 0094-8500
DD 660/.63
NLM W3 EN696 **CODEN** ENENDT
ENZYME ENGINEERING. [Enzym. eng.]. **Added/Corp** American Institute of Chemical Engineers. New York Academy of Sciences. Vol. 1 (1972)-. Monographic series. English. Irregular. Price varies per volume. Plenum Press, 233 Spring Street, New York NY 10013-1578. **Tel** (212)620-8000, (800)221-9369, FAX (212)463-0742, (212)807-1047, telex 23/421139.

Documents available from CASDDS.
Desc: Consists of papers presented at the Engineering Foundation Conference on Enzyme Engineering.
Ind/Abst AGRICOLA; BioBusiness; Chem. Abstr.; Dairy Sci. Abstr.; PESTDOC.

LC QD415
DD 574.192 US
ENZYME ENGINEERING AND BIOTECHNOLOGY. (19??)-. English. Eighteen times a year. $675.00 US; $765.00 other; combined with Molecular Biotechnology: $755.00 US, $855.00 other. Humana Press Inc., 999 Riverview Drive, Suite 208, Totawa NJ 07512. **Tel** (201)256-1699, FAX (201)256-8341. **ED** Howard H. Weetall. *Continues in part Applied Biochemistry and Biotechnology, 0273-2289.*

LC TP248
DD 660.6 NE
EUROPEAN BIOTECHNOLOGY INFORMATION SERVICE. (1991)-. Periodical. English. ASFRA BV, Voorhaven 33, 1135 BL Edam The Netherlands. **Tel** 011 31 02993 72751, FAX 011 31 02993 72877.
Ind/Abst Abstr. BioCommer.

LC TP248 **ISSN** 0765-2046
DD 660.6 FR
CCC
CODEN EBNWEI
Pr Rev.
EUROPEAN BIOTECHNOLOGY NEWSLETTER (PARIS). (EUROPEAN BIOTECHNOLOGY NEWSLETTER.). [Eur. biotechnol. newsl.]. **VFOAT** EBN. No. 1 (April 4, 1986)-. Newsletter. English. Twenty-two times a year. $684.00. Editions Scientifique Elsevier, 141 rue de Javel, 75747 Paris Cedex 15 France. **Tel** 011 33 1 45589067, FAX 011 33 1 45589424. (**Subscription address:** Editions Scientifiques Elsevier / for North America, PO Box 7247-7576, Philadelphia PA 19170-7576.) **ED** D. Butler. Documents available from CASDDS. *Continues Biotechnology Insight.*
Desc: Presents full length articles and short communications on various aspects of biotechnology.
Ind/Abst Abstr. BioCommer.; AGRICOLA [Select. Cov.]; BioBusiness (1988-); Chem. Abstr.; Chem. Ind. Notes (1986-); Curr. Biotechnol.

LC RV401 **ISSN** 1068-5324
DD 615 US
NLM W1; FD415
●F-D-C REPORTS. PRESCRIPTION PHARMACEUTICALS AND BIOTECHNOLOGY. **See** Pharmacy and Pharmacology.

LC TP248 **ISSN** 0237-0743
DD 660.6 HU
UDC 57.08
FOLIA BIOTECHNOLOGICA. [Folia biotechnol.]. (1984)-. Monographic series. English. Irregular. OMIKK, 1428 Budapest, PF 12, Hungary. **Tel** (361)-118-1994, FAX (361)-138-2414, telex 22-4944 omikk h. Documents available from CASDDS.
Ind/Abst Chem. Abstr.

LC TP248.65.F66 F66 **ISSN** 0890-5436
DD 664 US
CCC
NLM W1; FO435C **CODEN** FBIOEE
Pr Rev.
FOOD BIOTECHNOLOGY. [Food biotechnol.]. Vol. 1, No. 1 (1987)-. Periodical. English. Three times a year. $495.00. Marcel Dekker Inc., 270 Madison Avenue, New York NY 10016. **Tel** (212)696-9000, (800)228-1160, FAX (212)685-4540, telex 421419. (**Subscription address:** Marcel Dekker Inc., PO Box 5017, Monticello NY 12701. **Tel** (800)228-1160.) **ED** Dietrich Knorr. available on microfiche. Documents available from Article Express International, The Genuine Article, BIOSIS Document Express, CASDDS, Documents on Demand.
Desc: Brings together the current research on biotechnology in the areas of food production and processing. Subjects include chemicals, analytical methods, biopolymers, enzymes, fermentation technology, food additives, microbiology, molecular biology, nutrition, safety and toxicology, tissue culture, unit operations and novel food processes.
Ind/Abst AGRICOLA; BioBusiness; Biocont. News Inf.; Biodeter. Abstr.; Biol. Abstr. (1987-); Chem. Abstr.; Curr. Aware. Biol. Sci.; CABS; Curr. Biotechnol.; Curr. Contents Agric. Biol. Environ. Sci.; Ei Page One; Eng. Index Annu.; Environ. Abstr.; Food Sci. Technol. Abstr.; Microbiol. Abstr. Sect. A; Nutr. Abstr. Rev., Ser. B, Live Feeds and Feed.; Nutr. Abstr. Rev., Ser. A, Hum. Exp.; Ref. Upd. Deluxe Ed.; Res. Alert [Full Cov.]; Rev. Med. Vet. Mycology; SCISEARCH; Sug. Indus. Abstr.

LC TP248.65.F66 F65 **ISSN** 0952-357X
DD 664 UK
FOOD BIOTECHNOLOGY (LONDON). (FOOD BIOTECHNOLOGY.). [Food biotechnol.]. (1987)-. Academic Scholarly Publication. English. Elsevier Science Publishers Ltd., Crown House, Linton Road,

Barking Essex IG11 8JU United Kingdom. **Tel** 011 44 181 5947272, FAX 011 44 181 5945942, telex 896950. Documents available from CASDDS.
Ind/Abst AGRICOLA [Full Cov.]; Chem. Abstr.; PESTDOC.

LC RB46.5 .F76 **ISSN** 0893-6129
DD 616.07/56 US
NLM W1; FR945YK
CEASED
FRONTIERS IN IMMUNOASSAY AND BIOTECHNOLOGY. [Front. immunoass. biotechnol.]. Vol. 6, No. 1 (Jan. 1985)-(19??). Periodical. English. Scientific Newsletter Enterprises Inc., RD 4 Box 7, Middleton NY 10940. **ED** John F. Zack Jr. Index available. **Circ:** 500. *Continues Frontiers in Immunoassay.*
Desc: Contains developments in clinical biotechnology and non-isotopic immunoassay field, products, services, government regulations, books, calendar and bibliography.
Ind/Abst Abstr. BioCommer. (-199?).

LC R856 **ISSN** 0921-3775
DD 610.28 NE
NLM W1; FR946GN **CODEN** FMBEEQ
FRONTIERS OF MEDICAL AND BIOLOGICAL ENGINEERING. **See** Medical Sciences.

ISSN 1180-5668
DD 660./6/05 CN
FRONTIERS (POINTE-CLAIRE). (FRONTIERS.). [Frontiers]. **Added/Corp** STA Communications. Vol. 1, No. 1 (Aug. 1990)-. Periodical. English. Four times a year. Limited free distribution. STA Communications Inc., 955 St. John Boulevard, Suite 306, Pointe-Claire Quebec H9R 5K3 Canada. **Tel** (514)695-7623.

LC TP248 **ISSN** 0930-4320
DD 660 GW
NLM W1; GB22
GBF MONOGRAPHS. **Added/Corp** Gesellschaft fuer Biotechnologische Forschung (Braunschweig, Germany). **VFOAT** GBF Monographies. **VAT** Gesellschaft fuer Biotechnologische Forschung Monographs. Vol. 8 (1987)-. Monographic series. English (German). Price varies per volume. VCH Publishers Inc, 220 East 23rd Street, New York NY 10010. **Tel** (212)683-8333, FAX (212)481-0897. (**Subscription address:** VCH Publishers Inc., 303 Northwest 12th Avenue, Journals Department, Deerfield FL 33442. **Tel** (800)367-8249, (305)428-5566.) Documents available from CASDDS. *Continues GBF Monograph Series, 0930-4312.*
Ind/Abst Biodeter. Abstr.; Chem. Abstr.; Sug. Indus. Abstr.

LC TP248.17 .G46 **ISSN** 1063-0341
DD 338.7/6606/025 US
GEN GUIDE TO BIOTECHNOLOGY COMPANIES. [GEN guide biotechnol. co.]. **VFOAT** Guide to Biotechnology Companies; Genetic Engineering News Guide to Biotechnology Companies. (1985)-. English. One time a year. $197.00. Mary Ann Liebert Inc., 2 Madison Avenue, Larchmont NY 10538. **Tel** (914)834-3100, (800)M-LIEBERT, FAX (212)289-4697.

LC QH426 **ISSN** 1356-1308
DD 575.10 UK
●GENE THERAPY. (1995)-. Academic Scholarly Publication. English. Six times a year. £110.00. SUBIS, Mansion House 19 Kingfield Road, Sheffield S11 9AS United Kingdom. **Tel** 011 44 114 2554433, FAX 011 44 114 255 4626. available on diskette.
Desc: Aimed at clinical and life science researchers.

LC QH426
DD 575.1 US
Pr Rev.
●GENETIC ANALYSIS BIOMOLECULAR ENGINEERING. **See** Biology-Genetics.

LC QH426 .G44 **ISSN** 1050-3862
DD 574.87/328/05
CCC
NLM W1; GE277 **CODEN** GATAEVGANTONGANTDN
TITLE CHANGE
GENETIC ANALYSIS, TECHNIQUES AND APPLICATIONS. **See** Biology-Genetics.

LC TP248.13 **ISSN** 0959-020X
DD 660.6 UK
CCC
NLM W1; GE2785 **CODEN** GEBIER
Pr Rev.
GENETIC ENGINEER & BIOTECHNOLOGIST, THE. [Genet. eng. biotechnol.]. **VFOAT** Genetic Engineer and Biotechnologist. Vol. 10, Issue 1 (March/April 1990)-. Academic Scholarly Publication. English. Four times a year. $372.00. Carfax Publishing Company, PO Box 25, Abingdon, Oxfordshire OX14 3UE United Kingdom. **Tel** 011 44 1235 555335, FAX 011 44 1235 553559, telex 817484. **ED** Caroline MacDonald. **Bk Rev. Ad Acc. Circ:** 500. available on microfiche from University

Microfilms International (UMI). Documents available from The Genuine Article, CASDDS. ***Continues*** *International Industrial Biotechnology, 0269-7815.*
Desc: Covers business, finance and research and development.
Ind/Abst Abstr. BioCommer.; AgBiotech News Inf.; BioBusiness (1990-); Biodeter. Abstr. (1991-); Chem. Abstr.; Chem. Bus. Bull.; Chem. Bus. NewsBase (1990-); Chem. Bus. Update; Curr. Aware. Biol. Sci., CABS; Curr. Cit.; Food Sci. Technol. Abstr.; PESTDOC; Res. Alert [Full Cov.]; Rev. Plant Pathol.; Soc. Sci. Cit. Index [Select. Cov.]; Weed Abstr.

LC QH442 .G454 **ISSN** 0196-3716
DD 575.1 US
CCC
NLM W1 GE281 **CODEN** GENGDC
GENETIC ENGINEERING. (GENETIC ENGINEERING; PRINCIPLES AND METHODS.). [Genet. eng.]. (1979)-. Academic Scholarly Publication. English. Irregular. Price varies per volume. Plenum Press, 233 Spring Street, New York NY 10013-1578. **Tel** (212)620-8000, (800)221-9369, FAX (212)463-0742, (212)807-1047, telex 23/421139. **ED** Jane K. Setlow. Documents available from CASDDS.
Ind/Abst AGRICOLA [Select. Cov.]; Biotechnol. Res. Abstr.; Chem. Abstr.; Curr. Cit.; PESTDOC.

LC TP248
DD 660.65 AU
GENETIC ENGINEERING AND BIOTECHNOLOGY MONITOR. See Biology-Genetics.

ISSN 0890-0906
DD 660 US
NLM QH 442; G3285
GENETIC ENGINEERING AND BIOTECHNOLOGY RELATED FIRMS WORLDWIDE DIRECTORY. [Genet. eng. biotechnol. relat. firms worldw. dir.]. 5th Ed. (1986)-. Directory. English. One time a year (April). $299.00. Mega-Type Publications, 186 Route 571 Building 3A, PO Box 664, Princeton NJ 08550. **Tel** (800)962-7004, (609)275-6900, FAX (609)275-8011. Index available (free). ***Continues*** *Genetic Engineering and Biotechnology Firms Worldwide Directory, 0892-0710.*
Desc: Worldwide directory listing over 5500 firms in the US and sixty countries. Complete address information as well as free form text listings.

LC TP248.2 .G46 **ISSN** 0921-2604
DD 660/.6/05 NE
NLM TP 248.2; G328
Pr Rev.
GENETIC ENGINEERING AND BIOTECHNOLOGY YEARBOOK. [Genet. eng. biotechnol. yearb.]. (19??)-. Academic Scholarly Publication. English. One time a year. Price varies. Elsevier Science Publishers BV, PO Box 211, 1000 AE Amsterdam Netherlands. **Tel** 011 31 20 4853641, 011 31 20 4853642, FAX 011 31 20 4853598. **(Subscription address:** Elsevier Science Inc. / New York Books, 655 Avenue of the Americas, New York NY 10010. **Tel** (212)633-3650.**)**

LC TP248.6 .G4615 **ISSN** 0270-6377
DD 660/.65 US
NLM W1 GE281M **CODEN** GENNDX
GENETIC ENGINEERING NEWS. (GENETIC ENGINEERING NEWS : GEN.). [Genet. eng. news]. **VFOAT** GEN. Vol. 1, No. 1 (Jan./Feb. 1981)-. Academic Scholarly Publication. English. Twenty-six times a year (24 issues). $240.00. Mary Ann Liebert Inc., 2 Madison Avenue, Larchmont NY 10538. **Tel** (914)834-3100, (800)M-LIEBERT, FAX (212)289-4697. **ED** Joan Graf. **Bk Rev**. **Ad Acc**. Documents available from The Genuine Article, CASDDS, Documents on Demand. ***Absorbed*** *Agricultural Genetics Report, 0278-9736.*
Desc: The information source for the biotechnology/bioprocess industry that provides coverage of issues, regulatory and scale-up guidelines, R&D financial news (including public offerings, mergers, and venture capital), funding and government news, corporate profiles, university news, meeting reports, foreign reports, new product and literature information, and critical articles relating to the production of biotechnology products.
Ind/Abst Abstr. BioCommer.; AGRICOLA [Select. Cov.]; Arts Humanit. Citation Index [Select. Cov.]; BioBusiness (1984-); Chem. Abstr.; Chem. Ind. Notes; Energy Inf. Abstr.; Environ. Abstr.; F&S Index Plus Text, Int. [Select. Cov.]; Helminthol. Abstr.; PROMT; Protozoolog. Abstr.; Res. Alert [Full Cov.]; Soc. Sci. Cit. Index [Select. Cov.]; Trade Ind. Index.

ISSN 0740-9737
DD 363 US
CODEN GEWAE6
GENEWATCH. (GENEWATCH : A NEWSLETTER OF THE COMMITTEE FOR RESPONSIBLE GENETICS.). [Genewatch]. **Added/Corp** Committee for Responsible Genetics. **VFOAT** Gene Watch. (1984)-. Newsletter. English. Six times a year. $24.00 (individuals), $30.00 (institutions), $15.00 (students). Council for Responsible Genetics, 5 Upland Road, Suite 3, Cambridge MA 02140. **Tel** (617)868-0870, FAX (617)491-5344. **ED** Judith Glaubman. cum. index (brochure). **Bk Rev**, (Qty: varies). **Circ:** 900.
Desc: Analyzes politics, ethics and social impacts of genetic engineering and new biotechnology. Feature articles, news notes, reviews and resources.
Ind/Abst AGRICOLA [Select. Cov.]; Altern. Press Index (199?-); BioBusiness (1988-).

ISSN 0892-0036
DD 338 US
NLM W1; HE589K
HEALTH TECHNOLOGY CASE STUDY. [Health technol. case study]. **Added/Corp** United States. Congress. Office of Technology Assessment. **VFOAT** Case Study Series; OTA Case Studies. (March 1983)-. Monographic series. English. Price varies per volume. Iowa Department of Corrections, 523 East 12th Street, Capitol Annex, Des Moines IA 50319. **Tel** (515)281-4811, FAX (515)281-7345.

LC TP248
DD 660.6 US
IBA REPORTS. (19??)-. English. Six times a year. Free to members. Industrial Biotechnology Association, 1625 K Street NW, Suite 1100, Washington DC 20006.
Ind/Abst Abstr. BioCommer.

LC R856.A1 E54 **ISSN** 0739-5175
DD 610/.28 US
CCC
NLM W1 IE222H **CODEN** IEMBDE
Pr Rev.
IEEE ENGINEERING IN MEDICINE AND BIOLOGY MAGAZINE. (IEEE ENGINEERING IN MEDICINE AND BIOLOGY MAGAZINE : THE QUARTERLY MAGAZINE OF THE ENGINEERING IN MEDICINE & BIOLOGY SOCIETY.). [IEEE eng. med. biol. mag.]. **Added/Corp** IEEE Engineering in Medicine and Biology Society. **VFOAT** I.E.E.E. Engineering in Medicine and Biology Magazine; E.M.B. Magazine; EMB Magazine. **VAT** Institute of Electrical and Electronics Engineers Engineering in Medicine and Biology Magazine. Vol. 1, No. 2 (June 1982)-. Periodical. English. Six times a year. $125.00. IEEE / Institute of Electrical and Electronics Engineers Inc., 345 East 47th Street, New York NY 10017-2394. **Tel** (908)981-1393, FAX (908)981-9667. **(Subscription address:** IEEE / Institute of Electrical and Electronics Engineers, 445 Hoes Lane, PO Box 1331, Piscataway NJ 08855-1331. **Tel** (800)701-IEEE, (908)981-0060, FAX (908)981-9667, telex 833233.**)** Documents available from Article Express International, The Genuine Article, Ask*IEEE. ***Continues*** *Engineering in Medicine & Biology, 0278-0054.*
Desc: Covers general and technical articles on current technologies and methods used in biomedical and clinical engineering; societal implications of medical technologies, current news items; patent descriptions, and correspondence. Special interest departments, students, law, clinical engineering, ethics, new products, society news, historical features, government.
Ind/Abst Bioeng. Abstr.; Curr. Cit.; Curr. Contents Clin. Med.; Ei Page One; EMBASE; Eng. Index Annu.; Index IEEE Publ.; INSPEC (June 1982-); Pollut. Abstr. Indexes; Res. Alert [Full Cov.]; SCISEARCH; Soc. Sci. Cit. Index [Select. Cov.].

LC R895.A1 I25 **ISSN** 0018-9294
DD 610/.28 US
CCC
NLM W1 I223 **CODEN** IEBEAX
Pr Rev.
IEEE TRANSACTIONS ON BIO-MEDICAL ENGINEERING. [IEEE trans. biomed. eng.]. **Added/Corp** Institute of Electrical and Electronics Engineers. Bio-Medical Engineering Group. IEEE Engineering in Medicine and Biology Group. IEEE Engineering in Medicine and Biology Society. **VFOAT** IEEE Transactions on Biomedical Engineering; Transactions on Bio-Medical Engineering. **VAT** Institute of Electrical and Electronics Engineers Transactions on Bio-Medical Engineering. Vol. BME-11, No. 1 & 2 (Jan./April 1964)-. Academic Scholarly Publication. English. Twelve times a year. $385.00. IEEE / Institute of Electrical and Electronics Engineers Inc., 345 East 47th Street, New York NY 10017-2394. **Tel** (908)981-1393, FAX (908)981-9667. **(Subscription address:** IEEE / Institute of Electrical and Electronics Engineers, 445 Hoes Lane, PO Box 1331, Piscataway NJ 08855-1331. **Tel** (800)701-IEEE, (908)981-0060, FAX (908)981-9667, telex 833233.**)** available on microfiche. Documents available from Article Express International, The Genuine Article, BIOSIS Document Express, Ask*IEEE, CASDDS. ***Continues*** *IEEE Transactions on Bio-Medical Electronics, 0096-0616.*
Desc: Covers basic and applied papers dealing with biomedical engineering and applied biophysics. Papers range from practical/clinical applications through experimental science and technological development to formalized mathematical theory.
Ind/Abst Appl. Sci. Technol. Index; Bioeng. Abstr.; Biol. Abstr.; Biostatistica; Ceram. Abstr. (19??-); Chem. Abstr. (1964-1982); CSA Neuro. Abstr. (?-?); Curr. Aware. Biol. Sci., CABS; Curr. Cit.; Curr. Contents Eng. Comput. Technol.; Curr. Contents Life Sci.; Ei Page One; EMBASE; Energy Res. Abstr.; Eng. Index Annu.; Ergon. Abstr.; Expand. Acad. Index; Health Plan. Adminis.; Index Med.; Index IEEE Publ.; INSPEC (1968-); Int. Aerosp. Abstr.; Life Sci. Collect.; Psychol. Abstr.; Ref. Upd. Deluxe Ed.; Res. Alert [Full Cov.]; Sci. Cit. Index; SCISEARCH; Soc. Sci. Cit. Index [Select. Cov.].

LC TA2001 .I18a **ISSN** 0093-3813
DD 621 US
CCC
CODEN ITPSBD
Pr Rev.
IEEE TRANSACTIONS ON PLASMA SCIENCE. [IEEE trans. plasma sci.]. **Main/Corp** IEEE Nuclear and Plasma Sciences Society. **Added/Corp** IEEE Nuclear and Plasma Sciences Society. Transactions on Plasma Science. **VFOAT** Transactions on Plasma Science; Plasma Science. Vol. PS-1 (Mar. 1973)-. Academic Scholarly Publication. English. Six times a year. $265.00. IEEE / Institute of Electrical and Electronics Engineers Inc., 345 East 47th Street, New York NY 10017-2394. **Tel** (908)981-1393, FAX (908)981-9667. **(Subscription address:** IEEE / Institute of Electrical and Electronics Engineers, 445 Hoes Lane, PO Box 1331, Piscataway NJ 08855-1331. **Tel** (800)701-IEEE, (908)981-0060, FAX (908)981-9667, telex 833233.**)** Documents available from Article Express International, The Genuine Article, Ask*IEEE, CASDDS.
Desc: Covers all aspects of plasma science and engineering.
Ind/Abst Bioeng. Abstr.; Chem. Abstr.; Curr. Cit.; Curr. Contents Phys. Chem. Earth Sci.; Ei Page One; Energy Res. Abstr. (March 1975-); Eng. Index Annu.; Expand. Acad. Index (1992-); Index IEEE Publ.; INIS Atomindex [Micro.]; INSPEC (June 1973-); Int. Aerosp. Abstr.; Math. Rev.; Res. Alert [Full Cov.]; Sci. Cit. Index; SCISEARCH.

ISSN 1063-6528
DD 617 US
CCC
NLM W1; IE4463
IEEE TRANSACTIONS ON REHABILITATION ENGINEERING. (TRANSACTIONS ON REHABILITATION ENGINEERING.). [IEEE trans. rehabil. eng.]. **Added/Corp** Institute of Electrical and Electronics Engineers. **VAT** Institute of Electrical and Electronics Engineers Transactions on Rehabilitation Engineering. (1993)-. Periodical. English. Four times a year. $155.00. IEEE / Institute of Electrical and Electronics Engineers Inc., 345 East 47th Street, New York NY 10017-2394. **Tel** (908)981-1393, FAX (908)981-9667. **(Subscription address:** IEEE / Institute of Electrical and Electronics Engineers, 445 Hoes Lane, PO Box 1331, Piscataway NJ 08855-1331. **Tel** (800)701-IEEE, (908)981-0060, FAX (908)981-9667, telex 833233.**)**
Desc: Focuses on rehabilitation aspects of biomedical engineering and covers topics including functional electrical stimulation, acoustic dynamics, human performance measurement and analysis, nerve stimulation, electromyography, motor control and stimulation, and hardware and software applications for rehabilitation engineering and assistive devices.

LC SB950 **ISSN** 0964-069X
DD 632.9 UK
CEASED
IMPACT AGBIOINDUSTRY. (19??)-(Jan. 1993). English. CAB International Centre, Wallingford, Oxfordshire OX10 8DE United Kingdom. **Tel** 011 44 1491 832111, FAX 011 44 1491 833508, telex 847964 COMAGG G. Documents available from Documents on Demand. ***Continues*** *AgBioBusiness.*
Desc: Contains information on commerical opportunities and prospects based on technical innovations in the areas of nonchemical crop protection and related biotechnology.
Ind/Abst Abstr. BioCommer.; Environ. Abstr.

LC R856 **ISSN** 0243-7228
DD 610.28 FR
NLM W1 IN455AM
INNOVATION ET TECHNOLOGIE EN BIOLOGIE ET MEDECINE. See Medical Sciences.

LC TP248.13 .I59 **ISSN** 0888-7225
DD 660/.6 US
NLM W1; IN71Q
INTERNATIONAL BIOTECHNOLOGY LABORATORY. [Int. biotechnol. lab.]. **Added/Corp** International Scientific Communications, Inc. **VFOAT** Biotechnology Laboratory. (1983)-. Trade Publication. English. Four times a year. $135.00. International Scientific Communications Inc, PO Box 870, 30 Controls Drive, Shelton CT 06484-0870. **Tel** (203)926-9300, FAX (203)926-9310, telex 964292. **ED** Brian Howard. **Circ:** 32,796.
Ind/Abst Abstr. BioCommer.; Anal. Abstr.; BioBusiness; Curr. Biotechnol.; Mass Spect. Bull.; PESTDOC.

UK
INTERNATIONAL JOURNAL OF RESOURCE AND ENVIRONMENTAL BIOTECHNOLOGY. (19??)-. English. Four times a year. £99.00. AB Academic Publishers, PO Box 42 Bicester, Oxfordshire OX6 7NW United Kingdom. **Tel** 011 44 1869 320949, FAX 011 44 1869 320949. ***Continues*** *Biorecovery.*

LC TP248.13 .I86 **ISSN** 0208-2330
DD 660.6 RU
CODEN INSBE6

ITOGI NAUKI I TEHNIKI - VSESOUZNYJ INSTITUT NAUCNOJ I TEHNICESKOJ INFORMACII. SERIA BIOTEHNOLOGIA. (ITOGI NAUKI I TEKHNIKI. SERIIA BIOTEKHNOLOGIIA.). [Itogi nauki teh. - Vses. inst. nauEcn. teh. inf., Ser. biotehnol.]. **Added/Corp** Vsesoiuznyi Institut Nauchnoi i Tekhnicheskoi Informatsii (Soviet Union). **VFOAT** Seriia Biotekhnologiia; Biotekhnologiia; Itogi Nauki i Tekhniki. Biotekhnologiia. (1983)-. Monographic series. Russian. Irregular. Price varies per volume. VINITI - Vsesoyuznyi Institut Nauchno-Tekhnicheskoi Informatsii, All-Union Scientific and Technical Information Institute, Baltiiskaia ulitsa 14, 125219 Moscow Russia. **Tel** 011 7 95 2384600, FAX 011 7 95 9430060, telex 411160. Documents available from CASDDS.
Ind/Abst Chem. Abstr.

LC TP248 **ISSN** 0021-3292
DD 660.6 JA
NLM W1; IY585 v. 1-26; W1; BE97 v. 27- **CODEN** IYSEAK

IYO DENSHI TO SEITAI KOGAKU. (IYO DENSHI TO SEITAI KOGAKU = JAPANESE JOURNAL OF MEDICAL ELECTRONICS AND BIOLOGICAL ENGINEERING.). [Iyo denshi to seitai kogaku]. **Added/Corp** Nihon Emu I Gakkai. **VFOAT** JJME; Japanese Journal of Medical Electronics and Biological Engineering. Volume 1 (Feb. 1963)-. Academic Scholarly Publication. Japanese (summaries and/or abstracts in English; table of contents in English). Four times a year. Nihon ME Gakkai, (Japan Soc. of Medical Electronics & Biological Engineering), Dai 31 Kowa Biru 7F, 19-1 Shiroganedai 3 Chome, Minatoku Tokyo 108 Japan. **(Subscription address:** Maruzen Company Ltd., PO Box 5050, Import & Export Department, Tokyo 100 31 Japan. **Tel** 011 81 3 32789224.) **Ad Acc. Circ:** 10,000 (ctrl). Documents available from Ask*IEEE, CASDDS.
Desc: A journal which has an object of mutual cooperation between medical science and technology.
Ind/Abst Chem. Abstr. (1985-); Ei Page One; EMBASE; Index Med.; INSPEC (April 1971-).

LC TP248.13 .J35 **ISSN** 0930-9152
DD 660/.6/05 GW

JAHRBUCH BIOTECHNOLOGIE. [Jahrb. Biotechnol.]. **VFOAT** Biotechnologie Jahrbuch. (1986/1987)-. Trade Publication. German. Every 2 years. Carl Hanser Verlag, Postfach 860420, D-81631 Munich Germany. **Tel** 011 49 89 998300, FAX 011 49 89 981264. Documents available from The Genuine Article.
Ind/Abst AGRICOLA; Res. Alert [Full Cov.].

SP
NLM W1; JA981VL

JAPANESE TECHNOLOGY AND INDUSTRY. REPORT SERIES. BIOTECHNOLOGY. **VFOAT** Biotechnology. (Jan. 1989)-. Periodical. English. Twelve times a year. $430.00. Newmedia International Japan, AV Infanta Carlota 123 5 A, 08029 Barcelona Spain. **Tel** 011 34 3 4195690, FAX 011 34 3 4144213. **(Subscription address:** Newmedia International Japan Midland, Bank 196 Oxford Street, London W1A 1 EZ United Kingdom.)
Ind/Abst PROMT [Full Txt.]; PTS Newsl. Database [Full Txt.].

ISSN 1058-7330
US
CCC

JAPANESE TECHNOLOGY REVIEWS. SECTION E, BIOTECHNOLOGY. **VFOAT** Biotechnology. (1992)-. Periodical. English. Two times a year (1 volume). $185.00 (academic institutions), $289.00 (corporate institutions). Gordon & Breach Science Publishers, Inc., PO Box 786, Cooper Station, New York NY 10276. **Tel** (212)206-8900, FAX (212)645-2459. ***Continues in part*** *Japanese Technology Reviews, 0898-5693.*

ISSN 1065-8483
DD 612 US
CCC

•JOURNAL OF APPLIED BIOMECHANICS. [J. appl. biomech.]. **Added/Corp** International Society of Biomechanics. International Society for the Biomechanics of Sport. **VFOAT** JAB. Vol. 9, No. 1 (Feb. 1993)-. Periodical. English. Four times a year (Feb., May, Aug., Nov.). $90.00. Human Kinetics Publishers Inc., 1607 North Market Street, PO Box 5076, Champaign IL 61825-5076. **Tel** (217)351-5076, FAX (217)351-2674. **ED** Robert J. Gregor. Index available (Included in Nov. issue). ***Continues*** *International Journal of Sport Biomechanics, 0740-2082.*
Desc: Devoted to the study of human biomechanics in sport, exercise, and rehabilitation. Includes research articles, clinical studies, and other pertinent information on current advances in the field.
Ind/Abst Curr. Cit.; Soc. Sci. Cit. Index [Select. Cov.]; SPORT Discus.

LC R856.A1 J64 **ISSN** 0885-3282
DD 610/.28 US
CCC
NLM W1; JO564KF

JOURNAL OF BIOMATERIALS APPLICATIONS. [J. biomater. appl.]. **VFOAT** Biomaterials Applications. Vol. 1, No. 1 (July 1986)-. Periodical. English. Four times a year (Jan.,Apr., July and Oct.). $315.00. Technomic Publishing Company, Inc., 851 New Holland Avenue, Box 3535, Lancaster PA 17604. **Tel** (717)291-5609, (800)233-9936, FAX (717)295-4538. **ED** Michael Szycher. cum. index. **Circ:** 100. available on microfilm from University Microfilms International (UMI). Documents available from Article Express International, The Genuine Article, CASDDS.
Desc: Contains original articles that emphasize the clinical applications of implantable biomaterials. Development, manufacture, and clinical uses of biomaterials most compatible with the human body are highlighted from a scientific viewpoint. Devoted to new and emerging technologies, particular focus is placed on the many applications under development at industrial, biomedical, and polymer research facilities, as well as ongoing activities in academic and medical research laboratories.
Ind/Abst Chem. Abstr.; Curr. Cit.; Ei Page One; Eng. Index Annu.; Index Med.; Res. Alert [Full Cov.].

ISSN 0920-5063
NE
NLM W1; JO564KT **CODEN** JBSEEA
Pr Rev.

JOURNAL OF BIOMATERIALS SCIENCE. POLYMER EDITION. [J. biomater. sci., Polym. ed.]. **VFOAT** Polymer Edition. Vol. 1, No. 1 (1989)-. Academic Scholarly Publication. English. Twelve times a year. DM960.00. VSP International Science Publishers, Godfried van Seystlaan 47, 3703 BR Zeist Netherlands. **Tel** 011 31 3404 25790, FAX 011 31 3404 32081, telex 40217 USP NL. **(Subscription address:** VSP International Science Publishers, PO Box 346, 3700 AH Zeist Netherlands. **Tel** 011 31 30 6925790, FAX 011 31 30 6932081.) **ED** C.H. Bamford, S.L. Cooper, and T. Tsuruta. **Ad Acc.** Documents available from The Genuine Article, BIOSIS Document Express, CASDDS.
Desc: Publishes research on mechanisms of interactions between biomaterials and living organisms with attention to molecular and cellular levels.
Ind/Abst Biol. Abstr. (1991-); Chem. Abstr.; Curr. Cit.; Curr. Contents Life Sci.; Eng. Mater. Abstr.; Index Med.; Res. Alert [Full Cov.]; Sci. Cit. Index; SCISEARCH; Soc. Sci. Cit. Index [Select. Cov.].

LC R856.A1 **ISSN** 0148-0731
DD 610/.28 US
CCC
NLM W1 JO564L **CODEN** JBENDY
Pr Rev.

JOURNAL OF BIOMECHANICAL ENGINEERING. (TRANSACTIONS OF THE ASME. JOURNAL OF BIOMECHANICAL ENGINEERING.). [J. biomech. eng.]. Vol. 99, No. 1 (Feb. 1977)-. Academic Scholarly Publication. English. Four times a year. $165.00. American Society of Mechanical Engineers, 22 Law Drive, Fairfield NJ 07007. **Tel** (201)882-1167, (212)705-7722 (editorial). **ED** Cornelia Monahan. **Bk Rev. Ad Acc. Circ:** 874. available on microfilm and microfiche from University Microfilms International (UMI). Documents available from Article Express International, The Genuine Article, BIOSIS Document Express, Ask*IEEE, CASDDS.
Desc: Bio-fluids, bio-solid mechanics, bio-materials, health care delivery systems, artificial organs and prostheses, bio-instrumentation and measurement simulation of physiological systems, etc.
Ind/Abst BioBusiness; Bioeng. Abstr.; Biol. Abstr. (1985-); Chem. Abstr. (1977-1986); Civ. Struct. Eng. Abstr.; Comput. Inf. Syst. Abstr. J. [Full Cov.]; Curr. Cit.; Curr. Contents Life Sci.; Ei Page One; EMBASE; Energy Res. Abstr. (April 1978-); Eng. Index Annu.; Expand. Acad. Index (1992-); Fluid Abstr., Civil Eng.; Fluid Abstr. Proc. Eng.; FLUIDEX (1978-); Health Devices Alerts; Index Med.; INSPEC (Feb. 1977-); Int. Aerosp. Abstr.; Mater. Sci. Eng. Abstr.; Mech. Eng. Abstr.; Proc. Chem. Eng.; Res. Alert [Full Cov.]; Sci. Cit. Index; SCISEARCH; SportSearch; Theor. Chem. Eng.

ISSN 0141-5425
UK
CCC
NLM W1 JO564N **CODEN** JBIEDR
Pr Rev. **TITLE CHANGE**

JOURNAL OF BIOMEDICAL ENGINEERING. [J. biomed. eng.]. **Added/Corp** Biological Engineering Society. Vol. 1 (Jan. 1979)-Vol. 15, No. 6 (Nov. 1993). Academic Scholarly Publication. English. Butterworth Heinemann Publishers, Linacre House Jordan Hill, Oxford OX2 8DP United Kingdom. **Tel** 011 44 1865 310366, FAX 011 44 1865 310898. **ED** G.H. Byford. Index available. **Bk Rev. Ad Acc.** available on microfilm and microfiche from University Microfilms International (UMI). Documents available from Article Express International, The Genuine Article, BIOSIS Document Express, Ask*IEEE, CASDDS. ***Continued by*** *Medical Engineering & Physics, 1350-4533.*
Desc: Provides clinicians with an awareness of technological developments which have potential applications in health care. Contributions to the journal deal not only with original progress in various disciplines, but also give speedy attention to short communications describing unique applications. Review established techniques for user's benefit.
Ind/Abst Appl. Sci. Technol. Index; Biol. Abstr.; Ceram. Abstr.; Chem. Abstr.; Curr. Aware. Biol. Sci., CABS; Curr. Biotechnol.; Curr. Contents Life Sci.; Ei Page One; EMBASE; Eng. Index Annu.; Index Med.; Index Vet.; INSPEC (Oct. 1979-); Pap. Board Abstr.; Ref. Upd. Deluxe Ed.; Res. Alert [Full Cov.]; Sci. Cit. Index; SCISEARCH; Soc. Sci. Cit. Index [Select. Cov.]; Vet. Bull.

LC R856 .J6 **ISSN** 0021-9304
DD 610/.28 US
CCC
NLM W1 JO564P **CODEN** JBMRBG

JOURNAL OF BIOMEDICAL MATERIALS RESEARCH. [J. biomed. materi. res.]. **Added/Corp** Society for Biomaterials. European Society for Biomaterials. Nihon Baiomateriaru Gakkai. Vol. 1, Mar. (1967)-. Periodical. English. Twelve times a year. $1648.00. John Wiley & Sons, Inc., 605 Third Avenue, New York NY 10158-0012. **Tel** (212)850-6000, (212)850-6645, FAX (212)850-6088, telex 12-7063. **(Subscription address:** John Wiley & Sons / UK, Baffins Lane, Chichester, West Sussex PO19 1UD United Kingdom. **Tel** 011 44 1243 779777, FAX 011 44 243 776128, telex 86290 WIBOOKG.) **ED** A. Norman Cranin. **Ad Acc. Circ:** 1,600. available on microfilm and microfiche from University Microfilms International (UMI). Documents available from Article Express International, The Genuine Article, BIOSIS Document Express, CASDDS. ***Absorbed*** *Journal of Applied Biomaterials.*
Desc: Published in two sections, the journal offers a monthly research publication. Part A, the monthly, features topics ranging from alloys, polymers and ceramics to surgery, dentistry and implanted devices. The new Applied Biomaterials section covers product and engineering, pioneering surgical techniques and details on government regulations.
Ind/Abst BioBusiness; Bioeng. Abstr.; Biol. Abstr.; Calcium Calcif. Tissue Abstr.; Ceram. Abstr.; Chem. Abstr.; Curr. Biotechnol.; Curr. Cit.; Curr. Contents Life Sci.; Curr. Titles Dent.; Ei Page One; EMBASE; Energy Res. Abstr.; Eng. Index Annu.; Health Devices Alerts; Index Med.; INIS Atomindex [Micro.]; Int. Aerosp. Abstr.; Life Sci. Collect.; Ref. Upd. Deluxe Ed.; Res. Alert [Full Cov.]; Sci. Cit. Index; SCISEARCH.

LC TP248 **ISSN** 0168-1656
DD 660.65 NE
CCC
NLM W1; JO568H **CODEN** JBITD4JBDITD4
Pr Rev.

JOURNAL OF BIOTECHNOLOGY. [J. biotechnol.]. Vol. 1, No. 1 (May 1984)-. Academic Scholarly Publication. English. Twenty-one times a year (7 volumes). $1989.00. Elsevier Science Publishers BV, PO Box 211, 1000 AE Amsterdam Netherlands. **Tel** 011 31 20 4853641, 011 31 20 4853642, FAX 011 31 20 4853598. **ED** A. Fiechter. available on microfilm and microfiche from University Microfilms International (UMI); available on an online database from Elsevier Electronic Subscriptions (EES). Documents available from Article Express International, The Genuine Article, CASDDS, ADONIS.
Desc: Provides a medium for the rapid publication of full articles as well as short communications on various aspects of biotechnology.
Ind/Abst ADONIS; AGRICOLA [Select. Cov.]; BioBusiness; Biodeter. Abstr. (1991-); Biol. Agric. Index; Biotechnol. Res. Abstr.; Chem. Abstr. (1984-); Chem. Titles; Curr. Aware. Biol. Sci., CABS; Curr. Biotechnol.; Curr. Cit.; Curr. Contents Agric. Biol. Environ. Sci.; Dairy Sci. Abstr.; Ei Page One; EMBASE; Eng. Index Annu.; Field Crop Abstr.; Food Sci. Technol. Abstr.; For. Prod. Abstr. (1991-); Genet. Abstr.; Microbiol. Abstr. Sect. B; Microbiol. Abstr. Sect. A; Microbiol. Abstr. Sect. C; Oncog. Growth Factors Abstr.; Life Sci. Collect.; PESTDOC; Plant Breed. Abstr.; Plant Genet. Resour. Abstr.; Ref. Upd. Deluxe Ed.; Res. Alert [Full Cov.]; Rev. Agric. Entomol.; Sci. Cit. Index; SCISEARCH; Seed Abstr.; Weed Abstr.; Wheat Barley Trit. Abstr.

LC R **ISSN** 1353-3010
DD 610 UK

•JOURNAL OF BIOTECHNOLOGY IN HEALTHCARE. (1995)-. Academic Scholarly Publication. English. Four times a year. Henry Stewart Publications, 28/30 Little Russell Street, London WC1A 2HN United Kingdom. **Tel** 011 44 171 4043040, FAX 011 44 171 4042081.

ISSN 1073-7774
DD 616 US
NLM W1; JO575J

•JOURNAL OF CARDIOVASCULAR DIAGNOSIS AND PROCEDURES. [J. cardiovasc. diagn. proced.]. Vol. 11, No. 2 (1993)-. Periodical. English. Four times a year. $222.00. Mary Ann Liebert Inc., 2 Madison Avenue, Larchmont NY 10538. **Tel** (914)834-3100, (800)M-LIEBERT, FAX (212)289-4697. **ED** Michele Nanna. ***Continues*** *Journal of Cardiovascular Technology, 1043-4356.*

Biology —Bioengineering

Desc: Clinically oriented; fulfills demand for physicians who need to understand the underlying technologies of new instruments and procedures.

DD 616   ISSN 1043-4356 US
NLM W1; JO577H   CODEN JCATE6
TITLE CHANGE

JOURNAL OF CARDIOVASCULAR TECHNOLOGY (NEW YORK, N.Y.). See Medical Sciences-Cardiology.

LC TP   ISSN 1357-5481
DD 660   UK

●JOURNAL OF CELLULAR ENGINEERING. (1995)-. Academic Scholarly Publication. English. Four times a year. Peter Peregrinus Ltd, Station House Nightingale Road, Hitchin Hertfordshire SG5 1RJ United Kingdom. **Tel** 011 44 1438 313311, FAX 011 44 1438 313465.

LC TP248.13 .J68   ISSN 0268-2575
DD 660/.6/05   UK
   CCC
NLM W1; JO581SU   CODEN JCTBED

JOURNAL OF CHEMICAL TECHNOLOGY AND BIOTECHNOLOGY (1986). See Chemistry and Chemicals-Chemical Technology.

LC R856.A1 J68   ISSN 0363-8855
DD 610/.28   US
   CCC
NLM W1 JO588C   CODEN JCEND7

JOURNAL OF CLINICAL ENGINEERING. [J. clin. eng.]. Vol. 1, No. 1 (Oct./Dec. 1976)-. Periodical. English. Six times a year (Jan., Mar., May, July, Sept., Nov.). $159.00. Quest Publishing Company, 1351 Titan Way, Brea CA 92621. **Tel** (714)738-6400, FAX (714)525-6258. **ED** Allan F. Pacela. Index available. **Bk Rev**. **Ad Acc**. **Circ:** 3,000. Documents available from Article Express International, BIOSIS Document Express, Ask*IEEE.
Desc: Features the latest technical and professional information in biomedical and clinical engineering.
Ind/Abst BioBusiness; Bioeng. Abstr.; Biol. Abstr.; Comput. Inf. Syst. Abstr. J. [Full Cov.]; Curr. Cit.; Ei Page One; EMBASE; Eng. Index Annu.; Environ. Eng. Abstr.; Health Devices Alerts; Hosp. Health Admin. Index; INSPEC (Jan./March 1979-); Mech. Eng. Abstr.

   ISSN 0922-338X
   JA
NLM W1; JO659F   CODEN JFBIEX
Pr Rev.

JOURNAL OF FERMENTATION AND BIOENGINEERING. See Biology-Microbiology.

LC TP248.27.M37 J68
DD 660/.6   US
NLM W1; JO748I   CODEN JMBOEW

●JOURNAL OF MARINE BIOTECHNOLOGY, THE. See Biology-Marine Biology.

LC R857.M3 J69   ISSN 0957-4530
DD 610/.28   UK
   CCC
NLM W1; JO748QR   CODEN JSMMEL
Pr Rev.

JOURNAL OF MATERIALS SCIENCE. MATERIALS IN MEDICINE. VFOAT Materials in Medicine. Vol. 1, No. 1 (June 1990)-. Academic Scholarly Publication. English. Twelve times a year. $495.00. Chapman & Hall, 2-6 Boundary Row, London SE1 8HN United Kingdom. **Tel** 011 44 171 8650066, FAX 011 44 171 5229623, telex 290164 CHAPMA G. Documents available from Article Express International, The Genuine Article, Ask*IEEE, CASDDS.
Desc: Publishes papers on the science and technology of biomaterials and their applications as medical or dental implants, prostheses and devices, and of biological materials. Publishes a wide range of topics from the basic underpinning science to clinical applications, around a central theme of materials in medicine or dentistry.
Ind/Abst Ceram. Abstr. (19??-); Chem. Abstr. (1990-); Curr. Cit.; Curr. Contents Eng. Comput. Technol.; Ei Page One; Eng. Index Annu.; INSPEC (June 1990-); Res. Alert [Full Cov.]; SCISEARCH.

LC R856.A1 J7   ISSN 0309-1902
DD 610/.28   UK
   CCC
NLM W1 JO75C   CODEN JMTEDN
Pr Rev.

JOURNAL OF MEDICAL ENGINEERING & TECHNOLOGY. [J. med. eng. technol.]. VFOAT Journal of Medical Engineering and Technology. Vol. 1, No. 1 (Jan. 1977)-. Academic Scholarly Publication. English. Six times a year. $215.00. Taylor & Francis Ltd. / UK, Rankine Road, Basingstoke, Hampshire RG24 8PR United Kingdom. **Tel** 011 44 1256 840366, FAX 011 44 1256 479438, telex 858540. **(Subscription address:** Taylor & Francis Inc., 1900 Frost Road, Suite 101, Bristol PA 19007-1598. **Tel** (215)785-5800, (800)821-8312, FAX (215)785-5515.) **ED** R. E. Trotman (editor's address: Medical Physics Department, Royal Postgraduate Medical School, Ducane Road, London W12 0HS United Kingdom). available on microfilm from University Microfilms International (UMI). Documents available from Article Express International, The Genuine Article, Ask*IEEE, CASDDS, ADONIS. **Continues** Biomedical Engineering (London, England), 0006-2898.
Desc: An international and independent publication for engineers and scientists, physicians and surgeons, hospital administrators and industry professionals, and all personnel concerned with the effective use of medical devices.
Ind/Abst ADONIS; Agric. Eng. Abstr.; BioBusiness; Bioeng. Abstr.; Chem. Abstr.; Curr. Cit.; Curr. Contents Clin. Med.; Curr. Technol. Index; Ei Page One; EMBASE; Energy Res. Abstr. (March 1978-);; Eng. Index Annu.; Health Devices Alerts; Index Med.; INSPEC (Jan. 1977-); Phys. Med. Biol. (19??-19??); Res. Alert [Full Cov.]; Sci. Cit. Index; SCISEARCH.

   ISSN 0256-8551
   II
   CODEN JMIBES

JOURNAL OF MICROBIAL BIOTECHNOLOGY. [J. microb. biotechnol.]. VFOAT JMB. Vol. 1, No. 1 (Jan. 1986)-. Academic Scholarly Publication. English. Two times a year. $40.00. Biotech Publications, 111/233 Harsh Nagar, Kanpur - 208, 012 UP India. **(Subscription address:** Prints India, 11 Darya Ganj, New Delhi 110002 India. **Tel** 011 91 11 3268465, FAX 011 91 11 3275542, telex 31-61087 PRIN-IN.) Documents available from The Genuine Article, BIOSIS Document Express, CASDDS, Documents on Demand.
Ind/Abst Biocont. News Inf. (1991-); Biodeter. Abstr. (1991-); Biol. Abstr. (1987-); Chem. Abstr. (1986-); Curr. Aware. Biol. Sci., CABS; Curr. Biotechnol.; Curr. Cit.; Curr. Contents Agric. Biol. Environ. Sci.; Curr. Environ. Abstr.; PESTDOC; Res. Alert [Full Cov.]; Rev. Med. Vet. Entomol.; SCISEARCH; Sug. Indus. Abstr.

   ISSN 0352-1311
   CI
UDC 577

JUGOSLAVENSKA MEDICINSKA BIOKEMIJA. VFOAT JMB. (1982)-. Periodical. Serbo-Croatian (Roman). Two times a year. Jugoslovenska Medicinska Biokemija, Petrova 13, 41000 Zagreb Croatia. Documents available from CASDDS.
Ind/Abst Chem. Abstr.; EMBASE [Select. Cov.].

LC QC   ISSN 0368-7368
DD 530   NE
UDC 53

LAB-INSTRUMENTEN AMSTERDAM. (1965)-. Periodical. Dutch. Twelve times a year. Fl92.50 Netherlands; Fl110.00 other. ADEX CV, PO Box 328, 3760 AH Soest Netherlands. **Tel** 011 31 2155 10034, FAX 011 31 2155 25576.

LC R895.A1 I55   ISSN 0140-0118
DD 610/.28   UK
   CCC
NLM W1 ME168M   CODEN MBECDY

MEDICAL & BIOLOGICAL ENGINEERING & COMPUTING. See Biology-Computer Applications.

   ISSN 1063-1178
DD 615   US

●MEDICAL & PHARMACEUTICAL BIOTECHNOLOGY ABSTRACTS. See Biology-Abstracting, Bibliographies and Statistics.

   ISSN 0194-147X
DD 629   US
NLM W1 ME309LR

MEDICAL ELECTRONIC PRODUCTS. [Med. electron. prod.]. **Added/Corp** Medical Electronics Society. Vol. 8, No. 5 (Oct. 1977)-. Periodical. English. Six times a year. Measurement & Data Corporation, 2994 West Liberty Avenue, Pittsburgh PA 15216. **Tel** (412)343-9666, FAX (412)343-9685. **Continues** Med News.

   ISSN 1350-4533
   UK
   CCC
NLM W1; ME3101M   CODEN MEPHEO

●MEDICAL ENGINEERING & PHYSICS. **Added/Corp** Biological Engineering Society. VFOAT Medical Engineering and Physics. Vol. 16, No. 1 (Jan. 1994)-. Periodical. English. Eight times a year. $652.00. Butterworth Heinemann Publishers, Linacre House Jordan Hill, Oxford OX2 8DP United Kingdom. **Tel** 011 44 1865 310366, FAX 011 44 1865 843355. **(Subscription address:** Elsevier Science Ltd. / Oxford Fulfillment Centre, PO Box 800, Kidlington OX5 1DX United Kingdom. **Tel** 011 44 1865 843355.) available on an online database from Elsevier Electronic Subscriptions (EES). **Continues** Journal of Biomedical Engineering, 0141-5425.
Ind/Abst Curr. Cit.

   ISSN 0047-6552
   NE
   CCC
NLM W1 ME4198   CODEN MDPTBG
Pr Rev.

MEDICAL PROGRESS THROUGH TECHNOLOGY. [Med. progr. technol.]. VFOAT Medical Progress Technology. Vol. 1 (Mar. 1972)-. Academic Scholarly Publication. English. Four times a year. $275.00. Kluwer Academic Publishers, Postbus 322, 3300 AH Dordrecht The Netherlands. **Tel** 011 31 78 524990, FAX 011 31 78 183273, telex 20083. **ED** H. Hutten. Index available in last issue of volume--attached. **Bk Rev**. **Ad Acc**. **Acid Free**. **Circ:** 1,000. available on microfilm and microfiche from University Microfilms International (UMI). Documents available from Article Express International, The Genuine Article, Ask*IEEE.
Desc: This publication supports the exchange of information between the medical sciences and the engineering and physical sciences. Promotes the understanding of interdisciplinary problems originating from applied medicine.
Ind/Abst BioBusiness (-1990); Bioeng. Abstr.; Cumul. Index Nurs. Allied Health Lit.; Curr. Cit.; Curr. Contents Clin. Med.; Ei Page One; EMBASE; Energy Res. Abstr. (July 1976-); Eng. Index Annu.; Index Med.; INSPEC (1974-); Life Sci. Collect.; Ref. Upd. Deluxe Ed.; Res. Alert [Full Cov.]; Sci. Cit. Index; SCISEARCH.

LC R   ISSN 1065-996X
DD 610   US

MEDICAL TECHNOLOGY STOCK LETTER. [Med. technol. stock lett.]. (198?)-. Periodical. English. Twenty-four times a year. $320.00. Piedmont Venture Group, PO Box 40460, Berkeley CA 94704. **Tel** (510)843-1857, FAX (510)843-0901. **ED** Jim McCamant (phone: (510)843-1857).
Desc: An investment newsletter covering biotechnologies and other medical companies, with specific buy and sell recommendations.
Ind/Abst Abstr. BioCommer.

   ISSN 0344-9416
   GW
   CCC
NLM W1 ME858A   CODEN MDZNDG

MEDIZINTECHNIK (STUTTGART). (MEDIZINTECHNIK.). [Medizintechnik.]. VFOAT Engineering in Medicine. (April 1978)-. Academic Scholarly Publication. German (English; summaries and/or abstracts in English). Six times a year. $103.41. AW Gentner Verlag, Postfach 101742, D-70015 Stuttgart Germany. **Tel** 011 49 711 636720, FAX 011 49 711 6367247, telex 841 722244. **ED** R.D. Bockman. **Bk Rev**. **Ad Acc**. **Circ:** 6,500. Documents available from CASDDS. **Continues** Medizinische Technik, 0025-8504.
Desc: Publication covering the general fields of medical technology, diagnosis, and therapeutic rehabilitation. Reviews are also contained.
Ind/Abst Chem. Abstr.; EMBASE.

LC TP200   ISSN 0958-2118
DD 660.284/24   UK
   CCC
NLM W1; ME8937L
Pr Rev.

MEMBRANE TECHNOLOGY. See Engineering-Chemical Engineering.

LC QH442 .M478
DD 575.1/0724/05   UK
NLM W1; ME9615KG
Pr Rev.

METHODS IN GENE TECHNOLOGY. VFOAT Gene Technology. Vol. 1 (1991)-. Academic Scholarly Publication. English. Irregular. £62.50 UK; £97.50 other. JAI Press Ltd., The Courtyard, 28 High Street, Hampton Hill Middlesex TW12 1PD United Kingdom. **Tel** 011 44 181 9439296, FAX 011 44 181 9439317. **ED** J. Dale and P. Sanders. **Acid Free**. Documents available from BLDSC.
Desc: Describes the techniques of genetic engineering, in particular the use of gene probes, that have played a central role in the rapid development of molecular biology. The wide variety of applications is matched by considerable diversity in the methods for carrying out genetic manipulations and generating probes.

LC TP248
DD 660.6   US

MINORITY BIOMEDICAL SUPPORT PROGRAM : A DIRECTORY OF THE RESEARCH PROJECTS. **Main/Corp** Research Resources Information Center. **Added/Corp** National Institues of Health. Division of Research Resources. (19??)-. Directory. English. US Department of Health and Human Services National Institutes of Health, 9000 Rockville Pike, Bethesda MD 20892. **Tel** (301)496-9291, FAX (301)496-2443. Each issue contains an index to its own contents (no volume index)--loose.

Biology — Bioengineering

MODELLING, SIMULATION & CONTROL. C. VFOAT Modelling, Simulation and Control . C. (1984)-. Periodical. English. Four times a year.
UDC 658.5:681.3
ISSN 0761-2524
FR
Ind/Abst Curr. Cit.

MOLECULAR BIOTECHNOLOGY. [Mol. biotechnol.]. (1994)-. Periodical. English. Six times a year. $235.00. Humana Press Inc., 999 Riverview Drive, Suite 208, Totawa NJ 07512. Tel (201)256-1699, FAX (201)256-8341. ED John M. Walker. *Separated from Applied Biochemistry and Biotechnology, 0273-2289.* Desc: Publishes the latest detailed laboratory protocols for molecular biology techniques, and reviews articles and other information on the application of these techniques in the laboratory.
DD 660
ISSN 1073-6085
US
CCC
NLM W1; MO196DB   CODEN MLBOEO
Ind/Abst Index Med.

MOLECULAR ENGINEERING. Vol. 1, No. 1 (1991)-. Academic Scholarly Publication. English. Four times a year. $287.00. Kluwer Academic Publishers, Postbus 322, 3300 AH Dordrecht The Netherlands. Tel 011 31 78 524400, FAX 011 31 78 183273, telex 20083. available on microfilm and microfiche from University Microfilms International (UMI). Documents available from CASDDS.
ISSN 0925-5125
NE
CCC
NLM W1; MO196GL   CODEN MOLEEV
Ind/Abst Chem. Abstr.

MOLECULAR MARINE BIOLOGY AND BIOTECHNOLOGY. See Biology-Marine Biology.
DD 576
ISSN 1053-6426
US
CCC
NLM W1; MO196LN   CODEN MMBBEQ

NANOBIOLOGY : JOURNAL OF RESEARCH ON NANOSCALE LIVING SYSTEMS. See Biology-Cytology.
LC QH506 .N36
DD 574.1
ISSN 0958-3165
UK
CCC
NLM W1; NA128N   CODEN NNOBE7

NEWSLETTER - CANADIAN MEDICAL AND BIOLOGICAL ENGINEERING SOCIETY. Main/Corp Canadian Medical and Biological Engineering Society. (Jan. 1966)-. Newsletter. English. Irregular. Free. Canadian Medical and Biological Engineering Society Wellington Crescent, Winnipeg Manitoba R3M 0A8 Canada. ctrl circ.
DD 610.28/06/271
ISSN 0384-1820
CN

NIHON IYO MASU SUPEKUTORU GAKKAI KOENSHU. See Chemistry and Chemicals-Analytical Chemistry.
DD 545.33
ISSN 0916-085X
JA

NIHON JIKI KYOMEI IGAKKAI ZASSHI. [Nihon Jiki Kyomei Igakkai zasshi]. VFOAT Japanese Journal of Magnetic Resonance in Medicine. (1987)-. Academic Scholarly Publication. Multiple languages. Four times a year. Nihon Jiki Kyomei Igakkai, (Japanese Soc. of Magnetic Resonance in Medicine), c/o Chiba Daigaku Igakubu, Hoshasen Igaku Kyoshitsu, 8-1 Inohana 1 Chome, Chibashi Chibaken 280, Japan. Documents available from CASDDS. *Continues NMR Igaku, 0286-1364.*
DD 616
ISSN 0914-9457
JA
Ind/Abst Chem. Abstr.

NIKKEI BAIOTEKU. [Nikkei baioteku]. VFOAT Nikkei Biotechnology. (1981)-. Trade Publication. Japanese. Twenty-four times a year. Nihon Keizai Shimbun Inc., 9-5 Otemachi 1 Chome, Chiyoda-ku Tokyo 100 Japan. Tel 011 81 3 32700251, 011 81 3 52108502 (Nikkei Business Publications Inc.), FAX 011 81 3 52552661, 011 81 3 52108119 (Nikkei Business Publications Inc.).
DD 620.8
ISSN 0285-4600
JA

NMR IN BIOMEDICINE. See Medical Sciences-Nuclear Medicine.
DD 574
ISSN 0952-3480
UK
CCC
NLM W1; N168G   CODEN NMRBEF

NOSTRUM. (19??)-. English. Four times a year. Free. Scottish Development Agency, 120 Bothwell Street, Glasgow G2 7JP United Kingdom.
UK
Desc: Pertains to the Scottish health care and biotechnology industry.
Ind/Abst Abstr. BioCommer.

NTIS ALERT. BIOMEDICAL TECHNOLOGY & HUMAN FACTORS ENGINEERING. Added/Corp United States. National Technical Information Service. (1992)-. Periodical. English. Twenty-four times a year. $145.00 US; $210.00 other. National Technical Information Service - NTIS, Room 2027S, 5285 Port Royal Road, Springfield VA 22161. Tel (703)487-4630, (703)487-4660, (703)487-4650, FAX (703)321-8547, telex 89-9405. Index available. *Continues Biomedical Technology & Human Factors Engineering / NTIS, 0163-1497.*
LC TA
DD 620
US
Desc: Provides information on instrumentation and bioengineering, bionics and artificial intelligence, human factors engineering, tissue preservation and storage, etc.

OLSEN'S BIOTECHNOLOGY REPORT. [Olsen's biotechnol. rep.]. Vol. 1, No. 1 (April 1986)-(19??). Periodical. English. G V Olsen Associates, 123 Picketts Ridge Road, West Redding CT 06896. Tel (203)938-4188, FAX (203)938-4186. ED Gus Olsen. Bk Rev, (Qty: 12). Circ: 150. *Continues Biotechnology.*
DD 660
ISSN 0889-616X
US
CEASED
Desc: Covers engineering of plants and animals and recombinant DNA gene manipulation.

PASCAL. 215, BIOTECHNOLOGIES. See Medical Sciences-Abstracting, Bibliographies and Statistics.
LC TP248
DD 660.6
NLM ZQ 1; B9355
ISSN 1146-5034
FR

PHARMACEUTICAL & BIOTECH DAILY. [Pharm. biotech dly.]. VFOAT Pharmaceutical and Biotech Daily. Vol. 1, No. 1 (Jan. 25, 1994)-(Nov. 1994). Periodical. English. King Publishing Group, 627 National Press Building, Washington DC 20045. Tel (202)638-4260, FAX (202)662-9744. *Formed by the union of Biotech Daily, 1067-1196 and Pharmaceutical Daily, 1071-5096. Merged into Washington Drug Letter, 0194-1291.*
DD 615
ISSN 1074-8636
US
CODEN PBDAEN
TITLE CHANGE

PHARMACEUTICAL DAILY. See Pharmacy and Pharmacology.
DD 338
ISSN 1071-5096
US
TITLE CHANGE

PHILIPPINE JOURNAL OF BIOTECHNOLOGY. [Philipp. j. biotechnol.]. (1990)-. Periodical. English. Two times a year (June, Dec.) $40.00, $20.00 per copy. BIOTECH-UPLB, College Lagune 4031, Philippines. Tel FAX 63 94 2721. ED Reynaldo E. Dela Cruz. Index available. cum. index. Bk Rev, (Qty: varies). Acid Free. Circ: 500.
DD 620.8
ISSN 0117-0503
PH
Pr Rev.

PHYSICAL TECHNIQUES IN MEDICINE. [Phys. tech. med.]. Vol. 1 (1977)-. English. Irregular. Price varies per volume. John Wiley & Sons Ltd., Baffins Lane, Chichester, West Sussex PO19 1UD United Kingdom. Tel 011 44 1243 779777, FAX 011 44 1243 776128 BTG:JWP001, telex 86290 WIBOOKG. (Subscription address: John Wiley & Sons Inc / New Jersey, PO Box 2575, Secaucus NJ 07096-2575.) ED J.T. McMullan.
ISSN 0162-2528
UK
NLM W1 PH748

PHYSIOLOGICAL MEASUREMENT. Added/Corp Institute of Physical Sciences in Medicine (Great Britain). Vol. 14, No. 1 (Feb. 1993)-. Periodical. English. Four times a year. $295.00. Institute of Physics, Techno House, Redcliffe Way, Bristol BS1 6NX United Kingdom. Tel 011 44 117 9297481, FAX 011 44 117 9294318, telex 449149 INSTP G. (Subscription address: American Institute of Physics, Publishing Sales, 500 Sunnyside Blvd., Woodbury NY 11797. Tel (516)576-2200.) ED D. H. Evans. Index available. *Continues Clinical Physics and Physiological Measurement., 0143-0815.*
ISSN 0967-3334
UK
CCC
NLM W1; PH926M   CODEN PMEAE3
Desc: Reports the applications of physical measurement to clinical practice and investigation, and serving the collaborative interests of biomedical engineers, medical physicists and clinical specialists.
Ind/Abst Curr. Cit.; Index Med.; Sci. Cit. Index.

PLANT BIOTECHNOLOGY. See Biology-Botany.
LC QK
DD 581
UK

PLANT BIOTECHNOLOGY. See Biology-Botany.
ISSN 0260-5902
UK
CCC

PLASMAS AND POLYMERS : AN INTERNATIONAL JOURNAL. See Chemistry and Chemicals-Organic Chemistry.
LC TP155
DD 660
US

PREHRAMBENO-TEHNOLOSKA I BIOTEHNOLOSKA REVIJA. See Food and Food Industry.
LC TP368
DD 664
ISSN 0352-9193
YU
CODEN PTBREK

PROCEEDINGS OF THE ANNUAL INTERNATIONAL CONFERENCE OF THE IEEE ENGINEERING IN MEDICINE AND BIOLOGY SOCIETY. Main/Corp IEEE Engineering in Medicine and Biology Society. Conference. 10th (1988)-. Periodical. English. One time a year. IEEE / Institute of Electrical and Electronics Engineers Inc., 345 East 47th Street, New York NY 10017-2394. Tel (908)981-1393, FAX (908)981-9667. *Continues IEEE Engineering in Medicine and Biology Society. Conference. Proceedings of the ... Annual Conference of the IEEE/Engineering in Medicine and Biology Society, 1049-3565.*
US
Ind/Abst Index IEEE Publ.

PROCEEDINGS OF THE ANNUAL ROCKY MOUNTAIN BIOENGINEERING SYMPOSIUM. [Proc. annu. Rocky Mt. Bioeng. Symp.]. Main/Conf Rocky Mountain Bioengineering Symposium. (19??)-. Academic Scholarly Publication. English. One time a year. Instrument Society of America, 67 Alexander Drive, Research Triangle NC 27709. Tel (919)549-8411, FAX (919)549-8288, telex 802 540. Documents available from CASDDS.
ISSN 0148-1002
US
CODEN RMBSAQ
Ind/Abst Chem. Abstr.

PROCEEDINGS OF THE ... IEEE ... ANNUAL NORTHEAST BIOENGINEERING CONFERENCE. [Proc. IEEE Annu. Northeast Bioeng. Conf.]. Added/Corp IEEE Engineering in Medicine and Biology Society. Whitaker Foundation. 17th (1991)-. English. Irregular. IEEE, Institute of Electrical and Electronics Engineers Inc., 445 Hoes Lane, Piscataway NJ 08855. Tel (908)981-0060. *Continues Northeast Bioengineering Conference. Proceedings of the ... Annual Northeast Bioengineering Conference.*
LC TA164 .N67a
DD 660/.6
ISSN 1071-121X
US
Ind/Abst Curr. Cit.

PROCEEDINGS OF THE INSTITUTION OF MECHANICAL ENGINEERS. PART H, JOURNAL OF ENGINEERING IN MEDICINE. [Proc. Inst. Mech. Eng., H J. eng. med.]. Added/Corp Institution of Mechanical Engineers (Great Britain). VFOAT Journal of Engineering in Medicine. Vol. 203, No. H1 (1989)-. Proceedings. English. Four times a year (Feb., May, Aug., Nov.). $309.00. Mechanical Engineering Publications, PO Box 24, Northgate Avenue, Bury St. Edmunds, Suffolk IP32 6BW United Kingdom. Tel 011 44 1284 763277, FAX 011 44 1284 704006, telex 817376. (Subscription address: Mechanical Engineering Publications / Western Hemisphere Subscriptions, Subscription Office, PO Box 361, Birmingham AL 35201-0361. Tel (800)633-4931 (US and Canada), (205)991-1177, FAX (205)995-1588.) ED D. Dowson. Bk Rev. available on microfilm and microfiche from University Microfilms International (UMI). Documents available from Article Express International, Ask*IEEE. *Continues Engineering in Medicine (Institution of Mechanical Engineers (Great Britain)), 0046-2039.*
LC R856.A1 P76
DD 610.28
ISSN 0954-4119
UK
CCC
NLM W1; PR5852D   CODEN PIHMEQ
Desc: Objectives of this journal are to record and encourage developments of further work in the field of engineering in medicine; report new work through the publication of research papers in good standing; publish review articles and relevant book reviews; illustrate the development and use of new and improved products and systems in the field of medicine.

Biology —Bioengineering

Ind/Abst Curr. Cit.; Eng. Index Annu.; Health Plan. Adminis.; Hosp. Health Admin. Index (1989); Index Med. (1989-); INSPEC (1989-).

LC TP248.13 .P76
DD 661.8 UK
NLM W1; PR588AB **CODEN** PBCHE5
PROCESS BIOCHEMISTRY. Vol. 26 No. 1 (Feb. 1991)-. Academic Scholarly Publication. English. Eight times a year. $388.00 The Americas; £260.00 other. Elsevier Applied Science, An Imprint of Elsevier Science Ltd., The Boulevard, Langford Lane, Kidlington, Oxford OX5 1GB United Kingdom. **Tel** 011 44 1865 843000, 011 44 1865 843699, FAX 011 44 1865 843010. **(Subscription address:** Elsevier Science Ltd. / Oxford Fulfillment Centre, PO Box 800, Kidlington OX5 1DX United Kingdom. **Tel** 011 44 865 843355.**) ED** C.M. Brown. available on an online database from Elsevier Electronic Subscriptions (EES). Documents available from The Genuine Article, CASDDS. **Continues** Process Biochemistry International, 0963-4940.
Desc: Industry-orientated research journal devoted to reporting advances in the science and technology of the application of living organisms to the production of materials for the benefit of mankind.
Ind/Abst BioBusiness; Chem. Abstr.; Curr. Aware. Biol. Sci., CABS; PESTDOC; Res. Alert [Full Cov.]; Sci. Cit. Index; SCISEARCH.

LC TP248.13 .P76
DD 574.19/2/05 US
NLM W1; PR666J **CODEN** PBBIE3
Pr Rev.
●**PROGRESS IN BIOCHEMISTRY AND BIOTECHNOLOGY. See** Biology-Biological Chemistry.

ISSN 0920-5438
NE
CCC
NLM W1; PR666M **CODEN** PRBEEZ
Pr Rev.
PROGRESS IN BIOMEDICAL ENGINEERING. [Prog. biomed. eng.]. Vol. 1 (1984)-. Academic Scholarly Publication. English. Irregular. Price varies per volume. Elsevier Science Publishers BV, PO Box 211, 1000 AE Amsterdam Netherlands. **Tel** 011 31 20 4853641, 011 31 20 4853642, FAX 011 31 20 4853598. **(Subscription address:** Elsevier Science Inc. / New York Books, 655 Avenue of the Americas, New York NY 10010. **Tel** (212)633-3650.**)** Documents available from BIOSIS Document Express, CASDDS.
Ind/Abst Biol. Abstr.; Chem. Abstr. (1984-).

LC TP248.P77 P763 ISSN 0269-2139
DD 660/.63 UK
CCC
NLM W1; PR787P **CODEN** PRENE9
Pr Rev.
PROTEIN ENGINEERING. [Protein eng.]. Vol. 1, No. 1 (Oct./Nov. 1986)-. Academic Scholarly Publication. English. Twelve times a year. $495.00. Oxford University Press / UK, Walton Street, Oxford OX2 6DP United Kingdom. **Tel** 011 44 1865 56767, FAX 011 44 1865 267773, telex 851/837330 OXPRES G. **(Subscription address:** Oxford University Press / USA, Journals Marketing Department, Oxford University Press, 2001 Evans Road, Cary NC 27513. **Tel** (800)451-7556, (919)677-0977, FAX (919)677-1714.**) ED** A. R. Rees. available on microfilm and microfiche from University Microfilms International (UMI). Documents available from The Genuine Article, BIOSIS Document Express, CASDDS.
Desc: Offers accelerated publication for full-length papers describing original research that advance the understanding of the structural and biochemical basis of protein function.
Ind/Abst Biol. Abstr. (1986-); Chem. Abstr. (1986-); CSA Neuro. Abstr. (?-?); Curr. Aware. Biol. Sci., CABS; Curr. Biotechnol.; Curr. Cit.; Curr. Contents Life Sci.; Dairy Sci. Abstr.; EMBASE; Food Sci. Technol. Abstr.; Genet. Abstr.; Index Med.; Index Vet.; Microbiol. Abstr. Sect. B (19??-19??); Oncog. Growth Factors Abstr.; PESTDOC; Ref. Upd. Deluxe Ed.; Res. Alert [Full Cov.]; Sci. Cit. Index; SCISEARCH; Trop. Dis. Bull.

LC TP248
DD 660.6 US
RAFI COMMUNIQUE. Added/Corp Rural Advancement Fund International. **VAT** Rural Advancement Fund International Communique. (19??)-. Periodical. English. Rural Advancement Fund International, PO Box 1029, Pittsboro NC 27312.
Ind/Abst Maize Abstr.; Plant Breed. Abstr.; Wheat Barley Trit. Abstr.; World Agric. Econ. Rural Sociol. Abstr.

LC QH442 ISSN 0196-0229
DD 574.87/3282 US
NLM W1 RE1109I **CODEN** RDTBD5
CEASED
RECOMBINANT DNA TECHNICAL BULLETIN. [Recomb. DNA tech. bull.]. **VAT** Recombinant Deoxyribonucleic Acid Technical Bulletin. (Summer 1977)-(1993). Bulletin. English. Superintendent of Documents, US Government Printing Office, Washington DC 20402. **Tel** (202)275-3328, FAX (202)786-2377. Documents available from BIOSIS Document Express, CASDDS. **Continues** Nucleic Acid Recombinant Scientific Memoranda, 0190-0714.
Desc: Provides scientific information and reports on recent progress in DNA research in the U.S. and abroad and a periodically updated listing of hostvector systems certified by NIH.
Ind/Abst BioBusiness; Biol. Abstr.; Biol. Dig.; Chem. Abstr.; Chem. Hazards Ind.; Curr. Biotechnol.; EMBASE; Index Med.; Lab. Hazards Bull.

ISSN 1183-7454
DD 610/.28 CN
NLM W1; RE1763
REHABILITATION TECHNOLOGY. [Rehabil. technol.]. **Added/Corp** University of New Brunswick. Institute of Biomedical Engineering. **VFOAT** Technologie de la Readaption. Vol. 1, No. 1 (Spring 1991)-. Periodical. English (French). Two times a year. Limited free distribution. Institute of Biomedical Engineering, University of New Brunswick, PO Box 4400, Fredericton New Brunswick E3B 5A3 Canada.

ISSN 1183-7454
DD 610/.28 CN
REHABILITATION TECHNOLOGY. (FRENCH ED.) (TECHNOLOGIE DE LA READAPTION.). [Rehabil. technol.]. **Added/Corp** University of New Brunswick. Institute of Biomedical Engineering. **VFOAT** Rehabilitation Technology. Vol. 1, No 1 (Spring 1991)-. Periodical. French (English). Two times a year. Limited free distribution. Institute of Biomedical Engineering, University of New Brunswick, PO Box 4400, Fredericton New Brunswick E3B 5A3 Canada.

LC S542.G72 A377 ISSN 0961-6071
DD 630/.72041 UK
REPORT / IGER. See Agriculture.

ISSN 0864-0300
CU
NLM W1; RE3597
REVISTA CUBANA DE INVESTIGACIONES BIOMEDICAS.
Added/Corp Centro Nacional de Informacion de Ciencias Medicas. **VFOAT** RCIB; IB. Vol. 1, No. 1 (1982)-. Periodical. Spanish (summaries and/or abstracts in English, French and Russian). Three times a year. $21.00 North America; $23.00 South America; $28.00 other. Ediciones Cubanas, Obispo 527 Altos ESQ Bernaza, CP 10100 Havana Cuba.
Desc: Magazine with a scientific and technical character. Publishes previously unpublished studies of Cuban authors, with a wide experience in biomedical researches.
Ind/Abst EMBASE [Select. Cov.].

ISSN 1068-3682
US
CCC
NLM W1; BI9189
●**RUSSIAN BIOTECHNOLOGY.** (1993)-. Periodical. English (translations available in Russian). Twelve times a year. $740.00. Allerton Press Inc., 150 Fifth Avenue, New York NY 10011. **Tel** (212)924-3950, FAX (212)463-9684, telex 427441 ALPRES. **Continues** Biotekhnologiia. English. Soviet Biotechnology, 0890-734X.
Ind/Abst Curr. Cit.

LC S ISSN 1052-6781
DD 630 US
NLM W1; SA104K
SAAS BULLETIN, BIOCHEMISTRY AND BIOTECHNOLOGY. [SAAS bull. biochem. biotechnol.]. **Added/Corp** Southern Association of Agricultural Scientists. Biochemistry and Biotechnology. **VFOAT** SAAS Bulletin of Biochemistry and Biotechnology. Vol. 1 (Jan. 1988)-. Bulletin. English. Documents available from CASDDS.
Ind/Abst AgBiotech News Inf.; AGRICOLA [Select. Cov.]; Biodeter. Abstr.; Chem. Abstr.; Hortic. Abstr.; Index Vet.; Maize Abstr.; Plant Breed. Abstr.; Rev. Agric. Entomol.

ISSN 1016-0884
KO
UDC 577.1
SAENGHWAHAK NYUSU. VFOAT
Biochemistry News; Saenghwahak Hoe Nyusu. (19??)-. Periodical. Multiple languages. Documents available from CASDDS.
Ind/Abst Chem. Abstr.

LC QR53 .S35 ISSN 0257-2389
DD 660.62 KO
NLM W1; SA783 **CODEN** SMHAEH
SANNEB MISAINMURHAG HOIJI. See Biology-Microbiology.

ISSN 1053-6868
DD 338 US
TITLE CHANGE
SECOND SOURCE BIOMEDICAL. [Second source biomed.]. **VFOAT** Biomedical. Vol. 1, No. 1 (May 1990)-(1993). Periodical. English. Second Source Publications Inc., 10 Risho Avenue, East Providence RI 02914. **Tel** (401)434-1050. Documents available from The Genuine Article. **Continues in part** Second Source, 0892-3426. **Continued by** Biomedical Technology Management, 1073-1210.
Ind/Abst Res. Alert.

ISSN 0919-3758
JA
CODEN SEKAEA
●**SEIBUTSU KOGAKKAI SHI = SEIBUTSU-KOGAKU KAISHI. Added/Corp**
Nihon Seibutsu Kogakukai. **VFOAT** Seibutsu-Kogaku Kaishi. (1993)-. Periodical. Japanese (summaries and/or abstracts in English; table of contents in English). Six times a year. $340.00. Nihon Hakko Kogakkai, (Society of Fermentation Technology Japan), Osaka Daigaku Kogakubu, 2-1 Yamadaoka Suitashi, Osakafu 565 Japan. **(Subscription address:** Maruzen Company Ltd., PO Box 5050, Import & Export Department, Tokyo 100 31 Japan. **Tel** 011 81 3 32789224.**) Continues** Hakko Kogakkai shi, 0385-6151.
Ind/Abst Chem. Abstr.; Curr. Cit.

LC RA409.5 .S33
DD 610.21 JA
SEITAI JOHO KAGAKU KENKYU. BIOMEDICAL INFORMATION SCIENCE.
Added/Corp Seitai Joho Shori Kenkyu Gurupu. **VFOAT** Biomedical Information Science. (1976)-. Japanese. Kobe Daigaku Igakubu, Dai-2 Seirigabu Kyoshitsu Kusunokicho 6-chome Ikuta-ku 650, Koba Japan.

ISSN 1000-3061
CC
CODEN SGXUED
Pr Rev.
SHENGWU GONGCHENG XUEBAO.
(SHENG WU KUNG CHENG HSUEH PAO.). [Shengwu gongcheng xuebao]. **Added/Corp** Chung-Kuo Wei Sheng Wu Hsueh Hui. Kuo Chia Ko Wei Sheng Wu Kung Cheng Kai Fa Chung Hsin (China). **VFOAT** Chinese Journal of Biotechnology. (198?)-. Academic Scholarly Publication. Chinese (summaries and/or abstracts in English). Four times a year. $66.80. Science Press, 16 Donghuangchenggen North Street, Beijing 100707, People's Republic of China. **Tel** 011 86 1 4019821, 011 86 1 4010642, FAX 011 86 1 4012180, 011 86 1 4019810, telex 210147. **Ad Acc. Circ:** 6,000. Documents available from CASDDS.
Desc: Covers research papers on genetic, fermentation, cell and enzyme engineering.
Ind/Abst Chem. Abstr.

ISSN 1000-8543
CC
NLM W1; SH287M **CODEN** SHZAE4
Pr Rev.
SHENGWU HUAXUE ZAZHI. (SHENG WU HUA HSUEH TSA CHIH.). [Shengwu huaxue zazhi].
Added/Corp Chung-Kuo Sheng Wu Hua Hsueh Hui. **VFOAT** Chinese Biochemical Journal. (1985)-. Periodical. Chinese (summaries and/or abstracts in English; table of contents in English). Six times a year. Beijing Yike Daxue / Shengwu Huaxue Xi, Beijing Medical University, Department of Biochemistry, No. 38 Xueyuan Lu, Beijing 100083, People's Republic of China. **Tel** 861 2091416, FAX 861 2015681. **ED** C. Changying. **Bk Rev. Ad Acc.** Documents available from CASDDS, BLDSC.
Ind/Abst Chem. Abstr.

ISSN 0295-1967
FR
NLM W1; SP314F
SPECTRA BIOLOGIE. Vol. 14 No. 116 (Nov./Dec. 1986)-. Academic Scholarly Publication. French (summaries and/or abstracts in English). Eight times a year. $122.48. Editions PCI, 24 rue de Dunkerque, 75010 Paris Cedex France. **Tel** 011 33 45 267865. Documents available from CASDDS. **Continues** Spectra 2000 Biologie.
Ind/Abst Anal. Abstr.; Chem. Abstr.

ISSN 1055-7318
DD 620 US
STRATEGIC DEVELOPMENTS IN BIOTECHNOLOGY. [Strateg. dev. biotechnol.].
Added/Corp Institute for Biotechnology Information (North Carolina Biotechnology Center) North Carolina Biotechnology Center. Information Division. Vol. 1, No. 1 (Feb. 1991)-. Periodical. English. Twelve times a year. $299.00. Institute of Biotechnology Information, PO Box 14569, Research Triangle Park NC 27709. **Tel** (919)544-5111. **ED** Pamela J. Bruns. **Circ:** 80.

LC TP368 ISSN 0253-9675
DD 664 SZ
NLM W1; SW406G **CODEN** SWBIED
SWISS BIOTECH. Added/Corp Swiss Coordination Committee for Biotechnology. (198?)-. Periodical. English (French, Italian and Spanish). Six times a year (Feb., Apr., June, Aug., Oct., Dec.). $188.58. Verlag Dr Felix Wuest AG, Seestrasse 5 Postfach, CH-8700 Kuesnacht Switzerland. **Tel** 011 41 1 9110055, FAX 011 41 1 9106080, telex 825705.
Desc: Information medium of the Swiss Coordination Committee for biotechnology.
Ind/Abst Curr. Biotechnol.; PESTDOC.

LC TP248.6 .T42 ISSN 0741-3661
DD 660/.6 US

TECHNICAL INSIGHTS ANNUAL REPORT ON GENETIC TECHNOLOGY. [Tech. Insights annu. rep. genet. technol.]. **Added/Corp** Technical Insights, Inc. **VFOAT** Annual Report on Genetic Technology. (1984)-. English. Four times a year. Free on request. Technical Insights Inc., PO Box 1304, Fort Lee NJ 07024-9967. **Tel** (201)568-4744, FAX (201)568-8247, telex 425900 SWIFT UI.

ISSN 0928-7329
NE
CCC
NLM W1; TE211CD

●**TECHNOLOGY AND HEALTH CARE : OFFICIAL JOURNAL OF THE EUROPEAN SOCIETY FOR ENGINEERING AND MEDICINE.** **Added/Corp** European Society for Engineering and Medicine. Vol. 1, No. 1 (Apr. 1993)-. Academic Scholarly Publication. English. Four times a year (1 volume). $313.00. Elsevier Science Publishers BV, PO Box 211, 1000 AE Amsterdam Netherlands. **Tel** 011 31 20 4853641, 011 31 20 4853642, FAX 011 31 20 4853598. available on an online database from Elsevier Electronic Subscriptions (EES).
Ind/Abst Index Med.

ISSN 1049-4324
DD 621 US

TECHTRANSFER NEWS. [TechTransfer news]. **VFOAT** Tech Transfer News. Vol. 1, No. 1 (Mar. 1990)-. Periodical. English. Irregular. $300.00. TechTransfer Services, 69 Midland Avenue, Tarrytown NY 10591. **Tel** (914)631-2699. **ED** Marvin Margothes.
Desc: Provides information on technology for medical diagnostics and laboratory instruments, offered by nonprofit research organizations and government agencies internationally.

IT

TECNOLOGIE BIOMEDICHE. (19??)-. Italian. Two times a year. L100000 Italy; L120000 Europe; L135000 other. Edizioni Protezione Civile SPA, Via dell Acqua Traversa 187/189, 00135 Rome Italy. **Tel** 011 39 6 3313000, FAX 011 39 6 3313212, telex 626462 EPCINFI. Index available. cum. index. **Circ:** 5,000. ***Continues*** *Elettromedicali.*

LC R856
DD 610.28 IT
NLM W1; TE211
SUSPENDED

TECNOLOGIEBIOMEDICHE. **VFOAT** Tecnologie Biomediche. (1987)-Suspended (Dec. 1994). Academic Scholarly Publication. Italian. Six times a year. Edizioni Protezione Civile SPA, Via dell Acqua Traversa 187/189, 00135 Rome Italy. **Tel** 011 39 6 3313000, FAX 011 39 6 3313212, telex 626462 EPCINFI. ***Continues*** *Elettromedicali.*

LC R856 ISSN 1076-3279
DD 610.28 US
NLM W1; TI844

●**TISSUE ENGINEERING.** (1995)-. Academic Scholarly Publication. English. Four times a year. $188.00. Mary Ann Liebert Inc., 2 Madison Avenue, Larchmont NY 10538. **Tel** (914)834-3100, (800)M-LIEBERT, FAX (212)289-4697.
Desc: Focuses on engineering new tissue. Applies principles and methods of engineering and the life sciences toward the fundamental understanding of structure-function relationships in normal and pathologic tissue and the development of biological substitutes.

CN

TORONTO BIOSCAN. (19??)-. English. Four times a year. Toronto Biotechnology Initiative, PO Box 446, Station A, Toronto Ontario M5W 1C2 Canada.
Ind/Abst Abstr. BioCommer.

ISSN 1051-9688
DD 660 US
NLM W1; TR228WT

●**TRANSGENICA (LEVITTOWN, PA).** (TRANSGENICA : THE JOURNAL OF CLINICAL BIOTECHNOLOGY.). [Transgenica]. **Added/Corp** Pharmaceutical Information Associates. Vol. 1, No. 1 (Spring 1994)-. Periodical. English. Four times a year. $60.00. Pharmaceutical Information Associates, Ltd., 2761 Trenton Road, Levittown PA 19056. **Tel** (215)949-0490.

ISSN 1061-6314
DD 615 US

TRENDS, BIOTECHNOLOGY : INFORMATION AND ISSUES FOR PHARMACISTS. See Pharmacy and Pharmacology.

LC TP248.13 ISSN 0167-7799
DD 660/.6/05 NE
CCC
NLM W1 TR3407 **CODEN** TRBIDM
Pr Rev.

TRENDS IN BIOTECHNOLOGY (PERSONAL EDITION). (TRENDS IN BIOTECHNOLOGY.). [Trends biotechnol.]. Vol. 1, No. 1 (March/April 1983)-. Academic Scholarly Publication. English. Twelve times a year. $125.00. Elsevier Science Publishers BV, PO Box 211, 1000 AE Amsterdam Netherlands. **Tel** 011 31 20 4853641, 011 31 20 4853642, FAX 011 31 20 4853598. **ED** J. Hodgson. **Bk Rev. Ad Acc. Circ:** 4,000. available in microform from University Microfilms International (UMI). Documents available from The Genuine Article, CASDDS.
Desc: Provides ideas and opinions on all facets of biotechnology from cell culture; gene cloning, protoplast fusion, and screening through fermentation technology, raw materials formulation and immobilization techniques, to down-stream processing and purification.
Ind/Abst Abstr. BioCommer.; AgBiotech News Inf.; BioBusiness; Biodeter. Abstr.; Biotechnol. Res. Abstr.; Chem. Abstr. (1983-); CSA Neuro. Abstr. (?-?); Curr. Aware. Biol. Sci., CABS; Curr. Contents Agric. Biol. Environ. Sci.; EMBASE; Food Sci. Technol. Abstr.; Genet. Abstr.; Maize Abstr.; Microbiol. Abstr. Sect. B; Microbiol. Abstr. Sect. A; Nematol. Abstr.; Oncog. Growth Factors Abstr.; Life Sci. Collect.; Plant Breed. Abstr.; Plant Grow. Reg. Abstr.; Protozoolog. Abstr.; Res. Alert [Full Cov.]; Rice Abstr.; Sci. Cit. Index; SCISEARCH; Seed Abstr.; Soils Fert.; Soyabean Abstr.

LC TP248.13 .T743 ISSN 0167-9430
DD 660/.6 NE
CCC
Pr Rev.

TRENDS IN BIOTECHNOLOGY (REFERENCE ED.). (TRENDS IN BIOTECHNOLOGY.). [Trends biotechnol.]. Vol. 1 (1983)-. Periodical. English. Twelve times a year. $614.00. Elsevier Trends Journals, An Imprint of Elsevier Science Ltd., The Boulevard, Langford Lane, Kidlington, Oxford OX5 1GB United Kingdom. **Tel** 011 44 1865 843000, 011 44 1865 843699, FAX 011 44 1865 843010. **(Subscription address:** Elsevier Science Ltd. / Oxford Fulfillment Centre, PO Box 800, Kidlington OX5 1DX United Kingdom. **Tel** 011 44 865 843355.**)** available on microfilm and microfiche from University Microfilms International (UMI); available on an online database from Elsevier Electronic Subscriptions (EES). Documents available from Article Express International, ADONIS.
Ind/Abst ADONIS; AGRICOLA [Select. Cov.]; Curr. Biotechnol.; Curr. Cit.; Curr. Contents Agric. Biol. Environ. Sci.; Ei Page One; EMBASE; Eng. Index Annu. [Select. Cov.]; Index Vet.; PESTDOC; Ref. Upd. Deluxe Ed.

ISSN 1066-2936
DD 616 US
CODEN UHMEE7
Pr Rev.

●**UNDERSEA & HYPERBARIC MEDICINE.** (UNDERSEA & HYPERBARIC MEDICINE : JOURNAL OF THE UNDERSEA AND HYPERBARIC MEDICAL SOCIETY.). [Undersea hyperb. med.]. **Added/Corp** Undersea and Hyperbaric Medical Society. **VFOAT** Undersea and Hyperbaric Medicine. (1993)-. Periodical. English. Four times a year. $85.00. Undersea and Hyperbaric Medical Society, 10531 Metropolitan Avenue, Kensington MD 20895. **Tel** (301)942-2980. Documents available from BIOSIS Document Express. ***Formed by the union of*** *Undersea Biomedical Research, 0093-5387* ***and*** *Journal of Hyperbaric Medicine, 0884-1225.*
Ind/Abst Biol. Abstr.; Curr. Cit.; Curr. Contents Life Sci.; Index Med.; Sci. Cit. Index; Soc. Sci. Cit. Index [Select. Cov.].

ISSN 1078-2893
US

●**UNIVERSITY BIOMED WEEKLY.** (1995)-. English. Forty-eight times a year (weekly). $995.00. CW Henderson, PO Box 5528, Atlanta GA 30307-0528. **Tel** (404)377-8895, FAX (404)378-5411. **(Subscription address:** CW Henderson, Subscription Office, PO Box 830409, Birmingham AL 35283-0409. **Tel** (800)633-4931, (205)995-1567 (outside US and Canada), FAX (205)995-1588.**)**
Desc: Bridges the research tracks of academia and industry. Geared toward both university-based researchers interested in pharmaceutical industry involvement in biomedical research, as well as pharmaceutical professionals interested in biotech activities at universities.

ISSN 1047-4730
DD 574 US
NLM W1; NO849L
CEASED

WORLD BIO LICENSING & PATENT REPORT. [World bio licens. pat. rep.]. **VFOAT** World Bio Licensing and Patent Report; World Biolicensing & Patent Report; World Biolicensing and Patent Report. (198?)-(1993). Periodical. English. Deborah Mysiewicz Publishers, PO Box 2009, Oak Harbor WA 98277. **Tel** (415)689-2972. ***Continues*** *World Biolicensing Report, 0883-5527.*

UK

WORLD BIOTECH REPORT. (19??)-. English. Irregular. Online Publications, Blenheim House, Ash Hill Drive, Pinner Middlesex HA5 2AE United Kingdom. **Tel** 011 44 181 8684466, FAX 011 44 181 8689933, telex 851/923498.
Ind/Abst PESTDOC.

LC QR53 .M58 ISSN 0959-3993
DD 660/.62/05 UK
CCC
NLM W1; WO88F **CODEN** WJMBEY

WORLD JOURNAL OF MICROBIOLOGY & BIOTECHNOLOGY. See Biology-Microbiology.

ISSN 0190-0617
US
NLM W 3.5 W929

WORLDWIDE BIOMEDICAL MEETINGS, CONFERENCES, AND EXHIBITIONS. Vol. 1 (Apr. 1977)-. Periodical. English. Four times a year. Robert First, Inc., 405 Lexington Avenue, New York NY 10017.

LC R856.A1 C4 ISSN 0258-8021
DD 610/.28 CC
NLM W1; CH991AR **CODEN** ZSYXEI

ZHONGGUO SHENGWU YIXUE, GONGCHENG XUEBAO. (CHUNG-KUO SHENG WU I HSUEH KUNG CHENG HSUEH PAO = CHINESE JOURNAL OF BIOMEDICAL ENGINEERING.). [Zhongguo shengwu yixue, gongcheng xuebao]. **Added/Corp** Chung-kuo i Hsueh ko Hsueh Yuan. Chung-kuo Sheng wu i Hsueh Kung Cheng Hsueh Hui. **VFOAT** Chinese Journal of Biomedical Engineering. Vol. 1, (Nov. 1982)-. Academic Scholarly Publication. Chinese (summaries and/or abstracts in English). Four times a year. $18.00. Chung-Kuo Tu Shu Shin Chu Kou Tsung Kung SSU, 137 Chao Nei Ta Chieh, Beijing, People's Republic of China. **Tel** 440731 203, FAX 401 5664, telex 22313 CPC CN. **Ad Acc.** Documents available from Article Express International, BIOSIS Document Express, Ask*IEEE, CASDDS.
Ind/Abst Biol. Abstr. (1987-); Chem. Abstr.; Ei Page One; EMBASE; Eng. Index Annu.; INSPEC (1985-).

BIOLOGICAL CHEMISTRY

LC QP501 .A18 ISSN 0237-6261
DD 574.19/2/05 HU
CCC
NLM W1; AC755H **CODEN** ABBHE5
Pr Rev. TITLE CHANGE

ACTA BIOCHIMICA ET BIOPHYSICA HUNGARICA. [Acta biochim. biophys. Hung.]. Vol. 21, No. 1-2 (1986)-(19??). Academic Scholarly Publication. English (German). Akademiai Kiado, Publishing House of the Hungarian Academy of Sciences, Prielle Kornelia u. 19-35, H-1117 Budapest Hungary. **Tel** 011 36 1 1811991, FAX 011 36 1 1811991, telex 22-6228 AKNYO H. **ED** Elodi Pal and Jozsef Tigyi. Index available. cum. index. **Ad Acc. Circ:** 800. Documents available from The Genuine Article, BIOSIS Document Express, CASDDS. ***Continues*** *Acta Biochimica et Biophysica, 0001-5253.* ***Merged into*** *Neurobiology.*
Desc: Publishes original papers on biochemistry and biophysics. Main topics are: proteins (structure and synthesis), enzymes, nucleic acids, regulatory and transport processes, bioenergetics, excitation, muscular contraction, radiobiology, biocybernetics, functional structure and ultrastructure.
Ind/Abst Anim. Breed. Abstr.; Biol. Abstr. (1986-); Chem. Abstr. (1986-); Crop Physiol. Abstr.; Dairy Sci. Abstr.; EMBASE; Field Crop Abstr.; Index Med. (1986-); Plant Breed. Abstr.; Res. Alert [Select. Cov.]; Sci. Cit. Index (19??-19??); SCISEARCH; Seed Abstr.; Soc. Sci. Cit. Index [Select. Cov.]; Wheat Barley Trit. Abstr.

LC QP501 .A2 ISSN 0001-527X
DD 612.015 PL
CODEN ABPLAF
Pr Rev.

ACTA BIOCHIMICA POLONICA. [Acta biochim. pol.]. **Added/Corp** United States. Dept. of Health, Education, and Welfare. National Science Foundation (U.S.) National Library of Medicine (U.S.) Polska Akademia Nauk. Komitet Biochemiczny I Biofizyczny. Polska Akademia Nauk. Komitet Biochemiczny. Vol. 1 (1954)-. Periodical. English (Polish; summaries and/or abstracts in Polish and Russian). Four times a year. $160.00 (institutions), $80.00 (individuals). **(Subscription address:** Ars Polona-Ruch, PO Box 1001, Krakowskie Przedmiescie 7, 00-068 Warsaw Poland. **Tel** 011 48 22 261201.**)** Documents available from The Genuine Article, BIOSIS Document Express, CASDDS.
Ind/Abst Anim. Breed. Abstr.; Biol. Abstr.; Chem. Abstr.; CSA Neuro. Abstr. (?-?); Curr. Cit.; Curr. Contents Life Sci.; Dairy Sci. Abstr.; EMBASE; Field Crop Abstr.; Food Sci. Technol. Abstr.; Grass. Forage Abstr.; Hortic. Abstr.;

Index Med.; NAPRALERT; Life Sci. Collect.; Plant Breed. Abstr.; Protozoolog. Abstr.; Res. Alert [Full Cov.]; Sci. Cit. Index; SCISEARCH.

LC QP **ISSN** 0325-2957
DD 612 AG
UDC 61
NLM W1 AC764 **CODEN** ABCLDL
Pr Rev.

ACTA BIOQUIMICA CLINICA LATINOAMERICANA. [Acta bioquim. clin. latinoam.]. **Added/Corp** Federacion de Especialistas de Analisis Biologicos de la Provicia de Buenos Aires. Confederacion Latinoamericana de Bioquimica Clinica. Vol. 9, No. 3 (Sept. 1975)-. Academic Scholarly Publication. Spanish (summaries and/or abstracts in English). Four times a year (Mar., June, Sept., Dec.). $105.00. Federacion de Bioquimica, Prov de Buenos Aires, Calle 6 #1344, 1900 LA Plata Argentina. **Tel** 011 54 21 38821, 011 54 21 42797. **ED** Juan Miguel Castagnino. cum. index. **Ad Acc. Circ:** 2,200 (ctrl). Documents available from BIOSIS Document Express, CASDDS. ***Continues*** *Bioquimica Clinica, 0006-3533.*
Desc: Refers to subjects in the field of clinical biochemistry.
Ind/Abst Biol. Abstr.; Chem. Abstr.; EMBASE; Life Sci. Collect.

LC QP501 .A33 **ISSN** 0208-614X
DD 574.1 PL
CODEN AUFBD3

ACTA UNIVERSITATIS LODZIENSIS. FOLIA BIOCHIMICA ET BIOPHYSICA. **Added/Corp** Uniwersytet Lodzki. **VFOAT** Folia Biochimica et Biophysica. (1981)-. Monographic series. Polish (English and Russian). Irregular. Price varies per volume. Wydawnictwo Uniwersytetu Lodzkiego, Ul. Jaracza 34, Lodz Poland. **Tel** 011 48 42 331671, 011 48 42 336541. **(Subscription address:** Ars Polona-Ruch, PO Box 1001, Krakowskie Przedmiescie 7, 00-068 Warsaw Poland. **Tel** 011 48 22 261201.) ***Continues in part*** *Acta Universitatis Lodziensis. Seria II. Nauki Matematyczno-Przyrodnicze, 0137-4605.*
Ind/Abst Chem. Abstr.

ISSN 1351-5268
UK

ACTIVIN & INHIBIN. (19??)-. English. £85.00. SUBIS, Mansion House 19 Kingfield Road, Sheffield S11 9AS United Kingdom. **Tel** 011 44 114 2554433, FAX 011 44 114 255 4626.

UK
NLM W1; AD435

ADVANCES IN APPLIED LIPID RESEARCH. **VFOAT** Applied Lipid Research. Vol. 1 (1992)-. Periodical. English. $78.50. JAI Press Ltd., The Courtyard, 28 High Street, Hampton Hill Middlesex TW12 1PD United Kingdom. **Tel** 011 44 181 9439296, FAX 011 44 181 9439317. **ED** Fred Padley.
Desc: Aimed at the applied area of lipid research.

LC QH345 .A43 **ISSN** 1057-8943
DD 574.19/05 US
NLM W1; AD449G **CODEN** ABCHEA

ADVANCES IN BIOPHYSICAL CHEMISTRY. [Adv. biophys. chem.]. Vol. 1 (1990)-. Academic Scholarly Publication. English. $90.25. JAI Press Inc., 55 Old Post Road, Suite 2, PO Box 1678, Greenwich CT 06836-1678. **Tel** (203)661-7602, FAX (203)661-0792. **ED** Allen C. Bush. Documents available from CASDDS.
Desc: Presents an overview of several recent topics in high-resolution nuclear magnetic resonance spectroscopy and molecular modeling along with structural chemistry crucial for protein design.
Ind/Abst Chem. Abstr.

LC QD321 .A2 **ISSN** 0065-2318
DD 547/.78 US
CCC
NLM W1 AD53 **CODEN** ACBYAP

ADVANCES IN CARBOHYDRATE CHEMISTRY AND BIOCHEMISTRY. [Adv. carbohydr. chem. biochem.]. Vol. 24 (1969)-. Academic Scholarly Publication. English. Irregular. Price varies per volume. Academic Press Inc., 6277 Sea Harbor Drive, Orlando FL 32887. **Tel** (800)543-9534, (407)345-4100, FAX (407)352-3445. **ED** Melville L. Wolfrom and R. Stuart Tipson. cum. index. Documents available from The Genuine Article, CASDDS. ***Continues*** *Advances in Carbohydrate Chemistry, 0096-5332.*
Ind/Abst Abstr. Bull. Inst. Pap. Sci. Tech.; Chem Inform; Chem. Abstr.; Curr. Chem. React.; Curr. Cit.; Dairy Sci. Abstr.; EMBASE; Food Sci. Technol. Abstr.; Foods Adlibra; Health Plan. Adminis.; Hortic. Abstr.; Index Med.; Index Sci. Rev. [Full Cov.]; Nutr. Abstr. Rev., Ser. B, Live Feeds and Feed.; Nutr. Abstr. Rev., Ser. A, Hum. Exp.; Life Sci. Collect.; Ref. Upd. Basic Ed.; Ref. Upd. Deluxe Ed.; Res. Alert [Full Cov.]; Sci. Cit. Index; SCISEARCH; Vitis Vitic. Enol. Abstr.

LC RB1 .A2 **ISSN** 0065-2423
DD 616.0756 US
UDC 616-098 **CCC**
NLM W1 AD54 **CODEN** ACLCA9
Pr Rev.

ADVANCES IN CLINICAL CHEMISTRY. **See** Chemistry and Chemicals.

LC QP501 .A36 **ISSN** 1064-2722
DD 591.19/2 US
NLM W1; AD547L **CODEN** ADEBEG

ADVANCES IN DEVELOPMENTAL BIOCHEMISTRY. [Adv. dev. biochem.]. **VFOAT** Developmental Biochemistry. Vol. 1 (1992)-. English. $90.25. JAI Press Inc., 55 Old Post Road, Suite 2, PO Box 1678, Greenwich CT 06836-1678. **Tel** (203)661-7602, FAX (203)661-0792. **ED** Paul Wasserman.

LC QP519.9.E434 A38 **ISSN** 0932-3031
DD 541.3/72 GW
UDC 543.545 **CCC**
NLM W1; AD554 **CODEN** ADELEC

ADVANCES IN ELECTROPHORESIS. **See** Chemistry and Chemicals-Physical and Theoretical Chemistry.

LC QP601.A1 A28 **ISSN** 0065-2571
DD 612.0151 UK
CCC
NLM W3 AD24 **CODEN** AEZRA2
Pr Rev.

ADVANCES IN ENZYME REGULATION. [Adv. enzyme regul.]. Vol. 1 (1963)-. English. One time a year. $493.00. Pergamon Press, An Imprint of Elsevier Science Ltd., The Boulevard, Langford Lane, Kidlington, Oxford OX5 1GB United Kingdom. **Tel** 011 44 1865 843000, 011 44 1865 843699, FAX 011 44 1865 843010. **(Subscription address:** Elsevier Science Ltd. / Oxford Fulfillment Centre, PO Box 800, Kidlington OX5 1DX United Kingdom. **Tel** 011 44 865 843355.) **ED** George Weber. cum. index. available on microfilm and microfiche from University Microfilms International (UMI); available on an online database from Elsevier Electronic Subscriptions (EES). Documents available from The Genuine Article, BIOSIS Document Express, CASDDS.
Desc: Covers subjects which have reached the stage of productive summarization and critical evaluation in the light of new results. Topics covered include metabolic regulation, inborn errors of metabolism, metabolic diseases, diabetes and cancer.
Ind/Abst AGRICOLA; Biol. Abstr.; Chem. Abstr.; Curr. Aware. Biol. Sci., CABS; Curr. Cit.; Index Med.; Index Sci. Rev. [Full Cov.]; Life Sci. Collect.; Res. Alert [Full Cov.]; Sci. Cit. Index; SCISEARCH.

LC QP601.A1 A3 **ISSN** 0065-258X
DD 612.0151 US
CCC
Pr Rev.

ADVANCES IN ENZYMOLOGY AND RELATED SUBJECTS. [Advan. enzymol. relat. subj.]. **VFOAT** Advances in Enzymology; Advances in Enzymology and Related Subjects of Biochemistry; Advances in Enzymology and Related Areas of Molecular Biology. Vol. 1 (1941)-. Academic Scholarly Publication. English. Irregular. $69.95. John Wiley & Sons, Inc., 605 Third Avenue, New York NY 10158-0012. **Tel** (212)850-6000, (212)850-6645, FAX (212)850-6088, telex 12-7063. **(Subscription address:** John Wiley & Sons / UK, Baffins Lane, Chichester, West Sussex PO19 1UD United Kingdom. **Tel** 011 44 1243 779777, FAX 011 44 243 776128, telex 86290 WIBOOKG.) Documents available from The Genuine Article, CASDDS.
Ind/Abst AGRICOLA [Select. Cov.]; Chem. Abstr.; Curr. Cit.; Dairy Sci. Abstr.; Energy Res. Abstr. (Aug. 1982-); Foods Adlibra; Index Med.; Index Sci. Rev. [Full Cov.]; Life Sci. Collect.; PESTDOC; Res. Alert [Full Cov.].

LC QP501 .A37 **ISSN** 0190-0218
DD 574.19/214 US
NLM W1 AD648L **CODEN** AIBIDM

ADVANCES IN INORGANIC BIOCHEMISTRY. [Adv. inorg. biochem.]. (1979)-. Academic Scholarly Publication. English. Irregular. Prentice Hall Simon & Schuster, PO Box 11071, Des Moines IA 50336. **Tel** (800)947-7700, (515)284-6751. **ED** G.L. Eichhorn and L.G. Marzilli. Documents available from The Genuine Article, CASDDS.
Ind/Abst AGRICOLA [Select. Cov.]; Chem. Abstr.; Index Med. (1983-1984; Index Sci. Rev. [Full Cov.]; Res. Alert [Full Cov.]; SCISEARCH.

LC QP751 .A35 **ISSN** 0065-2849
DD 612.015 US
UDC 577.115 **CCC**
NLM W1 AD656 **CODEN** ALPDAR
Pr Rev.

ADVANCES IN LIPID RESEARCH. [Adv. lipid res.]. Vol. 1 (1963)-. Academic Scholarly Publication. English. Irregular. $85.00 (Vol. 26). Academic Press Inc., 6277 Sea Harbor Drive, Orlando FL 32887. **Tel** (800)543-9534, (407)345-4100, FAX (407)352-3445. **ED** Rodolfo Paoletti and David Kritchevsky. Documents available from The Genuine Article, CASDDS.
Ind/Abst AGRICOLA [Select. Cov.]; Chem. Abstr.; Curr. Aware. Biol. Sci., CABS; Dairy Sci. Abstr.; Food Sci. Technol. Abstr.; Index Med.; Index Sci. Rev. [Full Cov.]; Nutr. Abstr. Rev., Ser. B, Live Feeds and Feed.; Nutr. Abstr. Rev., Ser. A, Hum. Exp.; Life Sci. Collect.; Ref. Upd. Deluxe Ed.; Res. Alert [Full Cov.]; Sci. Cit. Index; SCISEARCH.

LC QD **ISSN** 0145-4811
DD 540 US
UDC 54
NLM W1 AD679M **CODEN** AMSMDB

ADVANCES IN MASS SPECTROMETRY IN BIOCHEMISTRY AND MEDICINE. [Adv. mass spectrom. biochem. med.]. **VFOAT** Mass Spectrometry in Biochemistry and Medicine. Vol. 1 (1976)-. Academic Scholarly Publication. English. Irregular. Price varies per volume. John Wiley & Sons, Inc., 605 Third Avenue, New York NY 10158-0012. **Tel** (212)850-6000, (212)850-6645, FAX (212)850-6088, telex 12-7063. **(Subscription address:** John Wiley & Sons / UK, Baffins Lane, Chichester, West Sussex PO19 1UD United Kingdom. **Tel** 011 44 1243 779777, FAX 011 44 243 776128, telex 86290 WIBOOKG.) Documents available from CASDDS.
Ind/Abst Chem. Abstr.

LC QP535.O1 A38 **ISSN** 1044-4696
DD 574.19/214 US
CODEN ADOXEU

ADVANCES IN OXYGENATED PROCESSES. [Adv. oxyg. process.]. Vol. 1 (1988)-. Periodical. English. One time a year. $90.25. JAI Press Inc., 55 Old Post Road, Suite 2, PO Box 1678, Greenwich CT 06836-1678. **Tel** (203)661-7602, FAX (203)661-0792. Documents available from CASDDS.
Desc: Information on active oxygen, oxidation and chemistry radicals.
Ind/Abst Chem. Abstr.

LC QP609.P56 A39 **ISSN** 0775-051X
DD 574.19/253 BE
NLM W1; AD795

ADVANCES IN PROTEIN PHOSPHATASES. [Adv. protein phosphatases]. **Added/Corp** Koninklijke Academie voor Geneeskunde van Belgie. Vol. 1 (1985)-. English. Irregular. 1500F. Universitaire Pers Leuven, Leuven University Press, Krakenstraat 3, B-3000 Leuven Belgium. **Tel** 011 32 16 284175, FAX 011 32 16 284176. **ED** W. Merlevede and J. Di Salvo. Documents available from CASDDS.
Ind/Abst Chem. Abstr.; Curr. Cit.

LC QP501 .A64 **ISSN** 0003-2697
DD 612.015 US
CCC
NLM W1 AN1915 **CODEN** ANBCA2ANBCA
Pr Rev.

ANALYTICAL BIOCHEMISTRY. [Anal. biochem.]. Vol. 1 (June 1960)-. Academic Scholarly Publication. English. Twenty-two times a year. $1840.00. Academic Press Inc., 6277 Sea Harbor Drive, Orlando FL 32887. **Tel** (800)543-9534, (407)345-4100, FAX (407)352-3445. **ED** William B. Jakoby. Index available (bound in last issue). Documents available from The Genuine Article, BIOSIS Document Express, CASDDS.
Desc: Emphasizes methods and methodology in the biological and biochemical sciences and all fields impinging on them.
Ind/Abst Abstr. Bull. Inst. Pap. Sci. Tech.; AgBiotech News Inf.; Anal. Abstr.; Biol. Abstr.; Calcium Calcif. Tissue Abstr.; Chem. Abstr.; Chem. Titles; Crop Physiol. Abstr.; CSA Neuro. Abstr. (?-?); Curr. Aware. Biol. Sci., CABS; Curr. Biotechnol.; Curr. Cit.; Curr. Contents Life Sci.; Dairy Sci. Abstr.; EMBASE; Energy Res. Abstr.; Field Crop Abstr.; Food Sci. Technol. Abstr.; Genet. Abstr.; Grass. Forage Abstr.; Health Plan. Adminis.; Helminthol. Abstr. (1991-); Hortic. Abstr.; Hum. Genome Abstr.; Immunol. Abstr.; Index Med.; Index Vet.; Ind. Hyg. Dig. (19??-19??); INIS Atomindex [Micro.]; Int. Aerosp. Abstr.; Maize Abstr.; Mass Spect. Bull.; Microbiol. Abstr. Sect. B (19??-19??); Microbiol. Abstr. Sect. A; Microbiol. Abstr. Sect. C; Nucl. Acids Abstr.; Nutr. Abstr. Rev., Ser. B, Live Feeds and Feed.; Nutr. Abstr. Rev., Ser. A, Hum. Exp.; Oncog. Growth Factors Abstr.; Life Sci. Collect.; PESTDOC; Protozoolog. Abstr.; Ref. Upd. Basic Ed.; Ref. Upd. Deluxe Ed.; Res. Alert [Full Cov.]; Rev. Agric. Entomol.; Rev. Med. Vet. Entomol.; Sci. Cit. Index; SCISEARCH; Seed Abstr.; Soils Fert.; Soyabean Abstr.; Trop. Dis. Bull.; Virol. AIDS Abstr.; Wheat Barley Trit. Abstr.

LC QH650 **ISSN** 1358-6122
DD 574.191 UK

•**ANCIENT BIOMOLECULES.** (1996)-. Academic Scholarly Publication. English. Three times a year. £120.00 (institutions), £36.00 (individuals). Carfax Publishing Company, PO Box 25, Abingdon, Oxfordshire OX14 3UE United Kingdom. **Tel** 011 44 1235 555335, FAX 011 44 1235 553559, telex 817484. **(Subscription address:** Carfax Publishing Co., 875-81 Massachusetts Avenue, Cambridge MA 02139.)

ISSN 0709-8502
DD 574.19/2/05 CN
CODEN ABCQD2
Pr Rev.

ANNALES DE BIOCHIMIE CLINIQUE DU QUEBEC. [Ann. biochim. clin. Que.]. **Added/Corp** Societe Quebecoise de Biochimie Clinique. Vol. 19, No. 1- (Feb. 1980)-. Academic Scholarly Publication. French.

Three times a year (Apr., Aug., Dec.). Free on request. Hopital du Saint-Sacrement 1050, Chemin Sainte-Foy Quebec Quebec G1S 4L8 Canada. **Tel** (418)691-5135. **(Subscription address:** Hotel-Dieu de Quebec, c/o Pierre Douville, 11 Cote du Palais, Quebec G1R 2J6 Canada.) **ED** Dr. Marc Letellier (editor's address: Departement de Biochimie Clinique, Centre Hospitalier Universitaire de Sherbrooke, 3001 12e Avenue Nord, Sherbrooke Quebec J1H 5N4 Canada; telephone: (819)563-5555 poste 5574; Fax: (819)820-6414). **Ad Acc. Circ:** 900 (ctrl). Documents available from BIOSIS Document Express, CASDDS. ***Continues*** *Bulletin de l'Association des Biochimistes des Hopitaux du Quebec, 0706-0742.*
Desc: Scientific information on clinical biochemistry.
Ind/Abst Biol. Abstr.; Chem. Abstr.

ISSN 1012-1773
CM
CODEN AFSBDV

ANNALES DE LA FACULTE DES SCIENCES. SERIE III, BIOLOGIE -BIOCHIMIE : AFS. [Ann. Fac. sci. Univ. Yaounde, Ser. 3 Biol. biochim.]. **VFOAT** AFS; Biologie, Biochimie; Biologie-Biochemie. Vol. 1 (Jan. 1983)-. Academic Scholarly Publication. French (English). Universite de Yaounde, Faculte des Lettres et Sciences Humaines, Prof. Sondengam BP 812, Yaounde Cameroon. Documents available from CASDDS. ***Continues*** *Annales de la Faculte des Sciences (University of Yaounde).*
Ind/Abst Chem. Abstr. (1983-).

LC QP **ISSN** 0004-5632
DD 612 UK
UDC 61 **CCC**
NLM W1 AN57N **CODEN** ACBOBU
Pr Rev.

ANNALS OF CLINICAL BIOCHEMISTRY. [Ann. clin. biochem.]. **Added/Corp** Association of Clinical Biochemists. Nederlandse Vereniging voor Klinische Chemie. Vol. 6 (March 1969)-. Academic Scholarly Publication. English. Six times a year. $184.00. Royal Society of Medicine Press, PO Box 9002, London W1A 0ZA United Kingdom. **Tel** 011 44 171 2902927, 011 44 171 2902900, FAX 011 44 171 2902929. **ED** S. P. Halloran. Index available (bound in last issue). **Bk Rev. Ad Acc. Circ:** 3,700. available on microfilm and microfiche from University Microfilms International (UMI). Documents available from The Genuine Article, BIOSIS Document Express, CASDDS. ***Continues*** *Association of Clinical Biochemists. Proceedings.*
Desc: Publishes papers from throughout the world that contribute to existing knowledge in all fields of clinical biochemistry.
Ind/Abst Anal. Abstr.; Biol. Abstr.; Chem. Abstr.; Curr. Aware. Biol. Sci., CABS; Curr. Biotechnol.; Curr. Cit.; Curr. Contents Life Sci.; Dairy Sci. Abstr.; EMBASE; Health Plan. Adminis.; Index Med.; Index Vet.; Nutr. Abstr. Rev., Ser. B, Live Feeds and Feed.; Nutr. Abstr. Rev., Ser. A, Hum. Exp.; Life Sci. Collect.; Protozoolog. Abstr.; Res. Alert [Full Cov.]; Rev. Med. Vet. Mycology; Sci. Cit. Index; SCISEARCH; Soc. Sci. Cit. Index [Select. Cov.]; Vet. Bull.; Wheat Barley Trit. Abstr.

ISSN 0197-8969
UK
CODEN APPEDR

ANNUAL PROCEEDINGS OF THE PHYTOCHEMICAL SOCIETY OF EUROPE. [Annu. proc. Phytochem. Soc. Eur.]. **Main/Corp** Phytochemical Society of Europe. **Added/Corp** Phytochemical Society of Europe. Symposia series. **VFOAT** Phytochemical Society of Europe Symposia Series. (1978)-. Academic Scholarly Publication. English. One time a year. $45.00. Oxford University Press / UK, Walton Street, Oxford OX2 6DP United Kingdom. **Tel** 011 44 1865 56767, FAX 011 44 1865 267773, telex 851/837330 OXPRES G. **(Subscription address:** Oxford University Press / USA, Journals Marketing Department, Oxford University Press, 2001 Evans Road, Cary NC 27513. **Tel** (800)451-7556, (919)677-0977, FAX (919)677-1714.) **ED** P. J. Lea. **Circ:** 500. Documents available from BIOSIS Document Express, CASDDS. ***Continues*** *Annual Proceedings of the Phytochemical Society, 0309-9393.*
Desc: Covers all aspects of plant chemistry and biochemistry; plant and animal coevolution, phytochemistry, plant genetics, molecular biology, cell biology and associated disciplines.
Ind/Abst Biol. Abstr.; Chem. Abstr.; Curr. Cit.; Microbiol. Abstr. Sect. C.

LC QP501 .A7 **ISSN** 0066-4154
DD 612.015 US
CCC
NLM W1 AN77 **CODEN** ARBOAW
Pr Rev.

ANNUAL REVIEW OF BIOCHEMISTRY. [Ann. rev. biochem.]. Vol. 1 (1932)-. Academic Scholarly Publication. English. One time a year (July). $59.00. Annual Reviews Inc., 4139 El Camino Way, PO Box 10139, Palo Alto CA 94303-0139. **Tel** (415)493-4400, (800)523-8635, FAX (415)855-9815. **ED** Charles C. Richardson. Index available. cum. index. ctrl circ. available on microfilm and microfiche from University Microfilms International (UMI). Documents available from The Genuine Article, BIOSIS Document Express, CASDDS, Documents on Demand.
Desc: Covers the basic biological, biomedical, physical, social, and behavioral sciences.
Ind/Abst Abstr. Bull. Inst. Pap. Sci. Tech.; Anim. Breed. Abstr.; Biol. Agric. Index; Biol. Abstr.; Chem. Abstr.; Crop Physiol. Abstr.; Curr. Aware. Biol. Sci., CABS; Curr. Cit.; Curr. Contents Life Sci.; Dairy Sci. Abstr.; EMBASE; Energy Res. Abstr.; Environ. Abstr.; Field Crop Abstr.; Food Sci. Technol. Abstr.; Grass. Forage Abstr.; Hortic. Abstr.; Index Med.; Index Sci. Rev. [Full Cov.]; INIS Atomindex [Micro.]; Nutr. Abstr. Rev., Ser. B, Live Feeds and Feed.; Nutr. Abstr. Rev., Ser. A, Hum. Exp.; Life Sci. Collect.; PESTDOC; Plant Breed. Abstr.; Ref. Upd. Basic Ed.; Ref. Upd. Deluxe Ed.; Res. Alert [Full Cov.]; Sci. Cit. Index; SCISEARCH; Soc. Sci. Cit. Index [Select. Cov.]; Soils Fert.; Soyabean Abstr.; Vitis Vitic. Enol. Abstr.; Weed Abstr.

ISSN 1350-4541
UK

APOPTOSIS. See Medical Sciences.

LC TP248.3 .J68
DD 660/.63/05 US
NLM W1 AP5196D **CODEN** ABIBDL
Pr Rev. **TITLE CHANGE**

APPLIED BIOCHEMISTRY AND BIOTECHNOLOGY. [Appl. biochem. biotechnol.]. **VFOAT** Enzyme Engineering and Biotechnology. Vol. 6, No. 1 (Mar. 1981)-(19??). Academic Scholarly Publication. English. Humana Press Inc., 999 Riverview Drive, Suite 208, Totawa NJ 07512. **Tel** (201)256-1699, FAX (201)256-8341. **ED** Howard Weetall. Index available. **Bk Rev. Ad Acc. Circ:** 750. Documents available from The Genuine Article, CASDDS. ***Continues*** *Journal of Solid-Phase Biochemistry, 0146-0641.* ***Split into*** *Molecular Biotechnology, 1073-6085* ***and*** *Enzyme Engineering and Biotechnology, 0273-2289.*
Desc: Premier journal of research on all aspects of applied biochemistry and biotechnology.
Ind/Abst AgBiotech News Inf.; AGRICOLA [Select. Cov.]; Anal. Abstr.; Biocont. News Inf. (1991-); Biodeter. Abstr. (19??-19??); Biotechnol. Res. Abstr.; Chem. Abstr.; Chem. Titles; Coal Abstr.; Crop Physiol. Abstr.; Curr. Aware. Biol. Sci., CABS; Curr. Biotechnol.; Curr. Cit.; Curr. Contents Agric. Biol. Environ. Sci.; Curr. Contents Life Sci.; EMBASE; Field Crop Abstr.; Food Sci. Technol. Abstr.; For. Prod. Abstr. (19??-19??); For. Abstr.; Genet. Abstr.; Health Plan. Adminis.; Index Med. (1983-); Microbiol. Abstr. Sect. B; Microbiol. Abstr. Sect. A; Microbiol. Abstr. Sect. C; Life Sci. Collect.; PESTDOC; Ref. Upd. Deluxe Ed.; Res. Alert [Full Cov.]; Sci. Cit. Index; SCISEARCH; Soc. Sci. Cit. Index [Select. Cov.]; Soils Fert.; Sug. Indus. Abstr.

LC QH345 .P713 **ISSN** 0003-6838
US
CCC
NLM W1 AP521 **CODEN** APBMAC

APPLIED BIOCHEMISTRY AND MICROBIOLOGY. [Appl. biochem. microbiol.]. **Added/Corp** Consultants Bureau. Vol. 1 (Jan./Feb. 1965)-. Periodical. English (Russian). Six times a year. $1295.00. Consultants Bureau, A Division of Plenum Publishing Corporation, 233 Spring Street, New York NY 10013. **Tel** (212)620-8000, (212)620-8466, FAX (212)463-0742, telex 23/421139. **ED** V. L. Kretovich. Index available. available on microfilm and microfiche from University Microfilms International (UMI). Documents available from The Genuine Article, BIOSIS Document Express.
Ind/Abst AGRICOLA [Select. Cov.]; Biol. Abstr. (-1984); Curr. Biotechnol.; EMBASE; Food Sci. Technol. Abstr.; INIS Atomindex [Micro.]; Life Sci. Collect.; Pollut. Abstr. Indexes; Res. Alert [Full Cov.].

ISSN 1062-3345
DD 616 US
CCC
NLM W1; AP524FD

•**APPLIED IMMUNOHISTOCHEMISTRY.** (APPLIED IMMUNOHISTOCHEMISTRY : OFFICIAL PUBLICATION OF THE SOCIETY FOR APPLIED IMMUNOHISTOCHEMISTRY.). [Appl. immunohistochem.]. **Added/Corp** Society for Applied Immunohistochemistry. Vol. 1, No. 1 (Spring 1993)-. Periodical. English. Four times a year (quarterly). $133.00. Lippincott - Raven Publishers, 227 East Washington Square, Philadelphia PA 19106. **Tel** (215)238-4200, (800)777-2295, FAX (215)238-4227.
Desc: Discusses the diagnostic and prognostic applications of immunochemistry, contributions of immunochemistry to the understanding of tumor biology, and laboratory procedures and interpretation of results.

LC QH650 **ISSN** 0778-3124
DD 574.1 BE
UDC 57
NLM W1; AR3944 **CODEN** AIPBE4
TITLE CHANGE

ARCHIVES INTERNATIONALES DE PHYSIOLOGIE, DE BIOCHIMIE ET DE BIOPHYSIQUE. See Biology-Physiology.

LC QP501 .A77 **ISSN** 0003-9861
DD 574.1905 US
CCC
NLM W1 AR449 **CODEN** ABBIA4

ARCHIVES OF BIOCHEMISTRY AND BIOPHYSICS. [Arch. biochem. biophys.]. Vol. 31 (March 1951)-. Academic Scholarly Publication. English. Twenty-four times a year. $1900.00. Academic Press Inc., 6277 Sea Harbor Drive, Orlando FL 32887. **Tel** (800)543-9534, (407)345-4100, FAX (407)352-3445. cum. index. Documents available from The Genuine Article, BIOSIS Document Express, CASDDS, Documents on Demand. ***Continues*** *Archives of Biochemistry, 0096-9621.*
Desc: Presents articles in the developing areas of biochemistry and biophysics, especially those related to molecular biology, cell biology and developmental biology.
Ind/Abst Abstr. Bull. Inst. Pap. Sci. Tech.; AgBiotech News Inf.; AGRICOLA [Select. Cov.]; Anal. Abstr.; Anim. Breed. Abstr.; Biodeter. Abstr. (1991-); Biol. Abstr.; Calcium Calcif. Tissue Abstr.; Chem. Abstr.; Chem. Titles; Crop Physiol. Abstr.; CSA Neuro. Abstr.; Curr. Aware. Biol. Sci., CABS; Curr. Biotechnol.; Curr. Cit.; Curr. Contents Life Sci.; Curr. Ref. Fish Res.; Dairy Sci. Abstr.; EMBASE; Energy Res. Abstr.; Environ. Abstr.; Field Crop Abstr.; Fish Rev. (Jan. 1989-July 1992); Food Sci. Technol. Abstr.; For. Abstr.; Genet. Abstr.; GeoRef; Grass. Forage Abstr.; Health Plan. Adminis.; Helminthol. Abstr. (19??-19??); Hortic. Abstr.; Immunol. Abstr.; Index Med.; Index Vet.; INIS Atomindex [Micro.]; Int. Aerosp. Abstr.; Irr. Drain. Abstr.; Maize Abstr.; Mass Spect. Bull.; Microbiol. Abstr. Sect. B; Microbiol. Abstr. Sect. C; NAPRALERT; Nematol. Abstr.; Nucl. Acids Abstr.; Nutr. Abstr. Rev., Ser. B, Live Feeds and Feed.; Nutr. Abstr. Rev., Ser. A, Hum. Exp.; Oncog. Growth Factors Abstr.; Ornamental Hort. (1991-); Life Sci. Collect.; PESTDOC; Pig News Inf.; Plant Breed. Abstr.; Plant Grow. Reg. Abstr.; Postharvest News Inf.; Potato Abstr.; Poult. Abstr.; Protozoolog. Abstr.; Ref. Upd. Basic Ed.; Ref. Upd. Deluxe Ed.; Res. Alert [Full Cov.]; Rev. Agric. Entomol.; Rev. Med. Vet. Mycology; Rev. Plant Pathol.; Rice Abstr.; Saf. Health Work; Sci. Cit. Index; SCISEARCH; Seed Abstr.; Soils Fert.; Sorghum Mill. Abstr.; Stat. Theory Method Abstr. (1959-1963); Vet. Bull.; Vitis Vitic. Enol. Abstr.; Weed Abstr.; Wheat Barley Trit. Abstr.; Wildl. Rev. (Jan. 1989-July 1992).

LC QP1 .A67 **ISSN** 1381-3455
DD 571 BE
UDC 57
NLM W1; AR3944 **CODEN** APBIF5

•**ARCHIVES OF PHYSIOLOGY AND BIOCHEMISTRY.** See Biology-Physiology.

ISSN 0365-0871
AG
UDC 577.1
CODEN 54

ARCHIVOS DE BIOQUIMICA, QUIMICA Y FARMACIA TUCUMAN. [Arch. bioquim., quim, farm., Tucuman]. (1957)-. Periodical. Spanish. Irregular. ***Continues*** *Archivos de Farmacia y Bioquimica del Tucuman, 0365-2114.*
Ind/Abst Int. Pharm. Abstr.

LC R856.A1 B56 **ISSN** 1073-1199
DD 610.28 US
CCC
NLM W1; AR955G

•**ARTIFICIAL CELLS, BLOOD SUBSTITUTES, AND IMMOBILIZATION BIOTECHNOLOGY.** See Biology-Bioengineering.

LC QD431
DD 547.7 US
UDC 54

ATLAS OF PROTEIN SEQUENCE AND STRUCTURE. SUPPLEMENT. **Added/Corp** National Biomedical Research Foundation. (1973)-. Monographic series. English. Irregular. $25.00 US; $31.25 other. National Biomedical Research Foundation, 3900 Reservoir Road NW, Washington DC 20007. **Tel** (202)687-2121, FAX (202)687-1662. **ED** M.O. Dayhoff.
Desc: A supplement to the series which concentrates on the tabulation of published amino acid sequences of proteins, compositions, molecular weights, references, homologous protein structures, etc.

ISSN 0261-4553
UK

ATPASES. [ATPases]. (1982)-. English. Twelve times a year. £85.00. SUBIS, Mansion House 19 Kingfield Road, Sheffield S11 9AS United Kingdom. **Tel** 011 44 114 2554433, FAX 011 44 114 255 4626.

LC QD431 **ISSN** 0921-0687
DD 547.7 NE
CCC
NLM W1; BI619MD **CODEN** BMOLEY

BIOACTIVE MOLECULES. [Bioactive mol.]. Vol. 1 (1986)-. Monographic series. English. Irregular. Price varies per volume. Elsevier Science Publishers BV, PO Box 211, 1000 AE Amsterdam Netherlands. **Tel** 011 31 20 4853641, 011 31 20 4853642, FAX 011 31 20 4853598. Documents available from BIOSIS Document

Express, CASDDS.
Ind/Abst AGRICOLA [Select. Cov.]; Biol. Abstr. (1988-); Chem. Abstr. (1986-).

LC TP248.65.E59 B54 **ISSN** 0886-4454
DD 660/.634/05 SZ
CCC
NLM W1; BI619QH **CODEN** BIOCED
TITLE CHANGE

BIOCATALYSIS. [Biocatalysis]. **Added/Corp** European Federation of Biotechnology. Working Party on Applied Biocatalysis. Vol. 1, No. 1 (May 1987)-(1995). Periodical. English. Harwood Academic Publishers, PO Box 90, Reading RG1 8JL United Kingdom. **Tel** 011 44 1734 560080, FAX 011 44 1734 568211. **ED** David Best. **Bk Rev.** **Ad Acc.** Documents available from The Genuine Article, CASDDS. ***Continued by*** *Biocatalysis and Biotransformation.*
Ind/Abst Chem. Abstr.; Curr. Aware. Biol. Sci., CABS; Curr. Biotechnol.; Curr. Cit.; Food Sci. Technol. Abstr.; For. Prod. Abstr.; Microbiol. Abstr. Sect. A; PESTDOC; Res. Alert [Full Cov.].

LC TP248.65.E59 B54 **ISSN** 1024-2422
DD 660 UK
UDC 66
CODEN BOBOEQ

•**BIOCATALYSIS AND BIOTRANSFORMATION.** **Added/Corp** European Federation of Biotechnology. Working Party on Applied Biocatalysis. Vol. 12, No. 1 (1995)-. Academic Scholarly Publication. English. Irregular. Harwood Academic Publishers, PO Box 90, Reading RG1 8JL United Kingdom. **Tel** 011 44 1734 560080, FAX 011 44 1734 568211. ***Continues*** *Biocatalysis, 0886-4454.*
Ind/Abst Chem. Abstr. (1995-).

LC QH301 .B358 **ISSN** 0006-291X
DD 574.1/9/05 US
CCC
NLM W1 BI6198 **CODEN** BBRCA9
Pr Rev.

BIOCHEMICAL AND BIOPHYSICAL RESEARCH COMMUNICATIONS. [Biochem. biophys. res. commun.]. Vol. 1 (July 1959)-. Academic Scholarly Publication. English. Thirty-six times a year (plus index issue). $1562.00. Academic Press Inc., 6277 Sea Harbor Drive, Orlando FL 32887. **Tel** (800)543-9534, (407)345-4100, FAX (407)352-3445. cum. index. Documents available from The Genuine Article, BIOSIS Document Express, CASDDS.
Desc: A journal devoted to the rapid dissemination of timely and significant experimental results in the diverse fields of modern biology. Emphasis is placed on the innovative aspects of the research reports.
Ind/Abst Abstr. Bull. Inst. Pap. Sci. Tech.; AgBiotech News Inf.; AGRICOLA [Select. Cov.]; Anim. Breed. Abstr.; Art Archaeol. Tech. Abstr.; Biocont. News Inf. (1991-); Biodeter. Abstr. (1991-); Biol. Abstr.; Calcium Calcif. Tissue Abstr.; Chem. Abstr.; Chem. Titles; Chemorecept. Abstr.; Crop Physiol. Abstr.; CSA Neuro. Abstr.; Curr. Aware. Biol. Sci., CABS; Curr. Biotechnol.; Curr. Cit.; Curr. Contents Life Sci.; Dairy Sci. Abstr.; EMBASE; Energy Res. Abstr.; Field Crop Abstr.; Food Sci. Technol. Abstr.; Genet. Abstr.; Grass. Forage Abstr.; Health Plan. Adminis.; Helminthol. Abstr. (19??-19??); Hortic. Abstr.; Hum. Genome Abstr.; Immunol. Abstr.; Index Med.; Index Vet.; INIS Atomindex [Micro.]; Int. Aerosp. Abstr.; Maize Abstr.; Mass Spect. Bull.; Microbiol. Abstr. Sect. B; Microbiol. Abstr. Sect. A; Microbiol. Abstr. Sect. C; NAPRALERT; Nucl. Acids Abstr.; Nutr. Abstr. Rev., Ser. B, Live Feeds and Feed.; Nutr. Abstr. Rev., Ser. A, Hum. Exp.; Oncog. Growth Factors Abstr.; Ornamental Hort. (1991-); Life Sci. Collect.; PESTDOC; Pig News Inf.; Plant Breed. Abstr.; Plant Grow. Reg. Abstr.; Postharvest News Inf.; Potato Abstr.; Protozoolog. Abstr.; Ref. Upd. Basic Ed.; Ref. Upd. Deluxe Ed.; Res. Alert [Full Cov.]; Rev. Agric. Entomol.; Rev. Med. Vet. Entomol.; Rev. Med. Vet. Mycology; Rev. Plant Pathol.; Rice Abstr.; Sci. Cit. Index; SCISEARCH; Seed Abstr.; Soils Fert.; Soyabean Abstr.; Vet. Bull.; Virol. AIDS Abstr.; Weed Abstr.; Wheat Barley Trit. Abstr.

LC QD
DD 540 US

BIOCHEMICAL AND MOLECULAR ASPECTS OF SELECTED CANCERS. **See** Medical Sciences-Cancer and Neoplastic Syndromes.

ISSN 1077-3150
DD 612 US
CCC
NLM W1; BI621R **CODEN** BMMEF4

•**BIOCHEMICAL AND MOLECULAR MEDICINE.** [Biochem. mol. med.]. Vol. 54, No. 1 (Feb. 1995)-. Periodical. English. Six times a year. $475.00. Academic Press Inc., 6277 Sea Harbor Drive, Orlando FL 32887. **Tel** (800)543-9534, (407)345-4100, FAX (407)352-3445. **(Subscription address:** Academic Press Inc., PO Box 620000, Orlando FL 32891-8340. **Tel** (800)543-9534.) ***Continues*** *Biochemical Medicine and Metabolic Biology, 0885-4505.*
Ind/Abst Biol. Abstr.; Chem. Abstr.; Curr. Cit.; EMBASE; Energy Res. Abstr.; Index Med.; Life Sci. Collect.; PESTDOC; RINGDOC; VETDOC.

ISSN 0749-5331
DD 574 US
CCC
NLM W1; BI6198E **CODEN** BIAREM
Pr Rev.

BIOCHEMICAL ARCHIVES. [Biochem. arch.]. Vol. 1, No. 1 (Feb. 1985)-. Academic Scholarly Publication. English. Four times a year (Feb., May, Aug., Nov.). $50.00. MBR Press Inc, PO Box P, Kenyon MN 55946. **Tel** (507)798-6285. **ED** Robert F. Derr. Index available in last issue of volume--attached. cum. index. Documents available from The Genuine Article, BIOSIS Document Express, CASDDS.
Desc: Publishes manuscripts on the results of original research in biochemistry and its application to nutrition, pharmacology, physiology and toxicology. Mini reviews are published.
Ind/Abst Biol. Abstr. (1985-); Chem. Abstr. (1985-); Curr. Aware. Biol. Sci., CABS; Curr. Cit.; Curr. Contents Life Sci.; Nutr. Abstr. Rev., Ser. A, Hum. Exp.; Ref. Upd. Deluxe Ed.; Res. Alert [Full Cov.]; Sci. Cit. Index; SCISEARCH.

LC QP518 .B56 **ISSN** 0307-4412
DD 574.19/2/071 UK
CCC
NLM W1 BI62P **CODEN** BIEDDX

BIOCHEMICAL EDUCATION. (BIOCHEMICAL EDUCATION : A QUARTERLY PUBLICATION OF THE INTERNATIONAL UNION OF BIOCHEMISTRY.). [Biochem. educ.]. **Added/Corp** International Union of Biochemistry. Vol. 1 (Autumn 1972)-. Periodical. English. Four times a year. $167.00. Pergamon Press, An Imprint of Elsevier Science Ltd., The Boulevard, Langford Lane, Kidlington, Oxford OX5 1GB United Kingdom. **Tel** 011 44 1865 843000, 011 44 1865 843699, FAX 011 44 1865 843010. **(Subscription address:** Elsevier Science Ltd. / Oxford Fulfillment Centre, PO Box 800, Kidlington OX5 1DX United Kingdom. **Tel** 011 44 865 843355.) **ED** Edward Wood. available on microfilm and microfiche from University Microfilms International (UMI); available on an online database from Elsevier Electronic Subscriptions (EES). Documents available from The Genuine Article, CASDDS.
Ind/Abst Chem. Abstr.; Contents Pages Educ.; Curr. Aware. Biol. Sci., CABS; Curr. Cit.; Curr. Index J. Educ.; Educ. Index (1992-); Educ. Technol. Abstr.; EMBASE; Energy Res. Abstr. (Aug. 1980-); Res. Alert [Select. Cov.]; Res. High. Educ. Abstr.; SCISEARCH; Soc. Sci. Cit. Index [Select. Cov.]; Tech. Educ. Train. Abstr.

LC QH431 .B54 **ISSN** 0006-2928
DD 575.2/1 US
CCC
NLM W1 BI621 **CODEN** BIGEBA
Pr Rev.

BIOCHEMICAL GENETICS. **See** Biology-Genetics.

LC QD415 **ISSN** 0264-6021
DD 574.192 UK
CCC
NLM W1; BI621J **CODEN** BIJOAK
Pr Rev.

BIOCHEMICAL JOURNAL (LONDON. 1984). (THE BIOCHEMICAL JOURNAL.). [Biochem. j.]. **Added/Corp** Biochemical Society (Great Britain). Vol. 217, No. 1 (Jan. 1, 1984)-. Academic Scholarly Publication. English. Twenty-four times a year (includes index and reviews). $1637.00. Portland Press Ltd., PO Box 32 Commerce Way, Colchester CO2 8HP Essex United Kingdom. **Tel** 011 44 1206 796351, FAX 011 44 1206 799331, telex 987275 BIOSOC G. **ED** A. J. Turner. Index available. cum. index. **Bk Rev.** **Ad Acc.** **Circ:** 3,500 (ctrl). available on microfilm from University Microfilms International (UMI). Documents available from The Genuine Article, BIOSIS Document Express, CASDDS. ***Formed by the union of*** *Biochemical Journal. Molecular Aspects, 0306-3275* ***and*** *Biochemical Journal. Cellular Aspects, 0306-3283 w (DLC)sn 84010973.*
Desc: Contains original papers describing recent advances in all fields of biochemical research world-wide. Features full-length papers, rapid papers, reviews, and letters.
Ind/Abst Abstr. Bull. Inst. Pap. Sci. Tech.; AgBiotech News Inf.; AGRICOLA [Select. Cov.]; Anal. Abstr.; Anim. Breed. Abstr.; Biodeter. Abstr. (1991-); Biol. Abstr.; Calcium Calcif. Tissue Abstr.; Chem. Abstr.; Crop Physiol. Abstr.; CSA Neuro. Abstr.; Curr. Aware. Biol. Sci., CABS; Curr. Cit.; Curr. Contents Life Sci.; Curr. Ref. Fish Res.; Dairy Sci. Abstr.; EMBASE; Field Crop Abstr.; Food Sci. Technol. Abstr.; Genet. Abstr.; Health Plan. Adminis.; Helminthol. Abstr.; Immunol. Abstr.; Index Med.; Index Vet.; Maize Abstr.; Mass Spect. Bull.; Microbiol. Abstr. Sect. B; Microbiol. Abstr. Sect. A; Microbiol. Abstr. Sect. C; Nematol. Abstr.; Nucl. Acids Abstr.; Nutr. Abstr. Rev., Ser. B, Live Feeds and Feed.; Nutr. Abstr. Rev., Ser. A, Hum. Exp.; Oncog. Growth Factors Abstr.; Ornamental Hort. (1991-); Life Sci. Collect.; PESTDOC; Pig News Inf.; Plant Breed. Abstr.; Potato Abstr.; Poult. Abstr.; Protozoolog. Abstr.; Ref. Upd. Basic Ed.; Ref. Upd. Deluxe Ed.; Res. Alert [Full Cov.]; Rev. Agric. Entomol.; Rev. Med. Vet. Entomol.; Rev. Plant Pathol.; Saf. Health Work; Sci. Cit. Index; SCISEARCH; Soils Fert.; Vet. Bull.; Trop. Dis. Bull.; Virol. AIDS Abstr.; Wheat Barley Trit. Abstr.

LC QP501 .B474 **ISSN** 0885-4505
DD 612/.015 US
CCC
NLM W1; BI621R **CODEN** BMMBES
TITLE CHANGE

BIOCHEMICAL MEDICINE AND METABOLIC BIOLOGY. [Biochem. med. metabol. biol.]. Vol. 35, No. 1 (Feb. 1986)-(1994). Academic Scholarly Publication. English. Academic Press Inc., 6277 Sea Harbor Drive, Orlando FL 32887. **Tel** (800)543-9534, (407)345-4100, FAX (407)352-3445. **ED** Edward R.B. McCabe, Chandra Mohan, S.P. Bessman. Documents available from The Genuine Article, BIOSIS Document Express, CASDDS. ***Continues*** *Biochemical Medicine, 0006-2944.* ***Continued by*** *Biochemical and Molecular Medicine.*
Desc: Papers are published describing original research in biochemistry, physiologic chemistry, and metabolic biology. The primary emphasis is on the determination of the interrelations among reactions, sequences, and formed elements of the cell.
Ind/Abst AGRICOLA [Select. Cov.]; Anal. Abstr.; Biol. Abstr. (1986-); Chem. Abstr.; Chem. Titles; Curr. Aware. Biol. Sci., CABS; Curr. Cit.; Curr. Contents Life Sci.; EMBASE; Energy Res. Abstr. (1986-); Health Plan. Adminis.; Index Vet.; INIS Atomindex [Micro.]; Maize Abstr.; Mass Spect. Bull.; Nutr. Abstr. Rev., Ser. A, Hum. Exp.; Life Sci. Collect. (1986-); PESTDOC (1986-); Potato Abstr.; Protozoolog. Abstr.; Res. Alert [Full Cov.]; Sci. Cit. Index; SCISEARCH; Soc. Sci. Cit. Index [Select. Cov.].

LC QP901 .B5 **ISSN** 0006-2952
DD 615.7 UK
CCC
NLM W1 BI622 **CODEN** BCPCA6
Pr Rev.

BIOCHEMICAL PHARMACOLOGY. **See** Pharmacy and Pharmacology.

LC QH345 .B522 **ISSN** 0067-8694
DD 574.19/2/05 UK
CCC
NLM W1 BI629 **CODEN** BSSYAT
Pr Rev.

BIOCHEMICAL SOCIETY SYMPOSIA. [Biochem. Soc. Symp.]. **Main/Corp** Biochemical Society (Great Britain). Symposia. **VFOAT** Symposia. No. 1 (Feb. 15, 1947)-. Monographic series. English. Irregular. Price varies per volume. Portland Press Ltd., PO Box 32 Commerce Way, Colchester CO2 8HP Essex United Kingdom. **Tel** 011 44 1206 796351, FAX 011 44 1206 799331, telex 987275 BIOSOC G. **(Subscription address:** Ashgate Publishing Company / US, Old Post Road, Brookfield VT 05036-9704. **Tel** (800)535-9544, (802)276-3162, FAX (802)276-3837.) **ED** J. Kay. Index available. **Ad Acc.** **Circ:** 2,000 (ctrl). Documents available from The Genuine Article, CASDDS.
Desc: Proceedings of symposia held by the Biochemical Society; international contributors.
Ind/Abst AGRICOLA [Select. Cov.]; Chem. Abstr.; Curr. Biotechnol.; Curr. Cit.; EMBASE; Index Med.; Nat. Prod. Updates; Nutr. Abstr. Rev., Ser. B, Live Feeds and Feed.; Nutr. Abstr. Rev., Ser. A, Hum. Exp.; Life Sci. Collect.; Res. Alert [Full Cov.]; Sci. Cit. Index (19??-19??); SCISEARCH.

LC QH345 .B523a **ISSN** 0300-5127
DD 574.1/92/05 UK
CCC
NLM W1 BI63 **CODEN** BCSTB5
Pr Rev.

BIOCHEMICAL SOCIETY TRANSACTIONS. (TRANSACTIONS.). [Biochem. Soc. trans.]. **Main/Corp** Biochemical Society (Great Britain). Vol. 1 (Jan. 1973)-. English. Four times a year. $253.00. Portland Press Ltd., PO Box 32 Commerce Way, Colchester CO2 8HP Essex United Kingdom. **Tel** 011 44 1206 796351, FAX 011 44 1206 799331, telex 987275 BIOSOC G. Index available. **Bk Rev.** **Ad Acc.** **Circ:** 2,500 (ctrl). Documents available from The Genuine Article, BIOSIS Document Express, CASDDS.
Desc: Well-referenced but short reviews on wide variety of topics from colloquia; organised or sponsored by Biochemical Society. Recent advances in medical and plant biochemistry and reports on lectures.
Ind/Abst AgBiotech News Inf.; AGRICOLA [Select. Cov.]; Anal. Abstr.; Biodeter. Abstr.; Biol. Abstr.; Calcium Calcif. Tissue Abstr.; Chem. Abstr.; Chem. Titles; Crop Physiol. Abstr.; CSA Neuro. Abstr. (?-?); Curr. Biotechnol.; Curr. Cit.; Curr. Contents Life Sci.; Dairy Sci. Abstr.; EMBASE; Field Crop Abstr.; Food Sci. Technol. Abstr.; For. Prod. Abstr.; Genet. Abstr.; Helminthol. Abstr. (1991-); Immunol. Abstr.; Index Med.; Microbiol. Abstr. Sect. A; Microbiol. Abstr. Sect. C; Nat. Prod. Updates; Nematol. Abstr.; Nutr. Abstr. Rev., Ser. B, Live Feeds and Feed.; Nutr. Abstr. Rev., Ser. A, Hum. Exp.; Oncog. Growth Factors Abstr.; Life Sci. Collect.; Plant Breed. Abstr.; Plant Grow. Reg. Abstr.; Protozoolog. Abstr.; Ref. Upd. Basic Ed.; Ref. Upd. Deluxe Ed.; Res. Alert [Full Cov.]; Rev. Med. Vet. Entomol.; Rev. Med. Vet. Mycology; Sci. Cit. Index; SCISEARCH; Soyabean Abstr.; Trop. Dis. Bull.; Virol. AIDS Abstr.

LC QH83 .B55 **ISSN** 0305-1978
DD 574/.01/2 UK
CCC
NLM W1 BI63F **CODEN** BSECBU
Pr Rev.

BIOCHEMICAL SYSTEMATICS AND ECOLOGY. [Biochem. syst. ecol.]. Vol. 2 (1974)-. Periodical. English (French and German). Eight times a year. $767.00. Pergamon Press, An Imprint of Elsevier Science Ltd., The Boulevard, Langford Lane, Kidlington, Oxford OX5 1GB United Kingdom. **Tel** 011 44 1865 843000, 011 44 1865 843699, FAX 011 44 1865 843010. **(Subscription address:** Elsevier Science Ltd. / Oxford Fulfillment Centre, PO Box 800, Kidlington OX5 1DX United Kingdom. **Tel** 011 44 865 843355.**)** **ED** Ernst Schoffeniels and Mick Richardson. available on microfilm from Pergamon Press; and Microforms International; available on microfilm and microfiche from University Microfilms International (UMI); available on an online database from Elsevier Electronic Subscriptions (EES). Documents available from The Genuine Article, BIOSIS Document Express, CASDDS. ***Continues*** *Biochemical Systematics, 0045-2025.*
Desc: Devoted to the publication of original papers and reviews, both submitted and invited in two subject areas: the application of biochemistry to problems relating to systematic biology of organisms (biochemical systematics); and the role of biochemistry in interactions between organisms or between an organism and its environment (biochemical ecology).
Ind/Abst AgBiotech News Inf.; AGRICOLA [Select. Cov.]; Anim. Breed. Abstr.; Biocont. News Inf.; Biol. Abstr.; Chem. Abstr.; Chem. Titles; Chemorecept. Abstr.; Crop Physiol. Abstr.; Curr. Aware. Biol. Sci., CABS; Curr. Cit.; Curr. Contents Agric. Biol. Environ. Sci.; Curr. Ref. Fish Res.; Ecology Abstr.; Entomol. Abstr.; Field Crop Abstr.; Fish Rev.; For. Prod. Abstr.; For. Abstr.; Grass. Forage Abstr.; Microbiol. Abstr. Sect. C; NAPRALERT; Nutr. Abstr. Rev., Ser. B, Live Feeds and Feed.; Ornamental Hort.; Life Sci. Collect.; Plant Breed. Abstr.; Plant Genet. Resour. Abstr.; Res. Alert [Full Cov.]; Rev. Agric. Entomol.; Rev. Med. Vet. Entomol.; Rev. Med. Vet. Mycology; Rev. Plant Pathol.; Rice Abstr.; Sci. Cit. Index; SCISEARCH; Seed Abstr.; Soils Fert.; Weed Abstr.; Wildl. Rev.

ISSN 0954-982X
DD 574.19205 UK

BIOCHEMIST LONDON. (THE BIOCHEMIST.). [Biochem. Lond.]. (1988)-. Periodical. English. Six times a year. $85.56. Portland Press Ltd., PO Box 32 Commerce Way, Colchester CO2 8HP Essex United Kingdom. **Tel** 011 44 1206 796351, FAX 011 44 1206 799331, telex 987275 BIOSOC G. **ED** Robert Dale, The Biochemical Society, 59 Portland Place, London, W1N 3AJ United Kingdom (Editor's Phone: 0715 805530). **Bk Rev**, (Qty: 25+). **Ad Acc**, **Adv Mgr:** Samantha Burt, **Tel** 0225 442574. **Circ:** 8,337 (ctrl). ***Continues*** *Bulletin - Biochemical Society, 0953-4008.*
Desc: Membership magazine for the Biochemical Society. Contains news, reviews articles of professional interest and provides information on relevant scientific meetings.
Ind/Abst Abstr. BioCommer.

LC QD **ISSN** 1065-7509
DD 540 US
UDC 54

●**BIOCHEMISTRY & BIOPHYSICS CITATION INDEX.** See Biology-Abstracting, Bibliographies and Statistics.

LC QP501 .C32 **ISSN** 0829-8211
DD 574.19/2/05 CN
CCC
NLM W1; BI6305 **CODEN** BCBIEQ
Pr Rev.

BIOCHEMISTRY AND CELL BIOLOGY. [Biochem. cell biol.]. **Added/Corp** Canadian Biochemical Society. National Research Council Canada. Canadian Society for Cell Biology. **VFOAT** Biochimie et Biologie Cellulaire; Canadian Journal of Biochemistry and Cell Biology; Revue Canadienne de Biochimie et Biologie Cellulaire. Vol. 64, No. 1 (Jan. 1986)-. Academic Scholarly Publication. English (summaries and/or abstracts in French). Twelve times a year. 265.00Can$. National Research Council of Canada, Receiver General for Canada, Ottawa Ontario K1A 0R6 Canada. **Tel** (613)993-0362, FAX (613)952-7656. **ED** K. G. Scrimgeour and A. M. Zimmerman. Index available. **Ad Acc. Circ:** 2,200 (ctrl). available on microfilm and microfiche from University Microfilms International (UMI). Documents available from The Genuine Article, BIOSIS Document Express, CASDDS, Documents on Demand. ***Continues*** *Canadian Journal of Biochemistry and Cell Biology, 0714-7511.*
Desc: Publishes papers in all fields of general biochemistry and experimental cell biology. These include full length papers and rapid communications reporting original work or invited reviews on topical subjects, as well as certain symposia and special issues dedicated to a particular subject or occasion.
Ind/Abst Abstr. Bull. Inst. Pap. Sci. Tech.; AgBiotech News Inf.; AGRICOLA [Select. Cov.]; Anal. Abstr.; AQUAREF; Biol. Agric. Index; Biol. Abstr. (1986-); Calcium Calcif. Tissue Abstr.; Chem. Abstr. (1983-); Crop Physiol. Abstr.; CSA Neuro. Abstr. (?-?); Curr. Aware. Biol. Sci., CABS; Curr. Biotechnol.; Curr. Cit.; Curr. Contents Life Sci.; Dairy Sci. Abstr.; Energy Inf. Abstr.; Environ. Abstr.; Field Crop Abstr.; Food Sci. Technol. Abstr.; Genet. Abstr.; Immunol. Abstr.; Index Med. (1986-); Index Vet.; INIS Atomindex [Micro.]; Maize Abstr.; Microbiol. Abstr. Sect. B (19??-19??); Microbiol. Abstr. Sect. C; Nutr. Abstr. Rev., Ser. A, Hum. Exp.; Oncog. Growth Factors Abstr.; Life Sci. Collect.; PESTDOC; Pig News Inf.; Plant Breed. Abstr.; Protozoolog. Abstr.; Ref. Upd. Deluxe Ed.; Res. Alert [Full Cov.]; Rev. Agric. Entomol.; Rev. Med. Vet. Entomol.; Sci. Cit. Index; SCISEARCH; Seed Abstr.; Sorghum Mill. Abstr.; Soyabean Abstr.; Vet. Bull.; Trop. Dis. Bull.; Wheat Barley Trit. Abstr.; World Text. Abstr.

ISSN 1069-8302
DD 574 AT
NLM W1; BI635M **CODEN** BMBIES

●**BIOCHEMISTRY AND MOLECULAR BIOLOGY INTERNATIONAL.** [Biochem. mol. biol. int.]. **Added/Corp** International Union of Biochemistry and Molecular Biology. Vol. 29, No. 1 (1993)-. Academic Scholarly Publication. English. Eighteen times a year. 750.00Aus$. Academic Press Inc., 6277 Sea Harbor Drive, Orlando FL 32887. **Tel** (800)543-9534, (407)345-4100, FAX (407)352-3445. ***Continues*** *Biochemistry International, 0158-5231.*
Ind/Abst Curr. Cit.; Curr. Contents Life Sci.; Index Med. (1993-); Sci. Cit. Index.

LC QP501 .B525 **ISSN** 0006-2960
DD 612/.015 US
CCC
NLM W1 BI635 **CODEN** BICHAW
Pr Rev.

BIOCHEMISTRY (EASTON). (BIOCHEMISTRY.). [Biochemistry]. **Added/Corp** American Chemical Society. Vol. 1 (Jan. 1962)-. Academic Scholarly Publication. English. One time a week (51 issues). $1764.00. American Chemical Society, 1155 Sixteenth Street Northwest, Washington DC 20036. **Tel** (800)333-9511, (800)227-5558, (614)447-3776, FAX (202)447-3671. **(Subscription address:** American Chemical Society / Ohio, Department L 0011, Columbus OH 43268-0011.**)** **ED** Hans Neurath. Index available (bound in last issue). **Bk Rev. Ad Acc. Acid Free. Circ:** 6,256. available on microfilm and microfiche from University Microfilms International (UMI); available on an online database from STN International. Documents available from The Genuine Article, BIOSIS Document Express, UMI Article Clearinghouse, CASDDS, Documents on Demand.
Desc: Results of original research in recognized or developing areas of biochemistry. Emphasis is on the strong relationship between chemistry, biochemistry and other biological sciences. Topics include enzymes, proteins, carbohydrates, lipids, nucleic acids, viruses, immunochemistry, genetics, bioenergetics, membrane structure and function and protein biosynthesis.
Ind/Abst Abstr. Bull. Inst. Pap. Sci. Tech.; Acad. Search; AGRICOLA [Select. Cov.]; Biocont. News Inf.; Biol. Agric. Index; Biol. Abstr.; Biotechnol. Res. Abstr.; Calcium Calcif. Tissue Abstr.; Chem. Abstr.; Chemorecept. Abstr.; Crop Physiol. Abstr.; CSA Neuro. Abstr.; Curr. Aware. Biol. Sci., CABS; Curr. Biotechnol.; Curr. Cit.; Curr. Ref. Fish Res.; EMBASE; Energy Inf. Abstr.; Energy Res. Abstr.; Environ. Abstr.; EP Collect.; Field Crop Abstr.; Fish Rev. (Jan. 1989-July 1992); Food Sci. Technol. Abstr.; Gen. Sci. Index; Gen. Sci. Source; Genet. Abstr.; Health Plan. Adminis.; Helminthol. Abstr. (1991-); Homework Help.; Hum. Genome Abstr.; Immunol. Abstr.; Index Med.; Index Vet.; INFO-SOUTH Abstr.; INIS Atomindex [Micro.]; Int. Aerosp. Abstr.; Mag. Search; Mass Spect. Bull.; MasterFile FullTEXT 1000; MasterFile FullTEXT 350; MasterFile FullTEXT 650; MasterFile FullTEXT (July 1993-); Microbiol. Abstr. Sect. B; Microbiol. Abstr. Sect. A; Microbiol. Abstr. Sect. C; Newsp. Period. Abstr. (1992-); Nucl. Acids Abstr.; OCLC; Oncog. Growth Factors Abstr.; PESTDOC; Pig News Inf.; Potato Abstr.; Protozoolog. Abstr.; Res. Alert [Full Cov.]; Rev. Med. Vet. Mycology; Rice Abstr.; Sci. Cit. Index; SCISEARCH; Seed Abstr.; Soyabean Abstr.; Telebase; Vet. Bull.; Trop. Dis. Bull.; Virol. AIDS Abstr.; Wildl. Rev. (Jan. 1989-July 1992).

LC QH301 .A3433 **ISSN** 0006-2979
DD 574.072 US
CCC
NLM W1 BI64 **CODEN** BIORAK

BIOCHEMISTRY (NEW YORK). (BIOCHEMISTRY.). [Biochemistry]. **Added/Corp** Consultants Bureau Enterprises. Consultants Bureau. Vol. 21 (Jan./Feb. 1956)-. Periodical. English (Russian). Twelve times a year. $1560.00. Consultants Bureau, A Division of Plenum Publishing Corporation, 233 Spring Street, New York NY 10013. **Tel** (212)620-8000, (212)620-8466, FAX (212)463-0742, telex 23/421139. **ED** V. P. Skulachev. available on microfilm and microfiche from University Microfilms International (UMI). Documents available from The Genuine Article, BIOSIS Document Express, CASDDS.
Desc: Covers English translation of original Russian research by Academy of Science of the USSR in biochemistry.
Ind/Abst AGRICOLA [Select. Cov.]; Biodeter. Abstr.; Biol. Abstr. (?-1984); Chem. Abstr.; Crop Physiol. Abstr.; Curr. Cit.; Curr. Contents Life Sci.; Curr. Ref. Fish Res.; EMBASE; Field Crop Abstr.; Food Sci. Technol. Abstr.; INIS Atomindex [Micro.]; Life Sci. Collect.; Res. Alert [Full Cov.]; Rev. Plant Pathol.; Sci. Cit. Index; Sug. Indus. Abstr.; Weed Abstr.

LC QH **ISSN** 0194-0538
DD 574.192 US
UDC 57
NLM W1 BI635B

BIOCHEMISTRY (NEW YORK, N.Y. 1980). (BIOCHEMISTRY.). [Biochemistry]. Vol. 1 (1980)-. Monographic series. English. Irregular. Price varies per volume. John Wiley & Sons Inc / New Jersey, 1 Wiley Drive, Somerset NJ 08875. **Tel** (800)225-5945, (908)469-4400. **(Subscription address:** John Wiley & Sons / UK, Baffins Lane, Chichester, West Sussex PO19 1UD United Kingdom. **Tel** 011 44 1243 779777, FAX 011 44 243 776128, telex 86290 WIBOOKG.**)**
Ind/Abst Ref. Upd. Basic Ed.; Ref. Upd. Deluxe Ed.

LC QD **ISSN** 0146-5600
DD 574.192 US
NLM W1 BI64F **CODEN** BCYDBL

BIOCHEMISTRY OF DISEASE, THE. [Biochem. dis.]. Vol. 1 (1971)-. Monographic series. English. Irregular. Price varies per volume. Marcel Dekker Inc., 270 Madison Avenue, New York NY 10016. **Tel** (212)696-9000, (800)228-1160, FAX (212)685-4540, telex 421419. **(Subscription address:** Marcel Dekker Inc., PO Box 5017, Monticello NY 12701. **Tel** (800)228-1160.**)** Documents available from BIOSIS Document Express, CASDDS.
Desc: Each title presents a different aspect of the biochemistry of disease. Topics covered include nutritional pathology and the pathology of transcription and translation.
Ind/Abst Biol. Abstr.; Chem. Abstr.

ISSN 0887-6495
DD 574 US
CODEN BIELEO

BIOCHEMISTRY OF THE ELEMENTS. [Biochem. elem.]. Vol. 1 (1980)-. Monographic series. English. Irregular. Price varies per volume. Plenum Press, 233 Spring Street, New York NY 10013-1578. **Tel** (212)620-8000, (800)221-9369, FAX (212)463-0742, (212)807-1047, telex 23/421139. Documents available from BIOSIS Document Express, CASDDS.
Ind/Abst Biol. Abstr.; Chem. Abstr.

LC QD **ISSN** 0393-0564
DD 574.192 IT
UDC 61
Pr Rev.

BIOCHIMICA CLINICA. [Biochim. clin.]. (1983)-. Periodical. Multiple languages (English and French). Twelve times a year. L91970. Biomedia Srl, Via Carlo Farini 70, 20159 Milan Italy. **Tel** 011 39 2 69001316. **ED** N. Nontalbeca. **Bk Rev. Ad Acc. Circ:** 8,500 (ctrl). ***Continues*** *Notiziario - Societa Italiana di Biochimica Clinica, 0392-7091.*
Desc: Information on clinical biochemistry, laboratory medicine and related science.
Ind/Abst Curr. Aware. Biol. Sci., CABS.

LC QD1 .B55
DD 574.1905 NE
NLM W1 BI652 **CODEN** BBACAQ
Pr Rev.

BIOCHIMICA ET BIOPHYSICA ACTA. (BIOCHIMICA ET BIOPHYSICA ACTA. INTERNATIONAL JOURNAL OF BIOCHEMISTRY AND BIOPHYSICS.). [Biochim. biophys. acta]. **VFOAT** International Journal of Biochemistry and Biophysics. Vol. 1 (Jan. 1947)-. Academic Scholarly Publication. English (French and German; summaries and/or abstracts in English, French and German). Irregular (119 issues per year; 45 vols.). $8837.00. Elsevier Science Publishers BV, PO Box 211, 1000 AE Amsterdam Netherlands. **Tel** 011 31 20 4853641, 011 31 20 4853642, FAX 011 31 20 4853598. **ED** P Borst, P Cohen, K van Dam, L L M van Deenen, E P Kennedy, G K Radda, and E C Slater. cum. index. **Ad Acc. Circ:** 3,000 (ctrl). available on microfilm and microfiche from University Microfilms International (UMI); available on an online database from Elsevier Electronic Subscriptions (EES). Documents available from The Genuine Article, BIOSIS Document Express, CASDDS, Documents on Demand, ADONIS.
Desc: Includes sections on bioenergetics, biomembranes, cancer, gene structure, lipids, molecular cell research, protein structure, enzymology, and general.
Ind/Abst Abstr. Anthropol.; ADONIS; AGRICOLA [Select. Cov.]; Anim. Breed. Abstr.; Biodeter. Abstr. (1991-); Biol. Abstr.; Calcium Calcif. Tissue Abstr.; Chem. Abstr.; Chemorecept. Abstr.; CSA Neuro. Abstr.; Curr. Biotechnol.; Curr. Contents Life Sci.; EMBASE; Energy Inf. Abstr.; Entomol. Abstr.; Environ. Abstr.; Field Crop Abstr.; Food Sci. Technol. Abstr.; Genet. Abstr.; Grass. Forage Abstr.; Health Plan. Adminis.; Hum. Genome Abstr.; Immunol. Abstr.; Index Med.; Index Vet.; Int. Aerosp. Abstr.; Mass Spect. Bull.; Microbiol. Abstr. Sect. B; Microbiol. Abstr. Sect. C; Nucl. Acids Abstr.; Nutr. Abstr. Rev., Ser. B, Live Feeds and Feed.; Nutr. Abstr. Rev., Ser. A, Hum. Exp.; Oncog. Growth Factors Abstr.; Life Sci. Collect.; Postharvest News Inf.; Protozoolog. Abstr.; Res. Alert [Full Cov.]; Rev. Med. Vet. Entomol.; Rev. Med. Vet. Mycology; Rev. Plant Pathol.; Sci. Cit. Index; SCISEARCH; Vet. Bull.; Virol. AIDS Abstr.; Weed Abstr.

LC QD1 .B55 ISSN 0005-2728
NE
CCC

Pr Rev.

BIOCHIMICA ET BIOPHYSICA ACTA. BIOENERGETICS. [Biochim. biophys. acta, Bioenerg.]. **VFOAT** Bioenergetics. Vol. B1, No. 1 (1967)-. Academic Scholarly Publication. English. Fifteen times a year (5 vols.). $1406.00. Elsevier Science Publishers BV, PO Box 211, 1000 AE Amsterdam Netherlands. **Tel** 011 31 20 4853641, 011 31 20 4853642, FAX 011 31 20 4853598. **ED** P Borst, P Cohen, K van Dam, L L M van Deenen, E P Kennedy, G K Radda, and E C Slater. available on microfilm and microfiche from University Microfilms International (UMI); available on an online database from Elsevier Electronic Subscriptions (EES). Documents available from ADONIS.
Ind/Abst ADONIS; AgBiotech News Inf.; Crop Physiol. Abstr.; Curr. Aware. Biol. Sci., CABS; Dairy Sci. Abstr.; EMBASE; Field Crop Abstr.; Grass. Forage Abstr.; Helminthol. Abstr.; Hortic. Abstr.; Maize Abstr.; PESTDOC; Plant Breed. Abstr.; Potato Abstr.; Protozoolog. Abstr.; Ref. Upd. Basic Ed.; Ref. Upd. Deluxe Ed.; Rev. Med. Vet. Entomol.; Rev. Med. Vet. Mycology; Rev. Plant Pathol.; Soils Fert.; Weed Abstr.; Wheat Barley Trit. Abstr.

LC QD1 .B55 ISSN 0005-2736
NE
CCC

Pr Rev.

BIOCHIMICA ET BIOPHYSICA ACTA. BIOMEMBRANES. (BIOMEMBRANES.). [Biochim. biophys. acta, Biomembr.]. Vol. 1, No. 1 (1967)-. Academic Scholarly Publication. English. Nineteen times a year (9 volumes). $2530.00. Elsevier Science Publishers BV, PO Box 211, 1000 AE Amsterdam Netherlands. **Tel** 011 31 20 4853641, 011 31 20 4853642, FAX 011 31 20 4853598. **ED** G K Radda, P Cohen, U M Va Deaven, E G Kennedy, K Va Dan, P V D Uiet, P L Dutton, Y Kagawa. Index available. cum. index. **Ad Acc. Circ:** 2,000. available on microfilm and microfiche from University Microfilms International (UMI); available on an online database from Elsevier Electronic Subscriptions (EES). Documents available from ADONIS.
Desc: Main focus is on membrane structure and organization, membrane fluidity and lipid composition, membrane proteins (receptors, ATPases), channel proteins, model membranes, liposome studies, lipid-protein interactions, transport studies (sugar, ions, amino-acids, drugs, and others), membrane surface studies, and membrane biophysics (NMR, ESR, fluorescence, etc.).
Ind/Abst ADONIS; AgBiotech News Inf.; Anim. Breed. Abstr.; Crop Physiol. Abstr.; Curr. Aware. Biol. Sci., CABS; Curr. Cit.; Dairy Sci. Abstr.; EMBASE; Field Crop Abstr.; Hortic. Abstr.; Nutr. Abstr. Rev., Ser. A, Hum. Exp.; Life Sci. Collect.; PESTDOC; Plant Breed. Abstr.; Protozoolog. Abstr.; Ref. Upd. Basic Ed.; Ref. Upd. Deluxe Ed.; Rev. Agric. Entomol.; Rev. Med. Vet. Entomol.; Rev. Med. Vet. Mycology; Rev. Plant Pathol.; Wheat Barley Trit. Abstr.

LC QD ISSN 0304-4165
DD 574.192 NE
CCC

Pr Rev.

BIOCHIMICA ET BIOPHYSICA ACTA (G). (GENERAL SUBJECTS.). [Biochim. biophys. acta (G)]. (19??)-. Academic Scholarly Publication. English. Nine times a year (3 vols.). $843.00. Elsevier Science Publishers BV, PO Box 211, 1000 AE Amsterdam Netherlands. **Tel** 011 31 20 4853641, 011 31 20 4853642, FAX 011 31 20 4853598. **ED** P. Borst, P. Cohen, K. van Dam, L.L.M. van Deenen, E.P. Kennedy, G.K. Radda, and E.C. Slater. available on microfilm and microfiche from University Microfilms International (UMI); available on an online database from Elsevier Electronic Subscriptions (EES). Documents available from ADONIS.
Ind/Abst ADONIS; Crop Physiol. Abstr.; Curr. Aware. Biol. Sci., CABS; EMBASE; Helminthol. Abstr.; Hortic. Abstr.; Index Vet.; Maize Abstr.; Ornamental Hort. (1991-); PESTDOC; Poult. Abstr.; Protozoolog. Abstr.; Ref. Upd. Basic Ed.; Ref. Upd. Deluxe Ed.; Rev. Agric. Entomol.; Rev. Med. Vet. Mycology; Rev. Plant Pathol.; Seed Abstr.; Soils Fert.; Soyabean Abstr.

LC QD1 .B55 ISSN 0005-2760
NE
CCC

Pr Rev.

BIOCHIMICA ET BIOPHYSICA ACTA. LIPIDS AND LIPID METABOLISM. (LIPIDS AND LIPID METABOLISM.). [Biochim. biophys. acta, L Lipids lipid metab.]. Vol. 13, No. 1 (1965)-. Academic Scholarly Publication. English. Eighteen times a year (6 volumes). $1687.00. Elsevier Science Publishers BV, PO Box 211, 1000 AE Amsterdam Netherlands. **Tel** 011 31 20 4853641, 011 31 20 4853642, FAX 011 31 20 4853598. **ED** P Borst, P Cohen, K van Dam, L L M van Deenen, E P Kennedy, G K Radda, and E C Slater. available on microfilm and microfiche from University Microfilms International (UMI); available on an online database from Elsevier Electronic Subscriptions (EES). Documents available from ADONIS. ***Continues*** *Biochimica et Biophysica Acta. Specialized Section on Lipids and Related Subjects.*
Ind/Abst ADONIS; Crop Physiol. Abstr.; Curr. Aware. Biol. Sci., CABS; EMBASE; Hortic. Abstr.; Maize Abstr.; PESTDOC; Plant Breed. Abstr.; Potato Abstr.; Poult. Abstr.; Protozoolog. Abstr.; Ref. Upd. Basic Ed.; Ref. Upd. Deluxe Ed.; Rev. Agric. Entomol.; Rev. Med. Vet. Mycology.

LC QD ISSN 0925-4439
DD 574.192 NE
CCC
CODEN BBADEX

Pr Rev.

BIOCHIMICA ET BIOPHYSICA ACTA. MOLECULAR BASIS OF DISEASE. (BIOCHIMICA ET BIOPHYSICA ACTA. MOLECULAR BASIS OF DISEASE : BBA.). [Biochim. biophys. acta, Mol. basis dis.]. **VFOAT** Molecular Basis of Disease; BBA. Molecular Basis of Disease. Vol. 1096, No. 1 (Nov. 1990)-. Academic Scholarly Publication. English. Nine times a year (3 volumes). $843.00. Elsevier Science Publishers BV, PO Box 211, 1000 AE Amsterdam Netherlands. **Tel** 011 31 20 4853641, 011 31 20 4853642, FAX 011 31 20 4853598. Index available. cum. index. available on microfilm and microfiche from University Microfilms International (UMI); available on an online database from Elsevier Electronic Subscriptions (EES). Documents available from BIOSIS Document Express, CASDDS, ADONIS.
Desc: Fundamental biochemical and genetic approaches to understanding dysfunction in human disease states and their models.
Ind/Abst ADONIS; AgBiotech News Inf.; Anim. Breed. Abstr.; Biol. Abstr.; Chem. Abstr.; Curr. Aware. Biol. Sci., CABS; EMBASE; Index Vet.; PESTDOC; Protozoolog. Abstr.; Ref. Upd. Basic Ed.; Ref. Upd. Deluxe Ed.; Vet. Bull.

LC QD ISSN 0167-4838
DD 574.192 NE
CCC

Pr Rev.

BIOCHIMICA ET BIOPHYSICA ACTA. PROTEIN STRUCTURE AND MOLECULAR ENZYMOLOGY. (PROTEIN STRUCTURE AND MOLECULAR ENZYMOLOGY.). [Biochim. biophys. acta, Prot. struct. mol. enzymol.]. **VFOAT** BBA, Biochimica et Biophysica Acta (P). Protein Structure Molecular Enzymology; BBA, Protein Structure & Molecular Enzymology. Vol. 700, No. 1 (Jan. 4, 1982)-. Academic Scholarly Publication. English. Fourteen times a year. $1,968.00. Elsevier Science Publishers BV, PO Box 211, 1000 AE Amsterdam Netherlands. **Tel** 011 31 20 4853641, 011 31 20 4853642, FAX 011 31 20 4853598. **ED** P. Borst. **Ad Acc. Circ:** 1,920 (ctrl). available on microfiche from University Microfilms International (UMI); available on an online database from Elsevier Electronic Subscriptions (EES). Documents available from ADONIS. ***Formed by the union of*** *Enzymology (Amsterdam, Netherlands)* ***and*** *Protein Structure.*
Desc: Covers investigations on the isolation and covalent structure of proteins, molecular weight determinations, and solution properties.
Ind/Abst ADONIS; Crop Physiol. Abstr.; Curr. Aware. Biol. Sci., CABS; EMBASE; Field Crop Abstr.; Hortic. Abstr.; Index Vet.; Maize Abstr.; PESTDOC; Pig News Inf.; Potato Abstr.; Poult. Abstr.; Protozoolog. Abstr.; Ref. Upd. Basic Ed.; Ref. Upd. Deluxe Ed.; Rev. Plant Pathol.; Small Anim. Abstr. Bibliogr.; Soyabean Abstr.; Wheat Barley Trit. Abstr.

ISSN 0300-9084
DD 574.1/92/05 FR
CCC
NLM W1 BI6527 CODEN BICMBE

Pr Rev.

BIOCHIMIE. [Biochimie]. **Added/Corp** Societe de Chimie Biologique, Paris. Vol. 53 (1971)-. Academic Scholarly Publication. French (English and French; summaries and/or abstracts in German). Ten times a year (1 volume). $639.00. Editions Scientifique Elsevier, 141 rue de Javel, 75747 Paris Cedex 15 France. **Tel** 011 33 1 45589067, FAX 011 33 1 45589424. **(Subscription address:** Editions Scientifiques Elsevier / for North America, PO Box 7247-7576, Philadelphia PA 19170-7576. **)** available on microfilm and microfiche from University Microfilms International (UMI); available on an online database from Elsevier Electronic Subscriptions (EES). Documents available from The Genuine Article, BIOSIS Document Express, CASDDS. ***Continues*** *Bulletin de la Societe de Chimie Biologique, 0037-9042.*
Ind/Abst AgBiotech News Inf.; AGRICOLA [Select. Cov.]; Anim. Breed. Abstr.; Biol. Abstr.; Chem. Abstr.; Crop Physiol. Abstr.; CSA Neuro. Abstr. (?-?); Curr. Biotechnol.; Curr. Cit.; Curr. Contents Life Sci.; Curr. Ref. Fish Res.; Dairy Sci. Abstr.; EMBASE; Energy Res. Abstr. (Sept. 1971-); Food Sci. Technol. Abstr.; Genet. Abstr.; Health Plan. Adminis.; Immunol. Abstr.; Index Med.; Maize Abstr.; Microbiol. Abstr. Sect. B; Microbiol. Abstr. Sect. C; Nucl. Acids Abstr.; Life Sci. Collect.; PESTDOC; Pig News Inf.; Plant Breed. Abstr.; Plant Grow. Reg. Abstr.; Potato Abstr.; Protozoolog. Abstr.; Ref. Upd. Basic Ed.; Ref. Upd. Deluxe Ed.; Res. Alert [Full Cov.]; Rev. Agric. Entomol.; Rev. Plant Pathol.; Rice Abstr.; Sci. Cit. Index; SCISEARCH; Virol. AIDS Abstr.

ISSN 0888-4404
DD 543 US
CCC
NLM W1; BI654 CODEN BCHREF
TITLE CHANGE

BIOCHROMATOGRAPHY. [BioChromatography]. **VFOAT** Bio Chromatography. Vol. 1, No. 1 (May/June 1986)-(19??). Periodical. English. Eaton Publishing Company, 154 East Central Street, Natick MA 01760. **Tel** (508)655-8282, FAX (508)655-9910. **ED** James Ellingboe. cum. index. **Ad Acc. Circ:** 20,000 (ctrl). Documents available from BIOSIS Document Express, CASDDS. ***Merged into*** *Biotechniques, 0736-6205.*
Desc: Information on the chromatography of biomolecules.
Ind/Abst Anal. Abstr.; Biol. Abstr. (1987-); Chem. Abstr.; Curr. Biotechnol.

LC QP517.B49 B56 ISSN 1043-1802
DD 574.19/2 US
CCC
NLM W1; BI66L CODEN BCCHES

BIOCONJUGATE CHEMISTRY. [Bioconjug. chem.]. **Added/Corp** American Chemical Society. Vol. 1, No. 1 (Jan./Feb. 1990)-. Academic Scholarly Publication. English. Six times a year. $334.00. American Chemical Society, 1155 Sixteenth Street Northwest, Washington DC 20036. **Tel** (800)333-9511, (800)227-5558, (614)447-3776, FAX (202)447-3671. **(Subscription address:** American Chemical Society / Ohio, Department L 0011, Columbus OH 43268-0011. **) ED** Claude F. Meares and Paul S. Miller. **Acid Free.** available on microfilm and microfiche from University Microfilms International (UMI). Documents available from The Genuine Article, BIOSIS Document Express, CASDDS.
Desc: Chemists, biochemists, and molecular biologists finding the most important research in conjugate chemistry.
Ind/Abst Biol. Abstr. (1990-); Chem. Abstr. (1990-); Curr. Aware. Biol. Sci., CABS; Curr. Cit.; Curr. Contents Life Sci.; Index Med. (1990-); Res. Alert [Full Cov.]; Sci. Cit. Index; SCISEARCH.

LC QD415
DD 574.192 SZ

•BIOELECTROCHEMISTRY : PRINCIPLES AND PRACTICE. (1994)-. Monographic series. English. Irregular. Birkhaeuser Verlag Ag, Klosterberg 23, PO Box 133, CH-4010 Basel Switzerland. **Tel** 011 41 61 2717400, FAX 011 41 61 2717666, telex 963475 birk ch.

LC QP771 .B53 ISSN 0951-6433
DD 612.3/99 UK
CCC
NLM W1; BI664C CODEN BIFAEU

Pr Rev.

BIOFACTORS (OXFORD). (BIOFACTORS.). [BioFactors]. **Added/Corp** International Union of Biochemistry. **VAT** Bio Factors. Vol. 1, No. 1 (Jan. 1988)-. Academic Scholarly Publication. English. Four times a year. $274.07. IOS Press, Van Diemenstraat 94, 1013 CN Amsterdam Netherlands. **Tel** 011 31 20 6382189, FAX 011 31 20 6203419. Index available. **Bk Rev. Ad Acc. Circ:** 500. available in microform from University Microfilms International (UMI). Documents available from The Genuine Article, BIOSIS Document Express, CASDDS.
Desc: A research journal aimed at identifying and increasing understanding of the biochemical effects and roles of the large number of trace substances required by living organisms.
Ind/Abst Biol. Abstr. (1988-); Chem. Abstr.; Crop Physiol. Abstr.; Curr. Aware. Biol. Sci., CABS; Curr. Cit.; Curr. Contents Life Sci.; EMBASE; Hortic. Abstr.; Nutr. Abstr. Rev., Ser. A, Hum. Exp.; Postharvest News Inf.; Ref. Upd. Deluxe Ed.; Res. Alert [Full Cov.]; Sci. Cit. Index; SCISEARCH; Soils Fert.; Weed Abstr.

LC QP801.B66 B56 ISSN 0168-8561
DD 599/.0188 UK
CCC
NLM W1; BI665T CODEN BIAME7

Pr Rev.

BIOGENIC AMINES. [Biog. amines]. Vol. 1, No. 1 (March 1984)-. Academic Scholarly Publication. English. Six times a year. DM430.00. VSP International Science Publishers, Godfried van Seystlaan 47, 3703 BR Zeist Netherlands. **Tel** 011 31 3404 25790, FAX 011 31 3404 32081, telex 40217 USP NL. **(Subscription address:** VSP International Science Publishers, PO Box 346, 3700 AH Zeist Netherlands. **Tel** 011 31 30 6925790, FAX 011 31 30 6932081.**) ED** S.H. Parvez, T. Nagatsu. **Ad Acc. Circ:** 200. Documents available from The Genuine Article, BIOSIS Document Express, CASDDS.
Desc: Publishes regular papers and short communications on all aspects of biogenic amines and amino acid transmitters, their related compounds and interaction phenomena. Original research data on catecholamines, serotonin and interacting compounds is reported. Papers from both basic research and clinical research are published.
Ind/Abst Biol. Abstr. (1984-); Chem. Abstr. (1984-); Curr. Cit.; Curr. Contents Life Sci.; Dairy Sci. Abstr.; EMBASE; Res. Alert [Full Cov.]; Rev. Med. Vet. Entomol.; Sci. Cit. Index; SCISEARCH.

LC QD ISSN 0320-9725
DD 574.192 RU
CCC
NLM W1 BI668 CODEN BIOHAO
BIOHIMIJA (MOSKVA). (BIOKHIMIIA.). [Biohimija]. **Added/Corp** Akademiia Nauk SSSR. Rossiiskaia Akademiia Nauk. **VFOAT** Biochimia. (1936)-. Academic Scholarly Publication. Russian (summaries and/or abstracts in English, French and German; table of contents in English). Twelve times a year. $360.00. Izdatelstvo Obedinennoe Nauchno-Tekhnicheskoe, Moscow Russia. **(Subscription address:** East View Publications Inc., 3020 Harbor Lane North, Suite 110, Minneapolis MN 55447. **Tel** (800)477-1005, (612)550-0961, FAX (612)559-2931.) cum. index. Documents available from BIOSIS Document Express, CASDDS.
Ind/Abst Abstr. Bull. Inst. Pap. Sci. Tech.; AGRICOLA; Aquat. Sci. Fish. Abstr. [CD-ROM Ed.]; Biol. Abstr.; Chem. Abstr.; Chem. Titles; CSA Neuro. Abstr.; Curr. Biotechnol.; EMBASE; Energy Res. Abstr.; Index Med.; Microbiol. Abstr. Sect. B; Microbiol. Abstr. Sect. C; NAPRALERT; PESTDOC; Protozoolog. Abstr.; Rev. Med. Vet. Entomol.

LC QP1 .B47 ISSN 0136-9377
DD 612.005 UN
UDC 612.32
NLM W1 BI669T CODEN BZCHDI
BIOKHIMIHA ZHIVOTNYKH I CHELOVEKA. Vol. 1 (1977)-. Academic Scholarly Publication. Russian. Izdatelstvo Naukova Dumka / Ukrainian Academy of Sciences, Yu. A. Khramov, Dir., Ul. Repina 3, 252 601 Kiev Ukraine. **Tel** 011 7 44 4303441, 011 7 44 2254182, telex 131376. Documents available from CASDDS.
Ind/Abst Chem. Abstr.

LC QP501 .B566 ISSN 0918-6158
DD 615/.7/05 JA
CCC
NLM W1; BI738G CODEN BPBLEO
•**BIOLOGICAL & PHARMACEUTICAL BULLETIN.** See Pharmacy and Pharmacology.

LC QD ISSN 0177-3593
DD 574.192 GW
CCC
NLM W1; BI733H CODEN BCHSEI
Pr Rev.
BIOLOGICAL CHEMISTRY HOPPE-SEYLER. [Biol. chem. Hoppe-Seyler]. Vol. 366, No. 1 (Jan. 1985)-. Academic Scholarly Publication. English (German). Twelve times a year. $840.75. Walter de Gruyter Inc., PO Box 303421, D-10728 Berlin Germany. **Tel** 011 49 30 260050, FAX 011 49 30 26005251, telex 184027. **ED** K. Decker, W. Stoffel and H. G. Zachau. **Circ:** 1,400. available on microfilm and microfiche from University Microfilms International (UMI). Documents available from The Genuine Article, BIOSIS Document Express, CASDDS, Documents on Demand. ***Continues** Hoppe-Seyler's Zeitschrift fur Physiologische Chemie, 0018-4888.*
Desc: Publishes reports on the latest research in the fields of biological and physiological chemistry.
Ind/Abst AgBiotech News Inf.; AGRICOLA [Select. Cov.]; Anim. Breed. Abstr.; Biol. Abstr. (1985-); Chem Inform; Chem. Abstr. (1985-); Chem. Titles; CSA Neuro. Abstr. (?-?); Curr. Aware. Biol. Sci., CABS; Curr. Cit.; Curr. Contents Life Sci.; Dairy Sci. Abstr.; EMBASE (1985-); Energy Inf. Abstr. (1985-); Energy Res. Abstr. (1985-); Environ. Abstr. (1985-?); Fish Rev. (Jan. 1989-July 1992); Genet. Abstr.; Immunol. Abstr.; Index Med. (1985-); Index Vet.; Mass Spect. Bull.; NAPRALERT; Nutr. Abstr. Rev., Ser. B, Live Feeds and Feed.; Nutr. Abstr. Rev., Ser. A, Hum. Exp.; Life Sci. Collect. (1985-); PESTDOC (1985-); Pig News Inf.; Postharvest News Inf.; Ref. Upd. Deluxe Ed.; Res. Alert [Full Cov.]; Rev. Agric. Entomol.; Rev. Med. Vet. Entomol.; Sci. Cit. Index; SCISEARCH; Vet. Bull.; Wheat Barley Trit. Abstr.; Wildl. Rev. (Jan. 1989-July 1992).

LC QP534 .B56 ISSN 0163-4984
DD 574.1/33 US
CCC
NLM W1 BI761; W1 BI761 CODEN BTERDG
Pr Rev.
BIOLOGICAL TRACE ELEMENT RESEARCH. [Biol. trace elem. res.]. **Added/Corp** International Association of Bioinorganic Scientists. Vol. 1, March (1979)-. Academic Scholarly Publication. English. Twelve times a year. $580.00. Humana Press Inc., 999 Riverview Drive, Suite 208, Totawa NJ 07512. **Tel** (201)256-1699, FAX (201)256-8341. **ED** Gerhard Schrauzer, Charles H. Hill and Yashushi Kodama. Index available. **Bk Rev. Ad Acc.** Documents available from The Genuine Article, BIOSIS Document Express, CASDDS.
Desc: Forefront journal publishing on all aspects of biological research on trace elements, from biochemistry, toxicology, neurobiology, nutrition, pharmacology, epidemiology, pathology.
Ind/Abst AGRICOLA [Select. Cov.]; Art Archaeol. Tech. Abstr.; Biodeter. Abstr. (1991-); Biol. Abstr. (1989-); Chem. Abstr.; Chem. Titles; Crop Physiol. Abstr.; CSA Neuro. Abstr. (?-?); Curr. Cit.; Curr. Contents Life Sci.; Dairy Sci. Abstr.; EMBASE; Field Crop Abstr.; For. Abstr.; Health Plan. Adminis.; Hortic. Abstr.; Index Med.; Index Vet.; Nutr. Abstr. Rev., Ser. B, Live Feeds and Feed.; Nutr. Abstr. Rev., Ser. A, Hum. Exp.; Life Sci. Collect.; Pig News Inf.; Poult. Abstr.; Protozoolog. Abstr.; Ref. Upd. Deluxe Ed.; Res. Alert [Full Cov.]; Rice Abstr.; Sci. Cit. Index; SCISEARCH; Seed Abstr.; Soils Fert.; Vet. Bull.; Wheat Barley Trit. Abstr.

LC QD ISSN 0730-7918
DD 574.192 US
NLM W1 BI852M CODEN BICADE
BIOLOGY OF CARBOHYDRATES. [Biol. carbohydr.]. Vol. 1 (1981)-. Academic Scholarly Publication. English. Irregular. Price varies. John Wiley & Sons, Inc., 605 Third Avenue, New York NY 10158-0012. **Tel** (212)850-6000, (212)850-6645, FAX (212)850-6088, telex 12-7063. **(Subscription address:** John Wiley & Sons / UK, Baffins Lane, Chichester, West Sussex PO19 1UD United Kingdom. **Tel** 011 44 1243 779777, FAX 011 44 243 776128, telex 86290 WIBOOKG.) **ED** Victor Ginsburg and Phillips Robbins. Documents available from BIOSIS Document Express, CASDDS.
Ind/Abst Biol. Abstr.; Chem. Abstr.

LC QD415 ISSN 1353-8616
DD 574.192 UK
•**BIOMEDICAL PEPTIDES, PROTEINS & NUCLEIC ACIDS.** (1994)-. Academic Scholarly Publication. English. Five times a year. £125.00 (institutions), £95.00 (individuals). Mayflower Worldwide Ltd., PO Box 13, Kingswinford West Midlands DY6 0HQ United Kingdom. **Tel** 011 44 1384 294463. **ED** Roger Epton. Documents available from BLDSC.

LC QP532 .B57 ISSN 0966-0844
DD 574.19/214 US
CCC
NLM W1; BI858N CODEN BOMEEH
BIOMETALS. (1992)-. Periodical. English. Four times a year. $446.00. Rapid Science Publishers, The Old Malthouse, Paradise Street, Oxford OX1 1LD United Kingdom. **Tel** 011 44 1865 790447, FAX 011 44 1865 244012, telex 9403712. **Ad Acc. Acid Free.** Documents available from The Genuine Article. ***Continues** Biology of Metals, 0933-5854.*
Desc: Aims to provide an international, multidisciplinary forum for new research and clinical results on the structure and function of metal ions, metal chelates, siderophones, metal-containing proteins and biominerals in all biosystems. The scope of the journal covers humans, animals, microbes and plants.
Ind/Abst Curr. Aware. Biol. Sci., CABS; Curr. Contents Life Sci.; Index Med.; Res. Alert [Full Cov.]; Sci. Cit. Index.

GW
NLM W1 BI859P
BIOMETRIE IN DER CHEMISCH-PHARMAZEUTISCHEN INDUSTRIE. See Pharmacy and Pharmacology.

LC QD ISSN 0968-0896
DD 574.192 UK
CCC
NLM W1; BI876E
•**BIOORGANIC & MEDICINAL CHEMISTRY.** [Biomed. Chem.]. **VFOAT** Bioorganic and Medicinal Chemistry. Vol. 1, No. 1 (July 1993)-. Academic Scholarly Publication. English. Twelve times a year. $1035.28. Pergamon Press, An Imprint of Elsevier Science Ltd., The Boulevard, Langford Lane, Kidlington, Oxford OX5 1GB United Kingdom. **Tel** 011 44 1865 843000, 011 44 1865 843699, FAX 011 44 1865 843010. **(Subscription address:** Elsevier Science Ltd. / Oxford Fulfillment Centre, PO Box 800, Kidlington OX5 1DX United Kingdom. **Tel** 011 44 865 843355.) **ED** Chi-Huey Wong. available on an online database from Elsevier Electronic Subscriptions (EES).
Desc: Provides an international forum for the publication of full original research papers and critical reviews on molecular interactions in key biological targets such as receptors, channels, enzymes, nucleotides, lipids and saccharides.
Ind/Abst Index Med.

LC QP501 .B57 ISSN 0960-894X
DD 574.19/24/05 UK
CCC
NLM W1; BI876KE CODEN BMCLE8
BIOORGANIC & MEDICINAL CHEMISTRY LETTERS. **VFOAT** Bioorganic and Medicinal Chemistry Letters. Vol. 1, No. 1 (1991)-. Academic Scholarly Publication. English. Twenty-four times a year. $1193.00. Pergamon Press, An Imprint of Elsevier Science Ltd., The Boulevard, Langford Lane, Kidlington, Oxford OX5 1GB United Kingdom. **Tel** 011 44 1865 843000, 011 44 1865 843699, FAX 011 44 1865 843010. **(Subscription address:** Elsevier Science Ltd. / Oxford Fulfillment Centre, PO Box 800, Kidlington OX5 1DX United Kingdom. **Tel** 011 44 865 843355.) **ED** Dale L. Boger. available on microfilm and microfiche from University Microfilms International (UMI); available on an online database from Elsevier Electronic Subscriptions (EES). Documents available from The Genuine Article, BIOSIS Document Express, CASDDS, ADONIS. ***Continues** Bio-Organic and Medicinal Chemistry.*
Desc: Presents preliminary experimental or theoretical research results of outstanding significance and timeliness on all aspects of science at the interface of chemistry and biology, and on major advances in drug design and development.
Ind/Abst ADONIS; Biol. Abstr. (1991-); Chem. Abstr.; Curr. Aware. Biol. Sci., CABS; Curr. Cit.; Curr. Contents Life Sci.; EMBASE; Res. Alert [Full Cov.]; Sci. Cit. Index; SCISEARCH.

LC QP501 .B58 ISSN 0045-2068
DD 574.1/924/05 US
CCC
NLM W1 BI876K CODEN BOCMBM
Pr Rev.
BIOORGANIC CHEMISTRY. [Bioorg. chem.]. **VFOAT** Bio Organic Chemistry. Vol. 1 (Sept. 1971)-. Academic Scholarly Publication. English. Four times a year. $244.00. Academic Press Inc., 6277 Sea Harbor Drive, Orlando FL 32887. **Tel** (800)543-9534, (407)345-4100, FAX (407)352-3445. **ED** Gordon A. Hamilton. Documents available from The Genuine Article, BIOSIS Document Express, CASDDS.
Desc: Publishes articles in which the principles and techniques of organic and physical organic chemistry are used in attempting to solve problems of relevance to biology or that describe chemical studies inspired by some biological observation.
Ind/Abst Abstr. Bull. Inst. Pap. Sci. Tech.; AGRICOLA [Select. Cov.]; Biol. Abstr.; Chem. Abstr.; Curr. Cit.; Curr. Contents Life Sci.; Curr. Contents Phys. Chem. Earth Sci.; EMBASE; NAPRALERT; Nat. Prod. Updates; Life Sci. Collect.; PESTDOC; Ref. Upd. Deluxe Ed.; Res. Alert [Full Cov.]; Sci. Cit. Index; SCISEARCH.

LC QP550 .B562
DD 574.19/2/05 GW
NLM W1; BI89S CODEN BCFRE5
BIOORGANIC CHEMISTRY FRONTIERS. Vol. 1 (1990)-. Academic Scholarly Publication. English. Irregular. Price varies per volume. Springer-Verlag New York Inc., 175 Fifth Avenue, New York NY 10010. **Tel** (212)460-1500 ext 256, FAX (212)533-3503, telex 232 235 SPB UR. **(Subscription address:** Springer-Verlag New York Inc. / North America, PO Box 2485, Journal Fulfillment, Secaucus NJ 07096. **Tel** (201)348-4033, (800)777-4643, FAX (201)348-4505.) **ED** H. Dugas. Documents available from CASDDS.
Desc: This series attempts to bring together critical reviews in the fields of biological and biochemical research.
Ind/Abst Chem. Abstr.

LC QH345 .B54 ISSN 0301-4622
DD 574.1/92/05 NE
CCC
NLM W1 BI876N CODEN BICIAZ
Pr Rev.
BIOPHYSICAL CHEMISTRY. [Biophys. chem.]. Vol. 1 (Oct. 1973)-. Academic Scholarly Publication. English. Eighteen times a year. $1720.00. Elsevier Science Publishers BV, PO Box 211, 1000 AE Amsterdam Netherlands. **Tel** 011 31 20 4853641, 011 31 20 4853642, FAX 011 31 20 4853598. **ED** A. Watts. available on microfilm and microfiche from University Microfilms International (UMI); available on an online database from Elsevier Electronic Subscriptions (EES). Documents available from The Genuine Article, BIOSIS Document Express, CASDDS.
Desc: Devoted to the interpretation of biological phenomena in terms of the principles and methods of physical chemistry. It is receptive to reviews and research articles which deal with biological molecules and systems, and to papers which treat systems serving as models for these.
Ind/Abst Biol. Abstr.; Chem. Abstr.; Chem. Titles; CSA Neuro. Abstr. (?-?); Curr. Cit.; Curr. Contents Life Sci.; Curr. Contents Phys. Chem. Earth Sci.; Curr. Titles Electrochem.; Dairy Sci. Abstr.; EMBASE; Index Med.; Int. Aerosp. Abstr.; Life Sci. Collect.; Protozoolog. Abstr.; Ref. Upd. Deluxe Ed.; Res. Alert [Full Cov.]; Sci. Cit. Index; SCISEARCH.

LC QP801.P64 B56 ISSN 0006-3525
DD 574.19/24 US
CCC
NLM W1 BI88N CODEN BIPMAA
Pr Rev.
BIOPOLYMERS. [Biopolymers]. Vol. 1 (Feb. 1963)-. Academic Scholarly Publication. English. Twelve times a year. $2,196.00 US; $2,376.00 Canada and Mexico; $2,443.00 other. John Wiley & Sons, Inc., 605 Third Avenue, New York NY 10158-0012. **Tel** (212)850-6000, (212)850-6645, FAX (212)850-6088, telex 12-7063. **(Subscription address:** John Wiley & Sons / UK, Baffins Lane, Chichester, West Sussex PO19 1UD United Kingdom. **Tel** 011 44 1243 779777, FAX 011 44 243 776128, telex 86290 WIBOOKG.) **ED** Murray Goodman. **Ad Acc. Circ:** 1,000. available on microfilm and microfiche from University Microfilms International (UMI); available on an online database from STN International. Documents available from Article Express International, The Genuine Article, BIOSIS Document Express, CASDDS. ***Supersedes in part** Journal of Polymer Science, 0022-3832.*
Desc: Publishes innovative original research papers on the structure, properties, interactions and assemblies of biomolecules. Covers organic and physical chemistry, experimental and theoretical research, static and dynamic aspects of structure. Also includes an examination of the broad aspects of biospectroscopy.
Ind/Abst Abstr. Bull. Inst. Pap. Sci. Tech.; AGRICOLA

Biology—Biological Chemistry

[Select. Cov.]; Appl. Mech. Rev.; Biol. Abstr.; Chem. Abstr.; Chem. Titles; Comput. Inf. Syst. Abstr. J. [Full Cov.]; CSA Neuro. Abstr. (?-?); Curr. Aware. Biol. Sci., CABS; Curr. Cit.; Curr. Contents Life Sci.; Dairy Sci. Abstr.; Elect. Comm. Abstr.; EMBASE; Energy Res. Abstr.; Eng. Index Anu.; Food Sci. Technol. Abstr.; Index Med.; INIS Atomindex [Micro.]; Int. Aerosp. Abstr.; Mater. Sci. Eng. Abstr.; Mech. Eng. Abstr.; Life Sci. Collect.; Polymer Contents; Protozoolog. Abstr.; Ref. Upd. Basic Ed.; Ref. Upd. Deluxe Ed.; Res. Alert [Full Cov.]; Rev. Med. Vet. Entomol.; Rev. Plant Pathol.; Sci. Cit. Index; SCISEARCH.

LC QH301 .B56   ISSN 0916-8451
DD 574.05/6   JA
     CCC
NLM W1; BI91H   CODEN BBBIEJ

BIOSCIENCE, BIOTECHNOLOGY, AND BIOCHEMISTRY. See Biology-Bioengineering.

LC QD   ISSN 1075-4261
DD 574   US
     CODEN BIOSFS
Pr Rev.

●BIOSPECTROSCOPY (NEW YORK, N.Y.). (BIOSPECTROSCOPY.).
[Biospectroscopy]. Vol. 1, Issue 1 (1995)-. Academic Scholarly Publication. English. Six times a year. $175.00. John Wiley & Sons, Inc., 605 Third Avenue, New York NY 10158-0012. **Tel** (212)850-6000, (212)850-6645, FAX (212)850-6088, telex 12-7063. **(Subscription address:** John Wiley & Sons / UK, Baffins Lane, Chichester, West Sussex PO19 1UD United Kingdom. **Tel** 011 44 1243 779777, FAX 011 44 243 776128, telex 86290 WIBOOKG.) available in microform from University Microfilms International (UMI). Documents available from BLDSC, CASDDS.
Ind/Abst Chem. Abstr.

LC QP501 .J66   ISSN 0885-4513
DD 660/.6   US
     CCC
NLM W1; BI918MJ   CODEN BABIEC
Pr Rev.

BIOTECHNOLOGY AND APPLIED BIOCHEMISTRY. See Biology-Bioengineering.

LC QD415   ISSN 0938-5584
DD 574.192   GW
UDC 57.08

BIOTECHNOLOGY (FRANKFURT 1991). See Biology-Bioengineering.

     UK
NLM W1; BI919MR   CODEN BTRNE2

BIOTRANSFORMATIONS : A SURVEY OF THE BIOTRANSFORMATIONS OF DRUGS AND CHEMICALS IN ANIMALS.
Added/Corp Royal Society of Chemistry (Great Britain). Vol. 1 (1988)-. English. One time a year. £130.00. Royal Society of Chemistry, Thomas Graham House, Science Park, Cambridge CB4 4WF United Kingdom. **Tel** 011 44 1223 420066, FAX 011 44 1223 423623, telex 818293 ROYAL. **(Subscription address:** Royal Society of Chemistry, Turpin Distribution Services Ltd., Blackhorse Road, Letchworth, Hertfordshire SG6 1HN United Kingdom. **Tel** 011 44 1462 672555, FAX 011 44 1462 480947.) ED David R. Hawkins. Documents available from BIOSIS Document Express.
Desc: Provides a complete survey of the biotransformation, in vertebrates, of the following: pharmaceuticals, agrochemicals, food additives, environmental chemicals, and industrial chemicals.
Ind/Abst Biol. Abstr.

LC QD   ISSN 0250-4685
DD 540   TU
NLM W1 BI995   CODEN BIDEDV

BIYOKIMYA DERGISI. Added/Corp Biyokimya Dernegi.
(1976)-. Academic Scholarly Publication. Turkish (summaries and/or abstracts in English). Three times a year. Documents available from CASDDS.
Ind/Abst Chem. Abstr.

LC QD   ISSN 1078-0491
DD 574   US
NLM W1; BL649L   CODEN BCEBEK

BLOOD CELL BIOCHEMISTRY. See Medical Sciences-Hematology.

     SP

BOEHRINGER MANNHEIM INFORMA DE ACTUALIDADES EN ANALITICA CLINICA Y BIOQUIMICA. See Medical Sciences.

DD 574.19   ISSN 1197-6578
     CN
     CODEN BCSBEM

BULLETIN OF THE CANADIAN SOCIETY OF BIOCHEMISTRY AND MOLECULAR BIOLOGY.
(BULLETIN OF THE CANADIAN SOCIETY OF BIOCHEMISTRY AND MOLECULAR BIOLOGY = BULLETIN DE LA SOCIETE CANADIENNE DE BIOCHEMIE ET BIOLOGIE MOLECULAIRE.). [Bull. Can. Soc. Biochem. Mol. Biol.]. **Main/Corp** Canadian Society of Biochemistry and Molecular Biology. **VFOAT** Bulletin de la Societe Canadienne de Biochemie et Biologie Moleculaire. Vol. 31 (Dec. 1992)-. Bulletin. English (summaries and/or abstracts in French). Two times a year. Canadian Biochemical Society, University of West Ontario / Department of Biochemistry, London Ontario N6A 5C1 Canada. **Tel** (519)661-3055.
Continues Canadian Biochemical Society. Bulletin of the Canadian Biochemical Society, 0008-302X.

DD 574 016   ISSN 0007-5434
     FR

BULLETIN SIGNALETIQUE 320: BIOCHEMIE. BIOPHYSIQUE. CHEMIE ANALYTIQUE BIOLOGIQUE. BIOPHYSIQUE. GENIE BIOLOGIQUE ET MEDICAL.
Main/Corp France. Centre National de la Recherche Scientifique. Vol. 30 (1969)-. Bulletin. French. Twelve times a year. Centre National de la Recherche Scientifique, Informascience, 26 rue Boyer, 75971 Paris France. **Tel** 011 33 1 61411105, telex CNRSDOC 220880 F. **Continues** Centre National de la Recherche Scientifique. Bulletin Signaletique 12: Biophysique, Biochemie, Chemie Analytique Biologique.

     ISSN 0162-7694
     US
     CODEN CSLAD4

CA SELECTS: ANIMAL LONGEVITY & AGING. See Chemistry and Chemicals-Abstracting, Bibliographies and Statistics.

     ISSN 0162-7732
     US
     CODEN CBCODI

CA SELECTS: BLOOD COAGULATION.
See Chemistry and Chemicals-Abstracting, Bibliographies and Statistics.

LC QD   ISSN 0148-2408
DD 574.192   US
     CODEN CSCTDG

CA SELECTS: CARCINOGENS, MUTAGENS & TERATOGENS. See
Chemistry and Chemicals-Abstracting, Bibliographies and Statistics.

LC QD   ISSN 0895-5905
DD 574   US
     CODEN CAFRE2

CA SELECTS: FREE RADICALS (BIOCHEMICAL ASPECTS). See Chemistry and Chemicals-Abstracting, Bibliographies and Statistics.

LC QD   ISSN 1059-2784
DD 574.192   US

CA SELECTS: MOLECULAR MODELING (BIOCHEMICAL ASPECTS).
See Chemistry and Chemicals-Abstracting, Bibliographies and Statistics.

     ISSN 0148-2335
     US
     CODEN CSPHDB

CA SELECTS: PHOTOBIOCHEMISTRY.
See Chemistry and Chemicals-Abstracting, Bibliographies and Statistics.

     ISSN 0362-9848
     US
     CODEN CASPDQ

CA SELECTS: PSYCHOBIOCHEMISTRY.
See Chemistry and Chemicals-Abstracting, Bibliographies and Statistics.

     ISSN 0160-9173
     US
     CODEN CSBSDB

CA SELECTS: STEROIDS (BIOCHEMICAL ASPECTS). See Chemistry and Chemicals-Abstracting, Bibliographies and Statistics.

LC QH345 .B527   ISSN 8756-7504
DD 574.19/2   US
NLM Z 5322.C3; B615
     CEASED

CAMBRIDGE SCIENTIFIC BIOCHEMISTRY ABSTRACTS: PART 1 BIOLOGICAL MEMBRANES.
[Camb. Sci. biochem. abstr., 1, Biol. membr.]. **Added/Corp** Cambridge Scientific Abstracts, Inc. **VFOAT** Biological Membranes. No. 1 (Jan. 1985)-(1993). English. Cambridge Scientific Abstracts, 7200 Wisconsin Avenue, #601, Bethesda MD 20814-4823. **Tel** (301)961-6750, (800)843-7751, FAX (301)961-6720. **ED** David Cheyney. Index available. cum. index. available on magnetic tape; available on CD-ROM; available on an online database. **Continues** Biochemistry Abstracts. Part 1, Biological Membranes, 0143-330X.
Desc: Provides insights into the major aspects of cell membrane structure and function across the entire scope of biological systems. Specific coverage includes: membrane components; physical properties; receptors; model and reconstituted systems; methodology; ultrastructure, and more. Each issue provides practical information to help scientists solve difficult problems of isolation and characterization.

LC QP551   ISSN 8756-7512
DD 574.87/328/05   US
UDC 577.113(048.3)
NLM ZQU 58; N964
     TITLE CHANGE

CAMBRIDGE SCIENTIFIC BIOCHEMISTRY ABSTRACTS: PART 2 NUCLEIC ACIDS. See Biology-Abstracting, Bibliographies and Statistics.

LC QP551 .A468   ISSN 8756-7520
DD 574.19/245   US
NLM ZQU 55; A518
     CEASED

CAMBRIDGE SCIENTIFIC BIOCHEMISTRY ABSTRACTS: PART 3 AMINO-ACIDS, PEPTIDES & PROTEINS.
[Camb. Sci. biochem. abstr., 3, Amino-acids pept. prot.]. **Added/Corp** Cambridge Scientific Abstracts, inc. **VFOAT** Amino-Acids, Peptides & Proteins; Amino Acids, Peptides and Proteins. Vol. 14, No. 1 (Jan. 1985)-(1993). English. Cambridge Scientific Abstracts, 7200 Wisconsin Avenue, #601, Bethesda MD 20814-4823. **Tel** (301)961-6750, (800)843-7751, FAX (301)961-6720. **ED** David Cheyney. Index available. cum. index. **Bk Rev.** available on magnetic tape, an online database, and CD-ROM.
Continues Biochemistry Abstracts. Part 3, Amino-Acids, Peptides & Proteins, 0143-3326.
Desc: Contains expanded emphasis on protein chemistry methods, protein engineering, and post-translational modifications. Provides researchers with a summary of world reports relating to amino acids, peptides, and proteins. Topics receiving major coverage range from isolation and purification techniques to structural analysis to solution studies.

LC QD415   ISSN 0305-7232
DD 574.192   US
     CCC
NLM W1 CA673   CODEN CABCD4
Pr Rev.

CANCER BIOCHEMISTRY BIOPHYSICS. See Medical Sciences-Cancer and Neoplastic Syndromes.

LC QP701 .C29   ISSN 0301-8679
DD 599/.01/9248   UK
NLM ZQU 75 C264

CARBOHYDRATE CHEMISTRY & METABOLISM ABSTRACTS. See Medical Sciences-Endocrinology.

     ISSN 1073-5070
     SZ

●CARBOHYDRATE LETTERS. (1994)-.
Periodical. English. Four times a year. Gordon & Breach Science Publishers, PO Box 90, Reading, Berkshire RG1 8JL United Kingdom. **Tel** 011 44 1734 560080, FAX 011 44 1734 568211.

LC QD321 .C3   ISSN 0008-6215
DD 547.7805   NE
     CCC
NLM W1 CA762N   CODEN CRBRAT
Pr Rev.

CARBOHYDRATE RESEARCH. See Chemistry and Chemicals-Organic Chemistry.

     ISSN 0895-6499
DD 574   US
     CODEN CBUCE5

CAS BIOTECH UPDATES. ANTIBODY CONJUGATES.
[CAS biotech updates, Antib. conjug.]. **Added/Corp** American Chemical Society. Chemical Abstracts Service. **VFOAT** Antibody Conjugates. **VAT** Chemical Abstracts Service Biotech Updates. Antibody Conjugates. Vol. 1 (1988)-. Periodical. English. Twenty-six times a year. $220.00. Chemical Abstracts Service, (Subsidiary of The American Chemical Society), 2540 Olentangy River Road, PO Box 3012, Columbus OH 43210-0012. **Tel** (614)447-3731, (800)753-4227, FAX (614)447-3751. **(Subscription address:** Chemical Abstracts Service, Customer Service Department, PO Box 3012, Columbus OH 43210. **Tel** (800)848-6538, (614)447-3600.)
Desc: Provides information on the preparation and uses of antibody conjugates. Coverage includes the uses of these conjugates in disease diagnosis and therapy, including drug delivery systems and immunotoxins. Coverage also includes immunochemical techniques and antibody immobilization studies.

     ISSN 0895-6626
DD 574   US
     CODEN CBUREG

CAS BIOTECH UPDATES. BIOCHEMICAL IMMOBILIZATION & BIOCATALYTIC REACTORS.
[CAS biotech updates. Biochem. immobil. biocatal. react.]. **Added/Corp** American Chemical Society. Chemical Abstracts Service. **VFOAT** Biochemical Immobilization & Biocatalytic Reactors; Biochemical Immobilization and Biocatalytic

Reactors; CAS Biotech Updates. Biochemical Immobilization and Biocatalytic; CTORS. **VAT** Chemical Abstracts Service Biotech Updates. Biochemical Immobilization & Biocatalytic Reactors. (Jan. 1988)-. Periodical. English. Twenty-six times a year. $220.00. Chemical Abstracts Service, (Subsidiary of The American Chemical Society), 2540 Olentangy River Road, PO Box 3012, Columbus OH 43210-0012. **Tel** (614)447-3731, (800)753-4227, FAX (614)447-3751. **(Subscription address:** Chemical Abstracts Service, Customer Service Department, PO Box 3012, Columbus OH 43210. **Tel** (800)848-6538, (614)447-3600.**)**
Desc: Contains information on the preparation and use of biological reactors and of immobilized microorganisms, plant and animal cells, enzymes, and other biological molecules. Coverage includes fermentors, biological electrodes, affinity chromatography, and enzyme immunoassay.

ISSN 1045-859X
DD 574 US
CODEN CBNSEI
CAS BIOTECH UPDATES. NUCLEIC ACID & PROTEIN SEQUENCES. [CAS biotechnol. updates, Nucleic acid protein seq.]. **Added/Corp** American Chemical Society. Chemical Abstracts Service. **VFOAT** Nucleic Acid & Protein Sequences; Nucleic Acid and Protein Sequences. **VAT** Chemical Abstracts Service Biotech Updates. Nucleic Acid & Protein Sequences. (Jan. 8, 1990)-. English. Twenty-six times a year. $220.00. Chemical Abstracts Service, (Subsidiary of The American Chemical Society), 2540 Olentangy River Road, PO Box 3012, Columbus OH 43210-0012. **Tel** (614)447-3731, (800)753-4227, FAX (614)447-3751. **(Subscription address:** Chemical Abstracts Service, Customer Service Department, PO Box 3012, Columbus OH 43210. **Tel** (800)848-6538, (614)447-3600.**)** ***Continues*** *CAS BioTech Updates. Biopolymer Sequences, 0890-751X.*

LC QD415
DD 574.192 US
CATIONS OF BIOLOGICAL SIGNIFICANCE. Vol. 1 (1981)-. Monographic series. English. Irregular. Price varies per volume. CRC Press Inc., 2000 Corporate Boulevard Northwest, Boca Raton FL 33431. **Tel** (407)994-0555, (800)272-7737, FAX (407)998-9784, (800)374-3401, telex 568689.
Ind/Abst AGRICOLA [Select. Cov.].

LC QH611 .C42 **ISSN** 0263-6484
DD 574.87/6042 UK
CCC
NLM W1 CE128F **CODEN** CBFUDH
Pr Rev.
CELL BIOCHEMISTRY AND FUNCTION. [Cell biochem. funct.]. Vol. 1, No. 1 (April 1983)-. Academic Scholarly Publication. English. Four times a year. $675.00. John Wiley & Sons Ltd., Baffins Lane, Chichester, West Sussex PO19 1UD United Kingdom. **Tel** 011 44 1243 779777, FAX 011 44 1243 776128 BTG:JWP001, telex 86290 WIBOOKG. **(Subscription address:** John Wiley & Sons, Inc. / Philadelphia, PO Box 7247, Philadelphia PA 19170. **Tel** (212)850-6645, (800)225-5945.**) ED** E. M. Crook. Index available. cum. index. **Bk Rev. Ad Acc. Circ:** 1,500. available on microfilm and microfiche from University Microfilms International (UMI). Documents available from The Genuine Article, CASDDS.
Desc: Provides a forum for reporting and discussing the biochemistry of whole cells. Discusses the link between biochemistry and the functioning of cells in isolation, in assemblies and in tissues.
Ind/Abst Chem. Abstr. (1983-); Chem. Titles; Curr. Aware. Biol. Sci., CABS; Curr. Cit.; Curr. Contents Life Sci.; EMBASE; Health Plan. Adminis.; Index Med. (1983-); Life Sci. Collect.; Protozoolog. Abstr.; Ref. Upd. Deluxe Ed.; Res. Alert [Full Cov.]; Sci. Cit. Index; SCISEARCH.

ISSN 1052-5882
DD 616 US
CCC
NLM W1; CE1286 **CODEN** CMMIEQ
CELLULAR AND MOLECULAR MECHANISMS OF INFLAMMATION. [Cell. mol. mech. inflamm.]. Vol. 1 (1990)-. Academic Scholarly Publication. English. Irregular. Price varies per volume. Academic Press Inc., 6277 Sea Harbor Drive, Orlando FL 32887. **Tel** (800)543-9534, (407)345-4100, FAX (407)352-3445. **ED** Charles G. Cochrane and Michael A. Gimbrone Jr. Documents available from CASDDS.
Desc: Of interest to those in areas of biochemistry, cell biology and pharmacology.
Ind/Abst Chem. Abstr.

LC QH573 **ISSN** 1015-8987
DD 574.87 SZ
CCC
NLM W1; CE1293 **CODEN** CEPBEW
Pr Rev.
CELLULAR PHYSIOLOGY AND BIOCHEMISTRY. See Biology-Cytology.

LC QD415 **ISSN** 0009-2304
DD 574.192 US
CHEMICAL ABSTRACTS. BIOCHEMISTRY SECTIONS. Added/Corp American Chemical Society. Vol. 56 (Jan. 1962)-. Abstracting/Indexing Service. English. Twenty-six times a year. $2240.00. Chemical Abstracts Service, (Subsidiary of The American Chemical Society), 2540 Olentangy River Road, PO Box 3012, Columbus OH 43210-0012. **Tel** (614)447-3731, (800)753-4227, FAX (614)447-3751. **(Subscription address:** Chemical Abstracts Service, Customer Service Department, PO Box 3012, Columbus OH 43210. **Tel** (800)848-6538, (614)447-3600.**) ED** Dr. David W. Weisgerber. available with charts; available with illustrations; available on an online database from STN International.
Ind/Abst Dairy Sci. Abstr.

LC QP455 .C47 **ISSN** 0379-864X
DD 612/.86/05 UK
CCC
NLM W1 CH265J **CODEN** CHSED8
CHEMICAL SENSES. [Chem. senses]. **Added/Corp** Information Retrieval Limited. European Chemoreception Research Organization. Vol. 5 (March 1980)-. Academic Scholarly Publication. English. Six times a year. $295.00. Oxford University Press / UK, Walton Street, Oxford OX2 6DP United Kingdom. **Tel** 011 44 1865 56767, FAX 011 44 1865 267773, telex 851/837330 OXPRES G. **(Subscription address:** Oxford University Press / USA, Journals Marketing Department, Oxford University Press, 2001 Evans Road, Cary NC 27513. **Tel** (800)451-7556, (919)677-0977, FAX (919)677-1714.**) ED** A. Holley, J. H. A. Kroeze, R. J. O'Connell, I. J. Miller, S. F. Takagi. **Ad Acc. Circ:** 500. available on microfilm and microfiche from University Microfilms International (UMI). Documents available from The Genuine Article, BIOSIS Document Express, CASDDS. ***Continues*** *Chemical Senses & Flavour.*
Desc: Exclusive journal for research papers covering taste, smell and all aspects of chemoreception; supported by ECRO, ACHEMS and JASTS.
Ind/Abst Biol. Abstr.; Chem. Abstr.; Chemorecept. Abstr.; CSA Neuro. Abstr.; Curr. Aware. Biol. Sci., CABS; Curr. Cit.; Curr. Contents Agric. Biol. Environ. Sci.; Curr. Contents Life Sci.; Curr. Ref. Fish Res.; Dairy Sci. Abstr.; EMBASE; Food Sci. Technol. Abstr.; Foods Adlibra; Index Med.; Nutr. Abstr. Rev., Ser. B, Live Feeds and Feed.; Nutr. Abstr. Rev., Ser. A, Hum. Exp.; Life Sci. Collect.; Potato Abstr.; Psychol. Abstr. (1980-); PsycINFO; PsycLit; Ref. Upd. Deluxe Ed.; Res. Alert [Full Cov.]; Sci. Cit. Index; SCISEARCH; Soc. Sci. Cit. Index [Select. Cov.]; Sug. Indus. Abstr.

LC QP501 .C39 **ISSN** 0009-2797
DD 574.1/92/05 IE
CCC
NLM W1 CH29X **CODEN** CBINA8
Pr Rev.
CHEMICO-BIOLOGICAL INTERACTIONS. [Chem.-biol. interact.]. **VFOAT** Chem.-Biol. Interactions. Vol. 1 (Oct. 1969)-. Academic Scholarly Publication. English (French and German). Fifteen times a year (5 vols.). $1484.00. Elsevier Science Ireland Ltd., Bay 15, Shannon Industrial Estate, Co Clare Ireland. **Tel** 011 353 61 471944. **ED** T.A. Baillie, P. Moldeus. Index available. available on microfilm and microfiche from University Microfilms International (UMI); available on an online database from Elsevier Electronic Subscriptions (EES). Documents available from The Genuine Article, BIOSIS Document Express, CASDDS, ADONIS.
Desc: Publishes research reports, rapid communications, review articles and commentaries that examine: molecular aspects of cytotoxicity, carcinogenesis, mutagenesis and teratogenesis; molecular mechanisms by which drugs exert their therapeutic or toxic effects.
Ind/Abst ADONIS; Biol. Abstr.; Chem. Abstr.; Chem. Titles; CSA Neuro. Abstr. (?-?); Curr. Aware. Biol. Sci., CABS; Curr. Cit.; Curr. Contents Life Sci.; Dairy Sci. Abstr.; EMBASE; Health Plan. Adminis.; Helminthol. Abstr. (1991-); Index Med.; Index Vet.; NAPRALERT; Nutr. Abstr. Rev., Ser. B, Live Feeds and Feed.; Nutr. Abstr. Rev., Ser. A, Hum. Exp.; Life Sci. Collect.; PESTDOC; Protozoolog. Abstr.; Ref. Upd. Deluxe Ed.; Res. Alert [Full Cov.]; Rev. Med. Vet. Mycology; Rev. Plant Pathol.; Sci. Cit. Index; SCISEARCH; Vet. Bull.; Toxicol. Abstr.; Weed Abstr.

LC QD415 **ISSN** 0366-7154
DD 574.192 GW
CCC
NLM W1; CH291R **CODEN** CMTLBX
CHEMIE, MIKROBIOLOGIE, TECHNOLOGIE DER LEBENSMITTEL. See Food and Food Industry.

ISSN 0009-3084
DD 539 665 547 IE
CCC
NLM W1 CH36E **CODEN** CPLIA4
Pr Rev.
CHEMISTRY AND PHYSICS OF LIPIDS. [Chem. phys. lipids]. Vol. 1 (Nov. 1966)-. Academic Scholarly Publication. English. Ten times a year (5 vols.). $1422.00. Elsevier Science Ireland Ltd., Bay 15, Shannon Industrial Estate, Co Clare Ireland. **Tel** 011 353 61 471944. **ED** F. Paltauf and H.H.O. Schmid. Index available. available on microfilm and microfiche from University Microfilms International (UMI); available on an online database from Elsevier Electronic Subscriptions (EES). Documents available from The Genuine Article, BIOSIS Document Express, CASDDS.
Desc: Publishes papers and review articles in the field of molecular biology which emphasize chemical and physical aspects of lipids.
Ind/Abst Biol. Abstr.; Chem. Abstr.; Chem. Titles; Curr. Aware. Biol. Sci., CABS; Curr. Cit.; Curr. Contents Life Sci.; Dairy Sci. Abstr.; EMBASE; Index Med.; Mass Spect. Bull.; Life Sci. Collect.; Protozoolog. Abstr.; Ref. Upd. Deluxe Ed.; Res. Alert [Full Cov.]; Sci. Cit. Index; SCISEARCH; Weed Abstr.

LC QD415.A1 K453 **ISSN** 0009-3130
US
CCC
NLM W1 CH364N **CODEN** CHNCA8
CHEMISTRY OF NATURAL COMPOUNDS. [Chem. nat. compd.]. **Added/Corp** Consultants Bureau. Vol. 1 (Jan./Feb. 1965)-. Periodical. English (Russian). Six times a year. $1245.00. Consultants Bureau, A Division of Plenum Publishing Corporation, 233 Spring Street, New York NY 10013. **Tel** (212)620-8000, (212)620-8466, FAX (212)463-0742, telex 23/421139. **ED** S. Yu Yunusov. available on microfilm and microfiche from University Microfilms International (UMI). Documents available from BIOSIS Document Express, CASDDS.
Ind/Abst AgBiotech News Inf.; AGRICOLA [Full Cov.]; Anal. Abstr.; Biol. Abstr. (?-1984); Chem. Abstr.; Crop Physiol. Abstr.; Curr. Cit.; Field Crop Abstr.; For. Prod. Abstr.; For. Abstr.; Grass. Forage Abstr.; Helminthol. Abstr. (1991-); Hortic. Abstr.; INIS Atomindex [Micro.]; Maize Abstr.; Mass Spect. Bull.; Nat. Prod. Updates; Nutr. Abstr. Rev., Ser. A, Hum. Exp.; Ornamental Hort. (1991-); Plant Breed. Abstr.; Postharvest News Inf.; Protozoolog. Abstr.; Rev. Agric. Entomol.; Rev. Med. Vet. Entomol.; Rev. Med. Vet. Mycology; Rev. Plant Pathol.; Rice Abstr.; Seed Abstr.; Sug. Indus. Abstr.; Weed Abstr.; Wheat Barley Trit. Abstr.

LC QD415.A1 C48 **ISSN** 1045-2680
DD 574.19/2/05 US
CCC
NLM W1; CH41GR **CODEN** CMBIE5
CHEMTRACTS. BIOCHEMISTRY AND MOLECULAR BIOLOGY. See Biology-Abstracting, Bibliographies and Statistics.

LC QD415 **ISSN** 0392-839X
DD 574.192 IT
CODEN CHOGDS
CHIMICA OGGI. [Chim. oggi]. **VFOAT** Chemistry Today; Chimicaoggi. Vol. 1 (March 1983)-. Periodical. English (Italian). Ten times a year. L255000. Tekno Scienze, Via Vincenzo Gioberti 1, 20123 Milan Italy. **Tel** 011 39 2 4818118. **ED** Carla Scesa. Index available. Documents available from CASDDS.
Ind/Abst Anal. Abstr.; Chem. Abstr. (1983-); Chem. Bus. Bull.; Chem. Bus. NewsBase (1987-); Chem. Bus. Update; Curr. Biotechnol.; Curr. Cit.; Fluid Abstr., Civil Eng.; Fluid Abstr. Proc. Eng.; FLUIDEX; Int. Pharm. Abstr.; PESTDOC; Proc. Chem. Eng.; Soc. Sci. Cit. Index [Select. Cov.]; Theor. Chem. Eng.

LC QP501 .S46 **ISSN** 0898-512X
DD 574.19/05 US
CCC
NLM W1; SH2871P
CHINESE JOURNAL OF BIOCHEMISTRY AND BIOPHYSICS. [Chin. j. biochem. biophys.]. **VFOAT** Acta Biochimica et Biophysica Sinica; Sheng Wu Hua Hsueh Yu Sheng Wu Wu Li Hsueh Pao. Vol. 20, No. 1 (1988)-. Periodical. English (translations available in Chinese). Four times a year. $440.00. Allerton Press Inc., 150 Fifth Avenue, New York NY 10011. **Tel** (212)924-3950, FAX (212)463-9684, telex 427441 ALPRES.
Ind/Abst Crop Physiol. Abstr.; Index Vet.; Pig News Inf.; Potato Abstr.; Rev. Agric. Entomol.; Rev. Plant Pathol.; Sorghum Mill. Abstr.

LC QP517.C57 C48 **ISSN** 0899-0042
DD 574 US
CCC
NLM W1; CH801 **CODEN** CHRLEP
Pr Rev.
CHIRALITY (NEW YORK, N.Y.). See Pharmacy and Pharmacology.

ISSN 0964-7597
UK
CHOLESTEROL AND LIPOPROTEINS. (19??)-. English. Twenty-six times a year. £85.00. SUBIS, Mansion House 19 Kingfield Road, Sheffield S11 9AS United Kingdom. **Tel** 011 44 114 2554433, FAX 011 44 114 255 4626. **Bk Rev. Ad Acc.**
Desc: Current awareness service for researchers and clinicians.

LC QD415 ISSN 0300-5208
DD 574.192 NE
NLM W3 C161F CODEN CIBSB4

CIBA FOUNDATION SYMPOSIUM. (CIBA FOUNDATION SYMPOSIUM; NEW SERIES.). [Ciba Found. symp.]. **Added/Corp** Ciba Foundation. (19??)-. Academic Scholarly Publication. English. Irregular. Price varies per volume. Elsevier Science Publishers BV, PO Box 211, 1000 AE Amsterdam Netherlands. **Tel** 011 31 20 4853641, 011 31 20 4853642, FAX 011 31 20 4853598. Documents available from The Genuine Article, BIOSIS Document Express, CASDDS.
Ind/Abst Biol. Abstr.; Chem. Abstr.; Curr. Cit.; EMBASE; Index Med.; Nematol. Abstr.; Life Sci. Collect.; Res. Alert [Full Cov.]; Rev. Agric. Entomol.; Sci. Cit. Index; SCISEARCH; Soc. Sci. Cit. Index [Select. Cov.]; SportSearch.

LC RB1 .C5 ISSN 0009-8981
DD 612.015 NE
CCC
NLM W1 CL295 CODEN CCATAR
Pr Rev.

CLINICA CHIMICA ACTA. [Clin. chim. acta]. Vol. 1 (Jan. 1956)-. Academic Scholarly Publication. English (French and German). Twenty-two times a year. $3085.00. Elsevier Science Publishers BV, PO Box 211, 1000 AE Amsterdam Netherlands. **Tel** 011 31 20 4853641, 011 31 20 4853642, FAX 011 31 20 4853598. **ED** M. Werner, I.W. Percy-Robb. cum. index. **Bk Rev. Ad Acc. Circ:** 1,780 (ctrl). available on microfilm and microfiche from University Microfilms International (UMI); available on an online database from Elsevier Electronic Subscriptions (EES). Documents available from The Genuine Article, BIOSIS Document Express, CASDDS, ADONIS.
Desc: Publishes original research reports, invited critical reviews and brief technical notes (of about 1,000 words) in the field of clinical chemistry and medical biochemistry.
Ind/Abst ADONIS; AgBiotech News Inf.; Anal. Abstr.; Biol. Abstr.; Chem. Abstr.; Chem. Titles; Curr. Biotechnol.; Curr. Chem. React.; Curr. Cit.; Curr. Contents Life Sci.; Dairy Sci. Abstr.; EMBASE; Health Plan. Adminis.; Helminthol. Abstr. (1991-); Immunol. Abstr.; Index Chem.; Index Med.; Index Vet.; Mass Spect. Bull.; Nutr. Abstr. Rev., Ser. B, Live Feeds and Feed.; Nutr. Abstr. Rev., Ser. A, Hum. Exp.; Life Sci. Collect.; PESTDOC; Pig News Inf.; Potato Abstr.; Protozoolog. Abstr.; Ref. Upd. Basic Ed.; Ref. Upd. Deluxe Ed.; Res. Alert [Full Cov.]; Sci. Cit. Index; SCISEARCH; SportSearch; Vet. Bull.; Weed Abstr.

LC QD415 ISSN 0095-4861
DD 574.192 US
NLM W1 CL654 CODEN CBAND5
Pr Rev.

CLINICAL AND BIOCHEMICAL ANALYSIS. [Clin. biochem. anal.]. Vol. 1 (1974)-. Monographic series. English. Irregular. Price varies per volume. Marcel Dekker Inc., 270 Madison Avenue, New York NY 10016. **Tel** (212)696-9000, (800)228-1160, FAX (212)685-4540, telex 421419. **(Subscription address:** Marcel Dekker Inc., PO Box 5017, Monticello NY 12701. **Tel** (800)228-1160.) **ED** M. K. Schwartz. Documents available from BIOSIS Document Express, CASDDS.
Ind/Abst Biol. Abstr.; Chem. Abstr.

LC QD415 ISSN 0159-8090
DD 574.192 AT
NLM W1 CL668Q CODEN CBREEU

CLINICAL BIOCHEMIST REVIEWS. (THE CLINICAL BIOCHEMIST. REVIEWS.). [Clin. biochem. rev.]. **Added/Corp** Australian Association of Clinical Biochemists. Australian Association of Clinical Biochemists. Conference. Vol. 1, No. 1 (May 1980)-. Academic Scholarly Publication. English. Four times a year. 53.44Aus$. Australian Association of Clinical Biochemists, PO Box 118, Maylands 6052, West Australia. **Tel** 61 9 3705224, FAX 61 9 3704409. **ED** J Whitfield. Index available. **Ad Acc. Circ:** 1,100 (ctrl). Documents available from CASDDS.
Desc: Reviews current topics of wide or general importance; includes bibliographies, brief abstracts of hallmark and classic papers and scientific reports, to assist laboratories in their analytical performance.
Ind/Abst Chem. Abstr.; Curr. Biotechnol.; Curr. Cit.

LC RB40 .C55
DD 612/.015 NE
NLM ZW 1 E978I

CLINICAL BIOCHEMISTRY. (19??)-. Academic Scholarly Publication. English. Thirty-two times a year. Fl.2197.00 (section 29), Fl.37,553.00 (full set). Elsevier Science Publishers BV, PO Box 211, 1000 AE Amsterdam Netherlands. **Tel** 011 31 20 4853641, 011 31 20 4853642, FAX 011 31 20 4853598. available on microfilm from University Microfilms International (UMI).
Desc: Contains information on the biochemistry of lower organisms of interest to biomedicine, particularly experimental animals, and basic biochemical theory and techniques.
Ind/Abst Ref. Upd. Deluxe Ed.

LC QD415
DD 574.192 GW
NLM W1; CL668P

CLINICAL BIOCHEMISTRY. Vol. 1 (1989)-. Monographic series. English. Irregular. Price varies per volume. Walter de Gruyter Inc., PO Box 303421, D-10728 Berlin Germany. **Tel** 011 49 30 260050, FAX 011 49 30 26005251, telex 184027.

LC RB112.5 .C55 ISSN 0009-9120
DD 616.07/05 US
CCC
NLM W1 CL668R CODEN CLBIAS
Pr Rev.

CLINICAL BIOCHEMISTRY (NEW YORK, N.Y.). (CLINICAL BIOCHEMISTRY.). [Clin. biochem.]. **Added/Corp** Canadian Society of Clinical Chemists. Vol. 1 (June 1967)-. Academic Scholarly Publication. English (French). Six times a year. $272.00. Pergamon Press, An Imprint of Elsevier Science Ltd., The Boulevard, Langford Lane, Kidlington, Oxford OX5 1GB United Kingdom. **Tel** 011 44 1865 843000, 011 44 1865 843699, FAX 011 44 1865 843010. **(Subscription address:** Elsevier Science Ltd. / Oxford Fulfillment Centre, PO Box 800, Kidlington OX5 1DX United Kingdom. **Tel** 011 44 865 843355.) **ED** D. M. Goldberg and J. L. Wittliff. available on an online database from Elsevier Electronic Subscriptions (EES). Documents available from The Genuine Article, BIOSIS Document Express, CASDDS, ADONIS.
Desc: Articles relate to the applications of molecular biology, biochemistry, chemistry and immunology to clinical investigation and to the diagnosis, therapy and monitoring of human digest.
Ind/Abst ADONIS; Anal. Abstr.; Biol. Abstr.; Chem. Abstr.; Curr. Aware. Biol. Sci., CABS; Curr. Biotechnol.; Curr. Cit.; Curr. Contents Life Sci.; Dairy Sci. Abstr.; EMBASE; Health Plan. Adminis.; Index Med.; INIS Atomindex [Micro.]; Int. Aerosp. Abstr.; Nutr. Abstr. Rev., Ser. A, Hum. Exp.; Life Sci. Collect.; PESTDOC; Res. Alert [Full Cov.]; Sci. Cit. Index; SCISEARCH; Soc. Sci. Cit. Index [Select. Cov.].

LC RB1 .A28 ISSN 0009-9147
DD 615.05 US
CCC
NLM W1; CL685 CODEN CLCHAUCLCHA

CLINICAL CHEMISTRY (BALTIMORE, MD.). See Pharmacy and Pharmacology.

LC QD415 ISSN 0143-5221
DD 574.192 UK
CCC
NLM W1 CL783AB CODEN CSCIAE

CLINICAL SCIENCE (1979). (CLINICAL SCIENCE.). [Clin. sci.]. **Added/Corp** Medical Research Society (Great Britain) Biochemical Society (Great Britain). Vol. 56 (Jan. 1979)-. Academic Scholarly Publication. English. Twelve times a year (includes two supplements). $430.00. Portland Press Ltd., PO Box 32 Commerce Way, Colchester CO2 8HP Essex United Kingdom. **Tel** 011 44 1206 796351, FAX 011 44 1206 799331, telex 987275 BIOSOC G. **ED** I. G. McFarlane, R. Green, and M. J. Brown. Index available. **Bk Rev. Ad Acc. Circ:** 2,500 (ctrl). available on microfilm; available with illustrations. Documents available from The Genuine Article, BIOSIS Document Express, CASDDS, ADONIS. ***Continues*** *Clinical Science and Molecular Medicine, 0301-0538.*
Desc: Original papers, short communications, letters and editorial reviews relating to clinical studies utilising biochemical, physiological, immunological, pharmacological and similar approaches.
Ind/Abst ADONIS; Anal. Abstr.; Biol. Abstr.; Chem. Abstr.; Chem. Hazards Ind.; Chem. Titles; CSA Neuro. Abstr. (?-?); Curr. Adv. Ecol. Sci.; Curr. Aware. Biol. Sci., CABS; Curr. Cit.; Curr. Contents Life Sci.; Dairy Sci. Abstr.; Dent. Abstr.; EMBASE; Helminthol. Abstr.; IDIS; Index Med.; Index Sci. Rev.; INIS Atomindex INIS Atomindeks; Lab. Hazards Bull.; Med. Abstr. Newsl.; Nutr. Abstr. Rev., Ser. A, Hum. Exp.; Nutr. Res. Newsl.; Life Sci. Collect.; PESTDOC; Phys. Med. Biol. (19??-19??); Protozoolog. Abstr.; Ref. Upd. Basic Ed.; Ref. Upd. Deluxe Ed.; Res. Alert [Full Cov.]; Sci. Cit. Index; SCISEARCH; Soc. Sci. Cit. Index [Select. Cov.]; SportSearch; Trop. Dis. Bull.

LC QD415 ISSN 0366-5887
DD 574.192 GW
CODEN CGBCA9

COLLOQUIUM DER GESELLSCHAFT FUER BIOLOGISCHE CHEMIE. [Colloq. Ges. Biol. Chem.]. **Main/Corp** Gesellschaft fuer Biologische Chemie. (1968)-. Academic Scholarly Publication. German. Irregular. Price varies per volume. Springer-Verlag GmbH & Company KG, Heidelberger Platz 3, D-14197 Berlin Germany. **Tel** 011 49 30 8207223, FAX 011 49 30 8214091, telex 183 319 SPBLN D. **(Subscription address:** Springer-Verlag New York Inc. / North America, PO Box 2485, Journal Fulfillment, Secaucus NJ 07096. **Tel** (201)348-4033, (800)777-4643, FAX (201)348-4505.) Documents available from CASDDS. ***Continues*** *Colloquium der Gesellschaft fuer Physiologische Chemie, 0072-4246.*
Desc: Contains articles on biochemical studies.
Ind/Abst Chem. Abstr.; Life Sci. Collect.

LC QP33 .C664
DD 591.1/05 UK
NLM W1; CO435IG
TITLE CHANGE

COMPARATIVE BIOCHEMISTRY AND PHYSIOLOGY. B, BIOCHEMISTRY & MOLECULAR BIOLOGY : CBP. VFOAT Biochemistry & Molecular Biology; Biochemistry and Molecular Biology; CBP; Comparative Biochemistry & Molecular Biology; Comparative Biochemistry and Physiology. Comparative Biochemistry & Molecular Biology. Vol. 107, No. 1 (Jan. 1994)-Vol. 108B, No. 4 (Aug. 1994). Periodical. English. Pergamon Press, An Imprint of Elsevier Science Ltd., The Boulevard, Langford Lane, Kidlington, Oxford OX5 1GB United Kingdom. **Tel** 011 44 1865 843000, 011 44 1865 843699, FAX 011 44 1865 843010. **(Subscription address:** Elsevier Science Ltd. / Oxford Fulfillment Centre, PO Box 800, Kidlington OX5 1DX United Kingdom. **Tel** 011 44 865 843355.) ***Continues*** *Comparative Biochemistry and Physiology. B, Comparative Biochemistry, 0305-0491.* ***Continued by*** *Comparative Biochemistry and Physiology. Part B, Biochemistry & Molecular Biology.*
Ind/Abst Index Med.

LC QP33 .C664 ISSN 0305-0491
DD 591.1/05 UK
CCC
NLM W1; CO435B CODEN CBPBB8
Pr Rev. TITLE CHANGE

COMPARATIVE BIOCHEMISTRY AND PHYSIOLOGY. B, COMPARATIVE BIOCHEMISTRY. [Comp. biochem. physiol., B. Comp. biochem.]. **VFOAT** Comparative Biochemistry. Vol. 38, No. 1B (Jan. 15, 1971)-(199?). Academic Scholarly Publication. English. Pergamon Press, An Imprint of Elsevier Science Ltd., The Boulevard, Langford Lane, Kidlington, Oxford OX5 1GB United Kingdom. **Tel** 011 44 1865 843000, 011 44 1865 843699, FAX 011 44 1865 843010. **ED** Gerald A. Kerkut. Index Available in last issue of each volume--loose separately paged. **Bk Rev. Ad Acc.** available on microfilm and microfiche from University Microfilms International (UMI); available on microfiche from the publisher. Documents available from The Genuine Article, BIOSIS Document Express, CASDDS, ADONIS. ***Continues in part*** *Comparative Biochemistry and Physiology, 0010-406X.* ***Continued by*** *Comparative Biochemistry & Physiology. B, Biochemistry and Molecular Biochemistry.*
Desc: Publishes papers on enzymology; alloenzymes; cell metabolism; mitrochondrial respiration; serum proteins; DNA; RNA; porphyrins; blood pigments; lipids; sterols; carbohydrates; proteins; peptides; etc. of invertebrates and vertebrates.
Ind/Abst ADONIS; AgBiotech News Inf.; AGRICOLA [Select. Cov.]; Anim. Breed. Abstr.; AQUAREF; Aquat. Sci. Fish. Abstr. [CD-ROM Ed.]; Biodeter. Abstr.; Biol. Abstr.; Chem. Abstr.; Chem. Titles; Chemorecept. Abstr.; CSA Neuro. Abstr.; Curr. Aware. Biol. Sci., CABS; Curr. Cit.; Curr. Contents Life Sci.; Curr. Ref. Fish Res.; Dairy Sci. Abstr.; EMBASE; Entomol. Abstr.; Fish Rev.; Genet. Abstr.; GeoRef; Helminthol. Abstr. (19??-19??); Index Med.; Index Vet.; Int. Aerosp. Abstr.; Mar. Sci. Contents Tables; Microbiol. Abstr. Sect. C; Nematol. Abstr.; Nutr. Abstr. Rev., Ser. B, Live Feeds and Feed.; Nutr. Abstr. Rev., Ser. A, Hum. Exp.; Ocean. Abstr.; Life Sci. Collect.; Pig News Inf.; Poult. Abstr.; Protozoolog. Abstr.; Ref. Upd. Basic Ed.; Ref. Upd. Deluxe Ed.; Res. Alert [Full Cov.]; Rev. Agric. Entomol.; Rev. Med. Vet. Entomol.; Sci. Cit. Index; SCISEARCH; Small Anim. Abstr. Bibliogr.; Soc. Sci. Cit. Index [Select. Cov.]; Vet. Bull.; Wildl. Rev.

UK

•COMPARATIVE BIOCHEMISTRY AND PHYSIOLOGY. C, PHARMACOLOGY, TOXICOLOGY & ENDOCRINOLOGY : CBP. See Pharmacy and Pharmacology.

LC QP33 .C66 UK
NLM W1; CO435A
TITLE CHANGE

COMPARATIVE BIOCHEMISTRY AND PHYSIOLOGY. COMPARATIVE PHYSIOLOGY. See Biology-Physiology.

US

•COMPARATIVE BIOCHEMISTRY AND PHYSIOLOGY. PART A, PHYSIOLOGY. See Biology-Physiology.

LC QP33 .C664
DD 591.1/05 UK

•COMPARATIVE BIOCHEMISTRY AND PHYSIOLOGY. PART B, BIOCHEMISTRY & MOLECULAR BIOLOGY. VFOAT Biochemistry & Molecular Biology; Biochemistry and Molecular Biology; CBP, Comparative Biochemistry and Physiology. B, P. Biochemistry & Molecular Biology. Vol. 109B, No. 1 (Sept. 1994)-. Periodical. English. Twelve times a year. $2221.00 (regular subscription), $5677.00 (combination subscription with Comparative Biochemistry and Physiology Parts A and C) The Americas; £1490.00 (regular subscription), £3810.00 (combination subscription with Comparative Biochemistry and

Physiology Parts A and C) other. Pergamon Press, An Imprint of Elsevier Science Ltd., The Boulevard, Langford Lane, Kidlington, Oxford OX5 1GB United Kingdom. **Tel** 011 44 1865 843000, 011 44 1865 843699, FAX 011 44 1865 843010. **(Subscription address:** Elsevier Science Ltd. / Oxford Fulfillment Centre, PO Box 800, Kidlington OX5 1DX United Kingdom. **Tel** 011 44 865 843355.) ***Continues*** *Comparative Biochemistry and Physiology. Biochemistry and Molecular Biology.*
Ind/Abst Bibliogr. Agric.

LC QH501
DD 574.1 UK
NLM W1; CO435A
Pr Rev. TITLE CHANGE
COMPARATIVE BIOCHEMISTRY AND PHYSIOLOGY. PHYSIOLOGY. See Biology-Physiology.

ISSN 0069-8032
DD 574 NE
CCC
Pr Rev.
COMPREHENSIVE BIOCHEMISTRY. Vol. 1 (1962)-. Monographic series. English. Irregular. Price varies per volume. Elsevier Science Publishers BV, PO Box 211, 1000 AE Amsterdam Netherlands. **Tel** 011 31 20 4853641, 011 31 20 4853642, FAX 011 31 20 4853598. **ED** M. Florkin, E.H. Stotz.

LC QD415 **ISSN** 0265-6701
DD 574.192 UK
NLM W1; CO769MQC
CONTEMPORARY ISSUES IN CLINICAL BIOCHEMISTRY. [Contemp. issues clin. biochem.]. (1984)-. Monographic series. English. Irregular. Price varies per volume. Churchill Livingstone, 1-3 Baxter's Place, Leith Walk, Edinburgh EH1 3AF United Kingdom. **Tel** 011 44 131 5562424, FAX 011 44 131 5581278, telex 727511. **(Subscription address:** Churchill Livingstone Inc. / for North America, 5 South 250 Frontenac Road, Naperville IL 60563. **Tel** (800)553-5426, (708)416-3939.)
Ind/Abst Health Plan. Adminis.

LC QP501 .C387 **ISSN** 1040-9238
DD 574.19/2/05 US
CCC
NLM W1; CR216UCH **CODEN** CRBBEJ
CRITICAL REVIEWS IN BIOCHEMISTRY AND MOLECULAR BIOLOGY. [Crit. rev. biochem. mol. biol.]. **VFOAT** CRC Critical Reviews in Biochemistry and Molecular Biology. **VAT** Chemical Rubber Company Critical Reviews in Biochemistry and Molecular Biology. Vol. 24, Issue 1 (1989)-. Academic Scholarly Publication. English. Six times a year. $441.00. CRC Press Inc., 2000 Corporate Boulevard Northwest, Boca Raton FL 33431. **Tel** (407)994-0555, (800)272-7737, FAX (407)998-9784, (800)374-3401, telex 568689. **(Subscription address:** CRC Press Inc. / New York, PO Box 750, Pearl River NY 10965.) Documents available from The Genuine Article, BIOSIS Document Express, CASDDS. ***Continues*** *Critical Reviews in Biochemistry, 1040-8355.*
Desc: This rapidly advancing field includes research from a wide range of subjects, such as medicine, genetics, immunology, developmental biology, biophysics, etc.
Ind/Abst AgBiotech News Inf.; AGRICOLA [Select. Cov.]; Biol. Abstr. (1989-); Chem. Abstr.; Curr. Aware. Biol. Sci., CABS; Curr. Cit.; Curr. Contents Life Sci.; EMBASE; Energy Res. Abstr. (1989-); Food Sci. Technol. Abstr.; Index Med. (1989-); INIS Atomindex [Micro.]; Life Sci. Collect.; PESTDOC; Plant Breed. Abstr.; Ref. Upd. Basic Ed.; Ref. Upd. Deluxe Ed.; Res. Alert [Full Cov.]; Sci. Cit. Index; SCISEARCH.

LC QH324 .C9 **ISSN** 0011-2240
DD 574.19/167/05 US
CCC
NLM W1 CR997 **CODEN** CRYBAS
Pr Rev.
CRYOBIOLOGY. [Cryobiology]. **Added/Corp** Society for Cryobiology. Vol. 1 (Sept./Oct. 1964)-. Academic Scholarly Publication. English. Six times a year. $232.00. Academic Press Inc., 6277 Sea Harbor Drive, Orlando FL 32887. **Tel** (800)543-9534, (407)345-4100, FAX (407)352-3445. **ED** Arthur W. Rowe. Documents available from The Genuine Article, BIOSIS Document Express, CASDDS.
Desc: A journal devoted to research articles that treat any of the aspects of low temperature biology and medicine.
Ind/Abst ASTIS Curr. Aware. Bull. (1978-); AgBiotech News Inf.; AGRICOLA [Select. Cov.]; Anim. Breed. Abstr.; ASTIS Bibliogr. (1978-); Biol. Abstr.; Chem. Abstr.; Crop Physiol. Abstr.; CSA Neuro. Abstr. (?-?); Curr. Cit.; Curr. Contents Life Sci.; Dairy Sci. Abstr.; EMBASE; Energy Res. Abstr.; Fish Rev.; Health Plan. Adminis.; Hortic. Abstr.; Index Med.; Index Vet.; INIS Atomindex [Micro.]; Int. Aerosp. Abstr.; Life Sci. Collect.; Plant Genet. Resour. Abstr.; Plant Grow. Reg. Abstr.; Postharvest News Inf.; Ref. Upd. Deluxe Ed.; Res. Alert [Full Cov.]; Rev. Agric. Entomol.; Sci. Cit. Index; SCISEARCH; Vet. Bull.; Wildl. Rev.

LC Z5524.B54 C87 QH345 **ISSN** 0965-0504
DD 016.57419/2 UK
NLM ZQU 4; C976
CURRENT ADVANCES IN PROTEIN BIOCHEMISTRY. See Biology-Abstracting, Bibliographies and Statistics.

LC Z5524.B54 **ISSN** 0965-0504
DD 574.192 UK
CURRENT ADVANCES IN PROTEIN CHEMISTRY. See Biology-Abstracting, Bibliographies and Statistics.

LC QD415 **ISSN** 0300-1725
DD 574.192 SZ
CCC
NLM W3 CU61
CEASED
CURRENT PROBLEMS IN CLINICAL BIOCHEMISTRY. [Curr. probl. clin. biochem.]. Vol. 2 (1968)-Series complete with Vol. 14. Academic Scholarly Publication. English. Verlag Hans Huber Ag Bern, Laenggass Strasse 76, CH-3000 Bern 9 Switzerland. **Tel** 011 41 31 3004500. Documents available from CASDDS. ***Continues*** *Aktuelle Probleme in der Klinischen Biochemie, 0065-5597.*
Ind/Abst Chem. Abstr.; Health Plan. Adminis.; Index Med.; Life Sci. Collect.; SportSearch.

US
•**CURRENT PROTOCOLS IN PROTEIN SCIENCE.** (1995)-. English. Four times a year. $340.00. John Wiley & Sons, Inc., 605 Third Avenue, New York NY 10158-0012. **Tel** (212)850-6000, (212)850-6645, FAX (212)850-6088, telex 12-7063.

US
CURRENT PROTOCOLS IN PROTEIN SCIENCE. CD-ROM. (19??)-. English. Four times a year. $486.00. John Wiley & Sons, Inc., 605 Third Avenue, New York NY 10158-0012. **Tel** (212)850-6000, (212)850-6645, FAX (212)850-6088, telex 12-7063.

LC QH541.5.M3 C87 **ISSN** 1076-4674
DD 574.5/26325 US
•**CURRENT TOPICS IN WETLAND BIOGEOCHEMISTRY / WETLAND BIOGEOCHEMISTRY INSTITUTE.** [Curr. top. wetl. biogeochem.]. **Added/Corp** Louisiana State University (Baton Rouge, La.). Wetland Biogeochemistry Institute. Vol. 1 (1994)-. English. One time a year. $30.00. Wetland Biogeochemistry Institute, Louisiana State University, Baton Rouge LA 70803. **Tel** (504)388-8806.

LC QD415 **ISSN** 0142-8055
DD 574.192 UK
NLM ZQU 58; C9949
TITLE CHANGE
CYCLIC AMP (SHEFFIELD, ENGLAND). (CYCLIC AMP.). **Added/Corp** University of Sheffield. Biomedical Information Service. (1970)-(19??). Periodical. English. SUBIS, Mansion House 19 Kingfield Road, Sheffield S11 9AS United Kingdom. **Tel** 011 44 114 2554433, FAX 011 44 114 255 4626. **Bk Rev. Ad Acc.** available on diskette. ***Superseded by*** *Signal Transduction & Cyclic Nucleotides, 0964-7589.*
Desc: Current awareness service for researchers in clinical and life sciences.

LC QD415 **ISSN** 0165-1714
DD 574.192 NE
CCC
NLM DE997VG **CODEN** DEBIDR
Pr Rev.
DEVELOPMENTS IN BIOCHEMISTRY. [Dev. biochem.]. Vol. 1 (1978)-. Monographic series. English. Irregular. Price varies per volume. Elsevier Science Publishers BV, PO Box 211, 1000 AE Amsterdam Netherlands. **Tel** 011 31 20 4853641, 011 31 20 4853642, FAX 011 31 20 4853598. **(Subscription address:** Elsevier Science Inc. / New York Books, 655 Avenue of the Americas, New York NY 10010. **Tel** (212)633-3650.) Documents available from BIOSIS Document Express, CASDDS.
Ind/Abst Biol. Abstr.; Chem. Abstr.

LC QD415 **ISSN** 0167-4978
DD 574.192 NE
NLM W1 DE997VR **CODEN** DLCBDQ
DEVELOPMENTS IN CLINICAL BIOCHEMISTRY. [Dev. clin. biochem.]. Vol. 1 (1980)-. Academic Scholarly Publication. English. Irregular. Price varies per volume. Kluwer Academic Publishers, Postbus 322, 3300 AH Dordrecht The Netherlands. **Tel** 011 31 78 524400, FAX 011 31 78 183273, telex 20083. Documents available from CASDDS.
Ind/Abst Chem. Abstr.

LC QD415 **ISSN** 0167-9023
DD 574.192 NE
NLM W1 DE998D **CODEN** DMCBDX
DEVELOPMENTS IN MOLECULAR AND CELLULAR BIOCHEMISTRY. [Dev. mol. cell. biochem.]. (1981)-. Monographic series. English. Irregular. $39.95. Kluwer Academic Publishers, Postbus 322, 3300 AH Dordrecht The Netherlands. **Tel** 011 31 78 524400, FAX 011 31 78 183273, telex 20083. **ED** V. A. Najjar. Documents available from BIOSIS Document Express.
Ind/Abst Biol. Abstr.

ISSN 0142-8640
DD 016.574873282 UK
CCC
DNA SHEFFIELD. See Biology-Genetics.

ISSN 0012-4958
US
CCC
NLM W1 DO64BC **CODEN** DBIOAM
DOKLADY. BIOCHEMISTRY. [Dokl., Biochem.]. **Main/Corp** Akademiia Nauk SSSR. **Added/Corp** Consultants Bureau. Consultants Bureau Enterprises. **VFOAT** Biochemistry. Vol. 154/56 (Jan./June 1964)-. Periodical. English (Russian). Six times a year. $975.00. MAIK Nauka / Interperiodica, Ulitsa Profsoyuznaia 90, Moscow 117864 Russia. **ED** A.A. Baev. available on microfilm and microfiche from University Microfilms International (UMI). Documents available from BIOSIS Document Express, CASDDS. ***Continues in part*** *Akademia Nauk SSSR. Doklady. Biological Sciences Sections, 0886-7534.*
Ind/Abst AgBiotech News Inf.; AGRICOLA [Select. Cov.]; Anim. Breed. Abstr.; Biol. Abstr. (?-1984); Chem. Abstr.; Crop Physiol. Abstr.; Curr. Biotechnol.; Curr. Cit.; Dairy Sci. Abstr.; EMBASE; Energy Res. Abstr. (July 1974-); Field Crop Abstr.; INIS Atomindex [Micro.]; Maize Abstr.; Mass Spect. Bull.; NAPRALERT; Nat. Prod. Updates; Plant Grow. Reg. Abstr.; Potato Abstr.; Rev. Agric. Entomol.; Rev. Med. Vet. Entomol.; Rev. Plant Pathol.; Soyabean Abstr.; Wheat Barley Trit. Abstr.

LC QP501 .E38 **ISSN** 0937-7344
DD 574.19/2/05 GW
EJB REVIEWS. (EJB REVIEWS / EDITED BY THE FEDERATION OF EUROPEAN BIOCHEMICAL SOCIETIES.). [EJB rev.]. **Added/Corp** Federation of European Biochemical Societies. **VAT** European Journal of Biochemistry Reviews. (1989)-. Academic Scholarly Publication. English. One time a year. Springer-Verlag GmbH & Company KG, Heidelberger Platz 3, D-14197 Berlin Germany. **Tel** 011 49 30 8207223, FAX 011 49 30 8214091, telex 183 319 SPBLN D. **(Subscription address:** Springer-Verlag New York Inc. / North America, PO Box 19386 Books, Newark NJ 07195. **Tel** (201)348-4033.) available in microform from University Microfilms International (UMI).

UK
ELECTROLYTE SOLUTIONS BULLETIN. (19??)-. Bulletin. English. Irregular. $47.00. University Newcastle Upon Tyne, 1 Kensington Terrace, Newcastle Tyne NE1 7RU United Kingdom. **Tel** 011 44 191 2328511 ext. 6507.

LC QD415
DD 574.192 SZ
•**EMERGING BIOCHEMICAL AND BIOPHYSICAL TECHNIQUES.** (1994)-. Academic Scholarly Publication. English. Irregular. Birkhaeuser Verlag Ag, Klosterberg 23, PO Box 133, CH-4010 Basel Switzerland. **Tel** 011 41 61 2717400, FAX 011 41 61 2717666, telex 963475 birk ch.

LC Z6663.N85 **ISSN** 1072-3072
DD 660 US
NLM W1; EN98K
TITLE CHANGE
ENTREZ. REFERENCES. (ENTREZ. REFERENCES [COMPUTER FILE] / NCBI.). [Entrez, Ref.]. **Added/Corp** National Center for Biotechnology Information (U.S.). **VFOAT** References. (1993)-(1994). Government Publication. English. Superintendent of Documents, US Government Printing Office, Washington DC 20402. **Tel** (202)275-3328, FAX (202)786-2377. ***Merged with*** *Entrez. Sequences, 1065-707X* ***to form*** *Entrez Document Retrieval System, 1078-7712.*

LC QP601.A1 E5 **ISSN** 0013-9432
DD 574.1/925/05 SZ
CCC
NLM W1 EN986N **CODEN** ENZYBT
Pr Rev. TITLE CHANGE
ENZYME. [Enzyme]. Vol. 12 (1971)-(19??). Academic Scholarly Publication. English. S. Karger AG, Allschwilerstrasse 10, PO Box, CH-4009 Basel Switzerland. **Tel** 011 41 61 3061111, FAX 011 41 61 3061234, telex CH 962 652. **ED** J. P. Colombo, H. Eppenberger, O. Greengard, U. Wiesmann. **Ad Acc.** available on microfilm from University Microfilms International (UMI). Documents available from The Genuine Article, BIOSIS Document Express, CASDDS. ***Continues*** *Enzymologia Biologica et Clinica, 0425-1423.* ***Continued by*** *Enzyme and Protein, 1019-6773.*
Desc: Articles on both basic and applied enzymology are included in this journal to create a practical guide to current research in the fields of clinical and experimental medicine. Original papers and occasional brief reviews are supported by a section for short communications which provides a forum for prelimary reports of particularly interesting or unusual findings. Enzymologists, biochemists, physiologists, pharmacologists, and molecular biologists will all find

stimulating reading and valuable data in this journal. A separately edited section, Inborn Errors of Metabolism in Humans, also offers pediatricians and geneticists useful information on the characterization and pathogenetic consequences of inherited enzymatic defects.
Ind/Abst AGRICOLA [Select. Cov.]; Biol. Abstr.; Chem. Abstr.; Chem. Titles; Curr. Aware. Biol. Sci., CABS; Curr. Biotechnol.; Curr. Contents Life Sci.; Dairy Sci. Abstr.; EMBASE; Health Plan. Adminis.; Index Med.; Nutr. Abstr. Rev., Ser. B, Live Feeds and Feed.; Nutr. Abstr. Rev., Ser. A, Hum. Exp.; Life Sci. Collect.; Res. Alert [Full Cov.]; Sci. Cit. Index (19??-19??); SCISEARCH.

LC QP601.A1 E5 **ISSN** 1019-6773
DD 574.19/25/05 SZ
NLM W1; EN986NL **CODEN** EPROEA
•**ENZYME & PROTEIN.** **Added/Corp** International Society for Clinical Enzymology. **VFOAT** Enzyme and Protein; Enzyme Protein. (1993)-. Periodical. English. Six times a year. $380.60. S. Karger AG, Allschwilerstrasse 10, PO Box, CH-4009 Basel Switzerland. **Tel** 011 41 61 3061111, FAX 011 41 61 3061234, telex CH 962 652. **ED** C. Bachmann. ***Continues** Enzyme, 0013-9432.*
Desc: Focuses on the function of proteins and the structure-function relationship. Attention is given not only to enzymes but also to transport, ligand binding and receptors. Original papers and reviews are supported by a section for short communications which allows the rapid publication of hot issues.
Ind/Abst Curr. Cit.; Index Med.; Ref. Upd. Deluxe Ed.; Sci. Cit. Index.

ISSN 0142-8071
DD 016.5741925 UK
CCC
ENZYME REGULATION. [Enzyme regul.]. (1971)-. English. Twelve times a year. $128.34. SUBIS, Mansion House 19 Kingfield Road, Sheffield S11 9AS United Kingdom. **Tel** 011 44 114 2554433, FAX 011 44 114 255 4626.
Desc: Current awareness service for researchers and clinicians.

LC QD415 **ISSN** 0423-2607
DD 574.192 US
ENZYMES, THE. Vol. 1 (1970)-. Monographic series. English. Irregular. Price varies per volume. Academic Press Inc., 6277 Sea Harbor Drive, Orlando FL 32887. **Tel** (800)543-9534, (407)345-4100, FAX (407)352-3445.
Ind/Abst AGRICOLA.

LC QH345 .E8 **ISSN** 0071-1365
DD 574.19/2 UK
NLM W1 ES674R **CODEN** ESBIAVESBIAN
ESSAYS IN BIOCHEMISTRY. [Essays biochem.]. **Added/Corp** Biochemical Society (Great Britain). Vol. 1 (1965)-. English. One time a year. Portland Press Ltd., PO Box 32 Commerce Way, Colchester CO2 8HP Essex United Kingdom. **Tel** 011 44 1206 796351, FAX 011 44 1206 799331, telex 987275 BIOSOC G. **ED** P. N. Campbell and G. D. Greville. Documents available from The Genuine Article, BIOSIS Document Express, CASDDS.
Ind/Abst Biol. Abstr.; Chem. Abstr.; CSA Neuro. Abstr. (?-?); Curr. Cit.; Curr. Titles Dent.; Index Med.; Index Sci. Rev. [Full Cov.]; Life Sci. Collect.; Res. Alert [Full Cov.]; SCISEARCH.

LC QP501 .E87 **ISSN** 0014-2956
DD 612.015 GW
CCC
NLM W1 EU68 **CODEN** EJBCAI
Pr Rev.
EUROPEAN JOURNAL OF BIOCHEMISTRY. [Eur. j. biochem.]. **Added/Corp** Federation of European Biochemical Societies. Vol. 1 (March 1967)-. Academic Scholarly Publication. English (French and German). Twenty-four times a year. $2581.00. Springer-Verlag GmbH & Company KG, Heidelberger Platz 3, D-14197 Berlin Germany. **Tel** 011 49 30 8207223, FAX 011 49 30 8214091, telex 183 319 SPBLN D. **(Subscription address:** Springer-Verlag New York Inc. / North America, PO Box 2485, Journal Fulfillment, Secaucus NJ 07096. **Tel** (201)348-4033, (800)777-4643, FAX (201)348-4505.**)** **ED** P Christen, M J Clemens, C W Hilbers, E Hofmann, L Hue, H Joernvall, C Liebecq, W Neupert, G Nicholls, G Pettersson, and J F G Vliegenthart. available on microfilm and microfiche from University Microfilms International (UMI). Documents available from The Genuine Article, BIOSIS Document Express, CASDDS, Documents on Demand, ADONIS. ***Supersedes** Biochemische Zeitschrift.*
Desc: Reports research results to the entire biomedical sciences community.
Ind/Abst ADONIS; AgBiotech News Inf.; AGRICOLA [Select. Cov.]; Anal. Abstr.; Anim. Breed. Abstr.; Biocont. News Inf. (1991-); Biol. Abstr.; Calcium Calcif. Tissue Abstr.; Chem. Abstr.; Chem. Titles; Crop Physiol. Abstr.; CSA Neuro. Abstr.; Curr. Aware. Biol. Sci., CABS; Curr. Biotechnol.; Curr. Cit.; Curr. Contents Life Sci.; Curr. Ref. Fish Res.; Dairy Sci. Abstr.; EMBASE; Energy Inf. Abstr.; Energy Res. Abstr.; Entomol. Abstr.; Environ. Abstr.; Field Crop Abstr.; Fish Rev. (Jan. 1989-July 1992); Food Sci. Technol. Abstr.; Genet. Abstr.; Grass. Forage Abstr.; Health Plan. Adminis.; Helminthol. Abstr. (19??-19??); Hortic. Abstr.; Hum. Genome Abstr.; Immunol. Abstr.; Index Med.; Index Vet.; Maize Abstr.; Mass Spect. Bull.; Microbiol. Abstr. Sect. B; Microbiol. Abstr. Sect. A; Microbiol. Abstr. Sect. C; NAPRALERT; Nat. Prod. Updates; Nucl. Acids Abstr.; Nutr. Abstr. Rev., Ser. A, Hum. Exp.; Oncog. Growth Factors Abstr.; Ornamental Hort. (1991-); Life Sci. Collect.; PESTDOC; Phys. Briefs; Pig News Inf.; Plant Breed. Abstr.; Postharvest News Inf.; Potato Abstr.; Poult. Abstr.; Protozoolog. Abstr.; Ref. Upd. Basic Ed.; Ref. Upd. Deluxe Ed.; Res. Alert [Full Cov.]; Rev. Agric. Entomol.; Rev. Med. Vet. Entomol.; Rev. Med. Vet. Mycology; Rev. Plant Pathol.; Rice Abstr.; Sci. Cit. Index; SCISEARCH; Seed Abstr.; Soils Fert.; Sorghum Mill. Abstr.; Soyabean Abstr.; Vet. Bull.; Trop. Dis. Bull.; Virol. AIDS Abstr.; Weed Abstr.; Wheat Barley Trit. Abstr.; Wildl. Rev. (Jan. 1989-July 1992).

LC RB40.A1 Z4 **ISSN** 0939-4974
DD 616.07/56/05 GW
CCC
NLM W1; EU72BT **CODEN** EJCBEO
EUROPEAN JOURNAL OF CLINICAL CHEMISTRY AND CLINICAL BIOCHEMISTRY. **Added/Corp** Forum of European Clinical Chemistry Societies. Vol. 29, No. 1 (Jan. 1991)-. Periodical. English (French and German). Twelve times a year. $747.15. Walter de Gruyter Inc., PO Box 303421, D-10728 Berlin Germany. **Tel** 011 49 30 260050, FAX 011 49 30 26005251, telex 184027. Documents available from The Genuine Article, CASDDS. ***Continues** Journal of Clinical Chemistry and Clinical Biochemistry, 0340-076X.*
Ind/Abst Chem. Abstr.; Curr. Aware. Biol. Sci., CABS; Curr. Cit.; Curr. Contents Life Sci.; EMBASE; Health Plan. Adminis.; Index Med. (1991-); Res. Alert [Full Cov.]; Sci. Cit. Index; SCISEARCH.

LC QD415 **ISSN** 1121-760X
DD 574.192 IT
NLM W1; EU72DFG **CODEN** EJHIE2
EUROPEAN JOURNAL OF HISTOCHEMISTRY : EJH. [Eur. j. histochem.]. **Added/Corp** Societa Italiana di Istochimica. **VFOAT** EJH. (1992)-. Academic Scholarly Publication. English. Four times a year. L230000. Tipolitografia L Ponzio, Via D Da Catalogna 1 3, 27100 Pavia Italy. **Tel** 011 39 382 35000. Index available. Documents available from CASDDS. ***Continues** European Journal of Basic and Applied Histochemistry, 1121-4201.*
Ind/Abst Chem. Abstr.; Curr. Aware. Biol. Sci., CABS; Index Med.; Sci. Cit. Index; SCISEARCH.

LC Z5320 **ISSN** 0300-5372
DD 016.57 NE
CCC
NLM ZW 1 E978I **CODEN** CLBIDV
EXCERPTA MEDICA. SECTION 29. CLINICAL BIOCHEMISTRY. **See** Biology-Abstracting, Bibliographies and Statistics.

LC QP501 .F43 **ISSN** 0014-5793
DD 574.1/92/05 NE
CCC
NLM W1 F31 **CODEN** FEBLAL
Pr Rev.
FEBS LETTERS. [FEBS lett.]. **Added/Corp** Federation of European Biochemical Societies. **VAT** Federation of European Biochemical Societies Letters. Vol. 1, No. 1 (July 1968)-. Academic Scholarly Publication. English (French). Sixty-three times a year (21 volumes). $3573.00. Elsevier Science Publishers BV, PO Box 211, 1000 AE Amsterdam Netherlands. **Tel** 011 31 20 4853641, 011 31 20 4853642, FAX 011 31 20 4853598. **ED** G Semenza. Index available in last issue of volume--attached. cum. index. available on microfilm from University Microfilms International (UMI); available on an online database from Elsevier Electronic Subscriptions (EES). Documents available from The Genuine Article, BIOSIS Document Express, CASDDS, Documents on Demand, ADONIS.
Desc: Brings together the most important developments in biochemistry, biophysics, cell and molecular biology. Also provides an international forum for reviews, commentaries and research results which merit urgent publication.
Ind/Abst ADONIS; AgBiotech News Inf.; Biol. Abstr.; Calcium Calcif. Tissue Abstr.; Chem. Abstr.; Chem. Titles; Chemorecept. Abstr.; Crop Physiol. Abstr.; CSA Neuro. Abstr.; Curr. Aware. Biol. Sci., CABS; Curr. Biotechnol.; Curr. Cit.; Curr. Contents Life Sci.; Curr. Ref. Fish Res.; Dairy Sci. Abstr.; EMBASE; Energy Inf. Abstr.; Environ. Abstr.; Field Crop Abstr.; Food Sci. Technol. Abstr.; Genet. Abstr.; Grass. Forage Abstr.; Health Plan. Adminis.; Helminthol. Abstr. (1991-); Hortic. Abstr.; Hum. Genome Abstr.; Immunol. Abstr.; Index Med.; Index Vet.; Int. Aerosp. Abstr.; Maize Abstr.; Mass Spect. Bull.; Microbiol. Abstr. Sect. B; Microbiol. Abstr. Sect. A; Microbiol. Abstr. Sect. C; NAPRALERT; Nematol. Abstr.; Nucl. Acids Abstr.; Nutr. Abstr. Rev., Ser. B, Live Feeds and Feed.; Nutr. Abstr. Rev., Ser. A, Hum. Exp.; Oncog. Growth Factors Abstr.; Ornamental Hort.; Life Sci. Collect.; PESTDOC; Pig News Inf.; Plant Breed. Abstr.; Plant Grow. Reg. Abstr.; Potato Abstr.; Poult. Abstr.; Protozoolog. Abstr.; Ref. Upd. Basic Ed.; Ref. Upd. Deluxe Ed.; Res. Alert [Full Cov.]; Rev. Agric. Entomol.; Rev. Med. Vet. Entomol.; Rev. Med. Vet. Mycology; Rev. Plant Pathol.; Rice Abstr.; Sci. Cit. Index; SCISEARCH; Seed Abstr.; Soils Fert.; Sorghum Mill. Abstr.; Virol. AIDS Abstr.; Vitis Vitic. Enol. Abstr.; Weed Abstr.; Wheat Barley Trit. Abstr.

LC QD415
DD 574.192 GW
NLM W3 F15 **CODEN** FEBSDB
FEBS SYMPOSIUM. No. 42- 1977-. Academic Scholarly Publication. English. Price varies per volume. Documents available from BIOSIS Document Express, CASDDS.
Ind/Abst Biol. Abstr. (-1979); Chem. Abstr.

LC QP535.F1 F5 **ISSN** 0015-4725
DD 574.1/921 US
CCC
NLM W1 FL957 **CODEN** FLUOA4
Pr Rev.
FLUORIDE. [Fluoride]. **Added/Corp** International Society for Fluoride Research. Vol. 3, No. 3 (July 1970)-. Academic Scholarly Publication. English. Four times a year (Jan., Apr., July, Oct.). $50.00. International Society of Fluoride Research, 81A Landscape Road / Mount Eden, Auckland 4 New Zealand. **Tel** 011 64 9 6307114, FAX 011 64 9 6307114. **ED** Dr. John Colquhoun. cum. index. **Bk Rev. Circ:** 500 (ctrl). available on microfilm from University Microfilms International (UMI). Documents available from The Genuine Article, BIOSIS Document Express, CASDDS, Documents on Demand. ***Continues** Fluoride Quarterly Reports, 0370-5978.*
Desc: Publication of papers and reports on the biological, chemical, ecological, industrial, toxicological, clinical impacts of inorganic and organic fluoride compounds.
Ind/Abst AGRICOLA; Biol. Abstr.; Calcium Calcif. Tissue Abstr.; Chem. Abstr.; CSA Neuro. Abstr. (?-?); Curr. Cit.; Curr. Contents Agric. Biol. Environ. Sci.; Curr. Titles Dent.; Dairy Sci. Abstr.; EMBASE; Energy Inf. Abstr.; Environ. Abstr.; Food Sci. Technol. Abstr.; Index Vet.; Leadscan; Nutr. Abstr. Rev., Ser. B, Live Feeds and Feed.; Nutr. Abstr. Rev., Ser. A, Hum. Exp.; Life Sci. Collect.; Pollut. Abstr. Indexes; Res. Alert [Full Cov.]; Saf. Health Work; Sci. Cit. Index; SCISEARCH; Soc. Sci. Cit. Index [Select. Cov.]; Soils Fert.; Vet. Bull.

LC TX501 .F66 **ISSN** 0308-8146
DD 664/.001/54 UK
CCC
NLM W1 FO4455 **CODEN** FOCHDJ
Pr Rev.
FOOD CHEMISTRY. [Food chem.]. Vol. 1 (July 1976)-. Academic Scholarly Publication. English. Twelve times a year. $1503.00. Elsevier Applied Science, An Imprint of Elsevier Science Ltd., The Boulevard, Langford Lane, Kidlington, Oxford OX5 1GB United Kingdom. **Tel** 011 44 1865 843000, 011 44 1865 843699, FAX 011 44 1865 843010. **(Subscription address:** Elsevier Science Ltd. / Oxford Fulfillment Centre, PO Box 800, Kidlington OX5 1DX United Kingdom. **Tel** 011 44 865 843355.**)** **ED** G. G. Birch. **Bk Rev. Ad Acc.** available on microfilm and microfiche from University Microfilms International (UMI); available on an online database from Elsevier Electronic Subscriptions (EES). Documents available from The Genuine Article, BIOSIS Document Express, CASDDS.
Desc: Concerned mainly with the chemistry and biochemistry of foods and chemical and biochemical changes occurring in foods. It is also concerned with sensory and nutritional properties of food within a chemical or biochemical framework.
Ind/Abst AGRICOLA [Select. Cov.]; Agrofor. Abstr. (1991-); Anal. Abstr.; BioBusiness; Biol. Abstr.; Chem. Abstr.; Chem. Titles; Chemorecept. Abstr.; Crop Physiol. Abstr.; Curr. Biotechnol.; Curr. Cit.; Curr. Contents Agric. Biol. Environ. Sci.; Dairy Sci. Abstr.; EMBASE; Field Crop Abstr.; Food Sci. Technol. Abstr.; Foods Adlibra; For. Prod. Abstr.; Hortic. Abstr.; Int. Packag. Abstr.; Mass Spect. Bull.; Nutr. Abstr. Rev., Ser. B, Live Feeds and Feed.; Nutr. Abstr. Rev., Ser. A, Hum. Exp.; Ornamental Hort.; Life Sci. Collect.; Plant Breed. Abstr.; Plant Genet. Resour. Abstr.; Plant Grow. Reg. Abstr.; Postharvest News Inf.; Potato Abstr.; Ref. Upd. Deluxe Ed.; Res. Alert [Full Cov.]; Rice Abstr.; Sci. Cit. Index; SCISEARCH; Seed Abstr.; Soils Fert.; Sorghum Mill. Abstr.; Soyabean Abstr.; Wheat Barley Trit. Abstr.

LC QP527 .F7 **ISSN** 0891-5849
DD 574.19/283 US
CCC
NLM W1; FR598 **CODEN** FRBMEH
Pr Rev.
FREE RADICAL BIOLOGY & MEDICINE. [Free radic. biol. med.]. **VFOAT** Free Radical Biology and Medicine. Vol. 3, No. 1 (1987)-. Academic Scholarly Publication. English. Fourteen times a year. $975.00. Pergamon Press, An Imprint of Elsevier Science Ltd., The Boulevard, Langford Lane, Kidlington, Oxford OX5 1GB United Kingdom. **Tel** 011 44 1865 843000, 011 44 1865 843699, FAX 011 44 1865 843010. **(Subscription address:** Elsevier Science Ltd. / Oxford Fulfillment Centre, PO Box 800, Kidlington OX5 1DX United Kingdom. **Tel** 011 44 865 843355.**)** **ED** William A. Pryor. available on microfilm and microfiche from University Microfilms International (UMI); available on an online database from Elsevier Electronic Subscriptions (EES). Documents available from The Genuine Article, BIOSIS Document Express, CASDDS, ADONIS. ***Formed by the union of** Advances in Free Radical Biology and Medicine, 8755-9668 **and** Journal of Free Radicals in Biology & Medicine, 0748-5514.*
Desc: An international, interdisciplinary publication encompassing chemical, biochemical, physiological, pathological, pharmacological, toxicological and medical approaches to free-radical research.
Ind/Abst ADONIS; Biol. Abstr. (1988-); Chem. Abstr.;

CSA Neuro. Abstr. (?-?); Curr. Aware. Biol. Sci., CABS; Curr. Cit.; Curr. Contents Life Sci.; EMBASE; Foods Adlibra; Health Plan. Adminis.; Index Med. (1987-); INIS Atomindex [Micro.]; Nutr. Abstr. Rev., Ser. A, Hum. Exp.; Ref. Upd. Basic Ed.; Ref. Upd. Deluxe Ed.; Res. Alert [Full Cov.]; Sci. Cit. Index; SCISEARCH; Toxicol. Abstr.

LC RB170 .F74 **ISSN** 8755-0199
DD 574.19/283 SZ
NLM W1; FR5986 **CODEN** TRCOEC
Pr Rev. **TITLE CHANGE**
FREE RADICAL RESEARCH COMMUNICATIONS. See Biology-Biological Physics.

LC QD415 **ISSN** 0301-3073
DD 574.192 SZ
CCC
NLM W1 FR946F **CODEN** FHRSA7
Pr Rev.
FRONTIERS OF HORMONE RESEARCH. [Front. horm. res.]. Vol. 1 (1972)-. English. One time a year. 180.00F (approx. per volume). S. Karger AG, Allschwilerstrasse 10, PO Box, CH-4009 Basel Switzerland. **Tel** 011 41 61 3061111, FAX 011 41 61 3061234, telex CH 962 652. **ED** A. Grossman. Documents available from The Genuine Article, BIOSIS Document Express, CASDDS.
Desc: Areas of endocrinology undergoing active investigation provide the focus for this series, which consolidates findings from both experimental and clinical work. Individual volumes have been designed to help readers understand how new knowledge on the activity and functional significance of hormones can contribute to improvements in clinical medicine.
Ind/Abst Biol. Abstr.; Chem. Abstr.; Dairy Sci. Abstr.; Index Med.; Index Sci. Rev. [Full Cov.]; Ref. Upd. Deluxe Ed.; Res. Alert [Full Cov.]; Sci. Cit. Index (19??-19??); SCISEARCH.

LC QP501 .S437 **ISSN** 0288-3953
DD 612.015 JA
CODEN FJDKDW
FUKUOKA JOSHI DAIGAKU KASEI GAKUBU KIYO. **Added/Corp** Fukuoka Joshi Daigaku. Kasei Gakubu. **VFOAT** Bulletin of the Faculty of Home Life Science, Fukuoka Women's University. (1983)-. Bulletin. English (Japanese). One time a year. Fukuoka Joshi Daigaku Kasei Gakubu, 1 No 1, Kasumigaoka 1-Chome, Higashi-ku, Fukuoka-shi 813 Japan. Documents available from CASDDS. ***Continues*** *Seikatsu Kagaku (Fukuoka-Shi, Japan), 0559-3042.*
Ind/Abst Chem. Abstr.

LC QD1 .G45
DD 540.5 JA
CODEN GNKGAN
GENDAI KAGAKU. CHEMISTRY TODAY. See Chemistry and Chemicals.

ISSN 0957-3526
UK
GENE EXPRESSION. See Biology-Genetics.

LC QP552.G59 G69 **ISSN** 0959-6658
DD 612.01575 UK
CCC
NLM W1; GL364 **CODEN** GLYCE3
Pr Rev.
GLYCOBIOLOGY (OXFORD). (GLYCOBIOLOGY.). [Glycobiology]. Vol. 1, No. 1 (Sept. 1990)-. Academic Scholarly Publication. English. Eight times a year. $355.00. Oxford University Press / UK, Walton Street, Oxford OX2 6DP United Kingdom. **Tel** 011 44 1865 56767, FAX 011 44 1865 267773, telex 851/837330 OXPRES G. **(Subscription address:** Oxford University Press / USA, Journals Marketing Department, Oxford University Press, 2001 Evans Road, Cary NC 27513. **Tel** (800)451-7556, (919)677-0977, FAX (919)677-1714.**)** **ED** G. Hart. **Bk Rev. Ad Acc. Circ:** 250. available on microfilm and microfiche from University Microfilms International (UMI). Documents available from The Genuine Article, BIOSIS Document Express, CASDDS, ADONIS.
Desc: Original research papers on any aspect of structure/function of glycoconjugates or proteins which interact with them.
Ind/Abst ADONIS; Biol. Abstr. (1991-); Chem. Abstr.; Curr. Aware. Biol. Sci., CABS; Curr. Cit.; Curr. Contents Life Sci.; EMBASE; Index Med. (Sept. 1990-); Ref. Upd. Deluxe Ed.; Res. Alert [Full Cov.]; Sci. Cit. Index; SCISEARCH.

LC QD241 **ISSN** 1356-1316
DD 547 UK
•**GLYCOBIOLOGY RESEARCH.** (1995)-. Abstracting/Indexing Service. English. Two times a month. £115.00. SUBIS, Mansion House 19 Kingfield Road, Sheffield S11 9AS United Kingdom. **Tel** 011 44 114 2554433, FAX 011 44 114 255 4626. available on diskette.

LC QD415 **ISSN** 0164-081X
DD 574.192 US
NLM QU 55 G568
GLYCOCONJUGATES, THE. Vol. 1 (1977)-. Monographic series. English. Irregular. Price varies per volume. Academic Press Inc., 6277 Sea Harbor Drive, Orlando FL 32887. **Tel** (800)543-9534, (407)345-4100, FAX (407)352-3445.
Ind/Abst Sci. Cit. Index (19??-19??); SCISEARCH.

ISSN 0017-3495
SP
CCC
CODEN GRACAN
Pr Rev.
GRASAS Y ACEITES (SEVILLA). See Food and Food Industry-Abstracting, Bibliographies and Statistics.

ISSN 0364-2577
US
UDC 577.121; 57.088.6
CODEN GMTHDX
GUIDELINES TO METABOLIC THERAPY. [Guidel. metab. ther.]. **VFOAT** Metabolic Therapy. (1972)-. Academic Scholarly Publication. English. Four times a year. Documents available from CASDDS.
Ind/Abst Chem. Abstr.

LC QD415.A1 H36a **ISSN** 0368-4881
DD 574.192 KO
NLM W1 HA524D **CODEN** KBCJAK
HAN'GUK SAENGHWAHAKOE CHI. **Main/Corp** Han'guk Saenghwahakoe. **Added/Corp** Han'guk Saenghwahakoe. Korean Biochemical Journal. **VFOAT** Korean Biochemical Journal. (1968)-. Periodical. English (Korean). Documents available from CASDDS.
Ind/Abst Chem. Abstr.; Crop Physiol. Abstr.; Curr. Cit.; Hortic. Abstr.; Plant Breed. Abstr.; Rev. Med. Vet. Mycology; Rev. Plant Pathol.

LC QP514 .R4 **ISSN** 1043-9811
DD 612/.015 US
NLM W1; HA593
HARPER'S BIOCHEMISTRY. [Harper's biochem.]. 21st Ed. (1988)-. English. Every 2 years. $34.13. Appleton Century Crofts, Prentice Hall, 200 Old Tappan Road, Old Tappan NJ 07675. **Tel** (201)767-5188, (800)922-0579. ***Continues*** *Harper's Review of Biochemistry, 0734-9866.*

ISSN 0950-0510
DD 016.57419245 UK
HEAT SHOCK PROTEINS. [Heat shock proteins]. (1987)-. Periodical. English. Twelve times a year. £75.00. SUBIS, Mansion House 19 Kingfield Road, Sheffield S11 9AS United Kingdom. **Tel** 011 44 114 2554433, FAX 011 44 114 255 4626. **Ad Acc.**
Desc: Current awareness service for researchers and clinicians.

LC QD **ISSN** 1083-4389
DD 540 US
•**HELICOBACTER.** (1996)-. Academic Scholarly Publication. English. Four times a year. $150.00 (institutions), $75.00 (individuals). Blackwell Scientific Publishers, 238 Main Street, Cambridge MA 02142. **Tel** (617)547-7110, (800)835-6770, FAX (617)547-0789. available on diskette.

ISSN 0916-3786
DD 591.1 JA
HIKAKU SEIRI SEIKAGAKU. See Biology-Physiology.

LC QD415 **ISSN** 0130-5972
DD 574.192 RU
NLM W1 KH45 **CODEN** KHZHAZ
HIMIJA I ZIZN. (KHIMIIA I ZHIZN.). [Him. zizn]. **Added/Corp** Akademiia Nauk SSSR. (1965)-. Academic Scholarly Publication. Russian. Twelve times a year. $104.00. Izdatelstvo Nauka / Akademiia Nauk, (Publishing House of the Russian Academy of Sciences), Leninskii Porspekt 14, 117901 Moscow Russia. **Tel** 011 95 9542153, FAX 011 95 9382144, telex 411964. **(Subscription address:** East View Publications Inc., 3020 Harbor Lane North, Suite 110, Minneapolis MN 55447. **Tel** (800)477-1005, (612)550-0961, FAX (612)559-2931.**)** Documents available from CASDDS.
Ind/Abst Chem. Abstr.; Int. Aerosp. Abstr.

LC QH345 .H66 **ISSN** 0096-2708
DD 574.1/9/05 US
NLM W1 HO596T **CODEN** HZBBAO
CEASED
HORIZONS IN BIOCHEMISTRY AND BIOPHYSICS. [Horiz. biochem. biophys.]. Vol. 1 (1974)-Completed Series, Vol. 5 (19??). English. Addison Wesley Publishing Company, 350 Bridge Parkway, Suite 208, Redwood City CA 94065. **Tel** (415)594-4423, (800)447-2226. **ED** E. Quagliariello, F. Palmieri, and T.P. Singer. Documents available from BIOSIS Document Express, Ask*IEEE, CASDDS.
Ind/Abst Biol. Abstr.; Chem. Abstr.; Energy Res. Abstr. (Aug. 1982-); Index Med.; INSPEC.

LC QD415 **ISSN** 0952-1097
DD 574.192 UK
NLM W3; I325 **CODEN** ISREEB
ICSU SHORT REPORTS. [ICSU short rep.]. **Added/Corp** International Council of Scientific Unions. Vol. 1 (1984)-. Academic Scholarly Publication. English. Irregular. Price varies per volume. Cambridge University Press, The Edinburgh Building, Shaftesbury Road, Cambridge CB2 2RU United Kingdom. **Tel** 011 44 1223 312393, FAX 011 44 1223 315052, telex 851-817256. Documents available from BIOSIS Document Express, CASDDS. ***Continues*** *Miami Winter Symposia.*
Ind/Abst Biol. Abstr. (1985-); Chem. Abstr. (1984-).

LC S **ISSN** 0970-6399
DD 630 II
UDC 63 :577.1
INDIAN JOURNAL OF AGRICULTURAL BIOCHEMISTRY. See Agriculture.

LC QP501 .I42 **ISSN** 0301-1208
DD 612.015 II
NLM W1 IN206PR **CODEN** IJBBBQ
Pr Rev.
INDIAN JOURNAL OF BIOCHEMISTRY & BIOPHYSICS. [Ind. j. biochem. biophys.]. **Added/Corp** Council of Scientific & Industrial Research (India) Indian National Science Academy. Society of Biological Chemists (India). **VFOAT** Indian Journal of Biochemistry and Biophysics. Vol. 8, No. 1 (March 1971)-. Academic Scholarly Publication. English. Six times a year. $100.00. Council of Scientific & Industrial Research, Publications & Information Director, Hillside Road, New Delhi 110012 India. **Tel** FAX 011 91 11 5731353. **(Subscription address:** Prints India, 11 Darya Ganj, New Delhi 110002 India. **Tel** 011 91 11 3268645, FAX 011 91 11 3275542, telex 31-61087 PRIN-IN.**)** Documents available from The Genuine Article, BIOSIS Document Express, CASDDS. ***Continues*** *Indian Journal of Biochemistry, 0019-5081.*
Ind/Abst AGRICOLA; Anal. Abstr.; Anim. Breed. Abstr.; Biodeter. Abstr.; Biol. Abstr.; Chem. Abstr.; Chem. Titles; Cot. Trop. Fibr. Abstr. Bibliogr.; Crop Physiol. Abstr.; CSA Neuro. Abstr. (?-?); Curr. Biotechnol.; Curr. Cit.; Curr. Contents Life Sci.; Dairy Sci. Abstr.; EMBASE; Field Crop Abstr.; Food Sci. Technol. Abstr.; Genet. Abstr.; Hortic. Abstr.; Index Med.; Microbiol. Abstr. Sect. B (19??-19??); Microbiol. Abstr. Sect. C; NAPRALERT; Nat. Prod. Updates; Nutr. Abstr. Rev., Ser. B, Live Feeds and Feed.; Nutr. Abstr. Rev., Ser. A, Hum. Exp.; Life Sci. Collect.; PESTDOC; Plant Breed. Abstr.; Plant Grow. Reg. Abstr.; Protozoolog. Abstr.; Res. Alert [Select. Cov.]; Rev. Agric. Entomol.; Rev. Med. Vet. Entomol.; Rev. Med. Vet. Mycology; Rev. Plant Pathol.; Rice Abstr.; SCISEARCH; Seed Abstr.; Soc. Sci. Cit. Index [Select. Cov.]; Sorghum Mill. Abstr.; Trop. Dis. Bull.

LC QD415 **ISSN** 0970-1915
DD 574.192 II
NLM W1; IN207AV **CODEN** IJCBEY
INDIAN JOURNAL OF CLINICAL BIOCHEMISTRY. (INDIAN JOURNAL OF CLINICAL BIOCHEMISTRY : IJCB.). [Indian j. clin. biochemistry]. **Added/Corp** Association of Clinical Biochemists of India. **VFOAT** IJCB. Vol. 1, No. 1 (Jan. 1986)-. Periodical. English. Two times a year. $5.00. Association of Clinical Biochemists of India, Patna Medical College, 800 004 Patna India. Documents available from CASDDS.
Ind/Abst Chem. Abstr. (1986-); Curr. Aware. Biol. Sci., CABS; Curr. Cit.; EMBASE.

LC QP518 .I58A
DD 574.1/92/072082 AG
INSTITUTO DE INVESTIGACIONES BIOQUIMICAS, ANUARIO. Spanish. Instituto de Investigaciones Bioquimicas, Calle Obligado 2490, Buenos Aires Argentina.

LC QP501 .I48 **ISSN** 0020-711X
DD 574.1/92/05 UK
CCC
NLM W1 IN7655N **CODEN** IJBOBV
Pr Rev. **TITLE CHANGE**
INTERNATIONAL JOURNAL OF BIOCHEMISTRY, THE. [Int. j. biochem.]. Vol. 1, (Feb. 1970)-(19??). Academic Scholarly Publication. English. Pergamon Press, An Imprint of Elsevier Science Ltd., The Boulevard, Langford Lane, Kidlington, Oxford OX5 1GB United Kingdom. **Tel** 011 44 1865 843000, 011 44 1865 843699, FAX 011 44 1865 843010. **(Subscription address:** Elsevier Science Ltd. / Oxford Fulfillment Centre, PO Box 800, Kidlington OX5 1DX United Kingdom. **Tel** 011 44 865 843355.**)** **ED** Gerald A. Kerkut. **Bk Rev. Ad Acc.** available on microfilm and microfiche from University Microfilms International (UMI). Documents available from The Genuine Article, BIOSIS Document Express, CASDDS, ADONIS. ***Continued by*** *International Journal of Biochemistry and Cell Biology.*
Desc: Provides comprehensive coverage of new research in the growth areas of biochemistry.
Ind/Abst ADONIS; AGRICOLA [Select. Cov.]; Anim. Breed. Abstr.; Biol. Abstr.; Calcium Calcif. Tissue Abstr.; Chem. Abstr.; Chem. Titles; CSA Neuro. Abstr. (?-?); Curr. Aware. Biol. Sci., CABS; Curr. Biotechnol.; Curr. Cit.; Curr. Contents Life Sci.; Curr. Ref. Fish Res.; Dairy Sci. Abstr.; EMBASE; Fish Rev. (Jan. 1989-July 1992); Genet. Abstr.; Health Plan. Adminis.; Helminthol. Abstr.; Index Med.; Index Vet.; Microbiol. Abstr. Sect. B; Microbiol. Abstr. Sect. C; NAPRALERT; Nutr. Abstr. Rev., Ser. B, Live Feeds and Feed.; Nutr. Abstr. Rev., Ser. A, Hum. Exp.; Oncog. Growth Factors Abstr.; Life Sci. Collect.; PESTDOC; Pig News Inf.; Poult. Abstr.; Protozoolog. Abstr.; Ref. Upd. Deluxe Ed.; Res. Alert [Full

Cov.]; Sci. Cit. Index; SCISEARCH; Soc. Sci. Cit. Index [Select. Cov.]; Soyabean Abstr.; Vet. Bull.; Wildl. Rev. (Jan. 1989-July 1992).

LC QP501 .I48
DD 574.1/92/05 UK
NLM W1; IN7655N

•INTERNATIONAL JOURNAL OF BIOCHEMISTRY AND CELL BIOLOGY. (1995)-. Academic Scholarly Publication. English. Twelve times a year. $1567.00. Elsevier Science Publishers Ltd., Crown House, Linton Road, Barking Essex IG11 8JU United Kingdom. **Tel** 011 44 181 5947272, FAX 011 44 181 5945942, telex 896950. **(Subscription address:** Elsevier Science Ltd. / Oxford Fulfillment Centre, PO Box 800, Kidlington OX5 1DX United Kingdom. **Tel** 011 44 865 843355.) Index available (Bound in Dec. issue). available on an online database from Elsevier Electronic Subscriptions (EES). ***Continues*** *International Journal of Biochemistry.*
Ind/Abst Curr. Cit.

LC QP801.P64 I57 **ISSN** 0141-8130
DD 574.19/2/05 UK
CCC
NLM W1 IN76553 **CODEN** IJBMDR
Pr Rev.

INTERNATIONAL JOURNAL OF BIOLOGICAL MACROMOLECULES. [Int. j. biol. macromol.]. **VFOAT** Biological Macromolecules. Vol. 1 (April 1979)-. Academic Scholarly Publication. English. Eight times a year. $1132.00. Butterworth Heinemann Publishers, Linacre House Jordan Hill, Oxford OX2 8DP United Kingdom. **Tel** 011 44 1865 310366, FAX 011 44 1865 310898. **(Subscription address:** Elsevier Science Ltd. / Oxford Fulfillment Centre, PO Box 800, Kidlington OX5 1DX United Kingdom. **Tel** 011 44 865 843355.) **ED** Edward Atkins. Index available. **Ad Acc.** available on microfilm and microfiche from University Microfilms International (UMI); available on an online database from Elsevier Electronic Subscriptions (EES). Documents available from The Genuine Article, BIOSIS Document Express, CASDDS.
Desc: An international research journal of research into the structure of natural macromolecules. It publishes the latest findings of studies on the molecular structure of macromolecules such as proteins, polysaccharides, nucleic acids, their synthetic analogues and assemblies in relation to molecular function and interactions with other molecules.
Ind/Abst Abstr. Bull. Inst. Pap. Sci. Tech.; Biol. Abstr.; Chem. Abstr.; Chem. Titles; Curr. Aware. Biol. Sci., CABS; Curr. Biotechnol.; Curr. Cit.; Curr. Contents Life Sci.; Dairy Sci. Abstr.; EMBASE; Food Sci. Technol. Abstr.; Life Sci. Collect.; Polymer Contents; Res. Alert [Full Cov.]; Rev. Agric. Entomol.; Sci. Cit. Index; SCISEARCH.

LC QH345 .I53a
DD 574 US
CODEN IJQSAF

INTERNATIONAL JOURNAL OF QUANTUM CHEMISTRY. QUANTUM BIOLOGY SYMPOSIUM : PROCEEDINGS OF THE INTERNATIONAL SYMPOSIUM ON THE APPLICATION OF FUNDAMENTAL THEORY TO PROBLEMS OF BIOLOGY AND PHARMACOLOGY. **VFOAT** Quantum Biology Symposium; Problems of Biology and Pharmacology; Quantum Biology Symposia. No. 19 (1992)-. Proceedings. English. One time a year. John Wiley & Sons, Inc., 605 Third Avenue, New York NY 10158-0012. **Tel** (212)850-6000, (212)850-6645, FAX (212)850-6088, telex 12-7063. **(Subscription address:** John Wiley & Sons / UK, Baffins Lane, Chichester, West Sussex PO19 1UD United Kingdom. **Tel** 011 44 1243 779777, FAX 011 44 243 776128, telex 86290 WIBOOKG.) ***Continues*** *International Symposium on Quantum Biology and Quantum Pharmacology. International Journal of Quantum Chemistry. Quantum Biology Symposium, 0360-8832.*

LC QD415 **ISSN** 0197-887X
DD 574.192 US

ISOZYME BULLETIN, THE. [Isozyme bull.]. **Added/Corp** Laboratory of Viral Carcinogenesis (National Cancer Institute). University of Illinois at Urbana-Champaign. College of Medicine. (196?)-. Bulletin. English. One time a year (Feb.). $12.00. Isozyme Bulletin, Kennesaw State College, PO Box 444, Marietta GA 30061. **Tel** (404)423-6158, FAX (404)423-6625. **ED** Ronald H. Matson. **Circ:** 125.

LC QD415 **ISSN** 0021-2938
DD 574.192 IT
NLM W1 IT135 **CODEN** IJBIAC
Pr Rev. **CEASED**

ITALIAN JOURNAL OF BIOCHEMISTRY, THE. [Ital. j. biochem.]. (Jan./Feb. 1951)-Vol. 44 (1995). Academic Scholarly Publication. English. Il Pensiero Scientifico Editore s.r.l., Via Bradano 3C, 00199 Rome Italy. **Tel** 011 39 6 86207158, 011 39 6 86207159, 86207168, 86207169, FAX 011 39 6 86207160. **ED** Antonio De Flora. Index available. **Bk Rev.** **Ad Acc.** Full Page (B&W) L1.300.000. **Circ:** 700. Documents available from The Genuine Article, BIOSIS Document Express, FAXON Xpress, CASDDS.
Ind/Abst AGRICOLA; Biol. Abstr.; Chem. Abstr.; Chem. Titles; CSA Neuro. Abstr. (?-?); Curr. Aware. Biol. Sci., CABS; Curr. Cit.; Curr. Contents Life Sci.; Curr. Ref. Fish Res.; Dairy Sci. Abstr.; EMBASE; Index Med.; NAPRALERT; Nat. Prod. Updates; Nutr. Abstr. Rev., Ser. B, Live Feeds and Feed.; Nutr. Abstr. Rev., Ser. A, Hum. Exp.; Life Sci. Collect.; PESTDOC; Ref. Upd. Deluxe Ed.; Res. Alert [Full Cov.]; Sci. Cit. Index; SCISEARCH.

ISSN 1121-1709
IT
UDC 616-008

ITALIAN JOURNAL OF MINERAL & ELECTROLYTE METABOLISM. [Ital. j. miner. electrolyte metab.]. **VFOAT** Italian Journal of Mineral and Electrolyte Metabolism. (1990)-. Periodical. Multiple languages. Four times a year. L91970. Edizioni Minerva Medica, Corso Bramante 83-85, 10126 Turin Italy. **Tel** 011 39 11 678282, FAX 011 39 11 674502. ***Continues*** *Giornale Italiano di Metabolismo Minerale ed Elettrolitico, 0394-1566.*
Desc: Covers both mineral and electrolyte metabolism and calcified tissues. The official journal of the Italian Society of Mineral Metabolism.

LC QP501 .I8 **ISSN** 0202-795X
DD 612.015 RU
NLM W1; IT576AM **CODEN** INBKBD

ITOGI NAUKI I TEKHNIKI. SERIIA BIOLOGICHESKAIA KHIMIIA. **Added/Corp** Vsesoiuznyi Institut Nauchnoi i Tekhnicheskoi Informatsii (Russia). **VFOAT** Seriia Biologicheskaia Khimiia; Biologicheskaia Khimiia; Itogi Nauki i Tekhniki. Biologicheskaia Khimiia. (1981)-. Monographic series. Russian. Irregular. Price varies per volume. VINITI - Vsesoyuznyi Institut Nauchno-Tekhnicheskoi Informatsii, All-Union Scientific and Technical Information Institute, Baltiiskaia ulitsa 14, 125219 Moscow Russia. **Tel** 011 7 95 2384600, FAX 011 7 95 9430060, telex 411160. **(Subscription address:** East View Publications Inc., 3020 Harbor Lane North, Suite 110, Minneapolis MN 55447. **Tel** (800)477-1005, (612)550-0961, FAX (612)559-2931.) Documents available from CASDDS. ***Continues*** *Itogi Nauki i Tekhniki. Biologicheskaia Khimiia.*
Ind/Abst Chem. Abstr.

LC QD415 **ISSN** 0075-3696
DD 574.192 IS
NLM W3 JE56 **CODEN** JSQCA7

JERUSALEM SYMPOSIA ON QUANTUM CHEMISTRY AND BIOCHEMISTRY, THE. Vol.1 (1968)-. Monographic series. English. Israel Academy of Sciences and Humanities, Jerusalem Israel. Documents available from BIOSIS Document Express, CASDDS.
Ind/Abst Biol. Abstr.; Chem. Abstr.

LC QP519.7 .J68 **ISSN** 0165-022X
DD 574.19/2/028 NE
CCC
NLM W1 JO562 **CODEN** JBBMDG
Pr Rev.

JOURNAL OF BIOCHEMICAL AND BIOPHYSICAL METHODS. [J. biochem. biophys. methods]. **VFOAT** Biochemical and Biophysical Methods. Vol. 1 (March 1979)-. Academic Scholarly Publication. English. Nine times a year. $902.00. Elsevier Science Publishers BV, PO Box 211, 1000 AE Amsterdam Netherlands. **Tel** 011 31 20 4853641, 011 31 20 4853642, FAX 011 31 20 4853598. **ED** C. F. Chignell, S. Hjerten and T. Ooi. **Bk Rev.** **Ad Acc.** available on microfilm and microfiche from University Microfilms International (UMI); available on an online database from Elsevier Electronic Subscriptions (EES). Documents available from The Genuine Article, BIOSIS Document Express, Ask*IEEE, CASDDS, ADONIS.
Desc: Offers researchers a unique opportunity to keep abreast of the development of methods and novel application of existing methods to solve biological problems.
Ind/Abst ADONIS; Anal. Abstr.; Biol. Abstr.; Chem. Abstr.; Chem. Hazards Ind.; Chem. Titles; CSA Neuro. Abstr. (?-?); Curr. Aware. Biol. Sci., CABS; Curr. Biotechnol.; Curr. Cit.; Curr. Contents Life Sci.; Dairy Sci. Abstr.; EMBASE; Food Sci. Technol. Abstr.; Index Med.; INSPEC (May 1979-); Lab. Hazards Bull.; Life Sci. Collect.; Ref. Upd. Deluxe Ed.; Res. Alert [Full Cov.]; Sci. Cit. Index; SCISEARCH.

LC QP501 .J664 **ISSN** 1065-9668
DD 574.19/2/05 US
NLM W1; JO563BP **CODEN** JOBOEC

JOURNAL OF BIOCHEMICAL ORGANIZATION. [J. biochem. organ.]. (1992)-. Academic Scholarly Publication. English. Four times a year. $295.00. Nova Science Publishers Inc., 6080 Jericho Turnpike, Suite 207, Commack NY 11725-2808. **Tel** (516)499-3103, (516)499-3106, FAX (516)499-3146. Documents available from CASDDS.
Ind/Abst Chem. Abstr.

LC RV401 **ISSN** 0887-2082
DD 615 US
CCC
NLM W1; JO563C **CODEN** JBTOEB
Pr Rev.

JOURNAL OF BIOCHEMICAL TOXICOLOGY. **See** Toxicology.

LC QP501 .J67 **ISSN** 0021-924X
DD 574.1905 JA
CCC
NLM W1 JO563E **CODEN** JOBIAO
Pr Rev.

JOURNAL OF BIOCHEMISTRY (TOKYO). (THE JOURNAL OF BIOCHEMISTRY.). [J. biochem.]. **Added/Corp** Nihon Seikagakkai. Vol. 1 (Jan. 1922)-. Academic Scholarly Publication. English (French and German). Twelve times a year. $230.00. **(Subscription address:** Maruzen Company Ltd., PO Box 5050, Import & Export Department, Tokyo 100 31 Japan. **Tel** 011 81 3 32789224.) Documents available from The Genuine Article, BIOSIS Document Express, CASDDS.
Desc: Offers original research papers in the field of biochemistry.
Ind/Abst AgBiotech News Inf.; AGRICOLA [Select. Cov.]; Anal. Abstr.; Anim. Breed. Abstr.; Biol. Abstr.; Chem. Abstr.; Chem. Titles; Crop Physiol. Abstr.; CSA Neuro. Abstr. (?-?); Curr. Aware. Biol. Sci., CABS; Curr. Biotechnol.; Curr. Cit.; Curr. Ref. Fish Res.; Dairy Sci. Abstr.; EMBASE; Field Crop Abstr.; For. Abstr.; Genet. Abstr.; Hum. Genome Abstr.; Immunol. Abstr.; Index Med.; Microbiol. Abstr. Sect. B; Microbiol. Abstr. Sect. C; NAPRALERT; Nat. Prod. Updates; Nucl. Acids Abstr.; Oncog. Growth Factors Abstr.; Life Sci. Collect.; PESTDOC; Potato Abstr.; Ref. Upd. Basic Ed.; Ref. Upd. Deluxe Ed.; Res. Alert [Full Cov.]; Rev. Agric. Entomol.; Rev. Med. Vet. Entomol.; Rev. Plant Pathol.; Rice Abstr.; Sci. Cit. Index; SCISEARCH; SEA Abstr.; Seed Abstr.; Sorghum Mill. Abstr.; Soyabean Abstr.; Virol. AIDS Abstr.

LC QD415 **ISSN** 0021-924x
DD 574.192 US

JOURNAL OF BIOCHEMISTRY (TOKYO). (JOURNAL OF BIOCHEMISTRY.). **Added/Corp** Nihon Seikagakkai. Vol. 1 (Jan. 1922)-. Academic Scholarly Publication. English. Twelve times a year. $240.00. **(Subscription address:** Maruzen Company Ltd., PO Box 5050, Import & Export Department, Tokyo 100 31 Japan. **Tel** 011 81 3 32789224.) Documents available from BIOSIS Document Express, CASDDS.
Ind/Abst Biol. Abstr.; Calcium Calcif. Tissue Abstr.; Chem. Abstr.; For. Abstr.

LC QP501 .J7 **ISSN** 0021-9258
DD 574.1905 US
CCC
NLM W1 JO564C **CODEN** JBCHA3
Pr Rev.

JOURNAL OF BIOLOGICAL CHEMISTRY, THE. [J. biol. chem.]. **Added/Corp** American Society of Biological Chemists. Rockefeller Institute for Medical Research. American Society for Biochemistry and Molecular Biology. Vol. 1 (Oct. 1905)-. Academic Scholarly Publication. English. One time a week. $1150.00. American Society for Biochemistry and Molecular Biology, 9650 Rockville Pike, Bethesda MD 20814. **Tel** (301)530-7150, FAX (301)571-1824. **(Subscription address:** Fulco, 30 Broad Street, Denville NJ 07834. **Tel** (800)783-4903, (201)627-2427.) Index available (bound in last issue). **Ad Acc, Adv Mgr:** Linda Acuff, **Tel** (301)530-7107. **Circ:** 7,000. available on microfilm and microfiche from University Microfilms International (UMI); available on CD-ROM from the publisher. Documents available from The Genuine Article, BIOSIS Document Express, CASDDS.
Desc: Designed for the prompt publication of original investigations of a chemical nature in the biological sciences.
Ind/Abst Abstr. Bull. Inst. Pap. Sci. Tech.; AgBiotech News Inf.; AGRICOLA [Select. Cov.]; Anim. Breed. Abstr.; Biocont. News Inf. (1991-); Biodeter. Abstr. (19??-19??); Biol. Agric. Index; Biol. Abstr.; Biotechnol. Res. Abstr.; Calcium Calcif. Tissue Abstr.; Chem. Abstr.; Chem. Titles; Chemorecept. Abstr.; Crop Physiol. Abstr.; CSA Neuro. Abstr.; Curr. Aware. Biol. Sci., CABS; Curr. Biotechnol.; Curr. Cit.; Curr. Contents Life Sci.; Curr. Ref. Fish Res.; Dairy Sci. Abstr.; EMBASE; Energy Res. Abstr.; Entomol. Abstr.; Field Crop Abstr.; Fish Rev.; Food Sci. Technol. Abstr.; Genet. Abstr.; Grass. Forage Abstr.; Helminthol. Abstr. (19??-19??); Hortic. Abstr.; Hum. Genome Abstr.; Immunol. Abstr.; Index Med.; INIS Atomindex [Micro.]; Int. Aerosp. Abstr.; Maize Abstr.; Microbiol. Abstr. Sect. B; Microbiol. Abstr. Sect. A; Microbiol. Abstr. Sect. C; NAPRALERT; Nematol. Abstr.; Nucl. Acids Abstr.; Nutr. Abstr. Rev., Ser. A, Hum. Exp.; Oncog. Growth Factors Abstr.; Life Sci. Collect.; PESTDOC; Pig News Inf.; Plant Breed. Abstr.; Plant Grow. Reg. Abstr.; Potato Abstr.; Poult. Abstr.; Protozoolog. Abstr.; Ref. Upd. Basic Ed.; Ref. Upd. Deluxe Ed.; Res. Alert [Full Cov.]; Rev. Agric. Entomol.; Rev. Med. Vet. Entomol.; Rev. Med. Vet. Mycology; Rev. Plant Pathol.; Rice Abstr.; Sci. Cit. Index; SCISEARCH; Seed Abstr.; Small Anim. Abstr. Bibliogr.; Soils Fert.; Sorghum Mill. Abstr.; Soyabean Abstr.; Stat. Theory Method Abstr. (1959-1963); Trop. Dis. Bull.; Virol. AIDS Abstr.; Weed Abstr.; Wildl. Rev.

LC QH506 .J67 ISSN 0730-2312
DD 574.87/05 US
CCC
NLM W1 JO579C CODEN JCEBD5
Pr Rev.
JOURNAL OF CELLULAR BIOCHEMISTRY. [J. cell. biochem.]. Vol. 18, No. 1 (1982)-. Academic Scholarly Publication. English. Twelve times a year (includes supplement). $2185.00. John Wiley & Sons, Inc., 605 Third Avenue, New York NY 10158-0012. **Tel** (212)850-6000, (212)850-6645, FAX (212)850-6088, telex 12-7063. **(Subscription address:** John Wiley & Sons / UK, Baffins Lane, Chichester, West Sussex PO19 1UD United Kingdom. **Tel** 011 44 1243 779777, FAX 011 44 243 776128, telex 86290 WIBOOKG.) **ED** C. Fred Fox, Gary S. Stein, and Max M. Burger. available on microfilm and microfiche from University Microfilms International (UMI). Documents available from The Genuine Article, BIOSIS Document Express, CASDDS, ADONIS. ***Continues*** *Journal of Supramolecular Structure and Cellular Biochemistry, 0275-3723.*
Desc: Publishes timely reviews, commentaries, and descriptions of original research in areas where complex cellular, pathogenic, clinical, or animal model systems are studied by biochemical, genetic or quantitative ultrastructural approaches.
Ind/Abst ADONIS; Biol. Abstr.; Chem. Abstr.; Chem. Titles; Curr. Cit.; Curr. Contents Life Sci.; Curr. Ref. Fish Res.; Dairy Sci. Abstr.; EMBASE; Energy Res. Abstr. (Nov. 1982-); Helminthol. Abstr.; Immunol. Abstr.; Index Med.; INIS Atomindex [Micro.]; NAPRALERT; Life Sci. Collect.; PESTDOC; Protozoolog. Abstr.; Ref. Upd. Basic Ed.; Ref. Upd. Deluxe Ed.; Res. Alert [Full Cov.]; Sci. Cit. Index; SCISEARCH; Soc. Sci. Cit. Index [Select. Cov.].

ISSN 0733-1959
DD 574 US
NLM W1 JO579D
JOURNAL OF CELLULAR BIOCHEMISTRY. SUPPLEMENT. [J. cell. biochem., Suppl.]. **VFOAT** Journal of Cellular Biochemistry. Abstracts Supplement. (1982)-. Monographic series. English. One time a year. Price varies per volume. Wiley Liss, 605 3rd Avenue, New York NY 10158. **Tel** (212)850-8800, (212)850-6645. **(Subscription address:** John Wiley & Sons / UK, Baffins Lane, Chichester, West Sussex PO19 1UD United Kingdom. **Tel** 011 44 1243 779777, FAX 011 44 243 776128, telex 86290 WIBOOKG.) ***Continues*** *Journal of Supramolecular Structure and Cellular Biochemistry. Supplement, 0730-6652.*
Ind/Abst Curr. Cit.; Energy Res. Abstr. (Aug. 1982-); Fish Rev. (Jan. 1989-July 1992); Index Med.; Wildl. Rev. (Jan. 1989-July 1992).

LC QD502 .J68 ISSN 1058-5834
DD 541.3/94 US
CODEN JCBKEI
JOURNAL OF CHEMICAL AND BIOCHEMICAL KINETICS. See Chemistry and Chemicals-Physical and Theoretical Chemistry.

LC QD415 ISSN 0912-0009
DD 574.192 JA
NLM W1; JO587AH CODEN JCBNER
Pr Rev.
JOURNAL OF CLINICAL BIOCHEMISTRY AND NUTRITION. **Added/Corp** Institute of Applied Biochemistry (Japan). Vol. 1, No. 1 (1986)-. Academic Scholarly Publication. English. Six times a year. $150.00. Oyo Seikagaku Kenkyujo, (Inst. of Applied Biochemistry), Yagi Kinen Paku Mitakecho, Kanigun Gifuken 505-01 Japan. **(Subscription address:** Maruzen Company Ltd., PO Box 5050, Import & Export Department, Tokyo 100 31 Japan. **Tel** 011 81 3 32789224.) Documents available from The Genuine Article, BIOSIS Document Express, CASDDS.
Desc: Offers original research articles and review articles covering the research fields of clinical biochemistry and clinical nutrition based on biochemistry.
Ind/Abst Biol. Abstr.; Chem. Abstr. (1986-); CSA Neuro. Abstr. (?-?); Curr. Aware. Biol. Sci., CABS; Curr. Cit.; Curr. Contents Life Sci.; Dairy Sci. Abstr.; Helminthol. Abstr. (1991-); Nutr. Abstr. Rev., Ser. A, Hum. Exp.; Nutr. Res. Newsl.; Res. Alert [Full Cov.]; Sci. Cit. Index; SCISEARCH; Soyabean Abstr.

LC QH301 .J678 ISSN 0256-0011
DD 574/.05 II
NLM W1; JO612DF CODEN JCUBEI
JOURNAL OF CURRENT BIOSCIENCES. [J. curr. biosci.]. Vol. 1, No. 1 (1984)-. Periodical. English. Four times a year. $25.00. Premier Publications, 863 Sardarpura, Chopasani Road, Jodhpur-342 003 India. Documents available from CASDDS.
Ind/Abst Chem. Abstr.

LC QP1 .J725 ISSN 0022-0930
DD 591.1/05 US
CCC
NLM W1 JO644D CODEN JEBPA9
Pr Rev.
JOURNAL OF EVOLUTIONARY BIOCHEMISTRY AND PHYSIOLOGY. See Biology-Physiology.

LC QP501 .B557 ISSN 0162-0134
DD 574.1/92/05 US
CCC
NLM W1 JO71I CODEN JIBIDJ
Pr Rev.
JOURNAL OF INORGANIC BIOCHEMISTRY. [J. inorg. biochem.]. **VFOAT** Inorganic Biochemistry. Vol. 10 (Feb. 1979)-. Academic Scholarly Publication. English. Sixteen times a year (4 volumes). $942.00. Elsevier Science Publishing Company Inc, Madison Square Station, PO Box 882, New York NY 10159-0882. **Tel** (212)633-3950, FAX (212)633-3990. **ED** H A O Hill and J F Riordan. **Ad Acc. Circ:** 600. available on microfilm and microfiche from University Microfilms International (UMI); available on an online database from Elsevier Electronic Subscriptions (EES). Documents available from The Genuine Article, BIOSIS Document Express, CASDDS. ***Continues*** *Bioinorganic Chemistry, 0006-3061.*
Desc: Publishes research papers and short communications in inorganic biochemistry, biochemistry and chemistry.
Ind/Abst AGRICOLA [Select. Cov.]; Biol. Abstr.; Chem. Abstr.; Chem. Titles; Curr. Aware. Biol. Sci., CABS; Curr. Cit.; Curr. Contents Life Sci.; Curr. Contents Phys. Chem. Earth Sci.; Dairy Sci. Abstr.; EMBASE; Index Med.; Leadscan; Mass Spect. Bull.; Nutr. Abstr. Rev., Ser. B, Live Feeds and Feed.; Life Sci. Collect.; Refer. Z.; Ref. Upd. Deluxe Ed.; Res. Alert [Full Cov.]; Rev. Plant Pathol.; Sci. Cit. Index; SCISEARCH.

LC QD415 ISSN 0741-5400
DD 574.192 US
CCC
NLM W1; JO745HA
JOURNAL OF LEUKOCYTE BIOLOGY. SUPPLEMENT. (1990)-. Monographic series. English. Irregular. Wiley Liss, 605 3rd Avenue, New York NY 10158. **Tel** (212)850-8800, (212)850-6645.
Ind/Abst Index Med.

LC QP751 .J65 ISSN 0022-2275
DD 612.015 US
CCC
NLM W1 JO745L CODEN JLPRAW
Pr Rev.
JOURNAL OF LIPID RESEARCH. [J. lipid res.]. Vol. 1 (Oct. 1959)-. Academic Scholarly Publication. English. Twelve times a year. $275.00. Federation of American Societies for Experimental Biology, Room L-2310, 9650 Rockville Park, Bethesda MD 20814-3998. **Tel** (301)530-7027. **ED** Lewis I Gidez. available on microfilm and microfiche from University Microfilms International (UMI). Documents available from The Genuine Article, BIOSIS Document Express, CASDDS.
Desc: Publishes original articles and invited reviews on subjects involving lipids in any scientific discipline.
Ind/Abst AgBiotech News Inf.; AGRICOLA [Select. Cov.]; Anal. Abstr.; Anim. Breed. Abstr.; Biol. Abstr.; Biol. Dig.; Chem. Abstr.; Chem. Titles; Curr. Aware. Biol. Sci., CABS; Curr. Chem. React.; Curr. Cit.; Curr. Contents Life Sci.; Curr. Ref. Fish Res.; Dairy Sci. Abstr.; EMBASE; Energy Res. Abstr.; Fish Rev. (Jan. 1989-July 1992); Food Sci. Technol. Abstr.; Index Chem.; Index Med.; Index Vet.; INIS Atomindex [Micro.]; Int. Aerosp. Abstr.; Mass Spect. Bull.; Nat. Prod. Updates; Nutr. Abstr. Rev., Ser. B, Live Feeds and Feed.; Nutr. Abstr. Rev., Ser. A, Hum. Exp.; Nutr. Res. Newsl.; Life Sci. Collect.; PESTDOC; Pig News Inf.; Poult. Abstr.; Protozoolog. Abstr.; Ref. Upd. Basic Ed.; Ref. Upd. Deluxe Ed.; Res. Alert [Full Cov.]; Sci. Cit. Index; SCISEARCH; Soyabean Abstr.; Vet. Bull.; Wildl. Rev. (Jan. 1989-July 1992).

LC RS402 .J65 ISSN 0022-2623
DD 615.19 US
CCC
NLM W1 JO757G CODEN JMCMAR
JOURNAL OF MEDICINAL CHEMISTRY. [J. of med. chem.]. **Added/Corp** American Chemical Society. Vol. 6, No. 1 (Jan. 1963)-. Academic Scholarly Publication. English. Twenty-six times a year. $948.00. American Chemical Society, 1155 Sixteenth Street Northwest, Washington DC 20036. **Tel** (800)333-9511, (800)227-5558, (614)447-3776, FAX (202)447-3671. **(Subscription address:** American Chemical Society / Ohio, Department L 0011, Columbus OH 43268-0011.) **ED** Philip S. Portoghese. Index available (free). **Bk Rev. Ad Acc. Acid Free. Circ:** 4,319 (ctrl). available on microfilm and microfiche from University Microfilms International (UMI). Documents available from The Genuine Article, BIOSIS Document Express, CASDDS. ***Continues*** *Journal of Medicinal and Pharmaceutical Chemistry, 0095-9065.*
Desc: Publishes approximately 300 papers yearly with the relationship of chemistry to biological activity, and features rapid communication of major advances in drug design and development.
Ind/Abst BioBusiness; Biol. Abstr.; Calcium Calcif. Tissue Abstr.; Chem. Abstr.; Chem. Titles; Chemorecept. Abstr.; CSA Neuro. Abstr.; Curr. Aware. Biol. Sci., CABS; Curr. Chem. React.; Curr. Cit.; Curr. Contents Life Sci.; Dairy Sci. Abstr.; EMBASE; Energy Res. Abstr.; Helminthol. Abstr. (19??-19??); IDIS; Immunol. Abstr.; Index Chem.; Index Med.; INIS Atomindex [Micro.]; Int. Pharm. Abstr.; Methods Organ. Synth.; Microbiol. Abstr. Sect. B; Microbiol. Abstr. Sect. A; Microbiol. Abstr. Sect. C; Nat. Prod. Updates; Nutr. Abstr. Rev., Ser. B, Live Feeds and Feed.; Nutr. Abstr. Rev., Ser. A, Hum. Exp.; Life Sci. Collect.; PESTDOC; Protozoolog. Abstr.; Ref. Upd. Basic Ed.; Ref. Upd. Deluxe Ed.; Res. Alert [Full Cov.]; Rev. Med. Vet. Mycology; Rev. Plant Pathol.; Sci. Cit. Index; SCISEARCH; Virol. AIDS Abstr.

LC QP141.A1 J68 ISSN 0955-2863
DD 613.2 US
CCC
NLM W1; JO798HR CODEN JNBIEL
JOURNAL OF NUTRITIONAL BIOCHEMISTRY, THE. [J. nutr. biochem.]. **VFOAT** Nutritional Biochemistry. Vol. 1, No. 1 (Jan. 1990)-. Academic Scholarly Publication. English. Twelve times a year. $465.00. Butterworth Heinemann / Woburn, MA, 225 Wildwood Avenue, Unit B, Woburn MA 01801. **Tel** (800)366-2665, FAX (617)928-2620, telex 880052. **(Subscription address:** Elsevier Science Inc. / New York Books, 655 Avenue of the Americas, New York NY 10010. **Tel** (212)633-3650.) available on microfilm and microfiche from University Microfilms International (UMI). Documents available from The Genuine Article, BIOSIS Document Express, CASDDS. ***Continues*** *Nutrition Reports International, 0029-6635.*
Ind/Abst AGRICOLA [Full Cov.]; Biol. Abstr.; Chem. Abstr. (1990-); Curr. Aware. Biol. Sci., CABS; Curr. Cit.; Curr. Contents Agric. Biol. Environ. Sci.; Curr. Contents Life Sci.; Dairy Sci. Abstr.; EMBASE [Select. Cov.]; Food Sci. Technol. Abstr.; Foods Adlibra (1990-); Nutr. Abstr. Rev., Ser. B, Live Feeds and Feed.; Nutr. Abstr. Rev., Ser. A, Hum. Exp.; Life Sci. Collect.; Poult. Abstr.; Ref. Upd. Deluxe Ed.; Res. Alert [Full Cov.]; Sci. Cit. Index; SCISEARCH; Wheat Barley Trit. Abstr.

LC QP551 .J68 ISSN 0277-8033
DD 574.19/245/05 US
CCC
NLM W1 JO851H CODEN JPCHD2
Pr Rev.
JOURNAL OF PROTEIN CHEMISTRY. [J. protein chem.]. Vol. 1, No. 1 (May 1982)-. Academic Scholarly Publication. English. Eight times a year. $425.00. Plenum Press, 233 Spring Street, New York NY 10013-1578. **Tel** (212)620-8000, (800)221-9369, FAX (212)463-0742, (212)807-1047, telex 23/421139. **ED** M. Z. Atassi. Index available. available on microfilm and microfiche from University Microfilms International (UMI). Documents available from The Genuine Article, BIOSIS Document Express, CASDDS.
Desc: International journal devoted to the publication and communication of original research in all aspects of investigation concerned with the evaluation of the molecular basis for protein function.
Ind/Abst Biocont. News Inf. (1991-); Biol. Abstr. (1989-); Chem. Abstr.; Chem. Titles; Crop Physiol. Abstr.; CSA Neuro. Abstr. (?-?); Curr. Aware. Biol. Sci., CABS; Curr. Cit.; Curr. Contents Life Sci.; Dairy Sci. Abstr.; EMBASE; Field Crop Abstr.; Hortic. Abstr.; Index Med. (Vol. 7, No. 1, 1988-);; Index Vet.; Oncog. Growth Factors Abstr.; Life Sci. Collect. (1985-); Ref. Upd. Deluxe Ed.; Res. Alert [Full Cov.]; Rev. Agric. Entomol.; Rev. Med. Vet. Entomol.; Rev. Plant Pathol.; Sci. Cit. Index; SCISEARCH; Seed Abstr.

LC QP801.S6 J63 ISSN 0960-0760
DD 574.19/243/05 UK
CCC
NLM W1; JO904S CODEN JSBBEZ
Pr Rev.
JOURNAL OF STEROID BIOCHEMISTRY AND MOLECULAR BIOLOGY, THE. [J. steroid biochem. mol. biol.]. Vol. 37, No. 1 (Sept. 1990)-. Periodical. English. Twenty-four times a year. $2225.00. Pergamon Press, An Imprint of Elsevier Science Ltd., The Boulevard, Langford Lane, Kidlington, Oxford OX5 1GB United Kingdom. **Tel** 011 44 1865 843000, 011 44 1865 843699, FAX 011 44 1865 843010. **(Subscription address:** Elsevier Science Ltd. / Oxford Fulfillment Centre, PO Box 800, Kidlington OX5 1DX United Kingdom. **Tel** 011 44 865 843355.) **ED** J. R. Pasqualini. available on microfilm and microfiche from University Microfilms International (UMI); available on an online database from Elsevier Electronic Subscriptions (EES). Documents available from The Genuine Article, BIOSIS Document Express, CASDDS, ADONIS. ***Continues*** *Journal of Steroid Biochemistry, 0022-4731.*
Ind/Abst ADONIS; Anim. Breed. Abstr.; Biol. Abstr.; Chem. Abstr.; Curr. Aware. Biol. Sci., CABS; Curr. Cit.; Curr. Contents Life Sci.; Dairy Sci. Abstr.; EMBASE; Health Plan. Adminis.; Index Med. (Sept. 1990-); Index Vet.; INIS Atomindex [Micro.]; Nutr. Abstr. Rev., Ser. A, Hum. Exp.; Life Sci. Collect.; Poult. Abstr.; Ref. Upd. Basic Ed.; Ref. Upd. Deluxe Ed.; Res. Alert [Full Cov.]; Rev. Med. Vet. Mycology; Sci. Cit. Index; SCISEARCH; Soc. Sci. Cit. Index [Select. Cov.]; SPORT Discus.

LC QD415 ISSN 0379-7368
DD 574.192 CH
NLM W1; JO916M CODEN JCBSB5
JOURNAL OF THE CHINESE BIOCHEMICAL SOCIETY. [J. Chin. Biochem. Soc.]. **Added/Corp** Chung-kuo Sheng wu hua Hsueh hui. **VFOAT** Chung-kuo Sheng wu hua Hsueh hui chi. (1972)-. Academic Scholarly Publication. English. Two times a year. Chinese Biochemical Society, Institute of Biological Chemistry, Academia Sinica, PO Box 23-106, Taipei Taiwan. Documents available from BIOSIS

Document Express, CASDDS.
Ind/Abst AGRICOLA [Select. Cov.]; Biol. Abstr.; Chem. Abstr.; EMBASE.

LC QD415 **ISSN** 0931-2838
DD 574.192 GW
CCC
NLM W1; JO966KDR **CODEN** JTEDET
Pr Rev. **TITLE CHANGE**

JOURNAL OF TRACE ELEMENTS AND ELECTROLYTES IN HEALTH AND DISEASE. Vol. 1, No. 1 (Sept. 1987)-(19??). Periodical. English. Walter de Gruyter Inc., PO Box 303421, D-10728 Berlin Germany. **Tel** 011 49 30 260050, FAX 011 49 30 26005251, telex 184027. **(Subscription address:** Walter de Gruyter Inc. / North America, 200 Saw Mill River Road, Hawthorne NY 10532. **Tel** (914)747-0110.**) ED** P. Bratter, K.D. Kruse-Jarres, I. Lombeck, W. Paterno. **Bk Rev. Ad Acc. Circ:** 800. Documents available from The Genuine Article, CASDDS. ***Continued by** Journal of Trace Elements in Medicine and Biology, 0946-672X.*
Desc: Covers theoretical and applied aspects of trace elements and electrolytes in medicine. It covers the following topics: analytical methods, metabolism (biochemistry and pathobiochemistry), nutrition, toxicology, epidemiology, and clinical applications (diagnosis and therapy).
Ind/Abst Chem. Abstr. (?-?); Chem. Hazards Ind. (?-?); Curr. Cit.; Curr. Contents Life Sci. (?-?); Dairy Sci. Abstr. (?-?); EMBASE (?-?); Index Med. (1987-?); Lab. Hazards Bull. (?-?); Nutr. Abstr. Rev., Ser. B, Live Feeds and Feed. (?-?); Nutr. Abstr. Rev., Ser. A, Hum. Exp. (?-?); Pig News Inf. (?-?); Res. Alert (?-?) [Full Cov.]; Sci. Cit. Index (?-?); SCISEARCH (?-?).

LC QD415.A1 K35 **ISSN** 0453-073X
DD 574 JA
NLM W1 KA367E **CODEN** KASEAA

KAGAKU TO SEIBUTSU. [Kagaku To Seibutsu]. **Added/Corp** Nihon Nogei Kagakkai. (1962)-. Academic Scholarly Publication. Japanese. Twelve times a year. $156.50. Nippon Nogei Kagakkai, (Agricultural Chemical Soc. of Japan), Gakkai Senta Biru, 4-16 Yayoi 2 Chome, Bunkyoku Tokyo 113 Japan. Documents available from CASDDS.
Ind/Abst Chem. Abstr.

LC QD415 **ISSN** 0378-8512
DD 574.192 KO
NLM W1 KO608 **CODEN** KJBID3

KOREAN JOURNAL OF BIOCHEMISTRY. (THE KOREAN JOURNAL OF BIOCHEMISTRY : OFFICIAL JOURNAL OF THE KOREAN BIOCHEMICAL SOCIETY.). [Korean j. biochem.]. **Added/Corp** Taehan Saenghwahakhoe. (19??)-. Periodical. English. Four times a year. $38.00. Korean Biochemical Society, Catholic University College of Medicine, 505 Banpo-dong, Socho-ku Seoul 137-701 South Korea. **Bk Rev. Circ:** 500. Documents available from BIOSIS Document Express, CASDDS. ***Continues** Taehan Saenghwahakhoe Chapchi, 0377-9572.*
Ind/Abst Biol. Abstr.; Chem. Abstr.

LC QP519 .L2 **ISSN** 0075-7535
DD 574.19/2/028 NE
NLM W1 LA232K **CODEN** LTBBDT
Pr Rev.

LABORATORY TECHNIQUES IN BIOCHEMISTRY AND MOLECULAR BIOLOGY. [Lab. tech. biochem. mol. biol.]. Vol. 1 (1969)-. Monographic series. English. Irregular. Price varies per volume. Elsevier Science Publishers BV, PO Box 211, 1000 AE Amsterdam Netherlands. **Tel** 011 31 20 4853641, 011 31 20 4853642, FAX 011 31 20 4853598. **ED** P.C. van der Vliet, A.J. Levine. Documents available from CASDDS.
Desc: Covers all aspects of laboratory work in biochemistry and molecular biology.
Ind/Abst Chem. Abstr.

ISSN 0143-4217
DD 016.57419245 UK
CCC

LECTINS SHEFFIELD. (LECTINS.). [Lectins Sheff.]. (1980)-. English. Twelve times a year. £85.00. SUBIS, Mansion House 19 Kingfield Road, Sheffield S11 9AS United Kingdom. **Tel** 011 44 114 2554433, FAX 011 44 114 255 4626. **Bk Rev. Ad Acc.**
Desc: Current awareness service for researchers and clinicians.

LC QD1 .L7 **ISSN** 0170-2041
DD 540.5/6 GW
CCC
NLM W1 LI26 **CODEN** LACHDL
Pr Rev. **TITLE CHANGE**

LIEBIGS ANNALEN DER CHEMIE. See Chemistry and Chemicals-Organic Chemistry.

LC QP501 .L48 **ISSN** 0278-6281
DD 574.19/2/05 US
CCC
NLM W1; LI39M **CODEN** LCHRDM

LIFE CHEMISTRY REPORTS. [Life chem. rep.]. Vol. 1, No. 1 (1982)-. Academic Scholarly Publication. English. Irregular (2 volumes per year). $425.00 (academic institutions), $662.00 (corporate institutions). Harwood Academic Publishers / New York, PO Box 786, Cooper Station, New York NY 10276. **Tel** (212)206-8900, (201)643-7500. **ED** J. V. Bannister. **Bk Rev. Ad Acc.** Documents available from CASDDS. ***Absorbed** International Journal of Chronobiology, 0300-9998.*
Ind/Abst Chem. Abstr.; Life Sci. Collect.

II

LIFE SCIENCE ADVANCES. BIOCHEMISTRY : A JOURNAL OF THE COUNCIL OF SCIENTIFIC RESEARCH INTEGRATION. VFOAT Biochemistry; Biochemistry - Life Science Advances. Periodical. English. $30.00 (individuals), $60.00 (institutions). Compilers International, 1/25 Nagwa Lanka, Varanasi 221 005 India. ***Continues in part** Life Science Advances, 0255-6642.*

LC QD415 **ISSN** 0956-666X
DD 574.192 UK
CCC
CODEN LITEEI

LIPID TECHNOLOGY. [Lipid technol.]. Vol. 1, No. 1 (Aug. 1989)-. Periodical. English. Six times a year. $218.09. PJ Barnes & Associates, PO Box 345, Wycombe Buckinghamshire HP01 9HL United Kingdom. **Tel** 011 44 1628 520312, FAX 011 44 1628 850035.
Ind/Abst Curr. Cit.

LC QP501 .L5 **ISSN** 0024-4201
DD 574.1/92 US
CCC
NLM W1 LI647 **CODEN** LPDSAP
Pr Rev.

LIPIDS. [Lipids]. **Added/Corp** American Oil Chemists' Society. Vol. 1 (Jan. 1966)-. Academic Scholarly Publication. English. Twelve times a year. $215.00. American Oil Chemists Society, PO Box 3489, Champaign IL 61826-3489. **Tel** (217)359-2344, FAX (217)351-8091, telex 4938651 AOCS UI. **ED** Wolfgang Baumann. Index available (bound in Dec. issue). cum. index. **Circ:** 1,712. available on microfilm and microfiche from University Microfilms International (UMI). Documents available from The Genuine Article, BIOSIS Document Express, CASDDS.
Ind/Abst AGRICOLA [Select. Cov.]; Anal. Abstr.; Biocont. News Inf.; Biol. Abstr.; Chem. Abstr.; Chem. Titles; Crop Physiol. Abstr.; Curr. Aware. Biol. Sci., CABS; Curr. Cit.; Curr. Contents Agric. Biol. Environ. Sci.; Curr. Contents Life Sci.; Curr. Ref. Fish Res.; Dairy Sci. Abstr.; EMBASE; Energy Res. Abstr.; Field Crop Abstr.; Food Sci. Technol. Abstr.; Foods Adlibra; Index Med.; INIS Atomindex [Micro.]; Int. Aerosp. Abstr.; Maize Abstr.; Mass Spect. Bull.; NAPRALERT; Nat. Prod. Updates; Nutr. Abstr. Rev., Ser. B, Live Feeds and Feed.; Nutr. Abstr. Rev., Ser. A, Hum. Exp.; Nutr. Res. Newsl.; Life Sci. Collect.; Pig News Inf.; Plant Breed. Abstr.; Poult. Abstr.; Ref. Upd. Basic Ed.; Ref. Upd. Deluxe Ed.; Res. Alert [Full Cov.]; Rev. Med. Vet. Entomol.; Rice Abstr.; Sci. Cit. Index; SCISEARCH; Soc. Sci. Cit. Index [Select. Cov.]; Soyabean Abstr.; Weed Abstr.

ISSN 0264-9659
DD 016.5748734 UK

LIPOSOMES. [Liposomes]. (1984)-. Periodical. English. Twenty-six times a year. £105.00. SUBIS, Mansion House 19 Kingfield Road, Sheffield S11 9AS United Kingdom. **Tel** 011 44 114 2554433, FAX 011 44 114 255 4626. **Bk Rev. Ad Acc.**
Desc: Current awareness service for researchers and clinicians.

ISSN 0142-8179
DD 016.6110185 UK

LYMPHOCYTES SHEFFIELD. (LYMPHOCYTES.). [Lymphocytes Sheff.]. (1976)-. English. Twenty-six times a year. £75.00. SUBIS, Mansion House 19 Kingfield Road, Sheffield S11 9AS United Kingdom. **Tel** 011 44 114 2554433, FAX 011 44 114 255 4626. **Bk Rev. Ad Acc.**
Desc: Current awareness service for researchers and clinicians.

ISSN 1351-5322
UK

LYSOSOMES & ENDOCYTOSIS. (19??)-. English. $145.45. SUBIS, Mansion House 19 Kingfield Road, Sheffield S11 9AS United Kingdom. **Tel** 011 44 114 2554433, FAX 011 44 114 255 4626. ***Continues** Lysosomes.*

ISSN 0142-8195
DD 016.61242 UK
CCC

MACROPHAGES SHEFFIELD. (MACROPHAGES.). [Macrophages Sheff.]. (1976)-. English. Twelve times a year. £110.00. SUBIS, Mansion House 19 Kingfield Road, Sheffield S11 9AS United Kingdom. **Tel** 011 44 114 2554433, FAX 011 44 114 255 4626.

ISSN 0025-5270
GW
CCC
CODEN MOBHAK

MATERIAL UND ORGANISMEN; BEIHEFT. See Chemistry and Chemicals-Analytical Chemistry.

LC QP552.C6 M38 **ISSN** 0934-8832
DD 591.1/85 GW
CCC
NLM W1; MA974 **CODEN** MTRXEH
Pr Rev. **TITLE CHANGE**

MATRIX (STUTTGART). (MATRIX : COLLAGEN AND RELATED RESEARCH.). [Matrix]. **VFOAT** Collagen and Related Research. Vol. 9, Nr. 1 (Jan. 1989)-Vol. 13, No. 6 (Nov. 1993). Academic Scholarly Publication. English. Gustav Fischer Verlag Stuttgart, Postfach 720143, D-70577 Stuttgart Germany. **Tel** 011 49 711 458030, FAX 011 49 711 4580334, telex 2627-7111488. **ED** S. Gay, E.J. Miller. Documents available from The Genuine Article, BIOSIS Document Express, CASDDS. ***Continues** Collagen and Related Research, 0174-173X.* ***Continued by** Matrix Biology, 0945-053X.*
Desc: Provides an international and interdisciplinary forum for the publications of original articles on collagen. The scope of the journal covers the biochemistry, embryology, histology, immunology, pathology and physiology of collagen and related macromolecules as well as the pathology of the various connective tissues.
Ind/Abst Biol. Abstr. (1989-); Chem. Abstr. (1989-); Curr. Aware. Biol. Sci., CABS; Curr. Cit.; EMBASE; Index Med. (Jan. 1989-); Res. Alert [Full Cov.]; Sci. Cit. Index; SCISEARCH.

LC QH601 .M465 **ISSN** 0149-046X
DD 574.8/75/05 US
CCC
NLM W1; ME8934 **CODEN** MEBIDO
Pr Rev. **TITLE CHANGE**

MEMBRANE BIOCHEMISTRY. [Membr. biochem.]. (1978)-(1993). Academic Scholarly Publication. English. Taylor & Francis Ltd. / UK, Rankine Road, Basingstoke, Hampshire RG24 8PR United Kingdom. **Tel** 011 44 1256 840366, FAX 011 44 1256 479438, telex 858540. **(Subscription address:** Taylor & Francis Inc., 1900 Frost Road, Suite 101, Bristol PA 19007-1598. **Tel** (215)785-5800, (800)821-8312, FAX (215)785-5515.**) ED** Adil E Shamoo (editor's address: Department of Biological Chemistry, University of Maryland School of Medicine, 660 West Redwood Street, Baltimore, MD 21201). **Bk Rev. Ad Acc. Circ:** 600 (ctrl). available on microfilm and microfiche from University Microfilms International (UMI). Documents available from The Genuine Article, BIOSIS Document Express, CASDDS. ***Continued by** Molecular Membrane Biology, 0968-7688.*
Desc: Provides specialists in physiology, biochemistry, biophysics and medicine with a forum for research in the study of membranes. The journal publishes original full-length research papers, short communications, and reviews of current topics in membrane science.
Ind/Abst AGRICOLA; Biol. Abstr.; Chem. Abstr.; CSA Neuro. Abstr. (?-?); Curr. Cit.; Curr. Contents Life Sci.; EMBASE; Index Med.; Life Sci. Collect.; Res. Alert [Full Cov.]; Sci. Cit. Index; SCISEARCH.

ISSN 0952-0422
UK

MEMBRANE LIPIDS. [Membr. lipids]. (1988)-. Periodical. English. Twelve times a year. £75.00. SUBIS, Mansion House 19 Kingfield Road, Sheffield S11 9AS United Kingdom. **Tel** 011 44 114 2554433, FAX 011 44 114 255 4626. **Ad Acc.** ***Continues** Structural Lipids, 0142-8438.*
Desc: Current awareness service for researchers and clinicians.

ISSN 0143-4233
DD 016.574 UK
CCC

MEMBRANE PROTEINS. [Membr. proteins]. (1980)-. English. Twelve times a year. £75.00. SUBIS, Mansion House 19 Kingfield Road, Sheffield S11 9AS United Kingdom. **Tel** 011 44 114 2554433, FAX 011 44 114 255 4626. **Ad Acc.**
Desc: Current awareness service for researchers and clinicians.

LC QP532 .M47 **ISSN** 0161-5149
DD 574.1/9214 US
CCC
NLM W1 ME9611AT **CODEN** MIBSCD

METAL IONS IN BIOLOGICAL SYSTEMS. [Met. ions biol. syst.]. Vol. 1 (1973)-. Monographic series. English. Irregular. Price varies per volume. Marcel Dekker Inc., 270 Madison Avenue, New York NY 10016. **Tel** (212)696-9000, (800)228-1160, FAX (212)685-4540, telex 421419. **(Subscription address:** Marcel Dekker Inc., PO Box 5017, Monticello NY 12701. **Tel** (800)228-1160.**)** Documents available from The Genuine Article, CASDDS.
Desc: This is an ongoing series. Each title has a different subject.
Ind/Abst AGRICOLA [Select. Cov.]; Chem. Abstr.; Curr. Cit.; Index Sci. Rev. [Full Cov.]; Res. Alert [Full Cov.]; Sci. Cit. Index; SCISEARCH.

LC QD415 ISSN 0271-2911
DD 574.192 US
NLM W1 ME9611AU CODEN MIOBDS
METAL IONS IN BIOLOGY. [Metal ions biol.]. (1980). Academic Scholarly Publication. English. Irregular. Price varies per volume. John Wiley & Sons, Inc., 605 Third Avenue, New York NY 10158-0012. **Tel** (212)850-6000, (212)850-6645, FAX (212)850-6088, telex 12-7063. **(Subscription address:** John Wiley & Sons / UK, Baffins Lane, Chichester, West Sussex PO19 1UD United Kingdom. **Tel** 011 44 1243 779777, FAX 011 44 243 776128, telex 86290 WIBOOKG.**)** **ED** T G Spiro. Documents available from CASDDS.
Ind/Abst Chem. Abstr. (19??-).

UK
•METHODOLOGICAL SURVEYS IN BIOANALYSIS OF DRUGS. **Added/Corp** Royal Society of Chemistry (Great Britain). **VFOAT** Biochemistry; Analysis (Trace-Organic). (1993)-. Academic Scholarly Publication. English. Price varies per volume. Royal Society of Chemistry, Thomas Graham House, Science Park, Cambridge CB4 4WF United Kingdom. **Tel** 011 44 1223 420066, FAX 011 44 1223 423623, telex 818293 ROYAL. **(Subscription address:** Royal Society of Chemistry, Turpin Distribution Services Ltd., Blackhorse Road, Letchworth, Hertfordshire SG6 1HN United Kingdom. **Tel** 011 44 1462 672555, FAX 011 44 1462 480947.**)** **ED** Eric Reid. ***Continues*** *Methodological Surveys in Biochemistry and Analysis, 0748-6715.*
Ind/Abst Biol. Abstr.; Chem. Abstr.

LC QP601 .M49 ISSN 0076-6879
DD 574.19/25/0287 US
CCC
NLM W1 ME9615K CODEN MENZAU
Pr Rev.
METHODS IN ENZYMOLOGY. [Methods enzymol.]. Vol. 1 (1955)-. Monographic series. English. Irregular. Price varies per volume. Academic Press Inc., 6277 Sea Harbor Drive, Orlando FL 32887. **Tel** (800)543-9534, (407)345-4100, FAX (407)352-3445. **ED** Sidney P. Colowick and Nathan O. Kaplan. cum. index. available on CD-ROM. Documents available from The Genuine Article, BIOSIS Document Express, CASDDS.
Ind/Abst AGRICOLA; Biol. Abstr.; Biotechnol. Res. Abstr.; Chem. Abstr.; CSA Neuro. Abstr. (?-?); Curr. Biotechnol.; Curr. Cit.; Dairy Sci. Abstr.; EMBASE; Energy Res. Abstr. (Feb. 1976-); Genet. Abstr.; Index Med.; Index Sci. Rev. [Full Cov.]; Microbiol. Abstr. Sect. C; Nutr. Abstr. Rev., Ser. B, Live Feeds and Feed.; Life Sci. Collect.; Plant Breed. Abstr.; Ref. Upd. Basic Ed.; Ref. Upd. Deluxe Ed.; Res. Alert [Full Cov.]; Sci. Cit. Index; SCISEARCH; Trop. Dis. Bull.

LC QD271 .M46 ISSN 0076-6941
DD 543.8 US
CCC
NLM W1 ME9617 CODEN MBANAA
METHODS OF BIOCHEMICAL ANALYSIS. **See** Chemistry and Chemicals-Analytical Chemistry.

LC QP519.7 .M474 ISSN 1046-2023
DD 574.19/28 US
CCC
CODEN MTHDE9
METHODS (SAN DIEGO, CALIF.). (METHODS. A COMPANION TO METHODS IN ENZYMOLOGY.). [Methods]. Vol. 1, No. 1 (Aug. 1990)-. Academic Scholarly Publication. English. Six times a year. $215.00. Academic Press Inc., 6277 Sea Harbor Drive, Orlando FL 32887. **Tel** (800)543-9534, (407)345-4100, FAX (407)352-3445. **ED** John N. Abelson, Melvin I. Simon. Documents available from BIOSIS Document Express, CASDDS. ***Absorbed*** *Methods. GenoMethods, 1078-1501; Methods. ImmunoMethods, 1078-151X* ***and*** *NeuroProtocols, 1058-6741.*
Desc: The articles in the topic-oriented issues comprising this journal present new methods applicable to a number of disciplines. Each issue is devoted to a specific approach or technique and describes its theoretical basis. Emphasis is placed on clear descriptions of protocols which allow applications of these methods in any modern laboratory. Each issue is organized by a special editor and consists of a set of invited articles.
Ind/Abst Biol. Abstr. (1990-); Chem. Abstr. (1990-); Curr. Cit.

LC R ISSN 0294-0671
DD 615 FR
NLM W1 MI791QP CODEN MPBPDK
MISES AU POINT DE BIOCHIMIE PHARMACOLOGIQUE. **See** Pharmacy and Pharmacology.

LC RA421 .M76 ISSN 0026-6841
DD 613 SZ
NLM W1 MI945 CODEN MGLHAE
MITTEILUNGEN AUS DEM GEBIETE DER LEBENSMITTELUNTERSUCHUNG UND HYGIENE. [Mitt. Geb. Lebensmittelunters. hyg.]. **Added/Corp** Switzerland. Eidgenossisches Gesundheitsamt. Switzerland. Bundesamt fur Gesundheitswesen. Schweizerischer Verein Analytischer Chemiker. Schweizerische Gesellschaft fur Analytische und Angewandte Chemie. **VFOAT** Travaux de Chimie Alimentaire et d'Hygiene. Vol. 1 (1910)-. Periodical. French (German and Italian; summaries and/or abstracts in English). Four times a year. $62.21. Bundesamt fuer Gesundheitswesen, Haslerstrasse 16, Postfach CH-3000, Bern Switzerland. Documents available from BIOSIS Document Express, CASDDS.
Ind/Abst AGRICOLA; Alum. Ind. Abstr.; Anal. Abstr.; BioBusiness; Biodeter. Abstr. (1991-); Biol. Abstr.; Chem. Abstr.; Curr. Cit.; Dairy Sci. Abstr.; Food Sci. Technol. Abstr.; Maize Abstr.; Met. Abstr.; Nutr. Abstr. Rev., Ser. A, Hum. Exp.; Life Sci. Collect.; PESTDOC; Potato Abstr.; Poult. Abstr.; Vitis Vitic. Enol. Abstr.

LC QR151 .M7 ISSN 0300-8177
DD 574.8/76 NE
CCC
NLM W1 MO194T CODEN MCBIB8
Pr Rev.
MOLECULAR AND CELLULAR BIOCHEMISTRY. [Mol. cell. biochem.]. Vol. 1 (May 1973)-. English. Twenty-four times a year. $3256.00. Kluwer Academic Publishers / Massachusetts, PO Box 358, Accord Station, Hingham MA 02018. **Tel** (617)871-6600. **ED** Naranjan S Dhalla. **Acid Free.** available on microfilm and microfiche from University Microfilms International (UMI). Documents available from The Genuine Article, BIOSIS Document Express, CASDDS. ***Supersedes*** *Enzymologia, 0013-9424.*
Desc: Publishes original research articles in all areas of the biochemical sciences, the emphasis being on those papers which present novel findings relevant to the biochemical basis of cellular function and disease processes, as well as the mechanisms of action of hormones and chemical agents.
Ind/Abst AGRICOLA [Select. Cov.]; Biol. Abstr.; Calcium Calcif. Tissue Abstr.; Chem. Abstr.; Chem. Titles; CSA Neuro. Abstr.; Curr. Biotechnol.; Curr. Cit.; Curr. Contents Life Sci.; Curr. Ref. Fish Res.; Dairy Sci. Abstr.; EMBASE; Energy Res. Abstr. (Dec. 1974-); Food Sci. Technol. Abstr.; Genet. Abstr.; Immunol. Abstr.; Index Med.; Microbiol. Abstr. Sect. B (19??-19??); Microbiol. Abstr. Sect. C; Nat. Prod. Updates; Nutr. Abstr. Rev., Ser. A, Hum. Exp.; Life Sci. Collect.; PESTDOC; Protozoolog. Abstr.; Ref. Upd. Basic Ed.; Ref. Upd. Deluxe Ed.; Res. Alert [Full Cov.]; Sci. Cit. Index; SCISEARCH; Trop. Dis. Bull.

LC RB112 .M64 ISSN 0098-2997
DD 616.07 UK
CCC
NLM W1 MO195H CODEN MAMED5MAMED
MOLECULAR ASPECTS OF MEDICINE. **See** Medical Sciences-Pathology.

LC QH611 ISSN 1356-1324
DD 574.8 UK
•MOLECULAR BIOLOGY TECHNIQUES. (1995)-. Academic Scholarly Publication. English. Twenty-four times a year. £105.00. SUBIS, Mansion House 19 Kingfield Road, Sheffield S11 9AS United Kingdom. **Tel** 011 44 114 2554433, FAX 011 44 114 255 4626.

LC QH601 .M465 ISSN 0968-7688
DD 574.8/75/05 UK
NLM W1; MO196LS CODEN MMEBE7
•MOLECULAR MEMBRANE BIOLOGY. [Mol. membr. biol.]. **VFOAT** MMB. Vol. 11, No. 1 (Jan./Mar. 1994)-. Periodical. English. Four times a year. $175.00. Taylor & Francis Ltd. / UK, Rankine Road, Basingstoke, Hampshire RG24 8PR United Kingdom. **Tel** 011 44 1256 840366, FAX 011 44 1256 479438, telex 858540. **(Subscription address:** Taylor & Francis Inc., 1900 Frost Road, Suite 101, Bristol PA 19007-1598. **Tel** (215)785-5800, (800)821-8312, FAX (215)785-5515.**)** **ED** Adil E. Shamoo (editor's address: Department of Biological Chemistry, University of Maryland School of Medicine, 660 West Redwood Street, Baltimore, MD 21201). **Bk Rev. Ad Acc.** ***Continues*** *Membrane Biochemistry, 0149-046X.*
Ind/Abst Curr. Cit.; Index Med.

ISSN 1351-5292
UK
MYCOBACTERIA. (19??)-. English. $145.45. SUBIS, Mansion House 19 Kingfield Road, Sheffield S11 9AS United Kingdom. **Tel** 011 44 114 2554433, FAX 011 44 114 255 4626.

LC QD415.A1 N378 ISSN 1057-5634
DD 547.7/05 UK
CCC
CODEN NPLEEF
NATURAL PRODUCT LETTERS. [Nat. prod. lett.]. Vol. 1, No. 1 (1992)-. Academic Scholarly Publication. English. Four times a year. $226.00 (academic libraries), $352.00 (corporate libraries). Harwood Academic Publishers, PO Box 90, Reading RG1 8JL United Kingdom. **Tel** 011 44 1734 560080, FAX 011 44 1734 568211. Documents available from CASDDS.
Desc: Covers all aspects of research in the chemistry and biochemistry of naturally occuring compounds.
Ind/Abst Chem. Abstr.

LC QD415.A1 ISSN 0265-0568
DD 574.192 UK
CCC
NLM W1; NA805H CODEN NPRRDF
Pr Rev.
NATURAL PRODUCT REPORTS. (NATURAL PRODUCT REPORTS : A JOURNAL OF CURRENT DEVELOPMENTS IN BIO-ORGANIC CHEMISTRY.). [Nat. prod. rep.]. **Added/Corp** Royal Society of Chemistry (Great Britain). Vol. 1, No. 1 (Feb. 1984)-. Academic Scholarly Publication. English. Six times a year (plus an index). $615.00. Royal Society of Chemistry, Thomas Graham House, Science Park, Cambridge CB4 4WF United Kingdom. **Tel** 011 44 1223 420066, FAX 011 44 1223 423623, telex 818293 ROYAL. **(Subscription address:** Royal Society of Chemistry, Turpin Distribution Services Ltd., Blackhorse Road, Letchworth, Hertfordshire SG6 1HN United Kingdom. **Tel** 011 44 1462 672555, FAX 011 44 1462 480947.**)** Index available (free). available on microfilm and microfiche from University Microfilms International (UMI). Documents available from The Genuine Article, BIOSIS Document Express, CASDDS. ***Formed by the union of*** *Alkaloids, 0305-9707; Biosynthesis, 0301-0708; Aliphatic and Related Natural Product Chemistry, 0142-7318* ***and*** *Terpenoids and Steroids, 0300-5992.*
Desc: Covers such areas as chemotaxonomy, enzymology and biosynthetic aspects of biotechnology, and also advances in physical techniques used for structure determination, e.g.: n.m.r., h.p.l.c. mass spectrometry, and chiroptical data.
Ind/Abst AGRICOLA [Select. Cov.]; Biol. Abstr. (-1985); Chem. Abstr. (1984-); Curr. Aware. Biol. Sci., CABS; Curr. Chem. React.; Curr. Cit.; Curr. Contents Phys. Chem. Earth Sci.; Index Med. Feb. 1984-; Index Sci. Rev. [Full Cov.]; Methods Organ. Synth.; NAPRALERT; Nat. Prod. Updates; Res. Alert [Full Cov.]; Sci. Cit. Index; SCISEARCH.

ISSN 0142-8403
DD 016.574 UK
CCC
NEUROCHEMISTRY SHEFFIELD. (NEUROCHEMISTRY.). [Neurochemistry Sheff.]. (1973)-. English. Twelve times a year. £75.00. SUBIS, Mansion House 19 Kingfield Road, Sheffield S11 9AS United Kingdom. **Tel** 011 44 114 2554433, FAX 011 44 114 255 4626. **Ad Acc.**
Desc: Current awareness service for researchers and clinicians.

LC QD415 ISSN 0167-7306
DD 574.192 US
CCC
NLM W1 NE372F CODEN NCBIDL
Pr Rev.
NEW COMPREHENSIVE BIOCHEMISTRY. [New compr. biochem.]. Vol. 1 (1981)-. Monographic series. English. Irregular. Price varies per volume. Elsevier Science Publishing Company Inc, Madison Square Station, PO Box 882, New York NY 10159-0882. **Tel** (212)633-3950, FAX (212)633-3990. **ED** A. Neuberger and L.L.M. van Deenen. Documents available from BIOSIS Document Express, CASDDS.
Desc: Designed to keep scientists informed of developments in the biochemical sciences.
Ind/Abst Biol. Abstr. (1986-); Chem. Abstr.; Curr. Cit.

LC QD415 ISSN 1011-6672
DD 574.192 SZ
NLM W1; NE513FN CODEN NTLREE
NEW TRENDS IN LIPID MEDIATORS RESEARCH. [New trends lipid mediat. res.]. Vol. 1 (1988)-. Monographic series. English. One time a year. 200.00F (approx. per volume). S. Karger AG, Allschwilerstrasse 10, PO Box, CH-4009 Basel Switzerland. **Tel** 011 41 61 3061111, FAX 011 41 61 3061234, telex CH 962 652. **ED** P. Braquet. Index available. ctrl circ. Documents available from BIOSIS Document Express.
Desc: Aims to define and reevaluate the role of lipid mediators in various pathological situations. Considers the development of antagonists of PAF and new drugs used to modulate the effects of the mediator.
Ind/Abst Biol. Abstr.; Ref. Upd. Deluxe Ed.

BE
NEWSLETTER BIOCHEMICAL AND HEALTH RESEARCH. Newsletter. English. Three times a year. Free. Medical Research Division, Comm of European Communities, B-1049 Brussels Belgium.

ISSN 0913-3348
DD 574.192 JA
NIHON OYO KOSO KYOKAISHI. [Nihon Oyo Koso Kyokaishi]. (1966)-. Academic Scholarly Publication. Japanese. One time a year. Nihon Oyo Koso Kyokai, (Japan Foundation for Applied Enzymology), 16-89 Kashima 3 Chome, Yodogawaku Osakashi, Osakafu 532 Japan. Documents available from CASDDS.
Ind/Abst Chem. Abstr.

LC QD415 **ISSN** 0002-1407
DD 631 JA
CODEN NNKKAA
Pr Rev.
NIPPON NOGEI KAGAKU KAISHI. **See** Agriculture.

LC QD415 **ISSN** 0392-7091
DD 574.192 IT
CODEN NSICDE
NOTIZIARIO - SOCIETA ITALIANA DI BIOCHIMICA CLINICA. (NOTIZIARIO / SOCIETA ITALIANA DE BIOCHIMICA CLINICA.). [Not. - Soc. ital. biochim. clin.]. **Added/Corp** Societa Italiana di Biochimica Clinica. **VFOAT** Newsletter. (1978)-. Academic Scholarly Publication. Italian. Twelve times a year. Societa Italiana di Biochimica Clinica. Documents available from CASDDS.
Ind/Abst Chem. Abstr.

LC Z5320 **ISSN** 1070-2466
DD 16.574 US
NLM ZQU 58; N964
•**NUCLEIC ACIDS ABSTRACTS (1994).** **See** Biology-Abstracting, Bibliographies and Statistics.

LC QP620 .N795 **ISSN** 0933-1891
DD 574.87/328/05 GW
NLM W1; NU128U **CODEN** NAMBE8
NUCLEIC ACIDS AND MOLECULAR BIOLOGY. [Nucleic acids mol. biol.]. Vol. 1 (1987)-. Academic Scholarly Publication. English. One time a year. $190.38. Springer-Verlag GmbH & Company KG, Heidelberger Platz 3, D-14197 Berlin Germany. **Tel** 011 49 30 8207223, FAX 011 49 30 8214091, telex 183 319 SPBLN D. **(Subscription address:** Springer-Verlag New York Inc. / North America, PO Box 2485, Journal Fulfillment, Secaucus NJ 07096. **Tel** (201)348-4033, (800)777-4643, FAX (201)348-4505.) Documents available from BIOSIS Document Express, CASDDS.
Ind/Abst AGRICOLA [Select. Cov.]; Biol. Abstr. (1987-); Chem. Abstr.; Curr. Cit.; PESTDOC.

ISSN 0005-2787
NE
NUCLEIC ACIDS AND PROTEIN SYNTHESIS. (Dec. 4, 1960)-. Academic Scholarly Publication. English. Twelve times a year. Elsevier Science Publishers BV, PO Box 211, 1000 AE Amsterdam Netherlands. **Tel** 011 31 20 4853641, 011 31 20 4853642, FAX 011 31 20 4853598. available on microfilm from University Microfilms International (UMI).

LC QP620 .N8 **ISSN** 0305-1048
DD 574.8/732 UK
CCC
NLM W1 NU129 **CODEN** NARHAD
Pr Rev.
NUCLEIC ACIDS RESEARCH. [Nucleic acids res.]. Vol. 1 (Jan. 1974)-. Periodical. English. Irregular (25 issues). $1325.00. Oxford University Press / UK, Walton Street, Oxford OX2 6DP United Kingdom. **Tel** 011 44 1865 56767, FAX 011 44 1865 267773, telex 851/837330 OXPRES G. **(Subscription address:** Oxford University Press / USA, Journals Marketing Department, Oxford University Press, 2001 Evans Road, Cary NC 27513. **Tel** (800)451-7556, (919)677-0977, FAX (919)677-1714.) **ED** R. T. Walker. Index available. **Ad Acc. Circ:** 2,500. available on microfilm and microfiche from University Microfilms International (UMI). Documents available from The Genuine Article, CASDDS.
Desc: Covers nucleic acids, their constituents and analogues. Information on sequence data, NMR assignment data, and useful improvements to existing methods.
Ind/Abst AgBiotech News Inf.; AGRICOLA [Select. Cov.]; Biocont. News Inf. (19??-19??); Biodeter. Abstr. (1991-); Biotechnol. Res. Abstr.; Chem. Abstr.; Chem. Titles; Crop Physiol. Abstr.; CSA Neuro. Abstr. (?-?); Curr. Biotechnol.; Curr. Cit.; Curr. Contents Life Sci.; Dairy Sci. Abstr.; EMBASE; Entomol. Abstr.; Field Crop Abstr.; Food Sci. Technol. Abstr.; For. Abstr.; Genet. Abstr.; Helminthol. Abstr. (19??-19??); Hum. Genome Abstr.; Immunol. Abstr.; Index Med.; Microbiol. Abstr. Sect. B; Microbiol. Abstr. Sect. C; Nematol. Abstr.; Nucl. Acids Abstr.; Oncog. Growth Factors Abstr.; Life Sci. Collect.; PESTDOC; Pig News Inf.; Plant Breed. Abstr.; Plant Grow. Reg. Abstr.; Postharvest News Inf.; Potato Abstr.; Protozoolog. Abstr.; Ref. Upd. Basic Ed.; Ref. Upd. Deluxe Ed.; Res. Alert [Full Cov.]; Rev. Agric. Entomol.; Rev. Med. Vet. Entomol.; Rev. Med. Vet. Mycology; Rev. Plant Pathol.; Rice Abstr.; Sci. Cit. Index; SCISEARCH; Seed Abstr.; Soils Fert.; Soyabean Abstr.; Trop. Dis. Bull.; Virol. AIDS Abstr.; Weed Abstr.

LC QD415.A1 **ISSN** 0261-3166
DD 574.192 UK
CCC
NLM W3 NU36 **CODEN** NACSD8
NUCLEIC ACIDS SYMPOSIUM SERIES. [Nucleic acids symp. ser.]. **VFOAT** Nucleic Acids Research. Symposium Series. No. 6 (1979)-. Academic Scholarly Publication. English. Irregular (Two per year). $120.00. Oxford University Press / UK, Walton Street, Oxford OX2 6DP United Kingdom. **Tel** 011 44 1865 56767, FAX 011 44 1865 267773, telex 851/837330 OXPRES G. **(Subscription address:** Oxford University Press / USA, Journals Marketing Department, Oxford University Press, 2001 Evans Road, Cary NC 27513. **Tel** (800)451-7556, (919)677-0977, FAX (919)677-1714.) Documents available from BIOSIS Document Express, CASDDS. ***Continues*** *Nucleic Acids Research. Special Publication, 0309-1872.*
Desc: A record of nucleic acids research in laboratories around the world.
Ind/Abst Biol. Abstr. (1986-); Chem. Abstr.; Chem. Titles; Curr. Cit.; Index Med.

LC QD320 .N82 **ISSN** 0732-8311
DD 574.19/249/05 US
CCC
NLM W1 NU136M **CODEN** NUNUD5NUNUDS
Pr Rev.
NUCLEOSIDES & NUCLEOTIDES. [Nucleosides nucleotides]. **VFOAT** Nucleosides and Nucleotides. Vol. 1, No. 1 (1982)-. Academic Scholarly Publication. English (French and German). Twelve times a year. $995.00. Marcel Dekker Inc., 270 Madison Avenue, New York NY 10016. **Tel** (212)696-9000, (800)228-1160, FAX (212)685-4540, telex 421419. **(Subscription address:** Marcel Dekker Inc., PO Box 5017, Monticello NY 12701. **Tel** (800)228-1160.) **ED** John A. Secrist, III. **Bk Rev. Ad Acc.** ctrl circ. available on microfiche. Documents available from The Genuine Article, BIOSIS Document Express, CASDDS. ***Continues in part*** *Journal of Carbohydrates, Nucleosides, Nucleotides, 0094-0585.*
Desc: This all-inclusive journal features research articles; short notices; and concise, critical reviews of related topics in the organic and medicinal chemistry and biochemistry of nucleosides and nucleotides. Presenting the latest original research papers with complete experimental details. Emphasizes the synthesis, biological activities, new and improved synthetic methods, and significant observations relating to new compounds.
Ind/Abst Abstr. Bull. Inst. Pap. Sci. Tech.; Biol. Abstr.; Chem. Abstr.; Chem. Titles; Curr. Aware. Biol. Sci., CABS; Curr. Biotechnol.; Curr. Chem. React.; Curr. Cit.; Curr. Contents Life Sci.; EMBASE; Index Chem.; Ref. Upd. Deluxe Ed.; Res. Alert [Full Cov.]; Sci. Cit. Index; SCISEARCH.

LC QD415
DD 574.192 US
NUTRITIONAL BIOCHEMICALS.
Added/Corp ICN Nutritional Biochemicals. **VFOAT** ICN Nutritional Biochemicals. (19??)-. English. ICN Nutritional Biochemicals, PO Box 28050, Cleveland OH 44128.

ISSN 0950-057X
DD 016.57419258 UK
CCC
OXYGEN RADICALS. [Oxyg. radic.]. (1987)-. Periodical. English. Twenty-four times a year. $196.79. SUBIS, Mansion House 19 Kingfield Road, Sheffield S11 9AS United Kingdom. **Tel** 011 44 114 2554433, FAX 011 44 114 255 4626. **Bk Rev. Ad Acc.**
Desc: Current awareness service for researchers and clinicians.

LC QP501 .P34 **ISSN** 0300-8185
DD 574.1/92/05 PK
NLM W1 PA35 **CODEN** PJBIAL
PAKISTAN JOURNAL OF BIOCHEMISTRY. [Pak. j. biochem.]. Vol. 1 (April-Oct. 1968)-. Academic Scholarly Publication. English. University of Punjab / Pakistan Society of Biochemists, Lahore 1 Pakistan. Documents available from BIOSIS Document Express, CASDDS.
Ind/Abst AGRICOLA; Biodeter. Abstr.; Biol. Abstr.; Chem. Abstr.; Crop Physiol. Abstr.; EMBASE; Field Crop Abstr.; Index Vet.; Irr. Drain. Abstr.; Nutr. Abstr. Rev., Ser. A, Hum. Exp.; Poult. Abstr.; Seed Abstr.; Vet. Bull.

ISSN 1146-5255
FR
UDC 011
PASCAL. F 52, BIOCHIMIE, BIOPHYSIQUE MOLECULAIRE, BIOLOGIE MOLECULAIRE ET CELLULAIRE. **VFOAT** PASCAL. F 52, Biochemistry, Molecular Biophysics, Molecular and Cellular Biology; PASCAL. F Cinquante Deux, Biochimie, Biophysique Moleculaire, Biologie Moleculaire et Cellulaire. (1990)-. Periodical. Multiple languages. Ten times a year. 1720.00F France; 1820.00F other. CNRS / Institut d'Information Scientifique et Technique, (Centre National de la Recherche Scientifique), 15 Quai Anatole France, 75700 Paris France. **Tel** 011 33 1 47531515, FAX 011 33 1 45517307, telex 260034. ***Continues*** *Pascal Folio. F52: Biochimie, Biophysique, Moleculaire Biologie, Moleculaire et Cellulaire.*

ISSN 0268-1552
DD 016.612405 UK
CCC
PEPTIDE HORMONE RECEPTORS. [Pept. horm. recept.]. (1986)-. English. Twelve times a year. $128.34. SUBIS, Mansion House 19 Kingfield Road, Sheffield S11 9AS United Kingdom. **Tel** 011 44 114 2554433, FAX 011 44 114 255 4626. **Ad Acc.**
Desc: Current awareness service for researchers and clinicians.

LC QP552.P4 P467 **ISSN** 0196-9781
DD 599.01/92456 US
CCC
NLM W1 PE77 **CODEN** PPTDD5
Pr Rev.
PEPTIDES (NEW YORK, N.Y, : 1980). (PEPTIDES.). [Peptides]. Vol. 1 (Spring 1980)-. Academic Scholarly Publication. English. Eight times a year. $1250.00. Pergamon Press, An Imprint of Elsevier Science Ltd., The Boulevard, Langford Lane, Kidlington, Oxford OX5 1GB United Kingdom. **Tel** 011 44 1865 843000, 011 44 1865 843699, FAX 011 44 1865 843010. **(Subscription address:** Elsevier Science Ltd. / Oxford Fulfillment Centre, PO Box 800, Kidlington OX5 1DX United Kingdom. **Tel** 011 44 865 843355.) **ED** Abba J. Kastin. **Bk Rev. Ad Acc.** ctrl circ. available on microfilm and microfiche from University Microfilms International (UMI); available on an online database from Elsevier Electronic Subscriptions (EES). Documents available from The Genuine Article, BIOSIS Document Express, CASDDS, ADONIS.
Desc: Publishes original reports of systematic studies on the chemistry, biochemistry, neurochemistry, endocrinology, gastroenterology, physiology and the neurological and behavioral effects of the peptides.
Ind/Abst ADONIS; Anim. Breed. Abstr.; Biodeter. Abstr.; Biol. Abstr.; Chem. Abstr.; Chem. Titles; CSA Neuro. Abstr.; Curr. Aware. Biol. Sci., CABS; Curr. Cit.; Curr. Contents Life Sci.; Dairy Sci. Abstr.; EMBASE; Helminthol. Abstr.; Index Med.; Index Vet.; Nutr. Abstr. Rev., Ser. B, Live Feeds and Feed.; Nutr. Abstr. Rev., Ser. A, Hum. Exp.; Life Sci. Collect.; Pig News Inf.; Poult. Abstr.; Protozoolog. Abstr.; Psychol. Abstr. (1981-); PsycINFO; PsycLit; Ref. Upd. Basic Ed.; Ref. Upd. Deluxe Ed.; Res. Alert [Full Cov.]; Rev. Agric. Entomol.; Rev. Med. Vet. Entomol.; Sci. Cit. Index; SCISEARCH; Soc. Sci. Cit. Index [Select. Cov.]; Vet. Bull.

LC QP550 .P46 **ISSN** 1062-239X
DD 574.19/214/05 UK
NLM W1; PE872CL **CODEN** PBICEK
PERSPECTIVES ON BIOINORGANIC CHEMISTRY. [Perspect. bioinorg. chem.]. **VFOAT** Bioinorganic Chemistry. Vol. 1 (1991)-. Academic Scholarly Publication. English. Irregular. $90.25. JAI Press Inc., 55 Old Post Road, Suite 2, PO Box 1678, Greenwich CT 06836-1678. **Tel** (203)661-7602, FAX (203)661-0792. **ED** R.W. Hay, Jon R. Dilworth, Kevin B. Nolan. Documents available from CASDDS.
Ind/Abst Chem. Abstr.

LC QD415
DD 574.192 US
PHARMACOLOGY BIOCHEMISTRY & BEHAVIOR. SUPPLEMENT. **See** Pharmacy and Pharmacology.

ISSN 0264-9624
DD 016.54777 UK
PHOSPHOLIPIDS. [Phospholipids]. (1984)-. Periodical. English. Twelve times a year. £75.00. SUBIS, Mansion House 19 Kingfield Road, Sheffield S11 9AS United Kingdom. **Tel** 011 44 114 2554433, FAX 011 44 114 255 4626. **Ad Acc.**
Desc: Current awareness service for researchers and clinicians.

LC QH515 .P47 **ISSN** 0363-499X
DD 574.19/153 US
NLM W1 PH653 **CODEN** PPHRDL
PHOTOCHEMICAL AND PHOTOBIOLOGICAL REVIEWS. [Photochem. photobiol. rev.]. Vol. 1 (1976)-. Academic Scholarly Publication. English. Irregular. $85.00 US and Canada; $102.00 other. Plenum Press, 233 Spring Street, New York NY 10013-1578. **Tel** (212)620-8000, (800)221-9369, FAX (212)463-0742, (212)807-1047, telex 23/421139. Documents available from BIOSIS Document Express, CASDDS.
Ind/Abst Biol. Abstr. (-1980); Chem. Abstr.

LC QD601.A1 P48 **ISSN** 0031-8655
DD 574.192 UK
CCC
NLM W1 PH661 **CODEN** PHCBAP
Pr Rev.
PHOTOCHEMISTRY AND PHOTOBIOLOGY. [Photochem. photobiol.]. Vol. 1 (Jan./Mar. 1962)-. Academic Scholarly Publication. English. Twelve times a year. $525.00. American Society of Photobiology, PO Box 3271, Augusta GA 30914. **(Subscription address:** Allen Press, PO Box 1897, Lawrence KS 66044. **Tel** (800)627-0629.) **ED** Pill-Soon Song. **Ad Acc. Acid Free.** available on microfilm and microfiche from University Microfilms International (UMI). Documents available from The Genuine Article, BIOSIS Document Express, CASDDS.
Desc: Publishes papers on all aspects of photochemistry and photobiology.
Ind/Abst AGRICOLA [Select. Cov.]; Anal. Abstr.; Biol. Abstr.; Chem. Abstr.; Chem. Titles; Crop Physiol. Abstr.; Curr. Aware. Biol. Sci., CABS; Curr. Cit.; Curr. Contents Life Sci.; Ei Page One; EMBASE; Field Crop Abstr.; Genet. Abstr.; Hortic. Abstr.; Index Med.; Int. Aerosp. Abstr.; Microbiol. Abstr. Sect. B; Microbiol. Abstr. Sect. C; Nematol. Abstr.; Nucl. Acids Abstr.; Ornamental Hort. (1991-); Life Sci. Collect.; Protozoolog. Abstr.; Ref. Upd.

Deluxe Ed.; Res. Alert [Full Cov.]; Rev. Med. Vet. Entomol.; Rev. Plant Pathol.; Sci. Cit. Index; SCISEARCH; Weed Abstr.

LC QK882 .P563 **ISSN** 0300-3604
NE
CCC
NLM W1 PH672K **CODEN** PHSYB5
Pr Rev.
PHOTOSYNTHETICA. See Biology-Botany.

LC QP501 .P48 **ISSN** 0748-6642
DD 574.19/2/05 US
NLM W1; PH926K **CODEN** PCPNER
Pr Rev.
PHYSIOLOGICAL CHEMISTRY AND PHYSICS AND MEDICAL NMR. [Physiol. chem. phys. med. NMR]. **VFOAT** Medical NMR; PCP. Vol. 15, No. 1 (1983)-. Academic Scholarly Publication. English. Four times a year (Mar., June, Sept., Dec.). $80.00. Pacific Press Inc., PO Box 1452, Melville NY 11747. **Tel** (516)694-2929, Ext. 246, FAX (516)249-3734. **ED** Gilbert N. Ling (editor's address: Damadian Foundation for Basic and Cancer Research c/o Fonar 110 Marcus Drive Melville NY 11747). Index available (Bound in 4th issue). **Bk Rev. Ad Acc. Circ:** 400. Documents available from The Genuine Article, CASDDS. ***Continues** Physiological Chemistry and Physics, 0031-9325.*
Desc: Original articles (as well as reviews) on the widest range of approaches toward elucidating the basic mechanism of molecular and cellular physiology and medicine. It provides a forum for publications that deal with major issues in a way that agrees with, or disagrees with, traditional beliefs. It encourages freedom of expression and scientific excellence.
Ind/Abst Chem. Abstr. (1983-); Curr. Aware. Biol. Sci., CABS; Curr. Cit.; Curr. Contents Life Sci.; Index Med.; Life Sci. Collect.; Res. Alert [Full Cov.]; Sci. Cit. Index; SCISEARCH.

ISSN 0143-4225
DD 016.612405 UK
CCC
POLYPEPTIDES SHEFFIELD. (POLYPEPTIDES.). [Polypeptides Sheff.]. (1980)-. English. Twelve times a year. £75.00. SUBIS, Mansion House 19 Kingfield Road, Sheffield S11 9AS United Kingdom. **Tel** 011 44 114 2554433, FAX 011 44 114 255 4626.

LC QP501 .P6 **ISSN** 0032-5422
DD 574.19/2/05 PL
NLM W1 PO936 **CODEN** PSTBAH
POSTEPY BIOCHEMII. [Postepy biochem.]. **Added/Corp** Polska Akademia Nauk. Komitet Biochemiczny. Polskie Towarzystwo Biochemiczne. (1955)-. Periodical. Polish. Four times a year. $96.00. **(Subscription address:** Ars Polona-Ruch, PO Box 1001, Krakowskie Przedmiescie 7, 00-068 Warsaw Poland. **Tel** 011 48 22 261201.) Documents available from BIOSIS Document Express.
Ind/Abst AGRICOLA; Biol. Abstr.; Index Med.; Life Sci. Collect.

LC QH324 .P67 **ISSN** 0032-7484
DD 574.1/92/028 US
CCC
NLM W1 PR424 **CODEN** PRBCBQ
Pr Rev.
PREPARATIVE BIOCHEMISTRY. [Prep. biochem.]. Vol. 1 (Jan. 1971)-. Periodical. English. Four times a year. $450.00. Marcel Dekker Inc., 270 Madison Avenue, New York NY 10016. **Tel** (212)696-9000, (800)228-1160, FAX (212)685-4540, telex 421419. **(Subscription address:** Marcel Dekker Inc., PO Box 5017, Monticello NY 12701. **Tel** (800)228-1160.) **ED** Carel J. Van Oss, Darrell Doyle, Stellan Hjerten, Jack D. Klingman. **Bk Rev. Ad Acc.** ctrl circ. available on microfiche. Documents available from The Genuine Article, BIOSIS Document Express, CASDDS.
Desc: This distinguished journal is an essential source of new methods and combinations of methods devised for the isolation and purification of biochemical substances. Encompassing biological, immunological, pharmaceutical, and clinical chemistry; molecular biology; biochemistry; and biophysics. Details new techniques and applications that are directly relevant to work in these fields.
Ind/Abst AGRICOLA [Select. Cov.]; Biol. Abstr.; Chem. Abstr.; Chem. Titles; CSA Neuro. Abstr. (?-?); Curr. Aware. Biol. Sci., CABS; Curr. Cit.; Curr. Contents Life Sci.; EMBASE; Energy Res. Abstr. (March 1979-); Index Med.; Index Vet.; Microbiol. Abstr. Sect. C; Life Sci. Collect.; PESTDOC; Ref. Upd. Deluxe Ed.; Res. Alert [Full Cov.]; Sci. Cit. Index; SCISEARCH; Vet. Bull.

LC QH345 .P7 **ISSN** 0555-1099
DD 574.1/92/05 RU
NLM W1 PR52 **CODEN** PBMIAK
PRIKLADNAJA BIOHIMIJA I MIKROBIOLOGIJA. (PRIKLADNAIA BIOKHIMIIA I MIKROBIOLOGIIA.). [Prikl. biohim. mikrobiol.]. **Added/Corp** Akademiia Nauk SSSR. Vol. 1, (Jan./Feb. 1965)-. Academic Scholarly Publication. Russian (summaries and/or abstracts in English). Six times a year. $263.75. Izdatelstvo Nauka / Akademiia Nauk, (Publishing House of the Russian Academy of Sciences), Leninskii Porspekt 14, 117901 Moscow Russia. **Tel** 011 95 9542153, FAX 011 95 9382144, telex 411964. **(Subscription address:** East View Publications Inc., 3020 Harbor Lane North, Suite 110, Minneapolis MN 55447. **Tel** (800)477-1005, (612)550-0961, FAX (612)559-2931.) Documents available from BIOSIS Document Express, CASDDS.
Ind/Abst Abstr. Bull. Inst. Paper Chem.; Abstr. Bull. Inst. Pap. Sci. Tech.; AGRICOLA; Biol. Abstr.; Chem. Abstr.; Chem. Titles; Crop Physiol. Abstr.; Curr. Biotechnol.; EMBASE; Food Sci. Technol. Abstr.; Index Med.; Microbiol. Abstr. Sect. B; Microbiol. Abstr. Sect. A; Microbiol. Abstr. Sect. C; Life Sci. Collect.; PESTDOC; Plant Grow. Reg. Abstr.; Vitis Vitic. Enol. Abstr.

LC QD415
DD 574.192 AT
NLM W1; AU675 **CODEN** PSBBEX
PROCEEDINGS OF THE AUSTRALIAN SOCIETY FOR BIOCHEMISTRY AND MOLECULAR BIOLOGY : ABSTRACTS OF PAPERS PRESENTED AT THE ... ANNUAL CONFERENCE OF THE SOCIETY HELD ... . Main/Corp Australian Society for Biochemistry and Molecular Biology. Conference. **VFOAT** Proceedings. Vol. 23 (1991)-. Proceedings. English. One time a year. 45.00Aus$. Australian Society for Biochemistry and Molecular Biology, PO Box 2331, Kent Town South Australia 5071 Australia. **Tel** 011 61 8 3620009. **(Subscription address:** DA Information Services Pty., 648 Whitehorse Road, Mitcham 3132 Victoria Australia. **Tel** 011 61 3 8734411.) ***Continues** Australian Biochemical Society. Proceedings of Australian Biochemical Society.*

LC QD415 **ISSN** 0126-9208
DD 574.192 MY
CODEN PMBCDR
PROCEEDINGS OF THE MALAYSIAN BIOCHEMICAL SOCIETY CONFERENCE. (PROCEEDINGS OF THE ... MALAYSIAN BIOCHEMICAL SOCIETY CONFERENCE / PERSATUAN BIOKIMIA MALAYSIA.). [Proc. Malays. Biochem. Soc. Conf.]. **Main/Corp** Persatuan Biokimia Malaysia. Conference. **Added/Corp** University of Malaya in Kuala Lumpur. Faculty of Medicine. (1974)-. Academic Scholarly Publication. English. One time a year. Documents available from CASDDS.
Ind/Abst Chem. Abstr.

LC QH301 **ISSN** 0845-5066
DD 574./05 CN
PROGRAMME, PROCEEDINGS / CANADIAN FEDERATION OF BIOLOGICAL SOCIETIES. See Biology-Physiology.

LC RM **ISSN** 0079-6085
DD 615 US
CCC
NLM W1 PR666H **CODEN** PBPHAW
PROGRESS IN BIOCHEMICAL PHARMACOLOGY. See Pharmacy and Pharmacology.

LC TP248.13 .P76
DD 574.19/2/05 US
NLM W1; PR666J **CODEN** PBBIE3
Pr Rev.
•**PROGRESS IN BIOCHEMISTRY AND BIOTECHNOLOGY.** Vol. 2, No. 1/2 (1994)-. Periodical. English. Four times a year. $295.00. Nova Science Publishers Inc., 6080 Jericho Turnpike, Suite 207, Commack NY 11725-2808. **Tel** (516)499-3103, (516)499-3106, FAX (516)499-3146. **ED** E. Volkov. Index available. **Bk Rev. Circ:** 400. ***Continues** Journal of Nonlinear Biology, 1047-1200.*

LC QH505.A1 P76 **ISSN** 0079-6107
DD 574.1 US
CCC
NLM W1 PR667 **CODEN** PBIMAC
Pr Rev.
PROGRESS IN BIOPHYSICS AND MOLECULAR BIOLOGY. See Biology-Biological Physics.

LC QD415 **ISSN** 0921-0423
DD 574.192 NE
CCC
NLM W1; PR667C **CODEN** PBITE3
PROGRESS IN BIOTECHNOLOGY. [Prog. biotechnol.]. (1985)-. Monographic series. English. Irregular. Price varies per volume. Elsevier Science Publishers BV, PO Box 211, 1000 AE Amsterdam Netherlands. **Tel** 011 31 20 4853641, 011 31 20 4853642, FAX 011 31 20 4853598. Documents available from BIOSIS Document Express, CASDDS.
Desc: Series focusing on biotechnology and biological chemistry.
Ind/Abst AGRICOLA [Select. Cov.]; Biol. Abstr. (1986-); Chem. Abstr.; Curr. Cit.; PESTDOC.

LC RB112.5 .P76 **ISSN** 0177-8757
DD 610/.5 GW
NLM W1; PR668EM **CODEN** PCBMEM
PROGRESS IN CLINICAL BIOCHEMISTRY AND MEDICINE. [Prog. clin. biochem. med.]. **VFOAT** Clinical Biochemistry and Medicine. (1984)-. Academic Scholarly Publication. English. Irregular. Price varies per volume. Springer-Verlag GmbH & Company KG, Heidelberger Platz 3, D-14197 Berlin Germany. **Tel** 011 49 30 8207223, FAX 011 49 30 8214091, telex 183 319 SPBLN D. **(Subscription address:** Springer-Verlag New York Inc. / North America, PO Box 2485, Journal Fulfillment, Secaucus NJ 07096. **Tel** (201)348-4033, (800)777-4643, FAX (201)348-4505.) Documents available from CASDDS.
Ind/Abst Chem. Abstr. (1984-).

ISSN 0950-0588
DD 016.57419256 UK
CCC
PROTEASES & INHIBITORS. [Proteases inhib.]. (1987)-. Periodical. English. Twelve times a year. $128.34. SUBIS, Mansion House 19 Kingfield Road, Sheffield S11 9AS United Kingdom. **Tel** 011 44 114 2554433, FAX 011 44 114 255 4626.

LC QP551 .P69749 QD431.A1 P76 **ISSN** 1070-3667
DD 574.19/245/05 UK
NLM W1; PR788G **CODEN** PPGIEO
Pr Rev.
•**PROTEIN PROFILE.** [Protein profile]. (1994)-. Academic Scholarly Publication. English. Ten times a year. $540.00. Academic Press Ltd., A Division of Harcourt Brace & Company Ltd., 24-28 Oval Road, London NW1 7DX United Kingdom. **Tel** 011 44 171 2674466, FAX 011 44 171 4822293, 011 44 171 4854752, telex 25775 ACPRES G. **(Subscription address:** Harcourt Brace & Company, Ltd., Foots Cray High Street, Sidcup Kent DA14 5HP United Kingdom. **Tel** 011 44 181 3003322, FAX 011 44 181 3090807, telex 896 377 ACADEM.) **ED** Peter Sheterline. Documents available from BLDSC, CASDDS, SWETS.
Ind/Abst Chem. Abstr.; Index Med. (1995-).

LC QP551 .P697625 **ISSN** 0961-8368
DD 574.19/245 US
CCC
NLM W1; PR788J **CODEN** PRCIEI
Pr Rev.
PROTEIN SCIENCE : A PUBLICATION OF THE PROTEIN SOCIETY. Added/Corp Protein Society. American Society for Biochemistry and Molecular Biology. Innovative Technology Fund. Biophysical Society. Vol. 1, No. 1 (Jan. 1992)-. Academic Scholarly Publication. English. Twelve times a year. $705.00. Cambridge University Press / New York, 40 West 20th Street, New York NY 10011-4211. **Tel** (212)924-3900, (800)221-4512, FAX (212)691-3239. **(Subscription address:** Cambridge University Press / Outside of North America, United Kingdom. **Tel** 011 44 223 312 393, FAX 011 44 223 325 959.) **ED** Hans Neurath. Index available (Dec.). **Bk Rev,** (Qty: 40-60/yr). **Ad Acc, Adv Mgr:** James Alexander. **Circ:** 3,200. available on microfilm and microfiche from University Microfilms International (UMI); available on CD-ROM from Cambridge University Press; available via Internet. Documents available from The Genuine Article.
Desc: A forum for reports on proteins in the broadest sense. Includes the structure, function, and biochemical significance of proteins, their role in molecular and cell biology, genetics and evolution, as well as their regulation and mechanism of action.
Ind/Abst Curr. Aware. Biol. Sci., CABS; Curr. Contents Life Sci.; Food Sci. Technol. Abstr.; Index Med.; Res. Alert [Full Cov.]; Sci. Cit. Index; Soc. Sci. Cit. Index [Select. Cov.].

LC QD415 **ISSN** 0931-9506
DD 574.192 GW
CCC
NLM W1; PR788N **CODEN** PSDAE6
CEASED
PROTEIN SEQUENCES & DATA ANALYSIS. [Protein seq. data anal.]. **VFOAT** Protein Sequences and Data Analysis. Vol. 1, No. 1 (Aug. 1987)-Vol. 5 No. 6 (Dec. 1993). Academic Scholarly Publication. English. Springer-Verlag GmbH & Company KG, Heidelberger Platz 3, D-14197 Berlin Germany. **Tel** 011 49 30 8207223, FAX 011 49 30 8214091, telex 183 319 SPBLN D. **(Subscription address:** Springer-Verlag New York Inc. / North America, PO Box 2485, Journal Fulfillment, Secaucus NJ 07096. **Tel** (201)348-4033, (800)777-4643, FAX (201)348-4505.) **ED** A Tsugita, B Keil, W C Barker, A Henschen, and H W Mewes. available on microfilm and microfiche from University Microfilms International (UMI). Documents available from The Genuine Article, BIOSIS Document Express, CASDDS.
Desc: Devoted to the publication of newly determined sequence data and to the organization, retrieval and analysis of this information using data banks.
Ind/Abst Biol. Abstr.; Chem. Abstr.; Curr. Cit.; Index Med. (1987-); Res. Alert [Full Cov.]; Rev. Med. Vet. Entomol.

Biology—Biological Chemistry

LC QP551 .P69777
DD 574.19/245/05
ISSN 0887-3585
US
CCC
NLM W1; PR79E
CODEN PSFGEY
Pr Rev.
PROTEINS. [Proteins]. VFOAT Proteins, Structure, Function, and Genetics. Vol. 1, No. 1 (1986)-. Academic Scholarly Publication. English. Twelve times a year. $792.00. John Wiley & Sons, Inc., 605 Third Avenue, New York NY 10158-0012. **Tel** (212)850-6000, (212)850-6645, FAX (212)850-6088, telex 12-7063. **(Subscription address:** John Wiley & Sons / UK, Baffins Lane, Chichester, West Sussex PO19 1UD United Kingdom. **Tel** 011 44 1243 779777, FAX 011 44 243 776128, telex 86290 WIBOOKG.) ED Cyrus Levinthal and Eaton E. Lattman. Documents available from The Genuine Article, BIOSIS Document Express, CASDDS.
Desc: Concentrates on advances in all areas of protein biochemistry-structure, function, genetics, computation and design.
Ind/Abst Biol. Abstr. (1986-); Chem. Abstr. (1986-); Curr. Aware. Biol. Sci., CABS; Curr. Cit.; Curr. Contents Life Sci.; EMBASE; Food Sci. Technol. Abstr.; Index Med. (1986-); Microbiol. Abstr. Sect. B (19??-19??); Protozoolog. Abstr.; Ref. Upd. Deluxe Ed.; Res. Alert [Full Cov.]; Sci. Cit. Index; SCISEARCH.

ISSN 0952-0406
UK
CCC
PROTEINS, POST-TRANSLATIONAL PROCESSING. [Proteins post-transl. process.]. (1988)-. Periodical. English. Twelve times a year. $205.35. SUBIS, Mansion House 19 Kingfield Road, Sheffield S11 9AS United Kingdom. **Tel** 011 44 114 2554433, FAX 011 44 114 255 4626. **Continues** Protein Phosphorylation, 0142-8292.

FR
CEASED
PUBLICATIONS DE L'UNITE DE BIOCHIMIE DE LA NUTRITION. See Nutrition and Dietetics.

ISSN 0888-7500
DD 574
US
NLM W1; RE107KE
CODEN RBMEEY
RECEPTOR BIOCHEMISTRY AND METHODOLOGY. [Recept. biochem. methodol.]. Vol. 1 (1984)-. Academic Scholarly Publication. English. Irregular. Price varies per volume. John Wiley & Sons, Inc., 605 Third Avenue, New York NY 10158-0012. **Tel** (212)850-6000, (212)850-6645, FAX (212)850-6088, telex 12-7063. **(Subscription address:** John Wiley & Sons / UK, Baffins Lane, Chichester, West Sussex PO19 1UD United Kingdom. **Tel** 011 44 1243 779777, FAX 011 44 243 776128, telex 86290 WIBOOKG.) ED J. Craig Venter and Len C. Harrison. Documents available from CASDDS.
Ind/Abst Chem. Abstr. (1984-).

LC QH603.C43 R38
DD 574.87
ISSN 1052-8040
US
CCC
NLM W1; RE107KG
RECEPTOR (CLIFTON, N.J. JOURNAL). (RECEPTOR.). [Receptor]. Vol. 1, Nos. 1-2 (Winter 1990/1991)-. Periodical. English. Four times a year. $205.00. Humana Press Inc., 999 Riverview Drive, Suite 208, Totawa NJ 07512. **Tel** (201)256-1699, FAX (201)256-8341. ED Gerald Litwack. **Bk Rev**. **Ad Acc**. Documents available from The Genuine Article.
Desc: Focuses on all phases of research on receptors involving every class of organism. Covers neurotransmitters, hormones, antibodies, viruses, growth factors, vitamins, molecular modeling, endocrinology and many other facets of biological research on receptors.
Ind/Abst Curr. Cit.; Curr. Contents Life Sci.; Index Med. (winter 1990-1991-); Res. Alert [Full Cov.]; Sci. Cit. Index.

LC QD415
DD 574.192
ISSN 1351-0002
UK
●**REDOX REPORT.** (1994)-. Academic Scholarly Publication. English. Four times a year. $310.00. Churchill Livingstone, 1-3 Baxter's Place, Leith Walk, Edinburgh EH1 3AF United Kingdom. **Tel** 011 44 131 5562424, FAX 011 44 131 5581278, telex 727511. **(Subscription address:** Maruzen Company Ltd., PO Box 5050, Import & Export Department, Tokyo 100 31 Japan. **Tel** 011 81 3 32789224.) ED Board. **Bk Rev**. **Continues** Free Radicals and Oxidation.
Desc: Covers free radicals, activated oxygen and redox processes in biology/pathology.

LC QH650
DD 574.192
ISSN 0869-4095
RU
REFERATIVNYI ZHURNAL. 04, 04D, BIOLOGIIA. FIZIKO-KHIMICHESKAIA BIOLOGIIA. Added/Corp Vsesoiuznyi Institut Nauchnoi i Tekhnicheskoi Informatsii (Russia (Federation)). **VFOAT** Fiziko-Khimicheskaia Biologiia. (1992)-. Abstracting/Indexing Service. Russian. Twelve times a year. VINITI - Vsesoyuznyi Institut Nauchno-Tekhnicheskoi Informatsii, All-Union Scientific and Technical Information Institute, Baltiiskaia ulitsa 14, 125219 Moscow Russia. **Tel** 011 7 95 2384600, FAX 011 7 95 9430060, telex 411160. **Continues** Referativnyi Zhurnal. 26, Fiziko-Khimicheskaia Biologiia.

LC QD415
DD 574.192
RU
NLM ZQU 4 R332
REFERATIVNYI ZHURNAL. BIOLOGICHESKAIA KHIMIIA. (19??)-. Abstracting/Indexing Service. Russian. Twenty-four times a year. VINITI - Vsesoyuznyi Institut Nauchno-Tekhnicheskoi Informatsii, All-Union Scientific and Technical Information Institute, Baltiiskaia ulitsa 14, 125219 Moscow Russia. **Tel** 011 7 95 2384600, FAX 011 7 95 9430060, telex 411160.

DD 016.574
ISSN 0143-4284
UK
CCC
RENIN, ANGIOTENSIN & KININS. [Renin angiotensin kinins]. (1980)-. English. Twenty-four times a year. $179.67. SUBIS, Mansion House 19 Kingfield Road, Sheffield S11 9AS United Kingdom. **Tel** 011 44 114 2554433, FAX 011 44 114 255 4626. **Ad Acc**.
Desc: Current awareness service for researchers.

ISSN 1041-0589
US
SUSPENDED
RESEARCH REVIEWS IN BIOCHEMISTRY. Added/Corp Institute for Scientific Information. **VFOAT** ISI Atlas Biochem. (1989)-Suspended (1989). Periodical. English. Four times a year. Institute for Scientific Information, 3501 Market Street, Philadelphia PA 19104. **Tel** (215)386-0100, (800)523-1850, FAX (215)386-6362, telex 84-5305. **Continues** ISI Atlas of Science. Biochemistry, 0894-3753.

LC QP1 .E6
DD 612.005/6
ISSN 0303-4240
GW
CCC
NLM W1 RE257G
CODEN RPBEA5
REVIEWS OF PHYSIOLOGY, BIOCHEMISTRY AND PHARMACOLOGY. See Biology-Physiology.

ISSN 0301-7052
BL
UDC 61
REVISTA DE FARMACIA E BIOQUIMICA. BELO HORIZONTE. See Pharmacy and Pharmacology.

LC RS1 .S27
DD 615/.1/05
ISSN 0370-4726
BL
NLM W1 RE396F
CODEN RFBUBI
REVISTA DE FARMACIA E BIOQUIMICA DA UNIVERSIDADE DE SAO PAULO. See Pharmacy and Pharmacology.

LC QP501 .A83
DD 612.015
ISSN 0004-4768
AG
NLM W1 RE406
CODEN RABAAO
REVISTA DE LA ASOCIACION BIOQUIMICA ARGENTINA. Main/Corp Asociacion Bioquimica Argentina. (1936)-. Academic Scholarly Publication. Spanish. Four times a year. Asociacion Bioquimica Argentina, Venezuela 1823/3ER Piso, Buenos Aires 1096 Argentina. **Tel** 011 541 382907. Documents available from CASDDS.
Ind/Abst Chem. Abstr.

LC QD1 .R32915
DD 540.5/6
ISSN 0370-5943
MX
CODEN RLAQA8
Pr Rev.
REVISTA LATINOAMERICANA DE QUIMICA. See Chemistry and Chemicals-Organic Chemistry.

LC QP501 .R43
DD 612.015
ISSN 0001-4214
RM
NLM W1 RE963X
CODEN RRBCAD
REVUE ROUMAINE DE BIOCHIMIE. [Rev. roum. biochim.]. **Added/Corp** Academia Republicii Socialiste Romania. Academia Republicii Populare Romine. Vol. 1 (1964)-. Periodical. Multiple languages (English, French, German and Russian; summaries and/or abstracts in English, French, German and Russian). Four times a year. $138.00. **(Subscription address:** Orion Press SRL, SPL Independentei 202-A, Bucharest 6 Romania. **Tel** 011 401 3122425.) Documents available from CASDDS.
Desc: Publishes studies on biochemistry.
Ind/Abst Anal. Abstr.; Chem. Abstr.; Crop Physiol. Abstr.; Curr. Biotechnol.; Curr. Cit.; EMBASE; Maize Abstr.; Nat. Prod. Updates; Life Sci. Collect.; PESTDOC; Plant Breed. Abstr.; Plant Grow. Reg.; Potato Abstr.; Rev. Plant Pathol.

LC QD415.A1 B5513
DD 547/.7/05
ISSN 1068-1620
US
CCC
●**RUSSIAN JOURNAL OF BIOORGANIC CHEMISTRY.** (1993)-. Periodical. English. Twelve times a year. $1055.00. Consultants Bureau, A Division of Plenum Publishing Corporation, 233 Spring Street, New York NY 10013. **Tel** (212)620-8000, (212)620-8466, FAX (212)463-0742, telex 23/421139. **Continues** Soviet Journal of Bioorganic Chemistry, 0360-4497.

LC QD415
DD 574.192
ISSN 0724-8784
GW
NLM W1; SC343H
CODEN LELBD8
SCHRIFTENREIHE LEBENSMITTELCHEMIE, LEBENSMITTELQUALITAT. Added/Corp Gesellschaft Deutscher Chemiker. Arbeitsgruppe Zusatzstofftechnologie und -Analytik. **VFOAT** Lebensmittelchemie, Lebensmittelqualitat; Technologie der Lebensmittel-Zusatzstoffe. (1983)-. Monographic series. German (English). Behrs Verlag, Averhoffstr 10, D-22085 Hamburg Germany. **Tel** 011 49 40 22700818, FAX 011 49 40 2201091. Documents available from CASDDS.
Ind/Abst Chem. Abstr.

LC QP625.N89 J68
DD 574.87/05
ISSN 0895-7479
US
CCC
NLM W1; SE217M
CODEN SMEPED
Pr Rev.
TITLE CHANGE
SECOND MESSENGER AND PHOSPHOPROTEINS. Vol. 12, No. 1 (1988)-(19??). Periodical. English. Marcel Dekker Inc., 270 Madison Avenue, New York NY 10016. **Tel** (212)696-9000, (800)228-1160, FAX (212)685-4540, telex 421419. **(Subscription address:** Marcel Dekker Inc., PO Box 5017, Monticello NY 12701. **Tel** (800)228-1160.) ED R. W. Butcher. Documents available from The Genuine Article, BIOSIS Document Express, CASDDS. **Continues** Journal of Cyclic Nucleotide and Protein Phosphorylation Research, 0746-3898. **Merged into** Journal of Receptor and Signal Transduction Research, 1079-9893.
Desc: Provides an ongoing forum for pharmacologists and biochemists. Serving as an outlet for original papers, this journal covers inter- and intracellular communication, all second messenger systems, especially inositol phosphates, calcium, diacylglycerols, and cyclic nucleotides, plus all phases of phosphoprotein metabolism and function. Presents basic and applied research articles, reviews, short reports, conference papers, and letters to the editor on a wide variety of topics: cyclic AMP, adenylate cyclase, phosphodiesterase, GTP binding proteins, kinase, and more.
Ind/Abst Biol. Abstr.; Chem. Abstr.; Curr. Aware. Biol. Sci., CABS; Curr. Cit.; Curr. Contents Life Sci.; EMBASE; Index Med.; Ref. Upd. Deluxe Ed.; Res. Alert [Full Cov.]; Sci. Cit. Index (19??-19??); SCISEARCH.

LC QP501
DD 612.015
ISSN 0031-9082
JA
NLM W1 SE249NE
CODEN SBBKA4
SEIBUTSU-BUTSURI-KAGAKU. [Seibutsu-butsuri-kagaku]. **VFOAT** The Physico-Chemical Biology. (1951)-. Academic Scholarly Publication. Japanese (English). Four times a year. Tokyo Medical and Dental University, 5-45 Yushima 1 chome, Bunkyoku Tokyo 113 Japan. Documents available from BIOSIS Document Express, CASDDS.
Ind/Abst Anal. Abstr.; Biol. Abstr.; Chem. Abstr.

LC QD415
DD 574.192
ISSN 0037-1017
JA
NLM W1 SE2515
CODEN SEIKAQ
SEIKAGAKU. [Seikagaku]. **Added/Corp** Nippon Seikagakkai. Vol. 20 (1948)-. Academic Scholarly Publication. Japanese. Twelve times a year. $340.00. **(Subscription address:** Maruzen Company Ltd., PO Box 5050, Import & Export Department, Tokyo 100 31 Japan. **Tel** 011 81 3 32789224.) Documents available from CASDDS. **Continues** Nippon Seikagakkai Shi.
Ind/Abst AGRICOLA; Chem. Abstr.; Curr. Biotechnol.; Curr. Cit.; Index Med.; Life Sci. Collect.; Sci. Cit. Index (19??-19??); SCISEARCH.

LC QP501 .S45
DD 612.015
ISSN 0253-9918
CH
CODEN SHYCD4
SHENGWU HUAXUE YU SHENGWU WULI JINZHAN. (SHENG WU HUA HSUEH YU SHENG WU WU LI CHIN CHAN.). [Shengwu huaxue yu shengwu wuli jinzhan]. (1974)-. Academic Scholarly Publication. Chinese. Six times a year. $35.04. Chinese Academy of Sciences, Institute of Biophysics, Science Press, 15 Donghuangchenggen North Street, Beijing 100707, People's Republic of China. **Tel** 011 86 1 4019821, FAX 011 86 4012180, telex 210147. **(Subscription address:** China International Book Trading Corporation, PO Box 399, Library Service Department, Beijing 100044 People's Republic of China. **Tel** 011 86 1 8414284, FAX 011 86 1 8412023, telex 22496 CIBTC CN.) **Ad Acc**. **Circ**: 11,000. Documents

available from BLDSC, CASDDS, CASDDS.
Ind/Abst Art Archaeol. Tech. Abstr.; Chem. Abstr.; Curr. Biotechnol.

LC RB112.5 .S68 **ISSN** 0887-2392
DD 510/.1/53 SZ
CCC
CODEN SRBRE5
CEASED

SOVIET MEDICAL REVIEWS. SECTION B, PHYSICOCHEMICAL ASPECTS OF MEDICINE REVIEWS. [Sov. med. rev., B Physicochem. asp. med. rev.]. **Added/Corp** Soviet Medical Reviews (Firm : Chur, Switzerland). **VFOAT** Physicochemical Aspects of Medicine Reviews. Vol. 1 (1987)-(1993). Periodical. English. Harwood Academic Publishers, PO Box 90, Reading RG1 8JL United Kingdom. **Tel** 011 44 1734 560080, FAX 011 44 1734 568211.

LC QH301 .S783 **ISSN** 0734-9351
DD 574/.05 SZ
CCC
NLM W1; SO996WE **CODEN** SRDREF
CEASED

SOVIET SCIENTIFIC REVIEWS. SECTION D, PHYSICOCHEMICAL BIOLOGY REVIEWS. **See** Biology-Biological Physics.

LC QD415 **ISSN** 1077-3444
DD 574.192 US

•**STEREOCHEMICAL TECHNOLOGY NEWS.** [Stereochem. technol. news]. Vol. 1, No. 1 (May 1994)-. Newsletter. English. Twelve times a year. $375.00. Business Communications Inc., 25 Van Zant Street, Suite 13, Norwalk CT 06855. **Tel** (203)853-4266, FAX (203)853-0348. **ED** Philip Rotheim.

LC QP752.S7 **ISSN** 0039-128X
DD 599.01/9243 US
CCC
NLM W1 ST479 **CODEN** STEDAM
Pr Rev.

STEROIDS. [Steroids]. Vol. 1 (Jan. 1963)-. Academic Scholarly Publication. English. Twelve times a year. $620.00. Butterworth Heinemann / Woburn, MA, 225 Wildwood Avenue, Unit B, Woburn MA 01801. **Tel** (800)366-2665, FAX (617)928-2620, telex 880052. **(Subscription address:** Elsevier Science Inc. / New York Books, 655 Avenue of the Americas, New York NY 10010. **Tel** (212)633-3650.) **ED** H Leon Bradlow. Index available. **Bk Rev. Ad Acc. Circ:** 1,000 (ctrl). available on microfilm and microfiche from University Microfilms International (UMI). Documents available from The Genuine Article, BIOSIS Document Express, CASDDS.
Desc: International journal providing a forum for rapid publication of over 3,500 significant original papers in organic chemistry, biochemistry, physiology, pharmacology, and endocrinology.
Ind/Abst AGRICOLA; Anim. Breed. Abstr.; Biol. Abstr.; Chem. Abstr.; Curr. Aware. Biol. Sci., CABS; Curr. Chem. React.; Curr. Cit.; Curr. Contents Life Sci.; EMBASE; Energy Res. Abstr.; Index Chem.; Index Med.; NAPRALERT; Nat. Prod. Updates; Nematol. Abstr.; Nutr. Abstr. Rev., Ser. A, Hum. Exp.; Life Sci. Collect.; PESTDOC; Poult. Abstr.; Protozoolog. Abstr.; Ref. Upd. Deluxe Ed.; Res. Alert [Select. Cov.]; Rev. Agric. Entomol.; Rev. Med. Vet. Entomol.; Sci. Cit. Index.

RM

STUDII SI CERCETARI DE BIOCHIMIE. **Added/Corp** Academia Republicii Socialiste Romania. Academia Republicii Populare Romine. Institutul de Biochimie. (1958)-. Academic Scholarly Publication. Romanian (summaries and/or abstracts in French and Russian). Two times a year. $48.00. Editura Academia Republicii Socialiste Romania, Calea Victoriei Nr 125, R-79717 Bucuresti Romania. **Tel** 011 40 0 10376. **(Subscription address:** Rompresfilatelia, PO Box 12 201, Bucharest Romania. **Tel** 011 40 0 10376.) **ED** Mihai Serban. **Bk Rev.** available with charts; available with illustrations. Documents available from CASDDS.
Desc: Publishes original works on biochemistry, the origin of living matter, as well as on comparative biochemistry.
Ind/Abst Chem. Abstr.

LC QH611 .S84 **ISSN** 0306-0225
DD 574.8/76 UK
CCC
NLM W1; SU14 **CODEN** SBCBAG

SUB-CELLULAR BIOCHEMISTRY. **See** Biology-Cytology.

LC QD380 **ISSN** 0968-5677
DD 539 UK
Pr Rev.

•**SUPRAMOLECULAR SCIENCE.** (1994)-. Academic Scholarly Publication. English. Four times a year. $239.00. Butterworth Heinemann Publishers, Linacre House Jordan Hill, Oxford OX2 8DP United Kingdom. **Tel** 011 44 1865 310366, FAX 011 44 1865 310898. **(Subscription address:** Elsevier Science Ltd. / Oxford Fulfillment Centre, PO Box 800, Kidlington OX5 1DX United Kingdom. **Tel** 011 44 865 843355.) **ED** Board. available in microform from University Microfilms International (UMI); available on an online database from Elsevier Electronic Subscriptions (EES). Documents available from BLDSC, CASDDS, The UnCover Company, UMI Article Clearinghouse.

LC QD415 **ISSN** 0166-1167
DD 574.192 NE
NLM W3 SY1056 **CODEN** SGLFD9
Pr Rev.

SYMPOSIA OF THE GIOVANNI LORENZINI FOUNDATION. **See** Medical Sciences.

LC QP501 .T36 **ISSN** 0039-9450
DD 612.015 JA
NLM W1 TA553 **CODEN** TAKKAJ

TANPAKUSHITSU KAKUSAN KOSO. (TANPAKUSHITSU, KAKUSAN, KOSO = PROTEIN, NUCLEIC ACID, ENZYME.). [Tanpakushitsu kakusan koso]. **VFOAT** Protein, Nucleic Acid, Enzyme. (1956)-. Academic Scholarly Publication. Japanese. Fifteen times a year. $142.68. Kyoritsu Shuppan Company Ltd., 4 6 19 Kohinata Bunkyoku, Tokyo 112 Japan. **Tel** 011 81 3 39472511, FAX 011 81 3 39448182. Index available in last issue of volume--attached. Documents available from BIOSIS Document Express, CASDDS.
Ind/Abst Biol. Abstr. (1987-); Chem. Abstr.; Curr. Biotechnol.; Index Med.

LC QD241 .T42 **ISSN** 0040-4039
DD 547.05 UK
CCC
NLM W1 TE637 **CODEN** TELEAY
Pr Rev.

TETRAHEDRON LETTERS. **See** Chemistry and Chemicals-Organic Chemistry.

LC QD241 **ISSN** 0040-4039
DD 547 UK
CCC
CODEN TELEAY

TETRAHEDRON LETTERS. **See** Chemistry and Chemicals-Organic Chemistry.

LC QD415 **ISSN** 0160-3183
DD 574.192 UK
UDC 577.23
NLM W1 TO539H **CODEN** TBBIDC

TOPICS IN BIOELECTROCHEMISTRY AND BIOENERGETICS. [Top. bioelectrochem. bioenerg.]. Vol. 1 (1976)-. Academic Scholarly Publication. English. Irregular. Price varies per volume. John Wiley & Sons Ltd., Baffins Lane, Chichester, West Sussex PO19 1UD United Kingdom. **Tel** 011 44 1243 779777, FAX 011 44 1243 776128 BTG:JWP001, telex 86290 WIBOOKG. **(Subscription address:** John Wiley & Sons Inc / New Jersey, PO Box 2575, Secaucus NJ 07096-2575.) **ED** G Milazzo. Documents available from CASDDS.
Ind/Abst Chem. Abstr.

LC QP571 .T66 **ISSN** 0271-9282
DD 599/.01/927 UK
NLM W1 TO539MS **CODEN** THOCDX

TOPICS IN HORMONE CHEMISTRY. [Top. horm. chem.]. (1978)-. Academic Scholarly Publication. English. Irregular. Price varies per volume. John Wiley & Sons Ltd., Baffins Lane, Chichester, West Sussex PO19 1UD United Kingdom. **Tel** 011 44 1243 779777, FAX 011 44 1243 776128 BTG:JWP001, telex 86290 WIBOOKG. **(Subscription address:** John Wiley & Sons, Inc. / Philadelphia, PO Box 7247, Philadelphia PA 19170. **Tel** (212)850-6645, (800)225-5945.) **ED** W.R. Butt. Documents available from BIOSIS Document Express, CASDDS.
Ind/Abst Biol. Abstr.; Chem. Abstr.

LC QD415
DD 574.192 GW
NLM W1; TR108BL **CODEN** TEELEO

•**TRACE ELEMENTS AND ELECTROLYTES.** Vol. 11, No. 1 (1st Quarter, 1994)-. Periodical. English. Four times a year. $142.00. Dustri-Verlag, Postfach 49, D-82032 Deisenhofen Germany. **Tel** 011 49 89 6138610, FAX 011 49 89 6135412. ***Continues** Trace Elements in Medicine, 0174-7371.*
Ind/Abst Chem. Abstr.; Curr. Cit.

LC QD415 **ISSN** 0376-5067
DD 574.192 NE

TRENDS IN BIOCHEMICAL SCIENCES (AMSTERDAM. REFERENCE EDITION). (TRENDS IN BIOCHEMICAL SCIENCES.). [Trends biochem. sci.]. **Added/Corp** International Union of Biochemistry. **VFOAT** TIBS. Vol. 1 (1976)-. Academic Scholarly Publication. English. Elsevier Science Publishers BV, PO Box 211, 1000 AE Amsterdam Netherlands. **Tel** 011 31 20 4853641, 011 31 20 4853642, FAX 011 31 20 4853598. available on microfilm and microfiche from University Microfilms International (UMI). Documents available from UMI Article Clearinghouse.
Ind/Abst Curr. Cit.; EMBASE; Expand. Acad. Index (1992-); Food Sci. Technol. Abstr.; Index Vet.; Newsp. Period. Abstr. (1992-); Oncog. Growth Factors Abstr.; PESTDOC; Ref. Upd. Basic Ed.; Ref. Upd. Deluxe Ed.; Trop. Dis. Bull.

LC QH345 .T76 **ISSN** 0167-7640
DD 574.1/92/05 UK
NLM W1 TR3405 **CODEN** TBSCDB

TRENDS IN BIOCHEMICAL SCIENCES (AMSTERDAM. REGULAR ED.). (TRENDS IN BIOCHEMICAL SCIENCES.). [Trends biochem. sci.]. **Added/Corp** International Union of Biochemistry. **VFOAT** TIBS. Vol. 1 (Jan. 1976)-. Academic Scholarly Publication. English. Twelve times a year. $614.00. Elsevier Trends Journals, An Imprint of Elsevier Science Ltd., The Boulevard, Langford Lane, Kidlington, Oxford OX5 1GB United Kingdom. **Tel** 011 44 1865 843000, 011 44 1865 843699, FAX 011 44 1865 843010. **(Subscription address:** Elsevier Science Ltd. / Oxford Fulfillment Centre, PO Box 800, Kidlington OX5 1DX United Kingdom. **Tel** 011 44 865 843355.) **ED** R. A. Bradshaw and Mary Purton. **Bk Rev. Ad Acc. Circ:** 8,000. available on microfilm from University Microfilms International (UMI); available on an online database from Elsevier Electronic Subscriptions (EES). Documents available from The Genuine Article, BIOSIS Document Express, CASDDS, Documents on Demand, ADONIS.
Desc: Of interest to biochemists, molecular biologists and researchers in related disciplines such as biophysics, cell biology, genetics, virology, microbiology, plant pathology, clinical chemistry and medical science.
Ind/Abst Abstr. BioCommer.; ADONIS; AGRICOLA; Biol. Abstr.; Chem. Abstr.; CSA Neuro. Abstr. (?-?); Curr. Contents Life Sci.; Dairy Sci. Abstr.; EMBASE; Energy Inf. Abstr.; Environ. Abstr.; Fish Rev. (Jan. 1989-July 1992); Genet. Abstr.; Index Med.; Microbiol. Abstr. Sect. B (19??-19??); Nutr. Abstr. Rev., Ser. B, Live Feeds and Feed.; Life Sci. Collect.; Plant Breed. Abstr.; Res. Alert [Full Cov.]; Sci. Cit. Index; SCISEARCH; Soc. Sci. Cit. Index [Select. Cov.]; Virol. AIDS Abstr.; Wildl. Rev. (Jan. 1989-July 1992).

LC QH301 **ISSN** 0970-2504
DD 574./05 II
NLM W1; TR341CL **CODEN** TLSCEE

TRENDS IN LIFE SCIENCES. (TRENDS IN LIFE SCIENCES.). [Trends life sci.]. **Added/Corp** Indian Society of Life Sciences. Vol. 1, Pt. 1 (May 1986)-. Periodical. English. Two times a year. $75.00. Manu Publications, Kanpur U.P. India. **(Subscription address:** Prints India, 11 Darya Ganj, New Delhi 110002 India. **Tel** 011 91 11 3268645, FAX 011 91 11 3275542, telex 31-61087 PRIN-IN.)

LC QP501 .U58 **ISSN** 0201-8470
DD 612.015 UN
CCC
NLM W1 UK755 **CODEN** UBZHD4

UKRAINSKII BIOKHIMICHESKII ZHURNAL. [Ukr. biohim. z.]. **Added/Corp** Instytut Biokhimii im. O.V. Palladina. **VFOAT** Ukrainian Biochemical Journal. Vol. 50, (Jan./Feb. 1978)-. Academic Scholarly Publication. Russian (summaries and/or abstracts in English). Six times a year. $109.95. **(Subscription address:** East View Publications Inc., 3020 Harbor Lane North, Suite 110, Minneapolis MN 55447. **Tel** (800)477-1005, (612)550-0961, FAX (612)559-2931.) Documents available from BIOSIS Document Express, CASDDS. ***Continues** Ukrainskyi Biokhimichnyi Zhurnal (Kiev, Ukraine: 1946).*
Ind/Abst AGRICOLA; Biol. Abstr.; Chem. Abstr.; Chem. Titles; Coal Abstr.; Field Crop Abstr.; Index Med.; Index Vet.; Nutr. Abstr. Rev., Ser. B, Live Feeds and Feed.; Nutr. Abstr. Rev., Ser. A, Hum. Exp.; Life Sci. Collect.; PESTDOC; Pig News Inf.; Rev. Med. Vet. Entomol.; Sci. Cit. Index (19??-19??); SCISEARCH; Vet. Bull.

ISSN 0130-7371
RU
CODEN UBKHAS

USPEKHI BIOLOGICHESKOI KHIMII. [Usp. biol. him.]. **Added/Corp** Institut Biokhimii im. A.N. Bakha. Vsesoiuznoe Biokhimicheskoe Obshchestvo. (1950)-. Academic Scholarly Publication. Russian. Izdatelstvo Nauka / Akademiia Nauk, (Publishing House of the Russian Academy of Sciences), Leninskii Porspekt 14, 117901 Moscow Russia. **Tel** 011 95 9542153, FAX 011 95 9382144, telex 411964. Documents available from CASDDS.
Ind/Abst Chem. Abstr.

LC QH301 .A3653
DD 574 BW
CODEN VABNE9

VESCI AKADEMII NAVUK BELARUSI. SERYA BIALAGICNYH NAVUK. (VESTSI AKADEMII NAVUK BELARUSI. SERYIA BIIALAHICHNYKH NAVUK.). **Added/Corp** Akademiia Navuk Belarusi. **VFOAT** Seryia Biialahichnykh Navuk. (1992)-. Academic Scholarly Publication. Byelorussian. Four times a year. $99.95. **(Subscription address:** East View Publications Inc., 3020 Harbor Lane North, Suite 110, Minneapolis MN 55447. **Tel** (800)477-1005, (612)550-0961, FAX (612)559-2931.) Documents available from BIOSIS Document Express, CASDDS. ***Continues** Vestsi Akademii Navuk BSSR. Seryia Biialahichnykh Navuk, 0002-3558.*
Ind/Abst Abstr. Bull. Inst. Pap. Sci. Tech.; Biol. Abstr.; Chem. Abstr.

Biology —Biological Physics

LC QD415   ISSN 0042-8809
DD 574.192   RU
   CCC
NLM W1 VO638A   CODEN VMDKAM
Pr Rev.
VOPROSY MEDICINSKOJ HIMII.
(VOPROSY MEDITSINSKOI KHIMII.). [Vopr. med. him.]. **Added/Corp** Soviet Union. Ministerstvo Zravookhraneniia. Akademiia Meditsinskikh Nauk SSSR. Vol. 1 (1955)-. Academic Scholarly Publication. Russian. Six times a year. $139.95. Izdatelstvo Meditsina / Russian Academy of Medical Sciences, Ulitsa Solyanka 14, 109801 Moscow Russia. **Tel** 011 95 297-05-04. **(Subscription address:** East View Publications Inc., 3020 Harbor Lane North, Suite 110, Minneapolis MN 55447. **Tel** (800)477-1005, (612)550-0961, FAX (612)559-2931.) Index available. **Bk Rev.** Documents available from The Genuine Article, BIOSIS Document Express, CASDDS.
Ind/Abst Biol. Abstr.; Chem. Abstr.; Chem. Titles; Curr. Biotechnol.; Curr. Contents Life Sci.; EMBASE [Select. Cov.]; Index Med.; Int. Aerosp. Abstr.; Nutr. Abstr. Rev., Ser. A, Hum. Exp.; Life Sci. Collect.; PESTDOC; Res. Alert [Full Cov.]; Rev. Med. Vet. Mycology; Sci. Cit. Index (19??-19??); SCISEARCH.

   ISSN 0043-2989
DD 574.1/92/05   NR
NLM W1 WE329   CODEN WAJBAK
WEST AFRICAN JOURNAL OF BIOLOGICAL AND APPLIED CHEMISTRY. Added/Corp Biochemical Society of Nigeria. Nutritional Society of Nigeria. Nigerian Association of Basic Medical Scientists. (1963)-. Academic Scholarly Publication. English. Four times a year. N10.00. West African Journal of Biological and Applied Chemistry, PO Box 4021, University of Ibadan Post Office, Ibadan Nigeria. **ED** O Bassir. **Bk Rev. Ad Acc. Circ:** 1,000. Documents available from BIOSIS Document Express, CASDDS. **Continues** West African Journal of Biological Chemistry.
Desc: Covers microbiological chemistry, industrial chemistry, chemotherapy, agricultural and veterinary research.
Ind/Abst Biol. Abstr.; Chem. Abstr.

LC QD415   ISSN 0049-8254
DD 574.192   UK
   CCC
NLM W1 XE17   CODEN XENOBH
Pr Rev.
XENOBIOTICA. See Toxicology.

LC QH345.Z5   ISSN 0044-4529
DD 574   RU
   CCC
NLM W1 ZH418T   CODEN ZEBFAJ
ZHURNAL EVOLIUTSIONNOI BIOKHIMII I FIZIOLOGII. [Z. evol. biokhim. fiziol.]. **Added/Corp** Akademiia Nauk SSSR. **VFOAT** Journal of Evolutionary Biochemistry and Physiology. Vol. 1, No. 1 (Jan./Feb. 1965)-. Academic Scholarly Publication. Russian (summaries and/or abstracts in English; table of contents in English). Six times a year. $148.00. Izdatelstvo Nauka / Akademiia Nauk, (Publishing House of the Russian Academy of Sciences), Leninskii Porspekt 14, 117901 Moscow Russia. **Tel** 011 95 9542153, FAX 011 95 9382144, telex 411964. **(Subscription address:** East View Publications Inc., 3020 Harbor Lane North, Suite 110, Minneapolis MN 55447. **Tel** (800)477-1005, (612)550-0961, FAX (612)559-2931.) Index available. **Bk Rev** Documents available from BIOSIS Document Express, CASDDS.
Ind/Abst AGRICOLA; Biol. Abstr.; Chem. Abstr.; CSA Neuro. Abstr. (?-?); EMBASE; Index Med.; Int. Aerosp. Abstr.; Life Sci. Collect.

BIOLOGICAL PHYSICS

LC QP501 .A18   ISSN 0237-6261
DD 574.19/2/05   HU
   CCC
NLM W1; AC755H   CODEN ABBHE5
Pr Rev.   TITLE CHANGE
ACTA BIOCHIMICA ET BIOPHYSICA HUNGARICA. See Biology-Biological Chemistry.

LC QP501 .A33   ISSN 0208-614X
DD 574.1   PL
   CODEN AUFBD3
ACTA UNIVERSITATIS LODZIENSIS. FOLIA BIOCHIMICA ET BIOPHYSICA. See Biology-Biological Chemistry.

LC QH345 .A43   ISSN 1057-8943
DD 574.19/05   US
NLM W1; AD449G   CODEN ABCHEA
ADVANCES IN BIOPHYSICAL CHEMISTRY. See Biology-Biological Chemistry.

LC QH505.A1 A33   ISSN 0065-227X
DD 574.19/1/05   IE
   CCC
NLM W1 AD449K   CODEN ADVBAT
Pr Rev.
ADVANCES IN BIOPHYSICS. [Adv. biophys.]. Vol. 1 (1970)-. Academic Scholarly Publication. English. Two times a year. $458.00. Elsevier Science Ireland Ltd., Bay 15, Shannon Industrial Estate, Co Clare Ireland. **Tel** 011 353 61 471944. **ED** M Kotani and H Noda. Index available. cum. index. available on microfilm from University Microfilms International (UMI); available on an online database from Elsevier Electronic Subscriptions (EES). Documents available from The Genuine Article, BIOSIS Document Express, CASDDS.
Desc: An international journal presenting the year's achievements in the field of biophysics, accommodating theoretical and comprehensive treatises of experimental results rather than technical details among new developments in the field.
Ind/Abst Biol. Abstr.; Chem. Abstr.; EMBASE; Index Med.; Index Sci. Rev. [Full Cov.]; Life Sci. Collect.; Ref. Upd. Deluxe Ed.; Res. Alert [Full Cov.]; SCISEARCH.

LC QH650   ISSN 0378-6900
   SZ
   CCC
NLM W1 AD53F   CODEN ACAPDU
ADVANCES IN CARDIOVASCULAR PHYSICS. [Adv. cardiovasc. phys.]. Vol 1 (1979)-. Academic Scholarly Publication. English. One time a year. 200.00F (approx. per volume). S. Karger AG, Allschwilerstrasse 10, PO Box, CH-4009 Basel Switzerland. **Tel** 011 41 61 3061111, FAX 011 41 61 3061234, telex CH 962 652. **ED** D.N. Ghista. Documents available from BIOSIS Document Express, CASDDS.
Desc: Individual volumes offer fundamental as well as applied information on innovations in such areas as cardiovascular modelling of process and phenomena, monitoring, diagnosis and rehabilitation. Each work is organized to acquaint the student, teacher or researcher with the rigors of pertinent engineering-physics disciplines which characterize a particular process and are invoked in a medical procedure or device.
Ind/Abst Biol. Abstr.; Chem. Abstr. (1979-); Ref. Upd. Deluxe Ed.

LC QP535.O1 A38   ISSN 1044-4696
DD 574.19/214   US
   CODEN ADOXEU
ADVANCES IN OXYGENATED PROCESSES. See Biology-Biological Chemistry.

   ISSN 0250-5002
   II
NLM W1; AM9017   CODEN AMPBDV
   TITLE CHANGE
AMPI MEDICAL PHYSICS BULLETIN.
[AMPI med. phys. bull.]. **Added/Corp** Association of Medical Physicists of India. **VFOAT** Medical Physics Bulletin. (1976)-Vol. 18, No. 4 (Oct./Dec. 1993). Bulletin. English. Association of Medical Physicists of India, Trombay Bombay India. **(Subscription address:** Prints India, 11 Darya Ganj, New Delhi 110002 India. **Tel** 011 91 11 3268645, FAX 011 91 11 3275542, telex 31-61087 PRIN-IN.) **Continued by** Journal of Medical Physics.
Ind/Abst Chem. Abstr.; Energy Res. Abstr. (Oct. 1978-).

LC QH652.A1 A75a
DD 574.1/915/05   US
ANNUAL REPORT ON AFRRI RESEARCH. Main/Corp Armed Forces Radiobiology Research Institute (U.S.). (1991)-. English. One time a year. Armed Forces Radiobiology Research Institute, Defense Nuclear Agency, Washington DC 20814-5145. **Continues** Armed Forces Radiobiology Research Institute (U.S.). Annual Research Report.

LC QH505 .A55   ISSN 1056-8700
DD 574.19   US
   CCC
NLM W1; AN77EF   CODEN ABBSE4
ANNUAL REVIEW OF BIOPHYSICS AND BIOMOLECULAR STRUCTURE.
[Annu. rev. biophys. biomol. struct.]. Vol. 21 (1992)-. Academic Scholarly Publication. English. One time a year (June). $67.00. Annual Reviews Inc., 4139 El Camino Way, PO Box 10139, Palo Alto CA 94303-0139. **Tel** (415)493-4400, (800)523-8635, FAX (415)855-9815. **ED** Donald M. Engelman. Documents available from The Genuine Article, BIOSIS Document Express, Ask*IEEE, CASDDS. **Continues** Annual Review of Biophysics and Biological Chemistry, 0883-9182.
Ind/Abst Biol. Abstr.; Chem. Abstr.; Curr. Aware. Biol. Sci.; CABS; Curr. Contents Life Sci.; Index Med.; INIS Atomindex [Micro.]; INSPEC; Ref. Upd. Basic Ed.; Ref. Upd. Deluxe Ed.; Res. Alert [Full Cov.].

LC QH650   ISSN 0778-3124
DD 574.1   BE
UDC 57
NLM W1; AR3944   CODEN AIPBE4
   TITLE CHANGE
ARCHIVES INTERNATIONALES DE PHYSIOLOGIE, DE BIOCHIMIE ET DE BIOPHYSIQUE. See Biology-Physiology.

LC QP501 .A77   ISSN 0003-9861
DD 574.1905   US
   CCC
NLM W1 AR449   CODEN ABBIA4
ARCHIVES OF BIOCHEMISTRY AND BIOPHYSICS. See Biology-Biological Chemistry.

LC QH650   ISSN 0158-9938
DD 530   AT
NLM W1 AU335H   CODEN AUPMDI
Pr Rev.
AUSTRALASIAN PHYSICAL & ENGINEERING SCIENCES IN MEDICINE. See Biology-Bioengineering.

LC QH301 .B358   ISSN 0006-291X
DD 574.1/9/05   US
NLM W1 BI6198   CODEN BBRCA9
Pr Rev.
BIOCHEMICAL AND BIOPHYSICAL RESEARCH COMMUNICATIONS. See Biology-Biological Chemistry.

LC QD   ISSN 1065-7509
DD 540   US
UDC 54
●**BIOCHEMISTRY & BIOPHYSICS CITATION INDEX. See** Biology-Abstracting, Bibliographies and Statistics.

LC QD1 .B55
DD 574.1905   NE
NLM W1 BI652   CODEN BBACAQ
Pr Rev.
BIOCHIMICA ET BIOPHYSICA ACTA. See Biology-Biological Chemistry.

LC QD1 .B55   ISSN 0005-2736
   NE
   CCC
Pr Rev.
BIOCHIMICA ET BIOPHYSICA ACTA. BIOMEMBRANES. See Biology-Biological Chemistry.

LC QD   ISSN 0304-4165
DD 574.192   NE
   CCC
Pr Rev.
BIOCHIMICA ET BIOPHYSICA ACTA (G). See Biology-Biological Chemistry.

LC QP82.2.E43 B53   ISSN 0197-8462
DD 591.19/17   US
   CCC
NLM W1 BI663N   CODEN BLCTDO
Pr Rev.
BIOELECTROMAGNETICS.
[Bioelectromagnetics]. **Added/Corp** Bioelectromagnetics Society (Gaithersburg, Md.). Vol. 1 (1980)-. Academic Scholarly Publication. English. Six times a year. $540.00. John Wiley & Sons, Inc., 605 Third Avenue, New York NY 10158-0012. **Tel** (212)850-6000, (212)850-6645, FAX (212)850-6088, telex 12-7063. **(Subscription address:** John Wiley & Sons / UK, Baffins Lane, Chichester, West Sussex PO19 1UD United Kingdom. **Tel** 011 44 1243 779777, FAX 011 44 243 776128, telex 86290 WIBOOKG.) **ED** Ben Greenebaum, C. K. Chou, Kjell Hansson-Mild, Donald I. McRee. Documents available from The Genuine Article, BIOSIS Document Express, Ask*IEEE, CASDDS.
Desc: Devoted to research on biological systems influenced by natural or manufactured electric and/or magnetic fields at frequencies from DC to visible light. Devoted primarily to the publication of data from intensive experimental or clinical studies, but also includes theoretical papers, literature reviews, and brief experimental reports.
Ind/Abst Biol. Abstr.; Chem. Abstr.; Curr. Cit.; Curr. Contents Life Sci.; EMBASE; Health Plan. Adminis.; Index Med. (1980-); INIS Atomindex [Micro.]; INSPEC (1982-); Life Sci. Collect.; Ref. Upd. Deluxe Ed.; Res. Alert [Full Cov.]; Sci. Cit. Index; SCISEARCH; Soc. Sci. Cit. Index [Select. Cov.].

LC QH505.A1 B53   ISSN 0006-3029
DD 615.012   RU
   CCC
NLM W1 BI665   CODEN BIOFAI
Pr Rev.
BIOFIZIKA. [Biofizika]. **Added/Corp** Akademiia Nauk SSSR. Vol. 1 (1956)-. Academic Scholarly Publication. Russian. Six times a year. $287.50. Izdatelstvo Nauka / Akademiia Nauk, (Publishing House of the Russian Academy of Sciences), Leninskii Porspekt 14, 117901 Moscow Russia. **Tel** 011 95 9542153, FAX 011 95

9382144, telex 411964. **(Subscription address:** East View Publications Inc., 3020 Harbor Lane North, Suite 110, Minneapolis MN 55447. **Tel** (800)477-1005, (612)550-0961, FAX (612)559-2931.) Documents available from The Genuine Article, BIOSIS Document Express, Ask*IEEE, CASDDS.
Ind/Abst Biol. Abstr.; Chem. Abstr.; Chemorecept. Abstr.; CSA Neuro. Abstr.; Curr. Contents Life Sci.; Ei Page One; Energy Res. Abstr.; Index Med.; INSPEC (1973-); Int. Aerosp. Abstr. (1984-); Microbiol. Abstr. Sect. B; Life Sci. Collect.; PESTDOC; Res. Alert [Full Cov.]; Sci. Cit. Index; SCISEARCH; Vitis Vitic. Enol. Abstr.

LC R857.06 B55 **ISSN** 0966-9051
DD 574/.028 UK
NLM W1; BI666D
●**BIOIMAGING.** See Physics-Light, Optics, Radiation.

LC QP82.2.E43 B55 **ISSN** 0147-2372
DD 574.1/917/05 US
BIOLOGICAL EFFECTS OF ELECTROMAGNETIC RADIATION.
English. Four times a year. Franklin Institute Press, PO Box 2266, Philadelphia PA 19103.

LC QH650
DD 574.191 US
BIOLOGICAL EFFECTS OF NONIONIZING ELECTROMAGNETIC RADIATION. **Added/Corp** United States. National Telecommunications and Information Administration. Science Information Services, Inc. United States. Office of Telecommunications Policy. United States. Navy Dept. Franklin Institute (Philadelphia, Pa.). Science Information Service. Vol. 1 (Oct. 1976)-. Periodical. English. Four times a year. National Telecommunications and Information Administration, Washington DC 20230. Each issue contains an index to its own contents (no volume index)--loose. available on microfiche (Vols. for (Oct. 1980-June 1981--) distributed to depository libraries). ***Continues*** *Biological Effects of Electromagnetic Radiation.*

LC QH345 .B54 **ISSN** 0301-4622
DD 574.1/92/05 NE
CCC
NLM W1 BI876N **CODEN** BICIAZ
Pr Rev.
BIOPHYSICAL CHEMISTRY. See Biology-Biological Chemistry.

LC QH505.A1 B537 **ISSN** 0006-3495
DD 574.19/1/05 US
CCC
NLM W1 BI8765 **CODEN** BIOJAU
BIOPHYSICAL JOURNAL. [Biophys. j.]. **Added/Corp** Biophysical Society. New York Heart Association. Symposium. American Physical Society. Division of Biological Physics. Vol. 1 (Sept. 1960)-. Academic Scholarly Publication. English. Thirteen times a year. $720.00. Biophysical Society, 9650 Rockville Pike, Bethesda MD 20814. **Tel** (301)571-8338, FAX (301)530-7133. available on microfilm and microfiche from University Microfilms International (UMI). Documents available from The Genuine Article, BIOSIS Document Express, Ask*IEEE, CASDDS.
Desc: Publishes reports on the latest theoretical and experimental developments in biophysical research.
Ind/Abst AGRICOLA [Select. Cov.]; Biol. Abstr.; Calcium Calcif. Tissue Abstr.; Chem. Abstr.; CSA Neuro. Abstr.; Curr. Aware. Biol. Sci., CABS; Curr. Cit.; Curr. Contents Life Sci.; Ei Page One; EMBASE; Energy Res. Abstr.; Food Sci. Technol. Abstr.; Health Plan. Adminis.; Index Med. (Feb. 1974-); INIS Atomindex [Micro.]; INSPEC (Feb. 1974-); Int. Aerosp. Abstr.; Math. Rev.; Life Sci. Collect.; Ref. Upd. Basic Ed.; Ref. Upd. Deluxe Ed.; Res. Alert [Full Cov.]; Rev. Med. Vet. Entomol.; Sci. Cit. Index; SCISEARCH.

LC QH650 **ISSN** 0360-019X
US
NLM W1 BI879AC
BIOPHYSICS (BOSTON). (BIOPHYSICS.). Vol. 3 (1973)-. Periodical. English. Irregular. GK Hall & Co., 100 Front Street, Riverside NJ 08075. **Tel** (800)257-5755 ext. 2223.

LC QH505.A1 B54 **ISSN** 0006-3509
DD 574.1 UK
CCC
NLM W1 BI879 **CODEN** BIOPAE
BIOPHYSICS (OXFORD). (BIOPHYSICS.). [Biophysics (Oxford)]. Vol. 2 (1957)-. Periodical. English (Russian). Six times a year. $1718.00. Pergamon Press, An Imprint of Elsevier Science Ltd., The Boulevard, Langford Lane, Kidlington, Oxford OX5 1GB United Kingdom. **Tel** 011 44 1865 843000, 011 44 1865 843699, FAX 011 44 1865 843010. **(Subscription address:** Elsevier Science Ltd. / Oxford Fulfillment Centre, PO Box 800, Kidlington OX5 1DX United Kingdom. **Tel** 011 44 865 843355.) **ED** E. E. Fesenko. available on microfilm from Microfilms International Marketing Corp.; available on microfilm and microfiche from University Microfilms International (UMI); available on an online database from Elsevier Electronic Subscriptions (EES). Documents available from BIOSIS Document Express, Ask*IEEE, CASDDS.
Desc: Articles cover all aspects of biophysics including cell and molecular biophysics, subcellular structure and the physical-chemical properties of ultrastructure, the basis of neural and muscular activity, the control theory of living organisms at all levels, theoretical studies in genetics and immunology, photosynthesis, the effects of ultrasound, ionising and ultra-violet radiations on biological structure.
Ind/Abst AGRICOLA; Biol. Abstr.; Chem. Abstr.; Chemorecept. Abstr.; CSA Neuro. Abstr. (?-?); Curr. Aware. Biol. Sci., CABS; EMBASE; INSPEC (1972-); Toxicol. Abstr.

LC QH505 .B5 **ISSN** 0006-355X
DD 574.191 UK
CCC
NLM W1 BI892 **CODEN** BRHLAU
Pr Rev.
BIORHEOLOGY (OXFORD).
(BIORHEOLOGY.). [Biorheology (Oxford)]. **Added/Corp** International Society of Biorheology. Vol. 1 (July 1962)-. Periodical. English (French and German). Six times a year. $640.00. Pergamon Press, An Imprint of Elsevier Science Ltd., The Boulevard, Langford Lane, Kidlington, Oxford OX5 1GB United Kingdom. **Tel** 011 44 1865 843000, 011 44 1865 843699, FAX 011 44 1865 843010. **(Subscription address:** Elsevier Science Ltd. / Oxford Fulfillment Centre, PO Box 800, Kidlington OX5 1DX United Kingdom. **Tel** 011 44 865 843355.) **ED** Alexander Silberberg. available on microfilm from Microfilms International Marketing Corp.; available on microfilm and microfiche from University Microfilms International (UMI); available on an online database from Elsevier Electronic Subscriptions (EES). Documents available from The Genuine Article, BIOSIS Document Express, Ask*IEEE, CASDDS, ADONIS.
Desc: Publishes work concerned with processes in the living organisms (in vivo) and with materials originating from the organisms (extracorporeal).The interrelationship is stressed between rheological properties of biological systems and their various structural aspects.
Ind/Abst ADONIS; AGRICOLA; Appl. Mech. Rev.; Biol. Abstr.; Chem. Abstr.; Curr. Cit.; Curr. Contents Life Sci.; Dairy Sci. Abstr.; EMBASE; Health Plan. Adminis.; Index Med.; INSPEC (1978-); Int. Aerosp. Abstr. (1983-); Life Sci. Collect.; Res. Alert [Full Cov.]; Sci. Cit. Index; SCISEARCH.

ISSN 0007-5434
DD 574 016 FR
BULLETIN SIGNALETIQUE 320: BIOCHEMIE. BIOPHYSIQUE. CHEMIE ANALYTIQUE BIOLOGIQUE. BIOPHYSIQUE. GENIE BIOLOGIQUE ET MEDICAL. See Biology-Biological Chemistry.

LC QD415 **ISSN** 0305-7232
DD 574.192 US
CCC
NLM W1 CA673 **CODEN** CABCD4
Pr Rev.
CANCER BIOCHEMISTRY BIOPHYSICS. See Medical Sciences-Cancer and Neoplastic Syndromes.

LC QH573 .C393 **ISSN** 0163-4992
DD 574.87/6041 US
CCC
NLM W1 CE128I **CODEN** CBIODE
Pr Rev.
CELL BIOPHYSICS. [Cell biophys.]. Vol. 1 (Mar. 1979)-. Academic Scholarly Publication. English. Six times a year. $295.00. Humana Press Inc., 999 Riverview Drive, Suite 208, Totawa NJ 07512. **Tel** (201)256-1699, FAX (201)256-8341. **ED** Fred Sachs and Edward Massaro. Index available. **Bk Rev. Ad Acc. Circ:** 250. Documents available from The Genuine Article, BIOSIS Document Express, CASDDS.
Desc: The key periodical dealing with the biophysical aspects of cell biology, immunology, analytical cytology, and neurobiology.
Ind/Abst Biol. Abstr. (1989-); Chem. Abstr.; Curr. Cit.; Curr. Contents Life Sci.; EMBASE; Health Plan. Adminis.; Helminthol. Abstr.; Index Med. (1979-); Life Sci. Collect.; PESTDOC; Protozoolog. Abstr.; Res. Alert [Full Cov.]; Sci. Cit. Index (19??-19??); SCISEARCH.

LC QP501 .S46 **ISSN** 0898-512X
DD 574.19/05 US
CCC
NLM W1; SH2871P
CHINESE JOURNAL OF BIOCHEMISTRY AND BIOPHYSICS. See Biology-Biological Chemistry.

LC QH506 .C64 **ISSN** 0143-8123
DD 574.8/8 US
CCC
NLM W1 CO375M **CODEN** CMCBDM
COMMENTS ON MOLECULAR AND CELLULAR BIOPHYSICS. (COMMENTS ON MODERN BIOLOGY, PART A, COMMENTS ON MOLECULAR AND CELLULAR BIOPHYSICS.). [Comments mol. cell. biophys.]. **VFOAT** Comments on Molecular and Cellular Biophysics. Vol. 1, No. 1 (Dec. 1980)-. Academic Scholarly Publication. English. Six times a year (1 volume). $508.00 (academic institutions), $792.00 (corporate institutions). Gordon & Breach Science Publishers, Inc., PO Box 786, Cooper Station, New York NY 10276. **Tel** (212)206-8900, FAX (212)645-2459. Documents available from Ask*IEEE, CASDDS.
Ind/Abst Chem. Abstr.; INSPEC (1980-).

LC QH324 .C9 **ISSN** 0011-2240
DD 574.19/167/05 US
CCC
NLM W1 CR997 **CODEN** CRYBAS
Pr Rev.
CRYOBIOLOGY. See Biology-Biological Chemistry.

LC QH511.A1 C87 **ISSN** 0070-2129
DD 574.1908 US
CCC
NLM W1 CU82C **CODEN** CUTBAO
CURRENT TOPICS IN BIOENERGETICS.
[Curr. top. bioenerg.]. Vol. 1 (1966)-. Monographic series. English. Irregular. Price varies per volume. Academic Press Inc., 6277 Sea Harbor Drive, Orlando FL 32887. **Tel** (800)543-9534, (407)345-4100, FAX (407)352-3445. **ED** D. R. Sanadi. Documents available from The Genuine Article, CASDDS.
Ind/Abst AGRICOLA; Chem. Abstr. (1966-1981); Curr. Aware. Biol. Sci., CABS; Curr. Cit.; Index Sci. Rev. [Full Cov.]; Life Sci. Collect.; Res. Alert [Full Cov.]; Sci. Cit. Index (19??-19??); SCISEARCH.

LC QH505 .A316a **ISSN** 0012-4974
DD 574.191 US
CCC
NLM W1 DO64BP **CODEN** DOKBAG
Pr Rev.
DOKLADY. BIOPHYSICS. [Dokl., Biophys.]. **Main/Corp** Akademiia Nauk SSSR. **Added/Corp** Consultants Bureau Enterprises. Consultants Bureau. **VFOAT** Biophysics. Vol. 154/156 (Jan./June 1964)-. Academic Scholarly Publication. English (Russian). Two times a year. $475.00. MAIK Nauka / Interperiodica, Ulitsa Profsoyuznaia 90, Moscow 117864 Russia. **ED** V.A. Kabanov. available on microfilm and microfiche from University Microfilms International (UMI). Documents available from BIOSIS Document Express, Ask*IEEE, BLDSC, FAXON Xpress, SWETS, UMI Article Clearinghouse, The UnCover Company. ***Continues in part*** *Akademiia Nauk SSSR. Doklady. Biological Sciences Sections, 0886-7534.*
Desc: An English translation of Russian research by the Academy of Science of the USSR in biophysics.
Ind/Abst AGRICOLA [Select. Cov.]; Biol. Abstr. (?-1983); EMBASE; Energy Res. Abstr. (Feb. 1975-); INIS Atomindex [Micro.]; INSPEC (Jan./June 1972-1986).

LC QP341 .J66 **ISSN** 1061-9526
DD 574.19/17/05 US
CCC
NLM W1; EL299E **CODEN** ELAGE9
ELECTRO- AND MAGNETOBIOLOGY.
[Electro- magnetobiol.]. **Added/Corp** International Society for Bioelectricity. Vol. 11, No. 1 (1992)-. Academic Scholarly Publication. English. Three times a year. $475.00. Marcel Dekker Inc., 270 Madison Avenue, New York NY 10016. **Tel** (212)696-9000, (800)228-1160, FAX (212)685-4540, telex 421419. **(Subscription address:** Marcel Dekker Inc., PO Box 5017, Monticello NY 12701. **Tel** (800)228-1160.) Documents available from The Genuine Article, BIOSIS Document Express, Ask*IEEE, CASDDS. ***Continues*** *Journal of Bioelectricity, 0730-823X.*
Desc: Covers electrophysiology, electromagnetic fields, and radiation.
Ind/Abst Biol. Abstr.; Chem. Abstr.; Curr. Contents Life Sci.; EMBASE; INSPEC; Life Sci. Collect.; Res. Alert [Full Cov.]; Sci. Cit. Index.

LC QH505 .E93 **ISSN** 0175-7571
DD 574.19/1/05 GW
CCC
NLM W1; EU612M **CODEN** EBJOE8
Pr Rev.
EUROPEAN BIOPHYSICS JOURNAL.
(EUROPEAN BIOPHYSICS JOURNAL : EBJ.). [Eur. biophys. j.]. **VFOAT** EBJ. Vol. 11, No. 1 (July 1984)-. Academic Scholarly Publication. English. Six times a year. $826.00. Springer-Verlag GmbH & Company KG, Heidelberger Platz 3, D-14197 Berlin Germany. **Tel** 011 49 30 8207223, FAX 011 49 30 8214091, telex 183 319 SPBLN D. **(Subscription address:** Springer-Verlag New York Inc. / North America, PO Box 2485, Journal Fulfillment, Secaucus NJ 07096. **Tel** (201)348-4033, (800)777-4643, FAX (201)348-4505.) **ED** P Bayley, F Conti, R Rigler, and E Sackmann. **Circ:** 260. available on microfilm from University Microfilms International (UMI). Documents available from The Genuine Article, Ask*IEEE, CASDDS. ***Continues*** *Biophysics of Structure and Mechanism, 0340-1057.*
Desc: Covers topics such as: molecular structure and interactions, membrane and receptor biophysics, thermodynamics and energetics of biological processes, and theoretical biophysics.
Ind/Abst Chem. Abstr. (July 1984-); Curr. Aware. Biol. Sci., CABS; Curr. Cit.; Curr. Contents Life Sci.; EMBASE; Energy Res. Abstr. (July 1984-); Index Med.; INSPEC (July 1984-); Life Sci. Collect.; Ref. Upd. Deluxe Ed.; Res. Alert [Full Cov.]; Rev. Med. Vet. Mycology; Sci. Cit. Index; SCISEARCH; Soc. Sci. Cit. Index [Select. Cov.].

LC Z6658 ISSN 0014-4312
DD 016.61 NE
CCC
NLM ZW 1 E978E

EXCERPTA MEDICA. SECTION 27. BIOPHYSICS, BIOENGINEERING AND MEDICAL INSTRUMENTATION. See Medical Sciences-Abstracting, Bibliographies and Statistics.

LC QH650 ISSN 0178-9600
DD 574.191 GW
NLM W1; FO813

FORTSCHRITT-BERICHTE VDI. REIHE 17, BIOTECHNIK. [Fortscht.-Ber. VDI, 17 Biotech.]. **Added/Corp** Verein Deutscher Ingenieure. **VFOAT** Biotechnik. (198?)-. Monographic series. German. Irregular. Price varies per volume. VDI Verlag GmbH, Postfach 101054, D-40001 Dusseldorf Germany. **Tel** 011 49 211 6188313, FAX 011 49 211 6188133. ***Continues*** *Fortschritt-Berichte der VDI Zeitschriften. Reihe 17: Biotechnik, 0341-1702.*

LC RB170 .F74 ISSN 8755-0199
DD 574.19/283 SZ
NLM W1; FR5986 CODEN TRCOEC
Pr Rev. **TITLE CHANGE**

FREE RADICAL RESEARCH COMMUNICATIONS. [Free radic. res. commun.]. Vol. 1, No. 1 (1985)-(19??). Academic Scholarly Publication. English. Harwood Academic Publishers, PO Box 90, Reading RG1 8JL United Kingdom. **Tel** 011 44 1734 560080, FAX 011 44 1734 568211. **ED** J. V. Bannister. **Bk Rev. Ad Acc.** Documents available from The Genuine Article, CASDDS. ***Continued by*** *Free Radical Research.*
Ind/Abst Chem. Abstr. (1985-); Curr. Aware. Biol. Sci., CABS; Curr. Cit.; Curr. Contents Life Sci.; Health Plan. Adminis.; Index Med.; Nutr. Abstr. Rev., Ser. A, Hum. Exp.; Protozoolog. Abstr.; Ref. Upd. Deluxe Ed.; Res. Alert [Full Cov.]; Rev. Agric. Entomol.; Rev. Med. Vet. Mycology; Sci. Cit. Index; SCISEARCH.

LC QP1 .G46 ISSN 0231-5882
DD 591.1/05 XO
NLM W1; GE256 CODEN GPBIE2
Pr Rev.

GENERAL PHYSIOLOGY AND BIOPHYSICS. See Biology-Physiology.

LC QH650 ISSN 0266-1144
DD 574.191 UK
CCC
Pr Rev.

GEOTEXTILES AND GEOMEMBRANES. (GEOTEXTILES AND GEOMEMBRANES : AN OFFICIAL JOURNAL OF THE INTERNATIONAL GEOTEXTILE SOCIETY.). [Geotext. geomembr.]. **Added/Corp** International Geotextile Society. Vol. 1 (1984)-. Academic Scholarly Publication. English. Twelve times a year. $398.00. Elsevier Applied Science, An Imprint of Elsevier Science Ltd., The Boulevard, Langford Lane, Kidlington, Oxford OX5 1GB United Kingdom. **Tel** 011 44 1865 843000, 011 44 1865 843699, FAX 011 44 1865 843010. **(Subscription address:** Elsevier Science Ltd. / Oxford Fulfillment Centre, PO Box 800, Kidlington OX5 1DX United Kingdom. **Tel** 011 44 865 843355.**) ED** T. S. Ingold. available on microfilm and microfiche from University Microfilms International (UMI); available on an online database from Elsevier Electronic Subscriptions (EES). Documents available from Article Express International, The Genuine Article.
Desc: Provides a forum for the dissemination of information amongst research workers, designers, engineers and manufacturers.
Ind/Abst Curr. Cit.; Curr. Contents Eng. Comput. Technol.; Ei Page One; Eng. Index Annu.; Fluid Abstr., Civil Eng.; Fluid Abstr. Proc. Eng.; FLUIDEX; Geogr. Abstr. Phys. Geogr.; Geotech. Abstr.; Nonwovens Abstr.; Res. Alert [Select. Cov.]; SCISEARCH; Text. Technol. Dig.

LC QH650 ISSN 0073-0475
DD 574.191 US
CODEN HBBIAD

HARVARD BOOKS IN BIOPHYSICS. [Harv. books biophys.]. Academic Scholarly Publication. English. Irregular. Price varies per volume. Harvard University Press, 79 Garden Street, Cambridge MA 02138. **Tel** (617)496-1344, (800)448-2242. Documents available from BIOSIS Document Express, CASDDS.
Ind/Abst Biol. Abstr.; Chem. Abstr. (1965-1983).

LC QH505.A1 H4 ISSN 0017-9078
DD 612.01448 US
CCC
NLM W1 HE4705 CODEN HLTPAO
Pr Rev.

HEALTH PHYSICS (1958). (HEALTH PHYSICS : OFFICIAL JOURNAL OF THE HEALTH PHYSICS SOCIETY.). [Health phys.]. **Added/Corp** Health Physics Society. Vol. 1, No. 1 (June 1958)-. Academic Scholarly Publication. English. Twelve times a year. $689.00. Williams & Wilkins Company, 428 East Preston Street, Baltimore MD 21202-3993. **Tel** (410)528-4000, (800)638-6423, FAX (410)528-8596, telex 87669. **(Subscription address:** Williams & Wilkins, PO Box 64380, Baltimore MD 21264. **Tel** 800 638-6423.**) ED** Genevieve Roessler. cum. index. available on microfilm and microfiche from University Microfilms International (UMI). Documents available from , The Genuine Article, BIOSIS Document Express, Ask*IEEE, CASDDS, , Documents on Demand, ADONIS, Quick Copies.
Desc: The official journal of the Health Physics Society. Provides nuclear chemists and health physicists a practical and effective means for communicating with radiation professionals around the globe.
Ind/Abst ADONIS; AGRICOLA; Biol. Abstr.; Chem. Abstr.; Chem. Titles; CIS Abstr.; Coal Abstr.; Cumul. Index Nurs. Allied Health Lit.; Curr. Aware. Biol. Sci., CABS; Curr. Biotechnol.; Curr. Cit.; Curr. Contents Life Sci.; Dairy Sci. Abstr.; EMBASE; Energy Inf. Abstr.; Energy Res. Abstr.; Environ. Abstr.; Environ. Period. Bibliogr.; Field Crop Abstr.; Food Sci. Technol. Abstr.; GeoRef; Grass. Forage Abstr.; Health Saf. Sci. Abstr.; Health Devices Alerts; Health Plan. Adminis.; Index Med.; Index Vet.; Ind. Hyg. Dig. (19??-19??); INIS Atomindex [Micro.]; INSPEC (Jan. 1972-); Int. Aerosp. Abstr.; Maize Abstr.; MINPROC; Mintec, Min. Technol. Abstr.; Nucl. Sci. Abstr.; Nutr. Abstr. Rev., Ser. B, Live Feeds and Feed.; Nutr. Abstr. Rev., Ser. A, Hum. Exp.; Life Sci. Collect.; Phys. Med. Biol. (19??-19??); Pollut. Abstr. Indexes; Poult. Abstr.; Res. Alert [Full Cov.]; Risk Abstr.; Saf. Health Work; Sci. Cit. Index; SCISEARCH; Sel. Water Resour. Abstr.; Soc. Sci. Cit. Index [Select. Cov.]; Soils Fert.; Soyabean Abstr.; Vet. Bull.; Toxicol. Abstr.; Trop. Dis. Bull.; Wheat Barley Trit. Abstr.

ISSN 0367-6110
JA
CODEN HOKBAQ

HOKEN BUTSURI. (HOKEN BUTSURI : JOURNAL OF THE JAPAN HEALTH PHYSICS SOCIETY.). [Hoken butsuri]. **Added/Corp** Nihon Hoken Butsuri Gakkai. (1966)-. Academic Scholarly Publication. Japanese (summaries and/or abstracts in English; table of contents in English). Four times a year. $149.17. **(Subscription address:** Maruzen Company Ltd., PO Box 5050, Import & Export Department, Tokyo 100 31 Japan. **Tel** 011 81 3 32789224.**)** Documents available from CASDDS.
Ind/Abst Chem. Abstr.

LC QH345 .H66 ISSN 0096-2708
DD 574.1/9/05 US
NLM W1 HO596T CODEN HZBBAO
CEASED

HORIZONS IN BIOCHEMISTRY AND BIOPHYSICS. See Biology-Biological Chemistry.

ISSN 0245-8608
FR
UDC 574.191

ICHTYOPHYSIOLOGICA ACTA. [Ichtyophysiol. acta]. (1977)-. Periodical. French. One time a year.
Ind/Abst Aquat. Sci. Fish. Abstr. [CD-ROM Ed.].

LC QP501 .I42 ISSN 0301-1208
DD 612.015 II
NLM W1 IN206PR CODEN IJBBBQ
Pr Rev.

INDIAN JOURNAL OF BIOCHEMISTRY & BIOPHYSICS. See Biology-Biological Chemistry.

LC QP519.7 .J68 ISSN 0165-022X
DD 574.19/2/028 NE
CCC
NLM W1 JO562 CODEN JBBMDG
Pr Rev.

JOURNAL OF BIOCHEMICAL AND BIOPHYSICAL METHODS. See Biology-Biological Chemistry.

LC QH505 .J66 ISSN 0092-0606
DD 574.1/91/05 NE
CCC
NLM W1 JO564E CODEN JBPHBZ
Pr Rev.

JOURNAL OF BIOLOGICAL PHYSICS. [J. biol. phys.]. Vol. 1 (Nov. 1973)-. Academic Scholarly Publication. English. Four times a year. $234.00. Kluwer Academic Publishers / Massachusetts, PO Box 358, Accord Station, Hingham MA 02018. **Tel** (617)871-6600. **ED** Terence Barrett, P.L. Christiansen, A.C. Scott. **Bk Rev. Ad Acc. Acid Free. Circ:** 400 (ctrl). available on microfilm and microfiche from University Microfilms International (UMI). Documents available from BIOSIS Document Express, Ask*IEEE, CASDDS.
Desc: Research articles describing original research in biological physics emphasizing the applications and use of experimental and/or theoretical methods of physics.
Ind/Abst AGRICOLA [Select. Cov.]; Biol. Abstr.; Chem. Abstr.; CSA Neuro. Abstr. (?-?); EMBASE; INSPEC (1982-); Life Sci. Collect.

LC QH641 .J67 ISSN 0884-3996
DD 574.19/125/05 UK
CCC
NLM W1; JO564K CODEN JBCHE7
Pr Rev.

JOURNAL OF BIOLUMINESCENCE AND CHEMILUMINESCENCE. [J. biolumin. chemilumin.]. Vol. 1, No. 1 (June 1986)-. Academic Scholarly Publication. English. Six times a year. $495.00. John Wiley & Sons Ltd., Baffins Lane, Chichester, West Sussex PO19 1UD United Kingdom. **Tel** 011 44 1243 779777, FAX 011 44 1243 776128 BTG:JWP001, telex 86290 WIBOOKG. **(Subscription address:** John Wiley & Sons, Inc. / Philadelphia, PO Box 7247, Philadelphia PA 19170. **Tel** (212)850-6645, (800)225-5945.**) ED** L. J. Kricka. available on microfilm and microfiche from University Microfilms International (UMI). Documents available from The Genuine Article, BIOSIS Document Express, Ask*IEEE, CASDDS.
Desc: Devoted to fundamental and applied aspects of chemiluminescence and bioluminescence, including their uses as research tools in fields as chemistry, clinical sciences, environmental monitoring and microbiology.
Ind/Abst Anal. Abstr.; Biol. Abstr. (1989-); Chem. Abstr.; Curr. Aware. Biol. Sci., CABS; Curr. Biotechnol.; Curr. Cit.; Curr. Contents Life Sci.; Curr. Contents Phys. Chem. Earth Sci.; Index Med. (Vol. 1 No. 1, 1986-); INSPEC (June 1988-); Life Sci. Collect.; Res. Alert [Full Cov.]; Sci. Cit. Index; SCISEARCH.

LC QP303 .J6 ISSN 0021-9290
DD 591.1/852 US
CCC
NLM W1 JO564T CODEN JBMCBS
Pr Rev.

JOURNAL OF BIOMECHANICS. [J. biomech.]. **Added/Corp** University of Michigan. Highway Safety Research Institute. American Society of Biomechanics. European Society of Biomechanics. Vol. 1, No. 1 (1968)-. Academic Scholarly Publication. English. Twelve times a year. $1233.00. Pergamon Press, An Imprint of Elsevier Science Ltd., The Boulevard, Langford Lane, Kidlington, Oxford OX5 1GB United Kingdom. **Tel** 011 44 1865 843000, 011 44 1865 843699, FAX 011 44 1865 843010. **(Subscription address:** Elsevier Science Ltd. / Oxford Fulfillment Centre, PO Box 800, Kidlington OX5 1DX United Kingdom. **Tel** 011 44 865 843355.**) ED** Richard Brand and Rik Huiskes. available on microfiche from University Microfilms International (UMI); available on an online database from Elsevier Electronic Subscriptions (EES). Documents available from Article Express International, The Genuine Article, BIOSIS Document Express, Ask*IEEE.
Desc: Publishes original research concerning the application of mechanics to medical and biological problems. Analytical as well as experimental papers are accepted for publication.
Ind/Abst Abstr. Anthropol.; AGRICOLA; Biol. Abstr.; Civ. Struct. Eng. Abstr.; CSA Neuro. Abstr. (?-?); Curr. Aware. Biol. Sci., CABS; Curr. Cit.; Curr. Contents Life Sci.; Curr. Titles Dent.; Ei Page One; Elect. Comm. Abstr.; EMBASE; Energy Res. Abstr.; Eng. Index Annu.; Ergon. Abstr.; Index Med.; INIS Atomindex [Micro.]; INSPEC (May 1970-); Int. Aerosp. Abstr.; Mater. Sci. Eng. Abstr.; Math. Rev.; Life Sci. Collect.; Ref. Upd. Deluxe Ed.; Res. Alert [Full Cov.]; Sci. Cit. Index; SCISEARCH; Soc. Sci. Cit. Index [Select. Cov.]; SPORT Discus; SportSearch.

LC QP519.9.N83 J68 ISSN 0925-2738
DD 612.015 NE
CCC
NLM W1; JO564UL CODEN JBNME9
Pr Rev.

JOURNAL OF BIOMOLECULAR NMR. Vol. 1 No. 1 (May 1991)-. Academic Scholarly Publication. English. Six times a year. $658.00. ESCOM Science Publishers BV, PO Box 214, 2300 AE Leiden The Netherlands. **Tel** 011 31 71 127052. **ED** Kurt Wuethrich, Y Arata, A Bax, R Kaptein, and B D Sykes. Index available. cum. index. **Ad Acc.** Documents available from The Genuine Article, CASDDS.
Desc: Provides a forum for publishing research on technical developments and innovative applications of nuclear magnetic resonance spectroscopy for the study of structure and dynamic properties of biopolymers in solution, liquid crystals, solids, and mixed environments.
Ind/Abst Chem. Abstr.; Curr. Aware. Biol. Sci., CABS; Curr. Cit.; Curr. Contents Life Sci.; Index Med. (May 1991-); Res. Alert [Full Cov.]; Sci. Cit. Index.

LC QH506 .J66 ISSN 0739-1102
DD 574.19/2 US
CCC
NLM W1; JO564W CODEN JBSDD6
Pr Rev.

JOURNAL OF BIOMOLECULAR STRUCTURE & DYNAMICS. [J. biomol. struct. dyn.]. **VFOAT** Journal of Biomolecular Structure and Dynamics. Vol. 1, Issue No. 1 (Oct. 1983)-. Academic Scholarly Publication. English. Six times a year (Feb., Apr., June, Aug., Oct., Dec.). $775.00. Adenine Press, PO Box 355/340, Guilderland NY 12084. **Tel** (518)456-0784, FAX (518)452-4955. **ED** R. H. Sarma. Index available. cum. index. **Bk Rev. Ad Acc.** ctrl circ. Documents available from The Genuine Article, BIOSIS Document Express, CASDDS.
Desc: Biological structure, dynamics, interactions and expression; both experimental and theoretical studies.
Ind/Abst AGRICOLA [Select. Cov.]; Biol. Abstr.; Chem. Abstr. (1983-); Chem. Titles; Curr. Aware. Biol. Sci., CABS; Curr. Cit.; Curr. Contents Life Sci.; EMBASE; Index Med. (Vol. 1, No. 1, 1983-); Nucl. Acids Abstr.; Life Sci. Collect. (1985-); Ref. Upd. Deluxe Ed.; Res. Alert [Full Cov.]; Sci. Cit. Index; SCISEARCH.

LC QH650 ISSN 0992-3039 FR CCC
NLM W1; JO323P CODEN JMNBEJ
Pr Rev. TITLE CHANGE

JOURNAL OF MEDECINE NUCLEAIRE ET BIOPHYSIQUE. [J. med. nucl. biophys.]. **Added/Corp** Societe Francaise de Biophysique et Medecine Nucleaire. Vol. 12 (1988)-(199?). Academic Scholarly Publication. French (summaries and/or abstracts in English). Editions Scientifique Elsevier, 141 rue de Javel, 75747 Paris Cedex 15 France. **Tel** 011 33 1 45589067, FAX 011 33 1 45589424. Documents available from The Genuine Article, BIOSIS Document Express, Ask*IEEE, CASDDS. ***Continues*** *Journal de Biophysique et de Biomecanique, 0766-5717.* ***Continued by*** *Medecine Nucleaire, 0928-1258.*
Ind/Abst Biol. Abstr. (1988-); Chem. Abstr.; EMBASE; INSPEC; Res. Alert [Full Cov.]; Sci. Cit. Index (19??-19??); SCISEARCH.

II

NLM W1; AM9017

•**JOURNAL OF MEDICAL PHYSICS.** **Added/Corp** Association of Medical Physicists of India. Vol. 19, No. 1 (Jan./Mar. 1994)-. Academic Scholarly Publication. English. Four times a year. Association of Medical Physicists of India, Trombay Bombay India. (**Subscription address:** Prints India, 11 Darya Ganj, New Delhi 110002 India. **Tel** 011 91 11 3268645, FAX 011 91 11 3275542, telex 31-61087 PRIN-IN.) ***Continues*** *AMPI Medical Physics Bulletin, 0250-5002.*

LC QH505 .J67 ISSN 1047-1200
DD 574.19/1 US
NLM W1; JO795HR CODEN JNOBEV
Pr Rev. TITLE CHANGE

JOURNAL OF NONLINEAR BIOLOGY. [J. nonlinear biol.]. Vol. 1 No. 1 (1990)-(199?). Periodical. English. Nova Science Publishers Inc., 6080 Jericho Turnpike, Suite 207, Commack NY 11725-2808. **Tel** (516)499-3103, (516)499-3106, FAX (516)499-3146. **ED** E. Volkov. Index available. **Bk Rev. Circ:** 400. ***Continued by*** *Progress in Biochemistry and Biotechnology.*

LC QH301 ISSN 0385-1036
DD 574 JA
NLM W1; MA492YL CODEN MAKUD9

MAKU. (MAKU = MEMBRANE.). [Maku]. **Added/Corp** Maku Konwakai (Japan) Nihon Maku Gakkai. **VFOAT** Membrane. Vol. 1, No. 1 (1976)-. Academic Scholarly Publication. Japanese (English). Six times a year. ¥2800. Nihon Maku Gakkai / Membrane Society of Japan, 14-9 Hongo 4-chome, Bunkyo-ku Tokyo 113 Japan. Documents available from BIOSIS Document Express, CASDDS.
Ind/Abst Biol. Abstr.; Chem. Abstr.

ISSN 0928-1258 FR CCC
NLM W1; ME148B

•**MEDECINE NUCLEAIRE : IMAGERIE FONCTIONELLE ET METABOLIQUE.** See Medical Sciences-Nuclear Medicine.

LC QP ISSN 0143-0203
DD 612 UK
NLM W1 ME409V CODEN MPHAE6

MEDICAL PHYSICS HANDBOOKS. [Med. phys. handb.]. **Added/Corp** Hospital Physicists' Association. (1979)-. Monographic series. English. Irregular. Price varies per volume. Documents available from BIOSIS Document Express, Ask*IEEE.
Ind/Abst Biol. Abstr. (1985-); INSPEC.

LC R895.A1 M44 ISSN 0094-2405
DD 610/1/53 US CCC
NLM W1 ME409R CODEN MPHYA6
Pr Rev.

MEDICAL PHYSICS (LANCASTER). (MEDICAL PHYSICS.). [Med. phys.]. **Added/Corp** American Association of Physicists in Medicine. American Institute of Physics. Vol. 1 (1974)-. Academic Scholarly Publication. English. Twelve times a year. $475.00. American Institute of Physics, 500 Sunnyside Boulevard, Woodbury NY 11797-2999. **Tel** (516)576-2270, (800)344-6902, FAX (516)349-9704, telex 960983. available on microfiche; available on microfilm. Documents available from The Genuine Article, BIOSIS Document Express, Ask*IEEE, CASDDS. ***Continues*** *Quarterly Bulletin - American Association of Physicists in Medicine, 0001-0162.*
Desc: Covers medical physics and biophysics.
Ind/Abst Acoust. Abstr.; Biol. Abstr.; Chem. Abstr.; Curr. Cit.; Curr. Contents Clin. Med.; Curr. Contents Life Sci.; Curr. Phys. Index; EMBASE; Energy Res. Abstr. (Sept. 1974-); Health Devices Alerts; Index Med.; INIS Atomindex [Micro.]; INSPEC (1974-); Int. Aerosp. Abstr.; Life Sci. Collect.; Phys. Med. Biol. (19??-19??); Pollut. Abstr. Indexes; Res. Alert [Full Cov.]; Sci. Cit. Index; SCISEARCH; SPIN (1974-).

ISSN 0163-1802
DD 610/.1/53 US
NLM W1 ME409W

MEDICAL PHYSICS MONOGRAPH. **Added/Corp** American Association of Physicists in Medicine. American Institute of Physics. (1978)-. Monographic series. English. Irregular. Price varies per volume. American Institute of Physics, 500 Sunnyside Boulevard, Woodbury NY 11797-2999. **Tel** (516)576-2270, (800)344-6902, FAX (516)349-9704, telex 960983. ***Continues*** *AAPM Monograph.*

ISSN 0301-374X UK
NLM W1 NE512N CODEN NTBPAM

NEW TECHNIQUES IN BIOPHYSICS AND CELL BIOLOGY. [New tech. biophys. cell biol.]. Vol. 1 (1973)-. Monographic series. English. Irregular. Price varies per volume. John Wiley & Sons Ltd., Baffins Lane, Chichester, West Sussex PO19 1UD United Kingdom. **Tel** 011 44 1243 779777, FAX 011 44 1243 776128 BTG:JWP001, telex 86290 WIBOOKG. (**Subscription address:** John Wiley & Sons, Inc. / Philadelphia, PO Box 7247, Philadelphia PA 19170. **Tel** (212)850-6645, (800)225-5945.) **ED** R.H. Pain and B.J. Smith. Documents available from BIOSIS Document Express, BIOSIS Document Express.
Ind/Abst Biol. Abstr. (-1976).

ISSN 1146-5255 FR
UDC 011

PASCAL. F 52, BIOCHIMIE, BIOPHYSIQUE MOLECULAIRE, BIOLOGIE MOLECULAIRE ET CELLULAIRE. See Biology-Biological Chemistry.

ISSN 0272-6327
DD 574 SZ
NLM W3 PE871AG

PERSPECTIVES IN BIOMECHANICS. [Perspect. biomech.]. Vol. 1, Pt. A (1980)-. Periodical. English. Irregular. Price varies. Harwood Academic Publishers, PO Box 90, Reading RG1 8JL United Kingdom. **Tel** 011 44 1734 560080, FAX 011 44 1734 568211. (**Subscription address:** Harwood Academic Publishers, PO Box 786, Cooper Station, New York NY 10276. **Tel** (201)643-7500.) **ED** D.N. Ghista.

LC QH650 ISSN 1120-1797 SZ
NLM W1; PH682

PHYSICA MEDICA. (PHYSICA MEDICA : PM : AN INTERNATIONAL JOURNAL DEVOTED TO THE APPLICATIONS OF PHYSICS TO MEDICINE AND BIOLOGY : OFFICIAL JOURNAL OF THE ITALIAN ASSOCIATION OF BIOMEDICAL PHYSICS (AIFB).). [Phys. med.]. **Added/Corp** Associazione Italiana di Fisica Biomedica. **VFOAT** PM. (1987)-. Periodical. English. Four times a year. $204.38. Giardini Editori Stampatori, Via Santa Bibbiana 28, 56127 Pisa Italy. **Tel** 011 39 50 934242. ***Continues*** *Fisica in Medicina, 1120-1916.*
Ind/Abst EMBASE.

LC QH505 .P47 ISSN 0031-9155
DD 574.191 UK CCC
NLM W1 PH844 CODEN PHMBA7
Pr Rev.

PHYSICS IN MEDICINE & BIOLOGY. See Biology-Abstracting, Bibliographies and Statistics.

LC QP501 .P48 ISSN 0748-6642
DD 574.19/2/05 US
NLM W1; PH926K CODEN PCPNER
Pr Rev.

PHYSIOLOGICAL CHEMISTRY AND PHYSICS AND MEDICAL NMR. See Biology-Biological Chemistry.

LC QH505.A1 P76 ISSN 0079-6107
DD 574.1 US CCC
NLM W1 PR667 CODEN PBIMAC
Pr Rev.

PROGRESS IN BIOPHYSICS AND MOLECULAR BIOLOGY. [Prog. biophys. mol. biol.]. Vol. 13 (1963)-. Academic Scholarly Publication. English. Six times a year. $767.00. Pergamon Press, An Imprint of Elsevier Science Ltd., The Boulevard, Langford Lane, Kidlington, Oxford OX5 1GB United Kingdom. **Tel** 011 44 1865 843000, 011 44 1865 843699, FAX 011 44 1865 843010. (**Subscription address:** Elsevier Science Ltd. / Oxford Fulfillment Centre, PO Box 800, Kidlington OX5 1DX United Kingdom. **Tel** 011 44 865 843355.) **ED** Denis Noble and Tom Blundell. cum. index. available on microfilm and microfiche from University Microfilms International (UMI); available on an online database from Elsevier Electronic Subscriptions (EES). Documents available from The Genuine Article, BIOSIS Document Express, Ask*IEEE, CASDDS. ***Continues*** *Progress in Biophysics and Biophysical Chemistry, 0096-4174.*
Ind/Abst Anim. Breed. Abstr.; Biol. Abstr.; Chem. Abstr.; Curr. Aware. Biol. Sci., CABS; Curr. Cit.; Curr. Contents Life Sci.; EMBASE; Index Med.; Index Sci. Rev. [Full Cov.]; INSPEC (1975-); Life Sci. Collect.; Poult. Abstr.; Ref. Upd. Deluxe Ed.; Res. Alert [Full Cov.]; Sci. Cit. Index; SCISEARCH.

LC QH505.A1 Q36 ISSN 0033-5835
DD 574.19/1/05 UK CCC
NLM W1 QU526E CODEN QURBAW
Pr Rev.

QUARTERLY REVIEWS OF BIOPHYSICS. [Q. rev. biophys.]. **Added/Corp** International Union for Pure and Applied Biophysics. Vol. 1 (May 1968)-. Academic Scholarly Publication. English. Four times a year. $270.00. Cambridge University Press, The Edinburgh Building, Shaftesbury Road, Cambridge CB2 2RU United Kingdom. **Tel** 011 44 1223 312393, FAX 011 44 1223 315052, telex 851-817256. (**Subscription address:** Cambridge University Press / North America, 110 Midland Avenue, Port Chester NY 10573. **Tel** (800)431-1580, (914)937-9600.) **ED** R. Henderson, R. Rigler, J. C. Wang, C. Miller and C. I. Branden. Index available. **Ad Acc. Circ:** 1,000. available on microfilm and microfiche from University Microfilms International (UMI). Documents available from The Genuine Article, BIOSIS Document Express, CASDDS.
Desc: The official journal of the International Union for Pure and Applied Biophysics. Covers the whole field of biophysics from microscopic imaging of cells to enzyme biochemistry. All reviews published are invited from authors who have made significant contributions to the field. These authors give critical and sometimes controversial accounts of recent progress and problems in their specialty. Thematic issues are occasionally published.
Ind/Abst Biol. Abstr.; Chem. Abstr.; Curr. Cit.; Curr. Contents Life Sci.; EMBASE; Index Med.; Life Sci. Collect.; Ref. Upd. Deluxe Ed.; Res. Alert [Full Cov.]; Sci. Cit. Index; SCISEARCH.

LC QH505.A1 B57 ISSN 0301-634X
DD 574.1/91/05 GW CCC
NLM W1 RA149 CODEN REBPAT
Pr Rev.

RADIATION AND ENVIRONMENTAL BIOPHYSICS. [Radiat. environ. biophys.]. Vol. 11 (1974)-. Academic Scholarly Publication. Multiple languages (English and German). Four times a year. $744.00. Springer-Verlag GmbH & Company KG, Heidelberger Platz 3, D-14197 Berlin Germany. **Tel** 011 49 30 8207223, FAX 011 49 30 8214091, telex 183 319 SPBLN D. (**Subscription address:** Springer-Verlag New York Inc. / North America, PO Box 2485, Journal Fulfillment, Secaucus NJ 07096. **Tel** (201)348-4033, (800)777-4643, FAX (201)348-4505.) **ED** U Hagen. available on microfilm and microfiche from University Microfilms International (UMI). Documents available from The Genuine Article, BIOSIS Document Express, Ask*IEEE, CASDDS. ***Continues in part*** *Biophysik.*
Desc: Covers biophysics of ionizing radiations, biophysics of nonionizing radiation, biological effects of physical factors and biophysical aspects of environmental and space influence.
Ind/Abst Biol. Abstr.; Chem. Abstr.; Curr. Cit.; Curr. Contents Life Sci.; EMBASE; Energy Res. Abstr. (May 1974-); For. Abstr.; Health Saf. Sci. Abstr.; Index Med.; INSPEC (1974-); Life Sci. Collect.; Protozoolog. Abstr.; Res. Alert [Full Cov.]; Sci. Cit. Index; SCISEARCH.

US

RADIATION PHYSICS, BIOPHYSICS AND RADIATION BIOLOGY; PROGRESS REPORT. See Physics-Light, Optics, Radiation.

LC RM865 ISSN 0033-8192
DD 615.832 RU CCC
NLM W1 RA21 CODEN RADOA8
TITLE CHANGE

RADIOBIOLOGIIA. See Medical Sciences-Radiology.

LC QH650 ISSN 0869-4095
DD 574.192 RU

REFERATIVNYI ZHURNAL. 04, 04D, BIOLOGIIA. FIZIKO-KHIMICHESKAIA BIOLOGIIA. See Biology-Biological Chemistry.

LC Z7144.B5 R43 QH505
DD 016.53 RU

REFERATIVNYI ZHURNAL: BIOFIZIKA. **Added/Corp** Vsesoiuznyi Institut Nauchnoi i Tekhnicheskoi Informatsii (Soviet Union). **VFOAT** Biofizika. (19??)-. Russian. Twelve times a year. $299.95. VINITI - Vsesoyuznyi Institut Nauchno-Tekhnicheskoi Informatsii, All-Union Scientific and Technical Information Institute, Baltiiskaia ulitsa 14, 125219 Moscow Russia. **Tel** 011 7 95 2384600, FAX 011 7 95 9430060, telex 411160. (**Subscription address:** East View Publications Inc., 3020 Harbor Lane North, Suite 110, Minneapolis MN 55447. **Tel** (800)477-1005, (612)550-0961, FAX (612)559-2931.)

LC QP501 .S45 ISSN 0253-9918
DD 612.015 CH
CODEN SHYCD4

SHENGWU HUAXUE YU SHENGWU WULI JINZHAN. See Biology-Biological Chemistry.

LC RB112.5 .S68 ISSN 0887-2392
DD 510/.1/53 SZ
CCC
CODEN SRBRE5
CEASED

SOVIET MEDICAL REVIEWS. SECTION B, PHYSICOCHEMICAL ASPECTS OF MEDICINE REVIEWS. See Biology-Biological Chemistry.

LC QH301 .S783 ISSN 0734-9351
DD 574/.05 SZ
CCC
NLM W1; SO996WE CODEN SRDREF
CEASED

SOVIET SCIENTIFIC REVIEWS. SECTION D, PHYSICOCHEMICAL BIOLOGY REVIEWS. [Sov. sci. rev., D, Physicochem. biol. rev.]. **VFOAT** Physicochemical Biology Reviews. Vol. 4 (1984)-Vol. 12. English (translations available in Russian). Harwood Academic Publishers, PO Box 90, Reading RG1 8JL United Kingdom. **Tel** 011 44 1734 560080, FAX 011 44 1734 568211. **ED** V. P. Skulachev. Documents available from BIOSIS Document Express. ***Continues*** *Soviet Scientific Reviews. Section D, Biology Reviews, 0143-0424.*
Ind/Abst Biol. Abstr. (-1984).

ISSN 0742-4256
DD 574 SZ
NLM W1; SO996MW

SOVIET SCIENTIFIC REVIEWS SUPPLEMENT SERIES. PHYSICOCHEMICAL BIOLOGY. [Sov. sci. rev. suppl. ser., Physicochem. biol.]. **VFOAT** Physicochemical Biology. Vol. 2 (1984)-. Monographic series. English (Russian). Price varies per volume. Harwood Academic Publishers, PO Box 90, Reading RG1 8JL United Kingdom. **Tel** 011 44 1734 560080, FAX 011 44 1734 568211. **ED** V P Skulachev. ***Continues*** *Soviet Scientific Reviews Supplement Series. Biology, 0275-7826.*

LC QH650 ISSN 0932-2353
GW
NLM W1; SP685MD CODEN SSBIEJ

SPRINGER SERIES IN BIOPHYSICS. [Springer ser. biophys.]. (1987)-. Academic Scholarly Publication. English. Price varies per volume. Springer-Verlag GmbH & Company KG, Heidelberger Platz 3, D-14197 Berlin Germany. **Tel** 011 49 30 8207223, FAX 011 49 30 8214091, telex 183 319 SPBLN D. **(Subscription address:** Springer-Verlag New York Inc. / North America, PO Box 2485, Journal Fulfillment, Secaucus NJ 07096. **Tel** (201)348-4033, (800)777-4643, FAX (201)348-4505.**)** Documents available from BIOSIS Document Express, CASDDS.
Ind/Abst Biol. Abstr. (1986-); Chem. Abstr. (1987-).

LC QH505 ISSN 0081-6337
DD 574.19/1/05 SZ
CCC
NLM W1 ST881L CODEN STBIBN
Pr Rev. SUSPENDED

STUDIA BIOPHYSICA. [Stud. biophys.]. Vol. 1 (1966)-?. Academic Scholarly Publication. German (English). Irregular. DM54.00 (per volume). Deutscher Judo Verband, Redaktion Ippon Segewaldweg 40, D-12557 Berlin Germany. **Tel** 011 49 711 210770, telex 051 678. Documents available from The Genuine Article, BIOSIS Document Express, CASDDS.
Ind/Abst AGRICOLA; Biol. Abstr.; Chem. Abstr.; CSA Neuro. Abstr. (?-?); Curr. Biotechnol.; EMBASE; Energy Res. Abstr.; Life Sci. Collect.; Protozoolog. Abstr.; Res. Alert [Full Cov.]; Sci. Cit. Index; SCISEARCH.

LC QH505 .Z34 ISSN 0137-9690
DD 574.1 PL
CODEN ZBWSD9

ZAGADNIENIA BIOFIZYKI WSPOLCZESNEJ. **Added/Corp** Polskie Towarzystwo Biofizyczne. (1976)-. Academic Scholarly Publication. Polish (summaries and/or abstracts in English). zl.30.00. Panstwowe Wydawnictwo Naukowe / PWN, (Polish Scientific Publishers PWN Ltd.), Ul. Miodowa 10, PO Box 391, 00-251 Warsaw Poland. **Tel** 011 48 22 312738, FAX 011 48 22 267163. Documents available from CASDDS.
Ind/Abst Chem. Abstr.

LC QH650
GW

ZAHLENWERTE UND FUNKTIONEN AUS NATURWISSENSCHAFTEN UND TECHNIK NEUE SERIE, GRUPPE VII, BIOPHYSIK. **VFOAT** Numerical Data and Functional Relationships in Science and Technology; Biophysik; Biophysics; Landolt-Bornstein. Vol. 1 (1989)-. Monographic series. English (English). Price varies per volume. Springer-Verlag GmbH & Company KG, Heidelberger Platz 3, D-14197 Berlin Germany. **Tel** 011 49 30 8207223, FAX 011 49 30 8214091, telex 183 319 SPBLN D. **(Subscription address:** Springer-Verlag New York Inc. / North America, PO Box 2485, Journal Fulfillment, Secaucus NJ 07096. **Tel** (201)348-4033, (800)777-4643, FAX (201)348-4505.**)**

BOTANY

LC QK ISSN 0904-6453
DD 581 DK

AAU REPORTS. (1988)-. Periodical. English. Irregular (one or two issues per year). $16.00 (per copy). Aarhus University Press, Aarhus University, Building 170, DK-8000 Aarhus C Denmark. **Tel** 011 45 86 197033, FAX 011 45 86 198433, telex 16600. ***Continues*** *Reports from the Botanical Institute, University of Aarhus, 0105-4236.*

LC QK ISSN 0133-6215
DD 581 HU
CODEN ABBOEQ

ABSTRACTA BOTANICA. [Abstr. bot.]. **Added/Corp** Eotvos Lorand Tudomanyegyetem. (1971)-. Periodical. Hungarian (summaries and/or abstracts in English and Hungarian). **(Subscription address:** Opulus Press AB, PO Box 25 137, S 750 25 Uppsala Sweden. **Tel** 011 46 18 320662.**)** Documents available from BIOSIS Document Express.
Ind/Abst Biol. Abstr.; Ecol. Abstr.

LC SB13 .A48 ISSN 0065-0951
PL
CODEN AAGWAU

ACTA AGROBOTANICA. [Acta agrobot.]. **Added/Corp** Polskie Towarzystwo Botaniczne. Vol. 1 (1953)-. Periodical. Polish (summaries and/or abstracts in English and Russian). Irregular. **(Subscription address:** Ars Polona-Ruch, PO Box 1001, Krakowskie Przedmiescie 7, 00-068 Warsaw Poland. **Tel** 011 48 22 261201.**)** Documents available from BIOSIS Document Express, CASDDS.
Ind/Abst Biodeter. Abstr.; Biol. Abstr.; Chem. Abstr.; Crop Physiol. Abstr.; Field Crop Abstr.; Grass. Forage Abstr.; Hortic. Abstr.; Index Vet.; Maize Abstr.; Nutr. Abstr. Rev., Ser. B, Live Feeds and Feed.; Nutr. Abstr. Rev., Ser. A, Hum. Exp.; Ornamental Hort.; Plant Breed. Abstr.; Plant Grow. Reg. Abstr.; Postharvest News Inf.; Potato Abstr.; Protozoolog. Abstr.; Rev. Med. Vet. Mycology; Rev. Plant Pathol.; Seed Abstr.; Soyabean Abstr.; Weed Abstr.

LC QK ISSN 0001-5296
DD 581 PL
CODEN ABCBAM

ACTA BIOLOGICA CRACOVIENSIA. SERIES : BOTANICA. [Acta biol. crac., ser. bot.]. **Added/Corp** Polska Akademia Nauk. Komisja Biologiczna. Vol. 2 (1959)-. Periodical. English. Irregular. Price varies per volume. **(Subscription address:** Ars Polona-Ruch, PO Box 1001, Krakowskie Przedmiescie 7, 00-068 Warsaw Poland. **Tel** 011 48 22 261201.**)** Documents available from The Genuine Article, BIOSIS Document Express. ***Continues*** *Acta Biologica Cracovensia. Serie Botanique.*
Ind/Abst Biol. Abstr.; Curr. Contents Agric. Biol. Environ. Sci.; Life Sci. Collect.; Res. Alert [Select. Cov.]; SCISEARCH.

LC QK
DD 581 SP

ACTA BOTANICA BARCINONENSIA. **Added/Corp** Universidad de Barcelona. Departamento de Botanica. (1978)-. Monographic series. Multiple languages. Irregular. Price varies per volume. Universitat de Barcelona, Facultat de Biologia, Department de Botanica, Barcelona Spain. **ED** X. Llimona. **Circ:** 1,100. ***Formed by the union of*** *Acta Geobotanica Barcinonensia* ***and*** *Acta Phytotaxonomica Barcinonensia.*
Desc: Information on plant taxonomy and phytocenology, vascular plants and cryptograms of the Western Mediterranean region.
Ind/Abst Soils Fert.

LC QK ISSN 0365-0588
DD 581 CI
CODEN ABCRA2

ACTA BOTANICA CROATICA. [Acta Bot. Croat.]. **Added/Corp** Sveuciliste u Zagrebu. Botanicki Zavod. Sveuciliste u Zagrebu. Bioloski Odjel. Vol. 16 (1957)-. Academic Scholarly Publication. Serbo-Croatian (Roman) (summaries and/or abstracts in English, French and German). One time a year. Price varies. Botanicki Odjel Prirodoslovno, 41000 Zabreb, Division of Biology, Marulicev TRG 20 II Croatia. Documents available from BIOSIS Document Express, CASDDS. ***Continues*** *Acta Botanica Instituti Botanici Universitatis Zagrebensis.*
Ind/Abst Agrofor. Abstr. (1991-); Biodeter. Abstr.; Biol. Abstr.; Chem. Abstr.; For. Abstr.; Life Sci. Collect.; Plant Breed. Abstr.; Potato Abstr.; Weed Abstr.

LC QH7 .S76 ISSN 0001-5369
DD 580/.5 FI
CODEN ABFEAC

ACTA BOTANICA FENNICA. [Acta bot. Fenn.]. **Added/Corp** Societas Pro Fauna et Flora Fennica. Vol. 1 (1925)-. Monographic series. English (German). Irregular. Price varies per volume. **(Subscription address:** Academic Bookstore Akateeminen, Postilokero 23, FIN 00371 Helsinki Finland. **Tel** 011 358 0 12141.**)** cum. index. **Circ:** 1,100. Documents available from BIOSIS Document Express, CASDDS.
Ind/Abst Biol. Abstr.; Chem. Abstr.; Ecol. Abstr.; Ecology Abstr.; For. Prod. Abstr. (19??-19??); Geogr. Abstr. Human Geogr. (?-?); GeoRef; Life Sci. Collect.; Plant Breed. Abstr.; Pollut. Abstr. Indexes; Rev. Med. Vet. Mycology; Rev. Plant Pathol.; Soils Fert.; Vitis Vitic. Enol. Abstr.

LC QK1 .S662
FR
CODEN ABGAE9

•**ACTA BOTANICA GALLICA : BULLETIN DE LA SOCIETE BOTANIQUE DE FRANCE.** **Added/Corp** Societe Botanique de France. **VFOAT** Bulletin de la Societe Botanique de France. Vol. 140, No. 1 (1993)-. Bulletin. English (French). Six times a year. 900.00F. Societe Botanique de France, rue J B Clement, 92296 Chatenay Malabry France. **Tel** 011 33 1 46835520. **(Subscription address:** Centrale des Revues, 11 rue Gossin, 92543 Montrouge Cedex France. **Tel** 011 33 1 46565266.**)** Documents available from CASDDS. ***Formed by the union of*** *Actualites Botaniques, 0181-1789* ***and*** *Societe Botanique de France. Bulletin de la Societe Botanique de France. Lettres Botaniques, 0181-1797.*
Ind/Abst Chem. Abstr.; Curr. Cit.

LC QK1 .A25 ISSN 0236-6495
DD 580/.5 HU
CCC
CODEN ABOHE2

ACTA BOTANICA HUNGARICA. [Acta bot. Hung.]. **Added/Corp** Magyar Tudomanyos Akademia. **VFOAT** Acta Botanica. Vol. 29, No. 1-4 (1983)-. Academic Scholarly Publication. English (French, German, Spanish and Russian). Four times a year. $92.00. Akademiai Kiado, Publishing House of the Hungarian Academy of Sciences, Prielle Kornelia u. 19-35, H-1117 Budapest Hungary. **Tel** 011 36 1 1811991, FAX 011 36 1 1811991, telex 22-6228 AKNYO H. Documents available from The Genuine Article, CASDDS. ***Continues*** *Acta Botanica Academiae Scientiarum Hungaricae, 0001-5350.*
Ind/Abst Chem. Abstr. (1983-); Crop Physiol. Abstr.; Curr. Contents Agric. Biol. Environ. Sci.; EMBASE; For. Prod. Abstr.; Index Vet.; Life Sci. Collect.; Plant Breed. Abstr.; Plant Grow. Reg. Abstr.; Res. Alert [Select. Cov.]; SCISEARCH.

LC QK1 .A27 ISSN 0379-508X
DD 581/.05 II
CODEN ABOIB2

ACTA BOTANICA INDICA. [Acta bot. indica]. **Added/Corp** Society for Advancement of Botany. Vol. 1 (1973)-. Periodical. English. Two times a year. $51.33. Scientific Publishers, PO Box 91, Ratanada Road, Jodhpur 342011 India. **(Subscription address:** Prints India, 11 Darya Ganj, New Delhi 110002 India. **Tel** 011 91 11 3268645, FAX 011 91 11 3275542, telex 31-61087 PRIN-IN.**)** **ED** V Singh. **Bk Rev. Ad Acc. Circ:** 600 (ctrl). Documents available from BIOSIS Document Express.
Desc: Devoted to plant sciences and carries articles on phycology, mycology, microbiology, chemical taxonomy, genetics, cytology, physiology, ecology, etc.
Ind/Abst AGRICOLA [Full Cov.]; Agrofor. Abstr.; Biocont. News Inf. (1991-); Biol. Abstr.; Curr. Cit.; EMBASE; Field Crop Abstr.; For. Prod. Abstr. (1991-); For. Abstr.; Grass. Forage Abstr.; Hortic. Abstr.; Microbiol. Abstr. Sect. A; Microbiol. Abstr. Sect. C; Life Sci. Collect.; Plant Breed. Abstr.; Potato Abstr.; Protozoolog. Abstr.; Rev. Agric. Entomol.; Rev. Med. Vet. Mycology; Rev. Plant Pathol.; Rice Abstr.; Seed Abstr.; Soils Fert.; Weed Abstr.

LC QK325.5 .A27 ISSN 0374-5066
DD 581.9491/2 IC

ACTA BOTANICA ISLANDICA. [Acta bot. isl.]. **VFOAT** Timarit Um Islenzka Grasafrdi. (1972)-. English (French, German and Icelandic). Irregular (issued approximately every two years). $15.00. Akureyri Museum of Natural History, PO Box 580, Akureyri 602 Iceland. **Tel** 011 354 6 22983. **ED** Hordur Kristinsson. Index available. **Bk Rev. Ad Acc. Circ:** 180. ***Supersedes*** *Flora (Akureyri, Iceland).*
Ind/Abst Life Sci. Collect.

ISSN 0210-9506
SP
CODEN ABMAE5
Pr Rev.

ACTA BOTANICA MALACITANA. [Acta bot. malacit.]. **Added/Corp** Universidad de Malaga. Facultad de Ciencias. Vol. 1, (1975)-. Spanish (French, English, Italian and Portuguese). One time a year. 3500ptas. Universidad de Malaga Facultad de Ciencias, Departamento de Biologia Vegetal, Apartado 59, 29080 Malaga Spain. **ED** B Cabezudo. Index available. cum. index. **Ad Acc. Circ:** 500 (ctrl). Documents available

from BIOSIS Document Express.
Desc: Annual international journal to report results of original research studies from all areas of phytology, especially those concerning systematics and ecology, applicable to both criptogams and phanerogams.
Ind/Abst Biol. Abstr.

LC WMLC 93/1478 **ISSN** 0187-7151
DD 581 MX
Pr Rev.

ACTA BOTANICA MEXICANA. Added/Corp Instituto de Ecologia (Mexico). No. 1 (Apr. 1988)-. Periodical. Spanish (English, French and Portuguese; summaries and/or abstracts in English). Four times a year. $15.00. Acta Botanica Mexicana, Institute Ecologia, Center Bajio, PO 386, Patzcuaro Michoacan Mexico. **Tel** 011 52 434 22698, FAX 011 52 434 2 2699. **ED** Jerzy Rzedowski Rotter. Index available (every 10 issues, free). **Circ:** 1,000.
Desc: Purpose is to make public all the results of the scientific research in all the disciplines of botany, in particular the plants found in Mexico.

LC QK1 .N353 **ISSN** 0044-5983
DD 581/.05 NE
CCC
CODEN ABNRAN
Pr Rev.

ACTA BOTANICA NEERLANDICA. (ACTA BOTANICA NEERLANDICA : OFFICAL PUBLICATION OF THE NEDERLANDSE BOTANISCHE VERENIGING.). [Acta bot. neerl.]. **Added/Corp** Koninklijke Nederlandse Botanische Vereniging. Vol. 1, No. 1 (1952)-. Academic Scholarly Publication. English (French and German). Four times a year. $239.00. Blackwell Scientific Publications Ltd, Marston Book Services, PO Box 88, Oxford OX2 ONE United Kingdom. **Tel** 011 44 1865 206206, FAX 011 44 1865 206219, telex 837 515 MARDIS G. Index available. **Bk Rev.** available on microfilm and microfiche from University Microfilms International (UMI). Documents available from The Genuine Article, BIOSIS Document Express, CASDDS. ***Formed by the union of*** *Nederlandsch Kruidkundig Archief* ***and*** *Recueil des Travaux Botaniques Nederlandais.*
Desc: Covers general botany.
Ind/Abst AgBiotech News Inf.; Biocont. News Inf. (1991-); Biol. Abstr.; Chem. Abstr.; Crop Physiol. Abstr.; Curr. Aware. Biol. Sci., CABS; Curr. Cit.; Curr. Contents Agric. Biol. Environ. Sci.; Ecol. Abstr.; Field Crop Abstr.; For. Prod. Abstr.; For. Abstr.; Geogr. Abstr. Phys. Geogr. (?-?); GeoRef; Grass. Forage Abstr.; Hortic. Abstr.; Irr. Drain. Abstr.; Maize Abstr.; Ornamental Hort.; Life Sci. Collect.; Plant Breed. Abstr.; Plant Genet. Resour. Abstr.; Plant Grow. Reg. Abstr.; Potato Abstr.; Protozoolog. Abstr.; Res. Alert [Full Cov.]; Rev. Agric. Entomol.; Rev. Med. Vet. Mycology; Rev. Plant Pathol.; Sci. Cit. Index; SCISEARCH; Seed Abstr.; Soils Fert.; Soyabean Abstr.; Weed Abstr.

LC QK1 .A285 **ISSN** 0095-4195
DD 581.05 US
NLM W1 AC767 **CODEN** ABSIDO
Pr Rev.

ACTA BOTANICA SINICA. [Acta bot. Sin.]. (June 1974)-. Academic Scholarly Publication. English (Chinese). Twelve times a year. $169.50. Chinese Academy of Sciences / Institute of Botany, Science Press, 16 Donghuangchenggen North Street, Beijing 100707, People's Republic of China. **Tel** 011 86 1 4019821, FAX 011 86 4012180, telex 210147. **ED** Cheng Tsui. Index available. **Ad Acc. Circ:** 12,000. available with charts; available with illustrations. Documents available from CASDDS.
Desc: Original papers on the applications and theory of plant morphology, cytology, chemistry, physiology and botany.
Ind/Abst AgBiotech News Inf.; Agrofor. Abstr. (1991-); Chem. Abstr.; Crop Physiol. Abstr.; Ecol. Abstr.; Field Crop Abstr.; Food Sci. Technol. Abstr.; For. Prod. Abstr. (19??-19??); For. Abstr.; Geogr. Abstr. Phys. Geogr.; Geol. Abstr.; Grass. Forage Abstr.; Hortic. Abstr.; Maize Abstr.; Ornamental Hort. (19??-19??); Plant Breed. Abstr.; Plant Genet. Resour. Abstr.; Plant Grow. Reg. Abstr.; Rev. Agric. Entomol.; Rev. Med. Vet. Mycology; Rev. Plant Pathol.; Rice Abstr.; Seed Abstr.; Soils Fert.; Sorghum Mill. Abstr.; Weed Abstr.; Wheat Barley Trit. Abstr.

LC QK474.8 **ISSN** 0231-5335
DD 582.16/005 XO
CODEN ACTDDL

ACTA DENDROBIOLOGICA. [Acta dendrobiol.]. (1979)-. Academic Scholarly Publication. Slovak (summaries and/or abstracts in English, German and Russian). One time a year. 46.00. Veda, Publishing House of the Slovak Academy of Sciences, Klemensova 19, 814 30 Bratislava Slovakia. **Tel** (7)583-15. Documents available from BIOSIS Document Express, CASDDS.
Ind/Abst Biol. Abstr.; Chem. Abstr.; For. Prod. Abstr.; For. Abstr.; Hortic. Abstr.; Ornamental Hort. (1991-); Plant Breed. Abstr.; Plant Grow. Reg. Abstr.; Rev. Agric. Entomol.

ISSN 0524-2371
XO

ACTA FACULTATIS RERUM NATURALIUM UNIVERSITATIS COMENIANAE. BOTANICA. Main/Corp Univerzita Komenskeho v Bratislave. Prirodovedecka Fakulta. **Added/Corp** Univerzita Komenskeho v Bratislave. Prirodovedecka Fakulta. Botanica. **VFOAT** Botanica. (1956)-. Periodical. Slovak (German; summaries and/or abstracts in Czech, English, German, Russian and Slovak). Irregular. Slovenske Pedagogicke Nakladetelstvo, Sasinkova 5, 891 12 Bratislava, Slovakia.
Ind/Abst Plant Breed. Abstr.

ISSN 0373-8205
XO
CODEN AFPPCN

ACTA FACULTATIS RERUM NATURALIUM UNIVERSITATIS COMENIANAE. PHYSIOLOGIA PLANTARUM. [Acta Fac. rerum nat. Univ. Comen., Physiol. plant.]. **Main/Corp** Univerzita Komenskeho v Bratislave. Prirodovedeck a Fakulta. **Added/Corp** Univerzita Komenskeho v Bratislave. Prirodovedecka Fakulta. Physiologia Plantarum. **VFOAT** Physiologia Plantarum. (1970)-. Academic Scholarly Publication. English (German; summaries and/or abstracts in Russian and Slovak). Two times a year. Slovenske Pedagogicke Nakladetelstvo, Sasinkova 5, 891 12 Bratislava, Slovakia. Documents available from CASDDS.
Ind/Abst Chem. Abstr.; Field Crop Abstr.; Hortic. Abstr.; Life Sci. Collect.; Plant Breed. Abstr.; Seed Abstr.; Vitis Vitic. Enol. Abstr.; Weed Abstr.

LC QH166 .A75 **ISSN** 0365-4850
DD 508.4 IC
CODEN ANIRAE

ACTA NATURALIA ISLANDICA. See Natural History.

LC QE901 .A3 **ISSN** 0001-6594
DD 561.05 PL
CODEN APBCAG

ACTA PALAEOBOTANICA. See Paleontology.

ISSN 0137-5881
PL
CODEN APPLDE

ACTA PHYSIOLOGIAE PLANTARUM. [Acta physiol. plant.]. **Added/Corp** Polska Akademia Nauk. Komitet Fizjologii, Genetyki i Hodowli Roslin PAN. Vol. 1, No. 1 (1978)-. Academic Scholarly Publication. English. Four times a year. $44.00. Agencja Wydawnicza ARIES, Ul. Kolowa 4-60, 03-536 Warsaw Poland. **Tel** 011 48 22 6794242. **(Subscription address:** Ars Polona-Ruch, PO Box 1001, Krakowskie Przedmiescie 7, 00-068 Warsaw Poland. **Tel** 011 48 22 261201.) Documents available from The Genuine Article, BIOSIS Document Express, CASDDS.
Desc: Papers and reviews on theoretical and practical aspects of plant physiology and related sciences.
Ind/Abst AgBiotech News Inf.; Biol. Abstr. (-1987); Chem. Abstr.; Crop Physiol. Abstr.; Curr. Aware. Biol. Sci., CABS; Curr. Cit.; Curr. Contents Agric. Biol. Environ. Sci.; Field Crop Abstr.; Hortic. Abstr.; Irr. Drain. Abstr.; Maize Abstr.; Plant Breed. Abstr.; Plant Grow. Reg. Abstr.; Postharvest News Inf.; Potato Abstr.; Res. Alert [Select. Cov.]; Rev. Med. Vet. Mycology; Rev. Plant Pathol.; SCISEARCH; Seed Abstr.; Wheat Barley Trit. Abstr.

LC QK **ISSN** 0084-5914
DD 581 SW
CODEN APGSAL

ACTA PHYTOGEOGRAPHICA SUECICA. [Acta phytogeogr. suec.]. **Main/Corp** Svenska Vaztgeografiska Sallskapet. (1929)-. Monographic series. Multiple languages (English and Swedish). One time a year (Dec.). Kr240.00. Scandinavian University Press, PO Box 2959 Toeyen, N 0608 Oslo 6 Norway. **Tel** 011 47 2 2575400, FAX 011 47 2 2575353, telex 71896 UROR N. **(Subscription address:** Scandinavian University Press, 200 Meacham Ave., Elmont NY 11003. **Tel** (516)352-7300, FAX (516)352-7377.) Documents available from BIOSIS Document Express.
Ind/Abst Biol. Abstr.; Ecol. Abstr.; Field Crop Abstr.; For. Prod. Abstr.; For. Abstr.; Grass. Forage Abstr.; Life Sci. Collect.; Plant Breed. Abstr.; Soils Fert.

ISSN 0065-1567
GW
CODEN APYMBQ
CEASED

ACTA PHYTOMEDICA. [Acta phytomed.]. Vol. 1 (1973)-Series Completed Vol. 10 (19??). Academic Scholarly Publication. German (summaries and/or abstracts in English). Blackwell Wissenschafts-Verlag, Kurfuerstendamm 57, D-10707 Berlin Germany. **Tel** 011 49 30 32790623, 011 49 30 32790624, FAX 011 49 30 327 90610. **(Subscription address:** Blackwell Wissenschafts VLG, Postfach 800620, Koch Neff Oetinger, D 70506 Stuttgart Germany. **Tel** 011 49 711 78991337.) **ED** A. Bronnimann, J. Colhoun and R. Heitefuss. Index available. cum. index. **Bk Rev. Ad Acc. Circ:** 2,500. Documents available from BIOSIS Document Express, CASDDS.
Ind/Abst Biol. Abstr.; Chem. Abstr.

LC QK **ISSN** 0238-1249
DD 581 HU
NLM W1; AC9245 **CODEN** APEHEG

ACTA PHYTOPATHOLOGICA ET ENTOMOLOGICA HUNGARICA. [Acta phytopathol. entomol. Hung.]. **Added/Corp** Magyar Tudomanyos Akademia. **VFOAT** Acta Phytopathologica. Vol. 21, No. 1/2 (1986)-. Academic Scholarly Publication. English. Four times a year. $104.00. Akademiai Kiado, Publishing House of the Hungarian Academy of Sciences, Prielle Kornelia u. 19-35, H-1117 Budapest Hungary. **Tel** 011 36 1 1811991, FAX 011 36 1 1811991, telex 22-6228 AKNYO H. Documents available from The Genuine Article, BIOSIS Document Express, CASDDS. ***Continues*** *Acta Phytopathologica Academiae Scientiarum Hungaricae, 0001-6780.*
Ind/Abst Biocont. News Inf. (1991-); Biol. Abstr. (1986-); Chem. Abstr.; Curr. Aware. Biol. Sci., CABS; Curr. Cit.; Curr. Contents Agric. Biol. Environ. Sci.; Entomol. Abstr.; Hortic. Abstr.; Microbiol. Abstr. Sect. C; Nematol. Abstr.; Plant Breed. Abstr.; Plant Grow. Reg. Abstr.; Potato Abstr.; Res. Alert [Select. Cov.]; Rev. Agric. Entomol.; Rev. Med. Vet. Entomol.; Rev. Plant Pathol.; Rice Abstr.; SCISEARCH; Seed Abstr.; Soyabean Abstr.; Vitis Vitic. Enol. Abstr.; Wheat Barley Trit. Abstr.

LC QK **ISSN** 0001-6799
DD 581 JA
CODEN SHBCAM

ACTA PHYTOTAXONOMICA ET GEOBOTANICA. SHOKUBUTSU BUNRUI CHIRI. [Acta phytotaxon. geobot.]. **VFOAT** Shokubutsu Bunrui Chiri. Vol. 1 (April 1932)-. Periodical. English (Japanese). Six times a year. $120.00. Shokubutsu Bunrui Chiri Gakkai (Phytogeographical Society), c/o Department of Botany, Faculty of Science, Kyoto University, Kitashirakawa Oiwake-cho, Sakyo-ku Kyoto 606 Japan. **(Subscription address:** Maruzen Company Ltd., PO Box 5050, Import & Export Department, Tokyo 100 31 Japan. **Tel** 011 81 3 32789224.) Documents available from BIOSIS Document Express.
Ind/Abst Biol. Abstr.; GeoRef; NAPRALERT; Life Sci. Collect.; Plant Breed. Abstr.; Rev. Med. Vet. Mycology; Rev. Plant Pathol.

LC QK1 .P75 **ISSN** 0001-6977
DD 581/.05 PL
CODEN ASBNA2ASPN2
Pr Rev.

ACTA SOCIETATIS BOTANICORUM POLONIAE. [Acta soc. bot. pol.]. **Main/Corp** Polskie Towarzystwo Botaniczne. Vol. 1 (1923)-. Periodical. Polish (summaries and/or abstracts in English, French and German). Four times a year. $60.00. Panstwowe Wydawnictwo Naukowe / PWN, (Polish Scientific Publishers PWN Ltd.), Ul. Miodowa 10, PO Box 391, 00-251 Warsaw Poland. **Tel** 011 48 22 312738, FAX 011 48 22 267163. **(Subscription address:** Ars Polona-Ruch, PO Box 1001, Krakowskie Przedmiescie 7, 00-068 Warsaw Poland. **Tel** 011 48 22 261201.) **ED** B. Rodkiewicz. Index available. **Circ:** 1,200 (ctrl). available on microfilm; available on microfiche; available on CD-ROM; available on diskette; available on audiocassette; available on videocassette. Documents available from The Genuine Article, BIOSIS Document Express, CASDDS.
Ind/Abst Biol. Abstr.; Chem. Abstr. (-1989); Crop Physiol. Abstr.; Curr. Contents Agric. Biol. Environ. Sci.; Ecol. Abstr. (?-?); Ecology Abstr.; Field Crop Abstr.; For. Prod. Abstr.; For. Abstr.; Grass. Forage Abstr.; Hortic. Abstr.; Irr. Drain. Abstr.; Ornamental Hort. (19??-19??); Life Sci. Collect.; Plant Breed. Abstr.; Plant Grow. Reg. Abstr.; Postharvest News Inf.; Res. Alert [Select. Cov.]; Rev. Agric. Entomol.; Rev. Med. Vet. Mycology; Rev. Plant Pathol.; SCISEARCH; Seed Abstr.; Soils Fert.; Soyabean Abstr.; Weed Abstr.; Wheat Barley Trit. Abstr.

LC QK322 .A28 **ISSN** 0208-6174
DD 581.95 PL

ACTA UNIVERSITATIS LODZIENSIS. FOLIA BOTANICA. Added/Corp Uniwersytet Lodzki. **VFOAT** Folia Botanica. (1981)-. Monographic series. Polish (summaries and/or abstracts in English). Irregular. Price varies per volume. Wydawnictwo Uniwersytetu Lodzkiego, Ul. Jaracza 34, Lodz Poland. **Tel** 011 48 42 331671, 011 48 42 336541. **(Subscription address:** Ars Polona-Ruch, PO Box 1001, Krakowskie Przedmiescie 7, 00-068 Warsaw Poland. **Tel** 011 48 22 261201.) ***Continues in part*** *Acta Universitatis Lodziensis. Seria II, Nauki Matematyczno-Przyrodnicze, 0137-4605.*
Desc: Information on flora and vegetation of Poland, particularly plant cover synanthropization.

ISSN 0860-3111
PL
UDC 573

ACTA UNIVERSITATIS LODZIENSIS. FOLIA PHYSIOLOGICA, CYTOLOGICA ET GENETICA. (1986)-. Monographic series. Multiple languages. Irregular. Price varies per volume. Wydawnictwo Uniwersytetu Lodzkiego, Ul. Jaracza 34, Lodz Poland. **Tel** 011 48 42 331671, 011 48 42 336541. **(Subscription address:** Ars Polona-Ruch, PO Box 1001, Krakowskie Przedmiescie 7, 00-068 Warsaw Poland. **Tel** 011 48 22 261201.)

Desc: Plant physiology, biochemistry, cytology and cytogenetics. Also covers cultures in vitro and micropropagation of plants.

LC QK1 .A353 **ISSN** 0065-2296
DD 581 UK
NLM W1 AD468 **CODEN** ABTRAJ
Pr Rev.
ADVANCES IN BOTANICAL RESEARCH. [Adv. bot. res.]. Vol. 1 (1963)-. Monographic series. English. Irregular. Price varies per volume. Academic Press Inc., 6277 Sea Harbor Drive, Orlando FL 32887. **Tel** (800)543-9534, (407)345-4100, FAX (407)352-3445. **ED** R. D. Preston. Documents available from The Genuine Article, CASDDS.
Ind/Abst AGRICOLA [Full Cov.]; Biol. Agric. Index; Chem. Abstr.; Curr. Aware. Biol. Sci., CABS; Curr. Cit.; Index Sci. Rev. [Full Cov.]; Life Sci. Collect.; Ref. Upd. Deluxe Ed.; Res. Alert [Full Cov.]; Sci. Cit. Index; SCISEARCH; Vitis Vitic. Enol. Abstr.

LC QK532.4 .A38 **ISSN** 0253-6226
DD 588/.05 GW
CODEN ABRYDX
ADVANCES IN BRYOLOGY. [Adv. bryol.]. **Added/Corp** International Association of Bryologists. Vol. 1 (1981)-. Academic Scholarly Publication. English (French and German; summaries and/or abstracts in German). Irregular. Price varies. Lubrecht & Cramer Ltd, 38 County Route 48, Forestburgh NY 12777. **Tel** (914)794-8539. Index available. **Bk Rev.** Documents available from BIOSIS Document Express, CASDDS.
Ind/Abst Biol. Abstr.; Chem. Abstr.

LC QK
DD 581 NE
NLM W1; AD531RM
•**ADVANCES IN CELLULAR AND MOLECULAR BIOLOGY OF PLANTS.** (1994)-. Monographic series. English. Irregular. Kluwer Academic Publishers, Postbus 322, 3300 AH Dordrecht The Netherlands. **Tel** 011 31 78 524400, FAX 011 31 78 183273, telex 20083.
Ind/Abst Bibliogr. Agric.

ISSN 0741-8280
DD 581 US
CCC
Pr Rev.
ADVANCES IN ECONOMIC BOTANY. [Adv. econ. bot.]. **Added/Corp** New York Botanical Garden. Institute of Economic Botany (New York Botanical Garden). Vol. 1 (1984)-. Monographic series. English. Irregular. Price varies per volume. New York Botanical Garden, Scientific Publishing Department B, New York NY 10458-5126. **Tel** (718)817-8721, FAX (718)817-6504, telex 5106015451. **Acid Free. Circ:** 150.
Desc: Publishes original monograph-length research papers and symposia dealing with the uses and management of plants; an interdisciplinary series designed to integrate pure and applied studies.
Ind/Abst Agrofor. Abstr. (1991-); For. Prod. Abstr. (1991-); For. Abstr.; Hortic. Abstr.; Ornamental Hort. (1991-); Rev. Plant Pathol.; Seed Abstr.

GW
NLM W1; AD655L **CODEN** ALEREI
ADVANCES IN LECTIN RESEARCH. Vol. 1 (1988)-. Academic Scholarly Publication. English. Irregular. Price varies per volume. Springer-Verlag GmbH & Company KG, Heidelberger Platz 3, D-14197 Berlin Germany. **Tel** 011 49 30 8207223, FAX 011 49 30 8214091, telex 183 319 SPBLN D. **(Subscription address:** Springer-Verlag New York Inc. / North America, PO Box 2485, Journal Fulfillment, Secaucus NJ 07096. **Tel** (201)348-4033, (800)777-4643, FAX (201)348-4505.**)** **ED** Harmut Franz. Documents available from BIOSIS Document Express, CASDDS.
Ind/Abst Biol. Abstr. (1988-); Chem. Abstr. (1990-).

LC SB599 .A38 **ISSN** 0736-4539
DD 581.2/05 UK
CODEN APLPD6
ADVANCES IN PLANT PATHOLOGY. [Adv. plant pathol.]. Vol. 1 (1982)-. Academic Scholarly Publication. English. Irregular. $105.00 (Vol. 10). Academic Press Inc., 6277 Sea Harbor Drive, Orlando FL 32887. **Tel** (800)543-9534, (407)345-4100, FAX (407)352-3445. **ED** David Ingram. **Circ:** 1,100. Documents available from CASDDS.
Desc: Serial volumes on topics of current scientific research in plant pathology, microbiology and genetics.
Ind/Abst AGRICOLA [Full Cov.]; Chem. Abstr.

LC QK1 .A3535 **ISSN** 0970-3586
DD 581/.05 II
CODEN APTSEM
ADVANCES IN PLANT SCIENCES (MUZAFFARNAGAR, INDIA). (ADVANCES IN PLANT SCIENCES.). [Adv. plant sci.]. **Added/Corp** Academy of Plant Sciences, India. Vol. 1, No. 1 (Feb. 1988)-. Periodical. English. Two times a year. $50.00. Dr S K Gupta Secretary, Academy of Plant Sciences, 657/6 South Civil Lines, Muzaffarnagar 251002 India. **(Subscription address:** Prints India, 11 Darya Ganj, New Delhi 110002 India. **Tel** 011 91 11 3268645, FAX 011 91 11 3275542, telex 31-61087 PRIN-IN.**)** Documents available from BIOSIS Document Express.
Ind/Abst Agrofor. Abstr. (1991-); Biocont. News Inf. (1991-); Biodeter. Abstr.; Biol. Abstr.; Crop Physiol. Abstr.; Dairy Sci. Abstr.; Field Crop Abstr.; For. Prod. Abstr. (1991-); For. Abstr.; Hortic. Abstr.; Irr. Drain. Abstr.; Ornamental Hort. (1991-); Plant Breed. Abstr.; Plant Grow. Reg. Abstr.; Postharvest News Inf.; Rev. Agric. Entomol.; Rev. Plant Pathol.; Seed Abstr.; Soils Fert.; Sorghum Mill. Abstr.; Weed Abstr.; Wheat Barley Trit. Abstr.

ISSN 1052-5432
DD 580 US
ADVANCES IN PLANT SCIENCES SERIES. [Adv. plant sci. ser.]. Vol. 2 (1988)-. Monographic series. English. Irregular. Price varies per volume. Timber Press, 9999 Southwest Wilshire, Suite 124, Portland OR 97225. **Tel** (800)327-5680, (503)292-0745, FAX (503)227-3070. ***Continues*** *Advances in Plant Sciences.*
Ind/Abst AGRICOLA [Full Cov.].

LC QK658 .A34 **ISSN** 0376-480X
II
CCC
CODEN APSRDDADPRDG
ADVANCES IN POLLEN-SPORE RESEARCH. [Adv. pollen-spore res.]. **Added/Corp** East Asian Palynological Association. **VFOAT** Advances in Pollen Spore Research. Vol. 1 (1974)-. Monographic series. English. One time a year. Price varies. East Asian Palynological Society, New Delhi India. **(Subscription address:** Prints India, 11 Darya Ganj, New Delhi 110002 India. **Tel** 011 91 11 3268645, FAX 011 91 11 3275542, telex 31-61087 PRIN-IN.**)** Each issue contains an index to its own contents (no volume index)--loose. Documents available from CASDDS.
Desc: Topics covered include biochemistry of the bacterial spore, pollen biochemistry, pollen tube growth and pollen biotechnology in relation to crop growth.
Ind/Abst Chem. Abstr. (1974-1979); GeoRef.

LC QK **ISSN** 0168-8022
DD 581 NE
CODEN AVSCDA
ADVANCES IN VEGETATION SCIENCE. [Adv. veg. sci.]. (1980)-. Monographic series. English. Irregular. Price varies per volume. Kluwer Academic Publishers, Postbus 322, 3300 AH Dordrecht The Netherlands. **Tel** 011 31 78 524400, FAX 011 31 78 183273, telex 20083. **(Subscription address:** Kluwer Academic Publishers / US Subscriptions, PO Box 253, Accord Station, Hingham MA 02018. **Tel** (617)871-6600.**)** Documents available from BIOSIS Document Express.
Ind/Abst Biol. Abstr.

ISSN 0963-6420
UK
Pr Rev.
AFRO-ASIAN JOURNAL OF NEMATOLOGY. See Zoology.

ISSN 0942-5276
GW
AKTUELLE AUGENHEILKUNDE. (1992)-. Multiple languages. Six times a year. $98.00. Georg Thieme Verlag Stuttgart, Postfach 301120, D-70451 Stuttgart Germany. **Tel** 011 49 711 89310, FAX 011 49 711 8931298, telex 7 252 275 GTVD. **(Subscription address:** Thieme Medical Publishers Inc., 381 Park Avenue South, New York NY 10016. **Tel** (212)683-5088.**)** ***Continues*** *Folia Ophthalmologica, 0323-4932.*

LC QK1 .U38 **ISSN** 0375-9237
DD 580/.5 UA
CODEN EGJBAY
AL-MAGALLA AL-MISRIYYA LI-N-NABAT. (EGYPTIAN JOURNAL OF BOTANY.). [Egypt. j. bot.]. **Added/Corp** Jamiyah al-Nabatiyah al-Misriyah. (1972)-. Periodical. English. Irregular. $75.00. National Information & Documentation Center, A1-Tahrir St Dokki Awqaf PO, Cairo Egypt. **Tel** 011 20 2 701696, telex 93069. Documents available from BIOSIS Document Express, CASDDS. ***Continues*** *Journal of Botany of the United Arab Republic, 0021-9363.*
Ind/Abst AGRICOLA; Biol. Abstr.; Chem. Abstr.; Crop Physiol. Abstr.; Field Crop Abstr.; Hortic. Abstr.; Irr. Drain. Abstr.; Life Sci. Collect.; Plant Grow. Reg. Abstr.; Rev. Med. Vet. Mycology; Rev. Plant Pathol.; Soils Fert.

LC QK
DD 581 BL
ALBERTOA. Added/Corp Herbario Alberto Castellanos. Vol. 1, No. 1 (Jan. 15, 1986)-. Periodical. Portuguese (summaries and/or abstracts in English). Irregular. Free to institutions that can send reprints, serial works, herbarium sheets or photos in exchange. Jardim Botanico do Rio de Janeiro, rua Jardim Botanico 1008, 22460 Rio de Janeiro RJ Brazil. **Tel** 011 55 21 2748246. **ED** J. P. P. Carauta. Index available. **Circ:** 1,000 (ctrl).

LC QK564 **ISSN** 0094-6362
DD 589.3 US
NLM Z 5356.A6 A394
ALGAE ABSTRACTS. See Biology-Abstracting, Bibliographies and Statistics.

LC QK149 .A4 **ISSN** 0065-6275
DD 581.9794 US
CODEN ALSOA7
Pr Rev.
ALISO. [Aliso]. Vol. 1 (April 1948)-. English. Two times a year (two volumes per year, four issues per volume). $34.00 US; $36.00 other. Rancho Santa Ana Botanic Garden, 1500 North College Avenue, Claremont CA 91711. **Tel** (909)625-8767, FAX (909)626-7670. **ED** Richard Benjamin. **Bk Rev. Ad Acc. Acid Free. Circ:** 500 (ctrl). Documents available from BIOSIS Document Express.
Desc: Covers systematic and evolutionary botany. Contains original papers dealing with botanical systematics and evolution including related studies in cytology, ecology, cladistics, genetics, biogeography, morphology, anatomy and physiology.
Ind/Abst AGRICOLA [Full Cov.]; Biol. Abstr.; Ecol. Abstr.; Field Crop Abstr.; For. Prod. Abstr. (1991-); For. Abstr.; Geol. Abstr.; Grass. Forage Abstr.; Hortic. Abstr.; Ornamental Hort. (19??-19??); Life Sci. Collect.; Plant Breed. Abstr.; Plant Genet. Resour. Abstr.

LC QK1 .A3648 **ISSN** 0735-8032
DD 581 US
CODEN LLRTD5
ALLERTONIA. [Allertonia]. **Added/Corp** Pacific Tropical Botanical Garden. (1975)-. Academic Scholarly Publication. English. Irregular. Price varies per volume. National Tropical Botanical Garden, PO Box 340, Lawai HI 96765. **Tel** (808)332-7324, FAX (808)332-9765. **ED** A. C. Smith. Index available. **Circ:** 200 (ctrl). Documents available from BIOSIS Document Express, CASDDS.
Desc: A series of occasional papers presenting results of original botanical or horticultural research undertaken by the Pacific Tropical Botanical Garden.
Ind/Abst Biol. Abstr.; Chem. Abstr.; Life Sci. Collect.

LC QK **ISSN** 0065-6429
DD 581 IT
CODEN ALLIAM
ALLIONIA. (ALLIONIA : BOLLETTINO DELL'INSTITUTO ED ORTO BOTANICO DELL'UNIVERSITA DI TORINO.). [Allionia]. Vol. 1, No. 1 (1952)-. Academic Scholarly Publication. Italian. Arti Grafiche Pacini Mariotti, Via S Maria 36, 56100 Pisa Italy. Documents available from CASDDS.
Ind/Abst Biodeter. Abstr.; Chem. Abstr.; Nematol. Abstr.; Life Sci. Collect.

SA
ALOE. Added/Corp South African Aloe and Succulent Society. (19??)-. Periodical. English (Afrikaans). Four times a year. $29.82. Succulent Society of South Africa, Box 1193, Pretoria 0001 South Africa. **Tel** 011 27 12 983588. **ED** Niko Sauer. **Bk Rev. Ad Acc. Circ:** 1,300 (ctrl).
Desc: Description and cultivation of succulents.
Ind/Abst Hortic. Abstr.; Ornamental Hort. (1991-); Plant Breed. Abstr.; Plant Genet. Resour. Abstr.; Seed Abstr.

LC BS660 .N45A **ISSN** 0303-1500
DD 220 IS
ALON HA-ONATI - NEOT QEDUMIM, HA-. See Religions and Theology.

LC QK520 .A6 **ISSN** 0002-8444
DD 587.305 US
CODEN AMFJA2
Pr Rev.
AMERICAN FERN JOURNAL. [Am. fern j.]. **Added/Corp** American Fern Society. Report. Vol. 1 (Aug. 1910)-. Periodical. English. Four times a year. $20.00. American Fern Soceity, 456 McGill Place, Atlanta GA 30312. **Tel** (404)525-3147. **ED** Carol Peek and James Peek. Index available. cum. index. **Bk Rev. Ad Acc. Circ:** 1,300 (ctrl). Documents available from The Genuine Article, BIOSIS Document Express.
Desc: Scientific papers on ferns and fern allies (worldwide) including native and cultivated ferns.
Ind/Abst AGRICOLA [Full Cov.]; Biol. Abstr.; Curr. Aware. Biol. Sci., CABS; Curr. Contents Agric. Biol. Environ. Sci.; GeoRef; Hortic. Abstr.; Life Sci. Collect.; Ref. Sources; Res. Alert [Full Cov.]; Sci. Cit. Index; SCISEARCH; Soils Fert.

LC QK1 .B345 **ISSN** 0002-9122
DD 581 US
NLM W1 AM448E **CODEN** AJBOAA
AMERICAN JOURNAL OF BOTANY. [Am. j. bot.]. **Added/Corp** Botanical Society of America. Brooklyn Botanic Garden. Vol. 1 (Jan. 1914)-. Academic Scholarly Publication. English. Twelve times a year (published at end of the month). $165.00. American Journal of Botany, Office of Publications, 1735 Neil Avenue, Columbus OH 43210. **Tel** (614)292-3519, FAX (614)292-3519. **ED** Nels R. Lersten. Index available (bound in last issue). **Ad Acc. Acid Free. Circ:** 5,000 (ctrl). Documents available from The Genuine Article, BIOSIS Document Express, UMI Article Clearinghouse, CASDDS. ***Absorbed*** *Botanical Society of America. Meeting. Abstracts.* ***Continued in part by*** *Botanical Society of America. Abstracts of Papers.*
Desc: A pure science journal devoted to every aspect of scientific botany. Provides researchers and the inquiring public with the current work in all areas of the botanical sciences.
Ind/Abst Acad. Ind. [Computer File] (1992-); Acad.

Search; AgBiotech News Inf.; AGRICOLA [Full Cov.]; Biol. Agric. Index; Biol. Abstr.; Biol. Dig.; Chem. Abstr.; Cot. Trop. Fibr. Abstr. Bibliogr.; Crop Physiol. Abstr.; Curr. Aware. Biol. Sci., CABS; Curr. Cit.; Curr. Contents Agric. Biol. Environ. Sci.; Ecol. Abstr.; Ecology Abstr.; EMBASE; EP Collect.; Expand. Acad. Index (1989-); Field Crop Abstr.; For. Prod. Abstr. (19??-19??); For. Abstr.; Gen. Sci. Index; Gen. Sci. Source; Genet. Abstr.; Geogr. Abstr. Phys. Geogr.; Geol. Abstr.; GeoRef; Grass. Forage Abstr.; Homework Help.; Hortic. Abstr.; INFO-SOUTH Abstr.; INIS Atomindex [Micro.]; Int. Aerosp. Abstr.; Irr. Drain. Abstr.; Mag. Search; Maize Abstr.; MasterFile FullTEXT 1000; MasterFile FullTEXT 350; MasterFile FullTEXT 650; MasterFile FullTEXT (July 1994-); Microbiol. Abstr. Sect. C; NAPRALERT; Newsp. Period. Abstr. (1992-); Ocean. Abstr.; OCLC; Ornamental Hort. (19??-19??); Life Sci. Collect.; PESTDOC; Plant Breed. Abstr.; Plant Genet. Resour. Abstr.; Plant Grow. Reg. Abstr.; Potato Abstr.; Protozoolog. Abstr.; Ref. Upd. Deluxe Ed.; Res. Alert [Full Cov.]; Rev. Agric. Entomol.; Rev. Med. Vet. Mycology; Rev. Plant Pathol.; Rice Abstr.; Risk Abstr. (19??-19??); Sci. Cit. Index; SCISEARCH; Seed Abstr.; Soils Fert.; Sorghum Mill. Abstr.; Soyabean Abstr.; Telebase; Vitis Vitic. Enol. Abstr.; Weed Abstr.; Wheat Barley Trit. Abstr.

ISSN 0365-575X
RM
CODEN APSVBN

ANALELE - INSTITUTULUI DE CERCETARI PENTRU PROTECTIA PLANTELOR, ACADEMIA DE STIINTE AGRICOLE SI SILVICE. (ANALELE - INSTITUTULUI DE CERCETARI PENTRU PROTECTIA PLANTELOR.). [An. - Inst. cercet. prot. plant., Acad. stiinte agric. silv.]. **Main/Corp** Romania. Institutul de Cercetari Pentru Protectia Plantelor. **Added/Corp** Romania. Institutul Central de Cercetari Agricole. Sectie de Protectia Plantelor. Academia de Stiinte Agricole si Silvice. Vol. 1 (1963)-. Academic Scholarly Publication. Romany. One time a year. Documents available from BIOSIS Document Express, CASDDS. ***Supersedes in part*** *Romania. Institutul de Cercetari Pentru Cereale si Plante Tehnice - Fundulea. Analele. Ser. C.*
Ind/Abst Biol. Abstr. (-1987); Chem. Abstr.; Nematol. Abstr.; Potato Abstr.; Rev. Agric. Entomol.

ISSN 0185-254X
DD 581 MX

ANALES DEL INSTITUTO DE BIOLOGIA. SERIE BOTANICA. [An. Inst. Biol., Ser. bot.]. (1930)-. Monographic series. Spanish. One time a year.
Ind/Abst Hortic. Abstr.

LC QK **ISSN** 0374-5511
DD 581 MX
CODEN AMXSAH
Pr Rev.

ANALES DEL INSTITUTO DE BIOLOGIA, UNIVERSIDAD NACIONAL AUTONOMA DE MEXICO. SERIE BOTANICA. [An. Inst. Biol., Univ. Nac. Auton. Mex., Ser. bot.]. **Main/Corp** Mexico (City). Universidad Nacional. Instituto de Biologia. Vol. 38 (1967)-. Periodical. Spanish (English and Multiple languages; summaries and/or abstracts in English). One time a year. $40,000. Universidad Nacional Autonoma de Mexico Instituto de Biologia, Apdo Postal 70-233, Ciudad Universitaria 04510, Mexico D.F. Mexico. **Tel** FAX 548 82 07. **ED** Roberto Johansen Naime. Index available. **Bk Rev. Circ:** 600 (ctrl). available on photocopies. Documents available from BIOSIS Document Express. ***Supersedes in part*** *Anales del Instituto Biologia, 0076-7174.*
Ind/Abst Biol. Abstr.; Ecol. Abstr.; For. Prod. Abstr.; Geogr. Abstr. Phys. Geogr.; Grass. Forage Abstr.; Maize Abstr.; Life Sci. Collect. (1989-); Rev. Med. Vet. Mycology; Rev. Plant Pathol.; Soils Fert.; Weed Abstr.

LC QK1 .S854 **ISSN** 0211-1322
DD 581.946/05 SP
CODEN AJBMD7

ANALES DEL JARDIN BOTANICO DE MADRID (1979). (ANALES DEL JARDIN BOTANICO DE MADRID / CONSEJO SUPERIOR DE INVESTIGACIONES CIENTIFICAS.). [An. Jard. Bot. Madr. (1979)]. **Added/Corp** Jardin Botanico de Madrid. Vol. 36 (1979)-. Periodical. Spanish (English and French). Two times a year. 2500ptas Spain; 3750ptas other. Consejo Superior Investigacion Cientificas / CSIC, Vitruvio 8, 28006 Madrid Spain. **Tel** 011 34 1 5612833, FAX 011 34 1 4113077, telex 42182. available on CD-ROM. Documents available from BIOSIS Document Express. ***Continues*** *Anales del Instituto Botanico A.J. Cavanilles, 0365-0790.*
Desc: Publishes original research studies on systematics, morphology, vegetal ecology, and other themes relating to phytotaxonomy.
Ind/Abst Agrindex; Biol. Abstr.; Ecol. Abstr.; Field Crop Abstr.; For. Prod. Abstr.; For. Abstr.; Grass. Forage Abstr.; Hortic. Abstr.; Ornamental Hort. (1991-); Plant Breed. Abstr.; Rev. Med. Vet. Mycology; Rev. Plant Pathol.; Soils Fert.; Weed Abstr.

LC QK1 .A456 **ISSN** 0066-1759
DD 581/.05 GW
CCC
CODEN ANBTAJ
Pr Rev.

ANGEWANDTE BOTANIK. [Angew. Bot.]. **Added/Corp** Vereinigung fuer Angewandte Botanik. Vol. 1 (April/May 1919)-. Periodical. German (summaries and/or abstracts in English). Three times a year. $316.27. Blackwell Wissenschafts-Verlag, Kurfuerstendamm 57, D-10707 Berlin Germany. **Tel** 011 49 30 32790623, 011 49 30 32790624, FAX 011 49 30 327 90610. **ED** H.J. Jaeger. Index available. cum. index. **Bk Rev. Ad Acc. Circ:** 2,500. Documents available from The Genuine Article, BIOSIS Document Express, CASDDS. ***Supersedes*** *Jahresbericht der Vereinigung fur Angewandte Botanik, 0344-6220.*
Desc: Covers applied botany.
Ind/Abst Agric. Eng. Abstr. (1991-); Anim. Breed. Abstr.; Art Archaeol. Tech. Abstr.; Biol. Abstr.; Chem. Abstr.; Crop Physiol. Abstr.; Curr. Aware. Biol. Sci., CABS; Curr. Cit.; Curr. Contents Agric. Biol. Environ. Sci.; Ecology Abstr.; EMBASE; Energy Res. Abstr. (June 1971-); Field Crop Abstr.; For. Prod. Abstr. (19??-19??); For. Abstr.; Grass. Forage Abstr.; Hortic. Abstr.; Irr. Drain. Abstr.; Maize Abstr.; Microbiol. Abstr. Sect. A; Microbiol. Abstr. Sect. C; Ornamental Hort. (19??-19??); Life Sci. Collect.; PESTDOC; Plant Breed. Abstr.; Plant Grow. Reg. Abstr.; Res. Alert [Select. Cov.]; Rev. Plant Pathol.; SCISEARCH; Seed Abstr.; Soils Fert.; Sorghum Mill. Abstr.; Soyabean Abstr.; Vitis Vitic. Enol. Abstr.; Weed Abstr.; Wheat Barley Trit. Abstr.

LC QK **ISSN** 0517-8452
DD 581 IO
CODEN ABOGAT

ANNALES BOGORIENSES. [Ann. Bogor.]. **Added/Corp** Kebun Raja Indonesia. Treub Laboratory. Pusat Penelitian dan Pengembangan Bioteknologi (Indonesia). Vol. 1, No. 1 (Oct. 1950)- Vol. 8, No. 2 (Dec. 1984); New Series, Vol. 1, No. 1 (Mar. 1988)-. Periodical. English (Indonesian; summaries and/or abstracts in Indonesian). Irregular. $3.25. Center for Research Biotechnology, Lipi J1 IR H Juanda 18, POB 323, Bogor 16122 Indonesia. **Tel** 011 62 251 2103821039, telex DIRBIONAS. **ED** S. Saono. Index available. cum. index. **Circ:** 223. Documents available from BIOSIS Document Express. ***Continues*** *Annals of the Botanic Gardens, Buitenzorg.*
Desc: News and information on the tropical botany.
Ind/Abst AgBiotech News Inf.; Biol. Abstr.; Plant Breed. Abstr.; Plant Grow. Reg. Abstr.

LC QK1 .A458 **ISSN** 0003-3847
DD 581.0 FI
CODEN ABOFAQ
Pr Rev.

ANNALES BOTANICI FENNICI. [Ann. bot. fenn.]. **Added/Corp** Suomen Biologian Seura Vanamo. Suomalainen Elain- ja Kasvitieteellinen Seura Vanamo. Vol. 1 (1964)-. Periodical. English (German). Four times a year. Fmk1500.00. Academic Bookstore Akateeminen, Postilokero 23, FIN-00371 Helsinki Finland. **Tel** 011 358 0 12141. Documents available from The Genuine Article, BIOSIS Document Express, CASDDS. ***Supersedes*** *Suomalaisen Elain- ja Kasvitieteellisen Seuran Vanamon Kasvitieteellisia Julkaisuja;* ***Supersedes in part*** *Archivum Societatis Zoologae Botanicae Fennicae 'Vanamo'.*
Ind/Abst Biol. Abstr.; Chem. Abstr.; Curr. Aware. Biol. Sci., CABS; Curr. Cit.; Curr. Contents Agric. Biol. Environ. Sci.; Ecol. Abstr.; Ecology Abstr.; EMBASE; Field Crop Abstr.; For. Prod. Abstr.; For. Abstr.; Geogr. Abstr. Phys. Geogr.; Geogr. Abstr. Human Geogr. (?-?); GeoRef; Grass. Forage Abstr.; Hortic. Abstr.; Immunol. Abstr.; Microbiol. Abstr. Sect. C; Ocean. Abstr.; Life Sci. Collect.; Plant Breed. Abstr.; Plant Genet. Resour. Abstr.; Res. Alert [Full Cov.]; Rev. Med. Vet. Mycology; Rev. Plant Pathol.; Sci. Cit. Index; SCISEARCH; Seed Abstr.; Soils Fert.

LC SB29.T8 A3 **ISSN** 0365-4761
DD 630 TI

ANNALES DE L'INSTITUT NATIONAL DE LA RECHERCHE AGRONOMIQUE DE TUNISIE. See Agriculture.

LC SB599 .K5 **ISSN** 0365-5814
DD 632.05 GR
CODEN APYBAQ
Pr Rev.

ANNALES DE L'INSTITUT PHYTOPATHOLOGIQUE BENAKI. See Agriculture.

LC QK **ISSN** 0003-455X
DD 581 FI
CODEN AZOFAO
Pr Rev.

ANNALES ZOOLOGICI FENNICI. [Ann. zool. fenn.]. Vol. 1 (1964)-. Periodical. Finnish (English and German). Four times a year. Fmk350.00. Academic Bookstore Akateeminen, Postilokero 23, FIN-00371 Helsinki Finland. **Tel** 011 358 0 12141. Index available (bound in 4th issue). Documents available from The Genuine Article, BIOSIS Document Express, CASDDS. ***Supersedes*** *Annales Zoologici Societatis Zoologicae-Botanicae Fennicae Vanamo, 0365-8627;* ***Supersedes in part*** *Archivum Societatis Zoologicae-Botanicae Fennicae Vanamo, 0365-7280.*
Ind/Abst Anim. Behav. Abstr.; Anim. Breed. Abstr.; Biocont. News Inf.; Biol. Abstr.; Chem. Abstr.; Curr. Aware. Biol. Sci., CABS; Curr. Cit.; Curr. Contents Agric. Biol. Environ. Sci.; Curr. Ref. Fish Res.; Ecol. Abstr.; Ecology Abstr.; EMBASE; Fish Rev.; For. Prod. Abstr.; For. Abstr.; Geol. Abstr.; GeoRef; Helminthol. Abstr. (1991-); Hortic. Abstr.; Key Word Index Wildl. Res.; Ocean. Abstr.; Life Sci. Collect.; Plant Breed. Abstr.; Protozoolog. Abstr.; Res. Alert [Full Cov.]; Rev. Med. Vet. Entomol.; Sci. Cit. Index; SCISEARCH; Soils Fert.; Wildl. Rev.

LC QK1 **ISSN** 0305-7364
DD 580 UK
CCC
NLM W1 AN566 **CODEN** ANBOA4
Pr Rev.

ANNALS OF BOTANY. [Ann. bot.]. (1887)-. Academic Scholarly Publication. English. Twelve times a year. $480.00. Academic Press Ltd., A Division of Harcourt Brace & Company Ltd., 24-28 Oval Road, London NW1 7DX United Kingdom. **Tel** 011 44 171 2674466, FAX 011 44 171 4822293, 011 44 171 4854752, telex 25775 ACPRES G. **(Subscription address:** Harcourt Brace & Company, Ltd., Foots Cray High Street, Sidcup Kent DA14 5HP United Kingdom. **Tel** 011 44 181 3003322, FAX 011 44 181 3090807, telex 896 377 ACADEM.) cum. index. **Bk Rev.** Documents available from The Genuine Article, BIOSIS Document Express, CASDDS.
Desc: A journal that gives broad coverage to all aspects of botany. Emphasizes current research in growth, mathematical models of physiological processes, and plant ultrastructure. The journal attracts short communications, research papers, and longer articles that are essential reading for research workers who aim to keep abreast of their own and related subjects.
Ind/Abst AgBiotech News Inf.; AGRICOLA [Full Cov.]; Agrofor. Abstr. (1991-); Biol. Agric. Index; Biol. Abstr.; Chem. Abstr.; Cot. Trop. Fibr. Abstr. Bibliogr.; Crop Physiol. Abstr.; Curr. Aware. Biol. Sci., CABS; Curr. Cit.; Curr. Contents Agric. Biol. Environ. Sci.; Ecol. Abstr.; Ecology Abstr.; EMBASE; Field Crop Abstr.; Fish Rev. (Jan. 1989-July 1992); Food Sci. Technol. Abstr.; For. Prod. Abstr. (19??-19??); For. Abstr.; Geogr. Abstr. Phys. Geogr.; GeoRef; Grass. Forage Abstr.; Hortic. Abstr.; Int. Aerosp. Abstr.; Irr. Drain. Abstr.; Maize Abstr.; Ornamental Hort. (1991-); Life Sci. Collect.; PESTDOC; Plant Breed. Abstr.; Plant Genet. Resour. Abstr.; Plant Grow. Reg. Abstr.; Postharvest News Inf.; Potato Abstr.; Res. Alert [Full Cov.]; Rev. Agric. Entomol.; Rev. Med. Vet. Mycology; Rev. Plant Pathol.; Rice Abstr.; Sci. Cit. Index; SCISEARCH; Seed Abstr.; Soils Fert.; Sorghum Mill. Abstr.; Soyabean Abstr.; Vitis Vitic. Enol. Abstr.; Weed Abstr.; Wheat Barley Trit. Abstr.; Wildl. Rev. (Jan. 1989-July 1992).

ISSN 0970-9924
II
UDC 581.1

ANNALS OF PLANT PHYSIOLOGY AKOLA. [Ann. Plant Physiol.Akola]. (1987)-. Periodical. English. Two times a year. Dr. S. B. Lall, Editor-in-Chief, RDG College Hostel-1 Amt Road, Akola 444001, Maharashtra India.
Ind/Abst Agrofor. Abstr. (1991-); Crop Physiol. Abstr.; Field Crop Abstr.; For. Prod. Abstr. (1991-); Hortic. Abstr.; Plant Breed. Abstr.; Plant Grow. Reg. Abstr.; Rice Abstr.; Seed Abstr.; Soils Fert.; Sorghum Mill. Abstr.; Soyabean Abstr.

LC QK1 .M65 **ISSN** 0026-6493
DD 581 US
CODEN AMBGA7
Pr Rev.

ANNALS OF THE MISSOURI BOTANICAL GARDEN. [Ann. Mo. Bot. Gard.]. **Main/Corp** Missouri Botanical Garden. **Added/Corp** Henry Shaw School of Botany. Graduate Laboratory. Vol. 1 (1914)-. Periodical. English. Four times a year (Feb., May, Aug., Nov.). $110.00. Missouri Botanical Garden, PO Box 299, St. Louis MO 63166. **Tel** (314)577-9534, (314)577-5100, FAX (314)577-9594. **ED** George Rogers. cum. index. **Bk Rev. Circ:** 800. available on microfilm from University Microfilms International (UMI). Documents available from The Genuine Article, BIOSIS Document Express. ***Continues in part*** *Missouri Botanical Garden. Annual Report - Missouri Botanical Garden, 0893-3243.*
Desc: Publishes papers primarily in systematic botany with an emphasis on tropical botany.
Ind/Abst AgBiotech News Inf.; AGRICOLA [Full Cov.]; Biocont. News Inf. (1991-); Biol. Agric. Index; Biol. Abstr.; Curr. Aware. Biol. Sci., CABS; Curr. Cit.; Curr. Contents Agric. Biol. Environ. Sci.; Ecol. Abstr. (?-?); Field Crop Abstr.; For. Prod. Abstr. (19??-19??); For. Abstr.; Geol. Abstr.; GeoRef; Grass. Forage Abstr.; Hortic. Abstr.; Ornamental Hort. (1991-); Life Sci. Collect.; Plant Breed. Abstr.; Plant Genet. Resour. Abstr.; Res. Alert [Full Cov.]; Rev. Med. Vet. Mycology; Rev. Plant Pathol.; Sci. Cit. Index; SCISEARCH; Soc. Sci. Cit. Index [Select. Cov.]; Wildl. Rev.

LC QL1 .A49 ISSN 0570-202X
XO
CODEN AZBTAZ

ANNOTATIONES ZOOLOGICAE ET BOTANICAE. See Zoology.

LC QK ISSN 0570-2496
DD 581 JA

ANNUAL INDEX OF THE REPORTS ON PLANT CHEMISTRY. See Biology-Abstracting, Bibliographies and Statistics.

LC QK
DD 581 US

ANNUAL REPORT / BROOKLYN BOTANIC GARDEN. **Main/Corp** Brooklyn Botanic Garden. English. One time a year. Brookyln Botanic Garden, 1000 Washington Avenue, Brooklyn NY 11225. **Tel** (718)622-4433. ***Continues in part*** *Brooklyn Botanic Garden Record.*

LC QK
DD 581 US

ANNUAL REPORT / DESERT BOTANICAL GARDEN. **Main/Corp** Desert Botanical Garden (Ariz.). (1989/1990)-. English.

ISSN 0893-1674
DD 581 US

ANNUAL REPORT ... - MSU-DOE PLANT RESEARCH LABORATORY. [Annu. rep. - MSU-DOE Plant Res. Lab.]. **Main/Corp** MSU-DOE Plant Research Laboratory. **VFOAT** Annual Report of the MSU-DOE Plant Research Laboratory. 15th (1980)-. English. One time a year. Michigan State University Artificial Language Laboratory, 405 Computer Center, East Lansing MI 48824-1042. **Tel** (517)353-0870, FAX (517)353-4766. ***Continues*** *MSU-DOE Plant Research Laboratory. Plant Research, 0556-0403.*

LC QK73.C232 H33 ISSN 0300-3140
DD 580/.744/71352 CN

ANNUAL REPORT - ROYAL BOTANICAL GARDENS. **Main/Corp** Royal Botanical Gardens (Hamilton, Ont.). Periodical. English (French). One time a year. 60.03Can$. Royal Botanical Gardens/CCHHS, PO Box 399, Hamilton Ontario L8N 3H8 Canada. **Tel** (416)527-1158, FAX (416)577-0375. **ED** Susan Malcolm. **Circ:** 4,500.
Desc: Financial statements, departmental reports of the programmes and work of the gardens.

LC SB599 .A68 ISSN 0066-4286
DD 581.205873 US
CCC
NLM W1 AN779F CODEN APPYAG
Pr Rev.

ANNUAL REVIEW OF PHYTOPATHOLOGY. [Annu. rev. phytopathol.]. Vol. 1 (1963)-. English. One time a year (September). $54.00. Annual Reviews Inc., 4139 El Camino Way, PO Box 10139, Palo Alto CA 94303-0139. **Tel** (415)493-4400, (800)523-8635, FAX (415)855-9815. **ED** R. James Cook. Index available. cum. index. ctrl circ. available on microfilm and microfiche from University Microfilms International (UMI). Documents available from The Genuine Article, BIOSIS Document Express, CASDDS, Documents on Demand.
Desc: Comprehensive, thorough coverage of latest advances in phytopathology; written by acknowledged experts in the field. Extensive literature citations included.
Ind/Abst AGRICOLA [Full Cov.]; Biol. Agric. Index; Biol. Abstr.; Chem. Abstr.; Curr. Aware. Biol. Sci., CABS; Curr. Cit.; Curr. Contents Agric. Biol. Environ. Sci.; EMBASE; Environ. Abstr.; Field Crop Abstr.; For. Prod. Abstr.; For. Abstr.; Grass. Forage Abstr.; Hortic. Abstr.; Index Sci. Rev. [Full Cov.]; Nematol. Abstr.; Life Sci. Collect.; PESTDOC; Plant Breed. Abstr.; Plant Genet. Resour. Abstr.; Protozoolog. Abstr.; Ref. Upd. Deluxe Ed.; Res. Alert [Full Cov.]; Rev. Med. Vet. Mycology; Rev. Plant Pathol.; Sci. Cit. Index; SCISEARCH; Soils Fert.; Vitis Vitic. Enol. Abstr.; Weed Abstr.

ISSN 1040-2519
DD 581 US
CCC
CODEN ARPBEX
Pr Rev.

ANNUAL REVIEW OF PLANT PHYSIOLOGY AND PLANT MOLECULAR BIOLOGY. [Annu. rev. plant physiol. plant mol. biol.]. Vol. 39 (1988)-. Academic Scholarly Publication. English. One time a year (June). $52.00. Annual Reviews Inc., 4139 El Camino Way, PO Box 10139, Palo Alto CA 94303-0139. **Tel** (415)493-4400, (800)523-8635, FAX (415)855-9815. **ED** Winslow Briggs. Index available. cum. index. ctrl circ. Documents available from The Genuine Article, BIOSIS Document Express, CASDDS. ***Continues*** *Annual Review of Plant Physiology, 0066-4294.*
Ind/Abst Abstr. Bull. Inst. Pap. Sci. Tech.; AGRICOLA [Full Cov.]; Biol. Agric. Index; Biol. Abstr. (1988-); Chem. Abstr.; Curr. Aware. Biol. Sci., CABS; Curr. Cit.; Curr. Contents Agric. Biol. Environ. Sci.; Curr. Contents Life Sci.; Energy Res. Abstr.; For. Abstr.; Hortic. Abstr.; INIS Atomindex [Micro.]; Int. Aerosp. Abstr.; Irr. Drain. Abstr.; Maize Abstr.; Life Sci. Collect.; PESTDOC; Plant Breed. Abstr.; Plant Grow. Reg. Abstr.; Ref. Upd. Basic Ed.; Ref. Upd. Deluxe Ed.; Res. Alert [Full Cov.]; Rev. Plant Pathol.; Sci. Cit. Index; SCISEARCH; Soyabean Abstr.

ISSN 0373-4641
PO
UDC 58
CODEN ASBRA

ANUARIO DA SOCIEDADE BROTERIANA. [Anu. Soc. Broter.]. (1935)-. Periodical. Multiple languages. One time a year (Jan.). $7.00. Instituto Botanico da Universidade de Coimbra, Arcos do Jardim, P-3049 Coimbra Codex Portugal. **Tel** 011 351 39 22897.

ISSN 0309-1791
DD 581 UK
CODEN APBODL

APPLIED BOTANY. [Appl. bot.]. Academic Scholarly Publication. English. Irregular. Price varies per volume. Academic Press Ltd., A Division of Harcourt Brace & Company Ltd., 24-28 Oval Road, London NW1 7DX United Kingdom. **Tel** 011 44 171 2674466, FAX 011 44 171 4822293, 011 44 171 4854752, telex 25775 ACPRES G. **ED** D W Robinson and J G D Lamb. Documents available from CASDDS.
Ind/Abst Chem. Abstr.

LC QK
DD 581 II

APPLIED BOTANY ABSTRACTS. **Added/Corp** National Botanical Research Institute (India). Economic Botany Information Service. Vol. 1, No. 1 (Mar. 1981)-. Periodical. English. Four times a year. $150.00. National Botanical Research Institute, Economic Botany Information Service, Lucknow India. **(Subscription address:** Prints India, 11 Darya Ganj, New Delhi 110002 India. **Tel** 011 91 11 3268645, FAX 011 91 11 3275542, telex 31-61087 PRIN-IN.**)**

IR

APPLIED ENTOMOLOGY AND PHYTOPATHOLOGY. See Zoology-Entomology.

US

APPLIED PHYCOLOGY FORUM. **Added/Corp** Phycological Society of America. **VFOAT** Forum. Vol. 1, No. 1 (Oct. 1984)-. Newsletter. English. Three times a year (May, Sept., Dec.). $10.00 US and Canada; $14.00 other. Applied Phycology Forum, PO Box 18381, Boulder CO 80308. **Tel** (303)871-3455.
Desc: Contains the research and the studies on algae.

ISSN 1051-1113
DD 632 US
CODEN AMSEEM

APS MONOGRAPH SERIES. [APS monogr. ser.]. **Added/Corp** American Phytopathological Society. **VAT** American Phytopathological Society Monograph Series. (198?)-. Monographic series. English. Price varies per volume. American Phytopathological Society, 3340 Pilot Knob Road, St. Paul MN 55121. **Tel** (612)454-7250, (800)328-7560, FAX (612)454-0766, telex 6502439657 (MCI UW). Documents available from BIOSIS Document Express. ***Continues*** *Monograph (American Phytopathological Society), 0569-6992.*
Ind/Abst Biol. Abstr. (1987-); Life Sci. Collect.

ISSN 0893-7702
DD 632 US

AQUAPHYTE. (AQUAPHYTE : NEWSLETTER OF THE IPPC AQUATIC WEED PROGRAM OF THE UNIVERSITY OF FLORIDA, A PART OF THE INTERNATIONAL PLANT PROTECTION CENTER OF THE OREGON STATE UNIVERSITY, WHICH IS FUNDED BY THE UNITED STATES AGENCY FOR INTERNATIONAL DEVELOPMENT.). [Aquaphyte]. **Added/Corp** University of Florida. Center for Aquatic Plants. University of Florida. IPPC Aquatic Weed Program. University of Florida. Center for Aquatic Weeds. Vol. 1, No. 1 (Fall 1981)-. Newsletter. English. Two times a year. Free. Aquatic Plant Library, University of Florida, 2183 McCarthy Hall, Gainesville FL 32611. **Tel** (904)392-1799. **ED** Victor A. Ramey and Karen Brown. **Bk Rev. Circ:** 5,000 (ctrl).
Desc: A newsletter for aquatic plant managers and researchers, containing articles, book reviews, current literature reviews, and meeting announcements, pertaining to aquatic plants.

LC QK916 .A65 ISSN 0304-3770
DD 581.9/2/05 NE
CCC
CODEN AQBODS
Pr Rev.

AQUATIC BOTANY. [Aquat. bot.]. Vol. 1 (May 1975)-. Academic Scholarly Publication. English. Twelve times a year (3 vols.). $803.00. Elsevier Science Publishers BV, PO Box 211, 1000 AE Amsterdam Netherlands. **Tel** 011 31 20 4853641, 011 31 20 4853642, FAX 011 31 20 4853598. **ED** C den Hartog and J M A Brown. available on microfilm and microfiche from University Microfilms International (UMI); available on an online database from Elsevier Electronic Subscriptions (EES). Documents available from The Genuine Article, BIOSIS Document Express, CASDDS.
Desc: Concerned with fundamental studies on structure, function, dynamics and classification of plant dominated aquatic ecosystems.
Ind/Abst AgBiotech News Inf.; AGRICOLA; Aquat. Sci. Fish. Abstr. [CD-ROM Ed.]; Biocont. News Inf.; Biol. Abstr.; Chem. Abstr.; Curr. Cit.; Curr. Contents Agric. Biol. Environ. Sci.; Ecol. Abstr.; Ecology Abstr.; EMBASE; Energy Res. Abstr. (Aug. 1976-); Environ. Period. Bibliogr.; Fish Rev. (Jan. 1989-July 1992); Food Sci. Technol. Abstr.; For. Prod. Abstr.; For. Abstr.; Fresh. Aqua. Contents Tables; Geogr. Abstr. Phys. Geogr.; Geogr. Abstr. Human Geogr. (?-?); Geol. Abstr.; Grass. Forage Abstr.; Helminthol. Abstr.; Irr. Drain. Abstr.; Leadscan; Mar. Sci. Contents Tables; Microbiol. Abstr. Sect. C; Ocean. Abstr.; Life Sci. Collect.; Plant Breed. Abstr.; Plant Grow. Reg. Abstr.; Pollut. Abstr. Indexes; Res. Alert [Full Cov.]; Rev. Agric. Entomol.; Sci. Cit. Index; SCISEARCH; Seed Abstr.; Soils Fert.; Weed Abstr.; Wildl. Rev. (Jan. 1989-July 1992).

ISSN 0570-5169
FI
CODEN ASBOD8

AQUILO. SER. BOTANICA. [Aquilo, Ser. Bot.]. Vol. 1 (1963)-. Academic Scholarly Publication. Finnish (German and English). Irregular (one or two per year). Societas Amicorum Naturae Ouluensis, Oulun Luonnonystavain Yhdistys ry, c/o Department of Zoology, University of Oulu, Linnanmaa 90570 Oulu Finland. **Tel** 011 358 81 353133. **ED** Prof Seppo Eurola. Documents available from BIOSIS Document Express, CASDDS. ***Supersedes in part*** *Oulon Luonnonystavain Yjidistys. Julkaisuja. Sarja A.*
Ind/Abst Aquat. Sci. Fish. Abstr. [CD-ROM Ed.]; Biol. Abstr.; Chem. Abstr.; Ecol. Abstr.; Geogr. Abstr. Phys. Geogr.; Life Sci. Collect.; Soils Fert.

ISSN 1014-6334
LE

ARAB AND NEAR EAST PLANT PROTECTION NEWSLETTER. (AL-NASHRAH LA-IKHBARIYAH LI-WIQAYAT AL-NABAT FI AL-BULDAN AL-ARABIYAH WA-AL-SHARQ AK-ADNA.). [Arab Near East plant prot. newsl.]. **Added/Corp** Jamiyah Al-Arabiyah Li-Wiqayat al Nabat. FAO Near East Regional Office. **VFOAT** Al-Nashrah La-Ikhbariyah; ANNEPNEL. (1985)-. Periodical. Arabic (English). Two times a year.
Ind/Abst Nematol. Abstr.

LC QK1 .A493 ISSN 0066-5878
DD 581.05 PL
CODEN ARKOA9

ARBORETUM KORNICKIE. [Arbor. kornickie]. **Added/Corp** Zaklad Dendrologii i Pomologii w Korniku (Polska Akademia Nauk) Zaklad Dendrologii i Arboretum Kornickie (Polska Akademia Nauk) Instytut Dendrologii (Polska Akademia Nauk). Vol. 1- (1955)-. Polish (summaries and/or abstracts in English and Russian; table of contents in English and Russian). One time a year. **(Subscription address:** Ars Polona-Ruch, PO Box 1001, Krakowskie Przedmiescie 7, 00-068 Warsaw Poland. **Tel** 011 48 22 261201.**)** Documents available from CASDDS. ***Continues*** *Kornik. Zaklad Dendrologii i Pomologii. Prace.*
Ind/Abst Chem. Abstr.; Crop Physiol. Abstr.; For. Prod. Abstr.; For. Abstr.; Hortic. Abstr.; Life Sci. Collect.; Soils Fert.

LC QK480.U52 H643 ISSN 0518-2662
DD 580 US

ARBORETUM LEAVES. [Arbor. leaves]. **Added/Corp** Holden Arboretum. Vol. 1 (Spring 1959)-. Periodical. English. Four times a year. $2.00. The Holden Arboretum, 9500 Sperry Road, Mentor OH 44060. **Tel** (216)946-4400. **ED** Florence Mustric. **Bk Rev. Circ:** 8,000.
Desc: Articles on woody plants: trees and shrubs; native plants: wild flowers; and regional ecology.

ISSN 0323-5408
GW
CCC
CODEN APPZAJ

ARCHIV FUER PHYTOPATHOLOGIE UND PFLANZENSCHUTZ. [Arch. phytopathol. pflanzenschutz]. **Added/Corp** Akademie der Landwirtschaftwissenschaften der DDR. **VFOAT** Archives of Phytopathology and Plant Prtoection. Vol. 9 (1973)-. Academic Scholarly Publication. German (summaries and/or abstracts in English and Russian; table of contents in English and Russian). Six times a year. $353.00 (academic institutions), $550.00 (corporate institutions). Harwood Academic Publishers, PO Box 90, Reading RG1 8JL United Kingdom. **Tel** 011 44 1734 560080, FAX 011 44 1734 568211. **Bk Rev**. Documents available from BIOSIS Document Express, CASDDS. ***Continues*** *Archiv fur Pflanzenschutz.*
Desc: Papers on problems in virology, bacteriology, mycology, animal pest control, resistance research, weed control, plant protection technology and toxicology.
Ind/Abst AgBiotech News Inf.; Agric. Eng. Abstr.; Biocont. News Inf. (19??-19??); Biodeter. Abstr.; Biol. Abstr. (1987-); Chem. Abstr.; Crop Physiol. Abstr.; Curr. Cit.; EMBASE; Field Crop Abstr.; For. Abstr.; Hortic. Abstr.; INIS Atomindex [Micro.]; Maize Abstr.; Nematol. Abstr.; PESTDOC; Plant Breed. Abstr.; Plant Grow. Reg.

Abstr.; Potato Abstr.; Rev. Agric. Entomol.; Rev. Plant Pathol.; SCISEARCH; Seed Abstr.; Soils Fert.; Weed Abstr.

LC QK316 **ISSN** 1122-7214
DD 581 IT
UDC 58

•ARCHIVIO GEOBOTANICO. [Arch. geobot.]. (1993)-. Academic Scholarly Publication. Italian (English and French; summaries and/or abstracts in English and French). Two times a year. L90000. Universita di Pavia / Insituto di Botanica, Via S. Epifania 14, 27100 Pavia Italy. **ED** Augusto Pirola. Index available. **Bk Rev. Circ:** 600. ***Continues*** *Atti dell'Istituto di Botanica e del Laboratorio Crittogamico dell'Universita di Pavia, 0373-3947.*

LC QK479 .A7 **ISSN** 0004-2633
DD 582.1605 US
CODEN ARNOAO

ARNOLDIA (JAMAICA PLAIN). (ARNOLDIA.). [Arnoldia]. **Added/Corp** Arnold Arboretum. Vol. 1 (Mar. 14, 1941)-. Periodical. English. Four times a year (seasonally). $20.00. Arnold Arboretum Harvard University, The Arborway, Jamaica Plain MA 02130. **Tel** (617)524-1718, FAX (617)524-1418. **ED** Karen Madsen (editor's address: Arnold Arboretum, 125 Arborway, Jamaica Plain, MA 02130, phone: (617)524-1718 Ext. 114). Index available (bound in 4th issue). **Circ:** 4,000 (ctrl). Documents available from BIOSIS Document Express. ***Supersedes*** *Bulletin of Popular Information, 0196-6057.*
Desc: A magazine for amateur and professional horticulturists. News and information on articles dealing with botany, horticulture and plant and exploration.
Ind/Abst AGRICOLA [Full Cov.]; Biol. Abstr.; Crop Physiol. Abstr.; Garden Lit. (1992-); Hortic. Abstr.; Key Word Index Wildl. Res.; Ornamental Hort.; Plant Genet. Resour. Abstr.; Plant Grow. Reg. Abstr.

ISSN 0197-4033
US

AROIDEANA. [Aroideana]. **Added/Corp** International Aroid Society. Vol. 1 (May 1978)-. Periodical. English. Four times a year. $20.00. International Aroid Society, PO Box 43-1853, South Miami FL 33143. **Tel** (305)271-3767. **ED** John Banta. cum. index. **Bk Rev. Ad Acc. Circ:** 450 (ctrl).
Desc: Clearing house for information on culture, propagation and taxonomy of aroids and promotes interest in aroids.

ISSN 0309-1120
UK
CODEN ASHIDK

ASHINGTONIA. [Ashingtonia]. Vol. 1, No. 1 (July 1973)-. Academic Scholarly Publication. English. Four times a year. Holly Gate Cactur Nursery, Billinghurst Lane B2133, Ashington West Sussex RH20 3BA United Kingdom. **ED** John Donald. cum. index.
Desc: Brief scholarly articles on cacti and succulents (some bulbs) written by renowned experts and accompanied by stunning color photographs, line drawings, and hand drawn maps.

LC QK **ISSN** 0971-2402
DD 581 II
CODEN ASCIEU

ASIAN JOURNAL OF PLANT SCIENCE. [Asian j. plant sci.]. Vol. 1, No. 1 (June 1989)-. Periodical. English. Two times a year. $40.00. **(Subscription address:** Prints India, 11 Darya Ganj, New Delhi 110002 India. **Tel** 011 91 11 3268645, FAX 011 91 11 3275542, telex 31-61087 PRIN-IN.**)**

LC QK
DD 581 II

ASPECTS OF PLANT SCIENCES. Vol.1 (1976)-. Periodical. English. One time a year. Price varies. Today and Tomorrow's Printers and Publishers, 24-B/5 Desh Bandhu Gupta Road, Karol Bagh, New Delhi 110 005 India. **Tel** 011 91 11 5721928, 011 91 11 572770, FAX 011 91 11 7210073 (TTPP). **(Subscription address:** Prints India, 11 Darya Ganj, New Delhi 110002 India. **Tel** 011 91 11 3268645, FAX 011 91 11 3275542, telex 31-61087 PRIN-IN.**)** ***Continues*** *New Botanists Reviews.*
Desc: Contains articles of theoretical and methodological interest as well as studies that are based on empirical research.

LC QK **ISSN** 1048-7794
DD 581 US

ASPT NEWSLETTER. [ASPT newsl.]. **Added/Corp** American Society of Plant Taxonomists. **VAT** American Society of Plant Taxonomists Newsletter. Vol. 1, No. 1 (Fall 1987)-. Newsletter. English. Four times a year. American Society of Plant Taxonomists, Saint Mary's College, Biology Department, Notre Dame IN 46556. **Tel** (219)284-4674, FAX (219)284-4716. available via Internet (gopher://nmnhgoph.si.edu:70/00/.docs/ASPT_data).
Desc: Provides information on botany and plant taxonomy.

BL

ATAS DA SOCIEDADE BOTANICA DO BRASIL, SECCAO RIO DE JANEIRO. **Added/Corp** Sociedade Botanica do Brasil. Seccao Rio de Janeiro. **VFOAT** Seccao Rio de Janeiro. Vol. 1, No. 1 (Nov. 15, 1981)-. Portuguese (summaries and/or abstracts in English). Irregular. Jardim Botanico do Rio de Janeiro, rua Jardim Botanico 1008, 22460 Rio de Janeiro RJ Brazil. **Tel** 011 55 21 2748246. **ED** Dorothy Araujo, Marli Lima and Alexandre Pedrini.

LC QK1
DD 580.82 IT

ATTI - PAVIA. UNIVERSITA. ISTITUTO BOTANICO E LABORATORIO CRITTOGAMICO. **Main/Corp** Pavia. Universita. Istituto Botanico e Laboratorio Crittogamico. Series 2, Vol. 1-18 (1888-1921)-. Periodical. Italian. Irregular. Universita Pavia, Istituto Botanico E Laboratorio Crittogamico, Pavia Italy. ***Continues*** *Pavia. Universita. Laboratorio di Bottanica Crittogamica. Archivio.*
Ind/Abst Ornamental Hort.; Plant Breed. Abstr.

ISSN 0815-3191
AT
CODEN AAPPDN

AUSTRALASIAN PLANT PATHOLOGY. (AUSTRALASIAN PLANT PATHOLOGY : APP.). [Australas. plant pathol.]. **Added/Corp** Australasian Plant Pathology Society. **VFOAT** APP. Vol. 7, No. 2 (June 1978)-. Academic Scholarly Publication. English. Four times a year. 61.66Aus$. Plant Research Institute / R. Floyd, Department of Agriculture, Baron Hay Court, South Perth Western Australia, 6151 Australia. **Tel** 011 61 7 3710866. **ED** Dr. R Dodman. cum. index. **Bk Rev. Circ:** 550. Documents available from BIOSIS Document Express, CASDDS. ***Continues*** *Australian Plant Pathology Society. APPS Newsletter.*
Desc: Research notes on plant pathology in Australasia including studies on disease control and descriptions of new diseases.
Ind/Abst Biocont. News Inf.; Biodeter. Abstr.; Biol. Abstr. (1985-); Chem. Abstr. (1978-1983); Curr. Cit.; For. Prod. Abstr.; For. Abstr.; Hortic. Abstr.; Maize Abstr.; Nematol. Abstr.; Life Sci. Collect.; Rev. Med. Vet. Mycology; Rev. Plant Pathol.; Seed Abstr.; Weed Abstr.; Wheat Barley Trit. Abstr.

LC QK1 .A9 **ISSN** 0067-1924
DD 581/.05 AT
CCC
NLM W1 AU556 **CODEN** AJBTAP
Pr Rev.

AUSTRALIAN JOURNAL OF BOTANY. [Aust. j. bot.]. **Added/Corp** Commonwealth Scientific and Industrial Research Organization (Australia) Australian National Research Council. Australian Academy of Science. Vol. 1 (March 1953)-. Periodical. English. Six times a year. 220.00Aus$ Australia and New Zealand; $220.00 other. CSIRO Publications, PO Box 89, 314 Albert Street, East Melborne Victoria 3002 Australia. **Tel** 011 61 3 4187333, 4187217, FAX 011 61 3 4190459, telex AA 30236. **ED** Laurie W. Martinelli. **Ad Acc. Acid Free. Circ:** 1,000. available on microfilm and microfiche from University Microfilms International (UMI). Documents available from The Genuine Article, BIOSIS Document Express, CASDDS.
Desc: Covers the botany of the Southern Hemisphere, with particular reference to the Australian, western Pacific and Indian Ocean regions. The journal is multidisciplinary, covering anatomy, cell biology, development, ecology, genetics, morphology, pathology and reproductive biology.
Ind/Abst AgBiotech News Inf.; AGRICOLA [Full Cov.]; Agrofor. Abstr. (1991-); Biocont. News Inf.; Biol. Agric. Index; Biol. Abstr.; Chem. Abstr.; Crop Physiol. Abstr.; Curr. Aware. Biol. Sci., CABS; Curr. Cit.; Curr. Contents Agric. Biol. Environ. Sci.; Ecol. Abstr.; Ecology Abstr.; Environ. Period. Bibliogr.; Field Crop Abstr.; For. Prod. Abstr.; For. Abstr.; Geogr. Abstr. Phys. Geogr.; Geol. Abstr.; GeoRef; Grass. Forage Abstr.; Hortic. Abstr.; Irr. Drain. Abstr.; Microbiol. Abstr. Sect. C; Ornamental Hort. (19??-19??); Life Sci. Collect.; Plant Breed. Abstr.; Plant Genet. Resour. Abstr.; Plant Grow. Reg. Abstr.; Protozoolog. Abstr.; Ref. Upd. Deluxe Ed.; Res. Alert [Full Cov.]; Rev. Agric. Entomol.; Rev. Med. Vet. Mycology; Rev. Plant Pathol.; Sci. Cit. Index; SCISEARCH; Seed Abstr.; Soils Fert.; Vitis Vitic. Enol. Abstr.; Weed Abstr.

LC QK710 .A93 **ISSN** 0310-7841
DD 581.1/05 AT
CCC
CODEN AJPPCH
Pr Rev.

AUSTRALIAN JOURNAL OF PLANT PHYSIOLOGY. [Aust. j. plant physiol.]. **Added/Corp** Commonwealth Scientific and Industrial Research Organization (Australia). Vol. 1 (March 1974)-. Periodical. English. Six times a year. 260.00Aus$. CSIRO Publications, PO Box 89, 314 Albert Street, East Melborne Victoria 3002 Australia. **Tel** 011 61 3 4187333, 4187217, FAX 011 61 3 4190459, telex AA 30236. **ED** Laurie W. Martinelli. Index available. **Ad Acc. Acid Free. Circ:** 1,000 (ctrl). available on microfilm and microfiche from University Microfilms International (UMI). Documents available from The Genuine Article, BIOSIS Document Express, CASDDS. ***Absorbed in part*** *Australian Journal of Biological Sciences, 0004-9417.*
Desc: Journal of plant physiology. The scope includes biochemistry, biophysics, genetics, structure and molecular biology as related to plant function.
Ind/Abst Abstr. Bull. Inst. Pap. Sci. Tech.; AgBiotech News Inf.; AGRICOLA [Full Cov.]; Biol. Abstr.; Chem. Abstr.; Cot. Trop. Fibr. Abstr. Bibliogr.; Crop Physiol. Abstr.; Curr. Aware. Biol. Sci., CABS; Curr. Cit.; Curr. Contents Agric. Biol. Environ. Sci.; Curr. Contents Life Sci.; Ecol. Abstr.; EMBASE; Field Crop Abstr.; Food Sci. Technol. Abstr.; For. Prod. Abstr. (1991-); For. Abstr.; Geogr. Abstr. Phys. Geogr.; Grass. Forage Abstr.; Hortic. Abstr.; Irr. Drain. Abstr.; Maize Abstr.; NAPRALERT; Ornamental Hort.; Life Sci. Collect.; PESTDOC; Plant Breed. Abstr.; Plant Genet. Resour. Abstr.; Plant Grow. Reg. Abstr.; Ref. Upd. Deluxe Ed.; Res. Alert [Full Cov.]; Rev. Med. Vet. Mycology; Rev. Plant Pathol.; Rice Abstr.; Sci. Cit. Index; SCISEARCH; Seed Abstr.; Soils Fert.; Sorghum Mill. Abstr.; Soyabean Abstr.; Vitis Vitic. Enol. Abstr.; Weed Abstr.; Wheat Barley Trit. Abstr.

LC QV **ISSN** 0005-0008
DD 580 AT
UDC 582(94); 633/635(94)
CODEN ANPLAV

AUSTRALIAN PLANTS. **See** Gardening and Horticulture.

LC QK **ISSN** 1030-1887
DD 581 AT
CODEN ASBOE9
Pr Rev.

AUSTRALIAN SYSTEMATIC BOTANY. [Aust. syst. bot.]. **Added/Corp** Commonwealth Scientific and Industrial Research Organization (Australia) Australian Academy of Science. Vol. 1, No. 1 (1988)-. Periodical. English. Six times a year. 260.00Aus$. CSIRO Publications, PO Box 89, 314 Albert Street, East Melborne Victoria 3002 Australia. **Tel** 011 61 3 4187333, 4187217, FAX 011 61 3 4190459, telex AA 30236. **ED** Laurence W. Martinelli. Index available. **Ad Acc. Acid Free. Circ:** 500. available on microfilm and microfiche from University Microfilms International (UMI). Documents available from BIOSIS Document Express. ***Formed by the union of*** *Brunonia, 0313-4245* ***and*** *Australian Journal of Botany. Supplementary Series, 0365-3587.*
Desc: Devoted to the systematic botany of the Australian region in both theory and practice. Papers on all plant groups, including fossil plants, are considered for publication. Papers may be of universal interest or specifically relevant to Australia and biogeographically related areas.
Ind/Abst AgBiotech News Inf.; AGRICOLA [Full Cov.]; Biol. Abstr.; Curr. Aware. Biol. Sci., CABS; Ecol. Abstr.; For. Abstr.; Ornamental Hort. (1988-); Plant Breed. Abstr.; Plant Genet. Resour. Abstr.; Rev. Plant Pathol.

LC QK **ISSN** 1034-1218
DD 581 AT

AUSTRALIAN SYSTEMATIC BOTANY SOCIETY NEWSLETTER. **Added/Corp** Australian Systematic Botany Society. **VFOAT** Newsletter. (19??)-. Newsletter. English. Four times a year (March, June, Sept., Dec.). 35.00Aus$ Comes with Australian Systematic Botany Society membership. Australian Systematic Botany Society, Royal Botanic Gardens, Sydney 2000 Australia. **Tel** 011 61 02 231 8158, FAX 011 61 02 2517231. **ED** Dr. G. Leach. Index available. cum. index. **Bk Rev**, (Qty: 4-8). **Ad Acc, Adv Mgr:** Dr. G. Leach. **Circ:** 450.
Desc: Information on the society business, reports, general interests, botanical articles, and reviews in the field of botany.

LC QK **ISSN** 0155-4131
DD 581 AT
CODEN AUSTDK

AUSTROBAILEYA. [Austrobaileya]. **Added/Corp** Queensland Herbarium. Vol. 1 (1977)-. Periodical. English. One time a year. 32.88Aus$. Department of Primary Industries / Queensland Australia, GPO Box 46, Brisbane Queensland 4001 Australia. **Tel** 011 61 7 2393111, FAX 011 61 7 2212490, telex AA41620. Documents available from BIOSIS Document Express. ***Supersedes*** *Queensland Herbarium. Contributions from the Queensland Herbarium.*
Ind/Abst Biol. Abstr.; For. Abstr.; Plant Breed. Abstr.; Plant Genet. Resour. Abstr.

ISSN 0309-930X
UK

B.S.B.I. NEWS. **Main/Corp** Botanical Society of the British Isles. **Added/Corp** Botanical Society of the British Isles. News. **VAT** Botanical Society of the British Isles News. (1972)-. Periodical. English. Two times a year. Botanical Society of the British Isle, 68 Outwoods Road, Loughborough LE11 3LY United Kingdom. **Tel** 011 44 1509 215598.

LC QK322 .B3 **ISSN** 0867-2815
DD 581.97 PL
CODEN BFNBEI

BADANIA FIZJOGRAFICZNE NAD POLSKA ZACHODNIA. SERIA B : BOTANIKA. **Added/Corp** Poznanskie Towarzystwo Przyjaciol Nauk. Komitet Fizjograficzny. (1974)-. Monographic series. Polish (summaries and/or abstracts in English, French and German). Irregular. Price varies per volume. Poznanskie Towarzystwo Przyjaciol Nauk, Ul. Mielzynskiego 27-29, 61-725 Poznan Poland. **Tel** 011 48 61 527441. ***Supersedes in part*** *Badania Fizjograficzne nad Polska Zachodnia. Seria B : Biologia.*

LC SB1 .C76 **ISSN** 0005-4003
DD 634.05 US
CODEN BAILAI

BAILEYA. [Baileya]. Vol. 1 (March 1953)-. Periodical. English. Irregular. Cornell University / Bailey Hortorium, 467 Mann Library, Ithaca NY 14853. **Tel** (607)255-7976. cum. index. available on microfilm and microfiche from University Microfilms International (UMI). Documents available from BIOSIS Document Express.
Ind/Abst AGRICOLA [Full Cov.]; Biol. Abstr.; Hortic. Abstr.; Ornamental Hort. (1991-); Plant Breed. Abstr.; Plant Genet. Resour. Abstr.

LC QK358.7 .B35 **ISSN** 0253-5416
DD 580/.5 BG
CODEN BJBTB3

BANGLADESH JOURNAL OF BOTANY. [Bangladesh j. bot.]. **Added/Corp** Bangladesh Botanical Society. Bangladesh Botanical Society. (1972)-. Academic Scholarly Publication. English. Two times a year (June and Dec.). $66.00. University of Dacca Bangladesh Botanical Society, Department of Botany, Dacca 2 Bangladesh. **Tel** 011 880 506378. **ED** Proffesor syed Hadiuzzaman. **Circ:** 500 (ctrl). Documents available from The Genuine Article, BIOSIS Document Express, CASDDS.
Desc: Covers taxonomy, genetics, algae, physiology, mycology, plant pathology, biometry, ecology, microbiology, bryophyte, petridophyte, plant tissue culture, plant breeding, limnology, cytogenetics, plant anatomy, plant nutrition, horticulture and forestry.
Ind/Abst Biol. Abstr.; Chem. Abstr.; Curr. Cit.; Curr. Contents Agric. Biol. Environ. Sci.; Field Crop Abstr.; Food Sci. Technol. Abstr.; Grass. Forage Abstr.; Plant Breed. Abstr.; Potato Abstr.; Res. Alert [Select. Cov.]; Rev. Med. Vet. Mycology; Rev. Plant Pathol.; Rice Abstr.; SCISEARCH; Seed Abstr.; Soils Fert.; Weed Abstr.

LC QK **ISSN** 0198-7356
DD 581 US

BARTONIA. (BARTONIA; PROCEEDINGS OF THE PHILADELPHIA BOTANICAL CLUB ...). [Bartonia]. **Added/Corp** Philadelphia Botanical Club. No. 1 (1908)-. English. One time a year (May). $17.50. Philadelphia Botanical Club, 19th & Parkway, Philadelphia PA 19103. **Tel** (215)299-1192. **ED** Alfred E. Schuyler. **Bk Rev. Ad Acc. Circ:** 350 (ctrl).
Desc: Articles on systematic botany, plant ecology, and history of botany. Also contains obituaries and news of interest to club members.
Ind/Abst AGRICOLA [Full Cov.].

LC QK504 .N62 **ISSN** 0078-2238
GW
CODEN NOHBA9

BEIHEFTE ZUR NOVA HEDWIGIA. [Beih. Nova Hedwigia]. No. 1 (1962)-. Monographic series. German. Three times a year. $396.00. Gebruder Borntraeger Verlagsbuchhandlung, Johannesstrasse 3-A, D-70176 Stuttgart Germany. **Tel** 0711/62 50 01, FAX (0711)625005, telex 723363 SCHB D. Documents available from BIOSIS Document Express.
Ind/Abst Aquat. Sci. Fish. Abstr. [CD-ROM Ed.]; Biol. Abstr.; For. Prod. Abstr. (1991-); GeoRef; Life Sci. Collect.; Rev. Med. Vet. Mycology; Rev. Plant Pathol.

LC QK1 .B115 **ISSN** 0005-8041
DD 581 GW
CCC
NLM W1 BE191 **CODEN** BEPFAT

BEITRAEGE ZUR BIOLOGIE DER PFLANZEN. [Beitr. biol. pflanz.]. Vol. 1 (1870)-. Periodical. German (English and French; summaries and/or abstracts in French and English). Three times a year. DM320.00. Duncker und Humblot Verlag, Postfach 410329, D-12113 Berlin Germany. **Tel** 011 49 30 79000612, 011 49 30 79000613. **ED** D V Denffer, H Schraudolf and F Webeling. **Circ:** 300. Documents available from BIOSIS Document Express.
Desc: Study of botany.
Ind/Abst Biodeter. Abstr.; Biol. Abstr.; Crop Physiol. Abstr.; EMBASE; Energy Res. Abstr.; Field Crop Abstr.; For. Prod. Abstr. (1991-); For. Abstr.; Hortic. Abstr.; Ornamental Hort. (19??-19??); Life Sci. Collect.; Plant Breed. Abstr.; Rev. Agric. Entomol.; Rev. Med. Vet. Mycology; Rev. Plant Pathol.; Seed Abstr.; Weed Abstr.

SZ

BEITRAGE ZUR GEOBOTANISCHEN LANDESAUFNAHME DER SCHWEIZ (1935). (BEITRAEGE ZUR GEOBOTANISCHEN LANDESAUFNAHME DER SCHWEIZ.). 18 (Feb. 1938)-. Monographic series. German. Irregular. Price varies per volume. F Fluck-Wirth-International Booksellers for Botany and Natural History, CH-9053 Teufen Switzerland. ***Continues** Materiaux Pour le Leve Geobotanique de la Suisse (1932).*

LC QK1 .S8 **ISSN** 0778-4031
DD 581 BE
CODEN BJBOEP

BELGIAN JOURNAL OF BOTANY. (BELGIAN JOURNAL OF BOTANY : BULLETIN DE LA SOCIETE ROYALE DE BOTANIQUE DE BELGIQUE.). [Belg. j. bot.]. **Added/Corp** Societe Royale de Botanique de Belgique. Vol. 123, (1990)-. Bulletin. English (French, Dutch and German). Two times a year (June & Dec.). $74.63. Societe Royale de Botanique de Belgique, Nieusvelaan 38, B 1860 Meise Belgium. **Tel** 011 32 02 2693905. Documents available from The Genuine Article, BIOSIS Document Express. ***Continues** Bulletin de la Societe Royale de Botanique de Belgique, 0037-9557.*
Ind/Abst AgBiotech News Inf.; Biol. Abstr. (1990-); Curr. Aware. Biol. Sci., CABS; Curr. Contents Agric. Biol. Environ. Sci.; EMBASE; Field Crop Abstr.; Grass. Forage Abstr.; Life Sci. Collect.; Plant Breed. Abstr.; Res. Alert [Select. Cov.]; Rice Abstr.; Wheat Barley Trit. Abstr.

LC QK1 .B1158 **ISSN** 0169-4375
DD 581/.08 NE

BELMONTIA. [Belmontia]. Vol. 1; 1974-. English. One time a year. Agricultural University, Department of Plant Taxonomy, 37 Generaal Foulkesweg, PO Box 8010, 6700 ED Wageningen The Netherlands. **Circ:** 150 (ctrl). ***Formed by the union of** Belmontia; Miscellaneous Publications in Botany. I. Taxonomy; Belmontia; Miscellaneous Publications in Botany. III. Horticulture **and** Belmontia; Miscellaneous Publications in Botany. IV. Incidental.*
Ind/Abst Life Sci. Collect.

LC QK867 .K54A
DD 581.1 DK

BERETNING FOR PERIODEN .... . **Main/Corp** Kongelige Veterinr- Og Landbohjskole (Denmark). Afdelingen For Planternes Ernring. Danish. One time a year. Afdelingen for Planternes Ernring, Den Kgl Veterinr-Og Landbohjskole, Copenhagen DK 1871 Denmark.

LC QK **ISSN** 0373-7640
DD 581 GW

BERICHTE DER BAYERISCHEN BOTANISCHEN GESELLSCHAFT ZUR ERFORSCHUNG DER HEIMISCHEN FLORA. [Ber. Bayer. Bot. Ges. Erforsch. heim. Flora]. **Main/Corp** Bayerische Botanische Gesellschaft zur Enforschung der Heimischen Flora, Munich. **Added/Corp** Bayerische Botanische Gesellschaft zur Enforschung der Heimischen Flora. Vol. 1 (1891)-. Monographic series. German. One time a year. DM50.00. Bayerische Botanische Gesellschaft, Menzinger Strasse 67, D-80638 Munich Germany. **ED** W. Lippert. **Bk Rev. Circ:** 1,200.
Desc: Systematics, floristic, cytological articles about plants from Bavaria and surrounding countries; Italy, Germany, Austria and Switzerland. Higher plants, mosses, lichens and fungi are covered.
Ind/Abst Life Sci. Collect.; Rev. Med. Vet. Mycology; Rev. Plant Pathol.

LC QK1 .Z8 **ISSN** 0373-7896
DD 581/.05 SZ
CODEN BGBIAG

BERICHTE DES GEOBOTANISCHEN INSTITUTES DER EIDG. TECHN. HOCHSCHULE, STIFTUNG RUEBEL. [Ber. geobot. inst. eidg. techn. hochsch., stift. rubel]. **Added/Corp** Eidgenossische Technische Hochschule Zurich. Geobotanisches Institut, Stiftung Ruebel. (1959)-. German (English and French). One time a year. Price varies. Geobotanisches Institute ETH Zurich, Stiftung Ruebel Zuerichberg 38, CH-8092 Zurich Switzerland. **Tel** 011 41 1 2563877. Documents available from BIOSIS Document Express. ***Continues** Bericht Uueber das Geobotanische Forschungsinstitut Ruebel in Zuerich fuer das Jahr ... .*
Ind/Abst Biol. Abstr.; Ornamental Hort. (1991-); Seed Abstr.

ISSN 1051-8959
DD 582 US

BETWEEN THE VINES. (BETWEEN THE VINES : NEWSLETTER OF THE AMERICAN IVY SOCIETY, INC.). [Between vines]. **Added/Corp** American Ivy Society. Vol. 1, No. 1 (Dec. 1989)-. Newsletter. English. Four times a year. $25.00. American Ivy Society, PO Box 2123, Naples FL 33939. **ED** Rachel Cobb. Index available. cum. index. **Circ:** 400-500 (ctrl).

LC QK **ISSN** 0067-6586
DD 581 BL
UDC 016:581.9(81)

BIBLIOGRAFIA BRASILEIRA DE BOTANICA. Vol. 1 (1955)-. Portuguese. Irregular. Instituto Nacional de Estudos e Pesquisas Educacionais Coordenadoria de Editoracao e Divulgacao, Via N 2 Anexo I do MEC, Subsolo 70047, Brasilia D F Brazil. **Tel** 242-2915.

ISSN 0232-069X
XR
UDC 58(016)

BIBLIOGRAPHIA SYNTAXONOMICA CECHOSLOVACA. [Bibliogr. syntaxon. Cech.]. (1970)-. Multiple languages. Irregular. Czech Botanical Society, Czech Academy of Sciences, Prague Czech Republic.
Ind/Abst Ecol. Abstr.

LC Z6033.P2 B476 QE993 **ISSN** 0249-762X
DD 016.582/016 FR

BIBLIOGRAPHIE PALYNOLOGIE. **See** Science and Technology-Abstracting, Bibliographies and Statistics.

ISSN 0193-5720
US

BIBLIOGRAPHY OF AMERICAN PALEOBOTANY. **See** Paleontology.

LC QK **ISSN** 0067-7892
DD 581 GW
CCC

BIBLIOTHECA BOTANICA. (1886)-. German (English, French and German). One time a year. $143.00. E. Schweizerbartische Verlagsbuchhandlung, Johannesstrasse 3A, D-70176 Stuttgart Germany. **Tel** 011 49 711 625001, FAX 011 49 711 625005, telex 723363 SCHB D. **ED** W Greuter and H Merxmueller. **Bk Rev. Ad Acc.**
Desc: Covers botany, with original contributions.

ISSN 0067-8112
GW

BIBLIOTHECA PHYCOLOGICA. (1967)-. Academic Scholarly Publication. English. Irregular. Price varies. Gebrueder Borntraeger, Johannesstrasse 3A, D-70176 Stuttgart Germany. **Tel** 011 49 711 625001, FAX 011 49 711 625005. **ED** L. Kies and R. Schnetter.
Ind/Abst Biol. Abstr.

ISSN 0351-9430
YU

BILTEN ZA HMELJ, SIRAK I LEKOVITO BILJE. [Bilt. hmelj sirak lekov. bilje]. **Added/Corp** Zavod za Hmelj, Sirak i Lekovito Bilje, Backi Petrovac. (198?)-. Periodical. Serbo-Croatian (Roman) (summaries and/or abstracts in English and French; table of contents in English and French). Four times a year. Institut za Ratarstvo i Povrtarstvo, Poljoprivredni Fakultet, Lenjinova 5, Backi Petrovac, Vojvodina Yugoslavia. **ED** Jan Kisgeci. ***Continues** Bilten za Hmelj i Sirak, 0350-333X.*
Ind/Abst Plant Breed. Abstr.

LC QK1 .B56 **ISSN** 0006-3134
DD 581 XR
CCC
NLM W1 BI671P **CODEN** BPABAJ
Pr Rev.

BIOLOGIA PLANTARUM. [Biol. plant.]. **Added/Corp** Ceskoslovenska Akademie Ved. Biologicky Ustav (Ceskoslovenska Akademie Ved) Ustav Experimentalni Botaniky CSAV. Vol. 1 (1959)-. Periodical. English (French, German and Russian; summaries and/or abstracts in Czech). Four times a year. $370.00. Kluwer Academic Publishers, Postbus 322, 3300 AH Dordrecht The Netherlands. **Tel** 011 31 78 524400, FAX 011 31 78 183273, telex 20083. **ED** J. Catsky. **Bk Rev. Acid Free. Circ:** 1,200. Documents available from The Genuine Article, BIOSIS Document Express, CASDDS. ***Supersedes** Ceskoslovenska Biologie.*
Desc: Contains original scientific information as well as brief communications in the fields of plant physiology, genetics and pathology - including structural botany.
Ind/Abst AgBiotech News Inf.; Biol. Abstr.; Chem. Abstr.; Crop Physiol. Abstr.; Curr. Aware. Biol. Sci., CABS; Curr. Cit.; Curr. Contents Agric. Biol. Environ. Sci.; EMBASE; For. Abstr.; Grass. Forage Abstr.; Hortic. Abstr.; Irr. Drain. Abstr.; Maize Abstr.; Ornamental Hort.; Life Sci. Collect.; Plant Breed. Abstr.; Plant Genet. Resour. Abstr.; Plant Grow. Reg. Abstr.; Potato Abstr.; Res. Alert [Select. Cov.]; Rev. Plant Pathol.; Rice Abstr.; SCISEARCH; Seed Abstr.; Soc. Sci. Cit. Index [Select. Cov.]; Soils Fert.; Vitis Vitic. Enol. Abstr.; Weed Abstr.; Wheat Barley Trit. Abstr.

FI

BIOLOGICA. **Added/Corp** Oulun Yliopisto. **VFOAT** Biologica. (1974)-. Monographic series. English (Finnish and German). Irregular. Price varies per volume. Prof Sakari Piha, University of Oulu, 90100 Oulu 10 Finland. **Tel** 358-81-332133. **ED** Sirkka Kupila-Ahvenniemi. **Ad Acc. Circ:** 500 (ctrl).
Desc: Monographs, reviews, and dissertations in the fields of botany and zoology.

LC QK
DD 581 RU

BIOLOGICHESKAIA FLORA MOSKOVSKOI OBLASTI. **VFOAT** Biological Flora of the Moscow Region. Vol. 1 (1974)-. Periodical. Russian. Izdatelstvo Moskovskogo Universiteta, K-9 Ulitsa Gertsena 5/7, 103009 Moscow Russia. **Tel** (301)881-5973.
Ind/Abst AGRICOLA.

ISSN 0289-0011
JA

BIOTRONICS. [Biotronics]. **Added/Corp** Kyushu Daigaku. Biotron Institute. Vol. 1 (1971)-. English (Japanese). Kyushu Daigaku Seibutsu Kankyo Chosetsu Kenkyu Senta, (Biotron Inst. Kyushu University), 10-1 Hakozaki 6 Chome, Higashiku, Fukuokashi Fukuokaken 812 Japan.
Ind/Abst Agric. Eng. Abstr.; Crop Physiol. Abstr.; Field Crop Abstr.; Hortic. Abstr.; Irr. Drain. Abstr.; Ornamental Hort. (1991-); Weed Abstr.

ISSN 0893-3138
DD 581 US

BISHOP MUSEUM BULLETINS IN BOTANY. [Bishop Mus. bull. bot.]. **Added/Corp** Bernice Pauahi Bishop Museum. **VFOAT** Bishop Museum

Bulletins in Botany. (1988)-. Bulletin. English. Irregular. Price varies per volume. Bishop Museum Press, 1525 Bernice Street, Honolulu HI 96817. **Tel** (808)847-3511, FAX (808)841-8968. ***Continues in part*** *Bernice Pauahi Bishop Museum. Bernice P. Bishop Museum Bulletin, 0005-9439.*

LC QH198.H3 B45 **ISSN** 0893-1348
DD 996.9/005 US
CODEN BMOPEC

BISHOP MUSEUM OCCASIONAL PAPERS. [Bishop Mus. occas. pap.]. **Added/Corp** Bernice Pauahi Bishop Museum. Vol. 26 (May 1986)-. Monographic series. English. One time a year. Price varies per volume. Bishop Museum Press, 1525 Bernice Street, Honolulu HI 96817. **Tel** (808)847-3511, FAX (808)841-8968. Index available. Documents available from BIOSIS Document Express. ***Continues*** *Occasional Papers of Bernice P. Bishop Museum, 0067-6160.*
Desc: Presents original contributions in all phases of anthropology, history, botany, entomology, and zoology.
Ind/Abst Biol. Abstr. (1986-); GeoRef (1986-); Rev. Agric. Entomol.

LC S583
DD 631 PL

BIULETYN / INSTYTUT HODOWLI I AKLIMATYZACJI ROSLIN = BULLETIN / INSTITUTE OF PLANT BREEDING AND ACCLIMATIZATION. **See** Agriculture-Crop Production and Soils.

LC QK **ISSN** 0366-502X
DD 581 RU
CODEN BYGBAA

BIULLETEN GLAVNOGO BOTANICHESKOGO SADA. [Bjull. Gl. bot. sada]. **Main/Corp** Glavnyi Botanicheskii Sad (Akademiia Nauk SSSR). (1948)-. Academic Scholarly Publication. Russian. Four times a year. Izdatelstvo Nauka / Akademiia Nauk, (Publishing House of the Russian Academy of Sciences), Leninskii Porspekt 14, 117901 Moscow Russia. **Tel** 011 95 9542153, FAX 011 95 9382144, telex 411964. cum. index. Documents available from CASDDS.
Ind/Abst Chem. Abstr.; Field Crop Abstr.; For. Abstr.; Hortic. Abstr.; Maize Abstr.; Ornamental Hort. (1991-); Plant Genet. Resour. Abstr.; Plant Grow. Reg. Abstr.; Seed Abstr.; Soils Fert.

LC QK **ISSN** 0513-1634
DD 581 RU
CODEN BGNBAL

BIULLETEN GOSUDARSTVENNOGO NIKITSKOGO BOTANICHESKOGO SADA. [Biull. Gos. Nikitsk. bot. sada]. **Main/Corp** Nikitskii Botanicheskii Sad (Ialta, Ukraine). **Added/Corp** Vsesoiuznaia Akademiia Selskokhoziaistvennykh Nauk imeni V.I. Lenina. **VFOAT** Bulletin of the State Nikita Botanical Gardens. (196?)-. Monographic series. Russian (summaries and/or abstracts in English). Documents available from CASDDS. ***Continues*** *Nikitskii Botanicheskii Sad (Ialta, Ukraine.) Biulleten Nauchni Informacii.*
Ind/Abst Chem. Abstr. (-1975); For. Abstr.; Hortic. Abstr.; Postharvest News Inf.

ISSN 0459-0864
RU
CODEN BVZRAU

BIULLETEN VSESOIUZNOGO NAUCHNO-ISSLEDOVATELSKOGO INSTITUTA ZASHCHITY RASTENII. **Main/Corp** Leningrad. Vsesoiuznyi Institut Zashchity Rastenii. No. 1 (1956)-. Bulletin. Russian (summaries and/or abstracts in English; table of contents in English). Vsesoiuznyi Institut Zashchity Rastenii, St. Petersburg Russia. **(Subscription address:** Victor Kamkin, 4956 Boiling Brook Parkway, Rockville MD 20852. **Tel** (301)881-5973.**)**
Ind/Abst Nematol. Abstr.

LC QK1 .B18 **ISSN** 0006-5196
DD 580.5 NE
CODEN BLMAAE

Pr Rev.
BLUMEA. (BLUMEA : TIJDSCHRIFT VOOR DE SYSTEMATIEK EN DE GEOGRAFIE DER PLANTEN : A JOURNAL OF PLANT TAXONOMY AND PLANT GEOGRAPHY.). [Blumea]. **Added/Corp** Rijksherbarium (Netherlands). Vol. 1 (Aug. 1934)-. Periodical. English (French and German). Irregular. Price varies. Rijksherbarium, PO Box 9514, 2300 RA Leiden Netherlands. **Tel** 011 31 71 273500. Documents available from The Genuine Article, BIOSIS Document Express. ***Continues*** *Rijksherbarium (Netherlands) Mededeelingen.*
Ind/Abst AGRICOLA [Full Cov.]; Biol. Abstr.; Curr. Aware. Biol. Sci., CABS; Curr. Contents Agric. Biol. Environ. Sci.; Field Crop Abstr.; Grass. Forage Abstr.; Helminthol. Abstr. (1991-); Hortic. Abstr.; Ornamental Hort. (1991-); Life Sci. Collect.; Plant Breed. Abstr.; Plant Genet. Resour. Abstr.; Res. Alert [Select. Cov.]; SCISEARCH.

LC QK1 .B183 **ISSN** 0006-5269
DD 581/.05 NO
CCC
CODEN BLYTAT

BLYTTIA. [Blyttia]. **Added/Corp** Norsk Botanisk Forening. Vol. 1 (1943)-. Periodical. Norwegian (summaries and/or abstracts in English). Four times a year. $89.00. Scandinavian University Press, PO Box 2959 Toeyen, N 0608 Oslo 6 Norway. **Tel** 011 47 2 2575400, FAX 011 47 2 2575353, telex 71896 UROR N. **(Subscription address:** Scandinavian University Press, 200 Meacham Ave., Elmont NY 11003. **Tel** (516)352-7300, FAX (516)352-7377.**) ED** Inger Nordal. cum. index. **Bk Rev. Ad Acc. Circ:** 1,400 (ctrl). Documents available from BIOSIS Document Express.
Desc: Norwegian journal covering all aspects of botany with emphasis on the Norwegian flora.
Ind/Abst Biol. Abstr.; Ecol. Abstr.; Geogr. Abstr. Human Geogr.; Life Sci. Collect.

LC QK314.5 .B63 **ISSN** 1120-4060
DD 581.909/82/205 FR

BOCCONEA. **Added/Corp** Organization for the Phyto-Taxonomic Investigation of the Mediterranean Area. Herbarium Mediterraneum Panormitanum. (1991)-. Monographic series. French (English and French).

LC QK1 .G42 **ISSN** 0373-2975
DD 581 SZ
CODEN BOISB2

BOISSIERA. [Boissiera]. **Added/Corp** Conservatoire et Jardin Botaniques de la Ville de Geneve. Universite de Geneve. Institut de Botanique Systematique. No. 1 (1936)-. French (English, German and Spanish). One time a year. $70.72. Conservatoire et Jardin Botaniques, Case Postale 60, CH-1292 Cambesy Geneva Switzerland. **Tel** 011 41 22 346969. cum. index. **Bk Rev. Circ:** 200. Documents available from BIOSIS Document Express.
Desc: Systematic botany, chorology, ecology of plants.
Ind/Abst Biol. Abstr.; Field Crop Abstr.; For. Abstr.; Grass. Forage Abstr.

LC QK1 .S28 **ISSN** 0081-0657
DD 580/.5 PO
CODEN BBRTAQ

BOLETIM DA SOCIEDADE BROTERIANA. [Bol. soc. broter.]. **Main/Corp** Sociedade Broteriana. **Added/Corp** Universidade de Coimbra. Instituto Botanico. (1880)-. Bulletin. Portuguese (English, French, German, Italian and Spanish). One time a year. $62.03. Instituto Botanico da Universidade de Coimbra, Arcos do Jardim, P-3049 Coimbra Codex Portugal. **Tel** 011 351 39 22897. **ED** A. Fernandes, Jose F. Mesquita. Index available. cum. index. **Bk Rev. Circ:** 1,100 (ctrl). Documents available from BIOSIS Document Express.
Desc: Botanical research specially concerning plant systematics, ecology, cytology, and physiology.
Ind/Abst Biodeter. Abstr. (1991-); Biol. Abstr.; EMBASE; Field Crop Abstr.; For. Abstr.; Grass. Forage Abstr.; Hortic. Abstr.; Ornamental Hort. (1991-); Plant Breed. Abstr.; Plant Grow. Reg. Abstr.; Rev. Agric. Entomol.; Rev. Med. Vet. Mycology; Rev. Plant Pathol.; Soils Fert.; Weed Abstr.

LC QK
DD 581 US

BOLETIN BOTANICO LATINOAMERICANO. **Added/Corp** Asociacion Latinoamericana de Botanica. No. 1 (July 1978)-. Periodical. Spanish (Portuguese). Two times a year. $10.00. New York Botanical Gardens, 200 St. Southern Boulevard, Bronx NY 10458. **Tel** (718)817-8628, FAX (718)562-6780. **ED** Enrique Forero (phone: (718)817-8628). **Circ:** 1,100.
Desc: Aimed at the Latin American botanical community and to botanists worldwide. Contains events, publications, honors and awards.

LC WMLC L 83/1577 **ISSN** 0373-580X
DD 581 AG
CODEN BABOAQ

BOLETIN DE LA SOCIEDAD ARGENTINA DE BOTANICA. [Bol. Soc. Argent. Bot.]. **Main/Corp** Sociedad Argentina de Botanica. (Nov. 1945)-. Periodical. Spanish (summaries and/or abstracts in English). Twelve times a year. Dept Pub Cientificas Argentina, Corrientess 127, Buenos Aires Argentina. Documents available from BIOSIS Document Express.
Ind/Abst Biodeter. Abstr.; Biol. Abstr.; Field Crop Abstr.; Grass. Forage Abstr.; Life Sci. Collect.; Rev. Med. Vet. Mycology; Rev. Plant Pathol.

LC QK1 .S2749 **ISSN** 0366-2128
DD 581/.05 MX
CODEN BOOXAC

BOLETIN DE LA SOCIEDAD BOTANICA DE MEXICO. [Bol. Soc. Bot. Mex.]. **Main/Corp** Sociedad Botanica de Mexico. No. 1 (1944)-. Spanish (summaries and/or abstracts in English). Documents available from BIOSIS Document Express.
Ind/Abst Biol. Abstr.; Rev. Plant Pathol.

LC QH426 **ISSN** 0325-8319
DD 575.1 AG
NLM W1 BO23F **CODEN** BOGOAD

BOLETIN GENETICO. ENGLISH EDITION. **See** Biology-Genetics.

ISSN 0962-7448
DD 631.52 UK

BOTANIC GARDENS MICROPROPAGATION NEWS. [Bot. Gard. micropropag. news]. **Added/Corp** Royal Botanic Gardens (Kew, England). (1990)-. Periodical. English. Two times a year.
Ind/Abst Hortic. Abstr.; Ornamental Hort. (1991-); Plant Breed. Abstr.; Plant Genet. Resour. Abstr.

LC QK1 .D4 **ISSN** 0932-8629
DD 581/.05 GW
UDC 58 **CCC**
CODEN BOACEJ

Pr Rev.
BOTANICA ACTA. [Bot. acta]. **VFOAT** Journal of the German Botanical Society; Berichte der Deutschen Botanischen Gesellschaft. Vol. 101 (July 1988)-. Periodical. English (German). Six times a year. $354.00. Georg Thieme Verlag Stuttgart, Postfach 301120, D-70451 Stuttgart Germany. **Tel** 011 49 711 89310, FAX 011 49 711 8931298, telex 7 252 275 GTVD. **(Subscription address:** Thieme Medical Publishers Inc., 381 Park Avenue South, New York NY 10016. **Tel** (212)683-5088.**) ED** U Luttge. available on microfilm from University Microfilms International (UMI). Documents available from The Genuine Article, BIOSIS Document Express, CASDDS. ***Continues*** *Berichte der Deutschen Botanischen Gesellschaft.*
Ind/Abst AgBiotech News Inf.; Biol. Abstr.; Chem. Abstr.; Crop Physiol. Abstr.; Curr. Aware. Biol. Sci., CABS; Curr. Cit.; Curr. Contents Agric. Biol. Environ. Sci.; Curr. Contents Life Sci.; Field Crop Abstr.; For. Abstr.; Grass. Forage Abstr.; Hortic. Abstr.; Maize Abstr.; Nematol. Abstr.; Ornamental Hort. (1991-); Plant Breed. Abstr.; Plant Genet. Resour. Abstr.; Plant Grow. Reg. Abstr.; Res. Alert [Full Cov.]; Rev. Plant Pathol.; Rice Abstr.; Sci. Cit. Index; SCISEARCH; Seed Abstr.; Soils Fert.; Soyabean Abstr.; Weed Abstr.; Wheat Barley Trit. Abstr.

LC QK1 .S2 **ISSN** 0253-1453
DD 581/.05 SZ
CCC
CODEN BOHEDP

Pr Rev.
BOTANICA HELVETICA. (BOTANICA HELVETICA : BULLETIN DE LA SOCIETE BOTANIQUE SUISSE : BERICHTE DER SCHWEIZERISCHEN BOTANISCHEN GESELLSCHAFT.). [Bot. Helv.]. **Added/Corp** Schweizerische Botanische Gesellschaft. **VFOAT** Bulletin de la Societe Botanique Suisse; Berichte der Schweizerischen Botanischen Gesellschaft. Vol. 91 (1981)-. Bulletin. English (French and German). Two times a year. $267.70. Birkhaeuser Verlag Ag, Klosterberg 23, PO Box 133, CH-4010 Basel Switzerland. **Tel** 011 41 61 2717400, FAX 011 41 61 2717666, telex 963475 birk ch. **(Subscription address:** Birkhaeuser Verlag AG, PO Box 133, CH 4010 Basel Switzerland. **Tel** 011 41 61 2717400.**) ED** H. R. Hohl and Gian A. Nogler. available on microfilm and microfiche from University Microfilms International (UMI). Documents available from The Genuine Article, BIOSIS Document Express. ***Continues*** *Berichte der Schweizerischen Botanischen Gesellschaft.*
Desc: Provides a forum for the plant sciences and accepts original research papers from the molecular, cellular, whole plant and plant community levels.
Ind/Abst Biol. Abstr.; Crop Physiol. Abstr.; Curr. Aware. Biol. Sci., CABS; Curr. Contents Agric. Biol. Environ. Sci.; Ecology Abstr.; Field Crop Abstr.; GeoRef; Hortic. Abstr.; Life Sci. Collect.; Plant Breed. Abstr.; Plant Grow. Reg. Abstr.; Res. Alert [Select. Cov.]; Rev. Plant Pathol.; SCISEARCH; Soyabean Abstr.; Weed Abstr.

LC QH301 .B58 **ISSN** 0045-2629
DD 574 II
CODEN BTNCAD

BOTANICA (NEW DELHI, INDIA). (THE BOTANICA : MAGAZINE OF DELHI UNIVERSITY BOTANICAL SOCIETY.). [Botanica]. **Added/Corp** Delhi University Botanical Society. University of Delhi. Dept. of Botany. (1950)-. English. One time a year. $10.00. Delhi University Botanical Society, Department of Botany, Delhi 1100007 India. **Tel** 2511266. **(Subscription address:** Prints India, 11 Darya Ganj, New Delhi 110002 India. **Tel** 011 91 11 3268645, FAX 011 91 11 3275542, telex 31-61087 PRIN-IN.**) ED** Vijaya Raghavan. **Bk Rev. Ad Acc. Circ:** 500. Documents available from BIOSIS Document Express, CASDDS, Documents on Demand.
Desc: Covers tissue culture, histochemistry, economic botany, molecular genetics, and students' activities.
Ind/Abst Biol. Abstr.; Chem. Abstr. (1950-1980); Environ. Abstr.; Field Crop Abstr.; Grass. Forage Abstr.

LC QK1 .C585 **ISSN** 0006-8063
DD 581 CH
CODEN BBASA6

Pr Rev.
BOTANICAL BULLETIN OF ACADEMIA SINICA. [Bot. bull. acad. sin.]. **Main/Corp** Chung Yang Yen Chiu Yuan. Chih Wu Yen Chiu So. **Added/Corp** Chung Yang Yen Chiu Yuan. Chih Wu Yen Chiu So.

VFOAT Kuo Li Chung Yang Yen Chiu Yuan Chih Wu Hsueh Hui Pao; Chung Yang Yen Chiu Yuan Wu Hsueh Hui Kan. Vol. 1-3 (March 1947-Dec. 1949); New Series, Vol. 1 (June 1960)-. Bulletin. English (Chinese). Four times a year. $100.00. Institute of Botany, Academia Sinica, Nankang Taipei 11529 Taiwan. **Tel** 886-2-782-1605, FAX 886-2-7827954. **ED** Chou Chang-Hung. Index available. **Circ:** 400. available on microfilm from University Microfilms International (UMI); available on CD-ROM. Documents available from The Genuine Article, BIOSIS Document Express, CASDDS.
Desc: Open to papers from researchers in any branch of botany.
Ind/Abst AgBiotech News Inf.; Biocont. News Inf.; Biodeter. Abstr. (1991-); Biol. Abstr.; Chem. Abstr.; Crop Physiol. Abstr.; Curr. Aware. Biol. Sci., CABS; Curr. Biotechnol.; Curr. Cit.; Curr. Contents Agric. Biol. Environ. Sci.; Energy Res. Abstr.; Field Crop Abstr.; Food Sci. Technol. Abstr.; For. Prod. Abstr. (1991-); For. Abstr.; Grass. Forage Abstr.; Hortic. Abstr.; Leadscan; Maize Abstr.; Nematol. Abstr.; Ornamental Hort. (19??-19??); Life Sci. Collect.; Plant Breed. Abstr.; Plant Genet. Resour. Abstr.; Plant Grow. Reg. Abstr.; Protozoolog. Abstr.; Res. Alert [Full Cov.]; Rev. Med. Vet. Mycology; Rev. Plant Pathol.; Rice Abstr.; Sci. Cit. Index; SCISEARCH; Seed Abstr.; Soils Fert.; Sorghum Mill. Abstr.; Soyabean Abstr.; Weed Abstr.; Wheat Barley Trit. Abstr.

LC QK1 .B4
UK
CODEN BJSCE6

BOTANICAL JOURNAL OF SCOTLAND.

Added/Corp Botanical Society of Scotland. Vol. 46, Pt. 1 (1991)-. Periodical. English. Two times a year. £36.00 UK and Europe; $60.00 North America; £40.00 other. Edinburgh University Press Ltd., 22 George Square, Edinburgh EH8 9LF United Kingdom. **Tel** 011 44 131 6506207, FAX 011 44 131 6620053. ***Continues*** *Botanical Society of Edinburgh. Transactions, 0374-6607.*

LC QH1 .L53 **ISSN** 0024-4074
DD 581/.05 UK
UDC 581 **CCC**
CODEN BJLSAF
Pr Rev.

BOTANICAL JOURNAL OF THE LINNEAN SOCIETY.

[Bot. j. Linn. Soc.]. **Main/Corp** Linnean Society of London. Vol. 62 (Jan. 1969)-. Academic Scholarly Publication. English. Twelve times a year. $780.31. Academic Press Ltd., A Division of Harcourt Brace & Company Ltd., 24-28 Oval Road, London NW1 7DX United Kingdom. **Tel** 011 44 171 2674466, FAX 011 44 171 4822293, 011 44 171 4854752, telex 25775 ACPRES G. **(Subscription address:** Harcourt Brace & Company, Ltd., Foots Cray High Street, Sidcup Kent DA14 5HP United Kingdom. **Tel** 011 44 181 3003322, FAX 011 44 181 3090807, telex 896 377 ACADEM.**) ED** S. L. Jury. Documents available from The Genuine Article, BIOSIS Document Express, CASDDS. ***Continues*** *Journal of the Linnean Society of London. Botany.*
Desc: Publishes original research papers in the plant sciences and offers a wide range of plant scientists a forum for the publication of the latest research in a number of important areas.
Ind/Abst AGRICOLA [Full Cov.]; Biodeter. Abstr.; Biol. Abstr.; Chem. Abstr. (1969-1982); Curr. Aware. Biol. Sci., CABS; Curr. Cit.; Curr. Contents Agric. Biol. Environ. Sci.; Ecology Abstr.; Field Crop Abstr.; Fish Rev.; For. Prod. Abstr.; For. Abstr.; GeoRef; Grass. Forage Abstr.; Hortic. Abstr.; NAPRALERT; Ornamental Hort. (19??-19??); Life Sci. Collect.; Plant Breed. Abstr.; Plant Genet. Resour. Abstr.; Plant Grow. Reg. Abstr.; Res. Alert [Full Cov.]; Rev. Med. Vet. Mycology; Rev. Plant Pathol.; Risk Abstr. (19??-19??); Sci. Cit. Index; SCISEARCH; Seed Abstr.; Soils Fert.; Weed Abstr.; Wildl. Rev.

LC QK1
DD 581 US

BOTANICAL MUSEUM LEAFLETS.

Added/Corp Harvard University. Botanical Museum. Vol. 1 (1932/33)-. Periodical. English. **ED** Donald H. Pfister.
Ind/Abst NAPRALERT.

LC QK1 .B335 **ISSN** 0006-8101
DD 581/.05 US
CCC
NLM W1 BO913H **CODEN** BOREA4
Pr Rev.

BOTANICAL REVIEW, THE.

[Bot. rev.]. **Added/Corp** New York Botanical Garden. Vol. 1 (Jan. 1935)-. Periodical. English. Four times a year. $71.00. New York Botanical Garden, Scientific Publishing Department B, New York NY 10458-5126. **Tel** (718)817-8721, FAX (718)817-6504, telex 5106015451. **ED** Arthur Cronquist. cum. index. **Ad Acc. Circ:** 2,000 (ctrl). available on microfilm and microfiche from University Microfilms International (UMI). Documents available from The Genuine Article, BIOSIS Document Express, UMI Article Clearinghouse, CASDDS, Documents on Demand.
Desc: Systematics, phytogeography, cladistics, evolution, physiology, ecology, morphology, paleobotany, and anatomy have been covered.
Ind/Abst Acad. Search; AGRICOLA [Full Cov.]; Biol. Agric. Index; Biol. Abstr.; Chem. Abstr. (1935-1982); Crop Physiol. Abstr.; Curr. Aware. Biol. Sci., CABS; Curr. Contents Agric. Biol. Environ. Sci.; Ecol. Abstr.; Energy Inf. Abstr.; Energy Res. Abstr. (Mar. 1972-); Environ. Abstr.; Environ. Period. Bibliogr.; EP Collect.; Expand. Acad. Index (1989-); Field Crop Abstr.; For. Prod. Abstr.; For. Abstr.; Gen. Sci. Index; Gen. Sci. Source; Geogr. Abstr. Phys. Geogr.; GeoRef; Grass. Forage Abstr.; Homework Help.; Hortic. Abstr.; INFO-SOUTH Abstr.; INIS Atomindex [Micro.]; Mag. Search; MasterFile FullTEXT 1000; MasterFile FullTEXT 350; MasterFile FullTEXT 650; MasterFile FullTEXT (Jan. 1993-); Newsp. Period. Abstr. (1991-); OCLC; Ornamental Hort. (1991-); Life Sci. Collect.; Plant Breed. Abstr.; Protozoolog. Abstr.; Res. Alert [Full Cov.]; Rev. Med. Vet. Mycology; Rev. Plant Pathol.; Sci. Cit. Index; SCISEARCH; Seed Abstr.; Soc. Sci. Cit. Index [Select. Cov.]; Soils Fert.; Telebase; Vitis Vitic. Enol. Abstr.; Vocat. Search; Weed Abstr.

LC QK **ISSN** 0006-8136
DD 581 RU
CCC
CODEN BOTZA9

BOTANICESKIJ ZURNAL.

(BOTANICHESKII ZHURNAL.). [Bot. z.]. **Added/Corp** Vsesoiuznoe Botanicheskoe Obshchestvo. Akademiia Nauk SSSR. Vol. 33 (1948)-. Academic Scholarly Publication. Russian (table of contents in English). Twelve times a year. $288.00. Izdatelstvo Nauka / Akademiia Nauk, (Publishing House of the Russian Academy of Sciences), Leninskii Porspekt 14, 117901 Moscow Russia. **Tel** 011 95 9542153, FAX 011 95 9382144, telex 411964. **(Subscription address:** East View Publications Inc., 3020 Harbor Lane North, Suite 110, Minneapolis MN 55447. **Tel** (800)477-1005, (612)550-0961, FAX (612)559-2931.**)** Documents available from BIOSIS Document Express, CASDDS. ***Continues*** *Botanicheskii Zhurnal SSSR.*
Ind/Abst AgBiotech News Inf.; Biol. Abstr.; Chem. Abstr.; Crop Physiol. Abstr.; Ecol. Abstr. (?-?); EMBASE; Field Crop Abstr.; For. Prod. Abstr. (19??-19??); For. Abstr.; GeoRef; Grass. Forage Abstr.; Hortic. Abstr.; Int. Aerosp. Abstr. (1983-); Ornamental Hort. (19??-19??); Life Sci. Collect.; Plant Breed. Abstr.; Plant Genet. Resour. Abstr.; Plant Grow. Reg. Abstr.; Rev. Med. Vet. Mycology; Rev. Plant Pathol.; Rice Abstr.; Seed Abstr.; Soils Fert.; Weed Abstr.; Wheat Barley Trit. Abstr.

ISSN 0006-8144
HU
CODEN BOKOAX

BOTANIKAI KOEZLEMENYEK.

[Bot. koezl.]. **Added/Corp** Magyar Biologai Tarsasag. Botanikai Szakosztaly. (1909)-. Periodical. Hungarian (summaries and/or abstracts in German, French, English and Russian). Two times a year. $14.00 Eastern Europe; $17.00 other. **(Subscription address:** Kultura, PO Box 143, H-1300 Budapest 3 Hungary. **Tel** 011 36 1 2500194.**)** Documents available from BIOSIS Document Express, CASDDS. ***Continues*** *Noevenytani Koezlemenyek.*
Ind/Abst Biol. Abstr.; Chem. Abstr.; Crop Physiol. Abstr.; Energy Res. Abstr. (Feb. 1980-); Field Crop Abstr.; GeoRef; Hortic. Abstr.; Irr. Drain. Abstr.; Maize Abstr.; Life Sci. Collect.; Soils Fert.; Wheat Barley Trit. Abstr.

LH

BOTANISCH ZOOLOGISCHE GESELLSCHAFT.

(19??)-. German (summaries and/or abstracts in English). One time a year. 40.00F. Ramschwagweg 474, FL 9496 Blaze Liechtenstein.

LC QK **ISSN** 0006-8152
DD 581 GW
CCC
CODEN BJPPAQ

BOTANISCHE JAHRBUCHER FUER SYSTEMATIK, PFLANZENGESCHICHTE UND PFLANZENGEOGRAPHIE.

[Bot. Jahrb. Syst., Pflanzengesch. Pflanzengeogr.]. Vol. 1 (1880)-. Periodical. German (English and French). Four times a year. $432.00. E. Schweizerbartische Verlagsbuchhandlung, Johannesstrasse 3A, D-70176 Stuttgart Germany. **Tel** 011 49 711 625001, FAX 011 49 711 625005, telex 723363 SCHB D. **ED** W Greuter and H Merxmueller. cum. index. **Bk Rev. Ad Acc.** Documents available from BIOSIS Document Express.
Ind/Abst AGRICOLA (-1987); Biol. Abstr.; Field Crop Abstr.; Grass. Forage Abstr.; Life Sci. Collect.; Plant Breed. Abstr.

LC QK1 .B77 **ISSN** 0006-8241
DD 581 SA
CODEN BTHLAA
Pr Rev.

BOTHALIA.

[Bothalia]. **Added/Corp** Botanical Research Institute (South Africa) South Africa. Dept. of Agriculture. Division of Botany and Plant Pathology. South Africa. Dept. of Agriculture. Division of Botany. Botanical Survey of South Africa. Vol. 1 (1921)-. Periodical. Afrikaans (English). Two times a year. R88.40 South Africa; R90.40 other. National Botanical Institute, Private Bag X101, Pretoria 0001 South Africa. **Tel** 011 27 12 8043200, FAX 011 27 12 8043211. **ED** O. A. Leistner. Index available. **Bk Rev. Circ:** 450. Documents available from The Genuine Article, BIOSIS Document Express.
Desc: Botanical coverage includes taxonomy, ecology, anatomy and cytology.
Ind/Abst AGRICOLA [Full Cov.]; Biol. Abstr.; Curr. Aware. Biol. Sci., CABS; Curr. Contents Agric. Biol. Environ. Sci.; Field Crop Abstr.; For. Prod. Abstr.; For. Abstr.; Grass. Forage Abstr.; Life Sci. Collect.; Plant Genet. Resour. Abstr.; Res. Alert [Select. Cov.]; Rev. Med. Vet. Mycology; Rev. Plant Pathol.; SCISEARCH; Soils Fert.

LC QK1 **ISSN** 0084-800X
DD 581/.05 BL
UDC 581
CODEN BRADD8

BRADEA.

[Bradea]. Vol. 1 (Aug. 1969)-. Monographic series. Portuguese (English, German and Latin; summaries and/or abstracts in English and Portuguese). Price varies per volume. Documents available from BIOSIS Document Express.
Ind/Abst Biol. Abstr.

ISSN 0265-086X
UK
CEASED

BRADLEYA.

(BRADLEYA : YEARBOOK OF THE BRITISH CACTUS AND SUCCULENT SOCIETY.). [Bradleya]. **Added/Corp** British Cactus and Succulent Society. Vol. 1 (1983)-(199?). English. British Cactus & Succulent Society, 71 Lakes Lane, Newport Paonecc, Bucuingham Shore MK16 8HT United Kingdom. **Tel** 011 44 908 611650.

ISSN 0264-3405
UK
UDC 582.852

BRITISH CACTUS & SUCCULENT JOURNAL.

[Br. cactus succul. j.]. **VFOAT** British Cactus and Succulent Journal. Vol. 1, No. 1 (March 1983)-. Periodical. English. Four times a year (Mar., June, Sept., Dec.). £28.00. British Cactus & Succulent Society, 71 Lakes Lane, Newport Paonecc, Bucuingham Shore MK16 8HT United Kingdom. **Tel** 011 44 908 611650. ***Formed by the union of*** *National Cactus and Succulent Journal* ***and*** *Cactus and Succulent Journal of Great Britain, 0007-9375.*
Ind/Abst Crop Physiol. Abstr.; Hortic. Abstr.; Ornamental Hort. (19??-19??); Plant Breed. Abstr.

ISSN 0959-6879
DD 615.321 UK

BRITISH JOURNAL OF PHYTOTHERAPY, THE.

[Br. j. phytother.]. (1990)-. Periodical. English. Four times a year (Seasonally). $77.01. British Journal of Phytotherapy, 3 Kings Mill Way, Hermitage Lane, Mansfield Nottinghamshire NA18 5ER United Kingdom. **Tel** 011 44 1623 644334, FAX 011 44 1623 657232. **ED** Mr. C. Nicholls. **Bk Rev**, (Qty: 1-2). **Ad Acc.** ctrl circ.
Desc: Covers all aspects of herbal medicine; materia medica, current issues, phytotherapeutics, aromatic medicine, toxicology and more.

LC QK520 .B76a **ISSN** 0301-9195
DD 587/.31/05 UK
CODEN BPSBA7

BRITISH PTERIDOLOGICAL SOCIETY BULLETIN.

(BULLETIN.). [Br. Pteridol. Soc. bull.]. **Main/Corp** British Pteridological Society. Vol. 1 (1973)-. Bulletin. English. One time a year. comes with membership. British Pteridological Society, Natural History Museum - Botany, Cromwell Road, London SW7 5BD United Kingdom. **Tel** 011 44 171 9389497. **ED** A.R. Busby. **Circ:** 650. Documents available from BIOSIS Document Express. ***Supersedes*** *British Pteridological Society. Newsletter.*
Desc: Covers British Pteridological Society business and reports of meetings and obituaries.
Ind/Abst Biol. Abstr. (?-1988); Curr. Aware. Biol. Sci., CABS.

LC QK **ISSN** 0958-0956
DD 581 UK
CODEN BRWIEW

BRITISH WILDLIFE : THE MAGAZINE FOR THE MODERN NATURALIST.

See Natural History.

LC QK1 .B875 **ISSN** 0007-196X
DD 580.5 US
CCC
CODEN BRTAAN
Pr Rev.

BRITTONIA.

[Brittonia]. **Added/Corp** New York Botanical Garden. American Society of Plant Taxonomists. Vol. 1 (Feb. 1931)-. Periodical. English. Four times a year. $66.00. New York Botanical Garden, Scientific Publishing Department B, New York NY 10458-5126. **Tel** (718)817-8721, FAX (718)817-6504, telex 5106015451. **ED** Noel H. Holmgren. **Bk Rev. Ad Acc. Circ:** 800 (ctrl). available on microfilm and microfiche from University Microfilms International (UMI). Documents available from The Genuine Article, BIOSIS Document Express, Documents on Demand.
Desc: Primary research articles in all areas of systematic botany. Each issue contains articles by the staff of The New York Botanical Garden and outside contributors.
Ind/Abst AGRICOLA [Full Cov.]; Biol. Abstr.; Curr. Aware. Biol. Sci., CABS; Curr. Contents Agric. Biol. Environ. Sci.; Energy Inf. Abstr.; Environ. Abstr.; Field Crop Abstr.; For. Prod. Abstr.; For. Abstr.; Grass. Forage Abstr.; Hortic. Abstr.; Ornamental Hort. (1991-); Life Sci.

Collect.; Plant Breed. Abstr.; Plant Genet. Resour. Abstr.; Res. Alert [Select. Cov.]; Rev. Med. Vet. Mycology; Rev. Plant Pathol.; SCISEARCH; Seed Abstr.; Weed Abstr.

LC QK
DD 581 UK
BROMELIADS. **Added/Corp** British Bromeliad Society. Vol. 1 (Sept. 1968)-. Periodical. English. Four times a year. £2.50. British Bromeliad Society, Queen Mary College, London E1 4NS United Kingdom. **Bk Rev. Ad Acc. Circ:** 500.
Ind/Abst Life Sci. Collect.

US
BROOKLYN BOTANIC GARDEN 21ST CENTURY GARDENING SERIES. (19??)-. English. Four times a year (Mar., June, Sept., Dec.). $25.00 (subscribing), $50.00 (sustaining), $125.00 (supporting), $300.00 (contributing) Comes with Brooklyn Botanic Garden Subscribing membership. Brooklyn Botanic Garden, 1000 Washington Avenue, Brooklyn NY 11225. **Tel** (718)622-4433, FAX (718)857-2430. ***Continues*** *Plants and Gardens.*

ISSN 0723-2470
GW
BRYOLOGISCHE BEITRAEGE. **Added/Corp** Universitaat-Gesamthochschule-Duisburg. Arbeitsgruppe Brylogie. **VFOAT** Bryologische Beitraege. Vol. 1 (Oct. 1, 1982)-. Monographic series. German (English). Irregular. Price varies per volume. Bryologische Beitraege IDH, Funkenstr 13, D-5358 Bad Muenstereifel Germany. **Tel** 011 49 2257 3282.

ISSN 0007-2745
DD 588 US
CCC
CODEN BRYOAM
Pr Rev.
BRYOLOGIST, THE. [Bryologist]. **Added/Corp** American Bryological and Lichenological Society. American Bryological Society. Vol. 1 (1898)-. Periodical. English. Four times a year (Jan., Apr., July., Oct.). $55.00. American Bryological Lichenologica, University of Nebraska at Omaha, Biology Department, Omaha NE 68182. **Tel** (402)554-2491. **ED** W. Reese. Index Available in last issue of volume--loose--unpaged. cum. index. **Bk Rev. Ad Acc. Circ:** 1,000 (ctrl). available on microfilm and microfiche from University Microfilms International (UMI). Documents available from The Genuine Article, BIOSIS Document Express, CASDDS.
Desc: Devoted to the study of bryophytes and lichens.
Ind/Abst AGRICOLA [Full Cov.]; Biol. Abstr.; Chem. Abstr.; Curr. Aware. Biol. Sci., CABS; Curr. Cit.; Curr. Contents Agric. Biol. Environ. Sci.; Ecol. Abstr.; Ecology Abstr.; INIS Atomindex [Micro.]; Microbiol. Abstr. Sect. C; Life Sci. Collect.; Ref. Sources; Res. Alert [Full Cov.]; Rev. Med. Vet. Mycology; Rev. Plant Pathol.; Sci. Cit. Index; SCISEARCH; Soils Fert.

ISSN 0258-3348
GW
UDC 582.32
CODEN BRBIDS
BRYOPHYTORUM BIBLIOTHECA. [Bryophyt. bibl.]. Vol. 1 (1973)-. Academic Scholarly Publication. English (German and French). Irregular (two to three issues per year). Price varies per volume. Gebruder Borntraeger Verlagsbuchhandlung, Johannesstrasse 3-A, D-70176 Stuttgart Germany. **Tel** 0711/62 50 01, FAX (0711)625005, telex 723363 SCHB D. Documents available from BIOSIS Document Express, CASDDS.
Ind/Abst Biol. Abstr.; Chem. Abstr. (1973-1985).

LC QK **ISSN** 0307-2657
DD 581 UK
BSBI ABSTRACTS. [BSBI abstr.]. **Added/Corp** Botanical Society of the British Isles. **VFOAT** B.S.B.I. Abstracts; Abstracts. **VAT** Botanical Society of the British Isles Abstracts. Pt. 1 (May 1971)-. English. Irregular. $13.69. Botanical Society of the British Isle, 68 Outwoods Road, Loughborough LE11 3LY United Kingdom. **Tel** 011 44 1509 215598. ***Continues in part*** *Proceedings of the Botanical Society of the British Isles.*

LC QK710 .F494 **ISSN** 1310-4586
DD 581.1 BU
•**BULGARIAN JOURNAL OF PLANT PHYSIOLOGY.** **Added/Corp** Institut po Fiziologiia na Rasteniiata "Metodii Popov.". **VFOAT** Bulgarsko Spisanie po Fiziologiia na Rasteniiata. Vol. 19, No. 1-4 (1993)-. Periodical. Bulgarian (summaries and/or abstracts in English). Four times a year. Izdatelstvo na Bulgarskata Akademiia na Naukite, 6 Rouski Boulevard, Sofia Bulgaria. **Tel** FAX 011 359 2 801341, telex 22267 HEMKIK. **(Subscription address:** Kubon & Sagner, ABT Zeitschriftenimport, D 80328 Munich Germany. **Tel** 011 49 89 54218130.) ***Continues*** *Fiziologiia na Rasteniiata, 0324-0290.*

US
BULLETIN. (19??)-. Bulletin. English. Twelve times a year. $12.50. Cleveland Botanical Garden, 11030 East Boulevard, Cleveland OH 44106. **Tel** (216)721-1600. **ED** Marilyn Sommer. **Bk Rev**, (Qty: 6). **Ad Acc. Circ:** 4,250 (ctrl). ***Continues*** *Garden Center Bulletin, 0892-564X.*

LC QK975 **ISSN** 8755-0490
DD 585 US
BULLETIN / AMERICAN CONIFER SOCIETY. **See** Forests and Forestry.

US
BULLETIN - AMERICAN SOCIETY OF PLANT PHYSIOLOGISTS. **Main/Corp** American Society of Plant Physiologists. **Added/Corp** American Society of Plant Physiologists. Directory of the American Society of Plant Physiologists. (19??)-. Bulletin. English. Twelve times a year. $4.00. American Society of Plant Physiologists, 15501 A Monona Drive, Rockville MD 20855. **Tel** (301)251-0560 ext. 17, FAX (301)279-2996.

LC QK1 .A8613
DD 581.9/67/0601 NE
BULLETIN - ASSOCIATION POUR L'ETUDE TAXONOMIQUE DE LA FLORE D'AFRIQUE TROPICALE. **Main/Corp** Association pour l'Etude Taxomonique de la Flore d'Afrique Tropicale. (19??)-. Bulletin. Multiple languages (English and French). One time a year (Dec.). $10.00. Professor Dr Ljg Van der Maesen, PO Box 8010, Department of Plant Taxonomy, NL 6700 Ed Wageningen Netherlands. **Tel** 011 31 8370 83170, FAX 011 31 8370 84917. **Bk Rev. Circ:** 1,000.
Desc: This gives news on botany and botanists in Africa, literature lists, and new projects.

ISSN 0008-3046
CN
CCC
BULLETIN - CANADIAN BOTANICAL ASSOCIATION. **Main/Corp** Canadian Botanical Association. Vol. 1 (Jan. 1968)-. Bulletin. English (French). Four times a year. 36.02Can$. Canadian Botanical Association, University Guelph, Botany Department, Guelph Ontario NIG 2W1 Canada. **Tel** (519)824-4120 ext. 3277. **ED** J.F. Gerrath. **Bk Rev. Ad Acc. Circ:** 350.
Desc: Articles of botanical interest (all fields), botanical news (local and global), information on scientific meetings.

ISSN 1079-0764
DD 635 US
•**BULLETIN - CLEVELAND BOTANICAL GARDEN, THE.** (THE BULLETIN / CLEVELAND BOTANICAL GARDEN.). [Bull. - Clevel. Bot. Gard.]. **Added/Corp** Cleveland Botanical Garden. Vol. 60, No. 5 (May 1994)-. Bulletin. English. Twelve times a year. $12.50. Cleveland Botanical Garden, 11030 East Boulevard, Cleveland OH 44106. **Tel** (216)721-1600. ***Continues*** *Garden Center Bulletin (Cleveland, Ohio : 1968), 0892-564X.*

ISSN 0228-975X
DD 581/.05 CN
BULLETIN DE LA SOCIETE BOTANIQUE DU QUEBEC. [Bull. - Soc. bot. Que.]. **Added/Corp** Societe Botanique du Quebec. No. 2 (1981)-. Bulletin. French. Irregular. Societe Botanique du Quebec, Pavillon Comtois, Universite Laval, Quebec Quebec G1K 7P4 Canada. **Tel** (418)656-3857. **ED** Pierre Morisset. **Bk Rev. Circ:** 300. ***Continues*** *Bulletin (Societe Botanique du Quebec), 0228-975X.*
Desc: General information on botanical activities and research in Quebec. Bibliographical notes, comments and occasional review articles.

ISSN 0303-9153
BE
UDC 712
BULLETIN DU JARDIN BOTANIQUE NATIONAL DE BELGIQUE. **VFOAT** Bulletin van de Nationale Plantentuin van Belgie. (1967)-. Bulletin. Multiple languages. Four times a year. Jardin Botanique Nationale Belgique, Domaine de Bouchout, B-1860 Meise Belgium. **Tel** 011 32 2 2693905. **ED** A. Robyns. Index available. cum. index. **Bk Rev.**
Ind/Abst Ornamental Hort. (1991-).

LC QK1 .B9 **ISSN** 0524-7837
BE
CODEN JBNBA6
BULLETIN DU JARDIN BOTANIQUE NATIONAL DE BELGIQUE. [Bull. Jard. bot. natl. Belg.]. **Main/Corp** Jardin Botanique National de Belgique. **Added/Corp** Jardin Botanique National de Belgique. Bulletin van de Nationale Plantentuin van Belgiue. **VFOAT** Bulletin van de Nationale Plantentuin van Belgie. Vol. 37 (1967)-. Bulletin. English (French and German). One time a year. $165.30. Jardin Botanique National Belquice, Domaine de Bouchout, B-1860- Meise Belgique. **Tel** 011 32 2 2693905. **Bk Rev. Circ:** 750. Documents available from BIOSIS Document Express. ***Continues*** *Jardin Botanique de l'Etat (Belgium). Bulletin du Jardin Botanique de l'Etat a Bruxelles.*
Desc: Systematic botany, taxonomy vegetation ecology, phytosociology mainly of Central Africa and Western Europe.
Ind/Abst Biol. Abstr.; Field Crop Abstr.; For. Prod. Abstr.; For. Abstr.; GeoRef; Grass. Forage Abstr.; Hortic. Abstr.; Life Sci. Collect.; Plant Breed. Abstr.; Plant Genet. Resour. Abstr.; Rev. Med. Vet. Mycology; Rev. Plant Pathol.

LC QK1 .B993 **ISSN** 0240-8937
DD 581/.05 FR
CODEN BMNBDW
BULLETIN DU MUSEUM NATIONAL D'HISTOIRE NATURELLE. SECTION B : ADANSONIA, BOTANIQUE, PHYTOCHIMIE. [Bull. Mus. natl. hist. nat., Sect. B Adansonia]. **Added/Corp** Museum National d'Histoire Naturelle (France). **VFOAT** Adansonia, Botanique, Phytochimie. Vol. 3, No. 1 (Jan./March 1981)-. Bulletin. French (English). Four times a year. 420.00F. Bulletin du Museum National d'Histoire Naturelle, 57 rue Cuvier, 75005 Paris France. **Tel** 40.79.33.53. **ED** Joel Jeremie. Index available. **Bk Rev. Circ:** 1,000. Documents available from BIOSIS Document Express, CASDDS. ***Formed by the union of*** *Adansonia, 0181-0634* ***and*** *Bulletin du Museum National d'Histoire Naturelle. Section B, Botanique, Biologie et Ecologie Vegetales, Phytochimie.*
Desc: The journal publishes papers in French or English devoted to various aspects of botany : systematics, biology, ecology, anatomy, palynology, phytochemistry, etc.
Ind/Abst Biol. Abstr.; Chem. Abstr.; Ecol. Abstr.; For. Prod. Abstr.; For. Abstr.; Geogr. Abstr. Human Geogr.; GeoRef; Hortic. Abstr.; Ornamental Hort. (1991-); Life Sci. Collect.; Plant Breed. Abstr.; Plant Genet. Resour. Abstr.

LC QK1 .P135 **ISSN** 1057-3968
DD 581.9/9 US
SUSPENDED
BULLETIN / NATIONAL TROPICAL BOTANICAL GARDEN, THE. [Bull. - Natl. Trop. Bot. Gard.]. **Added/Corp** National Tropical Botanical Garden. Vol. 19, No. 2 (April 1989)-Suspended (19??). Bulletin. English. Four times a year (Jan., Apr., July, Oct.). $10.00. National Tropical Botanical Garden, PO Box 340, Lawai HI 96765. **Tel** (808)332-7324, FAX (808)332-9765. **ED** Diane Ragone and Janet L. Leopold. Index available. **Bk Rev**, (Qty: 4). **Circ:** 5,000 (ctrl). ***Continues*** *Pacific Tropical Botanical Garden. Bulletin, 0093-3996.*
Desc: Topics of general botanical or horticultural interest, and news of the National Tropical Botanical Garden.

LC QK1 .B9936
DD 580/.5 II
BULLETIN OF PURE & APPLIED SCIENCES. SEC. B, BOTANY. **VFOAT** Botany. (19??)-. Academic Scholarly Publication. English. Two times a year. $14.00 institutions; $9.00 individuals. Dr Ajay Kumar Sharma, PO Box 38, Modinagar 201204 India. **Bk Rev. Ad Acc.** Documents available from BLDSC. ***Continues*** *Bulletin of Pure & Applied Sciences. Sec. B, Plant Science.*

LC QK358 .I381 **ISSN** 0006-8128
DD 581 II
CODEN BBSUAY
BULLETIN OF THE BOTANICAL SURVEY OF INDIA. [Bull. bot. surv. India]. **Main/Corp** Botanical Survey of India. Vol. 1 (Oct. 1959)-. Bulletin. English. Four times a year. $45.00. Botanical Survey of India / Howrah, Howrah India. **(Subscription address:** Prints India, 11 Darya Ganj, New Delhi 110002 India. **Tel** 011 91 11 3268645, FAX 011 91 11 3275542, telex 31-61087 PRIN-IN.)

ISSN 1046-1442
DD 581 US
BULLETIN OF THE CALIFORNIA NATIVE PLANT SOCIETY. (BULLETIN.). [Bull. Calif. Native Plant Soc.]. **Added/Corp** California Native Plant Society. **VFOAT** Bulletin of the California Native Plant Society. (197?)-. Bulletin. English. Four times a year. $35.00 Comes with membership. California Native Plant Society, 1722 J Street 17, Sacramento CA 95814. **Tel** (916)447-2677.

LC Z **ISSN** 0192-3641
DD 002 US
BULLETIN OF THE HUNT INSTITUTE FOR BOTANICAL DOCUMENTATION. [Bull. Hunt Inst. Bot. Doc.]. **Main/Corp** Hunt Institute for Botanical Documentation. Vol. 1 (Spring 1979)-. Bulletin. English. Two times a year. $4.00 US; $5.00 other. Hunt Institute, Carnegie Mellon University, Pittsburgh PA 15213. **Tel** (412)268-2434, FAX (412)268-5677. **ED** Sharon M. Tomasie. **Circ:** 600.

LC QK1 .K64A **ISSN** 0385-2431
DD 581/.05 JA
UDC 581
CODEN BMBBD6
BULLETIN OF THE NATIONAL SCIENCE MUSEUM. SERIES B, BOTANY. [Bull. Natl. Sci. Mus., Ser. B]. **Main/Corp** Kokuritsu Kagaku Hakubutsukan. **VFOAT** Kokuritsu Kagaku Hakubutsukan Kenkyu Hokoku. Shokubutsugaku. Vol. 1; March 1975-. Bulletin. English (English). National Science Museum, Ueno Park, Tokyo 110 Japan. Documents available from

BIOSIS Document Express. ***Supersedes in part*** *Bulletin of the National Science Museum.*
Ind/Abst AGRICOLA [Full Cov.]; Biol. Abstr.; GeoRef; Rev. Med. Vet. Mycology; Rev. Plant Pathol.

LC QK1 .B874 **ISSN** 0968-0446
DD 581 UK

•BULLETIN OF THE NATURAL HISTORY MUSEUM. BOTANY SERIES.
Added/Corp British Museum (Natural History). **VFOAT** Botany Series; Botany; Bulletin of the Natural History Museum. Botany. Vol. 23, No. 1 (June 24, 1993)-. Bulletin. English. Two times a year (June and Nov.). $134.76. Intercept Ltd., PO Box 716, Andover Hampshire SP10 1YG United Kingdom. **Tel** 011 44 1264 334748, FAX 011 44 1264 334058, telex 41103 PEPSOS G. ***Continues*** *Bulletin of the British Museum (Natural History). Botany Series, 0068-2292.*

LC QK1 .T6 **ISSN** 0040-9618
DD 580/.5 US
CODEN BTBCAL
Pr Rev.

BULLETIN OF THE TORREY BOTANICAL CLUB, THE.
[Bull. Torrey Bot. Club]. **Main/Corp** Torrey Botanical Club. Vol. 1 (Jan. 1870)-. Bulletin. English. Four times a year. $55.00. New York Botanical Garden, Scientific Publishing Department B, New York NY 10458-5126. **Tel** (718)817-8721, FAX (718)817-6504, telex 5106015451. **(Subscription address:** Bulletin of the Torrey Botanical Club, PO Box 1897, Lawrence KS 66044-8897. **) ED** H. David Hammond. Index available. **Bk Rev**. **Ad Acc**. **Acid Free. Circ:** 1,350. available on microfilm and microfiche from University Microfilms International (UMI). Documents available from The Genuine Article, BIOSIS Document Express, CASDDS, Documents on Demand. ***Absorbed*** *Torreya, 0096-3844.*
Desc: Keeps researchers, teachers and librarians, especially foreign, abreast of current research in basic plant sciences in this hemisphere.
Ind/Abst AgBiotech News Inf.; AGRICOLA [Full Cov.]; Agrofor. Abstr. (1991-); Biol. Abstr.; Chem. Abstr.; Crop Physiol. Abstr.; Curr. Aware. Biol. Sci., CABS; Curr. Cit.; Curr. Contents Agric. Biol. Environ. Sci.; Ecol. Abstr. (?-?); Ecology Abstr.; Energy Inf. Abstr.; Environ. Abstr.; Field Crop Abstr.; For. Prod. Abstr.; For. Abstr.; GeoRef; Grass. Forage Abstr.; Hortic. Abstr.; Ornamental Hort.; Life Sci. Collect.; Plant Breed. Abstr.; Pollut. Abstr. Indexes; Res. Alert [Full Cov.]; Rev. Agric. Entomol.; Rev. Med. Vet. Mycology; Rev. Plant Pathol.; Sci. Cit. Index; SCISEARCH; Seed Abstr.; Soils Fert.; Weed Abstr.

ISSN 0197-6265
US

BULLETIN - THE MARIE SELBY BOTANICAL GARDENS.
Main/Corp Marie Selby Botanical Gardens. Vol. 1 (1974)-. Bulletin. English. Four times a year. Free to members. Marie Selby Botanical Gardens, 811 South Palm Avenue, Sarasota FL 34236. **Tel** (813)366-5730. **ED** Spencer Ketchum. **Circ:** 3,300 (ctrl).
Desc: A general interest bulletin primarily for membership, which publishes articles on botanical subjects and membership activities.

LC QK **ISSN** 1047-8108
DD 581 US
CODEN CSNFEU

CA SELECTS: NITROGEN FIXATION.
See Chemistry and Chemicals-Abstracting, Bibliographies and Statistics.

ISSN 0526-717X
MX
Pr Rev.

CACTACEAS Y SUCULENTAS MEXICANAS.
Added/Corp Sociedad Mexicana de Cactologia. Vol.1 (July 1955)-. Academic Scholarly Publication. Spanish (English). Four times a year. $12.00. Societe Mexicana de Cactologia, APDO 60 487, 03801 Mesico DF Mexico. **Tel** 011 52 5 6229048, 011 52 5 6229046. **ED** Jorge Meyran. Index available (Every four years). cum. index. **Circ:** 1,000.
Desc: Covers botany, phytogeography, physiology and ecology.

AT

CACTUS AND SUCCULENT JOURNAL.
Added/Corp Cactus and Succulent Society of New South Wales. Vol. 10, No. 1 (1975)-. Periodical. English. Six times a year. 12.33Aus$. Cactus Succulent Society of New South Wales, PO Box 36, Woollhara New South Wales 2025 Australia. **Tel** 011 61 2 3631107. Index Available in last issue of volume--loose--unpaged.

ISSN 0526-7196
AT
Pr Rev.

CACTUS AND SUCCULENT JOURNAL WOOLLAHRA.
(CACTUS AND SUCCULENT JOURNAL.). (1957)-. Periodical. English. Four times a year (Mar., June, Sept., Dec.). 12.33Aus$. Cactus & Succulent Society New South Wales, PO Box 36, Woollhara NSW 2025 Australia. **Tel** 011 61 2 3631107. **ED** R. Johnstone and M. Jansen. Index available. **Bk Rev**. **Ad Acc**. **Circ:** 400 (ctrl).

ISSN 0094-3800
US
Pr Rev. **SUSPENDED**

CALIFORNIA PLANT PATHOLOGY.
[Calif. plant pathol.]. **Added/Corp** California. University. Cooperative Extension. University of California Agricultural Extension Service. No. 1 (1971)-(Sept. 1992). Periodical. English. Four times a year. $4.00 US; $7.50 other. Department of Plant Pathology, University of California, Ms. E. Jeffery, Davis CA 95616. **ED** W D Gubler. cum. index.
Desc: Research updates of California Plant Pathology departments at Davis, Berkeley and Riverside.
Ind/Abst AGRICOLA [Full Cov.]; Rev. Med. Vet. Mycology; Rev. Plant Pathol.

ISSN 0008-4026
CN
CCC
NLM W1 CA578 **CODEN** CJBOAW
Pr Rev.

CANADIAN JOURNAL OF BOTANY.
[Can. j. bot.]. **Added/Corp** National Research Council of Canada. National Research Council Canada. **VFOAT** Journal Canadien de Botanique. Vol. 29 (Feb. 1951)-. Academic Scholarly Publication. English (French). Twelve times a year. 475.00Can$. National Research Council of Canada, Receiver General for Canada, Ottawa Ontario K1A 0R6 Canada. **Tel** (613)993-0362, FAX (613)952-7656. **ED** I. E. P. Taylor. Index available. **Ad Acc. Circ:** 2,000 (ctrl). available on microfilm and microfiche from University Microfilms International (UMI). Documents available from The Genuine Article, BIOSIS Document Express, CASDDS, Documents on Demand. ***Continues*** *Canadian Journal of Research. Section C. Botanical Sciences.*
Desc: An inclusive publication covering all fields of plant science. In general the contributors deal with basic or fundamental research, but it is recognized that the boundary between pure and applied science cannot be sharply drawn.
Ind/Abst ASTIS Curr. Aware. Bull. (1978-); Abstr. Bull. Inst. Pap. Sci. Tech.; AgBiotech News Inf.; AGRICOLA [Full Cov.]; Agrofor. Abstr. (1991-); AQUAREF; ASTIS Bibliogr. (1978-); Biocont. News Inf. (19??-19??); Biodeter. Abstr. (19??-19??); Biol. Agric. Index; Biol. Abstr.; Chem. Abstr.; Chemorecept. Abstr.; Coal Abstr.; Cot. Trop. Fibr. Abstr. Bibliogr.; Crop Physiol. Abstr.; Curr. Aware. Biol. Sci., CABS; Curr. Cit.; Curr. Contents Agric. Biol. Environ. Sci.; Ecol. Abstr.; Ecology Abstr.; Environ. Abstr.; Environ. Period. Bibliogr.; Field Crop Abstr.; Food Sci. Technol. Abstr.; For. Prod. Abstr. (19??-19??); For. Abstr.; Genet. Abstr.; Geogr. Abstr. Phys. Geogr.; Geol. Abstr.; GeoRef; Grass. Forage Abstr.; Hortic. Abstr.; Immunol. Abstr.; Index Vet.; Int. Aerosp. Abstr.; Irr. Drain. Abstr.; Maize Abstr.; Microbiol. Abstr. Sect. B (19??-19??); Microbiol. Abstr. Sect. A; Microbiol. Abstr. Sect. C; NAPRALERT; Nat. Prod. Updates; Nematol. Abstr.; Ocean. Abstr.; Ornamental Hort. (19??-19??); PESTDOC; Plant Breed. Abstr.; Plant Genet. Resour. Abstr.; Plant Grow. Reg. Abstr.; Potato Abstr.; Protozoolog. Abstr.; Ref. Upd. Deluxe Ed.; Res. Alert [Full Cov.]; Rev. Agric. Entomol.; Rev. Med. Vet. Entomol.; Rev. Med. Vet. Mycology; Rev. Plant Pathol.; Rice Abstr.; Risk Abstr. (19??-19??); Sci. Cit. Index; SCISEARCH; Seed Abstr.; Soils Fert.; Sorghum Mill. Abstr.; Soyabean Abstr.; Vitis Vitic. Enol. Abstr.; Weed Abstr.; Wheat Barley Trit. Abstr.

ISSN 0706-0661
DD 632/.05 CN
UDC 581.2; 632 **CCC**
CODEN CJPPD6
Pr Rev.

CANADIAN JOURNAL OF PLANT PATHOLOGY.
[Can. J. plant pathol.]. **VFOAT** Revue Canadienne de Phytopathologie. Vol. 1 (June 1979)-. Academic Scholarly Publication. English (French). Four times a year (Mar., June, Sept., Dec.). 68.03Can$. University of Guelph / Plant Pathology, Canadian Journal of Plant Pathology, Department of Environmental Biology, Guelph Ontario N1G 2W1 Canada. **Tel** (519)824-4120, Ext. 3631, FAX (519)837-0442. **ED** Dr. Robert Hall. cum. index (From Vol. 1, 1979 to present). **Circ:** 900. Documents available from The Genuine Article, CASDDS, Documents on Demand.
Desc: Original research in plant pathology including technological aspects of plant disease control.
Ind/Abst AgBiotech News Inf.; AGRICOLA [Full Cov.]; BioBusiness; Biocont. News Inf. (19??-19??); Biodeter. Abstr. (1991-); Biol. Agric. Index; Chem. Abstr.; Crop Physiol. Abstr.; Curr. Aware. Biol. Sci., CABS; Curr. Cit.; Curr. Contents Agric. Biol. Environ. Sci.; Environ. Abstr.; Field Crop Abstr.; For. Abstr.; Grass. Forage Abstr.; Hortic. Abstr.; Irr. Drain. Abstr.; Environ.; Maize Abstr.; Nematol. Abstr.; Ornamental Hort. (1991-); PESTDOC; Plant Breed. Abstr.; Plant Grow. Reg. Abstr.; Postharvest News Inf.; Potato Abstr.; Res. Alert [Select. Cov.]; Rev. Agric. Entomol.; Rev. Med. Vet. Mycology; Rev. Plant Pathol.; SCISEARCH; Seed Abstr.; Sorghum Mill. Abstr.; Soyabean Abstr.; Vitis Vitic. Enol. Abstr.; Weed Abstr.; Wheat Barley Trit. Abstr.

ISSN 0008-4220
CN
CCC
CODEN CPLSAY
Pr Rev.

CANADIAN JOURNAL OF PLANT SCIENCE.
[Can. j. plant sci.]. **Added/Corp** Agricultural Institute of Canada. Canadian Society of Agronomy. Canadian Society for Horticultural Science. National Committee on Agricultural Services. **VFOAT** Revue Canadienne de Phytotechnie. Vol. 37 (Jan. 1957)-. Periodical. English (French). Four times a year. 72.02Can$. Agricultural Institute of Canada, 151 Slater Street, Suite 907, Ottawa Ontario K1P 5H4 Canada. **Tel** (613)232-9459, (613)238-2271, FAX (613)594-5190. **ED** A. R. Maurer. **Ad Acc. Circ:** 1,600. available on microfilm and microfiche from University Microfilms International (UMI). Documents available from The Genuine Article, BIOSIS Document Express, CASDDS, Documents on Demand. ***Continues in part*** *Canadian Journal of Agricultural Science, 0366-6557.*
Desc: Contributions to the journal are primarily in the disciplines of agronomy (grains, forages, weeds), horticulture (fruits, vegetables, ornamentals) and pest management (pathology, entomology, nematology, weed science). Papers on breeding and genetics, physiology, microbiology, management, economics and plant production systems are also published.
Ind/Abst AgBiotech News Inf.; AGRICOLA [Full Cov.]; Agric. Eng. Abstr. (1991-); AQUAREF; BioBusiness; Biocont. News Inf.; Biodeter. Abstr.; Biol. Agric. Index; Biol. Abstr.; Chem. Abstr.; Crop Physiol. Abstr.; Curr. Aware. Biol. Sci., CABS; Curr. Cit.; Curr. Contents Agric. Biol. Environ. Sci.; EMBASE; Environ. Abstr.; Environ. Period. Bibliogr.; Field Crop Abstr.; Food Sci. Technol. Abstr.; For. Prod. Abstr.; For. Abstr.; Genet. Abstr.; Grass. Forage Abstr.; Hortic. Abstr.; Irr. Drain. Abstr.; Environ.; Maize Abstr.; Microbiol. Abstr. Sect. A; Microbiol. Abstr. Sect. C; Nematol. Abstr.; Nutr. Abstr. Rev., Ser. B, Live Feeds and Feed.; Nutr. Abstr. Rev., Ser. A, Hum. Exp.; Ornamental Hort. (19??-19??); Life Sci. Collect.; PESTDOC; Plant Breed. Abstr.; Plant Genet. Resour. Abstr.; Plant Grow. Reg. Abstr.; Postharvest News Inf.; Potato Abstr.; Protozoolog. Abstr.; Ref. Upd. Deluxe Ed.; Res. Alert [Full Cov.]; Rev. Agric. Entomol.; Rev. Med. Vet. Entomol.; Rev. Med. Vet. Mycology; Rev. Plant Pathol.; Rice Abstr.; Sci. Cit. Index; SCISEARCH; Seed Abstr.; Soils Fert.; Sorghum Mill. Abstr.; Soyabean Abstr.; Vitis Vitic. Enol. Abstr.; Weed Abstr.; Wheat Barley Trit. Abstr.; World Agric. Econ. Rural Sociol. Abstr.

ISSN 0008-476X
CN
CODEN CPDSAS
Pr Rev.

CANADIAN PLANT DISEASE SURVEY.
[Can. plant dis. surv.]. **Added/Corp** Canada. Dept. of Agriculture. Research Branch. Plant Research Institute (Canada). **VFOAT** Inventaire des Maladies des Plantes au Canada. Vol. 40 (Sept. 1960)-. Government Publication. English (French). Four times a year. Free on request. Agriculture Canada, Communications Branch, Ottawa Ontario K1A 0C7 Canada. Documents available from The Genuine Article, BIOSIS Document Express, Documents on Demand. ***Continues*** *Canada. Plant Research Institute. Annual Report of the Canadian Plant Disease Survey., 0381-3088.*
Ind/Abst AGRICOLA [Full Cov.]; Biodeter. Abstr. (1991-); Biol. Abstr.; Curr. Aware. Biol. Sci., CABS; Curr. Contents Agric. Biol. Environ. Sci.; Energy Inf. Abstr.; Environ. Abstr.; For. Abstr.; Microbiol. Abstr. Sect. A; Microbiol. Abstr. Sect. C; Nematol. Abstr.; Life Sci. Collect.; Plant Breed. Abstr.; Postharvest News Inf.; Potato Abstr.; Res. Alert [Select. Cov.]; Rev. Agric. Entomol.; Rev. Plant Pathol.; SCISEARCH; Seed Abstr.; Soyabean Abstr.; Weed Abstr.; Wheat Barley Trit. Abstr.

LC QK1 .C215 **ISSN** 0373-2967
DD 580.5 SZ
CODEN CNDLAR

CANDOLLEA.
[Candollea]. **Added/Corp** Conservatoire et Jardin Botaniques de la Ville de Geneve. Vol. 1 (1922)-. Periodical. French (German, English and Spanish). Two times a year. 100.00F. Conservatoire et Jardin Botaniques, Case Postale 60, CH-1292 Cambesy Geneva Switzerland. **Tel** 011 41 22 346969. **Circ:** 650. Documents available from BIOSIS Document Express. ***Supersedes*** *Annuaire du Conservatoire et du Jardin Botaniques de la Ville de Geneve, 0255-9676.*
Desc: Original articles on systemology, morphology, chorology, vegetal ecology and other subjects closely linked to taxonomy.
Ind/Abst Biol. Abstr.; Field Crop Abstr.; Grass. Forage Abstr.

ISSN 1018-1210
CR
UDC 63

CARAPHIN NEWS.
[Caraphin news]. **VFOAT** Caribbean Animal and Plant Health Information Network News. (1989)-. Periodical. English. One time a year.
Ind/Abst Index Vet.

ISSN 0190-9215
US

CARNIVOROUS PLANT NEWSLETTER.
Added/Corp California State University, Fullerton. Arboretum. Vol. 1 (April 1972)-. Newsletter. English. Four

times a year (Mar., Jun., Sept., Dec.). $15.00. Arborteum, California State University, Fullerton CA 92634. **Tel** (714)773-2766, FAX (714)773-3426. **ED** Joe Mazrimas, Leo Song, D. S. Schnell. Index available (Dec.). **Bk Rev. Ad Acc. Circ:** 850 (ctrl).
Desc: Journal of International Carnivorous Plant Society. Focuses on furthering communication among carnivorous plant enthusiasts, from hobbyists to professionals.

XR
CASOPIS SLEZSKEHO MUZEA. SERIE C. DENDROLOGIE. Main/Corp Opava, Czechoslovak Republic. Slezske Muzeum. Vol. 1 (1962)-. Czech (German; summaries and/or abstracts in Russian; table of contents in English and Russian). Two times a year. **(Subscription address:** Artia Pegas Press Ltd., Palac Metro Narodni Trida 25, 11210 Prague 1 Czech Republic. **Tel** 011 42 2 24196265, 011 42 2 24196266.)
Ind/Abst Numis. Lit.

LC QK1 .C27 **ISSN** 0008-7475
DD 581.974 US
CODEN CSTNAC
Pr Rev.
CASTANEA. (CASTANEA : THE JOURNAL OF THE SOUTHERN APPALACHIAN BOTANICAL CLUB.). [Castanea]. **Added/Corp** Southern Appalachian Botanical Club. Southern Appalachian Botanical Club. Journal. (1937)-. Periodical. English. Four times a year (Mar., June, Sept., Dec.). $25.00. Southern Appalachian Botanical Society, Department of Biology, 2100 College Street, Newberry SC 29108. **Tel** (803)321-5257, FAX (803)321-5232. **ED** Audrey Mellichamp (editor's address: Department of Biology UNC-Charlotte NC 28223; phone: (704)536-2704). Index available (Bound in the 4th issue publish in December). cum. index. **Bk Rev**, (Qty: 8). **Ad Acc, Adv Mgr:** Cynthia Aulbach-Smith, **Tel** (803)359-5027. **Circ:** 1,100. available on microfilm from University Microfilms International (UMI). Documents available from BIOSIS Document Express. ***Continues*** *Journal of the Southern Appalachian Botanical Club.*
Desc: Covers the botany of the southern Appalachians and the Southeastern United States.
Ind/Abst AGRICOLA [Full Cov.]; Biol. Agric. Index; Biol. Abstr.; Curr. Aware. Biol. Sci., CABS; Ecol. Abstr.; Ecology Abstr.; For. Prod. Abstr.; For. Abstr.; Grass. Forage Abstr.; Plant Genet. Resour. Abstr.; Soils Fert.; Vitis Vitic. Enol. Abstr.

ISSN 1062-5151
DD 589 US
CATALOGUE OF YEASTS. (CATALOGUE OF YEASTS / AMERICAN TYPE CULTURE COLLECTION.). [Cat. yeasts]. **Main/Corp** American Type Culture Collection. **VFOAT** ATCC Catalogue of Yeasts; ATCC Yeasts. 18th Ed. (1990)-. English. Irregular. American Type Culture Collection, 12301 Parklawn Drive, Rockville MD 20852. **Tel** (301)881-2600, FAX (301)231-5826, telex 898-055. ***Continues in part*** *American Type Culture Collection. Catalogue of Fungi/Yeasts, 1053-3370.*

LC QK **ISSN** 0969-0239
DD 581 UK
CCC
Pr Rev.
•**CELLULOSE.** Vol. 1, No. 1 (March 1994)-. Academic Scholarly Publication. English. Four times a year. $268.00. Chapman & Hall, 2-6 Boundary Row, London SE1 8HN United Kingdom. **Tel** 011 44 171 8650066, FAX 011 44 171 5229623, telex 290164 CHAPMA G. **(Subscription address:** International Thomson Publishing Services Ltd., North Way Andover, Hampshire SP10 5BE United Kingdom. **Tel** 011 44 1264 332424.) **ED** John C. Roberts. **Ad Acc.** Documents available from BLDSC.
Desc: Research on progress in the field of cellulose, with an emphasis on the chemistry, biochemistry, physics, and materials science of cellulose.

ISSN 0937-2148
GW
CODEN CPLPET
CHEMISTRY OF PLANT PROTECTION. [Chem. plant prot.]. (1986)-. Monographic series. English. Irregular. Price varies per volume. Springer-Verlag GmbH & Company KG, Heidelberger Platz 3, D-14197 Berlin Germany. **Tel** 011 49 30 8207223, FAX 011 49 30 8214091, telex 183 319 SPBLN D. **(Subscription address:** Springer-Verlag New York Inc. / North America, PO Box 2485, Journal Fulfillment, Secaucus NJ 07096. **Tel** (201)348-4033, (800)777-4643, FAX (201)348-4505.) **ED** W. Ebing, G. Haug, H. Hoffmann. Documents available from BIOSIS Document Express, CASDDS. ***Continues*** *Chemie der Pflanzenschutz- und Schadlingsbekampfungsmittel.*
Ind/Abst AGRICOLA [Full Cov.]; Biol. Abstr. (1985-); Chem. Abstr.; Curr. Cit.

LC QK355 .C4624 **ISSN** 0529-1526
DD 581/.012 CC
UDC 58.06
CHIH WU FEN LEI HSUEH PAO. [Chih wu fen lei hsueh pao]. **VFOAT** Acta Phytotaxonomica Sinica. (March 1951)-. Periodical. Chinese (summaries and/or abstracts in Latin and English). Six times a year. $58.40. Science Press, 16 Donghuangchenggen North Street, Beijing 100707, People's Republic of China. **Tel** 011 86 1 4019821, 011 86 1 4010642, FAX 011 86 1 4012180, 011 86 1 4019810, telex 210147. **(Subscription address:** China International Book Trading Corporation, PO Box 399, Library Service Department, Beijing 100044 People's Republic of China. **Tel** 011 86 1 8414284, FAX 011 86 1 8412023, telex 22496 CIBTC CN.)
Ind/Abst For. Abstr.; GeoRef; Hortic. Abstr.; NAPRALERT; Ornamental Hort. (1991-); Weed Abstr.

LC QK1 .C52
DD 581 CC
CHIH WU HSUEH CHI KAN = BOTANICAL RESEARCH : CONTRIBUTIONS FROM THE INSTITUTE OF BOTANY, ACADEMIA SINICA. Added/Corp Chung-kuo ko Hsueh Yuan. Chih wu yen Chiu so. **VFOAT** Botanical ReseaOrch. (1983)-. Periodical. Chinese (summaries and/or abstracts in English). Four times a year. RMBY4.20.
Ind/Abst Biodeter. Abstr.

LC QK1 .C526 **ISSN** 0577-7496
DD 581/.05 CC
CODEN CHWHAY
CHIH WU HSUEH PAO. [Chih wu hsueh pao]. **Added/Corp** Chung-Kuo Chih Wu Hsueh Hui. **VFOAT** Acta Botanica Sinica. (1952)-. Academic Scholarly Publication. English (Chinese; summaries and/or abstracts in English and Russian). Six times a year. $81.30. Science Press, 16 Donghuangchenggen North Street, Beijing 100707, People's Republic of China. **Tel** 011 86 1 4019821, 011 86 1 4010642, FAX 011 86 1 4012180, 011 86 1 4019810, telex 210147. **(Subscription address:** China International Book Trading Corporation, PO Box 399, Library Service Department, Beijing 100044 People's Republic of China. **Tel** 011 86 1 8414284, FAX 011 86 1 8412023, telex 22496 CIBTC CN.) Documents available from BIOSIS Document Express, CASDDS.
Ind/Abst Biol. Abstr.; Chem. Abstr.; Coal Abstr.; Curr. Cit.; GeoRef; Soyabean Abstr.

ISSN 0577-750X
DD 632 CH
CODEN PLPBBH
CHIH WU PAO HU HSUEH HUI HUI K'AN. [Chih wu pao hu hsueh hui hui k'an]. **Added/Corp** Chung-kuo Chih Wu Pao Hu Hsueh Hui. **VFOAT** Plant Protection Bulletin. Vol. 1 (1959)-. Bulletin. Chinese (summaries and/or abstracts in English; table of contents in English). Four times a year. 1200.00NT$ Taiwan; 2000.00NT$ other. Plant Protection Society of the Republic of China, Department of Plant Pathology, National Chung Hsing University, 250 Kuo Kuang Road Taichung, Taichung 402 Taiwan. **ED** Y. C. Liu. Documents available from BIOSIS Document Express, CASDDS.
Ind/Abst Biocont. News Inf.; Biol. Abstr.; Chem. Abstr.; Maize Abstr.; Plant Breed. Abstr.; Potato Abstr.; Soyabean Abstr.

ISSN 0577-7518
DD 581 CC
CHIH WU PAO HU HSUEH PAO. [Chih Wu Pao Hu Hsueh Pao]. **Added/Corp** Chung-kuo Chih Wu Pao Hu Hsueh Hui. Chung-kuo Chih Wu Pao Hu Hsueh Hui. "Chih Wu Pao Hu Hsueh Hui" Pien Wei Hui. Chung-kuo Nung Hsueh Hui. **VFOAT** Zhiwu Baohu Xuebao; Acta Phytophylacica Sinica. Vol. 1 (1962)-. Periodical. Chinese (summaries and/or abstracts in English; table of contents in English). Four times a year. $4.00. Chinese Society of Plant Protection / Zhongguo Zhiwi Baohu Xuehui, Department of Plant Protection, Beijing University of Agriculture, Beijing 100094 People's Republic of China. **Tel** 2582244.
Desc: Contains information on the protection of plants.
Ind/Abst Rev. Plant Pathol.; Rice Abstr.

LC SB599 .C52 **ISSN** 0412-0914
DD 581.2/05 CC
CHIH WU PING LI HSUEH PAO. [Chih Wu Ping Li Hsueh Pao]. **Added/Corp** Chung-Kuo Nung Hsueh Hui. Chung-Kuo Chih Wu Pao Hu Hsueh Hui. Chung-Kuo Chih Wu Ping Li Hsueh Hui. **VFOAT** Acta Phytopathologica Sinica. (June 1955)-. Periodical. Chinese (summaries and/or abstracts in English). Four times a year. $64.50. **(Subscription address:** China International Book Trading Corporation, PO Box 399, Library Service Department, Beijing 100044 People's Republic of China. **Tel** 011 86 1 8414284, FAX 011 86 1 8412023, telex 22496 CIBTC CN.)
Ind/Abst Nematol. Abstr.; Rev. Med. Vet. Mycology; Rev. Plant Pathol.; Rice Abstr.; Seed Abstr.

LC QK710 .C48 **ISSN** 0257-4829
DD 581.876 CC
UDC 581.1
CODEN CWSPDA
CHIH WU SHENG LI HSUEH PAO. [Zhiwu shengli xuebao]. **VFOAT** Acta Phytophysiologia Sinica; Chung-Kuo Chih Wu Sheng Li Hsueh Hui Chu Pien. (19??)-. Academic Scholarly Publication. Chinese (summaries and/or abstracts in English). Four times a year. $30.90. **(Subscription address:** China International Book Trading Corporation, PO Box 399, Library Service Department, Beijing 100044 People's Republic of China. **Tel** 011 86 1 8414284, FAX 011 86 1 8412023, telex 22496 CIBTC CN.) Documents available from BIOSIS Document Express, CASDDS.
Ind/Abst Biol. Abstr.; Chem. Abstr.; Crop Physiol. Abstr.; EMBASE; Field Crop Abstr.; For. Abstr.; Hortic. Abstr.; NAPRALERT; Plant Breed. Abstr.; Plant Grow. Reg. Abstr.; Potato Abstr.; Rev. Plant Pathol.; Rice Abstr.; Seed Abstr.; Soils Fert.; Sorghum Mill. Abstr.; Weed Abstr.

LC QK710 .C484 **ISSN** 0412-0914
DD 581.876/05 CC
CODEN CWSPDA
Pr Rev.
CHIH WU SHENG LI HSUEH TUNG HSUN. [Chih Wu Sheng Li Hsueh Tung Hsun]. **Added/Corp** Chung-kuo Chih wu Sheng li Hsueh Hui. **VFOAT** Plant Physiology Communications. (19??)-. Chinese. Four times a year. $1.80 (per issue). Zhongguo Zhiwu Bingli Xuehui / China Phytopathological Society, Department of Plant Protection, Beijing University of Agriculture, Beijing 100094, People's Republic of China. **Tel** 2582244. **ED** Q. Weifan. **Bk Rev. Ad Acc. Circ:** 1,500.
Desc: Publishes articles on plant physiology, progress of research and review of developments, both at home and abroad. It also gives publicity to new techniques and methods, apparatus and equipment, and exchange of experience in teaching.
Ind/Abst Crop Physiol. Abstr.; NAPRALERT; Plant Breed. Abstr.; Plant Genet. Resour. Abstr.; Plant Grow. Reg. Abstr.; Potato Abstr.

LC QK355 .C4626
DD 581.951 CC
CHIH WU YEN CHIU. Added/Corp Tung-pei lin Hsueh Yuan (China). **VFOAT** Bulletin of Botanical Research. Vol. 1, No. 1/2 (Apr. 1981)-. Bulletin. Chinese (English and Latin). Four times a year. RMBY1.20. Science Press, 16 Donghuangchenggen North Street, Beijing 100707, People's Republic of China. **Tel** 011 86 1 4019821, 011 86 1 4010642, FAX 011 86 1 4012180, 011 86 1 4019810, telex 210147. **ED** Yi-Ling Chou. **Bk Rev. Circ:** 3,000. ***Continues*** *Chih Wu Yen Chiu Shih Hui Kan.*
Desc: Publishes scientific papers about the research on plant taxonomy, flora, plant anatomy, plant ecology and geobotany.
Ind/Abst Rev. Plant Pathol.; Wheat Barley Trit. Abstr.

UK
CHILEANS, THE. Vol. 1, No. 1 (March 1966)-. Academic Scholarly Publication. English. Irregular. £10.40 UK; $26.00 North America; £11.90 other. H Middleditch ESQ, 5 Lyons Avenue, Hetton-Le-Hole Co Durham DH5 0HS United Kingdom. **Tel** 011 44 191 5263324. **ED** H. Middleditch. Index available. cum. index. **Bk Rev. Circ:** 600 (ctrl).
Desc: Devoted to a scholarly treatment of South American cacti and succulents. The major focus of the journal is field trips to South America. The publication is both a scholarly and literary delight that would be enjoyed by anyone seriously involved in the study of any group of plants.

LC QK1 .C543 **ISSN** 1001-0718
DD 581/.05 CC
CODEN CJBOE2
CHINESE JOURNAL OF BOTANY. [Chin. j. bot.]. **Added/Corp** Chung-Hua Chih Wu Hsueh Hui. Vol. 1, No. 1 (June 1989)-. Periodical. English. Two times a year. $78.00. Science Press, 16 Donghuangchenggen North Street, Beijing 100707, People's Republic of China. **Tel** 011 86 1 4019821, 011 86 1 4010642, FAX 011 86 1 4012180, 011 86 1 4019810, telex 210147. **(Subscription address:** Science Press Ltd., 63-117 Alderton Street, Rego Park NY 11374. **Tel** (718)459-4638.) **ED** Prof. Wang Fuxiong and Zhang Xinshi. **Bk Rev.** Documents available from BIOSIS Document Express.
Desc: Publishes original articles on all aspects of plant sciences with emphasis on basic research. Reviews or minireviews, mainly on Chinese works, notes, short communications, and institution briefs may be included.
Ind/Abst Biol. Abstr. (1991-).

ISSN 0264-9640
DD 016.5748733 UK
CHLOROPLASTS. [Chloroplasts]. (1984)-. Periodical. English. Twelve times a year. £85.00. SUBIS, Mansion House 19 Kingfield Road, Sheffield S11 9AS United Kingdom. **Tel** 011 44 114 2554433, FAX 011 44 114 255 4626.

LC QK355 .C523
DD 581 CC
CHUNG-KUO KO HSUEH YUAN HUA NAN CHIH WU YEN CHIU SO CHI KAN = ACTA BOTANICA AUSTRO SINICA. Added/Corp Chung-Kuo Ko Hsueh Yuan. Hua Nan Chih Wu Yen Chiu So. **VFOAT** Hua Nan Chih Wu Yen Chiu So Chi Kan; Acta Botanica Austro Sinica. (1983)-. Periodical. Chinese (summaries and/or abstracts in English).
Ind/Abst Crop Physiol. Abstr.; Field Crop Abstr.; Hortic. Abstr.; Plant Breed. Abstr.; Rice Abstr.

LC QK **ISSN** 0010-0730
DD 581 SP
CODEN COBOAX
COLLECTANEA BOTANICA. [Collect. bot.]. **Added/Corp** Instituto Botanico de Barcelona. Vol. 1 (1946)-. Spanish (English, French and German). One

time a year. 1200ptas. Ayuntamiento Barcelona Regidura, Edificio de Publicaciones, Plaza Cataluna 9 5, 08004 Barcelona Spain. **Tel** 011 34 3 3187987. Documents available from BIOSIS Document Express.
Ind/Abst AGRICOLA; Biol. Abstr. (?-1986).

ISSN 0279-4969
US

COLTSFOOT. (19??)-. Periodical. English. Six times a year. $10.00. Coltsfoot, Rt 1 Box 313A, Shipman VA 22971. **Tel** (804)263-4817. **ED** James Troy.

UK

CONFERENCE REPORTS. Main/Corp Botanical Society of the British Isles. No. 1 (1949)-. Monographic series. English. Irregular. Price varies per volume. E W Classey Ltd., PO Box 93, Faringdon Oxfordshire SN7 7DR United Kingdom. **Tel** 011 44 1367 82399.

LC QK **ISSN** 0069-9616
DD 581 RM
CODEN CBGBBV

CONTRIBUTII BOTANICE. [Contrib. bot.]. **Added/Corp** Universitatea "Babes-Bolyai." Gradina Botanica. (1958)-. Academic Scholarly Publication. Romanian (German and French). One time a year. Available on exchange basis only. Universitatea Gradina Botanica, Str. Republicii Nr. 42, Cluj-Napoca Romania. **ED** Onoriu Ratiu. Documents available from BIOSIS Document Express, CASDDS. ***Continues*** *Contributii Botanice din Cluj.*
Ind/Abst AGRICOLA; Biol. Abstr.; Chem. Abstr.; Crop Physiol. Abstr.; For. Abstr.; Maize Abstr.; Potato Abstr.; Rev. Agric. Entomol.; Seed Abstr.; Soils Fert.; Soyabean Abstr.; Wheat Barley Trit. Abstr.

LC QK1
US

CONTRIBUTIONS - BROOKLYN BOTANIC GARDEN. Main/Corp Brooklyn. Botanic Garden. Monographic series. English. Price varies per volume.
Desc: This series consists of papers originally published in botanical or other periodicals, re-issued as "separates" without change of paging, and numbered consecutively.

ISSN 0736-0509
DD 581 US
CCC
CODEN CNYGEJ

CONTRIBUTIONS FROM THE NEW YORK BOTANICAL GARDEN. [Contrib. N.Y. Bot. Gard.]. **Added/Corp** New York Botanical Garden. (1899)-. Monographic series. English. Irregular. Price varies per volume. New York Botanical Garden, Scientific Publishing Department B, New York NY 10458-5126. **Tel** (718)817-8721, FAX (718)817-6504, telex 5106015451. Documents available from BIOSIS Document Express.
Desc: An avenue for the publication of classical works in botany that are either rare or out-of-print translations and their original source, along with annotated bibliographies.
Ind/Abst Biol. Abstr. (1986-); Hortic. Abstr.; Ornamental Hort. (1991-).

ISSN 0735-3669
US
UDC 581.082

CONTRIBUTIONS FROM THE UNIVERSITY OF KANSAS HERBARIUM. [Contrib. Univ. Kans. Herb.]. No. 1 (May 25, 1982)-. Monographic series. English. Irregular. Price varies per volume. Herbarium University of Kansas, 2045 Constant Avenue, Campus West, Lawrence KS 66047. **Tel** (913)864-4493. **ED** Ralph E Brooks. ctrl circ.
Desc: Xerographic production of papers dealing with plant systematics, especially floristics and taxonomy, of the plants of the Great Plains of North America.

LC QK1 .M545a **ISSN** 0091-1860
DD 580/.5 US
CODEN CUMHDA

CONTRIBUTIONS FROM THE UNIVERSITY OF MICHIGAN HERBARIUM. [Contrib. Univ. Mich. Herb.]. **Main/Corp** University of Michigan. University Herbarium. **Added/Corp** University of Michigan. University Herbarium. Vol. 1, (1939)-. English. Irregular. Price varies per volume. University of Michigan Herbarium, North University Building, Ann Arbor MI 48109. **Tel** (313)764-2407. Documents available from BIOSIS Document Express.
Ind/Abst AGRICOLA [Full Cov.]; Biol. Abstr.; For. Prod. Abstr.; For. Abstr.; Plant Breed. Abstr.

LC QK1 .C77 **ISSN** 0735-2689
DD 580/.5 US
CCC
CODEN CRPSD3

CRITICAL REVIEWS IN PLANT SCIENCES. [Crit. rev. plant sci.]. **VFOAT** C.R.C. Critical Reviews in Plant Sciences; CRC Critical Reviews in Plant Sciences. **VAT** Chemical Rubber Company Critical Reviews in Plant Sciences. Vol. 1 (1983)-. Academic Scholarly Publication. English. Six times a year. $441.00. CRC Press Inc., 2000 Corporate Boulevard Northwest, Boca Raton FL 33431. **Tel** (407)994-0555, (800)272-7737, FAX (407)998-9784, (800)374-3401, telex 568689. **ED** B.V. Conger. Documents available from The Genuine Article, CASDDS.
Desc: Presents reviews in the basic and applied areas of plant science.
Ind/Abst AgBiotech News Inf.; AGRICOLA [Full Cov.]; Biocont. News Inf.; Chem. Abstr. (1983-); Cot. Trop. Fibr. Abstr. Bibliogr.; Crop Physiol. Abstr.; Curr. Aware. Biol. Sci., CABS; Curr. Cit.; Curr. Contents Agric. Biol. Environ. Sci.; Field Crop Abstr.; Food Sci. Technol. Abstr.; For. Prod. Abstr. (1991-); For. Abstr.; Hortic. Abstr.; Index Sci. Rev. [Full Cov.]; Maize Abstr.; Nematol. Abstr.; Ornamental Hort.; Life Sci. Collect.; Plant Breed. Abstr.; Plant Genet. Resour. Abstr.; Plant Grow. Reg. Abstr.; Potato Abstr.; Ref. Upd. Deluxe Ed.; Res. Alert [Full Cov.]; Rev. Agric. Entomol.; Rev. Plant Pathol.; Rice Abstr.; Sci. Cit. Index; SCISEARCH; Seed Abstr.; Weed Abstr.

ISSN 0891-9100
DD 580 US
Pr Rev.

CROSSOSOMA. [Crossosoma]. **Added/Corp** Southern California Botanists. (19??)-. Periodical. English. Two times a year. $15.00. Southern California Botanists, California State Department, Biological Science, Fullerton CA 92634. **Tel** (714)449-7034. **ED** Curtis Clark. Index available (bound in issue). **Bk Rev**, (Qty: 3-5). **Circ:** 400 (ctrl).
Desc: Articles of interest involving botanical subjects generally from Southern California. Letters from the editor, local flora's observed on field trips and scientific studies are included.

LC QK504 .C79 **ISSN** 0935-2147
DD 586/.005 GW
CODEN CRBOEO
SUSPENDED

CRYPTOGAMIC BOTANY. [Cryptogam. bot.]. (June 1989)-Suspended with Vol.5 (1994). Periodical. English (English). Four times a year. DM366.00 Germany; DM374.00 other. Gustav Fischer Verlag Stuttgart, Postfach 720143, D-70577 Stuttgart Germany. **Tel** 011 49 711 458030, FAX 011 49 711 4580334, telex 2627-7111488. **(Subscription address:** VCH Publishers Inc., 303 Northwest 12th Avenue, Journals Department, Deerfield FL 33442. **Tel** (800)367-8249, (305)428-5566.**)** **ED** W Julich. Index available. cum. index. **Bk Rev. Ad Acc. Circ:** 600. Documents available from BIOSIS Document Express.
Desc: Dedicated to the promotion of cryptogamic plant sciences and to the encouragement of international communication among phycologists, mycologists, lichenologists, bryologists, and pteridologists.
Ind/Abst AGRICOLA [Full Cov.]; Biol. Abstr.; Curr. Cit.

ISSN 0931-4113
GW
CODEN CRYSEF

CRYPTOGAMIC STUDIES. [Cryptogam. stud.]. Vol. 1 (1987)-. Monographic series. English. Irregular. Price varies per volume. Gustav Fischer Verlag Stuttgart, Postfach 720143, D-70577 Stuttgart Germany. **Tel** 011 49 711 458030, FAX 011 49 711 4580334, telex 2627-7111488. Documents available from BIOSIS Document Express.
Ind/Abst AGRICOLA [Select. Cov.]; Biol. Abstr.

ISSN 0257-9421
SW
CODEN CRHEEO

CRYPTOGAMICA HELVETICA. [Cryptogam. Helv.]. **Added/Corp** Schweizerische Naturforschende Gesellschaft. Kryptogamenkommission. Conservatoire et Jardin Botaniques de la Ville de Geneve. Vol. 16 (1985)-. Monographic series. English (French, German and Italian). Irregular. Price varies per volume. F Fluck Wirth, Intl Bookseller for Botany & Natural Science, CH-9053 Teufen AR Switzerland. **Tel** 011 41 71 331687. Documents available from BIOSIS Document Express. ***Continues*** *Beitrage zur Kryptogamenflora der Schweiz, 0258-1671.*
Desc: Information on cryptograms and botany.
Ind/Abst Biol. Abstr. (1985-).

LC QK532.4 .C79 **ISSN** 0181-1576
DD 588/.05 FR
CODEN CBLIDB
Pr Rev.

CRYPTOGAMIE. BRYOLOGIE, LICHENOLOGIE. [Cryptogam., Bryol., lichenol.]. **Added/Corp** Laboratoire de Cryptogamie (Museum National d'Histoire Naturelle). **VFOAT** Bryologie, Lichenologie. Vol. 1, Issue 1 (1980)-. Academic Scholarly Publication. French (English, German, Spanish and Italian). Four times a year. $83.11. Cryptogamie, 12 rue de Buffon, 75005 Paris France. **Tel** 33 1 40793184. **ED** Denis Lamy. Index available (bound in last issue). **Bk Rev**, (Qty: 4). **Circ:** 400 (ctrl). Documents available from The Genuine Article, BIOSIS Document Express, CASDDS. ***Continues*** *Revue Bryologique et Lichenologique, 0373-0913.*
Desc: Original bryological and lichenological research.
Ind/Abst Biol. Abstr.; Chem. Abstr.; Curr. Contents Agric. Biol. Environ. Sci.; Ecol. Abstr.; Ecology Abstr.; EMBASE; Geogr. Abstr. Phys. Geogr.; Microbiol. Abstr. Sect. C; Life Sci. Collect.; Res. Alert [Select. Cov.]; Rev. Med. Vet. Mycology; Rev. Plant Pathol.; SCISEARCH.

ISSN 0213-4128
SP
UDC 632

CUADERNOS DE FITOPATOLOGIA. [Cuad. fitopatol.]. (1984)-. Periodical. Spanish. Five times a year. 3.727ptas Spain; 5.300ptas (surface mail), 6.800ptas (airmail) other. Ediciones y Promociones Lav S.L., Apartado 473, 46080 Valencia Spain. **Tel** 011 34 6 963720261, FAX 011 34 6 963710516.
Ind/Abst PESTDOC.

LC QK445 .C86 **ISSN** 0727-9620
DD 581.9944 AT
UDC 581.5(944)
CODEN CUNNEY

CUNNINGHAMIA : ECOLOGICAL CONTRIBUTIONS FROM THE NATIONAL HERBARIUM OF NEW SOUTH WALES. [Cunninghamia]. Vol. 1 (1981)-. Periodical. English. Irregular. Royal Botanic Gardens Sydney, Macquaries Road, Sydney New South Wales 2000 Australia. **Tel** (02)231-8111, FAX (02)251-4403. **ED** Marilyn Fox, Ian Close and Bob Percival. Documents available from BIOSIS Document Express.
Desc: All aspects of vegetation mapping and plant community descriptions.
Ind/Abst Biol. Abstr. (1984-).

LC Z5353 .C86 **ISSN** 0306-4484
DD 016.58 UK
CODEN CAPSCJ

CURRENT ADVANCES IN PLANT SCIENCE. **See** Biology-Abstracting, Bibliographies and Statistics.

ISSN 0971-0116
II

CURRENT NEMATOLOGY. [Curr. Nematol.]. **Added/Corp** Bioved Research Society. Vol. 1, No. 1 (June 1990)-. Periodical. English. Two times a year. $100.00. Bioved Research Society, Allahabad India. **(Subscription address:** Prints India, 11 Darya Ganj, New Delhi 110002 India. **Tel** 011 91 11 3268645, FAX 011 91 11 3275542, telex 31-61087 PRIN-IN.**)**
Ind/Abst Crop Physiol. Abstr.; Field Crop Abstr.; Hortic. Abstr.; Ornamental Hort. (1991-); Plant Breed. Abstr.; Rev. Agric. Entomol.; Rev. Plant Pathol.; Seed Abstr.; Weed Abstr.; Wheat Barley Trit. Abstr.

US
CODEN CTPPE9

CURRENT TOPICS IN PLANT BIOCHEMISTRY AND PHYSIOLOGY : PROCEEDINGS OF THE ... PLANT BIOCHEMISTRY AND PHYSIOLOGY SYMPOSIUM HELD AT THE UNIVERSITY OF MISSOURI--COLUMBIA. Added/Corp University of Missouri--Columbia. Interdisciplinary Plant Biochemistry and Physiology Program. Vol. 1 (1983)-. Proceedings. English. One time a year. Documents available from CASDDS.
Ind/Abst Chem. Abstr.; Crop Physiol. Abstr.; Field Crop Abstr.; Grass. Forage Abstr.; Hortic. Abstr.; Maize Abstr.; Ornamental Hort. (1991-); Life Sci. Collect.; Plant Breed. Abstr.; Potato Abstr.; Rev. Plant Pathol.; Seed Abstr.; Soils Fert.; Sorghum Mill. Abstr.; Wheat Barley Trit. Abstr.

LC QK **ISSN** 0378-7540
DD 581 II
CCC
NLM W3 CU613 **CODEN** CTSCDI

CURRENT TRENDS IN LIFE SCIENCES. [Curr. trends life sci.]. **VFOAT** Current Trends in Life Science. (1977)-. Academic Scholarly Publication. English. One time a year. Price varies. Today and Tomorrow's Printers and Publishers, 24-B/5 Desh Bandhu Gupta Road, Karol Bagh, New Delhi 110 005 India. **Tel** 011 91 11 5721928, 011 91 11 572770, FAX 011 91 11 7210073 (TTPP). **(Subscription address:** Prints India, 11 Darya Ganj, New Delhi 110002 India. **Tel** 011 91 11 3268645, FAX 011 91 11 3275542, telex 31-61087 PRIN-IN.**)** **ED** O N Srivastava. Documents available from CASDDS.
Desc: Encourages individual initiative for the acquisition and dissemination of knowledge as well as the discovery of new knowledge.
Ind/Abst Chem. Abstr.

LC QK1 .K46 **ISSN** 1355-4905
DD 581 UK

●CURTIS'S BOTANICAL MAGAZINE. **Added/Corp** Royal Botanic Gardens, Kew. Bentham-Moxon Trust. Vol. 12, Pt. 1 (Feb. 1995)-. Academic Scholarly Publication. English. Four times a year. $142.00 North America; £75.00 UK and Europe; £91.50 other. Basil Blackwell Publishers Ltd., 108 Cowley Road, Oxford 0X4 1JF United Kingdom. **Tel** 011 44 1235 465500, FAX 011 44 1235 465556, telex 837022 OXBOOK G. **(Subscription address:** Blackwell Publishers / UK, 108 Cowley Road, Oxford OX4 1JF United Kingdom. **Tel** 011 44 1865 791100, FAX 011 44 1865 791347.**)** ***Continues*** *Kew Magazine., 0265-3842.*

LC QK1 .D3 **ISSN** 0011-6793
DD 580.5 AG
CODEN DARWAG

Pr Rev.

DARWINIANA. [Darwiniana]. **Added/Corp** Instituto de Botanica Darwinion (San Isidro, Argentina) Academia Nacional de Ciencias Exactas, Fisicas y Naturales (Argentina). (Dec. 1922)-. Periodical. Spanish (summaries and/or abstracts in English, French, German and Latin). Four times a year. $65.00. Instituto de Botanica Darwinion, Labarden 200, Casilla Correo 22, 1642 San Isidro Argentina. **Tel** 011 54 1 7434800, 011 54 1 7474748, FAX 011 54 1 7474748. **ED** Juan Carlos Gamerro. Index available. **Bk Rev**, (Qty: 2-3). **Circ:** 800 (ctrl). Documents available from BIOSIS Document Express, CASDDS.
Desc: Articles on plant taxonomy, anatomy, cytology, paleontology, embryology, evolution, phytogeography, ecology, etc.
Ind/Abst AGRICOLA; Biol. Abstr.; Chem. Abstr.; Ecol. Abstr.; EMBASE; Field Crop Abstr.; For. Abstr.; Grass. Forage Abstr.; Life Sci. Collect.; Plant Breed. Abstr.; Potato Abstr.; Refer. Z.; Rev. Med. Vet. Mycology; Rev. Plant Pathol.; Weed Abstr.

LC QK **ISSN** 0318-059X
DD 582/.0467/0216 CN

DELECTUS SEMINUM ET SPORARUM QUAE HORTUS BOTANICUS MONTIS-REGII PRO MUTUA COMMUTATIONE OFFERT. **Main/Corp** Montreal Botanical Garden. (1936/1937)-. Multiple languages (English, Latin and French). One time a year. Free to exchangists and professionals. Jardin Botanique de Montreal, 4101 Sherbrooke Street East, Montreal Quebec H1X 2B2 Canada. **Tel** (514)872-1430. **Circ:** 800 (ctrl).
Desc: Seeds offered to botanical gardens and scientific institutions for exchange.

LC QK474.8
DD 582.16 IT

DENDROCHRONOLOGIA. **Added/Corp** Istituto Italiano di Dendrocronologia. Vol. 1 (1983)-. Italian (English, German and English). One time a year (Mar.). L40000. Instituto Italian Dendrochronologia, via c Ederle 16, Laboratory Ecologia, 37121 Verona Italy. **Tel** 011 39 45 916610, 011 39 45 8005157.
Ind/Abst Geogr. Abstr. Phys. Geogr.; Rev. Agric. Entomol.

DD 581 UK

DESCRIPTIONS OF PLANT VIRUSES. **Added/Corp** Commonwealth Mycological Institute (Great Britain) Association of Applied Biologists. **VFOAT** CMI/AAB Descriptions of Plant Viruses. Vol. 1 No. 1 (June 1970)-. Periodical. English. Irregular. Price varies. Association of Applied Biologists, Institute of Horticultural Research, Wellesbourne, Warwick CV35 9EF United Kingdom. **Tel** 011 44 1789 470382, FAX 011 44 1789 470234.

LC QK938.D4 D47 **ISSN** 0734-3434
DD 581.909/54 US

DESERT PLANTS. [Desert plants]. **Added/Corp** Boyce Thompson Southwestern Arboretum. University of Arizona. Vol. 1, No. 1 (Aug. 1979)-. Periodical. English. Two times a year. $20.00. Boyce Thompson Arboretum, Desert Plants, 2120 East Allen Road, Tucson AZ 85719. **Tel** (602)621-3593, (602)621-7190, FAX (602)621-8558. **ED** Margaret Norem. Index available. cum. index. **Bk Rev. Circ:** 1,000.
Desc: Broadening knowledge of plants indigenous or adaptable to arid and sub-arid regions; studying their growth; and encouraging their use in the arid environment.
Ind/Abst AGRICOLA [Full Cov.]; Agrofor. Abstr.; Fish Rev.; Hortic. Abstr.; Ornamental Hort.; Plant Breed. Abstr.; Plant Grow. Reg. Abstr.; Rev. Agric. Entomol.; Soils Fert.; Wildl. Rev.

LC QK
DD 581 NE

•**DEVELOPMENTS IN PLANT BREEDING.** (1994)-. Monographic series. English. Irregular. Kluwer Academic Publishers, Postbus 322, 3300 AH Dordrecht The Netherlands. **Tel** 011 31 78 524400, FAX 011 31 78 183273, telex 20083.

ISSN 0168-7972
NE
CODEN DPGBD6

DEVELOPMENTS IN PLANT GENETICS AND BREEDING. [Dev. plant genet. breed.]. (1983)-. Monographic series. English. Irregular. Price varies per volume. Elsevier Science Publishers BV, PO Box 211, 1000 AE Amsterdam Netherlands. **Tel** 011 31 20 4853641, 011 31 20 4853642, FAX 011 31 20 4853598. Documents available from BIOSIS Document Express, CASDDS.
Desc: Series covering the breeding and genetics of plants. Topics have included chromosome engineering and isozymes.
Ind/Abst Biol. Abstr.; Chem. Abstr. (1983-); Life Sci. Collect.

ISSN 0871-5440
PO
UDC 630
TITLE CHANGE

DGF INFORMACAO. [DGF inf.]. **VFOAT** Direccao Geral das Florestas Informacao. (1990)-(1993). Periodical. Portuguese. ***Continued by** Informacao Florestal, 0872-5772.*
Ind/Abst For. Abstr.

LC QK569.D54 D52 **ISSN** 0269-249X
DD 589.4/81/05 UK
CCC
CODEN DIRSEU

DIATOM RESEARCH. (DIATOM RESEARCH : THE JOURNAL OF THE INTERNATIONAL SOCIETY FOR DIATOM RESEARCH.). [Diatom res.]. **Added/Corp** International Society for Diatom Research. Vol. 1, No. 1 (May 1986)-. Periodical. English (French, German and Spanish). Two times a year. $138.00. Gebruder Borntraeger Verlagsbuchhandlung, Johannesstrasse 3-A, D-70176 Stuttgart Germany. **Tel** 0711/62 50 01, FAX (0711)625005, telex 723363 SCHB D. Documents available from BIOSIS Document Express.
Ind/Abst Biol. Abstr. (1987-); GeoRef.

ISSN 0391-4119
IT
UDC 632

DIFESA DELLE PIANTE. [Dif. piante]. (1978)-. Periodical. Italian. Six times a year. Baiesi, via Broccaindosso 2-C, 40125 Bologna Italy. **Tel** 011 39 51 239584.
Ind/Abst Biocont. News Inf.; Nematol. Abstr.; Postharvest News Inf.; Potato Abstr.; Rev. Agric. Entomol.; Rev. Med. Vet. Mycology; Rev. Plant Pathol.; Weed Abstr.; Wheat Barley Trit. Abstr.

ISSN 0012-3013
DD 581 SA
UDC 581

DINTERIA. [Dinteria]. No. 1- Nov. 1968-. Periodical. Dutch (English, German and Afrikaans). South West Africa Scientific Society, PO Box 67, Windhoek 9000 South Africa. **Tel** 011 27 61 225372.
Ind/Abst For. Prod. Abstr.; For. Abstr.; Life Sci. Collect.

LC QK480.U52 A763A **ISSN** 8755-1799
DD 582.16/0074/01444 US

DIRECTOR'S REPORT FOR THE ARNOLD ARBORETUM, THE. (THE DIRECTOR'S REPORT FOR THE ARNOLD ARBORETUM IN FISCAL YEAR ...). **Main/Corp** Arnold Arboretum. **VFOAT** Director's Report. English. One time a year. Arnold Arboretum, Harvard University, The Arborway, Jamaica Plain MA 02130. ***Continues** Annual Report of the Director of the Arnold Arboretum to the President and Fellows of Harvard University for ... .*

LC TP248 **ISSN** 1060-4200
DD 660 US

DIRECTORY OF PLANT BIOTECHNOLOGY COMPANIES IN USA. [Dir. plant biotechnol. co. USA]. **Added/Corp** FORE (Firm). (1992)-. Directory. English. $29.95. Fore, 115 Wellington Court, Athens GA 30605.

LC QK710 .A54A **ISSN** 0271-9789
DD 581.1/06/073 US
UDC 581.1(058.7)(73)

DIRECTORY OF THE AMERICAN SOCIETY OF PLANT PHYSIOLOGISTS. **Main/Corp** American Society of Plant Physiologists. (19??)-. Directory. English. One time a year. $25.00. American Society of Plant Physiologists, 15501 A Monona Drive, Rockville MD 20855. **Tel** (301)251-0560 ext. 17, FAX (301)279-2996.

LC QK35 .C28A **ISSN** 0824-1996
DD 580/.6071 CN
UDC 581.1(058.7)(71)

DIRECTORY OF THE CANADIAN BOTANICAL ASSOCIATION & CANADIAN SOCIETY OF PLANT PHYSIOLOGISTS. [Dir. Can. Bot. Assoc. Can. Soc. Plant Physiol.]. **Main/Corp** Canadian Botanical Association. 1984-. Directory. English (French). Four times a year. 20.00Can$ Canada; $20.00 US. Dr Luis Oliveira, Department of Botany, University of British Columbia, Vancouver British Columbia V6T 2B1 Canada. **Tel** (604)228-6897. **ED** Luis Oliveira.
Desc: Articles of botanical interest (all fields); botanical news (local and global); information on scientific meetings.

LC QK1 .D49 **ISSN** 0070-6728
DD 581 GW
CODEN DIBOD5

DISSERTATIONES BOTANICAE. [Diss. bot.]. (1968)-. Monographic series. German. Irregular. $3990.00. E. Schweizerbartische Verlagsbuchhandlung, Johannesstrasse 3A, D-70176 Stuttgart Germany. **Tel** 011 49 711 625001, FAX 011 49 711 625005, telex 723363 SCHB D. Documents available from BIOSIS Document Express.
Ind/Abst Biol. Abstr.; GeoRef.

ISSN 0012-396X
UK

DISTRIBUTION MAPS OF PLANT DISEASES. **Added/Corp** Commonwealth Mycological Institute. (1974)-. Periodical. English. Two times a year. $108.00. CAB International Centre, Wallingford, Oxfordshire OX10 8DE United Kingdom. **Tel** 011 44 1491 832111, FAX 011 44 1491 833508, telex 847964 COMAGG G. **ED** J. E. M. Mordue. **Ad Acc.** ***Continues** Imperial Mycological Institute. Distribution Maps of Plant Diseases.*
Desc: Each map gives the world distribution of a plant pathogen, incorporating information from the literature and the unique records of the CMI herbarium.

LC QK981 .D58 **ISSN** 0744-8163
DD 581 US
CCC
NLM W1; DI887R **CODEN** DIVEE8

DIVERSITY. [Diversity]. **Added/Corp** Laboratory for Information Science in Agriculture (Fort Collins, Colo.) Genetic Resources Communications Systems. Vol. 1, No. 1 (Spring 1982)-. Periodical. English. Four times a year. $35.00. GRCS Inc., 4905 Del Ray Avenue, Suite 401, Bethesda MD 20814. **Tel** (301)907-9350. Documents available from The Genuine Article.
Ind/Abst Abstr. BioCommer.; AgBiotech News Inf.; AGRICOLA [Select. Cov.]; For. Abstr.; Hortic. Abstr.; Maize Abstr.; Ornamental Hort. (1991-); Plant Breed. Abstr.; Plant Genet. Resour. Abstr.; Potato Abstr.; Res. Alert [Select. Cov.]; Rev. Plant Pathol.; Rural Dev. Abstr.; Soc. Sci. Cit. Index [Select. Cov.]; Soyabean Abstr.; Wheat Barley Trit. Abstr.; World Agric. Econ. Rural Sociol. Abstr.

ISSN 1011-0887
TU

DOGA. TURK BOTANIK DERGISI. [Doga, Turk bot. derg.]. **VFOAT** Doga. Turkish Journal of Botany. (1987)-. Academic Scholarly Publication. Turkish (English). Six times a year. $150.00. Tubitak, Ataturk Bulvari, No: 221, 06100 Kavaklidere Ankara Turkey. **(Subscription address:** Tubitak, Bilimsel Dergiler, Yazi Isleri Mudurlugu, PO Box 5, Kizilay 06420 Ankara Turkey. **Tel** 011 90 312 4685300 ext. 1122, 011 90 312 4270493, FAX 011 90 312 4271336.) **ED** Adil Guner. **Circ:** 700. Documents available from CASDDS. ***Continues** Doga. Turk Biyoloji Dergisi, 1010-7576.*
Desc: Covers plant morphology, taxonomy, phytosociology and ecology.
Ind/Abst Biol. Abstr.; Chem. Abstr.; Crop Physiol. Abstr.; Field Crop Abstr.; Plant Genet. Resour. Abstr.; Plant Grow. Reg. Abstr.; Postharvest News Inf.; Potato Abstr.; Rev. Agric. Entomol.; Rev. Med. Vet. Entomol.; Seed Abstr.; Weed Abstr.; Wheat Barley Trit. Abstr.

LC QK **ISSN** 0012-4982
DD 581 US
CCC
CODEN DKBSBT

DOKLADY. BOTANICAL SCIENCES. [Dokl., Bot. sci.]. **Main/Corp** Akademii a Nauk SSSR. **Added/Corp** Consultants Bureau. Consultants Bureau Enterprises. **VFOAT** Botanical Sciences. Vol. 154/156 (Jan./June 1964)-. Periodical. English (Russian). Two times a year. $475.00. MAIK Nauka / Interperiodica, Ulitsa Profsoyuznaia 90, Moscow 117864 Russia. **ED** A.A. Baev. available on microfilm and microfiche from University Microfilms International (UMI). Documents available from BIOSIS Document Express, CASDDS. ***Continues in part** Doklady. Biological Sciences Sections, 0886-7534.*
Ind/Abst AgBiotech News Inf.; AGRICOLA [Full Cov.]; Biol. Abstr. (?-1984); Chem. Abstr.; Crop Physiol. Abstr.; EMBASE; Energy Res. Abstr. (May 1975-); Field Crop Abstr.; Hortic. Abstr.; INIS Atomindex [Micro.]; Irr. Drain. Abstr.; Maize Abstr.; Ornamental Hort. (1991-); Plant Breed. Abstr.; Plant Genet. Resour. Abstr.; Plant Grow. Reg. Abstr.; Potato Abstr.; Soyabean Abstr.; Weed Abstr.; Wheat Barley Trit. Abstr.

AG

DOMINGUEZIA. (1978)-. Spanish (summaries and/or abstracts in Spanish and English). Museo de Botanica Juan A Dominguez, Facultad de Farmacia y Bioquimica, Universidad de Buenos Aires, Junin 954 1 Q Piso, CP 1113, Buenos Aires Argentina.

ISSN 0153-8756
FR
CODEN EMEDDQ

ECOLOGIA MEDITERRANEA. **See** Environmental Issues-Ecology.

LC RS164 .E27 **ISSN** 1066-5080
DD 615/.32 UK
NLM W1; EC924H **CODEN** EMPLE4

ECONOMIC AND MEDICINAL PLANT RESEARCH. [Econ. med. plant res.]. (1985)-. English. Academic Press Ltd., A Division of Harcourt Brace & Company Ltd., 24-28 Oval Road, London NW1 7DX United Kingdom. **Tel** 011 44 171 2674466, FAX 011 44 171 4822293, 011 44 171 4854752, telex 25775 ACPRES G.
Ind/Abst Chem. Abstr.; Curr. Cit.

LC SB1 .E3 ISSN 0013-0001
DD 581.6/1/05 US
CCC
NLM W1 EC925 CODEN ECBOA5
Pr Rev.

ECONOMIC BOTANY. [Econ. bot.]. **Added/Corp** New York Botanical Garden. Society for Economic Botany (U.S.). Vol. 1 (Jan./Mar. 1947)-. Periodical. English. Four times a year. $77.00. New York Botanical Garden, Scientific Publishing Department B, New York NY 10458-5126. **Tel** (718)817-8721, FAX (718)817-6504, telex 5106015451. **ED** John Thieret. Index available. cum. index. **Bk Rev. Ad Acc. Circ:** 2,000 (ctrl). available on microfilm and microfiche from University Microfilms International (UMI). Documents available from The Genuine Article, BIOSIS Document Express, CASDDS, Documents on Demand.
Desc: Attempts to bridge the gap between pure and applied botany by focusing on the uses of plants by people.
Ind/Abst AgBiotech News Inf.; AGRICOLA [Full Cov.]; Agrofor. Abstr. (19??-19??); Art Archaeol. Tech. Abstr.; Biogr. Index; Biol. Agric. Index; Biol. Abstr.; Biol. Dig.; Chem. Abstr.; Cot. Trop. Fibr. Abstr. Bibliogr.; Crop Physiol. Abstr.; Curr. Aware. Biol. Sci., CABS; Curr. Cit.; Curr. Contents Agric. Biol. Environ. Sci.; Curr. Geogr. Publ. (199?-); EMBASE; Energy Inf. Abstr.; Energy Res. Abstr. (Dec. 1979-); Environ. Abstr.; Environ. Period. Bibliogr.; Field Crop Abstr.; Food Sci. Technol. Abstr.; For. Prod. Abstr. (19??-19??); For. Abstr.; Gen. Sci. Index; Grass. Forage Abstr.; Helminthol. Abstr. (1991-); Hortic. Abstr.; Index Vet.; Irr. Drain. Abstr.; Leis., Rec., Tour. Abstr.; Maize Abstr.; NAPRALERT; Nutr. Abstr. Rev., Ser. B, Live Feeds and Feed.; Nutr. Abstr. Rev., Ser. A, Hum. Exp.; Life Sci. Collect.; PESTDOC; Plant Breed. Abstr.; Plant Genet. Resour. Abstr.; Plant Grow. Reg. Abstr.; Potato Abstr.; Protozoolog. Abstr.; Res. Alert [Full Cov.]; Rev. Agric. Entomol.; Rev. Med. Vet. Entomol.; Rev. Med. Vet. Mycology; Rev. Plant Pathol.; Rural Dev. Abstr.; Sci. Cit. Index; SCISEARCH; Seed Abstr.; Soc. Sci. Cit. Index [Select. Cov.]; Soils Fert.; Vet. Bull.; Vitis Vitic. Enol. Abstr.; Weed Abstr.; Wheat Barley Trit. Abstr.; World Agric. Econ. Rural Sociol. Abstr.

LC QK1 .E3 ISSN 0960-4286
DD 581/.05 UK
CCC

EDINBURGH JOURNAL OF BOTANY. [Edinb. j. bot.]. **Added/Corp** Royal Botanic Garden, Edinburgh. Vol. 47, No. 1 (1990)-. Academic Scholarly Publication. English. Three times a year. $136.00. Cambridge University Press, The Edinburgh Building, Shaftesbury Road, Cambridge CB2 2RU United Kingdom. **Tel** 011 44 1223 312393, FAX 011 44 1223 315052, telex 851-817256. **(Subscription address:** Cambridge University Press / North America, 110 Midland Avenue, Port Chester NY 10573. **Tel** (800)431-1580, (914)937-9600.) Documents available from BIOSIS Document Express. ***Continues*** *Notes From the Royal Botanic Garden Edinburgh, 0080-4274.*
Desc: Emphasis is on the systematic botany of higher plants, but papers on lower plants (especially fungi and lichens), vegetational analysis, scientific horticulture and history of botany are accepted.
Ind/Abst AGRICOLA [Full Cov.]; Biol. Abstr. (1991-); Grass. Forage Abstr.; Hortic. Abstr.; Ornamental Hort. (1991-); Plant Breed. Abstr.; Plant Genet. Resour. Abstr.; Weed Abstr.

ISSN 0301-8180
UA
CODEN EJPPAP
SUSPENDED

EGYPTIAN JOURNAL OF PHYTOPATHOLOGY. [Egypt. j. phytopathol.]. Vol. 4 (1972)-?. Periodical. English. One time a year. National Information & Documentation Center, A1-Tahrir St Dokki Awqaf PO, Cairo Egypt. **Tel** 011 20 2 701696, telex 93069. Documents available from CASDDS. ***Continues*** *United Arab Republic Journal of Phytopathology.*
Ind/Abst AGRICOLA; Biocont. News Inf.; Biodeter. Abstr.; Chem. Abstr. (-1986); Cot. Trop. Fibr. Abstr. Bibliogr.; Irr. Drain. Abstr.; Nematol. Abstr.; Plant Grow. Reg. Abstr.; Potato Abstr.

AT

ENCYCLOPAEDIA OF AUSTRALIAN PLANTS. (19??)-. English. Irregular. 120.00Aus$. Lothian Books, 11 Munro Street 3207 Australia. **Tel** 03 645 1544, FAX 03 646 4882. **ED** W.R. Elliot, David Jones. Index available. cum. index. **Acid Free.**

GW
CODEN EPNSDZ
CEASED

ENCYCLOPEDIA OF PLANT PHYSIOLOGY. NEW SERIES. Vol. 1 (1975)-Series complete with Vol. 20. Academic Scholarly Publication. English. Springer-Verlag GmbH & Company KG, Heidelberger Platz 3, D-14197 Berlin Germany. **Tel** 011 49 30 8207223, FAX 011 49 30 8214091, telex 183 319 SPBLN D. **(Subscription address:** Springer-Verlag New York Inc. / North America, PO Box 2485, Journal Fulfillment, Secaucus NJ 07096. **Tel** (201)348-4033, (800)777-4643, FAX (201)348-4505.) Each issue contains an index to its own contents (no volume index)--loose. Documents available from CASDDS. ***Supersedes*** *Handbuch der Pflanzenphysiologie.*
Ind/Abst Chem. Abstr.

LC QK ISSN 0170-4818
DD 581 GW

ENGLERA. **Added/Corp** Botanischer Garten und Botanisches Museum (Berlin, Germany). (1979)-. German (English, French and Spanish). One time a year (June). DM120.00. Botanischer Garten u Botanisches Museum, Biblio Koenigin Luise Strabe 6-8, D-14195 Berlin Germany. **Tel** 011 49 30 8314041, telex 183 798 SEN D. **ED** H. Scholz. **Circ:** 800. ***Continues*** *Willdenowia. Beiheft.*
Desc: Information and articles on taxonomic and floristic botany.
Ind/Abst Ecol. Abstr.

LC QK757 .R22 ISSN 0098-8472
DD 581.5/05 UK
CCC
NLM W1 EN981FN CODEN EEBODM
Pr Rev.

ENVIRONMENTAL AND EXPERIMENTAL BOTANY. [Environ. exp. bot.]. Vol. 16, No. 1, (Apr. 1976)-. Periodical. English. Four times a year. $507.00 The Americas; £340.00 other. Pergamon Press, An Imprint of Elsevier Science Ltd., The Boulevard, Langford Lane, Kidlington, Oxford OX5 1GB United Kingdom. **Tel** 011 44 1865 843000, 011 44 1865 843699, FAX 011 44 1865 843010. **(Subscription address:** Elsevier Science Ltd. / Oxford Fulfillment Centre, PO Box 800, Kidlington OX5 1DX United Kingdom. **Tel** 011 44 865 843355.) **ED** Morton Miller. available on microfilm and microfiche from University Microfilms International (UMI); available on an online database from Elsevier Electronic Subscriptions (EES). Documents available from The Genuine Article, BIOSIS Document Express, Ask*IEEE, CASDDS. ***Continues*** *Radiation Botany, 0033-7560.*
Desc: Publishes research papers on the physical and biological mechanisms that relate to the working of plant systems and their interaction with the environment. Experimental areas covered include: (1) Radiation botany; (2) Photobotany; (3) Chemical mutagensis; (4) Anatomy and morphology; (5) Cytogenetics and (6) Somatic cell genetics. Environmental areas covered include pollution effects and more.
Ind/Abst AGRICOLA [Full Cov.]; AQUAREF; Biol. Agric. Index; Biol. Abstr.; Chem. Abstr.; Coal Abstr.; Cot. Trop. Fibr. Abstr. Bibliogr.; Crop Physiol. Abstr.; Curr. Aware. Biol. Sci., CABS; Curr. Cit.; Curr. Contents Agric. Biol. Environ. Sci.; Ecol. Abstr.; Ecology Abstr.; EMBASE; Environ. Period. Bibliogr.; Field Crop Abstr.; Food Sci. Technol. Abstr.; For. Prod. Abstr.; For. Abstr.; Geogr. Abstr. Phys. Geogr.; Grass. Forage Abstr.; Hortic. Abstr.; Index Vet.; INSPEC (Feb. 1978-); Irr. Drain. Abstr.; Maize Abstr.; Nutr. Abstr. Rev., Ser. B, Live Feeds and Feed.; Ornamental Hort. (1991-); Life Sci. Collect.; Plant Breed. Abstr.; Plant Genet. Resour. Abstr.; Plant Grow. Reg. Abstr.; Pollut. Abstr. Indexes; Res. Alert [Full Cov.]; Rev. Plant Pathol.; Rice Abstr.; Sci. Cit. Index; SCISEARCH; Seed Abstr.; Soils Fert.; Sorghum Mill. Abstr.; Soyabean Abstr.; Weed Abstr.; Wheat Barley Trit. Abstr.

ISSN 0071-2396
FR

EPPO PUBLICATIONS. SERIES B. **Main/Corp** European and Mediterranean Plant Protection Organization. **VFOAT** Plant Health Newsletter. No. 1 (1950)-. Monographic series. Multiple languages (English and French). Price varies per volume. European and Mediterranean Plant Protection Organization, 1 rue le Notre, 75016 Paris France. **Tel** 011 33 1 45207794.
Ind/Abst Nematol. Abstr.

LC SB ISSN 0374-7565
DD 630 FR
UDC 63
CODEN EURAB

EPPO PUBLICATIONS, SERIES C. [EPPO Publ., Ser. C]. **VFOAT** European and Mediterranean Plant Protection Organization, Publications Series C. (19??)-. French. European and Mediterranean Plant Protection Organization, 1 rue le Notre, 75016 Paris France. **Tel** 011 33 1 45207794.
Ind/Abst For. Abstr.; Rev. Agric. Entomol.

IT

ERBORISTERIA DOMANI. (19??)-. Italian. Twelve times a year. L94000.00 Italy; L160000.00 other. Studio Edizioni SAS, Piazza Wagner 1, 20145 Milan Italy. **Tel** 011 39 2 4818684.

ISSN 8755-2000
DD 581 US
UDC 581.9(773-13)

ERIGENIA. (ERIGENIA : JOURNAL OF THE SOUTHERN ILLINOIS NATIVE PLANT SOCIETY.). [Erigenia]. No. 1 (Aug. 1982)-. Periodical. English. Irregular. $10.00. Illinois Native Plant Society, Department of Botany, Southern Illinois University, Carbondale IL 62901-6509. **Tel** (618)536-2331. **ED** Mark Mohlenbrock. **Bk Rev. Ad Acc. Circ:** 250 (ctrl).
Desc: Flora and natural areas of Illinois.

II

ETHNOBOTANY : JOURNAL OF SOCIETY OF ETHNOBOTANISTS. **Added/Corp** Society of Ethnobotanists (India). Vol. 1, No. 1 & 2 (1989)-. Periodical. English. Two times a year. $50.00. **(Subscription address:** Prints India, 11 Darya Ganj, New Delhi 110002 India. **Tel** 011 91 11 3268645, FAX 011 91 11 3275542, telex 31-61087 PRIN-IN.)

ISSN 0014-2336
NE
CCC
CODEN EUPHAA
Pr Rev.

EUPHYTICA. (EUPHYTICA; NETHERLANDS JOURNAL OF PLANT BREEDING.). [Euphytica]. **Added/Corp** Netherlands Study Circle of Plant Breeding. **VFOAT** Netherlands Journal of Plant Breeding. Vol. 1 (1952)-. Periodical. Dutch (English). Eighteen times a year. $1364.00. Kluwer Academic Publishers, Postbus 322, 3300 AH Dordrecht The Netherlands. **Tel** 011 31 78 524400, FAX 011 31 78 183273, telex 20083. **ED** A C Zeven. cum. index. **Ad Acc. Acid Free. Circ:** 1,700. available on microfilm and microfiche from University Microfilms International (UMI). Documents available from The Genuine Article, BIOSIS Document Express, CASDDS.
Desc: Presents the results of scientific research on plant breeding and related fields such as genetics, pests and diseases, selection methods, cytogenetics and plant evolution. These cover a wide range of subjects such as domestication, genetic resources, variation, cytology, floral biology, and more.
Ind/Abst AgBiotech News Inf.; AGRICOLA; BioBusiness; Biol. Abstr.; Chem. Abstr.; Cot. Trop. Fibr. Abstr. Bibliogr.; Crop Physiol. Abstr.; Curr. Aware. Biol. Sci., CABS; Curr. Cit.; Field Crop Abstr.; Food Sci. Technol. Abstr.; For. Prod. Abstr.; For. Abstr.; Genet. Abstr.; Grass. Forage Abstr.; Hortic. Abstr.; Irr. Drain. Abstr.; Maize Abstr.; Microbiol. Abstr. Sect. A; Nematol. Abstr.; Ornamental Hort. (19??-19??); Life Sci. Collect.; PESTDOC; Plant Breed. Abstr.; Plant Genet. Resour. Abstr.; Plant Grow. Reg. Abstr.; Potato Abstr.; Protozoolog. Abstr.; Ref. Upd. Deluxe Ed.; Res. Alert [Full Cov.]; Rev. Agric. Entomol.; Rev. Med. Vet. Mycology; Rev. Plant Pathol.; Rice Abstr.; Sci. Cit. Index; SCISEARCH; Seed Abstr.; Soils Fert.; Sorghum Mill. Abstr.; Soyabean Abstr.; Stat. Theory Method Abstr. (1987); Vitis Vitic. Enol. Abstr.; Weed Abstr.; Wheat Barley Trit. Abstr.

LC QK564 .B74 ISSN 0967-0262
DD 589.3/05 UK
CCC
CODEN EJPHE5

●EUROPEAN JOURNAL OF PHYCOLOGY. **Added/Corp** British Phycological Society. Vol. 28, No. 1 (Feb. 1993)-. Academic Scholarly Publication. English. Four times a year. $238.00. Cambridge University Press, The Edinburgh Building, Shaftesbury Road, Cambridge CB2 2RU United Kingdom. **Tel** 011 44 1223 312393, FAX 011 44 1223 315052, telex 851-817256. **(Subscription address:** Cambridge University Press / North America, 110 Midland Avenue, Port Chester NY 10573. **Tel** (800)431-1580, (914)937-9600.) **ED** Christine A. Maggs. ***Continues*** *British Phycological Journal, 0007-1617.*
Desc: Publishes papers on all aspects of the ecology, physiology and biochemistry, cell biology, molecular biology and systematics of algae.
Ind/Abst Curr. Cit.; Sci. Cit. Index.

LC SB621 ISSN 0929-1873
DD 581.2 NE
CCC
CODEN EPLPEH
Pr Rev.

●EUROPEAN JOURNAL OF PLANT PATHOLOGY. **Added/Corp** European Foundation for Plant Pathology. Vol. 100, No. 1 (Apr. 1994)-. Periodical. English. Nine times a year. $565.00. Kluwer Academic Publishers, Postbus 322, 3300 AH Dordrecht The Netherlands. **Tel** 011 31 78 524400, FAX 011 31 78 183273, telex 20083. **ED** Bob Schippers. ***Continues*** *Netherlands Journal of Plant Pathology, 0028-2944.*
Desc: Presents information on the field of plant disease and pests, including mycological and virological topics, entomological, nematological, weed and plant protection problems.
Ind/Abst AGRICOLA; Curr. Cit.

LC QK533.8 .E9 ISSN 0747-9859
DD 588/.0973 US

EVANSIA. [Evansia]. **Added/Corp** American Bryological and Lichenological Society. Vol. 1, No. 1 (1984)-. Periodical. English. Three times a year. $15.00. American Bryological Lichenologica, University of Nebraska at Omaha, Biology Department, Omaha NE 68182. **Tel** (402)554-2491. **ED** William R. Buck and Claire K. Schmitt. **Bk Rev. Circ:** 200. available on microfilm from University Microfilms International (UMI).
Desc: Local floristic of mosses, hepatics and lichens; bryological and lichenological techniques.

ISSN 1011-3258
UK
CCC
CODEN ETPLEJ

Pr Rev.
EVOLUTIONARY TRENDS IN PLANTS. [Evol. trends plants]. **VFOAT** ETP. Vol. 1, No. 1 (May 1987)-. Periodical. English. Four times a year. $274.00. Evolutionary Trends in Plants, PO Box 74 Leamington Spa, Warwickshire CV31 1FS United Kingdom. **Tel** 011 44 1926 334209, FAX 011 44 1926 334209. **ED** M. Nichols. Index available. **Bk Rev**, (Qty: 10). **Ad Acc.** Documents available from The Genuine Article, BIOSIS Document Express.
Ind/Abst AGRICOLA [Full Cov.]; Biol. Abstr. (1987-); Curr. Aware. Biol. Sci., CABS; Curr. Cit.; Curr. Contents Agric. Biol. Environ. Sci.; For. Abstr.; Hortic. Abstr.; Maize Abstr.; Ornamental Hort. (1991-); Plant Breed. Abstr.; Plant Genet. Resour. Abstr.; Res. Alert [Select. Cov.]; Rev. Agric. Entomol.; SCISEARCH; Seed Abstr.; Weed Abstr.

LC QK495.L72 E93 ISSN 0301-441X
DD 584/.0915/4 RH
EXCELSA. [Excelsa]. **Added/Corp** Aloe, Cactus and Succulent Society of Rhodesia. Aloe, Cactus and Succulent Society of Zimbabwe. No. 1 (1971)-. English. One time a year. $25.00. Aloe Cactus and Succulent Society, PO Box 8514, Causeway Harare Rhodesia. **Tel** 011 263 4 39175.

LC QK ISSN 0014-4037
DD 581 GW
CCC
CEASED
EXCERPTA BOTANICA. SECTIO A. TAXONOMICA ET CHOROLOGICA. (EXCERPTA BOTANICA. SECTIO A, TAXONOMICA ET CHOROLOGICA.). [Excerpta bot. Sect. A. Taxon. chorol.]. **Added/Corp** International Association for Plant Taxonomy. **VFOAT** Taxonomica et Chorologica. (1959)-Vol. 64 (1995). Periodical. German (English and French). Gustav Fischer Verlag Stuttgart, Postfach 720143, D-70577 Stuttgart Germany. **Tel** 011 49 711 458030, FAX 011 49 711 4580334, telex 2627-7111488. **(Subscription address:** VCH Publishers Inc., 303 Northwest 12th Avenue, Journals Department, Deerfield FL 33442. **Tel** (800)367-8249, (305)428-5566.)
Desc: Publishes abstracts from articles as well as book reviews of new publications in the fields of plant taxonomy, phytogeography, paleobotany and ethnobotany.
Ind/Abst Rev. Med. Vet. Mycology; Rev. Plant Pathol.

ISSN 0259-2517
IT
UDC 502.75
CODEN NU052
FAO PLANT PRODUCTION AND PROTECTION PAPER. [FAO plant prod. prot. pap.]. **VFOAT** Food and Agriculture Organization of the United Nations Plant Production and Protection Paper. (1976)-. Periodical. English. Food Agriculture Organization (FAO) / Italy, GIPCI66 via Terme di Caracalla, 00100 Rome Italy. **Tel** 011 39 6 52252925, FAX 011 39 6 52253152.
Ind/Abst Agric. Eng. Abstr.; Curr. Cit.; Field Crop Abstr.; Hortic. Abstr.; Plant Grow. Reg. Abstr.; Potato Abstr.; Rev. Plant Pathol.; Rice Abstr.; Seed Abstr.; Soils Fert.; Sorghum Mill. Abstr.; Soyabean Abstr.; Weed Abstr.

LC QK
DD 581 II
FASCICLES OF FLORA OF INDIA. **Added/Corp** Botanical Survey of India. Issue 1 (1978)-. English. Irregular. Koeltz Scientific Books, PO Box 1360, D-61453 Koenigstein Germany. **Tel** 011 49 6174 93720, FAX 011 49 6174 1634.

ISSN 0014-8903
SW
CODEN FUOFAA
FAUNA OCH FLORA. [Fauna flora]. **Added/Corp** Naturhistoriska Riksmuseet,. Vol. 1 (1906)-. Periodical. English (Swedish). Six times a year (Feb., Apr., June, Aug., Oct., Dec.). Kr165.00 Sweden; Kr220.00 Nordic and Baltic countries; Kr275.00 other European countries; Kr300.00 other. Fauna Och Flora / Sweden, Swedish Museum of Natural History, Box 50007, S 104 05 Stockholm Sweden. **Tel** 011 46 8 6664089.
Ind/Abst Ecology Abstr.; GeoRef; Key Word Index Wildl. Res.; Rev. Med. Vet. Entomol.

LC QK ISSN 0014-8962
DD 581 GW
CODEN FRZBAW
FEDDES REPERTORIUM. [Feddes repert.]. Vol. 70 (1965/1966)-. Periodical. Multiple languages (English, French and German). Four times a year. $440.00. Akademie-Verlag GmbH, Postfach, D-13162 Berlin Germany. **Tel** 011 49 30 47889300, FAX 011 49 30 47889357. **(Subscription address:** VCH Publishers Inc., 303 Northwest 12th Avenue, Journals Department, Deerfield FL 33442. **Tel** (800)367-8249, (305)428-5566.) Documents available from BIOSIS Document Express. ***Continues** Feddes Repertorium Specierum Novarum Regni Vegetabilis.*
Ind/Abst AGRICOLA; Biol. Abstr.; Crop Physiol. Abstr.; Ecol. Abstr. (?-?); Field Crop Abstr.; For. Prod. Abstr. (1991-); For. Abstr.; GeoRef; Grass. Forage Abstr.; Hortic. Abstr.; Maize Abstr.; Ornamental Hort. (1991-); Life Sci. Collect.; Plant Breed. Abstr.; Plant Genet. Resour. Abstr.; Seed Abstr.; Soils Fert.; Vitis Vitic. Enol. Abstr.; Weed Abstr.; Wheat Barley Trit. Abstr.

LC QK914 .F46
YU
UDC 551.57
FENOLOGICKA ROCENKA SLOVENSKEJ SOCIALISTICKEJ REPUBLIKY / HYDROMETEOROLOGICKY USTAV BRATISLAVA. **VFOAT** Fenologicka Rocenka S.S.R.; Fenologicka Rocenka SSR. 1971-1975-. Slovak. One time a year. Hydrometeorologicky Ustav V Bratislave Jeseniova, 17 PSC 883 15, Bratislava Slovakia.

LC QK520 .B75 ISSN 0308-0838
DD 587/.05 UK
CODEN FEGADG
FERN GAZETTE, THE. [Fern gaz.]. **Added/Corp** British Pteridological Society. Vol. 11 (1974)-. English. Two times a year. Free to members of the British Pteridological Society; £20.00 membership. British Pteridological Society, Natural History Museum - Botany, Cromwell Road, London SW7 5BD United Kingdom. **Tel** 011 44 171 9389497. **ED** B. S. Parris. Index available. **Bk Rev. Ad Acc. Circ:** 600. Documents available from BIOSIS Document Express. ***Continues** British Fern Gazette, 0524-5826.*
Desc: Reports worldwide work on the distribution, ecology, taxonomy and physiology of ferns and fern allies.
Ind/Abst Biol. Abstr.; Ecol. Abstr. (?-?); Rev. Plant Pathol.

LC QK
DD 581 SW
FESPP NEWSLETTER. **Added/Corp** Federation of European Societies of Plant Physiology. **VFOAT** F.E.S.P.P. Newsletter. **VAT** Federation of European Societies of Plant Physiology Newsletter. No. 1 (1982)-. Newsletter. English. Two times a year. Free on request. University of Lund, Box 7007, Department of Plant Biology, S-22007 Lund Sweden. **Tel** 011 46 46 2227789, FAX 011 46 46 2224113. **ED** Ian M. Moller. **Bk Rev**, (Qty: 2-5). **Ad Acc, Adv Mgr:** Ian Max Moller, **Tel** 011 46 46 2227789. **Circ:** 3,200.

LC QK1 .F4 ISSN 0015-0746
DD 581 US
CODEN FLDBAG
FIELDIANA. BOTANY. [Fieldiana, Bot.]. **Added/Corp** Chicago Natural History Museum. Field Museum of Natural History. **VFOAT** Botany. (1949)-. Monographic series. English. Irregular. Price varies per volume. Field Museum of Natural History, Roosevelt Road at Lake Shore Drive, Chicago IL 60605-2496. **Tel** (312)922-9410 ext. 402, FAX (312)922-0671. **ED** Timothy Plowman. **Bk Rev. Ad Acc. Circ:** 500 (ctrl). Documents available from BIOSIS Document Express, CASDDS. ***Continues** Publication (Field Museum of Natural History : 1909). Botanical Series, 0096-2759.*
Desc: Systematics and geographical distribution studies on the flora of Central and South America.
Ind/Abst AGRICOLA; Biol. Abstr.; Chem. Abstr.; Ecol. Abstr.; For. Prod. Abstr.; For. Abstr.; Geogr. Abstr. Phys. Geogr.; Hortic. Abstr.; Int. Dev. Abstr.; Life Sci. Collect.

ISSN 0430-6155
PE
Pr Rev.
FITOPATOLOGIA. **Added/Corp** Asociacion Latinoamericana de Fitopatologia. Vol. 1 (Apr. 1966)-. Periodical. Spanish (Portuguese and Spanish; summaries and/or abstracts in Portuguese and English). Three times a year. $40.00. Asociacion Latinoamericana de Fitopathologia, Apartado 1558, Lima Peru. **ED** Teresa Ames de Icochea. **Bk Rev**, (Qty: 4). **Ad Acc, Adv Mgr:** Hebert Torres, **Tel** 011 51 14 366920-2048. **Circ:** 600. Documents available from BIOSIS Document Express, CASDDS.
Desc: Identification of fungi bacteria viruses and other pathogens that attack plants and the different strategies and procedures used to control them.
Ind/Abst Biol. Abstr.; Chem. Abstr.; For. Prod. Abstr.; For. Abstr.; Hortic. Abstr.; Maize Abstr.; Microbiol. Abstr. Sect. A; Microbiol. Abstr. Sect. C; Plant Breed. Abstr.; Potato Abstr.; Rev. Med. Vet. Mycology; Rev. Plant Pathol.; Virol. AIDS Abstr.; Wheat Barley Trit. Abstr.

ISSN 0100-4158
BL
CODEN FIBRD2
Pr Rev.
FITOPATOLOGIA BRASILEIRA. [Fitopatol. bras.]. Vol. 1 (Feb. 1976)-. Academic Scholarly Publication. Portuguese (English). Four times a year. $60.00. Societe Brasileira Fitopatologia, C Postal 15-2932, 70910 Brasilia DF Brazil. **Tel** 011 55 61 2740022 ext. 2424, telex 0611083. **ED** Elliot W. Kitajima. Index available. **Bk Rev. Ad Acc. Circ:** 1,000 (ctrl). Documents available from BIOSIS Document Express, CASDDS.
Desc: Reports of research data from plant disease studies (etiology, physiopathology, control, etc.).
Ind/Abst AGRICOLA; Biodeter. Abstr.; Biol. Abstr.; Chem. Abstr.; Curr. Cit.; EMBASE; For. Abstr.; Irr. Drain. Abstr.; Nematol. Abstr.; Potato Abstr.; Rev. Med. Vet. Mycology; Rev. Plant Pathol.; Rice Abstr.; Sorghum Mill. Abstr.; Soyabean Abstr.; Vitis Vitic. Enol. Abstr.; Wheat Barley Trit. Abstr.

ISSN 0120-0143
CK
CODEN FICODW
FITOPATOLOGIA COLOMBIANA. [Fitopatol. colomb.]. (197?)-. Academic Scholarly Publication. Spanish. Two times a year. Asociacion Colombiana et Fitopatologia y Ciencias Afines, Apartado Aereo 5004, Cali Colombia. Documents available from CASDDS. ***Continues** Revista Noticias Fitopatologicas.*
Ind/Abst Chem. Abstr. (1978-1980); Maize Abstr.; Nematol. Abstr.; Rev. Plant Pathol.; Soils Fert.

ISSN 0798-0035
VE
CODEN FIVEEU
FITOPATOLOGIA VENEZOLANA. (FITOPATOLOGIA VENEZOLANA : REVISTA DE LA SOCIEDAD VENEZOLANA DE FITOPATOLOGIA.). [Fitopatol. venez.]. **Added/Corp** Sociedad Venezolana de Fitopatologia. Vol. 1, No. 1 (Enero-Jun. 1988)-. Periodical. Spanish (summaries and/or abstracts in English; table of contents in English). Two times a year. Documents available from BIOSIS Document Express.
Ind/Abst Biol. Abstr. (1991-); Maize Abstr.; Nematol. Abstr.; Rev. Agric. Entomol.; Seed Abstr.

ISSN 0367-326X
IT
NLM W1 FI815 CODEN FTRPAE
FITOTERAPIA. (FITOTERAPIA : REVISTA DI STUDI ED APPLICAZIONI DELLE PIANTE MEDICINALI.). [Fitoterapia]. (1934)-. Academic Scholarly Publication. English (French and Italian; summaries and/or abstracts in English). Six times a year. Available only to Universities and specialized pharmaceutical firms. Inverni Della Beffa, Via Ripamonti 99, 20141 Milan Italy. **Tel** 02 536312, 02 5691641, FAX 02-57404620, telex 312535 IDEBEF-I. **ED** Attilio Bonati. Index available. **Bk Rev. Circ:** 4,500 (ctrl). available on microfilm and microfiche from University Microfilms International (UMI). Documents available from BIOSIS Document Express, CASDDS.
Desc: Intended to publish papers concerning chemistry, pharmacology and use of medicinal plants and their derivatives.
Ind/Abst AgBiotech News Inf.; Agrofor. Abstr. (19??-19??); Biol. Abstr.; Chem. Abstr.; Crop Physiol. Abstr.; Curr. Biotechnol.; Curr. Cit.; EMBASE; Field Crop Abstr.; Foods Adlibra; For. Prod. Abstr. (19??-19??); For. Abstr.; Grass. Forage Abstr.; Helminthol. Abstr. (19??-19??); Hortic. Abstr.; Index Vet.; Int. Pharm. Abstr.; Mass Spect. Bull. (?-?); NAPRALERT; Ornamental Hort. (19??-19??); PESTDOC; Plant Genet. Resour. Abstr.; Plant Grow. Reg. Abstr.; Protozoolog. Abstr.; Rev. Agric. Entomol.; Rev. Med. Vet. Entomol.; Rev. Plant Pathol.; Seed Abstr.; Vet. Bull.

LC QK710 .F5 ISSN 0015-3303
DD 581.1 RU
CODEN FZRSAV
FIZIOLOGIIA RASTENII. [Fiziol. rast.]. **Added/Corp** Akademiia Nauk SSSR. **VFOAT** Plant Physiology. Vol. 1, (Sept./Oct. 1954)-. Academic Scholarly Publication. Russian (summaries and/or abstracts in English; table of contents in English). Six times a year. $96.25. Izdatelstvo Nauka / Akademiia Nauk, (Publishing House of the Russian Academy of Sciences), Leninskii Porspekt 14, 117901 Moscow Russia. **Tel** 011 95 9542153, FAX 011 95 9382144, telex 411964. **(Subscription address:** East View Publications Inc., 3020 Harbor Lane North, Suite 110, Minneapolis MN 55447. **Tel** (800)477-1005, (612)550-0961, FAX (612)559-2931.) Index available. **Bk Rev.** Documents available from BIOSIS Document Express, CASDDS.
Ind/Abst AGRICOLA; Biol. Abstr.; Chem. Abstr.; Cot. Trop. Fibr. Abstr. Bibliogr.; Crop Physiol. Abstr.; For. Abstr.; Hortic. Abstr.; Maize Abstr.; Ornamental Hort. (1991-); Plant Breed. Abstr.; Plant Genet. Resour. Abstr.; Plant Grow. Reg. Abstr.; Postharvest News Inf.; Potato Abstr.; Rice Abstr.; Seed Abstr.; Sel. Water Resour. Abstr.; Soils Fert.; Sorghum Mill. Abstr.; Soyabean Abstr.; Vitis Vitic. Enol. Abstr.; Weed Abstr.

LC QK710 .F48 ISSN 0256-1425
DD 581.1 UN
CODEN FBKRAT
FIZIOLOGIJA I BIOHIMIJA KULTURNYH RASTENIJ. (FIZIOLOGIIA I BIOKHIMIIA KULTURNYKH RASTENII.). [Fiziol. biohim. kult. rast.]. **Added/Corp** Instytut Fiziolohii Roslyn (Akademiia Nauk Ukrahinskoi RSR). **VFOAT** Physiology and Biochemistry of Cultivated Plants. Vol. 1, (July/Aug. 1969)-. Academic Scholarly Publication. Ukrainian (Russian; summaries and/or abstracts in English; table of contents in English). Six times a year. $109.95. Izdatelstvo Naukova Dumka / Ukrainian Academy of Sciences, Yu. A. Khramov, Dir., Ul. Repina 3, 252 601 Kiev Ukraine. **Tel** 011 7 44 4303441, 011 7 44 2254182, telex 131376. **(Subscription address:** East View Publications Inc., 3020 Harbor Lane North, Suite 110, Minneapolis MN 55447. **Tel** (800)477-1005, (612)550-0961, FAX (612)559-2931.) Documents available from BIOSIS Document Express, CASDDS.

Ind/Abst Biol. Abstr.; Chem. Abstr.; Cot. Trop. Fibr. Abstr. Bibliogr.; Crop Physiol. Abstr.; EMBASE; Field Crop Abstr.; For. Abstr.; Hortic. Abstr.; Life Sci. Collect.; Plant Breed. Abstr.; Plant Genet. Resour. Abstr.; Plant Grow. Reg. Abstr.; Postharvest News Inf.; Potato Abstr.; Rev. Plant Pathol.; SCISEARCH; Seed Abstr.; Sorghum Mill. Abstr.; Soyabean Abstr.; Weed Abstr.

LC QK710 .F494 **ISSN** 0324-0290
DD 581.1 BU
CODEN FIRADV
TITLE CHANGE

FIZIOLOGIJA NA RASTENIJATA. (FIZIOLOGIIA NA RASTENIIATA.). [Fiziol. rast.]. **Added/Corp** Selskostopanska Akademiia Georgi Dimitrov. Institut po Fiziologiia na Rasteniiata "Metodii Popov.". **VFOAT** Plant Physiology. (1974)-(199?). Bulgarian (summaries and/or abstracts in English and Russian). Izdatelstvo na Bulgarskata Akademiia na Naukite, 6 Rouski Boulevard, Sofia Bulgaria. **Tel** FAX 011 359 2 801341, telex 22267 HEMKIK. **(Subscription address:** Kubon & Sagner, ABT Zeitschriftenimport, D 80328 Munich Germany. **Tel** 011 49 89 54218130.) Documents available from BIOSIS Document Express, CASDDS. ***Continues*** *Institut po Fiziologiia na Rasteniiata Metodii Popov Izvestiia.* ***Continued by*** *Bulgarian Journal of Plant Physiology, 1310-4586.*
Ind/Abst AGRICOLA (?-?); Agric. Eng. Abstr. (?-?); Biol. Abstr. (?-?); Chem. Abstr. (?-?); Crop Physiol. Abstr. (?-?); EMBASE (?-?); Hortic. Abstr. (?-?); Ornamental Hort. (?-?); Plant Grow. Reg. Abstr. (?-?); Seed Abstr. (?-?).

LC QK
DD 581 US

FLORA BUTTENSIS. Vol. 1, No. 1 (1980)-. Monographic series. English. Irregular. Price varies per volume. Flora Buttensis, PO Box 299, Botany Department, St Louis MO 63166. **Tel** (314)664-1382. **ED** Mary Susan Taylor (phone: (314)577-5177). **Circ:** 100 (ctrl).
Desc: Designed as a means of informing professional associates of recent nomenclatural changes concerning California plants. Subjects encompass floristic treatments, regional bibliographies concerning floristics, taxonomy and ethnobotany, and occasional indexing projects.

LC QK
DD 581 MX

FLORA DE VERACRUZ. **Added/Corp** Instituto de Investigaciones sobre Recursos Bioticos (Mexico). Issue 1 (April 1978)-. Spanish. Irregular (4 or 5 issues per year). $20.00 Mexico, South America; $18.00 North America, US; $30.00 Europe; $45.00 Asia, Africa. Inireb Unidad de Communication, Social Apdo Postal 63, 91000 Xalapa Veracruz Mexico. **Tel** 011 52 281 86000. **ED** Thomas Duncan, Lilia Gama, Arturo Gomez Pompa, Nancy P Moreno, Lorin Nevling, Michael Nee, Bernice G Schubert, Victoria Sosa, Margarito Sota, Billie L Turner. Index available. **Circ:** 1,000.
Desc: Each issues includes a family treatment; contains descriptions, keys, distribution maps, relevant references, illustrations, list of specimens examined and ecological data.
Ind/Abst For. Abstr.

LC QK
DD 581 GS

FLORA GRUZII. **Added/Corp** Akademiia Nauk Gruzinskoi SSR. Institut Botaniki. No. 1 (1971)-. Periodical. Multiple languages (Russian and Georgian). Izdatelstvo Metsniereba / Akademiya Nauk Gruzii, (Georgian Academy of Sciences), Ulitsa Kutuzova 19, 380060 Tbilisi 60 Georgia (Republic).

AU

FLORA IRANICA : FLORA DES IRANISCHEN HOCHLANDES UND DER UMRAHMENDEN GEBIRGE. (1963)-. Monographic series. German. Irregular. Price varies per volume. Akademische Druck & Verlagsanstalt, Schoenaugasse 6, Postfach 598, A 8010 Graz Austria. **Tel** 011 43 316 813460.

LC QK **ISSN** 0374-7778
DD 581 NE
CODEN FMSPA4

FLORA MALESIANA. SERIES I, SPERMATOPHYTA. (FLORA MALESIANA. SERIES I, SPERMATOPHYTA : BEING AN ILLUSTRATED SYSTEMATIC ACCOUNT OF THE MALAYSIAN FLORA INCLUDING KEYS FOR DETERMINATION, DIAGNOSTIC DESCRIPTIONS, REFERENCES TO THE LITERATURE, SYNONYMY, AND DISTRIBUTION, AND NOTES ON THE ECOLOGY OF ITS WILD AND COMMONLY CULTIVATED PLANTS.). [Flora males., ser. I, Spermatoph.]. **Added/Corp** Indonesia. Departemen Pertanian. **VFOAT** Spermatophyta. Vol. 1 (19??)-. Monographic series. English. Irregular. Price varies per volume. Rijksherbarium, PO Box 9514, 2300 RA Leiden Netherlands. **Tel** 011 31 71 273500. **ED** C. G. G. J. van Steenis. Documents available from BIOSIS Document Express.
Ind/Abst AGRICOLA; Biol. Abstr.

LC QK **ISSN** 0071-5786
DD 581 NE

FLORA MALESIANA. SERIES II, PTERIDOPHYTA. (FLORA MALESIANA. SERIES II, PTERIDOPHYTA = FERN AND FERN ALLIES.). [Flora males., ser. II, pteridophyta]. **VFOAT** Pteridophyta; Ferns and Fern Allies. Vol. 1 (Dec. 1959)-. Monographic series. English. Irregular. Price varies. Rijksherbarium, PO Box 9514, 2300 RA Leiden Netherlands. **Tel** 011 31 71 273500. **ED** R. E. Holttum.
Ind/Abst AGRICOLA.

LC QK **ISSN** 1120-4052
DD 581 IT

FLORA MEDITERRANEA. **Added/Corp** Organization for the Phyto-Taxonomic Investigation of the Mediterranean Area. Herbarium Mediterraneum Panormitanum. (1991)-. Monographic series. English (French).

LC QK205 .F58 **ISSN** 0071-5794
DD 581.98/012 US
CCC
CODEN FLNMAV

FLORA NEOTROPICA. [Flora neotrop.]. **Added/Corp** Organization for Flora Neotropica. New York Botanical Garden. (1967)-. Monographic series. English. Irregular. Price varies per volume. New York Botanical Garden, Scientific Publishing Department B, New York NY 10458-5126. **Tel** (718)817-8721, FAX (718)817-6504, telex 5106015451. **Bk Rev. Ad Acc. Circ:** 250. Documents available from BIOSIS Document Express.
Desc: Provides taxonomic treatments of plant groups or families growing spontaneously in the Americas between the Tropics of Cancer and Cancer. Information on economic botany, conservation, cytology, anatomy, and phytochemistry.
Ind/Abst AGRICOLA; Biol. Abstr. (1986-).

LC QK
DD 581 BG

FLORA OF BANGLADESH. No. 1 (Oct. 1972)-. English. Three times a year. $75.70. Bangladesh National Herbarium, House 52, Road No 8A Dhanmondi, Dhaka 1209 Bangladesh. **Tel** 311273. **ED** Salar Khan. Index available. cum. index. **Bk Rev.** ctrl circ.
Desc: The first fascicle published in 1972 with five Angiosperm families. Number four (which contains aims of Flora), and the rest include single families.

UK

FLORA OF BHUTAN. (19??)-. Academic Scholarly Publication. English. Irregular. Price varies per volume. Wheldon & Wesley Ltd, Lytton Lodge Codicote, Hitchin Hertfordshire SG4 8TE United Kingdom. **Tel** 011 44 1483 820370.

UK

FLORA OF CYPRUS. (1977)-. Monographic series. English. Irregular. Price varies per volume. Bentham Moxon Trust, Royal Botanic Gardens Kew, Richmond Surrey TW9 3AB United Kingdom. **Tel** 011 44 171 9401171. **ED** R. D. Meikle.
Desc: A descriptive account of the islands plants.

LC QK **ISSN** 0347-8742
DD 581 SW
UDC 581.9(866)
CODEN FLECDR

FLORA OF ECUADOR. [Flora Ecuad.]. No. 5-. Monographic series. English. Price varies per volume. Nordic Journal of Botany, Secretary Farimagsgade 2-D, DK-1353 Copenhagen K Denmark. **Tel** 011 45 45 3314 4906, FAX 011 45 45 3314 4960. Documents available from BIOSIS Document Express. ***Continues*** *Opera Botanica. Ser B: Flora of Ecuador.*
Ind/Abst AGRICOLA; Biol. Abstr.

GW
Pr Rev.

FLORA OF THE GUIANAS. SERIES A : PHANEROGAMAE. (19??)-. Monographic series. English. Irregular. Price varies per volume. Koeltz Scientific Books, PO Box 1360, D-61453 Koenigstein Germany. **Tel** 011 49 6174 93720, FAX 011 49 6174 1634. **Circ:** 150.
Desc: Scientific publication covering the flora of the Guianas.

ISSN 0451-7814
UK

FLORA OF TROPICAL EAST AFRICA. **Main/Corp** Royal Botanic Gardens (Kew, Surrey). (1952)-. English. Irregular. $65.00. AA Balkema, Box 1675, 3000 BR Rotterdam Netherlands. **Tel** 011 31 10 4145822, FAX 011 31 10 4135947, telex 41605.

LC QK **ISSN** 0892-9106
DD 581 US

FLORA ONLINE. (FLORA ONLINE [COMPUTER FILE].). [Flora online]. **Added/Corp** Buffalo Museum of Science. No. 1 (1987)-. Periodical. English. Irregular. Free. Buffalo Museum of Science, Clinton Herbarium, 1020 Humboldt Parkway, Buffalo NY 14211. **Tel** (716)896-5200, FAX (716)897-6723. available on an online database (electronic bulletin board) from TAXACOM; available on diskette; available via Internet (ftp huh.harvard.edu, cd /pub/newsletters/flora online/).
Desc: Covers systematic botany.

LC QK **ISSN** 0430-6651
DD 581 FR
UDC 581.9(44)
CODEN FLFRB7

FLORE DE FRANCE. [Flore Fr.]. French. **ED** P Jovet. Documents available from BIOSIS Document Express.
Ind/Abst Biol. Abstr.

FR

FLORE DE LA NOUVELLE CALEDONIE ET DEPENDANCES. (1967)-. French. Irregular. 595.00F (per volume). Association de Botanique Tropicale, 16 rue Buffon, 75005 Paris France. **Tel** 011 33 1 40 79 33 53, FAX 011 33 1 40 79 33 42. Documents available from FAXON Xpress.
Desc: Taxonomic revisions of plant families occuring in New Caledonia.

FR

FLORE DE MADAGASCAR ET DES COMORES. French. Museum of National d'Historie Naturelle Laboratory de Phanerogam, 16 rue de Buffon, 75005 Paris France. **Tel** 011 33 1 40793366.

ISSN 0071-5867
FR

FLORE DU CAMBODGE, DU LAOS ET DU VIETNAM. **Added/Corp** Museum National d'Histoire Naturelle (France) Centre National de la Recherche Scientifique (France). (1960)-. Monographic series. French. Irregular. Price varies per volume. Museum of National d'Historie Naturelle Laboratory de Phanerogam, 16 rue de Buffon, 75005 Paris France. **Tel** 011 33 1 40793366.
Desc: Flora of the angiosperms of Cambodge, Laos and Vietnam.

LC QK **ISSN** 0071-5875
DD 581 FR

FLORE DU CAMEROUN. **Added/Corp** Paris. Museum National d'Histoire Naturelle. Laboratoire de Phanerogamie. (1963)-. Periodical. French. Irregular. Herbier National Natl Herbariu, BP 1601, Yaounde Cameroon. **Circ:** 550. ***Continues*** *Flore du Cameroun.*
Desc: Covers the flora of the angiosperms of Cameroon.

LC QK
DD 581 FR

FLORE DU GABON. **Added/Corp** Laboratoire de Phanerogamie (Museum National d'Histoire Naturelle). (1961)-. Monographic series. French. Irregular. Price varies per volume. Museum of National d'Historie Naturelle Laboratory de Phanerogam, 16 rue de Buffon, 75005 Paris France. **Tel** 011 33 1 40793366.

ISSN 0741-1448
US
TITLE CHANGE

FLORIDA FOLIAGE. **Added/Corp** Florida Foliage Association. **VFOAT** Florida Foliage Magazine. (19??)-(Jan. 1993). Periodical. English. FGR Incorporated, 1331 North Mills Avenue, Orlando FL 32803-7194. **Tel** (407)894-6522, FAX (407)894-6511. **Ad Acc, Adv Mgr:** Elaine Hudson, **Tel** (407)886-1036. **Circ:** 3,000. ***Continues*** *Foliage Digest.* ***Merged into*** *Florida Growers Ornamental Outlook.*

LC SB292.A2 F63 **ISSN** 0899-7837
DD 632/.95 US

FOCUS ON PHYTOCHEMICAL PESTICIDES. [Focus phytochem. pestic.]. Vol. 1 (1988)-. Periodical. English. One time a year. CRC Press Inc., 2000 Corporate Boulevard Northwest, Boca Raton FL 33431. **Tel** (407)994-0555, (800)272-7737, FAX (407)998-9784, (800)374-3401, telex 568689.
Ind/Abst AGRICOLA [Full Cov.]; Agrofor. Abstr.; For. Prod. Abstr. (1991-); For. Abstr.; Maize Abstr.

LC QK1 .F667 **ISSN** 0015-5551
DD 581.5/05 XR
CCC
CODEN FGPBA7
Pr Rev.

FOLIA GEOBOTANICA & PHYTOTAXONOMICA. [Folia geobot. phytotaxon.]. **Added/Corp** Botanicky Ustav (Ceskoslovenska Akademie Ved). **VFOAT** Folia Geobotanica et Phytotaxonomica. Vol. 2, No. 1 (1967)-. Periodical. English (German). Four times a year. Czech Academy of Sciences Institute of Botany, CS 25243 Pruhonice Czech Republic. **(Subscription address:** Opulus Press AB, PO Box 25 137, S 750 25 Uppsala Sweden. **Tel** 011 46 18 320662.) **ED** Toma Herben and Zdenek Skala. Index available. **Bk Rev. Circ:** 350. Documents available from The Genuine Article, BIOSIS Document Express. ***Continues*** *Folia Geobotanica & Phytotaxonomica Bohemoslovaca.*
Desc: Presents articles devoted to geobotany (plant sociology, synecology and autecology, paleoecology, plant geography), plant taxonomy (algae, fungi, bryophytes, higher plants), nomenclature and cytotaxonomy.

Biology —Botany

Ind/Abst AGRICOLA; Biol. Abstr.; Coal Abstr.; Curr. Contents Agric. Biol. Environ. Sci.; Ecol. Abstr.; Ecology Abstr.; GeoRef; Life Sci. Collect.; Plant Breed. Abstr.; Res. Alert [Select. Cov.]; SCISEARCH.

ISSN 0532-3215
US

FOUR SEASONS, THE. Added/Corp Berkeley, Calif. Regional Parks Botanical Garden. Vol. 1 (Sept. 8, 1964)-. Periodical. English. One time a year. Regional Parks Botanic Garden, Tilden Regional Park, Berkeley CA 94708-1199. Tel (415)841-8732. ED Stephen W. Edwards. cum. index. Bk Rev. Circ: 300.
 Desc: Covers all aspects of botany and horticulture of plants native to California; contains both technical and popular articles.

LC QK1 .F69
DD 581
ISSN 0015-931X
PL
CODEN FRFGAF

FRAGMENTA FLORISTICA ET GEOBOTANICA. [Fragm. florist. geobot.]. Added/Corp Instytut Botaniki (Polska Akademia Nauk) Polskie Towarzystwo Botaniczne. VFOAT Material y Florystyczne i Geobotaniczne. Vol. 1 (1953)-. Periodical. English (Polish and Latin; summaries and/or abstracts in German and Multiple languages). Four times a year. Polish Academy of Sciences / Institute of Botany, (Polska Akademia Nauk Instytut Botaniki), Ul. Lubicz 46, 31-512 Krakow Poland. (Subscription address: Ars Polona-Ruch, PO Box 1001, Krakowskie Przedmiescie 7, 00-068 Warsaw Poland. Tel 011 48 22 261201.) ED Adam Jasiewicz. Documents available from BIOSIS Document Express.
 Ind/Abst AGRICOLA; Biol. Abstr.; Ecol. Abstr.; Geogr. Abstr. Phys. Geogr.; GeoRef; Grass. Forage Abstr.; Life Sci. Collect.; Plant Breed. Abstr.; Plant Genet. Resour. Abstr.; Soils Fert.

LC QK149 .F73
DD 581.9/794
ISSN 0092-1793
US

Pr Rev.

FREMONTIA (SACRAMENTO, CALIF.). (FREMONTIA.). [Fremontia]. Added/Corp California Native Plant Society. Vol. 1, No. 1 (Apr. 1972)-. Periodical. English. Four times a year (Jan., Apr., July, Oct.). $35.00. California Native Plant Society, 1722 J Street 17, Sacramento CA 95814. Tel (916)447-2677. ED Phyllis Faber (editor's address: (415)388-6002). Index available. cum. index. Bk Rev. Ad Acc. Circ: 9,000 (ctrl).
 Ind/Abst AGRICOLA; Garden Lit. (1992-); Rev. Agric. Entomol.; Rev. Plant Pathol.

ISSN 0435-1096
JA
CODEN GFSYAR

GAMMA FIELD SYMPOSIA. [Gamma field symp.]. Added/Corp Japan. Norinsho. Hoshasen Ikushujo. No. 1 (1962)-. English (Japanese). One time a year. Norin Suisansho Nogyo Seibutsu Shjigen kenkyujo Hoshasen Ikushujo, (Inst. of Radiation Breeding National Inst. of Agrobiological Resources Ministry of Agriculture Forestry & Fisheries), Omiyamachi Nakagun, Ibarakiken 319-22 Japan. Documents available from CASDDS.
 Ind/Abst Chem. Abstr. (1962-1980); Rev. Plant Pathol.; Rice Abstr.; Wheat Barley Trit. Abstr.

LC QK1 .G27
DD 581.9/09/712469
ISSN 0379-9506
PO
CODEN GOBTAO

GARCIA DE ORTA : SERIE DE BOTANICA. [Garcia de Orta, ser. bot.]. Added/Corp Portugal. Junta de Investigacoes do Ultramar. Portugal. Junta de Investigacoes Cientificas do Ultramar. VFOAT Serie de Botanica. Vol. 1 (1973)-. Portuguese (English, French, German and Portuguese). Two times a year. 300$00. Instituto de Investigacao Cientifica Tropical, Centro de Documentacao e Informacao, rua Jau 47, 1 300 Lisbon Portugal. Tel 645321. Index available. Circ: 1,000 (ctrl). Documents available from BIOSIS Document Express. Supersedes in part Garcia de Orta.
 Desc: Publishes articles on botany in a broad sense (cytology, anatomy, physiology, genetics, taxonomy, ecology, phytogeography, phytopaleontology, etc.) as well as articles on basic botany and historical/biographical articles.
 Ind/Abst AGRICOLA; Biol. Abstr.; Field Crop Abstr.; For. Prod. Abstr.; For. Abstr.; Grass. Forage Abstr.; Life Sci. Collect.; Rev. Med. Vet. Mycology; Rev. Plant Pathol.

LC QK1 .G3
DD 581
ISSN 0016-5301
CL
CODEN GBCBAK

GAYANA : BOTANICA. [Gayana, Bot.]. Added/Corp Universidad de Concepcion. Instituto de Biologia Universidad de Concepcion. Instituto Central de Biologia. No. 1 (1961)-. Monographic series. Spanish (summaries and/or abstracts in English). Price varies per volume. Universidad de Concepcion Publicaciones, M Arevalo, Casilla 1557, Concepcion Chile. Tel 011 56 41 234985 Ext 2591. Documents available from BIOSIS Document Express.
 Ind/Abst Biol. Abstr. (-1984); Life Sci. Collect.

CH

GENETIC MANIPULATION IN PLANTS. Vol. 5, 1 (1989)-. Periodical. English. Two times a year. $48.00 (institutions), $24.00 (individuals). Institute of Genetics, Academia Sinica, Beijing 100101, People's Republic of China. Continues Genetic Manipulation in Crops Newsletter.
 Ind/Abst Field Crop Abstr.; Hortic. Abstr.; Plant Breed. Abstr.; Potato Abstr.; Rev. Plant Pathol.; Rice Abstr.; Seed Abstr.; Wheat Barley Trit. Abstr.

LC SB123 .G42
DD 631.5
ISSN 0016-6715
PL
CCC

NLM W1 GE287K
CODEN GPOLA4
TITLE CHANGE

GENETICA POLONICA. See Biology-Genetics.

ISSN 1051-662X
US

●**GENOTYPE-BY-ENVIRONMENT, INTERACTION, AND PLANT BREEDING SYMPOSIUM.** (GENOTYPE-BY-ENVIRONMENT, INTERACTION, AND PLANT BREEDING SYMPOSIUM : [PROCEEDINGS].). (1993)-. English. $20.00. Louisiana State University / 177 Pleasant Hall, Baton Rouge LA 70803.

ISSN 0072-0879
US

UDC 58.082.5
CODEN GEHEA7
SUSPENDED

GENTES HERBARUM. [Gentes herb.]. Vol. 1 (1920/25)-Suspended (1984). Periodical. English. Irregular. L H Bailey Hortorium, 467 Mann Library Building, Cornell University, Ithaca NY 14853. available on microfilm and microfiche from University Microfilms International (UMI). Documents available from BIOSIS Document Express.
 Ind/Abst AGRICOLA [Full Cov.]; Biol. Abstr.; Life Sci. Collect.

GW

UDC 631.45

GEOBOTANICA SELECTA. Vol. 1 (1961)-. Periodical. German. Irregular. VCH Publishers Inc, 220 East 23rd Street, New York NY 10010. Tel (212)683-8333, FAX (212)481-0897. (Subscription address: VCH Publishers Inc., 303 Northwest 12th Avenue, Journals Department, Deerfield FL 33442. Tel (800)367-8249, (305)428-5566.)

LC QE901 .G46
DD 561/.05
ISSN 0376-5156
II
CODEN GPHTAR

GEOPHYTOLOGY. See Paleontology.

LC QK1
DD 581
ISSN 0166-6495
NE

GEWASBESCHERMING. [Gewasbescherming]. Added/Corp Nederlandse Plantenziektenkundige Vereniging. Centrale Organisatie voor Toegepast-Natuurwetenschappelijkonderzoek. Coordinatiecommissie Onkruidbestrijding. (19??)-. Periodical. Dutch. Six times a year (Feb., Apr., Jun., Aug., Oct., Dec.). $30.83. Netherlands Society of Plant Pathology, Post Box 31, 6700 AA Wageningen Netherlands. Tel 011 31 8370 83051.
 Ind/Abst AGRICOLA; Biodeter. Abstr. (1991-); Hortic. Abstr.; Maize Abstr.; Nematol. Abstr.; Plant Breed. Abstr.; Postharvest News Inf.; Potato Abstr.; Rev. Agric. Entomol.; Rev. Med. Vet. Entomol.; Rev. Plant Pathol.; Weed Abstr.

ISSN 1074-0074
DD 583
US

GILLIFLOWER TIMES : THE QUARTERLY JOURNAL OF THE AMERICAN DIANTHUS SOCIETY, THE. Added/Corp American Dianthus Society. Vol. 1, No. 1 (Autumn 1991)-. Periodical. English. Four times a year. $15.00. American Dianthus Society, PO Box 22232, Santa Fe NM 87502. Tel (505)438-7038.

LC QK1 .N9
DD 580/.5
ISSN 0017-0070
IT
CODEN GBOIAX

Pr Rev.

GIORNALE BOTANICO ITALIANO (FLORENCE, ITALY : 1962). (GIORNALE BOTANICO ITALIANO.). [G. bot. ital.]. Added/Corp Societa Botanica Italiana. Consiglio Nazionale delle Ricerche (Italy). (1962)-. Academic Scholarly Publication. Italian (French and English). Six times a year. L163500. Societa Botanica Italiana, Via la Pira 4, 50121 Florence Italy. Tel 011 39 55 2757379. Index available. Circ: 1,300. Documents available from BIOSIS Document Express, CASDDS. Continues Nuovo Giornale Botanico Italiano.
 Desc: Diffusion of botanic knowledge.
 Ind/Abst AGRICOLA; Biol. Abstr.; Chem. Abstr.; Ecol. Abstr. (?-?); Field Crop Abstr.; For. Prod. Abstr.; For. Abstr.; Grass. Forage Abstr.; Hortic. Abstr.; Life Sci. Collect.; Plant Breed. Abstr.; Rev. Med. Vet. Mycology; Rev. Plant Pathol.; Weed Abstr.

LC QK
DD 581
ISSN 0332-0235
IE

GLASRA. [Glasra]. Added/Corp National Botanic Gardens (Ireland) Ireland. Dept. of Agriculture. (1978)-. English. One time a year. National Botanic Gardens, Glasnevin, Dublin 9 Ireland. Continues National Botanical Gardens (Ireland). Contributions from the National Botanic Gardens, Glasnevin.
 Ind/Abst AGRICOLA [Full Cov.].

LC QK
DD 581
GW

GLEDITSCHIA. Vol. 1 (1973)-. Periodical. German. Two times a year. $155.00. Akademie-Verlag GmbH, Postfach, D-13162 Berlin Germany. Tel 011 49 30 47889300, FAX 011 49 30 47889357. (Subscription address: VCH Publishers Inc., 303 Northwest 12th Avenue, Journals Department, Deerfield FL 33442. Tel (800)367-8249, (305)428-5566.) ED Von Walter Vent, Unter Mitwirkung, Von Gunther Natho and Dieter Benkert.

II

GLIMPSES IN PLANT RESEARCH. Vol. 1 (1973)-. Periodical. English. One time a year. Price varies. Today and Tomorrow's Printers and Publishers, 24-B/5 Desh Bandhu Gupta Road, Karol Bagh, New Delhi 110 005 India. Tel 011 91 11 5721928, 011 91 11 572770, FAX 011 91 11 7210073 (TTPP). (Subscription address: Prints India, 11 Darya Ganj, New Delhi 110002 India. Tel 011 91 11 3268645, FAX 011 91 11 3275542, telex 31-61087 PRIN-IN.) ED J N Govil.
 Desc: Carries scientific reviews and/or original research monographs on medicinal plants.

LC S
DD 631
ISSN 0017-1352
US

GLOXINIAN, THE. Added/Corp American Gloxinia and Gesneriad Society. American Gloxinia Society. Vol. 1 (June/July 1951)-. Periodical. English. Six times a year. Comes with American Gloxinia and Gesneriad Society membership. American Gloxinia and Gesneriad Society, PO Box 1598, Port Angeles WA 98362. Tel (360)417-2172. ED Anne C Crowley (editor's address: 88 Maynard, Rosindale MA 02131). Index available. Bk Rev. Ad Acc. ctrl circ.

UK

GOLDEN BOUGH, THE. No. 1 (Nov. 1982)-. Newsletter. English. Two times a year. Free. Dr Roger M Polhill, Herbarium / Royal Botanic Gardens, Kew Richmond Surrey TW9 3AB United Kingdom. Tel 011 44 181 3325233, 011 44 181 3225000, FAX 011 44 181 3325278, telex 296694 KEWGAR. ED R M Polhill. Circ: 300 (ctrl).
 Desc: Newsletter to foster the biosystematics of Loranthaceae and Viscaceae.

LC QK
DD 581
ISSN 0017-2294
NE

GORTERIA. [Gorteria]. Added/Corp Rijksherbarium (Netherlands). (1961)-. Monographic series. Dutch (summaries and/or abstracts in English). Price varies per volume. Rijksherbarium, PO Box 9514, 2300 RA Leiden Netherlands. Tel 011 31 71 273500.
 Ind/Abst Ecol. Abstr.

LC QK658 .G72
DD 582/.0463
ISSN 0017-3134
SW
CCC
CODEN GRNABF

Pr Rev.

GRANA. [Grana]. Vol. 10 (1970)-. Periodical. German (English). Six times a year. $277.00. Scandinavian University Press, PO Box 2959 Toeyen, N 0608 Oslo 6 Norway. Tel 011 47 2 2575400, FAX 011 47 2 2575353, telex 71896 UROR N. (Subscription address: Scandinavian University Press, 200 Meacham Ave., Elmont NY 11003. Tel (516)352-7300, FAX (516)352-7377.) Documents available from The Genuine Article, BIOSIS Document Express. Continues Grana Palynologica.
 Desc: Presents original articles, mainly on theoretical palynology and aerobiology.
 Ind/Abst AGRICOLA; Biocont. News Inf. (1991-); Biol. Abstr.; Curr. Aware. Biol. Sci.; CABS; Curr. Cit.; Curr. Contents Agric. Biol. Environ. Sci.; Ecol. Abstr.; For. Prod. Abstr.; Geogr. Abstr. Phys. Geogr.; GeoRef; Life Sci. Collect.; Plant Breed. Abstr.; Res. Alert [Select. Cov.]; Rev. Med. Vet. Mycology; Rev. Plant Pathol.; SCISEARCH; Weed Abstr.

ISSN 0167-2932
NE

UDC 574

GRASDUINEN. [Grasduinen]. (1979)-. Periodical. Dutch. Twelve times a year. $83.38. Medianet BV, Postbus 6298, 2001 LN Haarlem Netherlands. Tel 011 31 23 173311.

LC QK
DD 581
ISSN 0749-2138
US

GREEN THUMB NEWS. (GREEN THUMB NEWS.). Added/Corp Denver Botanic Gardens. Denver Botanic Gardens. Educational Dept. No. 83-4 (April 1983)-. Periodical. English. Twelve times a year. $25.00

(comes with membership). Denver Botanic Gardens, 909 York Street, Denver CO 80206. **Tel** (303)575-3751. **ED** Patricia A. Pachuta. **Bk Rev. Circ:** 7,000 (ctrl). ***Continues*** *Green Thumb Newsletter.*
Desc: Special gardens events and horticultural information.
Ind/Abst Garden Lit. (1992-).

NE

GROEI EN BLOEI. **Added/Corp** International Food Information Service. Commonwealth Agricultural Bureaux. Periodical. Dutch. Twelve times a year. Adservice, Nassau Odijckstraat 8, 2596 AH Den Haag The Netherlands.

ISSN 0072-8500
US

GUIDE TO GRADUATE STUDY IN BOTANY FOR THE UNITED STATES AND CANADA. See Education-Higher Education.

LC QK911 .H3 **ISSN** 0302-3141
NE
CODEN HVSCEK

HANDBOOK OF VEGETATION SCIENCE. [Handb. veg. sci.]. Pt. 1 (1974)-. Monographic series. English. Irregular. Price varies per volume. Kluwer Academic Publishers, Postbus 322, 3300 AH Dordrecht The Netherlands. **Tel** 011 31 78 524400, FAX 011 31 78 183273, telex 20083. **(Subscription address:** Kluwer Academic Publishers / US Subscriptions, PO Box 253, Accord Station, Hingham MA 02018. **Tel** (617)871-6600.) Documents available from BIOSIS Document Express.
Ind/Abst Biol. Abstr. (1988-).

GW

HANDBUCH DER PFLANZENANATOMIE. (19??)-. Monographic series. German. Irregular. E. Schweizerbartische Verlagsbuchhandlung, Johannesstrasse 3A, D-70176 Stuttgart Germany. **Tel** 011 49 711 625001, FAX 011 49 711 625005, telex 723363 SCHB D. **ED** H.J. Brann, S. Catlquist, P. Ozenda and O. Roth. **Bk Rev. Ad Acc.**
Desc: Covers plant anatomy as a fundamental part of botany. Aimed at anatomists as well as pharmacologists, agriculturists, and horticulturists.

ISSN 0091-7079
US
CODEN HLALAJ

HAROLD L. LYON ARBORETUM LECTURE. [Harold L. Lyon Arbor. lect.]. **Main/Corp** Harold L. Lyon Arboretum. **VFOAT** Lyon Arboretum Lecture. No. 1 (1970)-. English. One time a year. Price varies per volume. University of Hawaii Press, 2840 Kolowalu Street, Honolulu HI 96822. **Tel** (808)956-8833, (808)948-8697, FAX (808)988-6052. **ED** Yoneo Sagawa. **Circ:** 1,000 (ctrl). Documents available from BIOSIS Document Express.
Desc: Focuses on the Pacific as an area for biological research.
Ind/Abst Biol. Abstr. (1970-1988).

LC QK1 .H247 **ISSN** 1043-4534
DD 581/.05 US

HARVARD PAPERS IN BOTANY. [Harv. pap. bot.]. **VFOAT** Harvard Papers. No. 1 (May 1989)-. Periodical. English. Two times a year. Harvard University Botanical Museum, c/o K Harrow Publications Section, Oxford Street, Cambridge MA 02138. Documents available from BIOSIS Document Express. ***Formed by the union of*** *Occasional Papers of the Farlow Herbarium of Cryptogamic Botany, 0090-8754; Botanical Museum Leaflets, Harvard University, 0006-8098* ***and*** *Contributions from the Gray Herbarium of Harvard University, 0195-6094.*
Ind/Abst AGRICOLA [Full Cov.]; Biol. Abstr. (1989-); GeoRef (1989-).

LC QK533 .H365 **ISSN** 0073-0912
DD 588 JA
CODEN JHBLAI

HATTORI SHOKUBUTSU KENKYUJO HOKOKU. (THE JOURNAL OF THE HATTORI BOTANICAL LABORATORY.). **Main/Corp** Hattori Shokubutsu Kenkyusho. **Added/Corp** Hattori Shokubutsu Kenkyusho. **VFOAT** Hattori Shokubutsu Kenyusho Hokoku. No. 3 (Feb. 1948)-. Academic Scholarly Publication. English (Japanese and Latin). Two times a year. Price varies. Hattori Botanical Laboratory, OBI Nichinan-shi, Niyazaki-ken 889-25 Japan. **Tel** 0987 (25) 0110. **ED** Sinske Hattori. Documents available from BIOSIS Document Express, CASDDS. ***Continues*** *Hattori Shokubutsu Kenkyujo hokoku.*
Desc: A journal devoted to bryology and lichenology.
Ind/Abst AGRICOLA [Full Cov.]; Biol. Abstr.; Chem. Abstr. (-1988); Life Sci. Collect.; Plant Breed. Abstr.; Rev. Med. Vet. Mycology; Rev. Plant Pathol.

ISSN 0018-0599
PL

HERBA POLONICA. **Added/Corp** Instytut Przemysu Zielarskiego. Instytut Przemysu Zielarskiego. Biuletyn - Instytut Przemysu Zielarskiego Instytut Przemysu Zielarskiego. Biuletyn Instytutu Roslin Leczniczych. No. 1 (1955)-. Academic Scholarly Publication. Polish (summaries and/or abstracts in English and Russian). Four times a year. **(Subscription address:** Ars Polona-Ruch, PO Box 1001, Krakowskie Przedmiescie 7, 00-068 Warsaw Poland. **Tel** 011 48 22 261201.) Documents available from BIOSIS Document Express, CASDDS.
Ind/Abst AGRICOLA; Anal. Abstr.; Biol. Abstr.; Chem. Abstr.; EMBASE; Hortic. Abstr.; Int. Pharm. Abstr.; NAPRALERT; Life Sci. Collect.; PESTDOC; Soils Fert.

ISSN 0899-5648
DD 615 US
NLM W1; HE962
Pr Rev.

HERBALGRAM (AUSTIN, TEX.). (HERBALGRAM.). [HerbalGram]. **Added/Corp** Herb Research Foundation. American Herbal Products Association. American Botanical Council. **VFOAT** Herbal Gram. Vol. 3, No. 3 (Summer/Fall 1986)-. Periodical. English. Four times a year. $25.00. American Botanical Council, PO Box 201660, Austin TX 78720. **Tel** (512)331-8868, FAX (512)331-1924. **ED** Mark Blumenthal. Index available. cum. index. **Bk Rev. Ad Acc, Adv Mgr:** M. Wright. **Circ:** 20,000.
Desc: Research updates, literature reviews, legal and market updates, media coverage, book reviews, calendar, networking, conferences all about herbs and medicinal plants.
Ind/Abst Garden Lit. (1992-).

ISSN 0731-7824
US

HERBARIUM NEWS. [Herb. news]. **Added/Corp** Missouri Botanical Garden. Vol. 1, No. 1, (Sept. 1981)-. Periodical. English. Twelve times a year. $16.00. Missouri Botanical Garden, PO Box 299, St. Louis MO 63166. **Tel** (314)577-9534, (314)577-5100, FAX (314)577-9594. **ED** Nancy R. Morin. **Bk Rev. Circ:** 500.
Desc: Designed to provide rapid communication of current events in the herbarium community. Announcements include changes in staff, job openings, recent loans, requests for materials, developments in curatorial practices, and notices of publications.

LC QK1 .P67 **ISSN** 8756-9418
DD 584/.25/05 US
Pr Rev.

HERBERTIA (1984). (HERBERTIA.). [Herbertia]. **Added/Corp** American Plant Life Society. Vol. 40 (1984)-. English. One time a year. $30.00. International Bulb Society, PO Box 4928, Culver City CA 90230. **Tel** (310)827-3229. **ED** R. Mitchel Beauchamp. Index available. cum. index. **Bk Rev. Circ:** 850. ***Continues*** *Plant Life, 0275-0783.*
Desc: Covers the taxonomy and culture of bulbous plants.
Ind/Abst AGRICOLA [Full Cov.].

LC QK533.84.E8515 H47 **ISSN** 0018-0971
DD 588 GW
CCC
CODEN HRZGD4

HERZOGIA. [Herzogia]. **Added/Corp** Bryologich-Lichenologische Arbeitsgemeinschaft fuer Mitteileuropa. (1968)-. German. $35.00. Gebruder Borntraeger Verlagsbuchhandlung, Johannesstrasse 3-A, D-70176 Stuttgart Germany. **Tel** 0711/62 50 01, FAX (0711)625005, telex 723363 SCHB D. Documents available from BIOSIS Document Express.
Ind/Abst Biol. Abstr.; Rev. Med. Vet. Mycology; Rev. Plant Pathol.

LC QK **ISSN** 0439-0687
DD 581 GW
CODEN HFBRAY

HESSISCHE FLORISTISCHE BRIEFE. [Hess. florist. Briefe]. Vol. 26, No. 1- 1977-. Periodical. German. Four times a year. Documents available from BIOSIS Document Express.
Ind/Abst AGRICOLA; Biol. Abstr.

LC QK369 .H46 **ISSN** 0046-7413
DD 581.952 JA
CODEN HKBAAI

HIKOBIA / HIROSHIMA SHOKUBUTSUGAKU KENKYUKAI. **Added/Corp** Hiroshima Shokubutsugaku Kenkyukai. **VFOAT** Hikobia : Journal of the Hiroshima Botanical Club. Vol. 1 (1950)-. Periodical. Japanese (English). Irregular. Price varies. Hikobiakai, (Hiroshima Botanical Club), Hiroshima Daigaku Rigakubu, 1-89 Higashisendamachi 1 Chome, Nakaku Hiroshimashi, Hiroshimaken 730 Japan. **(Subscription address:** Japan Publications Trading Company Ltd., PO Box 5030, Tokyo International, Tokyo 100-31 Japan. **Tel** 011 81 3 3292 3753.) Documents available from BIOSIS Document Express.
Ind/Abst Biol. Abstr.; Life Sci. Collect.

LC QK
DD 581 II

HIMALAYAN PLANT JOURNAL. Vol. 1, No. 1 (June 1982)-. Periodical. English. Two times a year. $35.00 institutions, $25.00 individuals. Primulaceae Books, Abhijit Villa, BPO Ecchey, Kalimpong 734301 India. **Tel** 011 91 11 3552673. **(Subscription address:** Prints India, 11 Darya Ganj, New Delhi 110002 India. **Tel** 011 91 11 3268645, FAX 011 91 11 3275542, telex 31-61087 PRIN-IN.) **ED** Udai C. Pradhan, Tej K. Pradhan. Index available. **Bk Rev. Ad Acc. Circ:** 300 (ctrl).
Desc: A scientific journal devoted to the dissemination of knowledge on Himalayan Flora. Non-profit, supported by subscriptions and profits generated by primulaceae books.

LC SB413.H73 H68 **ISSN** 1041-553X
DD 635.9 US

HOSTA JOURNAL : A PUBLICATION OF THE AMERICAN HOSTA SOCIETY, THE. [Hosta j.]. Vol. 17, No. 1 (Spring 1986)-. Periodical. English. Two times a year. $12.50 (individual membership), $16.00 (family membership), $25.00 (sustaining membership). J Freedman, AHS Secretary, 3103 Heatherhill Road, Huntsville AL 35802. ***Formed by the union of*** *American Hosta Society, 0885-1905* ***and*** *American Hosta Society Newsletter.*

LC Z **ISSN** 0073-4071
DD 002 US
CCC
NLM Z 5351 H947
Pr Rev.

HUNTIA. [Huntia]. **Added/Corp** Hunt Institute for Botanical Documentation. Hunt Botanical Library. Vol. 1 (15 Apr. 1964)-. Periodical. English. Irregular (one to three issues). Price varies per volume. Hunt Institute, Carnegie Mellon University, Pittsburgh PA 15213. **Tel** (412)268-2434, FAX (412)268-5677. **ED** Sharon M. Tomasie. Index available. **Bk Rev. Circ:** 250.
Desc: Publishes intra- and extramural articles of varying lengths on all aspects of botanical history and documentation, including exploration, art, literature, biography and iconography.
Ind/Abst AGRICOLA [Full Cov.].

LC SB123.3 .I57
DD 631.54 II
TITLE CHANGE

IBPGR NEWSLETTER FOR ASIA AND THE PACIFIC. **Added/Corp** International Board for Plant Genetic Resources. Office for South and Southeast Asia. **VFOAT** Newsletter; IBPGR Newsletter for Asia, the Pacific and Oceania. **VAT** International Board for Plant Genetic Resources Newsletter for Asia and the Pacific. No. 1 (Sept. 1989)-No. 13 (Dec. 1993). Newsletter. English. IPGRI / International Plant Genetic Resources Institute, Office for South and Southeast Asia, New Delhi India. ***Continues*** *Newsletter (International Board for Plant Genetic Resources.; Regional Committee for Southeast Asia).* ***Continued by*** *IPGRI Newsletter for Asia, the Pacific and Oceania.*
Ind/Abst Plant Breed. Abstr.; Rev. Agric. Entomol.; Rev. Plant Pathol.; Rice Abstr.; Seed Abstr.; Wheat Barley Trit. Abstr.

LC QK **ISSN** 1021-5964
DD 581 IT
CODEN ICLSED

IBPGR TRAINING COURSES. LECTURE SERIES. [IBPGR train. courses: lect. ser.]. **Added/Corp** International Board for Plant Genetic Resources. **VFOAT** Training Courses; Lecture Series. **VAT** International Board for Plant Genetic Resources Training Courses. Lecture Series. No. 1 (1987)-. Monographic series. English. Irregular. Price varies per volume. International Board for Plant Genetic Resources, Via Delle Sette Chiese 142, 00145 Rome Italy. Documents available from BIOSIS Document Express.
Ind/Abst Biol. Abstr. (1987-).

LC QK1 .I25 **ISSN** 0073-4705
DD 581.981/65 BL
CODEN IHBOAG

IHERINGIA. SERIE BOTANICA. [Iheringia. Ser. bot.]. **Added/Corp** Fundacao Zoobotanica do Rio Grande do Sul. Museu de Ciencias Naturais. Museu Rio-Grandense de Ciencias Naturais. (19??)-. Periodical. English (Portuguese; summaries and/or abstracts in German). Two times a year. Price varies per volume. Fundacao Zoobotanica do Rio Grande do Sul Biblioteca, Museo de Ciencias Naturals, Caixa Postal 1188, 90690-000 Porto Alegre RS Brazil. **Tel** 011 55 51 336 1511. **ED** Teresia Strehl. Index available. **Circ:** 600 (ctrl). Documents available from BIOSIS Document Express. ***Continues*** *Iheringia. Botanica.*
Desc: Covers topics in botany such as the systematics, floristic, and ecology of Rio Grande do Sul Brazil.
Ind/Abst AGRICOLA; Biol. Abstr.

LC QK725 .I43 **ISSN** 1054-5476
DD 581/.0724 US
CCC
NLM W1; IN106G **CODEN** IVCPEO
Pr Rev.

IN VITRO CELLULAR & DEVELOPMENTAL BIOLOGY. PLANT. (IN VITRO CELLULAR & DEVELOPMENTAL BIOLOGY. PLANT : JOURNAL OF THE TISSUE CULTURE ASSOCIATION.). [In vitro cell. dev. biol., Plant]. **Added/Corp** Tissue Culture Association. **VFOAT** In Vitro Cellular and Developmental Biology. Plant; Plant. Vol. 27P, No. 1 Jan. (1991)-. Academic Scholarly Publication. English. Four times a year. $110.00. Society for In Vitro Biology, PO Box 73230, Baltimore MD 21273. **Tel** (410)992-0946. available on microfilm and microfiche from University Microfilms International (UMI). Documents available from The Genuine Article, BIOSIS Document Express, CASDDS. ***Continues in part*** *In Vitro Cellular &*

Developmental Biology, 0883-8364.
Ind/Abst AGRICOLA; Biol. Abstr.; Chem. Abstr.; Curr. Aware. Biol. Sci., CABS; Curr. Cit.; Curr. Contents Life Sci.; PESTDOC; Protozoolog. Abstr.; Res. Alert [Full Cov.]; Sci. Cit. Index; SCISEARCH.

SW

INDEX HOLMIENSIS. **VFOAT** Index Holmensis. (1969)-. English. Sveriges Entomologiska Forenin Naturhistoriska / Swedish Museum of Natural History, Box 50007, 104 05 Stockholm Sweden. **Tel** 011 46 8 6664089.
Desc: A world index of plant distribution maps.

SA

●**INDEX SEMINUM.** (1994)-. Government Publication. English. One time a year. Directorate of Plant and Quality Control, Private Bag X258, Pretoria South Africa.

HU

INDEX SEMINUM. **Main/Corp** Agrobotanikai Intezet. No. 14- 1971-. Periodical. Hungarian. ***Continues*** *Index Seminum.*

II
CODEN IBCOEH

INDIAN BOTANICAL CONTACTOR : IBC. **Added/Corp** Avichal Science Foundation (India). **VFOAT** IBC. (198?)-. Periodical. English. Four times a year. Indian Botanical Contractor, Sardar Patel University, Department of Biosciences, Vallabh Vidyanagar 388 120 India. Documents available from BIOSIS Document Express, CASDDS.
Ind/Abst Biol. Abstr.; Chem. Abstr.

ISSN 0970-1389
II
UDC 58

INDIAN BOTANICAL CONTRACTOR. [Indian Bot. Contract.]. **VFOAT** IBC Indian Botanical Contractor. (1984)-. Periodical. English. Four times a year. $70.00. **(Subscription address:** Prints India, 11 Darya Ganj, New Delhi 110002 India. **Tel** 011 91 11 3268645, FAX 011 91 11 3275542, telex 31-61087 PRIN-IN.**)**

LC QK358 .I48 **ISSN** 0254-4091
DD 581.954/05 II
CODEN IBREDR

INDIAN BOTANICAL REPORTER. (INDIAN BOTANICAL REPORTER : IBR.). [Indian bot. rep.]. **Added/Corp** Marathwada University. **VFOAT** IBR; I.B.R. Vol. 1, No. 1 (Aug. 1982)-. Periodical. English. Two times a year. $20.00. Marathwada University, Aurangabad 431004, Maharashtra India. **(Subscription address:** Prints India, 11 Darya Ganj, New Delhi 110002 India. **Tel** 011 91 11 3268645, FAX 011 91 11 3275542, telex 31-61087 PRIN-IN.**)** Documents available from CASDDS.
Ind/Abst AGRICOLA; Agrofor. Abstr. (1991-); Biodeter. Abstr. (1991-); Chem. Abstr.; Crop Physiol. Abstr.; Field Crop Abstr.; For. Abstr.; Grass. Forage Abstr.; Hortic. Abstr.; Maize Abstr.; Plant Breed. Abstr.; Plant Grow. Reg. Abstr.; Postharvest News Inf.; Rev. Agric. Entomol.; Rev. Plant Pathol.; Rice Abstr.; Seed Abstr.; Wheat Barley Trit. Abstr.

LC QK529.I4 I53 **ISSN** 0970-2741
DD 587/.310954 II
CODEN IFJOEC

INDIAN FERN JOURNAL. (INDIAN FERN JOURNAL : INTERNATIONAL JOURNAL OF PTERIDOLOGY PUBLISHED BY THE INDIAN FERN SOCIETY.). [Indian Fern J.]. **Added/Corp** Indian Fern Society (India). Vol. 1, No. 1 & 2 (1984)-. Periodical. English. Two times a year. $50.00. Indian Fern Society, Pteridophytic Taxonomy Laboratory, Department of Botany, Punjabi University, Patiala 147002 India. **(Subscription address:** Prints India, 11 Darya Ganj, New Delhi 110002 India. **Tel** 011 91 11 3268645, FAX 011 91 11 3275542, telex 31-61087 PRIN-IN.**)** Documents available from BIOSIS Document Express.
Ind/Abst AGRICOLA; Biol. Abstr. (1985-).

LC QK358 .I52 **ISSN** 0250-829X
DD 580/.5 II
CODEN IJBODX

INDIAN JOURNAL OF BOTANY. [Indian j. bot.]. Vol. 1 (1978)-. Academic Scholarly Publication. English. Two times a year. $20.00. Indian Journal of Botany, 6-1-127/2 Khairatabad, Hyderabad 500 004 India. **Tel** 234301. **(Subscription address:** Prints India, 11 Darya Ganj, New Delhi 110002 India. **Tel** 011 91 11 3268645, FAX 011 91 11 3275542, telex 31-61087 PRIN-IN.**) ED** A Satyanarayana. **Bk Rev. Ad Acc. Circ:** 500 (ctrl). Documents available from BIOSIS Document Express, CASDDS.
Desc: The journal deals with all aspects of research in plant science.
Ind/Abst Biol. Abstr.; Chem. Abstr.; Crop Physiol. Abstr.; Curr. Aware. Biol. Sci., CABS; Ecol. Abstr. (?-?); EMBASE; Energy Res. Abstr. (Feb. 1982-); Field Crop Abstr.; Geol. Abstr.; Grass. Forage Abstr.; Ornamental Hort.; Life Sci. Collect.; Plant Breed. Abstr.; Plant Grow. Reg. Abstr.; Rev. Plant Pathol.; Rice Abstr.; Sorghum Mill. Abstr.

LC SB123 .I6 **ISSN** 0019-5200
DD 631.52205 II
CODEN IJGBAG

INDIAN JOURNAL OF GENETICS & PLANT BREEDING, THE. **See** Biology-Genetics.

ISSN 0970-342X
II

INDIAN JOURNAL OF PLANT PATHOLOGY. [Indian j. Plant Pathol.]. **Added/Corp** Association of Plant Pathologists of India. **VFOAT** Indian J. Plant Path. Vol. 1, No. 1 (June 1983)-. Periodical. English. Two times a year. $60.00. Association of Plant Pathologists of India, Lucknow India. **(Subscription address:** Prints India, 11 Darya Ganj, New Delhi 110002 India. **Tel** 011 91 11 3268645, FAX 011 91 11 3275542, telex 31-61087 PRIN-IN.**)**
Ind/Abst Biocont. News Inf. (1991-); Curr. Aware. Biol. Sci., CABS; Curr. Cit.; Field Crop Abstr.; For. Prod. Abstr. (1991-); Hortic. Abstr.; Irr. Drain. Abstr.; Nematol. Abstr.; Plant Grow. Reg. Abstr.; Postharvest News Inf.; Potato Abstr.; Rev. Plant Pathol.; Seed Abstr.; Sorghum Mill. Abstr.; Soyabean Abstr.

LC QK710 .I5 **ISSN** 0019-5502
DD 581.1 II
NLM W1 IN226P **CODEN** IPPYA2
Pr Rev.

INDIAN JOURNAL OF PLANT PHYSIOLOGY. (INDIAN JOURNAL OF PLANT PHYSIOLOGY : OFFICIAL PUBLICATION OF THE INDIAN SOCIETY FOR PLANT PHYSIOLOGY.). [Indian j. plant physiol.]. **Added/Corp** Indian Society for Plant Physiology. Vol. 1 (1958)-. Periodical. English. Four times a year (Mar., July, Oct., Dec.). $60.00. Indian Society of Plant Physiology, Indian Agricultural Research Institute, New Delhi 110012 India. **Tel** 011 91 11 1 582815. **(Subscription address:** Prints India, 11 Darya Ganj, New Delhi 110002 India. **Tel** 011 91 11 3268645, FAX 011 91 11 3275542, telex 31-61087 PRIN-IN.**) ED** Dr. G. C. Srivastava (editor's address: Division of Plant Physiology, IARI, New Delhi 110012, India, phone: 011 91 11 1 5782815). Index available (bound in issue 4). **Bk Rev. Ad Acc. Circ:** 800 (ctrl). Documents available from BIOSIS Document Express, CASDDS.
Ind/Abst AgBiotech News Inf.; AGRICOLA; Agrofor. Abstr. (1991-); Biol. Abstr.; Chem. Abstr.; Crop Physiol. Abstr.; Curr. Cit.; Field Crop Abstr.; Food Sci. Technol. Abstr.; For. Abstr.; Grass. Forage Abstr.; Hortic. Abstr.; Index Vet.; Irr. Drain. Abstr.; Maize Abstr.; Ornamental Hort.; Plant Breed. Abstr.; Plant Genet. Resour. Abstr.; Plant Grow. Reg. Abstr.; Postharvest News Inf.; Potato Abstr.; Rev. Agric. Entomol.; Rev. Plant Pathol.; Rice Abstr.; Seed Abstr.; Soils Fert.; Sorghum Mill. Abstr.; Soyabean Abstr.; Vitis Vitic. Enol. Abstr.; Weed Abstr.; Wheat Barley Trit. Abstr.

ISSN 0253-4355
II
CODEN IPLPDQ

INDIAN JOURNAL OF PLANT PROTECTION. [Indian j. plant prof.]. **Added/Corp** Plant Protection Association of India. Vol. 1 (Oct. 1973)-. Academic Scholarly Publication. English. Two times a year. $30.00. Scientific Publishers, PO Box 91, Ratanada Road, Jodhpur 342011 India. **(Subscription address:** Prints India, 11 Darya Ganj, New Delhi 110002 India. **Tel** 011 91 11 3268645, FAX 011 91 11 3275542, telex 31-61087 PRIN-IN.**) ED** M Vasudevan Rao. **Bk Rev. Ad Acc. Circ:** 350. Documents available from BIOSIS Document Express, CASDDS.
Ind/Abst Agric. Eng. Abstr. (1991-); Agrofor. Abstr. (1991-); Biocont. News Inf. (19??-19??); Biodeter. Abstr. (19??-19??); Biol. Abstr. (1984-); Chem. Abstr.; Cot. Trop. Fibr. Abstr. Bibliogr.; Curr. Cit.; Field Crop Abstr.; For. Prod. Abstr. (19??-19??); For. Abstr.; Hortic. Abstr.; Maize Abstr.; Nematol. Abstr.; Plant Breed. Abstr.; Plant Genet. Resour. Abstr.; Postharvest News Inf.; Potato Abstr.; Rev. Agric. Entomol.; Rev. Med. Vet. Entomol.; Rev. Med. Vet. Mycology; Rev. Plant Pathol.; Rice Abstr.; Seed Abstr.; Soils Fert.; Sorghum Mill. Abstr.; Soyabean Abstr.; Weed Abstr.; Wheat Barley Trit. Abstr.

LC QK **ISSN** 0970-0404
DD 581 II
UDC 58
CODEN IPTSE8

INDIAN JOURNAL OF PLANT SCIENCES. [Indian j. plant sci.]. Vol. 1 (1983)-. English. Two times a year. $50.00. Scientific Publishers, PO Box 91, Ratanada Road, Jodhpur 342011 India. **(Subscription address:** Prints India, 11 Darya Ganj, New Delhi 110002 India. **Tel** 011 91 11 3268645, FAX 011 91 11 3275542, telex 31-61087 PRIN-IN.**)**

ISSN 0970-6380
II
UDC 635.65

INDIAN JOURNAL OF PULSES RESEARCH. [Indian J. Pulses Res.]. (1988)-. Periodical. English. Two times a year. $75.00. **(Subscription address:** Prints India, 11 Darya Ganj, New Delhi 110002 India. **Tel** 011 91 11 3268645, FAX 011 91 11 3275542, telex 31-61087 PRIN-IN.**)**
Ind/Abst Agrofor. Abstr.; Crop Physiol. Abstr.; Field Crop Abstr.; For. Abstr.; Irr. Drain. Abstr.; Nematol. Abstr.; Plant Breed. Abstr.; Plant Genet. Resour. Abstr.; Rev. Plant Pathol.; Seed Abstr.; Soils Fert.

LC QK564 .I48
DD 589.3/0954/05 II

INDIAN PHYCOLOGICAL REVIEW. Vol. 1 (1992)-. English. One time a year. $65.00. Bishen Singh Mahendra Pal Sing, 23A Connaught Place, PO Box 137, Dehra Dun 248 001 India. **Tel** 011 91 935 24048. **(Subscription address:** Prints India, 11 Darya Ganj, New Delhi 110002 India. **Tel** 011 91 11 3268645, FAX 011 91 11 3275542, telex 31-61087 PRIN-IN.**)**

LC SB599 .I53 **ISSN** 0367-973X
DD 582/02/0954 II
NLM W1 IN266S **CODEN** IPHYAU

INDIAN PHYTOPATHOLOGY. [Indian phytopathol.]. **Added/Corp** Indian Phytopathological Society. Vol. 1 (1948)-. Periodical. English. Four times a year. $80.00. Indian Phytopathological Society, New Delhi India. **(Subscription address:** Prints India, 11 Darya Ganj, New Delhi 110002 India. **Tel** 011 91 11 3268645, FAX 011 91 11 3275542, telex 31-61087 PRIN-IN.**)** Documents available from BIOSIS Document Express, CASDDS.
Ind/Abst AGRICOLA; Biocont. News Inf. (19??-19??); Biodeter. Abstr. (19??-19??); Biol. Abstr.; Chem. Abstr.; Cot. Trop. Fibr. Abstr. Bibliogr.; Crop Physiol. Abstr.; Field Crop Abstr.; Food Sci. Technol. Abstr.; For. Prod. Abstr.; For. Abstr.; Hortic. Abstr.; Maize Abstr.; Nematol. Abstr.; Life Sci. Collect.; PESTDOC; Plant Breed. Abstr.; Plant Genet. Resour. Abstr.; Plant Grow. Reg. Abstr.; Postharvest News Inf.; Potato Abstr.; Protozoolog. Abstr.; Rev. Agric. Entomol.; Rev. Med. Vet. Mycology; Rev. Plant Pathol.; Rice Abstr.; Seed Abstr.; Soils Fert.; Sorghum Mill. Abstr.; Soyabean Abstr.; Weed Abstr.

LC QK1 .I54 **ISSN** 0020-0697
IT
CODEN IBOIBM

INFORMATORE BOTANICO ITALIANO. (INFORMATORE BOTANICO ITALIANO : BOLLETTINO DELLA SOCIETA BOTANICA ITALIANA.). [Inf. bot. ital.]. **Added/Corp** Societa Botanica Italiana. (Jan./April 1969)-. Academic Scholarly Publication. Italian (English and French). Three times a year. L20000. Societa Botanica Italiana, Via la Pira 4, 50121 Florence Italy. **Tel** 011 39 55 2757379. Index available. **Circ:** 1,000. Documents available from BIOSIS Document Express, CASDDS.
Ind/Abst AGRICOLA; Biol. Abstr.; Chem. Abstr.

ISSN 0020-0735
IT
CODEN INFTAP

INFORMATORE FITOPATOLOGICO. [Inf. fitopatol.]. **Added/Corp** Italy. Direzione Generale della Produzione Agricola. Vol. 1 (1951)-. Periodical. Italian. Eleven times a year. L49740. Edagricole, PO Box 2157, 40100 Bologna Italy. **Tel** 011 39 51 492211 Ext. 22, FAX 011 39 51 493660, telex 510336 EDAGRI. Documents available from CASDDS.
Ind/Abst AGRICOLA; Biocont. News Inf. (1991-); Biodeter. Abstr. (1991-); Chem. Abstr.; Chem. Bus. Bull.; Chem. Bus. NewsBase (1989-); Chem. Bus. Update; Field Crop Abstr.; For. Prod. Abstr.; For. Abstr.; Hortic. Abstr.; Index Vet.; Maize Abstr.; Nematol. Abstr.; Ornamental Hort. (1991-); Plant Breed. Abstr.; Postharvest News Inf.; Potato Abstr.; Rev. Agric. Entomol.; Rev. Med. Vet. Entomol.; Rev. Med. Vet. Mycology; Rev. Plant Pathol.; Rice Abstr.; Soils Fert.; Soyabean Abstr.; Vitis Vitic. Enol. Abstr.; Weed Abstr.; Wheat Barley Trit. Abstr.

LC SB599 .I67
DD 632 NR

INTERAFRICAIN PHYTOSANITARY BULLETIN. **Added/Corp** Inter-African Phytosanitary Council. **VFOAT** Bulletin d'Informations Phytosanitaires Interafricain; Bulletin Interafricain d'Informations Phytosanitaires. (19??)-. Bulletin. Multiple languages (English and French). Interafricain Phytosanitary Council, BP 4170 Nglongkak, Yaounde Cameroon.

LC QK475 .I57a **ISSN** 0307-322X
DD 582/.16/005 UK

INTERNATIONAL DENDROLOGY SOCIETY YEARBOOK. (YEAR BOOK.). [Int. Dendrol. Soc. yearb.]. **Main/Corp** International Dendrology Society. **VFOAT** Yearbook - International Dendrology Society. (1966)-. English. One time a year. $26.53. International Dendrology Society, School House, Stannington Morpeth, Northumberland NE61 6HF United Kingdom. **Tel** 011 44 167 0789289, FAX 011 44 167 0789235. **ED** D.G. Jamison. Index available. **Bk Rev. Circ:** 1,200 (ctrl).
Desc: Contains articles on tours made by members and their study of trees throughout the world.
Ind/Abst Plant Genet. Resour. Abstr.

LC QK569.D54 I57 **ISSN** 0882-2093
DD 589.4/81/025 US

INTERNATIONAL DIATOMIST DIRECTORY. [Int. diatomist dir.]. **Added/Corp** Environmental Research & Technology, Inc. (19??)-. Directory. English. Environmental Research and Technology Inc, PO Box 2150, 1716 Heath Parkway, Fort Collins CO 80522.

LC QK1 .B3 ISSN 1058-5893
DD 580 US
CCC
CODEN IPLSE2

INTERNATIONAL JOURNAL OF PLANT SCIENCES. [Int. j. plant sci.]. **VFOAT** Plant Sciences; IJPS. Vol. 153, No. 1 (Mar. 1992)-. Academic Scholarly Publication. English. Six times a year. $182.00. University of Chicago Press / Journals Division, PO Box 37005, 5720 South Woodlawn, Chicago IL 60637. **Tel** (312)753-3347, FAX (312)753-0811. **ED** Edward D. Garber and Manfred Ruddat. **Acid Free.** available in microform. Documents available from The Genuine Article, BIOSIS Document Express, UMI Article Clearinghouse, CASDDS. ***Continues*** *Botanical Gazette (Chicago, Ill.), 0006-8071.*
Desc: Presents the results of original investigations in all areas of plant biology, including development, physiology, reproduction, evolution, cell biology, genetics, ecology, systematics and paleobotany.
Ind/Abst Abstr. Bull. Inst. Pap. Sci. Tech.; Acad. Search; AGRICOLA; Biol. Agric. Index; Biol. Abstr.; Chem. Abstr.; Curr. Aware. Biol. Sci., CABS; Curr. Contents Agric. Biol. Environ. Sci.; EMBASE; Energy Res. Abstr.; EP Collect.; Expand. Acad. Index (1992-); Gen. Sci. Index; Gen. Sci. Source; GeoRef; Homework Help.; INFO-SOUTH Abstr.; Int. Aerosp. Abstr.; MasterFile FullTEXT 1000; MasterFile FullTEXT 350; MasterFile FullTEXT 650; MasterFile FullTEXT (July 1993-); Newsp. Period. Abstr. (1991-); OCLC; Life Sci. Collect.; PESTDOC; Ref. Upd. Deluxe Ed.; Res. Alert [Full Cov.]; Sci. Cit. Index; Telebase; VETDOC.

LC SB724 .I57 ISSN 0254-0126
DD 632/.3/0913 II
CCC
CODEN IJTSEY

INTERNATIONAL JOURNAL OF TROPICAL PLANT DISEASES. [Int. j. trop. plant dis.]. Vol. 1, No. 1 (Jan./June 1983)-. Periodical. English. Two times a year. $90.00. Today and Tomorrow's Printers and Publishers, 24-B/5 Desh Bandhu Gupta Road, Karol Bagh, New Delhi 110 005 India. **Tel** 011 91 11 5721928, 011 91 11 572770, FAX 011 91 11 7210073 (TTPP). **(Subscription address:** Prints India, 11 Darya Ganj, New Delhi 110002 India. **Tel** 011 91 11 3268645, FAX 011 91 11 3275542, telex 31-61087 PRIN-IN.) **ED** S. P. Raychaudhuri and Anupam Varma. Index available (bound in last issue). **Bk Rev. Ad Acc, Adv Mgr:** S Jain. **Circ:** 500 (ctrl). Documents available from BIOSIS Document Express.
Desc: Strives to assist in the process of developing effective solutions to international plant disease problems on a global basis.
Ind/Abst Biodeter. Abstr.; Biol. Abstr. (1985-); Crop Physiol. Abstr.; Curr. Cit.; Food Sci. Technol. Abstr.; Irr. Drain. Abstr.; Maize Abstr.; Microbiol. Abstr. Sect. A; Microbiol. Abstr. Sect. C; Nematol. Abstr.; Life Sci. Collect. (1985-); Potato Abstr.; Soyabean Abstr.

ISSN 0731-2830
GW
UDC 582.29

INTERNATIONAL LICHENOLOGICAL NEWSLETTER. [Int. lichenol. newsl.]. Vol. 1 (Apr. 1967)-. Newsletter. English (French, German and Spanish). Two times a year. $20.00. International Association Lichenology, Department of Biology, University of Nebraska at Omaha, Omaha NE 68182-0040. **Tel** (402)554-2491. **(Subscription address:** International Association Lichenologica, University of Nebraska, Biology Department, Omaha NE 68182. **Tel** (402)554-2491.) **ED** Harrie Sipman. **Bk Rev. Ad Acc.** ctrl circ.

LC QK
DD 581 US

INTERNATIONAL PLANT BIOTECHNOLOGY NETWORK, THE. **Added/Corp** Colorado State University. Tissue Culture for Crops Project. United States. Agency for International Development. No. 4 (June 1985)-. Periodical. English. ***Continues*** *Tissue Culture for Crops.*
Ind/Abst Rev. Plant Pathol.; Sorghum Mill. Abstr.

LC SB108.R9 I454
DD 581 TK

INTRODUKTSIIA I EKOLOGIIA RASTENII. **Added/Corp** Merkezi Botanika Bagy (Turkmenistan SSR Ylymlar Akademiiasy). (1968)-. Russian. Izdatelstvo Ylym, Ulitsa Engelsa 6, 744000 Ashkhabad Turkmenistan. **Tel** 3632 9 04 84.

ISSN 1016-4928
US

IOP NEWSLETTER. See Paleontology.

ISSN 0141-2787
SZ

IOS BULLETIN. [IOS bull.]. **VFOAT** International Organization for Succulent Plant Study Bulletin. (1958)-. English. One time a year. Comes with membership. International Organization for Succulent Plant Study, Mythenquai 88, CH-8002 Zurich Switzerland. ***Continues*** *IOS Circular.*

LC SB123.3 .I57
DD 631.54 SI

•IPGRI NEWSLETTER FOR ASIA, THE PACIFIC AND OCEANIA. **Added/Corp** International Plant Genetic Resources Institute. Regional Office for Asia, the Pacific, and Oceania. **VFOAT** Newsletter for Asia, the Pacific and Oceania; APO Newsletter. **VAT** International Plant Genetic Resources Institute Newsletter for Asia, the Pacific and Oceania. No. 14 (Apr. 1994)-. Periodical. English. Three times a year. IPGRI / International Plant Genetic Resources Institute, Office for Asia, The Pacific and Oceania, Singapore. ***Continues*** *IBPGR Newsletter for Asia and the Pacific.*

ISSN 0921-2566
NE
NLM W1 I266G

IPO ANNUAL PROGRESS REPORT. [IPO annu. prog. rep.]. **Main/Corp** Institute for Perception Research. **Added/Corp** Instituut voor Perceptie Onderzoek. **VFOAT** Annual Progress Report. No. 1 (1966)-. Periodical. English. One time a year. Instituut voor Plantenziektekundig Onderzoek, Bibnnehaven 12, 6700 Wageningen Netherlands.
Ind/Abst Psychol. Abstr. (1974-); PsycINFO; PsycLit; Soc. Plann. Policy Dev. Abstr.

ISSN 0021-0838
IR
CODEN IJPLBO

IRANIAN JOURNAL OF PLANT PATHOLOGY. [Iran. j. plant pathol.]. **Added/Corp** Iranian Phytopathological Society. Plant Pests and Diseases Research Institute. (19??)-. Academic Scholarly Publication. Persian (summaries and/or abstracts in English). Four times a year. Iranian Phytopathological Society, Box 19395-1454, Teheran Iran. **Circ:** 2,000. Documents available from CASDDS.
Ind/Abst AGRICOLA; Biodeter. Abstr. (1991-); Chem. Abstr. (1964-1981); Postharvest News Inf.; Rev. Agric. Entomol.; Rev. Plant Pathol.; Rice Abstr.; Seed Abstr.; Wheat Barley Trit. Abstr.

LC QK
DD 581 US

ISELYA. **Added/Corp** X Club. Vol. 1 (Jan. 1979)-. Periodical. English. Two times a year. $10.00 institutions; $8.00 individuals. Iselya, Nicholls Street, University of Louisiana, Thibodaux LA 70310. **Tel** (504)446-8111 ext. 217.

LC QK1 .I93 ISSN 0792-9978
IS
CCC
Pr Rev.

•ISRAEL JOURNAL OF PLANT SCIENCES. Vol. 42, No. 1 (1994)-. Periodical. English. Four times a year. $205.00. Laser Pages Publishing Ltd., PO Box 50257, Jerusalem 91502 Israel. **Tel** 011 972 2 829770, 011 972 2 370699, FAX 011 972 2 818782. Index available. cum. index. **Bk Rev. Ad Acc.** ***Continues*** *Israel Journal of Botany, 0021-213X.*
Desc: Basic and applied plant sciences with emphasis on Israel and the surrounding areas. Special issues in pollination ecology, germination, physiology, and wheat.
Ind/Abst Curr. Cit.

ISSN 0213-8530
SP
UDC 58

ITINERA GEOBOTANICA. [Itinera geobot.]. **Added/Corp** Servicio Internationale de Phytosociologie. Seccion Espanola. (1987)-. Monographic series. Multiple languages. Irregular. Price varies per volume.
Ind/Abst Ecol. Abstr.

LC QK710 .I88 ISSN 0202-7186
DD 581.1 RU
CODEN ITFRDU

ITOGI NAUKI I TEKHNIKI. SERIIA FIZIOLOGIIA RASTENII. **Added/Corp** Vsesoiuznyi Institut Nauchnoi i Tekhnicheskoi Informatsii (Soviet Union). **VFOAT** Seriia Fiziologiia Rastenii; Fiziologiia Rastenii; Itogi Nauki i Tekhniki. Fiziologiia Rastenii. (1973)-. Monographic series. Russian. Price varies per volume. VINITI - Vsesoyuznyi Institut Nauchno-Tekhnicheskoi Informatsii, All-Union Scientific and Technical Information Institute, Baltiiskaia ulitsa 14, 125219 Moscow Russia. **Tel** 011 7 95 2384600, FAX 011 7 95 9430060, telex 411160.

LC SB123 .I88 ISSN 0202-716X
DD 631.5 RU

ITOGI NAUKI I TEKHNIKI. SERIIA RASTENIEVODSTVO. **Added/Corp** Vsesoiuznyi Institut Nauchnoi i Tekhnicheskoi Informatsii (Soviet Union). **VFOAT** Seriia Rastenievodstvo; Rastenievodstvo; Itogi Nauki i Tekhniki. Prastenievodstvo. (1979)-. Monographic series. Russian. Irregular. Price varies per volume. VINITI - Vsesoyuznyi Institut Nauchno-Tekhnicheskoi Informatsii, All-Union Scientific and Technical Information Institute, Baltiiskaia ulitsa 14, 125219 Moscow Russia. **Tel** 011 7 95 2384600, FAX 011 7 95 9430060, telex 411160. ***Continues*** *Itogi Nauki i Tekhniki. Rastenievodstvo.*

ISSN 0882-4142
DD 582 US

IVY JOURNAL. [Ivy j.]. **Added/Corp** American Ivy Society. Vol. 8, No. 1 (Mar. 1982)-. Periodical. English. Three times a year. comes with membership. American Ivy Society, PO Box 2123, Naples FL 33939. **ED** Rachel Cobb. Index available. **Bk Rev. Ad Acc. Circ:** 300. ***Continues*** *Ivy Bulletin.*
Desc: Life-size photos, feature articles on ivy culture, descriptions of new cultivars, hardiness testing, history, uses.
Ind/Abst Hortic. Abstr.; Ornamental Hort. (19??-19??); Plant Breed. Abstr.

LC QK
DD 581.652 US

IWSS. **Main/Corp** International Weed Science Society. **Added/Corp** Oregon State University. International Weed Science Society. **VFOAT** IWSS Newsletter. Vol. 1, No. 1 (June 1976)-. Newsletter. English. Two times a year (June, Dec.). $10.00. International Weed Science Society, OSU, Cordley Hall 2040, Corvallis OR 97331-2915. **Tel** (503)737-3541, FAX (503)737-3080. **ED** Susan Larson. **Bk Rev. Circ:** 450.
Desc: Newsletter of the International Weed Science Society. Dedicated to encourage, promote, and assist development of weed science and weed control technology.

LC QH109.J5 J36
DD 508.729 JM

JAMAICA NATURALIST. See Natural History.

LC QK ISSN 0183-5173
DD 581 FR
CODEN JATADT
SUSPENDED

JOURNAL D'AGRICULTURE TRADITIONNELLE ET DE BOTANIQUE APPLIQUEE. See Agriculture.

PL

•JOURNAL OF APPLIED GENETICS. See Biology-Genetics.

LC SH338.7 .J68 ISSN 0921-8971
DD 660/.62 NE
CCC
NLM W1; JO541V CODEN JAPPEL
Pr Rev.

JOURNAL OF APPLIED PHYCOLOGY. [J. appl. phycol.]. **VFOAT** Phycology. Vol. 1, No. 1 (April 1989)-. Periodical. English. Six times a year. $474.00. Kluwer Academic Publishers, Postbus 322, 3300 AH Dordrecht The Netherlands. **Tel** 011 31 78 524400, FAX 011 31 78 183273, telex 20083. **ED** B.A. Whitton. **Acid Free.** available on microfilm and microfiche from University Microfilms International (UMI). Documents available from The Genuine Article, BIOSIS Document Express.
Desc: The journal accepts submissions on fundamental research, development of techniques and practical applications in such areas as algal and cyanobacterial biotechnology and genetic engineering, tissues culture, culture collections, commercially useful micro-algae and their products, mariculture, algalization and soil fertility, pollution and fouling, monitoring , toxicity tests, toxic compounds, antibiotics and other biologically active compounds.
Ind/Abst Aquat. Sci. Fish. Abstr. [CD-ROM Ed.]; Biol. Abstr. (1991-); Curr. Aware. Biol. Sci., CABS; Curr. Cit.; Curr. Contents Soc. Behav. Sci.; Ecology Abstr.; Environ. Period. Bibliogr.; Fish Rev. (Jan. 1989-July 1992); Fresh. Aqua. Contents Tables; Mar. Sci. Contents Tables; Microbiol. Abstr. Sect. C (1991-); Ocean. Abstr.; PESTDOC; Res. Alert [Full Cov.]; Rev. Med. Vet. Mycology; Sci. Cit. Index; SCISEARCH; Wildl. Rev. (Jan. 1989-July 1992).

ISSN 0146-6623
US
CODEN JAPMDB
Pr Rev.

JOURNAL OF AQUATIC PLANT MANAGEMENT. (JOURNAL OF AQUATIC PLANT MANAGEMENT : A PUBLICATION OF THE AQUATIC PLANT MANAGEMENT SOCIETY, INC.). [J. aquat. plant manage.]. **Added/Corp** Aquatic Plant Management Society. (1976)-. Academic Scholarly Publication. English. Two times a year (Jan. & July). $70.00. Aquatic Plant Management Society, PO Box 121086, Clermont FL 34712-1086. **Tel** (202)272-1841, FAX (202)272-0907. **ED** Dr. W. T. Haller (editor's address: University of Florida Center for Aquatic Plants, 7922 Northwest 71st Street, Gainesville, FL 32606, phone: (904)392-9613). Index available. cum. index. **Circ:** 700 (ctrl). Documents available from The Genuine Article, CASDDS. ***Continues*** *Hyacinth Control Journal, 0146-9533.*
Desc: Management of aquatic plants, aquatic plant ecology, aquatic plant control.
Ind/Abst AGRICOLA; Aquat. Sci. Fish. Abstr. [CD-ROM Ed.]; Biocont. News Inf. (19??-19??); Chem. Abstr.; Curr. Aware. Biol. Sci., CABS; Curr. Cit.; Curr. Contents Agric. Biol. Environ. Sci.; Ecology Abstr.; Irr. Drain. Abstr.; Nutr. Abstr. Rev., Ser. B, Live Feeds and Feed.; Life Sci. Collect.; Plant Grow. Reg. Abstr.; Pollut. Abstr. Indexes; Res. Alert [Full Cov.]; Rev. Agric. Entomol.; Rev. Med. Vet. Entomol.; Sci. Cit. Index; SCISEARCH; Weed Abstr.

LC QK534 .B82 ISSN 0373-6687
DD 588 UK
CODEN JBRYAR

Pr Rev.

JOURNAL OF BRYOLOGY. [J. bryol.]. **Added/Corp** British Bryological Society. Vol. 7 (1972)-. English. Two times a year. $163.00. W. S. Maney and Son Ltd., Hudson Road, Leeds LS9 7DL United Kingdom. **Tel** 011 44 1532 497481, FAX 011 44 1532 486983. **ED** A Y E Smith. **Bk Rev. Ad Acc. Circ:** 900. available on microfilm and microfiche from University Microfilms International (UMI). Documents available from The Genuine Article, BIOSIS Document Express. ***Continues*** *British Bryological Society. Transactions.*
Desc: The study and classification of mosses and liverworts.
Ind/Abst AGRICOLA [Full Cov.]; Biol. Abstr.; Curr. Aware. Biol. Sci., CABS; Curr. Contents Agric. Biol. Environ. Sci.; Life Sci. Collect.; Res. Alert [Full Cov.]; Sci. Cit. Index; SCISEARCH.

LC QK ISSN 0022-0477
DD 581 UK
CCC
NLM W1 JO626R CODEN JECOAB

Pr Rev.

JOURNAL OF ECOLOGY, THE. [J. ecol.]. **Added/Corp** British Ecological Society. Vol. 1 (March 1913)-. Academic Scholarly Publication. English. Six times a year. $380.00. Blackwell Scientific Publications Ltd, Marston Book Services, PO Box 88, Oxford OX2 ONE United Kingdom. **Tel** 011 44 1865 206206, FAX 011 44 1865 206219, telex 837 515 MARDIS G. **ED** B. Moss, J. Lee and J. White. Index available. cum. index. **Bk Rev. Ad Acc. Circ:** 4,200. available on microfilm and microfiche from University Microfilms International (UMI). Documents available from The Genuine Article, BIOSIS Document Express, UMI Article Clearinghouse, CASDDS, Documents on Demand.
Desc: Original research papers on any aspect of plant ecology, provided they contain elements of general interest.
Ind/Abst Acad. Search; AGRICOLA [Select. Cov.]; Agrofor. Abstr.; AQUAREF; Aquat. Sci. Fish. Abstr. [CD-ROM Ed.]; Biocont. News Inf.; Biol. Agric. Index; Biol. Abstr.; Biostatistica (19??-19??); Br. Archaeol. Bibliogr.; Chem. Abstr.; Crop Physiol. Abstr.; Curr. Aware. Biol. Sci., CABS; Curr. Cit.; Curr. Contents Agric. Biol. Environ. Sci.; Curr. Ref. Fish Res.; Ecol. Abstr.; Ecology Abstr.; EMBASE; Energy Res. Abstr.; Environ. Abstr.; Environ. Period. Bibliogr.; EP Collect.; Expand. Acad. Index (1989-); Field Crop Abstr.; Fish Rev.; For. Prod. Abstr.; For. Abstr.; Fresh. Aqua. Contents Tables; Gen. Sci. Index; Gen. Sci. Source; Geogr. Abstr. Phys. Geogr.; Geogr. Abstr. Human Geogr.; Geol. Abstr.; Grass. Forage Abstr.; Homework Help.; INFO-SOUTH Abstr.; Int. Dev. Abstr.; Irr. Drain. Abstr.; Mag. Search; MasterFile FullTEXT 1000; MasterFile FullTEXT 350; MasterFile FullTEXT 650; MasterFile FullTEXT (Jan. 1994-); Nematol. Abstr.; Newsp. Period. Abstr. (1991-); Nutr. Abstr. Rev., Ser. B, Live Feeds and Feed.; OCLC; Ornamental Hort. (1991-); Life Sci. Collect.; Plant Breed. Abstr.; Plant Genet. Resour. Abstr.; Protozoolog. Abstr.; Res. Alert [Full Cov.]; Rev. Agric. Entomol.; Rev. Med. Vet. Mycology; Rev. Plant Pathol.; Rice Abstr.; Sci. Cit. Index; SCISEARCH; Seed Abstr.; Soils Fert.; Stat. Theory Method Abstr. (1959-1963, 1966-1970, 1976, 1978, 1980-1982); Telebase; Weed Abstr.; Wildl. Rev.; World Agric. Econ. Rural Sociol. Abstr.

LC QK ISSN 0250-9768
DD 581 II
CODEN JETBDQ

JOURNAL OF ECONOMIC AND TAXONOMIC BOTANY. [J. econ. taxon. bot.]. **Added/Corp** Society for Economic and Taxonomic Botany (India). **VFOAT** J. Econ. Tax. Bot. Vol. 1, No. 1 & 2 (1980)-. Academic Scholarly Publication. English. Irregular. Price varies. Arid Zone Research Association India, Jodhpur 342 003, Rajasthan India. **Tel** telex 218 CAZRI_IN_JU. **(Subscription address:** Prints India, 11 Darya Ganj, New Delhi 110002 India. **Tel** 011 91 11 3268645, FAX 011 91 11 3275542, telex 31-61087 PRIN-IN.) **ED** J K Maheshwari, M M Bhandari, Pawan Kumar. **Bk Rev. Ad Acc. Circ:** 300 (ctrl). Documents available from BIOSIS Document Express.
Desc: Economic botany, ethnobotany, medicinal plants, poisonous plants of economic importance and taxonomic botany which includes flora, phyto-geography, new records, new species, monographic work, revisionary work, and other aspects of taxonomic botany.
Ind/Abst Biol. Abstr.; EMBASE; Field Crop Abstr.; Grass. Forage Abstr.

LC QP958 .J68 ISSN 1041-2905
DD 668 US
CCC
CODEN JEOREG

JOURNAL OF ESSENTIAL OIL RESEARCH, THE. **See** Chemistry and Chemicals-Chemical Technology.

LC QK1 .J763 ISSN 0022-0957
DD 581 UK
CCC
CODEN JEBOA6

Pr Rev.

JOURNAL OF EXPERIMENTAL BOTANY. [J. exp. bot.]. **Added/Corp** Society for Experimental Biology (Great Britain). (March 1950)-. Periodical. English. Twelve times a year. $630.00. Oxford University Press / UK, Walton Street, Oxford OX2 6DP United Kingdom. **Tel** 011 44 1865 56767, FAX 011 44 1865 267773, telex 851/837330 OXPRES G. **(Subscription address:** Oxford University Press / USA, Journals Marketing Department, Oxford University Press, 2001 Evans Road, Cary NC 27513. **Tel** (800)451-7556, (919)677-0977, FAX (919)677-1714.) **ED** J. L. Hall. Index available. **Bk Rev. Ad Acc. Circ:** 1,500. available on microfilm and microfiche from University Microfilms International (UMI). Documents available from The Genuine Article, BIOSIS Document Express, CASDDS.
Desc: Papers in the field of plant physiology, biochemistry, and biophysics.
Ind/Abst Abstr. Bull. Inst. Pap. Sci. Tech.; AgBiotech News Inf.; AGRICOLA [Full Cov.]; Biol. Agric. Index; Biol. Abstr.; Chem. Abstr.; Cot. Trop. Fibr. Abstr. Bibliogr.; Crop Physiol. Abstr.; Curr. Cit.; Curr. Contents Agric. Biol. Environ. Sci.; PESTDOC; Curr. Contents Life Sci.; EMBASE; Field Crop Abstr.; Food Sci. Technol. Abstr.; For. Prod. Abstr. (19??-19??); For. Abstr.; Grass. Forage Abstr.; Hortic. Abstr.; Irr. Drain. Abstr.; Leadscan; NAPRALERT; Nematol. Abstr.; Ornamental Hort. (19??-19??); Life Sci. Collect.; PESTDOC; Plant Breed. Abstr.; Plant Genet. Resour. Abstr.; Plant Grow. Reg. Abstr.; Postharvest News Inf.; Potato Abstr.; Protozoolog. Abstr.; Ref. Upd. Deluxe Ed.; Res. Alert [Full Cov.]; Rev. Med. Vet. Mycology; Rev. Plant Pathol.; Rice Abstr.; Sci. Cit. Index; SCISEARCH; Seed Abstr.; Soils Fert.; Sorghum Mill. Abstr.; Soyabean Abstr.; Vitis Vitic. Enol. Abstr.; Weed Abstr.

UK

JOURNAL OF KEW GUILD. (19??)-. English. One time a year (May). £15.00. Kew Guild, Royal Botanic Gardens / Kew, Richmond Surrey TW9 3AB United Kingdom. **Tel** 011 44 181 3325116, FAX 011 44 181 3325197. **ED** Richard Ward (editor's telephone: 011 44 81 948 2970). **Ad Acc. Circ:** 600.
Desc: Annual reporting on activities of Kewites, awards made and activities at the Royal Botanic Gardens.

LC QE993 .J68 ISSN 0022-3379
DD 582/.0463 II
CCC
CODEN JPLYAR

JOURNAL OF PALYNOLOGY. [J. palynol.]. **Added/Corp** Palynological Society of India. Vol. 1, (1965)-. Periodical. English. Two times a year. $40.00. Today and Tomorrow's Printers and Publishers, 24-B/5 Desh Bandhu Gupta Road, Karol Bagh, New Delhi 110 005 India. **Tel** 011 91 11 5721928, 011 91 11 572770, FAX 011 91 11 7210073 (TTPP). **(Subscription address:** Prints India, 11 Darya Ganj, New Delhi 110002 India. **Tel** 011 91 11 3268645, FAX 011 91 11 3275542, telex 31-61087 PRIN-IN.) **ED** Sunirmal Chanda, Division of Palynology and Environmental Biology, Bose Institute, Calcutta 700 009 India. **Circ:** 400. Documents available from BIOSIS Document Express, CASDDS. ***Absorbed*** *Palynological Bulletin, 0031-0492.*
Desc: Dedicated to promoting the dissemination of palynological knowledge, covering all aspects of pollen spore studies, from algae to aniosperms.
Ind/Abst Biol. Abstr.; Chem. Abstr.; Ecol. Abstr. (?-?); Geogr. Abstr. Phys. Geogr. (?-?); Geol. Abstr.; GeoRef (1987-); Rev. Plant Pathol.

LC QK564 ISSN 0022-3646
DD 589/.3/05 US
UDC 582.26
CODEN JPYLAJ

Pr Rev.

JOURNAL OF PHYCOLOGY. [J. phycol.]. Vol. 1 (1965)-. Periodical. English. Six times a year. $250.00. Allen Press Inc., 810 East 10th Street, PO Box 1897, Lawrence KS 66044-8897. **Tel** (913)843-1221, (800)627-0629, FAX (913)843-1274. **(Subscription address:** Journal of Phycology, PO Box 1897, Lawrence KS 66044-8897.) **ED** Carole A. Lembi. Index available. cum. index. **Ad Acc. Acid Free. Circ:** 2,000 (ctrl). Documents available from The Genuine Article, BIOSIS Document Express, CASDDS. ***Supersedes*** *News Bulletin - Phycological Society of America.*
Desc: Publishes all aspects of research on algae to provide a common medium for the taxonomist, ecologist, morphologist, cytologist, physiologist, biochemist and molecular biologist.
Ind/Abst Abstr. Bull. Inst. Pap. Sci. Tech.; AGRICOLA; Aquat. Sci. Fish. Abstr. [CD-ROM Ed.]; Biol. Abstr.; Chem. Abstr.; Coal Abstr.; Curr. Aware. Biol. Sci., CABS; Curr. Cit.; Curr. Contents Agric. Biol. Environ. Sci.; Ecol. Abstr.; Ecology Abstr.; Energy Res. Abstr.; Genet. Abstr.; INIS Atomindex [Micro.]; Int. Aerosp. Abstr.; Mar. Sci. Contents Tables; Microbiol. Abstr. Sect. C; Ocean. Abstr.; Life Sci. Collect.; Res. Alert [Full Cov.]; Sci. Cit. Index; SCISEARCH.

ISSN 0970-5767
II
CODEN JPHREO

JOURNAL OF PHYTOLOGICAL RESEARCH. (JOURNAL OF PHYTOLOGICAL RESEARCH : A PUBLICATION OF PHYTOLOGICAL SOCIETY.). [J. phytol. res.]. **Added/Corp** Phytological Society. (1988)-. Periodical. English. Two times a year. $50.00. **(Subscription address:** Prints India, 11 Darya Ganj, New Delhi 110002 India. **Tel** 011 91 11 3268645, FAX 011 91 11 3275542, telex 31-61087 PRIN-IN.) Documents available from BIOSIS Document Express.
Ind/Abst Agrofor. Abstr.; Biocont. News Inf. (1991-); Biodeter. Abstr. (1991-); Biol. Abstr. (1991-); For. Abstr.; Hortic. Abstr.; Nematol. Abstr.; Plant Breed. Abstr.; Postharvest News Inf.; Rev. Agric. Entomol.; Rev. Plant Pathol.; Sorghum Mill. Abstr.; Weed Abstr.

LC QK640 .J68 ISSN 0256-436X
DD 581.4/05 II
CODEN JPMOE6

JOURNAL OF PLANT ANATOMY AND MORPHOLOGY. [J. plant anat. morphol.]. Vol. 1, No. 1 (Aug. 1984)-. Periodical. English (French). Two times a year. $70.00. Arid Zone Research Association India, Jodhpur 342 003, Rajasthan India. **Tel** telex 218 CAZRI_IN_JU. **(Subscription address:** Prints India, 11 Darya Ganj, New Delhi 110002 India. **Tel** 011 91 11 3268645, FAX 011 91 11 3275542, telex 31-61087 PRIN-IN.) **ED** Elizabeth G Cutter, M F Danilova, R B Knox, Y P S Bajaj, A N Rao, J A Inamdar. **Bk Rev. Ad Acc. Circ:** 300. Documents available from BIOSIS Document Express.
Desc: Journal provides rapid publication outlet for all types of research and review papers encompassing the descriptive and experimental studies on plants.
Ind/Abst AGRICOLA; Biol. Abstr. (1984-); For. Prod. Abstr.

LC QK
DD 581 KO
CODEN JPBIEZ

•**JOURNAL OF PLANT BIOLOGY = SINGMUL HAKHOE CHI. Added/Corp** Hanguk Singmul Hakhoe. **VFOAT** Singmul Hakhoe Chi; Plant Biology. Vol. 37, No. 1 (Mar. 1994)-. Periodical. English (Korean). Four times a year. $60.00. Botanical Society of Korea, Seoul National University, Department of Biology, Seoul 151-742 Korea. **Tel** 011 82 2 880 6676, FAX 011 82 872 6881. **ED** Kwang-Woong Lee. Index available (4th issue). **Ad Acc. Circ:** 800. ***Continues*** *Singmul Hakhoe Chi, 0583-421X.*
Desc: Devoted to all field of plant biology.

LC QK745 .J68 ISSN 0721-7595
DD 581.3/1 US
CCC
CODEN JPGRDI

Pr Rev.

JOURNAL OF PLANT GROWTH REGULATION. [J. plant growth reg.]. **Added/Corp** International Plant Growth Substances Association. Vol. 1, No. 1 (March 1982)-. Academic Scholarly Publication. English. Four times a year. $193.00. Springer-Verlag New York Inc., 175 Fifth Avenue, New York NY 10010. **Tel** (212)460-1500 ext 256, FAX (212)533-3503, telex 232 235 SPB UR. **(Subscription address:** Springer-Verlag New York Inc. / North America, PO Box 2485, Journal Fulfillment, Secaucus NJ 07096. **Tel** (201)348-4033, (800)777-4643, FAX (201)348-4505.) **ED** T C Moore. available on microfilm and microfiche from University Microfilms International (UMI). Documents available from The Genuine Article, CASDDS.
Desc: Focuses on both naturally occurring and synthetic growth substances-including herbicides and their effect on the growth and development of plants.
Ind/Abst Abstr. Bull. Inst. Paper Chem.; Abstr. Bull. Inst. Pap. Sci. Tech.; AgBiotech News Inf.; AGRICOLA [Full Cov.]; Agrofor. Abstr. (1991-); Chem. Abstr.; Crop Physiol. Abstr.; Curr. Cit.; Curr. Contents Agric. Biol. Environ. Sci.; Field Crop Abstr.; For. Abstr.; Hortic. Abstr.; Irr. Drain. Abstr.; Maize Abstr.; Ornamental Hort.; Life Sci. Collect.; PESTDOC; Plant Breed. Abstr.; Plant Genet. Resour. Abstr.; Plant Grow. Reg. Abstr.; Postharvest News Inf.; Potato Abstr.; Res. Alert [Full Cov.]; Rev. Plant Pathol.; Sci. Cit. Index; SCISEARCH; Seed Abstr.; Soils Fert.; Sorghum Mill. Abstr.; Soyabean Abstr.; Vitis Vitic. Enol. Abstr.; Weed Abstr.; Wheat Barley Trit. Abstr.

LC QK867 .J67 ISSN 0190-4167
DD 581.1/3/05 US
CCC
CODEN JPNUDS

Pr Rev.

JOURNAL OF PLANT NUTRITION. [J. plant nutr.]. Vol. 1 (June 1979)-. Academic Scholarly Publication. English. Twelve times a year. $950.00. Marcel Dekker Inc., 270 Madison Avenue, New York NY 10016. **Tel** (212)696-9000, (800)228-1160, FAX (212)685-4540, telex 421419. **(Subscription address:** Marcel Dekker Inc., PO Box 5017, Monticello NY 12701. **Tel** (800)228-1160.) **ED** J. Benton Jones, Jr. and Harry A. Mills. **Ad Acc.** ctrl circ. available on microfiche. Documents available from The Genuine Article, BIOSIS Document Express, CASDDS.
Desc: Devoted to the rapid communication of outstanding papers exploring the influence of the mineral elements on plant physiology and growth. Refereed by an

international editorial board, the original research articles and reviews published in this remarkably useful periodical provide a thorough yet concise source of current knowledge examining the influence of mineral elements on plant physiology and growth.
Ind/Abst AgBiotech News Inf.; AGRICOLA [Full Cov.]; Anal. Abstr.; BioBusiness; Biol. Agric. Index; Biol. Abstr.; Chem. Abstr.; Chem. Titles; Cot. Trop. Fibr. Abstr. Bibliogr.; Crop Physiol. Abstr.; Curr. Aware. Biol. Sci., CABS; Curr. Cit.; Curr. Contents Agric. Biol. Environ. Sci.; Environ. Period. Bibliogr.; Field Crop Abstr.; Grass. Forage Abstr.; Hortic. Abstr.; Irr. Drain. Abstr.; Maize Abstr.; Nematol. Abstr.; Nutr. Abstr. Rev., Ser. B, Live Feeds and Feed.; Ornamental Hort. (19??-19??); Plant Breed. Abstr.; Plant Grow. Reg. Abstr.; Postharvest News Inf.; Potato Abstr.; Ref. Upd. Deluxe Ed.; Res. Alert [Full Cov.]; Rev. Agric. Entomol.; Rice Abstr.; Sci. Cit. Index; SCISEARCH; Seed Abstr.; Soils Fert.; Sorghum Mill. Abstr.; Soyabean Abstr.; Vitis Vitic. Enol. Abstr.; Weed Abstr.; Wheat Barley Trit. Abstr.

LC QK1 .Z4 **ISSN** 0176-1617
DD 581.05/6 GW
CCC
CODEN JPPHEY
Pr Rev.

JOURNAL OF PLANT PHYSIOLOGY.

[J. plant physiol.]. Vol. 115 No. 1 (1984)-. Academic Scholarly Publication. English (French and German). Twelve times a year. $1240.00. Gustav Fischer Verlag Stuttgart, Postfach 720143, D-70577 Stuttgart Germany. **Tel** 011 49 711 458030, FAX 011 49 711 4580334, telex 2627-7111488. **(Subscription address:** VCH Publishers Inc., 303 Northwest 12th Avenue, Journals Department, Deerfield FL 33442. **Tel** (800)367-8249, (305)428-5566.**)** **ED** Martin Bopp, F B Salisbury. **Bk Rev. Ad Acc. Circ:** 750. Documents available from The Genuine Article, CASDDS. ***Continues*** *Zeitschrift fur Pflanzenphysiologie, 0044-328X.*
Ind/Abst Abstr. Bull. Inst. Pap. Sci. Tech.; AgBiotech News Inf.; Agrofor. Abstr. (1991-); Chem. Abstr. (1984-); Chem. Titles; Crop Physiol. Abstr.; Curr. Aware. Biol. Sci., CABS; Curr. Cit.; Curr. Contents Agric. Biol. Environ. Sci.; Curr. Contents Life Sci.; Ecol. Abstr. (?-?); EMBASE; Field Crop Abstr.; Food Sci. Technol. Abstr.; For. Prod. Abstr. (1991-); For. Abstr.; Genet. Abstr.; Grass. Forage Abstr.; Hortic. Abstr.; Index Vet.; Irr. Drain. Abstr.; Maize Abstr.; Microbiol. Abstr. Sect. B (19??-19??); Microbiol. Abstr. Sect. A; Microbiol. Abstr. Sect. C; Ornamental Hort. (19??-19??); PESTDOC; Plant Breed. Abstr.; Plant Genet. Resour. Abstr.; Plant Grow. Reg. Abstr.; Postharvest News Inf.; Potato Abstr.; Ref. Upd. Deluxe Ed.; Res. Alert [Full Cov.]; Rev. Plant Pathol.; Rice Abstr.; Sci. Cit. Index; SCISEARCH; Seed Abstr.; Soils Fert.; Sorghum Mill. Abstr.; Soyabean Abstr.; Stat. Theory Method Abstr. (1959-1963); Vitis Vitic. Enol. Abstr.; Weed Abstr.; Wheat Barley Trit. Abstr.

LC QK1 .B33 **ISSN** 0918-9440
DD 581.05 JA
CODEN JPLREA

•JOURNAL OF PLANT RESEARCH.

Added/Corp Nihon Shokubutsu Gakkai. **VFOAT** Shokubutsugaku Zasshi; J. Plant Res. Vol. 106, No. 1081 (Mar. 1993)-. Periodical. English. Four times a year. $240.00. Botanical Society of Japan, Toshin Bldg, Hongo 2-27-2 Bunkyo-ku, Tokyo 113 Japan. ***Continues*** *Botanical Magazine, Tokyo.*
Ind/Abst Curr. Cit.

LC QK **ISSN** 0970-2539
DD 581 II

JOURNAL OF PLANT SCIENCE RESEARCH, THE.

[J. plant sci. res.]. **Added/Corp** Society for the Promotion of Plant Science Research. Vol. 1, No. 1 (1985)-. Periodical. English. Four times a year. $60.00. Society for the Promotion of Plant Science Research, Punjab Agricultural University, Ludhiana-141004 India. **(Subscription address:** Prints India, 11 Darya Ganj, New Delhi 110002 India. **Tel** 011 91 11 3268645, FAX 011 91 11 3275542, telex 31-61087 PRIN-IN.**)** Documents available from CASDDS.
Ind/Abst Chem. Abstr.

LC Q77 .H5 **ISSN** 0075-4366
DD 506 JA
CODEN JHUBAF

JOURNAL OF SCIENCE OF THE HIROSHIMA UNIVERSITY. SERIES B. DIVISION 2. BOTANY.

[J. sci. Hiroshima Univ., Ser. B. Div. 2]. **Main/Corp** Hiroshima Daigaku. Vol. 1 (Dec. 1930)-. English (German and Japanese). Hiroshima University / Faculty of Science, 1-89 Higashisenda Machi 1-chome, Naka-ku Hiroshima 730 Japan. **Tel** 011 81 82 2411221. Documents available from BIOSIS Document Express.
Ind/Abst Biol. Abstr.; Ornamental Hort. (1991-); Life Sci. Collect.

LC QK431 .J68 **ISSN** 0313-4083
AT
CODEN JABGDP

JOURNAL OF THE ADELAIDE BOTANIC GARDENS.

[J. Adel.Bot. Gard.]. **Added/Corp** Adelaide Botanic Gardens. (Sept. 15, 1976)-. English. Irregular. Botanic Gardens of Adelaide State Herbarium, North Terrace, Adelaide 5000 South Australia. **Tel** 011 61 8 2282311, FAX 011 61 8 2514403. Documents available from BIOSIS Document Express.
Ind/Abst Biol. Abstr.; Hortic. Abstr.; Life Sci. Collect.; Plant Breed. Abstr.; Weed Abstr.

LC QK495.B76 B69a **ISSN** 0090-8738
DD 635.9/34/22 US

JOURNAL OF THE BROMELIAD SOCIETY.

[J. Bromel. Soc.]. **Main/Corp** Bromeliad Society. Vol. 21 (1971)-. Periodical. English. Six times a year (Jan., Mar., May, July, Sept., Nov.). $20.00. The Bromeliad Society Inc, 2488 East 49th, Tulsa OK 74105. **Tel** (918)742-5981. **ED** Thomas U. Lineham (editor's address: 1508 Lake Shore Drive, Orlando, FL 32803-1305 phone: (407)896-3722). Index available. **Bk Rev**, (Qty: 6). **Ad Acc. Circ:** 2,500 (ctrl). ***Continues*** *Bromeliad Society. Bromeliad Society Bulletin, 0007-2184.*
Ind/Abst AGRICOLA [Full Cov.].

LC QK1 .H49 **ISSN** 0368-2145
DD 581 JA
CODEN JFHBA4

JOURNAL OF THE FACULTY OF SCIENCE, HOKKAIDO UNIVERSITY, SERIES 5, BOTANY.

Added/Corp Hokkaido Daigaku. Rigakubu. **VFOAT** Botany; Hokkaido Daigaku Rigakubu Kiyo; Jour. Fac. Sci. Hokkaido Univ. Series 5, Botany. (19??)-. Periodical. English (German). Hokkaido University / Science, Faculty of Science, Sapporo Japan. ***Continues*** *Journal of the Faculty of Science, Hokkaido Imperial University. Series 5, Botany.*
Ind/Abst AGRICOLA [Full Cov.].

LC QK1 .T58 **ISSN** 0368-2196
JA
CODEN JFNBAY

JOURNAL OF THE FACULTY OF SCIENCE, UNIVERSITY OF TOKYO. SECTION 3, BOTANY.

(JOURNAL OF THE FACULTY OF SCIENCE, UNIVERSITY OF TOKYO. SECTION III, BOTANY.). [J. Fac. Sci., Univ. Tokyo, Sect. 3]. **Added/Corp** Tokyo Daigaku. Rigakubu. **VFOAT** Botany; Tokyo Daigaku Rigakubu Kiyo. Dai 3-Rui, Shokubutsugaku. Vol. 6, Pt. 1-3 (1952)-. Periodical. English (French and German). Tokyo Daigaku Rigakubu, (Faculty of Science University of Tokyo), 3-1 Hongo 7 Chome, Bunkyoku Tokyo 113 Japan. **Tel** 03 3812 2111. Documents available from BIOSIS Document Express. ***Continues*** *Journal of the Faculty of Science, Imperial University of Tokyo. Section III, Botany.*
Ind/Abst AGRICOLA [Select. Cov.]; Biol. Abstr.

LC QK1 **ISSN** 0371-7712
DD 581 JA
UDC 58

JOURNAL OF THE FACULTY OF SCIENCE, UNIVERSITY OF TOKYO. SECTION III : BOTANY.

Main/Corp Tokyo Daigaku. Rigakubu. Vol. 1, (1925)-. Periodical. English. $124.00. ***Supersedes*** *Journal of the College of Science.*
Ind/Abst AGRICOLA.

ISSN 0019-4468
II
CODEN JIBSAC

JOURNAL OF THE INDIAN BOTANICAL SOCIETY, THE.

[J. Indian Bot. Soc.]. **Main/Corp** Indian Botanical Society. Vol. 3, No. 6 (Apr. 1923)-. Academic Scholarly Publication. English. Four times a year. $75.00. Indian Botanical Society, Department of Botany, Lucknow University, Lucknow 226 007 India. **(Subscription address:** Prints India, 11 Darya Ganj, New Delhi 110002 India. **Tel** 011 91 11 3268645, FAX 011 91 11 3275542, telex 31-61087 PRIN-IN.**)** Documents available from BIOSIS Document Express, CASDDS. ***Continues*** *Journal of Indian Botany.*
Ind/Abst Biodeter. Abstr.; Biol. Abstr.; Chem. Abstr.; Field Crop Abstr.; For. Prod. Abstr.; For. Abstr.; Grass. Forage Abstr.; Nematol. Abstr.; Ornamental Hort.; Plant Breed. Abstr.; Potato Abstr.; Rev. Med. Vet. Mycology; Rev. Plant Pathol.; Rice Abstr.; Soils Fert.

LC QK495.C11 M24a **ISSN** 0464-8072
UK

JOURNAL OF THE MAMMILLARIA SOCIETY, THE.

[J. Mammill. Soc.]. **Main/Corp** Mammillaria Society. Vol. 1 (Aug. 1960)-. Periodical. English. Four times a year. $14.55. Mammillaria Society, 28 Winfield Grove, Newdigate SRY RH5 5AZ United Kingdom. **Tel** 011 44 1306 631682. **ED** W.F. Maddams. Index available (Free). **Bk Rev. Circ:** 500 (ctrl).
Desc: Covering the cultivation and study of cacti.

ISSN 0971-2976
II
UDC 58

JOURNAL OF THE NATIONAL BOTANICAL SOCIETY.

[J. Natl. Bot. Soc.]. (1990)-. Periodical. English. Four times a year. $23.00. **(Subscription address:** Prints India, 11 Darya Ganj, New Delhi 110002 India. **Tel** 011 91 11 3268645, FAX 011 91 11 3275542, telex 31-61087 PRIN-IN.**)** ***Continues*** *Bulletin of the Botanical Society of Bengal, 0006-811X.*

LC QK
DD 581 II

JOURNAL OF THE SWAMY BOTANICAL CLUB, THE.

Added/Corp Swamy Botanical Club. Madurai Kamaraj University. Dept. of Plant Morphology. Vol. 1, No. 1 (Mar. 1984)-. Periodical. English. Four times a year. $25.00. Department of Plant Morphology, Madurai India. **(Subscription address:** Prints India, 11 Darya Ganj, New Delhi 110002 India. **Tel** 011 91 11 3268645, FAX 011 91 11 3275542, telex 31-61087 PRIN-IN.**)**

ISSN 0378-8024
TU
CODEN JTUPD8

JOURNAL OF TURKISH PHYTOPATHOLOGY, THE.

[J. Turk. phytopathol.]. Vol. 1 (Oct. 1971)-. Academic Scholarly Publication. English (French and German). Three times a year. $6.00. Fitopatoloji Dernegi, Ege Universitesi Ziraat Fakultesi Fitopatoloji Ve Zirai Botanik Kursusu, Izmir Turkey. Documents available from CASDDS.
Ind/Abst AGRICOLA; Biodeter. Abstr. (1991-); Chem. Abstr. (1971-1987); Hortic. Abstr.; Microbiol. Abstr. Sect. A; Life Sci. Collect. (1985-); Plant Breed. Abstr.; Postharvest News Inf.; Rev. Plant Pathol.; Seed Abstr.; Soyabean Abstr.; Wheat Barley Trit. Abstr.

LC WMLC L 83/8770 **ISSN** 1100-9233
SW
CODEN JVESEK
Pr Rev.

JOURNAL OF VEGETATION SCIENCE.

(JOURNAL OF VEGETATION SCIENCE : OFFICIAL ORGAN OF THE INTERNATIONAL ASSOCIATION FOR VEGETATION SCIENCE.). [J. veg. sci.]. **Added/Corp** International Association for Vegetation Science. **VFOAT** JVS. Vol. 1, No. 1 (Feb. 1990)-. Periodical. English. Six times a year. $480.86. Opulus Press AB, PO Box 25 137, S-750 25 Uppsala Sweden. **Tel** 011 46 18320662, FAX 011 46 18321368. cum. index. **Bk Rev**, (Qty: 100). **Circ:** 1,200. Documents available from The Genuine Article.
Ind/Abst AGRICOLA [Full Cov.]; Curr. Aware. Biol. Sci., CABS; Curr. Cit.; Curr. Contents Agric. Biol. Environ. Sci.; Environ. Period. Bibliogr.; For. Abstr.; Res. Alert [Select. Cov.]; SCISEARCH.

ISSN 0022-7846
GW

KAKTEEN UND ANDERE SUKKULENTEN.

[Kakteen & andere Sukkulenten]. **Added/Corp** Deutsche Kakteen-Gesellschaft. Gesellschaft Oesterreichischer Kakteenfreunde. Schweizerische Kakteen-Gesellschaft. Vol. 1 (1937)-. Periodical. German. Twelve times a year. $24.00, $6.00 (registration fee for new members) other. Verlag Dieter Hoenig, Ahornweg 9, D-79822 Titisee Germany. **Tel** 011 49 7651 5000. **ED** Dieter Honig. ***Supersedes*** *Kakteenkunde;* ***Absorbed*** *Deutsche Kakteen-Gesellschaft E. V. Nachrichtenblatt.*
Desc: The journal is international in scope and contains more original descriptions of new species than any other journal.
Ind/Abst AGRICOLA.

ISSN 1055-419X
DD 581 US

KALMIOPSIS (ASHLAND, OR.).

(KALMIOPSIS : JOURNAL OF THE NATIVE PLANT SOCIETY OF OREGON.). **Added/Corp** Native Plant Society of Oregon. (1991)-. Periodical. English. $5.00. Native Plant Society of Oregon, c/o Membership Chair, 1920 Engel Court, Salem OR 97304.

LC QK1 .K4 **ISSN** 0075-5974
DD 581.05 UK
CODEN KEWBAF

KEW BULLETIN.

[Kew bull.]. **Added/Corp** Royal Botanic Gardens, Kew. (1946)-. Bulletin. English. Four times a year. £135.00. Her Majesty's Stationery Office, 51 Nine Elms Lane, London SW8 5DR United Kingdom. **Tel** 011 44 171 8738459, 011 44 171 8738499, FAX 011 44 171 8738499, 011 44 171 8738456, telex 297138. **(Subscription address:** Her Majesty's Stationery Office, PO Box 276, Public Centre, London SW8 5DT United Kingdom. **Tel** 011 44 171 8738499, 011 44 171 8738456.**)** **ED** J.M. Lock. available on microfilm and microfiche from University Microfilms International (UMI). Documents available from BIOSIS Document Express. ***Continues*** *Bulletin of Miscellaneous Information (Royal Botanic Gardens, Kew).*
Desc: Content is comprised almost entirely of original articles on vascular plants and macro-fungi. Papers on palynology, cytology, anatomy and phytochemistry are also included.
Ind/Abst AGRICOLA [Full Cov.]; Biol. Abstr.; Curr. Aware. Biol. Sci., CABS; Grass. Forage Abstr.; Ornamental Hort.; Life Sci. Collect.; Plant Breed. Abstr.; Plant Genet. Resour. Abstr.; Weed Abstr.

LC QK1 .K46 **ISSN** 0265-3842
DD 580/.5 UK
UDC 58 CCC
CODEN KEWMEI
TITLE CHANGE

KEW MAGAZINE, THE.

[Kew mag.]. Vol. 1, Pt. 1 (April 1984)-(199?). Academic Scholarly Publication. English. Basil Blackwell Publishers Ltd., 108 Cowley Road, Oxford 0X4 1JF United Kingdom. **Tel** 011 44 1235

465500, FAX 011 44 1235 465556, telex 837022 OXBOOK G. available on microfilm and microfiche from University Microfilms International (UMI). Documents available from BIOSIS Document Express. ***Continues*** *Curtis's Botanical Magazine, 0011-4073.* ***Continued by*** *Curtis's Botanical Magazine.*
Ind/Abst AGRICOLA (19??-19??) [Full Cov.]; Biol. Abstr. (19??-19??); Curr. Aware. Biol. Sci., CABS (19??-19??); Garden Lit. (19??-19??); Hortic. Abstr. (19??-19??); Ornamental Hort. (19??-19??); Plant Breed. Abstr. (19??-19??); Plant Genet. Resour. Abstr. (19??-19??); Seed Abstr. (19??-19??).

LC Z5354.C53 K48
DD 016.581 UK
KEW RECORD OF TAXONOMIC LITERATURE RELATING TO VASCULAR PLANTS FOR ... / ROYAL BOTANIC GARDENS, KEW, THE.
Added/Corp Royal Botanic Gardens, Kew. (1971)-. English. Four times a year. £115.00. Her Majesty's Stationery Office, 51 Nine Elms Lane, London SW8 5DR United Kingdom. **Tel** 011 44 171 8738459, 011 44 171 8738499, FAX 011 44 171 8738499, 011 44 171 8738456, telex 297138. **(Subscription address:** Her Majesty's Stationery Office, PO Box 276, Public Centre, London SW8 5DT United Kingdom. **Tel** 011 44 171 8738499, 011 44 171 8738456.) ***Continues*** *Index to European Taxonomic Literature for ..., 0073-5922;* ***Absorbed*** *Current Awareness List.*
Desc: Lists references to all publications relating to the taxonomy of flowering plants, gymnosperms and ferns. There are also references on phytogeography, nomenclature, chromosome surveys, chemotaxonomy, floras and botanical institutions.

ISSN 0961-4141
DD 580 UK
KEW RICHMOND. (KEW.). [KewRichmond]. (1991)-. Periodical. English. Three times a year. £9.00 UK; £18.00 other. Friends of the Royal Botanic Gardens, Kew, Richmond Surrey TW93AB United Kingdom. **Tel** 011 44 181 9401171, FAX 011 44 181 3325278.

LC QK
DD 581 RH
KIRKIA. Added/Corp Salisbury, Rhodesia. Federal Herbarium. Vol. 1 (1960/61)-. English. Irregular. $10.00. R & S S Information Services, PO Box 8108, Causeway Harare Zimbabwe. **Tel** 011 263 0 704531, telex 2455 AGRC ZW. **Bk Rev. Circ:** 500.
Desc: Covers taxonomy, flora, zambeziaca, vegetation, and survey.
Ind/Abst For. Abstr.; Grass. Forage Abstr.; Plant Breed. Abstr.; Soils Fert.; Weed Abstr.

LC QK
DD 581 RU
KOMAROVSKIE CHTENIIA. Added/Corp Botanicheskii Institut Im. V.L. Komarova. Vol. 1 (1949)-. Monographic series. Russian (English). Price varies per volume. Izdatelstvo Nauka / Akademiia Nauk, (Publishing House of the Russian Academy of Sciences), Leninskii Porspekt 14, 117901 Moscow Russia. **Tel** 011 95 9542153, FAX 011 95 9382144, telex 411964.

ISSN 0385-6410
JA
CODEN KBKKDW
KYUSHU BYOGAICHU KENKYUKAIHO. (HO.). [Kyushu Byogaichu Kenkyukaiho]. **Main/Corp** Kyushu Byogaichu Kenkyukai. **VAT** Kyushu Byogaichu Kenkyukai Ho. (19??)-. Japanese. Kyushu University / Faculty of Science, 10-1 Hakozaki 6 Chome Higasiku, Fukuokasi Fukuokaken 812 Japan. Documents available from CASDDS.
Ind/Abst Chem. Abstr.; Soyabean Abstr.

LC QK329 .L3 **ISSN** 0210-7708
SP
CODEN LAGAEL
LAGASCALIA. [Lagascalia]. **Added/Corp** Seville. Universidad. Departamento de Botanica. (1971)-. Multiple languages (English, Portuguese and Spanish). Two times a year. $13.32. Universidad de Sevilla / Servicio de Publicaciones, Valparaiso 5, 41013 Seville Spain. **Tel** 011 34 95 423-1958, 011 34 95 423-5976. Documents available from BIOSIS Document Express.
Ind/Abst Biol. Abstr. (1985-); Grass. Forage Abstr.; Hortic. Abstr.; Ornamental Hort. (1991-); Life Sci. Collect.; Plant Breed. Abstr.; Plant Genet. Resour. Abstr.; Seed Abstr.

LC QK329 .L38 **ISSN** 0210-9778
DD 581.946/05 SP
CODEN LAZAEE
LAZAROA. [Lazaroa]. **Added/Corp** Universidad Complutense de Madrid. Departamento de Botanica. Universidad Complutense de Madrid. Departamento de Biologia Vegetal II. Vol. 1 (1979)-. Periodical. Spanish (English and French). One time a year. $26.64. Editorial Universitaria SA de Chile, Casilla 10220, Santiago Chile. **Tel** 011 56 2 2325057, FAX 011 56 2 2322571. Documents available from BIOSIS Document Express.
Ind/Abst Biol. Abstr. (1987-); Ecol. Abstr.; Geogr. Abstr. Phys. Geogr.

LC QK
DD 581 NE
LEIDEN BOTANICAL SERIES. No. 3 (1976)-. Monographic series. English. Irregular. Price varies per volume. Rijksherbarium, PO Box 9514, 2300 RA Leiden Netherlands. **Tel** 011 31 71 273500.

LC QK **ISSN** 0457-4184
DD 581 BE
LEJEUNIA. [Lejeunia]. **Added/Corp** Societe Botanique de Liege. Societe des Naturalistes Namur-Luxembourg. Societe des Naturalistes de Charleroi. (1937)-. Monographic series. French (English; summaries and/or abstracts in English). Irregular. Price varies per volume. Societe Botanique de Liege ASBL, Department of Botanique, B 22 S Tilman, B 4000 Liege Belguim. **Tel** 011 32 41 563854. **Circ:** 500. Documents available from BIOSIS Document Express. ***Supersedes*** *Lejeunia. Memoire, 0773-3356.*
Desc: Covers all aspects of botany, but principally taxonomy, floristic, ecology, phytogeography, historical botany.
Ind/Abst AGRICOLA; Biol. Abstr.; Ecol. Abstr.; Life Sci. Collect.

ISSN 1193-767X
DD 581 CN
LIAISON - AMIS DU JARDIN BOTANIQUE DE MONTREAL. (LIAISON.). [Liaison - Amis Jard. bot. Montr.]. **Added/Corp** Amis du Jardin Botanique de Montreal. No. 58 (Autumn 1991)-. Periodical. French. Three times a year. Les Amis du Jardin Botanique, 4101 Est rue Sherbrooke 125, Montreal Quebec H1X 2B2 Canada. **Tel** (514)872-1493, FAX (514)872-3765. ***Continues*** *Societe d'Animation du Jardin et de l'Institut Botanique. Liaison - S A J I B., 0704-948X.*

LC QK580.7 .L53 **ISSN** 0024-2829
DD 589.1/05 UK
UDC 582.29 **CCC**
CODEN LCHNB8
Pr Rev.
LICHENOLOGIST (LONDON). (THE LICHENOLOGIST.). [Lichenologist]. (1958)-. Academic Scholarly Publication. English. Six times a year. $342.24. Academic Press Ltd., A Division of Harcourt Brace & Company Ltd., 24-28 Oval Road, London NW1 7DX United Kingdom. **Tel** 011 44 171 2674466, FAX 011 44 171 4822293, 011 44 171 4854752, telex 25775 ACPRES G. **(Subscription address:** Harcourt Brace & Company, Ltd., Foots Cray High Street, Sidcup Kent DA14 5HP United Kingdom. **Tel** 011 44 181 3003322, FAX 011 44 181 3090807, telex 896 377 ACADEM.) **ED** D. H. Brown. Documents available from The Genuine Article, BIOSIS Document Express, CASDDS.
Desc: Devoted exclusively to the study of lichen-forming fungi and reports on lichenology worldwide. All aspects of lichenology are considered for inclusion, and the editors endeavor to maintain a balance in the fields represented in each volume.
Ind/Abst Biol. Abstr.; Chem. Abstr.; Curr. Aware. Biol. Sci., CABS; Curr. Cit.; Curr. Contents Agric. Biol. Environ. Sci.; Ecol. Abstr. (?-?); Ecology Abstr.; EMBASE; For. Abstr.; Microbiol. Abstr. Sect. C; Life Sci. Collect.; Res. Alert [Full Cov.]; Sci. Cit. Index; SCISEARCH.

II
LIFE SCIENCE ADVANCES. PLANT PHYSIOLOGY : A JOURNAL OF COUNCIL OF SCIENTIFIC RESEARCH INTEGRATION. VFOAT Plant Physiology; Plant Physiology - Life Science Advances. Periodical. English. $30.00 (individuals), $60.00 (institutions). Publications Manager, Compliers International, 1/25 Nagwa, Lanka Varanasi-221 005 India. ***Continues in part*** *Life Science Advances, 0255-6642.*

LC QK1 .L73 **ISSN** 0075-9481
DD 580.5 AG
CODEN LLOAAW
LILLOA. (LILLOA / UNIVERSIDAD NACIONAL DE TUCUMAN, DEPARTMENTO DE INVESTIGACIONES REGIONALES, INSTITUTO MIGUEL LILLO.). [Lilloa]. **Added/Corp** Fundacion Miguel Lillo. Instituto Miguel Lillo. (1937)-. Periodical. Spanish (summaries and/or abstracts in English). Documents available from BIOSIS Document Express.
Ind/Abst Biol. Abstr.; Crop Physiol. Abstr.; Field Crop Abstr.; Life Sci. Collect.; Plant Breed. Abstr.; Seed Abstr.

LC QK533 .L5 **ISSN** 0105-0761
DD 588/.05 SW
CODEN LNBGAX
Pr Rev.
LINDBERGIA. [Lindbergia]. **Added/Corp** Nordisk Bryologisk Forening. Nederlandse Natuurhistorische Vereniging. Bryologische Wergroep. Vol. 1 (1971)-. Periodical. English (German, French, Danish, Dutch, Norwegian and Swedish; summaries and/or abstracts in English and Russian). Three times a year. $98.00. Department of Ecology / Sweden, Editorial Office, Ecology Building, S 223 62 Lund Sweden. **Circ:** 750 (ctrl). Documents available from The Genuine Article, BIOSIS Document Express, CASDDS.
Ind/Abst ASTIS Curr. Aware. Bull. (1978-); AGRICOLA [Full Cov.]; ASTIS Bibliogr. (1978-); Biol. Abstr.; Chem. Abstr.; EMBASE; Life Sci. Collect.; Res. Alert [Full Cov.]; Sci. Cit. Index; SCISEARCH.

LC SB **ISSN** 0889-258X
DD 635.9 US
CODEN LNDLES
LINDLEYANA : THE SCIENTIFIC JOURNAL OF THE AMERICAN ORCHID SOCIETY. [Lindleyana]. **Added/Corp** American Orchid Society. Vol. 1, No. 1 (Winter 1986)-. Periodical. English. Four times a year (March, June, Sept., Dec.). $24.00. American Orchid Society Inc, 6000 South Olive Avenue, West Palm Beach FL 33405. **Tel** (407)585-8666, FAX (407)585-0654. **ED** Gustavo A Romero and Heidi Hewis. Index available. cum. index (Bound in last issue). **Circ:** 1,200 (ctrl). Documents available from BIOSIS Document Express.
Desc: Serves botanists, researchers and serious orchid enthusiasts around the world as a central forum for the exchange of ideas and the concise presentation of ongoing debate and discussion It embraces all aspects of orchid research: systematics, physiology, phytochemistry, cytology, anatomy and morphology, pollination biology and evolution.
Ind/Abst Biol. Abstr. (1988-); Crop Physiol. Abstr.; Hortic. Abstr.; Ornamental Hort. (19??-19??); Plant Breed. Abstr.; Plant Genet. Resour. Abstr.; Plant Grow. Reg. Abstr.; Rev. Agric. Entomol.; Seed Abstr.

LC QK
DD 581 UK
LIST OF MEMBERS AND SUBSCRIBERS / BOTANICAL SOCIETY OF THE BRITISH ISLES. Main/Corp Botanical Society of the British Isles. (19??)-. English. Botanical Society of the British Isle, 68 Outwoods Road, Loughborough LE11 3LY United Kingdom. **Tel** 011 44 1509 215598.

ISSN 0782-050X
FI
UDC 58
LUTUKKA. [Lutukka]. (1985)-. Periodical. Finnish (English). Four times a year. $37.36. Botanical Museum / Finnish Museum of Natural History, PO Box 7, FIN 00014 Helsinki Univeristy Finland. **Tel** 011 358 0 1911, FAX 011 358 0 1918656. **ED** Arto Kurtto, Juha Suominen, Pertti Uotila, and Leena Helynranta. Index available. cum. index. **Bk Rev.** ctrl circ.
Desc: Contains small articles on Finnish flora, both flowering plants and cryptogams floristics, important plant finds, floristics mapping, threatened plants. working techniques, news and book reviews.

ISSN 0024-9637
US
CODEN MADRAU
Pr Rev.
MADRONO. (MADRONO: A WEST AMERICAN JOURNAL OF BOTANY.). [Madrono]. **Added/Corp** California Botanical Society. Vol. 1 (May 20, 1916)-. Periodical. English (Spanish). Four times a year (Jan., Apr., Jul., Oct.). $50.00. California Botanical Society, University Herbarium, University of California, Berkeley CA 94720. **Tel** (510)643-7008, FAX (510)643-5390. **ED** Robert Patterson. **Bk Rev. Circ:** 1,500 (ctrl). Documents available from BIOSIS Document Express, CASDDS.
Desc: A West American journal of botany.
Ind/Abst AGRICOLA [Full Cov.]; Biol. Abstr. (-1978); Chem. Abstr.; Ecology Abstr.; For. Abstr.; GeoRef; Life Sci. Collect.; Plant Breed. Abstr.; Plant Genet. Resour. Abstr.

ISSN 0127-0192
DD 639.99060595 MY
MAPPS NEWSLETTER. [MAPPS newsl.]. **VFOAT** Malaysian Plant Protection Society Newsletter. (1977)-. Periodical. English. Four times a year.
Ind/Abst Biocont. News Inf.; Nematol. Abstr.; Rev. Agric. Entomol.; Rev. Plant Pathol.; Rice Abstr.

LC QK **ISSN** 0250-4367
DD 581 II
NLM ZQV 766 M489
MEDICINAL & AROMATIC PLANTS ABSTRACTS. [Med. aromat. plants abstr.]. **Added/Corp** Council of Scientific & Industrial Research (India). Publications & Information Directorate. **VFOAT** Medicinal and Aromatic Plants Abstracts; M.A.P.A.; MAPA. (Feb. 1979)-. Abstracting/Indexing Service. English. Six times a year. $180.00. Publications & Information Directorate, CSIR, Dr. K.S. Krishnan Marg, New Delhi-110012 India. **Tel** 5726014, FAX 5731353, telex 031-77271 PID IN. **(Subscription address:** Prints India, 11 Darya Ganj, New Delhi 110002 India. **Tel** 011 91 11 3268645, FAX 011 91 11 3275542, telex 31-61087 PRIN-IN.) **ED** G. P. Phondke, H. C. Jain. **Bk Rev. Ad Acc. Circ:** 400. available on an online database. ***Continues*** *Bulletin of Indian Raw Materials and Their Utilization. Series A.*
Desc: Reports current world literature on medicinal and aromatic plants. Includes patents and papers presented at the national and international seminars and symposia in the field.

Ind/Abst Anal. Abstr.; For. Prod. Abstr.; Hortic. Abstr.; Protozoolog. Abstr.; Rev. Agric. Entomol.; Rev. Med. Vet. Entomol.

US

MEDICINAL PLANTS OF THE WORLD. (1???)-. Monographic series. English. Irregular. Price varies per volume. Reference Publications Inc., 218 St. Clair River Drive, Box 344, Algonac MI 48001. **Tel** (313)794-5722, FAX (313)794-7463.

LC QL254 .M4

SP

MEDITERRANEA. **See** Zoology.

LC QK1 .B344
DD 581 S 581/.025/73 US
UDC 58(060.21) (73)

MEMBERSHIP DIRECTORY AND HANDBOOK / BOTANICAL SOCIETY OF AMERICA. **Main/Corp** Botanical Society of America. **VFOAT** BSA Membership Directory and Handbook; BSA Membership Directory & Handbook. **VAT** Botanical Society of America Membership Directory and Handbook. (1986)-. Directory. English. Botanical Society of America, Inc., Office of Publications, 1735 Neil Avenue, Columbus OH 43210. **Tel** (614)292-3519. ***Continues*** *Directory / Botanical Society of America.*

LC QK
DD 581 US
UDC 58.006(799)

MEMOIR - PACIFIC TROPICAL BOTANICAL GARDEN. **Main/Corp** Pacific Tropical Botanical Garden. No. 1- Aug. 1973-. Monographic series. English. Irregular. Price varies per volume. National Tropical Botanical Garden, PO Box 340, Lawai HI 96765. **Tel** (808)332-7324, FAX (808)332-9765. **ED** Harold St John. **Circ:** 1,200 (ctrl).

LC QH3
DD 508.05 FR
UDC 58

MEMOIRES DE LA SOCIETE LINNEENNE DE NORMANDIE. SECTION BOTANIQUE. **Main/Corp** Societe Linneenne de Normandie, Caen. New Series, Vol. 1-15 (March 1926)-. French. ***Continues in part*** *Memoires de la Societe Linneenne de Normandie.*

LC QK
DD 581 SA

MEMOIRS OF THE BOTANICAL SURVEY OF SOUTH AFRICA. **Added/Corp** South Africa. Dept. of Agricultural Technical Services. Botanical Research Institute (South Africa). **VFOAT** Memoirs van die Botaniese Opname van Suid-Afrika. No. 40 (1975)-. Monographic series. English (summaries and/or abstracts in Afrikaans and French). ***Continues*** *Botanical Survey Memoir.*
Ind/Abst Grass. Forage Abstr.; Nutr. Abstr. Rev., Ser. B, Live Feeds and Feed.

LC QK1 .N525 **ISSN** 0077-8931
DD 581.08 US
CCC
CODEN MYBGAJ

MEMOIRS OF THE NEW YORK BOTANICAL GARDEN. [Mem. N. Y. Bot. Gard.]. **Added/Corp** New York Botanical Garden. (1900)-. Monographic series. English. Irregular. Price varies per volume. New York Botanical Garden, Scientific Publishing Department B, New York NY 10458-5126. **Tel** (718)817-8721, FAX (718)817-6504, telex 5106015451. **Circ:** 250. Documents available from BIOSIS Document Express, CASDDS.
Desc: A medium for the publication of lengthy, original research papers focusing on taxonomy and floristics with an emphasis on New World plants.
Ind/Abst Biol. Abstr.; Chem. Abstr.; Curr. Cit.; Life Sci. Collect.; Plant Breed. Abstr.; Rev. Plant Pathol.

LC QK1 .T62 **ISSN** 0097-3807
DD 581/.05 US

MEMOIRS OF THE TORREY BOTANICAL CLUB. **Main/Corp** Torrey Botanical Club. (1889)-. Monographic series. English. Irregular. Price varies per volume. New York Botanical Garden, Scientific Publishing Department B, New York NY 10458-5126. **Tel** (718)817-8721, FAX (718)817-6504, telex 5106015451.

LC QH7 .S722 **ISSN** 0373-6873
DD 574/.05 FI
CODEN MSFFAS

MEMORANDA SOCIETATIS PRO FAUNA ET FLORA FENNICA. [Memo. Soc. Fauna Flora Fenn.]. **Main/Corp** Societas Pro Fauna et Flora Fennica. Vol. 1 (1925)-. English (Finnish and German; summaries and/or abstracts in Finnish and German). Four times a year. Bookstore Tiedekirja, Kirkkokatu 14, Helsinki 00170 Finland. **Tel** 011 358 0 635177. cum. index. Documents available from BIOSIS Document Express. ***Supersedes*** *Meddelanden af Societatis Pro Fauna et Flora Fennica.*
Ind/Abst Biol. Abstr.; Ecol. Abstr.; Ecology Abstr.; GeoRef; Rev. Med. Vet. Entomol.; Wildl. Rev.

LC QK1 .S2825 **ISSN** 0081-0665
DD 580.624693 PO

MEMORIAS DA SOCIEDADE BROTERIANA. **Main/Corp** Sociedade Broteriana. **Added/Corp** Universidade de Coimbra. Instituto Botanico. Vol. 1 (1930)-. Monographic series. English (French, German and Portuguese). Irregular. Price varies per volume. Instituto Botanico da Universidade de Coimbra, Arcos do Jardim, P-3049 Coimbra Codex Portugal. **Tel** 011 351 39 22897. **ED** Jose F. Mesquita and Jorge Paiva. Index available. cum. index. **Bk Rev. Circ:** 1,000 (ctrl). Documents available from BIOSIS Document Express.
Desc: Floristic research concerning all the countries of the world.
Ind/Abst Biol. Abstr.

ISSN 1059-7522
DD 581 UK
CODEN MPBIEY

METHODS IN PLANT BIOCHEMISTRY. [Methods plant biochem.]. Vol. 1 (1989)-. Monographic series. English. Irregular. Price varies per volume. Academic Press Inc., 6277 Sea Harbor Drive, Orlando FL 32887. **Tel** (800)543-9534, (407)345-4100, FAX (407)352-3445. Documents available from CASDDS.
Ind/Abst Chem. Abstr.

LC QK1 .M55 **ISSN** 0026-203X
DD 581.9/774 US
CODEN MBOTAU
Pr Rev.

MICHIGAN BOTANIST. [Mich. bot.]. **Added/Corp** Michigan Botanical Club. Vol. 1 (Mar. 1962)-. Periodical. English. Four times a year. $16.00. Michigan Botanical Club / University of Michigan, 2001 North University Building, 1205 N University A, Ann Arbor MI 48109. **Tel** (313)845-9728, (313)747-2811. **ED** Jim and Nancy Weber. cum. index. **Bk Rev. Circ:** 1,000 (ctrl). Documents available from BIOSIS Document Express, CASDDS.
Desc: All aspects of botany in the Great Lakes region including systematics, ecology, distribution, life history, and anatomy of vascular plants, algae, mosses, lichens and fungi.
Ind/Abst AGRICOLA [Full Cov.]; Biol. Abstr.; Chem. Abstr.; Ecol. Abstr.; Ecology Abstr.; Life Sci. Collect.

LC QK1 .M63 **ISSN** 0026-6507
DD 580.744778/66 US

MISSOURI BOTANICAL GARDEN BULLETIN. [Mo. Bot. Gard. bull.]. **Main/Corp** Missouri Botanical Garden. Vol. 1 (Jan. 1913)-. Bulletin. English. Six times a year (Jan., Mar., May, July, Sept., Nov.). Comes with Missouri Botanical Gardens membership. Missouri Botanical Garden, PO Box 299, St. Louis MO 63166. **Tel** (314)577-9534, (314)577-5100, FAX (314)577-9594. cum. index. **Bk Rev. Circ:** 20,000 (ctrl). ***Continues in part*** *Missouri Botanical Garden. Annual Report - Missouri Botanical Garden, 0893-3243.* ***Continued in part by*** *Missouri Botanical Garden. Annual Report (1987), 1060-7854.*
Desc: Contains news and information about activities and events at Missouri Botanical Garden along with articles on gardening and botanical research.
Ind/Abst AGRICOLA; Life Sci. Collect. (19??-1985).

LC QK1 .S857A **ISSN** 0344-5615
DD 581/.05 GW
UDC 58
CODEN MIAHDA

MITTEILUNGEN AUS DEM INSTITUT FUER ALLGEMEINE BOTANIK HAMBURG. [Mitt. inst. allg. bot. Hamb.]. **Main/Corp** Hamburg. Institut fur Allgemeine Botanik. 15.- 1977-. Academic Scholarly Publication. German (summaries and/or abstracts in English). Documents available from BIOSIS Document Express, CASDDS. ***Continues*** *Mitteilungen aus dem Staatsinstitut fur Allgemeine Botanik Hamburg.*
Ind/Abst AGRICOLA; Biol. Abstr.; Chem. Abstr.; For. Abstr.; Life Sci. Collect.; Plant Breed. Abstr.; Rev. Plant Pathol.

ISSN 0934-5116
GW
UDC 631.41.9
CODEN 634

MITTEILUNGEN DER GESELLSCHAFT FUER PFLANZENBAUWISSENSCHAFTEN. (1988)-. Monographic series. German. Irregular.
Ind/Abst Crop Physiol. Abstr.; Postharvest News Inf.; Rev. Plant Pathol.; Seed Abstr.; Weed Abstr.

US

MN CROP NEWS. (19??)-. Newsletter. English. Thirty times a year. $30.00. University of Minnesota / Borlaug Hill, 495 Borlaug Hill, Plant Pathologist, St. Paul MN 55108. **Tel** (612)625-6290, FAX (612)625-9728. **ED** Debra Drange. **Circ:** 550 (ctrl). ***Continues*** *Plant Pest Newsletter.*

LC QK865 .M57 **ISSN** 0937-8340
DD 581.1334 GW
CCC
CODEN MMPSEB

MODERN METHODS OF PLANT ANALYSIS (1985). (MODERN METHODS OF PLANT ANALYSIS = MODERNE METHODEN DER PFLANZENANALYSE.). [Mod. methods plant anal.]. **VFOAT** Moderne Methoden der Pflanzenanalyse. Vol. 1-7 (1956); New Series Vol. 1 (1985)-. Monographic series. English (German). Price varies per volume. Springer-Verlag GmbH & Company KG, Heidelberger Platz 3, D-14197 Berlin Germany. **Tel** 011 49 30 8207223, FAX 011 49 30 8214091, telex 183 319 SPBLN D. **(Subscription address:** Springer-Verlag New York Inc. / North America, PO Box 2485, Journal Fulfillment, Secaucus NJ 07096. **Tel** (201)348-4033, (800)777-4643, FAX (201)348-4505.) Documents available from BIOSIS Document Express.
Ind/Abst AGRICOLA [Full Cov.]; Biol. Abstr. (1985-); Curr. Cit.

ISSN 1380-3743
NE
CCC
NLM W1; MO196DEK
Pr Rev.

●MOLECULAR BREEDING : NEW STRATEGIES IN PLANT IMPROVEMENT. **Added/Corp** International Society for Plant Molecular Biology. Vol. 1 No. 1 (1995)-. Academic Scholarly Publication. English. Four times a year. $344.00. Kluwer Academic Publishers, Postbus 322, 3300 AH Dordrecht The Netherlands. **Tel** 011 31 78 524400, FAX 011 31 78 183273, telex 20083.

ISSN 0894-0282
DD 580 US
NLM W1; MO197RH **CODEN** MPMIEL

MOLECULAR PLANT-MICROBE INTERACTIONS. (MOLECULAR PLANT-MICROBE INTERACTIONS : MPMI.). [Mol. plant-microb. interact.]. **Added/Corp** American Phytopathological Society. **VFOAT** Molecular Plant Microbe Interactions; MPMI. Vol. 1, No. 1 (Jan. 1988)-. Periodical. English. Six times a year. $285.00. American Phytopathological Society, 3340 Pilot Knob Road, St. Paul MN 55121. **Tel** (612)454-7250, (800)328-7560, FAX (612)454-0766, telex 6502439657 (MCI UW). available on microfilm and microfiche from University Microfilms International (UMI). Documents available from The Genuine Article, BIOSIS Document Express.
Desc: A new journal for plant science professionals studying the mechanistic aspects of pathogenic and symbiotic relationships of plants and microbes.
Ind/Abst AgBiotech News Inf.; AGRICOLA [Full Cov.]; Agrofor. Abstr.; Biodeter. Abstr.; Biol. Abstr.; Cot. Trop. Fibr. Abstr. Bibliogr.; Curr. Aware. Biol. Sci., CABS; Curr. Cit.; Curr. Contents Agric. Biol. Environ. Sci.; Curr. Contents Life Sci.; For. Abstr.; Grass. Forage Abstr.; Index Med.; Maize Abstr.; Plant Breed. Abstr.; Plant Grow. Reg. Abstr.; Potato Abstr.; Ref. Upd. Deluxe Ed.; Res. Alert [Select. Cov.]; Rev. Plant Pathol.; Rice Abstr.; Sci. Cit. Index; SCISEARCH; Soils Fert.; Soyabean Abstr.; Vitis Vitic. Enol. Abstr.; Wheat Barley Trit. Abstr.

LC QK **ISSN** 0077-0655
DD 581 PL

MONOGRAPHIAE BOTANICAE. [Monogr. bot.]. **Added/Corp** Polskie Towarzystwo Botaniczne. Vol. 1 (1953)-. Monographic series. Polish (summaries and/or abstracts in English and French). Irregular. Price varies per volume. **(Subscription address:** Ars Polona-Ruch, PO Box 1001, Krakowskie Przedmiescie 7, 00-068 Warsaw Poland. **Tel** 011 48 22 261201.)
Ind/Abst Life Sci. Collect.

LC QK **ISSN** 0161-1542
DD 581 US
UDC 582
CODEN MSBOE5

MONOGRAPHS IN SYSTEMATIC BOTANY FROM THE MISSOURI BOTANICAL GARDEN. [Monogr. syst. bot. Mo. Bot. Gard.]. **VFOAT** Monographs in Systematic Botany. Monographic series. English (Latin, French and Spanish). Irregular. Price varies per volume. New York Botanical Gardens, 200 St. Southern Boulevard, Bronx NY 10458. **Tel** (718)817-8628, FAX (718)562-6780. **Circ:** 85. Documents available from BIOSIS Document Express.
Desc: Monographic works in systematic and floristic botany, including reprints of important previously out-of-print publications.
Ind/Abst Biol. Abstr. (1987-).

ISSN 1037-1842
AT
Pr Rev.

MOOREANA : JOURNAL OF THE PALMETUM. **Added/Corp** Palmetum (Townsville, Qld.) Townsville Botanic Gardens. Vol. 1, No. 1 (June 1991)-. Periodical. English. Three times a year (Apr., Aug., Dec.). 20.55Aus$. Parks DIV Townsville Council, Botanic Gardens, PO Box 1268, Townsville Queensland 4810 Australia. **Tel** 011 61 77 251775, FAX 011 61 77 253290. **ED** John Dowe. **Bk Rev**, (Qty: 3). **Circ:** 250 (ctrl).

Desc: The aim is to provide a greater understanding, knowledge and appreciation of palms and their botany, ecology, conservation and cultivation.

LC QK227.7 .M67 **ISSN** 0254-6442
DD 581.97293 DR

MOSCOSOA : CONTRIBUCIONES CIENTIFICAS DEL JARDIN BOTANICO NACIONAL "DR. RAFAEL M. MOSCOSO". **Added/Corp** Jardin Botanico Nacional "Dr. Rafael M. Moscoso.". Vol. 1, No. 1 (Feb. 1976)-. Periodical. English (Spanish). One time a year. Jardin Botanico Nacional, Apartado 21-9, Santo Domingo Dominican Republic. **Tel** (809)565-2860, (809)567-6211. **ED** Thomas A. Zanoni. **Bk Rev. Circ:** 250 (ctrl).
Desc: Features technical articles on plants of the Dominican Republic, Haiti and other Caribbean islands, with coverage of taxonomy, distribution, ecology and ethnobotany.
Ind/Abst AGRICOLA [Full Cov.].

LC QK431 .M96 **ISSN** 0077-1813
DD 581/.05 AT
CODEN MAJBAC

MUELLERIA. [Muelleria]. **Added/Corp** Royal Botanic Gardens (Vic.) National Herbarium of Victoria. Vol. 1, No. 1 (Aug. 1955)-. Periodical. English. One time a year. National Herbarium of Victoria, Birwood Avenue South, Yarra Victoria 3141 Australia. Documents available from BIOSIS Document Express.
Ind/Abst AGRICOLA [Full Cov.]; Biol. Abstr.; Ecol. Abstr. (?-?); Life Sci. Collect.; Rev. Plant Pathol.

AU

MUTATION BREEDING REVIEW.
Added/Corp Joint FAO/IAEA Division of Isotope and Radiation Applications of Atomic Energy for Food and Agricultural Development. No. 1 (July 1982)-. Periodical. English. Irregular (7 issues per year). Free on request. International Atomic Energy Agency / IAEA, Wagramerstrasse 5, PO Box 100, A-1400 Vienna Austria. **Tel** 011 43 1 206021270, FAX 011 43 1 20607. **(Subscription address:** UNIPUB, 4611 F Assembly Drive, Lanham MD 20706. **Tel** (800)274-4888, (301)459-7666.**) ED** A. Micke. **Circ:** 300 (ctrl).
Ind/Abst Plant Breed. Abstr.; Seed Abstr.

LC QK1 .M94 **ISSN** 0027-5123
DD 580/.5 CK
CODEN MUTSAF

MUTISIA. [Mutisia]. **Added/Corp** Universidad Nacional de Colombia. Instituto de Ciencias Naturales. Universidad Nacional de Colombia. Departamento de Biologia. No. 1 (May 20, 1952)-. Periodical. Spanish (English, French, Dutch and Latin). Irregular. $5.00. Instituto de Ciencias Naturales, Apartado 7495, Bogota Colombia. **Tel** 011 57 1 2684336. **ED** Polidoro Pinto Escobar. **Ad Acc. Circ:** 1,000. Documents available from BIOSIS Document Express.
Ind/Abst Biol. Abstr.; Life Sci. Collect.

ISSN 0027-7479
GW
CCC
CODEN NDPBA6

NACHRICHTENBLATT DES DEUTSCHEN PFLANZENSCHUTZDIENSTES. [Nachrichtenbl. dtsch. Pflanzenschutzd.]. **Added/Corp** Biologische Bundesanstalt fuer Land- und Forstwirtschaft. Vol. 2 (1950)-. Academic Scholarly Publication. German (summaries and/or abstracts in English). Twelve times a year. $131.27. Verlag Eugen Ulmer, Postfach 700561, D-70574 Stuttgart Germany. **Tel** 011 49 711 4507108, FAX 011 49 711 4507120, telex 7-23634. Documents available from CASDDS. ***Continues*** *Nachrichtenblatt der Biologischen Zentralanstalt Braunschweig.*
Ind/Abst AgBiotech News Inf.; AGRICOLA; Agric. Eng. Abstr. (1991-); Biocont. News Inf. (19??-19??); Chem. Abstr.; EMBASE; For. Abstr.; Hortic. Abstr.; Irr. Drain. Abstr.; Maize Abstr.; Nematol. Abstr.; PESTDOC; Plant Breed. Abstr.; Plant Genet. Resour. Abstr.; Postharvest News Inf.; Potato Abstr.; Rev. Agric. Entomol.; Rev. Med. Vet. Entomol.; Rev. Plant Pathol.; Seed Abstr.; Soils Fert.; Vitis Vitic. Enol. Abstr.; Weed Abstr.; Wheat Barley Trit. Abstr.

LC Q **ISSN** 0363-0722
DD 500 US
CODEN NPSMD5

NATIONAL PARK SERVICE SCIENTIFIC MONOGRAPH SERIES. **See** Earth Sciences-Geology.

LC SB **ISSN** 0374-9525
DD 630 RU
UDC 631.52

NAUCNO-TEHNICESKIJ BULLETEN' VSESOUZNOGO SELEKCIONNO-GENETICESKOGO INSTITUTA. [Naucno-teh. bull. Vses. sel.- genet. inst.]. (1967)-. Bulletin. Russian.
Ind/Abst Plant Breed. Abstr.; Rev. Plant Pathol.

LC QK
DD 581 II

NBRI NEWSLETTER : A QUARTERLY HOUSE JOURNAL OF THE NATIONAL BOTANICAL RESEARCH INSTITUTE. (Jan. 1979)-. Newsletter. English. Four times a year. Economic Botany Information Service, National Botany Research Institute, Lucknow India. ***Continues*** *NBG Newsletter.*

LC SB998.N4 **ISSN** 0957-6797
DD 595.1 016.59 UK
NLM ZQX 200; H479B **CODEN** NEABEA

NEMATOLOGICAL ABSTRACTS. **See** Biology-Abstracting, Bibliographies and Statistics.

ISSN 0028-2944
NE
CODEN NJPPAM
Pr Rev. **TITLE CHANGE**

NETHERLANDS JOURNAL OF PLANT PATHOLOGY. [Neth. j. plant pathol.]. **Added/Corp** Nederlandse Planteziektenkundige Vereniging. **VFOAT** Tijdschrift Over Planteziekten. (1963)-(1993). Academic Scholarly Publication. English (Dutch). Netherlands Society of Plant Pathology, Post Box 31, 6700 AA Wageningen Netherlands. **Tel** 011 31 8370 83051. **ED** A B R Beemster. Index available. **Bk Rev.** ctrl circ. Documents available from The Genuine Article, BIOSIS Document Express, CASDDS. ***Continues*** *Tijdschrift over Planteziekten.* ***Continued by*** *European Journal of Plant Pathology, 0929-1873.*
Desc: Description of plant diseases, pests and their control measures. Mycological, virological, entomological, nematological topics, weed and plant protection problems.
Ind/Abst AgBiotech News Inf.; Biocont. News Inf. (19??-19??); Biodeter. Abstr. (1991-); Biol. Abstr.; Chem. Abstr.; Curr. Aware. Biol. Sci., CABS; Curr. Cit.; Curr. Contents Agric. Biol. Environ. Sci.; Field Crop Abstr.; Food Sci. Technol. Abstr.; For. Abstr.; Hortic. Abstr.; Microbiol. Abstr. Sect. A; Microbiol. Abstr. Sect. C; Nematol. Abstr.; Ornamental Hort. (1991-); Life Sci. Collect.; PESTDOC; Plant Breed. Abstr.; Plant Genet. Resour. Abstr.; Postharvest News Inf.; Potato Abstr.; Res. Alert [Full Cov.]; Rev. Agric. Entomol.; Rev. Med. Vet. Mycology; Rev. Plant Pathol.; Sci. Cit. Index; SCISEARCH; Seed Abstr.; Soc. Sci. Cit. Index [Select. Cov.]; Soils Fert.; Virol. AIDS Abstr.; Wheat Barley Trit. Abstr.

LC QK1 .N434 **ISSN** 0377-1741
DD 581/.05 II
CCC

NEW BOTANIST. [New bot.]. Vol. 1 (Jan./April 1974)-. Periodical. English. Four times a year. $40.00. Today and Tomorrow's Printers and Publishers, 24-B/5 Desh Bandhu Gupta Road, Karol Bagh, New Delhi 110 005 India. **Tel** 011 91 11 5721928, 011 91 11 572770, FAX 011 91 11 7210073 (TTPP). **(Subscription address:** Prints India, 11 Darya Ganj, New Delhi 110002 India. **Tel** 011 91 11 3268645, FAX 011 91 11 3275542, telex 31-61087 PRIN-IN.**) ED** J.N. Govil. Index available. cum. index. **Circ:** 300.
Desc: Deals with the higher reaches of knowledge in plant sciences.
Ind/Abst Irr. Drain. Abstr.; Nematol. Abstr.; Life Sci. Collect.

LC QK1 .N45 **ISSN** 0028-646X
DD 580.5 UK
CCC
CODEN NEPHAV
Pr Rev.

NEW PHYTOLOGIST, THE. [New phytol.]. Vol. 1 (Jan. 1902)-. Academic Scholarly Publication. English. Twelve times a year. $768.00. Cambridge University Press, The Edinburgh Building, Shaftesbury Road, Cambridge CB2 2RU United Kingdom. **Tel** 011 44 1223 312393, FAX 011 44 1223 315052, telex 851-817256. **(Subscription address:** Cambridge University Press / North America, 110 Midland Avenue, Port Chester NY 10573. **Tel** (800)431-1580, (914)937-9600.**) ED** D. H. Lewis. Index available (free). **Bk Rev.** available on microfilm from University Microfilms International (UMI). Documents available from The Genuine Article, BIOSIS Document Express, CASDDS, Documents on Demand.
Desc: Publishes research papers, review articles and book reviews on all aspects of the plant sciences. Covers physiology, biophysics, biochemistry, phytochemistry, biotechnology, ecology, lichenology, bryology, phycology (including cyanobacteriology), mutualistic symbioses, the history of vegetation, and the responses of plants to pathogens and pollutants.
Ind/Abst AgBiotech News Inf.; AGRICOLA [Full Cov.]; Agrofor. Abstr. (1991-); Aquat. Sci. Fish. Abstr. [CD-ROM Ed.]; Biocont. News Inf. (1991-); Biodeter. Abstr.; Biol. Abstr.; Biotechnol. Res. Abstr.; Br. Archaeol. Bibliogr.; Chem. Abstr.; Cot. Trop. Fibr. Abstr. Bibliogr.; Crop Physiol. Abstr.; Curr. Aware. Biol. Sci., CABS; Curr. Cit.; Curr. Contents Agric. Biol. Environ. Sci.; Ecol. Abstr.; Ecology Abstr.; EMBASE; Energy Inf. Abstr.; Environ. Abstr.; Environ. Period. Bibliogr.; Field Crop Abstr.; Food Sci. Technol. Abstr.; For. Prod. Abstr.; For. Abstr.; Geogr. Abstr. Phys. Geogr.; Geol. Abstr.; GeoRef; Grass. Forage Abstr.; Hortic. Abstr.; Irr. Drain. Abstr.; Maize Abstr.; Microbiol. Abstr. Sect. A; Microbiol. Abstr. Sect. C; NAPRALERT; Ornamental Hort. (19??-19??); Life Sci. Collect.; PESTDOC; Plant Breed. Abstr.; Plant Genet. Resour. Abstr.; Plant Grow. Reg. Abstr.; Pollut. Abstr. Indexes; Potato Abstr.; Ref. Upd. Deluxe Ed.; Res. Alert [Full Cov.]; Rev. Plant Pathol.; Rice Abstr.; Sci. Cit. Index; SCISEARCH; Seed Abstr.; Soils Fert.; Soyabean Abstr.; Vitis Vitic. Enol. Abstr.; Weed Abstr.

LC QK1 .N56 **ISSN** 0028-825X
DD 580/.5 NZ
CCC
CODEN NZJBAS
Pr Rev.

NEW ZEALAND JOURNAL OF BOTANY. [N. Z. j. bot.]. **Added/Corp** New Zealand. Dept. of Scientific and Industrial Research. Vol. 1 (March 1964)-. Periodical. English. Four times a year (Mar., June, Sep., Dec.). $200.00. SIR Publishing, PO Box 399, Wellington New Zealand. **Tel** 011 64 4 472 7421, FAX 011 64 4 473 1841. **ED** Margaret Wassilieff. **Bk Rev. Ad Acc. Circ:** 800 (ctrl). Documents available from The Genuine Article, BIOSIS Document Express, CASDDS, Documents on Demand.
Desc: Concerned with the vegetation and flora of New Zealand and the sub-Antarctic/South Pacific region.
Ind/Abst AGRICOLA; Biol. Abstr.; Chem. Abstr.; Crop Physiol. Abstr.; Curr. Aware. Biol. Sci., CABS; Curr. Cit.; Curr. Contents Agric. Biol. Environ. Sci.; Ecol. Abstr.; Ecology Abstr.; Environ. Abstr.; For. Prod. Abstr. (19??-19??); For. Abstr.; Geogr. Abstr. Phys. Geogr.; Geol. Abstr.; Grass. Forage Abstr.; Hortic. Abstr.; Microbiol. Abstr. Sect. C; Ornamental Hort. (19??-19??); Life Sci. Collect.; Plant Breed. Abstr.; Plant Genet. Resour. Abstr.; Plant Grow. Reg. Abstr.; Res. Alert [Full Cov.]; Rev. Agric. Entomol.; Rev. Plant Pathol.; Sci. Cit. Index; SCISEARCH; Seed Abstr.; Soils Fert.; Weed Abstr.

ISSN 1180-1417
DD 581.9713/05 CN

NEWSLETTER. [Newsl. - Field Bot. Ont.]. **Added/Corp** Field Botanists of Ontario. **VFOAT** Field Botanists of Ontario Newsletter; FBO Newsletter. (1989)-. Newsletter. English. Four times a year. Sonja Gilbert / Sugar Town Mews, Sugar Town Mews, Suite 0-505, Devon PA 19333. ***Continues*** *The Plant Press, 0826-2268.*

ISSN 0569-2423
DD 580 US

NEWSLETTER / AMERICAN ASSOCIATION OF BOTANICAL GARDENS AND ARBORETA. [Newsl. - Am. Assoc. Bot. Gard. Arbor.]. **Added/Corp** American Association of Botanical Gardens and Arboreta. **VFOAT** AABGA Newsletter. **VAT** American Association of Botanical Gardens and Arboreta Newsletter. (Jan. 1975)-. Newsletter. English. Twelve times a year. $24.00 Public Garden only; $50.00 combined with Public Garden and Newsletter. American Association of Botanical Gardens, 786 Church Road, Wayne PA 19087. **Tel** (610)688-1120, FAX (215)293-0149. **ED** Elizabeth Sullian. **Bk Rev. Circ:** 1,800. ***Continues*** *Newsletter (American Association of Botanical Gardens and Arboretums), 0569-2423.*
Ind/Abst Garden Lit.

LC QK **ISSN** 1017-5679
DD 581 US

NEWSLETTER. ASSOCIATION OF PACIFIC SYSTEMATISTS. [Newsl. - Assoc. Pac. Syst.]. **Added/Corp** Association of Pacific Systematists. **VFOAT** Association of Pacific Systematists Newsletter. No. 1 (March 1984)-. Newsletter. English. One time a year. $20.00 institutions; $5.00 individuals. Botanical Research Institute of Texas, 509 Pecan Street, Fort Worth TX 76102. **Tel** (817)332-4441, FAX (817)332-4112.

LC QK
DD 581 US

NEWSLETTER / CALIFORNIA NATIVE PLANT SOCIETY, BRISTLECONE CHAPTER. **Added/Corp** California Native Plant Society. Bristlecone Chapter. Vol. 1, No. 1 (Apr. 1982)-. Newsletter. English. Six times a year (Jan., Mar., May, July, Sept., Nov.). $5.00. Bristlecone Chapter CNPS / California Native Plant Society, HCR 67 Box 35, Independence CA 93526. **Tel** (619)878-2389. **ED** Anne Halford, (editor's address: Route 2, Box 149, Round Valley Road, Bishop, CA 93514; phone: (619)387-2781). Index available. cum. index. **Bk Rev**, (Qty: 1-2). **Ad Acc. Circ:** 270.
Desc: Items of interest concerning native plants, including plants lists, field trip schedules, and news concerning botanists.

ISSN 1033-0003
AT

NEWSLETTER - EARLY MORN AFRICAN VIOLET GROUP. (1982)-. Periodical. English. Twelve times a year. Early Morn African Violet Group Inc, 1 Miller Crescent, Mount Waverly 3101 Australia. ***Continues*** *Early Morn African Violet Group of the Victoria Saintpaulia Society, 0811-0379.*

ISSN 0254-8844
SZ
UDC 582
NEWSLETTER - INTERNATIONAL ORGANIZATION OF PLANT BIOSYSTEMATISTS.
[Newsl. - Int. Organ. Plant Biosyst.]. **VFOAT** International Organization of Plant Biosystematists Newsletter; IOPB Newsletter. (1983)-. Newsletter. English. Irregular. $30.00 institutions, $25.00 individuals. International Organization of Plant Biosystematists, Trondheimsveien 23B, N Oslo 5 Norway. **Tel** 514 457 2000 Ext. 379.

ISSN 0550-6565
US
NEWSLETTER - NEW YORK BOTANICAL GARDEN.
(THE NEW YORK BOTANICAL GARDEN NEWSLETTER.). **Main/Corp** New York Botanical Garden. **Added/Corp** New York Botanical Garden. Newsletter. (1967)-. Newsletter. English. Irregular. Free for members on request. New York Botanical Garden, Scientific Publishing Department B, New York NY 10458-5126. **Tel** (718)817-8721, FAX (718)817-6504, telex 5106015451. **ED** Karl F. Lauby. **Circ:** 11,000 (ctrl).
Desc: Research projects, scientific profiles, special events, horticultural information, announcements and a calendar of events.

ISSN 0332-3285
DD 632 IE
NEWSLETTER - SOCIETY OF IRISH PLANT PATHOLOGISTS.
[Newsl. - Soc. Ir. Plant Pathol.]. **VFOAT** S.I.P.P. Newsletter; Annual Newsletter - Society of Irish Plant Pathologists; Newsletter of the Society of Irish Plant Pathologists. (1970)-. Periodical. English. One time a year.
Ind/Abst Rev. Plant Pathol.

ISSN 0031-9473
JA
CCC
CODEN NSBGAM
NIPPON SHOKUBUTSU BYORI GAKKAI.
(ANNALS OF THE PHYTOPATHOLOGICAL SOCIETY OF JAPAN.). [Nippon shokubutsu byori gakkai]. **Main/Corp** Nihon Shokubutsu Byori Gakkai, Tokyo. **Added/Corp** Nihon Shokubutsu Byori Gakkai. **VFOAT** Nippon Shokubutsu Byori Gakkai. Vol. 1 (1918)-. Periodical. Japanese (English and German; summaries and/or abstracts in English and German). Six times a year. $300.00. Nihon Shokubutsu Byori Gakkai, (Phytopathological Society of Japan), Nihon Shokubutsu Boeki Kyokai Biru, 43-11 Komagome 1 Chome, Toshimaku Tokyo 170 Japan. **(Subscription address:** Japan Publications Trading Company Ltd., PO Box 5030, Tokyo International, Tokyo 100-31 Japan. **Tel** 011 81 3 3292 3753.) **ED** Tetsu Wakimoto. **Circ:** 2,400 (ctrl). Documents available from BIOSIS Document Express, CASDDS.
Desc: Scholars and specialists in phytopathologic make announcements concerning their monographs through this journal.
Ind/Abst AgBiotech News Inf.; Biocont. News Inf. (19??-19??); Biodeter. Abstr.; Biol. Abstr.; Chem. Abstr.; Crop Physiol. Abstr.; Curr. Cit.; For. Prod. Abstr.; For. Abstr.; Hortic. Abstr.; Maize Abstr.; Nematol. Abstr.; Plant Breed. Abstr.; Plant Grow. Reg. Abstr.; Potato Abstr.; Protozoolog. Abstr.; Rev. Agric. Entomol.; Rev. Med. Vet. Mycology; Rev. Plant Pathol.; Rice Abstr.; Seed Abstr.; Soils Fert.; Soyabean Abstr.; Wheat Barley Trit. Abstr.

LC QK1 .N75 **ISSN** 0107-055X
DD 581/.05 DK
CCC
CODEN NJBODK
Pr Rev.
NORDIC JOURNAL OF BOTANY.
[Nord. j. bot.]. Vol. 1, No. 1 (Jan. 1981)-. Academic Scholarly Publication. English. Six times a year. $335.89. Nordic Journal of Botany, Secretary Farimagsgade 2-D, DK-1353 Copenhagen K Denmark. **Tel** 011 45 45 3314 4906, FAX 011 45 45 3314 4960. **ED** Kai Larsen (editor's address: Dept. of Systematic Botany, University of Arahus, Nordlandsvej 68, DK-8240 Risskov, Denmark; tlelphone: 011 45 86 210677; fax #: 011 45 86 211891). Index available (bounded in Nov. issue). **Bk Rev**, (Qty: 30). **Ad Acc. Acid Free. Circ:** 600. Documents available from The Genuine Article, BIOSIS Document Express, CASDDS. ***Formed by the union of*** *Botanisk Tidsskrift; Friesia; Norwegian Journal of Botany, 0300-1156* ***and*** *Botaniska Notiser.*
Desc: Original research in botany within taxonomy, structural botany, geobotany, mycology lichenology, and phycology.
Ind/Abst ASTIS Curr. Aware. Bull. (1981-); AgBiotech News Inf.; ASTIS Bibliogr. (1981-); Biodeter. Abstr. (1991-); Biol. Abstr.; Chem. Abstr.; Crop Physiol. Abstr.; Curr. Aware. Biol. Sci., CABS; Curr. Cit.; Ecol. Abstr.; Ecology Abstr.; EMBASE; For. Prod. Abstr.; Grass. Forage Abstr.; Hortic. Abstr.; Microbiol. Abstr. Sect. C; Ornamental Hort. (19??-19??); Life Sci. Collect.; Plant Breed. Abstr.; Plant Genet. Resour. Abstr.; Plant Grow. Reg. Abstr.; Res. Alert [Full Cov.]; Rev. Plant Pathol.; Sci. Cit. Index; SCISEARCH; Seed Abstr.; Weed Abstr.

LC QK110 .N85 **ISSN** 0078-1312
US
CCC
CODEN NAFLBY
NORTH AMERICAN FLORA.
[North Am. flora]. **Added/Corp** New York Botanical Garden. (1905)-. Monographic series. English. Irregular. Price varies per volume. New York Botanical Garden, Scientific Publishing Department B, New York NY 10458-5126. **Tel** (718)817-8721, FAX (718)817-6504, telex 5106015451. Each issue contains an index to its own contents (no volume index)--loose. **Circ:** 250. Documents available from BIOSIS Document Express.
Desc: A series that provides keys and descriptions of plants growing spontaneously in North America, Central America, and the West Indies (excluding those islands whose flora is essentially South American).
Ind/Abst Biol. Abstr.

ISSN 0468-9291
IT
UDC 581.2; 632
CODEN NOMPA8
NOTIZIARIO SULLE MALATTIE DELLE PIANTE.
[Not. mal. piante]. No. 1- June 1949-. Italian (summaries and/or abstracts in English). One time a year. Soc Italiana di Fitoiatria, Casella Postale 230, 27100 Pavia Italy. **Tel** 02/2362880. **Ad Acc. Circ:** 200 (ctrl). Documents available from CASDDS.
Ind/Abst Chem. Abstr.; PESTDOC; Vitis Vitic. Enol. Abstr.

LC QK504 .N6 **ISSN** 0029-5035
DD 586 GW
CCC
CODEN NOHEAI
Pr Rev.
NOVA HEDWIGIA.
[Nova Hedwigia]. Vol. 1 (1959)-. Periodical. English (French and German; summaries and/or abstracts in English and French). Two times a year. $462.00. Gebruder Borntraeger Verlagsbuchhandlung, Johannesstrasse 3-A, D-70176 Stuttgart Germany. **Tel** 0711/62 50 01, FAX (0711)625005, telex 723363 SCHB D. Index available in last issue of volume--attached. Documents available from The Genuine Article, BIOSIS Document Express. ***Continues*** *Hedwigia.*
Ind/Abst AQUAREF; Aquat. Sci. Fish. Abstr. [CD-ROM Ed.]; Biodeter. Abstr.; Biol. Abstr. (-1981); Curr. Aware. Biol. Sci., CABS; Curr. Contents Agric. Biol. Environ. Sci.; Life Sci. Collect.; Res. Alert [Full Cov.]; Rev. Med. Vet. Entomol.; Rev. Plant Pathol.; Sci. Cit. Index; SCISEARCH; Soils Fert.

LC S **ISSN** 0546-8191
DD 630 HU
CODEN NOVEAK
Pr Rev.
NOVENYTERMELES.
(NOVENYTERMELES. RASTENIEVODSTVO. CROP PRODUCTION.). [Novenytermeles]. **VFOAT** Crop Production; Rastenievodstvo. (Aug. 1952)-. Academic Scholarly Publication. Hungarian (summaries and/or abstracts in English and Russian; table of contents in English, French, German and Russian). Six times a year. $31.00. **(Subscription address:** Kultura, PO Box 143, H-1300 Budapest 3 Hungary. **Tel** 011 36 1 2500194.) **ED** Ivan Bocsa. **Bk Rev. Ad Acc. Circ:** 2,000. Documents available from The Genuine Article, CASDDS.
Desc: Covers plant breeding and genetics, genetics technics, crop production, plant nutrition and fertilization, and physiology.
Ind/Abst AgBiotech News Inf.; AGRICOLA; Agric. Eng. Abstr.; Chem. Abstr.; Crop Physiol. Abstr.; Curr. Contents Agric. Biol. Environ. Sci.; EMBASE; Field Crop Abstr.; Grass. Forage Abstr.; Irr. Drain. Abstr.; Maize Abstr.; Microbiol. Abstr. Sect. A; Nutr. Abstr. Rev., Ser. B, Live Feeds and Feed.; Life Sci. Collect.; Plant Breed. Abstr.; Plant Genet. Resour. Abstr.; Plant Grow. Reg. Abstr.; Potato Abstr.; Res. Alert [Select. Cov.]; Rev. Agric. Entomol.; Rev. Plant Pathol.; SCISEARCH; Seed Abstr.; Soils Fert.; Sorghum Mill. Abstr.; Soyabean Abstr.; Wheat Barley Trit. Abstr.

ISSN 0133-0829
HU
CODEN NVVDAW
NOVENYVEDELEM.
[Novenyvedelem]. **VFOAT** Plant Protection; Zashchita Rastenyi Pflanzenschutz. (1965)-. Academic Scholarly Publication. Hungarian (summaries and/or abstracts in English, German and Russian; table of contents in English, German and Russian). Twelve times a year. Documents available from CASDDS.
Ind/Abst Biocont. News Inf. (1991-); Chem. Abstr.; For. Abstr.; Hortic. Abstr.; Maize Abstr.; Nematol. Abstr.; Ornamental Hort. (1991-); Plant Breed. Abstr.; Postharvest News Inf.; Rev. Agric. Entomol.; Rev. Med. Vet. Entomol.; Rev. Plant Pathol.; Soils Fert.; Weed Abstr.; Wheat Barley Trit. Abstr.

ISSN 0862-5158
XR
UDC 58
NOVITATES BOTANICAE UNIVERSITATIS CAROLINAE.
[Nov. bot. Univ. Carol.]. (1982)-. Multiple languages. Irregular. Charles University / Univerzita Karlova, Ovocnytrh 5, 116 36 Prague 1 Czech Republic. **Tel** 228441.
Ind/Abst Rev. Plant Pathol.

LC QK96 .N68 **ISSN** 1055-3177
DD 581/.014 US
CODEN NOVOEK
NOVON (SAINT LOUIS, MO.).
(NOVON : A JOURNAL FOR BOTANICAL NOMENCLATURE.). [Novon]. **Added/Corp** Missouri Botanical Garden. Vol. 1, No. 1 (Winter 1991)-. Periodical. English. Four times a year (Mar., Jun., Sept., Dec.). Comes with Annals of Missouri Botanical Gardens. Missouri Botanical Garden, PO Box 299, St. Louis MO 63166. **Tel** (314)577-9534, (314)577-5100, FAX (314)577-9594. Documents available from BIOSIS Document Express.
Ind/Abst Biol. Abstr. (1991-); Plant Genet. Resour. Abstr.

LC QK1 .A3627 **ISSN** 0568-5443
DD 581 RU
NLM W1 NO961H
NOVOSTI SISTEMATIKI VYSSHIKH RASTENII.
Added/Corp Botanicheskii Institut Im V.L. Komarova. Novitates Systematicae Plantarum Vascularium. **VFOAT** Novitates Systematicae Plantarum Vascularium. (1964)-. Russian (Latin). Izdatelstvo Nauka St. Petersburg, Mendeleevskaia Liniia 1, 199034 St. Petersburg, B-34 Russia. **Tel** 011 7 812 2182612.
Ind/Abst Plant Breed. Abstr.

LC QK1 .N93 **ISSN** 0085-4417
DD 581.9/941 AT
CODEN NUYTDN
NUYTSIA.
(NUYTSIA : BULLETIN OF THE WESTERN AUSTRALIAN HERBARIUM.). [Nuytsia]. **Added/Corp** Western Australian Herbarium. Western Australia. Dept. of Agriculture. Vol. 1 (1970)-. Bulletin. English. Irregular. 10.69Aus$. Department of Conservation and Land Management, PO Box 104, Corp Relations Division, Como WA 6152 Australia. **Tel** 011 61 09 3670333. **ED** N. S. Lander. **Circ:** 500 (ctrl). Documents available from BIOSIS Document Express.
Desc: Botanical taxonomic papers of relevance to Western Australia.
Ind/Abst Biol. Abstr.; Life Sci. Collect.

LC SD399.5 .Y64 **ISSN** 0073-9294
KO
CODEN IYYYA8
Pr Rev.
NYENGU BOGO - RIMMOG NYUGJON NYENGUSO.
See Forests and Forestry.

XR
CODEN OCROET
OCHRANA ROSTLIN.
Added/Corp Ceskoslovenska Akademie Zemedelska. Ustav Vedeckotechnickych Informaci pro Zemedelstvi. Vol. 26, 1 (1990)-. Periodical. Czech (English and Slovak; summaries and/or abstracts in English, German and Russian; table of contents in English, German and Russian). Four times a year. $34.00. Ustav Vedecko Technickych Informaci pro Zemedelstvi, Slezska 7, 120 56 Prague 2, Czech Republic. **Tel** 011 42 2 257541, FAX 011 42 2 257090. **ED** Marcela Braunova. **Bk Rev. Circ:** 850. ***Continues*** *Sbornik UVTIZ. Ochrana Rostlin, 0036-5394.*
Ind/Abst Potato Abstr.; Vitis Vitic. Enol. Abstr.

LC QK1 .064 **ISSN** 0078-5237
DD 581/.05 DK
UDC 58
CODEN OPBOA2
Pr Rev.
OPERA BOTANICA.
[Opera bot.]. Vol. 1 (1953)-. Monographic series. English. Irregular. Price varies per volume. Botanisk Museum, Gothersgade 130, DK-1123 Copenhagen K Denmark. **Tel** +45 33 144906, FAX +45 86211891. **ED** Kai Larsen. **Circ:** 600. Documents available from BIOSIS Document Express, CASDDS. ***Supersedes*** *Botaniska Notiser. Supplement;* ***Absorbed*** *Dansk Botanisk Arkiv.*
Desc: More comprehensive papers of original research in botany within taxonomy, structural botany, geobotany, mycology, lichenology and phycology.
Ind/Abst AGRICOLA; Biol. Abstr.; Chem. Abstr.; Curr. Aware. Biol. Sci., CABS; For. Abstr.; Hortic. Abstr.; Ornamental Hort. (1991-); Life Sci. Collect.; Seed Abstr.; Weed Abstr.

ISSN 0775-9592
BE
UDC 58.006
OPERA BOTANICA BELGICA.
[Opera Bot. Belg.]. (1988)-. Monographic series. French (Dutch). Irregular. Price varies per volume. Jardin Botanique Nationale Belgique, Domaine de Bouchout, B-1860 Meise Belgium. **Tel** 011 32 2 2693905.

LC QK
DD 581 IT
OPERA BOTANICA SEZIONE A.
Added/Corp Museo Tridentino di Scienze Naturali. Comitato Onoranze Bresadoliane. Vol. 1 (1974)-.

Monographic series. Italian. Price varies per volume. Each issue contains an index to its own contents (no volume index)--loose.

LC QK
DD 581 UZ
OPREDELITEL RASTENII SREDNEI AZII. **Added/Corp** Institut Botaniki (Uzbekiston SSR Fanlar Akademiiasi) V.I. Lenin Nomidagi Toshkent Davlat Universiteti. **VFOAT** Conspectus Florae Asiae Mediae. Vol. 1 (1968)-. Russian. Irregular. **(Subscription address:** Victor Kamkin, 4956 Boiling Brook Parkway, Rockville MD 20852. **Tel** (301)881-5973.)

LC QK725 .O97 **ISSN** 0264-861X
DD 581.87/05 UK
CODEN OSPBEO
OXFORD SURVEYS OF PLANT MOLECULAR AND CELL BIOLOGY. [Oxf. surv. plant mol. cell bio.]. **VFOAT** Plant Molecular and Cell Biology. (1984)-. Academic Scholarly Publication. English. Irregular. Price varies per volume. Oxford University Press / UK, Walton Street, Oxford OX2 6DP United Kingdom. **Tel** 011 44 1865 56767, FAX 011 44 1865 267773, telex 851/837330 OXPRES G. **(Subscription address:** Oxford University Press / USA, Journals Marketing Department, Oxford University Press, 2001 Evans Road, Cary NC 27513. **Tel** (800)451-7556, (919)677-0977, FAX (919)677-1714.) **ED** B.J. Miflin and H.F. Miflin. available with illustrations. Documents available from BIOSIS Document Express, CASDDS.
Ind/Abst AGRICOLA [Full Cov.]; Biol. Abstr. (1986-); Chem. Abstr. (1984-); Plant Grow. Reg. Abstr.; Soyabean Abstr.

LC QK1 .P14 **ISSN** 0556-3321
DD 581/.05 PK
UDC 58 **CCC**
CODEN PJBOB6
Pr Rev.
PAKISTAN JOURNAL OF BOTANY. [Pak. j. bot.]. Vol. 1 (June/Dec. 1969)-. Periodical. English. Two times a year. $20.00. Pakistan Botanical Society, University of Karachi, Karachi 32 Pakistan. **Tel** 462828. **ED** Abdul Ghaffar. **Bk Rev. Ad Acc. Circ:** 2,000. Documents available from The Genuine Article, BIOSIS Document Express, CASDDS.
Desc: Research articles in the field of botany and agriculture.
Ind/Abst AGRICOLA; Agrofor. Abstr. (1991-); Biol. Abstr.; Chem. Abstr.; Coal Abstr.; Crop Physiol. Abstr.; Curr. Cit.; Curr. Contents Agric. Biol. Environ. Sci.; EMBASE; Field Crop Abstr.; Food Sci. Technol. Abstr.; For. Abstr.; Grass. Forage Abstr.; Hortic. Abstr.; Irr. Drain. Abstr.; Maize Abstr.; Life Sci. Collect.; Plant Breed. Abstr.; Plant Grow. Reg. Abstr.; Potato Abstr.; Res. Alert [Select. Cov.]; Rev. Plant Pathol.; Rice Abstr.; SCISEARCH; Seed Abstr.; Soils Fert.; Soyabean Abstr.; Vitis Vitic. Enol. Abstr.; Weed Abstr.; Wheat Barley Trit. Abstr.

LC QK358.5 .P34
DD 581.9/549/105 PK
PAKISTAN SYSTEMATICS. **Added/Corp** Quaid-i-Azam University. Herbarium. Vol. 1 (July 1977)-. Periodical. English. Four times a year. The Herbarium / Quaid-I-Azam University, PO Box 1090, Islamabad Pakistan. **Tel** 827253. **ED** Rizwana Aleem Qureshi and Mohammad Nazeer Chaudhri. **Bk Rev. Ad Acc. Circ:** 1,000 (ctrl).
Desc: Devoted to systematic botany, plant ecology, and other closely allied disciplines, and is available in exchange for publications of a similar nature in these fields.

LC QE901 .P3 **ISSN** 0031-0174
DD 561 II
CODEN PLBOAJ
PALAEOBOTANIST (LUCKNOW). **See** Paleontology.

LC QK
DD 581 US
PALM JOURNAL. **Added/Corp** International Palm Society. **VFOAT** Palm Journal of the Southern California Chapter of the International Palm Society. Vol. 9, No. 2 (Mar./May 1990)-. Periodical. English. Six times a year. Southern California Chapter of the International Palm Society, 15461 Devonshire Circle, Westminster CA 92683. ***Continues*** *California Newsletter (International Palm Society).*

ISSN 1321-2346
AT
PALMS AND CYCADS. (1984)-. Periodical. English. Four times a year. 30.00Aus$ Australia; 40.00Aus$ others. Palm & Cycad Society, PO Box 1134, Milton Queensland 4064 Australia. **Tel** 011 61 7 2219122, FAX 011 61 7 32985088. **ED** T.L. Turner. Index available. cum. index. **Ad Acc. Circ:** 1,000 (ctrl).

ISSN 0256-1670
DD 581 US
UDC 56:581.33; 902.67
PALYNOS. (PALYNOS : NEWSLETTER OF THE INTERNATIONAL FEDERATION OF PALYNOLOGICAL SOCIETIES.). [Palynos]. Vol. 7, No. 2 (Dec. 1984)-. Newsletter. English. Two times a year (June and December). $10.00 (includes airmail postage for overseas). Palynos, Department of Botany, Arizona State University, Tempe AZ 85287-1601. **Tel** (602)965-1762, FAX (602)965-1608, telex 156-1058 ASU UT. **ED** James E Canright. **Bk Rev. Circ:** 3,000 (ctrl). Documents available from BIOSIS Document Express. ***Continues*** *ICP Newsletter, 0737-5786.*
Desc: Newsletter of the International Federation of Palynological Societies. NB-Palynologists are specialists on modern and fossil pollen and related microfossils.
Ind/Abst Biol. Abstr.; GeoRef.

ISSN 0710-0469
DD 580/.74/471352 CN
PAPPUS. (PAPPUS : A QUARTERLY PUBLICATION FROM THE ROYAL BOTANICAL GARDENS.). [Pappus]. **Added/Corp** Royal Botanical Gardens (Hamilton, Ont.). Vol. 1, No. 1 (Summer 1981)-. Periodical. English. Four times a year. 30.00Can$ (individuals), 75.00 (institutions) Only available with Royal Botanical Gardens membership. Royal Botanical Gardens - CHTA, Box 399, Hamilton Ontario L8N 3H8 Canada. **Tel** (416)527-1158. **ED** Susan Malcolm. **Bk Rev. Circ:** 3,347 (ctrl). ***Absorbed*** *Royal Botanical Gardens (Hamilton, Ont.). Members' Association. Members' Association Newsletter, 0821-7130.*
Desc: Bulletin on technical matters related to Royal Botanical Gardens work and a list of topics are also available.
Ind/Abst Garden Lit. (1992-).

LC QK261 .P37 **ISSN** 0325-9684
DD 581.982 AG
CODEN PRDND3
PARODIANA. [Parodiana]. **Added/Corp** Centro de Estudios Farmacologicos y de Principios Naturales (Buenos Aires, Argentina). Unidad Botanica. Consejo Nacional de Investigaciones Cientificas y Tecnicas (Argentina). Vol. 1 (March 1981)-. Academic Scholarly Publication. Spanish. Two times a year. $50.00. CEFYBO, Serrano 669, 1414 Buenos Aires Argentina. **Tel** 011 54 1 8557194, FAX 011 54 1 8562751. Documents available from CASDDS.
Ind/Abst AGRICOLA; Chem. Abstr. (1981-1983).

LC QK **ISSN** 0761-1927
DD 581 FR
PASCAL FOLIO. F55, BIOLOGIE VEGETALE. [PASCAL folio. F55 Biol. v,eg.]. **Added/Corp** CNRS - PASCAL (Center). **VFOAT** Plant Biology; Biologie Vegetale; PASCAL Folio. F55, Plant Biology. No. 1 (1984)-. Periodical. French (English and French). Eleven times a year. F1195.00 France; F1270.00 other. CNRS / Institut d'Information Scientifique et Technique, (Centre National de la Recherche Scientifique), 15 Quai Anatole France, 75700 Paris France. **Tel** 011 33 1 47531515, FAX 011 33 1 45517307, telex 260034. **(Subscription address:** Institut d'Information Scientifique et Technique Diffusion, 2 Allee du Parc de Brabois, 54514 Vandoeuvre Nancy France. **Tel** 011 33 83 504664, FAX 011 33 83 504666, telex 961942.) ***Continues in part*** *Bulletin Signaletique. 370, Biologie et Physiologie Vegetales (1981), 0240-8546.*

ISSN 0373-840X
BL
PESQUISAS. BOTANICA. [Pesqui. Bot.]. (1957)-. Monographic series. Portuguese. Irregular. Price varies per volume. Sao Leopoldo, Praca Tiradentes, 35 Rio Grande Do Sul Brazil 93010-020. **Tel** FAX 051 5921035. Index available. cum. index. **Circ:** 500 (ctrl). Documents available from FAXON Xpress.

ISSN 0031-6733
AU
CODEN PFLZAQ
PFLANZENARZT, DER. [Pflanzenarzt]. **Added/Corp** Vienna. Bundesanstalt fuer Pflanzenschutz. (1948)-. Periodical. German. Eight times a year. $60.99. Oesterreichischer Agrarverlag, Inkustr 1 7 Bueropark Donau, A 3400 Klosterneuberg Austria. **Tel** 011 43 2243 33300. **ED** Waltraud Wudy. **Bk Rev. Ad Acc. Circ:** 8,000. Documents available from BIOSIS Document Express.
Ind/Abst AGRICOLA; Biol. Abstr. (1969-1984); PESTDOC; Rev. Plant Pathol.; Vitis Vitic. Enol. Abstr.

SZ
PFLANZENSCHUTZ. Vol. 27, No. 124 (Feb. 1962)-. Periodical. German.
Ind/Abst Biocont. News Inf. (1991-); Maize Abstr.; Nematol. Abstr.; Plant Breed. Abstr.; Plant Grow. Reg. Abstr.; Potato Abstr.; Rev. Agric. Entomol.; Rev. Plant Pathol.; Weed Abstr.; Wheat Barley Trit. Abstr.

GW
PFLANZENSOZIOLOGIE; EINE REIHE VEGETATIONSKUNDLICHER GEBIETSMONOGRAPHIEN. (19??)-. Monographic series. German. Irregular. Price varies per volume. Gustav Fischer Verlag Jena, Postfach 100537, D-07705 Jena Germany. **Tel** 011 49 3641 626444, FAX 011 49 3641 626500. **ED** Erich Oberdorfer. **Bk Rev.**

LC SB123.3 .P48 **ISSN** 1013-0314
DD 631.5/23/096305 ET
PGRC/E-ILCA GERMPLASM NEWSLETTER. **VAT** Plant Genetic Resource. Newsletter. English. Three times a year.
Ind/Abst Agrofor. Abstr.; For. Abstr.; Nematol. Abstr.; Plant Breed. Abstr.

ISSN 0115-0804
PH
CODEN PHPHD9
PHILIPPINE PHYTOPATHOLOGY. [Philipp. phytopathol.]. **Added/Corp** Philippine Phytopathological Society. (1965)-. Periodical. English. One time a year. $20.00. Philippine Phytopathological Society, University of the Philippines at Los Banos, Department of Plant Pathology, Laguna Philippines. **Tel** 3534. **ED** Narceo Bajet, Paul S. Teng and Avelino Raymundo. Index available. **Ad Acc. Circ:** 500 (ctrl). Documents available from BIOSIS Document Express, CASDDS.
Ind/Abst AGRICOLA; Biol. Abstr. (1986-); Chem. Abstr.; Food Sci. Technol. Abstr.; Life Sci. Collect.; Philip. Sci. Technol. Abstr.

ISSN 0166-8595
NE
CCC
CODEN PHRSDI
Pr Rev.
PHOTOSYNTHESIS RESEARCH. [Photosynth. res.]. Vol. 1, No. 1 (1980)-. Academic Scholarly Publication. English. Twelve times a year. $1022.00. Kluwer Academic Publishers, Postbus 322, 3300 AH Dordrecht The Netherlands. **Tel** 011 31 78 524400, FAX 011 31 78 183273, telex 20083. **ED** R.E. Blankenship. **Bk Rev. Ad Acc. Acid Free. Circ:** 500. available on microfilm and microfiche from University Microfilms International (UMI). Documents available from The Genuine Article, BIOSIS Document Express, Ask*IEEE, CASDDS.
Desc: Aims to provide a forum for original papers dealing with photosynthesis without imposing an artificial division between fundamental and applied research. It covers all aspects of photosynthesis research including light absorption and emission, excitation energy transfer, primary photophosphorylation, carbon assimilation, regulatory phenomena, molecular biology, environmental and ecological aspects, photorespiration, and bacterial and algal photosynthesis.
Ind/Abst AgBiotech News Inf.; Biol. Abstr. (Jan. 1988-); Chem. Abstr. (Jan. 1988-); Chem. Titles (Jan. 1988-); Crop Physiol. Abstr.; Curr. Aware. Biol. Sci., CABS; Curr. Cit.; Curr. Contents Agric. Biol. Environ. Sci.; Curr. Contents Life Sci.; Field Crop Abstr.; For. Abstr.; Grass. Forage Abstr.; Hortic. Abstr.; INSPEC (Jan. 1988-); Irr. Drain. Abstr.; Maize Abstr.; Ornamental Hort. (1991-); Plant Breed. Abstr.; Ref. Upd. Basic Ed.; Ref. Upd. Deluxe Ed.; Res. Alert [Full Cov.]; Sci. Cit. Index; SCISEARCH; Soils Fert.; Sorghum Mill. Abstr.; Soyabean Abstr.; Weed Abstr.; Wheat Barley Trit. Abstr.

LC QK882 .P563 **ISSN** 0300-3604
NE
CCC
NLM W1 PH672K **CODEN** PHSYB5
Pr Rev.
PHOTOSYNTHETICA. [Photosynthetica]. **Added/Corp** Ustav Experimentalni Botaniky CSAV. Vol. 1 (1967)-. Academic Scholarly Publication. Multiple languages (English, French and German). Four times a year. $370.00. Kluwer Academic Publishers, Postbus 322, 3300 AH Dordrecht The Netherlands. **Tel** 011 31 78 524400, FAX 011 31 78 183273, telex 20083. **ED** Zdenek Sestak. cum. index. **Bk Rev. Acid Free. Circ:** 1,000. Documents available from The Genuine Article, BIOSIS Document Express, CASDDS.
Desc: This publication is devoted entirely to photosynthesis investigations; combines the biochemical, biophysical and ecological approaches to the study of photosynthesis in plants.
Ind/Abst AgBiotech News Inf.; AGRICOLA; Agric. Eng. Abstr. (1991-); Biol. Abstr.; Chem. Abstr.; Crop Physiol. Abstr.; Curr. Aware. Biol. Sci., CABS; Curr. Cit.; Curr. Contents Agric. Biol. Environ. Sci.; EMBASE; Field Crop Abstr.; For. Abstr.; Grass. Forage Abstr.; Hortic. Abstr.; Irr. Drain. Abstr.; Maize Abstr.; Ornamental Hort. (1991-); Life Sci. Collect.; Plant Breed. Abstr.; Plant Grow. Reg. Abstr.; Potato Abstr.; Res. Alert [Full Cov.]; Rice Abstr.; Sci. Cit. Index; SCISEARCH; Seed Abstr.; Soils Fert.; Sorghum Mill. Abstr.; Soyabean Abstr.; Weed Abstr.

LC QK564 .P44 **ISSN** 0031-8884
DD 589.3 UK
CCC
CODEN PYCOAD
Pr Rev.
PHYCOLOGIA (OXFORD). (PHYCOLOGIA.). [Phycologia]. **Added/Corp** International Phycological Society. Vol. 1, No. 1 (Mar. 1961)-. Academic Scholarly Publication. English (French, German, Russian and Spanish). Six times a year. $350.00. Blackwell Scientific Publications Ltd, Marston Book Services, PO Box 88, Oxford OX2 ONE United Kingdom. **Tel** 011 44 1865 206206, FAX 011 44 1865 206219, telex 837 515 MARDIS G. Index available (bound in last issue). **Bk Rev. Ad Acc. Circ:** 1,400. available on microfilm and

microfiche from University Microfilms International (UMI). Documents available from The Genuine Article, BIOSIS Document Express, CASDDS.
Ind/Abst AGRICOLA; Aquat. Sci. Fish. Abstr. [CD-ROM Ed.]; Biol. Abstr.; Chem. Abstr.; Curr. Aware. Biol. Sci., CABS; Curr. Contents Agric. Biol. Environ. Sci.; Ecol. Abstr.; Ecology Abstr.; Fresh. Aqua. Contents Tables; GeoRef; Mar. Sci. Contents Tables; Microbiol. Abstr. Sect. C; Ocean. Abstr.; Life Sci. Collect.; Res. Alert [Full Cov.]; Sci. Cit. Index; SCISEARCH.

LC QK564 .P475 **ISSN** 0554-1174
US

PHYCOLOGICAL STUDIES. [Phycol. stud.]. **Added/Corp** University of Texas at Austin. (1960)-. Monographic series. English. Price varies per volume. University of Texas at Austin / Phycological Studies, Austin TX 78712.
Ind/Abst Aquat. Sci. Fish. Abstr. [CD-ROM Ed.].

LC QK564 .P48 **ISSN** 0554-1182
DD 589.3/05 II
CODEN PHKSBF

PHYKOS. (PHYKOS : JOURNAL OF THE PHYCOLOGICAL SOCIETY (INDIA).). [Phykos]. **Added/Corp** Phycological Society (India). Vol. 1, No. 1 (April 1962)-. Periodical. English. Two times a year. $40.00. **(Subscription address:** Prints India, 11 Darya Ganj, New Delhi 110002 India. **Tel** 011 91 11 3268645, FAX 011 91 11 3275542, telex 31-61087 PRIN-IN.) Index Available in last issue of volume--loose--unpaged. Documents available from BIOSIS Document Express, CASDDS.
Ind/Abst AGRICOLA; Aquat. Sci. Fish. Abstr. [CD-ROM Ed.]; Biol. Abstr.; Chem. Abstr.; Ecology Abstr.; Microbiol. Abstr. Sect. C; Life Sci. Collect.

LC QK1 **ISSN** 0031-9317
DD 580.5 DK
UDC 581.2 **CCC**
NLM W1 PH925K **CODEN** PHPLAI
Pr Rev.

PHYSIOLOGIA PLANTARUM. [Physiol. plant.]. (1948)-. Academic Scholarly Publication. English (French and German). Twelve times a year. $731.82. Munksgaard International Publishers Ltd, PO Box 2148, DK-1016 Copenhagen K Denmark. **Tel** 011 45 33 127030, FAX 011 45 33 129387, telex 19431 MUNKS DK. **ED** Anders Kylin. Index available. **Ad Acc. Circ:** 2,000 (ctrl). Documents available from The Genuine Article, BIOSIS Document Express, CASDDS. ***Absorbed*** *What's New in Plant Physiology, 0193-0648.*
Desc: All aspects of plant physiology from biochemistry and biophysics to classical plant physiology and ecology.
Ind/Abst Abstr. Bull. Inst. Pap. Sci. Tech.; AgBiotech News Inf.; AGRICOLA; Biol. Agric. Index; Biol. Abstr.; Chem. Abstr.; Cot. Trop. Fibr. Abstr. Bibliogr.; Crop Physiol. Abstr.; Curr. Aware. Biol. Sci., CABS; Curr. Biotechnol.; Curr. Cit.; Curr. Contents Agric. Biol. Environ. Sci.; Ecol. Abstr. (?-?); EMBASE; Energy Res. Abstr.; Field Crop Abstr.; Food Sci. Technol. Abstr.; For. Abstr.; Grass. Forage Abstr.; Hortic. Abstr.; Int. Aerosp. Abstr.; Irr. Drain. Abstr.; Leadscan; Maize Abstr.; Microbiol. Abstr. Sect. A; Microbiol. Abstr. Sect. C; Nat. Prod. Updates; Ornamental Hort. (1991-); Life Sci. Collect.; Plant Breed. Abstr.; Plant Genet. Resour. Abstr.; Plant Grow. Reg. Abstr.; Postharvest News Inf.; Potato Abstr.; Ref. Upd. Deluxe Ed.; Res. Alert [Full Cov.]; Rev. Agric. Entomol.; Rev. Plant Pathol.; Rice Abstr.; Sci. Cit. Index; SCISEARCH; Seed Abstr.; Soils Fert.; Sorghum Mill. Abstr.; Soyabean Abstr.; Vitis Vitic. Enol. Abstr.; Weed Abstr.

LC SB599 .P46 **ISSN** 0885-5765
DD 632 580 UK
UDC 581.2; 632 **CCC**
CODEN PMPPEZ
Pr Rev.

PHYSIOLOGICAL AND MOLECULAR PLANT PATHOLOGY. [Physiol. mol. plant pathol.]. Vol. 28, No. 1 (Jan. 1986)-. Academic Scholarly Publication. English. Twelve times a year. $564.69. Academic Press Ltd., A Division of Harcourt Brace & Company Ltd., 24-28 Oval Road, London NW1 7DX United Kingdom. **Tel** 011 44 171 2674466, FAX 011 44 171 4822293, 011 44 171 4854752, telex 25775 ACPRES G. **(Subscription address:** Harcourt Brace & Company, Ltd., Foots Cray High Street, Sidcup Kent DA14 5HP United Kingdom. **Tel** 011 44 181 3003322, FAX 011 44 181 3090807, telex 896 377 ACADEM.) **ED** D. D. Clarke. Documents available from The Genuine Article, BIOSIS Document Express, CASDDS. ***Continues*** *Physiological Plant Pathology, 0048-4059.*
Desc: A forum for original research papers and occasional review articles. Deals with all aspects of the physiology and biochemistry of the plant-host parasite relationship at all levels of complexity from the molecular to the whole organism.
Ind/Abst AgBiotech News Inf.; AGRICOLA [Full Cov.]; Biocont. News Inf.; Biol. Abstr. (1986-); Chem. Abstr. (1986-); Crop Physiol. Abstr.; Curr. Aware. Biol. Sci., CABS; Curr. Cit.; Curr. Contents Agric. Biol. Environ. Sci.; Field Crop Abstr.; Food Sci. Technol. Abstr.; For. Abstr.; Irr. Drain. Abstr.; Maize Abstr.; Nat. Prod. Updates; Nematol. Abstr.; Life Sci. Collect.; PESTDOC; Plant Breed. Abstr.; Plant Grow. Reg. Abstr.; Postharvest News Inf.; Potato Abstr.; Ref. Upd. Deluxe Ed.; Res. Alert [Full Cov.]; Rev. Plant Pathol.; Rice Abstr.; Sci. Cit. Index; SCISEARCH; Sorghum Mill. Abstr.; Soyabean Abstr.; Weed Abstr.; Wheat Barley Trit. Abstr.

ISSN 0326-1441
AG
Pr Rev.

PHYSIS. SECCIONES A, B Y C. **See** Zoology.

LC QK95 .P45
DD 581/.012 II

PHYTA : JOURNAL OF THE SOCIETY OF PLANT TAXONOMISTS. **Added/Corp** Society of Plant Taxonomists (India). **VFOAT** Journal of the Society of Plant Taxonomists. Vol. 1 (1978)-. Periodical. English. $32.00. Society of Plant Taxonomists, Allahabad India. **(Subscription address:** Prints India, 11 Darya Ganj, New Delhi 110002 India. **Tel** 011 91 11 3268645, FAX 011 91 11 3275542, telex 31-61087 PRIN-IN.)

LC QK
DD 581 II

PHYTA MONOGRAPH. **Added/Corp** Society of Indian Plant Taxonomists. **VFOAT** Phyta Monograph Series. No. 1 (1984)-. Monographic series. English. Price varies per volume. Society of Plant Taxonomists, Allahabad India. **(Subscription address:** Prints India, 11 Darya Ganj, New Delhi 110002 India. **Tel** 011 91 11 3268645, FAX 011 91 11 3275542, telex 31-61087 PRIN-IN.)

LC QK865 .P48 **ISSN** 0958-0344
DD 581/.05 UK
CCC
NLM W1; PH419UF **CODEN** PHANEL

PHYTOCHEMICAL ANALYSIS. (PHYTOCHEMICAL ANALYSIS : PCA.). [Phytochem. anal.]. **VFOAT** PCA. Vol. 1, No. 1 (Sept. 1990)-. Academic Scholarly Publication. English. Six times a year. $465.00. John Wiley & Sons Ltd., Baffins Lane, Chichester, West Sussex PO19 1UD United Kingdom. **Tel** 011 44 1243 779777, FAX 011 44 1243 776128 BTG:JWP001, telex 86290 WIBOOKG. **(Subscription address:** John Wiley & Sons, Inc. / Philadelphia, PO Box 7247, Philadelphia PA 19170. **Tel** (212)850-6645, (800)225-5945.) **ED** Barry V. Charlwood and A. Douglas Kinghorn. available on microfilm and microfiche from University Microfilms International (UMI). Documents available from The Genuine Article, CASDDS.
Desc: Publishes original articles on the application of analytical methodology in the plant sciences. Covers methods and techniques relevant to the extraction, separation, purification, identification and quantification of substances in plant biochemistry, plant cellular and molecular biology, plant biotechnology, food sciences, agriculture and horticulture.
Ind/Abst Anal. Abstr.; Chem. Abstr.; Curr. Aware. Biol. Sci., CABS; Curr. Cit.; Curr. Contents Agric. Biol. Environ. Sci.; EMBASE; Res. Alert [Select. Cov.]; SCISEARCH.

ISSN 0898-3437
DD 581 US
Pr Rev.

PHYTOCHEMICAL BULLETIN. [Phytochem. bull.]. **Added/Corp** Botanical Society of America. Phytochemical Section. Vol. 5, No. 4 (Oct./Dec. 1972)-. Bulletin. English. Four times a year. $6.00. Phytochemical Bulletin, Department of Botany, Arizona State University, Tempe AZ 85287. **Tel** (602)965-4482, FAX (602)965-6899. ***Continues*** *Newsletter (Botanical Society of America. Phytochemical Section).*

LC QK861 .P45 **ISSN** 0031-9422
DD 581.19205 UK
CCC
NLM W1 PH987K **CODEN** PYTCAS
Pr Rev.

PHYTOCHEMISTRY (OXFORD). (PHYTOCHEMISTRY.). [Phytochemistry (Oxford)]. Vol. 1 (Oct. 1961)-. Academic Scholarly Publication. English (French and German). Eighteen times a year. $2110.00. Pergamon Press, An Imprint of Elsevier Science Ltd., The Boulevard, Langford Lane, Kidlington, Oxford OX5 1GB United Kingdom. **Tel** 011 44 1865 843000, 011 44 1865 843699, FAX 011 44 1865 843010. **(Subscription address:** Elsevier Science Ltd. / Oxford Fulfillment Centre, PO Box 800, Kidlington OX5 1DX United Kingdom. **Tel** 011 44 865 843355.) **ED** Jeffrey Harborne. Index available. available on microfilm from Microfilms International Marketing Corp.; available on microfilm and microfiche from University Microfilms International (UMI); available on microfiche from the publisher; available on an online database from Elsevier Electronic Subscriptions (EES). Documents available from The Genuine Article, BIOSIS Document Express, CASDDS.
Desc: Covers research on all aspects of pure and applied plant biochemistry, especially that which leads to a deeper understanding of the factors underlying the growth, development and metabolism of plants and the chemistry of plant constituents.
Ind/Abst Abstr. Bull. Inst. Pap. Sci. Tech.; AgBiotech News Inf.; AGRICOLA [Full Cov.]; Agrofor. Abstr. (19??-19??); Biocont. News Inf. (1991-); Biodeter. Abstr. (19??-19??); Biol. Agric. Index; Biol. Abstr.; Chem Inform; Chem. Abstr.; Chem. Titles; Chemorecept. Abstr.; Cot. Trop. Fibr. Abstr. Bibliogr.; Crop Physiol. Abstr.; Curr. Aware. Biol. Sci., CABS; Curr. Biotechnol.; Curr. Chem. React.; Curr. Cit.; Curr. Contents Agric. Biol. Environ. Sci.; Curr. Contents Life Sci.; Dairy Sci. Abstr.; EMBASE; Entomol. Abstr.; Field Crop Abstr.; Food Sci. Technol. Abstr.; For. Prod. Abstr. (19??-19??); For. Abstr.; Grass. Forage Abstr.; Helminthol. Abstr. (19??-19??); Hortic. Abstr.; Index Chem.; Int. Aerosp. Abstr.; Irr. Drain. Abstr.; Maize Abstr.; Microbiol. Abstr. Sect. B (19??-19??); Microbiol. Abstr. Sect. A; Microbiol. Abstr. Sect. C; NAPRALERT; Nat. Prod. Updates; Nutr. Abstr. Rev., Ser. B, Live Feeds and Feed.; Nutr. Abstr. Rev., Ser. A, Hum. Exp.; Ornamental Hort. (19??-19??); Life Sci. Collect.; PESTDOC; Plant Breed. Abstr.; Plant Genet. Resour. Abstr.; Plant Grow. Reg. Abstr.; Postharvest News Inf.; Potato Abstr.; Protozoolog. Abstr.; Ref. Upd. Deluxe Ed.; Res. Alert [Full Cov.]; Rev. Agric. Entomol.; Rev. Med. Vet. Entomol.; Rev. Med. Vet. Mycology; Rev. Plant Pathol.; Rice Abstr.; Sci. Cit. Index; SCISEARCH; Seed Abstr.; Soils Fert.; Sorghum Mill. Abstr.; Soyabean Abstr.; Vitis Vitic. Enol. Abstr.; Weed Abstr.

LC QK911 .P46 **ISSN** 0340-269X
DD 581.5/2/05 GW
CCC
CODEN PYCEBI

PHYTOCOENOLOGIA. [Phytocoenologia]. **Added/Corp** International Society for Vegetation Science. (1973)-. Multiple languages (English and French). Four times a year. $384.00. Gebruder Borntraeger Verlagsbuchhandlung, Johannesstrasse 3-A, D-70176 Stuttgart Germany. **Tel** 0711/62 50 01, FAX (0711)625005, telex 723363 SCHB D. **ED** Wilmanns Gehu. Documents available from BIOSIS Document Express.
Ind/Abst AGRICOLA; Biol. Abstr.; Ecology Abstr.; For. Abstr.; GeoRef; Grass. Forage Abstr.; Irr. Drain. Abstr.; Life Sci. Collect.; Plant Genet. Resour. Abstr.; Seed Abstr.; Soils Fert.; Weed Abstr.

LC QK1 .P58 **ISSN** 0031-9430
DD 580.5 US
CODEN PYTLAL
Pr Rev.

PHYTOLOGIA. [Phytologia]. (Dec. 1933)-. Periodical. English (Latin and Spanish). Twelve times a year. $44.00. Phytologia, 185 Westridge Drive, Huntsville TX 77340. **Tel** (409)295-5410, FAX (409)291-0009. **ED** Michael Warnock. Index available in last issue of volume--attached. **Bk Rev**, (Qty: 12). **Circ:** 400 (ctrl). Documents available from BIOSIS Document Express.
Desc: Intended for speedy publication of botanical and phytoecological papers.
Ind/Abst AGRICOLA [Full Cov.]; Biol. Abstr.; Crop Physiol. Abstr.; Field Crop Abstr.; Microbiol. Abstr. Sect. C; Life Sci. Collect.; Potato Abstr.

US
Pr Rev.

PHYTOLOGIA MEMOIRS. Monographic series. English (Spanish). Irregular. Price varies per volume. Dr Harold Moldenke, 590 Hemlock Avenue NW, Corvallis OR 97330. Index available. cum. index. **Bk Rev. Circ:** 300.

ISSN 0370-2723
FR
CODEN PYTOAU

PHYTOMA. (PHYTOMA, DEFENSE DES CULTURES; REVUE MENSUELLE D'INFORMATION ET DE DOCUMENTATION.). [Phytoma]. (July 1948)-. Academic Scholarly Publication. French. Twelve times a year. Editions le Caroussel, 26 rue Daniel Casanova, 75002 Paris France. **Tel** 011 33 1 40209474. Documents available from BIOSIS Document Express, CASDDS. ***Absorbed*** *Defense des Vegetaux, 0011-7579.*
Ind/Abst Biol. Abstr.; Chem. Abstr.; Chem. Bus. Bull.; Chem. Bus. NewsBase (1989-); Chem. Bus. Update; EMBASE; Maize Abstr.; Life Sci. Collect.; PESTDOC (?-?); Soils Fert.

FR

PHYTOMA LA DEFENSE DES VEGETAUX. French. Eleven times a year. 285.00F France; 335.00F other. Editions le Caroussel, 26 rue Daniel Casanova, 75002 Paris France. **Tel** 011 33 1 40209474.

LC QK1 .P586 **ISSN** 0031-9449
DD 581 II
CODEN PHYMAW

PHYTOMORPHOLOGY. [Phytomorphology]. **Added/Corp** International Society of Plant Morphologists. (Aug. 1951)-. Periodical. English (German and French). Four times a year. $55.00. International Society of Plant Morphologist, Department of Botany, University of Delhi, Delhi 110007 India. **Tel** 2918983. **(Subscription address:** Prints India, 11 Darya Ganj, New Delhi 110002 India. **Tel** 011 91 11 3268645, FAX 011 91 11 3275542, telex 31-61087 PRIN-IN.) **ED** N N Bhandari. Index available. cum. index. **Bk Rev. Ad Acc. Circ:** 900. Documents available from BIOSIS Document Express, CASDDS.
Desc: Promotes international cooperation in the study and diffusion of useful knowledge in the fields of descriptive and experimental plant morphology, anatomy, embryology, histochemistry, ultrastructure, cytology, palaeobotany and ecology.
Ind/Abst Abstr. Bull. Inst. Pap. Sci. Tech.; AGRICOLA [Full Cov.]; Agrofor. Abstr. (1991-); Biol. Abstr.; Chem. Abstr.; Crop Physiol. Abstr.; Field Crop Abstr.; For. Prod. Abstr. (1991-); For. Abstr.; GeoRef; Grass. Forage Abstr.;

Hortic. Abstr.; Irr. Drain. Abstr.; Ornamental Hort. (19??-19??); Plant Breed. Abstr.; Plant Grow. Reg. Abstr.; Rev. Plant Pathol.; Rice Abstr.; Seed Abstr.; Sorghum Mill. Abstr.; Weed Abstr.

LC QK1 .P5864 **ISSN** 0031-9457
DD 581/.05 AG
CODEN PHYBAX
Pr Rev.

PHYTON (BUENOS AIRES). (PHYTON.). [Phyton]. **Added/Corp** Fundacion Romulo Raggio. Domus Plantarum. Instituto para Investigaciones Cientificas y Tecnologicas (Argentina). Vol. 1 (July 1951)-. Periodical. English (French, German, Italian, Portuguese and Spanish). Two times a year. $35.00. Fundacion Romulo Raggio, Gaspar Campos 861, 1638 Vicente Lopez Argentina. **Tel** 011 54 796 1456, FAX 011 54 796 1456. **ED** Miguel Raggio. Index available in last issue of volume--attached. **Bk Rev. Ad Acc. Circ:** 1,000. Documents available from The Genuine Article, BIOSIS Document Express, CASDDS.
Desc: Experimental botany including plant physiology, genetics, biochemistry, ecology (experimental), phytochemistry, agriculture.
Ind/Abst Abstr. Bull. Inst. Pap. Sci. Tech.; AGRICOLA [Full Cov.]; Biol. Abstr.; Chem. Abstr.; Curr. Cit.; Field Crop Abstr.; For. Abstr.; Hortic. Abstr.; Life Sci. Collect.; Plant Breed. Abstr.; Plant Grow. Reg. Abstr.; Potato Abstr.; Res. Alert [Full Cov.]; Sci. Cit. Index; Seed Abstr.; Soils Fert.; Vitis Vitic. Enol. Abstr.; Weed Abstr.

LC QK1 .P587 **ISSN** 0079-2047
DD 580/.5 AU
CODEN PHYNAZ
Pr Rev.

PHYTON (HORN). (PHYTON.). [Phyton]. Vol. 1-12, (Nov. 1948)-. Periodical. German (summaries and/or abstracts in English). One time a year. VLG Ferdinand Berger & Soehne, Wienerstrasse 21-23, A-3580 Horn Austria. **Tel** 011 43 2982 23170 41610. **ED** Dr. O. Hartel and Dr. Teppner. Index available. **Bk Rev.** ctrl circ. Documents available from The Genuine Article, BIOSIS Document Express, CASDDS.
Ind/Abst AgBiotech News Inf.; AGRICOLA [Full Cov.]; Biol. Abstr.; Chem. Abstr.; Crop Physiol. Abstr.; Curr. Aware. Biol. Sci., CABS; For. Prod. Abstr.; For. Abstr.; Hortic. Abstr.; Irr. Drain. Abstr.; Maize Abstr.; Ornamental Hort. (19??-19??); Life Sci. Collect.; Plant Breed. Abstr.; Plant Grow. Reg. Abstr.; Res. Alert [Select. Cov.]; SCISEARCH; Soils Fert.; Soyabean Abstr.

ISSN 0334-2123
IS
CODEN PHPRA2
Pr Rev.

PHYTOPARASITICA. (PHYTOPARASITICA; ISRAEL JOURNAL OF PLANT PROTECTION SCIENCES.). [Phytoparasitica]. **Added/Corp** Merkaz Volkani. Phytopathological Society of Israel. Ha-Aguda Ha-Yisreelit Le-Mada Ha-Asavim Ha-Raim. **VFOAT** Israel Journal of Plant Protection Sciences. Vol. 1 (June 1973)-. Academic Scholarly Publication. English. Four times a year (Jan., Apr., July, Oct.). $150.00. Priel Publishers, PO Box 2385, 76123 Rehovot Israel. **Tel** 011 972 8 451971, FAX 011 972 8 456001. **ED** Vivian R. Priel. Index available (Bound in the 4th iss.). **Circ:** 500 (ctrl). Documents available from The Genuine Article, BIOSIS Document Express, CASDDS.
Desc: Includes articles and other information on the plant protection sciences.
Ind/Abst AGRICOLA; Agrofor. Abstr.; Biocont. News Inf. (19??-19??); Biodeter. Abstr. (19??-19??); Biol. Abstr.; Chem. Abstr.; Chemorecept. Abstr. (Sept. 27, 1990); Cot. Trop. Fibr. Abstr. Bibliogr.; Curr. Cit.; Curr. Contents Agric. Biol. Environ. Sci.; EMBASE; Entomol. Abstr.; For. Prod. Abstr.; For. Abstr.; Hortic. Abstr.; Microbiol. Abstr. Sect. A; Microbiol. Abstr. Sect. C; Nematol. Abstr.; Life Sci. Collect.; PESTDOC; Plant Breed. Abstr.; Plant Genet. Resour. Abstr.; Plant Grow. Reg. Abstr.; Postharvest News Inf.; Potato Abstr.; Res. Alert [Full Cov.]; Rev. Agric. Entomol.; Rev. Med. Vet. Entomol.; Rev. Plant Pathol.; Sci. Cit. Index; SCISEARCH; Seed Abstr.; Soils Fert.; Sorghum Mill. Abstr.; Vitis Vitic. Enol. Abstr.; Weed Abstr.

ISSN 0031-9465
IT
CODEN PYMDAU
Pr Rev.

PHYTOPATHOLOGIA MEDITERRANEA. [Phytopathol. mediterr.]. **Added/Corp** Mediterranean Phytopathological Union. Vol. 1, No. 1 (Aug. 1960)-. Periodical. Italian (English, French, Portuguese and Spanish; summaries and/or abstracts in English and French). Three times a year. L102190. Mediterranean Phytopathological Union, P le Delle Cascine 28 Surico, 50144 Firenze Italy. **Tel** 011 39 55 360546, FAX 011 39 55 354786. Index available. cum. index. **Bk Rev**, (Qty: 3-4). ctrl circ. Documents available from CASDDS.
Ind/Abst AGRICOLA; Biocont. News Inf. (19??-19??); Biodeter. Abstr. (1991-); Chem. Abstr.; Field Crop Abstr.; For. Abstr.; Hortic. Abstr.; Maize Abstr.; Microbiol. Abstr. Sect. A; Microbiol. Abstr. Sect. C; Life Sci. Collect.; PESTDOC; Plant Breed. Abstr.; Plant Genet. Resour. Abstr.; Plant Grow. Reg. Abstr.; Potato Abstr.; Rev. Agric. Entomol.; Rev. Med. Vet. Mycology; Rev. Plant Pathol.; Rice Abstr.; Seed Abstr.; Soils Fert.; Virol. AIDS Abstr.; Vitis Vitic. Enol. Abstr.; Weed Abstr.

LC S **ISSN** 1230-0462
DD 630 PL
Pr Rev.

PHYTOPATHOLOGIA POLONICA. [Phytopathol. Pol.]. **Added/Corp** Polskie Towarzystwo Fitopatologiczne. Polska Akademia Nauk. Polish Phytopathological Society. No. 11 (1990)-. Academic Scholarly Publication. English. Two times a year. $10.00. Polskie Towarzystwo Fitopatologiczne / Polish Phytopathological Society, Ul. Wojska Polskiego 71 C, 60-625 Poznan Poland. **Tel** 011 48 61 4877131, FAX 011 48 61 487145. **ED** Malgorzata Manka. **Circ:** 1,000. ***Separated from*** *Zeszyty Problemowe Postepow Nauk Rolniczych, 0084-5477.*
Desc: Research on diseases caused by bacteria, viruses, and fungi on agricultural, horticultural and forest plants.

LC SB599 .P47 **ISSN** 0069-7141
DD 581 UK
CODEN CMPYAH

PHYTOPATHOLOGICAL PAPERS. [Phytopathol. pap.]. **Added/Corp** Commonwealth Mycological Institute (Great Britain). **VFOAT** Phytopathological Paper. No. 1 (Sept. 1956)-. Monographic series. English. Irregular. Price varies per volume. CAB International Centre, Wallingford, Oxfordshire OX10 8DE United Kingdom. **Tel** 011 44 1491 832111, FAX 011 44 1491 833508, telex 847964 COMAGG G. Documents available from BIOSIS Document Express.
Desc: Series on plant pathological subjects, including diseases of individual crops, country lists of plant diseases, etc.
Ind/Abst Biol. Abstr.; Nematol. Abstr.; Life Sci. Collect.; Rev. Plant Pathol.

LC SB599 .P935 **ISSN** 0031-949X
DD 632/.05 US
CCC
NLM W1 PH988 **CODEN** PHYTAJ
Pr Rev.

PHYTOPATHOLOGY. [Phytopathology]. **Added/Corp** American Phytopathological Society. Vol. 1 (Feb. 1911)-. Academic Scholarly Publication. English. Twelve times a year. $270.00. American Phytopathological Society, 3340 Pilot Knob Road, St. Paul MN 55121. **Tel** (612)454-7250, (800)328-7560, FAX (612)454-0766, telex 6502439657 (MCI UW). **ED** G E Shaner. Index available (bound in Dec. issue). cum. index. **Circ:** 5,243. available on microfilm and microfiche from University Microfilms International (UMI). Documents available from The Genuine Article, BIOSIS Document Express, CASDDS, Documents on Demand.
Desc: International journal of plant pathology for reports of original research. The most cited source in botany core journals. Each volume groups papers under subject matter category.
Ind/Abst AgBiotech News Inf.; AGRICOLA [Full Cov.]; BioBusiness; Biocont. News Inf. (19??-19??); Biodeter. Abstr. (19??-19??); Biogr. Index; Biol. Agric. Index; Biol. Abstr.; Biol. Dig.; Chem. Abstr.; Coal Abstr.; Cot. Trop. Fibr. Abstr. Bibliogr.; Crop Physiol. Abstr.; Curr. Aware. Biol. Sci., CABS; Curr. Biotechnol.; Curr. Cit.; Curr. Contents Agric. Biol. Environ. Sci.; EMBASE; Entomol. Abstr.; Environ. Abstr.; Field Crop Abstr.; Food Sci. Technol. Abstr.; For. Prod. Abstr.; For. Abstr.; Genet. Abstr.; Grass. Forage Abstr.; Hortic. Abstr.; Immunol. Abstr.; Irr. Drain. Abstr.; Maize Abstr.; Microbiol. Abstr. Sect. B; Microbiol. Abstr. Sect. A; Microbiol. Abstr. Sect. C; Nematol. Abstr.; Life Sci. Collect.; PESTDOC; Plant Breed. Abstr.; Plant Genet. Resour. Abstr.; Plant Grow. Reg. Abstr.; Postharvest News Inf.; Potato Abstr.; Ref. Upd. Deluxe Ed.; Res. Alert [Full Cov.]; Rev. Agric. Entomol.; Rev. Med. Vet. Mycology; Rev. Plant Pathol.; Rice Abstr.; Sci. Cit. Index; SCISEARCH; Seed Abstr.; Soils Fert.; Sorghum Mill. Abstr.; Soyabean Abstr.; Virol. AIDS Abstr.; Vitis Vitic. Enol. Abstr.; Weed Abstr.

ISSN 0748-6693
DD 580 UK

PHYTOPHTHORA NEWSLETTER. **Added/Corp** University of Wisconsin--Madison. Dept. of Plant Pathology. University of California, Riverside. Dept. of Plant Pathology. No. 1 (Jan. 1973)-. Newsletter. English. One time a year. Free on request. Food & Marketing Agri Victoria, 166 Wellington, East Melbourne Victoria, Bangor LL57 2UW United Kingdom. **Tel** 011 44 1248 351151. **ED** Richard Shattock. Index available. **Ad Acc.** ctrl circ.
Desc: Current research on any aspect of the genus Phytophthora - a major cause of plant disease worldwide.

ISSN 0370-1263
SA
UDC 632.9
CODEN PPPMA9
CEASED

PHYTOPHYLACTICA. (PHYTOPHYLACTICA. PLANTBESKERMINGSWETENSKAPPE EN MIKROBIOLOGIE.). [Phytophylactica]. **VFOAT** Plant Protection Sciences and Microbiologie. Vol. 1, (1969)-(Dec. 1993). Periodical. English. Agricultural Tech Service, Beatrix Street, Private Bag 116, Agricultural Building, Pretoria South Africa. Documents available from BIOSIS Document Express, CASDDS. ***Supersedes in part*** *Suid-Afrikaanse Tydskrif vir Landbouwetenskap, 0585-8860.*
Ind/Abst AGRICOLA; Biocont. News Inf. (19??-19??); Biodeter. Abstr. (19??-19??); Biol. Abstr.; Chem. Abstr. (1969-1982); Curr. Cit.; Entomol. Abstr.; For. Abstr.; Hortic. Abstr.; Maize Abstr.; Microbiol. Abstr. Sect. B (19??-19??); Microbiol. Abstr. Sect. C; Nematol. Abstr.; Ornamental Hort. (1991-); Life Sci. Collect.; PESTDOC (?-?); Plant Breed. Abstr.; Postharvest News Inf.; Rev. Agric. Entomol.; Rev. Plant Pathol.; Seed Abstr.; Soils Fert.; Sorghum Mill. Abstr.; Soyabean Abstr.; Virol. AIDS Abstr.; Vitis Vitic. Enol. Abstr.; Weed Abstr.

LC QK710 .P55 **ISSN** 0032-0781
DD 581.1/05 JA
NLM W1; PL105KP **CODEN** PCPHA5
Pr Rev.

PLANT AND CELL PHYSIOLOGY. [Plant and cell physiol.]. **Added/Corp** Japanese Society of Plant Physiologists. **VFOAT** Plant and Cell Physiology. (1959)-. Academic Scholarly Publication. English (German and Esperanto). Eight times a year. $250.00. Japanese Society Plant Physiologists, Shimotachiuri Ogawa Higashi, Kamikyoku Kyoto 602 Japan. **Tel** 075-441-3157, FAX 074-441-3159. **(Subscription address:** Maruzen Company Ltd., PO Box 5050, Import & Export Department, Tokyo 100 31 Japan. **Tel** 011 81 3 32789224.**)** **ED** Hidemasa Imaseki. Index available. cum. index. **Ad Acc. Circ:** 2,600 (ctrl). Documents available from The Genuine Article, BIOSIS Document Express, CASDDS.
Desc: Covers all areas of science that relate to the physiology of plants.
Ind/Abst Abstr. Bull. Inst. Pap. Sci. Tech.; AgBiotech News Inf.; AGRICOLA; Biol. Agric. Index; Biol. Abstr.; Chem. Abstr.; Chem. Titles; Crop Physiol. Abstr.; Curr. Aware. Biol. Sci., CABS; Curr. Cit.; Curr. Contents Agric. Biol. Environ. Sci.; Curr. Contents Life Sci.; EMBASE; Field Crop Abstr.; Food Sci. Technol. Abstr.; For. Abstr.; Genet. Abstr.; Grass. Forage Abstr.; Hortic. Abstr.; Index Med.; Int. Aerosp. Abstr.; Irr. Drain. Abstr.; Maize Abstr.; Microbiol. Abstr. Sect. B (19??-19??); Microbiol. Abstr. Sect. C; NAPRALERT; Ornamental Hort. (19??-19??); Life Sci. Collect.; PESTDOC; Plant Breed. Abstr.; Plant Grow. Reg. Abstr.; Postharvest News Inf.; Potato Abstr.; Ref. Upd. Basic Ed.; Ref. Upd. Deluxe Ed.; Res. Alert [Full Cov.]; Rev. Plant Pathol.; Rice Abstr.; Sci. Cit. Index; SCISEARCH; Seed Abstr.; Soils Fert.; Sorghum Mill. Abstr.; Soyabean Abstr.; Vitis Vitic. Enol. Abstr.; Weed Abstr.

ISSN 0886-683X
DD 631 US

PLANT BIBLIOGRAPHY. [Plant bibliogr.]. **Added/Corp** Council on Botanical and Horticultural Libraries (U.S.). **VFOAT** CBHL Plant Bibliography. No. 1 (Jan. 1978)-. Monographic series. English. Irregular. Price varies per volume. Council Botanical Horticulture Libraries, New York Botanical Garden, Bronx NY 10458. **Tel** (212)220-8728, FAX (212)220-6504. **ED** Meryl Miasek Barney. cum. index. **Circ:** 400.
Ind/Abst AGRICOLA.

ISSN 0894-4563
DD 581 US
CODEN PBIOEM

PLANT BIOLOGY. [Plant biol.]. Vol. 1 (1986)-. Monographic series. English. Irregular. Price varies per volume. Wiley Liss, 605 3rd Avenue, New York NY 10158. **Tel** (212)850-8800, (212)850-6645. **(Subscription address:** John Wiley & Sons, Inc. / Philadelphia, PO Box 7247, Philadelphia PA 19170. **Tel** (212)850-6645, (800)225-5945.**)** Documents available from BIOSIS Document Express.
Ind/Abst AGRICOLA [Full Cov.]; Biol. Abstr. (1986-).

US

PLANT BIOLOGY SERIES. Monographic series. English. Irregular. Price varies per volume. Wiley Liss, 605 3rd Avenue, New York NY 10158. **Tel** (212)850-8800, (212)850-6645. **(Subscription address:** John Wiley & Sons, Inc. / Philadelphia, PO Box 7247, Philadelphia PA 19170. **Tel** (212)850-6645, (800)225-5945.**)** cum. index.

LC QK
DD 581 UK

PLANT BIOTECHNOLOGY. VFOAT Plant Biotechnology Series. Vol. 1 (1991)-. Monographic series. English. Chapman & Hall, 2-6 Boundary Row, London SE1 8HN United Kingdom. **Tel** 011 44 171 8650066, FAX 011 44 171 5229623, telex 290164 CHAPMA G.
Ind/Abst AGRICOLA.

ISSN 0260-5902
UK
CCC

PLANT BIOTECHNOLOGY. [Plant biotechnol.]. **Added/Corp** University of Sheffield. Biomedical Information Service. (1981)-. Academic Scholarly Publication. English. Twenty-four times a year. $196.79. RSS Centre for Statistical Education, University Park, University of Nottingham, Nottingham NG7 2RD United Kingdom. **Tel** 011 44 115 9514962, 011 44 115 9514949, FAX 011 44 115 9514951. **Bk Rev. Ad Acc.** available on diskette.
Ind/Abst Abstr. Bull. Inst. Pap. Sci. Tech.

Biology —Botany

LC SB123 .Z4 **ISSN** 0179-9541
DD 631.5 GW
CCC
CODEN PLABED
Pr Rev.
PLANT BREEDING. [Plant breed.]. **VFOAT** Zeitschrift fuer Pflanzenzuchtung. Vol. 97 (July 1986)-. Academic Scholarly Publication. English (German and French). Eight times a year. $868.22. Blackwell Wissenschafts-Verlag, Kurfuerstendamm 57, D-10707 Berlin Germany. **Tel** 011 49 30 32790623, 011 49 30 32790624, FAX 011 49 30 327 90610. **ED** W.E. Weber, G. Robbelen. Index available. cum. index. **Bk Rev. Ad Acc. Circ:** 2,500. Documents available from The Genuine Article, BIOSIS Document Express, CASDDS. ***Continues*** *Zeitschrift fuer Pflanzenzuchtung (Berlin, Germany : 1939), 0044-3298.*
Desc: Publishes articles exclusively on conventional plant breeding methodologies.
Ind/Abst AgBiotech News Inf.; AGRICOLA [Full Cov.]; BioBusiness; Biol. Abstr. (1986-); Chem. Abstr. (1986-); Cot. Trop. Fibr. Abstr. Bibliogr.; Crop Physiol. Abstr.; Curr. Aware. Biol. Sci., CABS (1986-); Curr. Cit.; Curr. Contents Agric. Biol. Environ. Sci. (1986-); Energy Res. Abstr. (1986-); Field Crop Abstr.; Food Sci. Technol. Abstr.; Grass. Forage Abstr.; Hortic. Abstr.; Irr. Drain. Abstr.; Maize Abstr.; Nematol. Abstr.; Ornamental Hort. (1991-); Life Sci. Collect. (1986-); PESTDOC; Plant Breed. Abstr.; Plant Genet. Resour. Abstr.; Plant Grow. Reg. Abstr.; Potato Abstr.; Res. Alert [Full Cov.]; Rev. Agric. Entomol.; Rev. Plant Pathol.; Rice Abstr.; Sci. Cit. Index (1986-); SCISEARCH; Seed Abstr.; Soils Fert.; Sorghum Mill. Abstr.; Wheat Barley Trit. Abstr.

LC SB123 .P55 **ISSN** 0730-2207
DD 631.5/3/05 US
CODEN PBREE3
PLANT BREEDING REVIEWS. [Plant breed. rev.]. **Added/Corp** American Society for Horticultural Science. (1983)-. Academic Scholarly Publication. English. Irregular. $110.00. John Wiley & Sons, Inc., 605 Third Avenue, New York NY 10158-0012. **Tel** (212)850-6000, (212)850-6645, FAX (212)850-6088, telex 12-7063. **(Subscription address:** John Wiley & Sons / UK, Baffins Lane, Chichester, West Sussex PO19 1UD United Kingdom. **Tel** 011 44 1243 779777, FAX 011 44 243 776128, telex 86290 WIBOOKG.) Documents available from CASDDS.
Ind/Abst AgBiotech News Inf.; Chem. Abstr. (1983-); Maize Abstr.; Nematol. Abstr.; Life Sci. Collect.; Plant Breed. Abstr.; Rev. Agric. Entomol.; Seed Abstr.; Soyabean Abstr.; Wheat Barley Trit. Abstr.

LC QK725 .P5518 **ISSN** 1040-4651
DD 581.8/05 US
NLM W1; PL105LG **CODEN** PLCEEW
Pr Rev.
PLANT CELL, THE. **See** Biology-Cytology.

ISSN 0140-7791
UK
CCC
NLM W1; PL105LP **CODEN** PLCEDV
Pr Rev.
PLANT, CELL AND ENVIRONMENT. [Plant cell environ.]. Vol. 1, No. 1 (March 1978)-. Academic Scholarly Publication. English (French and German). Twelve times a year. $1167.00. Blackwell Scientific Publications Ltd, Marston Book Services, PO Box 88, Oxford OX2 ONE United Kingdom. **Tel** 011 44 1865 206206, FAX 011 44 1865 206219, telex 837 515 MARDIS G. **ED** Harry Smith. Index available (bound in last issue). **Bk Rev. Ad Acc. Circ:** 700. available on microfilm and microfiche from University Microfilms International (UMI). Documents available from The Genuine Article, BIOSIS Document Express, CASDDS, Documents on Demand.
Desc: Covers physiology of green plants including plant biochemistry, biophysics, cell physiology, crop physiology and structural, genetical and micrometeorological aspects of plant functions.
Ind/Abst AgBiotech News Inf.; AGRICOLA [Full Cov.]; Agric. Eng. Abstr. (1991-); Biol. Abstr.; Chem. Abstr.; Cot. Trop. Fibr. Abstr. Bibliogr.; Crop Physiol. Abstr.; Curr. Aware. Biol. Sci., CABS; Curr. Cit.; Curr. Contents Agric. Biol. Environ. Sci.; Curr. Contents Life Sci.; Ecol. Abstr.; EMBASE; Environ. Abstr.; Environ. Period. Bibliogr.; Field Crop Abstr.; For. Abstr.; Geogr. Abstr. Phys. Geogr.; Grass. Forage Abstr.; Hortic. Abstr.; Irr. Drain. Abstr.; Maize Abstr.; Nutr. Abstr. Rev., Ser. B, Live Feeds and Feed.; Ornamental Hort. (1991-); Life Sci. Collect.; PESTDOC; Plant Breed. Abstr.; Plant Grow. Reg. Abstr.; Postharvest News Inf.; Potato Abstr.; Ref. Upd. Basic Ed.; Ref. Upd. Deluxe Ed.; Res. Alert [Full Cov.]; Rice Abstr.; Sci. Cit. Index; SCISEARCH; Seed Abstr.; Soils Fert.; Sorghum Mill. Abstr.; Soyabean Abstr.; Vitis Vitic. Enol. Abstr.; Weed Abstr.; Wheat Barley Trit. Abstr.

US
PLANT CELL INCOMPATABILITY NEWSLETTER. **Added/Corp** State University College at Cortland. Dept. of Biological Sciences. **VFOAT** Incompatibility Newsletter; PCIN. (1984)-. Newsletter. English. State University, c/o Doney, PO Box 2000, Cortland NY 13045. ***Continues*** *Incompatibility Newsletter.*
Ind/Abst Agrofor. Abstr.; For. Abstr.; Hortic. Abstr.; Maize Abstr.; Ornamental Hort. (1991-); Plant Grow. Reg. Abstr.; Rev. Plant Pathol.

ISSN 0167-6857
NE
CCC
CODEN PTCEDJ
Pr Rev.
PLANT CELL, TISSUE AND ORGAN CULTURE. [Plant cell, tissue organ cult.]. Vol. 1, No. 1 (1981)-. Academic Scholarly Publication. English. Twelve times a year. $1102.00. Kluwer Academic Publishers, Postbus 322, 3300 AH Dordrecht The Netherlands. **Tel** 011 31 78 524400, FAX 011 31 78 183273, telex 20083. **ED** R.H. Zimmerman, A.H. Scragg, D.J. Gray. **Ad Acc. Acid Free. Circ:** 950. available on microfilm and microfiche from University Microfilms International (UMI). Documents available from The Genuine Article, BIOSIS Document Express, CASDDS, Documents on Demand.
Desc: Publishes original results of studies on the various results on the various aspects of the invitro culture of higher plants including fundamental, methodological and technical aspects. Topics covered include: growth, development and differentiation, anatomical, histological and ultrastructural aspects, genetics and breeding, physiology and biochemistry, micropropagation, protoplast, cell and tissue culture, secondary metabolism and biotechnology.
Ind/Abst Abstr. Bull. Inst. Pap. Sci. Tech.; AgBiotech News Inf.; Agrofor. Abstr. (1991-); Biol. Abstr.; Chem. Abstr.; Cot. Trop. Fibr. Abstr. Bibliogr.; Crop Physiol. Abstr.; Curr. Aware. Biol. Sci., CABS; Curr. Biotechnol.; Curr. Cit.; Curr. Contents Agric. Biol. Environ. Sci.; Environ. Abstr.; Field Crop Abstr.; Food Sci. Technol. Abstr.; For. Abstr.; Grass. Forage Abstr.; Hortic. Abstr.; Maize Abstr.; Ornamental Hort. (19??-19??); PESTDOC; Plant Breed. Abstr.; Plant Genet. Resour. Abstr.; Plant Grow. Reg. Abstr.; Potato Abstr.; Ref. Upd. Deluxe Ed.; Res. Alert [Full Cov.]; Rev. Plant Pathol.; Rice Abstr.; Sci. Cit. Index; SCISEARCH; Sorghum Mill. Abstr.; Soyabean Abstr.; Vitis Vitic. Enol. Abstr.; Weed Abstr.; Wheat Barley Trit. Abstr.

LC S **ISSN** 0970-4914
DD 631 II
UDC 632
PLANT DISEASE RESEARCH. [Plant Dis. Res.]. (1986)-. Periodical. English. Two times a year. Indian Society of Plant Pathologists, Punjab Agricultural University, Ludhiana 141 004 India. **ED** S. S. Chahal.
Ind/Abst Cot. Trop. Fibr. Abstr. Bibliogr.; For. Prod. Abstr. (1991-); Hortic. Abstr.; Maize Abstr.; Nematol. Abstr.; Ornamental Hort. (1991-); Plant Breed. Abstr.; Postharvest News Inf.; Potato Abstr.; Rev. Plant Pathol.; Rice Abstr.; Seed Abstr.; Soils Fert.; Sorghum Mill. Abstr.; Wheat Barley Trit. Abstr.

ISSN 0966-0100
DD 581.1505 UK
PLANT GENETIC RESOURCES ABSTRACTS. **See** Biology-Abstracting, Bibliographies and Statistics.

II
PLANT GENETICS AND BREEDING REVIEW. **Added/Corp** National Agricultural Technology Information Centre (India). **VFOAT** Plant Genetics & Breeding Review. Vol. 1, No. 1 (Sept. 1988)-. Periodical. English. Two times a year. $20.00. National Agricultural Technology Information Center, Ludhiana India. **(Subscription address:** Prints India, 11 Darya Ganj, New Delhi 110002 India. **Tel** 011 91 11 3268645, FAX 011 91 11 3275542, telex 31-61087 PRIN-IN.)

LC SB128 .P518 **ISSN** 0167-6903
DD 631.8 NE
CCC
CODEN PGRED3
Pr Rev.
PLANT GROWTH REGULATION. [Plant growth regul.]. Vol. 1, No. 1 (1982)-. Academic Scholarly Publication. English. Nine times a year. $541.00. Kluwer Academic Publishers, Postbus 322, 3300 AH Dordrecht The Netherlands. **Tel** 011 31 78 524400, FAX 011 31 78 183273, telex 20083. **ED** Tudor Thomas. **Ad Acc. Acid Free.** available on microfilm and microfiche from University Microfilms International (UMI). Documents available from The Genuine Article, BIOSIS Document Express, CASDDS.
Desc: Publishes original papers linking fundamental and applied research on the natural hormonal regulation of plant processes and the effects of growth regulating substances on plant growth and development. Topics covered include: metabolic aspects and action mechanisms of plant hormones; environmental and genetic influences on hormone systems; hormonal control of fundamental processes; and all aspects involving the development and application of synthetic plant growth regulators.
Ind/Abst Abstr. Bull. Inst. Pap. Sci. Tech.; AGRICOLA [Full Cov.]; Biol. Abstr. (1988-); Chem. Abstr.; Chem. Titles; Crop Physiol. Abstr.; Curr. Aware. Biol. Sci., CABS; Curr. Cit.; Curr. Contents Agric. Biol. Environ. Sci.; Field Crop Abstr.; Food Sci. Technol. Abstr.; For. Abstr.; Grass. Forage Abstr.; Hortic. Abstr.; Irr. Drain. Abstr.; Maize Abstr.; Ornamental Hort. (19??-19??); PESTDOC (1988-); Plant Genet. Resour. Abstr.; Plant Grow. Reg. Abstr.; Postharvest News Inf.; Potato Abstr.; Ref. Upd. Deluxe Ed.; Res. Alert [Full Cov.]; Rice Abstr.; Sci. Cit. Index; SCISEARCH; Seed Abstr.; Sorghum Mill. Abstr.; Soyabean Abstr.; Vitis Vitic. Enol. Abstr.; Weed Abstr.; Wheat Barley Trit. Abstr.

LC QK728 .P53 **ISSN** 0960-7412
DD 581.8/05 UK
CCC
NLM W1; PL105NE
Pr Rev.
PLANT JOURNAL : FOR CELL AND MOLECULAR BIOLOGY, THE. **Added/Corp** Society for Experimental Biology (Great Britain). **VFOAT** Plant Journal for Cell and Molecular Biology. Vol. 1, No. 1 (July 1991)-. Academic Scholarly Publication. English. Twelve times a year. $942.00. Blackwell Scientific Publications Ltd, Marston Book Services, PO Box 88, Oxford OX2 ONE United Kingdom. **Tel** 011 44 1865 206206, FAX 011 44 1865 206219, telex 837 515 MARDIS G. cum. index. **Ad Acc. Circ:** 3,000. available on microfilm and microfiche from University Microfilms International (UMI). Documents available from The Genuine Article.
Desc: Provides an international forum for the publication of high quality research papers which adopt a modern approach to plant research and utilize molecular techniques in the study of plant cell processes.
Ind/Abst AGRICOLA; Curr. Aware. Biol. Sci., CABS; Curr. Cit.; Ref. Upd. Deluxe Ed.; Res. Alert [Full Cov.]; Sci. Cit. Index.

ISSN 0167-4412
NE
CCC
NLM W1; PL105NG **CODEN** PMBIDB
Pr Rev.
PLANT MOLECULAR BIOLOGY. **See** Biology-Genetics.

LC QK981 .P57 **ISSN** 0735-9640
DD 581.87/322 US
CCC
CODEN PMBRD4
PLANT MOLECULAR BIOLOGY REPORTER. (PLANT MOLECULAR BIOLOGY REPORTER / ISPMB.). [Plant mol. biol. report.]. **Added/Corp** International Society for Plant Molecular Biology. Vol. 1, No. 1 (1983)-. Academic Scholarly Publication. English. Four times a year (February, May, August, November). $196.00. Transaction Publishers / Rutgers State University, Department 3091 or 3092, New Brunswick NJ 08903. **Tel** (908)932-2280 ext. 105, FAX (908)932-3138. **ED** C.A. Price. **Circ:** 2,800. available on labels; available on microfilm and microfiche from University Microfilms International (UMI). Documents available from CASDDS. ***Continues*** *Plant Molecular Biology Newsletter, 0733-0537.*
Desc: A journal of news and opinion about progress in the rapidly developing area of plant molecular biology. Principal features include reviews relating the plant sciences with molecular biology; descriptions of genetic resources, including cloned plant genes; accounts of the activities of plant molecular biologists at major institutions around the world; and news of meetings involving plant molecular biologists. The official publication of the International Society for Plant Molecular Biology.
Ind/Abst AgBiotech News Inf.; AGRICOLA [Full Cov.]; Chem. Abstr. (1983-); Curr. Cit.; Food Sci. Technol. Abstr.; Hortic. Abstr.; Ornamental Hort. (19??-19??); Life Sci. Collect.; Plant Breed. Abstr.; Rev. Plant Pathol.; Soils Fert.; Wheat Barley Trit. Abstr.

LC SB599 .P96 **ISSN** 0032-0862
DD 632.05 UK
CCC
CODEN PLPAAD
Pr Rev.
PLANT PATHOLOGY. [Plant pathol.]. **Added/Corp** Plant Pathology Laboratory (Harpenden, England) British Society for Plant Pathology. Vol. 1 (March 1952)-. Academic Scholarly Publication. English. Six times a year. $497.00. Blackwell Scientific Publications Ltd, Marston Book Services, PO Box 88, Oxford OX2 ONE United Kingdom. **Tel** 011 44 1865 206206, FAX 011 44 1865 206219, telex 837 515 MARDIS G. **ED** P. Scott. Index available (bound in last issue). **Bk Rev. Ad Acc. Circ:** 1,750. available on microfilm and microfiche from University Microfilms International (UMI). Documents available from The Genuine Article, BIOSIS Document Express, CASDDS.
Desc: Topics include fungi, viruses, virus-like organisms and bacteria. Also covers biochemical, ecological, genetic and economic aspects of plant pathology, disease appraisal and control and crop management.
Ind/Abst AgBiotech News Inf.; AGRICOLA [Full Cov.]; BioBusiness; Biocont. News Inf. (19??-19??); Biodeter. Abstr. (1991-); Biol. Agric. Index; Biol. Abstr.; Chem. Abstr.; Cot. Trop. Fibr. Abstr. Bibliogr.; Curr. Aware. Biol. Sci., CABS; Curr. Biotechnol.; Curr. Cit.; Curr. Contents Agric. Biol. Environ. Sci.; Field Crop Abstr.; Food Sci. Technol. Abstr.; For. Abstr.; Genet. Abstr.; Hortic. Abstr.; Irr. Drain. Abstr.; Maize Abstr.; Microbiol. Abstr. Sect. B (19??-19??); Microbiol. Abstr. Sect. A; Microbiol. Abstr. Sect. C; Nematol. Abstr.; Ornamental Hort. (19??-19??); Life Sci. Collect.; PESTDOC; Plant Breed. Abstr.; Plant

Genet. Resour. Abstr.; Plant Grow. Reg. Abstr.; Postharvest News Inf.; Potato Abstr.; Ref. Upd. Deluxe Ed.; Res. Alert [Full Cov.]; Rev. Agric. Entomol.; Rev. Plant Pathol.; Rice Abstr.; Sci. Cit. Index; SCISEARCH; Seed Abstr.; Soils Fert.; Soyabean Abstr.; Virol. AIDS Abstr.; Vitis Vitic. Enol. Abstr.; Wheat Barley Trit. Abstr.

ISSN 0032-0870
US
CODEN FPPCB6

PLANT PATHOLOGY CIRCULAR (GAINESVILLE). (PLANT PATHOLOGY CIRCULAR.). [Plant pathol. circ.]. **Main/Corp** Florida. Division of Plant Industry. (196?)-. English. Six times a year. Florida Department of Agriculture & Consumer Services, State Capitol, 10th Floor, Tallahassee FL 32399. **Tel** (904)488-6971, FAX (904)488-8087. Documents available from BIOSIS Document Express. ***Continues*** *Pathology Circular.*
Ind/Abst Biol. Abstr. (-1979); Hortic. Abstr.; Ornamental Hort. (1991-); Rev. Plant Pathol.; Weed Abstr.

US
TITLE CHANGE

PLANT PEST NEWSLETTER. (19??)-(19??). Newsletter. English. University of Minnesota / Borlaug Hill, 495 Borlaug Hill, Plant Pathologist, St. Paul MN 55108. **Tel** (612)625-6290, FAX (612)625-9728. **ED** Debra Drange. **Circ:** 550 (ctrl). ***Continued by*** *MN Crop News.*

LC QK710 .P57 **ISSN** 0981-9428
DD 581.1 FR
CCC

PLANT PHYSIOLOGY AND BIOCHEMISTRY. [Plant physiol. biochem.]. **Added/Corp** Societe Francaise de Physiologie Vegetale. Federation of European Societies of Plant Physiology. Vol. 25, No. 1 (Jan./Feb. 1987)-. Periodical. English (English). Six times a year. $448.38. Gauthier-Villars, 15 rue Gossin, 92543 Montrouge Cedex France. **Tel** 33 1 40 92 65 00, FAX 33 1 40 92 65 97. **(Subscription address:** Centrale des Revues, 11 rue Gossin, 92543 Montrouge Cedex France. **Tel** 011 33 1 46565266.**) ED** J.C. Kader & M. Jacobs. Documents available from The Genuine Article, BIOSIS Document Express. ***Continues*** *Physologie Vegetale, 0031-9368.*
Desc: Seeks to maintain communication between diverse areas of original research. It embraces physiology, biochemistry, biophysics, structure and genetics at different levels from the molecular to the whole plant and environment.
Ind/Abst AgBiotech News Inf.; Agric. Eng. Abstr.; Biol. Abstr. (1987-); Crop Physiol. Abstr.; Curr. Aware. Biol. Sci., CABS; Curr. Cit.; Ecol. Abstr.; Field Crop Abstr.; Food Sci. Technol. Abstr.; For. Abstr.; Grass. Forage Abstr.; Hortic. Abstr.; Maize Abstr.; Ornamental Hort. (19??-19??); Plant Breed. Abstr.; Plant Grow. Reg. Abstr.; Potato Abstr.; Res. Alert; Rev. Plant Pathol.; Rice Abstr.; Sci. Cit. Index; SCISEARCH; Seed Abstr.; Soils Fert.; Sorghum Mill. Abstr.; Soyabean Abstr.; Sug. Indus. Abstr.; Weed Abstr.; Wheat Barley Trit. Abstr.

LC QK1 .P68 **ISSN** 0032-0889
DD 581.1/05 US
CCC
NLM W1; PL105P **CODEN** PLPHAY
Pr Rev.

PLANT PHYSIOLOGY (BETHESDA). (PLANT PHYSIOLOGY.). [Plant physiol.]. **Added/Corp** American Society of Plant Physiologists. (Jan. 1926)-. Academic Scholarly Publication. English. Twelve times a year. $1150.00. American Society of Plant Physiologists, 15501 A Monona Drive, Rockville MD 20855. **Tel** (301)251-0560 ext. 17, FAX (301)279-2996. **(Subscription address:** Fulco, 30 Broad Street, Denville NJ 07834. **Tel** (800)783-4903, (201)627-2427.**)** available on microfilm and microfiche from University Microfilms International (UMI). Documents available from The Genuine Article, BIOSIS Document Express, CASDDS, Documents on Demand.
Desc: Reports on both basic and applied research in plant physiology, biochemistry, and molecular biology.
Ind/Abst Abstr. Bull. Inst. Pap. Sci. Tech.; AgBiotech News Inf.; AGRICOLA [Full Cov.]; Agrofor. Abstr. (1991-); Biogr. Index; Biol. Agric. Index; Biol. Abstr.; Chem. Abstr.; Cot. Trop. Fibr. Abstr. Bibliogr.; Crop Physiol. Abstr.; Curr. Aware. Biol. Sci., CABS; Curr. Biotechnol.; Curr. Cit.; Curr. Contents Agric. Biol. Environ. Sci.; Curr. Contents Life Sci.; EMBASE; Energy Res. Abstr.; Environ. Abstr.; Field Crop Abstr.; Food Sci. Technol. Abstr.; For. Abstr.; Genet. Abstr.; Grass. Forage Abstr.; Hortic. Abstr.; Index Med.; Int. Aerosp. Abstr.; Irr. Drain. Abstr.; Maize Abstr.; Mass Spect. Bull.; Microbiol. Abstr. Sect. B; NAPRALERT; Nat. Prod. Updates; Nematol. Abstr.; Ocean. Abstr.; Ornamental Hort. (19??-19??); Life Sci. Collect.; PESTDOC; Plant Breed. Abstr.; Plant Genet. Resour. Abstr.; Plant Grow. Reg. Abstr.; Postharvest News Inf.; Potato Abstr.; Ref. Upd. Basic Ed.; Ref. Upd. Deluxe Ed.; Res. Alert [Full Cov.]; Rev. Agric. Entomol.; Rev. Plant Pathol.; Rice Abstr.; Sci. Cit. Index; SCISEARCH; Seed Abstr.; Soils Fert.; Sorghum Mill. Abstr.; Soyabean Abstr.; Sug. Indus. Abstr.; Weed Abstr.; Wheat Barley Trit. Abstr.

LC QK861 .P5 **ISSN** 0254-3591
DD 581.1/05 II
CODEN PPHBD7

PLANT PHYSIOLOGY BIOCHEMISTRY. (PLANT PHYSIOLOGY & BIOCHEMISTRY.). [Plant physiol. biochem.]. **Added/Corp** Society for Plant Physiology and Biochemistry. **VFOAT** Plant Physiology and Biochemistry. Vol. 9, No. 1 (1982)-. Academic Scholarly Publication. English. Two times a year. $60.00. Biblia Impex Private Ltd, 2 18 Ansari Road, New Delhi 110002 India. **Tel** 91 11 278034. **(Subscription address:** Prints India, 11 Darya Ganj, New Delhi 110002 India. **Tel** 011 91 11 3268645, FAX 011 91 11 3275542, telex 31-61087 PRIN-IN.) Documents available from BIOSIS Document Express, CASDDS. ***Continues*** *Plant Biochemical Journal, 0379-5578.*
Ind/Abst Abstr. Bull. Inst. Pap. Sci. Tech.; AGRICOLA [Full Cov.]; Biol. Abstr. (?-1983); Chem. Abstr.; Curr. Cit.; Curr. Contents Agric. Biol. Environ. Sci.; Curr. Contents Life Sci.; Field Crop Abstr.; For. Prod. Abstr.; For. Abstr.; Geogr. Abstr. Phys. Geogr.; Irr. Drain. Abstr.; Nutr. Abstr. Rev., Ser. A, Hum. Exp.; Plant Breed. Abstr.; Plant Grow. Reg. Abstr.; Rev. Plant Pathol.; Seed Abstr.; Soils Fert.; Vitis Vitic. Enol. Abstr.; Wheat Barley Trit. Abstr.

CC

PLANT PHYSIOLOGY COMMUNICATIONS. (19??)-. Chinese.
Ind/Abst Cot. Trop. Fibr. Abstr. Bibliogr.; Field Crop Abstr.; Irr. Drain. Abstr.; Postharvest News Inf.; Rice Abstr.; Seed Abstr.

YU

PLANT PROTECTION. (19??)-. Periodical. English (Serbian). Four times a year (Feb., June, Sept., Dec.). $45.00. Institute for Plant Protection, Teodora Draiera 9, POB 936, 11001 Belgrad Yugoslavia. **Tel** 660 049. Index available (free).
Ind/Abst Biocont. News Inf.; Cot. Trop. Fibr. Abstr. Bibliogr.; For. Abstr.; Plant Breed. Abstr.; Rev. Agric. Entomol.

ISSN 0378-0449
II
CODEN PLPBAG

PLANT PROTECTION BULLETIN. [Plant prot. bull. (Faridabad)]. **Main/Corp** India (Republic). Directorate of Plant Protection, Quarantine and Storage. (1949)-. Bulletin. English. National Chung Hsing University, Plant Pathology, 250 Kuokuang Road, 40227 Taichung Taiwan.
Ind/Abst Biocont. News Inf. (1991-); Biodeter. Abstr. (1991-); Chemorecept. Abstr.; Field Crop Abstr.; Food Sci. Technol. Abstr.; Maize Abstr.; Nematol. Abstr.; Plant Breed. Abstr.; Plant Genet. Resour. Abstr.; Postharvest News Inf.; Potato Abstr.; Rev. Agric. Entomol.; Rev. Plant Pathol.; Rice Abstr.; Seed Abstr.; Soyabean Abstr.; Wheat Barley Trit. Abstr.

LC QK1 .P683 **ISSN** 0340-2843
DD 580/.5 GW
UDC 58

PLANT RESEARCH AND DEVELOPMENT. [Plant res. dev.]. Vol. 1 (1975)-. Periodical. English. Two times a year. Institute for Scientific Co-Operation, Landhausstrasse 18, W-7400 Tubingen Germany. **Tel** 07071/5066.
Ind/Abst AGRICOLA [Full Cov.]; Agrofor. Abstr.; Crop Physiol. Abstr.; Maize Abstr.; Plant Breed. Abstr.; Potato Abstr.

LC QK1 .P685 **ISSN** 0032-0919
US
CODEN PSBLAP

PLANT SCIENCE BULLETIN. [Plant sci. bull.]. **Added/Corp** Botanical Society of America. Vol. 1 (Jan. 1955)-. Bulletin. English. Irregular. Comes with American Journal of Botany. American Journal of Botany, Office of Publications, 1735 Neil Avenue, Columbus OH 43210. **Tel** (614)292-3519, FAX (614)292-3519. available on microfilm and microfiche from University Microfilms International (UMI). Documents available from BIOSIS Document Express.
Ind/Abst AGRICOLA; Biol. Abstr.

LC QK1 .P69 **ISSN** 0168-9452
DD 581/.05 IE
CCC
CODEN PLSCE4
Pr Rev.

PLANT SCIENCE (LIMERICK). (PLANT SCIENCE.). [Plant sci.]. Vol. 38, No. 1 (Feb. 1985)-. Academic Scholarly Publication. English. Sixteen times a year (8 volumes). $2010.00. Elsevier Science Ireland Ltd., Bay 15, Shannon Industrial Estate, Co Clare Ireland. **Tel** 011 353 61 471944. **ED** J.A. Schiff and J.H. Weil. Index available. **Ad Acc.** available on microfilm and microfiche from University Microfilms International (UMI); available on an online database from Elsevier Electronic Subscriptions (EES). Documents available from The Genuine Article, BIOSIS Document Express, CASDDS, Documents on Demand. ***Continues*** *Plant Science Letters, 0304-4211.*
Desc: Publishes papers in all areas of experimental plant biology. Papers describing experimental work with multicellular plants and plant-like microorganisms and blue-green algae are appropriate.
Ind/Abst Abstr. Bull. Inst. Pap. Sci. Tech.; AgBiotech News Inf.; AGRICOLA; Biol. Abstr. (1985-); Chem. Abstr. (1985-); Crop Physiol. Abstr.; Curr. Aware. Biol. Sci., CABS; Curr. Cit.; Curr. Contents Agric. Biol. Environ. Sci.; Curr. Contents Life Sci.; EMBASE; Energy Inf. Abstr.; Environ. Abstr.; Field Crop Abstr.; Food Sci. Technol. Abstr.; For. Prod. Abstr. (19??-19??); For. Abstr.; Genet. Abstr.; Grass. Forage Abstr.; Hortic. Abstr.; Irr. Drain. Abstr.; Maize Abstr.; Microbiol. Abstr. Sect. B (19??-19??); Microbiol. Abstr. Sect. A; Microbiol. Abstr. Sect. C; Ornamental Hort. (19??-19??); Life Sci. Collect.; PESTDOC; Plant Breed. Abstr.; Plant Genet. Resour. Abstr.; Plant Grow. Reg. Abstr.; Postharvest News Inf.; Potato Abstr.; Ref. Upd. Basic Ed.; Ref. Upd. Deluxe Ed.; Res. Alert [Full Cov.]; Rev. Agric. Entomol.; Rev. Plant Pathol.; Rice Abstr.; Sci. Cit. Index; SCISEARCH; Soils Fert.; Sorghum Mill. Abstr.; Soyabean Abstr.; Vitis Vitic. Enol. Abstr.; Weed Abstr.; Wheat Barley Trit. Abstr.

ISSN 0913-557X
JA
CODEN PSBIEK

PLANT SPECIES BIOLOGY. [Plant species biol.]. **Added/Corp** Society for the Study of Species Biology (Japan). Vol. 1, No. 1 (1986)-. Periodical. English. Two times a year. $200.00. **(Subscription address:** Japan Publications Trading Company Ltd., PO Box 5030, Tokyo International, Tokyo 100-31 Japan. **Tel** 011 81 3 3292 3753.**)** Documents available from BIOSIS Document Express.
Ind/Abst Biol. Abstr. (1989-).

LC QK1 .O26 **ISSN** 0378-2697
DD 581.0(5/6) AU
CCC
CODEN ESPFBP
Pr Rev.

PLANT SYSTEMATICS AND EVOLUTION. [Plant syst. evol.]. **VFOAT** Entwicklungsgeschichte und Systematik der Pflanzen. Vol. 123, No. 1 (1974)-. Academic Scholarly Publication. English (German and French). Twenty times a year. $1819.00. Springer-Verlag Vienna, Sachsenplatz 4 6, PO Box 89, A-1201 Vienna Austria. **Tel** 011 43 1 33024150, FAX 011 43 1 330242665. **(Subscription address:** Springer-Verlag New York Inc. / North America, PO Box 2485, Journal Fulfillment, Secaucus NJ 07096. **Tel** (201)348-4033, (800)777-4643, FAX (201)348-4505.**) ED** F. Ehrendorfer. available on microfilm from University Microfilms International (UMI). Documents available from The Genuine Article, BIOSIS Document Express, CASDDS. ***Continues*** *Osterreichische Botanische Zeitschrift, 0029-8948.*
Desc: Serves as a medium for world-wide scientific communication in the fields of plant morphology and systematics in the widest sense.
Ind/Abst AgBiotech News Inf.; AGRICOLA [Full Cov.]; Biol. Abstr.; Chem. Abstr.; Curr. Aware. Biol. Sci., CABS; Curr. Cit.; Curr. Contents Agric. Biol. Environ. Sci.; Ecology Abstr.; For. Abstr.; Genet. Abstr.; GeoRef; Grass. Forage Abstr.; Hortic. Abstr.; Microbiol. Abstr. Sect. C; Ornamental Hort. (1991-); Life Sci. Collect.; Plant Breed. Abstr.; Plant Genet. Resour. Abstr.; Res. Alert [Full Cov.]; Rev. Agric. Entomol.; Rev. Plant Pathol.; Sci. Cit. Index; SCISEARCH; Seed Abstr.; Sorghum Mill. Abstr.; Weed Abstr.; Wheat Barley Trit. Abstr.

UK

•**PLANT TALK.** (1995)-. English. Four times a year. $60.00. Botanical Information Company, PO Box 400, Richmond Surrey TW10 7XJ United Kingdom. **Tel** 011 44 181 5466725.

ISSN 1018-8029
BG
UDC 63

PLANT TISSUE CULTURE. [Plant tissue cult.]. **VFOAT** PTC. Plant Tissue Culture. (1991)-. Periodical. English. Two times a year. Bangladesh Association for Plant Tissue Culture, University of Dhaka, Department of Botany, Dhaka 1000 Bangladesh.

LC QK1 .P73 **ISSN** 0032-0935
DD 581 GW
CCC
NLM W1 PL105U **CODEN** PLANAB
Pr Rev.

PLANTA. [Planta]. Vol. 1, No. 3 (Dec. 1925)-. Academic Scholarly Publication. English (French and German). Twelve times a year. $2661.00. Springer-Verlag GmbH & Company KG, Heidelberger Platz 3, D-14197 Berlin Germany. **Tel** 011 49 30 8207223, FAX 011 49 30 8214091, telex 183 319 SPBLN D. **(Subscription address:** Springer-Verlag New York Inc. / North America, PO Box 2485, Journal Fulfillment, Secaucus NJ 07096. **Tel** (201)348-4033, (800)777-4643, FAX (201)348-4505.**) ED** A Lang, A Sievers and M B Wilkins. Index Available, published separately, free-automatically sent. available on microfilm and microfiche from University Microfilms International (UMI). Documents available from The Genuine Article, BIOSIS Document Express, CASDDS. ***Continues*** *Archiv fuer Wissenschaftliche Botanik.*
Desc: Publishes original articles covering all aspects of experimental plant biology, from ultrastructure and molecular biology to whole-plant physiology, including studies with cells, tissues, and organs.
Ind/Abst Abstr. Bull. Inst. Pap. Sci. Tech.; AgBiotech News Inf.; AGRICOLA [Full Cov.]; Biol. Abstr.; Chem. Abstr.; Chem. Titles; Cot. Trop. Fibr. Abstr. Bibliogr.; Crop

Physiol. Abstr.; Curr. Aware. Biol. Sci.; CABS; Curr. Contents Agric. Biol. Environ. Sci.; Curr. Contents Life Sci.; Energy Res. Abstr.; Field Crop Abstr.; Food Sci. Technol. Abstr.; For. Abstr.; Hortic. Abstr.; Irr. Drain. Abstr.; Maize Abstr.; Microbiol. Abstr. Sect. A; Microbiol. Abstr. Sect. C; NAPRALERT; Ornamental Hort. (19??-19??); Life Sci. Collect.; PESTDOC; Plant Breed. Abstr.; Plant Genet. Resour. Abstr.; Plant Grow. Reg. Abstr.; Potato Abstr.; Ref. Upd. Basic Ed.; Ref. Upd. Deluxe Ed.; Res. Alert [Full Cov.]; Rev. Plant Pathol.; Rice Abstr.; Sci. Cit. Index; SCISEARCH; Seed Abstr.; Soils Fert.; Soyabean Abstr.; Weed Abstr.; Wheat Barley Trit. Abstr.

LC RS164 .P7   ISSN 0032-0943
DD 615/.32/05   GW
    CCC
NLM W1 PL106   CODEN PLMEAA
Pr Rev.

PLANTA MEDICA. See Pharmacy and Pharmacology.

    GW
PLANTA MEDICA. SUPPLEMENT. See Pharmacy and Pharmacology.

ISSN 1010-1640
SA
CODEN PLAKE6

PLANTBESKERMINGSNUUS. (PLANTBESKERMINGSNUUS : BULLETIN VAN DIE NAVORSINGSINSTITUUT VIR PLANTBESKERMING.). [Plantbeskermingsnuus]. **Added/Corp** Plant Protection Research Institute (South Africa) South Africa. Dept. of Agriculture and Water Supply. **VFOAT** Plant Protection News. No. 1 (Sep. 1985)-. Bulletin. Afrikaans (English). Four times a year. Plant Protection Research Institute, Privaatsak X134/Private Bag, Pretoria 0001 South Africa.
Ind/Abst Biocont. News Inf.; Cot. Trop. Fibr. Abstr. Bibliogr.; For. Abstr.; Nematol. Abstr.; Sorghum Mill. Abstr.; Weed Abstr.

LC QK   ISSN 0032-0994
DD 581   FR
NLM W1 PL109   CODEN PLMPA9
    CEASED

PLANTES MEDICINALES ET PHYTOTHERAPIE. See Pharmacy and Pharmacology.

LC SB107 .P526
DD   US

PLANTS & PEOPLE : SOCIETY FOR ECONOMIC BOTANY NEWSLETTER. **Added/Corp** Society for Economic Botany (U.S.). **VFOAT** Plants and People; Society for Economic Botany Newsletter; Economic Botany Newsletter. Vol. 5 (Spring 1992)-. Newsletter. English. Irregular. Comes with Society for Economic Botany membership. Society for Economic Botany, New York Botanical Garden, Scientific Publications Department, Bronx NY 10458-5126. **Tel** (718)817-8721, FAX (718)220-6504. **(Subscription address:** Allen Press, PO Box 1897, Lawrence KS 66044. **Tel** (800)627-0629.**)** *Continues* Society for Economic Botany Newsletter.

LC QL104 .P64   ISSN 0722-4060
DD 574.909/1   GW
    CCC
    CODEN POBIDP
Pr Rev.

POLAR BIOLOGY. See Zoology.

LC SB599 .B4   ISSN 0408-9952
    YU
UDC 632
    CODEN MPIPEM

POSEBNA IZDANJA INSTITUTA ZA ZASTITU BILJA. [Poseb. izd. - Inst. zast. bilja]. **Main/Corp** Institut za Zastitu Bilja (Belgrade, Serbia). **VFOAT** Memoires Publies par l'Institut pour la Protection des Plantes; Memoirs Published by the Institut for Plant Protection; Posebna Izdanja; Memoirs. No. 1-. Monographic series. Serbo-Croatian (Roman) (English). Price varies per volume. Plant Protection Research Institute, Privaatsak X134/Private Bag, Pretoria 0001 South Africa. Index available. **Bk Rev. Ad Acc. Circ:** 1,000 (ctrl). Documents available from BIOSIS Document Express.
Ind/Abst Biol. Abstr.

ISSN 1037-5457
DD 631.5850994   AT
    TITLE CHANGE

PRACTICAL HYDROPONICS. [Pract. hydroponics]. (1991)-(19??). Periodical. English. Practical Hydroponics, PO Box 879 Bondi Junction, New South Wales 2022 Australia. **Tel** 011 61 2 3871559. **(Subscription address:** Federal Publishing Co. Pty Ltd., PO Box 199, Alexandria NSW 2015 Australia. **Tel** 011 61 2 3530666.**)** *Continued by* Practical Hydroponics International.

AT

PRACTICAL HYDROPONICS AND GREENHOUSES. (19??)-. Periodical. English. Six times a year (Jan., Mar., May, July, Sept., Nov.). 35.70Aus$ Australia; 63.90Aus$ US and Israel; 53.10Aus$ New Zealand and PNG; 54.90Aus$ Fiji Indonesia and Malaysia; 59.70Aus$ India and Japan; 67.90Aus$ other. Practical Hydroponics, PO Box 879 Bondi Junction, New South Wales 2022 Australia. **Tel** 011 61 2 3871559. *Continues* Practical Hydroponics International.

AT

PRACTICAL HYDROPONICS INTERNATIONAL. (19??)-. Periodical. English. Six times a year. Practical Hydroponics, PO Box 879 Bondi Junction, New South Wales 2022 Australia. **Tel** 011 61 2 3871559. *Continues* Practical Hydroponics, 1037-5457.

LC QK1 .C352   ISSN 0032-7786
    XR
    CODEN PRESAK

PRESLIA. [Preslia]. **Added/Corp** Ceskoslovenska Botanicka Spolecnost. (1914)-. Periodical. Czech (German; summaries and/or abstracts in English). Four times a year. $152.77. Czech Botanical Society, Czech Academy of Sciences, Prague Czech Republic. **(Subscription address:** Kubon & Sagner, ABT Zeitschriftenimport, D 80328 Munich Germany. **Tel** 011 49 89 54218130.**)** **ED** Zdenek Cernohorsky, Josef Holub, Jan Kirschner. **Bk Rev. Circ:** 1,550 (ctrl). Documents available from BIOSIS Document Express.
Desc: A journal of botanical studies. Contributions contain original work in various fields of botany, although emphasis is placed on plant morphology, plant taxonomy, geobotany and floristics.
Ind/Abst AGRICOLA; Biol. Abstr.; Ecol. Abstr.; For. Abstr.; Geogr. Abstr.; Plant Phys. Geogr.; Grass. Forage Abstr.; Life Sci. Collect.; Plant Genet. Resour. Abstr.; Potato Abstr.; Weed Abstr.

LC SB299.P3 P7   ISSN 0032-8480
DD 633.85   US
    CODEN PRNCAH

PRINCIPES. [Principes]. **Added/Corp** International Palm Society. Palm Society. Vol. 1 (Oct. 1956)-. Academic Scholarly Publication. English. Four times a year. $30.00. International Palm Society, Box 1897, Lawrence KS 66044. **Tel** (913)843-1234. **(Subscription address:** Principes, PO Box 1897, Lawrence KS 66044-8897. **)** **ED** Natalie Uhl. **Acid Free. Circ:** 2,200 (ctrl). available on microfilm from University Microfilms International (UMI). Documents available from BIOSIS Document Express, CASDDS. *Continues* Palm Society. Bulletin - Palm Society.
Desc: A non-profit corporation engaged in the study of palms and the dissemination of information about them.
Ind/Abst AGRICOLA; Biol. Abstr.; Chem. Abstr.; Crop Physiol. Abstr.; Hortic. Abstr.; Ornamental Hort. (1991-); Plant Breed. Abstr.; Rev. Agric. Entomol.; Seed Abstr.

ISSN 1057-2600
DD 581   US
NLM W1; PR551PT

PROBE (BELTSVILLE, MD.). (PROBE : NEWSLETTER FOR THE USDA PLANT GENOME RESEARCH PROGRAM.). [Probe]. **Added/Corp** USDA Plant Genome Research Program. Plant Genome Data and Information Center (U.S.). Vol. 1, No. 1/2 (Spring/Summer 1991)-. Newsletter. English. Four times a year. National Agricultural Library, 10301 Baltimore Boulevard, Beltsville MD 20705.
Ind/Abst AGRICOLA.

LC QK1 .P83   ISSN 0253-410X
DD 580/.5   II
    CODEN PIPLDS
    TITLE CHANGE

PROCEEDINGS OF THE INDIAN ACADEMY OF SCIENCES. PLANT SCIENCES. (PROCEEDINGS. PLANT SCIENCES.). [Proc. Indian Acad. Sci., Plant sci.]. **Added/Corp** Indian Academy of Sciences. **VFOAT** Plant Sciences; Proceedings of the Indian Academy of Sciences. Animal Sciences. Vol. 89 No. 1 (Jan. 1980)-(1993). Academic Scholarly Publication. English. Indian Academy of Sciences Circulation, PO Box 8005, Department of Sadashivanagar, Bangalore 560 080 India. **Tel** 011 91 812 342546, 342310, telex 0845-2178 ACAD IN. **ED** C. V. Subramanian. Index available. **Circ:** 750. available on microfilm and microfiche from University Microfilms International (UMI). Documents available from BIOSIS Document Express, CASDDS. *Continues* Proceedings. B, Plant Sciences. *Merged into* Journal of Bioscience, 0250-5991.
Desc: A journal with topics on plant sciences such as plant morphology, taxonomy, physiology, ecology, cytology and genetics, mycology and plant pathology, algology, agriculture and forestry.
Ind/Abst Agrofor. Abstr. (1991-); Biodeter. Abstr. (1991-); Biol. Abstr.; Chem. Abstr.; Crop Physiol. Abstr.; Ecology Abstr.; Energy Res. Abstr. (June 1981-); Field Crop Abstr.; For. Abstr.; GeoRef; Hortic. Abstr.; Irr. Drain. Abstr.; Microbiol. Abstr. Sect. A; Microbiol. Abstr. Sect. C; Ornamental Hort. (1991-); Life Sci. Collect.; Plant Breed. Abstr.; Refer. Z.; Rev. Agric. Entomol.; Rev. Plant Pathol.; Rice Abstr.; SCISEARCH; Seed Abstr.; Soils Fert.; Sorghum Mill. Abstr.; Soyabean Abstr.; Wheat Barley Trit. Abstr.

ISSN 1172-0719
    NZ
    CODEN PNZCEJ
Pr Rev.

PROCEEDINGS OF THE NEW ZEALAND PLANT PROTECTION CONFERENCE. [Proc. N. Z. Plant Prot. Conf.]. **Added/Corp** New Zealand Plant Protection Society. (1992)-. Proceedings. English. One time a year (Sept.). $53.73. New Zealand Plant Protection Society, Private Bag 3020, Rotorua New Zealand. **Tel** 011 64 73 700511. Documents available from CASDDS. *Continues* Proceedings of the New Zealand Weed and Pest Control Conference, 0370-2804.
Ind/Abst Chem. Abstr.; Curr. Cit.

LC SB128 .P55a   ISSN 0731-1664
DD 631.8   US
    CODEN PPGRDG

PROCEEDINGS OF THE PLANT GROWTH REGULATOR SOCIETY OF AMERICA. [Proc. Plant Growth Regul. Soc. Am.]. **Main/Corp** Plant Growth Regulator Society of America. Meeting. **VFOAT** Proceedings. 8th Annual Meeting (Aug. 3-6, 1981)-. Academic Scholarly Publication. English. One time a year. $20.00. Plant Growth Regulator Society of America, PO Box 12014, Research Triangle NC 27709. **Tel** (919)549-2408. Documents available from CASDDS. *Continues* Plant Growth Regulator Working Group. Proceedings of the Plant Growth Regulator Working Group.
Ind/Abst AGRICOLA [Full Cov.]; Chem. Abstr.; Crop Physiol. Abstr.; Curr. Cit.; Field Crop Abstr.; Grass. Forage Abstr.; Hortic. Abstr.; Ornamental Hort.; Plant Grow. Reg. Abstr.; Seed Abstr.; Vitis Vitic. Enol. Abstr.

LC QK1 .F67   ISSN 0340-4773
DD 581/.05   GW
NLM W1 PR667E   CODEN PRBODU

PROGRESS IN BOTANY. [Prog. bot.]. **VFOAT** Fortschritte der Botanik. (1974)-. Academic Scholarly Publication. Multiple languages (English and German). Irregular. Springer-Verlag GmbH & Company KG, Heidelberger Platz 3, D-14197 Berlin Germany. **Tel** 011 49 30 8207223, FAX 011 49 30 8214091, telex 183 319 SPBLN D. **(Subscription address:** Springer-Verlag New York Inc. / North America, PO Box 19386 Books, Newark NJ 07195. **Tel** (201)348-4033.**)** Documents available from BIOSIS Document Express, CASDDS. *Continues* Fortschritte der Botanik, 0071-7878.
Desc: Contains topics on: morphology, physiology, genetics, taxonomy, and geobotany.
Ind/Abst AGRICOLA; Biol. Abstr.; Chem. Abstr.; For. Abstr.; GeoRef; Irr. Drain. Abstr.; Life Sci. Collect.; Plant Breed. Abstr.; Plant Grow. Reg. Abstr.

LC QK564 .P76   ISSN 0167-8574
DD 589.3   UK
    CODEN PPREEX

PROGRESS IN PHYCOLOGICAL RESEARCH. [Prog. phycol. res.]. Vol. 1 (1982)-. Academic Scholarly Publication. English. Irregular. Price varies per volume. Lubrecht & Cramer Ltd, 38 County Route 48, Forestburgh NY 12777. **Tel** (914)794-8539. Documents available from BIOSIS Document Express, CASDDS.
Ind/Abst Biol. Abstr. (1986-); Chem. Abstr.

LC S   ISSN 0921-5506
DD 630   NE
UDC 582.4

PROPHYTA. See Gardening and Horticulture.

ISSN 0723-0311
    GW

PSP : PFLANZENSCHUTZ-PRAXIS. **VFOAT** Pflanzenschutz-Praxis. (19??)-. Periodical. German. Four times a year. $48.36. Deutsche Landwirtschafts Gesellschaft, Verlags GmbH, Eschborner Landstr 122, D-60489 Frankfurt Germany. **Tel** 011 49 69 247880, FAX 011 49 69 24788580.
Ind/Abst Maize Abstr.; Nematol. Abstr.; Plant Breed. Abstr.; Potato Abstr.; Rev. Agric. Entomol.; Rev. Plant Pathol.; Seed Abstr.; Soils Fert.; Weed Abstr.; Wheat Barley Trit. Abstr.

ISSN 0749-7741
DD 587   US
    CODEN PTRID4
Pr Rev.

PTERIDOLOGIA. (PTERIDOLOGIA : A PUBLICATION OF THE AMERICAN FERN SOCIETY.). [Pteridologia]. **Added/Corp** American Fern Society. No. 1 (1979)-. Monographic series. English. Irregular. Price varies per volume. Dr. David Lellinger, US National Herbarium Smithsonian, NHB 166, Washington DC 20560. **Tel** (202)357-2568. **ED** D. B. Lellinger. Index available. **Circ:** 250. Documents available from BIOSIS Document Express.
Desc: Scholarly fern monograph series.
Ind/Abst Biol. Abstr.

LC QK520 .P74 **ISSN** 0266-1640
DD 587/.3/05 UK
CODEN PTEREZ

PTERIDOLOGIST. (PTERIDOLOGIST / THE BRITISH PTERIDOLOGICAL SOCIETY.). [Pteridologist]. **Added/Corp** British Pteridological Society. Vol. 1, Pt. 1 (1984)-. English. One time a year. £20.00 Comes with British Pteridological Society membership. British Pteridological Society, Natural History Museum - Botany, Cromwell Road, London SW7 5BD United Kingdom. **Tel** 011 44 171 9389497. **ED** M. H. Rickard. **Circ:** 650. Documents available from BIOSIS Document Express.
Desc: Articles on growing ferns, fern varities and general pteridology.
Ind/Abst Biol. Abstr. (1987-).

ISSN 0951-418X
DD 581 UK
CCC
NLM W1; PH988H **CODEN** PHYREH

PTR. PHYTOTHERAPY RESEARCH. (PHYTOTHERAPY RESEARCH : PTR.). [PTR, Phytother. res.]. **VFOAT** PTR. Vol. 1, No. 1 (March 1987)-. Academic Scholarly Publication. English. Eight times a year. $695.00. John Wiley & Sons Ltd., Baffins Lane, Chichester, West Sussex PO19 1UD United Kingdom. **Tel** 011 44 1243 779777, FAX 011 44 1243 776128 BTG:JWP001, telex 86290 WIBOOKG. **(Subscription address:** John Wiley & Sons, Inc. / Philadelphia, PO Box 7247, Philadelphia PA 19170. **Tel** (212)850-6645, (800)225-5945.**)** **ED** Fred J. Evans and S. L. Croft. Index available. **Bk Rev. Ad Acc.** available on microfilm and microfiche from University Microfilms International (UMI). Documents available from The Genuine Article, CASDDS, ADONIS.
Desc: An international journal for the publication of original medical plant research, including biochemistry and molecular pharmacology, toxicology, pathology, and the clinical application of herbs and natural products to both human and animal medicine.
Ind/Abst ADONIS; AgBiotech News Inf.; AGRICOLA [Select. Cov.]; Agrofor. Abstr. (1991-); Chem. Abstr.; Curr. Aware. Biol. Sci., CABS; Curr. Cit.; Curr. Contents Life Sci.; EMBASE; Food Sci. Technol. Abstr.; For. Prod. Abstr. (1991-); For. Abstr.; Helminthol. Abstr. (1991-); Hortic. Abstr.; Nutr. Abstr. Rev., Ser. A, Hum. Exp.; Plant Genet. Resour. Abstr.; Protozoolog. Abstr.; Res. Alert [Full Cov.]; Rev. Agric. Entomol.; Rev. Med. Vet. Mycology; Sci. Cit. Index; SCISEARCH; Seed Abstr.; Soc. Sci. Cit. Index [Select. Cov.].

LC QK **ISSN** 0820-5515
DD 581 CN

QUATRE-TEMPS (MONTREAL). (QUATRE-TEMPS : BULLETIN DE LA SOCIETE D'ANIMATION DU JARDIN ET DE L'INSTITUT BOTANIQUES DE MONTREAL.). [Quatre-temps]. **Added/Corp** Societe d'Animation du Jardin et de l'Institut Botaniques de Montreal. **VFOAT** Quatre-Temps, SAJIB; SAJIB; Bulletin de la Societe d'Animation du Jardin et de l'Institut Botaniques de Montreal. Vol. 11, No. 1 (1987)-. Bulletin. French. Four times a year (Mar., June, Sept., Dec.). 28.42Can$. Societe d'Animation du Jardin et de l'Institut Botanique, Jardin Botanique, 4101 East rue Sherbrooke #125, Montreal Quebec H1X 2B2 Canada. **Tel** (514)872-1493, FAX (514)872-3765. **ED** Suzanne Forget. cum. index. **Ad Acc, Adv Mgr:** P. Feugere, **Tel** (514)872-0650. **Circ:** 7,000. ***Continues** Bulletin de la Societe d'Animation du Jardin et de l'Institut Botanique, 0383-0845.*
Desc: Living plant collections of the Montreal Botanical Garden; ecology of Quebec Province; ornamental plants cultivated in Eastern Canada; vegetation of various countries.

AT
CODEN QBBUEG

QUEENSLAND BOTANY BULLETIN. **Added/Corp** Queensland. Dept. of Primary Industries. Botany Branch. No. 1 (1982)-. Bulletin. English. Department of Primary Industries / Queensland Australia, GPO Box 46, Brisbane Queensland 4001 Australia. **Tel** 011 61 7 2393111, FAX 011 61 7 2212490, telex AA41620. ***Continues** Technical Bulletin (Queensland. Dept. of Primary Industries. Botany Branch).*
Ind/Abst For. Abstr.

LC SB **ISSN** 0348-7954
DD 630 SW

RAPPORT - SVERIGES LANTBRUKSUNIVERSITET. INSTITUTIONEN FOER SKOGLIG GENETIK OCH VAEXTFYSIOLOGI = REPORT - SWEDISH UNIVERSITY OF AGRICULTURAL SCIENCES, DEPARTMENT OF FOREST GENETICS AND PLANT PHYSIOLOGY. **Main/Corp** Sveriges Lantbruksuniversitet. Institutionen foer Skoglig Genetik och Vaextfysiologi. **VFOAT** Report - Swedish University of Agricultural Sciences, Department of Forest Genetics and Plant Physiology. No. 1 (1979)-. Monographic series. English.
Ind/Abst For. Abstr.; Plant Breed. Abstr.

LC QK **ISSN** 0033-9946
DD 581 RU
CODEN RRESA8

RASTITELNYE RESURSY. [Rastit. resur.]. **Added/Corp** Akademiia Nauk SSSR. (1965)-. Academic Scholarly Publication. Russian. Four times a year. $112.00. Izdatelstvo Nauka / Akademiia Nauk, (Publishing House of the Russian Academy of Sciences), Leninskii Porspekt 14, 117901 Moscow Russia. **Tel** 011 95 9542153, FAX 011 95 9382144, telex 411964. **(Subscription address:** East View Publications Inc., 3020 Harbor Lane North, Suite 110, Minneapolis MN 55447. **Tel** (800)477-1005, (612)550-0961, FAX (612)559-2931.**)** Index available. Documents available from BIOSIS Document Express, CASDDS.
Ind/Abst AGRICOLA; Biol. Abstr.; Chem. Abstr.; Crop Physiol. Abstr.; For. Prod. Abstr. (1991-); For. Abstr.; Hortic. Abstr.; NAPRALERT; Ornamental Hort. (1991-); Life Sci. Collect.; Plant Grow. Reg. Abstr.

LC QK861 .R38 **ISSN** 0079-9920
DD 581.1/92 US
CCC
NLM W1 RE105Y **CODEN** RAPHBE

RECENT ADVANCES IN PHYTOCHEMISTRY. [Recent adv. phytochem.]. **Added/Corp** Phytochemical Society of North America. Proceedings of the Annual Symposium. Plant Phenolics Group of North America. Proceedings of the Annual Symposium. Vol. 1 (1968)-. Monographic series. English. Irregular. Price varies per volume. Plenum Press, 233 Spring Street, New York NY 10013-1578. **Tel** (212)620-8000, (800)221-9369, FAX (212)463-0742, (212)807-1047, telex 23/421139. Documents available from BIOSIS Document Express, CASDDS.
Desc: Covers the annual symposiums of the associated organizations.
Ind/Abst AGRICOLA [Full Cov.]; Biol. Abstr.; Chem. Abstr.; Curr. Cit.

LC QK358 .A4 **ISSN** 0375-0728
DD 581.954 II
CODEN RBSIA4

RECORDS OF THE BOTANICAL SURVEY OF INDIA. [Rec. Bot. Surv. India]. **Added/Corp** Botanical Survey of India. Vol. 1 No. 1 (1893)-. Monographic series. English. Irregular. Price varies per volume. Botanical Survey of India, Indian Botanic Garden, Howrah-3 India. cum. index. Documents available from BIOSIS Document Express.
Ind/Abst Biol. Abstr. (?-1983).

LC QK96 .R4 **ISSN** 0080-0694
DD 581.012 GW

REGNUM VEGETABLE. **Added/Corp** International Bureau for Plant Taxonomy and Nomenclature. International Association for Plant Taxonomy. (1953)-. Monographic series. English. Irregular. Price varies per volume. Koeltz Scientific Books, PO Box 1360, D-61453 Koenigstein Germany. **Tel** 011 49 6174 93720, FAX 011 49 6174 1634.
Desc: A serial by botanical taxonomists.

LC QK1 .R32 **ISSN** 0034-365X
IO
CODEN RNWDAP

REINWARDTIA. [Reinwardtia]. **Added/Corp** Bogor, Indonesia. Kebun Raja. Herbarium Bogoriense. Vol. 1 (Dec. 1950)-. Periodical. English. Irregular. Center for Research Biotechnology, Lipi J1 IR H Juanda 18, POB 323, Bogor 16122 Indonesia. **Tel** 011 62 251 2103821039, telex DIRBIONAS. **ED** Soedarsono Riswan, M. A. Rifai and E. A. Widjata. **Circ:** 500 (ctrl). Documents available from BIOSIS Document Express. ***Continues** Bulletin du Jardin Botanique de Buitenzorg.*
Desc: Covers taxonomic botany, plant sociology and ecology of the Malesian region.
Ind/Abst AGRICOLA [Full Cov.]; Biol. Abstr.; Life Sci. Collect.

LC QK96 .R4 **ISSN** 0486-4271
DD 581.012 NE

REPERTORIUM PLANTARUM SUCCULENTARUM. [Repert. plant. suc.]. **Added/Corp** International Organisation for Succulent Plant Study. British Section. International Bureau for Plant Taxonomy and Nomenclature. International Association for Plant Taxonomy. International Organisation for Succulent Plant Research. Vol. 1 (1950)-. English. One time a year. Free to members. International Organization for Succulent Plant Study, Mythenquai 88, CH-8002 Zurich Switzerland.
Desc: Publishes a list of newly published names of succulent plants. The list contains the taxonomic recombinations, an indication of whether the new names are valid or invalid, and the name of the journal in which the name was published. It also contains an index to the new plant names and a taxonomic bibliography indexed both by plant name and publishing author.

LC QK
DD 581 AT

REPORT / CSIRO DIVISION OF PLANT INDUSTRY. **Main/Corp** Commonwealth Scientific and Industrial Research Organization (Australia). Division of Plant Industry. (1979/1980)-. English. Every 2 years. CSIRO Publications, PO Box 89, 314 Albert Street, East Melborne Victoria 3002 Australia. **Tel** 011 61 3 4187333, 4187217, FAX 011 61 3 4190459, telex AA 30236. ***Continues** Commonwealth Scientific and Industrial Research Organization (Australia). Division of Plant Industry. Annual Report.*

ISSN 0573-0791
DD 632 UK

REPORT OF WORK CARRIED OUT. **Main/Corp** Commonwealth Institute of Biological Control. (1958)-. Periodical. English. CAB International Centre, Wallingford, Oxfordshire OX10 8DE United Kingdom. **Tel** 011 44 1491 832111, FAX 011 44 1491 833508, telex 847964 COMAGG G.

LC QK **ISSN** 0970-3845
DD 581 II

RESEARCH JOURNAL OF PLANT AND ENVIRONMENT. **Added/Corp** International Society for Plant and Environment. **VFOAT** Plant and Environment. (19??)-. Periodical. English. Two times a year. $40.00. Pandley - International Society for Plant and Environment, Kanpur India. **(Subscription address:** Prints India, 11 Darya Ganj, New Delhi 110002 India. **Tel** 011 91 11 3268645, FAX 011 91 11 3275542, telex 31-61087 PRIN-IN.**)**

LC QK **ISSN** 1356-1421
DD 581 UK
NLM ZQV 766; R454

●**REVIEW OF AROMATIC AND MEDICINAL PLANTS.** **Added/Corp** C.A.B. International. Vol. 1, No. 1 (Feb. 1995)-. Abstracting/Indexing Service. English. Six times a year. $230.00. CAB International Centre, Wallingford, Oxfordshire OX10 8DE United Kingdom. **Tel** 011 44 1491 832111, FAX 011 44 1491 833508, telex 847964 COMAGG G. **(Subscription address:** CAB International, Subscriptions Department, Wallingford OX OX108DE United Kingdom. **Tel** 011 44 1491 832111.**)** available on an online database.

LC SB599 .R4 **ISSN** 0034-6438
DD 632 UK

REVIEW OF PLANT PATHOLOGY. **See** Biology-Abstracting, Bibliographies and Statistics.

II

REVIEW OF TROPICAL PLANT PATHOLOGY. English. One time a year. Price varies per volume. Today and Tomorrow's Printers and Publishers, 24-B/5 Desh Bandhu Gupta Road, Karol Bagh, New Delhi 110 005 India. **Tel** 011 91 11 5721928, 011 91 11 572770, FAX 011 91 11 7210073 (TTPP). **(Subscription address:** Prints India, 11 Darya Ganj, New Delhi 110002 India. **Tel** 011 91 11 3268645, FAX 011 91 11 3275542, telex 31-61087 PRIN-IN.**)** **ED** S. P. Raychaudhuri and J. P. Verma.
Desc: Presents contributions from international scientists specialised in various aspects of pathogenesis of disease control.
Ind/Abst Microbiol. Abstr. Sect. A; Microbiol. Abstr. Sect. C.

LC QK263 .R48 **ISSN** 0100-8404
DD 581.981/05 BL
CODEN RRBODIRBBOD8

REVISTA BRASILEIRA DE BOTANICA. [Rev. bras. bot.]. **Added/Corp** Sociedade Botanica do Brasil. Regional de Sao Paulo. **VFOAT** Brazilian Journal of Botany. Vol. 1 (May 1978)-. Academic Scholarly Publication. Portuguese (English, Portuguese and Spanish). Two times a year (July, and Dec.). $72.00. Sociedade Botanica Sao Paulo, Caixa Postal 11491, 05499 Sao Paulo Brazil. **Tel** 011 55 11 5846300 ext. 288. **ED** Gil Martins Felippe. **Circ:** 750. Documents available from BIOSIS Document Express, CASDDS.
Desc: Publishes results of original research in botanical science.
Ind/Abst Biol. Abstr.; Chem. Abstr.; Soils Fert.

ISSN 0103-3131
BL
CODEN RBFVEG

REVISTA BRASILEIRA DE FISIOLOGIA VEGETAL. **Added/Corp** Sociedade Brasileira de Fisiologia Vegetal. **VFOAT** Brazilian Journal of Plant Physiology. Vol. 1, No. 1 (1989)-. Periodical. Portuguese (English). Two times a year. Documents available from CASDDS.
Ind/Abst Abstr. Trop. Agric.; Agrindex; Agrofor. Abstr. (1991-); Chem. Abstr.; Crop Physiol. Abstr.; Field Crop Abstr.; For. Abstr.; Grass. Forage Abstr.; Rice Abstr.; Seed Abstr.; Sorghum Mill. Abstr.; Weed Abstr.

LC QK227 **ISSN** 0253-5696
DD 580/.5 CU
UDC 58.006(729.1); 581
CODEN RJBNDR

REVISTA DEL JARDIN BOTANICO NACIONAL. [Rev. Jard. Bot. Nac.]. Vol. 1, No. 1 (1980)-. Periodical. Spanish (summaries and/or abstracts in English). Three times a year. $18.00. Ediciones Cubanas, Obispo 527 Altos ESQ Bernaza, CP 10100 Havana Cuba. **Circ:** 10,000 (ctrl). Documents available from BIOSIS Document Express.
Desc: This is a university-level magazine publishing

original scientific papers in the field of botany and related branches: taxonomy, ecology, phytogeometry, biochemistry, physiology, genetics, anatomy and botanical gardens.
Ind/Abst Biol. Abstr.; GeoRef; Hortic. Abstr.; Ornamental Hort. (1991-); Plant Breed. Abstr.; Soils Fert.

ISSN 0185-3309 MX

REVISTA MEXICANA DE FITOPATOLOGIA. [Rev. mex. fitopatol.]. Periodical. Spanish. Two times a year. Documents available from BIOSIS Document Express.
Ind/Abst Biocont. News Inf. (1991-); Biodeter. Abstr. (1991-); Biol. Abstr.; Field Crop Abstr.; Nematol. Abstr.; Postharvest News Inf.; Rev. Agric. Entomol.; Rev. Plant Pathol.; Seed Abstr.; Sorghum Mill. Abstr.

ISSN 0181-7582 FR
UDC 581.17
CODEN RCBBDA

REVUE DE CYTOLOGIE ET DE BIOLOGIE VEGETALES - LE BOTANISTE. [Rev. cytol. biol. veg., Bot.]. (1978)-. Academic Scholarly Publication. French (summaries and/or abstracts in English; table of contents in English). Four times a year. $207.78. Revue de Cytologie et de Biologie Vegetales le Botaniste, 61 rue de Buffon, F-75005 Paris France. **Tel** 64 28 01 01. **(Subscription address:** Revue de Cytologie & De Biologie Vegetales, 3 rue Des Pliants, 77140 Numours France. **Tel** 011 33 1 64280101.**)** Documents available from BIOSIS Document Express, CASDDS. ***Formed by the union of*** *Revue de Cytologie et de Biologie Vegetales* ***and*** *Botaniste.*
Ind/Abst AGRICOLA; Biol. Abstr.; Chem. Abstr.; (1978-1981); GeoRef; Life Sci. Collect.

LC QK1 .R366 **ISSN** 0250-5517
DD 581/.05 GW
CODEN RRBVD5

REVUE ROUMAINE DE BIOLOGIE. SERIE DE BIOLOGIE VEGETALE. [Rev. roum. biol., ser. biol. veg.]. **Added/Corp** Academia Republicii Socialiste Romania. Vol. 21 (1976)-. Academic Scholarly Publication. English (French). Two times a year. $88.00. **(Subscription address:** Ilexim Press Department, PO Box 1, 136-1-137, Bucharest, Romania. **Tel** 011 40 1 173836.**)** Documents available from BIOSIS Document Express, CASDDS. ***Continues in part*** *Revue Roumaine de Biologie, 0250-6572.*
Ind/Abst AGRICOLA; Biol. Abstr.; Chem. Abstr.; Coal Abstr.; EMBASE; Grass. Forage Abstr.; Irr. Drain. Abstr.; Plant Grow. Reg. Abstr.; Rev. Plant Pathol.; Vitis Vitic. Enol. Abstr.

LC QK **ISSN** 0971-2313
DD 581 II

RHEEDEA (CALICUT). (RHEEDEA : OFFICIAL JOURNAL OF INDIAN ASSOCIATION FOR ANGIOSPERM TAXONOMY.). [Rheedea]. **Added/Corp** Indian Association for Angiosperm Taxonomy. Vol. 1, Nos. 1 & 2 (1991)-. Periodical. English. Two times a year. $80.00. Indian Association for Angiosperm Taxonomy, Calcutta India. **(Subscription address:** Prints India, 11 Darya Ganj, New Delhi 110002 India. **Tel** 011 91 11 3268645, FAX 011 91 11 3275542, telex 31-61087 PRIN-IN.**)**

ISSN 0482-9905 GW

RHODODENDRON UND IMMERGRUNE LAUBGEHOLZE. [Rhododendr. immergrune Laubgeholze]. German. One time a year.

LC QK1 .R47 **ISSN** 0035-4902
DD 581.974 US
CODEN RHODAB
Pr Rev.

RHODORA. [Rhodora]. **Added/Corp** New England Botanical Club. Vol. 1 (Jan. 1899)-. Periodical. English. Four times a year. $45.00. Allen Press Inc., 810 East 10th Street, PO Box 1897, Lawrence KS 66044-8897. **Tel** (913)843-1221, (800)627-0629, FAX (913)843-1274. **ED** Dr. Gordon Dewoef. Index available (bound in Oct. issue). cum. index. **Bk Rev. Circ:** 850. available on microfilm and microfiche from University Microfilms International (UMI). Documents available from The Genuine Article, BIOSIS Document Express, CASDDS.
Ind/Abst AGRICOLA [Full Cov.]; Biol. Abstr.; Chem. Abstr.; Curr. Aware. Biol. Sci., CABS; Curr. Contents Agric. Biol. Environ. Sci.; Ecol. Abstr. (?-?); For. Abstr.; Grass. Forage Abstr.; Hortic. Abstr.; Ornamental Hort. (1991-); Life Sci. Collect.; Plant Breed. Abstr.; Plant Genet. Resour. Abstr.; Ref. Sources; Res. Alert [Select. Cov.]; Rev. Agric. Entomol.; Sel. Water Resour. Abstr.; Weed Abstr.

ISSN 0035-6441 IT
CODEN RPVGA9

RIVISTA DI PATOLOGIA VEGETALE. [Riv. patol. veg.]. Vol. 1, No. 1 (Mar. 1892)-Vol. 10 (Mar. 1902);New Series Vol. 1, No. 1 (1905)-Vol. 33 (1943);New Series 3, Vol. 1 (1964)-Vol. 4 (1964); New Series 4, Vol. 1 (1965)-. Academic Scholarly Publication. Italian (English). Three times a year. L68130. Istituto di Patologia Vegetale, Via Celoria 2, 20133 Milan Italy. **Tel** 011 39 2 2664169. **Bk Rev. Ad Acc. Circ:** 200. Documents available from BIOSIS Document Express, CASDDS.
Ind/Abst AGRICOLA; Biol. Abstr.; Chem. Abstr.; For. Abstr.; Life Sci. Collect.; Plant Breed. Abstr.; Potato Abstr.; Soils Fert.; Vitis Vitic. Enol. Abstr.

LC SB599 .R68 **ISSN** 0080-3693
DD 632 PL
CODEN RNORAR

ROCZNIKI NAUK ROLNICZYCH. SERIA E : OCHRONA ROSLIN. [Rocz. nauk roln., ser. E]. **Added/Corp** Polska Akademia Nauk. Komitet Ochrony Roslin. **VFOAT** Annaly Sel'skokhoziaistvennykh Nauk. Seriia E : Zashchita Rastenii; Polish Agricultural Annual. Series E : Plant Protection. (1970)-. Monographic series. Polish (summaries and/or abstracts in English and Russian). Irregular. Price varies per volume. Instytutu Ochrony Roslin, Ul. Miczurina 20, 60-318 Poznan Poland. **(Subscription address:** Ars Polona-Ruch, PO Box 1001, Krakowskie Przedmiescie 7, 00-068 Warsaw Poland. **Tel** 011 48 22 261201.**)** Documents available from CASDDS. ***Continues in part*** *Roczniki Nauk Lesnych (1951).*
Ind/Abst Chem. Abstr.

LC QK **ISSN** 0212-9108
DD 581 SP
UDC 58.006(460); 58

RUIZIA. (RUIZIA : R : MONOGRAFIAS DEL REAL JARDIN BOTANICO, CONSEJO SUPERIOR DE INVESTIGACIONES CIENTIFICAS.). [Ruizia]. **VFOAT** R. Vol. 1 (1984)-. Monographic series. Spanish (English, French, German and Portuguese). Irregular. Price varies per volume. Oficina de Publicaciones del C S I C, Vitrubio 8, 28006 Madrid Spain. **Tel** 011 34 1 2629633, FAX 011 34 1 4113077, telex 42182 CSIC E.
Desc: Studies on botany and gardening.
Ind/Abst Ecol. Abstr. (?-?).

LC QK1 .F513 **ISSN** 1021-4437
DD 581 US
CCC

•RUSSIAN JOURNAL OF PLANT PHYSIOLOGY : A COMPREHENSIVE RUSSIAN JOURNAL ON MODERN PHYTOPHYSIOLOGY. Added/Corp Interperiodica Publishing. Vol. 40, No. 5 (Sept.-Oct. 1993)-. Periodical. English (translations available in Russian). Six times a year. $1345.00. Plenum Press, 233 Spring Street, New York NY 10013-1578. **Tel** (212)620-8000, (800)221-9369, FAX (212)463-0742, (212)807-1047, telex 23/421139. **(Subscription address:** Plenum Press Subscription Department, PO Box 730, Canal Street, Station NY 10013-1578. **Tel** (212)620-8000, (212)620-8466.**)** ***Continues*** *Fiziologiia Rastenii. English. Russian Plant Physiology, 1070-3292.*
Ind/Abst Curr. Cit.

LC QK1 .F513 **ISSN** 1070-3292
US
CODEN RPPHEK
TITLE CHANGE

RUSSIAN PLANT PHYSIOLOGY. [Russ. plant physiol.]. **Added/Corp** Consultants Bureau. (1993)-(1993). Academic Scholarly Publication. English (translations available in Russian). MAIK Nauka / Interperiodica, Ulitsa Profsoyuznaia 90, Moscow 117864 Russia. Documents available from CASDDS. ***Continues*** *Fiziologiia Rastenii. English. Soviet Plant Physiology, 0038-5719.* ***Continued by*** *Fiziologiia Rastenii. English. Russian Journal of Plant Physiology, 1021-4437.*
Ind/Abst Chem. Abstr.; Curr. Cit.; EMBASE; Sci. Cit. Index.

ISSN 1010-3902 CH
Pr Rev.

SABRAO JOURNAL. [SABRAO j.]. **Added/Corp** Society for the Advancement of Breeding Researches in Asia and Oceania. **VFOAT** S.A.B.R.A.O. Journal. **VAT** Society for the Advancement of Breeding Researches in Asia and Oceania Journal. (19??)-. Periodical. English. Two times a year. 28.00Aus$. SABRAO, Taichung District Agricultural Improvement, Tatsuen Changhua Taiwan S 15.
Ind/Abst AGRICOLA [Full Cov.]; Maize Abstr.; Life Sci. Collect.; Plant Breed. Abstr.; Rev. Plant Pathol.; Rice Abstr.; Weed Abstr.; Wheat Barley Trit. Abstr.

ISSN 0275-6919
DD 581 US
TITLE CHANGE

SAGUAROLAND BULLETIN. [Saguaroland bull.]. **Added/Corp** Arizona Cactus and Native Flora Society. Desert Botanical Garden (Ariz.). (1947)-(19??). Bulletin. English. Desert Botanical Garden, 1201 North Galvin Parkway, Phoenix AZ 85008. **Tel** (602)941-1225. **ED** Sondra Mesnik. Index available. **Bk Rev. Circ:** 3,000 (ctrl). ***Continued by*** *Sonoran Quarterly, 1075-1386.*
Desc: Newsletter to members of the Desert Botanical Garden. Contains brief news stories about collections and research activities.

LC QK1 .S183 **ISSN** 0373-2525
DD 581/.05 SZ
CODEN SAUSDH

SAUSSUREA. [Saussurea]. **Added/Corp** Societe Botanique de Geneve. (1970)-. French (English, German, Spanish, Italian and Latin). One time a year. $118.76. Societe Botanique de Geneve, Case Postale 60, CH-1292 Cha Geneva Switzerland. **Tel** 011 41 122 7330362. **ED** Patrick Perret. Index available. **Ad Acc. Circ:** 400. Documents available from BIOSIS Document Express, CASDDS. ***Supersedes*** *Societe Botanique de Geneve. Travaux.*
Desc: Original scientific papers on all botanical fields.
Ind/Abst Biol. Abstr.; Chem. Abstr. (1970-1979); Life Sci. Collect.

LC QK **ISSN** 0201-7997
DD 581 UN

SBORNIK NAUCHNYKH TRUDOV. Added/Corp Nikitskii Botanicheskii Sad (IAlta, Ukraine). Vol. 85 (1981)-. Monographic series. Russian (summaries and/or abstracts in English; translations available in English). ***Continues*** *Trudy (Nikitskii Botanicheskii Sad (IAlta, Ukraine)).*
Ind/Abst For. Abstr.; Soils Fert.

LC QK564 .H625 **ISSN** 0385-6054
DD 589.30952 JA

SCIENTIFIC PAPERS OF THE INSTITUTE OF ALGOLOGICAL RESEARCH, FACULTY OF SCIENCE, HOKKAIDO UNIVERSITY. [Sci. pap. Inst. Algol. Res., Fac. Sci., Hokkaido Univ.]. **Main/Corp** Hokkaido Daigaku, Sapporo, Japan. Rigakubu. Kaiso Kenkyujo, Muroran. Vol. 1 (March 1935)-. Periodical. English. Irregular. Hokkaido University Institute of Algological Research, Hokkaido Daigaku Rigakubu Kaiso Kenkyujo, Bokoi Muroran Hokkaido 051 Japan.
Ind/Abst Life Sci. Collect.

LC QK900 .S44 **ISSN** 0371-0548
DD 581.5 JA

SEITAIGAKU KENKYU. (ECOLOGICAL REVIEW = SEITAIGAKU KENKYU.). [Seitaigaku kenkyu]. **Added/Corp** Hakkodasan Shokubutsu Jikkenjo. **VFOAT** Seitaigaku Kenkyu; Seitaigaku Kenkyu. Vol. 15, No. 2 (Aug. 1959)-. English (German). Tohoku Daigaku Hakkodasan Shokubutsu Jikkenjo, (Mt. Hakkoda Botanical Lab. Tohoku University), Tohoku Daigaku Rigakubu Fuzoku Shokubutsuen, Kawauchi, Sendaishi Miyagiken 980 Japan. cum. index. ***Continues*** *Seitaigaku Kenkyu.*
Ind/Abst AGRICOLA [Select. Cov.]; For. Abstr.; Grass. Forage Abstr.; Life Sci. Collect.

LC QK1 .S272 **ISSN** 0361-185X
DD 581/.05 US
CODEN SELBDH

SELBYANA. [Selbyana]. **Added/Corp** Marie Selby Botanical Gardens. (Jan. 1975)-. English. Two times a year. $55.00. Allen Press Inc., 810 East 10th Street, PO Box 1897, Lawrence KS 66044-8897. **Tel** (913)843-1221, (800)627-0629, FAX (913)843-1274. **ED** W. John Kress. **Circ:** 250 (ctrl). Documents available from BIOSIS Document Express.
Desc: Devoted to original biological research on tropical plants, especially epiphytes, including floristic, taxonomic and biosystematic treatments.
Ind/Abst AGRICOLA [Full Cov.]; Biol. Abstr.; Life Sci. Collect.

LC QK **ISSN** 0375-1651
DD 581 BL

SELLOWIA. [Sellowia]. **Added/Corp** Herbario "Barbosa Rodrigues.". Vol. 6, No. 6 (June 22, 1954)-. Portuguese (English, German and Spanish). One time a year. $15.00. Herbario Barbosa Rodrigues, Av Cel Marcos Konder 800, 88301 122 Itajai SC Brazil. **Tel** 011 55 473 442725. **ED** Raulino Reitz. ***Continues*** *Anais Botanicos do Herbario "Barbosa Rodrigues".*
Ind/Abst For. Abstr.; Life Sci. Collect.; Weed Abstr.

LC QK95 .S46 **ISSN** 0944-0178
DD 581/.05 GW
CODEN SNDTER

•SENDTNERA : MITTEILUNGEN DER BOTANISCHEN STAATSSAMMLUNG UND DES INSTITUTS FUER SYSTEMATISCHE BOTANIK DER UNIVERSITAET MUENCHEN. Added/Corp Botanische Staatssammlung Munchen. Universitat Munchen. Institut fuer Systematische Botanik. (1993)-. Periodical. German (English). Irregular (publishes one or two times per year). Free on request on exchange basis only. Botan Staatssammlung / Munich, Menzinger Str 67, D-80638 Munich Germany. ***Continues*** *Botanische Staatssammlung Munchen. Mitteilungen der Botanischen Staatssammlung Munchen, 0006-8179.*

ISSN 0120-5099 CK

SERIE MEMORIAS DE EVENTOS CIENTIFICOS COLOMBIANOS. Added/Corp Instituto Colombiano para el Fomento de la Educacion Superior. **VFOAT** Memorias de Eventos Cientificos Colombianos.; Serie Eventos Cientificos

Colombianos. (19??)-. Monographic series. Spanish. Price varies per volume. Instituto Colombiano Para el Fomento de la Educacion Superior, Calle 17 No 3-40, Apartado Aero 6319 Nal 2868, Bogota de Colombia.

LC QK827 .S39 **ISSN** 0934-0882
DD 581.1/66 GW
CCC
CODEN SPLRE7

SEXUAL PLANT REPRODUCTION. [Sex. plant reprod.]. Vol. 1, No. 1 (Mar. 1988)-. Periodical. English. Six times a year. $536.00. Springer-Verlag GmbH & Company KG, Heidelberger Platz 3, D-14197 Berlin Germany. **Tel** 011 49 30 8207223, FAX 011 49 30 8214091, telex 183 319 SPBLN D. **(Subscription address:** Springer-Verlag New York Inc. / North America, PO Box 2485, Journal Fulfillment, Secaucus NJ 07096. **Tel** (201)348-4033, (800)777-4643, FAX (201)348-4505.**)** **ED** H F Linskens. available on microfilm and microfiche from University Microfilms International (UMI). Documents available from The Genuine Article, BIOSIS Document Express.
Desc: Focuses on the dynamics and mechanisms of sexual processes in all plant groups, including algae and fungi, mosses and ferns. The primary emphasis is placed on the experimental approach.
Ind/Abst AgBiotech News Inf.; AGRICOLA [Full Cov.]; Biol. Abstr.; Crop Physiol. Abstr.; Curr. Aware. Biol. Sci., CABS; Curr. Cit.; Curr. Contents Agric. Biol. Environ. Sci.; Curr. Contents Life Sci.; Field Crop Abstr.; For. Abstr.; Hortic. Abstr.; Maize Abstr.; Ornamental Hort. (19??-19??); Plant Breed. Abstr.; Plant Genet. Resour. Abstr.; Plant Grow. Reg. Abstr.; Potato Abstr.; Res. Alert [Full Cov.]; Rev. Plant Pathol.; Sci. Cit. Index; SCISEARCH; Seed Abstr.; Sorghum Mill. Abstr.; Weed Abstr.; Wheat Barley Trit. Abstr.

LC SB989.J3 N67a **ISSN** 0387-0707
DD 632.96 JA
CODEN SBCKA9

SHOKUBUTSU BOEKIJO CHOSA KENKYU HOKOKU. (SHOKUBUTSU BOEKIJO CHOSA KENKYU HOKOKU. RESEARCH BULLETIN OF THE PLANT PROTECTION SERVICE, JAPAN.). [Shokubutsu Boekijo chosa kenkyu hokoku]. **Main/Corp** Norinsho Yokohama Shokubutsu Boikijo. **Added/Corp** Norinsho Yokohama Shokubutsu Boekijo. Research Bulletin of the Plant Protection Service, Japan. (1961)-. Academic Scholarly Publication. Japanese (summaries and/or abstracts in English). Irregular. Norinsho Yokohama Shokubutsu Boekijo 57, Kitanakadori-5, Naka-ku 231, Yokohama Japan. Documents available from BIOSIS Document Express, CASDDS.
Ind/Abst Biodeter. Abstr.; Biol. Abstr.; Chem. Abstr.; For. Prod. Abstr. (1991-); Rev. Med. Vet. Entomol.

ISSN 0022-2062
JA
CODEN SHKZAY

SHOKUBUTSU KENKYU ZASSHI. [Journ. Jap. Bot.]. **Added/Corp** Tsumura Kenkyujo. **VFOAT** Journal of Japanese Botany. Vol. 1 (1916)-. Academic Scholarly Publication. Japanese (English and German). Six times a year. $150.00. Tsumura Kenkyujo, (Tsumura Lab.), 3586 Yoshiwara Amimachi, Inashikigun Ibarakiken 300-11, Japan. cum. index. Documents available from BIOSIS Document Express, CASDDS.
Ind/Abst AGRICOLA; Biol. Abstr.; Chem. Abstr.; For. Abstr.; Hortic. Abstr.; Ornamental Hort. (1991-); Life Sci. Collect.; Plant Genet. Resour. Abstr.; Seed Abstr.

LC QK **ISSN** 0388-9130
DD 581 JA
CODEN SKACD7

SHOKUBUTSU NO KAGAKU CHOSETSU. (SHOKUBUTSU NO KAGAKU CHOSETSU.). [Shokubutsu no kagaku chosetsu]. **Added/Corp** Shokubutsu Kagaku Chosetsu Kenkyukai (Japan). **VFOAT** Chemical Regulation of Plants. (1966)-. Academic Scholarly Publication. Japanese. Two times a year. $46.00. Shokubutsu Kagaku Chosetsu Gakkai, (Soc. for Chemical Regulation of Plants), 26-6 Taito 1 Chome, Taitoku Tokyo 110 Japan. Documents available from CASDDS.
Ind/Abst Chem. Abstr.; Crop Physiol. Abstr.; Hortic. Abstr.; Ornamental Hort. (1991-); PESTDOC.

ISSN 0883-1475
DD 581 US

SIDA, BOTANICAL MISCELLANY. [SIDA bot. misc.]. **Added/Corp** Southern Methodist University. Herbarium. No. 1 & 2 (May 1987)-. Monographic series. English. Irregular. Price varies per volume. Botanical Research Institute of Texas, 509 Pecan Street, Fort Worth TX 76102. **Tel** (817)332-4441, FAX (817)332-4112. Index available. **Bk Rev. Circ:** 150.

LC QK1 .S15 **ISSN** 0036-1488
DD 580/.8 US
CODEN SCBTA4
Pr Rev.

SIDA, CONTRIBUTIONS TO BOTANY. [SIDA contrib. bot.]. **VFOAT** Contributions To Botany. Vol. 1 (1962)-. Periodical. English. Four times a year. $35.00. Botanical Research Institute of Texas, 509 Pecan Street, Fort Worth TX 76102. **Tel** (817)332-4441, FAX (817)332-4112. **ED** Barney Lipscomb. **Bk Rev. Circ:** 550. Documents available from BIOSIS Document Express.
Desc: Taxonomic botany and systematic botany.
Ind/Abst AGRICOLA [Full Cov.]; Biol. Abstr.; Life Sci. Collect.

LC QK725 .S56
KO
UDC 581.8

SINGMUL CHOJIK PAEYANG HAKHOE CHI. **VFOAT** Korean Journal of Plant Tissue. Periodical. Korean (summaries and/or abstracts in English). One time a year. $30.00. Korean Society of Plant Tissue Culture, c/o Agricultural Biotechnology Division, Agricultural Sciences Institute RDA, Suweon 440-707 Korea. **Tel** 011 82 331 29262, FAX 011 82 331 2926222. **ED** Chung Jae-Dong. **Ad Acc. Circ:** 700. ***Continues*** *Singmul Chojik Paeyang.*

LC QK370 .H35a **ISSN** 0583-421X
DD 581 KO
NLM W1 SI53K **CODEN** KJBOAI
Pr Rev. **TITLE CHANGE**

SINGMUL HAKHOE CHI. [Singmul hakhoe chi]. **Main/Corp** Hanguk Singmul Hakhoe. **VFOAT** Korean Journal of Botany. (1958)-(March 1994). Periodical. English (Korean). Botanical Society of Korea, Seoul National University, Department of Biology, Seoul 151-742 Korea. **Tel** 011 82 2 880 6676, FAX 011 82 872 6881. **ED** Kwang Woong Lee. Index available (bound in last issue). **Bk Rev. Ad Acc, Adv Mgr:** Young Myung Kwon. **Circ:** 700. ***Continues in part*** *Saengmul Hakhoe Po.* ***Continued by*** *Journal of Plant Biology.*

LC QK370 .S55
DD 581 KO

SINGMUL PULLYU HAKHOE CHI. **Added/Corp** Hanguk Singmul Pullyu Hakhoe. **VFOAT** Journal of Korean Plant Taxonomy. (19??)-. Periodical. English (Korean).
Ind/Abst Hortic. Abstr.; Plant Breed. Abstr.

LC S **ISSN** 0253-5211
DD 630 SZ
CODEN SSLADA

SLZ. SCHWEIZERISCHE LABORATORIUMS-ZEITSCHRIFT. **See** Agriculture.

LC QK1 .S2747 **ISSN** 0081-024X
DD 581/.05 US
CODEN SCBYAJ

SMITHSONIAN CONTRIBUTIONS TO BOTANY. [Smithson. contrib. bot.]. **Added/Corp** Smithsonian Institution. No. 1 (1969)-. Government Publication. English. Irregular. Superintendent of Documents, US Government Printing Office, Washington DC 20402. **Tel** (202)275-3328, FAX (202)786-2377. Documents available from BIOSIS Document Express.
Ind/Abst Biol. Abstr.; Curr. Aware. Biol. Sci., CABS; Life Sci. Collect.

LC QE701 .S56 **ISSN** 0081-0266
DD 560/.8 S US
CODEN SPBYA8

SMITHSONIAN CONTRIBUTIONS TO PALEOBIOLOGY. **See** Paleontology.

ISSN 0800-6865
NO
CCC

SOMMERFELTIA. (1985)-. Monographic series. English. Irregular. Price varies per volume. Sommerfeltia, Trondheimsveien 23B, N-0562 Oslo 5 Norway.

LC QK564 .S63 **ISSN** 0038-1578
DD 589 JA
CODEN JJPHDP
TITLE CHANGE

SORUI = THE BULLETIN OF JAPANESE SOCIETY OF PHYCOLOGY. [Sorui]. **Added/Corp** Nihon Sorui Gakkai. Nihon Sorui Gakkai. Bulletin. **VFOAT** Bulletin of the Japanese Society of Phycology; Japanese Journal of Phycology. Vol. 1 (Mar. 1953)-(19??). Bulletin. Japanese (English; summaries and/or abstracts in English). Nihon Sorui Gakkai, (Japanese Society of Phycology), Kyoto Daigaku Nogakubu Nettai, Nogaku Senko Kitashirakawa, Oiwakecho Sakyoku, Kyotoshi Kyotofu 606, Japan. **(Subscription address:** Japan Publications Trading Company Ltd., PO Box 5030, Tokyo International, Tokyo 100-31 Japan. **Tel** 011 81 3 3292 3753.**)** cum. index. Documents available from BIOSIS Document Express, CASDDS. ***Split into*** *Sorui Japanese Journal of Phycology* ***and*** *Phycological Research.*
Ind/Abst Aquat. Sci. Fish. Abstr. [CD-ROM Ed.]; Biol. Abstr.; Chem. Abstr.; Life Sci. Collect.

LC QK396 .S67 **ISSN** 0254-6299
DD 581.96 SA
CCC
CODEN SAJBDD

SOUTH AFRICAN JOURNAL OF BOTANY. (SOUTH AFRICAN JOURNAL OF BOTANY : OFFICIAL JOURNAL OF THE SOUTH AFRICAN ASSOCIATION OF BOTANISTS.). [S. Afr. j. bot.]. **Added/Corp** South African Association of Botanists. Foundation for Education, Science, and Technology (South Africa). Bureau for Scientific Publications. **VFOAT** Suid-Afrikaanse Tydskrif vir Plantkunde : Amptelike Tydskrif van die Suid-Afrikaanse Genootskap van Plantkundiges; Botany; Plantkunde; Suid-Afrikaanse Tydskrif vir Plantkunde. Vol. 1, No. 1/2 (1982)-. Academic Scholarly Publication. English (Afrikaans). Six times a year. $51.60. Foundation for Education Science & Technology, PO Box 1758, Pretoria 0001 South Africa. **Tel** 011 27 12 3226404, FAX 011 27 12 3207803. **ED** J. N. Eloff. Index available. **Bk Rev. Circ:** 1,100 (ctrl). Documents available from The Genuine Article, CASDDS. ***Absorbed*** *Journal of South African Botany, 0022-4618.*
Desc: Original research in any field of botany including taxonomic papers on flora of Southern Africa or adjacent islands.
Ind/Abst AGRICOLA [Full Cov.]; Agrofor. Abstr. (1991-); Biocont. News Inf.; Chem. Abstr. (1986-); Crop Physiol. Abstr.; Curr. Aware. Biol. Sci., CABS; Curr. Cit.; Curr. Contents Agric. Biol. Environ. Sci.; Ecol. Abstr.; Ecology Abstr.; EP Collect.; Field Crop Abstr.; For. Abstr.; Grass. Forage Abstr.; Homework Help.; Hortic. Abstr.; Irr. Drain. Abstr.; MasterFile FullTEXT 1000; MasterFile FullTEXT 350; MasterFile FullTEXT 650; MasterFile FullTEXT; Microbiol. Abstr. Sect. C; OCLC; Ornamental Hort. (19??-19??); Life Sci. Collect.; Plant Breed. Abstr.; Plant Genet. Resour. Abstr.; Plant Grow. Reg. Abstr.; Res. Alert [Select. Cov.]; Rev. Agric. Entomol.; Rev. Plant Pathol.; Rice Abstr.; Rural Dev. Abstr.; Soils Fert.; Soyabean Abstr.; Telebase; Weed Abstr.; World Agric. Econ. Rural Sociol. Abstr.

LC QK1 .F513 **ISSN** 0038-5719
DD 581 US
CCC
CODEN SOPPAA
Pr Rev. **TITLE CHANGE**

SOVIET PLANT PHYSIOLOGY. [Sov. plant physiol.]. **Added/Corp** American Institute of Biological Sciences. Consultants Bureau. Vol. 8, No. 3 (Nov. 1961)-(199?). Academic Scholarly Publication. English (translations available in Russian). MAIK Nauka / Interperiodica, Ulitsa Profsoyuznaia 90, Moscow 117864 Russia. **ED** A T Mokronosov. available on microfilm and microfiche from University Microfilms International (UMI). Documents available from The Genuine Article, BIOSIS Document Express, CASDDS. ***Continues*** *Fiziologiia Rastenii. English. Plant Physiology, 0097-384X.* ***Continued by*** *Russian Plant Physiology.*
Desc: English translation of Russian research of the Academy of Science of the USSR in biology and physiology of plants.
Ind/Abst AGRICOLA [Full Cov.]; Biol. Abstr. (-1984); Chem. Abstr.; Crop Physiol. Abstr.; Curr. Aware. Biol. Sci., CABS; Curr. Contents Agric. Biol. Environ. Sci.; EMBASE; Field Crop Abstr.; For. Abstr.; Grass. Forage Abstr.; Hortic. Abstr.; Irr. Drain. Abstr.; Maize Abstr.; Microbiol. Abstr. Sect. B (19??-19??); Microbiol. Abstr. Sect. A; Microbiol. Abstr. Sect. C; Ornamental Hort.; Plant Breed. Abstr.; Plant Grow. Reg. Abstr.; Potato Abstr.; Res. Alert [Full Cov.]; Rice Abstr.; Sci. Cit. Index; SCISEARCH; Seed Abstr.; Soils Fert.; Soyabean Abstr.; Weed Abstr.; Wheat Barley Trit. Abstr.

LC QR79 .S65 **ISSN** 0306-2074
DD 589/.04/165 UK

SPORE RESEARCH. [Spore res.]. (1971)-. Monographic series. English. Irregular. Price varies per volume. Academic Press Inc., 6277 Sea Harbor Drive, Orlando FL 32887. **Tel** (800)543-9534, (407)345-4100, FAX (407)352-3445. **ED** A. N. Barker, L. J. Wolf, D. J. Ellar, G. J. Dring and G. W. Golild.
Ind/Abst Life Sci. Collect.

LC QK **ISSN** 0211-9714
DD 581 SP
CODEN STBOEA

STUDIA BOTANICA. [Studia botanica]. **Added/Corp** Universidad de Salamanca. Universidad de Salamanca. Departamento de Botanica. (1982)-. Spanish (summaries and/or abstracts in English and Spanish). One time a year. 1200ptas. Ediciones Universidad de Salamanca, Apartado Postal 325, 37080 Salamanca Spain. **Tel** 011 34 23 294598, FAX 011 34 23 263046. Documents available from BIOSIS Document Express.
Ind/Abst Biol. Abstr. (1984-); Grass. Forage Abstr.; Weed Abstr.

LC QK311 .S86 **ISSN** 0301-7001
HU
CODEN SBHUBV

STUDIA BOTANICA HUNGARICA. [Stud. bot. Hung.]. **Added/Corp** Termeszettudomanyi Muzeum. (1973)-. Hungarian (English, German and French). One time a year. Termeszettudomanyi Muzeum Konyvtara, Baross U 13, 1088 Budapest Hungary. **Tel** 011 36 1 130035. Documents available from BIOSIS Document Express. ***Continues*** *Fragmenta Botanica Musei Historico-Naturalis Hungarici.*
Ind/Abst Biodeter. Abstr.; Biol. Abstr.; Life Sci. Collect.

LC QK281 .S88
DD 581.945 IT
UDC 581.9(45)

STUDIA GEOBOTANICA. Vol. 1, No. 1-. Periodical. English (German and Italian).
Ind/Abst Art Archaeol. Tech. Abstr.; Biodeter. Abstr. (1991-).

LC QK **ISSN** 0282-8677
DD 581 SW
CODEN SPLEE2

STUDIES IN PLANT ECOLOGY. [Stud. plant ecol.]. **Added/Corp** Svenska Vaextgeografiska Saellskapet. (1985)-. Monographic series. English (German and Swedish; summaries and/or abstracts in English, German and Swedish). Irregular. Price varies per volume. Opulus Press AB, PO Box 25 137, S-750 25 Uppsala Sweden. **Tel** 011 46 18320662, FAX 011 46 18321368. **ED** Erik Sjoegren. Documents available from BIOSIS Document Express. ***Continues** Vaextekologiska Studier, 0346-735X.*
Ind/Abst Biol. Abstr.; Curr. Adv. Ecol. Sci.

NE

STUDIES IN PLANT SCIENCE. (1991)-. Academic Scholarly Publication. English. Elsevier Science Publishers BV, PO Box 211, 1000 AE Amsterdam Netherlands. **Tel** 011 31 20 4853641, 011 31 20 4853642, FAX 011 31 20 4853598.

ISSN 0377-8169
RM
CODEN SCBVDD

STUDII SI CERCETARI DE BIOLOGIE. SERIA BIOLOGIE VEGETALA. [Stud. cercet. biol., Ser. biol. veg.]. **VFOAT** Seria Biologie Vegatala. Academic Scholarly Publication. Romanian (summaries and/or abstracts in English). Two times a year. **(Subscription address:** Ilexim Press Department, PO Box 1, 136-1-137, Bucharest, Romania. **Tel** 011 40 1 173836.**)** Documents available from BIOSIS Document Express, CASDDS. ***Continues in part** Studii Si Cercetari de Biologie.*
Ind/Abst Biocont. News Inf.; Biol. Abstr.; Chem. Abstr.; Crop Physiol. Abstr.; Maize Abstr.; Life Sci. Collect.; Sorghum Mill. Abstr.

ISSN 0039-4467
NE

SUCCULENTA. [Succulenta]. **Added/Corp** Nederlands - Belgische Vereniging van Liefhebbers van Cactussen en Andere Vetplanten. Nederlandsche Vereeniging van vetplantenverzamelaars. Vol. 1 (1919)-. Periodical. Dutch. Six times a year. $44.54. Succulenta, Clarionlaan 12, 2082 HZ Santpoort Netherlands. Index Available, published separately, free-automatically sent. **Ad Acc.** ctrl circ.
Desc: Contains information on cactus and succulent plants.
Ind/Abst AGRICOLA.

LC QK1 .S93 **ISSN** 0039-646X
DD 580.5 SW
CODEN SBOTAS

SVENSK BOTANISK TIDSKRIFT. [Sven. bot. tidskr.]. **Added/Corp** Svenska Botaniska Foreningen. Vol. 1 (1907)-. Periodical. Swedish (English). Six times a year. $69.72. Svensk Botanisk Tidskrift, The Botanical Museum, Oestra Vallgatan 18, S-223 61 Lund Sweden. **Tel** (011-46-46)108965. **ED** Thomas Karlsson. Index available. cum. index. **Bk Rev. Circ:** 2,800. Documents available from BIOSIS Document Express.
Ind/Abst AGRICOLA (-1987); Biol. Abstr.; Ecol. Abstr.; Ecology Abstr.; Geogr. Abstr. Phys. Geogr.; Geogr. Abstr. Human Geogr.; Microbiol. Abstr. Sect. C; Life Sci. Collect.; Plant Breed. Abstr.; Plant Genet. Resour. Abstr.

LC SB113 **ISSN** 0039-6990
DD 631.521 SW
UDC 63

SVERIGES UTSADESFORENINGS TIDSKRIFT. See Agriculture-Crop Production and Soils.

LC QK **ISSN** 0082-0644
DD 581 SW
UDC 58

SYMBOLAE BOTANICAE UPSALIENSIS. (SYMBOLAE BOTANICAE UPSALIENSES : ARBEITEN FRAN BOTANICAE UPSALIENSIS.). [Symb. bot. Ups.]. (1932)-. Monographic series. English (German and Swedish). Irregular. Price varies. Almqvist & Wiksell International, PO Box 4627, S-11691 Stockholm Sweden. **Tel** 011 46 8 6408800.
Ind/Abst Ecol. Abstr. (?-?); For. Abstr.

LC QK623.A1 S94 **ISSN** 0280-8331
DD 589.2/3/012 UK
CODEN SYASEI

SYSTEMA ASCOMYCETUM. [Syst. Ascomycetum]. **Added/Corp** C.A.B. International. Mycological Institute. Vol. 1 (Dec. 1982)-. English. Two times a year. $68.45. CAB International Centre, Wallingford, Oxfordshire OX10 8DE United Kingdom. **Tel** 011 44 1491 832111, FAX 011 44 1491 833508, telex 847964 COMAGG G. Documents available from BIOSIS Document Express.
Desc: Published in collaboration with the University of Umea. Tracks the changing taxonomy of the ascomycetes by publishing: an alphabetical list of generic names; notes on ascomycete systematics; an annual "outline of the ascomycetes"; lists of genera by families (including synonyms); an additional index to families and orders; original papers on ascomycete systematics.
Ind/Abst AGRICOLA; Bibliogr. Agric. (Sept. 27, 1990); Biol. Abstr. (1989-).

ISSN 1017-5598
IT
CODEN SESGEY

SYSTEMATIC AND ECOGEOGRAPHIC STUDIES ON CROP GENEPOOLS. [Syst. ecogeogr. stud. crop genepools]. **VFOAT** Systematic and Ecogeographic Studies of Crop Genepools. 1 (1985)-. Periodical. English. International Board for Plant Genetic Resources, Via Delle Sette Chiese 142, 00145 Rome Italy. Documents available from BIOSIS Document Express.
Ind/Abst Biol. Abstr.; Maize Abstr.

LC QK95 .S97 **ISSN** 0363-6445
DD 581/.01/2 US
CCC
Pr Rev.

SYSTEMATIC BOTANY. [Syst. botany]. **Added/Corp** American Society of Plant Taxonomists. Vol. 1 (Spring 1976)-. Periodical. English. Four times a year (Jan., Apr., July, Oct.). $90.00. American Society of Plant Taxonomists, Saint Mary's College, Biology Department, Notre Dame IN 46556. **Tel** (219)284-4674, FAX (219)284-4716. **ED** Dr. Gerald Gastory, (editor's address: Jordan Hall, Indiana University, Bloomington, Indiana 47405-6801, phone: (812)855-3333). Index available (bound in 4th issue, Oct.). **Bk Rev**, (Qty: 6-8). **Circ:** 1,650 (ctrl). Documents available from The Genuine Article, Documents on Demand.
Desc: Original articles pertinent to modern and traditional aspects of systematic botany, including theory as well as applications.
Ind/Abst AgBiotech News Inf.; AGRICOLA [Full Cov.]; Biol. Agric. Index; Curr. Aware. Biol. Sci., CABS; Curr. Cit.; Curr. Contents Agric. Biol. Environ. Sci.; Energy Inf. Abstr.; Environ. Abstr.; For. Abstr.; GeoRef; Grass. Forage Abstr.; Hortic. Abstr.; Maize Abstr.; Ornamental Hort. (1991-); Life Sci. Collect.; Plant Breed. Abstr.; Plant Genet. Resour. Abstr.; Potato Abstr.; Res. Alert [Full Cov.]; Rev. Plant Pathol.; Sci. Cit. Index; SCISEARCH; Sorghum Mill. Abstr.; Weed Abstr.

LC QK95 .S973 **ISSN** 0737-8211
DD 581/.012 US

SYSTEMATIC BOTANY MONOGRAPHS. (SYSTEMATIC BOTANY MONOGRAPHS : MONOGRAPHIC SERIES OF THE AMERICAN SOCIETY OF PLANT TAXONOMISTS.). [Syst. bot. monogr.]. **Added/Corp** American Society of Plant Taxonomists. Vol. 1 (1980)-. Monographic series. English. Irregular. Price varies per volume. American Society of Plant Taxonomists, Saint Mary's College, Biology Department, Notre Dame IN 46556. **Tel** (219)284-4674, FAX (219)284-4716.

ISSN 0372-333X
CH
CODEN TWNAAM

TAIWANIA. [Taiwania]. **Added/Corp** T'ai-wan ta Hsueh, T'ai-pei. Li Hsueh Yuan. Chih wu Hsueh hsi. Yen Chiu pao kao. **VFOAT** Kuo Li T'ai-Wan Ta Hsueh Li Hsueh Yuan Chih Wu Hsueh Hsi Yen Chiu Pao Kao. No. 1 (May 1948)-. Academic Scholarly Publication. English. One time a year. College of Science, National Taiwan University, Department of Botany, Taipei Taiwan. Documents available from CASDDS. ***Supersedes** Acta Botanica Taiwanica.*
Ind/Abst AGRICOLA; Agrofor. Abstr. (1991-); Biocont. News Inf. (1991-); Chem. Abstr.; For. Abstr.; Index Vet.; Life Sci. Collect.; Vet. Bull.

LC QK **ISSN** 0167-9406
DD 581 US
CODEN TUSCD8

TASKS FOR VEGETATION SCIENCE. [Tasks veg. sci.]. **VFOAT** Tasks for Vegetation Sciences; T:VS. (198?)-. Academic Scholarly Publication. English. Irregular. Price varies per volume. Kluwer Academic Publishers / Massachusetts, PO Box 358, Accord Station, Hingham MA 02018. **Tel** (617)871-6600. **(Subscription address:** Kluwer Academic Publishers / Netherlands, PO Box 322, 3300 AH Dordrecht Netherlands. **Tel** 011 31 78 392392, FAX 011 31 78 546474.**)** Documents available from BIOSIS Document Express, CASDDS.
Ind/Abst AGRICOLA [Full Cov.]; Biol. Abstr.; Chem. Abstr.

LC QK1 .T34 **ISSN** 0040-0262
GW
CODEN TAXNAP
Pr Rev.

TAXON. [Taxon]. **Added/Corp** International Association for Plant Taxonomy. Vol. 1 (Sept. 1951)-. Periodical. English (French and German). Four times a year (Feb., May, Aug., Nov.). $130.00. International Association for Plant Taxonomy, Koenigin Luise Strasse 6-8, 14191 Berlin Germany. **Tel** 011 49 30 8316010, FAX 011 49 30 83006218. **ED** F. A. Stafleu. cum. index. **Bk Rev. Ad Acc. Circ:** 2,000 (ctrl). Documents available from The Genuine Article, BIOSIS Document Express, CASDDS.
Desc: Devoted to systematic and evolutionary botany. The principal aim of the IAPT is to consider measures for the future development of plant taxonomy and plant geography and to organize the execution of such plans as require international cooperation.
Ind/Abst AgBiotech News Inf.; AGRICOLA [Full Cov.]; Biol. Agric. Index; Biol. Abstr.; Chem. Abstr.; Curr. Aware. Biol. Sci., CABS; Curr. Cit.; Curr. Contents Agric. Biol. Environ. Sci.; Ecol. Abstr.; For. Abstr.; Geogr. Abstr. Phys. Geogr.; Geol. Abstr.; GeoRef; Grass. Forage Abstr.; Ornamental Hort. (19??-19??); Life Sci. Collect.; Plant Breed. Abstr.; Plant Genet. Resour. Abstr.; Res. Alert [Full Cov.]; Sci. Cit. Index; SCISEARCH; Weed Abstr.

LC QK710 **ISSN** 0110-0610
DD 581.1 NZ

TECHNICAL REPORT / PLANT PHYSIOLOGY DIVISION. **Added/Corp** New Zealand. Dept. of Scientific and Industrial Research. Plant Physiology Division. (19??)-. Monographic series. English. DSIR, Botany Division, Private Bag, Christchurch New Zealand. **Tel** 252-511, FAX 252-074, telex NZ4703.
Ind/Abst Agrofor. Abstr.; For. Abstr.

LC QK **ISSN** 0250-0787
DD 581 SA

TERRESTRIAL ECOSYSTEMS NEWSLETTERS. **VFOAT** Landekosisteme Nuusbrief. No. 1 (Dec. 1978)-. Newsletter. English (Afrikaans). Twelve times a year. PO Box 395, Pretoria 0001 South Africa. **Tel** (012)841-4062, FAX (012)841-2018, telex 3-21287 SA.

ISSN 0157-9711
AT
CODEN TATMD5

TM. TROPICAL AGRONOMY TECHNICAL MEMORANDUM. (TROPICAL AGRONOMY TECHNICAL MEMORANDUM.). [TM, Trop. agron. tech. memo.]. **Added/Corp** Commonwealth Scientific and Industrial Research Organization (Australia). Division of Tropical Crops and Pastures. **VFOAT** TM; T.M. No. 1 (Sept. 1976)-. Academic Scholarly Publication. English. Irregular. Price varies per volume. CSIRO Publications, PO Box 89, 314 Albert Street, East Melborne Victoria 3002 Australia. **Tel** 011 61 3 4187333, 4187217, FAX 011 61 3 4190459, telex AA 30236. Documents available from BIOSIS Document Express, CASDDS.
Ind/Abst Biol. Abstr.; Chem. Abstr. (1977-1983); Geogr. Abstr. Phys. Geogr.; Life Sci. Collect.; Plant Breed. Abstr.; Soyabean Abstr.

ISSN 0378-6099
NE
CODEN TOPHDY
Pr Rev.

TOPICS IN PHOTOSYNTHESIS. [Top. photosynth.]. Vol. 1 (1976)-. Monographic series. English. Irregular. Price varies per volume. Elsevier Science Publishers BV, PO Box 211, 1000 AE Amsterdam Netherlands. **Tel** 011 31 20 4853641, 011 31 20 4853642, FAX 011 31 20 4853598. **(Subscription address:** Elsevier Science Inc. / New York Books, 655 Avenue of the Americas, New York NY 10010. **Tel** (212)633-3650.**)** **ED** J. Barber. Documents available from CASDDS.
Ind/Abst Chem. Abstr.

ISSN 0075-9708
US
UDC 58

TRANSACTIONS OF THE LINNAEAN SOCIETY OF NEW YORK. **Main/Corp** Linnaean Society of New York. Vol. 1-. English. Irregular. The Linnaean Society of New York, 15 West 77th Street, New York NY 10024.

ISSN 0829-318X
DD 582.16/01/05 CN
CCC
CODEN TRPHEM
Pr Rev.

TREE PHYSIOLOGY. See Forests and Forestry.

LC QK **ISSN** 1360-1385
DD 581 UK

●**TRENDS IN PLANT SCIENCE.** (1996)-. Academic Scholarly Publication. English. Twelve times a year. $614.00. Elsevier Applied Science, An Imprint of Elsevier Science Ltd., The Boulevard, Langford Lane, Kidlington, Oxford OX5 1GB United Kingdom. **Tel** 011 44 1865 843000, 011 44 1865 843699, FAX 011 44 1865 843010. **(Subscription address:** Elsevier Science Ltd., PO Box 7247, Philadelphia PA 19170. **)** **Ad Acc.** available on an online database from Elsevier Electronic Subscriptions (EES).

LC QK463 .N43A **ISSN** 0548-9547
DD 581.9/931 NZ

TRIENNIAL REPORT - BOTANY DIVISION, DEPARTMENT OF SCIENTIFIC AND INDUSTRIAL RESEARCH. (TRIENNIAL REPORT - BOTANY DIVISION.). [Trienn. rep. - Bot. Div. Dep. Sci. Ind. Res.]. **Main/Corp** New Zealand. Botany Division. **VFOAT** Triennial Report of Botany Division. (1957/1959)-. English. Every 3 years. DSIR, Botany Division, Private Bag, Christchurch New Zealand. **Tel** 252-511, FAX 252-074, telex NZ4703. **Circ:** 750 (ctrl).
Desc: Reports and outlines the progress of research in specialist disciplines including taxonomy, plant ecology,

palynology, quaternary history of New Zealand vegetation, cytology, plant structure and biology, and ecophysiology.

ISSN 0935-5626
GW

TROPICAL BRYOLOGY. No. 1- (1989)-. Periodical. English. Irregular. University of Duisburg, Postfach 101 503, Fachbereich 6, W-4100 Duisburg Germany. available on diskette ((5 1/4", 360K), or ASCII-file).

LC QK **ISSN** 0372-0586
DD 581 RU

TRUDY PO PRIKLADNOJ BOTANIKE. GENETIKE I SELEKCII. (SBORNIK NAUCHNYKH TRUDOV PO PRIKLADNOI BOTANIKE, GENETIKE I SELEKTSII.). [Tr. prikl. bot., genet. sel.]. **Added/Corp** Vsesoiuznaia Akademiia Selskokhoziaistvennykh Nauk Imeni V.I. Lenina. Vsesoiuznyi Nauchno-Issledovatelskii Institut Rastenievodstva Imeni N.I. Vavilova. **VFOAT** Bulletin of Applied Botany, Genetics and Plant Breeding. (1984)-. Monographic series. Russian (summaries and/or abstracts in English; table of contents in English). Irregular. Price varies per volume. ***Continues*** *Trudy po Prikladnoi Botanike, Genetike i Selektsii, 0372-0586.*
Ind/Abst Cot. Trop. Fibr. Abstr. Bibliogr.; Crop Physiol. Abstr.; Field Crop Abstr.; Hortic. Abstr.; Nematol. Abstr.; Ornamental Hort. (1991-); Plant Breed. Abstr.; Plant Genet. Resour. Abstr.; Plant Grow. Reg. Abstr.; Postharvest News Inf.; Potato Abstr.; Rev. Agric. Entomol.; Rev. Plant Pathol.; Seed Abstr.; Soyabean Abstr.; Wheat Barley Trit. Abstr.

LC QK1 .T84 **ISSN** 0289-3568
DD 581/.05 JA

TSUKUBA JIKKEN SHOKUBUTSUEN KENKYU HOKOKU = ANNALS OF THE TSUKUBA BOTANICAL GARDEN.
Added/Corp Kokuritsu Kagaku Hakubutsukan (Japan). Tsukuba Jikken Shokubutsuen. **VFOAT** Annals of the Tsukuba Botanical Garden. No. 1 (1983)-. Periodical. English (Japanese). Irregular. Tsukuba Botanical Garden, National Science Museum, Ministry of Education, 1-1 Amakubo 4-chome, Tsukubashi Ibarakiken 305 Japan.

LC QL1 .T94 **ISSN** 0082-6782
DD 574/.05 US
CODEN TSZBAN
Pr Rev.

TULANE STUDIES IN ZOOLOGY AND BOTANY. [Tulanne stud. zool. bot.]. **Added/Corp** Tulane University. Dept. of Biology. Vol. 15, No. 1 (Oct. 16, 1968)-. Periodical. English. Two times a year. $8.00. Tulane University / Department of Ecological Evolution Organic Biology, New Orleans LA 70118. **Tel** (504)865-5191. **ED** Steven P. Darwin. Index available. **Circ:** 600. Documents available from BIOSIS Document Express. ***Continues*** *Tulane Studies in Zoology, 0090-9246.*
Desc: Ecology and taxonomy of plants and animals.
Ind/Abst Biol. Abstr.; Fish Rev.; Life Sci. Collect.; Wildl. Rev.

UN
CODEN UKBZAW

UKRAINSKII BOTANICHNII ZHURNAL. [Ukr. bot. z.]. **Main/Corp** Akadamiia Nauk URSR, Kiev. Botanichna Sektsiia. **VFOAT** Ukrainian Botanical Review. (1922)-. Periodical. Russian. Six times a year. $109.95. **(Subscription address:** East View Publications Inc., 3020 Harbor Lane North, Suite 110, Minneapolis MN 55447. **Tel** (800)477-1005, (612)550-0961, FAX (612)559-2931.) Documents available from CASDDS.
Ind/Abst Chem. Abstr.; Crop Physiol. Abstr.; For. Abstr.; Hortic. Abstr. (?-?); Plant Breed. Abstr.; Plant Genet. Resour. Abstr.; Plant Grow. Reg. Abstr.; Rice Abstr.; Seed Abstr.; Soils Fert.; Wheat Barley Trit. Abstr.

LC QK **ISSN** 0372-4123
DD 581 UN

UKRAINSKYI BOTANICHNYI ZHURNAL. **Added/Corp** Instytut Botaniky (Akademiia nauk Ukrainskoi RSR. **VFOAT** Journal Botanique de l'Academie des Sciences de la RSS d'Ukraine. No. 1 (1956)-. Academic Scholarly Publication. Ukrainian (Russian; summaries and/or abstracts in English and German). Six times a year. Izdatelstvo Naukova Dumka / Ukrainian Academy of Sciences, Yu. A. Khramov, Dir., Ul. Repina 3, 252 601 Kiev Ukraine. **Tel** 011 7 44 4303441, 011 7 44 2254182, telex 131376. Documents available from CASDDS. ***Continues*** *Botanichnyi Zhurnal.*
Ind/Abst AGRICOLA; Chem. Abstr.; Ornamental Hort. (1991-); Life Sci. Collect.

ISSN 0041-6118
UN
CODEN UKBZAW

UKRAINSKYI BOTANICHNYI ZHURNAL. **Added/Corp** Istytut Botaniky (Akademiia Nauk Ukrinskoi RSR). **VFOAT** Journal Botanique de l'Academie des Sciences de la RSS d'Ukraine. Vol. 1 (1940)-. Periodical. Russian (Ukrainian; summaries and/or abstracts in English and German). Six times a year. $499.95. Izdatelstvo Naukova Dumka / Ukrainian Academy of Sciences, Yu. A. Khramov, Dir., Ul. Repina 3, 252 601 Kiev Ukraine. **Tel** 011 7 44 4303441, 011 7 44 2254182, telex 131376. **(Subscription address:** East View Publications Inc., 3020 Harbor Lane North, Suite 110, Minneapolis MN 55447. **Tel** (800)477-1005, (612)550-0961, FAX (612)559-2931.) Documents available from CASDDS. ***Supersedes*** *Zhurnal Institutu Botaniki A.N U.S.S.R.*
Ind/Abst Chem. Abstr.; Life Sci. Collect.

LC QK1 .C2 **ISSN** 0068-6395
DD 580/.5 US
CODEN UCPBA8

UNIVERSITY OF CALIFORNIA PUBLICATIONS IN BOTANY. [Univ. Calif. publ. bot.]. **Main/Corp** University of California, Berkeley. **Added/Corp** University of California, Berkeley. Publications in Botany. **VFOAT** Publications in Botany. (1902)-. Monographic series. English. Irregular. Price varies per volume. Regents University of California Press, 2120 Berkeley Way, Berkeley CA 94720. **Tel** (510)642-4191. ctrl circ. Documents available from BIOSIS Document Express.
Ind/Abst Biol. Abstr.; Life Sci. Collect.

UK

USEFUL PLANTS OF WEST TROPICAL AFRICA, THE. English. University Press of Virginia, PO Box 3608, Charlottesville VA 22903. **Tel** (804)924-3469.

ISSN 0843-3461
DD 580/.74/471133 CN

VAN DUSEN BOTANICAL GARDEN BULLETIN. [Van Dusen Bot. Gard. bull.]. (Jan. 1988)-. Bulletin. English. Four times a year. Vancouver Botanical Garden Association, 5251 Oak Street, Vancouver British Columbia V6M 4H1 Canada. ***Continues*** *Bulletin (Vancouver Botanical Gardens Association), 0710-9660.*

LC QK **ISSN** 0347-3236
DD 581 SW
CODEN VAJODHVAJODR
CEASED

VAXTSKYDDSRAPPORTER. JORDBRUK. **Main/Corp** Sveriges Lantbruksuniversitet. Institutionen for Vaxt- Och Skogsskydd. Konsulentavdelningen/Vaxtskydd. (1978)-(1993). Monographic series. Swedish (English). Documents available from CASDDS. ***Continues*** *Vaxtskyddsrapporter. Jordbruk, 0347-3236.*
Ind/Abst Biocont. News Inf.; Chem. Abstr.; For. Abstr.; Nematol. Abstr.; Potato Abstr.; Rev. Agric. Entomol.; Rev. Plant Pathol.; Soils Fert.

ISSN 0506-449X
XR

VEGETACE CSSR. REIHE A. **Added/Corp** Ceskoslovenska Akademie Ved. (1965)-. Periodical. Czech (English and German). Irregular. Academia, Publishing House of the Czechoslovak Academy of Sciences, Vodickova 40, PO Box 896, 112 29 Prague 1, Czech Republic. **Tel** 011 42 2 245117. **ED** S. Hejny, R. Neuhausl. **Circ:** 500.
Desc: Monographic studies on vegetation structure, dynamics ecology and functions. Modelling of processes, over regional surveys of plant communities, synthetic results of vegetation mapping.

LC QK901 .V3 **ISSN** 0042-3106
DD 581.5/05 NE
CCC
CODEN VGTOA4
Pr Rev.

VEGETATIO. [Vegetatio]. **Added/Corp** International Society for Vegetation Science. International Society for Plant Geography and Ecology. International Society of Vegetation Science. (July 1948)-. Periodical. English (French, German, Italian and Spanish; summaries and/or abstracts in French, German and Spanish). Twelve times a year. $1833.00. Kluwer Academic Publishers, Postbus 322, 3300 AH Dordrecht The Netherlands. **Tel** 011 31 78 524400, FAX 011 31 78 183273, telex 20083. **ED** D.C. Glenn-Lewin, A. Miyawaki, and M.J.A. Werger. Index Available, published separately, free-automatically sent. **Bk Rev. Ad Acc. Acid Free. Circ:** 700. available on microfilm and microfiche from University Microfilms International (UMI). Documents available from The Genuine Article, BIOSIS Document Express.
Desc: Publishes articles in the field of geobotany, in particular contributions to the synthesis of methods and theories from the major approaches in vegetation science. Also publishes book reviews and notices of scientific meetings.
Ind/Abst AGRICOLA; Biol. Abstr.; Br. Archaeol. Bibliogr. (?-19??); Coal Abstr.; Crop Physiol. Abstr.; Curr. Aware. Biol. Sci., CABS; Curr. Cit.; Curr. Contents Agric. Biol. Environ. Sci.; Curr. Geogr. Publ. (199?-); Ecol. Abstr.; Ecology Abstr.; Geogr. Abstr. Phys. Geogr.; Geogr. Abstr. Human Geogr.; Geol. Abstr.; Grass. Forage Abstr.; Int. Dev. Abstr.; Life Sci. Collect.; Plant Breed. Abstr.; Plant Genet. Resour. Abstr.; Res. Alert [Full Cov.]; Sci. Cit. Index; SCISEARCH; Seed Abstr.; Wildl. Rev.

ISSN 0939-6314
GW
UDC 561 **CCC**

VEGETATION HISTORY AND ARCHAEOBOTANY. [Veg. hist. archaeobot.]. (1992)-. Periodical. English. Four times a year. $235.00. Springer-Verlag GmbH & Company KG, Heidelberger Platz 3, D-14197 Berlin Germany. **Tel** 011 49 30 8207223, FAX 011 49 30 8214091, telex 183 319 SPBLN D. **(Subscription address:** Springer-Verlag New York Inc. / North America, PO Box 2485, Journal Fulfillment, Secaucus NJ 07096. **Tel** (201)348-4033, (800)777-4643, FAX (201)348-4505.) available on microfilm and microfiche from University Microfilms International (UMI).
Desc: Covers the entire field of vegetation history, mainly the development of flora and vegetation during the Holocene (but also from the Pleistocene), and including related subjects such as palaeoecology.

LC WMLC L 83/5553 **ISSN** 0589-3747
DD 581 US

VEGETATION OF CONNECTICUT NATURAL AREAS, THE. **Added/Corp** State Geological and Natural History Survey of Connecticut. No. 1 (1965)-. Monographic series. English. Price varies per volume. Natural Resource Center / Publications and Sales, 165 Capitol Avenue, Room 555, Hartford CT 06106. **Tel** (203)566-7719.

LC QK **ISSN** 0042-3203
DD 581 SA

VELD & FLORA. [Veld flora]. **Added/Corp** Botanical Society of South Africa. Vol. 61 (June 1975)-. Periodical. Multiple languages (Afrikaans and English). Four times a year. $8.41. Botanical Soc South Africa, Kirstenbosch, Claremont 7735 South Africa. **Tel** 011 27 7972090, FAX 011 27 7972376. **ED** C. Voget. Index available (Free - publ. every five years). **Bk Rev. Ad Acc. Circ:** 14,500. ***Continues*** *Journal of the Botanical Society of South Africa, 0068-0419;* ***Absorbed*** *Veld & Flora, 0042-3203.*
Ind/Abst AGRICOLA (19??-); Garden Lit. (1992-); Hortic. Abstr. (19??-); Ornamental Hort. (1991-); Life Sci. Collect. (19??-); Rev. Plant Pathol. (19??-).

LC QK **ISSN** 0254-9433
DD 581 SW
CODEN VGRZAR

VEROFFENTLICHUNGEN DES GEOBOTANISCHEN INSTITUTS DER ETH, STIFTUNG RUBEL, ZURICH. [Veroff. Geobot. Inst. ETH, Stift. Rubel, Zurich]. **Added/Corp** Geobotanisches Institut der ETH, Stiftung Rubel, Zurich. **VFOAT** Veroffentlichungen des Geobotanischen Instituts der E.T.H., Stiftung Rubel, Zurich. Heft 39 (1967)-. Academic Scholarly Publication. German (English). Irregular. Price varies per volume. Geobotanisches Institute ETH Zurich, Stiftung Ruebel Zuerichberg 38, CH-8092 Zurich Switzerland. **Tel** 011 41 1 2563877. Documents available from BIOSIS Document Express. ***Continues*** *Veroffentlichungen des Geobotanischen Institutes der Eidg. Techn. Hochschule, Stiftung Rubel, in Zurich, 0254-9433.*
Ind/Abst Biol. Abstr. (19??-); EMBASE (19??-); Grass. Forage Abstr. (19??-); Irr. Drain. Abstr. (19??-); Life Sci. Collect. (19??-); Plant Genet. Resour. Abstr. (19??-); Seed Abstr. 919??-).

ISSN 0169-8346
NE
UDC 632

VERSLAGEN EN MEDEDEELINGEN VAN DE PLANTENZIEKTENKUNDIGE DIENST, WAGENINGEN. [Versl. meded. Plantenziektenkd. Dienst Wageningen]. **VFOAT** Verslagen en Mededelingen - Plantenziektenkundige Dienst, Wageningen. (1916)-. Monographic series. Dutch. Irregular.
Ind/Abst Rev. Plant Pathol.

LC QL235 .V53 **ISSN** 0889-3284
DD 574.98/05 CR
CODEN VSNEEW
Pr Rev.

VIDA SILVESTRE NEOTROPICAL. **See** Zoology.

LC QH132.C3 V55 **ISSN** 0210-945X
DD 508.64/9 SP

VIERAEA. **See** Natural History.

ISSN 0378-9454
II

VISTAS IN PLANT SCIENCES. [Vistas plant sci.]. (1975)-. Monographic series. English. One time a year. Price varies per volume. Today and Tomorrow's Printers and Publishers, 24-B/5 Desh Bandhu Gupta Road, Karol Bagh, New Delhi 110 005 India. **Tel** 011 91 11 5721928, 011 91 11 572770, FAX 011 91 11 7210073 (TTPP). **ED** T. M. Varghese.
Desc: Contains original articles from Indian workers on viruses, plant morphology, embryology, ecology, plant breeding and biometrics.

LC QK321 .V667
RU
VOPROSY BOTANIKI IUGO-VOSTOKA. **Added/Corp** Russian S.F.S.R. Ministerstvo Vysshego i Srednego Spetsialnogo Obrazovaniia. Saratovskii Gosudarstvennyi Universitet Im. N.G. Chernyshevskogo. Vol. 1 (1975)-. Periodical. Russian. Saratov N.G. Chernyshevskii State University, Astrakhanskaya Ulitsa 83, 410071 Saratov Russia. **Tel** 011 7 241696, FAX 011 7 240446, telex 241125.

ISSN 0723-7812
GW
VORTRAGE FUER PFLANZENZUCHTUNG. [Vortr. Pflanzenzucht.]. **Added/Corp** Gesellschaft fur Pflanzenbauwissenschaften (Germany). Arbeitsgemeinschaft Pflanzenzuchtung. **VFOAT** Vortrage Pflanzenzuchtung. (1982)-. Monographic series. German.
Ind/Abst For. Abstr.; Maize Abstr.; Rev. Agric. Entomol.; Soyabean Abstr.

LC Z5351
DD 016.581
NE
CEASED
WATER-IN-PLANTS BIBLIOGRAPHY. See Biology-Abstracting, Bibliographies and Statistics.

LC QK **ISSN** 0043-1532
DD 581 UK
WATSONIA. [Watsonia]. **Added/Corp** Botanical Society of the British Isles. Vol. 1 (1949)-. Periodical. English. Two times a year. $47.06. Botanical Society of the British Isle, 68 Outwoods Road, Loughborough LE11 3LY United Kingdom. **Tel** 011 44 1509 215598. ***Absorbed*** *Botanical Society of the British Isles. Proceedings of the Botanical Society of the British Isles.*
Ind/Abst AGRICOLA [Select. Cov.]; Curr. Aware. Biol. Sci., CABS; Curr. Cit.; Grass. Forage Abstr.; Hortic. Abstr.; Ornamental Hort. (1991-); Life Sci. Collect.; Plant Breed. Abstr.; Plant Genet. Resour. Abstr.; Weed Abstr.

LC QK **ISSN** 0083-7792
DD 581 IT
CODEN WBIAAJ
Pr Rev.
WEBBIA. [Webbia]. **Added/Corp** Universita di Firenze. Istituto Botanico. (1905)-. English (Italian). Two times a year. L170310. Museo Botanico Universita Firenze, Via G La Pira 4, 50121 Florence Italy. **Tel** 011 39 55 2757472, FAX 011 39 55 2757373. **ED** Guido Moggi. Index available. **Bk Rev**, (Qty: 2-4). **Circ:** 250. Documents available from BIOSIS Document Express.
Desc: Covers plant taxonomy, plant geography and ecology, and environment.
Ind/Abst Biol. Abstr.; Curr. Aware. Biol. Sci., CABS; Curr. Cit.; Ecol. Abstr.; Grass. Forage Abstr.; Life Sci. Collect.; Plant Breed. Abstr.; Plant Genet. Resour. Abstr.; Refer. Z.; Rev. Med. Vet. Entomol.; Seed Abstr.

LC SB611 .W37 **ISSN** 0043-1737
DD 632.5 UK
CCC
CODEN WEREAT
Pr Rev.
WEED RESEARCH. [Weed res.]. **Added/Corp** European Weed Research Society. European Weed Research Council. Vol. 1 (Mar 1961)-. Academic Scholarly Publication. English (French and German). Six times a year. $308.00. Blackwell Scientific Publications Ltd, Marston Book Services, PO Box 88, Oxford OX2 ONE United Kingdom. **Tel** 011 44 1865 206206, FAX 011 44 1865 206219, telex 837 515 MARDIS G. **ED** R. J. Hance. Index available (bound in last issue). **Ad Acc. Circ:** 1,600. available on microfilm and microfiche from University Microfilms International (UMI). Documents available from The Genuine Article, BIOSIS Document Express, CASDDS.
Desc: Study of weeds, their control and related topics.
Ind/Abst AGRICOLA [Full Cov.]; Agrofor. Abstr. (19??-19??); BioBusiness; Biocont. News Inf.; Biol. Agric. Index; Biol. Abstr.; Chem. Abstr.; Crop Physiol. Abstr.; Curr. Aware. Biol. Sci., CABS; Curr. Cit.; Curr. Contents Agric. Biol. Environ. Sci.; Ecol. Abstr.; Ecology Abstr.; EMBASE; Environ. Period. Bibliogr.; Field Crop Abstr.; Fresh. Aqua. Contents Tables; Hortic. Abstr.; Maize Abstr.; Nematol. Abstr.; Nutr. Abstr. Rev., Ser. B, Live Feeds and Feed.; Life Sci. Collect.; PESTDOC; Plant Grow. Reg. Abstr.; Potato Abstr.; Res. Alert [Full Cov.]; Rev. Agric. Entomol.; Rice Abstr.; Sci. Cit. Index; SCISEARCH; Seed Abstr.; Soils Fert.; Sorghum Mill. Abstr.; Weed Abstr.

ISSN 1358-6912
UK
●**WEEDS WORLD.** [Weeds world]. (1994)-. Periodical. English. Three times a year. Free. Nottingham Arabidopsis Stock Centre, Department of Life Science, Nottingham NG7 2RD United Kingdom. **Tel** 011 44 115 9791216. available via Internet (http://probe.nalusda.gov:8300/ww/home.html).

LC QK77.W48 W49B
DD 354/.941/00855 AT
UDC 58.082.5(047.31)(941)
WESTERN AUSTRALIAN HERBARIUM ANNUAL REPORT. Main/Corp Western Australian Herbarium. (19??)-. English. Irregular. Free. Western Australia Department of Agriculture / South Perth, Information Branch / Baron-Hay Court, South Perth Western Australia 6151 Australia. **Tel** 011 61 9 3683231, FAX 011 61 9 4742018, telex AA 93304. **Circ:** 70 (ctrl).

LC QK **ISSN** 0043-5090
DD 581 PL
CODEN WIBOA7
WIADOMOSCI BOTANICZNE. [Wiad. bot.]. **Added/Corp** Instytut Botaniki im. Wadysawa Szafera PAN. Polskie Towarzystwo Botaniczne. **VFOAT** Botanical News. Vol. 1 (1957)-. Academic Scholarly Publication. Polish (summaries and/or abstracts in English). Four times a year. $32.00. **(Subscription address:** Ars Polona-Ruch, PO Box 1001, Krakowskie Przedmiescie 7, 00-068 Warsaw Poland. **Tel** 011 48 22 261201.) Documents available from CASDDS.
Ind/Abst Chem. Abstr.; Life Sci. Collect.

LC QK1 .W57 **ISSN** 0511-9618
DD 580/.5 GW
WILLDENOWIA. [Willdenowia]. **Added/Corp** Botanischer Garten und Botanischer Museum (Berlin, Germany) Botanischer Garten und Museum (Berlin, Germany). Vol. 1, No. 2 (Nov. 1954)-. Periodical. German (English and French). Two times a year (June & Dec.). DM120.00. Botanischer Garten u Botanisches Museum, Biblio Koenigin Luise Strabe 6-8, D-14195 Berlin Germany. **Tel** 011 49 30 8314041, telex 183 798 SEN D. **ED** H. W. Lack. Index available. **Bk Rev. Circ:** 800. ***Continues*** *Mitteilungen aus dem Botanischen Garden und Museum.*
Desc: Plant taxonomy floristics.
Ind/Abst AGRICOLA; Ecol. Abstr.; Hortic. Abstr.; Ornamental Hort. (1991-); Life Sci. Collect.; Plant Breed. Abstr.

ISSN 0419-0041
GW
UDC 582.28(063)
WISSENSCHAFTLICHE TAGUNG; VORTRAGE. Main/Corp Deutschsprachige Mykologische Gesellschaft. Vol. 1 (1961)-. Periodical. German. Springer-Verlag GmbH & Company KG, Heidelberger Platz 3, D-14197 Berlin Germany. **Tel** 011 49 30 8207223, FAX 011 49 30 8214091, telex 183 319 SPBLN D. **(Subscription address:** Springer-Verlag New York Inc. / North America, PO Box 2485, Journal Fulfillment, Secaucus NJ 07096. **Tel** (201)348-4033, (800)777-4643, FAX (201)348-4505.)

LC QK658 .W65 **ISSN** 0346-4601
DD 581.4/6 SW
CCC
CODEN WPSFAC
WORLD POLLEN AND SPORE FLORA. [World pollen spore flora]. **Added/Corp** Scandinavian Palynological Collegium. (1973)-. Periodical. English. Irregular. Price varies; (Issues 1-16 priced at Kr75.00, $12.00; per issue; Issues 17 and 18 priced at Kr150.00, $23.00 per issue). Scandinavian University Press, PO Box 2959 Toeyen, N 0608 Oslo 6 Norway. **Tel** 011 47 2 2575400, FAX 011 47 2 2575353, telex 71896 UROR N. **(Subscription address:** Scandinavian University Press, 200 Meacham Ave., Elmont NY 11003. **Tel** (516)352-7300, FAX (516)352-7377.) **ED** Siwert Nilsson. Documents available from BIOSIS Document Express.
Desc: Serial containing general descriptions of pollen and spores in different plant families of spermatophytes, pteridophytes and fungi. Large plant families may be divided into suitable smaller taxonomic units.
Ind/Abst AGRICOLA; Biol. Abstr.; GeoRef; Life Sci. Collect.

LC QK1 .Y85 **ISSN** 0253-2700
DD 581/.05 CC
CODEN YCWCDP
YUNNAN ZHIWU YANJIU. (YUN-NAN CHIH WU YEN CHIU.). [Yunnan zhiwu yanjiu]. **Added/Corp** Chung-kuo ko Hsueh Yuan. Kun-ming Chih wu Yen Chiu so. **VFOAT** Yun Nan Zhi Wu Yan Jiu; Acta Botanica Yunnanica. (1979)-. Academic Scholarly Publication. Chinese (summaries and/or abstracts in English). Four times a year. Kunming Institute of Botany, Academia Sinica, Heilongtan Kunming, 650204 Yunnan People's Republic of China. **Tel** 0871-5150660, FAX 0871-5150227. **(Subscription address:** China International Book Trading Corporation, PO Box 399, Library Service Department, Beijing 100044 People's Republic of China. **Tel** 011 86 1 8414284, FAX 011 86 1 8412023, telex 22496 CIBTC CN.) **ED** Wu Zhengyi. Documents available from BIOSIS Document Express, CASDDS, BLDSC, CASDDS.
Desc: Contains information on the various fields of botany.
Ind/Abst Biol. Abstr.; Chem. Abstr.; Crop Physiol. Abstr.; For. Abstr.; Hortic. Abstr.; NAPRALERT; Ornamental Hort. (1991-); Rice Abstr.; Soils Fert.

ISSN 0044-1864
RU
ZASHCHITA RASTENII. Added/Corp Soviet Union. Ministerstvo Selskogo Khoziaistva. **VFOAT** Plant Protection. (Mar./Apr. 1956)-. Periodical. Russian. Twelve times a year. $119.95. **(Subscription address:** East View Publications Inc., 3020 Harbor Lane North, Suite 110, Minneapolis MN 55447. **Tel** (800)477-1005, (612)550-0961, FAX (612)559-2931.) Index available.
Ind/Abst AGRICOLA; Agric. Eng. Abstr. (1991-); Biodeter. Abstr. (1991-); Cot. Trop. Fibr. Abstr. Bibliogr.; Field Crop Abstr.; For. Abstr.; Maize Abstr.; Nematol. Abstr.; Ornamental Hort. (1991-); Plant Breed. Abstr.; Plant Grow. Reg. Abstr.; Postharvest News Inf.; Protozoolog. Abstr.; Rev. Plant Pathol.; Rice Abstr.; Seed Abstr.; Soils Fert.; Sorghum Mill. Abstr.; Soyabean Abstr.

ISSN 0372-798X
JA
CODEN ZASKAN
ZASSO KENKYU. [Zasso kenkyu]. **Added/Corp** Nihon Zasso Bojo Kenkyukai. **VFOAT** Weed Research. (1962)-. Academic Scholarly Publication. Japanese. Four times a year. $75.02. Nihon Zasso Bojo Kenkyukai / Weed Science Society of Japan, Shokucho Building 26-6, Taito 1-chome, Taito-ku Taito 110 Japan. Documents available from CASDDS.
Ind/Abst Chem. Abstr.; Hortic. Abstr.; PESTDOC; Plant Grow. Reg. Abstr.; Seed Abstr.; Soyabean Abstr.

ISSN 0514-5872
YU
CODEN ZABIAY
ZASTITA BILJA. [Zast. bilja]. **VFOAT** Plant Protection. Vol. 1 (1950)-. Academic Scholarly Publication. Serbo-Croatian (Cyrillic) (summaries and/or abstracts in English). Irregular. Price varies per volume. Institute for Plant Protection, Teodora Draiera 9, POB 936, 11001 Belgrad Yugoslavia. **Tel** 660 049. Documents available from BIOSIS Document Express, CASDDS.
Ind/Abst AGRICOLA; Biocont. News Inf. (1991-); Biodeter. Abstr. (1991-); Biol. Abstr.; Chem. Abstr.; EMBASE; For. Prod. Abstr. (1991-); For. Abstr.; Nematol. Abstr.; Plant Breed. Abstr.; Postharvest News Inf.; Potato Abstr.; Protozoolog. Abstr.; Rev. Agric. Entomol.; Seed Abstr.; Soils Fert.; Soyabean Abstr.; Weed Abstr.; Wheat Barley Trit. Abstr.

LC QK867 .Z43 **ISSN** 0044-3263
DD 581.1334 GW
CCC
CODEN ZPBOAL
Pr Rev.
ZEITSCHRIFT FUER PFLANZENERHAHRUNG UND BODENKUNDE. [Z. Pflanzenernahr. Bodenkd.]. **Added/Corp** Deutsche Bodenkundliche Gesellschaft. Deutsche Gesellschaft fuer Pflanzenernahrung. **VFOAT** Journal of Plant Nutrition and Soil Science. (1967)-. Academic Scholarly Publication. German (summaries and/or abstracts in English). Six times a year. $332.00. VCH Gesellschaft GmbH, Postfach 101161, D-69451 Weinheim Germany. **Tel** 011 49 6201 606459, FAX 011 49 6201 606184. **(Subscription address:** VCH Publishers Inc., 303 Northwest 12th Avenue, Journals Department, Deerfield FL 33442. **Tel** (800)367-8249, (305)428-5566.) Documents available from The Genuine Article, BIOSIS Document Express, CASDDS. ***Continues*** *Zeitschrift fuer Pflanzenernahrung, Dungung, Bodenkunde (1946), 0932-6707.*
Ind/Abst Agric. Eng. Abstr.; Biol. Abstr.; Chem. Abstr.; Crop Physiol. Abstr.; Curr. Cit.; EMBASE; Energy Res. Abstr.; Field Crop Abstr.; Food Sci. Technol. Abstr.; For. Abstr.; GeoRef; Hortic. Abstr.; Nematol. Abstr.; Life Sci. Collect.; Plant Breed. Abstr.; Plant Grow. Reg. Abstr.; Res. Alert [Full Cov.]; Rice Abstr.; Sci. Cit. Index; Soils Fert.; Sorghum Mill. Abstr.; Vitis Vitic. Enol. Abstr.

ISSN 0340-8159
GW
CCC
CODEN ZPFPAA
ZEITSCHRIFT FUER PFLANZENKRANKHEITEN UND PFLANZENSCHUTZ (1970). (ZEITSCHRIFT FUER PFLANZENKRANKHEITEN UND PFLANZENSCHUTZ.). [Z. Pflanzenkr. Pflanzenschutz]. **VFOAT** Journal of Plant Diseases and Plant Protection. Vol. 77, No. 1 (Jan. 1970)-. Periodical. English (German; summaries and/or abstracts in English and German). Twelve times a year. $612.36. Verlag Eugen Ulmer, Postfach 700561, D-70574 Stuttgart Germany. **Tel** 011 49 711 4507108, FAX 011 49 711 4507120, telex 7-23634. Documents available from The Genuine Article, BIOSIS Document Express, CASDDS. ***Continues*** *Zeitschrift fuer Pflanzenkrankheiten (Pflanzenpathologie) und Pflanzenschutz, 0044-3271.*
Ind/Abst Biol. Abstr.; Chem. Abstr.; Cot. Trop. Fibr. Abstr. Bibliogr.; Curr. Aware. Biol. Sci., CABS; Curr. Cit.; Curr. Contents Agric. Biol. Environ. Sci.; Ecol. Abstr.; Field Crop Abstr.; For. Abstr.; Geogr. Abstr. Phys. Geogr.; Hortic. Abstr.; Life Sci. Collect.; PESTDOC; Postharvest News Inf.; Res. Alert [Full Cov.]; Rev. Agric. Entomol.; Rev. Med. Vet. Mycology; Rev. Plant Pathol.; Rice Abstr.; Sci. Cit. Index; SCISEARCH; Seed Abstr.; Soils Fert.; Soyabean Abstr.; Weed Abstr.; Wheat Barley Trit. Abstr.

GW
ZEITSCHRIFT FUER PFLANZENKRANKHEITEN UND PFLANZENSCHUTZ. SONDERHEFT. (1975)-. German (English). Every 2 years. Verlag Eugen Ulmer, Postfach 700561, D-70574 Stuttgart Germany. **Tel** 011 49 711 4507108, FAX 011 49 711 4507120, telex 7-23634. ***Continues*** *Zeitschrift fuer Pflanzenkrankheiten (Pflanzenpathologie) und Pflanzenschutz. Sonderheft.*
Ind/Abst Agrofor. Abstr. (1991-).

LC QK322 **ISSN** 0302-8585
DD 581.97 PL
CODEN ZJPBDD

ZESZYTY KAUKOWE UNIWERYSTETU JAGIELLONSKIEGO. PRACE BOTANICZNE. [Zesz. nauk. Uniw. Jagiell., Pr. bot.]. **Main/Corp** Uniwersytet Jagiellonski. **VFOAT** Folia Botanica. No. 1; 1973-. Academic Scholarly Publication. Polish (summaries and/or abstracts in English). Irregular. Panstwowe Wydawnictwo Naukowe / PWN, (Polish Scientific Publishers PWN Ltd.), Ul. Miodowa 10, PO Box 391, 00-251 Warsaw Poland. **Tel** 011 48 22 312738, FAX 011 48 22 267163. Documents available from BIOSIS Document Express, CASDDS.
Ind/Abst Biol. Abstr.; Chem. Abstr. (1973-1985); Ecol. Abstr.; Geol. Abstr.

LC SB750 .C45 **ISSN** 0529-1542
DD 581.2 CC

ZHIWU BAOHU. (CHIH WU PAO HU.). **Added/Corp** Chung-kuo Nung Hsueh Hui. Chung-kuo Chih Wu Pao Hu Hsueh Hui. **VFOAT** Plant Protection; Journal of the Society of Plant Protection of China. (19??)-. Periodical. Chinese. Six times a year. $12.30. **(Subscription address:** China International Book Trading Corporation, PO Box 399, Library Service Department, Beijing 100044 People's Republic of China. **Tel** 011 86 1 8414284, FAX 011 86 1 8412023, telex 22496 CIBTC CN.**)**

ISSN 0255-7940
GR
CODEN ZIZADJ

ZIZANIOLOGIA. (ZIZANIOLOGIA : EPISTEMONIKO PERIODIKO TES HELLENIKES ZIZANIOLOGIKES HETAIREIAS.). [Zizaniologia]. **Added/Corp** Hellenike Zizaniologike Hetaireia. **VFOAT** Zizaniology. (1982)-. English (Greek, Modern). Documents available from BIOSIS Document Express, CASDDS.
Ind/Abst Biol. Abstr. (1984-); Chem. Abstr. (1982-1985); Maize Abstr.; Plant Grow. Reg. Abstr.; Soyabean Abstr.

LC SB107 .Z62 **ISSN** 0352-1346
DD 581 CI

ZNANOST I PRAKSA U POLJOPRIVREDI I PREHRAMBENOJ TEHNOLOGIJI = RESEARCH AND PRACTICE IN AGRICULTURE AND FOOD TECHNOLOGY. **Added/Corp** OOUR Poljoprivredni Institut (Osijek, Croatia) Biotehnicki Znanstveno-Nastavni Centar Osijek. **VFOAT** Research and Practice in Agriculture and Food Technology. (1970)-. Serbo-Croatian (Roman).
Ind/Abst Soyabean Abstr.

COMPUTER APPLICATIONS

ISSN 0266-304X
UK

BINARY. [Binary]. (1984)-. Periodical. English. Six times a year (Feb., Apr., June, Aug., Oct., Dec.). $50.00 (personal), $110.00 (library) US; £30.00 (personal), £67.00 (library) UK. Society for General Microbiology, Marlboro House Basingstoke Road, Spencers Wood, Reading RG7 1AE United Kingdom. **Tel** 011 44 1734 885577, FAX 011 44 1734 885656. **ED** Dr. Julian Wimpenny. **Bk Rev. Ad Acc, Adv Mgr:** Evans.
Desc: An international journal which publishes a broad range of articles related to all aspects of computing as applied to microbiology. This journal aims to provide a forum for information exchange between microbiologists, globally, who use computers, and is designed to appeal to a wide range of computer expertise among its readers, from novice to expert.
Ind/Abst Biodeter. Abstr.; Curr. Cit.

ISSN 1057-350X
DD 576 UK
NLM W1; BI6190 **CODEN** BCMIED
Pr Rev.

BINARY COMPUTING IN MICROBIOLOGY. [Bin. comput. microbiol.]. **Added/Corp** Society for General Microbiology. **VFOAT** Binary. Vol. 1, Issue 1 (Feb. 1989)-. Academic Scholarly Publication. English. Six times a year. $110.00. School of Pure and Applied Biology, University of Wales Cardiff, PO Box 915, Cardiff CF1 3TL United Kingdom. **Tel** 011 44 1222 874000, FAX 011 44 1222 874305. **ED** J.W.T. Wimpenny. Index available. **Bk Rev**, (Qty: 6). **Ad Acc, Adv Mgr:** J.B. Evans. Documents available from BIOSIS Document Express. ***Continues*** *Binary.*
Desc: Publishes a broad range of articles relating to all aspects of computing as applied to microbiology. Original papers and informal articles are welcomed from those working in general and clinical microbiology and biotechnology. Contains a papers section and an informal section containing review articles, software/hardware reviews, meetings reports, and a news section.
Ind/Abst Biol. Abstr.

LC QH301 **ISSN** 1058-4129
DD 574 US

BIOLOGICAL ABSTRACTS ON COMPACT DISC [COMPUTER FILE]. See Biology-Abstracting, Bibliographies and Statistics.

LC Q350 .K92 **ISSN** 0340-1200
DD 574 GW
CCC
NLM W1 BI742 **CODEN** BICYAF
Pr Rev.

BIOLOGICAL CYBERNETICS. [Biol. cybern.]. Vol. 17 (Jan. 1975)-. English (German). Twelve times a year. $2197.00. Springer-Verlag GmbH & Company KG, Heidelberger Platz 3, D-14197 Berlin Germany. **Tel** 011 49 30 8207223, FAX 011 49 30 8214091, telex 183 319 SPBLN D. **(Subscription address:** Springer-Verlag New York Inc. / North America, PO Box 2485, Journal Fulfillment, Secaucus NJ 07096. **Tel** (201)348-4033, (800)777-4643, FAX (201)348-4505.**) ED** W Reichardt. available on microfilm and microfiche from University Microfilms International (UMI). Documents available from Article Express International, The Genuine Article, BIOSIS Document Express, Ask*IEEE. ***Continues*** *Kybernetik, 0023-5946.*
Desc: Uses the concept of information transmission and processing and automatic control, which originated in technology and physics, and applies them to a broad range of fields of biology.
Ind/Abst ACM Guide Comput. Lit.; Biol. Abstr.; Biostatistica (19??-19??); Comput. Rev.; CSA Neuro. Abstr.; Curr. Cit.; Curr. Contents Life Sci.; EMBASE; Eng. Index Annu.; Index Med.; INSPEC (1975-); Int. Aerosp. Abstr.; Math. Rev. (-199?); Nematol. Abstr.; Life Sci. Collect.; Phys. Briefs; Ref. Upd. Deluxe Ed.; Res. Alert [Full Cov.]; Rev. Med. Vet. Entomol.; Sci. Cit. Index; SCISEARCH; Soc. Sci. Cit. Index [Select. Cov.]; Zentralbl. Math. Ihre Grenzgeb.

LC R **ISSN** 0194-2778
DD 610 US
CCC
NLM W1 BI854IH

BIOMEDICAL ENGINEERING AND COMPUTATION SERIES. See Biology-Bioengineering.

LC AZ **ISSN** 0749-0372
DD 001 US
NLM W1; BI918Y **CODEN** BSOFEO
TITLE CHANGE

BIOTECHNOLOGY SOFTWARE. See Biology-Bioengineering.

ISSN 1077-4890
DD 004 US
NLM W1; BI9182

●**BIOTECHNOLOGY SOFTWARE JOURNAL.** [Biotechnol. softw. j.]. **VFOAT** Biotechnology Software Report; BSR. (1994)-. Periodical. English. Six times a year. $129.00. Mary Ann Liebert Inc., 2 Madison Avenue, Larchmont NY 10538. **Tel** (914)834-3100, (800)M-LIEBERT, FAX (212)289-4697. **ED** Kevin Ahern and Indira Rajagopal. ***Continues*** *Biotechnology Software, 0749-0372.*

ISSN 0266-7061
UK
CCC
NLM W1; CO457FH **CODEN** COABER
Pr Rev.

COMPUTER APPLICATIONS IN THE BIOSCIENCES. (COMPUTER APPLICATIONS IN THE BIOSCIENCES : CABIOS.). [Comput. appl. biosci.]. **VFOAT** CABIOS. Vol. 1, No. 1 (1985)-. Academic Scholarly Publication. English. Six times a year. $320.00. Oxford University Press / UK, Walton Street, Oxford OX2 6DP United Kingdom. **Tel** 011 44 1865 56767, FAX 011 44 1865 267773, telex 851/837330 OXPRES G. **(Subscription address:** Oxford University Press / USA, Journals Marketing Department, Oxford University Press, 2001 Evans Road, Cary NC 27513. **Tel** (800)451-7556, (919)677-0977, FAX (919)677-1714.**) Bk Rev. Ad Acc. Circ:** 300. available on microfilm and microfiche from University Microfilms International (UMI). Documents available from The Genuine Article, BIOSIS Document Express, CASDDS.
Desc: Papers on new algorithms, programs, software and their applications; short reports for useful information; reviews and surveys covering all aspects of computer applications in life sciences; a section devoted to solutions to the problems experienced by students and newcomers; literature survey, news and views and product reviews to keep readers updated; book and software reviews.
Ind/Abst AgBiotech News Inf.; AGRICOLA [Select. Cov.]; Anal. Abstr.; Anim. Breed. Abstr.; Biol. Abstr. (1985-); Chem. Abstr. (1985-); Chem. Hazards Ind.; CompuMath Cit. Index [Full Cov.]; Comput. Abstr.; Curr. Biotechnol.; Curr. Cit.; Curr. Contents Life Sci.; Ei Page One; EMBASE; Genet. Abstr.; Health Plan. Adminis.; Index Med. (Vol. 1, No. 1, 1985-); Lab. Hazards Bull.; Nematol. Abstr.; Plant Breed. Abstr.; Ref. Upd. Deluxe Ed.; Res. Alert [Full Cov.]; Sci. Cit. Index; SCISEARCH; Soils Fert.

ISSN 0169-2607
NE
CCC
NLM W1; CO457I **CODEN** CMPBEK
Pr Rev.

COMPUTER METHODS AND PROGRAMS IN BIOMEDICINE. [Comput. methods programs biomed.]. Vol. 20, No. 1 (May 1985)-. Academic Scholarly Publication. English. Nine times a year (3 volumes). $910.00. Elsevier Science Ireland Ltd., Bay 15, Shannon Industrial Estate, Co Clare Ireland. **Tel** 011 353 61 471944. **ED** W. Schneider, R.E. Smith, S. Kaihara, and T. Groth. available on microfilm and microfiche from University Microfilms International (UMI); available on an online database from Elsevier Electronic Subscriptions (EES). Documents available from Article Express International, The Genuine Article, BIOSIS Document Express, Ask*IEEE. ***Continues*** *Computer Programs in Biomedicine, 0010-468X.*
Desc: Audience is all life science researchers, clinicians, statisticians, health scientists, computer scientists, programmers and bio-engineers, engaged in applying and teaching biomedical information processing.
Ind/Abst Anim. Breed. Abstr.; Biol. Abstr. (1985-); CompuMath Cit. Index [Full Cov.]; Comput. Rev.; Curr. Aware. Biol. Sci., CABS; Curr. Cit.; Curr. Contents Life Sci.; Ei Page One; EMBASE; Eng. Index Annu.; Health Plan. Adminis.; Helminthol. Abstr.; Index Med. (May 1985-); INSPEC (May 1985-); Ref. Upd. Deluxe Ed.; Res. Alert [Full Cov.]; Sci. Cit. Index; SCISEARCH; Soc. Sci. Cit. Index [Select. Cov.].

LC R858.A1 C65 **ISSN** 0010-4825
DD 610/.285/4 US
CCC
NLM W1 CO457T **CODEN** CBMDAW
Pr Rev.

COMPUTERS IN BIOLOGY AND MEDICINE. [Comput. biol. med.]. Vol. 1 (Aug. 1970)-. Academic Scholarly Publication. English. Six times a year. $722.00. Pergamon Press, An Imprint of Elsevier Science Ltd., The Boulevard, Langford Lane, Kidlington, Oxford OX5 1GB United Kingdom. **Tel** 011 44 1865 843000, 011 44 1865 843699, FAX 011 44 1865 843010. **(Subscription address:** Elsevier Science Ltd. / Oxford Fulfillment Centre, PO Box 800, Kidlington OX5 1DX United Kingdom. **Tel** 011 44 865 843355.**) ED** Robert S. Ledley. available on microfilm and microfiche from University Microfilms International (UMI); available on an online database from Elsevier Electronic Subscriptions (EES). Documents available from Article Express International, The Genuine Article, BIOSIS Document Express, Ask*IEEE, CASDDS, ADONIS.
Desc: A medium of international communication on the revolutionary advances being made in the application of the computer to the fields of bioscience and medicine. It encourages the exchange of research, instruction, ideas and information on all aspects of the growing use of computers.
Ind/Abst ADONIS; Bioeng. Abstr.; Biol. Abstr.; Biostatistica; Chem. Abstr.; CompuMath Cit. Index [Full Cov.]; Comput. Abstr.; Comput. Rev.; CSA Neuro. Abstr. (?-?); Cumul. Index Nurs. Allied Health Lit.; Curr. Aware. Biol. Sci., CABS; Curr. Cit.; Curr. Contents Eng. Comput. Technol.; Curr. Contents Life Sci.; Ei Page One; EMBASE; Energy Res. Abstr. (Sept. 1971-); Eng. Index Annu.; Health Saf. Sci. Abstr.; Health Plan. Adminis.; Index Med.; Inf. Sci. Abstr.; INSPEC (Aug. 1970-); Int. Aerosp. Abstr.; Life Sci. Collect.; Pollut. Abstr. Indexes; Protozoolog. Abstr.; Res. Alert [Full Cov.]; Sci. Cit. Index; SCISEARCH.

LC TP248
DD 660 UK

DERWENT BIOTECHNOLOGY ABSTRACTS DATABASE [COMPUTER FILE]. **Added/Corp** SilverPlatter Information, Inc. Derwent Publications, Ltd. **VFOAT** Derwent Biotechnology Abstracts Database on SilverPlatter; Biotechnology Abstracts; Derwent Biotechnology Abstracts. (19??)-. Abstracting/Indexing Service. English. Four times a year. $1,185.00 (academic institutions); $1,580.00 all other. Derwent Publications Ltd., Derwent House 14, Great Queen Street, London WC2B 5DF United Kingdom. **Tel** 011 44 171 3442800, FAX 011 44 171 3442899. **(Subscription address:** Derwent Inc., 1420 Spring Hill Road, Suite 525, McLean VA 22102. **Tel** (703)790-0400.**)**
Desc: Contains abstracts of major scientific publications, conference proceedings, and patent literature covering all aspects of biotechnology and includes all industrial uses of microorganisms, enzymes and cell culture, as well as plant micropropagation.

LC QA402.5 .E96 **ISSN** 1063-6560
DD 004/.05 US
CCC
CODEN EOCMEO

●**EVOLUTIONARY COMPUTATION.** [Evol. comput.]. Vol. 1, No. 1 (Spring 1993)-. Periodical. English. Four times a year. $145.00. Massachusetts Institute of Technology (MIT) Press, 55 Hayward Street, Cambridge MA 02142. **Tel** (617)253-2889, (617)625-8481, FAX (617)258-6779. **ED** Kenneth de Jong.
Desc: Forum for facilitating and enhancing the exchange of information among researchers involved in the theoretical and practical aspects of computational systems of an evolutionary nature. Publishes theoretical

and practical developments of computational systems drawing their inspiration from nature, with particular emphasis on evolutionary models of computation.

LC QH201 .J68 **ISSN** 1040-7286
DD 502 US
CCC
NLM W1; JO595KV **CODEN** JCMIEX
Pr Rev.

JOURNAL OF COMPUTER-ASSISTED MICROSCOPY. [J. comput.-assist. microsc.]. **VFOAT** Journal of Computer Assisted Microscopy. **VAT** Journal of Computer Assisted Microscopy. Vol. 1, No. 1 (Mar. 1989)-. Periodical. English. Four times a year. $225.00. Plenum Press, 233 Spring Street, New York NY 10013-1578. **Tel** (212)620-8000, (800)221-9369, FAX (212)463-0742, (212)807-1047, telex 23/421139. **ED** John C. Russ. **Ad Acc.** available on microfilm and microfiche from University Microfilms International (UMI). Documents available from Article Express International, Ask*IEEE.
Desc: An international interdisciplinary forum for the publication of peer-reviewed original papers in the field of computer use in microscopy. All types of microscopy are covered. Is of interest to both researchers and practitioner-technologists in all fields of science and technology-biology, materials science, geology, , medicine, biochemistry, astronomy, engineering, robotics, etc.
Ind/Abst Curr. Cit.; Ei Page One; Eng. Index Annu.; INSPEC (1989-).

LC QR69.A88 J68 **ISSN** 1060-3999
DD 576/.028 US
NLM W1; JO865D **CODEN** JRMMEE

JOURNAL OF RAPID METHODS AND AUTOMATION IN MICROBIOLOGY. [J. rapid methods autom. micribiol.]. Vol. 1, No. 1 (Mar. 1992)-. Academic Scholarly Publication. English. Four times a year (Jan., Apr., July, Oct.). $112.00. Food & Nutrition Press Inc., 6527 Main Street, PO Box 374, Trumbull CT 06611. **Tel** (203)261-8587, FAX (203)261-9724. Documents available from CASDDS.
Ind/Abst Chem. Abstr.

LC R895.A1 I55 **ISSN** 0140-0118
DD 610/.28 UK
CCC
NLM W1 ME168M **CODEN** MBECDY

MEDICAL & BIOLOGICAL ENGINEERING & COMPUTING. [Med. biol. eng. comput.]. **Added/Corp** International Federation for Medical and Biological Engineering. **VFOAT** Medical and Biological Engineering and Computing. **VAT** Medical and Biological Engineering and Computing. Vol. 15 (Jan. 1977)-. Academic Scholarly Publication. English (French and German; summaries and/or abstracts in French and German). Six times a year. $572.00. Peter Peregrinus Ltd, Station House Nightingale Road, Hitchin Hertfordshire SG5 1RJ United Kingdom. **Tel** 011 44 1438 313311, FAX 011 44 1438 313465. **(Subscription address:** Peter Peregrinus Ltd / IEE, PO Box 96, Stevenage Hertfordshire SG1 2SD, United Kingdom. **Tel** 011 44 1438 313311.**) ED** C. Roberts. **Bk Rev. Ad Acc. Circ:** 1,500. Documents available from Article Express International, The Genuine Article, BIOSIS Document Express, Ask*IEEE, CASDDS. ***Continues*** *Medical & Biological Engineering, 0025-696X.*
Desc: Research level publication describing work on medical engineering topics and computer applications.
Ind/Abst Bioeng. Abstr.; Biol. Abstr.; Chem. Abstr.; Comput. Inf. Syst. Abstr. J. [Full Cov.]; Curr. Aware. Biol. Sci., CABS; Curr. Cit.; Curr. Contents Eng. Comput. Technol.; Curr. Contents Life Sci.; Ei Page One; Elect. Comm. Abstr.; EMBASE; Energy Res. Abstr. (March 1978-); Eng. Index Annu.; Ergon. Abstr.; Index Med.; INSPEC (Jan. 1977-); Manuf. Process Eng. Abstr.; Mech. Eng. Abstr.; Life Sci. Collect.; Phys. Med. Biol. (19??-19??); Res. Alert [Full Cov.]; Sci. Cit. Index; SCISEARCH; Soc. Sci. Cit. Index [Select. Cov.].

CYTOLOGY

LC AS80.A1 E85 QH301 **ISSN** 0101-5354
DD 050 S 574/.05 BL
CODEN ABLEEC

ACTA BIOLOGICA LEOPOLDENSIA. **Added/Corp** Universidade do Vale do Rio dos Sinos. (1979)-. Periodical. Portuguese (English). Two times a year. Cr$20.00. Unisinos, CEP 93022-000, Sao Leopoldo Brazil RS. **Tel** 011 55 512 5926333, FAX 011 55 512 5920333, telex 515106 SAVS. cum. index. **Circ:** 600 (ctrl).
Desc: Research in cytology, histology, and genetics. Mostly laboratory research.

LC QH573 **ISSN** 0861-0509
DD 574.87 BU
NLM W1; AC7839 **CODEN** ACYME6

ACTA CYTOBIOLOGICA ET MORPHOLOGICA. **Added/Corp** Bulgarska Akademiia na Naukite. (1989)-. Periodical. English. Four times a year. Bulgarian Academy of Sciences, 1 rue 15 Noemvri, 1040 Sofia Bulgaria. **Tel** 011 359 2 803127. **ED** Editorial Board. Documents available from CASDDS. ***Continues*** *Acta Morphologica, 0204-9139.*
Ind/Abst Chem. Abstr.

LC RG1 .A23 **ISSN** 0001-5547
DD 618.1 US
CCC
NLM W1 AC7841 **CODEN** ACYTAN
Pr Rev.

ACTA CYTOLOGICA. [Acta cytol.]. **Added/Corp** International Academy of Cytology. International Academy of Gynecological Cytology. American Society of Cytology. Inter-Society Cytology Council. Vol. 1 (1957)-. Academic Scholarly Publication. English. Six times a year. $243.00. Science Printers and Publishers Inc., PO Drawer 12425, 8342 Olive Boulevard, St Louis MO 63132-2814. **Tel** (314)991-4440, FAX (314)991-4654. **ED** George L. Wied. Index available. cum. index. **Bk Rev. Ad Acc. Circ:** 6,500 (ctrl). available on microfilm and microfiche from University Microfilms International (UMI). Documents available from The Genuine Article, BIOSIS Document Express, CASDDS. ***Absorbed*** *Inter-Society Cytology Council. Annual Meeting of the Inter-Society Cytology Council, Transactions.*
Desc: Designed for the publication of scientific articles for the advancement of clinical cytology. Letters to the editors, original articles on case reports, new research and new methodology.
Ind/Abst Biol. Abstr.; Chem. Abstr.; Curr. Aware. Biol. Sci., CABS; Curr. Cit.; Curr. Contents Life Sci.; Dairy Sci. Abstr.; EMBASE; Health Plan. Adminis.; Helminthol. Abstr.; Index Med.; INIS Atomindex [Micro.]; Med. Abstr. Newsl.; Life Sci. Collect.; Protozoolog. Abstr.; Ref. Upd. Deluxe Ed.; Res. Alert [Full Cov.]; Rev. Med. Vet. Mycology; Rev. Plant Pathol.; Sci. Cit. Index; SCISEARCH.

LC QM551 .A25 **ISSN** 0044-5991
DD 591.8/05 JA
NLM W1 AC809D **CODEN** ACHCBO
Pr Rev.

ACTA HISTOCHEMICA ET CYTOCHEMICA. (ACTA HISTOCHEMICA ET CYTOCHEMICA : OFFICIAL JOURNAL OF THE JAPAN SOCIETY OF HISTOCHEMISTRY AND CYTOCHEMISTRY.). [Acta histochem. cytochem.]. **Added/Corp** Nihon Soshiki Saibo Kagakukai. Vol. 1, No. 1 (Mar. 1968)-. Academic Scholarly Publication. English (French and German). Six times a year. $236.00. Japan Society of Histochemistry and Cytochemistry, c/o Department of Anatomy, Faculty of Medicine, Kyoto University, Konoe-cho Yoshida, Sakyo-ku, Kyoto 606-01 Japan. **(Subscription address:** Maruzen Company Ltd., PO Box 5050, Import & Export Department, Tokyo 100 31 Japan. **Tel** 011 81 3 32789224.) ctrl circ. available on microfilm and microfiche from University Microfilms International (UMI). Documents available from The Genuine Article, BIOSIS Document Express, CASDDS.
Desc: Journal of histochemistry and cytochemistry.
Ind/Abst Biol. Abstr.; Chem. Abstr.; CSA Neuro. Abstr.; Curr. Aware. Biol. Sci., CABS; Curr. Cit.; Curr. Contents Life Sci.; Dairy Sci. Abstr.; Nutr. Abstr. Rev., Ser. B, Live Feeds and Feed.; Nutr. Abstr. Rev., Ser. A, Hum. Exp.; Oncog. Growth Factors Abstr.; Life Sci. Collect.; Protozoolog. Abstr.; Ref. Upd. Deluxe Ed.; Res. Alert [Full Cov.]; Sci. Cit. Index; SCISEARCH.

ISSN 0860-3111
PL
UDC 573

ACTA UNIVERSITATIS LODZIENSIS. FOLIA PHYSIOLOGICA, CYTOLOGICA ET GENETICA. See Biology-Botany.

LC QL801 .E67 **ISSN** 0301-5556
DD 574.4/08 GW
NLM W1 AD433K

ADVANCES IN ANATOMY, EMBRYOLOGY AND CELL BIOLOGY. See Medical Sciences-Anatomy.

LC QH601 .A382 **ISSN** 1074-7567
DD 574.87/5/05 US
NLM W1; AD53IPF **CODEN** ACBMER

•**ADVANCES IN CELL AND MOLECULAR BIOLOGY OF MEMBRANES.** [Adv. cell mol. biol. membr.]. Vol. 1 (1993)-. English. $180.50. JAI Press Inc., 55 Old Post Road, Suite 2, PO Box 1678, Greenwich CT 06836-1678. **Tel** (203)661-7602, FAX (203)661-0792. **ED** Alan M. Tartakoff.

LC QH601 .A39 **ISSN** 1042-4156
DD 574.87/5 US
NLM W1; AD679Q **CODEN** AMFLEC

ADVANCES IN MEMBRANE FLUIDITY. [Adv. membr. fluid.]. Vol. 1 (1988)-. Monographic series. English. Irregular. Price varies per volume. Wiley Liss, 605 3rd Avenue, New York NY 10158. **Tel** (212)850-8800, (212)850-6645. **(Subscription address:** John Wiley & Sons, Inc. / Philadelphia, PO Box 7247, Philadelphia PA 19170. **Tel** (212)850-6645, (800)225-5945.) Documents available from BIOSIS Document Express, CASDDS.
Ind/Abst Biol. Abstr.; Chem. Abstr.

LC QH573 .A26
DD 574.87/05 US
NLM W1; AD682TR

ADVANCES IN MOLECULAR AND CELL BIOLOGY. **VFOAT** Molecular and Cell Biology; Cell Biology. Vol. 4 (1992)-. English. Irregular. $90.25. JAI Press Inc., 55 Old Post Road, Suite 2, PO Box 1678, Greenwich CT 06836-1678. **Tel** (203)661-7602, FAX (203)661-0792. **ED** E. Edward Bittar. ***Continues*** *Advances in Cell Biology (Greenwich, Conn.), 0898-8455.*

LC QP625.N89 A36 **ISSN** 1040-7952
DD 574.87/328 US
CCC
NLM W1; AD843 **CODEN** ASMRE5

ADVANCES IN SECOND MESSENGER AND PHOSPHOPROTEIN RESEARCH. [Adv. second messenger phosphoprot. res.]. Vol. 21 (1988)-. Academic Scholarly Publication. English. Irregular. Price varies per volume. Lippincott - Raven Publishers, 227 East Washington Square, Philadelphia PA 19106. **Tel** (215)238-4200, (800)777-2295, FAX (215)238-4227. **ED** Paul Greengard and G. Alan Robinson. Documents available from The Genuine Article, BIOSIS Document Express, CASDDS. ***Continues*** *Advances in Cyclic Nucleotide and Protein Phosphorylation Research, 0747-7767.*
Desc: A forum for new research on all aspects of hormonal and physiologic regulation.
Ind/Abst Biol. Abstr. (1988-); Chem. Abstr. (1988-); Curr. Cit.; Energy Res. Abstr. (1988-); Index Med. (1988-); Ref. Upd. Basic Ed.; Ref. Upd. Deluxe Ed.; Res. Alert [Full Cov.]; Sci. Cit. Index; SCISEARCH.

LC QH573 .A27 **ISSN** 1064-6000
DD 574.87/05 US
NLM W1; AD875M **CODEN** ASBIEP

ADVANCES IN STRUCTURAL BIOLOGY. [Adv. struct. biol.]. Vol. 1 (1991)-. Consumer Publication. English. $90.25. JAI Press Inc., 55 Old Post Road, Suite 2, PO Box 1678, Greenwich CT 06836-1678. **Tel** (203)661-7602, FAX (203)661-0792. **ED** Suudarshan Malhotra.

LC RB43 .A52 **ISSN** 0884-6812
DD 616.07/582/05 US
CCC
NLM W1; AN1913R **CODEN** AQCHED
Pr Rev.

ANALYTICAL AND QUANTITATIVE CYTOLOGY AND HISTOLOGY. (ANALYTICAL AND QUANTITATIVE CYTOLOGY AND HISTOLOGY / THE INTERNATIONAL ACADEMY OF CYTOLOGY AND AMERICAN SOCIETY OF CYTOLOGY.). [Anal. quant. cytol. histol.]. **Added/Corp** International Academy of Cytology. American Society of Cytology. Vol. 7, No. 1 (March 1985)-. Academic Scholarly Publication. English. Six times a year. $332.00. Science Printers and Publishers Inc., PO Drawer 12425, 8342 Olive Boulevard, St Louis MO 63132-2814. **Tel** (314)991-4440, FAX (314)991-4654. **ED** George L. Wied. Index available. cum. index. **Bk Rev. Ad Acc. Circ:** 2,500 (ctrl). available on microfilm and microfiche from University Microfilms International (UMI). Documents available from The Genuine Article, BIOSIS Document Express, CASDDS. ***Continues*** *Analytical and Quantitative Cytology, 0190-0471.*
Desc: Covers applied analytical and quantitative cytology, cell research and its methodology. An official periodical of the International Academy of Cytology and the American Society of Cytology and is the sister periodical of Acta Cytologica.
Ind/Abst Biol. Abstr. (1985-); Chem. Abstr. (1985-); Curr. Aware. Biol. Sci., CABS; Curr. Cit.; Curr. Contents Life Sci.; EMBASE; Health Plan. Adminis.; Index Med. (Vol. 7, No. 1, 1985-); Life Sci. Collect.; Ref. Upd. Deluxe Ed.; Res. Alert [Full Cov.]; Sci. Cit. Index; SCISEARCH; Soc. Sci. Cit. Index [Select. Cov.].

ISSN 0921-8912
NE
CCC
NLM W1; AN1915M **CODEN** ACPAER
Pr Rev.

ANALYTICAL CELLULAR PATHOLOGY. (ANALYTICAL CELLULAR PATHOLOGY : THE JOURNAL OF THE EUROPEAN SOCIETY FOR ANALYTICAL CELLULAR PATHOLOGY.). [Anal. cell. pathol.]. **Added/Corp** European Society for Analytical Cellular Pathology. Vol. 1, No. 1 (Feb. 1989)-. Academic Scholarly Publication. English. Eight times a year (2 volumes). $626.00. Elsevier Science Ireland Ltd., Bay 15, Shannon Industrial Estate, Co Clare Ireland. **Tel** 011 353 61 471944. available on microfilm and microfiche from University Microfilms International (UMI); available on an online database from Elsevier Electronic Subscriptions (EES). Documents available from The Genuine Article, BIOSIS Document Express.
Ind/Abst Biol. Abstr. (1991-); Curr. Aware. Biol. Sci., CABS; Curr. Cit.; Curr. Contents Clin. Med.; Curr. Contents Life Sci.; EMBASE; Health Plan. Adminis.; Index Med.; Res. Alert [Full Cov.]; Sci. Cit. Index; SCISEARCH.

ISSN 1081-0706
US

•ANNUAL REVIEW OF CELL AND DEVELOPMENTAL BIOLOGY. **Added/Corp** Annual Reviews, Inc. (1995)-. English. One time a year (November). $56.00. Annual Reviews Inc., 4139 El Camino Way, PO Box 10139, Palo Alto CA 94303-0139. **Tel** (415)493-4400, (800)523-8635, FAX (415)855-9815. **ED** George E. Palade. Index available. ctrl circ. available on microfilm and microfiche from University Microfilms International (UMI). ***Continues*** *Annual Review of Cell Biology, 0743-4634.*
Desc: A critical analysis of the important literature in the rapidly advancing field of cell biology. The series is an important influence among cell biologists and those in other scientific disciplines who wish to keep abreast of advances in cell biology. Includes a selective bibliography.
Ind/Abst Anim. Breed. Abstr.; Biol. Agric. Index; Biol. Abstr.; Biol. Dig.; Chem. Abstr.; Curr. Aware. Biol. Sci., CABS; Curr. Contents Life Sci.; EMBASE; Index Med.; Ref. Upd. Basic Ed.; Ref. Upd. Deluxe Ed.; Res. Alert; Sci. Cit. Index; SCISEARCH.

LC QH573 .A56 **ISSN** 0743-4634
DD 574.87/05 US
CCC
NLM W1; AN77G **CODEN** ARCBE2
Pr Rev. TITLE CHANGE
ANNUAL REVIEW OF CELL BIOLOGY. [Annu. rev. cell biol.]. **Added/Corp** Annual Reviews, Inc. Vol. 1 (1985)-(19??). English. (November). Annual Reviews Inc., 4139 El Camino Way, PO Box 10139, Palo Alto CA 94303-0139. **Tel** (415)493-4400, (800)523-8635, FAX (415)855-9815. **ED** George E. Palade. Index available. cum. index. ctrl circ. available on microfilm and microfiche from University Microfilms International (UMI). Documents available from The Genuine Article, BIOSIS Document Express, CASDDS. ***Continued by*** *Annual Review of Cell & Developmental Biology, 1081-0706.*
Desc: A critical analysis of the important literature in the rapidly advancing field of cell biology. The series is an important influence among cell biologists and those in other scientific disciplines who wish to keep abreast of advances in cell biology. Includes a selective bibliography.
Ind/Abst Anim. Breed. Abstr.; Biol. Agric. Index; Biol. Abstr. (1985-); Biol. Dig.; Chem. Abstr.; Curr. Aware. Biol. Sci., CABS; Curr. Cit.; Curr. Contents Life Sci.; EMBASE; Index Med. (1985-); Ref. Upd. Basic Ed.; Ref. Upd. Deluxe Ed.; Res. Alert [Full Cov.]; Sci. Cit. Index; SCISEARCH.

LC RB155.6 .A67 **ISSN** 1056-5191
DD 611/.01816/05 US
NLM W1; AP516CL
Pr Rev.
APPLIED CYTOGENETICS. **See** Biology-Genetics.

LC RB **ISSN** 0395-501X
DD 616.07 FR
CCC
NLM W1 AR312E **CODEN** AACPDQ
ARCHIVES D'ANATOMIE ET DE CYTOLOGIE PATHOLOGIQUES. **See** Medical Sciences-Pathology.

LC QH573 **ISSN** 0914-9465
DD 574.87 JA
NLM W1; AR455BB **CODEN** AHCYEZ
ARCHIVES OF HISTOLOGY AND CYTOLOGY. [Arch. histol. cytol.]. **Added/Corp** Nihon Soshikigaku Kirokukai. Vol. 51, No. 1 (Mar. 1988)-. Periodical. English. Five times a year. $410.00. Niigata University / School of Medicine, Department of Anatomy, Asahi Machi, Niigata 951 Japan. **Tel** 011 81 25 2236161. **(Subscription address:** Japan Publications Trading Company Ltd., PO Box 5030, Tokyo International, Tokyo 100-31 Japan. **Tel** 011 81 3 3292 3753.) **ED** Tsuneo Fujita. Index available. **Bk Rev. Ad Acc.** Documents available from The Genuine Article, BIOSIS Document Express, CASDDS. ***Continues*** *Archivum Histologicum Japonicum, 0004-0681.*
Ind/Abst Biol. Abstr. (1988-); Chem. Abstr.; Curr. Cit.; EMBASE; Index Med. (1988-); Nutr. Abstr. Rev., Ser. A, Hum. Exp.; Res. Alert [Full Cov.]; Sci. Cit. Index; SCISEARCH.

US

ART TO SCIENCE IN TISSUE CULTURE. **Added/Corp** HyClone Laboratories. (1982)-. Periodical. English. Four times a year. Free on request. Hyclone Laboratories Inc, 1725 South Highway 89-91, Logan UT 84321. **Tel** (801)753-4584, FAX (801)753-4589. **ED** Richard F. Wilkinson. **Bk Rev. Circ:** 30,000 (ctrl).
Desc: Issues of interest to cell and tissue culture scientists.

US

ASC BULLETIN. (19??)-. Bulletin. English. Six times a year. $30.00. American Society of Cytology, 1015 Chestnut Street, Suite 1518, Philadelphia PA 19107. **Tel** (215)922-3880. **Ad Acc.** ***Continues*** *Cytotechnologists Bulletin.*

LC QH585 .A85
DD 599/.00724 US
ATCC QUALITY CONTROL METHODS FOR CELL LINES. **Added/Corp** American Type Culture Collection. **VFOAT** Quality Control Methods for Cell Lines. **VAT** American Type Culture Collection Quality Control Methods for Cell Lines. 1st Ed. (1985)-. English. Irregular. $40.00. American Type Culture Collection, 12301 Parklawn Drive, Rockville MD 20852. **Tel** (301)881-2600, FAX (301)231-5826, telex 898-055.

US

ATLAS AND TEXT ASPIRATION BIOPSY CYTOLOGY. (19??)-. English. Irregular. $79.50. Williams & Wilkins Company, 428 East Preston Street, Baltimore MD 21202-3993. **Tel** (410)528-4000, (800)638-6423, FAX (410)528-8596, telex 87669. **(Subscription address:** Williams & Wilkins, PO Box 64380, Baltimore MD 21264. **Tel** 800 638-6423.) Documents available from , , Quick Copies.

ISSN 0167-4889
NE
CCC
Pr Rev.
BIOCHIMICA ET BIOPHYSICA ACTA. MOLECULAR CELL RESEARCH. [Biochim. biophys. acta. Mol. cell res.]. **VFOAT** Molecular Cell Research; BBA, Biochimica et Biophysica Acta (C). Molecular Cell Research; BBA, Molecular Cell Research. Vol. 720, No. 1 (1982)-. Academic Scholarly Publication. English. Fifteen times a year (5 volumes). $1406.00. Elsevier Science Publishers BV, PO Box 211, 1000 AE Amsterdam Netherlands. **Tel** 011 31 20 4853641, 011 31 20 4853642, FAX 011 31 20 4853598. available on microfilm and microfiche from University Microfilms International (UMI); available on an online database from Elsevier Electronic Subscriptions (EES). Documents available from ADONIS.
Ind/Abst ADONIS; AgBiotech News Inf.; Anim. Breed. Abstr.; Crop Physiol. Abstr.; Curr. Aware. Biol. Sci., CABS; Dairy Sci. Abstr.; EMBASE; Field Crop Abstr.; Hortic. Abstr.; Maize Abstr.; Nutr. Abstr. Rev., Ser. A, Hum. Exp.; PESTDOC; Plant Breed. Abstr.; Plant Genet. Resour. Abstr.; Ref. Upd. Basic Ed.; Ref. Upd. Deluxe Ed.; Soyabean Abstr.

ISSN 0265-9247
UK
NLM W1; BI663P **CODEN** BIOEEJ
Pr Rev.
BIOESSAYS. [BioEssays]. **Added/Corp** International Council of Scientific Unions. Company of Biologists. **VFOAT** Bio Essays. Vol. 1, No. 1 (July 1984)-. Academic Scholarly Publication. English. Twelve times a year (1 volume, 12 parts). $350.00. The Company of Biologists Limited, Bidder Building, 140 Cowley Road, Cambridge CB4 4DL United Kingdom. **Tel** 011 44 1223 426164, FAX 011 44 1223 423353. **(Subscription address:** Kinokuniya Company Ltd., 38-1 Sakuragaoka 5, chome Setagaya-ku, Tokyo 156 Japan. **Tel** FAX 011 03 3439 0136.) **ED** Adam S. Wilkins. Index available. **Bk Rev. Ad Acc. Circ:** 1,000. available on microfilm and microfiche from University Microfilms International (UMI). Documents available from The Genuine Article, BIOSIS Document Express, UMI Article Clearinghouse, CASDDS.
Desc: Each issue consists of a set of review articles and discussion pieces on the latest advances in cellular, developmental and molecular biology, and their implications.
Ind/Abst AgBiotech News Inf.; Anim. Breed. Abstr.; Biol. Abstr. (1985-); Chem. Abstr. (1985-); Crop Physiol. Abstr.; Curr. Aware. Biol. Sci., CABS; Curr. Biotechnol.; Curr. Cit.; Curr. Contents Life Sci.; Expand. Acad. Index (1992-); Fish Rev.; Health Plan. Adminis.; Index Med. (Vol. 3, No. 1, 1985-); Nematol. Abstr.; Newsp. Period. Abstr. (1992-); Nutr. Abstr. Rev., Ser. A, Hum. Exp.; Plant Breed. Abstr.; Plant Genet. Resour. Abstr.; Plant Grow. Reg. Abstr.; Potato Abstr.; Protozoolog. Abstr.; Ref. Upd. Deluxe Ed.; Res. Alert [Full Cov.]; Rev. Agric. Entomol.; Rev. Med. Vet. Entomol.; Rev. Plant Pathol.; Sci. Cit. Index; SCISEARCH; Weed Abstr.; Wheat Barley Trit. Abstr.; Wildl. Rev. (Vol. 3, No. 1, 1985-).

ISSN 1016-0922
SZ
CCC
NLM W1; BI759C
BIOLOGICAL SIGNALS. **VFOAT** Biol Signals. (Jan./Feb. 1992)-. Periodical. English. Six times a year. $345.60. S. Karger AG, Allschwilerstrasse 10, PO Box, CH-4009 Basel Switzerland. **Tel** 011 41 61 3061111, FAX 011 41 61 3061234, telex CH 962 652. **ED** SF Pang, T. Fujita, PA Ward. Documents available from BIOSIS Document Express.
Desc: An international journal publishing original articles, reviews and communications in the broad field of production, transmission, processing, recognition, effects, modification and evolution of biological signals. Topics of discussion range from the subcellular to the cellular and organismal level. Areas of investigation are approached from the molecular to the socio-biological level, and the stimuli and responses examined may be both long term and short term in nature.
Ind/Abst Biol. Abstr.; Index Med.; Ref. Upd. Deluxe Ed.

ISSN 0887-3224
DD 611 US
BIOLOGY OF EXTRACELLULAR MATRIX. [Biol. extracell. matrix]. (1986)-. Academic Scholarly Publication. English. Irregular. Price varies per volume. Academic Press Inc., 6277 Sea Harbor Drive, Orlando FL 32887. **Tel** (800)543-9534, (407)345-4100, FAX (407)352-3445. Documents available from BIOSIS Document Express, CASDDS. ***Continues*** *International Review of Connective Tissue Research, 0074-767X.*
Ind/Abst Biol. Abstr.; Chem. Abstr.; EMBASE; Energy Res. Abstr.; Math. Rev.

LC QH212.E4 J6 **ISSN** 0248-4900
DD 574.87/05 FR
CCC
NLM W1 BI852NL **CODEN** BCELDF
Pr Rev.
BIOLOGY OF THE CELL. [Biol. cell]. **Added/Corp** Societe Francaise de Microscopie Electronique. European Cell Biology Organization. Centre National de la Recherche Scientifique (France) Institut National de la Sante et de la Recherche Medicale (France). Vol. 40, No. 1 (1981)-. Academic Scholarly Publication. English (French). Nine times a year (3 volumes). $653.00. Editions Scientifique Elsevier, 141 rue de Javel, 75747 Paris Cedex 15 France. **Tel** 011 33 1 45589067, FAX 011 33 1 45589424. **(Subscription address:** Editions Scientifiques Elsevier / for North America, PO Box 7247-7576, Philadelphia PA 19170-7576.) **ED** R. Charret and D. Szafarz. Index available. cum. index. **Bk Rev. Ad Acc. Circ:** 2,000 (ctrl). available on microfilm and microfiche from University Microfilms International (UMI); available on an online database from Elsevier Electronic Subscriptions (EES). Documents available from The Genuine Article, BIOSIS Document Express, CASDDS. ***Continues*** *Biologie Cellulaire, 0399-0311.*
Desc: Publishes original reports, review articles and rapid communications concerning the structure and function of cells in the context of developmental biology, genetics, immunology and physiology.
Ind/Abst Biocont. News Inf.; Biol. Abstr.; Chem. Abstr.; Curr. Aware. Biol. Sci., CABS; Curr. Cit.; Curr. Contents Life Sci.; EMBASE; Energy Res. Abstr. (Jan. 1981-); Index Med. (1983-); Nutr. Abstr. Rev., Ser. A, Hum. Exp.; Life Sci. Collect.; Plant Grow. Reg. Abstr.; Protozoolog. Abstr.; Ref. Upd. Deluxe Ed.; Res. Alert [Full Cov.]; Rev. Agric. Entomol.; Rev. Med. Vet. Entomol.; Rev. Med. Vet. Mycology; Rev. Plant Pathol.; Sci. Cit. Index; SCISEARCH.

LC QH601 .B53 **ISSN** 0067-8864
DD 574.8/75 US
NLM W1 BI858L **CODEN** BOMBB5
BIOMEMBRANES (NEW YORK, N.Y.). (BIOMEMBRANES.). [Biomembranes]. Vol. 1 (1971)-. Periodical. English. Irregular. Price varies per volume. Plenum Press, 233 Spring Street, New York NY 10013-1578. **Tel** (212)620-8000, (800)221-9369, FAX (212)463-0742, (212)807-1047, telex 23/421139. **ED** Morris Kates and Lionel A. Manson. Index available. Documents available from CASDDS.
Ind/Abst Chem. Abstr.; Energy Res. Abstr. (Sept. 1975-); INIS Atomindex [Micro.].

LC QP801.P69 B56 **ISSN** 0233-7657
UN
CODEN BIKLEK
BIOPOLIMERY I KLETKA. [Biopolim. kletka]. **Added/Corp** Akademiia Nauk Ukrainskoi RSR. Otdelenie Biokhimii, Fiziologii i Teoreticheskoi Meditsiny. **VFOAT** Biopolymers and Cell. Vol. 1, No. 1 (Jan./Feb. 1985)-. Academic Scholarly Publication. Russian (summaries and/or abstracts in English; table of contents in English and Russian). Twelve times a year. $149.95 US, Canada and Europe; $174.95 other. Izdatelstvo Naukova Dumka / Ukrainian Academy of Sciences, Yu. A. Khramov, Dir., Ul. Repina 3, 252 601 Kiev Ukraine. **Tel** 011 7 44 4303441, 011 7 44 2254182, telex 131376. **(Subscription address:** East View Publications Inc., 3020 Harbor Lane North, Suite 110, Minneapolis MN 55447. **Tel** (800)477-1005, (612)550-0961, FAX (612)559-2931.) Documents available from BIOSIS Document Express, CASDDS.
Ind/Abst AgBiotech News Inf.; Biol. Abstr. (1986-); Chem. Abstr. (1985-); Maize Abstr.; Plant Breed. Abstr.

LC QH506 .B557 **ISSN** 0144-8463
DD 574.8/8/05 US
CCC
NLM W1 BI91T **CODEN** BRPTDT
Pr Rev.
BIOSCIENCE REPORTS. [Biosci. rep.]. **Added/Corp** Biochemical Society (Great Britain). Vol. 1, No. 1 (Jan. 1981)-. Academic Scholarly Publication. English. Six times a year. $395.00. Plenum Press, 233 Spring Street, New York NY 10013-1578. **Tel** (212)620-8000, (800)221-9369, FAX (212)463-0742, (212)807-1047, telex 23/421139. **ED** Charles A. Pasternak and William J. Lennarz. **Bk Rev. Ad Acc. Circ:** 500. available on microfilm and microfiche from University Microfilms International (UMI). Documents available from The Genuine Article, BIOSIS Document Express, CASDDS, Documents on Demand, ADONIS.
Desc: High quality papers that advance new concepts in molecular and cellular biology.
Ind/Abst ADONIS; AGRICOLA [Select. Cov.]; Anal.

Abstr.; Biol. Abstr.; Chem. Abstr.; Chem. Titles; CSA Neuro. Abstr. (?-?); Curr. Aware. Biol. Sci., CABS; Curr. Biotechnol.; Curr. Cit.; Curr. Contents Life Sci.; Dairy Sci. Abstr.; EMBASE; Energy Inf. Abstr.; Environ. Abstr.; Index Med. (Jan. 1982-); Index Vet.; Nutr. Abstr. Rev., Ser. B, Live Feeds and Feed.; Nutr. Abstr. Rev., Ser. A, Hum. Exp.; Life Sci. Collect.; PESTDOC; Ref. Upd. Basic Ed.; Ref. Upd. Deluxe Ed.; Res. Alert [Full Cov.]; Sci. Cit. Index; SCISEARCH.

ISSN 0309-1805
UK
NLM W 3 BR459 **CODEN** BSCSD2
BRITISH SOCIETY FOR CELL BIOLOGY SYMPOSIUM. [Br. Soc. Cell Biol. symp.]. **Main/Corp** British Society for Cell Biology. (1976)-. Academic Scholarly Publication. English. Irregular. Price varies per volume. Cambridge University Press, The Edinburgh Building, Shaftesbury Road, Cambridge CB2 2RU United Kingdom. **Tel** 011 44 1223 312393, FAX 011 44 1223 315052, telex 851-817256. **(Subscription address:** Cambridge University Press / North America, 110 Midland Avenue, Port Chester NY 10573. **Tel** (800)431-1580, (914)937-9600.**)** Documents available from BIOSIS Document Express, CASDDS.
Ind/Abst Biol. Abstr.; Chem. Abstr.

LC QP88.2 .C35 **ISSN** 0008-0586
DD 599/.019214 UK
NLM ZWE 200; C144
TITLE CHANGE
CALCIFIED TISSUE ABSTRACTS. **See** Medical Sciences-Abstracting, Bibliographies and Statistics.

LC QP88.2 .C35 **ISSN** 1069-5540
DD 612/.01524 US
NLM ZWE 200; C144
•CALCIUM AND CALCIFIED TISSUE ABSTRACTS. **See** Medical Sciences-Abstracting, Bibliographies and Statistics.

LC QH1 .C25 **ISSN** 0008-7114
DD 574.8/7/05 IT
NLM W1 CA895 **CODEN** CARYAB
Pr Rev.
CARYOLOGIA. [Caryologia]. **Added/Corp** Universita di Firenze. (1948)-. Periodical. English (Italian, French, German and Spanish). Four times a year. L115810. Caryologia, Via P A Micheli 3, 50121 Florence Italy. **Tel** 011 39 55 210756, FAX 011 39 55 2757438. Documents available from The Genuine Article, BIOSIS Document Express, CASDDS.
Ind/Abst AgBiotech News Inf.; AGRICOLA; Anim. Breed. Abstr.; Biol. Abstr.; Chem. Abstr.; Crop Physiol. Abstr.; Curr. Aware. Biol. Sci., CABS; Curr. Contents Agric. Biol. Environ. Sci.; EMBASE; Genet. Abstr.; Hortic. Abstr.; Ornamental Hort. (1991-); Life Sci. Collect.; Pig News Inf.; Plant Breed. Abstr.; Plant Grow. Reg. Abstr.; Poult. Abstr.; Res. Alert [Full Cov.]; Rev. Agric. Entomol.; Rev. Med. Vet. Entomol.; Rev. Med. Vet. Mycology; Rev. Plant Pathol.; Sci. Cit. Index; SCISEARCH; Soils Fert.; Sorghum Mill. Abstr.; Wheat Barley Trit. Abstr.

LC RB155 .I527a **ISSN** 0737-7983
DD 616/.042 US
NLM QS 26 H918
CEASED
CATALOG OF CELL LINES. [Cat. cell lines]. **Added/Corp** National Institutes of Health (U.S.) National Institute of General Medical Sciences (U.S.) National Institute on Aging. Institute for Medical Research (Camden, N.J.) Coriell Institute for Medical Research (U.S.). (1982)-(1995). Catalog. English. US Department of Health and Human Services National Institutes of Health, 9000 Rockville Pike, Bethesda MD 20892. **Tel** (301)496-9291, FAX (301)496-2443. ***Continues*** *Human Genetic Mutant Cell Repository, 0148-835X.* ***Continued in part by*** *Catalog of Cell Lines (National Institute on Aging).*

LC QH **ISSN** 1061-5385
DD 574 SZ
CCC
NLM W1; CE126E **CODEN** CADCEF
•CELL ADHESION AND COMMUNICATION. [Cell adhes. commun.]. Vol. 1, Issue 1 (May 1993)-. Periodical. English. Four times a year. $440.00 (university and hospital libraries), $687.00 (all except university and hospital libraries). Harwood Academic Publishers, PO Box 90, Reading RG1 8JL United Kingdom. **Tel** 011 44 1734 560080, FAX 011 44 1734 568211.
Desc: Presents research, short communications, and reviews on all families of adhesion receptors and counter-recepters from diverse biological systems.
Ind/Abst Index Med.

ISSN 0737-1233
US
NLM W1 CE126H
CELL ANALYSIS. [Cell anal.]. (1982)-. Monographic series. English. Irregular. Price varies per volume. Plenum Press, 233 Spring Street, New York NY 10013-1578. **Tel** (212)620-8000, (800)221-9369, FAX (212)463-0742, (212)807-1047, telex 23/421139. **ED** Nicholal Catsimpoolas.

ISSN 0254-2935
II
NLM W1; CE126R **CODEN** CCREE3
CELL AND CHROMOSOME RESEARCH. [Cell chromosome res.]. **Added/Corp** Association for Cell and Chromosome Research (India). Vol. 5 (1982)-. Academic Scholarly Publication. English. Three times a year. $12.00. Association for Cell and Chromosome Research Centre for Advanced Study, Department of Botany, University of Calcutta, 35 Ballygunge Circular Road, Calcutta-700 019 India. **(Subscription address:** Prints India, 11 Darya Ganj, New Delhi 110002 India. **Tel** 011 91 11 3268645, FAX 011 91 11 3275542, telex 31-61087 PRIN-IN.**)** **ED** Sibdas Ghosh. **Bk Rev. Ad Acc. Circ:** 200 (ctrl). Documents available from BIOSIS Document Express, CASDDS. ***Continues*** *Cell and Chromosome Newsletter, 0253-6919.*
Ind/Abst Biol. Abstr.; Chem. Abstr.

LC QH301 .Z43 **ISSN** 0302-766X
DD 574.8/05 GW
CCC
NLM W1 CE128E **CODEN** CTSRCS
Pr Rev.
CELL AND TISSUE RESEARCH. [Cell tissue res.]. Vol. 148 (1974)-. Periodical. English. Twelve times a year. $3639.00. Springer-Verlag GmbH & Company KG, Heidelberger Platz 3, D-14197 Berlin Germany. **Tel** 011 49 30 8207223, FAX 011 49 30 8214091, telex 183 319 SPBLN D. **(Subscription address:** Springer-Verlag New York Inc. / North America, PO Box 2485, Journal Fulfillment, Secaucus NJ 07096. **Tel** (201)348-4033, (800)777-4643, FAX (201)348-4505.**)** **ED** H Altner, M J Cavey, D E Kelly, B Lofts, J F Morris, A Oksche, B Scharrer, N J Strausfeld, and L Vollrath. **Ad Acc.** available on microfilm and microfiche from University Microfilms International (UMI). Documents available from The Genuine Article, BIOSIS Document Express, CASDDS, ADONIS. ***Continues*** *Zeitschrift fur Zellforschung und Mikroskopische Anatomie, 0340-0336.*
Desc: Presents significant advances encompassing the broad field of cell biology and microscopical anatomy. Covers cell biology, endocrinology, neuroanatomy, neurology, neurobiology, neuroendocrinology, neuropathology, neurosurgery and pathology.
Ind/Abst ADONIS; AgBiotech News Inf.; AGRICOLA; Biocont. News Inf.; Biol. Abstr.; Chem. Abstr.; CSA Neuro. Abstr. (?-?); Curr. Cit.; Curr. Contents Life Sci.; Curr. Ref. Fish Res.; Dairy Sci. Abstr.; EMBASE; Energy Res. Abstr. (Oct. 1975-); Fish Rev.; Helminthol. Abstr. (1991-); Index Med.; Nutr. Abstr. Rev., Ser. B, Live Feeds and Feed.; Nutr. Abstr. Rev., Ser. A, Hum. Exp.; Life Sci. Collect.; Pig News Inf.; Postharvest News Inf.; Protozoolog. Abstr.; Ref. Upd. Basic Ed.; Ref. Upd. Deluxe Ed.; Res. Alert [Full Cov.]; Rev. Agric. Entomol.; Rev. Med. Vet. Entomol.; Rev. Med. Vet. Mycology; Sci. Cit. Index; SCISEARCH; Wildl. Rev.

LC QH611 .C42 **ISSN** 0263-6484
DD 574.87/6042 UK
CCC
NLM W1 CE128F **CODEN** CBFUDH
Pr Rev.
CELL BIOCHEMISTRY AND FUNCTION. **See** Biology-Biological Chemistry.

LC QH573 .C385 **ISSN** 0742-2091
DD 574.87/05 NE
NLM W1; CE128FH **CODEN** CBTOE2
Pr Rev.
CELL BIOLOGY AND TOXICOLOGY (PRINCETON SCIENTIFIC PUBLISHERS). (CELL BIOLOGY AND TOXICOLOGY.). [Cell biol. toxicol.]. **Added/Corp** Genetic Toxicology Association. Vol. 1, No. 1 (Oct. 1984)-. Periodical. English. Six times a year. $439.00. Kluwer Academic Publishers, Postbus 322, 3300 AH Dordrecht The Netherlands. **Tel** 011 31 78 524400, FAX 011 31 78 183273, telex 20083. **ED** Gary M Williams. Index available. **Bk Rev. Ad Acc, Adv Mgr:** M A Mehlman. **Acid Free. Circ:** 1,000. Documents available from The Genuine Article, BIOSIS Document Express, CASDDS. ***Continues*** *Cell Biology and Toxicology (Cell Biology and Toxicology, Inc.), 0742-2091.*
Desc: Publishes research findings in cellular systems, both prokaryotic and eukaryotic, as well as subcellular systems dealing with techniques of cell culture, fundamental cell processes, metabolism and biotransformation, and toxic effects including cytotoxicity, mutagenicity and carcinogenicity.
Ind/Abst Biol. Abstr. (1986-); Chem. Abstr. (1984-); Curr. Aware. Biol. Sci., CABS; Curr. Cit.; Curr. Contents Life Sci.; EMBASE; Health Plan. Adminis.; Index Med. (1984-); Res. Alert [Full Cov.]; Rev. Med. Vet. Entomol.

LC QH573 .C39 **ISSN** 1065-6995
DD 574.8/7/05 UK
NLM W1; CE128FM
•CELL BIOLOGY INTERNATIONAL. (1993)-. Academic Scholarly Publication. English. Twelve times a year. $410.69. Academic Press Ltd., A Division of Harcourt Brace & Company Ltd., 24-28 Oval Road, London NW1 7DX United Kingdom. **Tel** 011 44 171 2674466, FAX 011 44 171 4822293, 011 44 171 4854752, telex 25775 ACPRES G. **(Subscription address:** Harcourt Brace & Company, Ltd., Foots Cray High Street, Sidcup Kent DA14 5HP United Kingdom. **Tel** 011 44 181 3003322, FAX 011 44 181 3090807, telex 896 377 ACADEM.**)** **ED** G. Bullock and C. Hawes. **Bk Rev.** Documents available from BIOSIS Document Express. ***Continues*** *Cell Biology International Reports, 0309-1651.*
Desc: Official publication of the International Federation for Cell Biology. Promoting the aims of most cell biologists, papers relating structure and function, and particularly the use of new techniques, are welcome. Facilities to publish Abstracts from the meetings of constituent societies are provided where possible. Information on scientific activities such as meetings and courses is published in a regular calendar. An improved book-reviewing facility has recently been introduced.
Ind/Abst Biol. Abstr.; Curr. Cit.; Index Med.; Index Vet.; Sci. Cit. Index; Small Anim. Abstr. Bibliogr.

LC QH573 .C393 **ISSN** 0163-4992
DD 574.87/6041 US
CCC
NLM W1 CE128I **CODEN** CBIODE
Pr Rev.
CELL BIOPHYSICS. **See** Biology-Biological Physics.

ISSN 0142-8020
UK
CELL CALCIUM. **Added/Corp** University of Sheffield. Biomedical Information Service. **VFOAT** Monthly Bibliography on Cell Calcium. Vol. 1, No. 1 (Jan. 1976)-. Periodical. English. Twelve times a year. £120.00. SUBIS, Mansion House 19 Kingfield Road, Sheffield S11 9AS United Kingdom. **Tel** 011 44 114 2554433, FAX 011 44 114 255 4626.

ISSN 0143-4160
UK
CCC
NLM W1 CE128J **CODEN** CECADV
Pr Rev.
CELL CALCIUM (EDINBURGH). (CELL CALCIUM.). [Cell calcium]. Vol. 1 (Jan. 1980)-. Academic Scholarly Publication. English. Twelve times a year. $655.00. Churchill Livingstone, 1-3 Baxter's Place, Leith Walk, Edinburgh EH1 3AF United Kingdom. **Tel** 011 44 131 5562424, FAX 011 44 131 5581278, telex 727511. **(Subscription address:** Maruzen Company Ltd., PO Box 5050, Import & Export Department, Tokyo 100 31 Japan. **Tel** 011 81 3 32789224.**)** **ED** R M Case and A Scarpa. **Ad Acc. Circ:** 600. available on microfilm and microfiche from University Microfilms International (UMI). Documents available from The Genuine Article, BIOSIS Document Express, CASDDS.
Desc: Publishes work from all branches of science and medicine on the regulation of cell calcium or the regulation of cell function by calcium.
Ind/Abst Biol. Abstr. (1986-); Calcium Calcif. Tissue Abstr.; Chem. Abstr.; Chem. Titles; CSA Neuro. Abstr. (?-?); Curr. Aware. Biol. Sci., CABS; Curr. Cit.; Curr. Contents Life Sci.; EMBASE; Index Med.; Life Sci. Collect.; Ref. Upd. Basic Ed.; Ref. Upd. Deluxe Ed.; Res. Alert [Full Cov.]; Sci. Cit. Index; SCISEARCH.

LC QH573 .C38 **ISSN** 0092-8674
DD 574.8/7/05 US
NLM W1 CE126K **CODEN** CELLB5
Pr Rev.
CELL (CAMBRIDGE). (CELL.). [Cell]. Vol. 1 (Jan. 1974)-. Periodical. English. Twenty-six times a year. $395.00. Cell Press, 50 Church Street, Cambridge MA 02138. **Tel** (617)661-7060, FAX (617)661-7061. **ED** Benjamin Lewin. Index available (bound in last issue). **Bk Rev. Ad Acc. Circ:** 8,800. Documents available from The Genuine Article, BIOSIS Document Express, CASDDS, Documents on Demand.
Desc: Publishes original works of research in biology, molecular biology and biomedicine.
Ind/Abst Acad. Search; AgBiotech News Inf.; AGRICOLA; Biol. Agric. Index; Biol. Abstr.; Chem. Abstr.; Crop Physiol. Abstr.; CSA Neuro. Abstr.; Curr. Cit.; Curr. Contents Life Sci.; Curr. Ref. Fish Res.; EMBASE; Energy Inf. Abstr.; Energy Res. Abstr. (July 1977-); Entomol. Abstr.; Environ. Abstr.; EP Collect.; Food Sci. Technol. Abstr.; Gen. Sci. Index (1992-); Gen. Sci. Source; Genet. Abstr.; Health Plan. Adminis.; Homework Help.; Hortic. Abstr.; Hum. Genome Abstr.; Immunol. Abstr.; Index Med.; INFO-SOUTH Abstr.; INIS Atomindex [Micro.]; MasterFile FullTEXT 1000; MasterFile FullTEXT 350; MasterFile FullTEXT 650; MasterFile FullTEXT (July 1993-); Microbiol. Abstr. Sect. B; Microbiol. Abstr. Sect. C; Nematol. Abstr.; Nucl. Acids Abstr.; OCLC; Oncog. Growth Factors Abstr.; Ornamental Hort. (1991-); Life Sci. Collect.; PESTDOC; Plant Breed. Abstr.; Plant Grow. Reg. Abstr.; Protozoolog. Abstr.; Ref. Upd. Basic Ed.; Ref. Upd. Deluxe Ed.; Res. Alert [Full Cov.]; Rev. Plant Pathol.; Sci. Cit. Index; SCISEARCH; Seed Abstr.; Soc. Sci. Cit. Index [Select. Cov.]; Soils Fert.; Soyabean Abstr.; Telebase; Trop. Dis. Bull.; Virol. AIDS Abstr.; Weed Abstr.

ISSN 1351-5314
UK
•CELL CONTACT AND COMMUNICATION. (1993)-. English. Irregular. £120.00. SUBIS, Mansion House 19 Kingfield Road, Sheffield S11 9AS United Kingdom. **Tel** 011 44 114 2554433, FAX 011 44 114 255 4626. ***Continues*** *Cell Contact Phenomena, 0142-8039.*
Desc: Current awareness service for researchers in clinical and life sciences.

ISSN 0142-8039
DD 016.57487 UK
TITLE CHANGE
CELL CONTACT PHENOMENA. [Cell contact phenom.]. (1976)-(1993). English. SUBIS, Mansion House 19 Kingfield Road, Sheffield S11 9AS United Kingdom. **Tel** 011 44 114 2554433, FAX 011 44 114 255 4626. **Bk Rev. Ad Acc.** ***Continued by*** *Cell Contact and Communication, 1351-5314.*
Desc: Current awareness service for researchers and clinicians.

ISSN 0263-7251
DD 016.57487 UK
CELL CYCLE. [Cell cycle]. (1983)-. English. Twelve times a year. £75.00. SUBIS, Mansion House 19 Kingfield Road, Sheffield S11 9AS United Kingdom. **Tel** 011 44 114 2554433, FAX 011 44 114 255 4626. **Bk Rev. Ad Acc.**
Desc: Current awareness service for researchers and clinicians.

LC QH573 **ISSN** 1350-9047
DD 574.87 UK
NLM W1; CE128JG
•CELL DEATH AND DIFFERENTIATION. Vol. 1, No. 1 (July 1994)-. Academic Scholarly Publication. English. Four times a year. $192.00. Arnold, 338 Euston Road, London NW1 3BH United Kingdom. **Tel** 011 44 1732 450111, FAX 011 44 1732 461321. **(Subscription address:** Edward Arnold, PO Box 386, Avenel NJ 07001-0386. **) Bk Rev. Ad Acc.** Documents available from BLDSC.
Desc: Covers cell death, proliferation, differentiation and development in eukaryotic models.

ISSN 0263-726X
DD 016.57487612 UK
CELL DIFFERENTIATION SHEFFIELD. [Cell differ.Sheff.]. (1983)-. English. Twenty-six times a year. £85.00. SUBIS, Mansion House 19 Kingfield Road, Sheffield S11 9AS United Kingdom. **Tel** 011 44 114 2554433, FAX 011 44 114 255 4626. **Bk Rev. Ad Acc.**
Desc: Current awareness service for researchers and clinicians.

ISSN 1044-9523
DD 611 US
NLM W1; CE128KP **CODEN** CGDIE7
CELL GROWTH & DIFFERENTIATION. (CELL GROWTH & DIFFERENTIATION : THE MOLECULAR BIOLOGY JOURNAL OF THE AMERICAN ASSOCIATION FOR CANCER RESEARCH.). [Cell growth differ.]. **Added/Corp** American Association for Cancer Research. **VFOAT** Cell Growth and Differentiation. Vol. 1, No. 1 (Jan. 1990)-. Academic Scholarly Publication. English. Twelve times a year. $245.00. American Association of Cancer Research, 150 South Independence Mall, West Pub Ledger Building, Philadelphia PA 19106. **Tel** (215)440-9300, FAX (215)440-9354. **(Subscription address:** Fulco, 30 Broad Street, Denville NJ 07834. **Tel** (800)783-4903, (201)627-2427.**) Ad Acc.** Documents available from The Genuine Article, BIOSIS Document Express, CASDDS.
Desc: Original in vitro and in vivo studies of mechanisms underlying normal and abnormal cell behavior and cell growth control.
Ind/Abst Biol. Abstr. (1990-); Chem. Abstr.; Curr. Aware. Biol. Sci., CABS; Curr. Cit.; Curr. Contents Life Sci.; Index Med. (Jan. 1990-); Res. Alert [Full Cov.]; Sci. Cit. Index; SCISEARCH.

ISSN 0142-8047
UK
CCC
CELL MEMBRANES. (1970)-. Periodical. English. Twenty-four times a year. $205.35. SUBIS, Mansion House 19 Kingfield Road, Sheffield S11 9AS United Kingdom. **Tel** 011 44 114 2554433, FAX 011 44 114 255 4626. **Bk Rev. Ad Acc.**
Desc: Current awareness service for researchers and clinicians.

LC QH601 .C37 **ISSN** 0740-784X
DD 574.87/5/05 US
NLM W1; CE128L **CODEN** CEMBDG
CELL MEMBRANES, METHODS AND REVIEWS. [Cell membr., methods rev.]. **VFOAT** Cell Membranes. Vol. 1 (1983)-. Academic Scholarly Publication. English. Irregular. Price varies per volume. Plenum Press, 233 Spring Street, New York NY 10013-1578. **Tel** (212)620-8000, (800)221-9369, FAX (212)463-0742, (212)807-1047, telex 23/421139. **ED** Elliot Elson, William Frazier, and Luis Glaser. Documents available from The Genuine Article, CASDDS. ***Continues*** *Methods in Membrane Biology, 0093-4771.*
Ind/Abst Chem. Abstr.; EMBASE; Life Sci. Collect.; Res. Alert [Full Cov.]; SCISEARCH.

LC QH647 .C442 **ISSN** 0886-1544
DD 574 US
CCC
NLM W1; CE128R **CODEN** CMCYEO
Pr Rev.
CELL MOTILITY AND THE CYTOSKELETON. [Cell motil. cytoskelet.]. Vol. 6, No. 1 (1986)-. Academic Scholarly Publication. English. Twelve times a year (plus video supplement). $1380.00. John Wiley & Sons, Inc., 605 Third Avenue, New York NY 10158-0012. **Tel** (212)850-6000, (212)850-6645, FAX (212)850-6088, telex 12-7063. **(Subscription address:** John Wiley & Sons / UK, Baffins Lane, Chichester, West Sussex PO19 1UD United Kingdom. **Tel** 011 44 1243 779777, FAX 011 44 243 776128, telex 86290 WIBOOKG.**) ED** B. R. Brinkley. Documents available from The Genuine Article, BIOSIS Document Express, CASDDS. ***Continues*** *Cell Motility, 0271-6585.*
Desc: An international journal specializing in the rapid publication of articles concerning all phenomena related to cell motility, including structural, biochemical, biophysical, and theoretical research, the journal also publishes invited review articles, mini-reviews, brief rapid communications, and book reviews.
Ind/Abst Biol. Abstr. (1986-); Chem. Abstr. (1986-); CSA Neuro. Abstr. (?-?); Curr. Aware. Biol. Sci., CABS; Curr. Cit.; Curr. Contents Life Sci.; EMBASE; Helminthol. Abstr. (1991-); Index Med. (1986-); Microbiol. Abstr. Sect. C; Nematol. Abstr.; Life Sci. Collect. (1986-); Protozoolog. Abstr.; Ref. Upd. Deluxe Ed.; Res. Alert [Full Cov.]; Rev. Agric. Entomol.; Rev. Plant Pathol.; Sci. Cit. Index; SCISEARCH.

LC QH573 **ISSN** 0141-299X
DD 574.87 UK
NLM Z 5322.C3 C393
CELL NUCLEUS. Added/Corp University of Sheffield. Biomedical Information Service. Vol. 1 (Jan. 1978)-. Periodical. English. Twelve times a year. £85.00. SUBIS, Mansion House 19 Kingfield Road, Sheffield S11 9AS United Kingdom. **Tel** 011 44 114 2554433, FAX 011 44 114 255 4626. **Bk Rev.**
Desc: An economy bulletin containing references on genes, chromosomes, histones, and chromatin.
Ind/Abst Index Sci. Rev. [Full Cov.].

LC QH631 .C45 **ISSN** 0960-7722
DD 574.87/6 UK
CCC
NLM W1; CE128T **CODEN** CPROEM
CELL PROLIFERATION. [Cell prolif.]. **Added/Corp** Cell Kinetics Society. European Study Group for Cell Proliferation. International Cell Cycle Society. Vol. 24, No. 1 (Jan. 1991)-. Academic Scholarly Publication. English. Twelve times a year. $428.00. Blackwell Scientific Publications Ltd, Marston Book Services, PO Box 88, Oxford OX2 ONE United Kingdom. **Tel** 011 44 1865 206206, FAX 011 44 1865 206219, telex 837 515 MARDIS G. available on microfilm and microfiche from University Microfilms International (UMI). Documents available from The Genuine Article, BIOSIS Document Express, CASDDS. ***Continues*** *Cell & Tissue Kinetics, 0008-8730.*
Ind/Abst Biol. Abstr. (1991-); Chem. Abstr. (1991-); Curr. Aware. Biol. Sci., CABS; Curr. Cit.; Curr. Contents Life Sci.; EMBASE; Index Med. (1991-); Ref. Upd. Deluxe Ed.; Res. Alert [Full Cov.]; Sci. Cit. Index; SCISEARCH.

ISSN 0915-907X
DD 574.87 576 JA
CELL SCIENCE. [Cell sci.]. (1990)-. Periodical. Japanese. Twelve times a year. Documents available from CASDDS. ***Continues*** *Biseibutsu, 0911-2707.*
Ind/Abst Chem. Abstr.

LC QH573 .C397 **ISSN** 0386-7196
DD 574.8/7 JA
CCC
NLM W1 CE1282 **CODEN** CSFUDY
Pr Rev.
CELL STRUCTURE AND FUNCTION. [Cell struct. funct.]. **Added/Corp** Nihon Saibo Seibutsu Gakkai. Vol. 1 (Oct. 1975)-. Academic Scholarly Publication. English. Six times a year. $154.00. **(Subscription address:** Maruzen Company Ltd., PO Box 5050, Import & Export Department, Tokyo 100 31 Japan. **Tel** 011 81 3 32789224.**) ED** Y. Tashiro and K. Omori. **Ad Acc. Circ:** 403 (ctrl). Documents available from The Genuine Article, BIOSIS Document Express, CASDDS.
Desc: Reports on the biology of cells from the molecular level to the level of cell differentiation and cell interaction.
Ind/Abst Biol. Abstr.; Chem. Abstr.; CSA Neuro. Abstr. (?-?); Curr. Cit.; Curr. Contents Life Sci.; EMBASE; Index Med. (1983-); Life Sci. Collect.; Ref. Upd. Basic Ed.; Ref. Upd. Deluxe Ed.; Res. Alert [Full Cov.]; Sci. Cit. Index; SCISEARCH.

ISSN 0142-8063
UK
CELL TRANSFORMATION. Added/Corp University of Sheffield. Biomedical Information Service. (197?)-. Periodical. English. Twelve times a year. SUBIS, Mansion House 19 Kingfield Road, Sheffield S11 9AS United Kingdom. **Tel** 011 44 114 2554433, FAX 011 44 114 255 4626. **Bk Rev.**
Desc: Contains references on viral, chemical, physical and spontaneous transformation of cells also details of forthcoming meetings.

LC QH611 .C429 **ISSN** 1073-1180
DD 574 US
CCC
NLM W1; CE1283HM **CODEN** CEVIEF
Pr Rev.
•CELL VISION. (CELL VISION : JOURNAL OF ANALYTICAL MORPHOLOGY.). [Cell vis.]. **VFOAT** Journal of Analytical Morphology; CellVision. Vol. 1, No. 1 (May/June 1994)-. Academic Scholarly Publication. English. Six times a year. $125.00. Eaton Publishing Company, 154 East Central Street, Natick MA 01760. **Tel** (508)655-8282, FAX (508)655-9910.
Desc: Focuses on advancements in the science of structural biochemical visualization.
Ind/Abst Chem. Abstr.

LC R857.M3 C46 **ISSN** 1051-6794
DD 502 US
CCC
NLM W1; CE1283L **CODEN** CEMAEE
Pr Rev.
CELLS AND MATERIALS. [Cells mater.]. Vol. 1, No. 1 (1991)-. Periodical. English. Four times a year (Mar., June., Sept., Dec.). $95.00. Scanning Microscopy International, PO Box 66507, AMF O'Hare, Chicago IL 60666-0507. **Tel** (708)529-6677, FAX (708)980-6698. Documents available from The Genuine Article.
Ind/Abst Curr. Contents Life Sci.; Res. Alert [Full Cov.]; Sci. Cit. Index; SCISEARCH.

ISSN 1060-9989
DD 502 US
CCC
NLM W1; CE1283LA
CELLS AND MATERIALS. SUPPLEMENT. [Cells mater., Suppl.]. **Added/Corp** Scanning Microscopy International. **VFOAT** Cells and Materials Supplement. (1992)-. Periodical. English. $95.00. Scanning Microscopy International, PO Box 66507, AMF O'Hare, Chicago IL 60666-0507. **Tel** (708)529-6677, FAX (708)980-6698.

LC QH611 .A552
DD 574 FR
UDC 576.3
NLM W1; CE1285
Pr Rev.
CELLULAR AND MOLECULAR BIOLOGY. [Cell. mol. biol.]. Vol. 38, Nos. 5/6 (Aug./Sept. 1992)-. Academic Scholarly Publication. English. Eight times a year (Feb., Mar., May, June, July, Sept., Nov., Dec.). 2950.00F. CMB Association Loi 1901, 1 Avenue du Pave Neuf, 93160 Noisy le Grand France. **Tel** 011 33 1 45923719, FAX 011 33 1 43042030. **ED** Raymond J. Wegmann. Index available. **Bk Rev**, (Qty: 100). **Circ:** 750. available on microfilm and microfiche from University Microfilms International (UMI); available with illustrations. Documents available from BIOSIS Document Express, The Genuine Article.
Desc: An integrative discipline journal publishing original articles in the fields of cellular and molecular biology, biophysics, immunoenzymology, immunology, pathology, pharmacology, and physiology. Covers all these relevant areas from life sciences, for human, animal and plant tissues.
Ind/Abst AgBiotech News Inf.; Anim. Breed. Abstr.; Biol. Abstr.; Chem. Abstr.; Chem. Titles; CSA Neuro. Abstr.; Curr. Aware. Biol. Sci., CABS; Curr. Contents Life Sci.; Curr. Ref. Fish Res.; Dairy Sci. Abstr.; EMBASE; Energy Res. Abstr. (1982-); Fish Rev. (Jan. 1989-July 1992); Helminthol. Abstr.; Index Med.; Index Vet.; Microbiol. Abstr. Sect. C; Life Sci. Collect.; Pig News Inf.; Poult. Abstr.; Protozoolog. Abstr.; Ref. Upd. Deluxe Ed.; Res. Alert [Full Cov.]; Rev. Med. Vet. Entomol.; Sci. Cit. Index; SCISEARCH; Vet. Bull.; Wildl. Rev. (Jan. 1989-July 1992).

LC QH611 .A55 **ISSN** 0968-8773
US
NLM W1; CE12853
•CELLULAR & MOLECULAR BIOLOGY RESEARCH. VFOAT Cellular and Molecular Biology Research. Vol. 39, No. 1 (1993)-. Periodical. English. Six times a year. $386.00 The Americas; £259.00 other. Pergamon Press, An Imprint of Elsevier Science Ltd., The Boulevard, Langford Lane, Kidlington, Oxford OX5 1GB United Kingdom. **Tel** 011 44 1865 843000, 011 44 1865 843699, FAX 011 44 1865 843010. **(Subscription address:** Elsevier Science Ltd. / Oxford Fulfillment Centre, PO Box 800, Kidlington OX5 1DX United Kingdom. **Tel** 011 44 865 843355.**)** available on an online database from Elsevier Electronic Subscriptions (EES). ***Continues*** *Cellular and Molecular Biology, 0145-5680.*
Ind/Abst Curr. Cit.; Index Med.; Sci. Cit. Index.

LC QP351 .C37 **ISSN** 0272-4340
DD 599.01/88 US
CCC
NLM W1 CE1287 **CODEN** CMNEDI
Pr Rev.
CELLULAR AND MOLECULAR NEUROBIOLOGY. **See** Medical Sciences-Neurology.

ISSN 1049-0302
DD 574 US
NLM W1; CE1289 **CODEN** CECSEI
CELLULAR CLOCKS. [Cell. clocks]. **VFOAT** Cellular Clocks Series. Vol. 2 (1989)-. Monographic series. English. Price varies per volume. Marcel Dekker Inc., 270 Madison Avenue, New York NY 10016. **Tel** (212)696-9000, (800)228-1160, FAX (212)685-4540, telex 421419. **(Subscription address:** Marcel Dekker Inc., PO Box 5017, Monticello NY 12701. **Tel** (800)228-1160.**)** Documents available from BIOSIS Document Express.

Desc: Covers topics such as cell cycle clocks and biological rhythms.
Ind/Abst Biol. Abstr. (1989-).

LC QH573
DD 574.8/765 US
UDC 576.32
CELLULAR DYNAMICS. Main/Conf Conference on Cellular Dynamics. 1st/2nd- 1963/64-. English. Six times a year. Gordon & Breach Science Publishers, Inc., PO Box 786, Cooper Station, New York NY 10276. **Tel** (212)206-8900, FAX (212)645-2459. **ED** L D Peachey.

ISSN 1351-3214 UK CCC
NLM W1; CE1292
•**CELLULAR PHARMACOLOGY. See** Pharmacy and Pharmacology.

LC QH573 **ISSN** 1015-8987
DD 574.87 SZ CCC
NLM W1; CE1293 **CODEN** CEPBEW
Pr Rev.
CELLULAR PHYSIOLOGY AND BIOCHEMISTRY. [Cell. physiol. biochem.]. (Jan./Feb. 1991)-. Periodical. English. Six times a year. $322.60. S. Karger AG, Allschwilerstrasse 10, PO Box, CH-4009 Basel Switzerland. **Tel** 011 41 61 3061111, FAX 011 41 61 3061234, telex CH 962 652. **ED** F. Lang. Index available. cum. index. **Ad Acc. Circ:** 1,000. available on microfilm and microfiche. Documents available from BIOSIS Document Express, CASDDS.
Desc: Takes a role in the interdisciplinary effort to unravel the mechanisms of cellular function. Addresses scientists from both the physiological and biochemical disciplines and from related fields such as molecular biology, pathophysiology, pathobiochemistry, and pharmacology.
Ind/Abst Biol. Abstr.; Chem. Abstr.; Curr. Cit.; Curr. Contents Life Sci.; Ref. Upd. Deluxe Ed.

ISSN 0190-146X US
NLM W1 CE1295 **CODEN** CSSGDN
CELLULAR SENESCENCE AND SOMATIC CELL GENETICS. [Cell senescence somatic cell genet.]. **Added/Corp** Institute for Medical Research (Camden, N.J.). (1977)-. English. Plenum Press, 233 Spring Street, New York NY 10013-1578. **Tel** (212)620-8000, (800)221-9369, FAX (212)463-0742, (212)807-1047, telex 23/421139. **ED** W.W. Nichols and D.G. Murphy.

LC QH604.2 .C47 **ISSN** 0898-6568
DD 574.87/5/05 UK CCC
NLM W1; CE1298 **CODEN** CESIEY
Pr Rev.
CELLULAR SIGNALLING. [Cell. signal.]. Vol. 1, No. 1 (1989)-. Periodical. English. Eight times a year (1 volume). $650.00. Pergamon Press, An Imprint of Elsevier Science Ltd., The Boulevard, Langford Lane, Kidlington, Oxford OX5 1GB United Kingdom. **Tel** 011 44 1865 843000, 011 44 1865 843699, FAX 011 44 1865 843010. **(Subscription address:** Elsevier Science Ltd. / Oxford Fulfillment Centre, PO Box 800, Kidlington OX5 1DX United Kingdom. **Tel** 011 44 865 843355.**) ED** Miles Houslay. available on microfilm and microfiche from University Microfilms International (UMI); available on an online database from Elsevier Electronic Subscriptions (EES). Documents available from The Genuine Article, BIOSIS Document Express, CASDDS, ADONIS.
Desc: Publishes original papers covering all aspects of mechanisms, actions and structural components of cellular signalling systems.
Ind/Abst ADONIS; Biol. Abstr.; Chem. Abstr.; CSA Neuro. Abstr. (?-?); Curr. Aware. Biol. Sci., CABS; Curr. Cit.; Curr. Contents Life Sci.; EMBASE; Index Med. (1989-); Ref. Upd. Deluxe Ed.; Res. Alert [Full Cov.]; Sci. Cit. Index; SCISEARCH.

LC QH573 **ISSN** 0008-8757
DD 574.87 BE
UDC 576.3
NLM W1 CE13 **CODEN** CELLA4
SUSPENDED
CELLULE, LA. [Cellule]. Vol. 1 (1884)-?. Periodical. French. Three times a year. 3160F Europe; $90.00 US. Editions Nauwelaerts SA, rue de l'Eglise Street/Sulpice 19, 5998 Beauvechain Belgium. **Tel** 32-10-866737, FAX 32-2-7517408. **ED** JB Carnoy. Index available. cum. index. **Circ:** 880. Documents available from BIOSIS Document Express, CASDDS.
Ind/Abst AGRICOLA; Biol. Abstr. (19??-1983); Chem. Abstr.; EMBASE; Life Sci. Collect.; Plant Breed. Abstr.

LC QH301 .C55 **ISSN** 0009-5915
GW CCC
NLM W1 CH944 **CODEN** CHROAU
Pr Rev.
CHROMOSOMA. [Chromosoma]. **VFOAT** Abt. B. Zeitschrift fur Zellforschung und Mikroskopische Anatomie. Vol. 1 (1947)-. Academic Scholarly Publication. German (English, French and German). Ten times a year. $1219.00. Springer-Verlag GmbH & Company KG, Heidelberger Platz 3, D-14197 Berlin Germany. **Tel** 011 49 30 8207223, FAX 011 49 30 8214091, telex 183 319 SPBLN D. **(Subscription address:** Springer-Verlag New York Inc. / North America, PO Box 2485, Journal Fulfillment, Secaucus NJ 07096. **Tel** (201)348-4033, (800)777-4643, FAX (201)348-4505.**) ED** W Hennig and P B Moens. Documents available from The Genuine Article, BIOSIS Document Express, CASDDS. ***Continues*** *Zeitschrift fuer Zellforschung und Mikroskopische Anatomie. Abteilung B, Chromosoma, 0932-8920.*
Desc: Linking classical cytology and cytogenetics with research in molecular biology, it is a forum for contributions to the field of nuclear and chromosome research.
Ind/Abst AgBiotech News Inf.; AGRICOLA [Select. Cov.]; Anim. Breed. Abstr.; Biol. Abstr.; Biotechnol. Res. Abstr.; Chem. Abstr.; CSA Neuro. Abstr. (?-?); Curr. Aware. Biol. Sci., CABS; Curr. Cit.; Curr. Contents Life Sci.; EMBASE; Energy Res. Abstr.; Fish Rev. (Jan. 1989-July 1992); Genet. Abstr.; Helminthol. Abstr.; Hum. Genome Abstr.; Index Med.; Life Sci. Collect.; Pig News Inf.; Plant Breed. Abstr.; Poult. Abstr.; Protozoolog. Abstr.; Ref. Upd. Basic Ed.; Ref. Upd. Deluxe Ed.; Res. Alert [Full Cov.]; Rev. Med. Vet. Entomol.; Sci. Cit. Index; SCISEARCH; Seed Abstr.; Wheat Barley Trit. Abstr.; Wildl. Rev. (Jan. 1989-July 1992).

LC QH573
DD 574.87 PO
NLM W1; CI2193 **CODEN** CBMBEU
CIENCIA BIOLOGICA. MOLECULAR AND CELLULAR BIOLOGY. Added/Corp Universidade de Coimbra. Departamento de Zoologia. Universidade de Coimbra. Instituto de Zoologia. **VFOAT** Molecular and Cellular Biology. Vol. 3 No. 1 (Dec. 1978)-. Academic Scholarly Publication. English (French, German and Portuguese). Four times a year. $10.00. Universidade de Coimbra, 3049 Coimbra Codex Portugal. Index available in last issue of volume--attached. Documents available from BIOSIS Document Express, CASDDS. ***Continues*** *Ciencia Biologica. Biologia Molecular e Celular.*
Ind/Abst Biol. Abstr.; Chem. Abstr. (1982-); Crop Physiol. Abstr.; CSA Neuro. Abstr. (?-?); Ornamental Hort.; Plant Grow. Reg. Abstr.; Protozoolog. Abstr.

LC QH573 **ISSN** 0210-1130
DD 574.87 SP
NLM W1; CI963B **CODEN** CITOEH
CEASED
CITOLOGIA : REVISTA OFICIAL DE LE SOCIEDAD ESPANOLA DE CITOLOGIA, EN COLABORACION CON LAS SOCIEDADES LATINOAMERICANAS DE CITOLOGIA. Added/Corp Sociedad Espanola de Citologia. (197?)-(1993). Monographic series. Spanish (summaries and/or abstracts in English). Editorial Garsi SA, Avenida Principe Asturias 20, 08012 Barcelona Spain. **Tel** 011 34 1 4154544.
Ind/Abst Indice Med. Esp.

ISSN 0260-5872 UK CCC
CLINICAL CYTOGENETICS. [Clin. cytogenet.]. (1981)-. Periodical. English. Twenty-four times a year. $205.35. SUBIS, Mansion House 19 Kingfield Road, Sheffield S11 9AS United Kingdom. **Tel** 011 44 114 2554433, FAX 011 44 114 255 4626. **Bk Rev. Ad Acc.**
Desc: Current awareness service for researchers and clinicians.

LC QH506 .C64 **ISSN** 0143-8123
DD 574.8/8 US CCC
NLM W1 CO375M **CODEN** CMCBDM
COMMENTS ON MOLECULAR AND CELLULAR BIOPHYSICS. See Biology-Biological Physics.

ISSN 0913-8188
DD 574.87 JA
COMMUNICATIONS IN APPLIED CELL BIOLOGY. [Commun. appl. cell biol.]. **VFOAT** Oyo Saibo Seibutsugaku Kenkyu. (1983)-. Periodical. Multiple languages. Four times a year. Nihon Oyo Saibo Seibutsugaku Kenkyukai, (Japan Applied Cell Biology Research Association), c/o Eiken Kizai K. K., 12-9 Higashijujo 1 Chome, Kitaku Tokyo 114 Japan. Documents available from CASDDS.
Ind/Abst Chem. Abstr.

LC QH450 .C75 **ISSN** 1045-4403
DD 574.87/322 US CCC
NLM W1; CR216ZBE **CODEN** CRGEEJ
CRITICAL REVIEWS IN EUKARYOTIC GENE EXPRESSION. [Crit. rev. eukaryot. gene expr.]. **VFOAT** Eukaryotic Gene Expression. Vol. 1, Issue 1 (1990)-. Academic Scholarly Publication. English. Four times a year. $295.00. Begell House Inc., 79 Madison Avenue, New York NY 10016-7892. **Tel** (212)725-1999, FAX (212)213-8368. **(Subscription address:** Begell House Inc., PO Box 1109, Pearl River NY 10965. **Tel** (212)725-1999.**) ED** Gary S. Stein, Janet L. Stein, Jane B. Lian. Documents available from The Genuine Article, BIOSIS Document Express, CASDDS.
Desc: Provides current, critical evaluations of the newest concepts, methods, and results in the field of mammalian genes and gene expression.
Ind/Abst AGRICOLA [Select. Cov.]; Biol. Abstr. (1991-); Chem. Abstr.; Curr. Aware. Biol. Sci., CABS; EMBASE; Index Med. (1990-); Res. Alert [Full Cov.].

LC Z5322.C3 C87 QH573 **ISSN** 0741-1626
DD 016.57487 UK
NLM Z 5322.C3; C976
CURRENT ADVANCES IN CELL AND DEVELOPMENTAL BIOLOGY. See Biology-Abstracting, Bibliographies and Statistics.

ISSN 1063-8806
DD 574 US CCC
NLM W1; CU7871 **CODEN** CCCBEL
CURRENT COMMUNICATIONS IN CELL & MOLECULAR BIOLOGY. [Curr. commun. cell mol. biol.]. **VFOAT** Current Communications in Cell and Molecular Biology. (1990)-. Academic Scholarly Publication. English. $65.00. Cold Spring Harbor Laboratory, 10 Skyline Drive, Plainview NY 11803. **Tel** (516)349-1930, (800)843-4388, FAX (516)349-1946. Documents available from CASDDS. ***Continues*** *Current Communications in Molecular Biology, 0737-3708.*
Desc: This series examines topics on which the impact of the techniques and concepts of molecular and cell biology is particularly evident.
Ind/Abst Chem. Abstr.; Curr. Cit.

LC QP351 .C88 **ISSN** 0738-0720
DD 591.1/88/028 US
CODEN CMCNEP
CURRENT METHODS IN CELLULAR NEUROBIOLOGY. [Curr. methods cell. neurobiol.]. Vol. 1-. Academic Scholarly Publication. English. Price varies per volume. John Wiley & Sons, Inc., 605 Third Avenue, New York NY 10158-0012. **Tel** (212)850-6000, (212)850-6645, FAX (212)850-6088, telex 12-7063. **(Subscription address:** John Wiley & Sons / UK, Baffins Lane, Chichester, West Sussex PO19 1UD United Kingdom. **Tel** 011 44 1243 779777, FAX 011 44 243 776128, telex 86290 WIBOOKG.**)** Documents available from CASDDS.
Ind/Abst Chem. Abstr. (1983-).

LC QH573 .C87 **ISSN** 0955-0674
US CCC
NLM W1; CU799GCE **CODEN** COCBE3
CURRENT OPINION IN CELL BIOLOGY. [Curr. opin. cell biol.]. Vol. 1, No. 1 (Feb. 1989)-. Periodical. English. Six times a year. $488.50. Current Science, 20 North 3rd Street, Philadelphia PA 19106. **Tel** (215)574-2266, (800)552-5866, FAX (215)574-2270. **ED** Norton B. Gilula and Lewis Wolpert. **Circ:** 2,500. available on an online database (for PC's). Documents available from BIOSIS Document Express.
Desc: Directed toward researchers, educators and students of cell biology. Presents review articles from an area of concentration covering an entire year's literature with annotated references. Each issue features a bibliography of the current world literature published during the previous year.
Ind/Abst AgBiotech News Inf.; Anim. Breed. Abstr.; Biol. Abstr. (1990-); Curr. Aware. Biol. Sci., CABS; Curr. Cit.; Index Med. (1989-); Ref. Upd. Deluxe Ed.

LC QH573 .C86 **ISSN** 0070-2137
DD 574.8/76 US
UDC 576.32/.36 CCC
NLM W1 CU82D **CODEN** CTCRAE
Pr Rev.
CURRENT TOPICS IN CELLULAR REGULATION. [Curr. top. cell. regul.]. **VFOAT** Cellular Regulation. Vol. 1 (1969)-. Monographic series. English. Irregular. Price varies per volume. Academic Press Inc., 6277 Sea Harbor Drive, Orlando FL 32887. **Tel** (800)543-9534, (407)345-4100, FAX (407)352-3445. **ED** Bernard L. Horecker and Earl R. Stadtman. Documents available from The Genuine Article, BIOSIS Document Express, CASDDS.
Ind/Abst AGRICOLA; Biol. Abstr.; Chem. Abstr.; Curr. Aware. Biol. Sci., CABS; Energy Res. Abstr. (Aug. 1982-); Index Med.; Index Sci. Rev. [Full Cov.]; Res. Alert [Full Cov.]; Sci. Cit. Index; SCISEARCH.

LC QH601 .C84 **ISSN** 1063-5823
DD 574 US CCC
NLM W1; CU82IW **CODEN** CTMEET
CURRENT TOPICS IN MEMBRANES. [Curr. top. membr.]. **Added/Corp** Yale University. Dept. of Cellular and Molecular Physiology. Vol. 38 (1991)-. Monographic series. English. Irregular. Price varies per volume. Academic Press Inc., 6277 Sea Harbor Drive, Orlando FL 32887. **Tel** (800)543-9534, (407)345-4100, FAX (407)352-3445. Documents available from BIOSIS Document Express. ***Continues*** *Current Topics in Membranes and Transport, 0070-2161.*
Ind/Abst Biol. Abstr.; Curr. Aware. Biol. Sci., CABS; Sci. Cit. Index.

LC QH573 .C9 **ISSN** 0011-4529
DD 574.8/7/05 UK
CCC
NLM W1 CY754 **CODEN** CYTBAI
Pr Rev.

CYTOBIOS. [Cytobios]. Vol. 1 (Jan./Mar. 1969)-. Periodical. English (French and German). Sixteen times a year. $675.93. Faculty Press, 88 Regent Street, Cambridge CB2 1DP United Kingdom. **Tel** FAX 011 44 1553 840695. cum. index. Documents available from BIOSIS Document Express, CASDDS.
Ind/Abst AGRICOLA [Select. Cov.]; Anim. Breed. Abstr.; Biol. Abstr.; Biol. Dig.; Chem. Abstr.; Crop Physiol. Abstr.; CSA Neuro. Abstr. (?-?); Curr. Aware. Biol. Sci., CABS; Curr. Cit.; Dairy Sci. Abstr.; EMBASE; Field Crop Abstr.; Genet. Abstr.; Health Plan. Adminis.; Helminthol. Abstr. (1991-); Hortic. Abstr.; Index Med.; Index Vet.; Microbiol. Abstr. Sect. C; Nematol. Abstr.; Ornamental Hort. (1991-); Life Sci. Collect.; PESTDOC; Plant Breed. Abstr.; Protozoolog. Abstr.; Ref. Upd. Deluxe Ed.; Rev. Agric. Entomol.; Rev. Med. Vet. Entomol.; Rev. Plant Pathol.; Sci. Cit. Index (19??-19??); SCISEARCH; Seed Abstr.; Soyabean Abstr.; Vet. Bull.; Weed Abstr.; Wheat Barley Trit. Abstr.

LC QH431 .C95 **ISSN** 0301-0171
DD 575.2/1 SZ
CCC
NLM W1 CY755 **CODEN** CGCGBR
Pr Rev.

CYTOGENETICS AND CELL GENETICS.
See Biology-Genetics.

ISSN 1013-9982
SZ
NLM W1; CY757 **CODEN** CYTKEF

CYTOKINES. [Cytokines]. Vol. 1 (1989)-. Monographic series. English. One time a year. 180.00F (approx. per volume). S. Karger AG, Allschwilerstrasse 10, PO Box, CH-4009 Basel Switzerland. **Tel** 011 41 61 3061111, FAX 011 41 61 3061234, telex CH 962 652. **ED** C. Sorg. Documents available from BIOSIS Document Express.
Desc: This timely series on cytokines will cover the cellular and molecular biological aspects of cell regulatory factors, while especially considering the biological and clinical perspectives. Carefully selected articles will provide the latest information on cell regulation in physiological and pathological processes, from which direct therapeutic consequences for the treatment of a variety of diseases are expected to emerge.
Ind/Abst Biol. Abstr. (1989-); Index Med. (1992-); Ref. Upd. Deluxe Ed.

LC QH301 .C9 **ISSN** 0011-4545
DD 442.8 JA
NLM W1 CY775 **CODEN** CYTOAN

CYTOLOGIA. [Cytologia]. Vol. 1, No. 1 (Aug. 1, 1929)-. Periodical. English (German and French). Four times a year. $300.00. Kokusai Saibo Gakkai Kitorogia, (Cytologia), Toshin Biru, 27-2 Hongo 2 Chome, Bunkyoku Tokyo 113 Japan. **(Subscription address:** Maruzen Company Ltd., PO Box 5050, Import & Export Department, Tokyo 100 31 Japan. **Tel** 011 81 3 32789224.) ctrl circ. Documents available from BIOSIS Document Express, CASDDS.
Desc: Organ papers of Kokvsai-Saibo-Gakkai.
Ind/Abst AgBiotech News Inf.; AGRICOLA [Select. Cov.]; Agrofor. Abstr. (1991-); Anim. Breed. Abstr.; Biol. Abstr.; Chem. Abstr.; Cot. Trop. Fibr. Abstr. Bibliogr.; Crop Physiol. Abstr.; Curr. Aware. Biol. Sci., CABS; Curr. Cit.; EMBASE; Field Crop Abstr.; For. Abstr.; Genet. Abstr.; Grass. Forage Abstr.; Hortic. Abstr.; Maize Abstr.; Microbiol. Abstr. Sect. C; Ornamental Hort. (19??-19??); Life Sci. Collect.; Plant Breed. Abstr.; Plant Genet. Resour. Abstr.; Plant Grow. Reg. Abstr.; Potato Abstr.; Rev. Agric. Entomol.; Rev. Med. Vet. Entomol.; Rev. Plant Pathol.; Rice Abstr.; Seed Abstr.; Soils Fert.; Sorghum Mill. Abstr.; Weed Abstr.; Wheat Barley Trit. Abstr.

LC QH426 .C94 **ISSN** 0095-4527
DD 574.8/7/05 US
CCC
NLM W1 CY796 **CODEN** CYGEDX

CYTOLOGY AND GENETICS. [Cytol. genet.]. Vol. 8 (1974)-. Periodical. English (Russian). Six times a year. $975.00. Allerton Press Inc., 150 Fifth Avenue, New York NY 10011. **Tel** (212)924-3950, FAX (212)463-9684, telex 427441 ALPRES. Documents available from BIOSIS Document Express, CASDDS.
Ind/Abst AGRICOLA [Select. Cov.]; Biol. Abstr. (1983-); Chem. Abstr.; Curr. Cit.; EMBASE; Fish Rev.

LC QH573 .C95 **ISSN** 0196-4763
DD 574.87/05 US
CCC
NLM W1 CY799 **CODEN** CYTODQ
Pr Rev.

CYTOMETRY (NEW YORK, N.Y.). (CYTOMETRY.). [Cytometry]. **Added/Corp** Society for Analytical Cytology (U.S.) International Society for Analytical Cytology. Vol. 1 (July 1980)-. Academic Scholarly Publication. English. Sixteen times a year. $596.00 (US); $756.00 (Canada and Mexico); $816.00 (other). John Wiley & Sons, Inc., 605 Third Avenue, New York NY 10158-0012. **Tel** (212)850-6000, (212)850-6645, FAX (212)850-6088, telex 12-7063. **(Subscription address:** John Wiley & Sons / UK, Baffins Lane, Chichester, West Sussex PO19 1UD United Kingdom. **Tel** 011 44 1243 779777, FAX 011 44 243 776128, telex 86290 WIBOOKG.) **ED** Brian H. Mayall. Documents available from The Genuine Article, BIOSIS Document Express, CASDDS, ADONIS.
Desc: An influential and widely cited international journal embracing all aspects of analytical cytology, which is broadly defined as the characterization and measurement of cells and cellular constitutents for diagnostic and therapeutic purposes.
Ind/Abst ADONIS; AGRICOLA; Biol. Abstr.; Chem. Abstr.; Curr. Cit.; Curr. Contents Life Sci.; EMBASE; Health Plan. Adminis.; Immunol. Abstr.; Index Med. (July 1980-); Int. Aerosp. Abstr.; Life Sci. Collect.; Ref. Upd. Basic Ed.; Ref. Upd. Deluxe Ed.; Res. Alert [Full Cov.]; Sci. Cit. Index; SCISEARCH.

ISSN 1046-7386
DD 574 US
NLM W1; CY799A

CYTOMETRY. SUPPLEMENT. (CYTOMETRY. SUPPLEMENT : THE JOURNAL OF THE SOCIETY FOR ANALYTICAL CYTOLOGY.). **Added/Corp** Society for Analytical Cytology (U.S.). Vol. 1 (1987)-. Monographic series. English. Irregular. Price varies per volume. Wiley Liss, 605 3rd Avenue, New York NY 10158. **Tel** (212)850-8800, (212)850-6645. **(Subscription address:** John Wiley & Sons, Inc. / Philadelphia, PO Box 7247, Philadelphia PA 19170. **Tel** (212)850-6645, (800)225-5945.)
Ind/Abst Health Plan. Adminis.; Index Med. (1987-).

ISSN 1069-045X
DD 616 US
NLM W1; CY81

CYTOPATHOLOGY ANNUAL. [Cytopathol. annu.]. (1992)-. English. One time a year. $90.00. Williams & Wilkins Company, 428 East Preston Street, Baltimore MD 21202-3993. **Tel** (410)528-4000, (800)638-6423, FAX (410)528-8596, telex 87669. **(Subscription address:** Williams & Wilkins, PO Box 64380, Baltimore MD 21264. **Tel** 800 638-6423.) Documents available from , , Quick Copies.

ISSN 0956-5507
UK
CCC
NLM W1; CY799L **CODEN** CYTPEU
Pr Rev.

CYTOPATHOLOGY (OXFORD). (CYTOPATHOLOGY : OFFICIAL JOURNAL OF THE BRITISH SOCIETY FOR CLINICAL CYTOLOGY.). [Cytopathology (Oxf.)]. **Added/Corp** British Society for Clinical Cytology. Vol. 1, No. 1 (1990)-. Academic Scholarly Publication. English. Six times a year. $279.00. Blackwell Scientific Publications Ltd, Marston Book Services, PO Box 88, Oxford OX2 ONE United Kingdom. **Tel** 011 44 1865 206206, FAX 011 44 1865 206219, telex 837 515 MARDIS G. **ED** Dulcie V. Coleman and Peter Trott. Index available. **Bk Rev. Ad Acc. Circ:** 800. available on microfilm and microfiche from University Microfilms International (UMI). Documents available from The Genuine Article, ADONIS.
Desc: Publishes articles relating to those aspects of cytology which increase our knowledge and understanding of the etiology, diagnosis and management of human disease.
Ind/Abst ADONIS; Curr. Aware. Biol. Sci., CABS; Curr. Cit.; Curr. Contents Clin. Med.; EMBASE; Health Plan. Adminis.; Index Med. (1990-); Res. Alert [Full Cov.]; Sci. Cit. Index; SCISEARCH.

ISSN 0268-1625
DD 016.5748734 UK
CCC

CYTOSKELETON SHEFFIELD. (CYTOSKELETON.). [Cytoskeleton Sheff.]. (1986)-. English. Twelve times a year. £105.00. SUBIS, Mansion House 19 Kingfield Road, Sheffield S11 9AS United Kingdom. **Tel** 011 44 114 2554433, FAX 011 44 114 255 4626.

LC QH573 **ISSN** 0920-9069
DD 574.87 NE
CCC
NLM W1; CY88 **CODEN** CYTOER
Pr Rev.

CYTOTECHNOLOGY (DORDRECHT). (CYTOTECHNOLOGY.). [Cytotechnology]. Vol. 1, No. 1 (Oct. 1987)-. Periodical. English. Nine times a year. $814.00. Kluwer Academic Publishers, Postbus 322, 3300 AH Dordrecht The Netherlands. **Tel** 011 31 78 524400, FAX 011 31 78 183273, telex 20083. **ED** Editorial Board. **Bk Rev.** available on microfilm and microfiche from University Microfilms International (UMI). Documents available from The Genuine Article, BIOSIS Document Express.
Desc: Represents a central repository for information on both the infrastructure of cell technology and the applied use of cell cultures, thus providing a panoramic perspective of the many facets and disciplines needed to develop successful cell cultures. This is an international journal on news and developments, methods and techniques in fundamental cell culture research, and the applications of that research in human and veterinary medicine, toxicology and animal cell biotechnology. The journal publishes reviews, original papers, short communications and technical reports containing information on all forms of vertebrate and invertebrate in vitro cell cultures.
Ind/Abst AgBiotech News Inf.; Biol. Abstr. (1988-); Curr. Aware. Biol. Sci., CABS; Curr. Cit.; Curr. Contents Agric. Biol. Environ. Sci.; Index Vet.; PESTDOC; Ref. Upd. Deluxe Ed.; Res. Alert [Full Cov.]; Rev. Med. Vet. Entomol.; SCISEARCH; Vet. Bull.

LC QH573 **ISSN** 0165-2265
DD 574.87 US
NLM W1 DE997VN **CODEN** DCBIDD
Pr Rev.

DEVELOPMENTS IN CELL BIOLOGY. [Dev. cell biol.]. (1977)-. Academic Scholarly Publication. English. Irregular. Price varies per volume. Elsevier Science Publishing Company Inc, Madison Square Station, PO Box 882, New York NY 10159-0882. **Tel** (212)633-3950, FAX (212)633-3990. **(Subscription address:** Elsevier Science Inc. / New York Books, 655 Avenue of the Americas, New York NY 10010. **Tel** (212)633-3650.) Documents available from CASDDS.
Ind/Abst Chem. Abstr.

ISSN 8755-1039
DD 611 US
CCC
NLM W1; DI258EX **CODEN** DICYE7
Pr Rev.

DIAGNOSTIC CYTOPATHOLOGY. [Diagn. cytopathol.]. Vol. 1, No. 1 (Jan./March 1985)-. Periodical. English. Nine times a year. $594.00. John Wiley & Sons, Inc., 605 Third Avenue, New York NY 10158-0012. **Tel** (212)850-6000, (212)850-6645, FAX (212)850-6088, telex 12-7063. **(Subscription address:** John Wiley & Sons / UK, Baffins Lane, Chichester, West Sussex PO19 1UD United Kingdom. **Tel** 011 44 1243 779777, FAX 011 44 243 776128, telex 86290 WIBOOKG.) **ED** Carlos W. M. Bedrossian. Documents available from The Genuine Article, BIOSIS Document Express.
Desc: Highly successful, international forum for original research and review articles on clinical aspects of cytology, encompassing such areas as flow cytometry, electron microscopy, image analysis, and immunocytochemistry.
Ind/Abst Biol. Abstr. (1989-); Curr. Cit.; Curr. Contents Clin. Med.; EMBASE; Health Plan. Adminis.; Helminthol. Abstr. (1991-); Index Med. (1985-); Protozoolog. Abstr.; Res. Alert [Select. Cov.]; SCISEARCH.

LC QH573 .D53 **ISSN** 0301-4681
DD 574.8/761 GW
CCC
NLM W1 DI531 **CODEN** DFFNAW
Pr Rev.

DIFFERENTIATION (LONDON). (DIFFERENTIATION.). [Differentiation]. **Added/Corp** International Society of Differentiation. Vol. 1 (Feb. 1973)-. Periodical. English. Ten times a year. $1333.00. Springer-Verlag GmbH & Company KG, Heidelberger Platz 3, D-14197 Berlin Germany. **Tel** 011 49 30 8207223, FAX 011 49 30 8214091, telex 183 319 SPBLN D. **(Subscription address:** Springer-Verlag New York Inc. / North America, PO Box 2485, Journal Fulfillment, Secaucus NJ 07096. **Tel** (201)348-4033, (800)777-4643, FAX (201)348-4505.) **ED** W W Franke. available on microfilm and microfiche from University Microfilms International (UMI). Documents available from The Genuine Article, BIOSIS Document Express, CASDDS.
Desc: Reports the research results on problems of biological diversification of plants and animals and in embryology.
Ind/Abst AGRICOLA; Biol. Abstr.; Calcium Calcif. Tissue Abstr.; Chem. Abstr.; CSA Neuro. Abstr. (?-?); Curr. Cit.; Curr. Contents Life Sci.; EMBASE; Genet. Abstr.; Health Plan. Adminis.; Immunol. Abstr.; Index Med.; Microbiol. Abstr. Sect. C; Oncog. Growth Factors Abstr.; Life Sci. Collect.; Protozoolog. Abstr.; Ref. Upd. Basic Ed.; Ref. Upd. Deluxe Ed.; Res. Alert [Full Cov.]; Sci. Cit. Index; SCISEARCH.

LC QH573 **ISSN** 0256-1514
DD 574.87 GW
NLM W1; EN396SX

ENDOCYTOBIOSIS AND CELL RESEARCH. **Added/Corp** International Society of Endocytobiology. **VFOAT** ISE Letters; International Journal on Endocytobiosis and Cell Research. Vol. 1 (Nov. 1984)-. Periodical. English. Irregular (2-3 issues per year). Attempto Verlag Tubingen, Wilhelmstrasse 7, D-7400 Tubingen Germany. **Tel** 011 49 707121201. Documents available from The Genuine Article.
Ind/Abst Curr. Cit.; Curr. Contents Agric. Biol. Environ. Sci.; Plant Grow. Reg. Abstr.; Protozoolog. Abstr.; Res. Alert [Full Cov.]; Sci. Cit. Index; SCISEARCH; Soyabean Abstr.

ISSN 1062-3329
US
CCC
CODEN ENDTE9

ENDOTHELIUM (NEW YORK, N.Y.). (ENDOTHELIUM : JOURNAL OF ENDOTHELIAL CELL RESEARCH.). **VFOAT** Journal of Endothelial Cell Research. (1992)-. Periodical. English. Four times a year (1 volume). $242.00 (academic institutions), $378.00 (corporate institutions). Harwood Academic Publishers / New York, PO Box 786, Cooper Station, New York NY 10276. **Tel** (212)206-8900, (201)643-7500.
Desc: Reports on endothelial cell research.

ISSN 0940-9912
UK
CCC

NLM W1; EP462DH
EPITHELIAL CELL BIOLOGY. Vol. 1, No. 1 (1992)-. Periodical. English. Four times a year. $224.00. Springer-Verlag London Ltd., Springer House, 8 Alexandra Road Wimbledon, London SW19 7JZ United Kingdom. **Tel** 011 44 181 9471280, 011 44 181 9475885, FAX 011 44 181 9474651, telex 21531 SPRGB G. **(Subscription address:** Springer-Verlag New York Inc. / North America, PO Box 2485, Journal Fulfillment, Secaucus NJ 07096. **Tel** (201)348-4033, (800)777-4643, FAX (201)348-4505.)
Ind/Abst Index Med.; Sci. Cit. Index.

ISSN 0268-808X
UK

ERYTHROCYTES. (1979)-. English. Twenty-four times a year. $188.23. SUBIS, Mansion House 19 Kingfield Road, Sheffield S11 9AS United Kingdom. **Tel** 011 44 114 2554433, FAX 011 44 114 255 4626. **Bk Rev. Ad Acc.**
Desc: Current awareness service for researchers and clinicians.

ISSN 1148-5493
FR
NLM W1; EU62M **CODEN** ECYNEJ
EUROPEAN CYTOKINE NETWORK (MONTROUGE). (EUROPEAN CYTOKINE NETWORK.). [Eur. cytokine netw.]. (199?)-. Periodical. English. Six times a year. $398.07. John Libbey Eurotext Ltd., 127 avenue de la Republique, 92120 Montrouge France. **Tel** 011 33 1 46730660, FAX 011 33 1 40840999. **(Subscription address:** ATEI John Libbey Eurotext, 3 Avenue Pierre Kerautret, 93230 Romainville France. **Tel** 011 33 1 48408686.)
Ind/Abst Curr. Cit.; Health Plan. Adminis.; Index Med.; Ref. Upd. Deluxe Ed.

LC QH573 .C895 **ISSN** 0171-9335
DD 574.87 GW
CCC
NLM W1 EU72BJ **CODEN** EJCBDN
Pr Rev.
EUROPEAN JOURNAL OF CELL BIOLOGY. [Eur. j. cell biol.]. **Added/Corp** Deutsche Gesellschaft fuer Elektronenmikroskopie. Deutsche Gesellschaft fuer Zellbiologie. European Cell Biology Organization. Vol. 19 (April 1979)-. Academic Scholarly Publication. English (German). Six times a year. DM420.00. Wissenschaftliche Verlagsgesellschaft mbH, Postfach 101061, D-70009 Stuttgart Germany. **Tel** 011 49 711 258200, FAX 011 49 711 2582290, telex 723636 DAZ D. **ED** Volker Herzog. Index available. **Bk Rev. Ad Acc. Circ:** 900 (ctrl). Documents available from The Genuine Article, BIOSIS Document Express, CASDDS. ***Continues** Cytobiologie, 0070-2463.*
Desc: A journal of experimental cell research which publishes papers on the structure, function and macromolecular organization of cells and cell components. Aspects of cellular dynamics, differentiation, biochemistry and molecular biology in relation to structural data are preferred fields for contributions.
Ind/Abst AgBiotech News Inf.; AGRICOLA; Anim. Breed. Abstr.; Biol. Abstr.; Chem. Abstr.; Chemorecept. Abstr.; Crop Physiol. Abstr.; CSA Neuro. Abstr. (?-?); Curr. Aware. Biol. Sci., CABS; Curr. Cit.; Curr. Contents Life Sci.; Curr. Ref. Fish Res.; Dairy Sci. Abstr.; EMBASE; Genet. Abstr.; Helminthol. Abstr.; Index Med.; Microbiol. Abstr. Sect. C; Oncog. Growth Factors Abstr.; Life Sci. Collect.; PESTDOC; Plant Breed. Abstr.; Plant Grow. Reg. Abstr.; Protozoolog. Abstr.; Ref. Upd. Basic Ed.; Ref. Upd. Deluxe Ed.; Res. Alert [Full Cov.]; Rev. Agric. Entomol.; Rev. Med. Vet. Entomol.; Rev. Med. Vet. Mycology; Rev. Plant Pathol.; Sci. Cit. Index; SCISEARCH; Soyabean Abstr.; Virol. AIDS Abstr.

LC QH573 **ISSN** 0724-5130
DD 574.87 GW
NLM W1 EU72BJA **CODEN** EJBSE2
EUROPEAN JOURNAL OF CELL BIOLOGY. SUPPLEMENT. [Euro. j. cell biol., Suppl.]. (1983)-. Monographic series. English. Irregular. Price varies per volume. Wissenschaftliche Verlagsgesellschaft mbH, Postfach 101061, D-70009 Stuttgart Germany. **Tel** 011 49 711 258200, FAX 011 49 711 2582290, telex 723636 DAZ D. Documents available from BIOSIS Document Express.
Ind/Abst Biol. Abstr. (1986-); Curr. Aware. Biol. Sci., CABS; Index Med.

LC QH581 .I523 **ISSN** 0014-4827
DD 576.305 574.805* US
CCC
NLM W1 EX501 **CODEN** ECREAL
Pr Rev.
EXPERIMENTAL CELL RESEARCH. [Exp. cell res.]. **Added/Corp** International Society for Cell Biology. Vol. 1 (Jan. 1950)-. Academic Scholarly Publication. English. Sixteen times a year. $1825.00. Academic Press Inc., 6277 Sea Harbor Drive, Orlando FL 32887. **Tel** (800)543-9534, (407)345-4100, FAX (407)352-3445. **ED** N. R. Ringertz. Documents available from The Genuine Article, BIOSIS Document Express, CASDDS.
Desc: Promotes the understanding of cell biology by publishing experimental studies on the general organization and activity of cells. The scope of the journal includes all aspects of cell biology, from the molecular level to the level of cell interaction and differentiation.
Ind/Abst AgBiotech News Inf.; AGRICOLA [Select. Cov.]; Anim. Breed. Abstr.; Biol. Agric. Index; Biol. Abstr.; Calcium Calcif. Tissue Abstr.; Chem. Abstr.; Chem. Titles; CSA Neuro. Abstr. (?-?); Curr. Aware. Biol. Sci., CABS; Curr. Cit.; Curr. Contents Life Sci.; Curr. Ref. Fish Res.; Dairy Sci. Abstr.; EMBASE; Energy Res. Abstr.; Genet. Abstr.; Health Plan. Adminis.; Hortic. Abstr.; Immunol. Abstr.; Index Med.; Index Vet.; INIS Atomindex [Micro.]; Microbiol. Abstr. Sect. C; Nucl. Acids Abstr.; Oncog. Growth Factors Abstr.; Life Sci. Collect.; PESTDOC; Plant Breed. Abstr.; Protozoolog. Abstr.; Ref. Upd. Basic Ed.; Ref. Upd. Deluxe Ed.; Res. Alert [Full Cov.]; Rev. Agric. Entomol.; Rev. Med. Vet. Entomol.; Sci. Cit. Index; SCISEARCH; Soc. Sci. Cit. Index [Select. Cov.]; Vet. Bull.; Virol. AIDS Abstr.

ISSN 0268-1617
DD 016.57487 UK
CCC

EXTRACELLULAR MATRIX. [Extracell. matrix]. (1986)-. English. Twenty-four times a year. $188.23. SUBIS, Mansion House 19 Kingfield Road, Sheffield S11 9AS United Kingdom. **Tel** 011 44 114 2554433, FAX 011 44 114 255 4626. **Bk Rev. Ad Acc.** available on diskette.
Desc: Current awareness service for researchers.

LC QH573 **ISSN** 0239-8508
DD 574.87 PL
NLM W1; FO1812 **CODEN** FHCYEM
Pr Rev.
FOLIA HISTOCHEMICA ET CYTOBIOLOGICA. [Folia histochem. cytobiol.]. **Added/Corp** Polskie Towarzystwo Histochemikow I Cytochemikow. Vol. 22 No. 1 (1984)-. Academic Scholarly Publication. English (summaries and/or abstracts in Polish and Russian). Four times a year. $60.00 (institutions), $50.00 (individuals). **(Subscription address:** Ars Polona-Ruch, PO Box 1001, Krakowskie Przedmiescie 7, 00-068 Warsaw Poland. **Tel** 011 48 22 261201.) Documents available from The Genuine Article, BIOSIS Document Express, CASDDS. ***Continues** Folia Histochemica et Cytochemica, 0015-5586.*
Ind/Abst Biol. Abstr.; Chem. Abstr. (1984-); Curr. Cit.; Index Med. (Vol. 22, No. 1, 1984-); Res. Alert [Full Cov.]; Sci. Cit. Index; SCISEARCH.

LC QH573 **ISSN** 0732-8079
DD 574.873282 US
NLM W1 GE278 **CODEN** GCTEDM
GENETIC AND CELLULAR TECHNOLOGY. See Biology-Genetics.

LC QH611 .H53 **ISSN** 0018-2214
DD 574.8 UK
CCC
NLM W1 HI74 **CODEN** HISJAE
Pr Rev.
HISTOCHEMICAL JOURNAL. (THE HISTOCHEMICAL JOURNAL.). [Histochem. j.]. **Added/Corp** Royal Microscopical Society (Great Britain). Vol. 1 (Aug. 1968)-. Academic Scholarly Publication. English. Twelve times a year. $815.00. Chapman & Hall, 2-6 Boundary Row, London SE1 8HN United Kingdom. **Tel** 011 44 171 8650066, FAX 011 44 171 5229623, telex 290164 CHAPMA G. **ED** P. Stoward. Index available. **Bk Rev. Ad Acc. Circ:** 600. available on microfilm and microfiche from University Microfilms International (UMI). Documents available from The Genuine Article, BIOSIS Document Express, CASDDS, ADONIS.
Desc: A primary journal, publishing international papers in histochemistry and cytochemistry. Covers areas including biochemistry, histochemistry, pathology, immunocytochemistry, and cell biology.
Ind/Abst ADONIS; AgBiotech News Inf.; AGRICOLA; Anim. Breed. Abstr.; Biol. Abstr.; Calcium Calcif. Tissue Abstr.; Chem. Abstr.; CSA Neuro. Abstr. (?-?); Curr. Aware. Biol. Sci., CABS; Curr. Cit.; Curr. Contents Life Sci.; Dairy Sci. Abstr.; EMBASE; Health Plan. Adminis.; Helminthol. Abstr.; Index Med.; Int. Aerosp. Abstr.; Nematol. Abstr.; Nutr. Abstr. Rev., Ser. B, Live Feeds and Feed.; Life Sci. Collect.; Pig News Inf.; Plant Breed. Abstr.; Plant Genet. Resour. Abstr.; Poult. Abstr.; Protozoolog. Abstr.; Ref. Upd. Basic Ed.; Ref. Upd. Deluxe Ed.; Res. Alert [Full Cov.]; Rev. Agric. Entomol.; Rev. Med. Vet. Entomol.; Sci. Cit. Index; SCISEARCH; Trop. Dis. Bull.

LC QH611 .Z43
GW

NLM W1; HI748
•**HISTOCHEMISTRY AND CELL BIOLOGY.** **Added/Corp** Society for Histochemistry. **VFOAT** Histochemistry. Vol. 103, No. 1 (Jan. 1995)-. Periodical. English. Twelve times a year. $2136.00. Springer-Verlag GmbH & Company KG, Heidelberger Platz 3, D-14197 Berlin Germany. **Tel** 011 49 30 8207223, FAX 011 49 30 8214091, telex 183 319 SPBLN D. **(Subscription address:** Springer-Verlag New York Inc. / North America, PO Box 2485, Journal Fulfillment, Secaucus NJ 07096. **Tel** (201)348-4033, (800)777-4643, FAX (201)348-4505.) ***Continues** Histochemistry, 0301-5564.*
Ind/Abst Curr. Cit.; Index Med. (1995-).

LC QH611 .Z43 **ISSN** 0301-5564
DD 574.8/21 GW
CCC
NLM W1; HI748 **CODEN** HCMYAL
TITLE CHANGE
HISTOCHEMISTRY (BERLIN). (HISTOCHEMISTRY.). [Histochemistry]. Vol. 38 (1974)-(19??). Periodical. English (German; summaries and/or abstracts in German). Springer-Verlag GmbH & Company KG, Heidelberger Platz 3, D-14197 Berlin Germany. **Tel** 011 49 30 8207223, FAX 011 49 30 8214091, telex 183 319 SPBLN D. **(Subscription address:** Springer-Verlag New York Inc. / North America, PO Box 2485, Journal Fulfillment, Secaucus NJ 07096. **Tel** (201)348-4033, (800)777-4643, FAX (201)348-4505.) **ED** T. H. Schiebler. available on microfilm and microfiche from University Microfilms International (UMI). Documents available from The Genuine Article, BIOSIS Document Express, CASDDS, ADONIS. ***Continues** Histochemie, 0018-2222. **Continued by** Histochemistry and Cell Biology.*
Desc: Publishes original papers dealing with problems in all areas of cyto- and histochemistry. Special emphasis is placed on theory and methodology.
Ind/Abst ADONIS; Biol. Abstr.; Chem. Abstr.; Chem. Titles; CSA Neuro. Abstr.; Curr. Cit.; Curr. Contents Life Sci.; EMBASE; Energy Res. Abstr. (Jan. 1975-); Health Plan. Adminis.; Index Med.; Life Sci. Collect.; Pig News Inf.; Protozoolog. Abstr.; Ref. Upd. Deluxe Ed.; Res. Alert [Full Cov.]; Rev. Agric. Entomol.; Rev. Med. Vet. Entomol.; Sci. Cit. Index; SCISEARCH; Weed Abstr.

LC QH573 **ISSN** 0213-3911
DD 574.87 SP
NLM W1; HI77D **CODEN** HIHIES
Pr Rev.
HISTOLOGY AND HISTOPATHOLOGY. [Histol. histopath.]. **Added/Corp** Consejeria de Sanidad de la Comunidad Autonoma de Murcia (Spain). Vol. 1, No. 1 (Jan. 1986)-. Academic Scholarly Publication. English. Four times a year. $200.00. Histology and Histopathology, Plaza Fuensanta 2 7C, 30008 Murcia Spain. **ED** F. Hernandez. Index available. cum. index. **Ad Acc. Circ:** 3,000. Documents available from The Genuine Article, CASDDS.
Desc: Publishes original works in English in histology, histopathology and general morphology.
Ind/Abst Biol. Abstr.; Chem. Abstr. (1986-); Curr. Aware. Biol. Sci., CABS; Curr. Cit.; Curr. Contents Life Sci.; EMBASE; Helminthol. Abstr. (1991-); Index Med. (Jan. 1986-); Index Vet.; Pig News Inf.; Protozoolog. Abstr.; Res. Alert [Full Cov.]; Sci. Cit. Index; SCISEARCH; Small Anim. Abstr. Bibliogr.; Vet. Bull.

ISSN 0914-7470
JA

NLM W1; HU444WL
HUMAN CELL : OFFICIAL JOURNAL OF HUMAN CELL RESEARCH SOCIETY. **Added/Corp** Hito Saibo Kenkyukai (Japan). Vol. 1, No. 1 (1988)-. Periodical. Japanese (English; summaries and/or abstracts in English and Japanese). Four times a year. $134.00. **(Subscription address:** Maruzen Company Ltd., PO Box 5050, Import & Export Department, Tokyo 100 31 Japan. **Tel** 011 81 3 32789224.)
Ind/Abst Index Med.

ISSN 0144-3909
UK

NLM W1 HU448L
HUMAN LYMPHOCYTE DIFFERENTIATION. [Human lymph. differ.]. Vol. 1, No. 1 (Jan.-Mar. 1981)-. Academic Scholarly Publication. English. Four times a year. $75.00. Holt Saunders Ltd, High Street, Foots Cray Sidcup, Kent DA14 5HP United Kingdom. **Tel** 011 44 181 3003322.
Ind/Abst EMBASE.

LC QR185.8.H93 H9 **ISSN** 0272-457X
DD 574.2/9 US
NLM W1 HY26 **CODEN** HYBRDY
Pr Rev.
HYBRIDOMA. See Medical Sciences-Allergy and Immunologic Diseases.

LC QH585 .I52 **ISSN** 1071-2690
DD 574/.072 US
NLM W1; IN106C **CODEN** IVCAED
Pr Rev.
•**IN VITRO CELLULAR & DEVELOPMENTAL BIOLOGY. ANIMAL.** [In vitro cell. dev. biol., Anim.]. **Added/Corp** Tissue Culture Association. Society for In Vitro Biology. **VFOAT** In Vitro Cellular and Developmental Biology. Animal; In Vitro. Animal; Animal. Vol. 29A, No. 3, Pt. 2 (Mar. 1993)-. Academic Scholarly Publication. English. Twelve times a year. $245.00. Society for In Vitro Biology, PO Box 73230, Baltimore MD 21273. **Tel** (410)992-0946. Documents available from The Genuine Article, CASDDS. ***Continues in part** In Vitro Cellular & Developmental Biology, 0883-8364.*
Ind/Abst Chem. Abstr.; Curr. Aware. Biol. Sci., CABS; Curr. Contents Life Sci.; Res. Alert [Full Cov.]; Sci. Cit. Index; SCISEARCH.

LC RG316 **ISSN** 0363-521X
DD 618.1 US
NLM W1 IN106A **CODEN** IVMOD2
IN VITRO. MONOGRAPH. [In vitro, Monogr.]. **Added/Corp** Tissue Culture Association. (1970)-. Monographic series. English. Irregular. Price varies per volume. Society for In Vitro Biology, PO Box 73230, Baltimore MD 21273. **Tel** (410)992-0946. **ED** M.K. Patterson Jr. Documents available from BIOSIS Document Express.
Desc: Deals with standardization of vertebrate cell cultures including quality control applied to procedures in molecular and cell biology.
Ind/Abst Biol. Abstr.; Biotechnol. Res. Abstr.; CSA Neuro. Abstr. (?-?); Energy Res. Abstr. (Aug. 1982-); Oncog. Growth Factors Abstr.

LC QH573 **ISSN** 0250-0868
DD 574.87 SZ
CCC
NLM W1 IN797B
Pr Rev.
INTERNATIONAL JOURNAL OF TISSUE REACTIONS. [Int. j. tissue react.]. **VFOAT** Tissue Reactions. Vol. 2, No. 2 (June 1980)-. Periodical. English. Six times a year. 342.00F Europe; 355.00F other. Biosciences Ediprint Inc, rue Alexandre Gavard 16, 1227 Carouge Geneva Switzerland. **Tel** 011 42 22 3003383. **ED** A. Bertelli. available on microfilm from University Microfilms International (UMI). Documents available from The Genuine Article, CASDDS. ***Continues*** *International Journal on Tissue Reactions, 0250-0868.*
Ind/Abst Chem. Abstr.; CSA Neuro. Abstr. (?-?); Curr. Aware. Biol. Sci., CABS; Curr. Cit.; Curr. Contents Life Sci.; Dairy Sci. Abstr.; EMBASE; Index Med.; Int. Pharm. Abstr.; Nutr. Abstr. Rev., Ser. A, Hum. Exp.; Life Sci. Collect.; PESTDOC; Res. Alert [Full Cov.]; Sci. Cit. Index; SCISEARCH.

LC QH573 .I5 **ISSN** 0074-7696
DD 574.87/05 US
CCC
NLM W1 IN832 **CODEN** IRCYAJ
INTERNATIONAL REVIEW OF CYTOLOGY. [Int. rev. cyt.]. Vol. 1 (1952)-. Academic Scholarly Publication. English. Irregular. Price varies per volume. Academic Press Inc., 6277 Sea Harbor Drive, Orlando FL 32887. **Tel** (800)543-9534, (407)345-4100, FAX (407)352-3445. **ED** G. H. Bourne, K. W. Jeon and M. Friedlander. Documents available from The Genuine Article, BIOSIS Document Express, CASDDS.
Ind/Abst AGRICOLA [Select. Cov.]; Anim. Breed. Abstr.; Biol. Abstr.; Chem. Abstr.; CSA Neuro. Abstr. (?-?); Curr. Aware. Biol. Sci., CABS; Curr. Cit.; EMBASE; Energy Res. Abstr.; Genet. Abstr.; Index Med.; Index Sci. Rev. [Full Cov.]; INIS Atomindex [Micro.]; Microbiol. Abstr. Sect. C; Nematol. Abstr.; Life Sci. Collect.; Plant Breed. Abstr.; Ref. Upd. Basic Ed.; Ref. Upd. Deluxe Ed.; Res. Alert [Full Cov.]; Rev. Agric. Entomol.; Sci. Cit. Index; SCISEARCH.

LC QH601 .I65 **ISSN** 1059-7514
DD 574.87/5 US
NLM W1; IO105
ION CHANNELS. [Ion channels]. (1988)-. Monographic series. English. Irregular. Price varies per volume. Plenum Press, 233 Spring Street, New York NY 10013-1578. **Tel** (212)620-8000, (800)221-9369, FAX (212)463-0742, (212)807-1047, telex 23/421139. **ED** Toshio Narahashi.
Ind/Abst Index Med.

LC QH573 .I83 **ISSN** 0131-1751
RU
NLM W1 TS278B **CODEN** ITTKEC
ITOGI NAUKI I TEHNIKI - VSESOUZNYJ INSTITUT NAUCNOJ I TEHNICESKOJ INFORMACII. SERIJA CITOLOGIJA. (ITOGI NAUKI I TEKHNIKI. SERIIA TSITOLOGIIA.). [Itogi nauki i teh. - Vses. inst. nauc. teh. inf., Ser. Citol.]. **Added/Corp** Vsesoiuznyi Institut Nauchnoi i Tekhnicheskoi Informatsii (Soviet Union). **VFOAT** Seriia Tsitologiia; Tsitologiia; Itogi Nauki i Tekhniki. Tsitologiia. Vol. 1 (1971)-. Monographic series. Russian. Price varies per volume. VINITI - Vsesoyuznyi Institut Nauchno-Tekhnicheskoi Informatsii, All-Union Scientific and Technical Information Institute, Baltiiskaia ulitsa 14, 125219 Moscow Russia. **Tel** 011 7 95 2384600, FAX 011 7 95 9430060, telex 411160.

LC QH573 **ISSN** 0021-9525
DD 574.87 US
CCC
NLM W1 JO578B **CODEN** JCLBA3
Pr Rev.
JOURNAL OF CELL BIOLOGY, THE. [J. cell biol.]. Vol. 12 (Jan. 1962)-. Academic Scholarly Publication. English. Twenty-four times a year. $525.00. Rockefeller University Press, 222 East 70th Street, New York NY 10021. **Tel** (212)327-8572, FAX (212)327-7944. **(Subscription address:** Rockefeller University Press, Box 5108 GPO, New York NY 10087-5108. **) ED** Norton B. Gilula. Index available. cum. index. **Circ:** 5,055. available on microfilm and microfiche from University Microfilms International (UMI). Documents available from The Genuine Article, BIOSIS Document Express, UMI Article Clearinghouse, CASDDS. ***Continues*** *Journal of Biophysical and Biochemical Cytology, 0095-9901.*
Desc: Provides a forum to house the diversity of contemporary cell biology from the international community.
Ind/Abst Abstr. Bull. Inst. Pap. Sci. Tech.; Acad. Search; AgBiotech News Inf.; AGRICOLA [Select. Cov.]; Anim. Breed. Abstr.; Biol. Agric. Index; Biol. Abstr.; Calcium Calcif. Tissue Abstr.; Chem. Abstr.; Chem. Titles; Chemorecept. Abstr.; Crop Physiol. Abstr.; CSA Neuro. Abstr.; Curr. Aware. Biol. Sci., CABS; Curr. Cit.; Curr. Contents Life Sci.; Curr. Ref. Fish Res.; Dairy Sci. Abstr.; EMBASE; Energy Res. Abstr.; EP Collect.; Expand. Acad. Index (1992-); Field Crop Abstr.; Gen. Sci. Index; Gen. Sci. Source; Genet. Abstr.; Grass. Forage Abstr.; Helminthol. Abstr.; Homework Help.; Hortic. Abstr.; Immunol. Abstr.; Index Med.; Index Vet.; INFO-SOUTH Abstr.; Int. Aerosp. Abstr.; MasterFile FullTEXT 1000; MasterFile FullTEXT 350; MasterFile FullTEXT 650; MasterFile FullTEXT (July 1993-); Microbiol. Abstr. Sect. C; NAPRALERT; Nematol. Abstr.; Newsp. Period. Abstr. (1992-); Nucl. Acids Abstr.; Nutr. Abstr. Rev., Ser. B, Live Feeds and Feed.; Nutr. Abstr. Rev., Ser. A, Hum. Exp.; OCLC; Oncog. Growth Factors Abstr.; Ornamental Hort. (1991-); Life Sci. Collect.; PESTDOC; Pig News Inf.; Plant Breed. Abstr.; Poult. Abstr.; Protozoolog. Abstr.; Ref. Upd. Basic Ed.; Ref. Upd. Deluxe Ed.; Res. Alert [Full Cov.]; Rev. Agric. Entomol.; Rev. Med. Vet. Entomol.; Sci. Cit. Index; SCISEARCH; Soils Fert.; Soyabean Abstr.; Telebase; Vet. Bull.; Trop. Dis. Bull.; Virol. AIDS Abstr.

LC QH573 .J58 **ISSN** 0021-9533
UK
NLM W1 JO578S **CODEN** JNCSAI
Pr Rev.
JOURNAL OF CELL SCIENCE. [J. cell sci.]. **Added/Corp** Company of Biologists. Vol. 1 (March 1966)-. Academic Scholarly Publication. English. Thirteen times a year (1 volume of 12 parts plus 1 supplement). $1125.00. The Company of Biologists Limited, Bidder Building, 140 Cowley Road, Cambridge CB4 4DL United Kingdom. **Tel** 011 44 1223 426164, FAX 011 44 1223 423353. **(Subscription address:** Kinokuniya Company Ltd., 38-1 Sakuragaoka 5, chome Setagaya-ku, Tokyo 156 Japan. **Tel** FAX 011 03 3439 0136.**) ED** Fiona Watt, Daniel Louvard, and Gary Borisy. Index available. cum. index. **Bk Rev. Ad Acc. Circ:** 1,400 (ctrl). available on microfilm and microfiche from University Microfilms International (UMI). Documents available from The Genuine Article, BIOSIS Document Express, CASDDS. ***Supersedes*** *Quarterly Journal of Microscopical Science, 0370-2952.*
Desc: Papers published cover the full range of topics in contemporary cell biology. Each issue has a popular commentary section containing short reviews. The journal is aimed at researchers in cell biology and related fields.
Ind/Abst AgBiotech News Inf.; AGRICOLA [Select. Cov.]; Anim. Breed. Abstr.; Biol. Agric. Index; Biol. Abstr.; Chem. Abstr.; Chemorecept. Abstr.; Crop Physiol. Abstr.; CSA Neuro. Abstr. (?-?); Curr. Aware. Biol. Sci., CABS; Curr. Cit.; Curr. Contents Agric. Biol. Environ. Sci.; Curr. Contents Life Sci.; Curr. Ref. Fish Res.; Dairy Sci. Abstr.; EMBASE; Field Crop Abstr.; Genet. Abstr.; Helminthol. Abstr. (1991-); Hortic. Abstr.; Immunol. Abstr.; Index Med.; Microbiol. Abstr. Sect. C; Nematol. Abstr.; Nutr. Abstr. Rev., Ser. B, Live Feeds and Feed.; Nutr. Abstr. Rev., Ser. A, Hum. Exp.; Oncog. Growth Factors Abstr.; Life Sci. Collect.; Pig News Inf.; Plant Breed. Abstr.; Poult. Abstr.; Protozoolog. Abstr.; Ref. Upd. Basic Ed.; Ref. Upd. Deluxe Ed.; Res. Alert [Full Cov.]; Rev. Agric. Entomol.; Rev. Med. Vet. Entomol.; Rice Abstr.; Sci. Cit. Index; SCISEARCH; Soils Fert.; Soyabean Abstr.; Trop. Dis. Bull.

LC QH573 .J582 **ISSN** 0269-3518
UK
NLM W1; JO578SA **CODEN** JCSSEP
JOURNAL OF CELL SCIENCE. SUPPLEMENT. [J. cell sci., Suppl.]. **Added/Corp** Company of Biologists. Vol. 1 (1984)-. Academic Scholarly Publication. English. Irregular (Comes with subscription to journal). $1125.00 North America; £645.00 other (Price includes 1 volume of 12 parts plus 1 supplement). The Company of Biologists Limited, Bidder Building, 140 Cowley Road, Cambridge CB4 4DL United Kingdom. **Tel** 011 44 1223 426164, FAX 011 44 1223 423353. **(Subscription address:** Kinokuniya Company Ltd., 38-1 Sakuragaoka 5, chome Setagaya-ku, Tokyo 156 Japan. **Tel** FAX 011 03 3439 0136.**)** Documents available from BIOSIS Document Express, CASDDS.
Ind/Abst Biol. Abstr. (1987-); Chem. Abstr. (1984-); Curr. Cit.; Index Med. (1984-).

LC QP1 .W533 **ISSN** 0021-9541
DD 574.8/76/05 US
CCC
NLM W1 JO579M **CODEN** JCLLAX
Pr Rev.
JOURNAL OF CELLULAR PHYSIOLOGY. **See** Biology-Physiology.

LC QH573 **ISSN** 0253-7605
DD 574.87 II
NLM W1 JO6125 **CODEN** JCGEDO
JOURNAL OF CYTOLOGY AND GENETICS, THE. [J. cytol. genet.]. **Added/Corp** Society of Cytologists and Geneticists, India. Vol. 1 (1965)-. Academic Scholarly Publication. English. Two times a year. $25.00. Society of Cytologists and Geneticists, New Delhi India. **(Subscription address:** Prints India, 11 Darya Ganj, New Delhi 110002 India. **Tel** 011 91 11 3268645, FAX 011 91 11 3275542, telex 31-61087 PRIN-IN.**) ED** Dr. B.H.M. Nijalinappa. Documents available from CASDDS.
Ind/Abst Chem. Abstr.; Life Sci. Collect.; Plant Breed. Abstr.; Protozoolog. Abstr.

LC QP501 .H523 **ISSN** 0022-1554
US
CCC
NLM W1 JO671 **CODEN** JHCYAS
Pr Rev.
JOURNAL OF HISTOCHEMISTRY AND CYTOCHEMISTRY, THE. [J. Histochem. Cytochem.]. **Added/Corp** Histochemical Society. **VFOAT** Histochemistry and Cytochemistry. Vol. 1 (Jan. 1953)-. Periodical. English. Twelve times a year. $230.00. The Histochemical Society, PO Box 1023, Planetarium Station, New York NY 10024. **Tel** (212)362-1801, (212)362-2689. **Ad Acc.** Documents available from The Genuine Article, BIOSIS Document Express, CASDDS.
Desc: Publishes articles reporting original research in all fields of histochemistry and cytochemistry, provided the reported investigations contribute to the development, evaluation, or application of histo- and cytochemical methods.
Ind/Abst AgBiotech News Inf.; AGRICOLA; Biol. Abstr.; Chem. Abstr.; Chem. Titles; Crop Physiol. Abstr.; Curr. Cit.; Curr. Contents Life Sci.; Dairy Sci. Abstr.; EMBASE; Energy Res. Abstr.; Field Crop Abstr.; Index Med.; INIS Atomindex [Micro.]; Nucl. Sci. Abstr.; Life Sci. Collect.; Plant Breed. Abstr.; Protozoolog. Abstr.; Ref. Upd. Basic Ed.; Ref. Upd. Deluxe Ed.; Res. Alert [Full Cov.]; Rev. Med. Vet. Entomol.; Sci. Cit. Index; SCISEARCH.

LC RS201.L55 J68 **ISSN** 0898-2104
DD 574.87/34 US
CCC
NLM W1; JO745M
CODEN JLREE7
JOURNAL OF LIPOSOME RESEARCH. Vol. 1, No. 1 (1988)-. Periodical. English. Four times a year. $450.00. Marcel Dekker Inc., 270 Madison Avenue, New York NY 10016. **Tel** (212)696-9000, (800)228-1160, FAX (212)685-4540, telex 421419. **(Subscription address:** Marcel Dekker Inc., PO Box 5017, Monticello NY 12701. **Tel** (800)228-1160.**) ED** Marc J. Ostro. available in microform (from Research Publications). Documents available from CASDDS.
Desc: Presenting liposome research in an array of subjects ranging from biophysical analysis of liposome membranes to clinical applications of liposome-encapsulated drugs. This journal contains information on what important laboratory findings can mean in terms of clinical use. Offers basic research articles, clinical papers, review articles, and letters to the editor.
Ind/Abst Chem. Abstr.; Curr. Aware. Biol. Sci., CABS; Curr. Cit.; EMBASE; PESTDOC; Ref. Upd. Deluxe Ed.

LC QH631 .J63 **ISSN** 0091-6552
DD 574.8/764 US
NLM W1 JO749N **CODEN** JMCLAO
JOURNAL OF MECHANOCHEMISTRY & CELL MOTILITY. [J. mechanochem. cell motility]. **VFOAT** Mechanochemistry & Cell Motility. **VAT** Journal of Mechanochemistry and Cell Motility. Vol. 1 (Dec. 1971)-. Periodical. English. Four times a year. $49.50. Plenum Press, 233 Spring Street, New York NY 10013-1578. **Tel** (212)620-8000, (800)221-9369, FAX (212)463-0742, (212)807-1047, telex 23/421139. Documents available from BIOSIS Document Express, CASDDS.
Ind/Abst Biol. Abstr.; Chem. Abstr.

LC QH601 .J63 **ISSN** 0022-2631
DD 574.8/75/05 US
CCC
NLM W1 JO76H **CODEN** JMBBBO
Pr Rev.
JOURNAL OF MEMBRANE BIOLOGY, THE. [J. membr. bio.]. **VFOAT** Membrane Biology. Vol. 1 (1969)-. Periodical. English. Eighteen times a year. $1299.00. Springer-Verlag New York Inc., 175 Fifth Avenue, New York NY 10010. **Tel** (212)460-1500 ext 256, FAX (212)533-3503, telex 232 235 SPB UR. **(Subscription address:** Springer-Verlag New York Inc. / North America, PO Box 2485, Journal Fulfillment, Secaucus NJ 07096. **Tel** (201)348-4033, (800)777-4643, FAX (201)348-4505.**) ED** W R Loewenstein. available on microfilm and microfiche from University Microfilms International (UMI). Documents available from The Genuine Article, BIOSIS Document Express, CASDDS, ADONIS.
Desc: Contains information on pects; including chemical and physical structure, immunochemical properties and fingerprinting, colloid and surface chemistry, including natural and artificial transport carriers systems, diffusion, and pinocytosis; also includes coverage of electrical phenomena in excitable membranes.
Ind/Abst ADONIS; AGRICOLA [Select. Cov.]; Biol. Abstr.; Calcium Calcif. Tissue Abstr.; Chem. Abstr.; Chem. Titles; CSA Neuro. Abstr.; Curr. Cit.; Curr. Contents Life Sci.; Curr. Ref. Fish Res.; Dairy Sci. Abstr.; EMBASE; Energy Res. Abstr. (Jan. 1971-); Index Med.; INIS Atomindex [Micro.]; Microbiol. Abstr. Sect. C; Nucl. Sci. Abstr.; Life Sci. Collect.; Ref. Upd. Basic Ed.; Ref. Upd. Deluxe Ed.; Res. Alert [Full Cov.]; Sci. Cit. Index; SCISEARCH.

ISSN 0142-4319
UK
CCC
NLM W1; JO775R **CODEN** JMRMD3
Pr Rev.

JOURNAL OF MUSCLE RESEARCH AND CELL MOTILITY. [J. muscle res. cell motil.]. Vol. 1, No. 1 (March 1980)-. Academic Scholarly Publication. English. Six times a year. $625.00. Chapman & Hall, 2-6 Boundary Row, London SE1 8HN United Kingdom. **Tel** 011 44 171 8650066, FAX 011 44 171 5229623, telex 290164 CHAPMA G. Index available. **Bk Rev. Ad Acc. Circ:** 600. available on microfilm from University Microfilms International (UMI). Documents available from The Genuine Article, BIOSIS Document Express, CASDDS, ADONIS.
Desc: Papers on any aspect of muscle, contractile mechanisms and cell motility. Favors papers with a molecular bias in the field of cell motility and papers on non-muscle contractile systems and microtubule-based motility.
Ind/Abst ADONIS; Biol. Abstr.; Calcium Calcif. Tissue Abstr.; Chem. Abstr.; CSA Neuro. Abstr. (?-?); Curr. Aware. Biol. Sci., CABS; Curr. Cit.; Curr. Contents Life Sci.; EMBASE; Index Med.; Nematol. Abstr.; Life Sci. Collect.; Ref. Upd. Basic Ed.; Ref. Upd. Deluxe Ed.; Res. Alert [Full Cov.]; Sci. Cit. Index; SCISEARCH.

LC QP351 .J58 **ISSN** 0300-4864
DD 591.1/88 UK
CCC
NLM W1 JO787 **CODEN** JNCYA2
Pr Rev.

JOURNAL OF NEUROCYTOLOGY. [J. neurocytol.]. Vol. 1 (July 1972)-. Periodical. English. Twelve times a year. $835.00. Chapman & Hall, 2-6 Boundary Row, London SE1 8HN United Kingdom. **Tel** 011 44 171 8650066, FAX 011 44 171 5229623, telex 290164 CHAPMA G. **ED** A. R. Lieberman, M. Brightman. Index available. **Bk Rev. Ad Acc. Circ:** 600. available on microfilm from University Microfilms International (UMI). Documents available from The Genuine Article, BIOSIS Document Express, CASDDS, ADONIS.
Desc: Publishes research papers dealing with fine structural studies and associated cytochemical, biochemical, physiological and pharmacological studies of neurons, receptors, synapses, neuroeffector junctions, glia and other elements of the peripheral and central nervous systems. Studies of both vertebrate and invertebrate nervous systems under normal, experimental and pathological conditions are included.
Ind/Abst ADONIS; Biol. Abstr.; Chem. Abstr.; CSA Neuro. Abstr.; Curr. Cit.; Curr. Contents Life Sci.; EMBASE; Index Med.; Life Sci. Collect.; Ref. Upd. Basic Ed.; Ref. Upd. Deluxe Ed.; Res. Alert [Full Cov.]; Rev. Agric. Entomol.; Sci. Cit. Index; SCISEARCH.

LC QH603.C43 J675 **ISSN** 1079-9893
DD 574.87/6 US
NLM W1; JO865W

•**JOURNAL OF RECEPTOR AND SIGNAL TRANSDUCTION RESEARCH.** (1995)-. Periodical. English. Six times a year. $595.00. Marcel Dekker Inc., 270 Madison Avenue, New York NY 10016. **Tel** (212)696-9000, (800)228-1160, FAX (212)685-4540, telex 421419. **(Subscription address:** Marcel Dekker Inc., PO Box 5017, Monticello NY 12701. **Tel** (800)228-1160.**) ED** Ross B. Mikkelsen and Vladimir K. Pliska. **Bk Rev. Ad Acc.** ctrl circ. available on microfiche. ***Absorbed*** *Journal of Receptor Research, 0197-5110* ***and*** *Second Messengers and Phosphopteins, 0895-7479.*
Desc: This publication accommodates all aspects of cell surface, cytoplasmatic, and nuclear receptors for drugs, hormones, immunologically active ligands, growth factors, toxins, lectins, viruses, protozoans, and other cells, the properties of the receptors, and their interactions and normal responses. The field of receptor pathobiology and the role of receptors in diagnosis and therapy of disease are also included along with invited reviews, full research papers, and brief communications.
Ind/Abst Biol. Abstr.; Chem. Abstr.; CSA Neuro. Abstr.; Curr. Aware. Biol. Sci., CABS; Curr. Cit.; Curr. Contents Life Sci.; EMBASE; Index Med.; Life Sci. Collect.; PESTDOC; Ref. Upd. Deluxe Ed.; Res. Alert [Full Cov.]; Sci. Cit. Index; SCISEARCH; Soc. Sci. Cit. Index [Select. Cov.].

LC QH603.C43 J68 **ISSN** 0197-5110
DD 574.87/5 US
CCC
NLM W1 JO866 **CODEN** JRERDMJREDRM
TITLE CHANGE

JOURNAL OF RECEPTOR RESEARCH. [J. recept. res.]. Vol. 1 (1980)-(19??). Academic Scholarly Publication. English. Marcel Dekker Inc., 270 Madison Avenue, New York NY 10016. **Tel** (212)696-9000, (800)228-1160, FAX (212)685-4540, telex 421419. **(Subscription address:** Marcel Dekker Inc., PO Box 5017, Monticello NY 12701. **Tel** (800)228-1160.**) ED** Ross B. Mikkelsen and Vladimir K. Pliska. **Bk Rev. Ad Acc.** ctrl circ. available on microfiche. Documents available from The Genuine Article, BIOSIS Document Express, CASDDS. ***Merged into*** *Journal of Receptor and Signal Transduction Research, 1079-9893.*
Desc: This publication accommodates all aspects of cell surface, cytoplasmatic, and nuclear receptors for drugs, hormones, immunologically active ligands, growth factors, toxins, lectins, viruses, protozoans, and other cells, the properties of the receptors, and their interactions and normal responses. The field of receptor pathobiology and the role of receptors in diagnosis and therapy of disease are also included along with invited reviews, full research papers, and brief communications.
Ind/Abst Biol. Abstr.; Chem. Abstr.; CSA Neuro. Abstr.; Curr. Aware. Biol. Sci., CABS; Curr. Cit.; Curr. Contents Life Sci.; EMBASE; Index Med.; Life Sci. Collect.; PESTDOC; Ref. Upd. Deluxe Ed.; Res. Alert [Full Cov.]; Sci. Cit. Index; SCISEARCH; Soc. Sci. Cit. Index [Select. Cov.].

LC QH573 .J59
DD 574.87/05 IT
NLM W1; JO905CE **CODEN** JSCPEE

JOURNAL OF SUBMICROSCOPIC CYTOLOGY AND PATHOLOGY. **Added/Corp** Universita di Bologna. Consiglio Nazionale delle Ricerche (Italy). Vol. 20, No. 1 (Jan. 1988)-. Periodical. English. Four times a year. L150000. Editrice Compositori SRL, Viale Stalingrado 97 2, 40128 Bologna Italy. **Tel** 011 39 51 327811. **(Subscription address:** Journal of Submicroscopic Cytology and Pathology, Via Stalingrado 97 2, 40128 Bologna, Italy. **Tel** 011 39 51 327811.**)** Documents available from The Genuine Article, BIOSIS Document Express, CASDDS. ***Continues*** *Journal of Submicroscopic Cytology, 0022-4782.*
Ind/Abst Anim. Behav. Abstr.; Anim. Breed. Abstr.; Biol. Abstr. (1988-); Chem. Abstr.; CSA Neuro. Abstr. (?-?); Curr. Aware. Biol. Sci., CABS; Curr. Contents Life Sci.; Helminthol. Abstr. (19??-19??); Index Med. (1988-); Index Vet.; Microbiol. Abstr. Sect. C; Nematol. Abstr.; Pig News Inf.; Poult. Abstr.; Protozoolog. Abstr.; Ref. Upd. Deluxe Ed.; Res. Alert [Full Cov.]; Rev. Med. Vet. Entomol.; Sci. Cit. Index; SCISEARCH; Vet. Bull.

LC RC **ISSN** 1078-9553
DD 616 US
NLM W1; JO905N

•**JOURNAL OF SURGICAL PATHOLOGY : CYTOLOGY, HISTOPATHOLOGY.** **See** Medical Sciences-Surgery.

LC QH585 .T53a **ISSN** 0271-8057
DD 574/.07/24 NE
CCC
NLM W1 JO966JD **CODEN** JTCMDB
TITLE CHANGE

JOURNAL OF TISSUE CULTURE METHODS. [J. tissue cult. methods]. **Added/Corp** Tissue Culture Association. Society for In Vitro Biology. Vol. 6, No. 1 (1980)-Vol. 16, No. 3-4 (1994). Academic Scholarly Publication. English. Kluwer Academic Publishers, Postbus 322, 3300 AH Dordrecht The Netherlands. **Tel** 011 31 78 524400, FAX 011 31 78 183273, telex 20083. **ED** MK Patterson Jr. **Bk Rev. Ad Acc. Circ:** 1,000 (ctrl). available on microfilm from University Microfilms International (UMI). Documents available from CASDDS. ***Continues*** *TCA Manual, 0361-0268.* ***Continued by*** *Methods in Cell Science, 1381-5741.*
Desc: Laboratory protocols for plant and animal cell, tissue and organ culture. Publishes new or significant improvements in methods and techniques.
Ind/Abst AGRICOLA (?-1986); Chem. Abstr.; Curr. Aware. Biol. Sci., CABS; Curr. Cit.; EMBASE.

LC QR185.8.L93 L98 **ISSN** 1056-5477
DD 616 US
NLM W1; LY5266 **CODEN** LCREEY
TITLE CHANGE

LYMPHOKINE AND CYTOKINE RESEARCH. [Lymphokine cytokine res.]. Vol. 10, No. 1 & 2 (April 1991)-(19??). Academic Scholarly Publication. English. Mary Ann Liebert Inc., 2 Madison Avenue, Larchmont NY 10538. **Tel** (914)834-3100, (800)M-LIEBERT, FAX (212)289-4697. **ED** Lawrence Lachman. Documents available from The Genuine Article, BIOSIS Document Express, CASDDS. ***Continues*** *Lymphokine Research, 0277-6766.* ***Merged into*** *Journal of Interferon and Cytokine Research.*
Desc: Covers recent advancements in lymphokine and monokine research and provides researchers and clinicians with information on current laboratory findings, as well as application of lymphokines as immunotherapeutic agents.
Ind/Abst Biol. Abstr.; Chem. Abstr.; Curr. Aware. Biol. Sci., CABS; Curr. Cit.; Curr. Contents Life Sci.; EMBASE; Health Plan. Adminis.; Immunol. Abstr.; Index Med. (1991-); Life Sci. Collect.; Ref. Upd. Basic Ed.; Ref. Upd. Deluxe Ed.; Res. Alert [Full Cov.]; Sci. Cit. Index; SCISEARCH.

NE
CODEN LBPAE5
Pr Rev.

LYSOSOMES IN BIOLOGY AND PATHOLOGY. (1984)-. Monographic series. English. Irregular. Price varies per volume. Elsevier Science Publishers BV, PO Box 211, 1000 AE Amsterdam Netherlands. **Tel** 011 31 20 4853641, 011 31 20 4853642, FAX 011 31 20 4853598. **(Subscription address:** Elsevier Science Inc. / New York Books, 655 Avenue of the Americas, New York NY 10010. **Tel** (212)633-3650.**) ED** J.T. Dingle, R.T. Dean, and W. Sly. Documents available from BIOSIS Document Express, CASDDS. ***Continues*** *Dingle, J. T. Lysosomes in Biology and Pathology.*
Ind/Abst Biol. Abstr. (1984-); Chem. Abstr. (1984-).

IE

MECHANISMS OF DEVELOPMENT. SUPPLEMENT. (19??)-. Academic Scholarly Publication. English. Elsevier Science Ireland Ltd., Bay 15, Shannon Industrial Estate, Co Clare Ireland. **Tel** 011 353 61 471944.

US
NLM W1 ME8937 (P)
SUSPENDED

MEMBRANE STRUCTURE AND FUNCTION. Vol. 1 (1979)-Suspended (19??). Monographic series. English. Irregular. Price varies per volume. Kreiger Publications, PO Box 9542, Melbourne FL 32901. **Tel** (407)724-9542. **ED** E.E. Bittar.

LC QH585 .M47 **ISSN** 0091-679X
DD 574.8/7/028 US
CCC
NLM W1 ME9615D **CODEN** MCBLAG

METHODS IN CELL BIOLOGY. [Methods cell biol.]. Vol. 6 (1973)-. Monographic series. English. Irregular. Price varies per volume. Academic Press Inc., 6277 Sea Harbor Drive, Orlando FL 32887. **Tel** (800)543-9534, (407)345-4100, FAX (407)352-3445. **ED** David M. Prescott. Documents available from The Genuine Article, BIOSIS Document Express, CASDDS. ***Continues*** *Methods in Cell Physiology, 0091-6579.*
Ind/Abst Biol. Abstr.; Chem. Abstr.; Curr. Cit.; EMBASE; Energy Res. Abstr. (Oct. 1974-); Index Med.; Index Sci. Rev. [Full Cov.]; Life Sci. Collect.; Res. Alert [Full Cov.]; Sci. Cit. Index; SCISEARCH; Trop. Dis. Bull.

LC QH585 **ISSN** 1381-5741
DD 574/.07/24 NE

•**METHODS IN CELL SCIENCE.** **Added/Corp** Society for In Vitro Biology. Vol. 17, No. 1 (Mar. 1995)-. Periodical. English. Four times a year. $170.00. Kluwer Academic Publishers, Postbus 322, 3300 AH Dordrecht The Netherlands. **Tel** 011 31 78 524400, FAX 011 31 78 183273, telex 20083. ***Continues*** *Journal of Tissue Culture Methods, 0271-8057.*

LC QH506 .M435 **ISSN** 0898-7750
DD 574.8/05 US
CCC
NLM W1; ME9616D **CODEN** MMCBEV

METHODS IN MOLECULAR AND CELLULAR BIOLOGY. [Methods mol. cell. biol.]. (1989)-. Periodical. English. Six times a year. $240.00. Wiley Liss, 605 3rd Avenue, New York NY 10158. **Tel** (212)850-8800, (212)850-6645. **(Subscription address:** John Wiley & Sons, Inc. / Philadelphia, PO Box 7247, Philadelphia PA 19170. **Tel** (212)850-6645, (800)225-5945.**) ED** Bernard Perbal. Documents available from The Genuine Article, BIOSIS Document Express, CASDDS, ADONIS. ***Absorbed*** *DNA and Protein Engineering Techniques.*
Desc: Devoted to the rapid publication of original reports describing new methods and methodologies, improvements of common protocols, troubleshooting guides, and new simplified protocols related to broad aspects of molecular biology.
Ind/Abst ADONIS; Biol. Abstr. (1991-); Chem. Abstr.; Curr. Cit.; EMBASE; Genet. Abstr.; Res. Alert [Full Cov.].

US

METHODS OF CELL SEPARATION. (1977)-. Monographic series. English. Irregular. Price varies per volume. Plenum Press, 233 Spring Street, New York NY 10013-1578. **Tel** (212)620-8000, (800)221-9369, FAX (212)463-0742, (212)807-1047, telex 23/421139.

LC Z5322.C3 M57 **ISSN** 0142-8217
UK
CCC

MITOCHONDRIA / ISSUED MONTHLY BY UNIVERSITY OF SHEFFIELD BIOMEDICAL INFORMATION SERVICE. **Added/Corp** University of Sheffield. Biomedical Information Service. (197?)-. Periodical. English. Twenty-four times a year. $179.67. SUBIS, Mansion House 19 Kingfield Road, Sheffield S11 9AS United Kingdom. **Tel** 011 44 114 2554433, FAX 011 44 114 255 4626.

LC QH573 .M63 **ISSN** 0745-3000
DD 574.87/05 US
NLM W1 MO124T **CODEN** MOCBDA

MODERN CELL BIOLOGY. [Mod. cell biol.]. Vol. 1 (1983)-. Academic Scholarly Publication. English. Irregular. Price varies per volume. Wiley Liss, 605 3rd Avenue, New York NY 10158. **Tel** (212)850-8800, (212)850-6645. **(Subscription address:** John Wiley & Sons, Inc. / Philadelphia, PO Box 7247, Philadelphia PA 19170. **Tel** (212)850-6645, (800)225-5945.**) ED** Birgit H. Satir. Documents available from CASDDS.
Desc: News and information concerning cell biology.
Ind/Abst Chem. Abstr. (1983-); Curr. Cit.

LC QH573
DD 574.87 UK
NLM W1; MO194M CODEN MCBDEU

MOLECULAR AND CELL BIOLOGY OF HUMAN DISEASES SERIES. VFOAT Molecular and Cell Biology of Human Diseases. (1992)-. Monographic series. English. Price varies per volume. Chapman & Hall, 2-6 Boundary Row, London SE1 8HN United Kingdom. **Tel** 011 44 171 8650066, FAX 011 44 171 5229623, telex 290164 CHAPMA G.
Ind/Abst Index Med. (1992-).

LC QH506 .M64 ISSN 0270-7306
DD 574 US
CCC
NLM W1 MO194U CODEN MCEBD4
Pr Rev.

MOLECULAR AND CELLULAR BIOLOGY. See Biology-Microbiology.

LC QH573 ISSN 0167-6970
DD 574.87 NE
NLM W1 MO195D CODEN MACRDS
Pr Rev.

MOLECULAR ASPECTS OF CELLULAR REGULATION. [Mol. aspects cell. regul.]. Vol. 1 (1980)-. Academic Scholarly Publication. English. Price varies per volume. Elsevier Science Publishers BV, PO Box 211, 1000 AE Amsterdam Netherlands. **Tel** 011 31 20 4853641, 011 31 20 4853642, FAX 011 31 20 4853598. **ED** P. Cohen. Documents available from BIOSIS Document Express, CASDDS.
Ind/Abst Biol. Abstr.; Chem. Abstr.

LC QH604 .C442 ISSN 1059-1524
DD 574.87 US
NLM W1; MO195U CODEN MBCEEV
Pr Rev.

MOLECULAR BIOLOGY OF THE CELL. [Mol. biol. cell]. **Added/Corp** American Society for Cell Biology. **VFOAT** MBC. Vol. 3, No. 1 (Jan. 1992)-. Academic Scholarly Publication. English. Twelve times a year (plus ASCB Annual Meeting Abstracts issue). $300.00. The American Society for Cell Biology, 9650 Rockville Pike, Bethesda MD 20814-3992. **Tel** (301)530-7153, FAX (301)571-8304. **ED** Rosalba Kampman. **Ad Acc, Adv Mgr:** Edward Newman. **Acid Free. Circ:** 1200. Documents available from The Genuine Article, BIOSIS Document Express, CASDDS. ***Continues*** *Cell Regulation, 1044-2030.*
Desc: Contains original research in molecular aspects of cell structure and function. Papers describe substantial progress in full. The journal encourages works whose scope bridges several areas of biology.
Ind/Abst Biol. Abstr.; Chem. Abstr.; Curr. Aware. Biol. Sci., CABS; Curr. Contents Life Sci.; Index Med. (1992-); Ref. Upd. Deluxe Ed.; Res. Alert [Full Cov.]; Sci. Cit. Index; SCISEARCH; Soc. Sci. Cit. Index [Select. Cov.].

ISSN 1016-8478
KO
UDC 574

MOLECULES AND CELLS. [Mol. cells]. (1990)-. Academic Scholarly Publication. Multiple languages. Four times a year. Documents available from CASDDS.
Ind/Abst Chem. Abstr.

LC QR186.85 .M6563 ISSN 1047-871X
DD 616.07/93 US
NLM QW 539; M7505
TITLE CHANGE

MONOCLONAL ANTIBODIES (NEW YORK, N.Y.). (MONOCLONAL ANTIBODIES.). [Monoclon. antib.]. Vol. 8, No. 1 (1990)-(19??). Periodical. English. Mary Ann Liebert Inc., 2 Madison Avenue, Larchmont NY 10538. **Tel** (914)834-3100, (800)M-LIEBERT, FAX (212)289-4697. **ED** Zenon Steplewski. ***Continues*** *Monoclonal Antibody News, 0272-4588.* ***Absorbed by*** *Hybridoma.*
Desc: Prompt publication of current information on new hybrid cell lines, methodology, and other information arising from the use of monoclonal antibodies. It is a source of availability of new monoclonal antibodies for all researchers.

LC QH573 ISSN 0077-0809
DD 574.87 SZ
CCC
NLM W1 MO567KF
Pr Rev.

MONOGRAPHS IN CLINICAL CYTOLOGY. [Monogr. Clin. cytol.]. Vol. 2 (1969)-. Monographic series. English. One time a year. 200.00F (approx. per volume). S. Karger AG, Allschwilerstrasse 10, PO Box, CH-4009 Basel Switzerland. **Tel** 011 41 61 3061111, FAX 011 41 61 3061234, telex CH 962 652. **ED** G. L. Wied. Documents available from BIOSIS Document Express. ***Continues*** *Clinical Cytology.*
Desc: Volumes perform the function of correlating extensive basic and clinical findings and applying these to discuss how innovations in cytology can improve patient diagnosis and management. Readers will find descriptions of techniques offering simplicity, speed, patient comfort and cost effectiveness as well as improved diagnostic precision.
Ind/Abst Biol. Abstr.; Index Med.; Ref. Upd. Deluxe Ed.

LC QH506 .N36 ISSN 0958-3165
DD 574.1 UK
CCC
NLM W1; NA128N CODEN NNOBE7

NANOBIOLOGY : JOURNAL OF RESEARCH ON NANOSCALE LIVING SYSTEMS. Vol. I, No. 1 (1992)-. Academic Scholarly Publication. English. Four times a year. $298.00. Carfax Publishing Company, PO Box 25, Abingdon, Oxfordshire OX14 3UE United Kingdom. **Tel** 011 44 1235 555335, FAX 011 44 1235 553559, telex 817484. **ED** Martyn C. Davies & Saul J.B. Tendler. Index available. available on microfiche. Documents available from CASDDS.
Ind/Abst Chem. Abstr.

LC QH573 ISSN 1010-8793
DD 574.87 GW
CODEN NASBE4
Pr Rev.

NATO ASI SERIES. SERIES H, CELL BIOLOGY. [NATO ASI ser., Ser. H Cell biol.]. **Added/Corp** North Atlantic Treaty Organization. Scientific Affairs Division. **VFOAT** N.A.T.O. A.S.I. Series. Series H, Cell Biology; Cell Biology. **VAT** North Atlantic Treaty Organization Advanced Science Institutes Series. Series H, Cell Biology. Vol. 1 (1986)-. Academic Scholarly Publication. English. Price varies per volume. Springer-Verlag GmbH & Company KG, Heidelberger Platz 3, D-14197 Berlin Germany. **Tel** 011 49 30 8207223, FAX 011 49 30 8214091, telex 183 319 SPBLN D. **(Subscription address:** Springer-Verlag New York Inc. / North America, PO Box 2485, Journal Fulfillment, Secaucus NJ 07096. **Tel** (201)348-4033, (800)777-4643, FAX (201)348-4505.**)** Documents available from BIOSIS Document Express, CASDDS.
Ind/Abst AGRICOLA [Select. Cov.]; Biocont. News Inf. (1991-); Biol. Abstr. (1986-); Chem. Abstr. (1986-); CSA Neuro. Abstr. (?-?); Curr. Cit.; Nematol. Abstr.; Plant Grow. Reg. Abstr.; Rev. Agric. Entomol.

LC QH573 ISSN 0142-8225
DD 574.87 UK
CCC

NERVE CELL BIOLOGY. **Added/Corp** University of Sheffield. Biomedical Information Service. (19??)-. Bulletin. English. Twenty-four times a year. $205.35. SUBIS, Mansion House 19 Kingfield Road, Sheffield S11 9AS United Kingdom. **Tel** 011 44 114 2554433, FAX 011 44 114 255 4626. **Bk Rev. Ad Acc.**
Desc: Contains references on anatomy, development and membrane function of the nervous system also details of forthcoming events.

LC QH ISSN 1066-615X
DD 574 US
Pr Rev.

NEWSLETTER - NATIONAL CAPITAL AREA TISSUE CULTURE SOCIETY. (NEWSLETTER / NATIONAL CAPITAL AREA TISSUE CULTURE SOCIETY.). [Newsl. - Natl. Cap. Area Tissue Cult. Soc.]. **Added/Corp** National Capital Area Tissue Culture Society. **VFOAT** Newsletter. (1992)-. Newsletter. English. Six times a year. $25.00 per volume. Society for In Vitro Biology, PO Box 73230, Baltimore MD 21273. **Tel** (410)992-0946. **ED** Dr Mary Pat Moyer. **Ad Acc, Adv Mgr:** Marietta W Ellis, **Tel** (410)992-0946. **Circ:** 3600 (ctrl). ***Continues*** *Newsletter (Tissue Culture Association. National Capital Area Branch), 0273-0146.*
Desc: Newsletter of the TCA. It contains news and notes about branches and divisions of the TCA, placement service, notice of events, short articles, and a list of courses available.

LC QH573 .N8 ISSN 0029-568X
DD 574.87/05 II
NLM W1 NU137 CODEN NULSAK
Pr Rev.

NUCLEUS (CALCUTTA). (THE NUCLEUS.). [Nucleus (Calcutta)]. **Added/Corp** University of Calcutta. Dept. of Botany. Cytogenetics Laboratory. Vol. 1 (June 1958)-. Academic Scholarly Publication. English. Three times a year. $66.00. University of Calcutta, Department of Botany, PO Box 10254, Professor AK Sharma, Calcutta 700019 India. **Tel** 011/91/33/461802. **(Subscription address:** Prints India, 11 Darya Ganj, New Delhi 110002 India. **Tel** 011 91 11 3268645, FAX 011 91 11 3275542, telex 31-61087 PRIN-IN.**) ED** A.K. Sharma and A. Sharma. Index available in last issue of volume--attached. cum. index. **Bk Rev**, (Qty: 6-8). **Circ:** 400 (ctrl). Documents available from BIOSIS Document Express, CASDDS.
Desc: Genetics in plants, animals and humans. Effects of environmental mutagen, cytology of plants and animals, and ultrastructure and function of cells. Cytogenetics of plants, animals and humans, and the effects of gene and environment in populations.
Ind/Abst AGRICOLA; Anim. Breed. Abstr.; Biol. Abstr.; Chem. Abstr.; EMBASE; Energy Res. Abstr.; For. Abstr.; Ornamental Hort.; Life Sci. Collect.; Plant Breed. Abstr.; Plant Genet. Resour. Abstr.; Rev. Med. Vet. Entomol.; Rice Abstr.

LC QH426 .O92 ISSN 0265-0738
DD 574.87/3223 US
NLM W1; OX621TM CODEN OSEGEI

OXFORD SURVEYS ON EUKARYOTIC GENES. Vol. 1 (1984)-. Monographic series. English. One time a year. $65.00. Oxford University Press / New York, 200 Madison Avenue, New York NY 10016. **Tel** (212)679-7300, (919)677-0977, (800)451-7556, (800)445-9714, FAX (919)677-1303. **ED** Norman Maclean. Documents available from BIOSIS Document Express.
Ind/Abst Biol. Abstr. (1986-); Index Med. (1984-).

LC RB125 .P37 ISSN 1015-2008
SZ
CCC
NLM W1; PA8955 CODEN PATHEF

PATHOBIOLOGY (BASEL). See Medical Sciences-Pathology.

ISSN 0301-0139
SZ
CCC
NLM W1 PI24 CODEN PGTCA4

PIGMENT CELL. [Pigm. cell]. Vol. 1 (1973)-. English. One time a year. 170.00F (approx. per volume). S. Karger AG, Allschwilerstrasse 10, PO Box, CH-4009 Basel Switzerland. **Tel** 011 41 61 3061111, FAX 011 41 61 3061234, telex CH 962 652. **ED** R. M. MacKie. Documents available from BIOSIS Document Express, CASDDS.
Desc: Volumes in this series serve to centralize the significant amount of research which has been stimulated by the pigment cell. Based on congresses organized by the International Pigment Cell Group, these books report the results of fundamental biochemical and biological inquiries as well as task-oriented research in cancer and other pathological conditions of pigment-producing tissues.
Ind/Abst Biol. Abstr.; Chem. Abstr.; Ref. Upd. Deluxe Ed.

LC QL767 ISSN 0893-5785
DD 591/19/218/05 US
CCC
NLM W1; PI24K CODEN PCREEA
Pr Rev.

PIGMENT CELL RESEARCH. [Pigment cell res.]. Vol. 1, No. 1 (July/Aug. 1987)-. Periodical. English. Six times a year. $355.54. Munksgaard International Publishers Ltd, PO Box 2148, DK-1016 Copenhagen K Denmark. **Tel** 011 45 33 127030, FAX 011 45 33 129387, telex 19431 MUNKS DK. Documents available from The Genuine Article, BIOSIS Document Express.
Ind/Abst Anim. Breed. Abstr.; Biol. Abstr. (1988-); CSA Neuro. Abstr. (?-?); Curr. Cit.; Curr. Contents Life Sci.; Index Med. (Vol. 1, No. 1, 1987-); Res. Alert [Full Cov.]; Rev. Med. Vet. Entomol.; Sci. Cit. Index; SCISEARCH.

LC QK725 .P5518 ISSN 1040-4651
DD 581.8/05 US
NLM W1; PL105LG CODEN PLCEEW
Pr Rev.

PLANT CELL, THE. [Plant cell]. **Added/Corp** American Society of Plant Physiologists. Vol. 1, No. 1 (Jan. 1989)-. Periodical. English. Twelve times a year. $160.00. American Society of Plant Physiologists, 15501 A Monona Drive, Rockville MD 20855. **Tel** (301)251-0560 ext. 17, FAX (301)279-2996. **(Subscription address:** Fulco, 30 Broad Street, Denville NJ 07834. **Tel** (800)783-4903, (201)627-2427.**) ED** Robert B. Goldberg, Brian A. Larkins, and Judith E. Grollman. Index available. cum. index. **Ad Acc. Circ:** 5,000 (ctrl). available on microfilm and microfiche from University Microfilms International (UMI). Documents available from The Genuine Article, BIOSIS Document Express.
Desc: Research journal that reports novel insights into basic plant cellular processes, such as regulation of gene expression, molecular and genetic basis of plant development, plant-microbe interactions, and molecular aspects of plant cell organization and function.
Ind/Abst Abstr. Bull. Inst. Pap. Sci. Tech.; AgBiotech News Inf.; AGRICOLA [Full Cov.]; Biol. Abstr.; Crop Physiol. Abstr.; Curr. Aware. Biol. Sci., CABS; Curr. Cit.; Curr. Contents Agric. Biol. Environ. Sci.; Curr. Contents Life Sci.; Field Crop Abstr.; Food Sci. Technol. Abstr.; Grass. Forage Abstr.; Hortic. Abstr.; Index Med.; Irr. Drain. Abstr.; Maize Abstr.; Ornamental Hort. (19??-19??); PESTDOC; Plant Breed. Abstr.; Plant Grow. Reg. Abstr.; Postharvest News Inf.; Ref. Upd. Deluxe Ed.; Res. Alert [Full Cov.]; Rev. Agric. Entomol.; Rev. Plant Pathol.; Rice Abstr.; Sci. Cit. Index; SCISEARCH; Seed Abstr.; Soils Fert.; Soyabean Abstr.; Weed Abstr.; Wheat Barley Trit. Abstr.

LC QK725 .P555 ISSN 0721-7714
DD 581.87/05 GW
CCC
CODEN PCRPD8
Pr Rev.

PLANT CELL REPORTS. [Plant cell rep.]. Vol. 1, No. 1 (Aug. 1981)-. Academic Scholarly Publication. English. Twelve times a year. $928.00. Springer-Verlag GmbH & Company KG, Heidelberger Platz 3, D-14197 Berlin Germany. **Tel** 011 49 30 8207223, FAX 011 49 30 8214091, telex 183 319 SPBLN D. **(Subscription address:** Springer-Verlag New York Inc. / North America, PO Box 2485, Journal Fulfillment, Secaucus NJ 07096.

Tel (201)348-4033, (800)777-4643, FAX (201)348-4505.) **ED** K Hahlbrock and O L Gamborg. available on microfilm and microfiche from University Microfilms International (UMI). Documents available from The Genuine Article, BIOSIS Document Express, CASDDS.
Desc: Devoted to the rapid publication of short communications by investigators in all fields of plant cell research.
Ind/Abst Abstr. Bull. Inst. Pap. Sci. Tech.; AgBiotech News Inf.; AGRICOLA [Full Cov.]; Agrofor. Abstr. (1991-); BioBusiness; Biol. Abstr.; Chem. Abstr.; Chem. Titles; Cot. Trop. Fibr. Abstr. Bibliogr.; Crop Physiol. Abstr.; Curr. Aware. Biol. Sci., CABS; Curr. Biotechnol.; Curr. Cit.; Curr. Contents Agric. Biol. Environ. Sci.; EMBASE; Field Crop Abstr.; Food Sci. Technol. Abstr.; For. Abstr.; Grass. Forage Abstr.; Hortic. Abstr.; Irr. Drain. Abstr.; Maize Abstr.; Ornamental Hort. (19??-19??); PESTDOC; Plant Breed. Abstr.; Plant Genet. Resour. Abstr.; Plant Grow. Reg. Abstr.; Potato Abstr.; Protozoolog. Abstr.; Ref. Upd. Deluxe Ed.; Res. Alert [Full Cov.]; Rev. Agric. Entomol.; Rev. Plant Pathol.; Rice Abstr.; Sci. Cit. Index; SCISEARCH; Seed Abstr.; Soils Fert.; Sorghum Mill. Abstr.; Soyabean Abstr.; Vitis Vitic. Enol. Abstr.; Weed Abstr.; Wheat Barley Trit. Abstr.

LC QH452 .P55 **ISSN** 0147-619X
DD 574/8/734 US
CCC
NLM W1 PL114 **CODEN** PLSMDX
Pr Rev.
PLASMID. [Plasmid]. Vol. 1 (Nov. 1977)-. Academic Scholarly Publication. English. Six times a year. $265.00. Academic Press Inc., 6277 Sea Harbor Drive, Orlando FL 32887. **Tel** (800)543-9534, (407)345-4100, FAX (407)352-3445. **ED** Richard D. Kolodner and Francis L. Macrina. Documents available from The Genuine Article, CASDDS.
Desc: The primary focus of the journal is the biology of extrachromosomal gene systems in prokaryotic and eukaryotic organisms, including their biological behavior, their molecular structure and genetic function, and their specific products.
Ind/Abst AGRICOLA [Select. Cov.]; Biocont. News Inf.; Chem. Abstr.; Chem. Titles; Curr. Aware. Biol. Sci., CABS; Curr. Biotechnol.; Curr. Cit.; Curr. Contents Life Sci.; EMBASE; Food Sci. Technol. Abstr.; Genet. Abstr.; Index Med.; Microbiol. Abstr. Sect. B; Nematol. Abstr.; Life Sci. Collect.; PESTDOC; Plant Grow. Reg. Abstr.; Ref. Upd. Basic Ed.; Ref. Upd. Deluxe Ed.; Res. Alert [Full Cov.]; Rev. Agric. Entomol.; Rev. Med. Vet. Entomol.; Rev. Plant Pathol.; Sci. Cit. Index; SCISEARCH.

LC QH573 .P65 **ISSN** 0324-833X
PL
NLM W1 PO936L **CODEN** PBKODV
POSTEPY BIOLOGII KOMORKI. [Post. biol. komorki]. **Added/Corp** Polskie Towarzystwo Anatomiczne. Vol. 1 (1974)-. Polish. Four times a year. $40.00. **(Subscription address:** Ars Polona-Ruch, PO Box 1001, Krakowskie Przedmiescie 7, 00-068 Warsaw Poland. **Tel** 011 48 22 261201.) Documents available from BIOSIS Document Express, CASDDS.
Ind/Abst AGRICOLA; Biol. Abstr.; Chem. Abstr.

LC QH573 **ISSN** 0733-9003
DD 574.87 US
CCC
NLM W1; PR666EH **CODEN** PTCYDB
PROGRESS AND TOPICS IN CYTOGENETICS. [Prog. top. cytogenet.]. Vol. 1 (1981)-. Academic Scholarly Publication. English. Irregular (at least once a year, additional vols. as needed). Price varies per volume. Wiley Liss, 605 3rd Avenue, New York NY 10158. **Tel** (212)850-8800, (212)850-6645. **(Subscription address:** John Wiley & Sons, Inc. / Philadelphia, PO Box 7247, Philadelphia PA 19170. **Tel** (212)850-6645, (800)225-5945.) **ED** Avery A. Sandberg. Documents available from BIOSIS Document Express, CASDDS.
Ind/Abst Biol. Abstr.; Chem. Abstr.; Life Sci. Collect.

LC QH611 .P75 **ISSN** 0079-6336
GW
CCC
NLM W1 PR67G **CODEN** PHCCAS
Pr Rev.
PROGRESS IN HISTOCHEMISTRY AND CYTOCHEMISTRY. [Prog. histochem. cytochem.]. Vol. 1 (1970)-. Monographic series. English (German). Irregular. Price varies per volume. Gustav Fischer Verlag Stuttgart, Postfach 720143, D-70577 Stuttgart Germany. **Tel** 011 49 711 458030, FAX 011 49 711 4580334, telex 2627-7111488. **ED** Board. Documents available from The Genuine Article, BIOSIS Document Express, CASDDS.
Desc: Series providing information on histochemistry, cytochemistry and histocytochemistry.
Ind/Abst Biol. Abstr.; Chem. Abstr.; Curr. Cit.; EMBASE; Index Med.; Index Sci. Rev. [Full Cov.]; Res. Alert [Full Cov.]; Sci. Cit. Index; SCISEARCH.

LC QH573 .P68 **ISSN** 0033-183X
AU
CCC
NLM W1 PR812 **CODEN** PROTA5
Pr Rev.
PROTOPLASMA. [Protoplasma]. Vol. 1 (1926)-. Academic Scholarly Publication. English (French and German). Twenty-four times a year (semimonthly). $1982.00. Springer-Verlag Vienna, Sachsenplatz 4 6, PO Box 89, A-1201 Vienna Austria. **Tel** 011 43 1 33024150, FAX 011 43 1 330242665. **(Subscription address:** Springer-Verlag New York Inc. / North America, PO Box 2485, Journal Fulfillment, Secaucus NJ 07096. **Tel** (201)348-4033, (800)777-4643, FAX (201)348-4505.) **ED** D.J. Morre, B.E.S. Gunning, H. Ishikawa, T.W. Keenan, B.A. Palevitz, J. Pickett-Heaps, E. Schnepf, M. Tazawa and G. Wiche. available on microfilm and microfiche from University Microfilms International (UMI). Documents available from The Genuine Article, BIOSIS Document Express, CASDDS, ADONIS.
Desc: Covers all areas of biology of the cell-animal, plant, algal, protozoan, differentiation, cytoskeletal elements, membranes and membrane biogenesis, cell fractionation, cytochemistry and new methodologies in these areas.
Ind/Abst Abstr. Bull. Inst. Pap. Sci. Tech.; ADONIS; AgBiotech News Inf.; AGRICOLA [Select. Cov.]; Biol. Abstr.; Chem. Abstr.; Crop Physiol. Abstr.; CSA Neuro. Abstr. (?-?); Curr. Cit.; Curr. Contents Agric. Biol. Environ. Sci.; Curr. Contents Life Sci.; EMBASE; Field Crop Abstr.; For. Abstr.; Genet. Abstr.; Hortic. Abstr.; Irr. Drain. Abstr.; Microbiol. Abstr. Sect. C; NAPRALERT; Nucl. Sci. Abstr.; Ornamental Hort.; Life Sci. Collect.; PESTDOC; Plant Breed. Abstr.; Plant Grow. Reg. Abstr.; Potato Abstr.; Protozoolog. Abstr.; Ref. Upd. Deluxe Ed.; Res. Alert [Full Cov.]; Rev. Med. Vet. Entomol.; Rev. Plant Pathol.; Sci. Cit. Index; SCISEARCH; Seed Abstr.; Soyabean Abstr.; Wheat Barley Trit. Abstr.

ISSN 0934-8727
AU
CODEN PRSUEW
PROTOPLASMA. SUPPLEMENTUM. [Protoplasma, Suppl.]. (1988)-. Monographic series. English. Irregular. Price varies per volume. Springer-Verlag Vienna, Sachsenplatz 4 6, PO Box 89, A-1201 Vienna Austria. **Tel** 011 43 1 33024150, FAX 011 43 1 330242665. Documents available from BIOSIS Document Express.
Ind/Abst AGRICOLA [Select. Cov.]; Biol. Abstr. (1989-).

US
NLM W1; RA96F
RAVEN PRESS SERIES ON MOLECULAR AND CELLULAR BIOLOGY. Vol. 1 (1992)-. Monographic series. English. Irregular. Price varies per volume. Lippincott - Raven Publishers, 227 East Washington Square, Philadelphia PA 19106. **Tel** (215)238-4200, (800)777-2295, FAX (215)238-4227. **ED** Fred C. Fox.

ISSN 0742-4108
US
NLM W1 RE107LM **CODEN** RLICEA
RECEPTORS AND LIGANDS IN INTERCELLULAR COMMUNICATION. [Recept. ligands intercell. commun.]. Vol. 1 (1983)-. Academic Scholarly Publication. English. Irregular. Price varies per volume. Marcel Dekker Inc., 270 Madison Avenue, New York NY 10016. **Tel** (212)696-9000, (800)228-1160, FAX (212)685-4540, telex 421419. **(Subscription address:** Marcel Dekker Inc., PO Box 5017, Monticello NY 12701. **Tel** (800)228-1160.) Documents available from CASDDS.
Desc: Presents information on intercellular junctions and intercellular junctions.
Ind/Abst Chem. Abstr. (1983-).

LC QH607 .R4 **ISSN** 0080-1844
DD 575.2/1 US
CCC
NLM W1 RE248X **CODEN** RCLDAT
RESULTS AND PROBLEMS IN CELL DIFFERENTIATION. [Results probl. cell differ.]. (1968)-. Monographic series. English. Irregular. Price varies per volume. Springer-Verlag New York Inc., 175 Fifth Avenue, New York NY 10010. **Tel** (212)460-1500 ext 256, FAX (212)533-3503, telex 232 235 SPB UR. **(Subscription address:** Springer-Verlag New York Inc. / North America, PO Box 2485, Journal Fulfillment, Secaucus NJ 07096. **Tel** (201)348-4033, (800)777-4643, FAX (201)348-4505.) **ED** W. Beermann, et al. Documents available from BIOSIS Document Express, CASDDS.
Ind/Abst AGRICOLA; Biol. Abstr.; Chem. Abstr. (-1980); Index Med.

ISSN 0035-4007
RM
REVUE ROUMAINE D'EMBRYOLOGIE ET DE CYTOLOGIE. SERIE DE CYTOLOGIE. See Biology-Embryology.

ISSN 1220-0522
RM
NLM W1; RO327H **CODEN** RRMEEA
ROMANIAN JOURNAL OF MORPHOLOGY AND EMBRYOLOGY. See Biology-Embryology.

LC QH573 **ISSN** 0287-3796
DD 574.87 JA
NLM W1; SA138D **CODEN** SAKOEO
SAIBO KOGAKU. (SAIBO KOGAKU = CELL TECHNOLOGY.). [Saibo kogaku]. **VFOAT** Cell Technology. (1982)-. Periodical. Japanese. Twelve times a year. $278.00. Shujunsha, (Shujunsha Co. Ltd.), Dai 31 Kowa Biru 7F, 19-1 Shiroganedai 3 Chome, Minatoku Tokyo 108 Japan. Documents available from CASDDS.
Ind/Abst Chem. Abstr.

ISSN 1043-4682
DD 574 US
CCC
NLM W1; SE487E **CODEN** SCEBE3
SEMINARS IN CELL BIOLOGY. [Sem. cell biol.]. Vol. 1, Issue 1 (Feb. 1990)-. Academic Scholarly Publication. English. Six times a year. $196.79. Academic Press Ltd., A Division of Harcourt Brace & Company Ltd., 24-28 Oval Road, London NW1 7DX United Kingdom. **Tel** 011 44 171 2674466, FAX 011 44 171 4822293, 011 44 171 4854752, telex 25775 ACPRES G. **(Subscription address:** Harcourt Brace & Company, Ltd., Foots Cray High Street, Sidcup Kent DA14 5HP United Kingdom. **Tel** 011 44 181 3003322, FAX 011 44 181 3090807, telex 896 377 ACADEM.) ***Absorbed*** *Seminars in Developmental Biology.*
Ind/Abst Curr. Cit.; Index Med. (Feb. 1990-).

ISSN 0964-7589
UK
NLM ZQU 58; S578
SIGNAL TRANSDUCTION & CYCLIC NUCLEOTIDES. **Added/Corp** University of Sheffield. Biomedical Information Service. **VFOAT** Signal Transduction and Cyclic Nucleotides. (1992)-. Periodical. English. Twenty-four times a year. $196.79. SUBIS, Mansion House 19 Kingfield Road, Sheffield S11 9AS United Kingdom. **Tel** 011 44 114 2554433, FAX 011 44 114 255 4626. **Bk Rev. Ad Acc.** available on diskette. ***Supersedes*** *Cyclic Amp, 0142-8055.*
Desc: Current awareness service for researchers.

LC QH442.2 .I57 **ISSN** 1066-5099
DD 574.87/6/05 US
CCC
NLM W1; ST439L **CODEN** STCEEJ
•**STEM CELLS (DAYTON, OHIO).** (STEM CELLS.). [Stem cells]. Vol. 11, No. 1 (Jan. 1993)-. Periodical. English. Six times a year. $179.00. Alphamed Press Inc, 4100 South Kettering Boulevard, Dayton OH 45439-2092. **Tel** (513)293-8508, FAX (513)293-7652. **ED** M.J. Murphy Jr. Index available. **Ad Acc. Acid Free.** Documents available from CASDDS. ***Continues*** *International Journal of Cell Cloning, 0737-1454.*
Desc: Publishes original articles and concise reviews which has grown to embrace stem and progenitor cell biology. Read by clinical and basic scientists whose expertise encompasses the rapidly-expanding fields of stem and progenitor cell biology including their clinical applications.
Ind/Abst Chem. Abstr.; Curr. Aware. Biol. Sci., CABS; Curr. Cit.; Curr. Contents Life Sci.; EMBASE; Index Med.; Sci. Cit. Index.

ISSN 0142-8330
DD 016.612405 UK
CCC
STEROID RECEPTORS. [Steroid recept.]. (1976)-. English. Twenty-four times a year. $179.67. SUBIS, Mansion House 19 Kingfield Road, Sheffield S11 9AS United Kingdom. **Tel** 011 44 114 2554433, FAX 011 44 114 255 4626. **Bk Rev. Ad Acc.** available on diskette.
Desc: Current awareness service for researchers in clinical and life sciences.

LC QH506 .S87 **ISSN** 0969-2126
UK
NLM W1; ST81TM **CODEN** STRUE6
•**STRUCTURE.** Vol. 1, No. 1 (Sept. 15, 1993)-. Periodical. English. Twelve times a year. $545.00. Current Science / England, Middlesex House, 34-42 Cleveland Street, London W1P 6LB United Kingdom. **Tel** 011 44 171 5808393, 011 44 171 3230323, FAX 011 44 171 5805646. **(Subscription address:** Current Science, 20 North 3rd Street, Philadelphia PA 19106. **Tel** (800)552-5866.)

LC QH611 .S84 **ISSN** 0306-0225
DD 574.8/76 UK
CCC
NLM W1; SU14 **CODEN** SBCBAG
SUB-CELLULAR BIOCHEMISTRY. [Sub-cell. biochem.]. **VFOAT** Subcellular Biochemistry. (1971)-. Monographic series. English. Irregular. Price varies per volume. Plenum Press, 233 Spring Street, New York NY 10013-1578. **Tel** (212)620-8000, (800)221-9369, FAX (212)463-0742, (212)807-1047, telex 23/421139. **ED** J.R. Harris. Documents available from BIOSIS Document Express, CASDDS. ***Continued in part by*** *Blood Cell Biochemistry.*
Ind/Abst AGRICOLA [Select. Cov.]; Biol. Abstr.; Chem. Abstr.; Curr. Cit.; EMBASE; Index Med.; Life Sci. Collect.

LC QH573 .T56 **ISSN** 0040-8166
DD 574.8/05 UK
CCC
NLM W1 TI827 **CODEN** TICEBI
Pr Rev.
TISSUE & CELL. [Tissue cell]. **VAT** Tissue and Cell. Vol. 1 (1969)-. Academic Scholarly Publication. English. Six times a year. $449.00. Churchill Livingstone, 1-3 Baxter's Place, Leith Walk, Edinburgh EH1 3AF United Kingdom. **Tel** 011 44 131 5562424, FAX 011 44

131 5581278, telex 727511. **(Subscription address:** Maruzen Company Ltd., PO Box 5050, Import & Export Department, Tokyo 100 31 Japan. **Tel** 011 81 3 32789224.) **ED** D Spencer-Smith and U Ryan. Index available. **Bk Rev. Ad Acc. Circ:** 1,000 (ctrl). available on microfilm and microfiche from University Microfilms International (UMI). Documents available from The Genuine Article, BIOSIS Document Express, CASDDS.
Desc: Devoted to research on the organization of cells, their components and extracellular products at all levels including interrelations of cells and organs.
Ind/Abst AgBiotech News Inf.; AGRICOLA; Anim. Breed. Abstr.; Biol. Abstr.; Biol. Dig.; Chem. Abstr.; Chemorecept. Abstr.; Curr. Aware. Biol. Sci., CABS; Curr. Cit.; Curr. Contents Life Sci.; Curr. Ref. Fish Res.; Dairy Sci. Abstr.; EMBASE; Entomol. Abstr.; Helminthol. Abstr. (19??-19??); Index Med.; Nematol. Abstr.; Life Sci. Collect.; Pig News Inf.; Postharvest News Inf.; Poult. Abstr.; Protozoolog. Abstr.; Ref. Upd. Basic Ed.; Ref. Upd. Deluxe Ed.; Res. Alert [Full Cov.]; Rev. Agric. Entomol.; Rev. Med. Vet. Entomol.; Sci. Cit. Index; SCISEARCH; Wildl. Rev. (19??-199?).

ISSN 0142-8810
DD 016.5748 UK
CCC

TISSUE CULTURE SHEFFIELD. [Tissue cult.Sheff.]. (1975)-. English. Twenty-four times a year. $196.79. SUBIS, Mansion House 19 Kingfield Road, Sheffield S11 9AS United Kingdom. **Tel** 011 44 114 2554433, FAX 011 44 114 255 4626.

LC QH7 **ISSN** 0211-8343
DD 574/.05 SP
NLM W1; TR103F
SUSPENDED

TRABAJOS DEL INSTITUTO CAJAL. [Trab. Inst. Cajal]. Vol. 70, No. 10 (1980)-Suspended Vol. 76. Academic Scholarly Publication. English (French). Four times a year. Instituto Santiago Ramon y Cajal, C Velasquez 144, 28006 Madrid Spain. Documents available from CASDDS. ***Continues*** *Trabajos del Instituto Cajal de Investigaciones Biologicas, 0020-3696.*
Ind/Abst Chem. Abstr.

LC QH573 **ISSN** 0271-6208
DD 574.87 US
NLM W1 TR235V

TRANSPORT IN THE LIFE SCIENCES. [Transp. life sci.]. (1980)-. Monographic series. English. Irregular. Price varies per volume. John Wiley & Sons, Inc., 605 Third Avenue, New York NY 10158-0012. **Tel** (212)850-6000, (212)850-6645, FAX (212)850-6088, telex 12-7063. **(Subscription address:** John Wiley & Sons / UK, Baffins Lane, Chichester, West Sussex PO19 1UD United Kingdom. **Tel** 011 44 1243 779777, FAX 011 44 243 776128, telex 86290 WIBOOKG.) **ED** E E Bittar.

LC QH573
DD 574.87 UK
NLM W1; TR3407R **CODEN** TCBIEK
Pr Rev.

TRENDS IN CELL BIOLOGY. Vol. 1, No. 1 (July 1991)-. Academic Scholarly PublicationAcademic Scholarly Publication. English. Twelve times a year. $614.00. Elsevier Trends Journals, An Imprint of Elsevier Science Ltd., The Boulevard, Langford Lane, Kidlington, Oxford OX5 1GB United Kingdom. **Tel** 011 44 1865 843000, 011 44 1865 843699, FAX 011 44 1865 843010. **(Subscription address:** Elsevier Science Ltd. / Oxford Fulfillment Centre, PO Box 800, Kidlington OX5 1DX United Kingdom. **Tel** 011 44 865 843355.) **ED** Carolyn Ellis. available on microfilm and microfiche from University Microfilms International (UMI); available on an online database from Elsevier Electronic Subscriptions (EES). Documents available from ADONIS.
Desc: Comprehensive coverage of new research developments and theories in cell biology.
Ind/Abst ADONIS; Curr. Aware. Biol. Sci., CABS; EMBASE; Ref. Upd. Deluxe Ed.

LC QH573 .T8 **ISSN** 0041-3771
RU
CCC
NLM W1 TS278 **CODEN** TSITAQ
Pr Rev.

TSITOLOGIIA. [TSitologiia]. **Added/Corp** Akademiia Nauk SSSR. Vol. 1 (1959)-. Academic Scholarly Publication. Russian (summaries and/or abstracts in English; table of contents in English). Twelve times a year. $258.00. Izdatelstvo Nauka / Akademiia Nauk, (Publishing House of the Russian Academy of Sciences), Leninskii Porspekt 14, 117901 Moscow Russia. **Tel** 011 95 9542153, FAX 011 95 9382144, telex 411964. **(Subscription address:** East View Publications Inc., 3020 Harbor Lane North, Suite 110, Minneapolis MN 55447. **Tel** (800)477-1005, (612)550-0961, FAX (612)559-2931.) Index available. **Bk Rev.** Documents available from The Genuine Article, BIOSIS Document Express, CASDDS.
Ind/Abst AGRICOLA; Biol. Abstr.; Chem. Abstr.; Crop Physiol. Abstr.; CSA Neuro. Abstr. (?-?); Curr. Ref. Fish Res.; EMBASE; Index Med.; Index Dent. Lit.; Microbiol. Abstr. Sect. C; Life Sci. Collect.; PESTDOC; Plant Breed. Abstr.; Protozoolog. Abstr.; Res. Alert [Full Cov.]; Rev. Med. Vet. Entomol.; Sci. Cit. Index; SCISEARCH.

LC AS262.T22 A25 QH573
ER

UCHENYE ZAPISKI TARTUSKOGO GOSUDARSTVENNOGO UNIVERSITETA. TRUDY PO TSITOLOGII I GENETIKE = TARTU RIIKLIKU ULIKOOLI TOIMETISED. TSUTOLOOGIA- JA GENEETIKA-ALASED TOOD. **Added/Corp** Tartu Riikliku ÈUlikooli. **VFOAT** Tartu Riikliku Ulikooli Toimetised. Tsutoloogia- Ja Geneetika-Alased Tood; Trudy po Tsitologii I Genetike; Tsutoloogia- Ja Geneetika- Alased Tood. (1976)-. Periodical. Russian (summaries and/or abstracts in English). Irregular. 0.85rub (single issue). Tartu Riiklik Ulikool, Ulitsa Uilikooli 18, 202400 Tartu Estonia. **Tel** 30851. **ED** H Kallak, A Heinaru, and M Viikmaa. **Circ:** 400 (ctrl).

UK
NLM W1; WI53P **CODEN** WSMRE9

WILEY SERIES ON MOLECULAR PHARMACOLOGY OF CELL REGULATION. See Pharmacy and Pharmacology.

LC QH573 .H84 **ISSN** 0253-9977
DD 574.87 CC
NLM W1; HS787H **CODEN** XISZD3

XIBAO SHENGWUXUE ZAZHI. (HSI PAO SHENG WU HSUEH TSA CHIH.). [Xibao shengwuxue zazhi]. **Added/Corp** Chung-Kuo Hsi Pao Sheng Wu Hsueh Hsueh Hui. (1979)-. Academic Scholarly Publication. Chinese. Post Office / China, People's Republic of China. Documents available from CASDDS.
Ind/Abst Chem. Abstr.

EMBRYOLOGY

LC QL801 .A2 **ISSN** 0001-5180
DD 611.05 SZ
CCC
NLM W1 AC752 **CODEN** ACATA5
Pr Rev.

ACTA ANATOMICA. See Medical Sciences-Anatomy.

LC QL801 .E67 **ISSN** 0301-5556
DD 574.4/08 GW
NLM W1 AD433K

ADVANCES IN ANATOMY, EMBRYOLOGY AND CELL BIOLOGY. See Medical Sciences-Anatomy.

LC QH491 .A23
DD 574.3/05 US
NLM W1; AD547Q

ADVANCES IN DEVELOPMENTAL BIOLOGY. Vol. 1 (1992)-. Periodical. English. One time a year. $90.25. JAI Press Inc., 55 Old Post Road, Suite 2, PO Box 1678, Greenwich CT 06836-1678. **Tel** (203)661-7602, FAX (203)661-0792. **ED** Paul Wasserman.

LC QL951 .Z4 **ISSN** 0340-2061
DD 596/.03 GW
CCC
NLM W1 AN211 **CODEN** ANEMDG
Pr Rev.

ANATOMY AND EMBRYOLOGY. See Medical Sciences-Anatomy.

ISSN 0210-5799
SP
UDC 611

ARCHIVOS DE ANATOMIA Y EMBRIOLOGIA. See Medical Sciences-Anatomy.

LC QM601 **ISSN** 0004-1947
DD 611.013 RU
NLM W1 AR828 **CODEN** AAGEAA
TITLE CHANGE

ARKHIV ANATOMII, GISTOLOGII I EMBRIOLOGII. See Medical Sciences-Anatomy.

LC RJ251 .B5 **ISSN** 0006-3126
DD 612.6/52/05 SZ
CCC
NLM W1 BI852P **CODEN** BNEOBV
Pr Rev.

BIOLOGY OF THE NEONATE. [Biol. neonate]. Vol. 15 (1970)-. Academic Scholarly Publication. English (French and German). Twelve times a year. $775.00. S. Karger AG, Allschwilerstrasse 10, PO Box, CH-4009 Basel Switzerland. **Tel** 011 41 61 3061111, FAX 011 41 61 3061234, telex CH 962 652. **ED** J. P. Relier, A. Minkowski, F. C. Battaglia, G. Duc, J. Girard, B. Salle, M. Delivoria-Papadopoulos. Index available. **Ad Acc.** available on microfilm from University Microfilms International (UMI). Documents available from The Genuine Article, BIOSIS Document Express, CASDDS. ***Continues*** *Biologia Neonatorum.*
Desc: Concerned with developments in fetal and neonatal research. Presents laboratory findings from both human and animal studies covering the physiological and biochemical events taking place during the period leading up to and immediately following birth.
Ind/Abst Biol. Abstr.; Chem. Abstr.; Curr. Cit.; Curr. Contents Life Sci.; Dairy Sci. Abstr.; Dev. Med. Child Neurol.; EMBASE; Health Plan. Adminis.; Index Med.; Nutr. Abstr. Rev., Ser. B, Live Feeds and Feed.; Nutr. Abstr. Rev., Ser. A, Hum. Exp.; Life Sci. Collect.; Pig News Inf.; Ref. Upd. Deluxe Ed.; Res. Alert [Full Cov.]; Rev. Med. Vet. Mycology; Sci. Cit. Index; SCISEARCH.

LC QL951 **ISSN** 0070-2153
DD 574 US
CCC
NLM W1 CU82G **CODEN** CTDBA5

CURRENT TOPICS IN DEVELOPMENTAL BIOLOGY. [Curr. top. dev. biol.]. Vol. 1 (1966)-. Monographic series. English. Irregular. Price varies per volume. Academic Press Inc., 6277 Sea Harbor Drive, Orlando FL 32887. **Tel** (800)543-9534, (407)345-4100, FAX (407)352-3445. **ED** John H. Lawrence and J. G. Hamilton. Documents available from The Genuine Article, CASDDS.
Ind/Abst Chem. Abstr.; Curr. Aware. Biol. Sci., CABS; Curr. Cit.; Energy Res. Abstr. (Aug. 1982-); Index Med.; Index Sci. Rev. [Full Cov.]; Life Sci. Collect.; Res. Alert [Full Cov.]; Sci. Cit. Index; SCISEARCH.

LC QL951 .D38 **ISSN** 0950-1991
DD 611.013 UK
NLM W1; DE997NR **CODEN** DEVPED
Pr Rev.

DEVELOPMENT (CAMBRIDGE). (DEVELOPMENT.). [Development]. **Added/Corp** Company of Biologists. Vol. 99 (Jan. 1987)-. Academic Scholarly Publication. English. Thirteen times a year (Includes 1 volume of 12 parts plus 1 supplement). $1360.00. The Company of Biologists Limited, Bidder Building, 140 Cowley Road, Cambridge CB4 4DL United Kingdom. **Tel** 011 44 1223 426164, FAX 011 44 1223 423353. **(Subscription address:** Kinokuniya Company Ltd., 38-1 Sakuragaoka 5, chome Setagaya-ku, Tokyo 156 Japan. **Tel** FAX 011 03 3439 0136.) **ED** C. Wylie. Index available. **Bk Rev. Ad Acc. Circ:** 1,300 (ctrl). available on microfilm and microfiche from University Microfilms International (UMI). Documents available from The Genuine Article, BIOSIS Document Express, CASDDS. ***Continues*** *Journal of Embryology and Experimental Morphology, 0022-0752.*
Desc: Mechanisms of development or organization including molecular, cellular and tissue studies on differentiation, patterns, morphogenesis, growth, regeneration and ageing.
Ind/Abst AGRICOLA; Arts Humanit. Citation Index [Select. Cov.]; Biol. Agric. Index; Biol. Abstr. (1987-); Chem. Abstr. (1987-); Crop Physiol. Abstr.; Curr. Aware. Biol. Sci., CABS; Curr. Cit.; EMBASE; Entomol. Abstr.; Index Med. (Jan. 1987-); Nematol. Abstr.; Nucl. Acids Abstr.; Oncog. Growth Factors Abstr.; Life Sci. Collect. (1987-); Ref. Upd. Basic Ed.; Ref. Upd. Deluxe Ed.; Res. Alert [Full Cov.]; Sci. Cit. Index; SCISEARCH; Soc. Sci. Cit. Index [Select. Cov.]; Wheat Barley Trit. Abstr.

GW

•**DEVELOPMENT GENES AND EVOLUTION.** (1995)-. English. Eight times a year. $764.00. Springer-Verlag GmbH & Company KG, Heidelberger Platz 3, D-14197 Berlin Germany. **Tel** 011 49 30 8207223, FAX 011 49 30 8214091, telex 183 319 SPBLN D. **(Subscription address:** Springer-Verlag New York Inc. / North America, PO Box 19386 Books, Newark NJ 07195. **Tel** (201)348-4033.) ***Continues*** *Roux's Archives of Developmental Biology.*
Desc: Presents results of research on animal systems at the molecular, cellular, and organismic level. Fields of interest include: pattern formation, morphogenesis, developmental biology, cellular differentiation, morphogenetic substances and developmental hormones, cellular interaction, regulation of gene expression, developmental genetics, and in vitro systems.

ISSN 0012-1592
DD 574.3 JA
CCC
NLM W1 DE997P **CODEN** DGDFA5
Pr Rev.

DEVELOPMENT, GROWTH & DIFFERENTIATION. [Dev. growth differ.]. **Added/Corp** Nihon Hassei Seibutsu Gakkai. **VFOAT** Development, Growth and Differentiation. Vol. 11, No. 1 (June 1969)-. Academic Scholarly Publication. English. Six times a year. $320.00. Blackwell Scientific Publications Australia, 54 University Street, PO Box 378, Carlton Victoria 3053 Australia. **Tel** 011 61 3 3470300, FAX 011 61 3 3475001, telex 10716421. **ED** Chiaki Katagiri. Documents available from The Genuine Article, BIOSIS Document Express, CASDDS. ***Continues*** *Embryologia.*
Desc: Devoted to the publication of original research papers concerning developmental phenomena. All types of organisms, including plants and microorganisms, are within the scope of the journal.
Ind/Abst AGRICOLA [Select. Cov.]; Biol. Abstr.; Chem. Abstr.; CSA Neuro. Abstr. (?-?); Curr. Aware. Biol. Sci., CABS; Curr. Cit.; Curr. Contents Life Sci.; Dairy Sci.

Abstr.; EMBASE; Genet. Abstr.; Life Sci. Collect.; Ref. Upd. Deluxe Ed.; Res. Alert [Full Cov.]; Sci. Cit. Index; SCISEARCH.

UK
NLM W1; DE997NAD **CODEN** DESUED
Pr Rev.
DEVELOPMENT. SUPPLEMENT.
Added/Corp Company of Biologists. (1990)-. Monographic series. English. Irregular (Comes with subscription to journal). $1,360.00 North America; £778.00 other (Price includes 1 volume of 12 parts plus 1 supplement). The Company of Biologists Limited, Bidder Building, 140 Cowley Road, Cambridge CB4 4DL United Kingdom. **Tel** 011 44 1223 426164, FAX 011 44 1223 423353. **(Subscription address:** Kinokuniya Company Ltd., 38-1 Sakuragaoka 5, chome Setagaya-ku, Tokyo 156 Japan. **Tel** FAX 011 03 3439 0136.**) ED** C. C. Wylie. Index available (bound in December issue). **Ad Acc, Adv Mgr:** R Skaer, **Tel** 44 223 420482. **Circ:** 2,000. available on CD-ROM; available on microfilm (via University Microfilms Int.).
Desc: A reference source for scientists, students, and teachers of development courses. Acts as a forum for all research that offers a genuine insight into mechanisms of plant and animal development.
Ind/Abst Index Med. (1990-).

LC QL801 .A4 **ISSN** 1058-8388
DD 611 US
CCC
NLM W1; DE997NJH **CODEN** DEDYEI
DEVELOPMENTAL DYNAMICS. See Medical Sciences-Anatomy.

LC QM **ISSN** 0014-4053
DD 611 NE
CCC
NLM ZW 1 E954 **CODEN** AAEHA9
EXCERPTA MEDICA. SECTION 1. ANATOMY, ANTHROPOLOGY, EMBRYOLOGY AND HISTOLOGY. See Medical Sciences-Abstracting, Bibliographies and Statistics.

ISSN 0014-4258
NE
CCC
EXCERPTA MEDICA. SECTION 21. DEVELOPMENTAL BIOLOGY AND TERATOLOGY. See Medical Sciences-Abstracting, Bibliographies and Statistics.

LC QM1 .F86 **ISSN** 0862-8416
DD 596/.04 XR
CCC
NLM W1; FU518E **CODEN** FDMOEE
CEASED
FUNCTIONAL AND DEVELOPMENTAL MORPHOLOGY. See Medical Sciences-Anatomy.

ISSN 0268-1161
UK
CCC
NLM W1; HU461F **CODEN** HUREEE
Pr Rev.
HUMAN REPRODUCTION (OXFORD). (HUMAN REPRODUCTION.). [Hum. reprod.]. **Added/Corp** European Society of Human Reproduction and Embryology. Vol. 1, No. 1 (Jan. 1986)-. Academic Scholarly Publication. English. Twelve times a year. $750.00. Oxford University Press / UK, Walton Street, Oxford OX2 6DP United Kingdom. **Tel** 011 44 1865 56767, FAX 011 44 1865 267773, telex 851/837330 OXPRES G. **(Subscription address:** Oxford University Press / USA, Journals Marketing Department, Oxford University Press, 2001 Evans Road, Cary NC 27513. **Tel** (800)451-7556, (919)677-0977, FAX (919)677-1714.**) ED** R. G. Edwards. Index available. cum. index. **Ad Acc.** available on microfilm and microfiche from University Microfilms International (UMI). Documents available from The Genuine Article, BIOSIS Document Express, CASDDS.
Desc: Covers sexual differentiation, gametogenesis, sexuality, fertilization and early embryology, reproductive physiology, reproductive endocrinology, reproductive immunology, reproductive behaviour, pregnancy, ethics and society.
Ind/Abst Biol. Abstr. (1986-); Chem. Abstr. (1986-); CSA Neuro. Abstr. (?-?); Curr. Cit.; Curr. Contents Clin. Med.; Curr. Contents Life Sci.; EMBASE; Index Med. (1986-); Ref. Upd. Deluxe Ed.; Res. Alert [Select. Cov.]; Sci. Cit. Index; SCISEARCH; Soc. Sci. Cit. Index [Select. Cov.]; Virol. AIDS Abstr.

LC QL951 .I57 **ISSN** 0214-6282
SP
CCC
NLM W1; IN766GB **CODEN** IJDBE5
Pr Rev.
INTERNATIONAL JOURNAL OF DEVELOPMENTAL BIOLOGY, THE. Vol. 33, No. 1 (March 1989)-. Periodical. English. Six times a year (Mar., June, Sept., Dec.). $366.38. University of Basque Country Press, Apartado 1397, 48080 Bilbao Vizcaya Spain. **Tel** 011 34 4 4647700 Ext 2153, FAX 011 34 4 4801314. **ED** Juan Arechaga. Index available (Dec. iss.). **Ad Acc. Circ:** 1,000 (ctrl). Documents available from The Genuine Article. ***Continues** Anales del Desarrollo.*
Desc: Includes all animal or vegetal organisms, experimental methods and aspects ranging from manifestations of normal development to pathological phenomena.
Ind/Abst Curr. Aware. Biol. Sci., CABS; Curr. Cit.; Curr. Contents Life Sci.; EMBASE; Genet. Abstr.; Index Med.; Indice Med. Esp.; Res. Alert [Full Cov.]; Sci. Cit. Index.

LC QL494 .I5 **ISSN** 0020-7322
DD 595.7/04/05 UK
CCC
NLM W1 IN769E **CODEN** IJIMBQ
Pr Rev.
INTERNATIONAL JOURNAL OF INSECT MORPHOLOGY & EMBRYOLOGY. See Zoology-Entomology.

ISSN 1122-6714
IT
UDC 611-01
ITALIAN JOURNAL OF ANATOMY AND EMBRYOLOGY. See Medical Sciences-Anatomy.

ISSN 0141-9846
UK
NLM W1 JO619V **CODEN** JDPHDH
Pr Rev. **CEASED**
JOURNAL OF DEVELOPMENTAL PHYSIOLOGY. [J. dev. physiol]. **VFOAT** Developmental Physiology. Vol. 1 (Feb. 1979)-(1993). Academic Scholarly Publication. English. Caxton Communications Limited, Unit 8 Central Park Business Centre, Bellfield Road Buckinghamshire HP13 5HG United Kingdom. **Tel** 011 44 1494 473405, FAX 011 44 1494 535573. **ED** C. T. Jones. Index available. **Bk Rev. Ad Acc. Circ:** 500. available on microfilm and microfiche from University Microfilms International (UMI). Documents available from The Genuine Article, BIOSIS Document Express, CASDDS.
Desc: Papers describing the result of original research on aspects of the scientific study of the pregnancy, the fetus, or the neonate of man or experimental animals.
Ind/Abst AGRICOLA [Select. Cov.]; Biol. Abstr.; Chem. Abstr.; Curr. Contents Life Sci.; Curr. Ref. Fish Res.; Dev. Med. Child Neurol.; EMBASE; Index Med.; Index Vet.; Life Sci. Collect.; Ref. Upd. Deluxe Ed.; Res. Alert [Full Cov.]; Sci. Cit. Index; SCISEARCH; Soc. Sci. Cit. Index [Select. Cov.]; Vet. Bull.

LC QP251 .M554 **ISSN** 1040-452X
DD 574.1/6/05 US
CCC
NLM W1; MO197RS **CODEN** MREDEE
MOLECULAR REPRODUCTION AND DEVELOPMENT. [Mol. reprod. dev.]. (1988)-. Academic Scholarly Publication. English. Twelve times a year. $1644.00. John Wiley & Sons, Inc., 605 Third Avenue, New York NY 10158-0012. **Tel** (212)850-6000, (212)850-6645, FAX (212)850-6088, telex 12-7063. **(Subscription address:** John Wiley & Sons / UK, Baffins Lane, Chichester, West Sussex PO19 1UD United Kingdom. **Tel** 011 44 1243 779777, FAX 011 44 243 776128, telex 86290 WIBOOKG.**) ED** Ralph B. L. Gwatkin. Documents available from The Genuine Article, BIOSIS Document Express, CASDDS. ***Absorbed** Gamete Research, 0148-7280.*
Desc: Devoted to broad aspects of reproductive and developmental processes in humans, lower animals, and plants.
Ind/Abst AgBiotech News Inf.; AGRICOLA [Select. Cov.]; Anim. Breed. Abstr.; Biol. Abstr. (1990-); Chem. Abstr. (1988-); Curr. Aware. Biol. Sci., CABS; Curr. Cit.; Curr. Contents Life Sci.; EMBASE; Genet. Abstr.; Health Plan. Adminis.; Index Med. (1988-); Nematol. Abstr.; Pig News Inf.; Poult. Abstr.; Ref. Upd. Deluxe Ed.; Res. Alert [Full Cov.]; Sci. Cit. Index; SCISEARCH.

LC QL951 **ISSN** 0165-196X
DD 574.33 NE
NLM W1 MO567M **CODEN** MFPHDU
Pr Rev.
MONOGRAPHS IN FETAL PHYSIOLOGY. Vol. 1 (1976)-. Academic Scholarly Publication. English. Irregular. Price varies per volume. Elsevier Science Publishing Company Inc, Madison Square Station, PO Box 882, New York NY 10159-0882. **Tel** (212)633-3950, FAX (212)633-3990. **(Subscription address:** Elsevier Science Inc. / New York Books, 655 Avenue of the Americas, New York NY 10010. **Tel** (212)633-3650.**)** Documents available from CASDDS.
Ind/Abst Chem. Abstr.

LC QP281 **ISSN** 0143-4004
DD 599.01/6 UK
CCC
NLM W1 PL101C **CODEN** PLACDF
Pr Rev.
PLACENTA (EASTBOURNE). (PLACENTA.). [Placenta]. Vol. 1 (Jan./March 1980)-. Academic Scholarly Publication. English. Irregular (8 issues). $326.00. Harcourt Brace & Company Ltd., Foots Cray High Street, Sidcup Kent DA14 5HP United Kingdom. **Tel** 011 44 181 3003322, FAX 011 44 181 3090807. **(Subscription address:** W. B. Saunders Company / North America Subscriptions, c/o Periodicals, 6277 Sea Harbour Drive, 4th Floor, Orlando FL 32887. **Tel** (800)654-2452, (407)345-3668.**) ED** R. D. H. Boyd and K. L. Thornburg. **Bk Rev.** Documents available from The Genuine Article, BIOSIS Document Express, CASDDS.
Desc: Provides comprehensive coverage of placental research. Articles of high scientific quality examine relevant areas of placental morphology, physiology, endocrinology, immunology, pharmacology, cell biology, placental microbiology, pathology, and toxicology. Contributions may take the form of full-length papers or short communications. Invited review articles are also published together with information about meetings of placental interest, conference reports, and reviews of relevant books.
Ind/Abst Anim. Breed. Abstr.; Biol. Abstr.; Chem. Abstr.; CSA Neuro. Abstr. (?-?); Curr. Aware. Biol. Sci., CABS; Curr. Cit.; Curr. Contents Clin. Med.; Curr. Contents Life Sci.; EMBASE; Index Med.; Index Vet.; Life Sci. Collect.; Res. Alert [Full Cov.]; Sci. Cit. Index; SCISEARCH; Vet. Bull.

ISSN 0035-4007
RM
REVUE ROUMAINE D'EMBRYOLOGIE ET DE CYTOLOGIE. SERIE DE CYTOLOGIE. (19??)-. Periodical. Multiple languages (French and Romanian). Two times a year. Editura Academia Republicii Socialiste Romania, Calea Victoriei Nr 125, R-79717 Bucuresti Romania. **Tel** telex 10376 PRSFI R.

ISSN 1220-0522
RM
NLM W1; RO327H **CODEN** RRMEEA
ROMANIAN JOURNAL OF MORPHOLOGY AND EMBRYOLOGY. (ROMANIAN JOURNAL OF MORPHOLOGY AND EMBRYOLOGY = REVUE ROUMAINE DE MORPHOLOGIE ET EMBRYOLOGIE.). [Rom. j. morphol. embryol.]. **Added/Corp** Academia de Stiinte Medicale. **VFOAT** Revue Roumaine de Morphologie et Embryologie. (Apr./June 1990)-. Periodical. English (French). Four times a year. $125.00. **(Subscription address:** Orion Press SRL, SPL Independentei 202-A, Bucharest 6 Romania. **Tel** 011 401 3122425.**)** Documents available from CASDDS. ***Continues** Morphologie et Embryologie, 0377-5038.*
Desc: Information on morphology, embryology, and cytology.
Ind/Abst Chem. Abstr.; Index Med.

ISSN 0930-035X
GW
CCC
NLM W1; RO489T **CODEN** RADBE7
TITLE CHANGE
ROUX'S ARCHIVES OF DEVELOPMENTAL BIOLOGY. (ROUX'S ARCHIVES OF DEVELOPMENTAL BIOLOGY : THE OFFICIAL ORGAN OF THE EDBO.). [Roux's arch. dev. biol.]. **Added/Corp** EDBO (Organization). **VFOAT** Wilhelm Roux's Archives; Developmental Biology; Roux's Archives. Vol. 195, No. 1 (Jan. 1986)-(1995). Academic Scholarly Publication. English. Springer-Verlag GmbH & Company KG, Heidelberger Platz 3, D-14197 Berlin Germany. **Tel** 011 49 30 8207223, FAX 011 49 30 8214091, telex 183 319 SPBLN D. **(Subscription address:** Springer-Verlag New York Inc. / North America, PO Box 2485, Journal Fulfillment, Secaucus NJ 07096. **Tel** (201)348-4033, (800)777-4643, FAX (201)348-4505.**) ED** K. Sander. available on microfilm and microfiche from University Microfilms International (UMI). Documents available from The Genuine Article, BIOSIS Document Express, CASDDS. ***Continues** Wilhelm Roux's Archives of Developmental Biology, 0340-0794. **Continued by** Development Genes and Evolution.*
Desc: Presents results of research on animal systems at the molecular, cellular, and organismic level. Fields of interest include: pattern formation, morphogenesis, developmental biology, cellular differentiation, morphogenetic substances and developmental hormones, cellular interaction, regulation of gene expression, developmental genetics, and in vitro systems.
Ind/Abst Biol. Abstr. (1988-); Chem. Abstr. (1986-); Curr. Aware. Biol. Sci., CABS; Curr. Cit.; EMBASE; Energy Res. Abstr.; Fish Rev. (19??-199?); GeoRef; Nematol. Abstr.; Life Sci. Collect.; Ref. Upd. Deluxe Ed.; Res. Alert [Full Cov.]; Rev. Med. Vet. Entomol.; Sci. Cit. Index; SCISEARCH; Wildl. Rev. (19??-199?).

ISSN 0891-9925
DD 618 US
NLM W1; TR877 **CODEN** TRREEN
TROPHOBLAST RESEARCH. [Trophobl. res.]. Vol. 1 (1984)-. Monographic series. English. Price varies per volume. Plenum Press, 233 Spring Street, New York NY 10013-1578. **Tel** (212)620-8000, (800)221-9369, FAX (212)463-0742, (212)807-1047, telex 23/421139.
Ind/Abst Chem. Abstr. (1984-); Curr. Cit.

LC QH491 .Z94 **ISSN** 0967-1994
DD 574.3/33 UK
CCC
NLM W1; ZY979
Pr Rev.
●**ZYGOTE.** Vol. 1, Issue 1 (Feb. 1993)-. Academic Scholarly Publication. English. Four times a year. $166.00. Cambridge University Press, The Edinburgh Building, Shaftesbury Road, Cambridge CB2 2RU United Kingdom. **Tel** 011 44 1223 312393, FAX 011 44 1223 315052, telex 851-817256. **(Subscription address:** Cambridge University Press / North America, 110 Midland Avenue, Port Chester NY 10573. **Tel** (800)431-1580, (914)937-9600.) **ED** Brian Dale and William Jeffery (co-editor).
Desc: Aims to identify basic mechanisms that establish the architecture of the early embryo.
Ind/Abst Index Med.

GENETICS

LC GN289. A25 **ISSN** 0258-0357
DD 573.2/05 II
NLM W1 AC7524 **CODEN** ACANDO
ACTA ANTHROPOGENETICA. See Anthropology.

LC AS80.A1 E85 QH301 **ISSN** 0101-5354
DD 050 S 574/.05 BL
CODEN ABLEEC
ACTA BIOLOGICA LEOPOLDENSIA. See Biology-Cytology.

LC QH426 .A38
DD 575.105/6 XO
ACTA FACULTATIS RERUM NATURALIUM UNIVERSITATIS COMENIANAE. GENETICA ET BIOLOGIA MOLECULARIS. **VFOAT** Genetica et Biologia Molecularis. No. 22 (1991)-. English (summaries and/or abstracts in Czech and Russian; table of contents in Czech and Russian). Slovenske Pedagogicke Nakladetelstvo, Sasinkova 5, 891 12 Bratislava, Slovakia. ***Continues*** *Acta Facultatis Rerum Naturalium Universitatis Comenianae. Genetica, 0524-2320.*
Ind/Abst Plant Grow. Reg. Abstr.; Seed Abstr.

LC QH426 **ISSN** 0001-5660
DD 575.1 IT
CODEN AGMGAKAMAXBK
Pr Rev.
ACTA GENETICAE MEDICAE ET GEMELLOLOGIAE. [Acta genet. med. gemellol.]. **Added/Corp** Istituto "Gregorio Mendel". Societa Italiana di Genetica Medica. Permanent Committee for the International Congresses of Human Genetics. International Society for Twin Studies. **VFOAT** Twin Research. Vol. 1, No. 1 (Jan. 1952)-. Academic Scholarly Publication. English (French, German and Italian). Four times a year. L330000. Gregor Mendel Institute, Piazza Galeno 5, 00161 Rome Italy. **Tel** (06)864 658. **ED** Luigi Gedda. Index available. cum. index. ctrl circ. Documents available from The Genuine Article.
Ind/Abst Anthropol. Index; Curr. Cit.; Curr. Contents Life Sci.; Dev. Med. Child Neurol.; EMBASE; Genet. Abstr.; Index Med.; Life Sci. Collect.; Psychol. Abstr. (1979-); PsycINFO (1990-); PsycLit; Res. Alert [Select. Cov.]; SCISEARCH; Soc. Sci. Cit. Index [Select. Cov.].

LC QP624.7 .A38 **ISSN** 1067-568X
DD 574.87/322 US
NLM W1; AD549D **CODEN** ADNAEO
ADVANCES IN DNA SEQUENCE SPECIFIC AGENTS. [Adv. DNA seq. specif. agents]. **VFOAT** Advances in Deoxyribonucleic Acid Sequence Specific Agents. Vol. 1 (1992)-. Academic Scholarly Publication. English. One time a year. $90.25. JAI Press Inc., 55 Old Post Road, Suite 2, PO Box 1678, Greenwich CT 06836-1678. **Tel** (203)661-7602, FAX (203)661-0792. **ED** Lawrence Hurley. Documents available from CASDDS.
Desc: Examines the techniques used to study DNA sequence recognition and the interactions between DNA and protein and small molecular weight molecules which lead to sequence recognition.
Ind/Abst Chem. Abstr.

LC QH431.A1 A3 **ISSN** 0065-2660
DD 575.082 US
UDC 575 **CCC**
NLM W1 AD615
Pr Rev.
ADVANCES IN GENETICS. [Adv. genet.]. Vol. 1 (1947)-. Academic Scholarly Publication. English. One time a year. $59.00 (Vol. 31). Academic Press Inc., 6277 Sea Harbor Drive, Orlando FL 32887. **Tel** (800)543-9534, (407)345-4100, FAX (407)352-3445. **ED** M. Demerec. Documents available from The Genuine Article, BIOSIS Document Express, CASDDS. ***Absorbed*** *Molecular Genetic Medicine.*
Ind/Abst AGRICOLA [Select. Cov.]; Anim. Breed. Abstr.; Biol. Agric. Index; Biol. Abstr.; Chem. Abstr.; Curr. Aware. Biol. Sci., CABS; Curr. Cit.; Energy Res. Abstr.; Index Med.; Index Sci. Rev. [Full Cov.]; INIS Atomindex [Micro.]; Maize Abstr.; Life Sci. Collect.; PESTDOC; Plant Breed. Abstr.; Res. Alert [Full Cov.]; Sci. Cit. Index; SCISEARCH; Trop. Dis. Bull.; Vitis Vitic. Enol. Abstr.

LC QH431.A1 A32 **ISSN** 0065-275X
DD 573.2/1 US
CCC
NLM W1 AD64 **CODEN** ADHGA8
Pr Rev.
ADVANCES IN HUMAN GENETICS. [Adv. hum. genet.]. Vol. 1 (1970)-. Academic Scholarly Publication. English. Irregular. Price varies per volume. Plenum Press, 233 Spring Street, New York NY 10013-1578. **Tel** (212)620-8000, (800)221-9369, FAX (212)463-0742, (212)807-1047, telex 23/421139. **ED** H. Harris and K. Hirschhorn. Documents available from The Genuine Article, BIOSIS Document Express, CASDDS.
Desc: Investigations from various disciplines such as enzymology, immunology, protein chemistry, molecular biology, cytology, pediatrics, etc.
Ind/Abst Biol. Agric. Index; Biol. Abstr.; Chem. Abstr.; Curr. Aware. Biol. Sci., CABS; EMBASE; Energy Res. Abstr. (Jan. 1971-); Health Plan. Adminis.; Index Med.; Index Sci. Rev. [Full Cov.]; INIS Atomindex [Micro.]; Life Sci. Collect.; Ref. Upd. Basic Ed.; Ref. Upd. Deluxe Ed.; Res. Alert [Full Cov.]; Sci. Cit. Index; SCISEARCH.

ISSN 1033-8624
DD 616.04205 AT
AGSA NEWSLETTER. [AGSA newsl.]. **Added/Corp** Association of Genetic Support of Australasia. **VFOAT** Association of Genetic Support of Australasia Newsletter. (1989)-. English. Four times a year. 20.55Aus$. Association of Genetic Support of Australasia, C 44 Rawson Street, Epping New South Wales 2121 Australia. **Tel** 011 61 2 8682559.

LC QH431.A1 A5 **ISSN** 0002-9297
DD 575.05 US
CCC
NLM W1 AM462 **CODEN** AJHGAG
Pr Rev.
AMERICAN JOURNAL OF HUMAN GENETICS. [Am. j. hum. genet.]. **Added/Corp** American Society of Human Genetics. Vol. 1 (Sept. 1949)-. Academic Scholarly Publication. English. Twelve times a year. $300.00. University of Chicago Press / Journals Division, PO Box 37005, 5720 South Woodlawn, Chicago IL 60637. **Tel** (312)753-3347, FAX (312)753-0811. **ED** Peter H. Byers, M.D. **Acid Free.** available on microfilm and microfiche from University Microfilms International (UMI). Documents available from The Genuine Article, BIOSIS Document Express, CASDDS.
Desc: A record of research and review relating to heredity in man and to the application of genetic principles in medicine, psychology, anthropology, and the social sciences as well as in related areas of molecular and cell biology. Topics explored by AJHG include: behavioral genetics, biochemical genetics, clinical genetics, cytogenetics, dysmorphology, genetic counseling, immunogenetics, etc.
Ind/Abst Abstr. Anthropol. (19??-); Anim. Breed. Abstr.; Anthropol. Index; Biol. Agric. Index; Biol. Abstr.; Biostatistica (19??-19??); Chem. Abstr.; Chicano Index; Cumul. Index Nurs. Allied Health Lit.; Curr. Aware. Biol. Sci., CABS; Curr. Cit.; Curr. Contents Clin. Med.; Curr. Contents Life Sci.; Dairy Sci. Abstr.; Dev. Med. Child Neurol.; EMBASE; Energy Res. Abstr.; Genet. Abstr.; Health Plan. Adminis.; Hum. Genome Abstr.; Immunol. Abstr.; Index Med.; Index Vet.; INIS Atomindex [Micro.]; Linguist. Lang. Behav. Abstr.; Life Sci. Collect.; Plant Breed. Abstr.; Protozoolog. Abstr.; Ref. Upd. Basic Ed.; Ref. Upd. Clinical Ed.; Ref. Upd. Deluxe Ed.; Res. Alert [Full Cov.]; Sci. Cit. Index; SCISEARCH; Soc. Plann. Policy Dev. Abstr.; Soc. Sci. Cit. Index [Select. Cov.]; Sociol. Abstr.; Stat. Theory Method Abstr. (1959-1963, 1969); Trop. Dis. Bull.

LC RB155 .A53 **ISSN** 0148-7299
DD 616/.042 US
CCC
NLM W1; AM488B **CODEN** AJMGDA
Pr Rev.
AMERICAN JOURNAL OF MEDICAL GENETICS. [Am. j. med. genet.]. **VFOAT** Neuropsychiatric Genetics. Vol. 1 (1977)-. Periodical. English. Twenty-six times a year. $3990.00. John Wiley & Sons, Inc., 605 Third Avenue, New York NY 10158-0012. **Tel** (212)850-6000, (212)850-6645, FAX (212)850-6088, telex 12-7063. **(Subscription address:** John Wiley & Sons / UK, Baffins Lane, Chichester, West Sussex PO19 1UD United Kingdom. **Tel** 011 44 1243 779777, FAX 011 44 243 776128, telex 86290 WIBOOKG.) **ED** John M. Opitz. **Bk Rev. Ad Acc.** Documents available from The Genuine Article, BIOSIS Document Express.
Desc: Journal on all biological and medical aspects of genetic disorders. Reports original research on a variety of relevant topics, including clinical genetics, cytogenetics, nosology, prenatal diagnosis of genetic disorders, and molecular and biochemical genetics.
Ind/Abst Biol. Abstr.; Calcium Calcif. Tissue Abstr.; Curr. Cit.; Curr. Contents Life Sci.; Dev. Med. Child Neurol.; EMBASE; Energy Res. Abstr. (April 1982-); Genet. Abstr.; Hum. Genome Abstr.; Index Med.; Index Vet.; INIS Atomindex [Micro.]; Nutr. Abstr. Rev., Ser. B, Live Feeds and Feed.; Nutr. Abstr. Rev., Ser. A, Hum. Exp.; Oncog. Growth Factors Abstr.; Life Sci. Collect.; Protozoolog. Abstr.; Ref. Upd. Basic Ed.; Ref. Upd. Clinical Ed.; Ref. Upd. Deluxe Ed.; Res. Alert [Full Cov.]; Sci. Cit. Index; SCISEARCH; Soc. Sci. Cit. Index [Select. Cov.].

ISSN 1014-2339
IT
UDC 63
CODEN NU052
ANIMAL GENETIC RESOURCES INFORMATION. [Anim. genet. resour. inf.]. **VFOAT** Bulletin d'Information sur les Ressources Genetiques Animales; Boletin de Informacion Sobre Recursos Geneticos Animales. (1983)-. Bulletin. Multiple languages. Four times a year.
Ind/Abst Pig News Inf.; Poult. Abstr.

ISSN 0268-9146
UK
CCC
NLM W1; AN228P **CODEN** ANGEE3
Pr Rev.
ANIMAL GENETICS. [Anim. genet.]. **Added/Corp** International Society for Animal Blood Group Research. Vol. 17, No. 1 (1986)-. Academic Scholarly Publication. English. Six times a year. $282.00. Blackwell Scientific Publications Ltd, Marston Book Services, PO Box 88, Oxford OX2 ONE United Kingdom. **Tel** 011 44 1865 206206, FAX 011 44 1865 206219, telex 837 515 MARDIS G. **ED** Roger L. Spooner. **Ad Acc. Circ:** 500. available on microfilm and microfiche from University Microfilms International (UMI). Documents available from The Genuine Article, BIOSIS Document Express, CASDDS. ***Continues*** *Animal Blood Groups and Biochemical Genetics, 0003-3480.*
Desc: Reports research on genetic variation at the level of single genes, their product and function.
Ind/Abst AgBiotech News Inf.; Anim. Breed. Abstr.; Biol. Abstr. (1986-); Chem. Abstr. (1986-); Curr. Aware. Biol. Sci., CABS; Curr. Cit.; Curr. Contents Agric. Biol. Environ. Sci.; Curr. Contents Life Sci.; Dairy Sci. Abstr.; Fish Rev. (Jan. 1989-July 1992); Genet. Abstr.; Helminthol. Abstr.; Immunol. Abstr.; Index Med. (1986-); Index Vet.; Pig News Inf.; Poult. Abstr.; Protozoolog. Abstr.; Res. Alert [Full Cov.]; Sci. Cit. Index; SCISEARCH; Vet. Bull.; Wildl. Rev. (Jan. 1989-July 1992).

LC QH426 **ISSN** 0003-3995
DD 575.1 FR
CCC
NLM W1 AN336 **CODEN** AGTQAH
Pr Rev.
ANNALES DE GENETIQUE. [Ann. genet.]. **Added/Corp** Societe Francaise de Genetique. Vol. 1 (1958)-. Academic Scholarly Publication. French (English and French; summaries and/or abstracts in German, Italian and Spanish). Four times a year. $389.32. Semaine de Hopitaux, 31 boulevard de la Tour-Maubourg, 75007 Paris France. **Tel** 011 33 1 40626400, FAX 011 33 1 45556920. **ED** J. de Grouchy. **Bk Rev.** Documents available from The Genuine Article, BIOSIS Document Express, CASDDS.
Ind/Abst AgBiotech News Inf.; Anim. Breed. Abstr.; Biol. Abstr.; Chem. Abstr.; Curr. Aware. Biol. Sci., CABS; Curr. Cit.; Curr. Contents; Curr. Contents Life Sci.; Dairy Sci. Abstr.; Dev. Med. Child Neurol.; EMBASE; Index Med.; Life Sci. Collect.; Pig News Inf.; Protozoolog. Abstr.; Res. Alert [Full Cov.]; Sci. Cit. Index; SCISEARCH; Soc. Sci. Cit. Index [Select. Cov.]; Wildl. Rev.

LC HQ750.A1 A5 **ISSN** 0003-4800
DD 306 UK
CCC
NLM W1 AN597 **CODEN** ANHGAA
Pr Rev.
ANNALS OF HUMAN GENETICS. [Ann. hum. genet.]. **Added/Corp** Galton Laboratory. Vol. 19 (1954)-. Academic Scholarly Publication. English. Six times a year. $228.00. Cambridge University Press, The Edinburgh Building, Shaftesbury Road, Cambridge CB2 2RU United Kingdom. **Tel** 011 44 1223 312393, FAX 011 44 1223 315052, telex 851-817256. **(Subscription address:** Cambridge University Press / North America, 110 Midland Avenue, Port Chester NY 10573. **Tel** (800)431-1580, (914)937-9600.) **ED** EB Robson, CAB Smith, DA Hopkinson. cum. index. **Bk Rev. Ad Acc.** available on microfilm from University Microfilms International (UMI). Documents available from The Genuine Article, BIOSIS Document Express, CASDDS. ***Continues*** *Annals of Eugenics.*
Desc: Publishes both original papers and book reviews. The material published is directly concerned with human genetics or the application of scientific principles and techniques to any aspect of human inheritance. Most papers fall into one of the following broad categories: biochemical and molecular genetics, gene mapping, cytogenetics, clinical genetics or mathematical models applied to sets of family or population data.
Ind/Abst Anim. Breed. Abstr.; Anthropol. Index; Anthropol. Lit.; Biol. Abstr.; Biostatistica (19??-19??); Chem. Abstr. (?-1988); Curr. Aware. Biol. Sci., CABS; Curr. Cit.; Curr. Contents Life Sci.; Dev. Med. Child Neurol.; EMBASE; Genet. Abstr.; Health Plan. Adminis.; Hum. Genome Abstr.; Index Med.; Math. Rev. (?-199?); Oncog. Growth Factors Abstr.; Life Sci. Collect.; Plant Breed. Abstr.; Protozoolog. Abstr.; Ref. Upd. Basic Ed.; Ref. Upd. Deluxe Ed.; Res. Alert [Full Cov.]; Sci. Cit. Index; SCISEARCH; Soc. Sci. Cit. Index [Select. Cov.];

Stat. Theory Method Abstr. (1959-1963, 1968, 1971, 1979, 1982-1983); Trop. Dis. Bull.; Zentralbl. Math. Ihre Grenzgeb.

LC RA645.G4 M37A **ISSN** 0882-8997
DD 353.97520084/1 US

ANNUAL REPORT / MARYLAND COMMISSION ON HEREDITARY DISORDERS. [Annu. rep. - Md. Comm. Hered. Disord.]. **Main/Corp** Maryland Commission on Hereditary Disorders. English. One time a year. Maryland Commission on Hereditary Disorders, 201 West Preston Street, Baltimore MD 21201.

LC QH431.A1
DD 575.1 JA

ANNUAL REPORT / NATIONAL INSTITUTE OF GENETICS. Main/Corp National Institute of Genetics (Japan). (1950)-. English. One time a year. National Institute of Genetics, 1111 Yata, Mishima-shi, Shizuoka-ken 411 Japan.
Ind/Abst Anim. Breed. Abstr.; Plant Breed. Abstr.; Rev. Plant Pathol.; Rice Abstr.; Seed Abstr.

LC QH431.A1 A54 **ISSN** 0066-4197
DD 575.1/05 US
CCC
NLM W1 AN771N **CODEN** ARVGB7
Pr Rev.

ANNUAL REVIEW OF GENETICS. [Annu. rev. genet.]. Vol. 1 (1967)-. Academic Scholarly Publication. English. One time a year (December). $52.00. Annual Reviews Inc., 4139 El Camino Way, PO Box 10139, Palo Alto CA 94303-0139. **Tel** (415)493-4400, (800)523-8635, FAX (415)855-9815. **ED** Allan Campbell. Index available in last issue of volume--attached. cum. index. ctrl circ. available on microfilm and microfiche from University Microfilms International (UMI). Documents available from The Genuine Article, BIOSIS Document Express, CASDDS.
Desc: Comprehensive, thorough coverage of latest advances in genetics; written by acknowledged experts in the field. Extensive literature citations included.
Ind/Abst Acad. Search; AgBiotech News Inf.; AGRICOLA [Select. Cov.]; Anim. Breed. Abstr.; BioBusiness (-1989); Biol. Agric. Index; Biol. Abstr.; Biol. Dig.; Chem. Abstr.; Curr. Aware. Biol. Sci., CABS; Curr. Cit.; Curr. Contents Life Sci.; EMBASE; Energy Res. Abstr.; EP Collect.; For. Prod. Abstr.; For. Abstr.; Gen. Sci. Index (1992-); Gen. Sci. Source; Genet. Abstr.; Health Plan. Adminis.; Homework Help.; Index Med.; Index Sci. Rev. [Full Cov.]; Index Vet.; INFO-SOUTH Abstr.; INIS Atomindex [Micro.]; Int. Aerosp. Abstr.; Maize Abstr.; MasterFile FullTEXT 1000; MasterFile FullTEXT 350; MasterFile FullTEXT 650; MasterFile FullTEXT (July 1992-); OCLC; Life Sci. Collect.; PESTDOC; Plant Breed. Abstr.; Plant Grow. Reg. Abstr.; Protozoolog. Abstr.; Ref. Upd. Basic Ed.; Ref. Upd. Clinical Ed.; Ref. Upd. Deluxe Ed.; Res. Alert [Full Cov.]; Rev. Agric. Entomol.; Rev. Med. Vet. Mycology; Rev. Plant Pathol.; Sci. Cit. Index; SCISEARCH; Telebase; Trop. Dis. Bull.

LC RB155.6 .A67 **ISSN** 1056-5191
DD 611/.01816/05 US
NLM W1; AP516CL
Pr Rev.

APPLIED CYTOGENETICS. (APPLIED CYTOGENETICS : JOURNAL OF THE ASSOCIATION OF CYTOGENETIC TECHNOLOGISTS / THE ASSOCIATION OF CYTOGENETIC TECHNOLOGISTS INC., ACT.). [Appl. cytogenet.]. **Added/Corp** Association of Cytogenetic Technologists. Vol. 16, No. 1 (Feb. 1990)-. Periodical. English. Six times a year (Feb., Apr., June, Aug., Oct., Dec.). $105.00. Association Cytogenetic Technologists, PO Box 15945, Lenexa KS 66285. **Tel** (913)541-9077. **ED** Barbara Kaplan, (editor's address: 616 South Orchard Drive, Burbank, CA 91605). Index available (Bound in issues). **Ad Acc, Adv Mgr:** Leslee, **Tel** (913)541-9077. **Circ:** 2,000 (ctrl). ***Continues*** *Karyogram, 0732-8745.*

LC QH426 **ISSN** 0271-7107
DD 575.1 US
CCC
NLM W1; AP524F **CODEN** AGNEEN

APPLIED GENETICS NEWS. [Appl. genet. news]. Vol. 1 (Aug. 1980)-. Periodical. English. Twelve times a year. $375.00. Business Communications Inc., 25 Van Zant Street, Suite 13, Norwalk CT 06855. **Tel** (203)853-4266, FAX (203)853-0348. **ED** Jack T Miskell. **Bk Rev. Ad Acc. Circ:** 150. available on an online database from NEWSNET; DATA-STAR; and (files 16,636/Full-Text) DIALOG. Documents available from UMI Article Clearinghouse, BLDSC.
Desc: Identifies and examines markets where primary and radical changes are taking place. Provides readers with a digest of issues that exemplify changing marketplace by function, industry and technology.
Ind/Abst Abstr. BioCommer.; AGRICOLA [Select. Cov.]; BioBusiness (1986-); Pharm. News Index (Nov. 1984-); PROMT [Full Txt.]; PTS Newsl. Database [Full Txt.].

LC QH426 **ISSN** 0066-9830
DD 575.1 IT
NLM W1 AT752G **CODEN** AAGNA3

ATTI A.G.I. (ATTI - ASSOCIAZIONE GENETICA ITALIANA.). [Atti A.G.I.]. **Added/Corp** Associazione Genetica Italiana. **VFOAT** Atti A. G. I. (1959)-. Multiple languages (English and Italian). One time a year (Nov.). L40000. Associazione Genetica Italania, IST Genetica VLE Scienze, 43100 Parma Italy. **Tel** 011 39 521 905601. **ED** G.A. Danieli. Documents available from BIOSIS Document Express. ***Supersedes*** *Convegno di Genetica.*
Ind/Abst Biol. Abstr.; NAPRALERT.

ISSN 0001-8244
US
CCC
NLM W1 BE124 **CODEN** BHGNAT
Pr Rev.

BEHAVIOR GENETICS. [Behav. genet.]. **Added/Corp** Behavior Genetics Association. Vol. 1 (Feb. 1970)-. Academic Scholarly Publication. English. Six times a year. $435.00. Plenum Press, 233 Spring Street, New York NY 10013-1578. **Tel** (212)620-8000, (800)221-9369, FAX (212)463-0742, (212)807-1047, telex 23/421139. **ED** Jan H. Bruel. Index available. available on microfilm and microfiche from University Microfilms International (UMI). Documents available from The Genuine Article, BIOSIS Document Express, CASDDS.
Desc: A journal dealing with the inheritance and evolution of behavioral characters in man and other species. Deals with application of various perspectives of genetics in the study of genetics.
Ind/Abst Anim. Behav. Abstr.; Anim. Breed. Abstr.; Biol. Abstr.; Chem. Abstr.; Chemorecept. Abstr.; CSA Neuro. Abstr. (?-?); Curr. Aware. Biol. Sci., CABS; Curr. Cit.; Curr. Contents Life Sci.; Curr. Contents Soc. Behav. Sci.; EMBASE; Energy Res. Abstr. (Feb. 1982-); Entomol. Abstr.; Genet. Abstr.; Health Plan. Adminis.; Index Med.; Index Vet.; INIS Atomindex [Micro.]; Life Sci. Collect.; Poult. Abstr.; Psychol. Abstr. (1970-); PsycINFO; PsycLit; Ref. Upd. Deluxe Ed.; Res. Alert [Full Cov.]; Rev. Agric. Entomol.; Rev. Med. Vet. Entomol.; Sci. Cit. Index; SCISEARCH; Soc. Sci. Cit. Index [Full Cov.]; Wildl. Rev.

LC QH426 **ISSN** 0161-7656
DD 575.1 US
NLM W1 BE516 **CODEN** BPGEDR

BENCHMARK PAPERS IN GENETICS. [Benchmark pap. genet.]. Vol. 1 (1974)-. Monographic series. English. Irregular. Price varies per volume. Academic Press Inc., 6277 Sea Harbor Drive, Orlando FL 32887. **Tel** (800)543-9534, (407)345-4100, FAX (407)352-3445. **ED** D.L. Jameson. Documents available from BIOSIS Document Express.
Ind/Abst Biol. Abstr. (?-1986).

LC QH431 .B54 **ISSN** 0006-2928
DD 575.2/1 US
CCC
NLM W1 BI621 **CODEN** BIGEBA
Pr Rev.

BIOCHEMICAL GENETICS. [Biochem. genet.]. Vol. 1 (June 1967)-. Academic Scholarly Publication. English. Twelve times a year. $655.00. Plenum Press, 233 Spring Street, New York NY 10013-1578. **Tel** (212)620-8000, (800)221-9369, FAX (212)463-0742, (212)807-1047, telex 23/421139. **ED** Hugh S. Forrest. Index available. available on microfilm and microfiche from University Microfilms International (UMI). Documents available from The Genuine Article, BIOSIS Document Express, CASDDS.
Ind/Abst Abstr. Anthropol. (19??-); AgBiotech News Inf.; AGRICOLA [Select. Cov.]; Anim. Breed. Abstr.; Biol. Agric. Index; Biol. Abstr.; Biotechnol. Res. Abstr.; Chem. Abstr.; Chem. Titles; Crop Physiol. Abstr.; Curr. Aware. Biol. Sci., CABS; Curr. Biotechnol.; Curr. Cit.; Curr. Contents Life Sci.; Dairy Sci. Abstr.; EMBASE; Energy Res. Abstr.; Entomol. Abstr.; Fish Rev.; For. Abstr.; Grass. Forage Abstr.; Health Plan. Adminis.; Index Med.; Index Vet.; INIS Atomindex [Micro.]; Int. Aerosp. Abstr.; Maize Abstr.; Nematol. Abstr.; Nutr. Abstr. Rev., Ser. A, Hum. Exp.; Life Sci. Collect.; PESTDOC; Plant Breed. Abstr.; Poult. Abstr.; Protozoolog. Abstr.; Psychol. Abstr.; Ref. Upd. Deluxe Ed.; Res. Alert [Full Cov.]; Rev. Med. Vet. Entomol.; Rice Abstr.; Sci. Cit. Index; SCISEARCH; Seed Abstr.; Soyabean Abstr.; Vet. Bull.; Wheat Barley Trit. Abstr.; Wildl. Rev.

ISSN 0167-4781
NE
CCC
Pr Rev.

BIOCHIMICA ET BIOPHYSICA ACTA. GENE STRUCTURE AND EXPRESSION. [Biochim. biophys. acta. Gene struct. expr.]. **VFOAT** Gene Structure and Expression; BBA, Biochimica et Biophysica Acta (N). Gene Structure and Expression; BBA, Gene Structure & Expression. Vol. 696, No. 1 (Jan. 26, 1982)-. Academic Scholarly Publication. English. Fifteen times a year (5 vols.). $1406.00. Elsevier Science Publishers BV, PO Box 211, 1000 AE Amsterdam Netherlands. **Tel** 011 31 20 4853641, 011 31 20 4853642, FAX 011 31 20 4853598. **ED** P Borst, P Cohen, K van Dam, L L M van Deenen, E P Kennedy, G K Radda, and E C Slater. available on microfilm and microfiche from University Microfilms International (UMI); available on an online database from Elsevier Electronic Subscriptions (EES). Documents available from ADONIS. ***Continues*** *Biochimica et Biophysica Acta. Nucleic Acids and Protein Synthesis.*
Ind/Abst ADONIS; AgBiotech News Inf.; Anim. Breed. Abstr.; Crop Physiol. Abstr.; Curr. Aware. Biol. Sci., CABS; Dairy Sci. Abstr.; EMBASE; Field Crop Abstr.; Maize Abstr.; Nutr. Abstr. Rev., Ser. B, Live Feeds and Feed.; PESTDOC; Pig News Inf.; Plant Breed. Abstr.; Poult. Abstr.; Ref. Upd. Basic Ed.; Ref. Upd. Deluxe Ed.; Rev. Agric. Entomol.; Rev. Med. Vet. Entomol.; Soils Fert.; Wheat Barley Trit. Abstr.

LC QD **ISSN** 0925-4439
DD 574.192 NE
CCC
CODEN BBADEX
Pr Rev.

BIOCHIMICA ET BIOPHYSICA ACTA. MOLECULAR BASIS OF DISEASE. **See** Biology-Biological Chemistry.

LC QH471
DD 574.16 US

•**BIOLOGY OF REPRODUCTION MONOGRAPH SERIES.** (1995)-. Monographic series. English. Irregular. Price varies. Society for the Study of Reproduction, Subscription Department, 1526 Jefferson Street, Madison WI 53711-2106. **Tel** (608)256-2777, FAX (608)256-4610.

LC TP950 **ISSN** 0393-9146
DD 661.8 IT
CODEN BBRCED
Pr Rev.

BIOTEC : RIVISTA BIMESTRALE DI BIOTECNOLOGIA. **See** Biology-Bioengineering.

LC TP248 **ISSN** 0864-4551
DD 660.6 CU
NLM W1; BI918LB
Pr Rev.

BIOTECNOLOGIA APLICADA : REVISTA DE LA SOCIEDAD IBEROLATINOAMERICANA PARA INVESTIGACIONES SOBRE INTERFERON Y BIOTECNOLOGIA EN SALUD. **See** Biology-Bioengineering.

ISSN 0067-9720
AG
UDC 575:581

BOLETIN GENETICO. [Bol. genet.]. (1965)-. Periodical. Spanish. Irregular. $15.00. Instituto Nacional de Tecnologia Agropecuaria Centro de Investigaciones en Ciencias Agronomicas, Departamento de Genetica, Casilla de Correo No. 25, 1712 Castelar Argentina.
Ind/Abst Biocont. News Inf.; Potato Abstr.

LC QH426 **ISSN** 0325-8319
DD 575.1 AG
NLM W1 BO23F **CODEN** BOGOAD

BOLETIN GENETICO. ENGLISH EDITION. (BOLETIN GENETICO.). [Bol. genet., Engl. ed.]. **Added/Corp** Argentine Republic. Instituto de Fitotecnia. Centro de Investigaciones en Ciencias Agronomicas. No. 1 (May 1965)-. Periodical. English. Centro de Investigaciones Filosoficas, Casilla 5379, 1000 Buenos Aires Argentina. **Tel** 011 54 1 7870533. Documents available from BIOSIS Document Express, CASDDS.
Ind/Abst Biol. Abstr. (?-1986); Chem. Abstr.; Maize Abstr.; Life Sci. Collect.; Plant Breed. Abstr.; Rev. Plant Pathol.; Seed Abstr.; Weed Abstr.; Wheat Barley Trit. Abstr.; World Agric. Econ. Rural Sociol. Abstr.

LC QH426 .G475a **ISSN** 0316-4357
DD 575.1/05 CN
Pr Rev.

BULLETIN - GENETICS SOCIETY OF CANADA. Main/Corp Genetics Society of Canada. **VFOAT** Bulletin - Societe de Genetique du Canada. Vol. 1 (July 1969)-. Bulletin. English (French). Four times a year. 20.01Can$. Genetics Society of Canada, 151 Slater Street/Suite 907, Ottawa Ontario K1P 5H4 Canada. **Tel** (613)232-9459. **ED** Stephen J. Molnar. **Bk Rev. Ad Acc. Circ:** 450 (ctrl).
Desc: Newsletter for Society containing news, articles, and comments on genetics and society activities. Book reviews and general overviews are featured, as well as abstracts for annual meeting.

ISSN 0574-9549
DD 581 JA

C I S; CHROMOSOMES INFORMATION SERVICE. (1961)-. Periodical. English. Two times a year. $54.00. Senshokutai Gakkai, (Society of Chromosome Research), c/o Shinka Seibutsugaku Kenkyujo, 2-4 Kamiyoga, Setagayaku Tokyo 158 Japan. **(Subscription address:** Japan Publications Trading Company Ltd., PO Box 5030, Tokyo International, Tokyo 100-31 Japan. **Tel** 011 81 3 3292 3753.**)**

LC S583 **ISSN** 0890-7528
DD 631 US
CODEN CBAGEJ

CAS BIOTECH UPDATES. AGRICULTURE. **See** Agriculture.

ISSN 1045-8581
DD 574 US
CODEN CBDPER
CAS BIOTECH UPDATES. DNA & RNA PROBES. [CAS biotechnol. updates, DNA RNA probes]. **Added/Corp** American Chemical Society. Chemical Abstracts Service. **VFOAT** DNA & RNA Probes; DNA and RNA Probes. **VAT** Chemical Abstracts Service Biotech Updates. Deoxyribonucleic Acid and Ribonucleic Acid Probes. (Jan. 8, 1990)-. English. Twenty-six times a year. $220.00. Chemical Abstracts Service, (Subsidiary of The American Chemical Society), 2540 Olentangy River Road, PO Box 3012, Columbus OH 43210-0012. **Tel** (614)447-3731, (800)753-4227, FAX (614)447-3751. **(Subscription address:** Chemical Abstracts Service, Customer Service Department, PO Box 3012, Columbus OH 43210. **Tel** (800)848-6538, (614)447-3600.**)**

ISSN 0895-6618
DD 574 US
CODEN CUDREU
CAS BIOTECH UPDATES. DNA FORMATION & REPAIR. [CAS biotech updates, DNA form. repair]. **Added/Corp** American Chemical Society. Chemical Abstracts Service. **VFOAT** DNA Formation & Repair; Repair; DNA Information and Repair. **VAT** Chemical Abstracts Service Biotech Updates. DNA Formation & Repair. Vol. 1 (1988)-. Periodical. English. Twenty-six times a year. $220.00. Chemical Abstracts Service, (Subsidiary of The American Chemical Society), 2540 Olentangy River Road, PO Box 3012, Columbus OH 43210-0012. **Tel** (614)447-3731, (800)753-4227, FAX (614)447-3751. **(Subscription address:** Chemical Abstracts Service, Customer Service Department, PO Box 3012, Columbus OH 43210. **Tel** (800)848-6538, (614)447-3600.**)**

ISSN 0884-7460
DD 611 US
CODEN CBUEEB
CAS BIOTECH UPDATES. GENETIC ENGINEERING. [CAS biotech updates, Genet. eng.]. **Added/Corp** American Chemical Society. Chemical Abstracts Service. **VFOAT** Genetic Engineering. **VAT** Chemical Abstract Service Biotech Updates. Genetic Engineering. (1986)-. Periodical. English. Twenty-six times a year. $220.00. Chemical Abstracts Service, (Subsidiary of The American Chemical Society), 2540 Olentangy River Road, PO Box 3012, Columbus OH 43210-0012. **Tel** (614)447-3731, (800)753-4227, FAX (614)447-3751. **(Subscription address:** Chemical Abstracts Service, Customer Service Department, PO Box 3012, Columbus OH 43210. **Tel** (800)848-6538, (614)447-3600.**)**

LC QH426
DD 575.1 US
CATALOG OF CELL LINES. Added/Corp National Institute on Aging. National Institutes of Health (U.S.) Coriell Institute for Medical Research (U.S.). **VFOAT** National Institute on Aging ... Catalog of Cell Lines; NIA Aging Cell Repository. (198?)-. Catalog. English. Cornell Institute for Medical Research, 401 Haddon Avenue, Camden NJ 08103. ***Continues in part*** *Catalog of Cell Lines, 0737-7983.*

ISSN 0254-2935
II
NLM W1; CE126R CODEN CCREE3
CELL AND CHROMOSOME RESEARCH. See Biology-Cytology.

LC QH465.C5 C45 ISSN 0093-6855
DD 575.2/92 US
CCC
NLM W1 CH259T CODEN CMMUAO
CHEMICAL MUTAGENS. [Chem. mutagens]. **Added/Corp** Environmental Mutagen Society. (1971)-. Academic Scholarly Publication. English. Irregular. Price varies per volume. Plenum Press, 233 Spring Street, New York NY 10013-1578. **Tel** (212)620-8000, (800)221-9369, FAX (212)463-0742, (212)807-1047, telex 23/421139. **ED** Frederick J. de Serres. Documents available from The Genuine Article, BIOSIS Document Express, CASDDS.
Ind/Abst Biol. Abstr.; Chem. Abstr. (1971-1984); EMBASE; Pollut. Abstr. Indexes; Res. Alert [Full Cov.]; SCISEARCH.

ISSN 0961-0901
UK
NLM W1; CH939 CODEN CHOMED
SUSPENDED
CHROMATIN. Vol. 1, No. 1 (1992)-(19??). Academic Scholarly Publication. English. Four times a year. £150.00. Faculty Press, 88 Regent Street, Cambridge CB2 1DP United Kingdom. **Tel** FAX 011 44 1553 840695. Documents available from CASDDS.
Ind/Abst Chem. Abstr.; Curr. Aware. Biol. Sci., CABS.

ISSN 0967-3849
UK
CCC
NLM W1; CH994G CODEN CRRSEE
•CHROMOSOME RESEARCH. (CHROMOSOME RESEARCH : AN INTERNATIONAL JOURNAL ON THE MOLECULAR, SUPRAMOLECULAR AND EVOLUTIONARY ASPECTS OF CHROMOSOME BIOLOGY.). [Chromosom. res.]. Vol. 1, No. 1 (May 1993)-. Periodical. English. Eight times a year. $569.00. Rapid Science Publishers, The Old Malthouse, Paradise Street, Oxford OX1 1LD United Kingdom. **Tel** 011 44 1865 790447, FAX 011 44 1865 244012, telex 9403712. **(Subscription address:** Rapid Science Publishers, 400 Market Street, Philadelphia PA 19106. **)**
Ind/Abst Index Med.

LC QH600 .I57a ISSN 0069-3944
DD 574.87/322/05 US
NLM W3 C156M CODEN CHRTBC
CHROMOSOMES TODAY. [Chromosomes today]. Vol. 6 (1977)-. English. Irregular. $104.95 (latest volume). Routledge Chapman & Hall Inc., 29 West 35th Street, New York NY 10001. **Tel** (212)244-3336, (212)244-6412. ***Continues*** *Leiden Chromosome Conference. Chromosomes Today, 0069-3944.*
Ind/Abst Biol. Abstr. (1977-); Chem. Abstr. (1977-).

LC QH426 .C47 ISSN 0898-5138
DD 575.1/05 US
CCC
NLM W1; CH762
CHUAN HSUEH PAO. (CHINESE JOURNAL OF GENETICS.). [Chin. j. genet.]. **VFOAT** Acta Genetica Sinica. Vol. 15, No. 1 (1988)-. Periodical. English (translations available in Chinese). Four times a year. $495.00. Allerton Press Inc., 150 Fifth Avenue, New York NY 10011. **Tel** (212)924-3950, FAX (212)463-9684, telex 427441 ALPRES.
Ind/Abst Plant Grow. Reg. Abstr.; Rev. Agric. Entomol.; Rev. Plant Pathol.; Soyabean Abstr.

ISSN 1021-7967
CH
UDC 575.19
CHUAN SHUO ZU. VFOAT Fiction Star Monthly. (1988)-. Periodical. Chinese. Twelve times a year. $80.00. World Journal Bookstore, 231 Adrian Road, Millbrae CA 94030. **Tel** (415)692-9936.

ISSN 0574-9549
JA
NLM W1 C379 CODEN CISCB7
CIS : CHROMOSOME INFORMATION SERVICE. [CIS, Chromosome inf. serv.]. **Added/Corp** Society of Chromosome Research, Tokyo. **VFOAT** Chromosome Information Service. No. 1 (Dec. 1960)-. Academic Scholarly Publication. English. Two times a year. $54.00. Society of Chromosome Research Research Institute of Evolutionary Biology, 2-4 Kamiyoga, Setagaya-ku, Tokyo 158 Japan. **(Subscription address:** Japan Publications Trading Company Ltd., PO Box 5030, Tokyo International, Tokyo 100-31 Japan. **Tel** 011 81 3 3292 3753.**)** Documents available from BIOSIS Document Express, CASDDS.
Ind/Abst Biol. Abstr.; Chem. Abstr. (1961-1983); Genet. Abstr.; Life Sci. Collect.

LC QH426 ISSN 0564-3783
DD 575.1 UN
CCC
NLM W1 TS278F CODEN TGANAK
CITOLOGIJA I GENETIKA (KIEV). (TSITOLOGIIA I GENETIKA.). [Citol. genet.]. **Added/Corp** Akademiia Nauk Ukrainskoi RSR. Viddil Biokhimii, Biofizyky i Fiziolohii Akademiia Nauk Ukrainskoi RSR. Viddil Zahalnoi Biolohii. **VFOAT** Cytology and Genetics. Vol. 1, No. 1 (Jan./Feb. 1967)-. Periodical. Russian (summaries and/or abstracts in English). Six times a year. $109.95. **(Subscription address:** East View Publications Inc., 3020 Harbor Lane North, Suite 110, Minneapolis MN 55447. **Tel** (800)477-1005, (612)550-0961, FAX (612)559-2931.**) ED** I.A. Shevtov. Index available in last issue of volume--attached. Documents available from BIOSIS Document Express, CASDDS. ***Continues*** *Tsitologiia i Genetika.*
Ind/Abst AGRICOLA; Biol. Abstr.; Chem. Abstr.; Cot. Trop. Fibr. Abstr. Bibliogr.; Crop Physiol. Abstr.; EMBASE [Select. Cov.]; Hortic. Abstr.; Index Med.; Int. Aerosp. Abstr.; Maize Abstr.; Plant Breed. Abstr.; Plant Genet. Resour. Abstr.; Potato Abstr.; Poult. Abstr.; Rev. Med. Vet. Entomol.; Rev. Plant Pathol.

LC RB155 .C57 ISSN 0009-9163
DD 616/.042/05 DK
CCC
NLM W1 CL71 CODEN CLGNAY
Pr Rev.
CLINICAL GENETICS. [Clin. genet.]. (1970)-. Academic Scholarly Publication. English. Twelve times a year. $687.38. Munksgaard International Publishers Ltd, PO Box 2148, DK-1016 Copenhagen K Denmark. **Tel** 011 45 33 127030, FAX 011 45 33 129387, telex 19431 MUNKS DK. **ED** Jan Book, J Mohr, and K Berg Jan Book. Index available. **Bk Rev. Ad Acc. Circ:** 1,000 (ctrl). Documents available from The Genuine Article, BIOSIS Document Express, CASDDS.
Desc: Genetics and clinical medicine, genetic etiology of diseases or defects, gene-controlled pathogenesis, biochemical genetics, inborn errors of metabolism, immunogenetics, pharmacogenetics and research in human genetics.
Ind/Abst Biol. Abstr.; Chem. Abstr.; Curr. Aware. Biol. Sci., CABS; Curr. Cit.; Curr. Contents Clin. Med.; Curr. Contents Life Sci.; Dairy Sci. Abstr.; Dev. Med. Child Neurol.; EMBASE; Energy Res. Abstr. (Dec. 1973-); Genet. Abstr.; Health Plan. Adminis.; Hum. Genome Abstr.; Index Med.; INIS Atomindex [Micro.]; Nutr. Abstr. Rev., Ser. B, Live Feeds and Feed.; Nutr. Abstr. Rev., Ser. A, Hum. Exp.; Life Sci. Collect.; Res. Alert [Full Cov.]; Sci. Cit. Index; SCISEARCH; Soc. Sci. Cit. Index [Select. Cov.].

ISSN 0914-3505
JA
Pr Rev.
CONGENITAL ANOMALIES. Added/Corp Nihon Senten Ijo Gakkai. **VFOAT** Senten Ijo. (19??)-. Periodical. English (Japanese). Four times a year (Mar., June, Sept., Dec.). ¥8000.00. Japanese Teratology Society, Kinki University School of Medicine, Sayama cho Osaka 589 Japan. **Tel** 011 81 723 66 0221, FAX 011 81 723 66 0206. **ED** Mineo Yasuda (phone: 81-82-251-1111). Index available. cum. index. **Bk Rev**, (Qty: varies). **Ad Acc. Circ:** 1,600. Documents available from CASDDS. ***Continues*** *Senten Ijo, 0037-2285.*
Desc: Original reports of studies in all areas of abnormal development and related fields.
Ind/Abst Chem. Abstr.

ISSN 8756-9086
DD 616 US
CONNECTIVE ISSUES. See Medical Sciences.

LC QH359 .C73 ISSN 0738-6001
DD 575/.005 US
CREATION/EVOLUTION. [Creat./evol.]. **VFOAT** Creation Evolution. Issue 1 (Summer 1980)-. Periodical. English. Two times a year. $25.00 US; $32.00 (surface mail), $39.00 (airmail) other. National Center for Science Education, 1328 6th Street, Berkeley CA 94710-1404. **Tel** (510)526-1674, FAX (510)526-1675. **ED** John Cole. Index available. **Bk Rev. Circ:** 3,000.
Desc: Counters arguments of creationists in science, religion, education, law and social policy. Authorities in these areas bring their expertise to bear on the issue of 'scientific' creationism in public education.

LC Z5322.G4 C88 QH426 ISSN 0741-1642
DD 016.5751 UK
NLM Z 5322.G4; C9762
CURRENT ADVANCES IN GENETICS & MOLECULAR BIOLOGY. See Biology-Abstracting, Bibliographies and Statistics.

LC GN289 .C88 ISSN 0748-7819
DD 573.2 US
CURRENT DEVELOPMENTS IN ANTHROPOLOGICAL GENETICS. [Curr. dev. anthropol. genet.]. Vol. 1 (1980)-. Monographic series. English. Irregular. Price varies per volume. Plenum Press, 233 Spring Street, New York NY 10013-1578. **Tel** (212)620-8000, (800)221-9369, FAX (212)463-0742, (212)807-1047, telex 23/421139.

LC QH426 .C87 ISSN 0172-8083
DD 575.1/05 GW
CCC
NLM W1 CU788JAH CODEN CUGED5
Pr Rev.
CURRENT GENETICS. [Curr. genet.]. (Dec. 1979)-. Academic Scholarly Publication. English. Twelve times a year. $1329.00. Springer-Verlag GmbH & Company KG, Heidelberger Platz 3, D-14197 Berlin Germany. **Tel** 011 49 30 8207223, FAX 011 49 30 8214091, telex 183 319 SPBLN D. **(Subscription address:** Springer-Verlag New York Inc. / North America, PO Box 2485, Journal Fulfillment, Secaucus NJ 07096. **Tel** (201)348-4033, (800)777-4643, FAX (201)348-4505.**) ED** F Kaudewitz and C W Birky Jr. **Bk Rev. Ad Acc.** available on microfilm and microfiche from University Microfilms International (UMI). Documents available from The Genuine Article, CASDDS, Documents on Demand.
Desc: An international journal devoted to the rapid publication of original papers of importance on the genetics of eukaryotes. Emphasis is on the genetics of yeasts, other fungi, mitochondria, and chloroplasts.
Ind/Abst AgBiotech News Inf.; AGRICOLA [Select. Cov.]; Chem. Abstr.; Curr. Aware. Biol. Sci., CABS; Curr. Biotechnol.; Curr. Cit.; Curr. Contents Life Sci.; Dairy Sci. Abstr.; EMBASE; Energy Inf. Abstr.; Environ. Abstr.; For. Abstr.; Genet. Abstr.; Hortic. Abstr.; Index Med. (1985-); Maize Abstr.; Microbiol. Abstr. Sect. C; Nematol. Abstr.; Nucl. Acids Abstr.; Ornamental Hort. (19??-19??); Life Sci. Collect.; PESTDOC; Plant Breed. Abstr.; Ref. Upd. Basic Ed.; Ref. Upd. Deluxe Ed.; Res. Alert [Full Cov.]; Rev. Med. Vet. Entomol.; Rev. Plant Pathol.; Rice Abstr.; Sci. Cit. Index; SCISEARCH; Soyabean Abstr.; Wheat Barley Trit. Abstr.

LC QH426 .C88 ISSN 0959-437X
DD 575.1/05 UK
CCC
NLM W1; CU799GCR CODEN COGDET
CURRENT OPINION IN GENETICS AND DEVELOPMENT. VFOAT Current Opinion in Genetics and Development; Genetics & Development; Genetics and Development. Vol. 1, No. 1 (June 1991)-. Academic Scholarly Publication. English. Six times a year. $147.00 (individuals), $440.00 (institutions). Current Science / England, Middlesex House, 34-42 Cleveland Street, London W1P 6LB United Kingdom. **Tel** 011 44 171 5808393, 011 44 171 3230323, FAX 011 44 171 5805646. **(Subscription address:** Current Science, 20

North 3rd Street, Philadelphia PA 19106. **Tel** (800)552-5866.) **ED** M. P. Scott and R. A. Laskey. **Ad Acc. Circ:** 1,000 (ctrl). available on diskette. Documents available from The Genuine Article, CASDDS.
Desc: Directed toward researchers, educators and students of genetics and development. Presents review articles from an area of concentration covering an entire year's literature with annotated references.
Ind/Abst AgBiotech News Inf.; Anim. Breed. Abstr.; Chem. Abstr.; Curr. Aware. Biol. Sci., CABS; Curr. Cit.; Index Med.; Ref. Upd. Deluxe Ed.; Res. Alert [Full Cov.].

LC QH431 .C95 **ISSN** 0301-0171
DD 575.2/1 SZ
CCC
NLM W1 CY755 **CODEN** CGCGBR
Pr Rev.

CYTOGENETICS AND CELL GENETICS. [Cytogenet. cell genet.]. Vol. 12 (1973)-. Periodical. English (French and German). Sixteen times a year. $1721.00. S. Karger AG, Allschwilerstrasse 10, PO Box, CH-4009 Basel Switzerland. **Tel** 011 41 61 3061111, FAX 011 41 61 3061234, telex CH 962 652. **ED** H. P. Klinger. **Ad Acc.** available on microfilm from University Microfilms International (UMI). Documents available from The Genuine Article, BIOSIS Document Express, CASDDS. ***Continues** Cytogenetics, 0011-4537.*
Desc: Dedicated to the publication of important original reports. Emphasis is on molecular genetics, including recombinant DNA technology and molecular cytogenetics; particularly their use in gene cloning, gene mapping, clarification of genetic mechanisms in malignant transformation, development and differentiation, and in population and evolutionary genetics. The journal continues to publish papers on chromosome aberrations in somatic, meiotic and malignant cells of man and other animals, and in cytotaxonomy and comparative cytogenetics. Also featured are the annual reports of the International Workshop on Human Gene Mapping.
Ind/Abst Abstr. Anthropol.; AgBiotech News Inf.; Biol. Abstr.; Chem. Abstr.; Curr. Cit.; Curr. Contents Life Sci.; Dev. Med. Child Neurol.; EMBASE; Genet. Abstr.; Health Plan. Adminis.; Hum. Genome Abstr.; Index Med.; Oncog. Growth Factors Abstr.; Life Sci. Collect.; Pig News Inf.; Ref. Upd. Basic Ed.; Ref. Upd. Deluxe Ed.; Res. Alert [Full Cov.]; Sci. Cit. Index; SCISEARCH; Soc. Sci. Cit. Index [Select. Cov.].

LC QH426 .C94 **ISSN** 0095-4527
DD 574.8/7/05 US
CCC
NLM W1 CY796 **CODEN** CYGEDX

CYTOLOGY AND GENETICS. **See** Biology-Cytology.

LC QH573 **ISSN** 0920-9069
DD 574.87 NE
CCC
NLM W1; CY88 **CODEN** CYTOER
Pr Rev.

CYTOTECHNOLOGY (DORDRECHT). **See** Biology-Cytology.

LC QH453 .D48 **ISSN** 0192-253X
DD 575.1 US
CCC
NLM W1 DE997NM **CODEN** DGNTDW
Pr Rev.

DEVELOPMENTAL GENETICS. [Dev. genet.]. Vol. 1 (1979)-. Academic Scholarly Publication. English. Six times a year. $664.00. John Wiley & Sons, Inc., 605 Third Avenue, New York NY 10158-0012. **Tel** (212)850-6000, (212)850-6645, FAX (212)850-6088, telex 12-7063. **(Subscription address:** John Wiley & Sons / UK, Baffins Lane, Chichester, West Sussex PO19 1UD United Kingdom. **Tel** 011 44 1243 779777, FAX 011 44 243 776128, telex 86290 WIBOOKG.) **ED** Gerald M. Kidder. **Bk Rev.** Documents available from The Genuine Article, BIOSIS Document Express, CASDDS.
Desc: Provides a forum for research on all organisms, including prokaryotes, plants, insects, worms, and mammals. Dual coverage of molecular and developmental genetics.
Ind/Abst AgBiotech News Inf.; AGRICOLA [Select. Cov.]; Anim. Breed. Abstr.; Biol. Abstr.; Chem. Abstr.; Curr. Aware. Biol. Sci., CABS; Curr. Cit.; Curr. Contents Life Sci.; EMBASE; Genet. Abstr.; Index Med. (Vol. 6, No. 3, 1986-); Maize Abstr.; Nucl. Acids Abstr.; Oncog. Growth Factors Abstr.; Life Sci. Collect.; Plant Breed. Abstr.; Plant Grow. Reg. Abstr.; Ref. Upd. Deluxe Ed.; Res. Alert [Full Cov.]; Sci. Cit. Index; SCISEARCH; Seed Abstr.; Soyabean Abstr.; Wheat Barley Trit. Abstr.

LC QH426 **ISSN** 0167-6458
DD 575.1 NE
NLM W1 DE997VCY **CODEN** DEGNDX
Pr Rev.

DEVELOPMENTS IN GENETICS. [Dev. genet.]. Vol. 1 (1979)-. Academic Scholarly Publication. English. Irregular. Price varies per volume. Elsevier Science Publishers BV, PO Box 211, 1000 AE Amsterdam Netherlands. **Tel** 011 31 20 4853641, 011 31 20 4853642, FAX 011 31 20 4853598. Documents available from CASDDS.
Desc: Series covering genetics and genetic research.
Ind/Abst Chem. Abstr. (1979-1980).

LC QH442 .D59 **ISSN** 1044-5498
DD 574.87/3282 US
NLM W1; DN125B **CODEN** DCEBE8

DNA AND CELL BIOLOGY. [DNA cell biol.]. **VAT** Deoxyribonucleic Acid and Cell Biology. Vol. 9, No. 1 (Jan./Feb. 1990)-. Academic Scholarly Publication. English. Twelve times a year. $508.00. Mary Ann Liebert Inc., 2 Madison Avenue, Larchmont NY 10538. **Tel** (914)834-3100, (800)M-LIEBERT, FAX (212)289-4697. **ED** Mark Greene, David Weiner and Michael Kavin. Documents available from The Genuine Article, BIOSIS Document Express, CASDDS. ***Continues** DNA (Mary Ann Liebert, Inc.), 0198-0238.*
Desc: Publishes papers, short communications, reviews, laboratory methods, and editorials on any subject dealing with eukaryotic or prokaryotic gene structure, organization, expression, and evolution. Papers studying genes and their expression at the level of RNA or proteins and by cell biology approaches are as appropriate as papers dealing directly with DNA.
Ind/Abst AgBiotech News Inf.; Anim. Breed. Abstr.; Biol. Abstr.; Chem. Abstr. (1990-); Curr. Cit.; Curr. Contents Life Sci.; Dairy Sci. Abstr.; EMBASE; Genet. Abstr.; Index Med. (1990-); Nucl. Acids Abstr.; PESTDOC; Ref. Upd. Basic Ed.; Ref. Upd. Deluxe Ed.; Res. Alert [Full Cov.]; Sci. Cit. Index; SCISEARCH.

ISSN 0266-6308
DD 016.574873282 UK
CCC

DNA PROBES. (1985)-. Periodical. English. Twenty-four times a year. $188.23. SUBIS, Mansion House 19 Kingfield Road, Sheffield S11 9AS United Kingdom. **Tel** 011 44 114 2554433, FAX 011 44 114 255 4626. **Bk Rev. Ad Acc.** available on diskette.
Desc: Current awareness service for researchers.

ISSN 1340-2838
JA
NLM W1; DN125G **CODEN** DARSE8

•**DNA RESEARCH : AN INTERNATIONAL JOURNAL FOR RAPID PUBLICATION OF REPORTS ON GENES AND GENOMES.** **Added/Corp** Kazusa Di Enu E Kenkyujo. Vol. 1, No. 1 (1994)-. Periodical. English. Six times a year. $110.00. **(Subscription address:** Japan Publications Trading Company Ltd., PO Box 5030, Tokyo International, Tokyo 100-31 Japan. **Tel** 011 81 3 3292 3753.)
Ind/Abst Chem. Abstr.

LC QP624 .D177 **ISSN** 1042-5179
DD 574.87/3282 SZ
CCC
NLM W1; D126 **CODEN** DNSEES

DNA SEQUENCE. (DNA SEQUENCE : THE JOURNAL OF DNA SEQUENCING AND MAPPING.). [DNA seq.]. Vol. 1, No. 1 (1990)-. Academic Scholarly Publication. English. Six times a year (1 volume). $255.00 (academic institutions), $397.00 (corporate institutions). Harwood Academic Publishers, PO Box 90, Reading RG1 8JL United Kingdom. **Tel** 011 44 1734 560080, FAX 011 44 1734 568211. **ED** Bart G. Barrell. Documents available from The Genuine Article, CASDDS.
Ind/Abst AGRICOLA [Select. Cov.]; Chem. Abstr.; Curr. Aware. Biol. Sci., CABS; Curr. Cit.; Food Sci. Technol. Abstr.; Index Med.; Res. Alert [Full Cov.].

ISSN 0142-8640
DD 016.574873282 UK
CCC

DNA SHEFFIELD. (DNA.). [DNA Sheff.]. **VFOAT** Deoxyribonucleic Acid. (1975)-. English. Twelve times a year. $136.89. SUBIS, Mansion House 19 Kingfield Road, Sheffield S11 9AS United Kingdom. **Tel** 011 44 114 2554433, FAX 011 44 114 255 4626.

ISSN 0161-0716
US

DOWN SYNDROME NEWS. **Added/Corp** National Down Syndrome Congress. Vol. 8, No. 10 (Dec. 1984)-. Newsletter. English. Ten times a year (published monthly with Jan/Feb and Jul/Aug issues combined). $35.00. National Down Syndrome Congress, 1605 Chantilly Drive, Suite 250, Atlanta GA 30324. **Tel** (404)633-1555, (800)232-6372, FAX (404)633-2817. cum. index. **Bk Rev. Circ:** 6,000. ***Continues** Down's Syndrome News.*

ISSN 0149-7162
US
NLM ZWS 107.3 D751

DOWN'S SYNDROME. Vol. 1 (Jan. 1978)-. Periodical. English. Four times a year. $7.50. Children Brain Research Clinic, Washington DC 20008. **Tel** (202)483-0444. **ED** Mary Coleman and George Lentz Jr. **Bk Rev. Circ:** 1,000.
Desc: Review of literature on Down's Syndrome and original summary articles.

ISSN 0161-0716
US

DOWN'S SYNDROME NEWS. **VFOAT** DSN. (197?)-. Periodical. English. Ten times a year. $35.00. National Down Syndrome Congress, 1605 Chantilly Drive, Suite 250, Atlanta GA 30324. ***Continues** Down's Syndrome Congress News.*

LC QH465.C5 E58 **ISSN** 0893-6692
DD 575.1/31/05 US
CCC
NLM W1; EN981FNF **CODEN** EMMUEG

ENVIRONMENTAL AND MOLECULAR MUTAGENESIS. [Environ. mol. mutagen.]. **Added/Corp** Environmental Mutagen Society. (1987)-. Academic Scholarly Publication. English. Eight times a year. $390.00. John Wiley & Sons, Inc., 605 Third Avenue, New York NY 10158-0012. **Tel** (212)850-6000, (212)850-6645, FAX (212)850-6088, telex 12-7063. **(Subscription address:** John Wiley & Sons / UK, Baffins Lane, Chichester, West Sussex PO19 1UD United Kingdom. **Tel** 011 44 1243 779777, FAX 011 44 243 776128, telex 86290 WIBOOKG.) **ED** Richard J. Albertini and J. Patrick O'Neill. Documents available from The Genuine Article, BIOSIS Document Express, CASDDS, ADONIS. ***Continues** Environmental Mutagenesis, 0192-2521.*
Desc: Provides an international forum for research on basic mechanisms of mutation, the detection of mutagens, and the implications of environmental mutagens for human health.
Ind/Abst ADONIS; AGRICOLA; Biol. Abstr. (1987-); Chem. Abstr. (1987-); Chem. Hazards Ind.; Chem. Titles; Coal Abstr. (1987-); Curr. Aware. Biol. Sci., CABS; Curr. Cit.; Curr. Contents Life Sci.; EMBASE; Energy Res. Abstr. (1987-); Fish Rev.; Food Sci. Technol. Abstr.; Genet. Abstr.; Health Plan. Adminis.; Index Med. (1987-); Lab. Hazards Bull.; NAPRALERT; Nutr. Res. Newsl.; Life Sci. Collect. (1987-); Pollut. Abstr. Indexes; Ref. Upd. Basic Ed.; Ref. Upd. Deluxe Ed.; Res. Alert [Full Cov.]; Sci. Cit. Index; SCISEARCH; Toxicol. Abstr.; Weed Abstr.

LC QH426 **ISSN** 1018-4813
DD 575.1 SZ
CCC
NLM W1; EU72DFHH
Pr Rev.

EUROPEAN JOURNAL OF HUMAN GENETICS : EJHG. **Added/Corp** European Society of Human Genetics. **VFOAT** EJHG. Vol. 1, No. 1 (1992)-. Periodical. English. Four times a year. $531.60. S. Karger AG, Allschwilerstrasse 10, PO Box, CH-4009 Basel Switzerland. **Tel** 011 41 61 3061111, FAX 011 41 61 3061234, telex CH 962 652. **ED** G. Romeo.
Desc: Publishes scientific information relevant to the development of research, education and medical application in the field of human genetics. In addition to original papers, short communications, and review articles, the journal publishes announcements, information and articles concerning the activities of the European Society of Human Genetics and of other organizations.
Ind/Abst Index Med.; Ref. Upd. Deluxe Ed.

LC QH301 **ISSN** 0014-3820
DD 575.05 US
NLM W1 EV391 **CODEN** EVOLAO
Pr Rev.

EVOLUTION. [Evolution]. Vol. 1 (1947)-. Periodical. English. Six times a year. $160.00. Allen Press Inc., 810 East 10th Street, PO Box 1897, Lawrence KS 66044-8897. **Tel** (913)843-1221, (800)627-0629, FAX (913)843-1274. **(Subscription address:** Evolution, PO Box 1897, Lawrence KS 66044-8897.) **ED** John Endler. **Ad Acc. Acid Free. Circ:** 4,000 (ctrl). available on microfilm and microfiche from University Microfilms International (UMI). Documents available from The Genuine Article, BIOSIS Document Express, UMI Article Clearinghouse, CASDDS.
Desc: Articles, address problems, or controversies concerning phylogenetic relationships, modes of specification, rates of evolution, geographic variation, molecular evolution, the unit of selection, kin selection, group selection, sexual selection, punctuated equilibria, the determination of fitness, and many other topics in evolution.
Ind/Abst Acad. Ind. [Computer File] (1992-); Acad. Search; AgBiotech News Inf.; AGRICOLA [Select. Cov.]; Agrofor. Abstr.; Anim. Behav. Abstr.; Anim. Breed. Abstr.; Biocont. News Inf.; Biol. Agric. Index; Biol. Abstr.; Chem. Abstr.; CSA Neuro. Abstr. (?-?); Curr. Aware. Biol. Sci., CABS; Curr. Cit.; Curr. Contents Agric. Biol. Environ. Sci.; Curr. Contents Life Sci.; Curr. Ref. Fish Res.; Ecol. Abstr.; Ecology Abstr.; EMBASE; Entomol. Abstr.; EP Collect.; Expand. Acad. Index (1989-); Field Crop Abstr.; Fish Rev.; For. Prod. Abstr.; For. Abstr.; Gen. Sci. Index; Gen. Sci. Source; Genet. Abstr.; GeoRef; Grass. Forage Abstr.; Helminthol. Abstr.; Homework Help.; Hortic. Abstr.; INFO-SOUTH Abstr.; Key Word Index Wildl. Res.; Mag. Search; Maize Abstr.; MasterFile FullTEXT 1000; MasterFile FullTEXT 350; MasterFile FullTEXT 650; MasterFile FullTEXT (Jan. 1993-); Newsp. Period. Abstr. (1991-); OCLC; Ornamental Hort. (1991-); Life Sci. Collect.; Plant Breed. Abstr.; Plant Genet. Resour. Abstr.; Protozoolog. Abstr.; Ref. Upd. Deluxe Ed.; Res. Alert [Full Cov.]; Rev. Agric. Entomol.; Rev. Med. Vet. Entomol.; Rev. Plant Pathol.; Rice Abstr.; Sci. Cit. Index; SCISEARCH; Seed Abstr.; Soc. Sci. Cit. Index [Select. Cov.]; Soyabean Abstr.; Stat. Theory Method Abstr. (1959-1963); Telebase; Vitis Vitic. Enol. Abstr.; Weed Abstr.; Wheat Barley Trit. Abstr.; Wildl. Rev.

LC QH366.A1 E9 ISSN 0071-3260
DD 575/.005 US
CCC
NLM W1 EV64 CODEN EVBIAI
EVOLUTIONARY BIOLOGY. [Evol. biol.]. Vol. 1 (1967)-. Monographic series. English. Irregular. Price varies per volume. Plenum Press, 233 Spring Street, New York NY 10013-1578. **Tel** (212)620-8000, (800)221-9369, FAX (212)463-0742, (212)807-1047, telex 23/421139. Documents available from The Genuine Article, BIOSIS Document Express, CASDDS.
Desc: Topics range from anthropology to molecular evolution, population biology, and paleobiology.
Ind/Abst Abstr. Anthropol.; AGRICOLA [Select. Cov.]; Biol. Abstr.; Chem. Abstr.; Curr. Aware. Biol. Sci., CABS; Curr. Cit.; GeoRef; Index Sci. Rev. [Full Cov.]; Key Word Index Wildl. Res.; Res. Alert [Full Cov.]; Sci. Cit. Index; SCISEARCH; Soc. Sci. Cit. Index [Select. Cov.]; Wildl. Rev.

LC QA402.5 .E96 ISSN 1063-6560
DD 004/.05 US
CCC
CODEN EOCMEO
•**EVOLUTIONARY COMPUTATION.** See Biology-Computer Applications.

LC QH431 .H835 ISSN 0014-4266
DD 573.2/1 NE
CCC
NLM ZW 1 E976
EXCERPTA MEDICA. SECTION 22. HUMAN GENETICS. See Medical Sciences-Abstracting, Bibliographies and Statistics.

LC QH426
DD 575.1 II
EXPERIMENTAL GENETICS. Periodical. English. Two times a year. $15.00. Society of Geneticists and Breeders, Department of Genetics and Plant Breeding, Bidhan Chandra Krishi Viswavidyalaya, Kalyani 741235 West Bengal.
Ind/Abst Cot. Trop. Fibr. Abstr. Bibliogr.; Plant Grow. Reg. Abstr.

ISSN 0015-5578
IT
NLM W1 FO181
FOLIA HEREDITARIA ET PATHOLOGICA. [Folia hered. pathol.]. (1951)-. Periodical. Italian. Four times a year. $18.00. Inst di Anatomie Istologia, Via Francesco Sforza 38, Milan 20122 Italy. **Tel** 02-8135366. **Bk Rev. Ad Acc. Circ:** 50 (ctrl).
Desc: Information and news on congenital, malformations and hereditary diseases.
Ind/Abst EMBASE; Life Sci. Collect.

LC SD399.5 .F57 ISSN 1335-048X
XO
Pr Rev.
•**FOREST GENETICS.** See Forests and Forestry.

LC QK623.S73 N48 ISSN 0895-1942
DD 589.2/0415/05 US
NLM W1; FU54F CODEN FGNEEA
Pr Rev.
FUNGAL GENETICS NEWSLETTER. See Biology-Mycology.

ISSN 0435-1096
JA
CODEN GFSYAR
GAMMA FIELD SYMPOSIA. See Biology-Botany.

UK
GENBANK. (19??)-. Academic Scholarly Publication. English. Irregular. £165.00. Blackwell Scientific Publications Ltd, Marston Book Services, PO Box 88, Oxford OX2 ONE United Kingdom. **Tel** 011 44 1865 206206, FAX 011 44 1865 206219, telex 837 515 MARDIS G.

LC QH442 .G43 ISSN 0378-1119
DD 575.1 NE
CCC
NLM W1 GE184M CODEN GENED6
Pr Rev.
GENE. [Gene]. Vol. 1 (1976)-. Academic Scholarly Publication. English. Thirty-four times a year (16 vols.). $5069.00. Elsevier Science Publishers BV, PO Box 211, 1000 AE Amsterdam Netherlands. **Tel** 011 31 20 4853641, 011 31 20 4853642, FAX 011 31 20 4853598. **ED** W Szybalski. **Ad Acc. Circ:** 1,352 (ctrl). available on microfilm and microfiche from University Microfilms International (UMI); available on an online database from Elsevier Electronic Subscriptions (EES). Documents available from The Genuine Article, BIOSIS Document Express, CASDDS, Documents on Demand, ADONIS.
Desc: Devoted to gene cloning and gene structure and function.
Ind/Abst Abstr. Anthropol.; ADONIS; AgBiotech News Inf.; AGRICOLA [Select. Cov.]; Biocont. News Inf. (19??-19??); Biodeter. Abstr. (1991-); Biol. Abstr.; Biotechnol. Res. Abstr.; Chem. Abstr.; Chem. Titles; CSA Neuro. Abstr. (?-?); Curr. Biotechnol.; Curr. Cit.; Curr. Contents Life Sci.; Dairy Sci. Abstr.; EMBASE; Energy Inf. Abstr.; Energy Res. Abstr. (May 1978-); Environ. Abstr.; Fish Rev. (Jan. 1989-July 1992); Food Sci. Technol. Abstr.; Genet. Abstr.; Helminthol. Abstr.; Hum. Genome Abstr.; Immunol. Abstr.; Index Med.; Index Vet.; Microbiol. Abstr. Sect. B; Microbiol. Abstr. Sect. C; Nematol. Abstr.; Nucl. Acids Abstr.; Life Sci. Collect.; PESTDOC; Pig News Inf.; Plant Breed. Abstr.; Plant Grow. Reg. Abstr.; Potato Abstr.; Protozoolog. Abstr.; Ref. Upd. Basic Ed.; Ref. Upd. Deluxe Ed.; Res. Alert [Full Cov.]; Rev. Agric. Entomol.; Rev. Med. Vet. Entomol.; Rev. Med. Vet. Mycology; Rev. Plant Pathol.; Rice Abstr.; Sci. Cit. Index; SCISEARCH; Soils Fert.; Sorghum Mill. Abstr.; Soyabean Abstr.; Vet. Bull.; Trop. Dis. Bull.; Virol. AIDS Abstr.; Weed Abstr.; Wheat Barley Trit. Abstr.; Wildl. Rev. (Jan. 1989-July 1992).

ISSN 0275-2778
US
NLM W1 GE184N CODEN GAAND8
Pr Rev.
GENE AMPLIFICATION AND ANALYSIS. [Gene amplif. anal.]. Vol. 1 (1981)-. Academic Scholarly Publication. English. Irregular. Price varies per volume. Elsevier Science Publishing Company Inc, Madison Square Station, PO Box 882, New York NY 10159-0882. **Tel** (212)633-3950, FAX (212)633-3990. **(Subscription address:** Elsevier Science Inc. / New York Books, 655 Avenue of the Americas, New York NY 10010. **Tel** (212)633-3650.) **ED** Jack G. Chirikjian. Documents available from CASDDS.
Ind/Abst Chem. Abstr.; Health Plan. Adminis.; Index Med.

LC QH450 .S455 ISSN 1052-2166
DD 575 US
CCC
NLM W1; GE184PE CODEN GEEXEJ
Pr Rev.
GENE EXPRESSION. [Gene expr.]. Vol. 1, No. 1 (Apr. 1991)-. Periodical. English. Six times a year. $350.00. Cognizant Communication Corporation, 3 Hartsdale Road, Elmsford NY 10523-3701. **Tel** (914)592-7720, FAX (914)592-8981. **Ad Acc, Adv Mgr:** Carole Timkovich, **Tel** (708)578-3259. Documents available from The Genuine Article.
Desc: International journal focusing on all aspects of the gene, including structure, function, and regulation...with special emphasis on DNA replication, repair, gene transcription, RNA processing, protein synthesis, and post-translational control in prokaryotes, eukaryotes, and viruses.
Ind/Abst Index Med. (Apr. 1991-); Res. Alert [Full Cov.]; SCISEARCH.

ISSN 0957-3526
UK
GENE EXPRESSION. (19??)-. English. Twelve times a year. $128.34. SUBIS, Mansion House 19 Kingfield Road, Sheffield S11 9AS United Kingdom. **Tel** 011 44 114 2554433, FAX 011 44 114 255 4626. **Ad Acc.**
Desc: Current awareness service for researchers and clinicians.

ISSN 0394-249X
IT
NLM W1; GE184PH
GENE GEOGRAPHY : A COMPUTERIZED BULLETIN ON HUMAN GENE FREQUENCIES. Vol. 1, No. 1 (April 1987)-. Bulletin. English. Three times a year. L70000. Genegeography Tor Vergata University, Via O Raimondo C, 00173 Rome Italy. **Tel** 011 39 6 72594320. **ED** L. Terrenato, A. Piazza and G. Modiano. Documents available from The Genuine Article.
Ind/Abst Health Plan. Adminis.; Hum. Genome Abstr.; Index Med. (1987-); Res. Alert [Full Cov.].

LC QH301 ISSN 0969-7128
DD 574 UK
CCC
NLM W1; GE184Q CODEN GETHEC
•**GENE THERAPY.** Vol. 1, No. 1 (Jan. 1994)-. Academic Scholarly Publication. English. Twelve times a year. $453.47. Macmillan Magazines Ltd., Brunel Road, Basingstoke, Hampshire RG21 6XS United Kingdom. **Tel** 011 44 1256 29242, FAX 011 44 1256 812358, telex 858493. Documents available from BLDSC.
Ind/Abst EMBASE.

ISSN 1078-2842
US
•**GENE THERAPY WEEKLY.** (1994)-. English. Forty-eight times a year. $1195.00. CW Henderson, PO Box 5528, Atlanta GA 30307-0528. **Tel** (404)377-8895, FAX (404)378-5411. **(Subscription address:** CW Henderson, Subscription Office, PO Box 830409, Birmingham AL 35283-0409. **Tel** (800)633-4931, (205)995-1567 (outside US and Canada), FAX (205)995-1588.)
Desc: Features reporting on recent discoveries and innovations in human genetic research.
Ind/Abst EP Collect.; Homework Help.; MasterFile FullTEXT 1000; MasterFile FullTEXT 350; MasterFile FullTEXT 650; MasterFile FullTEXT; OCLC; Telebase.

LC QH426 .G466 ISSN 0890-9369
DD 575.1 US
CCC
NLM W1; GE273M CODEN GEDEEP
Pr Rev.
GENES & DEVELOPMENT. [Genes dev.]. **Added/Corp** Genetical Society (Great Britain). **VFOAT** Genes and Development. Vol. 1, No. 1 (March 1987)-. Academic Scholarly Publication. English. Thirteen times a year. $533.50. Cold Spring Harbor Laboratory, 10 Skyline Drive, Plainview NY 11803. **Tel** (516)349-1930, (800)843-4388, FAX (516)349-1946. **ED** Judy Cuddihy. Index available. **Ad Acc.** available on microfilm and microfiche from University Microfilms International (UMI). Documents available from The Genuine Article, BIOSIS Document Express, CASDDS.
Desc: Devoted to the molecular analysis of gene expression in eukaryotes, prokaryotes and viruses.
Ind/Abst Abstr. Anthropol.; AgBiotech News Inf.; Anim. Breed. Abstr.; Biol. Abstr. (1987-); Biol. Dig.; Chem. Abstr. (1987-); Cot. Trop. Fibr. Abstr. Bibliogr.; CSA Neuro. Abstr. (?-?); Curr. Aware. Biol. Sci., CABS; Curr. Cit.; Curr. Contents Life Sci.; EMBASE; Entomol. Abstr.; Genet. Abstr.; Health Plan. Adminis.; Immunol. Abstr.; Index Med. (1987-); Index Vet.; Maize Abstr.; Microbiol. Abstr. Sect. B (19??-19??); Microbiol. Abstr. Sect. C (1987-); Nematol. Abstr.; Nucl. Acids Abstr.; Oncog. Growth Factors Abstr.; Plant Breed. Abstr.; Plant Grow. Reg. Abstr.; Protozoolog. Abstr.; Ref. Upd. Basic Ed.; Ref. Upd. Deluxe Ed.; Res. Alert [Full Cov.]; Rev. Plant Pathol.; Sci. Cit. Index; SCISEARCH; Soc. Sci. Cit. Index [Select. Cov.]; Soils Fert.; Virol. AIDS Abstr.; Weed Abstr.

JA
•**GENES AND GENETIC SYSTEMS.** (1995)-. Japanese. Six times a year. $120.00. Nihon Ronen Igakkai, (Japan Geriatrics Soc.), c/o Tokyo Daigaku Igakubu, Ronenbyogaku Kyoshitsu, 3-1 Hongo 7 Chome, Bunkyoku Tokyo 113 Japan. **(Subscription address:** Maruzen Company Ltd., PO Box 5050, Import & Export Department, Tokyo 100 31 Japan. **Tel** 011 81 3 32789224.) ***Continues*** *Japanese Journal of Genetics.*

LC RC268.4 .C433 ISSN 1045-2257
DD 616.99/4042/05 US
CCC
NLM W1; GE274L CODEN GCCAES
Pr Rev.
GENES, CHROMOSOMES & CANCER. [Genes chromosomes cancer]. **VFOAT** Genes, Chromosomes, and Cancer. (1989)-. Academic Scholarly Publication. English. Twelve times a year. $576.00. John Wiley & Sons, Inc., 605 Third Avenue, New York NY 10158-0012. **Tel** (212)850-6000, (212)850-6645, FAX (212)850-6088, telex 12-7063. **(Subscription address:** John Wiley & Sons / UK, Baffins Lane, Chichester, West Sussex PO19 1UD United Kingdom. **Tel** 011 44 1243 779777, FAX 011 44 243 776128, telex 86290 WIBOOKG.) **ED** Felix Mitelman and Janet D. Rowley. Documents available from The Genuine Article, BIOSIS Document Express, CASDDS.
Desc: Offers rapid publication of original full-length research papers, short communications, and concise invited reviews, as well as editorial commentaries on all aspects of genomic abnormalities related to neoplasia.
Ind/Abst Biol. Abstr. (1990-); Chem. Abstr.; Curr. Aware. Biol. Sci., CABS; Curr. Cit.; Curr. Contents Life Sci.; EMBASE; Genet. Abstr.; Health Plan. Adminis.; Index Med. (Sept. 1989-); Oncog. Growth Factors Abstr.; Res. Alert [Full Cov.]; Sci. Cit. Index; SCISEARCH.

LC QH426
DD 575.1 US
Pr Rev.
•**GENETIC ANALYSIS BIOMOLECULAR ENGINEERING.** (1995)-. English. Six times a year. $244.00. Elsevier Science Publishers BV, PO Box 211, 1000 AE Amsterdam Netherlands. **Tel** 011 31 20 4853641, 011 31 20 4853642, FAX 011 31 20 4853598. **(Subscription address:** Elsevier Science BV / Maryland, PO Box 64698, Baltimore MD 21264.) available on an online database from Elsevier Electronic Subscriptions (EES).

LC QH426 .G44 ISSN 1050-3862
DD 574.87/328/05 US
CCC
NLM W1; GE277 CODEN GATAEVGANTONGANTDN
TITLE CHANGE
GENETIC ANALYSIS, TECHNIQUES AND APPLICATIONS. [Genet. anal. tech. appl.]. **VFOAT** Genetic Analysis. Vol. 7, No. 1 (Feb. 1990)-(1995). Academic Scholarly Publication. English. Elsevier Science Publishers BV, PO Box 211, 1000 AE Amsterdam Netherlands. **Tel** 011 31 20 4853641, 011 31 20 4853642, FAX 011 31 20 4853598. available on microfilm and microfiche from University Microfilms International (UMI). Documents available from The Genuine Article, BIOSIS Document Express, CASDDS. ***Continues*** *Gene Analysis Techniques, 0735-0651.* ***Continued by*** *Genetic Analysis Biomolecular Engineering.*
Ind/Abst AgBiotech News Inf.; AGRICOLA; Biol. Abstr.; Chem. Abstr.; Curr. Aware. Biol. Sci., CABS; Curr. Cit.; Curr. Contents Life Sci.; EMBASE; Index Med. (1990-); Life Sci. Collect.; Plant Breed. Abstr.; Ref. Upd. Deluxe Ed.; Res. Alert [Full Cov.]; Sci. Cit. Index; SCISEARCH.

LC QH573 **ISSN** 0732-8079
DD 574.873282 US
NLM W1 GE278 **CODEN** GCTEDM

GENETIC AND CELLULAR TECHNOLOGY. [Genet. cell. technol.]. Vol. 1-. Academic Scholarly Publication. English. Price varies per volume. Marcel Dekker Inc., 270 Madison Avenue, New York NY 10016. **Tel** (212)696-9000, (800)228-1160, FAX (212)685-4540, telex 421419. **(Subscription address:** Marcel Dekker Inc., PO Box 5017, Monticello NY 12701. **Tel** (800)228-1160.**) ED** L. Patrick Gage. Documents available from BIOSIS Document Express, CASDDS.
Ind/Abst Biol. Abstr. (-1982); Chem. Abstr.

US

GENETIC COUNSELING. (1973)-. Periodical. English.
Ind/Abst Index Med.

LC RB155.7 .G46 **ISSN** 1015-8146
DD 616/.042 SZ
NLM W1; GE2783 **CODEN** GECOEG

GENETIC COUNSELING (GENEVA, SWITZERLAND). (GENETIC COUNSELING.). [Genet. couns.]. Vol. 1, No. 1 (1990)-. Periodical. English. Four times a year. $252.61. Medecine et Hygiene, Case Postale 456, CH-1211 Geneva 4 Switzerland. **Tel** 011 41 22 7029311. Index available. Documents available from The Genuine Article, BIOSIS Document Express. ***Continues** Journal de Genetique Humaine, 0021-7743.*
Desc: Covers medical, psychological and ethical problems.
Ind/Abst Biol. Abstr.; Curr. Cit.; EMBASE; Health Plan. Adminis.; Index Med. (1990-); Res. Alert [Full Cov.]; Soc. Sci. Cit. Index [Select. Cov.].

LC TP248
DD 660.65 AU

GENETIC ENGINEERING AND BIOTECHNOLOGY MONITOR. **Added/Corp** United Nations Industrial Development Organization. Technology Programme. (19??)-. Periodical. English. Four times a year (Mar., June, Sept., Dec.). $40.00. United Nations Industrial Development Organization, PO Box 300, A-1400 Vienna Austria. **Tel** 011 43 1 211310.
Ind/Abst Abstr. BioCommer.

LC TP248.2 .G46 **ISSN** 0921-2604
DD 660/.6/05 NE
NLM TP 248.2; G328
Pr Rev.

GENETIC ENGINEERING AND BIOTECHNOLOGY YEARBOOK. **See** Biology-Bioengineering.

ISSN 0741-0395
DD 614 US
CCC
NLM W1; GE281P
Pr Rev.

GENETIC EPIDEMIOLOGY. **See** Medical Sciences-Epidemiology.

LC BF712 .G46 **ISSN** 0740-9583
DD 155.4/18/05 GW
Pr Rev.

GENETIC EPISTEMOLOGIST, THE. (THE GENETIC EPISTEMOLOGIST : THE QUARTERLY JOURNAL OF THE JEAN PIAGET SOCIETY.). **Added/Corp** Jean Piaget Society. (Oct. 1976)-. Periodical. English. Four times a year. $55.00. Jean Piaget Society, Harvard University Graduate School Ed., Cambridge MA 02138. **ED** Frank B. Murray. Index available. **Bk Rev. Ad Acc. Circ:** 500. ***Continues** Newsletter - Jean Piaget Society.*
Desc: Reviews of empirical or theoretical literature on current topics of genetic epistemology or practical applications.
Ind/Abst Child Dev. Abstr. Bibliogr.

CH

GENETIC MANIPULATION IN PLANTS. **See** Biology-Botany.

LC QH445.2 .G45 **ISSN** 0738-5269
DD 576/.64 US
NLM W1; GE281M

GENETIC MAPS. [Genet. maps]. **Added/Corp** Laboratory of Viral Carcinogenesis (National Cancer Institute) Cold Spring Harbor Laboratory. Vol. 1 (Mar. 1980)-. English. Every 2 years. Price varies per volume. Cold Spring Harbor Laboratory, 10 Skyline Drive, Plainview NY 11803. **Tel** (516)349-1930, (800)843-4388, FAX (516)349-1946.
Desc: A compilation of linkage and restriction maps of genetically studied organisms.
Ind/Abst AGRICOLA [Select. Cov.].

LC S **ISSN** 0925-9864
DD 630 NE
CCC
CODEN GRCEE9
Pr Rev.

GENETIC RESOURCES AND CROP EVOLUTION. **See** Agriculture-Crop Production and Soils.

US

GENETIC STUDIES OF GENIUS. **See** Psychology.

LC QH426 **ISSN** 0272-9032
DD 575.1 US
CCC
NLM W1; GE285 **CODEN** GTNEEA

GENETIC TECHNOLOGY NEWS. [Genet. technol. news]. Vol. 1, No. 1 (Feb. 1981)-. Periodical. English. Twelve times a year. $650.00. Technical Insights Inc., PO Box 1304, Fort Lee NJ 07024-9967. **Tel** (201)568-4744, FAX (201)568-8247, telex 425900 SWIFT UI. **ED** Albert S. Hester, Laurel A. Vanderkleed and Richard Consolas. available on an online database from NEXIS; and (files 16,636/Full-Text) DIALOG. Documents available from CASDDS.
Desc: Focuses on genetic engineering and its uses in the chemical, pharmaceutical, food processing, and energy industries as well as in agriculture, animal breeding and medicine.
Ind/Abst Abstr. BioCommer.; AGRICOLA [Select. Cov.]; BioBusiness (1984-); Chem. Abstr.; Chem. Ind. Notes; PROMT [Full Txt.]; PTS Newsl. Database [Full Txt.].

LC QH301 .G4 **ISSN** 0016-6707
NE
CCC
NLM W1 GE287 **CODEN** GENEA3
Pr Rev.

GENETICA. [Genetica]. Vol. 1 (1919)-. Periodical. English (French, German and Dutch). Six times a year. $795.00. Kluwer Academic Publishers, Postbus 322, 3300 AH Dordrecht The Netherlands. **Tel** 011 31 78 524400, FAX 011 31 78 183273, telex 20083. **ED** J.F. McDonald. Index Available, published separately, free-automatically sent. **Bk Rev. Ad Acc. Circ:** 700. available on microfilm and microfiche from University Microfilms International (UMI). Documents available from The Genuine Article, BIOSIS Document Express, CASDDS.
Desc: Publishes original papers in the fields of cytogenetics, cytotaxonomy, ecological and population genetics, speciation and evolution.
Ind/Abst AgBiotech News Inf.; AGRICOLA; Anim. Breed. Abstr.; Biol. Abstr.; Chem. Abstr.; Curr. Aware. Biol. Sci., CABS; Curr. Cit.; Curr. Contents Life Sci.; Curr. Ref. Fish Res.; EMBASE; Entomol. Abstr.; Fish Rev.; Genet. Abstr.; Hortic. Abstr.; Index Med. (Vol. 35, No. 4, 1964-Vol. 43, No. 4, 1972, Vol. 75, No. 1, 1987-); Ornamental Hort. (19??-19??); Life Sci. Collect.; Pig News Inf.; Plant Breed. Abstr.; Plant Genet. Resour. Abstr.; Plant Grow. Reg. Abstr.; Postharvest News Inf.; Ref. Upd. Deluxe Ed.; Res. Alert [Full Cov.]; Rev. Agric. Entomol.; Rev. Med. Vet. Entomol.; Sci. Cit. Index; SCISEARCH; Seed Abstr.; Soc. Sci. Cit. Index [Select. Cov.]; Sorghum Mill. Abstr.; Wheat Barley Trit. Abstr.; Wildl. Rev.

LC SB123 .G42 **ISSN** 0016-6715
DD 631.5 PL
CCC
NLM W1 GE287K **CODEN** GPOLA4
TITLE CHANGE

GENETICA POLONICA. (GENETICA POLONICA = POLISH JOURNAL OF GENETICS AND PLANT BREEDING.). [Genet. pol.]. **Added/Corp** Zaklad Genetyki Roslin PAN. Polska Akademia Nauk. Wydzial V. **VFOAT** Polish Journal of Theoretical and Applied Genetics; Polish Journal of Genetics and Plant Breeding. Vol. 1, No. 1 (Dec. 1960)-(1995). Academic Scholarly Publication. English (summaries and/or abstracts in Polish and Russian). Polska Akademia Nauk / Instytut Genetyki Roslin, Ul. Strzeszynska 34, 60-479 Poznan Poland. **Tel** 011 48 61 233511, FAX 011 48 61 221122. **(Subscription address:** Ars Polona-Ruch, PO Box 1001, Krakowskie Przedmiescie 7, 00-068 Warsaw Poland. **Tel** 011 48 22 261201.**)** Index available. **Circ:** 600. Documents available from BIOSIS Document Express, CASDDS. ***Continued by** Journal of Applied Genetics.*
Ind/Abst AgBiotech News Inf.; Anim. Breed. Abstr.; Biol. Abstr.; Chem. Abstr.; Curr. Cit.; Field Crop Abstr.; Grass. Forage Abstr.; Index Vet.; Maize Abstr.; Life Sci. Collect.; Pig News Inf.; Plant Breed. Abstr.; Plant Genet. Resour. Abstr.; Plant Grow. Reg. Abstr.; Potato Abstr.; Poult. Abstr.; Protozoolog. Abstr.; Rev. Agric. Entomol.; Rev. Plant Pathol.; Seed Abstr.; Soils Fert.; Vet. Bull.; Wheat Barley Trit. Abstr.

LC QH426 **ISSN** 0016-6723
DD 575.1 UK
CCC
NLM W1 GE288
Pr Rev.

GENETICAL RESEARCH. [Genet. res.]. Vol. 1 (Feb. 1960)-. Academic Scholarly Publication. English. Six times a year. $325.00. Cambridge University Press, The Edinburgh Building, Shaftesbury Road, Cambridge CB2 2RU United Kingdom. **Tel** 011 44 1223 312393, FAX 011 44 1223 315052, telex 851-817256. **(Subscription address:** Cambridge University Press / North America, 110 Midland Avenue, Port Chester NY 10573. **Tel** (800)431-1580, (914)937-9600.**) ED** Editorial Board. **Bk Rev.** available on microfilm and microfiche from University Microfilms International (UMI). Documents available from The Genuine Article, BIOSIS Document Express, CASDDS.
Desc: Publishes original work of wide interest on all aspects of genetics with a particularly strong interest in the molecular genetics of the mouse and Drosophila. Other major interests include population and quantitative genetics, both theoretical and experimental studies, and the genetics of development.
Ind/Abst Abstr. Anthropol.; AgBiotech News Inf.; AGRICOLA [Select. Cov.]; Biocont. News Inf.; Biol. Agric. Index; Biol. Abstr.; Biostatistica (19??-19??); Chem. Abstr.; Curr. Cit.; Curr. Contents Life Sci.; EMBASE; Entomol. Abstr.; Genet. Abstr.; Health Plan. Adminis.; Helminthol. Abstr. (1991-); Index Med.; Nematol. Abstr.; Life Sci. Collect.; PESTDOC; Plant Breed. Abstr.; Plant Genet. Resour. Abstr.; Protozoolog. Abstr.; Res. Alert [Full Cov.]; Rev. Agric. Entomol.; Rev. Med. Vet. Entomol.; Sci. Cit. Index; SCISEARCH; Seed Abstr.; Soils Fert.; Stat. Theory Method Abstr. (1978); Trop. Dis. Bull.; Weed Abstr.; Wheat Barley Trit. Abstr.; Wildl. Rev.

LC QH431 .G432 **ISSN** 0016-674X
DD 575.1/08 US
NLM Z 5322.G4 G328

GENETICS ABSTRACTS. **See** Biology-Abstracting, Bibliographies and Statistics.

LC QH431 .G43 **ISSN** 0016-6731
DD 575.1/05 US
CCC
NLM W1 GE293 **CODEN** GENTAE
Pr Rev.

GENETICS (AUSTIN). (GENETICS.). [Genetics]. **Added/Corp** Genetics Society of America. Vol. 1 (Jan. 1916)-. Academic Scholarly Publication. English. Twelve times a year. $380.00. Genetics Society of America, 9650 Rockville Pike, Bethesda MD 20814. **Tel** (301)530-7027, FAX (301)530-7001. **(Subscription address:** Genetics, Subscription Department, Room L-2310, 9650 Rockville Pike, Bethesda MD 20814-3998. **)** available on microfilm and microfiche from University Microfilms International (UMI). Documents available from The Genuine Article, BIOSIS Document Express, UMI Article Clearinghouse, CASDDS.
Desc: Original research papers on all aspects of genetics.
Ind/Abst Abstr. Anthropol. (19??-); Acad. Ind. [Computer File] (1992-); Acad. Search; AgBiotech News Inf. (19??-); AGRICOLA (19??-) [Select. Cov.]; Anim. Breed. Abstr. (19??-); Biocont. News Inf. (19??-); Biogr. Index (19??-); Biol. Agric. Index (19??-); Biol. Abstr. (19??-); Biol. Dig. (19??-); Biotechnol. Res. Abstr. (19??-); Chem. Abstr. (19??-); Chemorecept. Abstr. (19??-); CSA Neuro. Abstr. (?-?); Curr. Aware. Biol. Sci., CABS (19??-); Curr. Cit.; Curr. Ref. Fish Res. (19??-); Dairy Sci. Abstr. (19??-); EMBASE (19??-); Energy Res. Abstr. (19??-); Entomol. Abstr.; EP Collect.; Expand. Acad. Index (1992-); Fish Rev. (19??-); Food Sci. Technol. Abstr. (19??-); For. Prod. Abstr. (19??-); For. Abstr. (19??-); Gen. Sci. Index (19??-); Gen. Sci. Source; Genet. Abstr. (19??-); Health Plan. Adminis. (19??-); Homework Help.; Hum. Genome Abstr. (19??-); Immunol. Abstr. (19??-); Index Med. (19??-); Index Vet. (19??-); INFO-SOUTH Abstr. (19??-); INIS Atomindex [Micro.] (19??-); Maize Abstr. (19??-); MasterFile FullTEXT 1000; MasterFile FullTEXT 350; MasterFile FullTEXT 650; MasterFile FullTEXT (July 1993-); Math. Rev. (19??-); Microbiol. Abstr. Sect. B (19??-19??); Microbiol. Abstr. Sect. C (19??-); Nematol. Abstr. (19??-); Newsp. Period. Abstr. (1992-); Nucl. Acids Abstr. (19??-); OCLC; Oncog. Growth Factors Abstr. (19??-); Life Sci. Collect. (19??-); PESTDOC (19??-); Plant Breed. Abstr. (19??-); Plant Grow. Reg. Abstr. (19??-); Potato Abstr. (19??-); Ref. Upd. Basic Ed. (19??-); Ref. Upd. Deluxe Ed. (19??-); Res. Alert (19??-) [Full Cov.]; Rev. Agric. Entomol. (19??-); Rev. Plant Pathol. (19??-); Rice Abstr. (19??-); Sci. Cit. Index (19??-); SCISEARCH (19??-); Seed Abstr. (19??-); Soils Fert. (19??-); Soyabean Abstr. (19??-); Telebase; Virol. AIDS Abstr. (19??-); Weed Abstr. (19??-); Wildl. Rev. (19??-).

LC SF105 .A66
DD 636.08/2/05 FR
NLM W1; GE293T **CODEN** GSEVE9
Pr Rev.

GENETICS, SELECTION, EVOLUTION. **Added/Corp** Institut National de la Recherche Agronomique (France) Centre National de la Recherche Scientifique (France). **VFOAT** GSE. Vol. 21, No. 1 (1989)-. Academic Scholarly Publication. English (French). Six times a year. $302.00. Editions Scientifique Elsevier, 141 rue de Javel, 75747 Paris Cedex 15 France. **Tel** 011 33 1 45589067, FAX 011 33 1 45589424. **(Subscription address:** Editions Scientifiques Elsevier / for North America, PO Box 7247-7576, Philadelphia PA 19170-7576. **) ED** B. Bibe, J.R. David & L. Ollivier. available on an online database from Elsevier Electronic Subscriptions (EES). Documents available from The Genuine Article, BIOSIS Document Express, CASDDS. ***Continues** Genetique, Selection, Evolution, 0754-0264.*
Desc: Publishes original research papers in the field of animal genetics and evolution.
Ind/Abst Biol. Abstr. (1989-); Chem. Abstr.; Curr. Cit.; Curr. Contents Agric. Biol. Environ. Sci.; Helminthol.

Abstr. (1991-); Pig News Inf.; Res. Alert [Full Cov.]; Rev. Agric. Entomol.; Rev. Med. Vet. Entomol.; Sci. Cit. Index; SCISEARCH; Vet. Bull.

ISSN 0435-284X
DD 575 GW
NLM W1 GE298 **CODEN** GNTKAC

GENETIK. [Genetik]. (1963)-. Monographic series. German. Irregular. Price varies per volume. Gustav Fischer Verlag Jena, Postfach 100537, D-07705 Jena Germany. **Tel** 011 49 3641 626444, FAX 011 49 3641 626500. **ED** Hans Stubbe. Documents available from BIOSIS Document Express.
Ind/Abst Biol. Abstr.

LC QH431.A1 **ISSN** 0534-0012
YU
CODEN GNTKDF

GENETIKA. [Genetika]. **VFOAT** Acta Biologica Iugoslavica. Serija F: Genetika. Vol. 1 (1969)-. Academic Scholarly Publication. Serbo-Croatian (Cyrillic). Three times a year. Documents available from CASDDS.
Ind/Abst AGRICOLA; Chem. Abstr.; Curr. Contents Life Sci.; Life Sci. Collect.; Pig News Inf.; Plant Breed. Abstr.; Plant Genet. Resour. Abstr.; Soils Fert.

LC QH426 **ISSN** 0016-6758
DD 575.1 RU
CCC
NLM W1 GE299 **CODEN** GNKAA5
Pr Rev.

GENETIKA. [Genetika]. **Added/Corp** Akademiia Nauk SSSR. No. 1 (July 1965)-. Academic Scholarly Publication. Russian (summaries and/or abstracts in English; table of contents in English). Twelve times a year. $192.50. Izdatelstvo Nauka / Akademiia Nauk, (Publishing House of the Russian Academy of Sciences), Leninskii Porspekt 14, 117901 Moscow Russia. **Tel** 011 95 9542153, FAX 011 95 9382144, telex 411964. **(Subscription address:** East View Publications Inc., 3020 Harbor Lane North, Suite 110, Minneapolis MN 55447. **Tel** (800)477-1005, (612)550-0961, FAX (612)559-2931.) Index available. **Bk Rev.** Documents available from The Genuine Article, BIOSIS Document Express, CASDDS.
Ind/Abst AGRICOLA; Biocont. News Inf.; Biodeter. Abstr.; Biol. Abstr.; Chem. Abstr.; Cot. Trop. Fibr. Abstr. Bibliogr.; Curr. Contents Life Sci.; Ecol. Abstr. (?-?); EMBASE; Fish Rev.; For. Abstr.; Helminthol. Abstr. (1991-); Hortic. Abstr.; Index Med.; Ornamental Hort. (1991-); Life Sci. Collect.; PESTDOC; Plant Breed. Abstr.; Plant Genet. Resour. Abstr.; Plant Grow. Reg. Abstr.; Postharvest News Inf.; Potato Abstr.; Res. Alert [Full Cov.]; Rev. Agric. Entomol.; Rev. Med. Vet. Mycology; Rev. Plant Pathol.; Sci. Cit. Index; SCISEARCH; Soc. Sci. Cit. Index [Select. Cov.]; Wheat Barley Trit. Abstr.; Wildl. Rev.

LC S
DD 630 XR

GENETIKA A SLECHTENI. See Agriculture-Crop Production and Soils.

LC S494 .G37 **ISSN** 0320-0035
DD 630 AJ
CODEN GSAZDY

GENETIKA I SELEKTSIIA V AZERBAIDZHANE. [Genet. sel. azerb.]. **Added/Corp** Azarbaijan SSR Elmlar Akademiiasy. Obshchestvo Genetikov i Selektsionerov Azerbaidzhana. **VFOAT** Azarbaijanda Genetika va Seleksiia. (1971)-. Academic Scholarly Publication. Russian (summaries and/or abstracts in Azerbaijani; table of contents in Azerbaijani). Documents available from CASDDS.
Ind/Abst AGRICOLA; Chem. Abstr.

LC QH426 **ISSN** 0016-6766
DD 575.1 BU
NLM W3 ME959W **CODEN** GESKAC

GENETIKA I SELEKTSIYA. (GENETIKA I SELEKTSIIA = GENETICS AND PLANT BREEDING.). [Genet. sel.]. **Added/Corp** Akademiia na Selskostopanskite Nauki. **VFOAT** Genetics and Plant Breeding. Vol. 1 (1968)-. Academic Scholarly Publication. Bulgarian (summaries and/or abstracts in English, German and Russian). Six times a year. DM143.00. Academie Bulgare des Sciences, Bibliotheque, 1 rue 7 Noemvri, 1040 Sofia Bulgaria. **Tel** 70-40-54. **(Subscription address:** Kubon & Sagner, ABT Zeitschriftenimport, D 80328 Munich Germany. **Tel** 011 49 89 54218130.) **ED** Khristo Daskalov. **Bk Rev. Ad Acc. Circ:** 930 (ctrl). Documents available from BIOSIS Document Express, CASDDS.
Desc: Journal of the Bulgarian Academy of Sciences.
Ind/Abst AgBiotech News Inf.; AGRICOLA; Anim. Breed. Abstr.; BioBusiness; Biol. Abstr.; Chem. Abstr.; Field Crop Abstr.; Genet. Abstr.; Grass. Forage Abstr.; Hortic. Abstr.; Index Vet.; Maize Abstr.; Nematol. Abstr.; Ornamental Hort. (1991-); Life Sci. Collect.; Pig News Inf.; Plant Breed. Abstr.; Plant Genet. Resour. Abstr.; Plant Grow. Reg. Abstr.; Potato Abstr.; Poult. Abstr.; Rev. Agric. Entomol.; Rev. Plant Pathol.; Soyabean Abstr.; Wheat Barley Trit. Abstr.

LC QH431.A1 C25 **ISSN** 0831-2796
DD 575.1/01 CN
CCC
NLM W1; GE336 **CODEN** GENOE3
Pr Rev.

GENOME. [Genome]. **Added/Corp** National Research Council Canada. Genetics Society of Canada. **VFOAT** Genome. Vol. 29, No. 1 (Feb. 1987)-. Academic Scholarly Publication. English (summaries and/or abstracts in French). Six times a year. 300.00Can$. National Research Council of Canada, Receiver General for Canada, Ottawa Ontario K1A 0R6 Canada. **Tel** (613)993-0362, FAX (613)952-7656. **ED** P. B. Moens. Index available. **Ad Acc. Circ:** 1,800 (ctrl). available on microfilm and microfiche from University Microfilms International (UMI). Documents available from The Genuine Article, BIOSIS Document Express, CASDDS. ***Continues*** *Canadian Journal of Genetics and Cytology, 0008-4093.*
Desc: Publishes papers in all fields of genetics.
Ind/Abst Abstr. Anthropol.; AgBiotech News Inf.; AGRICOLA [Select. Cov.]; Anim. Breed. Abstr.; Biocont. News Inf.; Biodeter. Abstr.; Biol. Agric. Index; Biol. Abstr. (1987-); Chem. Abstr. (1987-); Curr. Aware. Biol. Sci., CABS; Curr. Cit.; Curr. Contents Agric. Biol. Environ. Sci.; Curr. Contents Life Sci.; EMBASE; Entomol. Abstr.; Fish Rev. (Jan. 1989-July 1992); For. Abstr.; Genet. Abstr.; Health Plan. Adminis.; Hortic. Abstr.; Index Med. (1987-); Index Vet.; Maize Abstr.; Microbiol. Abstr. Sect. C; Nematol. Abstr.; Ornamental Hort. (1991-); PESTDOC; Plant Breed. Abstr.; Plant Genet. Resour. Abstr.; Plant Grow. Reg. Abstr.; Postharvest News Inf.; Potato Abstr.; Poult. Abstr.; Protozoolog. Abstr.; Ref. Upd. Deluxe Ed.; Res. Alert [Full Cov.]; Rev. Agric. Entomol.; Rev. Med. Vet. Entomol.; Rev. Plant Pathol.; Rice Abstr.; Sci. Cit. Index; SCISEARCH; Seed Abstr.; Sorghum Mill. Abstr.; Soyabean Abstr.; Vet. Bull.; Wheat Barley Trit. Abstr.; Wildl. Rev. (Jan. 1989-July 1992).

ISSN 1050-8430
DD 575 US
CCC
NLM W1; GE336D **CODEN** GEANE3

GENOME ANALYSIS. [Genome anal.]. Vol. 1 (1990)-. Academic Scholarly Publication. English. Irregular. $49.00. Cold Spring Harbor Laboratory, 10 Skyline Drive, Plainview NY 11803. **Tel** (516)349-1930, (800)843-4388, FAX (516)349-1946. Documents available from BIOSIS Document Express, CASDDS.
Desc: Explores genome structure and function.
Ind/Abst Biol. Abstr. (1991-); Chem. Abstr.

LC QH426 QH470 **ISSN** 1021-6278
DD 575.1 SZ
NLM W1; GE336EP

●**GENOME PRIORITY REPORTS.** Vol. 1 (1993)-. Monographic series. English. 400.00F (approx. per volume). S. Karger AG, Allschwilerstrasse 10, PO Box, CH-4009 Basel Switzerland. **Tel** 011 41 61 3061111, FAX 011 41 61 3061234, telex CH 962 652. **ED** H.P. Klinger.
Desc: Dedicated to the rapid publication of genetic conference and workshop compilations.

ISSN 1070-2830
US

●**GENOME SCIENCE & TECHNOLOGY.** **VFOAT** Genome Science and Technology. (1994)-. Periodical. English. Two times a year. $312.00. Mary Ann Liebert Inc., 2 Madison Avenue, Larchmont NY 10538. **Tel** (914)834-3100, (800)M-LIEBERT, FAX (212)289-4697.

LC QH445.2 .G47 **ISSN** 0888-7543
DD 574.87/322/05 US
CCC
NLM W1; GE336G **CODEN** GNMCEP
Pr Rev.

GENOMICS (SAN DIEGO, CALIF.). (GENOMICS.). [Genomics]. Vol. 1, No. 1 (Sept. 1987)-. Academic Scholarly Publication. English. Eighteen times a year. $900.00. Academic Press Inc., 6277 Sea Harbor Drive, Orlando FL 32887. **Tel** (800)543-9534, (407)345-4100, FAX (407)352-3445. **ED** Victor A. McKusick and Frank H. Ruddle. Documents available from The Genuine Article, BIOSIS Document Express, CASDDS.
Desc: Emphasizes the integration of basic and applied research in human and comparative gene mapping, molecular cloning, large-scale restriction mapping, and DNA sequencing and computational analysis. The journal provides a common meeting ground for those involved in molecular biology and genetics. Technologic and methodologic advances in genomic analysis and interpretation are described, and analyses of the human genome in hereditary and neoplastic diseases are reported. Full-length and brief research communications, reviews, and editorial commentary are included.
Ind/Abst Abstr. Anthropol.; AgBiotech News Inf.; Anim. Breed. Abstr.; Biol. Abstr. (1987-); Chem. Abstr.; CSA Neuro. Abstr. (?-?); Curr. Aware. Biol. Sci., CABS; Curr. Cit.; Curr. Contents Life Sci.; Genet. Abstr.; Health Plan. Adminis.; Hum. Genome Abstr.; Index Med. (1987-); Nematol. Abstr.; Nucl. Acids Abstr.; Oncog. Growth Factors Abstr.; PESTDOC; Pig News Inf.; Plant Breed. Abstr.; Poult. Abstr.; Ref. Upd. Deluxe Ed.; Res. Alert [Full Cov.]; Sci. Cit. Index; SCISEARCH; Soc. Sci. Cit. Index [Select. Cov.].

ISSN 0956-523X
UK
CCC
NLM W1; GR919CH **CODEN** GREGEP

GROWTH REGULATION. [Growth regul.]. **Added/Corp** British Library. Medical Information Service. Vol. 1, No. 1 (March 1991)-. Periodical. English. Four times a year. $257.00. Churchill Livingstone, 1-3 Baxter's Place, Leith Walk, Edinburgh EH1 3AF United Kingdom. **Tel** 011 44 131 5562424, FAX 011 44 131 5581278, telex 727511. **(Subscription address:** Maruzen Company Ltd., PO Box 5050, Import & Export Department, Tokyo 100 31 Japan. **Tel** 011 81 3 32789224.) Documents available from The Genuine Article.
Ind/Abst Curr. Aware. Biol. Sci., CABS; Curr. Cit.; Curr. Contents Life Sci.; Index Med.; Res. Alert [Full Cov.]; Sci. Cit. Index; SCISEARCH.

LC QH426 **ISSN** 0254-5934
DD 575.1 KO
NLM W1; HA525E **CODEN** KJGEDG

HANGUG NYUJEN HAGHOI JI. (HANGUK YUJON HAKHOE CHI.). [Hangug nyujen haghoi ji]. **VFOAT** Korean Journal of Genetics. Vol. 1, No. 1 (Oct. 1979)-. Academic Scholarly Publication. English (Korean). Hanguk Yujon Hakhoe, c/o Hanyang Taehakkyo Uikwa Taehak Yujonhak Kyosil, 17 Haengdang-dong, Songdong-ku, Seoul South Korea. Documents available from BIOSIS Document Express, CASDDS.
Ind/Abst Biol. Abstr.; Chem. Abstr.

LC QH491 .H364A **ISSN** 0303-0377
JA
NLM W1 HA792

HATTATSU SHOGAI KENKYUJO NEMPO. **Main/Corp** Hattatsu Shogai Kenkyujo. No. 1 (1972)-. Japanese. Aichi-Ken Shinshin Shogaisha Koroni, 713-1 Kamiya-cho, Kasugai 480-03 Japan.

LC QH431.A1 **ISSN** 0018-0661
SW
NLM W1 HE974 **CODEN** HEREAY
Pr Rev.

HEREDITAS. [Hereditas]. Vol. 1; 1920-. Academic Scholarly Publication. Multiple languages (English, French and German). Six times a year. $254.05. Hereditas Distribution, PO Box 1601, S-221 01 Lund Sweden. **Tel** FAX 46-46 147874. **ED** Karl Fredga and Arne Lundgoist. Index available. cum. index. available on microfilm and microfiche from University Microfilms International (UMI). Documents available from The Genuine Article, BIOSIS Document Express, CASDDS.
Desc: Original research in all fields of genetics.
Ind/Abst Abstr. Anthropol.; AgBiotech News Inf.; AGRICOLA; Anim. Breed. Abstr.; Biol. Abstr.; Chem. Abstr.; Curr. Aware. Biol. Sci., CABS; Curr. Biotechnol.; Curr. Cit.; Curr. Contents Life Sci.; EMBASE; Entomol. Abstr.; Field Crop Abstr.; Fish Rev.; For. Abstr.; Genet. Abstr.; Grass. Forage Abstr.; Health Plan. Adminis.; Helminthol. Abstr.; Hum. Genome Abstr.; Index Med.; Key Word Index Wildl. Res.; Life Sci. Collect.; Pig News Inf.; Plant Breed. Abstr.; Plant Genet. Resour. Abstr.; Plant Grow. Reg. Abstr.; Protozoolog. Abstr.; Res. Alert [Full Cov.]; Rev. Med. Vet. Entomol.; Rev. Med. Vet. Mycology; Rev. Plant Pathol.; Rice Abstr.; Sci. Cit. Index; SCISEARCH; Seed Abstr.; Sorghum Mill. Abstr.; Soyabean Abstr.; Wildl. Rev.

LC QH431 .H43 **ISSN** 0018-067X
DD 575.105 UK
CCC
NLM W1 HE979 **CODEN** HDTYAT
Pr Rev.

HEREDITY. [Heredity]. **Added/Corp** Genetical Society (Great Britain). Vol. 1, Pt. 1 (July 1947)-. Academic Scholarly Publication. English. Twelve times a year. $332.00. Blackwell Scientific Publications Ltd, Marston Book Services, PO Box 88, Oxford OX2 ONE United Kingdom. **Tel** 011 44 1865 206206, FAX 011 44 1865 206219, telex 837 515 MARDIS G. **ED** J. S. Barker and M. J. Kearsey. **Bk Rev. Ad Acc.** available on microfilm and microfiche from University Microfilms International (UMI). Documents available from The Genuine Article, BIOSIS Document Express, CASDDS.
Desc: Contains original articles on population, biochemical genetics, plant and animal breeding, evolution theory and cytogenetics.
Ind/Abst AgBiotech News Inf.; AGRICOLA [Select. Cov.]; Anim. Breed. Abstr.; Biol. Agric. Index; Biol. Abstr.; Chem. Abstr.; Curr. Aware. Biol. Sci., CABS; Curr. Cit.; Curr. Contents Agric. Biol. Environ. Sci.; Curr. Contents Life Sci.; Curr. Ref. Fish Res.; Entomol. Abstr.; Fish Rev.; Food Sci. Technol. Abstr.; For. Abstr.; Genet. Abstr.; Health Plan. Adminis.; Index Med.; Ornamental Hort. (1991-); Life Sci. Collect.; Plant Breed. Abstr.; Plant Genet. Resour. Abstr.; Postharvest News Inf.; Potato Abstr.; Ref. Upd. Deluxe Ed.; Res. Alert [Full Cov.]; Rev. Agric. Entomol.; Rev. Med. Vet. Entomol.; Rice Abstr.; Sci. Cit. Index; SCISEARCH; Seed Abstr.; Trop. Dis. Bull.; Wildl. Rev.

LC RB155.8 .H85 **ISSN** 1043-0342
DD 616/.042 US
NLM W1; HU448B **CODEN** HGTHE3

HUMAN GENE THERAPY. [Hum. gene ther.]. Vol. 1, No. 1 (Spring 1990)-. Periodical. English. Twelve times a year. $645.00. Mary Ann Liebert Inc., 2 Madison

Avenue, Larchmont NY 10538. **Tel** (914)834-3100, (800)M-LIEBERT, FAX (212)289-4697. **ED** W. French Anderson, M.D. **Ad Acc.** Documents available from The Genuine Article.
Desc: Covers aspects of the field of human gene therapy. Publishes scientific papers on original investigations into the transfer and expression of genes in mammals, including man. Improvements in vector development, delivery systems, and animal models are covered.
Ind/Abst AgBiotech News Inf.; Curr. Aware. Biol. Sci., CABS; Curr. Cit.; Curr. Contents Life Sci.; Health Saf. Sci. Abstr.; Health Plan. Adminis.; Index Med. (Spring 1990-);(spring 1990-); Ref. Upd. Deluxe Ed.; Res. Alert [Full Cov.]; Risk Abstr.; Sci. Cit. Index; SCISEARCH.

ISSN 0340-6717 GW CCC
NLM W1 HU448C **CODEN** HUGEDQ
HUMAN GENETICS.
[Hum. genet.]. Vol. 31 (1976)-. Academic Scholarly Publication. English (German). Twelve times a year. $2802.00. Springer-Verlag GmbH & Company KG, Heidelberger Platz 3, D-14197 Berlin Germany. **Tel** 011 49 30 8207223, FAX 011 49 30 8214091, telex 183 319 SPBLN D. **(Subscription address:** Springer-Verlag New York Inc. / North America, PO Box 2485, Journal Fulfillment, Secaucus NJ 07096. **Tel** (201)348-4033, (800)777-4643, FAX (201)348-4505.**) ED** C J Epstein, G Flatz, A G Motulsky, F Vogel, and U Wolf. available on microfilm and microfiche from University Microfilms International (UMI). Documents available from The Genuine Article, BIOSIS Document Express, CASDDS, Documents on Demand. ***Continues** Humangenetik, 0018-7348.*
Desc: Reports new observations in the fields of medical genetics and cytogenetics in order to improve genetic diagnosis, prognosis, and counselling.
Ind/Abst AgBiotech News Inf.; Biol. Abstr.; Chem. Abstr.; Curr. Cit.; Curr. Contents Life Sci.; Dev. Med. Child Neurol.; EMBASE; Energy Inf. Abstr.; Energy Res. Abstr.; Environ. Abstr.; Genet. Abstr.; Hum. Genome Abstr.; Index Med.; Index Vet.; Oncog. Growth Factors Abstr.; Life Sci. Collect.; Ref. Upd. Basic Ed.; Ref. Upd. Clinical Ed.; Ref. Upd. Deluxe Ed.; Res. Alert [Full Cov.]; Sci. Cit. Index; SCISEARCH; Soc. Sci. Cit. Index [Select. Cov.]; Vet. Bull.

LC RB155 .N37a **ISSN** 0196-1543
DD 616/.042 US
NLM ZQZ 50 H918H
HUMAN GENETICS (ROCKVILLE).
(HUMAN GENETICS, INFORMATIONAL AND EDUCATIONAL MATERIALS.). **Added/Corp** National Clearinghouse for Human Genetic Diseases (U.S.) United States. Health Services Administration. Genetic Disease Services Branch. Vol. 1, No. 1 (1979)-. English. U.S. Public Health Service, 5600 Fishers Lane, Rockville MD 20857.

LC RB155 .N37a Suppl **ISSN** 0197-8160
DD 016.616/042 US
HUMAN GENETICS. SUPPLEMENT (ROCKVILLE).
(HUMAN GENETICS, INFORMATIONAL AND EDUCATIONAL MATERIALS. SUPPLEMENT.). [Hum. genet. Suppl.]. **Added/Corp** National Clearinghouse for Human Genetic Diseases (U.S.) United States. Health Services Administration. Genetic Disease Services Branch. No. 1 (1980)-. English. U.S. Public Health Service, 5600 Fishers Lane, Rockville MD 20857.

ISSN 1045-4470
DD 573 US
NLM Z 5322.H8; H918
HUMAN GENOME ABSTRACTS.
See Biology-Abstracting, Bibliographies and Statistics.

ISSN 1050-6101
DD 573 US
NLM W1; HU448DQ
HUMAN GENOME NEWS.
(HUMAN GENOME NEWS / NATIONAL CENTER FOR HUMAN GENOME RESEARCH, NATIONAL INSTITUTES OF HEALTH.). [Hum. genome news]. **Added/Corp** National Center for Human Genome Research (U.S.) United States. Dept. of Energy. Office of Health and Environmental Research. Oak Ridge National Laboratory. Health and Safety Research Division. Biomedical and Environmental Information Analysis Section. Vol. 2, No. 1 (May 1990)-. Periodical. English. Six times a year. Free on request. Oak Ridge National Library, PO Box 2008, Oak Ridge TN 37831. **Tel** (615)574-6755, (615)574-5845. **(Subscription address:** Oak Ridge National Laboratory, PO Box 2008, Building 2001, Oak Ridge TN 37831. **Tel** (615)576-6669.**)** Documents available from The Genuine Article. ***Continues** Human Genome Quarterly, 1044-0828.*
Ind/Abst Res. Alert; Soc. Sci. Cit. Index [Select. Cov.].

LC RB155 .A25 **ISSN** 0001-5652 SZ CCC
NLM W1 HU448F **CODEN** HUHEAS
Pr Rev.
HUMAN HEREDITY.
[Human hered.]. Vol. 19, No. 1 (1969)-. Academic Scholarly Publication. English. Six times a year. $392.60. S. Karger AG, Allschwilerstrasse 10, PO Box, CH-4009 Basel Switzerland. **Tel** 011 41 61 3061111, FAX 011 41 61 3061234, telex CH 962 652. **ED** J. Ott. Index available in last issue of volume--attached. **Ad Acc.** available on microfilm from University Microfilms International (UMI). Documents available from The Genuine Article, BIOSIS Document Express, CASDDS. ***Continues** Acta Genetica et Statistica Medica, 0365-2785.*
Desc: Devoted to methodological and applied research on the genetics of human populations, linkage analysis, and the genetic mechanisms of disease. The increasing possibilities for prenatal diagnosis also receive special attention, as do papers on new serological, biochemical and statistical methods.
Ind/Abst Anim. Breed. Abstr.; Anthropol. Index; Anthropol. Lit.; Biol. Abstr.; Biostatistica (19??-19??); Chem. Abstr.; Curr. Aware. Biol. Sci., CABS; Curr. Cit.; Curr. Contents Life Sci.; Dev. Med. Child Neurol.; EMBASE; Genet. Abstr.; Health Plan. Adminis.; Helminthol. Abstr. (1991-); Index Med.; Nutr. Abstr. Rev., Ser. B, Live Feeds and Feed.; Nutr. Abstr. Rev., Ser. A, Hum. Exp.; Life Sci. Collect.; Ref. Upd. Deluxe Ed.; Res. Alert [Full Cov.]; Sci. Cit. Index; SCISEARCH; SportSearch; Stat. Theory Method Abstr. (1971); Trop. Dis. Bull.

LC RB155.5 .H87 **ISSN** 0964-6906 UK CCC
NLM W1; HU448LK **CODEN** HMGEE5
HUMAN MOLECULAR GENETICS.
[Hum. mol. genet.]. Vol. 1, No. 1 (Apr. 1992)-. Academic Scholarly Publication. English. Thirteen times a year. $550.00. Oxford University Press / UK, Walton Street, Oxford OX2 6DP United Kingdom. **Tel** 011 44 1865 56767, FAX 011 44 1865 267773, telex 851/837330 OXPRES G. **(Subscription address:** Oxford University Press / USA, Journals Marketing Department, Oxford University Press, 2001 Evans Road, Cary NC 27513. **Tel** (800)451-7556, (919)677-0977, FAX (919)677-1714.**)** Documents available from The Genuine Article, CASDDS.
Ind/Abst Chem. Abstr.; Curr. Aware. Biol. Sci., CABS; Index Med.; Ref. Upd. Basic Ed.; Ref. Upd. Deluxe Ed.; Res. Alert [Full Cov.]; Sci. Cit. Index.

LC RB155.5 .H875 **ISSN** 1059-7794
DD 616/.042/05 US
NLM W1; HU448MH **CODEN** HUMUE3
HUMAN MUTATION.
[Human mutat.]. Vol. 1, No. 1 (1992)-. Academic Scholarly Publication. English. Eight times a year. $250.00. John Wiley & Sons, Inc., 605 Third Avenue, New York NY 10158-0012. **Tel** (212)850-6000, (212)850-6645, FAX (212)850-6088, telex 12-7063. **(Subscription address:** John Wiley & Sons / UK, Baffins Lane, Chichester, West Sussex PO19 1UD United Kingdom. **Tel** 011 44 1243 779777, FAX 011 44 243 776128, telex 86290 WIBOOKG.**) ED** R. G. H. Cotton and Haig H. Kazazian, Jr. Documents available from The Genuine Article, CASDDS.
Desc: Publishes original research articles, mutation updates, briefs on new mutations and reviews on broad aspects of mutation research.
Ind/Abst Chem. Abstr.; Curr. Aware. Biol. Sci., CABS; Index Med.; Res. Alert [Full Cov.].

ISSN 0732-1368 US
NLM W1 HY27
HYBRIDOMA PROFILES.
Apr. 1981-. English. National Cancer Institute, NCI Building Room, 10A 18, Bethesda MD 20892. **Tel** (800)422-6237, (301)496-8774.

LC QH431 .I17 CC
NLM W1 I125 **CODEN** ICHPCG
I CHUAN HSUEH PAO.
VFOAT Acta Genetica Sinica. (1974)-. Academic Scholarly Publication. Chinese (summaries and/or abstracts in English). Six times a year. $63.80. **(Subscription address:** China International Book Trading Corporation, PO Box 399, Library Service Department, Beijing 100044 People's Republic of China. **Tel** 011 86 1 8414284, FAX 011 86 1 8412023, telex 22496 CIBTC CN.**)** Documents available from BIOSIS Document Express, CASDDS.
Ind/Abst AGRICOLA; Biocont. News Inf.; Biol. Abstr.; Chem. Abstr.; Crop Physiol. Abstr.; Field Crop Abstr.; Index Med.; Life Sci. Collect.; Plant Breed. Abstr.; Rice Abstr.

LC QK **ISSN** 1021-5964
DD 581 IT
CODEN ICLSED
IBPGR TRAINING COURSES. LECTURE SERIES.
See Biology-Botany.

ISSN 0387-0022
DD 575.1 JA
IDEN.
[Iden]. **VFOAT** Heredity (Tokyo. 1947). (1947)-. Periodical. Japanese. Twelve times a year. $134.00. Shokabo, (Shokabo Publisher Co. Ltd.), 8-1 Yonbancho Chiyodaku, Tokyo 102 Japan. Documents available from CASDDS.
Ind/Abst Chem. Abstr.

ISSN 0388-8177 JA
CODEN ISAHD2
IKUSHUGAKU SAIKIN NO SHINPO.
(IKUSHUGAKU SAIKIN NO SHINPO : DAI ...-KAI NIHON IKUSHU GAKKAI SHINPOJIUMU HOKOKU.). [Ikushugaku saikin no shinpo]. **Main/Conf** Nihon Ikushu Gakkai. Shinpojiumu. (1958)-. Academic Scholarly Publication. Japanese. One time a year. ¥2600 (vol. 18 through vol. 27), ¥3200 (vol. 1 through vol. 27) Japan; $20.00 (vol. 18 through vol. 27), $25.00 (vol. 1 through 27) US. Yoken-do Ltd, 5-30-5 Hongo, Chiyoda-ku Tokyo 113 Japan. **Tel** 03-233-3731, FAX 03-233-3730. Documents available from CASDDS.
Desc: Contains the contributions of the annual symposium held by the Japanese Society of Breeding every autumn. The latest results of the studies of breeding in Japan.
Ind/Abst Chem. Abstr. (1958-1981).

LC QH321 **ISSN** 1077-3975
DD 574.072 US
Pr Rev.
•IN VITRO REPORT.
See Biology-Microbiology.

LC SB123 .I6 **ISSN** 0019-5200
DD 631.52205 II
CODEN IJGBAG
INDIAN JOURNAL OF GENETICS & PLANT BREEDING, THE.
[Indian j. genet. & plant breed.]. **Added/Corp** Indian Society of Genetics & Plant Breeding. Vol. 1 (Dec. 1941)-. Periodical. English. Four times a year. $75.00. **(Subscription address:** Prints India, 11 Darya Ganj, New Delhi 110002 India. **Tel** 011 91 11 3268645, FAX 011 91 11 3275542, telex 31-61087 PRIN-IN.**)** Documents available from BIOSIS Document Express, CASDDS.
Ind/Abst AGRICOLA; BioBusiness; Biol. Abstr.; Biotechnol. Res. Abstr.; Chem. Abstr.; Cot. Trop. Fibr. Abstr. Bibliogr.; Field Crop Abstr.; Genet. Abstr.; Grass. Forage Abstr.; Hortic. Abstr.; Irr. Drain. Abstr.; Maize Abstr.; Nematol. Abstr.; Life Sci. Collect.; Plant Breed. Abstr.; Plant Grow. Reg. Abstr.; Protozoolog. Abstr.; Rev. Agric. Entomol.; Rev. Med. Vet. Mycology; Rev. Plant Pathol.; Rice Abstr.; Seed Abstr.; Soils Fert.; Sorghum Mill. Abstr.; Soyabean Abstr.

LC QH426 **ISSN** 0374-826X
DD 575.1 II
NLM W1 IN209B **CODEN** INJHA9
Pr Rev.
INDIAN JOURNAL OF HEREDITY.
[Indian j. hered.]. **Added/Corp** Genetic Association of India. **VFOAT** Journal of Heredity. Vol. 1 (1969)-. Academic Scholarly Publication. English. Four times a year. $25.00. Professor of Animal Genetics, Head of Animal Genetics, Indian Veterinary Research Institute, Izatnagar U P India. **(Subscription address:** Prints India, 11 Darya Ganj, New Delhi 110002 India. **Tel** 011 91 11 3268645, FAX 011 91 11 3275542, telex 31-61087 PRIN-IN.**) ED** N. S. Sidhu. **Bk Rev. Ad Acc. Circ:** 300 (ctrl). Documents available from BIOSIS Document Express, CASDDS.
Desc: Covers human genetics, livestock genetics and breeding, plant genetics and breeding, anthropology and related subjects, e.g. evolution, eugenics, cytogenetics, adaptations, etc.
Ind/Abst Biol. Abstr.; Chem. Abstr.; Cot. Trop. Fibr. Abstr. Bibliogr.; Dairy Sci. Abstr.; EMBASE; Index Vet.; Plant Breed. Abstr.; Sorghum Mill. Abstr.; Soyabean Abstr.

LC GN49 .I53 **ISSN** 0378-8156
DD 573/.05 II
NLM W1 IN2255 **CODEN** IJPGDB
INDIAN JOURNAL OF PHYSICAL ANTHROPOLOGY AND HUMAN GENETICS.
[Indian j. phys. anthropol. hum. genet.]. **Added/Corp** Ethnographic and Folk-Culture Society (Uttar Pradesh, India). Vol. 1 (June 1975)-. Academic Scholarly Publication. English. Three times a year. $40.00. Ethographic and Folk Culture Society, PB 209, Fiazabad Road, Lucknow 226007 India. **Tel** 72362. **(Subscription address:** Prints India, 11 Darya Ganj, New Delhi 110002 India. **Tel** 011 91 11 3268645, FAX 011 91 11 3275542, telex 31-61087 PRIN-IN.**) ED** B R K Shukla. **Bk Rev. Ad Acc. Circ:** 500. Documents available from BIOSIS Document Express, CASDDS.
Desc: An international forum for issues concerning physical anthropology, human genetics. The journal is mainly devoted to biological aspects of human populations.
Ind/Abst Anthropol. Index; Anthropol. Lit.; Biol. Abstr.; Chem. Abstr.

LC QH447 .I58 **ISSN** 0218-1932
DD 574.87/322 SI CCC
NLM W1; IN766LM **CODEN** IJGREY
CEASED
INTERNATIONAL JOURNAL OF GENOME RESEARCH.
[Int. j. genome res.]. Vol. 1, No. 1 (1992)-Vol. 1 No. 4 (May 1993). Academic Scholarly Publication. English. World Scientific Publishing Company, PO Box 128, Farrer Road, Singapore 9128 Singapore. **Tel** 011 65 3825663, FAX 011 65 3825919, telex RS 28561 WSPC. Documents available from CASDDS.
Ind/Abst Chem. Abstr.; Soc. Sci. Cit. Index [Select. Cov.].

LC QM691 .I85 **ISSN** 0740-8242
DD 616/.043 US
CCC
NLM W1 IS6673 **CODEN** ISRTDL

ISSUES AND REVIEWS IN TERATOLOGY. [Issues rev. teratol.]. Vol. 1 (1983)-. Academic Scholarly Publication. English. Irregular. Price varies per volume. Plenum Press, 233 Spring Street, New York NY 10013-1578. **Tel** (212)620-8000, (800)221-9369, FAX (212)463-0742, (212)807-1047, telex 23/421139. **ED** Harold Kalter. Documents available from CASDDS.
Ind/Abst Chem. Abstr. (1983-).

LC QH431 .I85 **ISSN** 0360-0394
DD 573.2/1/05 US
NLM W1 HU448D

ITOGI, SUMMARIES OF SCIENTIFIC PROGRESS : HUMAN GENETICS. **VFOAT** Human Genetics. Vol. 1 (19??)-. English (Russian). GK Hall & Co., 100 Front Street, Riverside NJ 08075. **Tel** (800)257-5755 ext. 2223.

LC QH426
DD 575.1 JA
NLM W1; ID395
TITLE CHANGE

JAPANESE JOURNAL OF GENETICS. **Added/Corp** Nihon Iden Gakkai. **VFOAT** Idengaku Zasshi. (1961)-(1995). Periodical. English (Japanese). Nihon Ronen Igakkai, (Japan Geriatrics Soc.), c/o Tokyo Daigaku Igakubu, Ronenbyogaku Kyoshitsu, 3-1 Hongo 7 Chome, Bunkyoku Tokyo 113 Japan. **(Subscription address:** Maruzen Company Ltd., PO Box 5050, Import & Export Department, Tokyo 100 31 Japan. **Tel** 011 81 3 32789224.) Documents available from The Genuine Article. ***Continues** Idengaku Zasshi, 0021-504X.* ***Continued by** Genes and Genetic Systems.*
Ind/Abst AgBiotech News Inf.; Anim. Breed. Abstr.; Crop Physiol. Abstr.; Curr. Aware. Biol. Sci., CABS; Field Crop Abstr.; Index Med. (Feb. 1988-); Plant Genet. Resour. Abstr.; Res. Alert [Full Cov.]; Rev. Med. Vet. Entomol.; Sci. Cit. Index; SCISEARCH; Seed Abstr.; Wheat Barley Trit. Abstr.

LC QH426 **ISSN** 0916-8478
DD 575.1 JA
NLM W1; JA955

JAPANESE JOURNAL OF HUMAN GENETICS, THE. **Added/Corp** Nihon Jinrui Iden Gakkai. Vol. 37, No. 1 (Mar. 1992)-. Periodical. English. Four times a year. $97.00. Nihon Jinrui Iden Gakkai, (Japan Soc. of Human Genetics), Tokyo Ika Shika Daigaku Jinrui, Idengaku kenkyushitsu, 5-45 Yushima 1 Chome, Bunkyoku Tokyo 113 Japan. **(Subscription address:** Japan Publications Trading Company Ltd., PO Box 5030, Tokyo International, Tokyo 100-31 Japan. **Tel** 011 81 3 3292 3753.) Documents available from The Genuine Article. ***Continues** Jinrui Idengaku Zasshi.*
Ind/Abst Curr. Aware. Biol. Sci., CABS; Hum. Genome Abstr.; Index Med. (1992-); Res. Alert [Full Cov.]; Sci. Cit. Index; SCISEARCH.

LC QH429.5 .A43a **ISSN** 0883-4709
DD 575.1/06/073 US
NLM QH 429.5; A512j

JOINT MEMBERSHIP DIRECTORY - AMERICAN SOCIETY OF HUMAN GENETICS. (JOINT MEMBERSHIP DIRECTORY / AMERICAN SOCIETY OF HUMAN GENETICS ; GENETICS SOCIETY OF AMERICA.). [Jt. membsh. dir. - Am. Soc. Hum. Genet.]. **Main/Corp** American Society of Human Genetics. **Added/Corp** Genetics Society of America. (1983)-. Directory. English. One time a year. $50.00. Genetics Society of America, 9650 Rockville Pike, Bethesda MD 20814. **Tel** (301)530-7027, FAX (301)530-7001.

ISSN 0931-2668
GW
UDC 636 **CCC**

JOURNAL OF ANIMAL BREEDING AND GENETICS (1986). [J. anim. breed. genet. 1986]. **VFOAT** Zeitschrift fuer Tierzuchtung und Zuchtungsbiologie (1986). (1986)-. Periodical. Multiple languages. Six times a year. $746.93. Blackwell Wissenschafts-Verlag, Kurfuerstendamm 57, D-10707 Berlin Germany. **Tel** 011 49 30 32790623, 011 49 30 32790624, FAX 011 49 30 327 90610. **ED** F. Pirchner (executive editor). Documents available from The Genuine Article. ***Continues** Zeitschrift fuer Tierzuchtung und Zuchtungsbiologie, 0044-3581.*
Desc: Publishes original articles on the progress of research in animal production, quantitative genetics, biology, and evolution of domestic animals.
Ind/Abst Curr. Cit.; Res. Alert [Full Cov.]; Sci. Cit. Index; SCISEARCH.

PL

•JOURNAL OF APPLIED GENETICS. (1995)-. Academic Scholarly Publication. English (summaries and/or abstracts in Polish and Russian). Four times a year. $66.00. Polska Akademia Nauk / Instytut Genetyki Roslin, Ul. Strzeszynska 34, 60-479 Poznan Poland. **Tel** 011 48 61 233511, FAX 011 48 61 221122. **(Subscription address:** Ars Polona-Ruch, PO Box 1001, Krakowskie Przedmiescie 7, 00-068 Warsaw Poland. **Tel** 011 48 22 261201.) Index available. **Bk Rev. Circ:** 600. ***Continues** Genetica Polonica, 0016-6715.*

LC RG135 .J68 **ISSN** 1058-0468
DD 618.1/78/005 US
CCC
NLM W1; JO544R **CODEN** JARGE4

JOURNAL OF ASSISTED REPRODUCTION AND GENETICS. **See** Medical Sciences-Gynecology and Obstetrics.

LC QH573 **ISSN** 0253-7605
DD 574.87 II
NLM W1 JO6125 **CODEN** JCGEDO

JOURNAL OF CYTOLOGY AND GENETICS, THE. **See** Biology-Cytology.

LC QH359 .J68 **ISSN** 1010-061X
DD 575/.005 SZ
CCC
NLM W1; JO644E **CODEN** JEBIEQ
Pr Rev.

JOURNAL OF EVOLUTIONARY BIOLOGY. [J. evol. biol.]. **Added/Corp** European Society of Evolutionary Biology. Vol. 1, No. 1 (1987)-. Periodical. English. Six times a year. $670.23. Birkhaeuser Verlag Ag, Klosterberg 23, PO Box 133, CH-4010 Basel Switzerland. **Tel** 011 41 61 2717400, FAX 011 41 61 2717666, telex 963475 birk ch. **(Subscription address:** Birkhaeuser Verlag AG, PO Box 133, CH 4010 Basel Switzerland. **Tel** 011 41 61 2717400.) **ED** P. H. Gouyon. Index available. cum. index. **Bk Rev. Ad Acc. Circ:** 600. available on microfilm and microfiche from University Microfilms International (UMI). Documents available from The Genuine Article, BIOSIS Document Express.
Desc: Publishes original research on any interesting aspects of evolutionary biology from botany, zoology and theory, including evolutionary ecology, genetical ecology, ecological genetics, population genetics, the role of development in evolution, the evolution of developmental mechanisms, and the interplay of microevolution and macroevolution.
Ind/Abst Anim. Behav. Abstr.; Anim. Breed. Abstr.; Biol. Abstr. (1988-); Curr. Aware. Biol. Sci., CABS; Curr. Cit.; Curr. Contents Agric. Biol. Environ. Sci.; Ecol. Abstr.; Ecology Abstr.; Entomol. Abstr.; For. Abstr.; Geol. Abstr.; Helminthol. Abstr. (1991-); Key Word Index Wildl. Res.; Plant Breed. Abstr.; Plant Genet. Resour. Abstr.; Protozoolog. Abstr.; Res. Alert [Select. Cov.]; Rev. Med. Vet. Entomol.; SCISEARCH.

LC RB155.7 .J68 **ISSN** 1059-7700
DD 616/.042 US
CCC
CODEN JGCOET
Pr Rev.

JOURNAL OF GENETIC COUNSELING. [J. genet. couns.]. **Added/Corp** National Society of Genetic Counselors (U.S.). Vol. 1, No. 1 (Mar. 1992)-. Periodical. English. Four times a year. $145.00. Human Sciences Press, PO Box 735, Canal Street Station, New York NY 10013. **Tel** (212)620-8000, FAX (212)807-1047, telex 23421139. **(Subscription address:** Eurospan Ltd., 3 Henrietta Street Covent Garden, London WC2E 8LU United Kingdom. **Tel** 011 44 181 2400856, FAX 011 44 181 3790609.) **ED** Deborah Eunpu and Joan Fitzgerald.
Desc: New international forum addressing all aspects of genetic counseling. The journal focuses on the critical questions and problems that arise at the interface between rapidly advancing technical developments and the concerns of the individual at genetic risk.
Ind/Abst Soc. Plann. Policy Dev. Abstr.; Soc. Work Abstr. [Select. Cov.].

LC QH301 .J7 **ISSN** 0022-1333
II
NLM W1 JO669L **CODEN** JOGNAU
Pr Rev.

JOURNAL OF GENETICS. [J. genet.]. **Added/Corp** Indian Academy of Sciences. Vol. 1 (1910)-. Periodical. English. Three times a year. $75.00. Indian Academy of Sciences Circulation, PO Box 8005, Department of Sadashivanagar, Bangalore 560 080 India. **Tel** 011 91 812 342546, 342310, telex 0845-2178 ACAD IN. **(Subscription address:** Prints India, 11 Darya Ganj, New Delhi 110002 India. **Tel** 011 91 11 3268645, FAX 011 91 11 3275542, telex 31-61087 PRIN-IN.) **ED** H Sharat Chandra. Index available. cum. index. **Circ:** 500. Documents available from The Genuine Article, BIOSIS Document Express, CASDDS.
Desc: Covers all areas of genetics and evolution including molecular genetics and molecular evolution.
Ind/Abst AgBiotech News Inf.; Anim. Breed. Abstr.; Biol. Abstr. (1986-); Biostatistica (19??-19??); Chem. Abstr.; Curr. Cit.; Curr. Contents Life Sci.; Hortic. Abstr.; Index Vet.; Plant Breed. Abstr.; Plant Grow. Reg. Abstr.; Res. Alert [Full Cov.]; Rev. Med. Vet. Entomol.; Rev. Med. Vet. Mycology; Rev. Plant Pathol.; Rice Abstr.; Sci. Cit. Index; SCISEARCH; Soils Fert.; Soyabean Abstr.; Stat. Theory Method Abstr. (1969); Vet. Bull.

ISSN 0394-9257
IT
CODEN JGBREX
Pr Rev.

JOURNAL OF GENETICS & BREEDING. **Added/Corp** Istituto Sperimentale per la Cerealicoltura. **VFOAT** Journal of Genetics and Breeding. Vol. 43, No. 1 (Jan. 1989)-. Periodical. English. Four times a year. L136250. Istituto Sperim Cerealicoltura, Via Cassia 176, 00191 Rome Italy. **Tel** 011 39 6 3295705, FAX 011 39 6 3286022. **ED** A. Bianchi, R.A. Forsberg, A.J. Prior. Index available. cum. index. **Ad Acc. Circ:** 400. Documents available from BIOSIS Document Express. ***Continues** Genetica Agraria, 0016-6685.*
Ind/Abst AgBiotech News Inf.; Anim. Breed. Abstr.; BioBusiness; Biol. Abstr. (1989-); Cot. Trop. Fibr. Abstr. Bibliogr.; Crop Physiol. Abstr.; Curr. Aware. Biol. Sci., CABS; Curr. Cit.; Field Crop Abstr.; Food Sci. Technol. Abstr.; Grass. Forage Abstr.; Hortic. Abstr.; Irr. Drain. Abstr.; Maize Abstr.; Ornamental Hort. (1991-); Plant Breed. Abstr.; Plant Genet. Resour. Abstr.; Plant Grow. Reg. Abstr.; Potato Abstr.; Rev. Agric. Entomol.; Rev. Plant Pathol.; Rice Abstr.; Seed Abstr.; Sorghum Mill. Abstr.; Weed Abstr.; Wheat Barley Trit. Abstr.

ISSN 0022-1503
US
CCC
NLM W1 JO67J **CODEN** JOHEA8
Pr Rev.

JOURNAL OF HEREDITY, THE. [J. hered.]. **Added/Corp** American Genetic Association. Vol. 5 (Jan. 1914)-. Academic Scholarly Publication. English. Six times a year. $140.00. Oxford University Press / New York, 200 Madison Avenue, New York NY 10016. **Tel** (212)679-7300, (919)677-0977, (800)451-7556, (800)445-9714, FAX (919)677-1303. **(Subscription address:** Oxford University Press / USA, Journals Marketing Department, Oxford University Press, 2001 Evans Road, Cary NC 27513. **Tel** (800)451-7556, (919)677-0977, FAX (919)677-1714.) **ED** Barbara A. Kuhn. **Bk Rev. Ad Acc. Acid Free. Circ:** 4,000 (ctrl). available on microfilm and microfiche from University Microfilms International (UMI). Documents available from The Genuine Article, BIOSIS Document Express, UMI Article Clearinghouse, CASDDS. ***Continues** American Breeders' Magazine.*
Desc: Covers areas of heredity from plant breeding to molecular genetics.
Ind/Abst Acad. Ind. [Computer File] (1992-); Acad. Search; AgBiotech News Inf.; AGRICOLA [Select. Cov.]; Anim. Breed. Abstr.; Biocont. News Inf.; Biol. Agric. Index; Biol. Abstr.; Biostatistica (19??-19??); Chem. Abstr.; Cot. Trop. Fibr. Abstr. Bibliogr.; Curr. Aware. Biol. Sci., CABS; Curr. Cit.; Curr. Contents Agric. Biol. Environ. Sci.; Curr. Contents Life Sci.; Curr. Ref. Fish Res.; EMBASE; Energy Res. Abstr.; EP Collect.; Expand. Acad. Index (1989-); Fish Rev. (Jan. 1989-July 1992); For. Prod. Abstr.; For. Abstr.; Gen. Sci. Index; Gen. Sci. Source; Genet. Abstr.; GeoRef; Helminthol. Abstr. (1991-); Homework Help.; Hortic. Abstr.; Index Med.; INFO-SOUTH Abstr.; INIS Atomindex [Micro.]; Mag. Search; Maize Abstr.; MasterFile FullTEXT 1000; MasterFile FullTEXT 350; MasterFile FullTEXT 650; MasterFile FullTEXT (July 1993-); Nematol. Abstr.; Newsp. Period. Abstr. (1989-); OCLC; Ornamental Hort. (19??-19??); Life Sci. Collect.; PESTDOC; Pig News Inf.; Plant Breed. Abstr.; Plant Genet. Resour. Abstr.; Potato Abstr.; Poult. Abstr.; Protozoolog. Abstr.; Ref. Upd. Deluxe Ed.; Res. Alert [Full Cov.]; Rev. Agric. Entomol.; Rev. Med. Vet. Entomol.; Rev. Plant Pathol.; Sci. Cit. Index; SCISEARCH; Seed Abstr.; Soils Fert.; Sorghum Mill. Abstr.; Soyabean Abstr.; Stat. Theory Method Abstr. (1959-1963); Telebase; Wildl. Rev. (Jan. 1989-July 1992).

ISSN 0022-2593
UK
CCC
NLM W1 JO75N **CODEN** JMDGAE
Pr Rev.

JOURNAL OF MEDICAL GENETICS. [J. med. genet.]. **Added/Corp** British Medical Association. Vol. 1 (1964)-. Academic Scholarly Publication. English. Twelve times a year. $335.40. BMJ / British Medical Journal Publishing Group, British Medical Association House, Tavistock Square, London WC1H 9JR United Kingdom. **Tel** 011 44 171 3874499, FAX 011 44 171 383 6402, telex 290034 HBJ MN. **ED** Peter S. Harper. available on microfilm and microfiche from University Microfilms International (UMI). Documents available from The Genuine Article, BIOSIS Document Express, CASDDS.
Desc: Original work on the subject including molecular genetics of human inherited disorders, human gene mapping and dysmorphology.
Ind/Abst Anim. Breed. Abstr.; Biol. Abstr.; Calcium Calcif. Tissue Abstr.; Chem. Abstr.; Curr. Aware. Biol. Sci., CABS; Curr. Cit.; Curr. Contents Clin. Med.; Curr. Contents Life Sci.; Dev. Med. Child Neurol.; EMBASE; Genet. Abstr.; Hum. Genome Abstr.; Index Med.; Index Vet.; Nutr. Abstr. Rev., Ser. B, Live Feeds and Feed.; Nutr. Abstr. Rev., Ser. A, Hum. Exp.; Life Sci. Collect.; Protozoolog. Abstr.; Ref. Upd. Clinical Ed.; Ref. Upd. Deluxe Ed.; Res. Alert [Full Cov.]; Risk Abstr.; Sci. Cit. Index; SCISEARCH; Soc. Sci. Cit. Index [Select. Cov.]; Vet. Bull.; Trop. Dis. Bull.

LC QH366.A1 J68 ISSN 0022-2844
DD 575 GW
CCC
NLM W1 JO773K CODEN JMEVAU
Pr Rev.

JOURNAL OF MOLECULAR EVOLUTION. [J. mol. evol.]. Vol. 1 (1971)-. Periodical. English. Twelve times a year. $915.00. Springer-Verlag New York Inc., 175 Fifth Avenue, New York NY 10010. **Tel** (212)460-1500 ext 256, FAX (212)533-3503, telex 232 235 SPB UR. **(Subscription address:** Springer-Verlag New York Inc. / North America, PO Box 2485, Journal Fulfillment, Secaucus NJ 07096. **Tel** (201)348-4033, (800)777-4643, FAX (201)348-4505.) **ED** E Zuckerkandl. available on microfilm and microfiche from University Microfilms International (UMI). Documents available from The Genuine Article, CASDDS.
Desc: Publishes articles in several fields, including biogenetic evolution, evolution of informational macromolecules, evolution of genetic control mechanisms, evolution of enzyme systems and their products, evolution of macromolecular systems and molecular bases for organismal evolution.
Ind/Abst AgBiotech News Inf.; AGRICOLA [Select. Cov.]; Biol. Agric. Index; Chem. Abstr.; Chem. Titles; Curr. Cit.; Curr. Contents Life Sci.; Curr. Ref. Fish Res.; Dairy Sci. Abstr.; EMBASE; Energy Res. Abstr. (March 1976-); Fish Rev. (Jan. 1989-July 1992); Food Sci. Technol. Abstr.; Genet. Abstr.; GeoRef; Hortic. Abstr.; Index Med.; Int. Aerosp. Abstr.; Microbiol. Abstr. Sect. C; Nematol. Abstr.; Nutr. Abstr. Rev., Ser. B, Live Feeds and Feed.; Ornamental Hort. (1991-); Life Sci. Collect.; Phys. Briefs; Plant Breed. Abstr.; Potato Abstr.; Protozoolog. Abstr.; Ref. Upd. Deluxe Ed.; Res. Alert [Full Cov.]; Rev. Agric. Entomol.; Rev. Med. Vet. Entomol.; Sci. Cit. Index; SCISEARCH; Small Anim. Abstr. Bibliogr.; Soyabean Abstr.; Virol. AIDS Abstr.; Wildl. Rev. (Jan. 1989-July 1992).

ISSN 0167-7063
DD 591 SZ
CCC
NLM W1; JO787F CODEN JLNEDK
Pr Rev.

JOURNAL OF NEUROGENETICS. [J. neurogenet.]. Vol. 1, No. 1 (Sept. 1983)-. Academic Scholarly Publication. English. Four times a year. £312.00 universities and hospitals and libraries; £487.00 other. Gordon & Breach Science Publishers, Inc., PO Box 786, Cooper Station, New York NY 10276. **Tel** (212)206-8900, FAX (212)645-2459. **ED** Jeffrey C. Hall C. Hall, and Marcelle R. Morrison. Documents available from The Genuine Article, CASDDS.
Desc: Original papers in the broad field of neurogenetics. This covers papers on the genetic mechanisms underlying early embryonic development as well as aspects of cell differentiation, pattern formation and genetic disorders of the nervous system.
Ind/Abst Chem. Abstr. (1983-); CSA Neuro. Abstr. (1983-1987); Curr. Aware. Biol. Sci., CABS; Curr. Cit.; Curr. Contents Life Sci.; Genet. Abstr.; Index Med. (Vol. 1, No. 1, 1983-1987); Nematol. Abstr.; Oncog. Growth Factors Abstr.; Life Sci. Collect. (Vol. 1, No. 1, 1983-1987-); Ref. Upd. Deluxe Ed.; Res. Alert [Full Cov.]; Sci. Cit. Index; SCISEARCH.

LC QH440.8.J32 K643
JA
NLM W1 KO301T

KOKURITSU IDENGAKU KENKYUJO NEMPO. **Main/Corp** Kokuritsu Idengaku Kenkyujo, Mishima, Japan. Japanese. Free. Kokuritsu Idengaku Kenkyujo, 1111 Yata 411, Mishima Japan. **Tel** 0559-75-0771. **Circ:** 500.

II
NLM W1; LI4066

LIFE SCIENCE ADVANCES. MOLECULAR GENETICS : A JOURNAL OF THE COUNCIL OF SCIENTIFIC RESEARCH INTEGRATION. **VFOAT** Molecular Genetics; Molecular Genetics - Life Science Advances. Periodical. English. $30.00 (individuals), $60.00 (institutions). Compilers International, 1/25 Nagwa Lanka, Varanasi 221 005 India. ***Continues in part*** *Life Science Advances, 0255-6642.*

ISSN 1078-1501
US
CCC
TITLE CHANGE

METHODS. GENOMETHODS. **VFOAT** GenoMethods; Geno Methods. (1995)-(1995). Periodical. English. Academic Press Inc., 6277 Sea Harbor Drive, Orlando FL 32887. **Tel** (800)543-9534, (407)345-4100, FAX (407)352-3445. **(Subscription address:** Academic Press Inc., PO Box 620000, Orlando FL 32891-8340. **Tel** (800)543-9534.) ***Continues*** *GenoMethods, 1076-559X.* ***Merged into*** *Methods, 1046-2023.*

ISSN 1056-4497
US

MODERN GENETICS. (1992)-. English. Harwood Academic Publishers / New York, PO Box 786, Cooper Station, New York NY 10276. **Tel** (212)206-8900, (201)643-7500.

LC QH431 .M552 ISSN 0026-8925
DD 575.1/05 GW
CCC
NLM W1 MO195 CODEN MGGEAE
Pr Rev.

MOLECULAR & GENERAL GENETICS : MGG. [MGG, Mol. gen. genet.]. **VFOAT** MGG. **VAT** Molecular and General Genetics. Vol. 99, No. 1 (1967)-. Academic Scholarly Publication. English (French and German; summaries and/or abstracts in French, German and English). Twenty-four times a year. $3232.00. Springer-Verlag GmbH & Company KG, Heidelberger Platz 3, D-14197 Berlin Germany. **Tel** 011 49 30 8207223, FAX 011 49 30 8214091, telex 183 319 SPBLN D. **(Subscription address:** Springer-Verlag New York Inc. / North America, PO Box 2485, Journal Fulfillment, Secaucus NJ 07096. **Tel** (201)348-4033, (800)777-4643, FAX (201)348-4505.) **ED** H Saedler and H Bohme. available on microfilm and microfiche from University Microfilms International (UMI). Documents available from The Genuine Article, BIOSIS Document Express, CASDDS, Documents on Demand, ADONIS. ***Continues*** *Zeitschrift fur Vererbungslehre, 0372-8609.*
Desc: Covers molecular and general genetics in modern botany and zoology, biotechnology and genetic engineering, molecular biology, biochemistry, biophysics, developmental physiology, virology and microbiology.
Ind/Abst ADONIS; AgBiotech News Inf.; AGRICOLA [Select. Cov.]; Biocont. News Inf. (19??-19??); Biol. Agric. Index; Biol. Abstr.; Chem. Abstr.; Crop Physiol. Abstr.; Curr. Aware. Biol. Sci., CABS; Curr. Biotechnol.; Curr. Cit.; Curr. Contents Life Sci.; Dairy Sci. Abstr.; EMBASE; Energy Inf. Abstr.; Energy Res. Abstr.; Entomol. Abstr.; Environ. Abstr.; Food Sci. Technol. Abstr.; Genet. Abstr.; Hortic. Abstr.; Index Med.; Int. Aerosp. Abstr. (1983-); Maize Abstr.; Microbiol. Abstr. Sect. B; Nucl. Sci. Abstr.; Nucl. Acids Abstr.; Ornamental Hort. (1991-); Life Sci. Collect.; PESTDOC; Plant Breed. Abstr.; Plant Genet. Resour. Abstr.; Postharvest News Inf.; Potato Abstr.; Ref. Upd. Basic Ed.; Ref. Upd. Deluxe Ed.; Res. Alert [Full Cov.]; Rev. Agric. Entomol.; Rev. Med. Vet. Entomol.; Rev. Med. Vet. Mycology; Rev. Plant Pathol.; Sci. Cit. Index; SCISEARCH; Seed Abstr.; Soils Fert.; Soyabean Abstr.; Virol. AIDS Abstr.; Weed Abstr.

LC RB155 .M627 ISSN 1057-2805
DD 616/.042 US
NLM W1; MO196GP CODEN MGMEEE
TITLE CHANGE

MOLECULAR GENETIC MEDICINE. [Mol. genet. med.]. (1991)-(199?). Academic Scholarly Publication. English. Academic Press Inc., 6277 Sea Harbor Drive, Orlando FL 32887. **Tel** (800)543-9534, (407)345-4100, FAX (407)352-3445. ***Absorbed by*** *Advances in Genetics, 0065-2660.*
Ind/Abst Index Med. (1991-).

LC QH506 .M683 ISSN 0891-4168
DD 575/.05 US
CCC
NLM W1; MO196H

MOLECULAR GENETICS, MICROBIOLOGY AND VIROLOGY. **See** Biology-Microbiology.

LC QH367.5 .M65 ISSN 1055-7903
DD 575 US
CCC
NLM W1; MO197G CODEN MPEVEK

MOLECULAR PHYLOGENETICS AND EVOLUTION. [Mol. phylogenet. evol.]. Vol. 1, No. 1 (Mar. 1992)-. Academic Scholarly Publication. English. Six times a year. $222.00. Academic Press Inc., 6277 Sea Harbor Drive, Orlando FL 32887. **Tel** (800)543-9534, (407)345-4100, FAX (407)352-3445. **ED** Morris Goodman. Documents available from CASDDS.
Desc: Publishes high quality papers that result from or encourage the collaboration of molecular biologists and computer scientists with the community of systematic and evolutionary biologists.
Ind/Abst Chem. Abstr.; Index Med.

LC QR74 .M66 ISSN 0208-0613
RU
CODEN MGMVDU

MOLEKULIARNAIA GENETIKA, MIKROBIOLOGIIA I VIRUSOLOGIIA. **See** Biology-Microbiology.

LC QH431 .M5532 ISSN 0136-491X
UN
CODEN MGBID4

MOLEKULJARNAJA GENETIKA I BIOFIZIKA. (MOLEKULIARNAIA GENETIKA I BIOFIZIKA.). [Mol. genet. biofiz.]. **Added/Corp** Kyivskyi Derzhavnyi Universytet Im. T. H. Shevchenka. Vol. 1 (1976)-. Academic Scholarly Publication. Russian. Izdatelstvo Vysshaia Shkola Kiev, Kreshchatik 4, 252001 Kiev-1 Ukraine. Documents available from CASDDS.
Ind/Abst Chem. Abstr.

LC QH431 .M554 ISSN 0077-0876
SZ
CCC
NLM W1 MO567P CODEN MOHGAD

MONOGRAPHS IN HUMAN GENETICS. **VFOAT** Monographs in Genetics. Vol. 1 (1966)-. Monographic series. English. One time a year. 180.00F (approx. per volume). S. Karger AG, Allschwilerstrasse 10, PO Box, CH-4009 Basel Switzerland. **Tel** 011 41 61 3061111, FAX 011 41 61 3061234, telex CH 962 652. **ED** J. Ott. Documents available from BIOSIS Document Express, CASDDS.
Desc: Volumes in this series perform the important function of making the results of sophisticated genetic studies intelligible to the general medical community. Focused on problems relevant to human health, individual volumes have succeeded in collecting and interpreting information which both interests the specialist and instructs the newcomer who has no prior training in this field.
Ind/Abst Biol. Abstr.; Chem. Abstr.; Ref. Upd. Deluxe Ed.

LC QH426 ISSN 0341-5376
DD 575.1 GW
NLM W1 MO573N

MONOGRAPHS ON THEORETICAL AND APPLIED GENETICS. [Monogr. theor. appl. genet.]. **VFOAT** Theoretical and Applied Genetics. (1975)-. Monographic series. English. Irregular. Price varies per volume. Society of Hospital Pharmacists of Australia, 31 Coventry Street, Suite 2, South Melbourne Victoria 3205 Australia. **Tel** 61 3 6906733, FAX 61 3 6967634. **ED** HF Linskens. **Bk Rev.**
Desc: Covers genetic fundamentals of plant and animal breeding, physiological fundamentals of plant and animal breeding and the application of cell genetics to breeding.
Ind/Abst AGRICOLA [Select. Cov.]; EMBASE.

LC QH465.A1 M873 ISSN 0267-8357
DD 575.2/92/05 UK
CCC
NLM W1; MU972M CODEN MUTAEX
Pr Rev.

MUTAGENESIS. [Mutagenesis]. **Added/Corp** United Kingdom Environmental Mutagen Society. Vol. 1, No. 1 (Jan. 1986)-. Academic Scholarly Publication. English. Six times a year. $345.00. Oxford University Press / UK, Walton Street, Oxford OX2 6DP United Kingdom. **Tel** 011 44 1865 56767, FAX 011 44 1865 267773, telex 851/837330 OXPRES G. **(Subscription address:** Oxford University Press / USA, Journals Marketing Department, Oxford University Press, 2001 Evans Road, Cary NC 27513. **Tel** (800)451-7556, (919)677-0977, FAX (919)677-1714.) **ED** J. M. Parry and J. A. Heddle. **Bk Rev.** available on microfilm and microfiche from University Microfilms International (UMI). Documents available from The Genuine Article, BIOSIS Document Express, CASDDS.
Desc: Original papers covering studies on the induction of point, chromosomal and genomic mutations; papers on guidelines for mutagenicity testing of environmental agents; the results and conclusions of mutagenicity testing programs; letters to the editor on current topics in practical theoretical and social areas of mutational change; reviews of topics covering all aspects of mutagenic change; and book reviews.
Ind/Abst Biol. Abstr. (1986-); Chem. Abstr. (1986-); Curr. Aware. Biol. Sci., CABS; Curr. Cit.; Curr. Contents Life Sci.; EMBASE; Genet. Abstr.; Index Med. Vol. 1, No. 1, 1986-; Index Vet.; Nutr. Abstr. Rev., Ser. A, Hum. Exp.; Nutr. Res. Newsl.; Pollut. Abstr. Indexes; Ref. Upd. Deluxe Ed.; Res. Alert [Full Cov.]; Rev. Agric. Entomol.; Rev. Med. Vet. Entomol.; Sci. Cit. Index; SCISEARCH; Vet. Bull.; Vitis Vitic. Enol. Abstr.; Weed Abstr.

ISSN 0921-8734
NE
CCC
CODEN MUREAV
Pr Rev.

MUTATION RESEARCH. DNAGING : GENETIC INSTABILITY AND AGING. [Mutat. res., DNAging : genet. instab. aging]. **VFOAT** DNAging; DNA Aging. Vol. 219, No. 1 (Jan. 1989)-. Academic Scholarly Publication. English. Six times a year (1 volume). $233.00. Elsevier Science Publishers BV, PO Box 211, 1000 AE Amsterdam Netherlands. **Tel** 011 31 20 4853641, 011 31 20 4853642, FAX 011 31 20 4853598. available on microfilm from University Microfilms International (UMI); available on an online database from Elsevier Electronic Subscriptions (EES). Documents available from ADONIS.
Ind/Abst ADONIS; Anim. Breed. Abstr.; Curr. Aware. Biol. Sci., CABS; EMBASE; Ref. Upd. Basic Ed.; Ref. Upd. Deluxe Ed.; Rev. Med. Vet. Entomol.

NE
Pr Rev.

MUTATION RESEARCH. ENVIRONMENTAL MUTAGENESIS AND RELATED SUBJECTS. **VFOAT** Environmental Mutagenesis and Related Subjects; Environmental Mutagenesis and Related Subjects Including Methodology. Vol. 130, No. 1 (Feb. 1984)-. Academic Scholarly Publication. English. Nine times a year (2 volumes). Fl884.00; Fl9499.00 combined subscription including all sections of Mutation Research. Elsevier Science Publishers BV, PO Box 211, 1000 AE

Amsterdam Netherlands. **Tel** 011 31 20 4853641, 011 31 20 4853642, FAX 011 31 20 4853598. available on an online database from Elsevier Electronic Subscriptions (EES). Documents available from ADONIS. ***Continues*** *Mutation Research. Section on Environmental Mutagenesis and Related Subjects, 0165-1161.*
Ind/Abst ADONIS; Anim. Breed. Abstr.; Curr. Aware. Biol. Sci., CABS; EMBASE; Index Med.; Ref. Upd. Basic Ed.; Ref. Upd. Deluxe Ed.; Rev. Med. Vet. Mycology.

NE

MUTATION RESEARCH. GENETIC TOXICOLOGY. (19??)-. Academic Scholarly Publication. English. Twenty times a year (5 vols.). Fl2210.00. Elsevier Science Publishers BV, PO Box 211, 1000 AE Amsterdam Netherlands. **Tel** 011 31 20 4853641, 011 31 20 4853642, FAX 011 31 20 4853598. available on an online database from Elsevier Electronic Subscriptions (EES). ***Continues*** *Mutation Research. Genetic Toxicology Testing.*

ISSN 0165-7992
NE
CCC
NLM W1 MU973 **CODEN** MUREAVMRLEDH

MUTATION RESEARCH. MUTATION RESEARCH LETTERS. **VFOAT** Mutation Research Letters. Vol. 91 No. 1 (Jan. 1981)-. Academic Scholarly Publication. English. Twelve times a year (3 vols.). Fl1326.00; Fl9499.00 combined subscription with Mutation Research/DNAging, Mutation Research/DNA Repair, Mutation Research/Environmental Mutagenesis and Related Subjects Including Methodology, Mutation Research/Genetic Toxicology Testing, and Mutation Research/Reviews in Genetic Toxicology. Elsevier Science Publishers BV, PO Box 211, 1000 AE Amsterdam Netherlands. **Tel** 011 31 20 4853641, 011 31 20 4853642, FAX 011 31 20 4853598. available on microfilm from University Microfilms International (UMI); available on an online database from Elsevier Electronic Subscriptions (EES). Documents available from ADONIS. ***Continues*** *Mutation Research, 0027-5107.*
Ind/Abst ADONIS; Anim. Breed. Abstr.; Crop Physiol. Abstr.; Curr. Aware. Biol. Sci., CABS; EMBASE; Field Crop Abstr.; Food Sci. Technol. Abstr.; Index Med.; Maize Abstr.; Nutr. Abstr. Rev., Ser. B, Live Feeds and Feed.; Nutr. Abstr. Rev., Ser. A, Hum. Exp.; Protozoolog. Abstr.; Ref. Upd. Basic Ed.; Ref. Upd. Deluxe Ed.; Rev. Med. Vet. Mycology; Seed Abstr.; Sug. Indus. Abstr.

ISSN 0165-1110
NE
CCC
NLM W1 MU973 **CODEN** MRRTEP
Pr Rev.

MUTATION RESEARCH. REVIEWS IN GENETIC TOXICOLOGY. **See** Toxicology.

LC QH431 .N363 **ISSN** 1061-4036
DD 573.2/1
US
CCC
NLM W1; NA812J **CODEN** NGENEC

NATURE GENETICS. [Nat. genet.]. **VFOAT** Genetics. Vol. 1, No. 1 (Apr. 1992)-. Academic Scholarly Publication. English. Twelve times a year. $495.00. Nature Publishing Company, 65 Bleecker Street, 12th Floor, New York NY 10012. **Tel** (212)477-9600, (800)524-0328, FAX (212)477-8020. **(Subscription address:** Nature Genetics Order Department, PO Box 7620, Riverton NJ 08077-7620. **Tel** (800)524-0384.) **Ad Acc**. Documents available from The Genuine Article, CASDDS. ***Separated from*** *Nature (London, England), 0028-0836.*
Desc: Reporting the latest findings in human genetics with a broad spectrum of papers on gene mapping, linkage analysis, candidate genes, positional cloning of important chromosomal regions, clinical genetics, aspects of developmental biology, imprinting and gene therapy.
Ind/Abst AGRICOLA; Chem. Abstr.; Curr. Aware. Biol. Sci., CABS; Curr. Contents Life Sci.; Index Med.; Ref. Upd. Basic Ed.; Ref. Upd. Deluxe Ed.; Res. Alert [Full Cov.]; Sci. Cit. Index; Soc. Sci. Cit. Index [Select. Cov.].

LC SB **ISSN** 0374-9525
DD 630
RU
UDC 631.52

NAUCNO-TEHNICESKIJ BULLETEN' VSESOUZNOGO SELEKCIONNO-GENETICESKOGO INSTITUTA. **See** Biology-Botany.

II

NBPGR ANNUAL REPORT. **Added/Corp** National Bureau of Plant Genetic Resources. **VFOAT** Annual Report. **VAT** National Bureau of Plant Genetic Resources Annual Report. (19??)-. Periodical. English.

LC QP624.5.D73 N54
US

NIH REPOSITORY OF HUMAN AND MOUSE DNA PROBES AND LIBRARIES / AMERICAN TYPE CULTURE COLLECTION. **Added/Corp** American Type Culture Collection. National Institutes of Health (U.S.). **VFOAT** National Institutes of Health Repository of Human and Mouse DNA Probes and Libraries; ATCC/NIH Repository of Human and Mouse DNA Probes and Libraries. (198?)-. English. American Type Culture Collection, 12301 Parklawn Drive, Rockville MD 20852. **Tel** (301)881-2600, FAX (301)231-5826, telex 898-055. ***Continues*** *NIH Repository of Human DNA Probes and Libraries.*

ISSN 0950-0561
UK

ONCOGENES. (19??)-. English. Twenty-six times a year. £115.00. SUBIS, Mansion House 19 Kingfield Road, Sheffield S11 9AS United Kingdom. **Tel** 011 44 114 2554433, FAX 011 44 114 255 4626. **Bk Rev. Ad Acc.**
Desc: Current awareness service for researchers in clinical and life sciences.

NE
NLM W1; OP217M

●**OPHTHALMIC GENETICS.** **Added/Corp** International Society for Genetic Eye Disease. Ophthalmic Genetics Study Club. International Society of Paediatric Ophthalmology. Vol. 15, No. 1 (Mar. 1994)-. Periodical. English. Four times a year. $225.00. Aeolus Press, PO Box 740, 4116 ZJ Buren The Netherlands. **Tel** 011 31 34472055, FAX 011 31 34472562. ***Continues*** *Ophthalmic Paediatrics and Genetics, 0167-6784.*
Ind/Abst Curr. Cit.; Index Med. (1994-).

UK

OXFORD MONOGRAPHS ON MEDICAL GENETICS. (1966)-. Monographic series. English. Irregular. Price varies per volume. Oxford University Press / UK, Walton Street, Oxford OX2 6DP United Kingdom. **Tel** 011 44 1865 56767, FAX 011 44 1865 267773, telex 851/837330 OXPRES G. **(Subscription address:** Oxford University Press / USA, Journals Marketing Department, Oxford University Press, 2001 Evans Road, Cary NC 27513. **Tel** (800)451-7556, (919)677-0977, FAX (919)677-1714.) **ED** Martin Bobrow, Peter S. Harper, Arno G. Motulsky, Charles Scriver.

ISSN 1146-5549
FR
NLM ZQ 1; P927793

PASCAL. 68, GENETIQUE HUMAINE. **Added/Corp** Institut de l'Information Scientifique et Technique (France). **VFOAT** Genetique Humaine; Human Genetics. No. 1 (1991)-. Periodical. English (French). Ten times a year (plus cumulative index). 705.00F France; 745.00F other. CNRS / Institut d'Information Scientifique et Technique, (Centre National de la Recherche Scientifique), 15 Quai Anatole France, 75700 Paris France. **Tel** 011 33 1 47531515, FAX 011 33 1 45517307, telex 260034. **(Subscription address:** Institut d'Information Scientifique et Technique Diffusion, 2 Allee du Parc de Brabois, 54514 Vandoeuvre Nancy France. **Tel** 011 33 83 504664, FAX 011 33 83 504666, telex 961942.) Index available. cum. index. ***Continues*** *PASCAL. E68, Genetique Humaine.*

ISSN 1146-5484
FR
UDC 011

PASCAL. E 58, GENETIQUE. **VFOAT** PASCAL. E 58, Genetics; PASCAL. E Cinquante-Huit, Genetique. (1990)-. Periodical. Multiple languages. Eleven times a year (10 monthly issues and cumulative index). 970.00F France; 1,025.00F other. CNRS / Institut d'Information Scientifique et Technique, (Centre National de la Recherche Scientifique), 15 Quai Anatole France, 75700 Paris France. **Tel** 011 33 1 47531515, FAX 011 33 1 45517307, telex 260034. **(Subscription address:** Institut d'Information Scientifique et Technique Diffusion, 2 Allee du Parc de Brabois, 54514 Vandoeuvre Nancy France. **Tel** 011 33 83 504664, FAX 011 33 83 504666, telex 961942.) Index available. cum. index.

ISSN 0960-314X
UK
CCC
NLM W1; PH272QH

PHARMACOGENETICS. **See** Pharmacy and Pharmacology.

AT

PISUM GENETICS. (19??)-. English. One time a year. $20.00. University of Tasmania Plant Science Department, Box 252C, Hobart Tasmania 7001 Australia. ***Continues*** *Pisum Newsletter.*

US
TITLE CHANGE

PISUM NEWSLETTER, THE. **Added/Corp** New York (State). Agricultural Experiment Station, Geneva. Vol. 1 (1969)-(19??). Newsletter. English. Pisum Genetics Association, New York State Agriculture Experiment Station, Geneva NY 14456. **Tel** (315)787-2218. **ED** G. A. Marx. **Circ:** 200. ***Continued by*** *Pisum Genetics.*
Desc: Genetics of Pisum.

ISSN 0167-4412
NE
CCC
NLM W1; PL105NG **CODEN** PMBIDB
Pr Rev.

PLANT MOLECULAR BIOLOGY. [Plant mol. biol.]. **Added/Corp** International Society for Plant Molecular Biology. Vol. 1, No. 1 (1981)-. Academic Scholarly Publication. English. Eighteen times a year. $1685.00. Kluwer Academic Publishers, Postbus 322, 3300 AH Dordrecht The Netherlands. **Tel** 011 31 78 524400, FAX 011 31 78 183273, telex 20083. **ED** R A Schilperoort. **Ad Acc. Acid Free. Circ:** 750. available on microfilm and microfiche from University Microfilms International (UMI). Documents available from The Genuine Article, BIOSIS Document Express, CASDDS.
Desc: Covers research and genetic engineering; provides a rapid publication outlet for all types of research concerned and connected with plant molecular biology and plant molecular genetics. There are three sections included in each issue: update, plant molecular biology news and views, and sequence announcements.
Ind/Abst AgBiotech News Inf.; AGRICOLA [Full Cov.]; Biol. Abstr.; Biotechnol. Res. Abstr.; Chem. Abstr.; Chem. Titles; Cot. Trop. Fibr. Abstr. Bibliogr.; Crop Physiol. Abstr.; Curr. Aware. Biol. Sci., CABS; Curr. Biotechnol.; Curr. Cit.; Curr. Contents Agric. Biol. Environ. Sci.; Curr. Contents Life Sci.; Field Crop Abstr.; Food Sci. Technol. Abstr.; For. Abstr.; Genet. Abstr. Health Plan. Adminis.; Hortic. Abstr.; Index Med. (Jan. 1989-); Maize Abstr.; Microbiol. Abstr. Sect. B (19??-19??); Microbiol. Abstr. Sect. C; Nat. Prod. Updates; Nucl. Acids Abstr.; Oncog. Growth Factors Abstr.; Ornamental Hort. (19??-19??); PESTDOC; Plant Breed. Abstr.; Plant Genet. Resour. Abstr.; Plant Grow. Reg. Abstr.; Postharvest News Inf.; Potato Abstr.; Ref. Upd. Basic Ed.; Ref. Upd. Deluxe Ed.; Res. Alert [Full Cov.]; Rev. Plant Pathol.; Rice Abstr.; Sci. Cit. Index; SCISEARCH; Seed Abstr.; Soils Fert.; Sorghum Mill. Abstr.; Soyabean Abstr.; Virol. AIDS Abstr.; Vitis Vitic. Enol. Abstr.; Weed Abstr.; Wheat Barley Trit. Abstr.

ISSN 1057-2600
DD 581
US
NLM W1; PR551PT

PROBE (BELTSVILLE, MD.). **See** Biology-Botany.

LC RG136.6 **ISSN** 0277-3155
DD 613.94
UK

PROCEEDINGS OF THE ANNUAL SYMPOSIUM OF THE EUGENICS SOCIETY. [Proc. annu. symp. Eugen. Soc.]. **Added/Corp** Eugenics Society (London, England). (19??)-. Proceedings. English. One time a year. Academic Press Ltd., A Division of Harcourt Brace & Company Ltd., 24-28 Oval Road, London NW1 7DX United Kingdom. **Tel** 011 44 171 2674466, FAX 011 44 171 4822293, 011 44 171 4854752, telex 25775 ACPRES G. ***Continues*** *Eugenics Society Symposia.*
Ind/Abst Index Med.

LC RB155 .P698 **ISSN** 0733-124X
DD 616/.042/05
US
NLM W1 PR585IG

PROCEEDINGS OF THE GREENWOOD GENETIC CENTER. [Proc. Greenwood Genet. Cent.]. **Added/Corp** Greenwood Genetic Center. Vol. 1 (1982)-. Proceedings. English. One time a year. Price varies per volume. Greenwood Genetic Center, 1 Gregor Mendel Circle, Greenwood SC 29646. **Tel** (803)223-9411. **ED** R. Saul M.D. & Mary C. Phelan M.D. Index available. cum. index. ctrl circ.
Desc: Case reports of clinical genetics cases.

LC Q334 .I556
US

PROCEEDINGS OF THE ... INTERNATIONAL CONFERENCE ON GENETIC ALGORITHMS. **VFOAT** Genetic Algorithms. (1989)-. Proceedings. English. Every 2 years. Morgan Kaufmann Publishers, 340 Pine Street, 6th Floor, San Francisco CA 94014. **Tel** (415)578-9911, (800)745-7323. ***Continues*** *International Conference on Genetic Algorithms. Genetic Algorithms and Their Applications.*

ISSN 0731-2849
DD 575.2/92/05
US
CCC
NLM W1 PR6719M **CODEN** PMRSDJ
Pr Rev.

PROGRESS IN MUTATION RESEARCH. [Progr. mutat. res.]. Vol. 1 (1981)-. Academic Scholarly Publication. English. Irregular. Price varies per volume. Elsevier Science Publishing Company Inc, Madison Square Station, PO Box 882, New York NY 10159-0882. **Tel** (212)633-3990, FAX (212)633-3990. **(Subscription address:** Elsevier Science Inc. / New York Books, 655 Avenue of the Americas, New York NY 10010. **Tel** (212)633-3650.) Documents available from CASDDS.
Ind/Abst Chem. Abstr.

LC QP551 .P695818 **ISSN** 1046-5928
DD 574.19/245
US
CCC
NLM W1; PR787T **CODEN** PEXPEJ

PROTEIN EXPRESSION AND PURIFICATION. [Protein expr. purif.]. Vol. 1, No. 1 (Sept. 1990)-. Academic Scholarly Publication. English. Eight times a year. $225.00. Academic Press Inc., 6277 Sea Harbor Drive, Orlando FL 32887. **Tel** (800)543-9534, (407)345-4100, FAX (407)352-3445. Documents available from The Genuine Article, BIOSIS Document Express, CASDDS.

Desc: Reports novel or significantly improved procedures for the isolation of protein in highly purified form, proteins from genetically engineered sources and molecular biological methods for the over expression of specific proteins.
Ind/Abst Biol. Abstr. (1990-); Chem. Abstr. (1990-); Curr. Aware. Biol. Sci., CABS; Curr. Cit.; Curr. Contents Life Sci.; Food Sci. Technol. Abstr.; Index Med. (Sept. 1990-); Res. Alert [Full Cov.]; Sci. Cit. Index.

ISSN 0955-8829
UK
CCC
NLM W1; PS256T **CODEN** PSGEEX
PSYCHIATRIC GENETICS. Vol. 1 (1990)-. Periodical. English. Four times a year. $287.00. Rapid Science Publishers, The Old Malthouse, Paradise Street, Oxford OX1 1LD United Kingdom. **Tel** 011 44 1865 790447, FAX 011 44 1865 244012, telex 9403712. **Ad Acc. Acid Free.** Documents available from The Genuine Article.
Desc: Forum for novel approaches using new technologies better to understand the normal and abnormal brain; charges in neuronal gene expression during development or induced in vitro by psychotropic drugs; gene localization and chromosome markers; linkage genetics- all related to or complemented by reports of a clinical nature where genetic factors have a role: family/pedigree, twin, adoption, high risk studies, variant behavior, diseases of the CNS with genetic component.
Ind/Abst Index Med.; Res. Alert [Full Cov.]; Soc. Sci. Cit. Index [Select. Cov.].

ISSN 0261-4979
DD 016.574873282 UK
CCC
CEASED
RECOMBINANT DNA. [Recomb. DNA]. **VFOAT** Recombinant Deoxyribonucleic Acid. (1982)-(Dec. 1993). English. SUBIS, Mansion House 19 Kingfield Road, Sheffield S11 9AS United Kingdom. **Tel** 011 44 114 2554433, FAX 011 44 114 255 4626. **Bk Rev. Ad Acc.**
Desc: Current awareness service for researchers and clinicians.

US
RECOMBINANT DNA MATERIALS LISTING. (19??)-. English. American Type Culture Collection, 12301 Parklawn Drive, Rockville MD 20852. **Tel** (301)881-2600, FAX (301)231-5826, telex 898-055.

ISSN 0148-480X
US
NLM W2 A N206RB
RECOMBINANT DNA RESEARCH. **Added/Corp** National Institutes of Health (U.S.). Office of Recombinant DNA Activities. National Institutes of Health (U.S.). Office of the Director. **VAT** Recombinant Deoxyribonucleic Acid Research. (June 1976)-. English. Irregular. Free on request. Office Recombinant DNA Activities, NIH Building 31 4B11, 90 Rockville Pike, Bethesda MD 20892. **Tel** (301)496-9838.

LC QH431.A1 K6 **ISSN** 0077-4995
JA
REPORT OF THE NATIONAL INSTITUTE OF GENETICS. **Main/Corp** Kokuritsu Idengaku Kenkyujo (Japan). (1950)-. English. One time a year. National Institute of Genetics, 1111 Yata, Mishima-shi, Shizuoka-ken 411 Japan.
Ind/Abst Anim. Breed. Abstr.; Life Sci. Collect.

ISSN 0100-8455
BL
NLM W1 RE326 **CODEN** RBGED3
Pr Rev.
REVISTA BRASILEIRA DE GENETICA. [Rev. Bras. genet.]. **Added/Corp** Sociedade Brasileira de Genetica. **VFOAT** Brazilian Journal of Genetics. Vol. 1, (1978)-. Academic Scholarly Publication. English (Portuguese). Four times a year (Mar., June, Sept., Dec.). $90.00. Sociedade Brasileira Genetica, Fac Medicina Riberiraopreto, 14049 Ribeirao Preto SP Brazil. **Tel** 011 55 16 6331610, FAX 011 55 55 16 6231039, telex 166354. **ED** Francisco A. Moura Duarte. Index available. cum. index. **Bk Rev. Ad Acc. Circ:** 2,000 (ctrl). Documents available from The Genuine Article, BIOSIS Document Express, CASDDS.
Desc: Scientific papers in the general area of genetics and evolution.
Ind/Abst AgBiotech News Inf.; Anim. Breed. Abstr.; Biocont. News Inf. (1991-); Biol. Abstr.; Chem. Abstr.; Curr. Aware. Biol. Sci., CABS; Curr. Cit.; Curr. Contents Life Sci.; Dairy Sci. Abstr.; EMBASE; Energy Res. Abstr. (Feb. 1981-); Maize Abstr.; Life Sci. Collect.; PESTDOC; Pig News Inf.; Plant Breed. Abstr.; Plant Genet. Resour. Abstr.; Poult. Abstr.; Protozoolog. Abstr.; Refer. Z.; Res. Alert [Select. Cov.]; Rev. Med. Vet. Entomol.; Seed Abstr.; Soyabean Abstr.

ISSN 0952-0414
UK
CCC
RIBOSOMES & TRANSLATION. [Ribos. transl.]. **VFOAT** Ribosomes and Translation. (1988)-. Periodical. English. Twenty-four times a year. $145.45. SUBIS, Mansion House 19 Kingfield Road, Sheffield S11 9AS United Kingdom. **Tel** 011 44 114 2554433, FAX 011 44 114 255 4626. **Bk Rev. Ad Acc.** ***Continues*** *Ribosomes (Sheffield), 0142-8322.*
Desc: Current awareness service for researchers and clinicians.

LC QH426 **ISSN** 1355-8382
DD 575.1 US
CCC
Pr Rev.
•RNA. THE OFFICIAL PUBLICATION OF THE RNA SOCIETY. (March 1995)-. Academic Scholarly Publication. English. Twelve times a year. $360.00. Cambridge University Press, The Edinburgh Building, Shaftesbury Road, Cambridge CB2 2RU United Kingdom. **Tel** 011 44 1223 312393, FAX 011 44 1223 315052, telex 851-817256. **(Subscription address:** Cambridge University Press, Journals Department, 40 West 20th Street, New York NY 10011. **Tel** (212)924-3900, FAX (212)691-3239.) **ED** Timothy W. Nilsen. **Bk Rev. Ad Acc.** Documents available from BLDSC, CASDDS.
Desc: Covers research in all areas of RNA structure and function in eukaryotic, prokaryotic and viral systems. Also covers areas such as mRNA structure, function and biogenesis, and alternative processing.

LC QH431 .S677 **ISSN** 1022-7954
RU
CCC
NLM W1; GE299G **CODEN** RJGEEQ
•RUSSIAN JOURNAL OF GENETICS. [Russ. j. genet.]. Vol. 30, No. 1 (Jan. 1994)-. Periodical. English (translations available in Russian). Twelve times a year. $1375.00. Consultants Bureau, A Division of Plenum Publishing Corporation, 233 Spring Street, New York NY 10013. **Tel** (212)620-8000, (212)620-8466, FAX (212)463-0742, telex 23/421139. ***Continues*** *Soviet Genetics, 0038-5409.*

LC QH426
DD 575.1 RU
SBORNIK NAUCHNYKH TRUDOV (VSESOIUZNYI). (SBORNIK NAUCHNYKH TRUDOV.). **Added/Corp** Soviet Union. Ministerstvo Selskogo Khoziaistva. Vsesoiuznyi Selektsionno-Geneticheskii Institut. (19??)-. Monographic series. Russian. Price varies per volume. ***Continues*** *Nauchnye Trudy / Vsesoiuznyi Selektsionno-Geneticheskii Institut.*

LC QH359 .S44a
DD 575/.005 IT
SEMINARIO SULLA EVOLUZIONE BIOLOGICA E I GRANDI PROBLEMI DELLA BIOLOGIA : [ATTI]. **Added/Corp** Accademia Nazionale dei Lincei. (Feb. 28/29/March 10, 1980)-. Italian. One time a year. Price varies. Accademia Nazionale dei Lincei, Via Lungara 10 Uff Diff Pubbl., 00165 Rome Italy. **Tel** 011 39 6 6838831. **Circ:** 800. ***Continues*** *Seminario Sulla Evoluzione Biologica. Seminario Sulla Evoluzione Biologica : [Atti].*
Desc: Publication of the proceedings of the annual meetings organized by the Centro Linceo Interdisciplinare Beniamino Segre in the Accademia Nazionale Dei Lincei.

ISSN 0385-4655
JA
NLM W1 SE62 **CODEN** SNSHBT
SENSHOKU-TAI. **Added/Corp** Sensyokutai-Gakkai. Zaidanhozin Sensyokutai-Gakkai. **VFOAT** Kromosomo. (Sept. 1946)-. Academic Scholarly Publication. English (Japanese). Four times a year. $100.00. Senshokutai Gakkai, (Society of Chromosome Research), c/o Shinka Seibutsugaku Kenkyujo, 2-4 Kamiyoga, Setagayaku Tokyo 158 Japan. **(Subscription address:** Japan Publications Trading Company Ltd., PO Box 5030, Tokyo International, Tokyo 100-31 Japan. **Tel** 011 81 3 3292 3753.) cum. index. ctrl circ. Documents available from BIOSIS Document Express, CASDDS.
Desc: Includes original contributions on a specific subject in the related fields of chromosomics.
Ind/Abst AGRICOLA; Biol. Abstr.; Chem. Abstr.; Life Sci. Collect.

LC QH426 **ISSN** 1100-3456
DD 575.1 SW
UDC 575
SKRIFTER - NORDISKA GENBANKEN. (SKRIFTER.). [Skr. - Nord. genbanken]. **VFOAT** Publications - Nordic Gene Bank. (1989)-. Monographic series. English. Irregular. Price varies per volume.
Ind/Abst Seed Abstr.

LC QH426 .S64 **ISSN** 0740-7750
DD 599/.0873223 US
CCC
NLM W1; SO887JK **CODEN** SCMGDN
Pr Rev.
SOMATIC CELL AND MOLECULAR GENETICS. [Somat. cell mol. genet.]. Vol. 10, No. 1 (Jan. 1984)-. Academic Scholarly Publication. English. Six times a year. $485.00 (institutions), $87.00 (individuals) US; $565.00 (institutions), $102.00 (individuals) other. Plenum Press, 233 Spring Street, New York NY 10013-1578. **Tel** (212)620-8000, (800)221-9369, FAX (212)463-0742, (212)807-1047, telex 23/421139. **ED** Richard L. Davidson. Index available. available on microfilm and microfiche from University Microfilms International (UMI). Documents available from The Genuine Article, CASDDS. ***Continues*** *Somatic Cell Genetics, 0098-0366.*
Desc: Publishes reports on original research in the fields of somatic cell genetics and molecular genetics of higher systems. Primary emphasis is on studies with animal or plant cells in gene expression, gene isolation, and genetic recombination.
Ind/Abst AgBiotech News Inf.; Anim. Breed. Abstr.; Chem. Abstr. (1984-); Chem. Titles; Curr. Aware. Biol. Sci., CABS; Curr. Cit.; Curr. Contents Life Sci.; EMBASE; Energy Res. Abstr. (Jan. 1984-); Genet. Abstr.; Hum. Genome Abstr.; Index Med.; Nucl. Acids Abstr.; Life Sci. Collect.; PESTDOC; Ref. Upd. Basic Ed.; Ref. Upd. Deluxe Ed.; Res. Alert [Full Cov.]; Sci. Cit. Index; SCISEARCH.

LC QH431.A1 S7 **ISSN** 0081-4148
DD 575.1/05 US
NLM W3 ST233 **CODEN** SGSYBV
STADLER GENETICS SYMPOSIA. (STADLER GENETICS SYMPOSIA : PROCEEDINGS.). [Stadler genet. symp.]. **Main/Conf** Stadler Genetics Symposium. **Added/Corp** University of Missouri--Columbia. Agricultural Experiment Station. (1971)-. Academic Scholarly Publication. English. Irregular. Price varies per volume. Plenum Press, 233 Spring Street, New York NY 10013-1578. **Tel** (212)620-8000, (800)221-9369, FAX (212)463-0742, (212)807-1047, telex 23/421139. Documents available from BIOSIS Document Express, CASDDS.
Ind/Abst AGRICOLA [Select. Cov.]; Biol. Abstr.; Chem. Abstr.

LC TP248.6 .T42 **ISSN** 0741-3661
DD 660/.6 US
TECHNICAL INSIGHTS ANNUAL REPORT ON GENETIC TECHNOLOGY.
See Biology-Bioengineering.

LC SB123 .Z8 **ISSN** 0040-5752
GW
CCC
NLM W1 T103 **CODEN** THAGA6
Pr Rev.
THEORETICAL AND APPLIED GENETICS. [Theor. appl. genet.]. **VFOAT** TAG; Theoretische und Angewandte Genetik. Vol. 38 (1968)-. Academic Scholarly Publication. English (German). Sixteen times a year. $2982.00. Springer-Verlag GmbH & Company KG, Heidelberger Platz 3, D-14197 Berlin Germany. **Tel** 011 49 30 8207223, FAX 011 49 30 8214091, telex 183 319 SPBLN D. **(Subscription address:** Springer-Verlag New York Inc. / North America, PO Box 2485, Journal Fulfillment, Secaucus NJ 07096. **Tel** (201)348-4033, (800)777-4643, FAX (201)348-4505.) **ED** G Wenzel. Index available in last issue of volume--attached. cum. index. **Bk Rev.** available on microfilm from University Microfilms International (UMI). Documents available from The Genuine Article, BIOSIS Document Express, CASDDS, Documents on Demand. ***Continues*** *Zuchter.*
Desc: Contains original articles in the following areas: genetics fundamentals of plant and animal breeding, physiological fundamentals of plant and animal breeding, application of cell genetics to breeding.
Ind/Abst Abstr. Bull. Inst. Paper Chem.; Abstr. Bull. Inst. Pap. Sci. Tech.; AgBiotech News Inf.; AGRICOLA [Select. Cov.]; Anim. Breed. Abstr.; Biol. Abstr.; Biostatistica (19??-19??); Biotechnol. Res. Abstr.; Chem. Abstr.; Cot. Trop. Fibr. Abstr. Bibliogr.; Crop Physiol. Abstr.; Curr. Aware. Biol. Sci., CABS; Curr. Biotechnol.; Curr. Cit.; Curr. Contents Agric. Biol. Environ. Sci.; Curr. Contents Life Sci.; Dairy Sci. Abstr.; EMBASE; Energy Inf. Abstr.; Energy Res. Abstr.; Environ. Abstr.; Field Crop Abstr.; Fish Rev.; For. Abstr.; Genet. Abstr.; Grass. Forage Abstr.; Hortic. Abstr.; Index Vet.; Irr. Drain. Abstr.; Maize Abstr.; Microbiol. Abstr. Sect. A; Microbiol. Abstr. Sect. C; Nematol. Abstr.; Ornamental Hort. (19??-19??); Life Sci. Collect.; PESTDOC; Pig News Inf.; Plant Breed. Abstr.; Plant Genet. Resour. Abstr.; Plant Grow. Reg. Abstr.; Postharvest News Inf.; Potato Abstr.; Poult. Abstr.; Ref. Upd. Deluxe Ed.; Res. Alert [Full Cov.]; Rev. Agric. Entomol.; Rev. Med. Vet. Entomol.; Rev. Plant Pathol.; Rice Abstr.; Sci. Cit. Index; SCISEARCH; Seed Abstr.; Soils Fert.; Sorghum Mill. Abstr.; Soyabean Abstr.; Vet. Bull.; Weed Abstr.; Wheat Barley Trit. Abstr.

LC QH301 .T5 **ISSN** 0040-5809
DD 575.1 US
CCC
NLM W1 TH12K **CODEN** TLPBAQ
Pr Rev.
THEORETICAL POPULATION BIOLOGY. [Theor. popul. biol.]. Vol. 1 (May 1970)-. Academic Scholarly Publication. English. Six times a year. $422.00. Academic Press Inc., 6277 Sea Harbor Drive, Orlando FL 32887. **Tel** (800)543-9534, (407)345-4100, FAX (407)352-3445. **ED** P. Chesson, K. Dietz, J. Gillespie, S. Karlin and M. Feldman. Documents available from The Genuine Article, BIOSIS Document Express.
Desc: Presents articles on the theoretical aspects of the biology of populations, particularly in the areas of ecology, genetics, demography, and epidemiology. Primary emphasis is on developments of the theory, but also presented are experimental results directly impinging on

the theory.
Ind/Abst AGRICOLA; Anim. Breed. Abstr.; Biocont. News Inf.; Biol. Abstr.; Curr. Aware. Biol. Sci., CABS; Curr. Cit.; Curr. Contents Agric. Biol. Environ. Sci.; Curr. Contents Life Sci.; Ecology Abstr.; For. Abstr.; Genet. Abstr.; Geogr. Abstr. Human Geogr.; Index Med.; Key Word Index Wildl. Res.; Math. Rev.; Life Sci. Collect.; Plant Breed. Abstr.; Plant Genet. Resour. Abstr.; Popul. Index; Res. Alert [Full Cov.]; Rev. Agric. Entomol.; Rev. Med. Vet. Entomol.; Sci. Cit. Index; SCISEARCH; Soc. Sci. Cit. Index [Select. Cov.]; Wildl. Rev.; Zentralbl. Math. Ihre Grenzgeb.

LC QH442.6 **ISSN** 0962-8819
DD 575.1 UK
CCC
NLM W1; TR228WN **CODEN** TRSEES
TRANSGENIC RESEARCH. Vol. 1, No. 1 (Dec. 1991)-. Academic Scholarly Publication. English. Six times a year. $335.00. Chapman & Hall, 2-6 Boundary Row, London SE1 8HN United Kingdom. **Tel** 011 44 171 8650066, FAX 011 44 171 5229623, telex 290164 CHAPMA G. **ED** R. J. Robins, R. Forster, R. A. Dixon, C. A. Pinkert. Documents available from The Genuine Article, CASDDS, ADONIS.
Desc: Publishes studies in animals, plants and fungi in which genetic manipulation has been used to confer on the organism novel metabolic or developmental properties by the insertion of transgenes or by altering the expression of homogenes.
Ind/Abst ADONIS; Chem. Abstr.; Curr. Aware. Biol. Sci., CABS; Curr. Cit.; Curr. Contents Life Sci.; Index Med.; Res. Alert [Full Cov.].

LC QH426 .T74 **ISSN** 0168-9479
DD 575.1/05 NE
CCC
TRENDS IN GENETICS (LIBRARY ED.). (TRENDS IN GENETICS.). [Trends genet.]. **VFOAT** TIG. Vol. 1 (1985)-. Periodical. English. Twelve times a year. $614.00. Elsevier Trends Journals, An Imprint of Elsevier Science Ltd., The Boulevard, Langford Lane, Kidlington, Oxford OX5 1GB United Kingdom. **Tel** 011 44 1865 843000, 011 44 1865 843699, FAX 011 44 1865 843010. **(Subscription address:** Elsevier Science Ltd. / Oxford Fulfillment Centre, PO Box 800, Kidlington OX5 1DX United Kingdom. **Tel** 011 44 865 843355.**)** available on an online database from Elsevier Electronic Subscriptions (EES). Documents available from ADONIS.
Ind/Abst ADONIS; Nucl. Acids Abstr.; Sci. Cit. Index.

LC QH426 .T72 **ISSN** 0168-9525
DD 575.1/05 UK
CCC
NLM W1; TR341C **CODEN** TRGEE2
TRENDS IN GENETICS (PERSONAL ED.). (TRENDS IN GENETICS.). [Trends genet.]. **VFOAT** TIG. Vol. 1, No. 1 (Jan. 1985)-. Periodical. English. Twelve times a year. $125.00. Elsevier Applied Science, An Imprint of Elsevier Science Ltd., The Boulevard, Langford Lane, Kidlington, Oxford OX5 1GB United Kingdom. **Tel** 011 44 1865 843000, 011 44 1865 843699, FAX 011 44 1865 843010. available on an online database from Elsevier Electronic Subscriptions (EES).
Ind/Abst Bibliogr. Agric.; Biol. Abstr. (1985-); Chem. Abstr. (1985-); Curr. Cit.; Index Med.

ISSN 1080-3033
DD 155 US
•**TWINS FOUNDATION RESEARCH UPDATE, THE.** **See** Psychology.

ISSN 0566-3946
RU
NLM W1 US915 **CODEN** USSGAE
USPEHI SOVREMENNOJ GENETIKI. (USPEKHI SOVREMENNOI GENETIKI.). [Usp. sovrem. genet.]. **Added/Corp** Institut Obshchei Genetiki (Akademiia Nauk SSSR) Nauchnyi Sovet po Problemam Genetiki i Selektsii (Akademiia Nauk SSSR). (1967)-. Academic Scholarly Publication. Russian. Izdatelstvo Nauka / Akademiia Nauk, (Publishing House of the Russian Academy of Sciences), Leninskii Porspekt 14, 117901 Moscow Russia. **Tel** 011 95 9542153, FAX 011 95 9382144, telex 411964. Documents available from CASDDS.
Ind/Abst Chem. Abstr.

ISSN 0920-8569
US
CCC
NLM W1; VI834 **CODEN** VIGEET
Pr Rev.
VIRUS GENES. **See** Biology-Microbiology.

LC QH426 .I17 **ISSN** 0253-9772
DD 575.1/05 CC
NLM W1; I123 **CODEN** ICHUDW
YICHUAN. (I CHUAN.). [Yichuan]. **Added/Corp** Chung-kuo I Chuan Hsueh Hui. **VFOAT** Hereditas. (Jan. 1979)-. Academic Scholarly Publication. Chinese. Six times a year. $58.00. Science Press, 16 Donghuangchenggen North Street, Beijing 100707, People's Republic of China. **Tel** 011 86 1 4019821, 011 86 1 4010642, FAX 011 86 1 4012180, 011 86 1 4019810, telex 210147. **Bk Rev. Ad Acc. Circ:** 31,000. Documents available from CASDDS. ***Continues*** *I Chuan Yu Yu Chung, 0253-9594.*
Desc: Contains information on genetics from research reports.
Ind/Abst Chem. Abstr.; Crop Physiol. Abstr.; Plant Grow. Reg. Abstr.; Poult. Abstr.

ISSN 0379-4172
CC
UDC 575
Pr Rev.
YICHUAN XUEBAO. [Yichuan xuebao]. **VFOAT** Acta Genetica Sinica. (1974)-. Academic Scholarly Publication. Chinese (summaries and/or abstracts in English). Six times a year. $92.50. Science Press, 16 Donghuangchenggen North Street, Beijing 100707, People's Republic of China. **Tel** 011 86 1 4019821, 011 86 1 4010642, FAX 011 86 1 4012180, 011 86 1 4019810, telex 210147. **Ad Acc. Circ** 16,100. Documents available from CASDDS.
Desc: Contains information from genetic research in mainland China.
Ind/Abst Chem. Abstr.; NAPRALERT.

MARINE BIOLOGY

ISSN 0860-2611
PL
CODEN ATOPEG
ACTA ACADEMIAE AGRICULTURAE AC TECHNICAE OLSTENENSIS. PROTECTIO AQUARUM ET PISCATORIA. (PROTECTIO AQUARUM ET PISCATORIA.). [Acta Acad. Agric. Tech. Olst., Prot. aquar. piscat.]. **Added/Corp** Akademia Rolniczo-Techniczna w Olsztynie. (1985)-. Periodical. Polish (summaries and/or abstracts in English and Russian; table of contents in English and Russian). Irregular. Price varies per volume. Wydawnictwo Akademia Rolniczo-Techniczna w Olsztynie / Agricultural and Technical Academy in Olsztyn, Blok 21, 10-957 Olsztyn-Kortowo Poland. **Tel** 011 48 89 273310. **(Subscription address:** Ars Polona-Ruch, PO Box 1001, Krakowskie Przedmiescie 7, 00-068 Warsaw Poland. **Tel** 011 48 22 261201.**)** Documents available from CASDDS. ***Continues*** *Zeszyty Naukowe Akademii Rolniczo-Technicznej w Olsztynie. Ochrona wod i Rybactwo Srodladowe, 0324-9190.*
Ind/Abst Agric. Eng. Abstr.; Anim. Breed. Abstr.; Chem. Abstr.; Curr. Ref. Fish Res.; Fish Rev. (Jan. 1989-July 1992); Index Vet.; Nutr. Abstr. Rev., Ser. B, Live Feeds and Feed.; Pig News Inf.; Plant Grow. Reg. Abstr.; Postharvest News Inf.; Potato Abstr.; Sug. Indus. Abstr.; Wildl. Rev. (Jan. 1989-July 1992).

LC QH93 **ISSN** 0001-5113
DD 574.922 CI
CODEN AADRAY
ACTA ADRIATICA. [Acta Adriat.]. Vol. 1 (1932)-. Monographic series. Serbo-Croatian (Cyrillic) (English, French, German and Italian). One time a year. Price varies per volume. Institut za Oceanografiju I Ribarstvo, PO Box 114, Split Croatia. **Tel** (058)46688. **Bk Rev.** ctrl circ. Documents available from BIOSIS Document Express, CASDDS.
Desc: Original scientific papers in marine science, marine fisheries, mariculture, marine biology, physical oceanography, chemical oceanography, marine microbiology, marine biochemistry, and marine geology.
Ind/Abst Biol. Abstr.; Chem. Abstr.; Ecol. Abstr. (?-?); GeoRef; Helminthol. Abstr. (1991-); Life Sci. Collect.; Protozoolog. Abstr.; Rev. Med. Vet. Entomol.

LC QH301.P63 A3 **ISSN** 0065-132X
PL
CODEN AHBPAX
ACTA HYDROBIOLOGICA. [Acta hydrobiol.]. **Added/Corp** Polska Akademia Nauk. Zaklad Biologii Wod. Vol. 1 (1959)-. Periodical. English (French, German and Polish; summaries and/or abstracts in French, German and Polish). Irregular. **(Subscription address:** Ars Polona-Ruch, PO Box 1001, Krakowskie Przedmiescie 7, 00-068 Warsaw Poland. **Tel** 011 48 22 261201.**)** Index Available, published separately, free-automatically sent. Documents available from BIOSIS Document Express, CASDDS. ***Supersedes*** *Biuletyn - Zakladu Biologii Stawow, Polska Akademia Nauk.*
Ind/Abst Anim. Breed. Abstr.; Biol. Abstr.; Chem. Abstr.; Curr. Ref. Fish Res.; Ecol. Abstr.; Fish Rev.; Fresh. Aqua. Contents Tables; Geogr. Abstr. Phys. Geogr.; Helminthol. Abstr. (1991-); Nutr. Abstr. Rev., Ser. B, Live Feeds and Feed.; Soils Fert.

LC QH90.A1 S55 **ISSN** 0559-9385
DD 574.92 CC
CODEN SSWKDR
Pr Rev.
ACTA HYDROBIOLOGICA SINICA. (SHUI SHENG SHENG WU HSUEH CHI KAN.). [Acta hydrobiol. sin.]. **Added/Corp** Chung-kuo ko Hsueh Yuan. Shui Sheng Sheng wu yen Chiu so. **VFOAT** Acta Hydrobiologica Sinica. (1955)-. Periodical. Chinese (summaries and/or abstracts in English). Irregular. $33.60. Science Press, 16 Donghuangchenggen North Street, Beijing 100707, People's Republic of China. **Tel** 011 86 1 4019821, 011 86 1 4010642, FAX 011 86 1 4012180, 011 86 1 4019810, telex 210147. **(Subscription address:** China International Book Trading Corporation, PO Box 399, Library Service Department, Beijing 100044 People's Republic of China. **Tel** 011 86 1 8414284, FAX 011 86 1 8412023, telex 22496 CIBTC CN.**) Ad Acc. Circ:** 6,000.
Desc: Journal of the Chinese Academy of Sciences, Institute of Hydrobiology.
Ind/Abst Index Vet.; Nutr. Abstr. Rev., Ser. B, Live Feeds and Feed.; Protozoolog. Abstr.; Vet. Bull.

LC GC **ISSN** 0761-3962
DD 551.46 FR
CODEN ACIFE7
ACTES DE COLLOQUES (BREST). **See** Earth Sciences-Oceanography.

LC QH91.A1 A22 **ISSN** 0065-2881
DD 574.92082 574 UK
NLM W1 AD679 **CODEN** AMBYAR
Pr Rev.
ADVANCES IN MARINE BIOLOGY. [Adv. mar. biol.]. Vol. 1 (1963)-. Academic Scholarly Publication. English. Irregular. $99.95 (Vol. 30). Academic Press Inc., 6277 Sea Harbor Drive, Orlando FL 32887. **Tel** (800)543-9534, (407)345-4100, FAX (407)352-3445. Documents available from The Genuine Article, CASDDS.
Ind/Abst AQUAREF; Aquat. Sci. Fish. Abstr. [CD-ROM Ed.]; Biol. Agric. Index; Chem. Abstr.; Curr. Cit.; Fish Rev.; GeoRef; Index Sci. Rev. [Full Cov.]; Mar. Sci. Contents Tables; Life Sci. Collect.; Protozoolog. Abstr.; Res. Alert [Full Cov.]; Sci. Cit. Index; SCISEARCH; Wildl. Rev.

ISSN 0065-6364
DD 574 US
CODEN AHMBAC
ALLAN HANCOCK MONOGRAPHS IN MARINE BIOLOGY. [Allan Hancock monogr. mar. biol.]. **Added/Corp** Allan Hancock Foundation. University of Southern California. Institute for Marine and Coastal Studies. **VFOAT** Allan Hancock Foundation Monograph; Monographs of the Allan Hancock Foundation. No. 1 (1966)-. Monographic series. English. Irregular. Price varies per volume. University of Southern California Press / Allan Hancock Foundation, Orward Park, Los Angeles CA 90007. **Tel** (213)743-2053. Documents available from BIOSIS Document Express.
Ind/Abst Biol. Abstr.; GeoRef; Life Sci. Collect.

ISSN 8755-7894
DD 639 US
ALTERNATIVE AQUACULTURE NETWORK. [Altern. aquac. netw.]. **Added/Corp** Alternative Aquaculture Association (U.S.). (198?)-. Periodical. English. Four times a year (Jan., Apr., July, Oct.). $14.00. Alternative Aquaculture Association, PO Box 109, Breinigsville PA 18031. **Tel** (610)395-5854. **ED** Steven Van Gorder. **Bk Rev,** (Qty: 1-4). **Circ:** 700. ***Continues*** *Rodale Network News.*

LC QH117 .A46 **ISSN** 0065-6755
DD 574.99/981/1 GW
CODEN AMAZAP
AMAZONIANA. **See** Earth Sciences-Hydrology.

LC QH91.A1 A94
AT
AMSA HANDBOOK. **Main/Corp** Australian Marine Sciences Association. (1968)-. Monographic series. English. Irregular. Price varies per volume. University of Queensland / School of Marine Sciences, St. Lucia Queensland 4072 Australia.

LC QH91.A1 A56 **ISSN** 0185-3287
DD 574.92/05 MX
CODEN AICME6
ANALES DEL INSTITUTO DE CIENCIAS DEL MAR Y LIMNOLOGIA, UNIVERSIDAD NACIONAL AUTONOMA DE MEXICO. **See** Earth Sciences-Hydrology.

LC Q33 .I55 **ISSN** 0120-3959
DD 574.92 CK
Pr Rev.
ANALES DEL INSTITUTO DE INVESTIGACIONES MARINAS DE PUNTA DE BETIN. [An. Inst. Invest. Mar. Punta Betin]. **Main/Corp** Instituto de Investigaciones Marinas de Punta de Betin. **Added/Corp** Instituto de Investigaciones Marinas de Punta de Betin. Investigaciones Marinas: Punta de Betin. **VFOAT** Investigaciones Marinas: Punta de Betin. No. 9 (1977)-. Academic Scholarly Publication. English (Spanish). One time a year. $12.00. Invemar, Apartado 1016, Santa Marta Colombia. **Tel** 57 54 211380, 57 54 214774, FAX 57 54 211377. **ED** Jaime Garzon-Ferreira. Index available. **Bk Rev. Circ:** 500. ***Continues*** *Instituto Colombo-Aleman de Investigaciones Cientificas Punta de Betin. Mitteilungen.*
Desc: Research on the sea and estuaries in American tropical and subtropical zones.

Biology —Marine Biology

LC GC
DD 551.46
ISSN 0073-8565
FR
CODEN AIMPCT

ANNALES DE L'INSTITUT MICHEL PACHA. Added/Corp Institut Michel Pacha. No. 1 (1968)-. French (summaries and/or abstracts in English). Documents available from CASDDS.
Ind/Abst Chem. Abstr.

LC SH11.M2 D46A
DD 353.97410082/362
ISSN 0742-9061
US

ANNUAL REPORT - MAINE. DEPT. OF MARINE RESOURCES. (ANNUAL REPORT / DEPARTMENT OF MARINE RESOURCES.). [Annu. rep. - Me., Dept. Mar. Res.]. Main/Corp Maine. Dept. of Marine Resources. (19??)-. English. One time a year. Department of Marine Resources, Statehouse Station #21, Augusta ME 04333.

US

AQUARIUM. (19??)-. English. Twelve times a year. $159.00. Grumpfish, PO Box 17761, Salem OR 97305. Tel (503)588-1815. Bk Rev, (Qty: varies). Ad Acc, Adv Mgr: Mary Gries, Tel (503)588-1815. ctrl circ. available on diskette (Must specify 5 1/4 inch or 3 1/2 disk).

LC SH201
Pr Rev.
ISSN 1357-5325
UK

●AQUARIUM SCIENCES AND CONSERVATION. (1995)-. Academic Scholarly Publication. English. Four times a year. $282.35. Chapman & Hall, 2-6 Boundary Row, London SE1 8HN United Kingdom. Tel 011 44 171 8650066, FAX 011 44 171 5229623, telex 290164 CHAPMA G. (Subscription address: International Thomson Publishing Services Ltd., North Way Andover, Hampshire SP10 5BE United Kingdom. Tel 011 44 1264 332424.) ED Peter Burgess. Ad Acc.
Desc: Covers fish biology and conservation issues; aimed at professionals involved with aquaria.

LC QL
DD 591
Pr Rev.
ISSN 0167-5427
UK

AQUATIC MAMMALS. [Aquat. mamm.]. Added/Corp Dolfinarium Harderwijk. Netherlands Foundation for Aquatic Mammal Research. European Association for Aquatic Mammals. Vol. 1 (Jan. 1972)-. Periodical. English (French and German). Three times a year. $95.00. Aquatic Mammals, PO Box 1106, Kailua HI 96734. Tel (808)257-5256, FAX (808)257-5236. ED Paul Nachtigall. Bk Rev, (Qty: 6). Circ: 200.
Desc: Papers dealing with all aspects of the care, conservation, medicine, and science of aquatic mammals.
Ind/Abst Anim. Behav. Abstr.; Curr. Cit.; Dairy Sci. Abstr.; Fish Rev.; Index Vet.; Key Word Index Wildl. Res.; Ocean. Abstr.; Life Sci. Collect.; Vet. Bull.; Zool. Rec.; Wildl. Rev.

LC SB614.3.C2 B74A
DD 354.7110077/2
CN

AQUATIC PLANT MANAGEMENT PROGRAM PROPOSALS FOR ... . Main/Corp British Columbia. Aquatic Plant Management Program. English. Aquatic Plant Management Program of the Ministry of Environment, Parliament Buildings, Victoria British Columbia V8V 1X4 Canada.

LC GB651 .S35
DD 551.48/05
ISSN 1015-1621
SZ
CCC
CODEN AQSCEA

AQUATIC SCIENCES. See Earth Sciences-Hydrology.

LC QH301 .A4932
DD 574
ISSN 0341-2881
GW
CCC
CODEN AHBSA8

ARCHIV FUER HYDROBIOLOGIE. SUPPLEMENTBAND, MONOGRAPHISCHE BEITRAEGE. (ARCHIV FUER HYDROBIOLOGIE. SUPPLEMENT-BAND: ORGAN DER INTERNATIONALEN VEREINIGUNG FUER THEORETISCHE UND ANGEWANDTE LIMNOLOGIE.). [Arch. Hydrobiol., Suppl.bd. Monogr. Beitr.]. Added/Corp International Association of Theoretical and Applied Limnology. VFOAT Supplement-Band. (1921)-. Academic Scholarly Publication. German (English and French). Twelve times a year. $768.00. E. Schweizerbartsche Verlagsbuchhandlung, Johannesstrasse 3A, D-70176 Stuttgart Germany. Tel 011 49 711 625001, FAX 011 49 711 625005, telex 723363 SCHB D. Documents available from BIOSIS Document Express, CASDDS. Continues Archiv fur Hydrobiologie und Planktonkunde. Supplement-Band.
Ind/Abst Biol. Abstr.; Chem. Abstr.; Fish Rev.; GeoRef; Microbiol. Abstr. Sect. C; Rev. Med. Vet. Entomol.; Wildl. Rev.

LC SH1 .A66
DD 639.2/8
ISSN 0944-1921
GW
CODEN ARFMEG

●ARCHIVE OF FISHERY AND MARINE RESEARCH = ARCHIV FUER FISCHEREI- UND MEERESFORSCHUNG. See Fish and Fisheries.

LC TP248.27.M37 M37
DD 660/.6
NLM ZQT 34; A797
ISSN 1054-2027
US

ASFA MARINE BIOTECHNOLOGY ABSTRACTS. See Biology-Abstracting, Bibliographies and Statistics.

ISSN 1011-4041
HK
NLM W1; AS1395
CODEN AMABEP

ASIAN MARINE BIOLOGY. [Asian mar. biol.]. Added/Corp Marine Biological Association of Hong Kong. (1984)-. Monographic series. English. Irregular. $29.00. Hong Kong University Press, 139 Pokfulam Road, University of Hong Kong, Hong Kong. Tel 011 852 5 2502703, FAX 011 852 5 28750734. Circ: 500. Documents available from BIOSIS Document Express.
Ind/Abst Aquat. Sci. Fish. Abstr. [CD-ROM Ed.]; Biol. Abstr. (1987-); Ocean. Abstr.; Life Sci. Collect.

LC QH117 .A87
DD 574.92/05
ISSN 0102-1656
BL

ATLANTICA. [Atlantica]. Added/Corp Fundacao Universidade do Rio Grande. Base Oceanografica Atlantica. Fundacao Universidade do Rio Grande. Departamento de Oceanografia. Vol. 1 (1976)-. Periodical. Portuguese (English and Portuguese). Three times a year.
Ind/Abst Aquat. Sci. Fish. Abstr. [CD-ROM Ed.].

DK
CODEN ATREAS

ATLANTIDE-REPORT: SCIENTIFIC RESULTS OF THE DANISH EXPEDITION TO THE COASTS OF TROPICAL WEST AFRICA, 1945-1946. [Atl. Rep.]. Added/Corp Danish Expedition to the Coasts of Tropical West Africa, 1945-1946. Kbenhavns Universitet. British Museum (Natural History). No. 1 (1950)-. English. Irregular. Price varies. Apollo Books, Kirkeby Sand 19, DK 5771 Stenstrup Denmark. Tel 011 45 62 263737, telex 39296 BRILL NL. Bk Rev. Ad Acc.
Desc: Scientific results of the Danish expedition to the coasts of tropical West Africa 1945-1946.

LC GC1 .A85
DD 551.4
NLM W1 AU613
Pr Rev.
ISSN 0067-1940
AT
CCC
CODEN AJMFA4
TITLE CHANGE

AUSTRALIAN JOURNAL OF MARINE AND FRESHWATER RESEARCH. See Earth Sciences-Oceanography.

ISSN 0157-6429
AT

AUSTRALIAN MARINE SCIENCE BULLETIN. (1970)-. Periodical. English. Four times a year (Jan., Apr., July, Oct). 28.78Aus$. Australian Marine Sciences Association, Western Australian Museum, Perth WA 6000 Australia. Tel 011 61 9 3284411, FAX 011 61 9 3288686. ED Dr. I. Tibbetts (phone: 011 61 7 365 4333). Bk Rev, (Qty: 8). Ad Acc. Circ: 1,000.
Ind/Abst Aquat. Sci. Fish. Abstr. [CD-ROM Ed.]; Ocean. Abstr.

LC GC1 .B35
DD 551.4
ISSN 0067-5148
GW
CODEN BMEKAB

BEITRAEGE ZUR MEERESKUNDE. See Earth Sciences-Oceanography.

ISSN 0341-8561
GW
CODEN BIMKDQ

BERICHTE AUS DEM INSTITUT FUER MEERESKUNDE AN DER CHRISTIAN-ALBRECHTS-UNIVERSITAT KIEL. [Ber. Inst. Meereskd. Christian-Albrechts-Univ. Kiel]. Main/Corp Universitat Kiel. Institut fuer Meereskunde. (1973)-. Periodical. Multiple languages. Six times a year.
Ind/Abst Aquat. Sci. Fish. Abstr. [CD-ROM Ed.].

LC QH91.A1 B5
DD 574
ISSN 0320-9695
UN
CODEN BIMOAZ

BIOLOGIA MORA (KIEV). (BIOLOGIIA MORIA.). [Biol. mora]. Added/Corp Instytut Biolohii Pivdennykh Moriv im. O.O. Kovalevskoho. (1968)-. Monographic series. Russian (summaries and/or abstracts in English). $147.00. Documents available from The Genuine Article, CASDDS. Continues Trudy -Sevastopolskaia Biologicheskaia Stantsiia.
Ind/Abst Chem. Abstr. (?-1977); Ecol. Abstr.; Res. Alert [Full Cov.]; Sci. Cit. Index; SCISEARCH.

LC QH91.A1 B52
DD
ISSN 0134-3475
RU
CCC
CODEN BIMOD4
Pr Rev.

BIOLOGIA MORA (VLADIVOSTOK). (BIOLOGIIA MORIA.). [Biol. mora]. Added/Corp Akademiia Nauk SSSR. Otdelenie Obshchei Biologii. Akademiia Nauk SSSR. Dalnevostochnyi Nauchnyi Tsentr. VFOAT Marine Biology. (1975)-. Academic Scholarly Publication. Russian (summaries and/or abstracts in English). Six times a year. $168.00. Izdatelstvo Nauka / Akademiia Nauk, (Publishing House of the Russian Academy of Sciences), Leninskii Porspekt 14, 117901 Moscow Russia. Tel 011 95 9542153, FAX 011 95 9382144, telex 411964. (Subscription address: East View Publications Inc., 3020 Harbor Lane North, Suite 110, Minneapolis MN 55447. Tel (800)477-1005, (612)550-0961, FAX (612)559-2931.) ED V L Kasyanov. Index available. Bk Rev. Ad Acc. Circ: 1,100 (ctrl).
Documents available from BIOSIS Document Express, CASDDS.
Ind/Abst AGRICOLA; Aquat. Sci. Fish. Abstr. [CD-ROM Ed.]; Biol. Abstr.; Chem. Abstr.; Curr. Ref. Fish Res.; Helminthol. Abstr. (1991-); Ocean. Abstr.

LC SH293.P7 B58
ISSN 0209-0708
PL

BIULETYN MORSKIEGO INSTYTUTU RYBACKIEGO = BULLETIN OF THE SEA FISHERIES INSTITUTE = BIULLETEN' INSTITUTA MORSKOGO RYBOLOVSTVA. See Fish and Fisheries.

LC GC1 .B65
DD 551.46/4/05
BL

BOLETIM DE CIENCIAS DO MAR. Added/Corp Universidade Federal do Ceara. Laboratorio de Ciencias do Mar. No. 21 (1969)-. Bulletin. Portuguese (summaries and/or abstracts in English). RECCS / Revista do Centro de, CP 1258, Universidade Federal, Fortaleza Ceara Brazil. Tel 011 55 2392833. Continues Boletim da Estacao de Biologia Marinha da Universidade Federal do Ceara.
Ind/Abst Aquat. Sci. Fish. Abstr. [CD-ROM Ed.]; Ocean. Abstr.

LC QH91
DD 574.92
PO

BOLETIM DO INSTITUTO NACIONAL DE INVESTIGACAO DAS PESCAS. Main/Corp Instituto Nacional de Investigacao das Pescas. No. 1 (May 1979)-. Bulletin. Portuguese Portugal. Secretaria de Estudo das Pescas. Notas e Estudos. Serie Recursos e Ambiente Aquatico and Notas e Estudos do Instituto de Biologia Maritima.
Ind/Abst Ocean. Abstr.

LC QH1 .S339
DD 574.92/05
ISSN 0373-5524
BL
CODEN BOCNAO

BOLETIM DO INSTITUTO OCEANOGRAFICO. [Bol. Inst. Oceanogr.]. Added/Corp Universidade de Sao Paulo. Instituto Oceanografico. (1952)-. Bulletin. Portuguese. One time a year. $17.00. Instituto Oceanografico, University of Sao Paulo, CP 9075, 05508 Sao Paulo SP Brazil. Tel 011 55 1 2102122. cum. index. Documents available from BIOSIS Document Express. Continues Boletim do Instituto Paulista de Oceanografia.
Ind/Abst Biol. Abstr.; GeoRef; Life Sci. Collect.

LC QH1 .S339
ISSN 0080-6331
BL

BOLETIM DO INSTITUTO OCEANOGRAFICO. [Bol. Inst. Oceanogr.]. Main/Corp Universidade de Sao Paulo. Instituto Oceanografico. Added/Corp Instituto Paulista de Oceanografia. Boletim do Instituto Paulista de Oceanografia. (June 1950)-. Bulletin. Portuguese. Instituto Oceanografico, University of Sao Paulo, CP 9075, 05508 Sao Paulo SP Brazil. Tel 011 55 1 2102122. cum. index.
Ind/Abst Aquat. Sci. Fish. Abstr. [CD-ROM Ed.].

LC QK564 .B66
ISSN 0006-8055
GW
CCC
CODEN BOTNA7
Pr Rev.

BOTANICA MARINA. [Bot. mar.]. Vol. 1 (1959)-. Academic Scholarly Publication. German. Six times a year. $845.90. Walter de Gruyter Inc., PO Box 303421, D-10728 Berlin Germany. Tel 011 49 30 260050, FAX 011 49 30 26005251, telex 184027. ED W. Lehnberg. Index Available in last issue of volume-loose- unpaged. Bk Rev. Ad Acc. Circ: 520. Documents available from The Genuine Article, BIOSIS Document Express, CASDDS, Documents on Demand.
Desc: Covers the entire field of marine botany including marine microbiology and marine mycology. Its purpose is to disseminate original knowledge.
Ind/Abst AQUAREF; Aquat. Sci. Fish. Abstr. [CD-ROM Ed.]; Biol. Abstr.; Chem. Abstr.; Curr. Aware. Biol. Sci.; CABS; Curr. Cit.; Curr. Contents Agric. Biol. Environ. Sci.; Ecol. Abstr. (?-?); Ecology Abstr.; Energy Inf. Abstr.; Energy Res. Abstr. (Sept. 1973-); Environ. Abstr.; Mar.

Sci. Contents Tables; Microbiol. Abstr. Sect. C; Ocean. Abstr.; Life Sci. Collect.; PESTDOC; Res. Alert [Full Cov.]; Sci. Cit. Index; SCISEARCH.

LC QH90.A1 M34A **ISSN** 0579-7926
DD 551.4/6/005 TI
BULLETIN DE L'INSTITUT NATIONAL SCIENTIFIQUE ET TECHNIQUE D'OCEANOGRAPHIE ET DE PECHE. [Bull. Inst. nat. sci. tech. oceanogr. peche]. **Main/Corp** Al-Mahad Al-Qawmi Al-Ilmi Wa-Al-Fanni Lil-Uqyanus Wa-Al-Sayd. **VFOAT** Nashrat Al-Mahad Al-Qawmi Al-Ilmi Wa-Al-Fanni Lil-Uqyanus Wa-Al-Sayd Bi-Salambu. Vol. 1 (1966)-. Bulletin. French (English; summaries and/or abstracts in English). Documents available from BIOSIS Document Express. ***Supersedes*** *Bulletin - Station Oceanographique de Salammbo.*
Ind/Abst Biol. Abstr.; GeoRef.

LC QH91.A1 U54A **ISSN** 0970-9878
DD 574.92/05 II
UDC 574.5
BULLETIN OF THE DEPARTMENT OF MARINE SCIENCES. [Bull. Dep. Mar. Sci. Univ. Cochin]. **Main/Corp** University of Cochin. Dept. of Marine Sciences. Vol. 6 (Dec. 1973)-. Bulletin. English. University of Cochin Department of Marine Sciences, Ernakulam India. ***Continues*** *Bulletin of the Department of Marine Biology and Oceanography, University of Cochin.*
Ind/Abst GeoRef; Life Sci. Collect.

LC QH188 .B84
DD 574.92/05 JA
BULLETIN OF THE MARINE PARK RESEARCH STATIONS. **VFOAT** Kaichu Koen Kenkyujo Kenkyu Hokoku. Vol. 1 (March 1975)-. Bulletin. Multiple languages (English and Japanese). Sabiura Kaichu Koen Kenkyujo, 1157 Kushimotocho Arita Nishi-Muro Gun, Kushimoto Japan.

LC QH90 .C3 **ISSN** 0007-9723
FR
CODEN CBIMA5
Pr Rev.
CAHIERS DE BIOLOGIE MARINE. [Cah. biol. mar.]. **Added/Corp** Universite de Paris. Station Biologique, Roscoff. Vol. 1 (1960)-. Periodical. French (English, Spanish and German). Four times a year (Mar., June, Oct., Dec.). $220.91. Station Biologique, BP 74 Place, Georges Teissier, 29682 Roscoff Cedex France. **Tel** 011 33 98 292323, FAX 011 33 98 292324. **(Subscription address:** Cahiers de Biologie Marine, Station Biologie Roscoff, 29680 Roschoff France. **) ED** C. Jovin Toulmond. ctrl circ. Documents available from The Genuine Article, BIOSIS Document Express, CASDDS.
Desc: Marine biology, oceanography, reproduction, genetics, morphogenesis, marine, ecology, zoogeography, plankton, benthos, algology, sedimentology, reviews, notes.
Ind/Abst Biol. Abstr.; Chem. Abstr. (1960-1983); Curr. Aware. Biol. Sci., CABS; Curr. Cit.; Curr. Contents Agric. Biol. Environ. Sci.; Curr. Ref. Fish Res.; Fish Rev.; GeoRef; Mar. Sci. Contents Tables; Nematol. Abstr.; Life Sci. Collect.; Protozoolog. Abstr.; Res. Alert [Select. Cov.]; Rev. Med. Vet. Entomol.; SCISEARCH; Soils Fert.; Wildl. Rev.

LC QH91.A1 C36 **ISSN** 8756-6354
DD 333.7/2/05 US
CALYPSO LOG (LOS ANGELES, CALIF.). **See** Earth Sciences-Oceanography.

LC QH92 **ISSN** 0706-6457
DD 574.971 CN
CCC
CODEN CTRSDR
CANADIAN TECHNICAL REPORT OF FISHERIES AND AQUATIC SCIENCES. **See** Fish and Fisheries.

LC QH91.A1 C47
DD 574.92/05 RM
CERCETARI MARINE: RECHERCHES MARINES. **Added/Corp** Institutul Roman de Cercetari Marine. **VFOAT** Recherches Marines. (1971)-. Periodical. Multiple languages (English, French and German). Institutul Roman de Cercetari Marine, Bd Lenin 300, Constanta Romania.

LC GC858 .C53 **ISSN** 0185-3880
DD 551.4/66/1 MX
CODEN CIMAD7
Pr Rev.
CIENCIAS MARINAS. [Cienc. mar.]. **Added/Corp** Universidad Autonoma de Baja California. Instituto de Investigaciones Oceanologicas. Universidad Autonoma de Baja California. Unidad de Ciencias Marinas. Vol. 1 (June 1974)-. Academic Scholarly Publication. English (Spanish). Four times a year. $180.00. Inst Invest Oceanologicas UABC, Apartado Postal 423, Ensenada Baja California Mexico. **Tel** 011 52 617 44601, FAX 011 52 617 45303. **ED** Isai Pacheco Ruiz. Index available. **Ad Acc. Circ:** 1,000 (ctrl). Documents available from BIOSIS Document Express, CASDDS.
Desc: Developments in research concerning all areas of marine sciences.

Ind/Abst Anim. Breed. Abstr.; Aquat. Sci. Fish. Abstr. [CD-ROM Ed.]; Biol. Abstr. (1986-); Chem. Abstr.; Fish Rev.; For. Abstr.; GeoRef; Maize Abstr.; Mar. Sci. Contents Tables; Nutr. Abstr. Rev., Ser. B, Live Feeds and Feed.; Nutr. Abstr. Rev., Ser. A, Hum. Exp.

ISSN 0072-1328
DD 574 US
Pr Rev.
COLLECTED REPRINTS - UNIVERSITY OF GEORGIA MARINE INSTITUTE. **Main/Corp** University of Georgia. Marine Institute. Vol. 1 (1955/1958)-. Periodical. English. Irregular. Free on request. University of Georgia Marine Institute, Lorene Townsend, Sanpelo Island GA 31327. **Tel** (912)485-2276, FAX (912)485-2133. **ED** Lorene Townsend. **Circ:** 500 (ctrl).
Desc: Papers published by faculty of the marine institute.

LC QH301 .C5
DD 574.072 US
CONTRIBUTION - CHESAPEAKE BIOLOGICAL LABORATORY. **Main/Corp** Chesapeake Biological Laboratory. No. 1 (1927)-. Monographic series. English. Irregular. Price varies per volume. Chesapeake Biology Laboratory, University of Maryland, Solomons MD 20688.

US
UDC 574.6(759)
CONTRIBUTION - FLORIDA DEPARTMENT OF NATURAL RESOURCES MARINE RESEARCH LABORATORY. **Main/Corp** Marine Research Laboratory, St. Petersburg. (196?)-. Monographic series. English. Irregular. Price varies per volume. Department of Natural Resources / Florida, Marine Research Laboratory, St Petersburg FL 33731. **Tel** (813)896-8626. **ED** Karen Steidinger. **Circ:** 800. ***Continues*** *Contribution - Florida Board of Conservation Marine Laboratory, 0428-6499.*
Desc: Articles, monographs, bibliographies, synopses and educational summaries dealing with the marine resources of Florida and nearby areas.

LC HD1694.N8 N6
DD 333.9/1/009756 S 551.4/6/08 US
CONTRIBUTION (PAMLICO MARINE LABORATORY). **See** Earth Sciences-Oceanography.

LC QH301 .V5 **ISSN** 0083-6400
DD 574.92 639.2072 US
CONTRIBUTION - VIRGINIA INSTITUTE OF MARINE SCIENCE. **Main/Corp** Virginia Institute of Marine Science, Gloucester Point. No. 104 (1962)-. Monographic series. English. Price varies per volume. Virginia Institute of Marine Science, Gloucester Point VA 23062. **Tel** (804)642-7116. ***Continues*** *Contribution - Virginia Fisheries Laboratory.*

ISSN 0545-803X
DD 551.4 UK
CONTRIBUTIONS - THE DOVE MARINE LABORATORY. **Main/Corp** Dove Marine Laboratory. No. 1 (1955)-. Monographic series. English. Price varies per volume. Dove Marine Laboratory, Cullercoats North Shields, Tyne and Wear, NE30 4PZ United Kingdom. **Tel** 011 44 191 2524850, FAX 011 44 191 2521054.

DD 574 551 UK
CONTRIBUTIONS TO MARINE SCIENCE (MENAI BRIDGE). (CONTRIBUTIONS TO MARINE SCIENCE.). **Main/Corp** University of Wales. Marine Science Laboratories. (19??)-. Periodical. English. University of Wales, Department of Maritime Studies, Cardiff CFI 3NU United Kingdom. ***Continues*** *Contributions to Marine Science from the University of Wales.*

DD 551.4 574 PR
CODEN CUPSDO
CONTRIBUTIONS - UNIVERSITY OF PUERTO RICO, DEPARTMENT OF MARINE SCIENCES. **Main/Corp** University of Puerto Rico (Mayaguez Campus). Dept. of Marine Sciences. Vol. 7, No. 107 (1967)-. Monographic series. English. One time a year. Price varies per volume. University of Puerto Rico / Department of Marine Science, Mayaguez Puerto Rico 00708. **Tel** (809)892-2482. ***Continues*** *Contributions - Institute of Marine Biology, University of Puerto Rico, 0555-6740.*
Ind/Abst GeoRef.

LC GC491 .C85A **ISSN** 0590-3351
DD 551.46/005 VE
UDC 551.46
CODEN COUODT
CUADERNOS OCEANOGRAFICOS. **See** Earth Sciences-Oceanography.

LC QH90 .D27 **ISSN** 0106-553X
DD 639/.2/005 DK
CODEN DANADZ
Pr Rev.
DANA (DANMARKS FISKERI- OG HAVUNDERSGELSER). (DANA.). [Dana]. **Added/Corp** Danmarks Fiskeri- og Havundersgelser. Vol. 1 (1980)-. Monographic series. English. Irregular. Price varies per volume. Olsen & Olsen, Helstedsvej 10, DK 3480 Fredensborg Denmark. **Tel** 011 45 42 281393, FAX 011 45 42 281393. Index available. Documents available from BIOSIS Document Express. ***Continues*** *Meddelelser fra Danmarks Fiskeri- og Havundersgelser,, 0070-3435.*
Ind/Abst Aquat. Sci. Fish. Abstr. [CD-ROM Ed.]; Biol. Abstr.; Curr. Aware. Biol. Sci., CABS; Fish Rev. (Jan. 1989-July 1992); Mar. Sci. Contents Tables; Life Sci. Collect.; SCISEARCH; Wildl. Rev. (Jan. 1989-July 1992).

GW
DELAWARE SEA GRANT REPORTER. **Added/Corp** University of Delaware. Sea Grant College Program. **VFOAT** Sea Grant Reporter. Vol. 1, No. 1 (Winter 1982)-. Periodical. English. Four times a year. Free.
Ind/Abst Biol. Dig.

ISSN 0163-6995
US
CODEN DMBIDF
Pr Rev.
DEVELOPMENTS IN MARINE BIOLOGY. [Dev. mar. biol.]. Vol. 1 (1979)-. Monographic series. English. Irregular. Price varies per volume. Elsevier Science Publishing Company Inc, Madison Square Station, PO Box 882, New York NY 10159-0882. **Tel** (212)633-3950, FAX (212)633-3990. Documents available from CASDDS.
Ind/Abst Chem. Abstr. (1979-1980).

ISSN 0177-5103
GW
NLM W1; DI752D **CODEN** DAOREO
DISEASES OF AQUATIC ORGANISMS. [Dis. aquat. org.]. Vol. 1, No. 1 (Dec. 21, 1985)-. Academic Scholarly Publication. English. Twelve times a year. $961.10. Inter-Research Science Publishing, Nordbuente 23, D-21385 Oldendorf Germany. **Tel** 011 49 4132 7127, FAX 011 49 4123 8883. Documents available from The Genuine Article, BIOSIS Document Express, CASDDS.
Ind/Abst AgBiotech News Inf.; Aquat. Sci. Fish. Abstr. [CD-ROM Ed.]; Biol. Abstr. (1986-); Chem. Abstr. (1986-); CSA Neuro. Abstr. (?-?); Curr. Aware. Biol. Sci., CABS; Curr. Cit.; Curr. Contents Agric. Biol. Environ. Sci.; Curr. Ref. Fish Res.; Ecol. Abstr.; Fish Rev.; Fresh. Aqua. Contents Tables; Helminthol. Abstr. (19??-19??); Index Vet.; Mar. Sci. Contents Tables; Microbiol. Abstr. Sect. B; Microbiol. Abstr. Sect. C; Nutr. Abstr. Rev., Ser. B, Live Feeds and Feed.; Ocean. Abstr.; Protozoolog. Abstr.; Res. Alert [Full Cov.]; Rev. Agric. Entomol.; Rev. Med. Vet. Entomol.; Rev. Med. Vet. Mycology; Risk Abstr.; Sci. Cit. Index; SCISEARCH; Vet. Bull.; Virol. AIDS Abstr.; Wildl. Rev.

LC QH541.5.S3 E37
DD 574.5/2636/05 UN
CODEN EKMODH
EKOLOGIIA MORIA. [Ekol. morja]. **Added/Corp** Instytut Biolohii Pivdennykh Moriv im. O.O. Kovalevskoho. (1980)-. Periodical. Russian (summaries and/or abstracts in English). Six times a year. $136.00. Izdatelstvo Naukova Dumka / Ukrainian Academy of Sciences, Yu. A. Khramov, Dir., Ul. Repina 3, 252 601 Kiev Ukraine. **Tel** 011 7 44 4303441, 011 7 44 2254182, telex 131376. **(Subscription address:** East View Publications Inc., 3020 Harbor Lane North, Suite 110, Minneapolis MN 55447. **Tel** (800)477-1005, (612)550-0961, FAX (612)559-2931.) Documents available from CASDDS.
Ind/Abst Chem. Abstr.

LC WMLC 93/2339 **ISSN** 0765-5320
FR
CODEN EQUIEE
EQUINOXE (NANTES). (EQUINOXE.). [Equinoxe]. **Added/Corp** Institut Francais de Recherche pour l'Exploitation de la Mer. (Feb./March 1985)-. Periodical. French. Six times a year. $30.62. Institut Francais de Recherche pour l'Exploitation de la Mer, BP 1049 Centre DE Nantes, 44037 Nantes Cedex France. **Tel** (011) 33 40 374000. Documents available from BIOSIS Document Express. ***Continues*** *Science et Peche, 0036-8350.*
Ind/Abst Aquat. Sci. Fish. Abstr. [CD-ROM Ed.]; Biol. Abstr. (1985-); Food Sci. Technol. Abstr.

LC S932.C47 E85 **ISSN** 0160-8347
DD 574.92/05 US
CCC
CODEN ESTUDO
Pr Rev.
ESTUARIES. [Estuaries]. **Added/Corp** Chesapeake Biological Laboratory. Estuarine Research Federation. Vol. 1 (March 1978)-. Academic Scholarly Publication. English. Four times a year. $215.00. Estuarine Research Federation, 490 Chippingwood Drive, No. 2, Port Republic MD 20676-2140. **Tel** (318)475-5443, FAX

Biology —Marine Biology

(318)475-5675. **(Subscription address:** Estuaries, PO Box 1897, Lawrence KS 66044-8897. **) Bk Rev. Acid Free. Circ:** 1,200 (ctrl). available on microfilm and microfiche from University Microfilms International (UMI). Documents available from The Genuine Article, BIOSIS Document Express, CASDDS. *Continues Chesapeake Science, 0009-3262.*
Desc: Publishes original papers based on research in any aspect of natural science applied to estuaries, including selected interpretive review papers that lead to new and important generalization.
Ind/Abst Abstr. Bull. Inst. Pap. Sci. Tech.; AGRICOLA [Select. Cov.]; Aquat. Sci. Fish. Abstr. [CD-ROM Ed.]; Biol. Abstr.; Chem. Abstr.; Curr. Aware. Biol. Sci., CABS; Curr. Cit.; Curr. Contents Agric. Biol. Environ. Sci.; Curr. Ref. Fish Res.; Ecol. Abstr.; Ecology Abstr.; EMBASE; Energy Res. Abstr. (Feb. 1980-); Environ. Period. Bibliogr. (?-?); Fish Rev.; Fluid Abstr., Civil Eng.; Fluid Abstr. Proc. Eng.; FLUIDEX; For. Abstr.; Geogr. Abstr. Phys. Geogr.; Geogr. Abstr. Human Geogr. (?-?); Geol. Abstr.; GeoRef; INIS Atomindex [Micro.]; Meteorol. Geoastrophys. Abstr. (199?-); Ocean. Abstr.; Life Sci. Collect.; Pollut. Abstr. Indexes; Res. Alert [Full Cov.]; Rev. Med. Vet. Entomol.; Sci. Cit. Index; SCISEARCH; Wildl. Rev.

ISSN 0309-3964
UK

ESTUARIES AND COASTAL WATERS OF THE BRITISH ISLES : A BIBLIOGRAPHY OF RECENT SCIENTIFIC PAPERS. Added/Corp Marine Biological Association of the United Kingdom. Library and Information Services. No. 4 (1980-). Bibliography. English. *Continues Estuaries of the British Isles.*
Ind/Abst Ocean. Abstr.

LC SH315.S7   ISSN 1015-6186
DD 639.20968   SA

FISHERIES BULLETIN (PRETORIA). See Fish and Fisheries.

LC SH1 .N542   ISSN 0919-9268
   JA
   CODEN FSCIEH

●FISHERIES SCIENCE : FS. See Fish and Fisheries.

LC QH91   ISSN 0015-3117
DD 574.92   NO
   CODEN FDSHAJ

FISKERIDIREKTORATETS SKRIFTER. SERIE HAVUNDERSKELSER. See Fish and Fisheries.

LC QE39 .G35   ISSN 0276-0460
DD 551.46/08   US
   CCC
   CODEN GMLEDI
Pr Rev.

GEO-MARINE LETTERS. [Geo-mar. lett.]. Vol. 1, No. 1 (Mar. 1981)-. Academic Scholarly Publication. English. Four times a year. $337.00. Springer-Verlag GmbH & Company KG, Heidelberger Platz 3, D-14197 Berlin Germany. **Tel** 011 49 30 8207223, FAX 011 49 30 8214091, telex 183 319 SPBLN D. **(Subscription address:** Springer-Verlag New York Inc. / North America, PO Box 2485, Journal Fulfillment, Secaucus NJ 07096. **Tel** (201)348-4033, (800)777-4643, FAX (201)348-4505.**)** **ED** A H Bouma. available in microform from University Microfilms International (UMI). Documents available from The Genuine Article, CASDDS.
Desc: Presents topics of international interest, including marine geophysics, marine chemistry, marine geotechnique, and directly related dynamics, processes, stratigraphy, environmental problems and applications.
Ind/Abst Aquat. Sci. Fish. Abstr. [CD-ROM Ed.]; Chem. Abstr.; Curr. Cit.; Curr. Contents Phys. Chem. Earth Sci.; Geogr. Abstr. Phys. Geogr.; GeoRef; Ocean. Abstr.; Res. Alert [Full Cov.]; Sci. Cit. Index; SCISEARCH.

ISSN 0375-8990
UN
CODEN GBZUAM

GIDROBIOLOGICESKIJ ZURNAL. (GIDROBIOLOGICHESKII ZHURNAL). [Gidrobiol. z.]. **Added/Corp** Akademiia Nauk URSR, Kiev. Otdeleneie Obshchei Biologii. **VFOAT** Hydrobiological Journal. Vol. 1 (1965)-. Academic Scholarly Publication. Russian (summaries and/or abstracts in English; table of contents in English). Six times a year. $109.95. Izdatelstvo Naukova Dumka / Ukrainian Academy of Sciences, Yu. A. Khramov, Dir., Ul. Repina 3, 252 601 Kiev Ukraine. **Tel** 011 7 44 4303441, 011 7 44 2254182, telex 131376. **(Subscription address:** East View Publications Inc., 3020 Harbor Lane North, Suite 110, Minneapolis MN 55447. **Tel** (800)477-1005, (612)550-0961, FAX (612)559-2931.**)** Documents available from BIOSIS Document Express, CASDDS.
Ind/Abst AGRICOLA; Aquat. Sci. Fish. Abstr. [CD-ROM Ed.]; Biodeter. Abstr. (1991-); Biol. Abstr.; Chem. Abstr.; Coal Abstr.; Fish Rev. (Jan. 1989-July 1992); Fresh.

Aqua. Contents Tables; GeoRef; Index Vet.; Life Sci. Collect.; Rev. Med. Vet. Mycology; Wildl. Rev. (Jan. 1989-July 1992).

   US

GOLDEN GATE AQUARIST. (19??)-. English. Four times a year. $10.00. San Francisco Aquarium Society, PO Box 34069, San Francisco CA 94134.

   US
Pr Rev.

GULF OF MEXICO SCIENCE. See Earth Sciences-Oceanography.

LC GC1 .O23   ISSN 0072-9027
   US
   CODEN GURRA4
Pr Rev.

GULF RESEARCH REPORTS. [Gulf res. rep.]. **Added/Corp** Gulf Coast Research Laboratory (Ocean Springs, Miss.). Vol. 1 (1961)-. Monographic series. English. Price varies per volume. Gulf Coast Research Laboratory, PO Box 7000, Ocean Springs MS 39564. **Tel** (601)872-4200. **ED** Harold D. Howse. **Circ:** 800. Documents available from BIOSIS Document Express.
Desc: Devoted primarily to the data of the marine sciences and chiefly to the Gulf of Mexico and adjacent waters.
Ind/Abst Aquat. Sci. Fish. Abstr. [CD-ROM Ed.]; Biol. Abstr. (1989-); Fish Rev. (Jan. 1989-July 1992); GeoRef; Mar. Sci. Contents Tables; Wildl. Rev. (Jan. 1989-July 1992).

LC QH91.A1 H25   ISSN 0438-380X
   CC
   CODEN HYKHAC

HAIYANG KEXUE JIKAN. (HAI YANG KO HSUEH CHI KAN. STUDIA MARINA SINICA.). [Haiyang kexue jikan]. **Added/Corp** Chung-Kuo Ko Hsueh Yuan. Hai Yang Yen Chiu So, Tsingtan, China. **VFOAT** Studia Marina Sinica. (Aug. 1962)-. Periodical. Chinese (English, French and Russian). Four times a year. Documents available from CASDDS.
Ind/Abst Aquat. Sci. Fish. Abstr. [CD-ROM Ed.]; Chem. Abstr.; GeoRef; Ocean. Abstr.; Life Sci. Collect.

LC QH301 .H4   ISSN 0174-3597
DD 574.92/05   GW
   CODEN HEMEDC

HELGOLAENDER MEERESUNTERSUCHUNGEN. [Helgol. Meeresunters.]. **Added/Corp** Biologische Anstalt Helgoland. Vol. 33 (1980)-. Academic Scholarly Publication. English (French). Four times a year. DM176.00 Germany; DM178.00 other. Biologische Anstalt Helgoland, Notkestr 31, D-22607 Hamburg Germany. **Tel** 011 49 40 89693160, telex 274977 BAH D. **ED** H. P. Bulnheim. Index available. cum. index. **Bk Rev. Circ:** 750 (ctrl). Documents available from The Genuine Article, BIOSIS Document Express, CASDDS. *Continues Helgolander Wissenschaftlich Meeresuntersuchungen, 0017-9957.*
Desc: Marine biology, dynamics of coastal ecosystems, aquatic pollution, mariculture, morphology, ecology, physiology and biochemistry of marine and brackish water organisms.
Ind/Abst Aquat. Sci. Fish. Abstr. [CD-ROM Ed.]; Biol. Abstr.; Chem. Abstr. (1980-1983); Curr. Cit.; Curr. Contents Agric. Biol. Environ. Sci.; Curr. Ref. Fish Res.; Ecology Abstr.; EMBASE; Energy Res. Abstr. (Sept. 1982-); Fish Rev. (19??-199?); GeoRef; Mar. Sci. Contents Tables; Ocean. Abstr.; Life Sci. Collect.; Pollut. Abstr. Indexes; Protozoolog. Abstr.; Res. Alert [Full Cov.]; Sci. Cit. Index; SCISEARCH.

LC QH93.3 .H5   ISSN 0073-2087
DD 574.9   RM

HIDROBIOLOGIA. [Hidrobiologia]. **Added/Corp** Academia Republicii Socialiste Romine. Academia Republicii Populare Romine. Academia Republicii Populare Romine. Comisia de Hidrologie, Hidrobiologia si Ihtiologie. Vol. 1 (1958)-. Multiple languages (English, French, German, Romanian and Russian). Editura Academia Republicii Socialiste Romania, Calea Victoriei Nr 125, R-79717 Bucuresti Romania. **Tel** telex 10376 PRSFI R. cum. index.
Ind/Abst Aquat. Sci. Fish. Abstr. [CD-ROM Ed.]; Life Sci. Collect.

LC SH1 .I45   ISSN 0537-2003
   II
   CODEN IJFIAW

INDIAN JOURNAL OF FISHERIES. See Fish and Fisheries.

LC QH91.5 .W66a   ISSN 0192-2300
DD 574.92/07/1174492   US
   CEASED

INFORMATIONAL BULLETIN - MARINE BIOLOGICAL LABORATORY. **Main/Corp** Marine Biological Laboratory (Woods Hole, Mass.). (1979)-(19??). Bulletin. English. Marine Biological Laboratory, MBL Street, Woods Hole MA 02543. **Tel** (508)548-3705 ext. 402, FAX (508)457-1924. *Supersedes Marine Biological Laboratory, Woods Hole, Mass. Marine Biological Laboratory. [Annual Announcement]*
Ind/Abst CSA Neuro. Abstr. (?-?); Ecology Abstr. (?-?).

DD 574 551   ISSN 0458-7774
UDC 574.5   PE

INFORME - INSTITUTO DEL MAR DEL PERU. **Main/Corp** Instituto del Mar del Peru. No. 1 (1965)-. Monographic series. Spanish. Irregular (four or five issues per year). Price varies per volume. Instituto del Mar del Peru, Centro de Informacion, Apdo. 22, Callao Peru. *Supersedes Informe.*

   ISSN 0020-7918
   IT

INTERNATIONAL MARINE SCIENCE NEWSLETTER. **Added/Corp** Unesco Division of Oceanograpahy. Unesco Division of Marine Sciences. **VFOAT** IMS Newsletter. No. 1 (Feb. 1973)-. Newsletter. English. Four times a year. free. UNESCO / France, 31 rue Francois Bonvin, 75732 Paris Cedex 15 France. **Tel** 011 33 1 45684564, 011 33 1 45684565, FAX 011 33 1 45669270, telex 204461 Paris. **ED** Gary Wright. **Circ:** 8,000. *Supersedes International Marine Science.*

   ISSN 0020-9309
   GW
   CCC
   CODEN IGHYAZ
Pr Rev.

INTERNATIONALE REVUE DER GESAMTEN HYDROBIOLOGIE. [Int. Rev. gesamten Hydrobiol.]. Vol. 44, (1959)-. Academic Scholarly Publication. German (English, French and German). Four times a year. $530.00. Akademie-Verlag GmbH, Postfach, D-13162 Berlin Germany. **Tel** 011 49 30 47889300, FAX 011 49 30 47889357. **(Subscription address:** VCH Publishers Inc., 303 Northwest 12th Avenue, Journals Department, Deerfield FL 33442. **Tel** (800)367-8249, (305)428-5566.**) ED** P. Mauersberger. cum. index. Documents available from The Genuine Article, BIOSIS Document Express, CASDDS. *Continues Internationale Revue der Gesamten Hydrobiologie und Hydrographie.*
Desc: Provides an international medium for information on hydrobiology, the science of processes of life in water.
Ind/Abst AGRICOLA; Biol. Abstr.; Chem. Abstr.; Coal Abstr.; Curr. Aware. Biol. Sci., CABS; Curr. Cit.; Curr. Contents Agric. Biol. Environ. Sci.; Curr. Ref. Fish Res.; Ecol. Abstr.; Ecology Abstr.; EMBASE; Fresh. Aqua. Contents Tables; Geogr. Abstr. Phys. Geogr.; Geol. Abstr.; Helminthol. Abstr. (1991-); Mar. Sci. Contents Tables; Ocean. Abstr.; Life Sci. Collect.; Protozoolog. Abstr.; Res. Alert [Full Cov.]; Rev. Med. Vet. Entomol.; Rice Abstr.; Sci. Cit. Index; SCISEARCH; Weed Abstr.

LC QH92   ISSN 0186-5102
DD 574.92   MX
   CODEN IMCMEK

INVESTIGACIONES MARINAS CICIMAR. (INVESTIGACIONES MARINAS CICIMAR.). [Invest. mar. CICIMAR]. **Added/Corp** Instituto Politecnico Nacional (Mexico). Centro Interdisciplinario de Ciencias Marinas. **VFOAT** Inv. Mar. Cent. Interdis. Cien. Mar. **VAT** Investigaciones Marinas Centro Interdisciplinario de Ciencias Marinas. (1984)-. Periodical. Spanish (summaries and/or abstracts in English). Documents available from BIOSIS Document Express, CASDDS.
Ind/Abst Biol. Abstr.; Chem. Abstr.

LC GC1 .I74   ISSN 0078-320X
DD 551.4   SA
   CODEN ORIIAX
Pr Rev.

INVESTIGATIONAL REPORT - OCEANOGRAPHIC RESEARCH INSTITUTE (DURBAN). (INVESTIGATIONAL REPORT / SOUTH AFRICAN ASSOCIATION FOR MARINE BIOLOGICAL RESEARCH, OCEANOGRAPHIC RESEARCH INSTITUTE.). [Invest. rep. - Oceanogr. Res. Inst.]. **Main/Corp** Durban, Natal. **Added/Corp** Oceanographic Research Institute (South Africa). **VFOAT** Oceanographic Research Institute: Investigational Report. No. 1 (1961)-. Monographic series. English. Price varies per volume. South African Association for Marine Biological Research / Oceanographic Research Institute, PO Box 10712, Marine Parade, Durban 4056 South Africa. **Tel** 011 27 31 373536, FAX 011 27 31 372132. **ED** A.J. DeFreitas. **Circ:** 500. Documents available from BIOSIS Document Express.
Desc: Research and results of current marine biological data.
Ind/Abst Biol. Abstr.; Fish Rev. (19??-199?); Ocean. Abstr.; Life Sci. Collect.; Wildl. Rev.

LC SH315.S7
DD 639.20968   SA
   CODEN IRSIEL

INVESTIGATIONAL REPORT (SEA FISHERIES RESEARCH INSTITUTE (SOUTH AFRICA)). See Fish and Fisheries.

LC QH541.5.W5 J68
DD 574.5/263
ISSN 0925-1014
NE
CCC
CODEN JAQHE2

Pr Rev.

JOURNAL OF AQUATIC ECOSYSTEM HEALTH. **Added/Corp** Aquatic Ecosystem Health and Management Society. Vol. 1, No. 1 (1992)-. Periodical. English. Four times a year. $293.00. Kluwer Academic Publishers, Postbus 322, 3300 AH Dordrecht The Netherlands. **Tel** 011 31 78 524400, FAX 011 31 78 183273, telex 20083. **ED** M. Munawar. **Acid Free.** available in microform. Documents available from Documents on Demand. ***Continues** Journal of Aquatic Ecotoxicology.*
Desc: Publishes papers on timely topics, issues, subjects, concepts and strategies, dealing with the health of biotic components of the aquatic ecosystem.
Ind/Abst Curr. Aware. Biol. Sci., CABS; Environ. Abstr.; Environ. Period. Bibliogr.; Fresh. Aqua. Contents Tables; Mar. Sci. Contents Tables.

LC QL435.A1 J68
DD 595.3/05
UDC 595.3
ISSN 0278-0372
US
CODEN JCBIDB

Pr Rev.

JOURNAL OF CRUSTACEAN BIOLOGY. (JOURNAL OF CRUSTACEAN BIOLOGY : A QUARTERLY OF THE CRUSTACEAN SOCIETY FOR THE PUBLICATION OF RESEARCH ON ANY ASPECT OF THE BIOLOGY OF CRUSTACEA.). [J. crustac. biol.]. Vol. 1, No. 1 (Feb. 1981)-. Academic Scholarly Publication. English. Four times a year. $98.00. The Crustacean Society, 840 East Mulberry, San Antonio TX 78212-3194. **Tel** (512)732-8809, (202)357-2506. **(Subscription address:** Journal of Crustacean Biology, PO Box 1897, Lawrence KS 66044-8897. **) ED** Arthur G. Humes. Index available (last issue of year). cum. index. **Bk Rev. Acid Free. Circ:** 1,000. Documents available from The Genuine Article, BIOSIS Document Express, CASDDS.
Desc: Provides international exchange of information among all those interested in any aspect of the biology of crustaceans.
Ind/Abst Anim. Behav. Abstr.; Aquat. Sci. Fish. Abstr. [CD-ROM Ed.]; Biol. Abstr.; Chem. Abstr.; CSA Neuro. Abstr. (?-?); Curr. Aware. Biol. Sci., CABS; Curr. Cit.; Curr. Contents Agric. Biol. Environ. Sci.; Ecology Abstr.; Mar. Sci. Contents Tables; Ocean. Abstr.; Life Sci. Collect.; Pollut. Abstr. Indexes; Res. Alert [Full Cov.]; Rev. Med. Vet. Entomol.; Sci. Cit. Index; SCISEARCH.

LC QH91.A1 J6
DD 574.92/05
ISSN 0022-0981
NE
CCC
CODEN JEMBAM

Pr Rev.

JOURNAL OF EXPERIMENTAL MARINE BIOLOGY AND ECOLOGY. [J. exp. mar. biol. ecol.]. Vol. 1 (1967)-. Academic Scholarly Publication. English (French and German). Twenty times a year (10 vols.). $2445.00. Elsevier Science Publishers BV, PO Box 211, 1000 AE Amsterdam Netherlands. **Tel** 011 31 20 4853641, 011 31 20 4853642, FAX 011 31 20 4853598. **ED** Harold Barnes, Margaret Barnes, Brian L. Bayne, F. John Vernberg, R. Gibson, S. Stancyk, and R. Warwick. available on microfilm and microfiche from University Microfilms International (UMI); available on an online database from Elsevier Electronic Subscriptions (EES). Documents available from The Genuine Article, BIOSIS Document Express, CASDDS, Documents on Demand.
Desc: Provides a forum in the biochemistry, physiology, behaviour, and genetics of marine plants and animals in relation to their ecology.
Ind/Abst AGRICOLA; Anim. Behav. Abstr.; Aquat. Sci. Fish. Abstr. [CD-ROM Ed.]; Biodeter. Abstr. (1991-); Biol. Abstr.; Chem. Abstr.; Chemorecept. Abstr.; CSA Neuro. Abstr. (?-?); Curr. Cit.; Curr. Contents Agric. Biol. Environ. Sci.; Curr. Ref. Fish Res.; Ecol. Abstr.; Ecology Abstr.; EMBASE; Energy Inf. Abstr.; Energy Res. Abstr.; Environ. Abstr.; Environ. Period. Bibliogr.; Fish Rev.; Geogr. Abstr. Phys. Geogr.; Geol. Abstr.; GeoRef; Helminthol. Abstr. (1991-); Immunol. Abstr.; Mar. Sci. Contents Tables; Microbiol. Abstr. Sect. C; Nutr. Abstr. Rev., Ser. B, Live Feeds and Feed.; Nutr. Abstr. Rev., Ser. A, Hum. Exp.; Ocean. Abstr.; Life Sci. Collect.; Pollut. Abstr. Indexes; Protozoolog. Abstr.; Res. Alert [Full Cov.]; Sci. Cit. Index; SCISEARCH; Soc. Sci. Cit. Index [Select. Cov.]; Wildl. Rev.

LC QH181 .J68
DD 574.92/9/05
ISSN 0970-9517
II

JOURNAL OF FRESHWATER BIOLOGY. **Added/Corp** Freshwater Biological Association of India. **VAT** J. Freshwater Biol. Vol. 1, No. 1 (1989)-. Periodical. English. Four times a year. $100.00. Freshwater Biology Association of India, Post Grad Dept Zoology, Bhagalpur University, 812007 India. **(Subscription address:** Prints India, 11 Darya Ganj, New Delhi 110002 India. **Tel** 011 91 11 3268645, FAX 011 91 11 3275542, telex 31-61087 PRIN-IN.)
Ind/Abst Aquat. Sci. Fish. Abstr. [CD-ROM Ed.]; Ecology Abstr.; Entomol. Abstr.

LC TP248.27.M37 J68
DD 660/.6
NLM W1; JO748I
US
CODEN JMBOEW

•**JOURNAL OF MARINE BIOTECHNOLOGY, THE.** Vol. 1, No. 1 (1993)-. Periodical. English. Four times a year. $149.00. Springer-Verlag New York Inc., 175 Fifth Avenue, New York NY 10010. **Tel** (212)460-1500 ext 256, FAX (212)533-3503, telex 232 235 SPB UR. **(Subscription address:** Springer-Verlag New York Inc. / North America, PO Box 2485, Journal Fulfillment, Secaucus NJ 07096. **Tel** (201)348-4033, (800)777-4643, FAX (201)348-4505.)
Ind/Abst Bibliogr. Agric.

LC GC1 .J6
DD 574.92
ISSN 0022-2402
US
CODEN JMMRAO

Pr Rev.

JOURNAL OF MARINE RESEARCH. [J. mar. res.]. **Added/Corp** Sears Foundation for Marine Research. Bingham Oceanographic Laboratory. Vol. 1 (Nov. 1937)-. Academic Scholarly Publication. English. Six times a year. $100.00. Kline Geology Laboratory, Yale University, Room 217, PO Box 208109, New Haven CT 06520-8109. **Tel** (203)432-3131, (203)432-5668, FAX (203)432-5668. **ED** George Veronis. available on microfilm and microfiche from University Microfilms International (UMI). Documents available from Article Express International, The Genuine Article, BIOSIS Document Express, CASDDS.
Ind/Abst Abstr. Bull. Inst. Pap. Sci. Tech.; Acad. Search; AGRICOLA; AQUAREF; Aquat. Sci. Fish. Abstr. [CD-ROM Ed.]; Bioeng. Abstr.; Biol. Abstr.; Chem. Abstr.; Curr. Aware. Biol. Sci., CABS; Curr. Contents Agric. Biol. Environ. Sci.; Ei Page One; EMBASE; Eng. Index Annu.; EP Collect.; Fluid Abstr., Civil Eng.; Fluid Abstr. Proc. Eng.; FLUIDEX; Gen. Sci. Index; Gen. Sci. Source; Homework Help.; INFO-SOUTH Abstr.; Int. Aerosp. Abstr.; Mag. Search; MasterFile FullTEXT 1000; MasterFile FullTEXT 350; MasterFile FullTEXT 650; MasterFile FullTEXT (July 1993-); Meteorol. Geoastrophys. Abstr.; Ocean. Abstr.; OCLC; Life Sci. Collect.; Res. Alert [Full Cov.]; Sci. Cit. Index; SCISEARCH; Telebase.

LC GC1000
DD 551.46
ISSN 0948-4280
GW

•**JOURNAL OF MARINE SCIENCE AND TECHNOLOGY.** (1996)-. Academic Scholarly Publication. English. Five times a year. DM230.00. Springer-Verlag GmbH & Company KG, Heidelberger Platz 3, D-14197 Berlin Germany. **Tel** 011 49 30 8207223, FAX 011 49 30 8214091, telex 183 319 SPBLN D. **(Subscription address:** Springer-Verlag New York Inc. / North America, PO Box 2485, Journal Fulfillment, Secaucus NJ 07096. **Tel** (201)348-4033, (800)777-4643, FAX (201)348-4505.) **ED** H. Kato.

CC
CEASED

JOURNAL OF MARINE SCIENCES. (19??)-Vol. 4, No. 4 (Jan. 1993). English. International Academic Publishers, 137 Chaonei Dajie, Beijing 100010, People's Republic of China. **Tel** 011 86 4035533 217, FAX 011 86 10 5063101.

LC QH90.8.P5 J68
DD 574.92
ISSN 0142-7873
US
CCC
CODEN JPLRD9

Pr Rev.

JOURNAL OF PLANKTON RESEARCH. [J. plankton res.]. Vol. 1 (April 1979)-. Academic Scholarly Publication. English. Twelve times a year. $380.00. Oxford University Press / UK, Walton Street, Oxford OX2 6DP United Kingdom. **Tel** 011 44 1865 56767, FAX 011 44 1865 267773, telex 851/837330 OXPRES G. **(Subscription address:** Oxford University Press / USA, Journals Marketing Department, Oxford University Press, 2001 Evans Road, Cary NC 27513. **Tel** (800)451-7556, (919)677-0977, FAX (919)677-1714.) **ED** D. H. Cushing. **Ad Acc. Circ:** 600. available on microfilm from University Microfilms International (UMI). Documents available from The Genuine Article, BIOSIS Document Express, CASDDS.
Desc: Covers zoo- and phytoplankton in all environments, publishing original papers on ecology (larval and juvenile stages), physiology and distribution (life history and taxonomy).
Ind/Abst AQUAREF; Aquat. Sci. Fish. Abstr. [CD-ROM Ed.]; Biol. Abstr.; Chem. Abstr.; Curr. Aware. Biol. Sci., CABS; Curr. Cit.; Curr. Contents Agric. Biol. Environ. Sci.; Ecol. Abstr.; Ecology Abstr.; EMBASE; Fresh. Aqua. Contents Tables; Geogr. Abstr. Phys. Geogr.; GeoRef; Mar. Sci. Contents Tables; Microbiol. Abstr. Sect. C; Ocean. Abstr.; Life Sci. Collect.; Res. Alert [Full Cov.]; Sci. Cit. Index; SCISEARCH.

ISSN 0025-3146
II
CODEN JMBIAA

JOURNAL OF THE MARINE BIOLOGICAL ASSOCIATION OF INDIA. [J. Mar. Biol. Assoc. India]. **Main/Corp** Marine Biological Association of India. Vol. 1 (June 1959)-. Periodical. English. Two times a year. $60.00. Scientific Publishers, PO Box 91, Ratanada Road, Jodhpur 342011 India. **(Subscription address:** Prints India, 11 Darya Ganj, New Delhi 110002 India. **Tel** 011 91 11 3268645, FAX 011 91 11 3275542, telex 31-61087 PRIN-IN.) **ED** K Rangarajan. **Bk Rev. Circ:** 550 (ctrl). Documents available from CASDDS.
Ind/Abst Aquat. Sci. Fish. Abstr. [CD-ROM Ed.]; Chem. Abstr.; Ecology Abstr.; Mar. Sci. Contents Tables; Ocean. Abstr.; Life Sci. Collect.; Protozoolog. Abstr.

LC QH301 .M2
NLM W1 MA653E
ISSN 0025-3154
UK
CCC
CODEN JMBAAK

Pr Rev.

JOURNAL OF THE MARINE BIOLOGICAL ASSOCIATION OF THE UNITED KINGDOM. [J. Mar. Biol. Assoc. U. K.]. **Main/Corp** Marine Biological Association of the United Kingdom. Vol. 1-2, (Aug. 1887-Aug. 1888); New Series, Vol. 1, (1889/1890)-. Academic Scholarly Publication. English. Four times a year. $376.00. Cambridge University Press, The Edinburgh Building, Shaftesbury Road, Cambridge CB2 2RU United Kingdom. **Tel** 011 44 1223 312393, FAX 011 44 1223 315052, telex 851-817256. **(Subscription address:** Cambridge University Press / North America, 110 Midland Avenue, Port Chester NY 10573. **Tel** (800)431-1580, (914)937-9600.) **ED** Michael Whitfield. **Bk Rev.** available on microfilm from University Microfilms International (UMI). Documents available from The Genuine Article, BIOSIS Document Express, CASDDS.
Desc: Publishes original research from workers in many countries on all aspects of marine biology. Subjects covered include ecological and population studies of oceanic, coastal and shore communities in European and North Atlantic waters, physiology and experimental biology, taxonomy, morphology and life history of marine animals and plants, and chemical and physical oceanography. Papers are also published on the rapidly developing techniques used at sea for sampling, recording, capture and observation of marine organisms, and chemical analyses of sea water.
Ind/Abst Anim. Breed. Abstr.; AQUAREF; Aquat. Sci. Fish. Abstr. [CD-ROM Ed.]; Biol. Agric. Index; Biol. Abstr.; Chem. Abstr.; Curr. Aware. Biol. Sci., CABS; Curr. Cit.; Curr. Contents Agric. Biol. Environ. Sci.; Curr. Ref. Fish Res.; Ecol. Abstr.; Ecology Abstr.; EMBASE; Environ. Period. Bibliogr.; Fish Rev.; Geogr. Abstr. Phys. Geogr.; Helminthol. Abstr. (1991-); Leadscan; Mar. Sci. Contents Tables; Nematol. Abstr.; Nutr. Abstr. Rev., Ser. B, Live Feeds and Feed.; Nutr. Abstr. Rev., Ser. A, Hum. Exp.; Ocean. Abstr.; Life Sci. Collect.; Protozoolog. Abstr.; Res. Alert [Full Cov.]; Rev. Med. Vet. Entomol.; Sci. Cit. Index; SCISEARCH; Wildl. Rev.

LC QH91.A1 K53
DD 574.92/05
ISSN 0172-7893
GW
CODEN KMSODP

KIELER MEERESFORSCHUNGEN. SONDERHEFT. [Kiel. Meeresforsch., Sonderh.]. **Added/Corp** Universitat Kiel. Institut fuer Meereskunde. Vol. 1 (1962)-. Academic Scholarly Publication. German (English). Irregular. Walter G. Muhlau, Holtenauer Strasse 116, D-24105 Kiel Germany. **Tel** 011 49 431 85085. **Bk Rev.** Documents available from BIOSIS Document Express, CASDDS.
Ind/Abst Aquat. Sci. Fish. Abstr. [CD-ROM Ed.]; Biol. Abstr.; Chem. Abstr.; GeoRef.

LC QH96.A1 L5
DD 574.92
ISSN 0075-9511
GW
CODEN LMNOA8

LIMNOLOGICA. **See** Earth Sciences-Hydrology.

LC Z5322.M3 M35a QH105.F6
DD 016.639/2/09759
US

LIST OF PUBLICATIONS OF THE BUREAU OF MARINE SCIENCE & TECHNOLOGY, MARINE RESEARCH LABORATORY. **Main/Corp** Florida. Marine Research Laboratory. 1968-. Bibliography. English. One time a year. Free. Florida Dept of Natural Resources, Division of Marine Resources etc., 100 Eighth Avenue SE, St Petersburg FL 33701-5095. **Tel** (813)896-8626. **ED** Karen Steidinger. Index available. **Circ:** 600. ***Continues** Florida. State Board of Conservation. Marine Laboratory, St. Petersburg. List of Publications.*
Desc: Bibliography of those publications produced by the staff of the Bureau of Marine Research.

ISSN 0273-2130
US

MANATEE QUARTERLY. Vol. 3 (Sept. 1980)-. Periodical. English. Four times a year. $5.00. Pendragon Communications Corporation, 1027 Ninth Street West, Bradenton FL 33505. ***Continues** Manatee.*

LC GC
DD 551.46
US

MARINE ADVISORY BULLETIN. **See** Earth Sciences-Oceanography.

LC QH91.A1 M35 **ISSN** 0025-3162
DD 574.92 GW
CCC
NLM W1 MA653H **CODEN** MBIOAJ
Pr Rev.
MARINE BIOLOGY. [Mar. biol.]. Vol. 1 (June 1967)-. Academic Scholarly Publication. English (French and German). Twelve times a year. $3219.00. Springer-Verlag GmbH & Company KG, Heidelberger Platz 3, D-14197 Berlin Germany. **Tel** 011 49 30 8207223, FAX 011 49 30 8214091, telex 183 319 SPBLN D. **(Subscription address:** Springer-Verlag New York Inc. / North America, PO Box 2485, Journal Fulfillment, Secaucus NJ 07096. **Tel** (201)348-4033, (800)777-4643, FAX (201)348-4505.**)** **ED** O Kinne. available on microfilm and microfiche from University Microfilms International (UMI). Documents available from The Genuine Article, BIOSIS Document Express, UMI Article Clearinghouse, CASDDS, Documents on Demand.
Desc: Publishes contributions in plankton research, experimental biology, biochemistry, physiology and behavior, biosystem research, evolution, and theoretical biology related to the marine environment.
Ind/Abst AGRICOLA; Anim. Behav. Abstr.; AQUAREF; Aquat. Sci. Fish. Abstr. [CD-ROM Ed.]; Biodeter. Abstr.; Biol. Agric. Index; Biol. Abstr.; Chem. Abstr.; Chemorecept. Abstr.; CSA Neuro. Abstr. (?-?); Curr. Aware. Biol. Sci., CABS; Curr. Cit.; Curr. Contents Agric. Biol. Environ. Sci.; Curr. Ref. Fish Res.; Ecology Abstr.; EMBASE; Energy Res. Abstr.; Environ. Abstr.; Environ. Period. Bibliogr.; Expand. Acad. Index (1992-); Fish Rev. (Jan. 1989-July 1992); GeoRef; Leadscan; Mar. Sci. Contents Tables; Microbiol. Abstr. Sect. B (19??-19??); Microbiol. Abstr. Sect. C; Newsp. Period. Abstr. (1992-); Nutr. Abstr. Rev., Ser. B, Live Feeds and Feed.; Ocean. Abstr.; Life Sci. Collect.; Pollut. Abstr. Indexes; Ref. Upd. Deluxe Ed.; Res. Alert [Full Cov.]; Rice Abstr.; Sci. Cit. Index; SCISEARCH; Soyabean Abstr.; Wildl. Rev. (Jan. 1989-July 1992).

LC SH11 .A4463 **ISSN** 0090-1830
DD 338.3/72/7092 US
CODEN MFSRA4
Pr Rev.
MARINE FISHERIES REVIEW. **See** Fish and Fisheries.

LC GC1 .D55 **ISSN** 0079-0435
DD 551.46/57 IO
CODEN MRINAQ
MARINE RESEARCH IN INDONESIA. [Mar. res. Indones.]. **Added/Corp** Lembaga Oseanologi Nasional (Indonesia). No. 16 (1976)-. Periodical. English (Indonesian). Irregular. Centre for Oceanological Research and Development Alamat, Jl Pasir Putih I, Ancol Timur, PO Box 580, DAK Jakarta 11001 Indonesia. **Tel** 011 62 21 683850, telex 62875 PDII IA. **ED** Kasijan Romimohtarto, Mohammad Kasim Moosa, Nurzali Naamin, and Abdul Gani Ilahude. ctrl circ. Documents available from BIOSIS Document Express. ***Continues*** *Lembaga Oseanologi Nasional. Penelitian laut di Indonesia.*
Ind/Abst Aquat. Sci. Fish. Abstr. [CD-ROM Ed.]; Biol. Abstr.; Life Sci. Collect.

ISSN 0316-1633
DD 574.92 CN
MARINE SCIENCES RESEARCH LABORATORY TECHNICAL REPORT. (TECHNICAL REPORT - MARINE SCIENCES RESEARCH LABORATORY.). **Added/Corp** Memorial University of Newfoundland. Marine Sciences Research Laboratory. **VFOAT** M S R L Technical Report; Marine Sciences Research Laboratory Technical Report. No. 1 (1969)-. Monographic series. English. Irregular. Free on request. Marine Sciences Research Laboratory, Elizabeth Avenue, PO Box 4200, St. John Newfoundland A1C 557 Canada.

LC QH92.3 .M45 **ISSN** 0085-0683
DD 574.92/34 US
CODEN MHGCBGMHGCB6
Pr Rev.
MEMOIRS OF THE HOURGLASS CRUISES. [Mem. Hourglass cruises]. **Added/Corp** Florida. Marine Research Laboratory. Florida. Bureau of Marine Research. Florida Marine Research Institute. Vol. 1 Pt. 1 (Mar. 1969)-. Monographic series. English. Price varies per volume. Florida Marine Research Institute, Department of Natural Resources, Division of Marine Resources, 100 8th Avenue SE, St. Petersburg FL 33701-5095. **Tel** (813)896-8626, FAX (813)823-0166. **ED** Karen Steidinger. **Circ:** 800. Documents available from BIOSIS Document Express.
Desc: Analysis of Project Hourglass, a systematic sampling program for benthic and planktonic flora and fauna collected along the west Florida Shelf.
Ind/Abst Biol. Abstr. (1969-1986); Fish Rev. (Jan. 1989-July 1992); Life Sci. Collect.; Wildl. Rev. (Jan. 1989-July 1992).

LC QH152 **ISSN** 0390-492X
IT
CODEN MBMOA5
MEMORIE DI BIOLOGIA MARINA E DI OCEANOGRAFIA. [Mem. biol. mar. oceanogr.]. Vol. 1 (1971)-. Academic Scholarly Publication. Multiple languages (English and Italian). Irregular. 10000. Istituto di Zoologia dell Universita di Messina, Via dei Verdi 75, Messina 98100 Italy. Documents available from BIOSIS Document Express, CASDDS.
Ind/Abst Biol. Abstr.; Chem. Abstr.; Ocean. Abstr.

LC QL121 .M45 **ISSN** 0176-3296
DD 592.092/05 GW
CCC
CODEN MMAREZ
MICROFAUNA MARINA. [Microfauna mar.]. **Added/Corp** Akademie der Wissenschaften und der Literatur (Germany). Kommission fuer Zoologie. Vol. 1 (1984)-. Monographic series. German (English). One time a year. Price varies per volume. Gustav Fischer Verlag Stuttgart, Postfach 720143, D-70577 Stuttgart Germany. **Tel** 011 49 711 458030, FAX 011 49 711 4580334, telex 2627-7111488. **ED** Peter Ax. Documents available from BIOSIS Document Express. ***Continues*** *Mikrofauna des Meeresbodens, 0342-3247.*
Desc: Numbered series that intends to cover the spectrum of all aspects of ecology, systematics and evolution, of morphology and ultrastructure, just as the natural history of this faunal component of the seas.
Ind/Abst Biol. Abstr. (1988-).

ISSN 1053-6426
DD 576 US
CCC
NLM W1; MO196LN **CODEN** MMBBEQ
MOLECULAR MARINE BIOLOGY AND BIOTECHNOLOGY. [Mol. mar. biol. biotechnolog.]. Vol. 1, No. 1 Sept. (1991)-. Academic Scholarly Publication. English. Four times a year. $195.00. Blackwell Scientific Publishers, 238 Main Street, Cambridge MA 02142. **Tel** (617)547-7110, (800)835-6770, FAX (617)547-0789. available on microfilm and microfiche from University Microfilms International (UMI). Documents available from The Genuine Article, CASDDS.
Ind/Abst Chem. Abstr.; Curr. Aware. Biol. Sci., CABS; Genet. Abstr.; Index Med.; Res. Alert [Full Cov.].

LC QH96 .M8 **ISSN** 0368-8275
GW
MUNCHNER BEITRAEGE ZUR ABWASSER-, FISCHEREI- UND FLUSSBIOLOGIE. [Munch. Beitr. Abwasser-Fisch.- Flussbiol.]. **VFOAT** Munchener Beitraege zur Abwasser-, Fischerei- und Flussbiologie. No. 1 (1953)-. Academic Scholarly Publication. German. One time a year. $50.67. R Oldenbourg Verlag, Postfach 801360, D-81613 Munich Germany. **Tel** 011 49 89 450190, FAX 011 49 89 45019305. Documents available from CASDDS.
Ind/Abst Chem. Abstr.; Curr. Cit.

ISSN 0164-2057
US
CODEN NCSFDT
NATO CONFERENCE SERIES. IV. MARINE SCIENCES. [Nato conf. ser., IV, Mar. sci.]. **Added/Corp** North Atlantic Treaty Organization. Scientific Affairs Division. **VAT** North Atlantic Treaty Organization Conference Series. Four. Marine Sciences. Vol. 1 (197?)-. Monographic series. English. Irregular. Price varies per volume. North Atlantic Treaty Organization, Distribution Unit, 1110 Brussels Belgium. **Tel** 011 32 2 2414400. Documents available from Ask*IEEE.
Ind/Abst Aquat. Sci. Fish. Abstr. [CD-ROM Ed.]; INSPEC.

LC QH90.A1 H9
DD 574.5/263/05 NE
CODEN NJAEEK
NETHERLANDS JOURNAL OF AQUATIC ECOLOGY : JOURNAL OF THE NETHERLANDS SOCIETY OF AQUATIC ECOLOGY. **Added/Corp** Nederlandse Vereniging voor Aquatische Ecologie. Vol. 26, No. 1 (Nov. 1992)-. Academic Scholarly Publication. English. Four times a year. $143.88. Netherlands Society of Aquatic Ecology, PO Box 1 Rivm Lwd, J H Janse, 3720 Ba Bilthoven, Netherlands. **Tel** 011 31 30 743136. Documents available from CASDDS. ***Continues*** *Hydrobiological Bulletin, 0165-1404.*
Desc: Information on aquatic biology and ecology.
Ind/Abst Chem. Abstr.; Curr. Cit.

LC GC1 .N48 **ISSN** 0077-7579
NE
CODEN NJSRBA
Pr Rev.
NETHERLANDS JOURNAL OF SEA RESEARCH. [Neth. j. sea res.]. **Added/Corp** Nederlands Instituut voor Onderzoek der Zee. Vol. 1 (April 1961)-. Periodical. English (French and German). Four times a year. Fl.200.00. Netherlands Institute of Sea Research, PO Box 59, 1790 AB Texel Netherlands. **Tel** 011 31 2220 19541. Documents available from The Genuine Article, BIOSIS Document Express, CASDDS, Documents on Demand.
Ind/Abst AGRICOLA; Aquat. Sci. Fish. Abstr. [CD-ROM Ed.]; Biol. Abstr.; Chem. Abstr.; Curr. Aware. Biol. Sci., CABS; Curr. Cit.; Curr. Contents Agric. Biol. Environ. Sci.; Curr. Ref. Fish Res.; Ecol. Abstr.; Ecology Abstr.; EMBASE; Environ. Abstr.; Fluid Abstr., Civil Eng.; Fluid Abstr. Proc. Eng.; FLUIDEX (199?-); Geogr. Abstr. Phys. Geogr.; GeoRef; Helminthol. Abstr. (1991-); Mar. Sci. Contents Tables; Ocean. Abstr.; Life Sci. Collect.; Res. Alert [Full Cov.]; Sci. Cit. Index; SCISEARCH.

LC QH91.A1 N48 **ISSN** 0028-8330
NZ
CCC
CODEN NZJMBS
Pr Rev.
NEW ZEALAND JOURNAL OF MARINE AND FRESHWATER RESEARCH. [N. Z. j. mar. freshwater res.]. **Added/Corp** New Zealand. Dept. of Scientific and Industrial Research. **VFOAT** Journal of Marine and Freshwater Research; N.Z. Journal of Marine and Freshwater Research. Vol. 1 (March 1967)-. Academic Scholarly Publication. English. Four times a year (Mar., June, Sep., Dec.). $200.00. SIR Publishing, PO Box 399, Wellington New Zealand. **Tel** 011 64 4 472 7421, FAX 011 64 4 473 1841. **ED** Jaap Jasperse. **Bk Rev. Ad Acc. Circ:** 750 (ctrl). Documents available from The Genuine Article, BIOSIS Document Express, CASDDS, Documents on Demand.
Desc: Published for researchers and resource managers in research institutes, universities, museums, regional authorities, and other centers concerned with fisheries and aquatic sciences in New Zealand and the wider South Pacific region.
Ind/Abst AgBiotech News Inf.; AGRICOLA; Anim. Breed. Abstr.; Aquat. Sci. Fish. Abstr. [CD-ROM Ed.]; Biocont. News Inf. (1991-); Biol. Abstr.; Chem. Abstr.; Curr. Aware. Biol. Sci., CABS; Curr. Cit.; Curr. Contents Agric. Biol. Environ. Sci.; Curr. Ref. Fish Res.; Ecol. Abstr.; Ecology Abstr.; EMBASE; Entomol. Abstr.; Environ. Abstr.; Environ. Period. Bibliogr.; Fish Rev. (19??-199?); Fresh. Aqua. Contents Tables; Geogr. Abstr. Phys. Geogr.; Geol. Abstr.; GeoRef; Mar. Sci. Contents Tables; Microbiol. Abstr. Sect. C; Nutr. Abstr. Rev., Ser. B, Live Feeds and Feed.; Ocean. Abstr.; Life Sci. Collect.; Pollut. Abstr. Indexes; Res. Alert [Select. Cov.]; Rev. Med. Vet. Entomol.; SCISEARCH; Soils Fert.; Weed Abstr.; Wildl. Rev. (19??-199?).

LC GC1 .W39 S381 .A35 subser. **ISSN** 0083-7903
DD 551.4600 NZ
CODEN NZOMAI
NEW ZEALAND OCEANOGRAPHIC INSTITUTE MEMOIR. **See** Earth Sciences-Oceanography.

LC QH91
DD 574.92 JA
CODEN PSJBAZ
NIHON PURANKUTON GAKKAI HO. **Added/Corp** Nihon Purankuton Gakkai. Nihon Purankuton Gakkai. Bulletin. Nihon Purankuton Kenkyu Renrakukai. Information Bulletin on Planktology in Japan. **VFOAT** Bulletin of Plankton Society of Japan. (1953)-. Bulletin. Japanese (summaries and/or abstracts in English; table of contents in English). Two times a year. ¥6,000. Hiroshima University, Saijyo Higashi-Hiroshima, Hiroshima Japan. **Tel** 03-376-1251. **ED** Taku Onbe. **Bk Rev. Ad Acc. Circ:** 1,000 (ctrl). Documents available from BIOSIS Document Express.
Desc: Covers research in the development of plankton.
Ind/Abst Aquat. Sci. Fish. Abstr. [CD-ROM Ed.]; Biol. Abstr.; Ecology Abstr.; Microbiol. Abstr. Sect. B (19??-19??); Microbiol. Abstr. Sect. C.

LC SH1 .N5 **ISSN** 0021-5392
JA
CCC
CODEN NSUGAF
Pr Rev. **TITLE CHANGE**
NIHON SUISAN GAKKAI SHI. **See** Fish and Fisheries.

LC GC1000 .N67 **ISSN** 1066-8357
DD 547 US
NOR'EASTER (NARRAGANSETT, R.I.). (NOR'EASTER.). [Nor'easter]. **Added/Corp** University of Rhode Island. Sea Grant College Program. Vol. 1, No. 1, (Spring 1989)-. Periodical. English. Two times a year. Free on request. University of Rhode Island / Bay Campus, Narragansett RI 02882. **Tel** (401)792-1000. **ED** Carole Jaworski. **Circ:** 10,500 (ctrl).
Desc: Covers marine related issues.

ISSN 0332-7132
DD 639.3 NO
NORSK FISKEOPPDRETT. [Nor. fiskeoppdrett]. (1976)-. Periodical. Norwegian. Twenty-two times a year. $95.93. Norsk Fiskeppdrett A S, Slottsgatan 3, N 5000 Bergen Norway. **Tel** 011 47 5 5317554, FAX 011 47 5 5322663. **ED** Gustav Erik Blaalid. **Ad Acc, Adv Mgr:** Barresen.

LC GC1 .N64 **ISSN** 0148-9836
DD 574.92/34 US
CODEN NGSCDE
Pr Rev. **TITLE CHANGE**
NORTHEAST GULF SCIENCE. **See** Earth Sciences-Oceanography.

Biology — Marine Biology

LC GC1 .O24
DD 551.46/005
ISSN 0748-1489
US
CODEN OABTAE

OCEANIC ABSTRACTS (BETHESDA, MD.). See Earth Sciences-Abstracting, Bibliographies and Statistics.

LC GC1 .O32
DD 551.46/005
ISSN 0078-3218
UK
CODEN OCMBAT

OCEANOGRAPHY AND MARINE BIOLOGY. See Earth Sciences-Oceanography.

LC GC1 .O37
DD 551.4/6/005
ISSN 0392-6613
IT
CODEN OEBAEN

OEBALIA. [Oebalia]. **Added/Corp** Istituto Sperimentale Talassografico. Vol. 1 (1975)-. Italian (Italian and French; summaries and/or abstracts in English). Two times a year. Istituto Sperimentale Talassografico CNR, Via Rome 3, 74100 Taranto Italy. **Tel** (099)25434-94957, FAX (099)94811. Index available. **Bk Rev. Circ:** 600. Documents available from BIOSIS Document Express.
Desc: Covers marine biology, oceanography and pollution.
Ind/Abst Biol. Abstr. (1984-); Fish Rev. (Jan. 1989-July 1992); Wildl. Rev. (Jan. 1989-July 1992).

LC QH91.A1
ISSN 0078-5326
DK
CODEN OPHLAN
Pr Rev.
OPHELIA. [Ophelia]. Vol. 1 (May 1964)-. Periodical. English. Six times a year. Kr12440. Apollo Books, Kirkeby Sand 19, DK 5771 Stenstrup Denmark. **Tel** 011 45 62 263737, telex 39296 BRILL NL. **ED** Kirsten Muus. Index available. **Ad Acc. Circ:** 500. Documents available from The Genuine Article, BIOSIS Document Express, CASDDS.
Desc: Marine biology and ecology.
Ind/Abst AGRICOLA; Biol. Abstr.; Chem. Abstr.; Curr. Aware. Biol. Sci.; CABS; Curr. Cit.; Curr. Contents Agric. Biol. Environ. Sci.; Ecology Abstr.; Energy Res. Abstr. (July 1977-); Fish Rev.; GeoRef; Helminthol. Abstr. (1991-); Mar. Sci. Contents Tables; Nutr. Abstr. Rev., Ser. B, Live Feeds and Feed.; Ocean. Abstr.; Life Sci. Collect.; Res. Alert [Full Cov.]; Sci. Cit. Index; SCISEARCH; Wildl. Rev.

LC GC861 .O83
DD 551.46
IO

●**OSEANOLOGI DAN LIMNOLOGI DI INDONESIA.** See Earth Sciences-Oceanography.

LC GC861 .O83
DD 551.46
ISSN 0125-9830
IO
TITLE CHANGE

OSEANOLOGI DI INDONESIA. See Earth Sciences-Oceanography.

LC GC1 .O24
DD 551.46/005
US

OUR LIVING OCEANS : THE ... ANNUAL REPORT ON THE STATUS OF U.S. LIVING MARINE RESOURCES.
Added/Corp United States. National Marine Fisheries Service. **VFOAT** Annual Report on the Status of U.S. Living Marine Resources. 1st (1991)-. English. US Department of Commerce / National Marine Fisheries Service, 1335 East-West Highway, Silver Spring MD 20910. **Tel** (301)713-2239, FAX (301)713-2258.

LC AS36 .F57
DD 551.46082
US

PAPERS - FLORIDA STATE UNIVERSITY, TALLAHASSEE. OCEANOGRAPHIC INSTITUTE. See Earth Sciences-Oceanography.

ISSN 1146-5476
FR
UDC 011
CEASED

PASCAL. E 57, BIOLOGIE MARINE.
VFOAT PASCAL. E 57, Marine Biology; PASCAL. E Cinquante-Sept, Biologie Marine. (1990)-(199?). Periodical. Multiple languages. CNRS / Institut d'Information Scientifique et Technique, (Centre National de la Recherche Scientifique), 15 Quai Anatole France, 75700 Paris France. **Tel** 011 33 1 47531515, FAX 011 33 1 45517307, telex 260034. **Continues** Pascal Explore, E57: Biologie Marine.

LC QH193.T46 R47
DD 574.9593/05
ISSN 0858-1088
TH
CODEN RBPCE9
Pr Rev.
PHUKET MARINE BIOLOGICAL CENTER. (RESEARCH BULLETIN / PHUKET MARINE BIOLOGICAL CENTER.) [Phuket Mar. Biol. Cent.]. **Added/Corp** Sun Chiwawitthaya Thang Thale Phuket. No. 1 (1973)-. Bulletin. English. Irregular (1-2 issues), per volume. $10.00. Phuket Marine Biological Center, PO Box 60, Phuket 83000 Thailand. **Tel** 011 66 76 391128, FAX 011 66 76 391127. **ED** Samsak Chullasorn. **Circ:** 550.

available with illustrations. Documents available from BIOSIS Document Express.
Desc: Examines research results carried out at the Center and also independent research in Thailand.
Ind/Abst Biol. Abstr.; Ocean. Abstr.

LC QH301 .P67
DD 574.92/05
ISSN 0032-3764
PL
CODEN PAHYA2

POLSKIE ARCHIWUM HYDROBIOLOGII. (POLSKIE ARCHIWUM HYDROBIOLOGII. POLISH ARCHIVES OF HYDROBIOLOGY.). [Pol. arch. hydrobiol.]. **Added/Corp** Instytut Biologii Doswiadczalnej im. M. Nenckiego. Instytut Ekologii (Polska Akademia Nauk). **VFOAT** Polish Archives of Hydrobiology. Vol. 1 (1953)-. Academic Scholarly Publication. English (Polish; summaries and/or abstracts in Russian; table of contents in Russian). Four times a year. $60.00. **(Subscription address:** Ars Polona-Ruch, PO Box 1001, Krakowskie Przedmiescie 7, 00-068 Warsaw Poland. **Tel** 011 48 22 261201.) Documents available from BIOSIS Document Express, CASDDS. **Supersedes** Archiwum Hydrobiologii I Rybactwa.
Ind/Abst AGRICOLA; Aquat. Sci. Fish. Abstr. [CD-ROM Ed.]; Biol. Abstr.; Chem. Abstr.; Curr. Cit.; Curr. Ref. Fish Res.; Ecol. Abstr.; Ecology Abstr.; Fish Rev.; Fresh. Aqua. Contents Tables; Geogr. Abstr. Phys. Geogr.; Life Sci. Collect.; Wildl. Rev.

LC GC1005.2 .S8A
DD 551.46/005
ISSN 0270-1480
US

PROCEEDINGS OF THE ANNUAL STUDENT SYMPOSIUM ON MARINE AFFAIRS. [Proc. annu. Stud. Symp. Mar. Aff.]. **Main/Conf** Student Symposium on Marine Affairs. 1st-1976-. Proceedings. English. One time a year. University of Hawaii Sea Grant College Program, 1000 Pope Road, Room 200, Honolulu HI 96822. **Tel** (808)956-7410, FAX (808)956-2880.

LC QH95.58 .N56A
DD 574.998/9
ISSN 0914-563X
JA
CODEN PNSBEF

PROCEEDINGS OF THE NIPR SYMPOSIUM ON POLAR BIOLOGY. [Proc. NIPR Symp. Polar Biol.]. **Main/Conf** NIPR Symposium on Polar Biology. **Added/Corp** Kokuritsu Kyokuchi Kenkyujo. No. 1 (1987)-. Proceedings. English. National Institute of Polar Research, 9-10 Kaga 1-Chome, Itabashi-ku Tokyo 173 Japan. **Tel** 011 81 3 9624711, FAX 011 81 3 9622529. Documents available from BIOSIS Document Express. **Continues** Symposium on Polar Biology. Proceeding of the ... Symposium on Polar Biology.
Ind/Abst Biol. Abstr. (1989-1990); Curr. Geogr. Publ. (199?-).

LC GC1 .P7
DD 551.46082
ISSN 0079-6611
UK
CCC
NLM W1 PR675U
CODEN POCNA8
Pr Rev.
PROGRESS IN OCEANOGRAPHY. See Earth Sciences-Oceanography.

LC QH90
DD 574.92
ISSN 0166-106X
NE
CODEN NSRPDU

PUBLICATION SERIES / NETHERLANDS INSTITUTE FOR SEA RESEARCH. [Publ. ser. - Neth. Inst. Sea Res.]. **Added/Corp** Nederlands Instituut voor Onderzoek der Zee. No. 1 (1978)-. Monographic series. English. Irregular. Price varies per volume. Netherlands Institute of Sea Research, PO Box 59, 1790 AB Texel Netherlands. **Tel** 011 31 2220 19541. Documents available from BIOSIS Document Express, CASDDS.
Ind/Abst Biol. Abstr.; Chem. Abstr.; Ecol. Abstr.; Geogr. Abstr. Phys. Geogr.

ISSN 0389-6609
JA

PUBLICATIONS OF THE SETO MARINE BIOLOGICAL LABORATORY. SPECIAL PUBLICATION SERIES. **Added/Corp** Kyoto Daigaku. Seto Rinkai Jikkenjo. Vol. 6 (1981)-. Monographic series. English. Kyoto Daigaku Rigakubu Fuzoku Seto Rinkai Jikkenjo, (Seto Marine Biological Lab. Faculty of Science Kyoto University), Shirahamacho Nishimurogun, Wakayamaken 649-22 Japan. **Continues** Special Publications from the Seto Marine Biological Laboratory.
Ind/Abst Aquat. Sci. Fish. Abstr. [CD-ROM Ed.]; Ocean. Abstr.

LC QH92
DD 574.92
ISSN 0273-1355
US

QUARTERLY REPORT - MIT SEA GRANT PROGRAM. (QUARTERLY REPORT / MIT SEA GRANT.). [Q. rep. - MIT Sea Grant Prog.]. **Main/Corp** Massachusetts Institute of Technology. Sea Grant Program. **Added/Corp** Massachusetts Institute of Technology. Sea Grant College Program. **VAT** Quarterly Report - Massachusetts Institute of Technology Sea Grant Program. (Summer 1979)-. Periodical. English. Four times a year. Free on request. Massachusetts Institute of Technology (MIT) / Sea Grant College Program, 292 Main Street, Third Floor, Cambridge MA 02139. **Tel** (617)253-7041. **ED** Karen Hartley and Carolyn Levi. **Circ:** 2,000. Documents available from Documents on Demand.
Ind/Abst Environ. Abstr.; Ocean. Abstr.

LC QH91.A1 R47
ISSN 0080-2115
CL
Pr Rev.
REVISTA DE BIOLOGIA MARINA. [Rev. biol. mar.]. **Added/Corp** Universidad de Chile. Departamento de Oceanologia. Universidad de Chile. Estacion de Biologia Marina. Vol. 1 (April 1948)-. Periodical. Spanish (English; summaries and/or abstracts in English). Two times a year. $12.00. Universidad de Valparaiso / Instituto de Oceanologia, Casilla Postal 13-D, Vina del Mar Chile. **ED** Luis Ramorino. **Ad Acc. Circ:** 900 (ctrl). **Continues** Montemar, 0544-9103.
Desc: Original papers on marine biology, marine ecology and oceanography dealing mainly with the Southeastern Pacific Ocean.
Ind/Abst Aquat. Sci. Fish. Abstr. [CD-ROM Ed.]; Ecol. Abstr.; Fish Rev.; Geogr. Abstr. Phys. Geogr. (?-?); Geol. Abstr.; GeoRef; Ocean. Abstr.; Life Sci. Collect.

LC QH109.C9 R44
DD 574.97291/05
ISSN 0252-1962
CU
CODEN RIMAD2

REVISTA DE INVESTIGACIONES MARINAS. [Rev. invest. mar.]. **Added/Corp** Universidad de La Habana. **VFOAT** Revista Investigaciones Marinas. Vol. 1 No. 1 (1980)-. Periodical. Spanish (summaries and/or abstracts in English). Three times a year. $24.00. Ediciones Cubanas, Obispo 527 Altos ESQ Bernaza, CP 10100 Havana Cuba. **Bk Rev. Ad Acc. Circ:** 10,000. Documents available from BIOSIS Document Express. **Continues** Ciencias. Serie 8: Investigaciones Marinas.
Desc: Publishes original articles on research related to the aquatic and fishing sciences, ecology, cultures of aquatic organisms, fish biology, physiology, ichthyology, plankton, benthos, conservation, environmental projects, oceanography, physics and chemistry.
Ind/Abst Biol. Abstr.; GeoRef.

ISSN 0399-1075
FR

REVUE FRANCAISE D'AQUARIOLOGIE, HERPETOLOGIE. Periodical. French (English). Four times a year. $32.81. Mus de Zool, 34 R Ste Catherine, 54000 Nancy France. **Tel** 011 33 83 329997. Index available. **Bk Rev.**
Desc: Original papers dealing with marine and fresh water species of Fish and invertebrates, amphibians and reptiles.

LC QH91.A1 B5213
DD 574.92/05
ISSN 1063-0740
US
CCC

RUSSIAN JOURNAL OF MARINE BIOLOGY. (1992)-. Academic Scholarly Publication. English. Six times a year. $765.00. Consultants Bureau, A Division of Plenum Publishing Corporation, 233 Spring Street, New York NY 10013. **Tel** (212)620-8000, (212)620-8466, FAX (212)463-0742, telex 23/421139. **Continues** Soviet Journal of Marine Biology, 0145-1456.
Ind/Abst EMBASE; Life Sci. Collect.; Pollut. Abstr. Indexes.

LC QH91.A1 S17
ISSN 0036-4827
NO
CODEN SARIA3
Pr Rev.
SARSIA. [Sarsia]. **Added/Corp** Universitetet i Bergen. Vol. 1 (March 1961)-. Monographic series. English (German). Four times a year. $104.65. University of Bergen, Department of Fisheries and Marine Biology, Bergen High-Technology Center, N-5020 Bergen Norway. **Tel** 011 47 5 544400, FAX 011 47 5 544450. **ED** Ulf Bamstedt. **Circ:** 750. Documents available from The Genuine Article, CASDDS. **Supersedes** Publications / Universitetet I Bergen. Biologisk Stasjon, Espergrend.
Desc: Results of original research on all aspects of marine biology and ecology, specifically concentrating on Nordic and North Atlantic organisms and their environment.
Ind/Abst Chem. Abstr. (-1976); Curr. Aware. Biol. Sci.; CABS; Curr. Cit.; Curr. Contents Agric. Biol. Environ. Sci.; Curr. Ref. Fish Res.; EMBASE; Fish Rev.; GeoRef; Helminthol. Abstr.; Mar. Sci. Contents Tables; Nematol. Abstr.; Nutr. Abstr. Rev., Ser. B, Live Feeds and Feed.; Life Sci. Collect.; Res. Alert [Full Cov.]; Rev. Med. Vet. Entomol.; Sci. Cit. Index; SCISEARCH; Wildl. Rev.

LC SH285 .I6
DD 574.92
ISSN 0214-8358
SP
CODEN SCIMEM

SCIENTIA MARINA. [Sci. mar.]. **Added/Corp** Instituto de Ciencias del Mar (Barcelona, Spain). **VFOAT** Revista de Ciencias Marinas; Journal on Marine Sciences. Vol. 53, No. 1 (March 1989)-. Academic Scholarly Publication. Spanish (English). Four times a year. $133.17. Instituto de Ciencias del Mar, Paseo Nacional S N Biblioteca, 08039 Barcelona Spain. **Tel** 011 34 3 3106416, 011 34 3 3106450. Documents available from BIOSIS Document Express, CASDDS. **Continues** Investigacion Pesquera (Barcelona, Spain), 0020-9953.

Ind/Abst Aquat. Sci. Fish. Abstr. [CD-ROM Ed.]; Biol. Abstr. (1991-); Chem. Abstr.; Ecology Abstr.; Fish Rev. (Jan. 1989-July 1992); Food Sci. Technol. Abstr.; GeoRef; Mar. Sci. Contents Tables; Ocean. Abstr.; Life Sci. Collect.; Pollut. Abstr. Indexes; Refer. Z.; Wildl. Rev. (Jan. 1989-July 1992).

LC QL737.C4 S38 **ISSN** 0917-0537
DD 599.5/05 JA
CODEN SRCTEG
SCIENTIFIC REPORTS OF CETACEAN RESEARCH. **See** Zoology.

LC GC
DD 551.46 US
SEA GRANT PROGRAM REPORT. **See** Earth Sciences-Oceanography.

ISSN 0700-9275
DD 590/.744/971133 CN
SEA PEN. **Added/Corp** Vancouver Public Aquarium. Vol. 20, No. 1, (Jan. 1976)-. Periodical. English. Five times a year. 15.00Can$ Canada; $8.65 US. Vancouver Public Aquarium Association, PO Box 3232, Vancouver British Columbia V6B 3X8 Canada. **Tel** (604)685-3364, FAX (604)631-2529. **Bk Rev. Circ:** 19,000 (ctrl). ***Continues** Vancouver Public Aquarium Newsletter, 0042-2495.*
Desc: Membership news and activities, marine biology, new exhibits, field trips, photographs, research projects and new specimens.

ISSN 1011-1603
DD 551.46/005 CN
SEA WIND. (SEA WIND : BULLETIN OF THE INTERNATIONAL MARINELIFE ALLIANCE.). [Sea wind]. **Added/Corp** International Marinelife Alliance. Ocean Voice International. (Jan./Mar. 1987)-. Bulletin. English (summaries and/or abstracts in French). Four times a year. 50.00Can$. Ocean Voice International, 3332 McCarthy Road, Box 37026, Ottawa Ontrio K1V 0W0 Canada. **Tel** (613)990-2207, FAX (613)521-4205. **ED** S Ochinan. Index available. cum. index. **Bk Rev. Ad Acc. Circ:** 1,000.
Desc: Shares knowledge about sea life, conservation and equitable sustainable marine harvesting.

ISSN 0272-6084
US
CODEN SCSLDY
SEDIMENTA. [Sedimenta]. **Added/Corp** Rosenstiel School of Marine and Atmospheric Sciences. Comparative Sedimentology Laboratory. (1971)-. Monographic series. English. Irregular. Price varies per volume. University of Miami Comparative Sedimentology Lab, RSMAS - MGG, 4600 Rickenbacker Causeway, Miami FL 33139. **Tel** (305)672-1841, FAX (305)361-4632, telex 7401484.
Ind/Abst GeoRef.

LC QE39 .S4 **ISSN** 0080-889X
DD 551.46/08 GW
CCC
CODEN SEMADJ
SENCKENBERGIANA MARITIMA. **See** Earth Sciences-Oceanography.

LC QH90.A1 S53 **ISSN** 1000-0615
CC
SHUICHAN XUEBAO. (SHUI CHAN HSUEH PAO.). **Added/Corp** Chung-Kuo Shui Chan Hsueh Hui. **VFOAT** Shuichan Xuebao; Journal of Fisheries of China. (19??)-. Periodical. Chinese (summaries and/or abstracts in English and Russian). Four times a year. $25.70. **(Subscription address:** China International Book Trading Corporation, PO Box 399, Library Service Department, Beijing 100044 People's Republic of China. **Tel** 011 86 1 8414284, FAX 011 86 1 8412023, telex 22496 CIBTC CN.)
Ind/Abst Aquat. Sci. Fish. Abstr. [CD-ROM Ed.]; Index Vet.; Ocean. Abstr.; Vet. Bull.

LC SH315.S7 S59b
DD 574.968 SA
SOUTH AFRICAN JOURNAL OF MARINE SCIENCE / REPUBLIC OF SOUTH AFRICA, DEPARTMENT OF ENVIRONMENT AFFAIRS, SEA FISHERIES RESEARCH INSTITUTE. **Added/Corp** Sea Fisheries Research Institute (South Africa). **VFOAT** Suid-Afrikaanse Tydskrif vir Seewetenskap. (1983)-. Periodical. English (summaries and/or abstracts in Afrikaans). Documents available from The Genuine Article, BIOSIS Document Express. ***Continues** Fisheries Bulletin (Sea Fisheries Institute (South Africa)), 0254-3559.*
Ind/Abst Aquat. Sci. Fish. Abstr. [CD-ROM Ed.]; Biol. Abstr. (1983-); Curr. Aware. Biol. Sci., CABS; Curr. Cit.; Curr. Contents Agric. Biol. Environ. Sci.; Ecology Abstr.; Life Sci. Collect. (1985-); Res. Alert [Select. Cov.].

UK
Pr Rev.
STEREO-ATLAS OF OSTRACOD SHELLS; EDITED BY P.C. SYLVESTER-BRADLEY AND DAVID J. SIVETER. (1973)-. Periodical. English. Two times a year (July & Dec.). $140.00 US and Canada; £80.00 other. British Micropaleontological Society, British Museum of Natural History, London SW7 5BD United Kingdom. **Tel** 011 44 171 9388837, FAX 011 44 171 9389277. **ED** Dr. J. E. Whittaker. Index available. **Ad Acc. Circ:** 350.
Desc: Stereo photographs and line drawings of ostracods together with a brief taxonomic description.

ISSN 0362-2886
US
CODEN NYTRAH
TECHNICAL REPORT - MARINE SCIENCES RESEARCH CENTER, STATE UNIVERSITY OF NEW YORK. **See** Earth Sciences-Oceanography.

LC QH91.A1 T45
DD 574.92 SP
THALASSAS : REVISTA DE CIENCIAS DEL MAR. (1983)-. Periodical. Spanish (Spanish). Universidad de Santiago / Publicaciones, Servicio de Publicaciones e Intercambio Cientifico, Campus Universitario, Santiago de Compostela, E-15706 Santiago Spain. **Tel** 011 34 59-35-00.
Ind/Abst Aquat. Sci. Fish. Abstr. [CD-ROM Ed.].

LC GC
DD 551.46 FR
UNESCO REPORTS IN MARINE SCIENCE. **See** Earth Sciences-Oceanography.

MICROBIOLOGY

LC QR
DD 576 CN
ABSTRACTS OF THE CANADIAN SOCIETY OF MICROBIOLOGY. **See** Biology-Abstracting, Bibliographies and Statistics.

ISSN 1060-2011
DD 576 US
CCC
NLM W1; AM767 **CODEN** AGMME8
ABSTRACTS OF THE ... GENERAL MEETING OF THE AMERICAN SOCIETY FOR MICROBIOLOGY. **See** Biology-Abstracting, Bibliographies and Statistics.

ISSN 0204-8809
BU
CCC
NLM W1 AC8625M **CODEN** AMBUDI
ACTA MICROBIOLOGICA BULGARICA. [Acta microbiol. bulg.]. **Added/Corp** Bulgarska Akademiia na Naukite. Vol. 1 (1978)-. Academic Scholarly Publication. Bulgarian (summaries and/or abstracts in English and Russian). Irregular. **(Subscription address:** Hemus Foreign Trade Organization, 1B Raiko Daskalov Sq Books, 1000 Sofia Bulgaria. **Tel** 011 359 2 882544, 011 359 2 801575.) Documents available from BIOSIS Document Express, CASDDS. ***Formed by the union of** Prilozhna Mikrobiologiia, 0323-9853 **and** Acta Microbiologica, Virologica et Immunologica, 0324-0452.*
Ind/Abst Biocont. News Inf. (1991-); Biodeter. Abstr. (1991-); Biol. Abstr.; Chem. Abstr.; Curr. Cit.; Dairy Sci. Abstr.; EMBASE; Index Med.; Index Vet.; PESTDOC; Rev. Agric. Entomol.; Rev. Med. Vet. Entomol.; Sug. Indus. Abstr.; Vet. Bull.; Trop. Dis. Bull.

LC QR1 .A35 **ISSN** 1217-8950
DD 576 HU
NLM W1; AC8645NL
•**ACTA MICROBIOLOGICA ET IMMUNOLOGICA HUNGARICA.** (1994)-. Academic Scholarly Publication. English (French, German and Russian). Four times a year. $98.00. Akademiai Kiado, Publishing House of the Hungarian Academy of Sciences, Prielle Kornelia u. 19-35, H-1117 Budapest Hungary. **Tel** 011 36 1 1811991, FAX 011 36 1 1811991, telex 22-6228 AKNYO H. Index available (free). ***Continues** Acat Microbiologica Hungarica, 0231-4622.*

LC QR1 .A35 **ISSN** 0231-4622
DD 576/.05 HU
NLM W1; AC8625P **CODEN** AMHUEF
Pr Rev. **TITLE CHANGE**
ACTA MICROBIOLOGICA HUNGARICA. [Acta microbiol. Hung.]. **Added/Corp** Magyar Tudomanyos Akademia. Vol. 30, No. 1 (1983)-(1993). Academic Scholarly Publication. English. Akademiai Kiado, Publishing House of the Hungarian Academy of Sciences, Prielle Kornelia u. 19-35, H-1117 Budapest Hungary. **Tel** 011 36 1 1811991, FAX 011 36 1 1811991, telex 22-6228 AKNYO H. **ED** Istvan Nasz and Bela Lanyi (editorial address: Acta Microbiologica, Institute of Microbiology, Semmelweis University Medical School, PO Box 370, H-1445 Budapest Hungary). cum. index. **Bk Rev. Ad Acc.** Documents available from The Genuine Article, BIOSIS Document Express, CASDDS. ***Continues** Acta Microbiologica Academiae Scientiarum Hungaricae. **Continued by** Acta Microbiologica et Immunologica Hungarica.*
Desc: Devoted to the publication of research on medical and veterinary bacteriology, bacterial genetics, virology, mycology, parasitology, as well as on immunology and epidemiology, agricultural and industrial microbiology.
Ind/Abst AGRICOLA (1983-); Biodeter. Abstr. (1991-); Biol. Abstr. (1983-); Chem. Abstr. (1983-); Curr. Aware. Biol. Sci., CABS; Curr. Cit.; Curr. Contents Life Sci.; Dairy Sci. Abstr.; EMBASE; Health Plan. Adminis.; Immunol. Abstr.; Index Med.; Index Vet.; Microbiol. Abstr. Sect. B (19??-19??); Microbiol. Abstr. Sect. A; Microbiol. Abstr. Sect. C; Nat. Prod. Updates; Life Sci. Collect. (1983-); PESTDOC; Poult. Abstr.; Res. Alert [Full Cov.]; Rev. Med. Vet. Mycology; Sci. Cit. Index; SCISEARCH; Vet. Bull.; Trop. Dis. Bull.

ISSN 0001-6195
PL
NLM W1 AC862W **CODEN** AMPOAX
ACTA MICROBIOLOGICA POLONICA. [Acta microbiol. Pol.]. **Added/Corp** Polskie Towarzystwo Mikrobiologow. Vol. 25 (1976)-. Periodical. English (Polish). Four times a year. $54.00. **(Subscription address:** Ars Polona-Ruch, PO Box 1001, Krakowskie Przedmiescie 7, 00-068 Warsaw Poland. **Tel** 011 48 22 261201.) Index available. Documents available from The Genuine Article, BIOSIS Document Express, CASDDS. ***Formed by the union of** Acta Microbiologica Polonica. Series A. Microbiologia Generalis, 0567-7815 **and** Acta Microbiologica Polonica. Series B. Microbiologia Applicata, 0567-7823.*
Ind/Abst AgBiotech News Inf.; Anal. Abstr.; Biodeter. Abstr. (19??-19??); Biol. Abstr.; Chem. Abstr.; Curr. Biotechnol.; Curr. Cit.; Curr. Contents Agric. Biol. Environ. Sci.; Dairy Sci. Abstr.; EMBASE; Field Crop Abstr.; Food Sci. Technol. Abstr.; Genet. Abstr.; Grass. Forage Abstr.; Index Med.; Index Vet.; Microbiol. Abstr. Sect. B; Microbiol. Abstr. Sect. A; Microbiol. Abstr. Sect. C; Life Sci. Collect.; PESTDOC; Pig News Inf.; Plant Breed. Abstr.; Plant Grow. Reg. Abstr.; Protozoolog. Abstr.; Res. Alert [Select. Cov.]; Rev. Med. Vet. Mycology; Rev. Plant Pathol.; Rice Abstr.; SCISEARCH; Soils Fert.; Sorghum Mill. Abstr.; Vet. Bull.; Weed Abstr.

LC QR1 .A37 **ISSN** 0098-9150
DD 576/.05 US
NLM W1 AC863S **CODEN** AMSIDX
ACTA MICROBIOLOGICA SINICA. [Acta microbiol. sin.]. (Feb. 1975)-. Periodical. English (Chinese). Six times a year. $100.00. Science Press, 16 Donghuangchenggen North Street, Beijing 100707, People's Republic of China. **Tel** 011 86 1 4019821, 011 86 1 4010642, FAX 011 86 1 4012180, 011 86 1 4019810, telex 210147. Documents available from CASDDS.
Ind/Abst Biocont. News Inf. (1991-); Biodeter. Abstr. (19??-19??); Chem. Abstr.; Dairy Sci. Abstr.; Genet. Abstr.; Hortic. Abstr.; Index Vet.; Maize Abstr.; Microbiol. Abstr. Sect. B; Microbiol. Abstr. Sect. A; Microbiol. Abstr. Sect. C; NAPRALERT; Nutr. Abstr. Rev., Ser. B, Live Feeds and Feed.; Protozoolog. Abstr.; Rev. Agric. Entomol.; Rev. Med. Vet. Entomol.; Rev. Med. Vet. Mycology; Rev. Plant Pathol.; Soyabean Abstr.; Vet. Bull.; Virol. AIDS Abstr.

ISSN 0001-723X
XR
CCC
NLM W1 AC9562 **CODEN** AVIRA2
Pr Rev.
ACTA VIROLOGICA (ANGLICKA VERZE). (ACTA VIROLOGICA.). [Acta virol.]. **Added/Corp** Ceskoslovenska Akademie Ved. Vol. 1 (Jan./March 1957)-. Academic Scholarly Publication. English. Six times a year. $186.00. Slovak Academic Press Ltd, PO Box 57, 84005 Bratislava Slovakia. **Tel** 011 42 7 211729. **(Subscription address:** Harcourt Brace & Company, Ltd., Foots Cray High Street, Sidcup Kent DA14 5HP United Kingdom. **Tel** 011 44 181 3003322, FAX 011 44 181 3090807, telex 896 377 ACADEM.) **ED** D. Blaskovic. Index Available, published separately, free-automatically sent. **Bk Rev. Circ:** 1,200. available with charts; available with illustrations. Documents available from The Genuine Article, BIOSIS Document Express, CASDDS.
Desc: Articles are presented in basic and applied human, animal, and plant virology. Articles are published from all parts of the world and achieves particularly extensive coverage of the socialist countries.
Ind/Abst AgBiotech News Inf.; AGRICOLA [Select. Cov.]; Biol. Abstr.; Chem. Abstr.; CSA Neuro. Abstr. (?-?); Curr. Aware. Biol. Sci., CABS; Curr. Cit.; Curr. Contents Life Sci.; Dairy Sci. Abstr.; EMBASE; Fish Rev. (Jan. 1989-July 1992); Health Plan. Adminis.; Immunol. Abstr.; Index Med.; Index Vet.; Microbiol. Abstr. Sect. B (19??-19??); Microbiol. Abstr. Sect. A; NAPRALERT; Life Sci. Collect.; PESTDOC; Pig News Inf.; Poult. Abstr.; Ref. Upd. Deluxe Ed.; Res. Alert [Full Cov.]; Rev. Med. Vet. Entomol.; Rev. Plant Pathol.; Sci. Cit. Index; SCISEARCH; Vet. Bull.; Trop. Dis. Bull.; Virol. AIDS Abstr.; Wildl. Rev. (Jan. 1989-July 1992).

ISSN 0732-0574
DD 589 IT
NLM W1; AC97DAH **CODEN** ACTID2
Pr Rev.
ACTINOMYCETES (1982), THE. (THE ACTINOMYCETES.). [Actinomycetes]. **Added/Corp** Waksman Institute of Microbiology. International Centre

for Theoretical and Applied Ecology. Universita di Udine. Chair of Mycology. Vol. 16, No. 3 (1982)-. Academic Scholarly Publication. English. Three times a year. L95000. CETA Ctr Ecologia Teorica Applicata, Via Vittorio Veneto 19, 34170 Gorizia Italy. **Tel** 011 39 481 536466, FAX 011 39 481 536470. Index available. **Bk Rev. Circ:** 150. Documents available from CASDDS. ***Continues*** *Actinomycetes and Related Organisms (Augusta, GA. : 1979), 0892-0656.*
Desc: Scientific communications in microbiology.
Ind/Abst Chem. Abstr. (1982-1985/1986); Life Sci. Collect.

LC QR1 .A38 **ISSN** 0065-2164
DD 660.28449 US
UDC 579.6 **CCC**
NLM W1 AD436 **CODEN** ADAMAP
Pr Rev.
ADVANCES IN APPLIED MICROBIOLOGY. [Adv. appl. microbiol.]. Vol. 1 (1959)-. Academic Scholarly Publication. English. Irregular. Price varies per volume. Academic Press Inc., 6277 Sea Harbor Drive, Orlando FL 32887. **Tel** (800)543-9534, (407)345-4100, FAX (407)352-3445. **ED** Wayne W. Umbreit. Documents available from The Genuine Article, BIOSIS Document Express, CASDDS.
Ind/Abst AGRICOLA [Select. Cov.]; Biodeter. Abstr.; Biol. Abstr.; Chem. Abstr.; Curr. Aware. Biol. Sci., CABS; Curr. Biotechnol.; Curr. Cit.; Dairy Sci. Abstr.; EMBASE; Energy Res. Abstr.; Food Sci. Technol. Abstr.; Health Plan. Adminis.; Index Med.; Index Sci. Rev. [Full Cov.]; Index Vet.; Life Sci. Collect.; PESTDOC; Plant Grow. Reg. Abstr.; Ref. Upd. Basic Ed.; Ref. Upd. Deluxe Ed.; Res. Alert [Full Cov.]; Rev. Med. Vet. Mycology; Rev. Plant Pathol.; Sci. Cit. Index; SCISEARCH; Vet. Bull.

LC QR84 .A24 **ISSN** 0065-2911
DD 616.014 UK
UDC 579.22 616-095
NLM W1 AD681 **CODEN** AMIPB2
ADVANCES IN MICROBIAL PHYSIOLOGY. [Adv. microb. physiol.]. Vol. 1 (1967)-. Academic Scholarly Publication. English. Irregular. $99.00 (Vol. 36). Academic Press Inc., 6277 Sea Harbor Drive, Orlando FL 32887. **Tel** (800)543-9534, (407)345-4100, FAX (407)352-3445. **ED** A. H. Rose and J. F. Wilkinson. Documents available from The Genuine Article, BIOSIS Document Express, CASDDS.
Ind/Abst AGRICOLA [Select. Cov.]; Biol. Abstr.; Chem. Abstr.; Curr. Aware. Biol. Sci., CABS; Curr. Cit.; EMBASE; Index Med.; Index Sci. Rev. [Full Cov.]; Life Sci. Collect.; Ref. Upd. Basic Ed.; Ref. Upd. Deluxe Ed.; Res. Alert [Full Cov.]; Rev. Med. Vet. Mycology; Rev. Plant Pathol.; Sci. Cit. Index; SCISEARCH; Trop. Dis. Bull.

LC QR360 .A3 **ISSN** 0065-3527
DD 576.6 US
UDC 578 **CCC**
NLM W1 AD889 **CODEN** AVREA8
Pr Rev.
ADVANCES IN VIRUS RESEARCH. [Adv. virus res.]. Vol. 1 (1953)-. Academic Scholarly Publication. English. Irregular. $90.00 (Vol. 43). Academic Press Inc., 6277 Sea Harbor Drive, Orlando FL 32887. **Tel** (800)543-9534, (407)345-4100, FAX (407)352-3445. **ED** Kenneth M. Smith. cum. index. Documents available from The Genuine Article, BIOSIS Document Express, CASDDS.
Ind/Abst AgBiotech News Inf.; AGRICOLA [Select. Cov.]; Biol. Abstr.; Chem. Abstr.; Curr. Aware. Biol. Sci., CABS; Curr. Cit.; EMBASE; Energy Res. Abstr.; For. Prod. Abstr.; For. Abstr.; Health Plan. Adminis.; Hortic. Abstr.; Index Med.; Index Sci. Rev. [Full Cov.]; Index Vet.; Life Sci. Collect.; Pig News Inf.; Poult. Abstr.; Ref. Upd. Deluxe Ed.; Res. Alert [Full Cov.]; Rev. Med. Vet. Mycology; Rev. Plant Pathol.; Sci. Cit. Index; SCISEARCH; Vet. Bull.; Trop. Dis. Bull.; Virol. AIDS Abstr.

LC QR1 .A73
AG
ANALES. Main/Corp Argentine Republic. Instituto Nacional de Microbiologia. (1962)-. Periodical. Spanish. ***Supersedes*** *Argentine Republic. Instituto Nacional de Microbiologia. Revista.*

LC RS189 .A57 **ISSN** 0090-2284
DD 615/.3 US
ANALYTICAL MICROBIOLOGY. [Analyt. microbiol.]. Vol. 1 (1963)-. Academic Scholarly Publication. English. Academic Press Inc., 6277 Sea Harbor Drive, Orlando FL 32887. **Tel** (800)543-9534, (407)345-4100, FAX (407)352-3445.

ISSN 0358-4895
FI
NLM W1 AC954NM
ANATOMICA, PATHOLOGICA, MICROBIOLOGICA. **See** Medical Sciences-Anatomy.

ISSN 0390-5454
IT
NLM W1 AN486M
ANNALI DELL'OSPEDALE MARIA VITTORIA DI TORINO. [Ann. Osp. Maria Vittoria Torino]. **Added/Corp** Ospedale Maria Vittoria, Turin. Vol. 17 (1974)-. Periodical. Italian (summaries and/or abstracts in English). Two times a year. L15000 Italy; L21000 other. Ospedale Maria Vittoria, Via Cibrario 72, 10144 Turin Italy. ***Formed by the union of*** *Giornale di Batteriologia, Virologia ed Immunologia ed Annali dell'Ospedale Maria Vittoria di Torino. Parte 1: Sezione Microbiologia, 0301-1453* ***and*** *Giornale di Batteriologia, Virologia ed Immunologia ed Annali dell'Ospedale Maria Vittoria di Torino. Parte 2: Sezione Clinica, 0301-1445.*
Ind/Abst Index Med.; Life Sci. Collect.; Trop. Dis. Bull.

ISSN 0003-4649
IT
CODEN AMEZAB
Pr Rev.
ANNALI DI MICROBIOLOGIA ED ENZIMOLOGIA. [Ann. microbiol. enzimol.]. **Added/Corp** Societa Italiana di Microbiologia. (1957)-. Periodical. Italian (English and French; summaries and/or abstracts in English). Two times a year (July & Dec.). L136250. Annali di Microbiologia ed Enzimologia, Dipartimento di Scienze e Tecnologie, Alimentari e Microbiologiche, Universita degli Studi di Milan, Via G. Celoria 2, 20133 Milan Italy. **Tel** 011 39 2 70630829, 39 2 2367344, FAX 011 39 2 70638625. Index available. cum. index. **Bk Rev**, (Qty: 10). **Circ:** 500. Documents available from The Genuine Article, CASDDS. ***Continues*** *Annali di Microbiologia, 0301-5211.*
Desc: Covers microbiology fermentation, microbe transformation, enzymology, biochemistry, agriculture, and food.
Ind/Abst Biocont. News Inf. (19??-19??); Chem. Abstr.; Curr. Cit.; Dairy Sci. Abstr.; Food Sci. Technol. Abstr.; For. Abstr.; Maize Abstr.; Protozoolog. Abstr.; Res. Alert [Full Cov.]; Rev. Plant Pathol.; Rice Abstr.; Soils Fert.; Vitis Vitic. Enol. Abstr.

LC QR1 .A5 **ISSN** 0066-4227
DD 589.95058 US
CCC
NLM W1 AN778 **CODEN** ARMIAZ
Pr Rev.
ANNUAL REVIEW OF MICROBIOLOGY. [Annu. rev. microbiol.]. Vol. 1 (1947)-. Academic Scholarly Publication. English. One time a year (October). $53.00. Annual Reviews Inc., 4139 El Camino Way, PO Box 10139, Palo Alto CA 94303-0139. **Tel** (415)493-4400, (800)523-8635, FAX (415)855-9815. **ED** L. Nicholas Ornston. Index available. cum. index. ctrl circ. available on an online database; available on microfilm and microfiche from University Microfilms International (UMI). Documents available from The Genuine Article, BIOSIS Document Express, CASDDS.
Desc: Comprehensive, thorough coverage of latest advances in microbiology; written by acknowledged experts in the field. Extensive literature included.
Ind/Abst Abstr. Bull. Inst. Pap. Sci. Tech.; Acad. Search; AGRICOLA [Select. Cov.]; Biol. Agric. Index; Biol. Abstr.; Biol. Dig.; Chem. Abstr.; Curr. Aware. Biol. Sci., CABS; Curr. Biotechnol.; Curr. Cit.; Curr. Contents Life Sci.; Dairy Sci. Abstr.; EMBASE; Energy Res. Abstr.; EP Collect.; Food Sci. Technol. Abstr.; For. Prod. Abstr.; For. Abstr.; Gen. Sci. Index; Gen. Sci. Source; Health Plan. Adminis.; Helminthol. Abstr.; Homework Help.; Hortic. Abstr.; Index Med.; Index Sci. Rev. [Full Cov.]; Index Vet.; INFO-SOUTH Abstr.; INIS Atomindex [Micro.]; MasterFile FullTEXT 1000; MasterFile FullTEXT 350; MasterFile FullTEXT 650; MasterFile FullTEXT (July 1992-); Microbiol. Abstr. Sect. B; OCLC; Life Sci. Collect.; PESTDOC; Plant Breed. Abstr.; Protozoolog. Abstr.; Ref. Upd. Basic Ed.; Ref. Upd. Clinical Ed.; Ref. Upd. Deluxe Ed.; Res. Alert [Full Cov.]; Rev. Med. Vet. Entomol.; Rev. Med. Vet. Mycology; Rev. Plant Pathol.; Sci. Cit. Index; SCISEARCH; Soils Fert.; Telebase; Trop. Dis. Bull.; Vitis Vitic. Enol. Abstr.; Weed Abstr.

ISSN 1170-8875
DD 616.0105 NZ
TITLE CHANGE
ANTIMICROBIAL NEWSLETTER. [Antimicrob. newsl.]. (1991)-(1995). Periodical. English. Institute of Environmental Science and Research, PO Box 50 348, Porirua Wellington New Zealand. **Tel** 011 64 4 2370149. **ED** Maggie Bret. **Circ:** 140 (ctrl). ***Merged into*** *Lablink.*

ISSN 0738-1751
US
UDC 615.28 **CCC**
NLM W1; AN875F **CODEN** ANNLDO
TITLE CHANGE
ANTIMICROBIC NEWSLETTER, THE. [Antimicrob. newsl.]. **VFOAT** AMN. Vol. 1, No. 1 (Jan. 1984)-(1993). Newsletter. English. Elsevier Science Publishing Company Inc, Madison Square Station, PO Box 882, New York NY 10159-0882. **Tel** (212)633-3950, FAX (212)633-3990. **ED** Daniel Amsterdam. **Circ:** 1,200. available on microfilm and microfiche from University Microfilms International (UMI). Documents available from CASDDS. ***Continued by*** *Antimicrobics and Infectious Diseases Newsletter.*
Desc: Provides laboratory and clinical evaluation of antimicrobial agents in order to aid in the delivery of rational therapy.
Ind/Abst Chem. Abstr. (1984-); Trop. Dis. Bull.

ISSN 1069-417X
DD 616 US
CCC
CODEN AIDIEX
●**ANTIMICROBICS AND INFECTIOUS DISEASES NEWSLETTER.** [Antimicrob. infect. dis. newsl.]. Vol. 13, No. 1 (Jan. 1994)-. Newsletter. English. Twelve times a year (1 volume). $238.00. Elsevier Science Publishing Company Inc, Madison Square Station, PO Box 882, New York NY 10159-0882. **Tel** (212)633-3950, FAX (212)633-3990. ***Formed by the union of*** *Antimicrobic Newsletter, 0738-1751* ***and*** *Infectious Diseases Newsletter (New York, N.Y.), 0278-2316.*
Ind/Abst Curr. Cit.

ISSN 0166-3542
US
CCC
NLM W1 AN869Q **CODEN** ARSRDR
Pr Rev.
ANTIVIRAL RESEARCH. [Antiviral res.]. Vol. 1, No. 1 (March 1981)-. Academic Scholarly Publication. English. Twelve times a year (3 volumes). $1288.00. Elsevier Science Publishers BV, PO Box 211, 1000 AE Amsterdam Netherlands. **Tel** 011 31 20 4853641, 011 31 20 4853642, FAX 011 31 20 4853598. **ED** A. Billiau, E. De Clercq, R. Whitley, R. Dolin, G. Galasso, H. Schellekens. available on microfilm and microfiche from University Microfilms International (UMI); available on an online database from Elsevier Electronic Subscriptions (EES). Documents available from The Genuine Article, BIOSIS Document Express, CASDDS, ADONIS.
Desc: Publishes full-length original articles, short definitive papers and review articles, pertaining to the effective control of virus infections in animals and man as well as in plants or lower organisms.
Ind/Abst ADONIS; AgBiotech News Inf.; AGRICOLA; Biol. Abstr.; Chem. Abstr.; Curr. Aware. Biol. Sci., CABS; Curr. Cit.; Curr. Contents Life Sci.; EMBASE; For. Prod. Abstr. (19??-19??); For. Abstr.; Health Plan. Adminis.; Hortic. Abstr.; Immunol. Abstr.; Index Med.; Index Vet.; Microbiol. Abstr. Sect. A; NAPRALERT; Life Sci. Collect.; PESTDOC; Pig News Inf.; Potato Abstr.; Ref. Upd. Deluxe Ed.; Res. Alert [Full Cov.]; Rev. Med. Vet. Entomol.; Rev. Med. Vet. Mycology; Rev. Plant Pathol.; Sci. Cit. Index; SCISEARCH; Small Anim. Abstr. Bibliogr.; Vet. Bull.; Trop. Dis. Bull.; Virol. AIDS Abstr.

ISSN 0003-6072
NE
CCC
NLM W1 AN897R **CODEN** ALJMAO
Pr Rev.
ANTONIE VAN LEEUWENHOEK. [Antonie van Leeuwenhoek]. **Added/Corp** Nederlandse Vereniging voor Microbiologie. Vol. 1 (1934)-. Academic Scholarly Publication. English (German and French). Fourteen times a year. $853.00. Kluwer Academic Publishers, Postbus 322, 3300 AH Dordrecht The Netherlands. **Tel** 011 31 78 524400, FAX 011 31 78 183273, telex 20083. **ED** A. H. Stouthamer. **Ad Acc. Circ:** 800. available on microfilm and microfiche from University Microfilms International (UMI). Documents available from The Genuine Article, BIOSIS Document Express, CASDDS. ***Supersedes*** *Nederlandsch Tijdschrift voor Hygiene, Microbiologie en Serologie, 0369-3821.*
Desc: Covers fundamental and applied research. Provides a rapid publication outlet for all types of research concerned and connected with microbiology. Publishes studies of bacteria, yeasts and fungi, including studies of their development and the ecology of micro-organisms. The papers published cover the areas of general microbiology, food microbiology, and medical microbiology.
Ind/Abst Biodeter. Abstr. (1991-); Biol. Abstr.; Chem. Abstr.; Curr. Biotechnol.; Curr. Cit.; Dairy Sci. Abstr.; EMBASE; Food Sci. Technol. Abstr.; Genet. Abstr.; Health Plan. Adminis.; Immunol. Abstr.; Index Med.; Index Vet.; Int. Aerosp. Abstr.; Maize Abstr.; Microbiol. Abstr. Sect. B; Microbiol. Abstr. Sect. A; Microbiol. Abstr. Sect. C; NAPRALERT; Nematol. Abstr.; Nutr. Abstr. Rev., Ser. B, Live Feeds and Feed.; Life Sci. Collect.; PESTDOC; Plant Breed. Abstr.; Postharvest News Inf.; Protozoolog. Abstr.; Ref. Upd. Deluxe Ed.; Res. Alert [Full Cov.]; Rev. Med. Vet. Entomol.; Rev. Med. Vet. Mycology; Rev. Plant Pathol.; Sci. Cit. Index; SCISEARCH; Soils Fert.; Vet. Bull.

ISSN 0903-4641
DK
CCC
NLM W1; AP18
Pr Rev.
APMIS : ACTA PATHOLOGICA, MICROBIOLOGICA ET IMMUNOLOGICA SCANDINAVICA. **See** Medical Sciences-Allergy and Immunologic Diseases.

LC R81 .A312 ISSN 0903-465X
DK
CCC
NLM W1; AP18a CODEN AISSE2APSUEN

APMIS. ACTA PATHOLOGICA, MICROBIOLOGICA ET IMMUNOLOGICA SCANDINAVICA. SUPPLEMENTUM. See Medical Sciences-Allergy and Immunologic Diseases.

LC QR1 .A6 ISSN 0099-2240
DD 576/.05 US
CCC
NLM W1 AP498 CODEN AEMIDF
Pr Rev.

APPLIED AND ENVIRONMENTAL MICROBIOLOGY. [Appl. environ. microbiol.]. **Added/Corp** American Society for Microbiology. Vol. 31 (Jan. 1976)-. Academic Scholarly Publication. English. Twelve times a year. $310.00. American Society for Microbiology / DC, 1325 Massachusetts Avenue Northwest, Washington DC 20005-4171. **Tel** (202)737-3600, FAX (202)737-0367. **(Subscription address:** American Society for Microbiology, Journals Subscription Department, PO Box 11127, Birmingham AL 35201-1127. **Tel** (800)633-4931, FAX (205)995-1588.) **ED** Lars G. Ljungdahl, Robert A. Bender, Ronald L. Crawford, Robert B. Hespell, Robert J. Maier, and Robert P. Williams. **Ad Acc. Acid Free. Circ:** 8,600. available on microfilm and microfiche from University Microfilms International (UMI); available on CD-ROM. Documents available from The Genuine Article, BIOSIS Document Express, UMI Article Clearinghouse, Petroleum Abstracts Document Delivery Service, CASDDS, Documents on Demand. ***Continues** Applied Microbiology, 0003-6919.*
Desc: Addresses all aspects of applied microbiological research as well as applied and basic ecological research on bacteria and other microorganisms, including fungi, protozoa, and other simple eucaryotic organisms.
Ind/Abst Abstr. Bull. Inst. Pap. Sci. Tech.; AgBiotech News Inf.; AGRICOLA [Select. Cov.]; Agrofor. Abstr. (19??-19??); Anal. Abstr.; AQUAREF; Aquat. Sci. Fish. Abstr. [CD-ROM Ed.]; BioBusiness; Biocont. News Inf. (19??-19??); Biodeter. Abstr. (19??-19??); Biol. Agric. Index; Biol. Abstr.; Biotechnol. Res. Abstr.; Chem. Abstr.; Chemorecept. Abstr.; Coal Abstr.; Curr. Aware. Biol. Sci., CABS; Curr. Biotechnol.; Curr. Cit.; Curr. Contents Agric. Biol. Environ. Sci.; Curr. Contents Life Sci.; Dairy Sci. Abstr.; Ecol. Abstr.; Ecology Abstr.; EMBASE; Energy Inf. Abstr.; Energy Res. Abstr. (April 1976-); Environ. Abstr.; Environ. Period. Bibliogr.; Expand. Acad. Index (1992-); Field Crop Abstr.; Fish Rev.; Food Sci. Technol. Abstr.; Foods Adlibra; For. Prod. Abstr. (19??-19??); For. Abstr.; Gen. Sci. Index; Genet. Abstr.; Geogr. Abstr. Phys. Geogr.; GeoRef; Grass. Forage Abstr.; Health Saf. Sci. Abstr.; Helminthol. Abstr. (19??-19??); Hortic. Abstr.; Index Med.; Index Vet.; INIS Atomindex [Micro.]; Int. Aerosp. Abstr.; Maize Abstr.; Mass Spect. Bull. (?-?); Microbiol. Abstr. Sect. B; Microbiol. Abstr. Sect. A; Microbiol. Abstr. Sect. C; NAPRALERT; Nat. Prod. Updates; Nematol. Abstr.; Newsp. Period. Abstr. (1992-); Nucl. Acids Abstr.; Nutr. Abstr. Rev., Ser. B, Live Feeds and Feed.; Nutr. Abstr. Rev., Ser. A, Hum. Exp.; Ocean. Abstr.; PESTDOC; Pet. Abstr.; Pig News Inf.; Plant Breed. Abstr.; Plant Grow. Reg. Abstr.; Pollut. Abstr. Indexes; Postharvest News Inf.; Potato Abstr.; Poult. Abstr.; Protozoolog. Abstr.; Ref. Upd. Basic Ed.; Ref. Upd. Deluxe Ed.; Res. Alert [Full Cov.]; Rev. Agric. Entomol.; Rev. Med. Vet. Entomol.; Rev. Med. Vet. Mycology; Rev. Plant Pathol.; Rice Abstr.; Risk Abstr.; Sci. Cit. Index; SCISEARCH; Seed Abstr.; Soils Fert.; Soyabean Abstr.; Sug. Indus. Abstr.; Vet. Bull.; Toxicol. Abstr.; Trop. Dis. Bull.; Virol. AIDS Abstr.; Vitis Vitic. Enol. Abstr.; Weed Abstr.; Wheat Barley Trit. Abstr.; Wildl. Rev.

LC QH345 .P713 ISSN 0003-6838
US
CCC
NLM W1 AP521 CODEN APBMAC

APPLIED BIOCHEMISTRY AND MICROBIOLOGY. See Biology-Biological Chemistry.

LC QR53 .E87 ISSN 0175-7598
DD 660/.62/05 GW
CCC
NLM W1; AP528B CODEN AMBIDG
Pr Rev.

APPLIED MICROBIOLOGY AND BIOTECHNOLOGY. [Appl. microbiol. biotechnol.]. Vol. 19, No. 1 (1984)-. Academic Scholarly Publication. English. Eighteen times a year. $3400.00. Springer-Verlag GmbH & Company KG, Heidelberger Platz 3, D-14197 Berlin Germany. **Tel** 011 49 30 8207223, FAX 011 49 30 8214091, telex 183 319 SPBLN D. **(Subscription address:** Springer-Verlag New York Inc. / North America, PO Box 2485, Journal Fulfillment, Secaucus NJ 07096. **Tel** (201)348-4033, (800)777-4643, FAX (201)348-4505.) **ED** H J Rehm, K Esser, A L Demain, and A Kimura. **Ad Acc. Circ:** 869. available on microfilm and microfiche from University Microfilms International (UMI). Documents available from The Genuine Article, CASDDS, Documents on Demand, ADONIS. ***Continues** European Journal of Applied Microbiology and Biotechnology, 0171-1741.*
Desc: An international journal presenting research articles on topics; also features theoretical articles with direct relevance to experimental studies in applied microbiology and a special section of short communications.
Ind/Abst ADONIS; AgBiotech News Inf.; AGRICOLA [Select. Cov.]; Anal. Abstr.; BioBusiness; Biocont. News Inf. (19??-19??); Biodeter. Abstr. (19??-19??); Biol. Agric. Index; Biotechnol. Res. Abstr.; Chem. Abstr. (1984-); Chem. Titles; Coal Abstr.; Crop Physiol. Abstr.; Curr. Aware. Biol. Sci., CABS; Curr. Biotechnol.; Curr. Cit.; Dairy Sci. Abstr.; Ei Page One; EMBASE; Energy Inf. Abstr.; Energy Res. Abstr. (1984-); Environ. Abstr.; Field Crop Abstr.; Food Sci. Technol. Abstr.; For. Prod. Abstr.; Genet. Abstr.; Grass. Forage Abstr.; Hortic. Abstr.; Index Vet.; Microbiol. Abstr. Sect. B; Microbiol. Abstr. Sect. A; Microbiol. Abstr. Sect. C; Nutr. Abstr. Rev., Ser. B, Live Feeds and Feed.; Life Sci. Collect.; PESTDOC; Plant Breed. Abstr.; Plant Grow. Reg. Abstr.; Postharvest News Inf.; Potato Abstr.; Ref. Upd. Deluxe Ed.; Res. Alert [Full Cov.]; Rev. Agric. Entomol.; Rev. Med. Vet. Entomol.; Rev. Plant Pathol.; Rice Abstr.; Sci. Cit. Index; SCISEARCH; Soils Fert.; Soyabean Abstr.; Sug. Indus. Abstr.; Vitis Vitic. Enol. Abstr.; Weed Abstr.; Wheat Barley Trit. Abstr.

ISSN 1041-245X
DD 616 US
NLM W1; AP516R CODEN AVREEC

APPLIED VIROLOGY RESEARCH. [Appl. virol. res.]. Vol. 1 (1988)-. Monographic series. English. Irregular. Price varies per volume. Plenum Press, 233 Spring Street, New York NY 10013-1578. **Tel** (212)620-8000, (800)221-9369, FAX (212)463-0742, (212)807-1047, telex 23/421139. **ED** Edouard Kurstak, R.G. Marusyk, F.A. Murphy and M.H.V. Van Regenmortel. Documents available from BIOSIS Document Express.
Ind/Abst Biol. Abstr. (1988-); Index Vet.; Poult. Abstr.; Rev. Med. Vet. Entomol.; Vet. Bull.

ISSN 0948-3055
GW

AQUATIC MICROBIAL ECOLOGY. (19??)-. Academic Scholarly Publication. English. Six times a year. $414.54. Inter-Research Science Publishing, Nordbuente 23, D-21385 Oldendorf Germany. **Tel** 011 49 4132 7127, FAX 011 49 4123 8883. Documents available from BIOSIS Document Express. ***Continues** Marine Microbial Food Webs, 0297-8148.*
Ind/Abst Aquat. Sci. Fish. Abstr. [CD-ROM Ed.]; Biol. Abstr.; Chem. Abstr.; Curr. Aware. Biol. Sci., CABS; Ecology Abstr.

ISSN 0570-5118
DD 576 US
CODEN AQMNA

AQUATIC MICROBIOLOGY NEWSLETTER. (AQUATIC MICROBIOLOGY NEWSLETTER : FROM SECTION ON AQUATIC MICROBIOLOGY, AMERICAN SOCIETY FOR MICROBIOLOGY.). [Aquat. microbiol. newsl.]. **Added/Corp** American Society for Microbiology. Section on Aquatic Microbiology. American Society for Microbiology. Division of Aquatic Microbiology. American Society for Microbiology. Division of Aquatic and Terrestial Microbiology. American Society for Microbiology. Division of Microbial Ecology. (1962)-. Newsletter. English. Two times a year. Aquatic Microbiology, Box 19090-A LSU Station, Baton Rouge LA 70803. **Tel** (504)388-5180. **ED** Samuel P. Meufrs. ctrl circ.
Desc: Broadly based international communication newsletter in aquatic microbiology.

ISSN 0020-2460
AE
NLM W1 IN509P

ARCHIVES DE L'INSTITUT PASTEUR D'ALGERIE. See Medical Sciences-Communicable Diseases.

ISSN 0020-2509
TI
NLM W1 AR337D CODEN APTUAO

ARCHIVES DE L'INSTITUT PASTEUR DE TUNIS. See Medical Sciences.

LC QR1 .A74 ISSN 0302-8933
DD 576/.05 GW
CCC
NLM W1 AR455DM CODEN AMICCW

ARCHIVES OF MICROBIOLOGY. [Arch. microbiol.]. Vol. 95 (1974)-. Periodical. Multiple languages (English and French; summaries and/or abstracts in English and French). Twelve times a year. $2402.00. Springer-Verlag GmbH & Company KG, Heidelberger Platz 3, D-14197 Berlin Germany. **Tel** 011 49 30 8207223, FAX 011 49 30 8214091, telex 183 319 SPBLN D. **(Subscription address:** Springer-Verlag New York Inc. / North America, PO Box 2485, Journal Fulfillment, Secaucus NJ 07096. **Tel** (201)348-4033, (800)777-4643, FAX (201)348-4505.) **ED** G Drews, H G Schlegel, and D J Kushner. available on microfilm and microfiche from University Microfilms International (UMI). Documents available from The Genuine Article, BIOSIS Document Express, CASDDS, Documents on Demand, ADONIS. ***Continues** Archiv fur Mikrobiologie, 0003-9276.*
Desc: Publishes results of basic research on bacteria and other fundamental aspects of ecophysiology, physiological genetics, and biochemistry.
Ind/Abst ADONIS; AgBiotech News Inf.; AGRICOLA [Select. Cov.]; Biocont. News Inf.; Biodeter. Abstr. (19??-19??); Biol. Abstr.; Chem. Abstr.; Chem. Titles; Curr. Biotechnol.; Curr. Cit.; Curr. Contents Life Sci.; Dairy Sci. Abstr.; EMBASE; Energy Res. Abstr. (Jan. 1975-); Environ. Abstr.; Food Sci. Technol. Abstr.; Genet. Abstr.; GeoRef; Index Med.; Index Vet.; Microbiol. Abstr. Sect. B; Microbiol. Abstr. Sect. A; Microbiol. Abstr. Sect. C; NAPRALERT; Nutr. Abstr. Rev., Ser. B, Live Feeds and Feed.; Nutr. Abstr. Rev., Ser. A, Hum. Exp.; Life Sci. Collect.; PESTDOC; Plant Breed. Abstr.; Plant Grow. Reg. Abstr.; Protozoolog. Abstr.; Ref. Upd. Basic Ed.; Ref. Upd. Deluxe Ed.; Res. Alert [Full Cov.]; Rev. Med. Vet. Entomol.; Rev. Med. Vet. Mycology; Rev. Plant Pathol.; Sci. Cit. Index; SCISEARCH; Soils Fert.; Soyabean Abstr.; Vet. Bull.; Virol. AIDS Abstr.; Vitis Vitic. Enol. Abstr.; Weed Abstr.

LC QR360 .A7 ISSN 0304-8608
DD 616.01/94 AU
CCC
NLM W1; AR49L CODEN ARVIDF
Pr Rev.

ARCHIVES OF VIROLOGY. [Arch. virol.]. Vol. 47, (Feb. 1975)-. Multiple languages (English, French and German). Twelve times a year. $1768.00. Springer-Verlag Vienna, Sachsenplatz 4 6, PO Box 89, A-1201 Vienna Austria. **Tel** 011 43 1 33024150, FAX 011 43 1 330242665. **(Subscription address:** Springer-Verlag New York Inc. / North America, PO Box 2485, Journal Fulfillment, Secaucus NJ 07096. **Tel** (201)348-4033, (800)777-4643, FAX (201)348-4505.) **ED** J W Almond, D R Lowy, F A Murphy, Y Nagai, C Scholtissek, J H Strauss, A Vaheri, M H V Van Regenmortel, D O White. **Bk Rev.** available on microfilm and microfiche from University Microfilms International (UMI). Documents available from The Genuine Article, BIOSIS Document Express, CASDDS, ADONIS. ***Continues** Archiv fur die Gesamte Virusforschung, 0003-9012.*
Desc: Publishes original contributions from all branches of research on viruses, viruslike agents, and virus infections of humans, animals, plants, insects, and bacteria. Coverage includes the broadest spectrum of topics, from initial descriptions of newly discovered viruses, to studies of virus structure, composition, and genetics, to studies of virus interactions with host cells, host organisms, and host populations. Multidisciplinary studies are particularly welcome, as are studies employing molecular biologic, molecular genetic, and modern immunologic and epidemiologic approaches. Studies involving applied research, such as diagnostic technology, development, monoclonal antibody panel development, vaccine development, and antiviral drug development, are also encouraged.
Ind/Abst ADONIS; AgBiotech News Inf.; AGRICOLA [Select. Cov.]; Biol. Abstr.; Chem. Abstr.; CSA Neuro. Abstr. (?-?); Curr. Cit.; Curr. Contents Life Sci.; Dairy Sci. Abstr.; EMBASE; Fish Rev.; Food Sci. Technol. Abstr.; Genet. Abstr.; Immunol. Abstr.; Index Med.; Index Vet.; INIS Atomindex [Micro.]; NAPRALERT; Oncog. Growth Factors Abstr.; Life Sci. Collect.; PESTDOC; Pig News Inf.; Plant Breed. Abstr.; Potato Abstr.; Ref. Upd. Deluxe Ed.; Res. Alert [Full Cov.]; Rev. Agric. Entomol.; Rev. Med. Vet. Entomol.; Rev. Plant Pathol.; Sci. Cit. Index; SCISEARCH; Small Anim. Abstr. Bibliogr.; Vet. Bull.; Trop. Dis. Bull.; Virol. AIDS Abstr.; Wildl. Rev.

ISSN 0939-1983
AU
CCC
NLM W1; AR49La CODEN AVISE9

ARCHIVES OF VIROLOGY. SUPPLEMENTUM. [Arch. virol., Suppl.]. (1991)-. Monographic series. English. Irregular. Price varies. Springer-Verlag Vienna, Sachsenplatz 4 6, PO Box 89, A-1201 Vienna Austria. **Tel** 011 43 1 33024150, FAX 011 43 1 330242665. **(Subscription address:** Springer-Verlag New York Inc. / North America, PO Box 2485, Journal Fulfillment, Secaucus NJ 07096. **Tel** (201)348-4033, (800)777-4643, FAX (201)348-4505.)
Ind/Abst Bibliogr. Agric.; Chem. Abstr.; Index Med. (1991-).

ISSN 0365-2998
PO
NLM W1 LI706 CODEN AIBCAZ

ARQUIVOS DO INSTITUTO BACTERIOLOGICO CAMARA PESTANA (LISBOA). (ARQUIVOS DO INSTITUTO BACTERIOLOGICO CAMARA PESTANA.). [Arq. Inst. Bacteriol. C·am. Pestana]. **Added/Corp** Instituto Bacteriologico Camara Pestana. (191?)-. Portuguese (English and French; table of contents in French and Portuguese). Documents available from CASDDS. ***Continues** Archivos do Instituto Bacteriologico Camara Pestana.*
Ind/Abst Chem. Abstr. (-1977); Trop. Dis. Bull.

LC QR398 .A77 ISSN 0736-7899
DD 576 US
NLM W1 AR953Y

ARTHROPOD-BORNE VIRUS INFORMATION EXCHANGE. [Arthropod-borne virus inf. exch.]. **Added/Corp** American Committee on Arthropod-Borne Viruses. Subcommittee on Information Exchange. No. 1 (Apr. 1960)-. Periodical. English. Two times a year. Center for Disease Control,

1600 Clifton Road, Atlanta GA 30333. **Tel** (404)639-3311, (404)639-3534, FAX (404)939-3039.
Ind/Abst Trop. Dis. Bull.

ISSN 0044-7897
US
CCC
NLM W1 A152J **CODEN** ASMNBO
ASM NEWS. [ASM news]. **Main/Corp** American Society for Microbiology. **Added/Corp** American Society for Microbiology. News. **VAT** American Society for Microbiology News. Vol. 29 (Jan. 1963)-. Periodical. English. Twelve times a year. $36.00. American Society for Microbiology / DC, 1325 Massachusetts Avenue Northwest, Washington DC 20005-4171. **Tel** (202)737-3600, FAX (202)737-0367. **(Subscription address:** American Society for Microbiology, Journals Subscription Department, PO Box 11127, Birmingham AL 35201-1127. **Tel** (800)633-4931, FAX (205)995-1588.) **ED** Michael I. Goldberg. **Bk Rev. Ad Acc. Circ:** 34,000. available on microfilm and microfiche from University Microfilms International (UMI). ***Continues*** *Bacteriological News.*
Desc: Publishes items of general interest to microbiologists; letters on nonscientific as well as scientific topics, and reports of legislative activity that affects microbiology. Contains feature articles, written for an audience ranging from graduate students to doctoral scientists, announcements of forthcoming meetings, and an employment section.
Ind/Abst Abstr. BioCommer.; AgBiotech News Inf.; Biodeter. Abstr.; Curr. Cit.; Index Vet.; Life Sci. Collect.; Protozoolog. Abstr.; Soc. Sci. Cit. Index [Select. Cov.]; Soils Fert.

ISSN 0158-619X
DD 576.05 AT
AUSTRALIAN MICROBIOLOGIST. [Aust. microbiol.]. (1980)-. Periodical. English. Irregular. Australian Society for Microbiology, Unit 23 20 Commercial Road, Melbourne Victoria 3004 Australia. **Tel** 011 61 3 98678699. ***Continues*** *ASM News, 0314-0563.*
Ind/Abst Curr. Cit.

LC QR46 **ISSN** 1011-9981
DD 616 BG
NLM W1; BA642J **CODEN** BJMIES
BANGLADESH JOURNAL OF MICROBIOLOGY. (BANGLADESH JOURNAL OF MICROBIOLOGY.). [Banglad. j. microbiol.]. **Added/Corp** Bangladesh Society of Microbiologists. (198?)-. Periodical. English. Two times a year. Documents available from BIOSIS Document Express.
Ind/Abst Biodeter. Abstr.; Biol. Abstr. (1990-); Hortic. Abstr.; Rev. Med. Vet. Mycology; Seed Abstr.; Sug. Indus. Abstr.

LC QR171.I6 B53 **ISSN** 0286-9306
DD 589.9/2 JA
NLM W1; BI533 **CODEN** BIMIDK
BIFIDOBACTERIA AND MICROFLORA. (BIFIDOBACTERIA AND MICROFLORA : BM.). [Bifidobact. microflora]. **Added/Corp** Nihon Bifizusukin Senta. Nihon Bifizusukin Senta. Conference. **VFOAT** BM. Vol. 1, No. 1 (March 1982)-. Academic Scholarly Publication. English. Two times a year. $65.00. Business Center for Academic Societies Japan, Hon-Komagome 5-16-9, Bunkyo-ku, Tokyo 113 Japan. **Tel** 011 81 3 5814 5811, FAX 011 81 3 5814 5822. **(Subscription address:** Maruzen Company Ltd., PO Box 5050, Import & Export Department, Tokyo 100 31 Japan. **Tel** 011 81 3 32789224.) Documents available from CASDDS.
Ind/Abst Chem. Abstr.; Dairy Sci. Abstr.; Nutr. Abstr. Rev., Ser. B, Live Feeds and Feed.; Nutr. Abstr. Rev., Ser. A, Hum. Exp.; Life Sci. Collect.

ISSN 0266-304X
UK
BINARY. **See** Biology-Computer Applications.

ISSN 1057-350X
DD 576 UK
NLM W1; BI6190 **CODEN** BCMIED
Pr Rev.
BINARY COMPUTING IN MICROBIOLOGY. **See** Biology-Computer Applications.

ISSN 1000-8721
CC
NLM W1; PI313 **CODEN** BIXUEA
BINGDU XUEBAO. (PING TU HSUEH PAO.). [Bingdu xuebao]. **Added/Corp** Chung-kuo Wei Sheng Wu Hsueh Hui. **VFOAT** Chinese Journal of Virology. (1985)-. Periodical. Chinese (summaries and/or abstracts in English; table of contents in English). Four times a year. **(Subscription address:** China International Book Trading Corporation, PO Box 399, Library Service Department, Beijing 100044 People's Republic of China. **Tel** 011 86 1 8414284, FAX 011 86 1 8412023, telex 22496 CIBTC CN.) Documents available from BIOSIS Document Express, CASDDS.
Ind/Abst Biocont. News Inf.; Biol. Abstr. (1987-1989); Chem. Abstr. (1986-); Index Vet.; Potato Abstr.; Poult. Abstr.; Rev. Agric. Entomol.; Rev. Med. Vet. Entomol.; Rev. Plant Pathol.; Vet. Bull.; Trop. Dis. Bull.

ISSN 1000-3223
CC
CODEN BIZAES
BINGDUXUE ZAZHI. (PING TU HSUEH TSA CHIH.). [Bingduxue zazhi]. **Added/Corp** Chung-Kuo Ko Hsueh Yuan. Wu-Han Ping Tu Yen Chiu So. **VFOAT** Virologica Sinica. (198?)-. Academic Scholarly Publication. Chinese (summaries and/or abstracts in English). Four times a year. $49.20. Science Press, 16 Donghuangchenggen North Street, Beijing 100707, People's Republic of China. **Tel** 011 86 1 4019821, 011 86 1 4010642, FAX 011 86 1 4012180, 011 86 1 4019810, telex 210147. **(Subscription address:** China International Book Trading Corporation, PO Box 399, Library Service Department, Beijing 100044 People's Republic of China. **Tel** 011 86 1 8414284, FAX 011 86 1 8412023, telex 22496 CIBTC CN.) Documents available from BIOSIS Document Express, CASDDS.
Ind/Abst Biol. Abstr.; Chem. Abstr.

LC QR1 .F67
GW
NLM W1; BI665KB
BIOFORUM. **Added/Corp** Vereinigung fuer Allgemeine und Angewandte Mikrobiologie. Gesellschaft fuer Umwelt-Mutationsforschung. No. 1 (Feb. 1991)-. Periodical. German (summaries and/or abstracts in English). Ten times a year. $113.61. GIT Verlag GmbH, Roblerstrabe 90, Postfach 110564, D-64220 Darmstadt Germany. **Tel** 011 49 6151 80900, FAX 011 49 6151 809045. ***Continues*** *Forum Mikrobiologie, 0170-8244.*

LC QR53 .B56A
JA
BISEIBUTSU KOGYO GIJUTSU KENKYUJO NEMPO. **Main/Corp** Kogyo Gijutsuin Biseibutsu Kogyo Gijutsu Kenkyujo (Japan). (19??)-. Japanese. Kogyo Gijutsuin Biseibutsu Kogyo Gijutsu Kenkyujo, (Fermentation Research Institute), 1-3 Higashi 1 chome, Tsukubashi, Ibarakiken 305 Japan.

LC QR100 .B57a
DD 576.15 JA
BISEIBUTSU NO SEITAI. **Main/Corp** Biseibutsu Seitai Shimpojiumu. **Added/Corp** Biseibutsu Seitai Kenkyukai. Vol. 1, (1972)-. Japanese. Tokyo Daigaku Shuppankai, Todai Konai Hongo Bunkyo-ku, Tokyo 113 Japan.

ISSN 0394-9877
IT
CODEN BMILE4
BML : BOLLETTINO DI MICROBIOLOGIA E INDAGINI DI LABORATORIO. **VFOAT** Bollettino di Microbiologia e Indagini di Laboratorio. (1981)-. Academic Scholarly Publication. Italian. Four times a year. L54500. Brixia Academic Press, Viale Venezia NR 82, 25100 Brescia Italy. **Tel** 011 39 30 3995650. Documents available from CASDDS.
Ind/Abst Chem. Abstr.

ISSN 0021-2547
IT
NLM W1 IS865 **CODEN** BISMAP
CEASED
BOLLETTINO DELL'INSTITUTO SIEROTERAPICO MILANESE. **See** Medical Sciences-Allergy and Immunologic Diseases.

ISSN 0391-481X
IT
NLM W1 BU813 **CODEN** BMBMD5
BULLETIN OF MOLECULAR BIOLOGY AND MEDICINE. [Bull. mol. biol. med.]. Vol. 1 (1976)-. Bulletin. English. Four times a year. L150000. Casa Editrice Libraria Idelson Gnocchi, Via Alcide De Gasperi 55, 80133 Naples Italy. **Tel** 011 39 81 5524733, FAX 011 39 81 5518295. **ED** Ernesto Quagliariello. **Bk Rev.** Documents available from CASDDS.
Ind/Abst Chem. Abstr.; CSA Neuro. Abstr. (?-?); Curr. Cit.; EMBASE; Life Sci. Collect.; PESTDOC; Protozoolog. Abstr.; Sci. Cit. Index (19??-19??); SCISEARCH.

ISSN 0895-5808
DD 574 US
CODEN CSEAE4
CA SELECTS: ENZYME ASSAYS. **See** Chemistry and Chemicals-Abstracting, Bibliographies and Statistics.

LC QR1 .C25 **ISSN** 0008-4166
DD 576.05 CN
CCC
NLM W1 CA596 **CODEN** CJMIAZ
Pr Rev.
CANADIAN JOURNAL OF MICROBIOLOGY. [Can. j. microbiol.]. **Added/Corp** Canadian Society of Microbiologists. National Research Council Canada. National Research Council of Canada. **VFOAT** Journal Canadien de Microbiologie. Vol. 1, No. 1 (Aug. 1954)-. Academic Scholarly Publication. English (French). Twelve times a year. 320.00Can$. National Research Council of Canada, Receiver General for Canada, Ottawa Ontario K1A 0R6 Canada. **Tel** (613)993-0362, FAX (613)952-7656. **ED** G. M. Gaucher and K. E. Sanderson. Index available. **Ad Acc. Circ:** 2,300 (ctrl). available on microfilm and microfiche from University Microfilms International (UMI). Documents available from The Genuine Article, BIOSIS Document Express, CASDDS, Documents on Demand.
Desc: Publishes papers on all kinds of microorganisms (bacteria, algae, yeast, fungi, and viruses) and on all aspects of microbiology, including ultrastructure, physiology, molecular biology and genetics, microbial development, applied and industrial microbiology, infection and immunity.
Ind/Abst Abstr. Bull. Inst. Pap. Sci. Tech.; AgBiotech News Inf.; AGRICOLA [Select. Cov.]; Agrofor. Abstr. (1991-); Anal. Abstr.; AQUAREF; Biocont. News Inf. (19??-19??); Biodeter. Abstr. (19??-19??); Biol. Agric. Index; Biol. Abstr.; Chem. Abstr.; Chem. Titles; Coal Abstr.; Cot. Trop. Fibr. Abstr. Bibliogr.; Crop Physiol. Abstr.; Curr. Aware. Biol. Sci., CABS; Curr. Biotechnol.; Curr. Cit.; Curr. Contents Agric. Biol. Environ. Sci.; Curr. Contents Life Sci.; Dairy Sci. Abstr.; Ecol. Abstr.; Ecology Abstr.; EMBASE; Environ. Abstr.; Field Crop Abstr.; Food Sci. Technol. Abstr.; For. Prod. Abstr. (19??-19??); For. Abstr.; Genet. Abstr.; Grass. Forage Abstr.; Health Plan. Adminis.; Hortic. Abstr.; Immunol. Abstr.; Index Med.; Index Vet.; Int. Aerosp. Abstr.; Maize Abstr.; Microbiol. Abstr. Sect. B; Microbiol. Abstr. Sect. A; Microbiol. Abstr. Sect. C; NAPRALERT; Nematol. Abstr.; Nutr. Abstr. Rev., Ser. B, Live Feeds and Feed.; Nutr. Abstr. Rev., Ser. A, Hum. Exp.; PESTDOC; Pig News Inf.; Plant Breed. Abstr.; Plant Grow. Reg. Abstr.; Postharvest News Inf.; Potato Abstr.; Poult. Abstr.; Protozoolog. Abstr.; Ref. Upd. Basic Ed.; Ref. Upd. Deluxe Ed.; Res. Alert [Full Cov.]; Rev. Agric. Entomol.; Rev. Med. Vet. Entomol.; Rev. Med. Vet. Mycology; Rev. Plant Pathol.; Rice Abstr.; Sci. Cit. Index; SCISEARCH; Seed Abstr.; Small Anim. Abstr. Bibliogr.; Soils Fert.; Soyabean Abstr.; Sug. Indus. Abstr.; Vet. Bull.; Trop. Dis. Bull.; Virol. AIDS Abstr.; Vitis Vitic. Enol. Abstr.; Weed Abstr.; Wheat Barley Trit. Abstr.

LC QH585 .A57A
DD 574/.07/24 US
NLM QW 26; A512cb
CATALOGUE OF CELL LINES AND HYBRIDOMAS. **Main/Corp** American Type Culture Collection. **VFOAT** Cell Lines & Hybridomas; Cell Lines and Hybridomas; ATCC Cell Lines and Hybridomas; ATCC Cell Lines & Hybridomas. 5th Ed. (1985)-. English. Irregular. Free. ATCC, 12301 Parklawn Drive, Rockville MD 20852-1776. ***Continues in part*** *Catalogue of Strains II, 0363-2989.*

ISSN 0009-0522
XR
CCC
NLM W1; CE879K **CODEN** CKEMAE
TITLE CHANGE
CESKOSLOVENSKA EPIDEMIOLOGIE, MIKROBIOLOGIE, IMUNOLOGIE. **See** Medical Sciences-Epidemiology.

LC QR46 .C48A
JA
UDC 579.22; 631.81.036; 579.64
NLM W1 CH423P
CHIBA DAIGAKU SEIBUTSU KASSEI KENKYUJO HOKOKU. **Main/Corp** Chiba Daigaku. Seibutsu Kassei Kenkyujo. **VFOAT** Annual Report of Research Institute for Chemobiodynamics, Chiba University. No. 1 (Vol. 1973)-. Japanese (English and French; summaries and/or abstracts in Japanese, English and French). Chiba Daigaku Seibutsu Kassei Kenkyujo, (Research Inst. for Chemobiodynamics Chiba University), 8-1 Inohana 1 Chome, Chibashi Chibaken 280 Japan. ***Supersedes*** *Chiba Daigaku Fuhai Kenkyujo Hoko.*

ISSN 0928-0197
NE
CCC
NLM W1; CL654H
Pr Rev.
•**CLINICAL AND DIAGNOSTIC VIROLOGY.** Vol. 1/1 (Mar. 1993)-. Academic Scholarly Publication. English. Nine times a year. $849.00. Elsevier Science Publishers BV, PO Box 211, 1000 AE Amsterdam Netherlands. **Tel** 011 31 20 4853641, 011 31 20 4853642, FAX 011 31 20 4853598. available on an online database from Elsevier Electronic Subscriptions (EES).

LC QR **ISSN** 1198-743X
DD 616.01 FR
•**CLINICAL MICROBIOLOGY AND INFECTION.** (1995)-. Academic Scholarly Publication. English. Four times a year. 810F (institutions), 622F (individuals). Decker Europe, 67 rue St. Jacques, 75005 Paris France. **Tel** 011 33 1 43251178, FAX 011 33 1 43251254.

ISSN 1198-743X
CN
•**CLINICAL MICROBIOLOGY AND INFECTIOUS DISEASES.** (July 1995)-. English. Four times a year. $150.00 (institutions), $115.00 (individuals). Decker Periodicals Publishing Inc., PO Box 620, Station A, Hamilton Ontario L8N 3K7 Canada. **Tel**

(416)522-7017, (800)568-7281, FAX (416)522-7839.
Desc: Official publication of the European Society of Clinical Microbiology and Infectious Diseases.

ISSN 0196-4399
DD 616 US
CCC
NLM W1 CL731G **CODEN** CMNEEJ
Pr Rev.

CLINICAL MICROBIOLOGY NEWSLETTER. [Clin. microbiol. newsl.]. Vol. 1 (1979)-. Newsletter. English. Twenty-four times a year (1 volume). $199.00. Elsevier Science Publishing Company Inc, Madison Square Station, PO Box 882, New York NY 10159-0882. **Tel** (212)633-3950, FAX (212)633-3990. **ED** Mary Jane Ferraro, Paul A Granato, Josephine A Morello and R J Zabransky. **Circ:** 2,700. available on microfilm and microfiche from University Microfilms International (UMI). Documents available from BIOSIS Document Express.
Desc: Keeps clinical microbiologists apprised of new developments in identification, diagnosis, and interpretation of laboratory test results.
Ind/Abst Biol. Abstr. (1987-); Curr. Cit.; Helminthol. Abstr. (1991-); Microbiol. Abstr. Sect. B; Microbiol. Abstr. Sect. A; Life Sci. Collect.; Rev. Med. Vet. Mycology; Trop. Dis. Bull.; Virol. AIDS Abstr.

ISSN 1062-8150
US
CCC
NLM W1; CL73S

CLINICAL MICROBIOLOGY REPORTS. (1992)-. Periodical. English. Twelve times a year. $149.00. W. B. Saunders Company, A Subsidiary of Harcourt Brace Jovanovich Inc., The Curtis Center, Suite 300, Independence Square West, Philadelphia PA 19106-3399. **Tel** (215)238-7800 or, 5587, FAX (215)238-7883, telex 173146. **(Subscription address:** W. B. Saunders Company / North America Subscriptions, c/o Periodicals, 6277 Sea Harbour Drive, 4th Floor, Orlando FL 32887. **Tel** (800)654-2452, (407)345-3668.) **ED** Irving Nachamkin.

LC QR67 .C56 **ISSN** 0893-8512
DD 616/.01/05 US
CCC
NLM W1; CL731GJ **CODEN** CMIREX
Pr Rev.

CLINICAL MICROBIOLOGY REVIEWS. [Clin. microbiol. rev.]. **Added/Corp** American Society for Microbiology. Vol. 1, No. 1 (Jan. 1988)-. Periodical. English. Four times a year. $140.00. American Society for Microbiology / DC, 1325 Massachusetts Avenue Northwest, Washington DC 20005-4171. **Tel** (202)737-3600, FAX (202)737-0367. **(Subscription address:** American Society for Microbiology, Journals Subscription Department, PO Box 11127, Birmingham AL 35201-1127. **Tel** (800)633-4931, FAX (205)995-1588.) **ED** Josephine A. Morello. Index available. cum. index. **Ad Acc. Acid Free. Circ:** 7,400 (ctrl). available on microfilm and microfiche from University Microfilms International (UMI); available on CD-ROM. Documents available from The Genuine Article, BIOSIS Document Express.
Desc: Serves the specific interests and needs of clinical microbiologists, medical microbiologists and immunologists, public health workers, and infectious disease specialists. Covers all areas of clinical microbiology and immunology, including bacteriology, mycology, virology, and parasitology.
Ind/Abst Biol. Abstr. (1988-); Curr. Aware. Biol. Sci., CABS; Curr. Cit.; Curr. Contents Life Sci.; EMBASE; Food Sci. Technol. Abstr.; Health Plan. Adminis.; Index Med. (1988-); Index Vet.; Microbiol. Abstr. Sect. B; Microbiol. Abstr. Sect. A; Pig News Inf.; Protozoolog. Abstr.; Ref. Upd. Deluxe Ed.; Res. Alert [Select. Cov.]; Rev. Med. Vet. Mycology; SCISEARCH; Virol. AIDS Abstr. (Vol. 1 No. 1, 1988-).

ISSN 0728-4837
AT
NLM W1; CL731H

CLINICAL MICROBIOLOGY UPDATE PROGRAMME. **Added/Corp** Australian Society for Microbiology. N.S.W. Branch. University of New South Wales. School of Microbiology and Immunology. (19??)-. Periodical. English. Three times a year (Mar., July, Nov.). 49.34Aus$. Clinical Micro Update Program, School of Microbiology, University NSW, PO Box 1, Kensington NSW 2033 Australia. **Tel** 011 61 2 6972100, FAX 011 61 2 3136528. **ED** Nenssa Lee. **Circ:** 400.

ISSN 0147-9571
UK
CCC
NLM W1 CO435K **CODEN** CIMIDV
Pr Rev.

COMPARATIVE IMMUNOLOGY, MICROBIOLOGY AND INFECTIOUS DISEASES. [Comp. immunol., microbiol. infect. dis.]. Vol. 1, No. 1/2 (1978)-. Periodical. English. Four times a year. $535.00. Pergamon Press, An Imprint of Elsevier Science Ltd., The Boulevard, Langford Lane, Kidlington, Oxford OX5 1GB United Kingdom. **Tel** 011 44 1865 843000, 011 44 1865 843699, FAX 011 44 1865 843010. **(Subscription address:** Elsevier Science Ltd. / Oxford Fulfillment Centre, PO Box 800, Kidlington OX5 1DX United Kingdom. **Tel** 011 44 865 843355.) **ED** Charles Pilet. available on microfilm and microfiche from University Microfilms International (UMI); available on an online database from Elsevier Electronic Subscriptions (EES). Documents available from The Genuine Article, BIOSIS Document Express.
Desc: Provides a forum for physicians and veterinarians whose specialties include immunology, immunopathology, microbiology, and infectious diseases in both animals and humans. Publishes both original papers and reviews of current research relative to the above specialties, and diagnosis and treatment of infectious diseases in man and animals.
Ind/Abst AgBiotech News Inf.; AGRICOLA [Select. Cov.]; Biol. Abstr.; Curr. Aware. Biol. Sci., CABS; Curr. Cit.; Curr. Contents Agric. Biol. Environ. Sci.; Dairy Sci. Abstr.; EMBASE; Health Plan. Adminis.; Helminthol. Abstr.; Immunol. Abstr.; Index Med. (1978-); Index Vet.; Microbiol. Abstr. Sect. B; Life Sci. Collect.; Pig News Inf.; Poult. Abstr.; Protozoolog. Abstr.; Res. Alert [Full Cov.]; Rev. Med. Vet. Entomol.; Sci. Cit. Index; SCISEARCH; Small Anim. Abstr. Bibliogr.; Vet. Bull.; Virol. AIDS Abstr.

ISSN 0301-3081
SZ
CCC
NLM W1 CO778UK **CODEN** CMIMBF

CONTRIBUTIONS TO MICROBIOLOGY AND IMMUNOLOGY. **See** Medical Sciences-Allergy and Immunologic Diseases.

SP

CORREO BACTERIOLOGICO. (19??)-. Spanish. Twelve times a year. Lilly Indiana de Espana SA, Paseo de la Industria S/N, 28100 Alcobendas (Madrid) Spain.

US
CEASED

CRC HANDBOOK OF MICROBIOLOGY. **Added/Corp** Cleveland Rubber Company. **VFOAT** Handbook of Microbiology. (1973)-Vol. 9 (199?). English. CRC Press Inc., 2000 Corporate Boulevard Northwest, Boca Raton FL 33431. **Tel** (407)994-0555, (800)272-7737, FAX (407)998-9784, (800)374-3401, telex 568689. **ED** Allen Laskin and Hubert Lechevalier.

LC QR1 .C47 **ISSN** 1040-841X
DD 576/.05 US
CCC
NLM W1; C555H **CODEN** CRVMAC
Pr Rev.

CRITICAL REVIEWS IN MICROBIOLOGY. [Crit. rev. microbiol.]. **VFOAT** CRC Critical Reviews in Microbiology. **VAT** Chemical Rubber Company Critical Reviews in Microbiology. Vol. 7, Issue 4 (1980)-. Academic Scholarly Publication. English. Four times a year. $300.00. CRC Press Inc., 2000 Corporate Boulevard Northwest, Boca Raton FL 33431. **Tel** (407)994-0555, (800)272-7737, FAX (407)998-9784, (800)374-3401, telex 568689. **ED** Ronald M. Atlas. Documents available from The Genuine Article, BIOSIS Document Express, CASDDS. ***Continues*** *CRC Critical Reviews in Microbiology, 0045-6454.*
Desc: Presents reviews from the fields of microbiology.
Ind/Abst AgBiotech News Inf.; AGRICOLA [Select. Cov.]; Biol. Abstr.; Chem. Abstr.; Curr. Aware. Biol. Sci., CABS; Curr. Cit.; Curr. Contents Life Sci.; EMBASE; Energy Res. Abstr. (Mar. 1979-); Index Med.; Index Sci. Rev. [Full Cov.]; Index Vet.; Microbiol. Abstr. Sect. B; Life Sci. Collect.; PESTDOC; Ref. Upd. Basic Ed.; Ref. Upd. Deluxe Ed.; Res. Alert [Full Cov.]; Rev. Med. Vet. Mycology; Sci. Cit. Index; SCISEARCH; Vet. Bull.

ISSN 0160-1660
US
CCC
NLM W1 CU473

CUMITECH. **Added/Corp** American Society for Microbiology. **VFOAT** Cumulative Techniques and Procedures in Clinical Microbiology. **VAT** Cumulative Techniques. (1974)-. Monographic series. English. Irregular. Price varies per volume. American Society for Microbiology / DC, 1325 Massachusetts Avenue Northwest, Washington DC 20005-4171. **Tel** (202)737-3600, FAX (202)737-0367.

LC Z5180 .C87 **ISSN** 0964-8712
DD 016.576 UK
NLM ZQW 4; C976

CURRENT ADVANCES IN APPLIED MICROBIOLOGY & BIOTECHNOLOGY. **See** Biology-Abstracting, Bibliographies and Statistics.

LC QR1 .C87 **ISSN** 0343-8651
DD 576/.05 US
CCC
NLM W1 CU799CM **CODEN** CUMIDD
Pr Rev.

CURRENT MICROBIOLOGY. [Cur. microbiol.]. Vol. 1 (1978)-. Academic Scholarly Publication. English. Twelve times a year. $399.00. Springer-Verlag New York Inc., 175 Fifth Avenue, New York NY 10010. **Tel** (212)460-1500 ext 256, FAX (212)533-3503, telex 232 235 SPB UR. **(Subscription address:** Springer-Verlag New York Inc. / North America, PO Box 2485, Journal Fulfillment, Secaucus NJ 07096. **Tel** (201)348-4033, (800)777-4643, FAX (201)348-4505.) **ED** A Balows and P Baumann. available on microfilm and microfiche from University Microfilms International (UMI). Documents available from The Genuine Article, CASDDS.
Desc: Information on all areas of microbiology - medical and non-medical, general and applied. Includes scientist discussions of their research findings.
Ind/Abst AgBiotech News Inf.; AGRICOLA [Select. Cov.]; Biocont. News Inf.; Biodeter. Abstr. (1991-); Chem. Abstr.; Curr. Aware. Biol. Sci., CABS; Curr. Biotechnol.; Curr. Cit.; Curr. Contents Life Sci.; Dairy Sci. Abstr.; EMBASE; Food Sci. Technol. Abstr.; Genet. Abstr.; Immunol. Abstr.; Index Vet.; Microbiol. Abstr. Sect. B; Microbiol. Abstr. Sect. A; Microbiol. Abstr. Sect. C; NAPRALERT; Nutr. Abstr. Rev., Ser. B, Live Feeds and Feed.; Life Sci. Collect.; PESTDOC; Plant Grow. Reg. Abstr.; Protozoolog. Abstr.; Ref. Upd. Deluxe Ed.; Res. Alert [Full Cov.]; Rev. Med. Vet. Entomol.; Rev. Med. Vet. Mycology; Rev. Plant Pathol.; Sci. Cit. Index; SCISEARCH; Soils Fert.; Soyabean Abstr.; Vet. Bull.; Virol. AIDS Abstr.; Weed Abstr.; Wheat Barley Trit. Abstr.

ISSN 0937-2156
GW
NLM W1; CU82IME **CODEN** CTIDE6

CURRENT TOPICS IN INFECTIOUS DISEASES AND CLINICAL MICROBIOLOGY. **See** Medical Sciences-Communicable Diseases.

ISSN 0139-598X
XR
NLM ZWA 105 C998

CZECHOSLOVAK BIBLIOGRAPHY ON EPIDEMIOLOGY AND MICROBIOLOGY. **See** Medical Sciences-Epidemiology.

LC QR1 .T34 **ISSN** 0253-3162
DD 576 KO
CODEN TMHCDX

DAIHAN MISAINMUR HAGHOI JI. (TAEHAN MISAENGMUL HAKHOE CHI = THE JOURNAL OF THE KOREAN SOCIETY FOR MICROBIOLOGY.). [Daihan misainmur haghoi ji]. **Added/Corp** Taehan Misaengmul Hakhoe. **VFOAT** The Journal of the Korean Society for Microbiology; Journal of the Korean Society for Microbiology. (1966)-. Academic Scholarly Publication. Korean (summaries and/or abstracts in English). Six times a year. $100.00. Catholic Medical University, 505 Banpo Dong Socho Gu, Seoul 137 040 Korea. **Tel** 011 82 2 5901219. Documents available from BIOSIS Document Express, CASDDS.
Ind/Abst Biol. Abstr.; Chem. Abstr. (1966-1979); EMBASE [Select. Cov.]; Index Vet.; Pig News Inf.; Rev. Med. Vet. Mycology; Small Anim. Abstr. Bibliogr.

ISSN 0438-9573
GR
UDC 576.8
CODEN DHMHDW

DELTION ELLENIKES MIKROBIOLOGIKES ETAIREIAS. [Delt. Ell. Mikrobiol. Etair.]. **VFOAT** Acta Microbiologica Hellenica. (1956)-. Periodical. Greek, Modern. Six times a year. Free on request. Greek Microbiology Society, University of Athens, Microbiology Department, Athens 115 27 Greece. **(Subscription address:** Ascent, Vas Sophias 77, Athens 115 21 Greece. **Tel** 011 30 1 7247306.) Documents available from CASDDS.
Ind/Abst Chem. Abstr.

ISSN 0264-2670
UK
NLM W1 DE997VXD **CODEN** DFMIDL
Pr Rev.

DEVELOPMENTS IN FOOD MICROBIOLOGY. [Dev. food microbiol.]. (1982)-. Academic Scholarly Publication. English. Irregular. Price varies per volume. Elsevier Science Publishing Company Inc, Madison Square Station, PO Box 882, New York NY 10159-0882. **Tel** (212)633-3950, FAX (212)633-3990. **(Subscription address:** Elsevier Science Inc. / New York Books, 655 Avenue of the Americas, New York NY 10010. **Tel** (212)633-3650.) **ED** R. Davies. Documents available from BIOSIS Document Express, CASDDS.
Ind/Abst AGRICOLA [Full Cov.]; Biol. Abstr. (1986-); Chem. Abstr.

LC QR53 .D47 **ISSN** 0070-4563
DD 576 US
CCC
NLM W1 DE997X **CODEN** DIMCAL
CEASED

DEVELOPMENTS IN INDUSTRIAL MICROBIOLOGY. (DEVELOPMENTS IN INDUSTRIAL MICROBIOLOGY : A PUBLICATION OF THE SOCIETY FOR INDUSTRIAL MICROBIOLOGY.). [Dev. ind. microbiol.]. **Added/Corp** Society for Industrial Microbiology (U.S.) Society for Industrial Microbiology (U.S.). General Meeting. Proceedings of the General Meeting of the Society for Industrial Microbiology. **VFOAT** Industrial Microbiology. Vol. 1 (1960)-(19??). English. Elsevier Science Publishers BV, PO Box 211, 1000 AE Amsterdam Netherlands. **Tel** 011 31 20 4853641, 011 31 20 4853642, FAX 011 31 20 4853598. **ED** Claude H Nash III and Leland A Underkofler. cum. index. **Circ:** 2,000. Documents available from BIOSIS Document Express, CASDDS.

Desc: The proceedings of the 40th general meeting of the Society for Industrial Microbiology.
Ind/Abst BioBusiness (?-?); Biodeter. Abstr. (1991-?); Biol. Abstr.; Biotechnol. Res. Abstr. (?-?); Chem. Abstr. (?-?); Curr. Biotechnol. (?-?); Dairy Sci. Abstr.; EMBASE (?-?); Food Sci. Technol. Abstr. (?-?); Helminthol. Abstr. (1991-?); Hortic. Abstr.; Int. Aerosp. Abstr. (?-?); Maize Abstr.; Life Sci. Collect. (?-?); PESTDOC; Plant Breed. Abstr.; Rev. Agric. Entomol.; Rev. Med. Vet. Entomol.; Rev. Med. Vet. Mycology (?-?); Rice Abstr.; Seed Abstr.; Soils Fert.; Weed Abstr.

ISSN 0167-8256
NE
NLM W1 DE998DG **CODEN** DMVIDD

DEVELOPMENTS IN MOLECULAR VIROLOGY. [Dev. mol. virol.]. Vol. 1 (1981)-. Academic Scholarly Publication. English. Irregular. Price varies per volume. Kluwer Academic Publishers, Postbus 322, 3300 AH Dordrecht The Netherlands. **Tel** 011 31 78 524400, FAX 011 31 78 183273, telex 20083. **ED** Yechiel Becker. Documents available from CASDDS.
Ind/Abst Chem. Abstr.

LC RB37.A1 D5 **ISSN** 0732-8893
DD 616 US
CCC
NLM W1 DI258JD **CODEN** DMIDDZ
Pr Rev.

DIAGNOSTIC MICROBIOLOGY AND INFECTIOUS DISEASE. [Diagn. microbiol. infect. dis.]. Vol. 1, No. 1 (March 1983)-. Academic Scholarly Publication. English. Twelve times a year (3 volumes). $535.00 US; $597.00 other. Elsevier Science Publishing Company Inc, Madison Square Station, PO Box 882, New York NY 10159-0882. **Tel** (212)633-3950, FAX (212)633-3990. **ED** R.N. Jones. **Bk Rev. Ad Acc. Circ:** 1,400. available on microfilm and microfiche from University Microfilms International (UMI); available on an online database from Elsevier Electronic Subscriptions (EES). Documents available from The Genuine Article, BIOSIS Document Express, CASDDS, ADONIS.
Desc: Publishes full-length articles, critical reviews, unusual case studies, and commentaries in clinical microbiology and the diagnosis and treatment of infectious diseases.
Ind/Abst ADONIS; Biol. Abstr.; Chem. Abstr.; Curr. Aware. Biol. Sci., CABS; Curr. Cit.; Curr. Contents Clin. Med.; Curr. Contents Life Sci.; EMBASE; Health Plan. Adminis.; Helminthol. Abstr. (19??-19??); Index Med. (1983-); Index Vet.; Life Sci. Collect.; Pollut. Abstr. Indexes; Protozoolog. Abstr.; Ref. Upd. Deluxe Ed.; Res. Alert [Full Cov.]; Rev. Med. Vet. Entomol.; Rev. Med. Vet. Mycology; Sci. Cit. Index; SCISEARCH; Vet. Bull.

LC QR1.A47 A3 **ISSN** 0196-8254
DD 576/.06/073 US
NLM QW 22 AA1 A5D

DIRECTORY OF MEMBERS - AMERICAN SOCIETY FOR MICROBIOLOGY. **Main/Corp** American Society for Microbiology. (1977)-. Directory. English. One time a year. $34.95. American Society for Microbiology / DC, 1325 Massachusetts Avenue Northwest, Washington DC 20005-4171. **Tel** (202)737-3600, FAX (202)737-0367. ***Continues** Directory and Constitution - American Society for Microbiology, 0272-5142.*
Desc: This directory contains over 500 pages listing the names, addresses, degrees, and division affiliation of all ASM members in the United States. Descriptions of ASM programs, division, awards, and branch organizations are also included, as well as headquarters staff information.

LC QR1 **ISSN** 0301-8172
DD 576/.05 UA
UDC 579
NLM W1 EG913M **CODEN** EJMBA2

EGYPTIAN JOURNAL OF MICROBIOLOGY. [Egypt. j. microbiol.]. **VFOAT** Majallah Al-Misriyah Lil-Mikrubiyuluzhiya. Vol. 7 (1972)-. Academic Scholarly Publication. English (summaries and/or abstracts in Arabic). Two times a year. $37.00. National Information & Documentation Center, A1-Tahrir St Dokki Awqaf PO, Cairo Egypt. **Tel** 011 20 2 701696, telex 93069. Documents available from CASDDS. ***Continues** United Arab Republic Journal of Microbiology, 0303-1438.*
Ind/Abst AGRICOLA; Chem. Abstr.; Dairy Sci. Abstr.; Field Crop Abstr.; Food Sci. Technol. Abstr.; Grass. Forage Abstr.; Rev. Plant Pathol.; Sug. Indus. Abstr.; Weed Abstr.

LC QH **ISSN** 1023-4152
DD 574.88 INT
UDC 681.3:574

•**EMBNET NEWS ONLINE.** **VFOAT** European Molecular Biology Network News (Online); EMBnet News (Online); Embnet.News(Online). (1994)-. Periodical. English. Four times a year. Free. available via Internet (http://www.embnet.unibas.Ch/embnet.news/info.html).

ISSN 0213-005X
SP
CCC
NLM W1; EN5899 **CODEN** EIMCE2

ENFERMEDADES INFECCIOSAS Y MICROBIOLOGIA CLINICA. See Medical Sciences-Communicable Diseases.

LC QR1 .C36 **ISSN** 1210-7913
XR
NLM W1; EP452NLM **CODEN** EMIME6

•**EPIDEMIOLOGIE, MIKROBIOLOGIE, IMUNOLOGIE : CASOPIS SPOLECNOSTI PRO EPIDEMIOLOGII A MIKROBIOLOGII CESKE LEKARSKE SPOLECNOSTI J.E. PURKYNE.** See Medical Sciences-Epidemiology.

ISSN 0934-9723
GW
CCC
NLM W1; EU72CHJ **CODEN** EJCDEU
Pr Rev.

EUROPEAN JOURNAL OF CLINICAL MICROBIOLOGY & INFECTIOUS DISEASES. [Eur. j. clin. microbiol. infect. dis.]. **Added/Corp** European Society of Clinical Microbiology. **VFOAT** European Journal of Clinical Microbiology and Infectious Diseases. Vol. 7, No. 1 (Feb. 1988)-. Periodical. English. Twelve times a year. $334.00. Vieweg Publishing, PO Box 5829, D-65048 Wiesbaden Germany. **Tel** 011 49 611 160230, FAX 011 49 611 534430. **ED** I. Braveny. Index available. **Ad Acc.** Documents available from The Genuine Article, BIOSIS Document Express, CASDDS. ***Continues** European Journal of Clinical Microbiology, 0722-2211.*
Desc: Devoted to the publication of communications on infectious diseases of bacterial, viral, fungal or parasitic origin. The scope of the journal covers the pathogenesis, diagnosis epidemiology, therapy and prevention of infectious diseases.
Ind/Abst Biodeter. Abstr. (1991-); Biol. Abstr. (1988-); Chem. Abstr.; Curr. Aware. Biol. Sci., CABS; Curr. Cit.; EMBASE; Health Plan. Adminis.; Immunol. Abstr.; Index Med. (Feb. 1988-); Index Vet.; Microbiol. Abstr. Sect. B; Microbiol. Abstr. Sect. A; Microbiol. Abstr. Sect. C; Protozoolog. Abstr.; Ref. Upd. Basic Ed.; Ref. Upd. Clinical Ed.; Ref. Upd. Deluxe Ed.; Res. Alert [Full Cov.]; Rev. Med. Vet. Entomol.; Rev. Med. Vet. Mycology; Sci. Cit. Index; SCISEARCH; Trop. Dis. Bull.; Virol. AIDS Abstr.

LC QH274 .P7 **ISSN** 0932-4739
DD 576/.05 GW
CCC
NLM W1; EU72ECE **CODEN** EJPREZ
Pr Rev.

EUROPEAN JOURNAL OF PROTISTOLOGY. [Eur. j. protistol.]. Vol. 23, No. 1 (Nov. 1987)-. Periodical. English (French). Four times a year. $422.00. Gustav Fischer Verlag Stuttgart, Postfach 720143, D-70577 Stuttgart Germany. **Tel** 011 49 711 458030, FAX 011 49 711 4580334, telex 2627-7111488. **(Subscription address:** VCH Publishers Inc., 303 Northwest 12th Avenue, Journals Department, Deerfield FL 33442. **Tel** (800)367-8249, (305)428-5566.**)** **ED** Klaus Hausmann (editor's address: Institut fur Zoologie, Freie Universitat Berlin, Konigin-Luise-Strasse 1-3, 1000 Berlin 33 W. Germany). **Bk Rev. Ad Acc. Circ:** 550. Documents available from The Genuine Article, BIOSIS Document Express. ***Continues** Protistologica, 0033-1821.*
Desc: Studies on protists are becoming increasingly important in the development of many major areas of biology such as organismic and molecular evolution, parasitology, and ecology. Goals are to provide succinct accounts of recent advances in the subject.
Ind/Abst Biocont. News Inf.; Biol. Abstr. (1987-); Curr. Aware. Biol. Sci., CABS; Curr. Cit.; Curr. Contents Agric. Biol. Environ. Sci.; Ecol. Abstr.; Protozoolog. Abstr.; Res. Alert [Full Cov.]; Rev. Agric. Entomol.; Rev. Med. Vet. Entomol.; Sci. Cit. Index; SCISEARCH.

ISSN 1064-4725
DD 576 US
TITLE CHANGE

EUROPEAN MICROBIOLOGY. [Eur. microbiol.]. Vol. 1, No. 1 (Oct. 1992)-(Jan. 1994). Trade Publication. English. VCH Gesellschaft GmbH, Postfach 101161, D-69451 Weinheim Germany. **Tel** 011 49 6201 606459, FAX 011 49 6201 606184. **(Subscription address:** VCH Publishers Inc., 303 Northwest 12th Avenue, Journals Department, Deerfield FL 33442. **Tel** (800)367-8249, (305)428-5566.**)** ***Continued by** Microbiology Europe, 0945-8182.*
Desc: Provides a communication plattform for microbiologists throughout Europe. Articles focus on the latest developments, methods, and techniques in all areas of microbiology.

LC QR46 .F45 **ISSN** 0928-8244
DD 616.01 NE
CCC
NLM W1; FE548S **CODEN** FIMIEVFMIMEH

•**FEMS IMMUNOLOGY AND MEDICAL MICROBIOLOGY.** See Medical Sciences-Allergy and Immunologic Diseases.

ISSN 0921-8254
NE
Pr Rev.

FEMS MICROBIOLOGY. (19??)-. Academic Scholarly Publication. English. Irregular (69 times a year). $5025.00. Elsevier Science Publishers BV, PO Box 211, 1000 AE Amsterdam Netherlands. **Tel** 011 31 20 4853641, 011 31 20 4853642, FAX 011 31 20 4853598. **ED** C. Fewson. Index available. cum. index. **Bk Rev. Ad Acc. Circ:** 1,200 (ctrl). available on an online database from Elsevier Electronic Subscriptions (EES). Documents available from ADONIS.
Desc: Scientific journal publishing short stories, original research articles and review articles dealing with every aspect of microbiology.
Ind/Abst ADONIS.

LC QR1 **ISSN** 0168-6496
DD 576.05 NE
UDC 579 CCC
Pr Rev.

FEMS MICROBIOLOGY, ECOLOGY. **VFOAT** Federation of European Microbiological Societies Microbiology, Ecology. (1985)-. Academic Scholarly Publication. English. Twelve times a year (3 volumes). $845.00. Elsevier Science Publishers BV, PO Box 211, 1000 AE Amsterdam Netherlands. **Tel** 011 31 20 4853641, 011 31 20 4853642, FAX 011 31 20 4853598. available on an online database from Elsevier Electronic Subscriptions (EES). Documents available from The Genuine Article, ADONIS.
Ind/Abst ADONIS; Biocont. News Inf. (1991-); Curr. Aware. Biol. Sci., CABS; Curr. Cit.; Ecology Abstr.; EMBASE; Nematol. Abstr.; Pollut. Abstr. Indexes; Ref. Upd. Deluxe Ed.; Res. Alert [Full Cov.]; Rev. Agric. Entomol.; Rev. Med. Vet. Entomol.; Sci. Cit. Index; SCISEARCH; Soils Fert.

ISSN 0920-8534
NE
UDC 579 CCC
NLM W1; FE549B **CODEN** FMIMEH
TITLE CHANGE

FEMS MICROBIOLOGY IMMUNOLOGY. [FEMS microbiol. immunol.]. **VFOAT** Microbiology Immunology. **VAT** Federation of European Microbiological Societies Microbiology Immunology. Vol. 47/1 (Jan. 1988)-(1993). Academic Scholarly Publication. English. Elsevier Science Publishers BV, PO Box 211, 1000 AE Amsterdam Netherlands. **Tel** 011 31 20 4853641, 011 31 20 4853642, FAX 011 31 20 4853598. **ED** H M Dicks. available on microfilm from University Microfilms International (UMI). Documents available from The Genuine Article, BIOSIS Document Express. ***Continued by** FEMS Immunology and Medical Microbiology.*
Desc: Covers new, rapid diagnostic methods in virology, bacteriology and parasitology facilitating treatment and control of epidemics and outbreaks.
Ind/Abst Biol. Abstr.; Curr. Aware. Biol. Sci., CABS; Curr. Contents Life Sci.; EMBASE; Genet. Abstr.; Helminthol. Abstr.; Index Vet.; Ref. Upd. Deluxe Ed.; Res. Alert [Full Cov.]; Rev. Med. Vet. Entomol.; Sci. Cit. Index (19??-19??); SCISEARCH; Vet. Bull.

LC QR1 .F44a **ISSN** 0378-1097
DD 576/.05 NE
CCC
NLM W1; F316 **CODEN** FMLED7
Pr Rev.

FEMS MICROBIOLOGY LETTERS. [FEMS micro. biol. lett.]. **Main/Corp** Federation of European Microbiological Societies. **Added/Corp** Federation of European Microbiological Societies. Microbiology Letters. **VFOAT** Microbiology Letters; FEMS Microbiology Ecology; FEMS Microbiology Reviews; FEMS Microbiology Index; FEMS Microbiology Immunology. **VAT** Federation of European Microbiological Societies Microbiology Letters. Vol. 1 (Jan. 1977)-. Academic Scholarly Publication. English. Thirty times a year (10 volumes). $3059.00. Elsevier Science Publishers BV, PO Box 211, 1000 AE Amsterdam Netherlands. **Tel** 011 31 20 4853641, 011 31 20 4853642, FAX 011 31 20 4853598. **ED** E A Dawes. available on microfilm and microfiche from University Microfilms International (UMI); available on an online database from Elsevier Electronic Subscriptions (EES). Documents available from The Genuine Article, BIOSIS Document Express, CASDDS, Documents on Demand, ADONIS. ***Continued in part by** FEMS Immunology and Medical Microbiology.*
Desc: Provides a vehicle for the rapid publication of short reports on research in all aspects of microbiology and microbial chemistry.
Ind/Abst ADONIS; AgBiotech News Inf.; AGRICOLA [Select. Cov.]; Biocont. News Inf. (19??-19??); Biodeter. Abstr. (19??-19??); Biol. Abstr. (1985-); Chem. Abstr. (1985-); Chem. Titles; Curr. Biotechnol.; Curr. Cit.; Curr. Contents Life Sci.; Dairy Sci. Abstr.; Ecol. Abstr.; Ecology Abstr.; EMBASE; Energy Inf. Abstr.; Environ. Abstr.; Field Crop Abstr.; Fish Rev. (Jan. 1989-July 1992); Food Sci. Technol. Abstr.; For. Prod. Abstr. (19??-19??); Genet.

Abstr.; Geogr. Abstr. Phys. Geogr.; Geol. Abstr.; Helminthol. Abstr. (1991-); Immunol. Abstr.; Index Med.; Index Vet.; Microbiol. Abstr. Sect. B; Microbiol. Abstr. Sect. A; Microbiol. Abstr. Sect. C; NAPRALERT; Nucl. Acids Abstr.; Nutr. Abstr. Rev., Ser. B, Live Feeds and Feed.; Nutr. Abstr. Rev., Ser. A, Hum. Exp.; Life Sci. Collect.; PESTDOC; Pig News Inf.; Protozoolog. Abstr.; Ref. Upd. Basic Ed.; Ref. Upd. Deluxe Ed.; Res. Alert [Full Cov.]; Rev. Agric. Entomol.; Rev. Med. Vet. Entomol.; Rev. Med. Vet. Mycology; Rev. Plant Pathol.; Rice Abstr.; Sci. Cit. Index; SCISEARCH; Small Anim. Abstr. Bibliogr.; Soils Fert.; Vet. Bull.; Virol. AIDS Abstr.; Weed Abstr.; Wheat Barley Trit. Abstr.; Wildl. Rev. (Jan. 1989-July 1992).

LC QR1 .F45 **ISSN** 0168-6445
DD 576/.05 NE
CCC
CODEN FMREE4
Pr Rev.

●**FEMS MICROBIOLOGY REVIEWS.** [FEMS microbiol. rev.]. **Main/Corp** Federation of European Microbiological Societies. **Added/Corp** Federation of European Microbiological Societies. **VFOAT** Microbiology Reviews. **VAT** Federation of European Microbiological Societies Microbiology Reviews. (1993)-. English. Twelve times a year (3 volumes). $845.00. Elsevier Science Publishers BV, PO Box 211, 1000 AE Amsterdam Netherlands. **Tel** 011 31 20 4853641, 011 31 20 4853642, FAX 011 31 20 4853598. **(Subscription address:** Elsevier Science BV / Maryland, PO Box 64698, Baltimore MD 21264. **)** available on an online database from Elsevier Electronic Subscriptions (EES). Documents available from The Genuine Article, CASDDS, ADONIS. ***Continues in part*** *Federation of European Microbiological Societies. FEMS Microbiology Letters, 0378-1097.*
Ind/Abst ADONIS; Chem. Abstr.; Curr. Aware. Biol. Sci., CABS; Curr. Biotechnol.; Curr. Cit.; Curr. Contents Life Sci.; EMBASE; Index Sci. Rev. [Full Cov.]; PESTDOC; Ref. Upd. Deluxe Ed.; Res. Alert [Full Cov.]; Sci. Cit. Index; SCISEARCH.

LC QR1 **ISSN** 0163-9188
DD 576/.05 UK
CCC
NLM W3 F21 **CODEN** FEMSDW

FEMS SYMPOSIUM. [FEMS symp.]. **Added/Corp** Federation of European Microbiological Societies. Society for Applied Bacteriology. Society for General Microbiology. **VFOAT** F.E.M.S. Symposium. **VAT** Federation of European Microbiological Societies Symposium. (197?)-. Monographic series. English. Plenum Press, 233 Spring Street, New York NY 10013-1578. **Tel** (212)620-8000, (800)221-9369, FAX (212)463-0742, (212)807-1047, telex 23/421139. Documents available from CASDDS.
Ind/Abst Chem. Abstr.; Curr. Cit.

ISSN 0015-5632
XR
UDC 579
NLM W1 FO25M **CODEN** FOMIAZ
Pr Rev.

FOLIA MICROBIOLOGICA. [Folia microbiol.]. Vol. 4 (1959)-. Academic Scholarly Publication. English. Six times a year. $229.31. Academic Press Ltd., A Division of Harcourt Brace & Company Ltd., 24-28 Oval Road, London NW1 7DX United Kingdom. **Tel** 011 44 171 2674466, FAX 011 44 171 4822293, 011 44 171 4854752, telex 25775 ACPRES G. **(Subscription address:** Harcourt Brace & Company, Ltd., Foots Cray High Street, Sidcup Kent DA14 5HP United Kingdom. **Tel** 011 44 181 3003322, FAX 011 44 181 3090807, telex 896 377 ACADEM.**) ED** V. Krumphanzl and J. Cudlin. Documents available from The Genuine Article, BIOSIS Document Express, CASDDS. ***Continues*** *Ceskoslovenska Mikrobiologie.*
Desc: Provides a forum for the publication of papers in general and applied microbiology. With particular interest in the molecular aspects of microbiological processes, the journal accepts articles on fundamental and applied topics.
Ind/Abst AgBiotech News Inf.; AGRICOLA; BioBusiness; Biodeter. Abstr.; Biol. Abstr.; Chem. Abstr.; Chem. Titles; Curr. Biotechnol.; Curr. Cit.; Curr. Contents Agric. Biol. Environ. Sci.; Curr. Contents Life Sci.; Dairy Sci. Abstr.; EMBASE; Health Plan. Adminis.; Index Med.; Index Vet.; Microbiol. Abstr. Sect. B; Microbiol. Abstr. Sect. A; Microbiol. Abstr. Sect. C; NAPRALERT; Nutr. Abstr. Rev., Ser. B, Live Feeds and Feed.; Nutr. Abstr. Rev., Ser. A, Hum. Exp.; Life Sci. Collect.; PESTDOC; Pig News Inf.; Protozoolog. Abstr.; Res. Alert [Full Cov.]; Rev. Med. Vet. Mycology; Rev. Plant Pathol.; Sci. Cit. Index; SCISEARCH; Soils Fert.; Vet. Bull.; Weed Abstr.

LC RB37 **ISSN** 0954-0105
DD 616.075/6 UK
CCC
NLM W1; FO402L **CODEN** FAIMEZ

FOOD AND AGRICULTURAL IMMUNOLOGY. [Food agric. immunol.]. Vol. 1, No. 1 (1989)-. Academic Scholarly Publication. English. Four times a year. $498.00. Carfax Publishing Company, PO Box 25, Abingdon, Oxfordshire OX14 3UE United Kingdom. **Tel** 011 44 1235 555335, FAX 011 44 1235 553559, telex 817484. **ED** M R A Morgan. available on microfiche. Documents available from BIOSIS Document Express, CASDDS.
Desc: Presents original immunological research with food, agricultural, environmental, and veterinary applications...on research exploiting antibodies and the immune response with food and agricultural application.
Ind/Abst AgBiotech News Inf.; Biodeter. Abstr. (1991-); Biol. Abstr. (1989-); Chem. Abstr. (1989-); Curr. Aware. Biol. Sci., CABS; Curr. Cit.; Dairy Sci. Abstr.; Food Sci. Technol. Abstr.; Index Vet.; Maize Abstr.; Nutr. Abstr. Rev., Ser. B, Live Feeds and Feed.; Nutr. Abstr. Rev., Ser. A, Hum. Exp.; Pig News Inf.; Postharvest News Inf.; Rev. Med. Vet. Mycology; Rev. Plant Pathol.; Soyabean Abstr.; Vet. Bull.; Weed Abstr.; Wheat Barley Trit. Abstr.

LC QR115 **ISSN** 0740-0020
DD 664/.028 UK
UDC 579.67 **CCC**
NLM W1; FO471D **CODEN** FOMIE5

FOOD MICROBIOLOGY. [Food microbiol.]. Vol. 1, No. 1 (Jan. 1984)-. Academic Scholarly Publication. English. Six times a year. $342.24. Academic Press Ltd., A Division of Harcourt Brace & Company Ltd., 24-28 Oval Road, London NW1 7DX United Kingdom. **Tel** 011 44 171 2674466, FAX 011 44 171 4822293, 011 44 171 4854752, telex 25775 ACPRES G. **(Subscription address:** Harcourt Brace & Company, Ltd., Foots Cray High Street, Sidcup Kent DA14 5HP United Kingdom. **Tel** 011 44 181 3003322, FAX 011 44 181 3090807, telex 896 377 ACADEM.**) ED** C. Batt and C. Dennis. **Bk Rev.** Documents available from The Genuine Article, BIOSIS Document Express, CASDDS.
Desc: Provides a means of communication in the field of the microbiology of food, soft drinks, and alcoholic beverages and is designed to take into account the growing importance of biotechnology in the food-processing industry.
Ind/Abst AGRICOLA [Full Cov.]; BioBusiness; Biodeter. Abstr. (19??-19??); Biol. Abstr. (1985-); Chem. Abstr. (1984-); Curr. Aware. Biol. Sci., CABS; Curr. Cit.; Curr. Contents Agric. Biol. Environ. Sci.; Dairy Sci. Abstr.; Food Sci. Technol. Abstr.; Foods Adlibra; Index Vet.; Maize Abstr.; Nutr. Abstr. Rev., Ser. A, Hum. Exp.; Life Sci. Collect.; Pig News Inf.; Poult. Abstr.; Res. Alert [Full Cov.]; Sci. Cit. Index; SCISEARCH; Soyabean Abstr.; Vet. Bull.; Vitis Vitic. Enol. Abstr.

II

FRONTIERS IN APPLIED MICROBIOLOGY. Vol. 1 (1985)-. English. One time a year. Price varies. Print House, 5 Tej Bahadur Sapru Marg, Lucknow UP India. **(Subscription address:** Prints India, 11 Darya Ganj, New Delhi 110002 India. **Tel** 011 91 11 3268645, FAX 011 91 11 3275542, telex 31-61087 PRIN-IN.**)**

LC QH359 **ISSN** 1356-9597
DD 575 UK

●**GENES TO CELLS.** (1996)-. Academic Scholarly Publication. English. Twelve times a year. Blackwell Science Ltd., Osney Mead, Oxford OX2 OEL United Kingdom. **Tel** 011 44 1865 206206, FAX 011 44 1865 206219. **ED** Jun-ichi Iomizawa.

LC QR103 .G46 **ISSN** 0149-0451
DD 550/.1576 US
CCC
CODEN GEJODG
Pr Rev.

GEOMICROBIOLOGY JOURNAL. [Geomicrobiol. j.]. Vol.1 (1978)-. Academic Scholarly Publication. English. Four times a year. $180.00. Taylor & Francis Ltd. / UK, Rankine Road, Basingstoke, Hampshire RG24 8PR United Kingdom. **Tel** 011 44 1256 840366, FAX 011 44 1256 479438, telex 858540. **(Subscription address:** Taylor & Francis Inc., 1900 Frost Road, Suite 101, Bristol PA 19007-1598. **Tel** (215)785-5800, (800)821-8312, FAX (215)785-5515.**) ED** Henry L. Ehrlich (editor's address: Department of Biology, Rensselaer Polytechnic Institute, Troy, NY 12180-3590). **Bk Rev. Ad Acc. Circ:** 600. available on microfilm and microfiche from University Microfilms International (UMI). Documents available from The Genuine Article, BIOSIS Document Express, Petroleum Abstracts Document Delivery Service, CASDDS.
Desc: Provides a unified vehicle for the publication of research and review articles in the rapidly growing field of geomicrobiology. Articles deal with microbial transformations of materials comprising the earth's crust, including oceans, seas, lakes, bottom sediments, soils, mineral deposits and rocks and the geological impact which these transformations have at present or have had over geologic time.
Ind/Abst AGRICOLA; Biol. Abstr.; Chem. Abstr.; Curr. Aware. Biol. Sci., CABS; Curr. Cit.; Curr. Contents Agric. Biol. Environ. Sci.; Ecol. Abstr.; Ecology Abstr.; Ei Page One; Geogr. Abstr. Phys. Geogr.; Geol. Abstr.; GeoRef; Int. Aerosp. Abstr.; Irr. Drain. Abstr.; Microbiol. Abstr. Sect. B; Life Sci. Collect.; Pet. Abstr.; Res. Alert [Full Cov.]; Sci. Cit. Index; SCISEARCH; Soils Fert.

LC QR53 .K85 **ISSN** 1001-6678
DD 660/.62/05 CC
CODEN GOWEEK

GONGYE WEISHENGWU. (KUNG YEH WEI SHENG WU.). [Gongye weishengwu]. **Added/Corp** Chuan Kuo Kung Yeh Wei Sheng Wu Ko Chi Ching Pao Chan (China) Shang-Hai Shih Kung Yeh Wei Sheng Wu Yen Chiu So (China). **VFOAT** Industrial Microbiology. (1971)-. Academic Scholarly Publication. Chinese (summaries and/or abstracts in English). Six times a year. $80.00. Shanghai Gongye Weishengwu Yanjiusuo, Shanghai Institute of Industrial Microbiology, 1515 Xietu road, Shanghai 200041 People's Republic of China. **Tel** 4034400. **ED** L. Zhaozu. **Bk Rev. Ad Acc. Circ:** 10,000. Documents available from CASDDS, BLDSC, CASDDS.
Ind/Abst Chem. Abstr.

LC RG316 **ISSN** 0363-521X
DD 618.1 US
NLM W1 IN106A **CODEN** IVMOD2

IN VITRO. MONOGRAPH. See Biology-Cytology.

LC QH321 **ISSN** 1077-3975
DD 574.072 US
Pr Rev.

●**IN VITRO REPORT.** **Added/Corp** Society for In Vitro Biology. **VFOAT** Report. Vol. 30, No. 4 (July/Aug. 1994)-. Academic Scholarly Publication. English. Six times a year. $35.00. Society for In Vitro Biology, PO Box 73230, Baltimore MD 21273. **Tel** (410)992-0946. **ED** Collette Rudd. **Circ:** 2,100. ***Continues*** *Tissue Culture Association. TCA Report, 0163-772X.*
Desc: Features news and notes about branches, divisions, committees, and members of the society, placement service, and short articles of the field.

ISSN 0255-0857
II
NLM W1; IN2126 **CODEN** IJMMEF

INDIAN JOURNAL OF MEDICAL MICROBIOLOGY. [Indian j. med. microbiol.]. **Added/Corp** Indian Association of Medical Microbiologists. (198?)-. Periodical. English. Four times a year. $80.00. Postgraduate Institute of Medical Education and Research, 160012 Chandigarh India. **Tel** 32351 ext. 270. **(Subscription address:** Prints India, 11 Darya Ganj, New Delhi 110002 India. **Tel** 011 91 11 3268645, FAX 011 91 11 3275542, telex 31-61087 PRIN-IN.**)** Documents available from CASDDS.
Ind/Abst Chem. Abstr. (1986-); EMBASE [Select. Cov.].

LC QR1 .I48 **ISSN** 0046-8991
DD 576/.05 II
NLM W1 IN219 **CODEN** IJMBACIJMPAC

INDIAN JOURNAL OF MICROBIOLOGY. [Indian j. microbiol.]. **Added/Corp** Association of Microbiologists of India. Vol. 1 (Jan./Mar. 1961)-. Periodical. English. Four times a year. $60.00. Scientific Publishers, PO Box 91, Ratanada Road, Jodhpur 342011 India. **(Subscription address:** Prints India, 11 Darya Ganj, New Delhi 110002 India. **Tel** 011 91 11 3268645, FAX 011 91 11 3275542, telex 31-61087 PRIN-IN.**) ED** P Tuaro (editor's address: Department of Microbiology, 125004 India). **Ad Acc. Circ:** 700. Documents available from BIOSIS Document Express, CASDDS.
Desc: Relates to all aspects of microbiology.
Ind/Abst Biocont. News Inf. (1991-); Biodeter. Abstr. (19??-19??); Biol. Abstr.; Chem. Abstr.; Curr. Cit.; Dairy Sci. Abstr.; EMBASE; Field Crop Abstr.; Food Sci. Technol. Abstr.; For. Abstr.; Index Vet.; Microbiol. Abstr. Sect. B; Life Sci. Collect.; PESTDOC; Protozoolog. Abstr.; Rev. Agric. Entomol.; Rev. Med. Vet. Mycology; Rev. Plant Pathol.; Seed Abstr.; Soils Fert.; Soyabean Abstr.; Vet. Bull.

ISSN 0377-4929
II
NLM W1 IN224H **CODEN** IJPMDT

INDIAN JOURNAL OF PATHOLOGY & MICROBIOLOGY. See Medical Sciences-Pathology.

ISSN 0970-2822
II
NLM W1; IN241J **CODEN** IJVIEE

INDIAN JOURNAL OF VIROLOGY. [Indian J. Virol.]. **Added/Corp** Indian Virological Society. Vol. 1, No. 1 (Jan. 1985)-. Periodical. English. Two times a year. $60.00. Indian Virological Society, Hisar India. **(Subscription address:** Prints India, 11 Darya Ganj, New Delhi 110002 India. **Tel** 011 91 11 3268645, FAX 011 91 11 3275542, telex 31-61087 PRIN-IN.**)** Documents available from BIOSIS Document Express.
Ind/Abst Agrofor. Abstr. (1991-); Biol. Abstr. (1985-); For. Prod. Abstr. (1991-); Index Vet.; Microbiol. Abstr. Sect. A; Rev. Agric. Entomol.; Soyabean Abstr.; Vet. Bull.; Virol. AIDS Abstr.

LC QR1.A47 A35 **ISSN** 0019-9567
DD 576/.2/05 US
CCC
NLM W1 IN406 **CODEN** INFIBR
Pr Rev.

INFECTION AND IMMUNITY. [Infect. immun.]. **Added/Corp** American Society for Microbiology. Vol. 1 (Jan. 1970)-. Academic Scholarly Publication. English. Twelve times a year. $419.00. American Society for Microbiology / DC, 1325 Massachusetts Avenue Northwest, Washington DC 20005-4171. **Tel** (202)737-3600, FAX (202)737-0367. **(Subscription address:** American Society for Microbiology, Journals Subscription Department, PO Box 11127, Birmingham AL 35201-1127. **Tel** (800)633-4931, FAX (205)995-1588.**) ED** Joseph W. Shands, Jr., Phillip J. Baker, Edwin H. Beachey, Peter Bonventre, Roy Curtiss III, Dexter H. Howard, Stephen H. Leppla, and Stephen E. Mergenhagen. Index available. **Bk Rev. Ad Acc. Acid**

Free. Circ: 7,101 (ctrl). available on microfilm and microfiche from University Microfilms International (UMI); available on CD-ROM. Documents available from The Genuine Article, BIOSIS Document Express, CASDDS.
Desc: Covers a wide area of topics, directed toward immunologists, epidemiologists, pathologists, and clinicians, including: infections caused by pathogenic bacteria, fungi, and unicellular parasites; ecology and epidemiology of pathogenic microbes; virulence factors such as toxins and surface structures; nonspecific factors in host resistance and susceptibility to infection; and immunology of microbial infections.
Ind/Abst AgBiotech News Inf.; AGRICOLA [Select. Cov.]; Anim. Breed. Abstr.; Biol. Abstr.; Chem. Abstr.; Chemorecept. Abstr.; Curr. Aware. Biol. Sci., CABS; Curr. Cit.; Curr. Contents Life Sci.; Curr. Titles Dent.; Dairy Sci. Abstr.; EMBASE; Energy Res. Abstr. (Jan. 1971-); Food Sci. Technol. Abstr.; Genet. Abstr.; Helminthol. Abstr. (19??-19??); Immunol. Abstr.; Index Med.; INIS Atomindex [Micro.]; Int. Aerosp. Abstr.; Microbiol. Abstr. Sect. B; Microbiol. Abstr. Sect. A; Microbiol. Abstr. Sect. C; Nucl. Acids Abstr.; Nutr. Abstr. Rev., Ser. B, Live Feeds and Feed.; Nutr. Abstr. Rev., Ser. A, Hum. Exp.; Life Sci. Collect.; PESTDOC; Pig News Inf.; Poult. Abstr.; Protozoolog. Abstr.; Ref. Upd. Basic Ed.; Ref. Upd. Deluxe Ed.; Res. Alert [Full Cov.]; Rev. Med. Vet. Entomol.; Rev. Med. Vet. Mycology; Rev. Plant Pathol.; Sci. Cit. Index; SCISEARCH; Soils Fert.; Trop. Dis. Bull.

ISSN 0952-1127
UK

NLM W1; IN455AT

INNOVATION IN MICROBIOLOGY SERIES. [Innov. microbiol. ser.]. 1983-. Monographic series. English. Price varies per volume. John Wiley & Sons Ltd., Baffins Lane, Chichester, West Sussex PO19 1UD United Kingdom. **Tel** 011 44 1243 779777, FAX 011 44 1243 776128 BTG:JWP001, telex 86290 WIBOOKG. **(Subscription address:** John Wiley & Sons Inc / New Jersey, PO Box 2575, Secaucus NJ 07096-2575. **) ED** A N Sharpe.

ISSN 0965-2310
UK

NLM W1; IN703R **CODEN** IANWEL

INTERNATIONAL ANTIVIRAL NEWS. Vol 1, No 1 (Nov. 1992)-. Newsletter. English. Ten times a year. £214.00 Europe; £215.00 other (institutions). Churchill Livingstone, 1-3 Baxter's Place, Leith Walk, Edinburgh EH1 3AF United Kingdom. **Tel** 011 44 131 5562424, FAX 011 44 131 5581278, telex 727511. **(Subscription address:** Maruzen Company Ltd., PO Box 5050, Import & Export Department, Tokyo 100 31 Japan. **Tel** 011 81 3 32789224.)

ISSN 0168-1605
NE
CCC

NLM W1; IN766JM **CODEN** IJFMDD
Pr Rev.

INTERNATIONAL JOURNAL OF FOOD MICROBIOLOGY. See Food and Food Industry.

LC QR46 .Z456 **ISSN** 0937-1591
DD 616/01 GW
NLM ZQW 4; Z56
CEASED

INTERNATIONAL JOURNAL OF MEDICAL MICROBIOLOGY AND HYGIENE ABSTRACTS OF MICROBIOLOGY, VIROLOGY, PARASITOLOGY, PREVENTIVE MEDICINE AND ENVIRONMENTAL HYGIENE. [Zent. bl. Bakteriol. Mikrobiol. Hyg.. Abstr. microbiol. virol. parasitol.

prev. med. environ. hyg.]. **VFOAT** Abstracts of Microbiology, Virology, Parasitology, Preventive Medicine and Environmental Hygiene; Zentralblatt fur Bakteriologie, Mikrobiologie und Hygiene. Vol. 309, No. 1 (March 1989)-Vol. 332. Periodical. English. Gustav Fischer Verlag Stuttgart, Postfach 720143, D-70577 Stuttgart Germany. **Tel** 011 49 711 458030, FAX 011 49 711 4580334, telex 2627-7111488. **ED** G. Henneberg, H.D. Brede. **Bk Rev. Ad Acc. Circ:** 450. ***Continues*** *International Journal of Microbiology and Hygiene. Abstracts. Medical Microbiology, Virology, Parasitology, Hygiene, Preventive Medicine, 0177-3103.*

UDC 579
NLM W1; IN769Y

INTERNATIONAL JOURNAL OF MICROBIOLOGY. Vol. 1, No. 1 (Oct. 1983)-. Periodical. English. Six times a year. Academic International Publications, R7 Hauz Khas Enclave, New Delhi 110016 India.
Ind/Abst Biodeter. Abstr.; Dairy Sci. Abstr.

LC QR1 .I5 **ISSN** 0020-7713
DD 589 US
CCC

NLM W1 IN791K **CODEN** IJSBA8
Pr Rev.

INTERNATIONAL JOURNAL OF SYSTEMATIC BACTERIOLOGY. [Int. j. syst. bacteriol.]. **Added/Corp** International Union of Microbiological Societies. International Association of Microbiological Societies. International Committee of Microbiological Nomenclature. Judicial Commission. International Association of Microbiological Societies. International Committee of Microbiological Nomenclature. International Association of Microbiological Societies. International Committee on Nomenclature of Microbiology. Judicial Commission. International Association of Microbiological Societies. International Committee on Nomenclature of Microbiology. International Association of Microbiological Societies. International Committee on Systematic Bacteriology. International Union of Microbiological Societies. International Committee on Systematic Bacteriology. Vol. 16 (June 1966)-. Academic Scholarly Publication. English. Four times a year (Jan., Apr., July., Oct.). $164.00. American Society for Microbiology / DC, 1325 Massachusetts Avenue Northwest, Washington DC 20005-4171. **Tel** (202)737-3600, FAX (202)737-0367. **(Subscription address:** American Society for Microbiology, Journals Subscription Department, PO Box 11127, Birmingham AL 35201-1127. **Tel** (800)633-4931, FAX (205)995-1588.**) ED** R.G.E. Murray. **Ad Acc. Acid Free. Circ:** 1,900. available on microfilm and microfiche from University Microfilms International (UMI); available on CD-ROM. Documents available from The Genuine Article, BIOSIS Document Express, CASDDS. ***Continues*** *International Bulletin of Bacteriological Nomenclature and Taxonomy, 0096-266X.*
Desc: Official journal of the International Committee on Systematic Bacteriology of the International Union of Microbiological Societies. This journal publishes papers concerned with the systematics of bacteria, yeasts and yeast-like organisms, including taxonomy, nomenclature, indentification, characterization and culture preservation.
Ind/Abst Abstr. Bull. Inst. Pap. Sci. Tech.; AgBiotech News Inf.; AGRICOLA [Select. Cov.]; Biocont. News Inf.; Biodeter. Abstr. (19??-19??); Biol. Abstr.; Chem. Abstr.; Curr. Aware. Biol. Sci., CABS; Curr. Cit.; Curr. Contents Life Sci.; Dairy Sci. Abstr.; EMBASE; Food Sci. Technol. Abstr.; Index Med. (Jan. 1990-); Index Vet.; Microbiol. Abstr. Sect. B; Microbiol. Abstr. Sect. A; Nutr. Abstr. Rev., Ser. B, Live Feeds and Feed.; Life Sci. Collect.; Pig News Inf.; Potato Abstr.; Poult. Abstr.; Protozoolog. Abstr.; Ref. Upd. Deluxe Ed.; Res. Alert [Full Cov.]; Rev. Med. Vet. Entomol.; Rev. Med. Vet. Mycology; Rev. Plant Pathol.; Rice Abstr.; Sci. Cit. Index; SCISEARCH; Small Anim. Abstr. Bibliogr.; Soils Fert.; Sorghum Mill. Abstr.; Soyabean Abstr.; Sug. Indus. Abstr.; Vet. Bull.; Trop. Dis. Bull.; Vitis Vitic. Enol. Abstr.

ISSN 1070-6259
DD 589 US

INTERNATIONAL JOURNAL OF SYSTEMATIC BACTERIOLOGY (CD-ROM). (INTERNATIONAL JOURNAL OF SYSTEMATIC BACTERIOLOGY [COMPUTER FILE].). [Int. j. syst. bacteriol.]. **Added/Corp** American Society for Microbiology. Vol. 42 (1992)-. Academic Scholarly Publication. English. Four times a year (quarterly). $300.00. American Society of Microbiology / Birmingham, PO Box 11127, Birmingham AL 35201. **Tel** (800)633-4931 ext. 2723.

LC QR355 .I58 **ISSN** 0300-5526
DD 576/.64/05 SZ
CCC

NLM W1 IN983K **CODEN** IVRYAK
Pr Rev.

INTERVIROLOGY. [Intervirology]. **Added/Corp** International Association of Microbiological Societies. Section on Virology. Vol. 1 (1973)-. Periodical. English. Six times a year. $577.60. S. Karger AG, Allschwilerstrasse 10, PO Box, CH-4009 Basel Switzerland. **Tel** 011 41 61 3061111, FAX 011 41 61 3061234, telex CH 962 652. **ED** R.W. Braun. Index available. **Ad Acc.** available on microfilm from University Microfilms International (UMI). Documents available from The Genuine Article, BIOSIS Document Express, CASDDS.
Desc: Provides coverage of virology research. Discusses virus structure and replication, virus-cell relationship, medical virology, human and related retroviruses, plant and invertebrate virology, as well as bacteriophage. Also features studies on the genetics, ecology and epidemiology of viruses as well as related problems of immunology and oncology.
Ind/Abst AgBiotech News Inf.; Biol. Abstr.; Chem. Abstr.; Curr. Cit.; Curr. Contents Life Sci.; Dairy Sci. Abstr.; EMBASE; For. Prod. Abstr.; For. Abstr.; Genet. Abstr.; Immunol. Abstr.; Index Med.; Life Sci. Collect.; Potato Abstr.; Ref. Upd. Deluxe Ed.; Res. Alert [Full Cov.]; Rev. Med. Vet. Entomol.; Rev. Med. Vet. Mycology; Rev. Plant Pathol.; Sci. Cit. Index; SCISEARCH; Soyabean Abstr.; Trop. Dis. Bull.; Virol. AIDS Abstr.

LC QL386 **ISSN** 1354-2516
DD 595.1 UK

•**INVERTEBRATE NEUROSCIENCE. See** Zoology-Entomology.

LC QR6 .I862 **ISSN** 0130-6758
RU
CODEN INMKAX

ITOGI NAUKI I TEKHNIKI : SERIIA MIKROBIOLOGIIA. Added/Corp Vsesoiuznyi Institut Nauchnoi i Tekhnicheskoi Informatsii (Soviet Union). **VFOAT** Seriia Mikrobiologiia. (1972)-. Academic Scholarly Publication. Russian. Price varies per volume. VINITI - Vsesoyuznyi Institut Nauchno-Tekhnicheskoi Informatsii, All-Union Scientific and Technical Information Institute, Baltiiskaia ulitsa 14, 125219 Moscow Russia. **Tel** 011 7 95 2384600, FAX 011 7 95 9430060, telex 411160. Documents available from CASDDS. ***Continues in part*** *Itogi Nauki. Virusologiia i Mikrobiologiia.*
Ind/Abst Chem. Abstr.

LC QR1 .I862 **ISSN** 0360-0416
DD 576/.05 US
UDC 579
NLM W1 MI292G

ITOGI, SUMMARIES OF SCIENTIFIC PROGRESS : MICROBIOLOGY. VFOAT Microbiology. Vol. 1 (1974)-. English. One time a year. GK Hall & Co., 100 Front Street, Riverside NJ 08075. **Tel** (800)257-5755 ext. 2223.

LC QR355 .I842 **ISSN** 0360-0440
DD 576/.64/05 US
UDC 578

ITOGI, SUMMARIES OF SCIENTIFIC PROGRESS : VIROLOGY. VFOAT Virology. Monographic series. English. Price varies per volume. GK Hall & Co., 100 Front Street, Riverside NJ 08075. **Tel** (800)257-5755 ext. 2223.

LC QR46 .R47 **ISSN** 1054-2744
DD 616/.01 US
NLM W1; JA988

JAWETZ, MELNICK & ADELBERG'S MEDICAL MICROBIOLOGY. [Jawetz, Melnick Adelberg's med. microbiol.]. **VFOAT** Jawetz, Melnick, and Adelberg's Medical Microbiology; Medical Microbiology; Microbiology. 19th Ed. (1991)-. English. Irregular. Appleton & Lange, (A Subsidiary of Simon & Schuster), Four Stamford Plaza, 107 Elm Street, Stamford CT 06902-3851. **Tel** (203)406-4500, (800)451-3794. **(Subscription address:** Appleton & Lange, PO Box 86, Congers NY 10920-0086. **) *Continues*** *Medical Microbiology (Norwalk, Conn.), 1042-8089.*

LC QR1 .J57 **ISSN** 0021-8847
DD 589.9 UK
CCC

NLM W1 JO539B **CODEN** JABAA4
Pr Rev.

JOURNAL OF APPLIED BACTERIOLOGY, THE. [J. appl. bacteriol.]. **Added/Corp** Society for Applied Bacteriology. Vol. 17 (April 1954)-. Academic Scholarly Publication. English. Twelve times a year. $728.00. Blackwell Scientific Publications Ltd, Marston Book Services, PO Box 88, Oxford OX2 ONE United Kingdom. **Tel** 011 44 1865 206206, FAX 011 44 1865 206219, telex 837 515 MARDIS G. **ED** M. Sussman, F. A. Skinner and G. I. Barrow. Index available. **Bk Rev. Ad Acc. Circ:** 3,200 (ctrl). available on microfilm and microfiche from University Microfilms International (UMI). Documents available from The Genuine Article, BIOSIS Document Express, CASDDS, ADONIS. ***Continues*** *Society for Applied Bacteriology. Proceedings of the Society for Applied Bacteriology.*
Desc: Publishes papers on the systematics and ecology of grounds of micro-organisms.
Ind/Abst ADONIS; AgBiotech News Inf.; AGRICOLA [Select. Cov.]; BioBusiness; Biocont. News Inf. (1991-); Biodeter. Abstr. (1991-); Biol. Agric. Index; Biol. Abstr.; Chem. Abstr.; Chemorecept. Abstr.; Curr. Aware. Biol. Sci., CABS; Curr. Biotechnol.; Curr. Cit.; Curr. Contents Agric. Biol. Environ. Sci.; Curr. Contents Life Sci.; Dairy Sci. Abstr.; Ecology Abstr.; EMBASE; Food Sci. Technol. Abstr.; Foods Adlibra; For. Abstr.; Geogr. Abstr. Human Geogr.; Health Saf. Sci. Abstr.; Hortic. Abstr.; Immunol. Abstr.; Index Med.; Index Vet.; Microbiol. Abstr. Sect. B; Microbiol. Abstr. Sect. A; Microbiol. Abstr. Sect. C; Nematol. Abstr.; Nutr. Abstr. Rev., Ser. B, Live Feeds and Feed.; Nutr. Abstr. Rev., Ser. A, Hum. Exp.; Ornamental Hort. (1991-); Life Sci. Collect.; Pig News Inf.; Pollut. Abstr. Indexes; Postharvest News Inf.; Potato Abstr.; Poult. Abstr.; Protozoolog. Abstr.; Ref. Upd. Deluxe Ed.; Res. Alert [Full Cov.]; Rev. Agric. Entomol.; Rev. Med. Vet. Entomol.; Rev. Med. Vet. Mycology; Rev. Plant Pathol.; Rice Abstr.; Sci. Cit. Index; SCISEARCH; Seed Abstr.; Soils Fert.; Soyabean Abstr.; Vet. Bull.; Trop. Dis. Bull.; Vitis Vitic. Enol. Abstr.; Wheat Barley Trit. Abstr.

LC QR1 .J6 **ISSN** 0021-9193
DD 589 US
CCC

NLM W1 JO55 **CODEN** JOBAAY
Pr Rev.

JOURNAL OF BACTERIOLOGY. [J. bacteriol.]. **Added/Corp** American Society for Microbiology. Society of American Bacteriologists. Vol. 1 (1916)-. Periodical. English. Twenty-four times a year. $391.00 (print), $400.00 (CD-ROM) US. American Society for Microbiology / DC, 1325 Massachusetts Avenue Northwest, Washington DC 20005-4171. **Tel**

(202)737-3600, FAX (202)737-0367. **(Subscription address:** American Society for Microbiology, Journals Subscription Department, PO Box 11127, Birmingham AL 35201-1127. **Tel** (800)633-4931, FAX (205)995-1588.) **ED** Graham Walker. cum. index. **Ad Acc. Acid Free. Circ:** 8,400. available on microfilm and microfiche from University Microfilms International (UMI); available on CD-ROM. Documents available from The Genuine Article, BIOSIS Document Express, UMI Article Clearinghouse, CASDDS.
Desc: Publishes articles on a range of topics. Sections include structure and function, plant microbiology, genetics and molecular biology, plasmids and transposons, eukaryotic cells, cell surfaces, physiology and metabolism, enzymes and proteins, bacteriophages, and physical and genetic mapping of the escherichia coli chromosome.
Ind/Abst Abstr. Bull. Inst. Pap. Sci. Tech.; Acad. Ind. [Computer File] (1992-); Acad. Search; AgBiotech News Inf.; AGRICOLA [Select. Cov.]; Biocont. News Inf. (19??-19??); Biodeter. Abstr. (19??-19??); Biol. Agric. Index; Biol. Abstr.; Chem. Abstr.; Chem. Titles; Chemorecept. Abstr.; Curr. Biotechnol.; Curr. Cit.; Curr. Contents Life Sci.; Dairy Sci. Abstr.; EMBASE; Energy Res. Abstr.; EP Collect.; Expand. Acad. Index (1992-); Field Crop Abstr.; Food Sci. Technol. Abstr.; Gen. Sci. Index; Gen. Sci. Source; Genet. Abstr.; Grass. Forage Abstr.; Homework Help.; Hortic. Abstr.; Immunol. Abstr.; Index Med.; INFO-SOUTH Abstr.; INIS Atomindex [Micro.]; Int. Aerosp. Abstr.; MasterFile FullTEXT 1000; MasterFile FullTEXT 350; MasterFile FullTEXT 650; MasterFile FullTEXT (Jan. 1994-); Microbiol. Abstr. Sect. B; Microbiol. Abstr. Sect. A; Microbiol. Abstr. Sect. C; NAPRALERT; Newsp. Period. Abstr. (1992-); Nucl. Acids Abstr.; OCLC; Life Sci. Collect.; PESTDOC; Pig News Inf.; Plant Breed. Abstr.; Potato Abstr.; Protozoolog. Abstr.; Ref. Upd. Basic Ed.; Ref. Upd. Deluxe Ed.; Res. Alert [Full Cov.]; Rev. Agric. Entomol.; Rev. Med. Vet. Entomol.; Rev. Med. Vet. Mycology; Rev. Plant Pathol.; Sci. Cit. Index; SCISEARCH; Soils Fert.; Soyabean Abstr.; Telebase; Trop. Dis. Bull.; Virol. AIDS Abstr.; Weed Abstr.

ISSN 1067-8832
DD 589 US

JOURNAL OF BACTERIOLOGY (CD-ROM).

(JOURNAL OF BACTERIOLOGY [COMPUTER FILE].). [J. bacteriol.]. **Added/Corp** American Society for Microbiology. (1992)-. Academic Scholarly Publication. English. Two times a month. $500.00. American Society of Microbiology / Birmingham, PO Box 11127, Birmingham AL 35201. **Tel** (800)633-4931 ext. 2723.

LC QR1 .Z4 **ISSN** 0233-111X
DD 576/.05 GW
CCC
NLM W1; JO553 **CODEN** JBMIEQ
Pr Rev.

JOURNAL OF BASIC MICROBIOLOGY.

[J. basic microbiol.]. Vol. 25, No. 1, (1985)-. Academic Scholarly Publication. English (German). Six times a year. $360.00. Akademie-Verlag GmbH, Postfach, D-13162 Berlin Germany. **Tel** 011 49 30 47889300, FAX 011 49 30 47889357. **(Subscription address:** VCH Publishers Inc., 303 Northwest 12th Avenue, Journals Department, Deerfield FL 33442. **Tel** (800)367-8249, (305)428-5566.) Index Available in last issue of each volume--loose separately paged. Documents available from The Genuine Article, BIOSIS Document Express, CASDDS. ***Continues** Zeitschrift fuer Allgemeine Mikrobiologie, 0044-2208.*
Ind/Abst AgBiotech News Inf.; Biocont. News Inf. (1991-); Biodeter. Abstr. (1991-); Biol. Abstr. (1985-); Chem. Abstr. (1985-); Curr. Aware. Biol. Sci., CABS; Curr. Biotechnol.; Curr. Cit.; Curr. Contents Life Sci.; Dairy Sci. Abstr.; EMBASE (1985-); Genet. Abstr.; Grass. Forage Abstr.; Hortic. Abstr.; Index Med. (1985-); Index Vet.; Maize Abstr.; Microbiol. Abstr. Sect. B (1985-); Microbiol. Abstr. Sect. A (Sept. 27, 1990); Microbiol. Abstr. Sect. C (1985-); Nutr. Abstr. Rev., Ser. B, Live Feeds and Feed.; Life Sci. Collect.; PESTDOC; Plant Grow. Reg. Abstr.; Postharvest News Inf.; Poult. Abstr.; Ref. Upd. Deluxe Ed.; Res. Alert [Full Cov.]; Rev. Agric. Entomol.; Rev. Med. Vet. Entomol.; Rev. Med. Vet. Mycology; Rev. Plant Pathol.; Rice Abstr.; Sci. Cit. Index; SCISEARCH; Seed Abstr.; Soc. Sci. Cit. Index [Select. Cov.]; Soils Fert.; Vet. Bull.; Trop. Dis. Bull.; Virol. AIDS Abstr.; Wheat Barley Trit. Abstr.

LC QH511.A1 J68 **ISSN** 0145-479X
DD 574.1/9121/05 US
CCC
NLM W1 JO564BE **CODEN** JBBID4
Pr Rev.

JOURNAL OF BIOENERGETICS AND BIOMEMBRANES.

[J. bioenerg. biomembranes]. Vol. 8, No. 3 (July 1976)-. Academic Scholarly Publication. English. Six times a year. $325.00. Plenum Press, 233 Spring Street, New York NY 10013-1578. **Tel** (212)620-8000, (800)221-9369, FAX (212)463-0742, (212)807-1047, telex 23/421139. **ED** Peter L. Pedersen. Index available. available on microfilm and microfiche from University Microfilms International (UMI). Documents available from The Genuine Article, BIOSIS Document Express, Ask*IEEE, CASDDS. ***Continues** Journal of Bioenergetics, 0449-5705.*
Desc: This is an international journal devoted to the publication of original research that contributes to fundamental knowledge in the areas of bioenergetics membranes and transport.
Ind/Abst Abstr. Bull. Inst. Pap. Sci. Tech.; Biol. Abstr.; Chem. Abstr.; Chem. Titles; CSA Neuro. Abstr. (?-?); Curr. Cit.; Curr. Contents Life Sci.; EMBASE; Energy Res. Abstr. (Oct. 1980-); Index Med.; INIS Atomindex [Micro.]; INSPEC (Oct. 1976-); Microbiol. Abstr. Sect. B; Life Sci. Collect.; Ref. Upd. Deluxe Ed.; Res. Alert [Full Cov.]; Sci. Cit. Index; SCISEARCH.

LC QR46 .J87 **ISSN** 0095-1137
DD 616.01/05 US
CCC
NLM W1 JO5893M **CODEN** JCMIDW
Pr Rev.

JOURNAL OF CLINICAL MICROBIOLOGY.

[J. clin. microbiol.]. **Added/Corp** American Society for Microbiology. Vol. 1 (Jan. 1975)-. Periodical. English. Twelve times a year. $300.00. American Society for Microbiology / DC, 1325 Massachusetts Avenue Northwest, Washington DC 20005-4171. **Tel** (202)737-3600, FAX (202)737-0367. **(Subscription address:** American Society for Microbiology, Journals Subscription Department, PO Box 11127, Birmingham AL 35201-1127. **Tel** (800)633-4931, FAX (205)995-1588.) **ED** Richard Tilton. Index available (bound in last issue). cum. index. **Ad Acc. Acid Free. Circ:** 13,707 (ctrl). available on microfilm and microfiche from University Microfilms International (UMI); available on CD-ROM. Documents available from The Genuine Article, BIOSIS Document Express, CASDDS.
Desc: Concerned with microbiological aspects of human and animal infections and infestations. Coverage includes bacteria, viruses, rickettsiae, chlamydiae, yeasts and fungi, mycrobacteria, aerobic actinomycetes, and parasites.
Ind/Abst AgBiotech News Inf.; AGRICOLA [Select. Cov.]; Biodeter. Abstr. (1991-); Biol. Abstr.; Chem. Abstr.; Curr. Biotechnol.; Curr. Cit.; Curr. Contents Clin. Med.; Curr. Contents Life Sci.; Dairy Sci. Abstr.; EMBASE; Energy Res. Abstr. (April 1977-); Fish Rev.; Food Sci. Technol. Abstr.; Genet. Abstr.; Helminthol. Abstr. (19??-19??); Immunol. Abstr.; Index Med.; INIS Atomindex [Micro.]; Int. Nurs. Index; Microbiol. Abstr. Sect. B; Microbiol. Abstr. Sect. A; Microbiol. Abstr. Sect. C; Nutr. Abstr. Rev., Ser. A, Hum. Exp.; Oncog. Growth Factors Abstr.; Life Sci. Collect.; PESTDOC; Pig News Inf.; Protozoolog. Abstr.; Ref. Upd. Basic Ed.; Ref. Upd. Deluxe Ed.; Res. Alert [Full Cov.]; Rev. Med. Vet. Entomol.; Rev. Med. Vet. Mycology; Rev. Plant Pathol.; Sci. Cit. Index; SCISEARCH; Small Anim. Abstr. Bibliogr.; Trop. Dis. Bull.; Virol. AIDS Abstr.; Wildl. Rev.

ISSN 1070-633X
DD 616 US

JOURNAL OF CLINICAL MICROBIOLOGY (CD-ROM).

(JOURNAL OF CLINICAL MICROBIOLOGY [COMPUTER FILE].). [J. clin. microbiol.]. **Added/Corp** American Society for Microbiology. Vol. 30 (1992)-. Academic Scholarly Publication. English. Twelve times a year. $500.00. American Society of Microbiology / Birmingham, PO Box 11127, Birmingham AL 35201. **Tel** (800)633-4931 ext. 2723.

ISSN 0922-338X
JA
NLM W1; JO659F **CODEN** JFBIEX
Pr Rev.

JOURNAL OF FERMENTATION AND BIOENGINEERING.

Added/Corp Nihon Hakko Kogakkai. Vol. 67, No. 1 (1989)-. Academic Scholarly Publication. English. Twelve times a year (2 vols.). $735.00. Elsevier Science Publishers BV, PO Box 211, 1000 AE Amsterdam Netherlands. **Tel** 011 31 20 4853641, 011 31 20 4853642, FAX 011 31 20 4853598. available on microfilm and microfiche from University Microfilms International (UMI); available on an online database from Elsevier Electronic Subscriptions (EES). Documents available from Article Express International, The Genuine Article, BIOSIS Document Express, CASDDS, ADONIS. ***Continues** Journal of Fermentation Technology, 0385-6380.*
Ind/Abst ADONIS; AgBiotech News Inf.; BioBusiness; Biodeter. Abstr. (19??-19??); Biol. Abstr. (1989-); Chem. Abstr. (1989-); Civ. Struct. Eng. Abstr.; Comput. Inf. Syst. Abstr. J. [Full Cov.]; Curr. Aware. Biol. Sci., CABS; Curr. Biotechnol.; Curr. Cit.; Curr. Contents Agric. Biol. Environ. Sci.; Curr. Contents Life Sci.; Dairy Sci. Abstr.; Ei Page One; Elect. Comm. Abstr.; EMBASE; Eng. Index Annu.; Environ. Eng. Abstr.; Food Sci. Technol. Abstr.; Hortic. Abstr.; Maize Abstr.; PESTDOC; Pig News Inf.; Res. Alert [Full Cov.]; Sci. Cit. Index; SCISEARCH; Soils Fert.; Soyabean Abstr.; Sug. Indus. Abstr.; Vitis Vitic. Enol. Abstr.; Weed Abstr.

LC QR1 .J63 **ISSN** 0022-1260
DD 576.05 JA
NLM W1 JO664 **CODEN** JGAMA9
Pr Rev.

JOURNAL OF GENERAL AND APPLIED MICROBIOLOGY, THE.

[J. gen. appl. microbiol.]. **Added/Corp** Tokyo Daigaku. Oyo Biseibutsu Kenkyujo. (Jan. 1955)-. Academic Scholarly Publication. English. Six times a year. $125.00. **(Subscription address:** Japan Publications Trading Company Ltd., PO Box 5030, Tokyo International, Tokyo 100-31 Japan. **Tel** 011 81 3 3292 3753.) available on microfilm and microfiche from University Microfilms International (UMI). Documents available from The Genuine Article, BIOSIS Document Express, CASDDS.
Ind/Abst AgBiotech News Inf.; AGRICOLA [Select. Cov.]; Biodeter. Abstr. (1991-); Biol. Abstr.; Biotechnol. Res. Abstr.; Chem. Abstr.; Chem. Titles; Coal Abstr.; Curr. Aware. Biol. Sci., CABS; Curr. Biotechnol.; Curr. Cit.; Curr. Contents Life Sci.; Dairy Sci. Abstr.; EMBASE; Field Crop Abstr.; Food Sci. Technol. Abstr.; Grass. Forage Abstr.; Hortic. Abstr.; Immunol. Abstr.; Microbiol. Abstr. Sect. B; Microbiol. Abstr. Sect. A; Microbiol. Abstr. Sect. C; NAPRALERT; Nutr. Abstr. Rev., Ser. B, Live Feeds and Feed.; Life Sci. Collect.; PESTDOC; Plant Breed. Abstr.; Protozoolog. Abstr.; Res. Alert [Full Cov.]; Rev. Agric. Entomol.; Rev. Med. Vet. Entomol.; Rev. Med. Vet. Mycology; Rev. Plant Pathol.; Rice Abstr.; Sci. Cit. Index; SCISEARCH; Soils Fert.; Soyabean Abstr.

LC QR1 .J64 **ISSN** 0022-1287
DD 576.05 589.9505* UK
CCC
NLM W1 JO668 **CODEN** JGMIAN
Pr Rev. **TITLE CHANGE**

JOURNAL OF GENERAL MICROBIOLOGY, THE.

[J. gen. microbiol.]. **Added/Corp** Society for General Microbiology. Federation of European Microbiological Societies. **VFOAT** JGM; JGM. Vol. 1-139 (1947)-(Dec. 1993). Academic Scholarly Publication. English. Society for General Microbiology, Marlboro House Basingstoke Road, Spencers Wood, Reading RG7 1AE United Kingdom. **Tel** 011 44 1734 885577, FAX 011 44 1734 885656. cum. index. **Ad Acc.** Documents available from The Genuine Article, BIOSIS Document Express, UMI Article Clearinghouse, CASDDS. ***Continued by** Microbiology (Reading, England), 1350-0872.*
Desc: Publishes original work on micro-organisms in the laboratory and in the field.
Ind/Abst AgBiotech News Inf.; AGRICOLA [Select. Cov.]; Biocont. News Inf. (19??-19??); Biodeter. Abstr. (1991-); Biol. Agric. Index; Biol. Abstr.; Chem. Abstr.; Chem. Titles; CSA Neuro. Abstr. (?-?); Curr. Aware. Biol. Sci., CABS; Curr. Biotechnol.; Curr. Cit.; Curr. Contents Life Sci.; Dairy Sci. Abstr.; EMBASE; Expand. Acad. Index (1992-); Field Crop Abstr.; Food Sci. Technol. Abstr.; Gen. Sci. Index; Genet. Abstr.; Grass. Forage Abstr.; Hortic. Abstr.; Immunol. Abstr.; INFO-SOUTH Abstr.; Int. Aerosp. Abstr.; Maize Abstr.; Microbiol. Abstr. Sect. B; Microbiol. Abstr. Sect. A; Microbiol. Abstr. Sect. C; NAPRALERT; Newsp. Period. Abstr. (1992-); Nucl. Acids Abstr.; Nutr. Abstr. Rev., Ser. B, Live Feeds and Feed.; Nutr. Abstr. Rev., Ser. A, Hum. Exp.; Life Sci. Collect.; PESTDOC; Pig News Inf.; Plant Breed. Abstr.; Pollut. Abstr. Indexes; Poult. Abstr.; Protozoolog. Abstr.; Ref. Upd. Basic Ed.; Ref. Upd. Deluxe Ed.; Res. Alert [Full Cov.]; Rev. Agric. Entomol.; Rev. Med. Vet. Entomol.; Rev. Med. Vet. Mycology; Rev. Plant Pathol.; Rice Abstr.; Sci. Cit. Index; SCISEARCH; Soils Fert.; Soyabean Abstr.; Trop. Dis. Bull.; Virol. AIDS Abstr.; Weed Abstr.

LC QR360 .J6 **ISSN** 0022-1317
DD 576.64 UK
CCC
NLM W1 JO668L **CODEN** JGVIAY
Pr Rev.

JOURNAL OF GENERAL VIROLOGY, THE.

[J. gen. virol.]. **Added/Corp** Society for General Microbiology. Federation of European Microbiological Societies. Vol. 1 (Jan. 1967)-. Academic Scholarly Publication. English. Twelve times a year. $840.00. Society for General Microbiology, Marlboro House Basingstoke Road, Spencers Wood, Reading RG7 1AE United Kingdom. **Tel** 011 44 1734 885577, FAX 011 44 1734 885656. **ED** CR Pringle. Index available. **Ad Acc. Circ:** 2,200. Documents available from The Genuine Article, BIOSIS Document Express, CASDDS.
Desc: Publishes original work on viruses that infect hosts of any kind. Emphasis is on fundamental studies at the molecular level, but papers on other subjects and applied studies are also published.
Ind/Abst AgBiotech News Inf.; AGRICOLA [Select. Cov.]; Anim. Breed. Abstr.; Biocont. News Inf. (1991-); Biol. Abstr.; Chem. Abstr.; Chem. Titles; CSA Neuro. Abstr. (?-?); Curr. Aware. Biol. Sci., CABS; Curr. Biotechnol.; Curr. Cit.; Curr. Contents Life Sci.; Dairy Sci. Abstr.; EMBASE; Fish Rev.; Food Sci. Technol. Abstr.; Genet. Abstr.; Immunol. Abstr.; Index Med.; Maize Abstr.; Microbiol. Abstr. Sect. A; NAPRALERT; Nucl. Acids Abstr.; Nutr. Abstr. Rev., Ser. B, Live Feeds and Feed.; Nutr. Abstr. Rev., Ser. A, Hum. Exp.; Oncog. Growth Factors Abstr.; Life Sci. Collect.; PESTDOC; Pig News Inf.; Plant Breed. Abstr.; Potato Abstr.; Poult. Abstr.; Ref. Upd. Basic Ed.; Ref. Upd. Deluxe Ed.; Res. Alert [Full Cov.]; Rev. Agric. Entomol.; Rev. Med. Vet. Entomol.; Rev. Med. Vet. Mycology; Rev. Plant Pathol.; Rice Abstr.; Sci. Cit. Index; SCISEARCH; Small Anim. Abstr. Bibliogr.; Soils Fert.; Stat. Theory Method Abstr. (1969); Virol. AIDS Abstr.; Vitis Vitic. Enol. Abstr.; Wildl. Rev.

ISSN 0169-4146
NE
CCC
NLM W1; JO705E **CODEN** JIMIE7
Pr Rev.

JOURNAL OF INDUSTRIAL MICROBIOLOGY. [J. ind. microbiol.]. **Added/Corp** Society for Industrial Microbiology (U.S.). Vol. 1, No. 1 (March 1986)-. Academic Scholarly Publication. English. Twelve times a year. $840.20. Macmillan Magazines Ltd., Brunel Road, Basingstoke, Hampshire RG21 6XS United Kingdom. **Tel** 011 44 1256 29242, FAX 011 44 1256 812358, telex 858493. **ED** GE Pierce, JS Cooney, VP Gullo, Al Laskin, CH Ward. available on microfilm and microfiche. Documents available from Article Express International, The Genuine Article, BIOSIS Document Express, CASDDS.
Desc: Publishes original research articles, short communications, critical reviews and letters to the editor in the fields of biotechnology, fermentation, environmental microbiology, biodegradation, biodeterioration, quality control and other areas of applied microbiology.
Ind/Abst AgBiotech News Inf.; AGRICOLA [Select. Cov.]; BioBusiness; Biocont. News Inf. (19??-19??); Biodeter. Abstr. (19??-19??); Biol. Abstr. (1986-); Chem. Abstr. (1986-); Curr. Aware. Biol. Sci., CABS; Curr. Biotechnol.; Curr. Cit.; Curr. Contents Agric. Biol. Environ. Sci.; Dairy Sci. Abstr.; Ei Page One; EMBASE; Eng. Index Annu.; Food Sci. Technol. Abstr.; Genet. Abstr.; Helminthol. Abstr. (19??-19??); Index Vet.; Microbiol. Abstr. Sect. B; Microbiol. Abstr. Sect. A; Microbiol. Abstr. Sect. C; Nutr. Abstr. Rev., Ser. B, Live Feeds and Feed.; Nutr. Abstr. Rev., Ser. A, Hum. Exp.; PESTDOC; Pollut. Abstr. Indexes; Poult. Abstr.; Protozoolog. Abstr.; Res. Alert [Full Cov.]; Rev. Agric. Entomol.; Rev. Med. Vet. Entomol.; Rev. Med. Vet. Mycology; Rev. Plant Pathol.; Rice Abstr.; SCISEARCH; Vet. Bull.; Vitis Vitic. Enol. Abstr.; Weed Abstr.

LC QR187.5 .J68 **ISSN** 1079-9907
DD 616.07/9 US
NLM W1; JO716KM **CODEN** JIREDJ
Pr Rev.

●**JOURNAL OF INTERFERON AND CYTOKINE RESEARCH.** **Added/Corp** International Society for Interferon Research. (1995)-. Academic Scholarly Publication. English. Twelve times a year. $510.00. Mary Ann Liebert Inc., 2 Madison Avenue, Larchmont NY 10538. **Tel** (914)834-3100, (800)M-LIEBERT, FAX (212)289-4697. **ED** Philip I. Marcus. **Bk Rev.** **Ad Acc.** Documents available from The Genuine Article. ***Formed by the union of*** *Journal of Interferon Research, 0197-8357* ***and*** *Lymphokine and Cytokine Research, 1056-5477.*
Desc: Journal for original articles, mini-reviews, and topical papers on basic and clinical aspects of research, encompassing the activity of interferons as antiviral, antitumor, and immunomodulatory molecules, with new studies pointing to their activity as antiparasitic agents.
Ind/Abst AgBiotech News Inf.; Chem. Abstr.; Chem. Titles; CSA Neuro. Abstr. (?-?); Curr. Aware. Biol. Sci., CABS; Curr. Contents; Curr. Contents Life Sci.; EMBASE; Energy Inf. Abstr.; Environ. Abstr.; Genet. Abstr.; Immunol. Abstr.; Index Med.; Index Vet.; Life Sci. Collect.; PESTDOC; Protozoolog. Abstr.; Ref. Upd. Deluxe Ed.; Res. Alert [Full Cov.]; Sci. Cit. Index; SCISEARCH; Vet. Bull.; Virol. AIDS Abstr.

LC QR187.5 .J68 **ISSN** 0197-8357
DD 616.07/9 US
NLM W1 JO716L **CODEN** JIREDJ
Pr Rev. **TITLE CHANGE**

JOURNAL OF INTERFERON RESEARCH. [J. interf. res.]. **Added/Corp** International Society for Interferon Research. Vol. 1, No. 1 (1980)-(19??). Academic Scholarly Publication. English. Mary Ann Liebert Inc., 2 Madison Avenue, Larchmont NY 10538. **Tel** (914)834-3100, (800)M-LIEBERT, FAX (212)289-4697. **ED** Philip I. Marcus. **Bk Rev.** **Ad Acc.** Documents available from The Genuine Article, CASDDS, Documents on Demand. ***Merged into*** *Journal of Interferon and Cytokine Research.*
Desc: Journal for original articles, mini-reviews, and topical papers on basic and clinical aspects of research, encompassing the activity of interferons as antiviral, antitumor, and immunomodulatory molecules, with new studies pointing to their activity as antiparasitic agents.
Ind/Abst AgBiotech News Inf.; Chem. Abstr.; Chem. Titles; CSA Neuro. Abstr. (?-?); Curr. Aware. Biol. Sci., CABS; Curr. Cit.; Curr. Contents; Curr. Contents Life Sci.; EMBASE; Energy Inf. Abstr.; Environ. Abstr.; Genet. Abstr.; Immunol. Abstr.; Index Med.; Index Vet.; Life Sci. Collect.; PESTDOC; Protozoolog. Abstr.; Ref. Upd. Deluxe Ed.; Res. Alert [Full Cov.]; Sci. Cit. Index; SCISEARCH; Vet. Bull.; Virol. AIDS Abstr.

LC QR46 .J88 **ISSN** 0022-2615
DD 616.01/05 UK
CCC
NLM W1 JO753 **CODEN** JMMIAV
Pr Rev.

JOURNAL OF MEDICAL MICROBIOLOGY. [J. med. microbiol.]. **Added/Corp** Pathological Society of Great Britain and Ireland. **VFOAT** Medical Microbiology. Vol. 1 (Aug. 1968)-. Periodical. English. Twelve times a year. $480.00. Churchill Livingstone, 1-3 Baxter's Place, Leith Walk, Edinburgh EH1 3AF United Kingdom. **Tel** 011 44 131 5562424, FAX 011 44 131 5581278, telex 727511. **(Subscription address:** Maruzen Company Ltd., PO Box 5050, Import & Export Department, Tokyo 100 31 Japan. **Tel** 011 81 3 32789224.) **ED** J Collee, B Duerden, M Parker and H Stern. available on microfilm and microfiche from University Microfilms International (UMI). Documents available from The Genuine Article, BIOSIS Document Express, CASDDS, ADONIS. ***Supersedes in part*** *Journal of Pathology and Bacteriology, 0368-3494.*
Desc: A journal of the Pathological Society of Great Britain and Northern Ireland.
Ind/Abst ADONIS; AgBiotech News Inf.; AGRICOLA; Biodeter. Abstr. (19??-19??); Biol. Abstr.; Chem. Abstr.; Curr. Cit.; Curr. Contents Life Sci.; Dairy Sci. Abstr.; EMBASE; Food Sci. Technol. Abstr.; Immunol. Abstr.; Index Med.; Microbiol. Abstr. Sect. B; Microbiol. Abstr. Sect. A; Microbiol. Abstr. Sect. C; NAPRALERT; Nutr. Abstr. Rev., Ser. B, Live Feeds and Feed.; Nutr. Abstr. Rev., Ser. A, Hum. Exp.; Life Sci. Collect.; PESTDOC; Pig News Inf.; Protozoolog. Abstr.; Ref. Upd. Basic Ed.; Ref. Upd. Deluxe Ed.; Res. Alert [Full Cov.]; Rev. Med. Vet. Mycology; Sci. Cit. Index; SCISEARCH; Small Anim. Abstr. Bibliogr.; Trop. Dis. Bull.

LC RC114.5 .J68 **ISSN** 0146-6615
DD 616.01/94/05 US
CCC
NLM W1 JO756V **CODEN** JMVIDB
Pr Rev.

JOURNAL OF MEDICAL VIROLOGY. [J. med. virol.]. Vol. 1 (1977)-. Academic Scholarly Publication. English. Twelve times a year. $1488.00. John Wiley & Sons, Inc., 605 Third Avenue, New York NY 10158-0012. **Tel** (212)850-6000, (212)850-6645, FAX (212)850-6088, telex 12-7063. **(Subscription address:** John Wiley & Sons / UK, Baffins Lane, Chichester, West Sussex PO19 1UD United Kingdom. **Tel** 011 44 1243 779777, FAX 011 44 243 776128, telex 86290 WIBOOKG.) **ED** Arie J. Zuckerman. Documents available from The Genuine Article, BIOSIS Document Express, CASDDS, ADONIS.
Desc: An international forum publishing original reports of major research developments and reviews of important progress in all aspects of medical virology.
Ind/Abst ADONIS; Biol. Abstr.; Chem. Abstr.; CSA Neuro. Abstr. (?-?); Curr. Cit.; Curr. Contents Clin. Med.; Curr. Contents Life Sci.; Dairy Sci. Abstr.; EMBASE; Energy Res. Abstr. (Sept. 1981-); Immunol. Abstr.; Index Med.; Index Vet.; INIS Atomindex [Micro.]; Microbiol. Abstr. Sect. A; Oncog. Growth Factors Abstr.; Life Sci. Collect.; Pig News Inf.; Ref. Upd. Basic Ed.; Ref. Upd. Deluxe Ed.; Res. Alert [Full Cov.]; Rev. Med. Vet. Entomol.; Risk Abstr.; Sci. Cit. Index; SCISEARCH; Soc. Sci. Cit. Index [Select. Cov.]; Vet. Bull.; Trop. Dis. Bull.; Virol. AIDS Abstr.

LC QR65 .J65 **ISSN** 0167-7012
DD 576/.028 NE
CCC
NLM W1; JO762C **CODEN** JMIMDQ
Pr Rev.

JOURNAL OF MICROBIOLOGICAL METHODS. [J. microbiol. methods]. Vol. 1, No. 1 (Feb. 1983)-. Academic Scholarly Publication. English. Twelve times a year. $1259.00. Elsevier Science Publishers BV, PO Box 211, 1000 AE Amsterdam Netherlands. **Tel** 011 31 20 4853641, 011 31 20 4853642, FAX 011 31 20 4853598. **ED** D C White, C J Knowles, and A Fox. available on microfilm and microfiche from University Microfilms International (UMI); available on an online database from Elsevier Electronic Subscriptions (EES). Documents available from The Genuine Article, CASDDS, ADONIS.
Desc: Publishes original papers and short reviews covering methods on all aspects of microbiology, excluding virology.
Ind/Abst Abstr. Bull. Inst. Pap. Sci. Tech.; ADONIS; AgBiotech News Inf.; AGRICOLA [Select. Cov.]; Biocont. News Inf.; Chem. Abstr. (1983-); Chem. Hazards Ind.; Curr. Aware. Biol. Sci., CABS; Curr. Biotechnol.; Curr. Cit.; Curr. Contents Life Sci.; Ecology Abstr.; EMBASE; Food Sci. Technol. Abstr.; For. Abstr.; Index Vet.; Lab. Hazards Bull.; Mass Spect. Bull.; Microbiol. Abstr. Sect. B; Microbiol. Abstr. Sect. A; Microbiol. Abstr. Sect. C; Nutr. Abstr. Rev., Ser. B, Live Feeds and Feed.; Life Sci. Collect.; PESTDOC; Ref. Upd. Deluxe Ed.; Res. Alert [Full Cov.]; Rev. Agric. Entomol.; Rev. Med. Vet. Entomol.; Rev. Med. Vet. Mycology; Rev. Plant Pathol.; Sci. Cit. Index; SCISEARCH; Soyabean Abstr.; Vet. Bull.; Trop. Dis. Bull.; Vitis Vitic. Enol. Abstr.

ISSN 1017-7825
KO
NLM W1; JO762E **CODEN** JOMBES

JOURNAL OF MICROBIOLOGY AND BIOTECHNOLOGY. **Added/Corp** Hanguk Sanop Misaengmul Hakhoe. (199?)-. Periodical. English. Four times a year. Korean Society of Applied Microbiology, 93 1 Mojin Dong Sungdong Ku, Seoul Korea. **Tel** 011 82 1 4471487.
Ind/Abst Rev. Plant Pathol.

LC QR69.A88 J68 **ISSN** 1060-3999
DD 576/.028 US
NLM W1; JO865D **CODEN** JRMMEE

JOURNAL OF RAPID METHODS AND AUTOMATION IN MICROBIOLOGY. **See** Biology-Computer Applications.

ISSN 0166-0934
NE
CCC
NLM W1 JO97T **CODEN** JVMEDH
Pr Rev.

JOURNAL OF VIROLOGICAL METHODS. [J. virol. methods]. Vol. 1 (1980)-. Academic Scholarly Publication. English. Twelve times a year. $1767.00. Elsevier Science Publishers BV, PO Box 211, 1000 AE Amsterdam Netherlands. **Tel** 011 31 20 4853641, 011 31 20 4853642, FAX 011 31 20 4853598. **ED** A J Zuckerman. available on microfilm and microfiche from University Microfilms International (UMI); available on an online database from Elsevier Electronic Subscriptions (EES). Documents available from The Genuine Article, BIOSIS Document Express, CASDDS, ADONIS.
Desc: Publishes original papers and invited reviews covering techniques on all aspects of virology.
Ind/Abst ADONIS; AgBiotech News Inf.; AGRICOLA [Select. Cov.]; Biol. Abstr.; Chem. Abstr.; CSA Neuro. Abstr. (?-?); Curr. Aware. Biol. Sci., CABS; Curr. Cit.; Curr. Contents Life Sci.; EMBASE; Immunol. Abstr.; Index Med.; Index Vet.; Microbiol. Abstr. Sect. A; Life Sci. Collect.; Pig News Inf.; Plant Genet. Resour. Abstr.; Potato Abstr.; Poult. Abstr.; Ref. Upd. Deluxe Ed.; Res. Alert [Full Cov.]; Rev. Agric. Entomol.; Rev. Med. Vet. Entomol.; Rev. Plant Pathol.; Sci. Cit. Index; SCISEARCH; Vet. Bull.; Trop. Dis. Bull.; Virol. AIDS Abstr.; Vitis Vitic. Enol. Abstr.

LC QR360 .J62 **ISSN** 0022-538X
DD 576/.64/05 US
CCC
NLM W1 JO97V **CODEN** JOVIAM
Pr Rev.

JOURNAL OF VIROLOGY. [J. virol.]. **Added/Corp** American Society for Microbiology. Vol. 1 (Feb. 1967)-. Periodical. English. Twelve times a year. $443.00. American Society for Microbiology / DC, 1325 Massachusetts Avenue Northwest, Washington DC 20005-4171. **Tel** (202)737-3600, FAX (202)737-0367. **(Subscription address:** American Society for Microbiology, Journals Subscription Department, PO Box 11127, Birmingham AL 35201-1127. **Tel** (800)633-4931, FAX (205)995-1588.) **ED** Arnold J. Levine. Index available. cum. index. **Ad Acc.** **Acid Free.** **Circ:** 5,042 (ctrl). available on microfilm and microfiche from University Microfilms International (UMI); available on CD-ROM. Documents available from The Genuine Article, BIOSIS Document Express, CASDDS.
Desc: Devoted to the dissemination of fundamental knowledge concerning viruses of bacteria, plants and animals. Publishes reports of original research in all areas of basic virology, including biochemistry and biophysics, immunology, morphology, physiology, and pathogenesis and immunity.
Ind/Abst AgBiotech News Inf.; AGRICOLA [Select. Cov.]; Biocont. News Inf.; Biol. Abstr.; Chem. Abstr.; Chem. Titles; CSA Neuro. Abstr. (?-?); Curr. Cit.; Curr. Contents Life Sci.; Dairy Sci. Abstr.; EMBASE; Energy Res. Abstr.; Fish Rev. (Jan. 1989-July 1992); Genet. Abstr.; Helminthol. Abstr.; Immunol. Abstr.; Index Med.; INIS Atomindex [Micro.]; Int. Aerosp. Abstr.; Microbiol. Abstr. Sect. B (19??-19??); NAPRALERT; Nucl. Acids Abstr.; Oncog. Growth Factors Abstr.; Life Sci. Collect.; PESTDOC; Pig News Inf.; Protozoolog. Abstr.; Ref. Upd. Basic Ed.; Ref. Upd. Deluxe Ed.; Res. Alert [Full Cov.]; Rev. Agric. Entomol.; Rev. Med. Vet. Entomol.; Rev. Plant Pathol.; Sci. Cit. Index; SCISEARCH; Small Anim. Abstr. Bibliogr.; Trop. Dis. Bull.; Virol. AIDS Abstr.; Wildl. Rev. (Jan. 1989-July 1992).

LC TP500 **ISSN** 0368-5365
JA
NLM W1 KO289S **CODEN** KGBKBK

KOGYO GIJUTSUIN BISEIBUTSU KOGYO GIJUTSU KENKYUSHO KENKYU HOKOKU. (KENKYU HOKOKU.). [Kogyo Gijutsuin Biseibutsu Kogyo Gijutsu Kenkyusho kenkyu hokoku]. **VFOAT** Report of the Fermentation Research Institute. (1969)-. Periodical. Japanese (summaries and/or abstracts in English; table of contents in English). Kogyo Gijutsuin Biseibutsu Kogyo Gijutsu Kenkyujo, (Fermentation Research Institute), 1-3 Higashi 1 chome, Tsukubashi, Ibarakiken 305 Japan. Documents available from BIOSIS Document Express, CASDDS. ***Continues*** *Kenkyu Hokoku (Kogyo Gijutsuin Hakko Kenkyujo (Japan)), 0015-0061.*
Ind/Abst Abstr. Bull. Inst. Pap. Sci. Tech.; Biol. Abstr.; Chem. Abstr.; Microbiol. Abstr. Sect. A.

NZ

●**LABLINK.** (1995)-. English. Four times a year. Free on request. Institute of Environmental Science and Research, PO Box 50 348, Porirua Wellington New Zealand. **Tel** 011 64 4 2370149. ***Absorbed*** *Antimicrobial Newsletter.*

LC QR1 .L45 **ISSN** 0266-8254
DD 660/.62/05 UK
CCC
NLM W1; LE889T **CODEN** LAMIE7
Pr Rev.

LETTERS IN APPLIED MICROBIOLOGY. [Lett. appl. microbiol.]. **Added/Corp** Society for Applied Bacteriology. **VFOAT** LAM. Vol. 1, No. 1 (1985)-. Academic Scholarly

Publication. English. Twelve times a year. Comes with subscription to Journal of Applied Bacteriology. Blackwell Scientific Publications Ltd, Marston Book Services, PO Box 88, Oxford OX2 ONE United Kingdom. **Tel** 011 44 1865 206206, FAX 011 44 1865 206219, telex 837 515 MARDIS G. Index available in last issue of volume--attached. Documents available from The Genuine Article, BIOSIS Document Express, CASDDS.
Ind/Abst AgBiotech News Inf.; AGRICOLA [Select. Cov.]; Biocont. News Inf. (1991-); Biodeter. Abstr. (19??-19??); Biol. Abstr. (1985-); Chem. Abstr. (1985-); Curr. Aware. Biol. Sci., CABS; Curr. Biotechnol.; Curr. Cit.; Curr. Contents Agric. Biol. Environ. Sci.; Curr. Contents Life Sci.; Dairy Sci. Abstr.; EMBASE; Food Sci. Technol. Abstr.; Foods Adlibra; For. Prod. Abstr. (1991-); Geogr. Abstr. Human Geogr.; Index Vet.; Maize Abstr.; Microbiol. Abstr. Sect. B; Microbiol. Abstr. Sect. A; Microbiol. Abstr. Sect. C; Nutr. Abstr. Rev., Ser. B, Live Feeds and Feed.; Nutr. Abstr. Rev., Ser. A, Hum. Exp.; PESTDOC; Pig News Inf.; Postharvest News Inf.; Poult. Abstr.; Protozoolog. Abstr.; Res. Alert [Full Cov.]; Rev. Agric. Entomol.; Rev. Med. Vet. Entomol.; Rev. Med. Vet. Mycology; Rev. Plant Pathol.; Sci. Cit. Index; SCISEARCH; Seed Abstr.; Small Anim. Abstr. Bibliogr.; Vet. Bull.; Trop. Dis. Bull.; Weed Abstr.; Wheat Barley Trit. Abstr.

LC QR106 .M38 **ISSN** 0297-8148
DD 574.5/2636 FR
CCC
CODEN MMFWE7
TITLE CHANGE

MARINE MICROBIAL FOOD WEBS.
Added/Corp Institut Oceanographique. Vol. 1, No. 1 (1985)-(19??). Academic Scholarly Publication. English. Institut Oceanographique, 195 rue Saint Jacques, 75005 Paris France. **Tel** 011 33 1 43256310, FAX 011 33 1 40517316. **(Subscription address:** Centrale des Revues, 11 rue Gossin, 92543 Montrouge Cedex France. **Tel** 011 33 1 46565266.) Documents available from BIOSIS Document Express, CASDDS. ***Continued by*** *Aquatic Microbial Ecology.*
Ind/Abst Aquat. Sci. Fish. Abstr. [CD-ROM Ed.]; Biol. Abstr. (1987-); Chem. Abstr. (1985-1988); Curr. Aware. Biol. Sci., CABS; Ecology Abstr.

LC QR46 .M466 **ISSN** 0739-5868
DD 616/.01/05 UK
NLM W1 ME387 **CODEN** MEMIEC

MEDICAL MICROBIOLOGY. [Med. microbiol.]. Vol. 1 (1982)-. Academic Scholarly Publication. English. Irregular. Price varies per volume. Academic Press Ltd., A Division of Harcourt Brace & Company Ltd., 24-28 Oval Road, London NW1 7DX United Kingdom. **Tel** 011 44 171 2674466, FAX 011 44 171 4822293, 011 44 171 4854752, telex 25775 ACPRES G. **ED** C S F Easmon and J Jeljaszewicz. Documents available from CASDDS.
Ind/Abst Chem. Abstr.

ISSN 0300-8584
GW
CCC
NLM W1 ME389 **CODEN** MMIYAO
Pr Rev.

MEDICAL MICROBIOLOGY AND IMMUNOLOGY. [Med. microbiol. immunol.]. **VFOAT** Zeitschrift fur Medizinische Mikrobiologie und Immunologie. Vol. 157 (1971)-. Academic Scholarly Publication. Multiple languages (English and German). Four times a year. $618.00. Springer-Verlag GmbH & Company KG, Heidelberger Platz 3, D-14197 Berlin Germany. **Tel** 011 49 30 8207223, FAX 011 49 30 8214091, telex 183 319 SPBLN D. **(Subscription address:** Springer-Verlag New York Inc. / North America, PO Box 2485, Journal Fulfillment, Secaucus NJ 07096. **Tel** (201)348-4033, (800)777-4643, FAX (201)348-4505.) **ED** S Bhakdi, B Fleisher, and R Rott. available on microfilm and microfiche from University Microfilms International (UMI). Documents available from The Genuine Article, BIOSIS Document Express, CASDDS, ADONIS. ***Continues*** *Zeitschrift fur Medizinische Mikrobiologie und Immunologie.*
Desc: Medical microbiology and medical immunology with special emphasis to mechanisms of pathogenesis in virus and micro-organisms.
Ind/Abst ADONIS; AGRICOLA; Biol. Abstr.; Chem. Abstr.; Curr. Aware. Biol. Sci., CABS; Curr. Cit.; Curr. Contents Life Sci.; Dairy Sci. Abstr.; EMBASE; Energy Res. Abstr. (May 1972-); Immunol. Abstr.; Index Med.; Index Vet.; Microbiol. Abstr. Sect. B; Nucl. Sci. Abstr.; Life Sci. Collect.; Protozoolog. Abstr.; Res. Alert [Full Cov.]; Rev. Med. Vet. Mycology; Sci. Cit. Index; SCISEARCH; Vet. Bull.; Trop. Dis. Bull.; Virol. AIDS Abstr.

ISSN 1018-4627
SZ
CCC
NLM W1; ME389M **CODEN** MMLEEH

MEDICAL MICROBIOLOGY LETTERS : AN INTERNATIONAL JOURNAL FOR RAPID COMMUNICATIONS ON ALL ASPECTS OF MEDICAL AND CLINICAL MICROBIOLOGY. Vol. 1, No. 1 (Mar. 15, 1992)-. Academic Scholarly Publication. English. Eight times a year. $300.79. Birkhaeuser Verlag Ag, Klosterberg 23, PO Box 133, CH-4010 Basel Switzerland. **Tel** 011 41 61 2717400, FAX 011 41 61 2717666, telex 963475 birk ch. **(Subscription address:** Birkhaeuser Verlag AG, PO Box 133, CH 4010 Basel Switzerland. **Tel** 011 41 61 2717400.) **ED** A. von Graevenitz. Documents available from The Genuine Article, CASDDS, ADONIS.
Desc: An international journal aiming at the prompt publication of short original papers and mini-reviews in all field of medical microbiology, with emphasis on clinical bacteriology, mycology, parasitology, virology, infectious serology, and antimicrobials. Papers in infectious disease are acceptable if their main emphasis is on microbiological aspects.
Ind/Abst ADONIS; Chem. Abstr.; Curr. Aware. Biol. Sci., CABS; Curr. Contents Life Sci.; Res. Alert; SCISEARCH; Soc. Sci. Cit. Index [Select. Cov.].

LC R91 .M428 **ISSN** 0025-8601
PL
NLM W1 ME866 **CODEN** MDMIAZ

MEDYCYNA DOSWIADCZALNA I MIKROBIOLOGIA. See Medical Sciences-Experimental Medicine.

LC QR65 .M45 **ISSN** 0580-9517
DD 576/.028 UK
NLM QW 25 M592 **CODEN** MMICEU

METHODS IN MICROBIOLOGY. [Methods microbiol.]. (1969)-. Monographic series. English. Irregular. Price varies per volume. Academic Press Inc., 6277 Sea Harbor Drive, Orlando FL 32887. **Tel** (800)543-9534, (407)345-4100, FAX (407)352-3445. **ED** J. R. Norris and D. W. Ribbons. Documents available from The Genuine Article, BIOSIS Document Express, CASDDS.
Ind/Abst Biol. Abstr. (1990-); Chem. Abstr.; Curr. Biotechnol.; Index Sci. Rev. [Full Cov.]; Res. Alert [Full Cov.]; Sci. Cit. Index; SCISEARCH.

ISSN 0966-6796
DD 576.162 UK
CEASED

MICROBIAL CLEAN-UP. [Microb. clean-up]. (1992)-Vol. 2 No. 6 (Dec. 1993). Periodical. English. Henry Stewart Publications, 28/30 Little Russell Street, London WC1A 2HN United Kingdom. **Tel** 011 44 171 4043040, FAX 011 44 171 4042081. **(Subscription address:** Allen Press, PO Box 1897, Lawrence KS 66044. **Tel** (800)627-0629.)
Ind/Abst Abstr. BioCommer.

LC QR100 .M5 **ISSN** 0095-3628
DD 576/.15/05 US
CCC
NLM W1 MI263 **CODEN** MCBEBU
Pr Rev.

MICROBIAL ECOLOGY. See Environmental Issues-Ecology.

LC QR171.A1 M53 **ISSN** 0891-060X
DD 616/.01/05 UK
CCC
NLM W1; MI263G **CODEN** MEHDE6

MICROBIAL ECOLOGY IN HEALTH AND DISEASE. [Microb. ecol. health dis.]. **Added/Corp** Society for Intestinal Microbial Ecology and Disease. Society for Microbial Ecology and Disease. Vol. 1 (1988)-. Periodical. English. Six times a year. $475.00. John Wiley & Sons Ltd., Baffins Lane, Chichester, West Sussex PO19 1UD United Kingdom. **Tel** 011 44 1243 779777, FAX 011 44 1243 776128 BTG:JWP001, telex 86290 WIBOOKG. **(Subscription address:** John Wiley & Sons, Inc. / Philadelphia, PO Box 7247, Philadelphia PA 19170. **Tel** (212)850-6645, (800)225-5945.) **ED** S.P. Borriello. Index available. **Bk Rev**. **Ad Acc**. available on microfilm and microfiche from University Microfilms International (UMI). Documents available from BIOSIS Document Express.
Desc: Presents research on different human microbial ecosystems and their role in health and disease. Topics include: investigative methods, animal and in vitro models, the effect of antibiotics or diet on the commensal flora or its development, alterations in the host environment, the role of immunological and other mechanisms that help maintain a stable flora, and the clinical application of the commensal flora in treatment and prevention of disease.
Ind/Abst Biol. Abstr. (1990-); Curr. Aware. Biol. Sci., CABS; Curr. Cit.; Dairy Sci. Abstr.; Environ. Period. Bibliogr. (?-?); Food Sci. Technol. Abstr.; Microbiol. Abstr. Sect. B; Nutr. Abstr. Rev., Ser. A, Hum. Exp.; Rev. Med. Vet. Mycology; Sci. Cit. Index.

LC QR175 .M53 **ISSN** 0882-4010
DD 616/.01 UK
CCC
NLM W1; MI265 **CODEN** MIPAEV
Pr Rev.

MICROBIAL PATHOGENESIS. See Medical Sciences-Communicable Diseases.

ISSN 0940-9653
GW
CCC
NLM W1; MI265E **CODEN** MRELE4
CEASED

MICROBIAL RELEASES : VIRUSES, BACTERIA, FUNGI. (June 1992)-Vol. 2, No. 4. Academic Scholarly Publication. English. Springer-Verlag GmbH & Company KG, Heidelberger Platz 3, D-14197 Berlin Germany. **Tel** 011 49 30 8207223, FAX 011 49 30 8214091, telex 183 319 SPBLN D. **(Subscription address:** Springer-Verlag New York Inc. / North America, PO Box 2485, Journal Fulfillment, Secaucus NJ 07096. **Tel** (201)348-4033, (800)777-4643, FAX (201)348-4505.) **ED** Walter Klingmuller. Documents available from CASDDS.
Desc: Devoted to the rapid publication of original articles and comments on viral, bacterial, or fungal releases. Release will be defined as placing microorganisms, manipulated or not, outdoors in small or large quantities, for a well-defined purpose.
Ind/Abst Chem. Abstr.

LC QR51 .Z45 **ISSN** 0944-5013
GW
NLM W1; MI274W **CODEN** MCRSEJ

•**MICROBIAL RESEARCH.** Vol. 149, 1 (Apr. 1994)-. Academic Scholarly Publication. English. Four times a year. $308.00. Gustav Fischer Verlag Jena, Postfach 100537, D-07705 Jena Germany. **Tel** 011 49 3641 626444, FAX 011 49 3641 626500. **(Subscription address:** VCH Publishers Inc., 303 Northwest 12th Avenue, Journals Department, Deerfield FL 33442. **Tel** (800)367-8249, (305)428-5566.) Documents available from CASDDS. ***Continues*** *Zentralblatt fuer Mikrobiologie, 0323-4393.*
Ind/Abst Chem. Abstr.; Curr. Cit.; Index Med.

ISSN 0213-4101
SP
NLM W1; MI266 **CODEN** MICBE3MCRBE2

MICROBIOLOGIA (MADRID).
(MICROBIOLOGIA : PUBLICACION DE LA SOCIEDAD ESPANOLA DE MICROBIOLOGIA.). [Microbiologia]. **Added/Corp** Sociedad Espanola de Microbiologia. Vol. 1, No. 1 & 2 (Sept. 1985)-. Periodical. English (Spanish). Two times a year. 8000ptas. Sociedad Espanola De Microbiologia, Hobtaleza 104 2 JZDA, 28004 Madrid Spain. **Tel** 011 34 1 3802511, 011 34 1 3082322. Documents available from BIOSIS Document Express, CASDDS.
Ind/Abst Biol. Abstr.; Chem. Abstr.; Curr. Cit.; Food Sci. Technol. Abstr.; Index Med.; Indice Med. Esp.

LC QR1 .B25 **ISSN** 0146-0749
DD 576/.05 US
CCC
NLM W1 MI275 **CODEN** MBRED3
Pr Rev.

MICROBIOLOGICAL REVIEWS. [Microbiol. rev.]. **Added/Corp** American Society for Microbiology. Vol. 42 (March 1978)-. Academic Scholarly Publication. English. Four times a year (Mar., June, Sept., Dec.). $130.00 (print), $155.00 (CD-ROM) US. American Society for Microbiology / DC, 1325 Massachusetts Avenue Northwest, Washington DC 20005-4171. **Tel** (202)737-3600, FAX (202)737-0367. **(Subscription address:** American Society for Microbiology, Journals Subscription Department, PO Box 11127, Birmingham AL 35201-1127. **Tel** (800)633-4931, FAX (205)995-1588.) **ED** W.K. Joklik. Index available. **Ad Acc**. **Acid Free**. **Circ:** 14,646. available on microfilm and microfiche from University Microfilms International (UMI); available on CD-ROM. Documents available from The Genuine Article, BIOSIS Document Express, UMI Article Clearinghouse, CASDDS. ***Continues*** *Bacteriological Reviews, 0005-3678.*
Desc: Review journal covering all aspects of microbiology, including bacteriology, virology, mycology, and parasitology. Some articles focus on the biology of the organisms, including their physiology, molecular biology, and genetics, whereas other articles address interactions with the environment, including host-parasite relationships which lead to disease. Busy scientists can find the bulk of the information that they need gathered together in a single article.
Ind/Abst Abstr. Bull. Inst. Pap. Sci. Tech.; Acad. Ind. [Computer File] (1992-); Acad. Search; AgBiotech News Inf.; AGRICOLA [Select. Cov.]; Biocont. News Inf. (1991-); Biodeter. Abstr. (19??-19??); Biol. Agric. Index; Biol. Abstr.; Chem. Abstr.; Curr. Aware. Biol. Sci., CABS; Curr. Biotechnol.; Curr. Cit.; Curr. Contents Life Sci.; EMBASE; Energy Res. Abstr. (Dec. 1981-); EP Collect.; Expand. Acad. Index (1992-); Food Sci. Technol. Abstr.; Foods Adlibra; Gen. Sci. Index; Gen. Sci. Source; Genet. Abstr.; Homework Help.; Index Med.; Index Sci. Rev. [Full Cov.]; Index Vet.; INFO-SOUTH Abstr.; MasterFile FullTEXT 1000; MasterFile FullTEXT 350; MasterFile FullTEXT 650; MasterFile FullTEXT (Jan. 1994-); Microbiol. Abstr. Sect. B; Microbiol. Abstr. Sect. A; Microbiol. Abstr. Sect. C; Newsp. Period. Abstr. (1992-); OCLC; Oncog. Growth Factors Abstr.; Life Sci. Collect.; PESTDOC; Protozoolog. Abstr.; Ref. Upd. Basic Ed.; Ref. Upd. Deluxe Ed.; Res. Alert [Full Cov.]; Rev. Agric. Entomol.; Rev. Med. Vet. Entomol.; Rev. Med. Vet. Mycology; Sci. Cit. Index; SCISEARCH; Telebase; Vet. Bull.; Trop. Dis. Bull.

ISSN 0889-3381
DD 576 US

MICROBIOLOGICAL UPDATE, THE. [Microbiolog. update]. **VFOAT** Microbiological Update For Pharmaceuticals, Medical Devices, and Cosmetics. Vol. 1, No. 1 (Apr. 1983)-. Periodical. English. Twelve times a year. $160.00. Microbiological Applications Inc, 132 San Remo Drive, Islamorada FL 33036. **Tel** (305)664-8513, FAX (305)664-8597. **ED** Murray S Cooper. **Bk Rev**. ctrl

circ.
Desc: Microbiological quality control for the pharmaceutical, medical device, and cosmetic industries.

LC S **ISSN** 0759-0644
DD 630 FR

MICROBIOLOGIE, ALIMENTS, NUTRITION = MICROBIOLOGY, FOODS AND FEEDS, NUTRITION. [M.A.N. microbiol. aliment. nutr.]. **Added/Corp** Societe I.E.E.N.A. Association A. Tessier. **VFOAT** Microbiology, Foods and Feeds, Nutrition; M.A.N.; Microbiology, Foods and Feeds, Nutrition. (198?)-. Periodical. French (English). Four times a year. 511.85F France; 540.00F other. IEENA, 2 Avenue Roger Salengro, 92290 Chatenay Malabry, France. **Tel** 011 33 1 47023688. Documents available from CASDDS.
Ind/Abst AGRICOLA; Biodeter. Abstr. (1991-); Chem. Abstr.; Curr. Cit.; Dairy Sci. Abstr.; Food Sci. Technol. Abstr.; Index Vet.; Nutr. Abstr. Rev., Ser. A, Hum. Exp.; Postharvest News Inf.; Potato Abstr.; Rev. Med. Vet. Entomol.; Rev. Med. Vet. Mycology; Rev. Plant Pathol.; Wheat Barley Trit. Abstr.

LC QR1 .J64 **ISSN** 1350-0872
DD 576.05 589.9505* UK
CCC
NLM W1; MI289 **CODEN** MROBEO

●**MICROBIOLOGY.** **Added/Corp** Society for General Microbiology. Vol. 140, Pt. 1 (Jan. 1994)-. Periodical. English. Twelve times a year. $840.00. Society for General Microbiology, Marlboro House Basingstoke Road, Spencers Wood, Reading RG7 1AE United Kingdom. **Tel** 011 44 1734 885577, FAX 011 44 1734 885656. ***Continues*** *Journal of General Microbiology, 0022-1287.*
Ind/Abst Acad. Search; Curr. Cit.; EP Collect.; Gen. Sci. Source; Homework Help.; Index Med.; MasterFile FullTEXT 1000; MasterFile FullTEXT 350; MasterFile FullTEXT 650; MasterFile FullTEXT (Jan. 1994-); OCLC; Telebase.

LC QR53 .I532 **ISSN** 0300-838X
DD 660/.62/05 US
NLM ZQW 4 M625Z

MICROBIOLOGY ABSTRACTS. SECTION A : INDUSTRIAL & APPLIED MICROBIOLOGY. See Biology-Abstracting, Bibliographies and Statistics.

LC QR1 .M62 **ISSN** 0300-8398
DD 576/.05 US
NLM ZQW 4 M626

MICROBIOLOGY ABSTRACTS. SECTION B, BACTERIOLOGY. **See** Biology-Abstracting, Bibliographies and Statistics.

LC QK564 .M5 **ISSN** 0301-2328
DD 589/.08 US
NLM ZQW 4 M626A

MICROBIOLOGY ABSTRACTS. SECTION C, ALGOLOGY, MYCOLOGY & PROTOZOOLOGY. **See** Biology-Abstracting, Bibliographies and Statistics.

LC QR1 .J36 **ISSN** 0385-5600
DD 616/.01 JA
NLM W1 MI292K **CODEN** MIIMDV
Pr Rev.

MICROBIOLOGY AND IMMUNOLOGY. **See** Medical Sciences-Allergy and Immunologic Diseases.

ISSN 0945-8182
GW
UDC 61

●**MICROBIOLOGY EUROPE.** (1993)-. Periodical. English. Six times a year. $104.00. VCH Gesellschaft GmbH, Postfach 101161, D-69451 Weinheim Germany. **Tel** 011 49 6201 606459, FAX 011 49 6201 606184. **(Subscription address:** VCH Publishers Inc., 303 Northwest 12th Avenue, Journals Department, Deerfield FL 33442. **Tel** (800)367-8249, (305)428-5566.) ***Continues*** *European Microbiology, 1064-4725.*

LC QR1 .M653 **ISSN** 0026-2617
DD 576.05 US
CCC
NLM W1 MI292 **CODEN** MIBLAO

MICROBIOLOGY (NEW YORK). (MICROBIOLOGY.). [Microbiol.]. **Added/Corp** Consultants Bureau. American Institute of Biological Sciences. Consultants Bureau Enterprises. National Science Foundation (U.S.). Vol. 26 (Jan./Feb. 1957)-. Academic Scholarly Publication. English (Russian). Six times a year. $1395.00. Consultants Bureau, A Division of Plenum Publishing Corporation, 233 Spring Street, New York NY 10013. **Tel** (212)620-8000, (212)620-8466, FAX (212)463-0742, telex 23/421139. **ED** M. V. Iranov. available on microfilm and microfiche from University Microfilms International (UMI). Documents available from The Genuine Article, BIOSIS Document Express, CASDDS.
Desc: English translations of Russian research by the Academy of Science of the USSR in microbiology.
Ind/Abst AGRICOLA [Select. Cov.]; Biocont. News Inf.; Biodeter. Abstr.; Biol. Abstr. (?-1984); Chem. Abstr.; Crop Physiol. Abstr.; Curr. Cit.; Field Crop Abstr.; Food Sci. Technol. Abstr.; For. Prod. Abstr. (1991-); For. Abstr.; Hortic. Abstr.; Maize Abstr.; Microbiol. Abstr. Sect. B (19??-19??); Nematol. Abstr.; Nutr. Abstr. Rev., Ser. B, Live Feeds and Feed.; Plant Breed. Abstr.; Plant Grow. Reg. Abstr.; Poult. Abstr.; Res. Alert [Full Cov.]; Rev. Agric. Entomol.; Rev. Med. Vet. Entomol.; Rev. Med. Vet. Mycology; Rev. Plant Pathol.; Rice Abstr.; Sci. Cit. Index; SCISEARCH; Soils Fert.; Soyabean Abstr.; Weed Abstr.

LC QR46 **ISSN** 0092-6027
DD 616/01 US
NLM W1 MI292S **CODEN** MSERDS

MICROBIOLOGY SERIES. [Microbiol. ser.]. Vol. 1 (1973)-. Monographic series. English. Irregular. Price varies per volume. Marcel Dekker Inc., 270 Madison Avenue, New York NY 10016. **Tel** (212)696-9000, (800)228-1160, FAX (212)685-4540, telex 421419. **(Subscription address:** Marcel Dekker Inc., PO Box 5017, Monticello NY 12701. **Tel** (800)228-1160.) **ED** Allen I. Laskin and Richard I. Mateles. Documents available from BIOSIS Document Express, CASDDS.
Desc: Each volume covers aspects of microbiology. Topics include fermentation and mycobacteria.
Ind/Abst AGRICOLA [Select. Cov.]; Biol. Abstr. (1987-); Chem. Abstr.; GeoRef.

LC QR46 .M55 **ISSN** 0026-2633
UK
CCC
NLM W1 MI294 **CODEN** MCBIA7
Pr Rev.

MICROBIOS. [Microbios]. Vol. 1 (Jan./Mar. 1969)-. Academic Scholarly Publication. English (French and German). Sixteen times a year. $675.93. Faculty Press, 88 Regent Street, Cambridge CB2 1DP United Kingdom. **Tel** FAX 011 44 1553 840695. cum. index. Documents available from The Genuine Article, BIOSIS Document Express, CASDDS.
Ind/Abst AgBiotech News Inf.; AGRICOLA (Vol. 71, No. 286, 1992) [Select. Cov.]; Biodeter. Abstr. (19??-19??); Biol. Abstr.; Biol. Dig.; Chem. Abstr.; Curr. Aware. Biol. Sci., CABS; Curr. Biotechnol.; Curr. Cit.; Curr. Contents Life Sci.; Dairy Sci. Abstr.; EMBASE; Grass. Forage Abstr.; Index Med.; Index Vet.; Int. Aerosp. Abstr.; Microbiol. Abstr. Sect. B; Microbiol. Abstr. Sect. A; Microbiol. Abstr. Sect. C; Nutr. Abstr. Rev., Ser. B, Live Feeds and Feed.; Life Sci. Collect.; PESTDOC; Poult. Abstr.; Protozoolog. Abstr.; Ref. Upd. Deluxe Ed.; Res. Alert [Full Cov.]; Rev. Agric. Entomol.; Rev. Med. Vet. Entomol.; Rev. Med. Vet. Mycology; Sci. Cit. Index; SCISEARCH; Soils Fert.; Sorghum Mill. Abstr.; Vet. Bull.; Virol. AIDS Abstr.; Vitis Vitic. Enol. Abstr.

LC QR1 .M64
DD 576 UN
NLM W1; MI407B **CODEN** MZHUDX
TITLE CHANGE

MIKROBIOLOGICHESKII ZHURNAL. [Mikrobiol. z.]. **Added/Corp** Akademiia Nauk URSR. Instytut Mikrobiolohii I Virusolohii. **VFOAT** Microbiological Journal. Vol. 40 (1978)-(1993). Academic Scholarly Publication. Russian (summaries and/or abstracts in English). Izdatelstvo Naukova Dumka / Ukrainian Academy of Sciences, Yu. A. Khramov, Dir., Ul. Repina 3, 252 601 Kiev Ukraine. **Tel** 011 7 44 4303441, 011 7 44 2254182, telex 131376. **(Subscription address:** East View Publications Inc., 3020 Harbor Lane North, Suite 110, Minneapolis MN 55447. **Tel** (800)477-1005, (612)550-0961, FAX (612)559-2931.) Documents available from BIOSIS Document Express, CASDDS. ***Continues*** *Mikrobiolohichnyi Zhurnal, 0026-3664.* ***Continued by*** *Mikrobiolohichnyi Zhurnal (Kiev, Ukraine : 1993).*
Ind/Abst AGRICOLA; Art Archaeol. Tech. Abstr.; Biocont. News Inf. (1991-); Biodeter. Abstr. (19??-19??); Biol. Abstr.; Chem. Abstr.; EMBASE; GeoRef; Immunol. Abstr.; Index Vet.; Microbiol. Abstr. Sect. B (19??-19??); Microbiol. Abstr. Sect. A; Microbiol. Abstr. Sect. C; Life Sci. Collect.; Pig News Inf.; Potato Abstr.; Rev. Med. Vet. Mycology; Rev. Plant Pathol.; Soils Fert.; Vet. Bull.; Wheat Barley Trit. Abstr.

RU
NLM W1 MI409B

MIKROBIOLOGIIA. [Mikrobiologija]. **Added/Corp** Vsesoiuznyi Institut Nauchnoi i Tekhnicheskoi Informatsii. (1972)-. Monographic series. English (Russian). Price vaies per volume. VINITI - Vsesoyuznyi Institut Nauchno-Tekhnicheskoi Informatsii, All-Union Scientific and Technical Information Institute, Baltiiskaia ulitsa 14, 125219 Moscow Russia. **Tel** 011 7 95 2384600, FAX 011 7 95 9430060, telex 411160.
Ind/Abst PESTDOC.

LC QR1 **ISSN** 0581-1538
DD 576/.005 YU
NLM W1 MI409G **CODEN** MIKJAT

MIKROBIOLOGIJA. [Mikrobiologija]. **VFOAT** Acta Biologica Iugoslavica. Mikrobiologija. (1964)-. Academic Scholarly Publication. Serbo-Croatian (Roman) (English). One time a year. Unija Bioloskih Nauchih, Drustava Jugoslavie Beograd ZM, 1108 Nemanjina 6 Yugoslavia. Documents available from BIOSIS Document Express, CASDDS.
Ind/Abst Biodeter. Abstr. (1991-); Biol. Abstr.; Chem. Abstr.; Index Vet.; Irr. Drain. Abstr.; Maize Abstr.; Life Sci. Collect.; Pig News Inf.; Plant Grow. Reg. Abstr.; Poult. Abstr.; Protozoolog. Abstr.; Rev. Med. Vet. Mycology; Rev. Plant Pathol.; Soyabean Abstr.; Vet. Bull.

LC QR1 .M65 **ISSN** 0026-3656
RU
CCC
NLM W1 MI409 **CODEN** MIKBA5

MIKROBIOLOGIJA (MOSKVA. 1932). (MIKROBIOLOGIIA.). [Mikrobiologija]. **VFOAT** Microbiology. (1932)-. Periodical. Russian (summaries and/or abstracts in English; table of contents in English). Six times a year. $173.00. Academy of Sciences of USSR, Library Exchange Department, 199034 St. Petersburg, Birgevaja Linia 1 Russia. **(Subscription address:** East View Publications Inc., 3020 Harbor Lane North, Suite 110, Minneapolis MN 55447. **Tel** (800)477-1005, (612)550-0961, FAX (612)559-2931.) Documents available from BIOSIS Document Express, CASDDS.
Ind/Abst AGRICOLA; Biocont. News Inf.; Biodeter. Abstr.; Biol. Abstr.; Chem. Abstr.; Coal Abstr.; Curr. Biotechnol.; EMBASE; NAPRALERT; Nematol. Abstr.; Soils Fert.

UN
NLM W1; MI407S

●**MIKROBIOLOHICHNYI ZHURNAL.** **Added/Corp** Instytut Mikrobiolohii i Virusolohii im. D.K. Zabolotnoho. **VFOAT** Mikrobiologichny Zhurnal. Vol. 55, No. 4 (1993)-. Periodical. Russian (Ukrainian; summaries and/or abstracts in English; table of contents in English). Six times a year. $109.95. Izdatelstvo Naukova Dumka / Ukrainian Academy of Sciences, Yu. A. Khramov, Dir., Ul. Repina 3, 252 601 Kiev Ukraine. **Tel** 011 7 44 4303441, 011 7 44 2254182, telex 131376. **(Subscription address:** East View Publications Inc., 3020 Harbor Lane North, Suite 110, Minneapolis MN 55447. **Tel** (800)477-1005, (612)550-0961, FAX (612)559-2931.) ***Continues*** *Mikrobiologicheskii Zhurnal, 0201-8462.*
Ind/Abst Index Med. (1993-).

ISSN 0374-9096
TU
NLM W1 MI409K **CODEN** MIBUBI

MIKROBIYOLOJI BULTENI. [Mikrobiyol. buel.]. **Added/Corp** Ankara Mikrobiyoloji Dernegi. Vol. 1 (1966)-. Academic Scholarly Publication. Turkish (summaries and/or abstracts in English and French; table of contents in English). Four times a year (Jan., Apr., July, Oct.). $60.00. Ankara Microbiology Society, Hacettepe University, Faculty of Medicine, Ankara Turkey. **Tel** 011 90 0312-3103545 1560. **ED** Professor Dr. Ayfer Gunalp, M. D. Documents available from BIOSIS Document Express, CASDDS.
Desc: News and information on infectious diseases and medical microbiology.
Ind/Abst Biol. Abstr.; Chem. Abstr.; Curr. Cit.; EMBASE [Select. Cov.]; Trop. Dis. Bull.

ISSN 0720-0536
GW
NLM W1 MI424 **CODEN** MITHE4

MIKROOEKOLOGIE UND THERAPIE. (MIKROOEKOLOGIE UND THERAPIE. MICROECOLOGY AND THERAPY.). [Mikroolog. Ther.]. **Added/Corp** Institut fuer Mikrooekologie. **VFOAT** Microecology and Therapy. Vol. 7 (1977)-. Academic Scholarly Publication. German (English and German; summaries and/or abstracts in English and German). Irregular. DM79.00 Europe. Institut fuer Mikrooekologie, Postfach 1765, D-35727 Herborn Germany. **Tel** 011 49 27722404. Documents available from CASDDS. ***Continues*** *Uber die Behandlungen mit Physiologischen Bakterien, 0720-1648.*
Ind/Abst Chem. Abstr. (1984-); Curr. Cit.; Protozoolog. Abstr.

LC QR1 .M68 **ISSN** 0440-2413
RU
UDC 579
CODEN MIHCAR

MISAENGMUL HAKHOE CHI. [Misainmurhag hoiji]. **VFOAT** Korean Journal of Microbiology; Kor. Jour. Microbiol. Academic Scholarly Publication. English (Korean). Hanguk Misaengmul Hakhoe, c/o Department of Microbiology, Seoul National University, Seoul 151 Korea. Documents available from BIOSIS Document Express, CASDDS.
Ind/Abst Biol. Abstr.; Chem. Abstr.

LC QR151 .M58
KO
UDC 579.266

MISAENGMUL KWA PARHYO. **VFOAT** Microorganisms and Fermentation. (19??)-. Academic Scholarly Publication. English (Korean). Hanguk Chonggun Hyophoe, 134 Sinchon-dong Sodaemun-ku, Seoul 1 Korea. Documents available from CASDDS.
Ind/Abst Chem. Abstr.

LC QR46 .M65
DD 616.01 JA
NLM W1 MO112N

MODAN MEDIA. **VFOAT** Modern Media. (1955)-. Periodical. Japanese. Twelve times a year. ¥720. Eiken Chemical Co. Ltd., 1-33-8 Hongo Bunkyo-ku, Tokyo 113 Japan.

ISSN 1048-6593
DD 576 UK
MODERN MICROBIOLOGICAL METHODS. [Mod. microbiol. methods]. (1988)-. Monographic series. English. Price varies per volume. John Wiley & Sons Ltd., Baffins Lane, Chichester, West Sussex PO19 1UD United Kingdom. **Tel** 011 44 1243 779777, FAX 011 44 1243 776128 BTG:JWP001, telex 86290 WIBOOKG. **(Subscription address:** John Wiley & Sons Inc / New Jersey, PO Box 2575, Secaucus NJ 07096-2575. **)**

LC QH506 .M64 **ISSN** 0270-7306
DD 574 US
CCC
NLM W1 MO194U **CODEN** MCEBD4
Pr Rev.
MOLECULAR AND CELLULAR BIOLOGY. [Mol. cell. biol.]. **Added/Corp** American Society for Microbiology. **VFOAT** MCB. Vol. 1, No. 1 (Jan. 1981)-. Academic Scholarly Publication. English. Twelve times a year. $433.00. American Society for Microbiology / DC, 1325 Massachusetts Avenue Northwest, Washington DC 20005-4171. **Tel** (202)737-3600, FAX (202)737-0367. **(Subscription address:** American Society for Microbiology, Journals Subscription Department, PO Box 11127, Birmingham AL 35201-1127. **Tel** (800)633-4931, FAX (205)995-1588.**)** **ED** Alan M. Weiner. Index available. **Ad Acc. Acid Free. Circ:** 5,200. available on CD-ROM; available on microfilm and microfiche from University Microfilms International (UMI). Documents available from The Genuine Article, BIOSIS Document Express, CASDDS.
Desc: Covers the molecular biology of eucaryotic cells, of both microbial and higher organisms. Its scope includes cellular morphology and function, genome organization, regulation of genetic expression, morphogenesis, and somatic cell genetics. Contains articles concerning plasmid vectors and virus-infected cells in which emphasis is clearly on the cell.
Ind/Abst AgBiotech News Inf.; Anim. Breed. Abstr.; Biol. Abstr.; Chem. Abstr.; Chem. Titles; Chemorecept. Abstr.; CSA Neuro. Abstr.; Curr. Aware. Biol. Sci., CABS; Curr. Cit.; Curr. Contents Life Sci.; Curr. Ref. Fish Res.; Dairy Sci. Abstr.; EMBASE; Entomol. Abstr.; Genet. Abstr.; Helminthol. Abstr.; Hum. Genome Abstr.; Immunol. Abstr.; Index Med.; Index Vet.; Maize Abstr.; Microbiol. Abstr. Sect. C; Nematol. Abstr.; Nucl. Acids Abstr.; Oncog. Growth Factors Abstr.; Life Sci. Collect.; PESTDOC; Plant Breed. Abstr.; Poult. Abstr.; Protozoolog. Abstr.; Ref. Upd. Basic Ed.; Ref. Upd. Deluxe Ed.; Res. Alert [Full Cov.]; Rev. Agric. Entomol.; Rev. Med. Vet. Entomol.; Rev. Med. Vet. Mycology; Sci. Cit. Index; SCISEARCH; Soyabean Abstr.; Vet. Bull.; Trop. Dis. Bull.; Virol. AIDS Abstr.; Wheat Barley Trit. Abstr.

LC QH506 .M683 **ISSN** 0891-4168
DD 575/.05 US
CCC
NLM W1; MO196H
MOLECULAR GENETICS, MICROBIOLOGY AND VIROLOGY. [Mol. genet. microbiol. virol.]. **VFOAT** Molekulyarnaya Genetika, Mikrobiologiya i Virusologiya. No. 1 (1986)-. Periodical. English (translations available in Russian). Six times a year. $680.00. Allerton Press Inc., 150 Fifth Avenue, New York NY 10011. **Tel** (212)924-3950, FAX (212)463-9684, telex 427441 ALPRES.

LC QR74 .M65 **ISSN** 0950-382X
DD 576/.05 UK
CCC
NLM W1; MO196N **CODEN** MOMIEE
Pr Rev.
MOLECULAR MICROBIOLOGY. [Mol. microbiol.]. **Added/Corp** International Union of Microbiological Societies. Vol. 1, No. 1 (July 1987)-. Academic Scholarly Publication. English. Twenty-three times a year. $1490.00. Blackwell Scientific Publications Ltd, Marston Book Services, PO Box 88, Oxford OX2 ONE United Kingdom. **Tel** 011 44 1865 206206, FAX 011 44 1865 206219, telex 837 515 MARDIS G. Index available (bound in last issue). available on microfilm and microfiche from University Microfilms International (UMI). Documents available from The Genuine Article, BIOSIS Document Express, CASDDS, ADONIS. ***Absorbed** Microbiological Sciences, 0265-1351.*
Desc: Publishes research papers addressing any microbiological question at a molecular level.
Ind/Abst ADONIS; AgBiotech News Inf.; AGRICOLA [Select. Cov.]; Biocont. News Inf. (19??-19??); Biol. Abstr. (1988-); Chem. Abstr.; Curr. Aware. Biol. Sci., CABS; Curr. Cit.; Curr. Contents Life Sci.; Dairy Sci. Abstr.; EMBASE; Food Sci. Technol. Abstr.; Genet. Abstr.; Index Med. (1987-); Index Vet.; Microbiol. Abstr. Sect. B; Microbiol. Abstr. Sect. C; Nucl. Acids Abstr.; PESTDOC; Protozoolog. Abstr.; Ref. Upd. Deluxe Ed.; Res. Alert [Full Cov.]; Rev. Agric. Entomol.; Rev. Med. Vet. Entomol.; Rev. Med. Vet. Mycology; Rev. Plant Pathol.; Sci. Cit. Index; SCISEARCH; Soils Fert.; Trop. Dis. Bull.

LC QR74 .M66 **ISSN** 0208-0613
RU
CODEN MGMVDU
MOLEKULIARNAIA GENETIKA, MIKROBIOLOGIIA I VIRUSOLOGIIA. [Mol. genet. mikrobiol. virusol.]. **Added/Corp** Soviet Union. Ministerstvo Zdravookhraneniia. (1983)-. Academic Scholarly Publication. Russian (summaries and/or abstracts in English; table of contents in English). Six times a year. $89.95. Izdatelstvo Meditsina / Russian Academy of Medical Sciences, Ulitsa Solyanka 14, 109801 Moscow Russia. **Tel** 011 95 297-05-04. **(Subscription address:** East View Publications Inc., 3020 Harbor Lane North, Suite 110, Minneapolis MN 55447. **Tel** (800)477-1005, (612)550-0961, FAX (612)559-2931.**)** Documents available from BIOSIS Document Express, CASDDS.
Ind/Abst Biol. Abstr.; Chem. Abstr. (1984-); Index Med.

LC QR355.5 **ISSN** 0077-0965
DD 576.64 SZ
CCC
NLM W1 MO569P **CODEN** MONVAK
MONOGRAPHS IN VIROLOGY. [Monogr. virol.]. Vol. 1 (1968)-. Monographic series. English. One time a year. 150.00F (approx. per volume). S. Karger AG, Allschwilerstrasse 10, PO Box, CH-4009 Basel Switzerland. **Tel** 011 41 61 3061111, FAX 011 41 61 3061234, telex CH 962 652. **ED** W. P. Parks. Documents available from BIOSIS Document Express, CASDDS.
Desc: Each monograph, centered on an active area of virologic research, contributes a well-organized analysis of progress, a critical evaluation of the current state of research, and a useful commentary on the direction of future trends.
Ind/Abst Biol. Abstr.; Chem. Abstr.; Life Sci. Collect.; Ref. Upd. Deluxe Ed.

ISSN 0097-5249
US
NLM ZQW 143 M995
MYCOPLASMATALES. (MYCOPLASMATALES; A BIBLIOGRAPHY AND INDEX.). **VFOAT** Mycoplasmataceae; A Bibliography and Index. Vol. 1 (1852/1970)-. Periodical. English. Virginia Polytechnic Institute and State University, Research Division, Blacksburg VA 24061. **ED** C. H. Domermuth and J. G. Rittenhouse.

ISSN 0929-0176
NE
UDC 576.612.014
NEDERLANDS TIJDSCHRIFT VOOR MEDISCHE MICROBIOLOGIE. [Ned. Tijdschr. Med. Microbiol.]. (1993)-. Periodical. Dutch. Five times a year. $71.95. Reed Healthcare Communications, Postbus 1126, 1000 BC Amsterdam Netherlands. **Tel** 011 31 20 5153356.

ISSN 1121-7138
IT
UDC 579
NEW MICROBIOLOGICA, THE. [New microbiol.]. (1992)-. Periodical. English. Four times a year. L149880. Tipolitografia I Ponzio, via D da Catalogna 1/3, 27100 Pavia Italy. **Tel** 011 39 382 35000, FAX 011 39 382 304435. ***Continues** Microbiologica (Bologna), 0391-5352.*
Ind/Abst Curr. Cit.

ISSN 0316-4934
DD 576/.06/271 CN
NEWSLETTER - CANADIAN SOCIETY OF MICROBIOLOGISTS. (NEWSLETTER - CANADIAN SOCIETY OF MICROBIOLOGISTS = BULLETIN DE NOUVELLES - SOCIETET CANADIENNE DES MICROBIOLOGISTES.). [Newsl. - Can. Soc. Microbiol.]. **Main/Corp** Canadian Society of Microbiologists. **VFOAT** Bulletin de Nouvelles - Societe Canadienne des Microbiologists. (1952)-. Bulletin. English (French). Five times a year. Canadian Society of Microbiologists, Department of Bacteriology and Immunology, University of Western Ontario, London Ontario N6A 3K6 Canada. **ED** Raymond Marusyk. ***Formed by the union of** Canadian Society of Microbiologists. Newsletter, 0316-4934 **and** Canadian Society of Microbiologists. Bulletin de Nouvelles.*

ISSN 0794-1293
NR
CODEN NJMIEO
NIGERIAN JOURNAL OF MICROBIOLOGY. [Niger. j. microbiol.]. **Added/Corp** Nigerian Society for Microbiology. (1978)-. Periodical. English. Two times a year. Documents available from BIOSIS Document Express.
Ind/Abst Biol. Abstr.; Trop. Dis. Bull.

ISSN 0021-4930
JA
NLM W1 NI93W **CODEN** NSKZAM
NIHON SAIKINGAKU ZASSHI. [Nihon saikingaku zasshi]. **Added/Corp** Nihon Saikin Gakkai. **VFOAT** Japanese Journal of Bacteriology. (July 1944)-. Academic Scholarly Publication. Japanese. Six times a year. $121.72. Nihon Saikin Gakkai, (Japanese Soc. for Bacteriology), Nihon Gakkai Jimu Senta, 4-16 Yayoi 2 Chome, Bunkyoku Tokyo 113 Japan. **(Subscription address:** Maruzen Company Ltd., PO Box 5050, Import & Export Department, Tokyo 100 31 Japan. **Tel** 011 81 3 32789224.**)** Documents available from BIOSIS Document Express, CASDDS.
Ind/Abst AGRICOLA; Biol. Abstr.; Chem. Abstr.; EMBASE; Food Sci. Technol. Abstr.; Index Med.; Microbiol. Abstr. Sect. B; Life Sci. Collect.; Trop. Dis. Bull.

ISSN 1146-5492
FR
UDC 011
PASCAL. E 61, MICROBIOLOGIE. **VFOAT** PASCAL. E 61, Microbiology; PASCAL. E Soixante-et-Un, Microbiologie. (1990)-. Periodical. Multiple languages. Ten times a year. 1740.00F France; 1840.00F other. CNRS / Institut d'Information Scientifique et Technique, (Centre National de la Recherche Scientifique), 15 Quai Anatole France, 75700 Paris France. **Tel** 011 33 1 47531515, FAX 011 33 1 45517307, telex 260034. **(Subscription address:** Institut d'Information Scientifique et Technique Diffusion, 2 Allee du Parc de Brabois, 54514 Vandoeuvre Nancy France. **Tel** 011 33 83 504664, FAX 011 33 83 504666, telex 961942.**)** ***Continues** Pascal Explore. E61: Microbiologie, Bacteriologie, Virologie, Mycologie, Protozaires.*

ISSN 0115-0324
PH
NLM W1; PH419SF
PHILIPPINE JOURNAL OF MICROBIOLOGY AND INFECTIOUS DISEASES, THE. **Added/Corp** Philippine Society for Microbiology and Infectious Diseases. (19??)-. Periodical. English. Two times a year. $20.00. Office of Publication, Santo Tomas University Hospital.
Ind/Abst Philip. Sci. Technol. Abstr.

ISSN 0265-3400
UK
NLM W1; PH622
PHLS MICROBIOLOGY DIGEST. [PHLS microbiol. dig.]. **Added/Corp** Great Britain. Public Health Laboratory Service. **VAT** Public Health Laboratory Service Microbiology Digest. Vol. 1, No. 1 (Oct. 1983)-. Periodical. English. Four times a year (Jan., Apr., July, Oct.). $68.45. Public Health Lab Service Board, 61 Colindale Avenue, CDR Section, London NW9 5DF United Kingdom. **Tel** 011 44 181 2006868, 011 44 181 2004400, FAX 011 44 181 2007875, telex 8953942. **ED** Brian Guthrie. **Bk Rev. Ad Acc. Circ:** 1,000. ***Continues** What's New (Great Britain. Public Health Laboratory Service).*
Desc: Brief reviews of interest to medical microbiologists.
Ind/Abst Biodeter. Abstr. (1991-); Curr. Cit.; Dairy Sci. Abstr.; Food Sci. Technol. Abstr.; Index Vet.; Nutr. Abstr. Rev., Ser. B, Live Feeds and Feed.; Nutr. Abstr. Rev., Ser. A, Hum. Exp.; Protozoolog. Abstr.; Trop. Dis. Bull.

LC QR1 .P65 **ISSN** 0079-4252
DD 576/.05 PL
NLM W1 PO942M **CODEN** PMKMAV
POSTEPY MIKROBIOLOGII. [Post. mikrobiol.]. **Added/Corp** Polska Akademia Nauk. Komitet Mikrobiologiczny. Vol. 1 (1962)-. Academic Scholarly Publication. Polish (English; summaries and/or abstracts in Russian). Four times a year. $50.00. **(Subscription address:** Ars Polona-Ruch, PO Box 1001, Krakowskie Przedmiescie 7, 00-068 Warsaw Poland. **Tel** 011 48 22 261201.**)** Documents available from CASDDS.
Ind/Abst Chem. Abstr.; EMBASE.

ISSN 0743-6505
DD 576 US
PRECEPTROL. [Preceptrol]. English. Irregular. Free. American Type Culture Collection, 12301 Parklawn Drive, Rockville MD 20852. **Tel** (301)881-2600, FAX (301)231-5826, telex 898-055.

LC QH345 .P7 **ISSN** 0555-1099
DD 574.1/92/05 RU
NLM W1 PR52 **CODEN** PBMIAK
PRIKLADNAJA BIOHIMIJA I MIKROBIOLOGIJA. **See** Biology-Biological Chemistry.

LC SB608.C5 I6 **ISSN** 0074-7203
DD 634/.3598/05 US
Pr Rev.
PROCEEDINGS OF THE ... CONFERENCE OF THE INTERNATIONAL ORGANIZATION OF CITRUS VIROLOGISTS. **See** Agriculture-Crop Production and Soils.

ISSN 0733-6373
US
CCC
NLM W3 IN991 **CODEN** POCHES
PROGRAM AND ABSTRACTS. [Program abstr. - Intersci. Conf. Antimicrob. Agents Chemother.]. **Main/Conf** Interscience Conference on Antimicrobial Agents and Chemotherapy. **Added/Corp** American Society for Microbiology. **VFOAT** Program and Abstracts of the ... Interscience Conference on Antimicrobial Agents and Chemotherapy. No. 11 (1971)-. English. Irregular. $25.00. American Society for Microbiology / DC, 1325 Massachusetts Avenue Northwest, Washington DC 20005-4171. **Tel** (202)737-3600, FAX (202)737-0367. Documents available from BIOSIS Document Express. ***Continues** Interscience Conference on Antimicrobial Agents and Chemotherapy. Abstracts of Papers*

Presented at the ... Interscience Conference on Antimicrobial Agents and Chemotherapy, 0535-4544.
Ind/Abst Biol. Abstr. (1991-); Curr. Cit.

LC QR53 .P72 **ISSN** 0079-6352
DD 660/.62 UK
CCC
NLM W1 PR67J **CODEN** PIMRAS
Pr Rev.
PROGRESS IN INDUSTRIAL MICROBIOLOGY (AMSTERDAM, NETHERLANDS). (PROGRESS IN INDUSTRIAL MICROBIOLOGY.). [Prog. ind. microbiol.]. Vol. 1 (1959)-. Academic Scholarly Publication. English. Irregular. Price varies per volume. Elsevier Science Publishers BV, PO Box 211, 1000 AE Amsterdam Netherlands. **Tel** 011 31 20 4853641, 011 31 20 4853642, FAX 011 31 20 4853598. Documents available from BIOSIS Document Express, CASDDS.
Ind/Abst AGRICOLA [Select. Cov.]; Biol. Abstr. (1986-); Chem. Abstr.; Curr. Biotechnol.; Dairy Sci. Abstr.; Food Sci. Technol. Abstr.; PESTDOC.

LC RC114.5 .P7 **ISSN** 0079-645X
US
CCC
NLM W1 PR6712 **CODEN** PMVIA6
Pr Rev.
PROGRESS IN MEDICAL VIROLOGY. [Prog. med. virol.]. **VFOAT** Fortschritte der Medizinischen Virusforschung; Progres en Virologie Medicale. Vol. 1 (1958)-. Periodical. English. One time a year. 220.00F (approx. per volume). S. Karger AG, Allschwilerstrasse 10, PO Box, CH-4009 Basel Switzerland. **Tel** 011 41 61 3061111, FAX 011 41 61 3061234, telex CH 962 652. **ED** W. P. Parks. Index available. available on microfilm and microfiche. Documents available from The Genuine Article, BIOSIS Document Express, CASDDS.
Desc: New knowledge arising from virologic research is regularly consolidated and interpreted by volumes in this series, which acquaints scientists and clinicians with new developments described by top authorities in the field. Features overviews on topics deliberately selected for their diversity and timeliness.
Ind/Abst AGRICOLA; Biol. Abstr.; Chem. Abstr. (1958-1982); Curr. Aware. Biol. Sci., CABS; Index Med.; Index Sci. Rev. [Full Cov.]; Life Sci. Collect.; Ref. Upd. Deluxe Ed.; Res. Alert [Full Cov.]; Sci. Cit. Index; SCISEARCH; Trop. Dis. Bull.

ISSN 0136-7439
RU
NLM W1 PR813 **CODEN** PROTD8
PROTOZOOLOGIJA. (PROTOZOOLOGIIA.). [Protozoologija]. **Added/Corp** Vsesoiuznoe Obshchestvo Protozoologov. **VFOAT** Protozoology. (1976)-. Monographic series. Russian (summaries and/or abstracts in English). Price varies per volume. Izdatelstvo Nauka St. Petersburg, Mendeleevskaia Liniia 1, 199034 St. Petersburg, B-34 Russia. **Tel** 011 7 812 2182612.
Ind/Abst Protozoolog. Abstr.

ISSN 1058-0352
DD 576 US
PUBLICATIONS IN FOOD MICROBIOLOGY. [Publ. food microbiol.]. Vol. 1, No. 1 (Aug. 1991)-. Periodical. English. Twelve times a year. $96.00. American Research, 6612 Mineral Point Road, Madison WI 53705.

LC QR **ISSN** 0348-4041
DD 576 SW
RAPPORT / SVERIGES LANTBRUKSUNIVERSITET. INSTITUTIONEN FOR MIKROBIOLOGI.
See Agriculture.

ISSN 0743-6521
DD 576 US
UDC 575.08:577.21
RECOMBINANT DNA, VECTORS & HOSTS. [Recomb. DNA, vectors hosts]. **VFOAT** Recombinant DNA, Vectors and Hosts. English. Irregular. Free. American Type Culture Collection, 12301 Parklawn Drive, Rockville MD 20852. **Tel** (301)881-2600, FAX (301)231-5826, telex 898-055.

ISSN 0826-421X
DD 576 CN
UDC 579
REFERENCE SERIES. MICROBIOLOGY. [Ref. ser., Microbiol.]. MI-1-. Periodical. English. Toronto Institute of Medical Technology, 222 St. Patrick Street, Toronto Ontario M5T 1V4 Canada.

LC QR1 .N6 **ISSN** 0078-0944
JA
CODEN RNIRAV
REPORT OF THE NODA INSTITUTE FOR SCIENTIFIC RESEARCH. [Rep. Noda Inst. Sci. Res.]. **Main/Corp** Noda Sangyo Kagaku Kenkyujo. No. 1 (1957)-. English. One time a year. Free. Noda Institute for Scientific Research, Noda Sangyo Kagaku Kenkyusho, 399 Noda-shi Chiba-ken 278 Japan. **Tel** 0471-23-5585. **ED** Shigetaka Ishii. **Circ:** 600 (ctrl). Documents available from CASDDS.
Desc: The reports deal with subjects on biological chemistry, enzymology, microbiology, food science and related fields.
Ind/Abst Chem. Abstr.; Vitis Vitic. Enol. Abstr.

LC QR
DD 576 FR
NLM W1; RE212HK
REPORT ON THE DISEASE STATUS WORLDWIDE IN ... . **Added/Corp** International Office of Epizootics. (1986)-. French (English). One time a year. OIE - Office International des Epizooties, 12 rue de Prony, 75017 Paris France. **Tel** 011 33 1 44151888, FAX 011 33 1 42670987, telex EPIZOTI 642 285F.

LC QR1 .R44 **ISSN** 0923-2508
DD 576 FR
CCC
NLM W1; RE227GH **CODEN** ANMBCM
Pr Rev.
RESEARCH IN MICROBIOLOGY. Vol. 140, No. 1 (Jan. 1989)-. Academic Scholarly Publication. English (French). Nine times a year (1 volume). $456.00. Editions Scientifique Elsevier, 141 rue de Javel, 75747 Paris Cedex 15 France. **Tel** 011 33 1 45589067, FAX 011 33 1 45589424. **(Subscription address:** Editions Scientifiques Elsevier / for North America, PO Box 7247-7576, Philadelphia PA 19170-7576. **)** available on microfilm and microfiche from University Microfilms International (UMI); available on an online database from Elsevier Electronic Subscriptions (EES). Documents available from The Genuine Article, CASDDS, ADONIS. ***Continues*** *Annales de l'Institut Pasteur. Microbiology, 0769-2609.*
Ind/Abst ADONIS; AgBiotech News Inf.; Biocont. News Inf. (1991-); Chem. Abstr.; Curr. Aware. Biol. Sci., CABS; Curr. Cit.; Curr. Contents Life Sci.; Dairy Sci. Abstr.; EMBASE; Food Sci. Technol. Abstr.; Genet. Abstr.; Index Med.; Index Vet.; Microbiol. Abstr. Sect. B; PESTDOC; Poult. Abstr.; Ref. Upd. Deluxe Ed.; Res. Alert [Full Cov.]; Rev. Med. Vet. Entomol.; Rice Abstr.; Sci. Cit. Index; SCISEARCH; Vet. Bull.; Trop. Dis. Bull.

ISSN 0923-2516
FR
CCC
NLM W1; RE231D **CODEN** RESVEY
Pr Rev.
RESEARCH IN VIROLOGY (PARIS). (RESEARCH IN VIROLOGY.). [Res. virol.]. Vol. 140 No. 1 (Jan./Feb. 1989)-. Academic Scholarly Publication. English (summaries and/or abstracts in French). Six times a year (1 volume). $334.00. Editions Scientifique Elsevier, 141 rue de Javel, 75747 Paris Cedex 15 France. **Tel** 011 33 1 45589067, FAX 011 33 1 45589424. **(Subscription address:** Editions Scientifiques Elsevier / for North America, PO Box 7247-7576, Philadelphia PA 19170-7576. **)** available on microfilm and microfiche from University Microfilms International (UMI); available on an online database from Elsevier Electronic Subscriptions (EES). Documents available from The Genuine Article, BIOSIS Document Express, CASDDS, ADONIS. ***Continues*** *Annales de l'institut Pasteur. Virology, 0769-2617.*
Ind/Abst ADONIS; AgBiotech News Inf.; Biol. Abstr.; Chem. Abstr.; Curr. Aware. Biol. Sci., CABS; Curr. Cit.; Curr. Contents Life Sci.; EMBASE; Immunol. Abstr.; Index Med.; Index Vet.; Ref. Upd. Deluxe Ed.; Res. Alert [Full Cov.]; Rev. Agric. Entomol.; Rev. Med. Vet. Entomol.; Rev. Plant Pathol.; Sci. Cit. Index; SCISEARCH; Vet. Bull.; Trop. Dis. Bull.

ISSN 0954-139X
UK
CCC
NLM W1; RE257CFL **CODEN** RMEMER
REVIEWS IN MEDICAL MICROBIOLOGY : A JOURNAL OF THE PATHOLOGICAL SOCIETY OF GREAT BRITAIN AND IRELAND. **Added/Corp** Pathological Society of Great Britain and Ireland. (1990)-. Periodical. English. Four times a year. $275.00. Chapman & Hall, 2-6 Boundary Row, London SE1 8HN United Kingdom. **Tel** 011 44 171 8650066, FAX 011 44 171 5229623, telex 290164 CHAPMA G. available on microfilm and microfiche from University Microfilms International (UMI).
Desc: Reviews covering research and techniques. Provides reviews of topics in medical microbiology, virology, mycology, parasitology, clinical microbiology and hospital infection.
Ind/Abst Biodeter. Abstr. (1991-); Curr. Aware. Biol. Sci., CABS; Curr. Cit.; EMBASE; Helminthol. Abstr. (1991-); Index Vet.; Leis., Rec., Tour. Abstr.; Protozoolog. Abstr.; Rev. Med. Vet. Mycology; Small Anim. Abstr. Bibliogr.; Vet. Bull.; Trop. Dis. Bull.

ISSN 1052-9276
DD 616 UK
CCC
NLM W1; RE257CFR **CODEN** RMVIEW
REVIEWS IN MEDICAL VIROLOGY. [Rev. med. virol.]. Vol. 1 (1991)-. Periodical. English. Four times a year. $315.00. John Wiley & Sons Ltd., Baffins Lane, Chichester, West Sussex PO19 1UD United Kingdom. **Tel** 011 44 1243 779777, FAX 011 44 1243 776128 BTG:JWP001, telex 86290 WIBOOKG. **(Subscription address:** John Wiley & Sons, Inc. / Philadelphia, PO Box 7247, Philadelphia PA 19170. **Tel** (212)850-6645, (800)225-5945.**)** **ED** Paul Griffiths. available on microfilm and microfiche from University Microfilms International (UMI). Documents available from The Genuine Article.
Desc: Devoted to the publication of articles reviewing current research and new information on all viruses of medical importance.
Ind/Abst Curr. Aware. Biol. Sci., CABS; Curr. Contents Life Sci.; Res. Alert [Full Cov.]; Sci. Cit. Index; Trop. Dis. Bull.

LC QR1 .R45 **ISSN** 0325-7541
DD 576/.05 AG
NLM W1 RE271P **CODEN** RAMID4
Pr Rev.
REVISTA ARGENTINA DE MICROBIOLOGIA. [Rev. argent. microbiol.]. **Added/Corp** Asociacion Argentina de Microbiologia. (1979)-. Academic Scholarly Publication. Spanish (summaries and/or abstracts in English). Four times a year. $40.00. Asociacion Argentina de Microbiologia, Bulnes 44PBB, 1176 Buenos Aires Argentina. **Tel** 011 54 1 982-2220, FAX 011 54 1 982-8557. **Ad Acc. Circ:** 1,500 (ctrl). available on an online database from MEDLINE. Documents available from BIOSIS Document Express, CASDDS. ***Continues*** *Revista de la Asociacion Argentina de Microbiologia, 0325-1713.*
Desc: Covers microbiology, biotechnology, virology, immunology, genetics, veterinary medicine, metabolism, mycology, parasitology, and antimicrobial agents.
Ind/Abst AgBiotech News Inf.; Agrofor. Abstr. (1991-); Biodeter. Abstr. (19??-19??); Biol. Abstr.; Chem. Abstr.; Curr. Cit.; Dairy Sci. Abstr.; EMBASE; Food Sci. Technol. Abstr.; For. Abstr.; Index Med.; Index Vet.; Maize Abstr.; Life Sci. Collect.; Pig News Inf.; Protozoolog. Abstr.; Rev. Med. Vet. Entomol.; Soyabean Abstr.; Vet. Bull.; Trop. Dis. Bull.

LC QR6 .R46 **ISSN** 0001-3714
DD 576/.05 BL
NLM W1 RE445S **CODEN** RMBGBP
Pr Rev.
REVISTA DE MICROBIOLOGIA. (REVISTA DE MICROBIOLOGIA : ORGAO OFICIAL DA SOCIEDADE BRASILEIRA DE MICROBIOLOGIA.). [Rev. microbiol.]. **Added/Corp** Escola Paulista de Medicina. Departamento de Microbiologia e Parasitologia. Sociedade Brasileira de Microbiologia. Vol. 1, (July/Sept. 1970)-. Academic Scholarly Publication. Portuguese (English and Portuguese). Four times a year (Jan., Apr., July, Oct.). $30.00. Society Brasileira Microbioligia, AV Prof Lineu Prestes 1374, 05508 SAO Paulo SP Brazil. **Tel** 011 55 11 8139647, FAX 011 55 813 9641, telex 1135085. **ED** Professor Dr. Maria T. Martins. cum. index. **Bk Rev**, (Qty: 4). **Ad Acc. Circ:** 1,100. available on an online database (current contents). Documents available from The Genuine Article, BIOSIS Document Express, CASDDS.
Desc: Articles from research and development in all fields of microbiology.
Ind/Abst AgBiotech News Inf.; AGRICOLA; Biocont. News Inf.; Biodeter. Abstr. (1991-); Biol. Abstr.; Chem. Abstr.; Curr. Cit.; Curr. Contents Agric. Biol. Environ. Sci.; Dairy Sci. Abstr.; EMBASE [Select. Cov.]; Field Crop Abstr.; Food Sci. Technol. Abstr.; For. Prod. Abstr. (1991-); Index Vet.; Microbiol. Abstr. Sect. B; Microbiol. Abstr. Sect. A; Microbiol. Abstr. Sect. C; Nutr. Abstr. Rev., Ser. B, Live Feeds and Feed.; Life Sci. Collect.; Pig News Inf.; Postharvest News Inf.; Protozoolog. Abstr.; Res. Alert [Select. Cov.]; Rev. Med. Vet. Entomol.; Rev. Med. Vet. Mycology; Rev. Plant Pathol.; Soils Fert.; Vet. Bull.; Trop. Dis. Bull.; Virol. AIDS Abstr.

ISSN 0213-4829
SP
CCC
NLM W1; RE545AG
CEASED
REVISTA ESPANOLA DE MICROBIOLOGIA CLINICA. (198?)-Vol. 7, No. 10 (Jan. 1993). Spanish. Editorial Saned SA, Apolonio Morales 6, 28036 Madrid Spain. **Tel** 011 34 1 359-4092, FAX 011 34 1 457-9918.
Ind/Abst EMBASE; Indice Med. Esp.

ISSN 0187-4640
MX
NLM W1 RE597H **CODEN** RLMIAA
Pr Rev.
REVISTA LATINOAMERICANA DE MICROBIOLOGIA (1970). (REVISTA LATINOAMERICANA DE MICROBIOLOGIA.). [Rev. latinoam. microbiol.]. **Added/Corp** Asociacion Latinoamericana de Microbiologia. Asociacion Mexicana de Microbiologia. Vol. 12 (Jan./March 1970)-. Academic Scholarly Publication. Spanish (English and Portuguese). Four times a year (Jan., Apr., July, Oct.). $40.00. Asociacion Mexicana de Microbiologia, Apartado Postal 4 862, 06400 Mexico DF Mexico. **Tel** 011 52 5 3414795, FAX 011 52 5 3411683. **ED** Dr. Jorge Ortigoza-Ferado (editor's phone: 011 525 396 9028). Index available. **Bk Rev**, (Qty: 6 to 10). **Ad Acc. Circ:** 2,000 (ctrl). Documents available from BIOSIS Document Express, CASDDS. ***Continues*** *Revista Latinoamericana de Microbiologia y Parasitologia, 0370-5986;* ***Absorbed*** *Revista Latinoamericana de Microbiologia.*
Desc: Papers dealing with original research in microbiology covering all areas from basic knowledge to applied topics. Occasionally reviews on general interest

themes.
Ind/Abst AGRICOLA; Agrofor. Abstr. (1991-); Biol. Abstr.; Chem. Abstr.; Curr. Cit.; EMBASE; Food Sci. Technol. Abstr.; For. Abstr.; Helminthol. Abstr.; Index Med.; Maize Abstr.; Microbiol. Abstr. Sect. B; Microbiol. Abstr. Sect. A; Microbiol. Abstr. Sect. C; Nutr. Abstr. Rev., Ser. B, Live Feeds and Feed.; Life Sci. Collect.; Plant Grow. Reg. Abstr.; Pollut. Abstr. Indexes; Poult. Abstr.; Protozoolog. Abstr.; Rev. Med. Vet. Entomol.; Rev. Plant Pathol.; Soils Fert.; Soyabean Abstr.; Sug. Indus. Abstr.; Trop. Dis. Bull.; Virol. AIDS Abstr.

ISSN 1018-0532
RM
NLM W1; RE965FB **CODEN** RRVIEX
REVUE ROUMAINE DE VIROLOGIE (1990). (REVUE ROUMAINE DE VIROLOGIE.). [Rev. roum. virol.]. **Added/Corp** Academia de Stiinte Medicale. **VFOAT** Romanian Journal of Virology. Vol. 41, No. 1 (Jan./Mar. 1990)-. Periodical. English (French). Four times a year. $102.00. Editura Academia Republicii Socialiste Romania, Calea Victoriei Nr 125, R-79717 Bucuresti Romania. **Tel** telex 10376 PRSFI R. **(Subscription address:** Kubon & Sagner, ABT Zeitschriftenimport, D 80328 Munich Germany. **Tel** 011 49 89 54218130.) Documents available from BIOSIS Document Express. ***Continues** Virologie, 0377-8177.*
Desc: Information on virology and virus diseases.
Ind/Abst Biol. Abstr.; EMBASE [Select. Cov.]; Health Plan. Adminis.; Index Med. (1990-); Trop. Dis. Bull.

ISSN 1220-8485
RM
NLM W1; RO489H **CODEN** RAMIE5
ROUMANIAN ARCHIVES OF MICROBIOLOGY AND IMMUNOLOGY.
See Medical Sciences-Allergy and Immunologic Diseases.

LC QR355 .V66 **ISSN** 1068-3747
DD 616.9/25
US
CCC
NLM W1; VO6492
•**RUSSIAN PROGRESS IN VIROLOGY.**
[Russ. prog. virol.]. No. 1 (1993)-. Periodical. English (translations available in Russian). Six times a year. $875.00. Allerton Press Inc., 150 Fifth Avenue, New York NY 10011. **Tel** (212)924-3950, FAX (212)463-9684, telex 427441 ALPRES. ***Continues** Voprosy Virusologii. English. Soviet Progress in Virology, 0734-0311.*

LC QR53 .S35 **ISSN** 0257-2389
DD 660.62
KO
NLM W1; SA783 **CODEN** SMHAEH
SANNEB MISAINMURHAG HOIJI. (SANOP MISAENGMUL HAKHOE CHI.). [Sanneb misainmurhag hoiji]. **Added/Corp** Hanguk Sanop Misaengmul Hakhoe. **VFOAT** Korean Journal of Applied Microbiology and Bioengineering; Hanguk Sanop Misaengmul Hakhoe Chi. (197?)-. Academic Scholarly Publication. English (Korean). Six times a year. $40.00. Korean Society of Applied Microbiology, 93 1 Mojin Dong Sungdond Ku, Seoul Korea. **Tel** 011 82 1 4471487. Documents available from BIOSIS Document Express, CASDDS.
Ind/Abst BioBusiness; Biol. Abstr. (1985-); Chem. Abstr.

ISSN 0557-4129
UK
SELECTED LECTURES OF THE ROYAL SOCIETY. Main/Corp Royal Society of London. (1967)-. Monographic series. English. Irregular. Price varies per volume. Academic Press Inc., 6277 Sea Harbor Drive, Orlando FL 32887. **Tel** (800)543-9534, (407)345-4100, FAX (407)352-3445.

LC QR355 .S45 **ISSN** 1044-5773
DD 576/.64/05
US
CCC
NLM W1; SE489T **CODEN** SEVIEL
SEMINARS IN VIROLOGY. [Semin. virol.]. Vol. 1, Issue 1 (Jan. 1990)-. Academic Scholarly Publication. English. Six times a year. $196.79. Academic Press Ltd., A Division of Harcourt Brace & Company Ltd., 24-28 Oval Road, London NW1 7DX United Kingdom. **Tel** 011 44 171 2674466, FAX 011 44 171 4822293, 011 44 171 4854752, telex 25775 ACPRES G. **(Subscription address:** Harcourt Brace & Company, Ltd., Foots Cray High Street, Sidcup Kent DA14 5HP United Kingdom. **Tel** 011 44 181 3003322, FAX 011 44 181 3090807, telex 896 377 ACADEM.) Documents available from CASDDS.
Ind/Abst Chem. Abstr.; Curr. Cit.; Sci. Cit. Index; Trop. Dis. Bull.

UK
NLM W1; SG95
SGM QUARTERLY. (1992)-. Periodical. English. Four times a year. $65.00. Society for General Microbiology, Marlboro House Basingstoke Road, Spencers Wood, Reading RG7 1AE United Kingdom. **Tel** 011 44 1734 885577, FAX 011 44 1734 885656. ***Continues** Society for General Microbiology Quarterly, 0142-7547.*
Ind/Abst Curr. Cit.

ISSN 1043-4976
DD 660
US
SIM INDUSTRIAL MICROBIOLOGY NEWS. [SIM ind. microbiol. news]. Vol. 39, No. 1 (Jan./Feb. 1989)-. Periodical. English. Six times a year. $36.00 (nonmembers). SIM Headquarters, 4201 John Marr Drive, Annandale VA 22003. ***Continues** SIM News.*
Ind/Abst Abstr. BioCommer.

LC QR355 .S68 **ISSN** 0887-3496
DD 616/.0194
SZ
CCC
NLM W1; SO996LDB **CODEN** SMEREJ
CEASED
SOVIET MEDICAL REVIEWS. SECTION E, VIROLOGY REVIEWS. [Sov. med. rev., E Virol. rev.]. **Added/Corp** Soviet Medical Reviews (Firm : Chur, Switzerland). **VFOAT** Virology Reviews; Virology; Soviet Medical Reviews. Virology. Vol. 1 (1987)-(1993). Periodical. English. Harwood Academic Publishers, PO Box 90, Reading RG1 8JL United Kingdom. **Tel** 011 44 1734 560080, FAX 011 44 1734 568211.

LC QR46 **ISSN** 0197-1751
DD 616
UK
NLM W1 SP295G **CODEN** SPSMDQ
SPECIAL PUBLICATIONS OF THE SOCIETY FOR GENERAL MICROBIOLOGY. [Spec. publ. Soc. Gen. Microbiol.]. **Added/Corp** Society for General Microbiology. (1978)-. Academic Scholarly Publication. English. Irregular. Price varies per volume. Oxford University Press / UK, Walton Street, Oxford OX2 6DP United Kingdom. **Tel** 011 44 1865 56767, FAX 011 44 1865 267773, telex 851/837330 OXPRES G. Documents available from BIOSIS Document Express, CASDDS.
Ind/Abst AGRICOLA [Select. Cov.]; Biol. Abstr. (1985-); Chem. Abstr.; Genet. Abstr.

ISSN 0172-6331
US
UDC 579
SPRINGER SERIES IN MICROBIOLOGY. [Springer ser. microbiol.]. Monographic series. English. Irregular. Price varies per volume. Springer-Verlag New York Inc., 175 Fifth Avenue, New York NY 10010. **Tel** (212)460-1500 ext 256, FAX (212)533-3503, telex 232 235 SPB UR. **(Subscription address:** Springer-Verlag New York Inc. / North America, PO Box 2485, Journal Fulfillment, Secaucus NJ 07096. **Tel** (201)348-4033, (800)777-4643, FAX (201)348-4505.)
Desc: Study of microbiology.
Ind/Abst Life Sci. Collect.

DD 576/.05
UK
CODEN SSGMAI
SYMPOSIA OF THE SOCIETY FOR GENERAL MICROBIOLOGY. [Symp. Soc. Gen. Microbiol.]. **Added/Corp** Society for General Microbiology. 32nd (1982)-. Academic Scholarly Publication. English. Irregular. Price varies per volume. Cambridge University Press, The Edinburgh Building, Shaftesbury Road, Cambridge CB2 2RU United Kingdom. **Tel** 011 44 1223 312393, FAX 011 44 1223 315052, telex 851-817256. Documents available from BIOSIS Document Express, CASDDS. ***Continues** Symposia (Society for General Microbiology).*
Ind/Abst Biol. Abstr.; Chem. Abstr.; Curr. Cit.; Microbiol. Abstr. Sect. B (19??-19??); Life Sci. Collect.

UK
SYNTHETIC BIOTRANSFORMATIONS. (19??)-. English. Four times a year. 263.52Can$. Carfax Publishing Company, PO Box 25, Abingdon, Oxfordshire OX14 3UE United Kingdom. **Tel** 011 44 1235 555335, FAX 011 44 1235 553559, telex 817484.

LC QR1 .S94 **ISSN** 0723-2020
DD 576/.05
GW
CCC
NLM W1 SY695 **CODEN** SAMIDF
Pr Rev.
SYSTEMATIC AND APPLIED MICROBIOLOGY. [Syst. appl. microbiol.]. Vol. 4/1 (Jan. 1983)-. Academic Scholarly Publication. English. Four times a year. $540.00. Gustav Fischer Verlag Stuttgart, Postfach 720143, D-70577 Stuttgart Germany. **Tel** 011 49 711 458030, FAX 011 49 711 4580334, telex 2627-7111488. **(Subscription address:** VCH Publishers Inc., 303 Northwest 12th Avenue, Journals Department, Deerfield FL 33442. **Tel** (800)367-8249, (305)428-5566.) **ED** O Kandler. Documents available from The Genuine Article, CASDDS. ***Continues** Zentralblatt fur Bakteriologie, Mikrobiologie und Hygiene. 1. Abt. Originale C, Allgemeine, Angewandte und Okologische Mikrobiologie, 0721-9571.*
Desc: Publishes original papers in systematics, morphology and physiology, applied microbiology and ecology.
Ind/Abst AgBiotech News Inf.; AGRICOLA [Select. Cov.]; Biocont. News Inf. (19??-19??); Biodeter. Abstr. (1991-); Chem. Abstr. (1983-); Curr. Aware. Biol. Sci., CABS; Curr. Cit.; Curr. Contents Life Sci.; Dairy Sci. Abstr.; EMBASE; Food Sci. Technol. Abstr.; Genet. Abstr.; Index Vet.; Microbiol. Abstr. Sect. B; Microbiol. Abstr. Sect. A; Microbiol. Abstr. Sect. C; Nutr. Abstr. Rev., Ser. B, Live Feeds and Feed.; Life Sci. Collect. (1983-); PESTDOC; Pig News Inf.; Res. Alert [Full Cov.]; Rev. Med. Vet. Entomol.; Rev. Med. Vet. Mycology; Rev. Plant Pathol.; Sci. Cit. Index; SCISEARCH; Soils Fert.; Sug. Indus. Abstr.; Vet. Bull.; Trop. Dis. Bull.; Vitis Vitic. Enol. Abstr.; Weed Abstr.

LC QH **ISSN** 0163-772X
DD 574
US
TITLE CHANGE
TCA REPORT. Main/Corp Tissue Culture Association. **Added/Corp** Tissue Culture Association. Report. **VAT** Tissue Culture Association Report. Vol. 12 (Jan./Feb. 1978)-(199?). Periodical. English. Society for In Vitro Biology, PO Box 73230, Baltimore MD 21273. **Tel** (410)992-0946. ***Continues** TCA Newsletter, 0564-7584.* ***Continued by** In Vitro Report, 1077-3975.*

LC QR46
DD 616
UK
UDC 579.6
TITLE CHANGE
TECHNICAL SERIES (SOCIETY FOR APPLIED BACTERIOLOGY). (TECHNICAL SERIES / THE SOCIETY FOR APPLIED BACTERIOLOGY.). No. 1 (1966)-. Academic Scholarly Publication. English. Academic Press Inc., 6277 Sea Harbor Drive, Orlando FL 32887. **Tel** (800)543-9534, (407)345-4100, FAX (407)352-3445. **ED** C H Collins and J M Grange. Documents available from CASDDS.
Ind/Abst Chem. Abstr.; Dairy Sci. Abstr.; Food Sci. Technol. Abstr.; Nutr. Abstr. Rev., Ser. A, Hum. Exp.

LC QR180 .T55 **ISSN** 0001-2815
DD 591.2/92/05
DK
CCC
NLM W1 TI827K **CODEN** TSANA2TSANAZ
Pr Rev.
TISSUE ANTIGENS. [Tissue antigens]. Vol. 1 (Jan. 1971)-. Academic Scholarly Publication. English. Twelve times a year (monthly except June and Dec.). $483.93. Munksgaard International Publishers Ltd, PO Box 2148, DK-1016 Copenhagen K Denmark. **Tel** 011 45 33 127030, FAX 011 45 33 129387, telex 19431 MUNKS DK. **ED** Flemming Kissmeyer-Nielsen. Index available. **Bk Rev. Ad Acc. Circ:** 1,000 (ctrl). Documents available from The Genuine Article, BIOSIS Document Express, CASDDS.
Desc: Presents original full length articles, brief communications and occasional reviews on research in: immunogenetics of cell surface antigens, immunogentics of cell interactions, functional aspects of cell surface antigens and their natural ligands. Emphasis is on leukocyte differentiation antigens and transplantation antigens.
Ind/Abst AgBiotech News Inf.; Anim. Breed. Abstr.; Biol. Abstr.; Chem. Abstr.; Curr. Aware. Biol. Sci., CABS; Curr. Cit.; Curr. Contents Life Sci.; EMBASE; Energy Res. Abstr. (Dec. 1973-); Genet. Abstr.; Immunol. Abstr.; Index Med.; Life Sci. Collect.; Res. Alert [Full Cov.]; Rev. Med. Vet. Mycology; Sci. Cit. Index; SCISEARCH; Small Anim. Abstr. Bibliogr.; Trop. Dis. Bull.; Virol. AIDS Abstr.

LC QR1 .T74 **ISSN** 0966-842X
DD 576
UK
CCC
NLM W1; TR341CT
•**TRENDS IN MICROBIOLOGY (REGULAR ED.).** (TRENDS IN MICROBIOLOGY.). [Trends in microbiol.]. Vol. 1, No. 1 (Apr. 1993)-. Periodical. English. Twelve times a year. $614.00. Elsevier Trends Journals, An Imprint of Elsevier Science Ltd., The Boulevard, Langford Lane, Kidlington, Oxford OX5 1GB United Kingdom. **Tel** 011 44 1865 843000, 011 44 1865 843699, FAX 011 44 1865 843010. **(Subscription address:** Elsevier Science Ltd. / Oxford Fulfillment Centre, PO Box 800, Kidlington OX5 1DX United Kingdom. **Tel** 011 44 865 843355.) available on an online database from Elsevier Electronic Subscriptions (EES).
Ind/Abst Index Med.

ISSN 0202-1447
RU
NLM W1 TR951TI **CODEN** TIPAE6
TRUDY INSTITUTA IMENI PASTERA. See Medical Sciences-Epidemiology.

LC QR1 .U38a
UN
TRUDY SEZDA MIKROBIOLOGOV UKRAINY. Main/Corp Ukrainske Mikrobiolohichne Tovarystvo. **Added/Corp** Instytut Mikrobiolohii i Virusolohii Im. D.K. Zabolotnoho. (19??)-. Periodical. Russian. Izdatelstvo Naukova Dumka / Ukrainian Academy of Sciences, Yu. A. Khramov, Dir., Ul. Repina 3, 252 601 Kiev Ukraine. **Tel** 011 7 44 4303441, 011 7 44 2254182, telex 131376.

ISSN 0042-6857
DD 576
JA
NLM W1 UI332U **CODEN** UIRUAF
UIRUSU. (UIRUSU. VIRUS.). [Uirusu]. **Added/Corp** Nihon Uirusu Gakkai. **VFOAT** Virus. Vol. 1 (April 1951)-. Periodical. Japanese (summaries and/or abstracts in English). Two times a year. $150.00. Virusu / Virus, 1500

Josuihonmachi, Kodaira, Tokyo 187 Japan. **(Subscription address:** Maruzen Company Ltd., PO Box 5050, Import & Export Department, Tokyo 100 31 Japan. **Tel** 011 81 3 32789224.**)** Documents available from BIOSIS Document Express, CASDDS.
Ind/Abst Biol. Abstr.; Chem. Abstr.; EMBASE; Index Med.; Life Sci. Collect.

LC QR1 .U8 **ISSN** 0566-392X
RU

USPEKHI MIKROBIOLOGII. Added/Corp Vsesoiuznoe Mikrobiologicheskoe Obshchestvo. (1964)-. Academic Scholarly Publication. Russian. Izdatelstvo Nauka / Akademiia Nauk, (Publishing House of the Russian Academy of Sciences), Leninskii Porspekt 14, 117901 Moscow Russia. **Tel** 011 95 9542153, FAX 011 95 9382144, telex 411964. Documents available from CASDDS.
Ind/Abst Chem. Abstr.

ISSN 0720-9940
GW
UDC 616-076/-078
Pr Rev.

VERFAHRENSRICHTLINIEN FUER DIE MIKROBIOLOGISCHE DIAGNOSTIK. (DGHM VERFAHRENSRICHTLINIEN FUER DIE MIKROBIOLOGISCHE DIAGNOSTIK.). [Verfahr.richtlinien mikrobiol. Diagn.]. (1981)-. Multiple languages. Irregular. Gustav Fischer Verlag Stuttgart, Postfach 720143, D-70577 Stuttgart Germany. **Tel** 011 49 711 458030, FAX 011 49 711 4580334, telex 2627-7111488.
Desc: Standards of microbiological diagnostic according to the German Society for Microbiology.

ISSN 0378-1135
NE
CCC
NLM W1 VE933F **CODEN** VMICDQ
Pr Rev.

VETERINARY MICROBIOLOGY. See Veterinary Sciences.

LC QR360 .V5 **ISSN** 0042-6822
DD 632.3 632.8* US
CCC
NLM W1 VI828 **CODEN** VIRLAX
Pr Rev.

VIROLOGY (NEW YORK, N.Y.). (VIROLOGY.). [Virology]. Vol. 1 (May 1955)-. Academic Scholarly Publication. English. Eighteen times a year. $1600.00. Academic Press Inc., 6277 Sea Harbor Drive, Orlando FL 32887. **Tel** (800)543-9534, (407)345-4100, FAX (407)352-3445. cum. index. available on CD-ROM. Documents available from The Genuine Article, BIOSIS Document Express, CASDDS.
Desc: Dedicated to publishing original articles on the molecular, genetic, biophysical, immunological, and biological aspects of research on animal, insect, plant, and bacterial viruses. The emphasis is on pioneering fundamental, rather than applied, research directed at understanding the mechanisms by which viruses function.
Ind/Abst AgBiotech News Inf.; AGRICOLA [Select. Cov.]; Anim. Breed. Abstr.; Biol. Agric. Index; Biol. Abstr.; Chem. Abstr.; Chem. Titles; CSA Neuro. Abstr. (?-?); Curr. Aware. Biol. Sci., CABS; Curr. Cit.; Curr. Contents Life Sci.; Dairy Sci. Abstr.; EMBASE; Energy Res. Abstr.; Fish Rev. (Jan. 1989-July 1992); Food Sci. Technol. Abstr.; Genet. Abstr.; Immunol. Abstr.; Index Med.; Int. Aerosp. Abstr.; Microbiol. Abstr. Sect. A; Nucl. Acids Abstr.; Oncog. Growth Factors Abstr.; Life Sci. Collect.; PESTDOC; Pig News Inf.; Plant Breed. Abstr.; Potato Abstr.; Poult. Abstr.; Ref. Upd. Basic Ed.; Ref. Upd. Deluxe Ed.; Res. Alert [Full Cov.]; Rev. Agric. Entomol.; Rev. Plant Pathol.; Sci. Cit. Index; SCISEARCH; Small Anim. Abstr. Bibliogr.; Trop. Dis. Bull.; Virol. AIDS Abstr.; Wildl. Rev. (Jan. 1989-July 1992).

ISSN 0920-8569
US
CCC
NLM W1; VI834 **CODEN** VIGEET
Pr Rev.

VIRUS GENES. [Virus genes]. Vol. 1, No. 1 (Nov. 1987)-. English. Six times a year. $447.00. Kluwer Academic Publishers / Massachusetts, PO Box 358, Accord Station, Hingham MA 02018. **Tel** (617)871-6600. **ED** Yechiel Becker. **Bk Rev. Ad Acc. Acid Free. Circ:** 120. available on microfilm and microfiche from University Microfilms International (UMI). Documents available from The Genuine Article, BIOSIS Document Express.
Desc: Dedicated to the publication of studies on the structure and function of virus genes, providing a forum for the dissemination of data as well as for the analysis of developments in the field. It serves as a platform for the publication of experimental and computer studies on genes from all virus genera and families. The journal emphasizes evaluations of current developments as well as reviews and correspondence on scientific matters dealing with virus genes. Publishes original work on the following subjects: cloning and expression of viral genes from all virus families in prokaryotic and eukaryotic systems; studies on the sequence analysis of virus genes; computer programs for gene analysis; virus gene products; regulation of virus gene function; analysis of virus genes and their functions, based on sequence analyses; the role of virus genes in disease; antivirals affecting gene function; reviews and comparative aspects of virus genes.
Ind/Abst Biol. Abstr.; Curr. Aware. Biol. Sci., CABS; Curr. Cit.; Curr. Contents Life Sci.; EMBASE; Genet. Abstr.; Index Med. (1990-); Index Vet.; Ref. Upd. Deluxe Ed.; Res. Alert [Full Cov.]; Sci. Cit. Index; SCISEARCH; Vet. Bull.

ISSN 0168-1702
NE
CCC
NLM W1; VI836D **CODEN** VIREDF
Pr Rev.

VIRUS RESEARCH. (VIRUS RESEARCH : AN INTERNATIONAL JOURNAL OF MOLECULAR AND CELLULAR VIROLOGY.). [Virus res.]. Vol. 1, No. 1 (Jan. 1984)-. Academic Scholarly Publication. English. Twelve times a year. $1698.00. Elsevier Science Publishers BV, PO Box 211, 1000 AE Amsterdam Netherlands. **Tel** 011 31 20 4853641, 011 31 20 4853642, FAX 011 31 20 4853598. **ED** B W J Mahy and R W Compans. available on microfilm and microfiche from University Microfilms International (UMI); available on an online database from Elsevier Electronic Subscriptions (EES). Documents available from The Genuine Article, CASDDS, ADONIS.
Desc: Provides a means of rapid publication for original papers and occasional review articles on fundamental research concerning virus structure, replication, and pathogenesis.
Ind/Abst ADONIS; AgBiotech News Inf.; Chem. Abstr. (1984-); Chem. Titles; CSA Neuro. Abstr. (?-?); Curr. Aware. Biol. Sci., CABS; Curr. Cit.; Curr. Contents Life Sci.; EMBASE; Genet. Abstr.; Immunol. Abstr.; Index Med. (Vol. 1, No. 1, 1984-); Index Vet.; NAPRALERT; Nucl. Acids Abstr.; Life Sci. Collect.; Pig News Inf.; Potato Abstr.; Poult. Abstr.; Ref. Upd. Basic Ed.; Ref. Upd. Deluxe Ed.; Res. Alert [Full Cov.]; Rev. Med. Vet. Entomol.; Rev. Plant Pathol.; Sci. Cit. Index; SCISEARCH; Small Anim. Abstr. Bibliogr.; Vet. Bull.; Virol. AIDS Abstr.

ISSN 0921-2590
NE
NLM W1; VI836DA

VIRUS RESEARCH. SUPPLEMENT. [Virus res., Suppl.]. Vol. 1 (Sept. 1985)-. Academic Scholarly Publication. English. Elsevier Science Publishers BV, PO Box 211, 1000 AE Amsterdam Netherlands. **Tel** 011 31 20 4853641, 011 31 20 4853642, FAX 011 31 20 4853598. Documents available from ADONIS.
Ind/Abst ADONIS; Index Med. (1985-).

ISSN 0736-6647
US
NLM ZQW 80 V821

VIRUSES IN WASTE, RENOVATED, AND OTHER WATERS. See Environmental Issues-Pollution and Waste Management.

LC QR355 .V66 **ISSN** 0734-0311
DD 616.9/25 US
CCC
NLM W1; SO996S
TITLE CHANGE

VOPROSY VIRUSOLOGII. (SOVIET PROGRESS IN VIROLOGY.). [Sov. prog. virol.]. No. 1 (1956)-(1993). Periodical. English (Russian). Allerton Press Inc., 150 Fifth Avenue, New York NY 10011. **Tel** (212)924-3950, FAX (212)463-9684, telex 427441 ALPRES. ***Continued by*** *Russian Progress in Virology.*

ISSN 0507-4088
RU
CCC
NLM W1; VO649 **CODEN** VVIRAT

VOPROSY VIRUSOLOGII. [Vopr. virusol.]. **Added/Corp** Akademiia Meditsinskikh Nauk SSSR. Vsesoiuznoe Obshchestvo Epidemiologov i Mikrobiologov (Soviet Union) Vsesoiuznoe Obshchestvo Epidemiologov, Mikrobiologov i Infektsionov (Soviet Union) Soviet Union. Ministerstvo Zdravookhraneniia. Vol. 1, (1956)-. Academic Scholarly Publication. Russian (summaries and/or abstracts in English). Six times a year. $139.95. Izdatelstvo Meditsina / Russian Academy of Medical Sciences, Ulitsa Solyanka 14, 109801 Moscow Russia. **Tel** 011 95 297-05-04. **(Subscription address:** East View Publications Inc., 3020 Harbor Lane North, Suite 110, Minneapolis MN 55447. **Tel** (800)477-1005, (612)550-0961, FAX (612)559-2931.**)** Documents available from The Genuine Article, BIOSIS Document Express, CASDDS.
Ind/Abst AgBiotech News Inf.; Biol. Abstr.; Chem. Abstr.; Curr. Contents Life Sci.; EMBASE; Immunol. Abstr.; Index Med.; Microbiol. Abstr. Sect. A; Life Sci. Collect.; PESTDOC; Pig News Inf.; Plant Breed. Abstr.; Res. Alert [Full Cov.]; Rev. Agric. Entomol.; Rev. Med. Vet. Entomol.; Sci. Cit. Index; SCISEARCH; Small Anim. Abstr. Bibliogr.; Trop. Dis. Bull.; Virol. AIDS Abstr.

LC QR1 **ISSN** 0001-6209
DD 576/.05 CC
UDC 579
NLM W1 WE237 **CODEN** WSHPA8

WEI SHENG WU HSUEH PAO. [Wei sheng wu hsueh pao]. **VFOAT** Weishengwu Xuebao; Acta Microbiologica Sinica. (1953)-. Academic Scholarly Publication. Chinese (summaries and/or abstracts in English and Russian). Six times a year. $57.20. Science Press, 16 Donghuangchenggen North Street, Beijing 100707, People's Republic of China. **Tel** 011 86 1 4019821, 011 86 1 4010642, FAX 011 86 1 4012180, 011 86 1 4019810, telex 210147. **(Subscription address:** China International Book Trading Corporation, PO Box 399, Library Service Department, Beijing 100044 People's Republic of China. **Tel** 011 86 1 8414284, FAX 011 86 1 8412023, telex 22496 CIBTC CN.**)** available on microfilm from University Microfilms International (UMI). Documents available from BIOSIS Document Express, CASDDS.
Ind/Abst AGRICOLA (19??-); Biol. Abstr. (19??-); Chem. Abstr. (19??-); Curr. Cit.; Index Med. (Vol. 25, No. 1, 1985-).

LC QR1 .W44 **ISSN** 0253-2654
CC
CODEN WSWPDI

WEISHENGWUXUE TONGBAO. (WEI SHENG WU HSUEH TUNG PAO. WEISHENGWUXUE TONGBAO.). [Weishengwuxue tongbao]. **Added/Corp** Chung-kuo Wei Sheng Wu Hsueh Hui. **VFOAT** Weishengwuxue Tongbao. (19??)-. Academic Scholarly Publication. Chinese. Six times a year. $66.00. Chinese Academy of Sciences, Institute of Microbiology, Science Press, 16 Donghuangchenggen North Street, Beijing 100707, People's Republic of China. **Tel** 011 86 1 4019821, FAX 011 86 4012180, telex 210147. **Ad Acc. Circ:** 16,000. Documents available from CASDDS, CASDDS.
Desc: Contains information on microbiology.
Ind/Abst Chem. Abstr.; NAPRALERT.

ISSN 1002-056X
DD 576 CC

WEISHENGWUXUE ZAZHI. VFOAT Journal of Mirobiology. (1981)-. Academic Scholarly Publication. Chinese. Four times a year. Documents available from CASDDS.
Ind/Abst Chem. Abstr.

LC QR53 .M58 **ISSN** 0959-3993
DD 660/.62/05 UK
CCC
NLM W1; WO88F **CODEN** WJMBEY

WORLD JOURNAL OF MICROBIOLOGY & BIOTECHNOLOGY. [World j. microbiol. biotechnol.]. **Added/Corp** Unesco. International Union of Microbiological Societies. MIRCEN (Organization). **VFOAT** World Journal of Microbiology and Biotechnology. Vol. 6, No. 1 (Mar. 1990)-. Academic Scholarly Publication. English (summaries and/or abstracts in French). Six times a year. $470.50. Rapid Science Publishers, The Old Malthouse, Paradise Street, Oxford OX1 1LD United Kingdom. **Tel** 011 44 1865 790447, FAX 011 44 1865 244012, telex 9403712. **ED** Prof Colin Ratledge. Index available. cum. index. **Bk Rev. Ad Acc. Acid Free.** available on microfilm from University Microfilms International (UMI). Documents available from The Genuine Article, BIOSIS Document Express, CASDDS. ***Continues*** *MIRCEN Journal of Applied Microbiology and Biotechnology, 0265-0762.*
Desc: Publishes papers relating to all aspects of applied microbiology and biotechnology, encompassing management of culture collections, foodstuffs and biological control agents.
Ind/Abst AgBiotech News Inf.; AGRICOLA [Select. Cov.]; Biocont. News Inf. (1991-); Biodeter. Abstr. (1991-); Biol. Abstr.; Chem. Abstr.; Curr. Aware. Biol. Sci., CABS; Curr. Cit.; Curr. Contents Agric. Biol. Environ. Sci.; Food Sci. Technol. Abstr.; Helminthol. Abstr. (1991-); Nutr. Abstr. Rev., Ser. B, Live Feeds and Feed.; PESTDOC; Plant Genet. Resour. Abstr.; Postharvest News Inf.; Protozoolog. Abstr.; Res. Alert [Select. Cov.]; Rev. Med. Vet. Entomol.; Rev. Med. Vet. Mycology; Rev. Plant Pathol.; Rice Abstr.; SCISEARCH; Seed Abstr.; Soils Fert.; Sug. Indus. Abstr.; Trop. Dis. Bull.; Weed Abstr.; Wheat Barley Trit. Abstr.

LC QR46 .Y4 **ISSN** 1054-772X
DD 616/.01/05 US
NLM W1; YE114AK

YEAR BOOK OF CLINICAL MICROBIOLOGY. [Year b. clin. microbiol.]. **VFOAT** Yearbook of Clinical Microbiology. (1991)-. English. Irregular. Price varies per volume. CRC Press Inc., 2000 Corporate Boulevard Northwest, Boca Raton FL 33431. **Tel** (407)994-0555, (800)272-7737, FAX (407)998-9784, (800)374-3401, telex 568689.

LC QR151 .Y4 **ISSN** 0513-5222
DD 589.2/33/05 CN

YEAST (DAVIS, CALIF.). (YEAST.). [Yeast]. **Added/Corp** International Association of Microbiological Societies. International Commission on Yeasts and Yeast-Like Microorganisms. International Council of Yeasts and Yeast-Like Microorganisms. (1951)-. Periodical. English. Two times a year. 8.00Can$. University of Western Ontario Department of Plant Sciences, London Ontario N6A 5B7 Canada. **Tel** (519)661-3752, FAX (519)661-3292. **ED** M A Lachance. **Circ:** 500. Documents available from The Genuine Article.
Desc: An informal newsletter for persons interested in yeast.

Ind/Abst AgBiotech News Inf.; Curr. Contents Agric. Biol. Environ. Sci.; Curr. Contents Life Sci.; Ecology Abstr.; Genet. Abstr.; Microbiol. Abstr. Sect. A; Microbiol. Abstr. Sect. C; Nutr. Abstr. Rev., Ser. B, Live Feeds and Feed.; Res. Alert [Full Cov.].

LC QR **ISSN** 0724-9004
DD 576 GW
NLM W1; ZE234
TITLE CHANGE

ZAC, ZEITSCHRIFT FUER ANTIMIKROBIELLE, ANTINEOPLASTISCHE CHEMOTHERAPIE. (ZEITSCHRIFT FUER ANTIMIKROBIELLE, ANTINEOPLASTISCHE CHEMOTHERAPIE : ZAC.). [ZAC, Z. antimikrob. antineoplast. Chemother.]. **Added/Corp** Paul-Ehrlich-Gesellschaft. **VFOAT** ZAC; Zeitschrift fur Antimikrobielle und Antineoplastische Chemotherapie. Vol. 1, Nos. 1 & 2 (1983)-(Sept. 1994). Academic Scholarly Publication. German (summaries and/or abstracts in English). Futuramed GmbH, Postfach 830358, D-830358 Munich Germany. **Tel** 011 49 89 674047. Index available. **Bk Rev. Ad Acc.** Documents available from CASDDS. ***Continued by*** *Antiinfective Drugs and Chemotherapy ADC.*
Ind/Abst Chem. Abstr. (?-?); EMBASE (?-?).

LC QR46 .Z45 **ISSN** 0934-8840
GW
CCC
CODEN ZEBAE8

ZENTRALBLATT FUER BAKTERIOLOGIE. (INTERNATIONAL JOURNAL OF MEDICAL MICROBIOLOGY, VIROLOGY, PARASITOLOGY AND INFECTIOUS DISEASES.). [Zent.bl. Bakteriol.]. Vol. 275/1 (Apr. 1991)-. Periodical. English (summaries and/or abstracts in German). Eight times a year. DM976.00 Germany; DM992.00 other. Gustav Fischer Verlag Stuttgart, Postfach 720143, D-70577 Stuttgart Germany. **Tel** 011 49 711 458030, FAX 011 49 711 4580334, telex 2627-7111488. **(Subscription address:** VCH Publishers Inc., 303 Northwest 12th Avenue, Journals Department, Deerfield FL 33442. **Tel** (800)367-8249, (305)428-5566.) Documents available from The Genuine Article, BIOSIS Document Express. ***Continues*** *International Journal of Medical Microbiology, 0934-8840.*
Ind/Abst Biol. Abstr.; Curr. Aware. Biol. Sci., CABS; Health Plan. Adminis.; Res. Alert [Full Cov.]; Sci. Cit. Index (19??-19??); SCISEARCH.

ISSN 0941-018X
GW
NLM W1; ZE775BBD **CODEN** ZBASE2

ZENTRALBLATT FUER BAKTERIOLOGIE. SUPPLEMENT. [Zent.bl. Bakteriol., Suppl.]. **VFOAT** International Journal of Medical Microbiology. Supplement. (1989)-. Monographic series. English. Irregular. Price varies per volume. Gustav Fischer Verlag Stuttgart, Postfach 720143, D-70577 Stuttgart Germany. **Tel** 011 49 711 458030, FAX 011 49 711 4580334, telex 2627-7111488. Documents available from BIOSIS Document Express, CASDDS. ***Continues*** *Zentralblatt fuer Bakteriologie, Mikrobiologie und Hygiene. Supplemente, 0172-5629.*
Ind/Abst AGRICOLA [Select. Cov.]; Biol. Abstr. (1991-); Chem. Abstr.; Curr. Cit.

LC QR51 **ISSN** 0232-4393
DD 576/.16 GW
UDC 579 **CCC**
NLM W1 ZE779G **CODEN** ZEMIDI
Pr Rev. **TITLE CHANGE**

ZENTRALBLATT FUER MIKROBIOLOGIE. [Zentralbl. Mikrobiol.]. Vol. 137, No. 1 (1982)-(1993). Academic Scholarly Publication. English (German and French). Gustav Fischer Verlag Jena, Postfach 100537, D-07705 Jena Germany. **Tel** 011 49 3641 626444, FAX 011 49 3641 626500. **ED** W F Hirte. Index available. **Bk Rev. Ad Acc. Circ:** 580. Documents available from The Genuine Article, CASDDS. ***Continues*** *Zentralblatt fur Bakteriologie, Parasitenkunde, Infektionskrankheiten und Hygiene. Zweite, Naturwissenschaftliche Abteilung, Mikrobiologie der Landwirtschaft, der Technologie und des Umweltschutzes, 0323-6056.* ***Continued by*** *Microbiological Research.*
Desc: An international journal mainly publishing problems and aspects of applied microbiology as well as necessary basic knowledge. Publishes original papers, review articles, short communications and book reviews from the disciplines of biotechnology, agricultural microbiology, food and environmental microbiology under bacteriological, mycological and virological aspects.
Ind/Abst AgBiotech News Inf.; Agrofor. Abstr. (19??-19??); Biocont. News Inf. (19??-19??); Biodeter. Abstr. (1991-); Chem. Abstr.; Crop Physiol. Abstr.; Curr. Aware. Biol. Sci., CABS; Curr. Cit.; Curr. Contents Agric. Biol. Environ. Sci.; Dairy Sci. Abstr.; EMBASE; Field Crop Abstr.; Food Sci. Technol. Abstr.; For. Abstr.; Grass. Forage Abstr.; Index Med.; Index Vet.; Maize Abstr.; Microbiol. Abstr. Sect. B (19??-19??); Microbiol. Abstr. Sect. A; Microbiol. Abstr. Sect. C; Nematol. Abstr.; Nutr. Abstr. Rev., Ser. B, Live Feeds and Feed.; Life Sci. Collect.; PESTDOC; Pig News Inf.; Plant Breed. Abstr.; Plant Genet. Resour. Abstr.; Plant Grow. Reg. Abstr.; Postharvest News Inf.; Potato Abstr.; Res. Alert [Select. Cov.]; Rev. Agric. Entomol.; Rev. Med. Vet. Entomol.; Rev. Med. Vet. Mycology; Rev. Plant Pathol.; Seed Abstr.; Soils Fert.; Sorghum Mill. Abstr.; Soyabean Abstr.; Trop. Dis. Bull.; Virol. AIDS Abstr.; Weed Abstr.; Wheat Barley Trit. Abstr.

LC QH506 .K72a **ISSN** 0137-2351
PL
CODEN ZNUMDV

ZESZYTY NAUKOWE UNIWERSYTETU JAGIELLONSKIEGO. PRACE Z BIOLOGII MOLEKULARNEJ. (PRACE Z BIOLOGII MOLEKULARNEJ.). [Zesz. Nauk. Uniw. Jagiell., Pr. biol. md.]. **Added/Corp** Uniwersytet Jagiellonski. Instytut Biologii Molekularnej. **VFOAT** Schedae ad Biologiam Molecularem Pertinentes. (1974)-. Academic Scholarly Publication. Polish (summaries and/or abstracts in English). Irregular. Price varies per volume. Uniwersytet Jagiellonski, Ul. Golebia 24, 31-007 Krakow Poland. **(Subscription address:** Ars Polona-Ruch, PO Box 1001, Krakowskie Przedmiescie 7, 00-068 Warsaw Poland. **Tel** 011 48 22 261201.) Documents available from CASDDS.
Ind/Abst Chem. Abstr.

LC QR1 **ISSN** 0253-2662
DD 616/.01 CH
UDC 579
NLM W1 CH982T **CODEN** CKWCD9

ZHONGHUA MINGUO WEI SHENGWU JI MIANYIXUE ZAZHI. (CHUNG-HUA MIN KUO WEI SHENG WU CHI MIEN I HSUEH TSA CHIH.). [Zhonghua Minguo Wei Shengwu Ji Mianyixue Zazhi]. **VFOAT** Chinese Journal of Microbiology and Immunology; Chung-Hua Wei Mien Tsa Chih. (March 1980)-. Academic Scholarly Publication. English (Chinese). Four times a year. Chinese Journal of Microbiology and Immunology, No 1 Section 1, Jen-Ai Road, Taipei 100 Taiwan. Documents available from BIOSIS Document Express, CASDDS. ***Continues*** *Chinese Journal of Microbiology.*
Ind/Abst Biodeter. Abstr.; Biol. Abstr.; Chem. Abstr.; EMBASE; Helminthol. Abstr.; Immunol. Abstr.; Index Vet.; Microbiol. Abstr. Sect. B (19??-19??); Microbiol. Abstr. Sect. A; Life Sci. Collect.; Protozoolog. Abstr.; Trop. Dis. Bull.; Virol. AIDS Abstr.

ISSN 0254-5101
CC
NLM W1 CH985C **CODEN** ZWMZDP

ZHONGHUA WEISHENGWUXUE HE MIANYIXUE ZAZHI. **See** Medical Sciences-Allergy and Immunologic Diseases.

ISSN 0372-9311
RU
CCC
NLM W1; ZH421 **CODEN** ZMEIAV
Pr Rev.

ZHURNAL MIKROBIOLOGII, EPIDEMIOLOGII I IMMUNOBIOLOGII. **See** Medical Sciences-Epidemiology.

MICROSCOPY

LC QH201

DD 578 US

•ADVANCES IN ACOUSTIC MICROSCOPY. (1995)-. Monographic series. English. Irregular. Plenum Press, 233 Spring Street, New York NY 10013-1578. **Tel** (212)620-8000, (800)221-9369, FAX (212)463-0742, (212)807-1047, telex 23/421139.

LC QH201 .A2 **ISSN** 0065-3012
DD 578.4 UK
UDC 537.533.35; 57.086.2/.3
NLM W1 AD687 **CODEN** AOEMAK
TITLE CHANGE

ADVANCES IN OPTICAL AND ELECTRON MICROSCOPY. [Adv. opt. electron. microsc.]. Vol. 1 (1966)-(1994). Academic Scholarly Publication. English. Academic Press Inc., 6277 Sea Harbor Drive, Orlando FL 32887. **Tel** (800)543-9534, (407)345-4100, FAX (407)352-3445. **(Subscription address:** Academic Press Inc., PO Box 620000, Orlando FL 32891-8340. **Tel** (800)543-9534.) **ED** R. Barer and V. E. Cosslett. Documents available from BIOSIS Document Express, Ask*IEEE, CASDDS. ***Merged into*** *Advances in Imaging & Electron Physics, 0065-2539.*
Ind/Abst Biol. Abstr.; Chem. Abstr.; Curr. Cit.; GeoRef; INSPEC.

ISSN 0250-0418
DD 535.332506268 SA

ANNUAL CONFERENCE, PROCEEDINGS - ELECTRON MICROSCOPY SOCIETY OF SOUTHERN AFRICA. [Annu. conf., proc. - Electron. Microsc. Soc. South. Afr.]. **VFOAT** Verrigtings - Elektronmikroskopieveriging van Suidelike Afrika; Proceedings - Electron Microscopy Society of Southern Africa. (1973)-. Academic Scholarly Publication. Multiple languages. One time a year (Dec.). R127.00. Electron Micro Society of South Africa, PO Box 17039, Congella 4013 South Africa. Documents available from CASDDS. ***Continues*** *Conference Proceedings - Southern African Electron Microscopy Society.*
Ind/Abst Chem. Abstr.

AT

AUSTRALIAN ELECTRON MICROSCOPY NEWSLETTER. (1995)-. Newsletter. English. Four times a year. 16.44Aus$. Australian Society of Electron Microscopy, University of Adelaide, Adelaide 5005 Australia. **Tel** 011 61 8 3035855. ***Continues*** *CEMMSA.*

ISSN 0327-9545
AG
NLM W1; BI619QM

BIOCELL : OFFICIAL JOURNAL OF THE SOCIEDADES LATINOAMERICANAS DE MICROSCOPIA ELECTRONICA ... [ET AL.]. **Added/Corp** Sociedad Latinoamericana de Microscopia Electronica. Centro Regional de Investigaciones Cientificas y Tecnologicas (Argentina). (1994)-. Periodical. English (summaries and/or abstracts in Portuguese and Spanish). Three times a year. $100.00. Center Region Invest Cientif Tecn, Casilla de Correo 131, 5500 Mendoza Argentina. **Tel** 011 54 61 254400 ext. 441, telex 55438 CYTME AR. ***Continues*** *Microscopia Electronica y Biologia Celular, 0326-3142.*
Ind/Abst Curr. Cit.; Index Med. (1994-).

ISSN 1016-6505
BE
UDC 578

BIOTECH PRODUCTS INTERNATIONAL. **VFOAT** BPI. Biotech Products International. (1989)-. Periodical. English. Irregular (7 issues per year). $95.00. Pan European Publishing Company, rue Verte 216, 1210 Brussels 21 Belgium. **Tel** 011 32 2 2420611. **ED** Bas van Oosterhout and Sarah Soukias-Meredith. **Bk Rev. Ad Acc. Circ:** 30,000.
Ind/Abst Abstr. BioCommer.

ISSN 0383-1825
DD 502.8 CN
CODEN BMSCDQ

BULLETIN - MICROSCOPICAL SOCIETY OF CANADA. [Bull., Microsc. Soc. Can.]. **Main/Corp** Microscopical Society of Canada. Vol. 1 (Feb. 1973)-. Bulletin. English (summaries and/or abstracts in French). Four times a year. 30.42Can$. Microscopical Society of Canada, 1712 Avenue Road, PO Box 54560, Toronto Ontario M5M 4N5 Canada. **Tel** (416)483-3712, FAX (416)978-4761. **ED** F.W. Doane. **Bk Rev. Ad Acc. Circ:** 700 (ctrl). Documents available from CASDDS.
Desc: All aspects of light and electron microscopy.
Ind/Abst Chem. Abstr.

ISSN 0007-5663
FR

BULLETIN SIGNALETIQUE. [SECTION] 761. MICROSCOPIE ELECTRONIQUE, DIFFRACTION ELECTRONIQUE. **Main/Corp** France. Centre National de la Recherche Scientifique. **Added/Corp** Electron Microscope Society of America. France. Centre National de la Recherche Scientifique. Bulletin Signaletique. Section 6ME. Microscopie Electronique, Diffraction Electronique. Vol. 22 (1961)-. Bulletin. French. Irregular. $113.75. Editions du CNRS, 22 rue Saint Armand, F 75015 Paris France. **Tel** 011 33 1 45075050, telex 200 356 F. ***Continues*** *France. Centre National de la Recherche Scientifique. Bulletin Signaletique.*

ISSN 1132-1989
SP
UDC 573/578

CUADERNOS DE BIOETICA. (1990)-. Periodical. Spanish. Four times a year. $26.64. Francisco Javier Leon Correa, Plaza Cervantes 13 7, 14704 Santago Compostela Spain. **Tel** 011 34 81 599250. **Bk Rev.** (Qty: 40). **Ad Acc. Circ:** 2,000 (ctrl).

JA
NLM W1 DE158T **CODEN** DKENDV

DENSHI KENBIKYO (1974). (DENSHI KENBIKYO. ELECTRON-MICROSCOPY.). **Added/Corp** Nippon Denshi Kenbikyo Gakkai. **VFOAT** Electron-Microscopy; Electronmicroscopy. Vol. 9 (Nov. 1974)-. Academic Scholarly Publication. Japanese. $133.50. Nihon Denshi kenbikyo Gakkai, (Japanese Society of Electron-Microscopy), Gakkai Senta Biru, 4-16 Yayoi 2 Chome, Bunkyoku Tokyo 113 Japan. Documents available from Ask*IEEE, CASDDS. ***Continues in part*** *Journal of Electron Microscopy, 0022-0744.*
Ind/Abst Chem. Abstr.; INSPEC (1984-).

LC QH212.E4 E395 **ISSN** 0275-5262
DD 578/.45 US
NLM W1 EL333D **CODEN** EMBIDQ

ELECTRON MICROSCOPY IN BIOLOGY. [Electron microsc. biol.]. Vol. 1 (1981)-. Academic Scholarly Publication. English. Irregular. $120.00. John

Wiley & Sons, Inc., 605 Third Avenue, New York NY 10158-0012. **Tel** (212)850-6000, (212)850-6645, FAX (212)850-6088, telex 12-7063. **(Subscription address:** John Wiley & Sons / UK, Baffins Lane, Chichester, West Sussex PO19 1UD United Kingdom. **Tel** 011 44 1243 779777, FAX 011 44 243 776128, telex 86290 WIBOOKG.) **ED** Jack D. Griffith. Documents available from CASDDS.
Ind/Abst AGRICOLA; Chem. Abstr.

ISSN 0923-0475
US
NLM W1; EL33E **CODEN** EMBME5
ELECTRON MICROSCOPY IN BIOLOGY AND MEDICINE. [Electron microsc. biol. med.]. (1984)-. Monographic series. English. Irregular. Price varies per volume. Kluwer Academic Publishers / Massachusetts, PO Box 358, Accord Station, Hingham MA 02018. **Tel** (617)871-6600. **(Subscription address:** Kluwer Academic Publishers / US Subscriptions, PO Box 253, Accord Station, Hingham MA 02018. **Tel** (617)871-6600.) Documents available from BIOSIS Document Express.
Ind/Abst Biol. Abstr.; Index Vet.

ISSN 0936-6911
GW
NLM W1; EL453M
ELEKTRONENMIKROSKOPIE : MITTEILUNGEN DER DEUTSCHEN GESELLSCHAFT FUER ELEKTRONENMIKROSKOPIE E.V.
Added/Corp Deutsche Gesellschaft fuer Elektronenmikroskopie. No. 1 (Apr. 1990)-. Periodical. German. Irregular (two or three issues per year). DM32.00. Wissenschaftliche Verlagsgesellschaft mbH, Postfach 101061, D-70009 Stuttgart Germany. **Tel** 011 49 711 258200, FAX 011 49 711 2582290, telex 723636 DAZ D.

UK
EUREM ... : PROCEEDINGS OF THE ... EUROPEAN CONGRESS ON ELECTRON MICROSCOPY. Main/Conf European Congress on Electron Microscopy. **Added/Corp** Institute of Physics (Great Britain). (Sept. 1988)-. Proceedings. English. Institute of Physics, Techno House, Redcliffe Way, Bristol BS1 6NX United Kingdom. **Tel** 011 44 117 9297481, FAX 011 44 117 9294318, telex 449149 INSTP G. **(Subscription address:** American Institute of Physics, Publishing Sales, 500 Sunnyside Blvd., Woodbury NY 11797. **Tel** (516)576-2200.) ***Continues*** *Electron Microscopy.*

ISSN 0958-1952
DD 508.82 UK
EUROPEAN MICROSCOPY AND ANALYSIS. [Microsc. anal.]. (1987)-. Periodical. English. Six times a year (Jan., Mar., May, July, Sept., Nov.). $181.39. Rolston Gordon Communications, 1 Gable Cottage, Post House Lane, Great Bookham Surrey, KT23 3EA United Kingdom. **Tel** 011 44 1372 454891, FAX 011 44 1372 459957. **ED** Ian Watt. **Bk Rev**, (Qty: varies). **Ad Acc. Circ:** 7,000 UK, 18,000 Europe, 21,000 US (ctrl).
Desc: Information for users, buyers and those recommending microscopy equipment and products.

LC QL362 .I58 **ISSN** 1077-8306
DD 502 US
●**INVERTEBRATE BIOLOGY.** [Invertebr. biol.]. **Added/Corp** American Microscopical Society. American Society of Zoologists. Division of Invertebrate Zoology. Vol. 114, No. 1 (Winter 1995)-. Periodical. English. Four times a year. $75.00. American Microscopical Society. **(Subscription address:** Invertebrate Biology, PO Box 1897, Lawrence KS 66044-8897.) Index available (bound in Dec. issue). ***Continues*** *American Microscopical Society. Transactions of the American Microscopical Society, 0003-0023.*
Ind/Abst Curr. Cit.

LC QH201 .J68 **ISSN** 1040-7286
DD 502 US
CCC
NLM W1; JO595KV **CODEN** JCMIEX
Pr Rev.
JOURNAL OF COMPUTER-ASSISTED MICROSCOPY. See Biology-Computer Applications.

LC QC373.E4 J6 **ISSN** 0022-0744
JA
CCC
NLM W1 JO633 **CODEN** JELJA7
JOURNAL OF ELECTRON MICROSCOPY. [J. electron microsc.]. **Added/Corp** Nihon Denshi Kenbikyo Gakkai. **VFOAT** Journal of Electronmicroscopy; Denshi Kenbikyo Gakkai Shi. Vol. 13, No. 3 (1964)-. Academic Scholarly Publication. English (Japanese). Six times a year. $200.00. **(Subscription address:** Maruzen Company Ltd., PO Box 5050, Import & Export Department, Tokyo 100 31 Japan. **Tel** 011 81 3 32789224.) **Ad Acc. Circ:** 4,000 (ctrl). Documents available from The Genuine Article, BIOSIS Document Express, Ask*IEEE, CASDDS. ***Continues*** *Journal of Electronmicroscopy, 0022-0744.* ***Continued in part by*** *Denshi Kenbikyo.*
Ind/Abst Abstr. Bull. Inst. Pap. Sci. Tech.; Biol. Abstr.; Chem. Abstr.; CSA Neuro. Abstr. (?-?); Curr. Aware. Biol. Sci., CABS; Curr. Cit.; Curr. Contents Life Sci.; Dairy Sci. Abstr.; EMBASE; Helminthol. Abstr. (19??-19??); Index Med.; INSPEC (1968-); Life Sci. Collect.; Protozoolog. Abstr.; Res. Alert [Full Cov.]; Rev. Plant Pathol.; Rice Abstr.; Sci. Cit. Index; SCISEARCH.

ISSN 0022-2720
UK
CCC
NLM W1 JO763N **CODEN** JMICAR
Pr Rev.
JOURNAL OF MICROSCOPY (OXFORD). (JOURNAL OF MICROSCOPY.). [J. microsc.]. **Added/Corp** Royal Microscopical Society (Great Britain) International Society for Stereology. Vol. 89 (1969)-. Academic Scholarly Publication. English. Twelve times a year. $734.00. Blackwell Scientific Publications Ltd, Marston Book Services, PO Box 88, Oxford OX2 ONE United Kingdom. **Tel** 011 44 1865 206206, FAX 011 44 1865 206219, telex 837 515 MARDIS G. **ED** C. V. Howard. Index available (bound in last issue). **Bk Rev. Ad Acc.** available on microfilm and microfiche from University Microfilms International (UMI). Documents available from The Genuine Article, BIOSIS Document Express, Ask*IEEE, CASDDS, ADONIS. ***Continues*** *Journal of the Royal Microscopical Society, 0368-3974.*
Desc: Covers all branches of microscopy and microbeam analysis.
Ind/Abst Abstr. Bull. Inst. Pap. Sci. Tech.; ADONIS; AGRICOLA [Select. Cov.]; Alum. Ind. Abstr.; Anim. Breed. Abstr.; Biol. Abstr.; Ceram. Abstr.; Chem. Abstr.; Coal Abstr.; Curr. Aware. Biol. Sci., CABS; Curr. Cit.; Curr. Contents Life Sci.; EMBASE; Eng. Mater. Abstr.; Field Crop Abstr.; GeoRef; Grass. Forage Abstr.; Hortic. Abstr.; Index Med.; Index Vet.; INSPEC (Feb. 1972-); Maize Abstr.; Met. Abstr.; Nematol. Abstr.; Ornamental Hort. (1991-); Life Sci. Collect.; Pig News Inf.; Plant Breed. Abstr.; Protozoolog. Abstr.; Ref. Upd. Deluxe Ed.; Res. Alert [Full Cov.]; Rev. Agric. Entomol.; Rev. Plant Pathol.; Sci. Cit. Index; SCISEARCH; Soils Fert.; Sorghum Mill. Abstr.; Stat. Theory Method Abstr. (1986); Vet. Bull.; Trop. Dis. Bull.

ISSN 0196-5662
US
JOURNAL - TEXAS SOCIETY FOR ELECTRON MICROSCOPY. [J. - Tex. Soc. Electron Microsc.]. **Main/Corp** Texas Society for Electron Microscopy. **Added/Corp** Texas Society for Electron Microscopy. TSEM Journal. **VFOAT** Texas Society for Electron Microscopy Journal; TSEM Journal. Vol. 11 (Winter 1980)-. Periodical. English. Three times a year. Free on request. Texas Society for Electron Microscopy, Department of Biology, Baylor University, Waco TX 76798. **Tel** (817)755-2911. **Bk Rev. Ad Acc. Circ:** 550 (ctrl). ***Continues*** *Newsletter - Texas Society for Electron Microscopy, 0191-3360.*
Desc: Electron microscopy techniques and applications.

LC QH201 .M48 **ISSN** 0968-4328
DD 502/.8/205 UK
CCC
NLM W1; MI306MB **CODEN** MCONEN
MICRON : THE INTERNATIONAL RESEARCH AND REVIEW JOURNAL FOR MICROSCOPY. Vol. 24, No. 1 (Feb. 1993)-. Periodical. English. Six times a year. $692.00. Pergamon Press, An Imprint of Elsevier Science Ltd., The Boulevard, Langford Lane, Kidlington, Oxford OX5 1GB United Kingdom. **Tel** 011 44 1865 843000, 011 44 1865 843699, FAX 011 44 1865 843010. **(Subscription address:** Elsevier Science Ltd. / Oxford Fulfillment Centre, PO Box 800, Kidlington OX5 1DX United Kingdom. **Tel** 011 44 865 843355.) available on an online database from Elsevier Electronic Subscriptions (EES). ***Continues*** *Micron and Microscopica Acta, 0739-6260* ***and*** *Electron Microscopy Reviews, 0892-0354.*
Ind/Abst Curr. Cit.; Index Med.; Sci. Cit. Index.

LC QH201 .M585 **ISSN** 0026-282X
DD 502/.8/2 US
CCC
NLM W1; MI309H **CODEN** MICRAD
Pr Rev.
MICROSCOPE (LONDON). (THE MICROSCOPE.). [Microscope]. (July 1967)-. Academic Scholarly Publication. English. Four times a year. $65.00. Microscope Publications, 2820 South Michigan Avenue, Chicago IL 60616. **Tel** (312)842-7105, FAX (312)842-1078. **ED** Walter C. McCrone and David A. Stoney. Each issue contains an index to its own contents (no volume index)--loose. cum. index. **Bk Rev. Ad Acc. Circ:** 1,200 (ctrl). available on microfilm and microfiche from University Microfilms International (UMI). Documents available from BIOSIS Document Express, Ask*IEEE, CASDDS. ***Continues*** *Microscope and Crystal Front, 0368-8992.*
Desc: A journal for microscopists in industry, government research and universities, reviewing advances in microscopes, accessories, techniques and applications for study of particles, films, materials, surfaces.
Ind/Abst Abstr. Bull. Inst. Pap. Sci. Tech.; AGRICOLA; Biol. Abstr.; Chem. Abstr.; Curr. Cit.; EMBASE; GeoRef; INSPEC (July 1968-); Life Sci. Collect.; World Surf. Coat. Abstr.

ISSN 1041-0716
DD 502 US
CCC
TITLE CHANGE
MICROSCOPE TECHNOLOGY & NEWS. [Microsc. technol. news]. **VFOAT** Microscope Technology and News. (1989)-(19??). Periodical. English. The Cambrex Group, 33 Broad Street, Suite 1001, Boston MA 02109. **Tel** (617)742-8290, FAX (617)742-4942. **ED** Elinor Solit. Index available (bound in first issue). cum. index. **Bk Rev**, (Qty: 10). ***Continued by*** *Analytical Consumer, 1052-3065.*
Desc: Instrumentation, new product developments, applications, people and other news of interest.

LC QH201 **ISSN** 0326-3142
DD 578 AG
NLM W1; MI309LH **CODEN** MEBCE7
Pr Rev. **TITLE CHANGE**
MICROSCOPIA ELECTRONICA Y BIOLOGIA CELULAR : ORGANO OFICIAL DE LAS SOCIEDADES LATINOAMERICANA DE MICROSCOPIA ELECTRONICA E IBEROAMERICANA DE BIOLOGIA CELULAR. [Microsc. electron. biologia celular]. **Added/Corp** Sociedad Latinoamericana de Microscopia Electronica. Sociedad Iberoamericana de Biologia Celular. (198?)-(19??). Periodical. English (Spanish). Center Region Invest Cientif Tecn, Casilla de Correo 131, 5500 Mendoza Argentina. **Tel** 011 54 61 254400 ext. 441, telex 55438 CYTME AR. **ED** Mario H. Burgos and Ramon S. Piezzi. Index available. **Ad Acc.** ctrl circ. Documents available from BIOSIS Document Express, CASDDS. ***Continues*** *Revista de Microscopia Electronica, 0300-3426.* ***Continued by*** *Biocell.*
Desc: This journal publishes full length papers. Includes letters to the editors and reviews on subjects on a w ide range of topics regarding all aspects in areas of electron microscopy and of cell biology, from the molecular level to cell and tissue organization.
Ind/Abst Biol. Abstr. (1987-); Chem. Abstr.; Curr. Contents Life Sci.; Index Med. (1985-); SCISEARCH.

ISSN 0342-958X
GW
UDC 537.533.35
NLM W1 MI311A **CODEN** MACSDV
SUSPENDED
MICROSCOPICA ACTA. SUPPLEMENT. [Microsc. acta, Suppl.]. (1977)-(19??). Academic Scholarly Publication. English (German and French). Price varies per volume. S. Hirzel Verlag Stuttgart, Postfach 101061, D-70009 Stuttgart Germany. **Tel** 011 49 711 25820, FAX 0711/2582 290, telex 723636 daz d. Documents available from CASDDS.
Ind/Abst Chem. Abstr.

ISSN 0958-1952
UK
Pr Rev.
MICROSCOPY AND ANALYSIS. [Microsc. anal.]. **VFOAT** European Microscopy and Analysis. (198?)-. Periodical. English. Six times a year. $181.39. Rolston Gordon Communications, 1 Gable Cottage, Post House Lane, Great Bookham Surrey, KT23 3EA United Kingdom. **Tel** 011 44 1372 454891, FAX 011 44 1372 459957. **ED** Ian Watt. Index available. cum. index. **Bk Rev. Ad Acc. Circ:** 39,000 (ctrl).
Desc: Aims to inform and instruct those who wish to further their knowledge of microscopy, image analysis and associated techniques. Each issues contains articles from specialists in their field and industry news.
Ind/Abst Curr. Cit.

ISSN 0957-0365
US
CODEN MIHAEP
MICROSCOPY HANDBOOKS. [Microsc. handb.]. **Added/Corp** Royal Microscopical Society (Great Britain). **VFOAT** Microscopy Hand Books. (1984)-. Monographic series. English. Price varies per volume. Oxford University Press / New York, 200 Madison Avenue, New York NY 10016. **Tel** (212)679-7300, (919)677-0977, (800)451-7556, (800)445-9714, FAX (919)677-1303.
Ind/Abst Biol. Abstr. (1985-); Curr. Cit.

FR
NLM W1; MI313KM **CODEN** MMMIEY
MICROSCOPY, MICROANALYSIS, MICROSTRUCTURES : MMM. Added/Corp Societe Francaise de Microscopie Electronique. Centre National de la Recherche Scientifique (France). **VFOAT** MMM. Vol. 1 No. 1 (Feb. 1990)-. Academic Scholarly Publication. English (French and German; summaries and/or abstracts in English). Six times a year. $360.88. Les Editions de Physique, 7 Avenue du Hoggar, Z.I. de Courtaboeuf - BP 112, 91944 les Ulis Cedex A France. **Tel** 011 33 1 69187575, FAX 011 33 1 69288491, telex EDITPHY 692321F. Documents available from The

Genuine Article, Ask*IEEE, CASDDS. ***Continues*** *Journal de Microscopie et de Spectroscopie Electroniques, 0395-9279.*
Ind/Abst Chem. Abstr. (Feb. 1990-); Curr. Cit.; Curr. Contents Phys. Chem. Earth Sci. (19??-); INSPEC (Feb. 1990-); Res. Alert (19??-) [Full Cov.]; Sci. Cit. Index (19??-); SCISEARCH (19??-).

LC WMLC 93/1779 QH212.E4 J688 **ISSN** 1059-910X
DD 502 US
CCC
NLM W1; MI313KT **CODEN** MRTEEO
MICROSCOPY RESEARCH AND TECHNIQUE. [Microsc. res. tech.]. Vol. 20, No. 1 (Jan. 1, 1992)-. Periodical. English. Eighteen times a year. $1638.00. John Wiley & Sons, Inc., 605 Third Avenue, New York NY 10158-0012. **Tel** (212)850-6000, (212)850-6645, FAX (212)850-6088, telex 12-7063. **(Subscription address:** John Wiley & Sons / UK, Baffins Lane, Chichester, West Sussex PO19 1UD United Kingdom. **Tel** 011 44 1243 779777, FAX 011 44 243 776128, telex 86290 WIBOOKG.) **ED** John E. Johnson, Jr. Documents available from The Genuine Article. ***Continues*** *Journal of Electron Microscopy Technique, 0741-0581.*
Desc: Expanded scope to encompass all aspects of advanced microscopy, focusing on equipment, methodology, and applications in the biological, materials, and medical sciences.
Ind/Abst Abstr. Bull. Inst. Pap. Sci. Tech.; Curr. Aware. Biol. Sci., CABS; Curr. Contents Eng. Comput. Technol.; Curr. Contents Life Sci.; EMBASE; Index Med. (1992-); Ref. Upd. Deluxe Ed.; Res. Alert [Full Cov.]; Sci. Cit. Index; SCISEARCH.

LC QH212.E4 E413 **ISSN** 1062-9785
DD 502/.8 US
NLM W1; MI313KV
CEASED
MICROSCOPY SOCIETY OF AMERICA BULLETIN. **Added/Corp** Microscopy Society of America. **VFOAT** MSA Bulletin. (1993)-Vol. 24 No. 4 (19??). Bulletin. English. Microscopy Society of America, Business Office, PO Box MSA, Woods Hole MA 02543. **Tel** (508)540-7639. **ED** Joseph Warb. **Bk Rev**, (Qty: 15-20). **Ad Acc. Circ:** 6,000 (ctrl). ***Continues*** *EMSA Bulletin, 0146-6119.*

US
MICROSCOPY SOCIETY OF AMERICA PROCEEDINGS. (19??)-. English. One time a year (Aug.). $84.00. San Francisco Press Inc., PO Box 426800, San Francisco CA 94142. **Tel** (510)524-1000. ***Continues*** *Proceedings, Annual Meeting Electron Microscopy of America.*

LC QH201 .M74 **ISSN** 0026-3680
DD 578.05 GW
CCC
NLM W1 MI42 **CODEN** MKKSA2
MIKROKOSMOS (STUTTGART). (MIKROKOSMOS.). [Mikrokosmos]. **Added/Corp** Deutsche Mikrobiologische Gesellschaft Stuttgart. Mikrobiologische Vereinigung Hamburg. Mikrobiologische Arbeitsgemeinschaft Mannheim. Mikrobiologische Vereinigung Munchen. Mikrographische Gesellschaft Wien. Mikroskopische Gesellschaft Zurich. Vol. 1 (1907)-. Periodical. German. Six times a year. $82.00. Gustav Fischer Verlag Stuttgart, Postfach 720143, D-70577 Stuttgart Germany. **Tel** 011 49 711 458030, FAX 011 49 711 4580334, telex 2627-7111488. **(Subscription address:** VCH Publishers Inc., 303 Northwest 12th Avenue, Journals Department, Deerfield FL 33442. **Tel** (800)367-8249, (305)428-5566.) **ED** Dieter Krauter. Index available. cum. index. **Bk Rev. Ad Acc. Circ:** 3,000. Documents available from BIOSIS Document Express, CASDDS. ***Absorbed*** *Zeitschrift fur Angewandte Mikroskopie und Klinische Chemie.*
Desc: Covers protistology, microbiology, histology, plant anatomy.
Ind/Abst Biol. Abstr.; Chem. Abstr.; GeoRef; Life Sci. Collect.

LC QH201 **ISSN** 1355-185X
DD 578 UK
CCC
•**PROBE MICROSCOPY.** (1996)-. Academic Scholarly Publication. English. Four times a year. £146.00. Carfax Publishing Company, PO Box 25, Abingdon, Oxfordshire OX14 3UE United Kingdom. **Tel** 011 44 1235 555335, FAX 011 44 1235 553559, telex 817484. **(Subscription address:** Carfax Publishing Co., 875-81 Massachusetts Avenue, Cambridge MA 02139.) **ED** Mark Welland and Jim Gimzewski.

ISSN 0381-1751
DD 502.8 CN
UDC 57.086.3(060.55)(71)
CODEN PMSCDA
PROCEEDINGS OF THE MICROSCOPICAL SOCIETY OF CANADA. [Proc. Microsc. Soc. Can.]. **Main/Corp** Microscopical Society of Canada. **VFOAT** Resume des Communications de la Societe de Microscopie du Canada. (1974)-. Academic Scholarly Publication. English (French). One time a year. $20.00. Microscopical Society of Canada, 1712 Avenue Road, PO Box 54560, Toronto Ontario M5M 4N5 Canada. **Tel** (416)483-3712, FAX (416)978-4761. **Bk Rev. Ad Acc. Circ:** 600 (ctrl). Documents available from CASDDS.
Desc: All aspects of light and electron microscopy as applied to biological and material sciences.
Ind/Abst Chem. Abstr. (1974-1983); GeoRef.

LC QH201 .R77 **ISSN** 0035-9017
DD 578/.05 UK
CCC
NLM W1 PR586WM
PROCEEDINGS - ROYAL MICROSCOPICAL SOCIETY. [Proc. - R. Microsc. Soc.]. **Main/Corp** Royal Microscopical Society, London. Vol. 1 (1966)-. Academic Scholarly Publication. English. Six times a year. $212.00. Blackwell Scientific Publications Ltd, Marston Book Services, PO Box 88, Oxford OX2 ONE United Kingdom. **Tel** 011 44 1865 206206, FAX 011 44 1865 206219, telex 837 515 MARDIS G. **ED** P. J. Evennett. **Bk Rev. Ad Acc. Circ:** 2,950. available on microfilm and microfiche from University Microfilms International (UMI).
Desc: Covers microscopy and use of modern microscopes in life and materials science. Also contains notices, abstracts and reports of meetings and courses, articles, books and new equipment reviews.
Ind/Abst Curr. Aware. Biol. Sci., CABS; EMBASE; Life Sci. Collect.

LC QH201 .M589 **ISSN** 0969-3823
UK
CODEN QJMIEN
•**QUEKETT JOURNAL OF MICROSCOPY, THE.** **Added/Corp** Quekett Microscopical Club (London, Eng.). Vol. 37, Pt. 1 (Spring 1993)-. Periodical. English. Two times a year. $60.00. Quekett Microscopical Club, 31 High Street, Stanford in Vale, Farington Oxfordshire SN7 8LH United Kingdom. **Tel** 011 44 1367 710223. ***Continues*** *Microscopy, 0026-2838.*

LC QH212.S3 S26 **ISSN** 0161-0457
DD 502/.8/25 US
CCC
NLM W1 SC1565 **CODEN** SCNNDF
Pr Rev.
SCANNING. [Scanning]. **Added/Corp** Foundation for Advances in Clinical Medicine. Vol. 1, No. 1 (Feb. 1978)-. Academic Scholarly Publication. English. Eight times a year. $325.00. Foundation Advances in Medicine and Science Inc., Box 832, Mahwah NJ 07430. **Tel** (201)818-1010, FAX (201)818-0086, telex 220883 TAUR. **ED** A Boyde, L Reimer, and J Pawley. Index available. cum. index. **Bk Rev. Ad Acc. Circ:** 3,000 (ctrl). Documents available from The Genuine Article, BIOSIS Document Express, Ask*IEEE, CASDDS.
Desc: Latest developments in scanning electron microscopy.
Ind/Abst Abstr. Bull. Inst. Pap. Sci. Tech.; Biol. Abstr.; Ceram. Abstr.; Chem. Abstr.; Curr. Cit.; Curr. Contents Eng. Comput. Technol.; Curr. Contents Life Sci.; EMBASE; GeoRef; Index Med.; INSPEC (1979-); Res. Alert [Full Cov.]; Sci. Cit. Index; SCISEARCH.

LC QH212.S3 S28 **ISSN** X
DD 535/.3325 US
NLM W1; SC155MH **CODEN** SCMIEU
Pr Rev.
SCANNING MICROSCOPY. [Scanning microsc.]. **Added/Corp** Scanning Microscopy International. Vol. 1, No. 1 (March 1987)-. Academic Scholarly Publication. English. Four times a year (Mar., June, Sept., Dec.). $179.00. Scanning Microscopy International, PO Box 66507, AMF O'Hare, Chicago IL 60666-0507. **Tel** (708)529-6677, FAX (708)980-6698. **ED** Om. Johari, G. M. Roomau, R. P. Becker. Index available. cum. index. **Bk Rev. Circ:** 1,500. Documents available from Article Express International, The Genuine Article, BIOSIS Document Express, Ask*IEEE, CASDDS. ***Continues*** *Scanning Electron Microscopy, 0586-5581.*
Desc: Interdisciplinary journal devoted to various topics: scanning microscopies, SEM, and related techniques; science, instrumentation, theory, applications in physical, biological and biomedical sciences, and engineering. Includes surface analysis, microanalysis and characterization of materials.
Ind/Abst Abstr. Bull. Inst. Pap. Sci. Tech.; AGRICOLA; Anal. Abstr.; Anim. Breed. Abstr.; Bioeng. Abstr. (1987-); Biol. Abstr. (1987-); Chem. Abstr. (1987-); Coal Abstr. (1987-); Curr. Aware. Biol. Sci., CABS; Curr. Cit.; Curr. Contents Eng. Comput. Technol.; Curr. Contents Life Sci.; Ei Page One (1987-); EMBASE; Energy Res. Abstr. (1987-); Eng. Mater. Abstr.; Eng. Index Annu.; Field Crop Abstr.; Food Sci. Technol. Abstr.; For. Abstr.; GeoRef (1987-); Helminthol. Abstr.; Index Med. (1987-); Index Vet.; INSPEC (1987-); Mass Spect. Bull.; Met. Abstr. (1987-); Nematol. Abstr.; Poult. Abstr.; Ref. Upd. Deluxe Ed.; Res. Alert [Full Cov.]; Rev. Med. Vet. Entomol.; Rev. Med. Vet. Mycology; Rev. Plant Pathol.; Sci. Cit. Index; SCISEARCH; Soc. Sci. Cit. Index [Select. Cov.]; Vet. Bull.

ISSN 0892-953X
DD 502 US
CCC
NLM W1; SC155MHA **CODEN** SMSUEU
Pr Rev.
SCANNING MICROSCOPY. SUPPLEMENT. [Scanning microsc., Suppl.]. **Added/Corp** Scanning Microscopy International. (1987)-. Monographic series. English. One time a year. Price varies per volume. Scanning Microscopy International, PO Box 66507, AMF O'Hare, Chicago IL 60666-0507. **Tel** (708)529-6677, FAX (708)980-6698. **ED** J. Schore, P. Kruit, D. Newbury. Index available. cum. index. **Circ:** 700. Documents available from Article Express International, Ask*IEEE, CASDDS.
Desc: Devoted to topics of fundamental importance in microcopy and microanalysis.
Ind/Abst Chem. Abstr.; Curr. Cit.; Eng. Index Annu.; Index Med. (1987-); INSPEC (1990-).

ISSN 1183-8965
DD 579 CN
STUDIO NORTH. [Stud. North]. 1st Ed. (Summer 1991)-. Periodical. English. Irregular. Studio North, 78 Fox Run, Barrie, Ontario, L4N 5A8 Canada.

LC QH212.E4 T66A
DD 502/.8 JA
TOKYO DAIGAKU CHOKOATSU DENSHI KEMBIKYOSHITSU NEMPO. **Main/Corp** Tokyo Daigaku. Chokoatsu Denshi Kembikyoshitsu. Vol. 1 (1976)-. English (Japanese; summaries and/or abstracts in French, German and English). Tokyo Daigaku Kogakubu Sogo Shikenjo Chokoatsu Denshi Kembikyoshitsu, 11-16 Yayoi 2, Bunkyo-ku 113, Tokyo Japan.

LC QH212.E4 U57 **ISSN** 0304-3991
DD 502/.8 NE
CCC
NLM W1 UL73 **CODEN** ULTRD6
Pr Rev.
ULTRAMICROSCOPY. [Ultramicroscopy]. Vol. 1 (July 1975)-. Academic Scholarly Publication. English. Twenty times a year (5 vols.). $1497.00. Elsevier Science Publishers BV, PO Box 211, 1000 AE Amsterdam Netherlands. **Tel** 011 31 20 4853641, 011 31 20 4853642, FAX 011 31 20 4853598. **ED** P. Kruit. available on microfilm and microfiche from University Microfilms International (UMI); available on an online database from Elsevier Electronic Subscriptions (EES). Documents available from Article Express International, The Genuine Article, BIOSIS Document Express, Ask*IEEE, CASDDS.
Desc: Committed to the advancement of the tools and methods for the microscopic determination of ultrastructures.
Ind/Abst Alum. Ind. Abstr.; Bioeng. Abstr.; Biol. Abstr.; Chem. Abstr.; Civ. Struct. Eng. Abstr.; Comput. Inf. Syst. Abstr. J. [Full Cov.]; Curr. Aware. Biol. Sci., CABS; Curr. Cit.; Curr. Contents Life Sci.; Curr. Contents Phys. Chem. Earth Sci.; Ei Page One; Elect. Comm. Abstr.; EMBASE; Eng. Mater. Abstr.; Eng. Index Annu.; Environ. Eng. Abstr.; GeoRef; Index Med.; INSPEC (July 1975-); Manuf. Process Eng. Abstr.; Mater. Sci. Eng. Abstr.; Mech. Eng. Abstr.; Met. Abstr.; Life Sci. Collect.; Phys. Briefs; Ref. Upd. Deluxe Ed.; Res. Alert [Full Cov.]; Sci. Cit. Index; SCISEARCH; Solid State Supercond. Abstr.

MYCOLOGY

LC QK600 .A22 **ISSN** 0001-3617
DD 589/.2/08 US
NLM ZQW 180 A164 **CODEN** ABMYA5
ABSTRACTS OF MYCOLOGY. **See** Biology-Abstracting, Bibliographies and Statistics.

LC QK609.C6
DD 589.2 CH
ACTA MYCOLOGIA SINICA. (19??)-. Chinese. Four times a year. $81.20. Science Press, 16 Donghuangchenggen North Street, Beijing 100707, People's Republic of China. **Tel** 011 86 1 4019821, 011 86 1 4010642, FAX 011 86 1 4012180, 011 86 1 4019810, telex 210147.
Ind/Abst Biocont. News Inf. (1991-); Rev. Agric. Entomol.

LC QK600 .A23 **ISSN** 0001-625X
DD 589.2 PL
CODEN ACMYAC
ACTA MYCOLOGICA. [Acta mycol.]. **Added/Corp** Polskie Towarzystwo Botaniczne. Vol. 1 (1965)-. Periodical. Polish (summaries and/or abstracts in English and French). Irregular. $25.00. **(Subscription address:** Ars Polona-Ruch, PO Box 1001, Krakowskie Przedmiescie 7, 00-068 Warsaw Poland. **Tel** 011 48 22 261201.) Each issue contains an index to its own contents (no volume index)--loose. Documents available from BIOSIS Document Express, CASDDS.
Ind/Abst Biodeter. Abstr. (19??-19??); Biol. Abstr.; Chem. Abstr. (-1988); Microbiol. Abstr. Sect. C; Life Sci. Collect.; Rev. Med. Vet. Mycology; Rev. Plant Pathol.; Wheat Barley Trit. Abstr.

LC QK600 .S93 **ISSN** 1016-0019
AU
BEIHEFTE ZUR SYDOWIA. [Bei. Sydowia]. **VFOAT** Sydowia. (1957)-. Monographic series. English (Latin). Irregular. Price varies per volume. Verlag Ferdinand Berger & Soehne, Wienerstrasse 21-23, A-3580 Horn Austria. **Tel** 011 43 2982 4161232.
Ind/Abst Bibliogr. Agric.

LC Z5356.F97 C6 **ISSN** 0006-1573
DD 581 UK
NLM ZQW 180 B582
BIBLIOGRAPHY OF SYSTEMATIC MYCOLOGY. **Main/Corp** Commonwealth Mycological Institute (Great Britain). **Added/Corp** Commonwealth Mycological Institute (Great Britain) C.A.B. International. Mycological Institute. International Mycological Institute. (1957)-. Periodical. English. Two times a year. $90.00. CAB International Centre, Wallingford, Oxfordshire OX10 8DE United Kingdom. **Tel** 011 44 1491 832111, FAX 011 44 1491 833508, telex 847964 COMAGG G. **ED** P. Cannon. Index available.
Desc: Indexing publication listing articles on all aspects of the taxonomy of fungi.
Ind/Abst Plant Breed. Abstr.; Rev. Med. Vet. Mycology; Rev. Plant Pathol.

LC QK580
DD 589.1 GW
CODEN BLICD3
BIBLIOTHECA LICHENOLOGICA. Vol. 1 (1973)-. Monographic series. German (English, French and Spanish). Irregular. $414.54. Lubrecht & Cramer Ltd, 38 County Route 48, Forestburgh NY 12777. **Tel** (914)794-8539. Each issue contains an index to its own contents (no volume index)--loose. **Bk Rev**. Documents available from BIOSIS Document Express.
Desc: Science of lichens.
Ind/Abst Biol. Abstr.

GW
BIBLIOTHECA MYCOLOGIA. (19??)-. German (English). $330.00. Gebrueder Borntraeger, Johannesstrasse 3A, D-70176 Stuttgart Germany. **Tel** 011 49 711 625001, FAX 011 49 711 625005. **ED** A. Bresinsky, D. Regensburg, H. Butin, D. Braunschweig, H.O. Schwantes and D. Gieben. **Bk Rev. Ad Acc.** ctrl circ.

LC QK608.S7 B64 **ISSN** 0214-140X
DD 589.2/0946 SP
BOLETIN DE LA SOCIEDAD MICOLOGICA DE MADRID. **Added/Corp** Sociedad Micologica de Madrid. Real Jardin Botanico (Spain). Vol. 11 (1986)-. Periodical. Spanish (summaries and/or abstracts in English; table of contents in English). One time a year. ***Continues** Boletin de la Sociedad Micologica Castellana, 0210-7937.*
Ind/Abst For. Abstr.; Hortic. Abstr.

ISSN 0716-114X
CL
NLM W1; BO4294
BOLETIN MICOLOGICO. **Added/Corp** Universidad de Valparaiaso. Catedra de Micologia. **VFOAT** Mycologycal Bulletin. Vol. 1, No. 1 (1982)-. Bulletin. Spanish (summaries and/or abstracts in English). Two times a year. Universidad de Valparaiso / Facultad de Medicina, Catedra de Micologia, Casilla 92-V, Valparaiso Chile.
Ind/Abst Biocont. News Inf.; Maize Abstr.; Rev. Med. Vet. Mycology; Rev. Plant Pathol.; Wheat Barley Trit. Abstr.

LC QK600 .B32A **ISSN** 0270-4633
DD 589.2/005 US
UDC 582.28
BOSTON MYCOLOGICAL CLUB BULLETIN. [Boston Mycol. Club bull.]. **Main/Corp** Boston Mycological Club. Bulletin. English. Four times a year. $10.00 individual membership. Moselio Schaechter, 855 Commonwealth Avenue, Newton Center MA 02159. **ED** Moselio Schaechter. **Bk Rev. Circ:** 400.
Desc: Notices of club events plus articles about wild mushrooms and amateur mushroom collecting and study.

ISSN 0300-4562
UK
BRITISH LICHEN SOCIETY BULLETIN. [Br. Lichen Soc. bull.]. **Main/Corp** British Lichen Society. (1958)-. Bulletin. English. Two times a year. $25.67. British Lichen Society / Department of Botany, Natural Historical Museum, London SW7 5BD United Kingdom. **Tel** 011 44 171 9388852, FAX 011 44 171 9389260. **ED** Dr. P. D. Crittenden (editor's address: University of Nottingham, Nottingham N97 2RD UK). Index available. cum. index. **Circ:** 600.
Ind/Abst Life Sci. Collect.

ISSN 0275-0287
UK
UDC 582.28(063)
NLM W3 BR449 **CODEN** BMYSD2
BRITISH MYCOLOGICAL SOCIETY SYMPOSIUM SERIES. [Br. Mycol. Soc. symp. ser.]. **Main/Corp** British Mycological Society. **VFOAT** Symposium Series. No. 1 (1977)-. Academic Scholarly Publication. English. Price varies per volume. Academic Press Ltd., A Division of Harcourt Brace & Company Ltd., 24-28 Oval Road, London NW1 7DX United Kingdom. **Tel** 011 44 171 2674466, FAX 011 44 171 4822293, 011 44 171 4854752, telex 25775 ACPRES G. Documents available from BIOSIS Document Express, CASDDS.
Ind/Abst AGRICOLA [Full Cov.]; Biol. Abstr.; Chem. Abstr.

LC QK600 .S6 **ISSN** 0395-7527
DD 589.206244 FR
NLM W1 BU934J
BULLETIN TRIMESTRIEL DE LA SOCIETE MYCOLOGIQUE DE FRANCE. [Bull. trimest. soc. mycol. Fr.]. **Added/Corp** Societe Mycologique de France. **VFOAT** Bulletin de la Societe Mycologique de France. Vol. 46, No. 1 (1924)-. Bulletin. French (summaries and/or abstracts in English). Three times a year. $69.99. Societe Mycologique de France, 18 rue de l Ermitage, 75020 Paris France. **Tel** 011 33 1 43663540. cum. index. ***Continues** Bulletin de le Societe Mycologique de France.*
Ind/Abst Microbiol. Abstr. Sect. C; Life Sci. Collect.

LC QK580
DD 589 US
CATALOGUE OF FILAMENTOUS FUNGI. **Main/Corp** American Type Culture Collection. **VFOAT** ATCC Catalogue of Filamentous Fungi; ATCC Filamentous Fungi. 18th Ed. (1991)-. English. Irregular. American Type Culture Collection, 12301 Parklawn Drive, Rockville MD 20852. **Tel** (301)881-2600, FAX (301)231-5826, telex 898-055. ***Continues in part** Catalogue of Fungi/Yeasts., 1053-3370.*

LC S **ISSN** 1013-8609
DD 630 NE
CEREAL RUSTS AND POWDERY MILDEWS BULLETIN. **See** Agriculture-Crop Production and Soils.

LC SB353.3.C6 C5
DD 581.6/32/05 CC
CHUNG-KUO SHIH YUNG CHUN. **Added/Corp** Kun-Ming Shih Yung Chun Yen Chiu So. Chuan Kuo Shih Yung Chun Ko Chi Ching Pao Chung Hsin Chan (China). **VFOAT** Zhongguo Shiyongjun; Edible Fungi of China; Zhongguo Shiyong Jun. (198?)-. Periodical. Chinese. Six times a year.
Ind/Abst Agric. Eng. Abstr.; Biodeter. Abstr.; For. Prod. Abstr. (1991-); For. Abstr.; Hortic. Abstr.; Plant Breed. Abstr.; Postharvest News Inf.; Rev. Agric. Entomol.; Rev. Plant Pathol.; Wheat Barley Trit. Abstr.

ISSN 0525-6097
NE
CODEN COOLBM
COOLIA. **Added/Corp** Nederlandse Mycologische Vereniging. Vol. 1 (1954)-. Academic Scholarly Publication. Dutch (summaries and/or abstracts in English). Four times a year. Fl40.00. Nederlandse Mycolog Vereniging, Weverstraat 4, 9411 NC Beilin Netherlands. **Tel** 011 31 59 3024617. cum. index. Documents available from BIOSIS Document Express.
Ind/Abst Biol. Abstr.; EMBASE; Rev. Plant Pathol.; Soils Fert.

ISSN 0181-1584
FR
CODEN CRMYD6
Pr Rev.
CRYPTOGAMIE. MYCOLOGIE (1979). (CRYPTOGAMIE. MYCOLOGIE.). [Cryptogam., Mycol.]. **VFOAT** Mycologie. Vol.1, No.1 (1980)-. Academic Scholarly Publication. French (English, Spanish, German and Italian; summaries and/or abstracts in English). Four times a year. $83.11. Cryptogamie, 12 rue de Buffon, 75005 Paris France. **Tel** 33 1 40793184. **ED** Bruno Dennetiere. Index available (bound in last issue). **Bk Rev**, (Qty: 4). **Circ:** 400. Documents available from The Genuine Article, BIOSIS Document Express, CASDDS. ***Continues** Revue de Mycologie.*
Desc: Covers fungi, mycology, systematics, taxonomy, phytopathology, physiology, cytology and ecology.
Ind/Abst Biocont. News Inf.; Biodeter. Abstr. (19??-19??); Biol. Abstr.; Chem. Abstr. (1980-1983); Curr. Contents Agric. Biol. Environ. Sci.; Ecol. Abstr.; Ecology Abstr.; For. Prod. Abstr.; For. Abstr.; Maize Abstr.; Microbiol. Abstr. Sect. A; Microbiol. Abstr. Sect. C; Nutr. Abstr. Rev., Ser. B, Live Feeds and Feed.; Life Sci. Collect.; Plant Breed. Abstr.; Plant Grow. Reg. Abstr.; Res. Alert [Select. Cov.]; Rev. Med. Vet. Mycology; Rev. Plant Pathol.; SCISEARCH; Soils Fert.; Soyabean Abstr.

ISSN 0177-4204
US
CCC
NLM W1; CU82IT **CODEN** CTMMEJ
CURRENT TOPICS IN MEDICAL MYCOLOGY. [Curr. top. med. mycol.]. Vol. 1 (1985)-. Academic Scholarly Publication. English. Irregular. Prous Science Publishers, Apartado de Correos 540, 08080 Barcelona Spain. **Tel** 011 34 3 4592220, FAX 011 34 3 4581535. Documents available from BIOSIS Document Express, CASDDS.
Desc: Summarizes topics of current interest to medical mycologists and others working in microbiology and immunology.
Ind/Abst Biol. Abstr. (1985-); Chem. Abstr. (1985-); Health Plan. Adminis.; Index Med. (Vol. 1, 1985-).

LC QK600 .C4
XR
•**CZECH MYCOLOGY.** **Added/Corp** Ceska Vedecka Spolecnost pro Mykologii. Vol. 47, No. 1 (Dec. 1993)-. Periodical. English (French and German; summaries and/or abstracts in Czech and Slovak). Four times a year. $135.88. **(Subscription address:** Kubon & Sagner, ABT Zeitschriftenimport, D 80328 Munich Germany. **Tel** 011 49 89 54218130.) ***Continues** Ceska Mykologie, 0009-0476.*

LC QK600 .E95 **ISSN** 0147-5975
DD 589/.2/05 US
CCC
NLM W1; EX506R **CODEN** EXMYD2
Pr Rev.
EXPERIMENTAL MYCOLOGY. [Exp. mycol.]. Vol. 1 (Mar. 1977)-. Academic Scholarly Publication. English. Four times a year. $180.00. Academic Press Inc., 6277 Sea Harbor Drive, Orlando FL 32887. **Tel** (800)543-9534, (407)345-4100, FAX (407)352-3445. **ED** Robert Brambl. Documents available from The Genuine Article, CASDDS.
Desc: Devoted to the publication of experimental investigations that relate structure and function to growth, reproduction, morphogenesis, and differentiation of fungi and their traditional allies. Presents studies on the cellular, subcellular, and molecular levels of organization.
Ind/Abst AgBiotech News Inf.; AGRICOLA [Full Cov.]; Biocont. News Inf.; Biodeter. Abstr. (1991-); Chem. Abstr.; Curr. Cit.; Curr. Contents Agric. Biol. Environ. Sci.; Curr. Contents Life Sci.; EMBASE; Genet. Abstr.; Hortic. Abstr.; Microbiol. Abstr. Sect. A; Microbiol. Abstr. Sect. C; Life Sci. Collect.; PESTDOC; Plant Breed. Abstr.; Res. Alert [Full Cov.]; Rev. Agric. Entomol.; Rev. Med. Vet. Mycology; Rev. Plant Pathol.; Sci. Cit. Index; SCISEARCH; Soils Fert.

LC QK623.S73 N48 **ISSN** 0895-1942
DD 589.2/0415/05 US
NLM W1; FU54F **CODEN** FGNEEA
Pr Rev.
FUNGAL GENETICS NEWSLETTER. **Added/Corp** Reed College (Portland, Or.). Biology Dept. Fungal Genetics Stock Center (U.S.). **VFOAT** FGN. No. 33 (June 1986)-. Newsletter. English. One time a year (July). $7.00. Fungal Genetics Stock Center, Department of Microbiology, University of Kansas Medical Center, Kansas City KS 66103. **Tel** (913)588-7044, FAX (913)588-7295. **Circ:** 700. Documents available from BIOSIS Document Express. ***Continues** Neurospora Newsletter, 0028-3975.*
Ind/Abst Biol. Abstr. (1986-); Genet. Abstr.; Microbiol. Abstr. Sect. C.

LC QK600 .H35a **ISSN** 0253-651X
DD 589.2 KO
CODEN HKCHDD
HANGUG GYNNHAGHOI JI. (HAN'GUK KYUNHAKHOE CHI.). [Hangug gynnhaghoi ji]. **Main/Corp** Han'Guk Kyunhakhoe. **VFOAT** Korean Journal of Mycology. (19??)-. Periodical. English (Korean). Four times a year. Korean Society of Mycology, Department of Microbial Chemistry, College of Pharmacy, Seoul National University, Seoul 151 Korea Republic. Documents available from CASDDS.
Ind/Abst AGRICOLA; Biocont. News Inf.; Biodeter. Abstr.; Chem. Abstr.; Curr. Cit.; For. Abstr.; NAPRALERT; Life Sci. Collect.; Rev. Med. Vet. Mycology; Rev. Plant Pathol.; Rice Abstr.

LC SB733 .C24 **ISSN** 0009-9716
DD 589.2 UK
NLM W1; IM45725
IMI DESCRIPTIONS OF FUNGI AND BACTERIA. **Added/Corp** C.A.B. International. International Mycological Institute. **VFOAT** Descriptions of Fungi and Bacteria. **VAT** International Mycological Institute Descriptions of Fungi and Bacteria. Set 103 (1991)-. Periodical. English. Four times a year. $92.00 US. CAB International Centre, Wallingford, Oxfordshire OX10 8DE United Kingdom. **Tel** 011 44 1491 832111, FAX 011 44 1491 833508, telex 847964 COMAGG G. ***Continues** CMI Descriptions of Fungi and Bacteria.*

LC SB599 .C57 **ISSN** 0019-3895
UK
NLM ZQK 603 I39
INDEX OF FUNGI / COMMONWEALTH MYCOLOGICAL INSTITUTE. **Added/Corp** Imperial Mycological Institute (Great Britain) Commonwealth Mycological Institute (Great Britain) C-A-B International Mycological Institute. Vol. 1 (July 1940)-. Periodical. English. Two times a year. $110.00. CAB International Centre, Wallingford, Oxfordshire OX10 8DE United Kingdom. **Tel** 011 44 1491 832111, FAX 011 44 1491 833508, telex 847964 COMAGG G. **ED** P. M. Kirk. Bound Index published separately, free upon request. available on an online database from European Space Agency; DIALOG; DIMDI; CISTI; and BRS.
Desc: List names of new genera, species and varieties, new combinations and new names of fungi and lichens, compiled from world literature.
Ind/Abst Rev. Med. Vet. Mycology; Rev. Plant Pathol.

II
INDIAN JOURNAL OF MUSHROOMS. (19??)-. Periodical. English. Two times a year.
Ind/Abst Hortic. Abstr.; Nutr. Abstr. Rev., Ser. A, Hum. Exp.; Rice Abstr.

ISSN 0303-4097
II
CODEN IJMPAK
INDIAN JOURNAL OF MYCOLOGY AND PLANT PATHOLOGY. [Indian j. mycol. plant pathol.]. **Added/Corp** Society of Mycology and Plant Pathology. Vol. 1 (Jan. 1971)-. Periodical. English (summaries and/or abstracts in Hindi). Three times a year (Apr., Aug., Dec.). $100.00. Society of Mycology & Plant Pathology, Rajasthan College Agriculture, 313 001 Udaipur India. **Tel** 011 91 294 27760, 011 91 294 28612, FAX 011 91 294 524259. **(Subscription address:** Prints India, 11 Darya Ganj, New Delhi 110002 India. **Tel** 011 91 11 3268645, FAX 011 91 11 3275542, telex 31-61087 PRIN-IN.) **ED** Dr. O. Gemawat. Index available (Bound in 3rd issue in December.). **Bk Rev. Circ:** 1,000 (ctrl). Documents available from BIOSIS Document Express, CASDDS.
Ind/Abst AGRICOLA; Biocont. News Inf.; Biodeter. Abstr. (1991-); Biol. Abstr.; Chem. Abstr.; Cot. Trop. Fibr. Abstr. Bibliogr.; Field Crop Abstr.; For. Prod. Abstr.; For. Abstr.; Grass. Forage Abstr.; Hortic. Abstr.; Irr. Drain. Abstr.; Maize Abstr.; Microbiol. Abstr. Sect. B (19??-19??); Microbiol. Abstr. Sect. A; Microbiol. Abstr. Sect. C; Nematol. Abstr.; Ornamental Hort.; Life Sci. Collect.; Plant Breed. Abstr.; Plant Grow. Reg. Abstr.; Postharvest News Inf.; Potato Abstr.; Rev. Med. Vet. Mycology; Rev. Plant Pathol.; Rice Abstr.; Seed Abstr.; Soils Fert.; Sorghum Mill. Abstr.; Soyabean Abstr.; Virol. AIDS Abstr.

ISSN 1156-5233
FR
UDC 576.8
JOURNAL DE MYCOLOGIE MEDICALE PARIS. (JOURNAL DE MYCOLOGIE MEDICALE.). (1991)-. Periodical. French. Four times a year. $211.73. Masson Editeur, BP 22, 41354 Vineuil Cedex France. **Tel** 011 33 54 504612, FAX 011 33 54 504611. ***Continues*** *Bulletin de la Societe Francaise de Mycologie Medicale, 0037-9336.*
Ind/Abst Curr. Cit.

LC RC117 .S3 **ISSN** 0268-1218
DD 616.9/69/005 UK
CCC
NLM W1; JO749PC **CODEN** JMVMEO
Pr Rev.
JOURNAL OF MEDICAL AND VETERINARY MYCOLOGY. (JOURNAL OF MEDICAL AND VETERINARY MYCOLOGY : BI-MONTHLY PUBLICATION OF THE INTERNATIONAL SOCIETY FOR HUMAN AND ANIMAL MYCOLOGY.). [J. med. vet. mycol.]. **Added/Corp** International Society for Human and Animal Mycology. Vol. 24, No. 1 (Feb. 1986)-. Academic Scholarly Publication. English. Six times a year. $544.00. Blackwell Scientific Publications Ltd, Marston Book Services, PO Box 88, Oxford OX2 ONE United Kingdom. **Tel** 011 44 1865 206206, FAX 011 44 1865 206219, telex 837 515 MARDIS G. Index available in last issue of volume--attached. available on microfilm and microfiche from University Microfilms International (UMI). Documents available from The Genuine Article, BIOSIS Document Express, CASDDS, ADONIS. ***Continues*** *Sabouraudia, 0036-2174.*
Ind/Abst ADONIS; Biol. Abstr. (1986-); Chem. Abstr. (1986-); Curr. Aware. Biol. Sci., CABS; Curr. Cit.; Curr. Contents Life Sci.; Dairy Sci. Abstr.; EMBASE; Fish Rev. (Jan. 1989-July 1992); Immunol. Abstr.; Index Med.; Index Vet.; Microbiol. Abstr. Sect. A; Microbiol. Abstr. Sect. C; PESTDOC; Res. Alert [Full Cov.]; Rev. Med. Vet. Mycology; Sci. Cit. Index; SCISEARCH; Small Anim. Abstr. Bibliogr.; Soils Fert.; Vet. Bull.; Trop. Dis. Bull.; Wildl. Rev. (Jan. 1989-July 1992).

ISSN 0971-3719
II
JOURNAL OF MYCOPATHOLOGICAL RESEARCH. (1990)-. English. ***Continues*** *Indian Journal of Mycological Research, 0537-2054.*

LC QK600 **ISSN** 0453-3402
DD 589.2/05 FI
CODEN KRSTA4
KARSTENIA. [Karstenia]. Vol. 1 (1950)-. Periodical. English (Finnish, German and Swedish). Two times a year. $50.00. Societas Mycologica Fennica, Unioninkatu 44, SF-00170 Helsinki 17 Finland. **Tel** 358 0 799455 44. Documents available from BIOSIS Document Express, CASDDS.
Ind/Abst AgBiotech News Inf.; Biol. Abstr.; Chem. Abstr.; For. Prod. Abstr.; Life Sci. Collect.

LC QK609.I5 K37 **ISSN** 0379-5179
DD 589/.2/05 II
CODEN KVAKAH
KAVAKA. [Kavaka]. **Added/Corp** Mycological Society of India. Vol. 1 (1973)-. English. Two times a year. $20.00. Mycological Society of India, Treasurer K G Mukerji, Department of Botany, University of Delhi, Delhi 7 India. **(Subscription address:** Prints India, 11 Darya Ganj, New Delhi 110002 India. **Tel** 011 91 11 3268645, FAX 011 91 11 3275542, telex 31-61087 PRIN-IN.) **ED** C V Subramaniam. **Bk Rev. Ad Acc. Circ:** 500 (ctrl). Documents available from BIOSIS Document Express.
Ind/Abst Biol. Abstr.; Life Sci. Collect.; Postharvest News Inf.; Rev. Plant Pathol.; Rice Abstr.; Seed Abstr.; Soils Fert.

ISSN 0388-8266
JA
NLM W1 KI718H **CODEN** KJKKAH
KINJIN KENKYUJO KENKYU HOKOKU. (KINJIN KENKYUSHO KENKYU HOKOKU. REPORTS OF THE TOTTORI MYCOLOGICAL INSTITUTE.). [Kinjin Kenkyujo kenkyu hokoku]. **Main/Corp** Kinjin Kenkyusho. **Added/Corp** Kinjin Kenkyusho. Reports of the Tottori Mycological Institute. **VFOAT** Reports of the Tottori Mycological Institute. (1961)-. Periodical. Japanese (English). Nihon Kinoko Senta Kinjin Kenkyujo, (Tottori Mycological Institute), Japan Kinoko Research Centre, 211 Hirohata, Kokoge Tottorishi, Tottoriken 689-11 Japan. Documents available from BIOSIS Document Express.
Ind/Abst Biodeter. Abstr.; Biol. Abstr.; Rev. Plant Pathol.

LC QK600 .B25A **ISSN** 0377-0990
DD 589/.2/028 NE
LIST OF CULTURES. **Main/Corp** Koninklijke Nederlandse Akademie van Wetenschappen. Centraal Bureau voor Schimmelcultures. **Added/Corp** Koninklijke Nederlandse Akademie van Wetenschappen. (19??)-. English (Dutch). Irregular. Centraal Bureau voor Schimmelcultures, PO Box 273, 3740 AG Baarn Netherlands. **Tel** (02154)11841, FAX 16142. Index available.
Desc: Catalogue of living fungi in Centraal Bureau voor Schimmelcultures collection.

ISSN 0394-2597
IT
UDC 582.28
MICOLOGIA E VEGETAZIONE MEDITERRANEA. (1986)-. Periodical. Multiple languages. Two times a year.
Ind/Abst Rev. Plant Pathol.

LC QK600 .M52 **ISSN** 0390-0460
IT
CODEN MIITDI
MICOLOGIA ITALIANA. [Micol. ital.]. **Added/Corp** Unione Micologica Italiana. Vol. 1 (Apr./July 1972)-. Periodical. Italian (summaries and/or abstracts in English). Three times a year. L23850. Edagricole, PO Box 2157, 40100 Bologna Italy. **Tel** 011 39 51 492211 Ext. 22, FAX 011 39 51 493660, telex 510336 EDAGRI. Documents available from BIOSIS Document Express.
Ind/Abst AGRICOLA; Biodeter. Abstr. (1991-); Biol. Abstr.; For. Prod. Abstr. (1991-); Maize Abstr.; Microbiol. Abstr. Sect. C; Life Sci. Collect.; Rev. Plant Pathol.

ISSN 0187-8921
MX
MICOLOGIA NEOTROPICAL APLICADA. [Micol. neotrop. apl.]. **Added/Corp** Instituto de Investigaciones Sobre Recursos Bioticos (Mexico) Instituto de Micologia Neotropical Aplicada (Mexico) Consejo Nacional de Ciencia y Tecnologia (Mexico) O.R.S.T.O.M. (Agency : France) International Foundation for Science. Vol. 1 (Nov. 1988)-. Periodical. Spanish (English). One time a year. $15.00 Mexico; $20.00 other. Instituto de Micologia, Apartado Postal, 72001 Puebla Mexico. **Tel** 011 52 22 851442.

ISSN 0133-9095
HU
UDC 630.44
MIKOLOGIAI KOZLEMENYEK. [Mikol. k...ozl.]. (1963)-. Periodical. Hungarian. Three times a year.
Ind/Abst For. Abstr.; Rev. Plant Pathol.

ISSN 0026-3648
RU
CCC
NLM W1 MI372 **CODEN** MIFIB2
Pr Rev.
MIKOLOGIJA I FITOPATOLOGIJA. (MIKOLOGIIA I FITOPATOLOGIIA.). [Mikol. fitopatol.]. **Added/Corp** Akademiia Nauk SSSR. Vol. 1 (1967)-. Academic Scholarly Publication. Russian (English; table of contents in English). Six times a year. $216.25. **(Subscription address:** East View Publications Inc., 3020 Harbor Lane North, Suite 110, Minneapolis MN 55447. **Tel** (800)477-1005, (612)550-0961, FAX (612)559-2931.) Documents available from The Genuine Article, BIOSIS Document Express, CASDDS.
Ind/Abst Biodeter. Abstr.; Biol. Abstr.; Chem. Abstr.; Cot. Trop. Fibr. Abstr. Bibliogr.; Ecology Abstr.; For. Abstr.; Maize Abstr.; Microbiol. Abstr. Sect. A; Microbiol. Abstr. Sect. C; Life Sci. Collect.; PESTDOC; Plant Breed. Abstr.; Potato Abstr.; Poult. Abstr.; Res. Alert [Full Cov.]; Rev. Plant Pathol.; Rice Abstr.; Sci. Cit. Index; SCISEARCH.

ISSN 1078-4314
DD 589 US
MUSHROOM CULTURE, THE. [Mushroom cult.]. **Added/Corp** Florida Mycology Research Center. **VFOAT** Journal of Mushroom Cultivation. (Apr. 1984)-. Periodical. English. Four times a year. $20.00. Florida Mycology Research Center, PO Box 8104, Pensacola FL 32505. **Tel** (904)327-4378.

HK
SUSPENDED
MUSHROOM JOURNAL FOR THE TROPICS. **Added/Corp** International Mushroom Society for the Tropics. Vol. 7, No. 1 (Jan. 1987)-Suspended (Dec. 1991). Periodical. English. Four times a year. International Mushroom Society Tropics, Department of Biology, Chinese University, Shatin NT Hong Kong. **Tel** 011 852 0 26952286, 011 852 0 26952283, FAX 011 852 0 26035646. ***Continues*** *Mushroom Newsletter for the Tropics, 0258-8641.*
Ind/Abst Nematol. Abstr.

ISSN 0740-8161
US
MUSHROOM (MOSCOW, IDAHO). (MUSHROOM.). [Mushroom]. Vol. 1, No. 1 (Fall 1983)-. Periodical. English. Four times a year (Mar., June, Sept., Dec.). $16.00. Mushroom, Box 3156 University Station, Moscow ID 83843. **Tel** (208)882-8720. **ED** Don H. Coombs and Maggie Rogers. **Bk Rev. Ad Acc. Circ:** 2,100.

LC QK600 .M8 **ISSN** 0027-5514
DD 589/.2/05 US
CCC
NLM W1 MY734 **CODEN** MYCOAE
Pr Rev.
MYCOLOGIA. [Mycologia]. **Added/Corp** New York Botanical Garden. Mycological Society of America. Vol. 1 (Jan. 1909)-. Periodical. English. Six times a year. $99.00. New York Botanical Garden, Scientific Publishing Department B, New York NY 10458-5126. **Tel** (718)817-8721, FAX (718)817-6504, telex 5106015451. **(Subscription address:** Mycologia, PO Box 1897, Lawrence KS 66044-8897.) **ED** Ronald Peterson. Index available. cum. index. **Bk Rev. Ad Acc. Circ:** 3,000 (ctrl). available on microfilm and microfiche from University Microfilms International (UMI). Documents available from The Genuine Article, BIOSIS Document Express, CASDDS, Documents on Demand. ***Formed by the union of*** *Mycological Bulletin* ***and*** *Journal of Mycology, 1052-0368.*
Desc: Primary research and review articles on the fungi and lichens.
Ind/Abst AgBiotech News Inf.; AGRICOLA [Full Cov.]; Biocont. News Inf.; Biodeter. Abstr. (19??-19??); Biol. Agric. Index; Biol. Abstr.; Chem. Abstr.; Curr. Aware. Biol. Sci., CABS; Curr. Cit.; Curr. Contents Agric. Biol. Environ. Sci.; Ecol. Abstr.; Ecology Abstr.; Energy Inf. Abstr.; Energy Res. Abstr.; Environ. Abstr.; For. Prod. Abstr. (19??-19??); For. Abstr.; Geogr. Abstr. Phys. Geogr.; GeoRef; Hortic. Abstr.; Index Vet.; Maize Abstr.; Microbiol. Abstr. Sect. A; Microbiol. Abstr. Sect. C; Nematol. Abstr.; Life Sci. Collect.; PESTDOC; Plant Breed. Abstr.; Plant Genet. Resour. Abstr.; Plant Grow. Reg. Abstr.; Postharvest News Inf.; Res. Alert [Full Cov.]; Rev. Agric. Entomol.; Rev. Med. Vet. Entomol.; Rev. Med. Vet. Mycology; Rev. Plant Pathol.; Rice Abstr.; Sci. Cit. Index; SCISEARCH; Seed Abstr.; Soils Fert.; Sorghum Mill. Abstr.; Soyabean Abstr.; Vitis Vitic. Enol. Abstr.; Wheat Barley Trit. Abstr.

LC QK600 **ISSN** 0256-310X
DD 589.2 SZ
CODEN MYHEED
MYCOLOGIA HELVETICA. [Mycol. helv.]. **Added/Corp** Verband Schweizerischer Vereine fuer Pilzkunde. Schweizerische Mykologische Gesellschaft. (1983)-. Periodical. German (English, French and Italian). Two times a year. $75.44. Systematisch Geobotanisches, Altenbergrain 21 B Senn Irlet, CH-3013 Bern Switzerland. **Tel** 011 41 31 654511. Documents available from BIOSIS Document Express.
Ind/Abst Biodeter. Abstr.; Biol. Abstr. (1984-); For. Prod. Abstr. (1991-); Microbiol. Abstr. Sect. C.

ISSN 0580-3829
GW
NLM W1 MY734K
MYCOLOGIA MEMOIR. [Mycol. Mem.]. **Added/Corp** New York Botanical Garden. Mycological Society of America. (1965)-. Monographic series. English. Irregular. Price varies per volume. Lubrecht & Cramer Ltd, 38 County Route 48, Forestburgh NY 12777. **Tel** (914)794-8539.
Desc: Mycology.
Ind/Abst AGRICOLA [Full Cov.].

LC QK600 **ISSN** 0027-5522
DD 589.2 UK
CODEN CMIMAE
MYCOLOGICAL PAPERS. COMMONWEALTH MYCOLOGICAL INSTITUTE. (MYCOLOGICAL PAPERS.). [Mycol. pap., Commonw. Mycol. Inst.]. **Added/Corp** Imperial Mycological Institute (Great Britain) Imperial Bureau of Mycology (Great Britain) Commonwealth Mycological Institute (Great Britain) C.A.B. International. Mycological Institute. No. 1 (1925)-. Monographic series. English. Irregular. Price varies per volume. CAB International Centre, Wallingford, Oxfordshire OX10 8DE United Kingdom. **Tel** 011 44 1491 832111, FAX 011 44 1491 833508, telex 847964 COMAGG G. Documents available from BIOSIS Document Express.
Desc: Devoted to the systematics and taxonomy of fungi.
Ind/Abst AGRICOLA; Biodeter. Abstr.; Biol. Abstr.; Life Sci. Collect.

LC QK600 .B6 ISSN 0953-7562
DD 589.2/05 UK
CCC
NLM W1; MY734KM CODEN MYCRER
Pr Rev.

MYCOLOGICAL RESEARCH. [Mycol. res.]. **Added/Corp** Federation of European Microbiological Societies. British Mycological Society. Vol. 1, Pt. 1 (Jan. 1989)-. Academic Scholarly Publication. English. Twelve times a year. $752.00. Cambridge University Press, The Edinburgh Building, Shaftesbury Road, Cambridge CB2 2RU United Kingdom. **Tel** 011 44 1223 312393, FAX 011 44 1223 315052, telex 851-817256. **(Subscription address:** Cambridge University Press / North America, 110 Midland Avenue, Port Chester NY 10573. **Tel** (800)431-1580, (914)937-9600.**) ED** D. Moore. Index available (free). **Bk Rev.** available on microfilm and microfiche from University Microfilms International (UMI). Documents available from The Genuine Article, BIOSIS Document Express, CASDDS. ***Continues*** *Transactions of the British Mycological Society, 0007-1536.*
Desc: An international journal of fungal biology which covers ecology, physiology, plant pathology and systematics of fungi and is especially active in new areas such as ultrastructure, biochemistry, molecular biology, biodeterioration, biotechnology and genetics. The journal publishes full research papers, reviews on topical subjects, short communications and book reviews.
Ind/Abst AgBiotech News Inf.; AGRICOLA [Full Cov.]; Biocont. News Inf. (19??-19??); Biodeter. Abstr. (19??-19??); Biol. Abstr. (1989-); Chem. Abstr.; Curr. Aware. Biol. Sci., CABS; Curr. Cit.; Curr. Contents Agric. Biol. Environ. Sci.; Ecol. Abstr.; Ecology Abstr.; For. Prod. Abstr. (1991-); For. Abstr.; Genet. Abstr.; Hortic. Abstr.; Index Vet.; Irr. Drain. Abstr.; Maize Abstr.; Microbiol. Abstr. Sect. A; Microbiol. Abstr. Sect. C; Nematol. Abstr.; PESTDOC; Plant Breed. Abstr.; Plant Genet. Resour. Abstr.; Postharvest News Inf.; Potato Abstr.; Res. Alert [Full Cov.]; Rev. Agric. Entomol.; Rev. Med. Vet. Entomol.; Rev. Med. Vet. Mycology; Rev. Plant Pathol.; Rice Abstr.; Sci. Cit. Index; SCISEARCH; Seed Abstr.; Soils Fert.; Sorghum Mill. Abstr.; Soyabean Abstr.; Weed Abstr.; Wheat Barley Trit. Abstr.

LC QK600 .B622 ISSN 0269-915X
DD 589.2 UK
CCC
CODEN MYCOEI

MYCOLOGIST, THE. [Mycologist]. **Added/Corp** British Mycological Society. (1987)-. Academic Scholarly Publication. English. Four times a year. $50.00. Cambridge University Press, The Edinburgh Building, Shaftesbury Road, Cambridge CB2 2RU United Kingdom. **Tel** 011 44 1223 312393, FAX 011 44 1223 315052, telex 851-817256. **(Subscription address:** Cambridge University Press / North America, 110 Midland Avenue, Port Chester NY 10573. **Tel** (800)431-1580, (914)937-9600.**) ED** D. N. Pegler. Index available. **Bk Rev. Ad Acc. Circ:** 3,000. available on microfilm from University Microfilms International (UMI). Documents available from BIOSIS Document Express. ***Continues*** *Bulletin of the British Mycological Society, 0007-1528.*
Desc: Publishes material of interest to both specialists and non-professionals in mycology. It provides an outlet for news of international mycological activity and a forum for the exchange of views. A central pullout supplement details British Mycological Society and other activities. There are regular features for beginners, enthusiastic amateurs and professional scientists. Contributions also include pieces on mycotechnology, gastronomy, biographical accounts of individuals and organizations, and regular book reviews.
Ind/Abst Biocont. News Inf. (19??-19??); Biodeter. Abstr. (1991-); Biol. Abstr. (1987-); Curr. Aware. Biol. Sci., CABS; Ecol. Abstr.; Geogr. Abstr. Phys. Geogr.; Hortic. Abstr.; Microbiol. Abstr. Sect. A; Microbiol. Abstr. Sect. C; Ornamental Hort. (1991-); PESTDOC; Rev. Med. Vet. Mycology; Rev. Plant Pathol.

ISSN 0730-9597
US
CODEN MYSEDX

MYCOLOGY SERIES. [Mycol. ser.]. (1981)-. Academic Scholarly Publication. English. Irregular. Price varies per volume. Marcel Dekker Inc., 270 Madison Avenue, New York NY 10016. **Tel** (212)696-9000, (800)228-1160, FAX (212)685-4540, telex 421419. **(Subscription address:** Marcel Dekker Inc., PO Box 5017, Monticello NY 12701. **Tel** (800)228-1160.**) Bk Rev.** Documents available from BIOSIS Document Express, CASDDS.
Desc: Presents topics in mycology such as fungal protoplasts and the stress tolerance of fungi.
Ind/Abst AGRICOLA [Full Cov.]; Biol. Abstr.; Chem. Abstr.

LC QK600 .M95 ISSN 0301-486X
DD 589/.2/0469 NE
CCC
NLM W1 MY735 CODEN MYCPAH
Pr Rev.

MYCOPATHOLOGIA (1975). (MYCOPATHOLOGIA.). [Mycopathologia]. **Added/Corp** C.A.B. International. Mycological Institute. Vol. 55 (Feb. 1975)-. English (Multiple languages). Twelve times a year. $1130.00. Kluwer Academic Publishers, Postbus 322, 3300 AH Dordrecht The Netherlands. **Tel** 011 31 78 524400, FAX 011 31 78 183273, telex 20083. **ED** Arthur D. Salvo. **Acid Free.** available on microfilm and microfiche from University Microfilms International (UMI). Documents available from The Genuine Article, BIOSIS Document Express, CASDDS. ***Continues*** *Mycopathologia et Mycologia Applicata, 0027-5530.*
Desc: An international journal devoted to the study of the role of fungi in disease and biodeterioration. The journal covers a wide range of topics that is unique in breadth and depth, including original articles and critical reviews in the fields of medical and veterinary mycology, plant mycology (crop protection), mycotoxicosis, and applied industrial mycology. Also contains selected papers on systematics, taxonomy and basic biology of fungi involved in any of the above fields.
Ind/Abst AgBiotech News Inf.; AGRICOLA; Biocont. News Inf. (1991-); Biodeter. Abstr. (19??-19??); Biol. Abstr.; Chem. Abstr.; Curr. Aware. Biol. Sci., CABS; Curr. Cit.; Curr. Contents Agric. Biol. Environ. Sci.; Curr. Contents Life Sci.; Dairy Sci. Abstr.; EMBASE; Food Sci. Technol. Abstr.; Immunol. Abstr.; Index Med.; Index Vet.; Maize Abstr.; Microbiol. Abstr. Sect. A; Microbiol. Abstr. Sect. C; NAPRALERT; Nematol. Abstr.; Nutr. Abstr. Rev., Ser. B, Live Feeds and Feed.; Nutr. Abstr. Rev., Ser. A, Hum. Exp.; Life Sci. Collect.; PESTDOC; Plant Breed. Abstr.; Postharvest News Inf.; Poult. Abstr.; Ref. Upd. Deluxe Ed.; Res. Alert [Full Cov.]; Rev. Med. Vet. Entomol.; Rev. Med. Vet. Mycology; Rev. Plant Pathol.; Rice Abstr.; Sci. Cit. Index; SCISEARCH; Seed Abstr.; Small Anim. Abstr. Bibliogr.; Soils Fert.; Soyabean Abstr.; Vet. Bull.; Wheat Barley Trit. Abstr.

LC QK604.2.M92 M92 ISSN 0940-6360
GW
CCC
CODEN MCOREZ

MYCORRHIZA. Vol. 1, No. 1 (Sept. 1991)-. Periodical. English. Six times a year. $747.00. Springer-Verlag GmbH & Company KG, Heidelberger Platz 3, D-14197 Berlin Germany. **Tel** 011 49 30 8207223, FAX 011 49 30 8214091, telex 183 319 SPBLN D. **(Subscription address:** Springer-Verlag New York Inc. / North America, PO Box 2485, Journal Fulfillment, Secaucus NJ 07096. **Tel** (201)348-4033, (800)777-4643, FAX (201)348-4505.**) ED** W Julich. available on microfilm and microfiche from University Microfilms International (UMI).
Desc: International journal devoted to all aspects of mycorrhizal research, i.e. the symbiosis between higher plants and certain fungi or mushrooms.
Ind/Abst Sci. Cit. Index.

LC QK600 .N536 ISSN 1340-3540
JA

•**MYCOSCIENCE.** Vol. 35, No. 1 (Apr. 15, 1994)-. Periodical. English. Four times a year. $120.00. Nihon Kin Gakkai, (Mycological Soc. of Japan), Gakkai Senta Biru, 4-16 Yayoi 2 Chome, Bunkyoku Tokyo 113 Japan. **(Subscription address:** Japan Publications Trading Company Ltd., PO Box 5030, Tokyo International, Tokyo 100-31 Japan. **Tel** 011 81 3 3292 3753.) Documents available from BIOSIS Document Express, CASDDS. ***Continues*** *Nihon Kingakkai Kaiho, 0029-0289.*

ISSN 0933-7407
GW
CCC
NLM W1; MY735H CODEN MYCSEU

MYCOSES. [Mycoses]. **Added/Corp** Deutschsprachige Mykologische Gesellschaft. Vol. 31 No. 1 Jan. (1988)-. Periodical. English (German). Six times a year. $351.59. Blackwell Wissenschafts-Verlag, Kurfuerstendamm 57, D-10707 Berlin Germany. **Tel** 011 49 30 32790623, 011 49 30 32790624, FAX 011 49 30 327 90610. **ED** J. Mueller. available on microfilm from University Microfilms International (UMI). Documents available from The Genuine Article, BIOSIS Document Express, ADONIS. ***Continues*** *Mykosen, 0027-5557.*
Desc: Provides an international forum for original papers on the pathogenesis, diagnosis, therapy, prophylaxis, and epidemiology of fungal infectious diseases in humans and animals as well as on the biology of pathogenic fungi.
Ind/Abst ADONIS; Biol. Abstr. (1988-); Curr. Cit.; Curr. Contents Life Sci.; EMBASE; Immunol. Abstr.; Index Med. (Jan. 1988-); Index Vet.; Maize Abstr.; Microbiol. Abstr. Sect. B; Microbiol. Abstr. Sect. A; Microbiol. Abstr. Sect. C; PESTDOC; Res. Alert [Full Cov.]; Rev. Med. Vet. Mycology; Rice Abstr.; Sci. Cit. Index; SCISEARCH; Small Anim. Abstr. Bibliogr.; Soils Fert.; Vet. Bull.; Wheat Barley Trit. Abstr.

CC

MYCOSYSTEMA : ANNUAL REPORT OF SYSTEMATIC MYCOLOGY & LICHENOLOGY LABORATORY, INSTITUTE OF MICROBIOLOGY, ACADEMIA SINICA. **Added/Corp** Chung-kuo ko Hsueh Yuan. Chen Chun ti i hsi Tung Hsueh Kai Fang yen Chiu Shih Yen shih. **VFOAT** Chen Chun Hsi Tung. (1988)-. Periodical. English (summaries and/or abstracts in Chinese). One time a year. Science Press, 16 Donghuangchenggen North Street, Beijing 100707, People's Republic of China. **Tel** 011 86 1 4019821, 011 86 1 4010642, FAX 011 86 1 4012180, 011 86 1 4019810, telex 210147.
Ind/Abst Rev. Plant Pathol.

LC QK603.2 .M9 ISSN 0093-4666
DD 589/.2/012 US
CODEN MYXNAE
Pr Rev.

MYCOTAXON. [Mycotaxon]. (1974)-. Periodical. English (French). Four times a year (Feb., May, July, Oct.). $65.00 (multiuser), $30.00 (individuals) US; $67.00 (multiuser), $32.00 (individuals) Canada and Mexico; $70.00 (multiuser), $37.00 (individuals) other. Mycotaxon, PO Box 264, Ithaca NY 14851-0264. **Tel** (607)273-4357, FAX (607)273-4357. **ED** Richard P. Korf. Index available. cum. index. **Bk Rev. Circ:** 600. available on microfilm from University Microfilms International (UMI). Documents available from The Genuine Article, BIOSIS Document Express.
Desc: Taxonomy and nomenclature of fungi and lichens.
Ind/Abst AGRICOLA [Full Cov.]; Biocont. News Inf.; Biodeter. Abstr.; Biol. Abstr.; Curr. Aware. Biol. Sci., CABS; Curr. Cit.; Curr. Contents Agric. Biol. Environ. Sci.; For. Abstr.; Life Sci. Collect.; Ref. Upd. Deluxe Ed.; Res. Alert [Full Cov.]; Rev. Med. Vet. Entomol.; Rev. Med. Vet. Mycology; Rev. Plant Pathol.; Sci. Cit. Index; SCISEARCH; Seed Abstr.; Soils Fert.; Vitis Vitic. Enol. Abstr.; Weed Abstr.

ISSN 0178-7888
GW
NLM W1; MY735HG CODEN MYREET

MYCOTOXIN RESEARCH. [Mycotoxin res.]. Vol. 1, No. 1 (1985)-. Academic Scholarly Publication. English. Two times a year. $103.63. HWS / Hans W. Schmidt, PO Box 3628, D-55026 Mainz Germany. **Tel** 011 49 6131 320071. **ED** Rainer Schmidt. **Bk Rev. Ad Acc, Adv Mgr:** Rainer Schmidt. Documents available from CASDDS.
Desc: Contains scientific publications about molds and secondary metabolites (mycotoxins) produced by these molds, particularly in food and feed, and their toxicological effects.
Ind/Abst Biodeter. Abstr. (1991-); Chem. Abstr. (1985-); Curr. Aware. Biol. Sci., CABS; Curr. Cit.; Food Sci. Technol. Abstr.; Index Vet.; Maize Abstr.; Nutr. Abstr. Rev., Ser. B, Live Feeds and Feed.; Nutr. Abstr. Rev., Ser. A, Hum. Exp.; Pig News Inf.; Plant Genet. Resour. Abstr.; Postharvest News Inf.; Rev. Med. Vet. Mycology; Rev. Plant Pathol.; Vet. Bull.; Wheat Barley Trit. Abstr.

LC QK600 .M97 ISSN 0374-9436
XR

MYKOLOGICKY SBORNIK. [Mykol. sb.]. **Added/Corp** CS. Mykologicka Spolecnost v Praze. **VFOAT** Casopis CS. Houbaru (CCSH) Mykologicky Sbornik; Casopis CS. Houbaru Mykologicky Sbornik; Casopis Ceskoslovenskych Houbaru Mykologicky Sbornik; C.C.H. Mykologicky Sbornik; Acta Societatis Mycologicae Cechoslovenicae. (1935)-. Periodical. Czech (table of contents in English and Russian). Twelve times a year. $59.10. **(Subscription address:** Artia Pegas Press Ltd., Palac Metro Narodni Trida 25, 11210 Prague 1 Czech Republic. **Tel** 011 42 2 24196265, 011 42 2 24196266.**)** ***Continues*** *Casopis Ceskoslovenskych Houbaru.*
Ind/Abst AGRICOLA; Rev. Med. Vet. Mycology.

ISSN 0916-4804
JA
NLM W1; NI912T CODEN NIGZE4

NIHON ISHINKIN GAKKAI ZASSHI = JAPANESE JOURNAL OF MEDICAL MYCOLOGY. **Added/Corp** Nihon Ishinkin Gakkai. **VFOAT** Japanese Journal of Medical Mycology. Vol. 31, No. 1 (1990)-. Periodical. Japanese (English; summaries and/or abstracts in English; table of contents in English). Four times a year. $171.50. Japanese Journal of Medical Mycology, 4-16 Yayoi 2-chome, Bunkyo-ku 113 Tokyo Japan. **(Subscription address:** Japan Publications Trading Company Ltd., PO Box 5030, Tokyo International, Tokyo 100-31 Japan. **Tel** 011 81 3 3292 3753.**)** ***Continues*** *Shinkin to Shinkinsho, 0583-0516.*
Ind/Abst Chem. Abstr.; EMBASE.

ISSN 0029-0289
JA
CODEN NGKKAT
TITLE CHANGE

NIPPON KINGAKKAI KAIHO. (NIHON KINGAKKAI KAIHO = TRANSACTIONS OF THE MYCOLOGICAL SOCIETY OF JAPAN.). [Nippon Kingakkai kaiho]. **Main/Corp** Nihon Kingakkai. **Added/Corp** Nihon Kingakkai. Transactions of the Mycological Society of Japan. Nihon Kingakkai. Kaiho. **VFOAT** Transactions of the Mycological Society of Japan. Vol. 1 (May 1956)-(1993). Periodical. Japanese (English). Nihon Kin Gakkai, (Mycological Soc. of Japan), Gakkai Senta Biru, 4-16 Yayoi 2 Chome, Bunkyoku Tokyo 113 Japan. **(Subscription address:** Japan Publications Trading Company Ltd., PO Box 5030, Tokyo International, Tokyo 100-31 Japan. **Tel** 011 81 3 3292 3753.**)** Documents available from BIOSIS Document Express, CASDDS. ***Continued by*** *Mycoscience, 1340-3540.*
Ind/Abst Biocont. News Inf. (1991-); Biodeter. Abstr. (1991-); Biol. Abstr. (?-?); Chem. Abstr. (?-?); For. Prod. Abstr. (1991-); For. Abstr. (?-?); Hortic. Abstr. (?-?); Ornamental Hort. (1991-); Life Sci. Collect. (?-?); Potato Abstr. (?-?); Rev. Med. Vet. Mycology (?-?); Rev. Plant Pathol. (?-?); Rice Abstr. (?-?); Seed Abstr. (?-?); Soils Fert. (?-?).

LC QK600 .P4 **ISSN** 0031-5850
NE
NLM W1 PE8705
Pr Rev.
PERSOONIA. [Persoonia]. **Added/Corp** Rijksherbarium (Netherlands). Vol. 1, Pt. 1 (1959)-. Monographic series. English (French and German). Irregular. Fl.40.00. Rijksherbarium, PO Box 9514, 2300 RA Leiden Netherlands. **Tel** 011 31 71 273500. **ED** C. Bas and T. Van Brummelen. Index available. **Bk Rev. Circ:** 350. Documents available from The Genuine Article. ***Continues*** *Fungus.*
Desc: Morphology and taxonomy of fungi and lichen.
Ind/Abst AGRICOLA [Full Cov.]; Curr. Aware. Biol. Sci., CABS; Curr. Contents Agric. Biol. Environ. Sci.; For. Abstr.; Microbiol. Abstr. Sect. C; Life Sci. Collect.; Res. Alert [Select. Cov.]; Rev. Plant Pathol.; SCISEARCH.

LC QK600 .P42
NE
PERSOONIA. SUPPLEMENT. Added/Corp Rijksherbarium (Netherlands). **VFOAT** World-Monograph of the General Ascobolus and Saccobolus. Vol. 1 (1967)-. Monographic series. English. Price varies per volume. Rijksherbarium, PO Box 9514, 2300 RA Leiden Netherlands. **Tel** 011 31 71 273500.

ISSN 0034-6624
UK
REVIEW OF MEDICAL AND VETERINARY MYCOLOGY. **See** Veterinary Sciences-Abstracting, Bibliographies and Statistics.

ISSN 0325-4755
AG
NLM W1; RE271M
Pr Rev.
REVISTA ARGENTINA DE MICOLOGIA : ORGANO DE DIFUSION DE LA SOCIEDAD ARGENTINA DE MICOLOGIA. Added/Corp Sociedad Argentina de Micologia. Asociacion Argentina de Micologia. (197?)-. Periodical. Spanish (summaries and/or abstracts in English). Three times a year (Apr., Aug., Dec.). $25.00. Revista Argentina de Micologia, Juncal 3475 4 C, 1425 Buenos Aires Argentina. **Tel** 011 54 1 9627274. **ED** Finquelievich, Jorge (editor's phone: 54 1 9627274). Index available. **Bk Rev. Circ:** 1,000 (ctrl).
Ind/Abst Maize Abstr.; Rev. Med. Vet. Entomol.; Rev. Med. Vet. Mycology; Wheat Barley Trit. Abstr.

SP
CODEN RIMIER
REVISTA IBERICA DE MICOLOGIA. (1984)-. Periodical. Spanish (summaries and/or abstracts in English). Hospital General Htra Sra del Mar, Paseo Maritimo 25-29, 08003 Barcelona Spain. Documents available from BIOSIS Document Express.
Ind/Abst Biodeter. Abstr. (1991-); Biol. Abstr. (1984-); Index Vet.; Indice Med. Esp.; Rev. Med. Vet. Entomol.; Rev. Med. Vet. Mycology; Rev. Plant Pathol.; Soils Fert.

ISSN 1130-1406
SP
REVISTA IBEROAMERICANA DE MICOLOGIA. [Rev. iberoam. micol.]. **Added/Corp** Asociacion Espanola de Especialistas en Micologia. (1990)-. Periodical. Multiple languages. Four times a year. $48.85. Asociacion Espanola de Especialistas en Micologia, Apartado de Correos 2650, 08080 Barcelona Spain. **(Subscription address:** Publicidad Permanyer, Mallorca 310, 08037 Barcelona Spain. **Tel** 011 34 3 2075920.) ***Continues*** *Revista Iberica de Micologia, 0212-9523.*
Ind/Abst Biodeter. Abstr.; Index Vet.; Rev. Med. Vet. Mycology; Soils Fert.; Vet. Bull.

ISSN 0187-3180
MX
CODEN RMMIEL
REVISTA MEXICANA DE MICOLOGIA. (REVISTA MEXICANA DE MICOLOGIA : ORGANO OFICIAL DE LA SOCIEDAD MEXICANA DE MICOLOGIA.). [Rev. mex. micol.]. **Added/Corp** Sociedad Mexicana de Micologia. Vol. 1 (1985)-. Spanish (English; summaries and/or abstracts in English). One time a year. $10.00. Sociedad Mexicana de Micologia, Apartado Postal 26-378, Mexico DF 02860 Mexico. **ED** Conchita Toriello. Index available. cum. index. **Bk Rev. Ad Acc. Circ:** 500 (ctrl). available in microform from University Microfilms International (UMI); available on microfilm from Xerox. Documents available from BIOSIS Document Express. ***Continues*** *Sociedad Mexicana de Micologia. Boletin de la Sociedad Mexicana de Micologia, 0085-6223.*
Desc: Covers all aspects of fungi in the field of taxonomy, ecology, medicine, biochemistry, and microbiology.
Ind/Abst Biol. Abstr. (1985-); Potato Abstr.

ISSN 0373-2959
SZ
CODEN SZPLA7
SCHWEIZERISCHE ZEITSCHRIFT FUER PILZKUNDE. [Bull. suisse mycol.]. **VFOAT** Bulletin Suisse de Mycologie. Vol. 1 (1923)-. Bulletin. Multiple languages (French and German). Twelve times a year. Swiss Book Center / Schweizer Buchzentrum, Postfach 522, CH-4600 Olten 1 Switzerland. **Tel** 011 41 62 476161. Documents available from BIOSIS Document Express.
Ind/Abst AGRICOLA; Biol. Abstr.; Life Sci. Collect.

ISSN 0583-0516
JA
CODEN SHSHBL
TITLE CHANGE
SHINKIN TO SHINKINSHO. (SHINKIN TO SHINKINSHO = THE JAPANESE JOURNAL OF MEDICAL MYCOLOGY.). [Shinkin to shinkinshÂo]. **Added/Corp** Nihon Ishinkin Gakkai. **VFOAT** Japanese Journal of Medical Mycology. (1960)-(19??). Academic Scholarly Publication. Japanese. Kyorin Publishing Co, 3-46-10 Nishigahara Kita-ku, Tokyo 114 Japan. **(Subscription address:** Japan Publications Trading Company Ltd., PO Box 5030, Tokyo International, Tokyo 100-31 Japan. **Tel** 011 81 3 3292 3753.) Documents available from CASDDS. ***Continued by*** *Nihon Ishinkin Gakkai Zasshi, 0916-4804.*
Ind/Abst Chem. Abstr. (?-1989); EMBASE; Index Vet.; Rev. Med. Vet. Mycology; Small Anim. Abstr. Bibliogr.; Soils Fert.

LC QK600 .S93 **ISSN** 0166-0616
DD 589.2 NE
UDC 582.28
NLM W1; ST926 **CODEN** SMYCA2
Pr Rev.
STUDIES IN MYCOLOGY. [Stud. myrol.]. No. 1 (Sept. 1. 1972)-. Academic Scholarly Publication. English. Irregular. Price varies per volume. Centraal Bureau voor Schimmelcultures, PO Box 273, 3740 AG Baarn Netherlands. **Tel** (02154)11841, FAX 16142. **ED** W Gams, G S De Hoog, and R A Samson. Index available. ctrl circ. Documents available from The Genuine Article, BIOSIS Document Express, CASDDS.
Desc: Taxonomical studies concerning fungi and yeasts.
Ind/Abst Biocont. News Inf. (1991-); Biol. Abstr.; Chem. Abstr.; Curr. Aware. Biol. Sci., CABS; Curr. Contents Agric. Biol. Environ. Sci.; Life Sci. Collect.; Res. Alert [Full Cov.]; Rev. Plant Pathol.; Sci. Cit. Index (19??-19??); SCISEARCH.

LC QK600 .S92 **ISSN** 0082-0598
AU
CODEN SYAMAU
SYDOWIA. [Sydowia]. **VFOAT** Annales Mycologici, Ser. 2. Vol. 1 (1947)-. Periodical. English (French, German, Italian, Latin and Spanish). Six times a year. Price varies per volume. Verlag Ferdinand Berger & Soehne, Wienerstrasse 21-23, A-3580 Horn Austria. **Tel** 011 43 2982 4161232. Each issue contains an index to its own contents (no volume index)--loose. available on microfilm. Documents available from BIOSIS Document Express. ***Continues*** *Annales Mycologici.*
Ind/Abst AGRICOLA; Biocont. News Inf. (19??-19??); Biol. Abstr.; Life Sci. Collect.; Rev. Med. Vet. Mycology; Rev. Plant Pathol.; Soils Fert.

CN
UDC 582.28
TOPICS IN MYCOBIOLOGY. No. 1-. Monographic series. English. Irregular. Price varies per volume.

LC QK600 .Z4 **ISSN** 0170-110X
GW
CODEN ZEMYDW
ZEITSCHRIFT FUER MYKOLOGIE. [Z. Mykol.]. **Added/Corp** Deutsche Gesellschaft fuer Mykologie. Vol. 44 (May 1978)-. Academic Scholarly Publication. German (summaries and/or abstracts in English). Two times a year. $49.13. Deutsche Gesellschft Mykologie, Peter Dobbitsch, Rathausstr 16, 78594 Gunningen Germany. **Tel** 011 49 7424 7256. **Bk Rev. Ad Acc.** ctrl circ. Documents available from BIOSIS Document Express, CASDDS. ***Continues*** *Zeitschrift fur Pilzkunde.*
Desc: German with English table of contents and summaries. Many line drawings and color photographs.
Ind/Abst AGRICOLA; Biodeter. Abstr. (1991-); Biol. Abstr.; Chem. Abstr.; For. Abstr.; Microbiol. Abstr. Sect. A; Microbiol. Abstr. Sect. C; Life Sci. Collect.; Rev. Plant Pathol.

LC QK609.C6 C48 **ISSN** 0256-1883
DD 589.2 CC
CODEN ZHXUET
ZHENJUN XUEBAO. (CHEN CHUN HSUEH PAO.). [Zhenjun xuebao]. **Added/Corp** Chen Chun Hsueh Pao Pien Chi Wei Yuan Hui. **VFOAT** Acta Mycologica Sinica. (1982)-. Academic Scholarly Publication. Chinese (summaries and/or abstracts in English). Four times a year. $71.20. Science Press, 16 Donghuangchenggen North Street, Beijing 100707, People's Republic of China. **Tel** 011 86 1 4019821, 011 86 1 4010642, FAX 011 86 1 4012180, 011 86 1 4019810, telex 210147. Documents available from CASDDS.
Ind/Abst Biodeter. Abstr.; Chem. Abstr. (1984-); Hortic. Abstr.; Ornamental Hort. (1991-); Plant Breed. Abstr.; Rev. Plant Pathol.; Seed Abstr.; Sug. Indus. Abstr.

ISSN 1013-2732
CH
ZHONGHUA ZHENJUNXUEHUI HUIKAN. VFOAT Transactions of the Mycological Society of Republic of China. (1985)-. Periodical. Multiple languages. Four times a year.
Ind/Abst Rev. Plant Pathol.

PARASITOLOGY

LC QL757 .A12 **ISSN** 1230-2821
DD 591.5 PL
NLM W1; AC906J **CODEN** ACTPEO
ACTA PARASITOLOGICA. Added/Corp Polska Akademia Nauk. Instytut Parazytologii im. Witolda Stefanskiego. Vol. 37, No. 1 (1992)-. Academic Scholarly Publication. English. Four times a year. $100.00. W. Stefanski Institute of Parasitology, L. Pasteura 3, S.p. 153, 00-973 Warszawa, Poland. **(Subscription address:** Ars Polona-Ruch, PO Box 1001, Krakowskie Przedmiescie 7, 00-068 Warsaw Poland. **Tel** 011 48 22 261201.) Documents available from CASDDS. ***Continues*** *Acta Parasitologica Polonica, 0065-1478.*
Desc: Contains information on parasites and parasitology.
Ind/Abst Chem. Abstr.; Curr. Cit.

ISSN 0934-6112
US
CCC
NLM W1; AD548M **CODEN** ADVRED
ADVANCES IN DISEASE VECTOR RESEARCH. [Adv. dis. vector res.]. Vol. 5 (1988)-. Monographic series. English. Irregular. Price varies per volume. Springer-Verlag New York Inc., 175 Fifth Avenue, New York NY 10010. **Tel** (212)460-1500 ext 256, FAX (212)533-3503, telex 232 235 SPB UR. **(Subscription address:** Springer-Verlag New York Inc. / North America, PO Box 2485, Journal Fulfillment, Secaucus NJ 07096. **Tel** (201)348-4033, (800)777-4643, FAX (201)348-4505.) **ED** K.F. Harris. Documents available from BIOSIS Document Express. ***Continues*** *Current Topics in Vector Research, 0737-8491.*
Desc: Provides information on animals as carriers of disease and vector-pathogen relationships.
Ind/Abst AgBiotech News Inf.; Biol. Abstr. (1988-); Index Vet.; Maize Abstr.; Nematol. Abstr.; Protozoolog. Abstr.; Rev. Agric. Entomol.; Rev. Med. Vet. Entomol.; Rev. Plant Pathol.; Rice Abstr.

LC QH547 .A38 **ISSN** 0065-308X
DD 591.55 UK
NLM W1 AD71 **CODEN** ADPRAD
Pr Rev.
ADVANCES IN PARASITOLOGY. [Adv. parasitol.]. Vol. 1 (1963)-. Academic Scholarly Publication. English. Irregular. $79.00 (Vol. 33). Academic Press Inc., 6277 Sea Harbor Drive, Orlando FL 32887. **Tel** (800)543-9534, (407)345-4100, FAX (407)352-3445. **ED** Ben Dawes. Documents available from The Genuine Article, BIOSIS Document Express, CASDDS.
Ind/Abst AGRICOLA [Select. Cov.]; Biol. Agric. Index; Biol. Abstr.; Chem. Abstr.; Curr. Aware. Biol. Sci., CABS; Curr. Cit.; EMBASE; Energy Res. Abstr. (Aug. 1982-); Fish Rev. (19??-199?); Index Med.; Index Sci. Rev. [Full Cov.]; Index Vet.; Nutr. Abstr. Rev., Ser. B, Live Feeds and Feed.; Nutr. Abstr. Rev., Ser. A, Hum. Exp.; Life Sci. Collect.; Protozoolog. Abstr.; Ref. Upd. Basic Ed.; Ref. Upd. Deluxe Ed.; Res. Alert [Full Cov.]; Sci. Cit. Index; SCISEARCH; Vet. Bull.; Trop. Dis. Bull.; Wildl. Rev. (19??-199?).

LC QL757 .A14 **ISSN** 0003-4150
FR
CCC
NLM W1 AN374 **CODEN** APHCAC
Pr Rev. **TITLE CHANGE**
ANNALES DE PARASITOLOGIE HUMAINE ET COMPAREE. [Ann. parasitol. hum. comp.]. **VFOAT** Annales de Parasitologie. Vol. 1 (April 1923)-Vol. 68 (1993). Periodical. French (English). Masson Editeur, BP 22, 41354 Vineuil Cedex France. **Tel** 011 33 54 504612, FAX 011 33 54 504611. available on microfilm and microfiche from University Microfilms International (UMI). Documents available from The Genuine Article, BIOSIS Document Express. ***Continued by*** *Parasite.*
Ind/Abst Biocont. News Inf. (1991-?); Biol. Abstr. (?-?); Curr. Contents Agric. Biol. Environ. Sci. (?-?); Health Plan. Adminis. (?-?); Helminthol. Abstr. (19??-19??); Index Med. (?-?); Index Vet. (?-?); Microbiol. Abstr. Sect. C (?-?); Life Sci. Collect. (?-?); Pig News Inf. (?-?); Protozoolog. Abstr. (?-?); Res. Alert (?-?) [Full Cov.]; Rev. Agric. Entomol. (?-?); Rev. Med. Vet. Entomol. (?-?); Rev. Med. Vet. Mycology (?-?); Rev. Plant Pathol. (?-?); Sci. Cit. Index (?-?); SCISEARCH (?-?); Vet. Bull. (?-?); Trop. Dis. Bull. (?-?).

LC RC960 ISSN 0003-4983
DD 616.9883 UK
CCC
NLM W1 AN627P CODEN ATMPA2
Pr Rev.
ANNALS OF TROPICAL MEDICINE AND PARASITOLOGY. See Medical Sciences-Tropical Medicine.

ISSN 0943-0938
GW
NLM W1; AP528KM CODEN APPAEG
●**APPLIED PARASITOLOGY.** Vol. 34, No. 1 (1993)-. Periodical. English (German). Four times a year. $212.00. Gustav Fischer Verlag Jena, Postfach 100537, D-07705 Jena Germany. **Tel** 011 49 3641 626444, FAX 011 49 3641 626500. **(Subscription address:** VCH Publishers Inc., 303 Northwest 12th Avenue, Journals Department, Deerfield FL 33442. **Tel** (800)367-8249, (305)428-5566.) ***Continues*** *Angewandte Parasitologie, 0003-3162.*
Ind/Abst Curr. Cit.; Index Med. (1993-).

LC QR352.5
DD 589.9 RM
NLM W1; BA214
BACTERIOLOGIA, VIRUSOLOGIA, PARAZITOLOGIA, EPIDEMIOLOGIA. **Added/Corp** Uniunea Societatilor de Stiinte Medicale. Societatea Romana de Microbiologie. Vol. 35, 2 (Apr./June 1990)-. Periodical. Romanian (summaries and/or abstracts in English and Russian; table of contents in English, French and Russian). Four times a year. $88.00. Uniunea Societ Stiinte Medical, Str Progresului 8, Bucharest Romania. **(Subscription address:** Kubon & Sagner, ABT Zeitschriftenimport, D 80328 Munich Germany. **Tel** 011 49 89 54218130.) ***Continues*** *Revista de Igiena, Bacteriologie, Virusologie, Parazitologie, Epidemiologie, Pneumoftiziologie. Bacteriologia, Virusologia, Parazitologia, Epidemiologia, 0376-4494.*
Ind/Abst EMBASE [Select. Cov.]; Index Med. (1990-).

LC QL ISSN 0365-9402
DD 590 CL
NLM W1 BO204 CODEN BCPRAH
Pr Rev.
BOLETIN CHILENO DE PARASITOLOGIA. (BOLETIN CHILENO DE PARASITOLOGIA : PUBLICACION TRIMESTRAL DEL DEPARTAMENTO DE PARASITOLOGIA DE LA UNIVERSIDAD DE CHILE Y DE LA ASESORIA DE PARASITOLOGIA DEL SERVICIO NACIONAL DE SALUD.). [Bol. chil. parasitol.]. **Added/Corp** Universidad de Chile. Departamento de Parasitologia. Universidad de Chile. Departamento de Microbiologia y Parasitologia. Chile. Asesoria Tecnica de Parasitologia. Vol. 9, No. 1 (Feb./Mar. 1954)-. Academic Scholarly Publication. Spanish (summaries and/or abstracts in English). Two times a year (Mar. and Aug.). $20.00. University of Chile Facultad Medicina, Casilla 9183, Santiago Chile. **Tel** 011 56 2 7370081 ext. 5340, FAX 011 56 2 5510174. **ED** Hugo Schenone. Index available. **Bk Rev. Circ:** 1,000 (ctrl). Documents available from BIOSIS Document Express. ***Continues*** *Boletin de Informaciones Parasitarias Chilenas, 0366-0613.*
Desc: Contains original articles, current parasitological topics, practical notes, clinical cases, and communications.
Ind/Abst Biol. Abstr.; EMBASE; Fish Rev.; Helminthol. Abstr. (1991-); Index Med.; Index Vet.; Life Sci. Collect.; Protozoolog. Abstr.; Vet. Bull.; Wildl. Rev.

ISSN 0006-6176
CL
BOLETIN CHILENO DE PARASITOLOGIA. **Added/Corp** Universidad de Chile. Departamento de Microbiologia y Parasitologia. Universidad de Chile. Departamento de Parasitologia. Vol. 1 (1946)-. Periodical. Spanish (summaries and/or abstracts in English).
Ind/Abst Health Plan. Adminis.; Nutr. Abstr. Rev., Ser. A, Hum. Exp.; Trop. Dis. Bull.

ISSN 0761-8328
FR
NLM W1; BU518J CODEN BSFPE9
BULLETIN DE LA SOCIETE FRANCAISE DE PARASITOLOGIE. [Bull. Soc. fr. parasitol.]. **Added/Corp** Societe Francaise de Parasitologie. (1983)-. Bulletin. French (summaries and/or abstracts in English). Two times a year. $60.14. Laboratoire de Parasitologie, Faculte Medecine, 2 Ave du Prof L Bernard, 35043 Rennes Cedex France. **Tel** 33 99 336969. Documents available from CASDDS.
Ind/Abst Biocont. News Inf. (1991-); Chem. Abstr. (1985-); Curr. Cit.; Helminthol. Abstr. (1991-); Index Vet.; Poult. Abstr.; Protozoolog. Abstr.; Rev. Med. Vet. Entomol.; Small Anim. Abstr. Bibliogr.; Vet. Bull.; Trop. Dis. Bull.

ISSN 0007-4845
DD 616.9 IQ
NLM W1 BU757
BULLETIN OF ENDEMIC DISEASES. See Medical Sciences-Communicable Diseases.

LC Q60 .F553 QL757
FI
CONTRIBUTION - SUOMEN TIEDESEURA. PARASITOLOGIAN LAITOS. **Main/Corp** Suomen Tiedeseura. Parasitologian Laitos. English. Societas Scientiarum Fennica, (Finnish Society of Sciences and Letters), Marieg 5, SF 000170 Helsinki 17 Finland. **Tel** 011 358 633005.

ISSN 0091-049X
US
NLM W1 DY986H
DYNAMIC ASPECTS OF HOST-PARASITE RELATIONSHIPS. **Added/Corp** Hebrew University. Institute of Microbiology. Vol. 1 (1973)-. Monographic series. English. Irregular. Price varies per volume. Academic Press Inc., 6277 Sea Harbor Drive, Orlando FL 32887. **Tel** (800)543-9534, (407)345-4100, FAX (407)352-3445.

LC QL757 .E46 ISSN 0136-9121
RU
EKOLOGICHESKAIA I EKSPERIMENTALNAIA PARAZITOLOGIIA. **Added/Corp** Leningradskii Gosudarstvennyi Universitet Imeni A.A. Zhdanova. Russian S.F.S.R. Golovnoi Sovet po Biologii. Russian S.F.S.R. Ministerstvo Vysshego i Srednego Setsialnogo Obrazovzania. Vol. 1 (1975)-. Periodical. Russian (summaries and/or abstracts in English). St. Petersburg State University / Izdatelstvo Leningradskogo Universiteta, Universitetskaia Nab 7/9, 199034 St. Petersburg Russia. **Tel** 011 7 812 2189788, FAX 011 7 812 2185152, telex 121481.

LC QL757 .E9 ISSN 0014-4894
DD 616.96072 US
CCC
NLM W1 EX511 CODEN EXPAAA
Pr Rev.
EXPERIMENTAL PARASITOLOGY. [Exp. parasitol.]. Vol. 1 (Oct. 1951)-. Academic Scholarly Publication. English. Nine times a year. $533.00. Academic Press Inc., 6277 Sea Harbor Drive, Orlando FL 32887. **Tel** (800)543-9534, (407)345-4100, FAX (407)352-3445. Documents available from The Genuine Article, BIOSIS Document Express, CASDDS.
Desc: Original research papers on experimental parasitology. Emphasis is on the physiological, metabolic, immunologic, biochemical, nutritional, and chemotherapeutic aspects of parasites and host-parasite relationships.
Ind/Abst AgBiotech News Inf.; AGRICOLA [Select. Cov.]; Anim. Breed. Abstr.; AQUAREF; Biol. Abstr.; Chem. Abstr.; Curr. Aware. Biol. Sci., CABS; Curr. Cit.; Curr. Contents Life Sci.; Curr. Ref. Fish Res.; EMBASE; Energy Res. Abstr.; Fish Rev.; Genet. Abstr.; Helminthol. Abstr. (19??-19??); Immunol. Abstr.; Index Med.; Index Vet.; INIS Atomindex [Micro.]; Microbiol. Abstr. Sect. C; Nematol. Abstr.; Nutr. Abstr. Rev., Ser. B, Live Feeds and Feed.; Nutr. Abstr. Rev., Ser. A, Hum. Exp.; Life Sci. Collect.; PESTDOC; Pig News Inf.; Poult. Abstr.; Protozoolog. Abstr.; Ref. Upd. Deluxe Ed.; Res. Alert [Full Cov.]; Rev. Agric. Entomol.; Rev. Med. Vet. Entomol.; Sci. Cit. Index; SCISEARCH; Vet. Bull.; Trop. Dis. Bull.; Wildl. Rev.

ISSN 0015-5683
XR
CCC
NLM W1 FO277R CODEN FPARA9
Pr Rev.
FOLIA PARASITOLOGICA. [Folia parasitologica]. **Added/Corp** Parasitologicky Ustav (Ceskoslovenska Akademie Ved). Vol.13 (1966)-. Academic Scholarly Publication. English (Multiple languages; summaries and/or abstracts in Russian). Four times a year. $160.00. Czech Academy of Sciences, Branisovska 31, 37005 Ceske Budejovice, Czech Republic. **Tel** 011 42 38 817 ext. 213, 214. **ED** Jiri Lom. cum. index. **Bk Rev.** Documents available from The Genuine Article, BIOSIS Document Express, CASDDS. ***Continues*** *Ceskoslovenska Parasitologie.*
Desc: Publishes original papers from all branches of general medical and veterinary parasitology.
Ind/Abst AGRICOLA; Biol. Abstr.; Chem. Abstr.; Curr. Aware. Biol. Sci., CABS; Curr. Cit.; Curr. Contents Agric. Biol. Environ. Sci.; Curr. Ref. Fish Res.; For. Abstr.; Health Plan. Adminis.; Helminthol. Abstr. (19??-19??); Index Med.; Index Vet.; Microbiol. Abstr. Sect. C; Life Sci. Collect.; Pig News Inf.; Poult. Abstr.; Protozoolog. Abstr.; Refer. Z.; Res. Alert [Full Cov.]; Rev. Med. Vet. Entomol.; Sci. Cit. Index; SCISEARCH; Trop. Dis. Bull.; Virol. AIDS Abstr.

LC QL392 .H38 ISSN 0440-6605
XO
NLM W1 HE796B CODEN HMTGA4
HELMINTHOLOGIA. See Zoology.

LC QL392.A1 H42 ISSN 0957-6789
DD 595.1 UK
NLM ZQX 200; H479A CODEN HEABEC
HELMINTHOLOGICAL ABSTRACTS. See Zoology-Abstracting, Bibliographies and Statistics.

LC QL392.A1 B814 ISSN 0324-1947
BU
NLM W1 KH38 CODEN KHELDD
HELMINTOLOGIJA (SOFIJA). See Zoology.

ISSN 0255-4585
KE
NLM W1; IL946F
ILRAD REPORTS. See Veterinary Sciences.

LC OL386 .I5 ISSN 0019-5227
II
NLM W1 IN209
INDIAN JOURNAL OF HELMINTHOLOGY / HELMINTHOLOGICAL SOCIETY OF INDIA. See Zoology.

ISSN 0253-7168
II
NLM W1 IN224D CODEN IJPAES
INDIAN JOURNAL OF PARASITOLOGY. [Indian j. parasitol.]. **Added/Corp** Indian Society for Parasitology. Vol. 1, No. 1 (Jan. 1977)-. Academic Scholarly Publication. English. Two times a year. $80.00. Lucknow University / Department of Zoology, Lucknow 226 016 India. **(Subscription address:** Prints India, 11 Darya Ganj, New Delhi 110002 India. **Tel** 011 91 11 3268645, FAX 011 91 11 3275542, telex 31-61087 PRIN-IN.) Documents available from CASDDS.
Ind/Abst Biocont. News Inf.; Chem. Abstr.; Index Vet.; Protozoolog. Abstr.; Rev. Med. Vet. Entomol.; Vet. Bull.; Trop. Dis. Bull.

LC QL757 .A24 ISSN 0020-7519
DD 591.5/24 UK
CCC
NLM W1 IN7652G CODEN IJPYBT
Pr Rev.
INTERNATIONAL JOURNAL FOR PARASITOLOGY. [Int. j. parasitol.]. **Added/Corp** Australian Society for Parasitology. **VFOAT** Journal for Parasitology; International Journal of Parasitology. Vol. 1 (May 1971)-. Academic Scholarly Publication. English. Twelve times a year. $875.00. Pergamon Press, An Imprint of Elsevier Science Ltd., The Boulevard, Langford Lane, Kidlington, Oxford OX5 1GB United Kingdom. **Tel** 011 44 1865 843000, 011 44 1865 843699, FAX 011 44 1865 843010. **(Subscription address:** Elsevier Science Ltd. / Oxford Fulfillment Centre, PO Box 800, Kidlington OX5 1DX United Kingdom. **Tel** 011 44 865 843355.) **ED** J. F. A. Sprent. available on microfilm and microfiche from University Microfilms International (UMI); available on an online database from Elsevier Electronic Subscriptions (EES). Documents available from The Genuine Article, BIOSIS Document Express, CASDDS, ADONIS.
Ind/Abst ADONIS; AgBiotech News Inf.; AGRICOLA [Select. Cov.]; Anim. Breed. Abstr.; Biocont. News Inf. (19??-19??); Biol. Abstr.; Chem. Abstr.; CSA Neuro. Abstr. (?-?); Curr. Aware. Biol. Sci., CABS; Curr. Cit.; Curr. Contents Agric. Biol. Environ. Sci.; Curr. Contents Life Sci.; Curr. Ref. Fish Res.; Dairy Sci. Abstr.; Ecology Abstr.; EMBASE; Entomol. Abstr.; Fish Rev.; Food Sci. Technol. Abstr.; Helminthol. Abstr. (19??-19??); Immunol. Abstr.; Index Med.; Irr. Drain. Abstr.; Microbiol. Abstr. Sect. C; Nematol. Abstr.; Nutr. Abstr. Rev., Ser. B, Live Feeds and Feed.; Life Sci. Collect.; PESTDOC; Poult. Abstr.; Protozoolog. Abstr.; Res. Alert [Full Cov.]; Rev. Agric. Entomol.; Rev. Med. Vet. Entomol.; Sci. Cit. Index; SCISEARCH; Soils Fert.; Trop. Dis. Bull.; Wildl. Rev.

LC QR46 .Z456 ISSN 0937-1591
DD 616/01 GW
NLM ZQW 4; Z56
CEASED
INTERNATIONAL JOURNAL OF MEDICAL MICROBIOLOGY AND HYGIENE ABSTRACTS OF MICROBIOLOGY, VIROLOGY, PARASITOLOGY, PREVENTIVE MEDICINE AND ENVIRONMENTAL HYGIENE. See Biology-Microbiology.

LC QL757 .J68 ISSN 0022-3395
US
NLM W1 JO827H CODEN JOPAA2
Pr Rev.
JOURNAL OF PARASITOLOGY, THE. [J. parasitol.]. **Added/Corp** American Society of Parasitologists. Helminthological Society of Washington. Proceedings of the Helminthological Society of Washington. Vol. 1, (Sept. 1914)-. Academic Scholarly Publication. English. Six times a year (Feb., Apr., June, Aug., Oct., Dec.). $140.00. American Society of Parasitologists, Wake Forest University, Biology Department, Winston-Salem NC 27109. **Tel** (910)759-5323, FAX (910)759-6008. **(Subscription address:** Journal of Parasitology, PO Box 1897, Lawrence KS 66044-8897.) **Acid Free.** available on microfilm from University Microfilms International (UMI). Documents available from The Genuine Article, BIOSIS Document Express, CASDDS.
Desc: This magazine contain sections called Second International Congress of Parasitology.
Ind/Abst AgBiotech News Inf.; AGRICOLA [Select. Cov.]; Aquat. Sci. Fish. Abstr. [CD-ROM Ed.]; Biocont.

News Inf.; Biol. Agric. Index; Biol. Abstr.; Chem. Abstr.; CSA Neuro. Abstr. (?-?); Curr. Aware. Biol. Sci., CABS; Curr. Cit.; Curr. Contents Agric. Biol. Environ. Sci.; Curr. Contents Life Sci.; Curr. Ref. Fish Res.; Ecol. Abstr.; Ecology Abstr.; EMBASE; Energy Res. Abstr.; Entomol. Abstr.; Fish Rev.; Helminthol. Abstr. (19??-19??)(1991-); Immunol. Abstr.; Index Med.; Index Vet.; INIS Atomindex [Micro.]; Microbiol. Abstr. Sect. C; Nematol. Abstr.; Life Sci. Collect.; PESTDOC; Pig News Inf.; Poult. Abstr.; Protozoolog. Abstr.; Ref. Upd. Deluxe Ed.; Res. Alert [Full Cov.]; Rev. Agric. Entomol.; Rev. Med. Vet. Entomol.; Sci. Cit. Index; SCISEARCH; Small Anim. Abstr. Bibliogr.; Soc. Sci. Cit. Index [Select. Cov.]; Vet. Bull.; Trop. Dis. Bull.

ISSN 0253-5890
UA
NLM W1 JO92FC

JOURNAL OF THE EGYPTIAN SOCIETY OF PARASITOLOGY. [J. Egypt. Soc. Parasitol.]. **Added/Corp** Egyptian Society of Parasitology. (1970)-. Periodical. English. Two times a year. Egyptian Society Parasitology, 1 Ozoris Tager Building, Garden City Cairo Egypt.
Ind/Abst Biocont. News Inf. (19??-19??); Curr. Cit.; Index Med.; Index Vet.; Protozoolog. Abstr.; Rev. Agric. Entomol.; Rev. Med. Vet. Entomol.; Trop. Dis. Bull.

LC QL **ISSN** 1049-233X
DD 595 US
NLM W1; JO928G **CODEN** JHSWE4

JOURNAL OF THE HELMINTHOLOGICAL SOCIETY OF WASHINGTON. See Zoology.

ISSN 0021-5171
JA
NLM W1 KI844 **CODEN** KISZAR

KISEICHUGAKU ZASSHI. (JAPANESE JOURNAL OF PARASITOLOGY. KISEICHUGAKU ZASSHI.). [Kiseichugaku zasshi]. **Added/Corp** Japanese Society of Parasitology. **VFOAT** Kiseichugaku Zasshi. Vol. 1 (Oct. 1951)-. Academic Scholarly Publication. Japanese (English). Six times a year. $234.00. Nihon Kiseichu Gakkai, (Japanese Soc. of Parasitology), Tokyo Gaigaku Ikagaku Kenkyujo, Kiseichu Kenkyubu, 6-1 Shirokanedai 4 Chome, Minatoku Tokyo 108 Japan. available on microfilm from University Microfilms International (UMI). Documents available from BIOSIS Document Express, CASDDS.
Ind/Abst Biol. Abstr.; Chem. Abstr.; EMBASE; Helminthol. Abstr. (1991-); Index Vet.; Microbiol. Abstr. Sect. C; Nutr. Abstr. Rev., Ser. B, Live Feeds and Feed.; Life Sci. Collect.; PESTDOC; Pig News Inf.; Poult. Abstr.; Protozoolog. Abstr.; Rev. Med. Vet. Entomol.; Rice Abstr.; Small Anim. Abstr. Bibliogr.; Vet. Bull.; Trop. Dis. Bull.

KO
NLM W1; KO608F
Pr Rev.

●**KOREAN JOURNAL OF PARASITOLOGY, THE.** **Added/Corp** Taehan Kisaengchung Hakhoe. **VFOAT** Kisaengchunghak Chapchi. Vol. 31, No. 1 (1993)-. Periodical. English (Korean). Four times a year. Korean Department of Parasitology, 28 Yeon-Keon dong Chong-ro ku, 110799 Seoul Korea. **Tel** 011 82 2 7603317, 011 82 2 7408348, FAX 011 82 2 7656142. ***Continues*** *Kisaengchunghak Chapchi, 0023-4001.*
Ind/Abst Index Med.

LC RC960 .M4 **ISSN** 0025-8326
RU
CCC
NLM W1 ME796 **CODEN** MPPBAB

MEDICINSKAJA PARAZITOLOGIJA I PARAZITARNYE BOLEZNI. See Medical Sciences-Tropical Medicine.

ISSN 0074-0276
BL
NLM W1 ME903T **CODEN** MIOCAS

MEMORIAS DO INSTITUTO OSWALDO CRUZ. [Mem. Inst. Oswaldo Cruz]. **Added/Corp** Instituto Oswaldo Cruz. Vol. 1 (April 1909)-. Periodical. English (French, Portuguese and Spanish); summaries and/or abstracts in French, German, Portuguese and Spanish). Four times a year. Library Instituto Oswaldo Cruz, PO Box 926, Rio de Janeiro Brazil. **Tel** 011 55 21 2808787, FAX 011 55 21 5903545. **ED** Eloy Garcia. **Circ:** 1,000. Documents available from The Genuine Article, BIOSIS Document Express.
Ind/Abst AGRICOLA; Anim. Behav. Abstr.; Biocont. News Inf. (1991-); Biol. Abstr.; Curr. Cit.; Curr. Contents Life Sci.; Ecology Abstr.; Entomol. Abstr.; Fish Rev.; GeoRef; Helminthol. Abstr. (19??-19??); Immunol. Abstr.; Index Med.; Index Vet.; Microbiol. Abstr. Sect. B (19??-19??); Microbiol. Abstr. Sect. A; Microbiol. Abstr. Sect. C; Pig News Inf.; Poult. Abstr.; Protozoolog. Abstr.; Res. Alert [Full Cov.]; Rev. Med. Vet. Entomol.; Rev. Med. Vet. Mycology; Sci. Cit. Index; SCISEARCH; Small Anim. Abstr. Bibliogr.; Soc. Sci. Cit. Index [Select. Cov.]; Trop. Dis. Bull.; Virol. AIDS Abstr.; Wildl. Rev.

ISSN 0166-6851
NE
CCC
NLM W1 MO194P **CODEN** MBIPDP
Pr Rev.

MOLECULAR AND BIOCHEMICAL PARASITOLOGY. [Mol. biochem. parasitol.]. Vol. 1 (Mar. 1980)-. Academic Scholarly Publication. English. Fourteen times a year (7 volumes). $2527.00. Elsevier Science Publishers BV, PO Box 211, 1000 AE Amsterdam Netherlands. **Tel** 011 31 20 4853641, 011 31 20 4853642, FAX 011 31 20 4853598. **ED** Win Gutteridge, George Cross and C C Wang. available on microfilm and microfiche from University Microfilms International (UMI); available on an online database from Elsevier Electronic Subscriptions (EES). Documents available from The Genuine Article, BIOSIS Document Express, CASDDS, ADONIS.
Desc: Provides a medium for the rapid publication of investigations of the molecular biology, molecular immunology and biochemistry of parasitic protozoa and helminths and their interactions with the host.
Ind/Abst ADONIS; AgBiotech News Inf.; AGRICOLA [Select. Cov.]; Biol. Abstr.; Chem. Abstr.; Chem. Titles; Curr. Aware. Biol. Sci., CABS; Curr. Cit.; Curr. Contents Life Sci.; EMBASE; Genet. Abstr.; Helminthol. Abstr. (19??-19??); Immunol. Abstr.; Index Med.; Index Vet.; Microbiol. Abstr. Sect. C; NAPRALERT; Nematol. Abstr.; Life Sci. Collect.; PESTDOC; Protozoolog. Abstr.; Ref. Upd. Basic Ed.; Ref. Upd. Deluxe Ed.; Res. Alert [Full Cov.]; Rev. Med. Vet. Entomol.; Sci. Cit. Index; SCISEARCH; Trop. Dis. Bull.

ISSN 1252-607X
FR
NLM W1; PA635TM **CODEN** PASIED

●**PARASITE : JOURNAL DE LA SOCIETE FRANCAISE DE PARASITOLOGIE.** **Added/Corp** Societe Francaise de Parasitologie. Vol. 1, No 1 (Mar. 1994)-. Periodical. English (French). Four times a year. $360.88. PDG Communications, 30 rue d'Armaille, F-75017 Paris France. **Tel** 011 33 1 40550595. **(Subscription address:** Princeps Eds G Gilkes Dumas, 64 Ave. Charles de Gaulle, 92130 Issy Moulineaux France. **Tel** 011 33 1 46382414.) Index available (Bound in Mar. issue). ***Continues*** *Annales de Parasitologie Humaine et Comparee, 0003-4150.*
Ind/Abst Curr. Cit.; Index Med. (1994-).

LC RC119 .P344 **ISSN** 0730-9562
DD 616.9/6/005 US
NLM W1 PA635V **CODEN** PDISDD

PARASITIC DISEASES. [Parasit. dis.]. Vol. 1 (1981)-. Academic Scholarly Publication. English. Price varies per volume. Marcel Dekker Inc., 270 Madison Avenue, New York NY 10016. **Tel** (212)696-9000, (800)228-1160, FAX (212)685-4540, telex 421419. **(Subscription address:** Marcel Dekker Inc., PO Box 5017, Monticello NY 12701. **Tel** (800)228-1160.) Documents available from CASDDS.
Ind/Abst Chem. Abstr. (-1981).

ISSN 0031-1812
BE
NLM W1 PA635W **CODEN** PARGAW

PARASITICA. [Parasitica]. **Added/Corp** Association Pour les Etudes et les Recherches de Zoologie Appliquee et de Phytopathologie. (1945)-. Periodical. French (Dutch, English and German). Four times a year. $275.00. Parasitica, rue du Bordia 11, B-5030 Gembloux Belgium. Index available in last issue of volume--attached. **Bk Rev. Ad Acc. Circ:** 350. Documents available from CASDDS.
Desc: Covers phytopathology, zoology and phytopharmacy.
Ind/Abst Chem. Abstr.; Entomol. Abstr.; Maize Abstr.; Life Sci. Collect.; PESTDOC; Plant Breed. Abstr.; Postharvest News Inf.; Potato Abstr.; Poult. Abstr.; Rev. Agric. Entomol.

LC RC119 .P349 **ISSN** 0716-0720
DD 616.9/6/005 CL
NLM W1; PA636D

PARASITOLOGIA AL DIA : REVISTA DE LA SOCIEDAD CHILENA DE PARASITOLOGIA. **Added/Corp** Sociedad Chilena de Parasitologia. (19??)-. Periodical. Spanish. Two times a year (June & Dec.). $40.00. University of Chile Facultad Medicina, Casilla 9183, Santiago Chile. **Tel** 011 56 2 7370081 ext. 5340, FAX 011 56 2 5510174.
Ind/Abst Trop. Dis. Bull.

ISSN 0303-688X
HU
NLM W1 PA636K **CODEN** PAHUAO

PARASITOLOGIA HUNGARICA. [Parasitol. Hung.]. **Added/Corp** Magyar Parazitologusok Tarsasag. Termeszettudomanyi Muzeum (Hungary). (1968)-. Academic Scholarly Publication. Multiple languages (English, Hungarian, German and Russian). **(Subscription address:** Kultura, PO Box 143, H-1300 Budapest 3 Hungary. **Tel** 011 36 1 2500194.) Documents available from BIOSIS Document Express.
Ind/Abst Biol. Abstr.; Dairy Sci. Abstr.; EMBASE; Helminthol. Abstr. (1991-); Index Vet.; Poult. Abstr.; Protozoolog. Abstr.; Rev. Med. Vet. Entomol.; Small Anim. Abstr. Bibliogr.; Trop. Dis. Bull.

ISSN 0964-7570
UK

PARASITOLOGY. (19??)-. English. Six times a year. $196.79. SUBIS, Mansion House 19 Kingfield Road, Sheffield S11 9AS United Kingdom. **Tel** 011 44 114 2554433, FAX 011 44 114 255 4626.

LC QL **ISSN** 0031-1820
DD 590 UK
CCC
NLM W1 PA64 **CODEN** PARAAE
Pr Rev.

PARASITOLOGY. [Parasitology]. **VFOAT** Journal of Hygiene. Supplement. Vol. 1 (1908)-. Academic Scholarly Publication. English. Twelve times a year (plus 2 supplements). $540.00. Cambridge University Press, The Edinburgh Building, Shaftesbury Road, Cambridge CB2 2RU United Kingdom. **Tel** 011 44 1223 312393, FAX 011 44 1223 315052, telex 851-817256. **(Subscription address:** Cambridge University Press / North America, 110 Midland Avenue, Port Chester NY 10573. **Tel** (800)431-1580, (914)937-9600.) **ED** FEG. Cox, C Arme. **Bk Rev. Ad Acc. Circ:** 1,219 (ctrl). available on microfilm and microfiche from University Microfilms International (UMI). Documents available from The Genuine Article, BIOSIS Document Express, CASDDS, ADONIS. ***Absorbed*** *British Society for Parasitology. Symposia of the British Society for Parasitology, 0068-2497.*
Desc: Covers the latest advances in the subject. Publishes original papers on all aspects of parasitology and host-parasite relationships ranging from the latest discoveries in biochemical and molecular biology, to ecology and epidemiology in the context of the medical, veterinary and biological sciences. Each year the proceedings of the symposia of the British Society for Parasitology are published as an extra issue.
Ind/Abst ADONIS; AgBiotech News Inf.; AGRICOLA [Select. Cov.]; Biocont. News Inf.; Biol. Abstr.; Chem. Abstr.; CSA Neuro. Abstr. (?-?); Curr. Aware. Biol. Sci., CABS; Curr. Cit.; Curr. Contents Life Sci.; Curr. Ref. Fish Res.; Ecol. Abstr.; Ecology Abstr.; EMBASE; Entomol. Abstr.; Fish Rev.; Geogr. Abstr. Phys. Geogr.; Helminthol. Abstr. (19??-19??); Immunol. Abstr.; Index Med.; Int. Dev. Abstr.; Microbiol. Abstr. Sect. C; Nematol. Abstr.; Life Sci. Collect.; PESTDOC; Pig News Inf.; Potato Abstr.; Poult. Abstr.; Protozoolog. Abstr.; Ref. Upd. Deluxe Ed.; Res. Alert [Full Cov.]; Rev. Agric. Entomol.; Rev. Med. Vet. Entomol.; Sci. Cit. Index; SCISEARCH; Soc. Sci. Cit. Index [Select. Cov.]; Soils Fert.; Soyabean Abstr.; Trop. Dis. Bull.; Wildl. Rev.

LC QL757 .A48 **ISSN** 0932-0113
DD 574.5/249 GW
CCC
NLM W1; PA64EF **CODEN** PARREZ

PARASITOLOGY RESEARCH (1987). (PARASITOLOGY RESEARCH.). [Parasitol. res.]. **Added/Corp** Deutsche Gesellschaft fuer Parasitologie. Vol. 73, No. 1 (Jan. 1987)-. Academic Scholarly Publication. English. Eight times a year. $1709.00. Springer-Verlag GmbH & Company KG, Heidelberger Platz 3, D-14197 Berlin Germany. **Tel** 011 49 30 8207223, FAX 011 49 30 8214091, telex 183 319 SPBLN D. **(Subscription address:** Springer-Verlag New York Inc. / North America, PO Box 2485, Journal Fulfillment, Secaucus NJ 07096. **Tel** (201)348-4033, (800)777-4643, FAX (201)348-4505.) **ED** B M Honigberg, H Mehlhorn and W Wulker. Documents available from BIOSIS Document Express, CASDDS, ADONIS. ***Continues*** *Zeitschrift fur Parasitenkunde (Berlin, Germany), 0044-3255.*
Desc: Presents information on the latest developments in parasitology research, with special emphasis on practical aspects such as immunodiagnosis, chemotherapy, and epidemiology.
Ind/Abst ADONIS; Biol. Abstr. (1987-); Chem. Abstr. (1987-); Curr. Aware. Biol. Sci., CABS; Curr. Cit.; EMBASE (1987-); Energy Res. Abstr. (1987-); Helminthol. Abstr. (19??-19??); Index Med. (1987-); Life Sci. Collect. (1987-); PESTDOC (1987-); Rev. Med. Vet. Entomol.; Soc. Sci. Cit. Index [Select. Cov.]; Trop. Dis. Bull.

LC RC119-.7 **ISSN** 0169-4707
DD 616.96 UK
CCC
Pr Rev.

PARASITOLOGY TODAY (REFERENCE ED.). (PARASITOLOGY TODAY.). [Parasitol. today]. Vol. 1 (1985)-. English. Twelve times a year (includes library compendium and index). $614.00. Elsevier Trends Journals, An Imprint of Elsevier Science Ltd., The Boulevard, Langford Lane, Kidlington, Oxford OX5 1GB United Kingdom. **Tel** 011 44 1865 843000, 011 44 1865 843699, FAX 011 44 1865 843010. **(Subscription address:** Elsevier Science Ltd. / Oxford Fulfillment Centre, PO Box 800, Kidlington OX5 1DX United Kingdom. **Tel** 011 44 865 843355.) available on microfilm and microfiche from University Microfilms International (UMI); available on an online database from Elsevier Electronic Subscriptions (EES). Documents available from ADONIS.
Ind/Abst ADONIS; Curr. Cit.; EMBASE; Ref. Upd. Deluxe Ed.; Sci. Cit. Index.

Biology—Parasitology

LC QL757 .P35   **ISSN** 0048-2951
    IT
NLM W1 PA642   **CODEN** PSSGAR
PARASSITOLOGIA (ROMA).
(PARASSITOLOGIA.). [Parassitologia]. **Added/Corp** Rome (City). Universita. Istituto di Parassitologia. Societa Italiana di Parassitologia. Vol. 1 (Apr. 1959)-. Academic Scholarly Publication. Italian. Three times a year. L61310. Lombardo Editore, Via Verona 22, 00161 Rome Italy. **Tel** 011 39 6 44290974. Documents available from CASDDS.
Ind/Abst AGRICOLA; Biocont. News Inf. (1991-); Chem. Abstr.; Curr. Cit.; EMBASE; Helminthol. Abstr. (1991-); Index Med.; Index Vet.; Life Sci. Collect.; Protozoolog. Abstr.; Trop. Dis. Bull.

LC QL757 .A32
    RU
PARAZITOLOGICHESKII SBORNIK.
Added/Corp Akademiia Nauk SSSR. Zoologicheskii Institut. Akademiia Nauk SSSR. Zoologicheskii Institut. Otdel Parazitologii. **VFOAT** Magazin de Parasitologie. (1930)-. Monographic series. Russian. Price varies per volume. Izdatelstvo Nauka St. Petersburg, Mendeleevskaia Liniia 1, 199034 St. Petersburg, B-34 Russia. **Tel** 011 7 812 2182612.
Ind/Abst Index Vet.; Protozoolog. Abstr.; Rev. Med. Vet. Entomol.; Trop. Dis. Bull.

LC QL757 .A33   **ISSN** 0031-1847
    RU
    CCC
NLM W1 PA642P   **CODEN** PAZGA4
Pr Rev.
PARAZITOLOGIJA. (PARAZITOLOGIIA.).
[Parazitologija]. **Added/Corp** Akademiia Nauk SSSR. (1967)-. Academic Scholarly Publication. Russian (summaries and/or abstracts in English). Six times a year. $167.50. **(Subscription address:** East View Publications Inc., 3020 Harbor Lane North, Suite 110, Minneapolis MN 55447. **Tel** (800)477-1005, (612)550-0961, FAX (612)559-2931.) Documents available from The Genuine Article, BIOSIS Document Express, CASDDS.
Ind/Abst Biol. Abstr.; Chem. Abstr.; CSA Neuro. Abstr. (?-?); Curr. Ref. Fish Res.; Helminthol. Abstr. (1991-); Index Med.; Index Vet.; Microbiol. Abstr. Sect. C; Nematol. Abstr.; Life Sci. Collect.; Protozoolog. Abstr.; Res. Alert [Full Cov.]; Rev. Med. Vet. Entomol.; Sci. Cit. Index; SCISEARCH.

LC Z6900 .P64 QL757
    PL
NLM ZQX 4 P778
POLSKA BIBLIOGRAFIA PARAZYTOLOGICZNA.
(1965)-. Multiple languages. One time a year. **(Subscription address:** Ars Polona-Ruch, PO Box 1001, Krakowskie Przedmiescie 7, 00-068 Warsaw Poland. **Tel** 011 48 22 261201.)
Supersedes in part Wiadomosci Parazytologiczne.

    ISSN 0204-9155
    BU
NLM W1 PR574P   **CODEN** PIPDD4
PROBLEMS OF INFECTIOUS AND PARASITIC DISEASES. See Medical Sciences-Communicable Diseases.

    ISSN 1018-2500
    PK
PROCEEDINGS OF PARASITOLOGY.
(1985)-. Periodical. English. Two times a year.
Ind/Abst Index Vet.; Nematol. Abstr.; Protozoolog. Abstr.

    ISSN 1062-0338
DD 574   US
NLM W1; PR668GD
PROGRESS IN CLINICAL PARASITOLOGY.
[Prog. clin. parasitol.]. (1989)-. Monographic series. English. Springer-Verlag New York Inc., 175 Fifth Avenue, New York NY 10010. **Tel** (212)460-1500 ext 256, FAX (212)533-3503, telex 232 235 SPB UR.
Ind/Abst Index Med.

    US
REPORT - FOREST SERVICE. SOUTHEASTERN AREA. DIVISION OF FOREST PEST MANAGEMENT. See Forests and Forestry.

    VE
NLM W1; RE408RF
REVISTA DE LA FACULTAD DE CIENCIAS VETERINARIAS : ORGANO DE LA FACULTAD DE CIENCIAS VETERINARIAS. See Veterinary Sciences.

    ISSN 0187-4640
    MX
NLM W1 RE597H   **CODEN** RLMIAA
Pr Rev.
REVISTA LATINOAMERICANA DE MICROBIOLOGIA (1970). See Biology-Microbiology.

LC QL757 .R57   **ISSN** 0035-6387
    IT
NLM W1 RI591   **CODEN** RPSTAX
Pr Rev.
RIVISTA DI PARASSITOLOGIA. [Riv. parassitol.].
Vol. 1 (Jan. 1937)-. Periodical. Italian (English, French, German and Spanish). Three times a year. L72000. Rivista di Parassitologia, Via Cesare Battisti N 48, 98122 Messina Italy. **Tel** 011 39 90 673136, FAX 011 39 90 715022. cum. index. **Bk Rev. Ad Acc.** ctrl circ. Documents available from BIOSIS Document Express, CASDDS.
Ind/Abst Biocont. News Inf. (1991-); Biol. Abstr.; Chem. Abstr.; EMBASE; Helminthol. Abstr. (1991-); Nematol. Abstr.; Life Sci. Collect.; Pig News Inf.; Protozoolog. Abstr.; Rev. Agric. Entomol.; Small Anim. Abstr. Bibliogr.; Soils Fert.; Trop. Dis. Bull.

    RU
STROITELSTVO GELMINTOLOGICHESKOI NAUKI I PRAKTIKI V SSSR. See Zoology.

LC QL757 .S94   **ISSN** 0165-5752
DD 591.5/249   NE
    CCC
NLM W1 SY696   **CODEN** SYPAD4
Pr Rev.
SYSTEMATIC PARASITOLOGY. [Syst. parisitol.].
Added/Corp Junk (W.) (FIRM). Vol. 1 (Sept. 1979)-. Periodical. English. Nine times a year. $694.00. Kluwer Academic Publishers, Postbus 322, 3300 AH Dordrecht The Netherlands. **Tel** 011 31 78 524400, FAX 011 31 78 183273, telex 20083. **ED** D I Gibson. **Ad Acc.** **Acid Free. Circ:** 350. available on microfilm and microfiche from University Microfilms International (UMI). Documents available from The Genuine Article, BIOSIS Document Express.
Desc: Publishes papers on the systematics, taxonomy and nomenclature of the following groups: nematoda (including plant-parasitic), monogenea, digenea, cestoda, acanthocephala, aspidogastrea, cestodaria, arthropoda (parasitic copepods, hymenopterans, mites, ticks, etc.), protozoa (parasitic groups) and parasitic genera in other groups (mollusca, turbellaria, etc.).
Ind/Abst AGRICOLA [Select. Cov.]; Biol. Abstr.; Curr. Aware. Biol. Sci., CABS; Curr. Cit.; Curr. Contents Agric. Biol. Environ. Sci.; Helminthol. Abstr. (19??-19??); Index Vet.; Microbiol. Abstr.; Microbiol. Abstr. Sect. B; Microbiol. Abstr. Sect. C; Nematol. Abstr.; Protozoolog. Abstr.; Ref. Upd. Deluxe Ed.; Res. Alert [Full Cov.]; Rev. Agric. Entomol.; Rev. Med. Vet. Entomol.; Sci. Cit. Index; SCISEARCH; Trop. Dis. Bull.

    ISSN 0127-5720
    MY
NLM W1; TR88E   **CODEN** TRBIEN
TROPICAL BIOMEDICINE. See Medical Sciences-Tropical Medicine.

    ISSN 0177-2392
    GW
NLM W1; TR882   **CODEN** TMPAEY
Pr Rev.   **TITLE CHANGE**
TROPICAL MEDICINE AND PARASITOLOGY. See Medical Sciences-Tropical Medicine.

LC QR46 .Z45   **ISSN** 0934-8840
    GW
    CCC
    CODEN ZEBAE8
ZENTRALBLATT FUER BAKTERIOLOGIE. See Biology-Microbiology.

    ISSN 1000-7423
    CC
NLM W1; CH986H
ZHONGGUO JISHENGCHONGXUE YU JISHENGCHONGPING ZAZHI.
(CHUNG-KUO CHI SHENG CHUNG HSUEH YU CHI SHENG CHUNG PING TSA CHIH.). [Zhongguo jishengchongxue yu jishengchongping zazhi].
Added/Corp Chung-kuo yu Fang i Hsueh ko Hsueh Yuan. Chi Sheng Chung Ping yen Chiu so. **VFOAT** Chinese Journal of Parasitology and Parasitic Diseases. (1987)-. Periodical. Chinese (summaries and/or abstracts in English; table of contents in English). Four times a year. $10.60. **(Subscription address:** China International Book Trading Corporation, PO Box 399, Library Service Department, Beijing 100044 People's Republic of China. **Tel** 011 86 1 8414284, FAX 011 86 1 8412023, telex 22496 CIBTC CN.) **Continues** Chi Sheng Chung Hsueh Yu Chi Sheng Chung Ping Tsa Chih, 1000-1808.
Ind/Abst Biocont. News Inf.; Helminthol. Abstr.; Index Vet.; Nematol. Abstr.; Pig News Inf.; Protozoolog. Abstr.; Rev. Agric. Entomol.; Rev. Med. Vet. Entomol.; Rev. Med. Vet. Mycology.

PHYSIOLOGY

LC QP1 .M3329   **ISSN** 0236-5391
DD 599/.01/05   HU
    CCC
NLM W1 AC8643   **CODEN** AMHUDE
    CEASED
ACTA MORPHOLOGICA HUNGARICA.
See Medical Sciences-Experimental Medicine.

    ISSN 0323-9950
    BU
NLM W1 AC922   **CODEN** APPBDI
ACTA PHYSIOLOGICA ET PHARMACOLOGICA BULGARICA. [Acta physiol. pharmacol. Bulg.].
Added/Corp Bulgarska Akademiia na Naukite. Vol. 1 (1974)-. Periodical. English (summaries and/or abstracts in Russian and English). Four times a year. DM81.00. **(Subscription address:** Kubon & Sagner, ABT Zeitschriftenimport, D 80328 Munich Germany. **Tel** 011 49 89 54218130.) Documents available from BIOSIS Document Express, CASDDS.
Supersedes Izvestija na Instituta po Fiziologija, 0068-3922.
Ind/Abst Biol. Abstr.; Chem. Abstr.; Curr. Cit.; EMBASE; GeoRef; Health Plan. Adminis.; Index Med.

LC QP1 .M333   **ISSN** 0231-424X
DD 591.1/05   HU
    CCC
NLM W1 AC9226   **CODEN** APHHDU
Pr Rev.
ACTA PHYSIOLOGICA HUNGARICA.
[Acta physiol. Hung.]. **Added/Corp** Magyar Tudomanyos Akademia. Vol. 61, No. 1-2 (1983)-. Academic Scholarly Publication. English. Four times a year. $104.00. Akademiai Kiado, Publishing House of the Hungarian Academy of Sciences, Prielle Kornelia u. 19-35, H-1117 Budapest Hungary. **Tel** 011 36 1 1811991, FAX 011 36 1 1811991, telex 22-6228 AKNYO H. **ED** Peter Balint and Jeno Bartha (editor's address: Acta Physiologica Hungarica, PO Box 294, H-1445 Budapest Hungary). Documents available from The Genuine Article, BIOSIS Document Express, CASDDS. **Continues** Acta Physiologica Academiae Scientiarum Hungaricae, 0001-6756.
Desc: Provides a forum for important new research papers written by the most eminent scientists on experimental medical sciences. The subjects dealt with are from the domains of physiology, pathophysiology and pharmacology.
Ind/Abst Anim. Breed. Abstr.; Biol. Abstr.; Chem. Abstr. (1983-); Curr. Cit.; Curr. Contents Life Sci.; Curr. Ref. Fish Res.; Dairy Sci.; EMBASE; Health Plan. Adminis.; Helminthol. Abstr. (1991-); Index Med.; Index Vet.; Linguist. Lang. Behav. Abstr.; Maize Abstr.; Nutr. Abstr. Rev., Ser. A, Hum. Exp.; Life Sci. Collect. (1983-); PESTDOC; Pig News Inf.; Poult. Abstr.; Protozoolog. Abstr.; Res. Alert [Full Cov.]; Rev. Med. Vet. Entomol.; Rice Abstr.; Sci. Cit. Index; SCISEARCH; Soc. Plann. Policy Dev. Abstr.; Sociol. Abstr.

LC QP1 .A25
DD 599/.01/05   AG
NLM W1; AC9235   **CODEN** APTLEZ
ACTA PHYSIOLOGICA, PHARMACOLOGICA ET THERAPEUTICA LATINOAMERICANA : ORGANO DE LA ASOCIACION LATINOAMERICANA DE CIENCIAS FISIOLOGICAS Y [DE] LA ASOCIACION LATINOAMERICANA DE FARMACOLOGIA.
Added/Corp Asociacion Latinoamericana de Ciencias Fisiologicas. Asociacion Latinoamericana de Farmacologia. **VFOAT** APPTLA. Vol. 41, No. 1 (1991)-. Academic Scholarly Publication. English (Spanish). Four times a year. Acta Physiologica Pharmacol, Serrano 669, 1414 Buenos Aires Argentina. **Tel** 011 54 1 8557204. Documents available from CASDDS. **Continues** Acta Physiologica et Pharmacologica Latinoamericana, 0326-6656.
Ind/Abst Chem. Abstr.; Index Med. (1991-).

LC QP1 .A275   **ISSN** 0001-6772
DD 612/.05   UK
    CCC
NLM W1 AC9239   **CODEN** APSCAX
ACTA PHYSIOLOGICA SCANDINAVICA. [Acta physiol. Scand.].
Added/Corp Scandinavian Society for Physiology. No. 1 (1940)-. Academic Scholarly Publication. English (French and German). Twelve times a year. $288.00. Blackwell Scientific Publications Ltd, Marston Book Services, PO Box 88, Oxford OX2 ONE United Kingdom. **Tel** 011 44 1865 206206, FAX 011 44 1865 206219, telex 837 515 MARDIS G. cum. index. available on microfilm and microfiche from University Microfilms International (UMI). Documents available from The Genuine Article, BIOSIS Document Express, CASDDS, ADONIS. **Supersedes** Skandinavisches Archiv fur Physiologie.
Ind/Abst ADONIS; Anim. Breed. Abstr.; Biol. Abstr.; Calcium Calcif. Tissue Abstr.; Chem. Abstr.; CSA Neuro. Abstr.; Curr. Aware. Biol. Sci., CABS; Curr. Cit.; Curr.

Contents Life Sci.; Curr. Ref. Fish Res.; Dairy Sci. Abstr.; EMBASE; Energy Res. Abstr.; Fish Rev.; Health Plan. Adminis.; Index Med.; Index Vet.; Int. Aerosp. Abstr.; Nutr. Abstr. Rev., Ser. B, Live Feeds and Feed.; Nutr. Abstr. Rev., Ser. A, Hum. Exp.; Life Sci. Collect.; PESTDOC; Pig News Inf.; Protozoolog. Abstr.; Ref. Upd. Basic Ed.; Ref. Upd. Deluxe Ed.; Res. Alert [Full Cov.]; Saf. Health Work; Sci. Cit. Index; SCISEARCH; Small Anim. Abstr. Bibliogr.; SPORT Discus; SportSearch; Vet. Bull.; Wildl. Rev.

LC QP1 .A2752 **ISSN** 0302-2994
DD 612/.005 UK
NLM W1 AC9241 **CODEN** APSSAD
Pr Rev.
ACTA PHYSIOLOGICA SCANDINAVICA. SUPPLEMENTUM. [Acta physiol. scand. Suppl.]. No. 1 (1940)-. Academic Scholarly Publication. English (French and German). Irregular. Price varies per volume. Blackwell Scientific Publications Ltd, Marston Book Services, PO Box 88, Oxford OX2 ONE United Kingdom. **Tel** 011 44 1865 206206, FAX 011 44 1865 206219, telex 837 515 MARDIS G. Documents available from BIOSIS Document Express, CASDDS. ***Continues*** *Skandinavisches Archiv fur Physiologie. Supplementum.*
Ind/Abst Biol. Abstr.; Chem. Abstr.; Curr. Aware. Biol. Sci., CABS; Curr. Cit.; EMBASE; Fish Rev.; Health Plan. Adminis.; Index Med.; Nutr. Abstr. Rev., Ser. A, Hum. Exp.; Life Sci. Collect.; Wildl. Rev.

ISSN 0860-3111
PL
UDC 573
ACTA UNIVERSITATIS LODZIENSIS. FOLIA PHYSIOLOGICA, CYTOLOGICA ET GENETICA. See Biology-Botany.

LC QP33 .A38 **ISSN** 0938-2763
DD 591.1 GW
CCC
NLM W1; AD545 **CODEN** ACEPEH
ADVANCES IN COMPARATIVE AND ENVIRONMENTAL PHYSIOLOGY. [Adv. comp. environ. physiol.]. **VFOAT** Advances in Comparative & Environmental Physiology. (1988)-. Monographic series. English. Irregular. Price varies per volume. Springer-Verlag GmbH & Company KG, Heidelberger Platz 3, D-14197 Berlin Germany. **Tel** 011 49 30 8207223, FAX 011 49 30 8214091, telex 183 319 SPBLN D. **(Subscription address:** Springer-Verlag New York Inc. / North America, PO Box 2485, Journal Fulfillment, Secaucus NJ 07096. **Tel** (201)348-4033, (800)777-4643, FAX (201)348-4505.**)** Documents available from BIOSIS Document Express.
Ind/Abst Anim. Breed. Abstr.; Biol. Abstr.; Curr. Cit.; Nutr. Abstr. Rev., Ser. B, Live Feeds and Feed.; Poult. Abstr.; Rev. Med. Vet. Entomol.

LC R856 QC501
DD 610.28 537 US
Pr Rev.
●**ADVANCES IN ELECTROMAGNETIC FIELDS IN LIVING SYSTEMS.** See Biology-Bioengineering.

LC QL495 .A23 **ISSN** 0065-2806
DD 595.7 UK
UDC 595.7
NLM W1 AD651 **CODEN** AIPYAZ
ADVANCES IN INSECT PHYSIOLOGY. See Zoology-Entomology.

LC QR84 .A24 **ISSN** 0065-2911
DD 616.014 UK
UDC 579.22 616-095
NLM W1 AD681 **CODEN** AMIPB2
ADVANCES IN MICROBIAL PHYSIOLOGY. See Biology-Microbiology.

US
NLM W1; AD783G
ADVANCES IN PHYSIOLOGY. (1988)-. Monographic series. English. Price varies per volume. The Telford Press / New Jersey, 285 Bloomfield Avenue, Caldwell NJ 07006.

ISSN 1043-4046
DD 574 US
CCC
Pr Rev.
ADVANCES IN PHYSIOLOGY EDUCATION. [Adv. physiol. educ.]. **Added/Corp** American Physiological Society (1887-). Vol. 1, No. 1 (June 1989)-. Academic Scholarly Publication. English. Two times a year (June and Dec.). $22.00. American Physiological Society, 9650 Rockville Pike, Bethesda MD 20814. **Tel** (301)530-7180, FAX (301)571-1814. **ED** P.A. Hansen. **Ad Acc. Circ:** 2,500 to 6,500 (ctrl). available in reprints from University Microfilms International (UMI); available on microfilm and microfiche from University Microfilms International (UMI). Documents available from BIOSIS Document Express, CASDDS.
Desc: Dedicated to promoting improved education in the physiological sciences at all academic levels. Includes research reports, essays on the direction and scope of physiology training, and practical aids to teaching.
Ind/Abst Biol. Abstr.; Chem. Abstr.; Curr. Index J. Educ.; EMBASE.

LC QP360 .A326 **ISSN** 0892-7901
DD 152/.05 UK
NLM W1; AD798KH
ADVANCES IN PSYCHOPHYSIOLOGY. Vol. 1 (1985)-. English. Irregular. Price varies. Jessica Kingsley Publishers, 118 Pentonville Road, London N1 9JN United Kingdom. **Tel** 011 44 171 8332307, FAX 011 44 171 8372917. **(Subscription address:** Taylor & Francis Inc., 1900 Frost Road, Suite 101, Bristol PA 19007-1598. **Tel** (215)785-5800, (800)821-8312, FAX (215)785-5515.**)**

ISSN 1061-6306
DD 612 US
AGING & NEUROSCIENCE. [Aging neurosci.]. **Added/Corp** Philadelphia College of Pharmacy and Science. Office of Professional Programs. **VFOAT** Aging and Neuroscience. Vol. 1, No. 1 (Apr. 1992)-. Periodical. English. Four times a year. $40.00. Philadelphia College of Pharmacy and Science, 600 South 43rd Street, Philadelphia PA 19104.

LC QP1 .A5 **ISSN** 0002-9513
DD 612.05 US
CCC
NLM W1 AM507 **CODEN** AJPHAP
Pr Rev.
AMERICAN JOURNAL OF PHYSIOLOGY. [Am. j. physiol.]. **Added/Corp** American Physiological Society (1887-) American Physiological Society (1887-). Abstracts of Papers Presented at the Fall Meeting. American Physiological Society (1887-). Proceedings. Vol. 1 (Jan. 1898)-. Academic Scholarly Publication. English. Twelve times a year. $1466.00. American Physiological Society, 9650 Rockville Pike, Bethesda MD 20814. **Tel** (301)530-7180, FAX (301)571-1814. Index available (bound in last issue). cum. index. **Circ:** 2,800 (ctrl). available on microfilm and microfiche from University Microfilms International (UMI). Documents available from The Genuine Article, BIOSIS Document Express, CASDDS.
Desc: The consolidated journal contains all of the articles from eight individual journals plus "Advances in Physiology Education". The most economical way for institutions to subscribe to all eight sections of the "American Journal of Physiology".
Ind/Abst Acad. Search; AGRICOLA [Select. Cov.]; Biol. Agric. Index (1992-); Biol. Abstr.; Calcium Calcif. Tissue Abstr.; Chem. Abstr.; Chem. Titles; Chemorecept. Abstr.; CSA Neuro. Abstr.; Curr. Aware. Biol. Sci., CABS; Curr. Cit.; Curr. Contents Life Sci.; Curr. Ref. Fish Res.; EMBASE; Energy Res. Abstr.; EP Collect.; Fish Rev.; Gen. Sci. Index; Gen. Sci. Source; Health Plan. Adminis.; Helminthol. Abstr. (1991-); Homework Help.; Immunol. Abstr.; Index Med.; Index Vet.; INFO-SOUTH Abstr.; INIS Atomindex [Micro.]; Int. Aerosp. Abstr.; Mag. Search; Maize Abstr.; MasterFile FullTEXT 1000; MasterFile FullTEXT 350; MasterFile FullTEXT 650; MasterFile FullTEXT (July 1993-); Microbiol. Abstr. Sect. B; Nutr. Abstr. Rev., Ser. B, Live Feeds and Feed.; Nutr. Abstr. Rev., Ser. A, Hum. Exp.; OCLC; Oncog. Growth Factors Abstr.; Life Sci. Collect.; PESTDOC; Pig News Inf.; Poult. Abstr.; Protozoolog. Abstr.; Res. Alert [Full Cov.]; Rev. Agric. Entomol.; Rev. Med. Vet. Entomol.; Sci. Cit. Index; SCISEARCH; Soc. Sci. Cit. Index [Select. Cov.]; Soyabean Abstr.; SportSearch (1898-); Stat. Theory Method Abstr. (1959-1963); Telebase; Vet. Bull.; Wildl. Rev.

LC QH631 .A44 **ISSN** 0363-6143
DD 574.8/76/05 US
CCC
Pr Rev.
AMERICAN JOURNAL OF PHYSIOLOGY : CELL PHYSIOLOGY. [Am. j. physiol., Cell physiol.]. **Added/Corp** American Physiological Society (1887-). **VFOAT** AJP: Cell Physiology. Vol. 1 (Jan. 1977)-. Periodical. English. Twelve times a year. $286.00. American Physiological Society, 9650 Rockville Pike, Bethesda MD 20814. **Tel** (301)530-7180, FAX (301)571-1814. **ED** D.J. Benos. **Ad Acc. Circ:** 390 (ctrl). available on microfilm and microfiche from University Microfilms International (UMI).
Desc: Publishes original papers dealing with normal and abnormal cell function. Papers include function of cell membranes, contractile systems, and cellular organelles.
Ind/Abst EMBASE; Ref. Upd. Basic Ed.; Ref. Upd. Deluxe Ed.

LC QP145 .A45 **ISSN** 0193-1857
DD 616.3/3/005 US
CCC
AMERICAN JOURNAL OF PHYSIOLOGY : GASTROINTESTINAL AND LIVER PHYSIOLOGY. [Am. j. physiol.: gasterointest. liver physiol.]. **Added/Corp** American Physiological Society (Founded 1887-). (1980)-. Periodical. English. Twelve times a year. $210.00. American Physiological Society, 9650 Rockville Pike, Bethesda MD 20814. **Tel** (301)530-7180, FAX (301)571-1814. **ED** D.H. Alpers. **Ad Acc. Circ:** 400 (ctrl). available on microfilm from University Microfilms International (UMI). ***Continues in part*** *American Journal of Physiology. Endocrinology, Metabolism and Gastrointestinal Physiology, 0363-6100.*
Desc: Publishes original papers dealing with normal and abnormal functions of the alimentary canal and its accessory organs including the salivary glands, pancreas, gallbladder and liver.
Ind/Abst Dairy Sci. Abstr.; EMBASE; Ref. Upd. Basic Ed.; Ref. Upd. Deluxe Ed.

LC QP33 .A43 **ISSN** 0363-6119
DD 596/.01/05 US
CCC
AMERICAN JOURNAL OF PHYSIOLOGY : REGULATORY, INTEGRATIVE AND COMPARATIVE PHYSIOLOGY. [Am. j. physiol., Regul. integr. comp. physiol.]. **Added/Corp** American Physiological Society (1887-). **VFOAT** AJP: Regulatory, Integrative and Comparative Physiology. Vol. 1 (Jan. 1977)-. Periodical. English. Twelve times a year. $283.00. American Physiological Society, 9650 Rockville Pike, Bethesda MD 20814. **Tel** (301)530-7180, FAX (301)571-1814. **ED** W.H. Dantzler. **Ad Acc. Circ:** 250 (ctrl). available on microfilm and microfiche from University Microfilms International (UMI).
Desc: Publishes original articles that emphasize relationships between organ systems and the control of physiological processes in the whole organism and on comparative physiology.
Ind/Abst EMBASE; Ref. Upd. Basic Ed.; Ref. Upd. Deluxe Ed.

LC QP249 .A45 **ISSN** 0363-6127
DD 599/.01/43 US
CCC
AMERICAN JOURNAL OF PHYSIOLOGY RENAL, FLUID AND ELECTROLYTE PHYSIOLOGY. [Am. j. physiol., Renal fluid electrolyte physiol.]. **Added/Corp** American Physiological Society (Founded 1887-). **VFOAT** AJP Renal, Fluid and Electrolyte Physiology. Vol. 1 (Jan. 1977)-. Periodical. English. Twelve times a year. $236.00. American Physiological Society, 9650 Rockville Pike, Bethesda MD 20814. **Tel** (301)530-7180, FAX (301)571-1814. **ED** K.A. Hruska. **Ad Acc. Circ:** 600 (ctrl). available on microfilm from University Microfilms International (UMI).
Desc: Publishes original manuscripts encompassing a broad range of subject matter that relates to the kidney, urinary tract, and epithelial cell layers in general as well as to the control of body fluid volume and composition.
Ind/Abst EMBASE; Ref. Upd. Basic Ed.; Ref. Upd. Deluxe Ed.

LC GC **ISSN** 0073-8565
DD 551.46 FR
CODEN AIMPCT
ANNALES DE L'INSTITUT MICHEL PACHA. See Biology-Marine Biology.

LC QP1 .A535 **ISSN** 0066-4278
DD 599.01/05 US
CCC
NLM W1 AN779 **CODEN** ARPHAD
Pr Rev.
ANNUAL REVIEW OF PHYSIOLOGY. [Annu. rev. physiol.]. **Added/Corp** Annual Reviews, Inc. American Physiological Society (1887). Vol. 1 (1939)-. Academic Scholarly Publication. English. One time a year (March). $54.00. Annual Reviews Inc., 4139 El Camino Way, PO Box 10139, Palo Alto CA 94303-0139. **Tel** (415)493-4400, (800)523-8635, FAX (415)855-9815. **ED** Joseph F. Hoffman. Index available. cum. index. ctrl circ. available on microfilm and microfiche from University Microfilms International (UMI). Documents available from The Genuine Article, BIOSIS Document Express, CASDDS.
Desc: Comprehensive, thorough coverage of latest advances in physiology; written by acknowledged experts in the field. Extensive literature citations included.
Ind/Abst AGRICOLA [Select. Cov.]; Anim. Breed. Abstr.; Biol. Agric. Index; Biol. Abstr.; Chem. Abstr.; CSA Neuro. Abstr.; Curr. Aware. Biol. Sci., CABS; Curr. Cit.; Curr. Contents Life Sci.; Dairy Sci. Abstr.; EMBASE; Energy Res. Abstr.; Health Period. Database; Index Med.; Index Sci. Rev. [Full Cov.]; Index Vet.; INIS Atomindex [Micro.]; Int. Aerosp. Abstr.; Nutr. Abstr. Rev., Ser. B, Live Feeds and Feed.; Nutr. Abstr. Rev., Ser. A, Hum. Exp.; Protozoolog. Abstr.; Psychol. Abstr. (1939-); PsycINFO; PsycLit; Ref. Upd. Basic Ed.; Ref. Upd. Deluxe Ed.; Res. Alert [Full Cov.]; Sci. Cit. Index; SCISEARCH; SportSearch; Stat. Theory Method Abstr. (1959-1963); Vet. Bull.; Trop. Dis. Bull.

LC QP623.5.A58 A575 **ISSN** 1050-5261
DD 574.87/328 US
NLM W1; AN887 **CODEN** AREDEI
ANTISENSE RESEARCH & DEVELOPMENT. **VFOAT** Antisense Research and Development. Vol. 1, No. 1 (Spring 1991)-. Academic Scholarly Publication. English. Four times a year. $144.00. Mary Ann Liebert Inc., 2 Madison Avenue, Larchmont NY 10538. **Tel** (914)834-3100, (800)M-LIEBERT, FAX (212)289-4697. **ED** James Hawkins and Arthur Krieg. Documents available from The Genuine Article, CASDDS.
Desc: Deals with man-made substances and their effects on gene expression at the RNA and DNA levels both in vitro and in vivo. A forum for basic researchers in

molecular biology, cell biology, chemical synthesis, and applied therapeutics for the purpose of developing new concepts and experimental approaches to help understand and modulate gene activity.
Ind/Abst Anim. Breed. Abstr.; Chem. Abstr.; Curr. Cit.; Index Med. (Spring 1991-); Res. Alert [Full Cov.].

LC QH501 **ISSN** 1080-4757
DD 574.1 US

•**APSTRACTS (WORLD WIDE WEB VERSION).** (APSTRACTS [COMPUTER FILE].). **Added/Corp** American Physiological Society (1887-). (1995)-. Periodical. English. One time a week. Free. American Physiological Society, 9650 Rockville Pike, Bethesda MD 20814. **Tel** (301)530-7180, FAX (301)571-1814. available via Internet (http://www.uth.tmc.edu/apstracts); available in print.

LC QH650 **ISSN** 0778-3124
DD 574.1 BE
UDC 57
NLM W1; AR3944 **CODEN** AIPBE4
TITLE CHANGE

ARCHIVES INTERNATIONALES DE PHYSIOLOGIE, DE BIOCHIMIE ET DE BIOPHYSIQUE. [Arch. int. physiol. biochim. biophys.]. **Added/Corp** Association des Physiologistes (France). **VFOAT** Archives Internationales de Physiologie et de Biochimie. Vol. 99, No. 1 (Feb. 1991)-(199?). Academic Scholarly Publication. English (French). Vaillant Carmanne SA, Zeven Puttensraat 20, 3690 Zutendaal, Belgium. **Tel** 011 31 1122 3361. Documents available from The Genuine Article, CASDDS. ***Continues*** *Archives Internationales de Physiologie et de Biochimie, 0003-9799.* ***Continued by*** *Archives of Physiology and Biochemistry, 1381-3455.*
Ind/Abst Chem. Abstr.; Curr. Aware. Biol. Sci., CABS; Curr. Cit.; Dairy Sci. Abstr.; Index Med. (1991-); Index Vet.; Res. Alert [Full Cov.]; Sci. Cit. Index; SCISEARCH; Soc. Sci. Cit. Index [Select. Cov.]; Vet. Bull.

LC QP1 .A67 **ISSN** 1381-3455
DD 571 BE
UDC 57
NLM W1; AR3944 **CODEN** APBIF5

•**ARCHIVES OF PHYSIOLOGY AND BIOCHEMISTRY.** Vol. 103, No. 1 (Apr. 1995)-. Academic Scholarly Publication. English (French). Seven times a year. $465.23. Vaillant Carmanne SA, Zeven Puttensraat 20, 3690 Zutendaal, Belgium. **Tel** 011 31 1122 3361. **(Subscription address:** Swets Publishing Service, PO Box 825, 2160 SZ Lisse, The Netherlands. **Tel** 011 31 2521 35111.) Index available (bound in last issue). ***Continues*** *Archives Internationales de Physiologie, de Biochimie et de Biophysique, 0778-3124.*
Ind/Abst Chem. Abstr.

LC QP1 .A7 **ISSN** 0004-0096
IT
NLM W1 AR536 **CODEN** ARFIAY

ARCHIVIO DI FISIOLOGIA. [Arch. fisiol.]. **Added/Corp** Societa Italiana di Fisiologia. Vol. 1 (Nov. 1903)-. Academic Scholarly Publication. Italian (English; summaries and/or abstracts in English, Italian and French). Three times a year. Societa Italiana di Fisiologia / Casa Editrice Dott, Japelli 5, 35121 Padova Italy. Documents available from BIOSIS Document Express, CASDDS.
Ind/Abst Biol. Abstr.; Chem. Abstr.; EMBASE; Nutr. Abstr. Rev., Ser. B, Live Feeds and Feed.; Nutr. Abstr. Rev., Ser. A, Hum. Exp.

ISSN 0268-1641
DD 016.612173 UK
CCC

ATRIAL NATRIURETIC FACTORS. See Medical Sciences-Cardiology.

ISSN 0093-5557
DD 612 US
NLM W1 BE517 **CODEN** BPHPDV

BENCHMARK PAPERS IN HUMAN PHYSIOLOGY. [Benchmark pap. hum. physiol.]. Vol. 1 (1973)-. Monographic series. English (French and German). Irregular. Price varies per volume. Academic Press Inc., 6277 Sea Harbor Drive, Orlando FL 32887. **Tel** (800)543-9534, (407)345-4100, FAX (407)352-3445. Each issue contains an index to its own contents (no volume index)--loose. Documents available from BIOSIS Document Express.
Ind/Abst Biol. Abstr. (?-1979).

ISSN 0172-6897
GW
NLM W3 BE679S

BERLINER SEMINAR. See Pharmacy and Pharmacology.

ISSN 0142-8004
UK
CCC

BIOLOGICAL RHYTHMS. [Biol. rhythms]. (1972)-. English. Twenty-four times a year. $179.67. SUBIS, Mansion House 19 Kingfield Road, Sheffield S11 9AS United Kingdom. **Tel** 011 44 114 2554433, FAX 011 44 114 255 4626. **Bk Rev. Ad Acc.** ***Continues*** *Circadian Rhythms.*
Desc: Current awareness service for researchers and clinicians.

LC QP251.A1 B5 **ISSN** 0006-3363
DD 574.1/6/05 US
CCC
NLM W1 BI852N **CODEN** BIREBV
Pr Rev.

BIOLOGY OF REPRODUCTION. [Biol. reprod.]. **Added/Corp** Society for the Study of Reproduction. Vol. 1 (April 1969)-. Academic Scholarly Publication. English. Twelve times a year (plus one supplement sent with July issue). $180.00. Society for the Study of Reproduction, Subscription Department, 1526 Jefferson Street, Madison WI 53711-2106. **Tel** (608)256-2777, FAX (608)256-4610. **ED** Fuller W. Bazer (Editor-in-chief) and Judith Jansen (Managing Editor). **Ad Acc. Acid Free. Circ:** 3,700. Documents available from The Genuine Article, BIOSIS Document Express, CASDDS.
Desc: Publishes original research on a broad range of topics in the field of reproductive biology, as well as minireviews on topics of current importance or controversy.
Ind/Abst Abstr. Anthropol.; AgBiotech News Inf.; AGRICOLA [Select. Cov.]; Anim. Breed. Abstr.; Biol. Abstr.; Chem. Abstr.; CSA Neuro. Abstr.; Curr. Aware. Biol. Sci., CABS; Curr. Cit.; Curr. Contents Life Sci.; Dairy Sci. Abstr.; EMBASE; Energy Res. Abstr.; Fish Rev.; Health Plan. Adminis.; Index Med.; Index Vet.; INIS Atomindex [Micro.]; Key Word Index Wildl. Res.; NAPRALERT; Nucl. Sci. Abstr.; Nutr. Abstr. Rev., Ser. B, Live Feeds and Feed.; Nutr. Abstr. Rev., Ser. A, Hum. Exp.; Life Sci. Collect.; Pig News Inf.; Poult. Abstr.; Protozoolog. Abstr.; Ref. Upd. Basic Ed.; Ref. Upd. Deluxe Ed.; Res. Alert [Full Cov.]; Sci. Cit. Index; SCISEARCH; Small Anim. Abstr. Bibliogr.; Vet. Bull.; Wildl. Rev.

LC RG626 .B63 **ISSN** 0547-6844
DD 616/.043/05 611 US
NLM W1 BI966 **CODEN** BTHDAK

BIRTH DEFECTS ORIGINAL ARTICLE SERIES. See Medical Sciences-Gynecology and Obstetrics.

ISSN 0819-0739
DD 805 AT

BLAST MANUKA. [Blast Manuka]. (1987)-. Periodical. English. Four times a year (Mar., June, Sept., Dec.). 20.55Aus$. Blast, PO Box 3514, Nugent & Tully, Manuka ACT 2603 Australia. **Tel** 011 61 6 2621502. **ED** Bill Tully and Craig Cormick. **Bk Rev. Ad Acc, Adv Mgr:** Bill Tully.

LC QP31.2 .B64 **ISSN** 0101-4242
DD 591.1/05 BL
CODEN BFANDM

BOLETIM DE FISIOLOGIA ANIMAL. [Bol. fisiol. anim.]. **Added/Corp** Universidade de Sao Paulo. Departamento de Fisiologia Geral. (1977)-. Academic Scholarly Publication. Portuguese (English). One time a year. Universidade de Sao Paulo / Instituto de Biociencias, Departamento de Fisiologia Geral, Caixa Postal 11.176, CEP 05421 01000 Sao Paulo SP Brazil. Documents available from CASDDS.
Ind/Abst Chem. Abstr. (1977-1980).

LC QH671 **ISSN** 0286-2190
DD 574.2 JA
NLM W1; BY998J **CODEN** MDPHDG

BYOTAI SEIRI (OSAKA. 1982). See Medical Sciences-Pathology.

LC QP88 .C28 **ISSN** 0171-967X
DD 599/.01/852 US
CCC
NLM W1 CA162T **CODEN** CTINDZ
Pr Rev.

CALCIFIED TISSUE INTERNATIONAL. [Calcif. tissue int.]. Vol. 27 (1979)-. Academic Scholarly Publication. English. Twelve times a year. $659.00. Springer-Verlag New York Inc., 175 Fifth Avenue, New York NY 10010. **Tel** (212)460-1500 ext 256, FAX (212)533-3503, telex 232 235 SPB UR. **(Subscription address:** Springer-Verlag New York Inc. / North America, PO Box 2485, Journal Fulfillment, Secaucus NJ 07096. **Tel** (201)348-4033, (800)777-4643, FAX (201)348-4505.) **ED** L V Avioli. Documents available from The Genuine Article, BIOSIS Document Express, CASDDS. ***Continues*** *Calcified Tissue Research, 0008-0594.*
Desc: Publishes research emphasizing the structure and function of bone and other mineralized systems in living organisms.
Ind/Abst AGRICOLA (?-1987); Biol. Abstr.; Calcium Calcif. Tissue Abstr.; Chem. Abstr.; Curr. Cit.; Curr. Contents Life Sci.; Curr. Titles Dent.; Dairy Sci. Abstr.; EMBASE; Energy Res. Abstr. (May 1980-); GeoRef; Health Plan. Adminis.; Index Med.; Index Vet.; INIS Atomindex [Micro.]; Int. Aerosp. Abstr.; Nutr. Abstr. Rev., Ser. B, Live Feeds and Feed.; Nutr. Abstr. Rev., Ser. A, Hum. Exp.; Oncog. Growth Factors Abstr.; Life Sci. Collect.; Poult. Abstr.; Ref. Upd. Basic Ed.; Ref. Upd. Deluxe Ed.; Res. Alert [Full Cov.]; Sci. Cit. Index; SCISEARCH; Soc. Sci. Cit. Index [Select. Cov.]; Vet. Bull.

ISSN 1066-7814
DD 612 US
CCC
NLM W1; CA569EG **CODEN** CJAPEY

•**CANADIAN JOURNAL OF APPLIED PHYSIOLOGY.** [Can. j. appl. physiol.]. **Added/Corp** Canadian Society for Exercise Physiology. **VFOAT** Revue Canadienne de Physiologie Appliquee. Vol. 18, No. 1 (Mar. 1993)-. Periodical. English (French). Four times a year (Mar., June, Sept., Dec.). $110.00. Human Kinetics Publishers Inc., 1607 North Market Street, PO Box 5076, Champaign IL 61825-5076. **Tel** (217)351-5076, FAX (217)351-2674. **ED** Philip Gardiner & Francois Perronet. Index available. Documents available from BIOSIS Document Express. ***Continues*** *Canadian Journal of Sport Sciences, 0833-1235.*
Desc: Focuses on both basic and applied research articles that examine the relationship between the biological sciences and physical activity, fitness, and health.
Ind/Abst Biol. Abstr.; Curr. Cit.; Index Med.; Soc. Sci. Cit. Index [Select. Cov.]; SPORT Discus.

ISSN 0008-4212
CN
CCC
NLM W1 CA599H **CODEN** CJPPA3
Pr Rev.

CANADIAN JOURNAL OF PHYSIOLOGY AND PHARMACOLOGY. [Can. j. physiol. pharmacol.]. **Added/Corp** National Research Council of Canada. Canadian Physiological Society. Pharmacological Society of Canada. National Research Council Canada. **VFOAT** Journal Canadien de Physiologie et Pharmacologie. Vol. 42 (Jan. 1964)-. Academic Scholarly Publication. English (French). Twelve times a year. 390.00Can$. National Research Council of Canada, Receiver General for Canada, Ottawa Ontario K1A 0R6 Canada. **Tel** (613)993-0362, FAX (613)952-7656. **ED** H. L. Atwood and K. H. Jhamandas. Index available. **Ad Acc. Circ:** 1,500. available on microfilm and microfiche from University Microfilms International (UMI). Documents available from The Genuine Article, BIOSIS Document Express, CASDDS. ***Continues in part*** *Canadian Journal of Biochemistry and Physiology, 0576-5544.*
Desc: Publishes original research on all aspects of physiology, pharmacology, nutrition, and toxicology.
Ind/Abst AgBiotech News Inf.; Anim. Breed. Abstr.; Biol. Abstr.; Calcium Calcif. Tissue Abstr.; Chem. Abstr.; Chem. Titles; CSA Neuro. Abstr.; Curr. Aware. Biol. Sci., CABS; Curr. Cit.; Curr. Contents Life Sci.; Dairy Sci. Abstr.; EMBASE; Health Plan. Adminis.; Helminthol. Abstr. (1991-); Hortic. Abstr.; Index Med.; Index Vet.; INIS Atomindex [Micro.]; Int. Aerosp. Abstr.; Maize Abstr.; NAPRALERT; Nutr. Abstr. Rev., Ser. B, Live Feeds and Feed.; Nutr. Abstr. Rev., Ser. A, Hum. Exp.; Life Sci. Collect.; PESTDOC; Pig News Inf.; Potato Abstr.; Poult. Abstr.; Protozoolog. Abstr.; Ref. Upd. Basic Ed.; Ref. Upd. Deluxe Ed.; Res. Alert [Full Cov.]; Rev. Med. Vet. Entomol.; Sci. Cit. Index; SCISEARCH; Small Anim. Abstr. Bibliogr.; SportSearch; Vet. Bull.; Wheat Barley Trit. Abstr.

ISSN 0142-8012
DD 016.6121 UK

CARDIOVASCULAR PHYSIOLOGY. See Medical Sciences-Cardiology.

LC QP1 .P62 QP101.2 **ISSN** 0363-387X
DD 599/.01/1 US
NLM W1 IN834F v.9 etc. WG 102 C2672

CARDIOVASCULAR PHYSIOLOGY (LONDON, ENGLAND). See Medical Sciences-Cardiology.

ISSN 0142-8020
UK

CELL CALCIUM. See Biology-Cytology.

LC QP455 .C48 **ISSN** 0300-1261
DD 016.5911/826 US
NLM ZWL 102 C517

CHEMORECEPTION ABSTRACTS. See Biology-Abstracting, Bibliographies and Statistics.

ISSN 0258-6428
CC
UDC 612

CHINESE JOURNAL OF PHYSIOLOGICAL SCIENCES. [Chin. j. physiol. sci.]. (1985)-. Periodical. English. Four times a year. $245.00. Science Press, 16 Donghuangchenggen North Street, Beijing 100707, People's Republic of China. **Tel** 011 86 1 4019821, 011 86 1 4010642, FAX 011 86 1 4012180, 011 86 1 4019810, telex 210147. **ED** Hu Shutsu.
Desc: Publishes original papers in physiology and functionally oriented research contributions from biochemistry, biophysics, pharmacology, morphology and other related biomedical disciplines; provides coverage of work in the field.
Ind/Abst EMBASE.

LC QP1 .C633 ISSN 0304-4920
CH
NLM W1 CH765 CODEN CJPHDG

CHINESE JOURNAL OF PHYSIOLOGY, THE. [Chin. j. physiol.]. **Added/Corp** Chung-kuo Sheng li Hsueh Hui. **VFOAT** Chung-Kuo Sheng Li Hsueh Tsa Chih. Vol. 18 (1960)-. Academic Scholarly Publication. English. $80.00. Chinese Physiological Society, Taipei Taiwan. Documents available from CASDDS. ***Continues in part*** *Chinese Journal of Physiology.*
Ind/Abst Chem. Abstr.; Curr. Cit.; EMBASE [Select. Cov.]; Health Plan. Adminis.; Index Med.

LC QP84.6 .C44 ISSN 0390-0037
DD 574.1 IT
NLM W1 CH972 CODEN CBLGA2
Pr Rev. SUSPENDED

CHRONOBIOLOGIA. [Chronobiologia]. **Added/Corp** International Society for Chronobiology. Vol. 1-18 (Jan./Mar. 1974)-Suspended (1994). Academic Scholarly Publication. English (Italian). Four times a year (Jan., Apr., July, Oct.). Associated Chronobiologia Researchers, via R di Lauria 12 A, 20149 Milan Italy. **Tel** 011 39 2 324750, FAX 011 39 2 70635425. Index available. **Bk Rev.** available on microfilm from University Microfilms International (UMI). Documents available from The Genuine Article, BIOSIS Document Express, CASDDS.
Desc: Publishes results of original research, didactic material concerning patho-physiological and statistical evaluation of rhythms, growth, development, aging and other predictable changes in life forms.
Ind/Abst Anim. Breed. Abstr.; Biocont. News Inf.; Biol. Abstr.; Chem. Abstr.; CSA Neuro. Abstr. (?-?); Curr. Cit.; Curr. Contents Agric. Biol. Environ. Sci.; EMBASE; Index Med.; Index Vet.; Nutr. Abstr. Rev., Ser. B, Live Feeds and Feed.; Nutr. Abstr. Rev., Ser. A, Hum. Exp. (1977-); Life Sci. Collect.; Protozoolog. Abstr.; Psychol. Abstr. (1977-); PsycINFO; PsycLit; Res. Alert [Select. Cov.]; Rev. Med. Vet. Mycology; SCISEARCH; Soils Fert.; Vet. Bull.

ISSN 0305-1870
AT
CCC
NLM W1 CL664E CODEN CEXPB9
Pr Rev.

CLINICAL AND EXPERIMENTAL PHARMACOLOGY & PHYSIOLOGY. See Pharmacy and Pharmacology.

LC RB113 .C55 ISSN 0144-5979
DD 616.07/05 UK
CCC
NLM W1 CL766D CODEN CLPHDU
Pr Rev.

CLINICAL PHYSIOLOGY (OXFORD). (CLINICAL PHYSIOLOGY.). [Clin. physiol.]. **Added/Corp** Scandinavian Society of Clinical Physiology. Vol. 1, No. 1 (Feb. 1981)-. Academic Scholarly Publication. English. Six times a year. $468.00. Blackwell Scientific Publications Ltd, Marston Book Services, PO Box 88, Oxford OX2 ONE United Kingdom. **Tel** 011 44 1865 206206, FAX 011 44 1865 206219, telex 837 515 MARDIS G. **ED** J. Wahlen. **Ad Acc. Circ:** 250. available on microfilm and microfiche from University Microfilms International (UMI). Documents available from The Genuine Article, BIOSIS Document Express, CASDDS.
Desc: Publishes reports on clinical and experimental research pertinent to human physiology in health and disease.
Ind/Abst Biol. Abstr.; Chem. Abstr.; Curr. Aware. Biol. Sci., CABS; Curr. Cit.; Curr. Contents Clin. Med.; Curr. Contents Life Sci.; EMBASE; Health Plan. Adminis.; Index Med.; Nutr. Abstr. Rev., Ser. A, Hum. Exp.; Life Sci. Collect.; Ref. Upd. Deluxe Ed.; Res. Alert [Full Cov.]; Sci. Cit. Index; SCISEARCH; SportSearch.

US

COLLECTED PAPERS - FLORIDA. UNIVERSITY, GAINESVILLE. COLLEGE OF MEDICINE. DEPARTMENT OF PHYSIOLOGY. **Main/Corp** Florida. University, Gainesville. College of Medicine. Department of Physiology. Vol. 1 (1956-61)-. English.

LC QP33 .C664
DD 591.1/05 UK
NLM W1; CO435IG
TITLE CHANGE

COMPARATIVE BIOCHEMISTRY AND PHYSIOLOGY. B, BIOCHEMISTRY & MOLECULAR BIOLOGY : CBP. See Biology-Biological Chemistry.

LC QP33 .C664 ISSN 0305-0491
DD 591.1/05 UK
CCC
NLM W1; CO435B CODEN CBPBB8
Pr Rev. TITLE CHANGE

COMPARATIVE BIOCHEMISTRY AND PHYSIOLOGY. B, COMPARATIVE BIOCHEMISTRY. See Biology-Biological Chemistry.

UK

•COMPARATIVE BIOCHEMISTRY AND PHYSIOLOGY. C, PHARMACOLOGY, TOXICOLOGY & ENDOCRINOLOGY : CBP. See Pharmacy and Pharmacology.

LC QP33 .C66
UK
NLM W1; CO435A
TITLE CHANGE

COMPARATIVE BIOCHEMISTRY AND PHYSIOLOGY. COMPARATIVE PHYSIOLOGY. **VFOAT** Comparative Physiology; CBP. A, Physiology; Physiology; Comparative Biochemistry and Physiology. A, Comparative Physiology; Comparative Biochemistry and Physiology : CBP. A, Physiology. Vol. 101A, No. 2 (Feb. 1992)-Vol. 108A, No. 4 (Aug. 1994). Periodical. English. Pergamon Press, An Imprint of Elsevier Science Ltd., The Boulevard, Langford Lane, Kidlington, Oxford OX5 1GB United Kingdom. **Tel** 011 44 1865 843000, 011 44 1865 843699, FAX 011 44 1865 843010. **(Subscription address:** Elsevier Science Ltd. / Oxford Fulfillment Centre, PO Box 800, Kidlington OX5 1DX United Kingdom. **Tel** 011 44 865 843355.) ***Continues*** *Comparative Biochemistry and Physiology. A, Comparative Physiology, 0300-9629.* ***Continued by*** *Comparative Biochemistry and Physiology. Physiology.*
Desc: Publishes papers on respiration; metabolism; digestion; osmoregulation; excretion; blood, heart, and circulation; endocrinology; muscle; sense organs; neurophysiology etc. of invertebrates and vertebrates.
Ind/Abst Bibliogr. Agric.; Index Med. (1992-1994).

US

•COMPARATIVE BIOCHEMISTRY AND PHYSIOLOGY. PART A, PHYSIOLOGY. **VFOAT** Physiology; CBP, Comparative Biochemistry and Physiology. A, Physiology. Vol. 109A, No. 3 (Nov. 1994)-. Periodical. English. Twelve times a year. $2580.00. Elsevier Science Publishing Company Inc, Madison Square Station, PO Box 882, New York NY 10159-0882. **Tel** (212)633-3950, FAX (212)633-3990. Index Available in last issue of each volume--loose separately paged. **Bk Rev. Ad Acc.** available on microfilm and microfiche from University Microfilms International (UMI); available on microfiche from the publisher; available on an online database from Elsevier Electronic Subscriptions (EES). ***Continues*** *Comparative Biochemistry and Physiology. Physiology.*
Desc: Publishes papers on respiration; metabolism; digestion; osmoregulation; excretion; blood, heart, and circulation; endocrinology; muscle; sense organs; neurophysiology etc. of invertebrates and vertebrates.
Ind/Abst Bibliogr. Agric.

LC QP33 .C664
DD 591.1/05 UK

•COMPARATIVE BIOCHEMISTRY AND PHYSIOLOGY. PART B, BIOCHEMISTRY & MOLECULAR BIOLOGY. See Biology-Biological Chemistry.

LC QH501
DD 574.1 UK
NLM W1; CO435A
Pr Rev. TITLE CHANGE

COMPARATIVE BIOCHEMISTRY AND PHYSIOLOGY. PHYSIOLOGY. [Comp. biochem. physiol., A. Comp. physiol.]. **VFOAT** Physiology; CBP. A, Physiology; Comparative Biochemistry and Physiology : CBP. A, Physiology. Vol. 109A, No. 1 (Sept. 1994)-Vol. 109A, No. 2 (Oct. 1994). Academic Scholarly Publication. English. Pergamon Press, An Imprint of Elsevier Science Ltd., The Boulevard, Langford Lane, Kidlington, Oxford OX5 1GB United Kingdom. **Tel** 011 44 1865 843000, 011 44 1865 843699, FAX 011 44 1865 843010. **(Subscription address:** Elsevier Science Ltd. / Oxford Fulfillment Centre, PO Box 800, Kidlington OX5 1DX United Kingdom. **Tel** 011 44 865 843355.) **ED** Gerald A. Kerkut. Index Available in last issue of each volume--loose separately paged. **Bk Rev. Ad Acc.** available on microfilm and microfiche from University Microfilms International (UMI); available on microfiche from the publisher. Documents available from The Genuine Article, BIOSIS Document Express, CASDDS, ADONIS. ***Continues*** *Comparative Biochemistry and Physiology. Comparative Physiology.* ***Continued by*** *Comparative Biochemistry and Physiology. Part A, Physiology.*
Desc: Publishes papers on respiration; metabolism; digestion; osmoregulation; excretion; blood, heart, and circulation; endocrinology; muscle; sense organs; neurophysiology etc. of invertebrates and vertebrates.
Ind/Abst ADONIS; AGRICOLA [Select. Cov.]; Anim. Breed. Abstr.; AQUAREF; Aquat. Sci. Fish. Abstr. [CD-ROM Ed.]; Biol. Abstr.; Calcium Calcif. Tissue Abstr.; Chem. Abstr.; Chem. Titles; Chemorecept. Abstr.; CSA Neuro. Abstr.; Curr. Aware. Biol. Sci., CABS; Curr. Contents Agric. Biol. Environ. Sci.; Curr. Contents Life Sci.; Curr. Ref. Fish Res.; Dairy Sci. Abstr.; Ecol. Abstr. (?-?); Ecology Abstr.; EMBASE; Entomol. Abstr.; Fish Rev.; Helminthol. Abstr. (19??-19??); Index Med.; Index Vet.; Key Word Index Wildl. Res.; Mar. Sci. Contents Tables; NAPRALERT; Nematol. Abstr.; Nutr. Abstr. Rev., Ser. B, Live Feeds and Feed.; Nutr. Abstr. Rev., Ser. A, Hum. Exp.; Ocean. Abstr.; Life Sci. Collect.; Pig News Inf.; Potato Abstr.; Poult. Abstr.; Protozoolog. Abstr.; Ref. Upd. Basic Ed.; Ref. Upd. Deluxe Ed.; Res. Alert [Full Cov.]; Rev. Agric. Entomol.; Rev. Med. Vet. Entomol.; Sci. Cit. Index; SCISEARCH; Soyabean Abstr.; Vet. Bull.; Wildl. Rev.

LC QH540 .C63 ISSN 0379-0436
DD 574.1/05 II
CCC
NLM W1 CO436U CODEN CPECDM
Pr Rev. CEASED

COMPARATIVE PHYSIOLOGY AND ECOLOGY. [Comp. physiol. ecol.]. Vol. 1 (Jan. 1976)-Vol. 19 (1994). Academic Scholarly Publication. English. K.G. Purohit, Jodhpur India. **(Subscription address:** Prints India, 11 Darya Ganj, New Delhi 110002 India. **Tel** 011 91 11 3268645, FAX 011 91 11 3275542, telex 31-61087 PRIN-IN.) **ED** K. G. Purohit. **Bk Rev. Ad Acc.** Documents available from The Genuine Article, CASDDS.
Desc: Publish papers, short reports, and reviews on comparative physiology, environmental biology, physiological efficiencies, population, toxicology and etc.
Ind/Abst AGRICOLA; Chem. Abstr.; Crop Physiol. Abstr.; Curr. Cit.; Curr. Contents Agric. Biol. Environ. Sci.; Curr. Ref. Fish Res.; Ecology Abstr.; EMBASE; Energy Res. Abstr. (Dec. 1980-); Field Crop Abstr.; Helminthol. Abstr. (19??-19??); Hortic. Abstr.; Life Sci. Collect.; Protozoolog. Abstr.; Res. Alert [Select. Cov.]; Rev. Agric. Entomol.; Rev. Med. Vet. Entomol.; Rev. Med. Vet. Mycology; Rev. Plant Pathol.; SCISEARCH; Seed Abstr.; Soils Fert.; Weed Abstr.; Wheat Barley Trit. Abstr.

ISSN 0769-7996
FR
NLM W1; CO452F

COMPORTEMENTS. [Comportements]. **Added/Corp** Centre National de la Recherche Scientifique (France). No 1 (1984)-. Monographic series. French. Four times a year. Price varies per volume.
Ind/Abst PsycLit.

LC QP88.23 .C67 ISSN 0300-8207
DD 591.8/2 US
CCC
NLM W1 CO727M CODEN CVTRBC
Pr Rev.

CONNECTIVE TISSUE RESEARCH. [Connect. tissue res.]. Vol. 1 (March 1972)-. Periodical. English. Four times a year (Four issues per volume). $678.00 (academic institutions), $1058.00 (corporate institutions). Gordon & Breach Science Publishers, Inc., PO Box 786, Cooper Station, New York NY 10276. **Tel** (212)206-8900, FAX (212)645-2459. Documents available from The Genuine Article, BIOSIS Document Express, CASDDS.
Desc: Highlights the most significant and original contributions in the field of connective tissue research, to relate the many facets of the subject, and to afford easier communication amongst those who wish to remain informed of current development in the entire field while actively engaged in more narrowly focused studies.
Ind/Abst AGRICOLA; Biol. Abstr.; Calcium Calcif. Tissue Abstr.; Chem. Abstr.; Curr. Cit.; Curr. Contents Life Sci.; EMBASE; Health Plan. Adminis.; Index Med.; Nutr. Abstr. Rev., Ser. B, Live Feeds and Feed.; Nutr. Abstr. Rev., Ser. A, Hum. Exp.; Life Sci. Collect.; Ref. Upd. Deluxe Ed.; Res. Alert [Full Cov.]; Sci. Cit. Index; SCISEARCH.

LC QP364 .C87 ISSN 0747-5454
DD 599/.0188 US
NLM W1; CU821P CODEN CTRSES

CURRENT TOPICS IN RESEARCH ON SYNAPSES. [Curr. top. res. synap.]. Vol. 1 (1984)-. Academic Scholarly Publication. English. Irregular. Price varies per volume. Wiley Liss, 605 3rd Avenue, New York NY 10158. **Tel** (212)850-8800, (212)850-6645. **(Subscription address:** John Wiley & Sons, Inc. / Philadelphia, PO Box 7247, Philadelphia PA 19170. **Tel** (212)850-6645, (800)225-5945.) **ED** D. Gareth Jones. **Bk Rev. Ad Acc.** Documents available from CASDDS.
Ind/Abst Chem. Abstr. (1984-).

ISSN 0300-4015
KO

DAI HAN SENG RI HAK HUI JI. **Main/Corp** Dai Han Seng ri Hak Hui. **VFOAT** Korean Journal of Physiology. (1967)-. Academic Scholarly Publication. Korean (summaries and/or abstracts in English). Two times a year. $30.00. Korean Physiological Society, Seoul National University, 28 Yongon Dong, Congno Gu 110 460 Seoul Korea. **Tel** 011 82 2 7639667.
Ind/Abst EMBASE [Select. Cov.].

LC BF1074 .D72 ISSN 1053-0797
DD 154.6/3/05 US
CCC
NLM W1; DR26 CODEN DRMGEW
DREAMING (NEW YORK, N.Y.).
(DREAMING : JOURNAL OF THE ASSOCIATION FOR THE STUDY OF DREAMS.). [Dreaming]. **Added/Corp** Association for the Study of Dreams. Vol. 1, No. 1 (Mar. 1991)-. Periodical. English. Four times a year. $155.00. Human Sciences Press, PO Box 735, Canal Street Station, New York NY 10013. **Tel** (212)620-8000, FAX (212)807-1047, telex 23421139. **(Subscription address:** Eurospan Ltd., 3 Henrietta Street Covent Garden, London WC2E 8LU United Kingdom. **Tel** 011 44 181 2400856, FAX 011 44 181 3790609.) **ED** Ernest Hartmann.
Desc: An international forum for the publication of scholarly articles on various aspects of dreams and dreaming. Features biological/physiological research, psychological studies, clinical research, theoretical and sociological papers, and papers investigating the link between dreams and art, literature, or other human activities.
Ind/Abst Neuropsych. Abstr.; Psychoanal. Abstr.; PsycScan: Appl. Exp. Eng. Psych.; PsycScan: LD/MR.

LC QH301 .E425
DD 574/.05 UA
EGYPTIAN JOURNAL OF PHYSIOLOGICAL SCIENCES / EDITED BY THE EGYPTIAN PHYSIOLOGICAL SCIENCES SOCIETY. **Added/Corp** Jamiyah Al-Misriyah Lil-Ulum Al-Fisiyulujiyah. **VFOAT** Majallah Al-Misriyah Lil-Ulum Al-Fisiyulujiyah. Vol. 1, No. 2 (1974)-. Periodical. English (summaries and/or abstracts in Arabic). Two times a year. National Information & Documentation Center, A1-Tahrir St Dokki Awqaf PO, Cairo Egypt. **Tel** 011 20 2 701696, telex 93069. Documents available from CASDDS. ***Continues*** *Egyptian Journal of Physiological Science, 0301-8660.*
Ind/Abst Chem. Abstr.; Crop Physiol. Abstr.; Grass. Forage Abstr.; Hortic. Abstr.; Seed Abstr.; Weed Abstr.

ISSN 0168-5597
IE
UDC 616.831 CCC
ELECTROENCEPHALOGRAPHY AND CLINICAL NEUROPHYSIOLOGY EVOKED POTENTIALS. [Electroencephalogr. clin. neurophysiol., Evoked potentials]. (1984)-. Academic Scholarly Publication. English. Six times a year (1 volume). $172.00. Elsevier Science Ireland Ltd., Bay 15, Shannon Industrial Estate, Co Clare Ireland. **Tel** 011 353 61 471944. available on an online database from Elsevier Electronic Subscriptions (EES). Documents available from Ask*IEEE, ADONIS.
Ind/Abst ADONIS; Curr. Aware. Biol. Sci., CABS; EMBASE; INSPEC (Jan. 1985-); Psychol. Abstr. (1990-); PsycINFO; PsycLit; Ref. Upd. Deluxe Ed.

LC QP1 .A537 ISSN 0301-5548
DD 612/.005 GW
CCC
NLM W1 EU65 CODEN EJAPCK
Pr Rev.
EUROPEAN JOURNAL OF APPLIED PHYSIOLOGY AND OCCUPATIONAL PHYSIOLOGY. [Eur. j. appl. physiol. occup. physiol.]. Vol. 32 (1973)-. Academic Scholarly Publication. English (German). Twelve times a year. $2235.00. Springer-Verlag GmbH & Company KG, Heidelberger Platz 3, D-14197 Berlin Germany. **Tel** 011 49 30 8207223, FAX 011 49 30 8214091, telex 183 319 SPBLN D. **(Subscription address:** Springer-Verlag New York Inc. / North America, PO Box 2485, Journal Fulfillment, Secaucus NJ 07096. **Tel** (201)348-4033, (800)777-4643, FAX (201)348-4505.) **ED** R Goldsmith and W Isselhard. available on microfilm and microfiche from University Microfilms International (UMI). Documents available from The Genuine Article, BIOSIS Document Express, CASDDS. ***Continues*** *Internationale Zeitschrift fur Angewandte Physiologie Einschliesslich Arbeitsphysiologie, 0020-9376.*
Desc: Publishes original works on applied human physiology with emphasis on environmental and work physiology.
Ind/Abst Biol. Abstr.; Chem. Abstr.; Curr. Cit.; Curr. Contents Life Sci.; EMBASE; Energy Res. Abstr.; Ergon. Abstr.; Highw. Res. Abstr.; Index Med.; Int. Aerosp. Abstr.; Nutr. Abstr. Rev., Ser. B, Live Feeds and Feed.; Nutr. Abstr. Rev., Ser. A, Hum. Exp.; Life Sci. Collect.; Phys. Educ. Index; Ref. Upd. Deluxe Ed.; Res. Alert [Full Cov.]; Saf. Health Work; Sci. Cit. Index; SCISEARCH; Soc. Sci. Cit. Index [Select. Cov.]; Soyabean Abstr.; SPORT Discus; SportSearch.

ISSN 0367-1089
DD 016.612 NE
CCC
NLM ZW 1 E955
EXCERPTA MEDICA. SECTION 2A. PHYSIOLOGY. **See** Biology-Abstracting, Bibliographies and Statistics.

LC QP1 .Q3 ISSN 0958-0670
DD 591.L UK
NLM W1; EX511TK CODEN EXPHEZ
EXPERIMENTAL PHYSIOLOGY. [Exp. physiol.]. **Added/Corp** Physiological Society (Great Britain). Vol. 75, No. 1 (Jan. 1990)-. Academic Scholarly Publication. English. Six times a year. $306.00. Cambridge University Press, The Edinburgh Building, Shaftesbury Road, Cambridge CB2 2RU United Kingdom. **Tel** 011 44 1223 312393, FAX 011 44 1223 315052, telex 851-817256. **(Subscription address:** Cambridge University Press / North America, 110 Midland Avenue, Port Chester NY 10573. **Tel** (800)431-1580, (914)937-9600.) **ED** C. Kidd. **Bk Rev.** available on microfilm from University Microfilms International (UMI). Documents available from The Genuine Article, BIOSIS Document Express, CASDDS. ***Continues*** *Quarterly Journal of Experimental Physiology (Cambridge, England), 0144-8757.*
Desc: Original work on all facets of physiology are published. Integrative studies on man and animals are emphasized and contributions range from the molecular level, through systems physiology, to the whole animal. The Rapid Communications section provides for the publication of short papers in 2.5 months from each of six deadlines. A popular feature is the inclusion of critical reviews by active researchers in developing areas of physiology. Certain of the Physiological Society's Prize Lectures are also published.
Ind/Abst Biol. Abstr.; Chem. Abstr. (1990-); Curr. Aware. Biol. Sci., CABS; Curr. Cit.; Curr. Contents Life Sci.; Dairy Sci. Abstr.; EMBASE [Select. Cov.]; Health Plan. Adminis.; Index Med. (1990-); Index Vet.; Nutr. Abstr. Rev., Ser. B, Live Feeds and Feed.; Nutr. Abstr. Rev., Ser. A, Hum. Exp.; Ref. Upd. Deluxe Ed.; Res. Alert [Full Cov.]; Sci. Cit. Index; SCISEARCH; Vet. Bull.

ISSN 0428-2094
DD 612 US
FELS MONOGRAPH SERIES. No. 1 (1951)-. English. Fels Research Institute, Study of Human Development, Yellow Springs OH 45387.

US
FISH PHYSIOLOGY. Vol. 1 (1969)-. Monographic series. English. Irregular. Price varies per volume. Academic Press Inc., 6277 Sea Harbor Drive, Orlando FL 32887. **Tel** (800)543-9534, (407)345-4100, FAX (407)352-3445. **ED** William S. Hoar.

ISSN 0015-329X
RU
NLM W1; FI818M CODEN FZLZAM
FIZIOLOGICESKIJ ZURNAL SSSR IMENI I.M. SECENOVA. (FIZIOLOGICHESKII ZHURNAL SSSR IMENI I.M. SECHENOVA.). [Fiziol. z. SSSR im. I.M. Secenova]. **Added/Corp** Vsesoiuznoe Fiziologicheskoe Obshchestro Imeni I.P. Pavlova. Akademiia Nauk SSSR. **VFOAT** Journal of Physiology of USSR. (1992)-. Academic Scholarly Publication. Russian (summaries and/or abstracts in English, French and German). Twelve times a year. $256.00. **(Subscription address:** East View Publications Inc., 3020 Harbor Lane North, Suite 110, Minneapolis MN 55447. **Tel** (800)477-1005, (612)550-0961, FAX (612)559-2931.) Documents available from BIOSIS Document Express, CASDDS. ***Continues*** *Russkii Fiziologicheskii Zhurnal Imeni I.M. Sechenova.*
Ind/Abst Biol. Abstr.; Chem. Abstr.; CSA Neuro. Abstr. (?-?); Dairy Sci. Abstr.; EMBASE; Index Med.; Nutr. Abstr. Rev., Ser. B, Live Feeds and Feed.; Poult. Abstr.; PsycINFO (1990-).

LC QP1 .A453 ISSN 0201-8489
DD 612/.005 UN
CCC
NLM W1 FI817S CODEN FIZHDO
Pr Rev. TITLE CHANGE
FIZIOLOGICHESKII ZHURNAL. [Fiz.z.]. **Added/Corp** Instytut Fiziolohii im. O.O. Bohomoltsia. (Jan./Feb. 1978)-(1993). Academic Scholarly Publication. Russian (Ukrainian; summaries and/or abstracts in English; table of contents in English). Vidavnitstvo Naukova Dumka, Vul. Tereshchenkivska 3, 252 601 Kiev Ukraine. **Tel** 011 7 44 2444068, FAX 011 7 44 2447060, telex 131376. **(Subscription address:** East View Publications Inc., 3020 Harbor Lane North, Suite 110, Minneapolis MN 55447. **Tel** (800)477-1005, (612)550-0961, FAX (612)559-2931.) Documents available from The Genuine Article, BIOSIS Document Express, CASDDS. ***Continues*** *Fiziologichnyi Zhurnal.* ***Continued by*** *Fiziolohichnyi Zhurnal (Kiev, Ukraine : 1994).*
Ind/Abst Biol. Abstr. (?-?); Chem. Abstr. (?-?); Curr. Contents Life Sci. (?-?); Index Med. (?-?); Int. Aerosp. Abstr. (?-?); Nutr. Abstr. Rev., Ser. B, Live Feeds and Feed. (?-?); Nutr. Abstr. Rev., Ser. A, Hum. Exp. (?-?); Life Sci. Collect. (?-?); PsycLit (?-?); Res. Alert (?-?) [Full Cov.]; Rev. Med. Vet. Mycology (?-?); Sci. Cit. Index (?-?); SCISEARCH (?-?); Soc. Sci. Cit. Index (?-?) [Select. Cov.]; SportSearch (?-?).

LC QP34.5 .F5 ISSN 0131-1646
RU
NLM W1 FI82L CODEN FICHDB
FIZIOLOGIJA CELOVEKA. (FIZIOLOGIIA CHELOVEKA.). [Fiziol. celov.]. **Added/Corp** Akademiia Nauk SSSR. (1975)-. Academic Scholarly Publication. Russian. Six times a year. $300.00. Izdatelstvo Nauka / Akademiia Nauk, (Publishing House of the Russian Academy of Sciences), Leninskii Porspekt 14, 117901 Moscow Russia. **Tel** 011 95 9542153, FAX 011 95 9382144, telex 411964. **(Subscription address:** East View Publications Inc., 3020 Harbor Lane North, Suite 110, Minneapolis MN 55447. **Tel** (800)477-1005, (612)550-0961, FAX (612)559-2931.) Documents available from BIOSIS Document Express, CASDDS.
Ind/Abst Biol. Abstr.; Chem. Abstr.; Index Med. (Vol. 10, No. 1, 1984-); Int. Aerosp. Abstr.; SportSearch.

LC QH501
DD 574.1 UN
•**FIZIOLOHICHNYI ZHURNAL.** **Added/Corp** Instytut Fiziolohii im. O.O. Bohomoltsia. (1994)-. Periodical. Ukrainian (Russian; summaries and/or abstracts in English; table of contents in English). Six times a year. $109.95 US, Canada and Europe; $134.95 other. Vidavnitstvo Naukova Dumka, Vul. Tereshchenkivska 3, 252 601 Kiev Ukraine. **Tel** 011 7 44 2444068, FAX 011 7 44 2447060, telex 131376. **(Subscription address:** East View Publications Inc., 3020 Harbor Lane North, Suite 110, Minneapolis MN 55447. **Tel** (800)477-1005, (612)550-0961, FAX (612)559-2931.) ***Continues*** *Fiziologicheskii Zhurnal, 0201-8489.*

ISSN 0340-0840
GW
NLM W1 FU566N
FUNKTIONSANALYSE BIOLOGISCHER SYSTEME. **Added/Corp** Akademie der Wissenschaften und der Literatur (Germany). Mathematisch-Naturwissenschaftliche Klasse. (1974)-. Monographic series. German. Irregular. Price varies per volume. Franz Steiner Verlag GmbH, Postfach 101061, D-70009 Stuttgart Germany. **Tel** 011 49 711 2582372, FAX 011 49 711 2582290, telex 723636 daz d. **ED** Gerhard Thews. Documents available from CASDDS.
Ind/Abst Chem. Abstr.

LC QP1 .G46 ISSN 0231-5882
DD 591.1/05 XO
NLM W1; GE256 CODEN GPBIE2
Pr Rev.
GENERAL PHYSIOLOGY AND BIOPHYSICS. [Gen. physiol. biophys.]. **Added/Corp** Slovenska Akademia Vied. Vol. 1, No. 1 (Jan. 1982)-. Academic Scholarly Publication. English. Six times a year. $240.00. Veda, Publishing House of the Slovak Academy of Sciences, Klemensova 19, 814 30 Bratislava Slovakia. **Tel** (7)583-15. **(Subscription address:** Karger Libri AG, Petersgraben 31, CH 4009 Basel 11 Switzerland. **Tel** 011 41 61 3061500.) Documents available from The Genuine Article, BIOSIS Document Express, CASDDS.
Ind/Abst Biol. Abstr.; Chem. Abstr. (1984-); Curr. Cit.; Curr. Contents Life Sci.; Index Med.; Res. Alert [Full Cov.]; Sci. Cit. Index; SCISEARCH.

LC QP84 .G762 ISSN 0743-0779
DD 599/.031 US
NLM W1 GR919C CODEN GMFADA
GROWTH AND MATURATION FACTORS. [Growth matur. factors]. (1983)-. Academic Scholarly Publication. English. One time a year. Price varies per volume. John Wiley & Sons, Inc., 605 Third Avenue, New York NY 10158-0012. **Tel** (212)850-6000, (212)850-6645, FAX (212)850-6088, telex 12-7063. **(Subscription address:** John Wiley & Sons / UK, Baffins Lane, Chichester, West Sussex PO19 1UD United Kingdom. **Tel** 011 44 1243 779777, FAX 011 44 243 776128, telex 86290 WIBOOKG.) **ED** Gordon Guroff. Documents available from CASDDS.
Ind/Abst Chem. Abstr. (1983-).

ISSN 0964-7554
UK
GROWTH FACTORS & CYTOKINES. (19??)-. Bulletin. English. Twenty-four times a year. £120.00. SUBIS, Mansion House 19 Kingfield Road, Sheffield S11 9AS United Kingdom. **Tel** 011 44 114 2554433, FAX 011 44 114 255 4626. ***Continues*** *Growth Factors, 0268-1595.*

ISSN 0916-3786
DD 591.1 JA
HIKAKU SEIRI SEIKAGAKU. **VFOAT** Comparative Physiology and Biochemistry. (1990)-. Periodical. Japanese. Four times a year. Nihon Hikaku Seiri Seikagakkai, Tokyo Japan. Documents available from CASDDS. ***Continues*** *Dobutsu Seiri, 0289-6583.*
Ind/Abst Chem. Abstr.

LC QP34.5 .H85 ISSN 0362-1197
DD 612/.005 US
CCC
NLM W1 HU46P CODEN HUPHDC
HUMAN PHYSIOLOGY. [Hum. physiol.]. **Added/Corp** Consultants Bureau. Vol. 1 (Jan./Feb. 1975)-. Academic Scholarly Publication. English (Russian; translations available in Russian). Six times a year. $995.00. Consultants Bureau, A Division of Plenum Publishing Corporation, 233 Spring Street, New York NY 10013. **Tel** (212)620-8000, (212)620-8466, FAX (212)463-0742, telex 23/421139. **ED** V. I. Medvedev. Index available. available on microfilm and microfiche

from University Microfilms International (UMI). Documents available from BIOSIS Document Express, CASDDS.
Desc: Covers topics such as studies of the physiology of work, speech, and sport physiology of the brain and neurophysics of psychological activity.
Ind/Abst Biol. Abstr. (?-1983); Chem. Abstr.; EMBASE; Energy Res. Abstr. (Aug. 1982-); Index Med. (1978-1986); Psychol. Abstr. (1979-); PsycINFO; PsycLit; SportSearch.

ISSN 1355-4786
UK

•HUMAN REPRODUCTION UPDATE.
(1995)-. English. Six times a year. $545.00. Oxford University Press / UK, Walton Street, Oxford OX2 6DP United Kingdom. **Tel** 011 44 1865 56767, FAX 011 44 1865 267773, telex 851/837330 OXPRES G. **(Subscription address:** Oxford University Press / USA, Journals Marketing Department, Oxford University Press, 2001 Evans Road, Cary NC 27513. **Tel** (800)451-7556, (919)677-0977, FAX (919)677-1714.) ***Formed by the union of*** *Bibliography of Reproduction, 0006-1565* ***and*** *Oxford Reviews of Reproductive Biology, 0260-0854.*
Ind/Abst Curr. Cit.

LC BF575.S75 H84 **ISSN** 0885-1174
DD 155.9/05 US
NLM W1; HU464

HUMAN STRESS. See Psychology.

LC QP1 .I5 **ISSN** 0367-8350
DD 574.1/05 II
NLM W1 IN2259 **CODEN** IJPLAN

INDIAN JOURNAL OF PHYSIOLOGY AND ALLIED SCIENCES. [Indian j. physiol. allied sci.].
Added/Corp Physiological Society of India. (Jan. 1947)-. Periodical. English. Four times a year. $75.00. Physiological Society of India, Calcutta India. **(Subscription address:** Prints India, 11 Darya Ganj, New Delhi 110002 India. **Tel** 011 91 11 3268645, FAX 011 91 11 3275542, telex 31-61087 PRIN-IN.) Documents available from BIOSIS Document Express, CASDDS.
Ind/Abst Biol. Abstr.; Chem. Abstr.; NAPRALERT.

LC QP1 .I53 **ISSN** 0019-5499
II
NLM W1 IN226D **CODEN** IJPPAZ
Pr Rev.

INDIAN JOURNAL OF PHYSIOLOGY AND PHARMACOLOGY. [Indian j. physiol. pharmacol.].
Added/Corp Association of Physiologists and Pharmacologists of India. All-India Institute of Medical Sciences. Dept. of Physiology. (1957)-. Academic Scholarly Publication. English. Four times a year (Jan., Apr., July, Oct.). $75.00. All-India Institute of Medical Sciences, Department of Physiology, Ansari Nagar New Delhi 110029 India. **Tel** 661123-263. **(Subscription address:** Prints India, 11 Darya Ganj, New Delhi 110002 India. **Tel** 011 91 11 3268645, FAX 011 91 11 3275542, telex 31-61087 PRIN-IN.) **ED** Usha Nayar. Index available. **Bk Rev. Ad Acc. Circ:** 1,500 (ctrl). Documents available from BIOSIS Document Express, CASDDS.
Desc: Topics on physiology, pharmacology and allied sciences.
Ind/Abst Biol. Abstr.; Chem. Abstr.; Curr. Cit.; EMBASE [Select. Cov.]; Index Med.; Int. Pharm. Abstr.; NAPRALERT; SportSearch.

ISSN 1053-881X
DD 150 US
CCC
NLM W1; IN645T

INTEGRATIVE PHYSIOLOGICAL AND BEHAVIORAL SCIENCE. See Psychology.

ISSN 0167-8760
NE
CCC
NLM W1; IN777N **CODEN** IJPSEE
Pr Rev.

INTERNATIONAL JOURNAL OF PSYCHOPHYSIOLOGY. (INTERNATIONAL JOURNAL OF PSYCHOPHYSIOLOGY : OFFICIAL JOURNAL OF THE INTERNATIONAL ORGANIZATION OF PSYCHOPHYSIOLOGY.). [Int. j. psychophysiol.].
Vol. 1, No. 1 (Aug. 1983)-. Academic Scholarly Publication. English. Nine times a year (3 vols.). $1121.00. Elsevier Science Publishers BV, PO Box 211, 1000 AE Amsterdam Netherlands. **Tel** 011 31 20 4853641, 011 31 20 4853642, FAX 011 31 20 4853598. **ED** A F Ax, N P Bechtereva and J H Gruzelier. available on microfilm and microfiche from University Microfilms International (UMI); available on an online database from Elsevier Electronic Subscriptions (EES). Documents available from The Genuine Article.
Desc: Provides a forum for the publication of original contributions on all aspects of psychophysiology.
Ind/Abst CSA Neuro. Abstr. (?-?); Curr. Aware. Biol. Sci., CABS; Curr. Cit.; Curr. Contents Life Sci.; Curr. Contents Soc. Behav. Sci.; EMBASE; Index Med. (Vol. 1, No. 1 1983-); Life Sci. Collect.; Psychol. Abstr. (1983-); PsycINFO (1990-); PsycLit; Ref. Upd. Deluxe Ed.; Res. Alert [Full Cov.]; Sci. Cit. Index; SCISEARCH; Soc. Sci. Cit. Index [Full Cov.]; SportSearch.

LC QP1 .I85 **ISSN** 0134-2673
RU
CODEN INTFCL

ITOGI NAUKI I TEHNIKI - VSESOJUZNYI INSTITUT NAUCNOJ I TEHNICESKOJINFORMACI SERIJA FIZIOLOGIJA CELOVEKA I ZIVOTNYH.
(ITOGI NAUKI I TEKHNIKI: SERIIA FIZIOLOGIIA CHELOVEKA I ZHIVOTNYKH.). [Itogi nauki teh. - Vses. inst. naucn teh. inf., ser. Fiziol. cel. zivotn.]. **Added/Corp** Vsesoiuznyi Institut Nauchnoi i Tekhnicheskoi Informatsii (Soviet Union). **VFOAT** Itogi Nauki i Tekhniki; Fiziologiia Cheloveka i Zhivoinykh; Seriia Fiziologiia Cheloveka i Zhivotnykh. Vol. 9 (1972)-. Academic Scholarly Publication. Russian. Irregular. VINITI - Vsesoyuznyi Institut Nauchno-Tekhnicheskoi Informatsii, All-Union Scientific and Technical Information Institute, Baltiiskaia ulitsa 14, 125219 Moscow Russia. **Tel** 011 7 95 2384600, FAX 011 7 95 9430060, telex 411160. Documents available from CASDDS. ***Continues*** *Itogi Nauki: Fiziologiia Cheloveka i Zhivotnykh.*
Ind/Abst Chem. Abstr. (1972-1983).

LC QP509 .I84 **ISSN** 0021-3225
YU
NLM W1 IU753 **CODEN** IPPABX

IUGOSLAVICA PHYSIOLOGICA ET PHARMOCOLOGICA ACTA. [Iugoslav. physiol. pharmacol. acta].
Added/Corp Jugoslovensko Drustvo za Fiziologiju. Unija Bioloskih Naucnih Drustava Jugoslavije. **VFOAT** Acta Biologica Iugoslavica. Serija C: Iugoslavica Physiologica et Pharmocologica Acta. Vol. 1 (1965)-. Academic Scholarly Publication. English (summaries and/or abstracts in Russian and Serbian). Three times a year. $20.00. Unija Bioloskih Nauchih, Drustava Jugoslavie Beograd ZM, 1108 Nemanjina 6 Yugoslavia. **ED** V.M. Varagic (editor's address: Department of Pharmacology, PO Box 662, Blegrade Yugoslavia). Index available. cum. index. **Bk Rev. Circ:** 1,500. Documents available from BIOSIS Document Express, CASDDS.
Ind/Abst Biol. Abstr.; Chem. Abstr.; Curr. Cit.; Sci. Cit. Index (19??-19??); SCISEARCH.

LC QP1 .J3 **ISSN** 0021-521X
JA
NLM W1 JA972 **CODEN** JJPHAM
Pr Rev.

JAPANESE JOURNAL OF PHYSIOLOGY, THE. [Jpn. j. physiol.].
Added/Corp Nihon Seiri Gakkai. Vol. 1 (June 1950)-. Academic Scholarly Publication. English (Japanese). Seven times a year. $160.00. Nihon Seiri Gakkai, (Physiological Soc. of Japan), 4-16 Yayoi 2 Chome, Bunkyoku Tokyo 113 Japan. **(Subscription address:** Maruzen Company Ltd., PO Box 5050, Import & Export Department, Tokyo 100 31 Japan. **Tel** 011 81 3 32789224.) Documents available from The Genuine Article, BIOSIS Document Express, CASDDS. ***Supersedes*** *Japanese Journal of Medical Sciences. Part 3. Biophysics.*
Ind/Abst AGRICOLA; Biol. Abstr.; Calcium Calcif. Tissue Abstr.; Chem. Abstr.; CSA Neuro. Abstr.; Curr. Aware. Biol. Sci., CABS; Curr. Cit.; Curr. Contents Life Sci.; Dairy Sci. Abstr.; EMBASE; Index Med.; Int. Aerosp. Abstr.; Life Sci. Collect.; PsycINFO (?-?); PsycLit; Res. Alert [Full Cov.]; Sci. Cit. Index; SCISEARCH; Soc. Sci. Cit. Index [Select. Cov.]; SportSearch.

LC .J72 **ISSN** 8750-7587
DD 599/.01 US
CCC
NLM W1; JO542KB **CODEN** JAPHEV
Pr Rev.

JOURNAL OF APPLIED PHYSIOLOGY (1985). (JOURNAL OF APPLIED PHYSIOLOGY.). [J. appl. physiol.].
Added/Corp American Physiological Society (1887-). Vol. 58, No. 1 (Jan. 1985)-. Academic Scholarly Publication. English. Twelve times a year. $585.00. American Physiological Society, 9650 Rockville Pike, Bethesda MD 20814. **Tel** (301)530-7180, FAX (301)571-1814. **ED** N.S. Cherniack. **Bk Rev. Ad Acc. Circ:** 3,500 (ctrl). available on microfilm and microfiche from University Microfilms International (UMI). Documents available from The Genuine Article, BIOSIS Document Express, Ask*IEEE, CASDDS. ***Continues*** *Journal of Applied Physiology: Respiratory, Environmental and Exercise Physiology, 0161-7567.*
Desc: Applied physiology with emphasis on respiratory, cardiopulmonary, exercise, and environmental physiology.
Ind/Abst Biol. Agric. Index; Biol. Abstr.; Calcium Calcif. Tissue Abstr.; Chem. Abstr. (1985-); Chemorecept. Abstr.; CSA Neuro. Abstr.; Curr. Aware. Biol. Sci., CABS; Curr. Cit.; Curr. Contents Life Sci.; Dairy Sci. Abstr.; EMBASE; Fish Rev.; Helminthol. Abstr. (1991-); Immunol. Abstr.; Index Med. Jan. 1985-; Index Dent. Lit.; Index Vet.; INSPEC (1968-Aug. 1989); Med. Abstr. Newsl.; Nutr. Abstr. Rev., Ser. B, Live Feeds and Feed.; Nutr. Abstr. Rev., Ser. A, Hum. Exp.; PESTDOC; Phys. Educ. Index; Pig News Inf.; Ref. Upd. Basic Ed.; Ref. Upd. Deluxe Ed.; Res. Alert [Full Cov.]; Sci. Cit. Index; SCISEARCH; Small Anim. Abstr. Bibliogr.; Soc. Sci. Cit. Index [Select. Cov.]; SPORT Discus; SportSearch; Stat. Theory Method Abstr. (1959-1963); Vet. Bull.; Wildl. Rev.

ISSN 0792-6855
IS
NLM W1; JO552T **CODEN** JBPPES

JOURNAL OF BASIC AND CLINICAL PHYSIOLOGY AND PHARMACOLOGY.
Added/Corp Israel Physiological and Pharmacological Society. **VFOAT** Journal of Basic & Clinical Physiology & Pharmacology. Vol. 1, No. 1-4 (Jan./Dec. 1990)-. Periodical. English. Four times a year. $250.00. Freund Publishing House Ltd., PO Box 35010, 61 Nachmani Street, Tel Aviv 61350 Israel. **Tel** 011 972 3 5628540, FAX 011 972 3 5628538. **(Subscription address:** Freund Publishing House Ltd., Suite 500, Chesham House 150 Regent Street, London W1R 5FA United Kingdom. **Tel** 011 44 178 172811, FAX 011 972 3 615335.) **ED** M. Horowitz and Y. Oron. Documents available from BIOSIS Document Express. ***Continues*** *Reviews in Clinical & Basic Pharmacology, 0334-1534.*
Ind/Abst Bibliogr. Mission.; Biol. Abstr. (1991-); CSA Neuro. Abstr.; Curr. Cit.; EMBASE; Index Med. (1990-); Int. Pharm. Abstr. (199?-199?); PESTDOC.

LC QP1 .W533 **ISSN** 0021-9541
DD 574.8/76/05 US
CCC
NLM W1 JO579M **CODEN** JCLLAX
Pr Rev.

JOURNAL OF CELLULAR PHYSIOLOGY. [J. cell. physiol.].
Added/Corp Wistar Institute of Anatomy and Biology. Vol. 67, (Feb. 1966)-. Periodical. English. Twelve times a year. $2592.00. John Wiley & Sons, Inc., 605 Third Avenue, New York NY 10158-0012. **Tel** (212)850-6000, (212)850-6645, FAX (212)850-6088, telex 12-7063. **(Subscription address:** John Wiley & Sons / UK, Baffins Lane, Chichester, West Sussex PO19 1UD United Kingdom. **Tel** 011 44 1243 779777, FAX 011 44 243 776128, telex 86290 WIBOOKG.) **ED** Vittorio Defendi. Documents available from The Genuine Article, BIOSIS Document Express, CASDDS, ADONIS. ***Continues*** *Journal of Cellular and Comparative Physiology, 0095-9898.*
Desc: Publishes research papers concerned with physiology and pathology at the cellular level, including the biochemical and biophysical mechanisms concerned in the regulation of cellular growth, differentiation, and function.
Ind/Abst ADONIS; AgBiotech News Inf.; AGRICOLA; Biol. Agric. Index; Biol. Abstr.; Calcium Calcif. Tissue Abstr.; Chem. Abstr.; Chem. Titles; CSA Neuro. Abstr. (?-?); Curr. Cit.; Curr. Contents Life Sci.; Curr. Ref. Fish Res.; Dairy Sci. Abstr.; EMBASE; Energy Res. Abstr.; Genet. Abstr.; Immunol. Abstr.; Index Med.; INIS Atomindex [Micro.]; Int. Aerosp. Abstr.; Nutr. Abstr. Rev., Ser. B, Live Feeds and Feed.; Nutr. Abstr. Rev., Ser. A, Hum. Exp.; Oncog. Growth Factors Abstr.; Life Sci. Collect.; Protozoolog. Abstr.; Ref. Upd. Basic Ed.; Ref. Upd. Deluxe Ed.; Res. Alert [Full Cov.]; Rev. Med. Vet. Entomol.; Sci. Cit. Index; SCISEARCH; Soc. Sci. Cit. Index [Select. Cov.]; Virol. AIDS Abstr.

ISSN 0892-5070
DD 612 US

JOURNAL OF CLINICAL ELECTROPHYSIOLOGY. [J. clin. electrophysiol.].
Added/Corp American Physical Therapy Association (1921-). Section on Clinical Electrophysiology. (1989)-. Periodical. English. Two times a year. $100.00. Secretary Clinical Electrophysiology, Physical Therapy Department, Naval Hospital, Oakland CA 94627. **Tel** (510)633-5067.

LC QP1 .J724 **ISSN** 0340-7594
DD 591.1/88 GW
CCC
NLM W1; JO595JA **CODEN** JCPADN
Pr Rev.

JOURNAL OF COMPARATIVE PHYSIOLOGY. A, SENSORY, NEURAL, AND BEHAVIORAL PHYSIOLOGY. [J. comp. physiol., A].
VFOAT Sensory, Neural, and Behavioral Physiology. Vol. 154, No. 1 (Jan. 1984)-. Academic Scholarly Publication. English. Twelve times a year. $2659.00. Springer-Verlag GmbH & Company KG, Heidelberger Platz 3, D-14197 Berlin Germany. **Tel** 011 49 30 8207223, FAX 011 49 30 8214091, telex 183 319 SPBLN D. **(Subscription address:** Springer-Verlag New York Inc. / North America, PO Box 2485, Journal Fulfillment, Secaucus NJ 07096. **Tel** (201)348-4033, (800)777-4643, FAX (201)348-4505.) **ED** H. Autrum, W. Heiligenberg, F.G. Barth, G. Neuweiler. available on microfilm and microfiche from University Microfilms International (UMI). Documents available from The Genuine Article, BIOSIS Document Express, CASDDS. ***Continues in part*** *Journal of Comparative Physiology, 0302-9824.*
Desc: Concerned with the sense organs and all aspects of neuronal and neural processes as well as with the experimental analysis of behavior, especially neuroethology.
Ind/Abst AGRICOLA [Select. Cov.]; Anim. Behav. Abstr.; Anim. Breed. Abstr.; Biocont. News Inf. (1991-); Biol. Abstr.; Chem. Abstr. (1984-); Chemorecept. Abstr.; CSA Neuro. Abstr.; Curr. Aware. Biol. Sci., CABS; Curr. Cit.; Curr. Contents Life Sci.; Dairy Sci. Abstr.; EMBASE; Entomol. Abstr.; Fish Rev.; Helminthol. Abstr. (1991-); Index Med. (Vol. 157, No. 1, 1985-); Index Vet.; Key Word

Index Wildl. Res.; Life Sci. Collect.; Poult. Abstr.; Protozoolog. Abstr.; Ref. Upd. Deluxe Ed.; Res. Alert [Full Cov.]; Rev. Agric. Entomol.; Rev. Med. Vet. Entomol.; Sci. Cit. Index; SCISEARCH; Soc. Sci. Cit. Index [Select. Cov.]; Wildl. Rev.

LC QP33 .J68 **ISSN** 0174-1578
DD 591.1/05 GW
CCC
NLM W1; JO595JAB **CODEN** JPBPDL
Pr Rev.

JOURNAL OF COMPARATIVE PHYSIOLOGY. B, BIOCHEMICAL, SYSTEMIC, AND ENVIRONMENTAL PHYSIOLOGY. [J. comp. physiol., B Biochem. syst. environ. physiol.]. **VFOAT** Biochemical, Systemic, and Environmental Physiology. Vol. 154, No. 1 (Jan. 1984)-. Academic Scholarly Publication. English. Eight times a year. $1292.00. Springer-Verlag GmbH & Company KG, Heidelberger Platz 3, D-14197 Berlin Germany. **Tel** 011 49 30 8207223, FAX 011 49 30 8214091, telex 183 319 SPBLN D. **(Subscription address:** Springer-Verlag New York Inc. / North America, PO Box 2485, Journal Fulfillment, Secaucus NJ 07096. **Tel** (201)348-4033, (800)777-4643, FAX (201)348-4505.) **ED** H Langer, T Hirano, W T W Potts, and R B Reeves. available on microfilm and microfiche from University Microfilms International (UMI). Documents available from The Genuine Article, BIOSIS Document Express, CASDDS. ***Continues in part** Journal of Comparative Physiology, 0302-9824.*
Desc: Publishes articles concerning the 'machinery' of animals, from the molecular level up to the organismic level.
Ind/Abst AgBiotech News Inf.; AGRICOLA [Select. Cov.]; Biol. Abstr.; Chem. Abstr. (1984-); CSA Neuro. Abstr.; Curr. Aware. Biol. Sci., CABS; Curr. Cit.; Curr. Contents Agric. Biol. Environ. Sci.; Curr. Contents Life Sci.; EMBASE; Entomol. Abstr.; Fish Rev.; Helminthol. Abstr. (1991-); Index Med. (Vol. 155, No. 1, 1985-); Index Vet.; Key Word Index Wildl. Res.; Nutr. Abstr. Rev., Ser. B, Live Feeds and Feed.; Nutr. Abstr. Rev., Ser. A, Hum. Exp.; Life Sci. Collect.; Pig News Inf.; Poult. Abstr.; Protozoolog. Abstr.; Ref. Upd. Deluxe Ed.; Res. Alert [Full Cov.]; Rev. Agric. Entomol.; Rev. Med. Vet. Entomol.; Sci. Cit. Index; SCISEARCH; Vet. Bull.; Wildl. Rev.

ISSN 0141-9846
UK
NLM W1 JO619V **CODEN** JDPHDH
Pr Rev. **CEASED**

JOURNAL OF DEVELOPMENTAL PHYSIOLOGY. See Biology-Embryology.

ISSN 0307-5095
UK
NLM W1 JO633H

JOURNAL OF ELECTROPHYSIOLOGICAL TECHNOLOGY. [J. electrophysiol. technol.]. **Added/Corp** Electrophysiological Technologists' Association. Association Pour la Promotion des Techniques Eelectrophysiologiques. Fachvereinigung der Elektrophysiologischen Assistenten. Vol. 1 (March 1975)-. Academic Scholarly Publication. Multiple languages (English, French and German). Four times a year (March, June, Sept., Dec.). $42.78. EPTA, EEG Department, Leicester Royal, 1NF Leicester LE1 SWW United Kingdom. **ED** C. Green, R. Pottinger. cum. index. **Bk Rev. Ad Acc, Adv Mgr:** B. Bragg. **Circ:** 700.
Desc: Articles of interest to clinical electrophysiologists and technicians.
Ind/Abst Curr. Cit.; EMBASE.

LC QP1 .J725 **ISSN** 0022-0930
DD 591.1/05 US
CCC
NLM W1 JO644D **CODEN** JEBPA9
Pr Rev.

JOURNAL OF EVOLUTIONARY BIOCHEMISTRY AND PHYSIOLOGY. [J. evol. biochem. physiol.]. **Added/Corp** Consultants Bureau. **VFOAT** Evolutionary Biochemistry and Physiology. Vol. 5 (1969)-. Periodical. English (Russian). Six times a year. $1275.00. Consultants Bureau, A Division of Plenum Publishing Corporation, 233 Spring Street, New York NY 10013. **Tel** (212)620-8000, (212)620-8466, FAX (212)463-0742, telex 23/421139. **ED** V. L. Sviderskii. available on microfilm and microfiche from University Microfilms International (UMI). Documents available from The Genuine Article, BIOSIS Document Express, CASDDS.
Ind/Abst AGRICOLA [Select. Cov.]; Biocont. News Inf. (1991-); Biol. Abstr. (?-1984); Chem. Abstr.; CSA Neuro. Abstr. (?-?); Curr. Cit.; EMBASE; Helminthol. Abstr. (1991-); Index Vet.; Res. Alert [Select. Cov.]; Rev. Agric. Entomol.; Rev. Med. Vet. Entomol.; Sci. Cit. Index (19??-19??); SCISEARCH; Soyabean Abstr.

ISSN 0022-0949
UK
NLM W1 JO644H **CODEN** JEBIAM
Pr Rev.

JOURNAL OF EXPERIMENTAL BIOLOGY. [J. exp. biol.]. **Added/Corp** Company of Biologists. Society for Experimental Biology (Great Britain). Vol. 7 (1930)-. Academic Scholarly Publication. English. Twelve times a year. $1100.00. The Company of Biologists Limited, Bidder Building, 140 Cowley Road, Cambridge CB4 4DL United Kingdom. **Tel** 011 44 1223 426164, FAX 011 44 1223 423353. **(Subscription address:** Kinokuniya Company Ltd., 38-1 Sakuragaoka 5, chome Setagaya-ku, Tokyo 156 Japan. **Tel** FAX 011 03 3439 0136.) **ED** C. P. Ellington, R. G. Boutilier, W. A. Foster, and E. A. Howes. Index available in last issue of volume--attached. cum. index. **Bk Rev. Ad Acc. Circ:** 1,800 (ctrl). available on microfilm and microfiche from University Microfilms International (UMI). Documents available from The Genuine Article, BIOSIS Document Express, UMI Article Clearinghouse, CASDDS. ***Continues** British Journal of Experimental Biology, 0366-0788.*
Desc: A journal of comparative animal physiology. Gives papers a wide circulation amongst active scientists in all biological sciences. Increases the cross-fertilization of techniques and knowledge across specialization boundaries.
Ind/Abst Acad. Search; AgBiotech News Inf.; AGRICOLA; Biol. Agric. Index; Biol. Abstr.; Chem. Abstr.; Crop Physiol. Abstr.; Curr. Aware. Biol. Sci., CABS; Curr. Cit.; Curr. Contents Agric. Biol. Environ. Sci.; Curr. Contents Life Sci.; Curr. Ref. Fish Res.; Dairy Sci. Abstr.; EMBASE; EP Collect.; Expand. Acad. Index (1992-); Fish Rev.; Gen. Sci. Index; Homework Help.; Hortic. Abstr.; Index Med.; INFO-SOUTH Abstr.; Key Word Index Wildl. Res.; MasterFile FullTEXT 1000; MasterFile FullTEXT 350; MasterFile FullTEXT 650; MasterFile FullTEXT (July 1993-); Newsp. Period. Abstr. (1992-); Nutr. Abstr. Rev., Ser. B, Live Feeds and Feed.; Nutr. Abstr. Rev., Ser. A, Hum. Exp.; Ocean. Abstr.; OCLC; Life Sci. Collect.; Plant Breed. Abstr.; Pollut. Abstr. Indexes; Poult. Abstr.; Protozoolog. Abstr.; Psychol. Abstr.; Ref. Upd. Deluxe Ed.; Res. Alert [Full Cov.]; Rev. Agric. Entomol.; Rev. Med. Vet. Entomol.; Sci. Cit. Index; SCISEARCH; Soc. Sci. Cit. Index [Select. Cov.]; Soils Fert.; Telebase; Trop. Dis. Bull.; Weed Abstr.; Wildl. Rev.

LC QP1 .J73 **ISSN** 0022-1295
DD 591/.05 US
CCC
NLM W1 JO668C **CODEN** JGPLAD
Pr Rev.

JOURNAL OF GENERAL PHYSIOLOGY, THE. [J. gen. physiol.]. **Added/Corp** Society of General Physiologists. Rockefeller Institute for Medical Research. Rockefeller Institute. Vol. 1 No. 1 (Sept. 1918)-. Academic Scholarly Publication. English. Thirteen times a year (monthly plus one annual symposium). $245.00. Rockefeller University Press, 222 East 70th Street, New York NY 10021. **Tel** (212)327-8572, FAX (212)327-7944. **(Subscription address:** Rockefeller University Press, Box 5108 GPO, New York NY 10087-5108. **) ED** Dr. Paul Cranfield. available on microfilm and microfiche from University Microfilms International (UMI). Documents available from The Genuine Article, BIOSIS Document Express, UMI Article Clearinghouse, CASDDS.
Desc: Covers research of prime importance for cellular and molecular physiology.
Ind/Abst Acad. Search; AGRICOLA; Biol. Agric. Index; Biol. Abstr.; Calcium Calcif. Tissue Abstr.; Chem. Abstr.; Chem. Titles; CSA Neuro. Abstr.; Curr. Aware. Biol. Sci., CABS; Curr. Cit.; Curr. Contents Life Sci.; Curr. Ref. Fish Res.; Dairy Sci. Abstr.; EMBASE; Energy Res. Abstr.; EP Collect.; Expand. Acad. Index (1992-); Fish Rev.; Gen. Sci. Index; Gen. Sci. Source; Homework Help.; Index Med.; Index Vet.; INIS Atomindex [Micro.]; Int. Aerosp. Abstr.; MasterFile FullTEXT 1000; MasterFile FullTEXT 350; MasterFile FullTEXT 650; MasterFile FullTEXT (July 1993-); Newsp. Period. Abstr. (1992-); OCLC; Life Sci. Collect.; Ref. Upd. Basic Ed.; Ref. Upd. Deluxe Ed.; Res. Alert [Full Cov.]; Rev. Agric. Entomol.; Rev. Med. Vet. Entomol.; Sci. Cit. Index; SCISEARCH; Stat. Theory Method Abstr. (1959-1963); Telebase; Vet. Bull.; Trop. Dis. Bull.; Wildl. Rev.

LC QP301 .J67 **ISSN** 0300-8134
DD 612/.042/05 JA
NLM W1 JO673V **CODEN** JHEGAI

JOURNAL OF HUMAN ERGOLOGY. [J. hum. ergol.]. **Added/Corp** Human Ergology Research Association. Vol. 1 (Sept. 1972)-. Periodical. English. Two times a year. $74.00. **(Subscription address:** Maruzen Company Ltd., PO Box 5050, Import & Export Department, Tokyo 100 31 Japan. **Tel** 011 81 3 32789224.) Documents available from BIOSIS Document Express.
Ind/Abst Abstr. Anthropol.; Acoust. Abstr.; Biol. Abstr.; Curr. Cit.; EMBASE; Ergon. Abstr.; Index Med.; Psychol. Abstr. (1972-); PsycINFO; PsycLit; PsycScan: Appl. Psych.; SPORT Discus; SportSearch.

LC QP303 .J63 **ISSN** 0306-7297
DD 612/.76 UK
CCC
NLM W1 JO673VM **CODEN** JHMSDT
Pr Rev.

JOURNAL OF HUMAN MOVEMENT STUDIES. [J. hum. move. stud.]. **VFOAT** JHMS. Vol. 1 (Mar. 1975)-. Periodical. English. Twelve times a year. $875.00. Teviot Scientific Publications, 82 Great King Street, Edinburgh EH3 6QU United Kingdom. **Tel** 011 44 131 3328764, FAX 011 44 131 3432633. **ED** J. Irvine. **Ad Acc. Circ:** 500. Documents available from The Genuine Article, BIOSIS Document Express.
Desc: An international journal concerned with the development of human movement as a field of study including all aspects of sports medicine, therapy, psychology, kinesiology and biomechanics.
Ind/Abst Biol. Abstr.; Curr. Cit.; Curr. Contents Soc. Behav. Sci.; Dev. Med. Child Neurol.; EMBASE; Phys. Educ. Index (1978-1989); Res. Alert [Full Cov.]; Soc. Plann. Policy Dev. Abstr.; Sociol. Abstr. (?-?); SPORT Discus; SportSearch.

LC QL461 .J87 **ISSN** 0022-1910
DD 595.705 UK
CCC
NLM W1 JO714 **CODEN** JIPHAF
Pr Rev.

JOURNAL OF INSECT PHYSIOLOGY. See Zoology-Entomology.

LC QL801 .J9 **ISSN** 0362-2525
US
CCC
NLM W1 JO775 **CODEN** JOMOAT
Pr Rev.

JOURNAL OF MORPHOLOGY (1931). (JOURNAL OF MORPHOLOGY.). [J. morph.]. **Added/Corp** Wistar Institute of Anatomy and Biology. Vol. 52, No. 2 (Dec. 5, 1931)-. Academic Scholarly Publication. English. Twelve times a year. $1488.00. John Wiley & Sons, Inc., 605 Third Avenue, New York NY 10158-0012. **Tel** (212)850-6000, (212)850-6645, FAX (212)850-6088, telex 12-7063. **(Subscription address:** John Wiley & Sons / UK, Baffins Lane, Chichester, West Sussex PO19 1UD United Kingdom. **Tel** 011 44 1243 779777, FAX 011 44 243 776128, telex 86290 WIBOOKG.) **ED** Carl Gans. Documents available from The Genuine Article, BIOSIS Document Express, CASDDS. ***Continues** Journal of Morphology and Physiology, 0095-9626.*
Desc: Publishes original research in morphology as broadly defined, including the areas of cytology, protozoology, developmental biology, and general and functional morphology.
Ind/Abst AGRICOLA [Select. Cov.]; Biol. Abstr.; Chem. Abstr.; CSA Neuro. Abstr. (?-?); Curr. Cit.; Curr. Contents Life Sci.; Curr. Ref. Fish Res.; EMBASE; Energy Res. Abstr.; Fish Rev.; Helminthol. Abstr. (1991-); Index Med.; Index Vet.; INIS Atomindex [Micro.]; Int. Aerosp. Abstr.; Life Sci. Collect.; Postharvest News Inf.; Protozoolog. Abstr.; Ref. Upd. Deluxe Ed.; Res. Alert [Full Cov.]; Rev. Med. Vet. Entomol.; Sci. Cit. Index; SCISEARCH; Soc. Sci. Cit. Index [Select. Cov.]; Vet. Bull.; Wildl. Rev.

LC QP303 .J64 **ISSN** 0022-2895
DD 612.7/05 US
CCC
NLM W1; JO775K **CODEN** JMTBAB
Pr Rev.

JOURNAL OF MOTOR BEHAVIOR. [J. mot. behav.]. **Added/Corp** Helen Dwight Reid Educational Foundation. **VFOAT** JMB. Vol. 1 (Mar. 1969)-. Periodical. English. Four times a year. $116.00. Heldref Publications, 1319 Eighteenth Street Northwest, Washington DC 20036-1802. **Tel** (202)296-6267, (800)365-9753, FAX (202)296-5149. **ED** Wynne A Lee, Alan M Wing, and Howard Zelaznik. **Bk Rev. Ad Acc. Circ:** 1,200. available on microfilm and microfiche from University Microfilms International (UMI). Documents available from The Genuine Article, BIOSIS Document Express.
Desc: Devoted to an understanding of motor behavior as it is most broadly defined, this journal presents papers from various perspectives and differing levels of analysis. It encompasses all areas of motor behavior including psychology, kinesiology, neurophysiology, and biomechanics.
Ind/Abst Biol. Abstr. (1985-); Curr. Cit.; Curr. Contents Soc. Behav. Sci.; Dev. Med. Child Neurol.; EMBASE; Ergon. Abstr.; Phys. Educ. Index; Psychol. Abstr. (1970-); PsycINFO; PsycLit; Res. Alert [Full Cov.]; Soc. Sci. Cit. Index [Full Cov.]; Spec. Educ. Needs Abstr.; SPORT Discus; SportSearch.

ISSN 0867-5910
PL
NLM W1; JO837ABE **CODEN** JPHPEI

JOURNAL OF PHYSIOLOGY AND PHARMACOLOGY : AN OFFICIAL JOURNAL OF THE POLISH PHYSIOLOGICAL SOCIETY. **Added/Corp** Polskie Towarzystwo Fizjologiczne. Vol. 42, No. 1 (Mar. 1991)-. Periodical. English. Four times a year. $82.00. **(Subscription address:** Ars Polona-Ruch, PO Box 1001, Krakowskie Przedmiescie 7, 00-068 Warsaw Poland. **Tel** 011 48 22 261201.) ***Continues** Acta Physiologica Polonica, 0044-6033.*
Ind/Abst Curr. Cit.; Index Med. (1991-).

LC QP1 .J75 **ISSN** 0022-3751
DD 612.05 UK
NLM W1 JO837 **CODEN** JPHYA7
Pr Rev.

JOURNAL OF PHYSIOLOGY (LONDON). (THE JOURNAL OF PHYSIOLOGY.). [J. physiol.]. **Added/Corp** Physiological Society (Great Britain). Vol. 1 (March 12, 1878)-. Academic Scholarly Publication. English. Twenty-four times a year (plus 6 proceedings issues and index). $1864.00. Cambridge University Press, The Edinburgh Building, Shaftesbury Road, Cambridge CB2 2RU United Kingdom. **Tel** 011 44 1223 312393, FAX 011 44 1223 315052, telex 851-817256. **(Subscription address:** Cambridge

University Press / North America, 110 Midland Avenue, Port Chester NY 10573. **Tel** (800)431-1580, (914)937-9600.) **ED** C. A. R. Boyd. cum. index. available on microfilm and microfiche from University Microfilms International (UMI). Documents available from The Genuine Article, BIOSIS Document Express, CASDDS.
Desc: Original experimental works within the broad range of physiology are published. Human and mammalian physiology, including work at the level of the cell membrane, single cells, tissues or organs, are also published. All abstracts of scientific meetings of the Physiological Society, which are accepted by the members present at those meetings, are also published.
Ind/Abst AGRICOLA; Biol. Agric. Index; Biol. Abstr.; Calcium Calcif. Tissue Abstr.; Chem. Abstr.; Chemorecept. Abstr.; CSA Neuro. Abstr.; Curr. Aware. Biol. Sci., CABS; Curr. Cit.; Curr. Ref. Fish Res.; Dairy Sci. Abstr.; EMBASE; Ergon. Abstr. (?-?); Fish Rev. (Jan. 1989-July 1992); Geol. Abstr.; Helminthol. Abstr.; Index Med.; Int. Aerosp. Abstr.; Maize Abstr.; Nutr. Abstr. Rev., Ser. B, Live Feeds and Feed.; Life Sci. Collect.; PESTDOC; Pig News Inf.; Protozoolog. Abstr.; Ref. Upd. Basic Ed.; Ref. Upd. Deluxe Ed.; Res. Alert [Full Cov.]; Rev. Med. Vet. Entomol.; Rice Abstr.; Sci. Cit. Index; SCISEARCH; Soc. Sci. Cit. Index [Select. Cov.]; SportSearch; Wildl. Rev. (Jan. 1989-July 1992).

ISSN 0928-4257
FR
NLM W1; JO837ABG
Pr Rev.

JOURNAL OF PHYSIOLOGY, PARIS.
VFOAT Journal of Physiology. Vol. 86, No. 1/2/3 (1992)-. Academic Scholarly Publication. English. Six times a year. $394.00. Editions Scientifique Elsevier, 141 rue de Javel, 75747 Paris Cedex 15 France. **Tel** 011 33 1 45589067, FAX 011 33 1 45589424. **(Subscription address:** Editions Scientifiques Elsevier / for North America, PO Box 7247-7576, Philadelphia PA 19170-7576.) available on an online database from Elsevier Electronic Subscriptions (EES). ***Continues*** *Journal de Physiologie, 0021-7948.*
Ind/Abst Curr. Cit.; Index Med. (1992-); Sci. Cit. Index; Soc. Sci. Cit. Index [Select. Cov.].

LC QP188.P55 J68 **ISSN** 0742-3098
DD 599/.014 DK
CCC
NLM W1; JO837AC **CODEN** JPRSE9
Pr Rev.

JOURNAL OF PINEAL RESEARCH. [J. pineal res.]. Vol. 1, No. 1 (1984)-. Academic Scholarly Publication. English. Eight times a year. $910.58. Munksgaard International Publishers Ltd, PO Box 2148, DK-1016 Copenhagen K Denmark. **Tel** 011 45 33 127030, FAX 011 45 33 129387, telex 19431 MUNKS DK. **ED** Russel J. Reiter. Documents available from The Genuine Article, CASDDS.
Ind/Abst AgBiotech News Inf.; Anim. Breed. Abstr.; Chem. Abstr. (1984-); CSA Neuro. Abstr.; Curr. Aware. Biol. Sci., CABS; Curr. Cit.; Curr. Contents Life Sci.; Dairy Sci. Abstr.; EMBASE; Index Med. (Vol. 1, No. 1, 1984-); (Vol. 1, No. 1, 1984-);; Life Sci. Collect.; Ref. Upd. Deluxe Ed.; Res. Alert [Full Cov.]; Sci. Cit. Index; SCISEARCH.

ISSN 0269-8803
UK
CCC
NLM W1; JO858T

JOURNAL OF PSYCHOPHYSIOLOGY.
See Psychology.

ISSN 0916-8818
JA
NLM W1; JO868G **CODEN** JREDEF

JOURNAL OF REPRODUCTION AND DEVELOPMENT, THE. **Added/Corp** Kachiku Hanshoku Gakkai. (1992)-. Academic Scholarly Publication. English (Japanese). Four times a year. Japanese Society of Animal Reproduction, University of Tokyo, Department of Veterinary Physiology, 1-1-1 Yayoi, Bunkyo-ku Tokyo 113 Japan. **Tel** 011 81 3 38122111, FAX 011 81 3 38154266. **Bk Rev. Ad Acc. *Continues*** *Japanese Journal of Animal Reproduction, 0385-9932.*
Ind/Abst Chem. Abstr.; Curr. Cit.

LC QP251 .J75 **ISSN** 0022-4251
UK
CCC
NLM W1 JO868K **CODEN** JRPFA4
Pr Rev.

JOURNAL OF REPRODUCTION AND FERTILITY. [J. reprod. fertil.]. **Added/Corp** Society for the Study of Fertility. International Planned Parenthood Federation. Indian Society for the Study of Reproduction. Society for the Study of Fertility. Proceedings. **VFOAT** Journal of Reproduction & Fertility. Vol. 1 (Feb. 1960)-(19??). Academic Scholarly Publication. English. Six times a year. $455.00. Journals of Reproduction & Fertility Ltd., 22 Newmarket Rd., Cambridge CB5 8DT United Kingdom. **Tel** 011 44 1223 351809, FAX 011 44 1223 359754. **(Subscription address:** Portland Press Ltd., PO Box 32 Commerce Way, Colchester Essex CO2 8HP, United Kingdom. **Tel** 011 44 1206 796351, FAX 011 44 1206 799331.) **ED** Barbara Weir. Index available. cum. index. **Bk Rev. Ad Acc. Circ:** 2,200 (ctrl). available with charts; available with illustrations. Documents available from The Genuine Article, BIOSIS Document Express, CASDDS. ***Supersedes*** *Studies on Fertility, 0562-4142.* ***Continued in part by*** *Journal of Reproduction & Fertility. Abstract Series, 0954-0725.*
Desc: Covers reproductive morphology, physiology, biochemistry and pathology in man and other animals. Also veterinary problems of fertility and lactation.
Ind/Abst Abstr. Anthropol.; AgBiotech News Inf.; AGRICOLA [Select. Cov.]; Anim. Breed. Abstr.; Biol. Agric. Index; Biol. Abstr.; Chem. Abstr.; Curr. Aware. Biol. Sci., CABS; Curr. Biotechnol.; Curr. Cit.; Dairy Sci. Abstr.; EMBASE; Fish Rev.; Index Med.; Key Word Index Wildl. Res.; NAPRALERT; Nutr. Abstr. Rev., Ser. B, Live Feeds and Feed.; Life Sci. Collect.; PESTDOC; Pig News Inf.; Poult. Abstr.; Ref. Upd. Basic Ed.; Ref. Upd. Deluxe Ed.; Res. Alert [Full Cov.]; Sci. Cit. Index; SCISEARCH; Stat. Theory Method Abstr. (1986); Wildl. Rev.

LC QP251 .J74 **ISSN** 0954-0725
DD 591.1/6/05 UK
NLM W1; JO868KN

JOURNAL OF REPRODUCTION & FERTILITY. ABSTRACT SERIES / SOCIETY FOR THE STUDY OF FERTILITY. [J. reprod. fert. abstr. ser.]. **Added/Corp** Society for the Study of Fertility. **VFOAT** Journal of Reproduction and Fertility Abstract Series. No. 1, (July 1988)-. Academic Scholarly Publication. English. Two times a year. Journals of Reproduction & Fertility Ltd., 22 Newmarket Rd., Cambridge CB5 8DT United Kingdom. **Tel** 011 44 1223 351809, FAX 011 44 1223 359754. **(Subscription address:** Portland Press Ltd., PO Box 32 Commerce Way, Colchester Essex CO2 8HP, United Kingdom. **Tel** 011 44 1206 796351, FAX 011 44 1206 799331.) ***Continues in part*** *Journal of Reproduction and Fertility, 0022-4251.*
Desc: Abstracts papers presented at meetings.
Ind/Abst AGRICOLA [Select. Cov.]; Anim. Breed. Abstr.; Fish Rev.; Index Med. (July 1988-);; PESTDOC; Wildl. Rev.

LC QH516 .J68 **ISSN** 0306-4565
DD 574.1/916/05 UK
CCC
NLM W1 JO966H **CODEN** JTBIDS
Pr Rev.

JOURNAL OF THERMAL BIOLOGY. [J. therm. biol.]. Vol. 1 (Oct. 1975)-. Academic Scholarly Publication. English. Six times a year. $557.00. Pergamon Press, An Imprint of Elsevier Science Ltd., The Boulevard, Langford Lane, Kidlington, Oxford OX5 1GB United Kingdom. **Tel** 011 44 1865 843000, 011 44 1865 843699, FAX 011 44 1865 843010. **(Subscription address:** Elsevier Science Ltd. / Oxford Fulfillment Centre, PO Box 800, Kidlington OX5 1DX United Kingdom. **Tel** 011 44 865 843355.) **ED** K. Bowler and J. Heath. **Ad Acc.** available on microfilm and microfiche from University Microfilms International (UMI); available on an online database from Elsevier Electronic Subscriptions (EES). Documents available from The Genuine Article, BIOSIS Document Express, Ask*IEEE, CASDDS.
Ind/Abst ASTIS Curr. Aware. Bull. (1978-); AGRICOLA [Select. Cov.]; ASTIS Bibliogr. (1978-); Biol. Abstr.; Chem. Abstr.; CSA Neuro. Abstr. (?-?); Curr. Cit.; Curr. Contents Agric. Biol. Environ. Sci.; Curr. Contents Life Sci.; Curr. Ref. Fish Res.; EMBASE; Fish Rev.; Index Vet.; INSPEC (April 1984-); Key Word Index Wildl. Res.; Life Sci. Collect.; Res. Alert [Full Cov.]; Rev. Agric. Entomol.; Rev. Med. Vet. Entomol.; Sci. Cit. Index; SCISEARCH; Vet. Bull.

LC QP303 .K5 **ISSN** 0093-6960
DD 612/.76/05 US
NLM W1 KI635

KINESIOLOGY (WASHINGTON). (KINESIOLOGY.). 3- 1973-. English. One time a year. $4.50. American Alliance Publications, PO Box 704, Waldorf MD 20601. **Tel** (703)476-3481. ***Continues*** *Kinesiology Review.*

LC QP351 .S82a
RU

LENINSKAIA TEORIIA OTRAZHENIIA I PROBLEMY PSIKHOLOGII. **See** Psychology.

US
NLM W1; MA333 **CODEN** MLSEEB

MAGNES LECTURE SERIES. **See** Medical Sciences-Neurology.

LC RB113
DD 612 NE

•**MANUAL OF BIOLOGICAL MARKERS OF DISEASE.** **See** Medical Sciences-Allergy and Immunologic Diseases.

LC QL121 .M28 **ISSN** 0091-181X
DD 591.9/2 US
CCC
NLM W1 MA653D **CODEN** MBPHAX
Pr Rev.

MARINE BEHAVIOUR AND PHYSIOLOGY. [Mar. behav. physiol.]. Vol. 1 (Apr. 1972)-. English. Irregular (3 volumes per year). $764.00 (academic institutions), $1191.00 (corporate institutions). Gordon & Breach Science Publishers, Inc., PO Box 786, Cooper Station, New York NY 10276. **Tel** (212)206-8900, FAX (212)645-2459. **ED** M. Laverack. Index available. **Bk Rev. Ad Acc.** Documents available from The Genuine Article, BIOSIS Document Express, Ask*IEEE, CASDDS.
Desc: Papers on the physiology, behavior and neurobiology of marine animals.
Ind/Abst Anim. Behav. Abstr.; Aquat. Sci. Fish. Abstr. [CD-ROM Ed.]; Biol. Abstr. (-1984); Chem. Abstr. (1972-1983); CSA Neuro. Abstr. (?-?); Curr. Aware. Biol. Sci., CABS; Curr. Cit.; Curr. Ref. Fish Res.; Environ. Period. Bibliogr.; INSPEC (April 1972-); Mar. Sci. Contents Tables; Ocean. Abstr.; Life Sci. Collect.; Psychol. Abstr. (1972-); PsycINFO; PsycLit; Res. Alert [Full Cov.]; Sci. Cit. Index; SCISEARCH.

LC QP86 .M47 **ISSN** 0047-6374
DD 612.6/7/05 SZ
CCC
NLM W1 ME106A **CODEN** MAGDA3
Pr Rev.

MECHANISMS OF AGEING AND DEVELOPMENT. [Mech. ageing dev.]. **Added/Corp** Association for the Advancement of Aging Research. Vol. 1 (Apr./May 1972)-. Academic Scholarly Publication. English. Eighteen times a year. $1654.00. Elsevier Science Ireland Ltd., Bay 15, Shannon Industrial Estate, Co Clare Ireland. **Tel** 011 353 61 471944. **ED** B.L. Strehler. Index available. **Ad Acc.** available on microfilm and microfiche from University Microfilms International (UMI); available on an online database from Elsevier Electronic Subscriptions (EES). Documents available from The Genuine Article, BIOSIS Document Express, CASDDS.
Desc: An international journal devoted to the publication of experimental and theoretical articles that have a direct bearing on the mechanisms underlying the emergence and deterioration of structure and function in biological systems, including man.
Ind/Abst AgBiotech News Inf.; AGRICOLA; Biol. Abstr.; Chem. Abstr.; CSA Neuro. Abstr. (?-?); Curr. Cit.; Curr. Contents Life Sci.; Dairy Sci. Abstr.; EMBASE; Index Med.; Index Vet.; Int. Aerosp. Abstr.; Nematol. Abstr.; Life Sci. Collect.; Ref. Upd. Basic Ed.; Ref. Upd. Deluxe Ed.; Res. Alert [Full Cov.]; Rev. Med. Vet. Entomol.; Sci. Cit. Index; SCISEARCH; Soc. Sci. Cit. Index [Select. Cov.].

US

MINERAL METABOLISM : AN ADVANCED TREATISE. (1960)-. Monographic series. English. Irregular. Price varies per volume. Academic Press Inc., 6277 Sea Harbor Drive, Orlando FL 32887. **Tel** (800)543-9534, (407)345-4100, FAX (407)352-3445. **ED** C. L. Comar and Felix Bronner.

SZ
NLM W1; MO196DH **CODEN** MCHYEL
CEASED

MOLECULAR COMPARATIVE PHYSIOLOGY. Vol. 12 (1993)-(1993). Monographic series. English. S. Karger AG, Allschwilerstrasse 10, PO Box, CH-4009 Basel Switzerland. **Tel** 011 41 61 3061111, FAX 011 41 61 3061234, telex CH 962 652. **ED** R. K. H. Kinne, E. Kinne-Saffran and K. W. Beyenbach. ***Continues*** *Comparative Physiology, 1015-1702.*
Desc: Sets out to define and clarify the cellular and molecular aspects of cell function from a comparative physiological viewpoint. Goes beyond describing biological processes and functions to elucidating the molecular mechanisms leading to these events.
Ind/Abst Ref. Upd. Deluxe Ed.

ISSN 0079-2020
UK
NLM W1 MO569QW **CODEN** PHSMA2

MONOGRAPHS OF THE PHYSIOLOGICAL SOCIETY. [Monogr. Physiol. Soc.]. **Main/Corp** Physiological Society. **Added/Corp** Physiological Society (Great Britain). No. 1 (1953)-. Monographic series. English. Irregular. Price varies per volume. Documents available from BIOSIS Document Express.
Ind/Abst Biol. Abstr.

ISSN 0148-4427
US
NLM W1 MO569QY **CODEN** MPPADB

MONOGRAPHS OF THE PHYSIOLOGICAL SOCIETY OF PHILADELPHIA. [Monogr. Physiol. Soc. Philadelphia]. **Main/Corp** Physiological Society of Philadelphia. Academic Scholarly Publication. English. Halsted Press, 605 Third Avenue, New York NY 10016. **Tel** (718)658-0888. Documents available from BIOSIS Document Express, CASDDS.
Ind/Abst Biol. Abstr.; Chem. Abstr. (1976-1981).

LC QP341 .N45 **ISSN** 0047-942X
DD 612/.813 US
SUSPENDED

NEUROELECTRIC NEWS. Vol. 1, Oct. 1970-?. Periodical. English. Three times a year. $25.00. Neuroelectric Society, 8700 North Wisconsin Avenue, Milwaukee WI 53226. cum. index. ctrl circ. available on microfilm and microfiche from University Microfilms International (UMI).

Biology — Physiology

ISSN 0987-7053
NE
CCC
NLM W1; NE337U **CODEN** NCLIE4
Pr Rev.
NEUROPHYSIOLOGIE CLINIQUE. See Medical Sciences-Neurology.

ISSN 0090-2977
US
CCC
NLM W1 NE337V **CODEN** NPHYBI
NEUROPHYSIOLOGY (NEW YORK). See Medical Sciences-Neurology.

ISSN 0142-8241
UK
DD 016.6128 CCC
NEUROPHYSIOLOGY SHEFFIELD. See Medical Sciences-Neurology.

LC RC331 .N44 **ISSN** 0097-0549
DD 612/.8/05 US
CCC
NLM W1 NE342P **CODEN** NBHPBT
NEUROSCIENCE AND BEHAVIORAL PHYSIOLOGY. See Medical Sciences-Neurology.

LC QP1 .N48 **ISSN** 0886-1714
DD 599/.01/05 US
CCC
NLM W1; NE996V **CODEN** NEPSEY
Pr Rev.
NEWS IN PHYSIOLOGICAL SCIENCES. [News physiol. sci.]. **Added/Corp** International Union of Physiological Sciences. American Physiological Society (1887-). **VFOAT** NIPS. Vol. 1, No. 1 (Feb. 1986)-. Academic Scholarly Publication. English. Six times a year. $105.00. American Physiological Society, 9650 Rockville Pike, Bethesda MD 20814. **Tel** (301)530-7180, FAX (301)571-1814. available on microfilm and microfiche from University Microfilms International (UMI). Documents available from The Genuine Article, BIOSIS Document Express, CASDDS.
Desc: Review articles covering a broad range of topics familiar to all physiologists including information on the latest discoveries.
Ind/Abst Biol. Abstr. (1986-); Chem. Abstr. (1986-); Curr. Cit.; Curr. Contents Life Sci.; Res. Alert [Select. Cov.]; Sci. Cit. Index; SCISEARCH; Soc. Sci. Cit. Index [Select. Cov.].

ISSN 0794-859X
NR
NLM W1; NI394F
NIGERIAN JOURNAL OF PHYSIOLOGICAL SCIENCES : OFFICIAL PUBLICATION OF THE PHYSIOLOGICAL SOCIETY OF NIGERIA. **Added/Corp** Physiological Society of Nigeria. (198?)-. Periodical. English. Two times a year. Physiological Society of Nigeria, PO Box 14, Bendel State University, Ekpoma Bendel Nigeria. **Tel** (52)200250.
Ind/Abst EMBASE [Select. Cov.].

ISSN 0286-7052
JA
NLM W1; NI426WH
NIHON RINSHO SEIRI GAKKAI ZASSHI = JAPANESE JOURNAL OF APPLIED PHYSIOLOGY. [Nihon Rinsho Seiri Gakkai zasshi]. **Added/Corp** Nihon Rinsho Seiri Gakkai. **VFOAT** Japanese Journal of Applied Physiology. (1981)-. Academic Scholarly Publication. Japanese (English). Two times a year. Nihon Rinsho Seiri Gakkai, (Japanese Soc. of Applied Physiology), Dokkyo Ika Daigaku Dai 1 Naika, 880 Kitakobayashi Mibumachi, Shimotsugagun Tochigiken 321-02, Japan. **Continues** Myakuha, 0286-7044.
Ind/Abst Ocean. Abstr.

ISSN 0031-9341
JA
NLM W1 NI932P **CODEN** NISEAV
NIPPON SEIRIGAKU ZASSHI. [J. Physiol. Soc. Japan]. **Added/Corp** Nippon Seiri Gakkai. Dai Nippon Seiri Gakkai. **VFOAT** Journal of the Physiological Society of Japan. Vol. 1 (Feb. 1936)-. Academic Scholarly Publication. Japanese (English). Twelve times a year. $190.00. (**Subscription address:** Maruzen Company Ltd., PO Box 5050, Import & Export Department, Tokyo 100 31 Japan. **Tel** 011 81 3 32789224.) Documents available from BIOSIS Document Express, CASDDS. **Absorbed** Joken Hansha.
Ind/Abst AGRICOLA; Biol. Abstr.; Chem. Abstr.; EMBASE; Index Med.

LC QP251 .O94 **ISSN** 0260-0854
DD 599.01/6/05 UK
CCC
NLM W1 OX621T **CODEN** ORRBDQ
Pr Rev. TITLE CHANGE
OXFORD REVIEWS OF REPRODUCTIVE BIOLOGY. [Oxf. rev. reprod. biol.]. Vol. 1 (1979)-(19??). Academic Scholarly Publication. English. Oxford University Press / UK, Walton Street, Oxford OX2 6DP United Kingdom. **Tel** 011 44 1865 56767, FAX 011 44 1865 267773, telex 851/837330 OXPRES G. **ED** J. R. Clarke. available on microfilm from University Microfilms International (UMI). Documents available from The Genuine Article, BIOSIS Document Express, CASDDS. **Merged with** Bibliography of Reproduction, 0006-1565 **to form** Human Reproduction Update, 1355-4786.
Desc: Contains non-mammalian and mammalian topics and endocrinology. Also includes fertility and sterility problems.
Ind/Abst Anim. Breed. Abstr.; Biol. Abstr. (1984-199?); Chem. Abstr.; Curr. Cit.; Index Med. (Vol. 6, 1984-199?); Index Sci. Rev. [Full Cov.]; Res. Alert [Full Cov.]; Sci. Cit. Index; SCISEARCH; Soc. Sci. Cit. Index [Select. Cov.].

ISSN 1146-5263
FR
UDC 011
PASCAL. F 53, ANATOMIE ET PHYSIOLOGIE DES VERTEBRES. See Medical Sciences-Anatomy.

LC RB113 **ISSN** 0928-4680
DD 612 NE
CCC
NLM W1; PA963ET
Pr Rev.
●**PATHOPHYSIOLOGY : THE OFFICIAL JOURNAL OF THE INTERNATIONAL SOCIETY FOR PATHOPHYSIOLOGY.** See Medical Sciences-Pathology.

LC RB1 .P66 **ISSN** 0031-2991
RU
CCC
NLM W1 PA988 **CODEN** PAFEAY
PATOLOGICESKAJA FIZIOLOGIJA I EKSPERIMENTALNAJA TERAPIJA. (PATOLOGICHESKAIA FIZIOLOGIIA I EKSPERIMENTALNAIA TERAPIIA.). [Patol. fiziol. eksp. ter.]. **Added/Corp** Soviet Union. Ministerstvo Zdravookhraneniia. (1957)-. Academic Scholarly Publication. Russian (summaries and/or abstracts in English; table of contents in English). Four times a year. $109.95. Izdatelstvo Meditsina / Russian Academy of Medical Sciences, Ulitsa Solyanka 14, 109801 Moscow Russia. **Tel** 011 95 297-05-04. (**Subscription address:** East View Publications Inc., 3020 Harbor Lane North, Suite 110, Minneapolis MN 55447. **Tel** (800)477-1005, (612)550-0961, FAX (612)559-2931.) Index available.
Bk Rev. Documents available from BIOSIS Document Express, CASDDS.
Ind/Abst Biol. Abstr.; Chem. Abstr.; EMBASE [Select. Cov.]; Index Med.; Int. Aerosp. Abstr.; PESTDOC.

LC QP1 .A63 **ISSN** 0031-6768
DD 591.1/05 GW
CCC
NLM W1 PF482 **CODEN** PFLABK
PFLUGERS ARCHIV. (PFLUGERS ARCHIV. EUROPEAN JOURNAL OF PHYSIOLOGY.). [Pflugers Arch.]. **VFOAT** European Journal of Physiology. Vol. 302 (July 1968)-. Academic Scholarly Publication. English (French and German). Twelve times a year. $2236.00. Springer-Verlag GmbH & Company KG, Heidelberger Platz 3, D-14197 Berlin Germany. **Tel** 011 49 30 8207223, FAX 011 49 30 8214091, telex 183 319 SPBLN D. (**Subscription address:** Springer-Verlag New York Inc. / North America, PO Box 2485, Journal Fulfillment, Secaucus NJ 07096. **Tel** (201)348-4033, (800)777-4643, FAX (201)348-4505.) **ED** K Thurau. available on microfilm and microfiche from University Microfilms International (UMI). Documents available from The Genuine Article, BIOSIS Document Express, CASDDS, ADONIS. **Continues** Pfluger's Archiv fur die Gesamte Physiologie des Menschen und der Tiere, 0365-267X.
Desc: Keeps its readers abreast of developments in important subspecialties as well as the results of the extensive interdisciplinary collaboration with other fields such as biochemistry, biophysics and bioengineering.
Ind/Abst ADONIS; AGRICOLA; Biol. Abstr.; Calcium Calcif. Tissue Abstr.; Chem. Abstr.; CSA Neuro. Abstr.; Curr. Aware. Biol. Sci.; CABS; Curr. Cit.; Curr. Contents Life Sci.; Curr. Ref. Fish Res.; EMBASE; Fish Rev.; Index Med.; Int. Aerosp. Abstr.; Nucl. Sci. Abstr.; Life Sci. Collect.; PESTDOC; Pig News Inf.; Ref. Upd. Basic Ed.; Ref. Upd. Deluxe Ed.; Res. Alert [Full Cov.]; Rev. Med. Vet. Entomol.; Saf. Health Work; Sci. Cit. Index; SCISEARCH; SportSearch; Wildl. Rev.

ISSN 0358-4828
FI
NLM W1 AC954NM no.20 etc
PHARMACOLOGICA ET PHYSIOLOGICA (OULU). See Pharmacy and Pharmacology.

LC QK1 **ISSN** 0031-9317
DD 580.5 DK
UDC 581.2 CCC
NLM W1 PH925K **CODEN** PHPLAI
Pr Rev.
PHYSIOLOGIA PLANTARUM. See Biology-Botany.

ISSN 0736-4326
US
NLM W1 PH925N
PHYSIOLOGIC AND PHARMACOLOGIC BASES OF DRUG THERAPY. See Pharmacy and Pharmacology.

US
PHYSIOLOGICAL PHARMACOLOGY : A COMPREHENSIVE TREATISE. See Pharmacy and Pharmacology.

LC QP1 .C417
XR
NLM W1; PH926T **CODEN** PHRSEJ
PHYSIOLOGICAL RESEARCH / ACADEMIA SCIENTIARUM BOHEMOSLOVACA. **Added/Corp** Fysiologicky Ustav (Ceskoslovenska Akademie Ved). (1991)-. Academic Scholarly Publication. English. Six times a year. $208.77. Academic Press Ltd., A Division of Harcourt Brace & Company Ltd., 24-28 Oval Road, London NW1 7DX United Kingdom. **Tel** 011 44 171 2674466, FAX 011 44 171 4822293, 011 44 171 4854752, telex 25775 ACPRES G. (**Subscription address:** Harcourt Brace & Company, Ltd., Foots Cray High Street, Sidcup Kent DA14 5HP United Kingdom. **Tel** 011 44 181 3003322, FAX 011 44 181 3090807, telex 896 137 ACADEM.) **ED** K. Capek. Documents available from The Genuine Article, BIOSIS Document Express, CASDDS. **Continues** Physiologia Bohemoslovaca, 0369-9463.
Desc: Presents articles containing the results of original research and observations in the fields of normal and pathological, animal and human physiology, biochemistry, biophysics, and pharmacology. Developmental aspects of the research are emphasized.
Ind/Abst Biol. Abstr. (1991-); Chem. Abstr.; Curr. Aware. Biol. Sci.; CABS; Curr. Cit.; Curr. Contents Life Sci.; EMBASE [Select. Cov.]; Index Med. (1991-); Res. Alert [Full Cov.]; Sci. Cit. Index; SCISEARCH.

LC QP1 .P45 **ISSN** 0031-9333
US
CCC
NLM W1 PH927 **CODEN** PHREA7
Pr Rev.
PHYSIOLOGICAL REVIEWS. [Physiol. rev.]. **Added/Corp** American Physiological Society (1887-). Vol. 1 (Jan. 1921)-. Academic Scholarly Publication. English. Four times a year. $207.00. American Physiological Society, 9650 Rockville Pike, Bethesda MD 20814. **Tel** (301)530-7180, FAX (301)571-1814. **ED** G H Giebisch. Index available. cum. index. **Ad Acc. Circ:** 3,500. available on microfilm and microfiche from University Microfilms International (UMI). Documents available from The Genuine Article, BIOSIS Document Express, UMI Article Clearinghouse, CASDDS.
Desc: Contains reviews of physiological topics as well as reviews in biochemistry, nutrition, general physiology, biophysics and neuroscience.
Ind/Abst Acad. Search; Biol. Abstr.; Biol. Agric. Index; Biol. Abstr.; Chem. Abstr.; CSA Neuro. Abstr. (?-?); Curr. Aware. Biol. Sci., CABS; Curr. Cit.; Curr. Contents Life Sci.; Curr. Ref. Fish Res.; Dairy Sci. Abstr.; EMBASE; Energy Res. Abstr.; EP Collect.; Expand. Acad. Index (1992-); Fish Rev.; Gen. Sci. Index; Gen. Sci. Source; Homework Help.; Index Med.; Index Rev. [Full Cov.]; INFO-SOUTH Abstr.; Int. Aerosp. Abstr.; Mag. Search; MasterFile FullTEXT 1000; MasterFile FullTEXT 350; MasterFile FullTEXT 650; MasterFile FullTEXT (July 1993-); Newsp. Period. Abstr. (1991-); OCLC; Life Sci. Collect.; PESTDOC; Ref. Upd. Basic Ed.; Ref. Upd. Deluxe Ed.; Res. Alert [Full Cov.]; Rev. Agric. Entomol.; Rev. Med. Vet. Entomol.; Sci. Cit. Index; SCISEARCH; Soc. Sci. Cit. Index [Select. Cov.]; Telebase; Wildl. Rev.

LC QP1 .P55 **ISSN** 0031-9376
DD 599.01/05 US
NLM W1 PH948 **CODEN** PYSOAP
PHYSIOLOGIST, THE. [Physiologist].
Added/Corp American Physiological Society (1887-) American Physiological Society (1887-). Proceedings. Vol. 1 (Nov. 1957)-. Newsletter. English. Six times a year. $50.00. American Physiological Society, 9650 Rockville Pike, Bethesda MD 20814. **Tel** (301)530-7180, FAX (301)571-1814. **ED** M. Frank. **Ad Acc. Circ:** 500 to 6,500 (ctrl). available on microfilm and microfiche from University Microfilms International (UMI). Documents available from BIOSIS Document Express.
Desc: Newsletter of the American Physiological Society. Articles on Society affairs and announcements as well as articles of importance to physiologists.
Ind/Abst Biol. Abstr. (-1989); Curr. Cit.; Curr. Index J. Educ.; EMBASE; Energy Res. Abstr. (March 1976-); Index Med.; Int. Aerosp. Abstr.; SportSearch.

LC QP351 .P55 **ISSN** 0031-9384
DD 574 US
CCC
NLM W1 PH951H **CODEN** PHBHA4
Pr Rev.
PHYSIOLOGY & BEHAVIOR. [Physiol. behav.]. **VFOAT** Physiology and Behavior. Vol. 1 (Jan. 1966)-. Academic Scholarly Publication. English. Twelve times a year. $1750.00. Pergamon Press, An Imprint of Elsevier Science Ltd., The Boulevard, Langford Lane, Kidlington, Oxford OX5 1GB United Kingdom. **Tel** 011 44

1865 843000, 011 44 1865 843699, FAX 011 44 1865 843010. **(Subscription address:** Elsevier Science Ltd. / Oxford Fulfillment Centre, PO Box 800, Kidlington OX5 1DX United Kingdom. **Tel** 011 44 865 843355.) **ED** Matthew J. Wayner. available on microfilm and microfiche from University Microfilms International (UMI); available on microfiche from the publisher; available on an online database from Elsevier Electronic Subscriptions (EES). Documents available from The Genuine Article, BIOSIS Document Express, CASDDS, ADONIS.
Desc: Articles aim to integrate anatomy, biochemistry, endocrinology, pharmacology and neurobiology within a behavioral framework using species such as insects, reptiles, birds and mammals.
Ind/Abst ADONIS; AGRICOLA (Vol. 52, No. 4, 1992) [Select. Cov.]; Agric. Eng. Abstr. (1991-); Anim. Behav. Abstr.; Anim. Breed. Abstr.; Biol. Abstr.; Chem. Abstr.; Chemorecept. Abstr.; CSA Neuro. Abstr. (?-?); Curr. Aware. Biol. Sci., CABS; Curr. Cit.; Curr. Contents Life Sci.; Curr. Ref. Fish Res.; Dairy Sci. Abstr.; EMBASE; Energy Res. Abstr.; Fish Rev.; Index Med.; Int. Aerosp. Abstr.; Key Word Index Wildl. Res.; Maize Abstr.; Nutr. Abstr. Rev., Ser. B, Live Feeds and Feed.; Nutr. Abstr. Rev., Ser. A, Hum. Exp.; Life Sci. Collect.; Pig News Inf.; Potato Abstr.; Poult. Abstr.; Psychol. Abstr. (1966-); PsycINFO; PsycLit; Ref. Upd. Basic Ed.; Ref. Upd. Deluxe Ed.; Res. Alert [Full Cov.]; Rev. Agric. Entomol.; Sci. Cit. Index; SCISEARCH; Small Anim. Abstr. Bibliogr.; Soc. Sci. Cit. Index [Select. Cov.]; Soyabean Abstr.; SportSearch; Sug. Indus. Abstr.; Wildl. Rev.

LC QH188 .P48 **ISSN** 0370-9612
DD 574.5/0952 JA
CODEN PEJAE6

PHYSIOLOGY AND ECOLOGY JAPAN.
(1964)-. Periodical. English. Seiri Seitai Kenkokai, (Physiology & Ecology Japan Editorial Office), Kyoto Daigaku Rigakubu Dobutsugaku, Kyoshitsu Kitashirakawa, Sakyoku Kyotoshi Kyotofu 606, Japan.
Ind/Abst Anim. Breed. Abstr.; Ecol. Abstr.; Helminthol. Abstr. (1991-); Index Vet.; Life Sci. Collect.; Protozoolog. Abstr.; Rev. Med. Vet. Mycology.

ISSN 0822-9058
DD 612/.005 CN
NLM W1; PH9513

PHYSIOLOGY CANADA (1983).
(PHYSIOLOGY CANADA = PHYSIOLOGIE CANADA.). [Physiol. Can.]. **Added/Corp** Canadian Physiological Society. **VFOAT** Physiologie Canada. **VAT** Physiologie Canada (1983). Vol. 14, No. 2 (July 1983)-. Periodical. English (French). Two times a year. 9.61Can$. Canadian Physiological Society Inc., Western Ontario Medical Science Bl, London Ontario N6A 5C1 Canada. **Tel** (519)661-3475. **ED** T. Philip Hicks. **Bk Rev. Circ:** 600 (ctrl). ***Continues** Canada Physiology, 0226-8973.*
Desc: Articles, book reviews, and scientific abstracts concerning physiological and general interest to a physiological readership.

ISSN 0706-4284
DD 615'.8 CN

PHYSIOQUEBEC. [Physioquebec].
Added/Corp Corporation Professionnelle des Physiotherapeutes du Quebec. (1975)-. Periodical. French (English). Four times a year (Mar., July, Oct., Dec.). 37.40Can$. Corporation Professional Physiotheraphy of Quebec, 1100 Beaumont Avenue, Room 530 Town, Mount Royal Quebec H3P 3E5 Canada. **Tel** (514)737-2770.

LC QK1 **ISSN** 0032-5147
DD 580/.5 PO
NLM W1 PO851 **CODEN** PABAA2

PORTUGALIAE ACTA BIOLOGICA. SERIE A. MORFOLOGIA, FISIOLOGIA, GENETICA E BIOLOGIA GERAL. [Port. acta biol., Ser. A].
VFOAT Morfologia, Fisiologia, Genetica E Biologia Geral. Vol. 1 (1944)-. Academic Scholarly Publication. Portuguese (English, German and French). Irregular. Museu Laboratorio e Jardim Botanico, Rua da Escola Politecnica 58, 1294 Lisbon Codex Portugal. **Tel** 601997. **ED** F.M. Catarino. Index available. **Circ:** 210 (ctrl). Documents available from CASDDS.
Desc: Original contributions, critical reviews, morphology, physiology, genetics, and general biology.
Ind/Abst Chem. Abstr.; Field Crop Abstr.; Grass. Forage Abstr.; Life Sci. Collect.

ISSN 0067-2084
AT
NLM W1 PR5846R **CODEN** PAPPCH

PROCEEDINGS OF THE AUSTRALIAN PHYSIOLOGICAL AND PHARMACOLOGICAL SOCIETY. [Proc. Aust. Physiol. Pharmacol. Soc.].
Main/Corp Australian Physiological and Pharmacological Society. Vol. 1 (June 1970)-. Academic Scholarly Publication. English. Two times a year (Feb. & Oct.). 45.22Aus$. Australian Physiological and Pharmacological Society, Department of Physiology, Monash University, Sydney NSW 2006 Australia. **Tel** 011 61 2 6923477, FAX 011 61 2 6922058. **ED** Dr. I. C. McCance (editor's address: PO Box 459, Mt. Waverly, Victoria 3149 Australia, phone: 011 61 3 802 1838). Index available (bound in second issue). cum. index. **Bk Rev**, (Qty: 4). **Ad Acc, Adv Mgr:** Dr. I. McCance, **Tel** 011 61 3 802 1838. **Circ:** 600 (ctrl). Documents available from BIOSIS Document Express, CASDDS.
Desc: Proceedings of scientific meetings of the Australian National Society for Physiologists and Pharmacologists. Including abstracts of all communications and text of symposia, plus book review and invited lectures.
Ind/Abst Biol. Abstr. (-1987); Chem. Abstr.; Curr. Cit.; Life Sci. Collect.

LC QH301 **ISSN** 0845-5066
DD 574./05 CN

PROGRAMME, PROCEEDINGS / CANADIAN FEDERATION OF BIOLOGICAL SOCIETIES. [Programme proc. - Can. Fed. Biol. Soc., Annu. Meet.].
Main/Corp Canadian Federation of Biological Societies. Meeting. 30th (June 22/26, 1987)-. Proceedings. English. Limited free distribution. Federation of Biological Sciences, 575 King Edward Avenue, Ottawa Ontario K1N 7N5 Canada. ***Formed by the union of** Programme (Canadian Federation of Biological Societies), 0845-5058 **and** Proceedings (Canadian Federation of Biological Societies), 0714-8577.*
Desc: Abstracts of papers submitted to the meeting.

LC QP351 .P75 **ISSN** 0363-0951
DD 152/.05 US
CCC
NLM W1 PR6782 **CODEN** PPPPDL

PROGRESS IN PSYCHOBIOLOGY AND PHYSIOLOGICAL PSYCHOLOGY. [Prog. psychobiol. physiol. psychol.].
Vol. 6 (1976)-. Academic Scholarly Publication. English. Irregular. Academic Press Inc., 6277 Sea Harbor Drive, Orlando FL 32887. **Tel** (800)543-9534, (407)345-4100, FAX (407)352-3445. **ED** J. M. Sprague and A. N. Epstein. Documents available from The Genuine Article, CASDDS. ***Continues** Progress in Physiological Psychology, 0079-6670.*
Ind/Abst Chem. Abstr. (?-1987); Index Sci. Rev. [Full Cov.]; Res. Alert [Full Cov.]; Sci. Cit. Index; Soc. Sci. Cit. Index [Select. Cov.].

LC QP801.P68 P72 **ISSN** 0090-6980
DD 612/.0157/7 US
CCC
NLM W1 PR77 **CODEN** PRGLBA
Pr Rev.

PROSTAGLANDINS. [Prostaglandins].
Vol. 1 (Jan. 1972)-. Academic Scholarly Publication. English. Twelve times a year. $525.00. Butterworth Heinemann / Woburn, MA, 225 Wildwood Avenue, Unit B, Woburn MA 01801. **Tel** (800)366-2665, FAX (617)928-2620, telex 880052. **(Subscription address:** Elsevier Science Inc. / New York Books, 655 Avenue of the Americas, New York NY 10010. **Tel** (212)633-3650.) **ED** Peter W. Ramwell (editor's address: Georgetown University Medical Center, Washington, DC 20007). Index available. **Ad Acc. Circ:** 1,400 (ctrl). available on microfilm and microfiche from University Microfilms International (UMI). Documents available from The Genuine Article, BIOSIS Document Express, CASDDS, ADONIS.
Desc: The international journal of rapid communication encompassing all areas of prostaglandin research.
Ind/Abst ADONIS; AGRICOLA [Select. Cov.]; Anal. Abstr.; Anim. Breed. Abstr.; Biol. Abstr.; Chem. Abstr.; Curr. Aware. Biol. Sci., CABS; Curr. Chem. React.; Curr. Cit.; Curr. Contents Life Sci.; Dairy Sci. Abstr.; EMBASE; Energy Res. Abstr. (Dec. 1974-); Index Chem.; Index Med.; Index Vet.; Maize Abstr.; Mass Spect. Bull.; NAPRALERT; Nat. Prod. Updates; Life Sci. Collect.; PESTDOC; Pig News Inf.; Ref. Upd. Basic Ed.; Ref. Upd. Deluxe Ed.; Res. Alert [Full Cov.]; Sci. Cit. Index; SCISEARCH; Vet. Bull.

LC QP351 .P79 **ISSN** 0048-5772
DD 152/.05 US
CCC
NLM W1 PS78 **CODEN** PSPHAF
Pr Rev.

PSYCHOPHYSIOLOGY. [Psychophysiology].
Added/Corp Society for Psychophysiological Research (U.S.). Vol. 1 (July 1964)-. Academic Scholarly Publication. English. Six times a year. $105.00. Cambridge University Press / New York, 40 West 20th Street, New York NY 10011-4211. **Tel** (212)924-3900, (800)221-4512, FAX (212)691-3239. **(Subscription address:** Cambridge University Press / Outside of North America, United Kingdom. **Tel** 011 44 223 312 393, FAX 011 44 223 325 959.) **ED** Michael G. H. Coles (Editor-in-Chief). Index available. **Bk Rev. Ad Acc. Circ:** 2,100. available on microfilm and microfiche from University Microfilms International (UMI). Documents available from The Genuine Article, BIOSIS Document Express, CASDDS. ***Continues** Psychophysiology Newsletter.*
Desc: Publishes research findings on the identification and analysis of the physiological processes that underlie human behavior in health and psychosomatic and psychiatric diseases.
Ind/Abst Annals Behav. Med.; Biol. Abstr.; Chem. Abstr.; CSA Neuro. Abstr. (?-?); Curr. Aware. Biol. Sci., CABS; Curr. Cit.; Curr. Contents Life Sci.; EMBASE; Energy Res. Abstr. (Aug. 1982-); Ergon. Abstr.; Index Med.; Int. Aerosp. Abstr.; Life Sci. Collect.; Psychol. Abstr. (1964-); PsycINFO; PsycLit; Ref. Upd. Deluxe Ed.; Res. Alert [Full Cov.]; Sci. Cit. Index; SCISEARCH; Soc. Plann. Policy Dev. Abstr.; Soc. Sci. Cit. Index [Full Cov.]; SportSearch.

ISSN 1031-3613
AT
CCC
NLM W1; RE213KK **CODEN** RFDEEH
Pr Rev.

REPRODUCTION, FERTILITY, AND DEVELOPMENT. [Reprod. fertil. dev.].
Added/Corp Commonwealth Scientific and Industrial Research Organization (Australia) Fertility Society of Australia. Australian Academy of Science. Australian Society for Reproductive Biology. Vol. 1 (1989)-. Academic Scholarly Publication. English. Six times a year. 280.00Aus$. CSIRO Publications, PO Box 89, 314 Albert Street, East Melborne Victoria 3002 Australia. **Tel** 011 61 3 4187333, 4187217, FAX 011 61 3 4190459, telex AA 30236. **ED** A. Grant. Index available. **Ad Acc. Acid Free. Circ:** 900. available on microfilm and microfiche from University Microfilms International (UMI). Documents available from The Genuine Article, BIOSIS Document Express, CASDDS. ***Continues** Clinical Reproduction and Fertility, 0725-556X; **Continues in part** Australian Journal of Biological Sciences, 0004-9417.*
Desc: International journal for the publication of original work, review and comment in reproductive biology, reproductive endocrinology and developmental biology.
Ind/Abst AgBiotech News Inf.; AGRICOLA [Full Cov.]; Anim. Breed. Abstr.; Biol. Abstr.; Chem. Abstr.; Curr. Aware. Biol. Sci., CABS; Curr. Cit.; Curr. Contents Agric. Biol. Environ. Sci.; Curr. Contents Life Sci.; Dairy Sci. Abstr.; EMBASE [Select. Cov.]; Fish Rev. (Jan. 1989-July 1992); Index Med. (1989-); Index Vet.; Nutr. Abstr. Rev., Ser. B, Live Feeds and Feed.; Nutr. Abstr. Rev., Ser. A, Hum. Exp.; Pig News Inf.; Ref. Upd. Deluxe Ed.; Res. Alert [Full Cov.]; Sci. Cit. Index; SCISEARCH; Soc. Sci. Cit. Index [Select. Cov.]; Vet. Bull.; Trop. Dis. Bull.; Wildl. Rev. (Jan. 1989-July 1992).

LC QP1 .P62 QP251 **ISSN** 0266-6499
DD 599.01 S 599.01/66 US

REPRODUCTIVE PHYSIOLOGY. [Reprod. physiolog.].
Periodical. English. University Park Press, PO Box 4034, New York NY 10163.

LC QP356.3 .R46 **ISSN** 0096-2902
DD 612/.8/042 US
CCC
NLM W1 RE232D **CODEN** RMNUBP

RESEARCH METHODS IN NEUROCHEMISTRY.
See Medical Sciences-Neurology.

ISSN 0378-6129
NE
CCC
NLM W1 RE232GL **CODEN** RMTPD8
Pr Rev.

RESEARCH MONOGRAPHS IN CELL AND TISSUE PHYSIOLOGY. [Res. monogr. cell tissue physiol.].
Vol. 1 (1976)-. Academic Scholarly Publication. English. Irregular. Price varies per volume. Elsevier Science Publishers BV, PO Box 211, 1000 AE Amsterdam Netherlands. **Tel** 011 31 20 4853641, 011 31 20 4853642, FAX 011 31 20 4853598. **ED** J. T. Dingle. Documents available from CASDDS.
Ind/Abst Chem. Abstr.

LC QP121.A1 R4 **ISSN** 0034-5687
DD 591.1/2/05 NE
CCC
NLM W1 RE248H **CODEN** RSPYAK
Pr Rev.

RESPIRATION PHYSIOLOGY. [Respir. physiol.].
Vol. 1 (1966)-. Academic Scholarly Publication. English. Twelve times a year (4 vols.). $1210.00. Elsevier Science Publishers BV, PO Box 211, 1000 AE Amsterdam Netherlands. **Tel** 011 31 20 4853641, 011 31 20 4853642, FAX 011 31 20 4853598. **ED** Pierre Dejours. cum. index. available on microfilm and microfiche from University Microfilms International (UMI); available on an online database from Elsevier Electronic Subscriptions (EES). Documents available from The Genuine Article, BIOSIS Document Express, CASDDS.
Desc: Deals with the etiology, pathophysiology, diagnosis and treatment of acute disease.
Ind/Abst AGRICOLA; Biol. Abstr.; Chem. Abstr.; CSA Neuro. Abstr. (?-?); Curr. Aware. Biol. Sci., CABS; Curr. Cit.; Curr. Contents Life Sci.; EMBASE; Fish Rev.; Index Med.; Int. Aerosp. Abstr.; Life Sci. Collect.; Poult. Abstr.; Ref. Upd. Deluxe Ed.; Res. Alert [Full Cov.]; Saf. Health Work; Sci. Cit. Index; SCISEARCH; SportSearch; Wildl. Rev.

LC QP1 .R38 **ISSN** 0892-1253
DD 612 US
NLM W1 RE253ER

REVIEW OF MEDICAL PHYSIOLOGY.
[Rev. med. physiol.]. **VFOAT** Medical Physiology. 1st Ed. (1963)-. Monographic series. English (Spanish, Italian, Japanese, German, Turkish and Portuguese). Irregular. $29.95 (latest volume). Appleton Century Crofts, Prentice Hall, 200 Old Tappan Road, Old Tappan NJ 07675. **Tel** (201)767-5188, (800)922-0579. **ED** William F. Ganong.
Desc: Concise presentation of human physiology, discussing relevant anatomic considerations in each section. Offers examples from clinical medicine to illustrate physiologic points.
Ind/Abst Curr. Cit.

Biology — Physiology

LC QP1 .E6   **ISSN** 0303-4240
DD 612.005/6   GW
    CCC
NLM W1 RE257G   **CODEN** RPBEA5
REVIEWS OF PHYSIOLOGY, BIOCHEMISTRY AND PHARMACOLOGY. [Rev. physiol. biochem. pharmacol.]. Vol. 70 (1974)-. English. Irregular. Price varies. Springer-Verlag GmbH & Company KG, Heidelberger Platz 3, D-14197 Berlin Germany. **Tel** 011 49 30 8207223, **FAX** 011 49 30 8214091, telex 183 319 SPBLN D. (Subscription address: Springer-Verlag New York Inc. / North America, PO Box 2485, Journal Fulfillment, Secaucus NJ 07096. **Tel** (201)348-4033, (800)777-4643, **FAX** (201)348-4505.) Documents available from The Genuine Article, BIOSIS Document Express, CASDDS. *Continues* Ergebnisse der Physiologie, Biologischen Chemie, und Experimentellen Pharmakologie, 0080-2042.
Desc: Contains reviews of physiology, biochemistry, and pharmacology.
Ind/Abst Biol. Abstr.; Chem. Abstr.; Curr. Aware. Biol. Sci., CABS; Curr. Cit.; Index Med.; Index Sci. Rev. [Full Cov.]; Life Sci. Collect.; Res. Alert [Full Cov.]; Sci. Cit. Index; SCISEARCH.

LC QH501   **ISSN** 1359-6004
DD 574.1   UK
●**REVIEWS OF REPRODUCTION.** (1996)-. Academic Scholarly Publication. English. Three times a year. Journals of Reproduction & Fertility Ltd., 22 Newmarket Rd., Cambridge CB5 8DT United Kingdom. **Tel** 011 44 1223 351809, **FAX** 011 44 1223 359754. (Subscription address: Portland Press Ltd., PO Box 32 Commerce Way, Colchester Essex CO2 8HP, United Kingdom. **Tel** 011 44 1206 796351, **FAX** 011 44 1206 799331.) **ED** C.A. Doberska.

LC QP1 .R4   **ISSN** 0034-9402
DD 599/.01/05   SP
    CCC
NLM W1 RE534   **CODEN** REFIAS
Pr Rev.
REVISTA ESPANOLA DE FISIOLOGIA. (REVISTA ESPANOLA DE FISIOLOGIA / CONSEJO SUPERIOR DE INVESTIGACIONES CIENTIFICAS.). [Rev. Esp. fisiol.]. **Added/Corp** Consejo Superior de Investigaciones Cientificas (Spain) Instituto Espanol de Fisiologia y Bioquimica. Consejo Superior de Investigaciones Cientificas (Spain). Departamento de Investigaciones Fisiologicas. Vol. 1, No. 1 (March 1945)-. Academic Scholarly Publication. Spanish (English; summaries and/or abstracts in English and German). Four times a year. 14500ptas Spain; 18000ptas other. Consejo Superior Investigacion Cientificas / CSIC, Vitruvio 8, 28006 Madrid Spain. **Tel** 011 34 1 5612833, **FAX** 011 34 1 4113077, telex 42182. (Subscription address: Universidad DG Navarra, Apartado Correos 273, 31080 Pamplona Spain. **Tel** 011 34 48252150.) Index available in last issue of volume--attached. cum. index. Documents available from The Genuine Article, BIOSIS Document Express, CASDDS.
Ind/Abst Anim. Breed. Abstr.; Biol. Abstr.; Chem. Abstr.; Curr. Aware. Biol. Sci., CABS; Curr. Cit.; Curr. Contents Life Sci.; Dairy Sci. Abstr.; EMBASE [Select. Cov.]; Field Crop Abstr.; Index Med.; Indice Med. Esp.; Nutr. Abstr. Rev., Ser. B, Live Feeds and Feed.; Nutr. Abstr. Rev., Ser. A, Hum. Exp.; Life Sci. Collect.; Pig News Inf.; Poult. Abstr.; Res. Alert [Full Cov.]; Rev. Agric. Entomol.; Sci. Cit. Index; SCISEARCH.

LC HA1651 .A334 HA1634.S4 S47
DD 314   CI
ROENI U SR SRBIJI. *See* Biology-Abstracting, Bibliographies and Statistics.

    RM
NLM W1; RO327M
●**ROMANIAN JOURNAL OF PHYSIOLOGY : PHYSIOLOGICAL SCIENCES / [ACADEMIA DE STIINTE MEDICALE].** **Added/Corp** Academia de Stiinte Medicale. Vol. 30, 1/2 (Jan./June 1993)-. Periodical. English (French, German, Russian and Spanish). Four times a year. $125.00. (Subscription address: Orion Press SRL, SPL Independentei 202-A, Bucharest 6 Romania. **Tel** 011 401 3122425.) *Continues* Revue Roumaine de Physiologie (Bucharest, Romania : 1990).
Ind/Abst Index Med. (1993-).

LC QP53.J32 S447
    JA
SEIBUTSU KAGAKU SOGO KENKYU KIKO SEIRIGAKU KENKYUJO YORAN. **Main/Corp** Seirigaku Kenkyujo (Japan). (1977)-. Periodical. Japanese. Seibutsu Kagaku Sogo Kenkyo Kiko Seibutsugako, Aza Saigo, Myodaijicho 444 Okazaki Japan.

LC QP1 .S44
    JA
SEIRIGAKU KENKYUJO NENPO.
Added/Corp Seirigaku Kenkyujo (Japan). Vol. 1 (1980)-. English (Japanese). One time a year. Seibutsu Kagaku Sogo Kenkyo Kiko Seibutsugako, Aza Saigo, Myodaijicho 444 Okazaki Japan.

LC QP431 .S451123   **ISSN** 0894-4520
DD 591.1/82/05   US
    CCC
NLM W1; SE625J
SENSORY SYSTEMS. [Sens. syst.].
Added/Corp Consultants Bureau. **VFOAT** Sensornye Sistemy. Vol. 1, No. 1 (Jan./March 1987)-. Periodical. English (translations available in Russian). Four times a year. $625.00. Consultants Bureau, A Division of Plenum Publishing Corporation, 233 Spring Street, New York NY 10013. **Tel** (212)620-8000, (212)620-8466, **FAX** (212)463-0742, telex 23/421139. **ED** M. A. Ostrovskll. available on microfilm and microfiche from University Microfilms International (UMI).
Desc: Publishes recent Soviet research in sensory systems physiology involving processes of sensory reception - transduction and adaptation at the receptor level - mechanisms for processing information and for trait discrimination, and the study of higher cerebral processes.
Ind/Abst Chemorecept. Abstr.; CSA Neuro. Abstr. (?-?); Psychol. Abstr. (1987-); PsycINFO; PsycLit.

LC QP1 .S53   **ISSN** 0371-0874
    CC
NLM W1 SH287   **CODEN** SLHPAH
Pr Rev.
SHENG LI HSUEH PAO. [Sheng li hsueh pao].
Added/Corp Chung-Kuo Sheng Li K'o Hsueh Hui. **VFOAT** Acta Physiologica Sinica. Vol. 19 (1953)-. Academic Scholarly Publication. Chinese (summaries and/or abstracts in English, German and Russian). Six times a year. $66.00. Shanghai Institute of Physiology, Science Press, 16 Donghuangchenggen North Street, Beijing 100707, People's Republic of China. **Tel** 011 86 1 4019821, **FAX** 011 86 4012180, telex 210147. (Subscription address: China International Book Trading Corporation, PO Box 399, Library Service Department, Beijing 100044 People's Republic of China. **Tel** 011 86 1 8414284, **FAX** 011 86 1 8412023, telex 22496 CIBTC CN.) available on microfilm from University Microfilms International (UMI). Documents available from BIOSIS Document Express, CASDDS. *Continues in part* Chinese Journal of Physiology.
Ind/Abst Biol. Abstr.; Chem. Abstr.; Curr. Cit.; EMBASE; Index Med. (Vol. 37, No. 1, 1985-).

LC QP1 .S54   **ISSN** 0559-7765
    CC
NLM W1 SH287D   **CODEN** SLKHA8
SHENG LI KO HSUEH CHIN CHAN. [Sheng li ko hsueh chin chan]. **Added/Corp** Chung-Kuo Sheng Li Ko Hsueh Hui. (1957)-. Academic Scholarly Publication. Chinese. Four times a year. $13.56. Science Press, 16 Donghuangchenggen North Street, Beijing 100707, People's Republic of China. **Tel** 011 86 1 4019821, 011 86 1 4010642, **FAX** 011 86 1 4012180, 011 86 1 4019810, telex 210147. (Subscription address: China International Book Trading Corporation, PO Box 399, Library Service Department, Beijing 100044 People's Republic of China. **Tel** 011 86 1 8414284, **FAX** 011 86 1 8412023, telex 22496 CIBTC CN.) **ED** Ji-Sheng Han. **Bk Rev. Ad Acc. Circ:** 7,000. Documents available from CASDDS.
Desc: Publishes articles including physiology, biochemistry, pharmacology, biophysics, pathological physiology, and nutriology.
Ind/Abst Chem. Abstr.; Index Med.; SportSearch.

    ISSN 0234-9752
    RU
SIGNALNAYA INFORMATSIYA NEIROPEPTIDY. (1987)-. Periodical. Russian. Twelve times a year. 6.80rub. VINITI - Vsesoyuznyi Institut Nauchno-Tekhnicheskoi Informatsii, All-Union Scientific and Technical Information Institute, Baltiiskaia ulitsa 14, 125219 Moscow Russia. **Tel** 011 7 95 2384600, **FAX** 011 7 95 9430060, telex 411160. **Circ:** 190.

    ISSN 0379-6175
    SA
UDC 615.8
Pr Rev.
SOUTH AFRICAN JOURNAL OF PHYSIOTHERAPY. *See* Medical Sciences.

    ISSN 1040-3361
DD 574   UK
NLM W1; SO996WH
SOVIET SCIENTIFIC REVIEWS SUPPLEMENT SERIES. PHYSIOLOGY AND GENERAL BIOLOGY. [Sov. sci. rev. suppl. ser., Physiol. gen. biol.]. **VFOAT** Physiology and General Biology. (1990)-. Periodical. English. Two times a year. Harwood Academic Publishers, PO Box 90, Reading RG1 8JL United Kingdom. **Tel** 011 44 1734 560080, **FAX** 011 44 1734 568211.

LC QP355.2 .S96   **ISSN** 0324-0258
    BU
NLM W1 SU931   **CODEN** SPNEDB
SUVREMENNI PROBLEMI NA NEVROMORFOLOGIIATA. *See* Medical Sciences-Neurology.

LC QP1   **ISSN** 0372-1582
    KO
NLM W1; TA394UF   **CODEN** TSHCA4
TAEHAN SAENGNI HAKHOE CHI. [Taehan Saengni Hakhoe chi]. **Main/Corp** Taehan Saengni Hakhoe. **VFOAT** Korean Journal of Physiology. Academic Scholarly Publication. Korean (summaries and/or abstracts in English). Two times a year. Free to members. Taehan Saengni Hakhoe, 28 Yongno-ku Chongno-ku, Seoul Korea. **Tel** 02-765-2210. **ED** Jun Kim. **Circ:** 500 (ctrl). Documents available from CASDDS.
Ind/Abst Chem. Abstr.; EMBASE.

    ISSN 0882-3758
DD 616   US
NLM W1; TH68R
Pr Rev.
THERMOLOGY. (THERMOLOGY : THE JOURNAL OF THE AMERICAN ACADEMY OF THERMOLOGY.). [Thermology]. **Added/Corp** American Academy of Thermology. Vol. 1, No. 1 (April 1985)-. Periodical. English. Four times a year. Thermology, PO Box 1324, Vienna VA 22180. **Tel** (703)938-6140, **FAX** (703)938-1482. **ED** Sumio Vematsu. Index available. **Bk Rev. Ad Acc. Circ:** 3,000. *Continues* Thermology Quarterly, 0742-7050.
Desc: A medical journal presenting the most recent scientific studies involving liquid crystal and/or infrared imaging (thermography).

    ISSN 0301-1798
    RU
    CODEN UFZNAD
USPEHI FIZIOLOGICESKIH NAUK. (USPEKHI FIZIOLOGICHESKIKH NAUK.). [Usp. fiziol. nauk]. **Added/Corp** Akademiia Nauk SSSR. (1970)-. Academic Scholarly Publication. Russian. Four times a year. $112.44. Izdatelstvo Nauka / Akademiia Nauk, (Publishing House of the Russian Academy of Sciences), Leninskii Porspekt 14, 117901 Moscow Russia. **Tel** 011 95 9542153, **FAX** 011 95 9382144, telex 411964. (Subscription address: East View Publications Inc., 3020 Harbor Lane North, Suite 110, Minneapolis MN 55447. **Tel** (800)477-1005, (612)550-0961, **FAX** (612)559-2931.) Documents available from BIOSIS Document Express, CASDDS.
Ind/Abst Biol. Abstr.; Chem. Abstr.; Index Med.; Int. Aerosp. Abstr.

    US
WORLD DIRECTORY OF PHYSIOLOGISTS / INTERNATIONAL UNION OF PHYSIOLOGICAL SCIENCES. **Main/Corp** International Union of Physiological Sciences. (1977)-. Directory. English. Every 3 years. IUPS World Directory, American Physiological Society, 9650 Rockville Pike, Bethesda MD 20814. **Tel** (301)530-7180.

LC QH345.Z5   **ISSN** 0044-4529
DD 574   RU
    CCC
NLM W1 ZH418T   **CODEN** ZEBFAJ
ZHURNAL EVOLIUTSIONNOI BIOKHIMII I FIZIOLOGII. *See* Biology-Biological Chemistry.

    ISSN 0720-1842
    GW
NLM W1 ZO615M   **CODEN** ZOOPDH
ZOOPHYSIOLOGY. *See* Zoology.

    ISSN 0044-5401
    GW
    CCC
    CODEN ZUECAZ
Pr Rev.
ZUCHTUNGSKUNDE. [Zuchtungskunde]. Vol. 1 (1926)-. Periodical. German (English). Six times a year. $514.94. Verlag Eugen Ulmer, Postfach 700561, D-70574 Stuttgart Germany. **Tel** 011 49 711 4507108, **FAX** 011 49 711 4507120, telex 7-23634. Documents available from The Genuine Article, CASDDS.
Ind/Abst AgBiotech News Inf.; AGRICOLA; Anim. Breed. Abstr.; Chem. Abstr.; Curr. Cit.; Curr. Contents Agric. Biol. Environ. Sci.; Dairy Sci. Abstr.; Food Sci. Technol. Abstr.; Grass. Forage Abstr.; Maize Abstr.; Nutr. Abstr. Rev., Ser. B, Live Feeds and Feed.; Life Sci. Collect.; Pig News Inf.; Res. Alert [Full Cov.]; Sci. Cit. Index; SCISEARCH.

BIRTH CONTROL

    US
ADOLESCENT PREGNANCY PREVENTION AND SERVICES PROGRAM, ANNUAL REPORT / PREPARED BY THE NEW YORK STATE DEPARTMENT OF SOCIAL SERVICES. *See* Sociology-Social Services and Welfare.

ISSN 0267-4874
UK
CCC
NLM W1; AD546C **CODEN** ADCOEB
Pr Rev.

ADVANCES IN CONTRACEPTION. (ADVANCES IN CONTRACEPTION : THE OFFICIAL JOURNAL OF THE SOCIETY FOR THE ADVANCEMENT OF CONTRACEPTION.). [Adv. contracept.]. **Added/Corp** Society for the Advancement of Contraception. Vol. 1, No. 1 (March 1985)-. Academic Scholarly Publication. English (summaries and/or abstracts in French and Spanish). Four times a year. $252.00. Kluwer Academic Publishers, Postbus 322, 3300 AH Dordrecht The Netherlands. **Tel** 011 31 78 524400, FAX 011 31 78 183273, telex 20083. **ED** Gerald I. Zatuchni and Carolyn K. Williams. available on microfilm and microfiche from University Microfilms International (UMI). Documents available from BIOSIS Document Express, CASDDS.
Desc: Reproductive research aimed at both improving our understanding of the biological systems that govern our fertility and the development of methods of fertility regulation that will have an important impact on human behavior and fertility. The journal is the official journal of the Society for the Advancement of Contraception (SAC) and publishes papers concerned with reproductive research and clinical aspects of contraception. Letters to the Editor are welcome.
Ind/Abst Biol. Abstr. (1985-); Chem. Abstr. (1985-); Curr. Cit.; EMBASE; Health Plan. Adminis.; Index Med. (Vol. 1, No. 1, 1985-); Popul. Index (1994-); Ref. Upd. Deluxe Ed.

ISSN 1012-8689
US
NLM W1; AD546E **CODEN** ACDSEL
Pr Rev.

ADVANCES IN CONTRACEPTIVE DELIVERY SYSTEMS. (ADVANCES IN CONTRACEPTIVE DELIVERY SYSTEMS : CDS.). [Adv. contracept. deliv. syst.]. **Added/Corp** World Federation of Contraception & Health. World Academy of Population & Health Sciences. IVF/Andrology International, Inc. **VFOAT** Contraceptive Delivery Systems; CDS. (1985)-. Academic Scholarly Publication. English. Four times a year (Jan., Apr., July, Oct.). $200.00. Reproductive Health Center, 78 Surfsong Road, Kiawah Island SC 29455. **Tel** (803)768-5556, FAX (803)768-6494. **ED** Professor E. S. E. Hafet. Index available (Free). **Bk Rev. Ad Acc, Adv Mgr:** Professor E. Hafet. ctrl circ. Documents available from BIOSIS Document Express, CASDDS. ***Continues*** *Contraceptive Delivery Systems, 0143-6112.*
Desc: Scope of journal covers such topics as human sexuality, male contraception, oral contraceptives, IUD controversies, governmental and ethical aspects, etc.
Ind/Abst Biol. Abstr. (1986-); Chem. Abstr. (1985).

ISSN 0065-3179
NE
NLM W1 AD784 **CODEN** ADVPB4

ADVANCES IN PLANNED PARENTHOOD. [Adv. planned parent.]. **Added/Corp** Association of Planned Parenthood Physicians. Vol. 9 (1974)-. Periodical. English. Four times a year. Excerpta Medica Publishing Group, PO Box 548, 1000 AM Amsterdam Netherlands. **Tel** 011 31 20 5803243, FAX 011 31 20 5803222. ***Continues*** *Advances in Planned Parenthood, 0065-3179.*
Ind/Abst Med. Abstr. Newsl.

LC HQ766.5.E8 E35A
DD 362.8/2 ET

ANNUAL REPORT - FAMILY GUIDANCE ASSOCIATION OF ETHIOPIA. **Main/Corp** Family Guidance Association of Ethiopia. (19??)-. English. Family Guidance Association of Ethiopia, PO Box 5716, Addis Ababa Ethiopia.

LC HQ766.5.K4 F3A
DD 362.8/2 KE

ANNUAL REPORT - FAMILY PLANNING ASSOCIATION OF KENYA. **Main/Corp** Family Planning Association of Kenya. English. One time a year. Free. Phoenix House, Kenyatta Avenue, PO Box 30581, Nairobi Kenya. **Tel** 723940. **Circ:** 2,000.

LC HQ750.A3 I5 **ISSN** 0307-6857
DD 301.42/6/0621 UK
NLM W1 IN827PB

ANNUAL REPORT - INTERNATIONAL PLANNED PARENTHOOD FEDERATION. **Main/Corp** International Planned Parenthood Federation. (196?)-. Corporate Report. English (French, Spanish and Arabic). One time a year. Free on request. International Planned Parenthood Federation, Regent's College, Inner Circle Regent's Park, London NW1 4NS United Kingdom. **Tel** 011 44 171 4860741, FAX 011 44 171 4877950, telex 919573 IPEPEE G. **ED** Jeremy Hamand. **Circ:** 20,000 (ctrl). ***Continues*** *Report of the International Planned Parenthood Federation, 0309-2801.*
Desc: Seeks to inform the reader of what we are, what we do, and why we are deserving of continuing support internationally.

LC HQ766.5.H65 F34a
DD 362.8/2 CC

ANNUAL REPORT OF THE FAMILY PLANNING ASSOCIATION OF HONG KONG. **Main/Corp** Family Planning Association of Hong Kong. **Added/Corp** Family Planning Association of Hong Kong. Hsiang-Kang Chia Ting Chi Hua Chih Tao Hui Kang Tso Pao Kao. **VFOAT** Hsiang-Kang Chia Ting Chi Hua Chih Tao Hui Kung Tso Pao Kao. (19??)-. Multiple languages (Chinese and English). One time a year. $1.22. Family Planning Assn of Hong Kong, S Ctr 10 F, 130 Hennessy Road, Wanchai Hong Kong. **Tel** 011 852 25754477, FAX 011 852 28346767.

LC HQ763 .C47a
DD 354/.51/249008482 CH

ANNUAL REPORT - TAIWAN PROVINCIAL INSTITUTE OF FAMILY PLANNING. **Main/Corp** Taiwan Sheng Cia Ting Ci Ha Yen Chiu So. (1975)-. English. Taiwan Provincial Institute of Family Planning, PO Box 1020, Tsichung Taiwan. ***Continues*** *Taiwan. Wei Sheng Chu. Committee on Family Planning. Annual Report.*

LC K2000.A53 A5 **ISSN** 0364-3417
DD 344.04/8 US
NLM WA 33.1 A615

ANNUAL REVIEW OF POPULATION LAW. **See** Law.

LC HA4551 .A83 **ISSN** 0259-238X
DD 304.6/095 TH
NLM W1; AS1394

ASIA-PACIFIC POPULATION JOURNAL. **See** Population Studies.

ISSN 0144-8625
UK
NLM W1 BR531 **CODEN** BJFPDD

BRITISH JOURNAL OF FAMILY PLANNING, THE. [Br. j. fam. plann.]. **Added/Corp** National Association of Family Planning Doctors. (1975)-. Periodical. English. Four times a year. $77.01. Faculty of Family Planning, 27 Sussex Place, Regents Park, London NW1 4RG United Kingdom. **Tel** 011 44 171 7233175, FAX 011 44 171 7230575. Documents available from BIOSIS Document Express. ***Continues*** *Journal of Family Planning Doctors.*
Ind/Abst Appl. Soc. Sci. Index Abstr.; Biol. Abstr.; Curr. Cit.; Curr. Lit. Fam. Plan.; EMBASE.

ISSN 0842-9375
DD 613.9/4/097105 CN

BULLETIN - PLANNED PARENTHOOD FEDERATION OF CANADA. (BULLETIN / PLANNED PARENTHOOD FEDERATION OF CANADA = BULLETIN DE LA FEDERATION POUR LE PLANNING DES NAISSANCES DU CANADA.). [Bull. - Plan. Parenth. Fed. Can.]. **Added/Corp** Planned Parenthood Federation of Canada. **VFOAT** Bulletin de la Federation pour le Planning des Naissances du Canada. (1990)-. Bulletin. English (French). Four times a year. Free on request. Planned Parenthood Federation of Canada, Suite 430, 1 Nicholas Street, Ottawa Ontario K1N 7B7 Canada. ***Continues*** *PPFC News., 0836-1908.*

LC HQ766.5.K6 C54
DD 363.96 KO

CHONGUK KAJOK POGON SILTAE CHOSA POGO. Korean (English). Every 3 years. Free. Korea Institute for Population and Health, San 42-14 Bulgwangdong Eunpyungku, Seoul 122-040 Republic of Korea. **Tel** 355-8003-7, FAX 352-9129. **Circ:** 300 (ctrl).

LC HQ766.5.C6 C485
DD 363.9/6/0951 CC

CHUNG-KUO CHI HUA SHENG YU NIEN CHIEN. **Added/Corp** China. Kuo Chia Chi Hua Sheng Yu Wei Yuan Hui. Chung-kuo Jen Kou Ching Pao Chung Hsin. (1986)-. Chinese. One time a year. China National Publishing Import & Export Corporation, 16 Gongti E Rd., Chaoyang Dist., Beijing 100704, People's Republic of China. **Tel** 011 8601 50630169, 5066688, FAX 011 8601 5063101, 5063010, telex 22313.

ISSN 0740-6835
US

CONSCIENCE (WASHINGTON, D.C.). (CONSCIENCE.). [Conscience]. **Added/Corp** Catholics for a Free Choice (Organization). Vol. 1, No. 1 (Sept/Oct. 1980)-. Periodical. English. Four times a year (Summer, Fall and Winter). $10.00. Catholics For Free Choice, 1436 U Street Northwest, Suite 301, Washington DC 20009. **Tel** (202)986-6093, FAX (202)332-7995. **ED** Maggie Hume. **Bk Rev**, (Qty: 6). **Circ:** 12,000. available on microfilm.
Desc: Ethical discussion of reproductive health and rights and the role of women in the society and the Catholic church. Conscience and dissent in the church, and societal conditions affecting the women's choices in childbearing and child rearing years.
Ind/Abst Curr. Lit. Fam. Plan.

ISSN 1157-8181
FR
NLM W1; CO778CVC

CONTRACEPTION, FERTILITE, SEXUALITE. Vol. 19, No. 1 (Jan. 1991)-. Periodical. French (summaries and/or abstracts in English; table of contents in English). Twelve times a year. $284.34. Societe FSC, 55 rue des Petits Champs, F-75001 Paris France. **Tel** 011 33 1 42969725. ***Continues*** *Fertilite, Contraception, Sexualite, 0980-3904.*
Ind/Abst Curr. Cit.; Index Med. (1993-).

LC RG136.A1 C65 **ISSN** 0010-7824
DD 613.94/3/05 US
CCC
NLM W1 CO778CT **CODEN** CCPTAY
Pr Rev.

CONTRACEPTION (STONEHAM). (CONTRACEPTION.). [Contraception]. Vol. 1 (Jan. 1970)-. Academic Scholarly Publication. English. Twelve times a year. $425.00. Butterworth Heinemann / Woburn, MA, 225 Wildwood Avenue, Unit B, Woburn MA 01801. **Tel** (800)366-2665, FAX (617)928-2620, telex 880052. **(Subscription address:** Elsevier Science Inc. / New York Books, 655 Avenue of the Americas, New York NY 10010. **Tel** (212)633-3650.**) ED** David R Mishell (editor's address: Department of Obstetrics and Gynecology University of Southern California School of Medicine, Los Angeles, CA). **Ad Acc. Circ:** 900 (ctrl). available on microfilm and microfiche from University Microfilms International (UMI). Documents available from The Genuine Article, BIOSIS Document Express, CASDDS, ADONIS.
Desc: Publishes concise reports of original research in the experimental and clinical aspects of all areas of contraception. It is an international journal of communication of advances and new knowledge in this important field.
Ind/Abst ADONIS; Anim. Breed. Abstr.; Biol. Abstr.; Chem. Abstr.; Curr. Aware. Biol. Sci., CABS; Curr. Cit.; Curr. Contents Clin. Med.; Curr. Contents Life Sci.; Curr. Lit. Fam. Plan.; Dairy Sci. Abstr.; EMBASE; Health Plan. Adminis.; Index Med.; Index Vet.; Int. Pharm. Abstr.; NAPRALERT; Nutr. Abstr. Rev., Ser. B, Live Feeds and Feed.; Nutr. Abstr. Rev., Ser. A, Hum. Exp.; Life Sci. Collect.; PESTDOC; Popul. Index; Ref. Upd. Deluxe Ed.; Res. Alert [Full Cov.]; Risk Abstr. (19??-19??); Sci. Cit. Index; SCISEARCH; Soc. Sci. Cit. Index [Select. Cov.]; Vet. Bull.

LC RG136.A1 C67 **ISSN** 0091-9721
DD 613.9/4/05 US
NLM W1 CO778D

CONTRACEPTIVE TECHNOLOGY. (19??)-. English. Every 2 years. $39.95. Irvington Publishers Inc, Lower Mill Road, North Stratford NH 03590.
Desc: A practical manual covering the many new developments in the technology and delivery of birth control services for physicians, nurses, midwives, students, pharmacists, and educators.
Ind/Abst Curr. Lit. Fam. Plan.

ISSN 0274-726X
US
CCC
NLM W1 CO778DF

CONTRACEPTIVE TECHNOLOGY UPDATE. [Contracept. technol. update]. Vol. 1, No. 1 (April 1980)-. Periodical. English. Twelve times a year. $259.00. American Health Consultants, 3525 Piedmont Road, Suite 400, Atlanta GA 30305. **Tel** (800)688-2421, (404)262-7436, FAX (800)850-1232, (404)262-7837. **(Subscription address:** American Health Consultants, Dept. 5042, Box 71266, Chicago IL 60691. **) ED** E Marie Robertson. **Circ:** 2,200. available on microfilm from University Microfilms International (UMI); available on an online database from Lexis-Nexis. Documents available from BLDSC, UMI Article Clearinghouse.

LC HQ763 .D57 **ISSN** 0148-6322
DD 362.8/2 US

DIRECTORY OF PROVIDERS OF FAMILY PLANNING AND ABORTION SERVICES. **Added/Corp** Alan Guttmacher Institute. (19??)-. Directory. English. Alan Guttmacher Institute, 120 Wall Street, New York NY 10005. **Tel** (212)248-1111, (800)825-0061, FAX (212)248-1951.

LC HB3639 .D94
DD 304.6/0954 II
NLM W1; DY988H

DYNAMICS OF POPULATION AND FAMILY WELFARE. 1981-. Periodical. English. Every 2 years. Rs140.00. Himalaya Publishing House, Ramdoot Dr Bhalerao Marg, Kelewadi Girgaon, Bombay 400 004 India. **Tel** 011 91 22 3860171. **ED** K Srinivasan and S Mukerji. ***Continues*** *Dynamics of Population and Family Welfare in India.*
Desc: Presents a thorough study of conceptual and methodological significance, fertility and family planning, morbidity and mortality, migration, and studies of special population groups based on analytical data.

Birth Control

LC HQ766.5.E3 E38
DD 362.8/2
UA
EGYPTIAN POPULATION AND FAMILY PLANNING REVIEW, THE. See Population Studies.

LC HQ763 .F28   ISSN 0046-3213
DD 362.8/2   US
NLM W1 FA453BD
FAMILY PLANNING DIGEST. Added/Corp
United States. Health Services Administration. Bureau of Community Health Services. Alan Guttmacher Institute. Center for Family Planning Program Development (Planned Parenthood-World Population). (Jan. 1972)-. Periodical. English. Six times a year. Alan Guttmacher Institute, 120 Wall Street, New York NY 10005. **Tel** (212)248-1111, (800)825-0061, FAX (212)248-1951. available on microfilm and microfiche from University Microfilms International (UMI).

LC HQ763   ISSN 0742-1893
DD 363.9/6/02573   US
NLM HQ 766.5.U6; F198
FAMILY PLANNING GRANTEES, DELEGATES & CLINICS. VFOAT Family Planning Grantees, Delegates and Clinics. 1983-. English. Irregular. Family Information Exchange, PO Box 10716, Rockville MD 20850. **Tel** (301)770-3662. *Continues* Family Planning Grantees & Clinics, 0730-1375.

ISSN 1060-9172
DD 362   US
NLM W1; FA453CP
FAMILY PLANNING MANAGER, THE.
[Fam. plan. manag.]. **Added/Corp** United States. Agency for International Development. Family Planning Management Development (Firm). Vol. 1, No. 1 (Mar./Apr. 1992)-. Periodical. English. Six times a year. Free. Family Planning Management Development, 400 Centre Street, Newton Corner MA 02158.

LC HQ763 .F33   ISSN 0014-7354
DD 362.8/2   US
NLM W1 FA453T   CODEN FPGPA
Pr Rev.
FAMILY PLANNING PERSPECTIVES.
[Fam. plann. perspect.]. **Added/Corp** Alan Guttmacher Institute. Center for Family Planning Program Development (Planned Parenthood-World Population). **VFOAT** Perspectives. Vol. 1 (Spring 1969)-. Academic Scholarly Publication. English. Six times a year (Jan., Mar., May, July, Sept., Nov.). $52.00. Alan Guttmacher Institute, 120 Wall Street, New York NY 10005. **Tel** (212)248-1111, (800)825-0061, FAX (212)248-1951. **ED** Deirdre Wulf. cum. index ($30.00). **Bk Rev. Ad Acc.** Circ: 15,000 (ctrl). available on microfilm and microfiche from University Microfilms International (UMI). Documents available from The Genuine Article, UMI Article Clearinghouse, Documents on Demand.
  Desc: Professional journal focusing on pressing national reproductive health issues. Topics include teen pregnancy, contraception, abortion, sex education, fertility, population, reproductive health, and maternity.
  Ind/Abst Acad. Abstr.; Acad. Search; AGRICOLA [Select. Cov.]; Biol. Dig.; Chicano Index; Cumul. Index Nurs. Allied Health Lit.; Curr. Cit.; Curr. Contents Soc. Behav. Sci.; Curr. Lit. Fam. Plan.; EMBASE; Environ. Abstr.; EP Collect.; Expand. Acad. Index (1992-); Health Plan. Adminis.; Homework Help.; Hum. Resour. Abstr. (?-?); Index Med.; INFO-SOUTH Abstr.; Mag. Search; MasterFile FullTEXT 1000; MasterFile FullTEXT 350; MasterFile FullTEXT 650; MasterFile FullTEXT (Jan. 1991-); Middle East Abstr. Index; Multicult. Educ. Abstr.; Newsp. Period. Abstr. (1990-); OCLC; PAIS Int. Print (1991-); Popul. Index; Psychol. Abstr.; Res. Alert [Full Cov.]; Sage Fam. Stud. Abstr.; Soc. Plann. Policy Dev. Abstr.; Soc. Sci. Source; Soc. Sci. Cit. Index [Full Cov.]; Soc. Work Abstr. [Select. Cov.]; Sociol. Abstr.; Stat. Ref. Index; Stud. Women Abstr.; Telebase; Women Stud. Abstr.

ISSN 0093-352X
US
NLM W1 FA454BF
FAMILY PLANNING RESEARCH AND EVALUATION MANUAL. [Fam. plann. res. eval. man.]. VFOAT R.F.F.P.I. Family Planning Evaluation Manuals; Rapid Feedback for Family Planning Improvement Family Planning Evaluation Manuals. No. 1-1970-. Monographic series. English. Irregular. Price varies per volume. Community and Family Study Center, University of Chicago, 1411 East 60th Street, Chicago IL 60637.

LC HQ763 .C4A   ISSN 0094-4424
DD 362.8/2   US
FAMILY PLANNING SERVICES. ANNUAL SUMMARY. (FAMILY PLANNING SERVICES; ANNUAL SURVEY.). Main/Corp Center for Disease Control. (19??)-. English. One time a year. Centers for Disease Control, 1600 Clifton Road NE, Atlanta GA 30333. **Tel** (404)639-3311, FAX (404)639-3296.

ISSN 0309-1112
UK
NLM W1 FA454CD
FAMILY PLANNING TODAY. Added/Corp
Family Planning Association. (Sept. 1976)-. Periodical. English. Four times a year (Mar., June, Sept. Dec.). $30.80. Family Planning Association, 27-35 Mortimer Street, London W1N 7RJ United Kingdom. **Tel** 011 44 171 6367866, FAX 011 44 171 4363288. **ED** Helen Martins. **Bk Rev**. Circ: 33,000. *Supersedes* Family Planning, 0014-7338 #w (OCoIC)853054.
  Desc: Bulletin on fertility control, human relationships, population and related topics including abstracts, book reviews, comment section, and diary.
  Ind/Abst Curr. Lit. Fam. Plan.

US
FORUM. Added/Corp International Planned Parenthood Federation. Western Hemisphere Region. VFOAT Forum for Family Planners in the Western Hemisphere. Vol. 1 (May 1978)-. Periodical. English. International Planned Parenthood Federation / New York, Western Hemisphere Region Inc, 902 Broadway/10th Floor, New York NY 10010. **Tel** (212)995-8800, FAX (212)995-8853, telex 620661.
  Ind/Abst Curr. Lit. Fam. Plan. (19??-199?).

LC HQ766.5.G4 B76 1974
DD 613.9/4   GW
FRAUENHANDBUCH / BROT UND ROSEN. Main/Corp Brot und Rosen (Association). (1974)-. German.

ISSN 0253-5475
DD 363.9/6   BG
NLM W1 FR946I
FRP REPORT. See Medical Sciences-Gynecology and Obstetrics.

LC HQ767.5.G3 G47a
DD 301   GW
NLM W2 GG4 S773G
GESUNDHEITSWESEN. REIHE 3: SCHWANGERSCHAFTSABBRUECHE.
Main/Corp Germany (West). Statistisches Bundesamt. Added/Corp Germany (West). Statistisches Bundesamt. Schwangerschaftsabbrueche. (19??)-. German. Irregular. Metzler Poeschel Verlag Veroeffen, Statist Bundesamt Kernerstr 43, D-70182 Stuttgart Germany. **Tel** 011 49 7071 935350.

ISSN 0711-7388
DD 363.4/6/05   CN
HUMAN, THE. [Human]. Vol. 9, No. 4 (Oct. 1981)-. Periodical. English. Twelve times a year. $0.50 per issue. Uncertified Human Publishing, 1295 Gerrard Street East, Toronto Ontario M4L 1Y8 Canada. *Continues* Uncertified Human, 0319-2008.

LC HQ767 .H865   ISSN 0097-9783
DD 301   US
HUMAN LIFE REVIEW, THE. [Human life rev.].
Added/Corp Human Life Foundation. Vol. 1 (Winter 1975)-. English. Four times a year. $20.00. Human Life Foundation Inc, 150 East 35th Street, Room 840, New York NY 10016. **Tel** (212)685-5210. available on microfilm and microfiche from University Microfilms International (UMI). Documents available from UMI Article Clearinghouse.
  Ind/Abst Curr. Lit. Fam. Plan.; Expand. Acad. Index (1992-); Newsp. Period. Abstr. (1992-).

LC HQ763.6.I5 I54
DD 363.96   IO
INFORMATION, FAMILY PLANNING PROGRAM. Added/Corp Indonesia. Badan Koordinasi Keluraga Berencana Nasional. No. 1/1 (Aug. 1990)-. English.

LC HQ763 .I624   ISSN 0190-3187
DD 363.9/6/05   US
NLM W1 IN748MAT
Pr Rev.
INTERNATIONAL FAMILY PLANNING PERSPECTIVES. [Int. fam. plann. perspect.]. Added/Corp Alan Guttmacher Institute. Planned Parenthood Federation of America. Family Planning International Assistance Division. United States. Agency for International Development. (Mar. 1979)-. Periodical. English (summaries and/or abstracts in Spanish and French). Four times a year (Mar., June, Sept., Dec.). $46.00. Alan Guttmacher Institute, 120 Wall Street, New York NY 10005. **Tel** (212)248-1111, (800)825-0061, FAX (212)248-1951. **ED** Deirdre Wulf. Index available (back issues, $10.00). **Bk Rev**. Circ: 30,000. available on microfiche and microfiche from University Microfilms International (UMI). *Continues* International Family Planning Perspectives and Digest, 0162-2749.
  Desc: Articles dealing with fertility, family planning, maternal and infant health, and population policy, with an emphasis on Africa, Latin America, the Caribbean and Asia.
  Ind/Abst Biol. Dig.; Curr. Cit.; Curr. Lit. Fam. Plan.; EMBASE; PAIS Int. Print; Popul. Index; Rural Dev. Abstr.; Soc. Plann. Policy Dev. Abstr.; Stud. Women Abstr.; Trop. Dis. Bull.

LC HQ763   ISSN 0363-5155
DD 363.9/6/091724   US
NLM HQ 763.5; P831
INVENTORY OF POPULATION PROJECTS IN DEVELOPING COUNTRIES AROUND THE WORLD. See Population Studies.

LC HQ763 .P48
DD 301.32/1   IO
IPPA-NEWSLETTER. Main/Corp Perkumpulan Keluarga Berencana Indonesia. Added/Corp Perkumpulan Keluarga Berencana Indonesia. Newsletter. No. 1 (Sept. 1977)-. Newsletter. English. Four times a year. Indonesian Planned Parenthood Association, Jalan Hang Jebat III, F3 Kebayoran Baru, PO Box 18, Jakarta Selatan KBYB Indonesia. **Tel** (021)7394123, FAX 713904, telex 715905. **ED** Kustiniyati Mochtar. Circ: 1,000 (ctrl).
  Desc: Family planning and population activities in Indonesia.

ISSN 0019-0357
UK
NLM W1 I266M   CODEN IPPMAY
IPPF MEDICAL BULLETIN (ENGLISH EDITION). (IPPF MEDICAL BULLETIN.). [IPPF med. bull. (Engl. ed.)]. Main/Corp International Planned Parenthood Federation. VAT International Planned Parenthood Federation Medical Bulletin (English Edition). (Oct. 1966)-. Bulletin. English (French and Spanish). Six times a year. Free on request. International Planned Parenthood Federation, Regent's College, Inner Circle Regent's Park, London NW1 4NS United Kingdom. **Tel** 011 44 171 4860741, FAX 011 44 171 4877950, telex 919573 IPEPEE G. **ED** R. L. Kleinman. Circ: 27,000 (ctrl). Documents available from CASDDS.
  Desc: Provides health personnel with information on clinical aspects and developments in the field of family planning practice.
  Ind/Abst Chem. Abstr.; Curr. Lit. Fam. Plan.; EMBASE; Health Plan. Adminis.; Trop. Dis. Bull.

UK
IPPF OPEN FILE. Added/Corp International Planned Parenthood Federation. VFOAT Open File. (19??)-. Newsletter. English. Twelve times a year. Free. International Planned Parenthood Federation, Regent's College, Inner Circle Regent's Park, London NW1 4NS United Kingdom. **Tel** 011 44 171 4860741, FAX 011 44 171 4877950, telex 919573 IPEPEE G. **ED** Rupert Walder. **Bk Rev**, (Qty: 300). **Acid Free.** Circ: 2,500 (ctrl).
  Desc: New developments within the IPPF system, and information gathered at Central Office from correspondence, documents, journal, and the mass media.
  Ind/Abst Curr. Lit. Fam. Plan.

ISSN 0911-0755
DD 301.32   JA
JOICFP NEWS. [JOICFP news]. VFOAT Japanese Organization for International Cooperation in Family Planning News. (1974)-. Periodical. English. Twelve times a year. Free on request. Institute JOICFP Inc., 1 1 Sadoharacho Ichigaya, Shinjukuku Tokyo 162 Japan. **Tel** 011 81 3 32685875.
  Ind/Abst Trop. Dis. Bull.

LC HQ766.5.B7 R343
DD 304.6   BL
JORNAL DA REDE. Added/Corp Rede Nacional Feminista de Saude e Direitos Reprodutivos. (199?)-. Portuguese. Three times a year. SOS Corpo, Genero e Cidadania, Rua do Hospicio 859-14, 50050 Boa Bista, Recife PE Brazil. **Tel** 011 81 221-3018, FAX 011 81 221-3947. *Continues* Rede Nacional Feminista de Saude e Direitos Reprodutivos : [Boletim].

LC HQ750.A2 J65   ISSN 0022-1074
DD 363.92   II
NLM W1 JO6447
Pr Rev.
JOURNAL OF FAMILY WELFARE, THE.
[J. Fam. Welf.]. **Added/Corp** Family Planning Association of India. Vol. 1 (Nov. 1954)-. Periodical. English. Four times a year. $10.00. Family Planning Association of India, Bajaj Bhavan Nariman Point, Bombay 400021 India. **Tel** 011 91 22 2025174, 011 91 22 2029080. (**Subscription address:** Prints India, 11 Darya Ganj, New Delhi 110002 India. **Tel** 011 91 11 3268645, FAX 011 91 11 3275542, telex 31-61087 PRIN-IN.) **ED** Avabai B Wadia. Index available. cum. index. **Bk Rev. Ad Acc.** Circ: 3800 (ctrl). Documents available from The Genuine Article.
  Desc: Discusses views and provides information on all aspects of population and family planning including population education, human sexuality and women's development.
  Ind/Abst Curr. Contents Soc. Behav. Sci.; Popul. Index; Res. Alert [Full Cov.]; Soc. Sci. Cit. Index [Full Cov.]; Women Stud. Abstr.

Birth Control

LC HQ766.5.K6 K28
DD 301.32/1   KO
KAJOK KYEHOEK NONJIP. **VFOAT** Journal of Family Planning Studies. Periodical. English (Korean). Korean Institute of Family Planning, Seoul South Korea. **Ind/Abst** Popul. Index (?-?).

LC HQ766.5.I53 B3B
DD 363.96   IO
LAPORAN TAHUNAN BIRO PROYEK KHUSUS BKKBN. **Main/Corp** Badan Koordinasi Keluarga Berencana Nasional. Biro Proyek Khusus. Indonesian.

LC RG136.A1 M36
DD 613.94
NLM W1 MA622P   IO
MANTAP : MAJALAH ILMIAH PKMI : JOURNAL OF THE INDONESIAN ASSOCIATION FOR SECURE CONTRACEPTION. **VFOAT** Majalah Ilmiah Mantap; Maj. Ilmiah P.K.M.I.; Mag. Ilmiah PKMI. Day 1, No. 1 (Jan.-Apr. 1981)-. Periodical. Indonesian. Four times a year. Sekretariat Pkmi Pusat, Gedung LPPM, Jl Menteng Raya No 9, Jakarta Pusat Indonesia.

ISSN 1062-6573
DD 613   US
MARGARET SANGER PAPERS PROJECT NEWSLETTER. [Margaret Sanger Pap. Proj. newsl.]. **Added/Corp** Margaret Sanger Papers Project. No. 1 (Summer 1991)-. Newsletter. English. Margaret Sanger Papers Project, Department of History, New York University, 19 University Place, New York NY 10003.

ISSN 0270-3637
US
NETWORK (RESEARCH TRIANGLE PARK). (NETWORK.). [Network]. Oct. 1979-. Newsletter. English (French and Spanish). Four times a year. Free. Family Health International, PO Box 13950, Research Triangle Park NC 27709. **Tel** (919)544-7040, FAX (919)544-7261. **ED** Elizabeth Robinson. **Circ:** 4,000 (ctrl).
Desc: Newsletter on reproductive health and contraceptive research for health care providers in developing countries.

LC HQ766.5.I5 N43a
DD 363.9/6/0954   II
NEWS LETTER / POPULATION CENTRE BANGALORE. **Added/Corp** Population Centre Bangalore. (Jan. 1975)-. Newsletter. English. Four times a year. Free. Population Centre, India Population Project, KCG Hospital Complex Malleswaram, Bangalore-560003 India. **Tel** 364241. **ED** P.H. Reddy. **Bk Rev. Circ:** 800 (ctrl).

ISSN 1184-1478
DD 362.83/92/08352   CN
NEWSLETTER / B.C. ALLIANCE CONCERNED WITH EARLY PREGNANCY AND PARENTHOOD. See Sociology-Social Services and Welfare.

LC HQ766.5.N37 N56
DD 363.96   NP
NIYOJANA. Nepali. Four times a year. Rs1.00 single issue. Nepal Parivara Nijojana Sangha, Dillibajar, Kathmandu Nepal. **Tel** 410554, telex FPAN-NP 2307. **ED** Sharadha Sharma. **Ad Acc. Circ:** 2,000 (ctrl).
Desc: Editorials on MCH, population growth and family.

ISSN 0737-3732
NLM W1; OU552BR   US
OUTLOOK (SEATTLE, WASH. : 1983). (OUTLOOK.). [Outlook]. **Added/Corp** Program for the Introduction and Adaptation of Contraceptive Technology (U.S.) Program for Appropriate Technology in Health. **VFOAT** Out Look. Vol. 1, No. 1 (Mar. 1983)-. Periodical. English (Chinese, Portuguese, Spanish and Russian). Four times a year (March, June, Sept., Dec.). $40.00. Program for Appropriate Technology in Health, 4 Nickerson Street, Seattle WA 98109. **Tel** (206)285-3500, FAX (206)285-6619, telex 4740049. **ED** Jacqueline Sherris. Index available. cum. index (Issue 10 (3).). **Circ:** 16,000 (ctrl). available on an online database from Internet.
Desc: Provides information on new developments in contraceptive technology and reproductive health. Includes feature articles that explore aspects of family planning in depth; also included are brief summaries of current research findings, reports of new contraceptive products, and drug device regulatory announcements. **Ind/Abst** Int. Pharm. Abstr.

ISSN 1071-3158
DD 362   US
PASSAGES (WASHINGTON, D.C.). (PASSAGES.). [Passages]. **Added/Corp** International Center on Adolescent Fertility. (19??)-. Periodical. English. Three times a year (four qualified subscribers), $15.00 (other). Advocates for Youth, 1025 Vermont Avenue Northwest, Suite 200, Washington DC 20005. **Tel** (202)347-5700.
Desc: Works to reduce unintended teenage pregnancy and the spread of HIV/AIDS among adolescents by supporting programs worldwide to enhance decision making in key areas of their lives; and to improve access to health care.

ISSN 0190-3195
US
PERSPECTIVAS INTERNACIONALES EN PLANIFICACION FAMILIAR. **Added/Corp** Alan Guttmacher Institute. (1978)-. Periodical. Spanish (French). One time a year. $10.00. Alan Guttmacher Institute, 120 Wall Street, New York NY 10005. **Tel** (212)248-1111, (800)825-0061, FAX (212)248-1951.
Desc: Spanish- and French-language annual editions of International Family Planning Perspectives focusing on issues of particular concern to Latin America and francophone Africa.

ISSN 0197-6699
US
PIACT PAPERS. [Piact papers]. **Main/Corp** Program for the Introduction and Adaptation of Contraceptive Technology. (197?)-. Monographic series. English. Price varies per volume. Piact, 4000 NE 41St Street, PO Box C-5395, Seattle WA 98105. **Ind/Abst** Popul. Index (?-?).

ISSN 0198-7445
US
PIACT PRODUCT NEWS. [PIACT prod. news]. **Main/Corp** Program for the Introduction and Adaptation of Contraceptive Technology. **VAT** Program for the Introduction and Adaptation of Contraceptive Technology Product News. Periodical. English. Four times a year. Free. PIACT Product Reference Service, 4000 NE 41st Street, PO Box C-5395, Seattle WA 98105. **Continues** PIACT Product Newsletter, 0197-8489.

LC HQ766.5.B7 P54
DD 363.96   BL
PLANEJAMENTO AGORA. **Added/Corp** Associacao Brasileira de Entidades de Planejamento Familiar. (198?)-. Periodical. Portuguese. One time a week.
Ind/Abst Trop. Dis. Bull.

NLM W1; PL104M   UK
●**PLANNED PARENTHOOD CHALLENGES / INTERNATIONAL PLANNED PARENTHOOD FEDERATION.** **Added/Corp** International Planned Parenthood Federation. **VFOAT** Challenges. (1993)-. Periodical. English. Two times a year. Free on request. International Planned Parenthood Federation, Regent's College, Inner Circle Regent's Park, London NW1 4NS United Kingdom. **Tel** 011 44 171 4860741, FAX 011 44 171 4877950, telex 919573 IPEPEE G. **ED** Jeremy Hamand. **Circ:** 8,000-10,000 (ctrl).
Desc: Aims to debate and report on issues of topical interest to all those concerned with reproductive wellbeing, sexual health and family planning.

ISSN 0710-6343
DD 363.9/6/060713541   CN
PLANNED PARENTHOOD OF TORONTO. (PLANNED PARENTHOOD OF TORONTO : NEWSLETTER.). [Plann. Parent. Tor.]. **VAT** P.P.T. News; Planned Parenthood of Toronto News; Planned Parenthood. Newsletter. English. Six times a year. Free to members. Planned Parenthood of Toronto, 58 Shaftesbury Avenue, Toronto Ontario M4T 1A3 Canada.

LC HB848 .J68
DD 304.6/05   ISSN 0199-0039
NLM W1 PO597E   CCC
Pr Rev.   CODEN PENVDK
POPULATION AND ENVIRONMENT. See Population Studies.

LC RG136.5 .P66
DD 613
NLM W1 PO671R   ISSN 0097-9090
    US
    CEASED
POPULATION REPORT. SERIES I, PERIODIC ABSTINENCE (ENGLISH ED.). See Population Studies.

LC RG137.5 .P65
DD 613.9/432
NLM W1 PO671H   ISSN 0097-9074
    US
POPULATION REPORTS. SERIES A, ORAL CONTRACEPTIVES (ENGLISH ED.). See Population Studies.

LC RG137.3 .P63
DD 613.9/435
NLM W1 PO671I   ISSN 0092-9344
    US
POPULATION REPORTS. SERIES B, INTRAUTERINE DEVICES (ENGLISH ED.). See Population Studies.

DD 614
NLM W1; PO671KB   ISSN 0891-0030
    US
POPULATION REPORTS. SERIES C, FEMALE STERILIZATION (ENGLISH ED.). See Population Studies.

LC RG136 .P66 ser.D
DD 613
NLM W1; PO671MB   ISSN 0891-0049
    US
POPULATION REPORTS. SERIES D, MALE STERILIZATION (ENGLISH ED.). See Population Studies.

LC K2000.A13 P65
DD 344/.048 342.448
NLM W1 PO671ME   ISSN 0097-9082
    US
POPULATION REPORTS. SERIES E, LAW AND POLICY (ENGLISH ED.). See Population Studies.

LC RC888 .P67
DD 613
NLM W1 PO671Q   ISSN 0093-4496
    US
    CODEN PRSHDQ
POPULATION REPORTS. SERIES H, BARRIER METHODS (ENGLISH ED.). See Population Studies.

LC HQ763 .P616
DD 304
NLM W1 PO671S   ISSN 0091-925X
    US
    CODEN PLNRAK
POPULATION REPORTS. SERIES J, FAMILY PLANNING PROGRAMS (ENGLISH ED.). See Population Studies.

LC RG137.55 .P66
DD 613
NLM W1 PO671SC   ISSN 0097-9104
    US
    CODEN PRSIDT
POPULATION REPORTS. SERIES K, INJECTABLES AND IMPLANTS (ENGLISH ED.). See Population Studies.

LC RG136 .P6 Ser. M
DD 304
NLM W1 PO671SE
Pr Rev.   ISSN 0733-9135
    US
POPULATION REPORTS. SERIES M, SPECIAL TOPICS (ENGLISH ED.). See Population Studies.

LC RG136.A1 P66
DD 363.9/05   UA
POPULATION SCIENCES : JOURNAL OF INTERNATIONAL ISLAMIC CENTER FOR POPULATION STUDIES AND RESEARCH, AL-AZHAR UNIVERSITY, CAIRO. See Population Studies.

LC HQ763 .P62
DD 303.6/6/05   BG
POPULATION TIMES, THE. Vol. 1, No. 1 (March 1982)-. Periodical. English. Four times a year. TK80.00, TK20.00 (single issue) Bangladesh; $10.00, $2.00 (single issue) US. The Population Times, 54A 1st Floor Road, 6A, Dacca 1209 Bangladesh. **ED** M.A. Rub. Index available. **Bk Rev. Ad Acc. Circ:** 2,000 (ctrl).
Desc: Exists to strengthen networking of information, education, research and data-based findings on various development issues particularly on South-East-Asian region.

ISSN 0836-7221
DD 363.4/6/0971   CN
PRO-CHOICE NEWS. [Pro-choice news]. **Added/Corp** Canadian Abortion Rights Action League. (July 1985)-. Periodical. English. Four times a year. Comes with Canadian Abortion Rights Action League membership. Canadian Abortion Rights Action League, 344 Bloor Street, Suite 306, Toronto Ontario M5S 3A7 Canada. **Tel** (416)961-1507. ctrl circ. **Continues** Canadian Abortion Rights Newsletter.
Desc: A national forum of news and opinion on abortion rights.

LC HQ763 .A8a
DD 301   ISSN 1054-2531
    US
    CEASED
PROCEEDINGS OF THE ANNUAL CONFERENCE - ASSOCIATION FOR POPULATION/FAMILY PLANNING LIBRARIES AND INFORMATION CENTERS, INTERNATIONAL. CONFERENCE. (PROCEEDINGS OF THE ... ANNUAL CONFERENCE.). [Proc. annu. conf. - Assoc. Popul./Fam. Plann. Libr. Inf. Centers Int., Conf.]. **Main/Corp** Association for Population/Family Planning Libraries and Information Centers, International. Conference. 11th (1978)-(1994). Proceedings. English. Association for Population/Family Planning Libraries and Information Centers, c/o Population Council Library, 1 Dag Hammarskjold Plaza, New York NY 10017. **Tel** (212)339-0500. **Continues** Association for

Birth Control

Population/Family Planning Libraries and Information Centers. Proceedings of the Annual Conference - Association for Population/Family Planning Libraries and Information Centers, 0363-938X.

LC HQ766.5.I53 P7
DD 363.96 IO
PROGRAM KELUARGA BERENCANA NASIONAL DALAM GRAFIK DAN GAMBAR. **Added/Corp** Pusat Jaringan Informasi & Dokumentasi Keluarga Berencana Nasional (Indonesia). **VFOAT** Indonesian Family Planning Program through Charts and Pictures. (1983/1984)-. Indonesian (English). ***Continues*** *Program Nasional Kependudukan dan Keluarga Berencana Dalam Grafik dan Gambar.*

LC HQ763.I63 A367
DD 362.8/2 UK
PROGRAMME REVIEW AND FINANCIAL STATEMENTS. **Main/Corp** International Planned Parenthood Federation. (19??)-. English. International Planned Parenthood Federation, Regent's College, Inner Circle Regent's Park, London NW1 4NS United Kingdom. **Tel** 011 44 171 4860741, FAX 011 44 171 4877950, telex 919573 IPEPEE G.

BL
TITLE CHANGE
REDE NACIONAL FEMINISTA DE SAUDE E DIREITOS REPRODUTIVOS : BOLETIM. **Added/Corp** Rede Nacional Feminista de Saude e Direitos Reprodutivos. (1992)-(199?). Bulletin. Portuguese. Two times a year. SOS Corpo, Genero e Cidadania, Rua do Hospicio 859-14, 50050 Boa Bista, Recife PE Brazil. **Tel** 011 81 221-3018, FAX 011 81 221-3947. ***Continued by*** *Jornal da Rede.*

LC HQ766.5.I5 F33A
DD 362.8/2 II
REPORT - FAMILY PLANNING ASSOCIATION OF INDIA. **Main/Corp** Family Planning Association of India. (19??)-. English. One time a year. Free on request. Family Planning Association of India, Bajaj Bhavan Nariman Point, Bombay 400021 India. **Tel** 011 91 22 2025174, 011 91 22 2029080. **Circ:** 2,000 (ctrl). available with illustrations.

LC HQ766.5.U5 R47 **ISSN** 0275-2050
DD 363.9/6/0973 US
REPORT ON FAMILY PLANNING SERVICES AND POPULATION RESEARCH, A. [Rep. fam. plann. serv. popul. res.]. (19??)-. Government Publication. English. One time a year. Superintendent of Documents, US Government Printing Office, Washington DC 20402. **Tel** (202)275-3328, FAX (202)786-2377.
Desc: Report to the Congress of the United States pursuant to section 1009 public law 94-63.

ISSN 8756-2057
DD 344 US
REPORTER ON HUMAN REPRODUCTION AND THE LAW. **See** Law.

LC RG136.A1 S47 **ISSN** 0253-357X
DD 613.9/4/05 CC
CODEN SCYYDZ
SHENGZHI YU BIYUN. (SHENG CHIH YU PI YUN.). [Shengzhi yu biyun]. **VFOAT** Reproduction and Contraception. (1980)-. Academic Scholarly Publication. Chinese (English; summaries and/or abstracts in English). Six times a year. $25.80. Science Press, 16 Donghuangchenggen North Street, Beijing 100707, People's Republic of China. **Tel** 011 86 1 4019821, 011 86 1 4010642, FAX 011 86 1 4012180, 011 86 1 4019810, telex 210147. **(Subscription address:** China International Book Trading Corporation, PO Box 399, Library Service Department, Beijing 100044 People's Republic of China. **Tel** 011 86 1 8414284, FAX 011 86 1 8412023, telex 22496 CIBTC CN.) Documents available from CASDDS.
Ind/Abst Chem. Abstr.; NAPRALERT.

LC HQ750.A1 E84 **ISSN** 0037-766X
DD 613.9/4 US
NLM W1 SO104J **CODEN** SOBIAL
Pr Rev.
SOCIAL BIOLOGY. [Soc. biol.]. **Added/Corp** Society for the Study of Social Biology. American Eugenics Society. Vol. 16 (March 1969)-. Academic Scholarly Publication. English. Two times a year. $68.00. Social Biology, PO Box 2349, Port Angeles WA 98362. **Tel** (206)457-6530. **Bk Rev. Ad Acc. Circ:** 1,600. available on microfilm and microfiche from University Microfilms International (UMI). Documents available from The Genuine Article, BIOSIS Document Express, UMI Article Clearinghouse, CASDDS. ***Continues*** *Eugenics Quarterly, 0097-2762.*
Desc: Advancement and dissemination of knowledge about biological and sociocultural forces which affect the structure and composition of human populations.
Ind/Abst Acad. Search; Anthropol. Lit.; Appl. Soc. Sci. Index Abstr.; Biol. Abstr.; Biol. Dig.; Chem. Abstr.; Curr. Cit.; Curr. Contents Soc. Behav. Sci.; Curr. Lit. Fam. Plan.; EMBASE; Energy Res. Abstr.; EP Collect.; Expand. Acad. Index (1989-); Gen. Sci. Source; Homework Help.; Index Med.; INFO-SOUTH Abstr.; Int. Bibliogr. Sociol.; J. Plan. Lit.; Mag. Search; MasterFile FullTEXT 1000; MasterFile FullTEXT 350; MasterFile FullTEXT 650; MasterFile FullTEXT (Jan. 1993-); Newsp. Period. Abstr. (1991-); OCLC; Life Sci. Collect.; Popul. Index; Psychol. Abstr. (1969-); PsycINFO; PsycLit; Res. Alert [Full Cov.]; Soc. Plann. Policy Dev. Abstr.; Soc. Sci. Source; Soc. Sci. Cit. Index [Full Cov.]; Soc. Sci. Index Fulltext (Spring 1988-) [Full Txt.]; Sociol. Abstr.; SportSearch; Telebase; Trop. Dis. Bull.

US
CEASED
SOCIAL MARKETING FORUM. (198?)-Issue 20 (19??). Periodical. English. Dk Tyagi Fund/PSI, 1120 19th Street Northwest, Suite 600, Washington DC 20036. **Tel** (202)785-0072.

LC HB3663.4.A3 S685
DD 304.6/0968/021 SA
SOUTHERN AFRICAN JOURNAL OF DEMOGRAPHY = SUIDELIKE AFRIKAANSE TYDSKRIF VIR DEMOGRAFIE. **Added/Corp** Demographic Association of Southern Africa. **VFOAT** Suidelike Afrikaanse Tydskrif vir Demografie. Vol. 1, No. 1 (July 1987)-. Periodical. English (Afrikaans). One time a year (July). R16.95. Human Science Research Council / Demographic Association of Southern Africa, Private Bag X41, Pretoria 0001 South Africa. **Tel** 011 27 12 2022673.
Ind/Abst Popul. Index.

LC KF3771.Z95 S74 **ISSN** 1046-6703
DD 344.73/0419 347.304419 US
NLM WQ 32; AA1 S7
STATE REPRODUCTIVE HEALTH MONITOR. (STATE REPRODUCTIVE HEALTH MONITOR / PREPARED BY THE ALAN GUTTMACHER INSTITUTE.). [State reprod. health monit.]. **Added/Corp** Alan Guttmacher Institute. Issue 1 (Mar. 1990)-. Periodical. English. Four times a year. $96.00. Alan Guttmacher Institute, 120 Wall Street, New York NY 10005. **Tel** (212)248-1111, (800)825-0061, FAX (212)248-1951. Index available (Back issues $40.00).
Desc: Keep abreast of the latest developments at the state level. Each report begins with an analytic summary discussing emerging policy trends concerning, abortion, family planning services, sex education, teenage pregancy, infertility services, new reproductive technology, AIDS and STD's, maternal and infant health, and other related topics.

LC HQ763 **ISSN** 0039-3665
DD 363.9/6/05 US
NLM W1 ST919P **CODEN** SFPLA3
Pr Rev.
STUDIES IN FAMILY PLANNING. [Stud. fam. plann.]. Vol. 1 (July 1963)-. Academic Scholarly Publication. English. Six times a year. $24.00. Population Council, One Dag Hammarskjold Plaza, New York NY 10017. **Tel** (212)644-1300, FAX (212)755-6052, telex 9102900660 POPCO. **ED** Valeda Slade. Index available. cum. index. **Bk Rev. Circ:** 6,000 (ctrl). available on microfilm. Documents available from The Genuine Article, BIOSIS Document Express, UMI Article Clearinghouse, Documents on Demand.
Desc: Concerned with all aspects of fertility regulation and family planning, particularly in developing countries. Interests encompass contraceptive technology, the social context of reproductive behavior, and policies and programs affecting fertility.
Ind/Abst Acad. Search; Appl. Soc. Sci. Index Abstr.; Biol. Abstr.; Chicano Index; Cumul. Index Nurs. Allied Health Lit.; Curr. Cit.; Curr. Contents Soc. Behav. Sci.; Curr. Lit. Fam. Plan.; EMBASE; Environ. Abstr.; EP Collect.; Expand. Acad. Index (1992-); Geogr. Abstr. Human Geogr.; Homework Help.; Index Med.; INFO-SOUTH Abstr.; Int. Bibliogr. Sociol.; Int. Dev. Abstr.; Int. Pharm. Abstr. (199?-); Mag. Search; MasterFile FullTEXT 1000; MasterFile FullTEXT 350; MasterFile FullTEXT 650; MasterFile FullTEXT (July 1993-); Middle East Abstr. Index; Multicult. Educ. Abstr.; Newsp. Period. Abstr. (1989-); OCLC; PAIS Int. Print; Popul. Index; Res. Alert [Full Cov.]; Rural Dev. Abstr.; Sage Fam. Stud. Abstr.; Soc. Plann. Policy Dev. Abstr.; Soc. Sci. Cit. Index [Full Cov.]; Sociol. Abstr.; Spec. Educ. Needs Abstr.; Stud. Women Abstr.; Telebase; Trop. Dis. Bull.; Women Stud. Abstr.; World Agric. Econ. Rural Sociol. Abstr.

LC JK6 .W37a
DD 353.04/025 US
●**WHO KNOWS WHAT, A GUIDE TO EXPERTS / BY WASHINGTON RESEARCHERS, LTD.** **See** Public Administration.

LC LC5163.D44 W67 **ISSN** 0300-7006
DD 370.19/4/09172405 US
WORLD EDUCATION REPORTS. **See** Education.

LC HQ763.I63 A34 **ISSN** 0535-1774
DD 363.9/6/025 UK
WORLD LIST OF FAMILY PLANNING ADDRESSES. **Added/Corp** International Planned Parenthood Federation. (19??)-. English. Two times a year. Free. International Planned Parenthood Federation, Regent's College, Inner Circle Regent's Park, London NW1 4NS United Kingdom. **Tel** 011 44 171 4860741, FAX 011 44 171 4877950, telex 919573 IPEPEE G. **ED** Edda Ivan-Smith. **Circ:** 2,000. ***Continues*** *International Planned Parenthood Directory. World List of Family Planning Agencies.*
Desc: List of principal offices of family planning agencies world wide.

ABSTRACTING, BIBLIOGRAPHIES AND STATISTICS

LC Z7164.B5 B5 **ISSN** 0300-1598
DD 016.30132/1 UK
NLM Z 7164.B5 B5825
BIBLIOGRAPHY OF FAMILY PLANNING & POPULATION. [Bibliogr. fam. plann. popul.]. **VFOAT** Bibliography of Family Planning and Population. Vol. 1 (July 1972)-. Bibliography. English. Six times a year. $13.00 per issue. Simon Population Trust, 141 New Market Road, Cambridge United Kingdom.

LC Z7164.B5 K37a HQ766 **ISSN** 0092-6000
DD 016.3639/6 US
NLM Z 675.F4 C976
CEASED
CURRENT LITERATURE IN FAMILY PLANNING. [Curr. lit. fam. plann.]. **Main/Corp** Katharine Dexter McCormick Library. **Added/Corp** Planned Parenthood Federation of America. Dept. of Education. (1972)-(Aug. 1995). Abstracting/Indexing Service. English. Planned Parenthood, 810 7th Avenue, K Medical Division, New York NY 10019. **Tel** (212)541-7800. **ED** Gloria A. Roberts. **Bk Rev. Circ:** 600. available on microfilm from University Microfilms International (UMI). ***Continues*** *Acquisitions List - Katharine Dexter McCormick Library.*
Desc: Classified annotated list of books and articles in the field of family planning received in the Library of Planned Parenthood Federation of America.
Ind/Abst Curr. Lit. Fam. Plan.; Popul. Index (?-?).

LC HQ767.5.U5 N4A **ISSN** 0095-3105
DD 301 US
NEBRASKA STATISTICAL REPORT OF ABORTIONS. [Neb. stat. rep. abort.]. **Main/Corp** Nebraska. Division of Health Data and Statistical Research. 1974-. Statistical Publication. English. Nebraska Department of Health, Division of Health Data and Statistical Research, Lincoln NE. ***Continues*** *Nebraska Statistical Report of Abortions, 0095-3105.*

BOATS AND BOATING

LC KFC524.P5 A812
DD 343/.794/0965 US
ABCS OF THE CALIFORNIA BOATING LAW. **Added/Corp** California. Dept. of Navigation and Ocean Development. (19??)-. English. One time a year. Free. Department of Navigation and Ocean Developments, 1416 Ninth Street/Room 1336, Sacramento CA 95814. **ED** Carlton Moore. **Circ:** 250,000.

LC GV834 .A4629
DD 797.1/25/06073 US
AMERICAN POWER BOAT ASSOCIATION REFERENCE BOOK. **Main/Corp** American Power Boat Association. **VFOAT** APBA Reference Book. (19??)-. English. American Power Boat Association, 17640 East Nine Mile Road, PO Box 377, Detroit MI 48021. **Tel** (313)773-9700, FAX (313)773-6490.

LC GV834 .A463 **ISSN** 0278-7040
DD 797.1/4/02573 US
AMERICAN POWER BOAT ASSOCIATION ROSTER. **Main/Corp** American Power Boat Association. **VFOAT** Roster; APBA Roster; A.P.B.A. Roster. (19??)-. English. $3.00 (single issue). American Power Boat Association, 17640 East Nine Mile Road, PO Box 377, Detroit MI 48021. **Tel** (313)773-9700, FAX (313)773-6490. **ED** Hilary R. Spittle. **Ad Acc. Circ:** 2,500.

LC WMLC 93/3088 **ISSN** 0279-9553
DD 797 US
AMERICAN SAILOR. (AMERICAN SAILOR : NEWSLETTER OF THE UNITED STATES YACHT RACING UNION.). [Am. sail.]. **Added/Corp** United States Yacht Racing Union. Vol. 6, No. 2 (March/April 1981)-. Newsletter. English. Twelve times a year. $500.00 (benefactor member); $200.000 (sponsoring member); $100.00 (supporting member); $75.00 (sustaining member); $50.00 (contributing member); $35.00 (regular member) Comes with membership. US Yacht Racing

Boats and Boating

Union, PO Box 209, Newport RI 02840. **Tel** (401)849-5200, FAX (401)849-5208, telex 704592. **ED** Mark Smith. **Bk Rev. Ad Acc. Circ:** 30,000 (ctrl). **Continues** USYRU News, 0164-4351. **Desc:** Information pertaining to sailboat racing. **Ind/Abst** SPORT Discus.

LC VM351 .A18a **ISSN** 0097-8442
DD 623.82/2 US
ANCIENT INTERFACE, THE. [Anc. interface]. **Main/Conf** AIAA Symposium on the Aero/Hydronautics of Sailing. (1970)-. English. One time a year. Western Periodicals Company, 424 East Main Street, Ventura CA 93001. **Tel** (805)641-2665, FAX (805)643-4854. **Desc:** Covers boat design and aerodynamics of sailing vessels.

LC GV811.8 .A56
DD 797.1/05 FR
ANNEE BATEAUX (ENGLISH ED.). (L'ANNEE BATEAUX / THE WORLD OF YACHTING.). **VFOAT** World of Yachting; The World of Yachting. (19??)-. English. Six times a year. 200.00F. l'Annee Bateaux / The World of Yachting, 21 rue Pergolese, 75116 Paris France. **Tel** 011 33 1 45006350, telex 205-302 PUBLI BTI. Index available. **Bk Rev. Ad Acc. Circ:** 32,000.

LC GV811.8 .A55
DD 797.1/05 FR
ANNEE BATEAUX. THE WORLD OF YACHTING, L'. **VFOAT** World of Yachting. (1978)-. French. Editions de Messine, 21 rue Pergolese, 75016 Paris France.

LC GV776.W2 W35A **ISSN** 0097-7594
DD 353.9/797/00783 US
ANNUAL REPORT - OFFICE OF BOATING WATER SAFETY (WASHINGTON (STATE)). **Main/Corp** Washington (State). Office of Boating Water Safety. English. One time a year. Office of Boating Water Safety, Olympia WA 98504.

LC VK4 .A55
DD 387.5 SP
ANO DE LA NAUTICA, EL. See Naval Science, Navigation.

IT
AQUA (MILAN, ITALY). (AQUA.). **VFOAT** Aqva. (198?)-. Periodical. Italian. Eleven times a year. L41970. Editrice Portoria, Via Chiossetto 1, 20122 Milan Italy. **Tel** 011 39 2 76000099.

LC WMLC 93/4057
DD 387.2 US
ASH BREEZE, THE. **Added/Corp** Traditional Small Craft Association. (1978)-. Periodical. English. Four times a year. Traditional Small Craft Association, PO Box 350, Mystic CT 06355.

LC GV776.28.A2 A87
DD 797.1/097295 PR
ATLAS COSTERO DE PUERTO RICO. (19??)-. Spanish. M.J. Cerame Vivas, Inc., Apartado 523, Boqueron Puerto Rico, 00622.

ISSN 0313-766X
DD 623.8231 AT
AUSTRALIAN POWERBOAT. [Aust. powerboat]. (1976)-. Periodical. English. Six times a year. 25.49Aus$. Yaffa Publishing Group Pty Ltd., GPO Box 606, Sydney New South Wales 2001 Australia. **Tel** 011 61 2 2812333, FAX 011 61 2 2812750. **Ind/Abst** SPORT Discus.

ISSN 0726-5646
DD 797.1240994 AT
AUSTRALIAN SAILING. [Aust. sail.]. (1977)-. Periodical. English. Twelve times a year. 49.34Aus$. Yaffa Publishing Group Pty Ltd., GPO Box 606, Sydney New South Wales 2001 Australia. **Tel** 011 61 2 2812333, FAX 011 61 2 2812750. Index available. **Ind/Abst** SPORT Discus.

ISSN 1035-3852
DD 797.124605 AT
AUSTRALIAN YACHTING. [Aust. yacht.]. (1990)-. Periodical. English. Twelve times a year. 111.00Aus$. Yaffa Publishing Group Pty Ltd., GPO Box 606, Sydney New South Wales 2001 Australia. **Tel** 011 61 2 2812333, FAX 011 61 2 2812750. **Continues** Nautical News (South Yarra), 1034-4179.

ISSN 0392-2294
UDC 62 IT
Pr Rev.
AUTOMAZIONE NAVALE, L'. [Autom. Nav.]. (1970)-. Trade Publication. Italian (English). Eleven times a year. L40880. L'Automazione Navale, Via D. Ganduccio 7, PO Box 7463, 16167 Genoa Nervi Italy. **Tel** 011 39 10 372-4340, FAX 011 39 10 326447. **Bk Rev. Ad Acc. Circ:** 8,000. **Desc:** Establishes a meeting point between designers, builders, and users concerning advanced technologies as applied on board ships, in shipyards, in the ports, in the communications field, in the offshore sector and for marine operators in general.

ISSN 1184-9789
DD 797.1 CN
AVIRON CANADIEN. [Aviron can.]. **Added/Corp** Canadian Amateur Rowing Association. **VFOAT** Canadian Rowing. (Apr. 1991)-. Periodical. English (French; summaries and/or abstracts in French). Six times a year (Feb., Apr., June, Aug., Oct., Dec.). 13.60Can$. Canadian Amateur Rowing Association, 1600 James Naismith Drive, Gloucester Ontario K1B 5N4 Canada. **Tel** (613)748-5656, FAX (613)748-5712. **ED** Peter King (phone: (613)241-3816). Index available. **Ad Acc, Adv Mgr:** Barbara Lalonde, tel (613)748-5656. **Circ:** 5000. **Continues** Rowing Canada., 0832-1469.

VB
B.V.I. YACHT CLUB ... YEARBOOK. **Main/Corp** B.V.I. Yacht Club. **VFOAT** Yearbook. English. One time a year.

LC WMLC 93/4484
DD 796.95 US
●**BASS & WALLEYE BOATS.** **VFOAT** Bass and Walleye Boats. Vol. 1, No. 1 (Spring 1994)-. Trade Publication. English. Six times a year (Feb., April, June, Aug., Oct., Dec.). $11.97. Poole Publications Inc, 20700 Belshaw Avenue, Carson CA 90746. **Tel** (310)537-6322, FAX (310)537-8735. **(Subscription address:** Kable Publishers Aide / Illinois, 308 East Hitt Street, Subscription Department, Mt. Morris IL 61054-1473. **Tel** (815)734-1261.**)** **ED** Bruce Smith. **Ad Acc, Adv Mgr:** R. Holroyd. Full Page (B&W) $2,770.00. Full Page (Color) $4,395.00. **Circ:** 125,000. **Desc:** Contains articles on boat and motor maintenance, operation, outfitting, performance upgrades, marine electronics, do-it-yourself projects and fishing product reviews, boat, trailer and tow vehicle test.

LC WMLC L 83/6803 **ISSN** 0884-4739
DD 796 US
BASSIN'. See Fish and Fisheries.

FR
BATEAUX. (19??)-. French. Twelve times a year. Socpresse Bateaux, 14 rue Brunel, F 75017 Paris France.

ISSN 0212-632X
UDC 797 SP
Pr Rev.
BITACORA. [Bitacora]. (1976)-. Periodical. Spanish. Twelve times a year. 5500ptas. Bitacora, Velazquez 100, Madrid 28006 Spain. **Tel** 1-575-9452, FAX 1-578-2856. **Ad Acc. Circ:** 25,000.

LC HF6201.B3 B6 **ISSN** 0006-5366
DD 381/.4562382023/0973 US
BOAT AND MOTOR DEALER. **VFOAT** Boat & Motor Dealer. (1958)-. Trade Publication. English. Twelve times a year. $30.00. Preston Publications Inc., 7800 Merrimac Avenue, Niles IL 60714. **Tel** (708)965-0566, (708)967-1810, FAX (708)965-7639, telex 910-223-1780 PRESTON NILE. Index available. **Bk Rev. Ad Acc. Circ:** 32,000 (ctrl). **Continues** Boats & Motors. **Desc:** Trade magazine for the pleasure boat industry. Topics include merchandising, news, and case histories for marine retailers, boat builders, engine manufacturers and accessory manufacturers.

US
BOAT BUILDERS DIRECTORY. **Added/Corp** American Business Directory, Inc. (19??)-. Directory. English. American Business Directory, 5711 South 86th Circle, PO Box 27347, Omaha NE 68127. **Tel** (402)593-4600, FAX (402)331-5481.

LC HD9993.B633 U527
DD 381/.456238202/02573 US
BOAT DEALERS DIRECTORY. **Added/Corp** American Business Directories, Inc. **VFOAT** Boat Dealers. (19??)-. Directory. English. One time a year. American Business Directories, Inc. 5711 South 86th Street, Omaha NE 68127. **Tel** (402)593-4600, FAX (402)331-1505. **Continues** Directory. Boat Dealers, 0884-3163.

ISSN 0826-2802
DD 797.1/0971 CN
BOAT GUIDE. [Boat guide]. 1984-. English. One time a year. $3.00 per volume. L'Annuaire de l'Automobile Formula Publications, Bureau 105/1255 rue Yonge, Toronto Ontario M4T 1W6 Canada. **ED** Jan Mundu. **Ad Acc. Circ:** 55,000 (ctrl).

ISSN 0264-9136
UK
BOAT INTERNATIONAL. [Boat int.]. (19??)-. Periodical. English. Twelve times a year. $102.67. SF Publications Ltd, 120 126 Lavender Avenue, Mitcham Surrey, CR4 3HP United Kingdom. **Tel** 011 44 181 6870993, FAX 011 44 181 5471201. **Ad Acc. Circ:** 26,000. **Desc:** Articles on boating.

ISSN 0888-1561
DD 797 US
Pr Rev.
BOAT PENNSYLVANIA. [Boat Pa.]. **Main/Corp** Pennsylvania Fish Commission. **Added/Corp** Pennsylvania Fish Commission. Vol. 1, No. 1 (May/June 1984)-. Periodical. English. Four times a year. $6.00. Pennsylvania Fish Commission, PO Box 1673, Harrisburg PA 17105. **Tel** (717)657-4518. **ED** Art Michaels. cum. index. **Circ:** 12,000.

LC VM320 .B717 **ISSN** 0144-4034
DD 623.8/6/05 UK
BOAT TECHNOLOGY INTERNATIONAL. (Jan. 1980)-. Periodical. English. Six times a year. £15.00 UK; £17.00 Europe; £45.00 other. Mexrose Ltd., 147 Moorgreen Road West End, Southampton Hampshire S03 3HG United Kingdom.

LC HD9993.B63 B63
DD 629.2/26 US
BOAT TRAILER TRADE-IN GUIDE, BLUE BOOK. **Added/Corp** Intertec Publishing Corporation. Abos Marine Publications Division. **VFOAT** Blue Book. (19??)-. English. $9.95. Intertec Publishing Corporation, 9800 Metcalf, Overland Park KS 66212. **Tel** (913)341-1300.

ISSN 0886-0254
DD 623 US
BOATBUILDER (RIVERSIDE, CONN.). (BOATBUILDER.). [Boatbuilder]. **VFOAT** Boat Builder; Boatbuilder Magazine. (19??)-. Periodical. English. Six times a year. $30.00. Belvoir Publications Inc., 75 Holly Hill Lane, Greenwich CT 06836. **Tel** (203)661-6111, FAX (203)661-4802. **(Subscription address:** Palm Coast Data, PO Box 420163, Agency Department, Palm Coast FL 32142. **Tel** (904)445-4662 ext. 669, (800)829-5475.**)** **ED** Keith Lawrence. **Ad Acc. Circ:** 10,000. **Desc:** Provides plans, techniques and source-of-material information for amateur and professional boatbuilders and yacht designers.

ISSN 0702-7524
DD 338.4/7/62382310971 CN
BOATING BUSINESS (SCARBOROUGH). (BOATING BUSINESS.). (1976)-. Periodical. English. Four times a year. S S P Publications, 120 Barbados Boulevard, Scarborough ONT M1J 1L2 Canada.

ISSN 1189-9913
DD 917.13/7 CN
BOATING EAST (1991). (BOATING EAST.). [Boat. east]. **VFOAT** Cruising & Vacation Guide, Boating East. (1991)-. English. One time a year. Boating East, Marble Rock Road, RR #2, Gananoque ONT K7G 2V4 Canada. **Continues** Boating East Ports & Cruising Guide., 0845-4167.

LC HD9993.B633 .U52 **ISSN** 0006-5404
DD 338.4/7/62382 US
CCC
BOATING INDUSTRY, THE. [Boat. ind.]. (1929)-. Trade Publication. English. Twelve times a year (11 issues and one directory). $38.00. Argus Business, 6151 Powers Ferry Road Northwest, Atlanta GA 30339. **Tel** (404)995-2500, FAX (404)995-0400. **(Subscription address:** Hallmark Data Systems, PO Box 1147, Skokie IL 60076. **Tel** (708)647-6933.**)** **Ad Acc. Circ:** 27,000 (ctrl). available on microfilm and microfiche from University Microfilms International (UMI); available on an online database (file 648/Full-Text) from DIALOG. **Absorbed** Marine Business, 0147-8923. **Desc:** Trade publication serving the pleasure boating industry; management magazine for boat dealers, builders, manufacturers, distributors and manufacturer representatives. **Ind/Abst** Bus. ASAP (1990-) [Full Txt.]; Bus. Index (1985-); EP Collect.; Gen. BusinessFile (1985-); Gen. Period. Index (1985-); Homework Help.; Mag. Search; MasterFile FullTEXT 1000; MasterFile FullTEXT 350; MasterFile FullTEXT 650; MasterFile FullTEXT (Jan. 1993-); OCLC; Stat. Ref. Index; Telebase; Trade Ind. ASAP [Full Txt.]; Trade Ind. Index (1981-) [Full Txt.]; Vocat. Search.

US
BOATING INDUSTRY MARINE BUYERS' GUIDE. (1937)-. Consumer Publication. English. One time a year. $49.95. Argus Business, 6151 Powers Ferry Road Northwest, Atlanta GA 30339. **Tel** (404)995-2500, FAX (404)995-0400. **ED** Dick Porter, Barbara Katinsky. **Ad Acc. Circ:** 30,900. available in microform. **Desc:** Listings of suppliers, distributors and manufacturers, representatives of marine products/services, both alphabetically and by products and services. Also lists stock boat manufacturers and a calendar of boat shows, and publishes a supplement of manufacturers catalogs and literature.

Boats and Boating

LC HD9993.B633 U522   ISSN 0277-8378
DD 338.4/762382/0973   US
BOATING INDUSTRY STATISTICAL YEARBOOK. See Boats and Boating-Abstracting, Bibliographies and Statistics.

US
BOATING INFORMATION - A BIBLIOGRAPHY AND SOURCE LIST.
Bibliography. English. American Boat and Yacht Council Inc, PO Box 808, 190 Ketcham Avenue, Amityville NY 11701. Tel (519)598-0550.
 Desc: Contains over 1,350 descriptive, bibliographic entries of books, videos, pamphlets, posters, films, reports, articles, slide shows, training programs, etc.

LC Z7514.B6 B63 GV771
DD 016.7971/05   UK
BOATING MEDIA GUIDE. VFOAT IBI Boating Media Guide. (1987)-. English. One time a year. International Boat Industry Magazine, Link House, Dingwalll Avenue, Croydon CR9 2TA United Kingdom.

LC GV771 .P6   ISSN 0006-5374
DD 797   US
BOATING (NEW YORK, N.Y.). (BOATING.). [Boating]. Vol. 20, No. 1 (July 1966)-. Periodical. English. Twelve times a year. $26.00. Hachette Magazines Inc., 1633 Broadway, New York NY 10019. Tel (212)767-6000. **(Subscription address:** Neodata / Colorado, PO Box 2606, Boulder CO 80322. **) Ad Acc, Adv Mgr:** Peter Beckenbach, Tel (212)767-5571. available on microfilm and microfiche from University Microfilms International (UMI); available on an online database from DIALOG. Documents available from UMI Article Clearinghouse, Magazine Collection. **Continues** Popular Boating; **Absorbed** Motorboat, 0093-6782.
 Desc: The magazine for everyone who loves powerboats and boating. New boat tests, navigation and seamanship pointers, plus everything from sportfishing to cruising.
 Ind/Abst Access (1975-); Consum. Index Prod. Eval. Inf. Source; EP Collect.; Gen. Period. Index (1985-); Homework Help.; Mag. Index Plus (1989-); MasterFile FullTEXT 1000; MasterFile FullTEXT 350; MasterFile FullTEXT 650; MasterFile FullTEXT (July 1994-); Newsp. Period. Abstr. (1988-); OCLC; Pub. Lib. FullTEXT; Telebase; Mag. Index (1977-); Vocat. Search.

ISSN 0700-7388
CN
CEASED
BOATING NEWS (VANCOUVER). (BOATING NEWS.). (July 1970)-(Nov. 1995). English. BN Publishing, 201 1252 Burrard Street, Vancouver British Columbia V6Z 1Z1 Canada. Tel (604)684-1643. **ED** Don Tyrell. **Bk Rev. Ad Acc. Circ:** 21,000 (ctrl).
 Desc: Directed to members of yacht clubs and boating groups in British Columbia and Alberta.

ISSN 0190-4507
US
CEASED
BOATING PRODUCT NEWS. VFOAT BPN. (19??)-(19??). Periodical. English. Boating Industry, 390 5th Avenue, c/o CCI, New York NY 10018-8104. Tel (212)715-2600. **ED** Jim Pavia. **Ad Acc. Circ:** 24,288 (ctrl). available on microfilm from University Microfilms International (UMI).
 Desc: Mid-month tabloid serving the pleasure boating trade. Contains news and product stories.

LC GV776.A2 B6   ISSN 0163-7207
DD 353.9/3/87723   US
BOATING REGISTRATION STATISTICS. See Boats and Boating-Abstracting, Bibliographies and Statistics.

LC KEO571 .B63   ISSN 0840-8521
DD 363.12/3/09713   CN
BOATING REGULATIONS AND INFORMATION. (BOATING REGULATIONS AND INFORMATION = REGLEMENTS DE LA NAVIGATION DE PLAISANCE.). [Boat. regul. inf.]. **Added/Corp** Ontario. Ministry of Natural Resources. **VFOAT** Reglements de la Navigation de Plaisance. (1989)-. English (French). Ministry of Natural Resources / Ontario, Whitney Block, Parliament Buildings, Toronto Ontario M7A 1W3 Canada. **Continues** Boating Restriction Regulations, Ontario., 0823-4523.

LC KF2558.P5 A813   ISSN 0190-5481
DD 623.88/8   US
BOATING SAFETY TRAINING MANUAL. **Added/Corp** United States. Coast Guard. (19??)-. English. One time a year. US Coast Guard, 2100 2nd Street Southwest, Washington DC 20590. Tel (202)267-1408.

LC WMLC L 83/2213
DD 363.123   US
BOATING STATISTICS. See Boats and Boating-Abstracting, Bibliographies and Statistics.

LC VM320 .S6   ISSN 1059-5155
DD 797.1/05   US
BOATING WORLD. [Boat. world]. No. 80 (Sept. 1991)-. Periodical. English. Ten times a year. $18.00. Billian Publishing Inc., 2100 Powers Ferry Road, Atlanta GA 30339. Tel (404)955-5656, FAX (404)952-0669. **(Subscription address:** Kable News Co. Inc. / Illinois, 308 East Hitt Street, PO Box 564, Mt. Morris IL 61054-0564. **Tel** (800)967-6572.**) ED** Richard Lebovitz. **Ad Acc, Adv Mgr:** Jay Perkins, **Tel** same as publisher. **Circ:** 150,000. available on an online database, CD-ROM, magnetic tape, and microfilm from University Microfilms International (UMI). **Continues** Boat Journal, 1050-8945.
 Desc: Covers family boating/cruising adventures, fun watersports, best new boats and add-ons.

ISSN 0890-9202
DD 797   US
CEASED
BOATRACING. [Boatracing]. VFOAT Boat Racing; Boatracing Magazine. (19??)-(19??). Periodical. English. Muncey Productions Inc, PO Box 707, Monroe WA 98272.

LC WMLC L 83/8914   ISSN 1048-5244
DD 623   US
BOATS & GEAR. [Boats gear]. VFOAT Boats and Gear. No. 1 (Spring 1990)-. Periodical. English. One time a year. $20.00. Taunton Press, 63 South Main Street, PO Box 5506, Newtown CT 06470-5506. Tel (203)426-8171, (800)283-7252, FAX (203)426-4434, telex 5106004860. **ED** Roger Barnes.
 Desc: Emphasizes boat maintenance repair and improvement.

ISSN 0739-2257
US
BOATS & HARBORS. VFOAT Boats and Harbors. (19??)-. Periodical. English. Thirty-six times a year. $48.00. Boats & Harbors, PO Drawer 647, Crossville TN 38557. Tel (615)484-8708.

LC SH401 .Z9   ISSN 0277-531X
DD 799.1/05   US
BOB ZWIRZ' FISHING/BOATING GUIDE. See Fish and Fisheries.

ISSN 1121-3108
UDC 797.1   IT
BOLINA ROMA. [BolinaRoma]. (1985)-. Periodical. Italian. Eleven times a year. L36000 Italy; L46000 Europe; L80000 other. Editrice Incontri Nautici, Piazza Coppelle 62, 00186 Rome Italy. Tel 011 39 6 6867626.

ISSN 0743-8125
US
BOW WAVE'S BOATING. (19??)-. Periodical. English. Twelve times a year. $9.00 (one-year), $16.00 (two-year). Spencer Publications Inc. / Florida, 2554 Garden Court, Hollywood FL 33026. **Tel** (305)423-7833. **Continues** Bow Wave.

ISSN 0316-2532
DD 797.1/05   CN
BOWLINE (THORNHILL). (BOWLINE SAIL AND POWER.). [Bowline]. VFOAT Bowline. Vol. 1, No. 12 (Sept. 1973)-. Periodical. English. Twelve times a year. 35.00Can$. Flintcom Publishing Company Ltd., 57 Glencameron Road, Thornhill Ontario Canada. **Continues** Bowline News, 0316-2524.

LC HD9993.B633 U523a   ISSN 0195-346X
DD 623.8/2023/02973   US
CEASED
BUC ... NEW BOAT PRICE GUIDE. [BUC's new boat price guide]. **Added/Corp** BUC International Corporation. **VFOAT** B.U.C. ... New Boat Price Guide; New Boat Price Guide. (1980)-(1993). English. BUC International Corporation, 1314 Northeast, 17th Court, Fort Lauderdale FL 33305. Tel (305)565-6715, (8000327-6929, FAX (305)561-3095. **ED** Walter J Sullivan III. **Bk Rev.** ctrl circ. available on an online database. **Continues** BUC's New Boat Price Guide, 0195-346X.
 Desc: Boat and engine manufacturers' complete specifications and list prices for model line. Complete trade name, cross-referenced index of over 20,000 listings in 250 pages.

LC HD9993.B633 U515   ISSN 0735-973X
DD 623.8/2023/02973   US
BUC USED BOAT PRICE GUIDE. [BUC used boat price guide]. **Added/Corp** BUC International Corporation. **VFOAT** BUC Used Boat Price Guide; B.U.C. Used Boat Price Guide. **VAT** Boats Unlimited Corporation Used Boat Price Guide. (19??)-. Periodical. English. Two times a year (Summer & Winter). Price varies per volume. BUC International Corporation, 1314 Northeast, 17th Court, Fort Lauderdale FL 33305. Tel (305)565-6715, (8000327-6929, FAX (305)561-3095. **ED** Walter J. Sullivan III. **Bk Rev.** ctrl circ. available on an online database. **Continues** Statistically Authenticated Used Boat Price Guide, 0190-4795.
 Desc: Statistically, authenticated current market prices for pleasure boats with area, condition and equipment scale.

DD 797.12   ISSN 0045-4494
CN
CANADIAN BOATING. [Can. boat.]. VFOAT Boating (Mississauga); Canadian Boating Magazine; Boating (Toronto). (19??)-. Periodical. English. Twelve times a year. 19.20Can$. Arthurs Publications Ltd., 4141 Dixie Rd., PO Box 149, Mississauga Ontario, L4W 1V5 Canada. Tel (905)625-9660, FAX (905)625-7559. available on microfilm and microfiche from Micromedia Limited. **Absorbed** CPS. Canadian Power & Sail, 0700-8732.
 Ind/Abst Can. Index.

ISSN 1183-5990
DD 623.8   CN
CANADIAN OUTBOARD MOTOR DEALERS BLUE BOOK. [Can. outboard mot. deal. blue book]. (1991)-. English. $19.95. Canadian Outboard Motor Dealers Blue Book, PO Box 2508, Station R, Kelowna British Columbia V1X 6A6 Canada.

ISSN 0384-0999
DD 797.1/24/0971   CN
CANADIAN YACHTING. [Can. yacht.]. Vol. 1 (Sept. 1976)-. Periodical. English. Six times a year. 10.60Can$. Kerrwil Publications Ltd., 395 Matheson Boulevard E, Mississauga Ontario L4Z 2H2 Canada. Tel (905)890-1846. **ED** Doug Hunter. **Ad Acc. Circ:** 23,000. **Supersedes** Better Boating, 0045-1797.
 Desc: Power-boating and sailing in Canada.
 Ind/Abst Can. Index; Can. Period. Index (19??-); SPORT Discus.

LC GV781 .C18
DD 797.1   US
●**CANOE & KAYAK.** Added/Corp Canoe America Associates. VFOAT Canoe and Kayak. Vol. 22, Issue 1 (Mar. 1994)-. Periodical. English. Six times a year. $18.00 US; $21.00 Canada; $36.00 other. Canoe America Associates, Box 3146, Kirkland WA 98033. **Tel** (206)827-6363, FAX (206)827-1893. **(Subscription address:** CDS Agency Hard Copy, PO Box 4966, Des Moines IA 50340. **Tel** (515)247-7569.**) Continues** Canoe, 0360-7496.

LC GV781 .C18   ISSN 0360-7496
DD 797.1/22/0973   US
TITLE CHANGE
CANOE (CAMDEN, ME.). (CANOE.). [Canoe]. **Added/Corp** American Canoe Association. VFOAT Canoe Magazine. (April 1973)-(1993). Periodical. English. Canoe America Associates, Box 3146, Kirkland WA 98033. **Tel** (206)827-6363, FAX (206)827-1893. **(Subscription address:** CDS Agency Hard Copy, PO Box 4966, Des Moines IA 50340. **Tel** (515)247-7569.**) ED** David F. Harrison. Index available. **Bk Rev. Ad Acc. Circ:** 63,000. **Absorbed** American Canoeist (1941). **Continued by** Canoe & Kayak.
 Desc: Resource for canoeing and kayaking. Includes paddling adventures, trip tips, outfitting information and equipment evaluation, where to go paddling, what to take, and how to use it.
 Ind/Abst Phys. Educ. Index; SPORT Discus; SportSearch.

LC GV771 .C36   ISSN 0094-5889
DD 797.1/05   US
CAPTAIN'S MATE. (19??)-. Periodical. English. Twelve times a year. $9.00. Captain's Mate, 833 Dover Drive, Suite 3, Newport Beach CA 92660.

US
CARIBBEAN SPORTS TRAVEL QUARTERLY. (19??)-. English. Four times a year. $8.00 (one-year), $14.00 (two-year), $18.00 (three-year). Graphcom Publishing Inc., 1995 Northeast 150th Street, North Miami FL 33181. **Tel** (305)945-7403. **Continues** Pleasure Boating FL, 0191-7366.

ISSN 0045-656X
US
CHESAPEAKE BAY MAGAZINE. VFOAT Chesapeake Bay and Bay Country. Vol. 1 (May 1971)-. Periodical. English. Twelve times a year. $19.95. Chesapeake Bay Magazine, 1819 Bay Ridge Avenue, Annapolis MD 21403. Tel (301)263-2662. **ED** Betty Rigoli. Index available. **Bk Rev. Ad Acc. Circ:** 35,000. available on microfilm.
 Desc: Regional boating magazine covering the Chesapeake Bay.

LC GV776.M32 C474   ISSN 0164-808X
DD 797.1/09755/18   US
CHESAPEAKE BOATMAN, THE. Vol. 1 (July 1978)-. Periodical. English. Twelve times a year. $9.95. Whitney Publishing, 222 Severn Avenue, Annapolis MD 21403.

ISSN 1070-9290
DD 797   US
CLASSIC BOATING. (CLASSIC BOATING : THE MAGAZINE OF VINTAGE POWER BOATS.). [Class. boat.]. No. 18 (July-Aug. 1987)-. Periodical. English. Six times a year. Classic Boating, North Wangard, 208 Lac La Belle, Oconomowoc WI 53066. **Continues** Antique & Classic Boat.

Boats and Boating

COASTAL CRUISING. See Leisure and Recreation-Outdoor Recreation.

LC KFC3908.5.M67 C66
DD 343.74609/6 347.460396 US
CONNECTICUT BOATING SAFETY ENFORCEMENT MANUAL. Added/Corp Connecticut. Dept. of Environmental Protection. Bureau of Law Enforcement. Marine Patrol Division. Connecticut. Office of Boating Safety. **VFOAT** Connecticut Boating Safety Enforcement Manual. (19??)-. English. Connecticut Department of Environmental Protection Marine Headquarters, PO Box 280, 333 Ferry Road, Old Lyme CT 06371-0280.

ISSN 0812-4086
AT
CRUISING HELMSMAN. (19??)-. English. Twelve times a year. 49.34Aus$. Yaffa Publishing Group Pty Ltd., GPO Box 606, Sydney New South Wales 2001 Australia. **Tel** 011 61 2 2812333, **FAX** 011 61 2 2812750. **Ad Acc. Circ:** 7,000.
Desc: Covers all aspects of sailboat cruising.

LC GV771 .C86
DD 797.1/24/05 ISSN 0098-3519
US
CRUISING WORLD. [Cruis. world]. **VFOAT** Annual Cruising World; Sailboat Show Annual. (1975)-. Periodical. English. Twelve times a year. $28.00. Golf Digest- Tennis Inc., 5520 Park Avenue, Trumbull CT 06611. **Tel** (203)373-7256, **FAX** (203)371-2102. **(Subscription address:** CDS Agency Hard Copy, PO Box 4966, Des Moines IA 50340. **Tel** (515)247-7569.) **ED** George Day. Index available. **Bk Rev. Ad Acc. Circ:** 125,300. available on microfilm and microfiche from University Microfilms International (UMI). Documents available from UMI Article Clearinghouse, Magazine Collection.
Desc: For those who enjoy cruising their sailboats. Features first-person narratives by sailors involved in cruising. Articles on seamanship, safety, boat care and maintenance, navigation, new gear and equipment.
Ind/Abst EP Collect.; Gen. Period. Index (1985-); Homework Help.; Mag. Artic. Summar. Elite; Mag. Artic. Summar. Select; Mag. Artic. Summar. CD-ROM; Mag. Index Plus (1989-); Mag. Search; MasterFile FullTEXT 1000; MasterFile FullTEXT 350; MasterFile FullTEXT 650; MasterFile FullTEXT (Sept. 1984-June 1989); Newsp. Period. Abstr. (1988-); OCLC; Telebase; Mag. Index (1980-).

LC HD9993.B633 U528
DD 381/.4562382023/025794 US
DIRECTORY, LICENSED YACHT AND SHIP BROKERS, AND SALESPERSONS. Added/Corp California. Dept. of Boating and Waterways. **VFOAT** Directory of Licensed Yacht and Ship Brokers, and Salespersons. (19??)-. Directory. English. One time a year. Department of Boating and Waterways, 1629 S Street, Sacramento CA 95814-7291. **Continues** California. Dept. of Navigation and Ocean Development. Directory of Licensed Yacht and Ship Brokers and Salesmen.

ISSN 1048-1370
US
DIRECTORY OF NORTH AMERICAN GUIDE AND CHARTERBOAT SERVICES. Added/Corp North American Guide and Charterboat Federation. (1992). Directory. English. Two times a year. National Directory of Guide and Charterboat Services, PO Box 6506, Athens GA 30604.

LC GV777.4 .D57
DD 797.1/0973 ISSN 1048-4671
US
DIRECTORY OF RECREATIONAL MARINE PRODUCT DEALERS. [Dir. recreat. mar. prod. deal.]. **Added/Corp** Chain Store Guide (Firm). **VFOAT** Recreational Marine Product Dealers. 1st Ed (1991)-. Directory. English. Every 2 years. $349.00. Lebhar Friedman Inc., PO Box 31203, Tampa FL 33633. **Tel** (800)944-4676, (813)664-6707.
Desc: Complete profiles on 11,000+ marine dealers, boat dealers and marinas, and on approximately 400 major distributors. Listings include company name, address, telephone/fax numbers, names/titles of key executives, sales volume, year founded, and product lines. Dealers and marina listings include outboard motors sold, sales volume, services offered, boat brands carried, primary distributors, etc.

FR
DOCKS. English (French). Four times a year. 90.00F (per issue). Editions Nepe, Le Moulin de Ventabren, 13122 Ventabren France.

ISSN 1057-0187
DD 623 US
ELECTRIC TROLLING MOTOR REPAIR FOR MR. & MS. FIX-IT. (1991)-. Periodical. English. $19.95. G/M Publishing, 1901 North Bell Street, Kokomo IN 46901.

DD 797 ISSN 0744-3129
US
ENSIGN (SAN MATEO, CALIF.), THE. (THE ENSIGN : OFFICIAL PUBLICATION OF THE UNITED STATES POWER SQUADRONS.). [Ensign]. **Added/Corp** United States Power Squadrons. (19??)-. Periodical. English. Twelve times a year. $10.00. United States Power Squadrons, 1504 Blue Ridge Road, Raleigh NC 27622. **Tel** (919)821-0892. **ED** Carol Eddy. Index available ($5.00). cum. index. **Bk Rev**, (Qty: approx. 24/year). **Ad Acc. Circ:** 50,000.
Desc: Boating safety and education articles, as well as technical and how-to articles, all geared primarily for the members of United States Power Squadrons.

LC VM320 .E93a
DD 623.82/2/05 ISSN 0149-239X
US
EXPERIMENTAL YACHT SOCIETY JOURNAL. Main/Corp Experimental Yacht Society. **Added/Corp** Experimental Yacht Society. Journal. (Sept. 1977)-. Periodical. English. Four times a year. Experimental Yacht Society, 591 Island Avenue, Tarpon Springs FL 33589.

IT
FARE VELA. (19??)-. Italian. Ten times a year. L50000 Italy; L80000 other. Publiedit Srl, Via Margutta 47 A, 00187 Rome Italy. **Tel** 011 39 6 3212310.

LC VM362 .H65 ISSN 0954-3988
DD 623.8204 UK
FAST FERRY INTERNATIONAL. Vol. 28, No. 1 (Jan./Feb. 1989)-. Trade Publication. English. Ten times a year (monthly with Jan./Feb. & Jul./Aug. issues combined). $110.00. High-Speed Surface Craft, 69 Kings Road, Kingston Upon Thames, Surrey KT2 5JB United Kingdom. **Tel** 011 44 181 5491077, **FAX** 011 44 181 5472893. **ED** Alan Blunden, 24 Leaf Close, Northwood, Middlesex, HA6 2YY, United Kingdom. **Ad Acc, Adv Mgr:** D. Woodgate, **Tel** 81-549-1077. **Circ:** 5,000 (ctrl). available on microfilm from University Microfilms International (UMI). **Continues** High-Speed Surface Craft, 0144-7823.
Ind/Abst BMT Abstr.

LC SH401 .G29 ISSN 1040-9947
DD 799.1/05 US
FISHING & BOATING ILLUSTRATED. [Fish. boat. illus.]. **VFOAT** Fishing and Boating Illustrated. (1986)-. Periodical. English. Six times a year. Gallant Charger Publishing Inc., Box HH, 34249 Camino Capistrano, Capistrano Beach CA 92624. **Tel** (714)493-2101, **FAX** (714)240-8680. **Continues** Gallant/Charger's Fishing & Boating Annual.

ISSN 0705-1824
DD 797.1/09713 CN
FLAGSHIP. Added/Corp Civilian Marine Emergency Volunteers. Vol. 1 (May/June 1976)-. Periodical. English. 0.75Can$ per no. Flagship Publications, Suite 301/85 King Street East, Toronto Ontario M5C 1G3 Canada.
Ind/Abst HILITES.

IT
SUSPENDED
FORZA 7. (19??)-(Jan. 1993). Italian. Twelve times a year. L65000. Publimedia Editrice SRL, Corso Venezia 18, 20121 Milan Italy. **Tel** 011 39 2 77521.

ISSN 0016-4259
CN
GAM ON YACHTING. (1957)-. Periodical. English. Eight times a year. 16.01Can$. Gam on Yachting, 250 The Esplanade, Suite 202, Toronto Ontario M5A 1J2 Canada. **Tel** (416)363-1559, **FAX** (416)368-2831. **ED** Karin Larson. **Bk Rev**, (Qty: 8). **Ad Acc, Adv Mgr:** Craig Green. **Circ:** 22,300 (ctrl). **Continues** Gam on Lake Sailing, 0380-335X.
Desc: Covers sailing in Canada, racing and cruising, navigation, rules, equipment and gear, and vacations. Includes boat building and safety tips, classified ads, a service directory, and more.
Ind/Abst SportSearch (May 1987-).

IT
GIORNALE DELLA VELA, IL. (19??)-. Italian. Twelve times a year. L88000 Italy; L121000 Europe; L181500 other. Editrice Portoria, Via Chiossetto 1, 20122 Milan Italy. **Tel** 011 39 2 76000099.

LC HE566.E9 G73
DD 387.5/42/02577 US
GREAT LAKES CRUISE HANDBOOK : GUIDE TO PASSENGER CRUISES, EXCURSIONS, AND FERRY SERVICES ON THE GREAT LAKES AND ST. LAWRENCE RIVER. (19??)-. English. $5.25. Harbor House Publishers, 221 Water Street, Boyne City MI 49712. **Tel** (616)582-2814, **FAX** (615)582-3392.

ISSN 0194-4622
US
GREAT LAKES SAILING SCANNER. (19??)-. Periodical. English. Twelve times a year. Free on request. Morning Star Publications Inc. / Michigan, 1923 Crestwood, Muskegon MI 49441. **Tel** (616)726-2865.

ISSN 0017-4629
US
GROSSE POINTER, THE. See Travel and Tourism.

ISSN 0836-3137
DD 797.1/09714 CN
GUIDE NAUTIQUE (MONTREAL). (GUIDE NAUTIQUE). [Guide naut.]. (1986)-. French. Guide Nautique, 4464 Hotel-de-Ville, Montreal Quebec H2W 2H5 Canada.

LC VM325 .G85
DD 623.8/503/05 US
GUIDE TO BOAT ELECTRONICS. VFOAT Boat Electronics. (1988)-. Periodical. English. Cahners Publishing Company, 249 West 17th Street, New York NY 10011. **Tel** (212)645-0067, **FAX** (212)242-6987.

ISSN 1042-1009
DD 797 US
HEARTLAND BOATING. [Heartl. boat.]. **VFOAT** Heart Land Boating. Vol. 1, No. 1 (March/April 1989)-. Periodical. English. Seven times a year. $17.97. Inland Publications Inc., PO Box 1067, Martin TN 38237. **Tel** (901)587-6791, **FAX** (901)587-6893. **ED** Molly Lightfoot Blom. **Bk Rev**, (Qty: 6). **Ad Acc, Adv Mgr:** Kelly Smith. **Circ:** 15,000.
Desc: Published for those interested in inland boating and life on or near the lakes and rivers of Mid-America. Content is focused on useful and entertaining information for boat owners and users. Included in each issue are pictorial articles about boating life in the area.

ISSN 0745-1628
US
CEASED
HOBIE HOT LINE. Added/Corp World Hobie Class Association. **VFOAT** Hobie Hotline. (19??)-(1995). Periodical. English. Hot Line Publications, PO Box 1008, Oceanside CA 92054. **Tel** (619)758-1841. **Ad Acc. Circ:** 25,000.
Desc: The catamaran sailors magazine.

LC GV776.81.H66 H66
DD 797.1/0951/25 HK
HONG KONG BOATING ANNUAL. (1976)-. English. One time a year. $10.00. Hong Kong Boating Annual, 1908 Prince's Building, des Voeux Road, Hong Kong.

LC WMLC 93/1383 ISSN 0892-8320
DD 797 US
HOT BOAT. [Hot boat]. (198?)-. Periodical. English. Twelve times a year. $27.00. LFP Inc., 8484 Wilshire Boulevard, Suite 900, Beverly Hills CA 90210. **Tel** (213)651-5400. **(Subscription address:** Kable Publishers Aide / Illinois, 308 East Hitt Street, Subscription Department, Mt. Morris IL 61054-1473. **Tel** (815)734-1261.) **ED** Ron Piechota. **Ad Acc. Circ:** 95,000. **Continues** Hot Boat Magazine, 0745-6077.
Desc: Contains technical tips on performance boating, water skiing and water toys. Profiles on most inland (lake) boats and consumer reports.

US
●**HOUSEBOAT MAGAZINE.** (1993)-. English. Six times a year. $16.95 (one-year), $30.95 (two-year), $40.95 (three-year) US; $28.95 Canada; $31.95 other. Harris Publishing Inc, 520 Park Avenue, Idaho Falls ID 83402. **Tel** (208)524-7000, **FAX** (208)522-5241.

ISSN 1054-3856
DD 381 US
HOW TO BUY A NEW OR USED POWER BOAT WITHOUT GETTING BURNED. [How buy new used power boat without get. burn.]. **VFOAT** MacLean-Hunter Used Boat Valuation Guide. Vol. 1, No. 1 (1991)-. English. $15.95 (single issue). J & J Publishing Group, 3310 Richmond Avenue, Suite 102, Houston TX 77098.

LC VM349 .B55
DD 623.8/231/0294 US
INBOARD BOAT TRADE-IN GUIDE, BLUE BOOK. Added/Corp Intertec Publishing Corporation. Abos Marine Publications Division. **VFOAT** Blue Book. 23rd Ed. (1984)-. Periodical. English. Irregular. Intertec Publishing Corporation, 9800 Metcalf, Overland Park KS 66212. **Tel** (913)341-1300. **(Subscription address:** Intertec Publishing Corporation, PO Box 2901, Overland Park KS 66282. **Tel** 800 441-0294.) **Continues** Blue Book, Official Inboard/Outdrive Boat Trade-in Guide.

US
INLAND SEA COMBINED WITH RUDDER. VFOAT Inland Sea. Vol. 69, No. 7 (July 1977)-. Periodical. English. Twelve times a year. **Formed by the union of** Rudder and Sea, 0160-0214.

LC HD9999.B5 I58 ISSN 0020-6172
DD 338.4/7/62382005 UK
INTERNATIONAL BOAT INDUSTRY. [Int. boat ind.]. Trade Publication. Multiple languages (English, French and German). Six times a year. $66.00. Boating

Boats and Boating

Communications Ltd, Perrymount Road, Haywards Heath, West Sussex RH163BR United Kingdom. **Tel** 011 44 444 440421.

US

INTERNATIONAL MARINE BUSINESS JOURNAL. Trade Publication. English. Every 2 years. $15.00 US; (add $10.00 postage) other. International Marine Business Journal, 1766 Bay Road, Miami Beach FL 33139. **Tel** (305)538-0700, FAX (305)532-8657. **ED** Skip Allen. **Bk Rev. Ad Acc. Circ:** 12,000 (ctrl).
 Desc: Covers boating industry and export.

LC GV771 .I55
DD 797.12

GW

INTERNATIONALES BODENSEE JAHRBUCH DER SPORTSCHIFFAHRT. **Added/Corp** Bodensee--Segler--Verband. Internationaler Bodensee-Motorboot-Verband. (19??)-. German. Internationaler Verlag H Mann, Friedrichstrasse 53, Postfach 17 26, 7990 Friedrichshafen 1 Germany.

US

INTRACOASTAL WATERWAY FESTIVAL AND SERVICES DIRECTORY, THE. **VFOAT** ICW Festival and Services Directory; ICW Festival & Services Directory. (1992)-. Directory. English. Monkey's First Press, 16 Sevilla Street, Saint Augustine FL.

ISSN 0867-4337
PL

UDC 797.14
JACHTING WARSZAWA. (JACHTING.). [Jachting Warsz.]. (1991)-. Periodical. Polish. Twelve times a year. Price on request. **(Subscription address:** Ars Polona-Ruch, PO Box 1001, Krakowskie Przedmiescie 7, 00-068 Warsaw Poland. **Tel** 011 48 22 261201.**)**

LC GV835.8 .J63a   ISSN 0271-2040
DD 797.1   US
JOHNSON OUTBOARDS BOATING. **Main/Corp** Johnson Outboards. **VFOAT** Johnson Boating; Boating. (19??)-. Periodical. English. One time a year. $2.25 US; $2.75 other. Aqua Field Publications Inc., 66 West Gilbert Street, Shrewsbury NJ 07702. **Tel** (201)842-8300.

LC GV770.3
DD 797.127

GW

●**KANUMAGAZIN.** (1994)-. Consumer Publication. English. Six times a year. DM45.90. Rotpunkt Verlag, Ziegeleistr. 16, 71384 Weinstadt Germany. **Tel** 011 49 7151 999020, FAX 011 49 7151 999029. **ED** Stephan Glocker. **Ad Acc, Adv Mgr:** Karsten Heyder. Full Page (B&W) DM3680.00. Full Page (Color) DM6400.00. **Circ:** 50,000.

LC HE559.J3 K66
DD 386.8

JA

KOUN TOKEI SHIRYO: SHISETSU HOYU JOKYO. **Added/Corp** Japan. Unyusho. Kowankyoku. Koseika. (19??)-. Japanese. Koaji Hoancho Somubu, (Maritime Safety Agency Administration Dept.), 1-3 Kasumigaseki 2 chome, Chiyodaku Tokyo 100 Japan.

ISSN 0744-9194
US

LAKELAND BOATING (1982). (LAKELAND BOATING.). [Lakel. boat.]. (1982)-. Periodical. English. Eleven times a year. $16.94. Lakeland Boating, 1600 Orrington Avenue, Suite 500, Evanston IL 60201. **Tel** (312)869-5400. **(Subscription address:** Kable Publishers Aide / Illinois, 308 East Hitt Street, Subscription Department, Mt. Morris IL 61054-1473. **Tel** (815)734-1261.**)** **ED** Mike Hilts. **Bk Rev. Ad Acc. Circ:** 45,000. available on microfilm and microfiche from University Microfilms International (UMI). **Continues** Lakeland Boating Incorporating Sea, 0274-9076.
 Desc: The freshwater boating magazine.
 Ind/Abst Consum. Index Prod. Eval. Inf. Source.

ISSN 0790-4916
DD 623.8887   IE
LIFEBOATS IRELAND. [Lifeboats Irel.]. (1985)-. English (French). One time a year (Nov.). $3.49. Royal National Lifeboat Institute, 3 Clare Street, Dublin 2 Ireland. **Tel** 011 353 1 762217, telex 41328. **Continues** Irish Lifeboats, 0535-6768.

LC GV825 .R4
DD 929.9   UK
LLOYD'S REGISTER OF CLASSED YACHTS. **Added/Corp** Lloyd's Register of Shipping (Firm : 1914-). **VFOAT** Register of Classed Yachts. (1981)-. English. One time a year. $40.00. Lloyd's Register of Shipping / London, 71 Senchurch Street, London EC3 M4BS United Kingdom. **Tel** 011 44 171 7099166. **(Subscription address:** Lloyd's Register of Shipping, 17 Battery Place, New York NY 10004. **Tel** (212)425-8050.**) Continues** Lloyd's Register of Yachts.

 Desc: Contains details of all yachts classed with LR, and those built under LR's Building Certificate Schemes during recent years.

US

LOG AND SAN DIEGO LOG. (19??)-. Newsletter. English. Twenty-four times a year. $24.95. Log Newspapers Inc, 1025 Rosencrans Street, San Diego CA 92106. **Tel** (619)226-1608, FAX (619)226-0573. **Continues** San Diego Log.

ISSN 0025-0600
US

MAIN SHEET. **Added/Corp** Detroit Yacht Club. (19??)-. Periodical. English. Twelve times a year. $24.00. Kelvin Publishing, 27421 Harper Avenue, St Clair Shores MI 48081. **Tel** (313)774-3530. **ED** Don Topolsky. **Bk Rev. Ad Acc. Circ:** 1,200.

ISSN 1064-1688
US

MAINSHEET (SAN FRANCISCO, CALIF.). (MAINSHEET.). **Main/Corp** St. Francis Yacht Club (San Francisco, Calif.). (1992)-. Periodical. English. Twelve times a year. St. Francis Yacht Club, On the Marina, San Francisco CA 94123.

ISSN 1079-1930
DD 387   US
MARINA DOCK AGE. [Marina dock age]. **VFOAT** Marina/Dock Age. (19??)-. Trade Publication. English. Six times a year (Jan., Mar., May, July, Sept., Nov.). $24.00. Preston Publications Inc., 7800 Merrimac Avenue, PO Box 48312, Niles IL 60714. **Tel** (708)965-0566, (708)967-1810, FAX (708)965-7639, telex 910-223-1780 PRESTON NILE.
 Desc: Directed at owners and operators of marinas.

LC VM348 .M34   ISSN 1061-6772
DD 623.8/2313/0297   US
MARINE BLUE BOOK (OVERLAND PARK, KAN.). (MARINE BLUE BOOK.). [Mar. blue book]. **VFOAT** Abos Marine Blue Book. (19??)-. Periodical. English. One time a year. $149.95. Intertec Publishing Corporation, 9800 Metcalf, Overland Park KS 66212. **Tel** (913)341-1300. **(Subscription address:** Intertec Publishing Corporation, PO Box 2901, Overland Park KS 66282. **Tel** 800 441-0294.**)**

US

MARINE DOCK AGE. Trade Publication. English. Six times a year. $20.00 US; $40.00 other. Van Zevern Publications, 3949 Oakton Street, Skokie IL 60076. **Tel** (708)982-1810. **ED** George Van Zevern and Lisa Berman. Index available. **Bk Rev. Ad Acc. Circ:** 24,000 (ctrl).
 Desc: Trade magazine for marina owners, operators, designers, governmental agencies, suppliers and associations. Written to help marinas to become more profitable and efficient in operation. Environmental concerns are stressed.

LC VM325 .M35
DD 623.8/504/0244   US
MARINE ELECTRONICS ... BUYERS GUIDE. **VFOAT** Buyers Guide; Skipper Marine Electronics. (19??)-. English. One time a year. $35.00. Skipper Marine Electronics, 3170 Commercial Avenue, Northbrook IL 60062.

US

MARINE SERVICE CENTER. (19??)-. Trade Publication. English. Six times a year. $21.00 US; $27.00 other. Preston Publications Inc., 7800 Merrimac Avenue, PO Box 48312, Niles IL 60714. **Tel** (708)965-0566, (708)967-1810, FAX (708)965-7639, telex 910-223-1780 PRESTON NILE.
 Desc: Covers repairs and products in the marine service industry.

ISSN 0705-8993
DD 380.1/45/6238230971   CN
MARINE TRADES (1978). (MARINE TRADES.). Vol. 12, No. 2 (2nd Quarter 1978)-. Periodical. English. Four times a year. 15.21Can$. Arthurs Publications Ltd., 4141 Dixie Rd., PO Box 149, Mississauga Ontario, L4W 1V5 Canada. **Tel** (905)625-9660, FAX (905)625-7559. **ED** Gary Arthurs. **Bk Rev. Ad Acc. Circ:** 7,200 (ctrl). **Continues** Marine & Outdoor Trades, 0380-4690.
 Desc: News and technology referencing boating marine dealers.

US

●**MCKNEW & PARKER'S BUYER'S GUIDE TO FAMILY & EXPRESS CRUISERS.** **Added/Corp** American Marine Publishing. **VFOAT** McKnew and Parker's Buyer's Guide to Family and Express Cruisers; Buyer's Guide to Family & Express Cruisers; Family & Express Cruisers; Family and Express Cruisers. (1995)-. English. International Marine Publishing Company, PO Box 220, Camden ME 04843. **Tel** (207)236-4342. **Continues in part** Powerboat Guide, 1045-5434.

US

●**MCKNEW & PARKER'S BUYER'S GUIDE TO MOTOR YACHTS & TRAWLERS.** **Added/Corp** American Marine Publishing. **VFOAT** McKnew and Parker's Buyer's Guide to Motor Yachts and Trawlers; Buyer's Guide to Motor Yachts & Trawlers; Motor yachts & Trawlers; Motor Yachts and Trawlers. (1995)-. English. International Marine Publishing Company, PO Box 220, Camden ME 04843. **Tel** (207)236-4342. **Continues** Powerboat Guide, 1045-5434.

LC VM431 .M384
DD 623.8/231/0247991   US
●**MCKNEW & PARKER'S BUYER'S GUIDE TO SPORTFISHING BOATS.** **Added/Corp** American Marine Publishing. **VFOAT** McKnew and Parker's Buyer's Guide to Sportfishing Boats; Sportfishing Boats. (1995)-. English. International Marine Publishing Company, PO Box 220, Camden ME 04843. **Tel** (207)236-4342. **Continues** Powerboat Guide, 1045-5434.

FR

MEER & YACHTEN. (19??)-. German (English). Four times a year. DM57.00 Germany; DM66.00 Austria. Meer & Yachten, 107 rue du Point au Jou, 92100 Boulogne France. **Tel** 011 33 1 69103060, FAX 011 33 1 49103061. Index available. cum. index. **Bk Rev. Ad Acc. Circ:** 35,000. **Continues** Mer et Bateaux.
 Desc: Luxurious sailboats and motorboats from all over the world.

ISSN 0999-7148
FR

UDC 797.1
MER & BATEAUX PARIS. (MER & BATEAUX.). [Mer bateaux Paris]. **VFOAT** Mer et Bateaux (Paris). (1989)-. Periodical. French. Nine times a year. $89.68. Mer a Bateaux, 107 rue du Pointe du Jow, 92100 Boulogne France. **Tel** 011 33 1 49103060, FAX 33 1 49 10 30 61. Index available. cum. index. **Bk Rev. Ad Acc. Circ:** 32,000. **Continues** L'Annee Bateaux (Paris. 1977), 0184-5055.
 Desc: Covers sailboats and motor boats from over the world.

US

MESSING ABOUT IN BOATS. English. Twenty-four times a year (published on the 1st and 15th of each month). $20.00. Cycle Sport Publishing, 29 Burley Street, Wenham MA 01984. **Tel** (508)774-0906. **ED** Bob Hicks. **Bk Rev, (Qty: varies). Ad Acc. Circ:** 4,000.
 Desc: Articles relating to the enjoyment of small boating.

MX

MEXICO YATES Y VILLAS. (19??)-. Periodical. Spanish (English). Four times a year. JGY Servicios Profesionales, 101 Marina Vallarta, Puerto Vallarta Jalisco Mexico 48300. **ED** Heather Wilson, Madelyn Hernandez. **Ad Acc.**
 Desc: Provides information on yachts, marinas, resorts, etc. in Mexico.

ISSN 1078-1021
DD 797   US
●**MIAMI HERALD ... SOUTH FLORIDA OUTDOOR GUIDE, THE.** See Leisure and Recreation-Outdoor Recreation.

ISSN 0144-2910
DD 745   UK
MODEL BOATS. [Model boats]. (19??)-. Periodical. English. Twelve times a year. $50.00. Argus Specialist Publications, Argus House, Boundary Way / Hemel, Hempstead Herts HP27ST United Kingdom. **Tel** 011 44 181 6671033, FAX 011 44 181 6889573, telex 948669 TOPJNL G. **ED** John Cundell. **Bk Rev. Ad Acc. Circ:** 20,000. **Continues** Gem Craft, 0140-5977.
 Desc: Covers all aspects of boat modelling from steam to sail, and concentrates on the needs of scale boat modelling, both working and static. Includes full-color pages, regular full-size plan features, and twice yearly superplans.
 Ind/Abst Index Inf.

ISSN 0811-0697
AT

MODERN BOATING (1980). (1980)-. English. Six times a year. 24.67Aus$. Federal Publishing Co Pty Ltd., PO Box 199, 180 Bourke Road, Alexandria New South Wales 2015 Australia. **Tel** 011 61 2 3539992, FAX 011 61 2 66923059935.

IT

MONDO BARCA. Italian. Twelve times a year. L80000 Italy; L120000 other. Media Sea Communications, Via G A Amadeo 41, 20133 Milan Italy. **Tel** 011 39 2 70100020.

Boats and Boating

DD 797 **ISSN** 0027-1780
UK
MOTOR BOAT AND YACHTING. [Mot. boat yacht.]. **VFOAT** Motorboat and Yachting. (19??)-. Periodical. English. Twelve times a year. $60.00. IPC Magazines Ltd., Perrymount Road, Haywards Heath, West Sussex RH16 3DH United Kingdom. **Tel** 011 44 1444 440421, FAX 011 44 1444 445599. Index available (free). **Absorbed** Power & Sail.

LC VM320 .M92 **ISSN** 0027-1799
DD 623.8 US
MOTOR BOATING & SAILING. [Motor boat. sail.]. **VAT** Motor Boating and Sailing. Vol. 126, No. 4 (Oct. 1970)-. Periodical. English. Twelve times a year. $15.97. The Hearst Corporation, 250 West 55th Street, New York NY 10019. **Tel** (212)649-4014, (800)925-0485. **(Subscription address:** CDS Agency Hard Copy, PO Box 4966, Des Moines IA 50340. **Tel** (515)247-7569.) **ED** Peter A. Janssen. **Ad Acc. Circ:** 150,000. available on microfilm and microfiche from University Microfilms International (UMI). Documents available from UMI Article Clearinghouse. **Continues** Motor Boating.
Desc: Magazine for men and women who love boats and the adventure, challenge and romance of the sea.
Ind/Abst Acad. Abstr. Full Text Elite; Acad. Abstr.; Consum. Index Prod. Eval. Inf. Source; EP Collect.; Homework Help.; Mag. Artic. Summar. Elite; Mag. Artic. Summar. Select; Mag. Artic. Summar. CD-ROM; Mag. Search; MasterFile FullTEXT 1000; MasterFile FullTEXT 350; MasterFile FullTEXT 650; MasterFile FullTEXT (Jan. 1984-); Newsp. Period. Abstr. (1988-); OCLC; Pub. Lib. FullTEXT; Read. Guide Abstr. Select Ed.; Read. Guide Period. Lit.; Telebase; Mag. Index (1977-); Vocat. Search.

ISSN 0148-8740
US
MOTORBOAT & EQUIPMENT DIRECTORY. **VAT** Motorboat and Equipment Directory. (1978)-. Directory. English. One time a year. $2.75. Motorboat Inc, 38 Commercial Wharf, Boston MA 02110. **Supersedes in part** Motorboat.

LC GV811.8 .T72 **ISSN** 0735-5483
DD 797.1/25/05 US
MOTORYACHT. [Motoryacht]. **VFOAT** Motor Yacht. Vol. 3, No. 1 (1982)-. Periodical. English. Six times a year. Trawler Cruiser Yacht Inc., 524 Thames Street, Newport RI 02840. **Continues** Trawler Cruiser Yacht, 0270-3785.

ISSN 0749-4122
DD 797 US
MULTIHULLS. [Multihulls]. **VFOAT** Multihulls Magazine. (1975)-. Periodical. English. Six times a year. $21.00 US; $27.00 other. Chiodi Advertising & Publishing Inc, 421 Hancock Street, North Quincy MA 02171. **Tel** (617)328-8181, FAX (617)471-0118. **ED** Charles Chiodi. Index available. cum. index. **Bk Rev. Ad Acc. Circ:** 30,000.
Desc: Complete coverage of all size multihulls, design, racing, boat tests, cruising information and safety information.

LC HD9993.B63 N13 **ISSN** 1055-1972
DD 629.8/202/029473 US
N.A.D.A. LARGE BOAT APPRAISAL GUIDE. [N. A. D. A. large boat appraisal guide]. **Added/Corp** National Automobile Dealers Association. **VFOAT** NADA Large Boat Appraisal Guide; Large Boat Appraisal Guide. **VAT** National Automobile Dealers Association Large Boat Appraisal Guide. (Sept./Dec. 1990)-. Periodical. English. Three times a year. $65.00. NADA Appraisal Guides, PO Box 7800, Costa Mesa CA 92628. **Tel** (714)556-8511, (800)966-6232, FAX (714)556-8715.

LC HD9993.B63 N14 **ISSN** 1055-1964
DD 629.8/202/029473 US
N.A.D.A. SMALL BOAT APPRAISAL GUIDE. [N. A. D. A. small boat appraisal guide]. **Added/Corp** National Automobile Dealers Association. **VFOAT** NADA Small Boat Appraisal Guide; Small Boat Appraisal Guide. **VAT** National Automobile Dealers Association Small Boat Appraisal Guide. (Sept./Dec. 1990)-. Periodical. English. Three times a year. $95.00. NADA Appraisal Guides, PO Box 7800, Costa Mesa CA 92628. **Tel** (714)556-8511, (800)966-6232, FAX (714)556-8715.

ISSN 0828-1327
DD 797.1/22/0971 CN
NASTAWGAN. **Added/Corp** Wilderness Canoe Association. Vol. 9, No. 1 (Spring 1982)-. Periodical. English. Four times a year (Mar., June, Sept., Dec.). 20.01Can$. Wilderness Canoe Association, Box496 Station K, Toronto Ontario, M4P 2G9 Canada. **Tel** (416)964-2495. **ED** Antoni Harting. cum. index. **Bk Rev**, (Qty: 12). **Circ:** 1000 (ctrl). **Continues** The Wilderness Canoeist., 0828-1319.
Desc: This journal includes information and reviews of camp sites, trails, whitewater courses, etc.

LC HV8080.W38 N37 **ISSN** 1066-2383
DD 363.2/86/097305 US
NATIONAL ASSOCIATION OF STATE BOATING LAW ADMINISTRATORS' SMALL CRAFT ADVISORY. [Natl. Assoc. State Boat. Law Adm. small craft adv.]. **Added/Corp** National Association of State Boating Law Administrators. **VFOAT** Small Craft Advisory. (1985)-. Periodical. English. Six times a year. Outdoor Empire Publishing Company, 511 Eastlake Avenue, Box 19000, Seattle WA 98109. **Tel** (206)624-3845.

LC VM361 .N36 **ISSN** 0363-1354
DD 338.4/7/623820202573 US
NATIONAL BOAT BOOK. (1976)-. Periodical. English. One time a year. $110.00. Intertec Publishing Corp, 29 North Wacker Drive, Chicago IL 60606-3298. **Tel** (312)726-2802, FAX (312)726-3091. **(Subscription address:** Maclean Hunter Market Reports, 29 North Wacker Drive, Chicago IL 60606.)

LC GV776.A2 N38 **ISSN** 1048-1362
DD 387.5/42/0973 US
NATIONAL DIRECTORY OF GUIDE AND CHARTERBOAT SERVICES. [Natl. dir. guide chart.boat serv.]. **Added/Corp** Outdoor Statistical Resources (Firm) U.S. Guide & Charterboat Federation. **VFOAT** Guide & Charterboat Services; Guide and Charterboat Services; National Directory of Guide & Charterboat Services. (1990)-. Directory. English. Four times a year. $30.00 (single issue). National Directory of Guide and Charterboat Services, PO Box 6506, Athens GA 30604.

FR
NEPTUNE YACHTING. (19??)-. English. Eleven times a year. $84.86. Hachette Filipacchi, 10 rue Thierry le Luron, 92592 Levallois Perret France. **Tel** 011 33 1 41348500. **Continues** Cahiers du Yachting.

LC VM341 .N48 **ISSN** 0884-8378
DD 623.8/231/0294 US
NEW BOAT AND MOTOR PRICE GUIDE BLUE BOOK. [New boat mot. price guide blue book]. (19??)-. Periodical. English. One time a year. $22.95. Intertec Publishing Corporation, 9800 Metcalf, Overland Park KS 66212. **Tel** (913)341-1300. **(Subscription address:** Intertec Publishing Corporation, PO Box 2901, Overland Park KS 66282. **Tel** 800 441-0294.)

ISSN 0886-0955
US
NEW JERSEY BOATER. **VFOAT** NJ Boater; N.J. Boater. (198?)-. Periodical. English. Twelve times a year. Leitstein Publications Inc. / New Jersey Boater, 568 Cookman Avenue, Ashbury Park NJ 07712. **Continues** NJ Boater.

LC GV776.N74 N67 **ISSN** 0148-8090
DD 614.8/1 US
NORTH CAROLINA BOATING ACCIDENT STATISTICS. See Boats and Boating-Abstracting, Bibliographies and Statistics.

ISSN 0192-1169
US
NORTHWEST BOAT TRAVEL. (197?)-. Periodical. English. Four times a year (Jan., May, June, July). $18.00. Northwest Boat Travel, PO Box 220, Anacortes WA 98221. **Tel** (206)684-9786, FAX (206)293-6764. **ED** Phil Cole. **Bk Rev. Ad Acc. Circ:** 10,000 (ctrl).
Desc: Describes over 1,700 places to go, accommodations, ports of call along the Inside Passage from Olympia, Washington to Skagway and Alaska.

US
NORTHWEST SAILBOARD. (19??)-. English. Six times a year. $9.97 US; $16.00 Canada; $38.00 other. Gorge Publishing, PO Box 918, Hood River OR 97031. **Tel** (503)386-7440, FAX (503)386-7480. **ED** Carol York. **Bk Rev. Ad Acc, Adv Mgr:** Marie Cordell, **Tel** (503)386-7440. **Circ:** 25,000.
Desc: Magazine full of news and information about windsurfing in the Northwest. Equipment reviews, technical features, instructional tips, and action photos geared toward a wide range of readers, from the novice to the radical windsurfer.

ISSN 0739-747X
DD 797 US
NOR'WESTING. [Nor'westing]. **Added/Corp** Interclub Boating Association of Washington. (19??)-. Periodical. English. Twelve times a year. $15.00. Nor'Westing, PO Box 1027, Edmonds WA 98020. **Tel** (206)776-3138. **ED** Tom Kincard. **Bk Rev. Ad Acc**.
Desc: Pleasure boat magazine.

LC GV776.C47 N96
DD 797.1/09755/1805 US
NYNEX BOATERS DIRECTORY. CHESAPEAKE BAY EDITION. **VFOAT** Boaters Directory. Chesapeake Bay Edition. (1988)-. Directory. English. NYNEX Information Resources Co., 195 Market Street, Lynn MA 01901.

LC GV776.F6 N96
DD 797.1/09759/05 US
NYNEX BOATERS DIRECTORY. FLORIDA GOLD COAST/KEYS EDITION. **VFOAT** Boaters Directory. Florida Gold Coast/Keys Edition. (1988)-. Directory. English. NYNEX Information Resources Co., 195 Market Street, Lynn MA 01901.

LC GV776.F62 G856
DD 797.1/09759 US
NYNEX BOATERS DIRECTORY. FLORIDA GULF COAST EDITION. **VFOAT** Boaters Directory. Florida Gulf Coast Edition; Florida Gulf Coast Edition. (19??)-. Directory. English. NYNEX Information Resources Co., 195 Market Street, Lynn MA 01901.

LC GV776.M4 N96
DD 797.1/025/744 US
NYNEX BOATERS DIRECTORY. MASSACHUSETTS EDITION. **VFOAT** Boaters Directory. Massachusetts Edition. (1987)-. Directory. English. NYNEX Information Resources Co., 195 Market Street, Lynn MA 01901.

LC GV776.N35 N96 **ISSN** 1050-9305
DD 797.1/0974 US
NYNEX BOATERS DIRECTORY. NEW ENGLAND COASTAL EDITION. [NYNEX boat. dir. N. Engl. Coast. ed.]. **VFOAT** New England Coastal Edition; Boaters Directory. New England Coastal Edition. (19??)-. Directory. English. NYNEX Information Resources Co., 195 Market Street, Lynn MA 01901.

LC GV776.C22 N676
DD 797.1/09794/105 US
NYNEX BOATERS DIRECTORY. NORTHERN CALIFORNIA EDITION. **VFOAT** Boaters Directory. Northern California Edition. (1988)-. Directory. English. NYNEX Information Resources Co., 195 Market Street, Lynn MA 01901.

LC GV776.N76 N96
DD 797.1/09795/05 US
NYNEX BOATERS DIRECTORY. PACIFIC NORTHWEST EDITION. **VFOAT** Boaters Directory. Pacific Northwest Edition. (1988)-. Directory. English. NYNEX Information Resources Co., 195 Market Street, Lynn MA 01901.

LC GV776.C22 S675
DD 797.1/09794/905 US
NYNEX BOATERS DIRECTORY. SOUTHERN CALIFORNIA EDITION. **VFOAT** Boaters Directory. Southern California Edition. (1988)-. Directory. English. NYNEX Information Resources Co., 195 Market Street, Lynn MA 01901.

ISSN 0274-9394
US
OFFSHORE (WEST NEWTON). (OFFSHORE.). (1976)-. Periodical. English. Twelve times a year. $16.97. Offshore Publications Inc, PO Box 817, Needham Heights MA 02194. **Tel** (617)449-6204, FAX (617)449-9702. **ED** Herbert Gliick. **Bk Rev. Ad Acc. Circ:** 36,000 paid (ctrl). **Continues** New England Offshore, 0192-4885.
Desc: New England's boating magazine, for sailors and powerboaters who love the five state coast.

LC WMLC 91/734 **ISSN** 1056-8263
DD 797 US
OFFSHORE WORLDWIDE. [Offshore worldw.]. Vol. 1 (1991)-. Periodical. English. Twelve times a year. $40.00 US; $58.00 Canada. Offshore Worldwide Inc, 2000 South Dixie Highway, Suite 206-C, Miami FL 33133. **Tel** (305)858-0970. **ED** J. D. Berg.
Desc: International offshore powerboat racing.

LC HD9993.B633 U56 **ISSN** 0197-212X
DD 623.8/2023/029473 US
OLDER BOAT PRICE GUIDE. (OLDER BOAT PRICE GUIDE.). [Older boat price guide]. **Added/Corp** BUC International Corporation. **VFOAT** BUC Older Boat Price Guide. (1980)-. English. One time a year. $38.00. BUC International Corporation, 1314 Northeast, 17th Court, Fort Lauderdale FL 33305. **Tel** (305)565-6715, (8000327-6929, FAX (305)561-3095.

UK
OMEGA REPORT. (19??)-. English. Twelve times a year. $2566.81. Petrodata, Dock Gate House, York Place, Waterloo Quay, Aberdeen AB2 1DF United Kingdom. **Tel** 011 44 1224 572472, FAX 011 44 1224 580320. **(Subscription address:** Petrodata Ltd. Accounts Office, Lamdin Road, Bury Street, Edmunds IP32 6NU United Kingdom. **Tel** 011 44 1284 750326.)

LC SH344.8.B6 O85
DD 623.86 KO
OSON. See Fish and Fisheries.

LC VM348 .B52 VM348 .A2 ISSN 1070-3500
DD 623.8/2313/0294 US
OUTBOARD BOAT BLUE BOOK.
(OUTBOARD BOAT BLUE BOOK / ABOS.). [Outboard boat blue book]. **Added/Corp** Intertec Publishing Corporation. Abos Marine Publications Division. **VFOAT** ABOS Outboard Boat Blue Book. (1992)-. English. Intertec Publishing Corporation, 9800 Metcalf, Overland Park KS 66212. **Tel** (913)341-1300. ***Continues*** *Outboard Boat Trade-In Guide Blue Book.*

LC GV776.C2 S4 ISSN 0193-3515
DD 797.1/09794/1 US
PACIFIC BOATING ALMANAC. NORTHERN CALIFORNIA & NEVADA.
VAT Pacific Boating Almanac. Northern California and Nevada. English. One time a year. $13.95. Western Marine Enterprises Inc., 13468 Beach Avenue, Marina del Rey CA 92270. **Tel** (310)577-9575. **ED** William Berssen. Index available. **Bk Rev. Ad Acc. Circ:** 8,000. ***Continues*** *Sea Boating Almanac. Northern California & Nevada, 0363-7700.*
Desc: Illustrated with over 448 pages each describing marine facilities from Acupulco, Mexico to Skagway, Alaska. Includes tide and current tables, US coast pilot, radiotelephone and navigational data, fish identification, etc.

ISSN 0899-9368
DD 797 US
PACIFIC BOATING ALMANAC. PACIFIC NORTHWEST & ALASKA. [Pac. boat. alm. Pac. Northwest Alsk.]. **VAT** Pacific Boating Almanac. Pacific Northwest and Alaska. (1985)-. English. $11.95. Western Marine Enterprises Inc., 13468 Beach Avenue, Marina del Rey CA 92270. **Tel** (310)577-9575. **ED** William Berssen. ***Continues*** *Pacific Boating Almanac. Oregon, Washington, British Columbia and Southeastern Alaska Edition, 0276-8771.*

LC GV776.C22 S677 ISSN 0193-3507
DD 797.1/09794/9 US
PACIFIC BOATING ALMANAC. SOUTHERN CALIFORNIA, ARIZONA & BAJA. **VAT** Pacific Boating Almanac. Southern California, Arizona and Baja. (1977)-. English. One time a year (Dec.). $19.95. Western Marine Enterprises Inc., 13468 Beach Avenue, Marina del Rey CA 92270. **Tel** (310)577-9575. **ED** William Berssen. Index available. cum. index. **Bk Rev. Ad Acc. Circ:** 10,000 (ctrl). ***Continues*** *Sea Boating Almanac. Southern California, Arizona, Baja, 0363-6712.*
Desc: The how to and where to of boating, where to go, how to get there, where to stop, and refuel and get repairs.

LC GV776.N76 P33 ISSN 1076-1578
DD 797.1/09795/05 US
•**PACIFIC NORTHWEST WAGGONER.** [Pac. Northwest waggoner]. **VFOAT** Waggoner. (1994)-. English. One time a year. $9.95. Waggoner, Robert Hale and Co., Weatherly Press Division, Bellevue WA.

ISSN 0030-8986
CN
PACIFIC YACHTING. [Pac. yacht.]. Vol. 2, No. 6 (Sept. 1969)-. Periodical. English. Twelve times a year. 28.01Can$. Special Interest Publications / Canada, 1132 Hamilton Street/Suite 202, Vancouver BC V6B 2S2 Canada. **Tel** (604)687-1581, FAX (604)687-1925. **ED** Paul Burkhart. Index available. **Bk Rev. Ad Acc. Circ:** 18,000. ***Continues*** *Pacific Yachting Journal, 0380-6332.*
Desc: Regional yachting magazine covering all aspects of boating in British Columbia. How-to, history, geology, flora and fauna, navigation, piloting, seamanship, weather power and sailboat gear and equipment.
Ind/Abst AQUAREF; Can. Index; Can. Period. Index (19??-).

ISSN 0835-0310
DD 797.1/22/09713 CN
PADDLER. [Paddler]. Vol. 1, No. 1 (Spring 1986)-. Periodical. English. Four times a year. 10.00Can$. Paddler, 157 Silver Birch Avenue, Toronto Ontario M4E 3L3 Canada. **Tel** (416)690-5103. **ED** Kathy Fremes. **Ad Acc. Circ:** 23,000 (ctrl).
Desc: Appeals to the recreational and serious canoeist and kayaker. Along with articles on the sport, has regular columns on humor and fiction, heritage, photography and repair maintenance.
Ind/Abst Can. Index (?-?); SPORT Discus.

ISSN 0820-5086
DD 797.1/25/09714 CN
PLAISANCIERS. (LES PLAISANCIERS.). [Plaisanciers]. (Jan./Feb. 1986)-. Periodical. French. Five times a year (Jan., Mar., May, July, Sept.). 9.61Can$. CRV Publications, 2585 Skymark Ave, Suite 306, Mississauga Ontario L4W 4L5 Canada. **Tel** (416)624-8218, FAX (416)624-6764.

ISSN 0830-8705
DD 797.1/0971 CN
PORT HOLE (SCARBOROUGH). (THE PORT HOLE.). [Port hole]. **Added/Corp** Canadian Power Squadrons. (197?)-. Periodical. English (French; summaries and/or abstracts in French). Four times a year. 6.40Can$. Canadian Power & Sail Squadron, 26 Golden Gate Court, Scarborough Ontario M1P 3A5 Canada. **Tel** (800)268-3579, (905)293-2438.

ISSN 0886-4411
DD 797 US
POWER AND MOTORYACHT. [Power mot.yacht]. **VFOAT** Power and Motor Yacht. (198?)-. Periodical. English. Twelve times a year. $19.95. Cahners Publishing Company, 249 West 17th Street, New York NY 10011. **Tel** (212)645-0067, FAX (212)242-6987. **(Subscription address:** Power and Motoryacht, PO Box 2606, Boulder CO 80322-2606. **) Circ:** 150,000 (ctrl).
Desc: Edited for owners of large powerboats. Features include articles on cruising, sportfishing, gear, electronics, megayachts, etc.

ISSN 1018-1385
SA
UDC 797
POWER BOAT AND SKI. [Power boat ski]. (1991)-. Periodical. English. Six times a year. Yachting News Ltd, 4 Gordon Street, Gardens Cape Town 8001 South Africa. **Tel** (021)461-7472, FAX (021)461-3758. ***Continues*** *Power & Ski, 1012-3288.*

LC GV ISSN 0838-0872
DD 797.1/25/05 CN
POWER BOATING CANADA. [Power boat. Can.]. **VFOAT** Power Boating Magazine. Vol. 3, No. 1, (Jan./Feb. 1988)-. Periodical. English. Six times a year. 14.40Can$. CRV Publications, 2585 Skymark Ave, Suite 306, Mississauga Ontario L4W 4L5 Canada. **Tel** (416)624-8218, FAX (416)624-6764. **ED** Darryl Simmons. **Ad Acc. Circ:** 40,000. ***Continues*** *Power Boating Ontario, 0827-7710.*

ISSN 1039-0952
DD 623.823105 AT
POWERBOAT FISHING. [Powerb. fish]. (1992)-. Periodical. English. Six times a year. 29.70Aus$ Australia; 84.00Aus$ other. Yaffa Publishing Group Pty Ltd., GPO Box 606, Sydney New South Wales 2001 Australia. **Tel** 011 61 2 2812333, FAX 011 61 2 2812750.

ISSN 1040-3663
DD 623 US
POWERBOAT REPORTS. [Powerb. rep.]. (1988)-. Periodical. English. Twelve times a year. $68.00. Belvoir Publications Inc., 75 Holly Hill Lane, Greenwich CT 06836. **Tel** (203)661-6111, FAX (203)661-4802. **(Subscription address:** Palm Coast Data, PO Box 420163, Agency Department, Palm Coast FL 32142. **Tel** (904)445-4662 ext. 669, (800)829-5475.) **ED** Tim Cole.
Desc: Ratings, evaluations and tests of powerboats, accessories and equipment.

LC GV835.9 .P6 ISSN 0032-6089
DD 797.1/4 US
POWERBOAT (VAN NUYS, CALIF.). (POWERBOAT.). (19??)-. Periodical. English. Eleven times a year. $27.00. Powerboat Magazine, 15917 Strathern Street, Van Nuys CA 91406. **Tel** (818)989-1820, FAX (818)989-1823. **Bk Rev**, (Qty: 1-2 /year). **Ad Acc. Circ:** 40,000. ***Continues*** *Power Boat.*
Desc: Reports news and trends in high-performance boating. Coverage from stock outboards to superboats; dedicated to covering major national and international events.

LC VM320 .P85 ISSN 0032-6348
UK
CCC
PRACTICAL BOAT OWNER. (1967)-. Periodical. English. Twelve times a year. $64.90. IPC Magazines Ltd., Perrymount Road, Haywards Heath, West Sussex RH16 3DH United Kingdom. **Tel** 011 44 1444 440421, FAX 011 44 1444 445599.

LC WMLC L 83/131 ISSN 0161-8059
DD 623 US
PRACTICAL SAILOR, THE. [Pract. sail.]. (19??)-. Periodical. English. Twenty-four times a year. $96.00. Belvoir Publications Inc., 75 Holly Hill Lane, Greenwich CT 06836. **Tel** (203)661-6111, FAX (203)661-4802. **(Subscription address:** Palm Coast Data, PO Box 420163, Agency Department, Palm Coast FL 32142. **Tel** (904)445-4662 ext. 669, (800)829-5475.) **ED** Dan Spurr. Index available. **Circ:** 50,000.
Desc: Product evaluations of sailboats and sailing equipment.
Ind/Abst SPORT Discus.

ISSN 1043-2035
DD 623 US
PROFESSIONAL BOATBUILDER MAGAZINE. [Prof. boatbuild. mag.]. **VFOAT** Professional Boat Builder; Professional Boatbuilder. No. 1 (Oct./Nov. 1989)-. Trade Publication. English. Six times a year. $35.95. Woodenboat Publications, PO Box 78, Brooklin ME 04616. **Tel** (207)359-4651, FAX (207)359-8920. **ED** Paul Lazarus.
Desc: Designed for large boat manufacturing companies, small shops that specialize in new construction and top-level managers of repair yards.

ISSN 0194-6218
US
PROPELLER (EAST DETROIT). (PROPELLER.). **Added/Corp** American Power Boat Association. (19??)-. Periodical. English. Twelve times a year. $25.00. American Power Boat Association, 17640 East Nine Mile Road, PO Box 377, Detroit MI 48021. **Tel** (313)773-9700, FAX (313)773-6490. **ED** Renee J. Mahn. **Bk Rev. Ad Acc. Circ:** 9,000.
Desc: Update on American Power Boat Association racing news and technical information. Annual photo issue in November.

ISSN 0838-6080
DD 797.1/025/71133 CN
PROPWASH (VANCOUVER). (PROPWASH.). [Propwash]. **Main/Corp** Canadian Power and Sail Squadrons. Pacific Mainland District. (1986)-. English. Canadian Power & Sail Squadron, 26 Golden Gate Court, Scarborough Ontario M1P 3A5 Canada. **Tel** (800)268-3579, (905)293-2438.

ISSN 0833-918X
DD 797.1/24/09714 CN
QUEBEC YACHTIING, VOILE & MOTEUR. [Que. yacht. voile mot.]. Vol. 9, No. 6 (June 1986)-. Periodical. French. Six times a year. 11.80Can$. Publications Transcontinental Inc, 1100 Rene-Levesque, 24Fl boulevard West, Montreal Quebec H3B 4X9 Canada. **Tel** (514)392-9000, FAX (514)392-4724. **ED** Henri Rene de Cotret. **Bk Rev. Ad Acc. Circ:** 11,108 (ctrl). ***Continues*** *Quebec Yachting & Voile, 0829-3198.*
Desc: Covers the yachting scene, and power and sail in the province. Keeps readers up to date on all major sail races in the world. Includes regular features to help owners in their decision-making process including boat tests (power and sail), engine tests, cruising guides, navigation technique, new designs and new products.
Ind/Abst Repere (1986-).

LC HE554.A7 Q55 ISSN 0749-3754
DD 386/.8/0977 US
QUIMBY'S HARBOR GUIDE. [Quimby's harbor guide]. (19??)-. English. Waterways Journal, 319 North 4th Street, Suite 650, St Louis MO 63102. **Tel** (314)241-7354, FAX (314)241-4207.

LC GV776.48.A2 C66a
DD 797.1/0944 FR
RAPPORT ET DEBATS. **Main/Corp** Conseil Superieur de la Navigation de Plaisance et des Sports Nautiques (France). **VFOAT** Navigation de Plaisance, Sports Nautiques, Rapport et Debats. (19??)-. French. One time a year. 100F. Documentation Francaise, 29 quai Voltaire, 75344 Paris Cedex 7 France. **Tel** 011 33 1 40157000, FAX 011 33 1 40157230, telex 204 826 DOCFRAN.

LC GV777.55 U52a ISSN 0149-7286
DD 614.8/1 US
RECREATIONAL BOATING SAFETY, R & D ANNUAL REPORT. **Main/Corp** United States. Coast Guard. Office of Research and Development. **Added/Corp** United States. Coast Guard. Office of Research and Development. R & D Annual Report. **VAT** Recreational Boating Safety, Research and Development Annual Report. (19??)-. English. One time a year. US Department of Transportation / US Coast Guard, 2100 Second Street Southwest, Washington DC 20953-0001. **Tel** (202)267-2229.

ISSN 0989-6961
FR
UDC 797.1
REGATE INTERNATIONAL PARIS. (1987). (REGATE INTERNATIONALE.). (1987)-. Periodical. French. Six times a year. $50.31. ERI, 105 rue Mademoiselle, 75015 Paris France. **Tel** 011 33 1 43060000.

UK
Pr Rev.
REGATTA. **See** Leisure and Recreation-Outdoor Recreation.

LC GV811.8 .Y2 ISSN 1045-0416
DD 797 US
REGISTER OF AMERICAN YACHTS. [Regist. Am. yachts]. **Added/Corp** Yacht Owners Register, Inc. (1989)-. English. One time a year. $110.00. Yacht Owners Register Inc., 334 Beacon Street, Boston MA 02116. ***Continues*** *Yacht Owners Register, 0742-549X.*

LC WMLC L 83/287
US
RIVER RUNNER. **VFOAT** River Runner Magazine. (1982)-. Periodical. English. Four times a year. Juniper Publications, Powell Butte OR 97753. **Tel** (619)744-7170. **Bk Rev. Ad Acc. Circ:** 12,000 (ctrl). ***Continues*** *River Runner Magazine.*
Desc: A magazine for whitewater rafting, kayaking, and canoeing enthusiasts. Covers in the areas of sea and

Boats and Boating

kayak touring, new products, river trips, how-to articles and people profiles.
Ind/Abst SPORT Discus; SportSearch (May 1987).

UK

ROWING. (19??)-. English. Twelve times a year. $54.76. Rowing Magazine, PO Box 49E, Worchester Park, Surrey KT4 8UN United Kingdom.
Ind/Abst SPORT Discus.

ISSN 0342-8281
GW

UDC 797.123
RUDERSPORT. [Rudersport]. (1951)-. Periodical. German. Thirty-three times a year. $134.72. Limpert Verlag GmbH, Luisenplatz 2, D-65185 Wiesbaden Germany. **Tel** 011 49 611 373072.

LC GV835.9 .A46b **ISSN** 0272-3468
DD 797.1/4 US
RULES FOR INBOARD, INBOARD ENDURANCE, UNLIMITED RACING.
Main/Corp American Power Boat Association. (19??)-. English. One time a year (Nov.). $3.00. American Power Boat Association, 17640 East Nine Mile Road, PO Box 377, Detroit MI 48021. **Tel** (313)773-9700, FAX (313)773-6490. **ED** Hilary R. Spittle. **Ad Acc. Circ:** 2,500.
Desc: Technical and safety rules for inboard competition.

LC GV835.9 A46a **ISSN** 1045-4187
DD 797.1/4 US
RULES FOR OFFSHORE RACING, THE.
(THE ... RULES FOR OFFSHORE RACING.). [Rules offshore racing]. **Main/Corp** American Power Boat Association. Offshore Racing Commission. **VFOAT** Offshore Racing Rules. (1985)-. English. American Power Boat Association, 17640 East Nine Mile Road, PO Box 377, Detroit MI 48021. **Tel** (313)773-9700, FAX (313)773-6490. **Continues** American Power Boat Association. Offshore Racing Commission. Handbook for Offshore Racing, 0272-409X.

LC GV835.9 .A46C **ISSN** 0272-3514
DD 797.1/4 US
RULES FOR OUTBOARD PERFORMANCE, CRAFT AND DRAG RACING. Main/Corp American Power Boat Association. (19??)-. English. One time a year. American Power Boat Association, 17640 East Nine Mile Road, PO Box 377, Detroit MI 48021. **Tel** (313)773-9700, FAX (313)773-6490.

LC GV835.9 .A46d **ISSN** 0272-3476
DD 797.1/4 US
RULES FOR STOCK OUTBOARD, PRO OUTBOARD, MODIFIED OUTBOARD.
Main/Corp American Power Boat Association. **VFOAT** Rules for Stock Outboard, Pro Outboard, Modified Outboard, and Outboard Performance Craft. (19??)-. English. $3.00. American Power Boat Association, 17640 East Nine Mile Road, PO Box 377, Detroit MI 48021. **Tel** (313)773-9700, FAX (313)773-6490. **ED** Hilary R. Spittle. **Ad Acc. Circ:** 3,000.

LC VK200.U523 **ISSN** 0198-1501
DD 363.1/2375 US
SAFE BOATING. Added/Corp United States. Coast Guard. Office of Boating Safety. (19??)-. Periodical. English. Four times a year. Office of Boating Safety, US Coast Guard, Department of Transportation, Washington DC 20593. **Continues** Boating Safety Newsletter, 0145-109X.

LC GV811 .S24 **ISSN** 0036-2700
DD 797.1/24/05 US
CCC
SAIL. [Sail]. **Added/Corp** Institute for Advancement of Sailing. (1970)-. Periodical. English. Twelve times a year. $23.94. Cahners Publishing Company, 249 West 17th Street, New York NY 10011. **Tel** (212)645-0067, FAX (212)242-6987. **(Subscription address:** Sail, PO Box 2606, Boulder CO 80322-2606. **) ED** Patience Wales. **Ad Acc. Circ:** 175,000. available on microfilm and microfiche from University Microfilms International (UMI). Documents available from UMI Article Clearinghouse, Magazine Collection.
Desc: Monthly magazine that covers bareboat and crewed chartering, commissioning, boat shows, races, boardsailing, instruction, weather, navigation, new and used boats, gear, and how-to advice.
Ind/Abst Acad. Abstr. Full Text Elite; Acad. Abstr.; Acad. Search; EP Collect.; Gen. Period. Index (1985-); Health Source Plus; Health Source; Homework Help.; Mag. Artic. Summar. Elite; Mag. Artic. Summar. Select; Mag. Artic. Summar. CD-ROM; Mag. Index Plus (1989-); Mag. Search; MasterFile FullTEXT 1000; MasterFile FullTEXT 350; MasterFile FullTEXT 650; Newsp. Period. Abstr. (1988-); OCLC; Pub. Lib. FullTEXT; SPORT Discus; Telebase; Mag. Index (1970-).

LC GV810 .S26 **ISSN** 0733-0383
DD 797.1/24/05 US
SAIL INDEX. [Sail index]. (19??)-. English. $3.00. Magindex, 29328 40th Avenue South, Auburn WA 98002. **Tel** (206)839-2813. **ED** Stephen G. Stone. **Circ:** 10.
Desc: Complete index to sail magazine. 1979 and 1980 indexes are available.

ISSN 0148-8732
US
TITLE CHANGE
SAILBOAT & EQUIPMENT DIRECTORY.
VAT Sailboat and Equipment Directory. (19??)-(19??). English. Cahners Publishing Company, 249 West 17th Street, New York NY 10011. **Tel** (212)645-0067, FAX (212)242-6987. **Continued by** Sailboat Buyers' Guide.

LC VM351 .S228 **ISSN** 0738-5242
DD 623.8/223/05 US
SAILBOAT & SAILING JOURNAL. [Sailb. sail. j.]. **VFOAT** Sailboat and Sailing Journal. Vol. 1 (Mar. 1983)-. Periodical. English. Sailboat and Sailing Journal, PO Box 21176, San Jose CA 95151.

LC VM325 .S35
DD 623.8/504/0294 US
SAILBOAT INSTRUMENTS BUYERS GUIDE. Added/Corp Skipper Marine Electronics, Inc. (19??)-. English. $4.95. Skipper Marine Electronics, 3170 Commercial Avenue, Northbrook IL 60062.

LC HD9993.B633 U575 **ISSN** 0742-0447
DD 623.8/2023/029473 US
SAILBOAT TRADE-IN GUIDE, BLUE BOOK. (SAILBOAT TRADE-IN GUIDE, BLUE BOOK ...). **VFOAT** Sailboat Trade-In Guide; Blue Book. (19??)-. Periodical. English. One time a year. $9.95. Intertec Publishing Corporation, 9800 Metcalf, Overland Park KS 66212. **Tel** (913)341-1300. **ED** Tom Fournier.
Desc: Valuation guide for sailboats up to 30 feet; lists specifications, prices and trade-in values.

ISSN 0036-2719
US
SAILING. (19??)-. Periodical. English. Twelve times a year. $24.75. Port Publications Inc., 125 East Main Street, PO Box 249, Port Washington WI 53074. **Tel** (414)284-3494. **ED** William F. Schanen III. **Bk Rev. Ad Acc. Circ:** 28,000 (ctrl). available on microfilm and microfiche from University Microfilms International (UMI).
Desc: Articles of interest to those interested in wind sailing, nautical ads, supplies, etc.

ISSN 0709-4744
DD 797.1/24/05 CN
SAILING CANADA. [Sail. Can.]. **VFOAT** Sailing. **VAT** Sailing (Toronto). Vol. 1, No. 2 (March/April 1979)-(March 1993). Periodical. English. Six times a year. $37.14. Sailing Canada Magazine Ltd., 100 Eglinton Avenue E/404, Donmills Ontario M3C 1H9 Canada. **Tel** (416)366-3538. **ED** Paul Rumgay. **Bk Rev. Ad Acc. Circ:** 23,000. **Continues** Canadian Sail, 0709-4736.
Desc: Sailing in Canada.
Ind/Abst Can. Index (?-?); SportSearch (May 1987)-.

LC VK810 .S25
DD 623.89223 CN
SAILING DIRECTIONS. GENERAL INFORMATION. ATLANTIC COAST.
Added/Corp Canada. Dept. of Fisheries and Oceans. Canadian Hydrographic Service. **VFOAT** General Information. Atlantic Coast. 1st Ed. (1992)-. English. Fisheries & Oceans Canada, Scientific Information & Publications Branch, 200 Kent Street/12th Floor, Ottawa Ontario K1A 0E6 Canada. **Tel** (613)993-0600, (800)267-6677, telex 053-3585.

LC VK989 .L3 **ISSN** 0823-3799
DD 623.89/297182/05 CN
SAILING DIRECTIONS, LABRADOR AND HUDSON BAY. [Sail. dir. Labrador Hudson Bay]. **Added/Corp** Canada. Fisheries and Marine Service. Canada. Ocean and Aquatic Sciences. Scientific Information and Publications Branch. Canada. Dept. of Fisheries and Oceans. Canadian Hydrographic Service. 3rd Ed. (1974)-. English. Irregular. Canada Communication Group Publishers, Order Processing, Ottawa Ontario K1A 0S9 Canada. **Tel** (819)956-4800, (819)956-4800. **Continues** Labrador and Hudson Bay Pilot, 0576-2227.

ISSN 0821-4670
DD 797.1/24/09712 US
SAILING LIFE. [Sail. life]. Vol. 1, No. 1 (July 1982)-. Periodical. English. Twelve times a year. $16.95 Canada; $25.95 other. Kidd Publications, 216-1650 Duranleau Street, Granville Island Vancouver BC V6H 3S4 Canada.

ISSN 1071-1392
DD 797 US
SAILING QUARTERLY. (SAILING QUARTERLY. [VIDEORECORDING.]). [Sail. q.]. (1989)-. Periodical. English. Four times a year. $99.95 US; $114.95 Canada and Pan America; $137.95 other. Sailing Quarterly, 1623 Race Street, Denver CO 80206. **Tel** (303)393-1218, (800)783-7783. **ED** Patrick Bryant. cum.

index. **Ad Acc, Adv Mgr:** Bob Timm. **Circ:** 10,000.
Desc: A sailing journal distributed on VHS and Beta videocassettes.

LC GV811.8 .S23 **ISSN** 0889-4094
DD 797.1/05 US
SAILING WORLD. [Sail. world]. Vol. 25, No. 8 (August 1986)-. Periodical. English. Twelve times a year. $28.00. Golf Digest- Tennis Inc., 5520 Park Avenue, Trumbull CT 06611. **Tel** (203)373-7256, FAX (203)371-2102. **(Subscription address:** CDS Agency Hard Copy, PO Box 4966, Des Moines IA 50340. **Tel** (515)247-7569.) **Ad Acc, Adv Mgr:** Mark Herlyn. **Continues** Yacht Racing & Cruising, 0190-7956.
Desc: Emphasis on racing and performance cruising. Features include educational material on boat handling, equipment, navigation, safety, tactics, and racing and regatta reports.
Ind/Abst EP Collect.; Homework Help.; MasterFile FullTEXT 1000; MasterFile FullTEXT 350; MasterFile FullTEXT 650; MasterFile FullTEXT; OCLC; SPORT Discus; Telebase.

LC HD4966.B6 A26a **ISSN** 0147-2305
DD 331.2/82/3805 US
SALARIES & BENEFITS IN BOAT MANUFACTURING. See Business and Economics-Labor.

GW
SALING AKTIENFUHRER. German. Verlag Hoppenstedt & Company, Postfach 100139, D-64201 Darmstadt Germany. **Tel** 011 49 6151 380436, 011 49 6151 380361. **Ad Acc, Adv Mgr:** Susanne Kinhn, **Tel** 6151 380 260.

ISSN 0705-2065
DD 338.4/3/623823130971 CN
SANFORD EVANS GOLD BOOK OF OUTBOARD MOTOR DATA AND USED PRICES. (GOLD BOOK OF OUTBOARD MOTOR DATA.). **VFOAT** Gold Book of Outboard Motor Data and Used Prices. (1???)-. English. One time a year (Mar.). 6.50Can$. Sanford Evans Communications Ltd., Box 6900, 1700 Church Avenue, Winnipeg Manitoba R3C 3B1 Canada. **Tel** (204)694-2022, FAX (204)694-2347.

US
SEA COMBINED WITH RUDDER. VFOAT Sea for the Inland Boatman; Inland Sea. Vol. 70, No. 4 (Apr. 1978)-. Periodical. English. One time a year. **Continues** Inland Sea Combined with Rudder.

LC GV788.5 .S43 **ISSN** 0829-3279
DD 797.1/224 US
SEA KAYAKER. [Sea kayak.]. Vol. 1, No. 1 (Spring 1984)-. Periodical. English. Six times a year (Feb., April, June, Aug., Oct., Dec.). $21.00. Sea Kayaker Inc., 6327 Seaview Avenue Northwest, Seattle WA 98107. **Tel** (206)789-9536, (206)789-1326, FAX (206)789-6392. **ED** Christopher Cunningham (editor's address: PO Box 17170 Seattle WA 98107). Index available. **Bk Rev,** (Qty: 10). **Ad Acc, Adv Mgr Tel** (206)789-1326.
Ind/Abst SPORT Discus.

LC GV811.8 .S44 **ISSN** 0746-8601
DD 797.1/05 US
SEA (LOS ANGELES, CALIF.). (SEA.). [Sea]. **VFOAT** Sea Magazine. Vol. 76, No. 2 (Feb. 1984)-. Periodical. English. Twelve times a year. $19.94. Duncan McIntosh, 17782 Cowan, Irvine CA 92714. **Tel** (714)660-6150. **(Subscription address:** Kable Publishers Aide / Illinois, 308 East Hitt Street, Subscription Department, Mt. Morris IL 61054-1473. **Tel** (815)734-1261.) **ED** David Speer. **Ad Acc. Circ:** 45,339. available on microfilm and microfiche from University Microfilms International (UMI). **Continues** Sea & Pacific Skipper, 0274-905X.
Ind/Abst Pop. Mag. Rev. (1984).

ISSN 0711-379X
DD 797.1/09713 CN
SEAFARER (HAWKESBURY, ONT.). (THE SEAFARER.). [Seafarer]. Vol. 1, No. 1 (Apr./May 1977)-. Periodical. English. Six times a year. $2.00. Culloden House Publications, PO Box 456, Hawkesbury Ontario K6A 2S2 Canada.

ISSN 0143-246X
UK
SEAHORSE (LONDON). (SEASHORE : INTERNATIONAL YACHT RACING.). [Seahorse]. **Added/Corp** Royal Ocean Racing Club. (19??)-. Periodical. English. Twelve times a year. $77.01. Fairmead Communication Ltd., 120 126 Lavender Avenue, Mitcham Surrey CR4 3YZ United Kingdom. **Tel** 011 44 181 6461031.

ISSN 0734-0680
US
SHAVINGS. [Shavings]. **Added/Corp** Center for Wooden Boats (Seattle, Wash.). (19??)-. Periodical. English. Six times a year. Center for Wooden Boats, 1010 Valley Street, Seattle WA 98109.

Boats and Boating

DD 387   **ISSN** 0749-2952   US

SHOWBOATS INTERNATIONAL.
[Showboats int.]. (198?)-. Periodical. English. Six times a year. $28.00. Hachette Magazines Inc., 1633 Broadway, New York NY 10019. **Tel** (212)767-6000. **(Subscription address:** Neodata / Colorado, PO Box 2606, Boulder CO 80322. **) Continues** Showboats.
Desc: Covers luxury marine lifestyles. Focuses on the ultimate in mega-yachts.
Ind/Abst EP Collect.; Homework Help.; MasterFile FullTEXT 1000; MasterFile FullTEXT 350; MasterFile FullTEXT 650; MasterFile FullTEXT (July 1994-); OCLC; Pub. Lib. FullTEXT; Telebase.

ISSN 0306-0209   UK   TITLE CHANGE

SMALL CRAFT. Added/Corp Royal Institution of Naval Architects.
(198?)-(19??). Trade Publication. English. Royal Institution of Naval Architects, 10 Upper Belgrave Street, London SW1X 8BQ United Kingdom. **Tel** 011 44 71 2354622, FAX 011 44 71 245 6959, telex 265844 SINAI G. **Merged into** Ship & Boat International, 0037-3834.

DD 623.89/29/711   **ISSN** 1200-1694   CN

SMALL CRAFT GUIDE. BRITISH COLUMBIA.
[Small craft guide, B.C.]. **Added/Corp** Canada. Dept. of Fisheries and Oceans. Canada. Dept. of Fisheries and Oceans. Institute of Ocean Sciences. Canadian Hydrographic Service. Canada. Marine Sciences Directorate. Canada. Fisheries and Marine Service. Canada. Ocean and Aquatic Sciences. Scientific Information and Publications Branch. Canada. Ocean Science and Surveys. Scientific Information and Publications Branch. **VFOAT** British Columbia Small Craft Guide; Boundary Bay to Cortes Island; Vancouver Island, Port Alberni to Campbell River including the Gulf Islands. (19??)-. English. Department of Fisheries and Oceans / British Columbia, Hydrographic Chart Distribution Office, PO Box 8080, 1675 Russell Road, Ottawa ONT K1G 3H6 Canada. **Continues** British Columbia Small Craft Guide, 0826-1768.

DD 797.1/25/0971   **ISSN** 0841-2014   CN

SNOW GOER'S WATER GOER.
[Snow goer's water goer]. **VFOAT** Water Goer. Vol. 9, No. 4 (Spring/Summer 1989)-. English. Four times a year. 4.80Can$. Camar Publications Ltd., 130 Spy Court, Markham Ontario L3R 5H6 Canada. **Tel** (416)475-8440, FAX (416)475-9246.

LC GV   **DD** 797   US

SOUNDINGS (ESSEX, CONN.).
(SOUNDINGS.). (19??)-. Periodical. English. Twelve times a year. $19.97. Soundings Publications, 35 Pratt Street, Essex CT 06426. **Tel** (203)767-3200, FAX (203)767-1048. **ED** Marleah Ross. **Bk Rev**. **Ad Acc**. **Circ:** 80,000.
Desc: The nation's boating tabloid, with complete coverage of recreation boating - power and sail.

ISSN 0194-8369   US

SOUNDINGS. TRADE ONLY.
(197?)-. Periodical. English. Twelve times a year. $25.00. Soundings Publications, 35 Pratt Street, Essex CT 06426. **Tel** (203)767-3200, FAX (203)767-1048. **ED** David Eastman (phone: (203)767-3200). **Ad Acc**. **Circ:** 34,000.
Desc: The boating business newspaper, with coverage of industry and business news for the recreational boating field.
Ind/Abst F&S Index Plus Text, Int. [Select. Cov.]; PROMT.

ISSN 0192-3579   US

SOUTHERN BOATING.
[South. boat.]. (19??)-. Periodical. English. Twelve times a year. $15.00. Southern Boating and Yachting, 1766 Bay Road, Miami Beach FL 33139. **Tel** (305)538-0700, FAX (305)532-8657. **ED** David Strickland. **Ad Acc**, **Adv Mgr:** Steve Beck, **Tel** (305)538-0700. **Circ**, 33,000 (ctrl).
Desc: Boating publication throughout the Caribbean.

LC VM320 .S67   **DD** 623.8/223/028   **ISSN** 0272-619X   US

SPYGLASS.
[Spyglass]. Vol. 1 (1974)-. English. One time a year. $6.95. Spyglass, 2415 Mariner Square Drive, Alameda CA 94501.

LC VM331 .S78   **DD** 623.8/1821/05   **ISSN** 0744-8066   US

STEEL YACHT, THE.
[Steel yacht]. **VFOAT** Steel Yacht Quarterly. (19??)-. Periodical. English. Four times a year. $25.00 Canada, $20.00 other. Steel Yacht, 555 Fairview Avenue, Archadia CA 91006.

ISSN 1065-349X   US   CEASED

STEM TO STERN (CLAYTON, CALIF.).
See Naval Science, Navigation.

AT

TRADE-A-BOAT. See Business and Economics-Commerce.

LC GV776.A2 T7   **DD** 62388/2313/05   **ISSN** 0300-6557   US

TRAILER BOATS.
[Trailer boats]. **VFOAT** Trailer Boats Magazine. (1971)-. Periodical. English. Eleven times a year. $17.97. Poole Publications Inc, 20700 Belshaw Avenue, Carson CA 90746. **Tel** (310)537-6322, FAX (310)537-8735. **(Subscription address:** Kable Publishers Aide / Illinois, 308 East Hitt Street, Subscription Department, Mt. Morris IL 61054-1473. **Tel** (815)734-1261.) **ED** Wiley Poole. **Ad Acc**. **Circ:** 73,000. Documents available from UMI Article Clearinghouse.
Desc: An authority on mid-sized boats, featuring testing, tow tests, travel, how-to's, maintenance and new products.
Ind/Abst Mag. Index Plus (1989-); Newsp. Period. Abstr. (1988-); Mag. Index (1977-).

US

U S AIRBOAT.
English. Six times a year. $5.00 (one-year), $10.00 (two-year), $15.00 (three-year) library and institutions US; $8.95 (one-year), $17.90 (two-year), $26.85 (three-year) (individuals) US. Nichols Publishing, 9906 Old Dade City Rd., Lakeland FL 35201. **Tel** (813)858-6176. **ED** Ron Nichols. **Ad Acc**. **Circ:** 4000 (ctrl).
Desc: Contains technical reports and covers political issues affecting the sport of airboating.

LC GV811.8 .U58   **DD** 797.1/05   IT   CEASED

UOMO MARE.
(19??)-(19??). Periodical. Italian. Piazza Castello 27, 20121 Milan Italy.

ISSN 0751-5405   FR

UDC 629.125

VOILES ET VOILIERS PARIS.
(VOILES ET VOILIERS.). [Voiles voil. Paris]. (1971)-. Periodical. French. Twelve times a year. $94.05. SPER (Societe de Publications et D'Editions Reunies), 21 rue du Faubourg St. Antoine, 75550 Paris Cedex 11 France. **Tel** 011 33 1 40026262.

DD 797   US

●WATERCRAFT ACTION.
[Watercraft action]. (1993)-. Periodical. English. Ten times a year. Ehlert Publishing Group, 601 Lakeshore Parkway, Suite 600, Minnetonka MN 55305. **Tel** (612)476-2200. **ED** Joel Johnson. **Ad Acc**. **Circ:** 12,000.
Desc: Reports on events and news in racing and high performance watercraft news. Highlights racing series results and previews of upcoming competition.

LC WMLC L 83/9171

US

WATERCRAFT DEALER. VFOAT Water Craft Dealer.
Vol. 1, No. 3 (Fall 1990)-. English. Four times a year. Advanstar Data, 7500 Old Oak Boulevard, Cleveland OH 44130. **Tel** (800)225-4569.

ISSN 1073-3191   US

DD 797

●WATERCRAFT WORLD.
[Watercraft world]. Vol. 8, No. 1 (Dec. 1993)-. Periodical. English. Twelve times a year. $28.00. Ehlert Publishing Group, 601 Lakeshore Parkway, Suite 600, Minnetonka MN 55305. **Tel** (612)476-2200. **(Subscription address:** Kable Publishers Aide / Illinois, 308 East Hitt Street, Subscription Department, Mt. Morris IL 61054-1473. **Tel** (815)734-1261.) **ED** Michael Dapper. **Ad Acc**. **Circ:** 100,000 (ctrl). **Continues** Water Scooter, 0899-9775.

LC VK541   **DD** 623.88   **ISSN** 8756-0038   US

WATERFRONT NEWS.
(1984)-. Periodical. English. Twelve times a year. $12.00 (one-year), $20.00 (two-year), $30.00 (three-year). Waterfront News, 1523 South Andrews Avenue, Fort Lauderdale FL 33316. **Tel** (305)524-9450, FAX (305)524-9464. **ED** Jennifer Heit. **Bk Rev**, (Qty: 2). **Ad Acc**, **Adv Mgr:** Elana Stein, **Tel** (305)524-9450. **Circ:** 39,000.
Desc: A forum for the waterfront community of southeastern Florida covering boating, diving, fishing and related fields.

US

WATERWAY GUIDE (GREAT LAKES EDITION).
(WATERWAY GUIDE.). (19??)-. English. One time a year. $36.95. Argus Business, 6151 Powers Ferry Road Northwest, Atlanta GA 30339. **Tel** (404)995-2500, FAX (404)995-0400. **Supersedes** Inland Waterway Guide. Great Lakes Edition.
Desc: Navigational and travel advice for recreational boaters.

LC GV835 .W35   **DD** 797.1   **ISSN** 0509-917X   US

WATERWAY GUIDE. MID-ATLANTIC EDITION.
(WATERWAY GUIDE.). No. 1 (1963)-. English. One time a year. $36.95. Argus Business, 6151 Powers Ferry Road Northwest, Atlanta GA 30339. **Tel** (404)995-2500, FAX (404)995-0400.

ISSN 0090-712X   US

WATERWAY GUIDE. NORTHERN EDITION.
(WATERWAY GUIDE.). (19??)-. Periodical. English. One time a year. $36.95. Argus Business, 6151 Powers Ferry Road Northwest, Atlanta GA 30339. **Tel** (404)995-2500, FAX (404)995-0400. **ED** Queene Hooper. Index available. **Ad Acc**. **Circ:** 75,000. **Continues** Inland Waterway Guide. Northern Edition.
Desc: Navigational and travel advice for recreational boaters.

LC GV776.S65 W38   **DD** 797.1/0975   US

WATERWAY GUIDE. SOUTHERN. VFOAT Southern.
(19??)-. English. Communications Channels Inc, 6255 Barfield Road, Atlanta GA 30328-4369. **Tel** (404)256-9800, FAX (404)256-3116.

ISSN 0511-3806   US

DD 797

WATERWAY GUIDE. SOUTHERN EDITION.
(WATERWAY GUIDE.). [Waterway guide, South. ed.]. (19??)-. English. One time a year. $36.95. Argus Business, 6151 Powers Ferry Road, Atlanta GA 30339. **Tel** (404)995-2500, FAX (404)995-0400. **Continues** Inland WaterWay Guide. (Southern Edition).

ISSN 1188-5432   CN

DD 797.1/224/05

WAVE-LENGTH (GABRIOLA).
(WAVE-LENGTH.). [Wave-length]. Vol. 1, No. 1 (May/June 1991)-. Periodical. English. Six times a year. 12.01Can$. Consensus Communications, RR 1, Suite 17, Gabr Island BC V0R 1X0 Canada. **Tel** (604)247-8858. **ED** Alan Wilson. **Bk Rev**, (Qty:). **Ad Acc**. **Circ:** 10,000. available on an online database from Internet.
Desc: For sea kayakers, focused on the Pacific Northwest. We focus on safety and environmental conservation, while promoting the products and services of the paddling industry.

LC GV781 .W52   **DD** 797.1/22/05   **ISSN** 0273-0111   US

WIDE WORLD OF CANOEING.
[Wide world canoe.]. **VFOAT** Canoeing. (19??)-. Periodical. English. $1.95 US; $2.50 other. Aqua Field Publications Inc., 66 West Gilbert Street, Shrewsbury NJ 07702. **Tel** (201)842-8300.

UK   TITLE CHANGE

WINDSURF AND BOARD SAILING.
(19??)-(19??). English. The Blue Barn, Tew Lane Wootton, Woodstock Oxford, OX7 1HA United Kingdom. **Tel** 011 44 1993 811181, FAX 011 44 1993 811481. **Continued by** Windsurf Magazine.

UK

WINDSURF MAGAZINE.
(19??)-. Consumer Publication. English. Ten times a year. £2.25. The Blue Barn, Tew Lane Wootton, Woodstock Oxford, OX7 1HA United Kingdom. **Tel** 011 44 1993 811181, FAX 011 44 1993 811481. **ED** Mark Kasprowicz. **Bk Rev**, (Qty: 5). **Ad Acc**, **Adv Mgr:** Jim Peskett. **Circ:** 23,000. **Continues** Windsurf and Board Sailing.

LC WMLC L 83/6788   **ISSN** 0198-991X   US

WOODEN CANOE. Added/Corp Wooden Canoe Heritage Association.
No. 1 (Winter 1979/1980)-. Periodical. English. Six times a year. $20.00. Wooden Canoe Heritage Association, PO Box 226, Blue Mountain Lake NY 12812. **Tel** (803)648-7655. **ED** John Quenell. Index available. cum. index. **Ad Acc**. ctrl circ.
Desc: Dedicated to the preservation and celebration of wooden and birchbark canoes. Includes features from outings as well as how-to articles.

LC VM320 .W66   **DD** 623.82/07/405   **ISSN** 0095-067X   US

WOODENBOAT, THE. VAT Wooden Boat.
Vol. 1 (Sept./Oct. 1974)-. Trade Publication. English. Six times a year (Jan., Mar., May, July, Sept., Nov.). $24.95. Woodenboat Publications, PO Box 78, Brooklin ME 04616. **Tel** (207)359-4651, FAX (207)359-8920. **(Subscription address:** Woodenboat Subscription Department, PO Box 492, Mt Morris IL 61054. **Tel** (800)877-5284.) **ED** Jonathan A. Wilson. Index available. cum. index. **Bk Rev**. **Ad Acc**. **Circ:** 100,000.
Desc: Devoted to the building, care, design and use of wooden boats, both large and small, yachts and working vessels, traditional and modern. Emphasis is on craftsmanship and knowledge.
Ind/Abst Index Inf.

Building and Construction

LC VK1 .W6   **ISSN** 0043-8014
DD 386.205   US
WORK BOAT, THE. [Work boat]. Vol. 1 (1944)-. Periodical. English. Six times a year. $20.00 US; $35.00 other. Journal Publications, PO Box 1348, Mandeville LA 70470. **Tel** (504)626-0298, **FAX** (504)624-4801, telex 161698 JOURNAL UT. **(Subscription address:** Linda Bryant, PO Box 908, Rockland ME 04841-0908. **Tel** (207)594-6222.) **ED** Robert Carpenter. Index available. **Ad Acc**. **Circ:** 12,500 (ctrl). *Absorbed Southern Marine Review.*
 Desc: Analyzes national and international developments of interest to those in the work boat industry of the US.
 Ind/Abst Ocean. Abstr.

LC HE   **ISSN** 1037-3748
DD 387   UK
WORK BOAT WORLD. (1989)-. English. Twelve times a year. 65.00Aus$. Baird Publications Pty Ltd, 10 Oxford Street, South Yarra Victoria, 3141 Australia. **Tel** 011 61 3 8268741, FAX 011 61 3 827-0704, telex AA36720. *Continues Work and Patrol Boat World, 0812-1648.*
 Desc: Journal of small ships.
 Ind/Abst Fluid Abstr., Civil Eng.; Fluid Abstr. Proc. Eng.; FLUIDEX (19??-).

UK
WORKBOAT INTERNATIONAL. [Workboat int.]. English. Six times a year. $68.45. Rushton Marine Press, Burnhams Road Little Bookham, Letterhead Surrey, KT23 3BA United Kingdom. **Tel** 011 44 1372 453316, FAX 011 44 1372 59974. **ED** Iain Sutherland. **Ad Acc**, **Adv Mgr:** Marilyn Stansell. **Circ:** 6,500 (ctrl).
 Desc: Newspaper with up to date news and information developments over the interntional industry of workboats.

   ISSN 0043-9932
UDC 629.125   GW
   CCC
YACHT. (1904)-. Periodical. German. Twenty-five times a year. $145.85. Delius Klasing & Co GmbH, Postfach 101671, D-33516 Bielefeld Germany. **Tel** 011 49 521 559291, FAX 011 49 521 559113, telex 9 32 934 DEKLA.

   ISSN 0043-9983
   UK
   CCC
YACHTING MONTHLY, THE. [Yacht. mon.]. **VFOAT** Yachting. Vol. 29, No. 166 (Feb. 1920)-. Periodical. English. Twelve times a year. $78.03. IPC Magazines Ltd., Perrymount Road, Haywards Heath, West Sussex RH16 3DH United Kingdom. **Tel** 011 44 1444 440421, FAX 011 44 1444 445599. *Continues Yachting Monthly and Magazine of the R.N.V.R.*

LC GV771 .Y2   **ISSN** 0043-9940
DD 797.1/05   US
YACHTING (NEW YORK, N.Y.). (YACHTING.). [Yachting]. Vol. 1 (Jan. 1907)-. Periodical. English. Twelve times a year. $19.98. Times Mirror Magazines, Two Park Avenue, New York NY 10016. **Tel** (212)779-5000. **(Subscription address:** Neodata / Colorado, PO Box 2606, Boulder CO 80322.) **Ad Acc**, **Adv Mgr:** Rick Becker, **Tel** (212)779-5086. available on microfilm and microfiche from University Microfilms International (UMI); available on an online database (file 647/Full-Text) from DIALOG. Documents available from UMI Article Clearinghouse.
 Desc: Reports on new racers, cruisers, daysailers and motor yachts. Articles on design, cruising, navigation and electronics.
 Ind/Abst Book Rev. Index; Consum. Index Prod. Eval. Inf. Source; EP Collect.; Gen. Period. Index (1985-); Health Source Plus; Health Source; Homework Help.; Mag. Artic. Summar. Elite; Mag. Artic. Summar. Select; Mag. Artic. Summar. CD-ROM; Mag. Index Plus (1989-); Mag. Search; MasterFile FullTEXT 1000; MasterFile FullTEXT 350; MasterFile FullTEXT 650; MasterFile FullTEXT (July 1994-); Newsp. Period. Abstr. (1989-); OCLC; Pub. Lib. FullTEXT; Read. Guide Period. Lit.; Telebase; Mag. Index (1977-).

   ISSN 0192-1649
   US
YACHTING NEWS. (19??)-. Periodical. English. Twelve times a year. Duncan Publishing, PO Box 309, 4107 Ladoga Avenue, Lakewood CA 90714. **Tel** (310)429-8946. **ED** Hugh Duncan.
 Desc: The magazine for the boaters in the Southern California area.

   ISSN 0043-9991
   UK
YACHTING WORLD. [Yacht. world]. (19??)-. Periodical. English. Twelve times a year. $66.86. IPC Magazines Ltd., Perrymount Road, Haywards Heath, West Sussex RH16 3DH United Kingdom. **Tel** 011 44 1444 440421, FAX 011 44 1444 445599. **ED** B. Hayman. available on microfilm from University Microfilms International (UMI).

LC GV825 .Y117   **ISSN** 0094-8136
DD 797.1/09794   US
YACHTING YEAR BOOK OF NORTHERN CALIFORNIA. Added/Corp Pacific Inter-Club Yacht Association of Northern California. (19??)-. English. One time a year. $8.20. Pacific Inter-Club Yacht Association of Northern California, 1050 Sansom Street, San Francisco CA 94111.

   ISSN 0044-0000
   UK
YACHTS AND YACHTING. [Yachts and yacht.]. (1947)-. Periodical. English. Twenty-six times a year. $92.40. Yachting Press Ltd, 196 Eastern Esplanade, Southend-on-End Essex United Kingdom. **Tel** 011 44 1702 582245.
 Ind/Abst SPORT Discus.

LC GV811.8 .Y26   **ISSN** 0276-8917
DD 797.1/05   US
YACHTSMAN'S POCKET ALMANAC, THE. [Yachtsm. pocket alm.]. (19??)-. English. One time a year. Prentice Hall Simon & Schuster, PO Box 11071, Des Moines IA 50336. **Tel** (800)947-7700, (515)284-6751.

LC GV814 .R6A   **ISSN** 0307-868X
DD 797.1/25   UK
YEAR BOOK - ROYAL YACHTING ASSOCIATION. Main/Corp Royal Yachting Association (Great Britain). English. One time a year. Royal Yachting Association, 5 Buckingham Gate S.W. 1, London United Kingdom.

ABSTRACTING, BIBLIOGRAPHIES AND STATISTICS

LC HD9993.B633 U522   **ISSN** 0277-8378
DD 338.4/762382/0973   US
BOATING INDUSTRY STATISTICAL YEARBOOK. [Boat. ind. stat. yearb.]. **VFOAT** Statistical Yearbook, Boating Industry. 1981-. Statistical Publication. English. One time a year. Business Projects Group, 7 Canterbury Lane, Nesconset NY 11767.

LC GV776.A2 B6   **ISSN** 0163-7207
DD 353.9/3/87723   US
BOATING REGISTRATION STATISTICS. English. One time a year. $35.00. National Association of Engine and Boat Manufactures, PO Box 5555 Grand Central Station, New York NY 10017.

LC WMLC L 83/2213
DD 363.123   US
BOATING STATISTICS. Added/Corp United States. Coast Guard. (1966)-. Government Publication. English. One time a year. Free on request. US Coast Guard, 2100 2nd Street Southwest, Washington DC 20590. **Tel** (202)267-1408. *Continues Recreational Boating Statistics.*
 Desc: Lists data and statistics on boating accidents and provides information on boating safety education.

LC GV776.N74 N67   **ISSN** 0148-8090
DD 614.8/1   US
NORTH CAROLINA BOATING ACCIDENT STATISTICS. [N. C. boat. accid. stat.]. (1976)-. English. One time a year. North Carolina Wildlife Resources Commission, Raleigh NC 27611.

BUILDING AND CONSTRUCTION

   ISSN 0277-1659
   US
A-E-C AUTOMATION NEWSLETTER. See Architecture-Computer Applications.

   ISSN 0966-9647
DD 721   UK
ABC AND D. ARCHITECT BUILDER CONTRACTOR AND DEVELOPER. See Architecture.

   ISSN 1062-3698
   US
Pr Rev.
ABC TODAY. (ABC TODAY : THE NEWS MAGAZINE FOR MERIT SHOP CONTRACTORS.). **Added/Corp** Associated Builders and Contractors (U.S.). Vol. 1, No. 1 (Jan. 8, 1992)-. Trade Publication. English. Twenty-two times a year. $60.00. Associated Builders Contractors, 1300 North 17th Street, Rosslyn VA 22209. **Tel** (703)812-2000, FAX (703)812-8203. **ED** Pamela Hunter, (phone: (703)812-2069) or Heather Hunt (phone: (703)812-2063). **Bk Rev**. **Ad Acc**, **Adv Mgr:** Bob K., **Tel** (703)812-2087. **Circ:** 16,000. *Continues Newsline (Associated Builders & Contractors (U.S.)), 0888-014X.*
 Desc: Information on construction trade, industry news and legislative updates.

LC TA680 .C745   **ISSN** 1051-5526
DD 624.1/834   US
   CODEN ABCCET
ABERDEEN'S CONCRETE CONSTRUCTION. [Aberdeen's concr. constr.]. **VFOAT** Concrete Construction. Vol. 35, No. 2 (Feb. 1990)-. Trade Publication. English. Twelve times a year. $24.00. Aberdeen Group, 426 South Westgate, Addison IL 60101. **Tel** (312)543-0870, FAX (708)543-3112. **ED** William M. Avery. available on microfilm and microfiche from University Microfilms International (UMI). Documents available from Article Express International. *Continues Concrete Construction, 0010-5333.*
 Ind/Abst Appl. Sci. Technol. Index; Curr. Cit.; Ei Page One [Select. Cov.]; Eng. Index Annu. [Select. Cov.]; Highw. Res. Abstr.

   ISSN 1051-4821
DD 691   US
ABERDEEN'S CONCRETE REPAIR DIGEST. [Aberdeen's concr. repair dig.]. **Added/Corp** Aberdeen Group. **VFOAT** Concrete Repair Digest. (Spring 1990)-. Trade Publication. English. Six times a year. $18.00. Aberdeen Group, 426 South Westgate, Addison IL 60101. **Tel** (312)543-0870, FAX (708)543-3112. **ED** Ward Malisch. ctrl circ.
 Desc: How-to technical publication aimed at contractors specializing in concrete repair.

   ISSN 1055-0356
DD 338   US
ABERDEEN'S CONCRETE TRADER. [Aberdeen's concr. trader]. **VFOAT** Concrete Trader. (19??)-. Trade Publication. English. Twelve times a year. Free to qualified individuals. Aberdeen Group, 426 South Westgate, Addison IL 60101. **Tel** (312)543-0870, FAX (708)543-3112. available on microfilm. *Continues Concrete Trader, 1040-5321.*

LC WMLC 93/772   **ISSN** 1051-483X
DD 380   US
ABERDEEN'S CONSTRUCTION MARKETING TODAY. [Aberdeen's constr. mark. today]. **Added/Corp** Aberdeen Group. **VFOAT** Construction Marketing Today. Vol. 1 No. 1 (July/Aug. 1990)-. Trade Publication. English. Twelve times a year. $27.00. Aberdeen Group, 426 South Westgate, Addison IL 60101. **Tel** (312)543-0870, FAX (708)543-3112. **ED** Diana Granitto. **Circ:** Yes.
 Desc: Editorial covers marketing news and news of the industry, and is aimed at marketers in the construction industry.

LC TH1199 .M22   **ISSN** 1055-4408
DD 693/.1/05   US
   CODEN AMMCEK
ABERDEEN'S MAGAZINE OF MASONRY CONSTRUCTION. [Aberdeen's mag. mason. constr.]. **Added/Corp** Aberdeen Group. **VFOAT** Magazine of Masonry Construction; Masonry Construction. Vol. 3, No. 3 (March 1990)-. Trade Publication. English. Twelve times a year. $24.00. Aberdeen Group, 426 South Westgate, Addison IL 60101. **Tel** (312)543-0870, FAX (708)543-3112. **ED** Kenneth A. Hooker. available on microfilm from University Microfilms International (UMI). *Continues Magazine of Masonry Construction, 0898-6088.*
 Ind/Abst Ceram. Abstr. (19??-).

LC TH455 .A33   **ISSN** 1079-3356
DD 683   US
●**ACCESSIBLE BUILDING PRODUCT GUIDE, THE.** (THE ... ACCESSIBLE BUILDING PRODUCT GUIDE.). [Access. build. prod. guide]. **Added/Corp** John Wiley & Sons. (1995)-. English. Irregular. John Wiley & Sons, Inc., 605 Third Avenue, New York NY 10158-0012. **Tel** (212)850-6000, (212)850-6645, FAX (212)850-6088, telex 12-7063.

LC HD9000   **ISSN** 0810-0969
DD 338.476240994   AT
ACEL UPDATE. [ACEL update]. (1981)-. Newsletter. English. Four times a year. ACEL Information Pty Ltd., Locked Bag 2471, Crows Nest NSW 2065 Australia. **Tel** 011 61 2 9066096, FAX 011 61 2 9066049.

LC TA439 .A358   **ISSN** 0065-7875
DD 620.1/36   US
   CCC
ACI MANUAL OF CONCRETE PRACTICE. Added/Corp American Concrete Institute. **VFOAT** Manual of Concrete Practice. **VAT** American Concrete Institute manual of concrete practice. (19??)-. Periodical. English. One time a year. $445.00. American Concrete Institute, PO Box 19150, Detroit MI 48219. **Tel** (313)532-2600, FAX (313)533-4747. **(Subscription address:** American Concrete Institute, PO Box 32190, Detroit MI 48232.)
 Ind/Abst Curr. Cit.

Building and Construction

LC TA439.A36 **ISSN** 0889-325X
DD 620.1/36/05 US
  CCC
  CODEN AMAJEF
Pr Rev.
ACI MATERIALS JOURNAL. See
Engineering-Civil Engineering.
  US
ACI SPECIAL PUBLICATIONS. See
Engineering-Civil Engineering.

LC TA680 .A25 **ISSN** 0889-3241
DD 624.1/834/05 US
  CCC
  CODEN ASTJEG
Pr Rev.
ACI STRUCTURAL JOURNAL. See
Engineering-Civil Engineering.

  ISSN 0153-5471
  FR
ACIER POUR CONSTRUIRE, L'. (1977)-.
French.
Ind/Abst Archit. Period. Index (1977-).

LC TJ1480 **ISSN** 0860-2956
DD 631.3 PL
UDC 631.17
ACTA ACADEMIAE AGRICULTURAE AC TECHNICAE OLSTENENSIS. AEDIFICATIO ET MECHANICA. See
Agriculture-Agricultural Equipment.

  ISSN 0355-2705
  FI
  CODEN APCBAI
ACTA POLYTECHNICA SCANDINAVICA. CIVIL ENGINEERING AND BUILDING CONSTRUCTION SERIES. CI. See Engineering-Civil Engineering.

  ISSN 0896-8403
DD 693 US
ADOBE NEWS (1988). (ADOBE NEWS.). [Adobe news]. Vol. 1 (1988)-. Periodical. English. Twelve times a year. $10.00 per issue. Solar Earthbuilder International, PO Box 16119, Las Cruces NM 88004-6119. **Separated from** Solar Earthbuilder International's Earth & Sun, 0898-5065.

  ISSN 1065-7355
  US
  CCC
Pr Rev.
●**ADVANCED CEMENT-BASED MATERIALS. VFOAT** Advanced Cement Based Materials. (1993)-. Academic Scholarly Publication. English. Eight times a year (1 volume). $330.00. Elsevier Science Publishing Company Inc, Madison Square Station, PO Box 882, New York NY 10159-0882. **Tel** (212)633-3950, **FAX** (212)633-3990. available on an online database from Elsevier Electronic Subscriptions (EES).

  ISSN 0951-7197
  UK
  CCC
ADVANCES IN CEMENT RESEARCH. Vol. 1, No. 1 (Oct. 1987)-. Trade Publication. English. Four times a year (Jan., Apr., July, Oct.). £71.00 UK; £105.00 other. Thomas Telford Ltd, Thomas Telford House, 1 Heron Quay, London E14 9XF United Kingdom. **Tel** 011 44 171 9876999, **FAX** 011 44 171 5384101, telex 298105. **ED** J. N. Clarke. Index available. **Bk Rev.** available in microform from University Microfilms International (UMI). Documents available from Article Express International, CASDDS.
  Desc: An international journal on the fundamentals of cement science. The scope covers: cement manufacture and materials, hydration of cement compounds, properties and durability of cementitious materials and systems, interaction of cements with other materials, analysis and testing and special cements and applications.
  Ind/Abst Chem. Abstr.; Curr. Cit.; Eng. Index Annu.

  US
AED GREEN BOOK. (19??)-. English. One time a year (Feb). $58.00. K-III Directory Corporation, 1735 Technology Drive, Suite 410, San Jose CA 95110. **Tel** (800)669-3282, (408)467-6700, **FAX** (408)467-6795. **ED** C. David Loftus. Index available (bound in all issues). **Bk Rev. Circ:** 14,000.
  Desc: Nationally averaged monthly, weekly and daily rental rates and model specifications for construction equipment.

LC HD9715.A5 A37 SUPPL.
DD 338.4/7624/096 UK
AFRICA CONSTRUCTION. Issue No. 1-. Trade Publication. English. One time a year. £15.00. Africa Journal Ltd, Kirkman House, 54A Tottenham Court Road, London W1P 0BT United Kingdom. **Tel** 011 44 171 6379341, telex 8952670.

LC TH4911 .A45 **ISSN** 1046-7947
DD 690/.892 US
AGRICULTURAL BUILDING COST GUIDE (1987). (AGRICULTURAL BUILDING COST GUIDE.). **Agric. build. cost guide]. Added/Corp** American Appraisal Associates. E.H. Boeckh Co. (198?)-. English. One time a year. $42.00. E.H. Boeckh Company, 2885 South Calhoun Road, New Berlin WI 53151. **Tel** (800)285-1288, (414)780-2800. **Continues in part** Personal Lines Valuation Guide, 0742-440X.
  Desc: Provides replacement costs of agricultural occupancies for frame, masonry, pole frame, and pre-engineered construction types.

  ISSN 1080-2002
DD 624 US
AISC NEWS. See Metals and Metallurgy.

  SZ
  TITLE CHANGE
AKTUELLES BAUEN. See Architecture.

  ISSN 0846-3247
DD 338.4 CN
ALASKA CONTRACTOR : A PUBLICATION OF THE ASSOCIATED GENERAL CONTRACTORS OF ALASKA, THE. [Alsk. contract.]. **Added/Corp** Associated General Contractors of Alaska. **VFOAT** Associated General Contractors Magazine; AGC Magazine. (1991)-. English. Naylor Communications Ltd, 100 Sutherland Avenue, Winnipeg Manitoba R2W 3C7 Canada. **Tel** (204)947-0222, **FAX** (604)985-7399.

DD 338.4/7/690097123 **ISSN** 0709-2431
  CN
ALBERTA CONSTRUCTION. Added/Corp Alberta Construction Association. Vol. 1 (May/June 1978)-. Periodical. English. Six times a year. 16.77Can$. Naylor Communications Ltd, 100 Sutherland Avenue, Winnipeg Manitoba R2W 3C7 Canada. **Tel** (204)947-0222, **FAX** (604)985-7399.

DD 338.4/769/00257123 **ISSN** 0713-4045
  CN
ALBERTA CONSTRUCTION & RESOURCE INDUSTRIES DIRECTORY/PURCHASING GUIDE. [Alta. constr. resour. ind. dir./purch. guide]. 1982-. English. One time a year. 20.00Can$. Sanford Evans Communications Ltd., Box 6900, 1700 Church Avenue, Winnipeg Manitoba R3C 3B1 Canada. **Tel** (204)694-2022, **FAX** (204)694-2347. **Continues** Alberta Construction Industry Directory, Purchasing Guide, 0381-9663.
  Desc: Dedicated to contractors and firms engaged in construction, mining, forestry and oil and gas industries. Provides names, addresses and telephone numbers of suppliers, contractors and subcontractors.

LC KF581.Z9 A115 **ISSN** 0191-202X
DD 346/.73/0433 US
ALI-ABA COURSE OF STUDY. CONDOMINIUM CONVERSIONS: MATERIALS. See Law.

LC LAW **ISSN** 0190-387X
DD 343/.56/078 US
ALI-ABA COURSE OF STUDY. CONSTRUCTION CONTRACTING IN THE MIDDLE EAST, PROBLEMS AND SOLUTIONS: MATERIALS. See Law.

  ISSN 0705-4157
DD 693.8/3/05 CN
ALUMI-NEWS. Vol. 1 (Dec. 1976)-. Trade Publication. English (French). Six times a year (Jan., Mar., May, July, Sept., Nov.). 28.81Can$. Work 4 Projects Ltd, PO Box 400 Victoria Station, Westmount Quebec H3Z 2V8 Canada. **Tel** (514)489-4941, **FAX** (514)489-5505. **ED** Nachmi Artzy. **Ad Acc. Circ:** 19,000 (ctrl).
  Desc: Dedicated to the renovation, construction, and energy conservation industries in Canada.

  ISSN 0740-3607
  US
AMERICAN BUILDING CONTRACTOR, THE. Added/Corp American Building Contractors Association. (19??)-. Periodical. English. Twelve times a year. $35.00. American Building Contractors Association, 11100 Valley Boulevard 120, El Monte CA 91731-2533. **Tel** (801)401-0071. **ED** Michael E. Leeson. Index available. cum. index. **Bk Rev. Ad Acc. Circ:** 10,000.
  Desc: Primarily geared to the California remodeling industry.

LC TA401 .A454 **ISSN** 0002-7731
DD 338.4/7/69 US
AMERICAN BUILDING SUPPLIES. VFOAT ABS. Vol. 1 (Jan. 1967)-. Periodical. English. Twelve times a year. International Thomson Retail Press Inc, 345 Park Avenue South, New York NY 10010. **Tel** (212)887-8400. available on microfilm from University Microfilms International (UMI).

  ISSN 1055-0674
DD 728 US
AMERICAN BUNGALOW. Vol. 1, No. 1 (1991)-. Periodical. English. Four times a year. $29.95 US; $39.95 Canada. American Bungalow, 123 South Baldwin Avenue, PO Box 756, Sierra Madre CA 91025. **Tel** (818)355-3363. **ED** George Murray & Jill Ganon. **Bk Rev,** (Qty: 4). **Ad Acc, Adv Mgr:** Al Griffin. **Circ:** 5,000.

LC TA680.5 .A6
DD 666/.94/025 US
AMERICAN CEMENT DIRECTORY, THE. Added/Corp Bradley Pulverizer Co. (19??)-. Directory. English. One time a year (published in May or June). $64.00. Bradley Pulverizer Company, PO Box 1318, Allentown PA 18105-1318. **Tel** (610)434-5191, **FAX** (610)770-9400. **ED** Veronica M. Saylor. **Ad Acc, Adv Mgr:** Veronica Saylor, **Tel** (610)434-5191. **Circ:** 800.
  Desc: Listing of cement companies in the U.S., Canada, and Central and South America.

LC TH
DD 690 UK
●**AMERICAN CONSTRUCTION CATALOG.** (1995)-. Catalog. English. One time a year. $55.00. Data Distribution Publications, Apex House, London Road Northfleet Gravesend, Kent DA11 9JA United Kingdom. **Tel** 011 44 1322 277788, **FAX** 011 44 1322 569627.

LC HD9715.U5 A72 **ISSN** 0195-9484
  US
AMERICAN CONSTRUCTION INDUSTRY DIRECTORY. [Am. constr. ind. dir.]. Directory. English. One time a year. $14.75 post publication. Studio 4 Products, 4439 Village Road, Long Beach CA 90808.

LC HD9715.C33 Q46B **ISSN** 0317-5901
DD 338.4/7624/09714 CN
ANALYSE DE L'INDUSTRIE DE LA CONSTRUCTION AU QUEBEC. Main/Corp Office de la Construction du Quebec. 1974-. French. One time a year. 7.95Can$. Office de la Construction du Quebec, 5530 Jean Talon Ouest, Montreal Quebec H3R 2G3 Canada. **Tel** (514)341-7740. **Circ:** 3,000. **Continues** Analyse des Caracteristiques de la Population Active de la Construction, 0316-3970.

  ISSN 0896-9752
DD 343 US
ANALYSIS OF REVISIONS OF THE UNIFORM BUILDING CODE, U.B.C. STANDARDS ... . See Law.

LC TH2 .P3 **ISSN** 0020-2568
DD 624/.05 FR
  CODEN AITBAK
  CEASED
ANNALES DE L'INSTITUT TECHNIQUE DU BATIMENT ET DES TRAVAUX PUBLICS. [Ann. inst. tech. batim. trav. publics]. **Main/Corp** Institut Technique du Batiment et des Travaux Publics (Paris, France). Vol. 1 (Jan./Feb. 1936)-(1995). Periodical. French. Ten times a year. Sarl Sebtp, 7 rue la Perouse, 75116 Paris Cedex 16 France. **Tel** 011 33 1 40695309. cum. index. Documents available from Article Express International.
  Ind/Abst Bioeng. Abstr.; Coal Abstr.; Concr. Abstr.; Ei Page One; Energy Res. Abstr.; Eng. Index Annu.; GeoRef; Int. Civil Eng. Abstr.; Saf. Health Work; Soft. Abstr. Eng.; World Ceram. Abstr.

  ISSN 1186-6012
DD 693/.5/025714 CN
ANNUAIRE DES MEMBRES ... ET MANUEL DE REFERENCE. [Annu. memb. man. ref. - Assoc. Beton Que.]. **Main/Corp** Association Beton Quebec. **VFOAT** Annuaire des Membres et Manuel de Reference. **VAT** Annuaire des Membres ... et Manuel de Reference - ABQ. (1991)-. French. Every 2 years. Free for members. Association Beton Quebec, Bureau 120, 550 CH Chambly, Longueuil Quebec J4H 3L8 Canada.

LC HD9715.A1 U48
DD 338.4/7698/094021 SZ
ANNUAL BULLETIN OF HOUSING AND BUILDING STATISTICS FOR EUROPE AND NORTH AMERICA = BULLETIN ANNUEL DE STATISTIQUES DU LOGEMENT ET DE LA CONSTRUCTION POUR L'EUROPE ET L'AMERIQUE DU NORD = EZHEGODNYI BIULLETEN ZHILISHCHNOI I STROITELNOI STATISTIKI DLIA EVROPY I SEVERNOI AMERIKI. See Housing and Urban Development.

LC TH1 .Q35 **ISSN** 0376-6322
DD 690/.05 SI
ANNUAL JOURNAL - SINGAPORE POLYTECHNIC BUILDING SOCIETY. (QUANTIBUILD.). **Added/Corp** Singapore Polytechnic Building Society. Vol. 1, (1968)-. English. Singapore

Building and Construction

Polytechnic Department of Civil Engineering and Building, Civil Engineering and Building Club, Dover Road, 0513 Singapore. **Continues** Polybuild.

LC TH104.65 .H68a
DD 690/.0720549/22
BG
ANNUAL REPORT / HOUSING AND BUILDING RESEARCH INSTITUTE, DACCA. **Main/Corp** Housing and Building Research Institute, Dacca. (19??)-. English.

LC LD3841 .N49a
DD 338.4/73781962/0974743
US
ANNUAL REPORT / THE STATE UNIVERSITY CONSTRUCTION FUND.
Main/Corp New York State University Construction Fund. (1979)-. English. State University Construction Fund, State University Plaza, PO Box 1946, Albany NY 12201-1946. **Continues** New York State University Construction Fund. State University Construction Fund.

LC TH1715.A1 U54a **ISSN** 0195-4806
DD 363.5/82
US
ANNUAL REPORT TO THE PRESIDENT AND THE CONGRESS ON THE WEATHERIZATION ASSISTANCE PROGRAM. See Energy.

LC HD9715.I8 A65
IT
ANNUARIO DELL'EDILIZIA E ARREDAMENTO. Vol. 1 (19??)-. Italian. One time a year. SEAT, Via Aurelio Saffi 18, Turin 10138 Italy. **Tel** 011 39 2 33101, 011 39 2 212248, FAX 011 39 2 4472953, telex 212248 I.

LC HD9715.I8 A66
DD 338.4/7624/02545
IT
ANNUARIO SEAT. VOL. D, EDILIZIA.
Added/Corp SEAT (Firm). **VFOAT** Edilizia; Annuario S.E.A.T. Vol. D, Edilizia. (198?)-. Trade Publication. Italian. One time a year. L30000. ILTE, Via Aurelio Saffi 18-10138, Turin Italy. **Tel** 011-33301, telex 212248 I. **Bk Rev. Circ:** 30,200.
 Desc: Yearbook of Italian companies operating in building and construction materials, machines and equipment for the building industry. Additional information on specific market situation in Italy is available.

LC TH89 .A68
SW
ANSLAGSFRAMSTALLNING FOR BUDGETARET ... / STATENS RAD FOR BYGGNADSFORSKNING. See Finance-Taxation.

ISSN 1186-9119
DD 690
CN
APERCU - ASSOCIATION CANADIENNE DE LA CONSTRUCTION.
(L'APERCU.). [Apercu - Assoc. can. constr.]. **Main/Corp** Association Canadienne de la Construction. (1991)-. French. Association Canadienne de la Construction, 85 rue Albert, Ottawa Ontario K1P 6A4 Canada.

LC HD9622.U5 A66
DD 381/.4566694/0973021
US
APPARENT USE OF PORTLAND CEMENT BY STATE AND MARKET / MARKET AND ECONOMIC RESEARCH.
Added/Corp Portland Cement Association. Market and Economic Research Dept. (19??)-. English. One time a year. $500.00. Portland Cement Association, 5420 Old Orchard Road, Skokie IL 60077. **Tel** (708)966-6200.

US
APPLICATOR, THE. (19??)-. English. Three times a year. $1300.00 (manufacturers), $650.00 (contractors). Sealant, Water Proofing and Restoration Institute, 3101 Broadway, Suite 585, Kansas City MO 64111. **Tel** (816)561-8230. **Ad Acc, Adv Mgr:** Jan Burchett.
 Desc: Presents articles on sealants and sealant information along with other information relevant to contractors and other professionals.

ISSN 0003-7117
JA
APUROCHI. APPROACH. **Added/Corp** Takenaka Komuten. **VFOAT** Approach. (1964)-. Periodical. Japanese (English). Four times a year. Takenaka Komuten Kohobu, (Takenaka Komuten Co. Ltd.), 4-27 Honmachi Higashiku, Osakashi Osakafu 541 Japan.
 Ind/Abst Archit. Period. Index (Autumn 1977-Winter 1980); Avery Index Archit. Period. Suppl. Colum. Univ. (No. 6, 1989-).

LC N1 .A2627 **ISSN** 0308-8596
UK
TITLE CHANGE
ARCHITECT & SURVEYOR. See Architecture.

LC TH435 .A7 **ISSN** 0066-6157
DD 692/.5/0973
US
ARCHITECTS, CONTRACTORS, ENGINEERS GUIDE TO CONSTRUCTION COSTS. **VFOAT** Construction Costs; ACE Guide to Construction Costs. (1970)-. English. One time a year. $32.00. A C & E Publishing Company, 6129 Beard Avenue South, Minneapolis MN 55410. **Tel** (612)920-9699. **ED** D. S. Roth. Index available.
 Desc: A complete cost programmed book for estimating and cost accounting for contractors, engineers, and architects for use with or without computers.

ISSN 1071-4634
US
●ARCHITECTURAL & CONSTRUCTION MEDIA SOURCE. See Architecture.

ISSN 0169-4421
NE
UDC 72
Pr Rev.
ARCHITECTUUR, BONWEN. See Architecture.

IT
ARCHIVIO EDILE. (19??)-. Italian. One time a year. L160000. SAET Srl, Via Buonarroti 50, 20090 Trezzano S Nav Italy. **Tel** 011 39 2 48401223, FAX 011 39 2 48401229. **Circ:** 6,000 (ctrl).
 Desc: A systematic collection of MFR's catalogues in building and construction.

LC HD58 .A8 **ISSN** 1048-6534
DD 658.2/1/05
US
AREA DEVELOPMENT SITES & FACILITY PLANNING. See Real Estate.

LC TH4 .N28 **ISSN** 0235-7259
RU
ARKHITEKTURA I STROITELSTVO ROSSII : AS. See Architecture.

ISSN 0212-8578
SP
UDC 69
ARTE Y CEMENTO. (1959)-. Periodical. Spanish. Irregular (36 issues per year). 20000ptas. Arte y Cemento, Zancoeta 9, 48013 Bilbao Spain. **Tel** 011 34 4 441-0750.

ISSN 0004-4237
US
CODEN ASBSAH
ASBESTOS. [Asbestos]. (July 1919)-. English. Twelve times a year. $5.00 US; $6.00 other. D&B Enterprises Inc, PO Box B, Lakeville PA 18438. **Tel** (717)698-6337. available on microfilm and microfiche from University Microfilms International (UMI).
 Ind/Abst EMBASE; GeoRef.

LC KF1297.A73 A493 **ISSN** 0273-3048
DD 346.7303/82 347.306382
US
ASBESTOS LITIGATION REPORTER. See Law.

LC TD887.A8 A8 **ISSN** 1046-0438
DD 363.17/91
US
ASBESTOS MANAGEMENT SOURCEBOOK. [Asbestos]. (1989)-. Periodical. English. One time a year. $20.00 (institutions). Environmental Publications Inc, 1400 Front Avenue, PO Box 4357, Lutherville MD 21093. **Tel** (301)828-6618. **ED** S. Morris Murray. **Ad Acc.** Circ: 35,000 (ctrl).
 Desc: Contains the various opinions available when dealing with aspects in a facility, plus case histories, legal ramifications, etc. for the facility owner.

ISSN 1182-9982
DD 363.17/91
CN
ASBESTOS WATCH. (ASBESTOS WATCH / UNIVERSITY OF TORONTO). [Asbestos watch].
Added/Corp University of Toronto. Office of the Vice President, Human Resources. University of Toronto. Environmental Health and Safety. Director. No. 1 (July 24, 1990)-. Periodical. English. Limited free distribution. University of Toronto Office of the Vice-President Human Resources, Room 112, Simcoe Hall, 27 King's College Circle, Toronto Ontario M2L 2J3 Canada.

LC HD9715.A1 A75
DD 338.4/7624/095
HK
ASIAN ARCHITECT AND CONTRACTOR. See Architecture.

ISSN 0264-8164
HK
ASIAN BUILDING & CONSTRUCTION. See Architecture.

HK
ASIAN SOURCES HARDWARES FOR WORLD MARKETS. See Industry and Production.

LC HD9715.U5 A738 **ISSN** 0744-0340
DD 381/.45695
US
ASPHALT AND TAR ROOFING AND SIDING PRODUCTS. (CURRENT INDUSTRIAL REPORTS. MA-29A, ASPHALT AND TAR ROOFING AND SIDING PRODUCTS.). **Added/Corp** United States. Bureau of the Census. **VFOAT** Asphalt and Tar Roofing and Siding Products. (19??)-. Government Publication. English. One time a year. US Department of Commerce / Bureau of the Census, Data User Services Division, Customer Services, Washington DC 20233-0800. **Tel** (301)763-4100. (**Subscription address:** Superintendent of Documents, US Government Printing Office, Washington DC 20402.)
 Desc: Presents data on production, inventories, and orders.

ISSN 0197-3703
US
CODEN ERASDI
ASPHALT SALES. [Asphalt sales]. **Added/Corp** United States. Energy Information Administration. Office of Energy Data and Interpretation. United States. Bureau of Mines. Division of Fuels Data. **VFOAT** Sales of Asphalt. (19??)-. Periodical. English. One time a year. Dept of Energy, Energy Information Administration, 4800 Forbes Avenue, Pittsburgh PA 15213.

US
ASPHALT WEEKLY MONITOR. (19??)-. English. Fifty times a year (weekly except two weeks during Christmas). $1,650.00. Poten & Partners Inc., 885 3rd Avenue, New York NY 10022. **Tel** (212)230-2000, FAX (212)355-0295, telex 177118/420811. **ED** Jean Pierre Chovet (212)230-2087.
 Desc: A weekly report which provides information concerning pricing and market developments in the US and Canada.

US
ASTM STANDARDS IN BUILDING CODES. **Main/Corp** American Society for Testing and Materials. **Added/Corp** American Society for Testing Materials. **VFOAT** Standards in Building Codes; Building Codes. (1955)-. English. One time a year (Sept. or Oct.). Price varies. American Society for Testing and Materials, 1916 Race Street, Philadelphia PA 19103. **Tel** (215)299-5585, FAX (215)299-9679, telex 710 670 1037. **ED** Andrea Stanton. Index available.
 Desc: Contains 1,300 ASTM standards referenced by major building codes, Masterspec, Spectext, Army Corp of Engineers and Navfac.

ISSN 0211-8319
SP
UDC 621
ATEMCOP. [ATEMCOP]. **Added/Corp** Ociacion Espanola de Tecnicos de Maquinaria para la Construccion y Obras Publicas. Madrid. **VFOAT** Asociacion Espanola de Tecnicos de Maquinaria para la Construccion y Obras Publicas; Revista ATEMCOP. (1968)-. Periodical. Spanish. Twelve times a year. $79.90. Atemcop, Cruz del Sur 3, 28007 Madrid Spain. **Tel** 011 34 1 5749818.

ISSN 0842-9588
DD 338.4/769/009715
CN
ATLANTIC CONSTRUCTION JOURNAL.
[Atl. constr. j.]. Vol. 1, No. 1 (Aug. 1988)-. Periodical. English. Four times a year (Feb., May, Aug., Nov.). 14.40Can$. Bilby Holdings Ltd., 6029 Cunard Street, Halifax Nova Scotia B3K 1E5 Canada. **Tel** (920)420-0437, FAX (920)423-8212. **ED** Ken Patridge. **Ad Acc.** ctrl circ.
 Desc: Covers construction sector of Atlantic Canada.

LC HD9715.G3 A35
GW
AUSGEWAHLTE ZAHLEN FUER DIE BAUWIRTSCHAFT. **Main/Corp** Germany (West). Statistisches Bundesamt. (Jan. 1977)-. Trade Publication. German. Twelve times a year. DM219.60. Metzler Poeschel Verlag Veroeffen, Statist Bundesamt Kernerstr 43, D-70182 Stuttgart Germany. **Tel** 011 49 7071 935350. (**Subscription address:** Metzler Poeschel H Leins GmbH, Postfach 1152, D 72125 Kusterdingen Germany. **Tel** 011 49 7071 935350.) **Continues** Germany (West). Statistisches Bundesamt. Bauwirtschaft, Bautatigkeit, Wohnungen. Reihe 1: Ausgewahlte Zahlen fuer die Bauwirtschaft.
 Desc: Figures on the construction industry compiled from various statistical sources and presented in user-oriented form. Emphasis is on the data from construction reports and on building activity, supplemented by selected results of other statistics that provide information on the construction industry.

LC TH **ISSN** 1032-240X
DD 690.09944
AT
Pr Rev.
AUSTRALIAN BUILDING, CONSTRUCTION AND HOUSING. [Aust. build. hous. constr.]. (1988)-. Trade Publication. English. Ten times a year (monthly except Jan., Dec.). 49.34Aus$. Master Builders Association of New South Wales, Private Bag 9, Broadway New South Wales 2007 Australia. **Tel** 011 61 2 6607188, FAX 011 61 2 6604437. **ED** Juliet

Building and Construction

Pratley. **Bk Rev**, (Qty: 10). **Ad Acc**, **Adv Mgr Tel** 818 4111. **Circ:** 6,150 (ctrl). *Continues* Builder NSW, 0310-3544.

ISSN 1031-3249
AT
DD 620.13605
AUSTRALIAN CONCRETE CONSTRUCTION. [Aust. concr. constr.]. (1988)-.
Periodical. English. Six times a year. 42.00Aus$ Australia; 52.00Aus$ Asia and Oceania; 58.00Aus$ other. Intermedia Group Pty Ltd, 747 Darling Street, Rozelle New South Wales, 2039 Australia. **Tel** 011 61 2 8184111. **ED** Mark Cherrington. **Ad Acc. Circ:** 11,500 (ctrl).

LC TH437 .A95
DD 624/.0285
ISSN 0926-5805
NE
CCC
CODEN AUCOES
Pr Rev.
AUTOMATION IN CONSTRUCTION.
[Autom. constr.]. Vol. 1, No. 1 (May 1992)-. Academic Scholarly Publication. English. Six times a year. $360.00. Elsevier Science Publishers BV, PO Box 211, 1000 AE Amsterdam Netherlands. **Tel** 011 31 20 4853641, 011 31 20 4853642, FAX 011 31 20 4853598. **(Subscription address:** Elsevier Science BV / Maryland, PO Box 64698, Baltimore MD 21264.) available on an online database from Elsevier Electronic Subscriptions (EES). Documents available from Ask*IEEE.
Ind/Abst INSPEC (1992-).

LC HD9715.C5 A93
ISSN 0187-4950
MX
AVANCE DE INFORMACION ECONOMICA. INDUSTRIA DE LA CONSTRUCCION. **Added/Corp** Instituto Nacional de Estadistica, Geografia e Informatica (Mexico). **VFOAT** Industria de la Construccion; Avance de Informacion Economica. Encuesta Trimestral Sobre la Industria de la Construccion; Encuesta Trimestral Sobre la Industria de la Construccion. (19??)-. Spanish. Four times a year. $25.81. INEGI / Instituto Nacional de Estadistica, Geografia e Informatica, Avenida Patriotismo 711 Segundo Piso, 03730 Mexico DF Mexico. **Tel** 011 52 5 5639935, 011 52 5 5988935, FAX 011 52 55987941. **(Subscription address:** INEGI / Instituto Nacional de Estadistica, Geografia e Informatica, Avenida Heroe de Nacozari 2301 Sur, Fracc. Jardines del Parque, CP 20270, Aguascalientes Mexico. **Tel** 011 52 49 182998.) *Continues* Avance de Informacion Economica. Construccion.

ISSN 0728-4586
AT
DD 526.9060944
AZIMUTH. [Azimuth]. (1981)-. Periodical. English. Eleven times a year. 85.00Aus$. Institute of Surveyors / NSW Inc., 363 Pitt Street, Sydney NSW 2000 Australia. **Tel** 011 61 2 2642076. **ED** J. Abbott. **Ad Acc, Adv Mgr:** R. Phillips. **Circ:** 1,300. *Continues* N.S.W. Surveyors' Monthly Bulletin, 0726-4798.

LC TH12 .B18
DD 690/.025/42
UK
B & CJ BUILDING DIRECTORY. VFOAT
Building Directory. VAT B and CJ Building Directory. (1969)-. Directory. English.

LC TH
DD 690
ISSN 0968-9079
UK
BARBOUR INDEX BUILDING PRODUCT COMPENDIUM. [Barbour Index build. prod. compend.]. (198?)-. English. One time a year. Barbour Index PLC, New Lodge Drift Road, Windsor Berkshire SL4 4RQ United Kingdom. **Tel** 011 44 1344 884121, FAX 011 44 1344 884113. **Bk Rev**, (Qty: 2-3). **Ad Acc, Adv Mgr:** Barry Nutter. **Acid Free. Circ:** 21,000 (ctrl). Documents available from the publisher. *Continues* Barbour Compendium. Building Products, 0260-9169.
Desc: This publication is a building product reference source for buyers and specifiers in the construction industry. Contains a listing of 6,000 UK building product manufacturers and features 1,400 product ranges.

FR
BAREME DES COEFFICIENTS. SERIES 80. (19??)-. French. Twelve times a year. Editions Charles Massin & Cie, 16 18 rue de l'Amiral Mouchez, 75686 Paris Cedex 14 France. **Tel** 011 33 1 45654848.

FR
BAREME DES COEFFICIENTS. SERIES 85. (19??)-. French. Twelve times a year. Editions Charles Massin & Cie, 16 18 rue de l'Amiral Mouchez, 75686 Paris Cedex 14 France. **Tel** 011 33 1 45654848.

ISSN 1148-8859
FR
UDC 69
BATI HIGH TECH MAGAZINE. (1990)-.
Periodical. French. Eight times a year. 750.00F France; 850.00F airmail; 980.00F airmail. SEPP / Societe de Edition & de Publicites Professionnelles, 13 rue Ganneron, 75018 Paris France. **Tel** 011 33 1 42932243, FAX 011 33 1 42875024.

LC TH2 .B27
ISSN 0395-9376
FR
SUSPENDED
BATIMENT, BATIR, LE. [Batim.-batir]. No. 1- Sept. 1975-Suspended Jan. (1984). Periodical. French. Twelve times a year. 150.00. Le Batiment SA, 6 rue Paul-Valery, 75116 CCP 1078-10 Paris France. *Formed by the union of* Batiment and Batir.
Ind/Abst GeoRef; Int. Civil Eng. Abstr.; Soft. Abstr. Eng.

SZ
BAU. (19??)-. German. Twelve times a year. 87.00F Switzerland; 130.00F other. Editions Chantiers Monreux SA, Heinrichstr 17, CH-8031 Zurich Switzerland.

LC TH3 .B23
ISSN 0340-0271
GW
BAUANALYSIS. (1973)-. Periodical. German. 20.00. Verlag Moderne Industrie, Justus von Liebigstrasse 1, D-86899 Landsberg Lech Germany. **Tel** 011 49 8191 125453.

GW
BAUEN / ALTHAUS MODERNISIERUNG. (19??)-. Periodical. German. Six times a year. DM39.00 Germany; DM45.00 other. Fachschriften Verlag GmbH, Hoehenstrasse 17, D-70736 Fellbach Germany. **Tel** 011 49 711 5206256.

LC TH
DD 690
ISSN 0171-7952
GW
BAUEN FUER DIE LANDWIRTSCHAFT (ZEITSCHRIFT). (BAUEN FUER DIE LANDWIRTSCHAFT.). [Bauen Landwirtsch.]. Vol. 14, No. 2 (Sept. 1977)-. Trade Publication. German. Three times a year. DM40.00. Beton Verlag GmbH, Dusseldorferstr 8, Postfach 11034, D-40501 Dusseldorf Germany. **Tel** 0211 550090, FAX 0211 5500955. **ED** Loerg Brandt. **Bk Rev. Ad Acc. Circ:** 6,500. *Continues* Beton-Landbau.
Ind/Abst AGRICOLA.

LC TA681 .B29
DD 624.1/834
ISSN 0930-0252
GW
BAUEN IN BETON. VFOAT Construire en Beton. Vol. 1 (1986)-. Periodical. French (German). Vszkgf, Talstrasse 83, CH-8001 Zurich Switzerland.

GW
BAUEN MIT HOLZ. (1899)-. Trade Publication. German. One time a year. $147.39. Bruderverlag, Bismarckstr 21, D-76133 Karlsruhe Germany. **Tel** 011 49 721 23014, FAX 011 49 721 29396. **ED** Klaus Fritzen. Index available. **Bk Rev. Ad Acc. Circ:** 6,200 (ctrl).
Desc: Information for architects, master carpenters and civil engineers on outstanding projects, bimachinery, market innovations, research work, company management, etc.
Ind/Abst Int. Civil Eng. Abstr.; Soft. Abstr. Eng.

LC TH4805 .B37
GW
BAUEN + [I.E. UND] FERTIGHAUS.
(19??)-. Periodical. German. Six times a year. DM45.00 Germany; DM48.00 other. Fachschriften Verlag GmbH, Hoehenstrasse 17, D-70736 Fellbach Germany. **Tel** 011 49 711 5206256. **ED** Ottmar Strebel. **Bk Rev. Ad Acc.** ctrl circ.

LC TA3 .H33
ISSN 0005-6650
GW
CCC
CODEN BANGAS
BAUINGENIEUR, DER. See Engineering-Civil Engineering.

SZ
TITLE CHANGE
BAUKADER : AKTUELLES BAUEN = CONSTRUCTION ACTUELLE. See Architecture.

LC HA1173 .A27 HD9715.A9 A9
DD 314.36 S 338.4/7624/09436021
AU
BAUSTATISTIK. GERATEBESTAND IM HOCH- U. TIEFBAU AM ... . See Building and Construction-Abstracting, Bibliographies and Statistics.

LC HD9715.G3 B28
DD 338.4/7691/0943
ISSN 0343-5903
GW
BAUSTOFF UMSCHAU. (19??)-. Periodical. German. Nine times a year. Baader Verlag, Postfach 1220, 72522 Muensingen Germany. **Ad Acc. Circ:** 7,400.

ISSN 0323-4886
SZ
CODEN BIDABH
BAUSTOFFINDUSTRIE. AUSGABE A : PRIMARBAUSTOFFE. (1972)-. Academic Scholarly Publication. German. Six times a year. Deutscher Judo Verband, Redaktion Ippon Segewaldweg 40, D-12557 Berlin Germany. **Tel** 011 49 711 210770, telex 051 678. Documents available from CASDDS. *Supersedes in part* Baustoffindustrie.
Ind/Abst Chem. Abstr.; Coal Abstr.

ISSN 0170-9267
GW
CCC
CODEN BABADL
BAUTENSCHUTZ + BAUSANIERUNG.
[Bautenschutz + Bausanier.]. **Added/Corp** Wissenschaftlich-Technischer Arbeitskreis fuer Denkmalpflege und Bauwerksanierung. VFOAT Bautenschutz & Bausanierung; Bautenschutz und Bausanierung. (1978)-. Trade Publication. German. Eight times a year. $133.57. Verlagsgesellschaft Rudolf Mueller, Postfach 410949, D-50869 Cologne Germany. **Tel** 011 44 221 5497213, FAX 011 44 221 5497326. Documents available from CASDDS.
Ind/Abst Chem. Abstr.; Curr. Cit.; Int. Civil Eng. Abstr.

ISSN 0005-6847
GW
CCC
BAUVERWALTUNG. See Architecture.

LC TH435 .I13a
GW
BAUVORAUSSCHAETZUNG. Main/Corp
Ifo-Institut fuer Wirtschaftsforschung. Abteilung Bau- und Wohnungswirtschaft. (19??)-. German. One time a year. DM2000.00 Issue Westdeutschland; DM3500 Issue Regionen. Ifo-Institut fuer Wirtschaftsforschung, Poschingerstrasse 5, D-81679 Munich Germany. **Tel** (089)9224-0, FAX (089)985369, telex 5-22269. **ED** V. Russig, T. Goerhely. **Circ:** 200 (ctrl).
Desc: Contains forecasts of cyclical and tendency development.

LC HA1320.B2 A32 HD9715G3
GW
BAUWIRTSCHAFT, DIE. Main/Corp
Statistisches Landesamt Baden-Wuerttemberg. (1969/1970)-. Trade Publication. German. Eighteen times a year. $350.05. Bauverlag GmbH, Postfach 1460, D-65173 Wiesbaden Germany. **Tel** 011 49 6123 7000, FAX 011 49 6123 700122.
Desc: Publication providing information on the construction industry.
Ind/Abst Energy Res. Abstr. (Nov. 1978-); Infomat Int. Bus.; Int. Civil Eng. Abstr.; Soft. Abstr. Eng.

LC HD9715.G3 B3
ISSN 0341-3810
GW
BAUWIRTSCHAFT (HAUPTVERBAND DER DEUTSCHEN BAUINDUSTRIE).
(BAUWIRTSCHAFT : BW.). **Added/Corp** Hauptverband der Deutschen Bauindustrie. Bundesverband Steine und Erden. VFOAT BW : Bauwirtschaft. (Sept. 1947)-. Trade Publication. German. Twelve times a year. $261.77. Bauverlag GmbH, Postfach 1460, D-65173 Wiesbaden Germany. **Tel** 011 49 6123 7000, FAX 011 49 6123 700122. **ED** Martin A. Schmitt. **Bk Rev. Ad Acc. Circ:** 6,000 (ctrl).
Desc: Journal providing information on the building materials industry and the construction industry.

LC HA1320.N6 A32 HD9715.G3 G33
DD 314.3/55 S 338.4/7/690094355
GW
BAUWIRTSCHAFT UND BAUTATIGKEIT IN NORDRHEIN-WESTFALEN. See Building and Construction-Abstracting, Bibliographies and Statistics.

LC HD9715.G3 B34
ISSN 0721-6173
GW
BAUWIRTSCHAFTLICHE INFORMATIONEN / BETRIEBSWIRTSCHAFTLICHES INSTITUT DER WESTDEUTSCHEN BAUINDUSTRIE. Added/Corp
Betriebswirtschaftliches Institut der Westdeutschen Bauindustrie Dusseldorf. (1971)-. Proceedings. German. One time a year. Betriebswirtschaftliches Institut der Bauindustrie, Schillerstrasse 33, Dusseldorf Germany. **Tel** 0211 6703 0, FAX 0211 6703 282. Index available. cum. index. **Ad Acc, Adv Mgr:** Elvira Bodenmuller. **Circ:** 2,000 (ctrl).

ISSN 0005-6871
GW
BAUZEITUNG. [Bauzeitung]. Added/Corp
Germany (East). Ministerium fuer Bauwesen. Vol. 1 (1946)-. Periodical. German. Ten times a year. Verlag Fuer Bauwesen GmbH, AM Friedrichshain 22, D-10407 Berlin Germany. **Tel** 011 49 30 4287241. Documents available from Article Express International.
Ind/Abst Bioeng. Abstr.; Ei Page One; Eng. Index Annu.; Int. Civil Eng. Abstr.; Saf. Health Work; Soft. Abstr. Eng.

ISSN 0165-2540
NE
UDC 691
BEHEER EN ONDERHOUD. [Beheer onderh.].
(1975)-. Periodical. Dutch. Twelve times a year. Fl1377.50. Misset Uitgeverij BV / Doetinchem, Postbus 4, 7000 BA Doetinchem Netherlands. **Tel** 011 31 8340 49911, 011 31 8340 49562, FAX 011 31 8340 43839, 011 31 8340 40515. Index available. cum. index. ctrl circ.

LC HD9745.G7 B46 **ISSN** 0954-8548
DD 683/.029/441 UK

BENN'S GUIDE. **Added/Corp** Benn Business Information Services. 81st Ed. (1989)-. English. One time a year. £42.00 UK; £52.00 other. Miller Freeman Technical Ltd., Riverbank House, Angel Lane, Tonbridge Kent TN9 1SE United Kingdom. **Tel** 011 44 1732 362666, FAX 011 44 1732 770483, telex 95454 BBIS. **ED** Betty Chant. **Circ:** 1,500. ***Continues*** *Benn's Hardware & DIY Buyers' Guide.*
Desc: The most widely used information source in the fragmented industries of manufacturing, importing, distributing, wholesaling and retailing hardware products, housewares and gifts, do-it-yourself tools or professional instruments and items for the garden from furniture to seeds.

ISSN 0005-8866
GW
UDC 71 **CCC**
CODEN 69

BERATENDE INGENIEURE. **VFOAT** Beratende Ingenieur. (1947)-. Periodical. German. Twelve times a year. DM198.00. Springer-Verlag GmbH & Company KG, Heidelberger Platz 3, D-14197 Berlin Germany. **Tel** 011 49 30 8207223, FAX 011 49 30 8214091, telex 183 319 SPBLN D. **(Subscription address:** Springer-Verlag New York Inc. / North America, PO Box 2485, Journal Fulfillment, Secaucus NJ 07096. **Tel** (201)348-4033, (800)777-4643, FAX (201)348-4505.**)**

LC TH435 .B487 **ISSN** 0278-2146
DD 692/.5/0977 US

BERGER BUILDING & DESIGN COST FILE. UNIT PRICES. CENTRAL EDITION, THE. (THE ... BERGER BUILDING & DESIGN COST FILE. UNIT PRICES.). **VFOAT** Berger Building and Design Cost File. Unit Prices; Building & Design Cost File. Unit Prices. **VAT** Berger Building and Design Cost File. Unit Prices. Central Edition. (1981)-. English. One time a year. $34.95. Van Nostrand Reinhold Company Inc., 115 5th Avenue, New York NY 10003. **Tel** (212)254-3232, FAX (212)673-1239, telex 272562.

LC TH435 .B4873 **ISSN** 0732-4685
DD 692/.5/0975 US

BERGER BUILDING & DESIGN COST FILE. UNIT PRICES. SOUTHERN EDITION, THE. (THE ... BERGER BUILDING & DESIGN COST FILE. UNIT PRICES.). **VFOAT** Berger Building and Design Cost File. Unit Prices; Berger Building Cost File, Southern Edition. 1981-. English. One time a year. Van Nostrand Reinhold Company Inc., 115 5th Avenue, New York NY 10003. **Tel** (212)254-3232, FAX (212)673-1239, telex 272562. ***Formed by the union of*** *Berger Building Cost File. Unit Prices (Southern Edition), 0272-7676* ***and*** *Berger Design Cost File. Unit Prices.*

LC TH435 .B4874 **ISSN** 0278-2065
DD 692/.5/0978 US

BERGER BUILDING & DESIGN COST FILE. UNIT PRICES. WESTERN EDITION, THE. (THE ... BERGER BUILDING & DESIGN COST FILE. UNIT PRICES.). **VFOAT** Berger Building and Design Cost File. Unit Prices. **VAT** Berger Building and Design Cost File. Unit Prices. Western Edition. 1981-. Periodical. English. One time a year. $34.95. Van Nostrand Reinhold Company Inc., 115 5th Avenue, New York NY 10003. **Tel** (212)254-3232, FAX (212)673-1239, telex 272562.

LC TH435 .M147C **ISSN** 0272-5401
DD 692/.5/0977 US

BERGER BUILDING COST FILE, UNIT PRICES. CENTRAL EDITION, THE. (BERGER BUILDING COST FILE, UNIT PRICES.). **Main/Corp** Berger & Associates Cost Consultants. 1980-. English. One time a year. Van Nostrand Reinhold Company Inc., 115 5th Avenue, New York NY 10003. **Tel** (212)254-3232, FAX (212)673-1239, telex 272562. ***Continues*** *McKee-Berger-Mansueto. Building Cost File.*

LC TH435 .B484A **ISSN** 0271-3128
DD 338.4/369/0078 US

BERGER BUILDING COST FILE, UNIT PRICES. WESTERN EDITION. (BERGER BUILDING COST FILE, UNIT PRICES.). **Main/Corp** Berger & Associates Cost Consultants. (19??)-. English. Van Nostrand Reinhold Company Inc., 115 5th Avenue, New York NY 10003. **Tel** (212)254-3232, FAX (212)673-1239, telex 272562.

ISSN 0940-3825
GW
UDC 33

BERLIN-BRANDENBURGISCHE BAUWIRTSCHAFT. **VFOAT** BBW. Berlin-Brandenburgische Bauwirtschaft. (1991)-. Trade Publication. German. Twenty-four times a year. DM169.00 Germany; DM218.00 other. Bauverlag GmbH, Postfach 1460, D-65173 Wiesbaden Germany. **Tel** 011 49 6123 7000, FAX 011 49 6123 700122. ***Continues*** *Berliner Bauwirtschaft, 0405-5535.*

LC HD9715.H8 H83E **ISSN** 0139-3510
HU

BERUHAZASI, EPITOIPARI, LAKASEPITESI ZSEBKONYV. **Main/Corp** Hungary. Kozponti Statisztikai Hivatal. Beruhazasies Epitoipari Statisztikai Foosztaly. Hungarian. One time a year. 27.00ft. Statisztikai Kiado Vallalat, PO Box 99, H-1033 Budapest 3 Hungary. **Tel** 803-311, telex 22-6699-SKV-H. **Circ:** 1,500.
Desc: Statistical pocket-book on investments, construction and home-building of Hungary.

ISSN 0005-9846
GW
CCC
CODEN BTONAH

BETON. [Beton]. Vol. 7, No. 1 (Jan. 1957)-. Trade Publication. German. Twelve times a year. DM330.00. Beton-Verlag GmbH, Postfach 110134, D-40501 Duesseldorf Germany. **Tel** 011 49 211 550090. **Bk Rev. Ad Acc.** ***Continues*** *Beton-Zement-Markt.*
Ind/Abst Concr. Abstr.; Curr. Cit.; Ei Page One; EMBASE; Energy Res. Abstr. (Jan. 1972-); Int. Civil Eng. Abstr.; Soft. Abstr. Eng.

LC TA680 .B38 **ISSN** 0005-9889
RU
CODEN BTZBA2

BETON I ZELEZOBETON. (BETON I ZHELEZOBETON; NAUCHNO-TEKHNICHESKII I PROIZVODSTVENN I ZHURNAD.). [Beton zelezobeton]. **Added/Corp** Soviet Union. Gosudarstvennyi Komitet po Delam Stroitelstva. (1955)-. Academic Scholarly Publication. Russian. Six times a year. $129.95. **(Subscription address:** East View Publications Inc., 3020 Harbor Lane North, Suite 110, Minneapolis MN 55447. **Tel** (800)477-1005, (612)550-0961, FAX (612)559-2931.**)** Index available. **Bk Rev.** Documents available from Article Express International, CASDDS.
Ind/Abst Bioeng. Abstr.; Ceram. Abstr.; Chem. Abstr.; Concr. Abstr.; Ei Page One; Eng. Index Annu.; Int. Civil Eng. Abstr.; Soft. Abstr. Eng.

BE

BETON : REVUE DU BETON PREFABRIQUE. (19??)-. French (Dutch). Six times a year. 800.00F Belgium; 1200.00F other. Federation de l'Industrie du Beton, Blv Aug Reyerslaan 207-209, 1040 Brussels Belgium. **Tel** 32 2 7 35 8015, FAX 32 2 734 77 95. **ED** W. Simons. Index available. cum. index. **Bk Rev. Ad Acc, Adv Mgr:** M.R. Roisin, **Tel** 32/2-734-7795. Full Page (B&W) 20.500F. Full Page (Color) 49.00F. **Circ:** 8,500.
Desc: All aspects related to the precast concrete industry.

LC TA680 .B45 **ISSN** 0005-9900
GW
CCC
CODEN BESTAI

BETON- UND STAHLBETONBAU. [Beton-Stahlbetonbau]. **Added/Corp** Deutscher Beton- Verein (Wiesbaden Germany). Vol. 42, No. 1/2 (Jan. 1943)-. Academic Scholarly Publication. German. Twelve times a year. $323.00. Wilhelm Ernst & Sohn, Muehlenstr 33 34 170, D-13187 Berlin Germany. **Tel** 011 49 30 47889200. **(Subscription address:** VCH Publishers Inc., 303 Northwest 12th Avenue, Journals Department, Deerfield FL 33442. **Tel** (800)367-8249, (305)428-5566.**)** Documents available from Article Express International. ***Continues*** *Beton und Eisen.*
Ind/Abst Bioeng. Abstr.; Civ. Struct. Eng. Abstr.; Concr. Abstr.; Ei Page One; EMBASE; Energy Res. Abstr.; Eng. Index Annu.; Highw. Res. Abstr.; Int. Civil Eng. Abstr.; Mater. Sci. Eng. Abstr.; Soft. Abstr. Eng.

SW

BETONG. **Main/Corp** Swedish Concrete Association. **VFOAT** Concrete. (1991)-. Trade Publication. Swedish. Four times a year. Kr250.00. Byggfoerlaget, PO Box 5456, S-114 81 Stockholm Sweden. **Tel** 011 46 8 6635100, FAX 011 46 8 6677075, telex 14579 BYGGF S.

LC TH1491 .B47 **ISSN** 0373-4331
GW
CCC
CODEN BWFTAB

BETONWERK + [I.E. UND] FERTIGTEIL-TECHNIK / CONCRETE PRECASTING PLANT AND TECHNOLOGY. [Betonwerk + Fertigteil-Tech.]. **Added/Corp** Bundesverband Deutsche Beton- und Fertigteilindustrie. **VFOAT** Concrete Precasting Plant and Technology; Betonwerk und Fertigteil-Technik. Concrete Precasting Plant and Technology. Vol. 38, No. 1 (1972)-. Trade Publication. English (German). Twelve times a year. $280.96. Bauverlag GmbH, Postfach 1460, D-65173 Wiesbaden Germany. **Tel** 011 49 6123 7000, FAX 011 49 6123 700122. Documents available from CASDDS. ***Continues*** *Betonstein-Zeitung.*
Desc: Provides information on precast concrete and concrete plants.
Ind/Abst Chem. Abstr.; Concr. Abstr.; Curr. Cit.; Ei Page One; EMBASE; Int. Civil Eng. Abstr.; Saf. Health Work; Soft. Abstr. Eng.

ISSN 0744-530X
US

BETTER BUILDINGS. Vol. 1, No. 1 (Spring 1982)-. Trade Publication. English. Nine times a year. $50.00. Real Estate Forum, 111 8th Avenue, Suite 1511, New York NY 10011-5201. **Tel** (212)929-6900. **ED** John Salustri. **Ad Acc, Adv Mgr:** J. Schein, **Tel** same as publisher.
Ind/Abst Avery Index Archit. Period. Suppl. Colum. Univ. (Aug. 1989).

ISSN 8750-3077
US

BILDOR NEWS. **Added/Corp** Northeast Florida Builders Association. (19??)-. Periodical. English. Twelve times a year. Bildor News, PO Box 17339, Jacksonville FL 32245-7339.

LC NA5 .B55
PO

BINARIO. **See** Architecture.

LC TH13.P4 B58
DD 624/.029/47482 US

BLUE BOOK BUILDING AND CONSTRUCTION (EASTERN PENNSYLVANIA, SOUTHERN NEW JERSEY, DELAWARE ED.). (THE BLUE BOOK BUILDING AND CONSTRUCTION.). **VFOAT** Building and Construction. (1989)-. English. One time a year. Contractors Register Inc, Route 6, Box 500, Jefferson Valley NY 10535. **Tel** (914)245-0200. ***Continues*** *Blue Book Contractors Register (Eastern Pennsylvania, Southern New Jersey, Delaware Ed.).*

LC TA12 .B57 **ISSN** 1047-5443
DD 624/.029/4759 US

BLUE BOOK BUILDING AND CONSTRUCTION (FLORIDA ED.). (THE BLUE BOOK BUILDING AND CONSTRUCTION.). [Blue book build. constr.]. **VFOAT** Building and Construction. (1989)-. Trade Publication. English. One time a year. Free on request. Contractors Register Inc, Route 6, Box 500, Jefferson Valley NY 10535. **Tel** (914)245-0200. ***Continues*** *Blue Book Contractors Register (Florida Ed.), 0748-1667.*
Desc: Contains information on contractors and the construction industry.

US

BLUE BOOK BUILDING AND CONSTRUCTION. NEW YORK, THE. **VFOAT** New York; Building and Construction. (1992)-. English. Contractors Register Inc, Route 6, Box 500, Jefferson Valley NY 10535. **Tel** (914)245-0200. ***Continues in part*** *Blue Book Building and Construction. Metropolitan New York, Northern & Central New Jersey.*

LC NA705 .B54 **ISSN** 0742-0552
DD 720/.973 US

BLUEPRINTS - NATIONAL BUILDING MUSEUM (U.S.). **See** Architecture.

ISSN 0261-2933
DD 690.24 UK

BMCIS BUILDING MAINTENANCE PRICE BOOK. [BMCIS build. maint. price book]. **VFOAT** Building Maintenance Cost Information Service Building Maintenance Price book; Building Maintenance Price Book. (1980)-. English. One time a year. £32.50. Building Maintenance Information Ltd, 85-87 Clarence Street, Kingston upon Thames, Surrey KT1 1RB United Kingdom. **Tel** 011 44 181 5467555, FAX 011 44 181 5471238. Index available. **Ad Acc. Circ:** 3,000.
Desc: Building maintenance price book.

ISSN 0934-1773
GW

BMK. BAUEN MIT KUNSTSTOFFEN. [BmK, Bau. Kunstst.]. **VFOAT** Bauen mit Kunststoffen. (1986)-. Periodical. German. Six times a year. $69.09. IBK Inst Bauen Kunststoffen, Osannstrasse 37, W 6100 Darmstadt F R, Germany. **Tel** 11 49 6151 48097. ***Continues*** *Kunststoffe im Bau (1977), 0343-3129.*

LC TH3 .B24 **ISSN** 0942-1173
GW

BMT : BAUMASCHINENTECHNIK. **Added/Corp** Hauptverband der Deutschen Bauindustrie. Geraeteausschuss. **VFOAT** Baumaschinentechnik; Baumaschine + Bautechnik; Baumaschine und Bautechnik. (1991)-. Trade Publication. German (summaries and/or abstracts in English and French). Six times a year. $214.17. Bauverlag GmbH, Postfach 1460, D-65173 Wiesbaden Germany. **Tel** 011 49 6123 7000, FAX 011 49 6123 700122. ***Continues*** *Bau-Maschine und Bau-Technik, 0005-6693.*
Desc: Provides information on construction equipment commonly used in the building industries.
Ind/Abst Geotech. Abstr.; Int. Civil Eng. Abstr.

LC KF5701 .B8
DD 343/.73/078 US

BOCA BASIC HOUSING-PROPERTY MAINTENANCE CODE, THE. **See** Law.

Building and Construction

LC KF5701.A73 B8   ISSN 0897-0068
US
BOCA NATIONAL BUILDING CODE, THE. [BOCA natl. build. code]. **Main/Corp** Building Officials and Code Administrators International. **VFOAT** National Building Code. **VAT** Building Officials and Code Administrators National Building Code. 10th Edition (1987)-. English. Irregular (Every three years). $59.00. BOCA International, 4051 West Flossmoore Road, Country Club Hills IL 60478. **Tel** (708)799-2300, FAX (708)799-4981. **Continues** Building Officials and Code Administrators International. BOCA Basic/National Building Code.

DD 338.4/369052/0971   ISSN 0225-9389
CN
BOECKH BUILDING COST GUIDE. COMMERCIAL. [Boeckh bldg. cost guide, Commer.]. (1976)-. English. One time a year. $27.00. General Appraisal Corp, 310 Front Street West 8th Floor, Toronto Ontario M5V 3B5 Canada. **Tel** (416)593-4050. **Circ:** 500 (ctrl).
   Desc: General estimates of construction costs for commercial building types, such as offices, retail, etc.

DD 338.4/369/00971   ISSN 0225-9397
CN
BOECKH BUILDING COST GUIDE. INSTITUTIONAL. [Boeckh bldg. cost guide, Inst.]. (1976)-. English. One time a year. $27.00. American Appraisals Association Inc., Boeckh Customer Services, PO Box 664, Milwaukee WI 53201. **Tel** (800)558-8650. **Circ:** 300 (ctrl).
   Desc: General estimates of Canadian construction costs for institutional building types, such as schools, churches, etc.

DD 338.4/369054/0971   ISSN 0225-9400
CN
BOECKH BUILDING COST GUIDE. LIGHT INDUSTRIAL. [Boeckh bldg. cost guide, Light ind.]. (1976)-. English. One time a year. $27.00. General Appraisal Corp, 310 Front Street West 8th Floor, Toronto Ontario M5V 3B5 Canada. **Tel** (416)593-4050. **Circ:** 400 (ctrl).
   Desc: General estimates of Canadian construction costs for light industrial building types such as manufacturing, warehouses, etc.

DD 338.4/369083/0971   ISSN 0225-9419
CN
BOECKH BUILDING COST GUIDE. RESIDENTIAL. [Boeckh bldg. cost guide, Resid.]. (1976)-. English. One time a year. $27.00. General Appraisal Corp, 310 Front Street West 8th Floor, Toronto Ontario M5V 3B5 Canada. **Tel** (416)593-4050. **Circ:** 800 (ctrl).
   Desc: General estimates of Canadian construction costs for residential buildings.

ISSN 0090-8681
US
BOECKH BUILDING COST INDEX NUMBERS. Added/Corp American Appraisal Company. Boeckh Division. (Jan./Feb. 1969)-. Periodical. English. Six times a year. American Appraisal Associates Inc, 525 East Michigan Street, PO Box 664, Milwaukee WI 53201. **Tel** (414)271-7240. **Continues** Building Costs.

CK
BOLETIN DE PRECIOS. VFOAT Guia Lec de la Construccion. Periodical. Spanish. Legis LTDA, Apartado Aereo 98 888, Bogota Colombia. **Tel** 011 57 1 2632530, 011 57 1 2630718.

ISSN 0210-1947
SP
UDC 69
Pr Rev.
BOLETIN ECONOMICO DE LA CONSTRUCCION (1956). [Bol. econ. constr. 1956]. (1956)-. Periodical. Spanish. Four times a year (Feb., May, Aug, Nov.). $65.70. Boletin Economico de la Construccion, Suscripcion Emancipacion 28-30, 08022 Barcelona Spain. **Tel** 011 34 3 211-2121, FAX 011 34 3 211 2204. Index available. cum. index. **Bk Rev. Ad Acc, Adv Mgr:** J. L. Balcells Canela. **Circ:** 5,500.
Continues Nota de Precios del Ramo de la Construccion (1952), 0211-5328.
   Desc: News and information of materials, prices and other related fields in the construction business.

IT
BOLLETTINO DEGLI INGEGNERI. (19??)-. Italian. Ten times a year. L190.000 Italy; L270.000 other. Ad Agency, Lungarno Guicciardini 1, 50125 Florence Italy. **Tel** 011 39 55 211345.

NE
BOUKWOSTEN. Dutch. Eleven times a year. Fl1290.00 Netherlands. Misset Uitgeverij BV / Doetinchem, Postbus 4, 7000 BA Doetinchem Netherlands. **Tel** 011 31 8340 49911, 011 31 8340 49562, FAX 011 31 8340 43839, 011 31 8340 40515. Index available. cum. index. ctrl circ.

ISSN 0366-2330
NE
BOUW. [Bouw]. Vol. 1 (1946)-. Periodical. Dutch. Twenty-five times a year (publishes bi-weekly except in July with only one issue). Fl.225.00. Misset Uitgeverij BV / Doetinchem, Postbus 4, 7000 BA Doetinchem Netherlands. **Tel** 011 31 8340 49911, 011 31 8340 49562, FAX 011 31 8340 43839, 011 31 8340 40515. **ED** Stichting Bouw. **Bk Rev. Ad Acc. Circ:** 5,973.
   Desc: Reviews in the field of building in the Netherlands.
Ind/Abst Archit. Period. Index (1946-); Avery Index Archit. Period. Suppl. Colum. Univ. (1989-); Energy Res. Abstr. (Feb. 1980-); Int. Civil Eng. Abstr.; Saf. Health Work; Soft. Abstr. Eng.

ISSN 0006-8330
NE
UDC 69
BOUWBELANGEN. [Bouwbelanger]. **Added/Corp** Gemeen Verbond Bouwbedrijf. (1935)-. Trade Publication. Dutch. One time a week. $301.47. Ten Hagen and Stam BV, Postbus 34, 2501 AG The Hague Netherlands. **Tel** 011 31 70 3045700.

BE
Pr Rev.
BOUWKRONIEK : WEEKBLAD VOOR DE BOUW EN INDUSTRIE. (19??)-. Trade Publication. Dutch (Dutch). One time a week. 8.550F Belgium; $285.00 other. NV de Bouwkroniek, Zennestraat 37, 1000 Brussels Belgium. **Tel** 011 32 2 5138295, FAX 011 32 2 5117015. **ED** Leo Van Hoorick. **Bk Rev. Ad Acc, Adv Mgr:** Jan Van Hoorick, **Tel** (02)513-82-95. Full Page (Color) 2.259F. Half Page (Color) 1.445F. **Acid Free. Circ:** 12,500.
   Desc: A specialized weekly for the construction industry. Includes a weekly review of all public tenders in Belgium and the European Economic Community.

ISSN 0166-641X
NE
UDC 69
BOUWMARKT ROTTERDAM. See Industry and Production.

ISSN 0165-1528
NE
BOUWRECHT. See Law.

ISSN 0165-6457
NE
UDC 338
BOUWTIPS. ED. GRON, FRIESLAND, DRENTHE. (BOUWTIPS.). [Bouwtips, A, Ed. Gron Friesland Drenthe]. (1958)-. Periodical. Dutch. One time a week. Fl335.00. Studio Pit Bouwtips BV, Postbus 64, 7800 AB Emmen Netherlands. **Tel** 011 31 05910 11874.

ISSN 0165-6600
NE
UDC 338
BOUWTIPS. ED. NOORD-BRABANT, LIMBURG, ZEELAND. (BOUWTIPS.). [Bouwtips, D, Ed. Noord-Brabant Limbg. Zeel.]. (1958)-. Periodical. Dutch. One time a week. $354.14. Studio Pit Bouwtips BV, Postbus 64, 7800 AB Emmen Netherlands. **Tel** 011 31 05910 11874.

ISSN 0165-6554
NE
UDC 338
BOUWTIPS. ED. NOORD-HOLLAND EN ZUID-HOLLAND. (BOUWTIPS.). [Bouwtips, Ed. Noord-Holl. Zuid-Holl.]. (1958)-. Periodical. Dutch. One time a week. $354.14. Studio Pit Bouwtips BV, Postbus 64, 7800 AB Emmen Netherlands. **Tel** 011 31 05910 11874.

ISSN 0165-6503
NE
UDC 338
BOUWTIPS. ED. OVERIJSSEL, GELDERLAND, UTRECHT. (BOUWTIPS.). [Bouwtips, B, Ed. Overijssel Gelderland Utrecht]. (1958)-. Periodical. Dutch. One time a week. $354.14. Studio Pit Bouwtips BV, Postbus 64, 7800 AB Emmen Netherlands. **Tel** 011 31 05910 11874.

ISSN 0026-5942
NE
UDC 624
Pr Rev.
BOUWWERELD. [Bouwwereld]. (1956)-. Trade Publication. Dutch. Twenty-four times a year. Fl255.00. Misset Uitgeverij BV / Doetinchem, Postbus 4, 7000 BA Doetinchem Netherlands. **Tel** 011 31 8340 49911, 011 31 8340 49562, FAX 011 31 8340 43839, 011 31 8340 40515. Index available. cum. index. **Ad Acc.** ctrl circ.
Continues Vakblad Voor de Bouwbedrijven.

LC TH9111 .B3   ISSN 0006-9116
GW
UDC 614.84
BRANDWACHT. See Fire Prevention.

UK
CODEN BRIPEH
BRE INFORMATION PAPER. Added/Corp Building Research Establishment. **VFOAT** Building Research Establishment Paper. (June 1988)-. Periodical. English. Twelve times a year. $143.75. Building Research Establishment, BRE Bookshop, Garston Watford WD27JR United Kingdom. **Tel** 011 44 1923 664444, FAX 011 44 1923 664400. Documents available from BLDSC.
Continues Information Paper (Building Research Establishment).
Ind/Abst Curr. Cit.; J. Ferrocement.

ISSN 0265-9611
UK
BRE NEWS OF CONSTRUCTION RESEARCH. [BRE news constr. res.]. **Added/Corp** Building Research Establishment. (April 1984)-. Periodical. English. Five times a year. Free. Building Research Establishment, BRE Bookshop, Garston Watford WD27JR United Kingdom. **Tel** 011 44 1923 664444, FAX 011 44 1923 664400. **Circ:** 20,000 (ctrl).
Continues in part BRE News, 0144-8358.
   Desc: Features current projects of Building Research Establishment.
Ind/Abst Avery Index Archit. Period. Suppl. Colum. Univ. (1984-199?); Fluid Abstr., Civil Eng.; Fluid Abstr. Proc. Eng.; FLUIDEX (1984-); J. Ferrocement.

LC TH1301 .B7   ISSN 0307-9325
UK
BRICK BULLETIN. [Brick bull.]. **Added/Corp** National Federation of Clay Industries. Vol. 1 (1947)-. Bulletin. English. Four times a year. £10.00. Brick Development Association, Woodside House Winkfield Windsor, Berkshire SL4 2DX United Kingdom. **Tel** 011 44 1344 885651, FAX 011 44 1344 890129. Index available. cum. index. **Bk Rev. Ad Acc. Circ:** 240,000.
   Desc: Information on bricks and construction.
Ind/Abst Archit. Period. Index (1947-); Int. Civil Eng. Abstr.; Soft. Abstr. Eng. (1947-).

LC TH900 .B67
DD 681/.76   UK
BRITISH CONSTRUCTION EQUIPMENT AND CRANES. VFOAT Material de Construction et des Grues Britanniques; Directory of British Construction Equipment & Cranes. 1982-. Arabic (English, French and Spanish). Every 3 years. Federation of Manufacturers of Construction Equipment and Cranes, 8 Saint Bride Street, London EC4A 4DA United Kingdom. **Continues** British Construction Equipment.

LC NA7238.N6 B76   ISSN 0883-962X
DD 728   US
BROWNSTONER, THE. See Architecture.

UK
BRUSSELS BRIEFING. See Engineering-Civil Engineering.

ISSN 0953-9905
DD 332.3206041   UK
BSA ANNUAL REPORT. (ANNUAL REPORT OF THE BUILDING SOCIETIES ASSOCIATION.). [BSA annu. rep.]. **VFOAT** Building Societies Association Annual Report. (1988)-. English. One time a year. £500.00. Building Societies Association, The Bookshop, 3 Saville Row, London W1X 1AF United Kingdom. **Tel** 011 44 171 4370655, FAX 011 44 171 7346416. **Circ:** 1,500.
Continues Report of the Council - Building Societies Association, 0262-8155.
   Desc: Activities of the association during the year in review.

LC TH4 .B84   ISSN 0324-8674
PL
BUDOWNICTWO ROLNICZE. [Bud. roln.]. Vol. 29, No. 1- Jan. 1977-. Periodical. Polish. Centrala Kolportazu Prasy I Wydawnictw RSW Prasa-Ksiazka-Ruch, Ul Towarowa 28, 00-958 Warszawa Poland.

ISSN 0007-3229
DD 690 720   IE
BUILD; JOURNAL OF THE INDUSTRY. 1 (Jan. 1965)-. Periodical. English. Eleven times a year. $27.69. Build Magazine, 50 Fitzwilliam Square West, Dublin 2 Ireland. **Tel** 011 353 1 764587. **ED** Paddy Smith. **Bk Rev. Ad Acc. Circ:** 4,836 (ctrl). **Continues** Irish Architect and Contractor, 0535-6687.
Ind/Abst Int. Civil Eng. Abstr.; Soft. Abstr. Eng.

ISSN 0110-4381
DD 690   NZ
BUILD (WELLINGTON). [Build Wellingt.]. **VFOAT** Build Branz. (1978)-. Periodical. English. Six times a year (Feb., Apr., June, Aug., Oct., Dec.). $25.79. Building Research Association of New Zealand, Industrial Service Supervisor, Private Bag, Porirua New Zealand. **Tel** 011 64 4 357600, FAX 011 64 4 356070.

LC TH13.2.C2 C35   ISSN 0227-0595
DD 690/.029/471   CN
BUILDCORE INDEX. See Architecture.

Building and Construction

ISSN 0273-6225
US
BUILDER DEVELOPER WEST. Vol. 3, No. 11 (Sept. 1980)-. Periodical. English. Twelve times a year. $35.00. BDA News Inc, 440 South Anaheim Boulevard, Anaheim CA 92805. **Tel** (714)956-2680. **ED** Martin Barsky. **Ad Acc. Circ:** 24,351. **Continues** BDA News.

LC TH13.2.H6 H6
DD 690/.025/5125
HK
BUILDER DIRECTORY, HONG KONG. **VFOAT** Hong Kong Builder Directory. (19??)-. Directory. English (Chinese). One time a year. $85.00. Far East Trade Press Ltd., BL C 10 F Seaview E, 2 8 Watson, North Point Hong Kong. **Tel** 011 852 25668381, FAX 011 852 25710780, telex 83434. **ED** Kenneth Ho Kwik-yiu. **Ad Acc. Circ:** 6,000.
Desc: A complete guide to the building and conservation industry in Hong Kong.

LC HD9715.U5 B76
ISSN 0744-1193
DD 338.4/76908/0973
US
BUILDER (WASHINGTON, D.C. : 1981). (BUILDER.). [Builder]. **Added/Corp** National Association of Home Builders (U.S.). **VFOAT** NAHB Builder. (1981)-. Trade Publication. English. Twelve times a year. $29.95. Hanley-Wood Inc., 1 Thomas Circle Northwest, Suite 600, Washington DC 20005. **Tel** (202)452-0800, FAX (202)785-1974. **(Subscription address:** Palm Coast Data, PO Box 420163, Agency Department, Palm Coast FL 32142. **Tel** (904)445-4662 ext. 669, (800)829-5475.**)** **ED** Mitchell Rouda. **Ad Acc. Circ:** 220,000. available on microfilm and microfiche from University Microfilms International (UMI). **Continues in part** NAHB Builder, 0272-5347; **Absorbed** Housing, 0161-0619 **and** Sumichrast Report.
Desc: The magazine for the home-building industry. It's readers include builders, architects, subcontractors, manufacturers and dealers.
Ind/Abst Archit. Period. Index; Avery Index Archit. Period. Suppl. Colum. Univ. (19??-199?); Bus. ASAP (1992-) [Full Txt.]; Bus. Index (1985-); Bus. Period. Index; Bus. Source Plus; Bus. Source; EP Collect.; F&S Index Plus Text, Int. [Select. Cov.]; Gen. BusinessFile (1985-); Gen. Period. Index (1985-); Homework Help.; Mag. Search; MasterFile FullTEXT 1000; MasterFile FullTEXT 350; MasterFile FullTEXT 650; MasterFile FullTEXT (Jan. 1993-); OCLC; Predicasts Forecasts; Stat. Ref. Index; Telebase; Trade Ind. Index (1981-); Vocat. Search; Wilson Bus. Abstr.

LC NA7205 .B85
ISSN 1055-3460
DD 728/.37/0223
US
BUILDER'S BEST HOME DESIGNS. [Build. best home designs]. **VFOAT** Home Designs. Vol. 1, No. 1 (Spring 1991)-. Consumer Publication. English. Four times a year. $4.95 US; $5.95 other. Hanley-Wood Inc., 1 Thomas Circle Northwest, Suite 600, Washington DC 20005. **Tel** (202)452-0800, FAX (202)785-1974.
Desc: A consumer magazine that contains over 200 of today's most popular home plans. It features the work of top architects and designers who've appeared in Builder magazine.

LC HD9715.G7 B8
ISSN 0268-1323
DD 381/.4568
UK
BUILDERS MERCHANTS JOURNAL (TONBRIDGE AND MALLING, KENT : 1985). (BUILDERS MERCHANTS JOURNAL : BMJ.). **VFOAT** BMJ. (July 1985)-. Periodical. English. Twelve times a year. $128.34. Benn Publications Ltd., Sovereign Way, Tonbridge TN9 1RW United Kingdom. **Tel** 011 44 1732 364422, FAX 011 44 1732 361534, telex 95132 BENTON G. **ED** Eric Bignell. **Ad Acc. Circ:** 7,080 (ctrl). **Continues** Builders & Timber Merchant.
Desc: Information service for builders and merchants.

ISSN 0190-5996
US
BUILDERS (WASHINGTON, D.C. 1979), THE. (THE BUILDERS.). [Builders]. Vol. 1 (1979)-. Periodical. English. One time a week. The Builders, Room 603/815 16th Street NW, Washington DC 20006.

LC TH1061
ISSN 1351-010X
DD 693
UK
●**BUILDING ACOUSTICS.** [Build. acoust.]. **VFOAT** Journal of Building Acoustics. (1994)-. Academic Scholarly Publication. English. Four times a year. $136.89. Multi Science Publishing Company Ltd., 107 High Street, Brentwood, Essex CM14 4RX United Kingdom. **Tel** 011 44 1277 224632, FAX 011 44 1277 223453, telex 89-8452. **ED** B.M. Gibbs and D.J. Oldham. Documents available from BLDSC.
Desc: Concerned with acoustics in the environment. Strives to be a forum for scientists and engineers concerned with research and development for acoustic enhancement and noise control in the buildings.

LC HD9715.N4 B85
DD 338.4/76908/09931
NZ
BUILDING ACTIVITY BULLETIN. No. 1 (Apr. 1983)-. Bulletin. English. Twelve times a year. Department of Statistics / New Zealand, PO Box 2922, Wellington New Zealand. **Tel** 011 64 4 4954600.

AT
BUILDING AND CONSTRUCTION AND CAZALYS CONTRACT REPORTER. (19??)-. English. Irregular. 200Aus$. Building and Construction Publishing, 484 Station Street, Post Office Box 175, Box Hill Victoria 3128 Australia. **Tel** 011 61 3 8907892, FAX 011 61 3 8990621.

ISSN 0815-6050
DD 343.9407869
AT
BUILDING AND CONSTRUCTION LAW. See Law.

US
BUILDING AND CONSTRUCTION MARKET FORECAST. (19??)-. English. Nine times a year. $199.90. Cahners Publishing Company, 249 West 17th Street, New York NY 10011. **Tel** (212)645-0067, FAX (212)242-6987. **(Subscription address:** Cahners Publishing Company / Colorado, Paid Subscription Service Center, PO Box 7610, Highlands Ranch CO 80126-7610. **Tel** (303)470-4466, FAX (303)470-4691.**)**
Desc: Improve your planning with the monthly, six-page report that keeps you abreast of the latest market outlooks for the construction industry. Includes analyses and two-year forecasts for many types of US construction activity.

ISSN 0217-5541
DD 690
SI
BUILDING & CONSTRUCTION NEWS. [Build. constr. news]. **VFOAT** Building and Construction News. (1983)-. Trade Publication. English. One time a week (50 issues). $400.00. Al Hilal Publishing Fe Pte Ltd., 50 Jalan Sultan, 20-06 JS Centre, Singapore 0719 Singapore. **Tel** 011 65 2939233.

ISSN 1186-1398
DD 331.7
CN
BUILDING AND CONSTRUCTION TRADES TODAY. [Build. construct. trades today]. **VFOAT** Trades Today. (Winter 1991)-. Periodical. English. Four times a year. $10.00 Canada; $12.00 US. Heisey Publishing, 29 Bernard Avenue, Toronto Ontario M5R 1R3 Canada. **Tel** (416)923-5381. **ED** Beth Ryan. **Bk Rev. Ad Acc. Circ:** 4,000.
Desc: Serves unionized and non-unionized trades people in the more than 40 specialties of building and construction across Southern Ontario.

LC TH1 .B847
ISSN 0360-1323
DD 690/.05
UK
CCC
CODEN BUSCBC
Pr Rev.
BUILDING AND ENVIRONMENT. [Build. environ.]. Vol. 11 (1976)-. Periodical. English. Six times a year. $621.00. Pergamon Press, An Imprint of Elsevier Science Ltd., The Boulevard, Langford Lane, Kidlington, Oxford OX5 1GB United Kingdom. **Tel** 011 44 1865 843000, 011 44 1865 843699, FAX 011 44 1865 843010. **(Subscription address:** Elsevier Science Ltd. / Oxford Fulfillment Centre, PO Box 800, Kidlington OX5 1DX United Kingdom. **Tel** 011 44 1865 843355.**)** **ED** C. Wilson. available on microfilm and microfiche from University Microfilms International (UMI); and Microforms International; available on an online database from Elsevier Electronic Subscriptions (EES). Documents available from Article Express International, The Genuine Article, Documents on Demand. **Continues** Building Science, 0007-3628.
Ind/Abst Abstr. J. Earthq. Eng. (?-?); Archit. Period. Index (1977-)(1976-); Avery Index Archit. Period. Suppl. Colum. Univ. (1990-); Bioeng. Abstr.; Curr. Cit.; Curr. Contents Eng. Comput. Technol.; Curr. Technol. Index; Ei Page One; Energy Inf. Abstr.; Energy Res. Abstr. (April 1978-); Eng. Index Annu.; Environ. Abstr.; Environ. Period. Bibliogr.; Health Saf. Sci. Abstr.; Int. Build. Serv. Abstr.; Int. Civil Eng. Abstr.; J. Ferrocement; J. Plan. Lit.; Leadscan; Life Sci. Collect.; Res. Alert [Select. Cov.]; SCISEARCH; Soft. Abstr. Eng.; World Ceram. Abstr.

ISSN 0811-0913
AT
BUILDING AND RELATED STATISTICS, TASMANIA. See Building and Construction-Abstracting, Bibliographies and Statistics.

ISSN 0194-1569
US
BUILDING AND REMODELING. 1978-. Periodical. English. Six times a year. Hudson Home Publications, 175 S San Antonio Rd., Los Altos CA 94022. **Tel** (310)937-5486. **Continues** Home Building and Remodeling.

ISSN 1077-2030
US
●**BUILDING & REMODELING NEWS (NORTHERN/CENTRAL NEW JERSEY ED.).** (BUILDING & REMODELING NEWS.). (1994)-. Periodical. English. Twelve times a year. $22.00. DPH Communications Inc., PO Box 780, Pearl River NY 10965. **Tel** (201)327-1600. **Continues** Remodeling News (Northern / Central New Jersey ed.), 1053-1505.

IT
Pr Rev.
BUILDING AUTOMATION. (19??)-. Italian. Four times a year (Feb., May, Sept., Dec.). L60000 Italy; L80000 other. Tecnomedia SRL, via Sansovino 28, 20133 Milan Italy. **Tel** 011 39 2 70602276, FAX 011 39 2 26680468, telex 323047. **ED** Manuela Giabardo. **Ad Acc. Circ:** 4,200 (ctrl).

AT
BUILDING CODE OF AUSTRALIA. SUMMARY SHEETS. (19??)-. English. 110.00Aus$. BDAQ, PO Box 4, Miami Queensland 4220 Australia. **Tel** 011 61 7 5765996.

LC TH
ISSN 0143-2249
DD 690
UK
BUILDING CONSERVATION. [Build. conserv.]. (Summer 1978)-. Periodical. English. **Ind/Abst** Archit. Period. Index (Summer 1978-July/Aug. 1981); Art Archaeol. Tech. Abstr.

US
BUILDING CONSTRUCTION IN THE BUFFALO AREA / PREPARED BY RESEARCH AND STATISTICS DEPT., BUFFALO CHAMBER OF COMMERCE. See Building and Construction-Abstracting, Bibliographies and Statistics.

ISSN 1031-3745
DD 691.05
AT
BUILDING CONSTRUCTION MATERIALS AND EQUIPMENT. [Build. constr. mater. equip.]. **VFOAT** BCME. (1984)-. Periodical. English. Twelve times a year. 45.22Aus$. Federal Publishing Co Pty Ltd., PO Box 199, 180 Bourke Road, Alexandria New South Wales 2015 Australia. **Tel** 011 61 2 3539992, FAX 011 61 2 66923059935. **Continues** Australia/New Zealand Building Construction Materials and Equipment, 0811-0670.

ISSN 0192-7590
US
BUILDING CONSTRUCTION NEWS. (19??)-. Periodical. English. Ten times a year. $15.00. The Builders Exchange, 1737 Euclid Avenue/Suite 110, Cleveland OH 44115.

LC K1700
ISSN 0265-6493
DD 344.2037869
UK
BUILDING CONTROL. [Build. control]. (1983)-. Periodical. English. Six times a year. $68.45. Institute of Building Control, 21 High Street, Epsom Surrey KT17 1SB United Kingdom. **Tel** 011 44 181 3936860, FAX 011 44 181 3931083. **ED** Dr. A.C. Dennison. **Ad Acc.** **Continues** IBCO. Institution of Building Control Officers, 0264-8660.
Ind/Abst Curr. Cit.

LC TH435 .M147b
ISSN 0194-0295
DD 692/.5/0978
US
BUILDING COST FILE. WESTERN EDITION. (BUILDING COST FILE.). **Main/Corp** McKee-Berger-Mansueto. (1972)-. Trade Publication. English. One time a year. $42.00. Construction Publishing Company / Falls Church, 7297-Robert E Lee Highway, Falls Church VA 22042. **Tel** (703)536-5522. **ED** Jack C. Lewis. **Ad Acc. Circ:** 6,900 (ctrl).
Desc: Activities in highway, heavy construction, commercial and industrial building, surface mining and quarrying in MD, VA, WV, NC and DC. Local industry news, bid, award information, job features, new production and etc.

ISSN 0821-7327
DD 690/.892
CN
BUILDING COST GUIDE. AGRICULTURAL. [Build. cost guide, Agric.]. English. One time a year. $27.00. American Appraisals Association Inc., Boeckh Customer Services, PO Box 664, Milwaukee WI 53201. **Tel** (800)558-8650. **Circ:** 1,400 (ctrl).
Desc: General estimates of canadian construction costs for agricultural building types.

LC TH
ISSN 1320-4661
DD 692.509941
AT
BUILDING COST GUIDE. COMMERCIAL, INDUSTRIAL AND HOUSING, WESTERN AUSTRALIA. (1989)-. Periodical. English. Four times a year. 330.00Aus$ Australia. Cordell Building Publications, PO Box 124, St. Leonards NSW

Building and Construction

2065 Australia. **Tel** 011 61 2 9345555. *Continues* Cordell's Building Cost Guide. Commercial, Industrial and Housing. Western Australia, 0817-4210.

ISSN 1321-067X
AT

BUILDING COST GUIDE. COMMERCIAL INDUSTRIAL. QUEENSLAND. (1989)-. Periodical. English. Four times a year. 330.00Aus$ Australia; 389.00Aus$ New Zealand, Papua New Guinea; 406.00Aus$ Malaysia, Indonesia, Fiji; 414.00Aus$ Japan, India, Hong Kong; 426.00Aus$ US, Canada, Lebanon; 434.00Aus$ Europe, South Africa, former USSR. Cordell Building Publications, PO Box 124, St. Leonards NSW 2065 Australia. **Tel** 011 61 2 9345555. *Continues* Cordell's Building Cost Guide. Commercial and Industrial. Queensland, 0816-8865.

LC TH
DD 690
ISSN 1321-0688
AT

BUILDING COST GUIDE. COMMERCIAL INDUSTRIAL. VICTORIA. (1989)-. Periodical. English. Four times a year. Cordell Building Publications, PO Box 124, St. Leonards NSW 2065 Australia. **Tel** 011 61 2 9345555. *Continues* Cordell's Building Cost Guide. Commercial and Industrial. Victoria, 0816-8830.

LC TH
DD 692.509944
ISSN 1320-4300
AT

BUILDING COST GUIDE. HOUSING. NEW SOUTH WALES. (1989)-. Periodical. English. Four times a year. 330.00Aus$ Australia; 426.00Aus$ US, Canada, Lebanon and Israel. Cordell Building Publications, PO Box 124, St. Leonards NSW 2065 Australia. **Tel** 011 61 2 9345555. *Continues* Cordell's Building Cost Guide. Housing, New Construction. New South Wales, 0816-8822.

LC TH
DD 692.509943
ISSN 1320-4653
AT

BUILDING COST GUIDE. HOUSING, QUEENSLAND. (1989)-. Periodical. English. Four times a year (Feb., May, Aug., Nov.). 271.32Aus$. Cordell Building Publications, PO Box 124, St. Leonards NSW 2065 Australia. **Tel** 011 61 2 9345555. *Continues* Cordell's Building Cost Guide. Housing, New Construction. Queensland, 0816-8792.

ISSN 0821-7300
DD 690/.879
CN

BUILDING COST GUIDE. MOBILE HOME. (BUILDING COST GUIDE. MOBILE HOME / BOECKH, DIVISION OF GENERAL APPRAISAL OF CANADA LIMITED.). [Build. cost guide, Mob. home]. English. One time a year. 27.00Can$. American Appraisals Association Inc., Boeckh Customer Services, PO Box 664, Milwaukee WI 53201. **Tel** (800)558-8650. **Circ:** 500 (ctrl).
Desc: General estimate manual for supplied costs on mobile homes and related additional items for the Canadian market.

ISSN 0821-7319
DD 624.1/042
CN

BUILDING COST GUIDE. YARD IMPROVEMENTS. [Build. cost guide, Yard improv.]. English. One time a year. $22.00. American Appraisals Association Inc., Boeckh Customer Services, PO Box 664, Milwaukee WI 53201. **Tel** (800)558-8650.

LC TH435 .B843
DD 692/.5/0973
ISSN 0732-5789
US
TITLE CHANGE

BUILDING COST MANUAL. [Build. cost man.]. (19??)-(1993). English. Craftsman Book Company, PO Box 6500, 6058 Corte del Cedro, Carlsbad CA 92008. **Tel** (619)438-7828, (800)829-8123, FAX (619)438-0398. **ED** Lisa Andrews. Index available. ctrl circ. *Continued by* National Building Cost Manual, 1076-3953.
Desc: Covers construction costs per square foot for residential, commercial and industrial construction.

LC TH1 .M27
DD 721/.05
ISSN 0007-3407
US
CCC

BUILDING DESIGN & CONSTRUCTION. See Architecture.

ISSN 0007-3431
AT

BUILDING ECONOMIST, THE. [Build. econ.]. **Added/Corp** Australian Institute of Quantity Surveyors. Vol. 1 (March 1962)-. Periodical. English. Four times a year. 65.00Aus$ Australia. Australian Institute of Quantity Surveyors, 27-29 Napier Close, Deakin ACT 2600 Australia. **Tel** 011 61 6 2822222, FAX 011 61 6 2852427. **ED** George Freeman. cum. index. **Bk Rev**. **Ad Acc**. **Circ:** 3,800 (ctrl).
Desc: Features current construction costs in all mainland states, building cost indices, and cost planning features. Circulates to quantity surveyors, architects, builders and contractors, government and private owners.
Ind/Abst Archit. Period. Index (-1985); PAIS Bull. (1986-); Public Aff. Inf. Serv. Bull. (-1985).

LC NA1 .A14
DD 720/.5
UK

●**BUILDING ENGINEER : JOURNAL OF THE ASSOCIATION OF BUILDING ENGINEERS.** **Added/Corp** Association of Building Engineers. Vol. 68, No. 3 (Apr. 1993)-. Periodical. English. Ten times a year (monthly except Jan. and Aug.). $42.78. Association of Building Engineers, Jubilee House, Billing Brook Road, Northampton NN3 4NW United Kingdom. **Tel** 011 44 1604 404121, FAX 011 44 1604 784220. **ED** JV Scott. **Bk Rev**, (Qty: 50). **Ad Acc**. **Circ:** 5,000 (ctrl). *Continues* Architect and Surveyor, 0308-8596.
Ind/Abst Curr. Cit.

BUILDING ESTIMATOR'S REFERENCE BOOK, THE. 1st Ed. (1915)-. Periodical. English. Irregular (Every 2 to 3 years). Frank R. Walker Company, PO Box 3180, Lisle IL 60532. **Tel** (800)458-3737, FAX (708)971-8989. **ED** Scott Siddens.

LC NA7100 .B85
DD 728.3/7/0222
ISSN 0093-0938
US

BUILDING IDEAS (DES MOINES). See Architecture.

ISSN 1000-9507
CC
SUSPENDED

BUILDING IN CHINA. **Added/Corp** Chung Kuo Chien Chu Chi Shu Fa Chan Chung Hsing. Vol. 1, No. 1 (March 1988)-Suspended. Periodical. English. Irregular (2 double issues). $30.00. China Building Technology Development Centre, 19 Che Gong Zhuang Street, Beijing 100044, People's Republic of China. *Continues* China Building Selection.
Ind/Abst Avery Index Archit. Period. Suppl. Colum. Univ. (Mar., June, Sept. 1989, 1990-).

ISSN 1170-4527
DD 338.47690099305
NZ

BUILDING INDUSTRY NEWS. [Build. ind. news]. (1990)-. Periodical. English. Eleven times a year (11 issues). IPL Publishing Ltd., 17 Pipi Street Te Awanga, Hawkes Bay New Zealand. *Continues* Building News (Auckland), 0112-1456.

AT

BUILDING INDUSTRY REVIEW. (19??)-. English. Four times a year. 100.00Aus$. Q S Services (NSW Publis Works), Public Works Department, GPO Box 5280, Sydney New South Wales, 2001 Australia. **Tel** 011 61 2 37 23073, FAX 011 61 2 37 28077.

ISSN 0266-0628
DD 344.2037862402648
UK

BUILDING LAW MONTHLY. See Law.

LC KD1641.A38 B85
DD 343.41/078624/02643 344.1037862402643
ISSN 0141-5875
UK

BUILDING LAW REPORTS. See Law.

LC NA1 .B5
DD 720/.5
ISSN 0007-3318
UK
CODEN BULDBE

BUILDING (LONDON). (BUILDING.). [Build.]. (1966)-. Trade PublicationTrade Publication. English. One time a week. $222.45. Building Services Publications Ltd., Builder House, 1 Millharbour, London E14 9RA United Kingdom. **Tel** 011 44 171 5604000, telex 25212 BUILDA G. (**Subscription address:** Builder Group, Garrard House, 2-6 Homesdale Road, Bromley BR2 9WL United Kingdom. **Tel** 011 44 185 8468888.) **ED** Graham Rimmer. Index available. **Bk Rev**. **Ad Acc**. **Circ:** 21,000. available on microfilm and microfiche from University Microfilms International (UMI). Documents available from Ask*IEEE. *Continues* Builder (London, England).
Desc: News and features for the design and construction team.
Ind/Abst Agric. Eng. Abstr.; Archit. Period. Index (1977-); Avery Index Archit. Period. Suppl. Colum. Univ. (1989-); Br. Humanit. Index; Coal Abstr.; Curr. Cit.; Curr. Technol. Index; Eng. Mater. Abstr.; Infomat Int. Bus.; INSPEC (March 1972-); Int. Build. Serv. Abstr.; Saf. Health Work; Tech. Educ. Train. Abstr.; World Surf. Coat. Abstr.

ISSN 0267-2561
DD 338.476900941
UK

BUILDING MARKET REPORT. [Build. mark. rep.]. (1983)-. Trade Publication. English. Twelve times a year. $290.91. Building Publishers Ltd, Builder House, London E14 9BR United Kingdom.

US

BUILDING MATERIAL RETAILER. **Added/Corp** National Lumber and Building Material Dealers Association (U.S.). Vol. 1, No. 1 (July 1984)-. Periodical. English. Twelve times a year. $18.00. National Lumbermens Publishing Company, 1405 Lilac Drive North #130, Minneapolis MN 55422-4505. *Formed by the union of* Retail Lumberman *and* Northwestern Lumberman.

PH

BUILDING MATERIALS & EQUIPMENT SOUTHEAST ASIA. (19??)-. Periodical. English. Twelve times a year.
Ind/Abst Archit. Period. Index (Jan. 1981-June 1987).

US

BUILDING MATERIALS DIRECTORY / UNDERWRITERS' LABORATORIES, INC. **Added/Corp** Underwriters' Laboratories. (1972)-. Directory. English. One time a year. $10.00. Underwriters Laboratories Inc., 333 Pfingsten Road, Northbrook IL 60062. **Tel** (708)272-8800 ext.3542, FAX (708)272-8129, telex 6502543343. *Continues* Building Materials List, 0503-177X.

ISSN 0007-3547
US

BUILDING OFFICIAL AND CODE ADMINISTRATOR, THE. **Added/Corp** Building Officials and Code Administrators International. VFOAT BOCA International; BOCA; Building Official; Building Official and Code Administrator Magazine. Vol. 4, No. 2 (Feb. 1970)-. Periodical. English. Six times a year. $18.00. BOCA International, 4051 West Flossmoore Road, Country Club Hills IL 60478. **Tel** (708)799-2300, FAX (708)799-4981. *Continues* Building Official.
Ind/Abst Ei Page One.

ISSN 1071-2879
DD 380
US

BUILDING OKLAHOMA (OKLAHOMA CITY, OKLA. 1989). (BUILDING OKLAHOMA.). [Build. Okla.]. (1989)-. Trade Publication. English. Twelve times a year. $10.00. Oklahoma Retailer Publishing Company Inc, 4500 North Sewell, Oklahoma City OK 73118. **Tel** (405)528-0903. **ED** Fred Singleton. **Bk Rev**. **Ad Acc**. **Circ:** 3,200 (ctrl).
Desc: News of people, companies and products that make up Oklahoma's building business.

LC TH3301 .B4
DD 647/.05
ISSN 0007-3490
US

BUILDING OPERATING MANAGEMENT. [Build. oper. manag.]. Vol.17 (Jan. 1970)-. Trade Publication. English. Twelve times a year. $55.00. Trade Press Publishing Company, 2100 West Florist Avenue, Milwaukee WI 53209. **Tel** (414)228-7701, FAX (414)228-1134. **ED** Ed Sullivan. Index available. **Ad Acc**. **Circ:** 65,000 (ctrl). available on microfilm and microfiche from University Microfilms International (UMI). *Continues* Building Maintenance and Modernization.
Desc: Features, case histories, and news releases cover trends and developments in remodeling, replacement, retrofitting, renovation, maintenance and housekeeping products and services.
Ind/Abst Health Plan. Adminis.; Hosp. Health Admin. Index.

ISSN 0227-6631
DD 690/.24/05
CN

BUILDING OPERATING MANAGER. [Build. oper. manager]. VFOAT BOM. Vol. 1, No. 1 (Sept./Oct. 1980)-. Periodical. English. Six times a year. 5.00Can$. Building Operating Manager, 720 Spadina Avenue, Suite 308, Toronto Ontario M5S 2T9 Canada. **Tel** (416)922-8554. *Continues* Building Management Maintenance News, 0319-7018.

ISSN 0270-9317
US

BUILDING-PERMIT ACTIVITY IN FLORIDA (ANNUAL). (BUILDING-PERMIT ACTIVITY IN FLORIDA.). **Added/Corp** University of Florida. Bureau of Economic and Business Research. University of Florida. Computing Laboratory. **VAT** Building Permit Activity in Florida. (19??)-. English. One time a year (Mar.). $7.00. Bureau of Economic & Business Research / Florida, University of Florida, 221 Matherly Hall, Gainesville FL 32611. **Tel** (904)392-0171, FAX (904)392-4739. **ED** Susan Floyd. **Circ:** 300.
Desc: Number and value of building permits reported issued by Florida counties and cities for residential, nonresidential and public structures.

LC WMLC L 82/37
ISSN 0007-3555
US

BUILDING-PERMIT ACTIVITY IN FLORIDA (MONTHLY). (BUILDING-PERMIT ACTIVITY IN FLORIDA FOR THE MONTH OF ...). **Added/Corp** University of Florida. Bureau of Economic and Business Research. University of Florida. Computing Laboratory. **VFOAT** Building-Permit Activity in Florida. **VAT** Building Permit Activity in Florida. (19??)-. English. Twelve times a year. $45.00. Bureau of Economic & Business Research / Florida, University of Florida, 221 Matherly Hall, Gainesville FL 32611. **Tel** (904)392-0171, FAX (904)392-4739. ctrl circ. available on diskette from the publisher.

ISSN 0419-8174
US
BUILDING PERMITS. Periodical. English. Dun & Bradstreet / New York, 299 Park Avenue, 24th Floor, New York NY 10171. **Tel** (212)593-4173.

LC HD9715.C3 B84 **ISSN** 0575-7975
DD 354/.71/008242 CN
BUILDING PERMITS, ANNUAL SUMMARY. **See** Building and Construction-Abstracting, Bibliographies and Statistics.

LC TH26 .C37a **ISSN** 0318-8809
DD 338.4/769/00971 CN
BUILDING PERMITS (STATISTICS CANADA). (BUILDING PERMITS.). [Build. permits]. **Added/Corp** Statistics Canada. Business Finance Division. Statistics Canada. Construction Division. Statistics Canada. Building Permits Section. Statistics Canada. Current Investment Indicators Section. **VFOAT** Permis de Batir. Vol. 15, No. 8 (Aug. 1971)-. English (French). Twelve times a year. 288.00Can$. Statistics Canada Publications Sales and Services, R.H. Coats Building 6th Floor, Ottawa Ontario K1A 0T6 Canada. **Tel** (613)951-5078, (800)267-6677, FAX (613)951-1584, telex 053-3585. ***Continues*** *Building Permits (Canada. Dominion Bureau of Statistics), 0318-8809.*

AT
BUILDING PRODUCT NEWS. (19??)-. English. Twelve times a year. 77.00Aus$ Australia; 99.00Aus$ New Zealand, Papua New Guinea; 103.00Aus$ Malaysia, Indonesia, Fiji; 104.00Aus$ Japan, India, Hong Kong; 114.00Aus$ US, Canada, Lebanon; 124.00Can$ Europe, Africa, former USSR. Thomson Publications / Australia, 47 Chippen Street, Chippendale New South Wales 2008 Australia. **Tel** 011 61 2 6992411, FAX 011 61 2 6991184, telex 122226. **(Subscription address:** Thomson Publications Australia, PO Box 815, Strawberry Hills, New South Wales, 2012 Australia. **Tel** 011 61 2 6992411.)

ISSN 1041-9152
DD 338 US
BUILDING PRODUCTS (CLEVELAND, OHIO). (BUILDING PRODUCTS.). [Build. prod.]. **Added/Corp** Predicasts, Inc. (19??)-. Trade Publication. English. Twelve times a year. $225.00. Predicasts Inc., A Ziff Communications Company, 11001 Cedar Avenue, Cleveland OH 44106. **Tel** (800)321-6388, (216)795-3000, FAX (216)229-9944, telex 985 604. **(Subscription address:** Information Access Company, PO Box 61000, Department 1851, San Francisco CA 94161. **Tel** (800)321-6388.)

LC JK1651.W5 A37A
DD 353.97750086/2 US
BUILDING PROJECTS STATUS REPORT : A REPORT TO THE WISCONSIN LEGISLATURE. **Main/Corp** Wisconsin State Building Commission. 1977-1982-. English. Two times a year. State Building Commission, 101 South Webster Street, Madison WI 53702. ***Continues*** *Wisconsin State Building Commission. Building Action Report.*

ISSN 0957-5790
UK
BUILDING REFURBISHMENT. (1989)-. English. Four times a year. Morgan Grampian, 40 Beresford Street Woolwich, London SE18 6BQ United Kingdom. **Tel** 011 44 181 8557777, FAX 011 44 181 8555548, telex 896238. ***Continues*** *Building Refurbishment and Maintenance, 0141-0784.*

LC KFV2859.A1 A133
DD 343.755/07869/005 347.55037869005 US
BUILDING REGULATION. **See** Law.

ISSN 1070-5988
DD 338 US
BUILDING RENOVATION (CLEVELAND, OHIO). (BUILDING RENOVATION : BR.). [Build. renov.]. **VFOAT** BR. (Sept.-Oct. 1992)-. Periodical. English. Four times a year. $20.00 US; $25.00 Canada; $30.00 Mexico; $35.00 other. Penton Publishing, 1100 Superior Avenue, Cleveland OH 44114-2543. **Tel** (216)696-7000, FAX (216)696-0836.

LC TH1 .A86A **ISSN** 0312-617X
DD 690/.05 AT
BUILDING RESEARCH. [Build. res.]. **Main/Corp** Commonwealth Scientific and Industrial Research Organization (Australia). Division of Building Research. 1971/73-. English. One time a year. Building Research, 314 Albert Street, East Melbourne 3002 Australia. **Ind/Abst** Life Sci. Collect.

AT
BUILDING RESEARCH AND DEVELOPMENT IN AUSTRALIA / PREPARED BY BUILDING RESEARCH AND DEVELOPMENT ADVISORY COMMITTEE (BRDAC). **Added/Corp** Australia. Building Research and Development Advisory Committee. Australia. Dept. of Housing and Construction. **VFOAT** Better Building Through Research. (1986)-. English. Australia Department of Housing and Construction, PO Box 690, Canberra ACT 2601 Australia. ***Continues*** *Building Research in Australia (1973-74).*

LC TH1 .B38 **ISSN** 0961-3218
UK
CCC
CODEN BREIEA
Pr Rev.
BUILDING RESEARCH AND INFORMATION : THE INTERNATIONAL JOURNAL OF RESEARCH, DEVELOPMENT AND DEMONSTRATION. **Added/Corp** International Council for Building Research, Studies and Documentation. Vol. 19, No. 1 (Jan./Feb. 1991)-. Periodical. English. Six times a year. $299.00. E & FN Spon Ltd., 2 6 Boundary Row, London SE1 8HN United Kingdom. **Tel** 011 44 171 8650066. **ED** Anthony Kirk. available on microfilm from University Microfilms International (UMI). Documents available from Article Express International. ***Continues*** *Batiment International (Paris, France : 1975), 0182-3329.*
Desc: Devoted to the effective communication of international progress in the field of building research. Reflects the global concern of environmental issues in construction, how research is put into action, non-destructive investigation, the problems regarding healthy buildings, the increasingly complex issues involving legal and insurance matters and the dramatic rise in the use of expert systems. Each issue contains an editorial which reports on new research initiatives around the world. In addition to original research papers, technical papers and review articles, both invited and submitted are included.
Ind/Abst Archit. Period. Index (Vol. 19, No. 1, Jan./Feb. 1991-); Eng. Index Annu.; J. Ferrocement; World Ceram. Abstr.

UK
BUILDING RESEARCH ESTABLISHMENT UPDATE. English. Twelve times a year. £80.00 (add £12.00 airmail). Building Research Establishment, BRE Bookshop, Garston Watford WD27JR United Kingdom. **Tel** 011 44 1923 664444, FAX 011 44 1923 664400. Index available. cum. index. ctrl circ. Documents available from BLDSC.
Desc: Various aspects of building, construction problems, solutions and general information.

ISSN 1065-4968
DD 690 US
SUSPENDED
BUILDING RESEARCH JOURNAL. [Build. res. j.]. **Added/Corp** University of Illinois at Urbane-Champaign. Small Homes Council-Building Research Council. Vol. 1, No. 1 (Jan. 1992)-Suspended with Vol. 4, No. 1 (1995). Periodical. English. Two times a year. $80.00 (institutions). Building Research Journal, SHC-BRC, 1 East St. Mary's Road, Champaign IL 61820-6995.

LC HD9715.A8 A85a
DD 338.4/7/69080994 AT
BUILDING REVIEW. (Dec. 1977)-. Periodical. English. Four times a year. 100.00Aus$. QS Services New South Wales Public Works, GPO Box 5280, Sydney New South Wales, 2001 Australia. **Tel** 11 61 2 3728073. ***Continues*** *Building Industry Quarterly.*

LC TH1 .G3 **ISSN** 0007-3636
DD 690/.08 UK
BUILDING SCIENCE ABSTRACTS. **See** Building and Construction-Abstracting, Bibliographies and Statistics.

US
BUILDING SCIENCES. **Added/Corp** National Institute of Building Sciences. (1979)-. Periodical. English. Six times a year. $35.00. National Institute of Building Sciences, 1201 L Street Northwest, Suite 100, Washington DC 20005. **Tel** (202)289-7800, FAX (202)289-1092. **ED** Neil Sandler. **Bk Rev. Circ:** 1,500.
Desc: Covers a complete range of building industry issues, including reports on NIB's activities, information on industry concerns and industry research and technology.

LC TH1.B8473 **ISSN** 0143-6244
DD 690/.05 UK
CODEN BSETDF
Pr Rev.
BUILDING SERVICES ENGINEERING RESEARCH & TECHNOLOGY. (BUILDING SERVICES ENGINEERING RESEARCH & TECHNOLOGY : BSER & T.). [Build. serv. eng. res. technol.]. **Added/Corp** Chartered Institution of Building Services. **VFOAT** Building Services Engineering Research and Technology; BSER & T; BSER and T. Vol. 1, No. 1 (1980)-. Periodical. English. Four times a year. $169.41. Chartered Institution of Building Services Engineers, 222 Balham High Road, Delta House, London SW12 9BS United Kingdom. **Tel** 011 44 171 6755211, FAX 011 44 171 6756554. **ED** Barry W. Copping. Index available. cum. index. **Bk Rev. Circ:** 800. available on microfilm from University Microfilms International (UMI). Documents available from Article Express International, Ask*IEEE.
Desc: A high technology publication covering energy use and the environment in building. Its scope includes heating, ventilating, air conditioning, electrical services and other building services.
Ind/Abst Bioeng. Abstr.; Curr. Cit.; Ei Page One; Eng. Index Annu.; Ergon. Abstr.; Gas Abstr.; INSPEC (1980-); Int. Build. Serv. Abstr.; Int. Civil Eng. Abstr.; Soft. Abstr. Eng.

LC TH7201 .C47a **ISSN** 0951-9270
DD 697/.005 UK
BUILDING SERVICES : THE CIBSE JOURNAL. **Added/Corp** Chartered Institution of Building Services Engineers. Vol. 7, No. 5 (May 1985)-. Trade Publication. English. Twelve times a year. $140.32. Building Services Publications Ltd., Builder House, 1 Millharbour, London E14 9RA United Kingdom. **Tel** 011 44 171 5604000, telex 25212 BUILDA G. **ED** Roderic Bunn. Index available. cum. index. **Bk Rev. Ad Acc.** ctrl circ. available on microfilm from University Microfilms International (UMI). Documents available from Ask*IEEE. ***Continues*** *Journal of the Chartered Institution of Building Services, 0142-3630.*
Ind/Abst Archit. Period. Index; BMT Abstr.; Curr. Cit.; Gas Abstr. (?-?); INSPEC (June 1985-); Int. Build. Serv. Abstr.; Int. Civil Eng. Abstr.; PROMT.

LC TH1 .P3 **ISSN** 0270-1197
DD 690/.05 US
BUILDING STANDARDS. [Build. stand.]. **Added/Corp** International Conference of Building Officials. (1969)-. Trade Publication. English. Six times a year. $16.00. ICBO Evaluation Service Inc., 5360 South Workman Mill Road, Whittier CA 90601. **Tel** (213)699-0541, FAX (213)692-3853. **ED** Cheryl Melendez and Rhonda Reiseberg. Index available. cum. index. **Bk Rev. Ad Acc. Circ:** 12,500. Documents available from Article Express International. ***Continues*** *Building Standards Monthly.*
Desc: Published for building officials, engineers, architects and construction industry representatives. Provides information on building technology, and includes a complete index of evaluation reports. All code change amendments are published in this magazine.
Ind/Abst Ei Page One; Eng. Index Annu.; Urban Aff. Abstr.

LC HD9715.P23 P35A
DD 338.4/769/00953021 PP
BUILDING STATISTICS (PAPUA NEW GUINEA. NATIONAL STATISTICAL OFFICE). (BUILDING STATISTICS.). March Quarter (1980)-. Periodical. English. Four times a year. k6.00 Papua New Guinea; k7.00 (surface mail), k12.00 (airmail) other. National Statistical Office / New Guinea, PO Wards Strip NCO, Papua New Guinea. **Tel** 011 675 27182 271172, FAX 011 657 255057, telex FINANCE NE 22312. ***Continues*** *Building Statistics (Papua New Guinea. Bureau of Statistics).*

LC TA676 .B85 **ISSN** 0749-6133
DD 691/.2/05 US
BUILDING STONE MAGAZINE. [Build. stone mag.]. **Added/Corp** Building Stone Institute (New York, N.Y.). (Jan./Feb. 1980)-. Periodical. English. Six times a year. Building Stone Institute, 420 Lexington Avenue, New York NY 10017. **Tel** (212)490-2530.

LC TH1 .B86 **ISSN** 0890-9008
DD 381/.45683 US
CCC
TITLE CHANGE
BUILDING SUPPLY & HOME CENTERS. (BUILDING SUPPLY HOME CENTERS.). [Build. supply home cent.]. **VFOAT** BSHC. Vol. 148, No. 5 (May 1985)-(1993). Trade Publication. English. Cahners Publishing Company, 249 West 17th Street, New York NY 10011. **Tel** (212)645-0067, FAX (212)242-6987. **(Subscription address:** Cahners Publishing Company / Colorado, Paid Subscription Service Center, PO Box 7610, Highlands Ranch CO 80126-7610. **Tel** (303)470-4466, FAX (303)470-4691.) Index available. **Ad Acc. Circ:** 43,000 (ctrl). available on microfilm from University Microfilms International (UMI); available on an online database (file 648/Full-Text) from DIALOG. ***Continues*** *Building Supply & Home Centers, 0890-9008.* ***Split into*** *Building Supply Home Centers (Northeast ed.), 1075-802X; Building Supply Home Centers (Midwest ed.), 1075-8038; Building Supply Home Centers (South ed.), 1075-8054; Building Supply Home Centers (West ed.), 1075-8046.*
Desc: A magazine for retailers and wholesalers of lumber, building materials, hardware and home improvement products. Features new products and management, marketing and merchandising ideas for professional contractors and remodeling customers.
Ind/Abst Bus. Index (1985-); EP Collect.; F&S Index Plus Text, Int. [Select. Cov.]; Gen. BusinessFile (1985-); Gen. Period. Index (1985-); Homework Help.; Mag. Search; MasterFile FullTEXT 1000; MasterFile FullTEXT 350; MasterFile FullTEXT 650; MasterFile FullTEXT (July

1993-); OCLC; PROMT; Telebase; Trade Ind. ASAP [Full Txt.]; Trade Ind. Index (May 1985-) [Full Txt.]; Vocat. Search.

US

•BUILDING SUPPLY BUSINESS (MIDWEST EDITION). **VFOAT** BSHC. (1995)-. Periodical. English. Twelve times a year. $79.90 US; $112.06 Canada; $109.90 Mexico; $149.90 other. Cahners Publishing Company, 249 West 17th Street, New York NY 10011. **Tel** (212)645-0067, FAX (212)242-6987. **(Subscription address:** Cahners Publishing Company / Colorado, Paid Subscription Service Center, PO Box 7610, Highlands Ranch CO 80126-7610. **Tel** (303)470-4466, FAX (303)470-4691.) Index available. **Ad Acc.** ***Continues*** *Building Supply Home Centers BSHC (Midwest Ed.), 1075-8038.*
Desc: A magazine for retailers and wholesalers of lumber, building materials, hardware and home improvement products. Features new products and management, marketing and merchandising ideas for professional contractors and remodeling customers.

US

•BUILDING SUPPLY BUSINESS (NORTHEAST EDITION). **VFOAT** BSHC. (1995)-. Periodical. English. Twelve times a year. $79.90 US; $112.06 Canada; $109.90 Mexico; $149.90 others. Cahners Publishing Company, 249 West 17th Street, New York NY 10011. **Tel** (212)645-0067, FAX (212)242-6987. **(Subscription address:** Cahners Publishing Company / Colorado, Paid Subscription Service Center, PO Box 7610, Highlands Ranch CO 80126-7610. **Tel** (303)470-4466, FAX (303)470-4691.) Index available. **Ad Acc.** ***Continues*** *Building Supply Home Centers (Northeast Edition), 1075-802X.*
Desc: A magazine for retailers and wholesalers of lumber, building materials, hardware and home improvement products. Features new products and management, marketing and merchandising ideas for professional contractors and remodeling customers.

US

•BUILDING SUPPLY BUSINESS (SOUTH EDITION). **VFOAT** BSHC. (1995)-. Periodical. English. Twelve times a year. $79.90 US; $112.06 Canada; $109.90 Mexico; $149.90 others. Cahners Publishing Company, 249 West 17th Street, New York NY 10011. **Tel** (212)645-0067, FAX (212)242-6987. **(Subscription address:** Cahners Publishing Company / Colorado, Paid Subscription Service Center, PO Box 7610, Highlands Ranch CO 80126-7610. **Tel** (303)470-4466, FAX (303)470-4691.) Index available. **Ad Acc.** ***Continues*** *Building Supply Home Centers (South Edition), 1075-8054.*
Desc: A magazine for retailers and wholesalers of lumber, building materials, hardware and home improvement products. Features new products and management, marketing and merchandising ideas for professional contractors and remodeling customers.

US

•BUILDING SUPPLY BUSINESS (WEST EDITION). **VFOAT** BSHC. (1995)-. Periodical. English. Twelve times a year. $79.90 US; $112.06 Canada; $109.90 Mexico; $149.90 others. Cahners Publishing Company, 249 West 17th Street, New York NY 10011. **Tel** (212)645-0067, FAX (212)242-6987. **(Subscription address:** Cahners Publishing Company / Colorado, Paid Subscription Service Center, PO Box 7610, Highlands Ranch CO 80126-7610. **Tel** (303)470-4466, FAX (303)470-4691.) Index available. **Ad Acc.** ***Continues*** *Building Supply Home Centers (West Edition), 1075-8046.*
Desc: A magazine for retailers and wholesalers of lumber, building materials, hardware and home improvement products. Features new products and management, marketing and merchandising ideas for professional contractors and remodeling customers.

ISSN 1075-8038
DD 381 US
TITLE CHANGE

BUILDING SUPPLY HOME CENTERS (MIDWEST ED.). (BUILDING SUPPLY HOME CENTERS : BSHC.). [Build. supply home cent.]. **VFOAT** BSHC. (Jan. 1994)-(1995). Periodical. English. Cahners Publishing Company, 249 West 17th Street, New York NY 10011. **Tel** (212)645-0067, FAX (212)242-6987. **(Subscription address:** Cahners Publishing Company / Colorado, Paid Subscription Service Center, PO Box 7610, Highlands Ranch CO 80126-7610. **Tel** (303)470-4466, FAX (303)470-4691.) Index available. **Ad Acc.** ***Continues in part*** *Building Supply Home Centers, 0890-9008.* ***Continued by*** *Building Supply Business (Midwest Edition).*
Desc: A magazine for retailers and wholesalers of lumber, building materials, hardware and home improvement products. Features new products and management, marketing and merchandising ideas for professional contractors and remodeling customers.

LC HF **ISSN** 1075-802X
DD 381 US
TITLE CHANGE

BUILDING SUPPLY HOME CENTERS (NORTHEAST ED.). (BUILDING SUPPLY HOME CENTERS : BSHC.). [Build. supply home cent.]. **VFOAT** BSHC. (Jan. 1994)-(1995). Periodical. English. Cahners Publishing Company, 249 West 17th Street, New York NY 10011. **Tel** (212)645-0067, FAX (212)242-6987. **(Subscription address:** Cahners Publishing Company / Colorado, Paid Subscription Service Center, PO Box 7610, Highlands Ranch CO 80126-7610. **Tel** (303)470-4466, FAX (303)470-4691.) Index available. **Ad Acc.** ***Continues in part*** *Building Supply Home Centers, 0890-9008.* ***Continued by*** *Building Supply Business (Northeast Edition).*
Desc: A magazine for retailers and wholesalers of lumber, building materials, hardware and home improvement products. Features new products, and marketing and merchandising ideas for professional contractors and remodeling customers.

ISSN 1075-8054
DD 381 US
TITLE CHANGE

BUILDING SUPPLY HOME CENTERS (SOUTH ED.). (BUILDING SUPPLY HOME CENTERS : BSHC.). [Build. supply home cent.]. **VFOAT** BSHC. (Jan. 1994)-(1995). Periodical. English. Cahners Publishing Company, 249 West 17th Street, New York NY 10011. **Tel** (212)645-0067, FAX (212)242-6987. **(Subscription address:** Cahners Publishing Company / Colorado, Paid Subscription Service Center, PO Box 7610, Highlands Ranch CO 80126-7610. **Tel** (303)470-4466, FAX (303)470-4691.) Index available. **Ad Acc.** ***Continues in part*** *Building Supply Home Centers, 0890-9008.* ***Continued by*** *Building Supply Business (South Edition).*
Desc: A magazine for retailers and wholesalers of lumber, building materials, hardware and home improvement products. Features new products and management, marketing and merchandising ideas for professional contractors and remodeling customers.

ISSN 1075-8046
DD 381 US
TITLE CHANGE

BUILDING SUPPLY HOME CENTERS (WEST ED.). (BUILDING SUPPLY HOME CENTERS : BSHC.). [Build. supply home cent.]. **VFOAT** BSHC. (Jan. 1994)-(1995). Periodical. English. Cahners Publishing Company, 249 West 17th Street, New York NY 10011. **Tel** (212)645-0067, FAX (212)242-6987. **(Subscription address:** Cahners Publishing Company / Colorado, Paid Subscription Service Center, PO Box 7610, Highlands Ranch CO 80126-7610. **Tel** (303)470-4466, FAX (303)470-4691.) Index available. **Ad Acc.** ***Continues in part*** *Building Supply Home Centers, 0890-9008.* ***Continued by*** *Building Supply Business (West Edition).*
Desc: A magazine for retailers and wholesalers of lumber, building materials, hardware and home improvement products. Features new products and management, marketing and merchandising ideas for professional contractors and remodeling customers.

ISSN 0728-9820
DD 526.906094 AT

BUILDING SURVEYOR MELBOURNE. [Build. Surv. Melb.]. (1980)-. Periodical. English. Four times a year (Mar., June, Sept., Dec.). 49.34Aus$. Australian Institute of Building Surveyors, PO Box 1206, Cowandilla SA 5033 Australia. **Tel** 011 61 8 2342200, FAX 011 61 8 2342341. **ED** Drew Wadsworth (editor's address: PO Box 101, Hawthorn VIC 3122 Australia, phone: 018 586575). **Ad Acc, Adv Mgr:** D. Wadworth. **Circ:** 3,500 (ctrl).
Desc: For building control staff and anyone concerned with the building industry; contains technical information and articles.

ISSN 1064-5896
DD 690 US
TITLE CHANGE

BUILDING SYSTEMS BUILDER. [Build. sys. build.]. Vol. 13, No. 4 (May 1992)-(199?). Trade Publication. English. Twelve times a year. $39.00 (one-year), $59.00 (two-year), $75.00 (three-year). Building Systems Builder, 14 West South Street, Corry PA 16407. **Tel** (814)664-8624, FAX (814)664-7781. **ED** Terry Peterson. Index available. **Ad Acc, Adv Mgr:** Charles Mancino, **Tel** (814)838-0028. ctrl circ. ***Continues*** *Builder/Dealer, 0892-824X.* ***Continued by*** *Building Systems Magazine, 1079-7459.*
Desc: The magazine serving builders, dealers, and developers either using or considering the use of building systems components. It is written for those working with modular, log, panelized, pre-cut, timber frame and pre-engineered model-code complying homes.

ISSN 1079-7459
DD 690 US

BUILDING SYSTEMS MAGAZINE. [Build. sys. mag.]. **VFOAT** Building Systems. (199?)-. Periodical. English. Twelve times a year (includes directory). $39.00. Building Systems Builder, 14 West South Street, Corry PA 16407. **Tel** (814)664-8624. ***Continues*** *Building Systems Builder, 1064-5896.*

LC TH23 .C46A **ISSN** 0149-1679
DD 690/.07/2073 US
CODEN XNBSAV

BUILDING TECHNOLOGY PROJECT SUMMARIES. (BUILDING TECHNOLOGY PROJECT SUMMARIES / CENTER FOR BUILDING TECHNOLOGY, NATIONAL ENGINEERING LABORATORY, NATIONAL BUREAU OF STANDARDS, U.S. DEPARTMENT OF COMMERCE.). English. One time a year. National Bureau of Standards National Engineering Laboratory, Center for Building Technology, Washington DC 20402. available on microfiche (Vols. for (1981/1982-) distributed to depository libraries).

LC TH1 .C25
DD 338.4/7/6900971 CN

BUILDING : THE NEWSMAGAZINE FOR CANADA'S DEVELOPMENT INDUSTRY. **VFOAT** Canadian Building. Vol. 41, No. 7 (June/July 1991)-. Periodical. English. Seven times a year. 66.00Can$. Crailer Communications, 113 Davenport Road, Toronto Ontario M5R 1H8 Canada. **Tel** (416)966-9944. ***Continues*** *Canadian Building, 0008-3070.*

LC TA418.52 .B84
US

BUILDING THERMAL ENVELOPE SYSTEMS AND MATERIALS (BTESM) AND RESEARCH UTILIZATION/TECHNOLOGY TRANSFER PROGRESS REPORT FOR DOE OFFICE OF BUILDING AND COMMUNITY SYSTEMS : MONTHLY PROGRESS REPORT. Periodical. English. Twelve times a year. Oak Ridge National Laboratory, PO Box 2008, Oak Ridge TN 37831. **Tel** (615)574-6755, (615)574-5845, FAX (615)574-0334.

LC TH1 .B849
DD 690.05 UK
TITLE CHANGE

BUILDING TODAY. Vol. 194, No. 5727 (Oct. 15, 1987)-(19??). Periodical. English. International Thomson Business Publications, 42 Bedford Square, London WC1B 3SC United Kingdom. **Tel** 011 44 171 3236986. ***Continues*** *Building Trades Journal, 0306-3216.* ***Merged into*** *Construction News, 0010-6860.*
Ind/Abst Curr. Technol. Index; World Ceram. Abstr.

ISSN 0007-3717
US

BUILDING TRADESMAN, THE. **Added/Corp** Greater Detroit Building Trades Council. Michigan Building and Construction Trades Council. Vol. 1, (1952)-. Periodical. English. Irregular. $12.00. Building Tradesman, 1640 Porter Street, Detroit MI 48216. **Tel** (313)965-5080. ***Continues*** *Detroit Building Tradesman.*
Ind/Abst EP Collect.; Homework Help.; MasterFile FullTEXT 1000; MasterFile FullTEXT 350; MasterFile FullTEXT 650; MasterFile FullTEXT (July 1993-); OCLC; Telebase; Vocat. Search.

ISSN 0140-8488
UK

BUILDING WITH STEEL (LONDON. 1969). (BUILDING WITH STEEL.). (1969)-. English. British Steel Corporation, 151 Gower Street, London WCIE 6BB United Kingdom.
Ind/Abst Archit. Period. Index (1978-1984); Int. Civil Eng. Abstr.; Leadscan.

ISSN 0965-7231
DD 351.7130941 UK

•BUILDINGS & FACILITIES MANAGEMENT FOR THE PUBLIC SECTOR. [Build. Facilit. Manag. Public Sect.]. **VFOAT** Buildings and Facilities Management for the Public Sector. (1992)-. Periodical. English. Twelve times a year. £45.00 UK; £60.00 Europe; £75.00 other. Faversham House Group Ltd, Faversham House, 111 Saint James Road, Croydon Surrey CR9 2TH United Kingdom. **Tel** 011 44 81 684 4082.

LC TH **ISSN** 0007-3725
DD 690 US
CCC

BUILDINGS (CEDAR RAPIDS. 1947). (BUILDINGS.). [Buildings]. (1947)-. Trade Publication. English. Twelve times a year. $70.00. Stamats Communications Inc., 427 Sixth Avenue Southeast, Cedar Rapids IA 52406. **Tel** (319)364-6167, (800)553-8878, FAX (319)364-4278. **ED** Linda Monroe (editor's address: PO Box 1888, Cedar Rapids, IA 52406-1888). **Ad Acc, Adv Mgr Tel** (319)364-6167 ext. 744. **Circ:** 44,000 (ctrl). available on microfilm and

Building and Construction

microfiche from University Microfilms International (UMI); available on microfilm; and Information Access Company; available in microform from University Microfilms International (UMI); available on microfiche; available on CD-ROM; available on an online database from DIALOG. Documents available from Article Express International, UMI Article Clearinghouse. **Continues** *Buildings and Building Management; Absorbed National Real Estate and Building Journal.*
Desc: Serves the field of building management including development management, construction and operation of office, apartment or other commercial buildings.
Ind/Abst ABI/INFORM Glob. Ed.; ABI/INFORM [Computer File] (April 1973-March 1974); Avery Index Archit. Period. Suppl. Colum. Univ. (19??-199?); Bus. ASAP (1990-) [Full Txt.]; Bus. Index (1985-); Bus. Period. Index; Bus. Source Plus; Bus. Source; Eng. Index Annu. [Select. Cov.]; EP Collect.; Gen. BusinessFile (1985-); Gen. Period. Index (1985-); Homework Help.; Mag. Search; MasterFile FullTEXT 1000; MasterFile FullTEXT 350; MasterFile FullTEXT 650; MasterFile FullTEXT (Jan. 1993-); OCLC; Telebase; Trade Ind. ASAP [Full Txt.]; Trade Ind. Index (1981-) [Full Txt.]; Vocat. Search; Wilson Bus. Abstr.

ISSN 0891-3730
US
DD 697
BUILDINGS ENERGY TECHNOLOGY. See Energy.

LC HD4295.M9 A32
DD 338.4/7/690095487   II
BUILDINGS STATISTICS IN KARNATAKA STATE. See Building and Construction-Abstracting, Bibliographies and Statistics.

LC TH4 .B855
RM
BULETINUL STIINTIFIC SI TEHNIC AL INSTITUTULUI POLITEHNIC "TRAIAN VUIA" TIMISOARA. SERIA CONSTRUCTII. Added/Corp Instiutul Politehnic "Traian Vuia" Timisoara. VFOAT Buletinul Stiintific Si Tehnic Al Institutului Politehnic Traian Vuia Timisoara. Constructii; Seria Constructii. (19??)-. Periodical. English (French, German and Romanian). One time a year. DM164.00. (Subscription address: Kubon & Sagner, ABT Zeitschriftenimport, D 80328 Munich Germany. **Tel** 011 49 89 54218130.)

ISSN 0150-6021
FR
UDC 624
BULLETIN - ASSOCIATION FRANCIASE DES PONTS ET CHARPENTES. [Bull. - Assoc. fr. ponts charpentes]. (1969)-. Periodical. French. Two times a year. $284.34. Assn Francaise Construction, 46 Ave Aristide Briand, 92223 Bagneux France. **Tel** 011 33 1 42313290. **Continues** *Bulletin Annuel - Association Francaise des Ponts et Charpentes, 0150-603X.*

ISSN 1170-8395
NZ
BULLETIN - BRANZ. (BULLETIN.). VFOAT Bulletin - Building Research Association of New Zealand; BRANZ Bulletin. (1990)-. Bulletin. English. Twelve times a year. Building Research Association of New Zealand (BRANZ), 42 Vivian Street, Wellington 1 New Zealand.

CN
BULLETIN DE RECHERCHES DE LA DIVISION DES RECHERCHES SUR LE BATIMENT. Main/Corp Conseil National de Recherches du Canada. Division des Recherches sur le Batiment. Published since 1971?. Bulletin. French. Price varies per volume. Division des Recherches sur le Batimen CNR, Ottawa K1A 0G9 Ontario Canada.

ISSN 0378-9489
FR
BULLETIN D'INFORMATION - COMITE EURO-INTERNATIONAL DU BETON. (BULLETIN D'INFORMATION.). [Bull. inf. - Com. euro-int. beton]. Main/Corp Comite Euro-International du Beton. No. 113 (August 1976)-. Bulletin. French (English). Six times a year. $707.19. Comite Europ-International du Beton, Case Postale 88, CH-1015 Lausanne Switzerland. **Tel** 011 41 21 6932747, FAX 011 41 21 6935885, telex 45 44 78 EPFL CH. **Bk Rev**, (Qty: 5-6). **Continues** *Comite Europeen du Beton. Bulletin d'Information.*
Desc: Scientific reports in the fields of concrete research.
Ind/Abst GeoRef; Int. Civil Eng. Abstr.

ISSN 0701-0303
CN
DD 352/.992/09714
BULLETIN JURIDIQUE. See Law.

LC TH2416.A1 I5   ISSN 0304-3622
DD 624.1/7762/05   SP
CODEN BSSSCD
BULLETIN OF THE INTERNATIONAL ASSOCIATION FOR SHELL AND SPATIAL STRUCTURES. [Bull. Int. Assoc. Shell Spat. Struct.]. Main/Corp International Association for Shell and Spatial Structures. Vol.12, No.2 (Aug. 1971)-. Bulletin. English (French, German and Spanish). Three times a year. $103.72. International Association for Shell and Spatial Structures, Alfonso XII 3, 28104 Madrid Spain. **Tel** 011 34 1 3357409, FAX 011 34 1 5276013. Index available. **Circ:** 1,000 (ctrl). Documents available from Article Express International. **Continues** *International Association for Shell Structures. Bulletin.*
Desc: Related themes of theoretical and practical studies of shell and spatial structures.
Ind/Abst Bioeng. Abstr.; Civ. Struct. Eng. Abstr.; Comput. Inf. Syst. Abstr. J. [Full Cov.]; Concr. Abstr.; Ei Page One; Eng. Index Annu.; Geotech. Abstr.; Int. Civil Eng. Abstr.; J. Ferrocement; Mater. Sci. Eng. Abstr.; Mech. Eng. Abstr.; Soft. Abstr. Eng.

ISSN 0708-3912
CN
BULLETIN - OFFICE DE LA CONSTRUCTION DU QUEBEC. See Public Administration.

ISSN 0227-1044
CN
DD 690/.8/09714
BULLETIN TRIMESTRIEL ECONOMIQUE (MONTREAL). (BULLETIN TRIMESTRIEL ECONOMIQUE.). [Bull. trimest. econ.]. Main/Corp Association Provinciale des Constructeurs d'Habitations du Quebec. Vol. 3, No. 1 (March 1980)-. Bulletin. French. Four times a year. $50.00. Association Provinciale des Constructeurs d'Habitations du Quebec, 5930 Louis H. Lafontaine, Anjou Quebec H1M 1S7 Canada. **Tel** (514)353-9960, FAX (514)353-4825. **Continues** *Association Provinciale des Constructeurs d'Habitations du Quebec. Bulletin Economique, 0709-6720.*

ISSN 1187-4635
CN
DD 338.4   TITLE CHANGE
BUSINESS TODAY, CONSTRUCTION NEWS. [Bus. today constr. news]. Vol. 10, No. 57 (July 25, 1991)-(1993). Periodical. English. Con-Fax Publishing, 100-1847 West Broadway, Vancouver British Columbia V6J 1Y6 Canada. **Continues** *Business Today (Vancouver, B.C.), 0835-9407.* **Continued by** *Business Today -- For More Business Tomorrow, 1196-4332.*

UK
BUTTERWORTH'S CONSTRUCTION LAW MANUAL. See Law.

LC TH4 .B898   ISSN 0281-658X
SW
BYGG & TEKNIK. VFOAT Bygg och Teknik. Vol. 76, No. 1 (Feb. 1984)-. Periodical. Swedish. Eight times a year. Kr180.00 Sweden; $30.00 US. Forlags AB Bygg & Teknik, Sveavagen 116, 113 50 Stockholm Sweden. **Tel** 08 341760, FAX 08 345481. **ED** Stig Dahlin. **Ad Acc. Circ:** 6,500 (ctrl). **Continues** *Byggnadskonst.*

LC HD7347.A3 D4A
DK
BYGGE - OG BOLIGPOLITISKE UDVIKLING (DENMARK), DEN. Main/Corp Denmark. Boligministeriet. (19??)-. Danish.

ISSN 0348-6885
SW
UDC 72
BYGGNADSKULTUR. [Byggnadskultur]. VFOAT Meddelande - Svenska Foreningen for Byggnadsvard. (1977)-. Periodical. Swedish. Four times a year. $44.88. Svenska Fereningen Byggnadsvar, SV Road Linnegatan 81, PO Box 5405, S 114 84 Stockholm Sweden. **Tel** 011 46 8 6629115, FAX 011 46 8 7839165.
Ind/Abst BHA : Biblio. Hist. Art.

LC TD899.C5885 C2   ISSN 1078-3474
DD 690   US
●**C & D DEBRIS RECYCLING.** See Environmental Issues-Pollution and Waste Management.

US
CA QUICK SEARCH [COMPUTER FILE]. See Engineering-Abstracting, Bibliographies and Statistics.

ISSN 0871-8806
PO
UDC 741/744
CADERNOS DE DESIGN. See Architecture.

BE
CEASED
CAHIER GENERAL DES CHARGES POUR TRAVAUX DE CONSTRUCTION PRIVEE. (19??)-(19??). French. Centre Scientifique Tech Construction, rue de la Violette 21 23, 1000 Brussels Belgium. **Tel** 011 32 2 7164211.

LC TA192 .C32   ISSN 0010-244X
FR
CAHIERS DES COMITES DE PREVENTION DU BATIMENT ET DES TRAVAUX PUBLICS. See Industrial Health and Safety.

ISSN 0008-9850
FR
CAHIERS DU CENTRE SCIENTIFIQUE ET TECHNIQUE DU BATIMENT. [Cah. Cent. sci. tech. batim.]. Main/Corp Centre Scientifique et Technique du Batiment (France). No. 1 (July 1948)-. Periodical. French. Twenty times a year. 1374.37F France; 1630.00F other. Centre Scientifique et Technique du Batiment, 84 Avenue Jean Jaures, BP 2, 77421 Marne la Vallee Cedex 2 France. **Tel** 011 31 1 64688436, FAX 011 31 1 64688478. Index available. cum. index. **Bk Rev. Ad Acc. Circ:** 3,500 (ctrl).
Ind/Abst Archit. Period. Index; Int. Build. Serv. Abstr.; Int. Civil Eng. Abstr.; Saf. Health Work; Soft. Abstr. Eng.; World Ceram. Abstr.

ISSN 0241-6794
FR
UDC 69
CAHIERS TECHNIQUES DU BATIMENT. [Cah. tech. batim]. (1980)-. Periodical. French. Irregular (9 issues). 480.00F. Publications du Moniteur, 17 rue d'Uzes, 75108 Paris Cedex 02 France. **Tel** 011 33 1 40133030, FAX 011 33 1 40419495 customer service, 40133037 advertising, telex UPRESSE 680876 F. **Continues** *Cahiers Techniques du Moniteur, 0339-0810.*

ISSN 0527-2009
US
SUSPENDED
CALIFORNIA BUILDER. (1959)-Suspended (199?). Trade Publication. English. Six times a year (Feb., Apr., June, Aug., Oct., Dec.). $19.80 (one-year), $29.90 (two-year). Fellom Publishing Company, 170 South Spruce Avenue, Suite 120, South San Francisco CA 94080. **Tel** (415)588-8832, FAX (415)588-0901. **ED** Trisha Smith, managing editor. **Bk Rev. Ad Acc. Circ:** 10,000 (ctrl).
Desc: Home building and light commercial construction in the state of California.

LC HD9715.U53 C2335
US
CALIFORNIA CONSTRUCTION REVIEW. Added/Corp Construction Industry Research Board (Calif.). (198?)-. English. Twelve times a year. $75.00. Construction Industry Research Board, 2511 Empire Avenue, Burbank CA 91504. **Tel** (818)841-8210.

LC TH13.C2 C34   ISSN 0362-7136
DD 338.4/7/69000794   US
CALIFORNIA LICENSED CONTRACTOR, THE. Periodical. English. Four times a year. California Department of Consumer Affairs, 1020 North Street, Room 510, Sacramento CA 95814. **Tel** (916)445-4465, FAX (916)443-1601.

ISSN 0883-7880
US
CAM MAGAZINE. Added/Corp Construction Association of Michigan. VAT Construction Association of Michigan Magazine. (198?)-. Periodical. English. Twelve times a year. $36.00. Construction Association of Michigan, PO Box 33056, Detroit MI 48232. **Tel** (313)567-5500. **ED** Dewey Little. **Bk Rev. Ad Acc. Circ:** 4,000 (ctrl). **Continues** *Exchanger, 0274-7898.*
Desc: Construction related current issues, new products, new techniques, management topics, and features of new construction.

ISSN 1190-982X
CN
DD 382
●**CANADA'S EXPORT STRATEGY, THE INTERNATIONAL TRADE BUSINESS PLAN. 8, CONSTRUCTION PRODUCTS.** [Can. export strategy int. trade bus. plan, 8 Constr. prod.]. Added/Corp Canada. VFOAT Construction Products. (1996)-. Government Publication. English. **Continues** *Canada's International Trade Business Plan. 18, Minerals, Metals, Advanced Materials and Construction Products, 1200-1406.*

ISSN 1200-4855
CN
DD 382
●**CANADA'S EXPORT STRATEGY, THE INTERNATIONAL TRADE BUSINESS PLAN. N.17, MINERALS AND METALS.** See Metals and Metallurgy.

LC HB241   ISSN 0836-799X
DD 338.2/762/0971   CN
TITLE CHANGE
CANADIAN AGGREGATES. [Can. aggreg.]. Vol. 1, No. 1 (Oct. 1987)-Vol 1. 7, No. 8 (Dec. 1993). Periodical. English. Franmore Communications Inc., 4999 St. Catherine Street W., Suite 215, Westmount Quebec H3Z 1T3 Canada. **Tel** (514)482-9868, FAX (514)487-9276. **Continued by** *Canadian Aggregates & Roadbuilding contractor, 1196-7226.*

LC HB241   ISSN 1196-7226
DD 338.2/762/0971   CN
●**CANADIAN AGGREGATES & ROADBUILDING CONTRACTOR.** [Can. aggreg. roadbuild. contract.]. VFOAT Canadian

Building and Construction

Aggregates and Roadbuilding Contractor; Canadian Aggregates. Vol. 8, No. 1 (Jan./Feb. 1994)-. Periodical. English. Irregular. 28.01Can$. Franmore Communications Inc., 4999 St. Catherine Street W., Suite 215, Westmount Quebec H3Z 1T3 Canada. **Tel** (514)482-9868, FAX (514)487-9276. *Continues Canadian Aggregates, 0836-799X.*

ISSN 0824-4723
DD 692/.5   CN
CANADIAN BUILDING COST MODIFIER. [Can. build. cost modif.]. **Added/Corp** Boeckh Valuation and Cost Systems. (1976)-. Periodical. English. Four times a year. 60.03Can$. Boeckh Canada, 310 Front Street West, Suite 800, Toronto Ontario M5V 3B5 Canada. **Tel** (416)593-4050, FAX (416)593-5168. **Circ:** 500.
Desc: Index of Canadian building construction costs by classification of construction type, e.g. residential, agricultural, commercial, steel frame and r/c frame.

LC KE5270.F37 N37   **ISSN** 0700-1320
DD 343.71/078690892 347.10378690892   CN
CANADIAN FARM BUILDING CODE. [Can. farm build. code]. **Added/Corp** National Research Council of Canada. Associate Committee on the National Building Code. 4th Ed. (1975)-. English. Irregular. 15.00Can$. National Research Council of Canada, Receiver General for Canada, Ottawa Ontario K1A 0R6 Canada. **Tel** (613)993-0362, FAX (613)952-7656. *Continues Canadian Code for Farm Buildings (Farm Building Standards), 0826-645X.*

ISSN 0832-6533
DD 629.2/25/05   CN
CANADIAN HEAVY EQUIPMENT GUIDE. [Can. heavy equip. guide]. Vol. 1, No. 1 (June 1986)-. Periodical. English. Nine times a year (Jan./Feb., July/Aug., and Nov./Dec. issues combined). 31.21Can$. Baum Publications Ltd., 1625 Ingleton Avenue, Burnaby British Columbia V5C 4L8 Canada. **Tel** (604)291-9900, FAX (604)291-1906. **ED** Len Webster. **Ad Acc**, **Adv Mgr:** John. ctrl circ.

LC HD9715.C3 A37   **ISSN** 1201-057X
DD 338.4/769/00971   CN
CAPITAL EXPENDITURES BY TYPE OF ASSET. *See* Building and Construction-Abstracting, Bibliographies and Statistics.

ISSN 0847-4583
DD 690/.094/05   CN
CATALOGUE DE PUBLICATIONS EUROPEENNES. [Eur. publ. cat.]. **Main/Corp** Institut de Recherche en Construction (Canada). **VFOAT** European Publications Catalogue. (1990)-. French (English). Institute for Research in Construction, National Research Council Canada, Ottawa Ontario K1A 0R6 Canada. **Tel** (613)993-9960, FAX (613)952-4040, telex 053-3145 NRC ADMIN OTT.

ISSN 0277-0407
US
CEASED
CCAN. (CCAN : CONSTRUCTION COMPUTER APPLICATIONS NEWSLETTER.). [CCAN]. **VFOAT** Construction Computer Applications Newsletter. Vol. 1, No. 1 (1981)-(19??). Newsletter. English. Construction Industry Press, PO Box 9838, San Rafael CA 94912. **Tel** (415)927-2155.
Desc: Covers construction uses of computers for everyone in the industry. It is a source of the latest news on the fast changing technology and new applications for the computer.

ISSN 1188-0783
DD 691   CN
CCMC NEWS. [CCMC news]. **Added/Corp** Canadian Construction Materials Centre. National Research Council Canada. **VAT** Canadian Construction Materials Centre News. No. 1 (Spring 1992)-. Periodical. English (French). Four times a year. Free on request. Canadian Construction Materials Centre / CCMC, Institute of Research and Construction, National Research Council, Ottawa Ontario K1P 0R6 Canada. **Tel** (613)993-6189.

ISSN 0970-6720
II
UDC 666.8
CEMENT ABSTRACTS. (1980)-. Periodical. English. Four times a year. $60.00. **(Subscription address:** Prints India, 11 Darya Ganj, New Delhi 110002 India. **Tel** 011 91 11 3268645, FAX 011 91 11 3275542, telex 31-61087 PRIN-IN.)

ISSN 0008-8811
NE
UDC 691.54
CEMENT AMSTERDAM. [CementAmst.]. (1949)-. Periodical. Dutch. Eleven times a year. Fl168.00. Vereniging Nederlandse Cemntin, Postbus 3011, 5203 Da Den Bosch Netherlands. **Tel** 011 31 73 401150. **(Subscription address:** Stichting Betom Prisma, Postbus 3532, 5203 Hertogenbosch Netherlands. **Tel** 011 31 73 401150.) Index available.
Ind/Abst Concr. Abstr.; Highw. Res. Abstr.

LC TA680 .C43   **ISSN** 0008-8838
DD 624.1/834/05   II
CEMENT & CONCRETE. [Cem. concr.].
Added/Corp Sahu Cement Service. **VFOAT** Cement and Concrete. (1960)-. Periodical. English. Four times a year.
Ind/Abst Ceram. Abstr.; Geotech. Abstr.

ISSN 0958-9465
UK
CCC
CODEN CCOCEG
CEMENT & CONCRETE COMPOSITES.
VFOAT Cement and Concrete Composites. Vol. 12, No. 1 (1990)-. Academic Scholarly Publication. English. Six times a year. $470.00. Elsevier Applied Science, An Imprint of Elsevier Science Ltd., The Boulevard, Langford Lane, Kidlington, Oxford OX5 1GB United Kingdom. **Tel** 011 44 1865 843000, 011 44 1865 843699, FAX 011 44 1865 843010. **(Subscription address:** Elsevier Science Ltd. / Oxford Fulfillment Centre, PO Box 800, Kidlington OX5 1DX United Kingdom. **Tel** 011 44 865 843355.) available on microfilm and microfiche from University Microfilms International (UMI); available on an online database from Elsevier Electronic Subscriptions (EES). Documents available from Article Express International, CASDDS. *Continues International Journal of Cement Composites and Lightweight Concrete, 0262-5075.*
Ind/Abst Chem. Abstr. (1990-); Curr. Cit.; Eng. Index Annu.; Highw. Res. Abstr.

ISSN 0008-8803
II
CODEN CMNTDT
CEMENT (BOMBAY). (CEMENT.). [Cement].
Added/Corp Cement Manufacturers' Association (India). (19??)-. Periodical. English. Four times a year. $20.00. Cement Manufacturers Association, Bombay India. **(Subscription address:** Prints India, 11 Darya Ganj, New Delhi 110002 India. **Tel** 011 91 11 3268645, FAX 011 91 11 3275542, telex 31-61087 PRIN-IN.)

LC TA434 .C395   **ISSN** 0149-6123
DD 620.1/35/05   US
CCC
CODEN CCAGDP
CEMENT, CONCRETE AND AGGREGATES. (CEMENT, CONCRETE AND AGGREGATES / ASTM.). [Cem., concr. aggreg.].
Added/Corp American Society for Testing and Materials. Vol. 1, No. 1 (1979)-. Trade Publication. English. Two times a year (June and Dec.). $48.00. American Society for Testing and Materials, 1916 Race Street, Philadelphia PA 19103. **Tel** (215)299-5585, FAX (215)299-9679, telex 710 670 1037. **ED** Susan L. Gebremedhin. **Bk Rev**. **Circ:** 3,500. available on microfilm and microfiche from University Microfilms International (UMI). Documents available from Article Express International, CASDDS.
Desc: Provides information on new developments in testing, evaluation and standardization of cement, concrete, aggregate and admixtures.
Ind/Abst Ceram. Abstr. (19??-); Chem. Abstr.; Concr. Abstr.; Curr. Cit.; Ei Page One; Eng. Index Annu.

ISSN 0380-6898
DD 338.4/76620135/0971   CN
CEMENT (OTTAWA). (CEMENT.). [Cement].
Added/Corp Statistics Canada. Manufacturing and Primary Industries Division. Statistics Canada. Industry Division. **VFOAT** Ciments; Ciment. Vol. 24, No. 1 (Jan. 1972)-. Periodical. English (French). Twelve times a year. 72.00Can$. Statistics Canada Publications Sales and Services, R.H. Coats Building 6th Floor, Ottawa Ontario K1A 0T6 Canada. **Tel** (613)951-5078, (800)267-6677, FAX (613)951-1584, telex 053-3585. *Continues Cement (Canada. Dominion Bureau of Statistics)., 0380-6898.*
Desc: Includes information on production, shipments, stocks on hand and distribution of sales by region and type.
Ind/Abst Int. Civil Eng. Abstr.; Soft. Abstr. Eng.

ISSN 0008-8897
PL
CODEN CMWGAW
CEMENT, WAPNO, GIPS. [Cement, wapno, gips]. **VFOAT** Cement-Wapno-Gips; CWG. (1950)-. Academic Scholarly Publication. Polish (summaries and/or abstracts in English, Esperanto, French, German and Russian; table of contents in English, Esperanto, French, German and Russian). Twelve times a year. $171.00. **(Subscription address:** Ars Polona-Ruch, PO Box 1001, Krakowskie Przedmiescie 7, 00-068 Warsaw Poland. **Tel** 011 48 22 261201.) Documents available from CASDDS. *Continues Cement (Warsaw, Poland).*
Ind/Abst Ceram. Abstr. (19??-); Chem. Abstr.; Coal Abstr.; Concr. Abstr.

ISSN 0008-882X
CI
UDC 666.9
CODEN CEZAA7
CEMENT. ZAGREB. [CementZagreb]. (1959)-. Serbo-Croatian (Roman). Irregular. $20.00. JUCEMA, Association of the Yugoslav Cement and Asbestos-Cement Producers, Priloz JNA 30, 41000 Zagreb Croatia. **ED** S Zuliani. **Bk Rev**. **Ad Acc**. **Circ:** 650.
Ind/Abst Ceram. Abstr. (19??-); Concr. Abstr.

SZ
CEMENTBULLETIN. **Added/Corp** Technische Forschungs- und Beratungsstelle der E.G. Portland. (19??)-. Bulletin. German (French and Italian). Twelve times a year. 25.00F Switzerland; 50.00F other Europe; 80.00F other. Technische Forschungs und Beratungsstelle der Schweizerischen Zementindustrie, Lindenstrasse 10, CH-5103 Wildegg Switzerland. **Tel** 011 41 64 577272, FAX 011 41 64 531627. Index available. cum. index. ctrl circ.

ISSN 0393-6732
IT
UDC 691.328.1
TITLE CHANGE
CEMENTO (1945), IL. [Cemento 1945]. (1945)-(1995). Periodical. Italian. Servizio Italiano Pubblicazioni International, Viale Pasteur 6, 00144 Rome Italy. **Tel** 011 39 6 5920509, telex 614567 SIPIRM I. *Continues Il Cemento Armato , Le Industrie del Cemento, 0393-702X. Merged into Industria Italiana del Cemento.*

LC TA680 .C553   **ISSN** 0008-8919
SP
CODEN CMHOAF
CEMENTO HORMIGON. [Cem.-hormigon]. **VFOAT** Cemento. (1970)-. Trade Publication. Spanish. Twelve times a year. $195.00. Cemento Hormigon, Calle Maignon 26, Edicesa, 08024 Barcelona Spain. **Tel** 34 3 2844318. Documents available from CASDDS. *Continues Cemento (Barcelona, Spain).*
Ind/Abst Chem. Abstr.

LC Z5853.M4 C45 TP875   **ISSN** 0363-8642
DD 016.666/94   US
CCC
CODEN CRPRDY
SUSPENDED
CEMENTS RESEARCH PROGRESS. [Cem. res. prog.]. **Added/Corp** American Ceramic Society. Cements Division. (1974)-Suspended (1993). Academic Scholarly Publication. English. One time a year. $53.00. American Ceramic Society, 735 Ceramic Place, Westerville OH 43081-8720. **Tel** (614)890-4700, (614)794-5890, FAX (614)899-6109. **ED** J. Francis Young. Documents available from CASDDS.
Desc: A book devoted to updated information on cements.
Ind/Abst Chem. Abstr.; Ei Page One.

LC HD9715.F47 F54A
DD 338.4/7/690099611   FJ
CENSUS OF BUILDING AND CONSTRUCTION (FIJI). **Main/Corp** Fiji. Bureau of Statistics. 1970-. English. One time a year. 1.00Fij$ per copy. Government of Fiji / Bureau of Statistics, Box 2221, Suva Fiji Islands. **Tel** 011 679 315144. Index available. **Ad Acc**. **Circ:** 150 (ctrl).
Desc: Contains results of 1985 census of building and construction. Provides information for economic planning and provides data for the estimation of national income of Fiji.

ISSN 0770-7274
BE
UDC 711.6
Pr Rev.
CENTRE SCIENTIFIQUE ET TECHNIQUE DE LA CONSTRUCTION. [Cent. sci. tech. constr.]. **VFOAT** CSTC. Centre Scientifique et Technique de la Construction. (1966)-. Academic Scholarly Publication. French (French and Dutch). Four times a year. Price varies. Centre Scientifique Technique de la Construction, rue de la Violette 21-23, 1000 Brussels Belgium. **Tel** 011 32 2 7164211, FAX 011 32 2 7253212. Index available. **Bk Rev**, (Qty: 2). **Circ:** 15,000.
Desc: Articles from CSTC engineers concerning the results of their studies, research or practice in various building construction matters.
Ind/Abst Int. Civil Eng. Abstr.

ISSN 1062-0079
DD 692   US
CHANGE NOTICE, THE. [Change not.]. **Added/Corp** Means (Firm). (Jan. 1992)-. Periodical. English. Four times a year. RS Means Company Inc. / Trade Sales, 100 Construction Plaza, PO Box 800, Kingston MA 02364. **Tel** (617)585-7880, (800)448-8182, FAX (617)585-7466.
Desc: Information on regional and national trends, new technologies, building economies.

ISSN 0226-6210
DD 690/.8/05   CN
CHANTIER. [Chantier]. Vol. 1 (May 1978)-. Periodical. French. Six times a year. Free. Association Provinciale des Constructeurs d'Habitations du Quebec, 5930 Louis H. Lafontaine, Anjou Quebec H1M 1S7 Canada. **Tel** (514)353-9960, FAX (514)353-4825.

Building and Construction

ISSN 0397-4650
FR

CHANTIERS DE FRANCE. [Chantiers Fr.]. (1967)-. Trade Publication. French (German). Twelve times a year. 470.00F. Stepe, Bord de Seine, 202 Quai de Clichy, 92110 Clichy France. **Tel** 011 33 1 47561723. **Ad Acc.**
Ind/Abst Coal Abstr.; Energy Res. Abstr. (Feb. 1982-).

FR

CHARPENTE MENUISERIE METALLIQUES SERRURERIE. French. Nine times a year. 288.93F France; 408.00F other. Editions M Begassat, 17 rue du Louvre, 75001 Paris France. **Tel** 011 33 1 42360513, FAX 011 33 1 64595296.

ISSN 0311-1903
AT
DD 690.05
TITLE CHANGE

CHARTERED BUILDER. [Chart. build.]. (1972)-(1995). Periodical. English. Australian Institute of Building, GPO Box 1467, Camberra ACT 2601 Australia. **Tel** 011 61 62 477433. **ED** David Green (editor's address: PO Box 671, Dickson ACT 2602 Australia, phone: 011 61 6 2480963). **Bk Rev. Ad Acc, Adv Mgr:** Road Harrington, **Tel** 011 61 03 32995844. **Circ:** 2,800 (ctrl).
Continued by Chartered Building Professional.

ISSN 0957-8773
UK
Pr Rev.
TITLE CHANGE

CHARTERED BUILDER (ASCOT, 1989). (CHARTERED BUILDER : THE OFFICIAL JOURNAL OF THE CIOB.). [Chart. build.]. **Added/Corp** Chartered Institute of Building (Great Britain). (Sept./Oct. 1989)-(1995). Trade Publication. English. Chartered Institute of Building, Englemere Kings Ride, Ascot Berkshire SL5 8BJ United Kingdom. **Tel** 011 44 1344 23355, FAX 011 44 1344 23467. **ED** Connal Vickers. **Bk Rev,** (Qty: 30). **Ad Acc, Adv Mgr:** Pauline Sargent. **Circ:** 25,000 (ctrl). Documents available from BLDSC.
Continues Building Technology and Management, 0007-3709; **Absorbed** Chartered Builder News.
Continued by Construction Manager.
Ind/Abst Curr. Technol. Index; Int. Civil Eng. Abstr.

AT

CHARTERED BUILDING PROFESSIONAL. (19??)-. English. Four times a year. Free on request. Australian Institute of Building, GPO Box 1467, Camberra ACT 2601 Australia. **Tel** 011 61 62 477433.

ISSN 0142-5196
UK
CEASED

CHARTERED QUANTITY SURVEYOR. See Engineering-Civil Engineering.

LC HT435 .C47
DD 692/.5/05
UK

CHARTERED SURVEYOR : BUILDING AND QUANTITY SURVEYING QUARTERLY. **Added/Corp** Royal Institution of Chartered Surveyors. **VFOAT** Chartered Surveyor: BSQ Quarterly; Building and Quantity Surveying Quarterly. Vol. 1 (Sept. 1973)-. Periodical. English. Four times a year. £21.00. Royal Institution of Chartered Surveyors, 12 Great George Street, London SW1P 3AD United Kingdom. **Tel** 011 44 171 2227000, telex 25212 BUILDA-G. **ED** Mark Moore. **Bk Rev. Ad Acc. Circ:** 30,000 (ctrl).
Desc: Authorized magazine for members of the quantity surveyors division of the Royal Institution of Chartered Surveyors.
Ind/Abst Archit. Period. Index (Winter 1977/1978-Oct. 1978).

LC TH13.I3 C48 **ISSN 0732-0604**
DD 338.7/69/002577311 US

CHICAGO CONTRACTORS REGISTER. **VFOAT** Contractors Register. English. Index Publishing Corporation, 323 West Randolph Street, Chicago IL 60606. **Tel** (312)726-1477.

ISSN 8755-254X
US
DD 683
CCC

CHILTON'S HARDWARE AGE (1984). (CHILTON'S HARDWARE AGE.). [Chilton's hardw. age.]. **VFOAT** Hardware Age. Vol. 221, No. 1 (Jan. 1984)-. Periodical. English. Twelve times a year. $75.00. Chilton Company, One Chilton Way, Radnor PA 19089. **Tel** (610)964-4000, (800)695-1214, FAX (610)964-4978, telex 6851035 CHILTON UW. available on microfilm and microfiche from University Microfilms International (UMI); available on an online database from DIALOG. Documents available from UMI Article Clearinghouse.
Continues Hardware Age (1981), 8755-2558.
Desc: Hardware publication for do-it-yourselfers, home center retailers and wholesalers.
Ind/Abst Bus. ASAP (1990-) [Full Txt.]; Bus. Index (1985-); F&S Index Plus Text, Int. [Select. Cov.]; Gen. BusinessFile (1985-) Gen. Period. Index (1985-); Mag. Search; MasterFile FullTEXT (Jan. 1993-); PROMT; Trade Ind. ASAP [Full Txt.]; Trade Ind. Index (1984-) [Full Txt.].

LC HD9745.C54 C56 **ISSN 1012-3520**
DD 382/.45683/029451 CH

CHINA SOURCES. HARDWARE. **VFOAT** Hardware. Vol. 9, No. 6 (July 1988)-. Periodical. English. Twelve times a year. $50.00 (surface mail), $80.00 (airmail). Sino Communication Company Ltd, Block B 5-Fl Vita Tower, 29 Wong Chuk Hang Road, Hong Kong Hong Kong. **Tel** 011 852 25557355, telex 65932 SINOC HX.
Continues China Sources; **Absorbed** China Trader.

ISSN 0529-3294
CC

CHINE EN CONSTRUCTION, LA. Vol. 1 (April 1963)-. Periodical. French. Twelve times a year. $8.00. Peace Book Company Ltd, 903 Wing on House, 71 des Voeux Road C, Room 1502, Hong Kong Hong Kong. **Tel** 011 852 28046687, FAX 011 852 28046409, telex 76929.

LC HD9695.K82 C483
DD 338.47 KO

CHONGI KONGSAOP TONGGYE CHARYO. See Building and Construction-Abstracting, Bibliographies and Statistics.

LC TH153 .C48
JA

CHOSA KENKYU HOKOKUSHU / REPORTS OF THE HOKKAIDO PREFECTURAL COLD REGION BUILDING RESEARCH INSTITUTE. **Added/Corp** Hokkaidoritsu Kanchi Kenchiku Kenkyujo. **VFOAT** Reports of the Hokkaido Prefectural Cold Region Building Research Institute. (19??)-. Japanese. One time a year. Hokkaidoritsu Kanchi Kenchiku Kenkyujo, 3-36 1-chome, Nijuyonken 4 jo Nishiku, Sapporoshi Hokkaido 063 Japan.

LC HD9715.C54 C48
DD 338.4/769/00951 HK

CHUNG-KUO CHIEN CHU FA CHAN = CHINA BUILDING DEVELOPMENT. **VFOAT** China Building Development. (1983)-. Periodical. Chinese (English). One time a year. $10.00. Trend Publishing Ltd, Sup Tower, Room 603, 75-83 King's Road, North Point Hong Kong. **Tel** 011 852 5 28026299, FAX 011 852 5 28026458. **ED** Louis Fung. **Ad Acc. Circ:** 20,000 (ctrl).
Desc: Building projects in China.

LC TA401 .C47
DD 693/.05 CH

CHUNG-KUO CHIEN CHU TSAI LIAO NIEN CHIEN. Chinese. One time a year. NT$7.50. Chung-Kuo Chien Chu Kung Yeh Chu Pan She, Beijing, People's Republic of China.

ISSN 0254-4083
INT
UDC 69

CIB REPORT. [CIB report]. **VFOAT** International Council for Building Research, Studies and Documentation report; Council for Building Research Report. (19??)-. Periodical. English.
Ind/Abst Curr. Cit.

ISSN 0211-9919
SP
UDC 69

CIC INFORMA. [CIC inf.]. **VFOAT** Centro Informativo de la Construccion Informacion; Catalogo Informativo de la Construccion. Suplemento. (1968)-. Periodical. Spanish. Twenty-two times a year (Plus four special issues per year). 9775ptas. Centro Informativo de la Construccion, Calle Roger de Lluria 117, 08037 Barcelona Spain. **Tel** 011 34 3 487-0455.

LC KFX1242 .A1963
DD 343.773/1107869 347.7311037869 US

CITY OF CHICAGO BUILDING CODE. See Law.

US

CITY OF LOS ANGELES BUILDING CODE. See Law.

LC TP785 .B87
DD 666/.73/05 UK

CLAYWORKER. Vol. 82, No. 976 (Sept. 1973)-. Periodical. English. Twelve times a year. $27.00. available on microfilm from University Microfilms International (UMI). **Continues** British Clayworker.

ISSN 0143-0963
UK

CLEANING MAINTENANCE AND BIG BUILDING MANAGEMENT. [Clean. maint. big build. manage.]. Vol. 1 (1979)-. Trade Publication. English. Eleven times a year. Turret Group, 177 Hagden Lane, Watford Hertfordshire WD1 8LN United Kingdom. **Tel** 011 44 1923 228577, FAX 011 44 1923 221346.

Formed by the union of Cleaning and Maintenance *and* Building Maintenance Service.
Ind/Abst World Text. Abstr.

UK

●**CLEANING MAINTENANCE AND SUPPORT SERVICES.** (1995)-. Trade Publication. English. Eleven times a year. $133.48. Turret Group, 177 Hagden Lane, Watford Hertfordshire WD1 8LN United Kingdom. **Tel** 011 44 1923 228577, FAX 011 44 1923 221346. **Continues** Cleaning and Maintenance Journal.

ISSN 1051-5720
DD 658 CCC
TITLE CHANGE

CLEANING MANAGEMENT MAGAZINE. See Business and Economics-Management.

LC TH57 .C57 **ISSN 0020-2789**
DD 690/.068/5 UK

CLERK OF WORKS. **Added/Corp** Institute of Clerks of Works of Great Britain. (19??)-. Periodical. English. Twelve times a year. $20.53. Institute of Clerks of Works, 41 The Mall Ealing, London W5 3TJ United Kingdom. **Tel** 011 44 171 5792917.
Ind/Abst Archit. Period. Index (Dec. 1977-Mar. 1982); Concr. Abstr.

ISSN 0009-8779
US

CLEVELAND CITIZEN, THE. **Added/Corp** Cleveland Building and Construction Trades Council. United Trades and Labor Council. (1891)-. Newspaper. English. Twelve times a year. $6.50. Cleveland Building and Construction, 2012 West 25th Street, Suite 900, Cleveland OH 44113. **Tel** (216)861-4283.

US

CM : CLEANING MAINTENANCE MANAGEMENT. See Business and Economics-Management.

ISSN 0094-0372
US

COCKSHAW'S CONSTRUCTION LABOR NEWS & OPINION. **VFOAT** Construction Labor News & Opinion. (1971)-. Trade Publication. English. Twelve times a year. $229.00. Cockshaws Construction Labor, PO Box 427, Newton Square PA 19073. **Tel** (610)353-0123, FAX (215)353-0111. **ED** Peter A. Cockshaw. Index available (only upon request). **Circ:** 1,700.
Desc: News and trends from the construction labor-management field. Analysis of critical construction industry trends.

LC KFO459.A1 A133 **ISSN 0735-9330**
DD 343.771/07869005 347.71037869005 US

CODE NEWS (CLEVELAND, OHIO). (CODE NEWS : A NEWSLETTER ON BUILDING CONSTRUCTION LAW AND CODE ENFORCEMENT IN OHIO.). **Added/Corp** Banks-Baldwin Law Publishing Company. Vol. 1982, No. 1 (Jan./Feb. 1982)-. Newsletter. English. Six times a year. $60.00. Banks-Baldwin Law Publishing Company, PO Box 1974, University Center, Cleveland OH 44106. **Tel** (216)721-7373. ctrl circ.
Desc: Covers building construction, law and code enforcement in Ohio.

LC HD9715.U53 C624 **ISSN 0162-6744**
DD 338.4/7/624025788 US

COLORADO CONSTRUCTION INDUSTRY REFERENCE BOOK. **VFOAT** Colorado CIRB. (19??)-. English. $25.00. Colorado Construction Industry Reference Book, PO Box 10249, Phoenix AZ 85064.

ISSN 1070-4728
DD 690 US

COMMERCIAL BUILDER. [Commer. build.]. **Added/Corp** National Commercial Builders Council (U.S.). (Jan. 1990)-. Periodical. English. Six times a year. $55.00. National Association of Home Builders, 15th and M Street NW, Washington DC 20005. **Tel** (202)822-0203.
Desc: Issues of importance to the commercial contractor building smaller-scale projects are addressed in articles on business management, case studies, subcontractor relations, and cost estimating.

LC HD1393.25 .C63
DD 333.33/8 US

COMMERCIAL BUILDING VALUATION GUIDE. (1988)-. English. One time a year. E.H. Boeckh Company, 2885 South Calhoun Road, New Berlin WI 53151. **Tel** (800)285-1288, (414)780-2800.
Continues Commercial Lines Valuation Guide, 0740-9751.

LC TH3401 .C62 **ISSN 0747-0134**
DD 720/.28/605 US
CEASED

COMMERCIAL RENOVATION. [Commer. renov.]. Vol. 6, No. 1 (Feb. 1984)-(Nov./Dec. 1993). Periodical. English. PTN Publishing Company, 445 Broad Hollow Road, Melville NY 11747. **Tel** (516)845-2700, FAX

Building and Construction

(516)845-7109. **ED** Donald M Ferreira. **Ad Acc. Circ:** 45,000 (ctrl). *Continues Commercial Remodeling, 0163-8440.*
Desc: Renovation projects aimed at building owner, general contractor, and architect. Case histories, new techniques, and products are featured.
Ind/Abst Constr. Index.

DD 691   **ISSN** 1074-519X
US
CCC

●**COMPOSITES NEWS : INFRASTRUCTURE.** [Compos. news]. (Dec. 23, 1993)-. Periodical. English. Irregular. $199.00. Composites Worldwide Inc., 991 Lomas Santa Fe Drive, C469, Solana Beach CA 92075. **Tel** (619)755-1372.

LC TP875 .C65   **ISSN** 0045-8007
DD 666/.89
US
CCC
CODEN CNASB

CONCRETE ABSTRACTS. See Engineering-Abstracting, Bibliographies and Statistics.

UK

CONCRETE FORUM. (19??)-. English. Concrete Society Services Ltd., Framewood Road Wexham, Slough SL3 6PJ United Kingdom. **Tel** 011 44 1753 662226, FAX 011 44 1753 662126.
Ind/Abst Concr. Abstr.

ISSN 0010-535X
US

CONCRETE INDUSTRY BULLETIN.
Added/Corp Concrete Industry Board. (19??)-. Trade Publication. English. Five times a year. Free on request. Concrete Industry Board, 520 5th Avenue / 3rd Floor, New York NY 10017. **Tel** (212)302-6650.
Ind/Abst Concr. Abstr.

LC TA680 .C772   **ISSN** 0162-4075
DD 624/.1834
US
CCC
CODEN CIDCD2
TITLE CHANGE

CONCRETE INTERNATIONAL. (CONCRETE INTERNATIONAL : DESIGN & CONSTRUCTION.). [Concr. int.: des. constr.]. **Added/Corp** American Concrete Institute. **VAT** Concrete International: Design and Construction. Vol. 1 (Jan. 1979)-(19??). Academic Scholarly Publication. English. Twelve times a year. American Concrete Institute, PO Box 19150, Detroit MI 48219. **Tel** (313)532-2600, FAX (313)533-4747. (Subscription address: American Concrete Institute, PO Box 32190, Detroit MI 48232.) **ED** William J. Semioli. Index available. **Bk Rev. Ad Acc. Circ:** 20,000. available on microfiche. Documents available from Article Express International, CASDDS. *Continued by Concrete International, 1357-7336.*
Desc: Circulation is concentrated among the engineers, architects and contractors who design and build concrete structures of all kinds, 80 percent of readers have specifying/buying authority. Reaches 20,000 professionals worldwide, with 80 percent of those readers in North America.
Ind/Abst Abstr. J. Earthq. Eng.; Art Archaeol. Tech. Abstr.; Bioeng. Abstr.; Ceram. Abstr. (19??-); Chem. Abstr.; Coal Abstr.; Concr. Abstr.; Constr. Index; Curr. Cit.; Ei Page One; Eng. Index Annu.; Int. Civil Eng. Abstr.; J. Ferrocement; Soft. Abstr. Eng.

US
CODEN CNCIEH

CONCRETE INTERNATIONAL. Added/Corp American Concrete Institute. Vol. 12, No. 9 (Sept. 1990)-. Periodical. English. Twelve times a year. Documents available from CASDDS. *Continues Concrete International. Design & Construction.*
Ind/Abst Appl. Sci. Technol. Index; Chem. Abstr.; Geotech. Abstr.; Soils Fert.

LC TH   **ISSN** 0379-9824
DD 693.5
SA

CONCRETE (JOHANNESBURG). [Concrete Johannesbg.]. **VFOAT** Beton. (1971)-. Trade Publication. English. Five times a year. Concrete Society of South Africa, PO Box 1111, Halfway House, 1625 South Africa. **Tel** 011 27 805 7895833. **ED** G. Goyns.
Desc: Contains information about current innovations in the concrete industry.
Ind/Abst Concr. Abstr.

DD 693   **ISSN** 0010-5317
UK
CODEN CCRTAA

CONCRETE (LONDON). (CONCRETE.). [Concrete]. **Added/Corp** Concrete Society. Vol. 1 (Jan. 1967)-. Trade Publication. English. Six times a year. $94.11. Concrete Society Services Ltd., Framewood Road Wexham, Slough SL3 6PJ United Kingdom. **Tel** 011 44 1753 662226, FAX 011 44 1753 662126. **ED** R J Barfoot. **Bk Rev. Ad Acc. Circ:** 8,700. available on microfilm and microfiche from University Microfilms International (UMI). Documents available from Article Express International, CASDDS. *Formed by the union of Concrete and Constructional Engineering and Structural Concrete.*
Desc: Covers all aspects of concrete design and construction.

Ind/Abst Archit. Period. Index; Avery Index Archit. Period. Suppl. Colum. Univ. (19??-19??); Bioeng. Abstr.; Ceram. Abstr. (19??-); Chem. Abstr.; Coal Abstr.; Concr. Abstr.; Curr. Cit.; Ei Page One; EMBASE; Eng. Index Annu. (Select. Cov.); Geotech. Abstr.; Highw. Res. Abstr.; Int. Civil Eng. Abstr.; J. Ferrocement; Soft. Abstr. Eng.

LC TP885.P5 A45A   **ISSN** 0360-2877
DD 621.8/672
US

CONCRETE PIPE INDUSTRY STATISTICS. See Building and Construction-Abstracting, Bibliographies and Statistics.

US

CONCRETE PIPE NEWS. Added/Corp American Concrete Pipe Association. (19??)-. Periodical. English. Six times a year. American Concrete Pipe Association, 8300 Boone Boulevard, Suite 400, Vienna VA 22182.
Ind/Abst Concr. Abstr.

LC HD9715   **ISSN** 0264-0236
DD 338.47624183414
UK
TITLE CHANGE

CONCRETE PLANT AND PRODUCTION. Vol. 1, No. 1 (Nov. 1982)-(1994). Periodical. English. Concrete Plant and Production, 12 Grimsdells Lane, Amersham Buckinghamshire HP6 6HF United Kingdom. **Tel** 011 44 1494 726273, FAX 011 44 1494 722626, telex 838791. **ED** H. Jeffery. **Bk Rev. Ad Acc.** Documents available from Article Express International. *Continues Concrete Works International, 0262-4761. Continued by Quality Concrete, 1357-7336.*
Ind/Abst Concr. Abstr.; Curr. Cit.; Eng. Index Annu.

ISSN 0010-5368
US
CCC

CONCRETE PRODUCTS (1975). (CONCRETE PRODUCTS.). [Concr. prod.]. (1957)-. Periodical. English. Twelve times a year. $36.47. Intertec Publishing Corp, 29 North Wacker Drive, Chicago IL 60606-3298. **Tel** (312)726-2802, FAX (312)726-3091. available on microfilm from University Microfilms International (UMI); available on an online database (file 648/Full-Text) from DIALOG. *Separated from Rock Products (Chicago, Ill. : 1917), 0035-7464.*
Desc: Serves ready-mix, block, pipe and precast-prestressed concrete producers.
Ind/Abst Concr. Abstr.; F&S Index Plus Text, Int. [Select. Cov.]; PROMT; Trade Ind. ASAP [Full Txt.]; Trade Ind. Index [Full Txt.].

US

CONCRETE PUMPING. (19??)-. English. American Concrete Pumping Association, 279 East H Street, PO Box 1276, Bendicia CA 94510-3345.
Ind/Abst Concr. Abstr.

ISSN 0010-5376
UK
CEASED

CONCRETE QUARTERLY. [Concr. q.]. **Added/Corp** Cement and Concrete Association. No. 1 (July 1947)-No. 176 (1993). Periodical. English. British Cement Association, Wexham Springs, Slough SL3 6PL United Kingdom. **Tel** 011 44 1753 662727, FAX 011 44 1753 663727, telex 848352. **Circ:** 18,000.
Ind/Abst Archit. Period. Index (1947-?); ARTbibliogr. Mod.; Concr. Abstr.; Curr. Technol. Index; Int. Civil Eng. Abstr.; J. Ferrocement; Soft. Abstr. Eng.; World Ceram. Abstr.

JA

CONCRETE ROADS. (19??)-. English. Cement Association of Japan, Hattori Building 10-3, Kyobashi 1-Chome Chuo-ku, Tokyo 104 Japan.
Ind/Abst Concr. Abstr.

ISSN 0305-1986
CODEN CSTRDR

CONCRETE SOCIETY TECHNICAL REPORT. [Conc. Soc. tech. rep.]. **Main/Corp** Concrete Society. (19??)-. Monographic series. English. Concrete Society Services Ltd., Framewood Road Wexham, Slough SL3 6PJ United Kingdom. **Tel** 011 44 1753 662226, FAX 011 44 1753 662126.
Ind/Abst Chem. Abstr.; Curr. Cit.

ISSN 0069-8288
UK

CONCRETE YEAR BOOK, THE. 1st Ed.; 1926-. Trade Publication. English. One time a year. $70.00 (surface mail), $80.00 (airmail). Palladian Publications Ltd., The Old Forge, Surrey GU8 6DD United Kingdom. **Tel** 011 44 1252 703900. **ED** J Smith. **Ad Acc. Circ:** 1,000.
Desc: Directory of the UK concrete construction industry.

ISSN 1057-882X
DD 343
US

CONSTRUCCION DE VIVIENDAS CONFORME AL UNIFORM BUILDING CODE. Main/Corp International Conference of Building Officials. **VFOAT** Codigo Uniforme de Edificacion. (1991)-. Spanish (translations available in English). Every 3 years. $13.05 (nonmembers), $9.80 (members). ICBO Evaluation Service Inc., 5360 South Workman Mill Road, Whittier CA 90601. **Tel** (213)699-0541, FAX (213)692-3853.

ISSN 0187-7895
MX
CODEN CNTTEX

CONSTRUCCION Y TECNOLOGIA.
Added/Corp Instituto Mexicano del Cemento y del Concreto. Vol. 1, No. 1 (1988)-. Periodical. Spanish. Twelve times a year. Inst Mexicano Cemento Concreto, Insurgentes Sur 1844, 01030 Mexico DF Mexico. **Tel** 011 52 5 6625731, FAX 011 52 5 6614639. *Continues Instituto Mexicano del Cemento y del Concreto. Revista IMCYC.*

LC TS350 .C58   **ISSN** 1030-2581
DD 624.1/821 2 20
AT

CONSTRUCT IN STEEL. Added/Corp Australian Institute of Steel Construction. (Nov. 1987)-. Trade Publication. English. Four times a year (Feb., Mar., Aug., Nov.). 75.00Aus$ (indiviudal); 100.00Aus$ (institutions). Australian Institute of Steel Construction, PO Box 6366, North Sydney North South Wales 2059 Australia. **Tel** 011 61 2 9296666, FAX 011 61 2 9555406. **ED** Yvette Christianse. **Bk Rev.** (Qty: varies). **Ad Acc, Adv Mgr:** Micheal Carlton, **Tel** (02) 929-6666. **Circ:** 4,500. *Continues Steel Fabrication Journal, 0311-015X.*
Desc: Steel fabrication and allied technical and commercial matters.

LC HD9715.8.N4 N47A   **ISSN** 0168-3225
NE

CONSTRUCTIEWERKPLAATSEN, EXCL. TANK-, RESERVOIR- EN PIJPLEIDINGBOUW / CENTRAAL BUREAU VOOR DE STATISTIEK, HOOFDAFDELING STATISTIEK VAN INDUSTRIE EN BOUWNIJVERHEID.
VFOAT Constructiewerkplaatsen, Exclusief Tank-, Reservoir- en Pijpleidingbouw. Dutch (summaries and/or abstracts in English). One time a year. Fl14.00. Centraal Bureau voor de Statistiek, AFD ALG Zaken, Postbus 959, 2270 AZ Voorburg Netherlands. **Tel** 011 31 70 3373800, FAX 011 31 70 0387429, telex 32692 CBS NL. *Continues Constructiewerkplaatsen, Excl. Tank-, Reservoir- en Pijpleidingbouw Produktiestatistieken.*

ISSN 0373-7748
RM
CODEN CNTIBV

CONSTRUCTII. [Constructii]. **Added/Corp** Institutul Central de Cercetare. Proiectaire si Directivare in Constructii. Vol. 23, (1971)-. Academic Scholarly Publication. Romanian. Twelve times a year. (Subscription address: Ilexim Press Department, PO Box 1, 136-1-137, Bucharest, Romania. **Tel** 011 40 1 173836.) Documents available from CASDDS. *Continues in part Construcii si Materiale de Constructie.*
Ind/Abst Chem. Abstr. (1971-1982); Coal Abstr.; Int. Civil Eng. Abstr.; Soft. Abstr. Eng.

BE

CONSTRUCTION. (19??)-. French. Twenty-four times a year. 6250.00F. Confederation National Construction Asbl, rue de Lombard 34 32, 1000 Brussels Belgium. **Tel** 011 32 2 5104663.

ISSN 0700-9178
DD 338.4/7/690097123
CN

CONSTRUCTION ALBERTA NEWS.
[Constr. Alta. news]. Vol. 1 (Feb. 3, 1975)-. Periodical. English. Two times a week (Mon. & Thurs.). 180.08Can$. Construction Alberta News Limited, PO Box 8469 Station F, Edmonton Alberta T6H 5H3 Canada. **Tel** (403)424-1146, FAX (403)425-5886. **ED** Jack Turner. **Ad Acc. Circ:** 4,300 (ctrl).
Desc: Construction trade project news for Alberta and the Northwest Territory.

LC TA401 .C77   **ISSN** 0950-0618
DD 624.1/8
UK
CCC

CONSTRUCTION & BUILDING MATERIALS. [Constr. build. mater.]. **VFOAT** Construction and Building Materials. (1987)-. Periodical. English. Eight times a year. $398.00. Butterworth Heinemann Publishers, Linacre House Jordan Hill, Oxford OX2 8DP United Kingdom. **Tel** 011 44 1865 310366, FAX 011 44 1865 310898. (Subscription address: Elsevier Science Ltd. / Oxford Fulfillment Centre, PO Box 800, Kidlington OX5 1DX United Kingdom. **Tel** 011 44 865 843355.) available on microfilm and microfiche from University Microfilms International (UMI); available on an online database from Elsevier Electronic Subscriptions (EES). Documents available from The Genuine Article.
Ind/Abst Concr. Abstr.; Curr. Cit.; For. Prod. Abstr. (1991-); Res. Alert [Full Cov.].

Building and Construction

LC KF901.A75 C66   **ISSN** 8755-7568
DD 343   US
CONSTRUCTION AND DESIGN LAW DIGEST. See Law.

US
CONSTRUCTION AND DESIGN LITERATURE: CCL SUMMARIES. (19??)-. English. Twelve times a year. $490.00. CCL Construction Consultants, 4400 College Boulevard, Suite 150, Overland Park KS 66211.

US
CONSTRUCTION AND DEVELOPMENT FORMS. (19??)-. English. $160.00. Warren Gorham & Lamont Inc., Park Square Building, 31 St. James Avenue, Boston MA 02116-4112. **Tel** (617)423-2020, (800)950-1207, FAX (617)423-2026.

LC KFN5230.B8 A493   **ISSN** 0148-933X
DD 343/.747/078   US
CONSTRUCTION & SURETY LAW DIVISION NEWSLETTER. See Law.

ISSN 0010-6704
US
CONSTRUCTION (ARLINGTON).
(CONSTRUCTION.). (19??)-. Periodical. English. Twenty-four times a year. $50.00. Northeast Publishing Company, PO Box 362, 26 Long Hill Road, Guilford CT 06437. **Tel** (800)972-2001, (203)453-3717. **ED** Jack C. Lewis. **Ad Acc. Circ:** 6,900 (ctrl).
Desc: Covers activities in highway, heavy construction, commercial and industrial building, surface mining and quarrying in , VA, WV, NC and DC. Local industry news, bid, award information, job features, new production and more.

ISSN 0714-3133
DD 338.4/769/0025715   CN
CONSTRUCTION ATLANTIC. [Constr. Atl.].
(1979)-. English. One time a year. Free to members. Naylor Communications Ltd, 100 Sutherland Avenue, Winnipeg Manitoba R2W 3C7 Canada. **Tel** (204)947-0222, FAX (604)985-7399.

US
CONSTRUCTION BOXSCORE PLUS / SOFTWARE. (19??)-. English. Three times a year (update disks are issued three times in the year). $295.00. Gulf Publishing Company / Texas, PO Box 2608, Houston TX 77252. **Tel** (800)231-6275, (713)529-4301, FAX (713)520-4433.

ISSN 0162-3176
US
CONSTRUCTION BRIEFINGS. (June 1978)-. Periodical. English. Thirteen times a year. $576.64. Federal Publications Inc, 1120 20th Street Northwest, Washington DC 20036. **Tel** (202)337-7000, (800)922-4330, FAX (202)659-2233.

LC KF865.A15 C66   **ISSN** 0747-5233
DD 346.73/023 347.30623   US
CONSTRUCTION BRIEFINGS COLLECTION, THE. [Constr. brief. collect.].
Added/Corp Federal Publications Inc. **VFOAT** Construction Briefings. Vol. 1 (1981)-. Periodical. English. Twelve times a year. $320.00. Federal Publications Inc, 1120 20th Street Northwest, Washington DC 20036. **Tel** (202)337-7000, (800)922-4330, FAX (202)659-2233. **Ad Acc.**
Desc: Each volume accompanied by revision notes.

ISSN 0010-6720
US
CONSTRUCTION BULLETIN. (1893)-.
Bulletin. English. One time a week. $250.00. Chapin Publishing Company, 9443 Science Center Dr, New Hope MN 55428-3636. **Tel** (612)537-7730, (800)328-4827 1162, FAX (612)537-1363. **ED** George Rekela. Index available (Each iss.). **Ad Acc, Adv Mgr:** John Saunders, **Tel** (612)537-7730. **Circ:** 5,000. Absorbed Architect, Builder and Decorator; Street Railway and Electrical News and Midwest Construction News.
Desc: Articles on construction with buildings and highway and other related fields.

LC HD9715.A1 C66   **ISSN** 1059-406X
DD 624/.068   US
CONSTRUCTION BUSINESS REVIEW.
(CONSTRUCTION BUSINESS REVIEW : CBR.). [Constr. bus. rev.]. **VFOAT** CBR. Vol. 1, No. 1 (Jan./Feb. 1991)-. Periodical. English. Six times a year. $69.95. CBR Construction Business Review, PO Box 3835, McLean VA 22103. **Tel** (703)734-0017.

ISSN 0228-8788
DD 690/.05   CN
CONSTRUCTION CANADA.
(CONSTRUCTION CANADA (CONSTRUCTION SPECIFICATIONS CANADA). CONSTRUCTION CANADA.). [Constr. Can.]. **Added/Corp** Construction Specifications Canada. Vol. 22, No. 4 (July 1980)-. Trade Publication. English (summaries and/or abstracts in French). Six times a year. 24.01Can$. Construction Specs Canada, 100 Lombard Street, Suite 200, Toronto Ontario M5C 1M3 Canada. **Tel** (416)777-2198. **ED** Clifford Fowke. **Ad Acc. Circ:** 3,900 (ctrl). Continues Specification Associate, 0038-691X.
Desc: Articles related to various disciplines of the construction industry and construction specifications.

LC KF901.A53 C66   **ISSN** 0742-0889
DD 343.73/07869/02648 347.303786902648   US
CONSTRUCTION CLAIMS CITATOR, THE. Vol. 1, No. 1 (Sept./Oct. 1982)-. English. Twelve times a year. $350.00. Construction Industry Press, PO Box 9838, San Rafael CA 94912. **Tel** (415)927-2155. available on an online database from NEWSNET.
Desc: A case finder with construction contract claims and bid disputes. The most comprehensive available source for this specialized information.

LC KF901.A15 C66   **ISSN** 0272-4561
DD 343.73/07869 347.3037869   US
CCC
CONSTRUCTION CLAIMS MONTHLY.
VFOAT CCM. (19??)-. English. Twelve times a year. $233.00. Business Publishers Inc., 951 Pershing Drive, Silver Spring MD 20910-4464. **Tel** (301)587-6300, (800)274-0122, FAX (301)585-9075. **ED** Bruce Jervis. cum. index. available on an online database from NEWSNET.
Desc: Newsletter on current construction case law - summaries and expert legal commentaries on six to eight cases in each issue. Cross referenced and fully annotated.

ISSN 0899-5982
DD 346   US
CEASED
CONSTRUCTION CLAIMS TRAINING GUIDE. [Constr. claims train. guide]. Vol. 1, No. 1 (May 1988)-(March 1994). Periodical. English. Business Publishers Inc., 951 Pershing Drive, Silver Spring MD 20910-4464. **Tel** (301)587-6300, (800)274-0122, FAX (301)585-9075.
Desc: Each issue features five true to life construction contract disputes taken from actual cases, three different possible courses of action for each party involved, a detailed analysis of each course of action, its pros and its cons, references to actual cases posing the same or similar problems, and an explanation - in plain English - of pertinent legal terms and concepts.

US
CONSTRUCTION COMPLAINTS.
Government Publication. English. Irregular. US Department of Housing and Urban Development, 451 Seventh Street SW, Washington DC 20401. **Tel** (202)708-0980, FAX (202)708-0299.

LC KF865 .L482
DD 343/.73/078   US
CONSTRUCTION CONTRACT MODIFICATIONS; COURSE MANUAL. See Law.

LC TH425 .C598   **ISSN** 0146-9479
DD 343/.73/078   US
CONSTRUCTION CONTRACTOR, THE.
Vol. 1 (Jan. 10, 1977)-. Periodical. English. Twenty-six times a year. $678.40. Federal Publications Inc, 1120 20th Street Northwest, Washington DC 20036. **Tel** (202)337-7000, (800)922-4330, FAX (202)659-2233.

LC KF902.Z9 C673
DD 343.73/07869 347.3037869   US
TITLE CHANGE
CONSTRUCTION CONTRACTS AND LITIGATION. See Law.

ISSN 0194-2476
DD 338   US
CONSTRUCTION DIGEST. [Constr. dig.].
Trade Publication. English. Twenty-six times a year. Construction Digest Incorporated, PO Box 603, 7355 North Woodland Drive, Indianapolis IN 46206. **Tel** (317)297-5500. Continues in part Construction Digest.
Desc: Issues for 1977 includes annual buyers guide.

ISSN 0194-8903
DD 338   US
CONSTRUCTION DIMENSIONS. [Constr. dimens.]. **Added/Corp** Association of the Wall and Ceiling Industries-International. International Association of Wall and Ceiling Contractors/Gypsum Drywall Contractors International. (19??)-. Periodical. English. Twelve times a year. $15.00. Association of Wall and Ceiling Industries, 307 East Annandale Road, Falls Church VA 22042. **Tel** (703)534-8300, FAX (703)534-8307. **ED** Laura M. Potinchak. Index available (bound in January issue). cum. index. **Ad Acc, Adv Mgr:** B. Stone. **Circ:** 23,000 (ctrl).
Desc: Information on acoustical systems, asbestos, curtains, walls, drywall, fireproofing, insulation, lathing, plastering, steel framing and stucco.

ISSN 0161-3405
US
CONSTRUCTION EMPLOYMENT GUIDE IN THE NATIONAL AND INTERNATIONAL FIELD. (19??)-. Trade Publication. English. Irregular. Price varies per volume. World Trade Academy Press Inc, 50 East 42nd Street, Suite 509, New York NY 10017. **Tel** (212)697-4999, FAX (212)949-4001.
Desc: Tips on employment in the construction industry.

ISSN 0192-3978
DD 338   US
CCC
CONSTRUCTION EQUIPMENT (1970).
(CONSTRUCTION EQUIPMENT.). [Constr. equip.]. (1970)-. Trade Publication. English. Fourteen times a year. $95.90. Cahners Publishing Company, 249 West 17th Street, New York NY 10011. **Tel** (212)645-0067, FAX (212)242-6987. **(Subscription address:** Cahners Publishing Company / Colorado, Paid Subscription Service Center, PO Box 7610, Highlands Ranch CO 80126-7610. **Tel** (303)470-4466, FAX (303)470-4691.**)** **ED** Kirk Landers. **Ad Acc. Circ:** 80,195 (ctrl). available on microfilm and microfiche from University Microfilms International (UMI); available on an online database (file 648/Full-Text) from DIALOG. Continues Construction Equipment and Materials.
Desc: Heavy equipment and trucks; management, purchasing, maintenance, use and new product evaluation, and trends in industry, government and the economy.
Ind/Abst Bus. Index (1985-); Concr. Abstr.; EP Collect.; Gen. BusinessFile (1985-); Gen. Period. Index (1985-); Homework Help.; Int. Civil Eng. Abstr.; Mag. Search; MasterFile FullTEXT 1000; MasterFile FullTEXT 350; MasterFile FullTEXT 650; MasterFile FullTEXT (July 1993-); OCLC; Soft. Abstr. Eng.; Telebase; Trade Ind. ASAP [Full Txt.]; Trade Ind. Index (1981-) [Full Txt.]; Vocat. Search.

LC HD9715.U5 C6   **ISSN** 0010-6755
DD 380.1/45/6218   US
CONSTRUCTION EQUIPMENT DISTRIBUTION. **Added/Corp** Associated Equipment Distributors. **VFOAT** CE Distribution. Vol. 34, No. 4 (April 1968)-. English. Twelve times a year. $25.00. Associated Equipment Distributors, 615 West 22nd Street, Oak Brook IL 60521. **Tel** (312)574-0650, (800)388-0650. **ED** Edward P. Salek. **Circ:** 4,500. Continues Construction Equipment News.
Desc: Official publication of Association for Construction Equipment Distributors.

LC TH15 .C58   **ISSN** 0267-7768
UK
CONSTRUCTION HISTORY : JOURNAL OF THE CONSTRUCTION HISTORY GROUP. **Added/Corp** Chartered Institute of Building (Great Britain) Construction History Group. Construction History Society. Vol. 1 (1985)-. Academic Scholarly Publication. English. One time a year (November). $94.11. Chartered Institute of Building, Englemere Kings Ride, Ascot Berkshire SL5 8BJ United Kingdom. **Tel** 011 44 1344 23355, FAX 011 44 1344 23467. available on microfiche.
Desc: Covers all aspects of the history of building and construction and to the development of construction history as a scholarly discipline. Of interest to all concerned with the preservation, restoration or reconstruction of buildings.
Ind/Abst Am. Hist. Life (1985-); Archit. Period. Index; BHA : Biblio. Hist. Art.

LC HD9715.C3 A37   **ISSN** 0527-4974
DD 338.4/769/00971   CN
TITLE CHANGE
CONSTRUCTION IN CANADA (ANNUAL ED.). See Building and Construction-Abstracting, Bibliographies and Statistics.

ISSN 0069-9187
DD 338   US
CONSTRUCTION IN HAWAII. [Constr. Hawaii]. **Added/Corp** Bank of Hawaii. Dept. of Business Research. Bank of Hawaii. Economics Division. Bank of Hawaii. Economics Dept. (1967)-. English. Irregular. Bank of Hawaii, Economics Department, PO Box 2900, Honolulu HI 96846. **Tel** (808)537-8307, FAX (808)536-9433. Continues Housing Activity in Hawaii.
Ind/Abst F&S Index Plus Text, Int. [Select. Cov.].

LC Z7914.B9 C62 Th1   **ISSN** 0892-2047
DD 016.69   US
CONSTRUCTION INDEX. See Building and Construction-Abstracting, Bibliographies and Statistics.

US
CONSTRUCTION INDUSTRY ANNUAL FINANCIAL SURVEY. (19??)-. Trade Publication. English. One time a year. $99.00. Construction Financial Management Association, 707 State Road, Suite 223, Princeton NJ 08540. **Tel** (609) 683-5000, FAX (609) 683-4821.

LC HD9715.I69 C66
DD 338.4/7624/0941705   IE
CONSTRUCTION INDUSTRY IN IRELAND : REVIEW OF ... AND OUTLOOK FOR. (1984/85)-. English. One time a year. Government Publications, 4 5 Harcourt Road,

Building and Construction

Dublin 2 Ireland. **Tel** 011 353 1 6613111 ext.4005. *Continues* Building Industry in Ireland.

UK
CONSTRUCTION INDUSTRY THESAURUS UPDATE SERVICE. (19??)-. English. £13.00. Infodoc Services Ltd, 15 Holcrost Road, Hackney, London E9 7BA United Kingdom. **Tel** 011 44 171 9862088.

ISSN 1050-4060
DD 346 US
CONSTRUCTION INJURY LIABILITY MONTHLY. [Constr. inj. liabil. mon.]. **Added/Corp** Business Publishers. **VFOAT** Injury Liability. Vol. 1, No. 1 (Oct. 1989)-. Periodical. English. Twelve times a year. $173.00. Business Publishers Inc., 951 Pershing Drive, Silver Spring MD 20910-4464. **Tel** (301)587-6300, (800)274-0122, FAX (301)585-9075. available on an online database from NEWSNET.
 Desc: Helps you stay abreast of new construction safety law developments, from the OSHA and the Occupational Safety and Health Review Commission. Each monthly issue brings you a full dozen summaries of construction injury lawsuits against companies just like your own.

ISSN 0161-990X
DD 331 US
CONSTRUCTION LABOR NEWS. See Business and Economics-Labor.

LC HD8039.B892 U63 **ISSN** 0010-6836
DD 331.7/624/0973 US
 CCC
CONSTRUCTION LABOR REPORT. See Business and Economics-Labor.

ISSN 0827-3480
DD 343.71/07869005
CN
CONSTRUCTION LAW LETTER. See Law.

ISSN 0824-2593
DD 343.71/07869005 CN
CONSTRUCTION LAW REPORTS. See Law.

LC KD1641.A38 C66 **ISSN** 0950-3889
DD 343.41/07869/0264 3441.0378690264 UK
CONSTRUCTION LAW REPORTS (LONDON, ENGLAND). See Law.

LC KF1950.A15 C65 **ISSN** 0272-0116
DD 343.73/07869/0025 347.30378690025 US
Pr Rev.
CONSTRUCTION LAWYER, THE. See Law.

LC KF901.A75 C668
DD 343.73/07869 US
CONSTRUCTION LITIGATION LAW BULLETIN. See Law.

LC KF901.A75 C67 **ISSN** 0279-1102
DD 343.73/07869 347.3037869 US
CONSTRUCTION LITIGATION REPORTER. See Law.

LC TH57 .G7a **ISSN** 0142-0410
DD 624/.0941 UK
Pr Rev. SUSPENDED
CONSTRUCTION (LONDON, 1977). (CONSTRUCTION.). [Construction]. **Added/Corp** Great Britain. Dept. of the Environment. Great Britain. Dept. of Transport. (June 1977)-(19??). Periodical. English. Six times a year. £22.00 UK; £28.00 other. B & M Publications Ltd., PO Box 13, Hereford House, Bridle Path, Crydon CR9 4NL United Kingdom. **Tel** 011 44 181 6804200, FAX 011 44 181 6815049. **ED** Tony Kirk. Index available. **Ad Acc. Circ:** 10,000 (ctrl). *Continues* Great Britain. Dept. of the Environment. DOE Construction.
 Desc: An in-house technical journal for specifiers involved in the UK government's civil and military buildings.
 Ind/Abst Archit. Period. Index (1977-1980); Curr. Technol. Index; Int. Civil Eng. Abstr.; Soft. Abstr. Eng.

ISSN 0144-6193
UK
Pr Rev. CCC
CONSTRUCTION MANAGEMENT AND ECONOMICS. [Constr. manage. econ.]. Vol. 1, No. 1 (Spring 1983)-. Trade Publication. English. Six times a year. $435.00. E & FN Spon Ltd., 2 6 Boundary Row, London SE1 8HN United Kingdom. **Tel** 011 44 171 8650066. **ED** Ranko Bon, Will Hughes. **Bk Rev. Ad Acc. Circ:** 600. available on microfilm and microfiche from University Microfilms International (UMI). Documents available from UMI Article Clearinghouse.
 Desc: Brings together new ideas and developments in construction management and economics from around the world. Helps construction clients and owners find better ways of running and using their building and other constructed facilities. Publishes research papers, original reviews of current knowledge, case studies and reports of innovative practice as well as short notes commenting on issues of currrent interest.
 Ind/Abst ABI/INFORM Glob. Ed.; ABI/INFORM [Computer File] (Spring 1988-); Archit. Period. Index; Curr. Cit.; Int. Civil Eng. Abstr.; J. Ferrocement; Soft. Abstr. Eng.

ISSN 1056-7801
US
CONSTRUCTION MANAGEMENT JOURNAL. (1992)-. Periodical. English. Twelve times a year. $64.00. Management Consultants International, Inc., PO Box 2651, Cincinnati OH 45201.

UK
●**CONSTRUCTION MANAGER.** (1995)-. English. Ten times a year. £50.00. Chartered Institute of Building, Englemere Kings Ride, Ascot Berkshire SL5 8BJ United Kingdom. **Tel** 011 44 1344 23355, FAX 011 44 1344 23467. *Continues* Chartered Builder.

ISSN 0832-5804
DD 338.4/7624/097127 CN
CONSTRUCTION MANITOBA. [Constr. Manit.]. Vol. 1, No. 1 (1987)-. Trade Publication. English. Four times a year. 12.00Can$ Canada. Sanford Evans Communications Ltd, 1077 St James Street, Box 6900, Winnipeg Manitoba R3C 3B1 Canada. **Tel** (204)775-0201, FAX (204)783-7488. **ED** Jonathon Cote. **Circ:** 1,865 (ctrl).
 Desc: Features construction news, general topics, and items of interest providing an outlook on the construction industry as it develops and changes in the province of Manitoba.

ISSN 1078-862X
DD 690 US
●**CONSTRUCTION MARKET INTELLIGENCE, RUSSIA.** [Constr. mark. intell. Russ.]. Vol. 1, No. 1 (Apr./May 1994)-. Periodical. English. Six times a year. $202.90. RS Means Company Inc. / Trade Sales, 100 Construction Plaza, PO Box 800, Kingston MA 02364. **Tel** (617)585-7880, (800)448-8182, FAX (617)585-7466.

ISSN 0316-1064
DD 692/.3/0971 CN
CONSTRUCTION MATERIALS SPECIFIER, THE. **VFOAT** Specifier. Vol. 1 (Jan./Feb. 1975)-. Periodical. English. Six times a year. $8.00 Canada; $12.00 US; $30.00 other. Don Quick Publications, 297 Old Kingston Road, West Hill Ontario M1C 1B4 Canada.

ISSN 0010-6860
UK
CONSTRUCTION NEWS. [Constr. news]. (1871)-. Newspaper. English. One time a week. $316.58. Tower Publishing, Tower House, Sovereign Park Market Harborough, Leicester LE16 9EF United Kingdom. **Tel** 011 44 1858 468888, FAX 011 44 1462 480947. *Absorbed* Building Today.

LC TH1 .C813 **ISSN** 0160-5607
DD 338.4/769/00976 US
CONSTRUCTION NEWS (LITTLE ROCK). (CONSTRUCTION NEWS.). [Constr. news]. **VFOAT** Construction News. Construction Reports; Construction Reports. (1934-)-. Trade Publication. English. Twenty-four times a year. $65.00. Construction News / Little Rock, Arkansas, 10825 Financial Center Parkway 133, Little Rock AR 72211. **Tel** (501)227-8551, FAX (501)227-6856. (**Subscription address:** Construction News, PO Box 6132, Indianapolis IN 46206-6132. **Tel** (317)329-3100, FAX (317)329-3110.) **ED** Danny Strassle. **Ad Acc. Circ:** 7,100 (ctrl). available on an online database (files 771,772,799/Full-Text) from DIALOG.
 Desc: Bid and award news, national and local advertising for a five state area: Arkansas, Louisiana, Oklahoma, Mississippi and Western Tennessee.
 Ind/Abst Fluid Abstr., Civil Eng.; Fluid Abstr. Proc. Eng.; FLUIDEX; Infomat Int. Bus.

ISSN 0306-3232
UK
CONSTRUCTION NEWS MAGAZINE. [Constr. news mag.]. (1975)-. Trade Publication. English. Twelve times a year.
 Ind/Abst Archit. Period. Index (Dec. 1977-June 1983).

ISSN 0892-3337
DD 338 US
CONSTRUCTION NEWS WEST. [Constr. news west]. (198?)-. Periodical. English. One time a week. $378.00. Construction News West, 2050 East University Drive, Phoenix AZ 85034. **Tel** (602)258-1641, FAX (602)495-9730. *Continues* Construction Week, 0744-1568.

ISSN 1182-9818
DD 338.4/7624/0971312 CN
CONSTRUCTION NORTHWEST. (CONSTRUCTION NORTHWEST : THE OFFICIAL PUBLICATION OF THE CONSTRUCTION ASSOCIATION OF THUNDER BAY.). [Constr. northwest]. **Added/Corp** Construction Association of Thunder Bay. (1990/91)-. English. Naylor Communications Ltd, 100 Sutherland Avenue, Winnipeg Manitoba R2W 3C7 Canada. **Tel** (204)947-0222, FAX (604)985-7399.

US
CONSTRUCTION NOTEBOOK NEWS. English. One time a week (Published Fridays). $375.00. Construction Notebook Inc, 3131 Meade Avenue, Las Vegas NV 89102. **Tel** (702)876-8660, FAX (702)876-5683. **ED** Sheila L. Dickinson. **Ad Acc, Adv Mgr:** Paula. **Circ:** 1,500.

ISSN 0144-8587
UK
CONSTRUCTION PAPERS. **Added/Corp** Chartered Institute of Building (Great Britain). (198?)-. Periodical. English. Two times a year. Chartered Institute of Building, Englemere Kings Ride, Ascot Berkshire SL5 8BJ United Kingdom. **Tel** 011 44 1344 23355, FAX 011 44 1344 23467.
 Ind/Abst Archit. Period. Index (1980-1983).

LC TH900 .C66
DD 624/.028 UK
CONSTRUCTION PLANT & EQUIPMENT ANNUAL. **VAT** Construction Plant and Equipment Annual. English. Morgan Grampian, 40 Beresford Street Woolwich, London SE18 6BQ United Kingdom. **Tel** 011 44 181 8557777, FAX 011 44 181 8555548, telex 896238.

ISSN 0142-0550
UK
CONSTRUCTION PLANT & EQUIPMENT INTERNATIONAL ANNUAL. **VFOAT** Construction Plant and Equipment International Annual. 1978-. English. One time a year. Morgan Grampian, 40 Beresford Street Woolwich, London SE18 6BQ United Kingdom. **Tel** 011 44 181 8557777, FAX 011 44 181 8555548, telex 896238. *Continues* Construction Plant & Equipment Annual.

LC HD9715.C3 C66 **ISSN** 0833-238X
DD 338.4/3624/0971021 CN
CONSTRUCTION PRICE STATISTICS (QUARTERLY ED.). See Building and Construction-Abstracting, Bibliographies and Statistics.

CN
CONSTRUCTION PRODUCT AND SERVICE. English. Free. Construction Safety Association of Ontario, 74 Victoria Street, Toronto Ontario M5C 2A5 Canada.
 Desc: Construction service offering products such as manuals, data sheets, posters, stickers, films, and videotapes.

LC HE356.S6 C65
DD 353.97830072/22538 US
CONSTRUCTION PROGRAMS. See Transportation-Roads and Traffic.

ISSN 0746-8377
US
CONSTRUCTION PROJECT NEWS. GREATER DETROIT EDITION. (CONSTRUCTION PROJECT NEWS / CAM, CONSTRUCTION ASSOCIATION OF MICHIGAN.). **Added/Corp** Construction Association of Michigan. (19??)-. English. Seven times a week. $448.00 (members), $681.00 (nonmembers). Construction Association of Michigan, PO Box 33056, Detroit MI 48232. **Tel** (313)567-5500. *Continues* Construction News, 0195-0088.

ISSN 0967-0726
UK
CONSTRUCTION REPAIR. **VFOAT** Construction Repair Incorporating the Restoration of Ancient Buildings. Vol. 6, No. 4 (July/Aug. 1992)-. Trade Publication. English. Six times a year. *Continues* International Journal of Construction & Repair, 0959-5090.

LC TH113.S5 C65
DD 690/.05 SI
CONSTRUCTION REVIEW, THE. Vol. 1 (Sept. 1972)-. Periodical. English. $17.00 Singapore; $21.25 other.
 Desc: Lists virtually all of the Government's current statistics pertaining to construction.
 Ind/Abst Bus. Period. Index; F&S Index Plus Text, Int. [Select. Cov.]; Gen. Period. Index (1985-); PAIS Int. Print; Wilson Bus. Abstr.

Building and Construction

LC HD9715.U5 C66   **ISSN** 0010-6917
US

CONSTRUCTION REVIEW. (CONSTRUCTION
REVIEW / U.S. DEPARTMENT OF COMMERCE, INDUSTRY AND TRADE ADMINISTRATION.). [Constr. rev.]. **Added/Corp** United States. Dept. of Labor. United States. Dept. of Commerce. United States. Business and Defense Services Administration. United States. Bureau of Domestic Commerce. United States. Bureau of Competitive Assessment and Business Policy. United States. Industry and Trade Administration. United States. International Trade Administration. (Jan. 1955)-. Government Publication. English. Four times a year. $28.00. US Department of Commerce, 14th Street & Constitution Avenue NW, Washington DC 20230. **Tel** (202)482-2000, FAX (202)482-3772. **(Subscription address:** Superintendent of Documents, US Government Printing Office, Washington DC 20402.) available on an online database (files 15,648/Full-Text) from DIALOG. Documents available from UMI Article Clearinghouse, Documents on Demand, FAXON Xpress, The UnCover Company. **Formed by the union of** Construction Materials **and** Construction (United States. Bureau of Labor Statistics).
Desc: Compiled by the Bureau of Industrial Economics of the Department of Commerce; lists virtually all of the Government's current statistics pertaining to construction.
Ind/Abst ABI/INFORM Glob. Ed.; ABI/INFORM [Computer File] (Nov. 1990-); Am. Stat. Index; Bus. ASAP (1990-) [Full Txt.]; Bus. Index (1985-); Bus. Period. Index; Bus. Source Plus; Bus. Source; EP Collect.; Gen. BusinessFile (1985-); Homework Help.; Mag. Search; MasterFile FullTEXT 1000; MasterFile FullTEXT 350; MasterFile FullTEXT 650; MasterFile FullTEXT (Jan. 1993-); OCLC; Predicasts Forecasts; Telebase; Trade Ind. Index (1981-?); Vocat. Search; Wilson Bus. Abstr.

ISSN 0704-6766
DD 690/.22/0971   CN
SUSPENDED

CONSTRUCTION SAFETY JOURNAL.
Vol. 2, No. 1 (Fall 1976)-(1994). Periodical. English. Four times a year. 50.00Can$ (Canada); $42.00 (US). Construction Safety Association Ont, 74 Victoria Street-Communications Dept, Toronto Ontario M5C 2A5 Canada. **Tel** (416)366-1501. **Continues** Toronto Construction Safety Journal, 0704-6774.
Desc: Committed to helping the industry become accident-free.

UK

CONSTRUCTION SAFETY MANUAL.
English. One time a year. £52.00. Construction Safety, Crompton Way, Crawley Sussex RH10 2OP United Kingdom. **Tel** 011 44 1 6362862.

ISSN 0708-1073
DD 338.4/7/69009711   CN
CEASED

CONSTRUCTION SIGHTLINES. **Added/Corp**
Amalgamated Construction Association of British Columbia. Vol. 1 (July/Aug. 1978)-(Oct. 1993). Periodical. English. Naylor Communications Ltd, 100 Sutherland Avenue, Winnipeg Manitoba R2W 3C7 Canada. **Tel** (204)947-0222, FAX (604)985-7399. **ED** John Doyle. **Ad Acc. Circ:** 4,200 (ctrl).
Desc: Association magazine.

LC TH425 .C6   **ISSN** 0010-6925
DD 692
CODEN COSPAJ

CONSTRUCTION SPECIFIER, THE.
[Constr. specif.]. **Added/Corp** Construction Specifications Institute. Vol. 1 (1949)-. Trade Publication. English. Twelve times a year. $30.00. Construction Specifications, 601 Madison Street, Alexandria VA 22314-1791. **Tel** (703)684-0300, FAX (703)684-0465. **ED** Kimberly C. Young. available w/ mat. cum. index. **Bk Rev. Ad Acc. Circ:** 19,500 (ctrl). available on microfiche. Documents available from Article Express International.
Desc: Publication in the construction design field edited exclusively for architects, engineers and other professionals involved in construction specifications. Readers are involved in writing and/or supervising the specifications of commercial, industrial and institutional projects worth $110 billion.
Ind/Abst Avery Index Archit. Period. Suppl. Colum. Univ. (19??-199?); Bioeng. Abstr.; Ceram. Abstr. (19??-); Concr. Abstr.; Constr. Index; Curr. Cit.; Ei Page One; Eng. Index Annu. [Select. Cov.].

ISSN 0744-7167
US
CEASED

CONSTRUCTION SUPERVISION & SAFETY LETTER. **Added/Corp** National
Foremen's Institute (U.S.). **VFOAT** Construction Supervisor and Safety Letter. (198?)-(19??). Periodical. English. Bureau of Business Practice, 24 Rope Ferry Road, Waterford CT 06386. **Tel** (800)243-0876, (203)442-4365, (800)876-9105, FAX (203)443-1123. **ED** Deloris Hidestri, Winifred Bonney. **Continues** Construction Foreman's & Supervisor's Letter, 0010-678X.

LC TH1 .C832
DD 690/.05   SI

CONSTRUCTION TIMES, THE. Vol. 1, (May/June 1976)-. English.

UK
CODEN COWEEA
TITLE CHANGE

CONSTRUCTION WEEKLY. See
Engineering-Civil Engineering.

US

CONSTRUCTION Y OBRAS PUBLICAS.
(19??)-. Spanish. Six times a year. $90.00. MacDonald Communications / Texas, 3300 South Gessner, Suite 118, Houston TX 77063. **Tel** (713)266-0610, FAX (713)266-6657.

ISSN 0010-695X
AT
CCC

CONSTRUCTIONAL REVIEW. [Constr. rev.].
Vol. 1, (1927)-. Trade Publication. English. Four times a year (Feb., May, Aug., Nov.). 32.88Aus$. Cement and Concrete Association of Australia, PO Box 1889, 25 Berry Street, North Sydney New South Wales, 2059 Australia. **Tel** (02)923-1244, FAX 02 923 1925, telex 75575. **ED** Diane Kell. **Bk Rev. Ad Acc. Circ:** 3,000 (ctrl). available on an online database. **Continues** Highways.
Desc: Reviews buildings constructed of concrete.
Ind/Abst Archit. Period. Index (1982-); Concr. Abstr.; Int. Civil Eng. Abstr.; Soft. Abstr. Eng.

ISSN 0010-6968
US

CONSTRUCTIONEER. (19??)-. Periodical.
English. Twenty-four times a year. $50.00. Northeast Publishing Company, PO Box 362, 26 Long Hill Road, Guilford CT 06437. **Tel** (800)972-2001, (203)453-3717.
Ind/Abst Concr. Abstr.

DK
TITLE CHANGE

CONSTRUCTIS. (19??)-(19??). English. European
Construction Research, Hovedvejen 182, 2600 Glostrup Denmark. **Tel** 011 45 43436322, FAX 011 45 43430940. **ED** Sarah Leatherpatl. Index available. **Bk Rev. Ad Acc. Circ:** 350. **Continued by** Euro Build, 0905-913X.
Desc: Analysis of worldwide construction markets.

LC TH1 .C95   **ISSN** 0162-6191
US

CONSTRUCTOR (WASHINGTON).
(CONSTRUCTOR.). **Added/Corp** Associated General Contractors of America. Vol. 4, (Jan. 1922)-. Periodical. English. Eleven times a year. $36.00. Association of General Contractors of America, 1957 East Street Northwest, Washington DC 20006. **Tel** (202)393-2040. **ED** William F. Heavey. **Bk Rev. Ad Acc. Circ:** 36,500. **Continues in part** Associated General Contractors of America. Bulletin.
Ind/Abst Concr. Abstr.; Highw. Res. Abstr.; Int. Civil Eng. Abstr.; Soft. Abstr. Eng.; Urban Aff. Abstr.

ISSN 0833-0239
DD 338.4/7624/09714   CN

CONSTRUIRE (QUEBEC). (CONSTRUIRE :
PUBLICATION OFFICIELLE DE LA FEDERATION DE LA CONSTRUCTION DU QUEBEC.). [Construire]. **Added/Corp** Federation de la Construction du Quebec. Association de la Construction du Quebec. Vol. 1, No 1 (Oct. 1986)-Vol. 4, No 4 (July 1989); Vol. 1, No 1 (Sept./Oct. 1989)-. Periodical. French (English). Six times a year (Feb., Apr., June, Aug., Oct., Dec.). 19.96Can$. Association de la Construction au Quebec, 4970 Place de la Savane, 3rd Floor, Montreal Quebec H4P 1Z6 Canada. **Tel** (514)739-8565. **ED** Jasmin Girard. **Ad Acc. Adv Mgr:** Pierre Leduc, **Tel** (514)739-2381. **Circ:** 14,000 (ctrl). **Absorbed** Contact-CSST, 1182-1558.
Desc: Information of construction firms doing projects in the Province of Quebec, Canada. A forefront of major commerical industrial & residential construction projects.

LC NA105   **ISSN** 0958-2746
DD 363.69   UK

CONTEXT LETCHWORTH. See Housing and
Urban Development.

LC HD9715.G72 C66   **ISSN** 0010-7859
DD 692.8   UK
CCC

CONTRACT JOURNAL (SUTTON).
(CONTRACT JOURNAL.). [Contract j.]. (1879)-. Trade Publication. English. One time a week. $241.50. Reed Business Publishing / West Sussex, England, Perrymount Road, Haywards Heath, West Sussex RH16 3DH United Kingdom. **Tel** 011 44 1444 441212, FAX 011 44 1444 445447. available on microfilm from University Microfilms International (UMI). Documents available from UMI Article Clearinghouse. **Absorbed** Construction Weekly.
Ind/Abst ABI/INFORM Glob. Ed.; Archit. Period. Index; Coal Abstr.; Curr. Technol. Index; Infomat Int. Bus.; Saf. Health Work.

ISSN 0271-5511
US

CONTRACTOR BUSINESS REPORT.
Added/Corp MetaData Inc. Vol. 1, No. 1 (July 1981)-. Periodical. English. Twelve times a year. Metadata, PO Box 585, Locust NJ 07760. **Tel** (212)687-3836.

LC HD9715.U5 C66   **ISSN** 0897-7135
DD 338
US
CCC

CONTRACTOR (NEWTON, MASS.). See
Heating, Plumbing, and Refrigeration.

ISSN 0266-7045
UK

CONTRACTOR REPORT - TRANSPORT AND ROAD RESEARCH LABORATORY.
[Contract. rep. - Transp. Road Res. Lab.]. (1984)-. Monographic series. English. Irregular.
Ind/Abst Curr. Cit.; Geogr. Abstr. Human Geogr.; Int. Dev. Abstr.

ISSN 0273-5954
US

CONTRACTORS GUIDE (LOMBARD, ILL.). (CONTRACTORS GUIDE.). [Contract. guide].
(19??)-. Trade Publication. English. Twelve times a year. $26.00. Century Communications, 6201 Howard Street, Niles IL 60714-3435. **Tel** (708)647-1200, FAX (708)647-7055. **ED** Russell Gager. **Ad Acc. Circ:** 30,000 (ctrl). available on microfilm from University Microfilms International (UMI). **Continues** Insulator's Guide, 0192-8457.
Desc: Written for roofing, insulation and siding contractors.
Ind/Abst Constr. Index.

ISSN 0279-5566
US

CONTRACTORS HOT LINE EQUIPMENT ESTIMATOR. VFOAT Contractors Hot Line.
Periodical. English. Twenty-four times a year. Hot Line Inc, PO Box 1709, 1003 Central Avenue, Fort Dodge IA 50501.

ISSN 1058-7780
DD 690
US

CONTRACTORS JOURNAL, THE.
[Contract. j.]. (1991)-. Periodical. English. One time a week. Contractors Journal Publishing, 4045 East McDowell Road, Phoenix AZ 85008.

US

CONTRACTORS MANAGEMENT JOURNAL. See Architecture.

LC TH5615 .C66   **ISSN** 1074-0473
DD 694/.029/9   US

●CONTRACTOR'S PRICING GUIDE. FRAMING & ROUGH CARPENTRY (NATIONAL ED.). (CONTRACTOR'S PRICING
GUIDE. FRAMING AND ROUGH CARPENTRY.). [Contract. pricing guide, Fram. rough carpent.]. **VFOAT** Contractor's Pricing Guide. Framing and Rough Carpentry; Framing & Rough Carpentry; Framing and Rough Carpentry. (1994)-. Periodical. English. Irregular. $34.95. RS Means Company Inc. / Trade Sales, 100 Construction Plaza, PO Box 800, Kingston MA 02364. **Tel** (617)585-7880, (800)448-8182, FAX (617)585-7466. **Formed by the union of** Contractor's Pricing Guide. Framing & Rough Carpentry (Northeast ed.), 1057-5138; Southeast Regional Contractor's Pricing Guide. Framing & Rough Carpentry, 1057-5154; Western Regional Contractor's Pricing Guide. Framing & Rough Carpentry, 1057-5162; South Central Regional Contractor's Pricing Guide. Framing & Rough Carpentry, 1057-5170; Midwest Regional Contractor's Pricing Guide. Framing & Rough Carpentry, 1057-5189 **and** Contractor's Pricing Guide. Framing & Rough Carpentry (MidAtlantic ed.), 1057-5146.

ISSN 1074-0481
DD 690   US

●CONTRACTOR'S PRICING GUIDE. RESIDENTIAL DETAILED COSTS.
[Contract. pricing guide, Resid. detail. costs]. **VFOAT** Residential Detailed Costs. (1994)-. English. $36.95. RS Means Company Inc. / Trade Sales, 100 Construction Plaza, PO Box 800, Kingston MA 02364. **Tel** (617)585-7880, (800)448-8182, FAX (617)585-7466.

ISSN 1074-049X
DD 690   US

●CONTRACTOR'S PRICING GUIDE. RESIDENTIAL SQUARE FOOT COSTS.
[Contract. pricing guide, Resid. sq. foot costs]. **VFOAT** Residential Square Foot Costs. (1994)-. English. $39.95. RS Means Company Inc. / Trade Sales, 100 Construction Plaza, PO Box 800, Kingston MA 02364. **Tel** (617)585-7880, (800)448-8182, FAX (617)585-7466.

ISSN 0816-8903
DD 692.509944   AT

CORDELL'S BUILDING COST GUIDE. COMMERCIAL AND INDUSTRIAL. NEW SOUTH WALES. [Cordell's build. cost guide,
Commer. ind., N.S.W.]. **VFOAT** Cordell's Building Cost

Guide. New South Wales. (1985)-. Periodical. English. Four times a year. 271.32Aus$. Cordell Building Publications, PO Box 124, St. Leonards NSW 2065 Australia. **Tel** 011 61 2 9345555. ***Continues*** *Cordell's Building Cost Book. New Construction. New South Wales, 0725-8445.*

LC TH435 .C8 **ISSN** 0730-2436
DD 692/.5/05 US
COST FORECASTING SERVICE APPLICATIONS BULLETIN. [Cost Forecast. Serv. appl. bull.]. Vol. 1, No. 1-. Bulletin. English. DRI McGraw Hill, 24 Hartwell Avenue, Lexington MA 02173. **Tel** (617)863-5100, FAX (617)860-6464, (617)860-6416.

ISSN 0394-1590
IT
UDC 69
COSTRUIRE IN LATERIZIO. **See** Architecture.

LC TH **ISSN** 1121-6336
DD 690 IT
UDC 69
COSTRUIRE (MILANO). (COSTRUIRE.). [Costruire Milano]. (1987)-. Periodical. Italian. Twelve times a year. L63360. Editrice Abitare Segesta Spa, Corso Monforte 15, 20122 Milan Italy. **Tel** 011 39 2 76090214, FAX 011 39 2 791904, telex 315302 ABIT I. ***Continues*** *Costruire per Abitare, 1121-6328.*

IT
TITLE CHANGE
COSTRUIRE PER ABITARE. No. 1, (April/May 1982)-(19??). Periodical. Italian. Editrice Abitare Segesta Spa, Corso Monforte 15, 20122 Milan Italy. **Tel** 011 39 2 76090214, FAX 011 39 2 791904, telex 315302 ABIT I. ***Continued by*** *Costruire, 1121-6336.*

ISSN 0010-9665
IT
UDC 62
COSTRUZIONI. [Costruzioni]. (1952)-. Periodical. Italian. Twelve times a year. L81750. Casa Editrice la Fiaccola, Via C Ravizza 62, 20149 Milan Italy. **Tel** 011 39 2 481-4355, 481-4939, FAX 011 39 2 481-4834, telex 335512 COSTRU I. **ED** Giuseppe Saronni. **Bk Rev. Circ:** 8,000 (ctrl).
Desc: A monthly magazine on construction engineering in the building industry.

ISSN 0010-9673
IT
COSTRUZIONI METALLICHE. [Costr. Met.]. **Added/Corp** Associazione fra i Costruttori in Acciaio Italiani. (1949)-. Periodical. Italian (English). Six times a year (Jan., Mar., May, July, Sept., Nov.). L80000. Associazione Costruttori Acciaio Italiani, Viale Abruzzi 66, 20131 Milan Italy. **Tel** 011 39 2 29513413, 011 39 2 29513175, FAX 011 39 2 221324, telex 29513413. **ED** Giuseppe Coppadoro. cum. index. **Circ:** 2,000. ***Continues*** *Acciaio e Castruzioni Metalliche.*
Desc: Technical-scientific papers on topics concerning research, design and erection in the field of steel construction.
Ind/Abst Alum. Ind. Abstr.; Int. Civil Eng. Abstr.; Met. Abstr.; Soft. Abstr. Eng.

US
●**CRANE SAFETY REPORT.** **See** Industrial Health and Safety.

US
●**CRANES UK.** (1995)-. English. Four times a year. $77.01. KHL Publishing Ltd., Southview Road, Wadhurst, East Sussex TN5 6TP United Kingdom. **Tel** 011 44 1892 784088.

LC TH **ISSN** 0590-0581
DD 690 NZ
CRANWELLS BUILDING SUPPLIES CATALOGUE. [Cranwells build. supplies cat.]. **VFOAT** Building Supplies Catalogue. (1952)-. Catalog. English. One time a year. 59.95NZ$. Profile Publishing Ltd, PO Box 5544, Wellesley Street, Auckland New Zealand. **Tel** 011 64 9 3585455, FAX 011 64 9 3585462. ***Continues*** *Cranwells Building Supplies Register.*
Desc: A collation of building products available in and from New Zealand. Aimed at specifiers, especially architects and builders.

LC TA680 .C513
II
CRI ABSTRACTS. **See** Engineering-Abstracting, Bibliographies and Statistics.

ISSN 1062-6182
US
CRYPTIC SCHOLAR, THE. (Winter/Spring 1991)-. Periodical. English. Two times a year.

ISSN 0584-2840
DD 390 SA
CODEN CSIRB4
CSIR RESEARCH REPORT. **Main/Corp** South African Council for Scientific and Industrial Research. **Added/Corp** National Building Research Institute (South Africa). (19??)-. English. CSIR Publishing Division, PO Box 395, Pretoria 0001 South Africa. **Tel** 011 27 12 8412911 ext. 3765, FAX 011 27 12 8413789. Documents available from BIOSIS Document Express, CASDDS.
Ind/Abst Biol. Abstr.; Chem. Abstr.; Int. Civil Eng. Abstr.

LC NA
DD 720 BE
CSTC MAGAZINE : UNE EDITION DU CENTRE SCIENTIFIQUE ET TECHNIQUE DE LA CONSTRUCTION. **Added/Corp** Centre Scientifique et Technique de la Construction. **VFOAT** Centre Scientifique et Technique de la Construction Magazine. (199?)-. Periodical. French. Four times a year. Comes with Centre Scientifique et Technique de la Construction. Centre Scientifique Tech Construction, rue de la Violette 21 23, 1000 Brussels Belgium. **Tel** 011 32 2 7164211. ***Continues*** *CSTC Revue.*

LC NA
DD 720 BE
TITLE CHANGE
CSTC REVUE. **Main/Corp** Centre Scientific et Technique de la Construction. **Added/Corp** Centre Scientifique et Technique de la Construction. **VFOAT** Centre Scientifique et Technique de la Construction Revue. (Jan. 1966)-(199?). Periodical. French. Centre Scientifique Tech Construction, rue de la Violette 21 23, 1000 Brussels Belgium. **Tel** 011 32 2 7164211. ***Continued by*** *CSTC Magazine.*
Ind/Abst Archit. Period. Index; FLUIDEX (1973-); World Surf. Coat. Abstr.

LC HD9715.J2 J24h
DD 338.4/7/6240952 JA
CURRENT CONDITIONS & PROBLEMS IN THE CONSTRUCTION INDUSTRY. **Main/Corp** Japan. Kensetsusho. (1977)-. Periodical. English. International Engineering Consultants Association, New Kojimachi Building, 5-3-23 Kojimachi 5 chome, Chiyodaku Tokyo 102 Japan.

LC TH435 .L44a **ISSN** 0161-7257
DD 692/.5/05 US
CURRENT CONSTRUCTION COSTS. **Main/Corp** Lee Saylor, Inc. (19??)-. Trade Publication. English. One time a year (January). $59.70. Saylor Publications, Inc, 9420 Topanga Canyon Boulevard, Suite 203, Chatsworth CA 91311. **Tel** (818)718-5966, FAX (818)718-8024. **ED** Stanley Strychaz.

LC HD9715.U5 A275 **ISSN** 0896-6761
DD 338.4/76908/0973021 US
CURRENT CONSTRUCTION REPORTS. C20, HOUSING STARTS. (CURRENT CONSTRUCTION REPORTS. C20, HOUSING STARTS.). [Curr. constr. rep., C20 Hous. starts]. **Added/Corp** United States. Bureau of the Census. **VFOAT** Housing Starts. (Aug. 1987)-. Government Publication. English. Twelve times a year. $15.00. US Department of Commerce / Bureau of the Census, Data User Services Division, Customer Services, Washington DC 20233-0800. **Tel** (301)763-4100. **(Subscription address:** Superintendent of Documents, US Government Printing Office, Washington DC 20402. **)** Documents available from Documents on Demand. ***Continues*** *Construction Reports. C20, Housing Starts, 0498-8442.*
Desc: Provides data for the United States on new privately-owned housing units that have been started, authorized in permit-issuing places, or authorized but not started.
Ind/Abst Am. Stat. Index.

LC HD9715.U5 A275 **ISSN** 0896-6737
DD 338.4/76908/0973021 US
CURRENT CONSTRUCTION REPORTS. C21, NEW RESIDENTIAL CONSTRUCTION IN SELECTED METROPOLITAN STATISTICAL AREAS. [Curr. constr. rep., C21 New resid. constr. sel. metrop. stat. areas]. **Added/Corp** United States. Bureau of the Census. United States. Dept. of Housing and Urban Development. **VFOAT** New Residential Construction in Selected Metropolitan Statistical Areas. (2nd Quarter 1987)-. Government Publication. English. Four times a year. $9.00 US; $11.25 other. US Department of Commerce / Bureau of the Census, Data User Services Division, Customer Services, Washington DC 20233-0800. **Tel** (301)763-4100. **(Subscription address:** Superintendent of Documents, US Government Printing Office, Washington DC 20402. **)** ***Continues*** *Construction Reports. C21, New Residential Construction in Selected Standard Metropolitan Statistical Areas, 0145-0212.*
Desc: Presents estimates of the number of new, privately owned residential housing units authorized by building permits, authorized but not yet started, started, under construction, and completed.

LC HD9715.U5 A275 **ISSN** 0896-6702
DD 338.4/76908/0973021 US
CURRENT CONSTRUCTION REPORTS. C22, HOUSING COMPLETIONS. (CURRENT CONSTRUCTION REPORTS. C22, HOUSING COMPLETIONS / U.S. DEPT. OF COMMERCE, BUREAU OF THE CENSUS [AND] U.S. DEPT. OF HOUSING AND URBAN DEVELOPMENT.). [Curr. constr. rep., C22 Hous. complet.]. **Added/Corp** United States. Bureau of the Census. United States. Dept. of Housing and Urban Development. **VFOAT** Housing Completions. (July 1987)-. Government Publication. English. Twelve times a year. $20.00 US; $25.00 other. US Department of Commerce / Bureau of the Census, Data User Services Division, Customer Services, Washington DC 20233-0800. **Tel** (301)763-4100. **(Subscription address:** Superintendent of Documents, US Government Printing Office, Washington DC 20402. **)** ***Continues*** *Construction Reports. C22, Housing Completions, 0363-8804.*
Desc: Provides data on the number of new privately owned housing units completed and under construction.

LC HD7293.A1 C65
DD 381/.45690837/0973021 US
CURRENT CONSTRUCTION REPORTS. C25, NEW ONE-FAMILY HOUSES SOLD /U.S. DEPT. OF COMMERCE, BUREAU OF THE CENSUS [AND] U.S. DEPT. OF HOUSING AND URBAN DEVELOPMENT. **Added/Corp** United States. Bureau of the Census. United States. Dept. of Housing and Urban Development. **VFOAT** New One-Family Houses Sold; New One Family Houses Sold. (Jan. 1991)-. Government Publication. English. Twelve times a year. $25.00 US; $31.25 other. US Department of Commerce / Bureau of the Census, Data User Services Division, Customer Services, Washington DC 20233-0800. **Tel** (301)763-4100. **(Subscription address:** Superintendent of Documents, US Government Printing Office, Washington DC 20402. **)** ***Formed by the union of*** *Current Construction Reports. C25, New One-Family Houses Sold and for Sale, 0896-9256* ***and*** *Current Construction Reports. C27, Price Index of New One-Family Houses Sold, 0896-6710.*
Desc: Presents information on new privately owned one-family houses sold during the month and for sale at the end of the month.

ISSN 0896-6745
DD 338 US
CURRENT CONSTRUCTION REPORTS. C30, VALUE OF NEW CONSTRUCTION PUT IN PLACE (1987). (CURRENT CONSTRUCTION REPORTS. C30, VALUE OF NEW CONSTRUCTION PUT IN PLACE / U.S. DEPT. OF COMMERCE, BUREAU OF THE CENSUS.). [Curr. constr. rep., C30 Value new constr. put in place]. **Added/Corp** United States. Bureau of the Census. **VFOAT** Value of New Construction Put in Place; Construction Reports. C30, Value of New Construction Put in Place. (Apr. 1987)-. Government Publication. English. Twelve times a year. $24.00. US Department of Commerce / Bureau of the Census, Data User Services Division, Customer Services, Washington DC 20233-0800. **Tel** (301)763-4100. **(Subscription address:** Superintendent of Documents, US Government Printing Office, Washington DC 20402. **)** ***Continues*** *Construction Reports. C30, Value of New Construction Put in Place (Washington, D.C. : 1986), 0896-6753.*
Desc: Presents estimates of the value of total new construction put in place by type of construction and by type of owner.

LC HD7293.A1 C66 **ISSN** 0896-9221
DD 338.4/76908/0973021 US
CURRENT CONSTRUCTION REPORTS. C40, HOUSING UNITS AUTHORIZED BY BUILDING PERMITS. (CURRENT CONSTRUCTION REPORTS. C40, HOUSING UNITS AUTHORIZED BY BUILDING PERMITS.). [Curr. constr. rep., C40 Hous. units auth. build. permits]. **Added/Corp** United States. Bureau of the Census. **VFOAT** Housing Units Authorized by Building Permits. (Sept. 1987)-. Government Publication. English. Twelve times a year (Annual issue). $62.00 US; $77.50 other; $24.00 (annual issue), US; $30.00 (annual issue) other. US Department of Commerce / Bureau of the Census, Data User Services Division, Customer Services, Washington DC 20233-0800. **Tel** (301)763-4100. **(Subscription address:** Superintendent of Documents, US Government Printing Office, Washington DC 20402. **)** ***Continues*** *Construction Reports. C40, Housing Units Authorized by Building Permits, 0896-923X.*
Desc: Presents monthly statistics on the number of new housing units authorized by building permits and public contracts in the United States.

US
CURRENT CONSTRUCTION REPORTS. C50, EXPENDITURES FOR RESIDENTIAL IMPROVEMENTS AND REPAIRS. **Added/Corp** United States. Bureau of the Census. **VFOAT** Expenditures for Residential Improvements and Repairs. (2nd quarter 1990)-. Government Publication. English. Four times a year. $17.00. US Department of Commerce / Bureau of the Census, Data User Services Division, Customer Services, Washington DC 20233-0800. **Tel** (301)763-4100. **(Subscription address:** Superintendent of Documents, US Government Printing Office, Washington DC 20402. **)** ***Continues*** *Current Construction Reports. C50, Expenditures for Residential Upkeep and Improvement;* ***Absorbed*** *Current Construction Reports. C50, Expenditures for Residential Upkeep and Improvements (Annual).*

Building and Construction

Desc: Provides estimates of expenditures by property owners for maintenance and repairs, additions, alterations, and major replacements to residential properties.

UK
CEASED

CURRENT INFORMATION IN THE CONSTRUCTION INDUSTRY. (197?)-(Sept. 1993). Trade Publication. English. Building Research Establishment, BRE Bookshop, Garston Watford WD27JR United Kingdom. **Tel** 011 44 1923 664444, FAX 011 44 1923 664400. **Circ:** 400. **Continues** Library Bulletin.
Desc: Gives details of new publications. Journal articles and forthcoming courses, conferences and meetings relating to the construction industry.

LC TH89 .S93c
DD 690/.07/20485 SW

CURRENT PROJECTS - SWEDISH COUNCIL FOR BUILDING RESEARCH.
Main/Corp Sweden. Statens Rad for Byggnadsforskning. **VFOAT** (. (19??)-. English.

LC TJ810 .S4866 ISSN 0895-2493
DD 690/.83 US
CCC

CUSTOM BUILDER. [Cust. build.]. Vol. 2, No. 10, (Oct. 1987)-. Trade Publication. English. Six times a year. $23.00. Willows Publishing Group, 38 Lafayette Street, PO Box 998, Yarmouth ME 04096-0998. **Tel** (207)846-0970, FAX (207)846-1561. **ED** John Andrews. **Ad Acc. Circ:** 30,000 (ctrl). available on microfilm and microfiche from University Microfilms International (UMI); available on an online database (file 648/Full-Text) from DIALOG. **Continues** Progressive Builder (Peterborough, N.H. : 1986), 0888-9171.
Desc: A trade publication for builders of high-end, one-of-a-kind residential homes.
Ind/Abst Appl. Sci. Technol. Index (-1990); Bus. ASAP (1992-) [Full Txt.]; Bus. Index (1987-); Constr. Index (-199?); EP Collect.; Gen. BusinessFile (1987-); Homework Help.; MasterFile FullTEXT 1000; MasterFile FullTEXT 350; MasterFile FullTEXT 650; MasterFile FullTEXT (Jan. 1993-); OCLC; Pub. Lib. FullTEXT; Telebase; Vocat. Search.

ISSN 1065-8157
DD 728 US

CUSTOM HOME PLANS. [Custom home plans]. **Added/Corp** HomeStyles Source 1 Designers' Network. Vol. 1, No. 1 (Spring 1992)-. Periodical. English. Four times a year. $4.95 (single issue). Hanley-Wood Inc., 1 Thomas Circle Northwest, Suite 600, Washington DC 20005. **Tel** (202)452-0800, FAX (202)785-1974.

ISSN 0194-3324
US

CUSTOM HOMES. Periodical. English. Hudson Home Publications, 175 S San Antonio Rd., Los Altos CA 94022. **Tel** (310)937-5486.

LC TH2430 .D3 ISSN 0012-124X
GW
TITLE CHANGE

DACHDECKER-HANDWERK, DAS.
Added/Corp Zentralverband des Dachdeckerhandwerks. **VFOAT** DDH. (1971)-(19??). Periodical. German. Verlagsgesellschaft Rudolf Mueller, Postfach 410949, D-50869 Cologne Germany. **Tel** 011 44 221 5497213, FAX 011 44 221 5497326. Index available. **Bk Rev. Ad Acc. Continues** Deutsches Dachdecker-Handwerk. **Continued by** DDH Das Dachdecker Handwerk.

ISSN 0317-3178
DD 380.1 CN

DAILY COMMERCIAL NEWS AND CONSTRUCTION RECORD. [Dly. commer. news constr. rec.]. (1973)-. Periodical. English. Seven times a week. 410.57Can$. Daily Commercial News, 280 Yorkland Boulevard, Willowdale Ontario M2J 4Z6 Canada. **Tel** (416)494-4990, FAX (416)756-2767. **ED** Scott Button. **Ad Acc. Circ:** 6,500 (ctrl). **Continues** Daily Commercial News and Building Record, 0317-316X.
Desc: Covers the building and construction markets in Ontario, Quebec and the Atlantic provinces of Canada. Each issue contains reports on new and repair construction, building and engineering projects. Two daily news pages cover developments in business practices, technology, markets, manpower, domestic and international market conditions, the professions and new products.

ISSN 0011-5401
US

DAILY CONSTRUCTION SERVICE. (19??)-. Periodical. English. Seven times a week. $924.00. Wade Publishing Company, PO Box 3019, San Francisco CA 94119. **Tel** (415)781-8088. **ED** William B. Wallace. **Ad Acc. Circ:** 2,000.
Desc: Detailed reports on heavy and general engineering construction activity in the western United States.

ISSN 0931-1181
GW

DARMSTADT CONCRETE : ANNUAL JOURNAL ON CONCRETE AND CONCRETE STRUCTURES. **Added/Corp** Technische Hochschule Darmstadt. Institut fuer Massivbau. Vol. 1 (1986)-. Periodical. English. Technische Hochschule Darmstadt, Institut fuer Massivbau, Alexanderstrasse 5, 6100 Darmstadt Germany.
Ind/Abst Abstr. J. Earthq. Eng.; Concr. Abstr.

LC TA174 .D39 ISSN 1071-5975
DD 620/.0042/0685 US

DCQFORUM (SILVER SPRING, MD.).
(DCQFORUM : A PUBLICATION OF THE DESIGN & CONSTRUCTION QUALITY INSTITUTE.). [DCQForum]. **Added/Corp** Design & Construction Quality Institute. **VFOAT** DCQ Forum. (1991)-. Periodical. English. Four times a year (Jan., April, July, Oct.). $95.00. American Consulting Engineers Council, 1015 15th Street Northwest, Suite 802, Washington DC 20005. **Tel** (202)347-7474, FAX (202)898-0068.

ISSN 0172-1003
GW

UDC 69.024
DDH. DAS DACHDECKER-HANDWERK. [DDH, Dacchdecker-Handw.]. **VFOAT** Dachdecker-Handwerk (1978). (1978)-. Trade Publication. German. Twenty-four times a year. $198.05. Verlagsgesellschaft Rudolf Mueller, Postfach 410949, D-50869 Cologne Germany. **Tel** 011 44 221 5497213, FAX 011 44 221 5497326. **Continues** Das Dachdecker-Handwerk, 0341-5422.

ISSN 1148-4675
FR

UDC 681.3.002.52
DECISION MICRO PARIS. (DECISION MICRO.). (1990)-. Periodical. French. Irregular (43 per year). 548.48F France; 920.00F other. Groupe Tests, 26 rue d'Oradour sur Glane, 75504 Paris Cedex 15 France. **Tel** 011 33 1 44253001, FAX 011 33 1 45573506. **Continues** Decision Informatique (Paris), 0293-3896.

LC TH153 .D45 ISSN 0362-7772
DD 690/.26/05 CN

DEMOLITION AGE. (19??)-. Trade Publication. English. Twelve times a year. $36.00. National Association of Demolition Contractors, PO Box 2329, Doylestown PA 18901. **Tel** (215)348-8282, FAX (215)348-8422. **ED** Michael R. Taylor. **Ad Acc.** Full Page (B&W) $900.00. Half Page (B&W) $725.00. Full Page (Color) $1,575.00. Half Page (Color) $1,400.00.

ISSN 0820-778X
DD 696/.1/025714 CN

DES CHANTIERS ET DES HOMMES. [Des chantiers hommes]. **VFOAT** Projects and Men. Vol. 1, No 1 (Jan. 1983)-. Periodical. English (French). Four times a year. Free. Des Chantiers Et Des Hommes, Room 403A 5165 Sherbrooke Street West, Montreal Quebec H4A 1T6.

LC TA440 .P6 ISSN 0190-6755
DD 620.136 US

DESIGN AND CONTROL OF CONCRETE MIXTURES. **Main/Corp** Portland Cement Association. (19??)-. English. Irregular. Portland Cement Association, 5420 Old Orchard Road, Skokie IL 60077. **Tel** (708)966-6200. **ED** William C. Panarese and Steven H. Kosmatka. Index available. **Bk Rev. Circ:** 25,000.
Desc: Practical guidebook for anyone who designs concrete mixtures, prepares concrete and places it in construction or certifies and controls its quality.

LC NA7205 .D45
DD 728.3/7/0223 US

DESIGNER HOME PLANS. See Architecture.

ISSN 1046-6223
DD 602 CEASED

DESIGNSOURCE (1989). (DESIGNSOURCE.). [DesignSource]. **Added/Corp** American Society of Interior Designers. **VFOAT** Design Source. (198?)-(1995). English. K-III Press Inc., 424 West 33rd Street, New York NY 10001. **Tel** (212)714-3100, (800)221-5488. **Formed by the union of** DesignSource (Central Ed.), 0886-5442; DesignSource (East Ed.); DesignSource (Northeast Edition), 0886-5426; DesignSource (Southeast Ed.), 0886-5434; DesignSource (Southwest Edition), 0886-5469 **and** DesignSource (West Edition), 0886-5450.

ISSN 0171-7197
GW
CODEN DASBBR
CEASED

DEUTSCHER AUSSCHUSS FUER STAHLBETON. (DEUTSCHER AUSSCHUSS FUER STAHLBETON. SCHRIFTENREIHE.). [Dtsch. Aussch. Stahlbeton]. **Added/Corp** Deutscher Ausschuss Fur Stahlbeton. (1941)-Series complete with W 388. Academic Scholarly Publication. German. VCH Gesellschaft GmbH, Postfach 101161, D-69451 Weinheim Germany. **Tel** 011 49 6201 606459, FAX 011 49 6201 606184. Documents available from Article Express International, CASDDS.
Ind/Abst Bioeng. Abstr.; Chem. Abstr. (1941-1982); Ei Page One; Eng. Index Annu.

ISSN 0012-1215
GW

DEUTSCHES ARCHITEKTENBLATT. AUSGABE BADEN-WUERTTEMBERG. See Architecture.

UK
DEVELOPMENT AND MATERIALS BULLETIN. (1967)-. Bulletin. English.
Ind/Abst Archit. Period. Index (Oct./Nov. 1977-Sept. 1982).

ISSN 0847-1363
DD 338.4/769/00971128021 CN

DEVELOPMENT REVIEW (VICTORIA). See Real Estate.

NE
DHZ VAKHANDEL. See Interior Design and Decoration.

ISSN 0012-2467
FR

UDC 69 (089.2)
DICTIONNAIRE PERMANENT CONSTRUCTION. [Dict. perm. constr.]. (1962)-. French. Irregular. Editions Legislatives et Admin, 80 82 Avenue de la Marne, 92546 Montrouge Cedex France. **Tel** 011 33 1 40926868, FAX 011 33 1 46560015, telex 632 855 F.

ISSN 0701-5267
DD 690 CN

DIGEST DE LA CONSTRUCTION AU CANADA. [Dig. const. Can.]. **Added/Corp** Conseil National de Recherches du Canada. Division des Recherches sur le Batiment. Conseil National de Recherches Canada. Division des Recherches sur le Batiment. Institut de Recherche en Construction (Canada). **VFOAT** Digeste de la Construction au Canada. (1961)-. Monographic series. French. Irregular. Price varies per volume. Conseil National de Recherches du Quebec, Direction des Recherches Sur le Batiment, Ottawa Ontario Canada.

ISSN 0883-0258
DD 691 US
Pr Rev.

DIMENSIONAL STONE. [Dimens. stone]. Vol. 1, No. 1 (Spring 1985)-. Trade Publication. English. Twelve times a year. $50.00. Dimensional Stone, 20335 Ventura Boulevard #400, Woodland Hills CA 91364. **Tel** (818)704-5555, FAX (818)704-6500, telex 181545 TELE MAG CD. **ED** John Maynard. **Bk Rev. Ad Acc. Circ:** 15,289 (ctrl).
Desc: Published for all who quarry, fabricate, work, install, specify or sell dimensional stone.

LC KFX1238.1.C64 B85 ISSN 0190-4787
DD 344/.77311/018819 US

DIRECTORY AND GUIDE - BUILDING CONSTRUCTION EMPLOYERS' ASSOCIATION OF CHICAGO, INC. See Law.

ISSN 0228-1619
DD 690/.15/06071 CN

DIRECTORY - CANADIAN ROOFING CONTRACTORS' ASSOCIATION. [Dir. - Can. Roof. Contract. Assoc.]. **Main/Corp** Canadian Roofing Contractors' Association. **VFOAT** Annuaire - Association Canadienne des Entrepreneurs en Couverture. 1980-. Directory. English (French). One time a year. Canadian Roofing Contractors' Association, Suite 710/116 Albert Street, Ottawa Ontario K1P 5G3 Canada. **Continues** CRCA Directory, 0228-0876.

LC KF195.C58 A43 ISSN 0273-5180
DD 343.73/07869/0025 347.30378690025 US

DIRECTORY - FORUM COMMITTEE ON THE CONSTRUCTION INDUSTRY, AMERICAN BAR ASSOCIATION. See Law.

II
DIRECTORY OF BUILDERS AND CONTRACTORS. (19??)-. Directory. English. Every 2 years. $20.00. Architects Publishing Corporation of India, 51 Sujata/Ground Floor, Rani Sati Marg, Malad East, Bombay 400 097 India. **Tel** 840 4442 or 8405510, FAX 680 5510. **ED** A K Gupta. Index available. **Ad Acc. Circ:** 5,000.
Desc: Contains addresses of builders, contractors, manufacturers and dealers of building industry.

LC TH ISSN 1063-1232
DD 692 US

●DIRECTORY OF CALIFORNIA LICENSED CONTRACTORS. [Dir. North. Calif. licens. contract.]. 4th Ed. (1993)-. Directory. English.

Building and Construction

Every 2 years. $99.00. Database Publishing Company, PO Box 7440, Newport Beach CA 92658. **Tel** (714)646-1623, (800)-888-8434, FAX (714)631-8471. **Continues in part** Directory of California Licensed Contractors.

LC TH
DD 692 US

● **DIRECTORY OF CALIFORNIA LICENSED CONTRACTORS.** [Dir. South. Calif. licens. contract.]. 4th Ed. (1993)-. Directory. English. Every 2 years. $99.00. Database Publishing Company, PO Box 7440, Newport Beach CA 92658. **Tel** (714)646-1623, (800)-888-8434, FAX (714)631-8471. **Continues in part** Directory of California Licensed Contractors.

ISSN 0842-6589
DD 338.7/69/002571 CN

DIRECTORY OF CANADIAN CONSTRUCTION COMPANIES. (DIRECTORY OF CANADIAN CONSTRUCTION COMPANIES / [B.O.S.S.].). [Dir. Can. constr. co.]. **Added/Corp** Business Opportunities Sourcing System (Canada) Canada. Surface Transportation and Machinery Branch. Construction Division. Canada. Construction Industry and Capital Projects Directorate. **VFOAT** Directory of Construction Companies. (1987)-. Directory. English. One time a year (Jan.). 39.00Can$ Canada. Tyrell Press, Ltd., 2714 Fenton Road, Box 937, Gloucester Ontario K1G 3N3 Canada. **Tel** (800)574-0137, (613)822-0740, FAX (613)822-1089.

ISSN 0847-9720
DD 690/.025/71 CN

DIRECTORY OF CORPORATE MEMBER FIRMS AND MEMBER-ASSOCIATIONS / CANADIAN CONSTRUCTION ASSOCIATION. [Dir. corp. memb. firms memb.-assoc.]. **Main/Corp** Association Canadienne de la Construction. **VFOAT** Repertoire des Membres Corporatifs et des Associations-Membres. (1989)-. Directory. French (English). Canadian Construction Association, 85 Albert Street/2nd Floor, Ottawa Ontario K1P 6A4 Canada. **Tel** (613)236-9455, FAX (613)236-9526, telex 053-4436. **Continues** Directory of National Member Firms and Member-Associations., 0828-7031.

LC HD9745.U4 D52
DD 381/.4568/02573 US

DIRECTORY OF HARDLINES DISTRIBUTORS. **VFOAT** Chain Store Guide ... Directory of Hardlines Distributors. (1988)-. Directory. English. One time a year (June). $225.00 continental US; $235.00 other US; $250.00 other. Lebhar Friedman Inc., PO Box 31203, Tampa FL 33633. **Tel** (800)944-4676, (813)664-6707. Index available. available on magnetic tape. **Continues** Directory of Hardware & Housewares Distributors, 0882-536X.
Desc: Provides company profiles of houseware, paint and paint sundries, electrical, heating, cooling, plumbing, lumber, building supplies and lawn and garden distributors serving 6.5 million retailer, contractor and commercial accounts.

LC HD9745.U4 D485 ISSN 0272-0167
DD 381/.45683/02573 US

DIRECTORY OF HOME CENTER OPERATORS & HARDWARE CHAINS. [Dir. home cent. oper. hardw. chains]. **VFOAT** Home Center Operators & Hardware Chains. **VAT** Directory of Home Center Operators and Hardware Chains. (19??)-. Directory. English. One time a year. $255.00 continental US; $265.00 other US; $280.00 other. Lebhar Friedman Inc., PO Box 31203, Tampa FL 33633. **Tel** (800)944-4676, (813)664-6707. **ED** Christopher Warne. Index available. **Continues** Directory: Home Centers & Hardware Chains, Auto Supply Chains, 0094-8667.
Desc: Profiles on 6,300 home centers, lumber/building material companies and hardware chains, and 200 specialty paint/home decorating chains serving 22,700 units. Also covers 23 buying groups serving 85,000 stores.

LC HD9745.U4 D53 ISSN 0093-8718
DD 381/.45/68302573 US

DIRECTORY OF HOME CENTERS. (19??)-. English. One time a year. $90.00. Lebhar Friedman Inc., PO Box 31203, Tampa FL 33633. **Tel** (800)944-4676, (813)664-6707.

LC TH
DD 690 II

● **DIRECTORY OF MANUFACTURERS & DEALERS OF BUILDING INDUSTRY.** **VFOAT** Directory of Manufacturers and Dealers of Building Industry. (1994)-. Directory. English. Irregular. $15.00. Architects Publishing Corporation of India, 51 Sujata/Ground Floor, Rani Sati Marg, Malad East, Bombay 400 097 India. **Tel** 840 4442 or 8405510, FAX 680 5510. **ED** A.K. Gupta. **Ad Acc. Circ:** 5,000.

LC HD9993.S953 U53 ISSN 0884-3481
DD 381/.4569089 US

DIRECTORY. SWIMMING POOL DEALERS & CONTRACTORS. [Dir., Swim. pool deal. & contract.]. **VFOAT** Directory; Swimming Pool Dealers & Contractors; Swimming Pool Dealers and Contractors; Swimming Pool Dealers and Contractors Directory. (19??)-. Directory. English. One time a year. $300.00. American Business Directory, 5711 South 86th Circle, PO Box 27347, Omaha NE 68127. **Tel** (402)593-4600, FAX (402)331-5481. **ED** Andrew Bock. available on diskette.
Desc: A directory of 8,812 swimming pool dealers and contractors compiled from the yellow pages.

LC TA1 .D5 ISSN 0012-4281
DD 620.5 US

DIXIE CONTRACTOR, THE. See Engineering-Civil Engineering.

ISSN 0172-2867
GW

DLW-NACHRICHTEN. **VFOAT** Nachrichten der Deutsche Linoleum-Werke-AG. (19??)-. Trade Publication. Multiple languages.
Ind/Abst Archit. Period. Index (Vol. 39, No. 59, 1975-1982).

ISSN 0012-4370
DD 643 UK
CEASED

DO IT YOURSELF. [Do it yours.]. (1957)-(June 1994). Periodical. English. Link House Magazines Ltd., Link House, Dingwall Avenue, Croydon Surrey CR9 2TA United Kingdom. **Tel** 011 44 181 6862599, FAX 011 44 181 7600973, telex 947709.

LC TS200 .N3 ISSN 0889-2989
DD 338.4/7683/0973 US

DO-IT-YOURSELF RETAILING. [Do-it-yours. retail.]. **Added/Corp** National Retail Hardware Association (U.S.). **VFOAT** Do It Yourself Retailing. Vol. 150, No. 7 (June 1986)-. Trade Publication. English. Twelve times a year. $15.00. National Retailing Hardware Association, 5822 West 74th Street, Indianapolis IN 46278. **Tel** (317)297-1190. available on an online database (files 570,648/Full-Text) from DIALOG. **Continues** DIY Retailing, 8750-2569.
Ind/Abst Bus. ASAP (1990-) [Full Txt.]; Bus. Index (1986-); F&S Index Plus Text, Int. [Select. Cov.]; Gen. BusinessFile (1986-); Mark. Advert. Ref. Serv.; PROMT; Trade Ind. ASAP [Full Txt.]; Trade Ind. Index [Full Txt.].

DODGE BUILDING COST AND SPECIFICATION DIGEST. English. Two times a year. $176.50. McGraw Hill Publishing Company, Inc., 1221 Avenue of the Americas, New York NY 10020. **Tel** (212)512-6410, (800)525-5003, FAX (212)512-6111.

DD 338.4 US

DODGE BUILDING COST CALCULATOR & VALUATION GUIDE. **Added/Corp** McGraw Hill Information Systems Company. **VFOAT** Building Cost Calculator & Valuation Guide. **VAT** Dodge Building Cost Calculator and Valuation Guide. (1971)-. English. Four times a year. $80.00 US and Canada; $85.00 Pan America; $90.00 Europe; $95.00 other. Calculator Inc, PO Box 445, Occoquan VA 22125. **Tel** (703)379-4548. **ED** David Rosoff. **Continues** Dow Building Cost Calculator and Valuation Guide **and** Calculator Valuation Guide.
Desc: Guide used for preliminary estimates, budgeting, and backup in obtaining, financing for old or new buildings. Guide helps determine replacement costs and provides historical cost indexes.

ISSN 1053-3001
DD 692 US
TITLE CHANGE

DODGE REMODELING & RETROFIT COST DATA. [Dodge remodel. retrofit cost data]. **Added/Corp** McGraw-Hill Information Systems Company. **VFOAT** Dodge Remodeling and Retrofit Cost Data. (1987)-(19??). English. McGraw Hill Publishing Company, Inc., 1221 Avenue of the Americas, New York NY 10020. **Tel** (212)512-6410, (800)525-5003, FAX (212)512-6111. **Continues** McGraw Hill's Dodge Remodeling and Retrofit Cost Data. **Continued by** Repair & Remodel Quarterly.

● **DODGE REPAIR AND REMODEL COST BOOK.** (1995)-. English. One time a year. $65.95. Marshall & Swift, 911 Wilshire Boulevard, 16th Floor, Los Angeles CA 90026. **Tel** (800)544-2678, FAX (310)250-9811. **Continues** Repair and Remodel Quarterly.

US

DODGE REPORTS. English. Irregular. McGraw Hill Publishing Company, Inc., 1221 Avenue of the Americas, New York NY 10020. **Tel** (212)512-6410, (800)525-5003, FAX (212)512-6111.

US

DODGE/SWEET'S CONSTRUCTION OUTLOOK / MCGRAW-HILL CONSTRUCTION INFORMATION GROUP. **Added/Corp** McGraw-Hill Information Systems Company. Economics Dept. McGraw-Hill Construction Information Group. **VFOAT** Construction Outlook; Outlook. (19??)-. English. Four times a year. McGraw Hill Publishing Company, Inc., 1221 Avenue of the Americas, New York NY 10020. **Tel** (212)512-6410, (800)525-5003, FAX (212)512-6111. **Continues** F.W. Dodge Construction Outlook.
Ind/Abst F&S Index Plus Text, Int. [Select. Cov.]; Predicasts Forecasts.

LC TS200 .H85 ISSN 0361-5294
DD 338.4/7/683 US
Pr Rev.

DOORS AND HARDWARE. **Added/Corp** National Builders' Hardware Association. Door and Hardware Institute. Vol.35 (Sept. 1970)-. Trade Publication. English. Twelve times a year. $45.00. Doors & Hardware, 14170 Newbrook Drive, Chantilly VA 22021. **Tel** (703)222-2010, FAX (703)222-2410. **ED** Terre Simpson. Index available. cum. index. **Ad Acc, Adv Mgr:** R. Silverstein. **Circ:** 9,500. available on an online database (file 648/Full-Text) from DIALOG. **Continues** Hardware Consultant.
Desc: Covering the openings industry with articles on management, builders hardware, doors, educational programs, electronic security, codes, computerization and more.
Ind/Abst Constr. Index; Trade Ind. ASAP [Full Txt.]; Trade Ind. Index [Full Txt.].

US

DRAFTING CONSTRUCTION CONTRACTS AND HANDLING CONSTRUCTION LITIGATION. See Law.

ISSN 0264-4835
UK

DREDGING + PORT CONSTRUCTION. SERIES II. [DPC. Dredg. port constr.]. Vol. 5, No. 1 (Oct. 1977)-. Trade Publication. English. Twelve times a year. $208.00. Argus Press Group, Queensway House, 2 Queensway Redhill, Surrey RH1 1QS United Kingdom. **Tel** 011 44 1737 768611, 011 44 1737 761685, FAX 011 44 1737 760510, telex 948669 TOPJNL G. **Continues** International Dredging and Port Construction, 0579-546X.
Desc: Worldwide coverage of port construction and development and dredging projects.
Ind/Abst EMBASE; Fluid Abstr., Civil Eng.; Fluid Abstr. Proc. Eng.; FLUIDEX (1977-).

US

DREXEL INSULATION REPORT. English. Six times a year (Feb., Apr., June, Aug., Oct., Dec.). $50.00. Harold G. Lorsch / Drexel University, Philadelphia PA 19104. **Tel** (215)895-1833, FAX (215)895-1478. **Bk Rev,** (Qty: 4). **Circ:** 150.

US

DWELLING CONSTRUCTION UNDER THE UNIFORM BUILDING CODE. **Main/Corp** International Conference of Building Officials. **Added/Corp** International Conference of Building Officials. International Conference of Building Officials. Dwelling House Construction Under the Uniform Building Code. (19??)-. English. Irregular (Published every three years). $11.00 (members) of ICBO; $14.70 (nonmembers). ICBO Evaluation Service Inc., 5360 South Workman Mill Road, Whittier CA 90601. **Tel** (213)699-0541, FAX (213)692-3853.
Desc: Designed primarily for use in home building and apprentice training.

ISSN 0814-236X
DD 690.809945 AT

DWELLING UNIT COMMENCEMENTS REPORTED BY APPROVED AUTHORITIES, VICTORIA. [Dwell. unit commenc. rep. approv. auth. Vic.]. **Added/Corp** Australian Bureau of Statistics. Victorian Office. (1983)-. Periodical. English. Four times a year. $118.40. Australian Bureau of Statistics, PO Box 2796Y, Melbourne 3001 Australia. **Tel** 011 61 3 6157843. **Continues** Number of New Dwellings Commenced in Victoria, 0728-6538.

ISSN 1121-1180
IT
UDC 699.8

E T. EDIFICIO TECNOLOGICO. [E T, Edif. tecnol.]. **VFOAT** Edificio Tecnologico. (1991)-. Periodical. Italian. Six times a year. L74940. EPC Spa, Via dell'Acqua Traversa 187/189, 00135 Rome Italy. **Tel** 011 39 6 3313000, FAX 011 39 6 3313212.

US

EARTH SHELTER LIVING NEWSLETTER. No. 47 (Sept./Oct. 1986)-. Newsletter. English. Six times a year. Webco Publishing, 1701 East Cope, St. Paul MN 55109. **Tel** (612)430-1113. **Continues** Earth Shelter Living, 0744-1932.

Building and Construction

DD 338.430993021
ISSN 0114-6912
NZ
ECONOMY WIDE CENSUS. [Econ. wide census]. (1989)-. English. Five times a year. Department of Statistics / New Zealand, PO Box 2922, Wellington New Zealand. **Tel** 011 64 4 4954600. *Continues Census of Services, 0112-1413 and Census of Services, Finance and Insurance, 0112-9988.*
Desc: Information on business statistics in the building and construction industry.

ISSN 0013-3116
RU
EKONOMIKA STROITELSTVA. Added/Corp Soviet Union. Gosudarstvennyi Komitet po Delam Stroitelstva. (1959)-. Periodical. Russian. Twelve times a year. $79.95. **(Subscription address:** East View Publications Inc., 3020 Harbor Lane North, Suite 110, Minneapolis MN 55447. **Tel** (800)477-1005, (612)550-0961, FAX (612)559-2931.) Index available.

ISSN 0149-5771
US
CCC
ELECTRICAL MARKETING. See Engineering-Electrical Engineering.

LC HD9695.C2 A313
ISSN 0835-104X
DD 338.4/762131/0971021
CN
ELECTRICAL TRADE CONTRACTORS. (ELECTRICAL TRADE CONTRACTORS = ENTREPRENEURS EN METIERS ELECTRIQUES.). [Electr. trade contract.]. **Added/Corp** Statistics Canada. Industry Division. **VFOAT** Entrepreneurs en Metiers Electriques. (1984)-. English (French). One time a year. 22.00Can$ Canada; $26.00 US; $31.00 other. Statistics Canada Publications Sales and Services, R.H. Coats Building 6th Floor, Ottawa Ontario K1A 0T6 Canada. **Tel** (613)951-5078, (800)267-6677, FAX (613)951-1584, telex 053-3585. *Continues Electrical Contracting Industry, 0702-8083.*

LC TA401
ISSN 1062-9580
DD 624
US
ELECTRONIC SWEET'S. (ELECTRONIC SWEET'S [COMPUTER FILE] : DATABASES FOR CONSTRUCTION PROFESSIONALS.). [Electron. Sweet's]. (19??)-. English. Two times a year. McGraw-Hill Inc. Construction Information Services Group, Sweet's Group, 1221 Avenue of the Americas, New York NY 10020.

LC TH
ISSN 0210-2145
DD 690
SP
UDC 69
EME DOS. [Eme Dos]. (1976)-. Periodical. Spanish. Four times a year (Jan., Apr., July, Oct.). 10300ptas. Ert SL, Burdeaux 37 Entresuelo Primera, 08029 Barcelona Spain. **Tel** 93/4397873, FAX 93/4397902.
Desc: Publication covers general construction. Also provides information on the companies that intervene in the making of a project and decision making in the purchase of materials.

LC HD9715.E25 E5
DD 338.47624
EC
ENCUESTA DE EDIFICACIONES (PERMISOS DE CONSTRUCCION). Added/Corp Instituto Nacional de Estadistica (Ecuador) Ecuador. Division de Estadistica y Censos. **VFOAT** Encuesta de Permisos de Construccion; Estadisticas de Permisos de Construccion. (19??)-. Spanish. One time a year. Instituto Nacional de Estadistica y Censos, Avda 10 de Agosto 229, Quito Ecuador. **Tel** 011 593 2 581900, 011 593 2 581901, telex 21421 INFEC ED.

LC TJ163.5.B84 E523
ISSN 0378-7788
DD 690
SZ
CCC
CODEN ENEBDR
Pr Rev.
ENERGY AND BUILDINGS. [Energy build.]. Vol. 1 (May 1977)-. Academic Scholarly Publication. English. Three times a year (1 vols.). $812.00. Elsevier Sequoia SA, PO Box 564, CH-1001 Lausanne 1 Switzerland. **Tel** 011 41 21 3207381, FAX 011 41 21 3235444. **ED** Alan Meier, and B. Todorovic. **Ad Acc, Adv Mgr:** W. van Cattenburch (Amsterdam). available on microfilm and microfiche from University Microfilms International (UMI); available on an online database from Elsevier Electronic Subscriptions (EES). Documents available from Article Express International, The Genuine Article, Ask*IEEE.
Desc: Presents the results of research activities conducted by the building science community concerned with energy use, quality of the indoor environment and climatology. Covers all topics that can improve the energy efficiency in the built environment.
Ind/Abst AESIS Q.; Appl. Mech. Rev.; Archit. Period. Index (Oct. 1982-); Bioeng. Abstr.; Curr. Cit.; Curr. Contents Eng. Comput. Technol.; Educ. Adm. Abstr. (?-?); Ei Page One; EMBASE; Energy Inf. Abstr.; Energy Res. Abstr. (Aug. 1977-); Eng. Index Annu.; Environ. Period. Bibliogr.; Gas Abstr.; Health Saf. Sci. Abstr.; Hum. Resour. Abstr. (?-?); Infomat Int. Bus.; INSPEC (Aug. 1979-); Int. Aerosp. Abstr.; Int. Build. Serv. Abstr.; Int. Civil Eng. Abstr.; J. Plan. Lit.; Pollut. Abstr. Indexes; Res. Alert [Select. Cov.]; Sage Urban Stud. Abstr; SCISEARCH; Soft. Abstr. Eng.; World Ceram. Abstr.

LC TA684 .E65
ISSN 0013-8029
US
CODEN EJASAR
ENGINEERING JOURNAL (NEW YORK). (ENGINEERING JOURNAL.). [Eng. j.]. **Added/Corp** American Institute of Steel Construction. American Institute of Steel Construction. AISC Engineering Journal. **VFOAT** AISC Engineering Journal. **VAT** American Institute of Steel Construction Engineering Journal. Vol. 1, (Jan. 1964)-. Periodical. English. Four times a year. $25.00. American Institute of Steel Construction, 1 East Wacker Drive, Suite 3100, Chicago IL 60601. **Tel** (312)670-2400, FAX (312)670-5403. available on microfilm and microfiche from University Microfilms International (UMI). Documents available from Article Express International, The Genuine Article.
Ind/Abst Abstr. J. Earthq. Eng.; Appl. Sci. Technol. Index (Sept. 1974-); Bioeng. Abstr.; Ei Page One; Energy Res. Abstr.; Eng. Index Annu.; Geotech. Abstr.; Highw. Res. Abstr.; INIS Atomindex [Micro.]; J. Ferrocement; Life Sci. Collect.; Res. Alert [Full Cov.]; SCISEARCH; Soc. Sci. Cit. Index [Select. Cov.].

LC TA12 .E325
ISSN 1065-2205
DD 338
ENR DIRECTORY OF CONTRACTORS. MIDWEST REGION. [ENR dir. contract., Midwest reg.]. **VFOAT** Directory of Contractors. Midwest Region; Midwest Contractors; Directory. Midwest Contractors; ENR Directory. Midwest Contractors; ENR Contractors. Midwest. 9th Ed. (1991/1992)-. Directory. English. Every 2 years. ENR, 1221 Avenue of the Americas, New York NY 10020. **Tel** FAX (609)426-5472, telex 232 365 MGHPUBNET. *Continues in part ENR Directory of Contractors, 0098-6453.*

ISSN 1065-2213
DD 338
US
ENR DIRECTORY OF CONTRACTORS. SOUTH REGION. [ENR dir. contract., South reg.]. **VFOAT** Directory of Contractors. South Region; South Contractors; Directory. South Contractors; ENR Directory. South Contractors; ENR Contractors. South. 9th Ed. (1991/1992)-. Directory. English. Every 2 years. ENR, 1221 Avenue of the Americas, New York NY 10020. **Tel** FAX (609)426-5472, telex 232 365 MGHPUBNET. *Continues in part ENR Directory of Contractors, 0098-6453.*

ISSN 1065-2183
DD 338
US
ENR DIRECTORY OF CONTRACTORS. WEST REGION. [ENR dir. contract., West reg.]. **VFOAT** Directory of Contractors. West Region; West Contractors; Directory. West Contractors; ENR Directory. West Contractors; ENR Contractors. West. 9th Ed. (1991/1992)-. Directory. English. Every 2 years. ENR, 1221 Avenue of the Americas, New York NY 10020. **Tel** FAX (609)426-5472, telex 232 365 MGHPUBNET. *Continues in part ENR Directory of Contractors, 0098-6453.*

LC TA12 .E4
ISSN 0098-6305
DD 620/.004/2
US
ENR DIRECTORY OF DESIGN FIRMS. See Engineering.

LC HD9715.A1 E57
DD 338.4/7/624094
FR
ENTREPRISE EUROPEENNE, L'. See Industry and Production.

ISSN 0705-9272
DD 696
CN
ENVIRONMENT SYSTEMS & INDUSTRIES. [Environ. syst. ind.]. Vol. 7, No. 11 (Nov. 1976)-. Periodical. English. Twelve times a year. $5.00 Canada, $7.00 US. Wadham Publications, Division of Southam Communications Ltd, 1450 Don Mills Road, Don Mills Ontario M3B 2X7 Canada. **Tel** (416)445-6641, (416)442-2213. *Continues Environmental Systems Industries, 0046-2322.*

LC TA401 .E585
ISSN 1062-3957
DD 690
US
ENVIRONMENTAL BUILDING NEWS : A NEWSLETTER ON ENVIRONMENTALLY SUSTAINABLE DESIGN & CONSTRUCTION. [Environ. build. news]. (1992)-. Newsletter. English. Six times a year. $95.00. Environmental Building News, RR1, Box 161, Brattleboro VT 05301. **Tel** (802)257-7300, FAX (802)257-7304. **ED** Alex Wilson. Index available. cum. index. **Bk Rev**, (Qty: 15). **Circ:** 1,500.
Desc: A bi-monthly newsletter on environmentally sustainable design and construction. News, feature articles, new products, construction details and book reviews -- an essential resource for green building.

LC HD9718.5.A82 E58
ISSN 1047-336X
DD 363.17/91
US
ENVIRONMENTAL CONTRACTOR MAGAZINE. (ENVIRONMENTAL CONTRACTOR MAGAZINE : ECON.). [Environ. contract. mag.] **VFOAT** ECON; ECON, Environmental Contractor. (198?)-. Periodical. English. Twelve times a year. $45.00. PTN Publishing Company, 445 Broad Hollow Road, Melville NY 11747. **Tel** (516)845-2700, FAX (516)845-7109. *Continues Environmental Contractors, 1041-1372.*

LC TP785 .E63
ISSN 0013-970X
DD 666
HU
CODEN EPITAA
EPITOANYAG. See Glass and Ceramics.

LC HD9715.H8 H83A
HU
EPITOIPARI ARAK ALAKULASA, AZ. Main/Corp Hungary. Kozponti Statisztikai Hivatal. Beruhazasi Es Epitoipari Statisztikai Foosztaly. (19??)-. Hungarian. Statisztikai Kiado Vallalat, PO Box 99, H-1033 Budapest 3 Hungary. **Tel** 803-311, telex 22-6699-SKV-H.

LC HC800.A1 E68
DD 338.096
FR
EQUIP-AFRIC. French. Ediafric la Documentation Africaine, 10 rue Vineuse, 75116 Paris France. **Tel** 011 33 1 44308100, FAX 011 33 1 45208174.

ISSN 0700-432X
DD 690/.028
CN
EQUIPEMENT ET METHODES. Vol. 1 (Jan. 1977)-. Periodical. French. $12.00. Equipement et Methodes, rue Buies, Saint-Bruno Quebec J3V 2T5 Canada.

ISSN 0891-141X
DD 690
US
EQUIPMENT TODAY. [Equip. today]. Vol. 21, No. 10 (Oct. 1986)-. Trade Publication. English. Twelve times a year (plus special issue in March). $50.00. Johnson Hill Press Inc., (A Division of PTN Publishing Co.), 1233 Janesville Avenue, PO Box 803, Fort Atkinson WI 53538-0803. **Tel** (414)563-6388, FAX (414)563-1704. **ED** Jeff Ignaszak. **Ad Acc.** Full Page (B&W) $7090.00. Full Page (Color) $8690.00 (4-color). **Circ:** 81,018. *Continues Equipment Guide News, 0149-5240.*
Desc: Serves owners and managers of heavy construction contractor businesses. Provides equipment selection and maintenance information, as well as safety and preventive maintenance features.

ISSN 0308-8073
UK
ESTIMATING INFORMATION SERVICE. (1971)-. English. Four times a year.

LC TH435 .E7
DD 692/.5/05
US
ESTIMATOR'S HANDBOOK. English. One time a year. Balfour, 252 South Grant Avenue, Indianapolis IN 46201-4551.

ISSN 0905-913X
DD 690
DK
EURO-BUILD KBENHAVN. [Euro-build Kbh.]. **VFOAT** Euro-Build (Virum). (1990)-. Periodical. Danish. Twenty-six times a year. $540.00. European Construction Research, Hovedvejen 182, 2600 Glostrup Denmark. **Tel** 011 45 43436322, FAX 011 45 43430940. *Continues Constructis.*

ISSN 0941-5092
GW
UDC 62
CODEN 33
EUROPEAN ASPHALT MAGAZINE. **VFOAT** EAM. European Asphalt Magazine. (1990)-. Trade Publication. Multiple languages. Four times a year. DM76.00. Stein Verlag GmbH, Josef Herrmann Strasse 1-3, W-7557 Iffezheim FR Germany. **Tel** 011 49 7229 6060, FAX 011 49 7229 60610, telex 841/781328.

UK
EUROPEAN CONSTRUCTION DOCUMENTS. (19??)-. English. Four times a year. £99.00, £175.00 (new orders). Charles Knight & Company Ltd, Tolley House, 2 Addiscombe Road, Croydon Surrey CR9 5AF United Kingdom. **Tel** 011 44 181 6884163.

ISSN 0847-4583
DD 690/.094/05
CN
EUROPEAN PUBLICATIONS CATALOGUE. [Eur. publ. cat.]. **Main/Corp** Institute for Research in Construction (Canada). **VFOAT** Catalogue de Publications Europeennes. (1990)-. English (French). Institute for Research in Construction, National Research Council Canada, Ottawa Ontario K1A 0R6 Canada. **Tel** (613)993-9960, FAX (613)952-4040, telex 053-3145 NRC ADMIN OTT.

ISSN 0014-3995
US
SUSPENDED

EXCAVATING CONTRACTOR. Vol. 60 (Jan. 1966)-?. Periodical. English. Twelve times a year. $28.00 (one-year), $46.00 (two-year), $72.00 (three-year) US; $40.00 (one-year) Canada; $76.00 (one-year) other. Cummins Publishing, 26011 Evergreen Road/Suite 204, Southfield MI 48076. **Tel** (313)358-4900. **ED** Andrew J Cummins. **Ad Acc. Circ:** 27,000 (ctrl). available on microfilm and microfiche from University Microfilms International (UMI). ***Continues*** *Excavating Engineer.*
Desc: Publication deals with the owner operator contractor in the earthmoving field.

ISSN 0014-7702
SZ
CODEN FARAB7

FARBE UND RAUM. [Farbe Raum]. (19??)-. Academic Scholarly Publication. German. Twelve times a year. Deutscher Judo Verband, Redaktion Ippon Segewaldweg 40, D-12557 Berlin Germany. **Tel** 011 49 711 210770, telex 051 678. Documents available from CASDDS. ***Continues*** *Farbe und Glas, 0323-5238.*
Ind/Abst Art Archaeol. Tech. Abstr.; Biodeter. Abstr.; Chem. Abstr.; Surf. Treat. Technol. Abstr.; World Surf. Coat. Abstr.

ISSN 0265-5373
UK
CEASED

FARM BUILDINGS AND ENGINEERING : JOURNAL OF THE FARM BUILDINGS INFORMATION CENTRE AND THE FARM BUILDINGS ASSOCIATION. Vol. 10, No. 1 (1984)-(1993). Periodical. English. Farm & Rural Buildings Center, Agricultural Centre, Stoneleigh Kenilworth, Warwickshire CV8 2LG United Kingdom. **Tel** 011 44 1203 696503. Index available. cum. index. **Bk Rev. Ad Acc. Circ:** 2,000. ***Formed by the union of*** *Farm Buildings Digest (Kenilworth, Warwickshire : 1975)* ***and*** *Journal - Farm Buildings Association.*
Ind/Abst AgBiotech News Inf.; Agric. Eng. Abstr. (1991-); Dairy Sci. Abstr.; For. Prod. Abstr. (1991-); Hortic. Abstr.; Index Vet.; Pig News Inf.; Postharvest News Inf.; Potato Abstr.; Poult. Abstr.; Soils Fert.; World Agric. Econ. Rural Sociol. Abstr.; World Ceram. Abstr.

LC WMLC 93/1427 ISSN 0895-450X
DD 721 US
CCC

FENESTRATION (RIVERTON, N.J.). (FENESTRATION.). Vol. 1, No. 1 (Sept./Oct. 1987)-. Trade Publication. English. Six times a year. $15.00. Ashlee Publishing Company Inc, 310 Madison Avenue, New York NY 10017. **Tel** (212)682-7681, (800)360-1926, FAX (212)697-8331, telex 62-480. **ED** John G. Swanson. Index available. **Ad Acc. Circ:** 5,000 (ctrl).
Desc: Edited for manufacturers and fabricators of windows, doors, skylights, greenhouses, sunrooms and various framing areas made of wood, aluminum, steel and other standard materials.

LC TH1000 .F2 ISSN 0340-2967
GW
TITLE CHANGE

F+I-BAU. (F+I.E. UND I-BAU.). **VAT** F und I-Bau. (1973)-. Periodical. German. Element Verlag GmbH & Company Betriebs-KG, Redaktion F+I-bau, Zeppelin Strasse 3, 71332 Waiblingen Germany. **Tel** 011 07151 51871, FAX 011 07151 563343. **ED** Hans Schmid. Index available. cum. index. **Bk Rev. Ad Acc. Circ:** 6,200. ***Continues*** *Fertigteilbau & Industrialisiertes Bauen.* ***Continued by*** *F + I-bau Bauen mit Systemen.*

GW

F+I-BAU BAUEN MIT SYSTEMEN. (1966)-. German. Four times a year. DM7.00 (single issue). Element Verlag GmbH & Company Betriebs-KG, Redaktion F+I-bau, Zeppelin Strasse 3, 71332 Waiblingen Germany. **Tel** 011 07151 51871, FAX 011 07151 563343. **ED** Hans Schmid. Index available. cum. index. **Bk Rev. Ad Acc, Adv Mgr:** Brigitte Zugel. Full Page (B&W) DM2970.00. Half Page (B&W) DM1595.00. **Circ:** 6,200. Documents available from FAXON Xpress. ***Continues*** *F+I.E. und I-bau, 0340-2967.*

LC TH4805 .F55 ISSN 0273-1398
DD 690/.837/05 US

FINE HOMEBUILDING. [Fine homebuild.]. No. 1 (Feb./March 1981)-. Periodical. English. Seven times a year (includes special issue in Jan.). $29.00. Taunton Press, 63 South Main Street, PO Box 5506, Newtown CT 06470-5506. **Tel** (203)426-8171, (800)283-7252, FAX (203)426-3434, telex 5106004860. **ED** Mark Feirer, Kevin Freton and Bruce Greenlaw. Index available. cum. index. **Bk Rev. Ad Acc. Circ:** 243,000.
Desc: Publication about building new houses and rebuilding or improving older ones. Articles cover construction methods, techniques, tools and materials.
Ind/Abst Archit. Period. Index (1981-); Avery Index Archit. Period. Suppl. Colum. Univ.; Constr. Index; EP Collect.; Homework Help.; Index Inf. (1981-); Mag. Search; MasterFile FullTEXT 1000; MasterFile FullTEXT 350; MasterFile FullTEXT 650; MasterFile FullTEXT (Jan. 1993-); OCLC; Pub. Lib. FullTEXT; Telebase; Vocat. Search.

LC TH1092 .F55 ISSN 0308-0501
DD 620.1/1217/05 UK
CCC
CODEN FMATDV

FIRE AND MATERIALS. [Fire mater.]. Vol. 1 (Mar 1976)-. Academic Scholarly Publication. English. Six times a year. $695.00. John Wiley & Sons Ltd., Baffins Lane, Chichester, West Sussex PO19 1UD United Kingdom. **Tel** 011 44 1243 779777, FAX 011 44 1243 776128 BTG:JWP001, telex 86290 WIBOOKG. **(Subscription address:** John Wiley & Sons, Inc. / Philadelphia, PO Box 7247, Philadelphia PA 19170. **Tel** (212)850-6645, (800)225-5945.**) ED** John P. Redfern. **Circ:** 500. available on microfilm and microfiche from University Microfilms International (UMI). Documents available from Article Express International, BIOSIS Document Express, CASDDS.
Desc: Journal for scientific and technological communications on the fire properties of materials and the products into which they are made. Covers all aspects of the polymer field and the end uses where polymers find application; the important developments in the fields of natural products- wood and cellulosics; nonpolymeric materials- metals and ceramics are covered, as well as the chemistry and industrial applications of fire retardant chemicals.
Ind/Abst Bioeng. Abstr.; Biol. Abstr. (1991-); Chem. Abstr.; Civ. Struct. Eng. Abstr.; Coal Abstr.; Curr. Cit.; Curr. Contents Eng. Comput. Technol.; Curr. Contents Phys. Chem. Earth Sci.; Ei Page One; EMBASE; Eng. Mater. Abstr.; Eng. Index Annu.; Health Saf. Sci. Abstr.; Int. Aerosp. Abstr.; Int. Civil Eng. Abstr.; Mater. Sci. Eng. Abstr.; Mech. Eng. Abstr.; Life Sci. Collect.; SCISEARCH; Soft. Abstr. Eng.

ISSN 1079-4174
DD 338 US

FLOOR COVERING NEWS (1994). **See** Interior Design and Decoration-Home Furnishings.

ISSN 1045-5116
DD 338 US
TITLE CHANGE

FLOOR COVERING NEWS/U.S.A. **See** Interior Design and Decoration-Home Furnishings.

ISSN 1193-8781
DD 338.4 CN

FLOOR COVERING PLUS. [Floor cover. plus]. (1992)-. Trade Publication. English. Six times a year. 30.00Can$. Style Communications, 1448 Lawrence Avenue East, Suite 302, Toronto Ontario M4A 2V6 Canada. **Tel** (416)755-5199, FAX (416)755-9123. **ED** Jill Sawyer. **Ad Acc, Adv Mgr:** A. Thomas. **Circ:** 7,000 (ctrl). ***Continues*** *Floor Covering News., 0848-8339.*
Desc: News on the floor covering trade industry.

ISSN 1064-7627
DD 338 US
CODEN FLFOEZ

FLOOR FOCUS. [Floor focus]. **VFOAT** Focus. Vol. 1, No. 1 (June 1992)-. Trade Publication. English. Ten times a year (monthly except Feb. and Aug.). $29.95. Floor Focus, 28 Old Stone Hill Road, Pound Ridge NY 10576-1515. **Tel** (914)764-0556, FAX (914)764-0560. **ED** Frank O'Neill. **Ad Acc. Circ:** 6,400 (ctrl).

LC TH2521 .F62 ISSN 0162-881X
DD 694.605 US

FLOORING (NEW YORK, N.Y.). (FLOORING.). [Flooring]. (Aug. 1931)-. Trade Publication. English. Twelve times a year. $37.00. Douglas Publications Inc., 9609 Gayton Road, Suite 100, Richmond VA 23233. **Tel** (804)741-6704, FAX (804)750-2399. **(Subscription address:** Flooring Magazine, PO Box 39444, Greensboro NC 27438. **)** available on microfilm from University Microfilms International (UMI); available on an online database (file 16/Full-Text) from DIALOG.
Desc: Serving dealers, contractors and manufacturers in the flooring industry.
Ind/Abst F&S Index Plus Text, Int. [Full Txt.] [Select. Cov.]; PROMT [Full Txt.]; Text. Technol. Dig.

US

FLORIDA BUILDER. (19??)-. English. Six times a year (Jan., Mar., May, July, Sept., Nov.). $18.00. Florida Builder Magazine, PO Box 13167, Tampa FL 33681. **Tel** (813)835-4689, FAX (813)835-4689. **ED** Joan B. Antione. **Ad Acc, Adv Mgr:** D. Williams. **Circ:** 10,125 (ctrl). ***Continues*** *Florida Builder & Developer.*
Desc: Editorial coverage devoted to residential and commercial building, including technological developments, construction reports, contracts awarded, profile stories, marketing, personnel changes, and new products and trends in the Florida construction industry.

LC TH1 .F556
DD 690.0 US
CEASED

FLORIDA CONSTRUCTOR. **Added/Corp** Associated General Contractors of America. Florida Chapters. **VFOAT** Florida Constructor-FCI Magazine. Vol. 1, No. 2 (Sept./Oct. 1988)-(19??). Trade Publication. English. Thompson Cook, 1282 Timberline Road, Tallahasse FL 32312. **Tel** (904)893-3014. ***Continues*** *Florida Constructor and FCI Magazine.*

ISSN 0191-4618
US

FLORIDA FORUM. (FLORIDA FORUM : PUBLICATION OF THE FLORIDA ROOFING, SHEET METAL AND AIR CONDITIONING CONTRACTORS ASSOCIATION.). **Added/Corp** Florida Roofing, Sheet Metal and Air Conditioning Contractors Association. (19??)-. Trade Publication. English. Twelve times a year. $18.00 (one-year), $30.00 (two-year). Florida Roofing Sheet Metal & Air Conditioning Contractors Association, PO Drawer 4850, Winter Park FL 32793. **Tel** (407)671-3772. **ED** Glenda Arango. Index available. **Ad Acc. Circ:** 9,000.
Desc: News and items of interest to the roofing, sheet metal and air conditioning industries. Current technology products, systems, services and business-related items featured.

LC KF5701.A15 F64 ISSN 0198-7143
DD 343.73/07869/005 US

FOLIO. PUBLIC RELATIONS, THE. **See** Law.

ISSN 0015-7686
US

FORM & FUNCTION. **Added/Corp** United States Gypsum Company. **VAT** Form and Function. (1964)-. Trade Publication. English. Four times a year. Free on request. USG - United States Gypsum Corporation, 125 South Franklin Street, Chicago IL 60606. **Tel** (312)606-4181, FAX (312)606-5566. **ED** William D. Leavitt. Index available. **Circ:** 135,000 (ctrl).
Desc: Case histories of commercial, industrial and multi-family residential projects and technical features. Articles show how products of USG Corporation companies were used to solve construction problems.

UK
CEASED

FORTRESS. No. 1 (May 1989)-(19??). Periodical. English. Beaufort Publishing Ltd, PO Box 22, Liphood Hampshire GU30 7PJ United Kingdom.
Ind/Abst BHA : Biblio. Hist. Art.

ISSN 0274-5186
US

FOUNDATION DRILLING. [Found. drill.]. **Added/Corp** Association of Drilled Shaft Contractors (U.S.). Vol. 15, No. 5 (May 1980)-. Trade Publication. English. Eight times a year. $60.00. Association of Drilled Shaft Contractors, PO Box 280379, Dallas TX 75228. **Tel** (214)343-2091, FAX (214)343-2384. **ED** Susan Kins. **Bk Rev. Ad Acc, Adv Mgr:** Ted Ledgar, **Tel** (214)343-2091. **Circ:** 2,000. ***Continues*** *Drilled Shaft, 0192-9119.*

LC TH435 .G45 ISSN 1059-6046
DD 692/.5/0973 US

GENERAL CONSTRUCTION COSTBOOK. (GENERAL CONSTRUCTION ... COSTBOOK / BNI, BUILDING NEWS.). [Gen. constr. costb.]. **Added/Corp** Building News, Inc. **VFOAT** Costbook. 1st Ed. (1991)-. English. One time a year. $44.95. Building News, 77 Wexford Street, Needham Heights MA 02194. **Tel** (800)873-6797.

US

GENERAL CONSTRUCTION ESTIMATING STANDARDS: THE RICHARDSON RAPID SYSTEM. **Main/Corp** International Construction Analysts. **Added/Corp** Richardson Engineering Services. (1977)-. English. One time a year (Mar.). $227.00. Richardson Engineering Services, PO Box 9103, 1742 South Fraser Drive, Mesa AZ 85214-9103. **Tel** (602)497-2062, FAX (602)497-5529. Index available (Free). ***Continues*** *International Construction Analysts. Building Construction Estimating Standards.*

IT

GIORNALE DELL EDILIZIA E DEL RIVENDITORE EDILE, IL. (19??)-. Italian. Ten times a year. Free. Giornale Edilizia, Via Trezzo D Adda 16, 20144 Milan Italy. **Tel** 011 39 2 4238345.

UK

GLASS & GLAZING. **See** Architecture.

LC TH
DD 690 UK

●**GLOBAL CEMENT REPORT.** (1994)-. Trade Publication. English. One time a year. £125.00. Tradeship Publications Ltd., Old Kings Head Court, High Street, Dorking, Surrey RH4 1AR United Kingdom. **Tel** 011 44 1306 740363, FAX 011 44 1306 740660, telex 94016994.

LC TA4 .S753 ISSN 0205-0439
BU
CODEN GVISD6

GODISNIK NA VISSIJA INSTITUT PO ARHITEKTURA I STROITELSTVO. SVITK II HISROTEHNIKA. **See** Engineering.

Building and Construction

GOLD BOOK OF MULTI-HOUSING (SOUTH EDITION), THE. (THE GOLD BOOK OF MULTI-HOUSING.). 1st Ed. (1979)-Suspended with 1990-91 edition. English. One time a year. $155.00. F. W. Dodge Rsg., 24 Hartwell Avenue, Lexington MA 02172. **Tel** (617)863-5100. **ED** Jane Alex Mendleson. Index available. **Circ:** 500 (ctrl).
Desc: Reports on the owners, developers and managers of multifamily housing.
US SUSPENDED

GOOD BUILDING GUIDES. (19??)-. English. Irregular (up to 8 per year). £25.00. Building Research Establishment, BRE Bookshop, Garston Watford WD27JR United Kingdom. **Tel** 011 44 1923 664444, FAX 011 44 1923 664400. **Continues** Defect Action Sheets.
Desc: Provides practitioners with guidance on principles and practicalities of achieving quality building. Emphasis on practical solutions presented in a visual format.
UK

UDC 624
GRADBENI VESTNIK. [Gradb. vestn.]. (1952)-. Periodical. Slovenian (summaries and/or abstracts in English). Twelve times a year. $50.00. Zveza Drustev Gradbenih Inzenirjev in Tehnikov Slovenije, Erjavceva 15, Ljubljana Slovenia. **ED** Sergej Bubnov. Index available. **Bk Rev**. **Ad Acc**. **Circ:** 3,000. available with charts; available with illustrations.
Ind/Abst Concr. Abstr.; Int. Civil Eng. Abstr.
ISSN 1191-0879 XV

DD 338.4/7/000257135
GREATER TORONTO PROFESSIONAL AND SERVICE DIRECTORY. (GREATER TORONTO PROFESSIONAL AND SERVICE DIRECTORY / ROUTING SERVICES LIMITED.). [Gt. Tor. prof. serv. dir.]. **Added/Corp** Routing Services Limited. **VFOAT** Greater Toronto Area Professional & Service Directory. (198?)-. Directory. English. $100.00. Routing Services Ltd, 70 Silver Star Boulevard, Unit 137, Scarborough Ontario M1V 4W2 Canada. **Tel** (416)293-6664, FAX (416)293-7209.
CN

DD 728.3709944
GREGORY'S BEST PROJECT & KIT HOMES. See Architecture.
ISSN 1032-867X AT

UDC 69.057.7
GRONDVERZET & BOUWTRANSPORT. [Grondverzet bouwtransp.]. (1983)-. Trade Publication. Dutch. Twelve times a year. Uitgeverij Ten Hagen BV, Postbus 34, 2501 AG Den Haag Netherlands. **Tel** 011 31 70 3569100. **Continues** Machinepark, 0165-4012.
ISSN 0920-8380 NE

LC WMLC L 83/6782
GUIDE OFFICIEL DU BATIMENT / PUBLIE SOUS LE PATRONAGE OU AVEC LA COLLABORATION DE LA FEDERATION NATIONAL BELGE DU BATIMENT ET DES TRAVAUX PUBLICS ... [ET AL.]. **VFOAT** Officiele Gids der Bouwnijverheid. (19??)-. French. Guides Hallet, Brussels Belgium.
BE

LC TH4819.P7 N37A
DD 693.9/7
GUIDE TO MANUFACTURED HOMES. **Main/Corp** National Association of Home Manufacturers. **VFOAT** NAHM Guide to Manufactured Homes. **VAT** National Association of Home Manufacturers Guide to Manufactured Homes. Vol. 1 (Jan. 1978)-. English. One time a year. National Association of Home Manufacturers, 1619 Massachusetts Avenue NW, Washington DC 20036. **Tel** (202)234-1374.
ISSN 0160-7340 US

GUIDE TO QUALITY CONSTRUCTION PRODUCTS. **Added/Corp** Producers' Council. (19??)-. English. One time a year. Free. Producers Council Inc, 1717 Massachusetts Avenue Northwest, Washington DC 20036. **Tel** (202)667-8727.
ISSN 0197-6214 US

DD 338.4/76223635/0971
GYPSUM PRODUCTS. See Building and Construction-Abstracting, Bibliographies and Statistics.
ISSN 0380-7223 CN

DD 338.4/769/00971447
HABITABEC QUEBEC. [Habitabec Que.]. Vol. 4, No. 18 (Jan. 29, 1988). Periodical. French. One time a week. 80.00Can$. 3161 Chemin Sainte-Foy, Sainte-Foy Quebec G1X 1R3 Canada. **Continues** Habitabec (Sainte-Foy, Quebec), 0825-916X.
ISSN 0844-2487 CN

LC TH2430 .H36
DD 695
HANDBOOK OF COMMERCIAL ROOFING SYSTEMS. **VFOAT** Handbook. Trade Publication. English. One time a year. $18.00 US; $28.00 other.
Ind/Abst Constr. Index.
US

LC HD9937.U5 H35
DD 698/.9/029
HANDBOOK OF CONTRACT FLOOR COVERING. [Handb. contract floor cover.]. **VFOAT** Floor Covering Weekly. English. One time a year. Bart Publications, 919 3rd Avenue, New York NY 10022.
ISSN 0197-8209 US

DD 690
HANDY APPRAISAL CHART. [Handy appraisal chart]. **VFOAT** Market Appraisal Chart. (19??)-. Periodical. English. Two times a year. $19.95. Market Appraisal Chart Company, PO Box 42244, Cincinnati OH 45242. **Tel** (513)891-0890. **Bk Rev**. available on diskette.
Desc: Presents insurable values of residential and commercial buildings and structures.
ISSN 0891-2254 US

LC T174.3 .H35
DD 338.064
HANGUK KISUL. **Added/Corp** Hanguk Kisul Yongyok Hyophoe. (19??)-. Periodical. English (French, Korean and Spanish). Hanguk Kisul Yongyok Hyophoe, San 76-561 Yoksam-dong, Kangnam-ku Seoul Korea.
KO

DD 338.4/7684/00971
HARDWARE & HOME CENTRE MAGAZINE. [Hardw. home cent. mag.]. **VFOAT** Hardware and Home Centre Magazine; Centre. Vol. 12, No. 7 (Oct. 1988)-. Periodical. English. Eight times a year. 18.00Can$ Canada; 38.50Can$ other. Southam Information & Technical Group Inc, 1450 Don Mills Road, Don Mills Ontario M3B 2X7 Canada. **Tel** (416)445-6641, (800)668-2374, FAX (416)442-2261. **Continues** Hardware, Home, Building Supply Centre., 0847-995X.
ISSN 0847-9968 CN

DD 338.4
HARDWARE MERCHANDISING (1993). (HARDWARE MERCHANDISING.). [Hardw. merch.]. (199?)-. Periodical. English. Ten times a year. 29.61Can$. MacLean Hunter Ltd. Business Publishers / Canada, Box 9100, Station A, Toronto Ontario M5W 1A5 Canada. **Tel** (416)596-5000, , FAX (416)596-5552. **(Subscription address:** Indas Customer Service, 35 Riviera Drive, Building 17, Markham Ontario L3R 8N4 Canada. **Tel** (905)946-0406.) **Continues** Hardware Merchandising, Building Supply Dealer, 0831-0807.
ISSN 1199-2786 CN

DD 338.4/7683/0971
HARDWARE MERCHANDISING, BUILDING SUPPLY DEALER. [Hardw. merch. build. supply deal.]. **VFOAT** Hardware Merchandising. **VAT** Hardware Merchandising (1985). (August 1985)-(199?). Periodical. English. MacLean Hunter Canada / Montreal, 1001 bvd. de Maisonneuve W., Montreal Quebec H3A 3E1 Canada. **Tel** (514)845-5141, FAX (514)845-4302, telex 055-60604. **ED** Sally Praskey. **Ad Acc**. **Circ:** 17,000 (ctrl). available on microfilm from University Microforms International (UMI). **Continues** Hardware & Housewares Merchandising, 0827-1429. **Continued by** Hardware Merchandising (1993), 1199-2786.
Desc: Hardware and building supplies; including everything from lumber and insulation to upscale kitchen and bath furnishings.
ISSN 0831-0807 CN
TITLE CHANGE

LC TH6057.A6 H38
DD 696/.05
HAUS TECH. Periodical. German. Twelve times a year. $103.72. SHZ Forster Fachverlag AG, Seestrasse 37, CH-8027 Zurich Switzerland. **Tel** 011 41 1 2022046, FAX 011 44 1 9105155, telex 815 517. **Continues** Temperatur Technik, 0377-8363.
SZ

UDC 69
HAUSBAU-MAGAZIN, DAS. (1986)-. Periodical. German. Six times a year. $36.85. Fachschriften Verlag GmbH, Hoehenstrasse 17, D-70736 Fellbach Germany. **Tel** 011 49 711 5206256.
ISSN 0934-8026 GW

HAUSTECHNISCHE RUNDSCHAU. [Haustech. Rundsch.]. Vol. 12, No. 5 (Sept. 1907)-. Academic Scholarly Publication. German. Three times a month. $39.04. Carl Marhold Verlag, Postfach 191409, W-1000 Berlin 19 Germany. **Bk Rev**. **Ad Acc**. **Continues** Zeitschrift fur Heizung, Luftung und Beleuchtung.
Ind/Abst Coal Abstr.; EMBASE; Energy Res. Abstr. (April 1977-).
ISSN 0017-8438 GW

HEAVY CONSTRUCTION NEWS. [Heavy constr. news]. (Apr. 1957)-. Periodical. English. Twelve times a year. 38.42Can$. MacLean Hunter Ltd. Business Publishers / Canada, Box 9100, Station A, Toronto Ontario M5W 1A5 Canada. **Tel** (416)596-5000, , FAX (416)596-5552. **(Subscription address:** Indas Customer Service, 35 Riviera Drive, Building 17, Markham Ontario L3R 8N4 Canada. **Tel** (905)946-0406.) available on microfilm and microfiche from University Microfilms International (UMI). **Absorbed** Contractors Marketplace, 0714-6884.
Desc: Reaches contractors engaged in engineering construction, roads, sewers and excavation, plus industrial, commercial and institutional building.
Ind/Abst Can. Bus. Index.
ISSN 0017-9426 CN

HERB IRELAND'S SALES PROSPECTOR. CANADA. **Added/Corp** Prospector Research Services. **VFOAT** Sales Prospector. Canada. (19??)-. Periodical. English. Twenty-two times a year. $495.00. Intertec Publishing Corp, 29 North Wacker Drive, Chicago IL 60606-3298. **Tel** (312)726-2802, FAX (312)726-3091. **(Subscription address:** Sales Prospector, PO Box 9079, Waltham MA 02254.) **ED** Nora Galvin. available on an online database (files 16,636/Full-Text) from DIALOG.
Desc: Covers industrial, commercial, and institutional construction projects.
Ind/Abst PROMT [Full Txt.]; PTS Newsl. Database [Full Txt.].
ISSN 0270-8817 US

LC TE1 .R7
DD 625.7/05
HIGHWAY & HEAVY CONSTRUCTION PRODUCTS. See Transportation-Roads and Traffic.
ISSN 1062-5194 US
TITLE CHANGE

LC HD9717.5.R63 C33
DD 338.4/7624/0971021
HIGHWAY, ROAD, STREET AND BRIDGE CONTRACTORS. (HIGHWAY, ROAD, STREET, AND BRIDGE CONTRACTORS = ENTREPRENEURS DE GRANDE ROUTE, CHEMIN, RUE ET PONT.). [Highw. road street bridge contract.]. **Added/Corp** Statistics Canada. Industry Division. **VFOAT** Entrepreneurs de Grande Route, Chemin, Rue et Pont. (1984)-. English (French). One time a year. 22.00Can$ Canada; $26.00 US; $31.00 other. Statistics Canada Publications Sales and Services, R.H. Coats Building 6th Floor, Ottawa Ontario K1A 0T6 Canada. **Tel** (613)951-5078, (800)267-6677, FAX (613)951-1584, telex 053-3585. **Continues** Highway, Road, Street and Bridge Contracting Industry (Final), 0706-2451.
ISSN 0835-1058 CN

DD 690/.8/05
HOME BUILDER MAGAZINE. [Home build. mag.]. Vol. 1, No. 1 (Sept./Oct. 1988)-. Trade Publication. English (summaries and/or abstracts in French). Irregular. 29.17Can$. Home Builder Magazine, PO Box 400, Victoria Station, Westmount Quebec H3Z 2V8 Canada. **Tel** (514)489-4941, FAX (514)489-5505. **ED** Nachmi Artzy. **Ad Acc**. **Circ:** 16,500 (ctrl).
Desc: Covers the new residential construction market. Offers incisive, issues-oriented editorial content.
ISSN 0840-4348 CN

DD 728
HOME BUILDER'S JOURNAL, THE. [Home build. j.]. Vol. 1, Issue 1 (Aug. 1985)-. Periodical. English. Twelve times a year. Home Builders Association of Greater Kansas City, 600 East 103rd, Kansas City MO 64131. **Continues** Bits for Builders.
ISSN 0884-6774 US

LC TH4805 .H63
DD 690/.8/05
HOME BUILDING & REMODELING. **VAT** Home Building and Remodeling. (19??)-. English. $1.60. Hudson Home Publications, 175 S San Antonio Rd., Los Altos CA 94022. **Tel** (310)937-5486.
ISSN 0360-1382 US

LC TH4816 .H65
DD 690/.8/028
HOME IMPROVEMENT & REPAIR. **VAT** Home Improvement and Repair. English. $1.60. Hudson Home Publications, 175 S San Antonio Rd., Los Altos CA 94022. **Tel** (310)937-5486.
ISSN 0361-2813 US

LC TS800 .A5
DD 683/.05
ISSN 1045-9367 US
CCC CEASED

HOME IMPROVEMENT CENTER. [Home improv. cent.]. Issue No. 4089 (Aug. 1989)-(1993). Periodical. English. Vance Publishing Corporation, 400 Knightsbridge Parkway, Lincolnshire IL 60069. **Tel** (800)255-5113, (708)634-2600. available on microfilm and microfiche from University Microfilms International (UMI). **Continues** Home Center Magazine, 0194-1321.

Building and Construction

HOME IMPROVEMENTS JOURNAL.
ISSN 0142-0704 UK CEASED
(1978)-(19??). English. Six times a year. Newman Publishing Ltd, 48 Poland Street, London W1V 4PP United Kingdom. **Tel** 01-582 5266.
Ind/Abst Archit. Period. Index (Mar./Apr. 1978-June/July 1979).

HOME MAGAZINE'S BUILDING/REMODELING PLANNER.
ISSN 1061-6667 US
VFOAT Home Magazine's Building Remodeling Planner; Building Remodeling Planner. (1992)-. Periodical. English. $4.95. John J. Miller, 1653 Broadway, New York NY 10019.
LC TH4805 .H653
DD 728

HOME PLAN IDEAS.
ISSN 0194-0627 US
VFOAT Better Homes and Gardens Building Ideas Home Plan Ideas. (19??)-. English. Irregular. Meredith Corporation, Locust at 17th, Des Moines IA 50309. **Tel** (515)284-3000, FAX (515)284-2568.
LC NA7205 .H647
DD 728/.37/0222

HOME PLANNER.
ISSN 1040-547X US
[Home plan.]. Vol. 1, No. 1 (Spring 1989)-. Periodical. English. Two times a year. Home Planners Inc., 23761 Research Drive, Farmington Hills MI 48024. **Tel** (313)477-1850. **ED** Edward A. Spala. **Ad Acc. Circ:** 150,000.
Desc: Edited for the serious house planner and home builder. Every issue contains 150 to 200 home plans, each highlighted by detailed exterior illustrations, large floor plans, and planning pointers that zero in on the design's key features.
LC NA7205 .H653
DD 728.3/7/0223

HOME PLANS GUIDE. See Architecture.
ISSN 0899-4374 US CEASED

HOME PLANS TO BUILD. See Architecture.
ISSN 0899-4366 US
LC NA7205 .H656
DD 728

HOME RENOVATIONS. See Interior Design and Decoration.
ISSN 0714-8151 CN
DD 643/.7/05

HOMEOWNER, THE.
ISSN 0747-3176 US SUSPENDED
[Homeowner]. Vol. 8, No. 4 (July/Aug. 1983)-?. Periodical. English. Ten times a year. $18.00 (one-year), $54.00 (three-year). Family Media Inc., 3 Park Avenue, New York NY 10016. **Tel** (212)340-9200. **ED** Joe Carter. **Bk Rev. Ad Acc. Circ:** 700,000. available on microfilm and microfiche from University Microfilms International (UMI). Documents available from UMI Article Clearinghouse. **Continues** Homeowners How To, 0195-2196.
Desc: Covers home improvement ideas.
Ind/Abst Index Inf. (July 1983-); Mag. Search; Newsp. Period. Abstr. (1988-1991).
LC HD9715.H6 H65
DD 338.4/7/6240255125
HK

HONG KONG BUILDER DIRECTORY.
(19??)-. Directory. English. One time a year. HK$345.00 Hong Kong; $50.00 US. Far East Trade Press Ltd., BL C 10 F Seaview E, 2 8 Watson, North Point Hong Kong. **Tel** 011 852 25668381, FAX 011 852 25710780, telex 83434. **ED** Iris Stoner. Index available. **Ad Acc. Circ:** 6,000 (ctrl).
Desc: Directory (828 pages) to Hong Kong's building and construction industry.
LC HD
DD 338
ISSN 1047-4382 US

HOT LINE CONSTRUCTION EQUIPMENT MONTHLY UPDATE. [Hot line constr. equip. mon. update]. **VFOAT** Construction Equipment Monthly Update; Construction Equipment Guide Monthly Update. (1988)-. English. Twelve times a year. $79.95. Heartland Communications Group Inc., PO Box 916 1003 Central Ave, Fort Dodge IA 50501. **Tel** (800)247-2000, (515)955-1600, FAX (515)955-6636. **Bk Rev. Ad Acc. Circ:** 15,000.

HOUSE BEAUTIFUL'S HOME BUILDING.
US
VFOAT Home Building. (1990)-. Trade Publication. English. Two times a year. $2.95 (single copy). The Hearst Corporation, 250 West 55th Street, New York NY 10019. **Tel** (212)649-4014, (800)925-0485. **ED** Jim Kemp. **Ad Acc. Continues** Building Manual.
Desc: Edited for readers planning a custom-built house. This magazine surveys homes that illustrate fundamental design principles. It features cost-cutting techniques, siting problem solutions, product information and design ideas. Blueprints for home-style ideas are available through the magazine.

HOUSEMENDING NOTEBOOK.
ISSN 1054-6421 US
DD 643
[Housemending noteb.]. **Added/Corp** Housing Resource Center. **VFOAT** House Mending Notebook. (1987)-. Periodical. English. Twelve times a year. $85.00. Housing Resource Center, 1820 West 48 Street, Cleveland OH 44102. **Tel** (216)281-4663, FAX (216)651-0914. **ED** Alan Wasco. Index available. cum. index. **Bk Rev. Ad Acc. Circ:** 220.
Desc: Comprehensive collection of information on home construction, maintenance and improvement. Explains options and alternatives for a comprehensive range of topics.
LC HD7379.A3 H58
DD 301.5/4/0994
AT

HOUSING AND CONSTRUCTION QUARTERLY. See Housing and Urban Development.
LC HD7304.B2 H63
DD 338.4/769083/097526
ISSN 0742-6178 US

HOUSING PRODUCTION (BALTIMORE, MD.). See Housing and Urban Development.
LC TH4817.3 .H68
DD 643/.7/05
ISSN 0095-4705 US

HOW TO (INDIANAPOLIS). (HOW TO.). Vol. 1 (Fall 1974)-. Periodical. English. Four times a year. $0.95. National Retail Hardware Association, 770 North Highschool Road, Indianapolis IN 46224.
LC TH455 .H82
DD 690/.029/473
ISSN 0195-8941 US

HUDSON HOME PRODUCTS DIRECTORY. **VFOAT** Home Products Directory. (1980)-. English. One time a year. $2.95. Hudson Home Publications, 175 S San Antonio Rd., Los Altos CA 94022. **Tel** (310)937-5486.
LC TA4 .T34
NQ

I & I.E. Y A. See Engineering-Civil Engineering.
LC TH9116.5 .I57a
DD 363.3/78/025
ISSN 0743-0248 US

IAFC COMMITTEE LIST. (IAFC ... COMMITTEE LIST.). [IAFC comm. list]. **Main/Corp** International Association of Fire Chiefs. **VFOAT** I.A.F.C. ... Committee List. **VAT** International Association of Fire Chiefs Committee List. (19??)-. English. One time a year. International Association of Fire Chiefs, 4025 Fair Ridge Drive, Fairfax VA 22033. **Tel** (703)273-0911.
LC TH3 .A37A
GW

IBAC MITTEILUNGEN. Main/Corp Aachen. Technische Hochschule. Institut fur Bauforschung. Multiple languages (Czech, English and German).
DD 338.4/769/009714
ISSN 0713-6919 CN

IC. INFORMATION CONSTRUCTION. (INFORMATION CONSTRUCTION : IC.). [Inf. constr.]. **VFOAT** IC: Information Construction. Periodical. French (English). Twelve times a year. L'Association Provinciale Des Constructeurs D'Habitations Du Quebec, 14 Elgin place Bonaventure, CP 26, Montreal Quebec H5A 1A2.
ISSN 0019-1361 UK CCC

IDEAL HOME. [Ideal home]. Vol. 1 (Oct. 1919)-. Periodical. English. Twelve times a year. $42.36. IPC Magazines Ltd., Perrymount Road, Haywards Heath, West Sussex RH16 3DH United Kingdom. **Tel** 011 44 1444 440421, FAX 011 44 1444 445599.
Ind/Abst Archit. Period. Index (Dec. 1977-Feb. 1982).
ISSN 0380-0857 CN

IF. INDUSTRIALIZATION FORUM. (I. F. SYSTEMS CONSTRUCTION ANALYSIS RESEARCH.). [IF, Ind. forum]. **Added/Corp** Universite de Montreal. Harvard University. Massachusetts Institute of Technology. University of Illinois (Urbana-Champaign campus) Washington University (Saint Louis, Mo.). **VFOAT** if. Vol. 7 (1976)-. Periodical. English. Four times a year. $12.50 (individuals), $25.00 (institutions). **Continues** IF. Industrialization Forum, 0380-0857.
Ind/Abst Archit. Period. Index.
LC HD9715.E34 I37
UA

IHSA AL-TASHYID WA-AL-BINA. SHARIKAT AL-QITA AL-AMM. AL-JIHAZ AL-MARKAZI LIL-TABIAH AL-AMMAH WA-AL-IHSA. Added/Corp Egypt. Jihaz Al-Markazi Lil-Tabiah Al-Ammah Wa-Al-Ihsa. **VFOAT** Sharikat Al-Qita Al-Amm. (19??)-. Arabic. One time a year. Al-Jihaz Al-Markazi Lil-Tabiah Al-Ammah Wa-Al-Ihsa, Tariq Salahsalim Madinat Nasr, Al-Qahirah Egypt. Index available.
ISSN 8755-691X US

ILLINOIS CONSTRUCTION LAW. See Law.

IMPIANTISTICA ITALIANA. [Impiantistica ital.].
ISSN 0394-1582 IT
UDC 65.01
(1988)-. Periodical. Italian. Eleven times a year. L63700. Editoriale PEG Spa, Via Fratelli Bressan 2, 20126 Milan Italy. **Tel** 011 39 2 2579841, FAX 011 39 2 255-2779, telex 323088 PEGMOS I. **ED** Arrigo Pareschi. Index available. **Bk Rev. Ad Acc. Circ:** 6,500 (ctrl).
Desc: Industrial plant installation field and various aspects connected to industrial engineering and advanced production technologies.
LC HD9715.I642 I5a
DD 338.4767
IO

INDEKS HARGA PERDAGANGAN BESAR BAHAN BANGUNAN/KONSTRUKSI DI INDONESIA. Main/Corp Indonesia. Biro Pusat Statistik. (1977)-. Indonesian. $2.00. Biro Pusat Statistik / Central Bureau of Statistics, 8 Jalan Dr. Sutomo No. 8, Box 3, Jakarta Pusat 10710 Indonesia. **Tel** 011 62 21 372808, 011 62 21 374908 ext.342. ctrl circ.

INDIAN CONSTRUCTION : JOURNAL OF THE BUILDERS' ASSOCIATION OF INDIA. Added/Corp Builders' Association of India. Vol. 12, No. 1 (Jan. 1979)-. Periodical. English. Twelve times a year. $60.00. Builders Association of India Floor 3-B, Sir P M Road, Fort 400001 India. **(Subscription address:** Prints India, 11 Darya Ganj, New Delhi 110002 India. **Tel** 011 91 11 3268645, FAX 011 91 11 3275542, telex 31-61087 PRIN-IN.) **Continues** Bulletin of Builders' Association of India.
LC HD9715.B8 I53
BL

INDUSTRIA DA CONSTRUCAO : PRECOS DE MATERIAL DE CONSTRUCAO NO COMERCIO ATACADISTA - SALARIOS NA INDUSTRIA DA CONSTRUCAO. See Industry and Production.
IT

INDUSTRIA DEI LATERIZI, L'. Vol. 1, No. 1 (Jan./Feb. 1990)-. Periodical. Italian (summaries and/or abstracts in English). Six times a year. L30000. Faenza Editrice, Via P de Crescenzi 44, 48018 Faenza Italy. **Tel** 011 39 546 663488, FAX 011 39 546 660440, telex 550387. **Formed by the union of** Industria Italiana dei Laterizi, 0019-7610 **and** Refrattari e Laterizi.
ISSN 0579-4900 IT

INDUSTRIA DELLE COSTRUZIONI. (L'INDUSTRIA DELLE COSTRUZIONI : RIVISTA TECNICA DELL'ASSOCIAZIONE NAZIONALE COSTRUTTORI EDILI.). [Ind. costr.]. **Added/Corp** Associazione Nazionale Costruttori Edili. Periodical. Italian. Eleven times a year. L125000 Italy; L190000 Europe; L240000 other. CDP Editrice Srl, Via di Portonaccio 23 B, 00159 Rome Italy. **Tel** 011 39 6 4386447, FAX 011 39 6 43530186.
Ind/Abst Archit. Period. Index (Nov. 1977-); Avery Index Archit. Period. Suppl. Colum. Univ. (June 1989, Jan. 1990-).
ISSN 0019-7637 IT
CODEN IICEAW

INDUSTRIA ITALIANA DEL CEMENTO, L'. [Ind. ital. cem.]. **Added/Corp** Associazione Italiana Tecnico-Economica del Cemento. Associazione dell'Industria Italiana del cemento, Fibro-Cemento, Calce e Gesso. Associazione Italiana Cemento, Armato, e Precompresso. (1929)-. Periodical. Italian (English and French). Eleven times a year. L110.000. Servizio Italiano Pubblicazioni International, Viale Pasteur 6, 00144 Rome Italy. **Tel** 011 39 6 5920509, telex 614567 SIPIRM I. Documents available from Article Express International. **Absorbed** Il Cemento.
Ind/Abst Bioeng. Abstr.; Ceram. Abstr. (19??-); Concr. Abstr.; Ei Page One; Eng. Index Annu.; Int. Civil Eng. Abstr.; Soft. Abstr. Eng.
ISSN 0019-9036 GW CCC
CODEN IANZAQ

INDUSTRIE-ANZEIGER. [Ind.-Anz.]. **Added/Corp** Wirtschaftsverband Eisen, Blech und Metall Verarbeitende Industrie. Wirtschaftsverband Stahlverformung. Wirtschaftsvereinigung Ziehereien und Kaltwalzwerke. (1948)-. Academic Scholarly Publication. German. One time a week. $263.46. Konradin Verlags Gruppe, Robert Kohlhammer GmbH, Postfach 10 02 52, D-70765 Leinfelden Germany. **Tel** 011 49 711 7594070, 011 49 711 7594229, FAX 011 49 711 7894390. **ED** R. Langbein. **Bk Rev. Ad Acc. Circ:** 26,000 (ctrl). Documents available from Article Express International, Ask*IEEE, CASDDS. **Continues** Anzeiger fuer Maschinenwesen, 0365-5156; Eisen- und Metall-Verarbeitung.
Desc: Practice-related industrial magazine of the

Building and Construction

German market. For development, construction work, planning and production.
 Ind/Abst Acoust. Abstr.; Alum. Ind. Abstr.; Ceram. Abstr. (19??-); Chem. Abstr.; Coal Abstr.; Ei Page One; EMBASE; Energy Res. Abstr.; Eng. Index Annu.; Fluid Abstr., Civil Eng.; Fluid Abstr. Proc. Eng.; FLUIDEX (1973-); INSPEC (March 1971-); Met. Abstr.; Saf. Health Work; Surf. Treat. Technol. Abstr.

ISSN 0935-2023
GW
UDC 725.4
INDUSTRIEBAU HANNOVER.
(INDUSTRIEBAU.). [Industriebau Hann.]. (1988)-. Trade Publication. German. Six times a year. $138.18. Curt R. Vincentz Verlag, Postfach 6247, D-30062 Hannover Germany. **Tel** 011 49 511 990980, FAX 011 49 511 9909899, telex 923846. **ED** Juergen Muegge-Luttermann. **Bk Rev**. **Ad Acc**. **Circ**: 4,000. **Continues** *Zentralblatt fur Industriebau, 0044-4227.*

ISSN 1187-0303
DD 690 CN
INFO RENOVATION. SECTEUR EST DE MTL.
[Info renov., Sect. Est Mtl]. Vol. 1, No 1 (Spring 1991)-. Periodical. French. Four times a year. Limited free distribution. Info Renovation, Bureau 100, 5080 boulevard des Laurentides, Auteil Quebec H7K 2J6 Canada.

ISSN 1187-029X
DD 690 CN
INFO RENOVATION. SECTEUR RIVE-SUD.
[Info renov., Sect. Rive-Sud]. Vol. 1, No 1 (Spring 1991)-. Periodical. French. Four times a year. Limited free distribution. Info Renovation, Bureau 100, 5080 boulevard des Laurentides, Auteil Quebec H7K 2J6 Canada.

ISSN 0529-2263
DD 690 CL
INFORME.
Main/Corp Chile. Universidad, Santiago. Centro de la Vivienda y Construccion. (19??)-. Periodical. Spanish. Universidad de Santiago / Publicaciones, Servicio de Publicaciones e Intercambio Cientifico, Campus Universitario, Santiago de Compostela, E-15706 Santiago Spain. **Tel** 011 34 59-35-00.

ISSN 0020-0883
SP
INFORMES DE LA CONSTRUCCION.
Added/Corp Spain. Consejo Superior de Investigaciones Cientificas. Instituto Tecnico de la Construccion y del Cemento. No. 1 (May 1948)-. Periodical. Spanish. Six times a year. 8000ptas. Instituto Eduardo Torroja, Apartado 19002, 28080 Madrid Spain. **Tel** 011 34 1 3020440.
 Ind/Abst Archit. Period. Index (Oct. 1977-); Concr. Abstr.; Int. Civil Eng. Abstr.

LC NA722 .I54 **ISSN** 0020-1472
DD 720/.977 US
INLAND ARCHITECT. See Architecture.

ISSN 0275-6714
US
INSIDE CONGRESS.
Periodical. English. Four times a year. Free. Plasterers and Cement Mason's Action Committee, 1125 17th Street NW/6th Floor, Washington DC 20036.

ISSN 1049-9725
DD 728 US
INSIDE HOUSING.
(INSIDE HOUSING : THE DEFINITIVE GUIDE TO HOME BUILDING.). [Inside hous.]. Vol. 1, No 1 (Jan./Feb. 1990)-. Periodical. English. Six times a year. Levy Partnership Inc., 636 Broadway/Suite 1200, New York NY 10012.

ISSN 0212-8519
SP
UDC 725.85
INSTALACIONES DEPORTIVAS XXI.
VFOAT Instalaciones Deportivas Veintiuno. (1984)-. Periodical. Spanish. Seven times a year. $137.00. Elsevier Prensa SA, Avenida Paral Lel 180, 08015 Barcelona Spain. **Tel** 011 34 3 3255350, FAX 011 34 3 4252880. **Ad Acc**. Full Page (B&W) 130000ptas. Half Page (B&W) 90000ptas. Full Page (Color) 165000ptas. Half Page (Color) 110000ptas. **Circ**: 5,000.
 Desc: Covers building, equipment, maintenance, materials and accessories for sport installations.

LC TH1715 .I63
UK
INSULATION HANDBOOK, THE. (1959)-.
English. One time a year (Oct.). £11.50 UK; £12.50 other. Turret Group, 177 Hagden Lane, Watford Hertfordshire WD1 8LN United Kingdom. **Tel** 011 44 1923 228577, FAX 011 44 1923 221346.

LC TH1715.A1 I48 **ISSN** 0950-1940
DD 693.8/3/05 UK
CODEN INJOEY
INSULATION JOURNAL (RICKMARSWORTH).
(INSULATION JOURNAL.). [Insul. j.]. **VFOAT** Insulation. (198?)-. Periodical. English. Six times a year. $116.36. Turret Group, 177 Hagden Lane, Watford Hertfordshire WD1 8LN United Kingdom. **Tel** 011 44 1923 228577, FAX 011 44 1923 221346. **Continues** *Insulation, 0020-4552.*
 Ind/Abst Curr. Technol. Index; Ei Page One; F&S Index Plus Text, Int. [Select. Cov.]; Hortic. Abstr.; PROMT.

ISSN 0831-411X
DD 696/.2/060714 CN
INTER MECANIQUE DU BATIMENT.
[Inter-mec. batim.]. **Added/Corp** Corporation des Maitres Mecaniciens en Tuyauterie du Quebec. Vol. 1, No. 1 (Jan. 1986)-. Periodical. French. Seven times a year. Free on request. Corp des Maitres Mecaniciens, 8175 boulevard St Laurent, Montreal Quebec H2P 2M1 Canada. **Tel** (514)382-2668, FAX (514)954-8933. **Bk Rev**. **Ad Acc**. **Circ:** 5,900 (ctrl).
 Desc: Contains technical, juridical and administrative information appropriate for mechanical contractors, plus a description of corporative activities.

ISSN 0888-0387
DD 721 US
INTERIOR CONSTRUCTION. [Inter. constr.].
Added/Corp Ceilings & Interior Systems Construction Association. (19??)-. Trade Publication. English. Six times a year (Feb., Apr., June, Aug., Oct. Dec.). $35.00. C. I. S. C. A., 579 West North Avenue, Suite #301, Elmhurst IL 60126. **Tel** (708)833-1919, FAX (708)833-1940. **ED** John Sanger. **Bk Rev**. **Ad Acc, Adv Mgr:** Sharon Mathison. **Circ:** 8,500 (ctrl). **Continues** *Inside Contracting, 0193-2586.*
 Desc: For the interior systems specialist. Covers trends and techniques in all aspects of interior construction, and describes management techniques to make companies more efficient and profitable.

ISSN 0020-5656
US
INTERMOUNTAIN CONTRACTOR. (19??)-.
Trade Publication. English. One time a week. $381.00. Intermountain Contractor Inc., PO Box 26237, Salt Lake City UT 84126. **Tel** (801)972-4400. **ED** Michael Cannon. **Ad Acc**. **Circ:** 4,000.
 Desc: Construction jobs up for public bids throughout the intermountain area.

ISSN 0791-492X
DD 624 690 IE
INTERNATIONAL BUILDING SCIENCE & STRUCTURAL ABSTRACTS.
[Int. build. sci. struct. abstr.]. **VFOAT** International Building Science and Structural Abstracts. (1991)-. Periodical. English. Four times a year (plus Annual Index). $350.41. CITIS Ltd, 2 Rosemount Terrace, Blackrock Dublin Ireland. **Tel** 3531-886227, FAX 3531-885971, telex 30259 MSCH ET. **(Subscription address:** CITIS Ltd., 80 8th Avenue Suite 303, New York NY 10011. **)** Index available. available on CD-ROM. **Formed by the union of** *International Building Science and Construction Abstracts* **and** *International Structural Engineering Abstracts.*
 Desc: Provides coverage of topics such as concrete technology, construction practice, steel construction, properties of materials, building physics, dynamic structural analysis, computer applications, fracture mechanics, design and analysis of reinforced concrete, and concrete mix design.

ISSN 0791-492X
IE
INTERNATIONAL BUILDING SCIENCE & STRUCTURAL ABSTRACTS.
Abstracting/Indexing Service. English. Four times a year (plus Annual Index). £175.00 UK/Europe; $315.00 US and Canada; DM515.00 other. CITIS Ltd, 2 Rosemount Terrace, Blackrock Dublin Ireland. **Tel** 3531-886227, FAX 3531-885971, telex 30259 MSCH ET. **(Subscription address:** CITIS Ltd., 80 8th Avenue Suite 303, New York NY 10011. **)** Index available. available on CD-ROM. **Formed by the union of** *International Building Science and Construction Abstracts* **and** *International Structural Engineering Abstracts.*
 Desc: Provides coverage of topics such as concrete technology, construction practice, steel construction, properties of materials, building physics, dynamic structural analysis, computer applications, fracture mechanics, design and analysis of reinforced concrete, and concrete mix design.

LC TH7201 .T45 **ISSN** 0140-4237
DD 690/.05 UK
INTERNATIONAL BUILDING SERVICES ABSTRACTS. See Building and Construction-Abstracting, Bibliographies and Statistics.

ISSN 0959-6038
DD 338.4766694 UK
INTERNATIONAL CEMENT REVIEW. [Int. cem. rev.]. (1989)-.
Periodical. English. Twelve times a year. $196.79. Tradeship Publications Ltd., Old Kings Head Court, High Street, Dorking, Surrey RH4 1AR United Kingdom. **Tel** 011 44 1306 740363, FAX 011 44 1306 740660, telex 94016994. **ED** David Hargreaves & Ian Nuttall. **Ad Acc, Adv Mgr:** Paul Brown.
 Desc: Global reflections on cement industry and trade.

LC TA1 .I747 **ISSN** 0020-6415
UK
CODEN INCOBU
INTERNATIONAL CONSTRUCTION. See Engineering-Civil Engineering.

ISSN 1063-1135
US
INTERNATIONAL CONSTRUCTION DIRECTORY. INTERNATIONAL SECTION.
VFOAT International Section. (1992)-. Directory. English. One time a year. $70.00. Dataguide, Inc., PO Box 796307, Dallas TX 75379-6307. **Tel** (214)931-1160, FAX (214)712-3927. **ED** John Coakley.
 Desc: The ICD contains the following construction references: Subsidiary listings, Public/Listed Companies; State Owned (Nationalized) Companies, and Construction Contractor Associations.

ISSN 1063-1453
US
●INTERNATIONAL CONSTRUCTION DIRECTORY. USA SECTION. VFOAT USA
Section. (1994)-. Directory. English. Every 2 years. $65.00. Dataguide, Inc., PO Box 796307, Dallas TX 75379-6307. **Tel** (214)931-1160, FAX (214)712-3927. **ED** John E. Coakley.
 Desc: A listing of construction contractors both national and international. Includes the company rankings, cross references, indexes, and general statistical information on the construction industry.

LC K9 .N8155 **ISSN** 0265-1416
DD 343/.07869/005 342.37869005 UK
INTERNATIONAL CONSTRUCTION LAW REVIEW, THE. See Law-International Law.

ISSN 0149-5585
US
INTERNATIONAL CONSTRUCTION WEEK.
[Int. constr. week]. (19??)-. Periodical. English. One time a week. £725.00. ICW Publications Ltd., Chapter House, Hinderton Hall Estate, Neston S Wiral L64 7TS United Kingdom. **Tel** 011 44 151 3531234, FAX 011 44 151 3531011. **ED** Christopher J. Platt.
 Desc: Newsletter reporting major construction projects in developing regions worldwide.

ISSN 0791-4326
DD 620.0285 IE
INTERNATIONAL DIRECTORY OF CIVIL ENGINEERING/CONSTRUCTION SOFTWARE. See Engineering-Computer Applications.

LC HD69.C6 I587 **ISSN** 1053-2501
DD 338.7/61001/02547 US
INTERNATIONAL DIRECTORY OF CONSULTANTS AND CONTRACTORS ACTIVE IN EASTERN EUROPE, AN.
[Int. dir. consult. contract. active East. Eur.]. (1991)-. Directory. English. One time a year (Jan.). $25.00. Projects Research, Inc., PO Box 2558, Falls Church VA 22042. **Tel** (703)698-9330, FAX (703)698-9837.

LC TA12 .I566 **ISSN** 1056-1099
DD 624/.025/4 US
INTERNATIONAL DIRECTORY OF CONSULTANTS AND CONTRACTORS ACTIVE IN WESTERN EUROPE, AN.
[Intern. dir. consult. contract. act. West. Eur.]. **Added/Corp** Projects Research, inc. **VFOAT** Consultants and Contractors Active in Western Europe. (1991)-. Directory. English. Every 2 years. $60.00 US; $62.50 other. Projects Research, Inc., PO Box 2558, Falls Church VA 22042. **Tel** (703)698-9330, FAX (703)698-9837.

LC TS **ISSN** 1148-3555
DD 681 FR
UDC 681.3
CEASED
INTERNATIONAL DOMOTIQUE NEWS (PARIS).
(INTERNATIONAL DOMOTIQUE NEWS.). (1989)-(1993). Periodical. English. Maison du Futur Communications, CNIT BP 530, 92053 Paris-La-Defense France. **Tel** 011 33 1 46921830. **ED** Bruno De Latour. **Bk Rev**. **Ad Acc**. **Continues** *Home Bus Info.*
 Desc: Newsletter on home automation and the intelligent building industry.

LC TH **ISSN** 0947-4498
DD 690 GW
●INTERNATIONALE ZEITSCHRIFT FUER BAUINSTANDSETZEN. VFOAT International
Journal for Restoration of Buildings and Monuments. (1995)-. Trade Publication. German (English). Six times a year. DM180.00. IRB Verlag, Nobelstrasse 12, 70569 Stuttgart Germany. **Tel** 011 49 711 9702500, FAX 011 49 711 9702507, telex 7255168 IZS D. **ED** Folker Wittmann.

IT
ISOCLARE CTA.
Italian. BE MA Editrice, Via Teocrito 50, 20128 Milan Italy. **Tel** 011 39 2 2552451.

Building and Construction

LC TH3 .J33
DD 690/.05
GW
JAHRBUCH DER BAUTECHNIK, DAS.
(Aug. 1, 1982)-. Periodical. German. One time a year. Expert Verlag, Goethestr 5, Postfach 1262, 7044 Ehningen Bei Boblingen Germany.

LC TH105 .K35
DD 624/.0952
JA
JAPAN'S CONSTRUCTION TODAY.
Main/Corp Kaigai Kensetsu Kyoryokukai. (19??)-. English. Overseas Construction Association of Japan, 9-9 Hatchobori 1-chome, Chuo-ku, Tokyo 102 Japan. *Continues* Kaigai Kensetsu Kyoryokukai. *Japan's Construction.*

DD 621
ISSN 1068-0039
US
●JLC'S TOOLS OF THE TRADE. (JLC'S TOOLS OF THE TRADE.). [JLC's tools trade]. **VFOAT** Tools of the Trade; TT. (1993)-. Periodical. English. Four times a year. Builderburg Group, RR #2, Box 146, Richmond VA 05477. **Tel** (802) 434-4747, FAX (802) 434-4467. **ED** Clayton DeKorne. **Ad Acc, Adv Mgr:** Patti Tarbox.
Desc: Written and edited for tradesmen and professional builders, contains features on the tools and equipment in the construction and renovation industries.

ISSN 0047-2115
CN
JOURNAL CONSTRUCTO. (1964)-. Trade Publication. French. Irregular (85 times per year). 254.86Can$. Publications Transcontinental Inc, 1100 Rene-Levesque, 24Fl boulevard West, Montreal Quebec H3B 4X9 Canada. **Tel** (514)392-9000, FAX (514)392-4724. **ED** Patrick Rouleau and Raynald Fortier. **Circ:** 9,750 (ctrl).
Desc: Publishes all tender calls and subsequent information in the province of Quebec. Also, regular news coverage of investments and projects to come.

DD 620
ISSN 0887-381X
US
CCC
CODEN JCRGEI
JOURNAL OF COLD REGIONS ENGINEERING. See Engineering-Civil Engineering.

LC HF5686.B7 J66
DD 657/.869/0097305
ISSN 1054-3007
US
CCC
Pr Rev.
JOURNAL OF CONSTRUCTION ACCOUNTING & TAXATION. [J. constr. account. tax.] **VFOAT** Journal of Construction Accounting and Taxation. Vol. 1, No. 1 (Spring 1991)-. Trade Publication. English. Four times a year. $133.25. Warren Gorham & Lamont Inc., Park Square Building, 31 St. James Avenue, Boston MA 02116-4112. **Tel** (617)423-2020, (800)950-1207, FAX (617)423-2026. **ED** Steve Collins. **Ad Acc, Adv Mgr:** Phil Brady, **Tel** (212)971-5120. **Circ:** 3000.
Desc: For financial professionals in the construction industry and CPA's with construction company clients.

LC TA1 .A5236
DD 624/.05
ISSN 0733-9364
US
CCC
CODEN JCEMD4
JOURNAL OF CONSTRUCTION ENGINEERING AND MANAGEMENT. See Engineering-Civil Engineering.

ISSN 0143-974X
UK
CCC
CODEN JCSRDL
Pr Rev.
JOURNAL OF CONSTRUCTIONAL STEEL RESEARCH. (JOURNAL OF CONSTRUCTIONAL STEEL RESEARCH : JCSR.). [J. constr. steel res.]. **VFOAT** JCSR. Vol. 1, No. 1 (Sept. 1980)-. Academic Scholarly Publication. English. Fifteen times a year. $1193.00. Elsevier Applied Science, An Imprint of Elsevier Science Ltd., The Boulevard, Langford Lane, Kidlington, Oxford OX5 1GB United Kingdom. **Tel** 011 44 1865 843000, 011 44 1865 843699, FAX 011 44 1865 843010. **(Subscription address:** Elsevier Science Ltd. / Oxford Fulfillment Centre, PO Box 800, Kidlington OX5 1DX United Kingdom. **Tel** 011 44 865 843355.**) ED** Patrick J. Dowling, John E. Harding, and R. Bjorhovde. **Bk Rev. Ad Acc. Circ:** 400 (ctrl). available on microfilm and microfiche from University Microfilms International (UMI); available on an online database from Elsevier Electronic Subscriptions (EES). Documents available from Article Express International, The Genuine Article.
Desc: Provides an international forum for the presentation and discussion of the latest developments in structural steel research and their applications.
Ind/Abst Alum. J. Earthq. Eng.; Alum. Ind. Abstr.; Bioeng. Abstr.; BMT Abstr. (-199?); Civ. Struct. Eng. Abstr.; Curr. Cit.; Curr. Contents Eng. Comput. Technol.; Ei Page One; Energy Res. Abstr. (Apr. 1983-); Eng. Index Annu.; Environ. Eng. Abstr.; Fluid Abstr., Civil Eng. Fluid Abstr. Proc. Eng.; FLUIDEX (19??-); Int. Civil Eng. Abstr.;

Manuf. Process Eng. Abstr.; Mech. Eng. Abstr.; Met. Abstr.; Res. Alert [Full Cov.]; SCISEARCH; Solid State Supercond. Abstr.

LC TA444 .J68
DD 620.1/37
ISSN 0125-1759
TH
Pr Rev.
JOURNAL OF FERROCEMENT. See
Building and Construction-Abstracting, Bibliographies and Statistics.

DD 690
ISSN 1056-828X
US
JOURNAL OF LIGHT CONSTRUCTION (NATIONAL ED.), THE. (THE JOURNAL OF LIGHT CONSTRUCTION.). [J. light constr.]. Vol. 9, No. 10 (July 1991)-. Periodical. English. Twelve times a year. $27.50. Builderburg Partnership, PO Box 686, Holmes PA 19043. *Formed by the union of* Journal of Light Construction (Eastern Ed.), 1049-6033; Journal of Light Construction (Midwest Ed.), 1050-2629 *and* Journal of Light Construction (Western Ed.), 1050-2637.

DD 690
ISSN 1050-2610
US
JOURNAL OF LIGHT CONSTRUCTION (NEW ENGLAND ED), THE. (THE JOURNAL OF LIGHT CONSTRUCTION.). [J. light constr.]. **VFOAT** JLC. (1989)-. Trade Publication. English. Twelve times a year. $32.50. Journal of Light Construction, RR 2 Box 146, Richmond VA 05477. **Tel** (802)434-4747, FAX (802)434-4467. **ED** Steve Bliss. **Bk Rev** (Qty: 12). **Ad Acc, Adv Mgr:** Nellie Callahan, **Tel** (802)434-4747. **Circ:** 41,000. *Continues in part* Journal of Light Construction, 1040-5224.
Desc: An trade magazine serving builders, remodelers, general contractors and other such trades involved in the residential and light commercial construction industry.

LC HD890.67.A1 J68
DD 333.33/095957/05
SI
JOURNAL OF REAL ESTATE & CONSTRUCTION. See Real Estate.

LC TJ1480
DD 631.3
ISSN 0952-5513
UK
JOURNAL OF THE HISTORIC FARM BUILDINGS GROUP. **Added/Corp** Historic Farm Buildings Group. **VFOAT** H.F.B.G. Journal; HFBG Journal. No. 1 (1987)-. Periodical. English. One time a year. Historic Farm Buildings Group, University of Reading White Knights, Reading RG6 2AG United Kingdom. **Tel** 011 44 1734 318663.

LC TH1 .I5
ISSN 0027-8815
II
JOURNAL OF THE NATIONAL BUILDINGS ORGANISATION. **Main/Corp** National Buildings Organisation (India). Vol. 1 (Dec. 1955)-. Periodical. English. Two times a year. Rs10.00. National Buildings Organisation, G Wing Nirman Bhavan, Maulana Azad Road, New Delhi 11 India. **Bk Rev. Ad Acc.**
Ind/Abst Archit. Period. Index (Oct. 1978).

LC TH1715.A1 J68
DD 693.8/32/05
ISSN 1065-2744
US
CCC
CODEN JTIEEI
JOURNAL OF THERMAL INSULATION AND BUILDING ENVELOPES. [J. therm. insul. build. envel.]. **VFOAT** Thermal Insulation and Building Envelopes. (1992)-. Periodical. English. Four times a year. $245.00. Technomic Publishing Company, Inc., 851 New Holland Avenue, Box 3535, Lancaster PA 17604. **Tel** (717)291-5609, (800)233-9936, FAX (717)295-4538. Documents available from Article Express International. *Continues* Journal of Thermal Insulation, 0148-8287.
Ind/Abst Curr. Cit.; Ei Page One; Eng. Index Annu.

LC HD9715.J2 J85
JA
JUTAKU SANGYO HANDOBUKKU.
Added/Corp Jutaku Sangyo Joho Sabisu. (1976)-. Periodical. Japanese. One time a year. ¥3000. Jutaku Sengyo Joho Services, 23 Mori Building, 1-23-7 Toranomon Minatoku, Tokyo 105 Japan. **ED** Tsuneshi Miwa.

LC HD9715.I72 K32
IS
KABLAN VEHA-BONEH, HA-. (1952)-.
Periodical. Hebrew. Ha-Merkaz Ha-Artsi Shel, Irgune Ha-Kablanim Veha-Bonim Be-Yisrael, Rehov Mikveh Yisrael 18, Tel-Aviv Israel.

LC TH4809.J3 K35
DD 690.8
ISSN 0301-9934
JA
KANCHI KENCHIKU. **Added/Corp** Hokkaido Kenchiku Shido Senta. (19??)-. Japanese. ¥800. Hokkaido Kenchiku Shido Senta, 2-Chome Kitayojonishi, Chuo-Ku Sapporo.

LC TH105 .J35A
JA
KANCHO EIZEN. **Main/Corp** Japan. Kensetsusho. **VFOAT** Construction of Government Buildings. (1964)-. Japanese. Shikoku Chihi Kensetsukyoku, 26 32 Fukuokacho 760, Tokyo Japan.

ISSN 0368-5306
JA
CODEN KEYOBV
KEIKINZOKU YOSETSU. See Metals and Metallurgy-Welding.

LC HD9715.J2 J24F
JA
KENSETSU TOKEI GEPPO. **Main/Corp** Japan. Kensetsusho Keikagukyoku. Chosa Tokeika. **VFOAT** Monthly of Construction Statistics. Vol. 1, No. 1 (1973)-. Japanese. Kensetsusho Kensetsu Keizaikyoku, (Economic Affairs Bureau Ministry of Construction), 13-4 Nihonbashi Kodenmacho, Chuoku Tokyo 103 Japan.

JA
KENSETSUGYO ANZEN EISEI HOREI HYAKKA. **Main/Corp** Japan. **Added/Corp** Kensetsu Rodo Horei Kenkyukai. **VFOAT** Anzen Eisei Horei Hyakka. (19??)-. Periodical. Japanese. ¥2500. Tajima Building, No 101 1-6 Shinbashi 3-chome, Minato-ku 105 Tokyo Japan.

JA
KENSETSUGYO HOREI TSUTATSU ZENSHO. **Main/Corp** Japan. **Added/Corp** Japan. Laws, Statutes. etc. Kensetsugyoho. (1976)-. Japanese. Seibunsha / Osaka, 14-1 Minami Oquicho Kita-ku 530, Osaka Japan.

LC HD9715.K4 K45
DD 338.4/7/624096762
KE
KENYA BUILDER, THE. Vol. 1, No. 1 (1975)-. Periodical. English. $12.50. New Publishers, Norwich Union Building, PO Box 30339, Nairobi Kenya.

LC TS400
DD 683
NE
●KETENS IN KAART. (1994)-. Trade Publication. English. Two times a year. M'Xpress vof, PO Box 66, 5258 ZH Berlicum Netherlands. **Tel** 011 31 41034347.

LC TH7687.A1 K46
DD 697.9/3/05
ISSN 0945-0459
GW
●KI LUFT UND KAELTETECHNIK. (Jan. 1994)-. Trade Publication. German (summaries and/or abstracts in English and French). Twelve times a year. $178.00. Verlag CF Mueller, Verlags GS, D-69018 Heidelberg Germany. **Tel** 011 49 6221 4890. **(Subscription address:** WEPF Publishing Services GmbH, Auf dem Wolf 4, CH-4018 Basel Switzerland. **Tel** 011 41 61 3115125.**)** *Continues* Ki Klima Kaelte Heizung, 0172-1984 *and* Luft und Kaeltetechnik, 0024-7251.

UK
KNIGHT'S BUILDING REGULATIONS.
(19??)-. English. Two times a year. £159.00. Charles Knight & Company Ltd, Tolley House, 2 Addiscombe Road, Croydon Surrey CR9 5AF United Kingdom. **Tel** 011 44 181 6884163. **ED** H.W. Clarke, J.I.'A. Nelson and E. Thompson.
Desc: Documentation and guidance for all those concerned with building construction and design who need a complete understanding of the regulations governing building work. Includes the Building Regulations 1985, associated Statutory Instruments, Approved Documents, and the DoE Manual to the Building Regulations. Contains text, annotations, commentary and practical explanation.

ISSN 0387-1061
JA
CODEN KOKODX
KONKURITO KOGAKU. (KONKURITO KOGAKU = CONCRETE JOURNAL.). [Konkurito Kogaku]. **Added/Corp** Nihon Konkurito Kogaku Kyokai. **VFOAT** Concrete Journal. (1975)-. Academic Scholarly Publication. English. Twelve times a year. $258.00. Nihon Konkurito Kogaku Kyokai, (Japan Concrete Inst.), Shuwa Kioicho TBR 708, 5-7 Kojimachi Chiyodaku, Tokyo 102 Japan. **Tel** 011 81 3 3263 1571, FAX 011 81 3 3263 2115. Index available. **Bk Rev. Ad Acc.** Documents available from CASDDS. *Continues* Konkurito Jaanaru, 0023-3544.
Ind/Abst Chem. Abstr.; Coal Abstr.; Concr. Abstr.; Corros. Abstr. (199?-); Int. Civil Eng. Abstr.

LI
KONSTRUKCIJU ILGAAMZIS KUMO IR STIPRUMO PRADIDINIMAS. (19??)-.
Lithuanian. Library of Vilnius Civil Engineering Institute, Gorkio 73, 232600 Vilnius Lithuania.
Ind/Abst Concr. Abstr.

Building and Construction

LC TA455.G7 K57   ISSN 0134-9392
RU
CODEN KMOUDN
KONSTRUKCIONNYE MATERIALY NA OSNOVE UGLERODA. (KONSTRUKTSIONNYE MATERIALY NA OSNOVE UGLERODA.). [Konstr. mater. osn. ugleroda]. No. 9 (1974)-. Academic Scholarly Publication. Russian. Izdatelstvo Metallurgiia, 2-I Obydenskii Per. 14 G-34, Moscow Russia. Documents available from CASDDS. **Continues** Konstruktsionnye Materialy na Osnove Grafita.
Ind/Abst Chem. Abstr. (?-1983).

LC TH13.2.I5 K66
IO
KONSTRUKSI : DIRECTORY PERUSAHAAN DKI JAKARTA. (1977)-. Directory. Indonesian. Kantor Sensus dan Statistik Dki Jakarta, Jl Medan Merdeka Selatan 8-9, Lantai XX, Jakarta Indonesia.

LC TH6014. K414
JA
KUKI CHOWA EISEI KOGAKKAI ROMBUNSHU. No. 1- June 1976-. Periodical. Japanese (English). ¥2000. Kuki Chowa Eisei Kogakkai, c/o Nakajima Building 8-1, Kita Shinjuku 1-chome, Shinjuku-ku 160 Tokyo Japan.

LC HD9715.K8 K85
KO
KUKTO WA KONSOL. See Industry and Production.

LC TH900 .K798
DD 621.8   CH
KUNG CHENG CHI HSIEH. VFOAT Construction Machinery and Equipment; Construction Machinery & Equipment. Periodical. Chinese. Twelve times a year. NT$8.40. Science Press, 16 Donghuangchenggen North Street, Beijing 100707, People's Republic of China. **Tel** 011 86 1 4019821, 011 86 1 4010642, **FAX** 011 86 1 4012180, 011 86 1 4019810, telex 210147. **ED** Gao Heng, Yan Qing-man, Wang Chen-ling, Xing Bao-Hua and Huang Chun-hua. **Ad Acc. Circ:** 30,000.
Desc: Design, test building, application and maintenance of construction machinery and equipment.

DD 344.71/01769/00264   ISSN 1194-4552
CN
LANCASTER'S CONSTRUCTION INDUSTRY EMPLOYMENT LAW NEWS. See Law-Labor Laws and Legislation.

DD 338.4/369/00971   ISSN 0821-6649
CN
LANSDOWNE LETTER, THE. [Lansdowne lett.]. Vol. 1, No. 1 (Jan. 1983)-. Periodical. English. Four times a year. David K. Lansdowne & Partners, 505 Consortium Court, London Ontario N6E 2S8 Canada. **Tel** (519)681-2282.

DD 338.4/369/00971   ISSN 0820-8794
CN
LANSDOWNE'S CONSTRUCTION COSTS HANDBOOK. [Lansdowne's constr. costs handb.]. **Added/Corp** David K. Lansdowne & Partners. **VAT** Construction Costs Handbook. (1974)-. Periodical. English. Five times a year. David K. Lansdowne & Partners, 505 Consortium Court, London Ontario N6E 2S8 Canada. **Tel** (519)681-2282.

ISSN 8756-5749
US
LATIN AMERICAN CONSTRUCTION INDUSTRY DIRECTORY. (1985)-. Directory. English. One time a year. Aurora International Consulting, PO Box 668, Norwalk CT 06856.

LC TH435 .L3
DD 692/.5/0941   UK
LAXTON'S NATIONAL BUILDING PRICE BOOK. VFOAT New Laxton's National Building Price Book. 159th Ed. (1987)-. English. One time a year. Thomas Skinner Directories, Windsor Court, East Grinstead House, East Grinstead West Sussex RH19 1XE United Kingdom. **Tel** 011 44 1256 840366, telex 858540. **Continues** Laxton's Building Price Book.

DD 690/.068   ISSN 0711-2564
CN
LECTURE NOTES SERIES (UNIVERSITY OF WATERLOO. CONSTRUCTION MANAGEMENT GROUP). (LECTURE NOTES SERIES.). [Lect. notes ser. - Constr. Manage. Group]. **Added/Corp** University of Waterloo. Construction Management Group. 1A (1974)-. English. Construction Management Group, Department of Civil Engineering, University of Waterloo, Waterloo Ontario N2L E61 Canada. **Continues** Lecture Notes Series (University of Waterloo. Construction Option Group), 0711-2556.

LC KF902 .L44   ISSN 0887-1183
DD 343.73/078624 347.30378624   US
LEGAL HANDBOOK FOR ARCHITECTS, ENGINEERS AND CONTRACTORS. See Law.

ISSN 0318-1340
DD 338.7/6/66940971   CN
LIAISON (CIMENTS CANADA LAFARGE). See Industry and Production.

ISSN 1069-0050
DD 621   US
●**LIGHTING ANSWERS.** (LIGHTING ANSWERS / NATIONAL LIGHTING PRODUCT INFORMATION PROGRAM.). [Light. answ.]. **Added/Corp** Rensselaer Polytechnic Institute. Lighting Research Center. National Lighting Product Information Program (United State). Vol. 1, No. 1 (Apr. 1993)-. Periodical. English. Irregular (4-6 issues per year). $8.00 (single issue). Rensselaer Polytechnic Institute, Lighting Research Centre, Greene Building Room 115, Troy NY 12180-3590. **Tel** (518)276-8716, **FAX** (518)276-2999.
Desc: Includes current information on lighting technology such as fluorescent lamps and light polarizers.

ISSN 0319-2318
DD 620.8/6   CN
LIST OF EQUIPMENT AND MATERIALS. **Main/Corp** Underwriters' Laboratories of Canada. Vol. 2 (1964)-. English. One time a year. Underwriters Laboratories of Canada, 7 Crouse Road, Scarborough Ontario M1R 3A9 Canada. **Continues** List of Inspected Appliances, Equipment and Materials, 0497-5936.

LC HD9715.N6 N65a
NO
LISTE OVER GODKJENTE ENTREPRENRER. See Industry and Production.

ISSN 0336-4933
FR
CODEN LITHDQ
LITHOCLASTIA. [Lithoclastia]. **Added/Corp** Centre de Recherches et d'Etudes Cceanographiques. (1975)-. Academic Scholarly Publication. English (French). Two times a year. Centre de Recherche d'Oceanographique, 1 Quai Branly, 75007 Paris France. Documents available from CASDDS.
Ind/Abst Chem. Abstr. (1975-1976); GeoRef.

LC TS26 .L58   ISSN 0456-3867
CN
CEASED
LLOYD'S CANADIAN HARDWARE, ELECTRICAL AND BUILDING SUPPLY DIRECTORY. VFOAT Canadian Hardware, Electrical & Building Supply Directory. (19??)-(1993). Directory. English. Sentinel Business Publications, 7575 Trans Canada Highway, Suite 500, St. Laurent Quebec H4T 1V6 Canada. **Tel** (514)333-1116, **FAX** (514)631-8858. **ED** Keith Fredericks. **Ad Acc, Adv Mgr:** P.Young. **Circ:** 13,000 (ctrl).
Desc: Detailed product listings of companies supplying hardware, electrical, building supply retailers, wholesalers, distributors and contractors.

LC WMLC 93/2844   ISSN 1072-6063
DD 729   US
●**LOG HOMES ILLUSTRATED.** [Log homes illus.]. Vol. 1, No. 1 (Aug./Sept. 1993)-. Periodical. English. Six times a year. $25.00. GCR Publishing Group, 1700 Broadway, 34th Floor, New York NY 10019. **Tel** (212)541-7100, (800)659-1395, **FAX** (212)245-1241. **(Subscription address:** Kable Publishers Aide / Illinois, 308 East Hitt Street, Subscription Department, Mt. Morris IL 61054-1473. **Tel** (815)734-1261.) **ED** John Leeper. **Ad Acc.**
Desc: Complete consumer guide to log home plans, building techniques, product reviews and beautiful decorating ideas.

ISSN 0195-7074
US
LOUISIANA CONTRACTOR. (19??)-. Trade Publication. English. Twelve times a year. $25.00. Louisiana Contractor, 2900 Westfork Drive, Suite 345, Baton Rouge LA 70827. **Tel** (504)292-8980, **FAX** (504)292-5089. **ED** Sam Barnes. **Ad Acc. Circ:** 6,750.
Desc: Serves the construction industry and allied fields primarily in the state of Louisiana.

US
LSI RESIDENTIAL CONSTRUCTION COSTS / LEE SAYLOR, INC. Added/Corp Lee Saylor, Inc. **VFOAT** Residential Construction Costs; Residential Costs; L.S.I. Residential Construction Costs. 1st Annual Ed. (1982)-. Trade Publication. English. One time a year. $59.70. Saylor Publications, Inc, 9420 Topanga Canyon Boulevard, Suite 203, Chatsworth CA 91311. **Tel** (818)718-5966, **FAX** (818)718-8024. **(Subscription address:** Saylor Publications, PO Box 4508, West Hills CA 91308.) **ED** Paul Felber. **Circ:** 10,000 (ctrl).
Desc: Current commercial and residential building costs.

LC TH7687.A1 L83   ISSN 0024-7251
GW
CODEN LUKAA7
TITLE CHANGE
LUFT- UND KALETECHNIK. [Luft- Kaltetech.]. **Added/Corp** Institut fuer Luft- und Kaltetechnik. Vol. 1 (1966)-(Jan. 1994). Academic Scholarly Publication. German. Verlag CF Mueller, Verlags GS, D-69018 Heidelberg Germany. **Tel** 011 49 6221 4890. Documents available from Article Express International, Ask*IEEE, CASDDS. **Merged into** Ki Luft und Kaeltetechnik, 0945-0459.
Ind/Abst Bioeng. Abstr.; Chem. Abstr.; Coal Abstr.; Curr. Cit.; Ei Page One; EMBASE; Eng. Index Annu.; Food Sci. Technol. Abstr.; INSPEC (April 1971-); Saf. Health Work.

LC TH9557 .N48a
NE
MAANDELIJKSE MEDEDELINGEN - INSPECTIE VOOR HET BRANDWEERWEZEN. Main/Corp Netherlands. Inspectie voor Het Brandweerwezen. (19??)-. Dutch. Ten times a year. Inspectie Voot Het Brandweerwezen, Postbus 200II, NL-2500 Gravenhage Netherlands. **ED** C. P. Henneman. **Bk Rev.** ctrl circ.

LC HD9715.N2 N48a
NE
MAANDSTATISTIEK BOUWNIJVERHEID. See Building and Construction-Abstracting, Bibliographies and Statistics.

LC TA680 .M27   ISSN 0024-9831
DD 693.505*   UK
CCC
CODEN MCORAV
Pr Rev.
MAGAZINE OF CONCRETE RESEARCH. [Mag. concr. res.]. **Added/Corp** Cement and Concrete Association. (Jan. 1949)-. Trade Publication. English. Four times a year (Mar., June, Sept., Dec.). £100.00 UK; £150.00 (airmail) other. Thomas Telford Ltd, Thomas Telford House, 1 Heron Quay, London E14 9XF United Kingdom. **Tel** 011 44 171 9876999, **FAX** 011 44 171 5384101, telex 298105. **ED** J. N. Clarke. cum. index. **Bk Rev. Circ:** 1,200. available on microfilm from University Microfilms International (UMI). Documents available from Article Express International, The Genuine Article, Ask*IEEE, CASDDS.
Desc: Covers all aspects of research on concrete and allied materials, including performance and evaluation of materials, design and testing and the use of concrete in conjunction with other materials.
Ind/Abst Abstr. J. Earthq. Eng. (?-?); Bioeng. Abstr.; Ceram. Abstr.; Chem. Abstr.; Coal Abstr.; Concr. Abstr.; Curr. Cit.; Curr. Technol. Index; Ei Page One; Eng. Index Annu.; Geotech. Abstr.; Highw. Res. Abstr.; INSPEC (1968-1985); Int. Civil Eng. Abstr.; J. Ferrocement; Res. Alert [Full Cov.]; Sci. Cit. Index; SCISEARCH; Soft. Abstr. Eng.; World Ceram. Abstr.

ISSN 1072-3560
DD 690   US
●**MAINTENANCE SOLUTIONS.** [Maint. solut.]. Vol. 1, No. 1 (Sept./Oct. 1993)-. Periodical. English. Six times a year. $45.00. Trade Press Publishing Company, 2100 West Florist Avenue, Milwaukee WI 53209. **Tel** (414)228-7701, **FAX** (414)228-1134.

ISSN 0899-5729
DD 696   US
MAINTENANCE TECHNOLOGY. [Maint. technol.]. Vol. 1, No. 1 (Jan. 1988)-. Trade Publication. English. Twelve times a year. $95.00. Applied Technology Publications, 1300 South Grove Avenue, Suite 205, Barrington IL 60010. **Tel** (708)382-8100, **FAX** (708)304-8603. **ED** Robert Baldwin. Index available. **Bk Rev. Ad Acc. Circ:** 80,000 (ctrl).
Desc: Contains instructional articles on standard maintenance subjects.
Ind/Abst Shock Vibr. Dig.

SZ
MAINTENANCE UPDATE. (19??)-. English. Kunst und Wissen Erich Bieber, Dufourstrasse 51, CH-8008 Zurich Switzerland. **Tel** 011 41 11 694420.

LC TH4 .M32
DD 690   IQ
MAJALLAT BUHUTH AL-BINA. Added/Corp Markaz Buhuth al-Bina (Iraq). **VFOAT** Journal of Building Research. (19??)-. Periodical. Arabic (English). Four times a year. Petroleum Research Center, PO Box 10039, Jadiriyah Baghdad Iraq.
Ind/Abst Concr. Abstr.

LC HD9715.M3 M34   ISSN 0377-1148
DD 338.4/7/62409595   MY
MALAYSIAN BUILDING & CONSTRUCTION. VAT Malaysian Building and Construction. (1974)-. Periodical. English. Twelve times a year. $2.50 single issue. Asian Trade and Industry, 60-B Jalan Mesjid India, PO Box 836, Kuala Lumpur Malaysia.

Building and Construction

DD 338.4/769/00257127　　　ISSN 0712-2594
CN
MANITOBA CONSTRUCTION & RESOURCE INDUSTRIES. [Manit. constr. resour. ind.]. 15th Annual (1982)-. English. One time a year. Sanford Evans Communications Ltd., Box 6900, 1700 Church Avenue, Winnipeg Manitoba R3C 3B1 Canada. **Tel** (204)694-2022, FAX (204)694-2347. **ED** Steve Steigerwald, Herb Krushel, George Gamvrelis, and Alan Cherniak. **Ad Acc. Circ:** 6,017 (ctrl). *Continues Manitoba Construction Industry, 0380-674X.*
Desc: Dedicated to contractors and firms engaged in construction, mining, forestry and oil and gas industries. Provides the names, addresses and telephone numbers of suppliers, contractors and subcontractors.

DD 331.7/69/00257127　　　ISSN 0714-3222
CN
MANITOBA WINNIPEG BUILDING AND CONSTRUCTION TRADES COUNCIL YEARBOOK. See Business and Economics-Labor.

US
MANUAL. NEW YORK BUILDING LAWS. See Law.

US
MANUAL OF ACCEPTABLE PRACTICES. See Housing and Urban Development.

LC HD9715.5.U6 M36　　　ISSN 0733-2351
DD 690/.879/029473
MANUFACTURED HOUSING INDUSTRY ... BUYER'S MANUAL. See Housing and Urban Development.

LC TH1199 .M3　　　ISSN 0025-4681
DD 693　　　US
MASONRY. [Masonry]. **Added/Corp** Mason Contractors' Association of America. (19??)-. Periodical. English. Six times a year. $20.00. Mason Contractors Association of America, 1550 Spring Road, Suite 320, Oak Brook IL 60521. **Tel** (708)782-6767, FAX (708)782-6786. **Ad Acc.** Full Page (B&W) $715.00. Half Page (B&W) $430.00.

ISSN 0950-2289
UK
MASONRY INTERNATIONAL. (1984)-. Periodical. English. Three times a year. British Masonry Society, c/o British Ceramic Research Ltd, Queens Road, Stoke on Trent ST4 7LQ United Kingdom. **Tel** 011 44 1782 45431.

LC WMLC 93/1540　　　ISSN 0741-1294
US
CODEN MSJUET
Pr Rev.
MASONRY SOCIETY JOURNAL, THE. **Added/Corp** Masonry Society (U.S.). **VFOAT** Journal. Vol. 1, No. 1 (Jan./June 1981)-. Periodical. English. Two times a year (Feb. and Aug.). $55.00. Masonry Society, 3775 Iris Avenue, Suite 6, Boulder CO 80301-2043. **Tel** (303)939-9700, FAX (303)541-9215. **ED** Rochelle Jaffe. **Bk Rev.** (Qty: 2-10); **Circ:** 2,000.
Ind/Abst Abstr. J. Earthq. Eng.; Ceram. Abstr. (19??-); Constr. Index.

LC TH33.J3 M3
DD 338.4/769/0097292　　　JM
MASTERBUILDER, THE. Vol. 1 (1962)-. Periodical. English.
Ind/Abst Curr. Technol. Index.

LC HD9715.8.U63 A1415　　　ISSN 8756-2812
DD 691/.029/477　　　US
MASTERGUIDE. CENTRAL. (MASTERGUIDE. CENTRAL : THE OFFICIAL SPECIFYING AND BUYING DIRECTORY OF THE AMERICAN INSTITUTE OF ARCHITECTS.). **Added/Corp** American Institute of Architects. **VFOAT** Master Guide Central; Masterguide ... Central Region. 1985-. Directory. English. One time a year. $25.50 single volume AIA members, $29.95 single volume non-AIA members. Pactel Publishing, 50 Fremont Street/#2000, San Francisco CA 94105-2235.

ISSN 1121-0516
IT
MATERIA : RASSEGNA TECNICA DI MOTIVI D'ARCHITETTURA = AN ARCHITECTURAL REVIEW. See Architecture.

ISSN 0253-0201
RM
CODEN MCTIBU
MATERIALE DE CONSTRUCTII. (MATERIALE DE CONSTRUCTII : ORGAN AL MINISTERULUI INDUSTRIALIZARII LEMNULUI SI MATERIALELOR DE CONSTRUCTII.). [Mater. constr.]. **Added/Corp** Romania. Ministerul Industrializarii Lemnului si Materialelor de Constructii. Institutul de Cercetare si Proiectare Pentru Industria Materialelor de Constructii. **VFOAT** MC. (19??)-. Academic Scholarly Publication. Romanian. Four times a year. DM223.00. (**Subscription address:** Kubon & Sagner, ABT Zeitschriftenimport, D 80328 Munich Germany. **Tel** 011 49 89 54218130.) Documents available from CASDDS. *Continues in part Constructii si Materiale de Constructie.*
Desc: Contains articles in the field of building materials.
Ind/Abst Ceram. Abstr.; Chem. Abstr.; Concr. Abstr.

LC TP875 .M36　　　ISSN 0465-2746
SP
CCC
CODEN MCUAAA
MATERIALES DE CONSTRUCCION (MADRID). (MATERIALES DE CONSTRUCCION.). [Mater. constr.]. **Added/Corp** Instituto Eduardo Torroja de la Construccion y del Cemento. (1949)-. Academic Scholarly Publication. Spanish. Four times a year. 5000ptas. Instituto Eduardo Torroja, Apartado 19002, 28080 Madrid Spain. **Tel** 011 34 1 3020440. (**Subscription address:** CSIC Servicio de Revistas, Calle Vitrubio 8, 28006 Madrid Spain. **Tel** 011 34 1 561 2833.) Documents available from CASDDS.
Ind/Abst Ceram. Abstr.; Chem. Abstr.; Coal Abstr.; Concr. Abstr.; Curr. Cit.; Int. Civil Eng. Abstr.; Soft. Abstr. Eng.

US
MCGRAW-HILL'S DODGE CONSTRUCTION SYSTEMS COSTS. **Main/Corp** McGraw-Hill Information Systems Company. **VFOAT** Data from Dodge. 1980-. English. One time a year. McGraw Hill Publishing Company, Inc., 1221 Avenue of the Americas, New York NY 10020. **Tel** (212)512-6410, (800)525-5003, FAX (212)512-6111. *Continues Dodge Construction Systems Costs, 0148-8988.*

LC TH435 .B848　　　ISSN 0894-4342
DD 692/.5/05　　　US
MEANS ASSEMBLIES COST DATA. [Means assem. cost data]. **Added/Corp** Robert Snow Means Company. 11th Annual Ed. (1986)-. English. One time a year. $143.72. RS Means Company Inc. / Trade Sales, 100 Construction Plaza, PO Box 800, Kingston MA 02364. **Tel** (617)585-7880, (800)448-8182, FAX (617)585-7466. *Continues Means Systems Costs, 0739-1498.*

LC TH435 .B84　　　ISSN 1066-0240
DD 692.5　　　US
MEANS BUILDING CONSTRUCTION COST DATA. [Means build. constr. cost data]. **Added/Corp** Means (Firm). **VFOAT** Means Construction Cost Data. 50th Annual Ed. (1992)-. English. One time a year. $85.15. RS Means Company Inc. / Trade Sales, 100 Construction Plaza, PO Box 800, Kingston MA 02364. **Tel** (617)585-7880, (800)448-8182, FAX (617)585-7466. *Continues Building Construction Cost Data, 0068-3531.*

LC TA682.26 .C66　　　ISSN 1075-0274
DD 693/.5　　　US
●**MEANS CONCRETE & MASONRY COST DATA.** [Means concr. mason. cost data]. **Added/Corp** Means (Firm). **VFOAT** Means Concrete and Masonry Cost Data; Concrete & Masonry Cost Data. 12th Annual Ed. (1994)-. English. One time a year. $83.02. RS Means Company Inc. / Trade Sales, 100 Construction Plaza, PO Box 800, Kingston MA 02364. **Tel** (617)585-7880, (800)448-8182, FAX (617)585-7466. *Continues Means Concrete Cost Data, 1075-0533.*

LC TA682.26 .C66　　　ISSN 1075-0533
DD 693/.5　　　US
TITLE CHANGE
MEANS CONCRETE COST DATA. [Means concr. cost data]. **Added/Corp** Means (Firm). **VFOAT** Concrete Cost Data. 5th Annual Ed. (1987)-(1993). English. RS Means Company Inc. / Trade Sales, 100 Construction Plaza, PO Box 800, Kingston MA 02364. **Tel** (617)585-7880, (800)448-8182, FAX (617)585-7466. **ED** William D. Mahoney. **Bk Rev. Ad Acc. Circ:** 5,000. *Continues Concrete & Masonry Cost Data, 0739-8298.*
Continued by Means Concrete & Masonry Cost Data, 1075-0274.
Desc: Includes unit and systems prices for concrete and masonry classifications.

ISSN 0361-9591
US
MEANS CONSTRUCTION COST INDEXES. **Added/Corp** Robert Snow Means Company. **VFOAT** Construction Cost Indexes. (1975)-. Periodical. English. Four times a year. $210.87. RS Means Company Inc. / Trade Sales, 100 Construction Plaza, PO Box 800, Kingston MA 02364. **Tel** (617)585-7880, (800)448-8182, FAX (617)585-7466. **ED** William D. Mahoney. **Bk Rev. Ad Acc. Circ:** 500 (ctrl).
Desc: Provides cost adjustment factors to complete construction estimates. Breakdowns for 209 US and Canadian cities, national average, historical data.

LC TK435 .M42　　　ISSN 0748-7002
DD 621.319/24　　　US
MEANS ELECTRICAL COST DATA. [Means electr. cost data]. **Added/Corp** Robert Snow Means Company. 7th Ed. (198?-). Periodical. English. One time a year. $89.41. RS Means Company Inc. / Trade Sales, 100 Construction Plaza, PO Box 800, Kingston MA 02364. **Tel** (617)585-7880, (800)448-8182, FAX (617)585-7466. **Bk Rev. Ad Acc. Circ:** 15,000 (ctrl). *Continues in part Mechanical & Electrical Cost Data, 0193-1954.*
Desc: Illustrated electrical construction and estimating procedures. Includes labor materials, square feet costs for typical installations, reference tables, codes, demolition work and all aspects of electrical work.

LC TH435 .M425　　　ISSN 1075-0789
DD 692/.5　　　US
●**MEANS FACILITIES CONSTRUCTION COST DATA.** [Means facil. constr. cost data]. **Added/Corp** Means (Firm). **VFOAT** Facilities Construction Cost Data. 9th Ed. (1994)-. English. One time a year. $212.95. RS Means Company Inc. / Trade Sales, 100 Construction Plaza, PO Box 800, Kingston MA 02364. **Tel** (617)585-7880, (800)448-8182, FAX (617)585-7466. *Continues Means Facilities Cost Data, 0888-6709.*

ISSN 1074-0953
DD 658　　　US
●**MEANS FACILITIES MAINTENANCE & REPAIR COST DATA.** [Means facil. maint. repair cost data]. **Added/Corp** Means (Firm). **VFOAT** Means Facilities Maintenance and Repair Cost Data; Facilities Maintenance & Repair Cost Data. (1994)-. English. Four times a year. $212.95. RS Means Company Inc. / Trade Sales, 100 Construction Plaza, PO Box 800, Kingston MA 02364. **Tel** (617)585-7880, (800)448-8182, FAX (617)585-7466.

LC TH435 .M429　　　ISSN 0893-5602
DD 692/.5/05　　　US
MEANS HEAVY CONSTRUCTION COST DATA. [Means heavy constr. cost data]. **Added/Corp** Means (Firm). **VFOAT** Heavy Construction Cost Data; Means Heavy Const. Cost Data. 1st Ed. (1987)-. English. One time a year. $92.60. RS Means Company Inc. / Trade Sales, 100 Construction Plaza, PO Box 800, Kingston MA 02364. **Tel** (617)585-7880, (800)448-8182, FAX (617)585-7466.

LC TH435 .M43　　　ISSN 0277-8610
DD 692/.5/0973　　　US
MEANS HISTORICAL COST INDEXES. [Means hist. cost indexes]. **Added/Corp** Robert Snow Means Company. **VFOAT** Historical Cost Indexes. (19??)-. English. One time a year. RS Means Company Inc. / Trade Sales, 100 Construction Plaza, PO Box 800, Kingston MA 02364. **Tel** (617)585-7880, (800)448-8182, FAX (617)585-7466. **ED** William D. Mahoney. **Bk Rev. Ad Acc. Circ:** 500 (ctrl).
Desc: For estimation of past projects in today's marketplace.

LC TH435 .I576　　　ISSN 8755-7541
DD 692/5/0973　　　US
MEANS INTERIOR COST DATA. **Added/Corp** Means (Firm). **VFOAT** Interior Cost Data. 5th Annual ed. (1988)-. Trade Publication. English. One time a year. $89.41. RS Means Company Inc. / Trade Sales, 100 Construction Plaza, PO Box 800, Kingston MA 02364. **Tel** (617)585-7880, (800)448-8182, FAX (617)585-7466. *Continues Interior Cost Data, 8755-7541.*

LC HD4966.B92 U43
DD 331.2/2　　　US
MEANS LABOR RATES FOR THE CONSTRUCTION INDUSTRY. **Added/Corp** Means (Firm). **VFOAT** Labor Rates for the Construction Industry; Means Labor Rates. 15th Annual Ed. (1988)-. English. One time a year. $184.95. RS Means Company Inc. / Trade Sales, 100 Construction Plaza, PO Box 800, Kingston MA 02364. **Tel** (617)585-7880, (800)448-8182, FAX (617)585-7466. *Continues Labor Rates for the Construction Industry, 0098-3608.*

LC TH4315 .M43　　　ISSN 0896-7601
DD 692/.5/0973　　　US
MEANS LIGHT COMMERCIAL COST DATA. [Means light commer. cost data]. **Added/Corp** Means (Firm). **VFOAT** Light Commercial Cost Data. 7th Annual ed. (1988)-. English. One time a year. $81.95. RS Means Company Inc. / Trade Sales, 100 Construction Plaza, PO Box 800, Kingston MA 02364. **Tel** (617)585-7880, (800)448-8182, FAX (617)585-7466. *Continues in part Residential/Light Commercial Cost Data, 0738-1239.*

LC TH6014 .M43　　　ISSN 1054-4798
DD 696/.029/9　　　US
CEASED
MEANS MECHANICAL CHANGE ORDER COST DATA. [Means mech. change order cost data]. **Added/Corp** Means (Firm). **VFOAT** Mechanical Change Order Cost Data. 1st Annual Ed. (1991)-(19??). Periodical. English. RS Means Company Inc. / Trade Sales, 100 Construction Plaza, PO Box 800, Kingston MA 02364. **Tel** (617)585-7880, (800)448-8182, FAX (617)585-7466.

LC TH435 .M435 ISSN 0748-2698
DD 690/.028 US
MEANS MECHANICAL COST DATA. [Means mech. cost data]. **Added/Corp** Robert Snow Means Company. **VFOAT** Mechanical Cost Data. 7th Ed. (1984)-. English. One time a year. $89.41. RS Means Company Inc. / Trade Sales, 100 Construction Plaza, PO Box 800, Kingston MA 02364. **Tel** (617)585-7880, (800)448-8182, FAX (617)585-7466. **ED** William D. Mahoney. **Circ:** 17,000. ***Continues in part*** *Robert Snow Means Company. Mechanical & Electrical Cost Data, 0193-1954.* ***Continued in part by*** *Means Plumbing Cost Data, 1042-3850.*
Desc: A complete source for mechanical units and systems. Prices for plumbing, fire protection and mechanical system design or estimating problems.

LC TH435 .O52
DD 692/.5/0973 US
MEANS OPEN SHOP BUILDING CONSTRUCTION COST DATA. **Added/Corp** Means (Firm). **VFOAT** Open Shop Building Construction Cost Data; Means Open Shop BCCD. 4th Annual ed. (1988)-. English. One time a year. $82.95. RS Means Company Inc. / Trade Sales, 100 Construction Plaza, PO Box 800, Kingston MA 02364. **Tel** (617)585-7880, (800)448-8182, FAX (617)585-7466. ***Continues*** *Open Shop Building Construction Cost Data, 0883-8127.*

LC TH3411 .R6a ISSN 0898-5006
DD 692/.5/0973 US
MEANS REPAIR & REMODELING COST DATA. [Means repair remodel. cost data]. **Added/Corp** Means (Firm). **VFOAT** Repair & Remodeling Cost Data; Repair and Remodeling Cost Data; Means Repair and Remodeling Cost Data; Means R and R Cost Data; Means R & R Cost Data. 9th Annual ed. (1988)-. English. One time a year. $85.15. RS Means Company Inc. / Trade Sales, 100 Construction Plaza, PO Box 800, Kingston MA 02364. **Tel** (617)585-7880, (800)448-8182, FAX (617)585-7466. ***Continues*** *Repair and Remodeling Cost Data, 0271-5945.*

LC TH4815.8 .M43 ISSN 0896-8624
DD 692/.5/0973 US
MEANS RESIDENTIAL COST DATA. [Means resid. cost data]. **Added/Corp** Means (Firm). **VFOAT** Residential Cost Data. 7th Annual ed. (1988)-. English. One time a year. $79.33. RS Means Company Inc. / Trade Sales, 100 Construction Plaza, PO Box 800, Kingston MA 02364. **Tel** (617)585-7880, (800)448-8182, FAX (617)585-7466. ***Continues in part*** *Residential/Light Commercial Cost Data, 0738-1239.*

LC TH435 .M4372 ISSN 1064-5128
DD 692 US
MEANS SITE WORK & LANDSCAPE COST DATA. [Means site work landsc. cost data]. **Added/Corp** Means (Firm). **VFOAT** Means Site Work and Landscape Cost Data. 11th ed. (1992)-. English. One time a year. $92.60. RS Means Company Inc. / Trade Sales, 100 Construction Plaza, PO Box 800, Kingston MA 02364. **Tel** (617)585-7880, (800)448-8182, FAX (617)585-7466. ***Formed by the union of*** *Means Site Work Cost Data, 0734-8479* ***and*** *Means Landscape Cost Data, 0898-4042.*

LC TH435 .M44 ISSN 0732-815X
DD 333.33/8 US
MEANS SQUARE FOOT COSTS : RESIDENTIAL, COMMERCIAL, INDUSTRIAL, INSTITUTIONAL. **Added/Corp** Robert Snow Means Company. **VFOAT** Square Foot Costs. (1982)-. English. One time a year. $102.19. RS Means Company Inc. / Trade Sales, 100 Construction Plaza, PO Box 800, Kingston MA 02364. **Tel** (617)585-7880, (800)448-8182, FAX (617)585-7466. **ED** William D. Mahoney. **Bk Rev. Ad Acc. Circ:** 11,000 (ctrl). ***Continues*** *Appraisal Manual.*
Desc: Construction data for typical buildings, residential, commercial, industrial and institutional structures. Details four classes of residential quality: economy, average, custom, and luxury.

LC TH6010 .M454 ISSN 1061-3374
DD 692.5 US
MECHANICAL/ELECTRICAL ... COSTBOOK / BNI, BUILDING NEWS. [Mech./electr. costb.]. **Added/Corp** Building News, Inc. **VFOAT** Mechanical Electrical ... Costbook; Costbook. (1991)-. English. BNI Building News, PO Box 3031, Terminal Annex, Los Angeles CA 90051.

LC HD9715.C3 M43 ISSN 0835-1031
DD 338.4/7624/0971021 CN
MECHANICAL TRADE CONTRACTORS. (MECHANICAL TRADE CONTRACTORS = ENTREPRENEURS EN METIERS MECHANIQUES.). [Mech. trade contract.]. **Added/Corp** Statistics Canada. Industry Division. **VFOAT** Entrepreneurs en Metiers Mechaniques. (1984)-. English (French). One time a year. 22.00Can$ Canada; $26.00 US; $31.00 other. Statistics Canada Publications Sales and Services, R.H. Coats Building 6th Floor, Ottawa Ontario K1A 0T6 Canada. **Tel** (613)951-5078, (800)267-6677, FAX (613)951-1584, telex 053-3585. ***Continues*** *Mechanical Contracting Industry, 0576-0097.*

LC TH4817 .M4 ISSN 0271-2210
DD 643/.7 US
MECHANICS & HOME REPAIR. **VAT** Mechanics and Home Repair. Periodical. English. One time a year. $1.95 each copy. University Settlement, 3553 Street, Urbain, Montreal Quebec H2X 2N6.

LC TH2430 .N32a ISSN 1053-8305
DD 695/.06073 US
MEMBERSHIP DIRECTORY - NATIONAL ROOFING CONTRACTORS' ASSOCIATION. (MEMBERSHIP DIRECTORY.). [Membersh. dir. - Natl. Roofing Contract. Assoc.]. **Main/Corp** National Roofing Contractors' Association. Directory. English. National Roofing Contractors Association- NRCA, PO Box 4752, Carol Stream IL 60197. **Tel** (800)872-7663, (708)299-9070.

LC TH12 .I57A
DD 690/.021 US
MEMBERSHIP ROSTER - INTERNATIONAL CONFERENCE OF BUILDING OFFICIALS. **Main/Corp** International Conference of Building Officials. English. One time a year. International Conference of Building Officials, 5360 South Workman Mill Road, Whittier CA 90601. **Tel** (310)669-0541. **ED** Karen L Zisko. **Circ:** 10,000.
Desc: Contains listing of members of International Conference of Building Officials.

LC TH1 .M4 ISSN 0885-5781
DD 721 US
METAL ARCHITECTURE. See Architecture.

ISSN 8756-2014
US
METAL CONSTRUCTION NEWS. [Metal constr. news]. Vol. 5, No. 11 (Nov. 1984)-. Periodical. English. Thirteen times a year. Free on request. Modern Trade Communications, 7450 North Skokie Boulevard, Skokie IL 60077. **Tel** (708)674-2200, FAX (708)674-3676. **Ad Acc, Adv Mgr:** J.Garvey, **Tel** (708)674-2200. **Circ:** 33,000 (ctrl). ***Continues*** *Metal Building News, 0274-8843.*

ISSN 0711-8015
DD 691/.029/471 CN
METRIC CONSTRUCTION PRODUCTS FILE. [Metr. constr. prod. file]. **VFOAT** Dossier de Produits Metriques en Construction. Vol. 1, No. 1 (May 1980)-. Periodical. English (French). Four times a year. $25.00. Department of Architecture, University of Toronto, 230 College Street, Toronto Ontario M5S 1A1 Canada.

US
MICHIGAN CONTRACTOR & BUILDER. (19??)-. English. $125.00. Contractor Publishing Co., 1629 West Lafayette Boulevard, Detroit MI 48216. **Tel** (313)962-3337.

ISSN 0026-3044
US
MID-WEST CONTRACTOR. (19??)-. Trade Publication. English. Twenty-four times a year. $39.00. Construction Digest Incorporated, PO Box 603, 7355 North Woodland Drive, Indianapolis IN 46206. **Tel** (317)297-5500. **ED** John Krane. **Bk Rev. Ad Acc. Circ:** 8,500 (ctrl). ***Continues*** *Western Contractor, 0097-4218.*
Desc: A four state construction news magazine (Kansas, Iowa, Nebraska, Western Missouri) featuring local construction projects. Bid award news, plus local and state legislation affecting the general and heavy contractor.

LE
MIDDLE EAST AND WORLD CONSTRUCTION DIRECTORY. Directory. English. Every 2 years. $70.00 Middle East and Africa; $80.00 other. Middle East Business Publishing and Distributing, PO Box 13-5121, Chouran Beirut Lebanon. **Tel** 011 961 1 3572476353 4, FAX 011 961 1 3572456252, telex 4990 FLYCY. **ED** Riyadh Chehab. Index available. cum. index. **Ad Acc. Circ:** 5,000.
Desc: Articles deal with construction and construction equipment, supplies and building materials.

LC HD9623.C2 C33a ISSN 0229-6098
DD 338.4/7620144 CN
MINERAL WOOL INCLUDING FIBROUS GLASS INSULATION. [Miner. wool incl. fibrous glass insul.]. **Added/Corp** Statistics Canada. Manufacturing and Primary Industries Division. Statistics Canada. Industry Division. **VFOAT** Laine Minerale y Compris les Isolants en Fibre de Verre. Vol. 33, No. 1 (Jan. 1981)-. Periodical. English (French). Twelve times a year. 60.00Can$ Canada; $72.00 US; $84.00 other. Statistics Canada Publications Sales and Services, R.H. Coats Building 6th Floor, Ottawa Ontario K1A 0T6 Canada. **Tel** (613)951-5078, (800)267-6677, FAX (613)951-1584, telex 053-3585. ***Continues*** *Statistics Canada. Manufacturing and Primary Industries Division. Mineral Wool., 0380-8203.*
Desc: Shows the production and factory shipments of mineral wool including fibrous glass insulation used in construction on a monthly and cumulative basis.

LC HD4903.3.B92 U535 ISSN 0090-855X
DD 331.1/33 US
MINORITY BUILDER. Periodical. English. Six times a year. $10.00. Minority Contractors Resource Center, 1750 K Street NW/Suite 350, Washington DC 20006.

ISSN 1056-7828
US
MINORITY BUILDER GAZETTE, THE. **Added/Corp** Project Management Consultants International Corp. **VFOAT** Minority Builder Monthly Journal. (1992)-. Periodical. English. Twelve times a year. $90.00. The Minority Builder Gazette, PO Box 2651, Cincinnati OH 98033.

ISSN 1059-4620
DD 690 US
CEASED
MISSISSIPPI CONSTRUCTION. [Miss. constr.]. Vol. 1, No. 1 (May 1991)-(19??). Trade Publication. English. Mississippi Construction Magazine, 2900 Westfork Drive, Suite 345, Baton Rouge LA 70827. **Tel** (204)292-8980.

LC TA680 .D38
GW
MITTEILUNGEN. **Main/Corp** Technische Hochschule Darmstadt. Lehrstuhl und Institut fuer Massivbau. No. 1 (1963)-. German. Irregular. ***Supersedes*** *Darmstadt. Technische Hochschule. Institut fur Massivbau. Mitteilungen.*

ISSN 0172-3006
GW
UDC 624 **CCC**
MITTEILUNGEN - INSTITUT FUER BAUTECHNIK. [Mitt. - Inst. Bautech.]. **VFOAT** Mitteilungen IfBt. (1970)-. Trade Publication. German. Six times a year. $129.00. Wilhelm Ernst & Sohn, Muehlenstr 33 34 170, D-13187 Berlin Germany. **Tel** 011 49 30 47889200. **(Subscription address:** VCH Publishers Inc., 303 Northwest 12th Avenue, Journals Department, Deerfield FL 33442. **Tel** (800)367-8249, (305)428-5566.**)**

LC TA472 .M68 ISSN 0026-8445
DD 624 US
MODERN STEEL CONSTRUCTION. [Mod. steel constr.]. **Added/Corp** American Institute of Steel Construction. Vol. 1, (Sept. 1961)-. Periodical. English. Twelve times a year. $30.00. American Institute of Steel Construction, 1 East Wacker Drive, Suite 3100, Chicago IL 60601. **Tel** (312)670-2400, FAX (312)670-5403. Documents available from Article Express International. ***Supersedes*** *Steel Construction Digest.*
Ind/Abst Alum. Ind. Abstr.; Ei Page One; Eng. Mater. Abstr.; Eng. Index Annu.; Geotech. Abstr.; Met. Abstr.

ISSN 0390-1025
IT
UDC 624
MODULO. [Modulo]. (1975)-. Periodical. Italian. Ten times a year. L109000. BE MA Editrice, Via Teocrito 50, 20128 Milan Italy. **Tel** 011 39 2 2552451.

ISSN 0026-9700
FR
UDC 69
MONITEUR DES TRAVAUX PUBLICS ET DU BATIMENT, LE. [Monit. trav. publics batim.]. (1903)-. Periodical. French. Fifty-two times a year (plus two special issues). 1520.00F. Publications du Moniteur, 17 rue d'Uzes, 75108 Paris Cedex 02 France. **Tel** 011 33 1 40133030, FAX 011 33 1 40419495 customer service, 40133037 advertising, telex UPRESSE 680876 F. **(Subscription address:** Le Moniteur, BP 104, 75060 Paris Cedex 02 France. **Tel** 011 33 1 40133121/22/27 or 28, FAX 011 33 1 40133389.**) ED** Nathalie Seyer. **Ad Acc, Adv Mgr:** Dominique Laneyrie, **Tel** 011 33 1 40133319. **Circ:** 602,000.

LC HD9715.I8 M65
IT
MONITOR. (Jan. 1968)-. Periodical. Italian. Twelve times a year. Monitor, Via Clisio 9, 00199 Rome Italy. **Tel** 011 39 2 862534.

SP
MONOGRAFIAS DEL INSTITUTO EDUARDO TORROJA DE LA CONSTRUCCION Y DEL CEMENTO. **Main/Corp** Instituto Eduardo Torroja de la Construccion y del Cemento. (19??)-. Periodical. Spanish. Six times a year. Instituto Eduardo Torroja, Apartado 19002, 28080 Madrid Spain. **Tel** 011 34 1 3020440.
Ind/Abst Ceram. Abstr. (19??-); Int. Civil Eng. Abstr.

ISSN 1168-4534
FR

MONUMENTAL. **Added/Corp** France. Direction du Patrimoine. Sous-Direction des Monuments Historiques. (199?)-. Periodical. French (English). Four times a year. $84.86. Monumental, 12 rue du Parc Royal, 75003 Paris France. **Tel** 011 33 1 40157630.

SZ

MOP : GEBAEUDEUNTERHALT & REINIGUNG. (19??)-. German (French). Four times a year. 30.00F Switzerland; 38.00F other. Graf & Neuhaus AG, Hermetschloostr 77, CH-8010 Zurich Switzerland. **Tel** 011 41 1 4320276. **ED** Ruth Neuhaur. **Bk Rev. Ad Acc. Circ:** 5,000.
Desc: Problems of cleaning: staff education, cleaning machinery and chemicals.

LC TH4818.W6 M84 **ISSN** 0844-3459
DD 691/.1 US
CEASED

MUIR'S ORIGINAL LOG HOME GUIDE FOR BUILDERS AND BUYERS. [Muir's orig. log home guide build. buy.]. **VFOAT** Log Home Guide for Builders and Buyers. (Jan./Feb. 1989)-(Fall 1994). Consumer Publication. English. Muir Publishing Company, Inc., 1 Pacific, St. Anne Bellevue, Quebec H9X 1C5 Canada. **Tel** (514)457-2045, FAX (514)457-6255. **(Subscription address:** Muir Publishing Co. Ltd., PO Box 580 Middle Creek Rd., Cosby TN 37722. **Tel** (615)487-2256, (615)487-2257.) **ED** Doris Muir and Allan Muir. **Bk Rev. Ad Acc. Circ:** 150,000 (ctrl). ***Continues*** *Original Log Home Guide for Builders & Buyers, 0844-3440;* ***Absorbed in part*** *Log Home Decor for Builders and Buyers, 0833-9686.*
Desc: An accurate source of information for log home dreamers, builders, dwellers, sellers and creators.

LC HD9715.F5 F56A **ISSN** 0355-2314
FI

MYONNETYT RAKENNUSLUVAT. **Main/Corp** Finland. Tilastokeskus. **VFOAT** Beviljade Byggnadstillstand. Periodical. Finnish (Swedish). Twelve times a year. Tilastokeskus, PL 504, Annankatu 44, 00101 Helsinki Finland. **Tel** 011 358 0 17341, FAX 011 358 0 17342474, telex 1002111 TILASTO SF.

LC TH4 .N2
II

N.B.O. ABSTRACTS. **Added/Corp** National Buildings Organisation (India). (1956)-. Periodical. English. Twelve times a year.

LC HD9622.J3 N34
DD 338.2/4 JA

NAMA KONKURITO TOKEI NEMPO. **See** Building and Construction-Abstracting, Bibliographies and Statistics.

ISSN 0700-1207
DD 343.71/07869 CN

NATIONAL BUILDING CODE OF CANADA. [Natl. build. code Can.]. **Added/Corp** National Research Council of Canada. Associate Committee on the National Building Code. National Research Council Canada. Associate Committee on the National Building Code. 2nd Ed. (1953)-. English (French). Irregular (every 5 years). 57.00Can$. National Research Council of Canada, Receiver General for Canada, Ottawa Ontario K1A 0R6 Canada. **Tel** (613)993-0362, FAX (613)952-7656. Each issue contains an index to its own contents (no volume index)--loose. ***Continues*** *National Building Code.*

LC TH435 .B843 **ISSN** 1076-3953
DD 692/.5/0973 US

●**NATIONAL BUILDING COST MANUAL.** [Natl. build. cost man.]. (1994)-. Trade Publication. English. One time a year. $18.00. Craftsman Book Company, PO Box 6500, 6058 Corte del Cedro, Carlsbad CA 92008. **Tel** (619)438-7828, (800)829-8123, FAX (619)438-0398. Each issue contains an index to its own contents (no volume index)--loose. ***Continues*** *Building Cost Manual, 0732-5789.*

LC TH435 .N3 **ISSN** 0547-5511
DD 692/.5/05 US

NATIONAL CONSTRUCTION ESTIMATOR / EDITED BY CAL PACIFIC ESTIMATORS. **Added/Corp** Cal Pacific Estimators. (19??)-. English. One time a year (December). $37.50. Craftsman Book Company, PO Box 6500, 6058 Corte del Cedro, Carlsbad CA 92008. **Tel** (619)438-7828, (800)829-8123, FAX (619)438-0398. **ED** Lisa Andrews. Each issue contains an index to its own contents (no volume index)--loose. **Circ:** 32,000 (ctrl). ***Continues*** *National Home Estimator.*
Desc: Current building costs in dollars and cents for residential, commercial, and industrial construction. Prices for every commonly used building material and the labor cost to install that material.

LC HC415.15 .N37 **ISSN** 0738-1670
DD 338.956/005 US

NATIONAL DEVELOPMENT. MIDDLE EAST/AFRICA. [Natl. dev., Middle East/Afr.]. **VFOAT** Middle East/Africa. (19??)-. Trade Publication. English (Spanish and Latin). Five times a year. $40.00 US, Canada and Mexico; $50.00 other. National Development, PO Box 3410, Milford CT 06460. **Tel** (203)874-1401, FAX (203)874-1448. **ED** Paul R. Green and Polly Frost. Index available. **Ad Acc, Adv Mgr:** John Storms, **Tel** (914)237-7297. **Circ:** 25,000 (ctrl). ***Continues in part*** *National Development, 0730-0123.*
Desc: Covers infrastructure development and technology in developing countries as well as new products and construction equipment.

LC TH12.5 .N38 **ISSN** 0092-668X
DD 338.4/7/69 US

NATIONAL DIRECTORY OF MODULAR BUILDING MANUFACTURERS. [Natl. dir. modul. build. manuf.]. (1974)-. Directory. English. Reference Development Corporation, PO Box 2331, Princeton NJ 08540.

ISSN 0192-6772
DD 380 US
CCC

NATIONAL HOME CENTER NEWS. [Natl. home cent. news]. (19??)-. Newspaper. English. Twenty-three times a year. $99.00. Lebhar Friedman Inc., PO Box 31203, Tampa FL 33633. **Tel** (800)944-4676, (813)664-6707. **ED** Ken Schept. **Ad Acc. Circ:** 52,000 (ctrl). available on microfilm and microfiche from University Microfilms International (UMI); available on an online database (files 16,570/Full-Text) from DIALOG.
Desc: Newspaper to retailers, manufacturers and wholesalers in cumber, building material, hardware industry.
Ind/Abst Bus. Source Plus; Bus. Source; EP Collect.; F&S Index Plus Text, Int. [Full Txt.] [Select. Cov.]; Homework Help.; Mark. Advert. Ref. Serv. [Full Txt.]; MasterFile FullTEXT 1000; MasterFile FullTEXT 350; MasterFile FullTEXT 650; MasterFile FullTEXT (Jan. 1995-); OCLC; PROMT [Full Txt.]; Stat. Ref. Index; Telebase.

ISSN 0229-2866
DD 690/.574/06071 CN

NATIONAL NEWSLETTER - CANSPA. (BULLETIN NATIONAL : AU SERVICE DE L'INDUSTRIE DU BAIN TOURBILLON ET DE LA PISCINE.). [Natl. newsl. - CANSPA]. **VFOAT** National Newsletter. Vol. 1, No. 3 (April 1980)-. Bulletin. French (English). Free. Association de Piscine Canadienne, CP 294, Kleinburg Ontario L0J 1C0 Canada. ctrl circ. ***Continues*** *National Newsletter (Association de Piscine Canadienne), 0229-2866.*

ISSN 0192-0359
US

NATIONAL UTILITY CONTRACTOR, THE. **Main/Corp** National Utility Contractors Association. **Added/Corp** National Utility Contractors Association. (197?)-. Periodical. English. Twelve times a year. $15.00. National Utility Contractors Association, 4301 North Fairfax Drive, Suite 360, Arlington VA 22203. **Tel** (703)358-9300, FAX (703)979-8628. **ED** James B. Gardner. **Bk Rev. Ad Acc. Circ:** 11,000.
Desc: Features on issues important to the underground utility (water and sewer lines) contractor. Features on legislation affecting contractors, safety, legal aids, and education/FYI.

ISSN 8750-6580
DD 338 US

NATION'S BUILDING NEWS. [Nation's build. news]. **Added/Corp** National Association of Home Builders (U.S.). Vol. 1, No. 1 (Feb. 18, 1985)-. Periodical. English. Twenty-six times a year. $10.00. National Association of Home Builders, 15th and M Street NW, Washington DC 20005. **Tel** (202)822-0203. **ED** William R. Legg, Daniel H. Street, Tim Ahern, Jay Shackford, Susan Elmendorf. **Ad Acc. Circ:** 147,000 (ctrl). ***Continues*** *NAHB News, 0278-8136.*
Desc: Interprets how current and pending events affect the housing industry; also informs members about association affairs, crucial housing legislation, and policy issues.

UK

NATURAL STONE DIRECTORY : DIMENSION STONE SOURCES FOR BRITAIN AND IRELAND. **VFOAT** Natural Stone Directory. (1972)-. Directory. English. Every 2 years. £35.00. Herald House Publishing, 96 Dominion Road, Worthing West Sussex, BN14 8JP United Kingdom. **Tel** 011 44 1903 821082, FAX 011 44 1903 821081. **ED** Colin Reeves. Index available. cum. index. **Bk Rev**, (Qty: 10-20). **Ad Acc. Circ:** 3,000. available on diskette.

UK

NATURAL STONE SPECIALISTS. English. Twelve times a year. £29.00 UK; £34.00 (surface mail), £46.00 (airmail) other. Herald House Publishing, 96 Dominion Road, Worthing West Sussex, BN14 8JP United Kingdom. **Tel** 011 44 1903 821082, FAX 011 44 1903 821081.

ISSN 0028-1026
GW
CCC

NATURSTEIN. [Naturstein]. (1946)-. Trade Publication. German. Twelve times a year. DM144.86 Germany; DM177.00 other. Ebner Verlag GmbH & Co KG, Postfach 3060, D-89020 ULM Donau Germany. **Tel** 011 49 731 152031.
Desc: Building and architecture involving stone masonry.

ISSN 0956-9081
UK

NB. NEW BUILDER. [NB, New build.]. **VFOAT** New Builder. (1989)-. Periodical. English. One time a week. £78.00 UK; £130.00 other. Thomas Telford Ltd, Thomas Telford House, 1 Heron Quay, London E14 9XF United Kingdom. **Tel** 011 44 171 9876999, FAX 011 44 171 5384101, telex 298105.

ISSN 0848-600X
DD 690/.0218 CN

NBC/NFC NEWS. [NBC/NFC news]. **Added/Corp** Institute for Research in Construction (Canada) National Research Council Canada. Associate Committee on the National Building Code. National Research Council Canada. Associate Committee on the National Fire Code. National Research Council Canada. Issue No. 121 (Sept. 1989)-. Periodical. English. Four times a year. Free on request. National Research Council of Canada, Receiver General for Canada, Ottawa Ontario K1A 0R6 Canada. **Tel** (613)993-0362, FAX (613)952-7656. ***Continues*** *NBC News NFC, 0380-8599.*

LC TA401 .N37
II
CODEN NCQUEV

NCB QUEST. **Added/Corp** National Council for Cement and Building Materials (India). **VAT** National Council for Cement and Building Materials Quest. Vol. 1, No. 1 (Aug. 1987)-. Periodical. English. Four times a year. $50.00. National Council for Cement and Building Materials, M-10 South Extension 11 Ring Road, New Delhi 110 049 India. **Tel** 011 91 11 6440133, FAX 011 91 11 6468868, telex 031-66261. **(Subscription address:** Prints India, 11 Darya Ganj, New Delhi 110002 India. **Tel** 011 91 11 3268645, FAX 011 91 11 3275542, telex 31-61087 PRIN-IN.)

LC HD9715.8.P18 N47
DD 338.4/3624/095491 PK

NESPAK PRICE INDEX : ESCALATION OF PRICES OF CONSTRUCTION INDUSTRY INPUTS. **VFOAT** Price Index. (July 1974)-. English. Two times a year. National Engineering Services, 417 Wapda House, PO Box 1351, Lahore Pakistan.

ISSN 0892-6344
DD 690 US

NEW CONSTRUCTION (INTERNATIONAL ED.). (NEW CONSTRUCTION : THE CLARK REPORTS.). [New constr.]. **Added/Corp** Clark Associates (Lake Bluff, Ill.). **VFOAT** Clark Reports. (19??)-. Periodical. English. One time a week. $840.00. Clark Associates, PO Box 185, 127 Scranton Building, Lake Bluff IL 60044. **Tel** (312)234-6665, (800)222-0255, telex 28-3493. **ED** Emily L. Metcalf. ctrl circ.
Desc: Advanced notification of new construction projects. All major forms of construction reported except residential.

ISSN 0028-470X
DD 338 US

NEW ENGLAND CONSTRUCTION. [New Engl. constr.]. (19??)-. Periodical. English. Twenty-six times a year. $50.00. Northeast Publishing Company, PO Box 362, 26 Long Hill Road, Guilford CT 06437. **Tel** (800)972-2001, (203)453-3717.

LC HD1361
DD 333.33 CN

●**NEW HOMES.** **See** Real Estate.

LC TA684 .N49 **ISSN** 0968-0098
UK

NEW STEEL CONSTRUCTION. **Added/Corp** British Constructional Steelwork Association. Steel Construction Institute (Great Britain). (1992)-. Trade Publication. English. Six times a year. $154.01. Kingslea Press Ltd., 137 Newhall Street, Birmingham B3 1SF United Kingdom. **Tel** 011 44 121 2368112, FAX 011 44 121 2001480. ***Formed by the union of*** *Steel Construction (British Constructional Steelwork Association)* ***and*** *Steel Construction Today, 0950-9216.*
Desc: Technical publication for those concerned with structural steelwork in the construction and building industry.
Ind/Abst Curr. Cit.

ISSN 0028-7164
US

NEW YORK CONSTRUCTION NEWS. **VFOAT** ; Construction News. (19??)-. Trade Publication. English. One time a week. $39.00. New York Construction News Inc., 135 East 65th Street, Fourth

Building and Construction

Floor, New York NY 10021. **Tel** (212)472-6400, FAX (212)472-6066. **ED** David Chartock. **Ad Acc, Adv Mgr Tel** (212)512-4775. **Circ:** 6,200 (ctrl).

ISSN 0549-0219
NZ
CCC
NEW ZEALAND CONCRETE CONSTRUCTION. [N.Z. concr. constr.].
Added/Corp New Zealand Portland Cement Association. Vol. 22 (Feb. 1978)-. Trade Publication. English. Six times a year. $57.29. Cement and Concrete Association of New Zealand, 13 Wall Place, Private Bag 50-902, Porirua New Zealand. **Tel** 011 64 4 2328379, FAX 011 64 4 2324393. **Continues** N.Z. Concrete Construction, 0469-4031.
Ind/Abst Concr. Abstr.; Highw. Res. Abstr.; J. Ferrocement.

LC TH213.7.S8 S94

ISSN 1102-3554
SW
TITLE CHANGE
NEWSLETTER OF SWEDISH BUILDING RESEARCH.
Added/Corp Statens Rad for Byggnadsforskning (Sweden). **VFOAT** Newsletter. (1990)-(1993). Newsletter. English. Swedish Council for Building Research, Sankt Goransgatan 66, International Section, S-112 33 Stockholm Sweden. **Tel** 011 46 8 540640, FAX 011 46 8 6537462. **Continues** Swedish Building Research News. **Merged** with Synopses from the Swedish Building Research, 0347-9935 **to form** Swedish Building Research, 0349-8387.

DD 690/.22/09714
ISSN 0317-5804
CN
NEWSLETTER. SAFETY. CONSTRUCTION ASSOCIATION OF MONTREAL AND THE PROVINCE OF QUEBEC. (NEWSLETTER : SAFETY.). **Main/Corp**
Construction Association of Montreal and the Province of Quebec. Vol. 2 (Feb. 27, 1975)-. Newsletter. English. Construction Association of Montreal and the Province of Quebec, 4970 place de la Savane, Montreal Quebec H4P 1Z6 Canada. **Tel** (514)739-2381. **Continues** Montreal Construction Association. Newsletter: Safety, 0317-5790.

ISSN 0910-8017
JA
CODEN NGKHEO
NIHON KENCHIKU GAKKAI KEIKAKUKEI RONBUN HOKOKUSHU.
Added/Corp Nihon Kenchiku Gakkai. **VFOAT** Journal of Architecture, Planning and Environmental Engineering. (1985)-. Periodical. Japanese (summaries and/or abstracts in English). Twelve times a year. Nihon Kenchiku Gakkai, (Architectural Inst. of Japan), 26-20 Shiba 5 Chome, Minatoku Tokyo 108 Japan. **Continues in part** Nihon Kenchiku Gakkai Ronbun Hokokushu, 0387-1185.
Ind/Abst Abstr. J. Earthq. Eng.; Avery Index Archit. Period. Suppl. Colum. Univ. (Feb., Sept. 1988, Jan. 1990-).

DD 690
ISSN 0915-3470
JA
NIKKEI KONSUTORAKUSHON. VFOAT
Nikkei Construction. (1989)-. Periodical. Japanese. Twenty-four times a year. ¥15900. Nihon Keizai Shimbun Inc., 9-5 Otemachi 1 Chome, Chiyoda-ku Tokyo 100 Japan. **Tel** 011 81 3 32700251, 011 81 3 52108502 (Nikkei Business Publications Inc.), FAX 011 81 3 52552661, 011 81 3 52108119 (Nikkei Business Publications Inc.). **ED** Shoji Tanabe.
Desc: Information for those involved with construction and civil engineering projects.

DD 690
ISSN 1049-7579
US
CODEN NBSSES
NIST BUILDING SCIENCE SERIES. [NIST build. sci. ser.]. **Added/Corp** National Institute of Standards and Technology (U.S.). **VFOAT** National Institute of Standards and Technology Building Science Series. (1989)-. Monographic series. English. Irregular. Price varies per volume. Superintendent of Documents, US Government Printing Office, Washington DC 20402. **Tel** (202)275-3328, FAX (202)786-2377. Documents available from Article Express International, Ask*IEEE. **Continues** NBS Building Science Series, 0885-7563.
Ind/Abst Ceram. Abstr. (19??-); Ei Page One; Eng. Index Annu.; INSPEC; World Surf. Coat. Abstr.

LC TH4 .N5A
ISSN 0376-6802
NE
NIVAG CONTOUR. [NIVAG contour]. **Main/Corp**
Nieuwe Vereniging Van Aannemers Grootbedrijf. **VAT** Nieuwe Vereniging Van Aannemers Grootbedrijf Contour. (Jan. 1976)-. Periodical. Dutch. Twelve times a year. $38.62. Druk Jacob V Campen/O Z, Voorburgwal 87-89, 1012 El Amsterdam Netherlands.
Ind/Abst EMBASE.

DD 696.2/021/2
CN
NORME. **Main/Corp** Association Canadienne du Gaz. Monographic series. French. Price varies per volume. Association Canadienne du Gaz, 55 Chemin Scarsdale, Don Mills Ontario M3B 2R3 Canada.

DD 338.4/7690/02571313
ISSN 0229-1983
CN
NORTHERN ONTARIO CONSTRUCTION & RESOURCE INDUSTRIES DIRECTORY, PURCHASING GUIDE.
[North. Ont. constr. resour. ind. dir., purch. guide]. 1981-. Directory. English. One time a year. $10.00. Sanford Evans Communications Ltd., Box 6900, 1700 Church Avenue, Winnipeg Manitoba R3C 3B1 Canada. **Tel** (204)694-2022, FAX (204)694-2347. **Continues** Northern Ontario Construction Industry Directory/Purchasing Guide, 0704-688X.

DD 690
ISSN 0701-5224
CN
NOTE D'INFORMATION SUR LA CONSTRUCTION. No. 1F (1976)-. Monographic series. French. Price varies per volume. Conseil National de Recherches du Canada, Chemin de Montreal, Ottawa Ontario K1A 0R6 Canada. **Tel** (613)993-2463, FAX (613)954-5984.

ISSN 0379-6264
FR
Pr Rev.
NOTE D'INFORMATION TECHNIQUE - CENTRE SCIENTIFIQUE ET TECHNIQUE DE LA CONSTRUCTION. (NOTE D'INFORMATION TECHNIQUE.). [Note inf. tech. - Cent. Sci. Tech. Constr.]. **Added/Corp** Centre Scientifique et Technique de la Construction. (19??)-. Monographic series. French. Six times a year. Price varies per volume. Centre Scientifique Technique de la Construction, rue de la Violette 21-23, 1000 Brussels Belgium. **Tel** 011 32 2 7164211, FAX 011 32 2 7253212. Index available. cum. index. **Bk Rev**, (Qty: 2). **Circ:** 15,000. available in bound issues from the publisher.
Desc: Provides information concerning a specific building activity.
Ind/Abst FLUIDEX (1973-).

ISSN 0300-371X
AT
CCC
CEASED
NOTES ON THE SCIENCE OF BUILDING.
[Notes sci. build.]. **Added/Corp** Commonwealth Experimental Building Station (Australia). (Aug. 1949)-(Spring 1994). Monographic series. English. CSIRO Publications, PO Box 89, 314 Albert Street, East Melborne Victoria 3002 Australia. **Tel** 011 61 3 4187333, 4187217, FAX 011 61 3 4190459, telex AA 30236. **ED** Geoffrey Bock. Index available. cum. index. **Circ:** 2,000 (ctrl).
Desc: A series of illustrated pamphlets each dealing with an item of practical interest to those engaged in the building industry and to students.
Ind/Abst Archit. Period. Index (1949-).

SP
NOTICIAS DE LA CONSTRUCCION.
(19??)-. Spanish. Eleven times a year. $200.00 (two-year). Comunyted SA, Corcega 381 387 5, 08037 Barcelona Spain. **Tel** 011 34 3 4592233.

LC TH4819.P7 N68
DD 690/.837
ISSN 0731-9592
US
NOUVEAU. Summer 1981-. Periodical. English (English). $2.50 per copy. Nouveau, 29901 Agoura Road, Agoura CA 91301.

ISSN 0029-4675
FR
UDC 674
NOUVEAU JOURNAL DE CHARPENTE MENUISERIE PARQUETS. (1959)-. Periodical. French. Ten times a year. $142.17. Editions M Begassat, 17 rue du Louvre, 75001 Paris France. **Tel** 011 33 1 42360513, FAX 011 33 1 64595296. **ED** Christophe Rovan. **Continues** Nouveau Journal de Charpente-Menuiserie, 1141-1945.

DD 690/.0218
ISSN 0848-6018
CN
NOUVELLES CNB/CNPI. [Nouv. CNB/CNPI].
Added/Corp Institut de Recherche en Construction (Canada) Conseil National de Recherches Canada. Comite Associe du Code National du Batiment. Conseil National de Recherches Canada. Comite Associe du Code National de Prevention des Incendies. Conseil National de Recherches Canada. No. 121 (Sept. 1989)-. Periodical. French. Four times a year. Free on request. National Research Council of Canada, Receiver General for Canada, Ottawa Ontario K1A 0R6 Canada. **Tel** (613)993-0362, FAX (613)952-7656. **Continues** C N B Nouvelles C N P I., 0382-1730.

DD 331/.049/009714
ISSN 0317-0977
CN
NOUVELLES. RELATIONS OUVRIERES. ASSOCIATION DE LA CONSTRUCTION DE MONTREAL ET DU QUEBEC. **See** Business and Economics-Labor.

DD 690/.22/09714
ISSN 0384-7470
CN
NOUVELLES. SECURITE. ASSOCIATION DE LA CONSTRUCTION DE MONTREAL ET DU QUEBEC.
(NOUVELLES: SECURITE.). **Main/Corp** Association de la Construction de Montreal et du Quebec. Vol. 2 (Feb. 1975)-. Periodical. French. Irregular. Association de la Construction de Montreal et du Quebec, 4970 place de la Savane, Montreal Quebec H4P 1Z6 Canada. **Continues** Association de la Construction de Montreal. Nouvelles: Securite., 0384-7489.

LC Z5853.N14 N68 TA403

RU
NOVOSTI TEKHNICHESKOI LITERATURY. STROITEL'STVO I ARKHITEKTURA. RAZDEL A. SERIIA VII. STROITEL'NYE MATERIALY I IZDELIIA, KHARAKTERISTIKA I PRIMENENIE.
Added/Corp Moscow. TSentral'nyi Institut Nauchnoi Informatsii po Stroitel'stvu i Arkhitekture. TSentral'naia Nauchno-Tekhnicheskaia Biblioteka po Stroitel'stvu i Arkhitekture. Informatsionno-Bibliograficheskii Otdel. **VFOAT** Stroitel'nyi Institut Nauchnoi Informatsii po Stroitel'stvu i Arkhitekture; Stroitel'stvu i Arkhitektura. Razdel A. Seriia VII : Stroitel'nye Materialy i Izdeliia, Kharakteristika i Primenenie. (1974)-. Multiple languages (Russian). Twelve times a year. Informatsii po Stroitel'stvu i Arkhitekture, A-47 Ulitsa Gorkogo Dom 38, Moscow 125047 Russia. **Continues** Novosti Tekhnicheskoi Literatury. Stroitel'stvu i Arkhitektura. Razdel A. Seriia X : Stroitel'nye Materialy i Izdeliia.

LC Z7914.B9 N64 TH145

RU
NOVOSTI TEKHNICHESKOI LITERATURY. STROITELSTVO I ARKHITEKTURA. RAZDEL A. SERIIA VIII: STROITELNYE KONSTRUKTSII, STROITELNAIA FIZIKA. **Added/Corp** Moscow.
Tsentralnyi Institut Nauchnoi Informatsii po Stroitelstvu i Arkhitekture. TSentralnaia Nauchno-Tekhnicheskaia Biblioteka po Stroitelstvu i Arkhitekture. Informatsionno-Bibliograficheskii Otdel. **VFOAT** Stroitelstvo I Arkhitektura. Razdel A. Stroitelnye Konstruktsii, Stroitelnaia Fizika; Stroitelnye Konstruktsii, Stroitelnaia Fizika. (1974)-. Multiple languages (Russian and Multiple languages). Twelve times a year. Informatsii po Stroitel'stvu i Arkhitekture, A-47 Ulitsa Gorkogo Dom 38, Moscow 125047 Russia. **Continues** Novosti Tekhnicheskoi Literatury. Stroitelstvo I Arkhitektura. Razdel A. Seriia IX: Stroitelnye Konstruktsii, Stroitelnaia Fizika.

LC Z7914.B9 N635 TH4911

RU
NOVOSTI TEKHNICHESKOI LITERATURY. STROITELSTVO I ARKHITEKTURA. RAZDEL SERIIA V: SELSKO-KHOZIAISTVENNYE KOMPLEKSY, PREDPRIIATIIA, ZDANIIA I SOORUZHENIIA. **Added/Corp** Moscow.
Tsentralnyi Institut Nauchnoi Informatsii po Stroitelstvu i Arkhitekture. Tsentralnaia Nauchno-Issledovatelskaia Biblioteka po Stroitelstvu i Arkhitekture. Informatsionno-Bibliograficheskii Otdel. **VFOAT** Stroitelstvo I Arkhitektura. Seriia V: Selsko-Khoziaistvennye Kompleksy, Predpriiatiia, Zdaniia I Sooruzheniia; Selsko-Khoziaistvennye Kompleksy, Predpriiatiia, Zdaniia I Sooruzheniia. (1974)-. Periodical. Multiple languages (Russian and Multiple languages). Twelve times a year. Informatsii po Stroitel'stvu i Arkhitekture, A-47 Ulitsa Gorkogo Dom 38, Moscow 125047 Russia. **Continues** Novosti Tekhnicheskoi Literatury. Stroitelstvo I Arkhitektura. Razdel A. Seriia IV: Selskokhoziaistvennye Kompleksy, Zdaniia I Sooruzheniia.

LC Z7914.B9 N639 TH145

RU
NOVOSTI TEKHNICHESKOI LITERATURY. STROITELSTVO I ARKHITEKTURA. RAZDEL SERIIA VI. ORGANIZATSIIA, MEKHANIZATSIIA I PROIZVODSTVO STROITELNO-MONTAZHNYKH RABOT.
Added/Corp Moscow. Tsntralnyi Institut Nauchnoi Informatsii po Stroitelstvu i Arkhitekture. Tsentralnaia Nauchno-Tekhnicheskaia Biblioteka po Stroitelstvu i Arkhitekture. Informatsionno-Bibliograficheskii Otdel. **VFOAT** Organizatsiia, Mekhanizatsiia I Proizvodstvo Stroitelno-Montazhnykh Rabot; Stroitelstvo I Arkhitektura. Seriia VI. Organizatsiia, Mekhanizatsiia I Proizvodstvo Stroitelno-Montazhnykh Rabot. (1974)-. Multiple languages (Russian and Multiple languages). Twelve times a year. Informatsii po Stroitel'stvu i Arkhitekture, A-47 Ulitsa Gorkogo Dom 38, Moscow 125047 Russia. **Continues** Novosti Tekhnicheskoi Literatury. Stroitelstvo I Arkhitektura. Razdel A. Seriia VIII: Organizatsiia, Mekhanizatsiia I Proizvodstvo Stroitelno-Montazhnykh Rabot.

Building and Construction

NUOVO CANTIERE, IL. Vol. 1, No. 1 (Feb. 1967)-. Periodical. Italian. Eleven times a year. L74940. Etas SRL, Via Mecenate 89, 20138 Milan Italy. **Tel** 011 39 2 580841.

LC TH4 .O27

OBRAS. Spanish. Grupo Editorial Expansion, Sinaloa 149 P9, Col Roma, 06700 Mexico DF Mexico. **Tel** 011 52 5 2072066, 2072619, FAX 011 52 5 5116351.

LC TH3 .O26   ISSN 0029-8891   AU

OESTERREICHISCHE BAUZEITUNG. [Osterr. Bau Ztg.]. Periodical. German. One time a week. $7.50 single issue. Osterreich Wirtschaftsverlag, Nikolsdorfergasse 7-11, A-1501 Vienna Austria. **Tel** 0222/55-55-85.
Ind/Abst Saf. Health Work.

LC TH3401 .O43   ISSN 0094-0178
DD 643/.7/05   US CCC

OLD-HOUSE JOURNAL, THE. [Old-house j.]. **VAT** Old House Journal. Vol. 1 (Oct. 1973)-. Periodical. English. Six times a year. $27.00. Dovetale Publishers, 2 Main Street, Gloucester MA 01930. **Tel** (508)283-3200, (508)281-8803, FAX (508)283-4629. **ED** Patricia Poore. Index available. cum. index. **Bk Rev. Ad Acc. Circ:** 165,000.
Desc: Publication devoted to pre-1939 houses. Carries how-to articles on repair, restoration, maintenance, and decoration with emphasis on retaining original charm and character.
Ind/Abst Acad. Abstr.; Archit. Period. Index (1973,1977-)(1973-); Art Archaeol. Tech. Abstr.; Avery Index Archit. Period. Suppl. Colum. Univ. (1990-); Constr. Index (199?-); EP Collect.; Garden Lit. (1992-); Homework Help.; Index Inf.; Mag. Artic. Summar. Elite; Mag. Artic. Summar. Select; Mag. Artic. Summar. CD-ROM; Mag. Search; MasterFile FullTEXT 1000; MasterFile FullTEXT 350; MasterFile FullTEXT 650; MasterFile FullTEXT (Jan. 1992-) [Full Txt.]; OCLC; Pub. Lib. FullTEXT; Telebase; Vocat. Search.

LC TH455 .O43   ISSN 0271-7220
DD 690/.029/473   US TITLE CHANGE

OLD-HOUSE JOURNAL CATALOG, THE. (THE OLD-HOUSE JOURNAL CATALOG / COMPILED BY THE EDITORS OF THE OLD-HOUSE JOURNAL NEWSLETTER.). **VFOAT** Old House Journal Buyer's Guide Catalog. **VAT** Old House Journal Catalog. (197?)-(1993). Newsletter. English. Dovetale Publishers, 2 Main Street, Gloucester MA 01930. **Tel** (508)283-3200, (508)281-8803, FAX (508)283-4629. **ED** Patricia Poore. Index available. **Ad Acc. Circ:** 25,000. **Continues** Old-House Journal Buyer's Guide. **Continued by** Old-House Journal Restoration Directory.
Desc: Sourcebook of hard-to-find items for restoring houses built before 1939. Lists over 1,400 companies supplying nearly 10,000 products that are appropriate for old houses.

LC TH455 .O43   ISSN 1077-2332
DD 690/.029/473   US

● **... OLD-HOUSE JOURNAL RESTORATION DIRECTORY, THE.** [Old house j. restor. dir.]. **VFOAT** Restoration Directory. **VAT** Old House Journal Restoration Directory. (1994)-. Directory. English. One time a year. $14.95. Dovetale Publishers, 2 Main Street, Gloucester MA 01930. **Tel** (508)283-3200, (508)281-8803, FAX (508)283-4629. **Continues** Old-House Journal Catalog, 0271-7220.

LC TH1 .H74   ISSN 0098-7727
DD 338.4/7/69009753   US

ON SITE (WASHINGTON, D.C.). (ON SITE.). [On site]. **Added/Corp** Metropolitan Washington Builders Association. (19??)-. Periodical. English. Twelve times a year. Metropolitan Washington Builders Association, 5100 Wisconsin Avenue NW/Suite 310, Washington DC 20016. **Continues** Insight on Site, 0090-9238.

US

ONE AND TWO FAMILY DWELLING CODE; UNDER THE NATIONALLY RECOGNIZED MODEL CODES. **Added/Corp** Southern Building Code Congress International. American Insurance Association. Building Officials and Code Administrators International. International Conference of Building Officials. (1971)-. Periodical. English. Irregular. $31.00. ICBO Evaluation Service Inc., 5360 South Workman Mill Road, Whittier CA 90601. **Tel** (213)699-0541, FAX (213)692-3853.
(Subscription address: International Conference of Building Officials, 6738 Northwest Tower Drive, Kansas City MO 64151. **Tel** (816)741-2241.)
Desc: Eliminates conflicts and duplications among the model codes to achieve national uniformity. Covers mechanical and plumbing requirements as construction and occupancy.

LC TH1715.A1 N37a   ISSN 0898-5766
DD 693/.832   US

OUTLOOK (WASHINGTON, D.C. 1988). (OUTLOOK.). [Outlook]. **Added/Corp** National Insulation Contractors Association (U.S.) National Insulation and Abatement Contractors Association (U.S.). **VFOAT** Insulation Outlook. Vol. 33, No. 4 (April 1988)-. Trade Publication. English. Twelve times a year. $45.00. NIAC / National Insulation Association of Contractors, 99 Canal Center Plaza, Suite 222, Alexandria VA 22314. **Tel** (703)683-6480, FAX (703)549-4838. **ED** Stuart C. Hales. **Ad Acc. Circ:** 6,000 (ctrl). **Continues** Insulation Outlook, 0270-3963.
Desc: Commercial and industrial insulation articles for owners, contractors, engineers, specifiers and manufacturers.

ISSN 1062-6921
DD 330   US

OVERSEAS BUILDER. (OVERSEAS BUILDER: INTERNATIONAL MARKETS FOR THE AMERICAN HOUSING INDUSTRY.). [Overseas build.]. **Added/Corp** Secant Communications. Vol. 1, No. 1 (Apr. 1992)-. Periodical. English. Twelve times a year. $125.00. Secant Communications, PO Box 340, Laurel MD 20725.

ISSN 0728-7275
DD 728.0994   AT

OWNER BUILDER MAGAZINE. [Own. build. mag.]. (1981)-. Periodical. English. Six times a year (Feb., April, June, Aug., Oct., Dec.). 19.74Aus$. Owner Builder Magazine, PO Box 974, Bendigo Victoria 3550 Australia. **Tel** 011 61 54 395667, FAX 011 61 54 395667. **ED** Russell Andrews. **Ad Acc, Adv Mgr:** Vallerie Andrews. **Circ:** 15,100.
Desc: Building information and suggestions on alternative building materials. Also includes articles on actual owner builders and their houses.

ISSN 1146-5093
FR

UDC 011
PASCAL. T 295, BATIMENT TRAVAUX PUBLICS. See Engineering-Abstracting, Bibliographies and Statistics.

ISSN 1036-3378
AT

PERIOD HOME RENOVATOR, THE. (198?)-. Periodical. English. Five times a year (Published quarterly for the magazine and the Buyers Guide is published in Nov.). 26.27Aus$. Publicity Press Pty Ltd., 252 Bay Street, Port Melbourne 3207 Australia. **Tel** 011 61 3 6466788, FAX 011 61 3 6467162. **ED** Michel Simmons. **Ad Acc. Circ:** 33,000 (magazines), 36,000 (guide) (ctrl).

US

● **PERMANENT BUILDING AND FOUNDATIONS.** (1995)-. English. Six times a year. $24.00. R.W. Nielsen Company, PO Box 11067, 5245 North Kensington, Kansas City MO 64119. **Tel** (816)453-0950.

LC HD9715.F73 N65A
DD 338.4/7/690094428   FR

PERSPECTIVES ECONOMIQUES DE LA PROFESSION DU BATIMENT DANS LA REGION NORD (NORD-PAS-DE-CALAIS). Main/Corp Institut National de la Statistique et des Etudes Economiques (France). (19??)-. French. Direction Regionale de Lille, 12 rue du bas Jardin 59, Lille France.

LC NA3 .P47
DD 720/.5   AU

PERSPEKTIVEN (VIENNA, AUSTRIA). (PERSPEKTIVEN.). **Added/Corp** Vienna (Austria). Vol. 43, No. 3 (May 1988)-. Periodical. German (summaries and/or abstracts in English). Ten times a year. $120.01. Compress Verlag, Jenullgasse 4, A 1141 Vienna Austria. **Tel** 011 43 1 8946449. Index available. **Bk Rev. Ad Acc. Circ:** 10,000-12,000. **Continues** Aufbau (Vienna, Austria), 0004-7805.
Ind/Abst Archit. Period. Index.

AT
CEASED

PETERSON REPORT - CONSTRUCTION. (19??)-(Aug. 1994). English. Australian Construction Report, PO Box 521, Blackburn Victoria 3130 Australia. **Tel** 011 61 008 335782, FAX 011 61 03 8973290.

LC HD9715.P6 P55
DD 338.7/624/025599   PH

PHILIPPINE CONSTRUCTION DIRECTORY. 1981-82-. Directory. English. One time a year. P500.00 Philippines; $25.00 US. Asean Journals, Warner Building/Mahesak Road, Bangkok Thailand. **Tel** 235-9722. **ED** William Ogan. **Ad Acc. Circ:** 5,000.
Desc: Listing of firms and suppliers involved in Philippine construction.

ISSN 0210-6868
SP

UDC 628.1
PISCINAS. (PISCINAS XXI.). (1976)-. Periodical. Spanish. Eight times a year. $115.00. Elsevier Prensa SA, Avenida Paral Lel 180, 08015 Barcelona Spain. **Tel** 011 34 3 3255350, FAX 011 34 3 4252880. **Ad Acc.** Full Page (B&W) 135000ptas. Half Page (B&W) 120000ptas. Full Page (Color) 165000ptas. Half Page (Color) 130000ptas. **Circ:** 6,500.
Desc: Covers building maintenance and swimming pool equipment, spas and saunas.

ISSN 0295-5725
FR

UDC 725.74
PISCINES, SPAS MAGAZINE. See Architecture.

LC HT395.S8 A58   ISSN 1100-0678
SW

PLANERA BYGGA BO. See Housing and Urban Development.

ISSN 0826-4392
DD 690/.8/05   CN

PLANS DE MAISONS DU QUEBEC. [Plans maisons Que.]. Vol. 7, No 3 (Jan./March 1984)-. Periodical. French. Twelve times a year. 10.67Can$. Publications Quebecor le Nordais, 5800 rue St. Denis Bar 605, Montreal Quebec H2S 3L5 Canada. **Tel** (514)272-6330, FAX (514)270-7079. **Continues** Maisons du Quebec, 0703-5683.
Ind/Abst Repere.

ISSN 0147-2429
US CCC

PLASTICS IN BUILDING CONSTRUCTION. Vol. 1 (Jan. 1975)-. Periodical. English. Twelve times a year. $215.00. Technomic Publishing Company, Inc., 851 New Holland Avenue, Box 3535, Lancaster PA 17604. **Tel** (717)291-5609, (800)233-9936, FAX (717)295-4538. **ED** Richard Dunn. cum. index. **Circ:** 225. available on microfilm from University Microfilms International (UMI).
Desc: Covers the complete range of building, construction, and civil engineering applications of plastics and other polymeric materials. A digest of current articles from worldwide literature is included.
Ind/Abst Curr. Cit.; Ei Page One; Eng. Mater. Abstr.

ISSN 0381-9620
DD 691/.92/05   CN

PLASTICS IN CONSTRUCTION. See Plastics.

ISSN 0965-8203
DD 627.3   UK

PORT ENGINEERING MANAGEMENT. [Port eng. manag.]. (1991)-. Periodical. English. Six times a year. $107.81. Publishing Consultancy Service, Blue Barn Cottages Goudhurst, Kent TN17 2PD United Kingdom. **Tel** 011 44 181 7868202, FAX 011 44 1737 814154. **Continues** World Port Construction & Ocean Technology, 0959-9320; **Absorbed** Port Construction and Ocean Technology.

ISSN 0032-5600
UDC 62   SP CCC

POTENCIA. [Potencia]. (1964)-. Periodical. Spanish. Twelve times a year. $137.67. Pedeca, Maria Auxiliadora 5, 28040 Madrid Spain. **Tel** 011 34 1 4508837.

US

POWER TOOLS. English. One time a year. $79.00. Orion Research Corporation, 14555 North Scottsdale Road, Suite 330, Scottsdale AZ 85260. **Tel** (800)844-0759, (602)951-1114, FAX (602)951-1117.
Desc: Gives used pricing information on 8,970 products.

LC TA630 .W34a   ISSN 0138-0796
PL
CODEN PITBDI

PRACE INSTYTUTU TECHNIKI BUDOWLANEJ. See Engineering-Civil Engineering.

LC TH4 .B74
PL

PRACE NAUKOWE INSTYTUTU BUDOWNICTWA POLITECHNIKI WROCLAWSKIEJ. SERIA KONFERENCJE. VFOAT Seria Konferencje; Scientific Papers of the Institute of Building of Wroclaw Technical University. Conferences. (19??)-. Monographic series. Polish (summaries and/or abstracts in English, German and Russian). Price varies per volume.
(Subscription address: Ars Polona-Ruch, PO Box 1001, Krakowskie Przedmiescie 7, 00-068 Warsaw Poland. **Tel** 011 48 22 261201.)
Ind/Abst Coal Abstr.

Building and Construction

LC TH4805 .P73
DD 643/.7
ISSN 1042-4601
US
CODEN PRAHE5
CEASED

PRACTICAL HOMEOWNER. [Pract. homeown.]. **VFOAT** Practical Home Owner; Rodale's Practical Homeowner. Vol. 2, No. 6 (July/Aug. 1987)-(March 1993). Periodical. English. Weststar Media, 656 Beir Island Road, Redwood City CA 94063. **Tel** (415)921-1001. **Ad Acc.** available on microfilm and microfiche from University Microfilms International (UMI). **Continues** Rodale's Practical Homeowner, 0888-1006. **Ind/Abst** Acad. Abstr.; EP Collect.; Homework Help.; Index Inf.; MasterFile FullTEXT 1000; MasterFile FullTEXT 350; MasterFile FullTEXT 650; MasterFile FullTEXT (Jan. 1992-Dec. 1992); OCLC; Pub. Lib. FullTEXT; Telebase.

DD 690
ISSN 1186-9100
CN

PREVIEW - CANADIAN CONSTRUCTION ASSOCIATION. (PREVIEW.). [Preview - Can. Constr. Assoc.]. **Main/Corp** Canadian Construction Association. (1991)-. English. Canadian Construction Association, 85 Albert Street/2nd Floor, Ottawa Ontario K1P 6A4 Canada. **Tel** (613)236-9455, FAX (613)236-9526, telex 053-4436.

IT

PREZZI INFORMATIVI DELL EDILIZIA MATERIALI ED OPERE COMPIUTE : IMPIANTI TECNICI. Italian. L80.000. Edizioni Dei, Via Nomentana 12, 00161 Rome Italy. **Tel** 011 39 6 4402046, FAX 011 39 06 4402034. **ED** Giuseppe Rufo. Index available. **Bk Rev. Ad Acc.** available on diskette. **Desc:** Dedicated to the works of new buildings, urbanization and facilities, reutilization, restructuring and maintenance of old edificies, plumbing and waterworks systems.

IT

PREZZI INFORMATIVI DELL EDILIZIA MATERIALI ED OPERE COMPIUTE : NUOVE COSTRUZIONI. (19??)-. Trade Publication. Italian. Two times a year. L80000. DEI srl Tipografia del Genio Civile, via Nomentana 16/20, 00161 Rome Italy. **Tel** 011 39 6 4402046, FAX 011 39 6 4403307. **ED** Giuseppe Rufo. Index available. **Bk Rev. Ad Acc. Desc:** Covers maintenance, renovation and restoration of buildings; marketing and management in the field of construction.

IT

PREZZIARIO OPERE EDILI PROVINCIA VERONA. Italian. One time a year. L15000. Camera Com Ind Art Agr Verona, Corso Porta Nuova 96, 37100 Verona Italy. **Tel** 011 39 45 591077.

ISSN 0890-829X
US

PRINCE WILLIAM NEWSLETTER. (198?)-. Newsletter. English. Twenty-six times a year. $205.00. Virginia Newsletters, Dulles International Airport, Box 17162, Washington DC 20041. **Tel** (703)860-2666.

LC HD9715.I96 C47a
DD 338.4/7/624096668
IV

PRINCIPALES ENTREPRISES IVOIRIENNES: TRAVAUX PUBLICS, GENIE-CIVIL, BATIMENT ET ACTIVITES CONNEXES. **Main/Corp** Chambre d'Industrie de Cote d'Ivoire. (19??)-. French. Chambre d'Industrie de Cote d'Ivoire, 11 Avenue Lamblin, BP No 1 758, Abidjan Ivory Coast.

LC TH95.P7 P7
PL

PROBLEMY ROZWOJU BUDOWNICTWA. **Added/Corp** Instytut Organizacji i Mechanizacji Budownictwa (Warsaw, Poland). (196?)-. Periodical. Polish (table of contents in English, French, German and Polish). Four times a year. $34.00. (**Subscription address:** Ars Polona-Ruch, PO Box 1001, Krakowskie Przedmiescie 7, 00-068 Warsaw Poland. **Tel** 011 48 22 261201.) **Continues** Problemy Inwestowania i Rozwoju.

LC TP881 .I5a
DD 666/.94/05
ISSN 0277-8211
US
CODEN PCESDK

PROCEEDINGS / INTERNATIONAL CEMENT SEMINAR. [Proc. - Int. Cem. Semin.]. **Main/Conf** International Cement Seminar. **VFOAT** I.C.S. Proceedings; Proceedings of the International Cement Seminar. (19??)-. Academic Scholarly Publication. English. One time a year. $40.00. Intertec Publishing Corp, 29 North Wacker Drive, Chicago IL 60606-3298. **Tel** (312)726-2802, FAX (312)726-3091. Documents available from CASDDS. **Ind/Abst** Chem. Abstr.

ISSN 0950-9615
UK

PROCEEDINGS OF THE BRITISH MASONRY SOCIETY. **VFOAT** Masonry. No. 1 (Nov. 1986)-. Proceedings. English. British Masonry Society, c/o British Ceramic Research Ltd, Queens Road, Stoke on Trent ST4 7LQ United Kingdom. **Tel** 011 44 1782 45431.

US

PROCESS PLANT CONSTRUCTION ESTIMATING STANDARDS: THE RICHARDSON RAPID SYSTEM. **Main/Corp** International Construction Analysts. **Added/Corp** Richardson Engineering Services. (19??)-. English. Four times a year. $457.00. Richardson Engineering Services, PO Box 9103, 1742 South Fraser Drive, Mesa AZ 85214-9103. **Tel** (602)497-2062, FAX (602)497-5529. Index available (Free). **Continues in part** International Estimating Services. Manual of Commercial and Industrial Construction Estimating and Engineering Standards.

ISSN 0478-4049
CN

PRODUCTEUR D'AMIANTE, LE. **VFOAT** Asbestos Producer. Vol. 1 (Oct. 1954)-. Periodical. English (French). Quebec Asbestos Mining Association, PO Box 1646 Station B, Montreal Quebec H3B 3L3 Canada.

LC TH1 .P7
DD 690
ISSN 1072-0561
US
CCC

●**PROFESSIONAL BUILDER (1993).** (PROFESSIONAL BUILDER.). [Prof. buil.]. Vol. 58, No. 8 (Aug. 1993)-. Trade Publication. English. Twenty times a year. $99.00. Cahners Publishing Company, 249 West 17th Street, New York NY 10011. **Tel** (212)645-0067, FAX (212)242-6987. (**Subscription address:** Cahners Publishing Company / Colorado, Paid Subscription Service Center, PO Box 7610, Highlands Ranch CO 80126-7610. **Tel** (303)470-4466, FAX (303)470-4691.) **Continues** Professional Builder & Remodeler, 1053-6353. **Desc:** Includes complete coverage of the residential construction industry, featuring legislation, news, market data, merchandising, technology, design, land development and new products. **Ind/Abst** MasterFile FullTEXT (Aug. 1993-).

LC TH1 .P7
DD 690
ISSN 1053-6353
US
CCC
TITLE CHANGE

PROFESSIONAL BUILDER & REMODELER. [Prof. build. remodel.]. **VFOAT** Professional Builder and Remodeler. Vol. 55, No. 17 (Oct. 1, 1990)-(1993). Trade Publication. English. Cahners Publishing Company, 249 West 17th Street, New York NY 10011. **Tel** (212)645-0067, FAX (212)242-6987. available on microfilm and microfiche from University Microfilms International (UMI); available on an online database (file 648/Full-Text) from DIALOG. Documents available from Documents on Demand. **Continues** Professional Builder (Newton, Mass. : 1985), 0885-8020. **Continued by** Professional Builder (Newton, Mass. : 1993), 1072-0561. **Desc:** Includes complete coverage of the residential construction and remodeling industries, featuring legislation, news, market data, merchandising, technology, design, land development and new products. **Ind/Abst** Bus. Index (1990-1993); Bus. Period. Index; Constr. Index; Energy Inf. Abstr.; Environ. Abstr.; EP Collect.; Gen. BusinessFile (1990-1993); Gen. Period. Index (1990-1993); Homework Help.; Mag. Search; MasterFile FullTEXT 1000; MasterFile FullTEXT 350; MasterFile FullTEXT 650; MasterFile FullTEXT (July 1993-July 1993); OCLC; Stat. Ref. Index; Telebase; Trade Ind. ASAP [Full Txt.]; Trade Ind. Index [Full Txt.]; Vocat. Search; Wilson Bus. Abstr.

LC TA658 .M49A
DD 690/.8/9
ISSN 0148-6632
US

PROFESSIONAL DESIGN SUPPLEMENT. **Main/Corp** Midwest Plan Service. English. $6.50. Midwest Plan Service, Iowa State University, 122 Davidson Hall, Ames IA 50011. **Tel** (515)294-4337.

LC TH2430 .P7
DD 695
ISSN 0896-5552
US

PROFESSIONAL ROOFING. [Prof. roof.]. **Added/Corp** National Roofing Contractors' Association. **VFOAT** Roofing. Vol. 15, No. 10 (Oct. 1987)-. Trade Publication. English. Twelve times a year. $25.00. National Roofing Service Corporation, PO Box 66454, Chicago IL 60666. **Tel** (708)299-9070, FAX (708)299-1183. **ED** Mari Ujka (editor's address: 10255 West Higgins Road, Suite 600, Rosemont, IL 60018). Index available. cum. index. **Ad Acc, Adv Mgr:** Mary Carravallah, **Tel** (708)299-9070. **Circ:** 18,000 (ctrl). **Continues** Roofing Spec, 0199-7742. **Desc:** Information on roofing industry trends and products. Provides current information on roof systems, application techniques, business management, and industry events. Includes news about technical developments and regulations affecting commerical and residential roofing. **Ind/Abst** Constr. Index.

ISSN 0364-2925
US

PROJECT REFERENCE FILE. **Main/Corp** Urban Land Institute. Vol. 1 (1971)-. Periodical. English. Twenty times a year. $90.00. Urban Land Institute, 625 Indiana Avenue Northwest, Washington DC 20004. **Tel** (202)624-7000, (800)321-5011, FAX (202)624-7152. **ED** John A. Casazza. **Circ:** 2,000. **Desc:** Provides developers, design professionals, public officials, and educators with examples of financially successful innovative designs.

LC TH23 .U55A
DD 690./07/2073
ISSN 0360-5051
US

PROJECT SUMMARIES OF THE CENTER FOR BUILDING TECHNOLOGY, NATIONAL BUREAU OF STANDARDS. (PROJECT SUMMARIES OF THE CENTER FOR BUILDING TECHNOLOGY.). **Main/Corp** United States. Institute for Applied Technology. Center for Building Technology. (19??)-. English. One time a year. US Department of Commerce / National Bureau of Standards / Maryland, Gaithersburg MD 20899.

ISSN 0033-1198
UN
CODEN PSIZAY

PROMYSLENNOE STROITELSTVO I INZENERNYE SOORUZENIJA. (PROMYSHELNNOE STROITELSTVO I INZHENERNYE SOORUZHENIIA.). [Prom. stroit. inz. sooruz.]. (1959)-. Academic Scholarly Publication. Russian. Four times a year. $13.00. (**Subscription address:** Victor Kamkin, 4956 Boiling Brook Parkway, Rockville MD 20852. **Tel** (301)881-5973.) Documents available from CASDDS. **Ind/Abst** Chem. Abstr. (1959-1982).

DD 338.4/76433/060714
ISSN 0821-1264
CN

PROPOS DE CUISINE. [Propos cuisine]. **Added/Corp** Association des Fabricants et Distributeurs de L'industrie de la Cuisine du Quebec. Vol. 1, No 1 (Jan./Feb. 1983)-. Trade Publication. French. Six times a year (Jan., Apr., June, Aug., Oct., Dec.). 37.40Can$. Editions CR Inc, CP PO Box 1010, Victoriaville G6P 8Y1 Canada. **Tel** (819)752-4243, FAX (819)758-8812. **Bk Rev. Ad Acc. Circ:** 1,100 (ctrl). **Desc:** Covers technical, legal and administrative concern for managers of kitchen cabinet manufacturers and distributors. Also includes news of the association and the industry.

LC TH
DD 690
UDC 69
CN

●**PROVEN AND POPULAR HOME PLANS.** (1994)-. Consumer Publication. English. One time a year. 5.95Can$. Giroux Publishing, 102 Ellis Street, Penticton British Columbia V2A 4L5 Canada. **Tel** (604)493-0942, FAX (604)493-7526. **ED** Michael Giroux. **Circ:** 10,000. **Desc:** Includes articles on recent developments in housing and design; the work of Canadian designers is featured.

DD 338.4/769/009713
ISSN 0714-3206
CN

PROVINCIAL BUILDING & CONSTRUCTION TRADES COUNCIL OF ONTARIO. (PROVINCIAL BUILDING & CONSTRUCTION TRADES COUNCIL OF ONTARIO : YEARBOOK.). [Prov. Build. Constr. Trades Counc. Ont.]. **Added/Corp** Provincial Building & Construction Trades Council of Ontario. **VFOAT** Building Trades Council of Ontario. **VAT** Provincial Building and Construction Trades Council of Ontario. (197?)-. English. One time a year. Free to members. Building Trades Council of Ontario Yearbook, c/o Naylor Communications, 100 Sutherland Avenue, Winnipeg Manitoba R2W 3C7 Canada. **Tel** (204)224-2267. **ED** Dennis Corcoran and Will Oliver. **Circ:** 600.

ISSN 0033-2038
PL

PRZEGLAD BUDOWLANY. (1929)-. Polish. Twelve times a year. $150.00 (latest edition). Wydawnictwa Czasopism i Ksiazek Technicznych SIGMA - NOT, Ul. Ratuszowa 11, PO Box 1004, 00-950 Warsaw Poland. **Tel** 011 48 22 180918, FAX 011 48 22 192187. (**Subscription address:** Ars Polona-Ruch, PO Box 1001, Krakowskie Przedmiescie 7, 00-068 Warsaw Poland. **Tel** 011 48 22 261201.) **Ind/Abst** Ceram. Abstr. (19??-); Concr. Abstr.

ISSN 0193-2527
US
CCC
CODEN PSAIDE

PUBLICATION SP. [Publ. SP]. **Main/Corp** American Concrete Institute. **Added/Corp** American Concrete Institute. **VFOAT** Publication; ACI Publication; ACI Publications; A.C.I. Publication; SP; Special

Building and Construction

Publication. (1958)-. Academic Scholarly Publication. English. Irregular. Price varies per volume. American Concrete Institute, PO Box 19150, Detroit MI 48219. **Tel** (313)532-2600, FAX (313)533-4747. **(Subscription address:** American Concrete Institute, PO Box 32190, Detroit MI 48232. **)** Documents available from Article Express International, CASDDS.
 Ind/Abst Bioeng. Abstr.; Ceram. Abstr.; Chem. Abstr.; Ei Page One; Eng. Index Annu.

DD 016.69/0072071
ISSN 1185-9628
CN
CEASED

PUBLICATIONS CATALOGUE / INSTITUTE FOR RESEARCH IN CONSTRUCTION. [Pub. cat. - Inst. Res. Constr.].
Main/Corp Institute for Research in Construction (Canada). **VFOAT** Catalogue des Publications. **VAT** Catalogue des Publications - Institut de Recherche en Construction (Ottawa). (Oct. 1991)-(March 1993). English (French). Institute for Research in Construction, National Research Council Canada, Ottawa Ontario K1A 0R6 Canada. **Tel** (613)993-9960, FAX (613)952-4040, telex 053-3145 NRC ADMIN OTT. **Continues** List of IRC Publications., 0840-2035. **Continued in part by** Institut de Recherche en Construction (Canada). Catalogue des Publications.

ISSN 1064-4733
US

PUBLICITY DIRECTORY FOR THE DESIGN, ENGINEERING, AND BUILDING INDUSTRIES, THE. (1992)-.
Directory. English. $195.00. IDPR Group, 596 Tremont Street, Boston MA 02118.

LC HD9715.A1 P84
KO

PULLAENTU KONSOL SUCHUL. Periodical.
Korean. Twelve times a year. Hanguk Kwahak Kisul Chongbo Sento, 206-9 Chongyangni-dong, Tongdaemun-ku, Seoul South Korea.

ISSN 1060-6009
US

PURCHASING PERFORMANCE BENCHMARKS FOR THE U.S. CONSTRUCTION/ENGINEERING INDUSTRY. Added/Corp Center for Advanced Purchasing Studies (Tempe, Ariz.). VFOAT Purchasing Performance Benchmarks. (1991)-. English. Free. Center for Advanced Purchasing Studies, PO Box 22160, Tempe AZ 85285. Tel (602)752-2277.

LC TH
DD 690
ISSN 1023-2451
SA

●PWV HOME OWNER BUILDING AND IMPROVEMENTS BUYERS GUIDE. (1994)-.
Consumer Publication. English. One time a year. Avonwold Publishing Company Pty Limited, PO Box 52068, Saxonwold 2132, South Africa. **Tel** 11 27 11 7881610.

LC TH4816 .Q33
DD 690/.2
ISSN 0098-9207
US

QUALIFIED REMODELER. [Qualif. remodel.].
Vol. 1 (Mar. 1975)-. Periodical. English. Twelve times a year. $30.00. PTN Publishing Company, 445 Broad Hollow Road, Melville NY 11747. **Tel** (516)845-2700, FAX (516)845-7109. **Absorbed** Kitchen & Bath Concepts, 8750-9504.

LC HD28
DD 658
Pr Rev.
ISSN 0893-360X
US

QUALITY BY DESIGN. [Qual. des.]. Vol. 1, No 1 (Mar. 1987)-. Periodical. English. Four times a year (Jan., Apr., July, Oct.). $104.00. William Hayden, Jr. Consultants Inc., PO Box 56022, Jacksonville FL 32241-6022. Tel (904)260-7700, FAX (904)260-7701. ED William Hayden, Jr. Bk Rev. (Qty: 6-8). Circ: 1,600 (ctrl).
 Desc: Written for and by consulting engineers, environmental service personnel, architects, and design and constructing firms.

LC HD9715
DD 338.47624183414
ISSN 1357-7336
UK

●QUALITY CONCRETE. [Qual. concr.]. (1995)-.
Periodical. English. Twelve times a year. $61.60. Concrete Plant and Production, 12 Grimsdells Lane, Amersham Buckinghamshire HP6 6HF United Kingdom. **Tel** 011 44 1494 726273, FAX 011 44 1494 722626, telex 838791. **ED** H. Jeffery. **Bk Rev. Ad Acc. Continues** Concrete Plant and Production, 0264-0236.
 Ind/Abst Concr. Abstr.; Eng. Index Annu.

DD 691/.09714
ISSN 0709-0692
CN

QUART DE ROND. VFOAT Quarter Round. First issue in 1959. Periodical. French (English). Six times a year. 20.00Can$. Association Des Detaillants De Materiaux De Construction, 4270 rue Jean-Talon Est, Montreal Quebec H1S 1J7 Canada. Ad Acc. Circ: 6,000 (ctrl).
 Desc: Official renovation magazine for building supply dealers, wholesalers, buying groups, buyers gardening retailers, economy topics, management, business events.

LC HD9715.B3 B34a
DD 338.4/7/690097296
BF

QUARTERLY BULLETIN OF CONSTRUCTION STATISTICS. See Building
and Construction-Abstracting, Bibliographies and Statistics.

CN

●QUEBEC CONSTRUCTION BATIMENT.
(1995)-. Trade Publication. French. Seven times a year. Groupe Constructo Publication, 1500 Boulevard Jules Poitras, 200 St. Laurent QUE H4N 1X7 Canada. **Tel** (514)856-6628, (514)745-5720. **Separated from** Quebec Construction.

DD 338.4/769/0009714
ISSN 0829-5263
CN
TITLE CHANGE

QUEBEC CONSTRUCTION (ED. MENSUELLE). (QUEBEC CONSTRUCTION.).
[Que. constr.]. (1984)-(1995). Trade Publication. French. Publications Transcontinental Inc, 1100 Rene-Levesque, 24Fl boulevard West, Montreal Quebec H3B 4X9 Canada. **Tel** (514)392-9000, FAX (514)392-4724. **ED** Patrick Rouleau and Johanne Rouleau. **Split into** Quebec Construction Batiment **and** Quebec Construction Grands Travaux.
 Desc: News about equipment, investments, new products and innovations for the construction industry in Quebec which represents a market of 25 billion dollars.

CN

●QUEBEC CONSTRUCTION GRANDS TRAVAUX. (1995)-. Trade Publication. French.
Seven times a year. Groupe Constructo Publication, 1500 Boulevard Jules Poitras, 200 St. Laurent QUE H4N 1X7 Canada. **Tel** (514)856-6628, (514)745-5720. **Separated from** Quebec Construction.

LC TH
DD 690
ISSN 0048-6361
AT

QUEENSLAND MASTER BUILDER.
(1963)-. English. Eleven times a year (Dec/Jan. issues combined). 49.74Aus$. Queensland Master Builders Association, 417-419 Wickham Terrace, Brisbane Queensland 4000 Australia. **Tel** 011 61 7 831 7033, FAX 011 61 7 832 2361. **ED** Schendell Mason. **Ad Acc, Adv Mgr:** Denis Manahan. **Circ:** 4,700 (ctrl).
 Desc: Articles on technical subjects and on any matter relating to the building and construction industry.

LC HF1 .P775
DD 381/.4568
ISSN 0318-8531
CN

QUINCAILLERIE, MATERIAUX. Vol. 89, No 2 (Feb. 1976)-. Periodical. French. Six times a year. 20.01Can$. MacLean Hunter Ltd. Business Publishers / Canada, Box 9100, Station A, Toronto Ontario M5W 1A5 Canada. Tel (416)596-5000, , FAX (416)596-5552. (Subscription address: Indas Customer Service, 35 Riviera Drive, Building 17, Markham Ontario L3R 8N4 Canada. Tel (905)946-0406.) available on microfilm and microfiche from University Microfilms International (UMI). Continues Quincaillier (Montreal), 0318-8515.

LC HD9715.F5 F57A
DD 338.4/3624/094897
FI

RAKENNUSKUSTANNUSINDEKSI, PIENTALON RAKENNUSKUSTANNUSINDEKSI JA MAATALOUDEN TUOTANTORAKENNUKSEN RAKENNUSKUSTANNUSINDEKSI. VFOAT
Byggnadskostnadsindex, Byggnadskostnadsindex for Smahus Och Byggnadskostnadsindex for Lantbruksbyggnader; Building Cost Index, Building Cost Index for Single-Unit Dwellings and Building Cost Index for Agricultural Building. English (Finnish and Swedish). One time a year. Government Printing Centre, PO Box 516, SF-00101 Helsinki 10 Finland. **Continues** Rakennuskustannusindeksi Ja Pientalon Rakennuskustannusindeksi.

LC TH7216.F5 R34
FI

RAKENNUSTEN LAMMITUSENERGIAN KAYTTO. (1980)-. Finnish (summaries and/or abstracts in English and Swedish).

LC TH4 .R358
FI

RAKENNUSTUOTANTO. VFOAT
Byggnadsproduktion; Building Production. Trade Publication. Finnish (summaries and/or abstracts in English and Swedish). Fmk120.00. Unionkatu 3C, Helsinki 00130 Finland. **Tel** 358-0-658211. **ED** Simo EW Laine. **Bk Rev. Ad Acc. Circ:** 38,000 (ctrl).
 Desc: Building and construction tabloid paper published by the Federation of the Finnish Building Industry.

LC TH95.F5 R36
ISSN 0355-550X
FI

RAKENTAJAIN KALENTERI. Added/Corp
Suomen Rakennusmestariliitto. Rakennusmestarien Keskusliitto (Finland). **VFOAT** R.K.; RK. (19??)-. Trade Publication. Finnish. One time a year. Fmk350.00. Fredrikinkatu, 53 A 00100 Helsinki 10, Finland. **Ad Acc.**

 Circ: 10,000.
 Desc: Of interest to those involved in the construction industry.

FI

RAKENTAMINEN = BYGGANDET.
Added/Corp Finland. Tilastokeskus. **VFOAT** Byggandet. (19??)-. Finnish (Swedish and English). Central Statistical Office, PO Box 504, SF-00101 Helsinki Finland. **Tel** 011 358 0 17347, FAX 011 358 0 17342279.

LC TX957 .R35
DD 658
ISSN 0147-9059
US

RAM DIGEST, THE. See Housing and Urban Development.

ISSN 0229-8643
CN

DD 354.7140082/42
RAPPORT ANNUEL ... . Main/Corp Regie des Entreprises de Construction du Quebec. (1978/79)-.
Periodical. French. One time a year. Editeur Officiel du Quebec, 1283 boulevard Charest Ouest, Quebec Quebec G1N 2C9 Canada. **Continues** Regie des Entreprises de Construction du Quebec. Rapport d'Activities, 0229-8635.

DD 692/.09714
ISSN 0822-5028
CN

RAPPORTS DE CONSTRUCTION SOUTHAM. [Rapp. constr. Southam]. No. 1-.
Periodical. French. Irregular. Communications Southam, Bureau 201/310 Av Victoria, Montreal Quebec H3Z 2M9 Canada. **Continues** Rapports de Construction et de Genie (Montreal et District et Province of Quebec Moins Montreal), 0822-501X.

UDC 648.5
ISSN 0173-9220
GW

RATIONELL REINIGEN. [Ration. reinig.].
(1976)-. Periodical. German. Twelve times a year. DM108.00. Lobrecht Verlag Kg, Postfach 1454, D 86817 BD Woerishofen Germany. **Tel** 011 49 8247 2061, FAX 011 49 8247 5894. **Continues** Gebaudereiniger-Handwerk, 0016-5727.

DD 692.50994
ISSN 0810-8064
AT

RAWLINSON'S AUSTRALIAN CONSTRUCTION HANDBOOK. [Rawlinson
Aust. constr. handb.]. (1983)-. English. One time a year (updates published in April, July, Oct.). 152.11Aus$. Rawlhouse Publishing Pty Limited, PO Box 145 West Perth, 1141 Hay Street, Western 6872 Australia. **Tel** 011 61 9 3218951, FAX 011 61 9 4811914. **ED** Iain A. Baillie. Index available. **Ad Acc, Adv Mgr:** Ron Murphy, **Tel** 011 61 2 2642644. **Circ:** 3,500.
 Desc: A national building cost reference book providing prices for stages of the building construction process and applicable generally to medium and larger sized projects.

LC TH
DD 690
ISSN 0112-9961
NZ

RAWLINSON'S NEW ZEALAND CONSTRUCTION HANDBOOK.
[Rawlinson's N. Z. constr. handb.]. **VFOAT** New Zealand Construction Handbook. (1986)-. English. One time a year. 128.00NZ$. Rawlhouse Publishing New Zealand Ltd, PO Box 9804, Auckland New Zealand. **Tel** 011 64 9 5290061. **ED** James McAfee. **Bk Rev. Ad Acc. Circ:** 1,500 (ctrl).
 Desc: Building and construction price guide covering many building types and over 50,000 individual construction materials.

ISSN 0377-8460
II
CODEN CRIRDX

RB. [RB]. Added/Corp Cement Research Institute of India. VAT Research Bulletin - Cement Research Institute of India. (1969)-. Academic Scholarly Publication. English. Price varies per volume. Documents available from Article Express International, CASDDS.
 Ind/Abst Bioeng. Abstr.; Ceram. Abstr. (19??-); Chem. Abstr.; Ei Page One; Eng. Index Annu.; Eng. Index Energy Abstr.

DD 620
ISSN 1081-8774
US
CODEN RMIXEC
TITLE CHANGE

READY MIX. (READY MIX : A PIT & QUARRY PUBLICATION.). [Ready mix]. Vol. 1, No. 1 (June 1991)-(199?). Periodical. English. Advanstar Communications Inc., 131 West First Street, Duluth MN 55802. Tel (218)723-9477, (800)346-0085, FAX (218)723-9437. Continues Concrete Producer News, 0899-8671. Merged into Pit & Quarry, 0032-0293.

LC HD266.C22 L63
DD 333.33/09794
ISSN 0147-9946
US

REAL ESTATE AND CONSTRUCTION REPORT. See Real Estate.

LC HG1 .E3
ISSN 0034-1045
US

REALTY AND BUILDING. See Real Estate.

Building and Construction

UDC 69
ISSN 0246-9561
FR
RECUEIL D'EVALUATIONS DES OUVRAGES COURANTS DU BATIMENT. (1979)-. Periodical. French. Four times a year. $170.60. Editions Charles Massin & Cie, 16 18 rue de l'Amiral Mouchez, 75686 Paris Cedex 14 France. **Tel** 011 33 1 45654848.

LC TH13.T2 R4
DD 338.4/7/62402576
ISSN 0148-0014
US
RED BOOK CONSTRUCTION REGISTER. (19??)-. English. One time a year. Red Book Construction Register, 5 Paddock Place, Brentwood TN 37027.

DD 690
ISSN 1188-2670
CN
REDACTEUR (MONTREAL). (LE REDACTEUR.). [Redacteur]. **Added/Corp** Devis de Construction Canada. Section de Montreal. Vol. 1, No. 1 (Fevr. 1992)-. Periodical. English. Gratuit pour les membres. Devis De Construction Canada, 4970 De La Savanne, Montreal (Quebec) H4P 1Z6.

UK
REDLAND GUIDE TO THE RECOMMENDATIONS, REGULATIONS AND STATUTORY AND ADVISORY BODIES OF THE CONSTRUCTION INDUSTRY. **VFOAT** Redland Guide to the Construction Industry. (1971)-. English.

US
REFERENCE GUIDE TO HOMEBUILDING ARTICLES. See Architecture.

LC TH13.2.G7 F24
DD 690/.06/21
UK
REGISTER OF MEMBERS - FACULTY OF BUILDING. **Main/Corp** Faculty of Building. (19??)-. English. £1.50. The Secretariat / England, 10 Manor Way, Boreham Wood WD6 IQQ United Kingdom.

UK
REGISTER OF VALVES. See Petroleum and Natural Gas.

LC TA12 .R39
DD 624/620
SP
RELACION DE LOS INGENIEROS DE CAMINOS, CANALES Y PUERTOS. See Engineering-Civil Engineering.

LC TH3411 .R45
DD 692/.5/0973
ISSN 1060-5797
US
REMODELING ... COSTBOOK / BNI, BUILDING NEWS. [Remodel. costbook]. **Added/Corp** Building News, Inc. **VFOAT** Costbook. (1991)-. English. One time a year. $44.95. Building News, 77 Wexford Street, Needham Heights MA 02194. **Tel** (800)873-6797.

LC TH4816 .B47
DD 643/.7
ISSN 0731-7409
US
REMODELING IDEAS. (19??)-. Periodical. English. Four times a year. $3.99. Meredith Publications / Special Interest Section, 1716 Locust Street, Des Moines IA 50309. **Tel** (515)284-3000.

LC TH4816 .R475
DD 643/.7/05
ISSN 0885-8039
US
REMODELING (WASHINGTON, D.C.). (REMODELING.). [Remodeling]. Vol. 1, No. 3 (Sept. 1985)-. Trade Publication. English. Twelve times a year. $44.95. Hanley-Wood Inc., 1 Thomas Circle Northwest, Suite 600, Washington DC 20005. **Tel** (202)452-0800, FAX (202)785-1974. **(Subscription address:** Remodeling, PO Box 1067, Skokie IL 60076.) **ED** Wendy Jordan. **Bk Rev**. **Ad Acc**. **Circ:** 85,000 (ctrl). **Continues** Remodeling World (Washington, D.C.).
Desc: Covers remodeling industry issues for the professional remodeler. Also includes design ideas, management techniques, construction tips, marketing and image issues.

ISSN 0214-3127
SP
UDC 69
RENOVATEC BARCELONA. [Renovatec Barc.]. (1987)-. Periodical. Spanish. Six times a year. 5247.00ptas. Elsevier Prensa SA, Avenida Paral Lel 180, 08015 Barcelona Spain. **Tel** 011 34 3 3255350, FAX 011 34 3 4252880. Index available. **Bk Rev**. **Ad Acc**. **Circ:** 7,000.
Desc: Specialized in present day facts and technology in building restoration.

ISSN 0381-0992
CN
RENOVATION BRICOLAGE. Vol. 1 (May 1976)-. Periodical. French. Twelve times a year. 23.48Can$. Publications Quebecor le Nordais, 5800 rue St. Denis Bar 605, Montreal Quebec H2S 3L5 Canada. **Tel** (514)272-6330, FAX (514)270-7079. Index available. **Ad Acc**.
Ind/Abst Repere (1983-).

DD 728.3/028/6
ISSN 0836-5857
CN
RENOVATOR, THE. [Renovator]. **VFOAT** Zone Heating News. Vol. 1, No. 1 (April/May 1987)-. Periodical. English. Six times a year. Limited free distribution to Ontario contractors; $30.00 other. **Continues** Home Energy, 0710-2984.

DD 728
ISSN 1187-0788
CN
CEASED
RENOVER (OUTREMONT). (RENOVER.). [Renover]. (1988)-(19??). Periodical. French. Publications Quebecor le Nordais, 5800 rue St. Denis Bar 605, Montreal Quebec H2S 3L5 Canada. **Tel** (514)272-6330, FAX (514)270-7079.

LC TA213 .R4
DD 690
ISSN 0484-4041
US
RENTAL RATE BLUE BOOK. **Added/Corp** Pacific Appraisal Company. National Research Division. **VFOAT** Rental Rate Blue Book for Construction Equipment. (1962/63)-. English. Irregular. $452.40. K-III Press Inc., 424 West 33rd Street, New York NY 10001. **Tel** (212)714-3100, (800)221-5488.

ISSN 0277-2000
US
RENTAL RATE BLUE BOOK FOR OLDER EQUIPMENT. **VFOAT** Rental Rate Blue Book for Older Construction Equipment. (19??)-. English. One time a year. K-III Press Inc., 424 West 33rd Street, New York NY 10001. **Tel** (212)714-3100, (800)221-5488.

US
TITLE CHANGE
REPAIR & REMODEL QUARTERLY. (19??)-(1995). English. Marshall & Swift, 911 Wilshire Boulevard, 16th Floor, Los Angeles CA 90026. **Tel** (800)544-2678, FAX (310)250-9811. **(Subscription address:** Marshall & Swift, PO Box 26307, Los Angeles CA 90026.) **Continues** Dodge Remodel and Retrofit Cost Data. **Continued by** Dodge Repair and Remodel Cost Book.

LC TH900 F36A
DD 624/.028
FR
REPERTOIRE ET CARACTERISTIQUES DES PRINCIPAUX MATERIELS DE GENIE CIVIL. **Main/Corp** Federation Nationale des Travaux Publics. **VFOAT** Repertoire des Principaux Materiels de Genie Civil. (19??)-. French. Federation Nationale des Travaux Publics, 3 rue de Berri, Paris 75008 France.

UK
RESEARCH AND ADVANCED STUDIES BULLETIN / UNIVERSITY OF STRATHCLYDE, DEPARTMENT OF ARCHITECTURE AND BUILDING SCIENCE. **VFOAT** Research and Advanced Studies Bulletin. Vol. 12 (1989)-. Bulletin. English. Every 2 years. $11.12. University of Strathclyde Abacus School of Architecture, Glasgow GA 0NG United Kingdom. **Tel** 011 44 141 5524400 ext. 3021. **Continues** Research Bulletin (University of Strathclyde. Dept. of Architecture and Building Science).

LC HD4965.3.B9 S74
DD 331.2/89/083/0973
ISSN 0735-5068
US
RESIDENTIAL BUILDERS COMPENSATION SURVEY. See Business and Economics-Labor.

LC TH4815.8 .R47
DD 333
ISSN 1053-2986
US
RESIDENTIAL BUILDING COST GUIDE. [Resid. build. cost guide]. **Added/Corp** E.H. Boeckh Co. (1986)-. English. One time a year. $37.00. E.H. Boeckh Company, 2885 South Calhoun Road, New Berlin WI 53151. **Tel** (800)285-1288, (414)780-2800. **Continues in part** Personal Lines Valuation Guide, 0742-440X.

LC HD9715.U53 M52
DD 338.4/7/690809774
ISSN 0362-3424
US
RESIDENTIAL CONSTRUCTION IN SOUTHEAST MICHIGAN. [Resid. constr. southeast Mich.]. **Main/Corp** Southeast Michigan Council of Governments. English. One time a year. Free. Southeast Michigan Council of Governments, 1900 Edison Plaza, Detroit MI 48226. **Tel** (313)961-4266, FAX (313)961-4869. **ED** Gerald Rowe. **Circ:** 3,000 (ctrl).
Desc: Tables and some text presenting residential building permit data for all local communities in southeast michigan.

LC HD9715.C3 C35f
DD 338.4/76908/0971021
ISSN 0835-1074
CN
RESIDENTIAL GENERAL CONTRACTORS AND DEVELOPERS. (RESIDENTIAL GENERAL CONTRACTORS AND DEVELOPERS = ENTREPRENEURS GENERAUX ET PROMOTEURS RESIDENTIELS.). [Resid. gen. contract. dev.]. **Added/Corp** Statistics Canada. Industry Division. **VFOAT** Entrepreneurs Generaux et Promoteurs Residentiels. (1984)-. English (French). One time a year. 22.00Can$ Canada; $26.00 US; $31.00 other. Statistics Canada Publications Sales and Services, R.H. Coats Building 6th Floor, Ottawa Ontario K1A 0T6 Canada. **Tel** (613)951-5078, (800)267-6677, FAX (613)951-1584, telex 053-3585. **Continues** Residential General Building Contracting Industry, 0705-5501.

SA
SUSPENDED
RESTORICA. **Added/Corp** Simon van der Stel Foundation. (Dec. 1975)- (Suspended (19??). Periodical. English (Afrikaans and English). Two times a year. R10.00. Simon van der Stel Foundation, PO Box 12293, Centralil 6006 South Africa. **Tel** 011 27 41 562849, FAX 011 27 41 562849. **ED** Elize Labuschagne. **Ad Acc**. **Circ:** 5,000 (ctrl). **Supersedes** Simon van der Stel Foundation. Bulletin.
Desc: Articles on conservation, restoration and history of building in Southern Africa.

BL
REVISTA ADEMI. **Main/Corp** Associacao de Dirigentes de Empresas do Mercado Imobiliario (Rio de Janeiro, Brazil). **VAT** Revista Associacao de Dirigentes de Empresas do Mercado Imobiliario. Periodical. Portuguese. Associacao de Dirigentes de Empresas do Mercado I Mobiliario, Avenida Almirante Barroso, 22 - Gr 1206, Rio de Janeiro Brazil.

ISSN 0325-1594
AG
REVISTA DE CERAMICA EN LA CONSTRUCCION. (1973)-. Spanish. Six times a year. **Continues** Boletin de Ceramica en la Construccion, 0006-6222.

LC TH27.Q4 R48
ISSN 0714-4237
CN
REVUE DE L'ACTIVITE DANS L'INDUSTRIE DE LA CONSTRUCTION. **Added/Corp** Office de la Construction du Quebec. Service de la Recherche. (198?)-. French. Four times a year. Office de la Construction du Quebec, 5530 Jean Talon Ouest, Montreal Quebec H3R 2G3 Canada. **Tel** (514)341-7740. **Continues** Revue de l'Activite dans l'Industrie de la Construction au Quebec.

ISSN 0744-9240
US
RICHARDSON CONSTRUCTION COST TREND REPORTER, THE. **Main/Corp** Richardson Engineering Services. **VFOAT** Labor Cost Escalation Index. (197?)-. Monographic series. English. Four times a year. $85.00. Richardson Engineering Services, PO Box 9103, 1742 South Fraser Drive, Mesa AZ 85214-9103. **Tel** (602)497-2062, FAX (602)497-5529. **Continues** International Construction Analysts. Richardson Construction Cost Trend Reporter.

US
RIEI INFORMATION LETTER. English. Four times a year. $12.00 (one-year), $21.00 (two-year), $30.00 (three-year). Roofing Industry Educational Institute Information Letter, 13 Inverness Drive East Building H/Suite 110, Englewood CO 80112. **Tel** (303)770-0613.
Ind/Abst Constr. Index.

LC KKH3067.A13 R58
IT
RIVISTA GIURIDICA DELL'EDILIZIA. See Law.

LC TH2391 .R66
DD 695/.05
ISSN 0279-4616
US
ROOFER MAGAZINE, THE. [Roof. mag.]. Vol. 1, Issue 1 (Sept./Oct. 1981)-. Trade Publication. English. Twelve times a year. $25.00. Construction Publications Inc., 12734 Kenwood Lane #73, Fort Myers FL 33907. **Tel** (813)489-2929, FAX (813)489-1747. **ED** Angela M. Hutto. **Ad Acc**, **Adv Mgr:** G. Abrell. **Circ:** 19,857 (ctrl).
Desc: Features roofing technology, equipment comparisons, product news, safety, legal and business columns. Format includes contractor interviews and photo essays.
Ind/Abst Constr. Index.

UK
Pr Rev.
ROOFING, CLADDING & INSULATION. English. Ten times a year. £35.00 UK; $80.00 US; £50.00 other. Patey Doyle Publishing Ltd, Wilmington House, Church Hill, Dartford Kent DA2 7EF United Kingdom. **Tel** 011 44 171 8371212, FAX 011 44 171 2784003. **ED** Martin James. Index available. **Ad Acc**. **Circ:** 11,500 (ctrl).
Desc: Tecnical journal for roofing, cladding, and insulation industry.
Ind/Abst Int. Civil Eng. Abstr.

Building and Construction

DD 729
ISSN 1061-8953
US
Pr Rev.
ROOFING MATERIALS GUIDE. [Roof. mater. guide]. **Added/Corp** National Roofing Contractors' Association. (198?)-. English. One time a year. $65.00 (members), $95.00 (nonmembers). NRCA National Roofing Contractors, PO Box 809261, Chicago IL 60680. **Tel** 800 872-7663, (708)299-9070. **Circ:** 3000.
Continues Commercial, Industrial and Institutional Roofing Materials Guide.

LC HD9715.U5 A7613
DD 338.7/624/025756
ISSN 8756-3800
US
ROSTER - ASSOCIATED GENERAL CONTRACTORS OF AMERICA. CAROLINAS BRANCH. (ROSTER.).
Main/Corp Associated General Contractors of America. Carolinas Branch. English. Carolinas Branch, Associated General Contractors of America, PO Box 30277, Charlotte NC 28230-0277.

LC TA12 .M76a
DD 624/025/762
US
ROSTER OF LICENSED CONTRACTORS IN THE STATE OF MISSISSIPPI. Main/Corp Mississippi State Board of Contractors. **VFOAT** Roster of Contractors. (1986)-. English. Mississippi State Board of Public Contractors, 2001 Airport Road/#101, Jackson MS 39208-9787.
Continues Roster of Licensed Contractors in the State of Mississippi.

LC HD9715.U53 S68
DD 338.4/76908/025757
US
ROSTER OF LICENSED RESIDENTIAL HOME BUILDERS IN THE STATE OF SOUTH CAROLINA. Added/Corp South Carolina Residential Home Builders Commission. (19??)-. English. One time a year. $25.00. South Carolina Residential Home Builders Commission, 2221 Devine Street, Columbia SC 29205. **Tel** (803)734-9174.

ISSN 0033-7129
US
CCC
RSI. ROOFING SIDING INSULATION. [Roof. siding insul.]. **VFOAT** Roofing Siding Insulation. (1945)-. Trade Publication. English. Twelve times a year. $36.00. Advanstar Communications Inc., 131 West First Street, Duluth MN 55802. **Tel** (218)723-9477, (800)346-0085, FAX (218)723-9437. **ED** Webb Shaw. **Circ:** 19,125. available on microfilm from University Microfilms International (UMI).
Ind/Abst Constr. Index; Eng. Mater. Abstr.; EP Collect.; F&S Index Plus Text, Int. [Select. Cov.]; Homework Help.; Leadscan; MasterFile FullTEXT 1000; MasterFile FullTEXT 350; MasterFile FullTEXT 650; MasterFile FullTEXT; OCLC; PROMT; Telebase.

US
RULES AND REGULATIONS. Main/Corp South Carolina. Residential Home Builders Commission. 1976-. Periodical. English. South Carolina Residential Home Builders Commission, 2221 Devine Street, Suite 312, Columbia SC 29205.

DD 728
ISSN 0888-3025
US
CCC
RURAL BUILDER. [Rural build.]. **Added/Corp** American Farm Building Services. (April 1986)-. Trade Publication. English. Seven times a year. $18.95 (one-year), $35.25 (two-year). Krause Publications, 700 East State Street, Iola WI 54990-0001. **Tel** (715)445-2214, FAX (715)445-4087, telex 55 6461. **ED** Frank Lessiter. **Bk Rev. Ad Acc. Circ:** 25,000 (ctrl).
Continues Farm Building News, 0014-7869.
Desc: Covers construction, sales and business management ideas of interest to rural builders involved with commercial, light industrial, farm, turn-key, recreational, grain systems, remodeling and residential work in rural America.

LC NA6 .A7274
RU
CODEN SPPAEA
S.-PETERBURGSKAIA PANORAMA. See Architecture.

SA
SA BUILDER. (19??)-. Periodical. English (Afrikaans). Eleven times a year. R92.00 South Africa; R160.00 other. Emden Publishing, PO Box 1123, Pinegowrie 2123 South Africa. **Tel** 011 27 11 7892258, FAX 011 27 11 7895223. *Continues* The South African Builder.

ISSN 0036-505X
FR
UDC 614.8:69
Pr Rev.
SAUVEGARDE DES CHANTIERS. VFOAT Sauvegarde. (1951)-. Trade Publication. French. Six times a year. $31.94. Organisme Professionnel de Prevention du Batiment et des Travaux Publics, 204 Rond Point du Pont Sevres, 92516 Boulgne Blnct CDX France. **Tel** 011 33 1 46092681, 011 33 1 4609698, FAX 011 33 1 46092740. **ED** M. Pierre Verges. cum. index. **Ad Acc. Adv Mgr:** M. Francais, **Tel** 33 1 46092651. **Circ:** 18,400 (ctrl).
Desc: Contains technical articles concerning problems of prevention and conditions of work in the sector of Building and public works; designed for artisans and architects.

ISSN 0036-102X
GW
UDC 62 :794/99
SB. SPORTSTATTENBAU UND BADERANLAGEN. VFOAT Equipement Sportif et Piscines; Sports Facilities and Swimming Pools; Construccion de Instalaciones Deportivas y Piscinas; Sportstattenbau und B…aderanlagen. (1967)-. Trade Publication. German (English, French and Spanish). Six times a year. $60.64. SB67 Verlags GmbH, Postfach 320340, 5000 Koeln 30 F R Germany. **Tel** 49 221 591017.

ISSN 0370-9906
RU
CODEN SGMKAQ
SBORNIK TRUDOV - GOSUDARSTVENNYJ VSESOJUZNYJ NAUCNO--ISSLEDOVATELSKIJ INSTITUT STROITELNYH MATERIALOV I KONSTRUKCIJ IM. P.P. BUDNIKOVA. (SBORNIK TRUDOV.). [Sb. tr. - Gos. vses. naucno-issled. inst. stroitel. mater. konstr. "VNII strom" im. P. P. Budnikova]. **Added/Corp** Soviet Union. Ministerstvo Promyshlennosti Stroitelnykh Materialov. Gosudarstvennyi Veseoiuznyi Nauchno-Issledovatelskii Institut Stroitelnykh Materialov i Konstruktsii Im. P.P. Budnikova. (1964)-. Academic Scholarly Publication. Russian. Irregular. Price varies per volume. Documents available from CASDDS.
Ind/Abst Chem. Abstr.

SZ
SCHWEIZER BAUBLATT. See Architecture.

ISSN 0376-6853
SZ
SCHWEIZER BAUWIRTSCHAFT. [Schweiz. Bauwirtsch.]. **Added/Corp** Schweizerischer Baumeisterverband. **VFOAT** Journal Suisse des Entrepreneurs; Giornale Svizzero Degli Impresari Costruttori. (197?)-. Trade Publication. German (French and Italian). One time a week. F140.00 Comes in combination with Schweizer Holzbau. Ag Verlag Hoch und Tiebau, Postfach, CH-8023 Zurich Switzerland. **Tel** 011 41 1 2588333, FAX 011 41 1 2588335. *Continues* Hoch + Tiefbau, 0046-7677.
Ind/Abst Saf. Health Work.

LC TH61 .S35
DD 624/.0941
ISSN 0085-6002
UK
SCOTTISH BUILDING AND CIVIL ENGINEERING YEAR BOOK. [Scott. build. civil eng. year book]. (19??)-. English. One time a year. $15.00 UK; $19.00 other. Edinburgh Pictorial Ltd., Smith Place House, Edinburgh 6 United Kingdom. **Tel** (031)554-1551. **ED** C.C. Cumming. **Bk Rev. Ad Acc. Circ:** 3,000 (ctrl).
Desc: Building and civil engineering.

ISSN 1120-7876
IT
UDC 691
SEC. SERRAMENTI & COMPONENTI. [SEC, Serram. Compon.]. **VFOAT** Serramenti e Componenti. (1991)-. Periodical. Italian. Twelve times a year. L65000 Italy; L130000 Europe; L175000 other. Tecniche Nuove SPA, Via Ciro Menotti 14, 20129 Milan Italy. **Tel** 011 39 2 75701, FAX 011 39 2 7570205, telex 334647 TECHS I.

LC HD9715.G7 S4
DD 338.4/7/69002524
ISSN 0966-0399
UK
SELL'S BUILDING & CONSTRUCTION INDEX. VFOAT Sell's Building and Construction Index; Building & Construction Index; Sell's Building and Construction Index. 68th Ed. (1992)-. English. £55.00. Miller Freeman Technical Ltd., Riverbank House, Angel Lane, Tonbridge Kent TN9 1SE United Kingdom. **Tel** 011 44 1732 362666, FAX 011 44 1732 770483, telex 95454 BBIS. *Continues* Sell's Building Index.

ISSN 0201-4211
RU
SELSKOE STROITELSTVO. Added/Corp Russian S.F.S.R. Gosudarstvennyi Komitet po Delam Stroitelstva. Russian S.F.S.R. Ministerstvo Selskogo Khoziaistva. Vol. 15, No. 1, (Jan. 1960)-. Periodical. Russian. Twelve times a year. $79.95. **(Subscription address:** East View Publications Inc., 3020 Harbor Lane North, Suite 110, Minneapolis MN 55447. **Tel** (800)477-1005, (612)550-0961, FAX (612)559-2931.)

ISSN 0371-0718
JA
CODEN SKONA5
SEMENTO KONKURITO. [Semento, konkurito]. **VFOAT** Cement & Concrete. (1947)-. Periodical. Japanese. Twelve times a year. Cement Association of Japan, Hattori Building 10-3, Kyobashi 1-Chome Chuo-ku, Tokyo 104 Japan. Index available in last issue of volume--attached. Documents available from CASDDS.
Ind/Abst Ceram. Abstr.; Chem. Abstr.; Coal Abstr.; Concr. Abstr.

LC TA680 .S44
ISSN 0916-3182
JA
CODEN SKROER
SEMENTO KONKURITO RONBUNSHU. Added/Corp Semento Kyokai (Japan). **VFOAT** Proceedings of Cement & Concrete; Proceedings of Cement and Concrete; CAJ Proceedings of Cement & Concrete. **VAT** Cement Association of Japan Proceedings of Cement & Concrete. (19??)-. Japanese (summaries and/or abstracts in English). Semento Kyokai, c/o Hattori Building, 4-Kai 10-Ban 3-Go, Kyobashi 1-Chome Chuo-to, Tokyo-to 104 Japan. Documents available from CASDDS.
Ind/Abst Chem. Abstr.

LC TH900 .S44
DD 621.8/0216
ISSN 8756-2987
US
SERIAL NUMBER GUIDE. (SERIAL NUMBER GUIDE, USED CONSTRUCTION EQUIPMENT.). [Ser. number guide]. **Added/Corp** AED Research & Services Corp. **VFOAT** Construction Equipment Serial Number Guide. 16th Ed. (1983/84)-. Trade Publication. English. One time a year. $25.00. K-III Press Inc., 424 West 33rd Street, New York NY 10001. **Tel** (212)714-3100, (800)221-5488. **Ad Acc.** *Continues* Used Construction Equipment Serial Number Guide.
Desc: Complete library of value, specifications rental rates. Data on all types of construction equipment also software for estimating system and cost data on construction equipment.

DD 331.7/69/009714
ISSN 0710-5630
CN
SERVICES AUX MEMBRES - ASSOCIATION DE LA CONSTRUCTION DE MONTREAL ET DU QUEBEC. See Business and Economics-Labor.

ISSN 0314-5956
AT
SHEET - CSIRO, DIVISION OF BUILDING RESEARCH. Main/Corp Commonwealth Scientific and Industrial Research Organization (Australia). Division of Building Research. (19??)-. Monographic series. English. Irregular. Price varies per volume. CSIRO Publications, PO Box 89, 314 Albert Street, East Melborne Victoria 3002 Australia. **Tel** 011 61 3 4187333, 4187217, FAX 011 61 3 4190459, telex AA 30236.

ISSN 0164-6559
US
SHELTER (GERMANTOWN). (SHELTER.). (19??)-. Periodical. English. Six times a year. $18.00. Target Magazine Group, 167 East Highway 72, Collierville TN 38017. **Tel** (901)853-7470, (901)853-7720, (901)853-0545, FAX (901)853-6437.

LC TH4 .S45
DD 690/.05
CC
SHIH KUNG CHI SHU. VFOAT Shigong Jishu. Periodical. Chinese. Six times a year. RMBY0.25. Pei-Ching Pao Kan Fa Hsing Chu, Beijing, People's Republic of China. **Tel** 011 86 1 483531.

UK
SHOP EQUIPMENT & SHOPFITTING NEWS. (19??)-. Periodical. English. Twelve times a year. £21.00 UK; £25.00 Europe; £42.00 other. EMAP Readerlink, Audit House, 260 Field End Road, Ruislip Middlesex HA4 9LT United Kingdom. **Tel** 011 44 1773 63100, FAX 011 44 1733 87367. **(Subscription address:** EMAP Business Publishing, 4 Admiral House Cardinal Way, Middlesex HA5 5SQ United Kingdom. **Tel** 011 44 181 8684499.)

DD 381/.456901823/09713
ISSN 0848-7677
CN
TITLE CHANGE
SIDING & WINDOW CONTRACTOR. [Siding window contract.]. **VFOAT** Siding and Window Contractor. (Spring 1990)-(19??)?. Periodical. English. National Home Improvements Inc., Suite 200, 809 Dundas Street East, London Ontario N5W 5P6 Canada. *Continued by* Siding, Windows and Remodelling, 1196-0841.

LC HD9715.S5 S54
DD 338.5/0255957
SI
SINGAPORE BUILDERS DIRECTORY. Directory. English. One time a year. Far East Media Representatives, 57B 2D Floor/President Building, 320 Serangoon Road, Singapore 8 Singapore. *Continues* Singapore Builder Directory.

DD 624
ISSN 0826-5356
CN
SITE. [Site]. Vol. 1, No. 1 (Jan. 1984)-. Periodical. English. Four times a year. Free. Foundation Group of Companies, 1 Yonge Street, Toronto Ontario M5E 1E8 Canada. ctrl circ.

Building and Construction

ISSN 0275-1488
US
CCC
CEASED

SITE REPORT, THE. See Industry and Production-Manufacturing.

ISSN 1156-2897
FR

UDC 69
SMFA ACTUALITES PARIS. (SMFA ACTUALITES.). **VFOAT** SMFA Structures Menuiseries Fermetures et Protections Solaires Actualites. (1988)-. Periodical. French. Six times a year. $99.00. Masson SA, Avenue Beauregard 12, CH-1701 Fribourg Switzerland. **Tel** 011 41 37 249585, FAX 011 41 37 247559, telex 942658 SEMI CH. **Continues** Structures Menuiseries Fermetures Actualites, 0761-9634.

ISSN 8756-3436
DD 721
SMITH'S TABLES. [Smith's tables]. **VFOAT** UBC Smith's Tables. **VAT** Uniform Building Code Smith's Tables. (19??)-. English. Every 3 years. Technical Publications, 19471 Madrone Court, Los Gatos CA 95030.

ISSN 0898-5065
DD 693
US
SOLAR EARTHBUILDER INTERNATIONAL'S EARTH & SUN. [Solar earthbuild. int. earth sun]. **VFOAT** Earth and Sun; Earth & Sun; Solar Earthbuilder International's Earth and Sun. Issue 49 (1987)-. Periodical. English. Solar Earthbuilder International, PO Box 16119, Las Cruces NM 88004-6119. **Continues** Solar Earthbuilder International, 0893-3324. **Continued in part by** Adobe News (1988), 0896-8403.

LC TH1601
DD 693.8/32/05
ISSN 0828-6574
CN
CODEN SREVEW
SOLPLAN REVIEW. [Solplan rev.]. **Added/Corp** Drawing-Room Graphic Services. (Feb. 1985)-. Periodical. English. Six times a year (Feb., Apr., June, Aug., Oct., Dec.). 30.42Can$. Drawing Room Graphic Services, PO Box 86627, North Vancouver BC V7L 4L2 Canada. **Tel** (604)689-1841, FAX (604)689-1401. **ED** Richard Kadulsky, (phone: (604)689-1841). cum. index. **Bk Rev. Ad Acc. Circ:** 5,000.

ISSN 0129-6175
SI
CEASED
SOUTHEAST ASIA BUILDING.
(19??)-(19??). Periodical. English. Safan APFi Publications Pte Ltd., 71 Robinson Road, #04-01 Singapore 0106 Singapore. **Tel** 011 65 2223422, FAX 011 65 2225587, telex RS 28366 SAFAN.
Ind/Abst Archit. Period. Index (July 1987-); Avery Index Archit. Period. Suppl. Colum. Univ. (Oct. 1989-); J. Ferrocement.

ISSN 0038-3864
US
SOUTHERN BUILDING. **Added/Corp** Southern Building Code Congress International. (19??)-. Periodical. English. Twelve times a year (magazine publishes even months and newsbrief publishes odd months). $12.00. Southern Building Code Congress International, 900 Montclair Road, Birmingham AL 35213. **Tel** (205)591-1853. **ED** Karla Price. **Ad Acc. Circ:** 8,000. **Desc:** Subjects relating to building codes and their enforcement activities.

US
SOUTHERN BUILDING CODE CONGRESS INTERNATIONAL COMPLIANCE REPORT. (19??)-. English. Irregular. $60.00 (members); $100.00 (nonmembers). Southern Building Code Congress International, 900 Montclair Road, Birmingham AL 35213. **Tel** (205)591-1853.

ISSN 1064-6914
DD 624
US
SOUTHWEST CONTRACTOR (PHOENIX, ARIZ.). (SOUTHWEST CONTRACTOR.). [Southwest contract.]. Vol. 46, No. 2 (Feb. 1984)-. Periodical. English. Twelve times a year. $19.95. Southwest Contractor, 2050 East University, Suite 1, Phoenix AZ 85034. **Tel** (602)258-1641, FAX (602)495-9407. **ED** Elaine Beall (editor's address: PO Box 60490, Phoenix AZ 85082). **Ad Acc, Adv Mgr:** Bill Davis, **Tel** same as publisher. **Circ:** 7,200 (ctrl). **Continues** Arizona, New Mexico Contractor-Engineer.
Desc: Highway and heavy construction, municipal works and mining structural engineering in Arizona, New Mexico, West Texas and Nevada.

LC HD9715.C3 S68
DD 338.4/7624/0971021
ISSN 0835-1090
CN
SPECIAL TRADE CONTRACTORS.
(SPECIAL TRADE CONTRACTORS = ENTREPRENEURS EN METIERS SPECIALISES.). [Spec. trade contract.]. **Added/Corp** Statistics Canada. Industry Division. **VFOAT** Entrepreneurs en Metiers Specialises. (1984)-. English (French). One time a year. 27.00Can$ Canada; $32.00 US; $38.00 other. Statistics Canada Publications Sales and Services, R.H. Coats Building 6th floor, Ottawa Ontario K1A 0T6 Canada. **Tel** (613)951-5078, (800)267-6677, FAX (613)951-1584, telex 053-3585. **Continues** Special Trades Contracting Industry, 0705-6125.

IT
SPECIALIZZATA. (19??)-. Trade Publication. Italian. Ten times a year. L90000 Itlay; L110000 other. BE MA Editrice, Via Teocrito 50, 20128 Milan Italy. **Tel** 011 39 2 2552451.

ISSN 0348-0593
SW
SPECIALMEDDELANDE. [Spec.medd. - Sver. lantbruksuniv. Inst. lantbr. byggn.tek.]. **Added/Corp** Sveriges Lantbruksuniversitet. Institutionen for Lantbrukets Byggnadsteknik. **VFOAT** Special Report. (1977)-. Monographic series. Swedish (summaries and/or abstracts in English). **Continues** Specialmeddelande (Lantbrukshogskolan. Institutionen for Lantbrukets Byggnadsteknik), 0346-7686.
Ind/Abst Agric. Eng. Abstr.; Dairy Sci. Abstr.; Index Vet.; Postharvest News Inf.; Potato Abstr.; Vet. Bull.; Wheat Barley Trit. Abstr.

LC TH425 .S65
DD 692.305
UK
SPECIFICATION. (1970)-. English. Irregular. Price varies per volume. The Architectural Press, 9 Queen Anne's Gate, London SW1H 9BY United Kingdom. **Tel** 011 44 171 2224333. **ED** Alastair Blyth. Index available. **Ad Acc. Circ:** 20,000 (ctrl). **Continues** Specification.
Desc: Comprehensive reference to building methods, products and specification clauses.

US
SPECIFIER'S GUIDE TO CONTRACT FLOOR COVERING. (19??)-. English. One time a year (Aug.). $18.50. Hearst Business Communications, 1790 Broadway, New York NY 10019. **Tel** (212)969-7500, FAX (212)969-7564.

UK
SPON'S ARCHITECT'S AND BUILDER'S PRICE BOOK. English. One time a year (includes three updates). £45.00. International Thompson Publishing Services Ltd., North Way, Cheriton House, Andover Hampshire SP10 5BE United Kingdom. **Tel** 011 44 1264 342840, FAX 011 44 1264 342761.

UK
SPON'S INTERNATIONAL CONSTRUCTION COSTS HANDBOOK.
1988-. English. **Separated from** Spon's Architects' and Builders' Price Book, 0306-3046.

LC TH65.4.S53 S5a
XO
SPRAVODAJCA MINISTERSTVA STAVEBNICTVA SLOVENSKEJ SOCIALISTICKEJ REPUBLIKY. **Main/Corp** Slovak Socialist Republic. Ministerstvo Stavebnictva. (19??)-. Slovak. Irregular. Ministerstvo Stavebnictva SSR vo Vydavatelstve Obzor, Ul Cs Armady 29/A, Bratislava Slovakia.

ISSN 1064-5500
DD 658
US
SRDS MEDIA & MARKET PLANNER. ARCHITECTURAL & CONSTRUCTION MARKETS. [SRDS media mark. plan., Archit. constr. mark.]. **Added/Corp** Standard Rate & Data Service. **VFOAT** SRDS Media and Market Planner. Architectural & Construction Markets; Media and Market Planner. Architectural & Construction Markets; Media & Market Planner. Architectural & Construction Markets; Architectural & Construction Markets; Architectural and Construction Markets. **VAT** Standard Rate & Data Service Media & Market Planner. Architectural & Construction Markets. Vol. 1 (1992)-. Trade Publication. English. SRDS / Standard Rate & Data Service, 3004 Glenview Road, Wilmette IL 60091. **Tel** (708)375-5049, (800)851-7737, FAX (708)375-5003.

LC TA684 .S68
ISSN 0038-9145
GW
CCC
CODEN STAHAE
STAHLBAU, DER. [Stahlbau]. Vol. 1 (1928)-. Trade Publication. German. Twelve times a year. $335.00. Wilhelm Ernst & Sohn, Muehlenstr 33 34 170, D-13187 Berlin Germany. **Tel** 011 49 30 47889200. **(Subscription address:** VCH Publishers Inc., 303 Northwest 12th Avenue, Journals Department, Deerfield FL 33442. **Tel** (800)367-8249, (305)428-5566.) cum. index. Documents available from Article Express International.
Ind/Abst Alum. Ind. Abstr.; Bioeng. Abstr.; Coal Abstr.; Ei Page One; EMBASE; Energy Res. Abstr. (Jan. 1971-); Eng. Index Annu.; Geotech. Abstr.; Int. Aerosp. Abstr.; Int. Civil Eng. Abstr.; Met. Abstr.; Soft. Abstr. Eng.; Surf. Treat. Technol. Abstr.

LC JK1651.M5 A32A
DD 353.97740086/2
US
STATE BUILDING AUTHORITY, MICHIGAN. **Main/Corp** Michigan. State Building Authority. **VFOAT** Report of the State Building Authority. English. State Building Authority, Stevens T Mason Building, PO Box 30026, Lansing MI 48909.

LC HD4186 .S73
DD 363/.0945/021
IT
STATISTICHE DELLE OPERE PUBBLICHE. **Added/Corp** Istituto Centrale di Statistica (Italy). Vol. 1 (1986)-. Periodical. Italian. One time a year. Istituto Nazionale Statistica, GBP SEZ4 Via Cesare Balbo 16, 00184 Rome Italy. **Tel** 011 39 6 46735118. **Continues in part** Statistiche dell'Attivita Edilizia e delle Opere Pubbliche.

LC HD9715.F7 F69A
DD 338.4/7624/0944
FR
STATISTIQUES DE LA CONSTRUCTION.
See Building and Construction-Abstracting, Bibliographies and Statistics.

LC HD9715.B4
DD 338.4/7/69009493
ISSN 0772-7712
BE
STATISTIQUES DE LA CONSTRUCTION ET DU LOGEMENT. See Building and Construction-Abstracting, Bibliographies and Statistics.

LC HD9715.I8 S7
IT
STATISTISCHE DELL'ATTIVITA EDILIZIA. No. 1 (1986)-. Italian. One time a year. 2500000L. Istituto Nazionale Statistica, GBP SEZ4 Via Cesare Balbo 16, 00184 Rome Italy. **Tel** 011 39 6 46735118. **Continues in part** Statistiche dell'Attivita Edilizia e delle Opere Pubbliche.

LC HD9715.S85 S73
DD 338.47624
ISSN 0085-6991
SW
STATISTISKA MEDDELANDEN. SERIE BO. (19??)-. Monographic series. Swedish. Price varies per volume. SCB Statistiska Centralbyran, 11581 Stockholm Sweden.

LC HD9715.D4 S72
ISSN 0108-5549
DK
STATISTISKE EFTERRETNINGER. BYGGE- OG ANLGSVIRKSOMHED. See Building and Construction-Abstracting, Bibliographies and Statistics.

LC TH4 .S774
XO
STAVEBNICKA ROCENKA. (19??)-. Slovak. One time a year. 24.00. Alfa / Slovakia, Hurbanovo Nam 3, 815 89 Bratislava Slovakia. **Tel** 7 331-441, FAX 7 594-43.

ISSN 0039-078X
XO
CODEN STVCA2
STAVEBNICKY CASOPIS. [Stavebnicky cas.]. **Added/Corp** Slovenska Akademia Vied. Vol. 1 (1953)-. Periodical. Slovak. Six times a year. DM150.00. Slovenska Akademia Vied / Slovak Academy of Sciences, PO Box 57, 81005 Bratislava Slovakia. **Tel** 011 42 7 3782715, 011 42 7 3782925, FAX 011 42 7 496849, telex 93261. **(Subscription address:** Kubon & Sagner, ABT Zeitschriftenimport, D 80328 Munich Germany. **Tel** 011 49 89 54218130.) Documents available from Article Express International.
Ind/Abst Bioeng. Abstr.; Concr. Abstr.; Ei Page One; Eng. Index Annu.

ISSN 0049-2205
AT
STEEL CONSTRUCTION : JOURNAL OF THE AUSTRALIAN INSTITUTE OF STEEL CONSTRUCTION. **Added/Corp** Australian Institute of Steel Construction. Vol. 1, No. 1 (1967)-. Periodical. English. Four times a year. $49.34. Australian Institute of Steel Construction Ltd, PO Box 6366, North Sydney New South Wales, 2059 Australia. **Tel** 011 62 2 9296666, FAX 011 62 2 9231799. **ED** A. Firkins. **Bk Rev.** ctrl circ.
Desc: A technical journal related to structural steel research, design and construction.
Ind/Abst Ei Page One.

ISSN 0585-2382
US
STEEL RESEARCH FOR CONSTRUCTION; BULLETIN. **Added/Corp** American Iron and Steel Institute, New York. American Iron and Steel Institute, New York. Committee of Structural Steel Producers. American Iron and Steel Institute, New York. Committee of Steel Plate Producers. No. 1 (1965)-. Bulletin. English. Irregular. Free on request. American Iron & Steel Institute, 1101 17th Street Northwest, Suite 1300, Washington DC 20036. **Tel** (202)452-7100, (202)452-7151.

ISSN 0701-0176
DD 721/.0447/105 CN
STELCO TENDANCES. **Main/Corp** Steel Company of Canada. No. 44 (1975)-. Periodical. French. Steel Company of Canada Ltd., 100 Kings Street, PO Box 2030, Hamilton Ontario L8N 3T1 Canada. ***Continues*** *STELCO Trend. [Ed. Francaise]. Steel Company of Canada, 0318-3432;* ***Absorbed*** *STELCO Tendances, Rapport sur la Construction, 0705-7253.*

ISSN 0039-1778
UK
TITLE CHANGE
STONE INDUSTRIES. **See** Mines and Mining-Mineralogy.

ISSN 1045-4519
DD 338 US
CEASED
STONE THROUGH THE AGES / MARBLE INSTITUTE OF AMERICA. [Stone ages]. **Added/Corp** Marble Institute of America. (1989)-(199?). Periodical. English. Marble Institute of America Inc., 33305 State Street, Farmington MI 48335. **Tel** (313)476-5558, FAX (313)476-1630. ***Continues*** *Through the Ages (Farmington, Mich.), 0896-2421.*

ISSN 0039-2375
RU
STROITEL. **Added/Corp** Soviet Union. Gosudarstvennyi Komitet po Delam Stroitelstva Profsoiuz Rabochnikh Stroitelstva i Promyshlennosti Stroitelnykh Materialov. Tsentralnyi Komitet. Vol. 1, (1955)-. Periodical. Russian. Twelve times a year. $54.00. Stroiizdat, Ulitsa Shchousseva rm. 60, 103001 Moscow Russia. **(Subscription address:** Victor Kamkin, 4956 Boiling Brook Parkway, Rockville MD 20852. **Tel** (301)881-5973.**)** Index available. **Bk Rev**.

ISSN 0562-1836
BU
CODEN SMSIAO
STROITELI MATERIALI I SILIKATNA PROMISLENOST. (STROITELNI MATERIALI I SILIKATNA PROMISHLENOST : [ORGAN NA MINISTERSTVOTO NA LEKATA PROMISHLENOST, MINISTERSTVOTO NA STROITELSTVOTO I ARKHITEKTURATA, SUIUZITE PO STROITELSTVO I PO KHIMIIA I KHIMICHESKA PROMISHLENOST PRI TSS NA NTS].). [Stroit. mater. silik. prom.]. **Added/Corp** Bulgaria. Ministerstvo na Lekata Promishlenost. Bulgaria. Ministerstvo na Stroitelstvoto i Arkhitekturata. Bulgaria. Suiuzite po Stratelstvo i po Khimiia i Khimicheska Promishlenost. (1960)-. Periodical. Bulgarian (table of contents in English, German and Russian). Twelve times a year. 4.10lv. **(Subscription address:** Hemus Foreign Trade Organization, 1B Raiko Daskalov Sq Books, 1000 Sofia Bulgaria. **Tel** 011 359 2 882544, 011 359 2 801575.**)** **Circ:** 2,500. Documents available from CASDDS.
Ind/Abst Ceram. Abstr.; Chem. Abstr. (1960-1984).

ISSN 0585-430X
RU
CODEN STRMAC
STROITEL'NYE MATERIALY. [Stroit. mater.]. **Added/Corp** Russia. Ministerstvo Promyshlennosti Stroitel'nykh Materialov. No. 11 (1956)-. Academic Scholarly Publication. Russian. Twelve times a year. $79.95. **(Subscription address:** East View Publications Inc., 3020 Harbor Lane North, Suite 110, Minneapolis MN 55447. **Tel** (800)477-1005, (612)550-0961, FAX (612)559-2931.**)** Documents available from CASDDS. ***Continues*** *Stroitel'nye Materialy, Izdeliia i Konstruktsii.*
Ind/Abst Ceram. Abstr.; Chem. Abstr.; Coal Abstr.

LC TA401 .S719 ISSN 0136-7773
RU
CODEN SMKOD5
STROITEL'NYE MATERIALY I KONSTRUKTSII. **Added/Corp** Ukraine. Derzhavnyi Komitet v Spravakh Budivnytstva. No. 1 (1977)-. Academic Scholarly Publication. Russian. Four times a year. $69.95. Izdatelstvo Ukrarkhstroyinform, Menzhinskogo 71, Kiev-135 Ukraine. **(Subscription address:** East View Publications Inc., 3020 Harbor Lane North, Suite 110, Minneapolis MN 55447. **Tel** (800)477-1005, (612)550-0961, FAX (612)559-2931.**)** Index available. **Ad Acc.** Documents available from CASDDS. ***Continues*** *Budivelni Materialy i Konstruksii.*
Ind/Abst Ceram. Abstr.; Chem. Abstr.

ISSN 0562-1852
BU
UDC 69
STROITELSTVO. [Stroitelstvo]. (1954)-. Periodical. Bulgarian. Twelve times a year. DM142.00. Ministerstvo na Stroezhite i Arkitekturata, Sofia Bulgaria. **(Subscription address:** Kubon & Sagner, ABT Zeitschriftenimport, D 80328 Munich Germany. **Tel** 011 49 89 54218130.**)**
Ind/Abst Ceram. Abstr. (19??-).

ISSN 0039-2421
RU
STROITELSTVO I ARKHITEKTURA MOSKVY. **Added/Corp** Moscow. Arkhitekturno-Planirovochnoe Upravlenie. Moscow. Ispolnitelnyi Komitet. (Nov. 1952)-. Periodical. Russian. Twelve times a year. $99.50 (latest editions). **(Subscription address:** East View Publications Inc., 3020 Harbor Lane North, Suite 110, Minneapolis MN 55447. **Tel** (800)477-1005, (612)550-0961, FAX (612)559-2931.**)**
Ind/Abst Archit. Period. Index (No. 1, Jan. 1987-).

ISSN 0167-4730
NE
CCC
Pr Rev.
STRUCTURAL SAFETY. [Struct. saf.]. Vol. 1, No. 1 (Sept. 1982)-. Academic Scholarly Publication. English. Four times a year (1 vol.). $404.00. Elsevier Science Publishers BV, PO Box 211, 1000 AE Amsterdam Netherlands. **Tel** 011 31 20 4853641, 011 31 20 4853642, FAX 011 31 20 4853598. **ED** E H Vanmarcke. available on microfilm and microfiche from University Microfilms International (UMI); available on an online database from Elsevier Electronic Subscriptions (EES). Documents available from Article Express International, The Genuine Article.
Desc: Devoted to integrated risk assessment for a wide range of constructed facilities such as buildings, bridges, earth structures, offshore structures, dams, lifelines and nuclear structural systems.
Ind/Abst Abstr. J. Earthq. Eng. (?-?); Archit. Period. Index (1982/1983-); Curr. Cit.; Curr. Contents Eng. Comput. Technol.; Ei Page One; Eng. Mater. Abstr.; Eng. Index Annu.; GeoRef; Health Saf. Sci. Abstr.; Pollut. Abstr. Indexes; Res. Alert [Full Cov.]; Risk Abstr.; Sci. Cit. Index; SCISEARCH; Soc. Sci. Cit. Index [Select. Cov.].

US
STRUCTURAL SURVEY. (19??)-. English. Four times a year. $369.00. MCB University Press, 60 62 Toller Lane, Bradford, West Yorkshire BD8 9BY United Kingdom. **Tel** 011 44 1274 785280, FAX 011 44 1274 785200, telex 51317-MCBUNI-G. **(Subscription address:** MCB University Press / US and Canada Subscriptions, PO Box 10812, Birmingham AL 35201-0812. **Tel** (205)995-1567, (800)633-4931, FAX (205)995-1588.**)** Index available. **Bk Rev. Ad Acc. Acid Free.**
Desc: A medium for those responsible for the appraisal and refurbishment of buildings. Topics regularly covered include: the survey and appraisal of commercial, residential and industrial buildings; case studies of refurbishment projects; engineering project surveys; building conservation; materials and components.
Ind/Abst Archit. Period. Index; Curr. Cit.; Int. Civil Eng. Abstr.; Soft. Abstr. Eng.; World Ceram. Abstr.

LC TH4911 .M52A ISSN 0149-1245
DD 690/.8/9 US
Pr Rev.
STRUCTURES AND ENVIRONMENT HANDBOOK. **Main/Corp** Midwest Plan Service. (1969)-. English. One time a year. $25.00 per issue. Midwest Plan Service, Iowa State University, 122 Davidson Hall, Ames IA 50011. **Tel** (515)294-4337. **ED** John H Pedersen. **Bk Rev. Circ:** 1,500.
Desc: A basic reference for planning farmstead buildings and facilities. Useful to students, teachers, and practicing engineers.

LC TH435 .S86 ISSN 0162-3508
DD 692/.5 US
STRUCTURES COST MANUAL; SQUARE FOOT COSTS FOR RESIDENTIAL, COMMERCIAL, INDUSTRIAL, AGRICULTURAL AND MILITARY BUILDINGS. **VFOAT** SCM. 1977-. English. $10.00. Craftsman Book Company, PO Box 6500, 6058 Corte del Cedro, Carlsbad CA 92008. **Tel** (619)438-7828, (800)829-8123, FAX (619)438-0398. **ED** G B Smith.

LC TA683 .S78
DD 624.1/8341/05 IT
STUDI E RICERCHE / POLITECNICO DI MILANO, SCUOLA DI SPECIALIZZAZIONE IN COSTRUZIONI IN CEMENTO ARMATO. No. 12 (1991)-. Italian (English). Giardini Editori Stampatori, Via Santa Bibbiana 28, 56127 Pisa Italy. **Tel** 011 39 50 934242. ***Continues*** *Studi e Ricerche (Politecnico di Milano. Corso di Perfezionamento per le Costruzioni in Cemento Armato F.lli Pesenti).*

ISSN 0195-1459
US
SUBCONTRACTOR, THE. **Added/Corp** American Subcontractors Association. (197?)-. Trade Publication. English. Twelve times a year. $40.00. American Subcontractors Association, 1004 Duke Street, Alexandria VA 22314. **Tel** (703)684-3450. **ED** Marsha Rhea. **Ad Acc. Circ:** 10,000. ***Continues*** *ASA Review.*
Desc: A news publication of the American Subcontractors Association. A newspaper of national construction industry news, and legislative, business and legal information for the subcontracting industry.

LC KF1950.Z95 S95
DD 343.73/078624 347.30378624 US
SUMMARY OF STATE REGULATIONS AND LAWS AFFECTING GENERAL CONTRACTORS. **See** Finance-Taxation.

LC TH1 .S9 ISSN 0744-8872
DD 338.4/769/00979 US
SUN/COAST ARCHITECT/BUILDER. **VFOAT** Sun Coast Architect Builder; Sun/Coast. Vol. 47 (July 1982)-. Periodical. English. Twelve times a year. $22.00. McKellar Publishers, 333 East Glenoaks Boulevard, Suite 204, Glendale CA 91207. **Tel** (818)241-0250, FAX (818)241-4406. **ED** Ceve Allsbrook. **Bk Rev. Ad Acc. Circ:** 56,000 (ctrl). ***Formed by the union of*** *Pacific Coast Builder, 0192-1703* ***and*** *Western Building Design, 0192-1568.*
Desc: Publication for builders, architects, interior architects, specification writers, engineers, contractors, developers, remodelers and others allied to the field.

ISSN 0826-6131
DD 343.71/07869 CN
SUPPLEMENT TO THE NATIONAL BUILDING CODE OF CANADA, THE. [Suppl. Natl. build. code Can.]. **Added/Corp** National Research Council Canada. Associate Committee on the National Building Code. **VFOAT** Climatic Information for Building Design in Canada; Fire-Performance Ratings; Measures for Fire Safety in High Buildings; Commentaries on Part 4 of the National Building Code of Canada; List of Standards Referenced in the National Building Code. 1st Ed. (1980)-. Periodical. English. 45.00Can$. National Research Council of Canada, Receiver General for Canada, Ottawa Ontario K1A 0R6 Canada. **Tel** (613)993-0362, FAX (613)952-7656. ***Formed by the union of*** *Climatic Information for Building Design in Canada, 0825-8325* ***and*** *Fire Performance Ratings Commentaries on Part 4 of the National Building Code of Canada, 0825-8317.*

LC HD9715.H6 S9
DD 338.4/7624/095125 HK
SURVEY OF BUILDING, CONSTRUCTION, AND REAL ESTATE SECTORS. **Added/Corp** Hong Kong. Census and Statistics Dept. Hong Kong. Census and Statistics Dept. Building, Construction, and Real Estate Statistics Section. **VFOAT** Report of the ... Survey of Building, Construction, and Real Estate Sectors. (19??)-. English. One time a year. $30.00. Hong Kong Government Information Service, Beaconsfield House, 4 Queens Road, Hong Kong Hong Kong. **Tel** 011 852 284288014, 011 852 259881947, FAX 011 852 28459078, 011 852 25987482, telex 61190 HKGIS.

LC TH213.7.S8 S94 ISSN 0349-8387
SW
•**SWEDISH BUILDING RESEARCH.** **Added/Corp** Statens Rad for Byggnadsforskning (Sweden). (March 1994)-. Periodical. English. Svensk Byggtjanst, Box 7853, 103 99 Stockholm Sweden. ***Formed by the union of*** *Synopses from the Swedish Building Research, 0347-9935* ***and*** *Newsletter of Swedish Building Research, 1102-3554.*

LC TH ISSN 1190-9072
DD 691.029471 CN
SWEET'S CANADIAN CONSTRUCTION CATALOGUE (1989). (SWEET'S CANADIAN CONSTRUCTION CATALOGUE FILE.). [Sweet's Can. constr. cat. file 1989]. (1989)-. Multiple languages. One time a year. Sweet's Catalogue Services, McGraw Hill Information Systems Company of Canada Ltd, 330 Progress Avenue, Scarborough Ontario M1P 2Z5 Canada. **Tel** (416)293-1931. ***Continues*** *Canadian Construction Catalogue File, 0082-0431.*

LC TH455 .S787
DD 691/.029/473 US
SWEET'S CATALOG FILE. CONTRACT INTERIORS. **Added/Corp** McGraw-Hill, inc. Sweet's Group. **VFOAT** Contract Interiors; Sweet's Contract Interiors Catalog File; Products for Contract Interiors. (1991)-. Catalog. English. McGraw Hill Publishing Company, Inc., 1221 Avenue of the Americas, New York NY 10020. **Tel** (212)512-6410, (800)525-5003, FAX (212)512-6111. ***Continues*** *Sweet's Catalog File. Products for Contract Interiors, 0743-9121.*

ISSN 1070-8324
DD 690 US
SWEET'S CATALOG FILE. HOMEBUILDING & REMODELING. **Added/Corp** McGraw-Hill, Inc. Sweet's Group. **VFOAT** Sweet's Homebuilding & Remodeling Catalog File; Sweet's Homebuilding and Remodeling Catalog File; Homebuilding & Remodeling; Homebuilding and Remodeling. (1991)-. Catalog. English. McGraw Hill Publishing Company, Inc., 1221 Avenue of the Americas, New York NY 10020. **Tel** (212)512-6410, (800)525-5003, FAX (212)512-6111. ***Continues*** *Sweets Catalog File.*

Building and Construction

Products for Home Building and Remodeling, 0743-5789.
Desc: Covers the materials and fittings involved in building.

LC TA215 .S78   **ISSN 0145-4889**
DD 690/.5/4   US
SWEET'S CATALOG FILE : PRODUCTS FOR INDUSTRIAL CONSTRUCTION AND RENOVATION, RENOVATION EXTENSION. **VFOAT** Products for Industrial Construction and Renovation, Renovation Extension. Catalog. English. One time a year. McGraw Hill Information Systems Company, 1221 Avenue of the Americas, New York NY 10020. **Tel** (212)512-2000, (800)525-5003, FAX (212)512-6111.

LC TH455 .S873
DD 338.4/7/690028   US
SWEET'S ENGINEERING CATALOG FILE. 1st- 1976-. Catalog. English. McGraw Hill Publishing Company, Inc., 1221 Avenue of the Americas, New York NY 10020. **Tel** (212)512-6410, (800)525-5003, FAX (212)512-6111.

LC TH455 .S7864   **ISSN 1082-2380**
DD 690/.029/473   US
● **SWEET'S GENERAL BUILDING & RENOVATION.** [Sweet's gen. build. renov.]. **Added/Corp** McGraw-Hill, Inc. Sweet's Group. **VFOAT** Sweet's General Building & Renovation; General Building and Renovation; Sweet's general Building & Renovation ... Catalog File. (1993)-. Catalog. English. McGraw Hill Publishing Company, Inc., 1221 Avenue of the Americas, New York NY 10020. **Tel** (212)512-6410, (800)525-5003, FAX (212)512-6111. **Continues** *Sweet's Catalog File. General Building & Renovation, 1082-2372.*

LC TH12.5 .S94   **ISSN 0146-8456**
DD 338.4/7/62402573   US
SWEET'S GENERAL BUILDING MARKET. 1977-. English. McGraw Hill Publishing Company, Inc., 1221 Avenue of the Americas, New York NY 10020. **Tel** (212)512-6410, (800)525-5003, FAX (212)512-6111.

LC TH12 .S93   **ISSN 0094-825X**
DD 338.4/7/69002573   US
SWEET'S INDUSTRIAL CONSTRUCTION & RENOVATION FILE WITH PLANT ENGINEERING EXTENSION MARKET LIST. **VAT** Sweet's Industrial Construction and Renovation File with Plant Engineering Extension Market List. (1974)-. English. McGraw Hill Publishing Company, Inc., 1221 Avenue of the Americas, New York NY 10020. **Tel** (212)512-6410, (800)525-5003, FAX (212)512-6111.

LC TH12.5 .S942   **ISSN 0146-8324**
DD 338.4/7/6702573   US
SWEET'S INDUSTRIAL CONSTRUCTION AND RENOVATION MARKET/RENOVATION EXTENSION. (1977)-. English. McGraw Hill Publishing Company, Inc., 1221 Avenue of the Americas, New York NY 10020. **Tel** (212)512-6410, (800)525-5003, FAX (212)512-6111.

LC TH12.5 .S943   **ISSN 0146-8308**
DD 338.4/7/690802573   US
SWEET'S LIGHT RESIDENTIAL CONSTRUCTION MARKET. 1977-. English. McGraw Hill Information Systems Company, 1221 Avenue of the Americas, New York NY 10020. **Tel** (212)512-2000, (800)525-5003, FAX (212)512-6111.

LC HD9715.U5 S95   **ISSN 0364-3654**
DD 381/.45/69   US
SWEET'S SHOWROOM MARKET LIST. English. One time a year. McGraw Hill Information Systems Company, 1221 Avenue of the Americas, New York NY 10020. **Tel** (212)512-2000, (800)525-5003, FAX (212)512-6111.

LC TH4763 .S82   **ISSN 0197-7997**
DD 688.7   US
SWIMMING POOL WEEKLY AND SWIMMING POOL AGE REPLACEMENT PARTS GUIDE. **VFOAT** Replacement Parts Guide. Vol. 1 (1980)-. English. One time a year. Hoffman Publications Inc, 3000 NE 30th Place, Ft Lauderdale FL 33306.

  ISSN 0989-2583
  FR
UDC 69
SYCODES PARIS. (SYCODES.). **Added/Corp** Agence pour la Prevention des Desordres et l'Amelioration de la Qualite de la Construction (Paris). **VFOAT** SYCODES Informations; Systeme de Collecte d'Informations sur les Desordres de la Construction. (1987)-. Periodical. French. Six times a year. $83.11. Agence Qualite Construction, 9 Bd Malesherbes, 75008 Paris Cedex 08 France. **Tel** 011 33 1 44510351. **(Subscription address:** Qualite Construction, 36 rue de Picpus, 75012 Paris France. **)**

LC TH213.7.S8 S96   **ISSN 0347-9935**
  SW
  TITLE CHANGE
SYNOPSES FROM THE SWEDISH BUILDING RESEARCH. **Added/Corp** Statens Rad for Byggnadsforskning (Sweden). **VFOAT** Synopses from Swedish Building Research; Synopses of Swedish Building Research. (1976)-(1993). Periodical. English. Svensk Byggtjanst, Box 7853, 103 99 Stockholm Sweden. Documents available from Documents on Demand. **Continues in part** *Synopses and Summaries from National Swedish Building Research.* **Merged with** *Newsletter of Swedish Building Research, 1102-3554* **to form** *Swedish Building Research, 0349-8387.*
Ind/Abst Environ. Abstr.

  AT
TASMANIAN BUILDING JOURNAL. (19??)-. English. Twelve times a year. 55.00Aus$. Master Builders Association of Tasmania, GP Box 992K, 59 Sandy Bay Road, Hobart Tasmania 7001 Australia. **Tel** 011 61 2 232377, FAX 011 61 2 234194. **ED** Wesley Phillips. **Ad Acc. Circ:** 800 (ctrl).
Desc: Provides practical legal and contractual information on building, design and new products.

  ISSN 0820-0653
DD 336.2/7869/00971   CN
TAX & TARIFF BULLETIN. See Finance-Taxation.

  ISSN 0262-6632
  UK
TECHNICAL INFORMATION SERVICE - CHARTERED INSTITUTE BUILDING. (1982)-. English. Chartered Institute of Building, Englemere Kings Ride, Ascot Berkshire SL5 8BJ United Kingdom. **Tel** 011 44 1344 23355, FAX 011 44 1344 23467. **Formed by the union of** *Estimating Information Service, 0308-8073; Site Management Information Service, 0308-8081; Maintenance Information Service, 0140-649X* **and** *Surveying Information Service, 0143-649X.*

  ISSN 0110-4403
  NZ
  CODEN BTPPDV
TECHNICAL PAPER P - BUILDING RESEARCH ASSOCIATION OF NEW ZEALAND. (BRANZ TECHNICAL PAPER P.). [Tech. pap. P - Build. Res. Assoc. N.Z.]. **VFOAT** Technical Paper P; B.R.A.N.Z. Technical Paper P; Technical Paper. (1974)-. Academic Scholarly Publication. English. Irregular. Price varies per volume. Building Research Association of New Zealand (BRANZ), 42 Vivian Street, Wellington 1 New Zealand. Documents available from CASDDS.
Ind/Abst Chem. Abstr. (1974-1979); Ei Page One.

  AT
TECHNICAL RECORD (NATIONAL BUILDING TECHNOLOGY CENTRE (AUSTRALIA)). (TECHNICAL RECORD / NATIONAL BUILDING TECHNOLOGY CENTRE, DEPT. OF HOUSING AND CONSTRUCTION.). **Added/Corp** National Building Technology Centre (Australia). **VFOAT** NBTC Technical Record. 511 (June 1985)-. Monographic series. English. Irregular. Price varies per volume. **Continues** *Technical Record (Experimental Building Station (Australia)).*

  ISSN 0730-6504
  US
TECHNIQUES AND COMMENTS. [Tech. comments]. (1980)-. Periodical. English. Twenty-four times a year. $100.00 US; $125.00 Canada; $150.00 other. Techniques & Comments, 4960 Hamilton Avenue, Suite 100, San Jose CA 95130. **Tel** (408)866-8488.

  ISSN 0245-9590
  FR
UDC 69
TECHNIQUES DE L'INGENIEUR. CONSTRUCTION. [Tech. ing., Constr.]. (1949)-. Trade Publication. French. Four times a year. Techniques de l'Ingenieur, 21 rue Cassette, 75006 Paris France. **Tel** 011 33 1 42223550. **(Subscription address:** Techniques de l'Ingenieur, 21 rue Cassette, 75006 Paris France. **Tel** 011 33 1 44390679, 011 33 1 44390670.**)**

LC GV1002 .T46
DD 624   US
TENNIS COURTS : CONSTRUCTION, MAINTENANCE, EQUIPMENT, GUIDELINE SPECIFICATIONS / COMPILED AND WRITTEN BY THE USTA FACILITIES COMMITTEE WITH THE COOPERATION OF THE U.S. TENNIS COURT AND TRACK BUILDERS ASSOCIATION. See Sports and Games.

LC TH13.T4 T49   **ISSN 0731-4035**
DD 338.4/769/0025764   US
TEXAS BUILDERS AND CONTRACTORS DIRECTORY. [Tex. build. contract. dir.]. (19??)-. English. One time a year. $75.00. Gulfstream Publishing Company, 8751 West Broward Blvd., Fort Lauderdale FL 33324. **Tel** (305)475-3999, (800)628-6228.

  ISSN 0192-9216
  US
TEXAS CONTRACTOR. (19??)-. Trade Publication. English. One time a week. $80.00. Peters Publishing Company, PO Box 551359, Dallas TX 75355. **Tel** (214)271-2693. **ED** Barbara Clay. **Circ:** 500.
Desc: Comprehensive daily coverage of Texas construction through categories of pre-bid, bids wanted, low bidder and contract award.

LC HD9715.T48 T46
DD 380.1/45/624025593   TH
THAI BUILDER DIRECTORY. **VFOAT** Khum Sathapanik Witsawakon L Naichang. (19??)-. Directory. English (Thai). One time a year. $15.00 Thailand; $18.00 other. Gemini International Services, 116/340 Mooban Pricha Soi 1, Bangkok 10110 Thailand. **Tel** 2519016. **Ad Acc.** ctrl circ.

  ISSN 1030-7036
DD 624.0994   AT
THOMSON'S CONSTRUCTION AUSTRALIA. [Thomson's constr. Aust.]. **VFOAT** Construction Australia. (1986)-. Periodical. English. Twelve times a year. 77.00Aus$ Australia; 95.00Aus$ New Zealand, Papua New Guinea; 100.00Aus$ Malaysia, Indonesia, Fiji; 101.00Aus$ Japan, India, Hong Kong; 110.00Aus$ US, Canada, Lebanon; 118.00Can$ Europe, Africa, former USSR. Thomson Publications / Australia, 47 Chippen Street, Chippendale New South Wales 2008 Australia. **Tel** 011 61 2 6992411, FAX 011 61 2 6991184, telex 122226. **(Subscription address:** Thomson Publications Australia, PO Box 815, Strawberry Hills, New South Wales, 2012 Australia. **Tel** 011 61 2 6992411.**)** **Continues** *Construction Equipment News, 0007-8247.*

LC TH4 .B897   **ISSN 0349-3733**
  SW
TIDNINGEN BYGGINDUSTRIN. (TIDNINGEN BYGG INDUSTRI.). [Tidn. byggind.]. **VFOAT** Byggindustrin. (1980)-. Trade Publication. Swedish. One time a week (38 issues). Kr690.00. Byggfoerlaget, PO Box 5456, S-114 81 Stockholm Sweden. **Tel** 011 46 8 6635100, FAX 011 46 8 6677075, telex 14579 BYGGF S. **Continues** *Byggnadsindustrin.*
Ind/Abst Saf. Health Work.

  ISSN 0938-9806
  GW
UDC 62
TILE & BRICK INTERNATIONAL. [Tile brick int.]. **VFOAT** Tile and Brick International; TBI. Tile & Brick International. (1990)-. Trade Publication. Multiple languages. Six times a year. $237.98. Verlag Schmid Journals GmbH, Postfach 6609, Hofackerstr 92, D-79042 Freiburg 1 Germany. **Tel** 011 49 761 82057, FAX 011 49 761 84863, telex 761 403 CARNEWS D. **Continues** *Interbrick, 0178-2223.*
Ind/Abst Ceram. Abstr. (199?-).

  ISSN 1054-1136
DD 694   US
TIMBER FRAME HOMES. (TIMBER FRAME HOMES : BUYER'S GUIDE.). [Timber frame homes]. **VFOAT** Timber Frame Homes Buyer's Guide. Vol. 1, No. 1 (1991)-. Periodical. English. $4.95. Home Buyer Publications Inc, PO Box 220039, Chantilly VA 22022. **Tel** (703)478-0435, (800)826-3893.

LC TH9585.T64 T63A
  JA
TOKYO SHOBOCHO JIMU NENKAN. **Main/Corp** Tokyo (Japan). Shobocho. Japanese. 3-5 Otemachi 1, Chiyoda-ku, Tokyo 100 Japan.

LC TH27.O52 T39   **ISSN 0712-5895**
DD 338.4/769/0060713541   CN
TORONTO CONSTRUCTION NEWS. [Tor. constr. news]. **VFOAT** TC News; TCN. Vol. 4, No. 2 (July/Aug. 1982)-. Trade Publication. English. Six times a year (Jan., Mar., May, July, Sept., Nov.). 33.37Can$. Daily Communications News, 580 Yorkland Boulevard, North York Ontario M2J 4Z6 Canada. **Tel** (905)494-4990. **ED** Janice Kray. **Ad Acc. Circ:** 3,600 (ctrl). **Continues** *TCA News.*
Desc: News and information of the construction industry and association.

  ISSN 0827-407X
DD 338.4/769/009713541   CN
TORONTO CONSTRUCTION TRENDS. (TORONTO CONSTRUCTION TRENDS : A QUARTERLY BULLETIN / PREPARED BY THE RESEARCH AND INFORMATION SECTION, CITY OF TORONTO, PLANNING AND DEVELOPMENT DEPARTMENT.). [Tor. constr. trends]. **Added/Corp** Toronto (Ont.). Planning and Development Dept. Research and Information Section. (Feb. 1984)-. Bulletin.

English. Four times a year. City of Toronto, Clerk's Office, City Hall, Toronto Ontario M5H 2N2 Canada. **Tel** (416)392-7185.

ISSN 0724-6234
GW

TRIALOG. [Trialog]. **Added/Corp** Vereinigung zur Wissenschaftlichen Erforschung des Planens und Bauens in Entwicklungslandern (Germany). (1983)-. Trade Publication. German (summaries and/or abstracts in English). Four times a year.
Ind/Abst Geogr. Abstr. Human Geogr.; Int. Dev. Abstr.

LC TH4 .N33a **ISSN** 0206-1074
RU
CODEN TNISDP

TRUDY INSTITUTA - NAUCHNO-ISSLEDOVATELSKII INSTITUT PROMYSHLENNOGO STROITELSTVA. [Tr. inst. - Naucno-issled. inst. prom. stroit.]. **Main/Corp** Nauchno-Issledovatelskii Institut Promyshlennogo Stroitelstva. (1974)-. Academic Scholarly Publication. Russian. Nauchno-Issledovatelskii Institut Promyshlennogo Stroitelstva, 103066 Kaliaevskaia D 23-A, Moscow Russia. Documents available from CASDDS. ***Continues*** *Nauchno-Issledovatelskii Institut Promyshlennogo Stroitelstva. TSbornik Trudov - Nauchno-Issledovatelskii Institut Promyshlennogo Stroitelstva.*
Ind/Abst Chem. Abstr.

ISSN 1075-3664
DD 333 US

●**TRW REDI REALTY REPORT.** See Real Estate.

LC TA680 .T7 **ISSN** 0041-4867
RU
CCC
CODEN TSMTAC

TSEMENT. **Added/Corp** Soviet Union. Narodnyi Komissariat Promyshlennosti Stroitelnykh Materialov. Soviet Union. Ministerstvo Promyshlennosti Stroitelnykh Materialov. Soviet Union. Gosudarstvennyi Komitet po Delam Stroitelstva Soviet Union. Gosudarstvennyi Komitet po Promyshlennosti Stroitelnykh Materialov. (1933)-. Academic Scholarly Publication. Russian (table of contents in English and German). Twelve times a year. $106.00. **(Subscription address:** Victor Kamkin, 4956 Boiling Brook Parkway, Rockville MD 20852. **Tel** (301)881-5973.) Documents available from CASDDS. ***Continues*** *Stroitelnye Materialy.*
Ind/Abst Ceram. Abstr.; Chem. Abstr.; Concr. Abstr.

ISSN 0041-3909
UK
CODEN TUSTAM

TUBULAR STRUCTURES. [Tubul. struct.]. Periodical. English. Two times a year. BSC Tubes Division, Publicity and Promotions, Weldon Road, Corby Northhamptonshire United Kingdom. **Tel** 011 44 1536 202121. **Circ:** 4,000 (ctrl). Documents available from Article Express International.
Desc: To promote the use of structural hollow sections in building and construction.
Ind/Abst Archit. Period. Index (1970-); Ei Page One; Eng. Index Annu.

ISSN 0394-9605
IT

U&C UNIFICAZIONE & CERTIFICAZIONE. (19??)-. Italian. Ten times a year. L62680. Editoriale PEG Spa, Via Fratelli Bressan 2, 20126 Milan Italy. **Tel** 011 39 2 2579841, FAX 011 39 2 255-2779, telex 323088 PEGMOS I. **ED** Walter Esposti. Index available. **Bk Rev. Ad Acc. Circ:** 7,000 (ctrl).
Desc: Deals with normative matters, certification and standardization of industrial products also in consideration of the European unification.

ISSN 0394-8293
IT
UDC 69

UFFICIO TECNICO, L'. (1979)-. Periodical. Italian. Twelve times a year. L152600. Maggioli Editore, Casella Postale 290, 47037 Rimini Italy. **Tel** 011 39 541 628666, FAX 011 39 541 742217.

LC KF5701.A39 I5 **ISSN** 0896-9655
DD 343.73/07869 347.3037869 US

UNIFORM BUILDING CODE. [Unif. build. code]. **Main/Corp** International Conference of Building Officials. **VFOAT** UBC. (1958)-. Periodical. English. Every 3 years. ICBO Evaluation Service Inc., 5360 South Workman Mill Road, Whittier CA 90601. **Tel** (213)699-0541, FAX (213)692-3853. ***Continues*** *Pacific Coast Building Officials Conference. Uniform Building Code, 0896-9655;* ***Absorbed*** *International Conference of Building Officials. Uniform Building Code Standards, 0896-9663.* ***Continued in part by*** *International Conference of Building Officials. Uniform Building Code Standards, 0896-9663* ***and*** *International Conference of Building Officials. Uniform Sign Code, 0896-9701.*

US

UNIFORM BUILDING CODE. **Main/Corp** International Conference of Building Officials. **Added/Corp** International Conference of Building Officials. (1927)-. English. Every 3 years (every 3 years). Price varies. ICBO Evaluation Service Inc., 5360 South Workman Mill Road, Whittier CA 90601. **Tel** (213)699-0541, FAX (213)692-3853. **(Subscription address:** Inter Conference Building Officials, 6738 Northwest Tower Drive, Kansas City MO 64151. **Tel** (816)741-2241.) **ED** Beverly Eicholtz. **Bk Rev. Ad Acc. Circ:** 200,000.
Desc: Provides complete regulations covering all major aspects of building design and construction relating to life and fire safety and structural safety.

LC KF5701.Z95 I584 **ISSN** 0501-1213
DD 343.73/07869 347.3037869 US

UNIFORM HOUSING CODE. [Unif. hous. code]. **Main/Corp** International Conference of Building Officials. (19??)-. English. Every 3 years (published every 3 year). $9.00 members, $11.95 nonmembers. ICBO Evaluation Service Inc., 5360 South Workman Mill Road, Whittier CA 90601. **Tel** (213)699-0541, FAX (213)692-3853.
Desc: Provides complete requirements affecting conservation and rehabilitation of housing. Its regulations are compatible with the uniform building code.

LC KF5708.Z95 I57 **ISSN** 0896-9671
DD 343.73/078697 347.30378697 US

UNIFORM MECHANICAL CODE. [Unif. mech. code]. **Main/Corp** International Conference of Building Officials. **Added/Corp** International Association of Plumbing and Mechanical Officials. **VFOAT** UMC. (1967)-. English. Irregular (Published every three years). $44.65. ICBO Evaluation Service Inc., 5360 South Workman Mill Road, Whittier CA 90601. **Tel** (213)699-0541, FAX (213)692-3853.
Desc: Contains requirements for the installation and maintenance of heating, insulating, cooling and refrigeration systems.

LC KF5710.Z95 I58 **ISSN** 0896-9701
DD 343.73/08 347.3038 US

UNIFORM SIGN CODE. [Unif. sign code]. **Main/Corp** International Conference of Building Officials. (19??)-. English. Every 3 years. $5.90 members, $7.65 nonmembers. ICBO Evaluation Service Inc., 5360 South Workman Mill Road, Whittier CA 90601. **Tel** (213)699-0541, FAX (213)692-3853. **Circ:** 5,000. ***Continues in part*** *International Conference of Building Officials. Uniform Building Code, 0896-9655.*
Desc: Provides regulations affecting signs and sign construction outside of building and is compatible with the uniform building code.

ISSN 1060-4014
DD 346 US

UNIFORM ZONING CODE. [Unif. zoning code]. **Added/Corp** International Conference of Building Officials. (1991)-. English. Every 3 years. ICBO Evaluation Service Inc., 5360 South Workman Mill Road, Whittier CA 90601. **Tel** (213)699-0541, FAX (213)692-3853.

LC TH89 .S83A
DD 690.09485 SW

VERKSAMHETEN. **Main/Corp** Stockholm. Statens Institut for Byggnadsforskning (Sweden). (19??)-. Swedish. One time a year. Statens Institut for Byggnadsforskning, Box 27 163 102 52 27, Stockholm Sweden.

LC TH8120 .C63 **ISSN** 0043-0161
DD 338.4/7/693605 US
CCC

WALLS & CEILINGS. [Walls ceil.]. **Added/Corp** Contracting Plasterers' and Lathers' International Association. Northwest Plaster Bureau. **VAT** Walls and Ceilings. (19??)-. Trade Publication. English. Twelve times a year. $42.00. Lee Rector, 8175 South Virginia Street, Suite 850 A, Reno NV 89511. **Tel** (702)828-1111, FAX (702)828-1503. **ED** Greg Campbell. **Bk Rev. Ad Acc, Adv Mgr:** Paula Graham, **Tel** (800)533-5653. **Circ:** 22,500 (ctrl). ***Continues*** *Plastering Industries.*
Desc: Publication for contractors engaged in drywall, lath, plaster, ceiling systems, partitions, steel fireproofing, acoustics and insulation.

ISSN 0043-3624
DD 338.4/769/009712 CN

WCI : WESTERN CONSTRUCTION AND INDUSTRY MAGAZINE. [WCI, West. constr. ind. mag.]. **VFOAT** Western Construction and Industry Magazine; Western Commerce and Industry Magazine. Vol. 27, No. 7 (Dec. 1975)-. Periodical. English. Irregular. Mercury Publications Ltd. / Manitoba, 945 King Edward Street, Winnipeg Manitoba R3H 0P8 Canada. **Tel** (204)775-0387, FAX (204)775-7830. ***Continues*** *Western Construction and Industry, 0820-8867.*

LC WMLC 91/1561 **ISSN** 1059-6712
US

WCOE (CARMICHAEL, CALIF.). (WCOE : WOMEN CONSTRUCTION OWNERS AND EXECUTIVES : AN OFFICIAL PUBLICATION OF WCOE CALIFORNIA CHAPTER.). **Added/Corp** Women Construction Owners & Executives, U.S.A. California State Chapter. **VFOAT** Women Construction Owners and Executives. Vol. 2, No. 9 (July 1991)-. English. Twelve times a year. ***Continues*** *WCOE Newsletter, 1056-9235.*

ISSN 0934-7321
GW
UDC 620.22
TITLE CHANGE

WERKSTOFF UND INNOVATION. [Werkst. Innov.]. (1988)-(Jan. 1993). Periodical. German. Umschau Verlag, Postfach 110262, D-60037 Frankfurt Germany. **Tel** 011 49 69 2600692, FAX 011 49 69 2600223, telex 411964. ***Merged into*** *Ingenieur Werkstoffe.*

ISSN 0043-3535
US

WESTERN BUILDER. (19??)-. Trade Publication. English. Seven times a week. $145.00. Western Builder Publishing Company, 6526 River Parkway, Milwaukee WI 53213. **Tel** (414)453-7700.

ISSN 0164-5803
US

WESTERN ROOFING INSULATION AND SIDING. **VFOAT** Western Roofing. Vol. 1, (Feb./Mar. 1978)-. Periodical. English. Six times a year. $12.00. Western Roofing Insulation, 546 Court Street, Reno NV 89501. **Tel** (702)333-1080, FAX (702)333-1081. **ED** Marc Dodson. Index available (Bound in Jan. iss.). **Bk Rev. Ad Acc. Circ:** 20,000 (ctrl). available on microfilm and microfiche.
Desc: For the building professional concerned with the design and specification of roofing insulation and siding. Includes industry-related news from throughout the western United States.

UK

WHAT'S NEW IN BUILDING. English. Twelve times a year. £48.00 UK and Northern Ireland; $90.00 other. Morgan Grampian, 40 Beresford Street Woolwich, London SE18 6BQ United Kingdom. **Tel** 011 44 181 8557777, FAX 011 44 181 8555548, telex 896238.

ISSN 0217-1260
DD 690 SI

WHAT'S NEW IN BUILDING SINGAPORE. (WHAT'S NEW IN BUILDING.). [What's new build. Singap.]. (1982)-. Trade Publication. English. Twelve times a year. $210.00. Toucan Publications PTE Ltd., 112 Lavender Street #02-00 Chuan B, Singapore 1233 Singapore. **Tel** 011 65 2958891. **ED** Stephen Tan. **Ad Acc, Adv Mgr:** Louis Lee. ctrl circ. available in microform from University Microfilms International (UMI).
Desc: Information, new products and new technology in the field of building and construction.

LC TH12 .W48 **ISSN** 0268-6325
DD 381/.45691/02541 UK
CEASED

WHERE TO BUY CONSTRUCTION & MAINTENANCE SERVICES FOR BUILDINGS. **VFOAT** Where to Buy Construction and Maintenance Services for Buildings. No. 66 (1985)-(1994). Trade Publication. English. Where to Buy Ltd, Queensway House, 2 Queensway, Redhill Surrey RH1 1QS United Kingdom. ***Continues*** *Where to Buy: Building Construction & Maintenance.*
Desc: Information on the construction industry and building materials.

US

WHITEACRE REPORT, THE. English. Six times a year. $99.75 Ohio, $95.00 other. DCW Associates, 1827 Wales Road NE, Massillon OH 44646. **Tel** (216)832-6282.
Desc: Deals with subjects related to ceramic tile flooring and materials and methods installation.
Ind/Abst Constr. Index.

LC TH2055 .W48 **ISSN** 0276-7813
DD 696/.029/473 US

WHOLESALER PRODUCTS CATALOG. (WHOLESALER PRODUCTS CATALOG : WPC.). **VFOAT** WPC; Orange Book. Catalog. English. $30.00 US; $35.00 other. Hutton Publishing Company Inc., 4300 West 62nd Street, Indianapolis IN 46268. **Tel** (516)935-2740.

LC HD9621.U4 W48 **ISSN** 0884-0229
DD 338.7/6912/02573 US

WHO'S WHO IN THE STONE BUSINESS. [Who's who stone bus.]. **Added/Corp** Building Stone Institute (New York, N.Y.). (19??)-. English. One time a year. Building Stone Institute, 420 Lexington Avenue, New York NY 10017. **Tel** (212)490-2530.

LC KF902 .W56 KF902 .W54 **ISSN** 1054-9331
DD 344 US

WILEY CONSTRUCTION LAW UPDATE. [Wiley constr. law update]. **VFOAT** Construction Law Update. (1991)-. English. One time a year (Feb.). $110.00. John Wiley & Sons, Inc., 605 Third Avenue, New York NY 10158-0012. **Tel** (212)850-6000, (212)850-6645, FAX (212)850-6088, telex 12-7063. **(Subscription address:** John Wiley & Sons / UK, Baffins Lane, Chichester, West Sussex PO19 1UD United Kingdom. **Tel** 011 44 1243 779777, FAX 011 44 243 776128, telex 86290 WIBOOKG.)

Building and Construction —Abstracting, Bibliographies and Statistics

ISSN 0271-6011
US

WILEY SERIES OF PRACTICAL CONSTRUCTION GUIDES. [Wiley ser. prac. constr. guides]. (19??)-. Monographic series. English. Irregular. Price varies per volume. John Wiley & Sons, Inc., 605 Third Avenue, New York NY 10158-0012. **Tel** (212)850-6000, (212)850-6645, FAX (212)850-6088, telex 12-7063. **(Subscription address:** John Wiley & Sons / UK, Baffins Lane, Chichester, West Sussex PO19 1UD United Kingdom. **Tel** 011 44 1243 779777, FAX 011 44 243 776128, telex 86290 WIBOOKG.**)**

LC HD9715.K8 W64

KO

WOLGAN KONSOL. VFOAT Konsol; The Construction Industry; Construction Industry. Korean (Korean). Twelve times a year. Free. Taehan Konsol Hyophoe, 31-23 1-ka Taepyong-Road, Chung-ku Seoul Korea. **Tel** (02)735-6101. **ED** Lee Jae-Joon. **Ad Acc. Circ:** 3,000.
Desc: Scientific essay for construction industry to improve construction methods and technical expertise.

ISSN 0040-7798
UK
CCC

WOOD BASED PANELS INTERNATIONAL. See Forests and Forestry-Lumber and Wood.

LC TP875 .C423
DD 666/.94/05
ISSN 0263-6050
UK
CODEN WOCEDR

WORLD CEMENT. [World cem.]. **VFOAT** World Cement Technology. Vol. 13, No. 2 (Mar. 1982)-. Academic Scholarly Publication. English. Twelve times a year. $200.00. Palladian Publications Ltd., The Old Forge, Surrey GU8 6DD United Kingdom. **Tel** 011 44 1252 703900. **ED** J. Smith. **Bk Rev. Ad Acc. Circ:** 1,300. available on microfilm from University Microfilms International (UMI); available on an online database (file 648/Full-Text) from DIALOG. Documents available from Article Express International, CASDDS. **Continues** World Cement Technology.
Desc: Manufacture of cement. Also covers plant and machinery installations.
Ind/Abst Bioeng. Abstr.; Ceram. Abstr.; Chem. Abstr.; Coal Abstr.; Concr. Abstr.; Curr. Cit.; Curr. Technol. Index; Ei Page One; EMBASE; Eng. Index Annu. [Select. Cov.]; F&S Index Plus Text, Int. [Select. Cov.]; Infomat Int. Bus.; Mintec, Min. Technol. Abstr.; PROMT; World Ceram. Abstr.

ISSN 1045-0343
DD 622
US

WORLD DREDGING, MINING & CONSTRUCTION. See Engineering-Hydraulic Engineering.

ISSN 1054-5115
DD 631
US

WORLD FENCE NEWS. [World fence news]. (1983)-. Periodical. English. Twelve times a year. $24.95. World Fencing Data Center, 6301 Manchacha Road Stem, Austin TX 78745. **Tel** (512)445-3388, FAX (512)445-3496.

LC HD69.C6 W67
DD 338.7/61001/025
ISSN 1058-5818
US

WORLDWIDE DIRECTORY OF CONSULTANTS AND CONTRACTORS. See Industry and Production-Trade and Industrial Directories.

ISSN 0043-9460
US

WRECKING AND SALVAGE JOURNAL. (1967)-. Trade Publication. English. Twelve times a year. $35.00. Duane Publishing, PO Box 9073, Raintree MA 02184. **Tel** (617)848-6150, FAX (617)848-6150. **ED** Diane Fitzgerald. **Ad Acc; Adv Mgr:** Karen Duane, **Tel** (617)848-6160. **Circ:** 3,000+.
Desc: Serves the demolition industry.

ISSN 0319-3438
DD 692/.5
CN

YARDSTICKS FOR COSTING. (1968)-. English. One time a year. 92.04Can$. Southnam Information & Technical Group Inc, 1450 Don Mills Road, Don Mills Ontario M3B 2X7 Canada. **Tel** (416)445-6641, (800)668-2374, FAX (416)442-2261.

LC TH13.2.G7 I5
DD 690/.06/242
UK

YEAR BOOK AND DIRECTORY OF MEMBERS - INSTITUTE OF BUILDING. Main/Corp Institute of Building. 1967/68-. Directory. English. One time a year. £10.00 single issue. J Morris Publicity Ltd, Publicity House, Streatham Hill, London SW2 4TP United Kingdom.

LC TA402.5.T28 Y56
DD 338.4/7691/02551249
CH

YING TSAO CHIEN TSAI TSUNG LAN. See Engineering-Civil Engineering.

LC HD9715.G3 Z33
ISSN 0342-7943
GW

ZDB FORDERUNGEN, ZIELVORSTELLUNGEN FUER DIE ... LEGISLATURPERIODE DES DEUTSCHEN BUNDESTAGES. See Business and Economics-Labor.

ISSN 0867-1788
PL
UDC 624

ZESZYT NAUKOWY - POLITECHNIKA KRAKOWSKA. INZYNIERIA LADOWA. (ZESZYT NAUKOWY INZYNIERIA LADOWA.). [Zesz. Nauk. - Politech. Krak., Inz. Lad.]. **VFOAT** Zeszyty Naukowy Politechniki Krakowskiej. Inzynieria Ladowa. (1988)-. Polish. Irregular. Politechnika Krakowska, Ul. Warszawska 24, 31-155 Krakow Poland. **Tel** 011 48 12 374289, FAX 011 48 12 335773, telex 322468 PK PL. **Continues** Zeszyt Naukowy - Politechnika Krakowska. Budownictwo Ladowe, 0454-4862.

DD 343.43/07869
GW

ZFBR, ZEITSCHRIFT FUER DEUTSCHES UND INTERNATIONALES BAURECHT. See Law.

ISSN 0044-4472
RU

ZHILISHCHNOE STROITELSTVO. [Zilis. stroit.]. **Added/Corp** Akademiia Stroitelstva i Arkhitektury SSSR. Soviet Union. Gosudarstvennyi Komitet po Delam Stroitelstva. Nauchno-Tekhnicheskoe Obshchestvo Stroitelnoi Industrii (Soviet Union). Tsentralnoe Pravlenie. Soviet Union. Gosudarstvennyi Komitet po Grazhdanskomu Stroitelstvu i Arkhitekture. Tsentralnoe Pravlenie VNTO Stroiindustrii. (1958)-. Periodical. Russian. Twelve times a year. $119.95. **(Subscription address:** East View Publications Inc., 3020 Harbor Lane North, Suite 110, Minneapolis MN 55447. **Tel** (800)477-1005, (612)550-0961, FAX (612)559-2931.) Index available. **Bk Rev. Supersedes** Gorodskoe I Selskoe Stroitelstvo.

LC TP785 .Z5
DD 666/.73/05
ISSN 0341-0552
GW
CCC
CODEN ZIIND7

ZI INTERNATIONAL. [ZI int.]. **Added/Corp** Bundesverband der Deutschen Ziegelindustrie. **VAT** Ziegelindustrie International. (1976)-. Trade Publication. English (German; summaries and/or abstracts in German, French and Italian; table of contents in French and Italian). Twelve times a year. DM313.00 Germany; DM373.00 other. Bauverlag GmbH, Postfach 1460, D-65173 Wiesbaden Germany. **Tel** 011 49 6123 7000, FAX 011 49 6123 700122. **ED** Hans Bloss and Klaus Gobel. **Bk Rev. Ad Acc. Circ:** 4,547 (ctrl). Documents available from Article Express International, CASDDS. **Continues** ZI. Ziegelindustrie, 0044-4693.
Desc: Journal for the brick, tile and structural ceramics industries.
Ind/Abst Ceram. Abstr.; Chem. Abstr.; Civ. Struct. Eng. Abstr.; Coal Abstr.; Curr. Cit.; Ei Page One; EMBASE; Eng. Index Annu.; GeoRef; Mater. Sci. Eng. Abstr.; Mech. Eng. Abstr.; World Ceram. Abstr.

ISSN 0722-4400
GW
UDC 666.9

ZKG INTERNATIONAL. EDITION B. [ZKG int., Ed. B]. **VFOAT** Zement, Kalk, Gips International. Edition B. (1980)-. Trade Publication. Multiple languages. Twelve times a year. DM621.00 Germany; DM641.00 other. Bauverlag GmbH, Postfach 1460, D-65173 Wiesbaden Germany. **Tel** 011 49 6123 7000, FAX 011 49 6123 700122. Documents available from CASDDS. **Continues** ZKG. Zement, Kalk, Gips. Edition B., 0341-0560.
Ind/Abst Ceram. Abstr. (19??-); Chem. Abstr.; Curr. Cit.; Ei Page One.

XR

ZPRAVODAJ MINISTERSTVA STAVEBNICTVI CESKE SOCIALISTICKE REPUBLIKY. Main/Corp Czech Socialist Republic, (Czechoslovakia). Ministerstvo Stavebnictvi. Vol. 1 (June/July 1969)-. Czech. Twenty-four times a year. kcs24.00. Ministerstvo Stavebnictvi Ceske Socialisticke Republiky, Legislativnia Pravni Oddelen, Na Porincim Prava C 1, Prague 2 Czech Republic.

ISSN 0514-4094
XR
UDC 069

ZPRAVY MUZEI ZAPADOCESKEHO KRAJE. [Zpr. muz. Zapadoces. kraje]. (1964)-. Periodical. Czech. One time a year.
Ind/Abst Biocont. News Inf.; Rev. Agric. Entomol.

ABSTRACTING, BIBLIOGRAPHIES AND STATISTICS

LC Z5941 .A69 NA1.A1
DD 016.72
ISSN 0266-4380
UK

API. ARCHITECTURAL PERIODICALS INDEX. See Architecture-Abstracting, Bibliographies and Statistics.

LC HA1173 .A27 HD9715.A9 A9
DD 314.36 S 338.4/7624/09436021
AU

BAUSTATISTIK. GERATEBESTAND IM HOCH- U. TIEFBAU AM ... . VFOAT Geratebestand im Hoch- U Tiefbau Am ... . Trade Publication. German. One time a year. S170.00.
Desc: A yearly inventory taken on the last day of December of the number of machines, tools and vehicles owned and operated by the construction firms.

LC HA1320.N6 A32 HD9715.G3 G33
DD 314.3/55 S 338.4/7/690094355
GW

BAUWIRTSCHAFT UND BAUTATIGKEIT IN NORDRHEIN-WESTFALEN. Main/Corp North Rhine-Westphalia (Germany). Landesamt fur Datenverarbeitung und Statistik. 1973-. German. One time a year. DM12.00. Landesamt fuer Datenverarbeitung und Statistik Nordrhein-Westfalen, Postfach 101105, 40002 Duesseldorf Germany. **Tel** (0211)944901, FAX (0211)442006, telex 8586654 LDST D. **Circ:** 250. **Continues** Bauwirtschaft und Bautatigkeit in Nordrhein-Westfalen.
Desc: Statistical returns on the building boom, building measures, planning and building permission and house building.

AT

BUILDING ACTIVITY, WESTERN AUSTRALIA. See Housing and Urban Development-Abstracting, Bibliographies and Statistics.

ISSN 0811-0913
AT

BUILDING AND RELATED STATISTICS, TASMANIA. Added/Corp Australian Bureau of Statistics. Tasmanian Office. (1981/82)-. English. One time a year. Australian Bureau Statistics / Tasmanian Office, Commonwealth Government Centre, 188 Collins Street, Hobart GPO Box 66A, Hobart Tasmania 7001 Australia. **Tel** 011 61 2 205889. **Continues** Building Industry, Tasmania, 0067-1010.

US

BUILDING CONSTRUCTION IN THE BUFFALO AREA / PREPARED BY RESEARCH AND STATISTICS DEPT., BUFFALO CHAMBER OF COMMERCE. Added/Corp Buffalo Area Chamber of Commerce. Research and Marketing Dept. Buffalo, N.Y. Chamber of Commerce. Research and Statistics Dept. (1???)-. Periodical. English. Twelve times a year. $6.00 (members); $12.00 (nonmembers). Buffalo Area Chamber of Commerce, 107 Delaware Avenue, Buffalo NY 14202. **Tel** (716)852-7100.
Desc: Contains three statistical sections: building construction in the Buffalo metropolitan area; building permits issued in the Buffalo metropolitan area; and conversions/demolitions in the Buffalo metropolitan area.

LC HD9715.C3 B84
DD 354/.71/008242
ISSN 0575-7975
CN

BUILDING PERMITS, ANNUAL SUMMARY. [Build. permits, Annu. summ.]. **Added/Corp** Canada. Dominion Bureau of Statistics. Business Finance Division. Statistics Canada. Business Finance Division. Statistics Canada. Construction Division. Statistics Canada. Science, Technology and Capital Stock Division. Statistics Canada. Current Investment Indicators Section. **VFOAT** Permis de Batir, Sommaire Annuel. (1966)-. English (French). One time a year. 72.00Can$. Statistics Canada Publications Sales and Services, R.H. Coats Building 6th Floor, Ottawa Ontario K1A 0T6 Canada. **Tel** (613)951-5078, (800)267-6677, FAX (613)951-1584, telex 053-3585. Index available. cum. index. **Bk Rev. Circ:** 500. available on diskette.
Desc: Statistics on the number, type and value of building permits issued monthly in some 2,400 Canadian municipalities. Various geographical aggregate totals are available up to Canada level.

LC TH1 .G3
DD 690/.08
ISSN 0007-3636
UK

BUILDING SCIENCE ABSTRACTS. [Build. sci. abstr.]. **Added/Corp** Building Research Station (Great Britain) Institute of Builders. Building Research Establishment. Vol. 1 (Jan. 1928)-. English. Twelve times a year. Her Majesty's Stationery Office, 51 Nine Elms Lane, London SW8 5DR United Kingdom. **Tel** 011 44 171 8738459, 011 44 171 8738499, FAX 011 44 171 8738499, 011 44 171 8738456, telex 297138. **(Subscription address:** Her Majesty's Stationery Office,

PO Box 276, Public Centre, London SW8 5DT United Kingdom. **Tel** 011 44 171 87384998456.)
Ind/Abst Ceram. Abstr.; World Ceram. Abstr.

LC HD4295.M9 A32
DD 338.4/7/690095487 II
BUILDINGS STATISTICS IN KARNATAKA STATE. **Main/Corp** Karnataka, India. Public Works Dept. Chief Engineer, Communications and Buildings. (19??)-. English. One time a year. Chief Engineer Communications and Buildings, Public Works Department, Central Office, 50001 Bangalori India. ***Continues*** *Building Statistics in Karnataka State.*

LC HD9715.C3 A37 **ISSN** 1201-057X
DD 338.4/769/00971 CN
CAPITAL EXPENDITURES BY TYPE OF ASSET. (CAPITAL EXPENDITURES BY TYPE OF ASSET = DEPENSES EN IMMOBILISATIONS PAR TYPE D'ACTIF.). [Cap. expend. type asset]. **Added/Corp** Statistics Canada. Investment and Capital Stock Division. **VFOAT** Depenses en Immobilisations par Type d'Actif. (1992)-. Trade Publication. English (French). One time a year. 47.00Can$. Statistics Canada Publications Sales and Services, R.H. Coats Building 6th Floor, Ottawa Ontario K1A 0T6 Canada. **Tel** (613)951-5078, (800)267-6677, FAX (613)951-1584, telex 053-3585. ***Continues*** *Construction in Canada, 0527-4974.*
Desc: Presents total value of construction work performed, with analyses in current and constant repair dollars, by type of structure, by type of construction, by industry and by province. Includes separate analyses of labor content and cost of materials, and a general annual review.

LC HD9695.K82 C483
DD 338.47 KO
CHONGI KONGSAOP TONGGYE CHARYO. **VFOAT** Electrical Construction Statistics Yearbook. English (Korean). Hanguk Chongi Kongsa Hyophoe, 533-2 Tungchon-dong Kangso-ku, Seoul Korea.

LC TP885.P5 A45A **ISSN** 0360-2877
DD 621.8/672 US
CONCRETE PIPE INDUSTRY STATISTICS. **Main/Corp** American Concrete Pipe Association. (1974)-. English. One time a year. $3.50. American Concrete Pipe Association, 8300 Boone Boulevard, Suite 400, Vienna VA 22182.

LC HD9715.C3 A37 **ISSN** 0527-4974
DD 338.4/769/00971 CN
TITLE CHANGE
CONSTRUCTION IN CANADA (ANNUAL ED.). (CONSTRUCTION IN CANADA.). [Constr. Can.]. **Added/Corp** Canada. Dominion Bureau of Statistics. Forecast Surveys Section. Canada. Dominion Bureau of Statistics. Capital Expenditures Section. Canada. Dominion Bureau of Statistics. Business Finance Division. Operations Section. Canada. Dominion Bureau of Statistics. Construction Section. Statistics Canada. Construction Section. Statistics Canada. Construction Division. Statistics Canada. Science, Technoloy and Capital Stock Division. Statistics Canada. Investment and Capital Stock Division. **VFOAT** Construction au Canada. **VAT** Construction au Canada (Ed. Annuelle). (1953)-(1993). Trade Publication. English (French). Statistics Canada Publications Sales and Services, R.H. Coats Building 6th Floor, Ottawa Ontario K1A 0T6 Canada. **Tel** (613)951-5078, (800)267-6677, FAX (613)951-1584, telex 053-3585. ***Continues*** *Canada. Bureau of Statistics. The Construction Industry in Canada.* ***Continued by*** *Capital Expenditures by Type of Asset, 1201-057X.*
Desc: Presents total value of construction work performed, with analyses in current and constant repair dollars, by type of structure, by type of construction, by industry and by province. Includes separate analyses of labor content and cost of materials, and a general annual review.

LC Z7914.B9 C62 Th1 **ISSN** 0892-2047
DD 016.69 US
CONSTRUCTION INDEX. [Constr. index]. Vol. 1 (1987)-. Abstracting/Indexing Service. English. One time a year (Feb.). $75.00. ArchiText, 410 South Michigan Avenue, Suite 1008, Chicago IL 60605. **Tel** (312)939-3202, FAX (312)939-1020. **ED** Susan Greenwald. **Circ:** 200. available on CD-ROM from SilverPlatter (US); available on an online database from STN International (Math) Database; and ORBIT.
Desc: Annotated index of journal articles of interest to architects and other construction industry professionals, arranged by CSI master format. Contains over 10,000 article annotations from over 50 architectural industry journals.

LC HD9715.C3 C66 **ISSN** 0833-238X
DD 338.4/3624/0971021 CN
CONSTRUCTION PRICE STATISTICS (QUARTERLY ED.). (CONSTRUCTION PRICE STATISTICS = STATISTIQUES DES PRIX DE LA CONSTRUCTION.). [Constr. price stat.]. **Added/Corp** Statistics Canada. Prices Division. **VFOAT** Statistiques des Prix de la Construction. Vol. 1, No. 1 (1st Quarter 1985)-. Periodical. English (French). Four times a year. 92.00Can$. Statistics Canada Publications Sales and Services, R.H. Coats Building 6th Floor, Ottawa Ontario K1A 0T6 Canada. **Tel** (613)951-5078, (800)267-6677, FAX (613)951-1584, telex 053-3585. cum. index. ***Continues*** *Construction Price Statistics, Monthly Bulletin, 0319-8243.*

ISSN 0970-7891
II
UDC 666.8
CRI CURRENT CONTENTS. (1969)-. Periodical. English. Six times a year. Rs50.00 India; $25.00 other. National Council for Cement and Building Materials, M-10 South Extension 11 Ring Road, New Delhi 110 049 India. **Tel** 011 91 11 6440133, FAX 011 91 11 6468868, telex 031-66261.
Desc: A documentation list of current literature about cement and building materials. Contains article titles, authors, and primary journal reference form over 400 journals.

ISSN 0380-7223
DD 338.4/76223635/0971 CN
GYPSUM PRODUCTS. [Gypsum prod.]. **Main/Corp** Canada. Statistique Canada. Division des Industries Manufacturieres et Primaires. **Added/Corp** Canada. Dominion Bureau of Statistics. Mining, Metallurgical & Chemical Section. Canada. Dominion Bureau of Statistics. Canada. Dominion Bureau of Statistics. Metal and Chemical Products Section. Canada. Bureau Federal de la Statistique. Division de l'Industrie et du Commerce. Canada. Bureau Federal de la Statistique. Division de l'Industrie. Canada. Bureau Federal de la Statistique. Division des Industries Manufacturieres et Primaires. Statistique Canada. Division des Industries Manufacturieres et Primaires. Statistique Canada. Division de l'Industrie. **VFOAT** Produits de Gypse. Vol. 2, No. 1 (Jan. 1951)-. Abstracting/Indexing Service. French (English). Twelve times a year. 48.02Can$. Statistics Canada Publications Sales and Services, R.H. Coats Building 6th Floor, Ottawa Ontario K1A 0T6 Canada. **Tel** (613)951-5078, (800)267-6677, FAX (613)951-1584, telex 053-3585. ***Continues*** *Production Shipments and Stocks of Gypsum Products.*
Desc: Production, factory shipments and factory stocks, monthly and cumulative.

LC HD7333.A3 H676 **ISSN** 0308-9819
DD 338.4/7624/0941 UK
CCC
HOUSING AND CONSTRUCTION STATISTICS (ANNUAL). (HOUSING AND CONSTRUCTION STATISTICS / DEPARTMENT OF THE ENVIRONMENT, SCOTTISH DEVELOPMENT DEPT., [AND] WELSH OFFICE.). **Added/Corp** Great Britain. Dept. of the Environment. Great Britain. Scottish Development Dept. Great Britain. Welsh Office. (19??)-. Trade Publication. English. One time a year. £40.00. Her Majesty's Stationery Office, 51 Nine Elms Lane, London SW8 5DR United Kingdom. **Tel** 011 44 171 8738459, 011 44 171 8738499, FAX 011 44 171 8738499, 011 44 171 8738456, telex 297138. **(Subscription address:** Her Majesty's Stationery Office, PO Box 276, Public Centre, London SW8 5DT United Kingdom. **Tel** 011 44 171 8738499, 011 44 171 8738456.)
Desc: Produced in two parts. Part 1 contains tables on housebuilding performance, housing finance and building materials. Part 2 contains tables on construction activity and employment, local authority housing loans and sales.

LC TH7201 .T45 **ISSN** 0140-4237
DD 690/.05 UK
INTERNATIONAL BUILDING SERVICES ABSTRACTS. **Added/Corp** Representatives of European Heating and Ventilating Associations. Vol. 13 (1978)-. Abstracting/Indexing Service. English. Six times a year. $167.69. Building Services Research and Information Association, Old Bracknell Lane West, Bracknell Berkshire RG12 7AH United Kingdom. **Tel** 011 44 1344 426511, FAX 011 44 1344 487575, telex 848288. **ED** M McCarthy. Index available. **Bk Rev. Circ:** 500. available on an online database. ***Continues*** *Thermal Abstracts.*
Desc: Covers heating, ventilation, air condition, plumbing, electrical installations, energy conservation, and lighting.
Ind/Abst Agric. Eng. Abstr.

LC TA444 .J68 **ISSN** 0125-1759
DD 620.1/37 TH
Pr Rev.
JOURNAL OF FERROCEMENT. [J. ferrocement]. **Added/Corp** International Ferrocement Information Center. New Zealand Ferro Cement Marine Association. **VAT** Journal of Ferro Cement. (1972)-. Abstracting/Indexing Service. English. Four times a year. $85.00. International Ferrocement Information Center, PO Box 2754, Bangkok Thailand. **Tel** 011 66 2 529-0100, FAX 011 66 2 529-0374, telex 84276 TH. **ED** Lilia Robles-Austriaco. cum. index. **Bk Rev. Ad Acc, Adv Mgr Tel** 66-2-524-5864. **Circ:** 400 (ctrl). available on microfilm and microfiche; available on diskette. Documents available from Article Express International.
Desc: Publication contains the following: IFIC editorial papers on research and development, papers on applications and techniques, bibliographic list, INFC database, news and notes, IFIC reference centers, author's profile, book reviews, abstracts, international meetings, IFIC publications and price list and advertisements.
Ind/Abst Abstr. AIT Rep. Publ. Energy; Bioeng. Abstr.; Civ. Struct. Eng. Abstr.; Concr. Abstr.; Curr. Cit.; Ei Page One; Eng. Index Annu.; Int. Civil Eng. Abstr.; Mater. Sci. Eng. Abstr.; Life Sci. Collect.; Pollut. Abstr. Indexes; Soft. Abstr. Eng.

LC Z7914.B9 S77A
DD 016 SW
LITTERATUR/PUBLICATIONS. **Main/Corp** Stockholm. Statens Institut for Byggnadsforskning. 1944/69-. Multiple languages (English and Swedish). Statens Institut for Byggnadsforskning, Box 27 163 102 52 27, Stockholm Sweden.

LC HD9715.N2 N48a
NE
MAANDSTATISTIEK BOUWNIJVERHEID. **Main/Corp** Netherlands (Kingdom, 1815-). Centraal Bureau Voor de Statistiek. **Added/Corp** Netherlands. Centraal Bureau voor de Statistiek. Monthly Bulletin on Construction Statistics. **VFOAT** Monthly Bulletin on Construction Statistics. (Jan. 1973)-. Bulletin. Dutch. Twelve times a year. $76.27. Centraal Bureau voor de Statistiek, AFD ALG Zaken, Postbus 959, 2270 AZ Voorburg Netherlands. **Tel** 011 31 70 3373800, FAX 011 31 70 0387429, telex 32692 CBS NL. ***Continues*** *Maandstatistiek van de Bouwnijverheid.*

ISSN 0964-4571
UK
MONTHLY BULLETIN OF INDICES PRICE ADJUSTMENT FORMULAE FOR CONSTRUCTION CONTRACTS. [Mon. bull. indices., Price adjust. formul. constr. contract.]. (19??)-. Bulletin. English. Twelve times a year. £66.00. Her Majesty's Stationery Office, 51 Nine Elms Lane, London SW8 5DR United Kingdom. **Tel** 011 44 171 8738459, 011 44 171 8738499, FAX 011 44 171 8738499, 011 44 171 8738456, telex 297138. **(Subscription address:** Her Majesty's Stationery Office, PO Box 276, Public Centre, London SW8 5DT United Kingdom. **Tel** 011 44 171 8738499, 011 44 171 8738456.) ***Formed by the union of*** *Monthly Bulletin of Indices. Price Adjustment Formulae for Building Contracts, 0262-0634* ***and*** *Monthly Bulletin Construction Indices for Use with National Economic Development Office Price Adjustment Formula. Civil Engineering Works, 0262-0642.*
Desc: Presents indices which allow for increases in the costs of labor and materials in formulating methods of adjusting building, specialist and civil engineering contracts.

LC HD9622.J3 N34
DD 338.2/4 JA
NAMA KONKURITO TOKEI NEMPO. **VFOAT** Year Book of Readymixed Concrete Statistics. 1971-. Japanese. ¥700. Tsusho Sangyosho Daijin Kanbo Chosa Tokeibu, (Research & Statistics Dept. Minister's Secretariat Ministry of International Trade & Industry), 3-1 Kasumigaseki 1 Chome, Chiyodaku Tokyo 100 Japan.

LC Z7914.B9 N66 TH145
DD 016 RU
NOVOSTI TEKHNICHESKOI LITERATURY. RAZDEL PROEKTIROVANIE I STROITELSTVO. STROITELSTVO I ARKHITEKTURA. **Added/Corp** Moscow. Tsentralnyi Institut nauchnoi Informatsii po Stroitelstvu i Arkhitekture. (19??)-. Russian. Proektirovanie I Stroitelstvo, A-47 Ulitsa Gorkogo 38, Moscow Russia.

LC HC186 .P73 **ISSN** 0101-1766
DD 338.981 BL
PROJETO. **See** Architecture.

DD 016.69/0072071 CN
PUBLICATIONS CATALOGUE - INSTITUTE FOR RESEARCH IN CONSTRUCTION (OTTAWA). (CATALOGUE DES PUBLICATIONS / INSTITUT DE RECHERCHE EN CONSTRUCTION.). [Pub. cat. - Inst. Res. Constr.]. **Main/Corp** Institut de Recherche en Construction (Canada). **VFOAT** Publications Catalogue. (Oct. 1991)-. French (English). Institute for Research in Construction, National Research Council Canada, Ottawa Ontario K1A 0R6 Canada. **Tel** (613)993-9960, FAX (613)952-4040, telex 053-3145 NRC ADMIN OTT. ***Continues*** *List of IRC Publications., 0840-2035.* ***Continued in part by*** *Institute for Research in Construction (Canada). Publications Catalogue, 1185-9628.*

LC HD9715.B3 B34a
DD 338.4/7/690097296 BF
QUARTERLY BULLETIN OF CONSTRUCTION STATISTICS. **Main/Corp** Bahamas. Dept. of Statistics. (19??)-. Statistical Publication. English. Four times a year. $1.00. Department of Statistics / Barbados, Cabinet Office, PO Box N 3904, Nassau Bahamas. **Tel** (809)325-5149, FAX (809)325-5149. **Circ:** 60 (ctrl).

LC HD9715.F7 F69A
DD 338.4/7624/0944 FR
STATISTIQUES DE LA CONSTRUCTION. **Main/Corp** France. Bureau des Systemes d'Information sur la Construction et l'Urbanisation. (197?)-. French. Twelve times a year. 225.00F France; 275.00F (surface mail), 365.00F (airmail) other. Documentation Francaise, 29 quai Voltaire, 75344 Paris Cedex 7 France. **Tel** 011 33 1 40157000, FAX 011 33 1 40157230, telex 204 826 DOCFRAN. available in microform.
Desc: Statistics on construction per department.

LC HD9715.B4 **ISSN** 0772-7712
DD 338.4/7/69009493 BE
STATISTIQUES DE LA CONSTRUCTION ET DU LOGEMENT. **Main/Corp** Belgium. Institut National de Statistique. 1971-. French (Dutch). One time a year. 375F Belgium; 425F other. Institut National de Statistique / Belgium, rue de Louvain 44, 1000 Brussels Belgium. **Tel** 011 32 2 5486211, FAX 011 32 2 5486367. **Bk Rev**. **Ad Acc. Circ:** 825 (ctrl).
Desc: Statistics about building, construction and housing.

LC HD9715.D4 S72 **ISSN** 0108-5549
DK
STATISTISKE EFTERRETNINGER. BYGGE- OG ANLGSVIRKSOMHED. **VFOAT** Bygee- og Anlgsvirksomhed. Vol. 1 (1983)-. Monographic series. Danish. Price varies per volume. Danmarks Statistik, Sejrgade 11, DK-2100 Copenhagen Denmark. **Tel** 011 45 3 9173917, FAX 011 45 31 18 48 01, telex 1 62 36. ***Continues in part*** *Danmarks Statistisk. Statistiske Efterretninger.*
Desc: Statistics on employment and labor costs, with building cost indexes, construction cost indexes for civil engineering projects, tendency surveys, accounts statistics and sales and assessments of real property.

CARPENTRY AND WOODWORK

ISSN 0824-0868
DD 338.4/7674/09714 CN
2 X 4. (2 X 4 [I.E. DEUX FOIS QUATRE] : TOUT SUR LE BOIS - 2 X 4 [I.E. TWO-BY-FOUR] : ALL ABOUT WOOD.). **VFOAT** Deux Fois Quatre; Two-by-Four; Tout Sur Le Bois; All About Wood. **VAT** Deux Par Quatre. Vol. 1, No 1 (Feb/Mar. 1985)-. Periodical. English (French). Six times a year. 37.40Can$. Editions CR Inc, CP PO Box 1010, Victoriaville G6P 8Y1 Canada. **Tel** (819)752-4243, FAX (819)758-8812.

LC TT **ISSN** 0895-9005
DD 684 US
AMERICAN WOODTURNER. (AMERICAN WOODTURNER : THE JOURNAL OF THE AMERICAN ASSOCIATION OF WOODTURNERS.). **Added/Corp** American Association of Woodturners. (198?)-. Trade Publication. English. Four times a year (Mar., June, Sept., Dec.). $25.00. American Association of Woodturners, 667 Harriet Avenue, Shoreview MN 55126. **Tel** (612)484-9094, FAX (612)484-1724. **Circ:** 4,000.

LC TT194 .A47 **ISSN** 8750-9318
DD 684/.08/05 US
TITLE CHANGE
AMERICAN WOODWORKER, THE. [Am. woodwork.]. Vol. 1, No. 1 (March 1985)-(199?). Periodical. English. Rodale Press Inc., 400 South 10th Street, Emmaus PA 18098. **Tel** (610)967-5171, (800)666-2503, FAX (610)967-8964, telex 847338. **(Subscription address:** CDS Agency Hard Copy, PO Box 4966, Des Moines IA 50340. **Tel** (515)247-7569.) available in microform. ***Continued by*** *Rodale's American Woodworker, 1074-9152.*
Ind/Abst Index Inf. (1989-199?).

ISSN 1077-7997
DD 684 US
●**AMERICAN WOODWORKER (1994).** (AMERICAN WOODWORKER.). [Am. woodwork.]. No. 42 (Dec. 1994)-. Periodical. English. Six times a year. $23.88 US; $36.48 others. Rodale Press Inc., 400 South 10th Street, Emmaus PA 18098. **Tel** (610)967-5171, (800)666-2503, FAX (610)967-8964, telex 847338. **(Subscription address:** CDS Agency Hard Copy, PO Box 4966, Des Moines IA 50340. **Tel** (515)247-7569.) available in microform. ***Continues*** *Rodale's American Woodworker, 1074-9152.*
Desc: The how-to magazine of woodwork.
Ind/Abst Index Inf.

ISSN 0380-5786
DD 338.4/7695 CN
ASPHALT ROOFING. [Asph. roof.]. **Added/Corp** Canada. Dominion Bureau of Statistics. Canada. Dominion Bureau of Statistics. Forestry Section. Canada. Dominion Bureau of Statistics. Industry and Merchandising Division. Canada. Dominion Bureau of Statistics. Industry Division. Canada. Dominion Bureau of Statistics. Manufacturing and Primary Industries Division. Statistics Canada. Manufacturing and Primary Industries Division. Statistics Canada. Industry Division. **VFOAT** Papier-Toiture Asphaltes; Papier-Toiture Asphalte. (Jan. 1950)-. Periodical. English (French). Twelve times a year. 60.00Can$ Canada; $72.00 US; $84.00 other. Statistics Canada Publications Sales and Services, R.H. Coats Building 6th Floor, Ottawa Ontario K1A 0T6 Canada. **Tel** (613)951-5078, (800)267-6677, FAX (613)951-1584, telex 053-3585. ***Continues*** *Asphalt Roofing New Classification.*
Desc: Provides production and shipments, domestic and export, of asphalt roofing shingles, sidings, tar and asphalt felts and sheathings on a monthly and cumulative basis.

ISSN 1039-9925
DD 684.1040994 AT
●**AUSTRALIAN WOOD REVIEW.** [Aust. wood rev]. (1993)-. Periodical. English. Four times a year. 21.37Aus$. Interwood Holdings Pty Ltd., 330 West Mount Cotton Road, Mount Cotton Queensland 4165 Australia. **Tel** 011 61 7 3419349. **ED** Linda Nathan. **Bk Rev**. **Ad Acc**. ***Continues*** *Australian Wood Magazine, 1038-7501.*

ISSN 0818-0261
DD 684.080994 AT
AUSTRALIAN WOODWORKER. [Aust. woodwork.]. (1985)-. Trade Publication. English. Six times a year. 18.91Aus$. Skills Book Publishing Pty. Ltd., Private Mail Bag 7, Red Lion Street, Rozelle NSW 2039, Australia. **Tel** 011 61 2 8106222, FAX 011 61 2 8185675.
Ind/Abst EP Collect.; Homework Help.; MasterFile FullTEXT 1000; MasterFile FullTEXT 350; MasterFile FullTEXT 650; MasterFile FullTEXT (Sept. 1994-); Telebase; World Mag. Bank.

ISSN 0820-5752
DD 694 CN
B. ALLAN MACKIE SCHOOL OF LOG BUILDING. (B. ALLAN MACKIE SCHOOL OF LOG BUILDING : NEWSLETTER.). [B. Allan Mackie Sch. Log. Build.]. Vol. 8, No. 6 (Dec. 1, 1986)-. Newsletter. English. Six times a year. $5.00. Mackie School of Log Building, PO Box 1205, Prince George British Columbia V2L 4V3 Canada. ***Continues*** *The Scribers & The Adze, 0820-5760.*

ISSN 1056-716X
DD 684 US
BETTER HOMES AND GARDENS DECORATIVE WOODCRAFTS. [Better homes gard. decor. woodcrafts]. **VFOAT** Decorative Woodcrafts. Issue 1 (Oct. 1991)-. Periodical. English. Six times a year. $29.97. Meredith Corporation, Locust at 17th, Des Moines IA 50309. **Tel** (515)284-3000, FAX (515)284-2568. **(Subscription address:** Neodata / Colorado, PO Box 2606, Boulder CO 80322. **)** **ED** Larry Clayton. **Circ:** 150,000.
Desc: Geared toward crafting enthusiasts who are looking for simple project designs for easy-to-make woodcrafts. Each issue contains between 12 and 14 projects.

ISSN 0933-2855
GW
UDC 747
BTH. BODENBELAGE, TAPETEN, HEIMTEXTILIEN. FUSSBODEN-ZEITUNG. [BTH, Bodenbelage Tapeten Heimtext., Fussboden-Ztg.]. **VFOAT** Bodenbelage, Tapeten, Heimtextilien. Fussboden-Zeitung. (1987)-. Periodical. German. Eleven times a year. DM158.00 Germany; DM176.00 other. SN Verlag Michael Steinert, An der Alster 21, W 2000 Hamburg 1 F R Germany. **Tel** 011 49 40 240852, FAX 011 49 40 2803788. ***Continues*** *Fussboden-Zeitung (1975), 0342-6181.*

ISSN 1220-9430
RM
UDC 674
BULLETIN OF THE TRANSYLVANIA UNIVERSITY OF BRASOV. SERIA B II, INDUSTRIA LEMNULUI. [Bull. Transylv. Univ. Bra–sov, Ser. B II Ind. lemn.]. (1990)-. Bulletin. Multiple languages. One time a year. Price varies. Universitatea Transilvania Brasov, 2200 Brasov B-Dul Eroilor Nr. 9, Brasov Romania. **Tel** 068 150786. Index available. **Circ:** 247. ***Continues*** *Buletinul Universitatii din Brasov. Seria BII, Industrializarea Lemnului, 1220-9457.*

ISSN 0318-2215
DD 694 CN
C W C DATAFILE. [CWC datafile]. **Main/Corp** Canadian Wood Council. (1971)-. Monographic series. English. Price varies per volume. Canadian Wood Council, 55 Metcalfe Street, Ottawa Ontario K1P 6L5 Canada. **Tel** (613)235-7221, telex 053-3138.

ISSN 1048-0196
DD 684 US
CCC
CABINETMAKER (CHICAGO, ILL.). (CABINETMAKER.). [CabinetMaker]. **VFOAT** Cabinet Maker. (198?)-. Trade Publication. English. Eight times a year. $59.90. Cahners Publishing Company, 249 West 17th Street, New York NY 10011. **Tel** (212)645-0067, FAX (212)242-6987. **(Subscription address:** Cahners Publishing Company / Colorado, Paid Subscription Service Center, PO Box 7610, Highlands Ranch CO 80126-7610. **Tel** (303)470-4466, FAX (303)470-4691.) **ED** Bruce Plantz and Jim Saul. **Ad Acc. Circ:** 27,000 (ctrl).
Desc: Edited for small cabinet shops serving the kitchen and commercial market. Geared expressly for the small cabinet manufacturer.

ISSN 0704-0717
DD 684/.08/05 CN
CANADIAN WORKSHOP. [Can. workshop]. Vol. 1 (Oct. 1977)-. Periodical. English. Eleven times a year. 20.77Can$. Camar Publications Ltd., 130 Spy Court, Markham Ontario L3R 5H6 Canada. **Tel** (416)475-8440, FAX (416)475-9246. **ED** Cindy Lister. **Bk Rev. Ad Acc. Circ:** 110,000. Documents available from Documents on Demand.
Desc: A how-to magazine covering all aspects of home maintenance and woodworking. Caters to the houseproud homeowner.
Ind/Abst Can. Index; Energy Inf. Abstr.; Environ. Abstr.; Index Inf. (1980-).

LC HD6350.C2 C3 **ISSN** 0008-6843
DD 694/.05 US
CARPENTER. **Added/Corp** United Brotherhood of Carpenters and Joiners of America. Vol. 1, (1881)-. Trade Publication. English. Six times a year. $10.00. The Carpenter / Washington DC, 101 Constitution Avenue Northwest, Washington DC 20001. **Tel** (202)546-6206, FAX (202)543-5724, telex 89561. **ED** David Ransom. **Ad Acc, Adv Mgr:** David Peterson, **Tel** (202)546-6206. **Circ:** 650,000 (ctrl).
Desc: Member publication for the United Brotherhood of Carpenters and Joiners of America covering news of importance to its various building trades and industrial members.
Ind/Abst Work Relat. Abstr.

ISSN 0882-9055
US
CARPENTER (NEW YORK, N.Y.), THE. (THE CARPENTER : OFFICIAL PUBLICATION OF THE NEW YORK DISTRICT COUNCIL OF CARPENTERS-AFL-CIO.). **Added/Corp** United Brotherhood of Carpenters and Joiners of America. District Council of New York and Vicinity. Vol. 1, No. 1 (Oct./Nov. 1984)-. Periodical. English. Twelve times a year. The Carpenter / New York, 204-8 East 23rd Street, New York NY 10010.

LC NE1183.3 .C528
DD 769.951 CC
CHING TSAO MU KO. (19??)-. Periodical. Chinese. Hsin Hua Shu Tien / Tien-Chin, Tien-Chin Shih, People's Republic of China.

LC TT199.7 .C46 **ISSN** 0577-9294
DD 731.4/62/06273 US
CHIP CHATS. [Chip chats]. **Added/Corp** National Wood Carvers' Association. (1954)-. Periodical. English. Six times a year. Comes with membership to National Wood Carvers Association $11.00. National Woodcarvers Association, 7424 Miami Avenue, Cincinnatti OH 45243. **Tel** (513)561-0627. **ED** Edward F. Gallenstein. **Bk Rev. Circ:** 43,500.
Desc: Contains information, photos, plans, and projects of interest to woodcarvers; listings of shows and carving events are included. Aims to promote woodcarving, fellowship among members.
Ind/Abst Index Inf. (March 1990-).

ISSN 1131-8694
SP
UDC 674
COMERCIO E INDUSTRIA DE LA MADERA. [Comer. ind. madera]. (1981)-. Periodical. Spanish. Eight times a year. $152.00. Elsevier Prensa SA, Avenida Paral Lel 180, 08015 Barcelona Spain. **Tel** 011 34 3 3255350, FAX 011 34 3 4252880. **Ad Acc.** Full Page (B&W) 115000ptas. Half Page (B&W) 85000ptas. Full Page (Color) 150000ptas. Half Page (Color) 95000ptas. **Circ:** 7,000.
Desc: Technical publication for the wood industry including manufacturing and trade. Primarily targeted at carpenters, furniture manufacturers, joiners, varnishers, etc.

ISSN 0770-111X
BE
UDC 58
COURRIER DU BOIS, LE. **VFOAT** Houtnieuws. (1961)-. Periodical. Multiple languages (French and Dutch). Four times a year. Free on request. Bureau National de Documentation, 111 rue Royale sur le Bois, 1000 Brussels Belgium. **Tel** 011 32 2 2192832, FAX 011 32 2 2173003. **ED** P. Calluy and A. De Beukelaer. **Ad Acc.**
Desc: Material wood and its possibilities and applications.

ISSN 1058-403X
DD 338 US
CUSTOM WOODWORKING BUSINESS. (CUSTOM WOODWORKING BUSINESS : CWB.). [Cust. woodwork. bus.]. **VFOAT** CWB. Vol. 1, No. 1 (Spring 1991)-. Periodical. English. Four times a year. $25.00. Vance Publishing Corporation, 400 Knightsbridge Parkway, Lincolnshire IL 60069. **Tel** (800)255-5113,

Building and Construction — Carpentry and Woodwork

(708)634-2600. **(Subscription address:** Vance Publishing Corporation, PO Box 421, Lincolnshire IL 60069. **Tel** (708)634-4347.**)**

DD 674

ISSN 0011-9008
RU
CODEN DVPYAN

DEREVOOBRABATYVAJUSCAJA PROMYSLENNOST. (DEREVOOBRABATYVAIUSHCHAIA PROMYSHLENNOST.). [Derevoobrab. prom.]. **Added/Corp** Russia (1923-U.S.S.R.) Ministerstvo Lesnoi i Derevoobrabatyvaiushchei Promyshlennost. Nauchno-Tekhnicheskoe Obshchestvo Bumazhnoi i Derevoobrabatyvaiushchei Promyshlennosti. (1955)-. Academic Scholarly Publication. Russian. Six times a year. $69.95. Izdatelstvo Lesnaia Promyshlennost, Ulitsa Kirova 40 A, Moscow Russia. **(Subscription address:** East View Publications Inc., 3020 Harbor Lane North, Suite 110, Minneapolis MN 55447. **Tel** (800)477-1005, (612)550-0961, FAX (612)559-2931.**)** Documents available from CASDDS. **Continues in part** Derevopererabatyvaiushchaia i Lesokhimicheskaia Promyshlennost.
 Ind/Abst Abstr. Bull. Inst. Pap. Sci. Tech.; AGRICOLA; Art Archaeol. Tech. Abstr.; Biodeter. Abstr.; Chem. Abstr.; For. Prod. Abstr. (19??-19??); Pap. Board Abstr.

ISSN 0012-6144
XR
CODEN DRVOAT

DREVO. [Drevo]. **Added/Corp** Drevarsky Vyskumny Ustav. (1946)-. Academic Scholarly Publication. Czech (Slovak). Twelve times a year. DM166.00. **(Subscription address:** Slovart GTG Ltd., Krupinska 4, 852 99 Bratislava Slovakia. **Tel** 011 42 7 839471 2.**)** Documents available from CASDDS.
 Ind/Abst Abstr. Bull. Inst. Pap. Sci. Tech.; AGRICOLA; Art Archaeol. Tech. Abstr.; Chem. Abstr.; For. Prod. Abstr.; Saf. Health Work.

LC TT180 .E2
DD 684/.08/05

ISSN 1058-3807
US

EASY-TO-BUILD WOOD PROJECTS. [Easy build wood proj.]. **VFOAT** Easy to Build Wood Projects. (1990)-. Periodical. English. Two times a year. $3.50 (single issue) US; $3.95 (single issue) Canada. Harris Publications, 1115 Broadway, 8th Floor, New York NY 10010. **Tel** (212)807-7100.

LC TS880 .F13
DD 749/.05

ISSN 0192-8058
US
CCC

FDM, FURNITURE DESIGN & MANUFACTURING. **VFOAT** Furniture Design & Manufacturing. **VAT** Furniture Design and Manufacturing; FDM, Furniture Design and Manufacturing. (19??)-. Trade Publication. English. Thirteen times a year. $75.90. Cahners Publishing Company, 249 West 17th Street, New York NY 10011. **Tel** (212)645-0067, FAX (212)242-6987. **(Subscription address:** Cahners Publishing Company / Colorado, Paid Subscription Service Center, PO Box 7610, Highlands Ranch CO 80126-7610. **Tel** (303)470-4466, FAX (303)470-4691.**)** **ED** Michael Chazin. Index available. **Ad Acc. Circ:** 42,000 (ctrl). available on microfilm and microfiche from University Microfilms International (UMI). **Desc:** Technical publication edited for manufacturing executives and designers producing furniture, kitchen cabinets, architectural woodwork and other types of secondary wood products.

LC TT180 .F55
DD 684/.08/05

ISSN 0361-3453
US

FINE WOODWORKING. [Fine woodwork.]. Vol. 1 (Winter 1975)-. Periodical. English. Six times a year (Jan., Mar., May, July, Sept., Nov.). $29.00. Taunton Press, 63 South Main Street, PO Box 5506, Newtown CT 06470-5506. **Tel** (203)426-8171, (800)283-7252, FAX (203)426-3434, telex 5106004860. **ED** Dick Burrows, Sander Nagyszalanczy and Jim Boesel. Index available. cum. index. **Bk Rev. Ad Acc. Circ:** 280,000. **Desc:** Covers techniques, traditions, tools, materials, machines, designs, and shop tricks for both the beginning and expert woodworker.
 Ind/Abst Art Archaeol. Tech. Abstr.; Art Index; BHA : Biblio. Hist. Art; Index Inf. (1976-).

DD 684

ISSN 1076-8327
US

●**FINE WOODWORKING'S HOME FURNITURE.** See Interior Design and Decoration-Home Furnishings.

ISSN 0016-3090
US

FURNITURE WORKERS PRESS. **Added/Corp** United Furniture Workers of America. Vol. 1 (Jan. 1939)-. Periodical. English. Twelve times a year. United Furniture Workers of America, 700 Broadway, New York NY 10003. available through film reproduction.

ISSN 0197-6559
US

HANDS ON! (DAYTON, OHIO). (HANDS ON.). **Added/Corp** Shopsmith, Inc. (1979)-. Periodical. English. Six times a year. Shopsmith Inc, 3931 Image Drive, Dayton OH 45414-2523. **Tel** (513)898-6070. **ED** John Clark. **Circ:** 800,000 (ctrl). **Desc:** Information and woodworking projects for the home workshop.
 Ind/Abst Curr. Index J. Educ. (March 1990).

LC TS810.G3 H64a

GW

HBG-MITTEILUNGEN. Main/Corp Holz-Berfusgenossenschaft. **Added/Corp** Holz-Berfusgenossenschaft. Ihre Holz-Berfusgenossenschaft Informiert. Holz-Berfusgenossenschaft. Mitteilungen. **VFOAT** Ihre Holz-Berufsgenossenschaft. **VAT** Holz-Berufsgenossenschaft- Mitteilungen. (19??)-. German. Four times a year. Holz-Berufsgenossenschaft, Am Knie 6, W-8000 Munich 60 Germany. **Tel** 011 49 89 88971. **Circ:** 105,000 (ctrl). **Desc:** Prevention and safety news and other information concerning the woodworking handicraft industries.

GW

HK, HOLZ- UND KUNSTSTOFFVERARBEITUNG. (199?)-. English. Eleven times a year. $177.33. DRW Verlag Weinbrenner GmbH and Company, Fasanenweg 18, D-70771 Leinfelden Germany. **Tel** 011 49 711 75911, FAX 011 49 711 7591266, telex 7 255609. **Continues** HK Holz und Mobelindustrie.

LC TS840 .M64

ISSN 0721-2585
GW
CCC
TITLE CHANGE

HK, HOLZ- UND MOBELINDUSTRIE. **VFOAT** Holz- und Mobelindustrie; HK International, Holz- und Mobelindustrie. (198?)-(Jan. 1994). Periodical. English (French and German). DRW Verlag Weinbrenner GmbH and Company, Fasanenweg 18, D-70771 Leinfelden Germany. **Tel** 011 49 711 75911, FAX 011 49 711 7591266, telex 7 255609. **Continues** Holz- und Kunststoffverarbeitung, 0721-2585. **Continued by** HK Holz und Kunststoffverabeitung.

LC T1 .M46
DD 605

ISSN 8755-0423
US

HOME MECHANIX. [Home mechanix]. **VFOAT** Home Mechanics. Vol. 80, No. 681 (Jan. 1985)-. Periodical. English. Ten times a year. $13.94. Times Mirror Magazines, Two Park Avenue, New York NY 10016. **Tel** (212)779-5000. **(Subscription address:** Neodata / Colorado, PO Box 2606, Boulder CO 80322. **)** available on microfilm and microfiche from University Microfilms International (UMI). Documents available from UMI Article Clearinghouse, Magazine Collection. **Continues** Mechanix Illustrated, 0025-6587. **Desc:** The how-to magazine with a mix of advice, ideas, product information, and easy to follow plans to help in home improvement, automotive, garden and remodeling projects.
 Ind/Abst Acad. Abstr. Full Text Elite; Acad. Abstr.; EP Collect.; Gen. Period. Index (1985-); Homework Help.; Index Inf. (1985-); Mag. Artic. Summar. Elite; Mag. Artic. Summar. Select; Mag. Artic. Summar. CD-ROM; Mag. Express (1988-) [Full Txt.]; Mag. Index Plus (1989-); Mag. Index Sel. Microfiche (1986-) [Full Txt.]; Mag. Index. Sel. (1986-); Mag. Search; MasterFile FullTEXT 1000; MasterFile FullTEXT 350; MasterFile FullTEXT 650; MasterFile FullTEXT (Nov. 1987-); Newsp. Period. Abstr. (1988-); OCLC; Pub. Lib. FullTEXT; Read. Guide Abstr. Select Ed.; Read. Guide Period. Lit.; Resource/One Ondisc; Telebase; Mag. Index (Jan. 1985-); TOM Gen. Index (1985-) [Full Txt.]; Vocat. Search; World Mag. Bank.

LC TH4817 .H66
DD 643/.7/0971

ISSN 0840-8106
CN

HOMEOWNER REPAIR AND RENOVATION EXPENDITURE IN CANADA. [Homeown. repair renov. expend. Can.]. **Added/Corp** Statistics Canada. Family Expenditure Survey. **VFOAT** Depenses sur les Reparations et Renovations Effectuees par Proprietaires de Logement au Canada. (1987)-. English (French). One time a year. 30.00Can$ Canada; $36.00 US; $42.00 other. Statistics Canada Publications Sales and Services, R.H. Coats Building 6th Floor, Ottawa Ontario K1A 0T6 Canada. **Tel** (613)951-5078, (800)267-6677, FAX (613)951-1584, telex 053-3585.

DD 684.0805

ISSN 1037-1354
AT

HOUSE & HOME WOODWORKER. [House home woodwork.]. **VFOAT** House and Home Woodworker.; House & Home. (1991)-. Trade Publication. English. Six times a year. 12.00Aus$ (Australia); 17.50Aus$ (New Zealand); 22.50Aus$ (other). Skills Book Publishing Pty. Ltd., Private Mail Bag 7, Red Lion Street, Rozelle NSW 2039, Australia. **Tel** 011 61 2 8106222, FAX 011 61 2 8185675. **Continues** The Australian Home Woodworker, 1035-1108.
 Ind/Abst EP Collect.; Homework Help.; MasterFile FullTEXT 1000; MasterFile FullTEXT 350; MasterFile FullTEXT 650; MasterFile FullTEXT (Sept. 1994-?); Telebase; World Mag. Bank.

NE

HOUTWERELD. (19??)-. Dutch. Twenty-four times a year. Fl172.00 (latest issue). Nijgh Periodieken BV, Postbus 122, 3100 AC Schiedam Netherlands. **Tel** 011 31 10 4274174.

UDC 674.2

ISSN 0750-0181
FR
CODEN 686.7

I.N. REVUE DES TECHNIQUES NOUVELLES EN SERRURERIE MENUISERIE MIROITERIE. **VFOAT** Techniques Nouvelles. Revue des Techniques Nouvelles en Serrurerie Menuiserie Miroiterie. (1967)-. Periodical. French. Ten times a year. 176.30F (one-year), 293.83F (two-year) France; 350.00F (one-year), 580.00F (two-year) other. Techniques Nouvelles / France, 28 rue Andre Bonnenfant, 78100 St. Germain Laye France. **Tel** 011 33 1 39735031.

IT

INDUSTRIA DEL LEGNO & DEL MOBILE, L'. **VFOAT** Industria del Legno e del Mobile; LM. No. 1 (Jan. 1971)-. Periodical. Italian. Six times a year. L54500. Centro Studi Ind Leggera, Via Gesu 17, 20121 Milan Italy. **Tel** 011 39 2 796630, FAX 011 39 2 780703. **Continues** Industria del Legno, Mobile & Ambiente.

ISSN 0392-9086
IT

UDC 674

INDUSTRIA DEL LEGNO & DEL MOBILE, L'. [Ind. legno & mob.]. **VFOAT** Industria del Legno e del Mobile. (1971)-. Periodical. Italian (English). Six times a year. L80000 Italy; L160000 other. Centro Studi Ind Leggera, Via Gesu 17, 20121 Milan Italy. **Tel** 011 39 2 796630, FAX 011 39 2 780703. **Bk Rev. Ad Acc. Adv Mgr:** Paola Govoni, **Tel** 76 02 16 48. **Circ:** 4,000. **Continues** Industria del Legno, Mobile e Ambiente, 0367-8695.
 Desc: Provides economic, technique, and organizational information for the wood and furniture industry.

IT

INDUSTRIA DEL MOBILE, L'. Vol. 1 (1959)-. Periodical. Italian. Eleven times a year. L177130. Editrice Industria del Mobile Srl, Via Giambologna 21, 20136 Milan Italy. **Tel** 011 39 2 8394780, 011 39 2 8394898. **Bk Rev. Ad Acc. Circ:** 6,000. **Desc:** Magazine of woodworking machines, tools and about problems in the wood and furniture field.

US

LOG HOME LIVING ANNUAL BUYER'S GUIDE. English. One time a year. $11.95. Home Buyer Publications Inc, PO Box 220039, Chantilly VA 22022. **Tel** (703)478-0435, (800)826-3893.

ISSN 1131-897X
SP

UDC 674

MADERPRESS BARCELONA. [Maderpress Barc.]. (1989)-. Periodical. Spanish. Six times a year. Free on request. Elsevier Prensa SA, Avenida Paral Lel 180, 08015 Barcelona Spain. **Tel** 011 34 3 3255350, FAX 011 34 3 4252880. **Ad Acc. Circ:** 12,000. **Desc:** New products publication for the wood industry.

LC HD999.B883 U65
DD 648/.5/068

ISSN 1055-9663
CCC
SUSPENDED

MAINTENANCE EXECUTIVE. See Interior Design and Decoration-Home Furnishings.

LC TS840 .M63
DD 684/.08

ISSN 1055-4440
US

MODERN WOODWORKING. [Mod. woodwork.]. Vol. 1, No. 1 (Aug. 1989)-. Periodical. English. Twelve times a year. $24.00. Target Magazine Group, 167 East Highway 72, Collierville TN 38017. **Tel** (901)853-7470, (901)853-7720, (901)853-0545, FAX (901)853-6437. **Absorbed** Furniture & Cabinet Manufacturing.

US

MODERN WOODWORKING DIRECTORY AND BUYERS GUIDE. Directory. English. One time a year. $10.00. Target Magazine Group, 167 East Highway 72, Collierville TN 38017. **Tel** (901)853-7470, (901)853-7720, (901)853-0545, FAX (901)853-6437.

LC TA419.A1 M64

ISSN 0285-7049
JA
CODEN MKSHDC

MOKUZAI KENKYU SHIRYO. [Mokuzai kenkyu shiryo]. **Added/Corp** Kyoto Daigaku. Mokuzai Kenkyujo. **VFOAT** Wood Research Review; Wood Research and Technical Notes. (1951)-. Academic Scholarly Publication. Japanese. Kyoto Mokuzai Kako Gijutsu Kyokai, (Wood Technological Assoc. of Japan),

Building and Construction — Carpentry and Woodwork

2-16 Shiba Koen 1 Chome, Minatoku Tokyo 105 Japan. Documents available from CASDDS.
Ind/Abst Chem. Abstr.

ISSN 0392-6443
IT

UDC 67/68
MONDO LEGNO. [Mondo legno]. (1977)-. Periodical. Italian. Twelve times a year. L72000 Italy. Masson SPA, via Statuto 2/4, 20121 Milan Italy. **Tel** 011 39 2 63671, FAX 011 39 2 6367211. **ED** Almerico Ribera. **Circ:** 4,000.
Desc: Covers the whole world of wood, analysing the different processes and the correct use of wood in the building fields.

US

NATIONAL ASSOCIATION OF HOME AND WORKSHOP WRITERS NEWSLETTER. (1973)-. Newsletter. English. Four times a year. $25.00 (members only). National Association of Home and Workshop Writers, Box 10, Palomar Mountain CA 92060. **ED** Richard Day. **Bk Rev**, (Qty: 5). **Circ:** 90 (ctrl).
Desc: Information of use to members, who are writers in the home and workshop field. Includes marketing helps, writing tips, humor, photo tips, and news about the Association and its members.

ISSN 0194-0910
US

NATIONAL HARDWOOD MAGAZINE. (1943)-. Trade Publication. English. Thirteen times a year (With an additional issue in December). $45.00. International Wood Trade Publications, PO Box 34908, Memphis TN 38184. **Tel** (901)372-8280 or (800)844-1280. **Continues** Memphis Lumberman and Southern Woodworker.

Pr Rev.
NUOVA FINESTRA. Vol. 2, No. 7/8 (July/Aug. 1981)-. Periodical. Italian. Twelve times a year. L64720. Tecnomedia SRL, via Sansovino 28, 20133 Milan Italy. **Tel** 011 39 2 70602276, FAX 011 39 2 26680468, telex 323047. Index available (published in Dec. issue). **Ad Acc. Circ:** 8,000 (ctrl). **Continues** Finestra.

IT

LC TS851 .C44 ISSN 1063-0414
DD 381 US
POWER EQUIPMENT TRADE. [Power equip. trade]. Vol. 41, No. 1 (Jan./Feb. 1992)-. Trade Publication. English. Ten times a year. $35.00. Hatton Brown Publishers Inc, PO Box 2268, Montgomery AL 36197. **Tel** (334)834-1170, FAX (334)834-4525, telex 782350. **Continues** Chain Saw Age & Power Equipment Trade, 1055-4734.

ISSN 0032-6488
UK
CCC

PRACTICAL WOOD WORKING. **VFOAT** Practical Woodworking; Wood Working. (1966)-. Periodical. English. Twelve times a year. $46.50. IPC Magazines Ltd., Perrymount Road, Haywards Heath, West Sussex RH16 3DH United Kingdom. **Tel** 011 44 1444 440421, FAX 011 44 1444 445599.
Ind/Abst EP Collect.; Homework Help.; MasterFile FullTEXT 1000; MasterFile FullTEXT 350; MasterFile FullTEXT 650; MasterFile FullTEXT; OCLC; Telebase; World Mag. Bank.

LC TS840 .P72 ISSN 0373-9856
PL

PRZEMYS DRZEWNY. [Przem. drzew.]. **Added/Corp** Stowarzyszenie Naukowo-Techniczne Inzynierow i Technikow Lesnictwa i Drzewnictwa. (May 1950)-. Periodical. Polish. Twelve times a year. $93.00. (**Subscription address:** Ars Polona-Ruch, PO Box 1001, Krakowskie Przedmiescie 7, 00-068 Warsaw Poland. **Tel** 011 48 22 261201.)
Ind/Abst AGRICOLA; Biodeter. Abstr.; For. Prod. Abstr. (1991-); For. Abstr.

ISSN 0953-0800
DD 749.22 UK
REGIONAL FURNITURE. See Antiques.

ISSN 1074-9152
DD 684 US
TITLE CHANGE
RODALE'S AMERICAN WOODWORKER. [Rodale's Am. woodwork.]. **VFOAT** American Woodworker. (19??)-(1994). Periodical. English. Rodale Press Inc, 400 South 10th Street, Emmaus PA 18098. **Tel** (610)967-5171, (800)666-2503, FAX (610)967-8964, telex 847338. (**Subscription address:** CDS Agency Hard Copy, PO Box 4966, Des Moines IA 50340. **Tel** (515)247-7569.) available in microform. **Continues** American Woodworker, 8750-9318. **Continued by** American Woodworker (Emmaus, Pa. : 1994), 1077-7997.
Desc: How-to magazine for woodworking enthusiasts. Edited with hands-on woodworking techniques, coverage of new tools and products, and tips for the serious amateur and professional woodworker.
Ind/Abst Index Inf.

UK

ROUTING. English. Four times a year. £10.00 UK; $26.00 other. Argus Specialist Publications, Argus House, Boundary Way / Hemel, Hempstead Herts HP27ST United Kingdom. **Tel** 011 44 181 6671033, FAX 011 44 181 6889573, telex 948669 TOPJNL G.
Desc: Covers the impact on woodworking made by the electric router, with information on the latest information on future developments, materials and methods of usage.

ISSN 0392-8063
IT

UDC 683.37
SERRAMENTI & FALEGNAMERIA.
VFOAT Serramenti e Falegnameria. (1981)-. Periodical. Italian. Ten times a year (monthly with July/Aug. and Nov./Dec. combined). L65000 Italy. Masson SPA, via Statuto 2/4, 20121 Milan Italy. **Tel** 011 39 2 63671, FAX 011 39 2 6367211. **ED** Almerico Ribera. **Circ:** 6,500.
Desc: Gives full coverage to all the problems of window and door frames, as well as carpentry in general. Analyzes in depth the increasingly diversified economic, commercial and technological realities of the sector.

ISSN 1181-9464
DD 338.4/76841/009714021 CN
STATISTIQUES SUR L'INDUSTRIE DU MEUBLE. [Stat. ind. meuble]. **Added/Corp** Association des Fabricants de Meubles du Quebec. (May 1990)-. Periodical. French. Limited free distribution. Association des Fabricants de Meubles de Quebec, CP 1002, Place Bonaventure, Montreal Quebec H5A 1E9 Canada.

LC TS840 .T43 ISSN 0321-382X
RU
CODEN TODPDW
TEKHNOLOGIA I OBORUDOVANIE DEREVOOBRABATYVAIUSHCHIKH PROIZVODSTV. **Added/Corp** Leningradskaia Lesotekhnicheskaia Akademiia Imeni S. M. Kirova. Vol. 1 (1973)-. Academic Scholarly Publication. Russian. Documents available from CASDDS.
Ind/Abst Abstr. Bull. Inst. Pap. Sci. Tech.; Chem. Abstr. (?-1982).

ISSN 1041-8113
DD 684 US
TODAY'S WOODWORKER. [Today's woodwork.]. Vol. 1 No. 1 (Jan./Feb. 1989)-. Periodical. English. Six times a year. $18.95. Today's Woodworker / Rockler Press, PO Box 44, Rogers MN 55374. **Tel** (612)428-4101.
Desc: Detailed plans and full color illustrations for beautiful projects. Geared to both the beginning and advanced woodworker.

LC TJ1195 .T6287 ISSN 0266-1756
DD 680/.9 UK
TOOLS & TRADES. **Added/Corp** Tool and Trades History Society. **VFOAT** Tools and Trades. (1983)-. English (summaries and/or abstracts in French and German). One time a year.
Ind/Abst BHA : Biblio. Hist. Art.

ISSN 0346-2846
SW
UDC 674
TRAINDUSTRIN (STOCKHOLM). [Traindustrin Stockh.]. (1975)-. Trade Publication. Swedish. Irregular. Kr485.00 Nordic countries; Kr520.00 other. Arbor Publishing AB, Box 26212, S 100 41 Stockholm Sweden. **Tel** 011 46 8 6799011, FAX 011 46 8 6643005.

ISSN 0384-1243
DD 691/.1/05 CN
TREATED WOOD PERSPECTIVES. P1-1973-. Periodical. English. Canadian Institute of Timber Construction, 200 Cooper Street, Ottawa K2P 0G1 Canada. **Supersedes** Modern Wood, 0077-0175.

AT

VICTORIAN HOMES. See Interior Design and Decoration.

LC WMLC 93/4859 ISSN 1058-3750
DD 694 US
WEEKEND WOOD PROJECTS. [Weekend wood proj.]. **VFOAT** Wood Projects. (1991)-. Periodical. English. Two times a year. $3.50 (U.S.), $3.95 (Can.). Harris Publications, 1115 Broadway, 8th Floor, New York NY 10010. **Tel** (212)807-7100.

LC TT180 .W3463 ISSN 1058-4072
DD 684/.08/05 US
WEEKEND WOODWORKER ANNUAL, THE. (THE WEEKEND WOODWORKER ANNUAL : ... EASY-TO-BUILD PROJECTS / SELECTED BY THE EDITORS OF RODALE BOOKS). [Weekend woodwork. annu.]. **Added/Corp** Rodale Books. (1991)-. English. One time a year. $17.95 US; $21.55 Canada. Rodale Press Inc., 400 South 10th Street, Emmaus PA 18098. **Tel** (610)967-5171, (800)666-2503, FAX (610)967-8964, telex 847338.

ISSN 1042-6094
DD 684 US
WEEKEND WOODWORKING PROJECTS. See Hobbies.

US

WIN FDM'S WOODWORKING INDUSTRY NEWSLETTER. (19??)-. Newsletter. English. Six times a year. $149.00 US and Canada; $199.00 other. Cahners Publishing Company, 249 West 17th Street, New York NY 10011. **Tel** (212)645-0067, FAX (212)242-6987. (**Subscription address:** Cahners Publishing Company / Colorado, Paid Subscription Service Center, PO Box 7610, Highlands Ranch CO 80126-7610. **Tel** (303)470-4466, FAX (303)470-4691.)
Desc: Offers woodworking industry executives up-to-date industry news.

LC TH2270 .W5
US

WINDOW & DOOR SPECIFIER. **Added/Corp** National Wood Window & Door Association (U.S.). **VFOAT** Window and Door Specifier. (19??)-. Periodical. English. Four times a year. $20.00. National Wood Window & Door Association, 125 S. Wacker Drive #300, Chicago IL 60606. **Tel** (312) 214-2545, FAX (312) 214-2546. **ED** James O. Ahtes. **Ad Acc. Circ:** 75,000.
Desc: Official publication of the National Wood Window & Door Association. Offers reporting on residential and commercial projects, niche marketing and changes in technology.

US

WOOD DESIGN FOCUS. See Architecture.

LC TS840 .F93 ISSN 1045-7348
DD 674/.8/05 US
WOOD DIGEST. [Wood dig.]. Vol. 20, No. 5 (August 1989)-. Periodical. English. Twelve times a year. $50.00. PTN Publishing Company, 445 Broad Hollow Road, Melville NY 11747. **Tel** (516)845-2700, FAX (516)845-7109. **Continues** Furniture/Wood Digest, 0746-1089.

ISSN 1063-7893
DD 684 US
WOOD MAGAZINE'S SUPER SCROLLSAW PATTERNS. [Wood mag. super scrollsaw patterns]. **VFOAT** Super Scrollsaw Patterns. Vol. 1, no. 1 (1992)-. Periodical. English. Six times a year. $30.00. Meredith Corporation, Locust at 17th, Des Moines IA 50309. **Tel** (515)284-3000, FAX (515)284-2568.

LC TH5601 ISSN 1058-3815
DD 694 US
TITLE CHANGE
WOOD PROJECTS (NEW YORK, N.Y. 1991). (WOOD PROJECTS.). [Wood proj.]. **VFOAT** Wood Projects Annual. (1991)-(19??). Periodical. English. Harris Publications, 1115 Broadway, 8th Floor, New York NY 10010. **Tel** (212)807-7100. **Continued by** Country Wood Projects, 1058-3769.

LC HD9767.S6 W6
DD 338.4767 SA
●**WOOD SOUTHERN AFRICA & TIMBER TIMES.** See Forests and Forestry-Lumber and Wood.

ISSN 1069-6962
DD 745 US
●**WOOD STROKES.** (WOOD STROKES : EASY PAINT DESIGNS FOR WOOD.). [Wood strokes]. (1993)-. Periodical. English. Six times a year. EGW Publishing Company, 1041 Shary Circle, Concord CA 94518. **Tel** (510)671-9852, (800)777-1164, FAX (510)671-0692. **ED** Sharon Mikkelson. **Ad Acc. Circ:** 101,260.
Desc: Highlights projects and craft ideas for painted wood figures and designs.

ISSN 0164-4114
US

WOODSMITH. (1979)-. Periodical. English. Six times a year. $19.95. Woodsmith Publishing, 2200 Grand Avenue, Des Moines IA 50312. **Tel** (515)282-7000, (800)333-5075, FAX (515)282-6741. (**Subscription address:** SIFD Agency Control, 1901 Bell Avenue, Des Moines IA 50312. **Tel** (515)246-6812.) **ED** Donald B. Peschke. Index available (bound in issue). cum. index. **Bk Rev. Circ:** 250,000 (ctrl).
Desc: Woodsmith is a step-by-step guide for woodworkers. Each issue shows complete woodworking plans with a whole series of illustrations and easy-to-follow instructions. High quality projects are designed and built by the woodsmith staff. Shop tips and techniques for both the novice and the experienced woodworker. Contains no advertising.
Ind/Abst Index Inf.

UK

WOODTURNING. (1990)-. Periodical. English. Six times a year. $65.00 US. Guild of Master Craftsman Publications Ltd., 166 High Street, Lewes East Sussex, BN7 1XU United Kingdom. **Tel** 011 44 1273 477374, FAX

Building and Construction —Carpentry and Woodwork

011 44 1273 478606. **ED** Nick Hough.
Desc: Designed for amateur, professional, and student woodturners. Icludes reviews of new tools, books and lathes with hints, techniques and ideas.
LC TT180 .W595 **ISSN** 1045-3040
DD 684/.08/05 US
WOODWORK (ROSS, CALIF.).
(WOODWORK.). [Woodwork]. **VFOAT** Woodwork Magazine. No. 1 (Spring 1989)-. Periodical. English. Six times a year (Jan., Mar. May, July, Sept., Nov.). $17.95. Woodwork, PO Box 1529, Ross CA 94957. **Tel** (415)382-0580, FAX (415)382-0587. **ED** Graham Blackburn. **Ad Acc. Circ:** 70,000.
Desc: An magazine covering simple to complex projects and techniques for woodworks.
Ind/Abst Index Inf.

ISSN 0043-776X
UK
WOODWORKER (HEMEL HEMPSTEAD. (1910)). (WOODWORK.). [Woodwork]. **VFOAT** Wood Worker. (19??)-. Periodical. English. Twelve times a year. $62.80. Argus Specialist Publications, Argus House, Boundary Way / Hemel, Hempstead Herts HP27ST United Kingdom. **Tel** 011 44 181 6671033, FAX 011 44 181 6889573, telex 948669 TOPJNL G. **ED** John Hemsley. Index available. **Bk Rev. Ad Acc. Circ:** 36,884. **Continues** Woodworker and Art Craftsman.
Desc: Information and ideas for the amateur craftsman and small professional woodworker; includes projects, new designs, and constructional details from craftsmen on furniture, turning, carving and related techniques.
Ind/Abst Art Archaeol. Tech. Abstr.; Work Relat. Abstr.

LC TT180 .W64 **ISSN** 0197-4149
DD 684/.08 US
CEASED
WOODWORKER (NEW YORK, N.Y. 1980). (WOODWORKER : PROJECTS AND TECHNIQUES.). [Woodwork.]. **VFOAT** Woodworker Projects and Techniques; Woodworker Projects & Techniques. (19??)-(June 1995). English. F&W Publications, 1507 Dana Avenue, Cincinnati OH 45207. **Tel** (513)531-2222, FAX (513)531-1843. (**Subscription address:** CDS Agency Hard Copy, PO Box 4966, Des Moines IA 50340. **Tel** (515)247-7569.)

LC NK **ISSN** 1080-0042
DD 745 US
●**WOODWORKER WEST.** [Woodwork. west.]. Vol. 7, No. 1 (Jan.-Feb. 1994)-. Periodical. English. Six times a year. $9.00. Southern California Woodworking, PO Box 66751, Los Angeles CA 90066. **Tel** (310)398-5931.
Continues Southern California Woodworker, 0898-3550.

ISSN 0199-1892
US
WOODWORKER'S JOURNAL (NEW MILFORD), THE. (THE WOODWORKER'S JOURNAL.). (1977)-. English. Six times a year. $19.95. PJS Publications Inc., News Plaza, PO Box 1790, Peoria IL 61656. **Tel** (309)682-6626, FAX (309)682-7394. **ED** James J. McQuillan. **Ad Acc. Circ:** 120,000 (ctrl).
Desc: Woodworking projects magazine with 70-plus plans yearly for the novice at advanced cabinet-making, with detailed instruction, illustrations and photos for furniture, toys, jigs, clocks, gifts.
Ind/Abst EP Collect.; Homework Help.; Index Inf.; Mag. Search; MasterFile FullTEXT 1000; MasterFile FullTEXT 350; MasterFile FullTEXT 650; MasterFile FullTEXT (July 1993-); OCLC; Pub. Lib. FullTEXT; Telebase; Vocat. Search.

ISSN 0177-7114
GW
UDC 621 :674
WOODWORKING INTERNATIONAL NURNBERG. [Woodwork. int. Nurnb.]. (1983)-. Trade Publication. English. Four times a year. $48.00. Harnisch Verlagsgesellschaft, Blumenstrasse 15, D-90402 Nuernberg Germany. **Tel** 011 49 911 203658, FAX 011 49 911 204579. **ED** Adrian Alecu. **Bk Rev. Ad Acc. Circ:** 11,000. **Continues** Ubersee-Post. Woodworking, 0177-7106.
Desc: The international magazine for the woodworking industry. Reports on aspects of woodworking from wood treatment to machines, tools and technical know-how, from timber engineering supplies to the latest developments in technologies and markets. Directly addresses the decision-makers within the industry, such as factory managers and production engineers.

ISSN 1180-5862
DD 621.9/029/471 CN
WOODWORKING SOURCER. [Woodwork. sourcer]. (1991)-. English. Action Communications Inc, 135 Spy Ct, Markham Ontario L3R 5H6 Canada. **Tel** (416)477-3222.

UK
WOODWORKS. English. Four times a year. £10.00 UK; $25.00 other. Argus Specialist Publications, Argus House, Boundary Way / Hemel, Hempstead Herts HP27ST United Kingdom. **Tel** 011 44 181 6671033, FAX 011 44 181 6889573, telex 948669 TOPJNL G.
Desc: Aimed at the home woodworker - includes projects and tips on saving time and money while yielding results.

LC GV1201 .W64 **ISSN** 0043-8057
US
WORKBENCH. [Workbench]. Vol. 13, No. 3 (March/April 1957)-. Periodical. English. Six times a year. $14.95. KC Publishing Inc., 700 West 47th Street, Suite 310, Kansas City MO 64112. **Tel** (816)531-5730, (800)444-0801. (**Subscription address:** CDS Agency Hard Copy, PO Box 4966, Des Moines IA 50340. **Tel** (515)247-7569.) **ED** Robert Hoffman. Index available. **Bk Rev. Ad Acc. Circ:** 835,000. available on microfilm and microfiche from University Microfilms International (UMI); available on an online database (file 647/Full-Text) from DIALOG. Documents available from UMI Article Clearinghouse, Magazine Collection. **Continues** Profitable Hobbies Workbench.
Desc: Publication provides detailed information on home maintenance, home improvement, woodworking and lots more.
Ind/Abst Acad. Abstr. Full Text Elite; Acad. Abstr.; Consum. Index Prod. Eval. Inf. Source; EP Collect.; Gen. Period. Index (1985-); Homework Help.; Index Inf.; Mag. Artic. Summar. Elite; Mag. Artic. Summar. Select; Mag. Artic. Summar. CD-ROM; Mag. Index Plus (1989-); Mag. Search; MasterFile FullTEXT 1000; MasterFile FullTEXT 350; MasterFile FullTEXT 650; MasterFile FullTEXT (Jan. 1989-) [Full Txt.]; Mid. Search; Newsp. Period. Abstr. (1988-); OCLC; Pub. Lib. FullTEXT; Read. Guide Abstr. Select Ed.; Read. Guide Period. Lit.; Telebase; Mag. Index (1977-); TOM Gen. Index (1985-) [Full Txt.]; Vocat. Search.

BUSINESS AND ECONOMICS

LC HD2709 **ISSN** 0897-5736
DD 338.74 US
501(C)(3) MONTHLY LETTER. [501(c)(3) mon. lett.]. **Added/Corp** American Association for Corporate Contributions. **VFOAT** Five Hundred One Three Monthly Letter. (198?)-. Corporate Report. English. Twelve times a year. $46.00. Insight Systems Limited, PO Box 192, Atlantic IA 50022. **Tel** (712)243-5257.

LC HD1407 .C67 **ISSN** 0545-4441
DD 630 US
TITLE CHANGE
A.E. RES. See Agriculture-Agricultural Economics.

LC HC800.A1 A16
DD 330.96/0021 US
A.I.D. ECONOMIC DATA BOOK.
AFRICA. Main/Corp United States. Agency for International Development. Statistics and Reports Division. **Added/Corp** United States. Agency for International Development. Office of Statistics and Reports. (No.223, June (1969)-. English. National Technical Information Service - NTIS, Room 2027S, 5285 Port Royal Road, Springfield VA 22161. **Tel** (703)487-4630, (703)487-4660, (703)487-4650, FAX (703)321-8547, telex 89-9405.

LC HB
DD 330 US
A.I.D. ECONOMIC DATA BOOK, EAST ASIA. Main/Corp United States. Agency for International Development. Statistics and Reports Division. No.264 (Jan. 1973)-. Periodical. English. Irregular. National Technical Information Service - NTIS, Room 2027S, 5285 Port Royal Road, Springfield VA 22161. **Tel** (703)487-4630, (703)487-4660, (703)487-4650, FAX (703)321-8547, telex 89-9405.

LC HB
DD 330 US
A.I.D. ECONOMIC DATA BOOK, LATIN AMERICA. Main/Corp United States. Agency for International Development. Statistics and Reports Division. (No.246- June 1974)-. Periodical. English. Irregular. National Technical Information Service - NTIS, Room 2027S, 5285 Port Royal Road, Springfield VA 22161. **Tel** (703)487-4630, (703)487-4660, (703)487-4650, FAX (703)321-8547, telex 89-9405. ctrl circ.
Desc: Lists a sampling of reports contained in the NTIS database in five categories: manufacturings processing industry, agriculture and food, construction, and management and economic development.

UK
A-Z BUSINESS INFORMATION SOURCES. (19??)-. English. Four times a year. £146.65. Croner Publ Ltd., Croner House London Road, Kingston Upon Thames, Surrey KT2 6SR United Kingdom. **Tel** 011 44 181 5473333, FAX 011 44 181 5472637.

UK
A-Z OF EUROPEAN BUSINESS INFORMATION SOURCES. (19??)-. Periodical. English. £139.15. Croner Publ Ltd., Croner House London Road, Kingston Upon Thames, Surrey KT2 6SR United Kingdom. **Tel** 011 44 181 5473333, FAX 011 44 181 5472637.

GW
ABC DER DEUTSCHEN WIRTSCHAFT. ORTSLEXIKON FUER WIRTSCHAFT UND VERKEHR. VFOAT Ortslexikon Fur Wirtschaft und Verkehr; ABC Ortslexikon Fur Wirtschaft und Verkehr. German. ABC Publishing Group, POB 100262, D 64202 Darmstadt Germany. **Tel** 011 49 6151 38920.

GW
ABC DER DEUTSCHEN WIRTSCHAFT. QUELLENWERK FUER EINKAUF-VERKAUF. VFOAT Quellenwerk Fur Einkauf-Verkauf; ABC Quellenwerk Fur Einkauf-Verkauf. (1949)-. German. ABC Publishing Group, POB 100262, D 64202 Darmstadt Germany. **Tel** 011 49 6151 38920.

ISSN 0959-2911
UK
ABC EXECUTIVE FLIGHT PLANNER. ASIA, PACIFIC. See Travel and Tourism.

ISSN 0959-1389
UK
TITLE CHANGE
ABC EXECUTIVE FLIGHT PLANNER EUROPE, MIDDLE EAST, AFRICA. See Travel and Tourism.

UK
ABECOR COUNTRY REPORTS. (19??)-. English. Irregular. £150.00 academic subscribers, £300.00 other all the countries, (the series covers reports of over 150 countries). Barclays Bank Ltd, PO Box 12, 1 Wimborne Road, Poole Dorset BH15 2BB United Kingdom. **Tel** 011 44 1202 671212, telex 887591.

ISSN 0814-5180
DD 026.3310994 AT
ABLATIVE. [ABLative]. **Added/Corp** Australian National University. Archives of Business and Labour. (1985)-. Periodical. English. Two times a year. Free. Noel Butlin Archives of Bussiness and Labor, Australian National University, Canberra ACT 0200 Australia. **Tel** 011 61 6 2492219, FAX 011 61 6 2490140, telex AA62694 SOPAC. **ED** Michael Saclier. **Circ:** 400 (ctrl).
Desc: Publication providing current news and detailed information on the Noel Butlin Archives Centre.
Ind/Abst Aust. Educ. Index; Aust. Libr. Inf. Sci. Abstr. (1985-).

AT
CEASED
ABM. (19??)-(June 1995). Periodical. English. Australian Consolidated Press Ltd., Private Bag 92615 Symonds St, Auckland New Zealand. **Tel** 011 64 9 3735408, FAX 011 64 9 3022889. **Continues** Australian Business.

LC HB1 .A27 **ISSN** 0951-0079
DD 330/.05 US
ABSTRACTS OF WORKING PAPERS IN ECONOMICS : THE OFFICIAL JOURNAL OF THE AWPE DATABASE. Added/Corp Cambridge University Press. Vol. 1, No. 1 (1986)-. Academic Scholarly Publication. English. Four times a year. Cambridge University Press / New York, 40 West 20th Street, New York NY 10011-4211. **Tel** (212)924-3900, (800)221-4512, FAX (212)691-3239. (**Subscription address:** Cambridge University Press / Outside of North America, United Kingdom. **Tel** 011 44 223 312 393, FAX 011 44 223 325 959.) **ED** Halbert White, University of California, San Diego. available on magnetic tape (as AWPE Database); available on diskette (as AWPE Database); available on microfilm and microfiche from University Microfilms International (UMI); available on an online database from BRS.
Desc: Point of access for thousands of working papers in all areas of economics, finance and econometrics. A network of over 70 research centers worlwide provides full bibliographic information including author addresses, price and availability. Plus, the publication contains abstracts for current working papers. Each issue includes about 400 of the latest papers, all of which are indexed by author, issuing institution, and keyword/permuted title index.

ISSN 1061-5547
DD 004 US
TITLE CHANGE
ABUI NETWORK NEWS. (ABUI NETWORK NEWS; JOURNAL OF THE ASSOCIATION OF BANYAN USERS INTERNATIONAL.). [ABUI netw. news]. **Added/Corp** Association of Banyan Users International (U.S.). **VAT** Association of Banyan Users International Network News. Vol. 5, No. 1 (Jan./Feb. 1992)-(19??). Periodical. English. Association of Banyan Users

International, 401 North Michigan Avenue, Chicago IL 60611. **Tel** (312)644-6610. ***Continues** Network News (Sudbury, Mass.), 1057-2082.* ***Continued by** Enterprise Networking.*

ISSN 1073-2012
US

●ACCEPTABLE RISK. (1995)-. Periodical. English. Six times a year. $120.00 US; $360.00 Canada. Portfolio Publications, PO Box 220251, Chantilly VA 22022-0251.

ISSN 1195-0889
CN

●ACCESS MAGAZINE (VANCOUVER). (ACCESS MAGAZINE.). (1993)-. English. British Columbia Hydro Information Center, 970 Burrard Street, Vancouver BC V6Z 1Y3 Canada. **Tel** (604)663-2618. ***Formed by the union of** B.C. Hydro. People., 1181-9626; B.C. Hydro. Directions., 1181-9367 **and** B.C. Hydro. Issues., 1181-6430.*

ISSN 0044-5894
SP

UDC 331

ACCION EMPRESARIAL. [Accion empres.]. (1971)-. Periodical. Spanish. Four times a year. $15.10. Accion Social Empresarial, C Alfonso XI 4, 28014 Madrid Spain. **Tel** 011 34 1 5932758, FAX 011 34 1 5932821. **ED** Alfonso Sanchez. cum. index. **Circ:** 5,000. ***Continues** Informaciones Sociales (Madrid), 0443-0999.*

LC HB235.U6 C58 **ISSN** 1070-9169
DD 339.4/2/097305 US

ACCRA COST OF LIVING INDEX. (ACCRA COST OF LIVING INDEX / PRODUCED BY ACCRA.). [ACCRA cost living index]. **Added/Corp** American Chamber of Commerce Researchers Association. **VFOAT** American Chamber of Commerce Researchers Association Cost of Living Index; Cost of Living Index. Vol. 25, No. 3 (3rd Quarter 1992)-. Periodical. English. Irregular (4 issues). $120.00. ACCRA - American Chamber of Commerce Researchers Association, PO Box 6749, Louisville KY 40206. **Tel** (502)897-2890, FAX (502)894-9917. ***Continues** Cost of Living Index (American Chamber of Commerce Researchers Association), 1048-2830.*

LC QD81
DD 544 GW

ACCREDITATION AND QUALITY ASSURANCE. (19??)-. Academic Scholarly Publication. English. Six times a year. $172.00. Springer-Verlag GmbH & Company KG, Heidelberger Platz 3, D-14197 Berlin Germany. **Tel** 011 49 30 8207223, FAX 011 49 30 8214091, telex 183 319 SPBLN D. **(Subscription address:** Springer-Verlag New York Inc. / North America, PO Box 2485, Journal Fulfillment, Secaucus NJ 07096. **Tel** (201)348-4033, (800)777-4643, FAX (201)348-4505.**)**

ISSN 1060-3182
DD 388 US

ACKERMAN WAREHOUSING FORUM. [Ackerman warehous. forum]. **Added/Corp** Ackerman Co. **VFOAT** Warehousing Forum. Vol. 1, No. 1 (Dec. 1985)-. Periodical. English. Twelve times a year. $96.00. K B Ackerman Co., 1328 Dublin Road, Columbus OH 43215. **Tel** (614)488-3165. **ED** Kenneth B Ackerman. Index available (published separately). cum. index. **Circ:** 600.
Desc: Newsletter on the warehousing business.

ISSN 1062-6670
DD 331 US

ACME ... SURVEY OF U.S. KEY MANAGEMENT INFORMATION. [ACME surv. U.S. key manag. inf.]. **Added/Corp** ACME, Inc. Industry Insights, Inc. Council of Consulting Organizations, Inc. **VFOAT** Survey of U.S. Key Management Information; ACME ... United States Survey of Key Management Information; Survey of US Key Management Information; ACME ... Survey of US Key Management Information. (19??)-. English. One time a year. $498.00. Association of Consulting Management Engineers, 521 5th Avenue, 35th Floor, New York NY 10175. **Tel** (212)697-9693. ***Continues** ACME ... Survey of Key Management Information, 1050-4540.*

LC HC59.69 .A26 **ISSN** 1015-213X
DD 330.9172/4 LU

ACP BASIC STATISTICS. See Business and Economics-Abstracting, Bibliographies and Statistics.

LC KF1477.Z9 A273
DD 346.73/06626 347.3066626 US
TITLE CHANGE

ACQUISITIONS AND MERGERS IN A TROUBLED ENVIRONMENT. Added/Corp Practising Law Institute. (1991)-(199?). English. Practising Law Institute, 810 Seventh Avenue, New York NY 10019-5818. **Tel** (212)765-5700, FAX (212)581-4670 general correspondence, (212)265-4742 orders and billing inquiries. ***Continues** Acquisitions and Mergers, 0883-4407.* ***Continued by** Acquisitions, Mergers, Spin-offs, and Other Restructurings, 1070-907X.*

ISSN 1070-907X
DD 343 US

●ACQUISITIONS, MERGERS, SPIN-OFFS, AND OTHER RESTRUCTURINGS. [Acquis. mergers spin-offs other restruct.]. **Added/Corp** Practising Law Institute. (1993)-. English. $100.00. Practising Law Institute, 810 Seventh Avenue, New York NY 10019-5818. **Tel** (212)765-5700, FAX (212)581-4670 general correspondence, (212)265-4742 orders and billing inquiries. ***Continues** Acquisitions and Mergers in a Troubled Environment.*

LC HD2746.5 .A27
DD 338.8/3/05 UK

ACQUISITIONS MONTHLY. (Nov 1984)-. Periodical. English. Twelve times a year. $397.00. Tudor House Publications Ltd., 78 Mount Ephraim Tunbridge Wls, Kent TN4 8BS United Kingdom. **Tel** 011 44 1892 515454, FAX 011 44 1892 511547. **(Subscription address:** Acquisitions Monthly, PO Box 48429, Washington DC 20002. **) ED** Philip Healey. Index available (Free). **Ad Acc. Circ:** 5,000.
Ind/Abst Curr. Cit.; F&S Index Plus Text, Int. [Select. Cov.]; PROMT; Trade Ind. ASAP [Full Txt.]; Trade Ind. Index.

LC HC101 .C64 **ISSN** 0147-1554
DD 330.9/73/092 US
CODEN ACBODW

ACROSS THE BOARD. [Across board]. **Added/Corp** Conference Board. Vol. 13, No. 10 (Oct. 1976)-. Trade Publication. English. Ten times a year. $40.00. Conference Board, 845 Third Avenue, New York NY 10022. **Tel** (212)759-0900 ext. 582, (800)872-6273, FAX (212)980-7014. **ED** Howard Muson. **Bk Rev. Ad Acc. Circ:** 35,000. available on microfilm and microfiche from University Microfilms International (UMI); available on an online database (full text) from DIALOG. Documents available from UMI Article Clearinghouse, Documents on Demand. ***Continues** Conference Board Record, 0010-5546;* ***Absorbed** Focus, 0015-5039.*
Ind/Abst ABI/INFORM Glob. Ed.; ABI/INFORM Ondisc: Expr. Ed. (Jan. 1987-); ABI/INFORM [Computer File] (Sept. 1971-); Anbar Account. Finan. Abstr. [Full Txt.]; Anbar Mark. Distr. Abstr. [Full Txt.]; Anbar Top Manage. Abstr. [Full Txt.]; Bus. ASAP (1990-) [Full Txt.]; Bus. Index (1985-); Bus. Period. Index; Coal Abstr.; Contents Pages Manage.; Curr. Cit.; Curr. Thoughts Trends; Energy Inf. Abstr.; Environ. Abstr.; F&S Index Plus Text, Int. [Select. Cov.]; Gen. BusinessFile (1985-); Gen. Period. Index (1985-); Health Plan. Adminis.; Hosp. Health Admin. Index (Vol. 15, No. 3, 1978-Vol. 25, No. 12, 1988); INFO-SOUTH Abstr.; Mag. Search; Manage. Market. Abstr.; Manage. Bibliogr. Rev.; Manage. Contents; MasterFile FullTEXT (July 1993-); Middle East Abstr. Index; Oper. Prod. Manage. Abstr. [Full Txt.]; PAIS Int. Print; Person. Train. Abstr. [Full Txt.]; Person. Manage. Abstr.; Predicasts Forecasts; SportSearch; Trade Ind. ASAP [Full Txt.]; Trade Ind. Index [Full Txt.]; UMI ABI/Inform--Bus. Period. Ondisc (Jan. 1987-) [Full Txt.]; Urban Aff. Abstr.; Wilson Bus. Abstr.; Women Manage. Rev. [Full Txt.]; Work Relat. Abstr.

LC HB9.M28 A27 **ISSN** 0001-6373
DD 330.05/6 HU
CCC

Pr Rev.

ACTA OECONOMICA. (ACTA OECONOMICA : PERIODICAL OF THE HUNGARIAN ACADEMY OF SCIENCES.). [Acta oecon.]. **Added/Corp** Magyar Tudomanyos Akademia. Magyar Tudomanyos Akademia. Kozgazdasagtudomanyi Intezet. Vol. 1 (1966)-. Academic Scholarly Publication. Multiple languages (German, Russian, English and French; summaries and/or abstracts in English and Russian). Four times a year. $104.00. Akademiai Kiado, Publishing House of the Hungarian Academy of Sciences, Prielle Kornelia u. 19-35, H-1117 Budapest Hungary. **Tel** 011 36 1 1811991, FAX 011 36 1 1811991, telex 22-6228 AKNYO H. **ED** Tamas Foldi (editor's address: Acta Oeconomica, PO Box 262, H-1502 Budapest Hungary). Index available. cum. index. **Ad Acc.** available on an online database. Documents available from The Genuine Article.
Desc: Publishes articles mainly on Hungary's economic development, economic policy and on some issues of economic management system and planning, on economic reforms and on mathematics applied in economics.
Ind/Abst AGRICOLA; Contents Recent Econ. J.; Econ. Lit. Index; Int. Labour Doc.; J. Econ. Lit.; LABORDOC; Middle East Abstr. Index; PAIS Int. Print; Res. Alert [Full Cov.]; Soc. Sci. Cit. Index [Full Cov.].

LC HB3 .A17 **ISSN** 0208-6018
PL

ACTA UNIVERSITATIS LODZIENSIS. FOLIA OECONOMICA. Added/Corp Uniwersytet Lodzki. **VFOAT** Folia Oeconomica. (1980)-. Monographic series. Polish (summaries and/or abstracts in English). Irregular. Price varies per volume. Wydawnictwo Uniwersytetu Lodzkiego, Ul. Jaracza 34, Lodz Poland. **Tel** 011 48 42 331671, 011 48 42 336541. **(Subscription address:** Ars Polona-Ruch, PO Box 1001, Krakowskie Przedmiescie 7, 00-068 Warsaw Poland. **Tel** 011 48 22 261201.**)** ***Continues in part** Acta Universitatis Lodziensis. Seria III, Nauki Ekonomiczne i Socjologiczne, 0076-0374.*
Desc: Political economics, statistics and econometrics, accounting, marketing, foreign trade, etc.

LC S
DD 630 FR

ACTES ET COMMUNICATIONS. See Agriculture.

ISSN 1067-1714
DD 613 US

ACTION (INDIANAPOLIS, IND.). See Health.

LC HB
DD 330 MX

ACTIVIDAD ECONOMICA. Added/Corp Centro de Estudios Economicos del Sector Privado, A.C. No. 1 (Sept./Oct. 1965)-. Periodical. Spanish. Six times a year. Centro de Estudios Economicos del Sector Privado, A.C. Homero 527, 5o Piso Mexico City Mexico.
Ind/Abst PAIS Int. Print.

LC HC **ISSN** 0001-771X
DD 330 CN

ACTUALITE ECONOMIQUE. (L'ACTUALITE ECONOMIQUE.). [Actual. econ.]. **Added/Corp** Ecole des Hautes Etudes Commerciales (Montreal, Quebec) Societe Canadienne de Science Economique. (1925)-. Academic Scholarly Publication. French (English; summaries and/or abstracts in English). Four times a year (Mar., June, Sept., Dec.). 48.02Can$. Ecole des Hautes Etudes Commerciales, 5255 Decelles Avenue, Montreal Quebec H3T 1V6 Canada. **Tel** (514)340-6437, FAX (514)340-6469. **ED** Gilles Grenier. **Bk Rev. Circ:** 1,200 (ctrl). Documents available from BLDSC.
Desc: Covers economic theory, econometrics, public policy, and political economy.
Ind/Abst AGRICOLA; Am. Hist. Life (1963-1978); Can. Period. Index; Econ. Lit. Index; Int. Bibliogr. Sociol.; Int. Labour Doc.; J. Econ. Lit.; PAIS Int. Print; Repere (1983-).

LC HC
DD 330 FR

ACTUALITE / LE MENSUEL DE L'ACTUALITE ECONOMIQUE & SOCIALE. (19??)-. French. Eleven times a year (monthly except Aug.). 340.00F France; 435.00F other. Maisonneuve / A I E S, BP 341, 75830 Paris Cedex 17 France. **Tel** 011 33 1 40542020.
Ind/Abst Am. Hist. Life (1963-1978).

ISSN 0335-3400
RE

UDC 33

ACTUALITES ECONOMIQUES DE LA REUNION. [Actual. econ. Reunion]. (1973)-. Periodical. French. One time a week. 3800.00F France; 4080.00F other. Societe Generale de Presse et d'Editions, 13 Avenue de l'Opera, 75001 Paris France. **Tel** 011 33 1 40151789.

ISSN 1145-8704
FR

UDC 656.2 (44)
CEASED

ACTUALITES SOCIALES. (1952)-(19??). Periodical. French. La Vie du Rail, 11 rue de Milan, 75440 Paris Cedex 09 France. **Tel** 011 33 1 49701263.

ISSN 1195-7468
DD 051 CN

●ACUMEN (TORONTO). (ACUMEN.). [Acumen]. **VFOAT** Acumen, Global Insight. (Oct./Nov. 1993)-. Periodical. English. Six times a year. 24.01Can$. Synergism Marketing and Comm., 199 Avenue Road, 3rd Floor, Toronto ONT M5R 2J3 Canada. **Tel** (416)962-9184. ***Continues** The Inside Guide., 0838-6269.*

PH

ADB BUSINESS OPPORTUNITIES. (19??)-. English. Twelve times a year. $30.00. Asian Development Bank / Information Office, PO Box 789, 1099 Manila Philippines. **Tel** 011 63 2 8344444, 011 63 2 7113851, FAX 011 63 2 7417961, 011 63 2 6326816, telex 63587 ADB PN ETPI, 42205 ADB PM ITT, 29066 ADB PH RCA.

ISSN 0165-0726
NE

UDC 659.1

ADFORMATIE. [Adformatie]. (1973)-. Periodical. German. One time a week. $151.90. Samsom Bedrijfsinformatie BV, Postbus 4, 2400 MA Alphen Rij Netherlands. **Tel** 011 31 1720 66633. **(Subscription address:** Intermedia BV, Postbus 4, 2400 MA Alphen AD Rijn Netherlands. **Tel** 011 31 1720 66481.**)**
Ind/Abst Child. Lit. Abstr. (19??-).

US

ADMINISTRATIVE ASSISTANT ADVISOR. (19??)-. English. Irregular. $230.00. Progressive Business Publications, 370 Technology Drive, PO Box 3019, Malvern PA 19355. **Tel** (617)527-8600, (800)220-5000, FAX (617)647-8089.

Business and Economics

DD 330
ISSN 0886-778X
US
CEASED
ADVANCE (WASHINGTON, D.C. 1986). (ADVANCE : THE JOURNAL OF THE AFRICAN DEVELOPMENT FOUNDATION.). [Advance]. **Added/Corp** African Development Foundation. Vol. 1, No. 1 (1986/87)-(19??). Government Publication. English. Superintendent of Documents, US Government Printing Office, Washington DC 20402. **Tel** (202)275-3328, FAX (202)786-2377.

NE
ADVANCED STUDIES IN THEORETICAL AND APPLIED ECONOMETRICS. See Business and Economics-Abstracting, Bibliographies and Statistics.

LC HC
DD 330
ISSN 0169-5568
NE
ADVANCED TEXTBOOKS IN ECONOMICS. [Adv. textb. econ.]. Vol. 1 (1971)-. Monographic series. English. Irregular. Price varies per volume. Elsevier Science Publishers BV, PO Box 211, 1000 AE Amsterdam Netherlands. **Tel** 011 31 20 4853641, 011 31 20 4853642, FAX 011 31 20 4853598. **Ind/Abst** Math. Rev.; Zentralbl. Math. Ihre Grenzgeb.

LC HB172 .A38
DD 338.5/05
ISSN 0278-0984
US
CCC
ADVANCES IN APPLIED MICROECONOMICS. [Adv. appl. microecon.]. Vol. 1 (1981)-. Periodical. English. Irregular. $75.95. JAI Press Inc., 55 Old Post Road, Suite 7, PO Box 1678, Greenwich CT 06836-1678. **Tel** (203)661-7602, FAX (203)661-0792.

US
ADVANCES IN AUSTRIAN ECONOMICS. (19??)-. Periodical. English. $73.25. JAI Press Inc., 55 Old Post Road, Suite 2, PO Box 1678, Greenwich CT 06836-1678. **Tel** (203)661-7602, FAX (203)661-0792. **ED** Peter J. Boettke and Mario J. Rizzo.

LC HB1 .A45
DD 330/.05
ISSN 0890-0159
US
ADVANCES IN BEHAVIORAL ECONOMICS. [Adv. behav. econ.]. Vol. 1 (1987)-. English. Irregular. Price varies per volume. Ablex Publishing Corporation, 355 Chestnut Street, Norwood NJ 07648. **Tel** (201)767-8450, (201)767-8455 (Customer Service), FAX (201)767-6717. **ED** Leonard Green and John H. Kagel.

LC HB139 .A33
DD 330/.028
ISSN 0731-9053
US
ADVANCES IN ECONOMETRICS. [Adv. econom.]. Vol. 1 (1982)-. English. One time a year. $73.25. JAI Press Inc., 55 Old Post Road, Suite 2, PO Box 1678, Greenwich CT 06836-1678. **Tel** (203)661-7602, FAX (203)661-0792. **ED** George F. Rhodes Jr.

LC HB615 .A37
US
●**ADVANCES IN ENTREPRENEURSHIP, FIRM EMERGENCE, AND GROWTH.** Vol. 1 (1993)-. English. Irregular. $73.25 US; $74.25 other. JAI Press Inc., 55 Old Post Road, Suite 2, PO Box 1678, Greenwich CT 06836-1678. **Tel** (203)661-7602, FAX (203)661-0792. **ED** Jerome Katz. **Desc:** Provides an annual examination of the major current research, in the field of entrepreneurship and its related disciplines of small business, family business, population ecology, as well as firm growth and emergence research. The goal of the series is to provide a bridge between established and promising newer methods of research in entrepreneurship with the established disciplines of the administrative and social sciences.

LC HB615 .A38
DD 338/.04/05
ISSN 1048-4736
US
ADVANCES IN THE STUDY OF ENTREPRENEURSHIP, INNOVATION, AND ECONOMIC GROWTH. [Adv. study entrep. innov. econ. growth]. Vol. 1 (1986)-. English. One time a year. $73.25. JAI Press Inc., 55 Old Post Road, Suite 2, PO Box 1678, Greenwich CT 06836-1678. **Tel** (203)661-7602, FAX (203)661-0792. **ED** Gary Libecap.

LC HG4028.W65 A34
DD 658.1/5244/05
ISSN 1041-6749
US
Pr Rev.
ADVANCES IN WORKING CAPITAL MANAGEMENT. [Adv. work. cap. manage.]. Vol. 1 (1988)-. Monographic series. English. Irregular. $73.25. JAI Press Inc., 55 Old Post Road, Suite 2, PO Box 1678, Greenwich CT 06836-1678. **Tel** (203)661-7602, FAX (203)661-0792. **ED** Yong H. Kim and Venkat Srinivasan.

Desc: Promotes theoretical, empirical and applied research in the analysis, management and control of working capital.

CN
AFFAIRES 500, LES. (19??)-. French (English). (Included in subscription to Les Affaires). Publications Transcontinental Inc, 1100 Rene-Levesque, 24Fl boulevard West, Montreal Quebec H3B 4X9 Canada. **Tel** (514)392-9000, FAX (514)392-4724. **Ind/Abst** Can. Period. Index (19??-).

CN
AFFAIRES TRIMESTRIEL, LES. (19??)-. French (English). (Included in subscription to Les Affaires). Publications Transcontinental Inc, 1100 Rene-Levesque, 24Fl boulevard West, Montreal Quebec H3B 4X9 Canada. **Tel** (514)392-9000, FAX (514)392-4724. **Ind/Abst** Can. Period. Index (19??-); Repere.

LC HG46 .A35
DD 332/.096
ISSN 0950-902X
UK
AFRICA ANALYSIS. No. 1 (July 11, 1986)-. English. Twenty-five times a year. $595.00. Africa Analysis Ltd, Suite 71 Ludgate House, 107 111 Fleet Street, London EC41 2AB United Kingdom. **Tel** 011 44 171 3531117, FAX 011 44 171 3531516. available on an online database (file 771/Full-Text) from DIALOG. **Continues** Sampson Letter. **Desc:** African financial newsletter, providing analytical reports for the entire continent. Includes surveys of official and parallel currencies, oil, minerals and commodities update and regional/topical review/news analysis.

SA
AFRICA ENTERPRISE UPDATE. (19??)-. English. Twelve times a year. $10.00 US, Canada and Africa; $12.50 other. Africa Enterprise, PO Box 647, Pietermaritzburg, 3200 South Africa. **Tel** 0331 56321. **ED** R. Jarvis. **Circ:** 40,000 (ctrl).

DD 338
ISSN 1065-0180
US
AFRICAN-AMERICAN BUSINESS. [Afr.-Am. bus.]. **Added/Corp** African-American Business Association. **VFOAT** African American Business. Vol. 1, No. 1 (Sept. 1992)-. Periodical. English. Twelve times a year. $12.00. African-American Business Association, 9 Hawthorne Court NE, Washington DC 20011.

ISSN 1055-0127
US
AFRICAN ANVIL AND BUSINESS NEWS, THE. (1992)-. Trade Publication. English. One time a week. $1.00 (single issue). Bankole Enterprise, Inc., PO Box 28856, Providence RI 02908.

LC HC1005.A1 A35
DD 330.966/0097541
FR
AFRIQUE NOIRE POLITIQUE ET ECONOMIQUE, L'. (1977)-. French. One time a year. 1,190F. Ediafric la Documentation Africaine, 10 rue Vineuse, 75116 Paris France. **Tel** 011 33 1 44308100, FAX 011 33 1 45208174.

DD 381
ISSN 0892-1121
US
CCC
AFTERMARKET BUSINESS. [Aftermark. bus.]. Vol. 96, No. 7 (July 1, 1986)-. Trade Publication. English. Twelve times a year. $37.00. Advanstar Communications Inc., 131 West First Street, Duluth MN 55802. **Tel** (218)723-9477, (800)346-0085, FAX (218)723-9437. available on an online database (file 16,648/Full-Text) from DIALOG. **Continues** Home & Auto, 0162-8801. **Ind/Abst** Bus. Index (1986-); Bus. Source Plus; Bus. Source; EP Collect.; F&S Index Plus Text, Int. [Full Txt.] [Select. Cov.]; Gen. BusinessFile (1986-); Homework Help.; MasterFile FullTEXT 1000; MasterFile FullTEXT 350; MasterFile FullTEXT 650; MasterFile FullTEXT (Jan. 1995-); OCLC; PROMT [Full Txt.]; Telebase; Trade Ind. ASAP [Full Txt.]; Trade Ind. Index (July 1, 1986-) [Full Txt.].

LC HG31 .A35
SW
AGARNA OCH MAKTEN I SVERIGES BORSFORETAG. **VFOAT** Owners and Power in Sweden's Listed Companies. (1985)-. English (Swedish). One time a year. Dagens Nyheter, Box 138, 10515 Stockholm Sweden. **Tel** 011 87381725. **ED** Sven-Ivan Sundqvist.

DD 332
ISSN 1051-7332
US
AGENCY EXAMINER, THE. [Agency exam.]. (July 1989)-. Periodical. English. Twelve times a year. $159.00. Resource Management Services, 9915 Pioneer Blvd., Santa Fe CA 90670. **Tel** (310)801-4504, FAX (310)801-4509. **Desc:** For credit and collection and recovery professionals providing information regarding collection agency auditing, evaluating, monitoring and other collecting concepts.

US
CEASED
AGENCY NEWS. (19??)-(19??). Periodical. English. National Register Publishing Company Inc., PO Box 31, 121 Chanlon Road, New Providence NJ 07974. **Tel** (800)521-8110, (800)323-6772, FAX (908)665-6688. **ED** Beverly Miller.

IT
AGENZIA ECONOMICA FINANZIARIA. (19??)-. Italian. L300000. Agenzia Economica Finanziaria Zambelli, Piazza Della Rotonda 7, 00186 Rome Italy. **Tel** 011 39 6 6869830.

IT
AGENZIA OMNIA PRESS. (19??)-. Italian. Irregular (230 issues). L3000000 Italy; L2400000 others. Omnia Press Teleservice, Viale Majno 38, 20129 Milan Italy. **Tel** 011 39 2 2046935, FAX 011 39 2 784070.

IT
AGGIORNAMENTI CODICI A SCHEDA PEM. (19??)-. Italian. Four times a year. Ist Geografico de Agostini, Via Giovanni da Verrazano 15, 28100 Novara Italy. **Tel** 011 39 321 4712015.

ISSN 0002-1024
UK
AGRA EUROPE (BRITISH EDITION). See Agriculture-Agricultural Economics.

LC HD101 .A416
ISSN 0002-1121
GW
CCC
AGRARWIRTSCHAFT. See Agriculture-Agricultural Economics.

ISSN 0256-6303
SZ
AGRARWIRTSCHAFTLICHE STUDIEN. [Agrarwirtsch. Stud.]. **VFOAT** Etudes d'Economie Rurale. (19??)-. Periodical. German. **Ind/Abst** World Agric. Econ. Rural Sociol. Abstr.

ISSN 0311-0370
AT
AGRIBUSINESS DECISION. See Agriculture-Agricultural Economics.

LC HD1401 .A333
DD 338.1/05
ISSN 0742-4477
US
CCC
CODEN AGRBEY
AGRIBUSINESS (NEW YORK, N.Y.). See Agriculture.

LC HD
DD 338
ISSN 0899-1294
US
Pr Rev.
AGRIBUSINESS NEWS FOR KENTUCKY. See Agriculture.

LC HD1773.A2 N67a
DD 338.1/0974
ISSN 1068-2805
USUS
●**AGRICULTURAL AND RESOURCE ECONOMICS REVIEW.** See Agriculture-Agricultural Economics.

ISSN 0169-5150
NE
CCC
CODEN AGECE6
Pr Rev.
AGRICULTURAL ECONOMICS. See Agriculture-Agricultural Economics.

AT
AGRICULTURAL ECONOMICS DISCUSSION PAPER. See Agriculture-Agricultural Economics.

LC HD1407 .M5
DD 630
ISSN 0065-4442
US
AGRICULTURAL ECONOMICS REPORT (MICHIGAN STATE UNIVERSITY. DEPT. OF AGRICULTURAL ECONOMICS). See Agriculture-Agricultural Economics.

LC SB205.S7 N64
DD 630
ISSN 0549-8295
US
AGRICULTURAL ECONOMICS REPORT (NORTH DAKOTA AGRICULTURAL EXPERIMENT STATIONS (FARGO)). See Agriculture-Agricultural Economics.

US
Pr Rev.
AGRICULTURAL ECONOMICS RESEARCH REPORT (MISSISSIPPI AGRICULTURAL AND FORESTRY EXPERIMENT STATION). See Agriculture-Agricultural Economics.

Business and Economics

ISSN 0883-0088
DD 338 US
Pr Rev.
AGRICULTURAL ECONOMICS TECHNICAL PUBLICATION. See Agriculture-Agricultural Economics.

LC HD1751 .D46a
DD 338.1/0973 **ISSN** 0099-1066
CODEN AGOUD7 US
AGRICULTURAL OUTLOOK (WASHINGTON, D.C. : 1975). See Agriculture-Agricultural Economics.

ISSN 0188-3070
DD 630 MX
Pr Rev.
AGROCIENCIA. SERIE SOCIOECONOMIA. [Agrocienc., Ser. socioecon.]. (1990)-. Periodical. Spanish. Three times a year. $25.00. Colegio de Postgraduados, Gen Lazardo Cardenas 24 La Paz, 56170 Texcoco Mexico. **Tel** 011 52 595 47011. **Continues** Agrociencia (Montecillo, Edo. Mex.), 0185-0288.

ISSN 0870-287X
UDC 66 PO
AIP INFORMACAO. (1975)-. Periodical. Portuguese. Twelve times a year. $40.00. Associacao Industrial Portuguesa, Apartado 3200, Praca das Industrias, 1304 Lisbon Codex Portugal. **Tel** 011 3620100, 011 3639047.

LC HE9761 **ISSN** 1072-1797
DD 387 US
●**AIRPORT BUSINESS.** (AIRPORT BUSINESS : INFORMATION FOR MANAGERS OF AIRPORTS & AIRPORT-BASED BUSINESSES.). [Airpt. bus.]. Vol. 7, No. 9 (Sept./Oct. 1993)-. Trade Publication. English. Nine times a year. $40.00. Johnson Hill Press Inc., (A Division of PTN Publishing Co.), 1233 Janesville Avenue, PO Box 803, Fort Atkinson WI 53538-0803. **Tel** (414)563-6388, FAX (414)563-1704. **ED** John F. Infanger. **Ad Acc.** Full Page (B&W) $4415.00. Full Page (Color) $5340.00 (4-color). **Circ**: 18,756. **Formed by the union of** FBO, 0893-3081 **and** Airport Services, 1041-4231.
Desc: Serves businesses involved in airport operations, airport-based businesses, major/regional/commuter airlines, consultants, contract service providers and aviation management schools. Includes coverage of business management, financing and funding, regulations, community relations, marketing operations, maintenance, security, fuel and ground services.

LC HC411 .A574
DD 330 JA
AJIA NO KEIKI DOKO SHISU. **Added/Corp** Ajia Keizai Kenkyujo (Japan). Tokei Chosabu. (19??)-. Japanese. Four times a year. Ajia Keizai Kenkyujo, 42 Ichigaya Honmura-cho, Shinjuku-ku Tokyo 162 Japan.

LC D880 .A39 **ISSN** 0389-0007
JA
AJIKEN NYUSU. **Added/Corp** Ajia Keizai Kenkyujo (Japan). (19??)-. Periodical. Japanese. Twelve times a year. ¥2000. Ajia Keizai Kenkyujo, 42 Ichigaya Honmura-cho, Shinjuku-ku Tokyo 162 Japan.

LC HC407.A1 A38
DD 330/338.9497 CI
AKTUALNI PROBLEMI PRIVREDNIH KRETANJA I EKONOMSKE POLITIKE HRVATSKE. **Added/Corp** Ekonomski Institut Zagreb. (199?)-. Periodical. Serbo-Croatian (Roman). **Continues** Aktuelni Problemi Privrednih Kretanja i Ekonomske Politike Jugoslavije.

LC HC407.A1 A38
DD 330/338.9497 CI
TITLE CHANGE
AKTUELNI PROBLEMI PRIVREDNIH KRETANJA I EKONOMSKE POLITIKE JUGOSLAVIJE. **Added/Corp** Savez Ekonomista Jugoslavije. Ekonomski Institut Zagreb. Univerzitet u Beogradu. Naucno-Istrazivacki Centar. Institut za Spoljnu Trgovinu (Belgrade, Serbia). **VFOAT** Problemi Provodjenja Drustveno-Ekonomske Reforme; Aktuelni Problemi Ekonomske Politike i Privrednog Sistema Jugoslavije; Aktuelni Problemi Privrednog Razvoja i Privrednog Sistema Jugoslavije; Aktuelni Problemi Ekonomske Politike i Privrednih Kretanja Jugoslavije; Aktuelni Problemi Privrednih Kretanja Jugoslavije; Crvena Knjiga. (1968)-(199?). Periodical. Serbo-Croatian (Roman). cum. index. **Continued by** Aktulni Problemi Privrednih Kretanja i Ekonomske Politike Hrvatske.

LC HD4343 .D34
TS
AL-DALIL AL-HADITH LIL-HAYAT WA-AL-MUASSASAT WA-AL-SHARIKAT. **Added/Corp** Markaz al-Qahirah al-Thaqafi. (19??)-. Arabic. Markaz al-Qahirah al-Thaqafi, PO Box 2216, Al-Qahirah United Arab Republic.

KU
AL-KJHALI AL-IQTISADI. **VFOAT** Alkhaleej Business Magazine. (19??)-. Periodical. Arabic. Twelve times a year. $75.00. Muassasat Al-Khaly Al-Iqtisadi, Lebanon. **Tel** 811103, telex 20680 JOEINTLE. **ED** Zulficar Kobeissi. **Bk Rev** **Circ**: 29,000.
Desc: Politics and business of the gulf, Middle East and the Arab World in general.

LC HC107.A4 A67 **ISSN** 1055-4645
DD 330.9761/005 US
ALABAMA BUSINESS & ECONOMIC INDICATORS. [Ala. bus. econ. indic.]. **Added/Corp** University of Alabama. Center for Business and Economic Research. **VFOAT** Alabama Business and Economic Indicators; Business & Economic Indicators; Business and Economic Indicators; Alabama Business. Vol. 59, No. 3 (Mar. 1990)-. Periodical. English. Twelve times a year. Free. Center for Business & Economic Research, PO Box 870221, University of Alabama, Tuscaloosa AL 35487. **Tel** (205)348-6191, FAX (205)248-2951. **Continues** Alabama Business, 0002-4163.
Ind/Abst Stat. Ref. Index.

ISSN 1235-1970
CODEN AARAEN FI
ALARA. **Added/Corp** Sateilyturvakeskus (Finland). (1992)-. Periodical. Finnish (summaries and/or abstracts in English). Four times a year. Valtion Painatuskeskus, PO Box 516, SF 00101 Helsinki Finland. **Tel** 011 358 0 5660266, FAX 011 358 0 5660374.

LC WMLC 93/98 **ISSN** 8756-4092
DD 330 US
ALASKA BUSINESS MONTHLY. [Alsk. bus. mon.]. Vol. 1, No. 1 (Jan. 1985)-. Periodical. English. Twelve times a year. $21.95. Alaska Business Monthly, PO Box 24-1288, Anchorage AK 99524-1288. **Tel** (907)276-4373, FAX (907)279-2900. **ED** Judith F Griffin. cum. index. **Ad Acc. Circ**: 10,000 (ctrl). available on microfilm and microfiche from University Microfilms International (UMI); available on an online database from Mead Data Central; and (files 635,648/Full-Text) DIALOG. Documents available from UMI Article Clearinghouse.
Desc: Objective analysis of issues and trends of Alaskan business climate. Focus on individuals and companies in Alaska.
Ind/Abst Acad. Search; Bus. Dateline (Jan. 1986-) [Full Txt.]; Bus. Index (1985-); Bus. Source Plus; Bus. Source; EP Collect.; Gen. BusinessFile (1985-); Gen. Period. Index (1985-); Homework Help.; INFO-SOUTH Abstr.; Mag. Search; MasterFile FullTEXT 1000; MasterFile FullTEXT 350; MasterFile FullTEXT 650; MasterFile FullTEXT (July 1993-); OCLC; Telebase; Trade Ind. ASAP [Full Txt.]; Trade Ind. Index [Full Txt.].

LC HC
US
ALASKA ECONOMIC REPORT, THE. **Added/Corp** Alaska Information Service. (April 18, 1975)-. Periodical. English. Twenty-two times a year. $245.00. Alaska Information & Research Service, 3037 South Circle, Anchorage AK 99507. **Tel** (907)349-7711. **ED** Mike Bradley. **Circ**: 650 (ctrl).
Desc: Alaska public and resource policy.

LC HC107.A45 A458a
DD 330.9/798/05 US
ALASKAN ECONOMY, THE. **Added/Corp** Alaska. Division of Economic Enterprise. Alaska. Economic Analysis Section. Alaska. Divison of Business Development. **VFOAT** Alaska Economy; Alaska Economy Year-End Performance Report. Vol. 4, No. 1 (1975)-. English. Every 2 years. Alaska Department of Commerce and Economic Development, PO Box D, Juneau AK 99811. **Tel** (907)465-2521, FAX (907)463-3841. **Continues** Performance Report of the Alaskan Economy.

LC HF3221 **ISSN** 0827-2603
DD 380.1/097123 CN
CODEN ALBBEN
ALBERTA BUSINESS (CALGARY). (ALBERTA BUSINESS.). [Alta. bus.]. Vol. 1, No. 1 (Mar./Apr. 1984)-. Trade Publication. English. Six times a year (six issues per year). 8.79Can$. Sunrise Publication Ltd., 2207 Hanselman Court, Saskatoon Sask S7L 6A8 Canada. **Tel** (306)244-5668, FAX (305)653-4515. **ED** Pat Rediger. **Ad Acc, Adv Mgr:** Twila Reddekopp. Full Page (Color) 2345.00Can$. **Pub. Size:** Standard. **Circ**: 10,901 (ctrl). available on microfiche from University Microfilms International (UMI); available in microform from Micromedia Limited; available on an online database from INFO ACCESS. Documents available from UMI Article Clearinghouse.
Desc: Devoted to regional business. Reports on trends, developments and economic news from around the province. Profiles companies, individuals and organizations.
Ind/Abst Bus. Dateline (Jan. 1985-) [Full Txt.]; Bus. Index (1985-); Can. Index; Can. Period. Index (19??-); Gen. BusinessFile (1985-); Gen. Period. Index (1985-); INFO-SOUTH Abstr.; Mag. Search; PROMT; Trade Ind. ASAP [Full Txt.]; Trade Ind. Index [Full Txt.].

US
ALERT. (19??)-. Newsletter. English. One time a week. $350.00. National Institute of Business Management, Inc., 1101 King Street, Alexandria VA 22133. **Tel** (800)543-2052, (703)548-3885, (800)543-2049, FAX (703)549-0182. ctrl circ.
Desc: Covers current issues of interest to those in the business world.

ISSN 0747-7813
DD 330 US
ALEXANDER PARIS REPORT, THE. [Alexander Paris rep.]. Vol. 1, No. 1 (Sept. 1984)-. Periodical. English. Twelve times a year. $195.00. The Alexander Paris Report, Editorial Office, 18-1 East Dundee Road, Suite 110, Barrington IL 60010. **Tel** (800)233-6205, (708)382-7788, FAX (708)382-7390. **(Subscription address:** Alexander Paris Report, Subscription Office, PO Box 11318, Birmingham AL 35202-1318. **Tel** (800)633-4931, (205)995-1567 (outside US and Canada), FAX (205)995-1588.) **ED** Alexander Paris. **Bk Rev. Circ**: 40,000.
Desc: Concise conclusions on the economy and business cycle trends-inflation, interest rates, stocks, and commodities. The latest changes from Washington, taxes, legislation and specific recommendations.

ISSN 1046-5480
DD 330 US
ALL ABOUT BUSINESS IN HAWAII. [All bus. Hawaii]. 1st Ed. (1972)-. English. $3.95. Crossroads Press Inc., PO Box 833, Honolulu HI 96808. **Tel** (808)521-0021, FAX (808)591-2321.
Ind/Abst PROMT.

LC HF5035 .A38 **ISSN** 1049-8257
DD 338.7/4/02573 US
ALL-IN-ONE BUSINESS CONTACTBOOK. [All-in-one bus. contactb.]. **VFOAT** ABC. (1990)-. English. Irregular. $52.95. Gale Research Inc., 835 Penobscot Building, 645 Griswold Street, Detroit MI 48226. **Tel** (800)877-GALE, (313)961-2242, FAX (313)961-6083, (800)414-5043, telex TWX 810-221-7086. **ED** Karen Hill.
Desc: Information on contacting firms within a particular industry or geographic area. Direct dial phone numbers are offered for most companies, including main office, toll-free, fax, telex, cable, special recordings and consumer information and/or hotlines.

US
ALLEGHENY BUSINESS NEWS. (19??)-. English. Twelve times a year. $12.00. Associated Business Publishing, 471 Lincoln Avenue, Suite 300, Pittsburgh PA 15202. **Tel** (412)734-2300. available on an online database (file 635/Full-Text) from DIALOG. Documents available from UMI Article Clearinghouse.
Ind/Abst Bus. Dateline (Dec. 1990-) [Full Txt.].

ISSN 1359-4621
NE
●**ALLIANCE CORPORATE CITIZENSHIP.** (1996)-. English. Four times a year. $87.00. Kluwer Law International / Netherlands, PO Box 85889, 2508 CN The Hague Netherlands. **Tel** 011 31 70 3081500, FAX 011 31 70 3081515.

LC HC **ISSN** 0734-2837
DD 330 US
ALLIANCE (NORWOOD, N.J.). (ALLIANCE.). **Added/Corp** National Alliance of Homebased Businesswomen (U.S.). (19??)-. Periodical. English. Six times a year. National Alliance Homebased Businesswomen, PO Box 306, Midland Park NJ 07432.

LC HF5681.R25 A45 **ISSN** 0747-9107
DD 338.7/4/0973 US
ALMANAC OF BUSINESS AND INDUSTRIAL FINANCIAL RATIOS. [Alm. bus. ind. financ. ratios]. (19??)-. English. One time a year. $89.95. Prentice-Hall / College & Adult Education, PO Box 11074, Des Moines IA 50336. **Tel** (800)947-7700. **ED** Leo Troy.
Desc: Provides comparative financial data on more than 3.6 million U.S. corporations in 181 fields of business and industry and ranks small, medium and large companies by 22 key financial factors.

FR
ALTERNATIVES ECONOMIQUES. (19??)-. Periodical. French. Twelve times a year. $48.12. Alternatives Economiques, 12 rue de Chaignot, 21000 Dijon France. **Tel** 011 33 1 80309776, FAX 011 33 1 80300878.

ISSN 0247-3739
FR

UDC 336
Pr Rev.
ALTERNATIVES ECONOMIQUES DIJON. [Altern. econ.Dijon]. **VFOAT** Alter Eco (Dijon). (1980)-. Periodical. French. Ten times a year (monthly except Aug. and Sep.). $48.12. Alternatives Economiques, 12 rue de Chaignot, 21000 Dijon France. **Tel** 011 33 1 80309776, FAX 011 33 1 80300878. **Bk Rev. Ad Acc. Circ:** 46,000 (ctrl). ***Continues*** *L'Economie en Questions (Paris), 0221-1300.*
Ind/Abst LABORDOC; PAIS Int. Print.

AG
AMBITO FINANCIERO. **VFOAT** Diario Ambito Financiero. (19??)-. Newspaper. Spanish. Seven times a week. $400.00 US and Canada; $480.00 Europe; $570.00 other. Editorial Amfin SA, Paseo Colon 1196, CP 1063, Buenos Aires Argentina. **Tel** 349 1500, FAX 349 1509. **Ad Acc, Adv Mgr:** Eduardo Ribas Somar. **Circ:** 120,000. available on microfilm; available on diskette.
Desc: Political/financial/business newspaper. Printed in Buenos Aires and in three other cities through satellite links.
Ind/Abst PROMT.

ISSN 1071-9105
DD 338 US
•AMERICA, BUSINESS TODAY. [Am., bus. today]. **VFOAT** America. (Mar./Apr. 1993)-. Periodical. English. Twelve times a year. $32.00. Link Frame Publishing International, 9524 Kearny Villa Road, Suite 117, San Diego CA 92126. **Tel** (619)566-9664.

LC HF5036.A47 A53 ISSN 0364-0833
DD 381/.025/73 US
AMERICAN BLACK DIRECTORY. **See** Industry and Production-Trade and Industrial Directories.

ISSN 0363-566X
US
AMERICAN BUSINESS. [Am. bus.]. Vol. 1 (Nov. 1976)-. Periodical. English. Four times a year. American Business / Avant-Garde Media, 1775 Broadway, New York NY 10019. **Tel** (212)581-2000. available on microfilm from University Microfilms International (UMI).
Ind/Abst Pop. Mag. Rev. (1984-).

US
AMERICAN BUSINESS CLIMATE AND ECONOMIC PROFILES. (Nov. 1993)-. English. One time a year. $129.00. Gale Research Inc., 835 Penobscot Building, 645 Griswold Street, Detroit MI 48226. **Tel** (800)877-GALE, (313)961-2242, FAX (313)961-6083, (800)414-5043, telex TWX 810-221-7086.
Desc: Allows readers to explore the business environments of more than 300 of the nation's biggest markets.

LC HF5035 ISSN 1062-5119
DD 338 US
AMERICAN BUSINESS DISK, THE. (THE AMERICAN BUSINESS DISK [COMPUTER FILE].). **Added/Corp** American Business Information, Inc. (19??)-. English. One time a year. $2515.00. American Business Information, 5711 South 86th Circle, PO Box 27347, Omaha NE 68127.
Desc: System requirements: IBM PC, AT or compatible 286 based machine or PS/2 Model 50, 60, 70, or 80. 640K RAM, MS-DOS or PC-DOS 3.0 or higher, fixed hard disk with minimum 1MB storage, CD-ROM drive and extensions.

LC HF3503 .A47 ISSN 0140-5799
DD 338.8/8973/042025 UK
AMERICAN BUSINESS IN BRITAIN. **Added/Corp** Clifton Data Research Services. (1977)-. Periodical. English. American Business in Britain, 21 Culver Road, St. Albans Hertfordshire United Kingdom.

LC HD9999.C27 A43 ISSN 0095-1811
DD 338.4/7/629287 US
CCC
AMERICAN CLEAN CAR. [Am. clean car]. (19??)-. Periodical. English. Six times a year. $33.00. Crain Associates Enterprises Inc, 500 North Dearborn Street, Chicago IL 60610. **Tel** (312)337-7700. **ED** Ren Rooney. **Ad Acc. Circ:** 18,000. available on microfilm from University Microfilms International (UMI).
Desc: Our magazine is devoted to the car wash operators in the U.S. and Canada: case histories and management features.

LC HD6983 .A67 ISSN 1071-099X
DD 339.4/2/097305 US
•AMERICAN COST OF LIVING SURVEY. [Am. cost living sur.]. **Added/Corp** Gale Research Inc. 1st Ed. (1993)-. Periodical. English. Every 2 years. $99.00. Gale Research Inc., 835 Penobscot Building, 645 Griswold Street, Detroit MI 48226. **Tel** (800)877-GALE, (313)961-2242, FAX (313)961-6083, (800)414-5043, telex TWX 810-221-7086. **ED** Arsen J. Darnay.
Desc: Collects cost and expense data covering approximately 350 American cities and Metropolitan Statistical Areas.

LC HB1 .E26 ISSN 0002-8282
DD 330.973/09 US
Pr Rev.
AMERICAN ECONOMIC REVIEW, THE. [Am. econ. rev.]. **Added/Corp** American Economic Association. American Economic Association. Bulletin. American Economic Association. Hand Book. American Economic Association. Papers and proceedings. Vol. 1 (March 1911)-. Periodical. English. Five times a year (March, May, June, Sep., Dec.). $130.00. American Economic Association / Tennessee, 2014 Broadway, Suite 305, Nashville TN 37203-2418. **Tel** (615)322-2595, FAX (615)343-7590. Index available (bound in Dec. issue). cum. index. available on microfilm and microfiche from University Microfilms International (UMI). Documents available from The Genuine Article, UMI Article Clearinghouse, Documents on Demand. ***Formed by the union of*** *Economic Bulletin / American Economic Association* ***and*** *American Economic Association Quarterly.*
Desc: The publication includes an annual list of doctoral dissertations in political economy that are currently being pursued by students in the universities and colleges of America.
Ind/Abst ABI/INFORM Glob. Ed.; ABI/INFORM Ondisc: Expr. Ed. (March 1987-); ABI/INFORM [Computer File] (Sept. 1971-); Acad. Abstr.; Acad. Ind. [Computer File] (1985-); Acad. Search; AGRICOLA [Select. Cov.]; Am. Hist. Life (1954-1981,1983-); Am. Bibliogr. Slavic East Europ. Stud.; Arts Humanit. Citation Index [Select. Cov.]; Bus. Index (1985-); Bus. Period. Index; Bus. Source Plus; Bus. Source; Contents Recent Econ. J.; Contents Pages Manage.; Curr. Cit.; Curr. Contents Soc. Behav. Sci.; Curr. Lit. Sci. Sci.; Econ. Lit. Index; Energy Res. Abstr. (1976-); Environ. Abstr.; EP Collect.; Expand. Acad. Index (1985-); Gen. BusinessFile (1985-); Gen. Period. Index (1985-); Geogr. Abstr. Human Geogr.; Geol. Abstr.; Health Plan. Adminis.; Health Serv. Abstr.; Homework Help.; Hum. Resour. Abstr. (?-?); Index Period. Artic. Relat. Law; INFO-SOUTH Abstr.; Int. Bibliogr. Sociol.; Int. Dev. Abstr.; J. Econ. Lit.; J. Plan. Lit.; LABORDOC; Leis., Rec., Tour. Abstr.; Mag. Index Plus (1989-); Mag. Search; Manage. Market. Abstr.; MasterFile FullTEXT 1000; MasterFile FullTEXT 350; MasterFile FullTEXT 650; MasterFile FullTEXT (July 1990-); Middle East Abstr. Index; Newsp. Period. Abstr. (1986-); OCLC; Oper. Res./Manage. Sci.; PAIS Int. Print (1991-); Popul. Index; Pub. Lib. FullTEXT; Qual. Control Appl. Stat.; Res. Alert [Full Cov.]; Risk Abstr.; Rural Dev. Abstr.; Sage Race Relat. Abstr.; Selec. Coop. Index Manage. Period.; Soc. Sci. Source; Soc. Sci. Cit. Index [Full Cov.]; Soc. Sci. Index; Soc. Sci. Index Fulltext (Sept. 1988-) [Full Txt.]; Stat. Theory Method Abstr. (1959-1963); Telebase; Mag. Index (1977-); UMI ABI/Inform--Bus. Period. Ondisc (Mar. 1987-) [Full Txt.]; Wilson Bus. Abstr.; Women Stud. Abstr.; Work Relat. Abstr.; World Agric. Econ. Rural Sociol. Abstr.

LC HB1 .A53 ISSN 0569-4345
DD 330/.05 US
AMERICAN ECONOMIST (NEW YORK, N.Y. 1960), THE. (THE AMERICAN ECONOMIST.). [Am. econ.]. **Added/Corp** Omicron Chi Epsilon. Omicron Delta Epsilon. Vol. 4 (May 1960)-. Periodical. English. Two times a year. $35.00. Omicron Delta Epsilon, PO Drawer A S, University of Alabama, Tuscaloosa AL 35486. **Tel** (205)758-9947. **ED** Michael Szenberg. **Bk Rev. Circ:** 6,000 (ctrl). available on microfilm and microfiche from University Microfilms International (UMI). Documents available from UMI Article Clearinghouse. ***Continues*** *Omicron Chi Epsilon Journal.*
Desc: Journal of Omicron Delta Epsilon. Outlet for essays and papers by students. To acquaint young economists with current developments in pure and applied economics.
Ind/Abst ABI/INFORM Glob. Ed. (Spring 1981-); ABI/INFORM Ondisc: Expr. Ed. (Spring 1987-); ABI/INFORM [Computer File] (Spring 1981-); Acad. Abstr.; Acad. Search; Bus. ASAP (1992-) [Full Txt.]; Bus. Index (1988-); Bus. Period. Index; Bus. Source Plus; Bus. Source; Curr. Cit.; Econ. Lit. Index; EP Collect.; Gen. BusinessFile (1988-); Gen. Period. Index (1988-); Homework Help.; INFO-SOUTH Abstr.; J. Econ. Lit.; Mag. Search; Manage. Contents (1974-); MasterFile FullTEXT 1000; MasterFile FullTEXT 350; MasterFile FullTEXT 650; MasterFile FullTEXT (July 1990-) [Full Txt.]; Newsp. Period. Abstr. (1988-); OCLC; Public Aff. Inf. Serv. Bull.; Pub. Lib. FullTEXT; Soc. Sci. Source; Telebase; UMI ABI/Inform--Bus. Period. Ondisc (Fall 1987-) [Full Txt.]; Wilson Bus. Abstr.; Work Relat. Abstr.

LC D839 .A383 ISSN 1047-3572
DD 909.82 US
AMERICAN ENTERPRISE (WASHINGTON, D.C.), THE. (THE AMERICAN ENTERPRISE.). [Am. enterp.]. **Added/Corp** American Enterprise Institute for Public Policy Research. Vol. 1, No. 1 (Jan./Feb. 1990)-. Periodical. English. Six times a year. $29.00. American Enterprise Institute, 1150 17th Street Northwest, Department 260, Washington DC 20036. **Tel** (202)862-5800, (800)269-6267. **(Subscription address:** American Enterprise Institute, PO Box 6827, Syracuse NY 20036. **)** **ED** Karlyn H. Keene. Index available. **Ad Acc, Adv Mgr:** Ashley Cooper, **Tel** (202)862-5870. **Circ:** 15,000 (ctrl). available on microfilm and microfiche from University Microfilms International (UMI). Documents available from UMI Article Clearinghouse. ***Formed by the union of*** *American Enterprise Institute for Public Policy Research. AEI Economist, 0149-9785* ***and*** *Public Opinion, 0149-9157 Regulation.*
Desc: Focuses on major domestic and international issues from the perspectives of international and US news makers. Within its pages, economists, legal scholars, political scientists and foreign policy experts explore the ideas that have shaped America and the issues and controversies facing the country in the 1990s. Each issue contains the "Public Opinion Report" section, a comprehensive examination of current public opinion. Examines public policy and provides in-depth analysis into the issues of economics, regulation, politics, foreign policy, and cultural trends. The magazine is devoted to free enterprise and limited government and its contributors include reknown journalists and academics.
Ind/Abst ABC POL SCI; Acad. Search; Bus. Source Plus; EP Collect.; Expand. Acad. Index (1990-); Homework Help.; INFO-SOUTH Abstr.; Mag. Search; MasterFile FullTEXT 1000; MasterFile FullTEXT 350; MasterFile FullTEXT 650; MasterFile FullTEXT (July 1993-); Newsp. Period. Abstr. (1990-); OCLC; Sage Public Adm. Abstr.; Soc. Sci. Source; Soc. Sci. Index; Soc. Sci. Index Fulltext (March 1990-) [Full Txt.]; Stat. Ref. Index; Telebase.

US
AMERICAN ENTREPRENEUR. (19??)-. English. Irregular. $24.50 Comes with American Entrepreneur Association membership. American Entrepreneur, 2311 Pontius Avenue, Los Angeles CA 90064. **Tel** (213)477-2996.

LC E838 .A52
US
•AMERICAN FORECASTER ALMANAC. (1994)-. English. One time a year. $14.95. Reference Press Inc., 6448 Highway 290 East, Suite E-104, Austin TX 78723-9828. **Tel** (800)486-8666, (512)454-7778, FAX (512)454-9401.

LC S560 .J6 ISSN 0002-9092
DD 338.1/05 US
CODEN AJAEBA
Pr Rev.
AMERICAN JOURNAL OF AGRICULTURAL ECONOMICS. **See** Agriculture-Agricultural Economics.

ISSN 0886-9707
DD 338 US
AMERICAN MOVER. [Am. mover]. **Added/Corp** American Movers Conference. Vol. 41, No. 1 (Jan. 1986)-. Periodical. English. Twelve times a year. $40.00. American Movers Conference, 1611 Duke Street, Alexandria VA 22314. **Tel** (703)683-7410, FAX (703)684-5720. **ED** Leslie L. Frank. **Circ:** 2,250. ***Continues*** *Movers Journal.*
Desc: Covers all facets of business that pertains to the moving industry.

LC PN1993.5.U6 A877 ISSN 0279-0041
DD 384/.8/0973 US
AMERICAN PREMIERE. **See** Motion Picture.

LC HG4057 .A146 ISSN 0740-4018
DD 338.7/4/02573 US
NLM HG 4057; A5122
AMERICA'S CORPORATE FAMILIES AND INTERNATIONAL AFFILIATES. [Am. corp. fam. int. affil.]. **Added/Corp** Dun's Marketing Services. (1983)-. English. One time a year (May). $495.00. Dun & Bradstreet Information Services, 3 Sylvan Way, Parsippany NJ 07054. **Tel** (201)605-6000, (800)526-0651.

ISSN 0883-7953
DD 332 US
CEASED
AMERICA'S FASTEST GROWING COMPANIES (1985). (AMERICAN'S FASTEST GROWING COMPANIES.). Vol. 27, No. 4 (Apr. 1985)-(Feb. 1994). Periodical. English. Financial Data Systems, 38 East 29th Street, New York NY 10016. **Tel** (212)689-2777, FAX (212)689-6663. **ED** Jonathan Steinberg. ***Continues*** *Johnson Survey, 0732-9466.*
Desc: Gives upcoming features on new companies with superior growth. Includes balance model portfolio, performance and other stocks.

LC HG4915 .A64 ISSN 1057-5642
DD 338.7/4/097305 US
AMERICA'S FINEST COMPANIES. [Am. finest co.]. (1991)-. English. One time a year. $17.95. Financial Training Group, 300 East Boulevard, B-4, Charlotte NC 28203. **Tel** (704)335-0276.

LC HF5068.A5 A52 ISSN 0742-7298
DD 338/.0025/79496 US
ANAHEIM ... BUSINESS AND INDUSTRIAL DIRECTORY. **VFOAT** Business and Industrial Directory; Anaheim Chamber of Commerce Business and Industrial Directory. Directory. English. One time a year. $10.00 member, $20.00 nonmember. Anaheim Chamber of Commerce, 100 South Anaheim Boulevard, #300, Anaheim CA 92805-3859.

Business and Economics

LC HB9 .U59a
RM

ANALELE UNIVERSITATII DIN CRAIOVA. SERIA: STIINTE ECONOMICE SI GEOGRAFIE. **Main/Corp** Universitatea Din Craiova. **VFOAT** Stiinte Economice si Geografie; Annales de l'Universite de Craiova. Seria: Stiinte Economice si Geografie; Annals of the University of Craiova. Seria: Stiinte Economice si Geografie; Annals of University of Cariova. Seria: Stiinte si Geografie; Stiinte Economice. No. 7 (1976)-. Romanian (summaries and/or abstracts in French, English, German, Italian and Spanish). One time a year. Annals of the University of Craiova, Al I Cuza Street Number 13, Craiova Romania. **Continues** Universitatea din Craiova. Analele Universitatii din Craiova: Stiinte Economice si Sociale.

ISSN 1221-4523
RM

ANALELE UNIVERSITATII DIN GALATI. FASCICULA I: MANAGEMENT, ECONOMIE SI STIINTE SOCIO-UMANE. (19??)-. Directory. English (French). One time a year. Varies. Universitatea "Dunarea de Jos" Redactia Analelor, Str. Domneasca Nr. 47, 6200 Galati Romania. **ED** Mihai Jascanu. **Ad Acc**. Documents available from BLDSC. **Continues** Buletinul Universitatii din Galati. Fascicula I, Stiinte Sociale si Umaniste.
Desc: Scientific papers written by the teachers of the University, as well as teachers or scientists abroad.

LC HC
DD 330
ISSN 0399-1245
FR

ANALYSES DE LA S.E.D.E.I.S. See Social Sciences.

ISSN 1130-4413
SP
UDC 33(468.1)

ANDALUCIA ECONOMICA. [Andal. econ.]. (1990)-. Periodical. Spanish. Twelve times a year. $41.52. Andalucia Economica, Republica Argentina 26 Bis, 41011 Seville Spain. **Tel** 011 34 95 42813624283909. Index available. **Bk Rev**. **Ad Acc**, **Adv Mgr:** Rosa Mafner, **Tel** 95-446-1775. **Circ:** 15,000 (ctrl).

LC HB
DD 338
ISSN 1067-7976
US

●**ANGOLA (SYRACUSE, N.Y.).** (ANGOLA : AN EXECUTIVE REPORT.). [Angola]. **Added/Corp** Political Risk Services (IBC USA (Publicaitons) Inc.). (1993)-. English. $110.00. Political Risk Services, 6320 Fly Road, Suite 102, PO Box 248, East Syracuse NY 13057-0248. **Tel** (315)431-0511, FAX (315)431-0200.
Desc: Focuses on the long-term outlook for business. Includes a brief review of recent events and current circumstances, background intelligence including geography, history, economics and social conditions, as well as the key political and economic forecasts.

LC HA1631 .A33 HC407.Z9
DD 314.971
YU

ANKETA O PRIHODIMA, RASHEDIMA I POTRESNJI DOMACINSTAVA. See Business and Economics-Abstracting, Bibliographies and Statistics.

ISSN 0773-4123
BE

ANNALEN - KONINKLIJKE MUSEUM VOOR MIDDEN-AFRIKA ECONOMISCHE WETENSCHAPPEN. **VFOAT** Annales - Musee Royal de l'Afrique Centrale. Sciences Economiques. (1964)-. Monographic series. Multiple languages. Irregular.
Ind/Abst Hortic. Abstr.

TI

ANNALES. See Agriculture-Agricultural Economics.

ISSN 0379-3699
FR

ANNALES DE L'ECONOMIE PUBLIQUE, SOCIALE ET COOPERATIVE, LES. [Ann. econ. publique, soc. coop.]. (1974)-. Periodical. French (English and German). Four times a year. $133.00. De Boeck Wesmael SA, 4 Fond Jean Paques, 1348 Louvain La Neuve Belgium. **Tel** 011 32 10 482509, FAX 011 32 2 6273650. **(Subscription address:** ACCES Plus, Fond Jean Paques 4, B 1348 Louvain La Neuve Belgium. **Tel** 011 32 10 482500.) **Continues** Annales de L'Economie Collective.
Ind/Abst Int. Labour Doc.; LABORDOC; PAIS Int. Print (1991-).

LC HC
DD 330
ISSN 0769-489X
FR

ANNALES D'ECONOMIE ET DE STATISTIQUE. [Ann. econ. stat.]. **Added/Corp** Association pour le Developpement de la Recherche en Economie et en Statistique. Institut National de la Statistique et des Etudes Economiques (France). Vol. 1 (Jan./March 1986)-. Periodical. French (English). Four times a year. 538.00F. CNGP INSEE - Institut National de la Statistique et des Estudes Economiques, BP 2718, 1 rue V Auriol, F 80027 Amiens Cedex 1 France. **Tel** 011 33 22 927322. available on microfiche. **Formed by the union of** Institut National de la Statistique et des Etudes Economiques (France). Annales de l'Insee, 0019-0209 **and** Seminaire d'Econometrie. Cahiers du Seminaire d'Econometrie, 0071-8343.
Ind/Abst Econ. Lit. Index (1986-); Int. Bibliogr. Sociol.; J. Econ. Lit.; Math. Rev.

LC HB9 .L9
ISSN 0459-9586
PL

ANNALES UNIVERSITATIS MARIAE CURIE-SKLODOWSKA. SECTIO H. OECONOMIA. **Main/Corp** Uniwersytet Marii Curie-Sklodowskiej. (1967)-. Academic Scholarly Publication. Polish (English, French and German; summaries and/or abstracts in Russian, French, English and Polish). One time a year. Price varies per volume. Uniwersytet Marii Curie-Sklodowskiej, Biuro Wydawnictwo, Pl. Marii Curie-Sklodowskiej 5, 20-031 Lublin Poland. **Tel** 011 48 81 375304, FAX 011 48 81 336699, telex 0643223.
Ind/Abst Potato Abstr.

LC H17 .F65
DD 055.1
ISSN 0531-9870
IT

ANNALI DELLA FONDAZIONE LUIGI EINAUDI. See Social Sciences.

LC HF5001 .K652
DD 650/.07/1152
ISSN 0085-2570
JA

ANNALS OF THE SCHOOL OF BUSINESS ADMINISTRATION, KOBE UNIVERSITY, THE. **Main/Corp** Kobe Daigaku. Keieigakubu. No. 1 (1957)-. Periodical. English (Multiple languages). One time a year. Kobe University / Business Administration, School of Business Administration, Rokkodaicho Nadaku, Kobe Hyogoken 657 Japan. **Tel** 011 81 78 881-1212, FAX 011 81 78 881-8100. **ED** Mr. Futatsugi, Mr. Kanai, Mr. Kuroda, Mr. Kato. **Circ:** 600 (ctrl).
Ind/Abst Account. Index Suppl.

LC HC279 .A65
DD 330
FR
SUSPENDED

ANNUAIRE DES ENTREPRISES D'OUTRE-MER. **VFOAT** Annuaire des Entreprises et Organismes d'Outre-Mer. (19??)-Suspended (1995). French. Every 2 years. 548.06F France; 650.00F other. Annuaire des Entreprises d'Outre-Mer, 190 boulevard Haussmann, F 75008 Paris France. **Tel** 011 33 1 44959992, telex NAVIMAR 290 131 F.

LC HC271 .A2512a
DD 354/.44/0072
FR

ANNUAIRE GENERAL. **Main/Corp** France. Ministere de l'Economie et des Finances. (19??)-. French. Imprimerie Nationale / France, BP 514, 79505 Douai Cedex France. **Tel** 011 33 27 937090.

LC HC
DD 330
BD

ANNUAIRE STATISTIQUE. See Business and Economics-Abstracting, Bibliographies and Statistics.

LC HF3369 .A14
MQ

ANNUAIRE STATISTIQUE (CHAMBRE DE COMMERCE ET D'INDUSTRIE DE LA MARTINIQUE. DIRECTION DE L'INFORMATION ET DES RELATIONS CONSULAIRES). (ANNUAIRE STATISTIQUE / CHAMBRE DE COMMERCE ET D'INDUSTRIE DE LA MARTINIQUE, DIRECTION DE L'INFORMATION ET DES RELATIONS CONSULAIRES, FICHIER CONSULAIRE.). French. One time a year. Chambre de Commerce et d'Industrie de la Martinique, 50 rue Ernest Deproge, BP 478, Fort-de-France Martinique.

LC HA1213 .A4
DD 314.4
NLM W2 GF7 I5A
ISSN 0066-3654
FR

ANNUAIRE STATISTIQUE DE LA FRANCE (PARIS, FRANCE : 1952). See Business and Economics-Abstracting, Bibliographies and Statistics.

DD 330.9/715/04
ISSN 0319-003X
CN

ANNUAL CONFERENCE OF THE ATLANTIC CANADA ECONOMICS ASSOCIATION. **Main/Corp** Atlantic Canada Economics Association. **VFOAT** C. E. A. Papers. Vol. 1 (1972)-. Periodical. English (French). One time a year. 20.01Can$. Acadia University, PO Box 298, Editions du Grade Pre, Wolfville Nova Scotia B0P 1X0 Canada. **Tel** (902)542-9872, (902)542-2201. **(Subscription address:** Atlantic Canada Economics Association, 325 McDonald Avenue, Oromocto NB E2V 1A8 Canada.) **ED** John Davies and Aynul Masan. **Ad Acc**. **Circ:** 200 (ctrl).
Desc: Papers delivered at annual meeting of Atlantic Canada Economic Association.

LC HC517.M3 A38
DD 338.096897
MW

ANNUAL ECONOMIC SURVEY (ZOMBA, MALAWI). (ANNUAL ECONOMIC SURVEY.). **Added/Corp** Malawi. National Statistical Office. (1979)-. English. Irregular. Malawi National Statistical Office, PO Box 333, Zomba Malawi. **Tel** 011 265 522377, FAX 011 265 523130. **Continues** Malawi. National Statistical Office. Annual Economic Survey, Larger Establishments.

JA

ANNUAL OF DISPLAY & COMMERCIAL SPACE DESIGNS IN JAPAN. **VFOAT** Annual of Display and Commercial Space Designs in Japan. 1983-. Japanese (English). One time a year. Rockport Publishers Inc, 5 Smith Street, PO Box 396, Rockport MA 01966. **Formed by the union of** Annual of Display Works in Japan **and** Annual of Commercial Space Designs in Japan.

LC HB79.9.T34 U55a
DD 330/.072067823
TZ

ANNUAL PROGRESS REPORT / ECONOMIC RESEARCH BUREAU, UNIVERSITY OF DAR ES SALAAM. **Main/Corp** University of Dar Es Salaam. Economic Research Bureau. (19??)-. English. One time a year. University of Dar es Salaam, PO Box 35189, Dar es Salaam Tanzania. **Tel** 011 255 51 48235.

LC HC117.A6 A5162A
DD 354.71230082/06
ISSN 0837-4163
CN

ANNUAL REPORT - ALBERTA ECONOMIC DEVELOPMENT AND TRADE. [Annu. rep. - Alta. Econ. Dev. Trade]. **Main/Corp** Alberta. Alberta Economic Development and Trade. (1986)-. English. One time a year. Alberta Economic Development and Trade, Communications Division, 407 Legislative Building, Edmonton Alberta T5K 2B6 Canada. **Tel** (403)427-5028. ctrl circ. **Continues** Annual Report / Alberta Economic Development, 0229-8732; **Continues in part** Annual Report / Alberta Tourism and Small Business, 0823-454X.

LC HC117.M35 A88a
DD 354/.715/0082
ISSN 0067-0162
CN

ANNUAL REPORT - ATLANTIC PROVINCES ECONOMIC COUNCIL. [Annu. rep. - Atl. Prov. Econ. Counc.]. **Main/Corp** Atlantic Provinces Economic Council. (19??)-. English (French). One time a year. Comes with Atlantic Provinces Economic Council membership. Atlantic Provinces Economic Council, 5121 Sackville Street, Suite 500, Halifax Nova Scotia B3J 1K1 Canada. **Tel** (902)422-6516, FAX (902)429-6803. available in microform from Micromedia Limited.

LC HC
DD 330
AT

ANNUAL REPORT FOR ... / THE AUSTRALIAN NATIONAL UNIVERSITY, DEPARTMENT OF ECONOMICS, RESEARCH SCHOOL OF PACIFIC STUDIES. **Main/Corp** Australian National University. Research School of Pacific Studies. Dept. of Economics. (1981)-. Periodical. English. One time a year. Free. Anutech Pty. Limited, GPO Box 4, Canberra ACT 2601 Australia. **Tel** 011 61 6 2492479, FAX 011 61 6 2575088. **ED** C. Kavanagh. **Acid Free**. **Circ:** 300 (ctrl). **Continues** Australian National University. Research School of Pacific Studies. Dept. of Economics. Research Report.
Desc: Summarizes the year's research activities. Includes a publications list.

LC H62.5 .I7E24a
DD 330/.0720415
IE

ANNUAL REPORT FOR THE YEAR ENDED 31 DECEMBER. **Main/Corp** Economic and Social Research Institute. Council. English. Economic & Social Research Institute / Dublin, 4 Burlington Road, Dublin 4 Ireland. **Tel** 011 353 1 6760115 Ext. 427. **Continues** Report to the Members / Economic and Social Research Institute. Council.

LC HC
DD 330
US

ANNUAL REPORT / HEWLETT-PACKARD COMPANY. **Main/Corp** Hewlett-Packard Company. (19??)-. English. One time a year. Free on request. Hewlett-Packard Company, 3000 Hanover Street, Palo Alto CA 94304. **Tel** (415)857-1501.

LC H11 .N2433
DD 330.72
US

ANNUAL REPORT - NATIONAL BUREAU OF ECONOMIC RESEARCH. **Main/Corp** National Bureau of Economic Research. **Added/Corp** National Bureau of Economic Research. Report of the President and Report of the Directors of Research. National Bureau of Economic Research. Annual Report of the Executive Director. National Bureau of Economic Research. Report of the Executive Director. National Bureau of Economic Research. Report of the

Director of Research. National Bureau of Economic Research. Annual Report of the Director of Research. (19??)-. English. One time a year. National Bureau of Economic Research / New York, 261 Madison Avenue, New York NY 10016.

LC QH76.5.N5 N48a
DD 333.78/4 US
ANNUAL REPORT / NEW JERSEY, PINELANDS COMMISSION. **Main/Corp** New Jersey. Pinelands Commission. English.

LC HB235.H75 A56
DD 338.5/28/095125 HK
ANNUAL REPORT ON THE CONSUMER PRICE INDEX. **Added/Corp** Hong Kong. Census and Statistics Dept. Consumer Price Index Section. (19??)-. English. One time a year. HK$32.00. Hong Kong Government Information Service, Beaconsfield House, 4 Queens Road, Hong Kong Hong Kong. **Tel** 011 852 284288014, 011 852 259881947, FAX 011 852 28459078, 011 852 25987482, telex 61190 HKGIS.

LC J905 .L3 HB236.A8
DD 328.94/01 S 354/.94/0082 AT
ANNUAL REPORT - PRICES JUSTIFICATION TRIBUNAL (AUSTRALIA). **Main/Corp** Australia. Prices Justification Tribunal. 1st- 1973/74-. English.

LC HC **ISSN** 0899-2231
DD 330 US
ANNUAL REPORT / THE CONFERENCE BOARD. [Annu. rep. - Conf. Board]. **Main/Corp** Conference Board. (1987)-. English. One time a year. Free on request. Conference Board, 845 Third Avenue, New York NY 10022. **Tel** (212)759-0900 ext. 582, (800)872-6273, FAX (212)980-7014. ***Continues in part*** *Conference Board. Annual Report and Directory.*

LC JX1977 .A2 HC59 **ISSN** 0252-2047
DD 330.8 S 330.9/6 US
ANNUAL REPORT - UNITED NATIONS, ECONOMIC COMMISSION FOR AFRICA. (ANNUAL REPORT - ECONOMIC COMMISSION FOR AFRICA.). [Annu. rep. - U. N., Econ. Comm. Afr.]. **Main/Corp** United Nations. Economic Commission for Africa. **VFOAT** Economic Commission for Africa Annual Report. (Dec. 29, 1958/Jan. 6, 1959)-. English. One time a year. United Nations Economic Commission for Africa, PO Box 3001, Addis Ababa Ethiopia. **Tel** (212)754-8302, telex 21029 VNECA ET. ***Continues*** *United Nations. Economic Commission for Africa. Report of the ... Session.*

LC HC111 .E24 **ISSN** 0070-8488
DD 330 CN
CEASED
ANNUAL REVIEW - ECONOMIC COUNCIL OF CANADA. **Main/Corp** Economic Council of Canada. (1964)-(199?). Periodical. English. Statistics Canada Publications Sales and Services, R.H. Coats Building 6th Floor, Ottawa Ontario K1A 0T6 Canada. **Tel** (613)951-5078, (800)267-6677, FAX (613)951-1584, telex 053-3585.
Ind/Abst LABORDOC.

ISSN 0891-8414
DD 339 US
ANNUAL U.S. ECONOMIC DATA. [Annu. U. S. econ. data]. **Added/Corp** Federal Reserve Bank of St. Louis. **VAT** Annual United States Economic Data. (1983)-. English. One time a year. Free. Federal Reserve Bank of St. Louis, PO Box 66953, Research and Publication Information, St. Louis MO 63166. **Tel** (314)444-8444, (314)444-8660, FAX (314)444-8731. **Circ:** 8,954 (ctrl). ***Continues*** *Federal Reserve Bank of St. Louis. Compounded Rates of Change, 0091-8334.*
Desc: Monetary and business data, including closely watched production, employment and price series in levels and compounded rates of changes.
Ind/Abst F&S Index Plus Text, Int. [Select. Cov.]; Predicasts Forecasts.

LC HC
JA
AOYAMA BUSINESS REVIEW. **Added/Corp** Aoyama Gakuin Daigaku, Tokyo. Institute of Business Research. No. 1 (Sept. 1969)-. Periodical. English. Aoyama-Gakuin University, 4-4-25 Shibuya Shibuya-ku, Tokyo 150 Japan.

AU
APA JOURNAL ECONOMIST. (19??)-. Periodical. German. Five times a week. S7.000 (per month). Austria Presse Agentur, Gundoldstrasse 14, A-1199 Vienna Austria. **Tel** 011 43 1 3605 261, FAX 011 43 1 3605 607. **ED** Susanne Obermayer. **Bk Rev. Ad Acc, Adv Mgr:** Lia Seidl. available on an online database.

LC HC311 .A2574a
DD 330 BE
•**APERCU TRIMESTRIEL DE L'ECONOMIE.** **Added/Corp** Belgium. Ministere des Affaires Economiques. Direction Generale des Etudes et de la Documentation. Vol. 10 No. 1 (Mar. 1993)-. Periodical. French. Four times a year. 1000F Belgium, 1250F other; 1250F Belgium, 1500F other Comes with combineation et Lettre de Conjocture. Direction Generales des Etudes et de la Documentation, 6 rue de l'Industrie, 1040 Brussels Belgium. **Tel** 02 506.51.11, 02 506.63.07, FAX 02 513.46.57. ***Continues*** *Apercu Economique Trimestriel.*

LC HF5548.4.A68 A67 **ISSN** 0898-1183
DD 005.369 US
APPLEWORKS JOURNAL. **See** Computers-Programs and Programming.

LC HB1 .A665 **ISSN** 0003-6846
DD 330/.05 UK
CCC
CODEN APPEBP
Pr Rev.
APPLIED ECONOMICS. [Appl. econ.]. Vol. 1 (Jan. 1969)-. Periodical. English. Irregular (30 issues). $1045.00. Chapman & Hall, 2-6 Boundary Row, London SE1 8HN United Kingdom. **Tel** 011 44 171 8650066, FAX 011 44 171 5229623, telex 290164 CHAPMA G. **ED** M. H. Peston. Index available. **Bk Rev. Ad Acc. Circ:** 1,200. available on microfilm and microfiche from University Microfilms International (UMI). Documents available from The Genuine Article, UMI Article Clearinghouse.
Desc: Encourages the application of economic analysis to specific problems in both the public and private sectors. Particularly hopes to foster quantitative studies, the results of which promise to be of use in the practical field, and thus help to bring economic theory nearer to reality. Covers areas including industry, macro- and micro-economics, commerce, finance, econometrics and public administration.
Ind/Abst ABI/INFORM Glob. Ed.; ABI/INFORM [Computer File] (Feb. 1982-); Acad. Search; AgBiotech News Inf.; Bus. ASAP (1992-) [Full Txt.]; Bus. Index (1985-); Bus. Period. Index; Bus. Source Plus; Bus. Source; Coal Abstr.; Contents Recent Econ. J.; Contents Pages Manage.; Curr. Cit.; Curr. Contents Soc. Behav. Sci.; Econ. Lit. Index; Energy Res. Abstr.; EP Collect.; Expand. Acad. Index (1992-); Gen. BusinessFile (1985-); Gen. Period. Index (1985-); Geogr. Abstr. Human Geogr.; Homework Help.; INFO-SOUTH Abstr.; Int. Bibliogr. Sociol.; Int. Dev. Abstr.; Int. Labour Doc.; J. Econ. Lit.; J. Plan. Lit.; Leis., Rec., Tour. Abstr.; Mag. Search; MasterFile FullTEXT 1000; MasterFile FullTEXT 350; MasterFile FullTEXT 650; MasterFile FullTEXT (Jan. 1994-); Newsp. Period. Abstr. (1992-); Nutr. Abstr. Rev., Ser. B, Live Feeds and Feed.; OCLC; PAIS Int. Print; Pig News Inf.; Poult. Abstr.; Res. Alert [Full Cov.]; Risk Abstr.; Rural Dev. Abstr.; Soc. Sci. Cit. Index [Full Cov.]; SportSearch; Telebase; Wilson Bus. Abstr.; World Agric. Econ. Rural Sociol. Abstr.

ISSN 0955-3096
UK
APPLIED ECONOMICS DISCUSSION PAPER - UNIVERSITY OF OXFORD. INSTITUTE OF ECONOMICS AND STATISTICS. (APPLIED ECONOMICS DISCUSSION PAPER.). [Appl. econ. discuss. pap. - Univ. Oxf., Inst. Econ. Stat.]. **VFOAT** Applied Economics Discussion Paper Series. (1986)-. Monographic series. English. University of Oxford / Institute of Economics and Statistics, St. Cross Building, Manor Road, Oxford OX1 3UL United Kingdom. **Tel** 011 44 1865 271073, FAX 011 44 1865 271094.
Ind/Abst Curr. Cit.

LC HB1 .A666 **ISSN** 1350-4851
DD 330/.05 UK
Pr Rev.
•**APPLIED ECONOMICS LETTERS.** Vol. 1, No. 1 (Jan. 1994)-. Academic Scholarly Publication. English. Twelve times a year. $242.00. Chapman & Hall, 2-6 Boundary Row, London SE1 8HN United Kingdom. **Tel** 011 44 171 8650066, FAX 011 44 171 5229623, telex 290164 CHAPMA G. **(Subscription address:** International Thomson Publishing Services Ltd., North Way Andover, Hampshire SP10 5BE United Kingdom. **Tel** 011 44 1264 332424.) **ED** Maurice Preston. **Ad Acc.** available via Internet.
Desc: Publishes short accounts of new original research within two months of receipt in the field of economics. Also carries news items including software reviews, book reviews, conference reports and announcements.
Ind/Abst Curr. Contents; MasterFile FullTEXT (Jan. 1994-).

LC WMLC 91/3439 **ISSN** 1058-7039
DD 338 US
CCC
AQUATICS INTERNATIONAL. [Aquat. int.]. (1991)-. Trade Publication. English. Six times a year. $42.00. Argus Business, 6151 Powers Ferry Road Northwest, Atlanta GA 30339. **Tel** (404)995-2500, FAX (404)995-0400. **(Subscription address:** Hallmark Data Systems, PO Box 1147, Skokie IL 60076. **Tel** (708)647-6933.) **ED** Terri Simmons. Index available. **Bk Rev. Ad Acc. Circ:** 30,000 (ctrl). available on microfilm and microfiche from University Microfilms International (UMI). ***Continues*** *Aquatics (Atlanta, Ga.), 1042-9697.*

LC HC498.A1 A733
DD 330.9/17/4927 LE
ARAB ECONOMIST, THE. **Added/Corp** Center for Economic, Financial and Social Research and Documentation. No. 25 (Jan. 1971)-. Periodical. English. Twelve times a year. Center for Economic, Financial and Social Research and Documentation, PO Box 11-6068, Clemenceau Street, Beirut Lebanon. ***Continues*** *Center for Economic, Financial and Social Research and Documentation. Monthly Survey of Arab Economies.*
Ind/Abst Leis., Rec., Tour. Abstr.; Rural Dev. Abstr.; World Agric. Econ. Rural Sociol. Abstr.

ISSN 0954-8912
DD 004.09536 UK
ARABIAN BUSINESS COMPUTING. **See** Computers.

IT
ARCHIVI E IMPRESSE : BOLLETTINO INFORMAZIONI STUDI E RICERCHE. (19??)-. Italian. Two times a year. L50000 (public libraries, universities and individuals), L300000 (institutions) other. Assimpresa, Archivi Imprese, Corso Porta Romana 57, 20122 Milan Italy. **Tel** 011 39 2 55191679.

LC Z7164.C81 A69
DD 016.33/0973 US
AREA BUSINESS DATABANK. PRINT INDEX. **VFOAT** Print Index. Vol. 2 (Jan./Dec. 1984)-. English. One time a year. Information Access Company, 362 Lakeside Drive, Foster City CA 94404. **Tel** (800)227-8431, (800)458-1565. ***Continues*** *ABD Index.*

ISSN 0267-9949
UK
ARGENTINA (LONDON, ENGLAND). (ARGENTINA.). **Added/Corp** Latin American Monitor Ltd. (1985)-. Periodical. English. One time a year. $435.00. Latin American Monitor Ltd., 56 60 St. John Street, London EC1M 4DT United Kingdom. **Tel** 011 44 171 6083646.

LC DK285 .A73 **ISSN** 0957-0020
DD 947.085/4/05 UK
CEASED
ARGUMENTS & FACTS INTERNATIONAL. [Argum. facts int.]. **VFOAT** Arguments and Facts International; Facts. Vol. 1, No. 1 (Jan. 1990)-Vol. 5, No. 29 (Jan.-Feb. 1994). Periodical. English. Arguments & Facts International, PO Box 35, Hastings East Sussex, TN34 2UX United Kingdom. **Tel** 011 44 1424 444142, FAX 011 44 1424 717498. **Bk Rev,** (Qty: 24). **Ad Acc. Circ:** 5,000.
Desc: Business intelligence newsletter containing economic/commercial intelligence and research on trade, industry, political and social matters in the USSR.
Ind/Abst Curr. Dig. Post Sov. Press.

ISSN 1042-6787
DD 330 US
ARIZONA BLUE CHIP ECONOMIC FORECAST. [Ariz. blue chip econ. forecast]. **Added/Corp** Arizona State University. Economic Outlook Center. **VFOAT** Arizona Blue Chip. (198?)-. Periodical. English. Twelve times a year. $99.00. Economic Outlook Center, PO Box 874406, College of Business, Arizona State University, Tempe AZ 85287-4406. **Tel** (602)965-5543, 800 448-9432, FAX (602)965-5458. **ED** Lee R. McPheters, Tracy Clark and Robert J. Eggert Sr. **Circ:** 700.
Desc: Economic forecasts for the state of Arizona based on a consensus of opinions by the state's economists.

LC HC107.A6 A766 **ISSN** 0093-0717
DD 330.9/791/05 US
CODEN ABBUA6
ARIZONA BUSINESS. [Ariz. bus.]. **Added/Corp** Arizona State University. Bureau of Business and Economic Research. (1972)-. Newsletter. English. Twelve times a year. $18.00. Arizona State University / Center for Business Research, College of Business-NBJ, Box 874406, Tempe AZ 85287-4406. **Tel** (602)965-3961, FAX (602)965-5458. **ED** Nan Beams. Index available. **Circ:** 2,000. available on microfilm from University Microfilms International (UMI); available on photocopies from University Microfilms International (UMI); available on CD-ROM; available on an online database from Information Access Company; and (files 16,648/Full-Text) DIALOG. Documents available from UMI Article Clearinghouse, BLDSC. ***Continues*** *Arizona Business Bulletin; Occasional Papers (Arizona State University. Bureau of Business and Economic Research).*
Desc: Presents Arizona economic data and analysis, including indicators, gross state product, quarterly economic forecasts, metro Phoenix CPI, and construction activity.
Ind/Abst ABI/INFORM Glob. Ed.; ABI/INFORM [Computer File] (June 1972-); Acad. Search; Bus. ASAP (1990-) [Full Txt.]; Bus. Index (1985-); Bus. Source Plus; Bus. Source; Chicano Index; EP Collect.; Gen. BusinessFile (1985-); Gen. Period. Index (1985-); Homework Help.; INFO-SOUTH Abstr.; MasterFile FullTEXT 1000; MasterFile FullTEXT 350; MasterFile FullTEXT 650; MasterFile FullTEXT (July 1993-); OCLC;

PAIS Int. Print (1991-); Stat. Ref. Index; Telebase; Trade Ind. ASAP [Full Txt.]; Trade Ind. Index [Full Txt.]; UMI ABI/Inform--Bus. Period. Ondisc (Dec. 1987-) [Full Txt.].

US
TITLE CHANGE
ARIZONA BUSINESS & DEVELOPMENT. (19??)-(19??). English. Arizona Business & Development, 3111 North Central Avenue, Suite 230, Phoenix AZ 85012. **Tel** (602)277-6045. ***Continued by** Arizona Business Magazine.*

ISSN 0273-6950
US
ARIZONA BUSINESS GAZETTE. Vol. 81, No. 6 (Sept. 30, 1980)-. Newspaper. English. One time a week. $45.00. Phoenix Newspapers Inc., PO Box 660, Phoenix AZ 85001. **Tel** (602)271-8503, (602)271-8000, FAX (602)271-8910. **ED** Steve Bergsman and Joe Kullman. **Bk Rev. Ad Acc. Circ:** 8,500. available on an online database from VU-TEXT; Dow Jones News/Retrieval; Mead Data Central; and (files 635,648/Full-Text) DIALOG. Documents available from UMI Article Clearinghouse. ***Continues** Arizona Weekly Gazette.*
Desc: Business and legal newspaper designed to provide timely and comprehensive news to individuals and businesses throughout the state.
Ind/Abst Bus. Dateline (June 2, 1986-) [Full Txt.]; Bus. Index (Jan. 1985-Dec. 1985); Gen. BusinessFile (Jan. 1985-Dec. 1985); Gen. Period. Index (Jan. 1985-Dec. 1985); PROMT; Trade Ind. ASAP [Full Txt.]; Trade Ind. Index [Full Txt.].

LC HD2321 **ISSN** 0193-7480
DD 338 US
ARIZONA BUSINESS/INDUSTRY. (19??)-. Periodical. English. Twelve times a year. $15.00. Trailbeau Publications, PO Box 15604, Phoenix AZ 85060.

US
ARIZONA BUSINESS MAGAZINE. (19??)-. English. Four times a year. $16.00 (one-year), $27.00 (two-year). Arizona Business & Development, 3111 North Central Avenue, Suite 230, Phoenix AZ 85012. **Tel** (602)277-6045. ***Continues** Arizona Business and Development.*

LC Discard **ISSN** 0743-9997
US
ARIZONA BUSINESS REPORTS. (19??)-. Periodical. English. One time a week. $195.00. Arizona Business Reports, PO Box 13716, Scottsdale AZ 85267.

US
ARIZONA'S ECONOMY. Added/Corp University of Arizona. Division of Economic and Business Research. (Jan. 1979)-. Periodical. English. Four times a year. Free on request. University of Arizona / Economics, Division of Economic & Business Research, College of Business & Public Administration, Tucson AZ 85721. **Tel** (602)621-2155, FAX (602)621-2150. **ED** Jo Marie Gellerman. **Circ:** 3,600 (ctrl). ***Separated from** Arizona Review, 0004-1629.*
Desc: Analysis of current business conditions and forecasts of future economic activity in Arizona.
Ind/Abst PAIS Int. Print; Urban Aff. Abstr.

ISSN 1053-6582
DD 330 US
Pr Rev.
ARKANSAS BUSINESS. [Ark. bus.]. Vol. 1, No. 1 (Mar. 19, 1984)-. Periodical. English. One time a week. $54.95. Arkansas Business, PO Box 3686, Little Rock AR 72203. **Tel** (501)372-1443, FAX (501)375-3623. **ED** Rex Nelson. **Ad Acc, Adv Mgr:** Karen Raley, **Tel** (501)372-1443. **Circ:** 8,000 (ctrl). available on an online database (files 635,648/Full-Text) from DIALOG. Documents available from UMI Article Clearinghouse.
Desc: Central Arkansas business news.
Ind/Abst Bus. Dateline (April 27, 1987-) [Full Txt.]; Gen. BusinessFile (1985-1990); Gen. Period. Index (1985-1990); PROMT; Trade Ind. ASAP [Full Txt.]; Trade Ind. Index [Full Txt.].

LC HC107.A8 A64 **ISSN** 0004-1742
DD 330 US
CODEN ABRVBM
Pr Rev.
ARKANSAS BUSINESS AND ECONOMIC REVIEW. [Ark. bus. econ. rev.]. Vol. 1 (Aug. 1968)-. Periodical. English. Irregular. Free on request. University of Arkansas / Business, College of Business Administration, Fayetteville AR 72701. **Tel** (501)575-4151, FAX (501)575-7687. Index available. cum. index. available on an online database from DIALOG. Documents available from UMI Article Clearinghouse, Ask*IEEE, FAXON Xpress, The UnCover Company. ***Supersedes** Arkansas Economist; Arkansas Business Bulletin.*
Ind/Abst ABI/INFORM Glob. Ed.; ABI/INFORM [Computer File] (Summer 1973-); Acad. Search; Bus. ASAP (1992-) [Full Txt.]; Bus. Index (1985-); Bus. Source Plus; Bus. Source; EP Collect.; Gen. BusinessFile (1985-); Gen. Period. Index (1985-); Homework Help.; INFO-SOUTH Abstr.; INSPEC (Summer 1981-); MasterFile FullTEXT 1000; MasterFile FullTEXT 350; MasterFile FullTEXT 650; MasterFile FullTEXT (July 1993-); OCLC; PAIS Int. Print; Person. Manage. Abstr.; Stat. Ref. Index; Telebase; Trade Ind. ASAP [Full Txt.]; Trade Ind. Index [Full Txt.].

ISSN 0893-3901
DD 705 US
Pr Rev.
ART CALENDAR (GREAT FALLS, VA.). **See** The Arts-Art.

LC Z7165.I6 A85 HC431
DD 016.330954 II
ARTHA SUCHI : AN INDEX TO INDIAN ECONOMIC LITERATURE. Added/Corp National Council of Applied Economic Research. Library. Vol. 1, No. 1 & 2 (July/Dec. 1983)-. Periodical. English. Four times a year. $30.00. Library - National Council of Applied Economic Research, New Delhi India. **(Subscription address:** Prints India, 11 Darya Ganj, New Delhi 110002 India. **Tel** 011 91 11 3268645, FAX 011 91 11 3275542, telex 31-61087 PRIN-IN.**)**

LC HB1 .A7 **ISSN** 0004-3575
II
ARTHANITI. Added/Corp University of Calcutta. Dept. of Economics. Vol. 1 (Nov. 1957)-. Periodical. English. One time a year. $5.00. Calcutta University, Department of Economics, Calcutta 700-050 India. **(Subscription address:** Prints India, 11 Darya Ganj, New Delhi 110002 India. **Tel** 011 91 11 3268645, FAX 011 91 11 3275542, telex 31-61087 PRIN-IN.**) Circ:** 200.

UK
TITLE CHANGE
ARTHUR ANDERSEN CORPORATE REGISTER, THE. Added/Corp Arthur Andersen (Firm). (1992)-(199?). Directory. English. Hemmington Scott Publishing Ltd, 25-31 Whiskin Street, City Innovation Centre, London EC1R OBP United Kingdom. **Tel** 011 44 171 2787769, FAX 011 44 171 2789808. ***Continues** Corporate Register, 0956-2893. **Continued by** Price Waterhouse Corporate Register, 1352-8157.*
Desc: Information for corporate executives.

AT
ASC DIGEST. VFOAT Australian Security Commission Digest. (19??)-. English. 695.00Aus$. Center for Professional Development, 100 Albert Road, 5th Floor, South Melbourne Victoria 3205 Australia. **Tel** 011 61 3 6903933, FAX 011 61 3 6906073.

LC HC441.A1 A72 **ISSN** 0217-4472
DD 330.959/005 SI
Pr Rev.
ASEAN ECONOMIC BULLETIN. Added/Corp Institute of Southeast Asian Studies. ASEAN Economic Research Unit. Vol. 1, No. 1 (July 1984)-. Bulletin. English. Three times a year (Mar., Jul., Nov,). $44.00. Institute of Southeast Asian Studies / Singapore, Heng Mui Keng Terrace, Pasir Panjang Road, Singapore 0511 Republic of Singapore. **Tel** 011 65 8702447, FAX 011 65 7781735, telex 37068. **ED** Joseph L H Tan, Shonkar Sharma. Index available. cum. index. **Bk Rev. Circ:** 900. Documents available from UMI Article Clearinghouse.
Desc: Emphasizes economic issues affecting the countries of the Association of Southeast Asian Nations; concerned with ASEAN's major trading partners and its relationship with the world political economy.
Ind/Abst ABI/INFORM Glob. Ed.; Asia.-Pac. Econ. Lit.; For. Abstr.; Hum. Resour. Abstr. (?-?); Int. Bibliogr. Sociol.; Leis., Rec., Tour. Abstr.; Newsp. Period. Abstr. (1989-); PAIS Int. Print; Rural Dev. Abstr.; Sage Public Adm. Abstr.; World Agric. Econ. Rural Sociol. Abstr.

ISSN 1058-6334
DD 005 US
ASHTON-TATE UPDATE. [Ashton-Tate update]. **Added/Corp** Ashton-Tate. **VFOAT** Ashton Tate Update. (Spring 1991)-. Periodical. English. Four times a year. Ashton-Tate, 20101 Hailton Avenue, PO Box 2833, Torrance CA 90509-2833.

LC HC411 .E324
DD 330.95/005 US
ASIA AND OTHER SELECTED COUNTRIES QUARTERLY REVIEW. Added/Corp DRI World Service. **VFOAT** Asian Economic Review. (June 1986)-. Periodical. English. Four times a year. DRI McGraw Hill, 24 Hartwell Avenue, Lexington MA 02173. **Tel** (617)863-5100, FAX (617)860-6464, (617)860-6416. **(Subscription address:** Data Resources, PO Box 5 0210, Woburn MA 01815. **)** ***Continues** Asian Review (Data Resources, Inc.).*

AT
ASIA BUSINESS REPORT. (19??)-. English. Forty-eight times a year. 640.00Aus$ Australia; 690.00Aus$ other. C R Publishing, 515 Kent Street, 1st Floor, Sydney 2000 Australia. **Tel** 011/61/02/2612123, FAX 011/61/02/2672261. **ED** Siam Loh Soh. **Ad Acc.**

ISSN 0004-4466
US
ASIA LETTER, THE. (1964)-. Periodical. English. One time a week. $195.00. Asia Letter Group, GPO Box 10874, Central Hong Kong. **Tel** 011 852 25262950, FAX 011 852 25267131, telex 61166. **(Subscription address:** Asia Letter Group, PO Box 88189, Los Angeles CA 90009. **) ED** Charles R. Smith. **Bk Rev.** ctrl circ.
Desc: An analysis of the political and economical developments in the various Asian countries for people doing business in Asia.

LC S
DD 630 US
ASIA-PACIFIC AGRIBUSINESS REPORT. **See** Agriculture.

ISSN 1351-0967
UK
ASIA PACIFIC CONSENSUS FORECASTS. (19??)-. English. Twelve times a year. £590.37. Consensus Economics Inc., 49 Berkeley Square, London W1X 6LT United Kingdom. **Tel** 011 44 171 4913211, FAX 011 44 171 4092331. available with charts.

ISSN 1020-1246
US
UDC 33
CODEN NU003
•**ASIA-PACIFIC DEVELOPMENT JOURNAL.** [Asia-Pac. dev. j.]. (1994)-. Monographic series. English. Irregular. Price varies per volume. United Nations Publications, 2 United Nations Plaza, Room DC2 0853, Department 007C, New York NY 10017. **Tel** (212)963-8303, (800)253-9646. ***Continues** Economic Bulletin for Asia and the Pacific, 0378-455X.*
Ind/Abst Contents Recent Econ. J.; Int. Labour Doc.; Middle East Abstr. Index; Rural Dev. Abstr.; World Agric. Econ. Rural Sociol. Abstr.

LC HB **ISSN** 1358-6653
DD 330 UK
•**ASIA - PACIFIC ECONOMIC REVIEW.** (1995)-. Academic Scholarly Publication. English. Three times a year. £75.00. Cambridge University Press, The Edinburgh Building, Shaftesbury Road, Cambridge CB2 2RU United Kingdom. **Tel** 011 44 1223 312393, FAX 011 44 1223 315052, telex 851-817256. **(Subscription address:** Cambridge University Press, Journals Department, 40 West 20th Street, New York NY 10011. **Tel** (212)924-3900, FAX (212)691-3239.**) ED** Colin Hargreaves and Peter C.B. Phillips. **Bk Rev. Ad Acc.**
Desc: Includes information on the economic expansion of the Asia-Pacific region.

ISSN 0966-0453
DD 332.095 UK
ASIA PACIFIC HANDBOOK. [Asia Pac. handb.]. **VFOAT** Extel Financial Asia Pacific Handbook. (1991)-. Directory. English. Two times a year. $325.13. Extel Financial Ltd., Fitzroy House, 13-17 Epworth Street, London EC2A 4DL United Kingdom. **Tel** 011 44 171 8258000, FAX 011 44 171 8258328, telex 884319 EXTELX G. Index available. **Ad Acc, Adv Mgr:** Kevin Brady. available on CD-ROM; available on microfiche; available on diskette.
Desc: Coverage of over 1000 companies in Australia, Japan, Hong Kong, Malaysia, Singapore, Thailand and Korea. Includes contact details, major shareholders, share price data, three years of profit and loss and balance sheet details, performance ratios and ordinary share record. Rankings across all companies, by country and industry sector are also provided.

ISSN 1018-5291
BG
UDC 711.3
ASIA-PACIFIC JOURNAL OF RURAL DEVELOPMENT. [Asia-pac. j. rural dev.]. (1991)-. Periodical. English. Two times a year. $24.00. Centre on Integrated Rural Development for Asia and the Pacific / CIRDAP, Chameli House, 17 Topkhana Road, GPO Box 2883, Dhaka-1000 Bangladesh. **Tel** 011 880 256704, 011 880 238651, FAX 011 880 2 833321, telex 612333 CIRDAP BJ. **ED** Leelangi Wanasundera. **Bk Rev. Ad Acc.**
Desc: News and information on rural development for Asia and the Pacific.

ISSN 1022-4696
HK
UDC 33
ASIA PACIFIC PRIVATE EQUITY BULLETIN. [Asia Pac. priv. equity bull.]. (1993)-. Bulletin. English. Ten times a year (publishes monthly except July & Dec.). $150.00. Asia Pacific Communications Ltd., 1209 Harcourt House, 39 Gloucester, Wanchai Hong Kong. **Tel** 011 852 28610102.

LC DS501 .A8333 **ISSN** 1036-3793
DD 338.99 AT
ASIA PACIFIC PROFILES. [Asia Pac. profiles]. **Added/Corp** Australian National University. National Centre for Development Studies. Australian National University. Asia-Pacific Economics Group. (Apr. 23/24 1990)-. English. One time a year. 500.00Aus$. Anutech Pty. Limited, GPO Box 4, Canberra ACT 2601 Australia. **Tel** 011 61 6 2492479, FAX 011 61 6 2575088.

ISSN 0813-2844
DD 382.0959094 AT
ASIA TODAY. [Asia today]. (1983)-. Periodical. English. Twelve times a year. 110.00Aus$. Asia Today, PO Box N7, Grosvenor Place, Sydney NSW 2000, Australia. **Tel** 011 61 2 9706477, FAX 011 61 2 9132003. **ED** Florence Chong. Index available. cum. index. **Ad Acc, Adv Mgr:** A.L. Mazey. **Circ:** 7,397.
Desc: Reports business opportunities and economic trends.

LC HC
HK
ASIA YEARBOOK. (1973)-. English. One time a year (Dec.). $42.00 (softcover). Review Publishing Company Ltd., 25 F Citicorp Center, 18 Whitfield Road, GPO Box 160, Hong Kong Hong Kong. **Tel** 011 852 25084337, FAX 011 852 25031549, 25031553, telex 66452 REVCD HX. **(Subscription address:** Review Publishing Company Ltd., PO Box 160, Hong Kong Hong Kong. **Tel** 011 852 25084300.) ***Continues*** *Far Eastern Economic Review. Yearbook.*
Desc: Covering 31 countries, this reference discusses politics, military strengths, social and foreign affairs, economy and infrastructure, and more.

LC HF3751 .A74 ISSN 0254-3729
DD 650/.095 HK
CCC
ASIAN BUSINESS. [Asian bus.]. Vol. 15, No. 6, (June 1979)-. Periodical. English. Twelve times a year. $55.00. Far East Trade Press Ltd., BL C 10 F Seaview E, 2 8 Watson, North Point Hong Kong. **Tel** 011 852 25668381, FAX 011 852 25710780, telex 83434. **ED** Jack Maisamo. Index available. **Ad Acc, Adv Mgr:** Katherina Chan. **Circ:** 87,500 (ctrl). available on microfilm and microfiche from University Microfilms International (UMI). Documents available from UMI Article Clearinghouse. ***Continues*** *Asian Business & Industry.*
Desc: Updates on economic developments and current business conditions in all major Asian markets.
Ind/Abst ABI/INFORM Glob. Ed.; ABI/INFORM [Computer File] (Jan. 1984-); Acad. Search; Bus. Period. Index; Bus. Source Plus; Bus. Source; Curr. Cit.; EP Collect.; F&S Index Plus Text, Int. [Select. Cov.]; Homework Help.; INFO-SOUTH Abstr.; LABORDOC; Mag. Search; MasterFile FullTEXT 1000; MasterFile FullTEXT 350; MasterFile FullTEXT 650; MasterFile FullTEXT (July 1993-); OCLC; PAIS Int. Print; PROMT; Telebase; UMI ABI/Inform--Bus. Period. Ondisc (Nov. 1987-) [Full Txt.]; Wilson Bus. Abstr.

AT
Pr Rev.
ASIAN BUSINESS REVIEW. (19??)-. Periodical. English. Eleven times a year. 39.46Aus$. Asian Business Review, GPO Box 3901, Sydney New South Wales 2001 Australia. **Tel** 011 61 2 2621400, FAX 011 61 2 2621304. **ED** Maggie Macrae. **Bk Rev**, (Qty: 33). **Ad Acc, Adv Mgr:** Andrew Powell. ctrl circ.
Ind/Abst MasterFile FullTEXT (Jan. 1995-).

ISSN 1074-0643
US
ASIAN CENTURY BUSINESS REPORT. **VFOAT** Asian Century. (199?)-. English. Eleven times a year. $185.00. Asian Century Business Report, PO Box 4, Provo UT 84603. **Tel** (801)373-3900, FAX (801)374-1357. **ED** Brooke Hanks. **Circ:** 100.
Desc: Keeping current with the most recent thinking and practice concerning business in Asia.

LC HF3820.5.A48 A85
DD 338.7/4/09505 JA
ASIAN COMPANY HANDBOOK. **Added/Corp** Toyo Keizai Shinposha. **VFOAT** ACH-Asian Company Handbook. (1990)-. English. One time a year (July). $87.81. Toyo Keizai Inc., 1-2-1 Nihonbashi Hongokucho, Chuo-ku Tokyo 103 Japan. **Tel** 011 81 3 3246 5470, FAX 011 81 3 32310629. **(Subscription address:** Japan Publications Trading Company Ltd., PO Box 5030, Tokyo International, Tokyo 100-31 Japan. **Tel** 011 81 3 3292 3753.)
Desc: Covers the latest financial information on 1,009 selected companies listed on the stock exchanges of six Asian countries: Hong Kong, Republic of Korea, Taiwan, Thailand, Malaysia, and Singapore. Some Indonesian companies are also covered.

UK
ASIAN INFRASTRUCTURE MONTHLY. (1995)-. English. Twelve times a year. $1026.72. Financial Times / UK, Maple House, 149 Tottenham Court Road, London W1P 9LL United Kingdom. **Tel** 011 44 171 8962276, FAX 011 44 171 8962275, 011 44 171 8962399. **(Subscription address:** Pearson Professional Ltd., PO Box 77, Fourth Avenue, Harlow Essex CM19 5BQ United Kingdom. **Tel** 011 44 1279 623924.)

HK
ASIAN INTELLIGENCE. **See** Political Science.

LC HB1 .A75
DD 330/.05 II
ASIAN JOURNAL OF ECONOMICS AND SOCIAL STUDIES. **Added/Corp** Society for Asian Development (Delhi, India). Vol. 3, No. 1 (Jan. 1984)-. Periodical. English. Four times a year. $60.00. Society for Asian Development, New Delhi India. **(Subscription address:** Prints India, 11 Darya Ganj, New Delhi 110002 India. **Tel** 011 91 11 3268645, FAX 011 91 11 3275542, telex 31-61087 PRIN-IN.) ***Continues*** *Asian Journal of Economics.*

LC HC411 .A733 ISSN 0818-9935
DD 330.95/005 UK
CODEN AELIEB
Pr Rev.
ASIAN-PACIFIC ECONOMIC LITERATURE. **See** Business and Economics-Abstracting, Bibliographies and Statistics.

ISSN 0956-3784
UK
ASIAN REVIEW OF BUSINESS AND TECHNOLOGY. (19??)-. Trade Publication. English. Eleven times a year. $88.00. Alain Charles Publishing Ltd., 27 Wilfred Street, London SW1E 6PR United Kingdom. **Tel** 011 44 171 8347676, FAX 011 44 171 9730076, telex 297165. ***Continues*** *Far Eastern Technical Review, 0144-8218.*

LC Newspaper ISSN 0377-9920
HK
CODEN AWSJD4
ASIAN WALL STREET JOURNAL. [Asian wall st. j.]. Vol. 1 (Sept. 1, 1976)-. Newspaper. English. Five times a week (Mon.-Fri.). $825.00. Dow Jones and Company Inc., 200 Burnett Road, Chicopee MA 01021. **Tel** (413)592-7761, (800)568-7625. **(Subscription address:** Asian Wall Street Journal, GPO Box 9825, Hong Kong, Hong Kong. **Tel** 011 852 25737121.) **ED** Barry Wain. **Ad Acc. Circ:** 35,000.
Desc: Asia's business newspaper.
Ind/Abst Chem. Ind. Notes; F&S Index Plus Text, Int. [Select. Cov.]; PROMT.

LC HG4234.85 .A85
DD 338.7/4/09505 UK
ASIA'S 7,500 LARGEST COMPANIES. **Added/Corp** Asia Pacific Marketing Services. **VFOAT** Asia's Seven Thousand, Five Hundred Largest Companies. (1985)-. English. One time a year. $400.50 libraries; $445.00 other. Dun & Bradstreet Information Services, 3 Sylvan Way, Parsippany NJ 07054. **Tel** (201)605-6000, (800)526-0651.

ISSN 0305-1641
UK
ASIDES. ABERDEEN STUDIES IN DEFENCE ECONOMICS. [ASIDES, Aberdeen stud. def. econ.]. **VFOAT** Aberdeen Studies in Defence Economics. (1973)-. English. Irregular. £4.00. University of Aberdeen / Centre for Defence Studies, Dunbar Street, Aberdeen AB9 2TY United Kingdom. **Tel** 011 44 1224 40241.

ISSN 1066-890X
DD 361 US
●**ASPEN'S NONPROFIT SURVIVAL NETWORK.** [Aspen's nonprofit surviv. netw.]. **VFOAT** Nonprofit Survival Network's Board Talk; Board Talk; Nonprofit Survival Network. Vol. 1, No. 1 (Mar. 1993)-. Periodical. English. Twelve times a year. $78.00. Aspen Publishers Inc., 7201 McKinney Circle, Frederick MD 21701. **Tel** (800)234-1660, (301)698-7100, FAX (301)251-5784, telex 5106014543. **(Subscription address:** Aspen Publishers Inc., PO Box 990, Frederick MD 21701. **Tel** (800)901-9074, (301)698-7100.)

ISSN 0275-5610
US
ASSETS. (19??)-. Trade Publication. English. Six times a year. American Society of Chartered Life Underwriters, PO Box 59, Bryn Mawr PA 19010. **Tel** (610)526-2500, FAX (610)527-1499. **ED** Richard I Isbell. **Circ:** 1,000.
Desc: Newsletter imprinted for individual society members for distribution to their clients, estate, business, employee benefit, tax, and financial planning.

LC HD4965.5.U6 A594A ISSN 0273-0367
DD 331.2/81658/00973 US
ASSOCIATION EXECUTIVE COMPENSATION STUDY. **Main/Corp** American Society of Association Executives. 1980-. English. Twelve times a year. $30.00 US; $45.00 other nonmembers. ASAE, 1575 Eye Street NW, Washington DC 20005. **Tel** (202)626-2723. **ED** Chris Condeelis. Index available. cum. index. **Bk Rev. Ad Acc. Circ:** 4,000. available on microfilm; available on microfiche. ***Formed by the union of*** *Compensation and Benefits for Association Executive Personnel* ***and*** *Association Executive Compensation Study, 0273-0367.*
Desc: Management magazine for association executives. Provides information on salary and benefits afforded to management personnel in associations.

ISSN 1055-9817
US
ASSOCIATION EXECUTIVE EXCHANGE. (1991)-. Periodical. English. One time a week. Inventure Publications / College Park, 4431 Lehigh Road, Suite 162, College Park MD 20740.

ISSN 1066-8691
DD 658 US
ASSOCIATION SOURCE. (ASSOCIATION SOURCE : THE MAGAZINE OF THE FLORIDA SOCIETY OF ASSOCIATION EXECUTIVES.). [Assoc. source]. **Added/Corp** Florida Society of Association Executives. (199?)-. Periodical. English. Twelve times a year. Florida Society of Association Executives, 1211 Semoran Boulevard, Suite 165, Casselberry FL 32707. **Tel** (407)678-9344, FAX (407)678-7635. ***Continues*** *Source (Tallahassee, Fla.), 0898-8811.*

ISSN 0196-1942
US
ASSOCIATION TRENDS. (1973)-. Periodical. English. Fifty times a year (weekly on Fri. except end of July and Christmas). $95.00. Martineau Corporation, 7910 Woodmont Avenue, #1150, Bethesda MD 20814. **Tel** (301)652-8666, FAX (301)656-8654. **ED** Lak Vohra. **Bk Rev. Ad Acc. Circ:** 7,000.
Desc: Covers national and regional association activities and association staff changes. Contains management tips, legislative ideas, membership programs, communications ideas, and marketing activities.
Ind/Abst Curr. Lit. Fam. Plan. (19??-199?).

LC HD2425 .A88 ISSN 1054-4070
DD 061/.3/025 US
CCC
ASSOCIATIONS YELLOW BOOK. **See** Business and Economics-Abstracting, Bibliographies and Statistics.

US
AT THE WHEEL POSTER. (19??)-. English. $102.96. Bureau of Business Practice, 24 Rope Ferry Road, Waterford CT 06386. **Tel** (800)243-0876, (203)442-4365, (800)876-9105, FAX (203)443-1123.

ISSN 0747-315X
DD 338 US
ATHLETIC BUSINESS. [Athl. bus.]. Vol. 8, No. 3 (March 1984)-. Trade Publication. English. Twelve times a year. $36.00. Athletic Business Publications, 1842 Hoffman Street, Madison WI 53704. **Tel** (800)722-8764, (608)249-0186, FAX (608)249-1153. **ED** Sue Schmid. Index available (Bound in Feb. issue). cum. index. **Ad Acc. Circ:** 40,000 (ctrl). ***Continues*** *Athletic Purchasing and Facilities, 0192-5482.*
Desc: The magazine for those whose responsibility is the business of planning, financing and operating athletic fitness programs and facilities.
Ind/Abst Phys. Educ. Index; SPORT Discus; SportSearch.

LC HB71 ISSN 0164-8071
DD 330 US
CCC
ATLANTA BUSINESS CHRONICLE. [Atlanta bus. chron.]. Vol. 1 (June 5, 1978)-. Periodical. English. One time a week. $54.00. Atlanta Business Chronicle, 1801 Peachtree Street, Suite 150, Atlanta GA 30309. **Tel** (404)249-1010, FAX (404)249-1048. **ED** Anita Sharpe, David Black. **Ad Acc. Circ:** 30,000 (ctrl). available on microfilm and microfiche from University Microfilms International (UMI); available on an online database (files 635,648/Full-Text) from DIALOG. Documents available from UMI Article Clearinghouse.
Desc: Atlanta's weekly business newspaper, presenting local business news and in-depth features in the 18-county metro area.
Ind/Abst Bus. Dateline; Bus. Index (1985-1990); Bus. Source Plus; Bus. Source; EP Collect.; Gen. BusinessFile (1985-1990); Gen. Period. Index (1985-1990); Homework Help.; MasterFile FullTEXT 1000; MasterFile FullTEXT 350; MasterFile FullTEXT 650; MasterFile FullTEXT (Jan. 1995-); OCLC; PROMT; Telebase; Trade Ind. Index.

LC HG4058.A85 A85 ISSN 1054-5182
DD 338.7/4/0294758231 US
ATLANTA BUSINESS MAKERS & SHAKERS SERIES. [Atlanta bus. makers shakers ser.]. **VFOAT** Atlanta Business Makers and Shakers Series; Atlanta's Top Decision Makers; A.Atlanta's top networking channels. 1st Edition (1991)-. Monographic series. English. Irregular (every 18 months). Price varies per volume. Resource Communications Group, 3011 North Lamar Boulevard, Austin TX 78705. **Tel** (512)458-2021, FAX (512)458-2059. **ED** Jeanne Graves. Index available. **Bk Rev**, (Qty: 2/yr). **Circ:** 800 (ctrl). available on labels.
Desc: Comprehensive collection of target marketing information that contains over 3,000 key corporate contacts.

ISSN 1064-3877
DD 051 US
ATLANTA TRIBUNE (ROSWELL, GA.), THE. (THE ATLANTA TRIBUNE.). [Atlanta trib.]. Vol. 1, No. 1 (1987)-. Periodical. English. Twenty-four times a year. $24.00. Atlanta Tribune, 875 Old Roswell Road, Suite C100, Roswell GA 30076. **Tel** (404)587-0501, FAX (404)642-6501. **ED** Renita Mathis. **Bk Rev**, (Qty: 24). **Ad Acc. Circ:** 30,000.
Desc: Focuses on corporate and entrepreneurial business issues, personal finance, marketing and legal matters. Lifestyle departments include travel, arts and entertainment, social, community and school news.

Business and Economics

ISSN 1192-0203
DD 381 CN
ATLANTIC BUSINESS REPORT. [Atl. bus. rep.]. **VFOAT** Brunswick Business Journal Atlantic Business Report; BBJ Atlantic Business Report. Vol. 1, Issue 1 (Feb. 1992)-. Periodical. English. Twelve times a year. 20.01Can$. ABJ Publishing Inc., 599 Mian Street, Suite 203, Moncton NB E1C 1C8 Canada. **Tel** (506)857-9696, FAX (506)859-7395. **ED** Lynda MacGibbon. **Bk Rev. Ad Acc. Circ:** 16,000 (ctrl). available on microfiche.
Desc: Covers business in Atlantic Canada. A business-to-business newspaper personally addressed to decision makers--CEO's managers, purchasing agents, and the government.

LC HB1 .A77 **ISSN 0197-4254**
US
Pr Rev.
ATLANTIC ECONOMIC JOURNAL :
AEJ. [Atl. econ. j.]. **Added/Corp** Atlantic Economic Society. **VFOAT** AEJ. Vol. 1, No. 1 (Nov. 1973)-. Periodical. English. Four times a year (Jan., Mar., June, Sept.). $147.00. Atlantic Economic Society, Southern Illinois University at Edwardsville, Campus Box 1101, Edwardsville IL 62026-1101. **Tel** (618)692-2291, FAX (618)692-3400. **ED** John M. Virgo. Index available. cum. index. **Bk Rev**, (Qty: 3-5). **Ad Acc. Circ:** 1,200. available on microfilm and microfiche from University Microfilms International (UMI); available on an online database (file 648/Full-Text) from DIALOG; available on CD-ROM from EBSCO Publishing - Peabody. Documents available from UMI Article Clearinghouse, BLDSC, FAXON Xpress, The UnCover Company, SWETS.
Desc: Articles concerning all economic interest areas, without regard to fields or methodological preferences.
Ind/Abst ABI/INFORM Glob. Ed.; ABI/INFORM [Computer File] (March 1980-); Acad. Search; Bus. ASAP (1990-) [Full Txt.]; Bus. Index (1985-); Bus. Source Plus; Bus. Source; Contents Recent Econ. J.; Curr. Cit.; Econ. Lit. Index (199?-); EP Collect.; Gen. BusinessFile (1985-); Gen. Period. Index (1985-); Homework Help.; Hum. Resour. Abstr.; INFO-SOUTH Abstr.; J. Econ. Lit.; Mag. Search; MasterFile FullTEXT 1000; MasterFile FullTEXT 350; MasterFile FullTEXT 650; MasterFile FullTEXT (July 1993-); OCLC; PAIS Int. Print (1991-); Sage Public Adm. Abstr.; Telebase; Trade Ind. ASAP [Full Txt.]; Trade Ind. Index [Full Txt.]; UMI ABI/Inform--Bus. Period. Ondisc (Dec. 1987-) [Full Txt.].

ISSN 0225-7629
DD 071/.15 CN
ATLANTIC LIFE BUSINESS. [Atl. life bus.]. Vol. 1 (1979)-. Periodical. English. Twelve times a year. $7.20 for 24 issues. Atlantic Life Business, PO Box 12, Fredericton New Brunswick E3B 4Y2 Canada. *Continues Atlantic Life, 0225-7629.*

ISSN 1184-051X
DD 338.7/09715/05 CN
ATLANTIC LIFESTYLE BUSINESS. [Atl. lifestyle bus.]. **VFOAT** AL Business. Vol. 1, No. 3 (July/Aug. 1990)-. Periodical. English. Six times a year. 12.01Can$. Atlantic Lifestyle Business, PO Box 2356 Station C, St. Johns Newfoundland A1C 6E7 Canada. **Tel** (709)726-9300, FAX (709)726-3013. **ED** Adrian D. Smith. **Ad Acc, Adv Mgr:** Hubert F. Hutton. **Circ:** 25,000 (ctrl) *Continues Newfoundland Lifestyle Business, 1184-0501.*
Desc: This magazine focuses on business people, businesses and related issues of interest to the people of the Atlantic region of Canada.

ISSN 1202-4562
DD 330.9715 330.9715/005 CN
●**ATLANTIC REVIEW (HALIFAX. 1994).**
(ATLANTIC REVIEW : NEWSLETTER OF THE ATLANTIC PROVINCES ECONOMIC COUNCIL.). [Atl. rev.]. **Added/Corp** Atlantic Provinces Economic Council. (June 1994)-. Periodical. English. Irregular. Comes with Atlantic Provinces Economic Council membership. Atlantic Provinces Economic Council, 5121 Sackville Street, Suite 500, Halifax Nova Scotia B3J 1K1 Canada. **Tel** (902)422-6516, FAX (902)429-6803. available in microform from Micromedia Limited. *Continues Atlantic Provinces Economic Council. APEC Newsletter, 0044-989X.*

ISSN 0226-2258
DD 330.971/0646 CN
AU COURANT (OTTAWA. EDITION FRANCAIS). (AU COURANT.). [Au courant]. **Added/Corp** Conseil Economique du Canada. Services des Communications. Vol. 1, No 1 (Spring 1980)-. Periodical. French. Four times a year. *Continues in part Conseil Economique du Canada. Bulletin., 0702-6633.*
Ind/Abst Can. Period. Index; Repere (1992).

ISSN 0961-124X
DD 657.450285 UK
CCC
AUDIT TUNBRIDGE WELLS. (AUDIT.). [AudIT Tunbridge Wells]. (1990)-. Trade Publication. English. Six times a year. $231.02. Cork Publishing Ltd., Granary House, Rutland Street, Cork Ireland. **Tel** 011-353-21-313855, FAX 011-353-21-313496. **ED** Brian O'Kane. **Ad Acc. Circ:** 750.
Desc: Focuses on issues raised by the audit process.

LC J335 .H26 **ISSN 0866-6865**
HU
TITLE CHANGE
AULA : TARSADALOM ES GAZDASAG : A BUDAPESTI KOZGAZDASAGTUDOMANYI EGYETEM FOLYOIRATA. Added/Corp
Budapesti Kozgazdasagtudomanyi Egyetem. (1990)-(1994). Periodical. Hungarian (English). *Continues Egyetemi Szemle, 0139-4045. Continued by Tarsadalom es Gazdasag Kozep- es Kelet-Europaban.*

GW
AUSGABE DER NEUEN BUNDESLANDER. (19??)-. German. One time a week. DM140.80. Ges Wirtschaftspublizistik GWP GmbH, Postfach 3752, D-90018 Nuernberg FR Germany. **Tel** 011 49 911 5325173.

ISSN 0892-869X
DD 330 US
CCC
AUSTIN BUSINESS JOURNAL. [Austin bus. j.]. Vol. 1, No. 1 (Feb. 1981)-. Periodical. English. One time a week. $51.00. Austin Business Journal, D Vedder, 1301 South Capital of Texas #200C, Austin TX 78746. **Tel** (512)328-0180, FAX (512)338-7304. **ED** Ken Martin. Index available. **Ad Acc, Adv Mgr:** Rebecca Melancon. **Circ:** 10,500. available on an online database from Mead Data Central; and (files 635,648/Full-Text) DIALOG. Documents available from UMI Article Clearinghouse.
Desc: Source of professional business journalism for and about the Austin, Texas community.
Ind/Abst Acad. Search; Bus. Dateline; Bus. Index (Jan. 1985-Dec. 1985); Bus. Source Plus; Bus. Source; EP Collect.; Gen. BusinessFile (Jan. 1985-Dec. 1985); Gen. Period. Index (Jan. 1985-Dec. 1985); Homework Help.; INFO-SOUTH Abstr.; Mag. Search; MasterFile FullTEXT 1000; MasterFile FullTEXT 350; MasterFile FullTEXT 650; MasterFile FullTEXT (July 1993-); OCLC; PROMT; Telebase; Trade Ind. ASAP [Full Txt.]; Trade Ind. Index [Full Txt.].

LC HF5382.75.A8 A87 **ISSN 1046-8080**
DD 650.1/4/099405 US
AUSTRALIA EMPLOYMENT DIRECTORY. See Occupations and Careers.

LC HC601 .A817 **ISSN 0278-3940**
DD 337.94073/05 US
AUSTRALIAN-AMERICAN BUSINESS REVIEW, THE. (THE AUSTRALIAN-AMERICAN BUSINESS.). [Austr.-Am. bus. rev.]. **VAT** The Australian American Business Review. (1980)-. Periodical. English. Eleven times a year. 45.00Aus$ Australia; 50.00Aus$ US. Kejash Pty Ltd., PO Box 405, Roseville NSW 2069 Australia. **Tel** 011 61 29226177. **ED** Ken McGregor.
Desc: The business-to-business international magazine for two-way trade and investment.

AT
TITLE CHANGE
AUSTRALIAN BUSINESS BRIEF AND HANSARD SERVICE. (19??)-(19??). English. Commerce Management Services, PO Box E162 Queen Victoria, Terrace ACT 2600 Australia. **Tel** 011 61 6 2951961, FAX 011 61 6 2590170. *Continued by Government Affairs Monitor.*

ISSN 0725-3109
DD 016.338005 AT
SUSPENDED
AUSTRALIAN BUSINESS INDEX. [Aust. bus. index]. (1981)-Suspended (Jan. 1995). Periodical. English. Twelve times a year. 880.00Aus$. Australian Business Index, PO Locked Bag 2100, South Yarra Victoria 3141 Australia. **Tel** 011 61 3 8827344, FAX 011 61 3 8826837, telex 70508. Index available (free). **Circ:** 350. available on microfiche. *Absorbed Austalasian Industry Reporter.*
Desc: Reference guide featuring news on all aspects of Australian industries.
Ind/Abst APAIS, Aust. Public Aff. Inf. Ser. (1977-19??).

AT
Pr Rev.
AUSTRALIAN COMPANY SECRETARY.
(19??)-. Periodical. English. Eleven times a year (published monthly except Jan.). 46.04Aus$. Chartered Institute of Company Secretaries in Australia, 70 Castlereagh Street, Level 9, Sydney, New South Wales 2000 Australia. **Tel** 011 61 2 2235744. Index available (bound in all issues). *Continues Journal of Corporate Management, 1038-2410.*

ISSN 1035-865X
DD 330.0994 AT
AUSTRALIAN ECONOMIC INDICATORS. [Aust. econ. indic.]. **Added/Corp** Australian Bureau of Statistics. (1991)-. Periodical. English. Eleven times a year (monthly except Jan.). 256.52Aus$. Australian Bureau of Statistics, PO Box 2796Y, Melbourne 3001 Australia. **Tel** 011 61 3 6157843.
Desc: Presents a statistical summary of recent developments in the Australian economy.

LC HC601 .A825 **ISSN 0004-9018**
DD 338.994 AT
Pr Rev.
AUSTRALIAN ECONOMIC REVIEW, THE. [Aust. econ. rev.]. **Added/Corp** University of Melbourne. Institute of Applied Economic Research. University of Melbourne. Institute of Applied Economic and Social Research. No. 1 (1968)-. Academic Scholarly Publication. English. Four times a year. 131.55Aus$. Institute of Applied Economic and Social Research / Australia, University of Melbourne, Economics Building, Parkville Victoria 3052 Australia. **Tel** 011 61 3 3445330, FAX 011 61 3 3445630, telex 35185. **ED** D. Johnon and P. Kenyon. **Ad Acc. Circ:** 1,050. available on microfilm and microfiche from University Microfilms International (UMI); available on an online database from University Microfilms International (UMI).
Desc: Contains articles on applied economic and social issues. The second and fourth issues of each year contain short term forecasts of the Australian economy.
Ind/Abst APAIS, Aust. Public Aff. Inf. Ser. (1969-); Contents Recent Econ. J.; Curr. Cit.; Econ. Lit. Index; Int. Labour Doc.; J. Econ. Lit.; PAIS Int. Print (1991-).

ISSN 1031-5810
DD 658.87080994 AT
TITLE CHANGE
AUSTRALIAN FRANCHISING. [Aust. franch.]. (1988)-(19??). Periodical. English. Hassel Hunt & Moore Pty Ltd, PO Box 900, Mona Vale 2103 Australia. **Tel** 011 61 02 9706688, FAX 011 61 02 4393959. *Continued by Franchising.*

ISSN 0812-129X
AT
AUSTRALIAN INVESTOR. (1984)-. English. Twelve times a year.

LC HD1401 .A9 **ISSN 0004-9395**
DD 338.1/0994 AT
Pr Rev.
AUSTRALIAN JOURNAL OF AGRICULTURAL ECONOMICS, THE. See Agriculture-Agricultural Economics.

AT
AUSTRALIAN PROFILE. (19??)-. English. Six times a year. 350.00Aus$. Commercial Economic Advisors Service of Australia, PO Box 104 St. Leonards, New South Wales 2065 Australia. **Tel** 011 61 2 4393790, 011 61 2 4393750, FAX 011 61 2 4383729. cum. index. **Ad Acc, Adv Mgr Tel** 02 439 3750. ctrl circ.

ISSN 0314-4275
AT
AUSTRALIAN SECRETARY. (1976)-. English. Four times a year (Mar., June, Sep., Dec.). 24.67Aus$. Institute of Professional Secretaries/ Australia, PO Box 373, East Kew Vic, 3102 Australia. **Tel** 011 61 3 8530923, FAX 011 61 3 8530919. *Continues IPSA Journal.*

LC HG4272.5 .A94 **ISSN 1036-3874**
DD 338.7/4/02594 AT
AUSTRALIA'S TOP 100. Added/Corp
Australian Stock Exchange. **VFOAT** Australia's Top One Hundred. (19??)-. English. One time a year. 20.51Aus$. Stock Exchange Melbourne Australia, GPO Box 1784 Q, Melbourne 3001 Australia. **Tel** 011 61 03 6178611.

LC HD9999.C27 A98 **ISSN 0005-0776**
DD 338 US
AUTO LAUNDRY NEWS. See Transportation-Automobiles.

ISSN 0192-186X
US
AUTO MERCHANDISING NEWS. See Transportation-Automobiles.

UK
AUTOMOTIVE BUSINESS NEWS. See Transportation-Automobiles.

LC TL1 .A885 **ISSN 0567-2317**
DD 658/.92/9287 US
AUTOMOTIVE REBUILDER. See Transportation-Automobiles.

ISSN 1198-8185
DD 658/.041/0971405 CN
●**AUTONOME (MONTREAL).** (L'AUTONOME.). [Autonome]. **VFOAT** Magazine Autonome. Vol. 1, No 1 (Oct. 1994)-. Periodical. French. Six times a year. 14.24Can$. Editions VB Mag ENR, 5253 boulevard Decarie, Bureau 515, Montreal QUE H3W 3C3 Canada. **Tel** (514)489-7254.

LC HF3231 .A95 ISSN 0187-4942
MX

AVANCE DE INFORMACION ECONOMICA. BALANZA COMERCIAL. **Added/Corp** Instituto Nacional de Estadistica, Geografia e Informatica (Mexico). **VFOAT** Balanza Comercial. (19??)-. Spanish. Twelve times a year. $187,000. INEGI / Instituto Nacional de Estadistica, Geografia e Informatica, Avenida Patriotismo 711 Segundo Piso, 03730 Mexico DF Mexico. **Tel** 011 52 5 5639935, 011 52 5 5988935, FAX 011 52 55987941.

LC HC
DD 330 MX

AVANCE DE INFORMACION ECONOMICA. INDUSTRIA MAQUILADORA DE EXPORTACION. **Added/Corp** Instituto Nacional de Estadistica, Geografia e Informatica (Mexico). **VFOAT** Industria Maquiladora de Exportacion. (19??)-. Spanish. Twelve times a year. $30.55. INEGI / Instituto Nacional de Estadistica, Geografia e Informatica, Avenida Patriotismo 711 Segundo Piso, 03730 Mexico DF Mexico. **Tel** 011 52 5 5639935, 011 52 5 5988935, FAX 011 52 55987941. **(Subscription address:** INEGI / Instituto Nacional de Estadistica, Geografia e Informatica, Avenida Heroe de Nacozari 2301 Sur, Fracc. Jardines del Parque, CP 20270, Aguascalientes Mexico. **Tel** 011 52 49 182998.**)**

LC TS2301.A7 F472 ISSN 1064-7112
DD 621.389/7 US
TITLE CHANGE

AVC PRESENTATION FOR THE VISUAL COMMUNICATOR. [AVC present. vis. commun.]. **VFOAT** Presentation for the Visual Communicator; Presentation; AVC; AVC Presentation. Vol. 26, No. 7 (July 1992)-(1993). Periodical. English. PTN Publishing Company, 445 Broad Hollow Road, Melville NY 11747. **Tel** (516)845-2700, FAX (516)845-7109. Documents available from UMI Article Clearinghouse. ***Continues*** *AVC Presentation Development & Delivery, 1062-2683.* ***Continued by*** *Advanced Imaging (Woodbury, N.Y.).*
Ind/Abst Bus. ASAP [Full Txt.]; Newsp. Period. Abstr. (1986-).

ISSN 1187-6611
DD 331.110971405 CN

AVENIR (MONTREAL. 1991). (AVENIR.). [Avenir Montr., 1991]. (1991)-. Periodical. French. Six times a year. 40.00Can$. Les Editions du Montreal Royal Inc, 3715 Avenue Lacombe, Bureau 200, Montreal Quebec H3T 1M3 Canada. **Tel** (514)341-7916, FAX (514)341-2644. **ED** Matthias Rioux. **Bk Rev. Ad Acc.** ctrl circ. ***Continues*** *Magazine Avenir, 0846-5274.*
Ind/Abst Repere (1991-).

LC HE9761 ISSN 0961-2513
DD 387.71 UK

AVMARK AVIATION ECONOMIST. **See** Aeronautics, Astronautics.

LC HD5100 .A25a
DD 331.2/2/0994 AT

AWARD RATES OF PAY INDEXES, AUSTRALIA. **Added/Corp** Australian Bureau of Statistics. (Sept. 1982)-. English. Twelve times a year. 147.99Aus$. Australian Bureau of Statistics, PO Box 2796Y, Melbourne 3001 Australia. **Tel** 011 61 3 6157843. **Circ:** 4,000. ***Continues*** *Wage Rates Indexes.*

NE

B & ID. (19??)-. Dutch. Six times a year. VNU Business Publications BV, Postbus 9194, 1006 AC Amsterdam Netherlands. **Tel** 011 31 20 4875879.

ISSN 1036-1723
DD 330.994063 AT

BACKGROUND PAPER - ECONOMIC PLANNING ADVISORY COUNCIL. (BACKGROUND PAPER.). [Backgr. pap. - Econ. Plan. Advis. Counc.]. **Added/Corp** Australia. Office of the Economic Planning Advisory Council Australia. Economic Planning Advisory Council. (1990)-. Government Publication. English. Irregular. 54.00Aus$. Australian Government Publishing Service, GPO Box 84, Canberra ACT 2601 Australia. **Tel** 011 61 6 2954411, FAX 011 61 6 2954455.

LC F1650 .B3 ISSN 0067-2912
BF

BAHAMAS HANDBOOK AND BUSINESSMAN'S ANNUAL. **See** Travel and Tourism.

LC HC188.B3 B38
DD 338.0981/42 BL

BAHIA ... RESENHA DE EMPRESAS / SECRETARIA DA INDUSTRIA E COMERCIO. 1981-. Portuguese. One time a year.

US

BAKER LIBRARY MINI-LIST. **Main/Corp** Baker Library. **VFOAT** Baker Library Mini List. (19??)-. Periodical. English. $10.00 complete set (add $1.50 for postage and handling). Harvard Business School Publishing Division, Operations Department, 60 Harvard Way, Boston MA 02163. **Tel** (617)495-6192, (617)495-8948, FAX (617)495-6891, telex 6817229.

LC HF1101 .B3 ISSN 0005-4232
DD 375 US

BALANCE SHEET (CINCINNATI, OHIO), THE. (THE BALANCE SHEET.). [Balance sheet]. Vol. 1 (Oct. 1919)-. Periodical. English. Five times a year. Southwestern Publishing Company, 5101 Madison Road, Cincinnati OH 45227. **Tel** (513)271-8811. **ED** Robert Nesbit. available on microfilm and microfiche from University Microfilms International (UMI).
Ind/Abst Account. Art.; Bus. Educ. Index; Curr. Index J. Educ.; Mat. Fact.

ISSN 0005-4259
NE
UDC 343.8

BALANS (DEN HAAG). (BALANS.). [Balans Den Haag]. (1970)-. Periodical. Dutch. Irregular (22 issues). $243.10. Uitgeverij Biblo, Brasschaatsesteenweg 200, 2920 Kalmthout Belgium. **Tel** 011 32 3 6200240 6200211, 011 32 3 6200211, FAX 011 32 3 6200361, telex 72080. Index available (free). ***Continues*** *Maandschrift voor het Gevangeniswezen.*

LC F189.B13 B35 ISSN 1052-0996
DD 975.2/6/0025 US

BALTIMORE/ANNAPOLIS. [Baltim./Annap.]. **Added/Corp** Columbia Books, Inc. (Washington, D.C.). **VFOAT** Baltimore, Annapolis. (1987)-. English. Every 2 years. $60.00. Columbia Books Inc, 1212 New York Avenue NW/Suite 330, Washington DC 20005. **Tel** (202)898-0662, FAX (202)898-0775. **ED** John J Russell. Index available. **Circ:** 2,000 (ctrl).
Desc: Lists 2,000 key public and private institutions of Baltimore and Annapolis areas and their 10,000 leaders. Arranged by subject in 17 chapters, including federal, state and local governments, businesses, association, educational and cultural institutions, media. Combined index of individuals and organizations shows miltiple affiliations and responsibilities of leaders.

ISSN 0747-1823
US
CCC
Pr Rev.

BALTIMORE BUSINESS JOURNAL. Vol. 1, No. 1 (June 20, 1983)-. Newspaper. English. One time a week. $51.00. Baltimore Business Journal, 117 Water Street, 9th Floor, Baltimore MD 21202. **Tel** (410)576-1161. **ED** Tom York. **Ad Acc, Adv Mgr:** Gary Press. **Circ:** 15,000. available on microfilm and microfiche; available on an online database (files 635,648/Full-Text) from DIALOG. Documents available from UMI Article Clearinghouse.
Desc: Contains the business news and advertising needs of Maryland's business community.
Ind/Abst Acad. Search; Bus. Dateline; Bus. Index (1985-1991); Bus. Source Plus; Bus. Source; EP Collect.; Gen. BusinessFile (1985-1990); Gen. Period. Index (1985-1990); Homework Help.; INFO-SOUTH Abstr.; Mag. Search; MasterFile FullTEXT 1000; MasterFile FullTEXT 350; MasterFile FullTEXT 650; MasterFile FullTEXT (July 1993-); OCLC; PROMT; Telebase; Trade Ind. ASAP [Full Txt.]; Trade Ind. Index [Full Txt.].

LC HC301 .B3 ISSN 0005-4607
DD 330.945/005 IT

BANCA NAZIONALE DEL LAVORO QUARTERLY REVIEW. (QUARTERLY REVIEW / BANCA NAZIONALE DEL LAVORO.). **Main/Corp** Banca Nazionale del Lavoro. No. 1 (April 1947)-. Periodical. English. Four times a year. Free. Banca Nazionale del Lavoni, Viaa Veneto 119, Rome Italy. **Tel** 47021, telex 610116. **ED** Luigi Ceriani, Alessandro Roncaglia. Index available. cum. index. **Circ:** 4,800. available on microfilm and microfiche from University Microfilms International (UMI).
Desc: Articles by economists on macroeconomic theory and policy, international trade and finance, the evolution of national monetary and financial institutions and allied topics.
Ind/Abst Bus. Index (1985-); Contents Recent Econ. J.; Contents Pages Manage.; Econ. Lit. Index; Gen. BusinessFile (1985-); Gen. Period. Index (1985-); J. Econ. Lit.; Leis., Rec., Tour. Abstr.; Rural Dev. Abstr.; Trade Ind. Index; World Agric. Econ. Rural Sociol. Abstr.

ISSN 0005-4895
SW
UDC 331.881

BANCOPOSTEN. [Bancoposten]. (1916)-. Swedish. Irregular.
Ind/Abst Numis. Lit.

DD 959 TH
UDC 95

BANGKOK POST WEEKLY REVIEW. (19??)-. Periodical. English. One time a week. $60.00 Thailand; $102.00 Asia; $142.00 other. Post Publishing Company Ltd., 136 Na Ranong Road, Klong Toey 10110 Bangkok Thailand. **Tel** 011 66 2 2403700. **ED** Anussorn Thavisin. **Ad Acc.**
Desc: Presents Thailand and the region to international business news.

LC HD2075.6 .B37
DD 338.1/09549/2 BG

BANGLADESH JOURNAL OF AGRICULTURAL ECONOMICS, THE. **See** Agriculture-Agricultural Economics.

ISSN 1067-7984
DD 338 US

•BANGLADESH (SYRACUSE, N.Y.). (BANGLADESH : AN EXECUTIVE REPORT.). [Bangladesh]. **Added/Corp** Political Risk Services (IBC USA (Publications) Inc.). (1993)-. English. $110.00. Political Risk Services, 6320 Fly Road, Suite 102, PO Box 248, East Syracuse NY 13057-0248. **Tel** (315)431-0511, FAX (315)431-0200.
Desc: Focuses on the long-term outlook for business. Includes a brief review of recent events and current circumstances, background intelligence including geography, history, economics and social conditions, as well as the key political and economic forecasts.

ISSN 0741-5729
US
TITLE CHANGE

BARBARA BRABEC'S NATIONAL HOME BUSINESS REPORT. [Barbara Brabec's Nat'l. home bus. rep.]. **VFOAT** National Home Business Report. (1984)-(19??). Trade Publication. English. Barbara Brabec Productions, PO Box 2137, Naperville IL 60567. **Tel** (708)717-0488. ***Continues*** *Sharing Barbara's Mail, 0730-7853.* ***Continued by*** *Barbara Brabec's Self Employment Survival Letter.*

ISSN 1075-1815
US

•BARBARA BRABEC'S SELF-EMPLOYMENT SURVIVAL LETTER. **Added/Corp** Barbara Brabec Productions. (1994)-. Periodical. English. Six times a year. $29.00. Barbara Brabec Productions, PO Box 2137, Naperville IL 60567. **Tel** (708)717-0488. ***Continues*** *Barbara Brabec's National Home Business Report, 0741-5729.*

LC HF1131 .B375 ISSN 1043-190X
DD 650/.071/173 US

BARRON'S GUIDE TO GRADUATE BUSINESS SCHOOLS. **VFOAT** Guide to Graduate Business Schools. (1984)-. Directory. English. Every 2 years. Barron's Educational Series Inc., 250 Wireless Boulevard, Hauppauge NY 11788. **Tel** (800)645-3476, FAX (516)434-3723. **ED** E Miller. ***Formed by the union of*** *Barron's Guide to Graduate Business Schools (Eastern Ed.), 1043-1926* ***and*** *Barron's Guide to Graduate Business Schools (Western Ed.), 1043-1934.*

LC HF5695 .E87 ISSN 0362-0670
DD 513/.93/076 US

BARRON'S REGENTS EXAMS AND ANSWERS : BUSINESS MATHEMATICS. **See** Mathematics.

ISSN 0199-7858
US

BAY STATE BUSINESS WORLD. (19??)-. Periodical. English. One time a week (except week before Christmas, alternate weeks in July and Aug.). $40.00. Bay State Business World, 314 Nahatan Street, Norwood MA 02062. **Tel** (617)762-7771.

ISSN 0739-1072
US

BAYLOR BUSINESS REVIEW. [Baylor bus. rev.]. **Added/Corp** Hankamer School of Business. Bureau of Business Research. Vol. 1, No. 1 (Summer 1983)-. Periodical. English. Three times a year. $14.00. Baylor University / Hankamer School of Business, Box 98009, Waco TX 76798. **Tel** (817)755-3495, FAX (817)755-1068. **ED** Judith Corwin. **Photos. Circ:** 18,000. available on microfilm and microfiche from University Microfilms International (UMI). Documents available from UMI Article Clearinghouse. ***Continues*** *Baylor Business Studies.*
Ind/Abst ABI/INFORM Glob. Ed.; ABI/INFORM [Computer File] (Winter 1985); Bus. Index (1979-?); Bus. Source Plus; EP Collect.; Homework Help.; MasterFile FullTEXT 1000; MasterFile FullTEXT 350; MasterFile FullTEXT 650; MasterFile FullTEXT; OCLC; Telebase; UMI ABI/Inform--Bus. Period. Ondisc (Summer 1988-) [Full Txt.].

US

BBP MANAGEMENT LETTER. (19??)-. English. Twenty-four times a year. $137.88 (US), $167.16 (Canada). Bureau of Business Practice, 24 Rope Ferry Road, Waterford CT 06386. **Tel** (800)243-0876, (203)442-4365, (800)876-9105, FAX (203)443-1123.

LC HC111 ISSN 0829-481X
DD 330.9711/04/05 CN

BC BUSINESS. [BC bus.]. **VFOAT** BC Business Magazine. Vol. 11, No. 9 (Sept. 1983)-. Periodical. English. Twelve times a year. 18.37Can$. Canada Wide Magazines Ltd., 401-4180 Lougheed Highway, Burnaby British Columbia V5C 6A7 Canada. **Tel** (604)299-7311, FAX (604)299-9188. **ED** Bonnie Irving. **Ad Acc, Adv Mgr:** Tim Kelley. available on microfiche (from Toronto,

Micromedia) from University Microfilms International (UMI); available on an online database (files 635,648/Full-Text) from Knight-Ridder Information, Inc.; available in microform from Micromedia Limited. Documents available from UMI Article Clearinghouse. **Continues** B.C. Business Magazine, 0384-0581; **Absorbed** Asia Pacific Business, 0829-4488.
Ind/Abst Acad. Search; Bus. Dateline; Bus. Index (1985-); Bus. Source Plus; Bus. Source; Can. Index; Can. Period. Index; EP Collect.; Gen. BusinessFile (1985-); Gen. Period. Index (1985-); Homework Help.; INFO-SOUTH Abstr.; MasterFile FullTEXT 1000; MasterFile FullTEXT 350; MasterFile FullTEXT 650; MasterFile FullTEXT (July 1993-); OCLC; PROMT; Telebase; Trade Ind. ASAP [Full Txt.]; Trade Ind. Index [Full Txt.].

ISSN 0005-2841
DD 700
US

BCA NEWS (NEW YORK, N.Y.). See The Arts.

GW

BEGLEITPAPIERE FUER AUSFUHRSENDUNGEN. (19??)-. German. Irregular (8-10 issues per year). DM126.00 (basic rate). VD Linnepe Verlagsgesellschaft GmbH & Co, Bahnhofstrasse 28, Postfach 2260, W 5800 Hagen 1 FR Germany. **Tel** 011 49 2331 32078 or 79. **(Subscription address:** Friederike Mendel Verlag, Robensstrasse 39, D-52070 Aachen Germany. **Tel** 011 49 241 154355.**)**

ISSN 0175-5676
GW

UDC 33:001.891
BEITRAEGE ZUR OKONOMISCHEN FORSCHUNG. [Beitr. okon. Forsch.]. (1974)-. Monographic series. Multiple languages. Irregular. Price varies per volume. Vandenhoeck & Ruprecht, Robert Bosch Breite 6, D-37079 Goettingen Germany. **Tel** 011 49 551 695911, FAX 011 49 551 695917, telex 965226 VAN d.
Ind/Abst Zentralbl. Math. Ihre Grenzgeb.

BE
BELGIAN BUSINESS. (19??)-. Periodical. French (Dutch). Ten times a year. 1600F Belgium; 2600F North America; 2200F Europe. Diligentia, Hulstlaan 42 Avenue du Houx, 1170 Brussels Belgium. **Tel** 011 32 2 6738170. **ED** Robert Verbeek. **Ad Acc. Circ:** 31,500.

BE
BELGIUM'S 500 LARGEST COMPANIES. **VFOAT** Les Principales Societes en Belgique; De Grootste Maatschappijen in Belgie. Periodical. Multiple languages (English, French and Dutch). One time a year.

ISSN 1354-8107
UK
CCC

●**BENCHMARK KEMPSTON.** (THE BENCHMARK.). [Benchmark Kempston.]. (1994)-. English. Four times a year (Feb., May, Aug., Nov.). $273.80. IFS Ltd., Wolseley Road, Kemps Business Park, Kemps Bedford MK42 7PW United Kingdom. **Tel** 011 44 1234 853605, FAX 011 44 1234 854499. **ED** Rory L. Chase. **Bk Rev.** available on photocopies.
Desc: Provides practitioners with proven strategies, tools and techniques for introducing and conducting competitive business benchmarking within their organizations.

ISSN 1351-5055
UK
CEASED
BENCHMARKING BRIEFING. (1994)-(Feb. 1995). English. Longman Group Ltd., Fourth Avenue, Longman House, Harlow Essex CM19 5SR United Kingdom. **Tel** 011 44 1279 429655, FAX 011 44 1279 431067, telex 81259.

GW
BERICHT ... DES BUNDESVERBANDES DER DEUTSCHEN INDUSTRIE E.V. **Added/Corp** Bundesverband der Deutschen Industrie. (1988). German. Every 2 years. **Continues** Jahresbericht ... des Bundesverbandes der Deutschen Industrie E.V., 0521-7741.

ISSN 1170-4861
NZ
DD 330.900112099305
BERL FORECASTS. [BERL forecasts]. **VFOAT** Business and Economic Research Ltd. Forecasts; Business Forecasts. (1985)-. English. Three times a year (March, July, Nov.). $283.67. BERL Forecasts, PO Box 10277, Wellington New Zealand. **Tel** 011/64/4/4705550, FAX 011/64/4/4733276. ctrl circ. Documents available.

UK
BEST BES ADVICE. (19??)-. English. Irregular. $213.90. Allenbridge Group, 29 Maddox Street, London U1R 9LD United Kingdom. **Tel** 011 44 171 4091111.

LC HG4028.B2 B43 **ISSN** 0360-8743
DD 658.1/512 US
BEST IN ANNUAL REPORTS, THE. (1975)-. Trade Publication. English. Every 2 years. $17.50. RC Publications Inc., 3200 Tower Oaks Boulevard, Rockville MD 20852. **Tel** (800)222-2654, (301)770-2900, FAX (301)984-3203.

ISSN 0959-2113
UK
CODEN BBUIEC
BEST OF BUSINESS INTERNATIONAL. [Best bus. int.]. **VFOAT** Best of Business. (1987)-. Periodical. English. Four times a year. Whittle Communications / London, 24 Conway Street, London W1P 5HP United Kingdom. Documents available from Ask*IEEE.
Ind/Abst HILITES; INSPEC (Summer 1989-).

ISSN 0889-3136
US
CEASED
BEST OF LONG RANGE PLANNING, THE. (1989)-Series complete with Vol. 12. Periodical. English. Pergamon Press, An Imprint of Elsevier Science Ltd., The Boulevard, Langford Lane, Kidlington, Oxford OX5 1GB United Kingdom. **Tel** 011 44 1865 843000, 011 44 1865 843699, FAX 011 44 1865 843010.
Desc: Provides for the papers on strategic and corporate planning from long range planning. Each issue will provide both industrialists and educators with a record of practice and theory in particular aspects of strategic planning.

LC HB21 .B47 **ISSN** 1058-4110
DD 330/.05 US
CEASED
BEST PAPERS PROCEEDINGS / ATLANTIC ECONOMIC SOCIETY. [Best pap. proc. - Atl. Econ. Soc.]. **Main/Corp** Atlantic Economic Society. **Added/Corp** Atlantic Economic Society. **VFOAT** Atlantic Economic Society Best Papers Proceedings; AES, Best Papers Proceedings. (Jan. 1991)-(1994). Proceedings. English. Southern Illinois University / Ewardsville - Economic Society, Campus Box 1101, Edwardsville IL 62026. **Tel** (618)692-2291, FAX (618)692-3400.

UK
●**BEST PRACTICE MAGAZINE.** (1993)-. English. Six times a year (Jan., Mar., May, July, Sept., Nov.). $299.46. IFS Ltd., Wolseley Road, Kemps Business Park, Kemps Bedford MK42 7PW United Kingdom. **Tel** 011 44 1234 853605, FAX 011 44 1234 854499. **ED** Rory L. Chase. **Bk Rev. Ad Acc.**
Desc: Provides executives and managers in business, government and services with information to assist them in the introduction of best practice procedures to their organizations.

UK
BET. (19??)-. Periodical. English. Six times a year (Jan., Mar., May, July, Sept., Nov.). £37.50 UK and Europe; £49.50 (airmail) other. Pitman Publishing Ltd, 12 14 Slaidburn Cres, Southport Merseyside, PR9 9YF United Kingdom. **Tel** 011 44 1704 26881, FAX 011 44 1704 231970, telex 261367. **ED** Jill Priest. Index available. cum. index. **Bk Rev** (Qty: 18). **Ad Acc. Circ:** 10,000 (ctrl). **Continues** Business Education Today.
Desc: A resource magazine for teachers, lecturers, and trainers of business - related courses.

ISSN 0342-7064
GW
CCC
BETRIEBSWIRTSCHAFT STUTTGART, DIE. [BetriebswirtschaftStuttg.]. **VFOAT** DBW. Die Betriebswirtschaft. (1930)-. Periodical. German. Six times a year. $150.16. C E Poeschel Verlag, Postfach 103241, Kernerstrasse 43, W-7000 Stuttgart 10 Germany. **Tel** 011 49 711 229020.
Ind/Abst Selec. Coop. Index Manage. Period.

ISSN 0523-1051
US
SUSPENDED
BETTER BEEF BUSINESS. See Agriculture-Livestock.

ISSN 1064-1270
US
BETTER BUSINESS BULLETIN (NORTH PALM BEACH, FLA.), THE. (THE BETTER BUSINESS BULLETIN). Vol. 1, No. 1 (1992)-. Bulletin. English. Twelve times a year. $25.00. Drumbeat Publications, 420 US Highway 1, Suite 15-V, North Palm Beach FL 33408.

LC HC79.155 B46 **ISSN** 1061-9216
DD 650 US
BEYOND COMPUTING. See Computers.

ISSN 1166-245X
FR
UDC 336.76
BFCE MULTIDEVISES. **VFOAT** Banque Francaise du Commerce Exterieur Mutidevises. (1991)-. Periodical. French. Twelve times a year. $251.53. Banque Francais Commerce Exterieur, 21 boulevard Haussmann, 75427 Paris Cedex 09 France. **Tel** 011 33 1 48004685.
Continues Cours des Changes (Paris), 0183-5009.

LC Z7164.O7 C67 HD60.5 .U5 **ISSN** 0160-8819
DD 016.6584/08/0973 US
BIBLIOGRAPHY OF CORPORATE SOCIAL RESPONSIBILITY. See Industry and Production.

US
BID PROTEST DECISIONS. English. Twelve times a year. $644.48. Federal Publications Inc, 1120 20th Street Northwest, Washington DC 20036. **Tel** (202)337-7000, (800)922-4330, FAX (202)659-2233.

ISSN 8756-6567
US
BIG SKY BUSINESS JOURNAL. (198?)-. Periodical. English. Twenty-four times a year. $25.00. Tanstaafl Enterprises, PO Box 3262, Billings MT 59103. **Tel** (406)259-2309. **ED** Evelyn Pyburn. **Ad Acc, Ad Mgr:** Dennis Pyburn. **Circ:** 5,000.
Desc: Focuses on local and statewide business news, information, and statistics of interest to Billings business people.

LC HF5001 .B5
JA
BIJINESU REBYU. BUSINESS REVIEW. **Added/Corp** Hitotsubashi Daigaku. Sangyo Keiei Kenkyujo. **VFOAT** Business Review. (19??)-. Japanese. Four times a year. $95.00. Chikura Shobo, Kyobashi Daiichi Seimei Building, 4-12, Kyobashi 2-chome, Chuo-ku, Tokyo 104 Japan. **(Subscription address:** Maruzen Company Ltd., PO Box 5050, Import & Export Department, Tokyo 100 31 Japan. **Tel** 011 81 3 32789224.**) Circ:** 1,000 (ctrl).
Desc: Introduces the results of theoretical and practical research about enterprises in Japan.

LC HC111 **ISSN** 1184-6259
DD 330.9714/17/05 CN
BILAN SOCIO-ECONOMIQUE, REGION DE LA COTE-NORD. [Bilan socio-econ. reg. Cote-Nord]. **Added/Corp** Office de Planification et de Developpement du Quebec. (1990)-. French. Every 3 years. **Continues** Bilan Socio-Economique ..., Cote-Nord., 1184-6240.

ISSN 0755-2238
FR
CCC
UDC 07 "53"
BILANS POLITIQUES ECONOMIQUES ET SOCIAUX HEBDOMADAIRES. [Bilans polit. econ. soc. hebd.]. **VFOAT** Bilans Hebdomadaires Politiques Economiques et Sociaux. (1945)-. Periodical. French. One time a week. 3500.00F France; 3780.00F other. Societe Generale de Presse et d'Editions, 13 Avenue de l'Opera, 75001 Paris France. **Tel** 011 33 1 40151789.

ISSN 0894-9697
DD 320 US
BILL SHIPP'S GEORGIA. See Public Administration.

ISSN 0832-5359
DD 338.4/7662669 CN
BIO FAX. [Bio fax]. **VFOAT** Biofax. Vol. 1, No. 1 (July 9, 1987)-. Periodical. English. One time a week. Free. Biopress, PO Box 441 Station E, Ottawa Ontario K1S 5B4 Canada.

US
BIOBUSINESS. See Business and Economics-Abstracting, Bibliographies and Statistics.

ISSN 0898-5227
DD 660 US
BIOBUSINESS SEARCH GUIDE. See Business and Economics-Abstracting, Bibliographies and Statistics.

LC TP248
DD 660.6 US
BIOCENTURY : THE BERNSTEIN REPORT ON BIOBUSINESS. See Biology-Bioengineering.

LC TP248 **ISSN** 0965-9595
DD 660.6 UK
BIOTECHNOLOGY BUSINESS NEWS. **See** Biology-Bioengineering.

LC JA **ISSN** 0032-3276
DD 320 US
BIPAC POLITICS. See Political Science.

ISSN 0889-2237
US
BIRMINGHAM BUSINESS JOURNAL. (198?)-. Periodical. English. Twelve times a year. $36.00. Birmingham Business Journal, 2101 Magnolia S/Suite 400, Birmingham AL 35205. **Tel** (205)322-0000, FAX (205)322-0040. **ED** Tina Verciglio. **Ad Acc, Adv Mgr:** Linda Geldolatt. **Circ:** 10,500 (ctrl). available on an online database (files 636,648/Full-Text) from DIALOG. Documents available from UMI Article Clearinghouse.
Desc: Provides business news and reference information.
Ind/Abst Acad. Search; Bus. Dateline; Bus. Index (Jan. 1985-Dec. 1985); Bus. Source Plus; Bus. Source; EP Collect.; Gen. BusinessFile (Jan. 1985-Dec. 1985); Gen. Period. Index (Jan. 1985-Dec. 1985); Homework Help.; INFO-SOUTH Abstr.; MasterFile FullTEXT 1000; MasterFile FullTEXT 350; MasterFile FullTEXT 650; MasterFile FullTEXT (July 1993-); OCLC; Telebase; Trade Ind. ASAP [Full Txt.]; Trade Ind. Index [Full Txt.].

ISSN 1065-1012
DD 621 US
BISHOP REPORT, THE. (THE BISHOP REPORT : CONNECTOR PERFORMANCE & FORECAST.). [Bish. rep.]. **Added/Corp** Bishop & Associates, Inc. (199?)-. Periodical. English. Twelve times a year. $295.00. Bishop & Associates Inc., 1065 Aster Lane, Chicago IL 60185. **Tel** (708)876-1041.
Desc: A market research firm that specializes in monitoring, analyzing, reporting on the Connector Industry.

LC HF3628.U6 B57
US
BISNIS BULLETIN. **Added/Corp** United States. Business Information Service for the Newly Independent States. **VFOAT** Business Information Service for the Newly Independent States Bulletin. (June 1992)-. Bulletin. English. Twelve times a year. Free on request. BISNIS Information Center, Room 7413, US Department of Commerce, Washington DC 20230. **Tel** (202)482-4655.

LC HB251 ISSN 1380-8206
DD 339 NE
UDC 339
●**BIZZ DOETINCHEM.** (BIZZ). [BIZZ Doetinchem]. (1994)-. Trade Publication. Dutch. Four times a year. Misset Uitgeverij BV / Doetinchem, Postbus 4, 7000 BA Doetinchem Netherlands. **Tel** 011 31 8340 49911, 011 31 8340 49562, FAX 011 31 8340 43839, 011 31 8340 40515.

US
BL BLANKET ORDER. **Main/Corp** OECD. (19??)-. Government Publication. English. Irregular. Price varies. OECD Publications and Information Center, 2 rue Andre-Pascal, 75775 Paris Cedex 16 France. **Tel** 011 33 1 49104262, US:(202)785-6323, FAX 011 33 1 45248500, 011 33 1 45248176, telex 620 160 OCDE. **(Subscription address:** OECD Publications Center, 2001 L Street, Suite 700, Washington DC 20036. **Tel** (202)822-3873, (202)785-6323.)

ISSN 0963-133X
UK
BLACK COUNTRY SOUTH BUSINESS DIRECTORY. (1990)-. Directory. English. One time a year. £23.00. Holcot Press Ltd, Station House, Station Road, Newport Pognell, Milton Keynes MK16 0AG United Kingdom. **Tel** 011 44 1908 614477, FAX 011 44 1908 217425. **ED** Hilda Knight. available on CD-ROM.

ISSN 1053-704X
DD 331 US
BLACK EMPLOYMENT & EDUCATION. [Black employ. educ.]. **VFOAT** Black Employment and Education; Black Employment & Education Magazine. (June 1990)-. Periodical. English. Ten times a year (4 times a year with 6 special issues). $19.95. Hamdani Communications inc., 2625 Piedmont, Building 56 Suite 282, Atlanta GA 30324. **Tel** (404)469-5891, FAX (404)469-8997. **ED** Barry Hamdani. cum. index. **Bk Rev**, (Qty: 20). **Ad Acc, Adv Mgr:** Dennis Matthews, **Tel** (404)469-5891. **Circ:** 153,287 (ctrl). available in bound issues from University Microfilms International (UMI).
Desc: Recruitment of blacks in the business world.

LC E185.8 .B5 ISSN 0006-4165
DD 338/.04 US
CCC
CODEN BLENDG
BLACK ENTERPRISE. [Black enterp.]. Vol. 1 (Aug. 1970)-. Periodical. English. Twelve times a year. $19.95. Earl G. Graves Publishing Company, 130 Fifth Avenue, New York NY 10011. **Tel** (212)242-8000, FAX (212)989-8410. **(Subscription address:** CDS Agency Hard Copy, PO Box 4966, Des Moines IA 50340. **Tel** (515)247-7569.) **ED** Earl G. Graves. **Bk Rev. Ad Acc, Adv Mgr:** Earl G. Graves, Jr., **Tel** (212)242-8000. **Circ:** 230,000. available on microfilm and microfiche from University Microfilms International (UMI); available on CD-ROM; available on microfiche; available on an online database (files 15,647,648/Full-Text) from DIALOG. Documents available from UMI Article Clearinghouse, Magazine Collection.
Desc: A business publication targeted to the upscale black professional, entrepreneur and manager. As a "how-to" guidebook, it covers topics ranging from money management to the current growth of black-owned businesses.
Ind/Abst ABI/INFORM Glob. Ed. (Oct. 1973-); ABI/INFORM Ondisc: Expr. Ed. (Jan. 1987-); ABI/INFORM [Computer File] (Oct. 1973-); Acad. Abstr. Full Text Elite; Acad. Abstr.; Acad. Ind. [Computer File] (1984-); Acad. Search; Book Rev. Index; Bus. ASAP (1992-) [Full Txt.]; Bus. Index (1985-); Bus. Period. Index; Bus. Source Plus; Bus. Source; Curr. Cit.; EP Collect.; Expand. Acad. Index (1984-); Gen. BusinessFile (1985-); Gen. Period. Index (1985-); Homework Help.; Index Period. Artic. Relat. Law; INFO-SOUTH Abstr.; Mag. Artic. Summar. Elite; Mag. Artic. Summar. Select; Mag. Artic. Summar. CD-ROM; Mag. Express (1986-) [Full Txt.]; Mag. Index Plus (1989-); Mag. Index. Sel. (1986-); Mag. Search; MasterFile FullTEXT 1000; MasterFile FullTEXT 350; MasterFile FullTEXT 650; MasterFile FullTEXT (May 1984-) [Full Txt.]; Newsp. Period. Abstr. (1986-); OCLC; PAIS Int. Print; Pub. Lib. FullTEXT; Read. Guide Abstr. Select Ed.; Read. Guide Period. Lit.; Resource/One Ondisc; Stat. Ref. Index; Telebase; Mag. Index (1978-); TOM Gen. Index (1993-) [Full Txt.]; Trade Ind. Index (1981-?); UMI ABI/Inform--Bus. Period. Ondisc (Jan. 1987-) [Full Txt.]; Vocat. Search; Wilson Bus. Abstr.; Work Relat. Abstr.; World Mag. Bank.

ISSN 1063-0449
DD 338 US
BLACK PAGES OF AMERICA (BALTIMORE METROPLITAN ED.). **See** Ethnic Interests.

ISSN 1063-0457
DD 338 US
BLACK PAGES OF AMERICA (HAMPTON ROADS METROPOLITAN ED.). **See** Ethnic Interests.

LC HA37 .F632
FR
BLOC NOTES DE L'OBSERVATOIRE ECONOMIQUE DE PARIS (MONTHLY). (BLOC NOTES DE L'OBSERVATOIRE ECONOMIQUE DE PARIS.). French. Eleven times a year. 135.00F France; 155.00F other. Observatoire Economique de Paris, 195 rue de Bercy, Tour Gamma A, 75582 Paris Cedex 12 France. **Tel** 011 33 1 43417141, FAX 011 33 1 43425843, telex 230541. **ED** Guy Stehle. Index available.

LC HF3223 .B59 ISSN 0381-7245
DD 338.7/4/0971 CN
BLUE BOOK OF CANADIAN BUSINESS, THE. (1976)-. English. One time a year. 159.95Can$. Canadian Newspaper Services Inc., 65 Overlea Boulevard, Suite 207, Toronto Ontario N4H 1P1 Canada. **Tel** (416)422-4742, FAX (416)422-4746. **ED** Lisa A. Browning, William A. Lewis and Philip B. Gurvich. Index available. available on diskette. ***Continues** National Reference Book, 0470-2190.*

LC HD5723 .J62 ISSN 1062-9327
DD 331.12/0973/021 US
BLUE CHIP JOB GROWTH UPDATE. [Blue chip job growth update]. **Added/Corp** Arizona State University. Economic Outlook Center. (1992)-. English. Twelve times a year. $79.00. Economic Outlook Center, PO Box 874406, College of Business, Arizona State University, Tempe AZ 85287-4406. **Tel** (602)965-5543, 800 448-9432, FAX (602)965-5458. **ED** Nan Beams,. ***Continues** Job Growth Update, 1051-5615.*
Desc: Presents nonagricultural establishment survey data gathered directly from the US Bureau of Labor. The states are ranked according to the percentage change in jobs for each of the major employment sectors.

ISSN 0777-9216
BE
UDC 686.8
BMB BURO INFORMATIKA. [BMB buro inform.]. **VFOAT** Belgisch Bulletijn Mecanografie Buro Informatika. (1990)-. Periodical. Dutch. Twelve times a year. Business & Management Editions, rue Stephanie 17, B 1020 Brussels Belgium. **Tel** 011 32 2 4266115, FAX 011 32 2 4258226. ***Continues** BMB Kantoor Magazine, 0777-9194.*

LC HF
DD 380 CN
SUSPENDED
BOARD OF TRADE OF METROPOLITAN TORONTO BUSINESS JOURNAL. (19??)-Suspended (Oct. 1995). Periodical. English. Ten times a year. Free to members of the Board; 27.50Can$ US; 17.50Can$ Canada; 22.50Can$ other. Board of Trade of Metropolitan Toronto, PO Box 60, 1 First Canadian Place, Toronto Ontario M5X 1C1 Canada. **Tel** (416)366-6811, (416)366-7139, FAX (416)366-5620. available on an online database from Knight-Ridder Information, Inc.; available on microfilm. ***Continues** Metropolitan Toronto Business Journal.*

ISSN 0730-7241
US
BODYSHOP BUSINESS. **See** Transportation-Automobiles.

LC HC1080.A1 B65
DD 330 PG
BOLETIM DE INFORMACAO SOCIO-ECONOMICA. **Added/Corp** Guinea-Bissau. Ministerio do Plano e Cooperacao Internacional. Gabinete de Estudos Economicos. Guinea-Bissau. Ministerio do Plano. Gabinete de Estudos Economicos. Centro de Estudos Socio-Economicos (Guinea-Bissau). **VFOAT** BISE. **VAT** Boletim de Informacao Socioeconomica. Vol. 1, No. 1 (Nov. 1985)-. Bulletin. Portuguese. Four times a year. Centro de Estudos Socio-Economicos, Instituto Nacional de Estudos e Pesquisas (INEP), Complexo Escolar 14 de Novembro, Bairro Cobornel, BP 112, Bissau Guinea Bissau.
Ind/Abst PAIS Int. Print.

LC HB9 .D452 ISSN 0006-6249
DD 330 SP
BOLETIN DE ESTUDIOS ECONOMICOS. [Bol. estud. econ.]. **Added/Corp** Universidad Comercial de Deusto. Asociacion de Licenciados en Ciencias Economicas. (19??)-. Periodical. Spanish (summaries and/or abstracts in English). Three times a year. $39.08. Association Licenciados Cienc Econo, University of Commerce Deusto, Apartado 20044, 18080 Bilbao Spain. **Tel** 011 34 94 4452212, FAX 011 34 94 4456345. **ED** Susana Rodriguez Vidarte and Fernanado Gomez-Bezares. Index available. cum. index. **Bk Rev. Ad Acc. Circ:** 5,000 (ctrl). Documents available from BLDSC, SWETS.
Desc: Theoretical and applied economics.
Ind/Abst Am. Hist. Life (1958-1975); Selec. Coop. Index Manage. Period.

LC HC152.5.A1 B6
DD 330.9 CU
BOLETIN DE INFORMACION SOBRE ECONOMIA CUBANA. **Added/Corp** Centro de Investigaciones de la Economia Mundial (Havana, Cuba). **VFOAT** BIEC. Vol. 1, No. 1 (January 1992)-. Bulletin. Spanish (table of contents in English and Spanish). Twelve times a year. $96.00 (institutions); $84.00 (individuals). Centro de Investigaciones de la Economia Mundial, Qunita Avenue North 2010, Esquina a 22 Miramar Playa, Havana Cuba. **ED** Jose Luis Rodriguez.
Desc: Features articles on the Cuban economy.

ISSN 0214-8307
SP
UDC 33
BOLETIN ICE ECONOMICO. [Bol. ICE econ.]. (1988)-. Periodical. Spanish. One time a week. Min Economia Hacienda Ctr Publ, Plaza Campillo Mundo Nuevo 3, 28005 Madrid Spain. **Tel** 011 34 1 5271437, or 5835665. ***Continues** Boletin Economico de Informacion Comercial Espanola, 0213-3768.*

AG
BOLETIN INFORMATIVO. **Added/Corp** Colegio de Graduados en Ciencias Economicas de Tucuman. (197?)-. Periodical. Spanish. ***Continues** Boletin Informativo Bimestral.*
Ind/Abst Hum. Rights Intern. Rep.

LC HC141 .P47a
DD 330 GT
BOLETIN INFORMATIVO. **Added/Corp** Permanent Secretariat of the General Treaty for Central American Economic Integration. **VFOAT** SIECA Boletin Informativo. (199?)-. Periodical. Spanish. Six times a year. Secretaria Permanente del Tratoad General de Integracion Economica Centroamericana, Apdo. 1237, 4 Avenida No. 10-25, Zona 14, Guatemala City Guatemala. ***Continues** Carta Informativa de la Secretaria Permanente de Integracion Economica Centroamericana.*

ISSN 0213-3415
SP
UDC 338.43
BOLETIN PRECIOS AGRARIOS ED. MENSUAL. (1980)-. Periodical. Spanish. Twelve times a year. $34.64. Ministerio Agricultura, Crto Publ, Calle Alfonso XII 56, 28014 Madrid Spain. **Tel** 011 34 1 3475551.

ISSN 0211-7614
SP
UDC 313.3
BOLETIN TRIMESTRAL DE COYUNTURA. (1981)-. Periodical. Spanish. Four times a year. 6500ptas. Libreria Lines Chiel, Plaza Virgen del Romero 6, 28007 Madrid Spain. **Tel** 011 34 1 40131211, 011 34 1 40131456.

LC HC307.A5 B64
DD 330.9/45/671 IT
BOLLETTINO ECONOMICO. **Added/Corp** Camera di Commercio, Industria, Artigianato e Agricoltura (Ancona, Italy) Camera di Commercio, Industria e Agricoltura (Ancona, Italy). (19??)-. Periodical. Italian. Twelve times a year. L45000. Camera di Commercio Industria Artigianato e Agricoltura Lucca, Provento Publ Corte Campana 10, 55100 Lucca Italy. **Tel**

Business and Economics

011 39 583 9765. **Ad Acc. Circ:** 1,000 (ctrl).
Ind/Abst Numis. Lit.; World Agric. Econ. Rural Sociol. Abstr.

IT

BOLLETTINO VARIAZIONI ANAGRAFICHE DITTE. Italian. Twelve times a year. L50000. Regione Autonoma Valle Aosta, Piazza della Repubblica 15, 11100 Aosta Italy. **Tel** 011 39 165 303524.

II

BOMBAY MARKET. Vol. 34 (1970)-. Periodical. English. Twelve times a year. Bombay Market, 505 Arun Chambers, Tardeo Road, Bombay 34 India. **ED** K. Multani. **Ad Acc**.

LC HF5065.A4 B66

US

BOOK OF LISTS: A REFERENCE GUIDE TO ALASKA'S LEADING INDUSTRIES, THE. (1992)-. English. Alaska Journal of Commerce Holdings Inc., 3710 Woodland Park Drive, Suite 2100, Anchorage AK 99517. **Tel** (907)249-1900, **FAX** (907)248-7454.

LC HD2709
DD 338.74

US

BOOK OF LISTS (LOS ANGELES, CALIF.). (THE ... BOOK OF LISTS.). **VFOAT** Los Angeles Business Journal Book of Lists. (1981?)-. Periodical. English. One time a year. $35.77. Los Angeles Business Journal, PO Box 469016, Escondido CA 90246. **Tel** (213)549-5225, (800)255-3302.

ISSN 1063-3561
DD 338

US

BOOTSTRAPPIN' ENTREPRENEUR. (BOOTSTRAPPIN' ENTREPRENEUR : THE NEWSLETTER FOR INDIVIDUALS WITH GREATER IDEAS AND A LITTLE BIT OF CASH.). [Bootstrapp. entrep.]. Vol. 1, No. 1 (Summer 1992)-. Newsletter. English. Four times a year (Feb., May, Aug., Nov.). $30.00. Research Done Write, 8726 South Sepulveda, Suite B261-ESSX, Los Angeles CA 90045. **Tel** (310)568-9861. **ED** Kimberly Stansell. Index available. cum. index. **Bk Rev**, (Qty: 2-4).
Desc: This magazine helps people move forward with their business ideas on a mini-budget. Each issue contains articles on low-cost marketing strategies, business building tips and ideas, nationwide networking contacts, free products and services, bootstrapper's success stories, and a problem and solution exchange with other self-employed people.

SW

BOSCH BUSINESS, DEN. Swedish. Six times a year. Regio Pers, Postbus 5005201AM, S-Hertogenbosch Netherlands. **Tel** 011 31 073 145981.

ISSN 0746-4975
US
CCC

BOSTON BUSINESS JOURNAL, THE. (THE BOSTON BUSINESS JOURNAL : BBJ.). **VFOAT** BBJ; B.B.J. Vol. 1, No. 1 (Oct. 19, 1981)-. Periodical. English. One time a week. $64.00. MCP Inc., 5500 Wayzata Boulevard, Suite 800, Minneapolis MN 55416. **Tel** (612)591-2700, **FAX** (612)591-2639. **ED** Bennie DiVaedo. **Circ**: 32,000. available on microfilm from University Microfilms International (UMI); available on an online database (files 635,648/Full-Text) from DIALOG. Documents available from UMI Article Clearinghouse.
Continues P & L, The Boston Business Journal.
Desc: Covers business and politics in greater Boston. Its coverage includes breaking news stories as well as in-depth analyses. Contains special sections dealing with subjects like technology, real estate, and banking.
Ind/Abst Acad. Search; Bus. Dateline; Bus. Index (Jan. 1985-Dec. 1985); Bus. Source Plus; Bus. Source; EP Collect.; Gen. BusinessFile (Jan. 1985-Dec. 1985); Gen. Period. Index (Jan. 1985-Dec. 1985); Homework Help.; INFO-SOUTH Abstr.; MasterFile FullTEXT 1000; MasterFile FullTEXT 350; MasterFile FullTEXT 650; MasterFile FullTEXT (July 1993-); OCLC; Telebase; Trade Ind. ASAP [Full Txt.]; Trade Ind. Index [Full Txt.].

ISSN 1067-7992
DD 338

US

●**BOTSWANA (SYRACUSE, N.Y.).** (BOTSWANA : AN EXECUTIVE REPORT.). [Botswana]. **Added/Corp** Political Risk Services (IBC USA (Publications) Inc.). (1993)-. English. $110.00. Political Risk Services, 6320 Fly Road, Suite 102, PO Box 248, East Syracuse NY 13057-0248. **Tel** (315)431-0511, **FAX** (315)431-0200.
Desc: Focuses on the long-term outlook for business. Includes a brief review of recent events and current circumstances, background intelligence including geography, history, economics and social conditions, as well as the key political and economic forecasts.

LC HF53 .B64

FR

BOTTIN ENTREPRISES. IDENTITES.
VFOAT Identites. (1989)-. French. **Continues** Bottin Entreprises. Rubriques Professionnelles.

ISSN 1056-7798
US

BOTTOM LINE, THE. (1991)-. Periodical. English. Twelve times a year. Barrow Publishing Co., 35633 Garner, Romulus MI 48174.

ISSN 1082-457X
DD 338
US

●**BOTTOM LINE BUSINESS.** [Bottom line bus.]. Vol. 24, No. 10 (May 15, 1995)-. Periodical. English. Twenty-four times a year. $49.00. Boardroom Reports Inc., 330 West 42nd Street, 14th Floor, New York NY 10036. **Tel** (212)239-9000. **(Subscription address:** Neodata / Colorado, PO Box 2606, Boulder CO 80322.) available on microfilm and microfiche from University Microfilms International (UMI). **Continues** Boardroom Reports, 0045-2300.
Desc: Management's source of inside information. A continuing education in running a business successfully in uncertain times. Inside ways to save taxes, cut costs, improve cash flow, increase productivity, and out-perform competition. Contains facts about banking, insurance, advertising, marketing, computers, credit, management, sales, etc.
Ind/Abst Pop. Mag. Rev.

US

BOULDER COUNTY BUSINESS REPORT. (19??)-. English. Twelve times a year. $18.00 Colorado; $22.00 US; $50.00 other. Boulder County Business Report, 4885 Riverbend Road, Boulder CO 80301. **Tel** (303)440-4950. available on an online database (file 635/Full-Text) from DIALOG. Documents available from UMI Article Clearinghouse.
Ind/Abst Bus. Dateline (May 1985-) [Full Txt.].

ISSN 1058-4234
DD 330
US

BOWERS BUSINESS BAROMETER. [Bowers bus. barom.]. **Added/Corp** Bowers-Havens Organization. Weatherhead School of Management. (July 15, 1991)-. Periodical. English. Twelve times a year. $156.00. Bowers-Haven Organization, PO Box 93801, Cleveland OH 44122. **Tel** (216)368-2165, **FAX** (216)368-4776.

ISSN 0006-8446
DD 794

BOWLING PROPRIETOR. See Sports and Games.

ISSN 1074-8113
DD 338
US

●**BRANSON BUSINESS JOURNAL.** [Branson bus. j.]. (1994)-. Periodical. English. Six times a year. $16.50. Branson Business Journal, PO Box 1449, Forsyth MO 65653. **Tel** (417)546-2520.

LC F2521 .B7582

BL

BRASILINFORM. EXECUTIVE NEWS BRIEFS. VFOAT Executive News Briefs. Vol. 9, No. 413 (Oct. 30, 1991)-. Periodical. English. One time a week. $350.00. Brasilinform, CAIXA Postal 37584, 22642 Rio de Janeiro RJ Brazil. **Tel** 011 55 21 3222109. **Continues** Brasilinform. News Briefs.

BL

BRASILINFORM. NEWS BRIEFS. VFOAT News Briefs. (198?)-. Periodical. English. Twenty-six times a year. $50.00. Edwin Taylor, Caixa Postal 37584, 22642 Rio de Janeiro RJ Brazil. **Tel** 011 55 21 3222109.
Desc: Summary of the principal economic and political development in Brazil for multinational firms, international banks, diplomats and universities.

ISSN 0889-1761
DD 330
US
CCC
TITLE CHANGE

BRAZIL SERVICE. (BRAZIL SERVICE : BR.). [Braz. serv.]. **Added/Corp** International Reports, inc. **VFOAT** BR; Financial Times Brazil Service. (19??)-(1995). Periodical. English. International Reports Inc., 11300 Rockville Pike 1100, Rockville MD 20852. **Tel** (212)685-6900, **FAX** (212)685-8566, telex 233139 RPTUR. **ED** Jaures Mazzone. available on an online database from NEWSNET; Lexis-Nexis; (file 636/Full-Text) DIALOG; and DATA-STAR. **Merged into** Brazil Watch.
Desc: Analysis of new political, social and economic forces about to surface in Brazil's complex and volatile business climate. In-depth analysis of major issues affecting business in Brazil, ranging from Brazil's economic program to the mechanics of the parallel market.
Ind/Abst PTS Newsl. Database [Full Txt.].

LC HC186 .B74
DD 330.9/81/05

ISSN 0100-2910
BL

BRAZILIAN ECONOMIC STUDIES. [Braz. econ. stud.]. **Added/Corp** Instituto de Planejamento Economico e Social. Instituto de Pesquisas. Instituto de Planejamento Economico e Social. No. 1 (1975)-. English (Portuguese). IPEA Servicio Editorial / Instituto de Pesquisa Economica y Aplicada, Avenue P Antonio Carlos 51-14 Andar, CP 2672, 20020 010 Rio de Janeiro Brazil. **Tel** 011 55 21 2925141 ext. 1118, **FAX** 011 55 21 2401920.
Ind/Abst Hisp. Am. Period. Index, HAPI; Int. Labour Doc.

ISSN 0006-9566
FR
UDC 669(449)

BREF RHONE ALPES. [Bref Rhone Alpes]. (1966)-. Periodical. French. One time a week. 1976.00F. Editions Sme, 55 Montee de Choulans, 69323 Lyon Cedex 05 France. **Tel** 011 33 78 422953.

ISSN 0889-5104
US

BREVARD BUSINESS NEWS. VFOAT BBN. (19??)-. Periodical. English. Twenty-six times a year. $13.00. BBN Enterprises, PO Box 1657, Cocoa FL 32923-1657.

TU

BRIEFING. See Political Science.

LC HF5415.12.B7 B75
DD 658.8/00981
BL

BRIEFING (SAO PAULO, BRAZIL). (BRIEFING.). Periodical. Portuguese (Portuguese). Twelve times a year.

LC HG4136.5 .B75
DD 338.7/4/02541
UK

BRITAIN'S TOP PRIVATELY OWNED COMPANIES. (1990)-. English. Irregular. £130.00. Jordan Publishing Ltd., 21 St. Thomas Street, Bristol BS1 6JS United Kingdom. **Tel** 011 44 117 9230600, **FAX** 011 44 117 230063, telex 499119. **Formed by the union of** Britain's Privately Owned Companies. Top 2000 **and** Britain's Privately Owned Companies. Second 2000, 0268-9529.

ISSN 1191-8640
DD 658/.041/09711
CN
TITLE CHANGE

BRITISH COLUMBIA & ALBERTA HOME BUSINESS REPORT. [B.C. Alta. home bus. rep.]. **VFOAT** Home Business Report; BC & Alberta Home Business Report. **VAT** British Columbia and Alberta Home Business Report. (Aug./Oct. 1992)-(1995). Periodical. English. HB Communications Group Incorporated, 2949 Ash Street, Abbotsford BC V2S 4GS Canada. **Tel** (604)857-1788, **FAX** (604)854-3087. **ED** Ted James. **Ad Acc. Circ**: 25,000 (ctrl). **Continues** The B.C. Home Business Report., 0847-5717. **Continued by** Home Business Report.
Desc: Aimed at the variety of people taking on the challenge of operating a business from the home.

ISSN 1184-9207
DD 338.09711
CN

BRITISH COLUMBIA BUSINESS INDICATORS. [B.C. bus. indic.]. **Added/Corp** British Columbia. Ministry of Finance and Corporate Relations. Planning and Statistics Division. Data Dissemination. 1st Quarter (1991)-. Periodical. English. Twelve times a year. 48.02Can$. Ministry of Finance, 553 Superior Street, Victoria BC V8V 1X4 Canada. **Tel** (604)387-1502.

LC HC117.B8 B6635 HC117.B8 B742 **ISSN** 0847-1525
DD 330.9711/005
CN

BRITISH COLUMBIA ECONOMIC AND STATISTICAL REVIEW. [B.C. econ. stat. rev.]. **Added/Corp** British Columbia. Ministry of Finance and Corporate Relations. **VFOAT** Economic and Statistical Review. (1989)-. Statistical Publication. English. One time a year. 18.41Can$. Ministry of Finance, 553 Superior Street, Victoria BC V8V 1X4 Canada. **Tel** (604)387-1502. **Formed by the union of** Financial and Economic Review (Victoria, B.C.), 0701-9882 **and** British Columbia Facts and Statistics, 0407-2340.

UK

BRITISH COMPANIES SECRETARY'S PRACTICE MANUAL. English. CCH Editions Ltd., Telford Road Bicester, Oxfordshire OX6 OXD United Kingdom. **Tel** 011 44 1869 253300, **FAX** 011 44 1869 245814.

ISSN 0263-3523
UK

BRITISH ECONOMY SURVEY. (197?)-. Periodical. English. Two times a year. $12.50. Longman Group Ltd., Fourth Avenue, Longman House, Harlow Essex CM19 5SR United Kingdom. **Tel** 011 44 1279 429655, **FAX** 011 44 1279 431067, telex 81259. available on microfilm and microfiche from University Microfilms International (UMI).

LC HB1 .B68 **ISSN** 0141-4739
DD 330/.05 UK
Pr Rev.

BRITISH REVIEW OF ECONOMIC ISSUES. [Br. rev. econ. issues]. **Added/Corp** Association of Polytechnic Teachers in Economics. No. 1 (Nov. 1977)-. Periodical. English. Three times a year (Feburary, June, and October). $77.01. Association Polytechnic Teachers Economics, Leek Road Staffordshire Polytech, Stoke on Trent ST4 2DF United Kingdom. **Tel** 011 44 1782 574085, **FAX** 011 44 1782

747006. **ED** Peter Reynolds, (phone: 011 44 782 412515 Ext. 4083). **Bk Rev**, (Qty: 20). **Ad Acc, Adv Mgr:** Allistair Dawson, **Tel** 011 44 782 412515 ext. 4079. **Circ:** 400.
Desc: Devoted to current issues in economics and to the teaching of economics.
Ind/Abst Contents Recent Econ. J.; Contents Pages Manage.; Curr. Cit.; Econ. Lit. Index; J. Econ. Lit. (1981-); Leis., Rec., Tour. Abstr.; PAIS Bull. (1986-); PAIS Int. Print (1991-); Public Aff. Inf. Serv. Bull. (?-1985); Rural Dev. Abstr. (1981-); World Agric. Econ. Rural Sociol. Abstr. (1986-).

LC HC101 .B785 **ISSN** 0007-2303
DD 330.973/092 US
CCC

BROOKINGS PAPERS ON ECONOMIC ACTIVITY. [Brookings pap. econ. act.]. **Added/Corp** Brookings Institution. **VFOAT** Economic Activity. (1970)-. Academic Scholarly Publication. English. Three times a year. $52.00. Brookings Institution, 1775 Massachusetts Avenue Northwest, Washington DC 20036-2188. **Tel** (202)797-6255, (800)275-1447. **(Subscription address:** Brookings Institution, PO Box 037, Washington DC 20042. **Tel** (202)797-6255.) **ED** William C. Brainard and George L. Perry. cum. index. available on microfilm and microfiche from University Microfilms International (UMI). Documents available from The Genuine Article, UMI Article Clearinghouse. ***Continued in part by*** *Brookings Papers on Economic Activity. Microeconomics, 1057-8641.*
Desc: Provides academic and business economists, government officials, and members of the financial and business community with timely analyses of current economic developments.
Ind/Abst ABI/INFORM Glob. Ed.; ABI/INFORM [Computer File] (1987); Acad. Abstr.; Acad. Ind. [Computer File] (1984-); Acad. Search; Asia.-Pac. Econ. Lit.; Bus. Index (1985-); Bus. Period. Index; Bus. Source Plus; Contents Recent Econ. J.; Contents Pages Manage.; Curr. Cit.; Curr. Contents Soc. Behav. Sci.; Econ. Lit. Index; EP Collect.; Expand. Acad. Index (1984-); Gen. BusinessFile (1985-); Gen. Period. Index (1985-); Homework Help.; Int. Bibliogr. Sociol.; Int. Labour Doc.; J. Econ. Lit.; J. Plan. Lit.; LABORDOC; MasterFile FullTEXT 1000; MasterFile FullTEXT 350; MasterFile FullTEXT 650; MasterFile FullTEXT (July 1990-); Newsp. Period. Abstr. (1990-); OCLC; PAIS Int. Print (1991-); Res. Alert [Full Cov.]; Soc. Sci. Source; Soc. Sci. Cit. Index [Full Cov.]; Soc. Sci. Index; Soc. Sci. Index Fulltext (1988-) [Full Txt.]; Telebase; UMI ABI/Inform--Bus. Period. Ondisc (1987-) [Full Txt.]; Urban Aff. Abstr.; Wilson Bus. Abstr.

LC HC101 .B787 **ISSN** 1057-8641
DD 338.973/005 US
CCC

BROOKINGS PAPERS ON ECONOMIC ACTIVITY. MICROECONOMICS. [Brookings pap. econ. act., Microecon.]. **Added/Corp** Brookings Institution. **VFOAT** Microeconomics. 2nd Ed. (1989)-. Academic Scholarly Publication. English. One time a year (June). $13.00. Brookings Institution, 1775 Massachusetts Avenue Northwest, Washington DC 20036-2188. **Tel** (202)797-6255, (800)275-1447. **(Subscription address:** Brookings Institution, PO Box 037, Washington DC 20042. **Tel** (202)797-6255.) **ED** Martin Neil Baily and Clifford Winston. ***Continues in part*** *Brookings Papers on Economic Activity, 0007-2303.*
Desc: Focuses on research drawn from theoretical and applied microeconomics, industrial organization, labor economics, and technological change.

LC H1 .B76 **ISSN** 0745-1253
DD 300/.5 US
CCC

BROOKINGS REVIEW, THE. [Brookings rev.]. **Added/Corp** Brookings Institution. Vol. 1, No. 1 (Fall 1982)-. Academic Scholarly Publication. English. Four times a year. $17.95. Brookings Institution, 1775 Massachusetts Avenue Northwest, Washington DC 20036-2188. **Tel** (202)797-6255, (800)275-1447. **(Subscription address:** Brookings Institution, PO Box 037, Washington DC 20042. **Tel** (202)797-6255.) available on microfilm and microfiche from University Microfilms International (UMI); available on an online database (file 15/Full-Text) from DIALOG. Documents available from UMI Article Clearinghouse. ***Continues*** *Brookings Bulletin (Washington, D.C. : 1962), 0007-229X.*
Desc: The public policy magazine of the Brookings Institution with articles on economics, foreign policy and government.
Ind/Abst ABI/INFORM Glob. Ed.; ABI/INFORM [Computer File] (Spring 1983-); Acad. Abstr.; Acad. Ind. [Computer File] (1984-); Acad. Search; Am. Bibliogr. Slavic East Europ. Stud.; Bus. ASAP (1992-) [Full Txt.]; Bus. Index (1985-); Energy Res. Abstr. (Oct. 1982-); EP Collect.; Expand. Acad. Index (1984-); Gen. BusinessFile (1985-); Gen. Period. Index (1985); Health Plan. Adminis.; Homework Help.; Hosp. Health Admin. Index; INFO-SOUTH Abstr.; J. Plan. Lit.; MasterFile FullTEXT 1000; MasterFile FullTEXT 350; MasterFile FullTEXT 650; MasterFile FullTEXT (July 1990-); Middle East Abstr. Index; Newsp. Period. Abstr. (1988-); OCLC; PAIS Int. Print (1991-); Pub. Lib. FullTEXT; Read. Guide Period. Lit.; Soc. Sci. Source; Telebase; UMI ABI/Inform--Bus. Period. Ondisc (Spring 1988-) [Full Txt.].

US

BROWARD DAILY BUSINESS REVIEW. (19??)-. Periodical. English. Seven times a week. $460.00. American Lawyer Media, L.P., 600 3rd Avenue, New York NY 10016. **Tel** (212)973-2800. **(Subscription address:** Broward Review, PO Box 14366, Ft. Lauderdale FL 33302. **Tel** (305)468-2600.) ***Continues*** *Broward Review.*

US

BROWARD ECONOMIC HANDBOOK. English. $38.00. Broward Economic Development Council, 200 East Las Olas Blvd., Ste 1850, Ft Lauderdale FL 33301. **Tel** (305)524-3113.

ISSN 0277-7541
US

BROWN COMPANY ANNUAL REPORT. **Main/Corp** Brown Company. English. One time a year. Treasurer Brown Company, 251 South Lake Avenue, Pasadena CA 91101.

ISSN 1066-2421
DD 338 US
CEASED

BROWN'S BUSINESS REPORTER. [Brown's bus. rep.]. (19??)-(Dec. 1994). Periodical. English. Browns Business Reporter, PO Drawer 1376, Eugene OR 97440. **Tel** (503)345-8665, FAX (503)683-6184. **ED** Dennis M. Hunt. **Bk Rev**, (Qty: 9). **Ad Acc. Circ:** 1,400.
Desc: Business news for Lane, Douglas, Linn, Benton & Marion counties in the state of Oregon.

LC HF3151 **ISSN** 0829-5239
DD 381/.09715 CN

BRUNSWICK BUSINESS JOURNAL, THE. [Brunswick bus. j.]. (July 12, 1984)-. Periodical. English. Twelve times a year. 25.00Can$ (Canada); 35.00Can$ (US); 50.00Can$ (other). The Brunswick Business Journal, 140 Baig Boulevard, Moncton NB E1E 1C8 Canada. **Tel** (506)857-9696, FAX (506)859-7395. **ED** Lynda MacGibbon. **Bk Rev**, (Qty: varies). **Ad Acc, Adv Mgr:** J. Matthews. **Circ:** 16,000 (ctrl). available on microfiche from University Microfilms International (UMI); available on an online database (file 635/Full-Text) from DIALOG. Documents available from UMI Article Clearinghouse.
Desc: Business to business newspaper personally addressed to decision-makers.
Ind/Abst Bus. Dateline (Jan. 1992-) [Full Txt.].

LC HF5001 .B79
AT
CEASED

BRW : THE MAGAZINE OF AUSTRALIAN & NEW ZEALAND BUSINESS. **VFOAT** Business Review Weekly; BRW International. (199?)-(March 1994). English. Business Review Weekly, 469 La Trobe Street, Melbourne Victoria 3000 Australia. **Tel** 011 61 3 6033888, FAX 011 61 3 6704328.

US

BUCKMASTER'S FORTUNE 500 [MICROFORM] : ANNUAL REPORTS. **Added/Corp** Buckmaster Publishing. **VFOAT** Fortune 500 : Annual Reports. (1986)-. Corporate Report. English. Four times a year. $570.00. Buckmaster Publishing - Virginia, Route 4, Box 1630, Mineral VA 23117. **Tel** (703)894-5777.

LC HC
DD 330 IT

●**BUDGET / ITALY.** (1995)-. Italian. Four times a year. L57910. Editrice IFAF, Largo Schuster 1, 20122 Milan Italy. **Tel** 011 39 2 72002170.

ISSN 0885-9930
DD 332 US

BUILDING ECONOMIC ALTERNATIVES. (BUILDING ECONOMIC ALTERNATIVES: A QUARTERLY PUBLICATION OF CO-OP AMERICA.). [Build. econ. altern.]. **Added/Corp** Co-Op America. (19??)-. Periodical. English. Four times a year (Mar., Jun., Sep., Dec.). $25.00 (individuals - includes membership); $60.00 (organizations - includes membership). Co-Op America, 1850 Main Street Northwest, Suite 700, Washington DC 20036. **Tel** (202)872-5307. **ED** Rosemary Brown. **Bk Rev. Ad Acc. Circ:** 50,000 (ctrl).
Ind/Abst Altern. Press Index (199?-).

ISSN 0742-5694
US

BUILDING PRODUCTS DIGEST. **See** Forests and Forestry-Lumber and Wood.

ISSN 0736-9050
DD 338 US
CODEN BUSHEU

BU$INESS OF HERBS, THE. **See** Gardening and Horticulture.

LC HF1371 **ISSN** 1183-0190
DD 382/.0971047/05 CN

BULLETEN - CANADA-USSR BUSINESS COUNCIL. (BIULLETEN = BULLETIN.). [Bull. - Can.-USSR Bus. Counc.]. **Added/Corp** Canada-USSR Business Council. **VAT** Bulletin - Canada-USSR Business Council. Vol. 1, No. 1 (1990)-. Periodical. English. Six times a year. Free to members. Canada-USSR Business Council, Suite 2125, 2 First Canadian Place, Toronto Ontario M5X 1A9 Canada.

LC HC **ISSN** 0896-307X
DD 330 US

BULLETIN / ASSOCIATION OF CHRISTIAN ECONOMISTS. [Bull. - Assoc. Christ. Econ.]. **Added/Corp** Association of Christian Economists. **VFOAT** Bulletin of the Association of Christian Economists. (198?)-. Bulletin. English. Two times a year. $15.00. Association of Christian Economists, Gordon College, Wenham MA 01984. **Tel** (617)927-2300.

LC WMLC 91/328
US

BULLETIN / BUREAU OF BUSINESS RESEARCH, COLLEGE OF BUSINESS ADMINISTRATION, UNIVERSITY OF TOLEDO. **Added/Corp** University of Toledo. Bureau of Business Research. No. 1 (Oct. 16, 1936)-. Bulletin. English. Price varies per volume.

ISSN 0265-7996
UK
Pr Rev.

BULLETIN (CENTRE FOR ECONOMIC POLICY RESEARCH (GREAT BRITAIN)). (BULLETIN : CENTRE FOR ECONOMIC POLICY RESEARCH.). **VFOAT** CEPR Bulletin. No. 1 (Feb. 1984)-. Bulletin. English. Six times a year. Free on request. Center for Economic Policy Research, 25 28 Old Burlington Street, London W1X 1LB United Kingdom. **Tel** 011 44 171 7349110, FAX 011 44 171 7348760.
Desc: This is issued to inform the academic, business and government policy communities of the current and forthcoming activities of the centre. It also summarizes Discussion Papers produced under the auspices of the Centre.

SP

BULLETIN COMITE ECONOMIQUE ET SOCIAL DES COMMUNAUTES. (19??)-. Bulletin. Spanish. Twelve times a year. 4049ptas. Mundi Prensa, Castello 37, Apartado 1123, 28001 Madrid Spain. **Tel** 011 34 1 4313222.

LC DT348 .B84 **ISSN** 0045-3501
DD 330.967/005 FR

BULLETIN DE L'AFRIQUE NOIRE. [Bull. Afr. noire]. (1957)-. Bulletin. French. One time a week. $1224.83. Ediafric la Documentation Africaine, 10 rue Vineuse, 75116 Paris France. **Tel** 011 33 1 44308100, FAX 011 33 1 45208174.
Desc: Analyses of the economy of black African countries: plans-budgets, economic and financial accounts, foreign trade, activities of public organizations, development programs, agriculture, and industry.
Ind/Abst Leis., Rec., Tour. Abstr.; Rural Dev. Abstr.; World Agric. Econ. Rural Sociol. Abstr.

ISSN 1153-2254
FR
UDC 368(44)

BULLETIN DE L'INSTITUT DES ACTUAIRES FRANCAIS. **VFOAT** Bulletin Trimestriel de l'Institut des Actuaires Francais; Bulletin Trimestriel - Institut des Actuaires Francais. (1890)-. Bulletin. French. Four times a year. $229.66. Institut Actuaires Francais, 243 rue Saint Honore, 75001 Paris France. **Tel** 011 33 1 42601694. ***Continues*** *La Lettre de l'Institut des Actuaires Francaise.*

ISSN 0770-4585
BE
UDC 330.191.5

BULLETIN DE L'IRES. [Bull. IRES]. **VFOAT** Bulletin de l'Institut de Recherches Economiques. (1981)-. Monographic series. French. Irregular. Price varies per volume. Univ Catholique Louvain / IRES, Place Montesquieu 3 Bte 4, B-1348 Louvain Belgium. **Tel** 011 32 10 474152.

LC HF **ISSN** 0588-6902
DD 382 BE

BULLETIN DES COMMUNAUTES EUROPEENNES. **Main/Corp** Commission of the European Communities. (Jan. 1968)-. Bulletin. French. Twenty-six times a year. ***Supersedes*** *European Coal and Steel Community. Bulletin de la Communaute Europeenne du Charbon et de l'Acier* ***and*** *European Economic Community. Bulletin de la Communaute Economique Europeenne.*
Ind/Abst LABORDOC.

ISSN 0226-5540
DD 330.9714/22 CN
BULLETIN D'INFORMATION - CONSEIL REGIONAL DE DEVELOPPEMENT DE L'OUTAOUAIS (07).
[Bull. inf. - Cons. reg. dev. Outaouais (07)]. **Main/Corp** Conseil Regional de Developpement de l'Outaouais. Jan. 1977-. Bulletin. French. Free. C.R.D.O., 131 rue Richer, Hull Quebec J8X 4V2. ctrl circ.

FR
BULLETIN D'INFORMATION DU CENTRE DE DOCUMENTATION SUR LE LAOS.
Added/Corp Cercle de Culture et de Recherche Laotiennes. No. 49 (1989)-. Bulletin. French. Four times a year. 12.00F. Centre de Documentation sur le Laos, 14 rue Dame Genette, 57070 Metz France. **Tel** 011 877 53783, FAX 011 873 72709. **ED** Crunelle Geoffroi. **Circ:** 300. available on diskette. ***Continues*** *Bulletin d'Information et de Liaison du C.C.R.L.*

ISSN 0989-5086
FR
UDC 351.77
BULLETIN D'INFORMATION ET DE DOCUMENTATION - CENTRE NATIONAL DE FORMATION, DOCUMENTATION ET COOPERATION INTERNATIONALE DE LA DIRECTION GENERALE DE LA CONCURRENCE, DE LA CONSOMMATION ET DE LA REPRESSION DES FRAUDES.
(BULLETIN D'INFORMATION ET DE DOCUMENTATION.). **VFOAT** Bulletin d'Information et de Documentation - Centre National de Formation, de Documentation et Cooperation Internationale. (1988)-. Bulletin. French. Eleven times a year. $207.78. Center National de Formation Documentation et Cooperation Internationale, BP 2048 2 rue St. Pierre, 34024 Montpellier Cedex France. **Tel** 011 33 67 604422. ***Continues*** *B.I.D. - Centre National de Formation, Documentation et Cooperation Internationale de la Direction de la Consommation et de la Repression des Fraudes, 0758-0304.*

CM
BULLETIN DU MARCHE MONETAIRE DE LA ZONE BEAC.
(19??)-. Bulletin. French. Twelve times a year. Banque des Etats de l'Afrique Centrale / Cameroon, BP 1917, Yaounde Cameroon. **Tel** 011 237 23 4695, 011 237 23 4696, FAX 011 237 23 4693.

FR
BULLETIN FISCAL & FEUILLET RAPIDE: BFFR.
(19??)-. Bulletin. French. Eleven times a year. Editions Lefebvre, 5 Rue Jacques Bingen, 75854 Paris Cedex 17 France. **Tel** 011 33 1 47631260, 011 33 1 41052200, FAX 011 33 1 46227266, telex 649 470 F.

LC HB235.I4 **ISSN** 0445-5983
II
UDC 338.5:63(540)
BULLETIN OF AGRICULTURAL PRICES (INDIA).
See Agriculture-Agricultural Economics.

LC HB1 **ISSN** 0307-3378
DD 330/.05 UK
CCC
BULLETIN OF ECONOMIC RESEARCH.
[Bull. econ. res.]. Vol. 23 (May 1971)-. Bulletin. English. Four times a year. $213.00. Basil Blackwell Publishers Ltd., 108 Cowley Road, Oxford 0X4 1JF United Kingdom. **Tel** 011 44 1235 465500, FAX 011 44 1235 465556, telex 837022 OXBOOK G. **(Subscription address:** Blackwell Publishers / UK, 108 Cowley Road, Oxford OX4 1JF United Kingdom. **Tel** 011 44 1865 791100, FAX 011 44 1865 791347.) **ED** John P Hutton and Peter J Lambert. **Bk Rev. Ad Acc.** available on microfilm and microfiche from University Microfilms International (UMI); available on an online database (file 648/Full-Text) from DIALOG. Documents available from UMI Article Clearinghouse. ***Continues*** *Yorkshire Bulletin of Economic and Social Research.*
Desc: International forum publishing results of research into all aspects of economics, theoretical and applied.
Ind/Abst ABI/INFORM Glob. Ed.; ABI/INFORM [Computer File] (May 1982-); Acad. Search; Am. Hist. Life (1955-1985, 1971-); Br. Humanit. Index; Bus. ASAP (1992-) [Full Txt.]; Bus. Index (1985-); Contents Recent Econ. J.; Curr. Cit.; Econ. Lit. Index; EP Collect.; Gen. BusinessFile (1985-); Gen. Period. Index (1985-); Geogr. Abstr. Human Geogr.; Homework Help.; INFO-SOUTH Abstr.; Int. Bibliogr. Sociol.; Int. Dev. Abstr.; J. Econ. Lit.; MasterFile FullTEXT 1000; MasterFile FullTEXT 350; MasterFile FullTEXT 650; MasterFile FullTEXT (Jan. 1994-); Middle East Abstr. Index; OCLC; PAIS Int. Print; Telebase; UMI ABI/Inform--Bus. Period. Ondisc (Oct. 1987-) [Full Txt.]; World Agric. Econ. Rural Sociol. Abstr.

LC HC **ISSN** 0007-4918
AT
Pr Rev.
BULLETIN OF INDONESIAN ECONOMIC STUDIES.
[Bull. Indones. econ. stud.]. **Added/Corp** Australian National University. Research School of Pacific Studies. Dept. of Economics. **VFOAT** Indonesian Economic Studies. Vol. 1 No. 1 (June 1965)-. Bulletin. English. Three times a year. 34.53Aus$. Indonesia Project Research, School of Pacific Studies, Australia National University, Canberra ACT 0200 Australia. **Tel** 011 61 6 2492760. **ED** A. Booth. **Bk Rev. Ad Acc. Circ:** 1,500 (ctrl). available on microfilm and microfiche from University Microfilms International (UMI). Documents available from The Genuine Article.
Desc: Surveys of recent developments, Indonesian agriculture, industries, national and regional income, household consumption, foreign investment.
Ind/Abst APAIS, Aust. Public Aff. Inf. Ser. (1966-); Asia.-Pac. Econ. Lit.; Contents Recent Econ. J.; Curr. Cit.; Curr. Contents Soc. Behav. Sci.; Econ. Lit. Index (19??-); Geogr. Abstr. Human Geogr.; Int. Dev. Abstr.; Int. Labour Doc.; J. Econ. Lit.; LABORDOC; Leis., Rec., Tour. Abstr.; Maize Abstr.; PAIS Int. Print (1991); Popul. Index; Postharvest News Inf.; Res. Alert [Full Cov.]; Rural Dev. Abstr.; Soc. Sci. Cit. Index [Full Cov.]; World Agric. Econ. Rural Sociol. Abstr.

ISSN 8756-1972
DD 658 US
TITLE CHANGE
BULLETIN OF THE ASSOCIATION FOR BUSINESS COMMUNICATION, THE.
[Bull. Assoc. Bus. Commun.]. **Added/Corp** Association for Business Communication (U.S.) Association for Business Communication (U.S.). Membership directory of the Association for Business Communication. Vol. 48, No. 1 (Mar. 1985)-(199?). Bulletin. English. Association for Business Communication, Department of Management, College of Business Administration, University of North Texas, Denton TX 76203. **Tel** (217)333-7891. **ED** Dr. N. L. Reinsch (phone: (202)687-5125) Journal; Dr. Kitty O. Locker (phone: (614)292-6556) Bulletin. Index available. **Bk Rev. Ad Acc. Circ:** 2,700. available on microfilm and microfiche from University Microfilms International (UMI). ***Continues*** *ABCA Bulletin, 0001-0383.* ***Continued by*** *Business Communication Quarterly, 1080-5699.*
Desc: Articles of general interest to teachers and practitioners of business communications.
Ind/Abst Acad. Search; Bus. Educ. Index; Bus. Index (1985-); Bus. Source Plus; Bus. Source; Curr. Index J. Educ.; EP Collect.; Gen. BusinessFile (1985-); Gen. Period. Index (1985-); Homework Help.; INFO-SOUTH Abstr.; Linguist. Lang. Behav. Abstr.; Mag. Search; MasterFile FullTEXT 1000; MasterFile FullTEXT 350; MasterFile FullTEXT 650; MasterFile FullTEXT (July 1993-); OCLC; Soc. Plann. Policy Dev. Abstr.; Sociol. Abstr.; Telebase.

LC HC
DD 330 FR
BULLETIN OFFICIEL DES IMPOTS.
(19??)-. Bulletin. French. Imprimerie Nationale / France, BP 514, 59505 Douai Cedex France. **Tel** 011 33 27 937090.

FR
BULLETIN OFFICIEL DES IMPOTS : FISCALITE DIRECTE DES ENTERPRISES 127.
(19??)-. Bulletin. French. Imprimerie Nationale / France, BP 514, 59505 Douai Cedex France. **Tel** 011 33 27 937090.

ISSN 1350-3197
UK
•BULLETPOINT REIGATE.
[Bulletpoint Reigate]. (1993)-. English. Ten times a year. $487.70. Bulletpoint Communications Ltd., 41 Effingham Road, Reigate, Surrey RH2 7JN United Kingdom. **Tel** 011 44 1737 247357.

ISSN 0889-7840
DD 332 US
BULLISH CONSENSUS, THE.
(19??)-. Periodical. English. Irregular (50 issues per year). $395.00 (one-year), $750.00 (two-year). Hadady Corporation, 1111 Arroyo Parkway, Suite 410, Pasadena CA 91109. **Tel** (818)441-3457, 441-8466. **ED** R Earl Hadady.
Desc: A futures market advisory service consisting of a weekly letter and telephone hotline. Its primary feature is a poll of other advisors including the major brokers which results in a percentage of bullish sentiment for each of over 30 of the most actively traded markets.

ISSN 0931-5918
GW
UDC 67/68(058)
BUNDESFIRMENREGISTER. BAND 1, NORD- UND WESTDEUTSCHLAND.
[Bundesfirmenregist., 1 Nord- Westdtschl. 1986]. **VFOAT** Bundesfirmenregister. Band 1, Nord- und Westdeutschland. A, Alphabetischer Teil; Bundesfirmenregister. Band 1, Nord- und Westdeutschland. B, Branchenteil. (1986)-. German. One time a year. Verlagsbetriebe Walter Dorn GmbH & Co. KG, Am Tuv 6 (Stadtadressbuchhaus), D-30519 Hannover Germany. **Tel** 0511 830351, FAX 0511 83 5444. ***Continues*** *Bundesregister ... der Handelsregisterlich Eingetragenen Firmen. Band 1, Nord- und Westdeutschland, 0723-0559.*

ISSN 0257-8328
SZ
UDC 651
TITLE CHANGE
BUREAUX ET SYSTEMES.
(1979)-(19??). Periodical. French. Fachpresse Goldach Hudson & Co, Abteilung Vertrieb 272, CH-9403 Goldach Switzerland. **Tel** 011 41 71 416611. ***Continued by*** *IB Suisse.*

ISSN 1067-800X
DD 338 US
•BURMA (SYRACUSE, N.Y.).
(BURMA : AN EXECUTIVE REPORT.). [Burma]. **Added/Corp** Political Risk Services (IBC USA (Publications) Inc.). (1993)-. English. $110.00. Political Risk Services, 6320 Fly Road, Suite 102, PO Box 248, East Syracuse NY 13057-0248. **Tel** (315)431-0511, FAX (315)431-0200.
Desc: Focuses on the long-term outlook for business. Includes a brief review of recent events and current circumstances, background intelligence including geography, history, economics and social conditions, as well as the key political and economic forecasts.

US
BURTON GROUP REPORT.
(19??)-. English. Twelve times a year. $1895.00. Burton Group, 2649 East Union Boulevard, Salt Lake City UT 84121. **Tel** (801)943-1966, (800)824-9924. ***Continues*** *Clarke Burton Report.*

LC HF1002.5 .B865 **ISSN** 0899-3726
DD 338.7/4/025 US
BUSINESS ACRONYMS.
[Bus. acron.]. **Added/Corp** Gale Research Inc. 1st Ed. (1988)-. English. Irregular. $75.00. Gale Research Inc., 835 Penobscot Building, 645 Griswold Street, Detroit MI 48226. **Tel** (800)877-GALE, (313)961-2242, FAX (313)961-6083, (800)414-5043, telex TWX 810-221-7086. **ED** Julie E. Towell.
Desc: Definitions for 25,000 abbreviations used in all aspects of business. Two arrangements of the definitions allow fast access to the meaning of any business related acronym and the appropriate acronym for any business related phrase or term.

UK
BUSINESS AFRICA.
Added/Corp Economist Intelligence Unit (Great Britain). (19??)-. English. Twenty-two times a year. $633.75 (schools and educational libraries), $845.00 (other) North America. The Economist Intelligence Unit, 40 Duke Street, London W1A 1DW United Kingdom. **Tel** 011 44 171 8301000. **(Subscription address:** Economist Intelligence Unit / North America Subscriptions, 111 West 57th Street, New York NY 10019. **Tel** 800 938-4685, (212)554-0600, FAX (212)586-1181, (212)586-1182.) available on an online database from Lexis-Nexis. ***Formed by the union of*** *South Africa Alert* ***and*** *Africa Markets Monitor.*
Desc: A concise report providing business intelligence and analysis of developments throughout the region and their impact on business operations. Includes case studies of companies' successes and failures.

ISSN 1050-091X
DD 338 US
BUSINESS ALABAMA MONTHLY.
[Bus. Ala. mon.]. Vol. 2, No. 1 (Jan. 1987)-. Periodical. English. Twelve times a year. $24.00. PMT Publishing, PO Box 66200, Mobile AL 36660. **Tel** (334)479-8722, (334)473-6269, FAX (334)473-6269. **ED** T.J. Potts. **Photos. Ad Acc.** ***Continues*** *Business Alabama, 0886-3024.*

ISSN 0738-7253
US
BUSINESS & ACQUISITION NEWSLETTER.
[Bus. acquis. newsl.]. **VFOAT** Business and Acquisition Newsletter. (19??)-. Newsletter. English. Twelve times a year. $300.00. Newsletters International, 2600 South Gessner, Suite 412, Houston TX 77063. **Tel** (713)783-0100. **ED** Len Fox. Index available. cum. index. **Bk Rev.**
Desc: Contains information about companies which want to buy or sell companies, divisions, subsidiaries, product lines, patents and patent licensing.

LC HF5343 .B9a **ISSN** 0894-6825
DD 338.0973 US
BUSINESS AND ECONOMIC HISTORY.
(BUSINESS AND ECONOMIC HISTORY : PAPERS PRESENTED AT THE ... ANNUAL MEETING OF THE BUSINESS HISTORY CONFERENCE.). [Bus. econ. hist.]. **Main/Conf** Business History Conference. **Main/Corp** Business History Conference. **Added/Corp** University of Illinois (Urbana-Champaign campus). Bureau of Economic and Business Research. University of Illinois at Urbana-Champaign. Bureau of Economic and Business Research. College of William and Mary. Dept. of Economics. (Feb. 28-March 1, 1975)-. English. Two times

a year. Business History Conference, Department of Economics, William and Mary College, Williamsburg VA 23185. **Tel** (804)221-2381. available on microfilm and microfiche from University Microfilms International (UMI). ***Continues*** *Business History Conference. Proceedings of the Business History Conference.*
Ind/Abst Am. Hist. Life (1987-).

LC HC107.K2 K38 **ISSN** 1043-6227
DD 330.9781/005 US
Pr Rev.
BUSINESS & ECONOMIC REPORT. [Bus. econ. rep.]. **Added/Corp** Wichita State University. Center for Business and Economic Research. Wichita State University. Center for Economic Development and Business Research. **VFOAT** Business and Economic Report. Vol. 14, No. 1, March (1984)-. Periodical. English. Irregular (Report is quarterly, Indicators 12 per year). $35.00. Center for Economic Development and Business Research, Wichita State University, 1845 Fairmount Street, Wichita KS 67260. **Tel** (316)689-3225, FAX (316)689-3950. **ED** S. Michelle Davis. **Circ:** 1,000. ***Continues*** *Quarterly Kansas Economic Indicators.*
Desc: Gathers, analyzes and publishes data describing economic conditions for Wichita and Kansas.
Ind/Abst PAIS Int. Print.

LC HC **ISSN** 0951-919X
DD 330 UK
BUSINESS & ECONOMICS REVIEW. [Bus. econ. rev.]. **Added/Corp** University of Wales. **VFOAT** Business and Economics Review; University of Wales Review. Business & Economics; Business and Economics; Business & Economics. No. 1 (Summer 1987)-. Periodical. English. Two times a year. $40.00. Welsh Development Agency, Pearl House, Greyfriars Road, Cardiff CF1 3XX United Kingdom. **Tel** 011 44 1222 222666, telex 497513. Documents available from UMI Article Clearinghouse.
Ind/Abst ABI/INFORM Glob. Ed.

UK
BUSINESS AND GOVERNMENT. English. Six times a year. £90.00. Business & Government, 35-37 Grosvenor Gardens, London SW1 WOBS United Kingdom. **Tel** 011 44 171 8286626.

LC HD7102.U4 B87 **ISSN** 0739-9413
DD 331.25/5 US
CCC
NLM W1; HU9734
BUSINESS AND HEALTH. [Bus. health]. **Added/Corp** Washington Business Group on Health. **VFOAT** Business & Health. Vol. 1, No. 1 (Nov. 1983)-. Periodical. English. Fourteen times a year. $99.00. Medical Economics Publishing, Five Paragon Drive, Second Floor, Montvale NJ 07645. **Tel** (800)432-4570, (201)358-2210. **(Subscription address:** Fulco, PO Box 3000, Denville NJ 07834. **Tel** (800)875-2997, (201)627-2427.**) ED** Jane Stein. **Ad Acc. Circ:** 10,000. available on an online database (files 15,149,648/Full-Text) from DIALOG. Documents available from UMI Article Clearinghouse.
Desc: Health care policy and cost strategies. Full coverage of current developments, critical analysis, insightful commentary on innovations legislative proposals and cost management strategies.
Ind/Abst ABI/INFORM Glob. Ed.; ABI/INFORM [Computer File] (January 1986); Acad. Abstr.; Acad. Search; Bus. Period. Index; Bus. Source Plus; Bus. Source; Curr. Cit.; EP Collect.; Health Index (1989-); Health Period. Database [Full Txt.]; Health Plan. Adminis.; Health Ref. Cent. (Jan. 1989-) [Full Txt.] [Full Cov.]; Health Source Plus; Health Source; Healthcare Leader. Rev.; Homework Help.; Hosp. Health Admin. Index; INFO-SOUTH Abstr.; Mag. Search; MasterFile FullTEXT 1000; MasterFile FullTEXT 350; MasterFile FullTEXT 650; MasterFile FullTEXT (Jan. 1992-); OCLC; PAIS Int. Print; Pub. Lib. FullTEXT; Telebase; Trade Ind. ASAP [Full Txt.]; Trade Ind. Index [Full Txt.]; UMI ABI/Inform--Bus. Period. Ondisc (Feb. 1987-) [Full Txt.]; Wilson Bus. Abstr.; Work Relat. Abstr.

LC HC **ISSN** 0021-0463
US
BUSINESS & INDUSTRY. [Bus. ind.]. **VFOAT** Business & Industry Magazine. **VAT** Business and Industry. (19??)-. Periodical. English. Twelve times a year. $24.00. Business & Industry, 1720 28th Street/#B, Des Moines IA 50265-1436. **Tel** (515)225-2545. **ED** James Snyder. **Ad Acc, Adv Mgr:** Robert Wagner. **Circ:** 12000 (ctrl).

LC HF5387 .B86 **ISSN** 0277-2027
DD 174/.4/05 US
Pr Rev.
BUSINESS & PROFESSIONAL ETHICS JOURNAL. [Bus. prof. ethics j.]. **Added/Corp** Rensselaer Polytechnic Institute. Human Dimensions Center. University of Delaware. University of Florida. **VFOAT** Business and Professional Ethics Journal. Vol. 1, No. 1 (Fall 1981)-. Periodical. English. Four times a year (published within the seasons). $85.00. University of Florida / Center for Applied Philosophy, 331 Griffin-Floyd Hall, Gainesville FL 32611. **Tel** (904)392-2084, FAX (904)392-5577. **(Subscription address:** Business & Professional Ethics Journal, PO Box 15017, Gainesville FL 32604. **) ED** Robert J. Baum. **Ad Acc. Acid Free. Circ:** 800. Documents available from UMI Article Clearinghouse.
Desc: Serves as a forum for the analysis of ethical issues that arise in practicing a profession or conducting business.
Ind/Abst Acad. Search; Bus. Index; Bus. Period. Index; Bus. Source Plus; Bus. Source; EP Collect.; Expand. Acad. Index (1989-); Homework Help.; INFO-SOUTH Abstr.; J. Plan. Lit.; Mag. Search; MasterFile FullTEXT 1000; MasterFile FullTEXT 350; MasterFile FullTEXT 650; MasterFile FullTEXT (Jan. 1994-); Newsp. Period. Abstr. (1991-); OCLC; PAIS Int. Print (1991-); Philos. Index; Soc. Sci. Source; Soc. Sci. Index; Soc. Sci. Index Fulltext (Spring 1987-) [Full Txt.]; Telebase; Wilson Bus. Abstr.

LC HF5001 .B7657 **ISSN** 0007-6503
DD 330 US
CCC
CODEN BUSOBE
Pr Rev.
BUSINESS AND SOCIETY. [Bus. soc.]. **Added/Corp** Roosevelt University. Business Research Center. Roosevelt University. College of Business Administration. Walter E. Heller College of Business Administration. **VFOAT** Business & Society. Vol. 1, No. 1 (Autumn 1960)-. Periodical. English. Three times a year (Apr., Aug., Dec.). $132.00. SAGE Periodical Press, 2455 Teller Road, Thousand Oaks CA 91320. **Tel** (805)499-0721, FAX (805)499-0871, telex 100799. **ED** Thomas M. Jones and Donna J. Wood. **Bk Rev. Acid Free. Circ:** 2,500 (ctrl). available on microfilm and microfiche from University Microfilms International (UMI). Documents available from UMI Article Clearinghouse.
Desc: Devoted exclusively to the field of business and society. Publishes original research and dissertation abstracts relating to business ethics, business-government relations, corporate governance, corporate social performance and environmental management.
Ind/Abst ABI/INFORM Glob. Ed.; ABI/INFORM [Computer File] (Winter 1980-); Acad. Search; Bus. Index (1985-); Bus. Period. Index; Bus. Source Plus; Bus. Source; EP Collect.; Gen. BusinessFile (1985-); Gen. Period. Index (1985-); Homework Help.; INFO-SOUTH Abstr.; Mag. Search; Manage. Contents; MasterFile FullTEXT 1000; MasterFile FullTEXT 350; MasterFile FullTEXT 650; MasterFile FullTEXT (Jan. 1994-); OCLC; Oper. Res./Manage. Sci.; Telebase; Trade Ind. ASAP [Full Txt.]; Trade Ind. Index; UMI ABI/Inform--Bus. Period. Ondisc (Spring 1988-) [Full Txt.]; Work Relat. Abstr.

ISSN 1065-5875
DD 338 US
CODEN BSBRET
TITLE CHANGE
BUSINESS AND SOCIETY BRIEFING. [Bus. soc. brief.]. **Added/Corp** Conference Board. Vol. 1, No. 1 (Fall 1992)-(1993). Periodical. English. Conference Board, 845 Third Avenue, New York NY 10022. **Tel** (212)759-0900 ext. 582, (800)872-6273, FAX (212)980-7014. ***Merged with*** *Quality Briefing, 1059-3918; Conference Board Briefing, 0899-6741* ***to form*** *Conference Board's Membership Update, 1072-0235.*

ISSN 0778-7588
BE
UDC 384
BUSINESS & TELECOM (NEDERLANDSE ED.). **VFOAT** Business and Telecom (Nederlandse Ed.). (1990)-. Periodical. Dutch (French). Twelve times a year. $55.98. Telecom Media SC, Sterstraat 95, 1620 Drogenbos Belgium. **Tel** 011 32 2 3310022. Index available. **Circ:** 16000 (ctrl).

LC HF1 .B866 **ISSN** 1062-6158
DD 330 GW
BUSINESS & THE CONTEMPORARY WORLD (WALTHAM, MASS. 1991). (BUSINESS & THE CONTEMPORARY WORLD.). [Bus. contemp. world]. **Added/Corp** Bentley College. York University (Toronto, Ont.). Faculty of Administrative Studies. Keio Gijuku Daigaku. **VFOAT** Business and the Contemporary World; BCW. Vol. 4, No. 1 (Autumn 1991)-. Periodical. English. Four times a year (Jan., Apr., July, Oct.). $108.00. Walter de Gruyter Inc., PO Box 303421, D-10728 Berlin Germany. **Tel** 011 49 30 260050, FAX 011 49 30 26005251, telex 184027. **ED** H. L. Sawyer. ***Continues*** *Business in the Contemporary World, 1041-8482.*
Desc: Offers global perspectives on ties between the corporation and society--ties that dramatically influence our changing world. Corporate leaders share the issues and opportunities they find most challenging, while authorities in education, technology, and government identify developing trends and their implications for domestic and international corporations.

LC HD59 .B869 **ISSN** 0270-3572
DD 302.2/34 US
BUSINESS AND THE MEDIA. **See** Communications.

LC HC **ISSN** 0572-7545
DD 330 HK
BUSINESS ASIA. [Bus. Asia]. **Added/Corp** Business International Asia/Pacific Ltd. (Oct. 1970)-. Newsletter. English. Twenty-six times a year. $695.00. The Economist Intelligence Unit, 40 Duke Street, London W1A 1DW United Kingdom. **Tel** 011 44 171 8301000. **(Subscription address:** Economist Intelligence Unit / North America Subscriptions, 111 West 57th Street, New York NY 10019. **Tel** 800 938-4685, (212)554-0600, FAX (212)586-1181, (212)586-1182.**)** available on an online database (file 627/Full-Text) from DIALOG. Documents available from UMI Article Clearinghouse.
Desc: Informs business managers with regional responsibility for Asia on political, economic, social and regulatory trends shaping Asian markets. Regular features include medium term business outlooks for each country in Asia/Pacific, case studies of individual firms' regional strategies, checklists and strategic planning perspectives.

LC HG1501 **ISSN** 0146-4744
DD 332.1 US
BUSINESS ASSISTANCE MONOGRAPH SERIES, THE. Monographic series. English. Price varies per volume. Federal Reserve Bank of Boston, 600 Atlantic Avenue, Research Library D, Boston MA 02106. **Tel** (617)973-3397, (617)973-3403.

DD 650 US
BUSINESS ASSOCIATION REVIEW. Vol. 11 No. 2 (Fall 1973)-. Periodical. English. School of Business Administration / California, San Diego CA 92115. ***Continues*** *Journal of Business.*
Ind/Abst Econ. Lit. Index (?-199?).

ISSN 0192-0855
US
CCC
TITLE CHANGE
BUSINESS ATLANTA. Vol. 7, No. 7 (Nov./Dec. 1978)-(Feb. 1994). Trade Publication. English. Argus Business, 6151 Powers Ferry Road Northwest, Atlanta GA 30339. **Tel** (404)995-2500, FAX (404)995-0400. **(Subscription address:** Hallmark Data Systems, PO Box 1147, Skokie IL 60076. **Tel** (708)647-6933.**) ED** Barrie Rissman. **Circ:** 24,049. available on microfilm and microfiche from University Microfilms International (UMI); available on an online database (files 635,648/Full-Text) from DIALOG. Documents available from UMI Article Clearinghouse. ***Continues*** *Real Estate & Business Atlanta.* ***Merged into*** *Georgia Trend.*
Ind/Abst Acad. Search; Bus. Dateline; Bus. Index (1985-); Bus. Source Plus; Bus. Source; EP Collect.; Gen. BusinessFile (1985-); Gen. Period. Index (1985-); Homework Help.; INFO-SOUTH Abstr.; MasterFile FullTEXT 1000; MasterFile FullTEXT 350; MasterFile FullTEXT 650; MasterFile FullTEXT (July 1993-Jan. 1994); OCLC; PROMT; Telebase; Trade Ind. ASAP [Full Txt.]; Trade Ind. Index [Full Txt.].

UK
BUSINESS BASICS - GUIDE TO BUSINESS FORMS. (19??)-. Periodical. English. £80.50. Croner Publ Ltd., Croner House London Road, Kingston Upon Thames, Surrey KT2 6SR United Kingdom. **Tel** 011 44 181 5473333, FAX 011 44 181 5472637.

UK
BUSINESS BASICS - GUIDE TO NATIONAL INSURANCE. (19??)-. Periodical. English. £80.40. Croner Publ Ltd., Croner House London Road, Kingston Upon Thames, Surrey KT2 6SR United Kingdom. **Tel** 011 44 181 5473333, FAX 011 44 181 5472637.

UK
BUSINESS BASICS - PROPERTY. (19??)-. Periodical. English. £80.20. Croner Publ Ltd., Croner House London Road, Kingston Upon Thames, Surrey KT2 6SR United Kingdom. **Tel** 011 44 181 5473333, FAX 011 44 181 5472637.

ISSN 1352-5581
UK
•**BUSINESS BASICS STAFF BULLETIN.** (1993)-. Bulletin. English. $138.26. Croner Publ Ltd., Croner House London Road, Kingston Upon Thames, Surrey KT2 6SR United Kingdom. **Tel** 011 44 181 5473333, FAX 011 44 181 5472637.

UK
BUSINESS BASICS - TAX. (19??)-. Periodical. English. £80.60. Croner Publ Ltd., Croner House London Road, Kingston Upon Thames, Surrey KT2 6SR United Kingdom. **Tel** 011 44 181 5473333, FAX 011 44 181 5472637.

SA
BUSINESS BLUE-BOOK OF SOUTH AFRICA. **VFOAT** Business Blue Book of South Africa; Business Blue Book of Southern Africa; Business Blue-Book of Southern Africa; Business Blue-Book of

Business and Economics

S.A. (1967)-. English. One time a year (Nov.). $99.90. National Publishing Pty. Ltd., 155 2nd Avenue, PO Box 2271, Kenilworth 7700 South Africa. **Tel** 011 27 21 611140, FAX 011 27 21 611389, telex 9555542+. *Continues Business Blue-Book of Southern Africa.*

ISSN 0741-8132
US

BUSINESS BOOK REVIEW. [Bus. book rev.]. **Added/Corp** Corporate Support Systems, Inc. Vol. 1, No. 1 (Nov/Dec. 1983)-. Periodical. English. Four times a year (Feb., May, Aug., Nov.). $80.00. Corporate Support Systems Inc, 1626 Mason Mill Road, Atlanta GA 30329. **Tel** (404)320-6972, FAX (404)325-0091. **ED** Jagdish N. Sheth. Index available in last issue of volume--attached. cum. index. **Bk Rev**, (Qty: 50-60). **Circ:** 3,000 (ctrl).
Desc: Review of books that reflects the most current business trends, philosophies, and practical information. Books categorized into major works, special topics, business histories, and references. Reviews are chapter-by-chapter summaries.
Ind/Abst Book Rev. Index (1984-).

UK

BUSINESS BRIEFING. English. One time a week. £94.00 UK; £106.00 Europe; £120.00 other. Association of British Chambers of Commerce, Border House, High Street Farndon, Chester CH3 6PT United Kingdom. **Tel** 011 44 1829 270714.

ISSN 0890-2178
DD 330
US

BUSINESS BRIEFS (DETROIT, MICH.). (BUSINESS BRIEFS.). [Bus. briefs]. **Added/Corp** Manufacturers National Corporation. Manufacturers National Bank (Detroit, Mich.). (19??)-. Periodical. English. Twelve times a year. Free on request. Manufacturers National Corporation, 411 West Lafayette, Detroit MI 48226. **Tel** (313)222-4000.

ISSN 0899-6830
US

BUSINESS BULLETIN (FRANKFORT, KY.). (BUSINESS BULLETIN.). (198?)-. Bulletin. English. Irregular (8 issues per year). $30.00. Kentucky Chamber of Commerce, Box 817, 464 Chenault Road, Frankfort KY 40602. **Tel** (502)695-4700, FAX (502)695-6824. *Continues Strictly Business, 8750-8303.*

ISSN 0969-3866
DD 658
UK
CCC
CODEN BCAREE

●**BUSINESS CHANGE & RE-ENGINEERING.** [Bus. change re-eng.]. **VFOAT** Business Change and Re-engineering; Business Change & Re Engineering. (1993)-. Periodical. English. Four times a year. $275.00. John Wiley & Sons, Inc., 605 Third Avenue, New York NY 10158-0012. **Tel** (212)850-6000, (212)850-6645, FAX (212)850-6088, telex 12-7063.
Desc: Features papers on practical issues surrounding organizational change and business re-engineering.

LC HC440.8.A1 B87
DD 330.9/549/205
II

BUSINESS CHRONICLE. No. 1 (June 1972)-. Periodical. English. Rs1.00 single issue. 49/6 R K Mission Road, Dacca 3 Bangladesh.

ISSN 1080-5699
DD 658
US

●**BUSINESS COMMUNICATION QUARTERLY : A PUBLICATION OF THE ASSOCIATON FOR BUSINESS COMMUNICATION.** **Added/Corp** Association for Business Communication (U.S.). **VFOAT** Quarterly. (1995)-. Bulletin. English. Four times a year. $40.00. Association for Business Communication, Department of Management, College of Business Administration, University of North Texas, Denton TX 76203. **Tel** (217)333-7891. **ED** Dr. N. L. Reinsch (phone: (202)687-5125) Journal; Dr. Kitty O. Locker (phone: (614)292-6556) Bulletin. *Continues Bulletin of the Association for Business Communication.*
Desc: Articles of general interest to teachers and practitioners of business communications.

UK

BUSINESS COMMUNICATIONS. English. Free. British Telcom, Intel House/Room 107, 24 Sthwrk Brg, London SE1 9HJ United Kingdom. **Tel** 011 44 171 9288686. *Continues Network User.*

JA

BUSINESS COMMUNICATIONS. (19??)-. Japanese. Twelve times a year. $155.00. Kikaku Senta, (Kikaku Center), Kimura Biru, 2-1 Kanda Ogawamachi, Chiyoda-ku Tokyo 101 Japan. **(Subscription address:** Maruzen Company Ltd., PO Box 5050, Import & Export Department, Tokyo 100 31 Japan. **Tel** 011 81 3 32789224.)

ISSN 1055-8217
US

BUSINESS CONCEPTS. **Added/Corp** Publishing and Business Consultants. (1992)-. Periodical. English. Four times a year. $29.99. Publishing & Business Consultants, PO Box 75392, Los Angeles CA 90075. **Tel** (213)732-3477, FAX (213)732-9123. **ED** Andeson Napoleon Atia. **Ad Acc.** Full Page (B&W) $5750.00. Half Page (B&W) $3575.00. Full Page (Color) $8750.00 (2 color). Half Page (Color) $5500.00 (2 color). **Circ:** 45,000.
Desc: Focused on the active entrepreneur. Features special articles on start-up business concepts, management, financing, taxes and international business.

ISSN 1193-9559
DD 330.971
CN

BUSINESS CONDITIONS BULLETIN (TORONTO). (BUSINESS CONDITIONS BULLETIN.). [Bus. cond. bull.]. **Added/Corp** Ernst & Young (Firm). Strategy Marketing & Economics Group. Ernst & Young (Firm). (Sept./Dec. 1991)-. Bulletin. English. Irregular. Limited free distribution. Ernst & Young / Canada, PO Box 251, Toronto Dominion Centre, Toronto Ontario, M5K 1J7 Canada. *Continues Business Conditions (Toronto, Ont.), 0710-3611.*

ISSN 1198-1261
DD 338.6
CN

BUSINESS CONNECTIONS (TORONTO). (BUSINESS CONNECTIONS.). [Bus. connect.]. Vol. 1, No. 1 (Sept. 1992)-. Periodical. English. Four times a year. 8.00Can$. Business Connections, 16 Phoebe Street, Toronto, Ontario M5T 2Z3. **Tel** (416)971-6911.

LC HF3223 .B8
CN
CEASED

BUSINESS CONNEXIONS. **VFOAT** Connexions d'Affaires. (19??)-(Jan. 1994). English (French). Globe Information Services, 444 Front Street West, Toronto Ontario M5V 2S9 Canada. **Tel** (800)268-9128, (416)585-5250.
Desc: National bilingual business to business communications directory. Contains phone, fax, telex and toll-free numbers and addresses for 80,000 Canadian businesses.

ISSN 0814-4273
AT

BUSINESS COUNCIL BULLETIN. [Bus. Counc. bull.]. **Added/Corp** Business Council of Australia. (1984)-. Bulletin. English. Ten times a year (Feb. thru Dec.). 36.18Aus$. Business Council of Australia, GPO Box 7225, Melbourne Victoria 3004 Australia. **Tel** 011 61 3 2747777, FAX 011 61 3 2747744. **ED** M. Bentley. Index Available Published separately--free--upon request. **Bk Rev. Circ:** 6,200. *Absorbed Business Council of Australia. Annual Report; Continues Bulletin - Australian Industries Development Association, 0312-9683.*
Ind/Abst APAIS, Aust. Public Aff. Inf. Ser. (1989-).

LC K623
DD 346
US

●**BUSINESS CRIMES BULLETIN.** See Law-Civil Law.

LC HF5001
ISSN 1320-971X
DD 650.07129405
AT

●**BUSINESS DATE.** [Bus. date]. (1993)-. Periodical. English. Four times a year (Mar., May, July, Sept.). 45.00Aus$. Warringal Productions, 114 Argyle Street, Fitzroy 3065 Australia. **Tel** 011 61 3 4160200, FAX 011 61 3 4160402. **(Subscription address:** Warringal Publications, PO Box 336, Fitzroy 3065 Australia. **Tel** 011 61 3 4160200.) **ED** Jan Arter. **Circ:** 1,200.
Desc: Provides teachers and students with information on business management, management and communications, human resource management, corporate management and other commerce-related subjects.
Ind/Abst Bus. Source Plus; EP Collect.; Homework Help.; MasterFile FullTEXT 1000; MasterFile FullTEXT 350; MasterFile FullTEXT 650; MasterFile FullTEXT; OCLC; Telebase; World Mag. Bank.

US

BUSINESS DATELINE. See Business and Economics-Abstracting, Bibliographies and Statistics.

UK

BUSINESS DIARY. (19??)-. Periodical. English. Four times a year. £86.00. Croner Publ Ltd., Croner House London Road, Kingston Upon Thames, Surrey KT2 6SR United Kingdom. **Tel** 011 44 181 5473333, FAX 011 44 181 5472637.

ISSN 8750-2305
US

BUSINESS DIGEST (BURLINGTON, VT.). See Business and Economics-Computer Applications.

ISSN 8750-9520
US

BUSINESS DIGEST (DANBURY, CONN.). (BUSINESS DIGEST.). **VFOAT** Greater Danbury Business Digest. Vol. 1, No. 1 (Mar. 1985)-. Periodical. English. Twelve times a year. $24.00. Business Digest / Connecticut, 275 Greenwood Avenue, Bethel CT 06801. **Tel** (203)798-7963. **ED** Don Waters. **Ad Acc. Circ:** 6,500 (ctrl).

ISSN 0895-3791
US

BUSINESS DIGEST (HYANNIS, MASS.). (BUSINESS DIGEST.). **VFOAT** Cape & Islands Business Digest; Southeastern Massachusetts/Cape & Islands Business Digest; Southeastern Massachusetts Cape & Islands Business Digest; Southeastern Massachusetts Cape and Islands Business Digest; Cape and Islands Business Digest. (Apr. 1986)-. Periodical. English. Twelve times a year. Cape & Islands Business Digest, 72 Winter Street, Hyannis MA 02601. **Tel** (508)778-5042, FAX (508)778-5063. Documents available from UMI Article Clearinghouse.
Ind/Abst Bus. Dateline (May 1986-) [Full Txt.].

ISSN 1167-2064
FR

UDC 336(44)

BUSINESS DIGEST PARIS. (BUSINESS DIGEST.). (1992)-. Periodical. French. Twelve times a year. $216.53. Business Digest / France, 1 rue Edgar Poe, 75019 Paris France. **Tel** 011 33 1 42030763, FAX 33 1 42030767.

ISSN 0747-1629
US
CEASED

BUSINESS DIGEST (PORTSMOUTH, N.H.). (BUSINESS DIGEST.). **VFOAT** Seacoast New Hampshire Business Digest; Seacoast Business Digest. Vol. 1, No. 1 (Feb. 1984)-(19??). Periodical. English. Business Digest / New Hampshire, PO Box 3128, Portsmouth NH 03801.

ISSN 1031-2315
DD 650.0994
AT

BUSINESS DIRECTIONS. [Bus. dir.]. (1987)-. Periodical. English. Eight times a year. 40.29Aus$. Business Directions, 868 Albany Highway, 1st Floor Victoria Park, PO Box 565, Victoria Park WA 6979 Australia. **Tel** 011 61 9 4702353, FAX 011 61 9 4702363. **ED** Richard Reeves and Jane Walker. Index available. cum. index. **Bk Rev**, (Qty: 8). **Ad Acc. Adv Mgr:** David Dell. **Circ:** 10,000 (ctrl).
Ind/Abst Bus. Source Plus; Bus. Source; EP Collect.; Homework Help.; MasterFile FullTEXT 1000; MasterFile FullTEXT 350; MasterFile FullTEXT 650; MasterFile FullTEXT; OCLC; Telebase; World Mag. Bank.

LC HF3851 .B88
DD 338.4/025/5125
HK

BUSINESS DIRECTORY OF HONG KONG. See Industry and Production-Trade and Industrial Directories.

US

BUSINESS DOCUMENTS. (19??)-. Trade Publication. English. Four times a year. $145.00. North American Publishing Company, 401 North Broad Street, Philadelphia PA 19108. **Tel** (215)238-5300, (800)777-8074, FAX (215)238-5383.
Desc: Serves the needs and interests of business forms managers, buyers, and users. Covers forms and systems design, applications and management. Keeps track of the latest industry developments, and professional association news; also profiles the largest forms buyers and users.

ISSN 0831-7291
DD 658/.005
CN
CEASED

BUSINESS DYNAMICS (100 MILE HOUSE). (BUSINESS DYNAMICS.). [Bus. dyn.]. Issue No. 1 (March 1983)-(1993). Periodical. English. Business Dynamics/Integrating, PO Box 964, 100 Mile House British Columbia V0K 2E0 Canada. **Tel** (604)395-2485, FAX (604)395-2143. **ED** Norman Smotler. **Bk Rev. Circ:** 1,000 (ctrl).
Desc: Demonstrating integrity in the world of business.

UK

BUSINESS EASTERN EUROPE. **Added/Corp** Business International S.A. Vol. 5, No. 26 (July 2, 1976)-. Periodical. English. One time a week (51 times per year). $1175.00. The Economist Intelligence Unit, 40 Duke Street, London W1A 1DW United Kingdom. **Tel** 011 44 171 8301000. **(Subscription address:** Economist Intelligence Unit / North America Subscriptions, 111 West 57th Street, New York NY 10019. **Tel** 800 938-4685, (212)554-0600, FAX (212)586-1181, (212)586-1182.) available on an online database (file 627/Full-Text) from DIALOG. *Continues Eastern Europe Report.*
Desc: A concise 12-page newsletter providing business information on Central and Eastern Europe and the former-Soviet Republics. Its emphasis is on covering practical day-to-day business issues, with a range of features.
Ind/Abst F&S Index Plus Text, Int. [Select. Cov.].

LC HC101 .B88 ISSN 0007-666X
DD 330 US
CCC
CODEN BECODS

BUSINESS ECONOMICS (CLEVELAND, OHIO). (BUSINESS ECONOMICS : THE JOURNAL OF THE NATIONAL ASSOCIATION OF BUSINESS ECONOMISTS.). [Bus. econ.]. **Added/Corp** National Association of Business Economists (U.S.). Vol. 1, No. 1 (Summer 1965)-. Periodical. English. Four times a year. $50.00. NABE / National Association of Business Economists, 1233 20th Street NW, Suite 505, Washington DC 20036. **Tel** (202)463-6223. **(Subscription address:** National Association of Business Economists, 1801 East Ninth Street, Suite 700, Cleveland OH 44114. **Tel** (216)241-6223.**) ED** Edmund A. Mennis. **Bk Rev. Ad Acc. Circ:** 4,600 (ctrl). available on microfilm and microfiche from University Microfilms International (UMI); available on CD-ROM. Documents available from UMI Article Clearinghouse, Magazine Collection.
Desc: Contains articles on applied business economics of interest to economists, financial analysts, market analysts and general business persons. Stresses practical business applications of economics.
Ind/Abst ABI/INFORM Glob. Ed. (Sept. 1972-); ABI/INFORM Ondisc: Expr. Ed. (Jan. 1987-); ABI/INFORM [Computer File] (Sept. 1972-); Acad. Search; Bus. ASAP (1990-) [Full Txt.]; Bus. Index (1985-); Bus. Period. Index; Bus. Source Plus; Bus. Source; Curr. Cit.; Econ. Lit. Index (Sept. 1972-); EP Collect.; Gen. BusinessFile (1985-); Gen. Period. Index (1985-); Homework Help.; Hum. Resour. Abstr. (?-?); INFO-SOUTH Abstr.; J. Econ. Lit.; J. Plan. Lit.; Mag. ASAP Plus [Full Txt.]; Mag. Index Plus (1989-); Mag. Search; MasterFile FullTEXT 1000; MasterFile FullTEXT 350; MasterFile FullTEXT 650; MasterFile FullTEXT (July 1993-) [Full Txt.]; Newsp. Period. Abstr. (1988-); OCLC; PAIS Int. Print (1991-); Telebase; Mag. Index (1977-); Trade Ind. ASAP [Full Txt.]; Trade Ind. Index (1981-) [Full Txt.]; UMI ABI/Inform--Bus. Period. Ondisc (Jan. 1988-) [Full Txt.]; Wilson Bus. Abstr.; World Mag. Bank.

LC HB ISSN 0306-5049
DD 330 UK

BUSINESS ECONOMIST. (THE BUSINESS ECONOMIST.). [Bus. econ.]. **Added/Corp** Business Economist's Group (Great Britain) Society of Business Economists (Great Britain). Vol. 1, No. 1 (Spring 1969)-. Academic Scholarly Publication. English. Three times a year (Apr., June, Nov.). $58.19. The Society of Business Economists, 11 Bay Tree Walk, Watford Hertfordshire WD1 3RX United Kingdom. **Tel** 011 44 1923 237287, FAX 011 44 1923 223947. **ED** Barry Naisbitt. Index available (Bound in 3rd iss.). cum. index. **Circ:** 900. Documents available from BLDSC.
Desc: Features worldwide economic development. Analyzes industries and markets, tests theories, and reviews the latest publications of interest to economists.
Ind/Abst Contents Pages Manage.; Curr. Cit.; Work Relat. Abstr.

LC HF1101.U57 A2 ISSN 0007-6678
DD 650 US

BUSINESS EDUCATION FORUM. (BUSINESS EDUCATION FORUM.). [Bus. educ. forum]. **Added/Corp** United Business Education Association (U.S.) National Business Education Association. **VFOAT** Business Education (UBEA) Forum; UBEA Business Education Forum. Vol. 4, No. 1 (Oct. 1949)-. Periodical. English. Four times a year (Oct., Dec., Feb., and April). Membership: $60.00 US; $70.00 other. National Business Education Association, 1914 Association Drive, Reston VA 22091-1596. **Tel** (703)860-8300, FAX (703)620-4483. **ED** Regina McDowell. Index available. **Ad Acc. Circ:** 17,000 (ctrl). available on microfilm and microfiche from University Microfilms International (UMI). ***Continues*** *UBEA Forum;* ***Absorbed*** *National Business Education Quarterly* ***and*** *National Business Education Yearbook, 1049-0256.* ***Continued in part by*** *National Business Education Yearbook (Reston, Va. : 1987), 1049-0256.*
Desc: Contains articles about processing communication, keyboarding/typewriting, basic business and economics, marketing, accounting and office procedures. It also contains information on current issues and general interest to business educators.
Ind/Abst Acad. Search; Bus. Educ. Index; Bus. Source Plus; Bus. Source; Contents Pages Educ.; Curr. Index J. Educ.; Educ. Index; EP Collect.; Homework Help.; INFO-SOUTH Abstr.; Mag. Search; MasterFile FullTEXT 1000; MasterFile FullTEXT 350; MasterFile FullTEXT 650; MasterFile FullTEXT (Jan. 1994-); OCLC; Tech. Educ. Train. Abstr.; Telebase.

ISSN 0710-7714
DD 651/.07/12715 CN

BUSINESS EDUCATION NEWS (FREDERICTON). (BUSINESS EDUCATION NEWS.). [Bus. educ. news]. Vol. 7, No. 1 (Dec. 1977)-. Periodical. English. Three times a year. Free. New Brunswick Teachers' Association, PO Box 752, Fredericton New Brunswick E3B 5R6 Canada. **Tel** (506)452-8921. ctrl circ. ***Continues*** *Business Education Observer, 0710-7706.*

ISSN 1068-2198
DD 330 US

BUSINESS-EDUCATION REPORT. [Bus.-educ. rep.]. **VFOAT** Business Education Report. (1989)-. Periodical. English. Twelve times a year. $175.00 US; $225.00 other. Info Media Inc., PO Box 210, Ellenton FL 34222-0210. **Tel** (813)776-2535. **ED** Don Adams, (phone: (813)776-2535).
Desc: Business involvement in K-12 education via partnerships.

ISSN 0951-1512
DD 651.07 UK
TITLE CHANGE

BUSINESS EDUCATION TODAY. [Bus. educ. today]. (1985)-(19??). Periodical. English. Pitman Publishing Ltd, 12 14 Slaidburn Cres, Southport Merseyside, PR9 9YF United Kingdom. **Tel** 011 44 1704 26881, FAX 011 44 1704 231970, telex 261367. **ED** Jill Priest. **Bk Rev. Ad Acc. Circ:** 6,000 (ctrl). ***Continues*** *Office Skills for the Business Studies Teacher.* ***Continued by*** *BET.*
Desc: A resource magazine for teachers, lecturers, and trainers of business - related courses.

ISSN 0731-0102
US

BUSINESS ELECTRONICS NETWORKS. [Bus. electron. netw.]. **Added/Corp** Alexander Hamilton Institute (U.S.). (198?)-. Periodical. English. Twenty-four times a year. Alexander Hamilton Institute, 70 Hilltop Road, Ramsey NJ 07446-1119. **Tel** (201)825-8161, (800)879-2441, FAX (201)825-8696.

JA
TITLE CHANGE

BUSINESS ENGLISH. (19??)-(19??). Japanese. **(Subscription address:** Kinokuniya Company Ltd., 38-1 Sakuragaoka 5, chome Setagaya-ku, Tokyo 156 Japan. **Tel** FAX 011 03 3439 0136.**)** ***Continued by*** *Yasashii Business Eigo.*

AT

BUSINESS ENVIRONMENTAL FORUM. (19??)-. English. Six times a year. 53.44Aus$. Australian Chamber of Commerce and Industry, PO Box E14, Queen Victoria Terrace, ACT 2600 Australia. **Tel** 011 61 62 732381, FAX 011 61 62 733646, telex 62507.

ISSN 0962-8770
UK
CCC

BUSINESS ETHICS: A EUROPEAN REVIEW. **See** Ethics.

ISSN 0894-6582
DD 174 US

BUSINESS ETHICS (MADISON, WIS.). **See** Ethics.

LC HF5387 .B8728 ISSN 1052-150X
DD 174/.4 US

BUSINESS ETHICS QUARTERLY. (BUSINESS ETHICS QUARTERLY : THE JOURNAL OF THE SOCIETY FOR BUSINESS ETHICS.). [Bus. ethics q.]. **Added/Corp** Society for Business Ethics. **VFOAT** BEQ. Vol. 1, No. 1 (Jan. 1991)-. Periodical. English. Four times a year. $98.00. Philosophy Documentation Center, Bowling Green State University, Bowling Green OH 43403-0189. **Tel** (419)372-2419, (800)444-2419, FAX (419)372-6987.
Ind/Abst Hum. Resour. Abstr.

LC HF5387 .B8753 ISSN 1064-0223
DD 174/.4/05 US

BUSINESS ETHICS RESOURCE. [Bus. ethics resour.]. Vol. 1, No. 1 (Mar. 1987)-. Periodical. English. Four times a year (Feb., May, Aug., Nov.). $29.00 US; $34.00 other. Revehen Consultants, 28 Marshal Street, Suite 3, Brookline MA 02146. **Tel** (617)232-1820, FAX (617)232-2775. **ED** William H. P. Smith (editor's address: 10 Turtle Lane, Dover, MA 02030, phone: (508)785-0067). **Bk Rev**, (Qty: 3-4). **Circ:** 1,400 (ctrl).
Desc: Published for executives and managers by an executive and manager with graduate school level training in both ethics and business. Short, thought provoking articles, cartoons, quips and quotables. Distinguishes between the business versus the ethical side of enterprises; separates morals and ethics; identifies microethical and macroethical issues.

ISSN 0966-3541
UK

BUSINESS EUROPA. Vol. 1, No. 1 (May/June 1992)-. Trade Publication. English. Six times a year. $45.00. Walden Publishing Ltd., 2 Market Street Shaffron, Walden Essex CB10 1HZ United Kingdom. **Tel** 011 44 1799 521150, FAX 011 44 1799 524805, telex 817197 JAXPRS G. **(Subscription address:** Business Europa / North America Subscriptions, Subscription Office, PO Box 830430, Birmingham AL 35283-0430. **Tel** (800)633-4931, FAX (205)995-1588.**) ED** Justin Keay. available on an online database from Information Access Company.
Desc: Provides a country-by-country look at the marketplace potential in the newly emergent economic region of Central Europe.

LC HF5001 ISSN 0007-6724
DD 650 UK

BUSINESS EUROPE. [Bus. Eur.]. **Added/Corp** Business International S.A. (Jan. 1960)-. Periodical. English. One time a week (50 times per year). $1150.00. The Economist Intelligence Unit, 40 Duke Street, London W1A 1DW United Kingdom. **Tel** 011 44 171 8301000. **(Subscription address:** Economist Intelligence Unit / North America Subscriptions, 111 West 57th Street, New York NY 10019. **Tel** 800 938-4685, (212)554-0600, FAX (212)586-1181, (212)586-1182.**)**
Desc: Coverage includes: briefings on major news items such as analysis of new EC policy initiatives, updates on national issues, "Eurowatch" and critical issues.
Ind/Abst F&S Index Plus Text, Int. [Select. Cov.].

US

BUSINESS EXPECTATIONS. **Added/Corp** Dun and Bradstreet, Inc. Business Economics Division. (19??)-. Periodical. English. Four times a year. $40.00. Dun & Bradstreet / New York, 299 Park Avenue, 24th Floor, New York NY 10171. **Tel** (212)593-4173. ***Continues*** *Businessmen's Expectations.*

US

BUSINESS FAILURE RECORD. **Added/Corp** Dun & Bradstreet Corporation. Economic Analysis Dept. (1982/83)-. English. One time a year. Free on request. Dun & Bradstreet / New York, 299 Park Avenue, 24th Floor, New York NY 10171. **Tel** (212)593-4173. ***Continues*** *Dun & Bradstreet Business Failure Record.*

LC HC340.2 .B87 ISSN 0785-5540
DD 338.094897/05 FI

BUSINESS FINLAND. (1989)-. Trade Publication. English. One time a year. Fmk170.00. Helsinki Media Asiakaspalvelu, PO Box 35, Fin 01771 Vantaa Finland. **Tel** 011 358 0 1201, FAX 011 358 0 205599, telex 125848.

US

BUSINESS FIRST. (19??)-. Periodical. English. Twelve times a year. $12.00. Business First, 400 Vestavia Parkway, Suite 111, Birmingham AL 35216. **Tel** (205)979-0004. available in microform from University Microfilms International (UMI). ***Formed by the union of*** *Commercial Real Estate; Health Care* ***and*** *Banking & Finance.*

ISSN 0749-9418
US
CCC

BUSINESS FIRST (BUFFALO, N.Y.). (BUSINESS FIRST.). **VFOAT** Business First of Buffalo, Inc.; Business First of Buffalo. (1984)-. Periodical. English. One time a week. $55.00. Business First / Buffalo, 472 Delaware Avenue, Buffalo NY 14202. **Tel** (716)882-6200, FAX (716)882-3020. **ED** Donna Collins. **Ad Acc. Circ:** 12,000. available on microfilm and microfiche from University Microfilms International (UMI); available on an online database from Lexis-Nexis; and (files 635,648/Full-Text) DIALOG. Documents available from UMI Article Clearinghouse.
Desc: Business newspaper covering Buffalo and Western New York.
Ind/Abst Acad. Search; Bus. Dateline; Bus. Index (1985-); Bus. Source Plus; Bus. Source; EP Collect.; Gen. BusinessFile (1985-); Gen. Period. Index (1985-1990); Homework Help.; INFO-SOUTH Abstr.; MasterFile FullTEXT 1000; MasterFile FullTEXT 350; MasterFile FullTEXT 650; MasterFile FullTEXT (July 1993-); OCLC; PROMT; Telebase; Trade Ind. ASAP [Full Txt.]; Trade Ind. Index [Full Txt.].

ISSN 0748-6146
US
CCC

BUSINESS FIRST (COLUMBUS, OHIO). (BUSINESS FIRST.). (1984)-. Newspaper. English. One time a week. $52.00. Business First of Columbus Inc, 471 East Broad Street, Suite 1500, Columbus OH 43216. **Tel** (614)461-4040, FAX (614)461-5480. **ED** James Breiner. Index available. cum. index. **Bk Rev. Ad Acc. Circ:** 13,500 (ctrl). available on an online database (files 635,648/Full-Text) from DIALOG. Documents available from UMI Article Clearinghouse.
Desc: The business newspaper of greater Columbus, reports and analyzes business news in Central Ohio.
Ind/Abst Acad. Search; Bus. Dateline; Bus. Index (1985-1991); Bus. Source Plus; Bus. Source; EP Collect.; Gen. BusinessFile (1985-1990); Gen. Period. Index (1985-1990); Homework Help.; INFO-SOUTH Abstr.; MasterFile FullTEXT 1000; MasterFile FullTEXT 350; MasterFile FullTEXT 650; MasterFile FullTEXT (July 1993-); OCLC; PROMT; Telebase; Trade Ind. ASAP [Full Txt.]; Trade Ind. Index [Full Txt.].

ISSN 0748-6138
US
CCC

BUSINESS FIRST (LOUISVILLE, KY.). (BUSINESS FIRST.). (198?)-. Periodical. English. One time a week. $49.00. Business First / Kentucky, PO Box 249, Louisville KY 40201. **Tel** (502)583-1731. **ED** Tom Monahan, (editor's address: 111 West Washington Street, Louisville, KY 40202). **Ad Acc, Adv Mgr:** Maureen O'Mearo. **Circ:** 15,000. available on microfilm from University Microfilms International (UMI); available

on an online database from DIALOG. Documents available from UMI Article Clearinghouse.
Ind/Abst Acad. Search; Bus. Dateline; Bus. Index (Jan. 1985-Dec. 1985); Bus. Source Plus; Bus. Source; EP Collect.; Gen. BusinessFile (Jan. 1985-Dec. 1985); Gen. Period. Index (Jan. 1985-Dec. 1985); Homework Help.; INFO-SOUTH Abstr.; MasterFile FullTEXT 1000; MasterFile FullTEXT 350; MasterFile FullTEXT 650; MasterFile FullTEXT (July 1993-); OCLC; PROMT; Telebase; Trade Ind. ASAP [Full Txt.]; Trade Ind. Index [Full Txt.].

ISSN 0893-3073
DD 387 US
TITLE CHANGE
BUSINESS FLYER, THE. [Bus. flyer]. (1986)-(199?). Periodical. English. Holcon, PO Box 276, Newton Centre MA 02159. **Tel** (203)782-2155, (800)359-3774. ***Continued by** Businessflyer Bulletin, 1082-6947.*

ISSN 1184-9223
DD 338.09711 CN
BUSINESS FORMATIONS AND FAILURES. [Bus. form. fail.]. **Added/Corp** British Columbia. Ministry of Finance and Corporate Relations. Planning and Statistics Division. Data Dissemination. (Jan. 1991)-. Periodical. English. Twelve times a year.

LC HD28 .L62 **ISSN** 0733-2408
DD 650/.05 US
CCC
Pr Rev.
BUSINESS FORUM (LOS ANGELES, CALIF.). (BUSINESS FORUM : THE JOURNAL OF THE SCHOOL OF BUSINESS AND ECONOMICS, CAL STATE L.A.). [Bus. forum]. **Added/Corp** California State University, Los Angeles. School of Business and Economics. Vol. 7, No. 1 (Winter 1982)-. Periodical. English. Four times a year (Feb., May, Aug., Nov.). $16.00 (one-year), $28.00 (two-year), $38.00 (three-year). California State University / School of Business and Economics, 5151 State University Drive, Los Angeles CA 90032. **Tel** (213)343-2806, FAX (213)343-2813. **ED** Tom H. Woods. **Bk Rev. Ad Acc. Circ:** 5,000. available on microfilm and microfiche from University Microfilms International (UMI). Documents available from UMI Article Clearinghouse. ***Continues** Los Angeles Business & Economics, 0278-3428.*
Desc: Magazine-style business journal featuring articles written by the experts--leaders in business, government, and academia. In-depth, analytical coverage of issues affecting business in a changing society. National audience of executives, scholars, and public officials. Articles, features, commentaries, and reviews useful in research on a wide range of current business topics. Published by the School of Business and Economics, California State University, Los Angeles.
Ind/Abst ABI/INFORM Glob. Ed.; ABI/INFORM [Computer File] (Winter 1982-); Bus. Index (1992-); Curr. Cit.; Gen. BusinessFile (1992-); PAIS Int. Print (1991-); UMI ABI/Inform--Bus. Period. Ondisc (Fall 1987-) [Full Txt.].

LC HF3550.5.Z6 B87 **ISSN** 0238-180X
DD 338.6/042/0943905 HU
BUSINESS GUIDE HUNGARY. VFOAT Business Guide. (1973)-. Periodical. English. Hungarian Chamber of Commerce, Kossuth Lajos Ter 6-8, 1055 Budapest Hungary. **ED** K. Multani.

LC HF3163.A84 B87 **ISSN** 1045-3822
DD 330.9758/231/005 US
BUSINESS GUIDE TO ATLANTA. [Bus. guide Atlanta]. (1990)-. English. One time a year. $4.95. Georgia Trend Magazine, PO Box 56447, Atlanta GA 30343.

LC HF5001 **ISSN** 0007-6791
DD 650 UK
Pr Rev.
BUSINESS HISTORY. [Bus. hist.]. Vol. 1 (1958)-. Periodical. English. Four times a year (Jan., Apr., July, Oct.). $185.00. Frank Cass & Company Ltd., Newbury House, 890-900 Eastern Avenue, Ilford Essex IG2 7HH United Kingdom. **Tel** 011 44 181 5998866, FAX 011 44 181 5990984, telex 897719. **ED** Charles Harvey and Geoffrey Jones. **Bk Rev. Ad Acc, Adv Mgr:** Anne Kidson. Full Page (B&W) £195.00. **Circ:** 689. available on microfilm and microfiche from University Microfilms International (UMI); available on CD-ROM from University Microfilms International (UMI); available on an online database from Information Access Company; and (file 648/Full-Text) DIALOG. Documents available from The Genuine Article, BLDSC, FAXON Xpress, The UnCover Company, SWETS, UMI Article Clearinghouse.
Desc: Provides an outlet for research articles in the field of business history, industrial management, commercial enterprise and cognate areas of economic development.
Ind/Abst Acad. Search; Am. Hist. Life (1958-); Arts Humanit. Citation Index [Select. Cov.]; Br. Humanit. Index; Bus. ASAP (1992-) [Full Txt.]; Bus. Index (1988-); Bus. Period. Index; Bus. Source Plus; Bus. Source; Curr. Cit.; Curr. Contents Soc. Behav. Sci.; Econ. Lit. Index; EP Collect.; Gen. BusinessFile (1988-); Gen. Period. Index (1988-); Geogr. Abstr. Human Geogr.; Homework Help.; INFO-SOUTH Abstr.; J. Plan. Lit.; Linguist. Lang. Behav. Abstr.; Mag. Search; MasterFile FullTEXT 1000; MasterFile FullTEXT 350; MasterFile FullTEXT 650; MasterFile FullTEXT (July 1993-); OCLC; Res. Alert [Full Cov.]; Soc. Plann. Policy Dev. Abstr.; Soc. Sci. Cit. Index [Full Cov.]; Sociol. Abstr.; Telebase; Wilson Bus. Abstr.; World Mag. Bank.

LC HF5001 .B8262 **ISSN** 0007-6805
DD 330 US
Pr Rev.
BUSINESS HISTORY REVIEW. [Bus. hist. rev.]. **Added/Corp** Harvard University. Graduate School of Business Administration. Vol. 28, No. 1 (Mar. 1954)-. Academic Scholarly Publication. English. Four times a year (Mar., June, Sept., Dec.). $75.00. Business History Review, Harvard Business School Publishing, Soldiers Field, Boston MA 02163. **Tel** (617)495-6154, FAX (617)496-8066. **ED** Jack High. Index available (4th issue). **Bk Rev**, (Qty: 125). **Ad Acc, Adv Mgr:** A. Chaney, **Tel** (617)495-6154. **Circ:** 2,100 (ctrl). available on microfilm from University Microfilms International (UMI); available on an online database (file 648/Full-Text) from DIALOG. Documents available from The Genuine Article. ***Continues** Bulletin of the Business Historical Society, 1065-9048.*
Desc: Contains articles, books reviews, review essays, and scholarly debates. It is directed to historians, economists, business people, and government administrators, and it is received by many academic and corporate libraries.
Ind/Abst Acad. Search; Am. Hist. Life (1954-); Am. Bibliogr. Slavic East Europ. Stud.; Book Rev. Digest (1974-); Book Rev. Index (1954-); Bus. ASAP (1990-) [Full Txt.]; Bus. Index (1985-); Bus. Period. Index (1981-); Bus. Source Plus; Bus. Source; Curr. Contents Soc. Behav. Sci.; Econ. Lit. Index; EP Collect.; Gen. BusinessFile (1985-); Gen. Period. Index (1985-); Homework Help.; Index Period. Artic. Relat. Law (19??-19??); INFO-SOUTH Abstr.; Int. Bibliogr. Sociol.; J. Econ. Lit.; J. Plan. Lit.; Mag. Search; MasterFile FullTEXT 1000; MasterFile FullTEXT 350; MasterFile FullTEXT 650; MasterFile FullTEXT (Jan. 1993-); OCLC; PAIS Int. Print; Res. Alert [Full Cov.]; Soc. Sci. Cit. Index [Full Cov.]; Soc. Sci. Index; Telebase; Trade Ind. Index (1954-?); Wilson Bus. Abstr.; Work Relat. Abstr.

LC HF5001 .B828 **ISSN** 0007-6813
DD 658/.005 US
CCC
CODEN BHORA
BUSINESS HORIZONS. [Bus. horiz.]. **Added/Corp** Indiana University. Graduate School of Business. Indiana University. Bureau of Business Research. Vol. 1 (Winter 1958)-. Periodical. English. Six times a year. $160.00. JAI Press Inc., 55 Old Post Road, Suite 2, PO Box 1678, Greenwich CT 06836-1678. **Tel** (203)661-7602, FAX (203)661-0792. **ED** Dennis W. Organ. Index available. cum. index. **Bk Rev. Circ:** 5,000. available on microfilm and microfiche from University Microfilms International (UMI); available on an online database (files 15,647,648/Full-Text) from DIALOG. Documents available from Ask*IEEE, UMI Article Clearinghouse, Documents on Demand.
Desc: Of interest to practitioners of business; articles emphasize subjects with economic, social, or political implications.
Ind/Abst ABI/INFORM Glob. Ed. (Aug. 1971-); ABI/INFORM Ondisc: Expr. Ed. (Jan. 1987-); ABI/INFORM [Computer File] (1971-); Acad. Search; Account. Art.; Anbar Account. Finan. Abstr. [Full Txt.]; Anbar Mark. Distr. Abstr. [Full Txt.]; Anbar Top Manage. Abstr. [Full Txt.]; Book Rev. Digest; Book Rev. Index; Bus. ASAP (1990-) [Full Txt.]; Bus. Index (1985-); Bus. Period. Index; Bus. Source Plus; Bus. Source; Commun. Abstr.; Comput. Lit. Index; Contents Recent Econ. J.; Contents Pages Manage.; Curr. Cit.; EMBASE; Energy Inf. Abstr.; Environ. Abstr.; EP Collect.; F&S Index Plus Text, Int. [Select. Cov.]; Fed. Tax Artic.; Foods Adlibra; Gen. BusinessFile (1985-); Gen. Period. Index (1985-); Health Plan. Adminis.; Homework Help.; INFO-SOUTH Abstr.; INSPEC (July/Aug. 1983-); Int. Exec.; Mag. ASAP Plus [Full Txt.]; Mag. Index Plus (1989-); Mag. Search; Manage. Market. Abstr.; Manage. Bibliogr. Rev.; MasterFile FullTEXT 1000; MasterFile FullTEXT 350; MasterFile FullTEXT 650; MasterFile FullTEXT (July 1993-) [Full Txt.]; Middle East Abstr. Index; Newsp. Period. Abstr. (1988-); OCLC; Oper. Prod. Manage. Abstr. [Full Txt.]; Oper. Res./Manage. Sci.; PAIS Int. Print (1991-); Person. Train. Abstr. [Full Txt.]; Person. Manage. Abstr.; PROMT; Sage Fam. Stud. Abstr.; Selec. Coop. Index Manage. Period.; Telebase; Mag. Index (1977-); Trade Ind. Index (1981-?); UMI ABI/Inform--Bus. Period. Ondisc (Jan. 1987-) [Full Txt.]; Wilson Bus. Abstr.; Women Manage. Rev. [Full Txt.]; Women Stud. Abstr.; Work Relat. Abstr.; World Mag. Bank.

ISSN 0738-7024
US
BUSINESS IDEAS NEWSLETTER. **Added/Corp** Dan Newman Co. (19??)-. Newsletter. English. Ten times a year (monthly except July and Aug.). $40.00. Dan Newman Company, 1051 Bloomfield Avenue, Clifton NJ 07011. **Tel** (201)778-6677. **ED** L. LaGalla and Dan Newman. **Circ:** 4,000 (ctrl).

ISSN 1082-3778
US
BUSINESS IN BROWARD. Series/Conf Broward's Committee of 100Broward Economic Development Board. (1987)-. Periodical. English. Six times a year. Palm Beach Publishing Inc., 2455 East Sunrise, Suite 300, Ft Lauderdale FL 33304. **Tel** (305)563-8805, FAX (305)563-8853. **ED** T. Constance Ciyne. Index available. **Bk Rev. Ad Acc. Circ:** 20,000 (ctrl). available on an online database from Lexis-Nexis.
Desc: Business to business magazine for upper and mid-management as well as owners.
Ind/Abst Bus. Dateline (Dec. 1990-) [Full Txt.].

ISSN 0007-683X
DD 330 US
BUSINESS IN NEBRASKA. [Bus. Neb.]. **Added/Corp** University of Nebraska (Lincoln campus). Dept. of Business Research. University of Nebraska--Lincoln. Bureau of Business Research. Association for University Business and Economic Research. No. 60 (Sept. 7, 1949)-. Periodical. English. Ten times a year (monthly with Dec./Jan.,Jul./Aug. combined). $10.00. University of Nebraska / Bureau of Business Research, 200 College Business Administration Building, Lincoln NE 68588-0407. **Tel** (402)472-2334, FAX (402)472-3878. **ED** John S. Austin, (402)472-7932. **Ad Acc. Circ:** 9,000. ***Continues in part** University of Nebraska News; Business in Nebraska Cities.*
Desc: Covers subjects of business and economic interest in Nebraska and plains states. Monthly reviews of retail sales, employment, and construction for Nebraska and its major cities.
Ind/Abst PAIS Int. Print; Stat. Ref. Index.

US
BUSINESS IN PALM BEACH COUNTY. (19??)-. English. Four times a year. $12.95. Palm Beach Publishing Inc., 2455 East Sunrise, Suite 300, Ft Lauderdale FL 33304. **Tel** (305)563-8805, FAX (305)563-8853. **ED** T. Constance Ciyne. Index available. **Bk Rev. Ad Acc. Circ:** 15,000 (ctrl).
Desc: Covers business to business in Palm Beach County. For business people upper-, mid- management to owners.

LC HF41 .B843 **ISSN** 0125-0140
DD 330.9/593/04 TH
BUSINESS IN THAILAND. (19??)-. Periodical. English. Twelve times a year. $52.00. Business Thailand Co Ltd, 972 Soi Saeng Cham Rama 9 Road, Bangkok 10310 Thailand. **Tel** 011 66 2 2483257. **ED** William Than. **Ad Acc. Circ:** 16,000 (ctrl).
Desc: Business magazine catering to a broad spectrum of topics covering economy, commerce, industry and trade as well as advertising, marketing and media.

ISSN 0849-5017
DD 380.1/09711/3305 CN
BUSINESS IN VANCOUVER. [Bus. Vanc.]. Issue No. 1 (Oct. 2, 1989)-. Periodical. English. One time a week. 51.23Can$. BIV Publications Ltd., 1235 West Pender, Lower Floor, Vancouver BC V6E 2V6 Canada. **Tel** (604)688-2398, FAX (604)688-1963. **ED** Peter Ladner. **Ad Acc, Adv Mgr:** Sandi Gilmer, **Tel** same as publisher. **Circ:** 16,000.
Desc: Provides information on local business news.

LC HB **ISSN** 0273-3684
DD 016.330 US
BUSINESS INDEX. **See** Business and Economics-Abstracting, Bibliographies and Statistics.

LC HF5001 .B8286 **ISSN** 0254-5268
DD 658.4/00954 II
BUSINESS INDIA. [BusinessIndia.]. **VFOAT** BusinessIndia. No. 1 (Feb./March 1978)-. Periodical. English. Twenty-six times a year. $110.00. A H Advani, Wadia Building, 17/19 Dalal Street, Bombay 400001 India. **Tel** 275388, FAX 022 2045446, telex 011-3557 BZIN. **(Subscription address:** Prints India, 11 Darya Ganj, New Delhi 110002 India. **Tel** 011 91 11 3268645, FAX 011 91 11 3275542, telex 31-61087 PRIN-IN.**) ED** Ashok H Advari. **Bk Rev. Ad Acc. Circ:** 90,000 (ctrl).
Desc: Provides an insight into the world of Indian commerce and industry. Information on economy, management, finance, investment markets, marketing trends and policies.
Ind/Abst Energy Res. Abstr. (Jan. 1982-); PROMT.

LC HC601 .A52
DD 330 AT
BUSINESS INDICATORS. Added/Corp Australia and New Zealand Banking Group. Economics Unit. Issue 193 (Summer 1987)-. Periodical. English. Four times a year. ANZ Bank Economics Department, 10/100 Queen Street, Melbourne Victoria 3000 Australia. **Tel** 011 61 3 273 6224, FAX 011 61 3 273 5711. **Circ:** 45,000 (ctrl). ***Continues** ANZ Business Indicators.*

ISSN 1042-0746
DD 025 US
CCC
BUSINESS INFORMATION ALERT. See Library and Information Sciences.

UK
BUSINESS INFORMATION BASICS. (1992)-. English. Two times a year. £129.00 UK; $259.00 other. Headland Business Information, 1 Henry Smiths Terrace, Headland Cleveland, TS24 0PD United Kingdom. **Tel** 011 44 429 231902, FAX 011 44 429 861403.

LC Z ISSN 0966-2138
DD 025.06658 UK
BUSINESS INFORMATION FROM GOVERNMENT. [Bus. inf. gov.]. (1992)-. English. One time a year. $204.00. Headland Business Information, 1 Henry Smiths Terrace, Headland Cleveland, TS24 0PD United Kingdom. **Tel** 011 44 429 231902, FAX 011 44 429 861403.

ISSN 0892-6034
DD 650 US
BUSINESS INFORMATION FROM YOUR PUBLIC LIBRARY. (BUSINESS INFORMATION FROM YOUR PUBLIC LIBRARY : Bl.). [Bus. inf. your public libr.]. **VFOAT** Bl. (19??)-. Periodical. English. Three times a year. Administrators Digest Press, PO Box 933, South San Francisco CA 94080. **Tel** (415)573-5474. **ED** Robert S. Alvarez.

LC HF5351 .B975
UK
BUSINESS INFORMATION YEARBOOK / EDITED BY GERRY SMITH. (1988/89)-. English. One time a year. $220.00. Headland Business Information, 1 Henry Smiths Terrace, Headland Cleveland, TS24 0PD United Kingdom. **Tel** 011 44 429 231902, FAX 011 44 429 861403. ***Continues*** *Business Information Sourcebook, 0953-9263.*

ISSN 1056-6244
US
BUSINESS INSIGHT. [Bus. insight]. Vol. 6, No. 4 (April 1991)-. Trade Publication. English. Twelve times a year. $24.00. Specialty Publications Inc, 4341 South Westnedge Avenue, Suite 2101, Kalamazoo MI 49008. **Tel** (616)345-1727, FAX (616)345-5581. **ED** Mary Buday. **Bk Rev. Ad Acc. Circ:** 9,000 (ctrl). ***Continues*** *Business Digest (Kalamazoo, Mich.), 0897-5221.*

LC WMLC 93/1914 ISSN 0270-2266
US
BUSINESS INSIGHTS : SCHOOL OF BUSINESS ADMINISTRATION QUARTERLY MAGAZINE, CALIFORNIA STATE UNIVERSITY, LONG BEACH. **Added/Corp** California State University, Long Beach. School of Business Administration. Vol. 1, No. 1 (Spring 1984)-. Periodical. English. Two times a year (Spring & Fall). $12.00. Business Insights, School of Business Administration, California State University / Long Beach, Long Beach CA 90840. **Tel** (213)985-7694, (213)985-2399. ***Continues*** *Current Business Perspectives, 0270-2266.*

LC HG4057 .A15633 ISSN 0747-7937
DD 368.8/1/00973 US
BUSINESS INSURANCE. DIRECTORY OF CORPORATE BUYERS OF INSURANCE, BENEFIT PLANS AND RISK MANAGEMENT SERVICES. VFOAT Directory of Corporate Buyers of Insurance, Benefit Plans and Risk Management Services; Business Insurance. Directory of Buyers. 1st Ed. (July 1983)-. Directory. English. One time a year. $95.00. Business Insurance, 740 North Rush Street, Chicago IL 60611-2590. **Tel** (312)649-5279, FAX (312)280-3174. **(Subscription address:** Crain Communications, 965 East Jefferson Avenue, Detroit MI 48207. **Tel** (800)678-9595, (313)446-1616.**)** **ED** Marilou C Jones. **Ad Acc. Circ:** 1,000. available on magnetic tape.
Desc: Names and titles of financial, insurance, employee benefits and related executives for over 2,000 major corporations.

LC HF1 .B867 ISSN 0007-6872
US
TITLE CHANGE
BUSINESS INTERNATIONAL. [Bus. int.]. **Added/Corp** Business International Corporation. 1 (1954)-Vol. 40, No. 13 (Apr. 5, 1993). Periodical. English. The Economist Intelligence Unit, 40 Duke Street, London W1A 1DW United Kingdom. **Tel** 011 44 171 8301000. ***Continued by*** *Crossborder Monitor.*
Desc: This publication interprets developments in international management, marketing, finance, licensing, exporting, taxation, law, accounting, personnel, planning, and government.

LC HF5001 .B8288
GW
BUSINESS JOURNAL. Periodical. German (German). DM42.00. Verlagsgesellschaft Intorgpress MBH, Savignystrasse 18, 6000 Frankfurt Am Main Germany.

LC HF5001 .B829 ISSN 0091-3537
DD 658.4/005 US
BUSINESS JOURNAL, THE. Added/Corp Kansas. State University, Wichita. College of Business Administration. (19??)-. English. One time a week (Friday). $53.00. Wichita Business Journal, 110 South Main, Suite 200, Wichita KS 67202. **Tel** (316)267-6406, FAX (316)267-8570. **ED** Kevin Bumgarner. **Ad Acc, Adv Mgr:** Teresa Moore. **Circ:** 6134.
Ind/Abst Bus. Dateline; MasterFile FullTEXT (Jan. 1995-); PROMT.

ISSN 0887-5588
DD 330 US
CCC
BUSINESS JOURNAL (CHARLOTTE, N.C.). (THE BUSINESS JOURNAL.). Vol. 1, No. 1 (April 14, 1986)-. Periodical. English. One time a week. $44.00. The Business Journal / North Carolina, 128 South Tryon Street, Suite 2250, Charlotte NC 28202-6001. **Tel** (704)347-2340, FAX (704)347-2350. **ED** Joanne Skoog. **Ad Acc, Adv Mgr:** Ann Sontag. **Circ:** 12,500. available on an online database from DIALOG; available on microfilm from University Microfilms International (UMI). Documents available from UMI Article Clearinghouse.
Ind/Abst AGRICOLA [Select. Cov.]; Bus. Dateline; Bus. Source Plus; Bus. Source; EP Collect.; Homework Help.; MasterFile FullTEXT 1000; MasterFile FullTEXT 350; MasterFile FullTEXT 650; MasterFile FullTEXT (Jan. 1995-); OCLC; PROMT; Telebase; Trade Ind. ASAP [Full Txt.]; Trade Ind. Index [Full Txt.].

ISSN 0740-2899
US
CCC
BUSINESS JOURNAL (MILWAUKEE, WIS.), THE. (THE BUSINESS JOURNAL.). [Bus. j.]. (1983)-. Periodical. English. One time a week. $64.95. Business Journal / Milwaukee, 2025 North Summit Avenue, Milwaukee WI 53202. **Tel** (414)278-7788, FAX (414)278-7028. **ED** Pat Wirth and Gary Miller. **Ad Acc, Adv Mgr:** Dan Meyer. **Circ:** 13,000. available on an online database from DIALOG. Documents available from UMI Article Clearinghouse.
Desc: Covers business news in Milwaukee and the surrounding areas.
Ind/Abst Bus. Dateline; Bus. Index (1985-1990); Bus. Source Plus; Bus. Source; EP Collect.; Gen. BusinessFile (1985-1990); Gen. Period. Index (1985-1990); Homework Help.; MasterFile FullTEXT 1000; MasterFile FullTEXT 350; MasterFile FullTEXT 650; MasterFile FullTEXT; OCLC; PROMT; Telebase; Trade Ind. ASAP [Full Txt.]; Trade Ind. Index [Full Txt.].

US
BUSINESS JOURNAL (NEW YORK). (19??)-. English. Twelve times a year. $10.00. Sheahan Publications, Suffolk County Airport, Westhampton Beach NY 11978. **Tel** (516)288-5400, FAX (516)288-5420. **ED** Dennis Sheahan (editor's address: PO Box 826, West Hampton Beach, NY 11978). **Bk Rev. Ad Acc, Adv Mgr:** Roy Dickinson, **Tel** (516)288-5400. **Circ:** 9,500.
Desc: News and general information on business matters in Long Island and the metro areas and how it is affecting the businesses in New York.

ISSN 0889-3403
DD 330 US
BUSINESS JOURNAL OF NEW JERSEY (JAMESBURG, N.J : 1985). (BUSINESS JOURNAL OF NEW JERSEY.). [Bus. j. N.J.]. Vol. 3, No. 1 (Sept. 1985)-. Periodical. English. Twelve times a year. $29.00 (one-year), $47.00 (two-year), $63.00 (three-year). Micromedia, 55 Park Place, Morristown NJ 07963. **Tel** (201)644-5554. **(Subscription address:** Business Journal of New Jersey, 307 Southgate Court, Brentwood TN 37027. **Tel** (615)377-3322.**)** available on an online database (files 635,648/Full-Text) from DIALOG. Documents available from UMI Article Clearinghouse. ***Formed by the union of*** *Business Journal of New Jersey Magazine* ***and*** *Business Journal of New Jersey Weekly.*
Ind/Abst Acad. Search; Bus. Dateline; Bus. Index (1985-); Bus. Source Plus; Bus. Source; EP Collect.; Gen. BusinessFile (1985-); Gen. Period. Index (1985-); Homework Help.; INFO-SOUTH Abstr.; MasterFile FullTEXT 1000; MasterFile FullTEXT 350; MasterFile FullTEXT 650; MasterFile FullTEXT (July 1993-July 1993); OCLC; PAIS Int. Print (1991-); PROMT; Telebase; Trade Ind. ASAP [Full Txt.]; Trade Ind. Index [Full Txt.].

ISSN 1040-6360
US
BUSINESS JOURNAL OF UPPER EAST TENNESSEE AND SOUTHWEST VIRGINIA. VFOAT Business Journal. (198?)-. Periodical. English. Twelve times a year. $22.00. The Business Journal, PO Box 643, Blountville TN 37617. **Tel** (615)232-7111. **ED** Angie Hickman. **Bk Rev. Ad Acc.** ctrl circ. available on microfilm and microfiche from University Microfilms International (UMI); available on an online database (file 635/Full-Text) from DIALOG. Documents available from UMI Article Clearinghouse.
Ind/Abst Bus. Dateline (Jan. 1992-) [Full Txt.].

ISSN 0895-1632
US
CCC
BUSINESS JOURNAL (PHOENIX, ARIZ.), THE. (THE BUSINESS JOURNAL.). Vol. 7, No. 37 (July 27, 1987)-. Periodical. English. One time a week. $52.45. American City Business Journal, PO Box 16718, Phoenix AZ 85011. **Tel** (602)230-8400, FAX (602)230-0955. **ED** John Genzale. **Ad Acc. Circ:** 19,000. available on an online database from DIALOG. Documents available from UMI Article Clearinghouse. ***Continues*** *Greater Phoenix Business Journal, 0890-9644.*
Desc: Covers all facets of business news pertaining to metropolitan Phoenix.
Ind/Abst Acad. Search; Bus. Dateline (198?-) [Full Txt.]; Bus. Index (1987-1990); Bus. Source Plus; Bus. Source; EP Collect.; Gen. BusinessFile; Gen. Period. Index (1987-1990); Homework Help.; INFO-SOUTH Abstr.; MasterFile FullTEXT 1000; MasterFile FullTEXT 350; MasterFile FullTEXT 650; MasterFile FullTEXT (July 1993-); OCLC; PROMT; Telebase; Trade Ind. ASAP [Full Txt.]; Trade Ind. Index [Full Txt.].

ISSN 0742-6550
DD 330 US
CCC
BUSINESS JOURNAL (PORTLAND, OR.), THE. (THE BUSINESS JOURNAL.). [Bus. j.]. **VFOAT** Business Journal Serving Greater Portland. Vol. 1, No. 1 (March 5/11, 1984)-. Periodical. English. One time a week. $52.00. The Business Journal / Oregon, PO Box 14490, Portland OR 97214. **Tel** (503)274-8733, FAX (503)227-2650. **ED** Steve Jones. cum. index. **Ad Acc. Circ:** 15,500. available on an online database from DIALOG; available on microfilm from University Microfilms International (UMI). Documents available from UMI Article Clearinghouse.
Desc: General business news and features, focus on Portland metro area, and the Pacific Northwest. It explores forces at the workplace in shaping business activity, and personalities involved in business activity.
Ind/Abst Acad. Search; Bus. Dateline; Bus. Index (1985-1990); Bus. Source Plus; Bus. Source; EP Collect.; Gen. BusinessFile (1985-1990); Gen. Period. Index (1985-1990); Homework Help.; MasterFile FullTEXT 1000; MasterFile FullTEXT 350; MasterFile FullTEXT 650; MasterFile FullTEXT (July 1993-); OCLC; PROMT; Telebase; Trade Ind. ASAP [Full Txt.]; Trade Ind. Index [Full Txt.].

ISSN 8756-5897
US
CCC
BUSINESS JOURNAL (SACRAMENTO, CALIF.). (THE BUSINESS JOURNAL.). **VFOAT** Sacramento Business Journal. Vol. 1, No. 37, (Dec. 17 1984)-. Periodical. English. One time a week. $59.95. Business Journal / Sacramento, 1401 21st Street, Sacramento CA 95814. **Tel** (916)447-7661, FAX (916)447-2243. **ED** Lee Wessman. Index available. cum. index. **Ad Acc. Circ:** 15,000. available on an online database from DIALOG. Documents available from UMI Article Clearinghouse. ***Continues*** *Capitol Business Journal.*
Desc: Covers business news for the greater Sacramento area.
Ind/Abst Acad. Search; Bus. Dateline; Bus. Index (1985-1990); Bus. Source Plus; Bus. Source; EP Collect.; Gen. BusinessFile (1985-1990); Gen. Period. Index (1985-1990); Homework Help.; INFO-SOUTH Abstr.; MasterFile FullTEXT 1000; MasterFile FullTEXT 350; MasterFile FullTEXT 650; MasterFile FullTEXT (July 1993-); OCLC; PROMT; Telebase; Trade Ind. ASAP [Full Txt.]; Trade Ind. Index [Full Txt.].

US
BUSINESS JOURNAL : SONOMA & MARIN. (19??)-. Newspaper. English. Twenty-four times a year. $14.00. Sloan Publications, 5550 Skylane Boulevard, Suite 201, Santa Rosa CA 95403. **Tel** (707)579-2900, FAX (707)579-8475. **ED** Shannon Swingle. **Ad Acc, Adv Mgr:** Ken Clark, **Tel** (707)579-2900. **Circ:** 8,500 (ctrl).
Desc: Local business coverage of Sonoma & Marin counties.

ISSN 1016-5304
KO
BUSINESS KOREA. [Bus. Korea]. (1983)-. Periodical. English. Twelve times a year. $95.00. Business Korea, Hanwool International Co. Ltd., Seocho PO Box 403, Seoul 137 604 Korea. **Tel** 011 82 2 5783220.

LC HC466 .B87
DD 330.9519/5/005 KO
BUSINESS KOREA. Vol. 1, No. 1 (June 1983)-. Periodical. English. Twelve times a year. $90.00 (one-year), $155.00 (two-year), $300.00 (three-year) North and South America, Oceania, Southwest Asia and Middle East; $75.00 (one-year), $125.00 (two-year), $160.00 (three-year) Southeast Asia; $100.00 (one-year), $170.00 (two-year), $220.00 (three-year) Japan, Taiwan, Hong Kong and Macao. Business Korea Ltd, Hanam Building/Suite 808, Yoido-dong, Yongdungpo-gu, Seoul 150 Korea. available on microfilm and microfiche from University Microfilms International (UMI); available on an online database (file 15/Full-Text) from DIALOG.
Ind/Abst Bus. Index (1992-); Curr. Cit.; F&S Index Plus Text, Int. [Select. Cov.]; Gen. BusinessFile (1992-); Int. Exec.; PAIS Int. Print; PROMT.

LC HF3830.5.A48 B87
DD 338.7/4/095195 KO
BUSINESS KOREA YEARBOOK ON KOREAN ECONOMY AND BUSINESS. **VFOAT** Business Korea Yearbook; Business Korea Yearbook on the Korean Economy and Business; Yearbook on the Korean Economy and Business. Vol. 1 (1986)-. Monographic series. English. Irregular. Price varies per volume. Business Korea, Hanwool International Co. Ltd., Seocho PO Box 403, Seoul 137

604 Korea. **Tel** 011 82 2 5783220. **ED** Kim Kyong-Hae. **Circ:** 3,500.
Desc: Details of approximately 320 major Korean firms, including their 5-year performances.

LC HC **ISSN** 0007-6880
DD 338 UK
BUSINESS LATIN AMERICA. [Bus. Lat. Am.]. **Added/Corp** Business International Corporation. Vol. 1 (Dec. 15, 1966)-. Newsletter. English. One time a week (50 times per year). $975.00. The Economist Intelligence Unit, 40 Duke Street, London W1A 1DW United Kingdom. **Tel** 011 44 171 8301000. **(Subscription address:** Economist Intelligence Unit / North America Subscriptions, 111 West 57th Street, New York NY 10019. **Tel** 800 938-4685, (212)554-0600, FAX (212)586-1181, (212)586-1182.**)** available on an online database from Lexis-Nexis; and (file 627/Full-Text) DIALOG. Documents available from SWETS.
Desc: Aimed at firms doing business with South and Central America, Mexico and the Caribbean. It analyzes economic, political and regulatory trends in the region and their effect on business. Market forecasts, in-depth looks at corporate strategies and tables of key economic and business indicators, exchange controls, licensing regulations and labor laws help the reader to locate information and compare conditions in countries throughout the region. It is produced by a team of regional specialists in New York, supported by a network of analysts and offices in 17 Latin American and Caribbean countries.

LC KF884 .B87 **ISSN** 0277-1713
DD 346.73/07/02648 347.306702648 US
BUSINESS LAW REPORTER. See Law-Banking Law.

ISSN 1060-8230
DD 338 US
BUSINESS LEADER (RALEIGH, N.C.). (BUSINESS LEADER.). [Bus. lead.]. **VFOAT** Raleigh-Durham-RTP Business Digest; Raleigh, Durham, RTP Business Digest. (1991)-. Periodical. English. Twelve times a year. $20.00. Business to Business, Inc., 4109 Wake Forest Road, Suite 102, Raleigh NC 27609. **Tel** (919)872-7077. ***Continues*** *Business Digest (Raleigh, N.C.), 1058-6490.*

ISSN 0190-6208
US
BUSINESS LEADS AND SALES TARGETS. (BLAST. BUSINESS LEADS AND SALES TARGETS.). [Bus. leads sales targets]. **Added/Corp** National Audio-Visual Association. **VFOAT** Business Leads and Sales Targets. No. 1, (Mar. 1979)-. Periodical. English. Four times a year. $1.00. National Audio-Visual Association Inc, 3150 Spring Street, Fairfax VA 22031.

ISSN 1050-5474
US
BUSINESS LEADS INTERNATIONAL. (1990)-. Periodical. English. Irregular. $595.00. Plymouth Associates, Box 3505, McLean VA 22103.

ISSN 0191-4006
US
BUSINESS LIBRARY NEWSLETTER. See Library and Information Sciences.

LC HG1 .B97 **ISSN** 1045-7798
DD 330/.05 US
CCC
CODEN BLRVE4
BUSINESS LIBRARY REVIEW. [Bus. libr. rev.]. Vol. 16, No. 1 (Oct. 1990)-. Periodical. English. Four times a year (1 volume). $156.00 (academic institutions), $243.00 (corporate institutions). Gordon & Breach Science Publishers, Inc., PO Box 786, Cooper Station, New York NY 10276. **Tel** (212)206-8900, FAX (212)645-2459. **(Subscription address:** Gordon & Breach Science Publishers / England, PO Box 90 Reading, Berkshire RG1 8JL United Kingdom. **Tel** 011 44 734 560080.**)** ***Formed by the union of*** *Wall Street Review of Books, 0091-1526* ***and*** *Economics and Business, 0884-8335.*
Ind/Abst Book Rev. Index.

ISSN 0714-8585
DD 330.9712/005 CN
BUSINESS LIFE (1980). (BUSINESS LIFE.). [Bus. life]. Vol. 8, No. 9 (Sept. 1980)-. Periodical. English. Twelve times a year (irregular). $2.00 per no., $15.00 per year. Business Life Publishing Company, 6299 Airport Road/Suite 705, Mississauga Ontario L4U 1N3 Canada. **Tel** (403)230-3131. available on microfilm from University Microfilms International (UMI). ***Continues*** *Business Life in Western Canada, 0380-9099.*

ISSN 0898-3526
DD 338 US
SUSPENDED
BUSINESS LINE (SYLMAR, CALIF.). (BUSINESS LINE.). Suspended with (Dec. 1990). Periodical. English. Six times a year. $24.00. Beth Smith and Associates, 12935 Chippewa Street, Sylmar CA 91342-4906.
Desc: The most complete homebased business newsletter in California. This is the source for all those interested in "how to" successfully start and run your own business from home.

LU
BUSINESS (LUXEMBOURG). (19??)-. Periodical. English (French). Twelve times a year. 3500F Europe; 4105F other. Business Luxembourg, 34 Victor Hugo, L-1750 Luxembourg Luxembourg. **Tel** 011 352 461122. **ED** Somon Grey and Pol Wirk. **Bk Rev. Ad Acc. Circ:** 6,000 (ctrl).

ISSN 0192-7450
US
BUSINESS (MADISON). (BUSINESS.). **VFOAT** In Business. (197?)-. Periodical. English. Twelve times a year. $29.00. Magna Publications Inc, 2718 Dryden Drive, Madison WI 53704. **Tel** (800)433-0499, (608)246-3591, FAX (608)246-3597.

ISSN 0925-0913
NE
UDC 658
BUSINESS MAGAZINE B'HERTOGENBOSCH. [Bus. mag. Hertogenbosch]. **VFOAT** Business. (1989)-. Periodical. Dutch. Two times a month. Business Publishers Nederland, Postbus 155, 6500 AD Nijmegen Netherlands. **Tel** 011 31 80 787444.

ISSN 0739-3873
US
BUSINESS MAILERS REVIEW. (19??)-. Periodical. English. Twenty-four times a year. $249.00. Business Mailers Review Inc, 1813 Shepherd Street Northwest, Washington DC 20011. **Tel** (202)723-3397, FAX (202)723-0953. **ED** Van H. Seagraves. **Circ:** 2,000.

LC HF5001 .B837 **ISSN** 8756-9639
DD 001.55/05 US
BUSINESS MEDIA WEEK. [Bus. media week]. Vol. 1, No. 1 (April 15, 1985). Periodical. English. One time a week. $297.00. Knowledge Industry Publications Inc, 701 Westchester Avenue, White Plains NY 10604. **Tel** (914)328-9157, (800)800-5474, FAX (914)328-9093. ***Continues*** *Software Publishing Report.*

LC HF3231 .B88 **ISSN** 0187-1455
MX
BUSINESS MEXICO. Added/Corp American Chamber of Commerce of Mexico. Vol. 1, No. 1 (March 1991)-. Periodical. English. Ten times a year (monthly plus one double issue in Jan./Feb.). $134.00 US; $114.00 Mexico; $150.00 other. American Chamber of Commerce of Mexico, Lucerna 78/ Col Juarez, Mexico DF 06600 Mexico. **Tel** 011 52 5 7243826, or 7243800, FAX 011 52 5 7032911, telex 1771300. **ED** Mary Witoshynsky and Joel Russell. **Bk Rev. Ad Acc, Adv Mgr:** Hector Abaroa, **Tel** 7243800. **Circ:** 10,000 (ctrl). available on microfilm and microfiche from University Microfilms International (UMI); available on CD-ROM from University Microfilms International (UMI). ***Formed by the union of*** *Business Mexico, 0187-1455* ***and*** *Mexico Update.*
Ind/Abst Acad. Search; Bus. Source Plus; Bus. Source; EP Collect.; Homework Help.; INFO-SOUTH Abstr.; MasterFile FullTEXT 1000; MasterFile FullTEXT 350; MasterFile FullTEXT 650; MasterFile FullTEXT (July 1993-); OCLC; PAIS Int. Print (1991-); Telebase.

UK
BUSINESS MIDDLE EAST. (19??)-. English. Twenty-two times a year. $633.75 (schools and educational libraries), $845.00 (other)'North America. The Economist Intelligence Unit, 40 Duke Street, London W1A 1DW United Kingdom. **Tel** 011 44 171 8301000. **(Subscription address:** Economist Intelligence Unit / North America Subscriptions, 111 West 57th Street, New York NY 10019. **Tel** 800 938-4685, (212)554-0600, FAX (212)586-1181, (212)586-1182.**)** available on an online database from Lexis-Nexis. ***Formed by the union of*** *Turkey Monitor, 0950-3234; Iran Monitor* ***and*** *Saudi Arabia Monitor.*
Desc: Focuses on the Middle East.

UK
BUSINESS MONITOR PRODUCTION SERIES. PRODUCTION MONITORS. (19??)-. English. Irregular. £25.00. Her Majesty's Stationery Office, 51 Nine Elms Lane, London SW8 5DR United Kingdom. **Tel** 011 44 171 8738459, 011 44 171 8738499, FAX 011 44 171 8738499, 011 44 171 8738456, telex 297138. **(Subscription address:** Her Majesty's Stationery Office, PO Box 276, Public Centre, London SW8 5DT United Kingdom. **Tel** 011 44 171 8738499, 011 44 171 8738456.**)**

LC HF5001 **ISSN** 1046-9575
DD 650 US
BUSINESS NEW HAMPSHIRE MAGAZINE. (BUSINESS NEW HAMPSHIRE. MAGAZINE : BNH.). [Bus. N. H. mag.]. **VFOAT** BNH. Vol. 6, No. 9 (Sept. 1989)-. Periodical. English. Twelve times a year. $24.00. Laurentian Business Publishing, 404 Chestnut Street, Suite 201, Manchester NH 03101. **Tel** (603)626-6354, FAX (603)626-6359. **ED** Robin Baskerville. **Ad Acc, Adv Mgr:** David Kruger. **Circ:** 13,000 (ctrl). available on an online database from DIALOG. Documents available from UMI Article Clearinghouse. ***Continues*** *Business of New Hampshire, 1042-7511.*
Desc: Business features and columns, solely devoted to New Hampshire's business community.
Ind/Abst Acad. Search; Bus. Dateline (August 1986-) [Full Txt.]; Bus. Source Plus; Bus. Source; EP Collect.; Homework Help.; MasterFile FullTEXT 1000; MasterFile FullTEXT 350; MasterFile FullTEXT 650; MasterFile FullTEXT (Oct. 1993-); OCLC; PROMT; Telebase.

US
BUSINESS NEWS CONFIDENTIAL. English. Irregular. $249.00 (annual); $299.00 (semi-annual); $399.00 (quarterly); $745.00 (monthly). TJFR Publishing Company, 545 North Maple Avenue, 2nd Floor, Ridgewood NJ 07450. **Tel** (201)444-6061, FAX (201)444-5919.

LC HB241 **ISSN** 1064-1661
DD 338 US
BUSINESS NEWS (EUGENE, OR.), THE. (THE BUSINESS NEWS : SERVING LANE COUNTY.). [Bus. news]. (1991)-. Periodical. English. Twenty-six times a year. $24.00. Northwest Media, 326 West 12th Avenue, Eugene OR 97401. **Tel** (503)343-6636, (800)777-6636, FAX (503)343-0177. **ED** Debra Woodruff. **Ad Acc. Circ:** 35,000 (ctrl).
Desc: Provides news for the Lane County business community.

PL
BUSINESS NEWS FROM POLAND. English. $200.00. Polish Press Agency, PO Box 898, Al Jerozolimskie 7, 00-950 Warsaw Poland. **Tel** 011 48 22 216306.

ISSN 0192-9461
US
BUSINESS NEWS (MACOMB). (BUSINESS NEWS.). (19??)-. Newspaper. English. One time a week. Park Newspapers of Illinois, 128 North Lafayette, Macomb IL 61455.

US
•**BUSINESS NEWS NEW JERSEY.** (1995)-. English. Twenty-five times a year. $39.00. Business News New Jersey, 391 George Street, New Brunswick NJ 08901. **Tel** (908)246-7677. ***Absorbed*** *Business for Central New Jersey.*

ISSN 0738-6869
US
BUSINESS NEWS, SAN DIEGO. VFOAT Business News. Periodical. English. Twenty-six times a year. $26.00. Business News, 4350 Lajolla Village Drive, San Diego CA 92122. **Tel** (619)565-2636. **ED** Harold Betancourt. **Circ:** 10,000. available on an online database from DIALOG. Documents available from UMI Article Clearinghouse.
Ind/Abst Bus. Dateline.

LC HC
DD 330 US
BUSINESS NEWSBANK PLUS. [COMPUTER FILE]. (19??)-. Periodical. English. Twelve times a year. Newsbank Inc., 58 Pine Street, New Canaan CT 06840. **Tel** (800)243-7694, (800)762-8182, FAX (203)966-6254.

LC HC107.N8 B87 **ISSN** 0279-4276
DD 338.09756 US
BUSINESS, NORTH CAROLINA. Vol. 1, No. 1 (Oct. 1981)-. Periodical. English. Twelve times a year (monthly). $30.00. The News & Observer Publishing Company, 5435 77 Center Drive, Suite 50, Charlotte NC 28217. **Tel** (704)523-6987, FAX (704)523-4211. **ED** David Mildenberg. **Ad Acc, Adv Mgr:** Glenn Benton. **Circ:** 26,000 (ctrl). available on an online database from Lexis-Nexis; and DIALOG. Documents available from UMI Article Clearinghouse.
Desc: For executives in North Carolina. Focuses on people, trends, events, and companies that shape the state's business environment.
Ind/Abst Acad. Search; AGRICOLA [Select. Cov.]; Bus. Dateline; Bus. Index (1985-); Bus. Source Plus; Bus. Source; EP Collect.; Gen. BusinessFile (1985-); Gen. Period. Index (1985-); Homework Help.; MasterFile FullTEXT 1000; MasterFile FullTEXT 350; MasterFile FullTEXT 650; MasterFile FullTEXT (July 1993-); OCLC; PAIS Int. Print; PROMT; Telebase; Trade Ind. ASAP [Full Txt.]; Trade Ind. Index [Full Txt.].

ISSN 0846-1058
DD 650 CN
BUSINESS NORTHWEST. [Bus. northwest]. Vol. 1, No. 1 (Nov. 1990)-. Periodical. English. Six times a year. $25.00 for 10 no. $35.00, U.S.A. and other countries. Northern Insights, 72 Jean Street, Thunderbay Ontario P7A 5E9 Canada. **Tel** (807)345-5538.

LC HF5003 .D68a **ISSN** 1057-5014
DD 330 US
TITLE CHANGE
... BUSINESS ONE IRWIN BUSINESS AND INVESTMENT ALMANAC, THE. [Bus. One Irwin bus. investm. alm.]. **Added/Corp** Business One Irwin. **VFOAT** Business and Investment Almanac. (1991)-(1993). English. Irwin Professional Publishing,

1333 Burr Ridge Parkway, Burr Ridge Parkway IL 60521. **Tel** (800)634-3966, (708)789-5480. ***Continues*** *Dow Jones-Irwin Business and Investment Almanac, 0733-2610.* ***Continued by*** *Irwin Business and Investment Almanac, 1072-6136.*

NZ

BUSINESS OPINION. **Added/Corp** New Zealand Institute of Economic Research. New Zealand Institute of Economic Research. Report on Survey of Industrial Opinion. New Zealand Institute of Economic Research. Report on the Survey of Business Opinion. New Zealand Institute of Economic Research. Report on the Quarterly Survey of Business. **VFOAT** Quarterly Survey of Business Opinion. 1st (June 1961)-. Periodical. English. Four times a year (Mar., June., Sep., Dec.). $177.30. New Zealand Institute for Economic Research, PO Box 3479, Wellington New Zealand. **Tel** 011 64 4 721880. **ED** R. Bowie. **Ad Acc. Circ:** 1,000 (ctrl).
Desc: Data regarding intentions and outcomes of business and monitoring of economic activity in New Zealand.

LC HF3902 .A15
DD 330.96891/005 RH
BUSINESS OPINION SURVEY. **Added/Corp** University of Zimbabwe. MBA Programme. (19??)-. English. Four times a year. University of Zimbabwe / Publications Department, PO Box MP 45, Mount Pleasant Harare Zimbabwe. **Tel** 011 263 4 303211, FAX 011 263 4 333407, telex 26580 UNIVZ ZW.

LC HF5429.235.U5 B87 **ISSN** 1042-6175
DD 381/.1/02573 US
Pr Rev.
BUSINESS OPPORTUNITIES HANDBOOK. [Bus. oppor. handb.]. **VFOAT** Business Opportunities. (19??)-. English. Four times a year (Seasonally). $15.95 US; $25.95 Canada and Mexico; $33.95 Europe and Western Hemisphere; $40.95 other. Enterprise Magazines Inc., 1020 North Broadway, Suite 111, Milwaukee WI 53202. **Tel** (414)272-9977, FAX (414)272-9973. **ED** Micheal McDermott. Index available. **Ad Acc, Adv Mgr:** Andrea Freedman, **Tel** (414)272-9977. **Circ:** 55,000.
Desc: Contains basic information on franchisors and other non-franchising companies offering business opportunities to the general public.

ISSN 1051-0273
DD 382 US
CCC
BUSINESS OPPORTUNITIES IN EASTERN EUROPE. [Bus. oppor. East. Eur.]. **Added/Corp** Atlantic Information Services. Georgetown University. Center for International Business & Trade. (1990)-. Periodical. English. Twenty-six times a year. $411.00. Buraff Publications Inc., 714 Church Street, Alexandria VA 22314. **Tel** (800)333-1291, (703)739-8500.

LC HG450 **ISSN** 0193-3221
DD 332.6 US
BUSINESS OPPORTUNITIES JOURNAL. See Business and Economics-Investments.

LC HF **ISSN** 0849-3901
DD 380.1/097127 CN
BUSINESS PEOPLE MAGAZINE (WINNIPEG. 1990). (BUSINESS PEOPLE MAGAZINE.). [Bus. people mag.]. Vol. 6, No. 2 (Apr./May 1990)-. Trade Publication. English. Four times a year (Feb., June, Sept., Nov.). 10.00Can$ Canada; $15.00Can$ US. McCaine-Davies Commun Limited, 232 Henderson Highway, Winnipeg Manitoba R2L 1L9 Canada. **Tel** (204)982-4002, FAX (204)982-4001. **ED** Heather McCaine-Davies. **Ad Acc, Adv Mgr:** (204)982-4000. **Circ:** 11,000 (ctrl). available on an online database from University Microfilms International (UMI). Documents available from UMI Article Clearinghouse. ***Continues*** *Winnipeg's Business People., 0848-8827.*
Ind/Abst Bus. Dateline (1990-) [Full Txt.].

ISSN 0896-3703
DD 330 US
BUSINESS PERSPECTIVES (MEMPHIS, TENN.). (BUSINESS PERSPECTIVES.). [Bus. perspect.]. **Added/Corp** Fogelman College of Business and Economics. Bureau of Business & Economic Research. Vol. 1, No. 1 (Oct. 1987)-. Trade Publication. English. Four times a year (Jan., Apr., July, Oct.). Free on request. Bureau of Business and Economic Research / Tennessee, Memphis State University, Fogelman College, Memphis TN 38152. **Tel** (901)678-2281, FAX (901)678-2281. available on microfilm and microfiche from University Microfilms International (UMI); available on an online database (file 648/Full-Text) from DIALOG. Documents available from UMI Article Clearinghouse. ***Continues*** *Mid-South Business Journal, 0279-8174.*
Ind/Abst ABI/INFORM Glob. Ed.; ABI/INFORM [Computer File] (1987-); Acad. Search; Bus. ASAP (1990-) [Full Txt.]; Bus. Index (1987-); Bus. Source Plus; Bus. Source; EP Collect.; Gen. BusinessFile (1987-); Gen. Period. Index (1985-); Homework Help.; INFO-SOUTH Abstr.; Mag. Search; MasterFile FullTEXT 1000; MasterFile FullTEXT 350; MasterFile FullTEXT 650; MasterFile FullTEXT (July 1993-); OCLC; Stat. Ref. Index; Telebase; Trade Ind. ASAP [Full Txt.]; Trade Ind. Index [Full Txt.].

ISSN 1051-7510
DD 330 US
BUSINESS PHILADELPHIA. [Bus. Phila.]. (1990)-. Periodical. English. Twelve times a year. $32.10. Geographic Business Publishing, The Atlantic Building, 260 South Broad Street, Philadelphia PA 19102. **Tel** (215)735-6969, FAX (215)735-6965.
Ind/Abst Acad. Search; Bus. Source Plus; Bus. Source; EP Collect.; Homework Help.; MasterFile FullTEXT 1000; MasterFile FullTEXT 350; MasterFile FullTEXT 650; MasterFile FullTEXT (July 1994-); OCLC; Telebase.

ISSN 1064-2471
DD 332 US
BUSINESS PICTURE, THE. [Bus. pict.]. **Added/Corp** Gilman Research Corporation. (19??)-. Periodical. English. Four times a year (Jan. Apr., July, Oct.). $240.00. Gilman Research Corporation, PO Box 20567, Oakland CA 94620. **Tel** (510)655-3103. **ED** George Gilman.
Desc: A collection of economic and financial long term charts.

US
●**BUSINESS PLANS HANDBOOK.** (Feb. 1994)-. English. One time a year. $99.00. Gale Research Inc., 835 Penobscot Building, 645 Griswold Street, Detroit MI 48226. **Tel** (800)877-GALE, (313)961-2242, FAX (313)961-6083, (800)414-5043, telex TWX 810-221-7086. **ED** Karin Koek.
Desc: Provides entrepreneurs and small businesses with a starting point for developing their own strategies and goals.

ISSN 1045-8697
DD 338 US
BUSINESS PRESS (FORT WORTH, TEX.), THE. (THE BUSINESS PRESS.). [Bus. press]. Vol. 1, No. 1 (May 16, 1988)-. Periodical. English. One time a week. $42.00. The Business Press, 303 Main Street, Ft Worth TX 76102. **Tel** (817)336-8300, FAX (817)332-3038. **ED** Jack Flanders III. **Ad Acc, Adv Mgr:** Carolyn Ashford, **Tel** (817)336-8300. **Circ:** 9,500.
Ind/Abst Bus. Source Plus; EP Collect.; Homework Help.; MasterFile FullTEXT 1000; MasterFile FullTEXT 350; MasterFile FullTEXT 650; MasterFile FullTEXT; OCLC; PROMT; Telebase.

HK
BUSINESS PROFILE SERIES. THE PEOPLE'S REPUBLIC OF CHINA. **Added/Corp** Hongkong and Shanghai Banking Corporation. **VFOAT** People's Republic of China. (19??)-. English. Irregular. Free. Hongkong and Shanghai Banking Corporation, 1 Queen's Road Central, Hong Kong.

ISSN 1071-4642
US
●**BUSINESS PUBLICATION ADVERTISING SOURCE.** See Business and Economics-Advertising and Public Relations.

LC HF5905 .S723 **ISSN** 0038-948X
DD 659.132058 US
CODEN BPRDB9
TITLE CHANGE
BUSINESS PUBLICATION RATES AND DATA. [Bus. publ. rates data]. **Added/Corp** Standard Rate & Data Service. **VFOAT** SRDS Business Publication; SRDS Business. Vol. 34, No. 3 (Mar. 21, 1952)-Vol. 75, No. 9 (Sept. 1993). Periodical. English. SRDS / Standard Rate & Data Service, 3004 Glenview Road, Wilmette IL 60091. **Tel** (708)375-5049, (800)851-7737, FAX (708)375-5003. **(Subscription address:** Neodata / Colorado, PO Box 2606, Boulder CO 80322. **)** ***Continues*** *Business Publication Advertising Rates and Data.* ***Continued by*** *Business Publication Advertising Source, 1071-4642.*
Desc: Catalog of over 4,900 business publications arranged by market classifications. Includes advertising rates, closing dates, and circulation statements.

US
BUSINESS PUBLISHER. (19??)-. English. Twenty-three times a year. $335.00. JK Publisher, PO Box 71020, Milwaukee WI 53211. **Tel** (414)332-1625, FAX (414)962-0084. **ED** John Kenney. available on an online database (files 16,636/Full-Text) from DIALOG; and Predicasts, Inc.
Ind/Abst PROMT [Full Txt.]; PTS Newsl. Database [Full Txt.].

LC HF3351 .B87
DD 338.7/097295/05 PR
BUSINESS PUERTO RICO. (Winter 1981)-. Periodical. English. Six times a year. $30.70. Puerto Rico Almanacs Inc, PO Box 9582, Santurce Puerto Rico 00908. **Tel** (809)725-3155.

ISSN 1038-1430
AT
BUSINESS QUEENSLAND. (1990)-. Periodical. English. One time a week. 81.40Aus$. Business Queensland, Locked Bag 1900, Spring Hill Queensland 4004 Australia. **Tel** 011 61 07 8310022, FAX 011 61 07 831 0044. **ED** Bob MacDonald. **Ad Acc, Adv Mgr:** Mario Salvadori. **Circ:** 14,000 (ctrl).

LC HG4050 .B88 **ISSN** 1043-7908
DD 338.7/4/097305 US
BUSINESS RANKINGS ANNUAL. (BUSINESS RANKINGS ANNUAL / COMPILED BY BROOKLYN PUBLIC LIBRARY, BUSINESS LIBRARY STAFF.). [Bus. rank. annu.]. **Added/Corp** Business Library (Brooklyn Public Library). (1989)-. English. One time a year. $160.00. Gale Research Inc., 835 Penobscot Building, 645 Griswold Street, Detroit MI 48226. **Tel** (800)877-GALE, (313)961-2242, FAX (313)961-6083, (800)414-5043, telex TWX 810-221-7086. available on magnetic tape; available on diskette. ***Continues*** *Business Rankings and Salaries Index.*
Desc: Features a simplified, easy-to-use subject arrangement, a listing of the top ten names in each ranking, a source list and one master index to every name in every list.

LC HD **ISSN** 1068-2899
DD 380 US
●**BUSINESS RECORD, THE.** [Bus. rec.]. **VFOAT** Greater Cincinnati Business Record; Record. Vol. 5, No. 26 (Jan. 4-10, 1993)-. Periodical. English. One time a week. $52.00. Paige Maren Corporation, 708 Walnut Street, Suite 400, Cincinnati OH 45202. **Tel** (513)421-9300. ***Continues*** *Greater Cincinnati Business Record, 1044-9264.*

ISSN 0833-062X
CN
BUSINESS REPORT. See Education.

LC HF1134 .N4 **ISSN** 0362-823X
DD 338/.008 US
BUSINESS RESEARCH BULLETIN. No. 73- 1972-. Bulletin. English. University of Nebraska / Bureau of Business Research, 200 College Business Administration Building, Lincoln NE 68588-0407. **Tel** (402)472-2334, FAX (402)472-3878. ***Continues*** *Business Research Bulletin.*

ISSN 0957-9869
DD 016.65805 UK
BUSINESS RESEARCH GUIDE HEADLAND. (BUSINESS RESEARCH GUIDE.). [Bus. res. guide Headland]. (1989)-. Monographic series. English. Irregular. $220.74. Headland Business Information, 1 Henry Smiths Terrace, Headland Cleveland, TS24 0PD United Kingdom. **Tel** 011 44 429 231902, FAX 011 44 429 861403.

LC HF5001 .B86 **ISSN** 0125-0477
DD 330.9/593/04 TH
BUSINESS REVIEW. [Bus. rev.]. (19??)-. Periodical. English. Twelve times a year. $80.00. Nation Publishing Group, 44 MOO 10, Bangna-Taad Road, Bangkok 10260 Thailand. **Tel** 011 66 2 3171366, 011 66 2 3171378.
Ind/Abst Asia.-Pac. Econ. Lit.; F&S Index Plus Text, Int. [Select. Cov.]; PROMT.

LC HD2709 **ISSN** 1354-1110
DD 338.7 UK
●**BUSINESS REVIEW DEDDINGTON.** (BUSINESS REVIEW.). [Bus. Rev. Deddington]. Vol. 1 (Sept. 1994)-. Periodical. English. Four times a year. $48.76. Philip Allan Publishers Ltd., Market Place, Deddington, Oxfordshire OX15 0SE United Kingdom. **Tel** 011 44 1869 338652, FAX 011 44 1869 338803. **ED** Ceri Jenkins.

LC HC107.A12 A2 **ISSN** 0007-7011
DD 330.973/005 US
CODEN FRBPBN
Pr Rev.
BUSINESS REVIEW (PHILADELPHIA). (BUSINESS REVIEW.). [Bus. rev.]. **Added/Corp** Federal Reserve Bank of Philadelphia. (July 1, 1923)-. Periodical. English. Six times a year. Free on request. Federal Reserve Bank of Philadelphia, Research Department, 100 North 6th Street, Philadelphia PA 19105-1574. **Tel** (215)574-6448. **ED** Sarah A. Burke (editor's telephone: (215)574-3805). **Circ:** 20,000 (ctrl). available on microfilm and microfiche from University Microfilms International (UMI). Documents available from UMI Article Clearinghouse. ***Continues*** *Business and Financial Conditions in the Third Federal Reserve District.*
Desc: Articles for the general economists on banking, regional and macro economics, and monetary policy.
Ind/Abst ABI/INFORM Glob. Ed.; ABI/INFORM [Computer File] (May 1980-); Acad. Search; Bus. Period. Index; Bus. Source Plus; Bus. Source; EP Collect.; Expand. Acad. Index (1992-); Gen. BusinessFile (1992-); Homework Help.; MasterFile FullTEXT 1000; MasterFile FullTEXT 350; MasterFile FullTEXT 650; MasterFile FullTEXT (July 1993-) [Full Txt.]; Mat. Fact; Newsp. Period. Abstr. (1992-); OCLC; PAIS Int. Print (1991-); Telebase; Wilson Bus. Abstr.

LC HB **ISSN** 1078-1056
DD 330 US
BUSINESS REVIEW (PHILADELPHIA, PA.), THE. (THE BUSINESS REVIEW.). [Bus. rev.]. (199?)-. Periodical. English. Twelve times a year. $36.00.

Fly Communication Ltd., PO Box 50386, Philadelphia PA 19132. **Tel** (215)235-7727. ***Continues*** *Philadelphia Business Review.*

ISSN 0727-758X
AT

BUSINESS REVIEW WEEKLY : BRW. **VFOAT** BRW. Vol. 3, No. 17 (July 25-31, 1981)-. Trade Publication. English. Fifty times a year. 111.00Aus$. Business Review Weekly, 469 La Trobe Street, Melbourne Victoria 3000 Australia. **Tel** 011 61 3 6033888, FAX 011 61 3 6704328. **ED** David Uren. **Bk Rev. Ad Acc. Circ:** 78,000. available on an online database (files 771,772,799/Full-Text) from DIALOG. Documents available from UMI Article Clearinghouse. ***Continues*** *Weekly Business Review (Melbourne, Vic.)*; ***Absorbed*** *Rydge's, 0725-5640.*
Ind/Abst ABI/INFORM Glob. Ed.; Bus. Source Plus; Bus. Source; EP Collect.; Homework Help.; Infomat Int. Bus.; MasterFile FullTEXT 1000; MasterFile FullTEXT 350; MasterFile FullTEXT 650; MasterFile FullTEXT (Sept. 1994-); SPORT Discus; Telebase; World Mag. Bank.

US

BUSINESS REVIEWS. Vol. 1 (June 1978)-. Periodical. English. Twelve times a year. $9.00 US and Canada; $12.00 other. Roscommon Publications, 666 North Broadway, Hastings-on-Hudson NY 10706.

GW

BUSINESS RISK SERVICE. (19??)-. English. Three times a year. DM1720.00 (includes supplements). Societaet Unternehmensplanung, Weinfeldstrasse 24, W 6200 Wiesbaden Germany. **Tel** 011 49 611 86979.

UK

●**BUSINESS RUSSIA.** (1995)-. English. Twelve times a year. $695.00. The Economist Intelligence Unit / New York, 111 West 57th Street, New York NY 10019. **Tel** (800)938-4685, (212)554-0600. available on an online database from Lexis-Nexis.

ISSN 1056-3512
US

●**BUSINESS SERIALS.** (1993)-. Periodical. English. Every 2 years. $129.00. SovaComm Inc, PO Box 64697, Virginia Beach VA 23464. **Tel** (804)420-3564, FAX (804)420-0840.

ISSN 1181-8131
US

BUSINESS SOURCE, THE. (1991)-. English. Business Source Inc., Ste. 300 219 Colonnade Rd., Nepean K2E 7K3 Ontario.

UK

BUSINESS SPAIN. (19??)-. English. Twelve times a year. £345.00 Europe; £355.00 other. Business Spain, 5 Newton Road Wimbledon, London SW19 3PJ United Kingdom. **Tel** 011 44 81 5408520, FAX 011 44 81 5429185. **ED** Graham Faiella. Index available. cum. index. **Bk Rev.**
Desc: A business report about Spain, in English, covering the economy; manufacturing and service industries; retailing and consumer markets; financial services sectors; company news and results; and statistics.

ISSN 1055-3568
DD 808 US

BUSINESS SPEAKER'S DIGEST. [Bus. speak. dig.]. (19??)-. Periodical. English. Six times a year (Feb., Apr., June, Aug., Oct., Dec.). $349.00. Lime Rock Press, Inc., 200 Route 126, Falls Village CT 06031. **Tel** (203)824-1411, FAX (203)824-1210.

LC HC101 .A13122 **ISSN** 0083-2545
DD 338.9 US

BUSINESS STATISTICS (BIENNIAL). See Business and Economics-Abstracting, Bibliographies and Statistics.

US

BUSINESS STATISTICS, NEW YORK STATE. See Business and Economics-Abstracting, Bibliographies and Statistics.

LC HF5001
DD 650 US

BUSINESS STRATEGIES. **Added/Corp** Commerce Clearing House. (1984)-. Periodical. English. Irregular. Commerce Clearing House Inc., 4025 West Peterson Avenue, Chicago IL 60646-6085. **Tel** (312)583-8500, FAX (708)940-4600. **ED** Sidney Kess and Bertil Westlin.
Desc: Explains the legal, tax and accounting ramifications of management decision-making.

ISSN 0964-4733
DD 333.7205 UK

BUSINESS STRATEGY AND THE ENVIRONMENT. [Bus. strategy environ.]. (1992)-. Periodical. English. Four times a year. $235.00. John Wiley & Sons Ltd., Baffins Lane, Chichester, West Sussex PO19 1UD United Kingdom. **Tel** 011 44 1243 779777, FAX 011 44 1243 776128 BTG:JWP001, telex 86290 WIBOOKG.

LC HD28 .B845 **ISSN** 0955-6419
DD 658.4/012/05 UK
CCC

BUSINESS STRATEGY REVIEW. **Added/Corp** London Business School. Centre for Business Strategy. Vol. 1, No. 1 (Spring 1990)-. Periodical. English. Four times a year. $120.00. Oxford University Press / UK, Walton Street, Oxford OX2 6DP United Kingdom. **Tel** 011 44 1865 56767, FAX 011 44 1865 267773, telex 851/837330 OXPRES G. **(Subscription address:** Oxford University Press / USA, Journals Marketing Department, Oxford University Press, 2001 Evans Road, Cary NC 27513. **Tel** (800)451-7556, (919)677-0977, FAX (919)677-1714.**)** **ED** John Cubbin and John Kay. available on microfilm and microfiche from University Microfilms International (UMI). Documents available from UMI Article Clearinghouse.
Desc: Encompasses all aspects of business strategy, including profitability and performance, global and national markets, and industry standards and product positioning. Aims to translate research findings, models, and ideas into forms that can readily be applied in business situations.
Ind/Abst ABI/INFORM Glob. Ed.; Curr. Cit.

LC HF11 .B8 **ISSN** 0953-685X
UK

BUSINESS STUDIES. (19??)-. Periodical. English. Four times a year (Feb., Apr., Oct., Dec.). $32.42. Anforme Business Publications Ltd., 2/3 Dukes Court, Princess Way, Prudhoe North Umberland NE42 6DA United Kingdom. **Tel** 11 44 0661 836635, FAX 11 44 0661 836265. **ED** Nigel Tree, David Parker and Professor John Burton. Index available. cum. index. **Ad Acc. Circ:** 10,000.
Desc: A variety of articles on all the main areas of business studies including management, accounting, business policy, marketing, business economics, commercial law and information technology. Aimed at all those taking business studies and professional and management courses.

AT

●**BUSINESS STUDIES REVIEW.** (1995)-. English. Six times a year. 50.00Aus$. Tim Riley Publications, PO Box 455, Dee Why NSW 2099 Australia. **Tel** 011 61 2 9722059.

LC KF6457 .H3 **ISSN** 0146-0587
DD 343/.73/06705 US

BUSINESS TAX INTERPRETATIONS. See Finance-Taxation.

AT
CEASED

BUSINESS TECHNOLOGY SOLUTIONS. (1995)-(March 1995). English. Presentation Solutions, PO Box 221, Elwood VIC 3184 Australia. **Tel** 011 61 3 5254804. ***Continues*** *Presentation Solutions.*

ISSN 0744-172X
US

BUSINESS TIMES (EAST HARTFORD, CONN.), THE. (THE BUSINESS TIMES.). Periodical. English. Twenty-four times a year. $18.00. MacClaren Press, 315 Peck Street, New Haven CT 06513. **Tel** (203)782-1420. **ED** Joy Esterson. **Ad Acc. Circ:** 30,000 (ctrl). available on an online database from DIALOG. Documents available from UMI Article Clearinghouse. ***Continues*** *Connecticut Business Times, 0161-6102.*
Ind/Abst Acad. Search; Bus. Dateline; Bus. Index (Jan. 1985-Dec. 1985); Bus. Source Plus; Bus. Source; EP Collect.; Gen. BusinessFile (Jan. 1985-Dec. 1985); Gen. Period. Index (Jan. 1985-Dec. 1985); Homework Help.; INFO-SOUTH Abstr.; MasterFile FullTEXT 1000; MasterFile FullTEXT 350; MasterFile FullTEXT 650; MasterFile FullTEXT (July 1994-); OCLC; Telebase.

SI

BUSINESS TIMES SINGAPORE. See Newspapers.

LC HF3321 .B87
CU

Pr Rev.

BUSINESS TIPS ON CUBA. **Added/Corp** Technological Information Promotion System. Cuba Office. (199?)-. Periodical. English (Spanish, French, German, Russian and Portuguese). Twelve times a year. $100.00. Tips Devnet, Calle 30 NRO 302, Esquina 3RA, Miramar Ciudad Havana Cuba. **Tel** 011 53 7 331797. Index available (bound in all issues).

ISSN 0897-9065
US

BUSINESS TO BUSINESS (PITTSFORD, N.Y.). (BUSINESS TO BUSINESS : ROCHESTER RIVERSIDE CONVENTION CENTER NEWS.). (1985)-. Periodical. English. Twenty-six times a year. $25.00. Business to Business Publishers, 1 Grove Street, Pittsford NY 14534. **Tel** (716)385-4960.

ISSN 1186-0340
DD 381 CN
CEASED

BUSINESS TO BUSINESS QUINTE. [Bus. bus. Quinte]. (Oct. 1990)-(199?). Periodical. English. Kirby Communications Group, Rural Route 7, Belleville Ontario K8N 4Z7 Canada.

LC HD28 **ISSN** 1033-9612
DD 658.005 AT

BUSINESS TO BUSINESS SOUTH AUSTRALIA. [Bus. bus. S. Aust.]. **VFOAT** Business to Business. (1988)-. Periodical. English. Twelve times a year. 22.50Aus$. Business Communications Pty. Ltd., 137 Rundle Street, Kent Town SA 5067 Australia. **Tel** 011 61 08 362 4677.
Ind/Abst AESIS Q.

LC HF5001 .P692 **ISSN** 0007-7100
DD 650/.05 US

BUSINESS TODAY. **Added/Corp** Princeton University. Vol. 1 (Spring 1968)-. Periodical. English. Three times a year. $9.00. Federation for Student Communication, Princeton University, 305 Aaron Burr Hall, Princeton NJ 08544. **Tel** (609)258-1111, FAX (609)258-1222. **ED** Brent Kawahara. **Ad Acc. Circ:** 200,000 (ctrl). available on an online database from DIALOG; available on microfilm and microfiche from University Microfilms International (UMI). ***Supersedes*** *Princeton Business Today.*
Desc: Articles concern current trends in industry, career opportunities for graduating students, features on student entrepreneurs, and ethics. Also addressed are student opinions on business issues. Regular features include annual career survey listing available career positions, general topics of interest and concern to students, and business innovations and contributions to society.

LC HF5001 .B8837a
DD 650/.0954/05 II

BUSINESS TODAY. Vol. 1, No. 1 (Jan. 7/21, 1992)-. Periodical. English. Twenty-four times a year. $72.00. Living Media India Ltd., F 14-15 Connaught Place, New Delhi 110001 India. **Tel** 011 91 11 3714059. **(Subscription address:** Living Media India Ltd., 404 Park Avenue South, Suite 1205, New York NY 10016. **Tel** (212)481-0040.**)**

ISSN 0708-5842
DD 331.4/81/658 CN

BUSINESS (TORONTO). (BUSINESS.). **Added/Corp** Women's Conference Institute. Vol. 1 (June 1979)-. Periodical. English. Twelve times a year. $8.00 Canada; $10.00 US and UK. Women's Conference Institute, Suite 30, 43 Victoria Street, Toronto Ontario M5C 2A2.

ISSN 1046-5057
DD 658 US

BUSINESS TRAVEL MANAGEMENT. [Bus. travel manage.]. Vol. 1, No. 1 (Sept. 1989)-. Trade Publication. English. Twelve times a year. Coastal Communications Corporation, 488 Madison Avenue, New York NY 10022. **Tel** (212)888-1500. **ED** Michael Billing. **Ad Acc. Circ:** 40,000 (ctrl).
Desc: Targeted to corporate executives, business travel managers and travel professionals servicing commercial accounts. Offers a balanced mix of management- and operations-oriented news, specialty features, and a selection of tabular material for policies and practices.

ISSN 8750-3670
DD 338 US
CCC

BUSINESS TRAVEL NEWS. [Bus. travel news]. (19??)-. Periodical. English. Irregular (29 issues). $95.00. Miller Freeman Inc., 600 Harrison Street, San Francisco CA 94107. **Tel** (415)905-2337, (415)905-2200, FAX (415)905-2240, telex 278273. **Ad Acc. Circ:** 52,462 (ctrl). available on an online database from NEWSNET; (file 16/Full-Time) DIALOG; and DATA-STAR.
Desc: Brings timely, hard-hitting news and information on helping to arrange, purchase, or supply business travel. Each issue reports on travel management, car rentals, hotel, airlines, travel agency business, meetings, and group travel.
Ind/Abst Curr. Lit. Fam. Plan. (19??-199?); F&S Index Plus Text, Int. (19??-) [Full Txt.] [Select. Cov.]; PROMT (19??-) [Full Txt.].

ISSN 0834-0552
DD 380.1/459104/05 CN

BUSINESS TRAVELLER AND LEISURE TIME PLANNER. See Travel and Tourism.

ISSN 0897-1781
DD 657 US

BUSINESS VALUATION REVIEW. [Bus. valuat. rev.]. Periodical. English. Four times a year. $50.00. American Society of Appraisers, PO Box 24222, Denver CO 80224. **Tel** (303)758-6148, (303)758-8818, FAX (303)758-6164. **ED** James H Schilt. Index available. cum. index. **Bk Rev. Ad Acc. Circ:** 650 (ctrl). ***Continues*** *Business Valuation News, 0882-2875.*
Desc: Technical journal of business valuation and appraisal, articles, treaties, book reviews, bibliographies, changes in related laws and taxes, current events relating to valuation, etc.

LC HC236 .B87 ISSN 1013-2120
DD 330.987/005 VE

BUSINESS VENEZUELA. [Bus. Venez.]. **Added/Corp** American Chamber of Commerce of Venezuela. Venezuelan-American Chamber of Commerce and Industry. (19??)-. Periodical. English. Twelve times a year. $80.00. Venezuelan-American Chamber of Commerce and Industry, 2 Avenida Campo Alegre Credival 10, Caracas 1010-A Venezuela. **Tel** 011 58 2 2630833, telex 23627 UACCI UC. **ED** Michael E. Heggie. **Ad Acc. Circ:** 6,500.
Desc: Focus on Venezuela's economy from a business perspective.

LC HF5001 .B89 ISSN 0007-7135
DD 650 US
CCC
CODEN BUWEA3

BUSINESS WEEK. [Bus. week]. No. 1 (Sept. 7, 1929)-. Academic Scholarly Publication. English. One time a week. $46.95. McGraw Hill Publishing Company, Inc., 1221 Avenue of the Americas, New York NY 10020. **Tel** (212)512-6410, (800)525-5003, FAX (212)512-6111. **(Subscription address:** McGraw Hill Book Company, Princeton Road, Hightstown NJ 08520. **Tel** (717)794-5461.) **Ad Acc.** available on microfilm from University Microfilms International (UMI); available on an online database from NEWSNET; Lexis-Nexis; Dow Jones News/Retrieval; and DIALOG. Documents available from CASDDS, CIS, Documents on Demand, FAXON Xpress, UMI Article Clearinghouse. ***Supersedes*** *Magazine of Business;* ***Absorbed*** *Annalist.*
Ind/Abst ABI/INFORM [Computer File] (Nov. 1972-); Abr. Read. Guide Period. Lit.; Abstr. Bull. Inst. Pap. Sci. Tech.; Acad. Abstr. Full Text Elite; Acad. Abstr.; Acad. Search; BioBusiness (1986-); Book Rev. Index; Bus. Period. Index; Bus. Source Plus; Bus. Source; Chem. Abstr.; Comput. Lit. Index; Energy Inf. Abstr.; Environ. Abstr.; EP Collect.; GeoRef; Health Plan. Adminis.; Homework Help.; Infobank (Jan. 1969-); Mag. Artic. Summar. Elite; Mag. Artic. Summar. Select; Mag. Artic. Summar. CD-ROM; MasterFile FullTEXT 1000; MasterFile FullTEXT 350; MasterFile FullTEXT 650; MasterFile FullTEXT (Jan. 1984-); OCLC; Pub. Lib. FullTEXT; Read. Guide Period. Lit.; Stat. Ref. Index; Telebase; Mag. Index (1959-); Trade Ind. Index (1981-); Vocat. Search; World Mag. Bank.

ISSN 0739-8395
DD 338 US
CODEN BWITEU

BUSINESS WEEK (INDUSTRIAL ED.). (BUSINESS WEEK.). [Bus. week]. (19??)-. Periodical. English. One time a week. McGraw Hill Publishing Company, Inc., 1221 Avenue of the Americas, New York NY 10020. **Tel** (212)512-6410, (800)525-5003, FAX (212)512-6111. **Circ:** 892,168. available on microfilm and microfiche from University Microfilms International (UMI); available on an online database from NEXIS. Documents available from UMI Article Clearinghouse, CASDDS, Documents on Demand.
Desc: Provides insights into our competitive economy, with thought-provoking coverage of new business strategies, trends in the marketplace and timely articles on all the topics that affect our personal and professional lives.
Ind/Abst ABI/INFORM Glob. Ed. (Nov. 1972-); ABI/INFORM Ondisc: Expr. Ed. (Jan. 1987-); ABI/INFORM [Computer File] (Nov. 1972-); Abr. Read. Guide Period. Lit.; Acad. Ind. [Computer File] (1984-); AGRICOLA [Select. Cov.]; Aviat. Tradescan [Select. Cov.]; BioBusiness; Book Rev. Index; Bus. Index (1985-); Bus. Period. Index; Chem. Abstr.; Chem. Ind. Notes (1985-); Chicano Index; Comput. Bus.; Curr. Lit. Fam. Plan. (19??-199?); Energy Inf. Abstr.; Environ. Abstr.; Expand. Acad. Index (1984-); F&S Index Plus Text, Int. [Select. Cov.]; Foods Adlibra; GATFWORLD (1984); Gen. BusinessFile (1985-); Gen. Period. Index (1985-); Health Ref. Cent. (1987-) [Select. Cov.]; Index Bus. Reports; Index Period. Artic. Relat. Law; Int. Exec.; Int. Labour Doc.; Mag. Express (1986-) [Full Txt.]; Mag. Index Plus (1989-); Mag. Index. Sel. (1986-); Mag. Search; Manage. Market. Abstr.; Middle East Abstr. Index; Newsp. Period. Abstr. (1986-); Oper. Res./Manage. Sci.; PAIS Int. Print; Peace Res. Abstr. J. (1963-1966, 1972-1973); PROMT; Read. Guide Abstr. Select Ed.; Read. Guide Period. Lit.; Resource/One Ondisc; Text. Technol. Dig. (19??-199?); Mag. Index (1977-); TOM Gen. Index (1985-); Trade Ind. Index; UMI ABI/Inform--Bus. Period. Ondisc [Full Txt.]; Urban Aff. Abstr.; Wilson Bus. Abstr.; Work Relat. Abstr.

ISSN 1031-1343
DD 338.0029494 AT

BUSINESS WHO'S WHO PRODUCTS AND TRADENAMES GUIDE. See Business and Economics-Abstracting, Bibliographies and Statistics.

US

BUSINESS WIRE NEWSLETTER. (19??)-. Newsletter. English. Twelve times a year. Business Wire, 44 Montgomery Street, Suite 2185, San Francisco CA 94104. **Tel** (415)986-4422. Documents available from UMI Article Clearinghouse.
Ind/Abst Bus. Dateline (July 28, 1988-) [Full Txt.].

ISSN 0738-8977
US

BUSINESS WORCESTER. Periodical. English. Twelve times a year. $26.00. Worcester Business Journal, 172 Shrewsbury Street, Worcester MA 01604. **Tel** (508)755-8004. **ED** Michael Warshaw. **Ad Acc. Circ:** 16,000 (ctrl). available on an online database (file 635/Full-Text) from DIALOG. Documents available from UMI Article Clearinghouse.
Ind/Abst Bus. Dateline; Bus. Index (Jan. 1985-Dec. 1985); Gen. BusinessFile (Jan. 1985-Dec. 1985); Gen. Period. Index (Jan. 1985-Dec. 1985); INFO-SOUTH Abstr.

CN
CEASED

BUSINESS YELLOW PAGES OF AMERICA ON CD-ROM. (19??)-(19??). English. Innotech Inc., 2001 Sheppard Avenue East 118, North York Ontario M2J 4Z7 Canada. **Tel** (416)492-3838.
Desc: Contains over 200,000 American businesses from coast to coast.

ISSN 1082-6947
DD 387 US

●**BUSINESSFLYER BULLETIN.** [Bus.fly. bull.]. **VFOAT** Business Flyer Bulletin; Businessflyer Fax. (May 1, 1995)-. Bulletin. English. Twelve times a year. $50.00. Holcon, PO Box 276, Newton Centre MA 02159. **Tel** (203)782-2155, (800)359-3774. ***Continues*** *Business Flyer, 0893-3073.*

ISSN 1064-2412
DD 338 US
CEASED

BUSINESSGRAM (TAMPA, FLA.). (BUSINESSGRAM.). [BusinessGram]. (19??)-(Dec. 1994). Periodical. English. BG Publishing, PO Box 273390, Tampa FL 33688. **Tel** (813)968-2979. **ED** Joseph R. McAuliffe. **Bk Rev.** ctrl circ.
Desc: Addresses business and news from a Christian standpoint.

DD 338 US

●**BUSINESSJOURNAL.** (July 1995)-. Periodical. English. Twenty-six times a year. $36.00. CNY Business Review Inc., 231 Walton Street, Syracuse NY 13202. **Tel** (315)446-3510. ***Continues*** *CNY Business Journal, 1050-3005.*
Ind/Abst Trade Ind. ASAP [Full Txt.]; Trade Ind. Index.

US
CEASED

BUSINESSLINK. **Added/Corp** Resources for Child Care Management (Organization). **VFOAT** Business Link. (19??)-Vol. 5 No. 3 (1993). Periodical. English. Resources Child Care Management, 16 South Street, Suite 300, Morristown NJ 07960. **Tel** (201)267-9100.

ISSN 0275-1690
US

BUSINESSMAN'S GUIDE TO THE ARAB WORLD. [Bus.man guide Arab world]. 4th Ed. (1980)-. English. One time a year. Arab World Business Guides Inc, A Service of Guides to Multinational Business Inc, Harvard Square Box 92, Cambridge MA 02138. ***Supersedes*** *Businessman's Guide.*

ISSN 1049-9822
DD 330 US

BUSINESSWEST (SPRINGFIELD, MASS.). (BUSINESSWEST.). [BusinessWest]. **VFOAT** Business West. Vol. 5, No. 12 (April 1989)-. Periodical. English. Twelve times a year. $15.00. BusinessWest, 625 Front Street, Chicopee MA 01013. **Tel** (413)598-8600. **ED** Gregory Sandler. Index available. cum. index. **Bk Rev. Ad Acc. Circ:** 12,000 (ctrl). available on microfilm and microfiche from University Microfilms International (UMI); available on an online database from the publisher. Documents available from UMI Article Clearinghouse. ***Continues*** *Western Massachusetts Business Journal, 0891-7302.*
Desc: Comprehensive analysis of business and economic trends in western Massachusetts and northern Connecticut.
Ind/Abst Acad. Search; Bus. Dateline (Jan. 1992-) [Full Txt.]; Bus. Source Plus; Bus. Source; EP Collect.; Homework Help.; INFO-SOUTH Abstr.; MasterFile FullTEXT 1000; MasterFile FullTEXT 350; MasterFile FullTEXT 650; MasterFile FullTEXT (July 1993-); OCLC; PROMT; Telebase.

US

BUYERISM NEWSLETTER. (19??)-. Newsletter. English. Twelve times a year. $35.00 (one-year); $65.00 (two-year). WWWWW / Information Services Inc, Box 10046, Rochester NY 14610. **Tel** (716)482-2022. **ED** Robert Fowler.
Desc: News and information about starting, buying and operating an business.

ISSN 1040-0990
DD 332 US
CCC

BUYOUTS (WELLESLEY HILLS, MASS.). (BUYOUTS.). **Added/Corp** Venture Economics, Inc. Vol. 1, Issue 1 (June 20, 1988)-. Periodical. English. Twenty-five times a year. $695.00. Securities Data Company, 40 West 57th Street, 11th Floor, New York NY 10019. **Tel** (212)765-5311. **ED** Steven P. Galante. available on an online database (files 16,636/Full-Text) from DIALOG.
Ind/Abst PROMT [Full Txt.]; PTS Newsl. Database [Full Txt.].

DD 338.9 US

C. E. D. PRESS REACTION. Main/Corp Committee for Economic Development. (19??)-. Periodical. English. Twelve times a year. Free on request. Committee for Economic Development, 477 Madison Avenue, New York NY 10022. **Tel** (212)688-2063.

ISSN 0213-8093
UDC 334 SP

C.I.R.I.E.C. ESPANA. (SOCIAL Y COOPERATIVA.). [C.I.R.I.E.C. Esp.]. **VFOAT** Centro de Investigacion e Informacion Sobre la Economia Publica, Social y Cooperativa Espana. (1987)-. Periodical. Spanish. Three times a year. $50.00. Escuela Univ Estudios Empresar, Calle Artes Graficas 13, 46010 Valencia Spain. **Tel** 011 34 6 369-1508.

ISSN 0258-3577
AU

CA QUARTERLY. [CA q.]. **Added/Corp** Creditanstalt-Bankverein (Austria). **VAT** Creditanstalt Quarterly. (1982)-. Periodical. English. Four times a year. ***Continues*** *Wirtschaftsberichte (Vienna, Austria), 0590-0727.*
Ind/Abst F&S Index Plus Text, Int. [Select. Cov.]; Predicasts Forecasts.

PO

CADERNOS DE ECONOMIA. REVISTA DE ANALISE. (19??)-. Spanish. Promeios, Prod Meois Com Lda Re, Adm Publ Serv Assin Franc Lobo, 2R C DTO 1000 Lisbon Portugal.
Ind/Abst PAIS Int. Print.

LC HC ISSN 0714-5659
DD 330/.05 CN
Pr Rev.

CAHIER - DEPARTEMENT D'ECONONOMIQUE, FACULTE DES SCIENCES SOCIALES, UNIVERSITE LAVAL. (CAHIER.). [Cah. - Dep. econ., Fac. sci. soc., Univ. Laval]. Monographic series. French (English). Irregular (35 a year). Price varies per volume. Universite Laval / Economique, Departement d'Economique, Faculte des Sciences Sociales, Quebec Quebec G1K 7P4 Canada. **Tel** (418)656-1926. Index available. cum. index. **Circ:** 150.
Desc: Consists of working papers written by the professors and researchers of the Department of Economics.

LC HB3 .C3 ISSN 0709-9231
DD 330/.01/8 CN

CAHIER (UNIVERSITE DE MONTREAL. DEPARTEMENT DE SCIENCES ECONOMIQUES). (CAHIER - DEPARTEMENT DES SCIENCES ECONOMIQUES, UNIVERSITE DE MONTREAL.). [Cah. - Dep. sci. econ., Univ. Montr.]. Monographic series. English (French). Price varies per volume. Presses de l'Universite de Montreal, PO Box 6128 Station A, Montreal Quebec H3C 3J7 Canada. **Tel** (514)343-6933. ***Continues*** *Cahier (Universite de Montreal. Departement des Sciences Economiques).*

ISSN 0983-1851
UDC 330.191.6 FR

CAHIERS DE LA FONDATION, LES. [Cah. Fond.]. (1986)-. Periodical. French. Four times a year. $109.36. Fondation Europe et Societe, 14 Avenue Victor Hugo, 75116 Paris France. **Tel** 011 33 1 45015547, FAX 011 33 1 45016523. Index available. cum. index. **Bk Rev. Ad Acc.** ctrl circ.

ISSN 0294-4049
UDC 368 FR

CAHIERS DE LA MUTUALITE DANS L'ENTREPRISE, LES. [Cah. mutual. entrep.]. **VFOAT** Cahier de la Mutualite dans l'Entreprise. (1982)-. Periodical. French. Four times a year.
Ind/Abst Int. Labour Doc.

LC HN49.C6 C34 ISSN 0755-9208
DD 307.1/412/05 FR

CAHIERS D'ECONOMIE ET SOCIOLOGIE RURALES. See Agriculture-Crop Production and Soils.

LC HC311 .C3 ISSN 0008-0195
DD 330.9493/005 BE
Pr Rev.

CAHIERS ECONOMIQUES DE BRUXELLES. [Cah. econ. Brux.]. **Added/Corp** Universite Libre de Bruxelles. Departement d'Economie Appliquee. No. 1, (Oct. 1958)-. Periodical. French (English and Dutch). Four times a year. $92.79. Editions du Dulbea, AV F D Roosevelt 50 - CP 140, B 1050

Brussels Belgium. **Tel** 32 2 6424119, FAX 32 2 6504012. **ED** Peter Praet. Index available. **Ad Acc. Circ:** 1,000.
Desc: Applied economics and econometrics.
Ind/Abst Econ. Lit. Index; Int. Labour Doc.; J. Econ. Lit.

ISSN 1167-5217
FR
UDC 330
•CAHIERS VERTS DE L'ECONOMIE PARIS, LES.
(LES CAHIERS VERTS DE L'ECONOMIE.). [Cah. verts econ.Paris]. **Added/Corp** Sociation Nationale des Docteurs es Sciences Economiques (France). (1992)-. Periodical. French. Twelve times a year. $1093.61. Socofi SA, 79 Avenue Marceau, 75116 Paris France. **Tel** 011 33 1 40701590, FAX 011 31 1 47235629. **ED** Sofie Tedesco. **Circ:** 400 (ctrl). ***Continues*** *Le Cahier de Conjoncture de l'ANDESE, 0986-7236.*

US
CAHNERS ECONOMIC OUTLOOK.
(19??)-. English. Six times a year. Free on request. Cahners Publishing Company, 249 West 17th Street, New York NY 10011. **Tel** (212)645-0067, FAX (212)242-6987.
Ind/Abst Predicasts Forecasts.

ISSN 0277-2949
US
CAI NEWS.
Added/Corp Community Associations Institute. Washington Metropolitan Chapter. **VAT** Community Associations Institute News - Community Associations Institute. Washington Metropolitan Chapter. (19??)-. Periodical. English. Twelve times a year. Free. Washington Metropolitan Chapter, Community Associations Institute, 9514 Hunt Square Court, Springfield VA 22153. **Tel** (062)732311. **ED** Susan Vale. **Circ:** 3,000 (ctrl).
Desc: Eight page newsletter covering topical economic and political events that effect Australian business development.

LC HE9761 **ISSN** 1183-7853
DD 387.7 CN
CALGARY & AREA AVIATION BUSINESS DIRECTORY.
See Aeronautics, Astronautics.

LC HC107.C2 C3 **ISSN** 0008-0926
DD 330 US
CALIFORNIA BUSINESS.
[Calif. bus.]. (Dec. 7, 1965)-. Periodical. English. Six times a year. $18.00. CABCO, 1427 Bay Street, Suite 200, San Francisco CA 94123. **Tel** (415)776-9966, FAX (415)776-1472. **(Subscription address:** Pub Data, 5615 West Cermak Road, Cicero IL 60650. **Tel** (312)762-2193.**) ED** Michael T. Harris. **Ad Acc. Circ:** 70,000 (ctrl). available on an online database from DIALOG; available on microfilm and microfiche from University Microfilms International (UMI). Documents available from BLDSC, The UnCover Company, UMI Article Clearinghouse.
Desc: Opportunities in the Golden State.
Ind/Abst Acad. Search; Bus. Index (1985-); Bus. Source Plus; Bus. Source; Calif. Period. Index (19??-); Calif. Period. Microfi. (19??-); EP Collect.; Gen. BusinessFile (1985-); Gen. Period. Index (1985-); Homework Help.; INFO-SOUTH Abstr.; Mag. Artic. Summar. Elite; Mag. Artic. Summar. Select; Mag. Artic. Summar. CD-ROM; MasterFile FullTEXT 1000; MasterFile FullTEXT 350; MasterFile FullTEXT 650; MasterFile FullTEXT (Sept. 1984-June 1989); OCLC; PAIS Int. Print (1991-); PROMT; Telebase; Trade Ind. ASAP [Full Txt.]; Trade Ind. Index [Full Txt.].

LC KFC442 .A5514 **ISSN** 0362-1804
DD 343/.794/088 US
CALIFORNIA COMMISSIONER OF CORPORATIONS CURRENT OFFICIAL OPINIONS ISSUED PURSUANT TO THE FRANCHISE INVESTMENT LAW.
Main/Corp California. Dept. of Corporations. **Added/Corp** California. Laws, Statutes, etc. Franchise Investment Law. (19??)-. English. Irregular. $312.00 (13 volume set of Opinions and 1969-1971 Policy Letters), $75.00 (Update service). California Continuing Education of the Bar, 2300 Shattuck Avenue, Berkeley CA 94704. **Tel** (510)642-8000, (800)232-3444, FAX (510)642-3788, (800)640-6994.
Desc: Includes opinions, a subject index and a list of citations.

LC HC107.C2 C345
DD 330 US
CALIFORNIA ECONOMIC UPDATE.
Added/Corp California State Library. California Research Bureau. (199?)-. Periodical. English. Twelve times a year. $60.00. Economic Sciences Corp, 2120 University Avenue, Suite 600, Berkeley CA 94704. **Tel** (510)841-6869, FAX (510)644-1943.

US
CALIFORNIA EXECUTIVE. SOUTHERN CALIFORNIA, THE.
VFOAT Southern California. Vol. 12, No. 9 (Sept. 1987)-. Periodical. English. Twelve times a year. $24.00. The Executive, 1888 Century Park East, Suite 830, Los Angeles CA 90067-1712. **Tel** (916)924-9815. Documents available from UMI Article Clearinghouse. ***Continues*** *Executive. Southern California.*
Ind/Abst Bus. Dateline.

US
CALIFORNIA PERSONAL LINES.
(19??)-. English. Twenty-four times a year. $178.69. Merritt Company, 1661 Ninth Street, PO Box 955, Santa Monica CA 90406. **Tel** (310)450-7234, (800)638-7597, FAX (310)396-4563.

LC HD9981.7.C2 C34 **ISSN** 0271-6615
DD 338.4/7/0025794 US
CALIFORNIA SERVICES REGISTER.
[Calif. serv. regist.]. 2nd Ed. (1981)-. Directory. English. One time a year (January). $172.00. Database Publishing Company, PO Box 7440, Newport Beach CA 92658. **Tel** (714)646-1623, (800)-888-8434, FAX (714)631-8471. Index Bound in First Issue. **Ad Acc, Adv Mgr:** D Pearce. **Circ:** 1,500 (ctrl). available on diskette. ***Continues*** *California Industrial Services Register, 0197-3347.*
Desc: Contains information on 20,000 California service businesses and 60,000 key executives by name and title.

ISSN 0961-0480
UK
CAMBRIDGE FUTURES CHARTS.
(19??)-. English. One time a week. $1694.09. Investment Research, 28 Panton Street, Cambridge CB2 1DH United Kingdom. **Tel** 011 44 1223 356251, FAX 011 44 1223 329806, telex 81247. **ED** Elli Gifford. ctrl circ.
Desc: Analysis and comprehensive charts covering all major international futures markets.

ISSN 0829-0814
DD 971/.005 CN
CANADA JOURNAL (DEUTSCHE AUSG.).
(CANADA JOURNAL.). [Can. j.]. (1983)- Vol. 11 (Jan. 1993)-. Periodical. German (English). Six times a year (Jan., Mar., May, July, Sept., Nov.). 20.81Can$. Canada Journal, 12 Lawton Boulevard, Toronto Ontario M4V 1Z4 Canada. **Tel** (416)485-5795, FAX (416)485-6354. **ED** Joseph Ruland (editor's phone: (416)927-9129). **Bk Rev**, (Qty: 8). **Ad Acc, Adv Mgr:** E. Tolles. **Circ:** 14,000 (ctrl).
Desc: Provides vacation and business information about Canada.

ISSN 0828-170X
DD 332.63/23/0971 CN
CANADIAN BOND PRICES.
[Can. bond prices]. **Added/Corp** Financial Post Corporation Service Group. Canadian Daily Quotation Service. 1st Ed. (1984)-. English. One time a year. 79.99Can$. Financial Post Company Ltd., 333 King Street East, Toronto Ontario M5A 4N2, Canada. **Tel** (416)350-6500, FAX (416)350-6601.
Desc: Lists monthly closing bid prices and yields for more than 900 Canadian federal, provincial and corporate debt issues.

CN
CANADIAN BUSINESS. 500.
VFOAT 500; Five Hundred. (June 1985)-. English. $3.50. CB Media Ltd., 777 Bay Street, Toronto Ontario M5W 1A7 Canada. **Tel** (416)596-5100, (416)596-5999, FAX (416)364-2783, (416)362-4505. ***Continues*** *Canadian Business. Top 500 Companies.*
Ind/Abst Can. Period. Index (19??-).

LC HF1 .C22 **ISSN** 0008-3100
DD 380.1/0971 CN
CCC
CODEN CABUAL
CANADIAN BUSINESS (1977).
(CANADIAN BUSINESS.). [Can. bus.]. Vol. 50 No. 9 (Sept. 1977)-. Periodical. English. Twelve times a year. 19.96Can$. CB Media Ltd., 777 Bay Street, Toronto Ontario M5W 1A7 Canada. **Tel** (416)596-5100, (416)596-5999, FAX (416)364-2783, (416)362-4505. **(Subscription address:** Indas Customer Service, 35 Riviera Drive, Building 17, Markham Ontario L3R 8N4 Canada. **Tel** (905)946-0406.**) ED** Randall Litchfield. **Ad Acc. Circ:** 85,000. available on microfiche from Micromedia Limited; available in microform from University Microfilms International (UMI). Documents available from UMI Article Clearinghouse, Ask*IEEE. ***Continues*** *Canadian Business Magazine, 0820-9529;* ***Absorbed*** *Energy (Calgary, Alta.), 0711-6381.*
Desc: Award-winning team of writers and artists bring readers in-depth, behind-the-scenes coverage of business in Canada. Features information on investment trends and opportunities; offers practical advice for big and small businesses; analyzes winning and losing business strategies; and profiles the enterprising personalities behind entrepreneurial success stories and corporate disasters alike.
Ind/Abst ABI/INFORM Glob. Ed.; ABI/INFORM [Computer File] (Sept. 1977-); Acad. Abstr. Full Text Elite; Acad. Abstr.; Acad. Search; BioBusiness (1986-); Bus. Index (1985-); Bus. Period. Index; Bus. Source Plus; Bus. Source; Can. Index; Can. Period. Index; Coal Abstr.; EP Collect.; Gen. BusinessFile (1985-); Gen. Period. Index (1985-); Homework Help.; INFO-SOUTH Abstr.; INSPEC (June 1983-); Mag. Artic. Summar. Elite; Mag. Artic. Summar. Select; Mag. Artic. Summar. CD-ROM; Mag. Index Plus (1989-); Mag. Search; Manage. Market. Abstr.; MasterFile FullTEXT 1000; MasterFile FullTEXT 350; MasterFile FullTEXT 650; MasterFile FullTEXT (Jan. 1990-) [Full Txt.]; Newsp. Period. Abstr. (1989-); OCLC; PAIS Int. Print (1991-); PROMT; Pub. Lib. FullTEXT; SPORT Discus; SportSearch; Telebase; Mag. Index (1983-)(1977-); Trade Ind. ASAP [Full Txt.]; Trade Ind. Index; Wilson Bus. Abstr.; Work Relat. Abstr.

ISSN 1082-3905
DD 338 US
CANADIAN BUSINESS & CURRENT AFFAIRS (CD-ROM).
(CANADIAN BUSINESS & CURRENT AFFAIRS [COMPUTER FILE].). [Can. bus. curr. aff.]. **VFOAT** Canadian Business and Current Affairs. (19??)-. English. Six times a year. Knight Ridder Information Inc., 2440 El Camino Real, Mountain View CA 94040. **Tel** (415)254-7000.

LC HC
DD 330 CN
CANADIAN BUSINESS CHARTBOOK.
Added/Corp Conference Board in Canada. 14th Ed.(1970)-. Periodical. English. One time a year. ***Continues*** *Chartbook of Current Business Trends in Canada.* ***Superseded in part by*** *Quarterly Business Indicators, 0319-3985.*

ISSN 0383-9893
DD 330.971/005 CN
CANADIAN BUSINESS CONDITIONS.
[Can. bus. cond.]. **Added/Corp** Canadian Imperial Bank of Commerce. Economics Division. Periodical. English. Canadian Imperial Bank of Commerce Economic Division, Commerce Court North, 7th Floor, Toronto Ontario M5L 1A2 Canada. **Tel** (416)980-2211, (416)980-3721. available on microfilm and microfiche from University Microfilms International (UMI); available on an online database (file 15/Full-Text) from DIALOG.
Ind/Abst Can. Period. Index.

LC HC111 **ISSN** 0705-8330
DD 330.9/71/0644 CN
CANADIAN BUSINESS ECONOMICS.
Added/Corp Canadian Association for Business Economics. No. 1 (1977)-. Periodical. English. Four times a year. 48.02Can$. Informetrica Limited, PO Box 828 Station B, Ottawa Ontario K1P 5P9 Canada. **Tel** (613)238-4831, FAX (613)238-7698.

LC HC111 .C1916 **ISSN** 0317-4026
DD 330.9/71/064 CN
CCC
CODEN CBREDT
CANADIAN BUSINESS REVIEW, THE.
[Can. bus. rev.]. Vol. 1 (Winter 1974)-. Periodical. English. Four times a year (Mar., June, Sept., Dec.). 40.39Can$. Conference Board of Canada, 255 Smyth Road, Ottawa Ontario K1H 8M7 Canada. **Tel** (613)526-3280, FAX (613)526-4857, telex 053-3034. **ED** S. Scott Hatfield. **Bk Rev. Circ:** 10,000 (ctrl). available on microfilm and microfiche from University Microfilms International (UMI); available on an online database (files 15,648/Full-Text) from DIALOG. Documents available from UMI Article Clearinghouse.
Desc: Provides a forum to examine and understand current trends and issues in the economy, management, public affairs and business both in Canada and internationally.
Ind/Abst ABI/INFORM Glob. Ed.; ABI/INFORM [Computer File] (Winter 1974-); Acad. Search; Bus. ASAP (1990-) [Full Txt.]; Bus. Index (1985-); Bus. Period. Index; Bus. Source Plus; Bus. Source; Contents Recent Econ. J.; Curr. Cit.; EP Collect.; F&S Index Plus Text, Int. [Select. Cov.]; Gen. BusinessFile (1985-); Gen. Period. Index (1985-); Homework Help.; INFO-SOUTH Abstr.; INIS Atomindex [Micro.]; Mag. Search; Manage. Contents; MasterFile FullTEXT 1000; MasterFile FullTEXT 350; MasterFile FullTEXT 650; MasterFile FullTEXT (July 1993-); OCLC; PAIS Int. Print; Person. Manage. Abstr.; Telebase; Trade Ind. ASAP [Full Txt.]; Trade Ind. Index (1981-) [Full Txt.]; UMI ABI/Inform--Bus. Period. Ondisc [Full Txt.]; Wilson Bus. Abstr.

ISSN 1192-845X
DD 016.330971 CN
CANADIAN BUSINESSDISC.
(CANADIAN BUSINESSDISC [COMPUTER FILE] = CD AFFAIRES.). [Can. bus.disc]. **Added/Corp** Societe Nationale d'Information. **VFOAT** Canadian Business Disc; CD Affaires. (1992)-. Periodical. English (French). Four times a year. 575.00Can$ community colleges, schools, and libraries; 975.00Can$ public libraries; 2020.00Can$ other. Southham Information & Technical Group Inc, 1450 Don Mills Road, Don Mills Ontario M3B 2X7 Canada. **Tel** (416)445-6641, (800)668-2374, FAX (416)442-2261. **(Subscription address:** Infomart on CD, 1450 Don Mills Road, Don Mills ONT M3B 2X7 Canada. **Tel** (416)445-6641.**)**

ISSN 0045-4575
DD 338.4762982 CN
CANADIAN COIN BOX MAGAZINE.
(CANADIAN COIN BOX.). [Can. coin box mag.]. (196?)-. Periodical. English. Ten times a year. 24.01Can$. NCC Publishing, 222 Argyle Avenue, Delhi Ontario N4B 2Y2 Canada. **Tel** (519)582-2513, FAX (519)582-4040. **Ad Acc, Adv Mgr:** Peter Wilkinson, **Tel** (416)271-1366.

LC KE1369 ISSN 1188-2026
DD 346.7106605 CN

CANADIAN CORPORATE COUNSEL. [Can. corp. couns.]. (1991)-. Periodical. English. Eight times a year (Jan., Mar., May, June, July, Sept., Oct., Nov.). 220.09Can$. Emond Montgomery Publiding Ltd., 58 Shaftesbury Avenue, Toronto Ontario, M4T 1A3 Canada. **Tel** (416)975-3925, FAX (416)975-3924. **Bk Rev.**

LC HC111 .C1975 ISSN 0835-9148
DD 330.971/0021 CN

CANADIAN ECONOMIC OBSERVER. [Can. econ. obs.]. **Added/Corp** Statistics Canada. **VFOAT** Observateur Economique Canadien. Vol. 1, No. 1 (Jan. 1988)-. Periodical. English (French). Twelve times a year. 264.00Can$. Statistics Canada Publications Sales and Services, R.H. Coats Building 6th Floor, Ottawa Ontario K1A 0T6 Canada. **Tel** (613)951-5078, (800)267-6677, FAX (613)951-1584, telex 053-3585. **Circ:** 3,400. ***Formed by the union of*** *Canadian Statistical Review (Ottawa, Ont.), 0008-509X; Revue Statistique du Canada, 0315-2073; Current Economic Indicators (Statistics Canada), 0828-0851; Quarterly Economic Summary, 0828-086X; Quarterly Economic Summary, Statistical Supplement, 0828-0878* ***and*** *Apercu Economique Trimestriel, Supplement Statistique, 0828-0894.*
Desc: A monthly publication for economic statistics. Each issue contains a monthly summary of the economy, major economic and statistical events, a feature article and technical note. A statistical summary contains a wide range of tables and graphs on the principle economic indicators for Canada, the provinces and the major industrial nations.
Ind/Abst Can. Period. Index (19??-); PAIS Int. Print (1991-).

LC HC ISSN 0008-3976
DD 338.1/0971 CN
CCC
Pr Rev.

CANADIAN JOURNAL OF AGRICULTURAL ECONOMICS. See Agriculture-Agricultural Economics.

LC HC111 .C225 ISSN 0008-4085
DD 330 CN
CCC
Pr Rev.

CANADIAN JOURNAL OF ECONOMICS, THE. [Can. j. econ.]. **Added/Corp** Canadian Economics Association. **VFOAT** Revue Canadienne d'Economique. Vol. 1 (Feb. 1968)-. Periodical. English (French). Four times a year (Feb., May, Aug., Nov.). 90.00Can$. University of Toronto Press, 5201 Dufferin Street, Downsview Ontario M3H 5T8 Canada. **Tel** (416)667-7781, (416)667-7810, FAX (416)667-7881. **ED** Lorne Carmichael. **Ad Acc.** available on microfilm and microfiche from University Microfilms International (UMI). Documents available from The Genuine Article, UMI Article Clearinghouse. ***Supersedes in part*** *Canadian Journal of Economics and Political Science., 0315-4890.*
Desc: Publishes original and significant contributions in all areas of economics. Papers range across the purely theoretical, the applied, the historical and the policy-oriented. Widely recognized internationally, it also publishes timely articles pertinent to problems of the Canadian economy.
Ind/Abst ABI/INFORM Glob. Ed.; ABI/INFORM [Computer File] (Nov. 1978-); Acad. Abstr.; Acad. Search; AGRICOLA; Bus. Index (1985-); Bus. Source Plus; Bus. Source; Can. Period. Index; Curr. Cit.; Curr. Contents Soc. Behav. Sci.; Econ. Lit. Index; EP Collect.; Expand. Acad. Index (1984-); Gen. BusinessFile (1985-); Gen. Period. Index (1985-); Homework Help.; Hum. Resour. Abstr.; INFO-SOUTH Abstr.; Int. Bibliogr. Sociol.; Int. Labour Doc.; J. Econ. Lit.; J. Plan. Lit.; Mag. Search; MasterFile FullTEXT 1000; MasterFile FullTEXT 350; MasterFile FullTEXT 650; MasterFile FullTEXT (Jan. 1992-); Newsp. Period. Abstr. (1991-); OCLC; PAIS Int. Print (1991-); Pub. Lib. FullTEXT; Res. Alert [Full Cov.]; Soc. Sci. Source; Soc. Sci. Cit. Index [Full Cov.]; Soc. Sci. Index; Soc. Sci. Index Fulltext (Nov. 1988-) [Full Txt.]; Telebase; Work Relat. Abstr.

ISSN 1187-919X
DD 382/.097105/05 CN

•CANADIAN MAPLE LEAF MAGAZINE. (1994)-. Periodical. English. Twelve times a year. First Generation Financial Group, Suite 850, 999 West Hastings Street, Vancouver British Columbia V6C 2W2 Canada. ***Continues*** *Canadian Maple Leaf Report, 1187-919X.*

ISSN 1187-919X
DD 382/.097105/05 CN
TITLE CHANGE

CANADIAN MAPLE LEAF REPORT, THE. [Can. maple leaf rep.]. **Added/Corp** First Generation Financial Group. (1992)-(199?). Periodical. English. First Generation Financial Group, Suite 850, 999 West Hastings Street, Vancouver British Columbia V6C 2W2 Canada. ***Continues*** *The Canadian Maple Leaf Business Report., 1187-7375.* ***Continued by*** *Canadian Maple Leaf Magazine, 1202-5887.*

ISSN 1195-1729
DD 658/.048/05 CN

•CANADIAN NOT-FOR-PROFIT NEWS. [Can. not-profit news]. **VFOAT** Not-for-profit News. Vol. 1, No. 1 (July 1993)-. Periodical. English. Twelve times a year. 135.00Can$. Carswell / Canada, 2075 Kennedy Road, Scarborough Ontario M1T 3V4 Canada. **Tel** (416)298-5092, (800)387-5164, FAX (416)298-5094.

ISSN 0832-0500
DD 330.971/0647/05 CN

CANADIAN OUTLOOK, EXECUTIVE SUMMARY. [Can. outlook exec. summ.]. **Added/Corp** Conference Board of Canada. (Oct. 1985)-. Periodical. English. Four times a year. Conference Board of Canada, 255 Smyth Road, Ottawa Ontario K1H 8M7 Canada. **Tel** (613)526-3280, FAX (613)526-4857, telex 053-3034. ***Continues*** *Quarterly Canadian Forecast. Executive Summary, 0829-1128.*

LC HC111 .C28 ISSN 0317-0861
DD 338.971/005 CN
CCC
Pr Rev.

CANADIAN PUBLIC POLICY. [Can. public policy]. **VFOAT** Analyse de Politiques. Vol. 1 (Winter 1975)-. Periodical. English (French). Four times a year. 53.85Can$. Canadian Public Policy, Room 039/MacKinnon Building, University of Guelph, Guelph Ontario N1G 2W1 Canada. **Tel** (519)824-4120 ext.3330, FAX (519)837-9953. **ED** Nancy Olewiler. Index available. cum. index. **Bk Rev**, (Qty: 4). **Ad Acc, Adv Mgr:** J.R. Vanderkamp. **Circ:** 2,000. available on microfiche from Micromedia Limited; available on microfilm and microfiche from University Microfilms International (UMI). Documents available from The Genuine Article, UMI Article Clearinghouse.
Desc: Covers economic and social policy in Canada. Provides a forum for discussion of ideas and results of research for criticism of policy and policy proposals. Features government reports and budgets.
Ind/Abst ABI/INFORM Glob. Ed.; ABI/INFORM [Computer File] (March 1988); Acad. Search; Am. Hist. Life (1983-); Can. Index; Can. Period. Index; Contents Recent Econ. J.; Curr. Cit.; Curr. Contents Soc. Behav. Sci.; Econ. Lit. Index; EP Collect.; Geogr. Abstr. Human Geogr.; Homework Help.; Hum. Resour. Abstr. (?-?); Index Can. Leg. Period. Lit.; Int. Dev. Abstr.; Int. Polit. Sci. Abstr.; J. Econ. Lit.; Leis., Rec., Tour. Abstr.; Linguist. Lang. Behav. Abstr.; MasterFile FullTEXT 1000; MasterFile FullTEXT 350; MasterFile FullTEXT 650; MasterFile FullTEXT (July 1994-); Middle East Abstr. Index; OCLC; PAIS Int. Print (1991-); Res. Alert [Full Cov.]; Rural Dev. Abstr.; Sage Public Adm. Abstr.; Sage Race Relat. Abstr.; Sage Urban Stud. Abstr (?-?); Soc. Plann. Policy Dev. Abstr.; Soc. Sci. Source; Soc. Sci. Cit. Index [Full Cov.]; Sociol. Abstr.; Telebase; Vocat. Search; World Agric. Econ. Rural Sociol. Abstr.

ISSN 1195-8650
DD 333.79/4/097105 CN

•CANADIAN RENEWABLE ENERGY NEWS (PINK MOUNTAIN). (CANADIAN RENEWABLE ENERGY NEWS.). [Can. renew. energy news]. **Added/Corp** Northern Alternate Power Systems. **VFOAT** R.E.N. Issue #4 (Summer 1993)-. Periodical. English. Four times a year. 11.89Can$. Renewable Energy News / Canadian Edition, PO Box 14, Pink Mountain British Columbia VOC2B0 Canada. **Tel** (604)774-1088. ***Continues*** *Renewable Energy News (Pink Mountain, B.C.), 1199-6471.*

CN

CANADIAN TREND PERSPECTIVES. (19??)-. Newsletter. English. One time a week. 195.00Can$ Canada; 296.17Can$ (postage included) other. Hencor Publications, PO Box 5057 Station A, Toronto Ontario M52 1N4 Canada. **Tel** (416)869-7299. **ED** Henry Cieszynski. **Circ:** not disclosed.
Desc: Highlights key trends from a fundamental point of view.

LC HD ISSN 1181-3385
DD 338.7/4/0971 CN

CANCORP DOCUMENTS SERVICE. (1990)-. Periodical. English. Micromedia Limited, 20 Victoria Street, Toronto Ontario M5C 2N8 Canada. **Tel** (416)362-5211, (800)387-2689, FAX (416)362-6161, telex 06524668. ***Continues*** *Insider (Toronto, Ont.)., 0820-8905.*

ISSN 1162-6704
FR

CAPITAL. (1991)-. French. Twelve times a year. $60.59. Prisma Presse, 6 rue Daru, 75379 Paris Cedex 08 France. **Tel** 011 33 1 44153000, FAX 011 33 1 47641042. **(Subscription address:** Captial Service Abonnements, B 190, 60732 S Genevieve Cedex 9 France. **Tel** 011 33 44895300.) **ED** Remy Dessarts. **Ad Acc.**
Desc: Articles cover both macroeconomics and microeconomics.

LC HB97.5 .C315 ISSN 0309-8168
DD 335.4/05 UK

CAPITAL & CLASS. [Cap. & cl.]. **Added/Corp** Conference of Socialist Economists. **VFOAT** Capital and Class. No. 1 (Spring 1977)-. Periodical. English. Three times a year (Feb., June, Oct.). $105.00. Conference Socialist Economist, 25 Horsell Road, London N5 1XL United Kingdom. **Tel** 011 44 181 6079615. **Bk Rev. Ad Acc. Circ:** 2,000. available on microfilm and microfiche from University Microfilms International (UMI). Documents available from UMI Article Clearinghouse. ***Supersedes*** *Conference of Socialist Economists. Bulletin of the Conference of Socialist Economists.*
Desc: The journal of the Conference of Socialist Economists. Committed to the development of a materialist critique of capitalism in the Marxist tradition.
Ind/Abst Altern. Press Index; Curr. Cit.; Expand. Acad. Index (1989-); INFO-SOUTH Abstr.; Int. Bibliogr. Sociol.; Left Index; Linguist. Lang. Behav. Abstr.; Mag. Search; MasterFile FullTEXT (Jan. 1992-); Newsp. Period. Abstr. (1991-); Soc. Plann. Policy Dev. Abstr.; Soc. Sci. Index; Soc. Sci. Index Fulltext (Summer 1988-) [Full Txt.]; Sociol. Abstr.; Stud. Women Abstr.

LC HC
GW

CAPITAL; DAS DEUTSCHE WIRTSCHAFTS MAGAZIN. (19??)-. Periodical. German. Twelve times a year. Gruner und Jahr Ag & Co, Abonnenten Service, D-20080 Hamburg Germany. **Tel** 011 49 40 37030, FAX 011 49 40 37035657.

ISSN 0747-3699
US
CCC

CAPITAL DISTRICT BUSINESS REVIEW. **VFOAT** Business Review. Vol. 10, No. 12 (Feb. 1984)-. Periodical. English. One time a week. $53.00. Capital District Business Review, PO Box 15081, Albany NY 12212. **Tel** (518)437-9855. **ED** Marlene Kennedy. **Ad Acc. Circ:** 10400. available on microfilm from University Microfilms International (UMI); available on an online database (files 635,648/Full-Text) from DIALOG. Documents available from UMI Article Clearinghouse. ***Continues*** *Business Review, 0192-527X.*
Ind/Abst Acad. Search; Bus. Dateline; Bus. Index (Jan. 1985-Dec. 1985); Bus. Source Plus; Bus. Source; EP Collect.; Gen. BusinessFile (Jan. 1985-Dec. 1985); Gen. Period. Index (Jan. 1985-Dec. 1985); Homework Help.; INFO-SOUTH Abstr.; MasterFile FullTEXT 1000; MasterFile FullTEXT 350; MasterFile FullTEXT 650; MasterFile FullTEXT (July 1993-); OCLC; PROMT; Telebase; Trade Ind. ASAP [Full Txt.]; Trade Ind. Index [Full Txt.].

SP

CAPITAL HUMANO. (19??)-. Spanish. Twelve times a year. 19000.00ptas Spain; 19069.00ptas other. Groupo Especial Directivos, Orense 39, 28020 Madrid Spain. **Tel** 011 34 91 556-6411, FAX 011 34 91 555-5118. **(Subscription address:** Capital Humano, C Orense 39, 28020 Madrid, Spain. **Tel** 011 34 1 5566411.)

ISSN 0891-9836
DD 330 US

CAPITAL JOURNAL (ALBANY, N.Y.). (CAPITAL JOURNAL.). [Cap. j.]. **Added/Corp** Business Council of New York State. (198?)-. Periodical. English. Irregular. Business Council of New York State, 152 Washington Avenue, Albany NY 12210-2289. **Tel** (518)465-7511, (800)692-5483.

IT

CAPITAL (MILAN, ITALY). (CAPITAL.). (19??)-. Periodical. Italian. Twelve times a year. $143.00. RCS Rizzoli Periodici, Via A Rizzoli 2, 20132 Milan Italy. **Tel** 011 39 2 27200720.

IT
CEASED

CAPITALE SUD. Vol. 1, No. 1 (Nov. 1987)-Vol. 7, No. 25 (1993). Periodical. Italian. Capitale Sud Spa, Corso Italia 22, 20122 Milan Italy.

ISSN 0954-8564
DD 332.76 UK

CARD WORLD. [Card world]. (1988)-. Periodical. English. Twelve times a year. $675.93. Card World Publications Ltd., PO Box 222, Weybridge Surrey KT13 8YL United Kingdom. **Tel** 011 44 1932 841688, FAX 011 44 1932 845542.

ISSN 0956-5558
US

CARDS INTERNATIONAL. (CARDS INTERNATIONAL : THE WORLDWIDE BRIEFING ON THE PLASTIC CARD INDUSTRY.). [Cards int.]. (1989)-. Trade Publication. English. Six times a year (23 issues). $879.00. Lafferty Publications Ltd., Tower Ida Centre Pearse Street, Dublin 2 Ireland. **Tel** 011 353 1 6718022, FAX 011 353 1 718520. **ED** Michael Lafferty, Steve Ledford. **Bk Rev. Circ:** 1,000.
Desc: Worldwide briefing on the plastic card industry.

US

CAREERS AND THE MBA. **Added/Corp** Harvard University. Graduate School of Business Administration. **VAT** Careers and the Masters in Business Administration. (19??)-. English. Two times a year (Feb. & Oct.). $14.95. Adams Media Corporation, 260 Center Street, Holbrook MA 02343. **Tel** (617)767-8100, (800)872-5627, FAX (617)767-0994. **ED** Gigi Ranno.

LC HC **ISSN** 0576-7334
DD 371.4 US
CAREERS IN BUSINESS. See Occupations and Careers.

ISSN 0968-2732
UK
•CARIBBEAN AND CENTRAL AMERICA REPORT. **VFOAT** Caribbean Report; Central America Report; Latin American Regional Reports. Caribbean and Central America report; Caribbean & Central America Report; Caribbean and Central America Report. (Jan. 21, 1993)-. Periodical. English. Ten times a year. $185.00. Lettres UK Ltd, 61 Old Street, London EC1V 9HX United Kingdom. **Tel** 011 44 171 2510012, FAX 011 44 171 2538193. available on an online database from Lexis-Nexis. ***Continues in part*** *Latin America Regional Reports. Caribbean, 0143-523X* ***and*** *Latin America Regional Reports. Mexico & Central America.*

ISSN 0194-8326
US
CARIBBEAN BUSINESS. [Caribb. bus.]. (1973)-. Periodical. English. One time a week (51 issues). $45.00. Casiano Communications, PO Box 12130, Loiza St. Station, San Juan Puerto Rico 00914. **Tel** (809)728-3000, (800)462-2185, FAX (809)268-1001, (809)728-7325. **ED** Mr. Sergio Camero. **Ad Acc, Adv Mgr:** Patricia Eaves. **Circ:** 45,000. available on an online database (file 648/Full-Text) from DIALOG.
Desc: Concentrates on the finanical news in the caribbean region and surrounding areas.
Ind/Abst Acad. Search; Bus. Index (Jan. 1985-Dec. 1985); Bus. Source Plus; Bus. Source; EP Collect.; Gen. BusinessFile (Jan. 1985-Dec. 1985); Gen. Period. Index (Jan. 1985-Dec. 1985); Homework Help.; INFO-SOUTH Abstr.; MasterFile FullTEXT 1000; MasterFile FullTEXT 350; MasterFile FullTEXT 650; MasterFile FullTEXT (July 1993-); OCLC; PROMT; Telebase.

LC HF3351 .C35
DD 330./025/7299 PR
CARIBBEAN BUSINESS TO BUSINESS GUIDE. **VFOAT** Business to Business Guide.; Official Business Guide to Puerto Rico. (1988)-. English. One time a year. $12.00. Casiano Communications, PO Box 12130, Loiza St. Station, San Juan Puerto Rico 00914. **Tel** (809)728-3000, (800)462-2185, FAX (809)268-1001, (809)728-7325. ***Continues*** *Caribbean Business, 0194-8326.*

ISSN 1061-3897
DD 338 US
SUSPENDED
CARIBBEAN RESOURCE MAGAZINE. [Caribb. resour. mag.]. Vol. 1, No. 1 (Jan-Mar 1992)-Suspended (199?). Periodical. English. Six times a year. Free. Caribbean Resource Magazine, 12855 SW 136th Avenue, Suite 221, Miami FL 33186.

ISSN 8756-324X
DD 917 US
CCC
CARIBBEAN UPDATE. [Caribb. update]. (1985)-. Periodical. English. Twelve times a year. $188.00. Mexico Business Monthly, 52 Maples Avenue, Department M, Maplewood NJ 07040. **Tel** (201)762-1565, (800)766-3949, FAX (201)762-9585. **ED** Kal Wagenheim. **Bk Rev. Circ:** 1,000. available on an online database (file 636/Full-Text) from DIALOG.
Desc: Focuses on business and economic news in Central America and Caribbean.
Ind/Abst F&S Index Plus Text, Int. [Select. Cov.]; PROMT.

AQ
CARIBBEAN YELLOW PAGES. **VFOAT** Caribbean Business Telephone Directory; Caribbean Yellow Pages Telephone Directory; A.Caribbean Publishing Company's Caribbean yellow pages. (1990)-. English. Irregular. Caribbean Publshing Company, 9500 South Dadeland Boulevard, Suite 500, Miami FL 33156. ***Continues*** *Caribbean Business Directory (George Town, Cayman Islands : 1987).*

LC HC151.A1 C375
DD 337.1/729/05 GY
CARICOM PERSPECTIVE. **Added/Corp** Caribbean Community. Secretariat. **VFOAT** Caribbean Community in the 1980's. No. 1 (March 1980)-. Periodical. English. Six times a year. Free on request. Caribbean Community Secretariat, PO Box 10827, Bank of Guyana Building, Georgetown Guyana. **Tel** 011 592 2 69281-9, FAX 011 592 2 67816, 011 592 2 58039, telex 2263 CARISEC GY. **Bk Rev. Circ:** 6,000 (ctrl).
Desc: Reports on the work achievements and problems of the 13-nation Caribbean Community.
Ind/Abst LABORDOC.

ISSN 0890-7609
DD 658 US
CARN (CHICAGO, ILL.). (CARN : THE CORPORATE ANNUAL REPORT NEWSLETTER.). [CARN]. **VFOAT** Corporate Annual Report Newsletter. (19??)-. Newsletter. English. Twelve times a year. $329.00. Ragan Communications Inc., 212 West Superior Street, Suite 200, Chicago IL 60610. **Tel** (312)335-0037, (800)878-5331, FAX (312)335-9583.
Desc: Designed to aid those responsible for creating, designing and editing their company's annual report.

LC HD87 .C37 **ISSN** 0167-2231
DD 338.9 NE
CCC
Pr Rev.
CARNEGIE-ROCHESTER CONFERENCE SERIES ON PUBLIC POLICY. [Carnegie-Rochester conf. ser. public policy]. **Added/Corp** University of Rochester. Center for Research in Government Policy and Business. Carnegie-Mellon University. Graduate School of Industrial Administration. William E. Simon Graduate School of Business Administration. Vol. 1 (1976)-. Academic Scholarly Publication. English. Two times a year (2 volumes). $195.00. Elsevier Science Publishers BV, PO Box 211, 1000 AE Amsterdam Netherlands. **Tel** 011 31 20 4853641, 011 31 20 4853642, FAX 011 31 20 4853598. **ED** Karl Brunner, Allan Meltzer. available on microfilm and microfiche from University Microfilms International (UMI); available on an online database from Elsevier Electronic Subscriptions (EES). Documents available from UMI Article Clearinghouse.
Desc: Surveys selected policy problems and explores the nature and weight of important issues confronting policy makers.
Ind/Abst ABI/INFORM Glob. Ed.; ABI/INFORM [Computer File] (1980); Contents Recent Econ. J.; Curr. Cit.; Econ. Lit. Index; J. Econ. Lit.

US
CAROLINA BUSINESS & FINANCE. (19??)-. Periodical. English. Twelve times a year. Fortune Media Inc, PO Box 36639, Charlotte NC 28236-6639. **Tel** (704)332-0148, FAX (704)332-0165.

LC HB **ISSN** 1245-0820
DD 338 FR
UDC 338(47+57)
CODEN 339.96
•CARREFOURS FRANCE-RUSSIE. (1993)-. Periodical. French. Twelve times a year. CCFS, 22 Ave F D Roosevelt, F-75008 Paris France. **Tel** 011 33 1 42259710.

LC HD38.25.B7 C27
BL
•CARTA CAPITAL. No. 1 (Aug. 1994)-. Portuguese. Twelve times a year. Carta Editorial Ltda., avenue de Basil 1456, CEP 01430 Sao Paulo Brazil. **Tel** 011 55 11 2677988.

ISSN 0187-7674
MX
CARTA ECONOMICA REGIONAL : CER. **Added/Corp** Universidad de Guadalajara. Instituto de Estudios Economicos y Regionales. **VFOAT** CER. (198?)-. Periodical. Spanish. Six times a year. Instituto de Estudios Economicos y Regionales, Universidad de Guadalajara, Avs. Alcalde y Maestros, Tercer Piso del Edificio de la Facultad de Derecho, Aptdo. 2-738, 44280 Guadalajara Jalisco Mexico.
Ind/Abst PAIS Int. Print.

HO
CARTA INFORMATIVA. **Main/Corp** Nicaragua. Secretaria de Informacion y Prensa. (19??)-. Periodical. Spanish. Irregular. Banco Centroamericano de Intergracion Economica, Apartado Postal 772, Tegucigalpa Honduras.

LC HD9506.V4 A33
VE
SUSPENDED
CARTA SEMANAL. **Added/Corp** Venezuela. Ministerio de Energia y Minas. Direccion de Informacion y Relaciones. (19??)- Suspended (199?). Periodical. Spanish. One time a week. ***Continues*** *Venezuela. Ministerio de Energia y Minas. Carta Semanal - Ministerio de Energia y Minas.*

ISSN 0731-4507
US
CASH MANAGEMENT ANALYST, THE. [Cash manage. anal.]. (Feb. 1983)-. Periodical. English. Fifteen times a year. $245.00. Card Research Inc., PO Box 514, Forest Hills NY 11375. **Tel** (212)263-2084.

US
CATALIST BUSINESS AND HOUSEHOLD DIGEST OF ITHACA. **Added/Corp** US West Marketing Resources (Firm). **VFOAT** Business and Household Digest of Ithaca; Catalist Business and Household Digest Ithaca, New York. (1991)-. English. ***Continues*** *Ithaca, New York City Directory.*

LC HF5483 .C38 **ISSN** 0069-1011
DD 381 US
CATALOG FOR COLLEGE STORES, THE. [Cat. coll. stores]. 1970-. Catalog. English. One time a year. College Store Catalog, Inc., 299 Madison Avenue, New York NY 10017.

LC HF5465.5 .C37 **ISSN** 1042-6167
DD 381/.142/02573 US
CATALOG HANDBOOK. [Cat. handb.]. (Summer 1989)-. Catalog. English. Four times a year (Seasonally). $19.95. Enterprise Magazines Inc., 1020 North Broadway, Suite 111, Milwaukee WI 53202. **Tel** (414)272-9977, FAX (414)272-9973. **ED** Micheal McDermott. Index available. **Ad Acc, Adv Mgr:** Andrea Freedman, **Tel** (414)272-9977. **Circ:** 55,000.
Desc: Contains all pertinent information about all known mail order catalogs available to the public. It is indexed both alphabetically by business category and alphabetically by company name. It contains information on over 5,000 available catalogs and useful articles.

IT
CATALOGO GENERALE DELLE ASTE: SOTHEBY'S. (19??)-. Italian. Eight times a year. L235295. Sothebys Italia, Via Broggi 19 Pal Broggi, 20122 Milan Italy. **Tel** 011 39 2 295001.

LC HG4528 .C37 **ISSN** 0742-6534
US
CEASED
CATALYST (MONTPELIER, VT.). (CATALYST.). **Added/Corp** Center for Economic Revitalization (U.S.) Institute for Gaean Economics. (Feb./Mar. 1984)-(Mar. 1993). Periodical. English. Catalyst, PO Box 1308, Montpelier VT 05601. **Tel** (802)223-7943. **Bk Rev**, (Qty: 8-10/yr). **Ad Acc.**
Desc: Ecological, community-based economics with articles on actual enterprises in the US and around the world. Also articles on corporate (lack of) accountability.

LC HB3711 .C386
DD 338.542 US
CAUSE AND CONTROL OF THE BUSINESS CYCLE. (1932)-. Monographic series. English. American Institute for Economic Research, Division Street, Great Barrington MA 01230. **Tel** (413)528-1216, FAX (413)528-0103.

LC HF3349.C3 A2a
DD 338/.097292/1 BF
CAYMAN ISLANDS HANDBOOK AND BUSINESSMAN'S GUIDE. (19??)-. English. British West Indies Northwester, PO Box 243, Grand Cayman, Georgetown Bahamas.

ISSN 0715-5956
DD 705 CN
CBAC NEWS. See The Arts-Art.

US
CBEF REVIEW OF THE COLORADO ECONOMY. FORECAST SUMMARY, THE. **Added/Corp** University of Denver. Center for Business and Economic Forecasting. **VFOAT** Review of the Colorado Economy. Forecast Summary; Forecast Summary. (19??)-. Periodical. English. Four times a year. Colorado Business and Economic Forecasting, University of Denver, Center for Business and Economic Forecasting, Denver CO.

ISSN 0199-686X
US
CBIA NEWS. **Main/Corp** Connecticut Business and Industry Association. **VFOAT** CBIANews. **VAT** Connecticut Business and Industry Association News. Vol. 55 No. 10 (Oct. 1977)-. Periodical. English. Ten times a year. $9.00. Connecticut Business and Industry Association, 370 Asylum Street, Hartford CT 06103. **Tel** (203)547-1661, FAX (203) 278-8562. **ED** Diane Friend Edwards (editor's telephone: 203-244-1900). **Ad Acc. Circ:** 8,000. available on microfilm from University Microfilms International (UMI). ***Continues*** *CBI Magazine.*
Desc: Newspaper covering business, economics, investments, etc.

LC HC59.69 .C46a
DD 330 DK
CDR IN ... . **Main/Corp** Centret for Udviklingsforskning (Denmark). (1985-1986)-. English. One time a year. Free. Centre for Development Research, Gammel Kongeuej 5, DK-1610 Copenhagen Denmark. **Tel** 011 45 33 251200, FAX 011 45 33 258110. **Bk Rev. Ad Acc. Circ:** 2,000 (ctrl). ***Continues*** *Centret for Udviklingsforskning (Denmark). CDR Annual Report.*
Desc: A report on the research activities performed and publications issued.

LC HC307.A4 C4
DD 330.945/14/005 IT
CE.D.R.E.S. DOCUMENTI. See Business and Economics-Abstracting, Bibliographies and Statistics.

ISSN 0008-9958
MX
CEMLA BOLETIN MENSUEL. **Main/Corp** Centro de Estudios Monetarios Latinoamericanos. (1955)-. Periodical. Spanish. Twelve times a year. Centro Estudios Monetarios Latinoamericanos (CEMLA), Durango 54, 06700 Mexico DF Mexico. **Tel** 011 52 5

Business and Economics

5330300, FAX 011 52 5 2072847, telex 1771229. **Continues** Boletin Quincenal. Suplemento. **Ind/Abst** PAIS Int. Print.

IT
CENSIS : NOTE E COMMENTI. (19??)-. Italian. Twelve times a year. L75000. Censis, Piazza Di Novella 2, 00199 Rome Italy. **Tel** 011 39 6 860911. **Circ:** 5000.

LC HF3901.Z8 L423
DD 338.09682
SA
CENSUS OF BUSINESSES, PROFESSIONS, AND TRADES, NATIONAL STATES LEBOWA. **Added/Corp** South Africa. Dept. of Statistics. **VFOAT** Sensus van Besighede, Beroepe en Handelsbedrywe, Nasionale State Lebowa. (1980)-. Afrikaans (English). Government Printer / South Africa, Bosman Street, Private Bag X85, Pretoria 0001 South Africa. **Tel** 011 27 12 3239731 ext. 262.

ISSN 0967-8689
DD 958
UK
SUSPENDED
CENTRAL ASIA AND THE CAUCASUS IN WORLD AFFAIRS. [Cent. Asia Cauc. World Aff.]. (1992)-Suspended (November 1994). Periodical. English. Twelve times a year. Arguments & Facts International, PO Box 35, Hastings East Sussex, TN34 2UX United Kingdom. **Tel** 011 44 1424 444142, FAX 011 44 1424 717498.
Desc: Opportunities for the cultivation and growth of commercial links, whether import-export, joint ventures or other investment projects.

ISSN 1053-9263
DD 330
US
CENTRAL BUSINESS REVIEW. [Cent. bus. rev.]. **Added/Corp** University of Central Oklahoma. College of Business Administration. **VFOAT** Business Review. Vol. 10, No. 2 (Summer 1991)-. Periodical. English. Two times a year. Free. Central State University / Oklahoma, 100 North University Drive, Edmond OK 73034. **Tel** (405)341-2980 ext.2821. **Continues** Central State Business Review, 8756-4521.

ISSN 1058-3599
DD 330
US
CENTRAL PENN BUSINESS JOURNAL. [Cent. Penn bus. j.]. (Feb. 1988)-. Trade Publication. English. Fifty-two times a year. $49.95. CPNC Inc., 1500 North 2nd Street, Harrisburg PA 17102. available on an online database (file 635/Full-Text) from DIALOG. Documents available from UMI Article Clearinghouse. **Continues** Strictly Business.
Ind/Abst Bus. Dateline (June 1990-) [Full Txt.].

LC HC244.A1 C46
ISSN 0749-6508
DD 338.5/443/091717
US
CENTRALLY PLANNED ECONOMIES OUTLOOK. (19??)-. English. Two times a year. $16,000. Wharton Centrally Planned Economies Service, Wharton Econometric Forecasting Associates Inc, 1110 Vermont Avenue NW/Suite 1100, Washington DC 20005. **Tel** (202)775-0610, FAX (202)833-3673. **Ad Acc.** ctrl circ.

US
CEO UPDATE. (19??)-. Periodical. English. Twelve times a year. Free on request to qualified subscribers. Securities Industry Association, 120 Broadway/35th Floor, New York NY 10271. **Tel** (212)608-1500, FAX (212)608-1604. ctrl circ.
Desc: Designed to address the information overload faced by CEOs. Provides capsules on selected developments that could affect the business of SIA members.

LC WMLC 93/428
ISSN 0898-4328
DD 330
US
CEP RESEARCH REPORT. (RESEARCH REPORT.). [CEP res. rep.]. **Added/Corp** Council on Economic Priorities. **VFOAT** CEP Research Report. **VAT** Council on Economic Priorities Research Report. (Sept. 1987)-. Periodical. English. Twelve times a year. Council on Economic Priorities, 30 Irving Place, New York NY 10003. **Tel** (212)420-1133, FAX (212)420-0988. **Circ:** 4,500 (ctrl). **Continues** Newsletter (Council on Economic Priorities), 8755-3538.
Desc: Highlights immediate policy concerns. It provides updated information and evaluates recent developments in such areas as corporate social responsibility, national security, arms control, energy and the environment.

LC HC270.2 .C47
DD 330
XR
●**CESKOMORAVSKY PROFIT.** (1993)-. Periodical. Czech. One time a week. $222.62. Ringier CR AS, Domazlicka 11, 13089 Prague 2 Czech Republic. **Tel** 011 42 2 6440066. **Continues** Cesky a Slovensky Profit.

LC HC
DD 330
PR
CETERIS PARIBUS. **Added/Corp** University of Puerto Rico (Mayaguez Campus). Dept. of Economics. Vol. 1, No. 1 (Apr. 1991)-. Periodical. Spanish (English). Two times a year. $20.00 individuals; $25.00 institutions.

Universidad de Puerto Rico / Departamento de Economia, Box 5000, Mayaguez Puerto Rico, 00709-50000.
Ind/Abst PAIS Int. Print.

LC HF5439.D75 C52
ISSN 0164-9914
DD 338
US
CHAIN DRUG REVIEW. [Chain drug rev.]. Vol. 1, No. 1 (Sept. 11, 1978)-. Periodical. English. Twenty-four times a year. $59.00. Racher Press, 220 Fifth Avenue, New York NY 10001. **Tel** (212)213-6000, FAX (212)213-6106. **Ad Acc. Circ:** 43,000 (ctrl). available on an online database (file 648/Full-Text) from DIALOG.
Desc: Serves the chain drug store retailing community. Articles cover business (sales and earnings), competition, new products, trends, and people in the industry.
Ind/Abst F&S Index Plus Text, Int. [Select. Cov.]; PROMT; Trade Ind. ASAP [Full Txt.]; Trade Ind. Index [Full Txt.].

LC HC
ISSN 0577-5132
DD 330
US
CODEN CHLGBB
CHALLENGE (WHITE PLAINS). (CHALLENGE.). [Challenge]. **Added/Corp** New York University. Institute of Economic Affairs. Vol. 2, No. 5 (Feb. 1954)-. Periodical. English. Six times a year. $97.00. M. E. Sharpe Inc., 80 Business Park Drive, Armonk NY 10504. **Tel** (914)273-1800, (800)541-6563, FAX (914)273-2106. **ED** Richard D. Bartel. **Bk Rev. Ad Acc.** 4,500 (ctrl). Documents available from UMI Article Clearinghouse. **Continues** Challenge Magazine.
Desc: The magazine of economic affairs. Written in a clear, readable style for everyone concerned about the how's and why's of today's economy. Covers both the domestic and international scene. Contains penetrating commentary written by the people who are shaping today's economic environment - top economists, labor leaders, business and government decision makers. In-depth analysis sets 'Challenge' apart from other publications on economic affairs. Examines the historical and political background of changes in the economy - the events, the issues, and the controversies behind the headlines.
Ind/Abst ABI/INFORM Glob. Ed.; ABI/INFORM [Computer File] (Sept. 1973-); Acad. Abstr. Full Text Elite; Acad. Abstr.; Acad. Search; Bus. ASAP (1992-) [Full Txt.]; Bus. Period. Index; Curr. Cit.; Econ. Lit. Index (199?-); Energy Res. Abstr. (Feb. 1977-); EP Collect.; Homework Help.; Humanit. Source; INFO-SOUTH Abstr.; INIS Atomindex [Micro.]; J. Econ. Lit.; Mag. Search; MasterFile FullTEXT 1000; MasterFile FullTEXT 350; MasterFile FullTEXT 650; MasterFile FullTEXT (July 1990-) [Full Txt.]; Newsp. Period. Abstr. (1988-); OCLC; PAIS Int. Print (1991-); Pub. Lib. FullTEXT; Soc. Sci. Source; Soc. Sci. Index; Soc. Sci. Index Fulltext (Nov. 1988-) [Full Txt.]; Telebase; Trade Ind. ASAP [Full Txt.]; Trade Ind. Index (1981-) [Full Txt.]; UMI ABI/Inform--Bus. Period. Ondisc (Nov. 1987-) [Full Txt.]; Vocat. Search; Wilson Bus. Abstr.; Work Relat. Abstr.

FR
CHALLENGES : LE PLUS EUROPEEN DES MAGAZINES DE L'ENTREPRISE. (19??)-. French. Twelve times a year. 293.83F France; 385.00F other. Challenges, 10 12 place de la Bourse, 75002 Paris France. **Tel** 011 33 1 44883403.
(Subscription address: Challenges, 8 rue d'Aboukir, 75002 Paris France. **Tel** 011 33 43425800.)
Ind/Abst LABORDOC.

LC T58.7
ISSN 1042-0088
DD 338
US
CHALLENGES (WASHINGTON, D.C. 1987). (CHALLENGES.). [Challenges]. **Added/Corp** Council on Competitiveness (U.S.). Vol. 1, No. 1 (Nov. 1987)-. Periodical. English. Ten times a year. $50.00. Council of Competitiveness, 900 17th Street Northwest, Suite 1050, Washington DC 20006. **Tel** (202)662-8760 or 785-3990.
Desc: Developments affecting the American competitiveness from public policy to private action in the US and around the world.

FR
CHAMPAGNE ECONOMIQUE. French. Ten times a year. Chambre Commerce d'Industrie, BP 2511 51070 Reims France. **Tel** 011 33 26 471515. **Ad Acc. Circ:** 17000.
Desc: Economic information on the department of Marne (commerce, industry, services).

LC HB95 .C49
ISSN 0741-3408
DD 330.12/2/05
US
CHAMPIONS OF FREEDOM. Vol. 1 (1974)-. English. One time a year. $5.00 (per volume). Hillsdale College Press, 33 East College Street, Hillsdale MI 49242. **Tel** (517)437-7341, (517)439-1524. **ED** Ronald Trawbridge. Index available. cum. index. **Circ:** 1,000 (ctrl). available on audiocassette; available on

videocassette.
Desc: Collection of essays on various economic topics from Hillsdale College's Ludwig Von Mises lecture series.

US
CHARLOTTE BUSINESS QUARTERLY. (19??)-. Periodical. English. Four times a year. Fortune Media Inc, PO Box 36639, Charlotte NC 28236-6639. **Tel** (704)332-0148, FAX (704)332-0165.

AT
CHARTAC PRACTICE MANAGEMENT NEWS. English. Eleven times a year (Jan./Feb. issues combined). 395.00Aus$ Australia, 415.00Aus$ other (with binder); 275.00 Aus$ Australia, 295.00Aus$ other (without binder). Professional Information Pty., 196 Drummond Street, Carlton VIC 3053 Australia. **Tel** 011 61 3 6622822, FAX 011 61 3 6623191.

UK
CHARTERED DESIGNERS' NEWSLETTER, THE. (19??)-. Newsletter. English. Chartered Society of Designers, 29 Bedford Square, London WC1B 3EG United Kingdom. **Tel** 011 44 171 6311510, FAX 011 44 171 5802338. **ED** Louella Miles. **Ad Acc.**

UK
CHARTERED INSTITUTE OF PURCHASING AND SUPPLY REPORT ON BUSINESS. Vol. 2 (1993)-. English. Twelve times a year. £160.00 UK; £375.00 other. NTC Publications Ltd., PO Box 69, Henley-on-Thames, Oxfordshire RG9 1GB United Kingdom. **Tel** 011 44 1491 574671, FAX 011 44 1491 571188.

ISSN 1171-9117
DD 330.9934905
NZ
CHATHAM ISLANDER. [Chatham Isl.]. (1992)-. Periodical. English. Twelve times a year. $19.34. Chatham Islander, PO Box 343, Napier New Zealand. **Tel** 011 64 6 8351075.

FR
CHEF DES VENTES INFOS. French. Twenty-two times a year (semimonthly except Aug.). 1490.00F. Editions Pratiques, BP 148, F-74941 Annecy Le Vieux France. **Tel** 011 33 16 50640439, FAX 011 33 16 50640320, telex 385060.

LC HF5468 .C47
KO
CHEIN SUTOO. **VFOAT** Chain Store; Monthly, The Chain Store. Periodical. Korean (Korean). Twelve times a year.

UK
CHEMICAL BUSINESS BULLETINS. See Business and Economics-Abstracting, Bibliographies and Statistics.

UK
●**CHEMICAL BUSINESS NEWSBASE [ONLINE DATABASE].** See Business and Economics-Abstracting, Bibliographies and Statistics.

ISSN 0950-6144
DD 016.3384766
UK
CHEMICAL BUSINESS UPDATE. See Chemistry and Chemicals-Abstracting, Bibliographies and Statistics.

LC HF5001 .C56
DD 330
CH
CHI YEH TIEN TI. **VFOAT** Union Enterprise. (1973)-. Periodical. Chinese (Chinese). $10.00. Union Enterprise / Taiwan, 99 4th Floor, Taipei Taiwan.

US
●**CHIEF EXECUTIVE OFFICER'S NEWSLETTER.** (1995)-. English. Twelve times a year. $71.00. Center for Entrepreneurial Management, 180 Varick Street/Penthouse, New York NY 10014. **Tel** (212)633-0060, FAX (212)633-0063. **Continues** Entrepreneurial Manager's Newsletter.
Desc: A source of entrepreneurial information on taxes, finance, banking, venture capital, business planning and smaller business problems.

LC HC10 .C44
DD 330
US
CODEN CEXOE9
CHIEF EXECUTIVE OPINION. **Added/Corp** Conference Board. No. 1 (July 1989)-. Monographic series. English. Irregular. $15.00 (non-associates), $5.00 (associates). Conference Board, 845 Third Avenue, New York NY 10022. **Tel** (212)759-0900 ext. 582, (800)872-6273, FAX (212)980-7014. **ED** Fabian Linden. ctrl circ.
Desc: An occasional publication analyzing the views of US CEO's on major policy issues and business trends.

LC HC462.9 .J25a
DD 330
JA
CHIIKI KEIKI DOKO CHOSA ITAKU HOKOKUSHO. **Added/Corp** Japan. Keizai Kikakucho. Naikoku Chosa Dai 2-ka. (19??)-. Japanese.

Business and Economics

Four times a year. Keizai Kikakucho Chosakyoku Naikoku, Chosa Dai 2-ka, Japan. **Continues** *Chiiki Keiki Doko Chosa Hokoku*.

LC LB1555 **ISSN** 1357-4019
DD 372 UK

●**CHILDREN'S SOCIAL AND ECONOMICS EDUCATION.** See Social Sciences.

ISSN 0711-6225
DD 330.983/005 CN

CHILE BUSINESS UPDATE. [Chile bus. update]. Vol. 1 (March 10, 1982)-. Periodical. English. Twelve times a year. $197.00. Information International, PO Box 1717, Victoria BC V8W 2Y1 Canada. **Continues** *Chilean Digest, 0228-3646*.

CL

CHILE NEWS. VFOAT Economic & Financial Survey. (1???)-. Periodical. English. **ED** Ruben Corvalan Vera.
Ind/Abst Hum. Rights Intern. Rep.

LC HD936 .C48
DD 333.73/13/0951249 CH

CHIN JIH TI CHENG. (1980)-. Periodical. Chinese. Twelve times a year. $600.00. Chin Jih Ti Cheng Yueh Kan Tsa Chih She, PO Box 128202, Taipei Taiwan.

US

CHINA BUSINESS JOURNAL. (19??)-. English. $180.00. China Business Journal, 142 36 38 Avenue 6B, Flushing NY 11354. **Tel** (719)321-7141.

ISSN 1056-4500
US

●**CHINA BUSINESS MONITOR.** (1993)-. Periodical. English. Twelve times a year. $160.00. Sun Communications, PO Box 500, Palisades Park NJ 07650.

ISSN 0143-9405
UK

CHINA BUSINESS REPORT. [Chin. bus. rep.]. **Added/Corp** Institute for International Research. **VFOAT** Zhong Guo Mao Yi Hui Bao. (1979)-. Periodical. English. Twelve times a year. Institute for International Research / New York, 95 Madison Avenue, New York NY 10016.

ISSN 1080-4080
US

●**CHINA BUSINESS UPDATE. AUTOMOTIVE.** (CHINA BUSINESS UPDATE. AUTOMOTIVE = CHUNG-KUO CH'I CH'E YAO WEN.). **VFOAT** Chung-kuo Ch'i Ch'e Yao Wen. (1995)-. Periodical. English. Twelve times a year. $495.00. GNIX Transpacific Co., 5 Rolling Green Drive, PO Box 1368, Amherst MA 01004. **Tel** (413)253-5477.

ISSN 1023-9685
UDC 38 HK

●**CHINA COMMERCIAL NEWS.** [China commer. news]. **VFOAT** Zhongguo Shangxun. (1994)-. Periodical. English. Six times a year. HK210.00 Hong Kong; $54.00 Asia; $66.00 other. CCN Network, (A Subsidiary of Pro & Pub Ltd.), 12/B Vincent House, 515 Lockhart Road, Causeway Bay, Hong Kong. **Tel** 011 852 8336055, FAX 011 852 8327826, 011 852 8336156. **ED** Keith Chan. **Photos. Ad Acc, Adv Mgr:** Dick Ip, **Tel** 011 852 8336055. Full Page (B&W) HK$7,800. Half Page (B&W) HK$5,500. Full Page (Color) HK$9,800. Half Page (Color) HK$7,000. ctrl circ.
Desc: A pro-business publication which disseminates information pertinent to China. Its aim is to promote and facilitate Sino-World business, especially with the English speaking international business communities.

HK

CHINA ECONOMIC NEWS. VFOAT Chung-Kuo Ching Chi Hsin Wen. (19??)-. Periodical. English (Chinese). Fifty times a year (published Mondays). $410.00. Economic Information and Agency Consultancy, 342 Hennessy Road, 12th Floor, Hong Kong Hong Kong. **Tel** 011 852 25739208, 011 852 25738217, FAX 011 852 258336889. **ED** Lo Chi Keung, and Lo King Fai. Index available.
Desc: Covers Chinese economic news, policies, rules, regulations, development trends, statistical data, tenders, and investment opportunities.

LC HC426 .C4823 **ISSN** 0967-8182
DD 330.951/005 UK

CHINA ECONOMIC REVIEW. (19??)-. Periodical. English. Twelve times a year. $212.00. Alain Charles Publishing Ltd., 27 Wilfred Street, London SW1E 6PR United Kingdom. **Tel** 011 44 171 8347676, FAX 011 44 171 9730076, telex 297165.

LC HC426 .C482 **ISSN** 1043-951X
DD 330.951/005 US
Pr Rev.

CHINA ECONOMIC REVIEW. [China econ. rev.]. Vol. 1, No. 1 (Spring 1989)-. Periodical. English. Two times a year. $165.00. JAI Press Inc., 55 Old Post Road, Suite 2, PO Box 1678, Greenwich CT 06836-1678. **Tel** (203)661-7602, FAX (203)661-0792. **ED** Weijian Shan and Mao Yu-Shi.

Desc: Publishes original academic works in the fields of economics and management sciences, especially those relevant, but not necessarily limited, to the Chinese economies under different systems.
Ind/Abst Econ. Lit. Index; Int. Labour Doc.; LABORDOC.

LC JA **ISSN** 0943-7533
DD 320 GW

●**CHINA MONTHLY DATA.** See Political Science.

LC HF5260.A3 C498
DD 650 HK
NLM TK 6011; C536

CHINA PHONE BOOK & BUSINESS DIRECTORY, THE. Added/Corp Chung-kuo Tien Hua Pu Kung Ssu. **VFOAT** China Phone Book and Business Directory; Chung-KuoTien Hua Pu. (Jan./June 1988)-. Directory. English (Chinese). Two times a year (Jan., July). $158.00. China Phone Book Company Ltd, GPO Box 11581, Hong Kong Hong Kong. **Tel** 011 852 25084448, FAX 011 852 25031526, telex 84958. **ED** K.S. Tang. Index available. **Ad Acc. Circ:** 15,000. **Continues** *China Phone Book & Address Directory, 0250-4170*.

LC HF3831 .C476
DD 380.1/0951/021 CC

CHINA TRADE AND PRICE STATISTICS. Added/Corp China. Kuo Chia Tung Chi Chu. China Statistical Information and Consultancy Service Centre. **VFOAT** China Trade and Price Statistics in ... . 1st Ed. (1987)-. English. One time a year. $68.00. China Statistical Information & Consultancy, 38 Yeutan Nanjie Sanlihe, Beijing 100826, People's Republic of China. **Tel** 011 86 1 8515074, FAX 011 86 1 8515078. **(Subscription address:** Greenwood Press Inc., 88 Post Road West, Box 5007, Westport CT 06881. **Tel** (203)226-3571.**)**

US

CHINESE BUSINESS HISTORY. (19??)-. English. Two times a year (Mar. and Nov.). $8.00. University of Louisville / History Department, Louisville KY 40292. **Tel** (502)588-6817, FAX (502)588-0770. **ED** Andrea McElderry and Robert Gardella. **Ad Acc, Adv Mgr:** A. McElderry, **Tel** same as publisher. **Circ:** 100.
Desc: Covers business and economics in China.

LC HC426 .C485 **ISSN** 0009-4552
DD 330 US
CCC

CHINESE ECONOMIC STUDIES. [Chin. econ. stud.]. **Added/Corp** M.E. Sharpe, Inc. International Arts and Sciences Press. Vol. 1 (Fall 1967)-. Periodical. English (Chinese). Six times a year. $572.00. M. E. Sharpe Inc., 80 Business Park Drive, Armonk NY 10504. **Tel** (914)273-1800, (800)541-6563, FAX (914)273-2106. **ED** George C. Wang. **Bk Rev. Ad Acc. Circ:** 400 (ctrl). available on microfilm from University Microfilms International (UMI). Documents available from The Genuine Article.
Desc: Contains translations on everything from a standard PRC textbook on political economy to reports on the management in Chinese enterprises.
Ind/Abst Asia.-Pac. Econ. Lit.; Contents Recent Econ. J.; Econ. Lit. Index; Int. Labour Doc.; J. Econ. Lit.; LABORDOC; Leis., Rec., Tour. Abstr.; PAIS Int. Print (1991-); Res. Alert [Full Cov.]; Rural Dev. Abstr.; Soc. Sci. Cit. Index [Full Cov.]; World Agric. Econ. Rural Sociol. Abstr.

LC HB9 .C462
DD 330 CC

CHING CHI KO HSUEH. Added/Corp Pei-Ching ta Hsueh. Ching Chi Hsi. Pei-Ching ta Hsueh. Ching Chi ko Hsueh Pien Chi Wei Yuan Hui. **VFOAT** Jingji Kexue; Economic Science. No. 1 (Nov. 1979)-. Periodical. Chinese. Six times a year. $47.60. **(Subscription address:** China International Book Trading Corporation, PO Box 399, Library Service Department, Beijing 100044 People's Republic of China. **Tel** 011 86 1 8414284, FAX 011 86 1 8412023, telex 22496 CIBTC CN.**)**

LC HC427.92 .C46823
DD 330.951/05/05 CC

CHING CHI TSUNG HENG. Added/Corp Chi-Lin Sheng Ching chi Hsueh Tuan ti Lien ho Hui. **VFOAT** Economic Review; Jing ji Zong Heng. (1985)-. Periodical. Chinese. Twelve times a year. International Commerical Bank of China, 100 Chi-lin Road, Taipei 10424 Taiwan.
Ind/Abst PAIS Int. Print.

LC HB9 .C472
CH

CHING CHI YEN CHIU. (19??)-. Periodical. Chinese.

LC HC
CC

CHING CHI YEN CHIU. VFOAT Jing Ji Yan Jiu; Ekonomicheskoe Issledovanie; Economic Research. (1955)-. Periodical. Chinese. Twelve times a year. $38.80. **(Subscription address:** China International Book Trading Corporation, PO Box 399, Library Service Department, Beijing 100044 People's Republic of China. **Tel** 011 86 1 8414284, FAX 011 86 1 8412023, telex 22496 CIBTC CN.**)**
Desc: Contains economic research.

LC HB235.K6 C48
KO

CHONGBU KUMAE MULCHA KAGYOK CHONGBO. VFOAT Price Information on Procurement. Korean (Korean). Four times a year. Chodalchong, 48-26 Inui-dong 4-ka Chongno-ku, Seoul Korea.

LC HC461 .N33a
DD 330 JA

CHOSA SHIRYO. Main/Corp Nagoya, Japan. Shikai. Jimukyoku. Chosaka. (19??)-. Periodical. Japanese. Nagoya Shikai Jimukyoku, 1-1 Sannomaru 3-chome Naka-ku, Nagoya Japan.

ISSN 1054-8874
US

CHRONICLE OF LATIN AMERICAN ECONOMIC AFFAIRS. (CHRONICLE OF LATIN AMERICAN ECONOMIC AFFAIRS [COMPUTER FILE].). [Chron. Lat. Am. econ. aff.]. **Added/Corp** University of New Mexico. Latin America Database. **VFOAT** Chronicle of Latin Am. Economic Affairs. (Sept. 6, 1990)-. Newsletter. English. One time a week. $225.00 (institutions), $125.00 (individuals). Latin America Data Base, 801 Yale Northeast, University of Mexico, Albuquerque NM 87131. **Tel** (505)277-6839, FAX (505)277-5989. ctrl circ. available on CD-ROM from National Information Service Corporation (NISC); available on an online database from Lexis-Nexis; NEWSNET; Internet; DATA-STAR; and DIALOG. **Continues** *Latin American Debt Chronicle*.
Ind/Abst PTS Newsl. Database [Full Txt.].

ISSN 1145-1408
FR

UDC 3:001

CHRONIQUE INTERNATIONALE PARIS. (LA CHRONIQUE INTERNATIONALE DE L'IRES.). (1989)-. Periodical. French. Six times a year. $40.46. Institut de Recherches Economiques & Sociales, 16 Bld du Mont d'Est, 93192 Noisy Grand Cdx France. **Tel** 011 33 1 48151890. **Ad Acc.**

LC HC
DD 330 FR

CHRONIQUES DE LA S.E.D.E.I.S. Added/Corp Societe d'Etudes et de Documentation, Economiques, Industrielles, et Sociales. **VFOAT** Chroniques de la SEDEIS. **VAT** Chroniques de la Societe d'Etudes et de Documentation, Economiques, Industrielles, et Sociales. Vol. 41, No 1 (15 Jan. 1992)-. Periodical. French. Twelve times a year. Sedeis, 141 boulevard Haussmann, 75008 Paris France. **Tel** 011 33 1 42563739, FAX 011 33 1 45638679. **Continues** *Chroniques d'Actualite de la S.E.D.E.I.S.*

LC HB3 .C48
FR

●**CHRONIQUES ECONOMIQUES / S.E.D.E.I.S. Added/Corp** Societe d'Etudes et de Documentation Economiques, Industrielles, et Sociales. **VFOAT** Chroniques Economiques S.E.D.E.I.S.; Chroniques Economiques SEDEIS; Chroniques Economiques Societe d'Etudes et de Documentation Economiques, Industrielles, et Sociales. (Jan. 1994)-. Periodical. French. Twelve times a year. $224.93. S E D E I S, 34 Avenue Charles de Caulle, 92200 Neuilly Sur Seine France. **Tel** 011 33 1 47228561. **Continues** *Chroniques de la S.E.D.E.I.S., 1164-8759*.

LC HF5500.3.T3 C48
DD 658.4/0092/2 B CH

CHUNG-HUA MIN KUO CHI YEH MING JEN LU. VFOAT Taiwan Who's Who in Business. (19??)-. Chinese (English). One time a year. $128.00. Harvard Management Service Inc, 9th Floor 166 Fu Shing N Road, Taipei Taiwan. **Tel** 011 886 2 7150471.

LC HC430.5.A1 C576
DD 330 CH

CHUNG-HUA MIN KUO CHING CHI NIEN CHIEN. VFOAT Economic Yearbook of the Republic of China. Chinese (English). One time a year. NT$1,000.00 single issue. Ching Chi Jih Pao, Kung Shang Fu Wu Pu 555, Chung Hsiao East Road, 4 Section/8th Floor, Taipei Shih Taiwan.

LC HC430.5 .C64 **ISSN** 0529-5920
DD 330.951/24905 CH

CHUNG-KUO CHING CHI = THE CHINA ECONOMIST. VFOAT The China Economist; Chung-Kuo Ching Chi Yueh Kan. (Oct. 1950)-. Periodical. Chinese. Twelve times a year. Chung-Kuo Ching Chi Yueh Kan She, PO Box 478, Taipei Taiwan.

ISSN 1013-5375
HK

CHUNGGUK KYONGJE SOKPO. VFOAT China Economic Express (Korean Ed.); Chungguk Kyongje Sokpo. Jogan. (1988)-. Periodical. Korean. Fifty times a year. $430.00. Economic Information & Agency, 342 Hennessy Road, 10-16th Floor, Hong Kong Hong Kong. **Tel** 011 852 25738217, FAX 011 852 8388304, telex 60647 EICC HX.

ISSN 1183-0409
DD 338.9/006/071428 CN
CIDEM EXPRESS. [CIDEM express]. **Main/Corp** Commission d'Initiative et de Developpement Economiques de Montreal. **VFOAT** Commission d'Initiative et de Developpement Economiques de Montreal, Express. Vol. 1, No 1 (Nov. 1990)-. Periodical. French. Four times a year. Limited free distribution. Commission d'Initiative et de Developpement Economiques de Montreal, Bureau 1100, 770 Ouest rue Sherbrook, Montreal Quebec H3A 1G1 Canada.

LC HG4009 .C54 ISSN 1060-8710
DD 338.7/4/05 US
CIFAR'S GLOBAL COMPANY HANDBOOK. (CIFAR'S GLOBAL COMPANY HANDBOOK : [AN ANALYSIS OF THE FINANCIAL PERFORMANCE OF THE WORLD'S LEADING 7,500 COMPANIES].). [CIFAR's glob. co. handb.]. **Added/Corp** Center for International Financial Analysis and Research (Princeton, N.J.). **VFOAT** Global Company Handbook. **VAT** Center for International Financial Analysis and Research's Global Company Handbook. (1992)-. English. One time a year (Apr.). $519.00. CIFAR, 3490 US Route 1, Princeton NJ 08540. **Tel** (609)520-9333, FAX (609)520-0905. available on CD-ROM.

LC HD ISSN 1061-3714
DD 338 US
•**CIFAR'S GLOBAL COMPANY NEWS DIGEST.** [CIFAR's glob. co. news dig.]. **Added/Corp** Center for International Financial Analysis and Research (Princeton, N.J.). **VFOAT** Global Company News Digest. (Nov. 1993)-. Periodical. English. Twelve times a year. $345.00. CIFAR, 3490 US Route 1, Princeton NJ 08540. **Tel** (609)520-9333, FAX (609)520-0905.

ISSN 0882-8881
DD 330 US
CINCINNATI BUSINESS COURIER. Vol. 1, No. 1 (May 14-20, 1984)-. Periodical. English. One time a week. $49.00. Cincinnati Business Courier, 35 East 7th Street, Suite 700, Cincinnati OH 45202. **Tel** (513)621-6665. **ED** Brain Settle. available on microfilm from University Microfilms International (UMI); available on an online database (files 635,648/Full-Text) from DIALOG. Documents available from UMI Article Clearinghouse.
Ind/Abst Acad. Search; Bus. Dateline; Bus. Index (1985-1990); Bus. Source Plus; Bus. Source; EP Collect.; Gen. BusinessFile (1985-1990); Gen. Period. Index (1985-1990); Homework Help.; INFO-SOUTH Abstr.; MasterFile FullTEXT 1000; MasterFile FullTEXT 350; MasterFile FullTEXT 650; MasterFile FullTEXT (July 1993-); OCLC; PROMT; Telebase; Trade Ind. ASAP [Full Txt.]; Trade Ind. Index [Full Txt.].

ISSN 8756-6249
US
CITYBUSINESS (NEW YORK, N.Y.). (CITYBUSINESS.). **VFOAT** City Business; New York City Business. (198?)-. Periodical. English. Twenty-six times a year. $20.00. Citybusiness/New York, Inc., 38 West Chestnut Street, Souderton NY 18964. Documents available from UMI Article Clearinghouse. ***Continues*** *New York Citybusiness, 8750-7056.*
Ind/Abst Bus. Dateline (Feb. 25, 1985-June 17, 1985) [Full Txt.]; Gen. BusinessFile (Jan. 1985-July 1985); Gen. Period. Index (Jan. 1985-April 1985); INFO-SOUTH Abstr.

US
CLEANING BUSINESS. (19??)-. Trade Publication. English. Four times a year. $20.00. Service Business Magazine, 1512 Western Avenue, Seattle WA 98101. **Tel** (206)622-4241. ***Continues*** *Service Business, 0736-5764.*
Desc: News and information on the cleaning business.

ISSN 1059-3055
DD 338 US
CLEVELAND ENTERPRISE (CLEVELAND, OHIO. 1991). (CLEVELAND ENTERPRISE.). [Clevel. enterp.]. **Added/Corp** Weatherhead School of Management. Enterprise Development, Inc. **VFOAT** Cleveland enterprise magazine. Vol. 1, No. 1 (Spring 1991)-. Periodical. English. Four times a year (Mar., June, Sept., Dec.). $9.95. Enterprise Development Inc, 11000 Cedar Avenue, Cleveland OH 44106. **Tel** (216)229-9445, FAX (216)229-3236. **ED** Sandra K. Seibenschuh. **Ad Acc, Adv Mgr:** Lee Kuegsegger. **Circ:** 30,000.
Desc: The purpose of the journal is to help entrepreneurs, senior managers and business owners in Northeast Ohio grow their businesses and thereby strengthen the regional economy.

ISSN 1061-6020
US
CLS MARKET PLACE. (1992)-. Periodical. English. Two times a year (Jan. and June). $ .75. Clemmons Creative Literacy Service and Company, Inc, 2346 A Lorillard Place, Bronx NY 10458. **Tel** (212)733-4529. **ED** Lorene Clemmons. Index available (June). cum. index. **Ad Acc. Acid Free. Circ:** 500.
Desc: Contains two features: one that explores some new development in the world of business, and another that profiles a person or sketch a new business venture.

ISSN 0747-8283
DD 613 US
CLUB INDUSTRY. **See** Health.

ISSN 0939-0359
GW
UDC 33
CM. CONTROLLER-MAGAZIN (1988). [CM. Control.-Mag. 1988]. **VFOAT** Controller-Magazin (1988); CM. Controller-Magazin. Controller's Thementafel. (1988)-. Periodical. German. Six times a year. Management Service Verlag, Postfach 1168, Untertaxetwes 76, W-8035 Gauting Germany. ***Continues*** *Controller-Magazin, 0343-267X.*

LC HC241.A1 C18 ISSN 0300-4406
DD 330.94/005 UK
CMN. COMMON MARKET NEWS. (THE COMMON MARKET NEWS.). [CMN, Common Mark. news]. **VFOAT** CMN. Vol. 2, No. 1 (Dec. 29, 1972)-. Periodical. English. Twelve times a year. $85.00. The European Economic Data, 19 Pemmaen Terrace, Seansea SA1 6HZ United Kingdom. **Tel** 011 44 171 7239681. **ED** Ivor B. N. Evans. **Bk Rev.** ***Continues*** *Common Market News Letter, 0300-4457.*
Desc: All matters concerning European Communities and its institutions.

ISSN 1050-3005
DD 338 US
TITLE CHANGE
CNY BUSINESS JOURNAL : CENTRAL NEW YORK'S LEADING BUSINESS NEWSPAPER, THE. [CNY bus. j.]. **VFOAT** Businessjournal; CNY Businessjournal; Business Journal. **VAT** Central New York Business Journal. Vol. 4, No. 3 (Aug. 1989)-(July 1995). Periodical. English. CNY Business Review Inc., 231 Walton Street, Syracuse NY 13202. **Tel** (315)446-3510. ***Continues*** *Business Journal (DeWitt, N.Y.), 0894-5675.* ***Continued by*** *Businessjournal.*
Ind/Abst Acad. Search; Bus. Source Plus; Bus. Source; EP Collect.; Homework Help.; MasterFile FullTEXT 1000; MasterFile FullTEXT 350; MasterFile FullTEXT 650; MasterFile FullTEXT (July 1993-); OCLC; Telebase; Trade Ind. ASAP (?-?) [Full Txt.]; Trade Ind. Index (?-?).

ISSN 1060-3417
DD 330 US
COAST BUSINESS. [Coast bus.]. **VFOAT** Coast Business Journal. (19??)-. Periodical. English. Twenty-six times a year. $16.00. Coast Business, Markham Hotel Building, Suite 900, Gulfport MS 39501. available on microfilm and microfiche from University Microfilms International (UMI); available on an online database (file 635/Full-Text) from DIALOG. Documents available from UMI Article Clearinghouse.
Ind/Abst Bus. Dateline (March 2, 1992-) [Full Txt.].

IT
CODICINI MORONI. Italian. Twelve times a year. L14000. Sole 24 Ore Libri, Via Parabiago 19, 20151 Milan Italy. **Tel** 011 39 2 66030288.

LC HC59.8 .C64
DD 330 CU
COLABORACION INTERNACIONAL. Periodical. Spanish. Four times a year. Ediciones Cubanas, Obispo 527 Altos ESQ Bernaza, CP 10100 Havana Cuba. ***Continues*** *Colaboracion (Havana, Cuba).*

LC HB51 .B3
AG
COLECCION METODOLOGICA; PUBLICACION. **Main/Corp** Bahia Blanca, Argentine Republic. Universidad Nacional del Sur. Instituto de Economia. No. 1 (1962)-. Spanish. Universidad del Sur, Instituto de Economia, 1800 Bahia Blanca Argentina.

US
COLORADO BUSINESS. **Added/Corp** Boulder Public Library. No. 1 (1979)-. English. One time a year. $5.00. Boulder Public Library Foundation, PO Drawer H, Boulder CO 80306. **Tel** (303)441-3195. Documents available from UMI Article Clearinghouse.
Ind/Abst Bus. Dateline (June 1986-) [Full Txt.].

LC HC107.C7 C587 ISSN 0898-6363
DD 330.9788/005 US
COLORADO BUSINESS MAGAZINE : CBM. [Colo. bus. mag.]. **VFOAT** CBM. Vol. 13, No. 7 (July 1986)-. Periodical. English. Twelve times a year. $24.00. Wiesner Publishing, 7009 South Potomac Street, Englewood CO 80112. **Tel** (303)397-7600, (800)945-0973, FAX (303)397-7619. **ED** Jeff Rundles and Carson Reed. **Ad Acc. Circ:** 22,000 (ctrl). available on an online database (files 647,648/Full-Text) from DIALOG. Documents available from UMI Article Clearinghouse. ***Continues*** *Colorado Business, 0092-5071.*
Desc: A magazine edited for executives and professionals throughout the state. Articles cover economic trends, politics, personalities and business profiles
Ind/Abst Acad. Search; Bus. ASAP (1990-) [Full Txt.]; Bus. Index (1986-); Bus. Source Plus; Bus. Source; EP Collect.; Gen. BusinessFile (1986-); Gen. Period. Index (1986-1990); Homework Help.; INFO-SOUTH Abstr.; Mag. ASAP Plus [Full Txt.]; Mag. Index Plus (1989-); MasterFile FullTEXT 1000; MasterFile FullTEXT 350; MasterFile FullTEXT 650; MasterFile FullTEXT (July 1993-) [Full Txt.]; Newsp. Period. Abstr. (1988-); OCLC; PAIS Int. Print (1991-); Telebase; Mag. Index (1986-); Trade Ind. ASAP [Full Txt.]; Trade Ind. Index (1986-) [Full Txt.].

LC HC107.C7 C59 ISSN 0010-1524
DD 330 US
COLORADO BUSINESS REVIEW. **Added/Corp** University of Colorado (Boulder campus). Bureau of Business Research. (1951)-. Periodical. English. Six times a year. Free on request. Business Research Division, University of Colorado, Campus Box 420, Boulder CO 80309-0420. **Tel** (303)492-8227, FAX (303)492-3620. ***Continues*** *Better Business.*
Ind/Abst Public Aff. Inf. Serv. Bull.

ISSN 1062-810X
DD 330 US
COLORADO SPRINGS BUSINESS JOURNAL, THE. [Colo. Springs bus. j.]. (1989)-. Trade Publication. English. Twenty-four times a year. $19.50. Colorado Springs Business Journal, PO Box 1541, Colorado Springs CO 80901. **Tel** (719)634-5905, FAX (719)634-5157.
Ind/Abst PROMT.

ISSN 1062-273X
US
COLUMBIA HEIGHTS BUSINESS NEWS. **Added/Corp** Development Corporation of Columbia Heights. Columbia Heights Association of Merchants and Professionals. (1992)-. Periodical. English. Free. The Corporation and the Association, 3419-14th Street NW, Washington DC 20010.

LC HF5001 .C64 ISSN 0022-5428
DD 330.9/04 US
CCC
CODEN CJWBAU
Pr Rev.
COLUMBIA JOURNAL OF WORLD BUSINESS, THE. [Columbia j. world bus.]. **Added/Corp** Columbia University. Graduate School of Business. Vol. 1 (Fall 1965)-. Periodical. English. Four times a year. $160.00. JAI Press Inc., 55 Old Post Road, Suite 2, PO Box 1678, Greenwich CT 06836-1678. **Tel** (203)661-7602, FAX (203)661-0792. **ED** Cynthia Howells. cum. index. **Bk Rev. Ad Acc. Circ:** 5,000 (ctrl). available on microfilm and microfiche from University Microfilms International (UMI); available on an online database (file 648/Full-Text) from DIALOG. Documents available from The Genuine Article, UMI Article Clearinghouse.
Desc: Perspectives on global business.
Ind/Abst ABI/INFORM Glob. Ed. (Sept. 1971-); ABI/INFORM Ondisc: Expr. Ed. (Spring 1987-); ABI/INFORM [Computer File] (Sept. 1971-); Acad. Abstr.; Acad. Search; Account. Art.; Am. Bibliogr. Slavic East Europ. Stud.; Anbar Account. Finan. Abstr. [Full Txt.]; Anbar Mark. Distr. Abstr. [Full Txt.]; Anbar Top Manage. Abstr. [Full Txt.]; Bus. ASAP (1990-) [Full Txt.]; Bus. Index (1985-); Bus. Period. Index; Bus. Source Plus; Bus. Source; Commun. Abstr. (?-?); Contents Pages Manage.; Curr. Cit.; Curr. Contents Soc. Behav. Sci.; EP Collect.; Gen. BusinessFile (1985-); Gen. Period. Index (1985-); Homework Help.; Index Period. Artic. Relat. Law; INFO-SOUTH Abstr.; Int. Aerosp. Abstr.; Int. Bibliogr. Sociol.; Leis., Rec., Tour. Abstr.; Mag. Search; Manage. Market. Abstr.; Manage. Bibliogr. Rev.; MasterFile FullTEXT 1000; MasterFile FullTEXT 350; MasterFile FullTEXT 650; MasterFile FullTEXT (July 1993-); Middle East Abstr. Index; OCLC; Oper. Prod. Manage. Abstr. [Full Txt.]; PAIS Int. Print (1991-); Person. Train. Abstr. [Full Txt.]; Person. Manage. Abstr.; Res. Alert [Full Cov.]; Rural Dev. Abstr.; Selec. Coop. Index Manage. Period.; Soc. Sci. Cit. Index [Full Cov.]; Telebase; Trade Ind. ASAP [Full Txt.]; Trade Ind. Index [Full Txt.]; UMI ABI/Inform--Bus. Period. Ondisc [Full Txt.]; Wilson Bus. Abstr.; Women Manage. Rev. [Full Txt.]; Work Relat. Abstr.; World Agric. Econ. Rural Sociol. Abstr.; World Mag. Bank.

LC HC ISSN 0069-6331
DD 330 US
COLUMBIA STUDIES IN ECONOMICS. Vol. 1 (1968)-. Monographic series. English. Irregular. Price varies per volume. Columbia University Press, 136 South Broadway, Irvington NY 10533. **Tel** (914)591-9111.

Business and Economics

ISSN 0817-5837
DD 330.5
AT
COMCISE. [Comcise]. (1981)-. Periodical. English. Twelve times a year. 349.43Aus$. Comert Business Economists Pty, Level 20, 100 Miller Street, North Sydney 2060 Australia. **Tel** 011 61 2 9564208, FAX 011 61 2 9595364.

BO
COMENTARIOS ECONOMICOS DE ACTUALIDAD : BOLETIN INFORMATIVO DEL CENTRO DE INVESTIGACION Y CONSULTORIA. Added/Corp Centro de Investigacion y Consultoria (La Paz, Bolivia). **VFOAT** CEA. (19??)-. Periodical. Spanish. Twenty-six times a year. Cinco, Casilla 12097, La Paz Bolivia.

HO
COMERCIO EXTERIOR. Added/Corp Honduras. Direccion General de Estadistica y Censos. Spanish. Irregular. Direccion General de Estadistica y Censos / Honduras, Republica de Honduras, Tegucigalpa DC Honduras. **Continues** Comercio Exterior de Honduras.

ISSN 0964-8585
DD 338.7638010942443
UK
COMMERCE BUSINESS DIRECTORIES REDDITCH ED. [Commer. bus. dir. Redditch ed.]. (1991)-. Periodical. English. Holcot Press Ltd, Station House, Station Road, Newport Pognell, Milton Keynes MK16 0AG United Kingdom. **Tel** 011 44 1908 614477, FAX 011 44 1908 217425. **Continues** Redditch & District Business Directory, 0957-1094.

ISSN 0745-077X
US
Pr Rev.
COMMERCE (HACKENSACK, N.Y.). (COMMERCE.). **Added/Corp** Commerce and Industry Association of Northern New Jersey. Commerce and Industry Association of New Jersey. (1971)-. Directory. English. Twelve times a year. $20.00. Commerce Magazine, PO Box 768, Paramus NJ 07653-0768. **Tel** (201)487-4600, FAX (201)261-8616. **ED** Jim Cowen. **Ad Acc. Circ:** 15,000 (ctrl). **Continues** Bergen.

US
TITLE CHANGE
COMMODITY YEAR BOOK STATISTICAL SUPPLEMENT. Added/Corp Commodity Research Bureau (U.S.). **VFOAT** Commodity Yearbook Statistical Supplement. Vol. 26, No. 1 (July 1988)-Vol. 30, No. 3 (Jan. 1993). Statistical Publication. English. Knight Ridder Financial Publishing, 30 South Wackler Drive, Suite 1820, Chicago IL 60606. **Tel** (312)454-1801, (800)621-5271, FAX (312)454-0239. **Continues** Commodity Year Book Statistical Abstract Service, 0010-3241. **Continued by** Knight-Ridder CRB Commodity Yearbook Statitsical Supplement.

US
COMMON SENSE NEGOTIATIONS. (19??)-. Periodical. English. Thirty-six times a year. $3.25 per copy. Economics Press Inc, 12 Daniel Road, Fairfield NJ 07004. **Tel** (201)227-1224, (800)526-2554, FAX (201)227-9742.
Desc: Geared for managers, supervisors, financial officers, salespeople, purchasing professionals, and others who must know how to negotiate intelligently for themselves or on behalf of the company.

CC
COMMONWEALTH. (19??)-. Chinese. Twelve times a year. $109.00 (US); 126.00 (Canada and Mexico). Evergreen Publ & Stationery, 136 S Atlantic Boulevard, Monterey Park CA 91754. **Tel** (818)281-3622, (818)284-9066, FAX (818)284-1571. **Acid Free.**
Desc: Covers current news on enterprises, provides information about business, management, finance based on different cases around the world.

ISSN 0893-9136
DD 332
US
COMMONWEALTH LETTERS. [CommonW. lett.]. **VFOAT** Common Wealth Letters; Jack Miller's Commonwealth Letters. (19??)-. Periodical. English. Twelve times a year. $70.00. National Capital Corp, PO Box 21172, Tampa FL 33523. **Tel** (813)287-1075.

ISSN 0819-7091
DD 338.740994
AT
COMMONWEALTH OF AUSTRALIA GAZETTE. BUSINESS. [Commonw. Aust. gaz., Bus.]. (1987)-. Government Publication. English. One time a week (50 issues). 220.00Aus$. Australian Government Publishing Service, GPO Box 84, Canberra ACT 2601 Australia. **Tel** 011 61 6 2954411, FAX 011 61 6 2954455.

ISSN 0223-3053
FR
UDC 382(4)
COMMUNAUTE EUROPEENNE INFORMATIONS. [Communaute eur. inf.]. (1970)-. Periodical. French. Eleven times a year. 75.00F. Communaute Europeenne Informations, 61 rue des Belles Feuilles, 75116 Paris France. **Tel** 011 33 1 45015885.

US
COMMUNICATIONS BUSINESS AND FINANCE. See Communications-Telecommunication.

UK
COMMUNITY MARKETS. Added/Corp Financial Times Limited. Issue No. 1 (Oct. 1979)-. Periodical. English. Financial Times Magazines, Greystoke Place, Fetter Lane, London EC4A 1ND United Kingdom. **Tel** 011 44 171 8316577. **Continues** European Community Information, 0046-2748.

ISSN 1185-5800
DD 330.97123/3/05
CN
COMMUNITY PROFILE, STETTLER. (STETTLER, COMMUNITY PROFILE.). [Community profile Stettler]. **Added/Corp** Stettler Economic Development Board. **VFOAT** Community Profile; Stettler, the Heart of Alberta, Alberta, Canada; Stettler, a Community Profile. (1991)-. English. Irregular. Stettler Economic Deveolpment Board, PO Box 280, Stettler Alberta T0C 2L0 Canada.

LC HG4050
DD 338
ISSN 1062-8525
US
COMPACT D/SEC. (COMPACT D/SEC [COMPUTER FILE].). [Compact D/SEC]. **Added/Corp** Disclosure Incorporated. **VFOAT** Compact D SEC; Compact Disclosure SEC. (July 1990)-. English. Twelve times a year. Disclosure Incorporated, 5161 River Road, Bethesda MD 20816. **Tel** (800)638-8241. **Continues** Compact Disclosure.

AT
COMPANIES AND SECURITIES BULLETIN. Bulletin. English. Twelve times a year. 595.00Aus$. Corporate Adviser Pty. Ltd., 161 Collins Street, 2nd Floor, Melbourne VIC 3000 Australia. **Tel** 011 61 3 288 5210, FAX 011 61 3 288 6666.

LC HD2848.A1 I73a
DD 338.7/4/09417
IE
COMPANIES / BY THE DEPARTMENT OF INDUSTRY, COMMERCE, AND TOURISM. Main/Corp Ireland. Dept. of Industry, Commerce, and Tourism. (19??)-. Periodical. English. One time a year. $45.00. Government Publications, 4 5 Harcourt Road, Dublin 2 Ireland. **Tel** 011 353 1 6613111 ext.4005. **Circ:** 1,000.

US
COMPANIES INTERNATIONAL [COMPUTER FILE]. (Dec. 1993)-. English. One time a year. $1995.00 DOS single version, $2945.00 DOS network version. Gale Research Inc., 835 Penobscot Building, 645 Griswold Street, Detroit MI 48226. **Tel** (800)877-GALE, (313)961-2242, FAX (313)961-6083, (800)414-5043, telex TWX 810-221-7086. available in print (as Ward's Business Directory and World Trade Centers Association World Business Directory).
Desc: Aims to help businesses, consultants, students and other researchers assess markets, appraise competition, find clients, target promotions, examine company backgrounds, form business partnerships, recruit new talent, conduct job searches and more.

ISSN 0816-5521
DD 658.4006094
AT
COMPANY DIRECTOR. [Co. dir.]. (1985)-. Periodical. English. Eleven times a year (publishes monthly with Dec./Jan. issues combined). 164.44Aus$. Australian Institute of Company Directors, Level 3, 71 York Street, Sydney NSW 2001 Australia. **Tel** 011 61 2 2998788.

NE
COMPANY GUIDE FOR BUSINESS IN EUROPE. (19??)-. Trade Publication. English. Four times a year. Fl120.00. Klynveld Main Goerdeler, EC Desk PO 72001, 1007 TB Amsterdam Netherlands. **Tel** 011 31 20 6461992. **(Subscription address:** KPMG Peat Marwick McClintock, PO Box 433, Truda Lansdowne, Watford Herts WD2 5QP United Kingdom. **Tel** 011 44 1923 210260.)
Desc: Designed to give business people a guide to community law.

ISSN 0967-635X
UK
COMPANY INFORMATION. (19??)-. English. Irregular (September 1993). $224.00. Headland Business Information, 1 Henry Smiths Terrace, Headland Cleveland, TS24 0PD United Kingdom. **Tel** 011 44 429 231902, FAX 011 44 429 861403.

LC HD2709
DD 338.74
UK
COMPANY LIQUIDITY. Added/Corp Great Britain. Central Statistical Office. Great Britain. Government Statistical Service. Quarter 1 (1991)-. Statistical Publication. English. Four times a year. The Librarian, Central Statistical Office, Government Buildings, Cardiff Road, Newport Gwent NP9 1XG United Kingdom. **Continues** Company Liquidity Survey.

UK
COMPANY SECRETARY'S FACTBOOK. (19??)-. English. Twelve times a year. £96.00 UK; £106.00 other. Gee & Company Limited, 183 Marsh Wall, South Quay Plaza, London E14 9FS United Kingdom. **Tel** 011 44 171 5385386, FAX 011 44 171 5388623. **(Subscription address:** Professional Publishing Ltd., South Quay Plaza 183 Marsh Wall, London E14 9FS United Kingdom. **Tel** 011 44 181 5385386.)

ISSN 0952-9977
UK
COMPANY SECRETARY'S REVIEW. SURVEY OF COMPANY CAR SCHEMES. [Co. secr. rev., Surv. co. car schemes]. (198?)-. Periodical. English. One time a year. £47.50. Tolley Publishing Company Ltd., Tolley House, 2 Addiscombe Road, Croydon, Surrey CR9 5AF United Kingdom. **Tel** 011 44 181 6869141, FAX 011 44 181 6863155. **ED** Peter Burgess.
Desc: Provides full statistical analysis with commentary on car schemes in 600 different companies with a total of 35,000 cars.

LC HC701 .A17
DD 330/.05
ISSN 0888-7233
US
Pr Rev.
COMPARATIVE ECONOMIC STUDIES. [Comp. econ. stud.]. **Added/Corp** Association for Comparative Economic Studies (U.S.). Vol. 27, No. 1 (Spring 1985)-. Academic Scholarly Publication. English. Four times a year (Mar., June, Sept., Dec.). $40.00. Association of Comparative Economic Studies, Department of Economics, Queens College of the City, University of New York, 65-30 Kissena Boulevard, Flushing NY 11367. **Tel** (718)997-5461, FAX (718)997-5535. **ED** Susan Linz. **Bk Rev,** (Qty: 18). **Ad Acc, Adv Mgr:** Michael R. Dohan, Ph.D., **Tel** (718)997-5461. **Circ:** 1,000. available on microfilm and microfiche from University Microfilms International (UMI). Documents available from UMI Article Clearinghouse. **Continues** Association for Comparative Economic Studies (U.S.). ACES Bulletin, 0360-5930.
Desc: The purpose is to promote scholarly exchange among persons interested in comparative studies of economic systems, planning, and economic development and to further the growth of systematic knowledge in these areas by facilitating research, instruction, and publication.
Ind/Abst Acad. Search: Am. Bibliogr. Slavic East Europ. Stud.; Bus. Index (1985-); Econ. Lit. Index; EP Collect.; Expand. Acad. Index (1992-); Gen. BusinessFile (1985-); Gen. Period. Index (1985-); Homework Help.; INFO-SOUTH Abstr.; J. Econ. Lit.; Mag. Search; MasterFile FullTEXT 1000; MasterFile FullTEXT 350; MasterFile FullTEXT 650; MasterFile FullTEXT (July 1993-); Middle East Abstr. Index; Newsp. Period. Abstr. (1992-); OCLC; PAIS Int. Print (1991-); Telebase; Trade Ind. Index; UMI ABI/Inform--Bus. Period. Ondisc [Full Txt.]; World Agric. Econ. Rural Sociol. Abstr.

LC HA1 .C57
DD 310/.5
US
COMPENDIUM OF SOCIAL STATISTICS AND INDICATORS = RECUEIL DE STATISTIQUES ET D'INDICATEURS SOCIAUX. See Business and Economics-Abstracting, Bibliographies and Statistics.

ISSN 1061-1576
DD 658
US
CEASED
COMPENSATION & BENEFITS ALERT. [Compens. benefits alert]. **VFOAT** Compensation and Benefits Alert; C&B Alert. Vol. 1, No. 1 (Jan. 27, 1992)-(1993). Periodical. English. Warren Gorham & Lamont Inc., Park Square Building, 31 St. James Avenue, Boston MA 02116-4112. **Tel** (617)423-2020, (800)950-1207, FAX (617)423-2026. **(Subscription address:** Warren Gorham & Lamont, PO Box 4966, Chicago IL 60680.) **ED** Pat Lenihan.

ISSN 1254-4906
FR
●**COMPETENCES PARIS.** (COMPETENCES.). (1994)-. Periodical. French. Twelve times a year. $141.07. Generation Formation, 27 rue du Chemin Vert, F-75011 Paris France. **Tel** 011 33 1 48074141, FAX 011 33 1 48074317. **(Subscription address:** Development Info Presse / DIP, 70 rue Compans, 75019 Paris France. **Tel** 011 33 1 44848511.) **Continues** Formation (Paris), 1167-2560.

Business and Economics

ISSN 0897-3881
US

COMPETITIVE EDGE (BEVERLY HILLS, CALIF.), THE. (THE COMPETITIVE EDGE.). (1988)-. Periodical. English. Twelve times a year. $145.00. Morton D. Bohn, 8530 Wilshire Boulevard, Suite 404, Beverly Hills CA 90211.

ISSN 1058-0247
DD 338
US
CODEN CINREU

COMPETITIVE INTELLIGENCE REVIEW. (COMPETITIVE INTELLIGENCE REVIEW : PUBLICATION OF THE SOCIETY OF COMPETITOR INTELLIGENCE PROFESSIONALS.). [Compet. intell. rev.]. **Main/Corp** Society of Competitive Intelligence Professionals. **Added/Corp** Society of Competitive Intelligence Professionals. Society of Competitive Intelligence Professionals. Vol. 1, No. 1 (Summer 1990)-. Periodical. English. Four times a year. $112.00. John Wiley & Sons, Inc., 605 Third Avenue, New York NY 10158-0012. **Tel** (212)850-6000, (212)850-6645, FAX (212)850-6088, telex 12-7063. **(Subscription address:** John Wiley & Sons / UK, Baffins Lane, Chichester, West Sussex PO19 1UD United Kingdom. **Tel** 011 44 1243 779777, FAX 011 44 243 776128, telex 86290 WIBOOKG.) **ED** Bonnie Hohhof. cum. index. **Bk Rev**. **Ad Acc**. **Circ:** 1,700 (ctrl). **Continues** Competitive Intelligencer, 1040-9645.
Desc: Reports intelligence/analysis concepts and presents the Society to external observers.
Ind/Abst Trade Ind. Index.

ISSN 0953-9239
DD 344.10682
UK

COMPLIANCE MONITOR. [Compliance monit.]. (1988)-. Periodical. English. Twelve times a year. $527.05. Tolley Publishing Company Ltd., Tolley House, 2 Addiscombe Road, Croydon, Surrey CR9 5AF United Kingdom. **Tel** 011 44 181 6869141, FAX 011 44 181 6863155.
Desc: Covers all aspects of financial services compliance.

US

COMPOSITE INDEXES OF LEADING, COINCIDENT, AND LAGGING INDICATORS. **Added/Corp** United States. Bureau of Economic Analysis. (19??)-. English. Twelve times a year. $24.00. Bureau of Economic Analysis, US Department of Commerce, 1401 K Street Northwest, Washington DC 20230. **Tel** (202)523-0777.

FR

COMPTES DE LA NATION, LES. (19??)-. French. Irregular. Observatoire Economique de Paris, 195 rue de Bercy Tour Gamma A, 75582 Paris Cedex 12 France.

FR

COMPTES ET RATIOS DES SOCIETES. **Added/Corp** Institut National de la Statistique et des Etudes Economiques (France). (1985)-. French. **Continues** Tableau de Bord Financier des Societes, les Comptes Intermediaires.

ISSN 1194-305X
DD 004
CN

COMPUTER POST. See Computers.

SP

●**COMPUTING ESPANA.** (1995)-. Spanish. Four times a year. 31500ptas. Business Publications Espana, J Camarillo, 29 Diapason D 1 3, 28037 Madrid Spain. **Tel** 011 34 1 3043344. **Continues** Tribuna Informatica.

US

COMSTOCK'S. Trade Publication. English. Twelve times a year. $30.00 US; $50.00 other. Comstock Publishing Inc, 1770 Tribute Road/Suite 205, Sacramento CA 95815. **Tel** (916)924-9815, FAX (916)924-9034. **ED** Janice Fillip. Index available. **Bk Rev**. **Ad Acc**. **Circ:** 16,000 (ctrl).
Desc: A regional business magazine covering the Sacramento Capital Region, its people, and community issues.

MX

COMUNIMEF. Periodical. Spanish. $20.00. Ruben Carranza, Patricio Sanz 1516, Mexico 12 DF Mexico. **Tel** 5/575-19-77. **Bk Rev**. **Ad Acc**. ctrl circ.
Desc: Articles on financial and economic subjects concerning current corporate, social and national programs.

LC HC905.A1 C66
DD 338.0968
SA

CONDENSER (TONGAAT, SOUTH AFRICA). (THE CONDENSER.). **Added/Corp** Tongaat Group Ltd. (19??)-. Periodical. English. One time a year. Free to qualified subscribers. Tongaat-Hulett Group Ltd., PO Box 3, Tongaat 4400, Natal South Africa. **Tel** 011 27 322 21000, FAX 011 27 322 21094. **ED** G.Y. Balfour. **Circ:** 18,000 (ctrl).

LC HC121 .C57
DD 330
UY

CONEXION. **Added/Corp** Asesoramiento en Comunicacion Social (Uruguay) Fundacion Banco de Boston. Vol. 1, No. 1 (Sept. 1991)-. Periodical. Spanish. Four times a year. Fundacion Banco de Boston, Bulivar Artigas, 934-902 Montevideo Uruguay. **Tel** 986342. **ED** Claudio Trobo.

ISSN 0885-9043
DD 332
US

CONFIDENTIAL, REPORT FROM ZURICH. [Confid. rep. Zur.]. Vol. 1, No. 1 (Oct. 1985)-. Periodical. English. Twelve times a year. $150.00. Oxford Club, PO Box 3064, Boca Raton FL 33431-0907. **Tel** 800 678-3300.
Desc: Analysis and specific advice based on information gathered directly from specialists on gold, silver, currencies, etc.

ISSN 1067-8018
US

●**CONGO (SYRACUSE, N.Y.).** (CONGO : AN EXECUTIVE REPORT.). **Added/Corp** Political Risk Services (IBC USA (Publications) Inc.). **VFOAT** Executive Report. (1993)-. English. $110.00. Political Risk Services, 6320 Fly Road, Suite 102, PO Box 248, East Syracuse NY 13057-0248. **Tel** (315)431-0511, FAX (315)431-0200.
Desc: Focuses on the long-term outlook for business. Includes a brief review of recent events and current circumstances, background intelligence including geography, history, economics and social conditions, as well as the key political and economic forecasts.

ISSN 0275-746X
US

CONGRESSIONAL DISTRICT BUSINESS PATTERNS. [Congr. dist. bus. patterns]. 1981-. English. One time a year. Economic Information Systems, 310 Madison Avenue, New York NY 10017.

ISSN 0714-7635
DD 330.971/064
CN
TITLE CHANGE

CONJONCTURE DES AFFAIRES. (CONJONCTURE DES AFFAIRES : BULLETIN ECONOMIQUE DE WOODS GORDON.). [Conjonct. aff.]. **Added/Corp** Woods, Gordon & Cie. Caron Belanger Ernst & Young (Firme). **VFOAT** Bulletin Economique de Woods Gordon. (Feb. 1981)-(199?). Bulletin. French. Conjoncture des Affaires, a/s Woods Gordon & Cie, 630 boulevard Dorchester, Suite 2000, Montreal Quebec H3B 1T9 Canada. **Continues** Andersen, Peter R. Bulletin Economique, 0714-7627. **Continued by** Bulletin Economique (Caron, Belanger Ernst & Young), 1197-6373.

LC HC186 .C75
DD 330
ISSN 0010-5945
BL

CONJUNTURA ECONOMICA (RIO DE JANEIRO, BRAZIL : 1986). (CONJUNTURA ECONOMICA.). [Conjunt. econ.]. **Added/Corp** Instituto Brasileiro de Economia. Vol. 40, No. 2 (Feb. 1986)-. Periodical. Portuguese. Twelve times a year. $235.00. Fundacao Getulio Vargas, Praia de Botafogo, 190 6 Andar, 22253-900 Rio de Janeiro RJ Brazil. **Tel** 011 5521 551 0698, FAX 011 5521 551 1596, 011 5521 551 5755. **Continues** Conjuntura, 0010-5945.
Desc: Analysis of the national economy, profile of national accounts, price indices for different sectors and the latest researches in the economic area.
Ind/Abst Int. Labour Doc.; LABORDOC; PAIS Int. Print (1991-).

LC HC107.C8 C564a
DD 330.9746/005
ISSN 0573-665X
US

CONNECTICUT MARKET DATA. See Business and Economics-Abstracting, Bibliographies and Statistics.

LC LC67.65.N49 C66
DD 378.74/05
ISSN 0895-6405
US

CONNECTION (BOSTON, MASS.). See Education-Higher Education.

UK

CONNEXION. (19??)-. Periodical. English. Twenty-six times a year. $136.89. VNU Business Publications BV, 32-34 Broadwick Street, London W1A 2HG United Kingdom. **Tel** 011 44 171 4394242 ext. 2222, FAX 011 44 171 4379638, telex 23918 VNU G, 8952440. Documents available from Ask*IEEE.
Ind/Abst Infomat Int. Bus.; INSPEC (July 1989-).

ISSN 1059-6623
DD 381
US

CONSCIOUS CONSUMER, THE. See Environmental Issues.

LC HC10 .C587
DD 330.9/001/12
ISSN 0957-0950
UK

CONSENSUS FORECASTS. **Added/Corp** Consensus Economics, Inc. (19??)-. Periodical. English. Twelve times a year. $565.00. Consensus Economics Inc., 49 Berkeley Square, London W1X 6LT United Kingdom. **Tel** 011 44 171 4913211, FAX 011 44 171 4092331. available with charts.

LC HC
DD 330/.05
ISSN 1043-4062
US
Pr Rev.

CONSTITUTIONAL POLITICAL ECONOMY. See Law-Constitutional Law.

ISSN 0964-0665
DD 338.47624094
UK

CONSTRUCTION EUROPE. [Constr. Eur.]. (1990)-. Periodical. English (summaries and/or abstracts in French and German). Twelve times a year. $162.57. KHL Publishing Ltd., Southview Road Wadhurst, East Sussex TN5 6TP United Kingdom. **Tel** 011 44 1892 784088.

ISSN 0045-8201
US

CONSULTANTS NEWS. (1970)-. Periodical. English. Eleven times a year. $188.00. Kennedy Publications, Templeton Road, Fitzwilliam NH 03447. **Tel** (603)585-6544, (800)531-0007, FAX (603)585-9555. **ED** James H. Kennedy. Index available. **Bk Rev**. available on microfilm and microfiche from University Microfilms International (UMI); available on an online database (file 485/Full-Text) from DIALOG.
Desc: Newsletter regularly covering trends and developments in the field.
Ind/Abst Account. Tax Datab. (Mar. 1992-) [Full Txt.].

ISSN 0273-4613
US

CONSULTING OPPORTUNITIES JOURNAL. [Consult. oppor. j.]. Vol. 1, No. 1 (Spring 1981)-. Periodical. English. Six times a year. $49.00. Consultants National Resource Center, PO Box 430, Clear Spring MD 21722. **Tel** (301)791-9332. **ED** J. Stephen Lanning. **Bk Rev**. **Ad Acc**.
Desc: Tells how to establish and market a successful consulting practice and develop information profit centers.

ISSN 1170-747X
NZ

CONSUMER EXPENDITURE STATISTICS. **Added/Corp** New Zealand. Dept. of Statistics. **VFOAT** Consumer Expenditure. (1991)-. Periodical. English. Department of Statistics / New Zealand, PO Box 2922, Wellington New Zealand. **Tel** 011 64 4 4954600.

LC HB235.H75 C66
DD 338.5/28/095125
HK

CONSUMER PRICE INDEX REPORT. **Added/Corp** Hong Kong. Census and Statistics Dept. Consumer Price Index Section. (19??)-. Periodical. English. Twelve times a year. $12.00. Hong Kong Government Information Service, Beaconsfield House, 4 Queens Road, Hong Kong Hong Kong. **Tel** 011 852 284288014, 011 852 259881947, FAX 011 852 28459078, 011 852 25987482, telex 61190 HKGIS.

LC HB235.P37 C66
DD 338.5/28/09953
PP

CONSUMER PRICE INDEXES (PORT MORESBY, PAPUA NEW GUINEA). (CONSUMER PRICE INDEXES.). (19??)-. Periodical. English. Four times a year. k8.00 Papua New Guinea; k9.00 (surface mail); k14.00 (airmail) other. National Statistical Office / New Guinea, PO Wards Strip NCO, Papua New Guinea. **Tel** 011 675 27182 271172, FAX 011 657 255057, telex FINANCE NE 22312. **Continues** Consumer Price Index (Konedobu, Papua New Guinea).

LC TX335
DD 640.73
ISSN 1053-1416
US

CONSUMER REPORTS ON CD-ROM (ADVANCED USER'S ED.). (CONSUMER REPORTS ON CD-ROM [COMPUTER FILE].). **Added/Corp** National Information Services Corporation. (1990)-. Consumer Publication. English. Four times a year. $711.00 US; $725.00 other. Consumer Reports Books, 101 Truman Avenue, Yonkers NY 10703. **Tel** (800)288-7898, FAX (914)378-2900. available on CD-ROM from National Information Service Corporation (NISC).

ISSN 1053-1408
US

CONSUMER REPORTS ON CD-ROM (BEGINNER'S ED.). (CONSUMER REPORTS ON CD-ROM. [COMPUTER FILE].). **Added/Corp** National Information Services Corporation. (1990)-. Consumer Publication. English. Two times a year. $711.00 US; $725.00 other. Consumer Reports Books, 101 Truman Avenue, Yonkers NY 10703. **Tel** (800)288-7898, FAX (914)378-2900.
Desc: Designed for first-time users of database search software or CD-ROM in a library or general reference setting. Full-text search and retrieval of the entire database is also available.

LC HF5035 .C67
DD 338.7/4/02573
ISSN 0098-7344
US
CEASED

CONSUMER'S REGISTER OF AMERICAN BUSINESS, THE. **Added/Corp** National Register Publishing Co. (19??)-(19??). English.

National Register Publishing Company Inc., PO Box 31, 121 Chanlon Road, New Providence NJ 07974. **Tel** (800)521-8110, (800)323-6772, FAX (908)665-6688.

ISSN 1193-7521
DD 658.85097105 CN
CONTACT - ASSOCIATION CANADIENNE DES PROFESSIONNELS DE LA VENTE. (CONTACT.). [Contact - Assoc. can. prof. vente]. **Added/Corp** Association Canadienne des Professionnels de la Vente. (1991)-. Periodical. French (English). Five times a year. Free to members of the Canadian Professional Sales Association. Contact, 145 Wellington Street West, Suite 310, Toronto Ontario, M5J 1H8 Canada. **Tel** (416)408-2685, FAX (416)408-2684. **ED** Corrine James. **Bk Rev**, (Qty: varies). **Ad Acc, Adv Mgr:** Corrine James. **Circ:** 30,000 (ctrl). Documents available. ***Continues*** *Contact - Commercial Travellers' Association of Canada, 0834-3845.* ***Continued in part by*** *Contact - Canadian Professional Sales Association, 1193-7513.*
Desc: Published for the Canadian Professional Sales Association members. Discusses issues of relevancy to the sales industry, such as sales force automation and management and government relations.

ISSN 1193-7513
DD 658.8/5/097105 CN
CONTACT - CANADIAN PROFESSIONAL SALES ASSOCIATION. (CONTACT.). [Contact - Can. Prof. Sales Assoc.]. **Added/Corp** Canadian Professional Sales Association. **VFOAT** Contact. (June 1991)-. Periodical. English (French). Five times a year. Free to members of the Canadian Professional Sales Association. Contact, 145 Wellington Street West, Suite 310, Toronto Ontario, M5J 1H8 Canada. **Tel** (416)408-2685, FAX (416)408-2684. **ED** Corrine James. **Bk Rev**, (Qty: varies). **Ad Acc, Adv Mgr:** Corrine James. **Circ:** 30,000 (ctrl). Documents available. ***Continues*** *Contact (Commercial Travellers' Association of Canada)., 0834-3845.* ***Continued in part by*** *Contact (Canadian Professional Sales Association). French., 1193-7521.*
Desc: Published for the Canadian Professional Sales Association members. Discusses issues of relevancy to the sales industry, such as sales force automation and management and government relations.

ISSN 0713-5009
DD 658/.005 CN
CONTACT (SOCIETE DE RELATIONS D'AFFAIRES, ECOLE DES HAUTES ETUDES COMMERCIALES. 1981). (LE CONTACT : JOURNAL DE LA SOCIETE DE RELATIONS D'AFFAIRES-ECOLE DES HAUTES ETUDES COMMERCIALES INC.). [Contact]. **Added/Corp** Societe de Relations d'Affaires H.E.C. Vol. 6, No. 1 (Nov./Dec. 1981)-. Periodical. French. One time a week. 56.02Can$. Les Editions Contact, 5255 Avenue Decelles, Local 2025 A, Montreal Quebec H3T 1V6 Canada. **Tel** (514)340-6227. ctrl circ. ***Continues*** *Journal le Contact, 0713-4037.*

LC HF5065.C2 C66 **ISSN** 0743-2682
DD 338.7/4/0257946 US
CONTACTS INFLUENTIAL. EAST BAY. (CONTACTS INFLUENTIAL. EAST BAY : CI.). **VFOAT** East Bay. ?. English. One time a year. Contacts Influential, 5711 South 86th Circle, Omaha NE 68127. **Tel** (402)593-4578. ***Continued in part by*** *Contacts Influential. Oakland Metro, 0888-6466.*

LC HF5068.F67 C66 **ISSN** 0884-9722
DD 338.7/4/025764531 US
CONTACTS INFLUENTIAL. FORT WORTH, TEXAS, TARRANT COUNTY : CI. **VFOAT** Fort Worth, Texas, Tarrant County. (1985)-. English. One time a year. Contacts Influential, 5711 South 86th Circle, Omaha NE 68127. **Tel** (402)593-4578. ***Continues*** *Contacts Influential Commerce and Industry Directory. Fort Worth, Tarrant County, 0743-0582.*

LC HF5065.C2 C666 **ISSN** 8756-0119
DD 338.7/4/02579493 US
CONTACTS INFLUENTIAL. LOS ANGELES COUNTY, SOUTHEAST L.A. : CI. **VFOAT** Los Angeles County, Southeast L.A. (19??)-. Directory. English. One time a year. $535.18. Contacts Influential, 5711 South 86th Circle, Omaha NE 68127. **Tel** (402)593-4578.
Desc: Directory of all businesses in Southeast Los Angeles, referenced by size, SIC, type of location and zip code, with all data verified by phone.

LC HF5065.C2 C667 **ISSN** 8756-064X
DD 338.7/4/02579496 US
CONTACTS INFLUENTIAL. NORTH ORANGE COUNTY. (CONTACTS INFLUENTIAL. NORTH ORANGE COUNTY : CI.). **VFOAT** North Orange County. (1984/85)-. Directory. English. One time a year. $600.00. Contacts Influential, 5711 South 86th Circle, Omaha NE 68127. **Tel** (402)593-4578. **(Subscription address:** Contacts Influential, PO Box 27346, Omaha NE 68127. **Tel** (402)593-4578.) ***Continues*** *Contacts Influential. North Orange County, Firms Only, 8756-0984.*
Desc: Directory of all businesses in northern Orange County, referenced by size, SIC, type of location and zip code, with all data verified by phone.

LC HF5068.W3 C66 **ISSN** 0743-264X
DD 338.7/4/025753 US
CONTACTS INFLUENTIAL. WASHINGTON, D.C. (CONTACTS INFLUENTIAL. WASHINGTON, D.C. : COMMERCE AND INDUSTRY DIRECTORY.). **VFOAT** Washington, D.C. Directory. English. One time a year. Contacts Influential, 5711 South 86th Circle, Omaha NE 68127. **Tel** (402)593-4578.

LC HD72 .C66 **ISSN** 1074-3529
DD 338.973/005 US
•**CONTEMPORARY ECONOMIC POLICY.** [Contemp. econ. policy]. **Added/Corp** Western Economic Association International. Vol. 12, No. 1 (Jan. 1994)-. Periodical. English. Four times a year. $110.00. Allen Press Inc., 810 East 10th Street, PO Box 1897, Lawrence KS 66044-8897. **Tel** (913)843-1221, (800)627-0629, FAX (913)843-1274. ***Continues*** *Contemporary Policy Issues, 0735-0007.*
Ind/Abst Curr. Cit.

LC HD72 .C66 **ISSN** 0735-0007
DD 338.973/005 US
Pr Rev. **TITLE CHANGE**
CONTEMPORARY POLICY ISSUES. [Contemp. policy issues]. **Added/Corp** Western Economic Association International. California State University, Long Beach. No. 1 (Oct. 1982)-Vol. 11, No. 4 (Oct. 1993). Periodical. English. Allen Press Inc., 810 East 10th Street, PO Box 1897, Lawrence KS 66044-8897. **Tel** (913)843-1221, (800)627-0629, FAX (913)843-1274. **ED** Eldon J. Dvorak. Index available. **Ad Acc.** **Acid Free. Circ:** 3,000. available on microfilm and microfiche from University Microfilms International (UMI); available on CD-ROM; available in microform. Documents available from The Genuine Article, UMI Article Clearinghouse. ***Continued by*** *Contemporary Economic Policy, 1074-3529.*
Desc: Focuses economic research and analysis on issues of concern to business, government and other decision makers and communicates that research to non-economists and economists.
Ind/Abst ABI/INFORM Glob. Ed.; ABI/INFORM [Computer File] (Spring 1985-?); Am. Hist. Life (1982-?); Crim. Justice Abstr.; Curr. Cit.; Curr. Contents Soc. Behav. Sci.; Econ. Lit. Index; Geogr. Abstr. Human Geogr.; Index Period. Artic. Relat. Law; Int. Bibliogr. Sociol.; Int. Dev. Abstr.; J. Econ. Lit.; Newsp. Period. Abstr. (1992-?); PAIS Int. Print (1991-?); Res. Alert [Full Cov.]; Sage Public Adm. Abstr.; Soc. Sci. Cit. Index [Full Cov.]; UMI ABI/Inform--Bus. Period. Ondisc [Full Txt.].

US
CONTEMPORARY STUDIES IN ECONOMIC AND FINANCIAL ANALYSIS. (19??)-. Periodical. English. Irregular. $73.25. JAI Press Inc., 55 Old Post Road, Suite 2, PO Box 1678, Greenwich CT 06836-1678. **Tel** (203)661-7602, FAX (203)661-0792. **ED** Robert Thornton and Richard Aronson.
Desc: Illustrates how statistical classification techniques should have been used in business, banking and finance. Discrimination techniques are discussed including their potential and pitfalls with regard to their latest analytical aspects. Specific fields covered include failure predication, credit analysis, security analysis, banking regulating and marketing within financial institutions.

LC HC
DD 330 US
CONTEMPORARY STUDIES IN ECONOMIC AND FINANCIAL ANALYSIS. **See** Finance.

LC HN398.W26 C65 **ISSN** 0951-4937
DD 306/.9429 UK
CONTEMPORARY WALES : AN ANNUAL REVIEW OF ECONOMIC AND SOCIAL RESEARCH. **Added/Corp** University of Wales. Board of Celtic Studies. Vol. 1 (1987)-. English. Irregular. £7.50. University of Wales Press, 6 Gwennyth Street, Cathays Cardiff CF2 4YD United Kingdom. **Tel** 011 44 1222 231919, FAX 011 44 1222 230908. **ED** Graham Day and Gareth Rees. **Bk Rev.** **Ad Acc. Circ:** 650.
Desc: An account of economic and social development in Wales. Draws upon empirical research and theoretical innovation.

UK
CONTENTS OF CURRENT JOURNALS. **See** Business and Economics-Abstracting, Bibliographies and Statistics.

UK
CEASED
CONTENTS OF RECENT ECONOMICS JOURNALS. **See** Business and Economics-Abstracting, Bibliographies and Statistics.

LC HC301 .C635 **ISSN** 0390-6434
DD 330 IT
CONTI ECONOMICI NAZIONALI. **Added/Corp** Istituto Centrale di Statistica (Italy) Istituto Nazionale di Statistica (Italy). (19??)-. Italian. One time a year. L50000. Istituto Nazionale Statistica, GBP SEZ4 Via Cesare Balbo 16, 00184 Rome Italy. **Tel** 011 39 6 46735118. ***Continues*** *Annuario di Contabilita Nazionale / Instituto Centrale di Statistica, 0390-6531.*

IT
CEASED
CONTI ECONOMICI TRIMESTRALI. (19??)-(1995). Italian. Istituto Nazionale Statistica, GBP SEZ4 Via Cesare Balbo 16, 00184 Rome Italy. **Tel** 011 39 6 46735118.

ISSN 0045-8376
US
CONTINENTAL FRANCHISE REVIEW. **VFOAT** CFR, Continental Franchise Review. (19??)-. Newsletter. English. Twenty-six times a year. $195.00. Continental Franchise Review, PO Box 3283, Englewood CO 80155. **Tel** (303)470-7744, FAX (303)740-7745. **ED** Ron Vlieger. Index available. cum. index. **Bk Rev. Circ:** 1,000.
Desc: Investigates and reports on marketing, financial and legal trends affecting franchising.

LC HC
DD 330 AT
•**CONTINUUM.** (1995)-. English. Four times a year. 42.76Aus$. Sector Publications Pty Ltd., 462 Hawthorn Road, South Caulfield, VIC 3162 Australia. **Tel** 011 61 3 5300558.

ISSN 0271-5511
US
CONTRACTOR BUSINESS REPORT. **See** Building and Construction.

US
CONTRACTORS DATA REPORT : NATIONWIDE TABULATED BID RESULTS. (19??)-. Periodical. English. Twelve times a year. $95.00. Contractors Data Reports, PO Box 2700, Southfield MI 48037-2700. **Tel** (517)864-3238. **Circ:** 200.

ISSN 0770-8521
BE
UDC 330.191.5
CODEN 331.831
CONTRADICTIONS BRUXELLES. (1972)-. Periodical. French. Four times a year. $44.77. Contradictions Asbl, Avenue des Grenadiers 2 Bte 1, B-1050 Brussels Belgium. **Tel** 011 32 2 6606598. Index available. cum. index.
Ind/Abst Geogr. Abstr. Human Geogr.; Int. Dev. Abstr.; PAIS Int. Print.

ISSN 1356-0239
DD 354.4100711 UK
•**CONTRAX WEEKLY.** [Contrax wkly]. (1994)-. Periodical. English. One time a week. £396.00. Business Information Publications, Freepost 15 Woodlands Terrace, Glasgow G3 6BR United Kingdom. **Tel** 011 44 141 3328247, FAX 011 44 141 3312652. **ED** Leslie Burges. **Ad Acc, Adv Mgr:** E. Regan. ctrl circ.

LC HC **ISSN** 0573-8555
DD 330 NE
Pr Rev.
CONTRIBUTIONS TO ECONOMIC ANALYSIS. [Contrib. econ. anal.]. (1952)-. Monographic series. English. Irregular. Price varies per volume. Elsevier Science Publishers BV, PO Box 211, 1000 AE Amsterdam Netherlands. **Tel** 011 31 20 4853641, 011 31 20 4853642, FAX 011 31 20 4853598. Documents available from Ask*IEEE.
Ind/Abst Curr. Cit.; INSPEC; Math. Rev.

LC HB1 .C59 **ISSN** 0277-5921
DD 330/.05 UK
CCC
CONTRIBUTIONS TO POLITICAL ECONOMY. [Contrib. polit. econ.]. Vol. 1 (March 1982)-. Academic Scholarly Publication. English. One time a year. $30.00. Academic Press Ltd., A Division of Harcourt Brace & Company Ltd., 24-28 Oval Road, London NW1 7DX United Kingdom. **Tel** 011 44 171 2674466, FAX 011 44 171 4822293, 011 44 171 4854752, telex 25775 ACPRES G. **(Subscription address:** Harcourt Brace & Company, Ltd., Foots Cray High Street, Sidcup Kent DA14 5HP United Kingdom. **Tel** 011 44 181 3003322, FAX 011 44 181 3090807, telex 896 377 ACADEM.) **ED** John Eatwell, Murray Milgate, and Giancarlo De Vivo. **Bk Rev.** Documents available from The Genuine Article.
Desc: Articles are published on the theory and history of political economy that fall broadly within a critical tradition in economic thought and are associated with the work of the old classical economists, Marx, Keynes, and Sraffa.
Ind/Abst Curr. Contents Soc. Behav. Sci.; Res. Alert [Full Cov.]; Soc. Sci. Cit. Index [Select. Cov.].

Business and Economics

ISSN 0266-1713
UK
CONTROL SAWBRIDGEWORTH. VFOAT
BPICS Control. (1983)-. English. *Continues* BPICS News.
Ind/Abst Curr. Cit.; Oper. Prod. Manage. Abstr.

ISSN 0194-8733
DD 658 US
Pr Rev.
CONVENIENCE STORE NEWS. [Conven. store news]. VFOAT CSN. (19??)-. Trade Publication. English. Irregular (16 issues per year). $72.00. BMT Publications, Inc., 7 Penn Plaza, New York NY 10001. **Tel** (212)594-4120, (800)223-9638. **Ad Acc. Circ:** 118,000 (ctrl). *Continues* CSN. Convenience Store News, 0045-8422.
Ind/Abst Foods Adlibra.

ISSN 0928-3048
NE
UDC 631.1(492)
COOPERATIE MAGAZINE. [Coop. mag.]. (1991)-. Periodical. Dutch. Four times a year. $23.98. NCR, Postbus 29774, 2502Lt Den Haag Netherlands. **Tel** 011 31 70 3382780. *Continues* Cooperatie, 0009-9783.

LC HC108.W3 C59 **ISSN** 1043-7800
DD 330.9753/001/12 US
COOPERATIVE FORECASTING. TECHNICAL REPORT. [Coop. forecast., Tech. rep.]. **Added/Corp** Metropolitan Washington Council of Governments. VFOAT Technical Report. English. $50.00. Metropolitan Washington Council of Governments, 777 North Capitol Street Northeast, Washington DC 20002-4239. **Tel** (202)962-3256.

ISSN 1130-2682
SP
UDC 334.73
COOPERATIVISMO E ECONOMIA SOCIAL. [Coop. econ. soc.]. (1990)-. Periodical. Gallegan. Two times a year. $8.88. Universidade de Vigo, Esc Univ Empresariales, Vigo Pontevedra Spain. **Tel** 011 34 86813748. **(Subscription address:** Galaxia, Reconquista Entresuelo, Vigo Pontevedra Spain. **)**
Ind/Abst LABORDOC.

BE
CORE DISCUSSION PAPERS. Main/Corp Universite Catholique de Louvain (1425-). Center for Operations Research and Econometrics. (19??)-. Academic Scholarly Publication. English (French). Irregular. Price varies per volume. Universite Catholique de Louvain Core, 34 Voie du Roman Pays, B 1348 Louvain Belgium. **Tel** 011 32 10 474321, FAX 011 32 10 474301. available on diskette.

LC HG4057 **ISSN** 1075-9948
DD 338 US
●**CORPORATE AFFILIATIONS PLUS.** (CORPORATE AFFILIATIONS PLUS [COMPUTER FILE].). [Corp. affil. plus]. (1993)-. English. Four times a year. National Register Publishing Company Inc., PO Box 31, 121 Chanlon Road, New Providence NJ 07974. **Tel** (800)521-8110, (800)323-6772, FAX (908)665-6688. **(Subscription address:** Reed Reference Publishing Company / New Jersey, 131 Chanlon Road, PO Box 31, New Providence NJ 07974. **Tel** 800 223-1797, (908)464-6802.**)**

ISSN 0739-1587
US
CORPORATE & INCENTIVE TRAVEL.
VFOAT Corporate and Incentive Travel. Vol. 1, No. 1 (Sept. 1983)-. Trade Publication. English. Twelve times a year. Coastal Communications Corporation, 488 Madison Avenue, New York NY 10022. **Tel** (212)888-1500.

LC KF1477 .C67 **ISSN** 0897-6740
DD 346.73/06626 347.3066626 US
CORPORATE ANTI-TAKEOVER DEFENSES. (CORPORATE ANTI-TAKEOVER DEFENSES, THE POISON PILL DEVICE / CHARLES E. SIMON & COMPANY.). [Corp. anti-takeover def.]. **Added/Corp** Charles E. Simon & Company. VFOAT Corporate Antitakeover Defenses. (1987)-. English. One time a year. $110.00. Clark Boardman Callaghan, 155 Pfingsten Road, Deerfield IL 60015. **Tel** (800)323-8067.

ISSN 0746-8652
US
CCC
CORPORATE BOARD, THE. [Corp. board]. Vol. 4, No. 24 (Nov./Dec. 1983)-. Periodical. English. Six times a year. $370.00. Vanguard Publications, 6604 West Saginaw Highway, Lansing MI 48917. **Tel** (517)321-0667, FAX (517)321-1015. **ED** Ralph D. Ward. Each issue contains an index to its own contents (no volume index)--loose. cum. index. **Bk Rev**, (Qty: 30 per year). **Circ:** 2,500. available on an online database (file 648/Full-Text) from DIALOG. *Continues* Corporate Director (New York, N.Y. : 1980), 0196-2116.
Desc: Written and read by CEO's, directors, consultants, and legal advisors of major corporations. Covers today's business world from the director's point of view.
Ind/Abst Acad. Search; Bus. ASAP (1990-) [Full Txt.]; Bus. Index (1985-); Bus. Source Plus; Bus. Source; EP Collect.; Gen. BusinessFile (1985-); Gen. Period. Index (1985-); Homework Help.; INFO-SOUTH Abstr.; Mag. Search; Manage. Contents; MasterFile FullTEXT 1000; MasterFile FullTEXT 350; MasterFile FullTEXT 650; MasterFile FullTEXT (July 1993-) [Full Txt.]; OCLC; Telebase.

ISSN 0831-9774
DD 332.63/234/0971 CN
CORPORATE BOND RECORD, THE.
[Corp. bond rec.]. **Added/Corp** Financial Post Corporation Service Group. 8th Ed. (1985)-. English. One time a year. 56.78Can$. Financial Post Company Ltd., 333 King Street East, Toronto Ontario M5A 4N2, Canada. **Tel** (416)350-6500, FAX (416)350-6601. *Continues* The Bond Record II., 0709-5066.
Desc: Information on Canadian corporate debt issues. Covers public offerings and private placements, conversion priveleges, DBRS rating, and more.

ISSN 1055-5978
US
CEASED
CORPORATE CLEVELAND. (1991)-(March 1994). Trade Publication. English. Business Journal Publishing Company, 1720 Euclid Avenue, Third Floor, Cleveland OH 44115. **Tel** (216)621-1644. available on an online database (files 635,648/Full-Text) from DIALOG. Documents available from UMI Article Clearinghouse.
Ind/Abst Bus. Dateline (March 1985-) [Full Txt.].

LC HG4028.C6 B53
US
CORPORATE CONTRIBUTIONS.
Added/Corp Conference Board. (1989)-. English. One time a year. $100.00. Conference Board, 845 Third Avenue, New York NY 10022. **Tel** (212)759-0900 ext. 582, (800)872-6273, FAX (212)980-7014. *Continues* Survey of Corporate Contributions, 1043-5344.

LC HF5686.C7 C653 **ISSN** 0899-0174
DD 658.1/5/05 US
CEASED
CORPORATE CONTROLLER. [Corp. control.]. Vol. 1, No. 1 (Sept./Oct. 1988)-(Spring 1993). Corporate Report. English. Faulkner & Gray Inc., 11 Penn Plaza, 17th Floor, New York NY 10001. **Tel** (212)967-7000, (800)535-8403. **ED** Pamela Goett. **Bk Rev. Ad Acc. Circ:** 2,500 (ctrl). available on microfilm and microfiche from University Microfilms International (UMI); available on an online database (files 15,485/Full-Text) from DIALOG.
Ind/Abst Account. Tax Datab. (1988-) [Full Txt.].

LC HC **ISSN** 0589-784X
DD 658 US
CORPORATE COUNSEL'S ANNUAL. See Law-Corporation Law.

ISSN 1062-368X
US
CORPORATE DETROIT. VFOAT Corporate Detroit Magazine,. Vol. 8, No. 2 (Feb. 1991)-. Periodical. English. Twelve times a year. $30.00. Corporate Detroit, 3031 West Grand Boulevard, Suite 624, Detroit MI 48202. **Tel** (313)872-6000. available on an online database (files 635,648/Full-Text) from DIALOG. Documents available from UMI Article Clearinghouse. *Continues* Business Detroit, 1062-3671.
Ind/Abst Acad. Search; Bus. Dateline (199?-) [Full Txt.]; Bus. Index (1991-); Bus. Source Plus; Bus. Source; EP Collect.; Gen. BusinessFile (1991-); Gen. Period. Index (1991-); Homework Help.; INFO-SOUTH Abstr.; MasterFile FullTEXT 1000; MasterFile FullTEXT 350; MasterFile FullTEXT 650; MasterFile FullTEXT (Jan. 1994-); OCLC; Telebase.

LC HD4965.5.U6 C678 **ISSN** 0885-1360
DD 331.2/81658422/0973021 US
CORPORATE DIRECTORS' COMPENSATION. (CORPORATE DIRECTORS' COMPENSATION / BY JEREMY BACON.). [Corp. dir. compens.]. **Added/Corp** Conference Board. American Society of Corporate Secretaries. (1985)-. English. One time a year. $120.00. Conference Board, 845 Third Avenue, New York NY 10022. **Tel** (212)759-0900 ext. 582, (800)872-6273, FAX (212)980-7014. *Continues* Corporate Directorship Practices. Compensation, 0884-2183.

ISSN 0841-1956
DD 174/.4/05 CN
CORPORATE ETHICS MONITOR, THE.
[Corp. ethics monit.]. (1989)-. Periodical. English. Six times a year. 237.70Can$. Ethicscan Canada Ltd., PO Box 165 Station S, Toronto Ontario M5M 4L6 Canada. **Tel** (416)783-6776, FAX (416)783-7569. **ED** Len Brooks, (416)828-3916. **Bk Rev. Circ:** 400.
Desc: A source of information on ethics in corporate Canada, designed to help Canada's senior executive groups improve their management of corporate ethics issues.

LC HC **ISSN** 0361-2309
DD 330 US
CORPORATE EXAMINER, THE.
Added/Corp Interfaith Center on Corporate Responsibility. National Council of the Churches of Christ in the United States of America. Corporate Information Center. National Council of the Churches of Christ in the United States of America. Corporate Information Center. CIC Brief. Interfaith Center on Corporate Responsibility. ICCR Brief. (Nov. 1971). English. Ten times a year. $12.50. Corporate Examiner, 475 Riverside Drive/Room 566, New York NY 10115. **Tel** (212)870-2296. **ED** Diane Bratcher. **Bk Rev. Circ:** 2000 (ctrl).
Desc: Newsletter of Corporate Social Responsibility Movement. Covers South Africa, nuclear and space weapons, world debt crisis, comparable worth, alternative investing, pharmaceuticals and toxics.
Ind/Abst Hum. Rights Intern. Rep.

CN
CORPORATE EXPLORATION STRATEGIES. See Mines and Mining.

US
CORPORATE FEDERAL INCOME TAX SPECIMEN RETURNS COMPLETELY FILLED OUT FOR FILING IN. (1989)-. English. One time a year. $51.00. Maxwell Macmillan Professional Business Division, 910 Sylvan Avenue, Englewood Cliffs NJ 07632-3310. **Tel** (800)431-9025. *Continues in part* Corporation, Partnership and Fiduciary Federal Income Tax Specimen Returns Completely Worked Out for Filing in ... .

LC HV89 .C68
DD 361.7/632/02573 US
CORPORATE FOUNDATION PROFILES. See Philanthropy.

ISSN 1061-4273
DD 361 US
CORPORATE FUNDERS OPERATING IN MISSOURI. [Corp. funders oper. Mo.]. **Added/Corp** Grants Link, Inc. 1st Ed. (1992)-. English. $50.00. Grants Link, T-16 Research Park, Columbia MO 65211.

US
CORPORATE GROWTH REPORT WEEKLY. No. 701 (July 13, 1992)-. Corporate Report. English. Fifty times a year. $795.00 US; $835.00 Canada and Mexico; $895.00 other. Quality Services Company, 5290 Overpass Road, Santa Barbara CA 93111. **Tel** (805)964-7841. **ED** Carl Shrager. Index available (published separately). cum. index. **Bk Rev**, (Qty: 5). **Ad Acc. Circ:** 1,000+. available on microfilm and microfiche from University Microfilms International (UMI); available on an online database from NEWSNET. Formed by the union of Acquisition/Divestiture Weekly Report, 0279-4160 and Corporate Growth Report, 1050-320X.

ISSN 0070-0282
DD 336.2/43/0971 CN
CORPORATE MANAGEMENT TAX CONFERENCE. [Corp. Manage. Tax Conf.]. **Main/Corp** Corporate Management Tax Conference. **Added/Corp** Canadian Tax Foundation. (1965)-. Periodical. English. One time a year. 38.02Can$. Canadian Tax Foundation, 1 Queen Street East, Suite 1800, Toronto Ontario M5C 2Y2 Canada. **Tel** (416)863-9784. *Continues* International Corporate Tax Conference. Conference: Papers, 0837-7502.
Ind/Abst Account. Tax Datab. (1991-); Curr. Law Index (1980-); Leg. Resour. Index (1980-); LegalTrac (1980-).

LC HD5260 .C67 **ISSN** 0745-1636
DD 910/.2/02 US
CCC
CORPORATE MEETINGS AND INCENTIVES. See Travel and Tourism.

ISSN 0889-941X
US
CORPORATE MONTHLY. (CORPORATE MONTHLY : PHILADELPHIA & DELAWARE VALLEY.). (198?)-. Periodical. English. Twelve times a year. Corporate Monthly, 105 Chestnut Street, PO Box 40168, Philadelphia PA 19106.
Ind/Abst Bus. Dateline (Jan. 1985-Dec. 1985); Gen. BusinessFile (Jan. 1985-Dec. 1985); Gen. Period. Index (Jan. 1985-Dec. 1985); Mag. Search.

ISSN 0589-7904
US
CORPORATE PLANNING IDEAS.
Main/Corp Institute for Business Planning, Inc. (1963)-. Periodical. English. Twenty-four times a year. $240.00. Institute for Business Planning Inc., Subscription Service Center, IBP Plaza, Englewood Cliffs NJ 07632.

ISSN 0730-5192
US
CORPORATE PUBLIC ISSUES AND THEIR MANAGEMENT. [Corp. Public Issues Their Manage.]. VFOAT Corporate Public Issues. (1977)-. Periodical. English. Twenty-four times a year. $215.00. Issue Action Publications Inc, 207 Loudoun Street Southeast, Leesburg VA 22075. **Tel** (703)777-8450, FAX (703)777-8484. **ED** Teresa Yancey Crane. Index available. cum. index. **Circ:** 4,000 (ctrl). *Absorbed* Public Affair Review.

Desc: Reports on issues and trends important to policy makers. Focus on programs, methodologies, case histories and coming events. Corporate audience.

UK
TITLE CHANGE
CORPORATE REGISTER, THE. (Sept. 1991)-(199?). Periodical. English. Hemmington Scott Publishing Ltd, 25-31 Whiskin Street, City Innovation Centre, London EC1R OBP United Kingdom. **Tel** 011 44 171 2787769, FAX 011 44 171 2789808. ***Continues*** *Hambro Corporate Register, 0956-2893.* ***Continued by*** *Arthur Andersen Corporate Register.*

LC HC107.M6 C63 **ISSN** 0279-5299
DD 338.7/4/0977 US
CCC
CODEN CRPMEK
CORPORATE REPORT MINNESOTA. [Corp. rep. Minn.]. **Added/Corp** Dorn Communications. **VFOAT** Corporate Report. Vol. 12, No. 1 (Feb. 1981)-. Corporate Report. English. Twelve times a year. $29.00. MCP Inc., 5500 Wayzata Boulevard, Suite 800, Minneapolis MN 55416. **Tel** (612)591-2700, FAX (612)591-2639. **Bk Rev. Ad Acc. Circ:** 24,000. available on an online database (files 635,648/Full-Text) from DIALOG. Documents available from UMI Article Clearinghouse. ***Continues*** *Corporate Report (Edina, Minn.), 0190-9517.*
Desc: Business news and features from Minnesota and surrounding states.
Ind/Abst Acad. Search; Bus. Dateline; Bus. Index (1985-); Bus. Source Plus; Bus. Source; EP Collect.; Foods Adlibra; Gen. BusinessFile (1985-); Gen. Period. Index (1985-); Homework Help.; INFO-SOUTH Abstr.; MasterFile FullTEXT 1000; MasterFile FullTEXT 350; MasterFile FullTEXT 650; MasterFile FullTEXT (July 1993-); OCLC; PROMT; Telebase; Trade Ind. ASAP [Full Txt.]; Trade Ind. Index [Full Txt.].

LC HC107.W63 I5325 **ISSN** 0890-4278
DD 338.7/4/0977505 US
CORPORATE REPORT WISCONSIN. [Corp. rep. Wis.]. **VFOAT** Corporate Report. Vol. 1, No. 1, Sept. (1985)- Vol. 8 (Sept. 1992)- Vol. 9 (Sept. 1993)-. Corporate Report. English. Twelve times a year. $18.00. Corporate Report Wisconsin, PO Box 878, Menommomee Falls WI 53052. **Tel** (414) 255-9077, FAX (414)255-3388. **ED** Pete Millard. **Ad Acc, Adv Mgr:** Christine Schramek, **Tel** (414)255-9077. **Circ:** 28,000 (ctrl). available on an online database (file 635/Full-Text) from DIALOG. Documents available from UMI Article Clearinghouse.
Desc: Statewide business publication with the following mission: advocate a strong business climate; provide advisory information, and promote economic development.
Ind/Abst Bus. Dateline (Jan. 1991-) [Full Txt.].

UK
CORPORATE RESTRUCTURING. (19??)-. Periodical. English. One time a year. $245.00. Euromoney Publications PLC, Nestor House, Playhouse Yard, London EC4Z 5EX United Kingdom. **Tel** 011 44 171 7798888, FAX 011 44 171 7798630, telex 290700 EUROMON G.

US
CORPORATE SYNDICATE PERSONNEL. (19??)-. Periodical. English. Two times a year. $102.83 New York; $95.00 other. Investment Dealers Digest Inc., Two World Trade Center, 18th Floor, New York NY 10048. **Tel** (212)227-1200, FAX (212)432-1039.

ISSN 0882-8709
DD 338 US
CCC
CORPORATE TRAVEL. **See** Travel and Tourism.

LC HD2798.M6 C67 **ISSN** 0747-6701
DD 338.7/4/025776 US
CORPORATE VIEW, MINNESOTA, A. **Added/Corp** Corporate View, Inc. (1983)-. English. One time a year. A Corporate View Inc, PO Box 10525, Chicago IL 60610.

LC HG4057 .A15646 **ISSN** 1058-2908
DD 338.7/4/02573 US
CCC
CORPORATE YELLOW BOOK. **See** Biographies.

LC KF6450.A73 C6 **ISSN** 0572-9785
DD 343.7305/26 347.303526 US
CORPORATION, PARTNERSHIP, FIDUCIARY FILLED-IN TAX RETURN FORMS. **See** Finance-Taxation.

ISSN 8750-5460
US
CORPUS CHRISTI MAGAZINE (1984). (CORPUS CHRISTI MAGAZINE.). (1984)-. Periodical. English. Twelve times a year. South Texas Financial Corporation, 2820 South Padre Island Drive, Corpus Christi TX 78415. ***Continues*** *Corpus Christi Magazine Business Monthly, 0745-4686.*

ISSN 0010-9118
DD 330 MX
CORREO ECONOMICO. **Added/Corp** Informacion Nacional y Publicidad. (1963)-. Periodical. Spanish. One time a week. $10.00. El Correo Economico, Cadiz 53, Mexico 13 DF Mexico.

LC HF5686.C7 C6 **ISSN** 0574-1831
US
COST OF DOING BUSINESS : CORPORATIONS. **Added/Corp** Dun & Bradstreet Corporation. Dun & Bradstreet Corporation. Economic Analysis Dept. **VFOAT** Corporations. (19??)-. English. Every 2 years. Free on request. Dun & Bradstreet / New York, 299 Park Avenue, 24th Floor, New York NY 10171. **Tel** (212)593-4173.

LC HC143.A1 E96
DD 330.97286/005 CR
TITLE CHANGE
COSTA RICA, PANORAMA ECONOMICO EN ... Y PERSPECTIVAS PARA ... / MINISTERIO DE PLANIFICACION NACIONAL Y POLITICA ECONOMICA, DIRECCION DE PLANIFICACION GLOBAL, DEPARTAMENTO DE ANALISIS ECONOMICO. **Added/Corp** Costa Rica. Ministerio de Planificacion Nacional y Politica Economica. Costa Rica. Direccion de Planificacion Global. Departamento de Analisis Economico. **VFOAT** Panorama Economico en ... y Perspectivas para ... . (1989/1990)-(199?). Spanish. ***Continues*** *Evolucion Economica y Social de Costa Rica.* ***Continued by*** *Panorama Economico de Costa Rica (Annual).*

ISSN 0327-5345
AG
UDC 657.471
Pr Rev.
COSTOS Y GESTION. (1991)-. Periodical. Spanish. Four times a year. $50.00. Instituto Argentino de Profesores, Universidad Costos Montevideo 771 7C, 1019 Buenos Aires Argentina. **Tel** 011 54 1 8115411, FAX 011 54 1 8026962. Index available. cum. index. **Ad Acc. Circ:** 1,500.

FR
COTE D'IVOIRE SELECTION. (19??)-. Periodical. French. Six times a year. $1137.35. IC Publications Ediafric, 10 rue Vineuse, 75116 Paris France. **Tel** 011 33 1 44308100.
Desc: Information on restructuring and reorganization of the economy of the Ivory Coast at the beginning of a new expansion phase. Covers national politics, economy, agriculture, industry, energy, banks and credits.

ISSN 0816-4991
DD 330.994063 AT
COUNCIL PAPER - ECONOMIC PLANNING ADVISORY COUNCIL. [Counc. pap. - Econ. Plan. Advis. Counc.]. **Added/Corp** Australia. Economic Planning Advisory Council Australia. Office of the Economic Planning Advisory Council. (1985)-. Government Publication. English. Irregular. 37.00Aus$. Australian Government Publishing Service, GPO Box 84, Canberra ACT 2601 Australia. **Tel** 011 61 6 2954411, FAX 011 61 6 2954455.

LC HC10 .C66 **ISSN** 1041-3553
DD 330.9/00112 US
CCC
COUNTRY FORECASTS. [Ctry. forecasts]. **Added/Corp** Frost & Sullivan. Political Risk Services. Vol. 8, No. 1 (Dec. 1988)-. Periodical. English. Two times a year (Jan., & July). $570.00. Political Risk Services, 6320 Fly Road, Suite 102, PO Box 248, East Syracuse NY 13057-0248. **Tel** (315)431-0511, FAX (315)431-0200. available on diskette (full/text version on IBM compatible diskettes); available on an online database from Information Access Company; DIALOG; and DATA-STAR. ***Formed by the union of*** *Political Climate for International Business, 0887-7637* ***and*** *Five-Year Forecast of Business Climate Trends in 85 Countries, 0897-0653.*
Desc: Each issue contains country-by-country facts, forecasts, and comparisons, concise analysis of the climate for international business and trade in 85 countries.

LC HC950.A1 C68
DD 330.9 UK
•**COUNTRY REPORT. ANGOLA.** **Added/Corp** Economist Intelligence Unit (Great Britain). **VFOAT** Angola; EIU Country Report. (1993)-. Periodical. English. Four times a year. $335.00 (per country), $100.00 (single issue) North America. The Economist Intelligence Unit, 40 Duke Street, London W1A 1DW United Kingdom. **Tel** 011 44 171 8301000. **(Subscription address:** Economist Intelligence Unit / North America Subscriptions, 111 West 57th Street, New York NY 10019. **Tel** 800 938-4685, (212)554-0600, FAX (212)586-1181, (212)586-1182.**)** ***Continues in part*** *Country Report. Angola, Sao Tome & Principe.*
Desc: Evaluates growth prospects, assesses opportunities, and examines problems. Provides concise and lucid business-oriented analysis of the latest economic and political indicators.

LC HC171 .C75 **ISSN** 0269-4212
DD 330.982/005 UK
COUNTRY REPORT. ARGENTINA. [Ctry. rep., Argent.]. **Added/Corp** Economist Intelligence Unit (Great Britain). **VFOAT** Argentina. No. 2 (1986)-. Periodical. English. Four times a year. $335.00 (per country), $100.00 (single issue) North America. The Economist Intelligence Unit, 40 Duke Street, London W1A 1DW United Kingdom. **Tel** 011 44 171 8301000. **(Subscription address:** Economist Intelligence Unit / North America Subscriptions, 111 West 57th Street, New York NY 10019. **Tel** 800 938-4685, (212)554-0600, FAX (212)586-1181, (212)586-1182.**)** available on an online database from Lexis-Nexis; and DIALOG. Documents available from BLDSC. ***Continues in part*** *Quarterly Economic Review of Argentina, 0142-4149.*
Desc: Evaluates growth prospects, assesses opportunities, and examines problems. Provides concise and lucid business-oriented analysis of the latest economic and political indicators.

LC HC601 .C7
DD 330.994/005 UK
COUNTRY REPORT. AUSTRALIA. **Added/Corp** Economist Intelligence Unit (Great Britain). **VFOAT** Australia. No. 2 (1986)-. Periodical. English. Four times a year. $335.00 (per country), $100.00 (single issue) North America. The Economist Intelligence Unit, 40 Duke Street, London W1A 1DW United Kingdom. **Tel** 011 44 171 8301000. **(Subscription address:** Economist Intelligence Unit / North America Subscriptions, 111 West 57th Street, New York NY 10019. **Tel** 800 938-4685, (212)554-0600, FAX (212)586-1181, (212)586-1182.**)** ***Continues in part*** *Quarterly Economic Review of Australia, 0266-9587.*
Desc: Evaluates growth prospects, assesses opportunities, and examines problems. Provides concise and lucid business-oriented analysis of the latest economic and political indicators.

LC HC261 .C653 **ISSN** 0269-5170
DD 330.9436/005 UK
COUNTRY REPORT. AUSTRIA. [Ctry. rep., Austria]. **Added/Corp** Economist Intelligence Unit (Great Britain). **VFOAT** Austria. No. 2 (1986)-. Periodical. English. Four times a year. $335.00 (per country), $100.00 (single issue) North America. The Economist Intelligence Unit, 40 Duke Street, London W1A 1DW United Kingdom. **Tel** 011 44 171 8301000. **(Subscription address:** Economist Intelligence Unit / North America Subscriptions, 111 West 57th Street, New York NY 10019. **Tel** 800 938-4685, (212)554-0600, FAX (212)586-1181, (212)586-1182.**)** available on an online database from Lexis-Nexis; and DIALOG. ***Continues in part*** *Quarterly Economic Review of Austria, 0142-3711.*
Desc: Evaluates growth prospects, assesses opportunities, and examines problems. Provides concise and lucid business-oriented analysis of the latest economic and political indicators.

LC HC415.38.A1 C69
DD 330.9 UK
COUNTRY REPORT. BAHRAIN, QATAR. **Added/Corp** Economist Intelligence Unit (Great Britain). **VFOAT** Bahrain, Qatar. No. 4 (1990)-. Periodical. English. Four times a year. $335.00 (per country), $100.00 (single issue) North America. The Economist Intelligence Unit, 40 Duke Street, London W1A 1DW United Kingdom. **Tel** 011 44 171 8301000. **(Subscription address:** Economist Intelligence Unit / North America Subscriptions, 111 West 57th Street, New York NY 10019. **Tel** 800 938-4685, (212)554-0600, FAX (212)586-1181, (212)586-1182.**)** ***Continues in part*** *Country Report. Bahrain, Qatar, Oman, The Yemens, 0269-5707.*
Desc: Evaluates growth prospects, assesses opportunities, and examines problems. Provides concise and lucid business-oriented analysis of the latest economic and political indicators.

LC HC243.A1 C682
DD 330.9 UK
•**COUNTRY REPORT. BALTIC REPUBLICS: ESTONIA, LATVIA, LITHUANIA.** **Added/Corp** Economist Intelligence Unit (Great Britain). **VFOAT** Baltic Republics: Estonia, Latvia, Lithuania; Estonia, Latvia, Lithuania; Country Report. Estonia, Latvia, Lithuania. 2nd Quarter (1993)-. Periodical. English. Four times a year. $335.00 (per country), $100.00 (single issue) North America. The Economist Intelligence Unit, 40 Duke Street, London W1A 1DW United Kingdom. **Tel** 011 44 171 8301000. **(Subscription address:** Economist Intelligence Unit / North America Subscriptions, 111 West 57th Street, New York NY 10019. **Tel** 800 938-4685, (212)554-0600, FAX (212)586-1181, (212)586-1182.**)** ***Continues in part*** *Country Report. Baltic Republics: Lithuania, Latvia, Estonia.*
Desc: Evaluates growth prospects, assesses opportunities, and examines problems. Provides concise and lucid business-oriented analysis of the latest economic and political indicators.

LC HC440.8.A1 C683 **ISSN** 0269-431X
DD 330.9549/2/005 UK
COUNTRY REPORT. BANGLADESH. [Ctry. rep., Bangladesh]. **Added/Corp** Economist Intelligence Unit (Great Britain). **VFOAT** Bangladesh. No. 2 (1986)-. Periodical. English. Four times a year. $335.00 (per country), $100.00 (single issue) North America. The Economist Intelligence Unit, 40 Duke Street, London W1A 1DW United Kingdom. **Tel** 011 44 171 8301000. **(Subscription address:** Economist Intelligence Unit / North America Subscriptions, 111 West 57th Street, New York NY 10019. **Tel** 800 938-4685, (212)554-0600, FAX (212)586-1181, (212)586-1182.) available on an online database from Lexis-Nexis; and DIALOG. ***Continues in part*** *Quarterly Economic Review of Bangladesh, 0266-9668.*
Desc: Evaluates growth prospects, assesses opportunities, and examines problems. Provides concise and lucid business-oriented analysis of the latest economic and political indicators.

LC HC311 .C685 **ISSN** 0269-4158
DD 330.9493/0005 UK
COUNTRY REPORT. BELGIUM, LUXEMBOURG. [Ctry. rep., Belg. Luxemb.]. **Added/Corp** Economist Intelligence Unit (Great Britain). **VFOAT** Belgium, Luxembourg. No. 2 (1986)-. English. Four times a year. $335.00 (per country), $100.00 (single issue) North America. The Economist Intelligence Unit, 40 Duke Street, London W1A 1DW United Kingdom. **Tel** 011 44 171 8301000. **(Subscription address:** Economist Intelligence Unit / North America Subscriptions, 111 West 57th Street, New York NY 10019. **Tel** 800 938-4685, (212)554-0600, FAX (212)586-1181, (212)586-1182.) available on an online database from Lexis-Nexis; and DIALOG. Documents available from BLDSC. ***Continues in part*** *Quarterly Economic Review of Belgium, Luxemburg, 0142-372X.*
Desc: Evaluates growth prospects, assesses opportunities, and examines problems. Provides concise and lucid business-oriented analysis of the latest economic and political indicators.

LC HC181
DD 330.9 UK
•**COUNTRY REPORT. BOLIVIA. Added/Corp** Economist Intelligence Unit (Great Britain). **VFOAT** Peru, Bolivia. (1995)-. Periodical. English. Four times a year. The Economist Intelligence Unit, 40 Duke Street, London W1A 1DW United Kingdom. **Tel** 011 44 171 8301000. **(Subscription address:** Economist Intelligence Unit / North America Subscriptions, 111 West 57th Street, New York NY 10019. **Tel** 800 938-4685, (212)554-0600, FAX (212)586-1181, (212)586-1182.) ***Continues in part*** *Country Report. Peru, Bolivia, 0269-543X.*

LC HC407.A1 C688
DD 330.9497/005 UK
•**COUNTRY REPORT. BOSNIA-HERCEGOVINA, CROATIA, MACEDONIA, SERBIA-MONTENEGRO, SLOVENIA. Added/Corp** Economist Intelligence Unit (Great Britain). **VFOAT** Bosnia-Hercegovina, Croatia, Macedonia, Serbia-Montenegro, Slovenia. No. 1 (1993)-. Periodical. English. Four times a year. $335.00 (per country), $100.00 (single issue) North America. The Economist Intelligence Unit, 40 Duke Street, London W1A 1DW United Kingdom. **Tel** 011 44 171 8301000. **(Subscription address:** Economist Intelligence Unit / North America Subscriptions, 111 West 57th Street, New York NY 10019. **Tel** 800 938-4685, (212)554-0600, FAX (212)586-1181, (212)586-1182.) ***Continues*** *Country Report. Yugoslav Republics.*
Desc: Evaluates growth prospects, assesses opportunities, and examines problems. Provides concise and lucid business-oriented analysis of the latest economic and political indicators.

LC HD996 **ISSN** 1356-4021
DD 330.9 UK
•**COUNTRY REPORT. BOTSWANA, LESOTHO. Added/Corp** Economist Intelligence Unit (Great Britain). **VFOAT** Botswana, Lesotho. (1995)-. Periodical. English. Four times a year. The Economist Intelligence Unit, 40 Duke Street, London W1A 1DW United Kingdom. **Tel** 011 44 171 8301000. ***Continues*** *Country Report. Namibia, Botswana, Lesotho, Swaziland, 0269-6746.*

LC HC186 .C79 **ISSN** 0269-5731
DD 330.981/005 UK
COUNTRY REPORT. BRAZIL. [Ctry. rep., Braz.]. **Added/Corp** Economist Intelligence Unit (Great Britain). **VFOAT** Brazil. No. 2 (1986)-. Periodical. English. Four times a year. $335.00 (per country), $100.00 (single issue) North America. The Economist Intelligence Unit, 40 Duke Street, London W1A 1DW United Kingdom. **Tel** 011 44 171 8301000. **(Subscription address:** Economist Intelligence Unit / North America Subscriptions, 111 West 57th Street, New York NY 10019. **Tel** 800 938-4685, (212)554-0600, FAX (212)586-1181, (212)586-1182.) available on an online database from Lexis-Nexis; and DIALOG. Documents available from BLDSC. ***Continues in part*** *Quarterly Economic Review of Brazil, 0142-4165.*
Desc: Evaluates growth prospects, assesses opportunities, and examines problems. Provides concise and lucid business-oriented analysis of the latest economic and political indicators.

LC HC403.A1 C68 **ISSN** 1356-4110
DD 330.9496/005 UK
•**COUNTRY REPORT. BULGARIA, ALBANIA. Added/Corp** Economist Intelligence Unit (Great Britain). **VFOAT** Bulgaria, Albania. (1995)-. Periodical. English. Four times a year. The Economist Intelligence Unit, 40 Duke Street, London W1A 1DW United Kingdom. **Tel** 011 44 171 8301000. ***Continues*** *Country Report. Romania, Bulgaria, Albania, 0269-5669.*

LC HC995.A1 C68 **ISSN** 0269-4336
DD 330.967/11/005 UK
COUNTRY REPORT. CAMEROON, CAR, CHAD. [Ctry. rep., Cameroon CAR Chad]. **Added/Corp** Economist Intelligence Unit (Great Britain). **VFOAT** Cameroon, CAR, Chad. No. 2 (1986)-. Periodical. English. Four times a year. $335.00 (per country), $100.00 (single issue) North America. The Economist Intelligence Unit, 40 Duke Street, London W1A 1DW United Kingdom. **Tel** 011 44 171 8301000. **(Subscription address:** Economist Intelligence Unit / North America Subscriptions, 111 West 57th Street, New York NY 10019. **Tel** 800 938-4685, (212)554-0600, FAX (212)586-1181, (212)586-1182.) ***Continues in part*** *Quarterly Economic Review of Cameroon, CAR, Chad, 0266-9757.*
Desc: Evaluates growth prospects, assesses opportunities, and examines problems. Provides concise and lucid business-oriented analysis of the latest economic and political indicators.

LC HC111 .C64 **ISSN** 0269-4166
DD 330.971/005 UK
COUNTRY REPORT. CANADA. [Ctry. rep., Can.]. **Added/Corp** Economist Intelligence Unit (Great Britain). **VFOAT** Canada. No. 2 (1986)-. Periodical. English. Four times a year. $335.00 (per country), $100.00 (single issue) North America. The Economist Intelligence Unit, 40 Duke Street, London W1A 1DW United Kingdom. **Tel** 011 44 171 8301000. **(Subscription address:** Economist Intelligence Unit / North America Subscriptions, 111 West 57th Street, New York NY 10019. **Tel** 800 938-4685, (212)554-0600, FAX (212)586-1181, (212)586-1182.) available on an online database from Lexis-Nexis; and DIALOG. ***Continues in part*** *Quarterly Economic Review of Canada, 0142-3762.*
Desc: Evaluates growth prospects, assesses opportunities, and examines problems. Provides concise and lucid business-oriented analysis of the latest economic and political indicators.

LC HC191 .C69 **ISSN** 0269-5197
DD 330.983/005 UK
COUNTRY REPORT. CHILE. [Ctry. rep., Chile]. **Added/Corp** Economist Intelligence Unit (Great Britain). **VFOAT** Chile. No. 2 (1986)-. English. Four times a year. $335.00 (per country), $100.00 (single issue) North America. The Economist Intelligence Unit, 40 Duke Street, London W1A 1DW United Kingdom. **Tel** 011 44 171 8301000. **(Subscription address:** Economist Intelligence Unit / North America Subscriptions, 111 West 57th Street, New York NY 10019. **Tel** 800 938-4685, (212)554-0600, FAX (212)586-1181, (212)586-1182.) available on an online database from Lexis-Nexis; and DIALOG. ***Continues in part*** *Quarterly Economic Review of Chile, 0142-3789.*
Desc: Evaluates growth prospects, assesses opportunities, and examines problems. Provides concise and lucid business-oriented analysis of the latest economic and political indicators.

LC HC427.92 .C68
DD 330.9 UK
•**COUNTRY REPORT. CHINA, MONGOLIA. Added/Corp** Economist Intelligence Unit (Great Britain). **VFOAT** China, Mongolia. No. 1 (1993)-. Periodical. English. Four times a year. $335.00 (per country), $100.00 (single issue) North America. The Economist Intelligence Unit, 40 Duke Street, London W1A 1DW United Kingdom. **Tel** 011 44 171 8301000. **(Subscription address:** Economist Intelligence Unit / North America Subscriptions, 111 West 57th Street, New York NY 10019. **Tel** 800 938-4685, (212)554-0600, FAX (212)586-1181, (212)586-1182.) ***Continues in part*** *Country Report. China, North Korea, 0269-6231.*
Desc: Evaluates growth prospects, assesses opportunities, and examines problems. Provides concise and lucid business-oriented analysis of the latest economic and political indicators.

LC HC196 .C644 **ISSN** 0269-7157
DD 330.9861/005 UK
COUNTRY REPORT. COLOMBIA. [Ctry. rep., Colomb.]. **Added/Corp** Economist Intelligence Unit (Great Britain). **VFOAT** Colombia. No. 2 (1986)-. English. Four times a year. $335.00 (per country), $100.00 (single issue) North America. The Economist Intelligence Unit, 40 Duke Street, London W1A 1DW United Kingdom. **Tel** 011 44 171 8301000. **(Subscription address:** Economist Intelligence Unit / North America Subscriptions, 111 West 57th Street, New York NY 10019. **Tel** 800 938-4685, (212)554-0600, FAX (212)586-1181, (212)586-1182.) available on an online database from Lexis-Nexis; and DIALOG. ***Continues in part*** *Quarterly Economic Review of Colombia, 0266-9633.*
Desc: Evaluates growth prospects, assesses opportunities, and examines problems. Provides concise and lucid business-oriented analysis of the latest economic and political indicators.

LC HC980.A1 C684
DD 330.9 UK
•**COUNTRY REPORT. CONGO, SAO TOME & PRINCIPE, GUINEA-BISSAU, CAPE VERDE. Added/Corp** Economist Intelligence Unit (Great Britain). **VFOAT** Congo, Sao Tome & Principe, Guinea-Bissau, Cape Verde; Congo, Sao Tome and Principe, Guinea-Bissau, Cape Verde. No. 1 (1993)-. Periodical. English. Four times a year. $335.00 (per country), $100.00 (single issue) North America. The Economist Intelligence Unit, 40 Duke Street, London W1A 1DW United Kingdom. **Tel** 011 44 171 8301000. **(Subscription address:** Economist Intelligence Unit / North America Subscriptions, 111 West 57th Street, New York NY 10019. **Tel** 800 938-4685, (212)554-0600, FAX (212)586-1181, (212)586-1182.) ***Continues in part*** *Country Report. Congo, Gabon, Equatorial Guinea; Country Report. Senegal, The Gambia, Guinea-Bissau, Cape Verde, 0269-719X* ***and*** *Country Report. Angola, Sao Tome & Principe.*
Desc: Evaluates growth prospects, assesses opportunities, and examines problems. Provides concise and lucid business-oriented analysis of the latest economic and political indicators.

LC HC143.A1 C69
DD 330.9 UK
•**COUNTRY REPORT. COSTA RICA, PANAMA. Added/Corp** Economist Intelligence Unit (Great Britain). **VFOAT** Costa Rica, Panama. No. 1 (1993)-. Periodical. English. Four times a year. $335.00 (per country), $100.00 (single issue) North America. The Economist Intelligence Unit, 40 Duke Street, London W1A 1DW United Kingdom. **Tel** 011 44 171 8301000. **(Subscription address:** Economist Intelligence Unit / North America Subscriptions, 111 West 57th Street, New York NY 10019. **Tel** 800 938-4685, (212)554-0600, FAX (212)586-1181, (212)586-1182.) ***Continues in part*** *Country Report. Nicaragua, Costa Rica, Panama, 0269-4247.*
Desc: Evaluates growth prospects, assesses opportunities, and examines problems. Provides concise and lucid business-oriented analysis of the latest economic and political indicators.

LC HC152.5.A1 C68 **ISSN** 0269-5251
DD 330.9729/005 UK
COUNTRY REPORT. CUBA, DOMINICAN REPUBLIC, HAITI, PUERTO RICO. [Ctry. rep., Cuba Domin. Repub. Haiti P.R.]. **Added/Corp** Economist Intelligence Unit (Great Britain). **VFOAT** Cuba, Dominican Republic, Haiti, Puerto Rico. No. 2 (1986)-. Periodical. English. Four times a year. $335.00 (per country), $100.00 (single issue) North America. The Economist Intelligence Unit, 40 Duke Street, London W1A 1DW United Kingdom. **Tel** 011 44 171 8301000. **(Subscription address:** Economist Intelligence Unit / North America Subscriptions, 111 West 57th Street, New York NY 10019. **Tel** 800 938-4685, (212)554-0600, FAX (212)586-1181, (212)586-1182.) available on an online database from Lexis-Nexis; and DIALOG. ***Continues in part*** *Quarterly Economc Review of Cuba, Dominican Republic, Haiti, Puerto Rico, 0142-3819.*
Desc: Evaluates growth prospects, assesses opportunities, and examines problems. Provides concise and lucid business-oriented analysis of the latest economic and political indicators.

LC HC415.2 .C68
DD 330 UK
•**COUNTRY REPORT. CYPRUS, MALTA. Added/Corp** Economist Intelligence Unit (Great Britain). **VFOAT** Cyprus, Malta. No. 1 (1993)-. Periodical. English. Four times a year. $335.00 (per country), $100.00 (single issue) North America. The Economist Intelligence Unit, 40 Duke Street, London W1A 1DW United Kingdom. **Tel** 011 44 171 8301000. **(Subscription address:** Economist Intelligence Unit / North America Subscriptions, 111 West 57th Street, New York NY 10019. **Tel** 800 938-4685, (212)554-0600, FAX (212)586-1181, (212)586-1182.) ***Continues in part*** *Country Report. Lebanon, Cyprus, 0269-5693; Country Report. Tunisia, Malta, 0269-7238.*
Desc: Evaluates growth prospects, assesses opportunities, and examines problems. Provides concise and lucid business-oriented analysis of the latest economic and political indicators.

LC HC270.2 .C68
DD 330.9437/005 UK
•**COUNTRY REPORT. CZECH REPUBLIC AND SLOVAKIA. Added/Corp** Economist Intelligence Unit (Great Britain). **VFOAT** Country Report. The Czech Republic, Slovakia; Czech Republic and Slovakia; Czech Republic, Slovakia. No. 1 (1993)-. Periodical. English. Four times a year. $335.00 (per country), $100.00 (single issue) North America. The Economist Intelligence Unit, 40 Duke Street, London W1A 1DW United Kingdom. **Tel** 011 44 171 8301000. **(Subscription address:** Economist Intelligence Unit / North America Subscriptions, 111 West 57th Street, New

York NY 10019. **Tel** 800 938-4685, (212)554-0600, FAX (212)586-1181, (212)586-1182.) ***Continues*** *Country Report. Czechoslovakia, 0269-4298.*
Desc: Evaluates growth prospects, assesses opportunities, and examines problems. Provides concise and lucid business-oriented analysis of the latest economic and political indicators.

LC HC351 .C68 **ISSN** 0269-574X
DD 330.9489/005 UK
COUNTRY REPORT. DENMARK, ICELAND. [Ctry. rep., Den. Icel.]. **Added/Corp** Economist Intelligence Unit (Great Britain). **VFOAT** Denmark, Iceland. No. 2 (1986)-. Periodical. English. Four times a year. $335.00 (per country), $100.00 (single issue) North America. The Economist Intelligence Unit, 40 Duke Street, London W1A 1DW United Kingdom. **Tel** 011 44 171 8301000. **(Subscription address:** Economist Intelligence Unit / North America Subscriptions, 111 West 57th Street, New York NY 10019. **Tel** 800 938-4685, (212)554-0600, FAX (212)586-1181, (212)586-1182.) available on an online database from Lexis-Nexis; and DIALOG. Documents available from BLDSC. ***Continues in part*** *Quarterly Economic Review of Denmark, Iceland, 0142-4181.*
Desc: Evaluates growth prospects, assesses opportunities, and examines problems. Provides concise and lucid business-oriented analysis of the latest economic and political indicators.

LC HC201 .C68 **ISSN** 0269-7165
DD 330.9866/005 UK
COUNTRY REPORT. ECUADOR. [Ctry. rep., Ecuad.]. **Added/Corp** Economist Intelligence Unit (Great Britain). **VFOAT** Ecuador. No. 2 (1986)-. English. Four times a year. $335.00 (per country), $100.00 (single issue) North America. The Economist Intelligence Unit, 40 Duke Street, London W1A 1DW United Kingdom. **Tel** 011 44 171 8301000. **(Subscription address:** Economist Intelligence Unit / North America Subscriptions, 111 West 57th Street, New York NY 10019. **Tel** 800 938-4685, (212)554-0600, FAX (212)586-1181, (212)586-1182.) available on an online database from Lexis-Nexis; and DIALOG. ***Continues in part*** *Quarterly Economic Review of Ecuador, 0266-9641.*
Desc: Evaluates growth prospects, assesses opportunities, and examines problems. Provides concise and lucid business-oriented analysis of the latest economic and political indicators.

LC HC830.A1 C68 **ISSN** 0269-526X
DD 330.962/005 UK
COUNTRY REPORT. EGYPT. [Ctry. rep., Egypt]. **Added/Corp** Economist Intelligence Unit (Great Britain). **VFOAT** Egypt. No. 2 (1986)-. Periodical. English. Four times a year. $335.00 (per country), $100.00 (single issue) North America. The Economist Intelligence Unit, 40 Duke Street, London W1A 1DW United Kingdom. **Tel** 011 44 171 8301000. **(Subscription address:** Economist Intelligence Unit / North America Subscriptions, 111 West 57th Street, New York NY 10019. **Tel** 800 938-4685, (212)554-0600, FAX (212)586-1181, (212)586-1182.) available on an online database from Lexis-Nexis; and DIALOG. ***Continues in part*** *Quarterly Economic Review of Egypt, 0142-3827.*
Desc: Evaluates growth prospects, assesses opportunities, and examines problems. Provides concise and lucid business-oriented analysis of the latest economic and political indicators.

LC HC340.2.A1 C68
DD 330.94897/005 UK
COUNTRY REPORT. FINLAND. **Added/Corp** Economist Intelligence Unit (Great Britain). **VFOAT** Finland. No. 2 (1986)-. Periodical. English. Four times a year. $335.00 (per country), $100.00 (single issue) North America. The Economist Intelligence Unit, 40 Duke Street, London W1A 1DW United Kingdom. **Tel** 011 44 171 8301000. **(Subscription address:** Economist Intelligence Unit / North America Subscriptions, 111 West 57th Street, New York NY 10019. **Tel** 800 938-4685, (212)554-0600, FAX (212)586-1181, (212)586-1182.) ***Continues in part*** *Quarterly Economic Review of Finland, 0142-419X.*
Desc: Evaluates growth prospects, assesses opportunities, and examines problems. Provides concise and lucid business-oriented analysis of the latest economic and political indicators.

LC HC271 .C75 **ISSN** 0269-5286
DD 330.944/005 UK
COUNTRY REPORT. FRANCE. [Ctry. rep., Fr.]. **Added/Corp** Economist Intelligence Unit (Great Britain). **VFOAT** France. No. 2, (1986)-. Periodical. English. Four times a year. $335.00 (per country), $100.00 (single issue) North America. The Economist Intelligence Unit, 40 Duke Street, London W1A 1DW United Kingdom. **Tel** 011 44 171 8301000. **(Subscription address:** Economist Intelligence Unit / North America Subscriptions, 111 West 57th Street, New York NY 10019. **Tel** 800 938-4685, (212)554-0600, FAX (212)586-1181, (212)586-1182.) available on microfiche; available on an online database from Lexis-Nexis; and DIALOG. Documents available from BLDSC. ***Continues in part*** *Quarterly Economic Review of France, 0142-3843.*
Desc: Evaluates growth prospects, assesses opportunities, and examines problems. Provides concise and lucid business-oriented analysis of the latest economic and political indicators.

UK
•**COUNTRY REPORT. GABON, EQUATORIAL GUINEA.** **Added/Corp** Economist Intelligence Unit (Great Britain). **VFOAT** Gabon, Equatorial Guinea; EIU Country Report. No. 1 (1993)-. Periodical. English. Four times a year. $335.00 (per country), $100.00 (single issue) North America. The Economist Intelligence Unit, 40 Duke Street, London W1A 1DW United Kingdom. **Tel** 011 44 171 8301000. **(Subscription address:** Economist Intelligence Unit / North America Subscriptions, 111 West 57th Street, New York NY 10019. **Tel** 800 938-4685, (212)554-0600, FAX (212)586-1181, (212)586-1182.) ***Continues in part*** *Country Report. Congo, Gabon, Equatorial Guinea.*
Desc: Evaluates growth prospects, assesses opportunities, and examines problems. Provides concise and lucid business-oriented analysis of the latest economic and political indicators.

LC HC281 .C678
DD 330.943/005 UK
COUNTRY REPORT. GERMANY. **Added/Corp** Economist Intelligence Unit (Great Britain). **VFOAT** Germany; EIU Country Report. Germany. **VAT** Economist Intelligence Unit Country Report. Germany. No. 1 (1991)-. English. Four times a year. $335.00 (per country), $100.00 (single issue) North America. The Economist Intelligence Unit, 40 Duke Street, London W1A 1DW United Kingdom. **Tel** 011 44 171 8301000. **(Subscription address:** Economist Intelligence Unit / North America Subscriptions, 111 West 57th Street, New York NY 10019. **Tel** 800 938-4685, (212)554-0600, FAX (212)586-1181, (212)586-1182.) ***Formed by the union of*** *Country Report. West Germany, 0269-5499* ***and*** *Country Report. East Germany, 0269-6207.*
Desc: Evaluates growth prospects, assesses opportunities, and examines problems. Provides concise and lucid business-oriented analysis of the latest economic and political indicators.

LC HC1060.A1 C687
DD 330/338 UK
•**COUNTRY REPORT. GHANA.** **Added/Corp** Economist Intelligence Unit (Great Britain). **VFOAT** Ghana. No. 1 (1993)-. Periodical. English. Four times a year. $335.00 (per country), $100.00 (single issue) North America. The Economist Intelligence Unit, 40 Duke Street, London W1A 1DW United Kingdom. **Tel** 011 44 171 8301000. **(Subscription address:** Economist Intelligence Unit / North America Subscriptions, 111 West 57th Street, New York NY 10019. **Tel** 800 938-4685, (212)554-0600, FAX (212)586-1181, (212)586-1182.) ***Continues in part*** *Country Report. Ghana, Sierra Leone, Liberia, 0269-7181.*
Desc: Evaluates growth prospects, assesses opportunities, and examines problems. Provides concise and lucid business-oriented analysis of the latest economic and political indicators.

LC HC291 .C685 **ISSN** 0269-591X
DD 330.9495/005 UK
COUNTRY REPORT. GREECE. [Ctry. rep., Greece]. **Added/Corp** Economist Intelligence Unit (Great Britain). **VFOAT** Greece. No. 2 (1986)-. Periodical. English. Four times a year. $335.00 (per country), $100.00 (single issue) North America. The Economist Intelligence Unit, 40 Duke Street, London W1A 1DW United Kingdom. **Tel** 011 44 171 8301000. **(Subscription address:** Economist Intelligence Unit / North America Subscriptions, 111 West 57th Street, New York NY 10019. **Tel** 800 938-4685, (212)554-0600, FAX (212)586-1181, (212)586-1182.) available on an online database from Lexis-Nexis; and DIALOG. ***Continues in part*** *Quarterly Economic Review of Greece, 0142-4203.*
Desc: Evaluates growth prospects, assesses opportunities, and examines problems. Provides concise and lucid business-oriented analysis of the latest economic and political indicators.

LC HC144.A1 C72
DD 330.9 UK
•**COUNTRY REPORT. GUATEMALA, EL SALVADOR.** **Added/Corp** Economist Intelligence Unit (Great Britain). **VFOAT** Guatemala, El Salvador. No. 1 (1993)-. Periodical. English. Four times a year. $335.00 (per country), $100.00 (single issue) North America. The Economist Intelligence Unit, 40 Duke Street, London W1A 1DW United Kingdom. **Tel** 011 44 171 8301000. **(Subscription address:** Economist Intelligence Unit / North America Subscriptions, 111 West 57th Street, New York NY 10019. **Tel** 800 938-4685, (212)554-0600, FAX (212)586-1181, (212)586-1182.) ***Continues in part*** *Country Report. Guatemala, El Salvador, Honduras, 0269-4220.*
Desc: Evaluates growth prospects, assesses opportunities, and examines problems. Provides concise and lucid business-oriented analysis of the latest economic and political indicators.

LC HC1030.A1
DD 330.9 UK
•**COUNTRY REPORT. GUINEA, SIERRA LEONE, LIBERIA.** **Added/Corp** Economist Intelligence Unit (Great Britain). **VFOAT** Guinea, Sierra Leone, Liberia. No. 1 (1993)-. Periodical. English. Four times a year. $335.00 (per country), $100.00 (single issue) North America. The Economist Intelligence Unit, 40 Duke Street, London W1A 1DW United Kingdom. **Tel** 011 44 171 8301000. **(Subscription address:** Economist Intelligence Unit / North America Subscriptions, 111 West 57th Street, New York NY 10019. **Tel** 800 938-4685, (212)554-0600, FAX (212)586-1181, (212)586-1182.) ***Continues in part*** *Country Report. Guinea, Mali, Mauritania, 0269-7203; Country Report. Ghana, Sierra Leone, Liberia, 0269-7181.*
Desc: Evaluates growth prospects, assesses opportunities, and examines problems. Provides concise and lucid business-oriented analysis of the latest economic and political indicators.

LC HC470.3.A1 C68 **ISSN** 0269-6762
DD 330.951/25/005 UK
COUNTRY REPORT. HONG KONG, MACAU. [Ctry. rep., Hong Kong Macau]. **Added/Corp** Economist Intelligence Unit (Great Britain). **VFOAT** Hong Kong, Macau. No. 2 (1986)-. Periodical. English. Four times a year. $335.00 (per country), $100.00 (single issue) North America. The Economist Intelligence Unit, 40 Duke Street, London W1A 1DW United Kingdom. **Tel** 011 44 171 8301000. **(Subscription address:** Economist Intelligence Unit / North America Subscriptions, 111 West 57th Street, New York NY 10019. **Tel** 800 938-4685, (212)554-0600, FAX (212)586-1181, (212)586-1182.) available on an online database from Lexis-Nexis; and DIALOG. ***Continues in part*** *Quarterly Economic Review of Hongkong, Macau, 0265-6906.*
Desc: Evaluates growth prospects, assesses opportunities, and examines problems. Provides concise and lucid business-oriented analysis of the latest economic and political indicators.

LC HC300.2 .C68 **ISSN** 0269-4301
DD 330.9439/005 UK
COUNTRY REPORT. HUNGARY. [Ctry. rep., Hung.]. **Added/Corp** Economist Intelligence Unit (Great Britain). **VFOAT** Hungary. No. 2 (1986)-. Periodical. English. Four times a year. $335.00 (per country), $100.00 (single issue) North America. The Economist Intelligence Unit, 40 Duke Street, London W1A 1DW United Kingdom. **Tel** 011 44 171 8301000. **(Subscription address:** Economist Intelligence Unit / North America Subscriptions, 111 West 57th Street, New York NY 10019. **Tel** 800 938-4685, (212)554-0600, FAX (212)586-1181, (212)586-1182.) available on an online database from Lexis-Nexis; and DIALOG. Documents available from BLDSC. ***Continues in part*** *Quarterly Economic Review of Hungary, 0144-8986.*
Desc: Evaluates growth prospects, assesses opportunities, and examines problems. Provides concise and lucid business-oriented analysis of the latest economic and political indicators.

LC HC435.2.A1 C68 **ISSN** 0269-5294
DD 330.954/005 UK
COUNTRY REPORT. INDIA, NEPAL. [Ctry. rep., India, Nepal]. **Added/Corp** Economist Intelligence Unit (Great Britain). **VFOAT** India, Nepal. No. 2 (1986)-. Periodical. English. Four times a year. $335.00 (per country), $100.00 (single issue) North America. The Economist Intelligence Unit, 40 Duke Street, London W1A 1DW United Kingdom. **Tel** 011 44 171 8301000. **(Subscription address:** Economist Intelligence Unit / North America Subscriptions, 111 West 57th Street, New York NY 10019. **Tel** 800 938-4685, (212)554-0600, FAX (212)586-1181, (212)586-1182.) available on an online database from Lexis-Nexis; and DIALOG. Documents available from BLDSC. ***Continues in part*** *Quarterly Economic Review of India, Nepal, 0142-3851.*
Desc: Evaluates growth prospects, assesses opportunities, and examines problems. Provides concise and lucid business-oriented analysis of the latest economic and political indicators.

LC HC444.A1 C68 **ISSN** 0269-5677
DD 330.959/005 UK
COUNTRY REPORT. INDOCHINA, VIETNAM, LAOS, CAMBODIA. [Ctry. rep., Indochina Vietnam Laos Cambodia]. **Added/Corp** Economist Intelligence Unit (Great Britain). **VFOAT** Indochina, Vietnam, Laos, Cambodia; Vietnam, Laos, Cambodia. (1986)-. Periodical. English. Four times a year. $335.00 (per country), $100.00 (single issue) North America. The Economist Intelligence Unit, 40 Duke Street, London W1A 1DW United Kingdom. **Tel** 011 44 171 8301000. **(Subscription address:** Economist Intelligence Unit / North America Subscriptions, 111 West 57th Street, New York NY 10019. **Tel** 800 938-4685, (212)554-0600, FAX (212)586-1181, (212)586-1182.) available on an online database from Lexis-Nexis; and DIALOG. ***Continues in part*** *Quarterly Economic Review of Indochina, Vietnam, Laos, Cambodia, 0142-4076.* ***Continued in part by*** *Country Report. Vietnam, 1356-403X; Country Report. Cambodia, Laos, Myanmar.*
Desc: Evaluates growth prospects, assesses opportunities, and examines problems. Provides concise and lucid business-oriented analysis of the latest economic and political indicators.

LC HC446 .C68 **ISSN** 0269-5413
DD 330.9598/005 UK
COUNTRY REPORT. INDONESIA. [Ctry. rep., Indones.]. **Added/Corp** Economist Intelligence Unit (Great Britain). **VFOAT** Indonesia. No. 2 (1986)-. Periodical. English. Four times a year. $335.00 (per country), $100.00 (single issue) North America. The Economist Intelligence Unit, 40 Duke Street, London W1A 1DW United Kingdom. **Tel** 011 44 171 8301000. **(Subscription address:** Economist Intelligence Unit / North America Subscriptions, 111 West 57th Street, New York NY 10019. **Tel** 800 938-4685, (212)554-0600, FAX (212)586-1181, (212)586-1182.**)** available on an online database from Lexis-Nexis; and DIALOG. Documents available from BLDSC. ***Continues in part*** *Quarterly Economic Review of Indonesia, 0142-3878.*
Desc: Evaluates growth prospects, assesses opportunities, and examines problems. Provides concise and lucid business-oriented analysis of the latest economic and political indicators.

LC HC471 .C68 **ISSN** 0269-5448
DD 330.955/005 UK
COUNTRY REPORT. IRAN. (COUNTRY REPORT. IRAN.). [Ctry. rep., Iran]. **Added/Corp** Economist Intelligence Unit (Great Britain). **VFOAT** Iran. No. 2 (1986)-. English. Four times a year. $335.00 (per country), $100.00 (single issue) North America. The Economist Intelligence Unit, 40 Duke Street, London W1A 1DW United Kingdom. **Tel** 011 44 171 8301000. **(Subscription address:** Economist Intelligence Unit / North America Subscriptions, 111 West 57th Street, New York NY 10019. **Tel** 800 938-4685, (212)554-0600, FAX (212)586-1181, (212)586-1182.**)** available on an online database from Lexis-Nexis; and DIALOG. ***Continues in part*** *Quarterly Economic Review of Iran, 0142-3924.*
Desc: Evaluates growth prospects, assesses opportunities, and examines problems. Provides concise and lucid business-oriented analysis of the latest economic and political indicators.

LC HC415.4.A1 C68 **ISSN** 0269-5502
DD 330.9567/005 UK
COUNTRY REPORT. IRAQ. [Ctry. rep., Iraq]. **Added/Corp** Economist Intelligence Unit (Great Britain). **VFOAT** Iraq. No. 2 (1986)-. English. Four times a year. $335.00 (per country), $100.00 (single issue) North America. The Economist Intelligence Unit, 40 Duke Street, London W1A 1DW United Kingdom. **Tel** 011 44 171 8301000. **(Subscription address:** Economist Intelligence Unit / North America Subscriptions, 111 West 57th Street, New York NY 10019. **Tel** 800 938-4685, (212)554-0600, FAX (212)586-1181, (212)586-1182.**)** available on an online database from Lexis-Nexis; and DIALOG. ***Continues in part*** *Quarterly Economic Review of Iraq, 0142-4009.*
Desc: Evaluates growth prospects, assesses opportunities, and examines problems. Provides concise and lucid business-oriented analysis of the latest economic and political indicators.

LC HC260.5.A1 C68 **ISSN** 0269-5278
DD 330.9415/005 UK
COUNTRY REPORT. IRELAND. [Ctry. rep., Irel.]. **Added/Corp** Economist Intelligence Unit (Great Britain). **VFOAT** Ireland. No. 2 (1986)-. Periodical. English. Four times a year. $335.00 (per country), $100.00 (single issue) North America. The Economist Intelligence Unit, 40 Duke Street, London W1A 1DW United Kingdom. **Tel** 011 44 171 8301000. **(Subscription address:** Economist Intelligence Unit / North America Subscriptions, 111 West 57th Street, New York NY 10019. **Tel** 800 938-4685, (212)554-0600, FAX (212)586-1181, (212)586-1182.**)** available on an online database from Lexis-Nexis; and DIALOG. ***Continues in part*** *Quarterly Economic Review of Ireland, 0142-3835.*
Desc: Evaluates growth prospects, assesses opportunities, and examines problems. Provides concise and lucid business-oriented analysis of the latest economic and political indicators.

LC HC415.25.A1 C68
DD 330.95694/005 UK
TITLE CHANGE
COUNTRY REPORT. ISRAEL. Added/Corp Economist Intelligence Unit (Great Britain). **VFOAT** Israel. No. 2 (1986)-(1993). Periodical. English. **(Subscription address:** Economist Intelligence Unit / North America Subscriptions, 111 West 57th Street, New York NY 10019. **Tel** 800 938-4685, (212)554-0600, FAX (212)586-1181, (212)586-1182.**)** ***Continues in part*** *Quarterly Economic Review of Israel, 0142-4238.* ***Continued by*** *Country Report. Israel, the Occupied Territories, 0269-5928.*
Desc: Evaluates growth prospects, assesses opportunities, and examines problems. Provides concise and lucid business-oriented analysis of the latest economic and political indicators.

LC HC415.25.A1 C68 **ISSN** 1353-3142
DD 330.0 UK
•**COUNTRY REPORT. ISRAEL, THE OCCUPIED TERRITORIES / EIU, THE ECONOMIST INTELLIGENCE UNIT.** [Ctry rep., Isr. Occupied Territ.]. **Added/Corp** Economist Intelligence Unit (Great Britain). **VFOAT** Israel, the Occupied Territories. (1993)-. Periodical. English. Four times a year. $315.00. **(Subscription address:** Economist Intelligence Unit / North America Subscriptions, 111 West 57th Street, New York NY 10019. **Tel** 800 938-4685, (212)554-0600, FAX (212)586-1181, (212)586-1182.**)** ***Continues in part*** *Country Report. Israel.*

LC HC301 .C65 **ISSN** 0269-5421
DD 330.945/005 UK
COUNTRY REPORT. ITALY. (COUNTRY REPORT. ITALY.). [Ctry. rep., Italy]. **Added/Corp** Economist Intelligence Unit (Great Britain). **VFOAT** Italy. No. 2 (1986)-. Periodical. English. Four times a year. $335.00 (per country), $100.00 (single issue) North America. The Economist Intelligence Unit, 40 Duke Street, London W1A 1DW United Kingdom. **Tel** 011 44 171 8301000. **(Subscription address:** Economist Intelligence Unit / North America Subscriptions, 111 West 57th Street, New York NY 10019. **Tel** 800 938-4685, (212)554-0600, FAX (212)586-1181, (212)586-1182.**)** available on an online database from Lexis-Nexis; and DIALOG. Documents available from BLDSC. ***Continues in part*** *Quarterly Economic Review of Italy, 0142-3886.*
Desc: Evaluates growth prospects, assesses opportunities, and examines problems. Provides concise and lucid business-oriented analysis of the latest economic and political indicators.

LC HC154.A1 C683 **ISSN** 1351-8674
DD 330 UK
TITLE CHANGE
COUNTRY REPORT. JAMAICA, BELIZE, BAHAMAS, BERMUDA, BARBADOS. [Ctry. rep., Jam. Belize Bahamas Bermuda Barbados]. **Added/Corp** Economist Intelligence Unit (Great Britain). **VFOAT** Jamaica, Belize, Bahamas, Bermuda, Barbados. (1993)-(1993). Periodical. English. The Economist Intelligence Unit, 40 Duke Street, London W1A 1DW United Kingdom. **Tel** 011 44 171 8301000. **(Subscription address:** Economist Intelligence Unit / North America Subscriptions, 111 West 57th Street, New York NY 10019. **Tel** 800 938-4685, (212)554-0600, FAX (212)586-1181, (212)586-1182.**)** available on an online database from Lexis-Nexis; and DIALOG. Documents available. ***Continues in part*** *Country Report. Jamaica, Belize, Bahamas, Bermuda, 0269-7130* ***and*** *Country Report. Trinidad & Tobago, Guyana, Barbados, Windward & Leeward Islands, 0269-7149.* ***Continued by*** *Country Report. Jamaica, Belize, Bahamas, Bermuda, Barbados, Cayman Islands.*
Desc: Evaluates growth prospects, assesses opportunities, and examines problems. Provides concise and lucid business-oriented analysis of the latest economic and political indicators.

LC HC154.A1 C682
DD 330 UK
•**COUNTRY REPORT. JAMAICA, BELIZE, BAHAMAS, BERMUDA, BARBADOS.** (1994)-. Periodical. English. The Economist Intelligence Unit, 40 Duke Street, London W1A 1DW United Kingdom. **Tel** 011 44 171 8301000. **(Subscription address:** Economist Intelligence Unit / North America Subscriptions, 111 West 57th Street, New York NY 10019. **Tel** 800 938-4685, (212)554-0600, FAX (212)586-1181, (212)586-1182.**)** ***Continues*** *Country Report. Jamaica, Belize, Bahamas, Bermuda, Barbados, Cayman Islands.*

LC HC154.A1 C682 **ISSN** 1351-8674
DD 330 UK
TITLE CHANGE
COUNTRY REPORT. JAMAICA, BELIZE, BAHAMAS, BERMUDA, BARBADOS, CAYMAN ISLANDS. Added/Corp Economist Intelligence Unit (Great Britain). **VFOAT** Jamaica, Belize, Bahamas, Bermuda, Barbados, Cayman Islands; Country Report. Jamaica, Belize, Bahamas, Bermuda, Barbados. (1994)-(1994). Periodical. English. The Economist Intelligence Unit, 40 Duke Street, London W1A 1DW United Kingdom. **Tel** 011 44 171 8301000. **(Subscription address:** Economist Intelligence Unit / North America Subscriptions, 111 West 57th Street, New York NY 10019. **Tel** 800 938-4685, (212)554-0600, FAX (212)586-1181, (212)586-1182.**)** ***Continues*** *Country Report. Jamaica, Belize, Bahamas, Bermuda, Barbados.* ***Continued by*** *Country Report. Jamaica, Belize, Bahamas, Bermuda, Barbados (1994).*

LC HC461 .C68 **ISSN** 0269-6681
DD 330.952/005 UK
COUNTRY REPORT. JAPAN. [Ctry. rep., Jpn.]. **Added/Corp** Economist Intelligence Unit (Great Britain). **VFOAT** Japan. No. 2 (1986)-. Periodical. English. Four times a year. $335.00 (per country), $100.00 (single issue) North America. The Economist Intelligence Unit, 40 Duke Street, London W1A 1DW United Kingdom. **Tel** 011 44 171 8301000. **(Subscription address:** Economist Intelligence Unit / North America Subscriptions, 111 West 57th Street, New York NY 10019. **Tel** 800 938-4685, (212)554-0600, FAX (212)586-1181, (212)586-1182.**) ED** Penelope Plowden. available on an online database from Lexis-Nexis; and DIALOG. ***Continues in part*** *Quarterly Economic Review of Japan, 0144-8897.*
Desc: Evaluates growth prospects, assesses opportunities, and examines problems. Provides concise and lucid business-oriented analysis of the latest economic and political indicators.

LC HC415.26.A1 C68 **ISSN** 0269-722X
DD 330.95691/005 UK
COUNTRY REPORT. JORDAN. [Ctry. rep., Jordan]. **Added/Corp** Economist Intelligence Unit (Great Britain). **VFOAT** Jordan. No. 2 (1986)-. English. Four times a year. $335.00 (per country), $100.00 (single issue) North America. The Economist Intelligence Unit, 40 Duke Street, London W1A 1DW United Kingdom. **Tel** 011 44 171 8301000. **(Subscription address:** Economist Intelligence Unit / North America Subscriptions, 111 West 57th Street, New York NY 10019. **Tel** 800 938-4685, (212)554-0600, FAX (212)586-1181, (212)586-1182.**)** available on an online database from Lexis-Nexis; and DIALOG. ***Continues in part*** *Quarterly Economic Review of Jordan, 0266-9714.*
Desc: Evaluates growth prospects, assesses opportunities, and examines problems. Provides concise and lucid business-oriented analysis of the latest economic and political indicators.

LC HC865.A1 C68 **ISSN** 0269-4239
DD 330.9676/2/005 UK
COUNTRY REPORT. KENYA. [Ctry. rep., Kenya]. **Added/Corp** Economist Intelligence Unit (Great Britain). **VFOAT** Kenya. No. 2 (1986)-. English. Four times a year. $335.00 (per country), $100.00 (single issue) North America. The Economist Intelligence Unit, 40 Duke Street, London W1A 1DW United Kingdom. **Tel** 011 44 171 8301000. **(Subscription address:** Economist Intelligence Unit / North America Subscriptions, 111 West 57th Street, New York NY 10019. **Tel** 800 938-4685, (212)554-0600, FAX (212)586-1181, (212)586-1182.**)** available on an online database from Lexis-Nexis; and DIALOG. Documents available from BLDSC. ***Continues in part*** *Quarterly Economic Review of Kenya, 0142-4254.*
Desc: Evaluates growth prospects, assesses opportunities, and examines problems. Provides concise and lucid business-oriented analysis of the latest economic and political indicators.

LC HC415.39.A1 C68 **ISSN** 0269-5715
DD 330.953/67/005 UK
COUNTRY REPORT. KUWAIT. (COUNTRY REPORT. KUWAIT.). [Ctry. rep., Kuwait]. **Added/Corp** Economist Intelligence Unit (Great Britain). **VFOAT** Kuwait. No. 2 (1986)-. Periodical. English. Four times a year. $335.00 (per country), $100.00 (single issue) North America. The Economist Intelligence Unit, 40 Duke Street, London W1A 1DW United Kingdom. **Tel** 011 44 171 8301000. **(Subscription address:** Economist Intelligence Unit / North America Subscriptions, 111 West 57th Street, New York NY 10019. **Tel** 800 938-4685, (212)554-0600, FAX (212)586-1181, (212)586-1182.**)** available on an online database from Lexis-Nexis; and DIALOG. Documents available from BLDSC. ***Continues in part*** *Quarterly Economic Review of Kuwait, 0142-4122.*
Desc: Evaluates growth prospects, assesses opportunities, and examines problems. Provides concise and lucid business-oriented analysis of the latest economic and political indicators.

LC HC415.24.A1 C692
DD 330 UK
•**COUNTRY REPORT. LEBANON.**
Added/Corp Economist Intelligence Unit (Great Britain). **VFOAT** Lebanon. No. 1 (1993)-. Periodical. English. Four times a year. $335.00 (per country), $100.00 (single issue) North America. The Economist Intelligence Unit, 40 Duke Street, London W1A 1DW United Kingdom. **Tel** 011 44 171 8301000. **(Subscription address:** Economist Intelligence Unit / North America Subscriptions, 111 West 57th Street, New York NY 10019. **Tel** 800 938-4685, (212)554-0600, FAX (212)586-1181, (212)586-1182.) ***Continues*** *Country Report. Lebanon, Cyprus, 0269-5693.*
Desc: Evaluates growth prospects, assesses opportunities, and examines problems. Provides concise and lucid business-oriented analysis of the latest economic and political indicators.

LC HC825.A1 C683
DD 330.961/2/005 UK
COUNTRY REPORT. LIBYA. Added/Corp Economist Intelligence Unit (Great Britain). **VFOAT** Libya. No. 2 (1986)-. Periodical. English. Four times a year. $335.00 (per country), $100.00 (single issue) North America. The Economist Intelligence Unit, 40 Duke Street, London W1A 1DW United Kingdom. **Tel** 011 44 171 8301000. **(Subscription address:** Economist Intelligence Unit / North America Subscriptions, 111 West 57th Street, New York NY 10019. **Tel** 800 938-4685, (212)554-0600, FAX (212)586-1181, (212)586-1182.**)** ***Continues in part*** *Quarterly Economic Review of Libya.*
Desc: Evaluates growth prospects, assesses opportunities, and examines problems. Provides concise and lucid business-oriented analysis of the latest economic and political indicators.

LC HC445.5.A1 C68 **ISSN** 0269-6703
DD 330.9595/005 UK
COUNTRY REPORT. MALAYSIA, BRUNEI. [Ctry. rep., Malays. Brunei]. **Added/Corp** Economist Intelligence Unit (Great Britain). **VFOAT** Malaysia, Brunei. No. 2 (1986)-. Periodical. English. Four times a year. $335.00 (per country), $100.00 (single issue) North America. The Economist Intelligence Unit, 40 Duke Street, London W1A 1DW United Kingdom. **Tel** 011

44 171 8301000. **(Subscription address:** Economist Intelligence Unit / North America Subscriptions, 111 West 57th Street, New York NY 10019. **Tel** 800 938-4685, (212)554-0600, FAX (212)586-1181, (212)586-1182.**)** available on an online database from Lexis-Nexis; and DIALOG. Documents available from BLDSC. ***Continues in part*** *Quarterly Economic Review of Malaysia, Brunei, 0144-8919.*
Desc: Evaluates growth prospects, assesses opportunities, and examines problems. Provides concise and lucid business-oriented analysis of the latest economic and political indicators.

LC HC597.5.A1 C68
DD 330.9 UK
●COUNTRY REPORT. MAURITIUS, MADAGASCAR, SEYCHELLES.
Added/Corp Economist Intelligence Unit (Great Britain). **VFOAT** Mauritius, Madagascar, Seychelles. No. 1 (1993)-. Periodical. English. Four times a year. $335.00 (per country), $100.00 (single issue) North America. The Economist Intelligence Unit, 40 Duke Street, London W1A 1DW United Kingdom. **Tel** 011 44 171 8301000. **(Subscription address:** Economist Intelligence Unit / North America Subscriptions, 111 West 57th Street, New York NY 10019. **Tel** 800 938-4685, (212)554-0600, FAX (212)586-1181, (212)586-1182.**)** ***Continues in part*** *Country Report. Madagascar, Mauritius, Seychelles, Comoros, 0269-5154.*
Desc: Evaluates growth prospects, assesses opportunities, and examines problems. Provides concise and lucid business-oriented analysis of the latest economic and political indicators.

LC HC131 .C67 **ISSN** 0269-5936
DD 330.972/005 UK
COUNTRY REPORT. MEXICO. [Ctry. rep., Mex.]. **Added/Corp** Economist Intelligence Unit (Great Britain). **VFOAT** Mexico. No. 2 (1986)-. Periodical. English. Four times a year. $335.00 (per country), $100.00 (single issue) North America. The Economist Intelligence Unit, 40 Duke Street, London W1A 1DW United Kingdom. **Tel** 011 44 171 8301000. **(Subscription address:** Economist Intelligence Unit / North America Subscriptions, 111 West 57th Street, New York NY 10019. **Tel** 800 938-4685, (212)554-0600, FAX (212)586-1181, (212)586-1182.**)** available on an online database from Lexis-Nexis; and DIALOG. ***Continues in part*** *Quarterly Economic Review of Mexico, 0142-4270.*
Desc: Evaluates growth prospects, assesses opportunities, and examines problems. Provides concise and lucid business-oriented analysis of the latest economic and political indicators.

LC HC810.A1 C7 **ISSN** 0269-6126
DD 330.964/005 UK
COUNTRY REPORT. MOROCCO. [Ctry. rep., Morocco]. **Added/Corp** Economist Intelligence Unit (Great Britain). **VFOAT** Morocco. No. 2 (1986)-. Periodical. English. Four times a year. $335.00 (per country), $100.00 (single issue) North America. The Economist Intelligence Unit, 40 Duke Street, London W1A 1DW United Kingdom. **Tel** 011 44 171 8301000. **(Subscription address:** Economist Intelligence Unit / North America Subscriptions, 111 West 57th Street, New York NY 10019. **Tel** 800 938-4685, (212)554-0600, FAX (212)586-1181, (212)586-1182.**)** available on an online database from Lexis-Nexis; and DIALOG. ***Continues in part*** *Quarterly Economic Review of Morocco, 0142-4289.*
Desc: Evaluates growth prospects, assesses opportunities, and examines problems. Provides concise and lucid business-oriented analysis of the latest economic and political indicators.

LC HC890.A1 C69
DD 330.9 UK
●COUNTRY REPORT. MOZAMBIQUE, MALAWI. **Added/Corp** Economist Intelligence Unit (Great Britain). **VFOAT** Mozambique, Malawi. No. 1 (1993)-. Periodical. English. Four times a year. $335.00 (per country), $100.00 (single issue) North America. The Economist Intelligence Unit, 40 Duke Street, London W1A 1DW United Kingdom. **Tel** 011 44 171 8301000. **(Subscription address:** Economist Intelligence Unit / North America Subscriptions, 111 West 57th Street, New York NY 10019. **Tel** 800 938-4685, (212)554-0600, FAX (212)586-1181, (212)586-1182.**)** ***Continues in part*** *Country Report. Tanzania, Mozambique, 0269-6630; Country Report. Zimbabwe, Malawi, 0269-4255.*
Desc: Evaluates growth prospects, assesses opportunities, and examines problems. Provides concise and lucid business-oriented analysis of the latest economic and political indicators.

LC HC940.A1 C68 **ISSN** 0269-6746
DD 330.9681 UK
TITLE CHANGE
COUNTRY REPORT. NAMIBIA, BOTSWANA, LESOTHO, SWAZILAND.
[Ctry. rep., Namib. Botsw. Lesotho Swazil.]. **Added/Corp** Economist Intelligence Unit (Great Britain). **VFOAT** Namibia, Botswana, Lesotho, Swaziland; Country Report. Botswana, Namibia, Lesotho, Swaziland; Botswana, Namibia, Lesotho, Swaziland. (1986)-(1994). English. The Economist Intelligence Unit, 40 Duke Street, London W1A 1DW United Kingdom. **Tel** 011 44 171 8301000. **(Subscription address:** Economist Intelligence Unit / North America Subscriptions, 111 West 57th Street, New York NY 10019. **Tel** 800 938-4685, (212)554-0600, FAX (212)586-1181, (212)586-1182.**)** ***Continues in part*** *Quarterly Economic Review of Namibia, Botswana, Lesotho, Swaziland, 0144-896X.* ***Split into*** *Country report. Namibia, Swaziland, 1356-4218* ***and*** *Country Report. Botswana, Lesotho, 1356-4021.*
Desc: Evaluates growth prospects, assesses opportunities, and examines problems. Provides concise and lucid business-oriented analysis of the latest economic and political indicators.

LC HC940.A1 C68 **ISSN** 1356-4218
DD 330 UK
●COUNTRY REPORT. NAMIBIA, SWAZILAND. **Added/Corp** Economist Intelligence Unit (Great Britain). **VFOAT** Namibia, Swaziland. (1995)-. Periodical. English. Four times a year. The Economist Intelligence Unit, 40 Duke Street, London W1A 1DW United Kingdom. **Tel** 011 44 171 8301000. ***Continues in part*** *Country Report. Namibia, Botswana, Lesotho, Swaziland, 0269-6746.*
Desc: Evaluates growth prospects, assesses opportunities, and examines problems. Provides business-oriented analysis of the latest economic and political indicators.

LC HC321 .C68 **ISSN** 0269-6134
DD 330.9492/005 UK
COUNTRY REPORT. NETHERLANDS. [Ctry. rep., Neth.]. **Added/Corp** Economist Intelligence Unit (Great Britain). **VFOAT** Netherlands. No. 2 (1986)-. Periodical. English. Four times a year. $335.00 (per country), $100.00 (single issue) North America. The Economist Intelligence Unit, 40 Duke Street, London W1A 1DW United Kingdom. **Tel** 011 44 171 8301000. **(Subscription address:** Economist Intelligence Unit / North America Subscriptions, 111 West 57th Street, New York NY 10019. **Tel** 800 938-4685, (212)554-0600, FAX (212)586-1181, (212)586-1182.**)** available on an online database from Lexis-Nexis; and DIALOG. ***Continues in part*** *Quarterly Economic Review of Netherlands, 0142-4297.*
Desc: Evaluates growth prospects, assesses opportunities, and examines problems. Provides concise and lucid business-oriented analysis of the latest economic and political indicators.

LC HC661 .C68 **ISSN** 0269-7114
DD 330.9931/005 UK
COUNTRY REPORT. NEW ZEALAND. [Ctry. rep., N.Z.]. **Added/Corp** Economist Intelligence Unit (Great Britain). **VFOAT** New Zealand. No. 2 (1986)-. Periodical. English. Four times a year. $335.00 (per country), $100.00 (single issue) North America. The Economist Intelligence Unit, 40 Duke Street, London W1A 1DW United Kingdom. **Tel** 011 44 171 8301000. **(Subscription address:** Economist Intelligence Unit / North America Subscriptions, 111 West 57th Street, New York NY 10019. **Tel** 800 938-4685, (212)554-0600, FAX (212)586-1181, (212)586-1182.**)** available on an online database from Lexis-Nexis; and DIALOG. Documents available from UMI Article Clearinghouse. ***Continues in part*** *Quarterly Economic Review of New Zealand, 0266-9595.*
Desc: Evaluates growth prospects, assesses opportunities, and examines problems. Provides concise and lucid business-oriented analysis of the latest economic and political indicators.

LC HC146.A1 C69
DD 330.97283/005 UK
●COUNTRY REPORT. NICARAGUA, HONDURAS. **Added/Corp** Economist Intelligence Unit (Great Britain). **VFOAT** Nicaragua, Honduras. No. 1 (1993)-. Periodical. English. Four times a year. $335.00 (per country), $100.00 (single issue) North America. The Economist Intelligence Unit, 40 Duke Street, London W1A 1DW United Kingdom. **Tel** 011 44 171 8301000. **(Subscription address:** Economist Intelligence Unit / North America Subscriptions, 111 West 57th Street, New York NY 10019. **Tel** 800 938-4685, (212)554-0600, FAX (212)586-1181, (212)586-1182.**)** ***Continues in part*** *Country Report. Nicaragua, Costa Rica, Panama, 0269-4247; Country Report. Guatemala, El Salvador, Honduras, 0269-4220.*
Desc: Evaluates growth prospects, assesses opportunities, and examines problems. Provides concise and lucid business-oriented analysis of the latest economic and political indicators.

LC HC1055.A1 C68 **ISSN** 0269-4204
DD 330.9669/005 UK
COUNTRY REPORT. NIGERIA. [Ctry. rep., Niger.]. **Added/Corp** Economist Intelligence Unit (Great Britain). **VFOAT** Nigeria. No. 2 (1986)-. Periodical. English. Four times a year. $335.00 (per country), $100.00 (single issue) North America. The Economist Intelligence Unit, 40 Duke Street, London W1A 1DW United Kingdom. **Tel** 011 44 171 8301000. **(Subscription address:** Economist Intelligence Unit / North America Subscriptions, 111 West 57th Street, New York NY 10019. **Tel** 800 938-4685, (212)554-0600, FAX (212)586-1181, (212)586-1182.**)** available on an online database from Lexis-Nexis; and DIALOG. Documents available from BLDSC. ***Continues in part*** *Quarterly Economic Review of Nigeria.*
Desc: Evaluates growth prospects, assesses opportunities, and examines problems. Provides concise and lucid business-oriented analysis of the latest economic and political indicators.

LC HC361 .C68
DD 330.9481/005 UK
COUNTRY REPORT. NORWAY.
Added/Corp Economist Intelligence Unit (Great Britain). **VFOAT** Norway. No. 2 (1986)-. Periodical. English. Four times a year. $335.00 (per country), $100.00 (single issue) North America. The Economist Intelligence Unit, 40 Duke Street, London W1A 1DW United Kingdom. **Tel** 011 44 171 8301000. **(Subscription address:** Economist Intelligence Unit / North America Subscriptions, 111 West 57th Street, New York NY 10019. **Tel** 800 938-4685, (212)554-0600, FAX (212)586-1181, (212)586-1182.**)** ***Continues in part*** *Quarterly Economic Review of Norway, 0142-3908.*
Desc: Evaluates growth prospects, assesses opportunities, and examines problems. Provides concise and lucid business-oriented analysis of the latest economic and political indicators.

LC HC415.35.A1 C68
DD 330.9 UK
COUNTRY REPORT. OMAN, YEMEN.
Added/Corp Economist Intelligence Unit (Great Britain). **VFOAT** Oman, Yemen. No. 1 (1991)-. English. Four times a year. $335.00 (per country), $100.00 (single issue) North America. The Economist Intelligence Unit, 40 Duke Street, London W1A 1DW United Kingdom. **Tel** 011 44 171 8301000. **(Subscription address:** Economist Intelligence Unit / North America Subscriptions, 111 West 57th Street, New York NY 10019. **Tel** 800 938-4685, (212)554-0600, FAX (212)586-1181, (212)586-1182.**)** available on microfilm. ***Continues in part*** *Country Report. Bahrain, Qatar, Oman, the Yemens, 0269-5707.*

LC HC681.A1 C68 **ISSN** 0269-7122
DD 330.99 UK
COUNTRY REPORT. PACIFIC ISLANDS--PAPUA NEW GUINEA, FIJI, SOLOMON ISLANDS, WESTERN SAMOA, VANUATU, TONGA. [Ctry. rep., Pac. Isl. Papua New Guinea Fiji Solomon Isl. West. Samoa Vanuatu Tonga]. **Added/Corp** Economist Intelligence Unit (Great Britain). **VFOAT** Pacific Islands--Papua New Guinea, Fiji, Solomon Islands, Western Samoa, Vanuatu, Tonga; Papua New Guinea, Fiji, Solomon Islands, Western Samoa, Vanuatu, Tonga. No. 2 (1986)-. Periodical. English. Four times a year. $335.00 (per country), $100.00 (single issue) North America. The Economist Intelligence Unit, 40 Duke Street, London W1A 1DW United Kingdom. **Tel** 011 44 171 8301000. **(Subscription address:** Economist Intelligence Unit / North America Subscriptions, 111 West 57th Street, New York NY 10019. **Tel** 800 938-4685, (212)554-0600, FAX (212)586-1181, (212)586-1182.**)** available on an online database from Lexis-Nexis; and DIALOG. ***Continues in part*** *Quarterly Economic Review of Pacific Islands, 0266-9609.*
Desc: Evaluates growth prospects, assesses opportunities, and examines problems. Provides concise and lucid business-oriented analysis of the latest economic and political indicators.

LC HC440.5.A1 C68 **ISSN** 0269-7173
DD 330.9549/1/005 UK
COUNTRY REPORT. PAKISTAN, AFGHANISTAN. [Ctry. rep., Pak. Afghan.]. **Added/Corp** Economist Intelligence Unit (Great Britain). **VFOAT** Pakistan, Afghanistan. (1986)-. Periodical. English. Four times a year. $335.00 (per country), $100.00 (single issue) North America. The Economist Intelligence Unit, 40 Duke Street, London W1A 1DW United Kingdom. **Tel** 011 44 171 8301000. **(Subscription address:** Economist Intelligence Unit / North America Subscriptions, 111 West 57th Street, New York NY 10019. **Tel** 800 938-4685, (212)554-0600, FAX (212)586-1181, (212)586-1182.**)** available on an online database from Lexis-Nexis; and DIALOG. Documents available from BLDSC. ***Continues in part*** *Quarterly Economic Review of Pakistan, Afghanistan (London, England : 1985), 0266-965X.*
Desc: Evaluates growth prospects, assesses opportunities, and examines problems. Provides concise and lucid business-oriented analysis of the latest economic and political indicators.

LC HC226
DD 330.9 UK
●COUNTRY REPORT. PERU. **Added/Corp** Economist Intelligence Unit (Great Britain). **VFOAT** Peru, Bolivia. (1995)-. Periodical. English. Four times a year. The Economist Intelligence Unit, 40 Duke Street, London W1A 1DW United Kingdom. **Tel** 011 44 171 8301000. **(Subscription address:** Economist Intelligence Unit / North America Subscriptions, 111 West 57th Street, New York NY 10019. **Tel** 800 938-4685, (212)554-0600, FAX (212)586-1181, (212)586-1182.**)** ***Continues in part*** *Country Report. Peru, Bolivia.*

LC HC226 .C65 **ISSN** 0269-543X
DD 330.984/005 UK
TITLE CHANGE
COUNTRY REPORT. PERU, BOLIVIA.
[Ctry. rep., Peru Bolivia]. **Added/Corp** Economist Intelligence Unit (Great Britain). **VFOAT** Peru, Bolivia.

(1986)- No. 2 (1994). Periodical. English. The Economist Intelligence Unit, 40 Duke Street, London W1A 1DW United Kingdom. **Tel** 011 44 171 8301000. **(Subscription address:** Economist Intelligence Unit / North America Subscriptions, 111 West 57th Street, New York NY 10019. **Tel** 800 938-4685, (212)554-0600, FAX (212)586-1181, (212)586-1182.**)** available on an online database from Lexis-Nexis; and DIALOG. Documents available from BLDSC. ***Continues in part*** *Quarterly Economic Review of Peru, Bolivia, 0142-3916.* ***Split into*** *Country Report. Peru* ***and*** *Country Report. Bolivia.*
Desc: Evaluates growth prospects, assesses opportunities, and examines problems. Provides concise and lucid business-oriented analysis of the latest economic and political indicators.

LC HC451 .C67 **ISSN** 0269-428X
DD 330.9599/005 UK
COUNTRY REPORT. PHILIPPINES. [Ctry. rep., Philipp.]. **Added/Corp** Economist Intelligence Unit (Great Britain). **VFOAT** Philippines. No. 2 (1986)-. Periodical. English. Four times a year. $335.00 (per country), $100.00 (single issue) North America. The Economist Intelligence Unit, 40 Duke Street, London W1A 1DW United Kingdom. **Tel** 011 44 171 8301000. **(Subscription address:** Economist Intelligence Unit / North America Subscriptions, 111 West 57th Street, New York NY 10019. **Tel** 800 938-4685, (212)554-0600, FAX (212)586-1181, (212)586-1182.**)** available on an online database from Lexis-Nexis; and DIALOG. Documents available from BLDSC. ***Continues in part*** *Quarterly Economic Review of Philippines, 0144-8935.*
Desc: Evaluates growth prospects, assesses opportunities, and examines problems. Provides concise and lucid business-oriented analysis of the latest economic and political indicators.

LC HC340.3.A1 C68 **ISSN** 0269-6193
DD 330.9438/005 UK
COUNTRY REPORT. POLAND. (COUNTRY REPORT. POLAND.). [Ctry. rep., Pol.]. **Added/Corp** Economist Intelligence Unit (Great Britain). **VFOAT** Poland. No. 2 (1986)-. Periodical. English. Four times a year. $335.00 (per country), $100.00 (single issue) North America. The Economist Intelligence Unit, 40 Duke Street, London W1A 1DW United Kingdom. **Tel** 011 44 171 8301000. **(Subscription address:** Economist Intelligence Unit / North America Subscriptions, 111 West 57th Street, New York NY 10019. **Tel** 800 938-4685, (212)554-0600, FAX (212)586-1181, (212)586-1182.**)** available on an online database from Lexis-Nexis; and DIALOG. Documents available from BLDSC. ***Continues in part*** *Quarterly Economic Review of Poland, 0144-8870.*
Desc: Evaluates growth prospects, assesses opportunities, and examines problems. Provides concise and lucid business-oriented analysis of the latest economic and political indicators.

LC HC391 .C68 **ISSN** 0269-5456
DD 330.9469/005 UK
COUNTRY REPORT. PORTUGAL. [Ctry. rep., Port.]. **Added/Corp** Economist Intelligence Unit (Great Britain). **VFOAT** Portugal. No. 2 (1986)-. English. Four times a year. $335.00 (per country), $100.00 (single issue) North America. The Economist Intelligence Unit, 40 Duke Street, London W1A 1DW United Kingdom. **Tel** 011 44 171 8301000. **(Subscription address:** Economist Intelligence Unit / North America Subscriptions, 111 West 57th Street, New York NY 10019. **Tel** 800 938-4685, (212)554-0600, FAX (212)586-1181, (212)586-1182.**)** available on an online database from Lexis-Nexis; and DIALOG. Documents available from BLDSC. ***Continues in part*** *Quarterly Economic Review of Portugal, 0142-3932.*
Desc: Evaluates growth prospects, assesses opportunities, and examines problems. Provides concise and lucid business-oriented analysis of the latest economic and political indicators.

LC HC405.A1 C68 **ISSN** 1356-4102
DD 330.9496/005 UK
●**COUNTRY REPORT. ROMANIA.** **Added/Corp** Economist Intelligence Unit (Great Britain). **VFOAT** Romania. (1995)-. Periodical. English. Four times a year. The Economist Intelligence Unit, 40 Duke Street, London W1A 1DW United Kingdom. **Tel** 011 44 171 8301000. ***Continues*** *Country Report. Romania, Bulgaria, Albania, 0269-5669.*

LC HC405.A1 C68 **ISSN** 0269-5669
DD 330.9496/005 UK
TITLE CHANGE
COUNTRY REPORT. ROMANIA, BULGARIA, ALBANIA. [Ctry. rep., Rom. Bulg. Albania]. **Added/Corp** Economist Intelligence Unit (Great Britain). **VFOAT** Romania, Bulgaria, Albania. No. 2 (1986)-(1994). Periodical. English. The Economist Intelligence Unit, 40 Duke Street, London W1A 1DW United Kingdom. **Tel** 011 44 171 8301000. **(Subscription address:** Economist Intelligence Unit / North America Subscriptions, 111 West 57th Street, New York NY 10019. **Tel** 800 938-4685, (212)554-0600, FAX (212)586-1181, (212)586-1182.**)** available on an online database from Lexis-Nexis; and DIALOG. ***Continues in part*** *Quarterly Economic Review of Romania, Bulgaria, Albania, 0142-4068.* ***Continued in part by*** *Country Report. Romania, Bulgaria, Albania, 1356-4102* ***and*** *Country Report. Bulgaria, Albania, 1356-4110.*
Desc: Evaluates growth prospects, assesses opportunities, and examines problems. Provides concise and lucid business-oriented analysis of the latest economic and political indicators.

LC HC340.12.A1 C68
DD 330/338.947 UK
●**COUNTRY REPORT. RUSSIA.** **Added/Corp** Economist Intelligence Unit (Great Britain). **VFOAT** Russia. No. 1 (1993)-. Periodical. English. Four times a year. $335.00 (per country), $100.00 (single issue) North America. The Economist Intelligence Unit, 40 Duke Street, London W1A 1DW United Kingdom. **Tel** 011 44 171 8301000. **(Subscription address:** Economist Intelligence Unit / North America Subscriptions, 111 West 57th Street, New York NY 10019. **Tel** 800 938-4685, (212)554-0600, FAX (212)586-1181, (212)586-1182.**)** ***Continues in part*** *Country Report. Commonwealth of Independent States.*
Desc: Evaluates growth prospects, assesses opportunities, and examines problems. Provides concise and lucid business-oriented analysis of the latest economic and political indicators.

LC HC415.33.A1 C68 **ISSN** 0269-6215
DD 330.953/8/005 UK
COUNTRY REPORT. SAUDI ARABIA. [Ctry. rep., Saudi Arab.]. **Added/Corp** Economist Intelligence Unit (Great Britain). **VFOAT** Saudi Arabia. No. 2, (1986)-. Periodical. English. Four times a year (with and annual update). $335.00 (per country), $100.00 (single issue) North America. The Economist Intelligence Unit, 40 Duke Street, London W1A 1DW United Kingdom. **Tel** 011 44 171 8301000. **(Subscription address:** Economist Intelligence Unit / North America Subscriptions, 111 West 57th Street, New York NY 10019. **Tel** 800 938-4685, (212)554-0600, FAX (212)586-1181, (212)586-1182.**)** available on microfilm from World Microfilm Publications Ltd; available on an online database from Lexis-Nexis; and DIALOG. ***Continues in part*** *Quarterly Economic Review of Saudi Arabia, 0142-4491.*
Desc: Evaluates growth prospects, assesses opportunities, and examines problems. Provides concise and lucid business-oriented analysis of the latest economic and political indicators.

LC HC1045.A1 C682
DD 330.9 UK
●**COUNTRY REPORT. SENEGAL, THE GAMBIA, MAURITANIA.** **Added/Corp** Economist Intelligence Unit (Great Britain). **VFOAT** Senegal, The Gambia, Mauritania. No. 1 (1993)-. Periodical. English. Four times a year. $335.00 (per country), $100.00 (single issue) North America. The Economist Intelligence Unit, 40 Duke Street, London W1A 1DW United Kingdom. **Tel** 011 44 171 8301000. **(Subscription address:** Economist Intelligence Unit / North America Subscriptions, 111 West 57th Street, New York NY 10019. **Tel** 800 938-4685, (212)554-0600, FAX (212)586-1181, (212)586-1182.**)** ***Continues in part*** *Country Report. Guinea, Mali, Mauritania, 0269-7203; Country Report. Senegal, The Gambia, Guinea-Bissau, Cape Verde, 0269-719X.*
Desc: Evaluates growth prospects, assesses opportunities, and examines problems. Provides concise and lucid business-oriented analysis of the latest economic and political indicators.

LC HC445.8.A1 C683 **ISSN** 0269-6711
DD 330.9595/7/005 UK
COUNTRY REPORT. SINGAPORE. [Ctry. rep., Singap.]. **Added/Corp** Economist Intelligence Unit (Great Britain). **VFOAT** Singapore. No. 2 (1986)-. Periodical. English. Four times a year. $335.00 (per country), $100.00 (single issue) North America. The Economist Intelligence Unit, 40 Duke Street, London W1A 1DW United Kingdom. **Tel** 011 44 171 8301000. **(Subscription address:** Economist Intelligence Unit / North America Subscriptions, 111 West 57th Street, New York NY 10019. **Tel** 800 938-4685, (212)554-0600, FAX (212)586-1181, (212)586-1182.**)** available on an online database from Lexis-Nexis; and DIALOG. ***Continues in part*** *Quarterly Economic Review of Singapore, 0144-8927.*
Desc: Evaluates growth prospects, assesses opportunities, and examines problems. Provides concise and lucid business-oriented analysis of the latest economic and political indicators.

LC HC905.A1 C68 **ISSN** 0269-6738
DD 330.968/005 UK
COUNTRY REPORT. SOUTH AFRICA. (COUNTRY REPORT. SOUTH AFRICA.). [Ctry. rep., South Afr.]. **Added/Corp** Economist Intelligence Unit (Great Britain). **VFOAT** South Africa. No. 2 (1986)-. English. Four times a year. $335.00 (per country), $100.00 (single issue) North America. The Economist Intelligence Unit, 40 Duke Street, London W1A 1DW United Kingdom. **Tel** 011 44 171 8301000. **(Subscription address:** Economist Intelligence Unit / North America Subscriptions, 111 West 57th Street, New York NY 10019. **Tel** 800 938-4685, (212)554-0600, FAX (212)586-1181, (212)586-1182.**)** available on an online database from Lexis-Nexis; and DIALOG. ***Continues in part*** *Quarterly Economic Review of South Africa, 0144-8951.*
Desc: Evaluates growth prospects, assesses opportunities, and examines problems. Provides concise and lucid business-oriented analysis of the latest economic and political indicators.

LC HC466
DD 330.9 UK
●**COUNTRY REPORT. SOUTH KOREA, NORTH KOREA.** **Added/Corp** Economist Intelligence Unit (Great Britain). **VFOAT** South Korea, North Korea. No. 1 (1993)-. Periodical. English. Four times a year. $335.00 (per country), $100.00 (single issue) North America. The Economist Intelligence Unit, 40 Duke Street, London W1A 1DW United Kingdom. **Tel** 011 44 171 8301000. **(Subscription address:** Economist Intelligence Unit / North America Subscriptions, 111 West 57th Street, New York NY 10019. **Tel** 800 938-4685, (212)554-0600, FAX (212)586-1181, (212)586-1182.**)** ***Formed by the union of*** *Country Report. South Korea, 0269-669X* ***and*** *Country Report. China, North Korea, 0269-6231.*
Desc: Evaluates growth prospects, assesses opportunities, and examines problems. Provides concise and lucid business-oriented analysis of the latest economic and political indicators.

LC HC381 .C68 **ISSN** 0269-4263
DD 330.946/005 UK
COUNTRY REPORT. SPAIN. [Ctry. rep., Spain]. **Added/Corp** Economist Intelligence Unit (Great Britain). **VFOAT** Spain. No. 2 (1986)-. Periodical. English. Four times a year. $335.00 (per country), $100.00 (single issue) North America. The Economist Intelligence Unit, 40 Duke Street, London W1A 1DW United Kingdom. **Tel** 011 44 171 8301000. **(Subscription address:** Economist Intelligence Unit / North America Subscriptions, 111 West 57th Street, New York NY 10019. **Tel** 800 938-4685, (212)554-0600, FAX (212)586-1181, (212)586-1182.**)** available on an online database from Lexis-Nexis; and DIALOG. Documents available from BLDSC. ***Continues in part*** *Quarterly Economic Review of Spain, 0142-4394.*
Desc: Evaluates growth prospects, assesses opportunities, and examines problems. Provides concise and lucid business-oriented analysis of the latest economic and political indicators.

LC HC424.A1 C68 **ISSN** 0269-4174
DD 330.9549/3/005 UK
COUNTRY REPORT. SRI LANKA. [Ctry. rep., Sri Lanka]. **Added/Corp** Economist Intelligence Unit (Great Britain). **VFOAT** Sri Lanka. No. 2 (1986)-. Periodical. English. Four times a year. $335.00 (per country), $100.00 (single issue) North America. The Economist Intelligence Unit, 40 Duke Street, London W1A 1DW United Kingdom. **Tel** 011 44 171 8301000. **(Subscription address:** Economist Intelligence Unit / North America Subscriptions, 111 West 57th Street, New York NY 10019. **Tel** 800 938-4685, (212)554-0600, FAX (212)586-1181, (212)586-1182.**)** available on an online database from Lexis-Nexis; and DIALOG. Documents available from BLDSC. ***Continues in part*** *Quarterly Economic Review of Sri Lanka (Ceylon), 0142-3770.*
Desc: Evaluates growth prospects, assesses opportunities, and examines problems. Provides concise and lucid business-oriented analysis of the latest economic and political indicators.

LC HC835.A1 C69 **ISSN** 0269-6150
DD 330.9624/005 UK
COUNTRY REPORT. SUDAN. [Ctry. rep., Sudan]. **Added/Corp** Economist Intelligence Unit (Great Britain). **VFOAT** Sudan. No. 2 (1986)-. English. Four times a year. $335.00 (per country), $100.00 (single issue) North America. The Economist Intelligence Unit, 40 Duke Street, London W1A 1DW United Kingdom. **Tel** 011 44 171 8301000. **(Subscription address:** Economist Intelligence Unit / North America Subscriptions, 111 West 57th Street, New York NY 10019. **Tel** 800 938-4685, (212)554-0600, FAX (212)586-1181, (212)586-1182.**)** available on an online database from Lexis-Nexis; and DIALOG. Documents available from BLDSC. ***Continues in part*** *Quarterly Economic Review of Sudan, 0142-4408.*
Desc: Evaluates growth prospects, assesses opportunities, and examines problems. Provides concise and lucid business-oriented analysis of the latest economic and political indicators.

LC HC371 .C68 **ISSN** 0269-6142
DD 330.9485/005 UK
COUNTRY REPORT. SWEDEN. [Ctry. rep., Swed.]. **Added/Corp** Economist Intelligence Unit (Great Britain). **VFOAT** Sweden. No. 2 (1986)-. Periodical. English. Four times a year. $335.00 (per country), $100.00 (single issue) North America. The Economist Intelligence Unit, 40 Duke Street, London W1A 1DW United Kingdom. **Tel** 011 44 171 8301000. **(Subscription address:** Economist Intelligence Unit / North America Subscriptions, 111 West 57th Street, New York NY 10019. **Tel** 800 938-4685, (212)554-0600, FAX (212)586-1181, (212)586-1182.**)** available on an online database from Lexis-Nexis; and DIALOG. ***Continues in part*** *Quarterly Economic Review of Sweden, 0142-4416.*
Desc: Evaluates growth prospects, assesses opportunities, and examines problems. Provides concise and lucid business-oriented analysis of the latest economic and political indicators.

LC HC395 .C685 **ISSN** 0269-6169
DD 330.9494/005 UK
COUNTRY REPORT. SWITZERLAND. [Ctry. rep., Switz.]. **Added/Corp** Economist Intelligence Unit (Great Britain). **VFOAT** Switzerland. No. 2 (1986)-. Periodical. English. Four times a year. $335.00 (per country), $100.00 (single issue) North America. The Economist Intelligence Unit, 40 Duke Street, London W1A 1DW United Kingdom. **Tel** 011 44 171 8301000. **(Subscription address:** Economist Intelligence Unit / North America Subscriptions, 111 West 57th Street, New York NY 10019. **Tel** 800 938-4685, (212)554-0600, FAX (212)586-1181, (212)586-1182.**)** available on an online database from Lexis-Nexis; and DIALOG. ***Continues in part*** *Quarterly Economic Review of Switzerland, 0142-4424.*
Desc: Evaluates growth prospects, assesses opportunities, and examines problems. Provides concise and lucid business-oriented analysis of the latest economic and political indicators.

LC HC415.23.A1 C68 **ISSN** 0269-7211
DD 330.95691/005 UK
COUNTRY REPORT. SYRIA. [Ctry. rep., Syr.]. **Added/Corp** Economist Intelligence Unit (Great Britain). **VFOAT** Syria. No. 2 (1986)-. Periodical. English. Four times a year. $335.00 (per country), $100.00 (single issue) North America. The Economist Intelligence Unit, 40 Duke Street, London W1A 1DW United Kingdom. **Tel** 011 44 171 8301000. **(Subscription address:** Economist Intelligence Unit / North America Subscriptions, 111 West 57th Street, New York NY 10019. **Tel** 800 938-4685, (212)554-0600, FAX (212)586-1181, (212)586-1182.**)** available on an online database from Lexis-Nexis; and DIALOG. ***Continues in part*** *Quarterly Economic Review of Syria, 0266-9706.*
Desc: Evaluates growth prospects, assesses opportunities, and examines problems. Provides concise and lucid business-oriented analysis of the latest economic and political indicators.

LC HC430.5.A1 C68 **ISSN** 0269-672X
DD 330.951/249/005 UK
COUNTRY REPORT. TAIWAN. [Ctry. rep., Taiwan]. **Added/Corp** Economist Intelligence Unit (Great Britain). **VFOAT** Taiwan. No. 2 (1986)-. Periodical. English. Four times a year. $335.00 (per country), $100.00 (single issue) North America. The Economist Intelligence Unit, 40 Duke Street, London W1A 1DW United Kingdom. **Tel** 011 44 171 8301000. **(Subscription address:** Economist Intelligence Unit / North America Subscriptions, 111 West 57th Street, New York NY 10019. **Tel** 800 938-4685, (212)554-0600, FAX (212)586-1181, (212)586-1182.**)** available on an online database from Lexis-Nexis; and DIALOG. ***Continues in part*** *Quarterly Economic Review of Taiwan, 0144-8943.*
Desc: Evaluates growth prospects, assesses opportunities, and examines problems. Provides concise and lucid business-oriented analysis of the latest economic and political indicators.

LC HC885.A1 C68
DD 330.9 UK
●**COUNTRY REPORT. TANZANIA, COMOROS.** **Added/Corp** Economist Intelligence Unit (Great Britain). **VFOAT** Tanzania, Comoros. No. 1 (1993)-. Periodical. English. Four times a year. $335.00 (per country), $100.00 (single issue) North America. The Economist Intelligence Unit, 40 Duke Street, London W1A 1DW United Kingdom. **Tel** 011 44 171 8301000. **(Subscription address:** Economist Intelligence Unit / North America Subscriptions, 111 West 57th Street, New York NY 10019. **Tel** 800 938-4685, (212)554-0600, FAX (212)586-1181, (212)586-1182.**)** ***Continues in part*** *Country Report. Tanzania, Mozambique, 0269-6630; Country Report. Madagascar, Mauritius, Seychelles, Comoros, 0269-5154.*
Desc: Evaluates growth prospects, assesses opportunities, and examines problems. Provides concise and lucid business-oriented analysis of the latest economic and political indicators.

LC HC445.A1 C682 **ISSN** 1356-4056
DD 330 UK
●**COUNTRY REPORT. THAILAND.** **Added/Corp** Economist Intelligence Unit (Great Britain). **VFOAT** Thailand. 1st Quarter (1995)-. Periodical. English. Four times a year. $335.00 (per country); $100.00 (single issue). The Economist Intelligence Unit, 40 Duke Street, London W1A 1DW United Kingdom. **Tel** 011 44 171 8301000. **(Subscription address:** Economist Intelligence Unit / North America Subscriptions, 111 West 57th Street, New York NY 10019. **Tel** 800 938-4685, (212)554-0600, FAX (212)586-1181, (212)586-1182.**)** ***Continues in part*** *Country Report. Thailand, Myanmar (Burma), 1350-7117.*

LC HC445.A1 C68 **ISSN** 1350-7117
DD 330.9591/005 UK
COUNTRY REPORT. THAILAND, MYANMAR (BURMA). (COUNTRY REPORT.). [Ctry. rep., Thail. Myanmar (Burma)]. **Added/Corp** Economist Intelligence Unit (Great Britain). **VFOAT** Country Report. Thailand, Myanmar; Thailand, Myanmar (Burma); Thailand, Myanmar. (1992)-. Periodical. English. Four times a year. $335.00 (per country), $100.00 (single issue) North America. The Economist Intelligence Unit, 40 Duke Street, London W1A 1DW United Kingdom. **Tel** 011 44 171 8301000. **(Subscription address:** Economist Intelligence Unit / North America Subscriptions, 111 West 57th Street, New York NY 10019. **Tel** 800 938-4685, (212)554-0600, FAX (212)586-1181, (212)586-1182.**)** ***Continues*** *Country Report. Thailand, Burma, 0269-5189.* ***Continued in part by*** *Country Report. Thailand, 1356-4056* ***and*** *Country Report. Cambodia, Laos, Myanmar, 1356-4048.*
Desc: Evaluates growth prospects, assesses opportunities, and examines problems. Provides concise and lucid business-oriented analysis of the latest economic and political indicators.

LC HC1000.A1 C68
DD 320.9 UK
COUNTRY REPORT. TOGO, NIGER, BENIN, BURKINA. **Added/Corp** Economic Intelligence Unit (Great Britain). **VFOAT** Togo, Niger, Benin, Burkina; Country Report. Togo, Niger, Benin, Burkina Faso. (199?)-. Periodical. English. Four times a year. The Economist Intelligence Unit, 40 Duke Street, London W1A 1DW United Kingdom. **Tel** 011 44 171 8301000. ***Continues*** *Country Report. Togo, Benin, Niger, Burkina.*

LC HC151.A1 C682
DD 330.9 UK
●**COUNTRY REPORT. TRINIDAD AND TOBAGO, GUYANA, WINDWARD AND LEEWARD ISLANDS, SURINAME, NETHERLANDS ANTILLES, ARUBA.** **Added/Corp** Economist Intelligence Unit (Great Britain). **VFOAT** Trinidad and Tobago, Guyana, Windward and Leeward Islands, Suriname, Netherlands Antilles, Aruba; Country Report. Trinidad and Tobago, Guyana, Suriname, Netherlands Antilles, Aruba, Windward and Leeward Islands. No. 1 (1993)-. Periodical. English. Four times a year. $335.00 (per country), $100.00 (single issue) North America. The Economist Intelligence Unit, 40 Duke Street, London W1A 1DW United Kingdom. **Tel** 011 44 171 8301000. **(Subscription address:** Economist Intelligence Unit / North America Subscriptions, 111 West 57th Street, New York NY 10019. **Tel** 800 938-4685, (212)554-0600, FAX (212)586-1181, (212)586-1182.**)** ***Continues in part*** *Country Report. Trinidad & Tobago, Guyana, Barbados, Windward & Leeward Islands, 0269-7149; Country Report. Venezuela, Suriname, Netherlands Antilles, 0269-6754.*
Desc: Evaluates growth prospects, assesses opportunities, and examines problems. Provides concise and lucid business-oriented analysis of the latest economic and political indicators.

LC HC820.A1 C682
DD 330.9 UK
●**COUNTRY REPORT. TUNISIA.** **Added/Corp** Economist Intelligence Unit (Great Britain). **VFOAT** Tunisia. No. 1 (1993)-. Periodical. English. Four times a year. $335.00 (per country), $100.00 (single issue) North America. The Economist Intelligence Unit, 40 Duke Street, London W1A 1DW United Kingdom. **Tel** 011 44 171 8301000. **(Subscription address:** Economist Intelligence Unit / North America Subscriptions, 111 West 57th Street, New York NY 10019. **Tel** 800 938-4685, (212)554-0600, FAX (212)586-1181, (212)586-1182.**)** ***Continues in part*** *Country Report. Tunisia, Malta, 0269-7238.*
Desc: Evaluates growth prospects, assesses opportunities, and examines problems. Provides concise and lucid business-oriented analysis of the latest economic and political indicators.

LC HC491 .C68 **ISSN** 0269-5464
DD 330.9561/005 UK
COUNTRY REPORT. TURKEY. [Ctry. rep., Turk.]. **Added/Corp** Economist Intelligence Unit (Great Britain). **VFOAT** Turkey. No. 2 (1986)-. Periodical. English. Four times a year. $335.00 (per country), $100.00 (single issue) North America. The Economist Intelligence Unit, 40 Duke Street, London W1A 1DW United Kingdom. **Tel** 011 44 171 8301000. **(Subscription address:** Economist Intelligence Unit / North America Subscriptions, 111 West 57th Street, New York NY 10019. **Tel** 800 938-4685, (212)554-0600, FAX (212)586-1181, (212)586-1182.**)** available on an online database from Lexis-Nexis; and DIALOG. ***Continues in part*** *Quarterly Economic Review of Turkey, 0142-3940.*
Desc: Evaluates growth prospects, assesses opportunities, and examines problems. Provides concise and lucid business-oriented analysis of the latest economic and political indicators.

LC HC870.A1 C69
DD 330.96757/005 UK
●**COUNTRY REPORT. UGANDA, RWANDA, BURUNDI.** **Added/Corp** Economist Intelligence Unit (Great Britain). **VFOAT** Uganda, Rwanda, Burundi. No. 1 (1993)-. Periodical. English. Four times a year. $335.00 (per country), $100.00 (single issue) North America. The Economist Intelligence Unit, 40 Duke Street, London W1A 1DW United Kingdom. **Tel** 011 44 171 8301000. **(Subscription address:** Economist Intelligence Unit / North America Subscriptions, 111 West 57th Street, New York NY 10019. **Tel** 800 938-4685, (212)554-0600, FAX (212)586-1181, (212)586-1182.**)** ***Continues in part*** *Country Report. Uganda, Ethiopia, Somalia, Djibouti; Country Report. Zaire, Rwanda, Burundi, 0269-5510.*
Desc: Evaluates growth prospects, assesses opportunities, and examines problems. Provides concise and lucid business-oriented analysis of the latest economic and political indicators.

LC HC415.36.A1 C69 **ISSN** 0269-5162
DD 330.953/57/005 UK
COUNTRY REPORT. UNITED ARAB EMIRATES. [Ctry. rep., United Arab Emir.]. **Added/Corp** Economist Intelligence Unit (Great Britain). **VFOAT** United Arab Emirates. No. 2 (1986)-. Periodical. English. Four times a year. $335.00 (per country), $100.00 (single issue) North America. The Economist Intelligence Unit, 40 Duke Street, London W1A 1DW United Kingdom. **Tel** 011 44 171 8301000. **(Subscription address:** Economist Intelligence Unit / North America Subscriptions, 111 West 57th Street, New York NY 10019. **Tel** 800 938-4685, (212)554-0600, FAX (212)586-1181, (212)586-1182.**)** available on an online database from Lexis-Nexis; and DIALOG. Documents available from BLDSC. ***Continues in part*** *Quarterly Economic Review of United Arab Emirates, 0141-8416.*
Desc: Evaluates growth prospects, assesses opportunities, and examines problems. Provides concise and lucid business-oriented analysis of the latest economic and political indicators.

LC HC251 .C68 **ISSN** 0269-5472
DD 330.941/005 UK
COUNTRY REPORT. UNITED KINGDOM. [Ctry. rep., U.K.]. **Added/Corp** Economist Intelligence Unit (Great Britain). **VFOAT** United Kingdom. No. 2 (1986)-. Periodical. English. Four times a year. $335.00 (per country), $100.00 (single issue) North America. The Economist Intelligence Unit, 40 Duke Street, London W1A 1DW United Kingdom. **Tel** 011 44 171 8301000. **(Subscription address:** Economist Intelligence Unit / North America Subscriptions, 111 West 57th Street, New York NY 10019. **Tel** 800 938-4685, (212)554-0600, FAX (212)586-1181, (212)586-1182.**)** available on an online database from Lexis-Nexis; and DIALOG. Documents available from BLDSC. ***Continues in part*** *Quarterly Economic Review of United Kingdom, 0142-3959.*
Desc: Evaluates growth prospects, assesses opportunities, and examines problems. Provides concise and lucid business-oriented analysis of the latest economic and political indicators.

LC HC231 .C68 **ISSN** 0269-6177
DD 330.9892/005 UK
COUNTRY REPORT. URUGUAY, PARAGUAY. [Ctry. rep., Urug. Parag.]. **Added/Corp** Economist Intelligence Unit (Great Britain). **VFOAT** Uruguay, Paraguay. No. 2 (1986)-. Periodical. English. Four times a year. $335.00 (per country), $100.00 (single issue) North America. The Economist Intelligence Unit, 40 Duke Street, London W1A 1DW United Kingdom. **Tel** 011 44 171 8301000. **(Subscription address:** Economist Intelligence Unit / North America Subscriptions, 111 West 57th Street, New York NY 10019. **Tel** 800 938-4685, (212)554-0600, FAX (212)586-1181, (212)586-1182.**)** available on an online database from Lexis-Nexis; and DIALOG. ***Continues in part*** *Quarterly Economic Review of Uruguay, Paraguay, 0142-4440.*
Desc: Evaluates growth prospects, assesses opportunities, and examines problems. Provides concise and lucid business-oriented analysis of the latest economic and political indicators.

LC HC236 .C699
DD 330.987/005 UK
●**COUNTRY REPORT. VENEZUELA.** **Added/Corp** Economist Intelligence Unit (Great Britain). **VFOAT** Venezuela. No. 1 (1993)-. Periodical. English. Four times a year. $335.00 (per country), $100.00 (single issue) North America. The Economist Intelligence Unit, 40 Duke Street, London W1A 1DW United Kingdom. **Tel** 011 44 171 8301000. **(Subscription address:** Economist Intelligence Unit / North America Subscriptions, 111 West 57th Street, New York NY 10019. **Tel** 800 938-4685, (212)554-0600, FAX (212)586-1181, (212)586-1182.**)** ***Continues in part*** *Country Report. Venezuela, Suriname, Netherlands Antilles, 0269-6754.*
Desc: Evaluates growth prospects, assesses opportunities, and examines problems. Provides concise and lucid business-oriented analysis of the latest economic and political indicators.

LC IN PROCESS HC444.A1 C68 **ISSN** 1356-403X
DD 330 UK
●**COUNTRY REPORT. VIETNAM.** **Added/Corp** Economist Intelligence Unit (Great Britain). **VFOAT** Vietnam. 1st Qtr. (1995)-. Periodical. English. Four times a year. $335.00 (per country), $100.00 (single issue) North America. The Economist Intelligence Unit, 40 Duke Street, London W1A 1DW United Kingdom. **Tel** 011 44 171 8301000. **(Subscription address:** Economist Intelligence Unit / North America Subscriptions, 111 West 57th Street, New York NY 10019. **Tel** 800 938-4685, (212)554-0600, FAX (212)586-1181, (212)586-1182.**)** ***Continues in part*** *Country Report. Indochina, Vietnam, Laos, Cambodia, 0269-5677.*

LC HD992
DD 330.96894/005 UK
●**COUNTRY REPORT. ZAMBIA, ZAIRE.** **Added/Corp** Economist Intelligence Unit (Great Britain). **VFOAT** Zambia, Zaire; EIU Country Report. No. 1

(1993)-. Periodical. English. Four times a year. $335.00 (per country), $100.00 (single issue) North America. The Economist Intelligence Unit, 40 Duke Street, London W1A 1DW United Kingdom. **Tel** 011 44 171 8301000. **(Subscription address:** Economist Intelligence Unit / North America Subscriptions, 111 West 57th Street, New York NY 10019. **Tel** 800 938-4685, (212)554-0600, FAX (212)586-1181, (212)586-1182.) ***Formed by the union of*** *Country Report. Zambia, 0269-4271* ***and*** *Country Report. Zaire, Rwanda, Burundi, 0269-5510.*
Desc: Evaluates growth prospects, assesses opportunities, and examines problems. Provides concise and lucid business-oriented analysis of the latest economic and political indicators.

LC HC910.A1 C692
DD 330.9 UK
•COUNTRY REPORT. ZIMBABWE.
Added/Corp Economist Intelligence Unit (Great Britain). **VFOAT** Zimbabwe. No. 1 (1993)-. Periodical. English. Four times a year. $335.00 (per country), $100.00 (single issue) North America. The Economist Intelligence Unit, 40 Duke Street, London W1A 1DW United Kingdom. **Tel** 011 44 171 8301000. **(Subscription address:** Economist Intelligence Unit / North America Subscriptions, 111 West 57th Street, New York NY 10019. **Tel** 800 938-4685, (212)554-0600, FAX (212)586-1181, (212)586-1182.) ***Continues in part*** *Country Report. Zimbabwe, Malawi, 0269-4255.*
Desc: Evaluates growth prospects, assesses opportunities, and examines problems. Provides concise and lucid business-oriented analysis of the latest economic and political indicators.

UK
COUNTRY REPORTS. English. One time a year. $79.00. Walden Publishing Ltd., 2 Market Street Shaffron, Walden Essex CB10 1HZ United Kingdom. **Tel** 011 44 1799 521150, FAX 011 44 1799 524805, telex 817197 JAXPRS G. **(Subscription address:** Business Europa / North America Subscriptions, Subscription Office, PO Box 830430, Birmingham AL 35283-0430. **Tel** (800)633-4931, FAX (205)995-1588.)
Desc: Geared toward persons who are involved in business with other countries. Each annual report gives you the following contents: demographics, public holidays, political structure, investments, natural resources, transportation, education, health & welfare, armed forces, local customs, geography & climate, banking & finance, agriculture, useful addresses, media & communications and maps.

LC HC101 .A184
DD 330 US
COUNTY BUSINESS PATTERNS.
Main/Corp United States. Bureau of the Census. **Added/Corp** United States. Bureau of Old-Age and Survivors Insurance. United States. National Production Authority. (1946)-. Government Publication. English. Irregular (approximately 53 reports). $296.00. US Department of Commerce / Bureau of the Census, Data User Services Division, Customer Services, Washington DC 20233-0800. **Tel** (301)763-4100. **(Subscription address:** Superintendent of Documents, US Government Printing Office, Washington DC 20402.)
Desc: Provides summary data by standard industrial classification code.

US
COUNTY BUSINESS PATTERNS, ALABAMA. **Added/Corp** United States. Bureau of the Census. (1964)-. Government Publication. English. One time a year. $8.00. US Department of Commerce / Bureau of the Census, Data User Services Division, Customer Services, Washington DC 20233-0800. **Tel** (301)763-4100. **(Subscription address:** Superintendent of Documents, US Government Printing Office, Washington DC 20402.) available on microfiche. ***Continues in part*** *County Business Patterns. Pt. 7, East South Central States, Alabama, Kentucky, Mississippi, Tennessee.*
Desc: Presents state and county data, by two-, three-, and four-digit levels of the standard industrial classification (SIC) system.

US
COUNTY BUSINESS PATTERNS, LOUISIANA. **Added/Corp** United States. Bureau of the Census. (1964)-. Government Publication. English. One time a year. $7.00. US Department of Commerce / Bureau of the Census, Data User Services Division, Customer Services, Washington DC 20233-0800. **Tel** (301)763-4100. **(Subscription address:** Superintendent of Documents, US Government Printing Office, Washington DC 20402.) available on microfiche. ***Continues in part*** *County Business Patterns. Pt. 8A, West South States, Arkansas, Louisiana, Oklahoma.*
Desc: Presents state and county data, by two-, three-, and four-digit levels of the standard industrial classification (SIC) system.

US
COUNTY BUSINESS PATTERNS, MINNESOTA. **Added/Corp** United States. Bureau of the Census. (1964)-. Government Publication. English. One time a year. $9.00. US Department of Commerce / Bureau of the Census, Data User Services Division, Customer Services, Washington DC 20233-0800. **Tel** (301)763-4100. **(Subscription address:** Superintendent of Documents, US Government Printing Office, Washington DC 20402.) ***Continues in part*** *County Business Patterns. Pt. 5A, West North Central States, Iowa, Minnesota, Missouri.*
Desc: Presents state and county data, by two-, three-, and four-digit levels of the standard industrial classification (SIC) system.

US
COUNTY BUSINESS PATTERNS, NEVADA. **Added/Corp** United States. Bureau of the Census. (1964)-. Government Publication. English. One time a year. $3.00. US Department of Commerce / Bureau of the Census, Data User Services Division, Customer Services, Washington DC 20233-0800. **Tel** (301)763-4100. **(Subscription address:** Superintendent of Documents, US Government Printing Office, Washington DC 20402.) available on microfiche. ***Continues in part*** *County Business Patterns. Pt. 9, Mountain States, Arizona, Colorado, Idaho, Montana, Nevada, New Mexico, Utah, Wyoming.*
Desc: Presents state and county data, by two-, three-, and four-digit levels of the standard industrial classification (SIC) system.

US
COUNTY BUSINESS PATTERNS, RHODE ISLAND. **Added/Corp** United States. Bureau of the Census. (1964)-. Government Publication. English. One time a year. $2.75. US Department of Commerce / Bureau of the Census, Data User Services Division, Customer Services, Washington DC 20233-0800. **Tel** (301)763-4100. **(Subscription address:** Superintendent of Documents, US Government Printing Office, Washington DC 20402.) available on microfiche. ***Continues in part*** *County Business Patterns. Pt. 2, New England States, Connecticut, Maine, Massachusetts, New Hampshire, Rhode Island, Vermont.*
Desc: Presents state and county data, by two-, three-, and four-digit levels of the standard industrial classification (SIC) system.

US
COUNTY BUSINESS PATTERNS, UNITED STATES. **Added/Corp** United States. Bureau of the Census. (1973)-. Government Publication. English. One time a year. $5.50. US Department of Commerce / Bureau of the Census, Data User Services Division, Customer Services, Washington DC 20233-0800. **Tel** (301)763-4100. **(Subscription address:** Superintendent of Documents, US Government Printing Office, Washington DC 20402.) ***Continues in part*** *County Business Patterns, U.S. Summary.*
Desc: Presents state and county data, by two-, three-, and four-digit levels of the standard industrial classification (SIC) system.

US
COUNTY BUSINESS PATTERNS, UTAH.
Added/Corp United States. Bureau of the Census. (1964)-. Government Publication. English. One time a year. $3.75. US Department of Commerce / Bureau of the Census, Data User Services Division, Customer Services, Washington DC 20233-0800. **Tel** (301)763-4100. **(Subscription address:** Superintendent of Documents, US Government Printing Office, Washington DC 20402.) available on microfiche. ***Continues in part*** *County Business Patterns. Pt. 9, Mountain States, Arizona, Colorado, Idaho, Montana, Nevada, New Mexico, Utah, Wyoming.*
Desc: Presents state and county data, by two-, three-, and four-digit levels of the standard industrial classification (SIC) system.

US
COUNTY BUSINESS PATTERNS, WYOMING. **Added/Corp** United States. Bureau of the Census. (1964)-. Government Publication. English. One time a year. $3.00. US Department of Commerce / Bureau of the Census, Data User Services Division, Customer Services, Washington DC 20233-0800. **Tel** (301)763-4100. **(Subscription address:** Superintendent of Documents, US Government Printing Office, Washington DC 20402.) available on microfiche. ***Continues in part*** *County Business Patterns. Pt. 9, Mountain States, Arizona, Colorado, Idaho, Montana, Nevada, New Mexico, Utah, Wyoming.*
Desc: Presents state and county data, by two-, three-, and four-digit levels of the standard industrial classification (SIC) system.

ISSN 0220-6994
FR
UDC 33
COURRIER CADRES. (COURRIER DES CADRES.). **Added/Corp** Association pour l'Emploi des Cadres (France). (1977)-. Periodical. French. One time a week. $118.11. Courrier des Cadres, 51 boulevard Brune, 75869 Paris Cedex 14 France. **Tel** 011 33 1 40522000.

LC HC **ISSN** 0590-0239
DD 330 FR
COURRIER DES PAYS DE L'EST. (LE COURRIER DES PAYS DE L'EST.). [Courr. pays est]. **Added/Corp** Groupe d'Etudes Prospectives Internationales du C.F.C.E. Centre d'Etudes sur l'U.R.S.S., la Chine et l'Europe Orientale (France) Ecole Pratique des Hautes Etudes (France). Centre de Documentation sur l'U.R.S.S. et les Pays Slaves. Centre National du Commerce Exterieur (France) France. Direction de Documentation. Centre d'Etudes et de Documentation sur l'U.R.S.S., la Chine et l'Europe de l'Est (France) Groupe d'Etudes Prospectives sur les Echanges Internationaux du C.F.C.E. Groupe d'Etudes Prospectives sur les Echanges Internationaux du C.N.C.E. Centre d'Etudes Prospectives et d'Information Internationales (France). (March 1964)-. Periodical. French. Ten times a year. 600.00F Europe; 870.00F other. Documentation Francaise, 29 quai Voltaire, 75344 Paris Cedex 7 France. **Tel** 011 33 1 40157000, FAX 011 33 1 40157230, telex 204 826 DOCFRAN. **(Subscription address:** Documentation Francaise, 124 rue Henri Barbusse, 93308 Aubervilliers Cedex France. **Tel** 011 33 1 48395600.) **ED** Jean Jenger. Index available. cum. index. **Bk Rev**. **Ad Acc. Circ:** 1,300. available in microform. Documents available from BLDSC, SWETS.
Desc: Politics of economics of eastern planified countries.
Ind/Abst Coal Abstr.; Int. Labour Doc.; LABORDOC; Repere.

LC HC196 .C65 **ISSN** 0120-3576
DD 330.9/861/063 CK
Pr Rev.
COYUNTURA ECONOMICA. **Added/Corp** Fundacion para la Educacion Superior y el Desarrollo. (April 1971)-. Periodical. Spanish. Four times a year. $220.00. Fedesarrollo, Apartado Aereo 75074, Bogota Colombia. **Tel** 011 57 1 2118018, 2116714, FAX 011 57 1 2126073. **ED** Cristina Lanzetta. **Ad Acc, Adv Mgr:** Cecilia Urtubey, **Tel** 011 57 1 3125300. **Circ:** 1,500 (ctrl).
Desc: Information and analysis of economic policies.
Ind/Abst Int. Labour Doc.; LABORDOC; Leis., Rec., Tour. Abstr.; PAIS Int. Print (1991-?); Rural Dev. Abstr.; World Agric. Econ. Rural Sociol. Abstr.

ISSN 0889-7395
DD 330 US
CRA REVIEW, THE. [CRA rev.]. **Added/Corp** Charles River Associates. **VAT** Charles River Associates Review. (19??)-. Periodical. English. Four times a year (Published 3 to 6 times per year). Free on request. Charles River Associates Inc., 200 Clarendon Street, T 43, Boston MA 02116. **Tel** (617)266-0500, FAX (617)266-0698, telex 706922. **ED** Harriet Ullman. **Circ:** 15,000 (ctrl). ***Continues*** *Charles River Associates. CRA Research Review.*
Desc: Descriptions of recent consulting assignments performed by Charles River Associates.

LC HF5549.5.E45 D56 **ISSN** 1058-3904
DD 910/.2/02 US
•CRAIGHEAD'S INTERNATIONAL BUSINESS, TRAVEL, AND RELOCATION GUIDE TO 71 COUNTRIES. **See** Travel and Tourism.

US
TITLE CHANGE
CRAIGHEAD'S INTERNATIONAL EXECUTIVE TRAVEL AND RELOCATION SERVICE. **See** Travel and Tourism.

ISSN 0149-6956
US
CCC
CRAIN'S CHICAGO BUSINESS. **VFOAT** Chicago Business. Vol. 1, No. 1 (June 5, 1978)-. Newspaper. English. One time a week. $81.00. Crain Communications Inc., 1400 Woodbridge, Detroit MI 48207-3187. **Tel** (313)446-6000, (800)992-9970. available on microfilm and microfiche from University Microfilms International (UMI); available on an online database from Lexis-Nexis; and (files 16,635/Full-Text) DIALOG. Documents available from UMI Article Clearinghouse.
Ind/Abst Acad. Search; Bus. Dateline; Bus. Index (1985-1990); Bus. Source Plus; Bus. Source; EP Collect.; F&S Index Plus Text, Int. [Full Txt.] [Select. Cov.]; Gen. BusinessFile (1985-1990); Gen. Period. Index (1985-1990); Homework Help.; INFO-SOUTH Abstr.; MasterFile FullTEXT 1000; MasterFile FullTEXT 350; MasterFile FullTEXT 650; MasterFile FullTEXT (July 1993-); OCLC; PROMT [Full Txt.]; Telebase; Trade Ind. Index.

ISSN 0197-2375
US
CCC
CRAIN'S CLEVELAND BUSINESS.
[Crain's Cleveland bus.]. Vol. 1 (Mar. 31, 1980)-. Periodical. English. One time a week. $45.00. Crain Communications Inc., 1400 Woodbridge, Detroit MI 48207-3187. **Tel** (313)446-6000, (800)992-9970. **(Subscription address:** Crain Communications, 965 East Jefferson Avenue, Detroit MI 48207. **Tel** (800)678-9595, (313)446-1616.) **ED** Brian Tucker. **Ad Acc. Circ:** 25,000 (ctrl). available on microfilm and microfiche from University Microfilms International (UMI); available on an online database from Lexis-Nexis; and (files 16,635,648/Full-Text) DIALOG. Documents available from UMI Article Clearinghouse.
Desc: Focusing on important business news and information in the seven-county Cleveland market.

Business and Economics

Ind/Abst Acad. Search; Bus. Dateline; Bus. Index (1985-1990); Bus. Source Plus; Bus. Source; EP Collect.; F&S Index Plus Text, Int. [Full Txt.] [Select. Cov.]; Gen. BusinessFile (1985-1990); Gen. Period. Index (1985-1990); Homework Help.; INFO-SOUTH Abstr.; MasterFile FullTEXT 1000; MasterFile FullTEXT 350; MasterFile FullTEXT 650; MasterFile FullTEXT (July 1993-); OCLC; PROMT [Full Txt.]; Telebase; Trade Ind. ASAP [Full Txt.]; Trade Ind. Index [Full Txt.].

ISSN 0882-1992
US
CCC

CRAIN'S DETROIT BUSINESS. VFOAT
Detroit Business. Vol. 1, No. 1 (Feb. 4-10, 1985)-. Periodical. English. One time a week. $40.00. Crain Communications Inc., 1400 Woodbridge, Detroit MI 48207-3187. **Tel** (313)446-6000, (800)992-9970. **(Subscription address:** Crain Communications, 965 East Jefferson Avenue, Detroit MI 48207. **Tel** (800)678-9595, (313)446-1616.**)** available on microfilm and microfiche from University Microfilms International (UMI); available on an online database (files 16,635/Full-Text) from DIALOG. Documents available from UMI Article Clearinghouse.
Ind/Abst Acad. Search; Bus. Dateline; Bus. Index (1985-1990); Bus. Source Plus; Bus. Source; EP Collect.; F&S Index Plus Text, Int. [Full Txt.] [Select. Cov.]; Gen. BusinessFile (1985-1990); Gen. Period. Index (1985-1990); Homework Help.; INFO-SOUTH Abstr.; MasterFile FullTEXT 1000; MasterFile FullTEXT 350; MasterFile FullTEXT 650; MasterFile FullTEXT (July 1993-); OCLC; PROMT [Full Txt.]; Telebase; Trade Ind. Index.

LC HC107.N7 C68   **ISSN** 8756-789X
DD 330.974/005   US
CCC

CRAIN'S NEW YORK BUSINESS. [Crain's N.Y. bus.]. Added/Corp Crain Communications Inc. VFOAT New York Business. Vol. 1, No. 1 (Jan. 7, 1985)-.
Periodical. English. One time a week. $52.00. Crain Communications Inc., 1400 Woodbridge, Detroit MI 48207-3187. **Tel** (313)446-6000, (800)992-9970. available on microfilm and microfiche from University Microfilms International (UMI); available on an online database (files 16,635/Full-Text) from DIALOG. Documents available from UMI Article Clearinghouse.
Ind/Abst Acad. Search; Bus. Dateline; Bus. Index (1985-1990); Bus. Source Plus; Bus. Source; EP Collect.; F&S Index Plus Text, Int. [Full Txt.] [Select. Cov.]; Gen. BusinessFile (1985-1990); Gen. Period. Index (1985-1990); Homework Help.; INFO-SOUTH Abstr.; MasterFile FullTEXT 1000; MasterFile FullTEXT 350; MasterFile FullTEXT 650; MasterFile FullTEXT (July 1993-); OCLC; PROMT [Full Txt.]; Telebase; Trade Ind. Index.

ISSN 1073-8444
DD 658   US

CREATIVE BUSINESS. [Creat. bus.]. (19??)-.
Periodical. English. Ten times a year. $79.00. Creative Business, 275 Newbury Street, Boston MA 02116. **Tel** (617)424-1368, FAX (617)353-1391. **ED** Cameron S. Foote. **Circ:** 3,000.

ISSN 1048-275X
DD 658   US

CREDIT & COLLECTION MANAGEMENT BULLETIN. [Credit collect. manage. bull.]
Added/Corp Bureau of Business Practice. **VFOAT** Credit and Collection Management Bulletin. (198?)-. Bulletin. English. Twenty-four times a year. $159.36 US; $208.80 Canada. Bureau of Business Practice, 24 Rope Ferry Road, Waterford CT 06386. **Tel** (800)243-0876, (203)442-4365, (800)876-9105, FAX (203)443-1123. Index available. **Formed by the union of** *Commercial Credit & Collection Management Bulletin, 0273-9623* **and** *Consumer Credit & Collection Management Bulletin, 0746-1232.*

ISSN 1078-0149
DD 650   US

●CREDITLINE (WATERFORD, CONN.).
(CREDITLINE). [CreditLine]. **Added/Corp** Bureau of Business Practice. **VFOAT** Credit Line. No. 101 (Sept. 1994)-. Periodical. English. Twelve times a year. $72.60. Bureau of Business Practice, 24 Rope Ferry Road, Waterford CT 06386. **Tel** (800)243-0876, (203)442-4365, (800)876-9105, FAX (203)443-1123.

LC HC59.8 .C74   **ISSN** 1023-8875
DD 337/.09172/405   FR

CREDITOR REPORTING SYSTEM GAZETTE. QUARTERLY REPORT ON INDIVIDUAL AID COMMITMENTS = SYSTEME DE NOTIFICATION DES PAYS CREANCIERS. RAPPORT TRIMESTRIEL SUR LES ENGAGEMENTS INDIVIDUELS D'AIDE.
See Sociology-Social Services and Welfare.

ISSN 0764-7611
FR
UDC 008(469)

CRISOL NANTERRE. (CRISOL.). (1983)-.
Periodical. French. Two times a year. 100.00F France; 120.00F other. Publidix, 200 Avenue de la Republique, 78001 Nanterre Cedex France. **Tel** 011 33 1 40977590.

LC HC121 .C75
DD 330.98/005   MX
SUSPENDED

CRITICAS DE LA ECONOMIA POLITICA.
(Oct.-Dec. 1976)-?. Periodical. Spanish. Four times a year. $30.00 Mexico; $32.00 US; $40.00 Europe; $43.00 Africa; $46.00 Asia; $32.00 South America. Criticas de la Economia Politica, Alejandro Galvez Cancino, Apart Postal 70-176, Mexico 20 DF Mexico. **Tel** 677 58 98. **ED** Alejandro Galvez Cancino. **Circ:** 5,000.
Desc: Review of Marxist orientation dedicated to the theocratic analysis of the principal topicals of economics, political sciences and social sciences in capitalism and socialism.

LC HC301   **ISSN** 0011-1775
DD 330   IT
SUSPENDED

CRONACHE ECONOMICHE.
(1947)-Suspended with Vol. 3 (1986). Periodical. Italian (English and French). Four times a year. L9000 Italy; L55000 other. Camera Commercio Ind Agr, C P No 413, 10100 Turin Italy. **Tel** (011)57161, telex 211247 CCIAAI. **ED** Attesa Di Nomina. cum. index. **Circ:** 3,500 (ctrl).
Desc: Articles by experts of economic problems regarding the 'local productive system' in relation to the Italian and international context.

UK
CRONER'S EUROPE. (19??)-. Periodical.
English. Twelve times a year. £235.05. Croner Publ Ltd., Croner House London Road, Kingston Upon Thames, Surrey KT2 6SR United Kingdom. **Tel** 011 44 181 5473333, FAX 011 44 181 5472637. **ED** Michael Gilliat.
Desc: Provides a balance of reports from Brussels with more in-depth analysis of developments and their practical implications for UK industry and commerce.

UK
CRONER'S MODEL BUSINESS CONTRACTS. (19??)-. Periodical. English. Two
times a year. £152.00. Croner Publ Ltd., Croner House London Road, Kingston Upon Thames, Surrey KT2 6SR United Kingdom. **Tel** 011 44 181 5473333, FAX 011 44 181 5472637.

UK
CRONER'S REFERENCE BOOK FOR THE SELF EMPLOYED & SMALLER BUSINESS. (19??)-. Periodical. English. Twelve
times a year. £147.50. Croner Publ Ltd., Croner House London Road, Kingston Upon Thames, Surrey KT2 6SR United Kingdom. **Tel** 011 44 181 5473333, FAX 011 44 181 5472637.

LC HC   **ISSN** 0319-843X
DD 330   CN

CROSS-CANADA COMMENT. Added/Corp
Canadian Association of Business Education Teachers. (Nov. 1971)-. Periodical. English (French). Four times a year. 2.40Can$. Canadian Association of Business Education Teachers, 184 Bonnechare Street South, Renfrew Ontario K7V 3ZF Canada.

ISSN 1066-6419
DD 658   US

CROSS SALES REPORT. [Cross sales rep.].
(1992)-. Periodical. English. Twenty-four times a year. $319.00. Siefer Consultants Inc., PO Box 1384, 525 Cayuga Street, Storm Lake IA 50588. **Tel** (712)732-7340, (712)747-7342, FAX (712)732-7906.

US
CROSSE CITY BUSINESS, LA. VFOAT
CityBusiness. Vol. 2, No. 9 (Feb. 6, 1984)-. Periodical. English. Twenty-four times a year. available on an online database (file 635/Full-Text) from DIALOG. Documents available from UMI Article Clearinghouse. **Continues** *La Crosse Citibusiness.*
Ind/Abst Bus. Dateline (Jan. 14, 1986-March 1987) [Full Txt.]; Bus. Index (Jan. 1985-Dec. 1985); Gen. BusinessFile (Jan. 1985-Dec. 1985).

ISSN 1038-2062
AT
CTC NEWSLETTER. VFOAT Competitive
Tendering and Contracting Newsletter. (19??)-. Periodical. English. Four times a year. Free on request. University of Sydney / School of Business, Sydney New South Wales, 2006 Australia. **Tel** 011 61 2 5508613, FAX 011 61 2 5570740.

ISSN 0955-2758
UK
CTN LONDON. [CTN Lond.]. VFOAT Confectioner
Tobacconist Newsagent (London). (198?)-. Trade Publication. English. One time a week. $143.75. Demographic, 4 Admiral House, Cardinal Way, Middlesex HA3 5FQ United Kingdom. **Tel** 011 44 181 8610960. **Continues** *CTN. Confectioner, Tobacconist, Newsagent, 0261-4278.*
Ind/Abst Infomat Int. Bus.

LC HD85.S7 S62a
DD 338.9   CK
CUADERNOS. Main/Corp Sociedad Colombiana
de Planificacion. (19??)-. Spanish. Sociedad Colombiana de Planificacion, Apartado Aereo 12029, Bogota Colombia.

LC HC   **ISSN** 0716-0046
DD 330   CL
CUADERNOS DE ECONOMIA (SANTIAGO). (CUADERNOS DE ECONOMIA.).
[Cuad. econ.]. **Added/Corp** Universidad Catolica de Chile. Facultad de Ciencias Economicas y Sociales. Universidad Catolica de Chile. Instituto de Economia. No. 1, (Sept./Dec. 1963)-. Periodical. Spanish (English). Three times a year. $48.00. Instituto de Economia, Casilla 274V, Correo 21, Santiago Chile. **Tel** 011 56 2 5522375 Ext. 4314, FAX 011 56 2 5521310, telex 240395. **ED** Ana Maria Aguirre. Index available in last issue of volume--attached. cum. index. **Bk Rev. Ad Acc.**
Desc: Theoretical articles about economic issues with special emphasis in Latin American problems.
Ind/Abst Hisp. Am. Period. Index, HAPI; J. Econ. Lit. (1984-); Leis., Rec., Tour. Abstr.; PAIS Int. Print (1991-); Rural Dev. Abstr.; World Agric. Econ. Rural Sociol. Abstr.

LC HC236 .C84
DD 330   VE
CUADERNOS DEL CENDES. Added/Corp
Universidad Central de Venezuela. Centro de Estudios del Desarrollo. Vol. 1 (Sept./Dec. 1983)-. Spanish (summaries and/or abstracts in English). Three times a year. $97.00. Centro Estudios de Desarollo, Apartado 6622 1010A, Caracas Venezuela. **Tel** 011 58 2 7523089, FAX 011 58 2 7512691. **ED** Nelson Prato Barbosa. **Bk Rev. Ad Acc. Circ:** 2,000 (ctrl).

SP
Pr Rev.
CUADERNOS ECONOMICOS DE I.C.E.
No. 1 (1977)-. Periodical. Spanish. Four times a year. $53.30. Industria Comercio Editores, Castellana 162, 28071 Madrid Spain. **Tel** 011 34 1 5641313. **(Subscription address:** BBR Action Ice, Goya 115, 28009 Madrid Spain. **Tel** 011 34 1 3090352.**)**

ISSN 0951-4708
UK
CUBA BUSINESS. Vol. 1, No. 1 (Oct. 1987)-.
Periodical. Spanish. Nine times a year. $547.59. Cuba Business, 254 258 Goswell Road, 3rd Floor, London EC1V 7EB United Kingdom. **Tel** 011 44 171 4901997, FAX 011 44 171 2537358, telex 931213217. **ED** Lila Haines. **Bk Rev,** (Qty: varies): **Circ:** 800.
Desc: Provides news and analysis of the Cuban economy. Covers trade, investment, political events and policy relevant to business; includes coverage of key sectors e.g. sugar.

LC HC152.5.A1 C78   **ISSN** 0864-1420
DD 330   CU
CUBA, ECONOMIA PLANIFICADA.
Added/Corp Cuba. Junta Central de Planificacion. **VFOAT** Economia Planificada. Vol. 1, No. 1 (Jan./March 1986)-. Periodical. Spanish (summaries and/or abstracts in English, French and Russian; table of contents in English and Russian). Four times a year. Junta Central de Planificacion, 11 y C, Vedado, Havana Cuba. **ED** Fernando Jimenez Gomez. Index available. cum. index. **Circ:** 2,000 (ctrl). **Continues** *Cuestiones de la Economia Planificada.*
Desc: Exposes theoretic, methodologic studies, investigations, experiences and criteria about the specific aspects of the economic sciences, preferably referring to themes such as the economic theory and politics.
Ind/Abst LABORDOC.

LC HC152.5.A1 C823   **ISSN** 0138-7766
DD 330   CU
CUBA, HALF-YEARLY ECONOMIC REPORT. Added/Corp Banco Nacional de Cuba.
Cuba. Comite Estatal de Estadisticas. **VFOAT** Cuba. (1990)-. Periodical. English. Two times a year. Banco Nacional de Cuba, Comite Estatal de Estadisticas, Gaveta Postal 6016, LaHabana Cuba. **Continues** *Cuba, Quarterly Economic Report.*

ISSN 1067-8026
US
●CUBA (SYRACUSE, N.Y.). (CUBA : AN
EXECUTIVE REPORT.). **Added/Corp** Political Risk Services (IBC USA (Publications) Inc.). **VFOAT** Executive Report. (1993)-. English. $110.00. Political Risk Services,

Business and Economics

6320 Fly Road, Suite 102, PO Box 248, East Syracuse NY 13057-0248. **Tel** (315)431-0511, FAX (315)431-0200. **Desc:** Focuses on the long-term outlook for business. Includes a brief review of recent events and current circumstances, background intelligence including geography, history, economics and social conditions, as well as the key political and economic forecasts.
US

CURRENCY FORECASTERS DIGEST.
(19??)-. Trade Publication. English. Twelve times a year. $650.00. Teck Enterprises Inc., Box 139, Gedney Station, White Plains NY 10605. **Tel** (914)949-6364, FAX (914)949-0303. **Bk Rev**, (Qty: 12/yr). **Absorbed** Blue Chip Economic Worldscan, 0741-8337.
Desc: Receives monthly currency forecasts from two groups of carefully selected organizations. Provides indications of the forecasting risks. Summarizes the key assumptions underlying the US economic outlook as well as the forecasts for each currency. Permits the reader to compare the expectations of a group of users of currency forecasts.

ISSN 1039-9275
AT

●CURRENT AWARENESS SERVICE.
(1993)-. Periodical. English. Three times a year. Australian Centre for Industrial Relations, Research and Teaching, University of Sydney, L02L Sydney NSW 2006 Australia. **Tel** 011 02 5199400, FAX 011 02 5199263. **ED** Merilyn Bryce.

LC HC
ISSN 0070-1858
UK

CURRENT BRITISH DIRECTORIES. See
Industry and Production-Trade and Industrial Directories.

LC HF105 .A667
ISSN 0363-8553
DD 381/.2/0973
US

CURRENT BUSINESS REPORTS. MONTHLY WHOLESALE TRADE, SALES, AND INVENTORIES.
[Curr. bus. rep., Mon. wholes. trade sales inventories]. **Added/Corp** United States. Bureau of the Census. **VFOAT** Monthly Wholesale Trade, Sales, and Inventories. (Mar. 1968)-. Government Publication. English. Twelve times a year. $25.00. US Department of Commerce / Bureau of the Census, Data User Services Division, Customer Services, Washington DC 20233-0800. **Tel** (301)763-4100. (**Subscription address:** Superintendent of Documents, US Government Printing Office, Washington DC 20402.) Documents available from Documents on Demand. **Continues** Monthly Wholesale Trade Report. Sales and Inventories.
Desc: Contains wholesaler's sales and inventories, by kinds of business and geographic divisions.
Ind/Abst Am. Stat. Index; Predicasts Forecasts.

UK
CURRENT CONTROVERSIES. Added/Corp
Institute of Economic Affairs (Great Britain). (1992)-. Monographic series. English. Irregular. Price varies per volume. Institute of Economic Affairs / IEA, 2 Lord North Street, London SW1P 3LB United Kingdom. **Tel** 011 44 171 7993745.

LC HC687.F5 A23
DD 330.9/96/11
FJ

CURRENT ECONOMIC STATISTICS. See
Business and Economics-Abstracting, Bibliographies and Statistics.

ISSN 0964-8518
DD 330.071
UK

CURRENT ECONOMICS.
[Curr. econ.]. (1991)-. Periodical. English. Twelve times a year. $320.00. Consensus Economics Inc., 49 Berkeley Square, London W1X 6LT United Kingdom. **Tel** 011 44 171 4913211, FAX 011 44 171 4092331.
Desc: Reviews the latest research produced by leading international economists from around the world. Includes the economic outlook for a selection of countries, analysis of topical issues and, periodically, the outlook for exchange rates and interest rates.

ISSN 0145-8450
DD 658
US

CUSTOMER COMMUNICATOR, THE.
[Cust. commun.]. (19??)-. Periodical. English. Twelve times a year. $137.00 US, Canada and Mexico; $187.00 other (minimum order - 10 copies). Alexander Research & Communications, Inc, 215 Park Avenue South, Suite 1301, New York NY 10003. **Tel** (212)228-0246, FAX (212)228-0376. **ED** Warren Beanding.
Desc: The training and motivation source for front-line customer service representatives.

ISSN 1068-154X
DD 658
US

CUSTOMER SERVICE MANAGER'S LETTER.
[Cust. serv. manag. lett.]. **Added/Corp** Bureau of Business Practice. Vol. 1, No. 1 (1989)-. Periodical. English. Twenty-four times a year. $191.47. Bureau of Business Practice, 24 Rope Ferry Road, Waterford CT 06386. **Tel** (800)243-0876, (203)442-4365, (800)876-9105, FAX (203)443-1123.
Desc: For the customer service manager who wants to make it big in one of today's fastest growing fields.
US

CUSTOMER SERVICE POSTING. English.
Twelve times a year. $53.28 (US); $65.04 (Canada). Bureau of Business Practice, 24 Rope Ferry Road, Waterford CT 06386. **Tel** (800)243-0876, (203)442-4365, (800)876-9105, FAX (203)443-1123.

LC TT950
ISSN 0274-8851
DD 646.72
US

CUTTER, THE. See Beauty and Cosmetics.

ISSN 0308-2237
IT

CV NEWS LETTER. Added/Corp Corpus
Vitrearum Technical Committee. **VAT** Corpus Vitrearum News Letter. (19??)-. Periodical. English (French and German). Two times a year. Centre Suisse Recherche & Info, Grand rue 46 sur le Vitrail, CH-1680 Romont Switzerland. **Tel** 011 41 37 521834.

ISSN 1055-1700
DD 332
US

CYCLE PROJECTIONS. (CYCLE
PROJECTIONS : PROJECTIONS IN STOCKS, REAL ESTATE, AND THE ECONOMY.). [Cycle proj.]. **Added/Corp** Foundation for the Study of Cycles (U.S.). (Aug. 1990)-. Periodical. English. Twelve times a year. $175.00. Foundation for the Study of Cycles Inc., 900 West Valley Road, Suite 502, Wayne PA 19087-1821. **Tel** (610)995-2120, FAX (610)995-2130.

ISSN 0822-8205
DD 339.37
CN

CYCLES ET TENDANCES. [Cycles tend.].
Main/Corp Caisse de Depot et Placement du Quebec. Direction des Etudes Economiques. **Added/Corp** Caisse de Depot et Placement du Quebec. Direction des Affaires Publiques. (198?)-. Periodical. French. Two times a year. Caisse Depot Placement Quebec, 1981 McGill College Avenue, Montreal Quebec H3A 3C7 Canada. **Tel** (514)842-3261. **Continues** Caisse de Depot et Placement du Quebec. Departement des Etudes Economiques. Cycles et Tendances., 0822-8205.

LC HC
ISSN 1013-3224
DD 330
CY
Pr Rev.

CYPRUS JOURNAL OF ECONOMICS, THE. Added/Corp Cyprus Economic Society. Vol. 1,
No. 1 (June 1988)-. Academic Scholarly Publication. English. Two times a year. $45.00. Cyprus Economic Society, PO Box 8724, Nicosia Cyprus. **Tel** 445281, FAX 472012, telex 2424. **ED** G.M. Georgiou and P. Demetriades. Index available. cum. index. **Bk Rev**. **Ad Acc. Circ:** 600.
Desc: The journal aims to cover a wide spectrum of areas in economics. These areas include finance, development economics, econometrics, history of economic thought, and the political economy.
Ind/Abst Econ. Lit. Index.

ISSN 1015-2881
CY

CYPRUS REVIEW, THE. See Political Science.

XR

CZECH & SLOVAK MARKETS. (19??)-.
English. Irregular (22 issues per year). $110.00 Europe; $120.00 other. Bonus Company Limited, Samova 8, 101 47 Prague Czech Republic. **Tel** 011 42 2 724573, FAX 011 42 2 724573. **Continues** Czechoslovak Market, 0862-9897.

LC HF37.C9 C93
ISSN 1210-5546
DD 382
XR
TITLE CHANGE

CZECH FOREIGN TRADE. Added/Corp Czech
Republic. Ministry of Industry and Trade. Czech Chamber of Commerce and Industry. **VFOAT** CFT. (1993)-(1993). Periodical. English. (**Subscription address:** Artia Pegas Press Ltd., Palac Metro Narodni Trida 25, 11210 Prague 1 Czech Republic. **Tel** 011 42 2 24196265, 011 42 2 24196266.) **Continues** Czechoslovak Foreign Trade, 0011-460X. **Continued by** Czech Business and Trade.

LC HF3550.3.A48 C9
ISSN 0964-0401
UK

CZECHOSLOVAKIA, MAJOR BUSINESSES. Added/Corp Dun & Bradstreet
International. (1992)-. English. Dun & Bradstreet / Business Reference Services, Business Reference Services, 26-32 Clifton Street, London EC2P 2LY United Kingdom. **Tel** 011 44 181 3774377, FAX 011 44 181 2473836, telex 886697 DEANBE G.

LC HG4132.Z5 D18
UK
DD 338.7/4/09405

●D & B EUROPA. VFOAT D and B Europa. (1993)-.
English. One time a year (Oct.). $650.00. Dun & Bradstreet Information Services, 3 Sylvan Way, Parsippany NJ 07054. **Tel** (201)605-6000, (800)526-0651. **Continues** Duns Europa.

LC HF5001 .D86A
ISSN 0746-6110
DD 330/.05
US
CCC
CODEN DBRED6
CEASED

D & B REPORTS. [D&B rep.]. Main/Corp Dun and
Bradstreet, Inc. Vol. 27, No. 3, (May/June 1979)-(March/April 1994). Periodical. English. Dun & Bradstreet / New York, 299 Park Avenue, 24th Floor, New York NY 10171. **Tel** (212)593-4173. **ED** Patricia W Hamilton. **Ad Acc. Circ:** 73,165. available on microfilm and microfiche from University Microfilms International (UMI). Documents available from UMI Article Clearinghouse. **Continues** Dun & Bradstreet Reports Magazine, 0164-517X.
Desc: Edited for top managers of small businesses. The publication contains how-to articles that deal with daily management problems and successful small-company profiles.
Ind/Abst ABI/INFORM Glob. Ed.; ABI/INFORM Ondisc: Expr. Ed. (Jan. 1987-); ABI/INFORM [Computer File] (Sept. 1983-); Acad. Search; Account. Tax Datab. (Sept. 1983-) [Full Txt.]; BioBusiness; Bus. Index (1984-); Bus. Period.; Bus. Source Plus; Bus. Source; EP Collect.; F&S Index Plus Text, Int. [Select. Cov.]; Gen. BusinessFile (1984-); Gen. Period. Index (1985-); Homework Help.; INFO-SOUTH Abstr.; Mag. Artic. Summar. Elite; Mag. Artic. Summar. Select; Mag. Artic. Summar. CD-ROM; Mag. Search; Manage. Contents; MasterFile FullTEXT 1000; MasterFile FullTEXT 350; MasterFile FullTEXT 650; MasterFile FullTEXT (Mar. 1984-June 1989); Newsp. Period. Abstr. (1992-); OCLC; PROMT; Telebase; Trade Ind. Index; UMI ABI/Inform--Bus. Period. Ondisc (Jan. 1988-) [Full Txt.]; Wilson Bus. Abstr.

LC Discard
ISSN 0346-640X
SW

DAGENS INDUSTRI. No. 15 (April 1, 1975)-.
Periodical. Swedish. Irregular (276 issues). $857.85. Dagens Industri, Box 3177, 103 63 Stockholm Sweden. **Tel** 011 46 8 7230670, FAX 011 46 8 7898896 205133, telex 19373. **ED** Hasse Olsson. **Ad Acc. Circ:** 65,000. Formed by the union of Modern Kemi and Modern Ytbehandling.
Desc: Newspaper providing information on business and finance.
Ind/Abst F&S Index Plus Text, Int. [Select. Cov.]; Infomat Int. Bus.; PROMT.

ISSN 1060-2240
DD 330
US

DAILY JAPAN DIGEST, THE. See Political
Science.

ISSN 0148-8155
US
CCC

DAILY REPORT FOR EXECUTIVES. [Dly.
rep. exec.]. **Added/Corp** Bureau of National Affairs (Washington, D.C.). (Nov. 1, 1943)-. Periodical. English. Five times a week (260 issues). $5811.00. Bureau of National Affairs Inc., 9435 Key West Avenue, Rockville MD 20850. **Tel** (800)372-1033, (301)258-1033, FAX (301)948-5823. **ED** Mike Cavanagh. available on an online database from NEXIS. **Continues** Daily Report on Tax Laws, War Contracts, Business Trends.
Desc: A notification service covering legislative, regulatory, legal, tax, and economic developments which affect both national and international businesses.

LC HG4245 .D33
JA

DAIYAMONDO KIGYO RANKINGU.
VFOAT Diamond Ranking. 1979-. Japanese. ¥2000. Daiyamondo Sha, (Diamond Inc.), 4-2 1-chome Kasumigaseki, Chiyoda-ku Tokyo 100 Japan. **Continues** Daiyamondo Rankingu Sohenshu.

ISSN 0899-4129
DD 330
US
CCC

DALLAS BUSINESS JOURNAL. [Dallas bus.
j.]. 11th Year, No. 37 (May 9, 1988)-. Periodical. English. One time a week. $52.00 US; $98.00 Hawaii, Mexico, Canada; $140.00 South America; $160.00 Europe; $180.00 Africa; $200.00 other. Dallas Business Journal, 4131 North Central Expressway, Suite 310, Dallas TX 75204. **Tel** (214)520-1010, FAX (214)522-5606. **ED** John Carroll and Huntley Daton. **Ad Acc. Circ:** 19,000. available on an online database (files 635,648/Full-Text) from DIALOG. Documents available from UMI Article Clearinghouse. **Continues in part** Dallas/Fort Worth Business Journal, 8750-6084.
Desc: Business news and information for Dallas, Texas.
Ind/Abst Acad. Search; Bus. ASAP (1990-) [Full Txt.]; Bus. Dateline; Bus. Index (1988-1990); Bus. Source Plus; Bus. Source; EP Collect.; Gen. BusinessFile

Business and Economics

(1988-1990); Homework Help.; MasterFile FullTEXT 1000; MasterFile FullTEXT 350; MasterFile FullTEXT 650; MasterFile FullTEXT (July 1993-); OCLC; PROMT; Telebase; Trade Ind. ASAP [Full Txt.]; Trade Ind. Index [Full Txt.].

DD 380.1/09716/22   ISSN 0824-2682   CN
DARTMOUTH BUSINESS NEWS.
[Dartmouth bus. news]. **Added/Corp** Dartmouth Chamber of Commerce. Vol. 1, Issue 1 (Apr. 1983)-. Periodical. English. Four times a year. Free. Dartmouth Chamber of Commerce, 12 Portland Street, Dartmouth Nova Scotia B2Y 1G9 Canada. **Tel** (902)469-7110. **Ad Acc.** ctrl circ. Documents available from UMI Article Clearinghouse. **Continues** *Chamber Chronicle, 0383-6975*.
Ind/Abst Bus. Dateline (June 1990-) [Full Txt.].

US
DARTNELL SALES MANAGER'S HANDBOOK, THE. See Business and Economics-Management.

LC QA76 .D3155   ISSN 0095-0033
DD 658/.05/405   US
   CODEN DTBSAN
Pr Rev.   TITLE CHANGE
DATA BASE. See Computers-Electronic Data Processing.

LC QA76 .D3155   US
DD 658/.05/405
   CODEN DTBSAN
●**DATA BASE FOR ADVANCES IN INFORMATION SYSTEMS : A QUARTERLY PUBLICATION OF SIGBIT, THE.** See Computers-Electronic Data Processing.

US
DATABASE SEARCHSHEETS. English. $19.50. Information Today Inc., 143 Old Marlton Pike, Medford NJ 08055-8750. **Tel** (609)654-6266, (609)654-4888 (editorial), FAX (609)654-4309. **ED** Frank Ryan.
Desc: Provides information that is needed for most searches on PTS PROMT, a database linking technology and business.

UK
   SUSPENDED
DATALINK. VFOAT Data Link. Suspended with (July 1990). Periodical. English. One time a week. VNU Business Publications BV, 32-34 Broadwick Street, London W1A 2HG United Kingdom. **Tel** 011 44 171 4394242 ext. 2222, FAX 011 44 171 4379638, telex 23918 VNU G, 8952440. available on an online database (files 771,772/Full-Text) from DIALOG. Documents available from Ask*IEEE.
Ind/Abst INSPEC (Nov. 1978-); World Text. Abstr.

US
DATAPRO BROADBAND NETWORKING. See Communications.

US
DATAPRO LAN INTERNETWORKING. See Communications.

LC HF5548.2 .D37   GW
DD 658/.054/05
DATENVERARBEITUNG, STEUER, WIRTSCHAFT, RECHT : DSWR : ORGAN DER DATEV. Added/Corp
Datenverarbeitungsorganisation des Steuerberatenden Berufes in der Bundesrepublik Deutschland. **VFOAT** DSWR; D.W.S.R. (19??)-. Periodical. German. Twelve times a year. DM89.00. CH Beck Verlagsbuchhandlung, D-80791 Munich Germany. **Tel** 011 49 89 381891.
Continues *Datenverarbeitung in Steuer, Wirtschaft und Recht*.

US
DATES & DEADLINES. (19??)-. English. Twelve times a year. $19.68 (US); $30.96 (Canada). Bureau of Business Practice, 24 Rope Ferry Road, Waterford CT 06386. **Tel** (800)243-0876, (203)442-4365, (800)876-9105, FAX (203)443-1123.

   ISSN 1063-3413
DD 330   US
   CCC
DAYTON BUSINESS REPORTER. [Dayton bus. report.]. (1991)-. Periodical. English. Twelve times a year. $21.00. Hannover Publishing Co., 6356 Far Hills Avenue, Dayton OH 45459. **Tel** (513)436-2342, FAX (513)436-3426. **ED** Gene Fox (513)291-1100. **Ad Acc.** ctrl circ.
Desc: A business-to-business publication serving the Dayton and Miami Valley areas.

US
   SUSPENDED
DAYTON-SPRINGFIELD BUSINESS LIFE. (19??)-Suspended (19??). English. Eleven times a year (monthly with combined Jan. / Feb.). Ohio Communications Corp., 6159 Far Hills Avenue, Centreville OH 45459. **Tel** (513)435-7273. available on an online database (file 635/Full-Text) from DIALOG. Documents available from UMI Article Clearinghouse.
Continues *Dayton Business Journal*.
Ind/Abst Bus. Dateline (Feb. 1987-July 1991) [Full Txt.].

BE
DE LLOYD. See Transportation.

FR
DECIMAL. See Business and Economics-Abstracting, Bibliographies and Statistics.

LC HD30.23 .D378   ISSN 0732-6823
   US
DECISION LINE. (DECISION LINE / THE DECISION SCIENCES INSTITUTE.). [Decis. line]. **Added/Corp** American Institute for Decision Sciences. Decision Sciences Institute. (198?)-. Periodical. English. Five times a year. $6.00. Decision Sciences Institute, Georgia State University, College of Business Administration, University Plaza, Atlanta GA 30303. **Tel** (404)651-4000, FAX (404)651-2804. **ED** Bernard W. Taylor III. **Bk Rev.** **Ad Acc.** **Circ:** 5,000 (ctrl).

LC HD30.23 .D4   ISSN 0011-7315
DD 658.4/03/05   US
   CODEN DESCDQ
Pr Rev.
DECISION SCIENCES. [Decis. sci.].
Added/Corp American Institute for Decision Sciences. Decision Sciences Institute. (Jan./Apr. 1970)-. Periodical. English. Six times a year. $75.00. Decision Sciences Institute, Georgia State University, College of Business Administration, University Plaza, Atlanta GA 30303. **Tel** (404)651-4000, FAX (404)651-2804. **ED** James C. Hershauer. **Ad Acc. Circ:** 4,000 (ctrl). available on microfilm and microfiche from University Microfilms International (UMI). Documents available from The Genuine Article, UMI Article Clearinghouse, Ask*IEEE.
Ind/Abst ABI/INFORM Glob. Ed.; ABI/INFORM [Computer File] (Jan. 1972-); Acad. Search; Account. Art.; Bus. Index (1985-); Bus. Period. Index; Contents Pages Manage. (Jan. 1972-); Curr. Cit.; Curr. Contents Soc. Behav. Sci.; EP Collect.; Fish Rev. (Jan. 1989-July 1992); Gen. BusinessFile (1985-); Gen. Period. Index (1985-); Homework Help.; INFO-SOUTH Abstr.; INSPEC (April 1977-); Int. Abstr. Oper. Res. [Full Cov.]; Mag. Search; MasterFile FullTEXT 1000; MasterFile FullTEXT 350; MasterFile FullTEXT 650; MasterFile FullTEXT (July 1993-); OCLC; Oper. Res./Manage. Sci. (1974-); Pig News Inf.; Pollut. Abstr. Indexes; Res. Alert [Full Cov.]; Selec. Coop. Indice Manage. Period.; Soc. Sci. Cit. Index [Full Cov.]; SportSearch (1974-); Telebase; Trade Ind. Index; UMI ABI/Inform--Bus. Period. Ondisc [Full Txt.]; Wildl. Rev. (Jan. 1989-July 1992).

   ISSN 0702-9578
DD 344.714/017   CN
DECISIONS DISCIPLINAIRES CONCERNANT LES CORPORATIONS PROFESSIONNELLES. [Decis. discip. concern. corp. prof.]. **Main/Corp** Societe Quebecoise d'Information Juridique. (1986)-. Periodical. French. Two times a year. 98.00Can$. Office des Professions du Quebec, 320 rue St. Joseph Est, Quebec G1K 8G5 Canada. **Continues** *Decisions Disciplinaires Concernant les Corporations Professionnelles, 0702-9578*.
Desc: Publishes decisions by disciplinary committees of Quebec professional corporations as well as judgements by the professional court. Decisions are grouped by jurisdiction and profession.

   ISSN 0364-9008
   US
   TITLE CHANGE
DEFENSE & ECONOMY : WORLD REPORT AND SURVEY. See Political Science-International Relations.

US
DEFENSE BUSINESS BRIEFING. See Military and Defense.

   ISSN 1064-3583
DD 338   US
DEFENSE MERGERS & ACQUISITIONS.
[Def. mergers acquis.]. **VFOAT** Defense Mergers and Acquisitions. Vol. 1, No. 1 (Jan. 1989)-. Periodical. English. Twelve times a year. $1295.00. Ardak Corporation, 6849 Old Dominion Drive, Suite 370, McLean VA 22101. **Tel** (703)893-3828, FAX (703)893-4010. **ED** Mac McCutchon. cum. index. available on diskette from the publisher.
Desc: Tracking merger and acquisition activity in the defense and aerospace industries. Providing a more comprehensive, timely, and accurate summary of industry-specific M&A activity than is available from any other single source. Informed on transactions at all states, from rumor to final agreement. Quantitative market analyses are included in each issue of the newsletter.

   ISSN 1061-4605
DD 338   US
DELAWARE BUSINESS REVIEW. [Del. bus. rev.]. (19??)-. English. One time a week. $48.00. Delaware Business Review, PO Box 3350, Wilmington DE 19804. **Tel** (302)998-9580, FAX (302)998-1276. **ED** Paul Wilke. **Bk Rev.** **Ad Acc.** **Adv Mgr:** Nancy Carney. **Circ:** 11,000 (ctrl). available on microfilm and microfiche from University Microfilms International (UMI); available on an online database (file 635/Full-Text) from DIALOG. Documents available from UMI Article Clearinghouse.
Ind/Abst Bus. Dateline (Jan. 20, 1992-) [Full Txt.].

LC HC   ISSN 0011-8052
DD 650   US
DELTA PI EPSILON JOURNAL. [Delta Pi Epsil. j.]. **Main/Corp** Delta Pi Epsilon. Vol. 1 (Sept. 1957)-. Periodical. English. Four times a year. $48.00. Delta Pi Epsilon National Office, PO Box 4340, Little Rock AR 72214. **Tel** (501)562-1233, FAX (501)562-1293. **ED** Marianne D Onofrio. **Ad Acc.** **Circ:** 10,000 (ctrl). available on microfilm and microfiche from University Microfilms International (UMI).
Desc: A publication devoted to research, scholarship, and leadership in business education.
Ind/Abst Bus. Educ. Index; Curr. Index J. Educ.; Educ. Index (1992-).

   ISSN 0160-3949
   US
DELTA PI EPSILON RAPID READER. See Education-Teaching and Curriculum.

US
DEMAND-SIDE REPORT. (19??)-. Newsletter. English. $545.00 US and Canada; $595.00 other. McGraw Hill Publishing Company, Inc., 1221 Avenue of the Americas, New York NY 10020. **Tel** (212)512-6410, (800)525-5003, FAX (212)512-6111.

LC HB1 .D44   ISSN 0301-9047
DD 330/.05   II
DEMOCRATIC WORLD. Vol. 1 (Nov. 23, 1972)-. Periodical. English. One time a week. $4.00. M. Gulab Singh & Sons Ltd., 6 Bahadur Shah Zafar Marg, New Delhi 110002 India. **Tel** 011 91 110002. **Formed by the union of** *Parliamentary Studies*.

LC HB3572.5.A3 D455   SR
DEMOGRAFISCHE DATA VOOR SURINAME. Dutch.

LC RK1 .O7   ISSN 0011-8583
DD 338.4/7/6176005   US
NLM W1 DE194P   CCC
DENTAL ECONOMICS (PITTSBURGH. 1968). See Dentistry.

   ISSN 0827-1305
DD 617.6/0068   CN
NLM W1; DE322H
DENTAL PRACTICE MANAGEMENT (DON MILLS, ONT.). See Dentistry.

   ISSN 0746-2964
   US
   CCC
   SUSPENDED
DENVER BUSINESS. Vol. 6, No. 1 (Sept. 1983)-Suspended (199?). Periodical. English. Six times a year. Tall Oaks Publishing Inc., 60 Golden Eagle Lane, Littleton CO 80127. **Tel** (303)973-6600, (800)662-1660, FAX (303)973-5327. **(Subscription address:** Tall Oaks Publishing Company, PO Box 621669, Littleton CO 80162. **Tel** (303)973-6700.) **ED** Glen Richardson. **Ad Acc. Circ:** 17,700 (ctrl). available on an online database (files 635,648/Full-Text) from DIALOG. Documents available from UMI Article Clearinghouse. **Continues** *Denver Business World, 0199-1922*.
Desc: The business magazine for Metro Denver. Focusing on local business trends and the people making them.
Ind/Abst Bus. Dateline; Bus. Index (1985-1991); Gen. BusinessFile (1985-1991); Gen. Period. Index (1985-1991); PROMT.

   ISSN 0893-7745
DD 330   US
   CCC
DENVER BUSINESS JOURNAL, THE.
[Denver bus. j.]. **VFOAT** Denver Business Journal. Vol. 38, No. 3 (Oct. 1986)-. Periodical. English. One time a week. $55.89. Denver Business Journal, 1700 Broadway Suite 515, Denver CO 80290. **Tel** (303)837-3500, FAX (303)433-4718. **ED** Dougald MacDonald. **Ad Acc, Adv Mgr:** Jill Hess. available on microfilm from University Microfilms International (UMI); available on an online database (files 635,648/Full-Text) from DIALOG. Documents available from UMI Article Clearinghouse. **Continues** *Rocky Mountain Business Journal, 0279-0769*.
Ind/Abst Bus. Dateline; Bus. Index (1986-1990); Bus. Source Plus; Bus. Source; EP Collect.; Gen. BusinessFile (1986-1990); Homework Help.; INFO-SOUTH Abstr.; MasterFile FullTEXT 1000; MasterFile FullTEXT 350;

Business and Economics

MasterFile FullTEXT 650; MasterFile FullTEXT (Jan. 1995-); OCLC; PROMT; Telebase; Trade Ind. ASAP [Full Txt.]; Trade Ind. Index [Full Txt.].

LC HF5068.D4 D46   **ISSN** 0736-7562
DD 338/.0025/78883   US

DENVER DOWNTOWN DIRECTORY, THE. (1983)-. Directory. English. One time a year. Downtown Data Co., PO Box 11605, Denver CO 80211.

ISSN 1068-6681
US

DES MOINES BUSINESS RECORD. (1974)-. Newspaper. English. Fifty-two times a year (Mon.). $39.95. Business Record, The Depot at Fourth, 100 4th Street, Des Moines IA 50309. **Tel** (515)288-3336, FAX (515)288-0309. **ED** Petro Kotz. **Ad Acc, Adv Mgr:** Mary Day. **Circ:** 9,300 (ctrl). *Continues Business Record (Des Moines, Iowa), 0746-410X.*
Desc: The highlights and analysis events, trends, and people in Central Iowa business.

LC HF3099 .S45   **ISSN** 0932-2973
DD 338.74   GW

DEUTSCH-AMERIKANISCHE GESCHAFTSBEZIEHUNGEN. VFOAT German American Business Contacts. (1987)-. German (English). One time a year. DM360.00. Verlag Hoppenstedt & Company, Postfach 100139, D-64201 Darmstadt Germany. **Tel** 011 49 6151 380436, 011 49 6151 380361. **ED** Klaus Schneider. Index available. **Ad Acc. Circ:** 1,200. *Continues Directory of American Business in Germany.*

LC HC282 .D4
DD 338/.0025/43   GW

DEUTSCHES BUNDES-ADRESSBUCH. BUND, LANDER UND GEMEINDEN. (19??)-. Directory. German. One time a year. DM145.00. Deutscher Adressbuch-Verlag fur Wirtschaft und Verkehr GmbH, Dav-Verlagshaus, Arheilger Weg 17, D-64380 Rossdorf Germany. **Tel** 06154 699500, FAX 06154 6995490, telex 4191324 DAV D. *Continues Deutsches Bundes-Adressbuch. Industrien, Gross und Aussenhandel, Dienstleistungen, Organisationen.*
Desc: Serves as a mediator for contacts in industry and local planning. Provides a current view of the market according to Laender, districts, counties, towns and communities.

LC HD72 .D485
DD 338.9/005   US

DEVELOPMENT BUSINESS. Added/Corp United Nations. Division for Economic and Social Information. United Nations. Dept. of Public Information. (1984)-. Periodical. English. Twenty-four times a year. $495.00. United Nations Development Forum, PO Box 5850, Grand Central Station, New York NY 10163. **Tel** (212)963-1515. **(Subscription address:** John Hopkins University Press, Journals Publishing Division, PO Box 19966, Baltimore MD 21211. **Tel** (410)516-6987, (800)548-1784, FAX (410)516-6968.) *Continues Development Forum; Absorbed International Business Opportunities Services.*
Desc: Lists procurement notices and bid invitations that alert readers to consulting, contracting, and supply opportunities as soon as projects are proposed. Publishes articles on transacting business and securing contracts in developing countries.

UK

DEVELOPMENT NEWS. (19??)-. English. Twelve times a year. £450.00. Mintel International Group Ltd., 18-19 Long Lane, London EC1A 9HE United Kingdom. **Tel** 011 44 171 6064533, FAX 011 44 171 6065932, telex 21405.

ISSN 0926-5589
NE

DEVELOPMENTS IN AGRICULTURAL ECONOMICS. See Agriculture-Agricultural Economics.

LC HC
DD 330   NE
NLM W1; DE997VZE

DEVELOPMENTS IN HEALTH ECONOMICS AND PUBLIC POLICY. See Public Health and Safety.

II

DEVOLOPMENT ALTERNATIVES NEWSLETTER. (19??)-. Newsletter. English. Twelve times a year. $50.00. **(Subscription address:** Prints India, 11 Darya Ganj, New Delhi 110002 India. **Tel** 011 91 11 3268645, FAX 011 91 11 3275542, telex 31-61087 PRIN-IN.)

ISSN 0950-8473
UK

DIA LONDON. [DiaLondon]. (1986)-. Periodical. Spanish. Twelve times a year. $188.00. Lettres UK Ltd, 61 Old Street, London EC1V 9HX United Kingdom. **Tel** 011 44 171 2510012, FAX 011 44 171 2538193. **ED** Miguel Angel Diez.

Desc: Monthly newsletter in Spanish with political, economic and current affairs in Europe, USA and Japan. Deals with international issues and topics.

ISSN 1055-7431
DD 338   US

DIABLO BUSINESS. (DIABLO BUSINESS : DB.). [Diablo bus.]. **VFOAT** DB. (1989)-. Consumer Publication. English. Four times a year. Diablo Country Magazine Inc, 2520 Camino Diablo, Suite 200, Walnut Creek CA 94596. **Tel** (510)943-1111, FAX (510)943-1045. **ED** Grant R. Opperman. **Ad Acc. Circ:** 15,000 (ctrl). Documents available from UMI Article Clearinghouse.
Desc: Regional business coverage of San Francisco's East Bay and Contra Costa County.
Ind/Abst Bus. Dateline (Oct. 1989-) [Full Txt.].

ISSN 0954-1837
DD 338.47681761   UK

DIAGNOSTICS BUSINESS. [Diagn. bus.]. (1988)-. Periodical. English. Twelve times a year.
Ind/Abst PTS Newsl. Database [Full Txt.].

ISSN 0872-1696
UDC 33   PO

DIARIO ECONOMICO. [D. econ.]. (1989)-. Newspaper. Portuguese. Seven times a week. Proinfec Lim, R Sta Marta 47, Ras Chao Esq, 1100 Lisbon Portugal. **Tel** 011 351 1 3151832, FAX 011 351 1 3151841.

ISSN 0889-5953
DD 658   US
TITLE CHANGE

DICKINSON'S PSAO. [Dickinson's PSAO]. **VAT** Dickinson's Pharmaceutical Services Administrative Organizations. Vol. 1, No. 1 (July 1986)-(19??). Periodical. English. Ferdic Inc., PO Box 367, Las Cruces NM 88004. **Tel** (505)527-8634, FAX (505)527-8858. **ED** James G. Dickinson. *Continued by Dickinson's Pharmacy, 1063-2441.*

FR

DICTIONNAIRE DE L'INDUSTRIE FRANCAISE. (19??)-. Directory. French. One time a year. 750.00F. U F A P, 13 Av Hennequin, BP 36, 78192 Trappes Cedex France. **Tel** 011 33 1 30506148, FAX 011 30 50 48 27. **Ad Acc.** available on magnetic tape from the publisher; available on diskette.

ISSN 0341-3683
UDC 519.68 + 681.3   GW

DIEBOLD-MANAGEMENT-REPORT. [Diebold-Manage.-Rep.]. (1971)-. Trade Publication. German. Twelve times a year. DM318.00 Germany; DM325.00 other. FBO Fachverlag GmbH, Postfach 316, D-76482 Baden-Baden Germany. **Tel** 011 49 7221 271066, 011 49 7221 271067, 011 49 7221 271068, FAX 011 49 7221 33228.

LC HF5166 .A3
AU

DIENSTLEISTUNGEN UND BEHORDEN-COMPASS. Added/Corp Bundeskammer der Gewerblichen Wirtschaft (Austria). **VFOAT** Dienstleistungs- Und Behorden-Compass Osterreich. (19??)-. German. One time a year. Compass Verlag, Wipplingerstrabe 32, 1013 Vienna Austria. **Ad Acc.**

LC HA1161 .A3
DD 318.5   UK

DIGEST OF WELSH STATISTICS. See Business and Economics-Abstracting, Bibliographies and Statistics.

IT
SUSPENDED

DIPCO. (19??)-Suspended (19??). Italian. Forty-three times a year. Organizzazione RAB SRL, via Crocifisso 51, 00165 Rome Italy. **Tel** 011 39 6 632595, 011 39 6 6381177. *Continues Dipco Notizie.*

ISSN 0210-0908
UDC 658   SP

DIRECCION Y PROGRESO. [Dir. prog.]. (1972)-. Periodical. Spanish. Six times a year. $97.70. Association Para Progreso Direccion, Montalban 3 2, 28014 Madrid Spain. **Tel** 011 34 1 5323407.
Ind/Abst Selec. Coop. Index Manage. Period.

ISSN 0012-320X
Pr Rev.   FR

DIRECTION ET GESTION DES ENTREPRISES. Added/Corp Institut National de Gestion Previsionelle et de Controle de Gestion. Vol. 1, (1965)-. Periodical. French. Six times a year. 288.71. Direction Gestion Enterprises, 29 rue de Corbeil BP 49, 91360 Epinay Sur Orge France. **Tel** 11 33 1 69099339, FAX 011 33 1 69093897. **ED** Gravier Jean-Pierre. Index available (6th iss.). cum. index. **Bk Rev**, (Qty: 6). **Ad Acc. Circ:** 2,800 (ctrl).
Ind/Abst Repere (1979-1986); Selec. Coop. Index Manage. Period.

ISSN 1188-6064
DD 332.1   CN

DIRECTIONS, EXECUTIVE BRIEFING. [Dir. exec. brief.]. **Added/Corp** Financial Services Institute. Vol. 1, No. 1 (Mar./Apr. 1992)-. Periodical. English. Six times a year. 316.13Can$. Financial Services Institute, 200 Bay Street, 1640 RB Plaza, Toronto, Ontario M5J 2J3 Canada. **Tel** (416)862-8329, FAX (416)863-5227.

LC HD28   **ISSN** 0012-3250
II

DIRECTOR, THE. Vol. 1 (1964)-. Periodical. English. Four times a year. Rs400.00. India International News Service, 12 India Exchange Place, Calcutta 700001 India. **Tel** 011 91 33 209563. **ED** H Kothari. **Bk Rev. Ad Acc.**
Desc: Articles about top management, new inventions, industrial and financial news, etc. Official organ of the Institute of Directors.
Ind/Abst Bus. Index (Jan. 1985-Dec. 1985); Gen. BusinessFile (Jan. 1985-Dec. 1985).

ISSN 0012-3242
UK

DIRECTOR (LONDON. 1935). (THE DIRECTOR.). [Director]. **Added/Corp** Institute of Directors. Vol. 35, No. 9 (Apr. 1983)-. Periodical. English. Twelve times a year. $107.81. Director Publications, 6-20 Elizabeth Street, Mountbarrow, London SW1W 9RB United Kingdom. **Tel** 011 44 171 7306060, FAX 011 44 171 2355627, telex 918802. **ED** Stewart Rock and Carol Kennedy. Index available. cum. index. **Bk Rev. Ad Acc. Circ:** 36,000 (ctrl). *Continues Director Magazine., 0012-3242.*
Desc: Runs political interviews and reporting on the role player by company directors, company profiles, and analyses of management practice.
Ind/Abst Contents Pages Manage.; EP Collect.; Homework Help.; MasterFile FullTEXT 1000; MasterFile FullTEXT 350; MasterFile FullTEXT 650; MasterFile FullTEXT; OCLC; PAIS Bull. (1986-); Public Aff. Inf. Serv. Bull. (?-1985); Telebase.

LC HC431 .D57
DD 650.1/0954   II

DIRECTOR'S DIGEST PORTFOLIO. **VFOAT** Director's Portfolio; Director Digest; Director Portfolio. Periodical. English. One time a year. Rs20.00. 34 Mittal Chambers Nariman Point, Bombay 400021 India.

LC HF5585.R46 A46A   **ISSN** 0149-5216
DD 338.7/61/3327   US

DIRECTORY - AMERICAN RECOVERY ASSOCIATION, INC. See Industry and Production-Trade and Industrial Directories.

ISSN 0266-1152
UK

DIRECTORY OF FRANCHISING. [Dir. franch.]. **VFOAT** Directory of Franchising and Franchise Year Book. (1984)-. English. Six times a year. $85.56. Franchise World Publications, James House, 37 Nottingham Road, London SW17 7EA United Kingdom. **Tel** 011 44 01 767-1371.

LC HD69.C6 D54   **ISSN** 0732-4723
DD 338.7/6165846/02573   US

DIRECTORY OF HUMAN RESOURCE SERVICES & PRODUCTS, THE. [Dir. hum. resour. serv. prod.]. (19??)-. Directory. English. One time a year. $12.00. Human Resource Communications Group, 2355 East Stadium Blvd., Ann Arbor MI 48104.

LC TH
DD 690   II

●**DIRECTORY OF MANUFACTURERS & DEALERS OF BUILDING INDUSTRY.** See Building and Construction.

LC HD2346.U52 T43   **ISSN** 0094-8004
DD 338.7/6/025764   US

DIRECTORY OF MINORITY OWNED BUSINESSES IN TEXAS. See Industry and Production-Trade and Industrial Directories.

LC HD4285.8 .D56
DD 338.7/4/0255493   CE

DIRECTORY OF STATE CORPORATIONS. See Industry and Production-Trade and Industrial Directories.

US

DIRECTORY OF WOMEN IN SPORTS BUSINESS, THE. (1991)-. Directory. English. Women's Sports Guide, PO Box 1417, Princeton NJ 08524.

ISSN 0394-8366
IT
UDC 33
Pr Rev.

DIRITTO ED ECONOMIA. (1988)-. Periodical. Italian. Three times a year. L81750. Maggioli Editore, Casella Postale 290, 47037 Rimini Italy. **Tel** 011 39 541 628666, FAX 011 39 541 742217. Index available. **Circ:** 1,000.
Desc: Contains information on economic problems and jurisprudence.

Business and Economics

LC HC
DD 330   AT
DISCUSSION PAPER. **Added/Corp** University of Queensland. Dept. of Economics. **VFOAT** Discussion Papers. No. 67 (July 1991)-. Monographic series. English. Irregular (at least 15 per year). 50.00Aus$. University of Queensland / Department of Economics, St Lucia Queensland 4072 Australia. **Tel** 011 61 7 365 1111.
Continues Discussion Paper in Economics, 1033-4661.

LC HD1483   **ISSN** 0113-4507
DD 338.109931   NZ
DISCUSSION PAPER - AGRIBUSINESS & ECONOMICS RESEARCH UNIT, LINCOLN COLLEGE. **See** Agriculture.

LC HC   **ISSN** 0924-7815
DD 330   NE
UDC 33
DISCUSSION PAPER / CENTER FOR ECONOMIC RESEARCH. [Discuss. pap. - Cent. Econ. Res.]. (1988)-. Monographic series. English. Irregular. Price varies per volume.
Ind/Abst World Agric. Econ. Rural Sociol. Abstr.

     ISSN 0956-7895
     UK
DISCUSSION PAPER - ECONOMICS RESEARCH CENTRE. (DISCUSSION PAPER.). [Discuss. pap. - Econ. Res. Cent.]. (198?)-. Monographic series. English. **Continues** Discussion Paper - University of East Anglia, 0956-7887.
Ind/Abst World Agric. Econ. Rural Sociol. Abstr.

     ISSN 09695698
     UK
DISCUSSION PAPER - LONDON BUSINESS SCHOOL. CENTRE FOR ECONOMIC FORECASTING. (DISCUSSION PAPER.). (1983)-. English. London Business School, Centre for Economic Forecasting, Basil Blackwell Journals, 108 Cowley Road, Oxford OX4 1JF United Kingdom. **Tel** 011 44 1865 791100, FAX 011 44 1865 791347.
Ind/Abst Curr. Cit.

     UK
DISCUSSION PAPER - NATIONAL INSTITUTE OF ECONOMIC AND SOCIAL RESEARCH. (19??)-. English. National Institution of Economic and Social Research, 2 Dean French Street Smith Square, London SWIP 3HE United Kingdom. **Tel** 011 44 171 17665.
Ind/Abst Curr. Cit.

LC HC   **ISSN** 0265-8003
DD 330.1   UK
DISCUSSION PAPER SERIES. [Disc. pap. ser. - Cent. Econ. Policy Res.]. **Added/Corp** Centre for Economic Policy Research (Great Britain). No. 1 (Jan. 1984)-. Monographic series. English. Irregular. Price varies per volume. Center for Economic Policy Research, 25 28 Old Burlington Street, London W1X 1LB United Kingdom. **Tel** 011 44 171 7349110, FAX 011 44 171 7348760.
Desc: Information on economic policy.
Ind/Abst Curr. Cit.

     ISSN 0702-0643
     CN
DISCUSSION PAPER SERIES - ONTARIO ECONOMIC COUNCIL. Monographic series. English. Price varies per volume. Ontario Economic Council, 81 Wellesley Street East, Toronto Ontario M4Y 1H6 Canada.

     ISSN 0952-8490
     UK
DISCUSSION PAPER SERIES - SURREY ENERGY ECONOMICS CENTRE. **See** Energy.

LC HC   **ISSN** 0317-0144
DD 330   CN
DISCUSSION PAPER (UNIVERSITY OF BRITISH COLUMBIA. DEPT. OF ECONOMICS). (DISCUSSION PAPER - DEPARTMENT OF ECONOMICS, UNIVERSITY OF BRITISH COLUMBIA.). **Added/Corp** University of British Columbia. Dept. of Economics. (19??)-. English. Irregular. Free on request to educational institutions. University of British Columbia, Department of Economics, Vancouver British Columbia, V6T 1W5 Canada. **Tel** (604)228-2876.

     ISSN 0725-430X
DD 330.994063   AT
DISCUSSION PAPERS - AUSTRALIAN NATIONAL UNIVERSITY, CENTRE FOR ECONOMIC POLICY RESEARCH. [Discuss. pap. - Aust. Natl. Univ., Cent. Econ. Policy Res.]. (1980)-. Monographic series. English. Three times a week. Anutech Pty. Limited, GPO Box 4, Canberra ACT 2601 Australia. **Tel** 011 61 6 2492479, FAX 011 61 6 2575088.
Ind/Abst Leis., Rec., Tour. Abstr.; World Agric. Econ. Rural Sociol. Abstr.

LC HC   **ISSN** 1014-9066
DD 330   US
DISCUSSION PAPERS / ECONOMIC COMMISSION FOR EUROPE. **Added/Corp** United Nations. Economic Commission for Europe. **VFOAT** UN ECE Discussion Papers. Vol. 1, No. 1 (1991)-. Monographic series. English. Four times a year. Price varies per volume. United Nations Publishers / Geneva, Palais des Nations, C115 Services Ventes, CH-1211 Geneva 10 Switzerland. **Tel** 011 41 22 7988400, FAX 011 41 22 7332673, telex 415465.
Separated from Economic Bulletin for Europe.

LC HC   **ISSN** 1235-2209
DD 330   FI
DISCUSSION PAPERS / HELSINKI SCHOOL OF ECONOMICS, DEPARTMENT OF ECONOMICS. **Added/Corp** Helsingin Kauppakorkeakoulu. Kansantaloustieteen Laitos. No. 1 (1992)-. Monographic series. English. Price varies per volume. Helsinki School of Economics Library, Uneberginkatu 22-24 Scimp, 00100 Helsinki Finland. **Tel** 011 358 0 43131, telex 122220 ECON SF.

LC HC
DD 330   SZ
DISCUSSION : STUDIES OF THE ECONOMIC COMMISSION FOR EUROPE. (19??)-. English. Irregular. ADECO, CP 465, La Cuez-Blonay, 1211 Geneva 19 Switzerland. **Tel** FAX 41 21 943 36 05.

LC HE   **ISSN** 0743-7269
DD 388   US
DISPATCH (ROCKVILLE, MD.). **See** Transportation.

LC HF5437.A2 D57
DD 658.72   AU
DISPO. (19??)-. Periodical. German. Twelve times a year. S280.00. J L Bondi, Zollergasse 17, Vienna Austria.

LC HF1134.M394 D58   **ISSN** 0046-0400
DD 658.4/009774   US
DIVIDEND. Spring 1969-. Periodical. English. Three times a year. University of Michigan Graduate School of Business, Room 2010, Ann Arbor MI 48109.

     US
●**DIVIDEND MONITOR AND OUTLOOK.** (1995)-. English. Four times a year. $160.00. CA Turner Monitor and Outlook, PO Box 1050, Morristown NJ 08057. **Tel** (800)925-4287.

     ISSN 0046-0419
     CN
     TITLE CHANGE
DIVIDEND RECORD. **Added/Corp** Financial Post Corporation Service. **VFOAT** Dividend Record and Investors' Diary. (19??)-(19??). Periodical. English. Financial Post DataGroup, 333 King Street East, Toronto Ontario M5A 4N2 Canada. **Tel** (800)661-7678, FAX (416)350-6501. **ED** D Jones. ctrl circ. **Continued by** Financial Post Investment Report Service Annual Dividend Record.
Desc: A permanent, year-end record of all dividends paid and/or declared on all Canadian public companies.

LC K4 .J63
     DK
DJF BLADET. **See** Law.

     ISSN 0264-9691
     UK
DOCKLANDS NEWS. (1983)-. English. Twelve times a year. £10.00. London Docklands Development Corp, Mastmaker Ct, 20 Mastmaker Road ISL Dogs, London E14 9TJ United Kingdom. **Tel** 011 44 171 5123000, FAX 011 171 5384414. **ED** Carole Lyplus. **Bk Rev. Ad Acc. Circ:** 140,000 (ctrl).
Desc: Reports on business, community leisure, arts, sport activities in London's docklands.

     ISSN 0733-2262
     US
DOCTOR'S OFFICE, THE. **See** Medical Sciences-Physicians and Medical Personnel.

     UK
DOG CAREER GUIDES. (19??)-. English. One time a year. £2.20. VNU Business Publications BV, 32-34 Broadwick Street, London W1A 4PN United Kingdom. **Tel** 011 44 171 4394242 ext. 2222, FAX 011 44 171 4379638, telex 23918 VNU G, 8952440.

     FR
DOGE. (19??)-. French. Two times a year. 610.00F France; 678.00F other. CPG, 1 rue Voltaire, 38000 Grenoble France. **Tel** 011 33 1 76 443457.
Desc: A bibliographic file covering the management of firms analyzing the thesis of doctorates, reports, research publications, and congress communiques. Subjects covered include international affairs, corporate environment, finance, accounting, production management, human resources management, public administration, marketing, information and decision systems.

LC KE450.B87 D65   **ISSN** 0734-4422
DD 346.71/07/05   US
DOING BUSINESS IN CANADA (NEW YORK, N.Y.). (DOING BUSINESS IN CANADA.). [Doing bus. Can.]. **Added/Corp** Price, Waterhouse & Co. (Sept. 1975)-. English. Irregular. Price Waterhouse & Company, 1177 Avenue of the Americas, New York NY 10020. **Tel** (212)596-7000. **Continues** Information Guide for Doing Business in Canada.

LC KJN7.3.B86 D65   **ISSN** 1059-1265
DD 346.5645/07 345.645067   US
DOING BUSINESS IN CYPRUS. [Doing bus. Cyprus]. **Added/Corp** Price Waterhouse (Firm). **VFOAT** Cyprus. Aug. (1980)-. English. Irregular. Price Waterhouse & Company, 1177 Avenue of the Americas, New York NY 10020. **Tel** (212)596-7000. **Continues** Information Guide for Doing Business in Cyprus.

     US
DOING BUSINESS IN EASTERN EUROPE. (1982)-. English. Irregular. Price Waterhouse & Company, 1177 Avenue of the Americas, New York NY 10020. **Tel** (212)596-7000. available on an online database (file 627/Full-Text) from DIALOG.
Continues East West Trade.

     ISSN 1057-3844
DD 338   US
DOING BUSINESS IN INDIA. [Doing bus. India]. **Added/Corp** Price, Waterhouse & Co. Price Waterhouse (Firm). **VFOAT** India. Jan. (1975)-. English. Irregular. Price Waterhouse & Company, 1177 Avenue of the Americas, New York NY 10020. **Tel** (212)596-7000.
Continues Information Guide for Doing Business in India.

     ISSN 1057-3879
DD 338   US
DOING BUSINESS IN MALAYSIA. [Doing bus. Malays.]. **Added/Corp** Price, Waterhouse & Co. Price Waterhouse (Firm). **VFOAT** Malaysia. Aug. (1977)-. English. Irregular. Price Waterhouse & Company, 1177 Avenue of the Americas, New York NY 10020. **Tel** (212)596-7000. **Continues** Information Guide for Doing Business in Malaysia.

     ISSN 1062-8029
DD 989   US
DOING BUSINESS IN PARAGUAY. [Doing bus. Parag.]. **Added/Corp** Price Waterhouse (Firm), Waterhouse & Co. **VFOAT** Paraguay. July (1976)-. English. Irregular. Price Waterhouse & Company, 1177 Avenue of the Americas, New York NY 10020. **Tel** (212)596-7000. **Continues** Information Guide for Doing Business in the Republic of Paraguay.

LC KPP97.75.A13 D65   **ISSN** 1057-3909
DD 338   US
DOING BUSINESS IN SINGAPORE. [Doing bus. Singap.]. **Added/Corp** Price, Waterhouse & Co. Price Waterhouse (Firm). **VFOAT** Singapore. Oct. (1975)-. English. Irregular. Price Waterhouse & Company, 1177 Avenue of the Americas, New York NY 10020. **Tel** (212)596-7000. **Continues** Information Guide for Doing Business in Singapore.

LC KKX78.B86 D65
DD 346.561/07 345.61067   US
DOING BUSINESS IN TURKEY. **Added/Corp** Price, Waterhouse Center for Transnational Taxation. Price Waterhouse (Firm). (1985)-. English. Irregular. $1,148.00 libraries, schools and universities, $1,350.00 other. Price Waterhouse & Company, 1177 Avenue of the Americas, New York NY 10020. **Tel** (212)596-7000.

     ISSN 1057-381X
DD 338   US
DOING BUSINESS IN ZIMBABWE. [Doing bus. Zimb.]. **Added/Corp** Price, Waterhouse Center for Transnational Taxation. Price Waterhouse (Firm). **VFOAT** Zimbabwe. (1984)-. English. Irregular. Price Waterhouse & Company, 1177 Avenue of the Americas, New York NY 10020. **Tel** (212)596-7000.

     ISSN 1044-1093
     UK
DOING BUSINESS WITH THE USSR. (1989)-. Periodical. English. Twelve times a year. Business International Ltd., 151 Dartford Trade Parkway, Hawley Dartford Kent DA1 1QB United Kingdom. **Tel** 011 44 1322 289194, FAX 011 44 1322 223803. (**Subscription address:** Business International Ltd., PO Box 154 Unit 151, Dartford Kent DA1 1QB United Kingdom. **Tel** 011 44 322 289194.)

     ISSN 1070-678X
DD 650   US
DOING RIGHT THINGS RIGHT. [Doing right things right]. **Added/Corp** Keeping Customers for Life Corp. (199?)-. Periodical. English. Twelve times a year. $60.00. DRTR Company / Keeping Customers for Life, 1359 Centre Street, Newton Centre MA 02159. **Tel**

Business and Economics

(617)332-0534, (800)366-5235, FAX (617)969-9472. **ED** Donald Caplin. Index available. cum. index.
 Desc: Provides information on customer service.
LC HD2346.U52 C516 **ISSN** 0884-5611
DD 330.973/008996073 US
DOLLARS & SENSE (CHICAGO, ILL.).
(DOLLARS & SENSE.). [Dollars & sense]. **VFOAT** Dollars and Sense. (197?)-. Periodical. English. Six times a year. $14.95. National Publications Sales Agency, 1610 East 79th Street, Chicago IL 60649. **Tel** (312)375-6800.

LC HC106.7 .D64 **ISSN** 0012-5245
DD 330.9/73/092 US
CCC
DOLLARS & SENSE (SOMERVILLE, MASS.).
(DOLLARS & SENSE.). [Dollars sense]. **Added/Corp** Union for Radical Political Economics. Economic Affairs Bureau. **VAT** Dollars and Sense. No. 1 (Nov. 1974)-. Periodical. English. Six times a year (issues are combined). $42.00. Dollars & Sense, 1 Summer Street, Somerville MA 02143. **Tel** (617)628-8411, FAX (617)628-2025. **ED** Bobby Reed. **Bk Rev**, (Qty: 10). **Ad Acc, Adv Mgr:** Debbie Dover, **Tel** (617)628-8411. **Circ:** 8,000. available on microfilm and microfiche from University Microfilms International (UMI); available on an online database. Documents available from UMI Article Clearinghouse.
 Desc: Covers current economic issues and trends of interest to people working for progressive social change. Simple explanations and analysis presented in everyday language for non-experts.
 Ind/Abst Altern. Press Index; Chicano Index; Expand. Acad. Index (1992-); Left Index; Newsp. Period. Abstr. (1992-); PAIS Int. Print (1991-); Soc. Plann. Policy Dev. Abstr.; Sociol. Abstr.

LC HD **ISSN** 0989-8107
DD 333 FR
UDC 333
DOMOTIQUE NEWS (PARIS). (DOMOTIQUE
NEWS.). (1988)-. Periodical. French. Eleven times a year (monthly with July/Aug. issues combined). $538.05. Maison du Futur Communications, CNIT BP 530, 92053 Paris-La-Defense France. **Tel** 011 33 1 46921830. **ED** Bruno de Latour.

ISSN 0894-1882
US
DON LARSON'S BUSINESS NEWSLETTER.
[Don Larson's bus. newsl.]. **Added/Corp** Business Newsletter, Inc. **VFOAT** Business Newsletter. (1980)-. Newsletter. English. Twenty-two times a year (twice monthly with one issue in Aug. & Dec.). $39.00. Don Larson's Business Newsletter, 537 East Vine Street, Owatonna MN 55060. **Tel** (507)455-3220.

ISSN 0379-3109
UDC (4) LU
CODEN CE
DOSSIER DE L'EUROPE.
[Doss. Eur.]. (1979)-. Periodical. French. Irregular (20 issues per year). 40.00F. Office for Official Publications of the European Communities, 2 rue Mercier, 2985 Luxembourg Luxembourg. **Tel** 011 352 499281, FAX 011 352 292942763. **(Subscription address:** Moniteur Belge Belg Staatsblad, rue de Louvain 40-42, 1000 Brussels Belgium. **Tel** 011 32 2 5120026.)

LC HC **ISSN** 0012-5822
DD 658.8 US
DOWNTOWN IDEA EXCHANGE.
Added/Corp Downtown Idea Exchange. Downtown Research and Development Center. (Sept. 1, 1954)-. Periodical. English. Twenty-four times a year. $143.00. Alexander Research & Communications, Inc, 215 Park Avenue South, Suite 1301, New York NY 10003. **Tel** (212)228-0246, FAX (212)228-0376. **ED** Laurence A. Alexander.
 Desc: Basic source of ideas on revitalizing central business districts including funding, planning, organization, development, etc.
 Ind/Abst Urban Aff. Abstr.

LC HT175 .D68 **ISSN** 0145-1715
DD 309.2/62/0973 US
DOWNTOWN PLANNING & DEVELOPMENT ANNUAL. See Housing and
Urban Development.

LC HF **ISSN** 0836-6659
DD 650/.05 CN
CODEN DBURER
DRAKE BUSINESS REVIEW. [Drake bus.
rev.]. **Added/Corp** Drake International. (Winter 1986)-. Periodical. English. Four times a year. Free on request. Drake International, PO Box 800, Station F, Toronto Ontario M4Y 2N8 Canada. **Tel** (416)216-1000. **ED** Colin Longhurst. **Circ:** 250,000.
 Ind/Abst INSPEC (Vol. 1, No. 2-).

ISSN 0848-7642
DD 338.7/6165845/09713 CN
DRH COMMUNICATIONS QUARTERLY, THE.
[DRH commun. q.]. **Added/Corp** D.R. Harley Consultants Limited. **VFOAT** Bulletin de Liaison Trimestriel de DRH. **VAT** D.R. Harley Communications Quarterly; Bulletin de Liaison Trimestriel de D.R. Harley. Vol. 1, No. 1 (Oct. 1990)-. Bulletin. English (French). Four times a year. Limited free distribution. D R Harley Consultants Limited, Suite 604, 294 Albert Street, Ottawa Ontario K1P 6E6 Canada.

LC HC **ISSN** 0419-814X
DD 330 US
DULUTH BUSINESS INDICATORS.
Added/Corp University of Minnesota, Duluth. Bureau of Business and Economic Research. Minnesota. Dept. of Economic Security. (19??)-. Periodical. English. Twelve times a year. $15.00. Bureau of Business and Economic Research, University of Minnesota, School of Business and Economics, Duluth MN 55812. **ED** Jerrold M Peterson. **Circ:** 800 (ctrl).
 Desc: Economic information on Duluth and Northeastern Minnesota.

ISSN 1063-0635
DD 330 US
CODEN DBCEEY
DUN & BRADSTREET COMMENTS ON THE ECONOMY.
[Dun Bradstreet comments econ.]. **Added/Corp** Dun & Bradstreet Corporation. Economic Analysis Dept. **VFOAT** Comments on the Economy; Dun and Bradstreet Comments on the Economy. (1990)-. Periodical. English. Six times a year. Free on request. Dun & Bradstreet / New York, 299 Park Avenue, 24th Floor, New York NY 10171. **Tel** (212)593-4173.

LC HF5573 .D7
US
DUN & BRADSTREET REFERENCE BOOK OF AMERICAN BUSINESS, THE.
Added/Corp Dun and Bradstreet, inc. **VFOAT** Dun and Bradstreet Reference Book of American Business; Reference Book of American Business; Reference Book. Vol. 612 (July-Aug. 1991)-. English. Six times a year. Dun & Bradstreet Information Services, 3 Sylvan Way, Parsippany NJ 07054. **Tel** (201)605-6000, (800)526-0651. **Continues** Reference Book (Dun and Bradstreet, Inc.), 0896-016X.

LC HD2771 .D86a **ISSN** 0270-7713
DD 338.7/4/0973 US
DUN & BRADSTREET'S KEY BUSINESS RATIOS.
[Dun & Bradstreet's key bus. ratios]. **Main/Corp** Dun and Bradstreet, Inc. Business Economics Division. **Added/Corp** Dun and Bradstreet, Inc. Business Economics Division. Key Business Ratios. **VFOAT** Key Business Ratios. (1979)-. English. One time a year. $440.00. Dun & Bradstreet Information Services, 3 Sylvan Way, Parsippany NJ 07054. **Tel** (201)605-6000, (800)526-0651. **Continues** Key Business Ratios, 0735-8601.

US
DUN'S 5000 SURVEY.
(19??)-. English. Irregular. Free. Dun & Bradstreet / New York, 299 Park Avenue, 24th Floor, New York NY 10171. **Tel** (212)593-4173.
 Desc: Provides information on 5,000 US firms.

LC HG4234.85.Z65 D86 **ISSN** 1050-5172
DD 338.7/4/09505 US
DUN'S ASIA/PACIFIC KEY BUSINESS ENTERPRISES.
[Dun's Asia Pac. key bus. enterp.]. **Added/Corp** Dun & Bradstreet International. **VFOAT** Dun's Asia Pacific Key Business Enterprises. (1991)-. English. Irregular. $575.00; $435.00 (libraries). Dun & Bradstreet Information Services, 3 Sylvan Way, Parsippany NJ 07054. **Tel** (201)605-6000, (800)526-0651.

DD 338.7/4/02573 US
DUN'S BUSINESS IDENTIFICATION SERVICE [MICROFORM]. **Added/Corp** Dun's
Marketing Services. Dun and Bradstreet, Inc. **VFOAT** Business Identification Service. (19??)-. Periodical. English. Two times a year. $1,850. Dun & Bradstreet Information Services, 3 Sylvan Way, Parsippany NJ 07054. **Tel** (201)605-6000, (800)526-0651. **Continues** D-U-N-S Account Identification Service.

LC HG4057 .A237 **ISSN** 0734-2845
DD 338.7/4/02573 US
DUN'S BUSINESS RANKINGS. (DUN'S
BUSINESS RANKINGS.). [Dun's bus. rank.]. **Added/Corp** Dun's Marketing Services. **VFOAT** Business Rankings. (1982)-. English. One time a year (June). $485.00; $355.00 (libraries). Dun & Bradstreet Information Services, 3 Sylvan Way, Parsippany NJ 07054. **Tel** (201)605-6000, (800)526-0651. **Bk Rev**.
 Desc: Rankings of over 7,500 top US companies in 152 industries. Ranks market leaders within state and within industry. Separate sections rank public and private companies by the number of employees and sales.

LC HF5343 .D8a **ISSN** 0196-8610
DD 338.0973 US
DUN'S CENSUS OF AMERICAN BUSINESS. See Business and
Economics-Abstracting, Bibliographies and Statistics.

ISSN 1082-8397
DD 338 US
●DUPAGE BUSINESS LEDGER. [DuPage bus.
ledger]. **VFOAT** Business Ledger. (1993)-. Periodical. English. Twelve times a year. $17.00. Ledger Publishing Inc., 709 Enterprise Drive, Oak Brook IL 60521. **Tel** (708)571-8911, FAX (708)571-4053.

LC HF5548.2 .D372
DD 658/.05/4 GW
DV [I.E. DATENVERARBEITUNG]-MAGAZIN.
Added/Corp IBM Deutschland. (19??)-. Periodical. German. Twelve times a year. IBM Deutschland GmbH, Postfach 80 0880, 7000 Stuttgart 80 Germany.

LC Discard **ISSN** 0279-4039
US
Pr Rev.
DYNAMIC BUSINESS : A PUBLICATION OF THE SMALLER MANUFACTURER'S COUNCIL.
Added/Corp Smaller Manufacturer's Council. (19??)-. Trade Publication. English. Ten times a year (Jan./Feb. & July/Aug. issues combined). $25.00. TEC/Pennsylvania Small Business United, 1400 South Braddock Avenue, Pittsburgh PA 15218. **Tel** (412)371-1500, FAX (412)371-0460. **ED** Mary L. Heindl. **Bk Rev**, (Qty: varies). **Ad Acc. Circ:** 5,300 (ctrl). **Continues** Smaller Manufacturer, 0164-9833.
 Desc: Dedicated to the management needs of all small business and firms employing less than 500 people.

US
DYNAMIC SELLING.
(19??)-. Newsletter. English. Twenty-six times a year. $41.34. Economics Press Inc, 12 Daniel Road, Fairfield NJ 07004. **Tel** (201)227-1224, (800)526-2554, FAX (201)227-9742.
 Desc: Devoted exclusively to techniques that make sales happen.

LC HC **ISSN** 0012-7396
US
DYNAMIC SUPERVISION. **Added/Corp**
Bureau of Business Practice. **VFOAT** Dynamic Supervision in the Office. No. 1 (1966)-. Periodical. English. Twenty-four times a year. $39.32. Bureau of Business Practice, 24 Rope Ferry Road, Waterford CT 06386. **Tel** (800)243-0876, (203)442-4365, (800)876-9105, FAX (203)443-1123.

LC HF5001 .D94
SA
DYNAMICA.
1964-. Periodical. Multiple languages (Afrikaans and English). One time a year. R4.00 South Africa; $3.20 other. University of South Africa, PO Box 392, Pretoria 0001 South Africa. **Tel** 011 27 12 4293111, FAX 011 27 12 4293221. **ED** B Lubbe. **Circ:** 5,300 (ctrl).
 Desc: Articles relating to business economics, advertising and marketing.

BE
DYNAMICS.
(19??)-. French (Dutch). Four times a year (Feb., Apr., Sep., Dec.). 1250.00F Belgium; 1850.00F other. Socorema, rue du Merlo 84 A, 1180 Brussels Belgium. **Tel** 011 32 2 3323421, 011 32 2 376 62 28, 011 32 2 3323421. **Bk Rev. Ad Acc, Adv Mgr:** J. Laffineur. **Circ:** 7,000. **Continues** Nieuw Neuf.
 Desc: Discusses topics such as management, products and quality labels, office and workshop equipment, design and trends, and events.

KE
EAER BULLETIN. **VFOAT** Eastern Africa
Economic Review Bulletin. Issue No. 1 (Dec. 1986)-. Bulletin. English. Two times a year. Eastern Africa Economic Review, PO Box 47678, Nairobi Kenya. **Tel** 011 254 2 334244 ext. 2122 2166.

ISSN 0733-0138
US
CCC
EARLY WARNING FORECAST. (19??)-.
Periodical. English. Twelve times a year. $259.00. Cahners Publishing Company, 249 West 17th Street, New York NY 10011. **Tel** (212)645-0067, FAX (212)242-6987. **(Subscription address:** Cahners Economics, PO Box 59, New Town Branch, Boston MA 02258. **Tel** (800)445-0678, (617)630-2124.)
 Desc: Features forecasts of the most widely-followed economic indicators and industry-specific indicators.

ISSN 0193-3655
US
CCC
EARLY WARNING REPORT. **VFOAT** Retail
Sales & Inventory Early Warning Report. **VAT** Retail Sales and Inventory Early Warning Report. (19??)-. Periodical. English. Twelve times a year. $1118.00. Warren Publishing, Inc., 2115 Ward Court Northwest, Washington DC 20037. **Tel** (202)872-9200, FAX

Business and Economics

(202)293-3435. **ED** David Lachenbruch.
 Desc: Monthly recap of national sales and inventory of TV sets, VCRs, projection TV, and stereo units.

AT
EARNINGS POWER. English. Six times a year. 120.00Aus$. Center for Professional Development, 100 Albert Road, 5th Floor, South Melbourne Victoria 3205 Australia. **Tel** 011 61 3 6903933, FAX 011 61 3 6906073.

ISSN 0961-2793
DD 330.950 UK
CEASED
EAST ASIA EXPRESS. [East Asia express]. (1990)-(199?). Periodical. English. International Industrial Information Ltd, PO Box 12, Monmouth Gwent NP5 3YL United Kingdom. **Tel** 011 44 1600 890274, FAX 011 44 1600 890774. **Continues** China Express, 0267-9345.
 Ind/Abst PTS Newsl. Database (19??-19??) [Full Txt.].

ISSN 1060-6157
DD 947 US
CCC
EAST EUROPE & THE REPUBLICS. [East Eur. repub.]. **Added/Corp** Political Risk Services (IBC USA (Publications) Inc.). 1st Edition (1992)-. English. One time a year (June). $440.00. Political Risk Services, 6320 Fly Road, Suite 102, PO Box 248, East Syracuse NY 13057-0248. **Tel** (315)431-0511, FAX (315)431-0200.
 Desc: Current information on the new countries and new markets evolving from old economic systems. Includes a background and five-year forecasts of political and economic risk.

ISSN 0966-7970
UK
EAST EUROPEAN BUSINESS INFORMATION. (199?)-. English. One time a year. $224.00. Headland Business Information, 1 Henry Smiths Terrace, Headland Cleveland, TS24 0PD United Kingdom. **Tel** 011 44 429 231902, FAX 011 44 429 861403.

LC HC244.A1 E28a
DD 330.947/0005 BE
EAST EUROPEAN STATISTICS SERVICE. See Business and Economics-Abstracting, Bibliographies and Statistics.

ISSN 0170-0243
AT
EAST-WEST EUROPEAN ECONOMIC INTERACTION. **Added/Corp** Wiener Institut fuer Internationale Wirtschaftsvergleiche. (1976)-. Monographic series. English. Irregular. Price varies per volume. St. Martin's Press, 175 Fifth Avenue, New York NY 10010. **Tel** (800)221-7945, (212)982-3900, FAX (212)777-6359.

ISSN 1014-6911
SZ
CODEN NU002
EAST-WEST JOINT VENTURES NEWS. [East-West Jt. Ventures News]. (1989)-. Periodical. English. Four times a year. $80.00. United Nations Publications, 2 United Nations Plaza, Room DC2 0853, Department 007C, New York NY 10017. **Tel** (212)963-8303, (800)253-9646.
 Desc: A newsletter of new laws permitting foreign enterprises to establish joint venture with domestic enterprises and to set up fully owned subsidiaries in the six European CMEA countries.

LC HC501 .E25 ISSN 1011-4750
DD 330.9676 KE
EASTERN AFRICA ECONOMIC REVIEW. [East. Afr. econ. rev.]. **Added/Corp** Oxford University Press. University of Nairobi. Vol. 1 (June 1969)-Vol. 8, No. 2 (Dec. 1976); New Series Vol. 1, No. 1 (Dec. 1985)-. Periodical. English. Two times a year (June & Dec). $70.00. Eastern Africa Economic Review, PO Box 47678, Nairobi Kenya. **Tel** 011 254 2 334244 ext. 2122 2166. **ED** M. S. Mukras. **Bk Rev**. **Circ:** 500. **Continues** East African Economics Review, 0424-0790.
 Desc: An academic economics journal specializing in policy studies and developmental issues. Focuses on sub-Saharan Africa but spans all third world countries; includes general theoretical analyses.
 Ind/Abst Econ. Lit. Index (199?-); Int. Bibliogr. Sociol.; J. Econ. Lit.; Leis., Rec., Tour. Abstr.; Nutr. Abstr. Rev., Ser. A, Hum. Exp.; Rural Dev. Abstr.; Soils Fert.; World Agric. Econ. Rural Sociol. Abstr.

LC HF1410 .E22 ISSN 0346-8186
DD 382/.09171/301717 SW
EASTERN BUSINESS MAGAZINE. (1976)-. Periodical. English (summaries and/or abstracts in German, Russian and Swedish). 360. Eastern Business Magazine, Rosenlundsgatan 54, Stockholm Sweden. **ED** E Kallgren.

LC HB1 .E13 ISSN 0094-5056
DD 330 US
EASTERN ECONOMIC JOURNAL. [East. econ. j.]. **Added/Corp** Eastern Economic Association (U.S.). Vol. 1, (Jan. 1974)-. English. Four times a year (Mar., June, Sept., Dec). $75.00. Eastern Economic Association, Koffler Center Bryant College, Smithfield RI 02917. **Tel** (401)232-6307, FAX (401)232-6720. **ED** Harold Hochman (phone: (215)250-5315). **Bk Rev**. **Ad Acc**. **Circ:** 1,000 (ctrl). Documents available from UMI Article Clearinghouse.
 Desc: Professional journal publishing quality articles on a broad range of topics in the field of economics. Of interest to economists in academia, business and industry, and government.
 Ind/Abst ABI/INFORM Glob. Ed.; Curr. Cit.; Econ. Lit. Index; J. Econ. Lit.

ISSN 0965-0350
US
EASTERN EUROPE ANALYST. Vol. 7, No. 1 (Summer 1992)-. Periodical. English. Four times a year. £200.00 (UK and Ireland); $500.00 other. World Reports Ltd., 108 Horse Ferry Road, Westminster, London SW1P 2EF United Kingdom. **Tel** 011 44 171 2223836, FAX 11 44 171 2330185. **Continues** Comecon Reports, 0142-0763.

ISSN 0950-7450
UK
EASTERN EUROPE NEWSLETTER. See Political Science.

LC HC244.A1 E3 ISSN 0012-8775
DD 330.9/47 US
CCC
Pr Rev.
EASTERN EUROPEAN ECONOMICS. [East. Europ. econ.]. Vol. 1 (Fall 1962)-. Periodical. English. Six times a year. $572.00. M. E. Sharpe Inc., 80 Business Park Drive, Armonk NY 10504. **Tel** (914)273-1800, (800)541-6563, FAX (914)273-2106. **ED** Laura D'Andrea. **Bk Rev**. **Ad Acc**. **Circ:** 450 (ctrl). available on microfilm and microfiche from University Microfilms International (UMI). Documents available from The Genuine Article.
 Desc: A unique survey of current economic scholarship from Albania, Bulgaria, Czechoslovakia, the German Democratic Republic, Hungary, Poland, Romania, and Yugoslavia.
 Ind/Abst Contents Recent Econ. J.; Curr. Contents Soc. Behav. Sci.; Econ. Lit. Index; Int. Labour Doc.; J. Econ. Lit.; LABORDOC; PAIS Int. Print (1991-); Res. Alert [Full Cov.]; Soc. Sci. Cit. Index [Full Cov.].

HK
EASTERN EUROPEAN OPPORTUNITIES. (19??)-. English. Twelve times a year. $600.00. Asiavox Limited, 1CD Aguilar Street, Hing Wai Building, Central Hong Kong. **Tel** 011 852 9819918, FAX 011 852 29814234.

ISSN 1074-9624
DD 330 US
EASTERN PENNSYLVANIA BUSINESS JOURNAL. [East. Pa. bus. j.]. (199?)-. Periodical. English. Twelve times a year. $39.00. Eastern Pennsylvania Business Jouranl, 5000 Tilghman Street, Suite 215, Allentown PA 18104.

ISSN 1186-690X
DD 333.79 CN
EASTMAIN 1 HYDROELECTRIC DEVELOPMENT. [Eastmain 1 hydroelectr. dev.]. **Added/Corp** Hydro-Quebec. **VAT** Eastmain One Hydroelectric Development. No. 1 (Jan. 1991)-. Periodical. English. Hydro-Quebec, 14E Etage, 75 Ouest boulevard Dorchester, Montreal Quebec H2Z 1A4 Canada.

ISSN 1072-9356
US
●**EASY MONEY (WESTPORT, CONN.).** (EASY MONEY.). (1994)-. Periodical. English. Six times a year. $29.95. Blue-Chip Capitol, 1771 Post Road East, Westport CT 06880.

US
EBSCO BUGLE. **Added/Corp** EBSCO Industries. **VFOAT** Bugle. (19??)-. Periodical. English. Four times a year. EBSCO Industries Inc., PO Box 1943, Birmingham AL 35201-1943. **Tel** (205)991-1465, FAX (205)991-1479. **ED** Karen Ingram. **Circ:** 3,000 (ctrl).
 Desc: Published by and for members of the EBSCO organization. Issued by a staff representing all departments of the company. It contains news and information concerning business, as well as personal activities of EBSCO employees.

LC HC241.2 .A1E2 ISSN 1054-4003
DD 338.094/05 US
EC INDUSTRIAL REPORT. (EC INDUSTRIAL REPORT : EUROPEAN COMMUNITY INDUSTRIAL REPORT.). [EC ind. rep.]. **VFOAT** A.E.C. Industrial Report. **VAT** European Community Industrial Report. Vol. 1, No. 1 (Jan. 1991)-. Periodical. English. Twelve times a year. Free to qualified subscribers. Tucker/Wilson, Inc., PO Box 1168, Skokie IL 60676-9796.

ISSN 0811-5842
DD 382.9142 AT
EC NEWS. [EC news]. **VFOAT** Economic Community News. (1983)-. Periodical. English. Six times a year.
 Ind/Abst AESIS Q.

IT
EC NEWSLETTER. (19??)-. Newsletter. English. Three times a year. L90000.00. Edizioni F Lli Laterza, Via Crisanzio 20, 70122 Bari Italy. **Tel** 011 39 80 5237936.

ISSN 0749-5749
DD 382 US
EC UPDATE. [EC update]. **Added/Corp** United States Council for International Business. **VFOAT** E.C. Update. **VAT** European Community Update. No. 1 (Dec. 1982)-. Periodical. English. Four times a year. United States Council of the International Chamber of Commerce, 1212 Avenue of the Americas, New York NY 10036. **Tel** (212)354-4480.
 Desc: Reports on policies and actions of the European community as they affect international business operations.

ISSN 1184-7239
DD 650/.071/171428 CN
ECHANGES - ECOLE DES HAUTES ETUDES COMMERCIALES, MONTREAL, QUEBEC. (ECHANGES : JOURNAL DE L'ECOLE DES HAUTES ETUDES COMMERCIALES.). [Echanges - Ec. hautes etud. commer. Montr. Que.]. **Added/Corp** Ecole des Hautes Etudes Commerciales (Montreal, Quebec). Vol. 7, No 1 (Sept. 1990)-. Periodical. French. Twelve times a year. Ecole des Hautes Etudes Commerciales, 5255 Decelles Avenue, Montreal Quebec H3T 1V6 Canada. **Tel** (514)340-6437, FAX (514)340-6469. **Continues** HEC Echanges., 0842-0599.

BE
ECHO : QUOTIDIEN DE L'ECONOMIE ET DE LA BOURSE, L'. (19??)-. French. Five times a week (Tues. - Sat.). 7800F Belgium; 9710F Luxembourg; 14920F other. Editeco S.A., 131 rue de Birmingham, 1070 Brussels Belgium. **Tel** 011 32 2 5265511, FAX 011 32 2 5265526, telex 23396. **ED** Freddy Mecaet. **Ad Acc**, **Adv Mgr:** Francine Mirmovitch, **Tel** 011 32 2 526 5566. Full Page (B&W) 259.20F. Half Page (B&W) 129.60F. **Circ:** 49,700.
 Desc: Business daily.

AT
ECODATE. (19??)-. English. Four times a year (Mar., May, July, Sept.). 45.00Aus$. Warringal Productions, 114 Argyle Street, Fitzroy 3065 Australia. **Tel** 011 61 03 4160200, FAX 011 61 03 4160402. **(Subscription address:** Warringal Publications, PO Box 336, Fitzroy 3065 Australia. **Tel** 011 61 3 4160200.)
 Desc: Provides commentary and issues and events and the problems facing the managers of the economy, including the government, business and unions.

LC HB1 ISSN 0296-4449
DD 330.05 FR
UDC 31 : 33
ECOFLASH. (1985)-. Periodical. French. Ten times a year. 112.63F (France); 130.00F (other). Centre National Documentation Pedagogique, 29 Square St. Charles, BP 7, 75012 Paris France. **Tel** 011 33 1 40020333, 011 33 1 46349425. **(Subscription address:** CNDP Abonnements, B 750, 60732 Genevieve Cedex 9 France. **Tel** 011 33 44 033237, FAX 011 33 44 074336.**)**

LC HC
DD 330 US
ECON/STATS I. [CD-ROM]. See Business and Economics-Abstracting, Bibliographies and Statistics.

LC Z7164.E2 E266
DD 016.3 US
ECONLIT [COMPUTER FILE]. See Business and Economics-Abstracting, Bibliographies and Statistics.

ISSN 0890-166X
DD 332 US
ECONOCLAST (HOUSTON, TEX.), THE. (THE ECONOCLAST.). [Econoclast]. (19??)-. Periodical. English. Twenty-six times a year (published monthly plus 4 special issues and monthly updates). $1250.00. The Econoclast, 3419 West Minster, Office 251, Dallas TX 75205. **Tel** (214)890-7877.
 Desc: Economic and strategy service on the US and global economy. Special emphasis on equity and fixed income markets.

LC HB139 .C64 ISSN 0747-4938
DD 330/.028 US
CCC
CODEN ECREEP
ECONOMETRIC REVIEWS. [Econom. rev.]. Vol. 3, No. 1 (1984)-. Periodical. English. Four times a year. $450.00. Marcel Dekker Inc., 270 Madison Avenue, New York NY 10016. **Tel** (212)696-9000, (800)228-1160, FAX (212)685-4540, telex 421419. **(Subscription address:** Marcel Dekker Inc., PO Box 5017, Monticello NY 12701. **Tel** (800)228-1160.) **ED** Esfandiar Maasoumi. **Bk Rev**. **Ad Acc**. available on microfiche. **Continues** Communications in Statistics. Econometric

Reviews, 0731-1761.
Desc: Each issue of this journal probes the limits of econometric knowledge, featuring retrospective, critical, and readable surveys of current economic conditions that determine where future efforts should be directed. Internationally known experts present controversial papers followed by insightful commentaries - affording readers a unique perspective of state-of-the-art information in this rapidly changing science.
Ind/Abst Curr. Cit.; Curr. Index Stat.; Econ. Lit. Index; J. Econ. Lit.; Math. Rev.; Stat. Theory Method Abstr. (1987); Zentralbl. Math. Ihre Grenzgeb.

LC HB139 .E284 **ISSN** 0266-4666
DD 330/.028 US
CCC
Pr Rev.
ECONOMETRIC THEORY. [Econ. theory]. Vol. 1, No. 1 (Apr. 1985)-. Academic Scholarly Publication. English. Eleven times a year. $194.00. Cambridge University Press / New York, 40 West 20th Street, New York NY 10011-4211. **Tel** (212)924-3900, (800)221-4512, FAX (212)691-3239. **(Subscription address:** Cambridge University Press / Outside of North America, United Kingdom. **Tel** 011 44 223 312 393, FAX 011 44 223 325 959.**)** **ED** Peter C. B. Phillips. **Bk Rev.** available on microfilm from University Microfilms International (UMI). Documents available from The Genuine Article.
Desc: Provides an outlet for contributions in major areas of econometrics. Includes book reviews and articles on theoretical research, historical studies on the evolution of econometric thought and on major scholars.
Ind/Abst Contents Recent Econ. J. (1989-); Curr. Cit.; Curr. Contents Soc. Behav. Sci.; Curr. Index Stat. (1989-); Econ. Lit. Index (199?-); J. Econ. Lit.; Math. Rev.; Res. Alert [Full Cov.]; Soc. Sci. Cit. Index [Full Cov.]; Soc. Res. Methodol. Abstr. (1990-).

LC HB1 **ISSN** 0012-9682
DD 330.5 US
CODEN ECMTA7
Pr Rev.
ECONOMETRICA. (ECONOMETRICA : JOURNAL OF THE ECONOMETRIC SOCIETY.). [Econometrica]. (Jan. 1933)-. Academic Scholarly Publication. English (French). Six times a year. $169.00. Basil Blackwell Publishers Ltd., 108 Cowley Road, Oxford 0X4 1JF United Kingdom. **Tel** 011 44 1235 465500, FAX 011 44 1235 465556, telex 837022 OXBOOK G. **(Subscription address:** Blackwell Publishers / UK, 108 Cowley Road, Oxford OX4 1JF United Kingdom. **Tel** 011 44 1865 791100, FAX 011 44 1865 791347.**)** **ED** Robert Gordon. Index available. cum. index. **Ad Acc. Circ:** 6,300. available on microfilm and microfiche from University Microfilms International (UMI). Documents available from The Genuine Article, UMI Article Clearinghouse.
Desc: Published by the Econometric Society, an international society for the advancement of economic theory in its relation to statistics and mathematics.
Ind/Abst ABI/INFORM Glob. Ed.; ABI/INFORM [Computer File] (March 1972-March 1973); Acad. Search; Biostatistica; Bus. Index (1985-); Bus. Source Plus; Bus. Source; CompuMath Cit. Index [Full Cov.]; Contents Recent Econ. J.; Contents Pages Manage.; Curr. Cit.; Curr. Contents Soc. Behav. Sci.; Econ. Lit. Index; EP Collect.; Expand. Acad. Index (1984-); Gen. BusinessFile (1985-); Gen. Period. Index (1985-); Homework Help.; INFO-SOUTH Abstr.; Int. Polit. Sci. Abstr.; J. Econ. Lit.; J. Plan. Lit.; MasterFile FullTEXT 1000; MasterFile FullTEXT 350; MasterFile FullTEXT 650; MasterFile FullTEXT (July 1993-); Math. Rev.; Newsp. Period. Abstr. (1991-); OCLC; Oper. Res./Manage. Sci.; Qual. Control Appl. Stat.; Res. Alert [Full Cov.]; Risk Abstr. (19??-19??); Selec. Coop. Index Manage. Period.; Soc. Sci. Source; Soc. Sci. Cit. Index [Full Cov.]; Soc. Sci. Index; Soc. Sci. Index Fulltext (Sept. 1988-) [Full Txt.]; Stat. Theory Method Abstr. (1959-1963, 1968-1973, 1976, 1978-1981, 1983, 1986-1987); Telebase; Zentralbl. Math. Ihre Grenzgeb.

ISSN 0012-978X
IT
ECONOMIA & LAVORO (1967). (ECONOMIA & LAVORO.). [Econ. lav.]. **Added/Corp** Fondazione Giacomo Brodolini. **VFOAT** Economia e Lavoro. Vol. 1 (Jan./Feb. 1967)-. Periodical. Italian. Four times a year. L81750. Marsilio Editori, Marittima Fabbricato 205, 30135 Venice Italy. **Tel** 011 39 41 5227822. **ED** Renato Brunetta. Index available. **Bk Rev. Ad Acc. Circ:** 4,000 (ctrl).
Desc: Articles about economics and industrial relations.
Ind/Abst Econ. Lit. Index; Int. Bibliogr. Sociol.; Int. Labour Doc.; J. Econ. Lit.; LABORDOC.

ISSN 1120-5032
IT
UDC 33
ECONOMIA & MANAGEMENT. [Econ. Manag.]. **VFOAT** Economia e Management. (1988)-. Periodical. Italian. Six times a year. L110360. Etas SRL, Via Mecenate 89, 20138 Milan Italy. **Tel** 011 39 2 580841.

LC HC171 .E13 **ISSN** 0424-2378
DD 330.982/05 AG
ECONOMIA ARGENTINA / THE ARGENTINE ECONOMY, LA. Added/Corp Consejo Tecnico de Inversiones (Argentina). **VFOAT** Argentine Economy; Anuario de la Economia Argentina; Year-End Report on the Argentine Economy. (1962)-. Spanish (English). One time a year. $120.00. Consejo Technical Inversiones SA, Esmeralda 320 6 Piso, 1343 Buenos Aires Argentina. **Tel** 011 54 1 350184.

LC HC
DD 330 IT
ECONOMIA AZIENDALE : FOUR MONTHLY REVIEW OF THE ACCADEMIA ITALIANA DI ECONOMIA AZIENDALE. Added/Corp Accademia Italiana di Economia Aziendale. Vol. 1, No. 1 (April 1982)-. Periodical. English (Italian). Three times a year. L61250. Giuffre Editore SPA, Via Busto Arsizio 40, 20151 Milan Italy. **Tel** 011 398 2 38089200. **ED** Vittorio Coda and Carlo Masini. **Bk Rev. Ad Acc. Circ:** 1,000.
Desc: This review of the Accademia Italiana di Economia Aziendale is dedicated to advancing the understanding and concern of economics.
Ind/Abst Contents Pages Manage.

LC HC186 . E275 **ISSN** 0424-2386
DD 330.981 BL
ECONOMIA BRASILEIRA E SUAS PERSPECTIVAS, A. Added/Corp APEC (Association). **VFOAT** Estudos Semestrals APEC; Estudos APEC. (1962)-. Portuguese (English; summaries and/or abstracts in English). One time a year. $180.00. Assoc Prom Estudos de Econ, rua Sorocaba 295-Botafogo, 22271 Rio de Janeiro RJ Brasil. **Tel** 011 55 21 2664449 or, 4249. **ED** Mircea Buescv. Index available. cum. index. **Ad Acc. Circ:** 2,000 (ctrl).
Desc: Contains analysis of the behavior of the Brazilian economy.

IT
ECONOMIA CULTURA. (19??)-. Italian. Three times a year. L50000.00 Italy; L100000.00 (surface mail), L130000.00 (airmail) other. Societa Editrice il Mulino, Strada Maggiore 37, 40125 Bologna Italy. **Tel** 011 39 51 256011, FAX 011 39 51 256034.

ISSN 0012-9771
IT
UDC 33
ECONOMIA E CREDITO. [Econ. credito]. (1961)-. Periodical. Italian. Four times a year. Servizio Studi, Cassa Centrale di Risparmio, V.E. per le Province Siciliane, Piazza Cassa Pisparmio 10, 90133 Palermo Italy. ***Continues*** *Bolletino dell'Ufficio Studi della Cassa di Risparmio Vittorio Emanuele per le Provincie Siciliane in Palermo.*
Ind/Abst PAIS Int. Print.

ISSN 0391-2078
IT
ECONOMIA E POLITICA INDUSTRIALE. [Econ. polit. ind.]. (1974)-. Periodical. Italian. Three times a year. L102080. Franco Angeli Riviste SRL, Viale Monza 106, 20127 Milan Italy. **Tel** 011 39 2 2827651, 011 39 2 289562, FAX 011 39 2 258004, telex 051-511650. ***Continues*** *Bolletino di Economia e Politica Industriale.*
Ind/Abst PAIS Int. Print.

ISSN 0422-2784
SP
ECONOMIA INDUSTRIAL. [Econ. ind.]. (1964)-. Periodical. Spanish. Six times a year. Ctro Publ Min Industria Energi, Doctor Fleming 7-2, 28036 Madrid Spain. **Tel** 011 34 1 3440362, 011 34 1 3440553.
Ind/Abst GeoRef; Selec. Coop. Index Manage. Period.

ISSN 0185-0849
MX
ECONOMIA INFORMA. Added/Corp Escuela Nacional de Economia (Mexico). (19??)-. Periodical. Spanish. Twelve times a year. $105.00. University Nacional Autonoma de Mexico, EDIF Anexo Circuito Interior, Mexico DF Mexico. **Tel** 011 52 5 6222102. Index available. cum. index. **Ad Acc, Adv Mgr:** Ernesto Bartolucci. **Circ:** 2,000 (ctrl).
Ind/Abst PAIS Int. Print (1991-).

IT
ECONOMIA ITALIANA (ROME, ITALY). (ECONOMIA ITALIANA.). Vol. 1 (1979)-. Periodical. Italian. Three times a year. free on request. Banco di Roma, Ufficio Relazione Esterne, Viale Tupini 180, 00144 Rome Italy. **Tel** 011 39 6 54451.
Desc: Economic conditions in Italy.

LC HC226 .E39 **ISSN** 0254-4415
DD 330.985/005 PE
ECONOMIA (LIMA). (ECONOMIA : REVISTA DEL DEPARTAMENTO DE ECONOMIA, PONTIFICIA UNIVERSIDAD CATOLICA DEL PERU.). [Economia]. **Added/Corp** Pontificia Universidad Catolica del Peru. Departamento de Economia. No. 1 (Dec. 1977)-. Periodical. Spanish. Two times a year (July & Dec.). $34.00. Pontificia Universidad Catolica del Peru, Fondo Editorial, Apartado 1761, Lima 1 Peru. **Tel** 011 51 14 622540.
Ind/Abst J. Econ. Lit.; PAIS Int. Print (1991-).

LC HB1.A1 .E18 **ISSN** 0870-3531
PO
Pr Rev.
ECONOMIA (LISBOA). (ECONOMIA.). [Econ.]. **Added/Corp** Universidade Catolica Portuguesa. Faculdade de Ciencias Humanas. Vol. 1 (Jan. 1977)-. Periodical. English (French, Portuguese and Spanish). Three times a year. $40.00. Universidade Catolica Portuguesa, Caminho da Palma de Cima, 1600 Lisbon Portugal. **Tel** 011 351 1 7265550, FAX 011 351 1 7260256. **Bk Rev. Ad Acc. Circ:** 3,000 (ctrl).
Desc: Economy micro- and macroeconomics theory and policies. International capital movements, foreign exchange intervention policies, a vintage model of supply, inflation and production in Portugal.
Ind/Abst Econ. Lit. Index (19??-); J. Econ. Lit.; PAIS Int. Print.

MX
ECONOMIA NACIONAL. (198?)-. Periodical. Spanish. Twelve times a year. KEAL S.A. de C.V., Rio Nazas 137-Altos, Col. Cuauhtemoc, 06500 Mexico City Mexico.
Ind/Abst PAIS Int. Print.

LC WMLC 93/418
IT
ECONOMIA POLITICA. Vol. 1 No. 1 (Apr. 1984)-. Periodical. Italian (summaries and/or abstracts in English). Three times a year. L77660. Societa Editrice il Mulino, Strada Maggiore 37, 40125 Bologna Italy. **Tel** 011 39 51 256011, FAX 011 39 51 256034.
Ind/Abst Econ. Lit. Index (199?-); J. Econ. Lit. (1985-); PAIS Int. Print.

LC HC
DD 330 IT
ECONOMIA SOCIETA E ISTITUZIONI. Vol. 1, No. 1 (Jan./April 1989)-. Periodical. Italian. Three times a year. Maggioli Editore, Casella Postale 290, 47037 Rimini Italy. **Tel** 011 39 541 628666, FAX 011 39 541 742217.

LC HB9 .E377
MX
ECONOMIA, TEORIA Y PRACTICA. Added/Corp Universidad Autonoma Metropolitana. **VFOAT** Economia. (19??)-. Periodical. Spanish. Three times a year. $500.00. Direccion de Difusion Cultural, Universidad Autonoma Metropolitana (UAM), Medellin 28, Col. Roma, Mexico City Mexico.
Ind/Abst PAIS Int. Print.

IT
ECONOMIA TRENTINA. Added/Corp Camera di Commercio, Industria, e Agricoltura di Trento. (19??)-. Periodical. Italian. Four times a year. L25210. Camera di Commerico Industria e Agricoltura di Trento, Via Calepina 13, 38100 Trento Italy. **Tel** 011 39 461 986755.

LC HC
US
ECONOMIC ABSTRACT OF ALABAMA. Added/Corp University of Alabama. Center for Business and Economic Research. University of Alabama. Bureau of Business Research. (196?)-. English. Irregular. $28.00. Center for Business & Economic Research, PO Box 870221, University of Alabama, Tuscaloosa AL 35487. **Tel** (205)348-6191, FAX (205)248-2951. **ED** Annette Watters. Index available. **Circ:** 1,000.
Desc: A source of demographic and economic information on Alabama in 20 categories. Much of the data is presented at national, state, and county levels. The tables cover several years to facilitate comparisons and trend analysis. Some projections for the future are presented as well.

LC HC431 .E32 **ISSN** 0424-2513
DD 330 II
ECONOMIC AFFAIRS (CALCUTTA). (ECONOMIC AFFAIRS.). [Econ. aff.]. (July 1956)-. Periodical. English. Four times a year (Mar., June, Sept., Dec.). $22.50. Economic Affairs, BC/144 Sector I Salt Lake City, Calcutta 700064 India. **Tel** 91 33 373034. **(Subscription address:** Prints India, 11 Darya Ganj, New Delhi 110002 India. **Tel** 011 91 11 3268645, FAX 011 91 11 3275542, telex 31-61087 PRIN-IN.**)** **ED** Dr. Himansu Roy. Index available. **Bk Rev. Ad Acc. Circ:** 2,000.
Desc: Papers on theoretical and applied economics with special reference to India.
Ind/Abst Agric. Eng. Abstr.; Int. Labour Doc.; J. Econ. Lit. (1968-1984); LABORDOC; Leis., Rec., Tour. Abstr.; Maize Abstr.; Postharvest News Inf.; Potato Abstr.; Rice Abstr.; Rural Dev. Abstr.; Soils Fert.; Soyabean Abstr.; Wheat Barley Trit. Abstr.; World Agric. Econ. Rural Sociol. Abstr.

ISSN 0265-0665
UK
ECONOMIC AFFAIRS (LONDON, ENGLAND). (ECONOMIC AFFAIRS.). [Econ. aff.]. Vol. 4, No. 1 (Oct. 1983)-. Periodical. English. Six times a year. $95.00. City Publications Ltd, 3-4 St. Andrew's Hill, London EC4V 5BY United Kingdom. **Tel** 011 44 171 2488265. **ED** Robert Miller. Index available. **Bk Rev. Ad Acc. Circ:** 4,000. ***Continues*** *Journal of Economic Affairs,*

0260-8359.
Ind/Abst Br. Humanit. Index; Contents Pages Manage.; Curr. Cit.

LC HB1 .E244 **ISSN** 0313-5926
DD 330/.05 AT
ECONOMIC ANALYSIS AND POLICY. [Econ. anal. policy]. **Added/Corp** Economic Society of Australia and New Zealand. Queensland Branch. Vol. 1 (March 1970)-. Periodical. English. Two times a year. 20.55Aus$. Economic Analysis and Policy, School of Economics, Faculty of Business, GPO Box 2434, Brisbane 4001 Australia. **Tel** 011 61 7 8641312, FAX 011 61 7 8757750. **ED** Allan Brown, D.T. Nguyen and Christine Smith. **Bk Rev. Ad Acc. Circ:** 400 (ctrl).
Desc: Journal attempts to present economic policy issues in banking, agriculture, resources, mining and manufacture.
Ind/Abst Contents Recent Econ. J.; PAIS Int. Print (1991-); Poult. Abstr.; World Agric. Econ. Rural Sociol. Abstr.

LC HC **ISSN** 0824-3980
DD 330.9711/04 CN
ECONOMIC ANALYSIS OF BRITISH COLUMBIA. [Econ. anal. B.C.]. **Added/Corp** B.C. Central Credit Union. Economics Dept. Vol. 1, No. 1 (June 17, 1981)-. English (French). Eleven times a year (Nine regular copies plus 2 comprehensive issues). 44.02Can$. BC Central Credit Union, 1441 Creekside Drive, Vancouver British Columbia V6J 4S7 Canada. **Tel** (604)734-2511, FAX (604)737-5055, telex 0455291. **ED** Richard Allen and Robyn Allan. **Circ:** 100,000 (ctrl).
Desc: Covers issues of economic importance to the province of British Columbia, with in-depth analysis by a team of professional economists.

LC TS1 .B4
DD 338.9493/05 BE
ECONOMIC AND COMMERCIAL INFORMATION, BELGIUM. **Added/Corp** Office Belge du Commerce Exterieur. **VFOAT** Belgium; Belgium Economic and Commercial Information. (19??)-. Periodical. English. Four times a year. 500.00F (Belgium); Free (other). Office Belge du Commerce Exterior, Boulevard Emile Jacqmain 162, 1210 Brussels Belgium. **Tel** 011 32 2 2031886. ***Continues** Belgium, Economic and Commercial Information, 0775-1443.*

LC HC107.W2 E25 **ISSN** 1050-8627
DD 330 US
TITLE CHANGE
ECONOMIC AND DEMOGRAPHIC ALMANAC OF WASHINGTON COUNTIES AND CITIES. **See** Population Studies.

US
ECONOMIC AND FINANCIAL INFORMATION OF THE REPUBLIC OF PANAMA BANCO NACIONAL DE PANAMA. **Added/Corp** Banco Nacional de Panama. (19??)-. English. Irregular. Banco Nacional de Panama, Casilla Postal 5220, Panama 5 Panama. ***Continues** Economic, Financial, and Social Information Concerning the Republic of Panama.*

LC HB **ISSN** 1351-3621
DD 330.94 UK
UDC 33
Pr Rev.
•**ECONOMIC & FINANCIAL REVIEW (LONDON).** [Econ. financ. rev. Lond.]. **VFOAT** Economic and Financial Review (London). (1994)-. Academic Scholarly Publication. English. Four times a year. £190.00 Europe; £205.00 other. European Economics & Finance Center, PO Box 2498, London W2 4LE United Kingdom. **Tel** 011 44 171 2290402, FAX 011 44 171 2215118. **ED** H.M. Scobie. Documents available from BLDSC.
Desc: Covers both the private and public sectors of economics and finance.

LC HE561 .E25
DD 387.5/09598 IO
ECONOMIC & SHIPPING REVIEW. **See** Transportation-Ships and Shipping.

LC HC
UK
ECONOMIC AND SOCIAL STUDIES. **Added/Corp** National Institute of Economic and Social Research. No. 1 (1942)-. Monographic series. English. Irregular. Price varies per volume. Cambridge University Press, The Edinburgh Building, Shaftesbury Road, Cambridge CB2 2RU United Kingdom. **Tel** 011 44 1223 312393, FAX 011 44 1223 315052, telex 851-817256. **(Subscription address:** Cambridge University Press / North America, 110 Midland Avenue, Port Chester NY 10573. **Tel** (800)431-1580, (914)937-9600.)

LC JX1977 .A2 HC411
DD 300 S 330.95/042 TH
ECONOMIC AND SOCIAL SURVEY OF ASIA AND THE PACIFIC. **Main/Corp** United Nations. Economic and Social Commission for Asia and the Pacific. (1974)-. Government Publication. English. One time a year. Price varies per volume. United Nations Publications, 2 United Nations Plaza, Room DC2 0853, Department 007C, New York NY 10017. **Tel** (212)963-8303, (800)253-9646. ***Continues** Economic Survey of Asia and the Far East.*
Desc: Presents a collection of articles on topics such as; developments, energy supply, trade between developing countries and East European countries, economics and sociology of alternative energy sources, and individual country reports on economic performances and prospects.
Ind/Abst Int. Labour Doc.; Middle East Abstr. Index.

ISSN 0953-4997
DD 330 UK
Pr Rev.
ECONOMIC AWARENESS. [Econ. aware.]. (1988)-. English. Three times a year. £21.00 UK; £22.00 Europe; $47.00 US; £26.00 other (institutions). Longman Group Ltd., Fourth Avenue, Longman House, Harlow Essex CM19 5SR United Kingdom. **Tel** 011 44 1279 429655, FAX 011 44 1279 431067, telex 81259. **ED** Steve Hodkinson and Linda Thomas. **Bk Rev. Ad Acc. Circ:** 1,300. available on microfilm and microfiche from University Microfilms International (UMI).
Desc: Articles in this and previous issues contain the ideas, views, and conclusions of teachers working in their classrooms and together.
Ind/Abst Br. Educ. Index.

LC HG3166 .A32 **ISSN** 0029-1676
NO
CCC
ECONOMIC BULLETIN. [Econ. bull.]. **Main/Corp** Norges Bank. **Added/Corp** Norges Bank. Vol. 36 (1965)-. Bulletin. English. Four times a year. Free on request. Norges Bank, Postboks 1179 Sentrum, 0107 Oslo 1 Norway. **Tel** 011 47 2 31600, FAX 011 47 2 413105, telex 71369 N BANK N. Index available. cum. index. Documents available from UMI Article Clearinghouse. ***Continues** Bulletin - Norges Bank.*
Ind/Abst ABI/INFORM Glob. Ed.; ABI/INFORM [Computer File] (1983-); F&S Index Plus Text, Int. [Select. Cov.]; PAIS Int. Print (1991-); Predicasts Forecasts; Selec. Coop. Index Manage. Period.

LC HC381 .E37
DD 330.946/005 SP
ECONOMIC BULLETIN / BANCO DE ESPANA. **Added/Corp** Banco de Espana. (June 1990)-. Bulletin. English (translations available in Spanish). Four times a year. Banco de Espana, Alcala 50, 28014 Madrid Spain. **Tel** 011 34 1 4469055, 011 34 1 3385072.

LC JX1977 .A2 HC511
DD 300/.8 330.9/5/042 US
TITLE CHANGE
ECONOMIC BULLETIN FOR ASIA AND THE PACIFIC. **Added/Corp** United Nations. Economic and Social Commission for Asia and the Pacific. Vol. 25, No. 2/3 (Sept./Dec. 1974)-(19??). Bulletin. English. United Nations Publications, 2 United Nations Plaza, Room DC2 0853, Department 007C, New York NY 10017. **Tel** (212)963-8303, (800)253-9646. ***Continues** Economic Bulletin for Asia and the Far East.* ***Continued by** Asia Pacific Development Journal, 1020-1246.*
Desc: Analyzes recent economic and social developments in the region, with particular emphasis on economic and social policy issues and broad development strategies.
Ind/Abst Contents Recent Econ. J.; Int. Labour Doc.; Middle East Abstr. Index; Rural Dev. Abstr.; World Agric. Econ. Rural Sociol. Abstr.

US
ECONOMIC CENSUS. 1987. CD-ROM. (19??)-. Government Publication. English. Seven times a year. $150.00 (per volume). US Department of Commerce / Bureau of the Census, Data User Services Division, Customer Services, Washington DC 20233-0800. **Tel** (301)763-4100. **(Subscription address:** Superintendent of Documents, US Government Printing Office, Washington DC 20402.) available on microfiche.
Desc: Presents 1987 economic census data.

SZ
ECONOMIC COMMISSION FOR EUROPE. PRESS RELEASES. (19??)-. Periodical. English. Six times a week (312 issues). Free on request. United Nations Publishers / Geneva, Palais des Nations, C115 Services Ventes, CH-1211 Geneva 10 Switzerland. **Tel** 011 41 22 7988400, FAX 011 41 22 7332673, telex 415465.

LC HB1 .E366 **ISSN** 0928-5040
DD 330.1 NE
CCC
CODEN EDESE9
Pr Rev.
•**ECONOMIC DESIGN.** Vol. 1, No. 1 (Aug. 1994)-. Periodical. English. Four times a year. $198.00. Elsevier Science Publishers BV, PO Box 211, 1000 AE Amsterdam Netherlands. **Tel** 011 31 20 4853641, 011 31 20 4853642, FAX 011 31 20 4853598. **(Subscription address:** Elsevier Science BV / Maryland, PO Box 64698, Baltimore MD 21264. **)** available on an online database from Elsevier Electronic Subscriptions (EES).

NE
•**ECONOMIC DESIGN.** (1994)-. Academic Scholarly Publication. English. Four times a year (1 volume). Fl302.00. Elsevier Science Publishers BV, PO Box 211, 1000 AE Amsterdam Netherlands. **Tel** 011 31 20 4853641, 011 31 20 4853642, FAX 011 31 20 4853598. **ED** Murat Sertel, William Thomson, Lenoid Hurwicz. available on an online database from Elsevier Electronic Subscriptions (EES).
Desc: Of interest to researchers in the fields of economic theory, comparative economic systems, public economic, game theory, experimental economics and others.

ISSN 1041-9969
DD 330 US
ECONOMIC DEVELOPER. (ECONOMIC DEVELOPER AND JOB CREATION DIGEST.). [Econ. dev. job creat. dig.]. **VFOAT** Economic Developer. 198?-. Periodical. English. Twelve times a year. $48.00. The Economic Developer, 620 1st Avenue SE, Clarion IA 50525. **Tel** (402)592-1180. **Bk Rev,** (Qty: 12). ***Continues** Economic Developer, 0745-0559.*
Desc: The practice, trends and impact of economic development upon society.

LC HC10 .C453 **ISSN** 0013-0079
DD 309.2 US
CCC
CODEN EDCCAF
Pr Rev.
ECONOMIC DEVELOPMENT AND CULTURAL CHANGE. **See** Sociology.

ISSN 0891-7000
DD 330 US
ECONOMIC DEVELOPMENT BRIEFS. [Econ. dev. briefs]. **Added/Corp** National Alliance of Business. Vol. 1, No. 1 (Winter 1987)-. Periodical. English. Four times a year. Free on request. National Alliance of Business, 1201 New York Avenue Northwest, Suite 700, Washington DC 20005. **Tel** (202)289-2888.

ISSN 0835-9059
DD 338.9/005 CN
Pr Rev.
ECONOMIC DEVELOPMENT BULLETIN. [Econ. dev. bull.]. **Added/Corp** University of Waterloo. Faculty of Environmental Studies. Economic Development Program. (1987)-. Periodical. English. $8.00. Economic Development Program, University of Waterloo, Waterloo Ontario N2L 3G1 Canada. **Tel** (519)885-2437.

ISSN 1060-5339
DD 331 US
ECONOMIC DEVELOPMENT DIGEST (WASHINGTON, D.C.). (ECONOMIC DEVELOPMENT DIGEST: A MONTHLY REPORT FOR THE ECONOMIC DEVELOPMENT COMMUNITY.). [Eco. dev. dig.]. **Added/Corp** National Association of Development Organizations Research Foundation. **VFOAT** Digest. (1992)-. Periodical. English. Twelve times a year. Free. National Association of Development Organizations, Research Foundation, 444 North Capitol Street NW, Suite 630, Washington DC 20001.

ISSN 0891-2424
DD 338 US
CCC
ECONOMIC DEVELOPMENT QUARTERLY. [Econ. dev. q.]. **VFOAT** EDQ. Vol. 1, No. 1 (Feb. 1987)-. Periodical. English. Four times a year (Feb., May, Aug., Nov.). $186.00. SAGE Periodical Press, 2455 Teller Road, Thousand Oaks CA 91320. **Tel** (805)499-0721, FAX (805)499-0871, telex 100799. **ED** Richard D. Bingham, Sammis B. White and Gail Garfield Schwartz. Index available. cum. index. **Ad Acc. Acid Free. Circ:** 894. available on microfilm and microfiche from University Microfilms International (UMI).
Desc: Disseminates information on the latest research, programs, policies and trends in the field of economic development. Unique for its concern for all areas of development.
Ind/Abst Curr. Cit.; EP Collect.; Homework Help.; Hum. Resour. Abstr.; Int. Bibliogr. Sociol.; MasterFile FullTEXT 1000; MasterFile FullTEXT 350; MasterFile FullTEXT 650; MasterFile FullTEXT (Jan. 1995-); OCLC; PAIS Int. Print (1991-); Sage Public Adm. Abstr.; Sage Urban Stud. Abstr; Soc. Plann. Policy Dev. Abstr.; Telebase.

US
ECONOMIC DEVELOPMENTS IN THE MIDDLE EAST. **Added/Corp** United Nations. Dept. of Economic and Social Affairs. (1954/55)-. Government Publication. English. Irregular. United Nations Publications, 2 United Nations Plaza, Room DC2 0853, Department 007C, New York NY 10017. **Tel** (212)963-8303, (800)253-9646. ***Continues** Summary of Recent Economic Developments in the Middle East.*

LC HC267.B2 E28
DD 330.9/437/04 XR
ECONOMIC DIGEST. Added/Corp Ceskoslovenska Obchodni Komora. (19??)-. Periodical. English. Twelve times a year. DM147.00. Ceskoslovenska Obchodni a Prumyslova Komora, Argentinska 38, 17005 Prague 7 Czech Republic. **Tel** 0724111, FAX 121862. **(Subscription address:** Kubon & Sagner, ABT Zeitschriftenimport, D 80328 Munich Germany. **Tel** 011 49 89 54218130.)

LC H62 .J5843 **ISSN** 0070-8534
DD 300.7 US
ECONOMIC EDUCATION EXPERIENCES OF ENTERPRISING TEACHERS. Main/Corp Joint Council on Economic Education. Vol. 1, (1962)-. English. One time a year (May). $7.95. National Council on Economic Education, 432 Park Ave South, New York NY 10016. **Tel** (212)685-5499, (800)338-1192, FAX (212)213-2872. **ED** J. W. Clark and P. L. Guyton.

ISSN 0898-0829
DD 330 US
ECONOMIC FACT BOOK (DETROIT, MICH.). (ECONOMIC FACT BOOK.). [Econ. fact book]. **Added/Corp** Detroit Area Economic Forum. Greater Detroit Chamber of Commerce. Economic Development Group. Research Dept. (1986)-. English. One time a year. $16.00. Greater Detroit Chamber of Commerce, 600 West Lafayette Blouvard, Detroit MI 48226. **Tel** (313)596-0352, FAX (313)964-0531. **ED** Melissa Armstrong. **Circ:** 1,500. ***Continues*** *Economic Fact Book for the Detroit Area.*

US
ECONOMIC FORUM MINORITY BUSINESS REVIEW. (19??)-. Periodical. English. Twenty-four times a year. $20.00. Minority Business Review / New York, PO Box 2132, 416 Jerusalem Avenue, Hempstead NY 11550-2132. **Tel** (516)489-0120, (516)546-6992. **ED** Robert Hugo Adams. **Ad Acc.** ***Continues*** *Minority Business Review, 1041-0864.*

LC HF1021 .E4 **ISSN** 0013-0095
DD 330.9 US
Pr Rev.
ECONOMIC GEOGRAPHY. [Econ. geogr.]. **Added/Corp** Clark University (Worcester, Mass.). Vol. 1, (Mar. 1925)-. Periodical. English. Four times a year (Jan., Apr., July, Oct.). $35.00 (individuals), $45.00 (institutions) US; $37.00 (individuals), $47.00 (institutions) other. Clark University, 950 Main Street, Worcester MA 01610. **Tel** (508)793-7311, FAX (508)793-8881. **ED** Susan Hanson and Richard Peet. cum. index. **Bk Rev.** available on microfilm and microfiche from University Microfilms International (UMI); available on an online database (file 648/Full-Text) from DIALOG. Documents available from The Genuine Article, UMI Article Clearinghouse.
Desc: These are articles reporting significant theoretical and empirical advances in the field of economic geography. Will interest people working on environment and development, land use, urban/regional development, gender and economy, agriculture, industrial change, and global/economic systems. Theme and special issues, as well as general issues are included also.
Ind/Abst Acad. Abstr.; Acad. Ind. [Computer File] (1984-); Acad. Search; Am. Hist. Life (1955-); Book Rev. Index; Bus. ASAP (1992-) [Full Txt.]; Bus. Index (1985-); Contents Recent Econ. J.; Curr. Cit.; Curr. Contents Soc. Behav. Sci.; Curr. Geogr. Publ. (199?-); Econ. Lit. Index; Energy Res. Abstr. (April 1976-);; EP Collect.; Expand. Acad. Index (1984-); Field Crop Abstr.; Gen. BusinessFile (1985-); Gen. Period. Index (1985-); Geogr. Abstr. Human Geogr.; Grass. Forage Abstr.; Highw. Res. Abstr.; Homework Help.; Index Period. Artic. Relat. Law (19??-19??); INFO-SOUTH Abstr.; INIS Atomindex [Micro.]; Int. Bibliogr. Sociol.; Int. Dev. Abstr.; Int. Index; Int. Polit. Sci. Abstr.; J. Econ. Lit.; J. Plan. Lit.; Leis., Rec., Tour. Abstr.; Mag. Search; Manage. Contents (1974-); MasterFile FullTEXT 1000; MasterFile FullTEXT 350; MasterFile FullTEXT 650; MasterFile FullTEXT (July 1990-); Middle East Abstr. Index; Newsp. Period. Abstr. (1991-); OCLC; PAIS Int. Print; Popul. Index; Public Aff. Inf. Serv. Bull.; Recent. Publ. Artic.; Ref. Sources; Res. Alert [Full Cov.]; Rural Dev. Abstr.; Soc. Sci. Source; Soc. Sci. Humanit. Index; Soc. Sci. Cit. Index [Full Cov.]; Soc. Sci. Index; Soc. Sci. Index Fulltext (Jan. 1988-) [Full Txt.]; Telebase; West. Hist. Q.; World Agric. Econ. Rural Sociol. Abstr.; Writ. Am. Hist.

US
ECONOMIC INDICATORS. Added/Corp Virginia Employment Commission. Economic Information Services Division. Vol. 22, No. 1 (1st Quarter 1990)-. English. Four times a year. Virginia Employment Commission, 703 East Main Street, PO Box 1358, Richmond VA 23211. ***Continues*** *Virginia Economic Indicators, 0042-6490.*

ISSN 0263-7065
DD 330.9410858 UK
ECONOMIC INDICATORS, FORECASTS FOR COMPANY PLANNING. [Econ. indic. forecasts co. plann.]. (1982)-. English. Four times a year. £320.00. Staniland Hall Association Ltd, Mappin House, 4 Winsley Street, London W1N 7AR United Kingdom. **Tel** 011 44 171 630757, FAX 011 44 171 6310754. ***Continues*** *Economic Indicators for Company Planning, 0140-1831.*

ISSN 1075-3834
DD 330 US
ECONOMIC INDICATORS HANDBOOK. (ECONOMIC INDICATORS HANDBOOK : TIME SERIES, CONVERSIONS, DOCUMENTATION.). [Econ. indic. handb.]. **VFOAT** EIH. 1st Ed. (1992)-. English. $145.00. Gale Research Inc., 835 Penobscot Building, 645 Griswold Street, Detroit MI 48226. **Tel** (800)877-GALE, (313)961-2242, FAX (313)961-6083, (800)414-5043, telex TWX 810-221-7086. **ED** Arsen J. Darnay.
Desc: Source of aggregate national statistics on approximately 175 US economic indicators.

LC HD1751 .E296
DD 338.1/3/0973021 US
CEASED
ECONOMIC INDICATORS OF THE FARM SECTOR. STATE FINANCIAL SUMMARY. See Agriculture-Agricultural Economics.

ISSN 0325-2388
AG
ECONOMIC INFORMATION ON ARGENTINA. [Econ. inf. Argent.]. **Added/Corp** Argentina. Secretaria de Estado de Programacion y Coordinacion Economica. (197?)-. Periodical. English (Spanish and French). Twelve times a year. Free. Direccion Nacional de Prensa, Hipolito Irigoyen 250 6 PO 626, 1310 Buenos Aires Argentina. ***Continues*** *Economic Information of Argentina.*

LC HB1 .W47 **ISSN** 0095-2583
DD 330/.05 US
CODEN ECIND6
Pr Rev.
ECONOMIC INQUIRY. [Econ. inq.]. **Added/Corp** Western Economic Association. Western Economic Association International. Vol. 12 (Mar. 1974)-. Periodical. English. Four times a year. $135.00. Allen Press Inc., 810 East 10th Street, PO Box 1897, Lawrence KS 66044-8897. **Tel** (913)843-1221, (800)627-0629, FAX (913)843-1274. **(Subscription address:** Economic Inquiry, PO Box 1897, Lawrence KS 66044-8897. **) ED** Frank C. Wykoff. Index available. cum. index. **Ad Acc. Acid Free. Circ:** 3,400. available on microfilm and microfiche from University Microfilms International (UMI); available on CD-ROM; available in microform; available on an online database (file 648/Full-Text) from DIALOG. Documents available from The Genuine Article, UMI Article Clearinghouse. ***Continues*** *Western Economic Journal, 0043-3640.*
Desc: Presents the latest research on all economics topics.
Ind/Abst ABI/INFORM Glob. Ed.; ABI/INFORM [Computer File] (Jan. 1980-); Acad. Search; Am. Hist. Life (1978-); Bus. ASAP (1990-) [Full Txt.]; Bus. Index (1985-); Bus. Source Plus; Bus. Source; Contents Recent Econ. J.; Curr. Cit.; Curr. Contents Soc. Behav. Sci.; Econ. Lit. Index; EP Collect.; Expand. Acad. Index (1984-); Gen. BusinessFile (1985-); Gen. Period. Index (1985-); Health Plan. Adminis.; Homework Help.; Hosp. Health Admin. Index; Hum. Resour. Abstr. (?-?); Index Period. Artic. Relat. Law; INFO-SOUTH Abstr.; Int. Bibliogr. Sociol.; J. Econ. Lit.; Leis., Rec., Tour. Abstr.; Mag. Search; MasterFile FullTEXT 1000; MasterFile FullTEXT 350; MasterFile FullTEXT 650; MasterFile FullTEXT (July 1993-); Middle East Abstr. Index; Newsp. Period. Abstr. (1991-); OCLC; PAIS Int. Print (1991-); Res. Alert [Full Cov.]; Rural Dev. Abstr.; Sage Public Adm. Abstr.; Sage Urban Stud. Abstr; Soc. Sci. Source; Soc. Sci. Cit. Index [Full Cov.]; Soc. Sci. Index; Soc. Sci. Index Fulltext (Oct. 1988-) [Full Txt.]; SportSearch; Telebase; UMI ABI/Inform--Bus. Period. Ondisc [Full Txt.]; West. Hist. Q.; World Agric. Econ. Rural Sociol. Abstr.

UK
ECONOMIC INTELLIGENCE REVIEW. (19??)-. Periodical. English. Twelve times a year. $145.00 US and Canada; £73.00 UK; £97.00 other. Intelligence International Ltd., 17 Rodney Road, Cheltenham Gloucestershire, GL50 1HX United Kingdom. **Tel** 011 44 1452 864764, FAX 011 44 1452 864848. **ED** R. H. Buttery.
Desc: Review on international economic intelligence, featuring reports on major economic trends, country forecasts, investment briefings, energy and science reports.

LC HB1 .E3 **ISSN** 0013-0133
UK
CCC
CODEN ECJOAB
Pr Rev.
ECONOMIC JOURNAL (LONDON). (THE ECONOMIC JOURNAL : THE QUARTERLY JOURNAL OF THE ROYAL ECONOMIC SOCIETY.). [Econ. J.]. **Added/Corp** British Economic Association. Royal Economic Society (Great Britain). Vol. 1, No. 1 (Mar. 1891)-. Academic Scholarly Publication. English. Six times a year. $190.00. Basil Blackwell Publishers Ltd., 108 Cowley Road, Oxford 0X4 1JF United Kingdom. **Tel** 011 44 1235 465500, FAX 011 44 1235 465556, telex 837022 OXBOOK G. **(Subscription address:** Blackwell Publishers / UK, 108 Cowley Road, Oxford OX4 1JF United Kingdom. **Tel** 011 44 1865 791100, FAX 011 44 1865 791347.) **ED** W.H. Buiter, D. Collard, C.H. Feinstein, J.P. Hutton, D.G. Mayes, J P Neary, D.M.G. Newbery and S.J. Nickell. cum. index. **Bk Rev.** available on microfilm and microfiche from University Microfilms International (UMI). Documents available from The Genuine Article, UMI Article Clearinghouse. ***Absorbed*** *Royal Economic Society (Great Britain). Conference. Conference Papers.*
Desc: Covers all fields of economics, theoretical and applied. Includes original articles, notes and comments and an extended section of reviews and signed notes on new books.
Ind/Abst ABI/INFORM Glob. Ed.; ABI/INFORM [Computer File] (March 1978-); Acad. Search; AGRICOLA; Am. Hist. Life (1955-); Br. Humanit. Index (March 1978-); Bus. ASAP (1992-) [Full Txt.]; Bus. Index (1985-); Bus. Source Plus; Bus. Source; Coal Abstr.; Contents Pages Manage. (1955-); Curr. Cit.; Curr. Contents Soc. Behav. Sci.; Econ. Lit. Index (19??-); EMBASE; Energy Res. Abstr. (1975-); EP Collect.; Expand. Acad. Index (1984-); Gen. BusinessFile (1985-); Gen. Period. Index (1985-); Geogr. Abstr. Human Geogr.; Highw. Res. Abstr.; Homework Help.; Int. Bibliogr. Sociol.; Int. Dev. Abstr. (1974-); Int. Labour Doc.; J. Econ. Lit.; LABORDOC; Leis., Rec., Tour. Abstr.; Mag. Search; MasterFile FullTEXT 1000; MasterFile FullTEXT 350; MasterFile FullTEXT 650; MasterFile FullTEXT (July 1993-); Middle East Abstr. Index; Newsp. Period. Abstr. (1989-); OCLC; PAIS Int. Print (1991-); Postharvest News Inf.; Res. Alert [Full Cov.]; Selec. Coop. Index Manage. Period.; Soc. Sci. Source; Soc. Sci. Cit. Index [Full Cov.]; Soc. Sci. Index; Soc. Sci. Index Fulltext (Dec. 1988-) [Full Txt.]; Stat. Theory Method Abstr. (1959-1963,1969); Telebase; Trade Ind. ASAP [Full Txt.]; Wheat Barley Trit. Abstr.; World Agric. Econ. Rural Sociol. Abstr.

LC HB9 .H63a **ISSN** 0916-4650
DD 330/.05 JA
ECONOMIC JOURNAL OF HOKKAIDO UNIVERSITY. Added/Corp Hokkaido Daigaku. Keizai Gakubu. Vol. 19 (1990)-. Periodical. English. Hokkaido University / Economics, Faculty of Economics, Sapporo Japan. ***Continues*** *Hokudai Economic Papers, 0441-7410.*

LC HC107.F6 A13 **ISSN** 0013-0141
DD 330.9759 US
ECONOMIC LEAFLETS. [Econ. leafl.]. **Added/Corp** University of Florida. Bureau of Economic and Business Research. Vol. 1 (Dec. 1941)-. Periodical. English. Twelve times a year. $15.00. Bureau of Economic & Business Research / Florida, University of Florida, 221 Matherly Hall, Gainesville FL 32611. **Tel** (904)392-0171, FAX (904)392-4739.

US
ECONOMIC LITERATURE INDEX. See Business and Economics-Abstracting, Bibliographies and Statistics.

LC HB141 .E248 **ISSN** 0264-9993
DD 330/.01/5118 UK
CCC
Pr Rev.
ECONOMIC MODELLING. [Econ. model.]. Vol. 1, No. 1 (Jan. 1984)-. Periodical. English. Four times a year. $466.00. Butterworth Heinemann Publishers, Linacre House Jordan Hill, Oxford OX2 8DP United Kingdom. **Tel** 011 44 1865 310366, FAX 011 44 1865 310898. **(Subscription address:** Elsevier Science Ltd. / Oxford Fulfillment Centre, PO Box 800, Kidlington OX5 1DX United Kingdom. **Tel** 011 44 865 843355.) **ED** Homa Motamen. Index available. **Bk Rev. Ad Acc. Circ:** 800 (ctrl). available on microfilm and microfiche from University Microfilms International (UMI); available on an online database from Elsevier Electronic Subscriptions (EES). Documents available from The Genuine Article, UMI Article Clearinghouse.
Desc: Provides both theoretical and applied papers on economic modelling. The journal's prime objective is to provide an international forum for continuous review of the state-of-the-art in economic modelling.
Ind/Abst ABI/INFORM Glob. Ed.; Contents Recent Econ. J. (1985-); Curr. Cit.; Curr. Contents Soc. Behav. Sci.; Econ. Lit. Index (199?-); J. Econ. Lit.; Res. Alert [Full Cov.]; Soc. Sci. Cit. Index [Full Cov.].

SI
ECONOMIC MONTHLY. (19??)-. Chinese. Twelve times a year. Singapore International Chamber of Commerce, 50 Raffles PL#03-02, Shell Tower, Singapore 0104 Singapore. **Tel** 011 65 2241255.

LC HC407.B9 A12 **ISSN** 0205-1400
DD 330.9497/7/005 BU
ECONOMIC NEWS OF BULGARIA. [Econ. news Bulg.]. **Added/Corp** Bulgarska Turgovsko-Promishlena Palata. **VFOAT** Economic News. (1960)-. Periodical. English (French, German, Russian and Spanish). Twelve times a year. $24.00. Bulgarian Chamber of Commerce and Industry, 11A Alexander Stambolliski Boulevard, Sofia Bulgaria. **Tel** 011 359 2 800821, FAX 011 359 2 873209. **ED** Lyuben Mikhailov. **Circ:** 25,000.
Ind/Abst Predicasts.

LC HB1 .E34 ISSN 0391-5026
DD 330/.05 IT

ECONOMIC NOTES - MONTE PASCHI SIENA. (ECONOMIC NOTES.). [Econ. notes - Monte Paschi Siena]. **Added/Corp** Monte Dei Paschi di Siena. (1972)-. Periodical. English. Monte dei Paschi di Siena, Piazza Salimbeni 3, 53100 Siena Italy. **Tel** 011 39 577 294401, FAX 011 39 577 294084.
Ind/Abst Curr. Cit.; Index Econ. Artic. J. Collect. Vol. (1982-); J. Econ. Lit. (1982-).

ISSN 0140-489X
UK
CCC

ECONOMIC OUTLOOK (LONDON. 1977). (ECONOMIC OUTLOOK.). [Econ. outlook]. **Main/Corp** London Graduate School of Business Studies. Centre for Economic Forecasting. (1976)-. Academic Scholarly Publication. English. Four times a year. $458.00. Basil Blackwell Publishers Ltd., 108 Cowley Road, Oxford 0X4 1JF United Kingdom. **Tel** 011 44 1235 465500, FAX 011 44 1235 465556, telex 837022 OXBOOK G. **(Subscription address:** Blackwell Publishers / UK, 108 Cowley Road, Oxford OX4 1JF United Kingdom. **Tel** 011 44 1865 791100, FAX 011 44 1865 791347.**)** **ED** P. W. Robinson and G. R. Dicks. ***Formed by the union of*** *International Economic Outlook, 0960-8869* ***and*** *Financial Outlook.*
Desc: A rolling four year business forecast of the UK economy.
Ind/Abst Curr. Cit.; PAIS Int. Print; Selec. Coop. Index Manage. Period.

LC HC59.7 .W33a ISSN 0324-864X
DD 330.9/172/4 PL

ECONOMIC PAPERS. [Econ. pap.]. **Main/Corp** Szkola Glowna Planowania i Statystyki (Warsaw, Poland). Instytut Gospodarki Krajow Rozwijajacych Sie. (1973)-. English (French). Research Institute for Developing Countries, Rakowiecka 24, 02-521 Warsaw Poland.
Ind/Abst PAIS Int. Print.

LC HC
DD 330 AT

ECONOMIC PAPERS. **Added/Corp** Economic Society of Australia. Vol. 1, No. 1 (Apr. 1982)-. Academic Scholarly Publication. English. Four times a year. 23.02Aus$. Economic Society of Australia, 23 Wallis Avenue, E Ivanhoe VIC 3079 Australia. **Tel** 011 61 3 4974140. **ED** H. Harley and W. Junior. **Ad Acc, Adv Mgr:** C. Orchard. **Circ:** 2,200 (ctrl). ***Continues*** *Economic Society of Australia and New Zealand. New South Wales Branch) Economic Papers.*
Desc: Discussion of issues in business economics, applied economics and economic policy.
Ind/Abst APAIS, Aust. Public Aff. Inf. Ser. (1982-); PAIS Int. Print.

ISSN 1048-7573
DD 338 US

ECONOMIC PERSPECTIVES. AGRICULTURAL CREDIT OUTLOOK. **See** Agriculture-Agricultural Economics.

LC HB1 .E2516 ISSN 0142-5900
DD 330/.05 US

ECONOMIC PERSPECTIVES (CHUR). (ECONOMIC PERSPECTIVES.). Vol. 1 (1979)-. Monographic series. English. Irregular. Harwood Academic Publishers / New York, PO Box 786, Cooper Station, New York NY 10276. **Tel** (212)206-8900, (201)643-7500. **ED** M.B. Ballabon.
Desc: Economics.

LC S ISSN 1191-3576
DD 630 CN

ECONOMIC PLANNING IN FREE SOCIETIES. **See** Agriculture.

LC HD87 .E26 ISSN 0266-4658
DD 338.9/005 UK
CCC

ECONOMIC POLICY. [Econ. policy]. (Nov. 1985)-. Academic Scholarly Publication. English. Two times a year (April and October). $101.00. Basil Blackwell Publishers Ltd., 108 Cowley Road, Oxford 0X4 1JF United Kingdom. **Tel** 011 44 1235 465500, FAX 011 44 1235 465556, telex 837022 OXBOOK G. **(Subscription address:** Blackwell Publishers / UK, 108 Cowley Road, Oxford OX4 1JF United Kingdom. **Tel** 011 44 1865 791100, FAX 011 44 1865 791347.**)** available on microfilm from University Microfilms International (UMI).
Desc: Offers analysis of topical issues in economics. Articles provide non-technical analyses of research on policy questions. Discusses the entire range of macro- and microeconomic issues, emphasizing the possibilities for cross-country comparisons.
Ind/Abst Contents Recent Econ. J. (1989-); Curr. Cit.; Econ. Lit. Index (199?-); Geogr. Abstr. Human Geogr. (1989-); Int. Dev. Abstr.; J. Econ. Lit.; PAIS Int. Print (1991-); Sage Public Adm. Abstr.

LC HC
DD 330 US

ECONOMIC POLICY PAPERS (NEW YORK, N.Y.). (ECONOMIC POLICY PAPERS.). **Added/Corp** C.V. Starr Center for Applied Economics (New York University). (1981)-. Periodical. English. Irregular. $100.00. CV Starr Center for Applied Economics, New York University, Washington Square, New York NY 10003. **Tel** (212)998-1212. **ED** Michael Dobie. Index available. cum. index. **Circ:** 2,285 (ctrl).
Desc: Focus on the application of economic concepts to problems confronting policy-makers.

ISSN 0940-5151
GW

UDC 33
Pr Rev.

ECONOMIC QUALITY CONTROL. [Econ. qual. control]. **VFOAT** EQC. Economic Quality Control. (1986)-. Periodical. English. Four times a year (March, June, Sept., Dec.). $38.38. Inst Angewandte Math & Statistics, Sanderring 2, D-97070 Wuerzburg Germany. **Tel** 011 49 93131971, FAX 011 49 93115123. **ED** Elart von Colloni. **Bk Rev. Circ:** 200 (ctrl).

LC HC107 ISSN 1069-7225
DD 332 US

•ECONOMIC QUARTERLY. [Econ. q. - Fed. Reserve Bank Richmond]. **Added/Corp** Federal Reserve Bank of Richmond. Research Dept. Vol. 79, No. 1 (Winter 1993)-. Periodical. English. Four times a year. Free on request. Federal Reserve Bank of Richmond, PO Box 27622, Public Services, Richmond VA 23261. **Tel** (804)697-8000. **ED** Thomas M. Humprey. **Circ:** 15,000. available with charts; available in microform from University Microfilms International (UMI); available on microfiche. Documents available from UMI Article Clearinghouse, BLDSC, FAXON Xpress, The UnCover Company. ***Continues*** *Economic Review, 0094-6893.*
Ind/Abst ABI/INFORM [Computer File]; Acad. Search; Bus. Source Plus; Bus. Source; EP Collect.; Homework Help.; J. Econ. Lit.; MasterFile FullTEXT 1000; MasterFile FullTEXT 350; MasterFile FullTEXT 650; MasterFile FullTEXT (July 1993-) [Full Txt.]; OCLC; Telebase.

LC HC601 .E4 ISSN 0013-0249
DD 338.994 AT
CCC

Pr Rev.

ECONOMIC RECORD, THE. [Econ. rec.]. **Added/Corp** Economic Society of Australia and New Zealand. Vol. 1 (Nov. 1925)-. Periodical. English. Four times a year (Mar., June, Sept., Dec.). 42.76Aus$. Brown Prior Anderson Pty Ltd., 5 Evans Street, Burwood Victoria 3125 Australia. **Tel** 011 61 3 8086622, FAX 011 61 3 8080706. **ED** R.A. Williams. Index Available, published separately, free-automatically sent. **Bk Rev. Ad Acc. Circ:** 4,000 (ctrl). available on microfilm and microfiche from University Microfilms International (UMI); available on an online database from University Microfilms International (UMI). Documents available from The Genuine Article, UMI Article Clearinghouse, The UnCover Company, SWETS, BLDSC, FAXON Xpress.
Desc: General economics; relates particularly to the Australian economy. Feature articles mainly written by Australian economists.
Ind/Abst ABI/INFORM Glob. Ed.; Acad. Search; APAIS, Aust. Public Aff. Inf. Ser. (1963-); Bibliogr. Mission. (1981-); Bus. Index (1985-); Bus. Source Plus; Bus. Source; Contents Recent Econ. J.; Curr. Cit.; Curr. Contents Soc. Behav. Sci.; Econ. Lit. Index; EP Collect.; Expand. Acad. Index (1992-); Gen. BusinessFile (1985-); Gen. Period. Index (1985-); Geogr. Abstr. Human Geogr.; Homework Help.; INFO-SOUTH Abstr.; Int. Dev. Abstr. (?-?); Int. Labour Doc.; J. Econ. Lit.; Leis., Rec., Tour. Abstr.; Mag. Search; MasterFile FullTEXT 1000; MasterFile FullTEXT 350; MasterFile FullTEXT 650; MasterFile FullTEXT (Jan. 1993-); Middle East Abstr. Index; Newsp. Period. Abstr. (1992-); OCLC; Res. Alert [Full Cov.]; Rural Dev. Abstr.; Soc. Sci. Cit. Index [Full Cov.]; Stat. Theory Method Abstr. (1959-1963); Telebase; Trade Ind. Index (1981-?); Work Relat. Abstr.; World Agric. Econ. Rural Sociol. Abstr.

ISSN 1312-8388
AT

•ECONOMIC REFORM AUSTRALIA. (1995)-. English. Seven times a year. Economic Reform Australia, 14 Gallimore Avenue, Balmain New South Wales 2041 Australia. **Tel** 011 61 2 8107812.

ISSN 1058-661X
DD 330 US

ECONOMIC REFORM TODAY. [Econ. reform today]. **Added/Corp** Center for International Private Enterprise. Vol. 1, No. 1 (Summer 1991)-. Periodical. English. Four times a year. $25.00. Center for Internaitonal Private Enterprise, 1615 H Street NW, Washington DC 20062. **Tel** (202)463-5901.

ISSN 1187-080X
DD 336.3/0971/05 CN

ECONOMIC REFORM (TORONTO). (ECONOMIC REFORM : NEWSLETTER OF THE COMMITTEE ON MONETARY AND ECONOMIC REFORM.). [Econ. reform]. **Added/Corp** Committee on Monetary and Economic Reform (Waterloo, Ont.). Vol. 3, No. 4 (Apr. 1991)-. Newsletter. English. Twelve times a year. 16.01Can$. Committee on Monetary and Economic Reform, 3284 Yonge Street, Suite 500, Toronto Ontario M4N 3M7 Canada. **Tel** (416)486-4686. ***Continues*** *C.O.M.E.R. Comments., 0845-7301.*

ISSN 0738-7210
US

ECONOMIC REPORT (ALBUQUERQUE, N.M.), THE. (THE ECONOMIC REPORT.). [Econ. rep.]. **Added/Corp** American Classical College. Institute for Economic & Financial Research. American Classical College. Research Center for Economic Psychology. (19??)-. Periodical. English. Twelve times a year. $300.00. The Institute for Economic & Financial Research, PO Box 4526, Albuquerque NM 87106. **Tel** (505)843-7749. **ED** Carlo Maria Flumiani. **Bk Rev.** ctrl circ.
Desc: Covers economic anticipations.

LC HC106.5 .A272 ISSN 0193-1180
DD 330.973 US

ECONOMIC REPORT OF THE PRESIDENT TRANSMITTED TO THE CONGRESS. **See** Finance-Public Finance.

LC HF3831 .C47
HK
SUSPENDED

•ECONOMIC REPORTER. **VFOAT** Economic Reporter China Market; Ching Chi Tao Pao. No. 4 (1993)-(19??). Periodical. English (table of contents in Chinese). Twelve times a year. Economic Information and Agency Consultancy, 342 Hennessy Road, 12th Floor, Hong Kong Hong Kong. **Tel** 011 852 25739208, 011 852 25738217, FAX 011 852 258336889. ***Continues*** *China Market, 0258-3054.*

LC HC ISSN 0441-0025
DD 330 JA

ECONOMIC RESEARCH SERIES. **Main/Corp** Hitotsubashi Daigaku, Tokyo. Keizai Kenkyujo. **Added/Corp** Hitotsubashi Daigaku. Keizai Kenkyujo. (1957)-. Monographic series. English. Irregular. Price varies per volume. **(Subscription address:** Kinokuniya Company Ltd., 38-1 Sakuragaoka 5, chome Setagaya-ku, Tokyo 156 Japan. **Tel** FAX 011 03 3439 0136.**)**

AT

ECONOMIC REVIEW. **Added/Corp** Commercial Bank of Australia, Ltd. (19??)-. Periodical. English. Four times a year. Free on request. Commercial Bank of Australia, 114 William Street, Melbourne Victoria 3000 Australia.

LC HC865.A1 E277
DD 330.96762/005 KE

ECONOMIC REVIEW, THE. (Oct. 5, 1992)-. Periodical. English. One time a week. $260.00. Economic Review Ltd, PO Box 40894, Nairobi, Kenya. **Tel** 011 254 2 219603.

LC HC117.N4 N456
DD 330.9718/005 CN

•ECONOMIC REVIEW, THE. **Added/Corp** Newfoundland. Executive Council. Economic Research & Analysis Division. Newfoundland. Cabinet Secretariat. (1994)-. Periodical. English. Four times a year. Executive Council Newfoundland and Labrador, 10th Floor East Block, Confederation Building, PO Box 8700, St Johns Newfoundland A1B 4J6 Canada. **Tel** (709)729-3255, (709)729-3649, FAX (709)729-6944. ***Continues*** *Newfoundland & Labrador Economic Review, 1197-1738.*

LC HC915.A1 Z35a
DD 338.96894/005 ZA

ECONOMIC REVIEW AND ANNUAL PLAN. **Main/Corp** Zambia. National Commission for Development Planning. (198?)-. English. K12.00. National Commission for Development Planning, PO Box RW268, Lusaka Zambia. ***Continues*** *Annual Plan.*

LC HC517.S9 S93A
DD 330.9681/3/005 SQ

ECONOMIC REVIEW AND OUTLOOK. (198?)-. English. One time a year. E4.00. Economics Statistics Library, PO Box 456, Mbabane Swaziland. **Tel** 011 43765. **Ad Acc.** ***Continues*** *Economic Review (Mbabane, Swaziland).*

LC HC107.O3 E26 ISSN 0013-0281
DD 330.9771 US
CODEN ERFCBR

Pr Rev.

ECONOMIC REVIEW (CLEVELAND). (ECONOMIC REVIEW.). [Econ. rev.]. **Added/Corp** Federal Reserve Bank of Cleveland. (1964)-. Periodical. English. Four times a year (Mar., June, Sept., Dec.). Free. Federal Reserve Bank of Cleveland, PO Box 6387, Cleveland OH 44101. **Tel** (216)579-3079, FAX (216)579-2477. **ED** Robin Ratliff and Tess Ferg. Index Bound in First Issue. **Circ:** 15,000. available on microfilm and microfiche from University Microfilms International (UMI). Documents available from UMI Article Clearinghouse. ***Supersedes*** *Federal Reserve Bank of Cleveland. Monthly Business Review.*
Desc: Presents research and comment on international

issues, and on national and regional issues in the US economy.
Ind/Abst ABI/INFORM Glob. Ed.; ABI/INFORM [Computer File] (Winter 1981/1982-); Acad. Search; Bus. Source Plus; Bus. Source; EP Collect.; Expand. Acad. Index (1992-); Fed. Print Econ. Bank. Top.; Gen. BusinessFile (1992-); Homework Help.; MasterFile FullTEXT 1000; MasterFile FullTEXT 350; MasterFile FullTEXT 650; MasterFile FullTEXT (Jan. 1993-) [Full Txt.]; Newsp. Period. Abstr. (1992-); OCLC; PAIS Int. Print (1991-); Telebase.

LC HC424.A1 E32 **ISSN** 0259-9775
DD 330.9/549/303 CE

ECONOMIC REVIEW (COLOMBO). (ECONOMIC REVIEW.). [Econ. rev.]. **Added/Corp** People's Bank (Sri Lanka). Research Dept. Vol. 1 (April 1975)-. Periodical. English (Sinhalese and Tamil). Twelve times a year. $22.00 North America; $30.00 Middle East and Japan; $27.00 South East Asia and Africa; $24.00 South Asia; $33.00 other. People's Bank Research Department, Head Office, Colombo 2 Sri Lanka. **Tel** 011 94 1 36940. **ED** Susantha Goonatilake and Chrys Gunaratne. **Bk Rev. Ad Acc. Circ:** 12,000 (ctrl).
Desc: Covers development and business issues from a Sri Lankan and international perspective.
Ind/Abst Hortic. Abstr.

ISSN 0254-3214
CY

ECONOMIC REVIEW (CYPRUS POPULAR BANK). (19??)-. English. Six times a year. Cyprus Popular Bank Ltd, PO Box 2032, Nicosia Cyprus. **Tel** 2-450000, FAX 2-450631, telex 2494. **ED** Savvas Savvides and Yiannis Tirkides. Index available. cum. index. **Circ:** 2,800 (ctrl).
Desc: Review of topical economic issues of local and international concern.

LC HC **ISSN** 0265-0290
DD 330 UK

ECONOMIC REVIEW (DEDDINGTON). (THE ECONOMIC REVIEW.). [Econ. rev.]. (1983)-. Periodical. English. Irregular (4 issues). $48.76. Philip Allan Publishers Ltd., Market Place, Deddington, Oxfordshire OX15 0SE United Kingdom. **Tel** 011 44 1869 338652, FAX 011 44 1869 338803.
Ind/Abst Curr. Cit.; PAIS Int. Print (1991-).

LC HC107.A17 A2 **ISSN** 0161-2387
DD 330.9/73/092 US
CODEN ERKCDK

ECONOMIC REVIEW (KANSAS CITY). (ECONOMIC REVIEW.). [Econ. rev.]. **Added/Corp** Federal Reserve Bank of Kansas City. (Jan. 1978)-. Periodical. English. Four times a year. Free on request. Federal Reserve Bank of Kansas City, 925 Grand Avenue, Kansas City MO 64198. **Tel** (816)881-2683. **ED** Thomas E Davis. Index available. **Circ:** 30,000 (ctrl). available on microfilm and microfiche from University Microfilms International (UMI). Documents available from UMI Article Clearinghouse. ***Continues*** *Monthly Review (Federal Reserve Bank of Kansas City), 0014-9152.*
Desc: Includes articles which discuss a variety of economic and financial topics.
Ind/Abst ABI/INFORM Glob. Ed.; ABI/INFORM [Computer File] (Feb. 1981-); AGRICOLA [Select. Cov.]; Bus. Period. Index; Bus. Source Plus; Bus. Source; Coal Abstr.; Curr. Cit.; Econ. Lit. Index; Energy Res. Abstr. (Feb. 1979-); EP Collect.; Expand. Acad. Index (1992-); F&S Index Plus Text, Int. [Select. Cov.]; Fed. Print Econ. Bank. Top.; Gen. BusinessFile (1992-); Homework Help.; Index Period. Artic. Relat. Law; INFO-SOUTH Abstr.; Mag. Search; MasterFile FullTEXT 1000; MasterFile FullTEXT 350; MasterFile FullTEXT 650; MasterFile FullTEXT; Newsp. Period. Abstr. (1992-); OCLC; PAIS Int. Print (1991-); Soyabean Abstr.; Telebase; UMI ABI/Inform--Bus. Period. Ondisc (Jan. 1987-) [Full Txt.]; Wheat Barley Trit. Abstr.; Wilson Bus. Abstr.

LC HC **ISSN** 0013-032X
LE

ECONOMIC REVIEW OF THE ARAB WORLD. **Added/Corp** Bureau of Lebanese and Arab Documentations. Vol. 1 (Feb. 1967)-. Periodical. English. Twelve times a year. $300.00. Bureau of Documentation, Marcel Tawil, Postfach 2412, 79514 Loerrach Germany. **Tel** 011 49 7621 2472, FAX 011 49 7621 2472. ***Continues*** *Economic Survey of Lebanon and the Arab World; Argus Pharma Report.*
Desc: Survey of economic developments in the Arab world.

LC G155.U6 E32 **ISSN** 0733-642X
DD 380.1/4591730492 US

ECONOMIC REVIEW OF TRAVEL IN AMERICA, THE. **See** Travel and Tourism.

LC HC464.F7 C574 **ISSN** 0013-029X
DD 330/.05 CH

ECONOMIC REVIEW (TAIPEI, TAIWAN). (ECONOMIC REVIEW / BANK OF CHINA, HEAD OFFICE.). [Econ. rev.]. **VFOAT** Ying Wen Ching Chi Ping Lun. No. 73 (Jan.-Feb. 1960)-. Periodical. English. Six times a year. Free. International Commercial Bank of China, Head Office, 100 Chi Lin Road, Taipei Taiwan. **Tel** 011 886 2 5633156. **ED** Han-Ming Su. **Circ:** 2,100. ***Continues*** *Bi-Monthly Economic Review.*
Desc: A publication focusing on various aspects on Taiwan, the Republic's economy and development.
Ind/Abst Leis., Rec., Tour. Abstr.; Rural Dev. Abstr.; Soils Fert.; World Agric. Econ. Rural Sociol. Abstr.

ISSN 0431-6045
GW

ECONOMIC SITUATION IN THE FEDERAL REPUBLIC OF GERMANY, THE. **Main/Corp** Germany (West). Bundesministerium fuer Wirtschaft. (19??)-. Periodical. English. Twelve times a year. Free on request. Bundesminister fuer Wirtschaft, POB 140260, D-53107 Bonn Germany. **Tel** 011 49 228 6151.

ISSN 1184-9231
DD 330.9711 CN

ECONOMIC STATISTICS REPORT. [Econ. stat. rep.]. **Added/Corp** British Columbia. Ministry of Finance and Corporate Relations. Planning and Statistics Division. Data Dissemination. (1991)-. Periodical. English. Twelve times a year. Ministry of Finance, 553 Superior Street, Victoria BC V8V 1X4 Canada. **Tel** (604)387-1502.

LC HC370.I52 E35 WMLC 93/793 **ISSN** 0801-8324
DD 330 NO

ECONOMIC SURVEY. **Added/Corp** Norway. Statistisk Sentralbyra. (19??)-. Periodical. English. Four times a year. Central Bureau of Statistics / Norway, PO Box 8131 DEP, N-0033 Oslo 1 Norway. **Tel** 011 47 2 2864964, FAX 011 47 2 864973.
Ind/Abst PAIS Int. Print.

FI

ECONOMIC SURVEY ... FINLAND. **Added/Corp** Finland. Kansantalousosasto. (1984)-. English. ***Continues*** *Economic Survey (Helsinki, Finland), 0430-5221.*
Ind/Abst F&S Index Plus Text, Int. [Select. Cov.]; Predicasts Forecasts; Trade Ind. Index.

LC HC **ISSN** 0070-8682
US

ECONOMIC SURVEY OF AFRICA. **Added/Corp** United Nations. Economic Commission for Africa. (1966)-. Government Publication. English. One time a year. United Nations Publications, 2 United Nations Plaza, Room DC2 0853, Department 007C, New York NY 10017. **Tel** (212)963-8303, (800)253-9646.

LC JX1977 .A2 **ISSN** 0070-8712
US

ECONOMIC SURVEY OF EUROPE. **Main/Corp** United Nations. Economic Commission for Europe. **Added/Corp** United Nations. Dept. of Economic Affairs. United Nations. Dept. of Economic and Social Affairs. (1947)-. Government Publication. English. One time a year. Price vaies per volume. United Nations Publications, 2 United Nations Plaza, Room DC2 0853, Department 007C, New York NY 10017. **Tel** (212)963-8303, (800)253-9646.
Desc: An internationally recognized economic report, it covers a wide range or research on the changing patterns of trade and output in Europe, Canada and the United States.

LC HC161 .U525 **ISSN** 0257-2184
DD 330.98/0005 CL

ECONOMIC SURVEY OF LATIN AMERICA AND THE CARIBBEAN / ECONOMIC COMMISSION FOR LATIN AMERICA AND THE CARIBBEAN. **Added/Corp** United Nations. Economic Commission for Latin America and the Caribbean. (1982)-. Government Publication. English. Irregular. $45.00. United Nations Publications, 2 United Nations Plaza, Room DC2 0853, Department 007C, New York NY 10017. **Tel** (212)963-8303, (800)253-9646. ***Continues*** *Economic Survey of Latin America.*
Desc: Views trends in the Latin American economy as a whole including inflation, trade, output, external finance and foreign trade.

LC HA2171 .A33 **ISSN** 0303-853X
DD 330.9/666/203 LB

ECONOMIC SURVEY OF LIBERIA. **Main/Corp** Liberia. Ministry of Planning and Economic Affairs. English. Ministry of Planning and Economic Affairs, Monrovia Liberia. **Tel** 222082. **ED** J Charles Nyema. **Circ:** 500. ***Continues*** *Economic Survey.*
Desc: Focuses on economic performance, gross domestic output, fiscal performance, money and banking trade, transportation, communication, health education, and housing industry.

LC HC **ISSN** 0953-5314
DD 330 UK
CCC

Pr Rev.

ECONOMIC SYSTEMS RESEARCH. (ECONOMIC SYSTEMS RESEARCH : JOURNAL OF THE INTERNATIONAL INPUT-OUTPUT ASSOCIATION.). [Econ. syst. res.]. **Added/Corp** International Input-Output Association. Vol. 1, No. 1 (1989)-. Periodical. English. Four times a year. $444.00. Carfax Publishing Company, PO Box 25, Abingdon, Oxfordshire OX14 3UE United Kingdom. **Tel** 011 44 1235 555335, FAX 011 44 1235 553559, telex 817484. **ED** Jan Oosterhaven. Index available. **Bk Rev. Ad Acc, Adv Mgr:** Linda Salter. **Circ:** 550 (ctrl). available on microfiche.
Desc: Dedicated to the furtherance of theoretical and factual knowledge about economic systems, economic structures and their change and motion.
Ind/Abst Bus. Source Plus; Bus. Source; Econ. Lit. Index (199?-); EP Collect.; Geogr. Abstr. Human Geogr.; Homework Help.; Int. Dev. Abstr.; J. Econ. Lit. (1989-); MasterFile FullTEXT 1000; MasterFile FullTEXT 350; MasterFile FullTEXT 650; MasterFile FullTEXT (July 1994-); Telebase.

LC HB1.A1 E4 **ISSN** 0938-2259
GW
CCC
CODEN ECTHEA

Pr Rev.

ECONOMIC THEORY. **Added/Corp** Society for the Advancement of Economic Theory. **VFOAT** ET. Vol. 1, No. 1 (Jan. 1991)-. Periodical. English. Six times a year. $639.00. Springer-Verlag GmbH & Company KG, Heidelberger Platz 3, D-14197 Berlin Germany. **Tel** 011 49 30 8207223, FAX 011 49 30 8214091, telex 183 319 SPBLN D. **(Subscription address:** Springer-Verlag New York Inc. / North America, PO Box 2485, Journal Fulfillment, Secaucus NJ 07096. **Tel** (201)348-4033, (800)777-4643, FAX (201)348-4505.**)** **ED** Susan A Vogel. **Bk Rev. Ad Acc. Circ:** 800. available on microfilm and microfiche from University Microfilms International (UMI).
Desc: Presents research in all areas of economics based on rigorous theoretical reasoning, and on specific topics in mathematics which is motivated by the analysis of economic problems.
Ind/Abst Econ. Lit. Index; Math. Rev.

NP

ECONOMIC TIMES, THE. **Added/Corp** Institute for Development Studies (Kathmandu, Nepal). Vol. 1, No. 1 (Mar.-June 1991)-. Periodical. English. Four times a year. Rs55.00 ($10.00 U.S.). Economic Times, Editor, PO Box 2274, Kathmandu Nepal.

LC HC101 .E44 **ISSN** 1050-0200
DD 330 US
CODEN ECTIED

ECONOMIC TIMES (NEW YORK, N.Y.). (ECONOMIC TIMES.). [Econ. times]. **Added/Corp** Conference Board. Vol. 1, no. 1 (May 1990)-. Periodical. English. Ten times a year. $395.00. Conference Board, 845 Third Avenue, New York NY 10022. **Tel** (212)759-0900 ext. 582, (800)872-6273, FAX (212)980-7014. ***Formed by the union of*** *Business Executives' Expectations, 0889-6674.*

LC HC101 .E454 **ISSN** 0748-2922
DD 330.973/0021 US

ECONOMIC TRENDS (CLEVELAND, OHIO). (ECONOMIC TRENDS.). [Econ. trends]. (1981)-. Periodical. English. Twelve times a year. Free on request. Federal Reserve Bank of Cleveland, PO Box 6387, Cleveland OH 44101. **Tel** (216)579-3079, FAX (216)579-2477. **Circ:** 7,000. available on microfilm and microfiche from University Microfilms International (UMI).
Desc: Offers a chart-oriented analysis of various aspects of the US economy. Emphasis is placed on offering the latest current data.
Ind/Abst Acad. Search; Bus. Source Plus; Bus. Source; EP Collect.; Homework Help.; MasterFile FullTEXT 1000; MasterFile FullTEXT 350; MasterFile FullTEXT 650; MasterFile FullTEXT (Jan. 1994-) [Full Txt.]; OCLC; Telebase.

LC HC251 .E23 **ISSN** 0013-0400
DD 330 UK
CCC

ECONOMIC TRENDS (LONDON). (ECONOMIC TRENDS.). [Econ. trends]. **Added/Corp** Great Britain. Central Statistical Office. **VFOAT** CSO Economic Trends. No. 1 (Nov. 1953)-. Statistical Publication. English. Twelve times a year. £155.00. Her Majesty's Stationery Office, 51 Nine Elms Lane, London SW8 5DR United Kingdom. **Tel** 011 44 171 8738459, 011 44 171 8738499, FAX 011 44 171 8738499, 011 44 171 8738456, telex 297138. **(Subscription address:** Her Majesty's Stationery Office, PO Box 276, Public Centre, London SW8 5DT United Kingdom. **Tel** 011 44 171 8738499, 011 44 171 8738456.**)**
Desc: Features definitive figures supported by background articles, with three regular sections of tables and charts illustrating trends in the UK economy.
Ind/Abst PAIS Int. Print (1991-); Predicasts; Public Aff. Inf. Serv. Bull.

LC HB1 .E43 **ISSN** 0014-9470
DD 330/.05 II

ECONOMIC TRENDS (NEW DELHI). (ECONOMIC TRENDS.). **Added/Corp** Federation of Indian Chambers of Commerce and Industry. Vol. 1 (Oct. 1, 1971)-. Periodical. English. Four times a year. $90.00. Federation of Indian Chambers of Commerce, Federation House Tansen Marg, New Delhi 110001 India. **Tel** 3319251. **(Subscription address:** Prints India, 11 Darya Ganj, New Delhi 110002 India. **Tel** 011 91 11 3268645, FAX 011 91 11 3275542, telex 31-61087 PRIN-IN.**)** **ED** R S Bisht. **Bk Rev. Ad Acc. Circ:** 1,500 (ctrl).
Desc: All important economic policy decisions of government, economic indicators and a general

economic round-up of the world. During Parliament sessions, it covers important questions and answers. Tax matters are also featured.

ISSN 0824-3425
DD 330.971/0646 CN
ECONOMIC UPDATE - DOMINION SECURITIES AMES. ECONOMICS.
(ECONOMICS. ECONOMIC UPDATE.). [Econ. update - Dom. Secur. Ames, Econ.]. (1982)-. Periodical. English. Free. Dominion Securities Ames, PO Box 21 Commerce Court South, Toronto Ontario M5L 1A7 Canada. ctrl circ.

ISSN 1034-747X
DD 330.994 AT
ECONOMIC UPDATE ULTIMO.
(AUSTRALIAN FINANCIAL REVIEW COMMONWEALTH BANK ECONOMIC UPDATE FOR AUSTRALIA.). [Econ. update Ultimo]. **Added/Corp** Australian Financial Review. (1987)-. English. One time a year. 17.23Aus$. Financial Review Publications, PO Box N542, Grosvenor Place, NSW 2000 Australia. **Tel** 011 61 2 2415385, FAX 011 61 2 2415354.
Desc: Up-to-date working economics reference book.

LC HF3127 .E36 **ISSN** 0164-3525
DD 330.9 US
CEASED
ECONOMIC WORLD (LOS ANGELES).
(ECONOMIC WORLD.). [Econ. world]. (Apr. 1975)-(Dec. 1993). Periodical. English. Economic Salon Ltd, 60 East 42nd Street/Room 734, New York NY 10165. **Tel** (212)986-1588, FAX (212)557-7541. **ED** Larry Fisher, (212)989-1585. **Bk Rev. Ad Acc, Adv Mgr:** Herb Pressman, **Tel** (212)986-1588. **Circ:** 35,000. ***Continues** Economic Salon, 0885-1395.*
Desc: Covers Japanese business in the US.
Ind/Abst F&S Index Plus Text, Int. [Select. Cov.].

LC HC447 .E28
DD 330 IO
ECONOMICA.
Added/Corp Universita Indonesia. Bagan Otonom "Economica" Mahasiswa. **VFOAT** Ekonomika. (June 1979)-. Periodical. Indonesian. Twelve times a year. Badan Otonom Economica, Fakultas Ekonomi, Universitas Indonesia, Salemba Raya 4, Jakarta 10430 Indonesia. **Tel** 3101628. **ED** Azis Armand, Toto Pranoto, Devi Femina, A I Wayan Raimantera, Rizka Y Baely, M Chatib Basri, D A Rosmianingrum, A V Hardiyanto, Ivan Patmadiwiria, Wimpie F Panjaitan. Index available. **Ad Acc. Circ:** 2,500 (ctrl). ***Supersedes** Economica.*
Desc: Current issues on economics, social, and culture in Indonesia.

LC HC **ISSN** 0013-0419
DD 330 AG
ECONOMICA.
[Economica]. **Added/Corp** Universidad Nacional de la Plata. Facultad de Ciencias Economicas. Vol. 1 (July/Sept. 1954)-. Periodical. Spanish. Irregular. $30.00. Facultad de Ciencias Economica, Calle 48 N 555 5 / University Plaza, 1900 La Plata Argentina.
Ind/Abst Contents Recent Econ. J.; Econ. Lit. Index (19??-); Geogr. Abstr. Human Geogr.; J. Econ. Lit.

LC HB1 .E5 **ISSN** 0013-0427
DD 330.5 UK
CCC
Pr Rev.
ECONOMICA (LONDON).
(ECONOMICA.). [Economica]. **Added/Corp** London School of Economics and Political Science. No. 1 (Jan. 1921)-No. 42 (Nov. 1933); New Ser., No. 1 (Feb. 1934)-. Academic Scholarly Publication. English. Four times a year. $88.00. Basil Blackwell Publishers Ltd., 108 Cowley Road, Oxford 0X4 1JF United Kingdom. **Tel** 011 44 1235 465500, FAX 011 44 1235 465556, telex 837022 OXBOOK G. **(Subscription address:** Blackwell Publishers / UK, 108 Cowley Road, Oxford OX4 1JF United Kingdom. **Tel** 011 44 1865 791100, FAX 011 44 1865 791347.) **ED** Frank Cowell, David de Mega, Rick van der Ploeg. Index available. cum. index. **Bk Rev. Ad Acc. Circ:** 3,150. available on microfilm and microfiche from University Microfilms International (UMI). Documents available from The Genuine Article, UMI Article Clearinghouse.
Desc: Devoted to economics, economic history, statistics and closely related problems in theoretical and empirical economics.
Ind/Abst ABI/INFORM Glob. Ed.; ABI/INFORM [Computer File] (Nov. 1971-Aug. 1973); Acad. Search; Am. Hist. Life (1954-); Br. Educ. Index (1954-); Bus. Source Plus; Bus. Source; Contents Recent Econ. J.; Contents Pages Manage.; Curr. Cit.; Curr. Contents Soc. Behav. Sci.; Econ. Lit. Index (199?-); EP Collect.; Homework Help.; INFO-SOUTH Abstr.; Int. Dev. Abstr.; Int. Labour Doc.; Int. Polit. Sci. Abstr.; J. Econ. Lit.; J. Plan. Lit.; Leis., Rec., Tour. Abstr.; MasterFile FullTEXT 1000; MasterFile FullTEXT 350; MasterFile FullTEXT 650; MasterFile FullTEXT (Jan. 1994-); Middle East Abstr. Index; Newsp. Period. Abstr. (1991-); OCLC; Res. Alert [Full Cov.]; Rural Dev. Abstr.; Selec. Coop. Index Manage. Period.; Soc. Sci. Source; Soc. Sci. Cit. Index [Full Cov.]; Soc. Sci. Index; Soc. Sci. Index Fulltext (Nov. 1988-) [Full Txt.]; Stat. Theory Method Abstr. (1959-1963, 1969, 1980-1981); Telebase; World Agric. Econ. Rural Sociol. Abstr.

US
•ECONOMICLEE.
(1995)-. English. Twelve times a year. $49.95. Economiclee, 15650 Roberts Lane, Ft. Myers FL 33908. **Tel** (941)481-1222.

AT
ECONOMICS.
Vol. 29 (Mar. 2, 1993)-. English. Four times a year (March, June, Sept., Dec.). Economics and Business Ed NSW, PO Box 333 8, Lakemba 2195 New South Wales Australia. **Tel** 011 61 2 7598917. ***Absorbed** Ectacom, 0813-9423.*
Ind/Abst Aust. Educ. Index (Mar. 1993-).

LC HB1 .E32 **ISSN** 0969-2509
UK
•ECONOMICS AND BUSINESS EDUCATION : THE QUARTERLY JOURNAL OF THE ECONOMICS ASSOCIATION.
Added/Corp Economics Association. Vol. 1, Pt. 1, No. 1 (Spring 1993)-. Periodical. English. Four times a year. $77.01. Economics and Business Education Association, 1 A Keymer Road, Hassocks West Sussex BN6 8AD United Kingdom. **Tel** 011 44 1273 846033, FAX 011 44 1273 8446646. ***Continues** Economics, 0300-4287.*
Ind/Abst Curr. Cit.

LC HB1 .E526 **ISSN** 0266-2671
DD 330/.05 UK
CCC
Pr Rev.
ECONOMICS AND PHILOSOPHY.
[Econ. philos.]. Vol. 1, No. 1 (Apr. 1985)-. Academic Scholarly Publication. English. Two times a year (April and October). $78.00. Cambridge University Press, The Edinburgh Building, Shaftesbury Road, Cambridge CB2 2RU United Kingdom. **Tel** 011 44 1223 312393, FAX 011 44 1223 315052, telex 851-817256. **(Subscription address:** Cambridge University Press / North America, 110 Midland Avenue, Port Chester NY 10573. **Tel** (800)431-1580, (914)937-9600.) **ED** Michael S. McPherson and Daniel M. Hausman. **Bk Rev.** available on microfilm from University Microfilms International (UMI). Documents available from The Genuine Article, UMI Article Clearinghouse.
Desc: Papers explore the foundations of economics as both a predictive/explanatory enterprise and a normative one. They examine the relevance of economic techniques, methods and conclusions to philosophical questions in ethics and social theory. Designed to foster collaboration between economists and philosophers and to bridge the increasingly artificial boundaries between them.
Ind/Abst ABI/INFORM Glob. Ed.; Arts Humanit. Citation Index [Select. Cov.]; Contents Recent Econ. J. (1985-); Curr. Cit.; Curr. Contents Soc. Behav. Sci.; Econ. Lit. Index (19??-); Int. Bibliogr. Sociol.; J. Econ. Lit.; J. Plan. Lit.; Philos. Index; Res. Alert [Full Cov.]; Soc. Plann. Policy Dev. Abstr.; Soc. Sci. Cit. Index [Full Cov.].

LC HD72 .E26 **ISSN** 0954-1985
DD 338.9/005 UK
CCC
ECONOMICS & POLITICS (OXFORD, ENGLAND).
(ECONOMICS & POLITICS.). [Econ. polit.]. **VFOAT** Economics and Politics. Vol. 1, No. 1 (Spring 1989)-. Academic Scholarly Publication. English. Three times a year. $164.00. Basil Blackwell Publishers Ltd., 108 Cowley Road, Oxford 0X4 1JF United Kingdom. **Tel** 011 44 1235 465500, FAX 011 44 1235 465556, telex 837022 OXBOOK G. **(Subscription address:** Blackwell Publishers / UK, 108 Cowley Road, Oxford OX4 1JF United Kingdom. **Tel** 011 44 1865 791100, FAX 011 44 1865 791347.) **Bk Rev. Ad Acc. Circ:** 300. available on microfilm and microfiche from University Microfilms International (UMI).
Desc: Brings together internationally known theorists work on political economy.
Ind/Abst Econ. Lit. Index (199?-); J. Econ. Lit.; Sage Public Adm. Abstr.

LC HB1 .I627 **ISSN** 0960-152X
DD 016.33 UK
CEASED
ECONOMICS AND RELATED DISCIPLINES.
Added/Corp British Library of Political and Economic Science. International Current Awareness Services. **VFOAT** Economics and Related Disciplines; Economics. Vol. 1 No. 1 (Nov. 1990)-(March 1994). Periodical. English. Routledge, 11 New Fetter Lane, London EC4P 4EE United Kingdom. **Tel** 011 44 171 5839855, FAX 011 44 171 5830701. **(Subscription address:** Kinokuniya Company Ltd., 38-1 Sakuragaoka 5, chome Setagaya-ku, Tokyo 156 Japan. **Tel** FAX 011 03 3439 0136.)

ISSN 1058-1758
DD 330 US
ECONOMICS (BOCA RATON, FLA.).
(ECONOMICS.). [Economics]. **Added/Corp** Social Issues Resources Series, inc. **VFOAT** SirS Global Perspectives, Economics. (1991)-. English. $80.00. Social Issues Resources Series Inc, PO Box 2348, Boca Raton FL 33427. **Tel** (800)327-0513, (407)994-0079.

US
ECONOMICS CLASSICS - OLD AND RARE BOOKS ON ECONOMICS.
(19??)-. English. Twelve times a year. $47.00 US; $60.00 other. American Classical College, Box 4526, Albuquerque NM 87196-4526. **ED** C. M. Flumian. **Bk Rev. Ad Acc. Circ:** 100.
Desc: News on famous and rare books by past economists.

ISSN 1034-6376
DD 330.071294 AT
Pr Rev.
ECONOMICS EDUCATION REVIEW.
[Econ. educ. rev.]. (1990)-. Newsletter. English. Six times a year. 32.06Aus$. Center for Independent Studies, PO Box 92, St Leonards New South Wales 2065 Australia. **Tel** 11 61 2 4384377, FAX 11 61 2 4397310, telex 71944. **ED** Tim Riley.
Desc: Economics newsletter for high school students and teachers.

LC HB61 .E26 **ISSN** 0090-4422
DD 330/.03 US
ECONOMICS : ENCYCLOPEDIA.
(1974)-. English. One time a year. Times Mirror Higher Education Group, 2460 Kerper Boulevard, Dubuque IA 52001. **Tel** (800)338-5578.

US
ECONOMICS FOR KIDS.
English. Three times a year. $8.95. National Council on Economic Education, 432 Park Ave South, New York NY 10016. **Tel** (212)685-5499, (800)338-1192, FAX (212)213-2872. ***Continues** The Elementary Economist.*

AT
ECONOMICS FOR THE GLOBAL GOOD.
(19??)-. English. Four times a year. 16.44Aus$. Economic Reform Australia, 14 Gallimore Avenue, Balmain New South Wales 2041 Australia. **Tel** 011 61 2 8107812.

US
ECONOMICS ILLUSTRATED.
English. Twelve times a year. $100.00. Bank of America Investment Research, 300 South Grand Avenue / Suite 2500, Los Angeles CA 90071. **Tel** (800)284-6074. **ED** Drew Brahos (editor's phone: (213)229-1963). **Ad Acc, Adv Mgr:** J. Simone, **Tel** (213)229-1961. **Circ:** 500.
Desc: A survey of the 17 Wall Street economists for quarterly and year over year estimates of various economic indicators. Aims to aid in making asset allocation, industry exposure decisions or speech writing.

LC HB1 .E53 **ISSN** 0165-1765
DD 330/.05 NE
CCC
CODEN ECLEDS
Pr Rev.
ECONOMICS LETTERS.
[Econ. lett.]. Vol. 1, No. 1 (1978)-. Periodical. English. Twelve times a year (3 vols.). $1295.00. Elsevier Sequoia SA, PO Box 564, CH-1001 Lausanne 1 Switzerland. **Tel** 011 41 21 3207381, FAX 011 41 21 3235444. **ED** Jerry Green. available on microfilm and microfiche from University Microfilms International (UMI); available on an online database from Elsevier Electronic Subscriptions (EES). Documents available from The Genuine Article.
Desc: Consists of short communications (letters) that provide a means of rapid and efficient dissemination of new results, models and methods in all fields of economic research.
Ind/Abst Contents Recent Econ. J.; Curr. Cit.; Curr. Contents Soc. Behav. Sci.; Econ. Lit. Index (199?-); Int. Bibliogr. Sociol.; J. Econ. Lit.; Math. Rev.; Res. Alert [Full Cov.]; Soc. Sci. Cit. Index [Full Cov.]; World Agric. Econ. Rural Sociol. Abstr.; Zentralbl. Math. Ihre Grenzgeb.

LC HC **ISSN** 0300-4287
DD 330 UK
TITLE CHANGE
ECONOMICS (LONDON).
(ECONOMICS.). [Economics]. **Added/Corp** Economics Association. Vol. 1 (1949)-(19??). Periodical. English. Economics and Business Education Association, 1 A Keymer Road, Hassocks West Sussex BN6 8AD United Kingdom. **Tel** 011 44 1273 846033, FAX 011 44 1273 8446646. **ED** Peter Maunder. **Bk Rev. Ad Acc. Circ:** 3,200 (ctrl). available on microfilm and microfiche from University Microfilms International (UMI). ***Continued by** Economics and Business Education.*
Desc: The official journal of the Economics Association; devoted to the publication of material connected with the teaching and learning of economics and kindred subjects.
Ind/Abst APAIS, Aust. Public Aff. Inf. Ser.; Br. Educ. Index; Br. Humanit. Index; Contents Pages Manage.; Curr. Index J. Educ.; Econ. Lit. Index; PAIS Int. Print (1991-).

AT
ECONOMICS MONITOR.
(19??)-. English. Twelve times a year. 200.00Aus$ (high schools); 100.00Aus$ (universities and libraries and other educational institutions); 495.00Aus$ (other). Access Economics Pty. Ltd., PO Box E347, Queen Victoria

Business and Economics

Terrace, Barton ACT 2600 Australia. **Tel** 011 61 6 2731222, FAX 011 61 6 2731223. ctrl circ.
Desc: An economic and corporate brief covering trends in the Australian and international economy designed for financial markets and business markets.

ISSN 1183-899X
DD 971/.005 CN
ECONOMICS OF CONFEDERATION.
[Econ. confed.]. **Added/Corp** Informetrica Limited. No. 1.0 (July 1991)-. Periodical. English. $500.00 per no. Informetrica Ltd, PO Box 828 Station B, Ottawa Ontario K1P 5P9 Canada. **Tel** (613)238-4831, FAX (613)238-7698.

LC HC10 .E418 **ISSN** 0013-0451
DD 338.9/009171/7 NE
CCC
ECONOMICS OF PLANNING. [Econ. plann.].
Added/Corp University of Birmingham. Centre for Russian and East European Studies. Norsk Utenrikspolitisk Institutt. **VFOAT** Ekonomika Planirovaniia. Vol. 3, No. 1 April (1963)-. Periodical. English. Three times a year. $188.00. Kluwer Academic Publishers, Postbus 322, 3300 AH Dordrecht The Netherlands. **Tel** 011 31 78 524400, FAX 011 31 78 183273, telex 20083. **ED** Wojciech W. Charemza, David Kemme, Subrata Ghatak. **Bk Rev. Ad Acc. Circ:** 750 (ctrl). available in microform from University Microfilms International (UMI). **Continues** St-Konomi.
Desc: Devoted to the study of micro and macroeconomic planning, related techniques, and algorithms and analysis of recent changes in economies traditionally associated with central planning. The aim of the journal is to provide a forum for wide economic discussion for authors working with the problems of planning and planned economies, representing various orientations and schools.
Ind/Abst Contents Recent Econ. J.; Econ. Lit. Index; Geogr. Abstr. Human Geogr.; Int. Dev. Abstr.; Int. Polit. Sci. Abstr.; J. Econ. Lit.; J. Plan. Lit.; Zentralbl. Math. Ihre Grenzgeb.

ISSN 0967-0750
UK
●**ECONOMICS OF TRANSITION, THE.**
Added/Corp European Bank for Reconstruction and Development. (Jan. 1993)-. Periodical. English. Four times a year. $280.00. Oxford University Press / UK, Walton Street, Oxford OX2 6DP United Kingdom. **Tel** 011 44 1865 56767, FAX 011 44 1865 267773, telex 851/837330 OXPRES G. (**Subscription address:** Oxford University Press / USA, Journals Marketing Department, Oxford University Press, 2001 Evans Road, Cary NC 27513. **Tel** (800)451-7556, (919)677-0977, FAX (919)677-1714.)

LC HB5 .E27 **ISSN** 0341-616X
GW
ECONOMICS (TUBINGEN). (ECONOMICS.).
[Economics]. **Added/Corp** Institut fur Wissenschaftliche Zusammenarbeit mit Hochschulen der Entwicklungslander (Tubingen, Germany). Vol 1 (1970)-. Periodical. English. Two times a year. $34.54. Institut fuer Wissenschaftliche Zusammenarbeit, A Wirt Recht Street, Landhausstr 18, D-72074 Tuebingen Germany. **Tel** 011 49 7071 21882, FAX 011 49 711 26753. **ED** Karl-Heinz W Bechtold. **Circ:** 3,000 (ctrl).
Ind/Abst PAIS Int. Print.

ISSN 0899-6555
DD 330 US
ECONOMICS UPDATE. (ECONOMICS UPDATE : A NEWSLETTER FROM THE FEDERAL RESERVE BANK OF ATLANTA.). [Econ. update].
Added/Corp Federal Reserve Bank of Atlanta. Vol. 1, No. 1 (Mar. 1988)-. Newsletter. English. Twelve times a year. Free on request. Federal Reserve Bank of Atlanta, 104 Marietta Street Northwest, Atlanta GA 30303. **Tel** (404)521-8788. **Continues** Economic Insight, 0896-8918.

LC HC440.8.A1 E3
DD 330/.05 BG
ECONOMICUS. (Oct. 1970)-. Periodical. English (English).

ISSN 0981-8715
FR
UDC 664
ECONOMIE AND GESTION AGRO-ALIMENTAIRE. See
Agriculture-Agricultural Economics.

LC HC271 .A25 **ISSN** 0249-4744
DD 330.944/005 FR
ECONOMIE & PREVISION. (ECONOMIE ET PREVISION. STATISTIQUES & ETUDES FINANCIERES, SERIE ECONOMIQUE.). [Econ. previs.].
Added/Corp France. Ministere de l'Economie. Direction de la Prevision. France. Ministere de l'Economie et des Finances. Direction de la Prevision. **VFOAT** Economie et Prevision. Statistiques & Etudes Financieres. No. 46 (1981)-. French. Five times a year. $87.49. Imprimerie Nationale / France, BP 514, 59505 Douai Cedex France. **Tel** 011 33 27 937090. **Continues** Statistiques & Etudes Financieres. Serie Orange.
Ind/Abst Int. Labour Doc.

LC HB3 .E21 **ISSN** 0013-0494
DD 330.5 SZ
ECONOMIE APPLIQUEE. [Econ. appl.].
Added/Corp Institut de Science Economique Appliquee (Paris, France) Institut de Sciences Mathematiques et Economiques Appliquees (Paris, France). Vol. 1 (Jan./March 1948)-. Periodical. French. Four times a year. 625.59F France; 690.00F other. Presses Universite de Grenoble, BP 47, 38040 Grenoble, Cedex 9 France. **Tel** 011 33 76 825651, 011 33 76 825652. **ED** De Bernis. cum. index. **Bk Rev. Circ:** 1,000. **Supersedes** Institut de Science Economique Appliquee. Bulletin.
Desc: Mathematical economy.
Ind/Abst Econ. Lit. Index; Int. Bibliogr. Sociol.; Int. Labour Doc.; J. Econ. Lit.; Stat. Theory Method Abstr. (1959-1963).

ISSN 1188-4304
DD 330/.025/714 CN
●**ECONOMIE ET AFFAIRES AU QUEBEC.**
(REPERTOIRE DESCRIPTIF. ECONOMIE ET AFFAIRES AU QUEBEC.). [Econ. aff. Que.].
Added/Corp Quebec dans le Monde (Association). **VFOAT** Economie et Affaires au Quebec. (1992/1993)-. French. Every 2 years. 39.95Can$. Quebec Dans Le Monde, CP 8503, Sainte-Foy Quebec G1V 4N5 Canada. **Tel** (418)659-5540, FAX (418)659-4143. **Continues** Repertoire Descriptif. Le Monde de l'Economie et des Affaires au Quebec., 0847-4974.

ISSN 0070-8798
FR
ECONOMIE ET FINANCES AGRICOLES. See Agriculture-Agricultural Economics.

LC HB3 .E24 **ISSN** 0424-3218
FR
ECONOMIE ET POLITIQUE (PARIS. 1954). (ECONOMIE ET POLITIQUE.). [Econ. polit.].
VFOAT Economie & Politique. No. 1 (April 1954)-. Periodical. French. Six times a year. $104.98. Economie & Politique, 2 Place du Colonel Fabien, 75940 Paris Cedex 19 France. **Tel** 011 33 1 40401340. cum. index.
Ind/Abst Foreign Lang. Index.

LC HC **ISSN** 0424-3226
DD 330.9 FR
Pr Rev.
ECONOMIE ET SOCIALISME. (1964)-.
Monographic series. French. Four times a year. Price varies per volume. Revue Economie et Socialisme, BP 6330, Rabat Morocco. **Tel** 011 212 7 61380, FAX 011 212 7 73889. **ED** Thami El-Khyari. **Bk Rev. Ad Acc.**
Desc: Reports problems in economic development in Morocco, Africa, and the world.
Ind/Abst Int. Labour Doc.; LABORDOC; PAIS Int. Print.

ISSN 0336-1454
FR
ECONOMIE ET STATISTIQUE. See Business and Economics-Abstracting, Bibliographies and Statistics.

ISSN 0247-3372
FR
ECONOMIE PAPETIERE. [Econ. papet.].
(1980)-. Periodical. French. Twelve times a year. $601.48. Communication Conseil International, 5 rue des Gravilliers, F 75003 Paris France. **Tel** 011 33 1 42728066.

LC HC **ISSN** 0013-0559
FR
ECONOMIE RURALE. See Agriculture-Agricultural Economics.

LC HB3 .E27 **ISSN** 0013-0567
FR
ECONOMIES ET SOCIETES. [Econ. soc.].
Added/Corp Institut de Sciences Mathematiques et Economiques Appliquees (Paris, France) Institut de Science Economique Appliquee (Paris, France). Vol. 1 (1967)-. Periodical. French (English). Twelve times a year. 1224.29F France; 1350.00F other. Economies et Societes, 18 rue Pierre et Marie Curie, 75005 Paris France. (**Subscription address:** Presses Univ de Grenoble, BP 47, 38040 Grenoble Cedex 09 France.)
Bk Rev. Ad Acc. Circ: 1,000. **Absorbed** Cahiers de l'Institut de Science Economique Appliquee.
Ind/Abst Econ. Lit. Index; Int. Bibliogr. Sociol.; Int. Labour Doc.; J. Econ. Lit.; LABORDOC; PAIS Int. Print; Selec. Coop. Index Manage. Period.; Wheat Barley Trit. Abstr.; World Agric. Econ. Rural Sociol. Abstr.

LC HC **ISSN** 0820-8816
DD 330/.06/0714 CN
ECONOMIQUE (MONTREAL).
(L'ECONOMIQUE : BULLETIN DE LA FONDATION QUEBECOISE D'EDUCATION ECONOMIQUE.). [Economique]. Vol. 2, No. 1 (June 1980)-. Bulletin. French (English). Three times a year. Free. Fondation Quebecoise Loisir Litteraire, 4545 Av Pierre Coubertin Succ M CP 1000 Montreal, Quebec H1V 3R2 Canada. **Continues** Fondation Quebecoise d'Education Economique. Bulletin d'Informations, 0709-9827.

LC HC **ISSN** 0013-0575
BE
ECONOMISCH EN SOCIAAL TIJDSCHRIFT. [Econ. soc. tijdschr.]. Vol. 1 (Feb. 1947)-. Periodical. Dutch (English and French). Four times a year. $58.09. Economisch en Sociaal Tijdschrift, Kipdorp 19, 2000 Antwerpen Belgium. **Tel** 32 3 2204746, 32 3 2204747. **ED** E. Van de Voorde. Index available. **Bk Rev.** (Qty: 120). **Ad Acc, Adv Mgr:** E. Van de Voorde. **Circ:** 2,000. available on microfilm from University Microfilms International (UMI). **Absorbed** Vie Economique et Sociale.
Desc: Developments in economic and social sciences, their relevance for business practice, professional management, interdisciplinary treatment of subjects in an accessible language and approach and comments on socio-economic trends and developments.
Ind/Abst Int. Bibliogr. Sociol.; J. Econ. Lit. (1968-1985).

LC HC317.L4 G23
DD 330 BE
ECONOMISCH RAPPORT. Added/Corp Gewestelijke Ontwikkelingsmaatschappij (Limburg, Belgium). (1988)-. Dutch. Four times a year. Gewestelijke Ontwikkelingsmaatschappij, Kunstlaan 18, 3500 Hasselt Belgium. **Tel** (011)272966, FAX (011)221706, telex 39 265. **Continues** Economisch Situatierapport.

UK
ECONOMIST DESK DIARY. English. One time a year. £31.95, $60.00 UK; £31.00, $58.00 Europe; £35.00, $66.00 (surface mail), £39.00, $74.00 (airmail) other. Economist, Diary Department, 25 St. James Street, London SW1A 1HG United Kingdom. **Tel** 011 44 14023 81555, FAX 011 44 14023 81211, telex 927809.
Desc: Contains addresses, telephone and fax numbers of hotels throughout the world. Includes a table of international dialing codes, a chart of worldwide national holidays and a map of time zones.

UK
ECONOMIST QUARTERLY INDEX, THE.
See Business and Economics-Abstracting, Bibliographies and Statistics.

ISSN 0013-0648
AG
ECONOMISTA, EL. [Economista]. Vol. 1, No. 1 (1950)-. Periodical. Spanish. One time a week (Fri.). $130.00. Economista Empresa Editorial, Cordoba 632, Buenos Aires Argentina.

ISSN 0013-0656
SP
UDC 33
ECONOMISTA (MADRID. 1886), EL.
[Economista Madr., 1886]. (1886)-. Periodical. Spanish. One time a week (48 issues per year). $103.92. Economista, Calle Conde Aranda 8, Apartado 1024, Madrid 1 Spain. **Tel** 011 34 1 5771708, 577-1709.
Ind/Abst PROMT.

ISSN 0212-4386
SP
ECONOMISTAS (MADRID, SPAIN).
(ECONOMISTAS.). **Added/Corp** Colegio de Economistas de Madrid. No. 1 (April 1983)-. Periodical. Spanish. Six times a year. 4500ptas Spain; 7000ptas other Europe; 8000ptas other. Colegio de Economistas, Hermosilla 49, 28001 Madrid Spain. **Tel** 011 34 1 526-8064. **Ad Acc. Circ:** 11,000.
Desc: Articles concerning the Spanish economy.
Ind/Abst PAIS Int. Print (1991-).

ISSN 1063-1208
DD 330 US
ECONOMY AT A GLANCE, THE. (THE ECONOMY AT A GLANCE: A SUMMARY OF KEY ECONOMIC STATISTICS.). [Econ. glance]. **Added/Corp** J.E. Gross & Associates. Vol. 1, No. 1 (Apr. 1992)-. Periodical. English. Twelve times a year. $185.00. J E Gross & Associates, One Crosfield Avenue, West Nyack NY 10994. **Tel** (914)358-7019, FAX (914)358-8074.

UK
ECONOMY BULLETINS. (19??)-. Bulletin. English. Twenty-four times a year. £105.00. SUBIS, Mansion House 19 Kingfield Road, Sheffield S11 9AS United Kingdom. **Tel** 011 44 114 2554433, FAX 011 44 114 255 4626. **Ad Acc.**
Desc: A series of current awareness bulletins for researchers in clinical and life sciences.

LC HC
US
ECONOMY SPECTATOR. (19??)-. Periodical. English.

LC HC440.5.A1 P23A
DD 330.95491/005 PK
ECONOMY SURVEY. Main/Corp Pakistan. Economic Adviser's Wing. **VFOAT** Pakistan Economic Survey. (1982/83)-. English. One time a year. NGM Communication, 3-D-1 Gulberg III, Near TP Exchange, Lahore 54660 Pakistan. **Tel** 011 92 21 428625, FAX 011 92 21 613854. **Continues** Pakistan Economic Survey.

LC HC111 ISSN 0712-2012
DD 330.971/005 CN
ECONOSCOPE. [Econoscope]. **Added/Corp** Royal Bank of Canada. Royal Bank of Canada. Economics Dept. Vol. 1, No. 1 (Oct. 1977)-. Periodical. English. Twelve times a year. 160.06Can$. Royal Bank of Canada, 200 Bay Street, 18th Floor South Tower, Toronto Ontario M5J 2J5 Canada. **Tel** (416)974-7242. **ED** Dawn Aspinall. available on microfiche from University Microfilms International (UMI); available on an online database (file 636/Full-Text) from DIALOG.
Desc: Economic analysis for Canada and the United States.
Ind/Abst PTS Newsl. Database [Full Txt.].

LC HC331 .E33 ISSN 0733-5989
DD 330.947/005 SZ
CCC
CEASED
ECOTASS (ENGLISH EDITION). (ECOTASS / TASS.). [Ecotass]. **Added/Corp** Telegrafnoe Agentstvo SSSR. (19??)-(1993). Periodical. English (French, German and Italian). Pergamon Press, An Imprint of Elsevier Science Ltd., The Boulevard, Langford Lane, Kidlington, Oxford OX5 1GB United Kingdom. **Tel** 011 44 1865 843000, 011 44 1865 843699, FAX 011 44 1865 843010. **ED** Tass News Agency. available on microfilm and microfiche from University Microfilms International (UMI); available on an online database (file 649/Full-Text) from DIALOG.
Desc: Only regular source of economic and commercial information from the USSR. It gives exporters, importers, financial analysts, bankers and economists a weekly update on policy issues such as the Soviet Union's line towards business contracts with the West and practical developments such as new contracts signed or under discussion with the Soviet Union.
Ind/Abst F&S Index Plus Text, Int. [Select. Cov.]; Predicasts Forecasts.

US
ECOTRENDS. (19??)-. English. Twelve times a year. $575.00. ITR Associates Inc., PO Box 278, Contoocook NH 03229. **Tel** (603)746-3135.

ISSN 0813-9423
AT
TITLE CHANGE
ECTACOM. (19??)-Vol. 29 (Mar. 2, 1993). English. Economics and Commercial Teachers Association of New South Wales, PO Box 333 8, Lakemba 2195 NSW Australia. **Tel** 61 2 7598917. ***Merged into** Economics EFF.*
Ind/Abst Aust. Educ. Index (?-Mar. 1993).

GW
EDEKA HANDELSRUNDSCHAU. (19??)-. German. Twenty-four times a year. DM80.40. Edeka Verlag, New York Ring 6, W 2000 Hamburg 60 FR Germany. **Tel** 011 49 40 93771.

US
EDGE. (19??)-. Periodical. English. Four times a year. $14.95. Entrepreneurial Edge, 656 East Swedesford Road, Suite 220, Wayne PA 19087. **Tel** (610)975-9130, FAX (610)975-9094. **ED** Jill Bond. **Ad Acc.**

LC Z7164.C81 E34 H5548.33 ISSN 1045-5698
DD 016.004 US
SUSPENDED
EDI (DALLAS, TEX.). **See** Computers-Electronic Data Processing.

ISSN 1048-3047
DD 005 US
CODEN EDFOE2
Pr Rev.
EDI FORUM. (EDI FORUM: THE JOURNAL OF ELECTRONIC DATA INTERCHANGE.). [EDI forum]. **VAT** Electronic Data Interchange Forum. (1989)-. English. Four times a year (Apr., July, Oct., Dec.). $250.00. EDI Group, Ltd, 221 Lake Street, PO Box 710, Oak Park IL 60302. **Tel** (708)848-0135, FAX (708)848-0270. **ED** Fred Lenhoff. cum. index. **Bk Rev**, (Qty: 5-10/yr). **Ad Acc**, **Adv Mgr:** Trinda Gray O'Connor, **Tel** (708)848-0135. **Circ:** 5,000. Documents available from Ask*IEEE.
Desc: The goal is to help facilitate the conversion of business-to-business communication from paper- and mail-based processes to electric processes.
Ind/Abst INSPEC (1992-).

ISSN 1013-2015
US
EDI SEMINAR PAPER, AN. **VAT** Economic Development Institute Seminar Paper. No. 37 (1988)-. English. Irregular. World Bank Publications, 1818 H Street Northwest, Washington DC 20043. **Tel** (202)473-1155, (202)473-1155, FAX (202)522-3224, telex WUI 64145 WORLDBANK. ***Continues** Seminar Paper Series.*
Ind/Abst Rural Dev. Abstr.; World Agric. Econ. Rural Sociol. Abstr.

ISSN 0712-4546
DD 380.1/097123/3 CN
EDMONTON AND ALBERTA BUSINESS. [Edmont. Alta. bus.]. Vol. 3, No. 48 (Sept. 1981)-. Periodical. English. One time a week. $1.00 per no. Whiskey Jack Publications, PO Box 76844, Station S, Vancouver BC V5R 5S7 Canada. ***Continues** Alberta Business, 0709-0005.*

ISSN 0964-5292
UK
CCC
•EDUCATION ECONOMICS. **See** Education.

ISSN 0990-5413
FR
UDC 37
EDUCATION ECONOMIE (PARIS). (EDUCATION ECONOMIE.). [Educ. econ. Paris]. (1988)-. Periodical. French. Four times a year. $29.52. Centre National Documentation Pedagogique, 21 Square St. Charles, BP 7, 75012 Paris France. **Tel** 011 33 1 40020333, 011 33 1 46349425. **(Subscription address:** CNDP Abonnements, B 750, 60732 Genevieve Cedex 9 France. **Tel** 011 33 44 033237, FAX 011 33 44 074336.**)**

US
EEOC COMPLIANCE MANUAL (COMMERCE CLEARING HOUSE EDITION). (EEOC COMPLIANCE MANUAL.). **Added/Corp** United States. Equal Employment Opportunity Commission. Commerce Clearing House. (1975)-. English. Irregular. $228.00. Bureau of National Affairs Inc., 9435 Key West Avenue, Rockville MD 20850. **Tel** (800)372-1033, (301)258-1033, FAX (301)948-5823. **ED** Susan J Sala.
Desc: A two-binder monthly service containing the complete text of the Equal Employment Opportunity Commission, with monthly notification of related developments.

US
EFFECTIVE BUSINESS WRITING. (19??)-. English. Forty-six times a year. $135.70. Economics Press Inc, 12 Daniel Road, Fairfield NJ 07004. **Tel** (201)227-1224, (800)526-2554, FAX (201)227-9742.
Desc: Strives to tackle the breadth and depth of all the kinds of writing that are required to communicate effectively in business today.

LC HC531 .E4 ISSN 0013-239X
DD 330.962 UA
EGYPTE CONTEMPORAINE, L'. [Egypte contemp.]. **Added/Corp** Societe Egyptienne d'Economie Politique, de Statistique et de Legislation. Societe Fouad Premier d'Economie Politique, de Statistique et de Legislation. **VFOAT** Misr al-Muasir. Vol. 1, No. 1 (Jan. 1910)-. Periodical. French. Four times a year. $90.00. Societe d'Economie Politique Stat, Avenue Ramses, 16 Boite Postale 732, Cairo Egypt. **Tel** 011 20 2 52797.
Desc: Economic conditions and international law which relate to Egypt and Arab countries and statistical studies.
Ind/Abst Int. Labour Doc.; Int. Polit. Sci. Abstr.; PAIS Int. Print (1991-?).

LC AS182.T58 A2
PL
EKONOMIA I ORGANIZACJA. No. 1-. Monographic series. Polish. Price varies per volume.

LC HC ISSN 0013-3035
XO
Pr Rev.
EKONOMICKY CASOPIS. **Added/Corp** Slovenska Akademia Vied. Vol. 1 (1953)-. Periodical. Slovak (summaries and/or abstracts in English and Russian). Twelve times a year. DM259.00 Germany; DM319.00 other. Veda, Publishing House of the Slovak Academy of Sciences, Klemensova 19, 814 30 Bratislava Slovakia. **Tel** (7)583-15. **(Subscription address:** Kubon & Sagner, ABT Zeitschriftenimport, D 80328 Munich Germany. **Tel** 011 49 89 54218130.**)** **ED** Egon Hlavaty. **Bk Rev**. **Ad Acc. Circ:** 2,900 (ctrl). Documents available from The Genuine Article.
Desc: Deals with current problems of the political economy in socialism and capitalism. Bears upon theoretical questions having to do with the development of the national economy and with various problems of the diverse economical branches.
Ind/Abst Curr. Contents Soc. Behav. Sci.; Geogr. Abstr. Human Geogr.; Int. Bibliogr. Sociol.; Int. Dev. Abstr. (?-?); Res. Alert [Full Cov.]; Soc. Sci. Cit. Index [Full Cov.].

TU
EKONOMIK PANORAMA. Turkish. One time a week. Gelisim Yaynlar Buyukdere Cad, Ali Kaya Sok No1 8 A, 80720 Levent Istanbul Turkey. **Tel** 011 90 11 1 1696680.

LC HB74.M3 E52 ISSN 0424-7388
DD 330 RU
CODEN EMAMBV
EKONOMIKA I MATEMATICHESKIE METODY. [Ekon. mat. metody]. **Added/Corp** Tsentralnyi Ekonomiko-Matematicheskii Institut (Akademiia Nauk SSSR). **VFOAT** Economics and Mathematical Methods. (1965)-. Academic Scholarly Publication. Russian. Four times a year. $202.50. Izdatelstvo Nauka / Akademiia Nauk, (Publishing House of the Russian Academy of Sciences), Leninskii Porspekt 14, 117901 Moscow Russia. **Tel** 011 95 9542153, FAX 011 95 9382144, telex 411964. **(Subscription address:** East View Publications Inc., 3020 Harbor Lane North, Suite 110, Minneapolis MN 55447. **Tel** (800)477-1005, (612)550-0961, FAX (612)559-2931.**)** **ED** V.L. Makarov. **Circ:** 3,500. Documents available from BLDSC.
Ind/Abst Math. Rev. (?-199?).

RU
EKONOMIKA I ZHIZN. (Jan. 1990)-. Periodical. Russian. One time a week. $239.95. **(Subscription address:** Victor Kamkin, 4956 Boiling Brook Parkway, Rockville MD 20852. **Tel** (301)881-5973.**)** ***Continues** Ekonomicheskaia Gazeta, 0013-3132.*
Ind/Abst F&S Index Plus Text, Int. [Select. Cov.].

LC HC337.U5 E36
DD 330 UN
EKONOMIKA UKRAINY. **Added/Corp** Ukraine. Ministerstvo Ekonomiky. Akademiia Nauk Ukrainy. (1991)-. Periodical. Ukrainian. Twelve times a year. $95.00. **(Subscription address:** East View Publications Inc., 3020 Harbor Lane North, Suite 110, Minneapolis MN 55447. **Tel** (800)477-1005, (612)550-0961, FAX (612)559-2931.**)** ***Continues** Ekonomika Radianskoi Ukrainy, 0131-775X.*

LC HB135 .E432
RU
EKONOMIKO-MATEMATICHESKIE MODELI. **Added/Corp** Tsentralnyi Ekonomiko-Matematicheskii Institut (Akademiia Nauk SSSR). (19??)-. Russian. Nauka, 103717 GSP K-62, Podsosenskii Per 21, Moscow Russia. **Tel** 296-472.

LC HC ISSN 1100-3413
DD 330 SW
EKONOMISKA RADETS ARSBOK. **VFOAT** Ekonomiska Radet; Arsbok. (1980)-. Swedish. One time a year. Ekonomiska Radet, Box 3116, S 103 62 Stockholm Sweden. **Tel** 011 46 8 4535939.

LC HC ISSN 0013-3183
DD 330 FI
EKONOMISKA SAMFUNDETS TIDSKRIFT. [Ekon. samf. tidskr.]. **Added/Corp** Ekonomiska Samfundet I Finland. (1913)-(1921); New Series (1923)-(1947); 3rd Series (1948)-. Periodical. Swedish (summaries and/or abstracts in English). Four times a year. Fmk150.00. Ekonomiska Samfundets Tidskrift / Economic Society of Finland, Swedish School of Economics, Arkadiagatan 22, SF 00100 Helsinski Finland. **Tel** 011 358 0 601322, FAX 011 358 0 601753. **ED** Marianne Stenius. Index available. **Bk Rev**. **Ad Acc. Circ:** 1,400 (ctrl). Documents available from The Genuine Article. ***Supersedes** Foeredrag O. Foerhandlingar.*
Ind/Abst Curr. Contents Soc. Behav. Sci.; Econ. Lit. Index (19??-); J. Econ. Lit.; Res. Alert [Full Cov.]; Selec. Coop. Index Manage. Period.; Soc. Sci. Cit. Index [Full Cov.].

DK
EKONOMISKA UTSIKTER I NORDEN. (THE OUTLOOK FOR THE NORDIC ECONOMIES.). (198?)-. English (translations available in Swedish). One time a year.

LC HC331 .P52
DD 330 RU
CODEN EKONEP
EKONOMIST. **Added/Corp** Soviet Union. Ministerstvo Ekonomiki I Prognozirovaniia. (1991)-. Periodical. Russian. Twelve times a year. $99.95. Izdatelstvo Ekonomika, Berezhkovskaia Nab. 6, 121864 Moscow Russia. **(Subscription address:** East View Publications Inc., 3020 Harbor Lane North, Suite 110, Minneapolis MN 55447. **Tel** (800)477-1005, (612)550-0961, FAX (612)559-2931.**)** ***Continues** Planovoe Khoziaistvo, 0370-0356.*
Ind/Abst LABORDOC; World Agric. Econ. Rural Sociol. Abstr.

LC HC ISSN 0013-3191
DD 330 CI
EKONOMIST : ORGAN DRUSTVA EKONOMISTA SRBIJE. **Added/Corp** Savez Ekonomista Jugoslavije. Drustvo Ekonomista Srbije. Savez Drustava Ekonomista Jugoslavije. Vol. 1 (1948)-. Periodical. Serbo-Croatian (Roman). Four times a year. $290.00. **(Subscription address:** Jugoslovenska Knjiga, PO Box 36, YU 11001 Belgrade Yugoslovia. **Tel** 011 38 11 621055, FAX 011 38 11 325970.**)** Index available. cum. index.

ISSN 0013-0621
DD 330 JA
EKONOMISUTO (TOKYO. 1946). [Ekonomisuto Tokyo, 1946]. **VFOAT** Economist (Tokyo. 1946). (1946)-. Periodical. Japanese. One time a week. 3380.00F. Economist Intelligence Unit / Essex, PO Box 14 Harold Hill, Romford RM3 8EQ, Essex United Kingdom. **Tel** 011 44 1322 289194, FAX 011 44 1322 223803. ***Continues** Keizai Mainichi, 0386-0736.*

LC HB9 .D733 ISSN 0424-7558
DD 330 CI
EKONOMSKI PREGLED. [Ekon. pregl.]. **Added/Corp** Drustvo Ekonomista Hrvatske. Savez Ekonomista Hrvatske. (1950)-. Periodical. Serbo-Croatian (Roman) (summaries and/or abstracts in English and Russian; table of contents in English and Russian).

Business and Economics

Twelve times a year. $22.00. **(Subscription address:** Mladost Export Import, Borongajska 69, 41000 Zagreb Croatia. **Tel** 011 385 1 221488, 011 385 1 215853.) cum. index.
Ind/Abst Am. Hist. Life (1970-).

ISSN 0733-5997
FR
EKOTASS (DEUTSCHE AUSGABE).
(EKOTASS.). [Ekotass]. **Added/Corp** Telegrafnoe Agentstvo SSSR. (19??)-. Periodical. German. One time a week. Pergamon Press, An Imprint of Elsevier Science Ltd., The Boulevard, Langford Lane, Kidlington, Oxford OX5 1GB United Kingdom. **Tel** 011 44 1865 843000, 011 44 1865 843699, FAX 011 44 1865 843010. available on microfilm and microfiche from University Microfilms International (UMI).
Ind/Abst F&S Index Plus Text, Int. [Select. Cov.]; PROMT.

ISSN 8750-6033
DD 330
US
CEASED
EL PASO ECONOMIC REVIEW (1983), THE. (THE EL PASO ECONOMIC REVIEW.). [El Paso econ. rev.]. (1983)-(19??). Periodical. English. The El Paso Economic Review, The Bureau of Business & Economic Research, The University of Texas at El Paso. **Tel** (915)747-5122. **ED** David Schauer. Index available. **Circ:** 2,000. **Continues in part** Southwest Business and Economic Review, 0195-198X.
Desc: Economic and industrial development of the El Paso, Texas metroplex, including West Texas, Southern New Mexico, and the State of Chihuahua, Mexico.

ISSN 1070-8928
DD 333
US
●**ELECTRICITY DAILY REPORT, THE.**
[Electr. dly. rep.]. (June 1993)-. Periodical. English. Seven times a week (publishes daily except national holidays and the last two weeks of Dec.). $895.00. The Electricity Journal, 1501 Western Avenue, Suite 100, Seattle WA 98101. **Tel** (206)382-0195, (800)326-1676, FAX (206)382-0098. **ED** Robert O. Marritz. **Circ:** 200 (ctrl).

UK
ELECTRONIC ANBAR. English. Twelve times a year. $8,249.00. MCB University Press, 60 62 Toller Lane, Bradford, West Yorkshire BD8 9BY United Kingdom. **Tel** 011 44 1274 785280, FAX 011 44 1274 785200, telex 51317-MCBUNI-G. **(Subscription address:** MCB University Press / US and Canada Subscriptions, PO Box 10812, Birmingham AL 35201-0812. **Tel** (205)995-1567, (800)633-4931, FAX (205)995-1588.) **Continues** Floppy Anbar.

ISSN 1071-8524
DD 332
US
CCC
●**ELECTRONIC CLAIMS PROCESSING REPORT.** [Electron. claims process. rep.]. **Added/Corp** Phillips Business Information, Inc. (1993)-. Periodical. English. Twenty-five times a year. $495.00. Phillips Business Information Inc., 1201 Seven Locks Road, PO Box 61130, Potomac MD 20854. **Tel** (301)424-3338, (301)340-1520, (800)777-5005, FAX (301)424-4297, telex 358149.

ISSN 0954-0393
US
ELECTRONIC PAYMENTS INTERNATIONAL. [Electron. paym. int.]. (1988)-. Periodical. English. Ten times a year. $749.00. Lafferty Publications Ltd., Tower Ida Centre Pearse Street, Dublin 2 Ireland. **Tel** 011 353 1 6718022, FAX 011 353 1 718520. **Continues** RBI EFTPOS International, 0269-459X.
Desc: Business intelligence for all those involved in electronic payments. Covers the world of electronic banking, smart cards, electronic data interchange, automated payments and corporate EFT.

LC H62.5.A9 E5 ISSN 0340-8744
DD 330/.07/20436 GW
CCC
Pr Rev.
EMPIRICA. [Empirica]. **Added/Corp** Osterreichisches Institut fur Wirtschaftsforschung. (1974)-. Periodical. German (English). Three times a year. $175.00. Kluwer Academic Publishers, Postbus 322, 3300 AH Dordrecht The Netherlands. **Tel** 011 31 78 524400, FAX 011 31 78 183273, telex 20083. **ED** Peter Mooslechner. **Acid Free.**
Desc: Publishes articles and papers dealing with all kinds of problems relevant to economic policy, focusing principally on three areas of research: industrial economics, economic integration, and economic policy.
Ind/Abst Econ. Lit. Index; J. Econ. Lit.

LC HB1.A1 E46 ISSN 0377-7332
DD 330/.05 AU
CCC
EMPIRICAL ECONOMICS. [Empir. econ.].
Added/Corp Institut fuer Hohere Studien und Wissenschaftliche Forschung (Vienna, Austria). Vol. 1 (1976)-. Periodical. English. Four times a year. $453.00. Physica-Verlag GmbH & Company, Postfach 105280, D-69042 Heidelberg Germany. **Tel** 011 49 6221 487492,

011 49 6221 345186, FAX 011 49 6221 487177 und 487366, telex 461723 sphbd-d. **(Subscription address:** Springer-Verlag New York Inc. / North America, PO Box 2485, Journal Fulfillment, Secaucus NJ 07096. **Tel** (201)348-4033, (800)777-4643, FAX (201)348-4505.) **ED** W. Franz, B. Raj, and A. Worgotter. **Ad Acc. Circ:** 500. Documents available from UMI Article Clearinghouse.
Desc: Aims to publish papers of high quality dealing with the confrontation of relevant economic theory with observed data through the use of adequate econometric methods. Preference is given to contribution about industrialized market economies.
Ind/Abst ABI/INFORM Glob. Ed.; Curr. Cit.; Econ. Lit. Index; Geogr. Abstr. Human Geogr. (?-?); Int. Abstr. Oper. Res. [Select. Cov.]; J. Econ. Lit.; Oper. Res./Manage. Sci.; World Agric. Econ. Rural Sociol. Abstr.

ISSN 0899-8833
DD 331
US
EMPLOYEE OWNERSHIP REPORT, THE. (THE EMPLOYEE OWNERSHIP REPORT : A PUBLICATION OF THE NATIONAL CENTER FOR EMPLOYEE OWNERSHIP, INC.). [Empl. ownersh. rep.].
Added/Corp National Center for Employee Ownership (U.S.). (198?)-. Periodical. English. Six times a year (Feb., Apr., June, Aug., Oct., Dec.). $70.00 (institutions); $30.00 (individuals) Comes with National Center for Employee Ownership membership. National Center for Employee Ownership, 1201 Martin Luther King Jr. Way, 2nd Floor, Oakland CA 94612. **Tel** (510)272-9461, FAX (510)272-9510. **ED** Corey Roben and Karen Young. cum. index. **Bk Rev. Circ:** 1,600. **Continues** Employee Ownership.
Desc: News of employee ownership in businesses, legislative proposals and changes, events and new books.

US
EMPLOYEE OWNERSHIP RESOURCE GUIDE. Added/Corp National Center for Employee Ownership (U.S.). (19??)-. Periodical. English. Two times a year. National Center for Employee Ownership, 1201 Martin Luther King Jr. Way, 2nd Floor, Oakland CA 94612. **Tel** (510)272-9461, FAX (510)272-9510.

BO
ENCUESTAS DE COYUNTURA (BOLIVIA). Main/Corp Bolivia. Ministerio de Planeamiento y Coordinacion. Periodical. Spanish. Ministerio de Planeamiento y Coordinacion Direccion de Planeamiento y Politica Global, Bolivia.

IT
ENERGIA ED ECONOMIA. (19??)-. Italian. One time a year. L15000. ENEA, V le Regina Margherita 125, 00198 Rome Italy. **Tel** 011 39 6 85281.

ISSN 1079-5855
DD 333
US
●**ENERGY DAILY'S NUCLEAR REMEDIATION WEEK, THE.** [Energy dly. nucl. remediat. week]. **VFOAT** Nuclear Remediation Week. (1994)-. Periodical. English. One time a week. $734.96. King Publishing Group, 627 National Press Building, Washington DC 20045. **Tel** (202)638-4260, FAX (202)662-9744. **Continues** Nuclear Remediation Report.

LC HD9502.A1 E5345 ISSN 0140-9883
DD 333.7 UK
CCC
CODEN EECODR
Pr Rev.
ENERGY ECONOMICS. See Energy.

LC K ISSN 1059-5813
DD 344 US
CCC
CODEN EECCEQ
ENERGY, ECONOMICS AND CLIMATE CHANGE. See Energy.

ISSN 1059-6402
DD 323 US
ENLACE (WASHINGTON, D.C. 1991).
(ENLACE : POLITICA Y DERECHOS HUMANOS EN LAS AMERICAS.). [Enlace]. **Added/Corp** Washington Office on Latin America. Vol. 1, No. 1 (Nov. 1991)-. Periodical. Spanish. Four times a year. Washington Office on Latin America, 110 Maryland Avenue NE, Suite 404, Washington DC 20002.

US
ENRICH!. English. Six times a year. $35.00. National Chamber of Commerce for Women, 10 Waterside Plaza/ Suite 6H, New York NY 10010. **Tel** (212)685-3454. **ED** Maggie Rinaldi. Index available. cum. index. **Bk Rev. Ad Acc.** ctrl circ. available on diskette; available on labels.
Desc: Shows how to increase cash flow yet ease work flow.

ISSN 0101-1723
BL
ENSAIOS FEE. [Ensaios FEE]. **Added/Corp** Rio Grande do Sul (Brazil). Fundacao de Economia e Estatistica. **VFOAT** Ensaios F.E.E. **VAT** Ensaios

Fundacao de Economia e Estatistica. Vol. 1, No. 1 (Jun. 1980)-. Portuguese. Two times a year. Fundacao de Economia e Estatistica, Rua Duque de Caixias 1691, 90010 Porto Alegre, Rio Grande do Sul Brazil. **Tel** 0512-259455, FAX 0512-25006, telex 0515042. cum. index.
Ind/Abst PAIS Int. Print.

LC HC121 .P754a ISSN 0102-0617
DD 330.9/8/003 BL
ENSAYOS ECIEL. [Ens. ECIEL]. **Main/Corp** Programa de Estudios Conjuntos sobre Integracion Economica Latinoamericana. **Added/Corp** Organization of American States. No. 1 (Nov. 1974)-. Periodical. Spanish (summaries and/or abstracts in English and Portuguese). Four times a year. Free on request. ECIEL, Caixa Postal 740, Rio de Janeiro Brazil. **Tel** 011 55 11 212053198. **Circ:** 1,000 (ctrl).
Desc: Publishes the results of the program's research and aims to further intellectual exchange on the subjects studied.
Ind/Abst Hisp. Am. Period. Index, HAPI.

ISSN 1188-8482
DD 370.19/316/0971 CN
ENSEMBLE - CONFERENCE BOARD OF CANADA. NATIONAL BUSINESS AND EDUCATION CENTRE. See Education.

LC WMLC 93/3166
SA
ENTERPRISE. (19??). Periodical. English. Twelve times a year. R450.00. Black Enterprise, PO Box 91845, Aucklandpark 2006 South Africa. **Tel** 011 27 11 4833863. **ED** George Williams. **Ad Acc.**
Desc: Business magazine for black entrepreneurs and decision makers.

LC HF5001 .E63
KO
ENTOPURAIJU. VFOAT The Enterprise; Enterprise. Vol. 1 (1984)-. Periodical. Korean (Korean). Twelve times a year. W35,000.

LC HD ISSN 1145-5764
DD 331 FR
UDC 331.82(085.3)
ENTREPRENDRE (PARIS. 1990).
(ENTREPRENDRE.). (1990)-. Periodical. French. Twelve times a year. $91.05. Groupe Entreprende, 75015 Paris France. **Tel** 011 33 1 45774141. **Bk Rev,** (Qty: 10). **Ad Acc. Circ:** 65,230. **Continues** Le Journal Entreprendre, 0765-3301.

LC HF5001 .E64 ISSN 0364-7218
DD 338/.04/0973 US
ENTREPRENEUR. Vol. 1 (Summer 1976)-. Periodical. English. Four times a year. Entrepreneur, PO Box 5337, San Bernardino CA 92408.

ISSN 0775-7239
BE
UDC 631
ENTREPRENEUR MAGAZINE (BERTRIX). [Entrep. mag. Bertrix]. (1988)-. Periodical. French (Dutch). Six times a year. $29.86. Edition Recad, Geelseweg 47-A, B-2200 Herentals Belgium. **Tel** 011 32 14 214447.

ISSN 1073-046X
US
●**ENTREPRENEUR NEWSLETTER.** (1994)-. Newsletter. English. Four times a year. $12.50. K&A Publications, 4847 Hopyard Road, Suite 3201, Pleasanton CA 94588.

ISSN 0259-5559
SA
ENTREPRENEUR POTCHEFSTROOM.
[Entrepreneur Potchefstroom]. (1982)-. Periodical. Multiple languages. Ten times a year. $10.43. Small Business Advisory Bureau, PO Box 1880, Potchefstroom 2520 South Africa. **Tel** 011 27 148 991002, FAX 011 27 148 991394. **Circ:** 3,000 (ctrl).

ISSN 1054-4046
US
ENTREPRENEURIAL COUPLES. (1991)-. Periodical. English. Twelve times a year. $129.00. Larry Israel, 1625 Olympic Boulevard, Santa Monica CA 90404.

ISSN 0272-0396
US
TITLE CHANGE
ENTREPRENEURIAL MANAGER'S NEWSLETTER. Added/Corp Center for Entrepreneurial Management. **VFOAT** Entrepreneurial Manager. (1979)-(19??). Newsletter. English. Center for Entrepreneurial Management, 180 Varick Street/Penthouse, New York NY 10014. **Tel** (212)633-0060, FAX (212)633-0063. **ED** Joseph Mancuso. **Bk Rev. Ad Acc. Circ:** 3,000. **Continued by** Chief Executive Officer's Newsletter.
Desc: A source of entrepreneurial information on taxes, finance, banking, venture capital, business planning and smaller business problems.

Business and Economics

LC HD6054.4.U6 E58　　ISSN 1051-2624
DD 658.4/21/082　　US
ENTREPRENEURIAL WOMAN. See Women's Interests.

　　ISSN 0898-5626
DD 338　　UK
　　CCC
Pr Rev.
ENTREPRENEURSHIP AND REGIONAL DEVELOPMENT. [Entrep. reg. dev.]. **VFOAT** Entrepreneurship & Regional Development. Vol. 1 (1989)-. Periodical. English. Four times a year. $135.00. Taylor & Francis Ltd. / UK, Rankine Road, Basingstoke, Hampshire RG24 8PR United Kingdom. **Tel** 011 44 1256 840366, FAX 011 44 1256 479438, telex 858540. **(Subscription address:** Taylor & Francis Inc., 1900 Frost Road, Suite 101, Bristol PA 19007-1598. **Tel** (215)785-5800, (800)821-8312, FAX (215)785-5515.) **ED** Gerald P. Sweeney (editor's address: SICA Innovation Consultants Ltd., 44 Fitzwilliam Square, Dublin 2 Ireland); Alan L. Carsrud (editor's address: Enterpreneurial Studies Center, Anderson Graduate School of Management, University of California at Los Angeles, 405 Hilgard Avenue, Los Angeles, CA 90024-1481). **Bk Rev. Ad Acc. Circ:** 200. available on microfilm and microfiche from University Microfilms International (UMI).
  Desc: Creates a single forum at an international level for the convergence of academic, government, and private sector interest in the key role of the entrepreneur as the creator of new business in the promotion of economic growth and sustained prosperity. The journal is an outlet for research and evaluation on such topics as the characteristics of entrepreneurs, networking, technology transfer, entrepreneurial support programmes, venture capital and factors affecting the regional milieu for innovation and entrepreneurship.
  Ind/Abst Curr. Cit.; Geogr. Abstr. Human Geogr.; Int. Dev. Abstr.; Int. Labour Doc.; LABORDOC.

LC HB615 .E67　　ISSN 1059-0137
DD 338　　US
　　CCC
　　CODEN EICHEZ
ENTREPRENEURSHIP, INNOVATION AND CHANGE. [Entrep. innov. change]. Vol. 1, No. 1 (Mar. 1992)-. Periodical. English. Four times a year. $135.00. Plenum Press, 233 Spring Street, New York NY 10013-1578. **Tel** (212)620-8000, (800)221-9369, FAX (212)463-0742, (212)807-1047, telex 23/421139.
  Ind/Abst Hum. Resour. Abstr.

LC HF5001 .E65
DD 338.0944/05　　FR
ENTREPRISE, L'. No 80 (May 1992)-. Periodical. French. Twelve times a year. Societe des Publications de L'Entreprise, 25 rue Leblanc, 75015 Paris Cedex 15 France. **Tel** 40 60 40 60, FAX 40 60 41 20. **Continues** Entreprise/A pour Affaires, 1164-7027.

　　FR
UDC 65
ENTREPRISE A POUR AFFAIRES ECONOMIQUES, L'. French. Twelve times a year. 378.06F France and Tunisia; 489.00F other Europe; 526.00F the Americas; 600.00F other. Groupe Expansion, Le Ponant, 25 rue LeBlanc, 75842 Paris Cedex 15 France. **Tel** 011 33 1 40604115. **(Subscription address:** L'Entreprise, Service Abbonements B030, 60732 Sainte Genevieve France.) **Continues** Entreprise.

　　ISSN 0995-4945
UDC 331.5　　FR
ENTREPRISE & CARRIERES (PARIS). (ENTREPRISE & CARRIERES.). **VFOAT** Liaisons Enterprise & Carrieres; Entreprise et Carrieres (Paris). (1989)-. Periodical. French. Forty-seven times a year. $96.41. Liaisons Sociales, 1 Avenue Edouard Belin, F 92856 Rueil Malmaison France. **Tel** 011 33 1 41299878, 011 33 1 41299879.

　　ISSN 1059-390X
DD 338　　US
ENVIROBUSINESS REPORT. See Environmental Issues.

LC HC440.8.A1 E58
DD 330.9549/2/005　　BG
ENVIRONMENT & REGION. **VFOAT** Environment and Region. Vol. 1, No. 1 (Jan. 1981)-. Periodical. English. Two times a year. $5.00 US and Canada. Environment and Region, Department of Geography, Jahangirnagar University Savar, Dacca Bangladesh.

　　ISSN 1060-1414
DD 333　　US
　　CCC
ENVIRONMENT WATCH. LATIN AMERICA. (ENVIRONMENT WATCH. LATIN AMERICA : NEWS & ANALYSIS FOR BUSINESS AND POLICY PROFESSIONALS FROM CUTTER INFORMATION CORP.). [Environ. watch, Lat. Am.]. **Added/Corp** Cutter Information Corp. Vol. 1, No. 1 (Nov. 1991)-. Periodical. English. Twelve times a year. $537.00. Cutter Information Corporation, 37 Broadway, Arlington MA 02174-5539. **Tel** (617)648-8700, (800)964-5118, FAX (617)648-8707, (617)648-1950, telex 650 100 9891. available on an online database (file 636/Full-Text) from DIALOG. **Absorbed** Mexican Environmental Business.
  Ind/Abst PTS Newsl. Database [Full Txt.].

　　ISSN 1066-6001
DD 940　　US
ENVIRONMENT WATCH. WESTERN EUROPE. (ENVIRONMENT WATCH. WESTERN EUROPE : NEWS & ANALYSIS FOR BUSINESS AND POLICY PROFESSIONALS FROM CUTTER INFORMATION CORP.). [Environ. watch, West. Eur.]. **Added/Corp** Cutter Information Corp. **VFOAT** Western Europe. Vol. 1, No. 1 (Oct. 1992)-. Periodical. English. Twenty-four times a year. $657.00. Cutter Information Corporation, 37 Broadway, Arlington MA 02174-5539. **Tel** (617)648-8700, (800)964-5118, FAX (617)648-8707, (617)648-1950, telex 650 100 9891. available on an online database (file 636/Full-Text) from DIALOG.

LC HC79.E5 E576　　ISSN 0924-6460
DD 330　　NE
　　CCC
　　CODEN ERECEP
Pr Rev.
ENVIRONMENTAL AND RESOURCE ECONOMICS. See Environmental Issues.

　　US
EPR ANNUAL REVIEW. See Energy.

　　US
EPR QUARTERLY REVIEW. See Energy.

LC HB848 .E67　　ISSN 0090-7871
DD 301.32/9/73　　US
EQUILIBRIUM (WASHINGTON, D.C.). See Population Studies.

LC HC271 .A218 HC280.C6
DD 330　　FR
EQUIPEMENT DES MENAGES, L'. **Main/Corp** Instutut National de la Statistique et des Etudes Economiques (France). French (summaries and/or abstracts in English and Spanish). 10.00F.

LC HF5001　　ISSN 0823-6801
DD 650/.09711/33　　CN
EQUITY (VANCOUVER). (EQUITY.). [Equity]. Vol. 1, No. 1 (Apr./May 1983)-. Periodical. English. Ten times a year. 30.00Can$. Pacific West Equities Ltd., 1178 West Pender Street/Suite 200, Vancouver British Columbia V6E 3X4 Canada. **Tel** (604)684-1414, FAX (604)684-6907.
  Ind/Abst Can. Index (?-?); Can. Period. Index (19??-).

　　ISSN 0343-6705
UDC 622.753:338　　GW
ERDOL-INFORMATIONSDIENST. [Erdol-Inf.dienst]. **VFOAT** EID. Erdol-Informationsdienst. (1947)-. Trade Publication. German. One time a week. $520.47. Erdol Informationsdienst, Burchardstrasse 17, D-20095 Hamburg Germany. **Tel** 011 49 40 337161, 337161, FAX 011 49 40 926780. **(Subscription address:** Handelsblatt GmbH, Postfach 102716, D 40018 Dusseldorf Germany. **Tel** 011 49 211 8871711.) **ED** Heino Elfert. Index available. cum. index. **Bk Rev. Ad Acc.** ctrl avlbe.
  Desc: Information, analysis, comments on the oil and natural gas markets in Germany and Europe with important emphasis on price reporting.

　　ISSN 1068-6304
DD 332　　US
ERISA TOP 25,000 COMPANIES : THE RED BOOK OF PENSION FUNDS. [ERISA top 25,000 co.]. **Added/Corp** Dun's Marketing Services. **VFOAT** ERISA Top Twenty-Five Thousand Companies; Top 25,000 Companies; Top Twenty-Five Thousand Companies; Red Book of Pension Funds. **VAT** Employee Retirement Income Security Act Top 25,000 Companies. (1990/91)-. English. Irregular. $525.00. Dun & Bradstreet Information Services, 3 Sylvan Way, Parsippany NJ 07054. **Tel** (201)605-6000, (800)526-0651.

　　ISSN 1188-5831
DD 333.33　　CN
ESPACE MONTREAL (ENGLISH EDITION 1992). (ESPACE MONTREAL.). [Espace Montr.]. Vol. 1, No. 1 (Winter 1992)-. Periodical. English (French). Four times a year. 26.18Can$. Espace Montreal, 651 Notre-Dame Street West, Suite 101, Montreal Quebec H3C 1H8 Canada. **Tel** (514)879-1559.

LC HC381 .E78
DD 338/.0946　　SP
ESPANA AL DIA. (1972)-. Spanish. Consorcio Americano de Ediciones, Victor de la Serna 5, 16 Madrid Spain. available with illustrations.

　　ISSN 0186-0496
　　MX
ESTADISTICAS DEL COMERCIO EXTERIOR DE MEXICO. INFORMACION PRELIMINAR. See Business and Economics-Abstracting, Bibliographies and Statistics.

LC HC　　ISSN 0250-7323
DD 330　　US
　　CEASED
ESTATUTOS Y REGLAMENTO. [Estatutos reglam. - Fondo Monet. Int.]. **Main/Corp** International Monetary Fund. (19??)-(19??). Spanish (French and Spanish). International Monetary Fund, 700 19th Street Northwest, Publishing Unit, Washington DC 20431. **Tel** (202)623-7430, FAX (202)623-7201.

LC HC161 .U5253　　ISSN 0252-2217
DD 330.98/0005　　CL
ESTUDIO ECONOMICO DE AMERICA LATINA Y EL CARIBE / COMISION ECONOMICA PARA AMERICA LATINA Y EL CARIBE. **Added/Corp** United Nations. Economic Commission for Latin America and the Caribbean. (19??)-. Spanish. CEPAL / United Nations Economic Commission for Latin America / Chile, Publications Sales Section, CEPAL Casilla 179-D, Santiago Chile. **Continues** United Nations. Estudio Economico de America Latina.
  Ind/Abst LABORDOC.

LC HB9 .E76　　ISSN 0304-2758
　　CL
Pr Rev.
ESTUDIOS DE ECONOMIA. **Added/Corp** Universidad de Chile. Departamento de Economia. (19??)-. Periodical. Spanish (English). Two times a year (June and Dec.). $40.00. Universidad de Chile / Departamento de Economia, Casilla Postal 3861, Santiago Chile. **Tel** 011 562 2228521. **ED** Jorge Marshall. Each issue contains an index to its own contents (no volume index)--loose. **Ad Acc, Adv Mgr:** Jaime Vatter. **Circ:** 300 (ctrl). Documents available.
  Desc: The publication presents empirical and theoretical papers in economics; there is an emphasis on problems relevant to developing countries.

LC HC131 .E83　　ISSN 0186-7202
DD 330　　MX
ESTUDIOS ECONOMICOS DE EL COLEGIO DE MEXICO. (ESTUDIOS ECONOMICOS.). [Estud. econ. Col. Mex.]. **Added/Corp** Colegio de Mexico. **VFOAT** Estudios Economicos de el Colegio de Mexico. Vol. 1, No. 1 (1986)-. Periodical. Spanish (summaries and/or abstracts in English). Two times a year. $45.00. Colegio de Mexico AC, Camino Al Ajusco No 20, 10740 Mexico DF Mexico. **Tel** 011 52 5 6455955 ext. 3138, telex 1777585 COLME. **Continues in part** Demografia y Economia.
  Ind/Abst Index Econ. Artic. J. Collect. Vol. (1986-); J. Econ. Lit. (1986-).

LC HC175 .E73　　ISSN 0325-6928
DD 330　　AG
Pr Rev.　　SUSPENDED
ESTUDIOS - INSTITUTO DE ESTUDIO ECONOMICOS SOBRE LA REALIDAD ARGENTINA Y LATINOAMERICANA. (ESTUDIOS.). [Estud. - Inst. Estud. Econ. Real. Argent. Latinoam.]. **Added/Corp** Fundacion Mediterranea (Argentina). Instituto de Estudios Economicos Sobre la Realidad Argentina y Latinoamericana. Yearly Volume 1 No. 1 (Jan./Feb. 1978)-Suspended. Periodical. Spanish. Six times a year. 800.00AR$ Argentina; $18.00 other. IEERAL, Campillo 394/CC 1311, Cordoba 5000 Argentina. **Tel** 051-72-6523, 6525, telex 51811 IERAL-AR. **ED** Juan Carlos Kusznir. Index available. cum. index. **Bk Rev. Ad Acc. Circ:** 2,500 (ctrl).
  Desc: Of interest to specialists on economic issues, entrepreneurs, politicians, and those in other sectors of Argentine and Latin American management.

LC HC191 .E87
DD 330.983/005　　SP
ESTUDIOS PUBLICOS. No. 1 (Dec. 1980)-. Periodical. Spanish. Four times a year. Centrl de Estudios Publicos, Monsenor Sotero Sanz 175, Santiago 9 Chile.
  Ind/Abst Hisp. Am. Period. Index, HAPI; PAIS Int. Print (1991-).

LC HB9 .E775　　ISSN 0101-4161
DD 330.1　　BL
ESTUDOS ECONOMICOS - INSTITUTO DE PESQUISAS ECONOMICAS. (ESTUDOS ECONOMICOS.). [Estud. econ. - Inst. Pesqui. Econ.]. (19??)-. Periodical. Portuguese. Three times a year (Plus special issue). $35.00. Instituto Pesquisas Economicas, Av Prof Luciano Gualberto 908, 05508 Sao Paulo SP Brazil. **Tel** 011 55 11 2125483, FAX 011 55 11 8143379, telex 30170. **ED** Nelson H. Nozoe. Index available. cum.

Business and Economics

index. **Ad Acc, Adv Mgr:** Antonio Evaldo Comune, **Tel** (011) 212-5471. **Circ:** 500. available with charts.
Desc: Original papers in economic research.
Ind/Abst Hisp. Am. Period. Index, HAPI; PAIS Int. Print.

LC HD4010.Q4 Q43a   **ISSN** 0848-3663
DD 354.71409/2   CN

ETATS FINANCIERS DES ENTREPRISES DU GOUVERNEMENT DU QUEBEC (1988).
(ETATS FINANCIERS DES ENTREPRISES DU GOUVERNEMENT DU QUEBEC.). [Etats financ. entrep. gouv. Que.]. **Added/Corp** Quebec (Province). Ministere des Finances. (1988)-. Government Publication. French. One time a year. Free on request. Ministere des Finances, 12 rue St. Louis, Quebec Quebec G1R 5L3 Canada. **Tel** (418)691-2226. *Continues Entreprises du Gouvernement du Quebec, Etats Financiers, 0837-4066.*

LC K5 .T35   **ISSN** 0895-5026
DD 174   US
     CCC

ETHIKOS. See Ethics.

     ISSN 1062-3639
     US

ETHIOPIAN BUSINESS MAGAZINE.
VFOAT Ethiopian Business. (1992)-. Periodical. English. Six times a year. $3.00 (single issue). Ethiopian Business Magazine, PO Box 3625, Washington DC 20007.

LC Z7165.E74 E87 HC845.A1
DD 016.338963   ET

ETHIOPIA'S DEVELOPMENT CURRENT ABSTRACTS. See Business and
Economics-Abstracting, Bibliographies and Statistics.

     ISSN 0378-0376
     FR

ETUDES ECONOMIQUES DE L'O C D E: CANADA.
[Etud. econ. OCDE, Can.]. **Main/Corp** Organisation de Cooperation et de Developpement Economiques. **VFOAT** Canada. (1961)-. French. Irregular. $385.00. OECD Publications and Information Center, 2 rue Andre-Pascal, 75775 Paris Cedex 16 France. **Tel** 011 33 1 49104262, US:(202)785-6323, FAX 011 33 1 45248500, 011 33 1 45248176, telex 620 160 OCDE. (**Subscription address:** OECD Publications Center, 2001 L Street, Suite 700, Washington DC 20036. **Tel** (202)822-3873, (202)785-6323.) *Continues Organisation de Cooperation et de Developpement Economiques. Situation et Problemes de l'Economie des pays Membres et Associes de l'O C D E: Canada.*

LC HC
DD 330   IT

EUI WORKING PAPER. ECO. Added/Corp
European University Institute. Dept. of Economics. **VFOAT** ECO; EUI Working Papers in Economics. No. 90/1 (1990)-. Monographic series. English. Price varies per volume. European University Institute Badia Fiesolana, Via dei Roccettini 5, San Domenico di Fiesole Florence Italy. *Continues in part EUI Working Paper.*

     ISSN 1021-1667
     LU

UDC 655.55:341.17(4)

EUR-OP NEWS DEUTSCHE AUSG.
[EUR-OP news Dtsch. Ausg.]. (1992)-. Periodical. German. Four times a year. Free on request. Office for Official Publications of the European Communities, 2 rue Mercier, 2985 Luxembourg Luxembourg. **Tel** 011 352 499281, FAX 011 352 292942763. **ED** Alexander von Witzleben.
Desc: Information on Europe.

     BE

EUREKA NEWS.
(19??)-. English (French, German, Spanish and Italian). Four times a year. Free on request. Eureka Secretariat, 19th Avenue des Arts, BP 3, B-1040 Brussels Belgium. **Tel** 011 32 2 2292240, FAX 011 32 2 2187906. **ED** Kirsten Voje.
Desc: Explains overall objectives of the EUREKA Initiative, which seeks to strengthen the productivity and the competitive position of industry and national economies on the world market. Aims to further Europe-wide cooperation in advanced technology projects with civilian ends.

     ISSN 1355-2759
     UK

●EURO JAPANESE JOURNAL.
(1994)-. Periodical. English. Anglo-Japanese Economic Institute, Morely House, 314-322 Regent Street, London W1R 5AD United Kingdom. *Continues Anglo-Japanese Journal, 0955-5129.*

     ISSN 0953-0711
     UK

EUROBUSINESS (LONDON).
(EUROBUSINESS.). [EuroBusiness]. **VFOAT** Euro Business. Vol. 1, No. 1 (Oct. 1988)-. Periodical. English. Twelve times a year. £24.00 (one-year), £40.00 (two-year), £54.00 (three-year) UK; £27.00 (one-year), £45.00 (two-year), £61.00 (three-year), Europe; $45.00 (one-year) $50.00 (two-year), $66.00 (three-year) US and Canada; $48.00 (one-year), $82.50 (two-year), $112.50 (three-year) other. Transnational Business Magazines Limited, Stratton House, Stratton Street, London W1X 5FE United Kingdom. **Tel** 011 44 171 4097009, FAX 011 44 171 4093006. available on an online database (file 648/Full-Text) from DIALOG.
Desc: Coverage of business developments throughout Europe. Country-by-country reporting of events in 30 European countries, featuring timely issues along with company results and reports.
Ind/Abst Contents Pages Manage.; F&S Index Plus Text, Int. [Select. Cov.]; PROMT.

LC S
DD 630   FR

EUROLETTRE PARIS. See Agriculture.

     UK

EUROMARKET LETTER & REPORT.
English. One time a week. £759.00 UK; £825.00 other. Euromoney Publications PLC, Nestor House, Playhouse Yard, London EC4Z 5EX United Kingdom. **Tel** 011 44 171 7798888, FAX 011 44 171 7798630, telex 290700 EUROMON G.

     ISSN 1061-2874
DD 338   UK
     TITLE CHANGE

EUROMEDIA ACQUISITIONS.
[Euromedia acquis.]. (Jan. 30, 1992)-(June 1995). Newsletter. English. Kagan World Media Inc., 126 Clock Tower Place, Carmel CA 93923-8734. **Tel** (408)624-1536, FAX (408)625-3225. (**Subscription address:** Kagan World Media Ltd., 524 Fulham Road, London SW6 5NR United Kingdom. **Tel** 011 44 171 3718880, FAX 011 44 171 3718715.) available via fax. *Merged into Euromedia Acquisitions and Finance.*

     US

●EUROMEDIA ACQUISITIONS AND FINANCE.
(1995)-. English. Twelve times a year. $795.00. Kagan World Media Inc., 126 Clock Tower Place, Carmel CA 93923-8734. **Tel** (408)624-1536, FAX (408)625-3225. (**Subscription address:** Kagan World Media Ltd., 524 Fulham Road, London SW6 5NR United Kingdom. **Tel** 011 44 171 3718880, FAX 011 44 171 3718715.) *Absorbed Euromedia Acquisitions and Euromedia Finance.*
Desc: Tracking of mergers, sales and management buyouts of media companies. Features estimates of multiples of revenue and cash flow.

     UK

EUROMONEY INDEX.
(19??)-. English. One time a year. $18.00. Euromoney Publications PLC, Nestor House, Playhouse Yard, London EC4Z 5EX United Kingdom. **Tel** 011 44 171 7798888, FAX 011 44 171 7798630, telex 290700 EUROMON G.

     FR

EUROP.
(1978)-. Periodical. French (English). Three times a year. $52.49. Europ, 33 rue du Louvre, F-75002 Paris France. **Tel** 31 1 44822000, FAX 31 1 45084232, telex 240 586. **ED** Jacques Stoufflet. **Ad Acc, Adv Mgr:** Jacques Stoufflet. **Circ:** 2,500.

     ISSN 0928-0758
     NE

UDC 339.92

EUROPA REGIONAAL CUIJK.
(EUROPA REGIONAAL.). [Eur. reg. Cuijk]. (1990)-. Periodical. Dutch. Eleven times a year (monthly with Jul./Aug issue combined). Fl75.00. Europa Regionaal BV, Postbus 146, 5430 AC Cuijk Netherlands. **Tel** 011 31 08850 18008.

     NE

EUROPA VAN MORGEN.
Dutch. Irregular. Free. Tav Europa Van Morgen, Postbus 30465, 2500 GL Den Haag Netherlands. **Tel** 011 31 070 3469326.

LC JN12 .E85a   **ISSN** 0304-2782
DD 320   AU

EUROPAEISCHE RUNDSCHAU. See
Political Science-International Relations.

LC HC241.2 .E81217
DD 330   IT

EUROPAFORUM : MENSILE DI ECONOMIA E DIRITTO COMUNITARIO.
VFOAT Europa Forum. (1988)-. Periodical. Italian. Twelve times a year. European Forum Srl, Via G De Calvi 6, 00151 Rome Italy.

     ISSN 1191-4238
DD 914.04/55   CN

EUROPE BUSINESS TRAVEL ORGANIZER, THE.
[Eur. bus. travel organ.]. **VFOAT** Business Travel Organizer, Europe. (1992)-. English. Every 2 years. $35.00 (US) per volume. Austin House, PO Box 1051, Oakville Ontario L6S 5E9 Canada.

LC HB
DD 330   BE

EUROPE ENTREPRISES.
(19??)-. French (English). Eleven times a year. 19300.00F Belgium; 20250.00F Rest of Europe; 20450.00F other. Europe Information Service, rue de Geneve 6, 1140 Brussels Belgium. **Tel** 011 32 2 242 6020, FAX 011 32 2 242 9549.
Desc: Provides a monthly update on the coalition of the EEC's market and particularly for firms.

     UK

EUROPE SANS FRONTIERES.
English. Four times a year. £65.00 UK; $125.00 US; £100.00 Europe. Confederation of British Industry, Centre Point, 103 New Oxford Street, London WC1A 1DU United Kingdom. **Tel** 011 44 171 3797400, FAX 011 44 171 8365856. **ED** Clare Hollingsworth. Index available. **Circ:** 800.
Desc: Provides details and developments on key issues affecting business in the run-up to 1992, with editorials written by the head of the CBI Brussels office.

LC HD70.E8 E88   **ISSN** 1352-4518
     UK

EUROPEAN BUSINESS & ECONOMIC DIGEST.
VFOAT European Business and Economic Digest. (19??)-. Periodical. English. Six times a year. $244.00. MCB University Press, 60 62 Toller Lane, Bradford, West Yorkshire BD8 9BY United Kingdom. **Tel** 011 44 1274 785280, FAX 011 44 1274 785200, telex 51317-MCBUNI-G. (**Subscription address:** MCB University Press / US and Canada Subscriptions, PO Box 10812, Birmingham AL 35201-0812. **Tel** (205)995-1567, (800)633-4931, FAX (205)995-1588.) *Absorbed Training Digest Europe; Continues European Business and Economic Development, 0966-8004.*
Ind/Abst Curr. Cit.

LC HG4132.Z5 E95
DD 338.092/2 B   GW

EUROPEAN BUSINESS AND INDUSTRY.
VFOAT Who's Who Edition European Business and Industry. (1985/86)-. English. Irregular (15 issues). Price varies. Who's Who Management Edition Pty Ltd., 99 York Street Level 12, Sydney 2000 Australia. **Tel** 011 61 2 220 6710.
Desc: Information on corporations, executives and businessmen.

LC HF3493 .E82
DD 380.1/025/4   BN

EUROPEAN BUSINESS GUIDE.
VFOAT Europaischer Geschaftsfuhrer; Evropski Poslovni Vodic. (1976)-. Multiple languages (English, German and Serbo-Croatian (Roman)). Veselin Maslesa, Obala 4, Sarajevo, Bosnia and Hercegovina. **Tel** 011 71 455107, FAX 011 71 272369, telex 41154.

     UK

EUROPEAN BUSINESS INFORMATION.
(19??)-. Periodical. English. Four times a year. £139.15. Croner Publ Ltd., Croner House London Road, Kingston Upon Thames, Surrey KT2 6SR United Kingdom. **Tel** 011 44 181 5473333, FAX 011 44 181 5472637.

     ISSN 0964-8550
     UK

EUROPEAN BUSINESS INFORMATION SOURCEBOOK.
(19??)-. English. Two times a year. $304.00. Headland Business Information, 1 Henry Smiths Terrace, Headland Cleveland, TS24 0PD United Kingdom. **Tel** 011 44 429 231902, FAX 011 44 429 861403.

     ISSN 0957-0039
DD 338.70254   UK

EUROPEAN BUSINESS INTELLIGENCE BRIEFING.
[Eur. bus. intell. brief.]. (1989)-. English. Eleven times a year (monthly with combined July/Aug). $424.00. Headland Business Information, 1 Henry Smiths Terrace, Headland Cleveland, TS24 0PD United Kingdom. **Tel** 011 44 429 231902, FAX 011 44 429 861403. **ED** Gerry Smith. **Bk Rev. Circ:** 500 (ctrl).
Desc: An in-depth evaluation of information sources on European companies, markets and products.

     ISSN 0955-808X
     UK

Pr Rev.

EUROPEAN BUSINESS JOURNAL.
(1989)-. English. Four times a year. $175.00. Whurr Publishers Ltd., 19B Compton Terrace, London N1 2UN United Kingdom. **Tel** 011 44 171 3595979, FAX 011 44 171 2265290. (**Subscription address:** Turpin Distribution Services Limited, Blackhorse Road, Letchworth, Hertfordshire SH6 1HN United Kingdom. **Tel** 011 44 1462 672555, FAX 011 44 1462 480947.) **ED** Sir William Nicoll. **Ad Acc.** Full Page **B&W)** £200.00. Half Page (B&W) £125.00. Acid Free.
Desc: Meets the need for an independent forum for the presentation and discussion of the major issues affecting business in the European Community as it advances into the 21st century.
Ind/Abst Curr. Cit.

     ISSN 1352-903X
DD 338.0094   UK
     CEASED

EUROPEAN BUSINESS MONITOR.
[Eur. bus. monit.]. (1993)-Vol. 7, No. 3 (1994). Periodical. English. Tolley Publishing Company Ltd., Tolley House, 2 Addiscombe Road, Croydon, Surrey CR9 5AF United Kingdom. **Tel** 011 44 181 6869141, FAX 011 44 181 6863155. *Continues 1992 Single Market Monitor, 0954-9013.*

Desc: Provides an update on European related business developments and regulations in the UK and in other member states.

LC HG4132 .A2
DD 338.7/4/09405 UK
EUROPEAN BUSINESS RANKINGS. 1st Ed. (1992)-. English. $160.00. Gale Research International, 2-6 Boundary Row, London SE1 8HN United Kingdom. **(Subscription address:** Gale Research Co., 835 Penobscot Building, Detroit MI 48226. **Tel** (800)347-4253.**)** available on magnetic tape; available on diskette.
Desc: Displays 2,250 business statistics and rankings from throughout Europe. Each entry contains the top ten names in each list, and gives the ranking criteria, the total number of items listed in the original ranking, and the name, date and page of the source.

ISSN 0955-534X
UK
EUROPEAN BUSINESS REVIEW.
Added/Corp International Management Centres, Europe. **VFOAT** EBR. Vol. 1 (1989)-. Periodical. English (summaries and/or abstracts in French and German). Five times a year. $1999.00. MCB University Press, 60 62 Toller Lane, Bradford, West Yorkshire BD8 9BY United Kingdom. **Tel** 011 44 1274 785280, FAX 011 44 1274 785200, telex 51317-MCBUNI-G. **(Subscription address:** MCB University Press / US and Canada Subscriptions, PO Box 10812, Birmingham AL 35201-0812. **Tel** (205)995-1567, (800)633-4931, FAX (205)995-1588.**) ED** Paul Fifield. **Ad Acc.** Documents available from UMI Article Clearinghouse. ***Absorbed*** *New European, 0953-1432.*
Desc: Seeks to provide an in-depth analysis of the opportunities and threats posed to managers by ever increasing levels of European integration.
Ind/Abst ABI/INFORM Glob. Ed.; Curr. Cit.; Person. Manage. Abstr.

LC HA1107.5 .A14
DD 309.1/4/055 UK
EUROPEAN COMMUNITY : FACTS AND FIGURES, THE. See Business and Economics-Abstracting, Bibliographies and Statistics.

LC HC241.2 .E834118 **ISSN** 1045-3857
DD 330.94/001/12 US
EUROPEAN COMMUNITY (SYRACUSE, N.Y.), THE. (THE EUROPEAN COMMUNITY : ANNUAL FIVE-YEAR FORECAST FOR INTERNATIONAL BUSINESS.). [Eur. community]. **Added/Corp** Political Risk Services (IBC USA (Publications) Inc.). **VFOAT** Five Year EC Forecast; Five-Year EC Forecast. **VAT** Five-Year European Community Forecast. Vol. 1 (1989)-. English. One time a year (Sept.). $390.00. Political Risk Services, 6320 Fly Road, Suite 102, PO Box 248, East Syracuse NY 13057-0248. **Tel** (315)431-0511, FAX (315)431-0200. **ED** William D. Coplin and Michael K. O'Leary. available on an online database.
Desc: Describes the policy-making process and forecasts changes likely to become operational.

LC HB1 .E94 **ISSN** 0014-2921
DD 330/.05 NE
CCC
CODEN EERVAI
Pr Rev.
EUROPEAN ECONOMIC REVIEW. [Eur. econ. rev.]. **Added/Corp** European Scientific Association of Applied Economics. Vol. 1, No. 1 (Fall 1969)-. Academic Scholarly Publication. English. Nine times a year (1 volume). Fl.1715.00. Elsevier Science Publishers BV, PO Box 211, 1000 AE Amsterdam Netherlands. **Tel** 011 31 20 4853641, 011 31 20 4853642, FAX 011 31 20 4853598. **ED** Jean Waelbroeck, Herbert Glejser, J. Peter Neary, and Agnar Sandmo. available on microfilm and microfiche from University Microfilms International (UMI); available on an online database from Elsevier Electronic Subscriptions (EES). Documents available from The Genuine Article, UMI Article Clearinghouse. ***Supersedes*** *Western European Economics.*
Desc: An all-European economics journal which assembles work being done throughout Europe and makes it accessible to the entire continent and to English-speaking countries.
Ind/Abst ABI/INFORM Glob. Ed.; ABI/INFORM [Computer File] (Jan. 1981-); Acad. Search; Bus. Index (1985-); Bus. Source Plus; Bus. Source; Contents Recent Econ. J.; Contents Pages Manage.; Curr. Cit.; Curr. Contents Soc. Behav. Sci.; Econ. Lit. Index; Energy Res. Abstr. (April 1976-); EP Collect.; Expand. Acad. Index (1984-); Gen. BusinessFile (1985-); Gen. Period. Index (1985-); Geogr. Abstr. Human Geogr.; Homework Help.; INFO-SOUTH Abstr.; Int. Dev. Abstr.; Int. Labour Doc.; J. Econ. Lit.; J. Plan. Lit.; Leis., Rec., Tour. Abstr.; Mag. Search; MasterFile FullTEXT 1000; MasterFile FullTEXT 350; MasterFile FullTEXT 650; MasterFile FullTEXT (July 1993-); Middle East Abstr. Index; Newsp. Period. Abstr. (1991-); OCLC; PAIS Int. Print (1991-?); Res. Alert [Full Cov.]; Risk Abstr. (19??-19??); Rural Dev. Abstr.; Soc. Sci. Source; Soc. Sci. Cit. Index [Full Cov.]; Soc. Sci. Index; Soc. Sci. Index Fulltext (Oct. 1988-) [Full Txt.]; Telebase; Trade Ind. Index; World Agric. Econ. Rural Sociol. Abstr.

LC HC240.A1 E819 **ISSN** 0175-8330
DD 330.94/0021 GW
EUROPEAN ECONOMIES IN GRAPHS AND FIGURES, THE. Added/Corp Ifo-Institut fur Wirtschaftsforschung. **VFOAT** European Economies. (1991)-. English.

LC HC241.2 .E857 **ISSN** 0379-0991
DD 330.94/005 LU
EUROPEAN ECONOMY. (EUROPEAN ECONOMY / COMMISSION OF THE EUROPEAN COMMUNITIES.). [Eur. econ.]. **Added/Corp** Commission of the European Communities. Commission of the European Communities. Directorate-General for Economic and Financial Affairs. **VFOAT** Annual Economic Report (Commission of the European Communities. Directorate-General for Economic and Financial Affairs); Annual Economic Review (Commission of the European Communities). No. 1 (Nov. 1978)-. Periodical. English. Two times a year. $140.00. Office for Official Publications of the European Communities, 2 rue Mercier, 2985 Luxembourg Luxembourg. **Tel** 011 352 499281, FAX 011 352 292942763. ***Continues*** *Economic Situation in the Community, 0378-3634.*
Desc: Economic forecasts and articles on current microeconomic trends in the European communities.
Ind/Abst Curr. Cit.; Manage. Market. Abstr.; PAIS Int. Print (1991).

LU
●**EUROPEAN ECONOMY. REPORTS AND STUDIES. Added/Corp** Commission of the European Communities. Commission of the European Communities. Directorate-General for Economic and Financial Affairs. **VFOAT** Reports and Studies. (1993)-. English. Irregular. UNIPUB, 4611-F Assembly Drive, Lanham MD 20706-4391. **Tel** (800)274-4888, FAX (301)459-0056, telex 28787 GATT CH. ***Continues*** *European Economy. Special Edition.*

LC HC241.2 .E857 Suppl **ISSN** 0379-2056
DD 330.94/005 LU
EUROPEAN ECONOMY. SUPPLEMENT A, RECENT ECONOMIC TRENDS.
Added/Corp Commission of the European Communities. Directorate-General for Economic and Financial Affairs. **VFOAT** Recent Economic Trends; European Economy. Recent Economic Trends. (Jan. 1981)-. English. Eleven times a year (monthly except Aug.). £26.30 UK; 28.50p Ireland. Office for Official Publications of the European Communities, 2 rue Mercier, 2985 Luxembourg Luxembourg. **Tel** 011 352 499281, FAX 011 352 292942763. ***Continues*** *European Economy. Supplement--Series A, Recent Economic Trends.*
Desc: Describes recent trends of industrial production, consumer prices, unemployment, the balance of trade, exchange rates, and gross domestic product in the European Community.

LC HC241.2 .E8572 **ISSN** 0379-2110
DD 330.94/005 LU
EUROPEAN ECONOMY. SUPPLEMENT B, BUSINESS AND CONSUMER SURVEY RESULTS. Added/Corp Commission of the European Communities. Directorate-General for Economic and Financial Affairs. **VFOAT** Business and Consumer Survey Results. (March 1985)-. English. Twelve times a year. £26.30 UK; 28.50p Ireland. Office for Official Publications of the European Communities, 2 rue Mercier, 2985 Luxembourg Luxembourg. **Tel** 011 352 499281, FAX 011 352 292942763. ***Formed by the union of*** *European Economy. Supplement B, Business Survey Results* ***and*** *European Economy. Supplement C, Consumer Survey Results.*

ISSN 0966-4858
UK
EUROPEAN HANDBOOK. (1991)-. Directory. English. Two times a year (Jan. & June). £205.00, £144.00 (public libraries) 2 editions, £120.00 (single copy); £240.00, £168.00 (public libraries) 2 editions, £140.00 (single copy) US, Canada and Mexico. Extel Financial Ltd., Fitzroy House, 13-17 Epworth Street, London EC2A 4DL United Kingdom. **Tel** 011 44 171 8258000, FAX 011 44 171 8258328, telex 884319 EXTELX G. Index available. **Ad Acc, Adv Mgr:** Kevin Brady. available on CD-ROM; available on diskette.
Desc: Coverage of over 2,000 companies in Austria, Belgium, Denmark, Finland, France, Germany, Ireland, Italy, Luxembourg, Netherlands, Norway, Switzerland, Sweden, United Kingdom and Spain. Includes for each company: contact details, major shareholders, share data, three years of profit and loss and balance sheet data, performance ratios and ordinary share record. Includes rankings by country and industry sectors.

UK
EUROPEAN HOME VIDEO DATABOOK. See Communications-Video.

ISSN 0929-1261
US
CCC
EUROPEAN JOURNAL OF LAW AND ECONOMICS. See Law.

LC HB1.A1 E97 **ISSN** 0967-2567
UK
●**EUROPEAN JOURNAL OF THE HISTORY OF ECONOMIC THOUGHT, THE.** (1993)-. English. Three times a year. $145.00. Routledge, 11 New Fetter Lane, London EC4P 4EE United Kingdom. **Tel** 011 44 171 5839855, FAX 011 44 171 5830701.

ISSN 0966-8608
DD 302.23094 UK
CEASED
EUROPEAN MARKET & MEDIA FACT. [Eur. mark. media fact]. **VFOAT** European Market and Media Fact.; European Market and MediaFact. (1990)-(199?). English. NTC Publications Ltd., PO Box 69, Henley-on-Thames, Oxfordshire RG9 1GB United Kingdom. **Tel** 011 44 1491 574671, FAX 011 44 1491 571188.

ISSN 1071-1570
DD 332 US
CCC
EUROPEAN MEDIA BUSINESS & FINANCE. [Eur. media bus. financ.]. **VFOAT** European Media Business and Finance; EMB&F. (Jan. 1991)-. Periodical. English. Twenty-five times a year. $895.00. Phillips Business Information Inc., 1201 Seven Locks Road, PO Box 61130, Potomac MD 20854. **Tel** (301)424-3338, (301)340-1520, (800)777-5005, FAX (301)424-4297, telex 358149.

LC HD1401 **ISSN** 0165-1587
DD 338.1 NE
CCC
CODEN ERAEDA
EUROPEAN REVIEW OF AGRICULTURAL ECONOMICS. See Agriculture-Agricultural Economics.

UK
EUROPEAN TELEVISION DATABOOK. CHANNELS. See Communications-Television and Cable.

UK
EUROPEAN TELEVISION DATABOOK. COUNTRIES. See Communications-Television and Cable.

UK
EUROPEAN TOP 500. VFOAT European Top Five Hundred. (1992)-. English. Financial Times / UK, Maple House, 149 Tottenham Court Road, London W1P 9LL United Kingdom. **Tel** 011 44 171 8962276, FAX 011 44 171 8962275, 011 44 171 8962399. ***Continues*** *European 500.*

ISSN 0954-1675
UK
EUROPEAN VENTURE CAPITAL JOURNAL : EUROPEAN VCJ. Added/Corp Venture Economics Limited. Venture Economics Sarl. **VFOAT** Venture Capital Journal; European VCJ; VCJ; EVCJ. (1988)-. Periodical. English. Six times a year. £395.00 Europe; £425.00 other. Venture Economics Ltd, Quadrange 180, Wardourst Street, London W1A 4YG United Kingdom. **Tel** 011 44 171 4340411, FAX 011 44 171 4343918. available on an online database (files 16,636/Full-Text) from DIALOG.
Ind/Abst PROMT [Full Txt.]; PTS Newsl. Database [Full Txt.].

LC HD2356.E9 E93 **ISSN** 0800-0638
DD 338.7/4/094 UK
EUROPE'S 15,000 LARGEST COMPANIES = DIE 15,000 GROSSTEN UNTERNEHMEN EUROPAS = LES 15,000 PLUS GRANDES SOCIETES DE L'EUROPE. VFOAT Die 15,000 Grossten Unternehmen Europas; Les 15,000 Plus Grandes Societes de l'Europe; Europe's Fifteen Thousand Largest Companies; Funfzehntausend Grossten Unternehmen Europas; Quinze Mille Plus Grandes Societes de l'Europe; 15,000 Grossten Unternehmen Europas; 15,000 Plus Grandes Societes de l'Europe. (1985)-. English (French and German). One time a year. $475.00. Dun & Bradstreet Information Services, 3 Sylvan Way, Parsippany NJ 07054. **Tel** (201)605-6000, (800)526-0651. **Ad Acc. Circ:** 2,000. available on magnetic tape; available on diskette. ***Continues*** *Europe's 10,000 Largest Companies.*
Desc: Comparative financial data on companies located in 16 West European countries and Scandinavia. Details 8,500 largest industrials, 2,500 largest trading companies, largest transport companies, banks, insurance companies, motels, restaurant chains and ad agencies.

Business and Economics

LC Z ISSN 0252-8266
DD 330 LU
EUROSTATISTIK, DATEN ZUR KONJUNKTURANALYSE. See Business and Economics-Abstracting, Bibliographies and Statistics.

US
EVALUATING AND BUYING A FRANCHISE. English. $3.95. Pilot Books, 103 Cooper Street, Babylon NY 11702-2319. **Tel** (516)422-2225, FAX (516)422-2227. **ED** James A Meaney.
 Desc: Advice covering the search for a franchise, evaluating the franchisor, investigating earnings claims, negotiating the contract, protection under the Federal Trade and Commission and State laws, continuing relationships with the franchisor, etc.

CN
●**EVANS MARKET UPDATE.** (1995)-. English. Six times a year. 236.10Can$. Evans Research Corporation, 2005 Sheppard Avenue East, 4th Floor, Willowdale Ontario M2J 5B1 Canada. **Tel** (416)498-6664, (416)497-9562, FAX (416)498-7275.

US
EVENTS BUSINESS NEWS. (199?)-. Trade Publication. English. Six times a year. Free to members of the American Vendors Association. 21st Century Marketing, 523 Route 38, Suite 207, Cherryhill NJ 08002. **Tel** (609)488-5255. **Continues** Special Events News.

LC HF3691 .E95
PO
EXAME. (1989)-. Periodical. Portuguese. Twelve times a year. $49.93. Editore Exame Ltda, rua Marcos Portugal 16-A, Alges 1495 Lisbon Portugal. **Tel** 011 351 1 4105570, FAX 011 351 1 4107050. **Bk Rev. Ad Acc.** ctrl circ.

LC HF5001 .E913
DD 658.4/005 BL
EXAME (1983). (EXAME.). (19??)-. Periodical. Portuguese. Twenty-six times a year. $180.00. Editora Abril SA, Rua do Curtume 769 Lapa, 05066 900 Sao Paulo SP Brazil. **Tel** 011 55 11 8239222, 011 55 11 2623322, FAX 011 55 11 8643796. **Continues** Negocios em Exame.
 Ind/Abst PROMT.

BL
EXAME VIP. VFOAT VIP; VIP Exame. No. 1 (1981)-. Periodical. Portuguese. Twelve times a year. $64.00. Editora Abril SA, Rua do Curtume 769 Lapa, 05066 900 Sao Paulo SP Brazil. **Tel** 011 55 11 8239222, 011 55 11 2623322, FAX 011 55 11 8643796.

ISSN 1033-2014
AT
EXCHANGE LILYFIELD. (1989)-. Periodical. English. Forty-eight times a year. 653.63Aus$. Stuart Corner Information Services, Locked Bag 13, Rozelle NSW 2039 Australia. **Tel** 011 61 2 5557377, FAX 011 61 2 8182294. **ED** Stuart Corner. ctrl circ. available on an online database from AUSINET; NEWSNET; and Predicasts, Inc.
 Ind/Abst PROMT [Full Txt.]; PTS Newsl. Database [Full Txt.].

ISSN 0894-5748
DD 651 US
EXEC-U-TARY, THE. (THE EXEC-U-TARY : OFFICIAL JOURNAL OF THE NATIONAL ASSOCIATION OF EXECUTIVE SECRETARIES.). [Exec-u-tary]. **Added/Corp** National Association of Executive Secretaries (U.S.). (19??)-. Periodical. English. Twelve times a year. $20.00. National Association of Executive Secretaries, 900 South Washington Street, Suite G-13, Falls Church VA 22046. **Tel** (703)237-8616, FAX (703)533-1153.

UK
EXECUTIVE COMPANION. (19??)-. Periodical. English. Twelve times a year. £129.45. Croner Publ Ltd., Croner House London Road, Kingston Upon Thames, Surrey KT2 6SR United Kingdom. **Tel** 011 44 181 5473333, FAX 011 44 181 5472637.

ISSN 0733-3412
US
EXECUTIVE COMPENSATION. [Exec. compens.]. **Added/Corp** Financial Executives Institute. Arthur Young & Company. English. $275.00. Financial Executives Institute Publishers, 10 Madison Avenue, PO Box 1938, Morristown NJ 07960. **Tel** (201)898-4600, FAX (201)898-4649.
 Desc: Consists of a biennial survey of compensation of chief executive officers and financial and accounting management, with updating issue published in alternate years.

ISSN 1073-6026
DD 658 US
●**EXECUTIVE DIRECTIONS.** [Exec. dir.]. Vol. 1, Issue 1 (Apr. 1994)-. Periodical. English. Three times a year. $50.00 US; $70.00 Canada; $100.00 other. Peterson's Guides, 202 Carnegie Center, Department 2342, PO Box 2123, Princeton NJ 08543-2123. **Tel** (609)243-9111, (800)338-3282, FAX (609)243-9150, (609)452-0966. **ED** Jim Gish and Karen Petty.
 Desc: Looks exclusively at how executives are made and how they can change an organization. Contains feature articles, opinion pieces, survey results, and more.

ISSN 0733-9291
US
EXECUTIVE EDGE. [Exec. edge]. Vol. 1, No. 1 (Oct. 1982)-. Periodical. English. Twenty-four times a year. $48.00. Executive Fitness Newsletter, Hennessy Road, PO Box 20036, Hong Kong Hong Kong. **Tel** 011 852 25667937.

LC HD38.2 .E935
DD 338.7/61658407111/025 UK
EXECUTIVE GRAPEVINE : EG, THE.
 VFOAT EG; Directory of Executive Recruitment Consultants. (19??)-. English. Irregular. $109.52. Executive Grapevine Ltd., 79 Manor Way, Blackheath, London, SE3 9XG United Kingdom. **Tel** 011 44 181 3184462, FAX 011 44 181 3189456.
 Ind/Abst Curr. Cit.

HK
EXECUTIVE (HONG KONG EDITION). (THE EXECUTIVE.). Vol. 5, No. 4 (Apr. 1984)-. Periodical. English. Twelve times a year. $25.00. Executive Media Ltd., 233 Hollywood Road, 3/F Hollywood, Hong Kong Hong Kong. **Tel** 011 852 5 28155221, FAX 011 852 5 28542794. **ED** Gerald Delikhan. **Ad Acc, Adv Mgr:** Lesley Kelly. **Circ:** 19,000. **Continues** Young Executive (Asean Edition).
 Desc: Aimed at entrepreneurs and successful business people. Includes lifestyle leisure subjects ranging from fashion to the holidays along with personal investment opportunities and advice from the experts.

CL
EXECUTIVE NOTES ON ENVIRONMENT AND DEVELOPMENT : INFORMATION BULLETIN PREPARED JOINTLY BY THE ENVIRONMENT AND HUMAN SETTLEMENTS DIVISION AND THE INFORMATION SERVICE OF THE ECONOMIC COMMISSION FOR LATIN AMERICA AND THE CARIBBEAN, ECLAC. Added/Corp United Nations. Economic Commission for Latin American and the Caribbean. Environment and Human Settlements Division. United Nations. Economic Commission for Latin American and the Caribbean. Information Service. (1992)-. Bulletin. English.

LC HG
DD 332 ISSN 0279-1382
 US
 CCC
EXECUTIVE REPORT (PITTSBURGH, PA.). (EXECUTIVE REPORT.). (1981)-. Periodical. English. Twelve times a year. $30.00. Executive Report, Three Gateway Center, Fifth Floor, Pittsburgh PA 15222. **Tel** (412)471-4585, FAX (412)644-3006. **ED** Patty Tascarella. **Ad Acc, Adv Mgr:** Karen Schade. **Circ:** 24,000 (ctrl). available on an online database from DIALOG; available via Internet (http://www.execreport.com/er.html). Documents available from UMI Article Clearinghouse.
 Desc: Topics of interest to western Pennsylvania business executives.
 Ind/Abst Acad. Search; Bus. Dateline; Bus. Index (Jan. 1985-Dec. 1985); Bus. Source Plus; Bus. Source; EP Collect.; Gen. BusinessFile (Jan. 1985-Dec. 1985); Gen. Period. Index (Jan. 1985-Dec. 1985); Homework Help.; INFO-SOUTH Abstr.; Mag. Search; MasterFile FullTEXT 1000; MasterFile FullTEXT 350; MasterFile FullTEXT 650; MasterFile FullTEXT (Jan. 1994-); OCLC; Telebase.

LC WMLC 93/792 ISSN 0888-4110
DD 808 US
EXECUTIVE SPEECHES (DAYTON, OHIO). (EXECUTIVE SPEECHES.). [Exec. speeches]. Vol. 1, No. 1 (Aug. 1986)-. Trade Publication. English. Six times a year. $60.00. The Executive Speaker Company, PO Box 292437, Dayton OH 45429. **Tel** (513)294-8493, FAX (513)294-6044. **ED** Robert O. Skovgard. available on microfilm from University Microfilms International (UMI). Documents available from UMI Article Clearinghouse.
 Desc: Full-texts of speeches by executives on topics like change, leadership, health care, and philanthropy.
 Ind/Abst ABI/INFORM Glob. Ed.; ABI/INFORM [Computer File] (Oct. 1987-); Curr. Cit.; UMI ABI/Inform--Bus. Period. Ondisc [Full Txt.].

ISSN 0968-8803
UK
EXECUTIVE SYSTEMS INTERNATIONAL NEWSLETTER. [Exec. syst. int.]. (1988)-. Newsletter. English. Twenty-five times a year. £295.00 UK; £340.00 other. Business Intelligence Publishing, Forum House, 1 Graham Road, London SW19 3SW United Kingdom. **Tel** 011 44 181 5441830, FAX 011 44 181 5449020. **ED** Clive Couldwell. Index available. cum. index. **Bk Rev.** (Qty: 10). ctrl circ.
 Desc: Conducts a continuing program of research into management support technologies in the UK and overseas markets.

ISSN 0733-5512
US
EXECUTIVE UPDATE. Added/Corp Greater Washington Society of Association Executives. (19??)-. Periodical. English. Twelve times a year. Comes with membership to the Greater Washington Society of Association Executives. GWSAE / Greater Washington Society of Association Executives, 1426 21st Street, Suite 200, Washington DC 20036. **Tel** (202)429-9370.

US
CEASED
EXECUTIVE UPDATE NEWSLETTER. (19??)-(April 1994). Newsletter. English. Dartnell Corporation, 4660 North Ravenswood Avenue, Chicago IL 60640. **Tel** (312)561-4000, (800)621-5463, FAX (312)561-3801. **Absorbed** The Effective Manager.

ISSN 1073-2993
DD 658 US
EXECUTIVECITIZEN. [Exec.citiz.]. **VFOAT** Executive Citizen. (Fall 1992)-. Periodical. English. Six times a year. $63.00. Executive Citizen, 10 Rogers Street, Suite 604, Cambridge MA 02142.

ISSN 1073-8355
DD 658 US
CODEN EXPMEG
EXPANSION MANAGEMENT. [Expans. manag.]. (198?)-. Trade Publication. English. Six times a year (with extra issue in Feb.). $40.00. Expansion Management, 1301 Spruce Street, Boulder CO 80302. **Tel** (800)839-7263, FAX (303)939-9559. **ED** Victoria Cooper. **Ad Acc. Circ:** 40,000 (ctrl).

ISSN 0824-3131
DD 343.7105/23/024658 CN
EXPENSES OF SALES REPRESENTATIVES, TAX TREATMENT. (EXPENSES OF SALES REPRESENTATIVES.). English. Every 2 years. $6.00. CCH Canadian Ltd., 6 Garamond Court, Don Mills Ontario M3C 1Z5 Canada. **Tel** (416)441-2992, FAX (416)441-3418.
 Desc: A booklet describing the income tax provisions which apply to sales representatives, whether employees or self-employed.

LC HD9561 .I6 ISSN 0537-9741
DD 338.2/7282/0973 US
 CCC
 CODEN EEPIA3
EXPLORATION AND ECONOMICS OF THE PETROLEUM INDUSTRY. See Petroleum and Natural Gas.

ISSN 0312-3774
DD 382.60994 AT
EXPORT HANDBOOK SYDNEY. [Export handb. Syd.]. (1975)-. Periodical. English. Irregular. 95.00Aus$ 15th Edition; 65.00Aus$ 14th Edition. Australian Institute of Export, 281 Sussex Street, Suite 9, Sydney NSW 2000 Australia. **Tel** 011 61 2 2649322, FAX 011 61 2 2649387. **Bk Rev. Ad Acc, Adv Mgr:** Andrew Pomeroy.
 Desc: A comprehensive guide to practical aspects of exporting which is essential for both experienced and novice exports

PP
EXPORT PRICE INDEXES (PORT MORESBY, PAPUA NEW GUINEA). (EXPORT PRICE INDEXES.). (June Quarter 1976)-. Periodical. English. Four times a year. k6.00 Papua New Guinea; k7.00 (surface mail), k10.00 (airmail) other. National Statistical Office / New Guinea, PO Wards Strip NCO, Papua New Guinea. **Tel** 011 675 27182 271172, FAX 011 657 255057, telex FINANCE NE 22312.

PO
EXPRESSO. (19??)-. Periodical. Portuguese. One time a week. $400.00. Sociedade Journal Editorial, Rua Duque de Palmela, 1296 Lisbon Codex Portugal. **Tel** 011 351 1 3526141.
 Ind/Abst Infomat Int. Bus.; PROMT.

ISSN 0899-8485
US
EXTRA INCOME NEWS NEWSLETTER.
 VFOAT Extra Income News. Newsletter. English. Twelve times a year. M J Chambers, PO Box 2427, Orange TX 77630.

ISSN 0888-367X
US
EXTRA INCOME. VFOAT Extra Income. (198?)-. Periodical. English. Six times a year. $11.95. Business Concepts, 16 West Mission Sutie North, Santa Barbara CA 93101. **Tel** (805)569-1363. **(Subscription address:** Kable Publishers Aide / Illinois, 308 East Hitt Street, Subscription Department, Mt. Morris IL 61054-1473. **Tel** (815)734-1261.)

Business and Economics

ISSN 0162-3184
US

EXTRAORDINARY CONTRACTUAL RELIEF REPORTER. (1973)-. Periodical. English. One time a year. $243.80. Federal Publications Inc, 1120 20th Street Northwest, Washington DC 20036. **Tel** (202)337-7000, (800)922-4330, FAX (202)659-2233.

LC CURRENT ISSUES ONLY

US

●**F & S INDEX UNITED STATES.** VFOAT F and S Index United States; F & S Index United States. Vol. 34, No. 5 (May 1993)-. English. Twelve times a year. $1150.26. Predicasts Inc., A Ziff Communications Company, 11001 Cedar Avenue, Cleveland OH 44106. **Tel** (800)321-6388, (216)795-3000, FAX (216)229-9944, telex 985 604. **(Subscription address:** Information Access Company, PO Box 61000, Department 1851, San Francisco CA 94161. **Tel** (800)321-6388.) **Continues** Predicasts F & S Index United States, 0270-4544.
 Desc: Covers broad business and economic data, product, industry, company and market activities reported in business publications.

ISSN 0307-7523
UK

FABIAN PAMPHLET. Added/Corp Fabian Society (Great Britain). (1991)-. Monographic series. English. Irregular (minimum of 6, up to 12 per year). Price varies per volume. Fabian Society, 11 Dartmouth Street, London SW1H 9BN United Kingdom. **Tel** 011 44 171 2228877, FAX 011 44 171 9767153. **ED** Stephen Pollard. Index available. cum. index. **Circ:** 5,500 (ctrl) **Continues** Fabian Tract.

US

FACT BOOK : TABLES AND CHARTS ON THE NEW YORK METROPOLITAN REGION. See Business and Economics-Abstracting, Bibliographies and Statistics.

LC HJ
DD 336
UDC 336.2 + 34 + 351.83
ISSN 0926-4078
NE

FACT (DEVENTER). (FACT.). [Fact Deventer]. (1991)-. Periodical. Dutch. Twenty-six times a year. $181.92. Kluwer Berdijfswetenschappen, Postbus 4, 2400 Alphen Rijn Netherlands. **Tel** 011 31 01720 66855. **(Subscription address:** Intermedia BV, Postbus 4, 2400 MA Alphen AD Rijn Netherlands. **Tel** 011 31 1720 66481.) **Continues** Feiten en Cijfers, 0165-0238.

IT

FACTS AND FIGURES (MONTEDISON GROUP). Main/Corp Montedison Group. 1980-. English. One time a year. Montedison Group, Foro Buonaparte 31, 20121 Milan Italy. **Continues** Montedison S.P.A. Annual Report.

LC G
DD 900
ISSN 0014-6641
US

FACTS ON FILE. See History.

CN

FAIR SCOPE. English. Five times a year (Jan., Mar. June, Sept. Nov.). 20.00Can$ Canada; 25.00Can$ other. Canadian Association of Exhibitions, 11811 81st Street, Edmonton Alberta T5B 2R4 Canada. **Tel** (403)474-1902, FAX (403)471-4981. **ED** Elizabeth J. Hart. **Ad Acc. Circ:** 2,200 (ctrl).
 Desc: News and information on the Canadian fairs and exhibitions industry in Canada.

ISSN 0898-9818
DD 330
US

FAIRFIELD COUNTY BUSINESS JOURNAL. [Fairfld. Cty. bus. j.]. (1988)-. Periodical. English. One time a week. $52.00. Westfair Communications Inc., 22 Sawmill River Road, Hawthorne NY 10532. **Tel** (914)347-5200, FAX (914)327-5576. available on an online database (files 635,648/Full-Text) from DIALOG. Documents available from UMI Article Clearinghouse. **Continues** Southern Connecticut Business Journal, 0894-976X.
 Ind/Abst Bus. Dateline; Bus. Source Plus; Bus. Source; EP Collect.; Homework Help.; MasterFile FullTEXT 1000; MasterFile FullTEXT 350; MasterFile FullTEXT 650; MasterFile FullTEXT; OCLC; PROMT; Telebase; Trade Ind. ASAP [Full Txt.]; Trade Ind. Index [Full Txt.].

LC HC
DD 330
ISSN 0965-1403
UK

FAMILY SPENDING. Added/Corp Great Britain. Central Statistical Office. (1990)-. Statistical Publication. English. One time a year. £25.00. Her Majesty's Stationery Office, 51 Nine Elms Lane, London SW8 5DR United Kingdom. **Tel** 011 44 171 8738499, FAX 011 44 171 8738499, 011 44 171 8738456, telex 297138. **(Subscription address:** Her Majesty's Stationery Office, PO Box 276, Public Centre, London SW8 5DT United Kingdom. **Tel** 011 44 171 8738499, 011 44 171 8738456.) **Continues** Family Expenditure Survey (London, England), 0072-5927.

LC HC240.A1 P73
DD 330
US

●**F&S INDEX EUROPE. Added/Corp** Information Access Company. VFOAT F and S Index Europe; Information Access Company F&S Index Europe. Vol. 16, No. 5 (May 1993)-. Abstracting/Indexing Service. English. Seventeen times a year. $1075.00. Predicasts Inc., A Ziff Communications Company, 11001 Cedar Avenue, Cleveland OH 44106. **Tel** (800)321-6388, (216)795-3000, FAX (216)229-9944, telex 985 604. **(Subscription address:** Information Access Company, PO Box 61000, Department 1851, San Francisco CA 94161. **Tel** (800)321-6388.) **Continues** Predicasts F & S Index Europe, 0270-4536.

LC HC240.A1 .E8 P73
DD 016.338/0025/4
ISSN 1076-6596

●**F&S INDEX EUROPE ANNUAL (1993).** (F&S INDEX EUROPE ANNUAL.). [F&S index Eur. annu.]. **Added/Corp** Information Access Company. VFOAT F & S Index Europe Annual. (1993)-. English. $1,075.00. Predicasts Inc., A Ziff Communications Company, 11001 Cedar Avenue, Cleveland OH 44106. **Tel** (800)321-6388, (216)795-3000, FAX (216)229-9944, telex 985 604. **(Subscription address:** Information Access Company, PO Box 61000, Department 1851, San Francisco CA 94161. **Tel** (800)321-6388.) **Continues** Predicasts F & S Index Europe Annual, 0277-9684.
 Desc: Covers business activities in the Common Market, Scandinavia, other areas of Western Europe, the former Soviet Union and Eastern Europe.

LC HD2321
DD 338
US

●**F&S INDEX INTERNATIONAL. See** Business and Economics-Abstracting, Bibliographies and Statistics.

LC Z7164.C81 F132
DD 382
ISSN 1065-5956
US

F&S INDEX PLUS TEXT. INTERNATIONAL. See Business and Economics-Abstracting, Bibliographies and Statistics.

LC Z7165.U5 F232
DD 381
ISSN 1065-5964
US

F&S INDEX PLUS TEXT. UNITED STATES. See Business and Economics-Abstracting, Bibliographies and Statistics.

LC Z7165.U5 F23
DD 016.3380973
ISSN 1076-4941
US

●**F&S INDEX UNITED STATES ANNUAL.** (F&S INDEX UNITED STATES ANNUAL / INFORMATION ACCESS COMPANY.). [F&S index U.S. annu.]. **Added/Corp** Information Access Company. VFOAT F & S Index United States Annual; F and S Index United States Annual. (1993)-. English. One time a year. $1,075.00. Predicasts Inc., A Ziff Communications Company, 11001 Cedar Avenue, Cleveland OH 44106. **Tel** (800)321-6388, (216)795-3000, FAX (216)229-9944, telex 985 604. **(Subscription address:** Information Access Company, PO Box 61000, Department 1851, San Francisco CA 94161. **Tel** (800)321-6388.) **Continues** Predicasts F & S Index United States (Annual Edition), 0277-9676.

DD 338
ISSN 0886-5906
US

FARM ECONOMICS : FACTS AND OPINIONS. See Agriculture-Agricultural Economics.

DD 338
ISSN 0555-9456
US

FARM ECONOMICS (UNIVERSITY PARK, PA.). See Agriculture-Agricultural Economics.

LC HD2075.6 .A28
DD 338.1/09549/2
BG

FARM ECONOMY. See Agriculture-Agricultural Economics.

DD 338
ISSN 0883-2188
US

FARM FINANCIAL CONDITIONS REVIEW. See Agriculture-Agricultural Economics.

ISSN 1059-6844
US

FAXON BUSINESS INFORMATION CATALOG. (1992)-. Catalog. English. Free on request. Faxon Press, PO Box 9102, Boston MA 02132.

ISSN 0740-347X
US

FAXON INTERNATIONAL NEWSLETTER. [Faxon int. newsl.]. **Added/Corp** Faxon Company. Vol. 1, No. 1 (1983)-. Newsletter. English. Four times a year. FW Faxon Company Inc., Faxon Building, 15 Southwest Drive, Westwood MA 02090. **Tel** (617)329-3350.

DD 330
ISSN 1045-3334
US

FEDGAZETTE (MINNEAPOLIS, MINN.). (FEDGAZETTE : REGIONAL BUSINESS & ECONOMICS NEWSPAPER.). [Fedgazette]. **Added/Corp** Federal Reserve Bank of Minneapolis. (Mar. 1989)-. Periodical. English. Four times a year (Jan., Apr., July, Oct.). Free on request. Federal Reserve Bank of Minneapolis, 250 Marquette Avenue, Publ Affairs, Minneapolis MN 55480. **Tel** (612)340-2356. **Circ:** 12,000. **Continues** District Economic Conditions, 0882-410X.
 Desc: Describes and forecasts economic conditions in the 9th Federal Reserve System in areas of Montana, North and South Dakota, Minnesota, Wisconsin, and the upper peninsula of Michigan. Focuses on regional news of current interest, economic indicators, editorials and opinion survey results.
 Ind/Abst EP Collect.; Homework Help.; MasterFile FullTEXT 1000; MasterFile FullTEXT 350; MasterFile FullTEXT 650; MasterFile FullTEXT; OCLC; Telebase.

FR

FEEDBACK ELISE. (19??)-. English (French). Irregular. **Added/Corp** OECD Publications and Information Center, 2 rue Andre-Pascal, 75775 Paris Cedex 16 France. **Tel** 011 33 1 49104262, US:(202)785-6323, FAX 011 33 1 45248500, 011 33 1 45248176, telex 620 160 OCDE.

NE

FEESTELIJK ZAKENDOEN MAGAZINE. (19??)-. Periodical. Dutch. Six times a year. FI155.50. Misset Uitgeverij BV / Doetinchem, Postbus 4, 7000 BA Doetinchem Netherlands. **Tel** 011 31 8340 49911, 011 31 8340 49562, FAX 011 31 8340 43839, 011 31 8340 40515.

LC HB71
DD 330
ISSN 1354-5071
UK

●**FEMINIST ECONOMICS. Added/Corp** International Association for Feminist Economics. (Spring 1995)-. Academic Scholarly Publication. English. Three times a year. $90.00. Routledge, 11 New Fetter Lane, London EC4P 4EE United Kingdom. **Tel** 011 44 171 5839855, FAX 011 44 171 5830701. **(Subscription address:** International Thomson Publishing Services Ltd., North Way Andover, Hampshire SP10 5BE United Kingdom. **Tel** 011 44 1264 332424.) **ED** Diana Strassmann. **Ad Acc.** Full Page (B&W) £150.00. Documents available from BLDSC.
 Desc: Covers different perspectives and intellectual traditions in economics.

AG

FIDE : THE ARGENTINE ECONOMIC REVIEW. Added/Corp Fundacion de Investigaciones para el Desarrollo (Argentina). VFOAT Argentine Economic Review. No. 1 (August 1983)-. Periodical. English. Twelve times a year.

ISSN 0015-086X
HU

FIGYELO. [Figyelo]. (1957)-. Periodical. Hungarian. One time a week. $84.00. **(Subscription address:** Kultura, PO Box 143, H-1300 Budapest 3 Hungary. **Tel** 011 36 1 2500194.)
 Ind/Abst Energy Res. Abstr. (Nov. 1982-).

FR

FIL DIRECTEUR. (19??)-. Periodical. French. Five times a year. 244.86F France; 300.00F other. Centre de Perfectionnement des Enterprises / CEP, 46 rue Lafayette, 75009 Paris France. **Tel** 011 33 1 42461434.

LC PN1993.5.U6 F49
DD 384/.8/0973021
ISSN 1056-6945
US

... FILM FINANCIAL RECORD, THE. See Motion Picture.

LC HC
DD 330
US

FINANCIAL & COMMON STOCK INFORMATION. English. Four times a year. $175.00. Edward D. Jones & Company, 201 Progress Parkway, Maryland Heights MO 63043. **Tel** (314)851-4246, FAX (314)851-3710.

LC HG6024.3 .F57
DD 332.64/4
ISSN 0890-1309
US

FINANCIAL FUTURES. [Financ. futur.]. **Added/Corp** Data Lab Corporation. (1978)-. Periodical. English. One time a week. $285.00. Future Charts, PO Box 32309, Palm Beach FL 33420. **Tel** (800)331-1069. **ED** M.V. Girardi. **Ad Acc.**

ISSN 0962-1474
UK

FINANCIAL MARKETING UPDATE. [Financ. mark. updat.]. (1988)-. Newsletter. English. Twelve times a year. $381.59. IBC Publishing, 57-61 Mortimer St., London W1N 7TD United Kingdom. **Tel** 011 44 171 6374383, FAX 011 44 171 6366314. **Continues** Financial Marketing News, 0265-7465.

CN

FINANCIAL POST OUTLOOK. (19??)-. English. Financial Post Outlook, 333 King Street East, Toronto Ontario M5A 4N2 Canada.
 Ind/Abst Can. Period. Index (19??-).

Business and Economics

LC HG176 .O35
DD 332/.021   FR
FINANCIAL STATISTICS MONTHLY. INTERNATIONAL MARKETS. Added/Corp
Organisation for Economic Co-operation and Development. **VFOAT** International Markets; Marches Internationaux; Statistiques Financieres Mensuelles. Marches Internationaux; OECD Financial Statistics. Part 1, Financial Statistics Monthly. International Markets. (July 1983)-. Government Publication. English (French). Twenty-four times a year. $340.00. OECD Publications and Information Center, 2 rue Andre-Pascal, 75775 Paris Cedex 16 France. **Tel** 011 33 1 49104262, US:(202)785-6323, FAX 011 33 1 45248500, 011 33 1 45248176, telex 620 160 OCDE. (**Subscription address:** OECD Publications Center, 2001 L Street, Suite 700, Washington DC 20036. **Tel** (202)822-3873, (202)785-6323.) *Continues OECD Financial Statistics. Part 1, Financial Statistics Monthly. International Markets.*
Desc: Contains figures on the preceding month's operations in international financial markets (international and foreign bond issues; medium and long term international and foreign bank loans). Deals with domestic financial markets (security issues, summary of all borrowing and lending transactions in each country, consumer credit) and interest rates in international and domestic markets.

UK
FINANCIAL TIMES BUSINESS TRAVEL COSTS. VFOAT Business Travel Costs. 1981-. Trade
Publication. English. Financial Times / UK, Maple House, 149 Tottenham Court Road, London W1P 9LL United Kingdom. **Tel** 011 44 171 8962276, FAX 011 44 171 8962275, 011 44 171 8962399. *Continues Living Costs Overseas.*

ISSN 0174-7363
GW
CODEN FITIBT
FINANCIAL TIMES (FRANKFURT ED.).
(FINANCIAL TIMES.). [Financ. times]. (1979)-. Academic Scholarly Publication. English. Seven times a week. $450.00. Financial Times Europe GmbH, Nibelungenplatz 3, D-60318 Frankfurt Germany. **Tel** 011 49 69 156850, FAX 011 49 69 5964481. Documents available from CASDDS.
Ind/Abst Chem. Abstr.

DD 071

ISSN 0884-6782
US
CODEN FITIEW
FINANCIAL TIMES (NORTH AMERICAN EDITION). (FINANCIAL TIMES.). [Financ. times].
(July 8, 1985)-. Newspaper. English. Six times a week. $450.00. Financial Times - North America, 14 East 60th Street, New York NY 10022. **Tel** (212)752-4500, (800)628-8088, FAX (212)308-2397. cum. index. available on microfilm; available on an online database from WESTLAW. Documents available from CASDDS.
Desc: Covers business, economic and political developments.
Ind/Abst Br. Humanit. Index; Chem. Abstr.; Chem. Ind. Notes (1985-).

ISSN 0772-0890
BE
UDC 336
FINANCIEEL EKONOMISCHE TIJD, DE.
[Financ. ekon. tijd]. (1968)-. Periodical. Dutch. Irregular (250 issues). $625.01. Uitgeversbedrijf Tijd NV, Franklin Building, Posthoflei 3, 2600 Berchem Antwerp Belgium. **Tel** 011 32 3 2860301. available on CD-ROM. *Formed by the union of Avond-Echo, 0772-3652 and Tijd, 0772-361X.*
Ind/Abst Infomat Int. Bus.; PROMT.

IT
FINANZA ITALIANA. (19??)-. Italian. Eleven
times a year. L50000 Italy; L100000 other. La Finanza Editrice Srl, Via Tacito 41, 00193 Rome Italy. **Tel** 011 39 6 6878241, FAX 011 39 6 3724867.

LC HC
DD 330
ISSN 0430-4977
GW
FINANZWISSENSCHAFTLICHE FORSCHUNGSARBEITEN. No. 1 (1953)-.
Monographic series. German. Irregular. Price varies per volume. Duncker and Humblot Verlag, Postfach 410329, D-12113 Berlin Germany. **Tel** 011 49 30 79000612, 011 49 30 79000613. *Continues Finanzwissenschaftliche Forschungsarbeiten.*

FI
FINNISH BUSINESS REPORT. (19??)-.
Periodical. English. Eleven times a year. $75.00. Valtion Painatuskeskus, PO Box 516, SF 00101 Helsinki Finland. **Tel** 011 358 0 5660266, FAX 011 358 0 5660374. **ED** Kirgi Vanila. **Circ:** 20,000 (ctrl).
Ind/Abst Selec. Coop. Index Manage. Period.

LC HB1 .F54
DD 330.94897/05
ISSN 0784-5197
FI
FINNISH ECONOMIC PAPERS. [Finn. econ.
pap.]. **Added/Corp** Taloustieteellinen Seura (Finland) Kansandoulliten Yhdistys (Finland) Ekonomiska Aamfund i Finland. Vol. 1, No. 1 (Spring 1988)-.

Periodical. English. Two times a year. Fmk150.00 Finland; Fmk200.00 other. Finnish Society of Economic Studies, Rauhankatu 19, Helsinki FIN 00170 Finland. **Tel** 011 358 0 1832541, FAX 011 358 0 6221882.
Ind/Abst Econ. Lit. Index (199?-); J. Econ. Lit.

ISSN 8755-4372
US
FIREWORKS BUSINESS. (Feb. 1984)-.
Periodical. English. Twelve times a year. $29.95. American Fireworks News, SR Box 30, Dingmans Ferry PA 18328. **Tel** (717)828-8417, FAX (717)828-8695. **ED** J. M. Drewes (phone: (717)828-8417). **Bk Rev. Ad Acc.**
Desc: Covers materials for fireworks trade and fireworks enthusiasts.

LC HC
DD 330
ISSN 1047-9546
US
TITLE CHANGE
FIRST BOSTON WORKING PAPER SERIES. [First Boston work. pap. ser.]. Added/Corp
Columbia University. Graduate School of Business. First Boston Corporation. **VFOAT** Working Paper Series; First Boston Series. (19??)-(19??). Monographic series. English. Columbia University Graduate School of Business, J. Glazener Hall / 6N Uris Hall, New York NY 10027. **Tel** (212)854-8346. *Continued by Paine Webber Working Paper Series in Money Economics and Finance.*

LC HG4058.C5 F57
DD 338.7/4/097731
US
FIRST CHICAGO GUIDE : MAJOR PUBLICLY HELD CORPORATIONS AND FINANCIAL INSTITUTIONS HEADQUARTERED IN NORTHERN ILLINOIS. (1986)-. English. One time a year. $31.95.
Scholl Communications Inc., PO Box 560, Deerfield IL 60015. **Tel** (708)945-1891, FAX (708)945-1897. **ED** David E Scholl (editor's address: 56 Birchwood Avenue, Deerfield IL 60015). available on diskette. *Continues Becker Guide.*

US
FIRST-RATE CUSTOMER SERVICE.
(19??)-. Newsletter. English. Twenty-six times a year. $41.34. Economics Press Inc, 12 Daniel Road, Fairfield NJ 07004. **Tel** (201)227-1224, (800)526-2554, FAX (201)227-9742.
Desc: Not only addresses the "how-to" of customer service, but also helps employees develop enthusiastic, service-oriented attitudes. Helps customer service professionals see clearly how their actions affect the whole company.

FR
FISCALITE AFRICAINES. REVUE DU DROIT DES AFFARIES AFRICAINES.
French. Twenty-two times a year. 9500F France; 9700F other. Editions FFA, 51 rue Louis Blanc Cedex 75, 92037 Paris La Defns 1 France. **Tel** 011 33 1 46936901, FAX 011 33 1 47880096, telex 615200.

FR
FISCALITE DE L'INNOVATION ET DU CAPITAL RISQUE DANS LA CEE, LA.
French. 900.00F France; 950.00F other. Cahiers Fiscaux Europeens, 51 Avenue Reine Victoria, 06000 Nice France. **Tel** 011 33 93 810326.

ISSN 0015-2862
GW
UDC 656.1.03
FISCHERS TARIF-NACHRICHTEN FUER EISENBAHN UND KRAFTWAGEN.
(19??)-. Trade Publication. German. Twelve times a year. DM74.25. Verkehrs Verlag J Fischer, Postfach 140265, D-40072 Dusseldorf Germany. **Tel** 011 49 211 991930.

ISSN 0772-4837
BE
UDC 336.2
FISKOLOOG. [Fiskoloog]. VFOAT Nieuwsbrief over
Fiskaliteit en Geldbeheer. (19??)-. Periodical. Multiple languages (Dutch and French). Twenty-four times a year. 4450.00F (one-year), 8350.50F (two-year). Uitgeverij Biblo, Brasschaatsesteenweg 200, 2920 Kalmthout Belgium. **Tel** 011 32 3 6200240 6200211, 011 32 3 6200211, FAX 011 32 3 6200361, telex 72080. Index available.

DD 330
ISSN 0897-0653
US
TITLE CHANGE
FIVE-YEAR FORECAST OF BUSINESS CLIMATE TRENDS IN 85 COUNTRIES.
[Five-year forecast bus. clim. trends 85 ctries.].
Added/Corp Frost & Sullivan. Political Risk Services. **VFOAT** Five Year Forecast of Business Climate Trends in 85 Countries. (1993)-(1993). English. Frost and Sullivan, Political Risk Services, 106 Fulton Street, New York NY 10038. *Continues Trends Through ..., 0893-1976. Merged with Political Climate for International Business, 0887-7637 to form Country Forecasts, 1041-3553.*

LC HC
DD 330
ISSN 0429-9485
GW
FIW-SCHRIFTENREIHE. Main/Corp
Forschungsinstitut fur Wirtschaftsverfassung und Wettbewerb, Cologne. (1962)-. Monographic series. German. Irregular. Price varies per volume. Carl Heymanns Verlag KG, Luxemburger Strasse 449, D-50939 Cologne Germany. **Tel** 011 49 221 460100, telex 8 881 888.

DD 332
ISSN 1076-7215
US
●FLEDGLING NEWSLETTER, THE. (1993)-.
Periodical. English. Twelve times a year. $150.00. The Fledgling Newsletter, 8205-E Martin Way, Olympia WA 98516. **Tel** (206)456-3996.

DD 975
ISSN 1042-590X
US
FLORIDA BUSINESS (CLEVELAND, OHIO). (FLORIDA BUSINESS.). [Fla. bus.]. (1988)-.
Periodical. English. Twelve times a year. Florida Business, 1720 Euclid Avenue, Suite 300, Cleveland OH 44115-9743. *Continues Florida Business/Tampa Bay, 0898-0772.*

ISSN 0733-964X
US
FLORIDA BUSINESS GUIDE, THE. [Fla.
bus. guide]. **Added/Corp** Industries Guides, Inc. 1st Edition (1981)-. Directory. English. One time a year. $70.00. Industries Guides Inc / Altamonte Springs, PO Box 160158, Altamonte Springs FL 32716. **Tel** (407)682-5600. **ED** Richard J. McHenry. **Ad Acc. Circ:** 50,000.
Desc: Contains non-manufacturing firms listed alphabetically by cities and broken down by functions.

LC HC
DD 380
ISSN 0428-7088
US
FLORIDA BUSINESS LETTER. SPECIAL MAPS AND GRAPHS OF FLORIDA.
VFOAT Florida Maps and Graphs. (1956)-. English. First Research Corporation, 1450 Coral Way, Miami FL 33145.

ISSN 1047-6105
US
DD 330
FLORIDA BUSINESS SOUTHWEST. [Fla.
bus. Southwest]. **VFOAT** Florida Business/Southwest. Vol. 7, No. 10 (Oct. 1989)-. Periodical. English. Twelve times a year. Trade and Industry Publishing Group, 3706 North Ocean Boulevard, Ft Lauderdale FL 33308. **ED** Ken Gooderham. **Bk Rev. Ad Acc.** ctrl circ. Documents available from UMI Article Clearinghouse. *Continues Business View (Naples, Fla.), 0895-4836.*
Ind/Abst Bus. Dateline (Aug. 1985-) [Full Txt.]; INFO-SOUTH Abstr.; Trade Ind. ASAP [Full Txt.]; Trade Ind. Index [Full Txt.].

LC HF5382.75.U62 F645
DD 331.12/8/0975905
ISSN 1069-8981
US
FLORIDA JOB BANK, THE. See Occupations and Careers.

DD 330
ISSN 0886-2729
US
FLORIDA MARKET UPDATE. [Fla. mark.
update]. **Added/Corp** Data Directions, Inc. (1985)-. Periodical. English. Irregular (12-15 issues per year). Data Directions Inc., PO Box 1052, Port Washington NY 11050. **Tel** (516)876-2108, (516)333-7730. **ED** Hank Boerner and Harry Prior. cum. index. **Circ:** 3,000. *Continues Florida Marketing Update, 0886-2710. Continued in part by Carib Basin Trade Update, 0888-1065.*
Desc: Publication reaches senior corporate managers, investors, financiers, bankers, and government officials. Editorial emphasis is on trends and news which will have effect on future directions of state's economy.

ISSN 0193-502X
US
CEASED
FOCUS (BUSINESS NEWS, INC.). (FOCUS
: METROPOLITAN PHILADELPHIA'S BUSINESS NEWSWEEKLY.). **VFOAT** Metropolitan Philadelphia's Business Newsweekly. (Feb. 7, 1968)-(1993). Periodical. English. Metropolitan Business News, 201 N. Broad St., Philadelphia PA 19107. **Tel** (215)561-8866, FAX (215)561-8885. **ED** Vijay S Kothare. **Bk Rev. Ad Acc. Circ:** 17,176 (ctrl). available on microfilm and microfiche from University Microfilms International (UMI). Documents available from UMI Article Clearinghouse.
Desc: Delaware Valley news publication.
Ind/Abst Bus. Dateline; Bus. Index (Jan. 1985-Dec. 1985); Gen. Period. Index (Jan. 1985-Dec. 1985); PROMT.

LC G1 .F6
DD 910.5
ISSN 0015-5004
US
CODEN BLOFA5
FOCUS (NEW YORK, N.Y. 1950). See Geography.

IT
FOGLIO ANNUNCI LEGALI. MILANO.
Italian. Tipografia Tediolo, Via Corrado 30 / 40, 46100 Mantova Italy.

ISSN 0015-6035
SP

FOMENTO DE LA PRODUCCION. [Fom. prod.]. (1946)-. Periodical. Spanish. Twenty-six times a year. 13700ptas. Fomento de La Produccion, Casanova 57, Barceloa 11 Spain. **Tel** 011 34 3 4530697, FAX 011 34 3 3233885.
Ind/Abst Infomat Int. Bus.

ISSN 1057-6940
DD 338 US

FOOD BUSINESS OPPORTUNITIES. [Food bus. oppor.]. (198?)-. Periodical. English. Four times a year (Mar., June, Sept., Dec.). $160.00. F. R. I. Enterprises, PO Box 67, New Berlin WI 53151. **Tel** (414)782-3330, FAX (414)782-8228. **ED** Dr. T Shukla. ctrl circ.

ISSN 0951-7731
UK

FOOD FORECAST. **See** Food and Food Industry.

LC HF5001 .F6 ISSN 0015-6914
DD 650/.05 US
CCC
CODEN FORBA5

FORBES. [Forbes]. **VFOAT** Forbes Magazine. Vol. 2, No. 1, (Apr. 20. 1918)-. Academic Scholarly Publication. English. Twenty-seven times a year. $57.00. Forbes Magazine, 60 Fifth Avenue, New York NY 10011. **Tel** (212)620-2200, (800)825-0061. **(Subscription address:** CDS / SIFD Agency Control, 1901 Bell Avenue, Des Moines IA 50315. **Tel** (515)246-6812.) **ED** James Michaels. **Ad Acc. Circ:** 735,000. available on microfilm and microfiche from University Microfilms International (UMI); available on an online database from NEXIS; and (files 16,647,648,675/Full-Text) DIALOG. Documents available from UMI Article Clearinghouse, CASDDS, Documents on Demand, Magazine Collection. ***Continues** Forbes Magazine.*
Desc: Reports on approximately 15 companies each issue from the manager's viewpoint. Interviews business leaders for answers to business problems. Wall Street analysts interpret the stock market and make recommendations.
Ind/Abst ABI/INFORM Glob. Ed.; ABI/INFORM Ondisc: Expr. Ed.; ABI/INFORM [Computer File] (Sept. 1971-); Abstr. Bull. Inst. Pap. Sci. Tech.; Acad. Abstr. Full Text Elite; Acad. Abstr.; Acad. Ind. [Computer File] (1984-); Acad. Search; Account. Tax Datab. (Sept. 1971-); AGRICOLA [Select. Cov.]; Aviat. Tradescan [Select. Cov.]; BioBusiness; Bus. Index (1985-); Bus. Period. Index; Bus. Source Plus; Bus. Source; Chem. Abstr.; Chem. Ind. Notes; Coal Abstr.; Comput. Bus.; Comput. Lit. Index; Comput. Rev.; Energy Inf. Abstr.; Environ. Abstr.; EP Collect.; Expand. Acad. Index (1987-); F&S Index Plus Text, Int. [Full Txt.] [Select. Cov.]; Foods Adlibra; Gen. BusinessFile (1985-); Gen. Period. Index (1985-); Health Plan. Adminis.; Homework Help.; Index Period. Artic. Relat. Law; INFO-SOUTH Abstr.; Infobank (Jan. 1969-); Int. Exec.; Mag. Artic. Summar. Elite; Mag. Artic. Summar. Select; Mag. Artic. Summar. CD-ROM; Mag. Express (1986-) [Full Txt.]; Mag. Index Plus (1989-); Mag. Index. Sel. (1986-); Mag. Search; MasterFile FullTEXT 1000; MasterFile FullTEXT 350; MasterFile FullTEXT 650; MasterFile FullTEXT (Jan. 1984-) [Full Txt.]; Middle East Abstr. Index; Newsp. Period. Abstr. (1986-); OCLC; Oper. Res./Manage. Sci.; PROMT [Full Txt.]; Pub. Lib. FullTEXT; Qual. Control Appl. Stat.; Read. Guide Abstr. Select Ed.; Read. Guide Period. Lit.; Resource/One Ondisc; SPORT Discus; Stat. Ref. Index; Telebase; Mag. Index (1977-); TOM Gen. Index (1985-) [Full Txt.]; Trade Ind. ASAP [Full Txt.]; Trade Ind. Index (1981-) [Full Txt.]; UMI ABI/Inform--Bus. Period. Ondisc (Jan. 1987-) [Full Txt.]; Urban Aff. Abstr.; Vocat. Search; Wilson Bus. Abstr.; World Mag. Bank.

FR

FORCE DE VENTE INFOS. French. Twenty-four times a year. 727.74F France; 810.00F other. Editions Pratiques, BP 148, F-74941 Annecy Le Vieux France. **Tel** 011 33 16 50640439, FAX 011 33 16 50640320, telex 385060.

US

•**FORECAST.** **Added/Corp** Faulkner & Gray, Inc. Vol. 1, No. 1 (Sept./Oct. 1993)-. Periodical. English. Six times a year. $103.95 US, Canada and Mexico; $129.00 other. Faulkner & Gray Inc., 11 Penn Plaza, 17th Floor, New York NY 10001. **Tel** (212)967-7000, (800)535-8403.

JA

FOREIGN CAPITAL AFFILIATED ENTERPRISES IN JAPAN. **Main/Corp** Japan. Tsusho Sangyosho. Kigyokyoku. **Added/Corp** Business Intercommunications, Inc. (19??)-. Periodical. English. One time a year. Business Intercommunications, 3-21-13 Minamisoyama, Minatoku Tokyo 107 Japan. **(Subscription address:** Maruzen Company Ltd., PO Box 5050, Import & Export Department, Tokyo 100 31 Japan. **Tel** 011 81 3 32789224.)

ISSN 1063-8407
DD 658 US
TITLE CHANGE

FORESIGHT (RESTON, VA.). (FORESIGHT.). [Foresight]. **Added/Corp** Marek Enterprise, Inc. (19??)-(19??). Periodical. English. Marek Enterprise Inc., 11733 Bowman Green Drive, Reston VA 22090. **Tel** (800)575-2735, FAX (703)709-6171. **ED** Edward S Marek. **Circ:** 100. available on an online database from Compuserve Inc. ***Continued by** Bulletins, 1076-8939.*
Desc: Business perspectives about business leadership in the global marketplace.

US

FORMS AND DIRECT MAIL MANUFACTURERS MARKET PLACE. English. Six times a year (Jan., Mar., May, July, Sept., Nov.). $49.00 (one-year); $125.00 (two-year). Bulls Eye Communication, PO Box 7070, Fairfax Station VA 22039. **Tel** (80)327-7652. **ED** Marsha A. Thompson. **Ad Acc, Adv Mgr Tel** (800)327-7652. **Circ:** 4,600.
Desc: A resource magazine for manufacturers of business forms and direct mail printers.

ISSN 0730-2665
US

FORMS OF BUSINESS AGREEMENTS & RESOLUTIONS. **VFOAT** Forms of Business Agreements and Resolutions. (19??)-. English. Four times a year. $306.00. Institute for Business Planning Inc., Subscription Service Center, IBP Plaza, Englewood Cliffs NJ 07632. ***Continues** Forms of Business Agreements.*

ISSN 1042-3028
DD 658 US
TITLE CHANGE

FORMSMFG. (ARLINGTON, VA.). (FORMSMFG.). [Formsmfg.]. **Added/Corp** International Business Forms Industries. **VAT** FormsManufacturing. Vol. 1, No. 1 (Oct. 1987)-(19??). Periodical. English. International Business Forms Industries Inc, 2111 Wilson Boulevard, Suite 350, Arlington VA 22201-3008. **Tel** (703)841-9191, FAX (703)522-5750. **ED** Judith Polas and John Rosenberg. Index available. **Ad Acc. Circ:** 3,200. ***Formed by the union of** Informs, 0278-9841; Tech Roundup **and** Econoscope (Arlington, Va.). **Continued by** Papertronix.*
Desc: Contains articles for the manufacturer of business forms, labels, direct mail and information systems on technology, marketing, planning and production.
Ind/Abst Abstr. Bull. Inst. Pap. Sci. Tech.

LC HF5001 .F7 ISSN 0015-8259
DD 051 US
NLM HF 5353 F745 CODEN FORTAP
Pr Rev.

FORTUNE. [Fortune]. Vol. 1, (Feb. 1930)-. Periodical. English. Twenty-six times a year. $57.00. Time Inc. / New York, Time & Life Building, Rockefeller Center, New York NY 10020. **(Subscription address:** Time Customer Service, PO Box 60050, Tampa FL 33609. **Tel** (800)541-9955.) **Ad Acc.** available on an online database from DIALOG; available on microfilm and microfiche from University Microfilms International (UMI). Documents available from The Genuine Article, UMI Article Clearinghouse, CASDDS, Documents on Demand, Magazine Collection.
Desc: A blue chip source of useful information about big business and what makes it work. Personal finance and personalities, corporate and entrepreneurial strategies, industry trends and highly accurate economic forecasts are covered.
Ind/Abst ABI/INFORM Glob. Ed.; ABI/INFORM [Computer File] (Sept. 1971-); Abstr. Bull. Inst. Pap. Sci. Tech.; Acad. Abstr. Full Text Elite; Acad. Abstr.; Acad. Ind. [Computer File] (1984-); Acad. Search; Account. Tax Datab. (Sept. 1971-) [Full Txt.]; AGRICOLA [Select. Cov.]; Aviat. Tradescan [Select. Cov.]; BioBusiness; Book Rev. Index; Bus. ASAP (1992-) [Full Txt.]; Bus. Index (1985-); Bus. Period. Index; Bus. Source Plus; Bus. Source; Can. Period. Index (19??-); Chem. Abstr.; Chem. Ind. Notes; Coal Abstr.; Comput. Bus. (19??-19??); Comput. Lit. Index; Contents Pages Manage.; Curr. Contents Soc. Behav. Sci.; Curr. Lit. Fam. Plan. (19??-199?); EMBASE; Energy Inf. Abstr.; Energy Res. Abstr. (June 1971-); Environ. Abstr.; EP Collect.; Expand. Acad. Index (1984-); F&S Index Plus Text, Int. [Select. Cov.]; Foods Adlibra; Gas Abstr.; GATFWORLD (1984); Gen. BusinessFile (1985-); Gen. Period. Index (1985-); GeoRef; Homework Help.; Hosp. Health Admin. Index; Index Bus. Reports; Index Period. Artic. Relat. Law; INFO-SOUTH Abstr.; Infobank (Jan. 1969-); INIS Atomindex [Micro.]; Int. Aerosp. Abstr.; Int. Exec.; Int. Labour Doc.; Law Office Inf. Serv.; Mag. Artic. Summar. Elite; Mag. Artic. Summar. Select; Mag. Artic. Summar. CD-ROM; Mag. ASAP Plus [Full Txt.]; Mag. ASAP Sel. [Full Txt.]; Mag. Express (1986-) [Full Txt.]; Mag. Index Plus (1989-); Mag. Index Sel. Microfiche (1986-1991) [Full Txt.]; Mag. Index. Sel. (1986-); Mag. Search; MasterFile FullTEXT 1000; MasterFile FullTEXT 350; MasterFile FullTEXT 650; MasterFile FullTEXT (Jan. 1984-); Middle East Abstr. Index; Newsp. Period. Abstr. (1986-); OCLC; Oper. Res./Manage. Sci.; PAIS Int. Print (1991-) [Full Txt.]; PROMPT; Pub. Lib. FullTEXT; Qual. Control Appl. Stat.; Read. Guide Abstr. Select Ed.; Read. Guide Period. Lit.; Res. Alert [Full Cov.]; Resource/One Ondisc; Selec. Coop. Index Manage. Period.; Soc. Sci. Cit. Index [Full Cov.]; SportSearch; Stat. Ref. Index; Telebase; Text. Technol. Dig.; Mag. Index (1977-); TOM Gen. Index (1985-) [Full Txt.]; Trade Ind. ASAP [Full Txt.]; Trade Ind. Index (1981-) [Full Txt.]; UMI ABI/Inform--Bus. Period. Ondisc (Jan. 1987-) [Full Txt.]; Urban Aff. Abstr.; Vocat. Search; Wilson Bus. Abstr.; Work Relat. Abstr.; World Mag. Bank.

ISSN 1048-8065
US

FORTUNE DIGEST. (1991)-. Periodical. English. One time a year. $24.95. Oxmoor House, PO Box 1862, Birmingham AL 35201. **Tel** (205)877-6000.

ISSN 0989-2869
FR

FORTUNE FRANCE. **VFOAT** Fortune. (1988)-. French. Twelve times a year.
Ind/Abst Selec. Coop. Index Manage. Period.

LC HF5001 .F73 ISSN 0738-5587
DD 650/.05 US

FORTUNE INTERNATIONAL. [Fortune int.]. Vol. 107, No. 1 (Jan. 10, 1983)-. Periodical. English. Twenty-seven times a year. $106.00. Time Life International, Ottho Heldringstraat 5, 1066 AZ Amsterdam Netherlands. **Tel** 011 31 20 5104203. Documents available from UMI Article Clearinghouse.
Ind/Abst ABI/INFORM Glob. Ed.; Abstr. BioCommer.; Infomat Int. Bus.; Int. Labour Doc.; LABORDOC; Manage. Market. Abstr.

LC HB1 .F633 ISSN 0736-0932
DD 330/.05 US
Pr Rev.

FORUM FOR SOCIAL ECONOMICS, THE. [Forum soc. econ.]. **Added/Corp** Association for Social Economics. Temple University. School of Business Administration. Villanova University. College of Commerce and Finance. (Spring 1977)-. Periodical. English. Two times a year (Apr. and Oct.). $7.00. Forum for Social Economics, St. Louis University, Department of Economics, St. Louis MO 63108. **Tel** (314)977-3814, FAX (314)977-3897. **ED** Patrick J. Welch. Index available. cum. index. **Bk Rev**, (Qty: varies). **Ad Acc. Circ:** 500 (ctrl). ***Continues** Forum (Denton, Tex.), 0732-0426.*
Desc: Aims to facilitate communication and discussion in the field of social economics and the social economy. Encourages dialogue within the profession on humanistic, value-oriented issues as well as topics in current affairs and others.
Ind/Abst Am. Hist. Life (1984-).

ISSN 0340-7705
GW

FORUM WARE. (19??)-. German (English and Italian). Four times a year. S550.00 Austria; S600.00 other. Osterreichische Gesellschaft fur Warenkunde & Technologie, Augasse 2 6, Dr. Wagner, A-1090 Vienna Austria. **Tel** 4313 1336 4806.

ISSN 1081-2792
DD 361 US

•**FOUNDATION & CORPORATE FUNDING ADVANTAGE.** [Found. corp. funding advant.]. **VFOAT** Foundation and Corporate Funding Advantage. (Jan. 1995)-. Periodical. English. Twelve times a year. $240.00. Progressive Business Publications, 370 Technology Drive, PO Box 3019, Malvern PA 19355. **Tel** (617)527-8600, (800)220-5000, FAX (617)647-8089.

ISSN 0882-3723
US

FOURTH WORLD JOURNAL. **Added/Corp** New, Inc. International Movement ATD Fourth World. (198?)-. Periodical. English. Twelve times a year. $5.00. Fourth World Movement, 7600 Willow Hill Drive, Landover MD 20785. **Tel** (301)336-9489, FAX (301)336-0092.
Ind/Abst Hum. Rights Intern. Rep.

LC HG4151 .F72
FR

FRANCE 30,000. **Added/Corp** Dun & Bradstreet France. **VFOAT** France Trente Mille. (1983)-. French. One time a year. $475.00. Dun & Bradstreet Information Services, 3 Sylvan Way, Parsippany NJ 07054. **Tel** (201)605-6000, (800)526-0651. ***Continues** France 10,000.*

ISSN 1146-0024
FR
UDC 334.788.2

FRANCE ITALIE. **See** Political Science.

LC HF5429.3 .F69 ISSN 0318-8752
DD 658.8/7/002573 CN

FRANCHISE ANNUAL (LEWISTON), THE. (THE FRANCHISE ANNUAL.). **Added/Corp** International Franchise Opportunities. (1969)-. English. One time a year. $39.95. Info Franchise News, 728 Center Street, Box 550, Lewiston NY 14092. **Tel** (716)754-4669, FAX (905)688-7728. **ED** Ted Dixon. **Ad Acc, Adv Mgr:** D. Muir. **Circ:** 10,000.

Desc: Directory listing over 4,200 business format franchisors (McDonalds, etc.) with complete descriptions. Handbook section details pros and cons of franchising.

US

●**FRANCHISE BUYER.** (1995)-. English. Six times a year. $35.00. Crain Communications Inc., 1400 Woodbridge, Detroit MI 48207-3187. **Tel** (313)446-6000, (800)992-9970.

UK

●**FRANCHISE INTERNATIONAL.** (1995)-. English. Four times a year. $213.90. Franchise Development Services, Castle House / Castle Meadow, Norwich NR2 1PJ United Kingdom. **Tel** 011 44 1603 620301, FAX 011 44 1603 630174.
Desc: Provides information on the franchise business through editorial and advertisements.

ISSN 0268-8395
UK
TITLE CHANGE

FRANCHISE MAGAZINE. (19??)-(1995). Trade Publication. English. Franchise Development Services, Castle House / Castle Meadow, Norwich NR2 1PJ United Kingdom. **Tel** 011 44 1603 620301, FAX 011 44 1603 630174. **ED** Dennis Chaplin. Index available. cum. index. **Bk Rev. Ad Acc, Adv Mgr:** Wendy Sanders. **Circ:** 250,000. ***Continued by*** *Franchise International.*
Desc: Provides information on the franchise business through editorial and advertisements.

LC HF5429.3 .F694
DD 381/.13/02573 US

FRANCHISE OPPORTUNITIES HANDBOOK. **Added/Corp** United States. Bureau of Industrial Economics. United States. Bureau of Domestic Commerce. United States. Bureau of Competitive Assessment and Business Policy. United States. Office of Minority Business Enterprise. United States. Domestic and International Business Administration. United States. Industry and Trade Administration. United States. International Trade Administration. United States. Minority Business Development Agency. (1972)-. Government Publication. English. One time a year (July). $31.00. Superintendent of Documents, US Government Printing Office, Washington DC 20402. **Tel** (202)275-3328, FAX (202)786-2377. **(Subscription address:** US Government Bookstore, O'Neil Building, 2023 3rd Avenue North, Birmingham AL 35203. **)** ***Continues*** *Franchise Company Data for Equal Opportunity in Business.*

ISSN 1321-408X
AT

FRANCHISING. (19??)-. English. Six times a year. 41.11Aus$. Hassel Hunt & Moore Pty Ltd, PO Box 900, Mona Vale 2103 Australia. **Tel** 011 61 02 9706688, FAX 011 61 02 4393959. ***Continues*** *Australian Franchising, 1031-5810.*

LC HF5429.235.U5 F736 **ISSN** 0895-7274
DD 658.8/708/097305 US

FRANCHISING (PITTSBURGH, PA.). (FRANCHISING.). [Franchising]. **VFOAT** FBO; Franchise and Business Opportunities. 3rd Edition, (1981)-. English. One time a year. $23.95. Franchise and Business Opportunities Publishing Co, 1725 Washington Road, Suite 205, Pittsburgh PA 15241. **Tel** (412)831-2522. **ED** William A. Griser. ***Continues*** *Franchise Business Opportunities.*
Desc: Fanchise and business information for entrepreneurs wanting to own their own business.
Ind/Abst LegalTrac (1980-1984).

ISSN 1041-7311
DD 658 US

FRANCHISING WORLD. [Franch. world]. **Added/Corp** International Franchise Association. (19??)-. Periodical. English. Six times a year. $18.00. International Franchise Association, 1350 New York Avenue Northwest, Suite 900, Washington DC 20005. **Tel** (202)628-8000, telex 323175. **(Subscription address:** IFA Publications, Po Box 1060, Evans City PA 16033. **Tel** (412)772-0070.**)** **ED** John Reynolds, Polly Larson. **Ad Acc. Circ:** 50,000 (ctrl). available on microfilm from University Microfilms International (UMI); available on an online database (file 15/Full-Text) from DIALOG. ***Continues*** *Legal Bulletin.*
Desc: Reports on franchising trends, opportunities and related issues.
Ind/Abst Acad. Search; Bus. Period. Index; Bus. Source Plus; Bus. Source; EP Collect.; Homework Help.; INFO-SOUTH Abstr.; Mag. Search; MasterFile FullTEXT 1000; MasterFile FullTEXT 350; MasterFile FullTEXT 650; MasterFile FullTEXT (Jan. 1993-); OCLC; Telebase; Vocat. Search; Wilson Bus. Abstr.

LC Z7163 .E27 HB3 **ISSN** 1157-383X
DD 016.33 FR
CEASED

FRANCIS. 617, ECODOC / RESEAU D'INFORMATION EN ECONOMIE GENERALE. **Added/Corp** Reseau d'Information en Economie Generale (France) Institut de l'Information Scientifique et Technique (France). **VFOAT** Ecodoc. No. 1 (1991)-No. 4 (1993). Periodical. French. CNRS / Institut d'Information Scientifique et Technique, (Centre National de la Recherche Scientifique), 15 Quai Anatole France, 75700 Paris France. **Tel** 011 33 1 47531515, FAX 011 33 1 45517307, telex 260034. Index available (free). **Circ:** 500. available on magnetic tape; available on CD-ROM. ***Continues*** *Ecodoc, 0292-1782.*

LC HC
GW

FRANKFURTER WISSENSCHAFTLICHE BEITRAEGE. RECHTS- UND WIRTSCHAFTSWISSENSCHAFTLICHE REIHE. **See** Law.

LC WMLC 93/1470 **ISSN** 0827-7893
DD 330.971/005 CN

FRASER FORUM. [Fraser forum]. **Added/Corp** Fraser Institute (Vancouver, B.C.). (Jan. 1983)-. Periodical. English. Twelve times a year. 38.42Can$. Fraser Institute, 626 Bute Street/2nd Floor, Vancouver British Columbia, V6E 3M1 Canada. **Tel** (604)688-0221, FAX (604)688-8539. **ED** Kristin McCahon. **Circ:** 5,700.
Desc: A collection of radio commentaries, newspaper articles and other material produced by Fraser Institute authors.

ISSN 0740-0276
DD 338 US

FRASER OPINION LETTER, THE. [Fraser opin. lett.]. (19??)-. Periodical. English. Twenty-six times a year. $70.00. Fraser Management Association, PO Box 494, Burlington VT 05402. **Tel** (802)658-0322, FAX (802)658-0260.

ISSN 0890-927X
DD 330 US
Pr Rev.

FRB SF WEEKLY LETTER. [FRB SF wkly. lett.]. **Main/Corp** Federal Reserve Bank of San Francisco. Research Dept. **VAT** Federal Reserve Bank of San Francisco Weekly Letter. (19??)-. Periodical. English. Forty-eight times a year. Free on request. Federal Reserve Bank of San Francisco, PO Box 7702, San Francisco CA 94120. **Tel** (415)974-2163, FAX (415)974-3429. **ED** Judith Groff. **Circ:** 25,000 (ctrl).
Desc: A single economic issue.
Ind/Abst EP Collect.; Homework Help.; MasterFile FullTEXT 1000; MasterFile FullTEXT 350; MasterFile FullTEXT 650; MasterFile FullTEXT; OCLC; Telebase.

ISSN 0740-5170
US

FREE CASH FLOW. **Added/Corp** Stern, Stewart, Putnam & Macklis, Ltd. Vol. 1, No. 1 (Fall 1983)-. Periodical. English. Four times a year. Stern Stewart Putnam & Macklis Ltd, 520 Madison Avenue/40th Floor, New York NY 10022.

LC AP2 .F9155 **ISSN** 0016-0652
DD 051 US

FREEMAN (IRVINGTON-ON-HUDSON, N.Y.), THE. (THE FREEMAN.). [Freeman]. **Added/Corp** Foundation for Economic Education, inc. Vol. 1 (Oct. 2, 1950)-. Periodical. English. Twelve times a year. $30.00. Foundation for Economic Education, 30 South Broadway, Irvington-on-Hudson NY 10533. **Tel** (914)591-7230, FAX (914)591-8910. **ED** Beth A Hoffman and Brian Summers. Index available. **Bk Rev. Circ:** 35,000 (ctrl). available on microfilm and microfiche from University Microfilms International (UMI). ***Supersedes*** *Plain Talk, 0190-4140;* ***Absorbed*** *Ideas on Liberty, 0445-2259.*
Desc: A study journal on the positive case for freedom. Each month, articles explore the nature of our free market economy, limited government, and individual liberty.
Ind/Abst Am. Hist. Life (1970-1974); Mat. Fact; PAIS Int. Print.

LC HD2853 .F73
DD 338.7/4/0944 FR

FRENCH COMPANY HANDBOOK. **Added/Corp** International Business Development (Firm). (1981)-. Periodical. English. One time a year. $95.83. International Business Development, 181 Avenue Charles de Gaulle, 92521 Neuilly Cedex France. **Tel** 011 33 1 46379494. **ED** Barton Reichert and Irving Sedar. Index available. **Circ:** 15,000 (ctrl).
Desc: Guide to the French corporate world. Information on major companies, evaluations, introductions to Paris Stock Exchange, practical dictionary of English-French business and financial terminology.

US

FRM WEEKLY. Newsletter. English. One time a week. $115.00 US, Canada and Mexico; $165.00 other. Hoke Communications Inc, 224 7th Street, Garden City NY 11530. **Tel** (516)746-6700, (800)229-6700.
Desc: News pertaining to fund raising activities.

LC HF **ISSN** 1045-2443
DD 658 US

FROM ONE BUSINESS TO ANOTHER. (FROM ONE BUSINESS TO ANOTHER : FOBTA.). [From one bus. another]. **Added/Corp** B/E Productions (Oconomowoc, Wis.). FOBTA, Inc. **VFOAT** FOBTA. (198?)-. Periodical. English. Twelve times a year. FOBTA Inc., 155 East Capitol Drive, Hartland WI 53029. **Tel** (414)369-0400, (800)242-0704, FAX (414)369-0765.

ISSN 1061-9712
DD 338 US
TITLE CHANGE

FROM THE STATE CAPITALS. ECONOMIC DEVELOPMENT. [From state cap., Econ. dev.]. **VFOAT** Economic Development. (Jan. 1, 1990)-(1995). Periodical. English. Wakeman Walworth Inc., 300 North Washington Street #204, Alexandria VA 22314. **Tel** (703)549-8606. ***Continues*** *From the State Capitals. Industrial Development, 0734-1628;* ***Absorbed*** *From the State Capitals. Parks and Recreation Trends, 0749-2804.* ***Continued by*** *State Capitals. Economic Development.*

LC HD6993.F6 L48 **ISSN** 0276-9034
DD 975.9/005 US

FROMMER'S HOW TO LIVE IN FLORIDA ON $10,000 A YEAR. [Frommer's how live Fla. $10,000 year]. **VFOAT** How to Live in Florida on $10,000 a Year. **VAT** Frommer's How to Live in Florida on Ten Thousand Dollars a Year. (19??)-. English. Macmillan Publishing Company / Indiana, 201 West 103rd Street, Indianapolis IN 46290. **Tel** (800)428-5331, (800)858-7674.

LC HB615 .C563
US
Pr Rev.

FRONTIERS OF ENTREPRENEURSHIP RESEARCH : PROCEEDINGS OF THE ... ANNUAL BABSON COLLEGE ENTREPRENEURSHIP RESEARCH CONFERENCE. **Added/Corp** Babson Center for Entrepreneurial Studies. Wharton Entrepreneurial Center. Joseph M. Katz Graduate School of Business. (1985)-. English. One time a year. $50.00. Babson College, Center for Entrepreneurial Studies, Wellesley MA 02157. **Tel** (617)239-4332, FAX (617)239-5272. Index available. cum. index (1981-1987). **Circ:** 500 varies, 900 annually. ***Continues*** *Entrepreneurship Research Conference. Frontiers of Entrepreneurship Research.*
Desc: Collection of empirical research papers on entrepreneurship available. These papers are selected from those presented at the annual Babson College Entrepreneurship Research Conference, held each year since 1981. Summaries of these papers presented but not published in their entirety have been included to give the reader an overview of research in the field. These authors represent a cross section of universities, private businesses, and government agencies.

ISSN 1054-9986
DD 382 US

FULD & COMPANY LETTER, THE. [Fuld Co. lett.]. **VFOAT** Fuld and Company Letter. Vol. 1, No. 1 (Summer 1989)-. Periodical. English. Four times a year. Free. Fuld & Company, 80 Trowbridge Street, Cambridge MA 02138. **Tel** (617)492-5900, FAX (617)492-7108. **ED** Virginia O'Brien. **Circ:** 6,000 (ctrl).
Desc: Focuses on business intelligence topics. Gives advice on business intelligence strategy, information sources around the world.

LC HC **ISSN** 0191-1708
DD 330 SZ

FUNDAMENTALS OF PURE AND APPLIED ECONOMICS. [Fundam. pure appl. econ.]. Vol. 1 (1986)-. Monographic series. English. Irregular. Price varies per volume. Harwood Academic Publishers, PO Box 90, Reading RG1 8JL United Kingdom. **Tel** 011 44 1734 560080, FAX 011 44 1734 568211.
Desc: Appeals to economists in academia, government and business. Divided by discipline into sections, each with its own editor.
Ind/Abst Curr. Cit.; Math. Rev.; Zentralbl. Math. Ihre Grenzgeb.

ISSN 1197-4699
DD 658.8/34/097105 CN
CEASED

FUTURE CONSUMER NEWSLETTER. [Future consum. newsl.]. **Added/Corp** Glocal Marketing. (1993)-Vol. 14 (1995). Newsletter. English. Glocal Marketing Inc., 2316 Baynard Boulevard, Wilmington DE 19802. **Tel** (302)841-8008, FAX (302)841-8009. **ED** Frank Feather. **Circ:** 600. ***Continues*** *Canada Tomorrow (Toronto, Ont.), 0828-4474.*
Desc: Future trends/issues (social, technological, economic, political) impacting on Canada, and their implications for strategic planners, marketers, and other executives.

LC HD **ISSN** 1062-3280
DD 333 US

FUTURECAST (LA CANADA, CALIF.). (FUTURECAST.). [Futurecast]. **Added/Corp** Cat-Trax, Inc. **VFOAT** Future Cast. Vol. 1, No. 1 (May 1, 1992)-. Periodical. English. Six times a year. $60.00. Cat-Trx, Inc., PO Box 1333, La Canada CA 91012-5333.

Business and Economics

LC HB3730 .F8
DD 338.54/4
ISSN 0016-3287
UK
CCC
CODEN FUTUBD
Pr Rev.
FUTURES (LONDON). (FUTURES.). [Futures].
Added/Corp Institute for the Future. Vol. 1 (Sept. 1968)-. Periodical. English. Ten times a year. $528.00. Butterworth Heinemann Publishers, Linacre House Jordan Hill, Oxford OX2 8DP United Kingdom. **Tel** 011 44 1865 310366, FAX 011 44 1865 310898. **(Subscription address:** Elsevier Science Ltd. / Oxford Fulfillment Centre, PO Box 800, Kidlington OX5 1DX United Kingdom. **Tel** 011 44 865 843355.) **ED** Colin Blackman. Index available. **Bk Rev**. **Ad Acc**. available on microfilm and microfiche from University Microfilms International (UMI); available on an online database from Elsevier Electronic Subscriptions (EES). Documents available from Article Express International, The Genuine Article, UMI Article Clearinghouse.
Desc: Presents original material dealing with forecasting, planning and future studies. Publishes primary research papers, prospective and comment articles, book reviews, news and reports.
Ind/Abst ABC POL SCI; ABI/INFORM Glob. Ed.; ABI/INFORM [Computer File] (June 1972-); Agrofor. Abstr.; Arts Humanit. Citation Index [Select. Cov.]; Bioeng. Abstr.; Bus. ASAP (1990-) [Full Txt.]; Bus. Index (1985-); Coal Abstr.; Contents Pages Manage.; Curr. Cit.; Ei Page One; Eng. Index Annu.; Expand. Acad. Index (1984-); Field Crop Abstr.; Fut. Surv.; Gen. BusinessFile (1985-); Gen. Period. Index (1985-); Geogr. Abstr. Human Geogr.; Grass. Forage Abstr.; Inf. Sci. Abstr.; Int. Dev. Abstr.; Int. Labour Doc.; LABORDOC; Leis., Rec., Tour. Abstr.; Manage. Market. Abstr.; Newsp. Period. Abstr. (1991-); Res. Alert [Full Cov.]; Rural Dev. Abstr.; Saf. Health Work; Selec. Coop. Index Manage. Period.; Soc. Plann. Policy Dev. Abstr.; Soc. Sci. Cit. Index [Full Cov.]; Soc. Sci. Index; Soc. Sci. Index Fulltext (Oct. 1988-) [Full Txt.]; Sociol. Abstr.; Trade Ind. Index; World Agric. Econ. Rural Sociol. Abstr.

US
FUTURESCAN. (19??)-. Newsletter. English. $95.00. Futurescan, 2218 Wilshire Boulevard, No. 826, Santa Monica CA 90403. **Tel** (310)451-2990, FAX (310)838-0427. **ED** Dr. Roger Selbert.
Desc: Newsletter on future trends.

LC H3 .F88
ISSN 0337-307X
FR
CCC
FUTURIBLES (PARIS). See Sociology.

SP
FUTURO EMPRESARIAL. (19??)-. Spanish. Twelve times a year. 3800ptas Spain; 5450ptas other. Cempro, Plaza Conde Valle Suchil 20, 28015 Madrid Spain. **Tel** 011 34 1 4462050, 011 34 1 4472700.

ISSN 1050-0782
DD 332
US
FX WEEK. (FX WEEK : THE BUSINESS OF FOREIGN EXCHANGE.). [FX week]. **VAT** Foreign Exchange Week. (1990)-. Periodical. English. Forty-eight times a year (weekly except four times per year). $1295.00. Waters Information Services, PO Box 2248, Binghamton NY 13902-2248. **Tel** (607)770-8535, FAX (607)798-1692. available on an online database (file 636/Full-Text) from DIALOG.
Ind/Abst PTS Newsl. Database [Full Txt.].

US
FYI : NOTES FOR BUSINESS AND INDUSTRY. (19??)-. English. Twelve times a year. $20.00. National Retail Federation, 325 7th Street NW Suite 1000, Washington DC 20004. **Tel** (202)626-8146.

LC GE1 .G35
DD 363.7/005
ISSN 0940-5550
GW
GAIA : OKOLOGISCHE PERSPECTIVEN IN NATUR-, GEISTES- UND WIRTSCHAFTSWISSENSCHAFTEN. See Environmental Issues-Ecology.

LC QA269 .G36
DD 519.3/05
ISSN 0899-8256
US
CCC
CODEN GEBEEF
GAMES AND ECONOMIC BEHAVIOR.
See Mathematics.

ISSN 0391-6138
IT
UDC 67/68
CEASED
GAZZETTA DELLA PICCOLA INDUSTRIA. [Gazz. piccola ind.]. (19??)-(Dec. 1993). Periodical. Italian. Servizio Italiano Pubblicazioni International, Viale Pasteur 6, 00144 Rome Italy. **Tel** 011 39 6 5920509, telex 614567 SIPIRM I.

GW
GDR MARKET. **VAT** German Democratic Republic Market. (19??)-. Periodical. English. Twelve times a year. Interwerbung GmbH, W-1157 Berlin Germany.
Continues Trade + Technical Review, 0232-5780.

LC HF
DD 658.3
ISSN 0968-6673
UK
CCC
Pr Rev.
●**GENDER, WORK AND ORGANISATION.**
See Sociology.

LC HC241.2 .A17
DD 338.94/005
ISSN 0069-6749
BE
GENERAL REPORT ON THE ACTIVITIES OF THE COMMUNITIES. Main/Corp
Commission of the European Communities. **VFOAT** General Report on the Activities of the European Communities in ... . (1967)-. English (Danish, Dutch, French, German and Italian). One time a year. £14.20. Office for Official Publications of the European Communities, 2 rue Mercier, 2985 Luxembourg Luxembourg. **Tel** 011 352 499281, FAX 011 352 292942763. **(Subscription address:** UNIPUB, 4611 F Assembly Drive, Lanham MD 20706. **Tel** (800)274-4888, (301)459-7666.) **Continues in part** European Coal and Steel Community. High Authority. General Report on the Activities of the Community, 0423-6971; European Economic Community. Commission. General Report on the Activities of the Community, 0531-3759 and European Atomic Energy Community. Commission. General Report on the Activities of the Community, 0531-2809.
Desc: Review of community activities in connection with common policies and programs and their implementing legislation.

US
GENERAL SERIES REPRINT. Main/Corp
Brookings Institution. **VFOAT** Brookings General Series Reprint. (1973)-. English. Irregular. $20.00 (includes Technical Series Reprints). Brookings Institution, 1775 Massachusetts Avenue Northwest, Washington DC 20036-2188. **Tel** (202)797-6255, (800)275-1447.
(Subscription address: Brookings Institution, PO Box 037, Washington DC 20042. **Tel** (202)797-6255.)
Continues Brookings Institution, Washington, D.C. Reprint.

LC HF5001 .G36
DD 650/.05
US
GENERATION : THE MAGAZINE OF YOUNG BUSINESSMEN. (Sept. 1968)-.
Periodical. English. Twelve times a year. $12.00. Claretian Publications, 205 West Monroe Street, Chicago IL 60606. **Tel** (312)236-7782, (800)328-6515.

LC HB241
DD 338
ISSN 1061-2270
US
GENESIS REPORT/RX, THE. See Pharmacy and Pharmacology.

ISSN 0267-7563
DD 330.9048
UK
GEOFILE. [Geofile]. (1982)-. Periodical. English. One time a year. £36.00. Mary Glasgow Publications, Building One, Kineton Road Industrial Estate, Southam Warwickshire CV33 0DG United Kingdom. **Tel** 011 44 1926 815560, FAX 011 44 1926 815563.

LC HD6983 .G38
DD 331.2/973/04
ISSN 1061-7469
US
GEOGRAPHIC REFERENCE REPORT.
[Geogr. ref. rep.]. **Added/Corp** BTA Economic Research Institute. 6th Ed. (1992)-. English. One time a year (published in Oct.). $365.50. Economic Research Institute, 16770 Northeast 79th Street, Suite 104, Redmond WA 98052. **Tel** (800)627-3697, (206)627-3697, FAX (206)885-5091. **Continues** Geographic Reference (Newport Beach, Calif.), 1057-8498.

LC HC107.G4 A13
DD 330.9758/005
ISSN 0279-3857
US
Pr Rev.
GEORGIA BUSINESS AND ECONOMIC CONDITIONS. **Added/Corp** University of Georgia. Graduate School of Business Administration. Division of Research. Vol. 41, No. 4 (July/Aug. 1981)-. Periodical. English. Six times a year. Free on request. University of Georgia Economic Growth Center, Terry College of Business, Athens GA 30602. **Tel** (706)542-4085, FAX (706)542-3835. **ED** Lorena M. Akioka. Index available. **Circ:** 5,000 (ctrl). **Continues** Georgia Business, 0016-8173.
Desc: Articles concerning various facets of Georgia's business and economic scene.
Ind/Abst PAIS Int. Print (1991-); Stat. Ref. Index.

LC HC107.G4 G34
DD 338.5/443/09758
ISSN 0884-1179
US
GEORGIA ECONOMIC OUTLOOK. [Ga. econ. outlook]. **Added/Corp** University of Georgia. Georgia Economic Forecasting Project. (1984)-. English. One time a year (Dec.). $15.00. University of Georgia Economic Growth Center, Terry College of Business, Athens GA 30602. **Tel** (706)542-4085, FAX (706)542-3835. **ED** Lorena M. Akioka. **Circ:** 1,000 (ctrl).
Desc: Economic forecast for the state; features sector forecasts for manufacturing, construction, finance, public utilities, government, services, and agriculture.

DD 333
ISSN 0433-6054
US
GEORGIA OPERATOR, THE. [Ga. oper.].
Added/Corp Georgia Water and Pollution Control Association. (Summer 1963)-. Periodical. English. Four times a year. Free. Georgia Water & Pollution Control Association, PO Box 634, Jonesboro GA 30237. **Tel** (404)378-0127, FAX (404)370-1336. Documents available from Documents on Demand.
Ind/Abst Environ. Abstr.

LC HC107.G4 G465
DD 330.9758/005
ISSN 0882-5971
US
CCC
GEORGIA TREND. [Ga. trend]. Vol. 1, No. 1 (Sept. 1985)-. Periodical. English. Twelve times a year. $18.00. Williams Communication, 1770 Indian Trail Road, Suite 350, Norcross GA 30093. **Tel** (404)806-6700.
(Subscription address: Datamatx, 3146 NE Expressway, Atlanta GA 30329. **Tel** (404)936-5600.) available on microfilm and microfiche from University Microfilms International (UMI); available on an online database (file 635/Full-Text) from DIALOG. Documents available from UMI Article Clearinghouse.
Continues Georgia Living; **Absorbed** Business Atlanta Magazine.
Ind/Abst Bus. Dateline (19??-).

US
GERALD APPELS SYSTEMS AND FORECASTS. (19??)-. English. Twenty-four times a year. $225.00. Signalert Corporation, 150 Great Neck Road, Great Neck NY 11021. **Tel** (516)829-6444, FAX (516)829-9366. **Bk Rev**, (Qty: 3). **Circ:** 3,000.

GW
GERMAN BRIEF. (19??)-. English. Irregular (65 times a year). $695.00. Frankfurter Allgemeine Zeitung, Postfach Auslandsvertrieb, D-60267 Frankfurt Germany. **Tel** 011 49 69 75911637, FAX 011 49 69 75911445. **ED** David Hart. Index available. cum. index. **Bk Rev**.

LC HD2857 .G47
GW
GERMANY'S TOP 300 : A HANDBOOK OF GERMANY'S LARGEST CORPORATIONS. **Added/Corp** Frankfurter Allgemeine Zeitung GmbH. Informationsdienste. **VFOAT** Handbook of Germany's Largest Corporations; Germany's Top Three Hundred. (1991)-. English. One time a year. $120.00. Frankfurter Allgemeine Zeitung, Postfach Auslandsvertrieb, D-60267 Frankfurt Germany. **Tel** 011 49 69 75911637, FAX 011 49 69 75911445.
(Subscription address: European Business Publications, PO Box 891, Darien CT 06820. **Tel** (203)656-2701.)

US
CEASED
GET RICH NEWS. (19??)-(19??)-. English. Get Rich News Inc, Box 126, Lake Worth FL 33460. **Tel** (310)586-0978, FAX (310)582-8320. **ED** Brian Hogan. **Bk Rev**. **Ad Acc**. **Circ:** 125,000.
Desc: Business opportunity news for entrepreneurs. Rags-to-Riches stories, business start-up tips.

ISSN 1067-8034
US
●**GHANA (SYRACUSE, N.Y.).** (GHANA : AN EXECUTIVE REPORT.). **Added/Corp** Political Risk Services (IBC USA (Publications) Inc.). **VFOAT** Executive Report. (1993)-. English. $110.00. Political Risk Services, 6320 Fly Road, Suite 102, PO Box 248, East Syracuse NY 13057-0248. **Tel** (315)431-0511, FAX (315)431-0200.
Desc: Focuses on the long-term outlook for business. Includes a brief review of recent events and current circumstances, background intelligence including geography, history, economics and social conditions, as well as the key political and economic forecasts.

ISSN 1067-8719
DD 025
US
●**GILBANE REPORT ON OPEN INFORMATION & DOCUMENT SYSTEMS, THE.** See Computers.

LC HC
DD 330
ISSN 0017-0097
IT
CODEN GIAEAY
GIORNALE DEGLI ECONOMISTI E ANNALI DI ECONOMIA. [G. econ. ann. econ.].
Added/Corp Universita Commerciale Luigi Bocconi. (Jan./Feb. 1939)-. Periodical. Italian. Four times a year. L68130. Universita Bocconi, V Sarfatti 25, 20136 Milan Italy. **Tel** 011 39 2 58365320, FAX 011 39 2 58365318, telex 316003 UNIBOC I. **ED** Mario Monti. Index available. cum. index. **Bk Rev**. **Ad Acc**. **Circ:** 950. **Formed by the union of** Giornale Degli Economisti e Rivista di Statistica **and** Annali di Economia.
Ind/Abst Econ. Lit. Index; J. Econ. Lit.; Math. Rev.; Stat. Theory Method Abstr. (1959-1963).

ISSN 0021-2482
IT
GIORNALE DELL'ISTITUTO ITALIANO DEGLI ATTUARI. Main/Corp Istituto Italiano Degli Attuari, Rome. Anno 1 (1930)-. Periodical. Italian.

Business and Economics

Irregular. Istituto Italiano Attuari, Via del Corea 3, 00186 Rome Italy. **Tel** 011 39 6 3226056.
Ind/Abst Zentralbl. Math. Ihre Grenzgeb.

LC HC415.15.A1 G55   **ISSN** 1062-1261
DD 338.0956/05   US
    CODEN GBWBEM

GLOBAL BUSINESS WHITE PAPERS.
[Glob. bus. white pap.]. **Added/Corp** Conference Board. **VFOAT** White Papers. No. 1 (May 1991)-. Periodical. English. Six times a year. Free to associates of the Conference Board. Conference Board, 845 Third Avenue, New York NY 10022. **Tel** (212)759-0900 ext. 582, (800)872-6273, FAX (212)980-7014.

    ISSN 0820-5167
DD 330.971/005   CN

GLOBAL ECONOMIC OUTLOOK (TORONTO).
(GLOBAL ECONOMIC OUTLOOK.). [Glob. econ. outlook]. **Added/Corp** Bank of Nova Scotia. Economics Dept. (Oct. 1986)-. Periodical. English. Two times a year (Jan. and July). Free. Bank of Nova Scotia, 44 King Street, 8th Floor, Toronto Ontario M5H 1H1 Canada. **Tel** (416)866-6253, 866-3925. available on microfilm and microfiche from University Microfilms International (UMI). **Continues** Regional and Industrial Outlook, 0820-5159.
Ind/Abst Can. Period. Index.

    ISSN 1055-6648
DD 363   US

GLOBAL FUTURES.
[Glob. futur.]. (19??)-. Periodical. English. Twelve times a year. $100.00. California Futures, 801 Crocker Road, Sacramento CA 95864. **Tel** (916)482-5200. **ED** Mona Escudero. **Bk Rev**. **Ad Acc**. Circ: 8,000 (ctrl). **Continues** Green Futures.

    ISSN 0226-9465
DD 003.2/05   CN

GLOBAL FUTURES DIGEST.
[Global futures dig.]. **Added/Corp** Global Futures Network. Vol. 1, No. 1 (Spring 1983)-. Periodical. English. Four times a year. $25.00. Global Futures Network, 26 Gramercy Park 1E, New York NY 10003. **Tel** (212)673-9398.

LC K22 .U5   **ISSN** 0016-3570
    GW
    CCC

GMBH-RUNDSCHAU.
Added/Corp Centrale fuer GmbH Dr. Otto Schmidt. (Jan. 1963)-. Periodical. German. Twelve times a year. $177.33. Verlag Dr Otto Schmidt KG, Unter den Ulman 96/98, D-50968 Cologne Germany. **Tel** 011 49 221 9373801. **Continues** Rundschau fuer GmbH.

LC Discard

    US

GOALS & GUIDELINES.
VFOAT Goals and Guidelines. (19??)-. Periodical. English. Twelve times a year. $45.48. Bureau of Business Practice, 24 Rope Ferry Road, Waterford CT 06386. **Tel** (800)243-0876, (203)442-4365, (800)876-9105, FAX (203)443-1123. **ED** Mary Schantz.

LC HF3721 .G63

    BU

GODISHNIK NA IKONOMICHESKI UNIVERSITET GR. VARNA.
Added/Corp Ikonomicheski Universitet Gr. Varna. **VFOAT** Godishnikut na Ikonomicheskiia Universitet--Varna; Godishnik Za ...; Annual Book. Vol. 63 (1991)-. Periodical. Bulgarian. **Continues** Godishnik na Visshiia Institut za Narodno Stopanstvo "Dimitur Blagoev"--Varna.

    ISSN 0211-867X
    SP
UDC 339

GONDOLA.
(1980)-. Periodical. Spanish. Twelve times a year. $106.58. Editmex SL, Comercio 4 Esc 1 1A, 28007 Madrid Spain. **Tel** 011 34 1 4336700.

LC HJ55 .A296a

    RU

GOSUDARSTVENNYI BIUDZHET SSSR.
Main/Corp Soviet Union. Ministerstvo Finansov. Biudzhetnoe Upravlenie. (19??)-. Russian. Izdatelstvo Finansy I Statistika, Ulitsa Chernyshvskogo 7 K-142, 101000 Moscow Russia.

    GW

GOTTINGER WIRTSCHAFTSWISSENSCHAFTLICHE STUDIEN.
(19??)-. German. Irregular. Verlag Otto Schwartz & Company, Annastrasse 7, D-37075 Goettingen Germany. **Tel** 011 49 551 31051, 011 49 551 31052, FAX 011 49 551 372812. **Continues** Gottinger Wirtschafts- und Sozialwissenschaftliche Studien, 0436-1296.

    AT

GOVERNMENT AFFAIRS MONITOR.
(19??)-. Periodical. English. One time a week (Fri.). 310.00Aus$. Commerce Management Services, PO Box E162 Queen Victoria, Terrace ACT 2600 Australia. **Tel** 011 61 6 2951961, FAX 011 61 6 2590170. **ED** HC Grant.

    ISSN 1078-9812
DD 353   US

●GOVERNMENT AFFAIRS YELLOW BOOK.
See Public Administration.

    ISSN 1194-9414
DD 338.971/005   CN

●GOVERNMENT ASSISTANCE PROGRAMS IN CANADA.
[Gov. assist. programs Can.]. **Added/Corp** CCH Canadian Limited. KPMG Peat Marwick Thorne. 14th Ed. (1992/1993)-. English. CCH Canadian Ltd., 6 Garamond Court, Don Mills Ontario M3C 1Z5 Canada. **Tel** (416)441-2992, FAX (416)441-3418. **Continues** Industrial Assistance Programs in Canada., 0826-5828.

    ISSN 0017-2588
    US

GOVERNMENT BUSINESS WORLD REPORT.
(1969)-. English. Twenty-four times a year. $335.00. Government Business Worldwide Reports, PO Box 5997, Washington DC 20016. **Tel** (202)244-7050, FAX (202)244-5410. **ED** J Wagner. **Bk Rev**. **Ad Acc**. ctrl circ.
Desc: Report on political, government and security developments around the world, business opportunities and government projects, procurement, and contacts, with emphasis on advanced technology and infrastructure.

    ISSN 1045-4055
    US
    CCC

GRAND RAPIDS BUSINESS JOURNAL.
VFOAT Business Journal. Periodical. English. One time a week. Grand Rapids Business Journal, 40 Pearl Street NW/Suite 1040, Grand Rapids MI 49503. **Tel** (616)459-4545. available on an online database (file 635/Full-Text) from DIALOG. Documents available from UMI Article Clearinghouse.
Ind/Abst Bus. Dateline; Bus. Source Plus; Bus. Source; EP Collect.; Homework Help.; MasterFile FullTEXT 1000; MasterFile FullTEXT 350; MasterFile FullTEXT 650; MasterFile FullTEXT (Jan. 1995-); OCLC; PROMT; Telebase.

LC HG4109 .G72
DD 658.1509   BL

GRANDES COMPANHIAS, AS.
(19??)-. Portuguese. One time a year. Editora Banas SA, Av Presidente Castelo Branco 6241, CEP 05038, Sao Paulo Brazil. **Continues in part** Brasil Financeiro.

LC HG1623.U5 G73   **ISSN** 0748-8424
DD 332.8/2/097305   US

GRANT'S INTEREST RATE OBSERVER.
[Grant's Interest rate obs.]. **VFOAT** Interest Rate Observer; Grant's. (198?)-. Periodical. English. Twenty-four times a year. $555.00. Grant's Interest Rates Observer, 30 Wall Street, New York NY 10005. **Tel** (212)809-7994, FAX (212)809-5925. **ED** James Grant. **Ad Acc**. Circ: 2,100.
Desc: Review of debt, interest rates and the credit markets.

    ISSN 1071-0590
DD 338   US

GRASSROOTS ECONOMIC ORGANIZING NEWSLETTER.
[Grassroots econ. organ. newsl.]. **Added/Corp** PACE of Philadelphia (Association). **VFOAT** GEO; GEO newsletter. Issue #1 (Nov. 1991)-. Newsletter. English. Six times a year (Jan., Mar., May, July, Sept., Nov.). $30.00 (institutions), $15.00 (individuals and technical assistance groups, grassroot economic organizations and worker co-ops). GEO / CT, PO Box 5065, New Haven CT 06525. **Tel** (203)389-6194, FAX (302)239-4536. **Bk Rev**. (Qty: 5-10). **Ad Acc**. Circ: 1,200. **Formed by the union of** Changing Work (New Haven, Conn.), 0883-1416 **and** Workplace Democracy, 0738-6044.
Desc: Models of community-driven economic development. Includes a forum for collaboration among grassroots groups.

    ISSN 0747-4652
    US

GREATER BATON ROUGE BUSINESS REPORT, THE.
VFOAT Baton Rouge Business Report; Business Report. Vol. 1, No. 1 (Sept. 1982)-. Periodical. English. Twelve times a year. $34.00. Baton Rouge Business Report, PO Box 1949, Baton Rouge LA 70821. **Tel** (504)928-1700, FAX (504)923-3448. available on an online database (file 635/Full-Text) from DIALOG. Documents available from UMI Article Clearinghouse.
Ind/Abst Acad. Search; Bus. Dateline; Bus. Index (?-?); Bus. Source Plus; Bus. Source; EP Collect.; Gen. BusinessFile (Jan. 1985-Dec. 1985); Gen. Period. Index (Jan. 1985-Dec. 1985); Homework Help.; INFO-SOUTH Abstr.; MasterFile FullTEXT 1000; MasterFile FullTEXT 350; MasterFile FullTEXT 650; MasterFile FullTEXT (July 1993-); OCLC; PROMT; Telebase; Trade Ind. ASAP [Full Txt.]; Trade Ind. Index [Full Txt.].

    ISSN 1044-9264
    US
    TITLE CHANGE

GREATER CINCINNATI BUSINESS RECORD, THE.
VFOAT Business Record. Vol. 1, No. 1 (July 18-24, 1988)-(199?). Periodical. English. Greater Cincinnati Business Record, 36 East 7th Street, Suite 1500, Cincinnati OH 45202. **Tel** (513)421-9300. available on an online database (file 635/Full-Text) from DIALOG. Documents available from UMI Article Clearinghouse. **Continued by** Business Record, 1068-2899.
Ind/Abst Bus. Dateline (May 6, 1991-) [Full Txt.].

    US

GREATER GREENWOOD BUSINESS JOURNAL, THE.
(19??)-. English. Twelve times a year (Second Wed. of each month). $18.00. The Greater Greenwood Business Journal, 128 South Park Boulevard, Greenwood IN 46143. **Tel** (317)882-8796, FAX (317)882-8830. **ED** Maggie Kelly. **Bk Rev**. (Qty: 12). **Photos**. **Ad Acc**, **Adv Mgr:** Brian Kelly. Full Page (B&W) $495.00. Half Page (B&W) $290.00. Full Page (Color) $570.00. Half Page (Color) $365.00. **Pub. Size:** Tabloid.

    US

GREATER LANSING BUSINESS MONTHLY.
(19??)-. English. Twelve times a year. $25.00. Greater Lansing Business Monthly, 300 South Washington Square, Suite 580, Lansing MI 48933. **Tel** (517)487-1714, FAX (517)487-9597. **ED** Amy McClellan. **Bk Rev**. **Ad Acc**, **Adv Mgr:** Denise Parks. Circ: 10,000 (ctrl). available on an online database (file 635/Full-Text) from DIALOG. Documents available from UMI Article Clearinghouse.
Ind/Abst Bus. Dateline (April 1991-) [Full Txt.].

    US

GREATER SAN DIEGO CHAMBER OF COMMERCE ECONOMIC BULLETIN.
(19??)-. Bulletin. English. Twelve times a year. $50.00. Greater San Diego Chamber of Commerce, 402 West Broadway, Suite 1000, San Diego CA 92101. **Tel** (619)544-1342. **Continues** San Diego Economic Bulletin.

    GR

GREEK BUSINESS MONITOR.
(19??)-. English. Twenty-six times a year. $325.00. Athens Equity Management, PO Box 70201, Glyfada 16610, Athens Greece. **Tel** 011 30 1 9626 580. **Continues** Athens Stock Exchange. Investment Report.

LC HB1 .G73   **ISSN** 1010-9994
DD 330/.09495/05   GR

GREEK ECONOMIC REVIEW.
[Greek econ. rev.]. Vol. 1 (Aug. 1979)-. Periodical. English. Two times a year. $35.00. Greek Economic Review, Central Post Office Box 4085, GR 102 10 Athens Greece. **Tel** 011 30 1 320 2383.
Ind/Abst Econ. Lit. Index; J. Econ. Lit.

LC TD169 .G74   **ISSN** 0962-9467
    UK
Pr Rev.

GREENPEACE BUSINESS.
See Environmental Issues.

LC HC
    US

GREY MATTER.
(19??)-. Periodical. English. Twenty-four times a year. Free on request. Grey Advertising Inc., Third Avenue, New York NY 10017.

    ISSN 0928-754X
    NE
UDC 339.3 :635

GROENTEVEILING WESTLAND.
[Groenteveiling Westland]. (1992)-. Periodical. Dutch. Twelve times a year (July/Aug. issues combined). $51.39. Coop Groenteveiling Westland, Postbus 204, 2680 AE Monster Netherlands. **Tel** 011 31 1749 45959.

LC HC683.5.Z9 I514   **ISSN** 1017-639X
DD 339.3953/05   PP

GROSS DOMESTIC PRODUCT AND EXPENDITURE : NATIONAL ECONOMIC ACCOUNTS / NATIONAL STATISTICAL OFFICE.
Added/Corp Papua New Guinea. National Statistical Office. (1983/1988)-. English. One time a year. k200 New Guinea; k3.00 other. National Statistical Office / New Guinea, PO Wards Strip NCO, Papua New Guinea. **Tel** 011 675 27182 271172, FAX 011 657 255057, telex FINANCE NE 22312. **ED** Nick Suvulo. **Ad Acc**. Circ: 150. **Continues** Gross Domestic Product at Constant Prices.

Business and Economics

Desc: Provides an analysis of all economic activity in New Guinea. Includes tables, a six year time series of expenditure on cost structure, etc.

US
GROUND FLOOR. (19??)-. English. $115.00. Hirsch Organization, 6 Deer Trail, Old Tappan NJ 07675. **Tel** (201)664-3400.

GW
GRUYTER STUDIES IN ORGANIZATION, DE. VFOAT Studies in Organization. (1984)-. Monographic series. English. Walter de Gruyter Inc. / Hawthorne, 200 Saw Mill River Road, Hawthorne NY 10532. **Tel** (914)747-0110, GERMANY: 011/49/30/260050, FAX (914)747-1326, telex 646677. **Ind/Abst** Curr. Cit.

LC HF4031.5 .A19 ISSN 1045-053X
DD 380.9967 GU
GUAM BUSINESS NEWS. [Guam bus. news]. Vol. 1, No. 1 (Mar. 1983)-. Periodical. English. Twelve times a year. $36.00. Glimpses of Guam Company, PO Box 3191, Agana Guam 96910. **Tel** (671)477-7606, FAX (671)472-2163. **ED** Alison Russell (editor's telephone: (671)477-7606). **Bk Rev**. **Ad Acc, Adv Mgr:** Vicki Anderson. **Circ:** 2,500 (ctrl). **Desc:** International newsletter that features different articles on business in the country of Guam.

ISSN 0824-6696
DD 330.971/005 CN
GUARDIAN CAPITAL'S VIEWPOINT. [Guard. Cap. viewp.]. **Added/Corp** Guardian Capital Group. (Aug. 1976)-. Periodical. English. Free. Guardian Capital Group, 48 Yonge Street, Toronto Ontario M5E 1M3 Canada. ctrl circ.

ISSN 0211-8688
UDC 621.391 SP
GUIA CHIP. [Guia chip]. (1982)-. Periodical. Spanish. One time a year. $87.93. VNU Business Publications / Spain, Cinca 13, 28002 Madrid Spain. **Tel** 011 34 1 563-8100, FAX 011 34 1 563-7572.

IT
GUIDA AGLI ACQUISTI PER GLI ENTI PUBBLICI. Added/Corp Societa Italiana per lo Studio dei Problemi Regionali. Associazione Nazionale dei Comuni Italiani. (1991/1992)-. Italian. Societa Italiana per Lo Studio dei Problemi Regionali, Via Della Scrofa 14, 00186 Rome Italy. **Tel** 011 39 6 6879852.

LC PN4888.C59 G85
DD 071/.3/025 US
GUIDE TO BUSINESS AND FINANCIAL NEWS MEDIA. See Journalism.

ISSN 1058-4897
DD 338 US
GUIDE TO BUSINESS VALUATIONS. [Guide bus. valuat.]. **Added/Corp** Practioners Publishing Company (Fort Worth, Tex.). 1st Ed. (May 1991)-. Periodical. Irregular (2 volume set with annual updates). $143.00 (2 volume set), $81.00 (updates only). Practitioners Publishing Company, PO Box 966, Fort Worth TX 76101-0966. **Tel** (800)332-3709.

ISSN 1055-1174
US
GUIDE TO ORANGE COUNTY FREELANCE MARKETS. (1991)-. English. $9.95. Guide to Orange County Freelance Markets, PO Box 18498, Irvine CA 92714.

LC HV27 .F86 ISSN 1070-7964
DD 361.7/4/02573 US
●**GUIDE TO PRIVATE FORTUNES.** (GUIDE TO PRIVATE FORTUNES : DESCRIPTIVE PROFILES OF THE WEALTHIEST AND MOST PHILANTHROPIC INDIVIDUALS AND FAMILIES.). [Guide priv. fortunes]. **Added/Corp** Taft Group (Rockville, Md.). (1993)-. Monographic series. English. Irregular. $245.00 (latest volume). Taft Group, 835 Penobscott Building, Customer Service, Detroit MI 48226. **Tel** (800)877-8238, FAX (313)961-6083. **Continues** Fund Raiser's Guide to Private Fortunes, 1045-2133. **Desc:** Features in-depth profiles of 1,250 people whose wealth and generosity make them top prospects for philanthropies.

LC LB1027
DD 371.42 UK
●**GUIDE TO TRAINING IN SECRETARIAL AND OFFICE SKILLS, THE. See** Occupations and Careers.

ISSN 0953-5411
DD 909.09749270828 UK
GULF STATES NEWSLETTER. [Gulf States newsl.]. (1987)-. Newspaper. English. Twenty-five times a year. $560.00. Middle East Newsletters, PO Box 124 Crawley, West Sussex RH10 3YT United Kingdom. **Tel** 011 44 342 712929, FAX 011 44 342 712829. **(Subscription address:** Gulf States Newsletter / US and Canada Subscriptions, Subscription Office, PO Box 1584, Birmingham AL 35201-1584. **Tel** (800)633-4931, (205)995-1567 (outside US and Canada), FAX (205)995-1588.**) Formed by the union of** Gulf States and Saudi Arabia, 0142-9302. **Desc:** Political and economic coverage (including oil) of the six GCG Gulf States, plus Iraq, Iran and Yeman.

ISSN 1067-8042
US
●**GUYANA (SYRACUSE, N.Y.).** (GUYANA : AN EXECUTIVE REPORT.). **Added/Corp** Political Risk Services (IBC USA (Publications) Inc.). **VFOAT** Executive Report. (1993)-. English. $110.00. Political Risk Services, 6320 Fly Road, Suite 102, PO Box 248, East Syracuse NY 13057-0248. **Tel** (315)431-0511, FAX (315)431-0200. **Desc:** Focuses on the long-term outlook for business. Includes a brief review of recent events and current circumstances, background intelligence including geography, history, economics and social conditions, as well as the key political and economic forecasts.

LC HF
DD 658 TU
HACETTEPE UNIVERSITY BULLETIN ADMINISTRATIVE SCIENCES. (19??)-. Bulletin. Turkish. One time a year. Hacettepe University Turkish, Middle East Soc & Econ Research, Institute Beytepe Ankara Turkey.

LC HC470.3.A1 H66a
DD 330.951/275/005 HK
HALF-YEARLY ECONOMIC REPORT. **Main/Corp** Hong Kong. **Added/Corp** Hong Kong. Economic Report. (19??)-. English (Chinese). One time a year. HK$15.00 Hong Kong; $3.30 (surface mail) other. Hong Kong Government Information Service, Beaconsfield House, 4 Queens Road, Hong Kong Hong Kong. **Tel** 011 852 284288014, 011 852 259881947, FAX 011 852 28459078, 011 852 25987482, telex 61190 HKGIS. **Circ:** 500 (ctrl). **Supersedes** Hong Kong. Quarterly Economic Reports. **Desc:** An assessment of Hong Kong's economic developments, plus additional analyses of economy covering the external, financial and labor sectors.

ISSN 0849-2387
DD 330.9716/22/05 CN
HALIFAX METRO PROFILE. [Halifax metro profile]. **Added/Corp** Halifax Board of Trade. **VFOAT** Business Facts and Figures for Halifax, Dartmouth, Bedford & Halifax County; Metro Profile. (1989/1990)-. English. Halifax Board of Trade, Duke Tower 4th Floor, 525 Duke Street, Halifax Nova Scotia B3J 1P3 Canada. **Tel** (902)422-6447. **Continues** Metro Profile., 0849-2379.

ISSN 0833-384X
DD 380.1/09713/533 CN
HALTON BUSINESS JOURNAL (1986). (HALTON BUSINESS JOURNAL.). [Halton bus. j.]. Vol. 5, No. 4 (May 1986)-. Trade Publication. English. Twelve times a year. 24.00Can$ Canada; 30.00Can$ US. Halton Business Journal, 1492 Wallace, Oakville Ontario L6L 2Y2 Canada. **Tel** (416)847-1404, FAX (416)847-1406. **ED** Roy Wilson. **Ad Acc, Adv Mgr:** V. McKee. **Circ:** 15,000 (ctrl). **Continues** Canadian Business Journal, 0827-7303. **Desc:** Focuses on local business concerns throughout Halton and Peel Regions, including profiles, trade shows, insurance and finance.

ISSN 0144-2015
UK
HAMBRO COMPANY GUIDE, THE. [Hambro co. guide]. (1979)-. Periodical. English. Four times a year. £99.00 UK; £139.00 Europe; £155.00 Middle East; £165.00 other. Hemington Scott Publishing Ltd, 26-31 Whiskin Street, London EC1R 0PB United Kingdom. **Tel** 011 44 171 2787769, FAX 011 44 171 2789808. **Ad Acc. Circ:** 10,000. available on diskette.

LC HD72 .H35 ISSN 0072-9566
DD 338.9 GW
HAMBURGER JAHRBUCH FUER WIRTSCHAFTS- UND GESELLSCHAFTSPOLITIK. Vol. 1 (1956)-. Bulletin. German (summaries and/or abstracts in English). One time a year. Price varies. JCB Mohr / Paul Siebeck, Postfach 2040, D-72010 Tuebingen Germany. **Tel** 011 49 7071 9230, FAX 011 49 7071 51104, telex 7/262872 mohr d. cum. index. **Ind/Abst** Int. Bibliogr. Sociol.

ISSN 0834-0536
DD 380.1/09713/52 CN
HAMILTON REPORT. [Hamilt. rep.]. **VFOAT** Hamilton Business Report. Vol. 1, No. 1 (Winter 1986)-. Periodical. English. Four times a year (Jan., Apr., July, Oct.). 7.97Can$. Hamilton This Month, 361 King Street West, Hamilton Ontario L8P 1B4 Canada. **Tel** (416)522-6117, FAX (416)529-2242. **ED** Wayne Narciso and Susann Camus. **Ad Acc, Adv Mgr:** Heather Rose. **Circ:** 21,000 (ctrl). **Desc:** A business magazine focusing on economics, new businesses, banking and finances.

ISSN 0829-1373
DD 051 CN
HAMILTON THIS MONTH. [Hamilt. mon.]. **VFOAT** Interiors. (Nov. 1984)-. Periodical. English. Five times a year. 10.37Can$. Hamilton This Month, 361 King Street West, Hamilton Ontario L8P 1B4 Canada. **Tel** (416)522-6117, FAX (416)529-2242. **ED** Elizabeth Kelly. **Ad Acc, Adv Mgr:** Heather Rose. **Circ:** 42,000 (ctrl).

NE
HANDBOOK IN ECONOMICS. (19??)-. English. Elsevier Science Publishers BV, PO Box 211, 1000 AE Amsterdam Netherlands. **Tel** 011 31 20 4853641, 011 31 20 4853642, FAX 011 31 20 4853598.

US
HANDBOOK OF BUSINESS LETTERS. (19??)-. English. One time a year (September). $16.95. Prentice-Hall Law and Business, 270 Sylvan Avenue, Englewood Cliffs NJ 07632. **Tel** (800)223-0231, (201)894-8538, FAX (201)894-8666. **ED** L.E. Frailey. **Circ:** 1,000,000. **Desc:** Provides information on business letter writing. Contains model letters, including new sample letters, covering every business occasion. Each letter can be used "as is" or adapted to the writer's needs.

LC HD30.28 .H3663 ISSN 0894-4318
DD 658.4/012/05 US
HANDBOOK OF BUSINESS STRATEGY. YEARBOOK. [Handb. bus. strategy, Yearb.]. (1986)-. Periodical. English. One time a year. $169.95. Faulkner & Gray Inc., 11 Penn Plaza, 17th Floor, New York NY 10001. **Tel** (212)967-7000, (800)535-8403.

ISSN 1054-7681
DD 332 US
HANDBOOK OF COMPARATIVE ECONOMIC POLICIES. [Handb. comp. econ. policies]. Vol. 1 (1991)-. Monographic series. English. Greenwood Press Inc., PO Box 5007, Westport CT 06881-5007. **Tel** (203)226-3571, FAX (203)222-1502.

ISSN 0196-9366
US
HANDBOOK OF CYCLICAL INDICATORS. Added/Corp United States. Bureau of Economic Analysis. (May 1977)-. Government Publication. English. Irregular. $15.30. US Department of Commerce, 14th Street & Constitution Avenue NW, Washington DC 20230. **Tel** (202)482-2000, FAX (202)482-3772.

LC HA155 .H36
US
HANDBOOK OF INTERNATIONAL ECONOMIC STATISTICS / DIRECTORATE OF INTELLIGENCE, CENTRAL INTELLIGENCE AGENCY. **Added/Corp** United States. Central Intelligence Agency. Directorate of Intelligence. (1992)-. English. One time a year. $32.00. Documents Expediting Project, Exchange and Gift Division, Library of Congress, Washington DC 20540. **Tel** (202)707-9527. **(Subscription address:** National Technical Information Service, 5285 Port Royal Road, Springfield VA 22161. **) Continues** Handbook of Economic Statistics, 0195-9018.

UK
HANDBOOK OF RISK MANAGEMENT. (19??)-. English. Three times a year. £331.45. Croner Publ Ltd., Croner House London Road, Kingston Upon Thames, Surrey KT2 6SR United Kingdom. **Tel** 011 44 181 5473333, FAX 011 44 181 5472637.

US
HANDBOOK TO A FAST-GROWTH BUSINESS MARKET. (199?)-. Trade Publication. English. $29.95. Hispanic Business, 360 South Hope Avenue, Suite 300 C, Santa Barbara CA 93105. **Tel** (805)682-5843, FAX (805)563-1239, (805)687-4546. **Desc:** Analysis of the US Hispanic business market over the past twenty-five years, as well as where the market is today and where it is headed for the future. Tells where Hispanic entrepreneurs are finding success by industry and region.

LC HC281 .H28 ISSN 0073-0068
DD 338.058 GW
HANDBUCH DER GROSSUNTERNEHMEN. Added/Corp Spezial-Archiv der Deutschen Wirtschaft. **VFOAT** Yearbook of Large Enterprises in Germany; Annuaire des Grandes Entreprises en Allemagne. (1941)-. Directory. German (English). One time a year (Feb.). $575.74. Verlag Hoppenstedt & Company, Postfach 100139, D-64201 Darmstadt Germany. **Tel** 011 49 6151 380436, 011 49 6151 380361. **ED** Klaus Schneider. Index available. **Ad Acc. Circ:** 6,400. available on CD-ROM; available on diskette. **Desc:** The 2-volume manual provides detailed company profiles of 23,000 major German companies. It includes free entries of companies with a turnover of 10 million and above, and/or a minimum of 100 employees.

LC HG4247 .H32
KO

HANGUK KIOP CHONGNAM. **Added/Corp** Hanguk Saengsansong Ponbu. (1986)-. Korean. W98,000. Hanguk Saengsansong Ponbu, 10 2-ka Pil-dong, Chung-ku 110, Seoul South Korea. ***Continues*** *Hanguk Kiop Chosarok.*

ISSN 0897-697X
DD 071 US

HAN'GUK KYONGJE SINMUN. (HAN'GUK KYONGJE SINMUN = KOREA ECONOMIC DAILY.). [Han'guk kyongje sinmun]. **VFOAT** Korea Economic Daily. (19??)-. Periodical. Korean. Seven times a week. $540.00. Seven Trading Co. Inc., 136-58 39th Avenue, Room #A, Flushing NY 11354. **Tel** (718)353-7378, FAX (718)353-1104.
Ind/Abst PROMT [Full Txt.]; PTS Newsl. Database [Full Txt.].

GR

HARVARD BUSINESS MANAGER. (19??)-. German. Four times a year. $79.84. Manager Magazin Verlag GmbH, Postfach 111060, Brandstwiete 19, W2000 Hamburg 11 Germany. **Tel** 011 49 40 3007551, FAX 011 49 40 3007247, telex 841 2162477. ***Continues*** *Harvard Manager.*

LC HF5001 .H3 **ISSN** 0017-8012
DD 330.9/04 US
CODEN HABRAX
Pr Rev.

HARVARD BUSINESS REVIEW. [Harvard bus. rev.]. **Added/Corp** Harvard University. Graduate School of Business Administration. Vol. 1 (Oct. 1922)-. Periodical. English. Six times a year. $75.00 (one-year), $138.00 (two-year), $198.00 (three-year) US; $95.00 (one-year), $175.00 (two-year), $250.00 (three-year) Canada and Mexico; $145.00 (one-year), $261.00 (two-year), $386.00 (three-year) other. Harvard Business Review, Soldiers Field, Boston MA 02163. **Tel** (617)495-6801, (800)274-3214, FAX (617)496-8145. **(Subscription address:** Neodata / Colorado, PO Box 2606, Boulder CO 80322. **)** cum. index. available on microfilm and microfiche from University Microfilms International (UMI); available on an online database from NEXIS; and (file 122/Full-Text) DIALOG. Documents available from The Genuine Article, Ask*IEEE, UMI Article Clearinghouse, Documents on Demand, Magazine Collection.
Desc: Written for upper level management. Presents analysis of management problems and helpful commentary on advanced thinking and practice in all fields of management and administration.
Ind/Abst ABI/INFORM Glob. Ed.; ABI/INFORM Ondisc: Expr. Ed.; ABI/INFORM [Computer File] (Sept. 1971-); Abstr. Bull. Inst. Pap. Sci. Tech.; Acad. Abstr. Full Text Elite; Acad. Abstr.; Acad. Ind. [Computer File] (1984-); Acad. Search; Access (1980-?); Account. Art.; ACM Guide Comput. Lit.; AGRICOLA [Select. Cov.]; Anbar Account. Finan. Abstr. [Full Txt.]; Anbar Mark. Distr. Abstr. [Full Txt.]; Anbar Top Manage. Abstr. [Full Txt.]; Biogr. Index; Book Rev. Index; Bowne Dig. Corp. Sec. Lawyers; Bus. Index (1985-); Bus. Period. Index; Bus. Source Plus; Bus. Source; Coal Abstr.; Comput. Bus. (19??-19??); Comput. Lit. Index; Comput. Rev.; Contents Pages Manage.; Curr. Cit.; Curr. Contents Soc. Behav. Sci.; Curr. Lit. Fam. Plan.; Data Process. Dig.; Energy Res. Abstr.; Environ. Abstr.; EP Collect.; Expand. Acad. Index (1984-); F&S Index Plus Text, Int. [Select. Cov.]; Fed. Tax Artic.; Foods Adlibra; Gen. BusinessFile (1985-); Gen. Period. Index (1985-); Health Plan. Adminis.; Homework Help.; Hosp. Health Admin. Index; Hum. Resour. Abstr.; Index Period. Artic. Relat. Law (19??-19??); Ind. Arts Index; INFO-SOUTH Abstr.; Infobank (Jan. 1969-); INSPEC (March/April 1970-Nov./Dec. 1991); Int. Aerosp. Abstr.; Int. Bibliogr. Sociol.; Int. Exec.; J. Plan. Lit.; LABORDOC; Law Office Inf. Serv.; Mag. Artic. Summar. Elite; Mag. Artic. Summar. Select; Mag. Artic. Summar. CD-ROM; Mag. Index Plus (1989-); Mag. Index. Sel. (1986-); Mag. Search; Manage. Market. Abstr.; Manage. Bibliogr. Rev.; Mark. Advert. Ref. Serv.; MasterFile FullTEXT 1000; MasterFile FullTEXT 350; MasterFile FullTEXT 650; MasterFile FullTEXT (May 1984-); Middle East Abstr. Index; Newsp. Period. Abstr. (1986-); OCLC; Oper. Prod. Manage. Abstr. [Full Txt.]; PAIS Int. Print (1991-); Person. Train. Abstr. [Full Txt.]; Person. Manage. Abstr.; PROMT; Pub. Lib. FullTEXT; Read. Guide Period. Lit.; Res. Alert [Full Cov.]; Resource/One Ondisc (1986-); Selec. Coop. Index Manage. Period.; Soc. Sci. Cit. Index [Full Cov.]; Stat. Theory Method Abstr. (1959-1963); Telebase; Text. Technol. Dig.; Mag. Index (1977-); Trade Ind. Index; Urban Aff. Abstr.; Vocat. Search; Wilson Bus. Abstr.; Women Manage. Rev. [Full Txt.]; Work Relat. Abstr.; World Mag. Bank.

LC HF5001 .H32
US
TITLE CHANGE

HARVARD BUSINESS REVIEW CATALOG. **Added/Corp** Harvard University. Graduate School of Business Administration. Publishing Division. (1988)-(1994). Catalog. English. Harvard Business School Publishing Division, Operations Department, 60 Harvard Way, Boston MA 02163. **Tel** (617)495-6192, (617)495-8948, FAX (617)495-6891, telex 6817229. ***Continues*** *Harvard Business Review Ten-Year Index.* ***Continued by*** *Harvard Business Review. Five-Year Index.*

LC HF5001 .H32
US

•**HARVARD BUSINESS REVIEW. FIVE-YEAR INDEX.** **Added/Corp** Harvard Business School Publishing Corporation. **VFOAT** Harvard Business Review ... Five Year Index. (1994)-. English. Irregular. $10.00. Harvard Business School Publishing Division, Operations Department, 60 Harvard Way, Boston MA 02163. **Tel** (617)495-6192, (617)495-8948, FAX (617)495-6891, telex 6817229. ***Continues*** *Harvard Business Review Catalog.*

LC HF1134 .H26 **ISSN** 0017-8020
US

HARVARD BUSINESS SCHOOL BULLETIN. **Added/Corp** Harvard University. Graduate School of Business Administration. Harvard Business School Association. Harvard University. Graduate School of Business Administration. Harvard Business School Association. Bulletin. Harvard University. Graduate School of Business Administration. (1927)-. Bulletin. English. Six times a year (Feb., Apr., June, Aug., Oct., Dec.). $35.00. Harvard Business School Bulletin, Teele 3rd Floor, Soldiers Field, Boston MA 02163. **Tel** (617)495-6554, FAX (617)496-8180, telex 6817229. **ED** Deborah Blagg. **Bk Rev. Ad Acc. Circ:** 55,000 (ctrl).
Desc: Articles about Harvard Business School alumni or topics of interest to alumni.

LC HD30.4 D573 **ISSN** 1042-654X
DD 650/.07/1174461 US

HARVARD BUSINESS SCHOOL ... CATALOG OF TEACHING MATERIALS. [Harv. Bus. Sch. cat. teach. mater.]. **Added/Corp** Harvard University. Graduate School of Business Administration. **VFOAT** Catalog of Teaching Materials. (1988)-. Catalog. English. One time a year (Spring). $10.00. Harvard Business School Publishing Division, Operations Department, 60 Harvard Way, Boston MA 02163. **Tel** (617)495-6192, (617)495-8948, FAX (617)495-6891, telex 6817229. ***Continues*** *Directory of Harvard Business School Cases and Related Course Materials, 1046-8218.*

ISSN 0197-7636
US

HARVARD COLLEGE ECONOMIST. [Harvard coll. econ.]. **Added/Corp** Harvard Student Economics Association. Vol. 1, No. 2 (Spring 1977)-. Periodical. English. Irregular. $25.00. Harvard College Economist Tutorial Office, 1875 Cambridge Street, Litauer Hall, Cambridge MA 02138. **Tel** (617)495-2411. ***Continues*** *Harvard Undergraduate Journal of Economics, 0197-7644.*

ISSN 0210-900X
SP
UDC 658

HARVARD - DEUSTO BUSINESS REVIEW. [Harv. - Deusto Bus. Rev.]. (1980)-. Periodical. Spanish. Four times a year. $225.91. Ediciones Deusto, Alameda Recalde 27 7, 48009 Bilbao Spain. **Tel** 011 34 4 425-1525, FAX 011 34 4 423-4556.
Ind/Abst Selec. Coop. Index Manage. Period.

US

HARVARD INSTITUTE OF ECONOMIC RESEARCH DISCUSSION PAPERS. Monographic series. English. Irregular. Price varies per volume. Harvard Institute of Economic Research, Littauer Center Room 201, Cambridge MA 02138. **Tel** (617)495-4234.

LC HC687 .H3H33 **ISSN** 0440-5056
DD 380 US

HAWAII BUSINESS. [Hawaii bus.]. (1955)-. Periodical. English. Twelve times a year. $34.00. Hawaii Business Publishing Corporation, PO Box 913, Honolulu HI 96808. **Tel** (808)946-3978. **ED** Diane Chang. **Ad Acc. Circ:** 10,000. available on an online database (files 635,648/Full-Text) from DIALOG. Documents available from UMI Article Clearinghouse. ***Continues*** *Hawaii Business and Industry.*
Desc: In-depth articles about business in Hawaii.
Ind/Abst Acad. Search; Bus. ASAP (1990-) [Full Txt.]; Bus. Dateline; Bus. Index (1985-); Bus. Source Plus; Bus. Source; EP Collect.; Gen. BusinessFile (1985-); Gen. Period. Index (1985-); Homework Help.; INFO-SOUTH Abstr.; MasterFile FullTEXT 1000; MasterFile FullTEXT 350; MasterFile FullTEXT 650; MasterFile FullTEXT (Jan. 1994-); OCLC; PROMT; Telebase; Trade Ind. ASAP [Full Txt.]; Trade Ind. Index [Full Txt.].

ISSN 1041-2565
DD 382 US

HAWORTH SERIES IN INTERNATIONAL BUSINESS. [Haworth ser. int. bus.]. Vol. No. 1 (1990)-. Monographic series. English. One time a year. Price varies per volume. The Haworth Press Inc., 10 Alice Street, Binghamton NY 13904-1580. **Tel** (607)722-5857, (800)3-HAWORTH, FAX (607)722-1424. **Acid Free.** Documents available from Haworth Document Delivery Service.

ISSN 1183-6709
DD 658/.041/097105 CN

HEAD OFFICE AT HOME. [Head off. home]. Vol. 1, No. 1 (Apr. 1991)-. Periodical. English. Six times a year. 15.71Can$. Abaco Communications Ltd., 44 Carlton Road, Unionville Ontario L3R 1Z5 Canada. **ED** Elizabeth Harris, (phone: (905)477-4349). **Bk Rev. Ad Acc. Circ:** 52,000.
Desc: This magazine is for entrepreneurs who run their businesses from the home. Articles includes, legal, tax, sales, management, and computers.

ISSN 0116-1202
DD 331.255 658.382 PH

HEALTH ALERT MANILA. [Health Alert Manila]. (1985)-. Newsletter. English. Twenty-six times a year. $36.00. Health Action Information Network, 9 Cabanatuan Road, c/o Philam Homes, Quezon City 1104 Phillippines. **Tel** 011 63 978805. **ED** Michael L. Tan. Index available. cum. index.
Desc: Discusses health issues of current concern in the Phillipines.

LC RA410.A1 .H385 **ISSN** 1057-9230
DD 338.4/33621 US
CCC
NLM W1; HE318LW **CODEN** HEECEZ

HEALTH ECONOMICS. **See** Public Health and Safety.

FR
NLM W1; HE475F

HEALTH POLICY STUDIES. **See** Insurance.

ISSN 1049-4499
DD 362 US
CCC

HEALTHCARE TECHNOLOGY & BUSINESS OPPORTUNITIES. **See** Medical Sciences.

LC KF1074.N3
DD 346.73/0926 347.306926 US

HEARING BOARD DECISIONS AND SUMMARIES. [MICROFORM]. **Main/Corp** New York Stock Exchange. Office of the Hearing Board. **VFOAT** N.Y.S.E. Inc. Hearing Board Decisions; N.Y.S.E. Inc. Hearing Board Summaries of Decisions; NYSE Inc. Hearing Board Decisions; NYSE Inc. Hearing Board Summaries of Decisions. (1972)-. English. New York Stock Exchange Inc., 20 Broad Street, New York NY 10005. **Tel** (212)656-3000, FAX (212)656-5725.

ISSN 0957-1043
UK

HEMEL HEMPSTEAD & DISTRICT BUSINESS DIRECTORY. (1988)-. English. One time a year. £9.00. Holcot Press Ltd, Station House, Station Road, Newport Pognell, Milton Keynes MK16 0AG United Kingdom. **Tel** 011 44 1908 614477, FAX 011 44 1908 217425. **Ad Acc.**

US

HEMISFILE: PERSPECTIVES ON POLITICAL AND ECONOMIC TRENDS IN THE AMERICAS. **See** Political Science.

ISSN 1060-9431
DD 333 US
TITLE CHANGE

HEROLD'S OIL SHARE MARKET PERFORMANCE. [Herold's oil share mark. perform.]. **Added/Corp** John S. Herold, Inc. (Jan. 1992)-(1994). Periodical. English. John S. Herold, Inc., 5 Edgewood Avenue, Greenwich CT 06830. **Tel** (203)869-2585, FAX (203)869-4729. ***Merged into*** *Petroleum Outlook, 0031-6490.*

ISSN 0732-166X
US

HI-LITES OF NATIVE BUSINESS. (197?)-. Periodical. English. Twenty-four times a year. $120.00. Hi-Lites of Native Business, 3605 Arctic Boulevard, #1409, Anchorage AK 99503. **Tel** (907)243-7576.

LC HF3000 .H57 **ISSN** 0199-0349
DD 650/.0240368 US
CCC

HISPANIC BUSINESS. [Hisp. bus.]. Vol. 1, No. 1 (Apr./May 1979)-. Periodical. English. Twelve times a year. $18.00. Hispanic Business, 360 South Hope Avenue, Suite 300 C, Santa Barbara CA 93105. **Tel** (805)682-5843, FAX (805)563-1239, (805)687-4546. **(Subscription address:** Hutchins & Associates Inc, 1865 East Valley Parkway, Suite 206, Escondido CA 92072. **Tel** (619)745-0685.**)** **ED** Jesus Chavarria. **Bk Rev. Ad Acc. Circ:** 136,000. Documents available from UMI Article Clearinghouse.
Desc: Targeted to Hispanic businessmen and professionals, administrators and entrepreneurs. Special issues deal with careers, the nation's 500 largest Hispanic-owned firms and 100 influencers.
Ind/Abst ABI/INFORM Glob. Ed.; Chicano Index; Mark. Advert. Ref. Serv.; PAIS Int. Print (1991-).

Business and Economics

LC HB75 .H546   **ISSN** 0440-9884
DD 330/.09   UK
HISTORY OF ECONOMIC THOUGHT NEWSLETTER.
No. 1 (Nov. 1968)-. Newsletter. English. Two times a year (May, November). $11.98. University of Exeter, Reed Hall, Streatham Drive, Exeter EX4 4RJ United Kingdom. **Tel** 011 44 1392 263202, **FAX** 011 44 1392 263242. **ED** Dr. John Vint (editor's address: Department of Economics and Economic History, Faculty of Humanities and Social Science, Mabel Tylecote Building, Cavendish Street, Manchester M15 6BG United Kingdom). cum. index. **Bk Rev**, (Qty: 15). **Ad Acc**. **Circ:** 400. available on microfilm from University Microfilms International (UMI).
Desc: International medium of information on history of economic thought, research in progress, conferences and meetings past and forthcoming, bibliographical articles, and book reviews.

LC HB75 .H546   **ISSN** 1037-0196
    AT
HISTORY OF ECONOMICS REVIEW / HISTORY OF ECONOMIC THOUGHT SOCIETY OF AUSTRALIA. Added/Corp
History of Economic Thought Society of Australia. **VFOAT** HER. (1991)-. Periodical. English. Two times a year. 15.00Aus$. Curtin University, Department of Economics, GPO Box U1987, Perth Western Australia 6001 Australia. **Tel** 011 61 9 3517722. **Continues** HETSA Bulletin.

LC HC461.A1 H5   **ISSN** 0018-280X
DD 330/.05   JA
Pr Rev.
HITOTSUBASHI JOURNAL OF ECONOMICS. Added/Corp
Hitotsubashi Daigaku. Hitotsubashi Gakkai. (Oct. 1960)-. Periodical. English. Two times a year. $63.50. **(Subscription address:** Maruzen Company Ltd., PO Box 5050, Import & Export Department, Tokyo 100 31 Japan. **Tel** 011 81 3 32789224.) Documents available from The Genuine Article. **Continues in part** Annals of the Hitotsubashi Academy, 0439-2841.
Ind/Abst Contents Recent Econ. J.; Curr. Contents Soc. Behav. Sci.; Econ. Lit. Index; J. Econ. Lit.; PAIS Int. Print (1991-); Res. Alert [Full Cov.]; Soc. Sci. Cit. Index [Full Cov.].

    US
HOFSTRA UNIVERSITY BUSINESS REVIEW : A QUARTERLY PUBLICATION OF THE HOFSTRA UNIVERSITY BUSINESS RESEARCH INSTITUTE.
Added/Corp Hofstra University. Business Research Institute. (198?)-. Periodical. English. Four times a year. Free on request. Hofstra University / Business Research Institute, Hofstra University, Hampstead NY 11550. **Tel** (516)560-5706.

LC HD1401   **ISSN** 0073-2907
DD 650   US
HOFSTRA UNIVERSITY YEARBOOK OF BUSINESS. Added/Corp
Hofstra University. **VFOAT** Yearbook of Business. Ser. 1, Vol. 1 (Mar. 1964)-. Monographic series. English. Irregular. Price varies per volume. Hofstra University School of Business, 111 Heger Hall, Hempstead NY 11550. **Tel** (516)560-5678, **FAX** (516)463-5268.
Desc: Each volume in this series has a distinctive title. Topics are selected from the areas of business and industrial research.

LC HB
DD 330   JA
HOJINZEIHO SOMATOME. (1970)-. Japanese.
¥1500. Zeimer Kenkyukai Shyppankai, 2-7-15 Sarugakucho Chiyoda-ku, Tokyo Japan. **Continues** Hojinzeiho Yonshukan.

LC H8.J3 H62   **ISSN** 0389-6498
DD 300.5   JA
HOKEI RONSO (MORIOKA, 1980). See
Law.

LC HB
DD 330   UK
●HOLLIS BUSINESS ENTERTAINMENT.
See Hotels/Motels.

    ISSN 1061-4222
DD 338   US
HOME BASED HOMERUN. (HOME BASED
HOMERUN: THE MONTHLY BUSINESS NEWSLETTER DEDICATED TO PUTTING YOU IN BUSINESS.). [Home based homerun]. **Added/Corp** Dream Team Consultants. (1992)-. Newsletter. English. Twelve times a year. $18.95. Home Based Homerun, 1033 Nithsdale Drive, Salisbury MD 21801.

    ISSN 1197-2351
DD 658   CN
●HOME BUSINESS REPORT (BRITISH COLUMBIA & ALBERTA ED.). (HOME
BUSINESS REPORT.). [Home bus. rep.]. (May/July 1993)-. Periodical. English. Four times a year. 26.00Can$. HB Communications Group Incorporated, 2949 Ash Street, Abbotsford BC V25 4GS Canada. **Tel** (604)857-1788, **FAX** (604)854-3087. **Continues** British Columbia & Alberta Home Business Report., 1191-8640.

    ISSN 1077-0801
DD 332   US
HOME INCORPORATED. [Home inc.]. (199?)-.
Periodical. English. Twelve times a year. $39.00. Agora Publishing, 824 East Baltimore Street, Baltimore MD 21202. **Tel** (800)433-1528.

    ISSN 1053-0444
    US
HOME OFFICE WORKER. (1991)-. Periodical.
English. Six times a year. $12.00. Archetype Publishing Inc., PO Box 6567, Champaign IL 61826.

    HK
HONG KONG BUSINESS. English. Twelve
times a year. $77.00. Communication Management Ltd., 188 Connaught Road West, 1811 HK Place, Hong Kong Hong Kong. **Tel** 011 852 25477117, **FAX** 011 852 28582671.

    ISSN 0257-3636
    HK
UDC 33
HONG KONG COUNTDOWN. [Hong Kong
countdown]. (1984)-. Periodical. English. Eighteen times a year. $147.00. N&N International Ltd., GPO Box 8926, Hong Kong Hong Kong. **Tel FAX** 011 852 28565648.

LC HC   **ISSN** 0018-4578
DD 330   HK
Pr Rev.   TITLE CHANGE
HONG KONG ECONOMIC PAPERS.
Added/Corp Hong Kong Economic Association. **VFOAT** Hsiang-Kang Ching Chi Hsueh Hui Kan. (June 1961)-(1995). Academic Scholarly Publication. English. Asian Research Service, Sub Department, GPO Box 2232, Hong Kong Hong Kong. **Tel** 011 852 25707227, **FAX** 011 852 25128050, telex 63899 CONPA HX. **Circ:** 1,000. **Continued by** Pacific Economic Review.
Desc: Publication of the Hong Kong Economic Association.
Ind/Abst Contents Recent Econ. J. (1984-); Econ. Lit. Index (19??-); J. Econ. Lit.

    ISSN 0018-4586
    HK
HONG KONG ENTERPRISE. Added/Corp
Hongkong. Dept. of Commerce and Industry. Hongkong Trade Development Council. **VFOAT** Hong Kong Trade Bulletin. (1953)-. Bulletin. English. Twelve times a year. $300.00. Hong Kong Trade Development Council, 38th Floor/Office Tower, Convention Plaza, 1 Harbour Road, Hong Kong. **Tel** 011 852 25844333, **FAX** 011 852 28240249, telex 7395 CONHK HX. **(Subscription address:** Hong Kong Trade Development Council, 219 East 46th Street, New York NY 10017.) ctrl circ.

LC HA4651 .H66a
DD 330.951/2500212   HK
HONG KONG SOCIAL & ECONOMIC TRENDS. See Business and Economics-Abstracting, Bibliographies and Statistics.

    ISSN 0194-5319
    US
HOOSIER BUSINESS WOMAN, THE. See
Women's Interests.

LC HG4009 .H668 HF5035 .H668   **ISSN** 1073-6433
DD 338   US
●HOOVER'S GUIDE TO PRIVATE COMPANIES. [Hoover's guide priv. co.]. (1995)-.
English. One time a year. $79.95. Reference Press Inc., 6448 Highway 290 East, Suite E-104, Austin TX 78723-9828. **Tel** (800)486-8666, (512)454-7778, **FAX** (512)454-9401.

LC HG4009 .H66   **ISSN** 1055-7199
DD 338.7/4/025   US
HOOVER'S HANDBOOK OF WORLD BUSINESS. [Hoover's handb. world bus.]. VFOAT
Handbook of World Business. (1992)-. English. $41.45. Reference Press Inc., 6448 Highway 290 East, Suite E-104, Austin TX 78723-9828. **Tel** (800)486-8666, (512)454-7778, **FAX** (512)454-9401. **Continues in part** Hoover's Handbook, 1056-6279.

    ISSN 1066-291X
    US
●HOOVER'S MASTERLIST OF MAJOR U.S. COMPANIES. VFOAT Hoover's Master List of
Major U.S. Companies; Masterlist of Major U.S. Companies. (1993)-. English. $53.45. Reference Press Inc., 6448 Highway 290 East, Suite E-104, Austin TX 78723-9828. **Tel** (800)486-8666, (512)454-7778, **FAX** (512)454-9401.

    SZ
HORS LIGNE. (19??)-. English. Four times a year.
$48.00. Hors Ligne Publishing SA, Postfach 418, 1211 Geneva Switzerland. **Tel** 011 41 22 215666, **FAX** 011 41 22 622696, telex 419068. **ED** Pio Fontana. **Ad Acc**. **Circ:** 30,000.

Desc: For high scholar people who are active in the fields of business, politics, sports, and the arts with a very high purchasing power.

    ISSN 1034-1897
DD 338.5280994   AT
HOUSE PRICE INDEXES. EIGHT CAPITAL CITIES. [House price indexes, Eight cap.
cities]. **Added/Corp** Australian Bureau of Statistics. (1989)-. Periodical. English. Four times a year. 88.80Aus$. Australian Bureau of Statistics, PO Box 2796Y, Melbourne 3001 Australia. **Tel** 011 61 3 6157843.

LC HD7064.4 .P685
DD 339.4/2/0968   SA
HOUSEHOLD SUBSISTANCE LEVEL IN THE MAJOR URBAN CENTRES OF THE REPUBLIC OF SOUTH AFRICA, THE.
(19??)-. English. Two times a year (Apr. & Oct.). $37.28. Institute of Planning Research, University of Port Eliz, PO Box 1600, Port Eliz 6000 South Africa. **Tel** 011 27 41 5042336, **FAX** 011 27 41 531769.

    ISSN 0277-4976
DD 330   US
    CCC
HOUSTON BUSINESS JOURNAL. [Houston
bus. j.]. Vol. 1 (1973)-. Periodical. English. One time a week. $52.00. Houston Business Journal, One West Loop South, Suite 650, Houston TX 77027. **Tel** (713)688-8811, **FAX** (713)963-0482. **ED** Bill Shadwald. **Bk Rev**. **Ad Acc**, **Adv Mgr:** Linda Harris. **Circ:** 17,000. Documents available from UMI Article Clearinghouse.
Ind/Abst Acad. Search; Bus. Dateline; Bus. Index (1985-1990); Bus. Source Plus; Bus. Source; EP Collect.; Gen. BusinessFile (1985-1990); Gen. Period. Index (1985-1990); Homework Help.; INFO-SOUTH Abstr.; MasterFile FullTEXT 1000; MasterFile FullTEXT 350; MasterFile FullTEXT 650; MasterFile FullTEXT (July 1993-); OCLC; PROMT; Telebase; Trade Ind. ASAP [Full Txt.]; Trade Ind. Index [Full Txt.].

LC JK404 .W37   **ISSN** 1044-7784
    US
HOW TO FIND BUSINESS INTELLIGENCE IN WASHINGTON. [How
find bus. intell. Wash.]. 1986-. English. Three times a week. $125.00. Washington Researchers, PO Box 19005, 20th Street Station, Washington DC 20036. **Tel** (202)333-3533, (202)333-3499, **FAX** (202)625-0656. Index available. **Continues** Washington Information Workbook, 0192-8848.
Desc: Identifies the major federal departments and agencies and targets prime information sources. It also explains how to use the Freedom of Information Act, information during houses and Capital Hill.

LC HG4057 .A4755   **ISSN** 1041-8024
DD 016.3387/4/0973   US
    CEASED
HOW TO FIND COMPANY INTELLIGENCE IN STATE DOCUMENTS.
[How find co. intell. state doc.]. **Added/Corp** Washington Researchers Publishing. 8th Ed. (1986)-(19??). English. Washington Researchers, PO Box 19005, 20th Street Station, Washington DC 20036. **Tel** (202)333-3533, (202)333-3499, **FAX** (202)625-0656. **Continues** Sources of State Information on Corporations.

LC HD2771 .H68   **ISSN** 0278-372X
DD 338   US
NLM HD 2785; H847
HOW TO FIND INFORMATION ABOUT COMPANIES. [How find inf. co.]. Added/Corp
Washington Researchers. Washington Researchers Publishing. (1979)-. Monographic series. English. Irregular. Price varies per volume. Washington Researchers, PO Box 19005, 20th Street Station, Washington DC 20036. **Tel** (202)333-3533, (202)333-3499, **FAX** (202)625-0656. Index available. **Bk Rev**. **Circ:** 8,000. available on videocassette.
Desc: Information about companies, competitors, acquisition, targets, potential clients, etc.

LC HF5382.75.U62
DD 650.14/09747/1   US
HOW TO GET A JOB IN NEW YORK : THE INSIDER'S GUIDE. English. $15.95. Surrey
Books, 230 East Ohio Street, Suite 120, Chicago IL 60611. **Tel** (800)326-4430, (312)751-7330.

LC HC445.8.A1 H75
DD 330   CC
HSIN-CHIA-PO CHING CHI NIEN CHIEN. ALMANAC OF SINGAPORE ECONOMY.
VFOAT Almanac of Singapore Economy. (1976)-. Chinese. Irregular. $36.00 per copy. Shih Li Pao Yeh Chi Kou, 78-B Robinson Road 1, Hsin-Chia-Po, People's Republic of China.

LC HB9 .H8
DD 330/.05   CC
HSUEH PAO (SHAN-HSI TSAI CHING HSUEH YUAN, TAI-YUAN SHIH, CHINA).
(HSUEH PAO / SHANXICAIJINGXUEYUANXUEBAO / SHAN-HSI TSAI CHING HSUEH YUAN.). **Added/Corp**

Business and Economics

Shan-hsi Tsai Ching Hsueh Yuan (Tai-yuan Shih, China). **VFOAT** Shanxicaijingxueyuanxuebao; Shan-Hsi Tsai Ching Hsueh Yuan Hsueh Pao; Journal of Shanxi Finance and Economics College. (19??)-. Periodical. Chinese. Six times a year. RMBY0.35. Hsueh Pao, Post Office, Tai-Yuan Shih, People's Republic of China.

ISSN 1050-1096
US

HUDSON VALLEY BUSINESS JOURNAL (ORANGE COUNTY ED.). (HUDSON VALLEY BUSINESS JOURNAL). (198?)-. Periodical. English. Twenty-six times a year. $20.00. County Business Journals, PO Box 339, Pine Island NY 10990. **Tel** (914)258-4008. **ED** Ed Klein. **Ad Acc. Continues** Orange County Business Journal (Pine Island, N.Y.), 1040-3000.
Ind/Abst MasterFile FullTEXT (July 1993-).

UK

HUNGARIAN BUSINESS BRIEF. English. Twenty-six times a year. $190.00. Walden Publishing Ltd., 2 Market Street Shaffron, Walden Essex CB10 1HZ United Kingdom. **Tel** 011 44 1799 521150, FAX 011 44 1799 524805, telex 817197 JAXPRS G. **(Subscription address:** Business Europa / North America Subscriptions, Subscription Office, PO Box 830430, Birmingham AL 35283-0430. **Tel** (800)633-4931, FAX (205)995-1588.)
Desc: Newsletter on business developments in Hungary.

LC HF13 .H8 ISSN 1215-2439
DD 382/.6/0943905 HU
CODEN HECRE2

HUNGARIAN ECONOMIC REVIEW : HER. [Hung. econ. rev.]. **Added/Corp** Magyar Kereskedelmi Kamara. **VFOAT** HER. Vol. 1, No. 1 (Apr. 1991)-. Periodical. English. Six times a year (Feb., Apr., June, Aug., Oct., Dec.). $48.00. Forka Communications Ltd., 126 Budapest, Herman Otto U 41 Hungary. **Tel** 011 36 1 1562812. **ED** Endre Aczel. Index available. **Ad Acc. Circ:** 6,000. **Continues** Hungarian Trade Journal, 0238-602X.

LC HC300.282.A1 H86 ISSN 0865-8579
DD 330 HU

HUNGARIAN MARKET REPORT. VFOAT Market Report; HMR. (19??)-. Periodical. English (Hungarian and German). Twelve times a year. **(Subscription address:** Kultura, PO Box 143, H-1300 Budapest 3 Hungary. **Tel** 011 36 1 2500194.)

ISSN 0756-368X
FR

UDC 658.8:687
HYPER G.A.P. VFOAT Hyper Groupe Avant-Premiere. (1983)-. Periodical. French. Four times a year. $39.37. Amicale Ensp, 187 Ave de la Division LeClerc, 92290 Chatenay Malabry France. **Tel** 011 33 1 46611047.

US

HYUNDAI NEWSLETTER. Newsletter. English. Twelve times a year. Free on Request. Hyundai Corporation, 1 Bridge Plaza North, Suite 600, Fort Lee NJ 07024. **Tel** (201)346-2020.
Desc: The business newsletter of the Hyundai Corporation.

US
Pr Rev.
I. S. E. R. SECTOR REPORTS. (19??)-. English. free. Alaska Department of Commerce and Economic Development, PO Box D, Juneau AK 99811. **Tel** (907)465-2521, FAX (907)463-3841. Index available.
Desc: Economic information on the AK economy, fisheries, minerals and mining, forest products, and petroleum.

US

I WAY. See Computers.

ISSN 0332-1118
IE

IBAR. VFOAT Journal of Irish Business and Administrative Research. Vol. 1, Pt. 1 (1979)-. Periodical. English. Two times a year. $17.11. IBAR / Irish Business Administration Research, Department of Business Administration, University College, Belfield Dublin Ireland.
Ind/Abst Selec. Coop. Index Manage. Period.

LC HC451 .I26 ISSN 0115-8007
DD 330.9599/005 PH

IBON FACTS AND FIGURES. Added/Corp Ibon Databank Phil., Inc. **VFOAT** IBON Facts & Figures. (19??)-. Periodical. English. Twenty-six times a year.
Ind/Abst Hum. Rights Intern. Rep.

US

ICECAP REPORT. (19??)-. English. Twelve times a year. $445.00. Integrated Circuit Engineering Corporation, 15022 North 75th Street, Scottsdale AZ 85260. **Tel** (602)998-9780, FAX (602)948-1925. **ED** Bill McClean. Index available. cum. index.
Desc: Each of the articles looks in detail at the critical issues confronting the semiconductor industry utilizing technical expertise and market insight.

LC HD9801.6.P763 U62 ISSN 1043-8319
DD 658.5/6 US

ID SYSTEM BUYER'S GUIDE. [ID syst. buy. guide]. **VAT** Identification System Buyer's Guide. (1989)-. Directory. English. One time a year. $34.90. Helmers Publishing Inc., 174 Concord Street, PO Box 874, Peterborough NH 03458-0874. **Tel** (603)924-9631, FAX (603)924-7408. **ED** Carl Helmers. **Ad Acc. Continues** Automatic Identification Manufactures & Services Directory, 1042-4512.
Desc: Contains a complete listing of the companies which deliver bar code and related products/services. Name, type of product, notes. Indexed by company and product.

ISSN 8750-4022
US

IDAHO BUSINESS REVIEW, THE. VFOAT Idaho Business. (198?)-. Periodical. English. One time a week. $61.95. Idaho Business Review, PO Box 7193, Boise ID 83707. **Tel** (208)336-3768. **ED** Carl Miller. **Ad Acc, Adv Mgr:** Kitty Fleischman. available on an online database (file 635/Full-Text) from DIALOG. Documents available from UMI Article Clearinghouse. **Continues** Business Reporter, 0746-5513.
Ind/Abst Bus. Dateline (Sept. 16, 1991-) [Full Txt.].

ISSN 0940-7693
GW
UDC 33
IDEENBRIEF FUER DEN CHEF, DER. [Ideenbr. Chef]. (19??)-. Newsletter. German (English). Twelve times a year. DM19.50. Verlag Norbert Mueller AG & Co. KG, Postfach 450632, Munich 80906 Germany. **Tel** 011 44 89 35093-02, FAX 011 44 89 35093-218. **ED** Dr. Koschut. Index available. **Bk Rev. Circ:** 2,600 (ctrl).
Desc: Contains ideas for business decision makers.

LC H11 .I47
DD 330/.08 UK

IEA LECTURE. Main/Corp Institute of Economic Affairs (Great Britain). **Added/Corp** Institute of Economic Affairs (Great Britain) Lecture. **VAT** Institute of Economic Affairs Lecture. (19??)-. English. Institute of Economics Affairs, 2 Lord North Street, SW1P 3LB United Kingdom.

ISSN 1016-7560
NE
UDC 336
IFA CONGRESS SEMINAR SERIES.
VFOAT International Fiscal Association Congress Seminar Series; Proceedings of a Seminar Held ... During ... Congress of the International Fiscal Association. (1977)-. Monographic series. English. Irregular. Price varies per volume. Kluwer Law and Taxation Publishers / Netherlands, Staverenstraat 32015, PO Box 23, 7400 GA Deventer Netherlands. **Tel** 011 30 5700 47261.
(Subscription address: Libresso BV, Postbus 23, 7400 GA Deventer Netherlands. **Tel** 011 30 5700 47333, 011 31 5700 33155.)

ISSN 0018-974X
GW
CCC
IFO SCHNELLDIENST. [Ifo schnelld.]. **Added/Corp** Ifo-Institut fuer Wirtschaftsforschung. (1948)-. Periodical. German. Thirty-six times a year. $298.77. Duncker und Humblot Verlag, Postfach 410329, D-12113 Berlin Germany. **Tel** 011 49 30 79000612, 011 49 30 79000613. Index Available in last issue of each volume--loose separately paged. **Bk Rev. Ad Acc. Circ:** 2,500.
Desc: Presents specific results of IFO's studies of immediate use to the economic planner. Columns include picture of the week, branch reports, commentary reports and analysis, the economy abroad and key economic statistics.
Ind/Abst Coal Abstr.; Dairy Sci. Abstr.; Energy Res. Abstr. (Oct. 1978-); Rice Abstr.; World Agric. Econ. Rural Sociol. Abstr.

LC HB5 .I23 ISSN 0018-9731
DD 330 GW
CCC
IFO-STUDIEN. [IFO-Stud.]. **Added/Corp** IFO-Institut fuer Wirtschaftsforschung. Vol. 1 (1955)-. Academic Scholarly Publication. German. Four times a year. $144.93. Duncker und Humblot Verlag, Postfach 410329, D-12113 Berlin Germany. **Tel** 011 49 30 79000612, 011 49 30 79000613. **ED** K.H. Oppenkaender. **Bk Rev.** Documents available from SWETS.
Desc: Publishes basic examinations into economic continuity, theoretically based and empirically pursued. Articles from economists world-wide and from members of the institute.
Ind/Abst Econ. Lit. Index; J. Econ. Lit.; PAIS Int. Print; Stat. Theory Method Abstr. (1959-1966).

LC HC281 .W535
DD 330.943/005 GW

IFO WIRTSCHAFTSKONJUNKTUR : MONATSBERICHTE DES IFO INSTITUTS FUER WIRTSCHAFTSFORSCHUNG.
Added/Corp Ifo-Institut fuer Wirtschaftsforschung. Vol. 7 (July 1991)-. Periodical. German. Twelve times a year. DM265.00. IFO-Institut fuer Wirtschaftsforschung,

Postfach 860460, D-81631 Munich Germany. **Tel** 011 49 89 92241, telex 5-22269. **Continues** Wirtschaftskonjunktur, 0043-6283.

LC HD9000.1 .I49A ISSN 0272-3700
DD 338.1/9/05 US

IFPRI REPORT. See Agriculture-Agricultural Economics.

ISSN 0961-3153
UK
IFS COMMENTARY. [IFS comment.]. **VFOAT** Institute for Fiscal Studies Commentary. (198?)-. Monographic series. English. Institute of Fiscal Studies, 7 Ridgmount Street, London WC1E 7AE United Kingdom. **Tel** 011 44 171 6363784.

LC HC107.I3 I55 ISSN 0019-1922
DD 330.5 US
CODEN ILBRAJ
ILLINOIS BUSINESS REVIEW. [Ill. bus. rev.]. **Added/Corp** University of Illinois (Urbana-Champaign Campus). Bureau of Economic and Business Research. Vol. 1 (Jan. 1944)-. Periodical. English. Four times a year (Jan., Apr., July, Oct). $10.00. Bureau of Economic and Business Research / Illinois, 428 Commerce West, 1206 South 6th Street, Champaign IL 61820. **Tel** (217)333-2332, FAX (217)244-3118. **ED** Bill Bryan, Janet Fitch and Susan Hartter. **Circ:** 2,000. available on microfilm and microfiche from University Microfilms International (UMI); available on an online database (file 648/Full-Text) from DIALOG. Documents available from UMI Article Clearinghouse.
Ind/Abst ABI/INFORM Glob. Ed.; ABI/INFORM [Computer File] (May 1979-); Acad. Search; Bus. ASAP (1990-) [Full Txt.]; Bus. Index (1985-); Bus. Source Plus; Bus. Source; EP Collect.; Gen. BusinessFile (1985-); Gen. Period. Index (1985-); Homework Help.; INFO-SOUTH Abstr.; MasterFile FullTEXT 1000; MasterFile FullTEXT 350; MasterFile FullTEXT 650; MasterFile FullTEXT (July 1993-); OCLC; Pollut. Abstr. Indexes; Stat. Ref. Index; Telebase; Trade Ind. ASAP [Full Txt.]; Trade Ind. Index [Full Txt.]; UMI ABI/Inform--Bus. Period. Ondisc (Dec. 1987-) [Full Txt.]; Urban Aff. Abstr.

LC HC107.I3 I585
DD 330.9773/005 US

ILLINOIS ECONOMIC OUTLOOK.
Added/Corp University of Illinois at Urbana-Champaign. Bureau of Economic and Business Research. (19??)-. English. Irregular. $7.50 institutions, $10.00 individuals. Bureau Economics and Business Research, 428 Commerce West, 1206 South 6th Street, Champaign IL 61820. **Tel** (217)333-2332, FAX (217)244-3118. cum. index. ctrl circ.

LC HD30.25 .I43 ISSN 0953-0061
DD 650/.01/513 UK
CCC
CODEN IMJIE9
IMA JOURNAL OF MATHEMATICS APPLIED IN BUSINESS AND INDUSTRY.
See Mathematics.

LC HC276.3 .I47
DD 330 FR

IMAGES ECONOMIQUES DES ENTREPRISES AU ... . Added/Corp Institut National de la Statistique et des Etudes Economiques (France). (1992)-. French. Institut National de la Statistique et des Etudes Economiques, 18 Bd Adolphe Pinard, 75675 Paris 14 France. **Formed by the union of** Images Economiques des Entreprises au ... Energie, Biens Intermediaires **and** Images Economiques des Entreprises au ... Commerce, Transports et Telecommunications Images Economiques des Entreprises au ... Agro-Alimentaire, Biens de Consommation Images Economiques des Entreprises au ... Biens d'Equipement, BTP Images Economiques des Entreprises au ... Services au ... .

LC HA1631 .A33 HF5500.3.Y8
DD 314.971 YU

IMENOVANJE DIREKTORA RADNIH ORGANIZACIJA. Main/Corp Savezni Zavod Za Statistiku (Yugoslavia). (19??)-. Serbo-Croatian (Roman). 10.00. Savezni Zavod za Statistiku, Kneza Milosa 20, Belgrad Yugoslavia.

ISSN 1198-8681
DD 658 CN

●**IMPACT.** [Impact - Univ. West. Ont., West. Bus. Sch]. **Added/Corp** University of Western Ontario. Western Business School. Vol. 1, No. 1 (Sept. 1994)-. Periodical. English. Two times a year. Free. Western Business School, University of Western Ontario, London Ontario N6A 3K7 Canada. **Tel** (519)661-4031, FAX (519)661-3700. **ED** Ken Hardy.
Desc: Provides information on management research in action.

ISSN 0961-4745
UK

IMPACT AGBIOBUSINESS. See Agriculture-Agricultural Economics.

Business and Economics

IMPRESA PUBBLICA. CIVILTA POSTINDUSTRIALE, L'. (19??)-(Dec. 1993). Italian. Twelve times a year. L50000 Italy; L77000 other. Euroitalia Srl, Via della Scrofa 39, 00186 Rome Italy. **Tel** 011 39 6 68300831.

ISSN 0277-8432
US

IMPRIMIS. [Imprimis]. **Added/Corp** Hillsdale College. Center for Constructive Alternatives. Vol. 1 (May 1972)-. Periodical. English. Twelve times a year. Free. Hillsdale College / Imprimis, 33 East College Street, Hillsdale MI 49242. **Tel** (517)437-7341. **ED** Ronald L. Trowbridge and Lissa Roche. cum. index. **Circ:** 550,000 (ctrl). available on an online database.
Ind/Abst Educ. Adm. Abstr.; PAIS Int. Print.

IT

IMQ NOTIZIE. (19??)-. Italian. Four times a year. Free on request. IMQ, Via Quintiliano 43, 20138 Milan Italy. **Tel** 011 39 2 5073.

LC HF5001　　　　　　　ISSN 0848-1008
DD 650/.09713/32　　　　　　　　　　CN

IN BUSINESS WINDSOR. [In bus. Windsor]. Vol. 1, Issue 1 (May 1989)-. Periodical. English. Twelve times a year. $27.00. In Business Windsor, 4510 Rhodes Drive, Suite 805, Windsor Ontario N8W 5C2 Canada. **Tel** (519)253-1752.

ISSN 1046-1736
DD 332　　　　　　　　　　　　　　　US

INCOME PLU$. [Income plu$]. **VFOAT** Income Plus. Vol. 1, No. 1 (Nov. 1989)-. Periodical. English. Twelve times a year. $19.95. Opportunity Associates, 73 Spring Street, New York NY 10012. **Tel** (212)925-3180. (**Subscription address:** Palm Coast Data, PO Box 420163, Agency Department, Palm Coast FL 32142. **Tel** (904)445-4662 ext. 669, (800)829-5475.) **ED** Roxanne Farmanfarmaia.
Desc: How-to magazine that offers buyer's guides, reference materials and step-by-step instructions for starting one's own business, including charts and worksheets.

ISSN 0746-4754
US

INDEPANDANT PROFESSIONAL AND FLORIDA BUSINESS JOURNAL, THE. **VFOAT** Independent Professional. (198?)-. Periodical. English. Twelve times a year. $22.00. Independent Professional Inc., PO Box 13485, Gainesville FL 32604. *Continues Independent Professional, 0740-5693.*

ISSN 1033-9957
DD 994.05　　　　　　　　　　　　　AT

INDEPENDENT MONTHLY, THE. See Political Science.

LC Z7164.E2 I4812 HB1　　　ISSN 0536-647X
DD 016.33　　　　　　　　　　　　　US

INDEX OF ECONOMIC ARTICLES IN JOURNALS AND COLLECTIVE VOLUMES. See Business and Economics-Abstracting, Bibliographies and Statistics.

UK

INDEX TO BUSINESS REPORTS. See Business and Economics-Abstracting, Bibliographies and Statistics.

LC Z
DD 011.75　　　　　　　　　　　　　US

INDEX TO DOCTORAL DISSERTATIONS IN BUSINESS EDUCATION, 1900-1975. See Education-Abstracting, Bibliographies and Statistics.

LC Z7164.E2 I49　　　　　　ISSN 0019-4026
II

INDEX TO INDIAN ECONOMIC JOURNALS. **Added/Corp** Information Research Academy. Vol. 1 (Jan./June 1966)-. Periodical. English. Twelve times a year. Rs350.00 India; $150.00 other. Information Research Academy, 37 Syed Amir Ali Avenue, Calcutta 700018 India. **ED** Partha Subir Guha. **Ad Acc**.

ISSN 1352-8335
DD 338.70954　　　　　　　　　　　UK

●**INDIA BUSINESS INTELLIGENCE.** [India bus. intell.]. (1993)-. Periodical. English. Twenty-four times a year. $872.72. Financial Times / UK, Maple House, 149 Tottenham Court Road, London W1P 9LL United Kingdom. **Tel** 011 44 171 8962276, FAX 011 44 171 8962275, 011 44 171 8962399.

LC HB1.A1 I5　　　　　　ISSN 0019-4670
DD 330.954/005　　　　　　　　　　II

INDIAN ECONOMIC REVIEW. [Indian econ. rev.]. **Added/Corp** Delhi School of Economics. Vol. 1, No. 1 (Feb. 1952)-. Periodical. English. Two times a year. $41.50. University of Delhi / School of Economics, New Delhi 110007 India. **Tel** 011 91 11 7257540. **ED** V. Pandit. **Circ:** 600 (ctrl).
Ind/Abst Contents Recent Econ. J.; Econ. Lit. Index; J. Econ. Lit.; Leis., Rec., Tour. Abstr.; Rural Dev. Abstr.; Stat. Theory Method Abstr. (1959-1963); World Agric. Econ. Rural Sociol. Abstr.

II

INDIAN ECONOMY. **Added/Corp** Hind Mazdoor Sabha. Research and Training Programme. (19??)-. Periodical. English. Four times a year. $20.00. Research Training Programme, Hind Mazdoor Sabha, New Delhi India. (**Subscription address:** Prints India, 11 Darya Ganj, New Delhi 110002 India. **Tel** 011 91 11 3268645, FAX 011 91 11 3275542, telex 31-61087 PRIN-IN.)

LC HD101 .I533　　　　　　ISSN 0019-5014
II

INDIAN JOURNAL OF AGRICULTURAL ECONOMICS, THE. See Agriculture-Agricultural Economics.

LC HB9 .I4　　　　　　　　ISSN 0019-5170
DD 330　　　　　　　　　　　　　　　II

INDIAN JOURNAL OF ECONOMICS. **Added/Corp** Indian Economic Association. University of Allahabad. Dept. of Economics. University of Allahabad. Dept. of Commerce. Indian Economic Association. Papers Read at the Annual Conference of the Indian Economic Association. Vol. 1, Pt. 1 (Jan. 1916)-. Academic Scholarly Publication. English. Four times a year. $125.00. University of Allahabad / Department of Economics, PO Box 2005, Allahabad 211002 India. **Tel** 011 91 11 51940. **ED** Prof. V.K. Anand, Prof. G.C. Agrawal (Anand's phone: 011 91 11 600123; Agrawal's phone: 011 91 11 607088). Index available (July issue). **Bk Rev. Circ:** 500 (ctrl). available with charts; available with illustrations; available on microfiche.
Desc: Covers all aspects of economics.
Ind/Abst Contents Recent Econ. J.; Int. Labour Doc.; Leis., Rec., Tour. Abstr.; Maize Abstr.; Rural Dev. Abstr.; World Agric. Econ. Rural Sociol. Abstr.

LC HB1 .I37　　　　　　　ISSN 0970-1532
DD 330/.05　　　　　　　　　　　　　II

INDIAN JOURNAL OF QUANTITATIVE ECONOMICS. [Indian J. Quant. Econ.]. **Added/Corp** Punjab School of Economics. Vol. 1 No. 1 (1985)-. Periodical. English. Two times a year (Jan., July). $20.00. Guru Nanak Dev University, Punjab School of Economics, Amritsar India. (**Subscription address:** Prints India, 11 Darya Ganj, New Delhi 110002 India. **Tel** 011 91 11 3268645, FAX 011 91 11 3275542, telex 31-61087 PRIN-IN.)
Ind/Abst Econ. Cot. Trop. Fibr. Abstr. Bibliogr.; Econ. Lit. Index (199?-); J. Econ. Lit.; PAIS Int. Print; Wheat Barley Trit. Abstr.; World Agric. Econ. Rural Sociol. Abstr.

LC DT365 .I49　　　　　　ISSN 0294-6475
FR

INDIAN OCEAN NEWSLETTER = LA LETTRE DE L'OCEAN INDIEN, THE. **Added/Corp** Banque d'Information et de Documentation de l'Ocean Indien (Paris, France). **VFOAT** Lettre de l'Ocean Indien; I.O.N.; ION. No. 1 (Oct. 31, 1981)-. Newsletter. French. One time a week (48 issues per year). $853.01. Indigo Publications, 10 rue du Sentier, 75002 Paris France. **Tel** 011 33 1 44882610, FAX 011 33 1 44882615, telex 215405. **ED** Francis Soler. **Circ:** 48.
Desc: Politics and economy in eastern Africa and Indian Ocean islands.
Ind/Abst Hum. Rights Intern. Rep.

LC HF107.I6 I5　　　　　　ISSN 1060-4154
DD 338.09772　　　　　　　　　　　US

INDIANA BUSINESS MAGAZINE. [Indiana bus. mag.]. Vol. 35, No. 1 (Jan. 1991)-. Periodical. English. Twelve times a year. $19.00. Curtis Magazine Group Inc., 1200 Waterway Boulevard, Indianapolis IN 46202. **Tel** (317)692-1200, FAX (317)692-4250. **ED** Steve Kaelble. **Ad Acc, Adv Mgr** Amy Krieg. **Circ:** 36,000 (ctrl). available on an online database (file 648/Full-Text) from DIALOG; available on diskette. *Continues Indiana Business, 0273-7930.*
Desc: Statewide business news.
Ind/Abst Acad. Search; Bus. Index (1985-); Bus. Source Plus; Bus. Source; EP Collect.; Gen. BusinessFile (1985-); Gen. Period. Index (1985-); Homework Help.; MasterFile FullTEXT 1000; MasterFile FullTEXT 350; MasterFile FullTEXT 650; MasterFile FullTEXT; OCLC; Telebase; Trade Ind. ASAP [Full Txt.]; Trade Ind. Index [Full Txt.].

LC HC107.I6 I48　　　　　ISSN 0019-6541
DD 330.9772/005　　　　　　　　　　US
　　　　　　　　　　　　　CODEN IBREAO

INDIANA BUSINESS REVIEW. [Indiana bus. rev.]. **Added/Corp** Indiana University. Bureau of Business Research. Indiana University. School of Business. Division of Research. **VFOAT** IBR; I.B.R. Vol. 1 (Mar. 1926)-. Periodical. English. Four times a year. Free on request. Indiana University Business Research Center, Graduate School of Business, Bloomington IN 47405. **Tel** (812)855-5507, FAX (812)855-7763. **ED** Morton Marcus. available in microform from Photographic Sciences Corp.; available on microfilm and microfiche from University Microfilms International (UMI); available on an online database (file 15/Full-Text) from DIALOG. Documents available from UMI Article Clearinghouse.
Desc: Discusses business and economic issues of concern to residents of Indiana and the Midwest.
Ind/Abst ABI/INFORM Glob. Ed. (Oct. 1974-); ABI/INFORM [Computer File] (Oct. 1974-); Stat. Ref. Index; UMI ABI/Inform--Bus. Period. Ondisc (Oct. 1987-) [Full Txt.].

ISSN 0274-4929
US
Pr Rev.

INDIANAPOLIS BUSINESS JOURNAL. **VFOAT** Who's Who in Indianapolis Business. Vol. 1, No. 1, May 19 (1980)-. Periodical. English. One time a week. $59.00. IBJ Corporation, 431 North Pennsylvania Street, Indianapolis IN 46204. **Tel** (317)634-6200, FAX (317)263-5060. **ED** Tom Harton. **Ad Acc, Adv Mgr:** Greg Morris. **Circ:** 16,500. available in microform from University Microfilms International (UMI); available on an online database (files 635,648/Full-Text) from DIALOG. Documents available from UMI Article Clearinghouse.
Desc: Local and regional business news concerning Indianapolis and central Indiana. Includes investigative reporting features, financial information, new corporations, columns, classifieds and special sections weekly.
Ind/Abst Acad. Search; Bus. Dateline; Bus. Index (1985-1990); Bus. Source Plus; Bus. Source; EP Collect.; Gen. BusinessFile (1985-1990); Gen. Period. Index (1985-1990); Homework Help.; MasterFile FullTEXT 1000; MasterFile FullTEXT 350; MasterFile FullTEXT 650; MasterFile FullTEXT (July 1993-); OCLC; PROMT; Telebase; Trade Ind. Index.

LC HF3231 .S47
DD 382/.0972/00212　　　　　　　　MX

INDICADORES DEL SECTOR EXTERNO. Spanish. Twelve times a year. $168,000 Mexico; $120.00 US; $180.00 Europe; $240.00 other. Oficina de Divulgacion Condesa, 6 1er Piso, Col Centro, Delegacion Cuauhtemoc 06059 Mexico DF. **Tel** 518-0500. Index available. **Circ:** 2,200. available on diskette. *Continues Serie Informacion Economica. Sector Externo.*
Desc: Economic statistics of production, finances, prices and the external sector.

LC HC131 .B28a
DD 330.972　　　　　　　　　　　　MX

INDICADORES ECONOMICOS (BANCOO DE MEXICO (1925-). SUBDIRECCION DE INVESTIGACION ECONOMICA). See Business and Economics-Abstracting, Bibliographies and Statistics.

BE

INDICATEUR FISCAL. (19??)-. French. Irregular. CED Samsom, Kouterveld 14, B-1831 Diegem, Brussels Belgium. **Tel** 011 32 2 723-1111.

ISSN 0121-2613
DD 330　　　　　　　　　　　　　　CK

INDICE COLOMBIANO DE ECONOMIA Y NEGOCIOS. See Business and Economics-Abstracting, Bibliographies and Statistics.

CK

INDICE DE PRECIOS AL CONSUMIDOR. **Main/Corp** Colombia. Departamento Administrativo Nacional de Estadistica. (19??)-. Periodical. Spanish. Twelve times a year. $200.00 (microfiche). Fondo Rotativo Dane, Apartado 80043, Bogota Colombia. **Tel** 011 57 1 2221750.

IT

INDICI MENSILI PIROLA. (19??)-. Italian. L129.000. Pirola Editore, CP 10444, Via Parabiago 19, 20151 Milan Italy. **Tel** 011 39 2 3022888. **Ad Acc, Adv Mgr** Tel 3022.1. **Circ:** 9,000.

LC HC446 .I533
DD 330　　　　　　　　　　　　　　US

INDONESIA DEVELOPMENT NEWS MONTHLY STATISTICAL BULLETIN. **Added/Corp** National Development Information Office (Indonesia). **VFOAT** Indonesia Monthly Statistical Bulletin. (199?)-. Bulletin. English. Twelve times a year. Hill and Knowlton Inc., 420 Lexington Avenue, New York NY 10017. **Tel** (212)697-5600. *Continues in part Indonesia Development News.*

LC HC446 .I53
DD 330/.338.9598　　　　　　　　　US

INDONESIA DEVELOPMENT NEWS QUARTERLY. **Added/Corp** National Development Information Office (Indonesia). **VFOAT** Indonesia Quarterly. Vol. 15, No. 3 (Spring 1992)-. Periodical. English. Four times a year. Hill and Knowlton Inc., 420 Lexington Avenue, New York NY 10017. **Tel** (212)697-5600. *Continues in part Indonesia Development News.*

Business and Economics

INDONESIA LETTER, THE. Vol. 1, (1969)-. Periodical. English. Twelve times a year. $195.00. Asia Letter Group, GPO Box 10874, Central Hong Kong. **Tel** 011 852 25262950, FAX 011 852 25267131, telex 61166. **(Subscription address:** Asia Letter Group, PO Box 88189, Los Angeles CA 90009.**)**
Desc: An analysis of political and economical developments of Indonesia. Published for people doing business with Indonesia.
LC HF41 .I45
DD 380.1/09598
ISSN 0019-7297
HK

INDONESIAN COMMERCIAL NEWSLETTERS. (1974)-. Newsletter. English. Twenty-four times a year. $440.00. PT Data Consult Inc, PO Box 108, Ing Jakarta 13041, Indonesia. **Tel** 11 62 21 3904711, telex 44328 PIOLA JKT. **ED** D. Ganjar Sidik. cum. index. Circ: 2,000 (ctrl) available on an online database (file 16/Full-Text) from DIALOG.
Desc: A reference source containing information on economic conditions such as the economic climate, consumers, producers, and sectoral development. For anyone interested in doing business in Indonesia.
Ind/Abst F&S Index Plus Text, Int. [Full Txt.] [Select. Cov.].
LC HC446 .I693
DD 330.9598/005
ISSN 0377-0001
IO

INDONESIAN ECONOMY, THE. Added/Corp Center for Policy Studies (Jakarta, Indonesia). (19??)-. Periodical. English. Twelve times a year. $250.00. Indonesian Economy, JL. S. Parman 81 Slipi, Jakarta 11420 Indonesia.
ISSN 0215-1561
IO

INDONESIAN ECONOMY BULLETIN. (19??)-. Bulletin. English. JL Kesejahteraan No 98 -Arena Pekan Raya Jakarta, POB 2744 JKT, Jakarta 10110 Indonesia.
LC HD2907.A1 I578
JA

INDUSTRIAL GROUPINGS IN JAPAN. Added/Corp Dodwell Marketing Consultants. (1973)-. English. Every 2 years. $800.00. Dodwell Marketing Consultants, Kowa No 35, Building 14-14, Akasaka 1-chome Minato-ku 107, Japan. **Tel** 03 3589 0207, FAX 03 3589 0516. **(Subscription address:** International Publications Service, A Division of Taylor & Francis, 1900 Frost Road, Suite 101, Bristol PA 19007-1598. **Tel** (800)821-8312.**)** Index available. **Bk Rev. Circ:** 4,000 (ctrl).
Desc: Guide to the Japanese industrial environment. A survey of 3,000 companies shows a functioning of the Japanese Industrial Group System.
UK

INDUSTRIAL PERFORMANCE ANALYSIS. (19??)-. English. One time a year (October). £95.00. Field House, 72 Old Field Road, Hamperton TW12 28HQ United Kingdom. **Tel** 081 783 0932, FAX 081 783 1940. **ED** Marie Fernandes. Index available.
Desc: A three-year analysis of the financial performance of over 200 sectors of the UK economy.
LC HC10 .I614
DD 338/.0021
FR

INDUSTRIAL STRUCTURE STATISTICS / STATISTIQUES DES STRUCTURES INDUSTRIELLES. See Business and Economics-Abstracting, Bibliographies and Statistics.
LC HA1320.N6 A32 HC287.N6 N6
DD 330
GW

INDUSTRIE IN NORDHEIN-WESTFALEN, DIE. See Business and Economics-Abstracting, Bibliographies and Statistics.
GW

INDUSTRIE UND HANDELSREVUE AKTUELLE OSTHANDELS INFORMATIONEN. German. Twenty-four times a year. DM249.60 Germany; DM272.40 other. Guenter W Sorge Verlag, Hebbelstrasse 1, W-5020 Frechen 5 Germany. **Tel** 011 49 2234 31071, 011 49 2234 31072.
US

INDUSTRIES IN TRANSITION. Added/Corp Business Communications Co. (19??)-. Periodical. English. Twelve times a year. $325.00. Business Communications Inc., 25 Van Zant Street, Suite 13, Norwalk CT 06855. **Tel** (203)853-4266, FAX (203)853-0348. available on an online database (files 16,636/Full-Text) from DIALOG. **Continues** Growth Industry News.
Ind/Abst PROMT [Full Txt.]; PTS Newsl. Database [Full Txt.].
ISSN 0276-7317
US

INDUSTRY INTERNATIONAL. (INDUSTRY INTERNATIONAL : A LINEAL PUBLICATION.). [Ind. int.]. Vol. 1, No. 1 (1981)-. Periodical. Multiple languages (English and Spanish). Six times a year. $30.00 US. Lineal Publishing Company, 10842 Pine Bark Lane, Boca Raton FL 33428-2852. **Tel** (407)451-9429, FAX (407)776-6649, telex 522-265 LINEAL CO FL. **ED** Irv Lineal. Index available. cum. index. **Bk Rev. Ad Acc. Circ:** 57,000 (ctrl).
Desc: Technical journals for plant engineers and operating managers in industrial and manufacturing facilities in Asia, Africa, the Middle East and the Pacific. In Spanish for Mexico, Central America and South America.
LC HF5681.R25 I53
DD 338.0973
ISSN 8755-2396

INDUSTRY NORMS AND KEY BUSINESS RATIOS. [Ind. norms key bus. ratios]. **Added/Corp** Dun & Bradstreet Credit Services. (1982/1983)-. English. One time a year. Price varies. Dun & Bradstreet Information Services, 3 Sylvan Way, Parsippany NJ 07054. **Tel** (201)605-6000, (800)526-0651. **Continues** Selected Key Business Ratios in 125 Line of Business, 0735-3367.
LC HC451 .I643
DD 338.09599
PH

INDUSTRY PERFORMANCE IN ... AND PROSPECTS FOR ... . English. P3,200 Philippines; $80.00 other. PO Box 757 Makati, Metro Manila 3117 Philippines. **Tel** 810-02-31, telex RCA 22080 RCPI 2131. **ED** Dante M Liwanes. **Ad Acc. Circ:** 150 (ctrl).
DD 334
ISSN 0846-2917
CN

INFO CLUB (OTTAWA ED.). (INFO CLUB.). [Info club]. Vol. 4, No. 2 (Apr. 1991)-. Periodical. French (English). Irregular. Free limited distribution. Info Club, 3010 rue Jacques-Bureau, Laval Quebec H7P 5P8 Canada.
DD 334/.09714
ISSN 0826-8045
CN

INFO-COOP. [Info-coop]. Vol. 1, No. 1 (Dec. 1984)-. Periodical. French. Five times a year. Free. Min Lindustrie Commerce Tech, Dir Comun 710 Place D Youviue, Quebec Quebec G1R 4Y4 Canada. **Tel** (418)691-5950. ctrl circ.
UDC 336.76
ISSN 0926-5775
NE

INFOGRAPH NEDERLANDSE ED. (INFOGRAPH.). [Infograph Ned. ed.]. (1978)-. Periodical. Dutch. Six times a year. Fl117.92. ING Bank, Economisch Buro, HA0206 Postbus 1800, 1000 BV Amsterdam Netherlands. **Tel** 011 31 20 5634401, FAX 011 31 20 5634409.
GW

INFOMARKT. (19??)-. Periodical. German. Two times a year. DM166.00. Infomarkt GmbH, Grafenberger Allee 368, D-40235 Duesseldorf Germany. **Tel** 011 49 211 669070.
US

INFOMAT INTERNATIONAL BUSINESS [ONLINE DATABASE]. See Business and Economics-Abstracting, Bibliographies and Statistics.
LC HD1875.S3 I58A
DD 338.18
ISSN 0100-4409
BL

INFORMACOES ECONOMICAS - INSTITUTO DE ECONOMIA AGRICOLA. See Agriculture-Agricultural Economics.
DD 658
ISSN 1192-358X
CN

INFORMATEUR DES GENS D'AFFAIRES. (L'INFORMATEUR DES GENS D'AFFAIRES.). [Inf. gens aff.]. Vol. 1, no 1 (Oct./Nov. 1992)-. Periodical. French. Nine times a year. 39.98Can$. Tempo Marketing, 2013 Liebert, Montreal Quebec H1L 5P9 Canada. **Tel** (514)355-0474.
ISSN 0226-9961
CN

INFORMATEUR (LONGUEUIL). (INFORMATEUR.). [Informateur]. **Added/Corp** R.E.G.A.R.S. **VAT** R.E.G.A.R.S. Regroupement d'Entraide pour les Gens de la Rive-Sud. No. 1 (1981)-. Periodical. French. Irregular. $95.00. REGARS, 18 Ouest rue le Moyne, Longueuil Quebec J4H 1V3 Canada.
DD 380.1/09714
ISSN 0167-398X
NE

INFORMATIE VOOR DE VERKOOPBINNENDIENST. (19??)-. Dutch. Twelve times a year. Samsom Bedrijfsinformatie BV, Postbus 4, 2400 MA Alphen Rij Netherlands. **Tel** 011 31 1720 66633. **(Subscription address:** Intermedia BV, Postbus 4, 2400 MA Alphen AD Rijn Netherlands. **Tel** 011 31 1720 66481.**)**
LC HF5548.125 .I54
DD 505.06/65
ISSN 1050-1576
US

INFORMATION ADVISOR, THE. (1992)-. English. Twelve times a year. $130.00. Find/SVP, 625 Avenue of Americas, New York NY 10011. **Tel** (212)645-4500. available on an online database (file 648/Full-Text) from DIALOG.
Desc: Designed specially for hands-on business researchers. Identifies, describes, and provides contact information for sources on the new single European Market. Sources covered include periodicals, books, market research reports, online databases, associations, directories, embassies, and more.
Ind/Abst Trade Ind. ASAP [Full Txt.]; Trade Ind. Index [Full Txt.].
LC HF5477.U63 C355
US

INFORMATION BULLETIN / CALIFORNIA AUCTIONEER COMMISSION. Main/Corp California Auctioneer Commission. **Added/Corp** California Auctioneer Commission. Board of Governors. Minutes. No. 31 (Mar. 1991)-. Bulletin. English. **Continues** Information Bulletin.
LC HC462.9 .I54
DD 330/.06/052
ISSN 0289-8721
JA

INFORMATION BULLETIN OF THE UNION OF NATIONAL ECONOMIC ASSOCIATIONS IN JAPAN. Added/Corp Nihon Keizai Gakkai RengAo. No. 1 (1981)-. Bulletin. English. One time a year.
Ind/Abst Am. Hist. Life (1981)-.
DD 658
ISSN 1045-3652
US

INFORMATION CATALOG, THE. [Inf. cat.]. (19??)-. Catalog. English. Four times a year. Find/SVP, 625 Avenue of Americas, New York NY 10011. **Tel** (212)645-4500. **Absorbed** Research from Wall Street.
ISSN 0167-6245
NE
CCC

Pr Rev.
INFORMATION ECONOMICS AND POLICY. See Communications.

ISSN 0020-0050
TI
UDC 33 (6)

INFORMATION ECONOMIQUE AFRICAINE. [Inf. econ. afr.]. **VFOAT** IEA Information Economique Africaine. (1961)-. Periodical. French. Twelve times a year. $200.00. Information Economique Africaine, 16 rue de Rome, 1015 Tunis Tunisia. **Tel** 011 216 1 245318, 011 216 1 255740, FAX 011 216 1 353172, telex 14459.
Ind/Abst PAIS Int. Print.
ISSN 0930-5181
GW
UDC 519.68 :65

INFORMATION MANAGEMENT (MUNCHEN). [Inf. Manag. Munch.]. **VFOAT** IM. Information Management. (1986)-. Periodical. Multiple languages. Four times a year. DM155.00. IDG Communications Verlag AG / Germany, Rheinstrasse 26 28, D-80803 Munich Germany. **Tel** 011 49 89 360860.
LC JK404
DD 353
ISSN 0733-8961
US
CODEN IRPTD4

INFORMATION REPORT (WASHINGTON, D.C.), THE. See Public Administration.
ISSN 1259-1106
FR
UDC 658

●**INFORMATIQUE & STRATEGIE D'ENTREPRISE. VFOAT** Informatique et Strategie D'entreprise. (1994)-. Periodical. French. Six times a year. 3300.00F France; 3400.00 other. Bouhot & Le Gendre Publishers, 75 Bis rue de Bellevue, F 92100 Boulogne France. **Tel** 011 33 1 46040708. **(Subscription address:** Centrale des Revues, 11 rue Gossin, 92543 Montrouge Cedex France. **Tel** 011 33 1 46565266.**)**
IT

INFORMATORE INAZ. (19??)-. Italian. Twenty-four times a year. L310000. Inaz Paghe Editore, Via Sirtori 5, 20129 Milan Italy. **Tel** 011 39 2 29404040.
ISSN 0250-751X
US
CEASED

INFORME ANUAL DEL DIRECTORIO EJECUTIVO - FONDO MONETARIO INTERNACIONAL. See Industry and Production-Trade and Industrial Directories.
LC WMLC 90/0663
CL

INFORME DE ACTIVIDADES / CORPORACION DE INVESTIGACIONES ECONOMICAS PARA LATINOAMERICA. Main/Corp Corporacion de Investigaciones Economicas Para Latinoamerica. (1984)-. Corporate Report. Spanish (English). One time a year. Free. Corporacion de Investigaciones Economicas Para Latinoamerica, Casilla 16496, Correo 9, Santiago Chile. **Tel** 633 3836, FAX 56 2 633 4411, telex 340 412PBVTR. **Circ:** 1,000 (Spanish), 300 (English) (ctrl).

LC HC236 .B3 **ISSN** 0067-3250
DD 330.987/005 VE
INFORME ECONOMICO. Main/Corp Banco Central de Venezuela. **VFOAT** Informe Economico - Banco Central de Venezuela. (1962)-. Spanish. Irregular. Banco Central de Venezuela, Apartado 2017, Caracas Venezuela. **Tel** 011 58 2 8629811, 8629821, 8629831, telex 22875. ctrl circ.

ISSN 0266-2914
DD 980.03805 UK
INFORME ESPECIAL - LATIN AMERICAN NEWSLETTERS. [Inf. espec. - Latin Am. Newsl.]. (1984)-. Periodical. Spanish. Six times a year. $230.00. Lettres UK Ltd, 61 Old Street, London EC1V 9HX United Kingdom. **Tel** 011 44 171 2510012, FAX 011 44 171 2538193. **ED** Eduardo Crawley. available on an online database from Lexis-Nexis.
Desc: Six reports published each year covering the politics, economics and finance of Latin America. Each report is devoted to a specific subject area.

ISSN 0252-8754
GT
INFORPRESS CENTROAMERICANA (SERIES). (INFORPRESS CENTROAMERICANA.). **Added/Corp** INFORPRESS Centroamericana. (1972)-. Periodical. Spanish. One time a week. $439.00. Inforpress Centroamericana, 9 Calle 3-19/Zona 1, Guatemala City Guatemala. **Tel** 011 502 2 29432, or 81997, FAX 011 502 2 83859. Index available. **Circ:** 500. available on diskette.
Desc: Information and analysis of the economic and political developments in Central America.

LC HF **ISSN** 1352-8610
DD 380 UK
●**INFRASTRUCTURE YEARBOOK.** [Infrastruct. yearb.]. (1994)-. Trade Publication. English. One time a year. £95.00. Privatisation International Ltd., Butlers Wharf Business Centre, 45 Curlew Street, Suite 404, London SE1 2ND United Kingdom. **Tel** 011 44 171 3781620, FAX 011 44 171 4037876. **ED** Rodney Lord.
Desc: Covers private financing of infrastructure projects.

LC HF5549.5.M3 I53
KO
INGAN KAEBAL. VFOAT The Monthly Human Development; Monthly Human Development. Periodical. Korean (Korean). Twelve times a year. 20.000. Hanguk Ingan Kaebal Yonguwon, 10522 Youido-dong Yongdungpo-ku, Seoul Korea.

ISSN 0955-1697
DD 337.142 UK
INITIATIVE EUROPE MONITOR. [Initiat. Eur. monit.]. (1988)-. English. Six times a year. $812.82. Initiative Europe Ltd., 69/71 Bondway, London SW8 1SQ United Kingdom. **Tel** 011 44 171 7359838, FAX 011 44 171 8200802. **ED** Jennifer Jury. **Bk Rev. Ad Acc.**
Desc: Strives to provide timely and accurate information for professionals involved in Europe's venture capital and buyout markets.

US
INNSIDE ISSUES. See Real Estate.

LC HC360.I57 I56 **ISSN** 0902-7726
DD 330 DK
INPUT-OUTPUT TABELLER OG ANALYSER. VFOAT Input-Output Tables and Analyses. **VAT** Input Output Tabeller Og Analyser. 1983-. Danish (summaries and/or abstracts in English). One time a year. kr90.00. Danmarks Statistik, Sejrgade 11, DK-2100 Copenhagen Denmark. **Tel** 011 45 3 9173917, FAX 011 45 31 18 48 01, telex 1 62 36. ***Continues*** *Import-, Beskftigelses- Og Energimultiplikatorer;* ***Continues in part*** *Nationalregnskabsstatistik.*

ISSN 0998-4828
FR
UDC 31(44)
INSEE CADRAGE. ECONOMIE GENERALE. VFOAT Institut National de la Statistique et des Etudes Economiques Cadrage. Demographie-Societe. (1989)-. Monographic series. French. Twenty times a year. Price varies per volume. CNGP INSEE - Institut National de la Statistique et des Estudes Economiques, BP 2718, 1 rue V Auriol, F 80027 Amiens Cedex 1 France. **Tel** 011 33 22 927322.

ISSN 1140-5252
FR
UDC 336
INSEE ETUDES. [INSEE etud]. **VFOAT** Institut National de la Statistique et des Etudes Economiques Etudes. (1989)-. Monographic series. French. Irregular. Institut National de la Stastitique et des Etudes Economiques, 18 Bd Adolphe Pinard, 75675 Paris 14 France.

ISSN 1142-3080
FR
UDC 31(44)
INSEE METHODES. VFOAT Institut National de la Statistique et des Etudes Economiques Methodes. (1989)-. Monographic series. French. Irregular. Institut National de la Statistique et des Etudes Economiques, 18 Bd Adolphe Pinard, 75675 Paris 14 France.

LC HC158.A1 I57 **ISSN** 0997-3192
DD 330 FR
INSEE PREMIERE. Added/Corp Institut National de la Statistique et des Etudes Economiques (France). **VAT** Institut National de la Statistique et des Etudes Economiques Premiere. No. 1 (Feb. 1990)-. Periodical. French. Sixty times a year. 480.00F France; 600.00F other. CNGP INSEE - Institut National de la Statistique et des Estudes Economiques, BP 2718, 1 rue V Auriol, F 80027 Amiens Cedex 1 France. **Tel** 011 33 22 927322.

ISSN 0998-4895
FR
UDC 31(44)
INSEE RESULTATS. SYSTEME PRODUCTIF. VFOAT Institut National de la Statistique et des Etudes Economiques Resultats. Systeme Productif. (1989)-. French. Fifteen times a year. 1054.00F. CNGP INSEE - Institut National de la Statistique et des Estudes Economiques, BP 2718, 1 rue V Auriol, F 80027 Amiens Cedex 1 France. **Tel** 011 33 22 927322.

ISSN 0188-5340
DD 320 MX
INSEH INFORMA. See Sociology.

AT
INSIDE ENTERPRISE BARGAINING. (19??)-. English. Twelve times a year. 195.00Aus$. Newsletter Information Service, PO Box 693, Manly New South Wales 2095 Australia. **Tel** 011 61 2 9777500, FAX 011 61 2 9773310.

ISSN 1082-071X
US
●**INSIDE ITS. See** Transportation.

ISSN 1069-5184
US
INSIDE TUCSON BUSINESS. (19??)-. Periodical. English. Twelve times a year. Inside Tucson Business, One West Orange Grove Road, Tucson AZ 85704.
Ind/Abst Bus. Source Plus; Bus. Source; EP Collect.; Homework Help.; MasterFile FullTEXT 1000; MasterFile FullTEXT 350; MasterFile FullTEXT 650; MasterFile FullTEXT; OCLC; Telebase.

ISSN 0313-8496
DD 361.994 AT
INSIDE WELFARE BULLETIN. [Inside welf. bull.]. (1976)-. Periodical. English. Six times a year (Jan., Mar., May, July, Sept., Nov.). 37.00Aus$. Office of Economic Development / Australia, GPO Box 154, Brisbane Queensland 4001 Australia. **Tel** 011 61 7 2256638, FAX 011 61 7 2298051. **Ad Acc, Adv Mgr:** Mark Paddenburg, **Tel** 07 225 4058. **Circ:** 2,500 (ctrl).
Desc: The latest in tender and commercial information about the City of Brisbane.

ISSN 0020-1871
IT
UDC 33
Pr Rev.
INSIEME. [Insieme]. (1968)-. Periodical. Italian. Ten times a year. L70000 Italy; L125000 other. Editoriale Italiana, Via Vigliena 10, 00192 Rome Italy. **Tel** 011 39 6 3212653, FAX 011 39 6 3211359, telex 3230177. **Bk Rev. Ad Acc.** ***Continues*** *Rassegna dell'Economo Cattolico, 0392-8381.*
Desc: Information on accounting, management, personnel, technical subjects and administration.

LC HC
DD 330 US
INSTITUTE OF PUBLIC POLICY STUDIES DISCUSSION PAPER. Added/Corp University of Michigan. Institute of Public Policy Studies. **VFOAT** IPPS Discussion Paper. (19??)-. Monographic series. English.
Ind/Abst World Agric. Econ. Rural Sociol. Abstr.

ISSN 1072-1517
DD 338 US
INSTRUCTIONAL STRATEGIES. [Instr. strateg.]. **Added/Corp** Delta Pi Epsilon. (19??)-. Trade Publication. English. Irregular. $15.00. Delta Pi Epsilon National Office, PO Box 4340, Little Rock AR 72214. **Tel** (501)562-1233, FAX (501)562-1293.

LC HF3241 .P45a
GT
INTEGRACION EN CIFRAS. Added/Corp Permanent Secretariat of the General Treaty for Central American Economic Integration. (1972)-. Periodical. Spanish. Four times a year. $10.00. Secretaria Permanente del Tratoad General de Integracion Economica Centroamericana, Apdo. 1237, 4 Avenida No. 10-25, Zona 14, Guatemala City Guatemala. **ED** Eduardo Bolanos. available with charts. ***Continues in part*** *Carta Informativa de la Secretaria Permanente de Integracion Economica Centroamericana.*

ISSN 1046-932X
DD 004 US
INTEGRATED IMAGE. See Computers.

LC B945.R234 I58 **ISSN** 0730-2355
US
INTELLECTUAL ACTIVIST, THE. See Political Science.

LC D410 .R47 **ISSN** 0020-4900
DD 940.5305 UK
INTELLIGENCE DIGEST. See Political Science.

UK
SUSPENDED
INTELLIGENT ENTERPRISE, THE. Added/Corp Aslib. Vol. 1, No. 1 (March 1991)-Suspended (199?). Periodical. English. Ten times a year. ASLIB, Information House, 20-24 Old Street, London EC1V 9AP United Kingdom. **Tel** 011 44 171 2534488, FAX 011 44 171 4300514, telex 23667 AJLIB G. **(Subscription address:** ASLIB, 20 24 Old Street, London EC1V 9AP United Kingdom. **Tel** 011 44 171 2534488.)

ISSN 0020-9481
GW
UDC (334.746.3/.4 + 334.742) :(658 + 377)
CODEN 338 :(658 + 573)
INTENATIONALES GEWERBEARCHIV. (1953)-. Periodical. German. Four times a year. $62.02. Duncker und Humblot Verlag, Postfach 410329, D-12113 Berlin Germany. **Tel** 011 49 30 79000612, 011 49 30 79000613.
Ind/Abst Selec. Coop. Index Manage. Period.

ISSN 0242-2999
FR
UDC 01
Pr Rev.
INTER CDI ETAMPES. VFOAT Inter Centre d'Etude de la Documentation et de l'Information Scolaires (Etampes). (1974)-. Periodical. French. Six times a year. $77.64. Inter-CDI, 2 Residence de Guinette, 91150 Etampes France. **Tel** 011 33 1 64943951, FAX 011 33 1 64944935. **ED** Marie Noelle Michaut. **Bk Rev**, (Qty: 6). **Ad Acc. Circ:** 8,800. ***Continues*** *Inter SDI (Etampes), 1154-7758.*

ISSN 1065-299X
DD 338 US
CCC
TITLE CHANGE
INTERACTIVE MEDIA BUSINESS. See Communications.

LC HC121 .I65 **ISSN** 1055-9299
DD 338.98/005 US
INTERAMERICAN OPPORTUNITIES BRIEFING. [Interam. oppor. brief.]. **Added/Corp** International Freedom Foundation. **VFOAT** Inter American Opportunities Briefing; Opportunities Briefing. Vol. 1, No. 1 (Apr./May 1991)-. Periodical. English. Six times a year. $65.00. IFF International Freedom Foundation, 150 Regent Street, Suite 500, Ches House, London W1R 5FA United Kingdom. **Tel** 32 2 646 6561, FAX 32 2 646 6598, . available on an online database (file 636/Full-Text) from DIALOG.
Ind/Abst PTS Newsl. Database [Full Txt.].

ISSN 0823-9851
DD 658/.007/1171344 CN
SUSPENDED
INTERCHANGE - SCHOOL OF BUSINESS AND ECONOMICS. WILFRID LAURIER UNIVERSITY. (INTERCHANGE : A PUBLICATION OF THE SCHOOL OF BUSINESS AND ECONOMICS, WILFRID LAURIER UNIVERSITY.). [Interchange - Sch. Bus. Econ., Wilfrid Laurier Univ.]. **Added/Corp** Wilfrid Laurier University. School of Business and Economics. (Summer 1983)-Suspended (199?). Periodical. English. Two times a year. Free. Interchange, c/o A W Caston School of Business and Economics, Wilfrid Laurier University, Waterloo Ontario N2L 3C5 Canada. **ED** A. Wayne Caston. **Bk Rev. Circ:** 2,500 (ctrl).
Desc: A newsletter describing the activities of the School of Business and Economics, its faculty and the Laurier Institute.

ISSN 0955-4890
DD 338.476094 UK
CEASED
INTERFACE EUROPE. [Interface Eur.]. (1987)-(Sept. 1995). Periodical. English. Interface Europe, 142A The Broadway Didcot, Didcot Oxfordshire OX11 8RJ United Kingdom. **Tel** 011 44 1235 811542.
Ind/Abst HILITES.

Business and Economics

INTERNAL AUDITING. (19??)-(19??). English. IPSOA Editore SRL, Casella Postale 12055, Mastrangelo, 20120 Milan Italy. **Tel** 011 39 2 82476248.
IT
CEASED

LC Z7164.E2 I58   ISSN 0085-204X
DD 016.33   US
INTERNATIONAL BIBLIOGRAPHY OF ECONOMICS. See Business and Economics-Abstracting, Bibliographies and Statistics.

LC HD69.B7 I58   ISSN 1050-8376
DD 338   US
INTERNATIONAL BRANDS AND THEIR COMPANIES. [Int. brands their co.]. **Added/Corp** Gale Research Inc. 2nd Ed. (1992)-. English. $295.00. Gale Research Inc., 835 Penobscot Building, 645 Griswold Street, Detroit MI 48226. **Tel** (800)877-GALE, (313)961-2242, FAX (313)961-6083, (800)414-5043, telex TWX 810-221-7086. **ED** Susan Steter. **Continues** International Trade Names Dictionary, 0899-7586.
 Desc: Provides current information on approximately 70,000 consumer oriented products in countries other than the United States.

LC HF1371
DD 382   US
INTERNATIONAL BUSINESS. Vol. 4, No. 7 (Aug. 1991)-. Periodical. English. Twelve times a year. Free on request. American International Publishing Co, 410 Theodore Fremd Avenue, Rye NY 10580. **Tel** (914)381-7700. **(Subscription address:** Neodata / Colorado, PO Box 2606, Boulder CO 80322. **) Continues** North American International Business, 1054-1748.
 Ind/Abst PROMT; Trade Ind. ASAP [Full Txt.]; Trade Ind. Index [Full Txt.].

HK
INTERNATIONAL BUSINESS. English. Twelve times a year. $100.00. Global Media Rep. Ltd., 22A Westlands Road, Toppan Building, Quarry Bay Hong Kong.

US
INTERNATIONAL BUSINESS CHRONICLE : THE REPORT ON INTERNATIONAL BUSINESS IN FLORIDA AND THE SOUTHEAST. (1990)-. Periodical. English. Twenty-six times a year.
 Ind/Abst PROMT.

ISSN 1047-8698
INTERNATIONAL BUSINESS CLIMATE, THE. (1991)-. Periodical. English. Twelve times a year. $90.00. Channel Island Publications, PO Box 6852, Santa Barbara CA 93160.

HK
INTERNATIONAL BUSINESS MONTHLY. English. Twelve times a year. Earwick International Ltd, 35 Kimberley Road, Room 1201-1202, Hong Kong Hong Kong. **Tel** 011 852 237390688.

US
INTERNATIONAL BUSINESS OPPORTUNITIES SERVICE. English. $250.00. Johns Hopkins University Press, 2715 North Charles Street, Baltimore MD 21218-4319. **Tel** (410)516-6987, FAX (410)516-6968.
 Desc: Benefits World civil works contractors, subcontractors, suppliers, and consultants around the world by providing comprehensive information about the Bank's procurement operations and upcoming projects.

ISSN 0969-5931
UK
CCC
INTERNATIONAL BUSINESS REVIEW. (199?)-. English. Six times a year. $450.00. Pergamon Press, An Imprint of Elsevier Science Ltd., The Boulevard, Langford Lane, Kidlington, Oxford OX5 1GB United Kingdom. **Tel** 011 44 1865 843000, 011 44 1865 843699, FAX 011 44 1865 843010. **(Subscription address:** Elsevier Science Ltd. / Oxford Fulfillment Centre, PO Box 800, Kidlington OX5 1DX United Kingdom. **Tel** 011 44 865 843355.) available on an online database from Elsevier Electronic Subscriptions (EES). **Continues** Scandinavian International Business Review, 0962-1262.

ISSN 0739-8409
US
INTERNATIONAL BUSINESS WEEK. [Int. bus. week]. **VFOAT** Business Week. (Jan. 1981)-. Periodical. English. One time a week. $165.00. McGraw Hill Publishing Company, Inc., 1221 Avenue of the Americas, New York NY 10020. **Tel** (212)512-6410, (800)525-5003, FAX (212)512-6111. **(Subscription address:** McGraw Hill Book Company, Princeton Road, Hightstown NJ 08520. **Tel** (717)794-5461.)
 Ind/Abst Abstr. BioCommer.; Chem. Bus. Bull.; Chem. Bus. NewsBase (1985-); Chem. Bus. Update; Infomat Int. Bus.

DD 384   ISSN 1053-8194
US
INTERNATIONAL CO-PRODUCTIONS. See Motion Picture.

UK
INTERNATIONAL CO-PRODUCTIONS DATABOOK. See Motion Picture.

LC HF54.U5 I55   ISSN 1050-8384
DD 338.7/4/025   US
INTERNATIONAL COMPANIES AND THEIR BRANDS. [Int. co. their brands]. **Added/Corp** Gale Research Inc. 2nd Ed. (1991/1992)-. English. $260.00. Gale Research Inc., 835 Penobscot Building, 645 Griswold Street, Detroit MI 48226. **Tel** (800)877-GALE, (313)961-2242, FAX (313)961-6083, (800)414-5043, telex TWX 810-221-7086. **ED** Linda Irvin. available on an online database (File 116) from DIALOG. **Continues** International Trade Names Dictionary. Company Index, 0899-7594.
 Desc: Tracks over 20,000 international manufacturers, importers and distributors of over 70,000 consumer products.

LC HC59.69 .I57   ISSN 0262-0855
DD 909/09724   UK
   CCC
Pr Rev.
INTERNATIONAL DEVELOPMENT ABSTRACTS. See Business and Economics-Abstracting, Bibliographies and Statistics.

US
INTERNATIONAL ECONOMIC ASSOCIATION SERIES. Main/Corp International Economic Association. Vol. 1 (1977)-. Monographic series. English. Price varies per volume. Westview Press Inc., 5500 Central Avenue, Boulder CO 80301. **Tel** (303)444-3541, (800)456-1995, FAX (303)449-3356.

US
INTERNATIONAL ECONOMIC INDICATORS. (19??)-. English. Twelve times a year. $2500.00. Foundation for International Business Cycle Research, 475 Riverside Drive, Suite 834, New York NY 10027.

LC HC
DD 330   KO
INTERNATIONAL ECONOMIC JOURNAL. Added/Corp Korea International Economic Association. Vol. 1 No. 1 (Spring 1987)-. Periodical. English. Four times a year. $50.00. Department of International Economics, College of Social Science, Seoul University, Professor Wontack Hong, Seoul 151-742 Korea. **ED** Wontack Hong, Young Chin Kim. Index available. **Circ:** 1,500.
 Ind/Abst Asia.-Pac. Econ. Lit.; Curr. Cit.; Econ. Lit. Index (19??-); J. Econ. Lit.

LC HB1 .I65   ISSN 0020-6598
DD 330/.05   US
   CCC
   CODEN INERAE
Pr Rev.
INTERNATIONAL ECONOMIC REVIEW (PHILADELPHIA). (INTERNATIONAL ECONOMIC REVIEW.). [Int. econ. rev.]. **Added/Corp** Wharton School. Kansai Keizai Rengokai. Osaka Daigaku. Shakai Keizai Kenkyujo. Osaka Daigaku. Institute of Social and Economic Research Association. Vol. 1, (Jan. 1960)-. Periodical. English. Four times a year (Feb., May, Aug., Nov.). $165.00. International Economic Review, 3718 Locust Walk, University of Pennsylvania, Philadelphia PA 19104-6297. **Tel** (215)898-5841, FAX (215)573-2072. **ED** Wilfred J. Ethier and Hajime Oniki. Index available. own index. **Ad Acc. Circ:** 2,200. available on microfilm and microfiche from University Microfilms International (UMI). Documents available from The Genuine Article, UMI Article Clearinghouse.
 Desc: Articles on quantitative economics. Welcomes contributions of empirical works, as well as as those in mathematical economics and statistical theory related to quantitative aspects of economics. Quantitative economics is broadly interpreted as covering both obviously quantitative studies and ideas that can lead to quantitative studies.
 Ind/Abst ABI/INFORM Glob. Ed.; ABI/INFORM [Computer File] (June 1975-); Acad. Index; Acad. Search; Bus. Index (1985-); Contents Recent Econ. J.; Curr. Contents Soc. Behav. Sci.; Econ. Lit. Index; EP Collect.; Expand. Acad. Index (1984-); Gen. BusinessFile (1985-); Gen. Period. Index (1985-); Geogr. Abstr. Human Geogr.; GeoRef; Homework Help.; INFO-SOUTH Abstr.; Int. Dev. Abstr. (?-?); J. Econ. Lit.; Leis., Rec., Tour. Abstr.; Manage. Contents (1974-); MasterFile FullTEXT 1000; MasterFile FullTEXT 350; MasterFile FullTEXT 650; MasterFile FullTEXT (Jan. 1992-); Math. Rev.; Middle East Abstr. Index; Newsp. Period. Abstr. (1991-); OCLC; Public Aff. Inf. Serv. Bull.; Pub. Lib. FullTEXT; Res. Alert [Full Cov.]; Rural Dev. Abstr.; Soc. Sci. Source; Soc. Sci. Cit. Index [Full Cov.]; Soc. Sci. Index; Soc. Sci. Index Fulltext (Nov. 1988-) [Full Txt.]; Telebase; Trade Ind.

Index; UMI ABI/Inform--Bus. Period. Ondisc (Feb. 1987-) [Full Txt.]; World Agric. Econ. Rural Sociol. Abstr.; Zentralbl. Math. Ihre Grenzgeb.

ISSN 0276-413X
US
INTERNATIONAL ENTREPRENEUR FROM THE HEARTLAND OF THE U.S.A, THE. [Int. entrep. heartl. U. S. A.]. **Added/Corp** International Trade Council of Kansas. Kansas State University. International Trade Institute. **VFOAT** International Entrepreneur. **VAT** International Entrepreneur from the Heartland of the United States of America. Vol. I, No. 1 (Mar. 1981)-. Periodical. English. Twelve times a year. $28.00. Jenkins Group Inc., 121 East Front Street, Suite 401, Travers City MI 49684. **Tel** (800)706-4636.

US
Pr Rev.
INTERNATIONAL FINANCE SECTION PUBLICATIONS. (19??)-. English. Irregular (7 or 8 per year). $35.00. International Finance Section, Princeton University, Department of Economics, Princeton NJ 08544. **Tel** (609)258-4051, FAX (609)258-6419, telex 499-1258 TIGER. **ED** Margaret Riccardi. **Bk Rev. Circ:** 2,000. available on microfilm and microfiche.
 Desc: Topical monographs on issues of international economics and finance, directed toward academic, governmental and educated general audiences.

ISSN 0953-2714
UK
INTERNATIONAL INSIDER. [Int. insid.]. (1973)-. Periodical. English. One time a week (50 issues). $850.00. International Insider Publishing Compnay Ltd, Ludgate House, 107 Fleet Street, London EC4A 2AB United Kingdom. **Tel** 011 44 171 3537311, FAX 011 44 171 5831895. **ED** Chris Wilkins. **Ad Acc, Adv Mgr:** Mary Adams, **Tel** 071 353 7311.

US
●**INTERNATIONAL JOURNAL OF BUSINESS.** (1995)-. English. Two times a year. JAI Press Inc., 55 Old Post Road, Suite 2, PO Box 1678, Greenwich CT 06836-1678. **Tel** (203)661-7602, FAX (203)661-0792. **Continues** Review of Business Studies.

LC HB615 .I58   ISSN 1355-2554
DD 338/.04/05   UK
●**INTERNATIONAL JOURNAL OF ENTREPRENEURIAL BEHAVIOUR & RESEARCH. VFOAT** International Journal of Entrepreneurial Behaviour and Research. (1995)-. Academic Scholarly Publication. English. Three times a year. $149.00. MCB University Press, 60 62 Toller Lane, Bradford, West Yorkshire BD8 9BY United Kingdom. **Tel** 011 44 1274 785280, FAX 011 44 1274 785200, telex 51317-MCBUNI-G. **ED** John Pheby.
 Desc: Seeks to provide a forum for a fresh perspective in the area of entrepreneurship/small firm studies. Concerned with research into entrepreneurial and small business behavior, and aimed at economists, sociologists, psychologists and marketing academics.

LC HB9
DD 332   UK
●**INTERNATIONAL JOURNAL OF FINANCE & ECONOMICS.** See Finance.

LC H61.4 .I57   ISSN 0169-2070
DD 003/.2/05   NE
   CCC
   CODEN IJFOEK
Pr Rev.
INTERNATIONAL JOURNAL OF FORECASTING. [Int. j. forecast.]. **Added/Corp** International Institute of Forecasters. Vol. 1 No. 1 (1985)-. Academic Scholarly Publication. English. Four times a year (1/year). $333.00. Elsevier Science Publishers BV, PO Box 211, 1000 AE Amsterdam Netherlands. **Tel** 011 31 20 4853641, 011 31 20 4853642, FAX 011 31 20 4853598. **ED** Spyros Makridakis, J. Scott Armstrong, Estela Bee Dagum and Robert Fildes. available on microfilm and microfiche from University Microfilms International (UMI); available on an online database from Elsevier Electronic Subscriptions (EES). Documents available from The Genuine Article, UMI Article Clearinghouse, Ask*IEEE. **Continues** Journal of Forecasting, 0277-6693.
 Desc: Publishes papers covering all aspects of forecasting. Its objective is to unify the field, and to bridge the gap between theory and practice. Places strong emphasis on empirical studies, evaluation activities, implementation research and ways of improving the practice of forecasting.
 Ind/Abst ABI/INFORM Glob. Ed.; ABI/INFORM [Computer File] (1985-); Contents Recent Econ. J.; Contents Pages Manage.; Curr. Cit.; Curr. Contents Soc. Behav. Sci.; Curr. Index Stat.; Econ. Lit. Index (1986-); INSPEC (1987-); Int. Abstr. Oper. Res. [Select. Cov.]; J. Econ. Lit. (1986-); J. Plan. Lit.; Oper. Res./Manage. Sci.; Qual. Control Appl. Stat.; Res. Alert [Full Cov.]; Soc. Plann. Policy Dev. Abstr.; Soc. Sci. Cit. Index [Full Cov.]; Soc. Res. Methodol. Abstr. (1990-); Women Manage. Rev. [Full Txt.]; World Agric. Econ. Rural Sociol. Abstr.

Business and Economics

LC HD38.5 .I58
DD 658
ISSN 0957-4093
US
Pr Rev.
INTERNATIONAL JOURNAL OF LOGISTICS MANAGEMENT, THE. [Int. j. logist. manag.]. **Added/Corp** Andersen Consulting. International Logistics Research Institute. Vol. 1, No. 1 (1990)-. Periodical. English. Two times a year (May and November). $75.00. International Logistics Research Institute, PO Box 2166, Ponte Vedra Beach FL 32004-2166. **Tel** (904)273-9063, FAX (904)273-5020. **ED** Douglas M. Lambert. **Circ:** 1,000.
Desc: Provides a global forum for the exchange of new ideas and practices in the dynamic field of logistics management.

LC HD28 .I5257
DD 658/.005
ISSN 1055-3185
US
CCC
CODEN IJOAEN
●**INTERNATIONAL JOURNAL OF ORGANIZATIONAL ANALYSIS.** [Int. j. organ. anal.]. **VFOAT** IJOA. Vol. 1, No. 1 (Jan. 1993)-. Periodical. English. Four times a year. $129.00. Center for Advanced Studies in Management, 1574 Mallory Court, Bowling Green KY 42103. **Tel** (502)782-2601, FAX (502)782-2601.
Desc: Empirical and conceptual articles, case studies, teaching notes, simulations, and book reviews on business and society; organization theory; organizational behavior; strategic management; and related areas.

LC HB1 .I67
DD 330/.05
ISSN 0306-8293
UK
CCC
CODEN ISLEBC
Pr Rev.
INTERNATIONAL JOURNAL OF SOCIAL ECONOMICS. [Int. j. soc. econ.]. **VFOAT** Social Economics; SE. International Journal of Social Economics. Vol. 1 (1974)-. Periodical. English. Twelve times a year. $3699.00. MCB University Press, 60 62 Toller Lane, Bradford, West Yorkshire BD8 9BY United Kingdom. **Tel** 011 44 1274 785280, FAX 011 44 1274 785200, telex 51317-MCBUNI-G. (**Subscription address:** MCB University Press / US and Canada Subscriptions, PO Box 10812, Birmingham AL 35201-0812. **Tel** (205)995-1567, (800)633-4931, FAX (205)995-1588.) **ED** John Conway O'Brien. available on an online database (file 15/Full-Text) from DIALOG. Documents available from The Genuine Article, UMI Article Clearinghouse. **Absorbed** International Review of Economics & Ethics, 0268-392X.
Desc: Provides a digest of exclusive reports on the major aspects of the area and presents social economics and social planning as a distinct and accepted discipline.
Ind/Abst ABI/INFORM Glob. Ed.; ABI/INFORM [Computer File] (Feb. 1976-); Acad. Search; Appl. Soc. Sci. Index Abstr.; Bus. Index (1985-); Contents Recent Econ. J.; Curr. Cit.; Curr. Contents Soc. Behav. Sci.; Ecol. Abstr. (?-?); Econ. Lit. Index; EP Collect.; Gen. BusinessFile (1985-); Gen. Period. Index (1985-); Geogr. Abstr. Human Geogr.; Homework Help.; INFO-SOUTH Abstr.; Int. Bibliogr. Sociol.; Int. Dev. Abstr.; Int. Labour Doc.; J. Econ. Lit. (1980-); LABORDOC; Manage. Market. Abstr.; MasterFile FullTEXT 1000; MasterFile FullTEXT 350; MasterFile FullTEXT 650; MasterFile FullTEXT (July 1993-); OCLC; Res. Alert [Full Cov.]; Rural Dev. Abstr.; Selec. Coop. Index Manage. Period.; Soc. Sci. Source; Soc. Sci. Cit. Index [Full Cov.]; Sociol. Educ. Abstr.; Tech. Educ. Train. Abstr.; Telebase.

LC HB71
DD 330
ISSN 1357-1516
UK
CCC
●**INTERNATIONAL JOURNAL OF THE ECONOMICS OF BUSINESS.** (1994)-. Academic Scholarly Publication. English. Three times a year. £114.00 (institutions), £34.00 (individuals). Carfax Publishing Company, PO Box 25, Abingdon, Oxfordshire OX14 3UE United Kingdom. **Tel** 011 44 1235 555335, FAX 011 44 1235 553559, telex 817484. **ED** Eleanor Morgan and Mick Silver. Index available. **Bk Rev. Ad Acc.** available on microfiche. Documents available from UMI Article Clearinghouse.

LC HD60 .I66
DD 658/.005
ISSN 0895-8815
US
CCC
INTERNATIONAL JOURNAL OF VALUE BASED MANAGEMENT. [Int. j. value based manage.]. **Added/Corp** Hagan School of Business. St. Edmund Hall (University of Oxford). **VFOAT** International Journal of Value-Based Management; Value Based Management; Value-Based Management; IJVBM. Vol. 1, No. 1 (1988)-. English. Three times a year. $143.00. Kluwer Academic Publishers, Postbus 322, 3300 AH Dordrecht The Netherlands. **Tel** 011 31 78 524400, FAX 011 31 78 183273, telex 20083.
Desc: Seeks to develop on international forum for clarifying the role of valued in organizational behavior and decision making. It provides a definitive source of information in the field of values and management.
Ind/Abst PAIS Int. Print (1991-); Work Relat. Abstr.

ISSN 0965-0644
UK
Pr Rev.
INTERNATIONAL MARINE BUSINESS. (1991)-. Periodical. English. Four times a year. £100.00; £50.00 (first year). Mediaship Ltd, Watergate Buildings, New Crane Street, Chester CH1 4JE United Kingdom. **Tel** 011 44 1244 316555, FAX 011 44 1244 343616. **Ad Acc, Adv Mgr:** Madeline Lowe. **Circ:** 5,000 (ctrl). available on diskette.

LC K1362 .I57
DD 341.7/53
ISSN 1053-4660
US
CEASED
INTERNATIONAL MERGER LAW. [Int. merger law]. **Added/Corp** Washington Regulatory Reporting Associates. No. 1 (Sept. 1990)-(199?). Periodical. English. Washington Regulatory Reporting Association, PO Box 356, Basye VA 22810. **Tel** (703)856-2216.

ISSN 0266-0512
UK
NLM W1; IN8254
INTERNATIONAL MONOGRAPHS ON RISK. [Int. monogr. risk]. (1984)-. Monographic series. English. Irregular. Price varies per volume. John Libbey & Company Ltd., 13 Smiths Yard, Summerley Street, London SW18 4HR United Kingdom. **Tel** 011 44 171 9472777, FAX 011 44 171 9472664, telex 94013503 JOHN G. **ED** A J Jouhar.

US
INTERNATIONAL ORGANIZATIONS REGULATORY GUIDEBOOK, THE. See Law-International Law.

LC HF3751 .I57
DD 382/.095/005
ISSN 1055-8209
US
INTERNATIONAL POLICY CASE SERIES. [Int. policy case ser.]. **Added/Corp** Pacific Asian Consortium for International Business Education and Research. University of Hawaii at Manoa. Pacific Asian Management Institute. Vol. 1, No. 1 (1991)-. Monographic series. English. Irregular. $1.00 per issue. Pacific Asian Consortium for International Business Education and Research, College of Business Administration, University of Hawaii at Manoa, 2404 Maile Way C202, Honolulu HI 96822.

LC HD69.C6 I593
DD 001/.025
ISSN 0749-2685
US
INTERNATIONAL REGISTRY OF ORGANIZATION DEVELOPMENT PROFESSIONALS AND ORGANIZATION DEVELOPMENT HANDBOOK, THE. See Biographies.

LC HB1 .I68
DD 330/.05
ISSN 0269-2171
UK
INTERNATIONAL REVIEW OF APPLIED ECONOMICS. [Int. rev. appl. econ.]. Vol. 1, No. 1 (Jan. 1987)-. Periodical. English. Three times a year (January, May and September). $248.00. Arnold, 338 Euston Road, London NW1 3BH United Kingdom. **Tel** 011 44 1732 450111, FAX 011 44 1732 461321. (**Subscription address:** Edward Arnold, PO Box 386, Avenel NJ 07001-0386.) **ED** M. Sawyer and S. Gazioglu.
Desc: The journal is devoted to the application of economic ideas to the real world. Applied economics are interpreted to include both empirical work and evaluation and development of economic policies. The interaction between empirical work and economic policy is an important feature. The journal also seeks to draw multinational comparisons of economic experience.
Ind/Abst Contents Recent Econ. J.; Curr. Cit.; Econ. Lit. Index (199?-); Int. Bibliogr. Sociol.; J. Econ. Lit.; PAIS Int. Print (1991-).

ISSN 1073-9084
DD 382
US
●**INTERNATIONAL TRADE & BUSINESS JOURNAL.** [Int. trade bus. j.]. **VFOAT** International Trade and Business Journal; Trade & Business Journal. Vol. 2, Bo. 1 (Nov. 1, 1993)-. Periodical. English. Twenty-four times a year. $95.00. International Business Strategies Inc, 1537 Gadsden Street, Suite 102, Columbia SC 29201. **Tel** (803)551-8787.

ISSN 0968-4026
UK
INTERNATIONAL TRADE FINANCE. [Int. trade financ.]. (1989)-. English. Two times a year. Chiltern Publishing, 18 Burgess Wood Road, Beaconsfield Buckinghamshire HP9 1EQ United Kingdom. **Tel** 011 44 1494 673062, FAX 011 44 1494 678914.

Desc: Loose-leaf publication for anyone concerned with international finance, export, import, UK taxation, and the law.

US
INTERNATIONAL WHO'S WHO. English. One time a year. $260.00. Taft Group, 835 Penobscott Building, Customer Service, Detroit MI 48226. **Tel** (800)877-8238, FAX (313)961-6083.

INTERNET BUSINESS REPORT. See Computers.

ISSN 1082-1945
US
●**INTERNET MARKETING AND TECHNOLOGY REPORT.** See Computers-Online Computing and Information.

ISSN 1081-2474
US
●**INTERNET WEEK.** See Computers-Online Computing and Information.

ISSN 0394-087X
IT
UDC 382.5
INTERSCAMBIO. [Interscambio]. (1986)-. Periodical. Italian. Twelve times a year. L47690. Sydaco Editrice, Via Baldovinetti 56/55, 00142 Rome Italy. **Bk Rev. Ad Acc.**

LC HC
DD 330.9714
ISSN 0715-3570
CN
INTERVENTIONS ECONOMIQUES POUR UNE ALTERNATIVE SOCIALE. No. 8 (Spring 1982)-. Periodical. French. Two times a year. 33.62Can$. Interventions Economiques, CP 206 Succursale C, Montreal Quebec H2L 4K1 Canada. **Tel** (514)987-4877. **Bk Rev. Ad Acc. Circ:** 1,200 (ctrl). **Continues** Interventions (Montreal, Quebec), 0715-3589.
Desc: Academic economic review and radical economics.
Ind/Abst LABORDOC; Repere (1983-).

LC HG
DD 332
BO
INVERSION Y DESARROLLO. No. 1 (Mar 1991)-. Periodical. Spanish. Twelve times a year. $47.00 Central and North America; $38.00 South America; $60.00 other. Epoca Editores Srl, Casilla Postal 14327, La Paz Bolivia. **Tel** 011 591 2 391808, 011 591 2 328579.

US
INVESTEXT. (19??)-. English. One time a year. Technical Data International, 11 Farnsworth Street, Boston MA 02210. available on an online database (file 545/Full-Text) from DIALOG. Documents available from UMI Article Clearinghouse.
Ind/Abst Pharm. News Index (April 1990-).

LC HA1651 .A334 HC407.Z7S4 Z7S46
DD 314
CI
INVESTICIJE SR SRBIJE / SOCIJALISTICKA REPUBLIKA SRBIJA, REPUBLICKI ZAVOD ZA STATISTIKU. See Business and Economics-Abstracting, Bibliographies and Statistics.

LC HB9 .I48
DD 330.972
ISSN 0185-1667
MX
INVESTIGACION ECONOMICA - FACULTAD DE ECONOMIA DE LA UNIVERSIDAD NACIONAL AUTONOMA DE MEXICO. (INVESTIGACION ECONOMICA.). [Invest. econ. - Fac. Econ. Univ. Nac. Auton. Mex.]. **Added/Corp** Escuela Nacional de Economia (Mexico) Universidad Nacional Autonoma de Mexico. Facultad de Economia. Vol. 1, No. 1 (1941)-. Periodical. Spanish. Four times a year (Jan., May, Aug., Nov.). $80.00. Facultad Economia de la Unam, Edif Anexo Circuito Interior, 04510 Mexico DF Mexico. **Tel** 011 52 5 6222155. cum. index.
Ind/Abst Am. Hist. Life (1968-); Int. Labour Doc.; LABORDOC; PAIS Int. Print.

ISSN 1067-4551
DD 331
US
CCC
●**IOMA'S REPORT ON SALARY SURVEYS.** [IOMA's rep. salary surv.]. **Added/Corp** Institute of Management & Administration. **VFOAT** Salary Surveys; Report on Salary Surveys. (1993)-. Periodical. English. Twelve times a year. $245.00. Institute of Management and Administration, 29 West 35th Street, 5th Floor, New York NY 10001-2299. **Tel** (212)244-0360, FAX (212)564-0465.

LC HC59.69 .I59
DD 330.9172/4
ISSN 1040-8452
US
IOWA INTERNATIONAL PAPERS - CENTER FOR INTERNATIONAL AND COMPARATIVE STUDIES. (IOWA INTERNATIONAL PAPERS.). [Iowa int. pap. - Cent. Int. Comp. Stud.]. **Added/Corp** University of Iowa. Center for

International and Comparative Studies. University of Iowa. Libraries. **VFOAT** Iowa International Papers Series. (1989)-. Periodical. English. Irregular (published only after major conferences). University of Iowa / Publications Order Department, Oakdale Hall, Iowa City IA 52242. **Tel** (319)335-4589, FAX (319)335-4039. ***Continues*** *Occasional Paper (University of Iowa. Center for International and Comparative Studies).*

SP

IP MARK. (19??)-. Periodical. Spanish. Twenty times a year (includes 2 supplements). 20600ptas Spain; 35000ptas other. Ediciones Estudios Grupo IP, Enrique Larreta 7-7A, 28036 Madrid Spain. **Tel** 011 34 1 7339114, 011 34 1 7339263, FAX 011 34 1 3157415, telex 47714. Index available. **Bk Rev. Ad Acc.** ctrl circ.

LC HB1 .I6 **ISSN** 1030-4177
DD 330/.05 AT

IPA REVIEW (1986). (IPA REVIEW.). [IPA rev.]. **Added/Corp** Institute of Public Affairs (Melbourne, Vic.). **VFOAT** Institute of Public Affairs Review. Vol. 40, No. 3 (Spring 1986)-. Periodical. English. Four times a year. 40.00Aus$. Institute of Public Affairs / Australia, 128 36 Jolimont Road, Jolimont Victoria 3002 Australia. **Tel** 011 61 3 6547499, FAX 011 61 3 6507627. **ED** Ken Baker. **Bk Rev. Ad Acc. Circ:** 17,000. available on an online database from University Microfilms International (UMI). Documents available from The UnCover Company, UMI Article Clearinghouse. ***Continues*** *Review (Institute of Public Affairs (Melbourne, Vic.)), 1030-4169.*
Desc: Major vehicle for the publication of free enterprise opinion in Australia.
Ind/Abst APAIS, Aust. Public Aff. Inf. Ser.; Aust. Educ. Index; EP Collect.; Homework Help.; MasterFile FullTEXT 1000; MasterFile FullTEXT 350; MasterFile FullTEXT 650; MasterFile FullTEXT (Jan. 1994-); Telebase; World Mag. Bank.

ISSN 0866-1944
HU

IPARI ES KERESKEDELMI KOZLONY : AZ IPARI ES KERESKEDELMI MINISZTERIUM HIVATALOS LAPJA. **Added/Corp** Hungary. Ipari es Kereskedelmi Miniszterium. (1990)-. Hungarian. Pallas Lap es Konyvkiado Vallalat, Lenin Korut 9-11, H-1906 Budapest Hungary. **Tel** 011 36 1 2210285. ***Formed by the union of*** *Kereskedelmi Kozlony, 0238-7530* ***and*** *Ipari Kozlony.*

LC HC701 .I64
DD 330 KO

IPECK PUKPANG KYONGJE. **Added/Corp** Kukche Mingan Kyongje Hyobuihoe (Korea). **VFOAT** International Private Economic Council of Korea Pukpang Kyongje; Pukpang Kyongje; New Market Economies. First Volume (1991)-. Periodical. Korean. Twelve times a year.

LC HC471 .I66 **ISSN** 0161-0627
DD 330.9/55 US

IRAN ECONOMIC NEWS. Vol. 1 (Jan. 1975)-. Periodical. English. Twelve times a year. Iranian Economic Mission, 5530 Wisconsin Avenue, Washington DC 20015.

LC HC471 .I68 **ISSN** 0935-1531
DD 330/955/005 UK

IRAN FOCUS. **VFOAT** IranFocus. (1988)-. Periodical. English. Eleven times a year (monthly except Aug.). $725.00. Menas Associates Ltd., Gallipoli House, Outwell Wisbech Cambridgeshire, PE14 8TN United Kingdom. **Tel** 011 44 1945 772733, FAX 011 44 1945 5201688. **Circ:** 120.

LC HF5003 .D68a **ISSN** 1072-6136
DD 330 US

•**IRWIN BUSINESS AND INVESTMENT ALMANAC, THE.** [Irwin bus. invest. alm.]. **VFOAT** Business and Investment Almanac. (1994)-. English. One time a year. Price varies. Irwin Professional Publishing, 1333 Burr Ridge Parkway, Burr Ridge Parkway IL 60521. **Tel** (800)634-3966, (708)789-5480. ***Continues*** *Business One Irwin Business and Investment Almanac, 1057-5014.*

LC HF5003 .D682 **ISSN** 1074-8873
DD 338 US

•**IRWIN INTERNATIONAL ALMANAC, THE.** (THE IRWIN INTERNATIONAL ALMANAC : BUSINESS AND INVESTMENTS.). [Irwin int. alm.]. **VFOAT** International Almanac. (1994)-. English. One time a year. $95.00. Irwin Professional Publishing, 1333 Burr Ridge Parkway, Burr Ridge Parkway IL 60521. **Tel** (800)634-3966, (708)789-5480. ***Continues*** *Business One Irwin International Almanac, 1068-0942.*

LC HC117.N4 .I84 **ISSN** 0828-6868
DD 330 CN

ISER RESEARCH AND POLICY PAPERS. **Added/Corp** Memorial University of Newfoundland. Institute of Social and Economic Research. **VFOAT** Institute of Social and Economic Research Research and Policy papers; Research and Policy Papers; ISER Research and Policy Papers Series. (1986)-. Monographic series. English. Irregular. price varies. Institute of Social and Economic Research / Canada, University of Newfoundland, St. John's Newfoundland A1C 5S7 Canada. **Tel** (709)737-8156, (709)737-2041. **Bk Rev. Ad Acc. Circ:** 250.
Desc: Presents article length papers on a variety of basic scientific research related topics. Main emphasis is on research conducted under the auspices and focuses on Newfoundland and North Atlantic studies.

US

ISRAEL BUSINESS TODAY. Vol. 6, No. 252 (Nov. 22, 1991)-. Periodical. English. Twenty-four times a year. $199.00. Israel Business Today, 350 5th Avenue, Suite 1901, New York NY 10118. **Tel** (212)967-6675. available on an online database (files 648,771,772,799/Full-Text) from DIALOG. ***Continues*** *Israel Commercial Economic Newsletter, 0792-3465.*
Ind/Abst Bus. Index (1992-); Gen. BusinessFile (1992-); Trade Ind. ASAP [Full Txt.]; Trade Ind. Index [Full Txt.].

IS

ISRAEL ECONOMIC AND BUSINESS REVIEW, THE. 1985-. English. One time a year. Israel Economist, 6 Hazanovitch Street, PO Box 7052, Jerusalem Israel. **Tel** (011)972-2-234131.

LC HB1.A1

TU

ISTANBUL UNIVERSITESI IKTISAT FAKULTESI MECMUAS. **Main/Corp** Istanbul. Universite. Iktisat Fakultesi. **VFOAT** Revue de la Faculte des Sciences Economiques de l'Universite d'Istanbul. Periodical. Turkish (summaries and/or abstracts in French and German).

LC HC337 .U5182 **ISSN** 0320-4421
DD 330/338.947 UN

•**ISTORIIA NARODNOHO HOSPODARSTVA TA EKONOMICHNOI DUMKY UKRAINY.** **Added/Corp** Instytut Ekonomiky (Akademiia nauk Ukrainy). (1994)-. Ukrainian (summaries and/or abstracts in Russian). Izdatelstvo Naukova Dumka / Ukrainian Academy of Sciences, Yu. A. Khramov, Dir., Ul. Repina 3, 252 601 Kiev Ukraine. **Tel** 011 7 44 4303441, 011 7 44 2254182, telex 131376. ***Continues*** *Istoriia Narodnoho Hospodarstva ta Ekonomichnoi Dumky Ukrainskoi RSR.*

ISSN 0021-2776
IT

ITALIA FORESTALE E MONTANA. (L'ITALIA FORESTALE E MONTANA : REVISTA DI POLITICA ECONOMIA E TECNICA.). [Ital. for. mont.]. (1946)-. Periodical. Italian. Six times a year. L54500. ACC Italiana Scienze Forestali, Piazza Edison 11, 50133 Florence Italy. **Tel** 011 39 55 570348. **(Subscription address:** Licosa s.p.a., PO Box 552, 50125 Florence Italy. **Tel** 011 39 55 645415.)
Ind/Abst AGRICOLA; Agrofor. Abstr.; For. Prod. Abstr. (1991-); For. Abstr.; Plant Genet. Resour. Abstr.; Seed Abstr.

ISSN 1120-5997
MC

ITALIAN BUSINESS REVIEW. (19??)-. English. Eleven times a year. $425.00. Italian Business Review Incorporated, c/o BSM, 1 rue des Geraniums, Monte Carlo 98000 Monaco. **Tel** 011 33 93 877286, FAX 011 33 93 303118.

LC HC106.8 .I93
DD 338.5/443/0973 US

ITR'S ECONOMIC OUTLOOK. **Added/Corp** ITR Associates, Inc. (19??)-. English. ITR Associates Inc., PO Box 278, Contoocook NH 03229. **Tel** (603)746-3135.

LC HC371 .I84 **ISSN** 0283-8974
DD 338.5/44/09485 SW

IUI YEARBOOK. **VFOAT** I.U.I. Yearbook. English. One time a year. Industriens Utredningsinstitut, Grevgatan 34, Box 5037, S102 41 Stockholm Sweden. ***Continues*** *Industriens Utredningsinstitut (Sweden). IUI Research Program.*

ISSN 0730-9368
US

J. CROSS EXECUTIVE ALERT. [J. Cross exec. alert]. **VAT** Joseph Cross Executive Alert. Periodical. English. Twelve times a year. $60.00. J. Cross Consulting Service, 520 East Street, Suite 606, San Diego CA 92101.

US

JACKSON BUSINESS JOURNAL. (19??)-. Periodical. English. Six times a year. $18.00. Jackson Business Journal, PO Box 12727, Jackson MS 39236. **Tel** (601)956-0756. ***Continues*** *Metro Jackson Business News.*

LC HD **ISSN** 0885-453X
DD 338 US
CCC

JACKSONVILLE BUSINESS JOURNAL. (1985)-. Periodical. English. Fifty-two times a year (published on Fridays). $45.00. Jacksonville Business Journal, 1200 Riverplace Blvd, Suite 201, Jacksonville FL 32207. **Tel** (904)396-3502, FAX (904)396-5706. **ED** Ben Eubanks. **Ad Acc, Adv Mgr:** L Chasteen. **Circ:** 10,000 (ctrl). available on microfilm from University Microfilms International (UMI); available on an online database (file 648/Full-Text) from DIALOG. Documents available from UMI Article Clearinghouse.
Ind/Abst Bus. Dateline; Bus. Source Plus; Bus. Source; EP Collect.; Homework Help.; MasterFile FullTEXT 1000; MasterFile FullTEXT 350; MasterFile FullTEXT 650; MasterFile FullTEXT (Jan. 1995-); OCLC; PROMT; Telebase; Trade Ind. ASAP [Full Txt.]; Trade Ind. Index [Full Txt.].

LC HB5 .J29 **ISSN** 0722-5369
DD 330/.05 GW

JAHRBUCH FUER NEUE POLITISCHE OKONOMIE. (1982)-. Periodical. German. One time a year. DM118.00. JCB Mohr / Paul Siebeck, Postfach 2040, D-72010 Tuebingen Germany. **Tel** 011 49 7071 9230, FAX 011 49 7071 51104, telex 7/262872 mohr d.

LC HC **ISSN** 0021-4027
DD 330 GW
CCC

Pr Rev.

JAHRBUCHER FUER NATIONALOKONOMIE UND STATISTIK. [Jahrb. nationalokon. stat.]. Vol. 1, (1863)-. Periodical. German. Six times a year. $410.00. Gustav Fischer Verlag Stuttgart, Postfach 720143, D-70577 Stuttgart Germany. **Tel** 011 49 711 458030, FAX 011 49 711 4580334, telex 2627-7111488. **(Subscription address:** VCH Publishers Inc., 303 Northwest 12th Avenue, Journals Department, Deerfield FL 33442. **Tel** (800)367-8249, (305)428-5566.) cum. index. Documents available from The Genuine Article.
Ind/Abst Econ. Lit. Index (19??-); J. Econ. Lit.; Res. Alert [Full Cov.]; Soc. Sci. Cit. Index [Full Cov.]; Stat. Theory Method Abstr. (1959-1963, 1966, 1968-1982, 1984); World Agric. Econ. Rural Sociol. Abstr.

LC Discard **ISSN** 0250-7528
US
CEASED

JAHRESBERICHT DER EXECUTIVDIREKTOREN - INTERNATIONALER WAHRUNGSFONDS. (JAHRESBERICHT DER EXECUTIVDIREKTOREN FUR DAS AM ... ABGELAUFENE GESCHAFTSJAHR.). **Main/Corp** International Monetary Fund. (19??)-(19??). German (English). International Monetary Fund, 700 19th Street Northwest, Publishing Unit, Washington DC 20431. **Tel** (202)623-7430, FAX (202)623-7201. available on microfilm from University Microfilms International (UMI).
Desc: Reviews IMF's activities, policies, organization and administration and surveys the world economy, with special emphasis on balance of payments problems, exchange rates, world trade, international liquidity and developments in the international monetary system.

LC H62.5.G4 M86a
GW

JAHRESBERICHT - OSTEUROPA-INSTITUT. **See** Social Sciences.

LC HF5251.J3 J33
DD 338.7/6/0255982 IO

JAKARTA BUSINESS DIRECTORY. **See** Industry and Production-Trade and Industrial Directories.

LC HC461 .A8 **ISSN** 0916-877X
DD 330.9/52/04 JA

JAPAN 21ST. **Added/Corp** Nihon Kogyo Shinbunsha. **VFOAT** Japan Twenty First. Vol. 37, No. 1 (Jan. 1992)-. Periodical. English. Twelve times a year. $164.00. Nihon Kogyo Shimbun, Sankei Building, 7 2 1 Chome Ohtemachi, Chiyoda-Ku Tokyo 100 Japan. **Tel** 11 81 3 231 7111 ext. 3558, FAX 11 81 3 3295-3991. available on microfilm and microfiche from University Microfilms International (UMI). ***Continues*** *Business Japan, 0300-4341.*
Ind/Abst Acad. Search; Bus. Index (1992-); Bus. Period. Index; Bus. Source Plus; Bus. Source; EP Collect.; Gen. BusinessFile (1992-); Gen. Period. Index (1992-); Homework Help.; INFO-SOUTH Abstr.; Mag. Search; MasterFile FullTEXT 1000; MasterFile FullTEXT 350; MasterFile FullTEXT 650; MasterFile FullTEXT (July 1993-); OCLC; PAIS Int. Print; Predicasts Forecasts; Telebase; Trade Ind. Index; Wilson Bus. Abstr.

LC HC461 .J35
DD 332.6/7 JA

JAPAN COMPANY HANDBOOK. FIRST SECTION FIRMS. **Added/Corp** Toyo Keizai Shinposha. **VFOAT** JCH-First Section; First Section; First Section Firms; Japan Company Handbook. First Section. 1st Half (1986)-. Periodical. English. Four times a year. $250.00. Toyo Keizai Inc., 1-2-1 Nihonbashi Hongokucho, Chuo-ku Tokyo 103 Japan. **Tel** 011 81 3 3246 5470, FAX 011 81 3 32310629. **(Subscription address:** Toyo Keizai America Inc., 9401 James Avenue South, Suite 160, Minneapolis MN 55431.) ***Continues*** *Japan Company Handbook, 0288-9307.*
Desc: Information on the blue-chip Japanese companies.

JA

JAPAN COMPANY HANDBOOK. SECOND SECTION. **Added/Corp** Toyo Keizai Shinposha. (Spring 1987)-. Periodical. English. Four

times a year. $250.00. Toyo Keizai Inc., 1-2-1 Nihonbashi Hongokucho, Chuo-ku Tokyo 103 Japan. **Tel** 011 81 3 3246 5470, FAX 011 81 3 32310629. **(Subscription address:** Toyo Keizai America Inc., 9401 James Avenue South, Suite 160, Minneapolis MN 55431.**) Ad Acc, Adv Mgr:** W. Ito, **Tel** (81) 3 3246 5655. **Continues** Second Section Firms, 0288-9315.
Desc: Complete background, outlook, performance data on Japanese companies.

LC HC461 .I6   ISSN 0910-8300
DD 330.952/005   JA
JAPAN ECONOMIC ALMANAC. (1985)-.
English. One time a year. $59.50. Nihon Keizai Shimbun Inc., 9-5 Otemachi 1 Chome, Chiyoda-ku Tokyo 100 Japan. **Tel** 011 81 3 32700251, 011 81 3 52108502 (Nikkei Business Publications Inc.), FAX 011 81 3 52552661, 011 81 3 52108119 (Nikkei Business Publications Inc.). **(Subscription address:** Japan Economic Almanac, 1325 Avenue of the Americas, Suite 2500, New York NY 10019. **Tel** (212)261-6234.**) Continues** Industrial Review of Japan, 0537-5452.
Desc: Insightful analysis of the outlook of the Japanese economy, money market, foreign trade, stock market, banking, labor, prices and consumption, science and technology plus major developing fields.

LC HB9 .J37
DD 333.05/6   JA
JAPAN RESEARCH QUARTERLY.
Added/Corp Nihon Sogo Kenkyujo. (Summer 1992)-. Periodical. English. Four times a year. Free on request. Japan Research Institute, Economics Department, Kioicho Building, 3-12, Kioicho, Chiyoda-ku, Tokyo 102 Japan. **Tel** 011 81 3 32884658, FAX 011 81 3 32884690. **Circ:** 5,000.

JA
JAPAN SOURCE CARD INNOVATION NEWSLETTER. (19??)-.
Newsletter. Japanese. Twelve times a year. ¥95000.00. Japan Business Connection Co, Kita Aoyama 3-12-7, R904 Capric, Minato Ku Tokyo 107 Japan. **Tel** 011 81 3 34076481, FAX 011 81 3 34076542, telex 2422765. **ED** Toshi Morimoto.
Desc: Contains the latest information covering Japanese manufacturers, academic circles, market trends, new technology, new applications, etc.

LC HF1602.15.U6 J376   ISSN 0888-5702
DD 382   US
JAPAN-U.S. BUSINESS REPORT.
[Jpn.-U.S. bus. rep.]. **Added/Corp** Japan Economic Institute of America. **VFOAT** Japan U.S. Business Report. **VAT** Japan-United States Business Report. No. 196 (Jan. 29, 1986)-. Periodical. English. Twelve times a year. $160.00. Japan Economic Institute of America, 1000 Connecticut Avenue NW, Suite 211, Washington DC 20036. **Tel** (202)296-5633, FAX (202)296-8333. Index available. **Circ:** 250. **Continues** Japan Economic Institute of America. Japan Report.
Desc: Specific information on marketing and investment plans of US and Japanese companies.

ISSN 1062-3302
US
JAPAN WATCH, USA. Added/Corp Japan Watch, USA.
VFOAT Japan Watch. (1992)-. Periodical. English. Twelve times a year. $36.00. Japan Watch, USA, PO Box 1307, San Ramon CA 94583.

ISSN 1352-4739
UK
JAPANESE ECONOMIC REVIEW. (19??)-.
Academic Scholarly Publication. English. Four times a year. $82.00. Basil Blackwell Publishers Ltd., 108 Cowley Road, Oxford OX4 1JF United Kingdom. **Tel** 011 44 1235 465500, FAX 011 44 1235 465556, telex 837022 OXBOOK G. **(Subscription address:** Blackwell Publishers / UK, 108 Cowley Road, Oxford OX4 1JF United Kingdom. **Tel** 011 44 1865 791100, FAX 011 44 1865 791347.**) Absorbed** Economic Studies Quarterly.

LC HC461 .J44   ISSN 0735-6609
DD 330.952/005   US
JAPANESE REVIEW. [Jpn. rev.]. Added/Corp
Data Resources, Inc. Nihon Keizai Shinbunsha. **VFOAT** Data Resources Japanese Review. (19??)-. Periodical. English. Four times a year. $6300.00. DRI McGraw Hill, 24 Hartwell Avenue, Lexington MA 02173. **Tel** (617)863-5100, FAX (617)860-6464, (617)860-6416. **Continues** Japanese Review, 0148-5938.

LC HD70.J3 J395   ISSN 0910-2027
DD 650/.0952   JA
JAPANESE YEARBOOK ON BUSINESS HISTORY. [Jpn. yearb. bus. hist.]. Added/Corp Nihon
Keieishi Kenkyujo. (1984)-. English. One time a year. $85.00. **(Subscription address:** Japan Publications Trading Company Ltd., PO Box 5030, Tokyo International, Tokyo 100-31 Japan. **Tel** 011 81 3 3292 3753.**)**
Ind/Abst Am. Hist. Life (1987-).

ISSN 0931-3230
GW
UDC 91 :32
JAPANINFO. [Japaninfo]. (1980)-.
Periodical. German. Seventeen times a year (Published every 3 weeks with 2nd week in Jan.). $343.91. Japaninfo, Bismarckring 40, 89077 ULM Germany. **Tel** 011 49 731 68093, FAX 011 49 731 68095. Index available (Every 2 yrs.). cum. index. **Bk Rev**, (Qty: 10). **Ad Acc. Circ:** 600.

ISSN 1140-4264
FR
UDC 338(52)
JAPON ECONOMIE ET SOCIETE PARIS. (JAPON ECONOMIE ET SOCIETE.). (1989)-.
Periodical. French. Eleven times a year. Free on request. Office Franco Japonais Etudes Economiques, 14 rue Cimarose, 75116 Paris France. **Tel** 011 33 1 47273090. **Continues** Japon Economie, 0184-7740.

ISSN 0313-5934
AT
JASSA. (19??)-.
English. Four times a year. 29.60Aus$. Securities Institute of Australia, PO Box H99, Australia Square, Sydney NSW 2001 Australia. **Tel** 011 61 2 2516799.

ISSN 0744-6489
DD 330   US
JEI REPORT. [JEI rep.]. Added/Corp Japan
Economic Institute of America. **VAT** Japan Economic Institute Report. (Jan. 9, 1981)-. Periodical. English. One time a week. $80.00. Japan Economic Institute of America, 1000 Connecticut Avenue NW, Suite 211, Washington DC 20036. **Tel** (202)296-5633, FAX (202)296-8333. **Continues** United States-Japan Trade Council. Council Report; **Absorbed** Japan Insight, 0737-4593.
Ind/Abst Stat. Ref. Index.

FR
JEUNE AFRIQUE ECONOMIE (PARIS, FRANCE : 1986). (JEUNE AFRIQUE
ECONOMIE.). No. 89 (Oct. 1986)-. Periodical. French. Twenty-four times a year. $146.54. Gideppe SA, 30 Avenue de Messine, 75008 Paris France. **Tel** 011 33 1 49530602, FAX 011 33 1 49530604. **Continues** Journal de l'Economie Africaine, 0292-7357.
Ind/Abst LABORDOC; PAIS Int. Print.

LC HC462.9 .K322
DD 330   JA
JIGYOSHO MEIKAN. SONO 1, JIGYOSHO HEN. Added/Corp Japan. Sorifu.
Tokeikyoku. Shakai Chosa Kenkyujo. Konpyuta Jigyobu. (1982)-. Japanese. Somucho Management and Coordination Agency), 19-1 Wakamatsucho Shinjukuku, Tokyo 162 Japan.
Continues Kaisha Jigyosho Meikan. Sono 1, Jigyosho Hen.

LC HC462.9 .K323
DD 330   JA
JIGYOSHO MEIKAN. SONO 2, KAISHA KIGYO HEN. Added/Corp Japan. Sorifu.
Tokeikyoku. Shakai Chosa Kenkyujo. Konpyuta Jigyobu. (1982)-. Japanese. Somucho Management and Coordination Agency), 19-1 Wakamatsucho Shinjukuku, Tokyo 162 Japan.
Continues Kaisha Jigyosho Meikan. Sono 2, Kigyo Hen.

LC HF5001   ISSN 0021-7050
DD 650   CN
JOBBER NEWS (TORONTO). (JOBBER
NEWS.). (1932)-. Periodical. English. Twelve times a year. 38.4Can$. Southham Information & Technical Group Inc, 1450 Don Mills Road, Don Mills Ontario M3B 2X7 Canada. **Tel** (416)445-6641, (800)668-2374, FAX (416)442-2261. **ED** Bob Blans. **Ad Acc. Circ:** 11,500 (ctrl).
Desc: Aftermarket publication serving the key buying and selling personnel of WD's jobbers and new mass merchandisers, hardware chains and national accounts.

ISSN 0813-7455
DD 338.7402594   AT
CEASED
JOBSON'S QUARTERLY. [Jobson's q.].
(1982)-(Sept. 1994). Periodical. English. Riddell Information Services Pty Limited, PO Box 3942, Sydney New South Wales 2001 Australia. **Tel** 11 61 23682100, FAX 11 61 23682150, telex 126736. **ED** Fran De Biasi. **Ad Acc, Adv Mgr:** Max Cunningham.

AT
JOBSON'S YEAR BOOK. PUBLIC COMPANIES OF AUSTRALIA & NEW ZEALAND. (JOBSON'S YEAR BOOK; PUBLIC
COMPANIES OF AUSTRALIA & NEW ZEALAND.). **Main/Corp** Jobson's Publications. **VFOAT** Jobson's Year Book of Public Companies. (197?)-. English. One time a year. 295.00Aus$. Riddell Information Services Pty Limited, PO Box 3942, Sydney New South Wales 2001 Australia. **Tel** 11 61 23682100, FAX 11 61 23682150, telex 126736. **ED** Sue Francis. **Supersedes** Jobson's Yearbook: Public Companies of Australia & New Zealand.
Desc: Provides Australian and international business,

Business and Economics

government, academics and investors with the in-depth, comprehensive and relevant analysis of the nature of commerce and industry throughout Australia and the world.

ISSN 0712-8177
DD 331.1/0971   CN
CEASED
JOHN KETTLE'S FUTURELETTER. [John
Kettle's futurelett.]. **VFOAT** Futureletter. (April 30, 1982)-(Nov. 1995). Periodical. English. Futuresearch Publishing Inc., 208 Winona Avenue, Oshawa Ontario L1G 3H5 Canada. **Tel** (416)404-0405. **(Subscription address:** John Kettle's Futureletter, Subscription Office, PO Box 830350, Birmingham AL 35283-0350. **Tel** (800)633-4931, (205)995-1567 (outside US and Canada), FAX (205)995-1588.**) ED** John Kettle. Index available. cum. index. **Bk Rev. Circ:** 500.
Desc: Economic, social, demographic, political, and technological trend analysis and forecasts for senior managers in public and private sectors.

LC HF3221   ISSN 0838-1542
DD 380.1/09711   CN
TITLE CHANGE
JOHN TWIGG'S REPORT ON B.C. [John
Twigg's rep. B.C.]. **VFOAT** Report on B.C. Vol. 1, No. 1 (Feb. 1988)-(199?). Periodical. English. Maitland Publications, 7 Cook Street, Victoria BC V8V 3W6 Canada. **Tel** (604)360-4053, FAX (604)360-0548. **(Subscription address:** Monday Publications, 1609 Blanshard Street, Victoria, British Columbia, V8W 2J5 Canada. **Tel** (604)382-6188, (800)661-6335.**) ED** John Twigg. **Bk Rev**, (Qty: 3). **Ad Acc. Circ:** 300 (ctrl). **Continued by** Report on B.C, 1196-6688.
Desc: Focuses on the big-picture and macro-economic aspects of British Columbia, especially regarding business and economic development.

ISSN 0162-5888
US
JOINT ECONOMIC REPORT, THE. (THE
JOINT ECONOMIC REPORT : REPORT OF THE JOINT ECONOMIC COMMITTEE ON THE ECONOMIC REPORT OF THE PRESIDENT TOGETHER WITH ADDITIONAL VIEWS.). **Main/Corp** United States. Congress. Joint Economic Committee. (196?)-. Government Publication. English. One time a year. Superintendent of Documents, US Government Printing Office, Washington DC 20402. **Tel** (202)275-3328, FAX (202)786-2377. **ED** Lee H. Hamilton. available on microfiche (Vols. for (1985-) distributed to some depository libraries). **Continues in part** Annual Report on the Economic Report of the President.
Desc: Intended to assist the several Committees of the Congress and its Members as they deal with economic issues and legislation pertaining thereto.

ISSN 0319-7239
CN
JOINT VENTURES (OTTAWA). (JOINT
VENTURES.). **Main/Corp** Indian and Eskimo Affairs Program (Canada). **VFOAT** Coparticipation. **VAT** Fonds de Promotion Economique des Indiens. Revue Annuelle; Indian Economic Development Fund Annual Review. 1972-. English (French). Free. Park Canada, Department of Indian and Northern Affairs, Ottawa Ontario K1A 0H4 Canada.

UK
JORDANS REGIONAL DIRECTORIES OF KEY BUSINESS PROSPECTS. VARIOUS AREAS IN UK.
English. £150.00. Jordans & Sons Ltd, 21 St. Thomas Street, Bristol BS1 6JS United Kingdom. **Tel** 011 44 117 9230600, FAX 011 44 117 9230063, telex 449119. **Ad Acc.** available on diskette; available on labels.
Desc: Directory containing names, addresses and telephone numbers of key business plus financial information.

ISSN 1145-6396
FR
UDC 330
JOURNAL DES ECONOMISTES ET DES ETUDES HUMAINES. [J. econ. etud. hum.].
(1989)-. Periodical. Multiple languages. Four times a year. $54.68. Inst Europeen Etudes Humaines, 3 Ave Robert Schuman, 13628 Aix-en-Provence France.

LC HD241   ISSN 1061-8228
DD 338   US
JOURNAL / ECONOMIC POLICY INSTITUTE. [Journal - Econ. Policy Inst.].
Added/Corp Economic Policy Institute. **VFOAT** Economic Policy Institute Journal; EPI Journal. Vol. 1, No. 1 (Feb. 1991)-. Periodical. English. EPI, Economic Policy Institute, 1730 Rhode Island Avenue NW, Suite 200, Washington DC 20036.

ISSN 0344-9327
AU
Pr Rev.
JOURNAL FUER BETRIEBSWIRTSCHAFT. [J. Betriebswirtsch.].
(1975)-. Periodical. German. Five times a year. DM136.00. Linde Verlag Wien Gesellschaft Mbh,

Scheydgasse 24, A 1210 Vienna Austria. **Tel** 011 43 1 2780526, FAX 011 43 1 27805263. **Bk Rev**, (Qty: 20-30). ***Continues*** *Der Eosterreichische Betriebswirt, 0472-5417.*
Desc: Articles about marketing, management, and other problems of economy and business.
Ind/Abst Selec. Coop. Index Manage. Period.

ISSN 0831-0122
DD 338.09714/05 CN

JOURNAL INDUSTRIEL DU QUEBEC, LE. [J. ind. Qu,e.]. Vol. 1, No. 1 (May 1985)-. Periodical. French. Twelve times a year (Except Jan. and July). 32.01Can$. Division Information Industreil Inc., 2370 boulevard Henri Bourassa Est, Montreal Quebec H2B 1T6 Canada. **Tel** (514)388-8801.

LC HC111 **ISSN** 0823-8715
DD 330.97124/005 CN

JOURNAL (INSTITUTE FOR SASKATCHEWAN STUDIES). (JOURNAL / INSTITUTE FOR SASKATCHEWAN STUDIES.). [J. - Inst. Sask. Stud.]. **Added/Corp** Institute for Saskatchewan Studies. **VAT** Institute for Saskatchewan Studies Journal. (1983)-. Periodical. English. $10.00. Institute for Saskatchewan Studies, PO Box 1462, Saskatoon Saskatchewan, S7K 3R1 Canada. ***Continues*** *Institute for Saskatchewan Studies (Newsletter), 0715-4496.*

UK

JOURNAL OF ACCOUNTING, FINANCE AND BUSINESS HISTORY. (19??)-. English. Three times a year. £50.00. Routledge, 11 New Fetter Lane, London EC4P 4EE United Kingdom. **Tel** 011 44 171 5839855, FAX 011 44 171 5830701. **(Subscription address:** Kinokuniya Company Ltd., 38-1 Sakuragaoka 5, chome Setagaya-ku, Tokyo 156 Japan. **Tel** FAX 011 03 3439 0136.**)**

LC HC **ISSN** 0300-1717
PH

JOURNAL OF AGRICULTURAL ECONOMICS AND DEVELOPMENT. See Agriculture-Agricultural Economics.

LC HD101 .A425 **ISSN** 1043-3309
DD 338.1/05 US
CODEN JAERE6
CEASED

JOURNAL OF AGRICULTURAL ECONOMICS RESEARCH, THE. See Agriculture-Agricultural Economics.

ISSN 0892-7626
DD 658 US
Pr Rev.

JOURNAL OF APPLIED BUSINESS RESEARCH. [J. appl. bus. res.]. Vol. No. 1 (Fall 1985)-. Periodical. English. Four times a year. $186.00. Journal of Applied Business, PO Box 620760, Littleton CO 80162. **Tel** (303)972-6604, FAX (303)978-0413. **ED** Ronald C. Clute. Index available. cum. index. **Bk Rev**, (Qty: 5). **Ad Acc, Adv Mgr:** Ron Clute, **Tel** (303)972-6604. **Circ:** 600 (ctrl). available on microfilm and microfiche from University Microfilms International (UMI).
Desc: Covers the areas of accounting, economics, entrepreneurship, finance, information systems, management, and marketing.
Ind/Abst Curr. Cit.; EP Collect.; Homework Help.; MasterFile FullTEXT 1000; MasterFile FullTEXT 350; MasterFile FullTEXT 650; MasterFile FullTEXT; OCLC; Telebase.

LC HB139 .J66 **ISSN** 0883-7252
DD 330/.028 UK
CCC
CODEN JAECET
Pr Rev.

JOURNAL OF APPLIED ECONOMETRICS (CHICHESTER, ENGLAND). (JOURNAL OF APPLIED ECONOMETRICS.). [J. appl. econ.]. **VFOAT** Applied Econometrics. Vol. 1, No. 1 (Jan. 1986)-. Periodical. English. Five times a year. $495.00. John Wiley & Sons Ltd., Baffins Lane, Chichester, West Sussex PO19 1UD United Kingdom. **Tel** 011 44 1243 779777, FAX 011 44 1243 776128 BTG:JWP001, telex 86290 WIBOOKG. **(Subscription address:** John Wiley & Sons, Inc. / Philadelphia, PO Box 7247, Philadelphia PA 19170. **Tel** (212)850-6645, (800)225-5945.**) ED** M. Hashem Pesaran, Arie Kapteyn, Nicholas M. Kiefer, Adrian Pagan, and Mark Watson. available on microfilm and microfiche from University Microfilms International (UMI). Documents available from The Genuine Article, UMI Article Clearinghouse.
Desc: Publishes articles of dealing with the application of existing, as well as new, econometric techniques to a wide variety of problems in economics and related subjects. This journal also covers topics in measurement, estimation, testing, forecasting and policy analysis.
Ind/Abst Curr. Cit.; Curr. Contents Soc. Behav. Sci.; Curr. Index Stat.; J. Econ. Lit. (1986-); Oper. Res./Manage. Sci.; Qual. Control Appl. Stat.; Res. Alert [Full Cov.]; Soc. Sci. Cit. Index [Full Cov.]; Stat. Theory Method Abstr.

ISSN 1077-1158
DD 339 US
Pr Rev.

•JOURNAL OF APPLIED MANAGEMENT AND ENTREPRENEURSHIP, THE. [J. appl. manag. entrep.]. **Added/Corp** Nova Southeastern University. School of Business and Entrepreneurship. **VFOAT** Applied Management and Entrepreneurship. Vol. 1, No. 1 (Aug. 1994)-. Periodical. English. Four times a year. $50.00. Graduate School Entrepreneurship, Nova Southeast University, 3301 College Avenue, Ft. Lauderdale FL 33314. **Tel** (305)476-8911.

UK

•JOURNAL OF APPLIED MANAGEMENT STUDIES. (1995)-. English. Two times a year. $136.00. Carfax Publishing Company, PO Box 25, Abingdon, Oxfordshire OX14 3UE United Kingdom. **Tel** 011 44 1235 555335, FAX 011 44 1235 553559, telex 817484. ***Continues*** *Journal of Industrial Affairs.*

ISSN 1059-9231
DD 330 US

•JOURNAL OF ASIA-PACIFIC BUSINESS. [J. Asia-Pac. bus.]. **VFOAT** Journal of Asia Pacific Business. (1993)-. English. Four times a year. $95.00. The Haworth Press Inc., 10 Alice Street, Binghamton NY 13904-1580. **Tel** (607)722-5857, (800)3-HAWORTH, FAX (607)722-1424. **ED** Zahir A. Quraeshi. **Acid Free.** Documents available from Haworth Document Delivery Service.
Desc: Deals with Asia-Pacific region's business practices and covers marketing, management, finance, accounting, business law, manufacturing, service, and other areas.

LC HD **ISSN** 1354-7860
DD 330.9 UK

•JOURNAL OF ASIA PACIFIC ECONOMIES. (Autumn 1995)-. Academic Scholarly Publication. English. Three times a year. $130.00. Routledge, 11 New Fetter Lane, London EC4P 4EE United Kingdom. **Tel** 011 44 171 5839855, FAX 011 44 171 5830701. **(Subscription address:** Kinokuniya Company Ltd., 38-1 Sakuragaoka 5, chome Setagaya-ku, Tokyo 156 Japan. **Tel** FAX 011 03 3439 0136.**)**

LC HF3790.8 .A3 **ISSN** 1068-0055
DD 330.959/005 US
Pr Rev.

•JOURNAL OF ASIAN BUSINESS. [J. Asian bus.]. **Added/Corp** University of Michigan. Southeast Asia Business Program. Vol. 9, No. 1 (Winter 1993)-. Periodical. English. Four times a year. $40.00. Association for Asian Studies Inc., University of Michigan, 1 Lane Hall, Ann Arbor MI 48109. **Tel** (313)665-2490, FAX (313)665-3801. **(Subscription address:** Association for Asian Studies, 130 Lane Hall / SEABP, Ann Arbor MI 48109. **) Bk Rev**. available on an online database. ***Continues*** *Journal of Southeast Asia Business, 1055-2073.*
Ind/Abst MasterFile FullTEXT (July 1993-).

LC HC460.5.A1 J68 **ISSN** 1049-0078
DD 330.95/005 US

JOURNAL OF ASIAN ECONOMICS. [J. Asian econ.]. **Added/Corp** American Committee on Asian Economic Studies. Vol. 1, No. 1 (Spring 1990)-. Periodical. English. Four times a year. $180.00. JAI Press Inc., 55 Old Post Road, Suite 2, PO Box 1678, Greenwich CT 06836-1678. **Tel** (203)661-7602, FAX (203)661-0792. **ED** M. Dutta.
Desc: Designed for the purpose of supporting analytical research that brings comparative and international perspectives to bear on important economic developments within the Asian region, including impacts of technology and institutional reforms, economic development, industrial organization, financial market systems, market behavior, and economic integration.
Ind/Abst Econ. Lit. Index; Int. Labour Doc.; LABORDOC; PAIS Int. Print (1991-); Rural Dev. Abstr.; World Agric. Econ. Rural Sociol. Abstr.

ISSN 0156-5826
AT
Pr Rev.

JOURNAL OF AUSTRALIAN POLITICAL ECONOMY, THE. [J. Aust. polit. econ.]. **Added/Corp** Australian Political Economy Movement. No. 1 (Oct. 1977)-. Periodical. English. Two times a year. 25.00Aus$. Australian Political Economy Movement, Box 76, Wentworth Building, University of Sydney, Sydney 2006 Australia. **Tel** 011 61 2 692-3063. **ED** F. Stilwell. cum. index. **Bk Rev. Ad Acc. Circ:** 1,000.
Desc: Analysis of Australian society from a point of view sympathetic to the labor movement.
Ind/Abst APAIS, Aust. Public Aff. Inf. Ser. (1980-); Energy Res. Abstr. (Sept. 1982-); Int. Bibliogr. Sociol.

US

JOURNAL OF BUSINESS. Vol. 1, No. 1 (Feb. 6, 1986)-. Newspaper. English. Twenty-four times a year. $22.00. Northwest Business Press Inc., 112 East First Avenue, Spokane WA 99202. **Tel** (509)456-5257. **ED** Norman Thorpe. **Photos. Ad Acc, Adv Mgr:** Scott Crytser. Full Page (B&W) $1,700.00. Half Page (B&W) $1,100.00. Full Page (Color) $2,180.00. Half Page (Color) $1,580.00. **Pub. Size:** Tabloid. **Circ:** 15,200. Documents available from UMI Article Clearinghouse.
Desc: Local business news of Spokane and surrounding areas in Washington.
Ind/Abst Bus. Dateline (Jan. 31, 1991-) [Full Txt.].

LC HC **ISSN** 0021-941X
CN
CCC

JOURNAL OF BUSINESS ADMINISTRATION (VANCOUVER). (JOURNAL OF BUSINESS ADMINISTRATION.). [J. bus. adm.]. **Added/Corp** University of British Columbia. Faculty of Commerce and Business Administration. Journal of Business Administration. Vol. 1 (Summer 1969)-. Periodical. English. Four times a year. 12.81Can$. Faculty of Commerce and Business Administration, University of British Columbia, 2053 Main Mall, Vancouver British Columbia, V6T 1Z2 Canada. **Tel** (604)224-8443, FAX (604)822-8521. **ED** Peter N. Nemetz. **Bk Rev. Ad Acc. Circ:** 500. available on microfilm and microfiche from University Microfilms International (UMI). Documents available from UMI Article Clearinghouse.
Desc: International journal of administrative inquiry devoted to research in traditional areas of business and policy, applied economics and operations research.
Ind/Abst ABI/INFORM Glob. Ed.; ABI/INFORM Ondisc: Expr. Ed.; ABI/INFORM [Computer File] (Spring 1975-); Acad. Search; Anbar Account. Finan. Abstr. [Full Txt.]; Anbar Mark. Distr. Abstr. [Full Txt.]; Anbar Top Manage. Abstr. [Full Txt.]; Bus. Index (1985-); Bus. Source Plus; Bus. Source; Can. Period. Index (19??-); EP Collect.; Gen. BusinessFile (1985-); Gen. Period. Index (1985-); Homework Help.; Mag. Search; Manage. Bibliogr. Rev.; Manage. Contents; MasterFile FullTEXT 1000; MasterFile FullTEXT 350; MasterFile FullTEXT 650; MasterFile FullTEXT (Jan. 1992-); OCLC; Oper. Prod. Manage. Abstr. [Full Txt.]; Person. Train. Abstr. [Full Txt.]; Pollut. Abstr. Indexes; Telebase; Women Manage. Rev. [Full Txt.].

LC HC
DD 330 US

JOURNAL OF BUSINESS AND ECONOMIC PERSPECTIVES. Added/Corp University of Tennessee (Martin Campus). School of Business Administration. **VFOAT** Business and Economic Perspectives. Vol. 8, No. 2 (Fall 1982)-. Periodical. English. Two times a year. $26.00. University of Tennessee at Martin / Business Administration, 102 Business Administration Building, Martin TN 38238. **Tel** (901)587-5248, (901)587-7226. ***Continues*** *Business and Economic Perspectives, 0887-4360.*

LC HB137 .J68 **ISSN** 0735-0015
DD 330/.072 US
CCC
Pr Rev.

JOURNAL OF BUSINESS & ECONOMIC STATISTICS. See Business and Economics-Abstracting, Bibliographies and Statistics.

US

JOURNAL OF BUSINESS AND ECONOMIC STUDIES, THE. Added/Corp Fairfield University. School of Business. Northeast Business & Economic Association (U.S.). Vol. 1, No. 1 (Spring/Summer 1991)-. Periodical. English. Fairfield University School of Business, Fairfield CT 06430. **Tel** (203)254-4070. ***Continues*** *Northeast Journal of Business & Economics, 8755-5123.*

LC HC
DD 330 US

JOURNAL OF BUSINESS AND ECONOMIC STUDIES, THE. Added/Corp Northeast Business & Economic Association (U.S.) Fairfield University. School of Business. Vol. 1, No. 1 (Spring/Summer 1991)-. English. Four times a year. Fairfield University School of Business, Fairfield CT 06430. **Tel** (203)254-4070.

LC Z675.B8 J65 **ISSN** 0896-3568
DD 027.6/905 US
CODEN JBFLEY
Pr Rev.

JOURNAL OF BUSINESS & FINANCE LIBRARIANSHIP. See Library and Information Sciences.

LC WMLC 93/1687 **ISSN** 0889-3268
DD 158 US
CCC
NLM W1; JO57RS

JOURNAL OF BUSINESS AND PSYCHOLOGY. See Psychology.

LC HF5001 .J59 **ISSN** 0021-9428
DD 300/.5 NR

JOURNAL OF BUSINESS AND SOCIAL STUDIES, THE. Added/Corp University of Lagos. School of Administration. University of Lagos. School of Social Studies. Vol. 1 (Sept. 1968)-. Periodical. English.

Irregular. $25.00. Lagos University Press, Publishing Division, PO Box 132, Akoka-Yaba University Lagos, Lagos Nigeria. **Tel** 011 234 1 825048. **ED** Oyeleye Oyediram. **Bk Rev. Ad Acc.** available on microfilm and microfiche from University Microfilms International (UMI).

LC HF5717 .I595 **ISSN** 1050-6519
DD 658.4/5/05 US
CCC
CODEN JBTCE9

JOURNAL OF BUSINESS AND TECHNICAL COMMUNICATION. (JOURNAL OF BUSINESS AND TECHNICAL COMMUNICATION : JBTC.). [J. bus. tech. commun.]. **Added/Corp** Iowa State University. **VFOAT** JBTC. Vol. 2, No. 2 (Sept. 1988)-. English. Four times a year (Jan., Apr., July, Oct.). $144.00. SAGE Periodical Press, 2455 Teller Road, Thousand Oaks CA 91320. **Tel** (805)499-0721, FAX (805)499-0871, telex 100799. **ED** Thomas Kent (Iowa State University). **Acid Free. *Continues*** *Iowa State Journal of Business and Technical Communication, 0892-5720.*
Desc: Provides forum for discussion of communication practices, problems, and trends in business, scientific, and governmental fields.
Ind/Abst Abstr. Anthropol. (19??-); Bus. Source Plus; Commun. Abstr.; Curr. Index J. Educ.; EP Collect.; Homework Help.; Hum. Resour. Abstr.; MasterFile FullTEXT 1000; MasterFile FullTEXT 350; MasterFile FullTEXT 650; MasterFile FullTEXT (Jan. 1995-); OCLC; Soc. Plann. Policy Dev. Abstr.; Telebase.

LC HF5001 .J6 **ISSN** 0021-9398
DD 650/.05 US
CCC
CODEN JOBUAQ

Pr Rev.
JOURNAL OF BUSINESS (CHICAGO, ILL.), THE. (THE JOURNAL OF BUSINESS.). [J. bus.]. **Added/Corp** University of Chicago. School of Business. University of Chicago. Graduate School of Business. University of Chicago. Dept. of Economics. **VFOAT** Journal of Business of the University of Chicago. Vol. 27, No. 1 (Jan. 1954)-. Periodical. English. Four times a year. $54.00. University of Chicago Press / Journals Division, PO Box 37005, 5720 South Woodlawn, Chicago IL 60637. **Tel** (312)753-3347, FAX (312)753-0811. **ED** Douglas W. Diamond, John Huizinga, Abel P. Jeuland and B. Peter Pashigian. cum. index. **Acid Free.** available on microfilm and microfiche from University Microfilms International (UMI). Documents available from The Genuine Article, UMI Article Clearinghouse. ***Continues*** *Journal of Business of the University of Chicago, 0740-9168.*
Desc: Publishes research, analysis and inquiry into issues of theoretical and practical importance to the business community. The scope comprehends the entire range of business topics, including finance, security markets, banking, administration and management, marketing and industrial organization.
Ind/Abst ABI/INFORM Glob. Ed.; ABI/INFORM [Computer File] (Oct. 1972-); Acad. Abstr.; Acad. Search; Account. Art.; Am. Hist. Life (1967-); Bus. Index (1985-); Bus. Period. Index; Bus. Source Plus; Bus. Source; Commun. Abstr.; Comput. Lit. Index; Curr. Cit.; Econ. Lit. Index (199?-); EP Collect.; Fed. Tax Artic.; Gen. BusinessFile (1985-); Gen. Period. Index (1985-); Homework Help.; INFO-SOUTH Abstr.; Int. Aerosp. Abstr.; J. Econ. Lit.; Mag. Search; Manage. Market. Abstr.; Manage. Contents; MasterFile FullTEXT 1000; MasterFile FullTEXT 350; MasterFile FullTEXT 650; MasterFile FullTEXT (July 1990-); Newsp. Period. Abstr. (1989-); OCLC; Oper. Res./Manage. Sci.; Person. Manage. Abstr.; Pub. Lib. FullTEXT; Res. Alert [Full Cov.]; Soc. Sci. Cit. Index [Full Cov.]; Telebase; UMI ABI/Inform--Bus. Period. Ondisc (Jan. 1987-) [Full Txt.]; Wilson Bus. Abstr.; Work Relat. Abstr.

LC HF5387 .J68 **ISSN** 0167-4544
DD 174/.4/05 NE
CCC

Pr Rev.
JOURNAL OF BUSINESS ETHICS. **See** Ethics.

LC HB3730 .J65 **ISSN** 0278-6087
DD 338.5/442/05 US
CCC

JOURNAL OF BUSINESS FORECASTING METHODS & SYSTEMS, THE. [J. bus. forecast. methods syst.]. **VFOAT** Journal of Business Forecasting; Journal of Business Forecasting and Systems; Business Forecasting. **VAT** Journal of Business Forecasting Methods and Systems. Vol. 1, No. 1 (July/Sept. 1981)-. Periodical. English. Four times a year (seasonally). $60.00. Graceway Publishing Company, PO Box 159 Station C, Flushing NY 11367. **Tel** (718)463-3914, FAX (718)544-9086. **ED** Chaman L. Jain. Index available. cum. index. **Bk Rev. Circ:** 3,500. available on microfilm and microfiche from University Microfilms International (UMI); available on CD-ROM; available on videocassette; available on audiocassette; available on diskette; available in microform. Documents available from UMI Article Clearinghouse.
Desc: Business forecasting methods in easy to understand language. Includes forecasting packages and economic outlooks.
Ind/Abst ABI/INFORM Glob. Ed.; ABI/INFORM [Computer File] (Winter 1982-1983); Account. Tax Datab. (Winter 1982-Winter 1983); Curr. Cit.; EP Collect.; Gen. BusinessFile (1992-); Homework Help.; Manage. Market. Abstr.; MasterFile FullTEXT 1000; MasterFile FullTEXT 350; MasterFile FullTEXT 650; MasterFile FullTEXT; OCLC; Telebase; UMI ABI/Inform--Bus. Period. Ondisc (Fall 1987-) [Full Txt.]; Women Manage. Rev. [Full Txt.].

LC HD38.5 .J68 **ISSN** 0735-3766
DD 658.5/005 US

Pr Rev.
JOURNAL OF BUSINESS LOGISTICS. [J. bus. logist.]. **Added/Corp** Council of Logistics Management (U.S.) Ohio State University. College of Administrative Science. National Council of Physical Distribution Management. **VFOAT** Business Logistics. Vol. 1 (Spring 1978)-. Periodical. English. Two times a year. $25.00. Council of Logistics Management, 2803 Butterfield Road, Suite 380, Oak Brook IL 60521. **Tel** (708)574-0985, FAX (708)574-0989. **ED** Bernard J. La Londe. **Circ:** 5,000. available on microfilm and microfiche from University Microfilms International (UMI). Documents available from UMI Article Clearinghouse.
Desc: Provides information, new theory or techniques, and researched generalizations about thought and practice in transportation and distribution. Presents views and syntheses which impact the future.
Ind/Abst ABI/INFORM Glob. Ed.; ABI/INFORM [Computer File] (1987-); Curr. Cit.; EP Collect.; Homework Help.; MasterFile FullTEXT 1000; MasterFile FullTEXT 350; MasterFile FullTEXT 650; MasterFile FullTEXT; OCLC; Telebase; UMI ABI/Inform--Bus. Period. Ondisc (1987-) [Full Txt.].

LC HF5001 .J14 **ISSN** 0148-2963
DD 658.4/005 US
CCC
CODEN JBRED4

Pr Rev.
JOURNAL OF BUSINESS RESEARCH. (JBR, JOURNAL OF BUSINESS RESEARCH.). [J. bus. res.]. **Added/Corp** University of Georgia. College of Business Administration. **VFOAT** JBR. (Summer 1973)-. Academic Scholarly Publication. English. Nine times a year (3 volumes). $565.00. Elsevier Science Publishing Company Inc, Madison Square Station, PO Box 882, New York NY 10159-0882. **Tel** (212)633-3950, FAX (212)633-3990. **ED** Arch G Woodside. **Ad Acc.** available on microfilm and microfiche from University Microfilms International (UMI); available on an online database from Elsevier Electronic Subscriptions (EES). Documents available from The Genuine Article, UMI Article Clearinghouse. ***Continues*** *Southern Journal of Business, 0148-2963.*
Desc: Applies theory developed from business research to actual business situations. Examines a wide variety of business decisions, processes and activities within the actual business setting. Theoretical and empirical advances in buyer behaviour, finance, organizational theory and behaviour, marketing, risk and insurance and international business are evaluated on a regular basis.
Ind/Abst ABI/INFORM Glob. Ed.; ABI/INFORM [Computer File] (March 1977-); Acad. Search; Anbar Account. Finan. Abstr. [Full Txt.]; Anbar Mark. Distr. Abstr. [Full Txt.]; Anbar Top Manage. Abstr. [Full Txt.]; Bus. Index (1985-); Bus. Period. Index; Bus. Source Plus; Bus. Source; Commun. Abstr.; Contents Pages Manage.; Curr. Cit.; Curr. Contents Soc. Behav. Sci.; EP Collect.; Gen. BusinessFile (1985-); Gen. Period. Index (1985-); Homework Help.; INFO-SOUTH Abstr.; J. Plan. Lit.; Mag. Search; Manage. Bibliogr. Rev.; MasterFile FullTEXT 1000; MasterFile FullTEXT 350; MasterFile FullTEXT 650; MasterFile FullTEXT (July 1993-); Middle East Abstr. Index; OCLC; Oper. Prod. Manage. Abstr. [Full Txt.]; Oper. Res./Manage. Sci.; Person. Train. Abstr. [Full Txt.]; Person. Manage. Abstr.; Psychol. Abstr. (1983-); PsycINFO; PsycLit; Res. Alert [Full Cov.]; Risk Abstr.; Soc. Sci. Cit. Index [Full Cov.]; Telebase; Wilson Bus. Abstr.; Women Manage. Rev. [Full Txt.]; Work Relat. Abstr. (-19??).

LC HF5001 .J577 **ISSN** 0377-0419
DD 330/.05 SI

JOURNAL OF BUSINESS (SINGAPORE). (THE JOURNAL OF BUSINESS.). English. Three times a year. $20.00 (surface mail), $32.00 (airmail). Asia Pacific-Journal of Management, School of Management, National University of Singapore, Kent Ridge, 0511 Singapore. **Tel** 7723022. **ED** Knin Maung Kyi. **Bk Rev. Ad Acc.** ctrl circ.
Desc: Study of functions, processes and structures of management as practised in the countries of the Asia Pacific region.
Ind/Abst Middle East Abstr. Index.

LC WMLC 93/1685 **ISSN** 0883-9026
DD 338 US
CCC
CODEN JBVEEP

Pr Rev.
JOURNAL OF BUSINESS VENTURING. [J. bus. venturing]. **Added/Corp** Snider Entrepreneurial Center. New York University. Center for Entrepreneurial Studies. Vol. 1, No. 1 (Winter 1985)-. Academic Scholarly Publication. English. Six times a year (1 volume). $340.00. Elsevier Science Publishing Company Inc, Madison Square Station, PO Box 882, New York NY 10159-0882. **Tel** (212)633-3950, FAX (212)633-3990. **ED** Ian C MacMillan. **Ad Acc.** available on microfilm and microfiche from University Microfilms International (UMI); available on an online database from Elsevier Electronic Subscriptions (EES). Documents available from The Genuine Article, UMI Article Clearinghouse.
Desc: Publishes empirically-based research on the topic of entrepreneurship, either as independent start-ups or within existing corporations.
Ind/Abst ABI/INFORM Glob. Ed.; ABI/INFORM [Computer File] (Winter 1985-); Bus. Index (1992-); Contents Pages Manage.; Curr. Cit.; Curr. Contents Soc. Behav. Sci.; Gen. BusinessFile (1992-); Manage. Market. Abstr.; Res. Alert [Full Cov.]; Soc. Sci. Cit. Index [Full Cov.].

LC HB90 .J67 **ISSN** 0147-5967
DD 330/.05 US
CCC

Pr Rev.
JOURNAL OF COMPARATIVE ECONOMICS. [J. comp. econ.]. **Added/Corp** Association for Comparative Economic Studies (US). Vol. 1 (March 1977)-. Academic Scholarly Publication. English. Six times a year. $260.00. Academic Press Inc., 6277 Sea Harbor Drive, Orlando FL 32887. **Tel** (800)543-9534, (407)345-4100, FAX (407)352-3445. **ED** Josef C. Brada. Documents available from The Genuine Article, UMI Article Clearinghouse.
Desc: Devoted to the analysis and study of contemporary, historical, and hypothetical economic systems. Such analyses may involve comparisons of the performance of different economic systems or subsystems, studies linking outcomes to system characteristics in one economy, or investigations of the origin and evolution of one or more economic systems. Empirical, theoretical, and institutional approaches are also published.
Ind/Abst Acad. Abstr.; Acad. Search; Am. Bibliogr. Slavic East Europ. Stud.; Bus. Index (1985-); Bus. Source Plus; Bus. Source; Contents Recent Econ. J.; Curr. Cit.; Curr. Contents Soc. Behav. Sci.; Dairy Sci. Abstr.; Econ. Lit. Index; EP Collect.; Expand. Acad. Index (1984-); Gen. BusinessFile (1985-); Gen. Period. Index (1985-); Homework Help.; INFO-SOUTH Abstr.; J. Econ. Lit.; Leis., Rec., Tour. Abstr.; Mag. Search; MasterFile FullTEXT 1000; MasterFile FullTEXT 350; MasterFile FullTEXT 650; MasterFile FullTEXT (Jan. 1992-); Newsp. Period. Abstr. (1991-); OCLC; PAIS Int. Print (1991-?); Res. Alert [Full Cov.]; Rural Dev. Abstr.; Soc. Sci. Source; Soc. Sci. Cit. Index [Full Cov.]; Soc. Sci. Index; Soc. Sci. Index Fulltext (Dec. 1988-) [Full Txt.]; Telebase; World Agric. Econ. Rural Sociol. Abstr.; Zentralbl. Math. Ihre Grenzgeb.

LC HG4001 .J67 **ISSN** 0929-1199
DD 658.15/05 NE
CCC

Pr Rev.
•**JOURNAL OF CORPORATE FINANCE : CONTRACTING, GOVERNANCE, AND ORGANIZATION.** Vol. 1, No. 1 (Mar. 1994)-. Periodical. English. Four times a year. $210.00. Elsevier Science Publishers BV, PO Box 211, 1000 AE Amsterdam Netherlands. **Tel** 011 31 20 4853641, 011 31 20 4853642, FAX 011 31 20 4853598. **(Subscription address:** Elsevier Science BV / Maryland, PO Box 64698, Baltimore MD 21264. **)** available on an online database from Elsevier Electronic Subscriptions (EES).

LC K10 .O8587 **ISSN** 0094-0593
DD 336.2/43/0973 US
CCC

Pr Rev.
JOURNAL OF CORPORATE TAXATION, THE. **See** Finance-Taxation.

LC NX180.S6 J68 **ISSN** 0885-2545
DD 338.4/77 NE
CCC

JOURNAL OF CULTURAL ECONOMICS. **See** The Arts.

ISSN 1066-9868
US

Pr Rev.
•**JOURNAL OF EAST-WEST BUSINESS.** **VFOAT** Journal of East West Business. (1994)-. Periodical. English. Four times a year. $95.00. The Haworth Press Inc., 10 Alice Street, Binghamton NY 13904-1580. **Tel** (607)722-5857, (800)3-HAWORTH, FAX (607)722-1424. **ED** Stanley Paliwoda. **Bk Rev. Ad Acc. Acid Free.** available on microfiche. Documents available from Haworth Document Delivery Service.
Desc: This journal will treat business from comparitive, cross-cultural, and cross-national perspectives. An Editorial Advisory Board will represent Russian, Asian, Eastern Europe, and Baltic republics in this new business arena, and will include businessmen actively trading in these areas as well as academics.

LC HB139 .J67 **ISSN** 0304-4076
DD 330/.05 NE
CCC
CODEN JECMB6

Pr Rev.
JOURNAL OF ECONOMETRICS. [J. econom.]. Vol. 1 (Mar. 1973)-. Periodical. English. Twelve times a year. $1598.00. Elsevier Sequoia SA, PO Box 564, CH-1001 Lausanne 1 Switzerland. **Tel** 011 41 21

3207381, FAX 011 41 21 3235444. **ED** D.J. Aigner, T. Amemiya and A. Zellner. available on microfilm and microfiche from University Microfilms International (UMI); available on an online database from Elsevier Electronic Subscriptions (EES). Documents available from The Genuine Article, UMI Article Clearinghouse.
Desc: Designed to serve as an outlet for new research in both theoretical and applied economics.
Ind/Abst ABI/INFORM Glob. Ed.; ABI/INFORM [Computer File] (Jan. 1982-); Acad. Search; Bus. Index (1985-); Bus. Source Plus; Bus. Source; CompuMath Cit. Index [Full Cov.]; Contents Recent Econ. J.; Contents Pages Manage.; Curr. Cit.; Curr. Contents Soc. Behav. Sci.; Curr. Index Stat. (1974-); Econ. Lit. Index (Jan. 1982-); EP Collect.; Expand. Acad. Index (1984-); Gen. BusinessFile (1985-); Gen. Period. Index (1985-); Homework Help.; INFO-SOUTH Abstr.; J. Econ. Lit.; Leis., Rec., Tour. Abstr.; Mag. Search; MasterFile FullTEXT 1000; MasterFile FullTEXT 350; MasterFile FullTEXT 650; MasterFile FullTEXT (July 1993-); Math. Rev.; Newsp. Period. Abstr. (1991-); OCLC; Res. Alert [Full Cov.]; Rural Dev. Abstr.; Soc. Sci. Source; Soc. Sci. Cit. Index [Full Cov.]; Soc. Sci. Index; Soc. Sci. Index Fulltext (Sept. 1988-) [Full Txt.]; Stat. Theory Method Abstr.; Telebase; World Agric. Econ. Rural Sociol. Abstr.; Zentralbl. Math. Ihre Grenzgeb.

LC H62.A1 R47 **ISSN** 0747-9662
DD 300/.72073 US
CCC
CODEN JEMEEZ

JOURNAL OF ECONOMIC AND SOCIAL MEASUREMENT. See Business and Economics-Abstracting, Bibliographies and Statistics.

LC HD28 .J594 **ISSN** 0167-2681
DD 330/.05 NE
CCC
CODEN JEBOD9
Pr Rev.

JOURNAL OF ECONOMIC BEHAVIOR & ORGANIZATION. [J. econ. behav. organ.]. **VFOAT** Journal of Economic Behavior and Organization. Vol. 1, No. 1 (Mar. 1980)-. Academic Scholarly Publication. English. Nine times a year (3 volumes). $902.00. Elsevier Science Publishers BV, PO Box 211, 1000 AE Amsterdam Netherlands. **Tel** 011 31 20 4853641, 011 31 20 4853642, FAX 011 31 20 4853598. **ED** R H Day, S G Winter, and Timur Kuran. **Bk Rev. Ad Acc.** ctrl circ. available on microfilm and microfiche from University Microfilms International (UMI); available on an online database from Elsevier Electronic Subscriptions (EES). Documents available from The Genuine Article, UMI Article Clearinghouse, Ask*IEEE.
Desc: Devoted to theoretical and empirical research concerning economic decision, organization and behavior. Its specific purpose is to foster an improved understanding of how human cognitive, computational and characteristics influence the working of economic organizations and market economies.
Ind/Abst ABI/INFORM Glob. Ed.; ABI/INFORM [Computer File] (Sept. 1984-); Acad. Search; Bus. Index (1985-); Bus. Source Plus; Bus. Source; Contents Recent Econ. J.; Curr. Cit.; Curr. Contents Soc. Behav. Sci.; Econ. Lit. Index; EP Collect.; Gen. BusinessFile (1985-); Gen. Period. Index (1985-); Homework Help.; INSPEC (Jan. 1990-); J. Econ. Lit.; MasterFile FullTEXT 1000; MasterFile FullTEXT 350; MasterFile FullTEXT 650; MasterFile FullTEXT (July 1993-); Math. Rev.; OCLC; Res. Alert [Full Cov.]; Soc. Sci. Cit. Index [Full Cov.]; Telebase.

TU

JOURNAL OF ECONOMIC COOPERATION AMONG ISLAMIC COUNTRIES. **Added/Corp** Statistical, Economic, and Social Research and Training Centre for Islamic Countries. (1979)-. English (French and Arabic). Four times a year. $60.00. Journal of Economic / Turkey, Ataturk Bulvari 215, Ankara Turkey. **ED** Sadi Cindoruk. Index available. **Bk Rev. Ad Acc. Circ:** 2,500.
Desc: Statistical, economic and social studies and research aimed at promoting economic and technical cooperation among the 45 members of the organization of the Islamic Conference.
Ind/Abst Econ. Lit. Index; Index Islam. Lit.; Maize Abstr.; Rural Dev. Abstr.; Middle East J.; Wheat Barley Trit. Abstr.; World Agric. Econ. Rural Sociol. Abstr.

LC HC **ISSN** 0165-1889
DD 330 NE
CCC
CODEN JEDCDH
Pr Rev.

JOURNAL OF ECONOMIC DYNAMICS & CONTROL. [J. econ. dyn. control]. **VFOAT** Economic Dynamics & Control. **VAT** Journal of Economic Dynamics and Control. Vol. 1 (Feb. 1979)-. Academic Scholarly Publication. English. Ten times a year. $899.00. Elsevier Science Publishers BV, PO Box 211, 1000 AE Amsterdam Netherlands. **Tel** 011 31 20 4853641, 011 31 20 4853642, FAX 011 31 20 4853598. **ED** Masanao Aoki and Stephen J Turnovsky. **Bk Rev. Ad Acc.** available on microfilm and microfiche from University Microfilms International (UMI); available on an online database from Elsevier Electronic Subscriptions (EES). Documents available from The Genuine Article, UMI Article Clearinghouse, Ask*IEEE.
Desc: Provides an outlet for the publication of papers on economic dynamics and on economics and control theory. The journal encourages the submission of both theoretical and applications papers.
Ind/Abst ABI/INFORM Glob. Ed.; ABI/INFORM [Computer File] (Feb. 1981-); Abstr. AIT Rep. Publ. Energy; Acad. Search; Bus. Index (1985-); Bus. Source Plus; Bus. Source; Contents Recent Econ. J.; Curr. Cit.; Curr. Contents Soc. Behav. Sci.; Econ. Lit. Index; EP Collect.; Gen. BusinessFile (1985-); Gen. Period. Index (1985-); Homework Help.; INFO-SOUTH Abstr.; INSPEC (Feb. 1980-); J. Econ. Lit.; Leis., Rec., Tour. Abstr.; Mag. Search; MasterFile FullTEXT 1000; MasterFile FullTEXT 350; MasterFile FullTEXT 650; MasterFile FullTEXT (July 1993-); Math. Rev.; OCLC; Res. Alert [Full Cov.]; Rural Dev. Abstr.; Soc. Sci. Cit. Index [Full Cov.]; Telebase; World Agric. Econ. Rural Sociol. Abstr.; Zentralbl. Math. Ihre Grenzgeb.

LC H62.5.U5 J6 **ISSN** 0022-0485
DD 330/.07 US
CCC
Pr Rev.

JOURNAL OF ECONOMIC EDUCATION, THE. [J. econ. educ.]. **Added/Corp** Helen Dwight Reid Educational Foundation. Joint Council on Economic Education. Vol. 1 (Fall 1969)-. Periodical. English. Four times a year. $75.00. Heldref Publications, 1319 Eighteenth Street Northwest, Washington DC 20036-1802. **Tel** (202)296-6267, (800)365-9753, FAX (202)296-5149. **ED** William E Becker. **Bk Rev. Ad Acc. Circ:** 1,147. available on microfilm and microfiche from University Microfilms International (UMI). Documents available from The Genuine Article.
Desc: Promotes the teaching and learning of economics in colleges, high schools, and elementary schools. Features important research in economic education, stimulating innovations in teaching, and timely professional information, as well as newly expanded coverage of current economic issues by noteworthy contributors.
Ind/Abst Bus. Educ. Index; Contents Pages Educ.; Curr. Contents Soc. Behav. Sci.; Curr. Index J. Educ.; Econ. Lit. Index; Educ. Index; Educ. Adm. Abstr.; EP Collect.; High. Educ. Abstr. (1985-); Homework Help.; J. Econ. Lit.; MasterFile FullTEXT 1000; MasterFile FullTEXT 350; MasterFile FullTEXT 650; MasterFile FullTEXT; OCLC; PAIS Int. Print (1991-?); Res. Alert [Full Cov.]; Soc. Sci. Cit. Index [Full Cov.]; Telebase.

LC HC26 **ISSN** 1381-4338
DD 330.1 NE

•**JOURNAL OF ECONOMIC GROWTH.** (1996)-. Academic Scholarly Publication. English. Four times a year. $284.00. Kluwer Academic Publishers, Postbus 322, 3300 AH Dordrecht The Netherlands. **Tel** 011 31 78 524400, FAX 011 31 78 183273, telex 20083.

LC HB1 .J64 **ISSN** 0021-3624
DD 332 US
CODEN JECIAR
Pr Rev.

JOURNAL OF ECONOMIC ISSUES. [J. econ. issues]. **Added/Corp** Association for Evolutionary Economics. **VFOAT** JEE. Journal of Economic Issues; JEI. Vol. 1 (June 1967)-. Periodical. English. Four times a year. $40.00. Association of Evolutionary Economics, University of Nebraska, Department of Economics, Lincoln NE 68588. **Tel** (402)472-3867. **ED** Marc R. Tool. **Bk Rev. Ad Acc. Circ:** 2,000 (ctrl). available on microfilm and microfiche from University Microfilms International (UMI). Documents available from The Genuine Article, UMI Article Clearinghouse.
Desc: Covers the integration of social and political theory into economics.
Ind/Abst ABI/INFORM Glob. Ed.; ABI/INFORM [Computer File] (March 1980-); Acad. Abstr.; Acad. Search; Am. Bibliogr. Slavic East Europ. Stud.; Arts Humanit. Citation Index [Select. Cov.]; Bus. Index (1985-); Bus. Period. Index; Bus. Source Plus; Bus. Source; Contents Pages Manage.; Curr. Cit.; Curr. Contents Soc. Behav. Sci.; Econ. Lit. Index; EP Collect.; Expand. Acad. Index (1984-); Gen. BusinessFile (1985-); Gen. Period. Index (1985-); Homework Help.; INFO-SOUTH Abstr.; Int. Bibliogr. Sociol.; Int. Labour Doc.; J. Econ. Lit.; LABORDOC; Mag. Search; MasterFile FullTEXT 1000; MasterFile FullTEXT 350; MasterFile FullTEXT 650; MasterFile FullTEXT (Jan. 1992-); Middle East Abstr. Index; Newsp. Period. Abstr. (1991-); OCLC; PAIS Int. Print (1991-); Pollut. Abstr. Indexes; Res. Alert [Full Cov.]; Soc. Plann. Policy Dev. Abstr.; Soc. Sci. Source; Soc. Sci. Cit. Index [Full Cov.]; Soc. Sci. Index; Soc. Sci. Index Fulltext (Dec. 1988-) [Full Txt.]; Sociol. Abstr.; Telebase; UMI ABI/Inform--Bus. Period. Ondisc (Mar. 1987-) [Full Txt.]; U.S. Polit. Sci. Doc. (19??-); Wilson Bus. Abstr.

LC HB1 .J6 **ISSN** 0022-0515
DD 330 US
CODEN JECLB3
Pr Rev.

JOURNAL OF ECONOMIC LITERATURE. See Business and Economics-Abstracting, Bibliographies and Statistics.

LC HB131 .J68 **ISSN** 1350-178X
UK

•**JOURNAL OF ECONOMIC METHODOLOGY.** **Added/Corp** International Network for Economic Method. Vol. 1, No. 1 (June 1994)-. Periodical. English. Two times a year. $100.00. Routledge, 11 New Fetter Lane, London EC4P 4EE United Kingdom. **Tel** 011 44 171 5839855, FAX 011 44 171 5830701. **(Subscription address:** International Thomson Publishing Services Ltd., North Way Andover, Hampshire SP10 5BE United Kingdom. **Tel** 011 44 1264 332424.) ***Continues** Methodus.*

LC HB1 .J643 **ISSN** 0895-3309
DD 330/.05 US
Pr Rev.

JOURNAL OF ECONOMIC PERSPECTIVES, THE. (THE JOURNAL OF ECONOMIC PERSPECTIVES.). [J. econ. perspect.]. **Added/Corp** American Economic Association. **VFOAT** Economic Perspectives. Vol. 1, No. 1 (Summer 1987)-. Periodical. English. Four times a year. Free with membership. American Economic Association / Tennessee, 2014 Broadway, Suite 305, Nashville TN 37203-2418. **Tel** (615)322-2595, FAX (615)343-7590. available on microfilm and microfiche from University Microfilms International (UMI). Documents available from The Genuine Article, UMI Article Clearinghouse.
Ind/Abst Acad. Abstr.; Acad. Ind. [Computer File] (1992-); Acad. Search; Am. Hist. Life (1987-); Am. Bibliogr. Slavic East Europ. Stud.; Bus. Period. Index; Bus. Source Plus; Bus. Source; Curr. Cit.; Curr. Contents Soc. Behav. Sci.; Econ. Lit. Index (19??-); EP Collect.; Expand. Acad. Index (1992-); Homework Help.; INFO-SOUTH Abstr.; Int. Bibliogr. Sociol.; Int. Labour Doc.; J. Econ. Lit.; J. Plan. Lit.; LABORDOC; Mag. Search; MasterFile FullTEXT 1000; MasterFile FullTEXT 350; MasterFile FullTEXT 650; MasterFile FullTEXT (Jan. 1992-); Newsp. Period. Abstr. (1992-); OCLC; PAIS Int. Print (1991-); Res. Alert [Full Cov.]; Soc. Sci. Source; Soc. Sci. Cit. Index [Full Cov.]; Telebase; Wilson Bus. Abstr.

LC HB74.P8 J68 **ISSN** 0167-4870
DD 330/.01/9 NE
CCC
Pr Rev.

JOURNAL OF ECONOMIC PSYCHOLOGY. [J. econ. psychol.]. **Added/Corp** European Research in Economic Psychology (Society). **VFOAT** Economic Psychology. Vol. 1 No. 1 (Mar. 1981)-. Academic Scholarly Publication. English (French). Six times a year. $326.00. Elsevier Science Publishers BV, PO Box 211, 1000 AE Amsterdam Netherlands. **Tel** 011 31 20 4853641, 011 31 20 4853642, FAX 011 31 20 4853598. **ED** S.E.G. Lea. **Bk Rev. Ad Acc.** available on microfilm and microfiche from University Microfilms International (UMI); available on an online database from Elsevier Electronic Subscriptions (EES). Documents available from The Genuine Article, UMI Article Clearinghouse.
Desc: Presents research that improves the understanding of behavioral, especially socio-psychological, aspects of economic phenomena and processes.
Ind/Abst ABI/INFORM Glob. Ed.; ABI/INFORM [Computer File] (Dec. 1984-); Acad. Search; Bus. Index (1985-); Bus. Source Plus; Bus. Source; Contents Recent Econ. J.; Curr. Cit.; Curr. Contents Soc. Behav. Sci.; Econ. Lit. Index (1981-); EP Collect.; Gen. BusinessFile (1985-); Gen. Period. Index (1985-); Highw. Res. Abstr.; Homework Help.; INFO-SOUTH Abstr.; Int. Bibliogr. Sociol.; J. Econ. Lit.; Mag. Search; MasterFile FullTEXT 1000; MasterFile FullTEXT 350; MasterFile FullTEXT 650; MasterFile FullTEXT (July 1993-); OCLC; Psychol. Abstr. (1981-); PsycINFO; PsycLit; Res. Alert [Full Cov.]; Rev. Agric. Entomol.; Soc. Sci. Cit. Index [Full Cov.]; Telebase; World Agric. Econ. Rural Sociol. Abstr.

LC HB1 .J644 **ISSN** 0144-3585
DD 330/.05 UK
CCC
Pr Rev.

JOURNAL OF ECONOMIC STUDIES (BRADFORD). (JOURNAL OF ECONOMIC STUDIES.). [J. econ. stud.]. Vol. 1, No. 1 (May 1974)-. Periodical. English. Six times a year. $3289.00. MCB University Press, 60 62 Toller Lane, Bradford, West Yorkshire BD8 9BY United Kingdom. **Tel** 011 44 1274 785280, FAX 011 44 1274 785200, telex 51317-MCBUNI-G. **(Subscription address:** MCB University Press / US and Canada Subscriptions, PO Box 10812, Birmingham AL 35201-0812. **Tel** (205)995-1567, (800)633-4931, FAX (205)995-1588.) **ED** Frank H Stephen. **Bk Rev.** Documents available from UMI Article Clearinghouse. ***Continues** Economic Studies (Glasgow, Scotland).*
Desc: Articles deal with such issues as developments in the international monetary system, urban bias in developing countries, dependency theory, labor and regional economics.
Ind/Abst ABI/INFORM Glob. Ed.; ABI/INFORM [Computer File] (1983-); Acad. Search; Asia.-Pac. Econ. Lit.; Bus. Index (1985-); Bus. Source Plus; Bus. Source; Curr. Cit.; Econ. Lit. Index (1974-); EP Collect.; Gen. BusinessFile (1985-); Gen. Period. Index (1985-); Geogr. Abstr. Human Geogr.; Homework Help.; INFO-SOUTH Abstr.; Int. Dev. Abstr.; J. Econ. Lit.; J. Plan. Lit.; Leis., Rec., Tour. Abstr.; Mag. Search; MasterFile FullTEXT

1000; MasterFile FullTEXT 350; MasterFile FullTEXT 650; MasterFile FullTEXT (Jan. 1993-); Middle East Abstr. Index; OCLC; PAIS Int. Print (1991-); Rural Dev. Abstr.; Telebase; World Agric. Econ. Rural Sociol. Abstr.

LC HB1 .J645 **ISSN** 0022-0531
DD 330/.01/82 US
CCC
CODEN JECTAQ
Pr Rev.

JOURNAL OF ECONOMIC THEORY. [J. econ. theory]. Vol. 1 (June 1969)-. Academic Scholarly Publication. English. Eight times a year. $817.00. Academic Press Inc., 6277 Sea Harbor Drive, Orlando FL 32887. **Tel** (800)543-9534, (407)345-4100, FAX (407)352-3445. **ED** Karl Shell. cum. index. Documents available from The Genuine Article, UMI Article Clearinghouse.
Desc: Publishes original research on economic theory, emphasizing the theoretical analysis of economic models, including the study of related mathematical techniques.
Ind/Abst ABI/INFORM Glob. Ed.; Acad. Search; Bus. Index (1985-); Bus. Source Plus; Bus. Source; Contents Recent Econ. J.; Curr. Cit.; Curr. Contents Soc. Behav. Sci.; Econ. Lit. Index; EP Collect.; Expand. Acad. Index (1984-); Gen. BusinessFile (1985-); Gen. Period. Index (1985-); Homework Help.; INFO-SOUTH Abstr.; J. Econ. Lit.; Mag. Search; MasterFile FullTEXT 1000; MasterFile FullTEXT 350; MasterFile FullTEXT 650; MasterFile FullTEXT (July 1994-); Math. Rev.; Newsp. Period. Abstr. (1992-); OCLC; Pollut. Abstr. Indexes; Res. Alert [Full Cov.]; Soc. Sci. Source; Soc. Sci. Cit. Index [Full Cov.]; Soc. Sci. Index; Soc. Sci. Index Fulltext (Oct. 1988-) [Full Txt.]; Telebase; West. Hist. Q.; Zentralbl. Math. Ihre Grenzgeb.

LC HB1 .M56a **ISSN** 0361-6576
DD 330/.05 US

JOURNAL OF ECONOMICS. Main/Corp Missouri Valley Economic Association. Vol. 1 (1975)-. English. Two times a year (Spring & Fall). $32.00. Missouri Valley Economic Association, University of South Dakota, Department of Economics, Vermilion SD 57069. **Tel** (605)677-5552. **(Subscription address:** Journal of Economics, c/o Dr. G. Miller Morehead, State University 222, Combs UPO 1280, Morehead KY 40351.) Documents available from The Genuine Article.
Ind/Abst Acad. Search; Bus. Source Plus; Bus. Source; EP Collect.; Homework Help.; MasterFile FullTEXT 1000; MasterFile FullTEXT 350; MasterFile FullTEXT 650; MasterFile FullTEXT; OCLC; Res. Alert [Full Cov.]; Telebase.

LC HC101 .P452 **ISSN** 0148-6195
DD 330./05 US
CCC
CODEN JEBUDR
Pr Rev.

JOURNAL OF ECONOMICS AND BUSINESS. [J. econ. bus.]. **Added/Corp** Temple University. School of Business Administration. Vol. 25, No. 1 (Fall 1972)-. Academic Scholarly Publication. English. Five times a year (1 volume). $252.00. Elsevier Science Publishing Company Inc, Madison Square Station, PO Box 882, New York NY 10159-0882. **Tel** (212)633-3950, FAX (212)633-3990. **ED** Robert H Deans. **Ad Acc.** available on microfilm and microfiche from University Microfilms International (UMI); available on an online database from Elsevier Electronic Subscriptions (EES). Documents available from The Genuine Article, UMI Article Clearinghouse, Documents on Demand. ***Continues*** *Economic and Business Bulletin.*
Desc: Provides a prominent forum for the publication of scholarly research in applied economics, finance, and related business disciplines which focus on the domestic and international aspects of business and society.
Ind/Abst ABI/INFORM Glob. Ed.; ABI/INFORM [Computer File] (Spring 1972-); Acad. Search; Bus. Index (1985-); Bus. Period. Index; Bus. Source Plus; Bus. Source; Coal Abstr.; Contents Recent Econ. J.; Curr. Cit.; Curr. Contents Soc. Behav. Sci.; Econ. Lit. Index (1974-); Energy Inf. Abstr.; Energy Res. Abstr. (Aug. 1977-); Environ. Abstr.; EP Collect.; Gen. BusinessFile (1985-); Gen. Period. Index (1985-); Homework Help.; INFO-SOUTH Abstr.; INIS Atomindex [Micro.]; Int. Exec.; J. Econ. Lit.; J. Plan. Lit.; Mag. Search; MasterFile FullTEXT 1000; MasterFile FullTEXT 350; MasterFile FullTEXT 650; MasterFile FullTEXT (July 1993-); OCLC; PAIS Int. Print (1991-?); Person. Manage. Abstr.; Res. Alert [Full Cov.]; Soc. Sci. Cit. Index [Full Cov.]; Telebase; Wilson Bus. Abstr.

LC HC **ISSN** 0931-8658
DD 330 AU
CCC
Pr Rev.

JOURNAL OF ECONOMICS (VIENNA, AUSTRIA). (JOURNAL OF ECONOMICS.). **VFOAT** Zeitschrift fur Nationalokonomie. Vol. 46, No. 1 (1986)-. Periodical. English. Six times a year. $540.00. Springer-Verlag Vienna, Sachsenplatz 4 6, PO Box 89, A-1201 Vienna Austria. **Tel** 011 43 1 33024150, FAX 011 43 1 330242665. **(Subscription address:** Springer-Verlag New York Inc. / North America, PO Box 2485, Journal Fulfillment, Secaucus NJ 07096. **Tel** (201)348-4033, (800)777-4643, FAX (201)348-4505.**)** **ED** W. Weber. ***Continues*** *Zeitschrift fur Nationalokonomie, 0044-3158.*

Desc: Specializes in mathematical economic theory. The editorial centers on microeconomic theory, but also publishes papers on macroeconomic topics.
Ind/Abst Econ. Lit. Index; J. Econ. Lit.; Soc. Sci. Cit. Index [Full Cov.]; Zentralbl. Math. Ihre Grenzgeb.

LC HF1101 .J6 **ISSN** 0883-2323
DD 650/.07/1073 US
Pr Rev.

JOURNAL OF EDUCATION FOR BUSINESS. [J. educ. bus.]. **VFOAT** Education for Business. Vol. 61, No. 1 (Oct. 1985)-. Periodical. English. Six times a year. $56.00. Heldref Publications, 1319 Eighteenth Street Northwest, Washington DC 20036-1802. **Tel** (202)296-6267, (800)365-9753, FAX (202)296-5149. **ED** Marianne D'Onofrio, Karen A. Fortin, and James L. Morrison. **Bk Rev. Ad Acc. Circ:** 4,500 (ctrl). available on microfilm and microfiche from University Microfilms International (UMI). Documents available from UMI Article Clearinghouse. ***Continues*** *Journal of Business Education, 0021-9444.*
Desc: Features practical articles on business fundamentals, career education, consumer economics, distributive education, management, trends in communication, and rapid changes in computers and high technology. Covers visual aid, new books, and research to create an information network for all business trainers and educators.
Ind/Abst Acad. Abstr. Full Text Elite; Acad. Abstr.; Acad. Search; Bus. Educ. Index; Bus. Source Plus; Bus. Source; Contents Pages Educ.; Curr. Cit.; Curr. Index J. Educ.; Educ. Index; Educ. Adm. Abstr.; Educ. Technol. Abstr.; EP Collect.; Homework Help.; Hum. Resour. Abstr.; INFO-SOUTH Abstr.; Int. Labour Doc.; Mag. Artic. Summar. Elite; Mag. Artic. Summar. Select; Mag. Artic. Summar. CD-ROM; Mag. Search; MasterFile FullTEXT 1000; MasterFile FullTEXT 350; MasterFile FullTEXT 650; MasterFile FullTEXT (July 1990-) [Full Txt.]; Med. Rev. Dig.; Newsp. Period. Abstr. (1992-); OCLC; PAIS Int. Print (1991-); Pub. Lib. FullTEXT; Tech. Educ. Train. Abstr.; Telebase; Vocat. Search.

LC HB615 .J7 **ISSN** 0971-3557
DD 658.4/21/095405 II

JOURNAL OF ENTREPRENEURSHIP, THE. Vol. 1, No. 1 (Jan.-June 1992)-. Periodical. English. Two times a year (Mar. and Sept.). $70.00. Sage India, Sage Publications Inc., India Private Limited, PO Box 4215, New Delhi 110 048 India.
Desc: Provides an avenue for the publication of original contributions, both conceptual and empirical, and serve as a vehicle for the fast-growing literature on entrepreneurship in developing countries, particularly in South Asia.
Ind/Abst Hum. Resour. Abstr.

ISSN 1070-4965
DD 338 US

JOURNAL OF ENVIRONMENT & DEVELOPMENT, THE. [J. environ. dev.]. **Added/Corp** University of California, San Diego. Graduate School of International Relations and Pacific Studies. **VFOAT** Journal of Environment and Development; E & D. Vol. 1, No. 1 (Summer 1992)-. Periodical. English. Two times a year. $50.00. University of California San Diego, Graduate School of International Relations & Pacific Studies, 9500 Gilman Drive, Mail Code 0519, La Jolla CA 92093-0519. **Tel** (619)534-7617. **ED** Daniel L. Nielson. **Bk Rev. Ad Acc.** Documents available from Documents on Demand.
Ind/Abst Environ. Abstr.

LC HC79.P55 J68 **ISSN** 0095-0696
DD 301.31/05 US
CCC
CODEN JEEMDI
Pr Rev.

JOURNAL OF ENVIRONMENTAL ECONOMICS AND MANAGEMENT. See Environmental Issues-Pollution and Waste Management.

LC HB1.A1 J68 **ISSN** 0936-9937
DD 330 GW
CCC
CODEN JEECEN
Pr Rev.

JOURNAL OF EVOLUTIONARY ECONOMICS. VFOAT Evolutionary Economics; JEE. Vol. 1, No. 1 (1991)-. Periodical. English. Four times a year. $295.00. Springer-Verlag GmbH & Company KG, Heidelberger Platz 3, D-14197 Berlin Germany. **Tel** 011 49 30 8207223, FAX 011 49 30 8214091, telex 183 319 SPBLN D. **(Subscription address:** Springer-Verlag New York Inc. / North America, PO Box 2485, Journal Fulfillment, Secaucus NJ 07096. **Tel** (201)348-4033, (800)777-4643, FAX (201)348-4505.**)** **ED** H Hanusch, M Perlman. **Bk Rev. Ad Acc.** available in microform from University Microfilms International (UMI).
Desc: Aims to provide an international forum for a new approach to economics. Publishes articles with emphasis on dynamics, changing structures (including technologies, institutions, beliefs and behaviours) and desequilibrium processes with an evolutionary perspective (innovation, selection, imitation, etc.).
Ind/Abst Econ. Lit. Index.

ISSN 1351-0363
UK

•JOURNAL OF FAR EASTERN BUSINESS. Vol. 1 (1994)-. English. Four times a year. $145.00. Frank Cass & Company Ltd., Newbury House, 890-900 Eastern Avenue, Ilford Essex IG2 7HH United Kingdom. **Tel** 011 44 181 5998866, FAX 011 44 181 5990984, telex 897719.

LC H61.4 .J68 **ISSN** 0277-6693
DD 003/.2/05 UK
CCC
CODEN JOFODV
Pr Rev.

JOURNAL OF FORECASTING. See Sociology.

LC HC **ISSN** 0898-5510
DD 330 US
Pr Rev.

JOURNAL OF FORENSIC ECONOMICS. [J. forensic econ.]. **Added/Corp** National Association of Forensic Economists (U.S.). **VFOAT** JFE. Vol. 1, No. 1 (Sept. 1987)-. Periodical. English. Three times a year (Jan./Feb., May/June, Sept./Oct.). $100.00. National Association of Forensic Economists, PO Box 30067, Kansas City MO 64112. **Tel** (816)235-2833, FAX (816)235-5263. **ED** John O. Ward. Index available. cum. index. **Bk Rev**, (Qty: 2). **Ad Acc. Acid Free. Circ:** 750. available on CD-ROM.
Desc: An academic/ professional journal that features original articles on economic research in areas of protection of lost earnings and services, vocational rehabilitation business evaluation, medical economics and antitrust.
Ind/Abst Econ. Lit. Index.

ISSN 1053-7287
DD 337 US
Pr Rev.

JOURNAL OF GLOBAL BUSINESS (HARRISONBURG, VA.). (JOURNAL OF GLOBAL BUSINESS : JGB.). [J. glob. bus.]. **Added/Corp** Association for Global Business. **VFOAT** JGB. Vol. 1, No. 1 (Summer 1990)-. Periodical. English. Two times a year (Spring & Fall). $30.00. Association for Global Business, PO Box 1381, Harrisonburg VA 22801. **Tel** (703)568-3079, (703)433-7403, FAX (703)568-3299. **ED** Faramarz Damanpour. **Bk Rev. Ad Acc. Circ:** 2,000.

LC HC **ISSN** 0167-6296
DD 330 NE
CCC
NLM W1; JO67BF
Pr Rev.

JOURNAL OF HEALTH ECONOMICS. [J. health econ.]. Vol. 1, No. 1 (May 1982)-. Academic Scholarly Publication. English. Six times a year. $466.00. Elsevier Science Publishers BV, PO Box 211, 1000 AE Amsterdam Netherlands. **Tel** 011 31 20 4853641, 011 31 20 4853642, FAX 011 31 20 4853598. **ED** Joseph P Newhouse and A J Culyer. **Ad Acc.** available on microfilm and microfiche from University Microfilms International (UMI); available on an online database from Elsevier Electronic Subscriptions (EES). Documents available from The Genuine Article, UMI Article Clearinghouse.
Desc: Seeks articles especially related to the economics of health and medical care.
Ind/Abst ABI/INFORM Glob. Ed.; ABI/INFORM [Computer File] (Dec. 1984-); Appl. Soc. Sci. Index Abstr.; Contents Recent Econ. J.; Curr. Cit.; Curr. Contents Soc. Behav. Sci.; Econ. Lit. Index; EMBASE; EP Collect.; Gen. BusinessFile (1992-); Health Plan. Adminis.; Health Serv. Abstr.; Health Source Plus; Health Source; Homework Help.; Hosp. Health Admin. Index; Hum. Resour. Abstr. (?-?); Int. Bibliogr. Sociol.; J. Econ. Lit.; MasterFile FullTEXT 1000; MasterFile FullTEXT 350; MasterFile FullTEXT 650; MasterFile FullTEXT; Res. Alert [Full Cov.]; Soc. Sci. Cit. Index [Full Cov.]; Telebase; Trop. Dis. Bull.

LC HD7293.Z9 J68 **ISSN** 1051-1377
DD 333 US
CCC

JOURNAL OF HOUSING ECONOMICS. See Housing and Urban Development.

LC HC431 .J66
DD 330/.0954/05 II

JOURNAL OF INDIAN SCHOOL OF POLITICAL ECONOMY. Added/Corp Indian School of Political Economy. **VFOAT** Journal of the Indian School of Political Economy. Vol. 1, No. 1 (Jan.-June 1989)-. Periodical. English. Four times a year. $40.00. Indian School of Political Economy, Pune India. **(Subscription address:** Prints India, 11 Darya Ganj, New Delhi 110002 India. **Tel** 011 91 11 3268645, FAX 011 91 11 3275542, telex 31-61087 PRIN-IN.**)**

ISSN 0143-084X
UK
CCC
TITLE CHANGE

JOURNAL OF INDUSTRIAL AFFAIRS. [J. ind. aff.]. (1973)-(1995). Periodical. English. Carfax Publishing Company, PO Box 25, Abingdon, Oxfordshire OX14 3UE United Kingdom. **Tel** 011 44 1235 555335,

FAX 011 44 1235 553559, telex 817484. Index available. ***Continued by*** *Journal of Applied Management Studies.*
Ind/Abst Br. Humanit. Index.

LC H5 .Z4 **ISSN** 0932-4569
GW
CCC

JOURNAL OF INSTITUTIONAL AND THEORETICAL ECONOMICS : JITE. See Social Sciences.

LC HB1 .J646 **ISSN** 0260-1079
DD 330/.05 UK
CCC

JOURNAL OF INTERDISCIPLINARY ECONOMICS.
Vol. 1, No. 1 (1985)-. Periodical. English. Four times a year. £89.00. AB Academic Publishers, PO Box 42 Bicester, Oxfordshire OX6 7NW United Kingdom. **Tel** 011 44 1869 320949, FAX 011 44 1869 320949.
Ind/Abst Am. Hist. Life (1985-1987); Appl. Soc. Sci. Index Abstr.; Curr. Cit.; Int. Bibliogr. Sociol.

LC HC59.72.E44 J68 **ISSN** 0954-1748
DD 338.9/009172/405 UK
CCC
CODEN JINDEV

Pr Rev.

JOURNAL OF INTERNATIONAL DEVELOPMENT.
[J. int. dev.]. **Added/Corp** University of Manchester. Institute for Development Policy and Management. International Development Centre (University of Manchester). Vol. 1, No. 1 (Jan. 1989)-. Periodical. English. Six times a year (icludes two special issues). $345.00. John Wiley & Sons Ltd., Baffins Lane, Chichester, West Sussex PO19 1UD United Kingdom. **Tel** 011 44 1243 779777, FAX 011 44 1243 776128 BTG:JWP001, telex 86290 WIBOOKG. **(Subscription address:** John Wiley & Sons, Inc. / Philadelphia, PO Box 7247, Philadelphia PA 19170. **Tel** (212)850-6645, (800)225-5945.**) ED** Paul Mosley and John Harriss. available on microfilm and microfiche from University Microfilms International (UMI). ***Continues*** *Manchester Papers on Development (1985), 0260-8235.*
Desc: The purpose is make available the results of development related research.
Ind/Abst Curr. Cit.; Geogr. Abstr. Human Geogr.; Int. Bibliogr. Sociol.; LABORDOC; Maize Abstr.; PAIS Int. Print (1991-); Plant Genet. Resour. Abstr.; Rural Dev. Abstr.; Soc. Plann. Policy Dev. Abstr.; World Agric. Econ. Rural Sociol. Abstr.

UK
TITLE CHANGE

JOURNAL OF INTERNATIONAL SECURITIES MARKETS, THE.
(Autumn 1987)-(19??). Periodical. English. IFR Publishing Ltd., Aldgate House, 33 Aldgate High Street, London EC3N 1DL United Kingdom. **Tel** 011 44 171 369 7536, FAX 011 44 171 369 7395, telex 889365/8953051 IFRPUBG. **(Subscription address:** IFR Publishing, 90 Broad Street, Second Floor, New York NY 10004. **)** ***Continued by*** *Capital Markets Strategies.*
Ind/Abst Contents Pages Manage. (?-?).

LC HC462.9 .J68 **ISSN** 0285-9556
DD 330.952/005 JA
CCC

Pr Rev.

JOURNAL OF JAPANESE TRADE & INDUSTRY.
[J. Jap. trade ind.]. **Added/Corp** Japan Economic Foundation. **VFOAT** Journal of Japanese Trade and Industry. Vol. 1, No. 1 (Jan. 1982)-. Periodical. English. Six times a year. $65.00. Japan Economic Foundation, 11th Floor Fukoku Seimei Building, 2-2-2 Uchisaiwai-cho Chiyoda-ku, Tokyo 100 Japan. **Tel** 03-3580-9291/9728. **(Subscription address:** Maruzen Company Ltd., PO Box 5050, Import & Export Department, Tokyo 100 31 Japan. **Tel** 011 81 3 32789224.**) ED** Takashi Suetsune. **Bk Rev. Ad Acc. Circ:** 30,000. available on microfilm from University Microfilms International (UMI). Documents available from UMI Article Clearinghouse, Documents on Demand.
Desc: Presents a snapshot of the spectrum of economic issues in Japan. Clearly written and focused articles help readers understand and deepen their perception of the current state of the nation's economy.
Ind/Abst ABI/INFORM Glob. Ed.; Asia.-Pac. Econ. Lit.; Environ. Abstr.; F&S Index Plus Text, Int. [Select. Cov.]; Int. Labour Doc.; LABORDOC; Manage. Market. Abstr.; PROMT; Text. Technol. Dig.

LC PB5 .J68 **ISSN** 8755-0504
DD 418/.007 US
Pr Rev.

JOURNAL OF LANGUAGE FOR INTERNATIONAL BUSINESS, THE. See Linguistics.

LC HC **ISSN** 0022-2186
DD 330.5 US
CODEN JLLEA7

Pr Rev.

JOURNAL OF LAW & ECONOMICS, THE. See Law.

LC K10 .O8734 **ISSN** 8756-6222
DD 349.746/05 347.46005 US
CCC

JOURNAL OF LAW, ECONOMICS & ORGANIZATION. See Law.

LC K10 .O87347 **ISSN** 1054-3023
DD 346.7303/23 347.306323 US
CODEN JLECE4

Pr Rev.

JOURNAL OF LEGAL ECONOMICS.
[J. leg. econ.]. **Added/Corp** American Academy of Economic and Financial Experts. **VFOAT** Legal Economics. Vol. 1, No. 1 (Mar. 1991)-. Periodical. English. Three times a year (Mar., July, Dec.). $60.00. American Academy Economics Financial Experts, University of North Alabama, PO Box 5077, Florence AL 35623. **Tel** (205)760-4144, FAX (205)760-4170. **ED** Michael W. Butler Ph.D. cum. index. **Ad Acc. Circ:** 350.
Desc: Theoretical and practical articles of interest to attorneys and to economists that serve as expert witnesses in a wide variety of legal cases.

ISSN 1078-3873
US

•JOURNAL OF LEGAL STUDIES IN BUSINESS.
Added/Corp Southeastern Academy of Legal Studies in Business. (1995)-. Periodical. English. Two times a year. Free on request. Southeast Academy of Legal Studies, West Carolina University, College of Business, Cullowhee NC 28723. **Tel** (704)227-7401. ***Continues*** *Southeastern Journal of Legal Studies in Business, 1078-4209.*

LC HB1 .J67 **ISSN** 0164-0704
DD 339/.05 US
CCC

Pr Rev.

JOURNAL OF MACROECONOMICS.
[J. macroecon.]. Vol. 1 (Winter 1979)-. Periodical. English. Four times a year (Jan., Apr., July, Oct.). $75.00. Louisiana State University Press, PO Box 25053, Baton Rouge LA 70894. **Tel** (504)388-8271, FAX (504)388-6461. Index available (included in final issue of each volume.). **Ad Acc. Circ:** 900. available on microfilm and microfiche from University Microfilms International (UMI). Documents available from The Genuine Article, UMI Article Clearinghouse.
Desc: Surveys the behavior of the aggregate economy. The determination of the GNP, price level and its rate of change, and the determination of the level of employment and unemployment.
Ind/Abst ABI/INFORM Glob. Ed.; ABI/INFORM [Computer File] (Spring 1979-)(spring 1979-); Contents Recent Econ. J.; Curr. Cit.; Curr. Contents Soc. Behav. Sci.; Econ. Lit. Index; Gen. BusinessFile (1992-); J. Econ. Lit.; Res. Alert [Full Cov.]; Soc. Sci. Cit. Index [Full Cov.].

LC HB135 .J68 **ISSN** 0304-4068
DD 330/.01/51 NE
CCC
CODEN JMECDA

Pr Rev.

JOURNAL OF MATHEMATICAL ECONOMICS.
[J. math. econ.]. Vol. 1, No. 1 (March 1974)-. Periodical. English. Seven times a year (1 volume). $820.00. Elsevier Sequoia SA, PO Box 564, CH-1001 Lausanne 1 Switzerland. **Tel** 011 41 21 3207381, FAX 011 41 21 3235444. **ED** Truman Bewley, Wayne J. Shafer. available on microfilm and microfiche from University Microfilms International (UMI); available on an online database from Elsevier Electronic Subscriptions (EES). Documents available from The Genuine Article, UMI Article Clearinghouse.
Desc: Aim is to improve communication between economists and mathematicians.
Ind/Abst ABI/INFORM Glob. Ed.; ABI/INFORM [Computer File] (Jan. 1982-); Acad. Search; Bus. Index (1985-); CompuMath Cit. Index [Full Cov.]; Contents Recent Econ. J.; Curr. Contents Soc. Behav. Sci.; Curr. Index Stat.; Econ. Lit. Index; EP Collect.; Gen. BusinessFile (1985-); Gen. Period. Index (1985-); Homework Help.; INFO-SOUTH Abstr.; J. Econ. Lit.; Mag. Search; MasterFile FullTEXT 1000; MasterFile FullTEXT 350; MasterFile FullTEXT 650; MasterFile FullTEXT (July 1993-); Math. Rev.; OCLC; Res. Alert [Full Cov.]; Soc. Sci. Cit. Index [Full Cov.]; Telebase; Zentralbl. Math. Ihre Grenzgeb.

LC P96.E252 U645 **ISSN** 0899-7764
DD 380 US
Pr Rev.

JOURNAL OF MEDIA ECONOMICS. See Communications.

LC HD
DD 331 US

•JOURNAL OF PENSIONS MANAGEMENT.
(1995)-. English. Four times a year (Mar., June, Sept., Dec.). £130.00 (Europe); £145.00 (other). Henry Stewart Publications, 28/30 Little Russell Street, London WC1A 2HN United Kingdom. **Tel** 011 44 171 4043040, FAX 011 44 171 4042081.

LC HB1 .J7 **ISSN** 0022-3808
DD 330/.05 US
CCC
CODEN JLPEAR

Pr Rev.

JOURNAL OF POLITICAL ECONOMY, THE.
[J. polit. econ.]. **Added/Corp** University of Chicago. Dept. of Political Economy. University of Chicago. Western Economic Society. Vol. 1 (Dec. 1892)-. Periodical. English. Six times a year. $114.00. University of Chicago Press / Journals Division, PO Box 37005, 5720 South Woodlawn, Chicago IL 60637. **Tel** (312)753-3347, FAX (312)753-0811. **ED** Robert E. Lucas, Jr., Jose A. Scheinkman, Sherwin Rosen, Gary S. Becker and Robert H. Topel. **Acid Free.** available on microfilm and microfiche from University Microfilms International (UMI). Documents available from The Genuine Article, UMI Article Clearinghouse.
Desc: Publishes work in traditional areas- monetary theory, fiscal policy, labor economics, planning and development, micro- and macroeconomic theory, international trade and finance, industrial organization- as well as in such interdisciplinary fields as the history of economic thought and social economics.
Ind/Abst ABC POL SCI; ABI/INFORM Glob. Ed.; ABI/INFORM [Computer File] (Sept. 1971-); Acad. Abstr.; Acad. Ind. [Computer File] (1984-); Acad. Search; AGRICOLA [Select. Cov.]; Am. Hist. Life (1955-); Asia.-Pac. Econ. Lit.; Book Rev. Index; Bus. Index (1985-); Contents Recent Econ. J.; Contents Pages Manage.; Crim. Justice Abstr.; Curr. Cit.; Curr. Contents Soc. Behav. Sci.; Curr. Lit. Sci. Sci.; Econ. Lit. Index (Sept. 1971-); Energy Res. Abstr. (Apr. 1976-); EP Collect.; Expand. Acad. Index (1984-); Gen. BusinessFile (1985-); Gen. Period. Index (1985-); Geogr. Abstr. Human Geogr.; Homework Help.; Index Period. Artic. Relat. Law; INFO-SOUTH Abstr.; Int. Bibliogr. Sociol.; Int. Dev. Abstr. (1955-); Int. Labour Doc.; Int. Polit. Sci. Abstr.; J. Econ. Lit.; Mag. Search; MasterFile FullTEXT 1000; MasterFile FullTEXT 350; MasterFile FullTEXT 650; MasterFile FullTEXT (July 1990-); Middle East Abstr. Index; Newsp. Period. Abstr. (1989-); OCLC; PAIS Int. Print; Popul. Index; Pub. Lib. FullTEXT; Res. Alert [Full Cov.]; Selec. Coop. Index Manage. Period.; Soc. Sci. Source; Soc. Sci. Cit. Index [Full Cov.]; Soc. Sci. Index; Soc. Sci. Index Fulltext (Oct. 1988-) [Full Txt.]; Stat. Theory Method Abstr. (1959-1963); Stud. Women Abstr.; Telebase; UMI ABI/Inform--Bus. Period. Ondisc (Feb. 1987-) [Full Txt.]; U.S. Polit. Sci. Doc.; West. Hist. Q. (1955-); Women Stud. Abstr.; Work Relat. Abstr. (1974-); World Agric. Econ. Rural Sociol. Abstr.

LC HB1 .J72 **ISSN** 0160-3477
DD 330/.05 US
CCC

Pr Rev.

JOURNAL OF POST KEYNESIAN ECONOMICS.
[J. post Keynes. econ.]. **VFOAT** Post Keynesian Economics. Vol. 1 (Fall 1978)-. Periodical. English. Four times a year. $129.00. M. E. Sharpe Inc., 80 Business Park Drive, Armonk NY 10504. **Tel** (914)273-1800, (800)541-6563, FAX (914)273-2106. **ED** Paul Davidson. **Bk Rev. Ad Acc. Circ:** 2,000. available on microfilm and microfiche from University Microfilms International (UMI). Documents available from The Genuine Article, UMI Article Clearinghouse.
Desc: A forum for original articles, the journal is a continuous challenge to prevailing economic theory. The real world and useful public policy are JPKE's central concerns.
Ind/Abst ABI/INFORM Glob. Ed.; Acad. Search; Bus. ASAP (1992-) [Full Txt.]; Bus. Index (1985-); Bus. Source Plus; Bus. Source; Contents Recent Econ. J.; Curr. Cit.; Curr. Contents Soc. Behav. Sci.; Econ. Lit. Index; EP Collect.; Gen. BusinessFile (1985-); Gen. Period. Index (1985-); Homework Help.; J. Econ. Lit.; J. Plan. Lit.; MasterFile FullTEXT 1000; MasterFile FullTEXT 350; MasterFile FullTEXT 650; MasterFile FullTEXT (July 1993-) [Full Txt.]; OCLC; Res. Alert [Full Cov.]; Soc. Sci. Cit. Index [Full Cov.]; Telebase.

LC HB95 .J68 **ISSN** 0890-913X
DD 330 US

JOURNAL OF PRIVATE ENTERPRISE, THE.
[J. priv. enterp.]. **Added/Corp** Association of Private Enterprise Education (U.S.). Vol. 1, No. 1 (Fall 1985)-. English. Two times a year (June, Dec.). $14.00. Association of Private Enterprise Education, 206 Founders Hall UTC, Chattanooga TN 37403. **Tel** (615)755-4118.

LC HF5415.153 .J68 **ISSN** 0737-6782
DD 658.5/75/05 US
CCC
CODEN JPIMDD

Pr Rev.

JOURNAL OF PRODUCT INNOVATION MANAGEMENT, THE.
[J. prod. innov. manage.]. **Added/Corp** Product Development & Management Association. **VFOAT** Product Innovation Management. Vol. 1, No. 1 (Jan. 1984)-. Academic Scholarly Publication. English. Six times a year. $295.00. Elsevier Science Publishing Company Inc, Madison Square Station, PO Box 882, New York NY 10159-0882. **Tel** (212)633-3950, FAX (212)633-3990. **ED** Blair Little. **Ad Acc.** available on microfilm and microfiche from University Microfilms International (UMI); available on an online database from Elsevier Electronic Subscriptions

(EES). Documents available from The Genuine Article, UMI Article Clearinghouse, Ask*IEEE.
Desc: Dedicated to the advancement of management practice in all of the functions involved in the total process of product innovation.
Ind/Abst ABI/INFORM Glob. Ed.; ABI/INFORM [Computer File] (Jan. 1984-); Anbar Account. Finan. Abstr. [Full Txt.]; Anbar Mark. Distr. Abstr. [Full Txt.]; Anbar Top Manage. Abstr. [Full Txt.]; Commun. Abstr. (?-?); Contents Pages Manage.; Curr. Cit.; Curr. Contents Eng. Comput. Technol.; Curr. Contents Soc. Behav. Sci.; Ei Page One; Gen. BusinessFile (1992-); INSPEC (1985-); Manage. Market. Abstr.; Manage. Bibliogr. Rev.; Oper. Prod. Manage. Abstr. [Full Txt.]; Oper. Res./Manage. Sci.; Person. Train. Abstr. [Full Txt.]; Res. Alert [Full Cov.]; SCISEARCH; Soc. Sci. Cit. Index [Full Cov.]; Women Manage. Rev. [Full Txt.].

LC HD251 .L36 **ISSN** 0959-9916
DD 333.33/0941/05 UK
CCC
Pr Rev.
JOURNAL OF PROPERTY RESEARCH.
See Real Estate.

LC HB135 .J7
DD 330/.01/51 II
JOURNAL OF QUANTITATIVE ECONOMICS : JOURNAL OF THE INDIAN ECONOMETRIC SOCIETY.
Added/Corp Indian Econometric Society. Vol. 1, No. 1 (Jan. 1985)-. Periodical. English. Two times a year. $40.00. Indian Econometric Society, Institute of Economic Growth, University Enclave, Delhi 110007 India. **(Subscription address:** Prints India, 11 Darya Ganj, New Delhi 110002 India. **Tel** 011 91 11 3268645, FAX 011 91 11 3275542, telex 31-61087 PRIN-IN.)
Ind/Abst Econ. Lit. Index (19??-); J. Econ. Lit.; Rice Abstr.

LC K10 .O889 **ISSN** 1054-8939
DD 362.973/05 US
Pr Rev. **CEASED**
JOURNAL OF REGULATION AND SOCIAL COSTS. [J. regul. soc. costs].
Added/Corp National Chamber Foundation. (Sept. 1990)-Vol. 3, No. 1. Periodical. English. National Chamber Foundation, 1615 H Street Northwest, Washington DC 20062. **Tel** (202)463-5620. **ED** Robert Ragland. **Ad Acc, Adv Mgr:** T.Armstrong. **Circ:** 2,500.

LC HB1 .J55 **ISSN** 1053-5357
DD 330 US
CCC
JOURNAL OF SOCIO-ECONOMICS. [J. socio-econ.]. **Added/Corp** Western Illinois University. Vol. 20 No. 1 (Spring 1991)-. Periodical. English. Six times a year. $200.00. JAI Press Inc., 55 Old Post Road, Suite 2, PO Box 1678, Greenwich CT 06836-1678. **Tel** (203)661-7602, FAX (203)661-0792. **ED** Richard Hattwick. ***Continues** Journal of Behavioral Economics, 0090-5720.*
Desc: Aimed toward academians, inside and outside the economics discipline, and the practitioners in business and nonprofit organizations. The two goals are to further knowledge of real economic phenomena by integrating psychological and sociological variables into economic analysis and to promote interdisciplinary research by academians and practitioners dealing in economics, the behavioral sciences and public policy.
Ind/Abst Acad. Search; Bus. Index (1985-); Bus. Source Plus; Bus. Source; Econ. Lit. Index (199?-); EP Collect.; Gen. BusinessFile (1991-); Gen. Period. Index (1991-); Homework Help.; J. Econ. Lit.; Mag. Search; MasterFile FullTEXT 1000; MasterFile FullTEXT 350; MasterFile FullTEXT 650; MasterFile FullTEXT (July 1993-) [Full Txt.]; OCLC; Psychol. Abstr. (1984-); PsycINFO; Telebase.

LC HD58.8 .J684 **ISSN** 1057-9265
DD 658.4/012/05 US
CCC
CODEN JSCHEO
JOURNAL OF STRATEGIC CHANGE. [J. strateg. change]. (1992)-. Periodical. English. Six times a year. $225.00. John Wiley & Sons, Inc., 605 Third Avenue, New York NY 10158-0012. **Tel** (212)850-6000, (212)850-6645, FAX (212)850-6088, telex 12-7063. **(Subscription address:** John Wiley & Sons / UK, Baffins Lane, Chichester, West Sussex PO19 1UD United Kingdom. **Tel** 011 44 1243 779777, FAX 011 44 243 776128, telex 86290 WIBOOKG.) **ED** David Hussey.
Desc: Addresses the central concern of senior managers and consultants worldwide - the planning and implementation of organizational change to meet the demands of changing business, economic and social environments.

LC HD62.4 .J68 **ISSN** 0897-5930
DD 658/.049/071 US
CODEN JTIBE9
Pr Rev.
JOURNAL OF TEACHING IN INTERNATIONAL BUSINESS. See Education-Higher Education.

ISSN 0962-1369
DD _b330.05 UK
CCC
•JOURNAL OF THE ECONOMICS OF BUSINESS. [J. econ. bus.]. Vol. 1 (1994)-. English. Three times a year. £78.00. Carfax Publishing Company, PO Box 25, Abingdon, Oxfordshire OX14 3UE United Kingdom. **Tel** 011 44 1235 555335, FAX 011 44 1235 553559, telex 817484. **ED** Elanor Morgam & Mick Silver. Index available. available on microfiche.
Desc: Covers both the public and private sectors of business.
Ind/Abst Bus. Source Plus; Bus. Source; EP Collect.; Homework Help.; MasterFile FullTEXT 1000; MasterFile FullTEXT 350; MasterFile FullTEXT 650; MasterFile FullTEXT (July 1994-); Telebase; World Mag. Bank.

LC HC **ISSN** 1053-8372
DD 330 US
Pr Rev.
JOURNAL OF THE HISTORY OF ECONOMIC THOUGHT. [J. hist. econ. thought]. **Added/Corp** History of Economics Society. **VFOAT** JHET; J.H.E.T. Vol. 12, No. 1 (Spring 1990)-. Periodical. English. Two times a year (Spring & Fall). $40.00. History of Economics Society, Department of Economics, Bellarmine College, Louisville KY 40205. **ED** D.A. Walker. **Circ:** 500. ***Continues** History of Economics Society. History of Economics Society Bulletin, 1042-7716.*
Ind/Abst Am. Hist. Life; Econ. Lit. Index (199?-); J. Econ. Lit. (1990-).

LC HD **ISSN** 1052-6099
DD 338 US
JOURNAL OF THE INTERNATIONAL ACADEMY OF HOSPITALITY RESEARCH, THE. (THE JOURNAL OF THE INTERNATIONAL ACADEMY OF HOSPITALITY RESEARCH [COMPUTER FILE] : JIAHR.). [J. Int. Acad. Hosp. Res.]. **Added/Corp** International Academy of Hospitality Research. Virginia Polytechnic Institute and State University. Dept. of Hotel, Restaurant, and Institutional Management. **VFOAT** JIAHR. Issue 1 (Nov. 26, 1990)-. English. Free. Scholarly Communications Projects, Virginia Tech, PO Box 90001, Blacksburg VA 24062. **Tel** (703)231-4922, FAX (703)231-3694. available via Internet.
Ind/Abst Leis., Rec., Tour. Abstr.

UK
JOURNAL OF THE PUBLIC ENTERPRISE. (19??)-. English. Two times a year. £18.00 UK; £30.00 other. Public Enterprise Group, 15 Manor Drive, Shelia Zelenskyi, Aylesbury Buck HP201EW United Kingdom. **Tel** 011 44 296 85573.
Ind/Abst PAIS Int. Print (1991-).

LC HT321 .J68 **ISSN** 0094-1190
DD 330.9/173/2 US
CCC
CODEN JUECDW
Pr Rev.
JOURNAL OF URBAN ECONOMICS. [J. urban econ.]. Vol. 1 (Jan. 1974)-. Academic Scholarly Publication. English. Six times a year. $362.00. Academic Press Inc., 6277 Sea Harbor Drive, Orlando FL 32887. **Tel** (800)543-9534, (407)345-4100, FAX (407)352-3445. **ED** Jan K. Brueckner. Documents available from The Genuine Article.
Desc: Provides a focal point for the publication of articles that illustrate empirical, theoretical, positive, or normative approaches to urban economics. The journal also features brief notes that contain new information, provide commentary on published work, or make new theoretical suggestions.
Ind/Abst Acad. Search; Bus. Index (1985-); Bus. Period. Index; Contents Recent Econ. J.; Crim. Justice Abstr.; Curr. Cit.; Curr. Contents Soc. Behav. Sci.; Econ. Lit. Index; EMBASE; EP Collect.; Gen. BusinessFile (1985-); Gen. Period. Index (1985-); Homework Help.; INFO-SOUTH Abstr.; Int. Bibliogr. Sociol.; J. Econ. Lit.; J. Plan. Lit.; Mag. Search; Manage. Contents; MasterFile FullTEXT 1000; MasterFile FullTEXT 350; MasterFile FullTEXT 650; MasterFile FullTEXT (Jan. 1994-); OCLC; PAIS Int. Print (1991-); Res. Alert [Full Cov.]; Sage Race Relat. Abstr.; Soc. Sci. Cit. Index [Full Cov.]; Telebase; Trade Ind. Index (1981-?); World Agric. Econ. Rural Sociol. Abstr.; Zentralbl. Math. Ihre Grenzgeb.

LC HG4028.W65 J68 **ISSN** 1076-5654
DD 658.15/244/05 US
CCC
•JOURNAL OF WORKING CAPITAL MANAGEMENT. [J. work. cap. manage.]. Vol. 1, No. 1 (Summer 1994)-. Periodical. English. Four times a year. $131.75. Warren Gorham & Lamont Inc., Park Square Building, 31 St. James Avenue, Boston MA 02116-4112. **Tel** (617)423-2020, (800)950-1207, FAX (617)423-2026.

LC WMLC L 83/1624
FR
JOURNAL OFFICIEL DE LA REPUBLIQUE FRANCAISE. AVIS ET RAPPORTS DU CONSEIL ECONOMIQUE ET SOCIAL. Main/Corp France. **Added/Corp** France. Conseil Economique et Social. **VFOAT** Avis et Rapports du Conseil Economique et Social. (1959)-. Periodical. French. ***Continues** France. Journal Officiel de la Republique Francaise. Avis et Rapports du Conseil Economique.*
Ind/Abst LABORDOC.

LC K10 .O93 **ISSN** 0737-5468
DD 349.766/05 347.66005 US
JOURNAL RECORD (OKLAHOMA CITY, OKLA.), THE. (THE JOURNAL RECORD.). (19??)-. Newspaper. English. Seven times a week. $141.00. Journal Record Publishing, PO Box 26370, Oklahoma City OK 73126. **Tel** (405)235-3100, FAX (405)278-6907. **ED** David Page (editor's phone: (405)278-6051). **Ad Acc, Adv Mgr:** M. Dunbar, **Tel** (405)278-6077. **Circ:** 3,900 (ctrl).
Desc: Business newspaper covering the State of Oklahoma.
Ind/Abst Bus. Index (1984-Dec. 1985); Gen. BusinessFile (Jan. 1985-Dec. 1985); Gen. Period. Index (Jan. 1985-Dec. 1985); INFO-SOUTH Abstr.; Mag. Search; PROMT.

SA
JSE HANDBOOK, THE. Added/Corp Johannesburg Stock Exchange. **VFOAT** J.S.E. Handbook; Johannesburg Stock Exchange Handbook. (Feb. 1991)-. English. Two times a year. Johannesburg Stock Exchange, PO Box 1174, 2000 Johannesburg South Africa. **Tel** 011 27 11 833 6580, FAX 011 27 11 838 1463. ***Continues** Stock Exchange Handbook.*

LC HC
DD 330 JA
KAKEI CHOSA NENPO. Added/Corp Japan. Sorifu. Tokeikyoku. **VFOAT** Annual Report on the Family Income and Expenditure Survey. (1953)-. Japanese (English). Government Publications Service Center, 2-1 Kasumigaseki 1-Chome, Chiyoda-Ku Tokyo 100 Japan. **Tel** 011 81 3 3504 3885. ***Continues** Shohi Jittai Chosa Nenpo.*

US
KAMI STRATEGIC ASSUMPTIONS. Newsletter. English. Four times a year. $135.00. Corporate Planning Inc, 2456 Northeast 26th Street, Lighthouse Port FL 33064. **Tel** (305)942-3226. **ED** M. J. Kami. ctrl circ.
Desc: Socio-economic newsletter.

LC HC428.K4 K36
DD 330.951/222/005 CC
KAN-CHIANG CHING CHI. Added/Corp Chiang-Hsi Sheng Ching Chi Yen Chiu So. Chiang-Hsi Sheng Ching Chi Hsueh Hui. (19??)-. Periodical. Chinese. Twelve times a year. RMBY0.30. Jiangxi Shifan Daxue / Xuebao Bianjibu, Jiangxi Normal University, Journal Editorial Department, Beijing Xilu Nanchang, Jiangxi 330027 People's Republic of China. **Tel** 333993.

LC HB9 .K328
JA
KANAZAWA DAIGAKU KEIZAI GAKUBU RONSHU. Added/Corp Kanazawa Daigaku. Keizai Gakubu. **VFOAT** Economic Review. Vol. 1 (1980)-. Periodical. English (German and Japanese). Kanazawa Daigaku Keisai Gakubu, 920 Japan.

LC HB9 .K33A **ISSN** 0289-0615
JA
KANAZAWA DAIGAKU KEIZAI RONSHU. [Kanazawa Daigaku keizai ronshu]. (1961)-. Japanese. Irregular. Kanazawa Daigaku Keizaigakkai, c/o Kanazawa Daigaku, Hobungakubu, Marunouchi Kanazawa Japan.

LC HB9 .K36 **ISSN** 0022-8427
DD 330.05/6 FI
KANSANTALOUDELLINEN AIKAKAUSKIRJA. [Kansantal. aikak.]. **Added/Corp** Kansantaloudellinen Yhdistys (Finland). (1929)-. Periodical. Finnish (summaries and/or abstracts in German). Four times a year. $25.59. Kansantaloudellinen Aikakauski, ETLA, Lonnrotinkatu 4 B, SF-H12 Helsinki Finland. **Tel** 011 358 9 648112, FAX 011 358 0 601753. **ED** Mika Widgen. **Bk Rev. Ad Acc. Circ:** 2,000.
Desc: Contains research articles on economics, debates on economic policies, and review articles on economic theory.

LC HF3161.K2 K35 **ISSN** 0199-3607
DD 650/.09781 US
SUSPENDED
KANSAS BUSINESS NEWS. Vol. 1, No. 1 (Dec. 1979)-Suspended with Vol. 11, No. 2. Periodical. English. Twelve times a year. $25.00. Chuck Henry Publications Inc, PO Box 490, Augusta KS 67010-0490. **Tel** (316)775-3201. **ED** Chuck Henry. **Bk Rev. Ad Acc. Circ:** 15,000 (ctrl). available on an online database (file 635/Full-Text) from DIALOG. Documents available from UMI Article Clearinghouse.
Desc: Success stories, management tips/advise, main thrust article devotes ten to twelve pages on a particular industry or subject and the impact it has on the Kansas economic development, in-the-news, faces and firms, etc. All relate to the Kansas business scene.

Business and Economics

Ind/Abst Bus. Dateline; Bus. Index (Jan. 1985-Dec. 1985); Gen. BusinessFile (Jan. 1985-Dec. 1985); Gen. Period. Index (Jan. 1985-Dec. 1985); INFO-SOUTH Abstr.

LC HC107.K2 K243   **ISSN** 0164-8632
DD 330.9/781/03   US
Pr Rev.
KANSAS BUSINESS REVIEW (LAWRENCE. 1977). (KANSAS BUSINESS REVIEW.). [Kans. bus. rev.]. **Added/Corp** University of Kansas. Institute for Economic and Business Research. University of Kansas. Institute for Public Policy and Business Research. University of Kansas. Division of Business and Economic Research. (Sept. 1977)-. Periodical. English. Four times a year. $15.00. University of Kansas Institute for Public Policy and Business Research, 1 Jayhawk Boulevard, 607 Blake Hall, Lawrence KS 66044. **Tel** (913)864-3701, **FAX** (913)864-3683. **ED** Laura Kriegstrom Poracsky and Thelma Helyar. **Circ:** 2,000 (ctrl).
Desc: Provides a forum for the dissemination of research studies and reports in the fields of economics and business and related public policy that would be of interest to business people, public officials, and academicians in Kansas and the Plains region.
Ind/Abst PAIS Int. Print (1991-).

LC HF5001
DD 650   US
KANSAS BUSINESS TEACHER, THE. **Added/Corp** Kansas Business Teachers Association. (1948)-. Periodical. English. Two times a year (Apr, Sep). $5.00. Kansas Business Teacher, 2074 Fanestil, Emporia KS 66801. **Tel** (316)343-1200 ext. 5393. **ED** Nona Berghaus. **Ad Acc. Circ:** 400 (ctrl).
Desc: Includes articles concerning business education and professional meetings. Also information for Kansas business teachers.
Ind/Abst Bus. Educ. Index.

ISSN 0734-2748
US
CCC
KANSAS CITY BUSINESS JOURNAL. Vol. 1, No. 1 (1982)-. Periodical. English. One time a week (published on Friday). $54.00. Kansas City Business Journal, 324 East 11th Street, Suite 800, Kansas City MO 64106. **Tel** (816)421-5900, **FAX** (816)472-4010. **ED** Eric Palmer and Toni Cardarella. **Ad Acc. Circ:** 15,000. available on microfilm and microfiche from University Microfilms International (UMI); available on an online database (files 635,648/Full-Text) from DIALOG; available on CD-ROM. Documents available from UMI Article Clearinghouse.
Desc: Business news covering the Kansas City metropolitan area.
Ind/Abst Acad. Search; Bus. Dateline; Bus. Index (1985-1990); Bus. Source Plus; Bus. Source; EP Collect.; Gen. BusinessFile (1985-1990); Gen. Period. Index (1985-1990); Homework Help.; INFO-SOUTH Abstr.; MasterFile FullTEXT 1000; MasterFile FullTEXT 350; MasterFile FullTEXT 650; MasterFile FullTEXT (July 1993-); OCLC; PROMT; Telebase; Trade Ind. ASAP [Full Txt.]; Trade Ind. Index [Full Txt.].

LC HC107.K2 K38
DD 330.9/781/03   US
KANSAS ECONOMIC INDICATORS. **Added/Corp** Wichita State University. Center for Business and Economic Research. Vol. 1, (Feb. 1971)-. Periodical. English. Twelve times a year. Center for Economic Development and Business Research, Wichita State University, 1845 Fairmount Street, Wichita KS 67260. **Tel** (316)689-3225, **FAX** (316)689-3950. **ED** Jimmy Skaggs. **Circ:** 1,000. **Continues** Kansas Business Review, 0191-4189.
Desc: Gathers, analyzes and publishes data describing economic conditions for Wichita and Kansas.

ISSN 0929-7871
NE
UDC 651.2655.42
●**KANTOOR BUSINESSMAGAZINE.** [Kantoor bus.mag.]. (1993)-. Periodical. Dutch. Ten times a year (publishes with Jan./Feb. and July/Aug. issues combined). $151.97. Districomm, PO Box 38274, 6503 AG Nijmegen Netherlands. **Tel** 011 31 80 787070. **Formed by the union of** KBM. Kantoormarkt, 0169-7285 **and** Best of Seven, 0929-788X.

ISSN 0332-5423
DD 330   NO
KAPITAL. [Kapital]. (1971)-. Periodical. Norwegian. Twenty-two times a year. Kr1455.00. Forlagsentralen Tidsskriftavd, PB 150 Furuset, 1001 Oslo 10 Norway. **Tel** 011 47 2 2320995. **ED** T Hegnar. **Ad Acc. Circ:** 45,000.
Ind/Abst Infomat Int. Bus.

ISSN 0800-3173
DD 651.8   NO
KAPITAL DATA. [Kap. DATA]. (1983)-. Periodical. Norwegian. Four times a year.
Ind/Abst Infomat Int. Bus.

LC HF5565 .K38   **ISSN** 0022-9504
FI
KAUPPAREKISTERILEHTI. VFOAT Handelsregistertidning. Finnish (Swedish). One time a week. Valtion Painatuskeskus, PO Box 516, SF 00101 Helsinki Finland. **Tel** 011 358 0 5660266, **FAX** 011 358 0 5660374. **Continues** Kaupparekisteri.

ISSN 0738-7229
US
KEEPING SCORE. **Added/Corp** Salt Lake Area Chamber of Commerce (Utah). Economic Development. (19??)-. Periodical. English. Twelve times a year. $60.00. Salt Lake Area Chamber of Commerce, 175 E 400 South, Suite 600, Salt Lake City UT 84111. **Tel** (801)364-3631.

LC HF5001 .K34   **ISSN** 0453-4557
DD 330.952/005   JA
KEIO BUSINESS REVIEW. **Added/Corp** Keio Gijuku Daigaku. Shogakkai. (1962)-. Periodical. English. One time a year. $26.00. Society of Business and Commerce, Keio University, Mita 2, 15-45 Minato-ku, Tokyo Japan. **(Subscription address:** Japan Publications Trading Company Ltd., PO Box 5030, Tokyo International, Tokyo 100-31 Japan. **Tel** 011 81 3 3292 3753.**)**
Ind/Abst Anbar Account. Finan. Abstr. [Full Txt.]; Anbar Mark. Distr. Abstr. [Full Txt.]; Anbar Top Manage. Abstr. [Full Txt.]; Int. Bibliogr. Sociol.; Manage. Bibliogr. Rev.; Oper. Prod. Manage. Abstr. [Full Txt.]; Person. Train. Abstr. [Full Txt.]; Women Manage. Rev. [Full Txt.].

LC HB9 .K4144
DD 330.0(5/6)   JA
KEIZAI GAKKAI HO. **Added/Corp** Kansai Daigku. Keizai Gakkai. **VFOAT** Kansai Daigku Keizai Gakkai Ho; Keizai Gakkai-Ho. Ed. 1 (1980)-. Japanese. Kansai Daigkai Gakkai, c/o Kansai Daigaku, Keizaigakubu Senriyama, Suita-Shi Tokyo Japan.

JA
KEIZAI HENDO KANSOKU SHIRYONEMPO. **Added/Corp** Japan. Keizai Kikakucho. Chosakyoku. **VFOAT** Annual Report on Business Cycle Indicators. (19??)-. Japanese (translations available in English). One time a year. Government Publications Service Center, 2-1 Kasumigaseki 1-Chome, Chiyoda-Ku Tokyo 100 Japan. **Tel** 011 81 3 3504 3885.

LC HC59 .K412
DD 330   JA
KEIZAI KEIEI KENKYU. **VFOAT** Economics Today. Vol. 1- (July 1980)-. Periodical. Japanese. Nihon Kaihatsu Ginko Setsubi, Toshi Kenkyujo 9-1, Otemachi 1-chome, Chiyoda-ku Tokyo 100 Japan.

LC HB9 .K4148   **ISSN** 0022-9733
JA
KEIZAI KENKYU / HITOTSUBASHI DAIGAKU KEIZAI KENKYUJO HEN. **Added/Corp** Hitotsubashi Daigaku. Keizai Kenkyujo. **VFOAT** Economic Review. (1950)-. Periodical. Japanese (English). Four times a year. $133.00. **(Subscription address:** Japan Publications Trading Company Ltd., PO Box 5030, Tokyo International, Tokyo 100-31 Japan. **Tel** 011 81 3 3292 3753.**)**
Ind/Abst Am. Hist. Life (1958-1971); Econ. Lit. Index (199?-); Int. Labour Doc.; J. Econ. Lit.

LC HF5549.5.T7 K37
JA
KEIZAI KENKYUJO HO / KEIZAI DOYUKAI KEIZAI KENKYUJO. **Added/Corp** Keizai Doyukai. Keizai Kenkyujo. (19??)-. Japanese. Keizai Doyukai, 4-6 Marunouchi 1 Chiyoda-ku, Tokyo-to 100 Japan.

LC HB9 .K415
JA
KEIZAI RIRON. **VFOAT** Wakayama Economic Review. Japanese. Wakayama Daigaku Keizaigakkai, 7-1 Nishi Takamatsu, 1-chome, Wakayama Japan.

LC HB61 .K36   **ISSN** 0450-0040
JA
KEIZAI SHINGO JITEN. **Added/Corp** Nihon Keizai Shimbun Sha. (1955)-. Japanese. Nihon Keizai Shimbun Inc., 9-5 Otemachi 1 Chome, Chiyoda-ku Tokyo 100 Japan. **Tel** 011 81 3 32700251, 011 81 3 52108502 (Nikkei Business Publications), **FAX** 011 81 3 52552661, 011 81 3 52108119 (Nikkei Business Publications Inc.).

ISSN 0022-9741
DD 330   JA
KEIZAI SHIRIN. **VFOAT** Hosei University Economic Review. (1932)-. Periodical. Multiple languages. Four times a year. ¥3200.00. Hosei Daigaku Keizai Gakkai, 4342 Aihara-machi, Machida-shi Tokyo Japan. **Bk Rev**. **Continues** Hosei Daigaku Ronshu.
Ind/Abst Am. Hist. Life (1958-1961,1971).

LC HC461 .H65
DD 330   JA
KEIZAI TOKEI NEMPO. **See** Business and Economics-Abstracting, Bibliographies and Statistics.

LC HB9 .K423
JA
KEIZAIGAKU RONSAN. **Added/Corp** Chuo Daigaku Keizaigaku Kenkyukai. **VFOAT** Journal of Economics. (1960)-. Periodical. English (Japanese). Six times a year. Chuo Daigaku Keizaigaku Kenkyukai, (Chuo University Economic Society), 742 Higashinakano, Hachioji-shi Tokyo Japan.

ISSN 0387-3021
DD 330   JA
KEIZAIGAKU RONSO (KYOTO. 1949). [Keizaigaku ronso Kyoto. 1949] **VFOAT** Doshisha University Economic Review. (1949)-. Academic Scholarly Publication. Japanese. Six times a year. **(Subscription address:** Japan Publications Trading Company Ltd., PO Box 5030, Tokyo International, Tokyo 100-31 Japan. **Tel** 011 81 3 3292 3753.**)**
Ind/Abst Am. Hist. Life (1990-).

LC HB9 .K4245   **ISSN** 0451-6281
JA
KEIZAIGAKU ZASSHI. **Added/Corp** Osaka Shoka Daigaku. Keizai Kenkyukai. Osaka Shiritsu Daigaku. Keizai Kenkyukai. Osaka Shiritsu Daigaku. Keizai Gakkai. Osaka Shoka Daigaku. **VFOAT** Journal of Economics. (1937)-. Periodical. Japanese.
Ind/Abst Am. Hist. Life (1958-1971).

LC HC107.K4 K426   **ISSN** 0734-4058
DD 330/.05   US
KENTUCKY JOURNAL OF ECONOMICS AND BUSINESS, THE. [Ky. j. econ. bus.]. No. 1 (1979/80)-. Periodical. English. One time a year. $15.00 (includes Kentucky Economics Association Membership). Acting Editor, Department of Business Administration, Northern Kentucky University, Heighland Heights KY 41076. Documents available from UMI Article Clearinghouse.
Ind/Abst Bus. Dateline.

KE
KENYA CERTIFICATE OF BUSINESS EDUCATION. REGULATIONS AND SYLLABUSES. English. One time a year. $3.50 Kenya; $10.00 other. Secretary of Kenya National Examinations Council, PO Box 73598, Nairobi Kenya. **Tel** 337841, telex COXAM 22534. **Circ:** 10,000 (ctrl).

LC HC267.A2 K45
DD 330   HU
KERESKEDELMI SZEMLE. **Added/Corp** Belkereskedelmi Kutato Intezet (Budapest, Hungary). (19??)-. Periodical. Hungarian. Twelve times a year.
Ind/Abst Leis., Rec., Tour. Abstr.; World Agric. Econ. Rural Sociol. Abstr.

ISSN 1055-5544
DD 331   US
KERN REPORT, THE. (THE KERN REPORT : TRENDS AND ISSUES IN HOME-BASED BUSINESS AND TELECOMMUTING.). [Kern rep.]. Vol. 1, No. 1 (Jan./Feb./Mar. 1991)-. Periodical. English. Four times a year. $129.00. The Kern Report, PO Box 14850, Chicago IL 60614. **Tel** (312)472-8116.

LC Z5640   **ISSN** 0954-9153
DD 016.004   UK
KEY ABSTRACTS. BUSINESS AUTOMATION. **See** Computers-Abstracting, Bibliographies and Statistics.

US
KEYING IN. (19??)-. Newsletter. English. Four times a year (Sept., Nov., Jan., and March). Membership: $60.00 US; $70.00 other. National Business Education Association, 1914 Association Drive, Reston VA 22091-1596. **Tel** (703)860-8300, **FAX** (703)620-4483.
Desc: Newsletter devoted to a subject of special interest to business educators. Issues may deal with topics such as economic education, integrating business education and academics, and promoting education for and about business.

LC HC321 .K54   **ISSN** 0023-1363
DD 338   NE
KIJK OP HET NOORDEN. Vol. 1 (April 1969)-. Periodical. Dutch. Twelve times a year. $47.96. NV Noord Nederlandse Drukkerij, Postbus 6, 7940 AA Meppel Nederlands. **Tel** 05220-68600. **ED** B.P. Tammeling. **Ad Acc. Circ:** 10,000 (ctrl). Documents available from SWETS.

JA
CEASED
KIKAN NIHON KEIZAI SHIHYO. **Added/Corp** Japan. Keizai Kikakucho. **VFOAT** Japanese Economic Indicators Quarterly. (1987)-(1993). Periodical. Japanese (English). **(Subscription address:** Japan Publications Trading Company Ltd., PO Box 5030, Tokyo International, Tokyo 100-31 Japan. **Tel** 011 81 3 3292 3753.**) Continues** Nihon Keizai Shihyo.

Business and Economics

LC HB9 .K434 **ISSN** 0557-109X
DD 330.0
JA
CCC
TITLE CHANGE
KIKAN RIRON-KEIZAIGAKU. [Kikan riron-keizaigaku]. **Added/Corp** Riron Keiryo Keizai Gakkai. **VFOAT** Economic Studies Quarterly; Journal of the Japanese Association of Theoretical Economics; Riron-Keizaigaku. (19??)-(1995). Periodical. Japanese (English; table of contents in English). **(Subscription address:** Maruzen Company Ltd., PO Box 5050, Import & Export Department, Tokyo 100 31 Japan. **Tel** 011 81 3 32789224.) *Merged into Japanese Economic Review.* **Ind/Abst** Asia.-Pac. Econ. Lit.; Econ. Lit. Index (199?-); J. Econ. Lit.

LC HC101 .K5 **ISSN** 0023-1770
DD 330
US
KIPLINGER WASHINGTON LETTER, THE. See Political Science.

ISSN 0771-1522
BE
UDC 658.3.048
KNIPSELKRANT ECONOMIE. (1982)-. Periodical. Dutch. Twenty-four times a year. 1390.00F. Uitgeverij Cockaert, Boomlaarstraat 76-78, B-2500 Lier Belgium.

LC HD70.C87 K57
DD 658/.00972986/05
NE
KNOW-HOW BUSINESS REVIEW. **VAT** Know How Business Review. (198?)-. Periodical. English. Know-How Business Review, PO Box 473, Curacao Netherlands Antilles.

LC HC461 .K6 **ISSN** 0075-6407
DD 338.95
JA
KOBE ECONOMIC & BUSINESS REVIEW. [Kobe econ. bus. rev.]. **Added/Corp** Kobe Daigaku. Keizai Keiei Kenkyujo. **VFOAT** Kobe Economic and Business Review. Vol. 1 (1953)-. Periodical. English. One time a year. Exchange basis. Kobe University / Faculty of Economics, 1 1 Rokkodai Cho Nada Ku, Kobe 67 Japan. **Tel** 011 81 078 8811212, **FAX** 011 81 078 8616434. **ED** Editorial Board.

LC HD4313 .K62a
JA
KOEI KIGYO KINYU KOKO. **Main/Corp** Koei Kigyo Kinyu Koko. (19??)-. Periodical. Japanese. Zenkoku Choson Kaikan Building Chiyoda-ku, Tokyo 100 Japan.

LC HB9 .K468A
JA
KOKUGAKUIN DAIGAKU KEIZAIGAKU KENKYU. **Main/Corp** Kokugakuin Daigaku. Daigakuin. **VFOAT** Kokugakuin University Economic Studies. No. 11 (1979)-. Japanese. Kokugakuin Daigaku, 10-28 Higashi 4-chome, Shiuya-ku, Tokyo Japan. **Tel** (03)409-0111.

LC HD72 .K64
JA
KOKYO SENTAKU NO KENKYU. **Added/Corp** Gendai Keizai Kenkyu Senta (Tokyo, Japan). **VFOAT** Public Choice Studies. (1981)-. Periodical. Japanese (summaries and/or abstracts in English). One time a year. ¥1000. Gendai Keizai Kenkyu Senta, Keiso Shobo 23-15, Koraku 2 Bunkyo-ku, Tokyo-to Japan.

LC HC **ISSN** 0075-6733
DD 330
UK
KOMPASS. **VFOAT** CBI/UK Kompass; UK Kompass; Kompass, United Kingdom. 1st Ed. (1962)-. Directory. English (French, German, Spanish and Italian). One time a year. $645.00. Reed Information Services Ltd., Windsor Court, East Grinstead House, East Grinstead RH19 1BR United Kingdom. **Tel** 011 44 1342 326972, **FAX** 011 44 1342 335977, telex 95127 INFSER G. **(Subscription address:** Cahners Publishing / Connecticut, PO Box 2118, Westport CT 06880. **Tel** (203)454-4147.) **ED** Jan Brazier. **Circ:** 8,500. available on an online database from Reed Information Services Ltd.; available on CD-ROM.

LC HC272 .R38
DD 338.4/7/0002944
FR
KOMPASS-FRANCE. **VFOAT** Kompass, Annuaire Industriel. (19??)-. English (French, German and Spanish). One time a year. 22 Avenue Franklin D Roosevelt, 22 Avenue franklin D. Roosevelt, 75008 Paris France. *Continues Repertoire General de la Production Francaise, Kompass-France.*

AT
CEASED
KOMPASS JAPAN. (July 1991)-(19??). English. Peter Isaacson Publications Pty Ltd, PO Box 172, Prahran Victoria 3181 Australia. **Tel** 03 520 5555, **FAX** 03 525 2983.

LC HF5181.B3 K6 **ISSN** 0075-6636
DD 650
BE
KOMPASS; MANUEL D'INFORMATIONS SUR L'ECONOMIE DE LA BELGIQUE ET DU GRAND-DUCHE DE LUXEMBOURG. **VFOAT** Handbook of Information on the Economy of Belgium and the Grand Duchy of Luxemburg. 1st Ed. (1961)-. Directory. Multiple languages (English, Flemish, French, German and Italian). One time a year. $325.00. Reed Information Services Ltd., Windsor Court, East Grinstead House, East Grinstead RH19 1BR United Kingdom. **Tel** 011 44 1342 326972, **FAX** 011 44 1342 335977, telex 95127 INFSER G. **(Subscription address:** Cahners Publishing / Connecticut, PO Box 2118, Westport CT 06880. **Tel** (203)454-4147.) **Ad Acc. Circ:** 4,700. available on CD-ROM; available on an online database. Documents available from BLDSC.

AT
KOMPASS PHILIPPINES. Tagalog. One time a year. 280.00Aus$. Peter Isaacson Publications Pty Ltd, PO Box 172, Prahran Victoria 3181 Australia. **Tel** 03 520 5555, **FAX** 03 525 2983. **(Subscription address:** Kompass Philippines, 1227 Makati MM, PDCP Bank Centre 6th Floor, Herrera cor. Alfaro St., Salcedo Village, Philippines.)

LC HB848 .I4314
IO
KONGRES IPADI. **Main/Corp** Ikatan Peminat Dan Ahli Demografi Indonesia. **VAT** Kongres Ikatan Peminat Dan Ahli Demografi Indonesia. Vol. 1; 1974-. Multiple languages (English and Indonesian). Demographic Institute, PO Box 427, Jakarta 10002 Indonesia. **Tel** 011 62 21 336434, 011 62 21 336539, 33102457.

LC HC701 .K65
DD 330
KO
KONGSANKWON KYONGJE. **VFOAT** Economic Survey of Socialist Countries. Vol. 1, No. 1 (1984)-. Periodical. Korean (Korean). Four times a year. W2.000. Hanguk Sanop Kyongje Kisul Yonguwon, 206-9 Chongnyangni-dong Tongdaemun-ku, Seoul Korea. *Continues Kongsankwon Kyongje Tonghyang.*

LC HC268.V5 V523a
DD 330
AU
KONJUNKTURBERICHT. **Main/Corp** Vienna, Austria. Magistrat Abteilung Wirtschaftsangelegenheiten. (19??)-. German. Irregular. Magistrat der Stadt Wien, Magistrat der Stadt Wien, Magistratsabteilung 4, A-1082 Vienna Austria. *Continues Konjunkturbericht.*

LC HD6756 .P75 **ISSN** 1102-6065
SW
KONKURRENS/ UITGAVEN AV STATENS PRIS- OCH KONKURRENSVERK I SAMARBETE MED NARINGSFRIHETSOMBUDSMANNEN OCH MARKNADSDOMSTOLEN. **Added/Corp** Sweden. Statens Pris- Och Konkurrensverk. Sweden. Naringsfrihetsombudsmannen. Sweden. Marknadsdomstolen. (1992)-. Periodical. Swedish. Six times a year. John Wiley & Sons Ltd., Baffins Lane, Chichester, West Sussex PO19 1UD United Kingdom. **Tel** 011 44 1243 779777, **FAX** 011 44 1243 776128 BTG:JWP001, telex 86290 WIBOOKG. **(Subscription address:** John Wiley & Sons Inc / New Jersey, PO Box 2575, Secaucus NJ 07096-2575.) *Continues Pris Och Konkurrens.*

LC HC370.I52 O38
DD 330
NO
KONOMISKE ANALYSER. Periodical. Norwegian. Twelve times a year. Kr120.00, Kr15.00 (per issue) Norway; $18.00 US. Central Bureau of Statistics / Norway, PO Box 8131 DEP, N-0033 Oslo 1 Norway. **Tel** 011 47 2 2864964, **FAX** 011 47 2 864973. **Bk Rev. Circ:** 3,500. *Absorbed Okonomisk Utsyn-, 0078-1924.*
Desc: Presents short- and medium-term analysis on the Norwegian economy and related aspects such as demographics, oil and energy.

LC HC380.C63 K65
DD 330
SW
KONSUMENTRATT & I.E. OCH EKONOMI. 1977-. Periodical. Swedish. Irregular. Kr60.00. Konsumentverket, Box 503, 162 15 Vallingby Sweden. *Formed by the union of Konsumentratt and KO, Konsumentombudsmannen.*

ISSN 0935-0241
GW
UDC 330.341.44
KONZERNE IN SCHAUBILDERN. [Konzerne Schaubildern]. **VFOAT** Intercompany Relations on Charts; Groupes Sous Forme de Tableaux Synoptiques. (1974)-. German. Irregular. DM480.20. Verlag Hoppenstedt & Company, Postfach 100139, D-64201 Darmstadt Germany. **Tel** 011 49 6151 380436, 011 49 6151 380361.

KO
KOREA BUSINESS WORLD. **VFOAT** Korea Businessworld. Periodical. English. Twelve times a year. $1100.00 Korea; $600.00 other. Korea Business World Ltd, Suite 303/Shinsong Building, 25-4 Yoido-dong, Yongdungpo-gu Seoul Korea. **ED** Lee Kie-Hong, Shin Sang-Kap and Arnold Stockard. **Bk Rev. Ad Acc. Circ:** 28,000 (ctrl).
Desc: Economic journal with stories on Korea's major industries and business issues, plus monthly economic indicators and comments by world economists.

LC HC466 .K565
DD 330.95195/005
KO
KOREA ECONOMIC WEEKLY, THE. **Added/Corp** Hanguk Kyongje Sinmunsa. No. 155 (Sept. 9, 1991)-. Periodical. English. One time a week. Korea Economic Weekly, #441 Chungnim-Dong Shung-Gu, CPO Box 960, Seoul Korea. *Continues Korea Economic Journal.*

KO
CEASED
KOREAN BUSINESS REVIEW. **Added/Corp** Chonguk Kyongjein Yonhaphoe. **VFOAT** Business Review. (19??)-(Feb. 1993). Periodical. English. Federation Korean Industries, 28-11 Yoido-Dong Yeongdeungpo, Seoul 150 Korea. **Tel** 011 82 2 7800821. **ED** Cho Kyu-Hah. **Bk Rev. Ad Acc. Circ:** 20,000. **Ind/Abst** PAIS Int. Print.

LC HC
US
KOREAN ECONOMIST, THE. **Added/Corp** Korean Economic Society (U.S.). **VFOAT** Kyonje Yongu. (19??)-. Periodical. English. Every 2 years. Korean Economic Society, 6842 Strata Street, McLean VA 22101.

LC HC267.A2 A15 **ISSN** 0023-4346
DD 330
HU
KOZGAZDASAGI SZEMLE. [Kozgazd. szle.]. **Added/Corp** Magyar Tudomanyos Akademia Magyar Tudomanyos Akademia. Kozgazdasagtudomanyi Intezet. Vol. 1, (Oct. 1954)-. Academic Scholarly Publication. Hungarian (summaries and/or abstracts in Russian and English). Twelve times a year. $103.00. Akademiai Kiado, Publishing House of the Hungarian Academy of Sciences, Prielle Kornelia u. 19-35, H-1117 Budapest Hungary. **Tel** 011 36 1 1811991, **FAX** 011 36 1 1811991, telex 22-6228 AKNYO H. **(Subscription address:** Kultura, PO Box 143, H-1300 Budapest 3 Hungary. **Tel** 011 36 1 2500194.) **ED** K. Szabo. **Bk Rev. Ad Acc. Circ:** 15,000.
Desc: Macro and microeconomic theory, general economic policy, finance and banking, international economic analyses, economic planning, history of economic thought, and economic history.
Ind/Abst Am. Hist. Life (1971-); Int. Bibliogr. Sociol.; Int. Labour Doc.; World Agric. Econ. Rural Sociol. Abstr.

ISSN 0931-9077
GW
UDC 657.47
KRP. KOSTENRECHNUNGSPRAXIS (1977). [Krp, Kostenrechn.prax. 1977]. **VFOAT** Kostenrechnungspraxis (1977). (1977)-. Trade Publication. German. Six times a year. $118.22. Gabler Verlag, Postfach 1546, D-65005 Wiesbaden Germany. **Tel** 011 49 611 534129, **FAX** 011 49 611 534430. *Continues Kostenrechnungs-Praxis, 0023-4265.*

ISSN 0945-0084
GW
UDC 33
●**KUNSTSTOFFE, PLAST EUROPE.** **VFOAT** Kunststoffe (Munchen. Bilingual Ed. 1994). (1994)-. Periodical. Multiple languages. Twelve times a year. $335.77. Carl Hanser Verlag, Postfach 860420, D-81631 Munich Germany. **Tel** 011 49 89 998300, **FAX** 011 49 89 981264. *Absorbed Kunststoffe PE Plast Europe.*
Ind/Abst Curr. Cit.

ISSN 0937-6186
GW
UDC 669.1
KW HEUTE. See Metals and Metallurgy.

ISSN 0169-9261
NE
UDC 339.3
KWALITEIT IN BEDRIJF. [Kwal. bedr.]. (1985)-. Periodical. Dutch. Six times a year. $85.64. Koggeschip Vakbladen BV, Postbus 1198, 1000 BD Amsterdam Netherlands. **Tel** 011 31 20 6916666.

LC HB9 .K5912
DD 330
KO
KYONGJE NONJIP (CHUNGNAM TAEHAKKYO. PUSOL KYONGYONG KYONGJE YONGUSO). (KYONGJE NONJIP.). **Added/Corp** Chungnam Taehakkyo. Pusol Kyongyong Kyongje Yonguso. **VFOAT** Journal of Economics; Chungnam Taehakkyo Kyongsang Taehak Pusol Kyongyong; Ongje Yonguso Kyongje Nonjip. Vol. 1 (Dec. 1985)-. Periodical. Korean. Four times a year. Seoul

National University Institute of Economic Research, Seoul Daehakkyo Kyeongje Yeonguso, San 56-1, Sinlim-dong Kwanak-ku, Seoul 151-742 South Korea. ***Continues in part*** *Kyongsang Nonjip (Chungnam Taehakkyo. Pusol Kyongyong Kyongje Yonguso).*

LC HB9 .K95

JA

KYUSHU SANGYO DAIGAKU SHOKEI RONSO. **VFOAT** Shokei Ronso; Economic and Business Review. Japanese. 327 Kashii Shokadai 2-chome Higashi-ku, Fukuoka Japan.

LC HC121 .L2
DD 330.98/0038 US

LA/C BUSINESS BULLETIN. **Added/Corp** Latin America/Caribbean Business Development Center (U.S.) United States. Agency for International Development. United States. International Trade Administration. **VAT** Latin America/Caribbean Business Bulletin. Vol. 1, No. 1 (Dec. 1990)-. Bulletin. English. Twelve times a year. US Department of Commerce, 14th Street & Constitution Avenue NW, Washington DC 20230. **Tel** (202)482-2000, FAX (202)482-3772. ***Continues*** *CBI Business Bulletin.*

FR

LAMY SOCIAL. **See** Law.

US

LAND LETTER : THE NEWSLETTER FOR NATURAL RESOURCE PROFESSIONALS. Newsletter. English. WJ Chandler Associates / Virginia, 7410 Recard Ln, Alexandria VA 22307-1846.

LC HC **ISSN** 0436-399X
DD 333.73/05 UK

LAND RESOURCE STUDY. [Land resour. stud.]. No. 1 (1966)-. Monographic series. English (summaries and/or abstracts in French). Irregular. Price varies per volume. Land Resources Department, Tolworth Tower, Ewell Road, Surbiton Surrey KT6 7DY United Kingdom. **Tel** 01-399 5281, FAX 01-390 5138, telex 263907 LDN G.

LC HD101 .L36 **ISSN** 0264-8377
DD 333.79/17/05 UK
CCC

LAND USE POLICY. [Land use policy]. Vol. 1, No. 1 (Jan. 1984)-. Periodical. English. Four times a year. $387.00. Butterworth Heinemann Publishers, Linacre House Jordan Hill, Oxford OX2 8DP United Kingdom. **Tel** 011 44 1865 310366, FAX 011 44 1865 310898. **(Subscription address:** Elsevier Science Ltd. / Oxford Fulfillment Centre, PO Box 800, Kidlington OX5 1DX United Kingdom. **Tel** 011 44 865 843355.) **ED** Colin Blackman. Index available. **Bk Rev. Ad Acc.** available on microfilm and microfiche from University Microfilms International (UMI); available on an online database from Elsevier Electronic Subscriptions (EES).
Desc: A growing international and interdisciplinary journal concerned with the social, economic, political, scientific and planning aspects of urban and rural land use.
Ind/Abst Avery Index Archit. Period. Suppl. Colum. Univ. (Apr. 1989, Jan. 1990); Curr. Cit.; Curr. Contents Soc. Behav. Sci.; Curr. Geogr. Publ. (199?-); For. Abstr.; Geogr. Abstr. Phys. Geogr.; Geogr. Abstr. Human Geogr.; Int. Dev. Abstr.; Int. Polit. Sci. Abstr.; Irr. Drain. Abstr.; J. Plan. Lit.; Leis., Rec., Tour. Abstr.; PAIS Int. Print (1991-); Plant Genet. Resour. Abstr.; Rice Abstr.; Rural Dev. Abstr.; Soc. Sci. Cit. Index [Full Cov.]; Soils Fert.; World Agric. Econ. Rural Sociol. Abstr.

ISSN 0800-5974
DD 338.1 NO

LANDBRUKS KONOMISK FORUM. **See** Agriculture-Agricultural Economics.

ISSN 0377-0788
AU

LANDERBANK ECONOMIC BULLETIN. [Landerbank econ. bull.]. **Main/Corp** Osterreichische Landerbank. (19??)-. Bulletin. English. Osterreichersche Landerbank, Economic Department, 1010 Vienna AM Hof 2 Austria. **Tel** 01143/0222-6624/4744, telex 115561. ***Continues*** *Economic Bulletin (Vienna).*
Ind/Abst F&S Index Plus Text, Int. [Select. Cov.].

AU

LANDERBANK REPORT : REPORT ON THE AUSTRIAN ECONOMY. **Added/Corp** Osterreichische Landerbank. (Jan. 1984)-. Periodical. English. Four times a year. Free. Osterreichersche Landerbank, Economic Department, 1010 Vienna AM Hof 2 Austria. **Tel** 01143/0222-6624/4744, telex 115561. **Circ:** 6,000. ***Continues*** *Landerbank Economic Bulletin.*
Desc: Contains business, exchange and foreign trade information. Also includes statistical information, but does not include any political or ideological objectives.
Ind/Abst Predicasts Forecasts; Trade Ind. ASAP [Full Txt.]; Trade Ind. Index [Full Txt.].

ISSN 1063-925X
DD 338 US

LANE REPORT, THE. [Lane rep.]. (1985)-. Periodical. English. Twelve times a year. $24.00. Lane Communications Group, 269 West Main Street, Lexington KY 40507. **Tel** (606)244-3522, FAX (606)244-3544. **ED** Alan I. Kirschenbaum. **Ad Acc, Adv Mgr:** Joe Oliver. **Circ:** 11,000 (ctrl). available in microform from University Microfilms International (UMI); available on an online database (file 635/Full-Text) from DIALOG. Documents available from UMI Article Clearinghouse.
Desc: Features profiles on entrepreneurs, companies and women in business, as well as the Gallup Poll, index of stocks of local interest, updates on health care, finances, the equine industry and business travel. A spotlight on the arts community, and a guide to area restaurants suitable for business dining are also included.
Ind/Abst Bus. Dateline (Dec. 1991-) [Full Txt.].

UK

LANGUAGE TRAINING. Periodical. English. Four times a year. £18.00 Europe; £25.00 other. Language Training Services, 5 Belvedere, Lansdown Road, Bath Avon BA1 5ED United Kingdom. **Tel** 011 44 1225 448148, FAX 011 44 1225 448149. **ED** Adrian Pilbeam and Fiona Scott-Barrett. **Bk Rev. Ad Acc. Circ:** 500.
Desc: Language traning in industry and business.

LC HD891 .A38B
IO

LAPORAN TAHUN ANGGARAN DIREKTORAT JENDERAL TRANSMIGRASI. **Main/Corp** Indonesia. Direktorat Jenderal Transmigrasi. Indonesian. Departemen Tenaga Kerja, Jalan H Agus Salim No 58, Jakarta Indonesia.

LC HD1393.5 M27A
DD 338.7/69054/09595 MY

LAPURAN TAHUN DAN KIRA-KIRA - MALAYSIA INDUSTRIAL ESTATES SENDIRIAN BERHAD. **Main/Corp** Malaysian Industrial Estates Ltd. **VFOAT** Annual Report and Accounts - MIEL. **VAT** Lapuran Tahun Dan Kira-Kira - Malaysia Industrial Estates Sendirian Berhad; Annual Report and Accounts - Malaysian Industrial Estates Limited. Multiple languages (English and Malay). Malaysian Industrial Estates, Sendiran Berhad Malaysian Industrial Estates Ltd, Bangunan Midf 117 Jalan Ampang, Kuala Lumpur Malaysia. ***Continues*** *Malaysian Industrial Estates Ltd. Annual Report and Accounts.*

ISSN 1121-1385
IT
UDC 658.8

LARGO CONSUMO. [Largo consumo]. (1983)-. Periodical. Italian. Eleven times a year (monthly with Jul./Aug. issues combined). L350000 Italy. Largo Consumo Editoriale, Via Bodini 2, 20155 Milan Italy. **Tel** 011 39 2 3271646, FAX 011 39 2 3271840, telex 334497 LARCON I. Index available. **Bk Rev. Ad Acc. Circ:** 25,000 (ctrl). ***Continues*** *Largo Consumo. Multicanale, 0392-131X.*
Desc: Observes and analyzes cases and characteristics of this market and it promotes every year a series of meetings as support of the editorial activity. This initiative is addressed to all businessmen interested in new opportunities of debate and reflection.

SZ

LATEINAMERIKA-KURIER. (19??)-. German. Twenty-six times a year. 125.00F Switzerland; 160.00F other. Lateinamerikanische Handelskam, Hintere Hauptgasse 9, CH-4800 Zofingen Switzerland. **Tel** 011 47 62 523222, FAX 011 47 62 518553. **Ad Acc. Circ:** 250 (ctrl).

LC WMLC 93/3306
UK

LATIN AMERICA MONITOR. CENTRAL AMERICA. **VFOAT** Central America; Latin American Monitor. Central America. Vol. 8, No. 2 (Mar. 1991)-. Periodical. English. Twelve times a year. Business Monitor International, 56 60 St. John Street, London EC1M 4DT United Kingdom. **Tel** 011 44 171 6083646, FAX 011 44 171 6083620. ***Continues*** *Latin America Monitor. 2, Central America.*

UK
TITLE CHANGE

LATIN AMERICA MONITOR. MEXICO & BRAZIL. **VFOAT** Mexico & Brazil; Mexico and Brazil. Vol. 8, No. 2 (Mar. 1991)-Vol. 10, No. 2 (Feb. 1993). English. ***Continues*** *Latin American Monitor. 1, Mexico & Brazil, 0265-6841.* ***Split into*** *Latin America Monitor. Brazil* ***and*** *Latin America Monitor. Mexico.*

UK

LATIN AMERICA MONITOR. SOUTHERN CONE. **VFOAT** Latin American Monitor. Southern Cone; Southern Cone. Vol. 8, No. 2 (Mar. 1991)-. Periodical. English. Twelve times a year. Business Monitor International, 56 60 St. John Street, London EC1M 4DT United Kingdom. **Tel** 011 44 171 6083646, FAX 011 44 171 6083620. ***Continues*** *Latin American Monitor. 4, Southern Cone.*

ISSN 1062-4651
DD 658 US

LATIN AMERICAN ADVISOR, THE. [Lat. Am. advis.]. (1991)-. Periodical. English. One time a week. $520.00. The Lee Group, 2044 Reynolds Street, Falls Church VA 22043.

LC HC
DD 330 US

LATIN AMERICAN BUSINESS ADVISOR. **Added/Corp** University of Miami. Center for International Business Education and Research. Vol. 1 (1991)-. English. ***Continues*** *Caribbean Basin Business Advisor.*

UK

LATIN AMERICAN CABLE PROGRAM NETWORKS DATABOOK. **See** Communications-Television and Cable.

LC HC121 .L268 **ISSN** 0968-4972
DD 330 UK

•**LATIN AMERICAN CONSENSUS FORECASTS.** **Added/Corp** Consensus Economics, Inc. **VFOAT** LACF. (1993)-. Periodical. English. Six times a year. $495.00. Consensus Economics Inc., 49 Berkeley Square, London W1X 6LT United Kingdom. **Tel** 011 44 171 4913211, FAX 011 44 171 4092331. available with charts.

LC HC121 .L279 **ISSN** 0960-8702
DD 330.98/0005 UK

LATIN AMERICAN ECONOMY & BUSINESS. **VFOAT** Economy & Business; Latin American Economy and Business; Economy and Business. LAEB-90-01 (Oct. 1990)-. Periodical. English. Sixteen times a year. $660.00. Lettres UK Ltd, 61 Old Street, London EC1V 9HX United Kingdom. **Tel** 011 44 171 2510012, FAX 011 44 171 2538193. **ED** Will Ollard. ctrl circ. ***Formed by the union of*** *Latin American Economic Report, 0268-6864* ***and*** *Latin American Commodities Report.*
Desc: Includes country by country economic reports, economic indicators, business pages, industrial profiles and privatization and commodities sections for the continent. Plus quarterly statistical bulletin.

ISSN 1075-3869
US

•**LEADERSHIP DIRECTORIES ON CD-ROM.** (1994)-. Directory. English. Four times a year. $2800.00. Chadwyck Healey / Virginia, 1101 King Street, Alexandria VA 22314. **Tel** (800)752-0515 ext. 1000, FAX (703)683-7589.

LC HF5068.D63 L43
DD 338.7/4/02577434 US

LEADSOURCE. DETROIT METRO SOUTHEAST. **VFOAT** Detroit Metro Southeast. (1987/88)-. English. One time a year. Leadsource Inc., 2207 East Camelback Road #101, Phoenix AZ 85016. **Tel** (602)468-1070, FAX (602)468-1075. ***Formed by the union of*** *Contacts Influential. Detroit Metro Central, 0886-7224* ***and*** *Contacts Influential. Detroit Metro South, 0886-7240.*

ISSN 0888-8981
DD 330 US

LEASING AND FINANCIAL SERVICES MONITOR, THE. [Leas. financ. serv. monit.]. **VFOAT** Monitor; MA monitor. (19??)-. Periodical. English. Seven times a year (Jan., March., May, July, Sep., Oct., Nov.). $40.00. Molloy Associates, 700 Pont Reading Road Southeast, Ardmore PA 19003. **Tel** (610)649-7112, FAX (610)649-0834. **ED** Lisa H. Rafter. cum. index. **Ad Acc, Adv Mgr:** S. Angelucci. **Circ:** 18,000.
Desc: Covers trends and developments in the US leasing industry. Also includes a comprehensive "Newsline" section which updates readers on people and places.

LC HC196 .T44A **ISSN** 0120-2596
DD 330/.05 CK

LECTURAS DE ECONOMIA. [Lect. econ.]. **VFOAT** Revista Lecturas de Economia. Vol. 1, No. 2 (May-Aug. 1980)-. Periodical. Spanish. Three times a year. ***Continues*** *Temas Economicos (Universidad de Antioquia. Departamento de Economia).*
Ind/Abst Int. Labour Doc.; PAIS Int. Print (1991-).

LC HC **ISSN** 0075-8442
GW

LECTURE NOTES IN ECONOMICS AND MATHEMATICAL SYSTEMS. [Lect. notes econ. math. syst.]. Vol. 60 (1971)-. Monographic series. English. Irregular. Price varies per volume. Springer-Verlag GmbH & Company KG, Heidelberger Platz 3, D-14197 Berlin Germany. **Tel** 011 49 30 8207223, FAX 011 49 30 8214091, telex 183 319 SPBLN D. **(Subscription address:** Springer-Verlag New York Inc. / North America, PO Box 2485, Journal Fulfillment, Secaucus NJ 07096. **Tel** (201)348-4033, (800)777-4643, FAX (201)348-4505.) **ED** G. Fandel, W. Trockel. Documents available from The Genuine Article, Ask*IEEE. ***Continues*** *Lecture Notes in Operations Research and Mathematical Systems.*
Desc: Covers the fields of mathematical economics, econometrics, operations research and mathematical systems.

Business and Economics

Ind/Abst CompuMath Cit. Index [Full Cov.]; Curr. Cit.; INSPEC; Math. Rev.; Res. Alert [Full Cov.]; Soc. Sci. Cit. Index [Full Cov.]; Zentralbl. Math. Ihre Grenzgeb.

LC HD70.S8 L43   **ISSN** 0280-7823
DD 338   SW
LEDARSKAP, EKONOMEN. (19??)-. Periodical. Swedish. Nine times a year. Kr385.00 Sweden; kr370.00 other. Ledarskap Ekonomen Klara, Soedra Kyrkogata 1, Box 70497, 10726 Stockholm Sweden. **Tel** 011 46 8 7966500.

   ISSN 1042-0134
DD 338   US
LEFT BUSINESS OBSERVER. [Left bus. obs.]. **VFOAT** Business Observer. (Sept. 1986)-. Periodical. English. Eleven times a year. $55.00. Left Business Observer, 250 West 85th Street, New York NY 10024-3217. **Tel** (212)874-4020. **ED** Doug Henwood. **Bk Rev**, (Qty: 3). **Circ:** 3,000.
Desc: A newsletter covering business, economics and politics.
Ind/Abst Altern. Press Index (199?-).

LC HC   **ISSN** 0024-0362
   UK
LEGAL EXECUTIVE, THE. See Law.

   CK
LEGISLACION ECONOMICA; REVISTA QUINCENAL DE INFORMACION Y CONSULTA. Added/Corp Colombia. Laws, Statutes, etc. (19??)-. Periodical. Spanish. Twenty-two times a year. Legis LTDA, Apartado Aereo 98 888, Bogota Colombia. **Tel** 011 57 1 2632530, 011 57 1 2630718.

   ISSN 0263-7774
DD 338.477900941   UK
LEISURE FUTURES. [Leis. futures]. (1982)-. Periodical. English. Four times a year. Henly Centre for Forecasting, London, United Kingdom. **Continues** U.K. Leisure Markets, 0308-776X.
Ind/Abst Curr. Cit.

LC HF3564.5 .L4
   GW
LEITENDE MANNER UND FRAUEN DER WIRTSCHAFT. See Biographies.

   ISSN 0930-4460
UDC 377.4   GW
   TITLE CHANGE
LERNFELD BETRIEB. [Lernfeld Betr.]. **VFOAT** Bildung + Betrieb. (1986)-(1994). Trade Publication. German. Dr. Josef Raabe Verlags GmbH, Postfach 103922, D-70034 Stuttgart Germany. **Tel** 011 49 711 6290093, telex 722232. **Continues** Arbeiten + Lernen, die Berufsbildung, 0176-3709. **Continued by** Personalpotential.

LC HC517.L4 L43
DD 380.1/025/686   LO
LESOTHO BUSINESS DIRECTORY. See Industry and Production-Trade and Industrial Directories.

   LO
LESOTHO (LESOTHO TOURIST CORPORATION). (LESOTHO.). **VFOAT** Lesotho, Kingdom in the Sky. (1978)-. Periodical. English. One time a year. R25.00. Braby's, (A Subsidiary of Kohler Packaging Ltd.), PO Box 1426, Pinetown 3600 South Africa. **Tel** 011 27 31 7017021, FAX 011 27 31 7017036.

   FR
LETTRE BANQUE ET SECURITE, LA. French. Six times a year. 1327.30F. INSIG Inst Formation Intrbancaire, 40 rue de Monceau, 75008 Paris France. **Tel** 011 33 1 42250724.

   ISSN 0766-883X
UDC 36.058.74   FR
LETTRE - C.A.F. VFOAT Lettre - Caisse des Allocations Familiales. (19??)-. Periodical. French. Twelve times a year.
Ind/Abst Int. Labour Doc.

   ISSN 0752-5168
UDC 381.81   FR
LETTRE DE LA CONCURRENCE, LA. [Lett. concurrence]. (1982)-. Periodical. French. Twenty-two times a year. $529.30. Publications Alain Dumait, 42 rue de Jeuneurs, 75002 Paris France. **Tel** 011 33 1 40280327.

   ISSN 0399-8606
UDC 33   FR
LETTRE DE L'EXPANSION, LA. [Lett. Expans.]. (1970)-. Periodical. French. Fifty times a year. $1137.35. Groupe Expansion, Le Ponant, 25 rue LeBlanc, 75842 Paris Cedex 15 France. **Tel** 011 33 1 40604115.

LC JQ1879.A15 L47
DD 960.3/2/05   FR
LETTRE DU CONTINENT : LC, LA. Added/Corp Banque d'Information et de Documentation Internationales (Paris, France). **VFOAT** LC. (1985)-. Periodical. French. Twenty-three times a year. $743.65. Indigo Publications, 10 rue du Sentier, 75002 Paris France. **Tel** 011 33 1 44882610, FAX 011 33 1 44882615, telex 215405. **ED** Antoine Glaser. **Circ:** 23.
Desc: Reports on politics, finances, and diplomacy on the African continent.

   US
LICENSING ECONOMICS REVIEW. (19??)-. English. Twelve times a year. $295.00. CA Turner Utility Reports, PO Box 1050, Morestown NJ 08057. **Tel** (609)234-9200 Ext. 400, FAX (609)234-8371.
Ind/Abst Abstr. BioCommer.

LC HF5192.9.A3 L53
   LI
LIETUVOS IMONES IR ORGANIZACIJOS / LIETUVOS INFORMACIJOS INSTITUTAS. Added/Corp Lietuvos Informacijos Institutas. **VFOAT** Lietkom. (1992)-. Lithuanian. Irregular. Lietuvos Informacijos Institutas, Kalvariju 3, 2659 Vilnius Lietuva Lithuania.

LC HD2709   **ISSN** 0106-5408
DD 338.74   DK
LIGNINGSVEJLEDNINGEN. SELSKABER. Main/Corp Denmark. Statsskattedirektoratet. (19??)-. Danish. Statsskattedirektoratet Ligningsafdelingen, Meldahlsgade 5, 1613 Copenhagen V Denmark.

LC HF3760 .A26   **ISSN** 0792-9765
DD 338.095694/05   IS
LINK. VFOAT Link Magazine. (19??)-. Periodical. English. Six times a year. $49.00. Pick Communications, 15 Beit Oved Street, Tel Aviv 67211 Israel. **Tel** 011 972 3 5374025, FAX 011 972 3 5374037. **ED** Michael Eilan. Index available. cum. index. **Ad Acc. Circ:** 15,000.

   ISSN 0261-4014
   UK
   CEASED
LINKS. Added/Corp Third World First (Group). (1976)-(1994). Periodical. English. Links Publications, 232 Cowley Road, Oxford OX4 1UH United Kingdom. **Tel** 011 44 1865 245678, FAX 011 44 1865 790096, .
Ind/Abst Altern. Press Index (199?-).

LC HX6 .L48   **ISSN** 0024-404X
   GW
Pr Rev.
LINKS : SOZIALISTISCHE ZEITUNG. See Political Science-Socialism, Communism, Anarchism, Utopianism.

   ISSN 0727-3924
DD 016.338705   AT
LIST OF HOLDINGS - AUSTRALIAN NATIONAL UNIVERSITY, RESEARCH SCHOOL OF SOCIAL SCIENCES, ARCHIVES OF BUSINESS AND LABOUR. [List hold. - Aust. Natl. Univ. Res. Sch. Soc. Sci. Arch. Bus. Labour]. (1981)-. English. One time a year. 5.00Aus$. Noel Butlin Archives of Bussiness and Labor, Australian National University, Canberra ACT 0200 Australia. **Tel** 011 61 6 2492219, FAX 011 61 6 2490140, telex AA62694 SOPAC. **ED** Michael Saclier. **Circ:** 400 (ctrl). **Continues** List of Records Relating to Companies and Firms Held by the Archives and List of Records Relating to Employee, Employer and Professional Associations Held by the Archives, 0725-8860.
Desc: Lists the holdings of the Noel Butlin Archives Centre. The list is divided into four parts: records of organizations, records of companies, personal papers, and collections acquired for the National AIDS Archives project.

LC HC   **ISSN** 0005-8521
DD 330   BE
LISTE MENSUELLE. See Business and Economics-Abstracting, Bibliographies and Statistics.

   ISSN 0921-6154
   NE
UDC 658.3 (048.8)
LITERATUURINFORMATIE PERSONEELSBELEID EN ORGANISATIE. (1985)-. Periodical. Dutch. Twenty-six times a year. KML/AFD Informative & Document, Postbus 7700, 1117 ZL Shiphol Netherlands.

   UK
LITHUANIA BUSINESS PACK, THE. (1992)-. English. Irregular. £75.00 UK; £80.00 other. Arguments & Facts International, PO Box 35, Hastings East Sussex, TN34 2UX United Kingdom. **Tel** 011 44 1424 444142, FAX 011 44 1424 717498.
Desc: Details on dealing with Lithuanian business enterprises.

LC HF5415.7 .F62   **ISSN** 1350-6293
   UK
●**LOGISTICS FOCUS : THE JOURNAL OF THE INSTITUTE OF LOGISTICS. Added/Corp** Institute of Logistics (Corby, England). Vol. 1, No. 1 (Aug. 1993)-. Periodical. English. Twelve times a year. Institute of Materials Management, Cranfield Institute of Technology, Cranfield MK43 0AL United Kingdom. **Tel** 011 44 1234 750662. **Formed by the union of** Focus on Logistics and Distribution Management **and** Logistics Today.
Ind/Abst Curr. Cit.

   ISSN 0927-0590
UDC 65.012.34   NE
   TITLE CHANGE
LOGISTIEK SIGNAAL. [Logist. signaal]. (1991)-(19??). Periodical. Dutch. Misset Uitgeverij BV / Rotterdam, Postbus 30180, 3001 DD Rotterdam, Netherlands. **Tel** 011 31 10 4053130. **Merged into** Transport + Opslag, 1065-330X.

   ISSN 0173-6213
UDC 658.78   GW
LOGISTIK HEUTE. See Transportation.

   ISSN 0172-9047
   GW
UDC 658.3   CCC
LOHN + GEHALT. VFOAT Lohn und Gehalt. (1979)-. Periodical. German. Six times a year. $101.33. Datakontext Verlag GmbH, Postfach 400253, D5000 Cologne Germany. **Tel** 011 49 221 486503, FAX 011 49 221 484391. **ED** Berud Heutschel. Index available. cum. index. **Bk Rev. Ad Acc.** ctrl circ.

LC HD4291 .A253   **ISSN** 0024-5925
DD 338/.0954   II
LOK UDYOG. Added/Corp India. Bureau of Public Enterprises. **VFOAT** Public Enterprise. (1967)-. Periodical. English. Twelve times a year. $20.00. Bureau of Public Enterprises, New Delhi India. **(Subscription address:** Prints India, 11 Darya Ganj, New Delhi 110002 India. **Tel** 011 91 11 3268645, FAX 011 91 11 3275542, telex 31-61087 PRIN-IN.) **Continues** Public Enterprise.
Ind/Abst Coal Abstr.; Int. Polit. Sci. Abstr.

LC HF5001   **ISSN** 0820-5698
DD 650/.09713/26   CN
LONDON BUSINESS MONTHLY MAGAZINE. [Lond. bus. mon. mag.]. Vol. 1, No. 1 (Mar. 1987)-. Trade Publication. English. Twelve times a year. 13.60Can$. Bowes Publishers, PO Box 7400 Station E, London Ontario N5Y 4X3 Canada. **Tel** (519)472-7601, FAX (519)473-2256. available on an online database (file 635/Full-Text) from DIALOG. Documents available from UMI Article Clearinghouse. **Continues** Western Ontario Business, 0383-6193.
Ind/Abst Bus. Dateline (May 6, 1985-) [Full Txt.].

   ISSN 0894-4806
   US
LONG ISLAND BUSINESS NEWS. VFOAT Long Island Business. (1987)-. Periodical. English. One time a week. $59.00. Long Island Business News, 2150 Smithtown Avenue, Ronkonkoma, Long Island NY 11779. **Tel** (516)737-1700. **ED** Paul Townsend. **Ad Acc, Adv Mgr:** T. Masterson. **Circ:** 11,000. Documents available from UMI Article Clearinghouse. **Continues** Long Island Business (Ronkonkoma, N.Y.), 0893-5734.
Ind/Abst Acad. Search; Bus. Dateline (Dec. 1990-) [Full Txt.]; Bus. Index (1987-1988); Bus. Source Plus; Bus. Source; EP Collect.; Gen. BusinessFile (1987-1988); Gen. Period. Index (1987-1988); Homework Help.; INFO-SOUTH Abstr.; MasterFile FullTEXT 1000; MasterFile FullTEXT 350; MasterFile FullTEXT 650; MasterFile FullTEXT (July 1993-); OCLC; PROMT; Telebase; Trade Ind. ASAP [Full Txt.]; Trade Ind. Index [Full Txt.].

LC HF5549.5.E45 L66   **ISSN** 1052-7664
DD 650.14   US
LOOKING FOR EMPLOYMENT IN FOREIGN COUNTRIES. [Look. employ. foreign ctries.]. **VFOAT** Looking for Employment in Foreign Countries Reference Handbook. English. $16.50. World Trade Academy Press Inc, 50 East 42nd Street, Suite 509, New York NY 10017. **Tel** (212)697-4999, FAX (212)949-4001.
Desc: Those seeking the adventure of living and working overseas can explore opportunities in private industry, with the US government, or with religious or other non-profit organizations. Special information for students who want to make money while spending the summer abroad.

   ISSN 0194-2603
DD 330   US
LOS ANGELES BUSINESS JOURNAL. [Los Angel. bus. j.]. (1979)-. Periodical. English. One time a week. $59.95. Los Angeles Business Journal, PO Box 469016, Escondido CA 90246. **Tel** (213)549-5225, (800)255-3302. **ED** David Yochum. **Ad Acc. Circ:** 40,000 (ctrl). available on microfilm from University Microfilms International (UMI); available on an online database (files 635,648/Full-Text) from DIALOG.

Documents available from UMI Article Clearinghouse.
Desc: Business journal covering Los Angeles and surrounding counties, with middle to upper management demographics. Part of a nationwide network of business publications.
Ind/Abst Acad. Search; Bus. Dateline; Bus. Index (1985-1990); Bus. Source Plus; Bus. Source; EP Collect.; Gen. BusinessFile (1985-1990); Gen. Period. Index (1985-); Homework Help.; INFO-SOUTH Abstr.; MasterFile FullTEXT 1000; MasterFile FullTEXT 350; MasterFile FullTEXT 650; MasterFile FullTEXT (July 1993-); OCLC; PROMT; Telebase; Trade Ind. ASAP [Full Txt.]; Trade Ind. Index [Full Txt.].

ISSN 0165-0335
NE
LOSBLADIG FISCAAL WEEKBLAD FED. [Losbl. fisc. weekbl. Fed]. (1940)-. Periodical. Dutch. Fifty-two times a year. Kluwer BV, Postbus 23, 7400 GA Deventer Netherlands. **Tel** 011 31 5700 33155, 011 31 5700 47421, FAX 011 31 5700 11504, telex 42829. **(Subscription address:** Libresso BV, Postbus 23, 7400 GA Deventer Netherlands. **Tel** 011 30 5700 47333, 011 31 5700 33155.**)**

LC HD2771 HD2771 .L68 **ISSN** 1060-2178
DD 338 US
LOTUS ONE SOURCE. CD/CORPORATE. U.S. PUBLIC COS. (LOTUS ONE SOURCE. CD/CORPORATE. U.S. PUBLIC COS. [COMPUTER FILE].). [Lotus one source, CD/corp., U. S. public cos.]. **Added/Corp** Lotus Development Corporation. **VFOAT** Lotus One Source. US Public Companies; Lotus One Source. United States Public Companies; CD/Corporate. U.S. Public Cos.; CD/Corporate. US Public Companies; CD Corporate. United States Public Companies; U.S. Public Cos.; US Public Companies; United States Public Companies; Lotus One Source. U.S. Public Companies. (July 1990)-. Periodical. English. Twelve times a year. Lotus Development Corporation, CD-ROM Information Services, 55 Cambridge Parkway, Cambridge MA 02142. ***Continues*** *Lotus One Source. CD/Corporate, 1065-7592.*

LC HD1775.L8 L75 **ISSN** 8756-6273
DD 338 US
LOUISIANA RURAL ECONOMIST. See Agriculture-Agricultural Economics.

ISSN 1056-7070
DD 330 US
LOWER COLUMBIA BUSINESS. [Low. Columbia bus.]. **VFOAT** Business. Vol. 1, No. 1 (July, 1991)-. Periodical. English. Six times a year. $15.00. Nextstep Publications, 1485 3rd Street, Astoria OR 97103-5305. **Tel** (503)325-8828.

ISSN 0956-8549
UK
LSE FINANCIAL MARKETS GROUP DISCUSSION PAPER SERIES. [LSE Financ. Mark. Group discuss. pap. ser.]. **VFOAT** London School of Economics Financial Markets Group Discussion Paper Series; Discussion Paper - LSE Financial Markets Group. (198?)-. Monographic series. English. Irregular (published 22-25 times a year). Free on request. London School of Economics, Houghton Street, London WC2A 2AE United Kingdom. **Tel** 011 44 171 9557438, FAX 011 44 171 9557446.

LC HB1 .L78 **ISSN** 0023-639X
DD 330/.05 UK
LSE MAGAZINE. [LSE mag.]. **Added/Corp** London School of Economics and Political Science. **VAT** London School of Economics Magazine. (Autumn/Winter 1989/90)-. Periodical. English. Four times a year. London School of Economics, Houghton Street, London WC2A 2AE United Kingdom. **Tel** 011 44 171 9557438, FAX 011 44 171 9557446.

ISSN 0460-0029
SW
LUND ECONOMIC STUDIES. (1962)-. Monographic series. English. Irregular. Price varies per volume. Liber International, S-205 10 Malmo Sweden. **Tel** 011 46 40 70650.

ISSN 1186-608X
DD 371.2/0097127 CN
M.A.S.B.O. NEWS. See Education-School Management and Organization.

ISSN 0381-6788
DD 650/.07 CN
M. B. E. T. A. NEWSLETTER. Main/Corp Manitoba Business Education Teachers Association. No. 1- 1975-. Newsletter. English. Manitoba Business Education Teachers Association, 47 Weinberg Road, Winnipeg Manitoba R2V 1M7 Canada.

LC HF5470 .M23 **ISSN** 0093-0482
DD 381 US
M.E. MEETINGS & EXPOSITIONS. (M. E.). **VFOAT** Meetings & Expositions. English. $15.00. Meetings and Expositions, 270 Madison Avenue, New York NY 10016.

LC AP9 .M5
DD 330.956/005 UA
M.E.N. ECONOMIC WEEKLY. Added/Corp Anba al-Sharq al-Awsat. **VFOAT** M.E.N. Economic Weekly; M.E.W. **VAT** Middle East News Economic Weekly. Vol. 12, Issue No. 3 (Jan. 20, 1973)-. Periodical. English. One time a week. $110.00 Egypt; $150.00 other. Middle East News Agency, PO Box 1165 Hoda Sha Rawy Str, Attaba 11511 Cairo Egypt. **Tel** 741102 741223 ext. 264. **ED** Zeinab M. Wahby. **Circ:** 300 (ctrl). ***Continues*** *Middle East News Economic Weekly.*
Desc: Publishes the current economic news of the Middle East, especially Egypt. Also provides news stories and features.

AT
Pr Rev.
M-SERIES MONOGRAPHS. See Travel and Tourism.

LC HB9 .M2 **ISSN** 0013-0486
NE
MAANDSCHRIFT ECONOMIE. [Maandschr. econ.]. (Oct. 1935)-. Academic Scholarly Publication. Dutch. Six times a year. $154.17. Wolters Noordhoff BV, Postbus 567, 9700 AN Groningen Netherlands. **Tel** 011 31 50 226886, FAX 011 31 50 264866. **ED** H.A. Kaag.
Ind/Abst EMBASE; Int. Bibliogr. Sociol.

LC HB235.N2 N47a
DD 338.52 NE
MAANDSTATISTIEK VAN DE PRIJZEN. See Business and Economics-Abstracting, Bibliographies and Statistics.

LC HB172.5 .M3353
DD 339/.05 US
MACROECONOMICS (GUILFORD, CONN.). (MACROECONOMICS.). **VFOAT** Annual Editions : Macroeconomics. (198?)-. Monographic series. English. Irregular. Price varies per volume. Dushkin Publishing Group Inc., Sluice Dock, Guilford CT 06437. **Tel** (203)453-4351, (800)243-6532, FAX (203)453-6000. **ED** Don Cole.
Desc: Examines the broad spectrum of aggregate economics addressing areas such as fiscal policy, monetary policy, inflation, and employment.

ISSN 0889-0838
US
MADDUX REPORT, THE. (198?)-. Periodical. English. Twelve times a year. $75.00. Maddux Publishing Inc., PO Box 202, St. Petersburg FL 33701. **Tel** (813)823-4394, FAX (813)821-1645. **ED** John Koenig. **Ad Acc, Adv Mgr:** Marcia Turner. **Circ:** 15,776 (ctrl).
Desc: Business publication covering 6-county Tampa Bay area.

LC HF3221 **ISSN** 1201-8589
DD 381.130971 CN
●**MAGAZINE QUEBE FRANCHISE.** (1995)-. English (French). Four times a year (Mar., June, Sept., Dec.). 20.00Can$. Magazine Quebec Franchise inc, CP 535 SUCC Place du Parc, Montreal Que H2W 2P1 Canada. **Tel** (514)287-9827, FAX (514)287-9684.

ISSN 1150-4447
FR
UDC 070.2(1-4)
MAGHREB CONFIDENTIEL PARIS. See Political Science.

ISSN 1071-7579
DD 961 US
MAGHREB REPORT. See Political Science.

ISSN 1040-1296
DD 650 US
MAIL ORDER PRODUCT GUIDE. [Mail order prod. guide]. 1st Ed. (1989)-. English. $23.00. B. Klein Publications, PO Box 8503, Coral Springs FL 33065. **Tel** (305)752-1708, FAX (305)752-2547. **ED** Barry T. Klein. Index available. **Ad Acc. Circ:** 2,000.
Desc: Lists 1500 manufacturers, importers and distributors of products for the mail order catalog industry.

LC HB9 .M29
IQ
MAJALLAT AL-BUHUTH AL-IQTISADIYAH WA-AL-IDARIYAH. Added/Corp Jamiat Baghdad. Markaz al-Buhuth al-Iqtisadiyah Wa-al-Idariyah. **VFOAT** Iraqi Journal of Economic and Administrative Research. (19??)-. Periodical. Arabic (English). Three times a year. Economic and Administrative Research Centre Al-Adhamiya, PO Box 4095, Baghdad Iraq.

LC HF3500.7.A48 M24
UK
MAJOR BUSINESS ORGANISATIONS OF EASTERN EUROPE AND THE SOVIET UNION. (1991)-. English. $599.00. Graham & Trotman Ltd., Sterling House, 66 Wilton Road, London SW1V 1DE United Kingdom. **Tel** 011 44 171 8211123, FAX 011 44 171 8288935.
Desc: Provides essential information on approximately 4,000 of the more important Eastern European and Soviet business organizations. This includes Ministries with which Western business people may have to deal, such as chambers of commerce, financial institutions, manufacturing companies, and trading organizations. For each commercial organization, whether it's still state owned or has been privatized, the following data is provided (as available): address, fax and telex, name of the President, General Director, Director of Imports, Director of Exports, Director of Joint Ventures with Foreign Companies, parent organizations and subsidiaries, bankers, number of employees and financial data.

LC HC241.2 .P667
DD 338.7/4/0254 UK
MAJOR COMPANIES OF EUROPE. (1982)-. English. One time a year. $1280.00. Graham & Trotman Ltd., Sterling House, 66 Wilton Road, London SW1V 1DE United Kingdom. **Tel** 011 44 171 8211123, FAX 011 44 171 8288935. **(Subscription address:** Gale Research Co., 835 Penobscot Building, Detroit MI 48226. **Tel** (800)347-4253.**) Bk Rev.** ***Continues*** *Principal Companies of the European Economic Community;* ***Absorbed*** *Major Companies of Scandinavia.*
Desc: Three volumes cover more than 6,200 of Europe's major companies. Each volume is arranged by country with indexes to company names, business activities and countries.

LC HF3866 .M3 **ISSN** 0144-0594
DD 338.4/025/174927 UK
MAJOR COMPANIES OF THE ARAB WORLD. [Major co. Arab world]. (1977)-. English. One time a year. $720.00. Graham & Trotman Ltd., Sterling House, 66 Wilton Road, London SW1V 1DE United Kingdom. **Tel** 011 44 171 8211123, FAX 011 44 171 8288935. **(Subscription address:** Gale Research Co., 835 Penobscot Building, Detroit MI 48226. **Tel** (800)347-4253.**) ED** G. C. Bricault. **Ad Acc.** ***Supersedes in part*** *Major Companies of the Arab World and Iran.*
Desc: Provides details of over 6,000 major Arab companies in 20 Arab countries. Gives information about each company's finances, personnel, structure, products, and profitability. Identifies the key decision-makers and executives.

LC HG4244.6 .M35 **ISSN** 0961-3226
DD 338.7/4/0255 UK
MAJOR COMPANIES OF THE FAR EAST AND AUSTRALASIA. (1990/1991)-. Directory. English. One time a year. $1140.00. Graham & Trotman Ltd., Sterling House, 66 Wilton Road, London SW1V 1DE United Kingdom. **Tel** 011 44 171 8211123, FAX 011 44 171 8288935. ***Continues*** *Major Companies of the Far East.*
Desc: Provides information on nearly 4,500 major companies of the Far East and Australasia.

LC HC107.W22 P864
DD 330 US
TITLE CHANGE
MAJOR EMPLOYERS, CENTRAL PUGET SOUND. Added/Corp Greater Seattle Chamber of Commerce. **VFOAT** Central Puget Sound Major Employers Directory. (1993)-(199?). Directory. English. ***Continues*** *Major Employers Directory, Central Puget Sound Region.* ***Continued by*** *Major Employers Directory, Central Puget Sound area.*

ISSN 1192-2427
DD 338.9 CN
Pr Rev.
MAKING WAVES (PORT ALBERNI). (MAKING WAVES : A NEWSLETTER FOR CED PRACTITIONERS IN CANADA.). [Mak. waves]. **Added/Corp** Westcoast Development Group (Port Alberni, B.C.) Centre for Community Enterprise (Port Alberni, B.C.). **VFOAT** Newsletter for CED Practitioners in Canada. Vol. 1, No. 1 (Oct. 1989)-. Newsletter. English. Four times a year (Feb., May, Aug., Nov.). 32.01Can$. Westcoast Development Group, 163 West Hastings, Suite 337, Vancouver British Columbia, V6B 1H5 Canada. **Tel** (604)542-7057, FAX (604)542-7229. **ED** Mike Lewis, (phone: (604)685-5058). **Bk Rev**, (Qty: 2). **Ad Acc. Circ:** 150 (ctrl).
Desc: The community developments strategies, anaylsis, and resources.

LC HC445.5.A1 M33
DD 338/.09595 MY
MALAYSIAN BUSINESS. (19??)-. Periodical. English. Twenty-four times a year. $211.78. New Straits Times Press, Balai Berita 31 Jalan Riong, 59100 Kuala Lumpur Malaysia. **Tel** 011 60 3 2823131, 011 60 3 2823322, FAX 011 60 3 2825502. **ED** Shaik Osman Majid. **Bk Rev. Ad Acc. Circ:** 18,000.
Desc: Complete business magazine.

LC HF5415.5 .M16 **ISSN** 0960-4529
DD 658.8/12/05 UK
CCC
CODEN MSQUEU
MANAGING SERVICE QUALITY. (19??)-. Periodical. English. Six times a year. $499.00. MCB University Press, 60 62 Toller Lane, Bradford, West Yorkshire BD8 9BY United Kingdom. **Tel** 011 44 1274 785280, FAX 011 44 1274 785200, telex 51317-MCBUNI-G. **(Subscription address:** Managing

Business and Economics

Service Quality, Subscription Office, PO Box 10812, Birmingham AL 35201. **Tel** (205)995-1567.**)**
Ind/Abst Curr. Cit.

LC HC **ISSN** 0025-2034
DD 330 UK
  CCC
Pr Rev.
MANCHESTER SCHOOL OF ECONOMIC AND SOCIAL STUDIES, THE. [Manch. sch. econ. soc. stud.]. **Added/Corp** University of Manchester. Dept. of Economics. **VFOAT** Manchester School. (1939)-. Academic Scholarly Publication. English. Five times a year. $161.00. Basil Blackwell Publishers Ltd., 108 Cowley Road, Oxford OX4 1JF United Kingdom. **Tel** 011 44 1235 465500, FAX 011 44 1235 465556, telex 837022 OXBOOK G. **(Subscription address:** Blackwell Publishers / UK, 108 Cowley Road, Oxford OX4 1JF United Kingdom. **Tel** 011 44 1865 791100, FAX 011 44 1865 791347.**)** available on microfilm and microfiche from University Microfilms International (UMI). Documents available from The Genuine Article, UMI Article Clearinghouse. **Continues** Manchester School.
Ind/Abst Acad. Search; Am. Hist. Life (1967-1978); Appl. Soc. Sci. Index Abstr.; Bus. Source Plus; Bus. Source; Contents Pages Manage.; Curr. Contents Soc. Behav. Sci.; Econ. Lit. Index (19??-); EP Collect.; Expand. Acad. Index (1989-); Homework Help.; INFO-SOUTH Abstr.; Int. Bibliogr. Sociol.; J. Econ. Lit.; MasterFile FullTEXT 1000; MasterFile FullTEXT 350; MasterFile FullTEXT 650; MasterFile FullTEXT (July 1993-); Middle East Abstr. Index; Newsp. Period. Abstr. (1991-); OCLC; Res. Alert [Full Cov.]; Risk Abstr.; Soc. Sci. Source; Soc. Sci. Cit. Index [Full Cov.]; Soc. Sci. Index; Soc. Sci. Index Fulltext [Dec. 1988-] [Full Txt.]; Stat. Theory Method Abstr. (1969, 1971, 1973); Telebase; Work Relat. Abstr. (1967-1978, 19??-); World Mag. Bank.

  ISSN 0709-2423
DD 380/.097127 CN
MANITOBA BUSINESS. [Manit. bus.]. (Jan./Feb. 1979)-. Periodical. English. Ten times a year. 13.57Can$. Canada Wide Magazines Ltd., 401-4180 Lougheed Highway, Burnaby British Columbia V5C 6A7 Canada. **Tel** (604)299-7311, FAX (604)299-9188. **ED** Ritchie Gage. **Ad Acc, Adv Mgr:** Louise Ayre, **Tel** (204)477-4620. **Circ:** 10,000. available on an online database (files 635,648/Full-Text) from DIALOG. Documents available from UMI Article Clearinghouse.
Desc: Local business profiles. Memorandum gives business tips and hands-on information to assist the executive in his/her working environment.
Ind/Abst Acad. Search; Bus. Dateline; Bus. Index (1985-); Bus. Source Plus; Bus. Source; Can. Bus. Index; Can. Index; Can. Period. Index (19??-); EP Collect.; Gen. BusinessFile (1985-); Gen. Period. Index (1985-); Homework Help.; INFO-SOUTH Abstr.; MasterFile FullTEXT 1000; MasterFile FullTEXT 350; MasterFile FullTEXT 650; MasterFile FullTEXT (July 1993-); OCLC; PROMT; Telebase; Trade Ind. ASAP [Full Txt.]; Trade Ind. Index [Full Txt.].

LC HF5001 **ISSN** 0318-2118
DD 650/.07/12 CN
MANITOBA SPECTRA. [Manit. spectra]. **Added/Corp** Manitoba Business Education Teachers Association. Vol. 2 (Feb. 1975)-. Periodical. English. Seven times a year. Manitoba Teachers Society, 191 Harcourt Street, Winnipeg Manitoba R3J 3H2 Canada. **Tel** (204)888-7961 ext.254, FAX (204)831-0877. **Continues** B.E.E.P., Business Education's Exciting Publication, 0315-2197.

  ISSN 0700-2971
  CN
MANITOBA STATISTICAL REVIEW. See Business and Economics-Abstracting, Bibliographies and Statistics.

  ISSN 0885-4149
DD 330 US
MANUFACTURERS HANOVER ECONOMIC REPORT, THE. Added/Corp Manufacturers Hanover Trust Company. **VFOAT** Economic Report. (19??)-. Periodical. English. Ten times a year. Free on request. Manufacturers Hanover Trust, Church Street Station, 270 Park Avenue, New York NY 10017. **Tel** (212)286-7346. Documents available from UMI Article Clearinghouse.
Ind/Abst ABI/INFORM [Computer File] (Nov. 1980-); Gen. BusinessFile (1992-).

  FR
MARCHES EST EUROPEENS. French. Forty-Five times a year. 5778.65F France; 5900.00F other. IC Publications Ediafric, 10 rue Vineuse, 75116 Paris France. **Tel** 011 33 1 44308100.

  ISSN 0887-851X
DD 338 US
  SUSPENDED
MARGIN (COLORADO SPRINGS, COLO.), THE. (THE MARGIN.). [Margin]. (1985)-(19??). Periodical. English. Two times a year (Spring & Fall). $11.00 (one-year); $19.95 (two-year). University of Colorado / Colorado, PO Box 7150, Colorado Springs CO 80933. **Tel** (719)593-3305, FAX (719)593-3328. **ED** Timothy Tregarthen and Suzanne Tregarthen. **Bk Rev. Circ:** 6,000.
Desc: Contains articles which analyze current events using economic tools, graduate school and career profiles, interviews, biographies, book reviews and current economic data.

  US
MARION COUNTY DEED REPORT. English. Irregular. $660.00. Sunday Missal Service, 1012 Vermont Street, Quincy IL 62301. **Tel** (217)222-4030, FAX (217)222-6808.

LC HC92 .M37 **ISSN** 0308-8839
DD 333.9/1/005 UK
  CCC
MARITIME POLICY AND MANAGEMENT. See Transportation-Ships and Shipping.

  ISSN 1122-8873
  IT
●**MARK UP.** Vol. 1, No. 1 (1994)-. Consumer Publication. Italian. Twelve times a year. L100.000. Quasar Editoriale s.r.l., Via Santa Lucia 2, 20122 Milan Italy. **Tel** 011 39 2 58301946, FAX 011 39 2 58303803. **Ad Acc.**
Desc: For entrepreneurs and managers of production, marketing, retailing, and service sectors.

  ISSN 0947-787X
  GW
MARKENBLATT. See Encyclopedias and General Reference Books.

  IT
MARKET INTELLIGENCE BULLETIN. (19??)-. Bulletin. English. Trade Development Authority, 16 Parliament Street, New Delhi 1 India.

  ISSN 1059-1923
  US
MARKET NICHES IN ... . (1991)-. English. Whitehaven Publishing, PO Box 20587, Oklahoma City OK 73156.

  IT
Pr Rev. CEASED
MARKETING TRIBUNE. (19??)-(1995). Italian. Esi Stampa Medica Srl, Casella Postale 42, 20097 San Donato Mil Italy. **Tel** 11 39 2 5274241, FAX 11 39 2 55600670, telex 324894. Index available. cum. index. **Circ:** 3,000 (ctrl).
Desc: Articles on marketing and sales on the pharmaceutical market. Dedicated to the top managers of pharmaceutical companies and advertising agencies.

  ISSN 0199-7130
  US
MARKETPLACE (SCOTTDALE), THE. (THE MARKETPLACE.). **Added/Corp** Mennonite Industry and Business Associates. Vol. 10 (Mar. 1980)-. Periodical. English. Six times a year (Jan., Mr., May, July, Sept., Nov.). $15.00. Mennonite Economic Developmebt Association, 280 Smith Street, Suite 302, Winnipeg Manitoba R3C 1K2 Canada. **Tel** (204)944-1995. **Continues** Mennonite Industry and Business Associates. MIBA Newsletter.

  ISSN 1055-5579
DD 333 US
MARKETSOURCE (CHICAGO, ILL.). (MARKETSOURCE : A STATISTICAL BULLETIN FROM THE APPRAISAL INSTITUTE.). [MarketSource]. **Added/Corp** Appraisal Institute (U.S.). **VFOAT** Market Source. Vol. 1, No. 1, 2nd Quarter (1991)-. Bulletin. English. Four times a year (Jan., Apr., July, Oct.). $150.00. Appraisal Institute, 875 North Michigan Avenue, Suite 2400, Chicago IL 60611. **Tel** (312)335-4100, FAX (312)335-4400.

  ISSN 0279-960X
DD 338 CCC
MARPLE'S BUSINESS NEWSLETTER. [Marple's. bus. newsl.]. **Added/Corp** Marple's Business Newsletter. Marple's Business Roundup, Inc. No. 640 (Aug. 14, 1974)-. Newsletter. English. Twenty-six times a year. $72.00. Newsletter Publishing Corporation, 117 W Mercer Street Suite 200, Seattle WA 98119. **Tel** (206)281-9609, FAX (206)281-8535. **ED** Michael J. Parks. Index available (Feb.). **Circ:** 4,000. **Continues** Marple's Business Roundup, 0025-391X.
Desc: A bi-weekly regional business newsletter focusing on the economy and companies of the Pacific Northwest and Alaska.

LC HC US
MARSHALL VALUATION SERVICE. **Main/Corp** Marshall and Stevens Publication Company. (19??)-. English. Twelve times a year. $189.95. Marshall & Swift, 911 Wilshire Boulevard, 16th Floor, Los Angeles CA 90026. **Tel** (800)544-2678, FAX (310)250-9811. **(Subscription address:** Marshall & Swift, PO Box 26307, Los Angeles CA 90026. **)**

  ISSN 0882-0589
  US
MARTIN BROWER'S ORANGE COUNTY REPORT. VFOAT Orange County Report. Vol. 1, No. 1 (May 1985)-. Periodical. English. Twelve times a year. $265.00. Martin Browers Orange County, 180 Newport Center Drive, Suite 180, Newport Beach CA 92660. **Tel** (714)720-0209. **ED** Martin A. Brower; Telephone: (714)720-8414. Index available (Bound in December issue). cum. index.
Desc: Published for business, professional, governmental and institutional leaders who need to understand Orange County, California.

  ISSN 0747-0320
  US
MARYLAND BUSINESS & LIVING. (MARYLAND BUSINESS & LIVING : B & L.). **VFOAT** B & L; B and L; B&L; Maryland Business and Living. Vol. 9, No. 1 (March/April 1984)-. Periodical. English. Twelve times a year. $12.00. Philos Publications, 7 Church Lane/Suite 16, Baltimore MD 21208. available on an online database (file 635/Full-Text) from DIALOG. Documents available from UMI Article Clearinghouse. **Continues** Maryland Business & Living Journal, 0746-5629.
Ind/Abst Bus. Dateline; Bus. Index (Jan. 1985-Dec. 1985); Gen. BusinessFile (Jan. 1985-Dec. 1985); Gen. Period. Index (Jan. 1985-Dec. 1985); INFO-SOUTH Abstr.

LC HC107.M3 M266 **ISSN** 0465-1057
DD 330.9/752/04 US
MARYLAND ECONOMY, THE. (THE MARYLAND ECONOMY : STATUS AND OUTLOOK.). [Md. econ.]. **Main/Corp** Maryland. Dept. of Economic and Community Development. English. One time a year. Maryland Department of Economic and Community Development, 45 Calvert Street, Annapolis MD 21401. **Tel** (312)337-1084.

LC HC107.M4 M39a **ISSN** 0360-5744
DD 330.9/744/04 US
MASSACHUSETTS ECONOMIC ASSUMPTIONS. Main/Corp Massachusetts. Division of Employment Security. Research Dept. (19??)-. English. Division of Employment Security / Boston, Charles F. Hurley Building, Government Center, Boston MA 02114. **Tel** (617)727-6531.

  US
MATCHING GIFT NOTES : NOTES OF INTEREST FROM CASE, THE NATIONAL CLEARINGHOUSE FOR CORPORATE MATCHING GIFT INFORMATION. See Education.

LC HB135 .M367 **ISSN** 0025-1127
DD 330/.01/51 US
  CCC
MATEKON. (MATEKON : TRANSLATIONS OF RUSSIAN & EAST EUROPEAN MATHEMATICAL ECONOMICS.). [Matekon]. **VFOAT** Translations of Russian & East European Mathematical Economics. Vol. 6 (Fall 1969)-. Periodical. English. Four times a year. $463.00. M. E. Sharpe Inc., 80 Business Park Drive, Armonk NY 10504. **Tel** (914)273-1800, (800)541-6563, FAX (914)273-2106. **ED** Martin Cave. **Bk Rev. Ad Acc. Circ:** 250 (ctrl). available on microfilm from University Microfilms International (UMI). Documents available from The Genuine Article. **Continues** Mathematical Studies in Economics and Statistics in the USSR and Eastern Europe.
Desc: Focuses on Soviet mathematical economics, programming, and applied control theory.
Ind/Abst CompuMath Cit. Index [Full Cov.]; Contents Recent Econ. J.; Econ. Lit. Index; J. Econ. Lit.; Res. Alert [Full Cov.]; Soc. Sci. Cit. Index [Full Cov.].

  GW
MATERIALANGEBOT, DAS. Periodical. German. Twenty-six times a year. Deutscher Judo Verband, Redaktion Ippon Segewaldweg 40, D-12557 Berlin Germany. **Tel** 011 49 711 210770, telex 051 678.

  ISSN 0344-3302
  GW
MATHEMATICAL SYSTEMS IN ECONOMICS. See Mathematics.

  UK
MBA COURSE, THE DPBA COURSE, THE. See Education-Higher Education.

  ISSN 1055-0534
DD 378 US
MBA NEWSLETTER, THE. [MBA newsl.]. **VAT** Masters of Busines Administration Newsletter. Vol. 1, No. 1 (Apr. 1991)-. Newsletter. English. Fourteen times a year (published monthly with 2 special issues). $267.00. Kwartler Communications Inc., 79 Verbena Avenue, Floral Park NY 11001. **Tel** (516)488-2010, FAX (516)488-2025. Index available (Free).

Business and Economics

LC HD38.2 .M22
ISSN 0954-4836
UK
CEASED

MBA REVIEW. See Education-Higher Education.

ISSN 0892-9831
US

MBEA TODAY. See Education.

LC HB1 .M38
DD 330/.05
ISSN 0712-1148
CN

MCGILL JOURNAL OF POLITICAL ECONOMY, THE. [McGill j. polit. econ.]. **Added/Corp** McGill University. Economics Students' Association. McGill University. Dept. of Political Economy. **VFOAT** Journal d'Economie Politique de McGill.; Revue d'Economie Politique de McGill. **VAT** Revue d'Economie Politique de McGill. Vol. 1, No. 1 (Feb. 1977)-. Periodical. English. One time a year. 6.00Can$. McGill Journal of Political Economy, c/o Department of Economics, McGill University, 855 Sherbrooke Street West, Montreal Quebec H3A 2T7 Canada. **Tel** (514)392-5239. Index available. cum. index. **Circ:** 500 (ctrl).
Desc: The journal consists of a collection of economic academic articles on issues ranging from historical reviews, statistical analysis, theoretical reviews and practical interpretations.

LC HG4264.3 .A19
DD 338.8/025/68
SA

MCGREGOR'S WHO OWNS WHOM. **VFOAT** Investors' Handbook; Who Owns Whom. 7th Ed. (1987)-. English. One time a year. R443.00. Purdey Holdings CC, PO Box 3434, Rustenburg 0300 South Africa. **Tel** 011 27 142 92609. **ED** Robin McGregor. Index available. **Ad Acc. Circ:** 2,500. **Continues** McGregor, Robin. McGregor's Investors Handbook.
Desc: A thorough, exhaustive and easy to use analysis of relevant data on all companies listed on the Johannesburg Stock Exchange.

US

MEDIA GENERAL INDUSTRY SCOPE. (Dec. 31, 1991)-. English. Twelve times a year. $324.00. Media General Inc., PO Box 85333, Richmond VA 23293. **Tel** (800)446-7922.
Desc: Tracks from database 7,000 publicly held stocks. Grouped within industry for easy comparison.

ISSN 0895-4550
DD 336
US

MEDIA MERGERS & ACQUISITIONS. See Communications.

ISSN 0934-4217
GW

UDC 33

MEDIA SELECTION. [Media sel.]. (1988)-. Trade Publication. German. Twenty-four times a year. DM148.00. Dr Horst Kerlikowsky Verlag, Konradstr 16, W-8000 Munich 40 Germany. **Tel** 089/34401201, FAX 089/390662, telex 335015. **ED** Horst Kevlihowsky. **Bk Rev. Ad Acc. Circ:** 1,000. available on diskette.
Desc: Abstracts of business and economic views.

ISSN 1120-1932
IT

UDC 655.5
SUSPENDED

MEDIAPLUSNEWS. [Mediaplusnews]. (1986)-Suspended (1993). Periodical. Italian. Twelve times a year. L50.000 Italy; L100.000 elsewhere Europe. Media Plus Srl, Via Ausonio 5, 20123 Milan Italy. **Tel** 011 39 2 8322832, FAX 011 39 2 58100311. **Bk Rev. Ad Acc. Circ:** 12,000.
Desc: Information, culture, and current technology news for the world of small business, with new technologies in particular.

ISSN 0743-8079
DD 368
NLM W1; ME228M
US

MEDICAL BENEFITS. See Insurance.

LC HB235.I78 M39
IT

MEDIE MENSILI ED ANNUALE DELLE QUOTAZIONI RIPORTATE NEI LISTINI SETTIMANALI DEI PREZZI ALL'INGROSSO SULLA PIAZZA DI MILANO PER L'ANNO. **Added/Corp** Universita Commerciale Luigi Bocconi. Camera di Commercio, Industria, Artigianato e Agricoltura di Milano. (19??)-. Italian. One time a year. Camera di Commercio Industria Artigianato E Agricoltura di Milano, via Meravigli 9 B, 20123 Milan Italy. **Tel** 011 39 2 85154516.

LC HF5152.A3 M43
DD 338.7/4/0254
ISSN 0960-1449
UK

MEDIUM COMPANIES OF EUROPE. (1991)-. English. $1198.00. Graham & Trotman Ltd., Sterling House, 66 Wilton Road, London SW1V 1DE United Kingdom. **Tel** 011 44 171 8211123, FAX 011 44 171 8288935.
Desc: Describes Europe's many privately-owned and fast-growing medium-sized firms. Provides information on over 7,000 rising stars in European business, finance and industry.

US

MEDVIN P-H-C- TRADELETTER. See Heating, Plumbing, and Refrigeration.

ISSN 8750-7218
DD 659
US

MEETING MANAGER, THE. [Meet. manager]. **Added/Corp** Meeting Planners International. (July 1984)-. Periodical. English. Twelve times a year. $35.00. Meeting Planners International, 1950 Stemmons Freeway, Suite 5018, Dallas TX 75207-3109. **Tel** (214)712-7735, FAX (214)712-7796. **ED** Tina Berres Filipski (editor's phone: (214)712-7733). **Ad Acc, Adv Mgr:** B. McGlynn, **Tel** (214)712-7733. **Circ:** 12,000 (ctrl). **Continues** Meetingplace.
Desc: Indepth articles on topics pertinent to experienced meeting professionals.

ISSN 0145-630X
DD 338
CCC

MEETING NEWS. [Meet. news]. Vol. 1 (Jan. 1977)-. Periodical. English. Twelve times a year. $70.00. Miller Freeman Inc., 600 Harrison Street, San Francisco CA 94107. **Tel** (415)905-2337, (415)905-2200, FAX (415)905-2240, telex 278273. **(Subscription address:** JCI, PO Box 1766, Riverton NJ 08077.)

LC AS6 .M44
DD 658.4/563
ISSN 0025-8652
US

MEETINGS AND CONVENTIONS. [Meet. conv.]. **VFOAT** M and C; Meetings & Conventions; M & C; M&C. Vol. 1, No. 1 (June 1966)-. Periodical. English. Thirteen times a year. $79.90. Cahners Publishing Company, 249 West 17th Street, New York NY 10011. **Tel** (212)645-0067, FAX (212)242-6987. **(Subscription address:** Cahners Publishing Company / Colorado, Paid Subscription Service Center, PO Box 7610, Highlands Ranch CO 80126-7610. **Tel** (303)470-4466, FAX (303)470-4691.) available on microfilm and microfiche from University Microfilms International (UMI); available on an online database (file 648/Full-Text) from DIALOG. Documents available from UMI Article Clearinghouse.
Desc: Magazine for meeting planners with world wide coverage. Whether the meeting is in Sydney, Australia or Tyler, Texas, the needed information is included. Every March, a 13th issue, Gavel, is published. This is the most frequently consulted, and relied on "encyclopedia" of meeting destinations, facilities and services.
Ind/Abst ABI/INFORM Glob. Ed.; ABI/INFORM [Computer File] (Jan. 1972-May 1978); Acad. Search; Bus. Index (1985-); Bus. Source Plus; Bus. Source; Curr. Lit. Fam. Plan. (19??-199?); EP Collect.; Gen. BusinessFile (1985-); Gen. Period. Index (1985-); Homework Help.; INFO-SOUTH Abstr.; Mag. Search; MasterFile FullTEXT 1000; MasterFile FullTEXT 350; MasterFile FullTEXT 650; MasterFile FullTEXT (Jan. 1994-); OCLC; Telebase; Trade Ind. Index (1981-).

ISSN 1048-0528
US

MEGABUCKING (STERLING HEIGHTS, MICH.). (MEGABUCKING). **VFOAT** Mega Bucking; DBA in America. **VAT** Doing Business As in America. (1992)-. Periodical. English. Twelve times a year. $48.00. The Grace Publishing Company, Sterling Office Plaza, 38900 Van Dyke Avenue, Sterling Heights MI 48077.

ISSN 1240-9863
FR

UDC 66

MEILLEURES ADRESSES DES TRAITEMENTS DE SURFACE, LES. (1991)-. French. One time a year. 227.49F France; 390.00F other. Revue Francaise des Metallurgistes, 32 rue Saint Marc, 75002 Paris France. **Tel** 011 31 1 42603151, FAX 011 31 1 42603842.

ISSN 0992-2164
FR

UDC 669.01 (058)

MEILLEURES ADRESSES DES TRAITEMENTS THERMIQUES, LES. (1988)-. Periodical. French. One time a year. 170.62F France; 295.00F other. Revue Francaise des Metallurgistes, 32 rue Saint Marc, 75002 Paris France. **Tel** 011 31 1 42603151, FAX 011 31 1 42603842.

ISSN 0734-3558
US
CEASED

MELLON ECONOMIC BRIEFING. **Added/Corp** Mellon Bank. Economics Dept. (Jan. 1982)-(June 1993). Periodical. English. Mellon Bank, 5222 One Mellon Bank Center, Pittsburgh PA 15258. ctrl circ. **Continues** Economic & Financial Briefing.

ISSN 1070-9177
US

●**MEMBERSHIP DIRECTORY & BUYERS' GUIDE - CHAMBER OF COMMERCE OF GREATER PHILADELPHIA.** (MEMBERSHIP DIRECTORY & BUYERS' GUIDE). **Main/Corp** Chamber of Commerce of Greater Philadelphia. **VFOAT** Membership Directory and Buyers' Guide. 1st Ed. (1992/1993)-. Consumer Publication. English. Greater Philadelphia Chamber of Commerce, 1346 Chestnut Street/Suite 800, Philadelphia PA 19107. **Tel** (215)545-1234. **Formed by the union of** Business Firms Directory of the Delaware Valley, 0091-2581 **and** Buyers' Guide of Greater Philadelphia-Delaware-South Jersey.

LC DS36 .A58
DD 909/.04927
LE

MEMO. **Added/Corp** Middle East Economic Consultants (Beirut, Lebanon). Vol. 10, No. 5 (Feb. 28, 1986)-. Periodical. English. Twenty-six times a year. $400.00. MEEC Publications Cyprus Limited, PO Box 4351, Limassol Cyprus. **Tel** 11 357 5 377095, FAX 011 347 5 375099, telex 5060. Index available. **Ad Acc.** ctrl circ. **Continues** Nahar Arab Report & Memo.
Desc: Newsletter of oil, business, and finance. Focuses on the economic data and activities in the Middle East countries.

LC HC
DD 330
NE

MEMORANDUM FROM INSTITUTE OF ECONOMIC RESEARCH, FACULTY OF ECONOMICS, UNIVERSITY OF GRONINGEN. **Added/Corp** Rijksuniversiteit te Groningen. Instituut voor Economisch Onderzoek. **VFOAT** Memorandum van het Instituut voor Economisch Onderzoek, Faculteit der Economische Wetenschappen, Rijksuniversiteit te Groningen. No. 1 (1974)-. Monographic series. English (Dutch). Irregular. Price varies per volume. University of Groningen, Institute of Economic Research Groningen Netherlands.
Ind/Abst Poult. Abstr.

ISSN 0747-167X
US
CCC

MEMPHIS BUSINESS JOURNAL. Vol. 5, No. 44 (March 26-30, 1984)-. Periodical. English. One time a week. $45.00. Mid South Communications, 88 Union/Suite 105, Memphis TN 38103-5195. **Tel** (901)526-2007. **(Subscription address:** Memphis Business Journal, 88 Union Center, Suite 102, Memphis TN 38103. **Tel** (901)523-1000.) **ED** Barney and Debby Dubois and Bill Wellborn. **Bk Rev. Ad Acc. Circ:** 15,000. available on microfilm from University Microfilms International (UMI); available on an online database (files 635,648/Full-Text) from DIALOG. Documents available from UMI Article Clearinghouse. **Continues** Mid-South Business, 0274-8525.
Ind/Abst Acad. Search; Bus. Dateline; Bus. Index (1984-1990); Bus. Source Plus; Bus. Source; EP Collect.; Gen. BusinessFile (1984-1990); Gen. Period. Index (1985-1990); Homework Help.; INFO-SOUTH Abstr.; MasterFile FullTEXT 1000; MasterFile FullTEXT 350; MasterFile FullTEXT 650; MasterFile FullTEXT (July 1993-); OCLC; PROMT; Telebase; Trade Ind. ASAP [Full Txt.]; Trade Ind. Index [Full Txt.].

LC HC
DD 330
US

MEMPHIS ECONOMY. **Added/Corp** Memphis State University. Bureau of Business and Economic Research. (19??)-. Periodical. English. Twelve times a year. Free on request. Bur Business & Economy Research, Memphis State University, Fogelman College, Memphis TN 38152. **Tel** (901)678-2281, FAX (901)678-2281.

UK

MENTOR. (19??)-. English. Irregular. $154.01. Contemporary Manage Publ Ltd, 121 Cambridge Street, London SW1V 4PZ United Kingdom. **Tel** 011 44 171 8345429.

LC HF1 .T74
DD 380.1/09749/65
ISSN 0194-9101
US

MERCER BUSINESS : A PUBLICATION OF MERCER COUNTY CHAMBER. **Added/Corp** Mercer County Chamber of Commerce. Vol. 55, No. 6 (June 1979)-. Periodical. English. Twelve times a year. $20.00. Mercer County Chamber of Commerce, PO Box 8307, 2550 Kuser Road, Trenton NJ 08650. **Tel** (609)586-2056, FAX (609)586-8052. **ED** Gene J. Sayko. **Ad Acc, Adv Mgr:** Donna Hill. **Circ:** 8,300. available on an online database from Business Dateline; and (file 635/Full-Text) DIALOG. Documents available from UMI Article Clearinghouse. **Continues** Trenton.
Desc: Covers business and financial topics in the Princeton-Trenton, New Jersey market area.
Ind/Abst Bus. Dateline.

ISSN 0739-9723
US

MERCHANT MAGAZINE, THE. See Forests and Forestry-Lumber and Wood.

LC HB1.A1 M35
DD 330/.05
ISSN 0543-5099
SA

MERCURIUS. Multiple languages (Afrikaans and English). $0.50 each issue. University of South Africa Department of Economics, PO Box 392, Pretoria South Africa.

LC HD2746.5 .M43 ISSN 0742-602X
DD 338.8/3/0973 US

MERGER AND ACQUISITION SOURCEBOOK. [Merger acquis. sourceb.]. **Added/Corp** Quality Services Company. (1983)-. English. One time a year (Mar.). $325.00. Quality Services Company, 5290 Overpass Road, Santa Barbara CA 93111. **Tel** (805)964-7841. **ED** Carl Shrager. **Ad Acc. Circ:** 1,000. ***Continues*** *Directory of Acquisitions.*
Desc: A guide to merger and acquisition activity contains details of over 3,000 transactions occurring in 1987. This includes takeovers, mergers, and geveraged buyouts. It also reports full financial data whenever available on both seller and buyer. Analyzes each transaction, traces its history and compares it to other acquisitions within the target's industry.

LC HD22746.5 .M439 ISSN 1076-3600
DD 338.8/3/05 US

●**MERGER YEARBOOK, THE.** [Merger yearb.]. **VFOAT** Merger Yearbook, U.S./International Edition; Merger Yearbook, US/International Edition. 15th Ed. (1993)-. Trade Publication. English. One time a year (May or June). $445.00. Securities Data Company, 40 West 57th Street, 11th Floor, New York NY 10019. **Tel** (212)765-5311. ***Formed by the union of*** *US Merger Yearbook, 1076-3619* ***and*** *International Merger Yearbook, 1052-9942.*
Desc: Provides information on the consolidation and merger of corporations. Also covers joint ventures, leveraged buyouts and corporate divestiture.

LC HD2807 .M47 ISSN 0843-5421
DD 338.8/3/097105 CN

MERGERS AND ACQUISITIONS IN CANADA (RICHMOND HILL, ONT.). (MERGERS AND ACQUISITIONS IN CANADA.). [Mergers acquis. Can.]. **Added/Corp** Harris-Bentley Limited. Venture Economics Canada. **VFOAT** Mergers & Acquisitions in Canada, the Monthly; M & A. (1986)-. Periodical. English. One time a year. 225.00Can$. Crosbie and Company, 1 First Canadian Place, 9th Place, Toronto Ontario M5X 1A4 Canada. **Tel** (416)362-7726, FAX (416)362-3447. **ED** Patricia Kelly. **Circ:** 200. available on an online database (file 636/Full-Text) from DIALOG. ***Continued in part by*** *Directory of Mergers & Acquisitions in Canada, 1186-6047.*
Ind/Abst PROMT [Full Txt.]; PTS Newsl. Database [Full Txt.].

LC HD2746.5 .M445 ISSN 1066-3525
DD 338.8/3/05 UK

MERGERS & ACQUISITIONS INTERNATIONAL. [Mergers + acquisit. int.]. **Added/Corp** Financial Times Business Information Ltd. Investment Dealers' Digest, Inc. **VFOAT** Mergers and Acquisitions International; Financial Times Mergers and Acquisitions International; FT Mergers & Acquisitions International. (1988)-. Periodical. English. Twenty-six times a year. $595.00. Investment Dealers Digest Inc., Two World Trade Center, 18th Floor, New York NY 10048. **Tel** (212)227-1200, FAX (212)432-1039. ***Absorbed*** *M & A Europe, 1017-5229.*
Ind/Abst PTS Newsl. Database [Full Txt.].

US

MERGERS & ACQUISITIONS REPORT. (19??)-. Periodical. English. One time a week. $980.00. Investment Dealers Digest Inc., Two World Trade Center, 18th Floor, New York NY 10048. **Tel** (212)227-1200, FAX (212)432-1039. available on an online database (files 15,485,636,648/Full-Text) from DIALOG.
Ind/Abst Account. Tax Datab. (Aug. 1991-) [Full Txt.]; PTS Newsl. Database [Full Txt.].

LC HD2746.5 .M48 ISSN 1071-4065
DD 338.8/3/0973 US

MERGERSTAT REVIEW. (MERGERSTAT REVIEW / W.T. GRIMM & CO.). [Mergerstat rev.]. **Added/Corp** Merrill Lynch Business Brokerage and Valuation. W.T. Grimm & Co. **VFOAT** W.T. Grimm & Co. Mergerstat Review. (1981)-. English. One time a year. $235.00. Merrill Lynch, 854 East Algonquin Road, Schaumburg IL 60173. **Tel** (708)981-9800. **ED** Merrill Lynch. **Circ:** 1,000. ***Continues*** *Merger Summary.*
Desc: A analysis of merger and acquisition activity.

ISSN 0194-7575
US

METRO BUSINESS. Vol. 1, No. 10 (May 15, 1979)-. Periodical. English. Twenty-four times a year. $18.00. Metro Business Monthly, Inc., 1012 14th Street NW, Washington DC 20005. Documents available from UMI Article Clearinghouse. ***Continues*** *Metro Business Monthly, 0191-0604.*
Ind/Abst Bus. Dateline (June 1990-Oct. 1990) [Full Txt.].

US
TITLE CHANGE

METRO JACKSON BUSINESS NEWS. (19??)-(19??). English. Jackson Business Journal, PO Box 12727, Jackson MS 39236. **Tel** (601)956-0756. ***Continues*** *Jackson Journal of Business.* ***Continued by*** *Jackson Business Journal.*

LC HB ISSN 1042-6825
DD 330 US

METRO PHOENIX BLUE CHIP ECONOMIC FORECAST. [Metro Phoenix blue chip econ. forecast]. **Added/Corp** Arizona State University. Economic Outlook Center. Phoenix Metropolitan Chamber of Commerce. Economic Research Group. **VFOAT** Metro Phoenix Blue Chip. Vol. 1, No. 1 (Fall 1988)-. Periodical. English. Four times a year. $39.00 (nonmembers), $30.00 (members). Phoenix Chamber of Commerce, 201 North Central Avenue, Suite 2700, Phoenix AZ 85073. **Tel** (602)254-5521. **ED** Nan Beams.

LC HB1.A1 ISSN 0026-1386
IT
CCC

METROECONOMICA. (METROECONOMICA; RIVISTA INTERNAZIONALE DI ECONOMICA.). Vol. 1 (1949)-. Academic Scholarly Publication. English (Italian and French). Three times a year. $119.00. Basil Blackwell Publishers Ltd., 108 Cowley Road, Oxford 0X4 1JF United Kingdom. **Tel** 011 44 1235 465500, FAX 011 44 1235 465556, telex 837022 OXBOOK G. **(Subscription address:** Blackwell Publishers / UK, 108 Cowley Road, Oxford OX4 1JF United Kingdom. **Tel** 011 44 1865 791100, FAX 011 44 1865 791347.) cum. index.
Ind/Abst Econ. Lit. Index; J. Econ. Lit.; Zentralbl. Math. Ihre Grenzgeb.

LC HA1 .M4 ISSN 0026-1424
DD 310/.5 IT
CODEN MRONAM

METRON. See Mathematics.

LC HD58 .M374 ISSN 1055-4165
DD 338.6/042/097471 US

METROPOLITAN NEW YORK BUSINESS AND MARKET GUIDE, THE. [Metrop. N. Y. bus. mark. guide]. **Added/Corp** New York Board of Trade (New York, N.Y.). **VFOAT** Business and Market Guide. (1992)-. English. $60.00. New York Board of Trade, 1328 Broadway, Suite 1033, New York NY 10001.

ISSN 0709-003X
DD 380.1/09713/541 CN
TITLE CHANGE

METROPOLITAN TORONTO BUSINESS JOURNAL, THE. [Metrop. Tor. bus. j.]. **Added/Corp** Board of Trade of Metropolitan Toronto. Communications Division. **VAT** Business Journal (Toronto. Christmas 1978). Vol. 68, No. 10 (Christmas 1978)-(19??). Periodical. English. Board of Trade of Metropolitan Toronto, PO Box 60, 1 First Canadian Place, Toronto Ontario M5X 1C1 Canada. **Tel** (416)366-6811, (416)366-7139, FAX (416)366-5620. **ED** Peter Carter. **Circ:** 16,000 (ctrl). available on an online database (file 635/Full-Text) from DIALOG. Documents available from UMI Article Clearinghouse. ***Continues*** *Business Journal, 0823-4671.* ***Continued by*** *Board of Trade of Metropolitan Toronto Business Journal.*
Desc: Toronto business magazine.
Ind/Abst Bus. Dateline; Can. Period. Index (19??-); PAIS Int. Print.

ISSN 0887-8528
US

METROWEST BUSINESS REVIEW, THE. [MetroWest bus. rev.]. **VFOAT** Metro West Business Review. (198?)-. Periodical. English. Twelve times a year. Bay State Publishing, 199 Newbury Street, Danvers MA 01923.

LC HC131 .C842
DD 330 MX

MEXICAN BULLETIN OF STATISTICAL INFORMATION. **Added/Corp** Instituto Nacional de Estadistica, Geografia e Informatica (Mexico). No. 1 (July/Sept. 1991)-. Bulletin. Spanish. Four times a year. National Institute of Statistics, Geography and Informatics, Central Office, Avenue Prolongacion Heroe de Nacozari Number 2301, Sur CP 20290 Ciudad Industrial, Aguascalientes AGS Mexico.

ISSN 1075-9034
DD 363 US
TITLE CHANGE

MEXICAN ENVIRONMENTAL BUSINESS. [Mex. environ. bus.]. (1994)-(Sept. 1995). Periodical. English. Pasha Publications Inc., 1616 North Fort Myer Drive, Suite 1000, Arlington VA 22209. **Tel** (800)424-2908, (703)528-1244, FAX (703)528-3742, (703)528-1253. ***Merged into*** *Environment Watch.*

ISSN 1077-7326
DD 346 US

●**MEXICO BUSINESS LAW ALERT.** [Mex. bus. law alert]. **Added/Corp** Peyton, Muriel & Associates. (1994)-. Periodical. English. Twelve times a year. $227.00. M. Lee Smith Publishers and Printers, PO Box 198867, Nashville TN 37219. **Tel** (615)242-7395, (800)274-6774, FAX (615)256-6601.
Desc: For US companies doing business in Mexico.

LC HG4092.Z65 M43
BL

MEXICO COMPANY HANDBOOK. **Added/Corp** Bolsa Mexicana de Valores. Asociacion Mexicana de Casas de Bolsa. **VFOAT** MCH. (1989)-. Trade Publication. English. One time a year. $38.45. Reference Press Inc., 6448 Highway 290 East, Suite E-104, Austin TX 78723-9828. **Tel** (800)486-8666, (512)454-7778, FAX (512)454-9401.

MX

MEXICO FINANCE & OIL REPORT, THE. (1984)-. Periodical. English. Twenty-four times a year. Mexico Finance and Oil Report, PO Box 15213, Calexico CA 92231. ***Continues*** *Mexico Report.*

ISSN 0277-0946
US

MEXICO REPORT (EL PASO, TEX.). (THE MEXICO REPORT.). [Mex. rep.]. (19??)-. Periodical. English. Irregular. $75.00. The Mexico Report, PO Box 848, El Paso TX 79945. **Tel** (915)533-5251. **ED** Wayne McClintock. **Bk Rev. Circ:** 900.
Desc: Review, analysis, and perspective of events in Mexico of business, finance, government, in-bond industry, petroleum, transportation, agriculture, and tourism.

LC HC307.S69 M492 ISSN 0394-3933
DD 330.945/7/005 IT

MEZZOGIORNO D'EUROPA. (JOURNAL OF REGIONAL POLICY.). [J. reg. policy]. **Added/Corp** Isveimer. (1985)-. Periodical. English. Four times a year. Free. Mezzogiorno d'Europa, Via S. Giacomo 19, 80133 Naples Italy. **Tel** 011 39 81 7853640. ***Continues*** *Mezzogiorno d'Europa (Naples, Italy : 1984).*
Ind/Abst Geogr. Abstr. Human Geogr.; Int. Bibliogr. Sociol.; Int. Dev. Abstr.; Leis., Rec., Tour. Abstr.; PAIS Int. Print; World Agric. Econ. Rural Sociol. Abstr.

LC HC107.O32 M51 ISSN 0026-1947
DD 330.9771 US

MIAMI BUSINESS REVIEW. (MIAMI BUSINESS REVIEW; PUBLISHED BY THE SCHOOL OF BUSINESS ADMINISTRATION, MIAMI UNIVERSITY ...). **Added/Corp** Miami University, Oxford, O. School of Business Administration. Vol. 1 (Jan. 1929)-. Periodical. English. Twelve times a year. Miami University, 302 Bachelor Hall, Oxford OH 45056. **Tel** (513)529-5253.

ISSN 1057-3089
DD 338 US

MICHIGAN ALLEGAN-MUSKEGON-OTTAWA COUNTIES BUSINESS REGISTER. **VFOAT** Michigan Allegan, Muskegon, Ottawa Counties Business Register; Allegan-Muskegon-Ottawa Counties Business Register; Allegan, Muskegon, Ottawa Counties Business Register. (1991)-. English. One time a year. $215.00. Pick Publications Inc, 24151 Telegraph Rd, Suite 280, Southfield MI 48034-7916. **Tel** (800)247-1558, (313)827-7111, FAX (313)827-7119. available on magnetic tape.

ISSN 1057-3054
DD 338 US

MICHIGAN BAY-MIDLAND-SAGINAW COUNTIES BUSINESS REGISTER. **VFOAT** Michigan Bay, Midland, Saginaw Counties Business Register; Bay-Midland-Saginaw Counties Business Register; Bay, Midland, Saginaw Counties Business Register. (1991)-. English. One time a year. $210.00. Pick Publications Inc, 24151 Telegraph Rd, Suite 280, Southfield MI 48034-7916. **Tel** (800)247-1558, (313)827-7111, FAX (313)827-7119. available on magnetic tape.

ISSN 1057-3097
DD 338 US

MICHIGAN BERRIEN-CASS-ST. JOSEPH BUSINESS REGISTER. **VFOAT** Michigan Berrien, Cass, St. Joseph Business Register; Berrien-Cass-St. Joseph Business Register; Berrien, Cass, St. Joseph Business Register. (1991)-. English. One time a year. $195.00. Pick Publications Inc, 24151 Telegraph Rd, Suite 280, Southfield MI 48034-7916. **Tel** (800)247-1558, (313)827-7111, FAX (313)827-7119. available on magnetic tape.

ISSN 1057-3135
DD 338 US

MICHIGAN BRANCH-HILLSDALE-LENAWEE-MONROE COUNTIES BUSINESS REGISTER. **VFOAT** Michigan Branch, Hillsdale, Lenawee, Monroe Counties Business Register; Branch-Hillsdale-Lenawee-Monroe Counties Business Register; Branch, Hillsdale, Lenawee, Monroe Counties Business Register. (1991)-. English. One time a year. $190.00. Pick Publications Inc, 24151 Telegraph Rd, Suite 280, Southfield MI 48034-7916. **Tel** (800)247-1558, (313)827-7111, FAX (313)827-7119. available on magnetic tape.

ISSN 1057-3100
DD 338 US
MICHIGAN CALHOUN-KALAMAZOO COUNTIES BUSINESS REGISTER. **VFOAT** Michigan Calhoun, Kalamazoo Counties Business Register; Calhoun-Kalamazoo Counties Business Register; Calhoun, Kalamazoo Counties Business Register. (1991)-. English. One time a year. $215.00. Pick Publications Inc, 24151 Telegraph Rd, Suite 280, Southfield MI 48034-7916. **Tel** (800)247-1558, (313)827-7111, FAX (313)827-7119. available on magnetic tape.

ISSN 1057-3062
DD 338 US
MICHIGAN CENTRAL REGION BUSINESS REGISTER. [Mich. Cent. Reg. bus. regist.]. **VFOAT** Central Region Business Register. (1991)-. English. One time a year. $190.00. Pick Publications Inc, 24151 Telegraph Rd, Suite 280, Southfield MI 48034-7916. **Tel** (800)247-1558, (313)827-7111, FAX (313)827-7119. available on magnetic tape.

ISSN 1057-3194
DD 338 US
MICHIGAN CITY OF DETROIT BUSINESS REGISTER. [Mich. City Detroit bus. regist.]. **VFOAT** City of Detroit Business Register. (1991)-. English. One time a year. $285.00. Pick Publications Inc, 24151 Telegraph Rd, Suite 280, Southfield MI 48034-7916. **Tel** (800)247-1558, (313)827-7111, FAX (313)827-7119. available on magnetic tape.

ISSN 1057-3151
DD 338 US
MICHIGAN GENESEE COUNTY BUSINESS REGISTER. **VFOAT** Genesee County Business Register. (1991)-. English. One time a year. $215.00. Pick Publications Inc, 24151 Telegraph Rd, Suite 280, Southfield MI 48034-7916. **Tel** (800)247-1558, (313)827-7111, FAX (313)827-7119. available on magnetic tape.

ISSN 1057-3119
DD 338 US
MICHIGAN INGHAM-JACKSON COUNTIES BUSINESS REGISTER. **VFOAT** Michigan Ingham, Jackson Counties Business Register; Ingham, Jackson Counties Business Register; Ingham, Jackson Counties Business Register. (1991)-. English. One time a year. $225.00. Pick Publications Inc, 24151 Telegraph Rd, Suite 280, Southfield MI 48034-7916. **Tel** (800)247-1558, (313)827-7111, FAX (313)827-7119. available on magnetic tape.

ISSN 1057-3143
DD 338 US
MICHIGAN KENT COUNTY BUSINESS REGISTER. [Mich. Kent Cty. bus. regist.]. **VFOAT** Kent County Business Register. (1991)-. English. One time a year. $235.00. Pick Publications Inc, 24151 Telegraph Rd, Suite 280, Southfield MI 48034-7916. **Tel** (800)247-1558, (313)827-7111, FAX (313)827-7119. available on magnetic tape.

ISSN 1057-3127
DD 338 US
MICHIGAN LIVINGSTON-WASHTENAW COUNTIES BUSINESS REGISTER. **VFOAT** Michigan Livingston, Washtenaw Counties Business Register; Livingston-Washtenaw Counties Business Register; Livingston, Washtenaw Counties Business Register. (1991)-. English. One time a year. $215.00. Pick Publications Inc, 24151 Telegraph Rd, Suite 280, Southfield MI 48034-7916. **Tel** (800)247-1558, (313)827-7111, FAX (313)827-7119. available on magnetic tape.

ISSN 1057-316X
DD 338 US
MICHIGAN MACOMB COUNTY BUSINESS REGISTER. **VFOAT** Macomb County Business Register. (1991)-. English. One time a year. $285.00. Pick Publications Inc, 24151 Telegraph Rd, Suite 280, Southfield MI 48034-7916. **Tel** (800)247-1558, (313)827-7111, FAX (313)827-7119. available on magnetic tape.

ISSN 1057-3178
DD 338 US
MICHIGAN NORTH OAKLAND COUNTY BUSINESS REGISTER. [Mich. North Oakl. Cty. bus. regist.]. **VFOAT** North Oakland County Business Register. (1991)-. English. One time a year. $285.00. Pick Publications Inc, 24151 Telegraph Rd, Suite 280, Southfield MI 48034-7916. **Tel** (800)247-1558, (313)827-7111, FAX (313)827-7119. available on magnetic tape.

ISSN 1057-3046
DD 338 US
MICHIGAN NORTHEASTERN REGION COUNTIES BUSINESS REGISTER. [Mich. Northeast. Reg. cties. bus. regist.]. **VFOAT** Northeastern Region Counties Business Register. (1991)-. English. One time a year. $215.00. Pick Publications Inc, 24151 Telegraph Rd, Suite 280, Southfield MI 48034-7916. **Tel** (800)247-1558, (313)827-7111, FAX (313)827-7119. available on magnetic tape.

ISSN 1057-3038
DD 338 US
MICHIGAN NORTHWESTERN REGION BUSINESS REGISTER. [Mich. Northwest. Reg. bus. regist.]. **VFOAT** Northwestern Region Business Register. (1991)-. English. One time a year. $235.00. Pick Publications Inc, 24151 Telegraph Rd, Suite 280, Southfield MI 48034-7916. **Tel** (800)247-1558, (313)827-7111, FAX (313)827-7119. available on magnetic tape.

ISSN 1057-3186
DD 338 US
MICHIGAN SOUTH OAKLAND COUNTY BUSINESS REGISTER. [Mich. South Oakl. Cty. bus. regist.]. **VFOAT** South Oakland County Business Register. (1991)-. English. One time a year. $285.00. Pick Publications Inc, 24151 Telegraph Rd, Suite 280, Southfield MI 48034-7916. **Tel** (800)247-1558, (313)827-7111, FAX (313)827-7119. available on magnetic tape.

ISSN 1057-3070
DD 338 US
MICHIGAN THUMB REGION BUSINESS REGISTER. [Mich. Thumb Reg. bus. regist.]. **VFOAT** Thumb Region Business Register. (1991)-. English. One time a year. $190.00. Pick Publications Inc, 24151 Telegraph Rd, Suite 280, Southfield MI 48034-7916. **Tel** (800)247-1558, (313)827-7111, FAX (313)827-7119. available on magnetic tape.

ISSN 1057-302X
DD 338 US
MICHIGAN UPPER PENINSULA BUSINESS REGISTER. [Mich. Up. Penins. bus. regist.]. **VFOAT** Upper Peninsula Business Register. (1991)-. English. One time a year. $195.00. Pick Publications Inc, 24151 Telegraph Rd, Suite 280, Southfield MI 48034-7916. **Tel** (800)247-1558, (313)827-7111, FAX (313)827-7119. available on magnetic tape.

ISSN 1057-3208
DD 338 US
MICHIGAN WESTERN WAYNE COUNTY BUSINESS REGISTER. [Mich. West. Wayne Cty. bus. regist.]. **VFOAT** Western Wayne County Business Register. (1991)-. English. One time a year. $285.00. Pick Publications Inc, 24151 Telegraph Rd, Suite 280, Southfield MI 48034-7916. **Tel** (800)247-1558, (313)827-7111, FAX (313)827-7119. available on magnetic tape.

ISSN 0883-4296
DD 338 US
MICRO ECONOMICS. [Micro econ.]. **Added/Corp** Boston Computer Society. Consultants and Entrepreneurs Group. (19??)-. Periodical. English. The Boston Computer Society, One Kendall Square, Cambridge MA 02139-1562. **Tel** (617)367-8080. **ED** John Chetterloy and Beth Andrus. **Bk Rev**. **Ad Acc. Circ:** 4,500 (ctrl).
Desc: Information on management and business methods to help entrepreneurs, consultants, managers, owners, financers and providers for series of businesses and consulting firms in the microcomputer and related fields.

ISSN 1198-3558
DD 330.9/005 CN
●**MICRO (OTTAWA).** (MICRO : THE MICRO-ECONOMIC RESEARCH BULLETIN.). [Micro]. **VFOAT** MICRO. Vol. 1, No. 1 (winter 1994)-. Periodical. English (French). Four times a year (March, June, Sept., Dec.). Free on request. Public Office of Micro Economic Policy Analysis, 235 Queen Street, 5th Floor West Tower, Ottawa K1A OH5 Canada. **Tel** (613)947-2068, FAX (613)991-1261. ctrl circ.

US
MICROECONOMICS. (1992)-. English. Dushkin Publishing Group Inc., Sluice Dock, Guilford CT 06437. **Tel** (203)453-4351, (800)243-6532, FAX (203)453-6000.

LC HD28 .M53 ISSN 0895-1772
DD 650/.05 US
Pr Rev.
MID-AMERICAN JOURNAL OF BUSINESS. [Mid-Am. j. bus.]. **Added/Corp** Mid-American Business Conference. **VFOAT** Midamerican Journal of Business. **VAT** Mid American Journal of Business. Vol. 1, No. 1 (Mar. 1986)-. Periodical. English. Two times a year (Mar., Sept.). $12.00. Mid-American Journal of Business, Bureau of Business Research, Ball State University, Muncie IN 47306. **Tel** (317)285-5926, FAX (317)285-8024. **ED** Danielle Vetter. Index available (bound in fourth issus). cum. index. **Bk Rev**, (Qty: 3). **Circ:** 1,500. Documents available from the publisher.
Desc: Provides a medium for business researches and theorists to inform other business professionals including executives, consultants, and teachers. Covers recent research developments and their practical implications.
Ind/Abst Gen. BusinessFile (1992-).

LC HF5001 .J58 ISSN 0732-9334
DD 650/.05 US
CCC
Pr Rev.
MID-ATLANTIC JOURNAL OF BUSINESS, THE. (THE MID-ATLANTIC JOURNAL OF BUSINESS / DIVISION OF RESEARCH, STILLMAN SCHOOL OF BUSINESS, SETON HALL UNIVERSITY.). [Mid-Atl. j. bus.]. **Added/Corp** Stillman School of Business. Division of Research. Vol.19, No. 1 (Winter 1980/81)-. Periodical. English. Three times a year. $45.00. Stillman School of Business, Seton Hall University, South Orange Avenue, South Orange NJ 07079. **Tel** (201)761-9231, FAX (201)761-9217. **ED** A. D. Amar (editor's phone: (201)761-9684). Index available (bound in third issue). cum. index. **Bk Rev. Ad Acc. Circ:** 1,000. available on microfilm and microfiche from University Microfilms International (UMI); available on an online database (file 648/Full-Text) from DIALOG. Documents available from UMI Article Clearinghouse. ***Continues*** *Journal of Business (South Orange, N.J.), 0021-9401.*
Desc: Strives to serve a diverse audience by providing a forum for the presentation and discussion of original contributions in all fields of business and economics.
Ind/Abst ABI/INFORM Glob. Ed.; ABI/INFORM [Computer File] (Winter 1980-); Acad. Search; Bus. ASAP (1990-) [Full Txt.]; Bus. Index (1985-); Bus. Source Plus; Bus. Source; Curr. Cit.; EP Collect.; Gen. BusinessFile (1985-); Gen. Period. Index (1985-); Homework Help.; INFO-SOUTH Abstr.; MasterFile FullTEXT 1000; MasterFile FullTEXT 350; MasterFile FullTEXT 650; MasterFile FullTEXT (Jan. 1994-); OCLC; Telebase; Trade Ind. ASAP [Full Txt.]; Trade Ind. Index [Full Txt.]; UMI ABI/Inform--Bus. Period. Ondisc (Nov. 1988-) [Full Txt.].

ISSN 0918-4422
JA
MID-TERM ECONOMIC FORECAST. [Mid-term econ. forecast]. (1990)-. Periodical. English. One time a year (Mar.). ¥13500.00. Japan Center of Economic Research, 6 1 Nihombashi Kayabacho 2 Cho, Chuoku Tokyo 103 Japan. **Tel** FAX 011 81 3 36392839. ***Continues*** *Five-Year Economic Forecast.*
Desc: Forecasts general economic trends and changes in Japan's economic structure. Aims to provide guidelines for policy formation by both government and the private sector.
Ind/Abst Predicasts Forecasts.

LC HC435.2 .M524
DD 330.954/005 II
MID YEAR REVIEW OF THE ECONOMY. **Added/Corp** Lancer International. India International Centre. **VFOAT** Midyear Review of the Economy; Mid-Year Review of the Indian Economy; Review of the Economy. (198?)-. English. One time a year. Price varies. Lancer International, PO Box 3802, New Delhi 110 049 India. **Tel** 664933, FAX 6862077. **(Subscription address:** Prints India, 11 Darya Ganj, New Delhi 110002 India. **Tel** 011 91 11 3268645, FAX 011 91 11 3275542, telex 31-61087 PRIN-IN.) ***Continues*** *Mid-Year Review of the Indian Economy.*

LC HC410.7.A1 M47
DD 330.956/005 UK
MIDDLE EAST (LONDON, ENGLAND : 1985). (THE MIDDLE EAST.). No. 125 (March 1985)-. Periodical. English. Twelve times a year. $90.00 US; £36.00 UK; £50.00 other. IC Publications Ltd., 7 Coldbath Square, London EC1R 4LQ United Kingdom. **Tel** 011 44 171 7137711, FAX 011 44 171 7137898, telex 8811757. **ED** Graham Benton. **Bk Rev**, (Qty: 12-24). **Ad Acc, Adv Mgr:** Chris Irwin. **Circ:** 10,500. available on microfilm; available on an online database from Predicasts, Inc. ***Continues*** *Middle East Magazine.*
Desc: English-language business and current affairs magazine. Major source of unbiased and objective information on this volatile region, with comprehensive coverage and in-depth analysis of developments in the area.
Ind/Abst Expand. Acad. Index (1992-); F&S Index Plus Text, Int. [Select. Cov.]; Index Islam. Lit.; Infobank (March 1985-).

ISSN 0961-8724
UK
MIDDLE EAST MONITOR. **VFOAT** MEM. Vol. 1, No. 1 (Jan. 1991)-. Periodical. English. Twelve times a year. $470.00. Business Monitor International, 56 60 St. John Street, London EC1M 4DT United Kingdom. **Tel** 011 44 171 6083646, FAX 011 44 171 6083620.

LC HC
DD 330 UA
MIDDLE EAST OBSERVER. SPECIAL SERVICES = AL-KHADAMAT AL-KHASSAH LIL-MIDIL IST UBZIRFAR, THE. **VFOAT** Al-Khadamat Al-Khassah Lil-Midil Ist Ubzirfar. (19??)-. Periodical.

English. Irregular. $300.00. Middle East Observer, 8 Shawarby Street, Cairo Egypt. **Tel** 011 20 2 711141, FAX 011 20 2 3606804. Index available.

US

MIDDLE MARKET FOCUS. (19??)-. Periodical. English. Twenty-four times a year. $495.00. Investment Dealers Digest Inc., Two World Trade Center, 18th Floor, New York NY 10048. **Tel** (212)227-1200, FAX (212)432-1039.

UK

MIDEAST MIRROR. English. Five times a week (Mon.-Fri.). £900.00 UK and US; £100.00 other. Mediagen Ltd, 18 Danvers Street/1st Floor, London SW3 5AT United Kingdom. **ED** F.C. Najia (Editor's Phone: (44)71-3512399).
Desc: A daily digest of the major business and political news and views in the Arabic, Hebrew, Turkish and Persian press, with the day-of-publication delivery. Available by private subscription only.

ISSN 0194-4525
US

MIDLANDS BUSINESS JOURNAL. (19??)-. Periodical. English. One time a week. $50.00. Midlands Business Journal, 11918 Poppleton Plaza, Omaha NE 68144. **Tel** (402)330-1760. **ED** Robert Hoig. **Ad Acc.**

ISSN 1070-0765
DD 658 US

●**MILITARY EXCHANGE MAGAZINE.** [Mil. exch. mag.]. **VFOAT** Exchange Magazine; Military Exchange. Vol. 1, No. 1 (Oct. 1993)-. Periodical. English. Four times a year. $40.00. Downey Communications Inc, Circulation Department, 4800 Montgomery Lane, Suite 710, Bethesda MD 20814. **Tel** (301)718-7600, FAX (301)718-7652.

LC HG4244.655 .A24
DD 338.7/4/09593 TH

MILLION BAHT BUSINESS INFORMATION, THAILAND. Added/Corp Pan Siam Communications Company. 1st, (1980)-. English. Pan Siam Communications, 138/1 Pansak Building/4th Floor, Petchburi Road Phyathai, Bangkok 4 Thailand.

ISSN 0143-1374
UK

MIND YOUR OWN BUSINESS. (1978)-. English. Twelve times a year. £20.00 UK; £45.00 other. Cairnmarh Ltd, 106 Church Road, London SE19 2UB United Kingdom. Documents available from Ask*IEEE.
Ind/Abst Curr. Cit.; HILITES; Inf. Manage. Technol.; INSPEC (June 1981-).

LC HD242 .R69A
DD 333.33/9 US

MINERAL REVENUES : THE ... REPORT ON RECEIPTS FROM FEDERAL AND INDIAN LEASES. See Environmental Issues-Conservation and Natural Resources.

LC HF5487 .A285 **ISSN** 0273-5822
DD 658.7/85 US

MINI STORAGE MESSENGER, THE. [Mini storage messenger]. **VFOAT** Mini-Storage Messenger. (198?)-. Trade Publication. English. Twelve times a year. $49.95. Minico Inc, 2531 West Dunlap Avenue, Phoenix AZ 85021. **Tel** (800)824-6864. Index available. **Ad Acc.** **Circ:** 4,000.

LC HC **ISSN** 0883-3044
DD 330 US
CCC

MINNEAPOLIS/ST. PAUL CITYBUSINESS. **VFOAT** Minneapolis St. Paul Citybusiness; Minneapolis/St. Paul City Business; Citybusiness; City Business. Vol. 3, No. 2 (May 8-21, 1985)-. Consumer Publication. English. One time a week (special book of lists in Jan.). $54.00. MCP Inc., 5500 Wayzata Boulevard, Suite 800, Minneapolis MN 55416. **Tel** (612)591-2700, FAX (612)591-2639. **ED** Beth Ewen (phone: (612)591-2644). **Ad Acc, Adv Mgr Tel** 591-2659. Full Page (B&W) $3275.00. **Circ:** 18,000. available on an online database (files 635,648/Full-Text) from DIALOG. Documents available from UMI Article Clearinghouse. Formed by the union of Minneapolis CityBusiness, 0742-809X and St. Paul CityBusiness.
Desc: Newsbased articles about businesses active in the Twin Cities and the people who run them, and issues of public importance.
Ind/Abst Acad. Search; Bus. Dateline; Bus. Index (May 1985-Dec. 1985); Bus. Source Plus; Bus. Source; EP Collect.; Gen. BusinessFile (May 1985-Dec. 1985); Gen. Period. Index (May 1985-Dec. 1985); Homework Help.; INFO-SOUTH Abstr.; MasterFile FullTEXT 1000; MasterFile FullTEXT 350; MasterFile FullTEXT 650; MasterFile FullTEXT (July 1993-); OCLC; PROMT; Telebase; Trade Ind. ASAP [Full Txt.]; Trade Ind. Index [Full Txt.].

LC HJ4655.M57 M56 HJ4655.M567
DD 336.24/09776 S 336.24/3/09776 US

MINNESOTA CORPORATION INCOME TAX. See Finance-Taxation.

ISSN 1058-3653
DD 330 US
CODEN MIVEE5

MINNESOTA VENTURES. [Minn. ventur.]. (Fall 1989)-. English. Four times a year. $18.00. MN Ventures Magazine Inc., 10 South 5th Street, Minneapolis MN 55402. **Tel** (612)338-4288. available on microfilm and microfiche from University Microfilms International (UMI). Documents available from UMI Article Clearinghouse.
Ind/Abst Bus. Dateline (Sept. 1991-) [Full Txt.]; Foods Adlibra.

LC WMLC 93/1309 **ISSN** 1048-0919
DD 658 US
Pr Rev.

MINORITY BUSINESS ENTREPRENEUR. (MINORITY BUSINESS ENTREPRENEUR : MBE.). [Minor. bus. entrep.]. **VFOAT** MBE. (1984)-. Trade Publication. English. Six times a year. $15.00. Minority Business Entrepreneur, 3528 Torrance Boulevard #101, Torrance CA 90503-4803. **Tel** (310)540-9398, FAX (310)792-8263. **ED** Jeanie M. Barnett. **Bk Rev. Ad Acc, Adv Mgr:** Barbara Daley. **Circ:** 40,000 (ctrl).
Desc: Targets minority and women business owners with special coverage of litigation, legislation and issues relevant to their businesses.

US

MINORITY BUSINESS NEWS U.S.A. English. Twelve times a year. $18.00. Minority Business News, 11333 North Central Expressway, Suite 201, Dallas TX 75243. **Tel** (214)369-3500, FAX (214)265-9393. **ED** Don Mckneely. **Bk Rev,** (Qty: 6). **Ad Acc, Adv Mgr:** Sharon Davis, **Tel** (214)221-5501. **Circ:** 75,000 (ctrl).
Desc: Focuses on ethnic minority business entrepreneurs and corporate America.

ISSN 1041-0864
DD 338 US
TITLE CHANGE

MINORITY BUSINESS REVIEW (HEMPSTEAD, N.Y.). (MINORITY BUSINESS REVIEW.). (1981)-(19??). Periodical. English. Minority Business Review / New York, PO Box 2132, 416 Jerusalem Avenue, Hempstead NY 11550-2132. **Tel** (516)489-0120, (516)546-6992. **Continued by** Economic Forum Minority Business Review.

ISSN 1071-8877
DD 650 US
TITLE CHANGE

MINORITY BUSINESS TIMES. [Minor. bus. times]. (1993)-(199?). Periodical. English. Minority Business Times, 40 Underhill Blvd. Ste. 2D, Syosset NY 11791. **Tel** (516)921-9264. **ED** Trevor Pearson. **Bk Rev,** (Qty: 3). **Ad Acc. Circ:** 15,000. available on an online database. **Continued by** Minority Times & Small Business News, 1078-1846.

US

MINORITY BUSINESS TODAY. Periodical. English. Four times a year. Free. Minority Business Development Agency, US Department of Commerce, Washington DC 20006. **ED** Lewis Giles.
Desc: Carries news and information on issues, opportunities, problems and prospects for minority business enterprise development.

US

MINORITY ENTRPRENEUR. A CLEARINGHOUSE FOR BUSINESS DEVELOPMENT. English. Twelve times a year. $30.00. Minority Entrepreneur, PO Box 661, Chicago IL 60690. **Tel** (312)939-7222, FAX (312)324-2927. **ED** Rita Jakes. Index available. **Bk Rev. Ad Acc, Adv Mgr:** Francois Leach, **Tel** (312)939-7222. ctrl circ.
Desc: Information on minority and women's business development, such as, laws, bids, programs and organizations.

ISSN 1040-1547
DD 650 US

MINORITY MBA. [Minor. MBA]. **VAT** Minority Master of Business Administration. (1988)-. Periodical. English. Two times a year (Sept., Dec.). $33.80. Petersons / COG Publishing, 1606 Ventura Boulevard, Suite 560, Encino CA 91436. **Tel** (818)789-5293, FAX (818)789-5488. **ED** Al Austin. **Ad Acc.** ctrl circ.

CN

MISSISSAUGA BUSINESS REPORT. English. Irregular. 32.00Can$. Mississauga News, 3125 Wolfdale Road, Mississauga Ontario, L5C 3A9 Canada. **Tel** (416)273-8236. **ED** Judy Hughes. **Ad Acc, Adv Mgr:** Bob Leuschner, **Tel** (416)273-8241. **Circ:** 16,000.

ISSN 1185-2186
DD 380.1/09713/535 CN

MISSISSAUGA BUSINESS TIMES. [Mississauga bus. times]. (Mar. 1991)-. Periodical. English. Irregular. North Island Publishing, 1605 Sedlescomb Drive, Unit 3, Mississauga Ontario L4X 1M6 Canada. **Tel** (905)625-7070. **Continues** Mississauga Business., 0826-4139.

US
Pr Rev.

MISSISSIPPI BUSINESS EDUCATION ASSOCIATION JOURNAL. Periodical. English. Every 2 years. $5.00. Mississippi State University / Department of Technology and Education, PO Drawer NU, Mississippi State MS 39762. **Tel** (601)325-2280. **ED** Judy Fleming. **Ad Acc. Circ:** 275 (ctrl).
Desc: Aimed toward professional development in business education.

ISSN 0195-0002
US

MISSISSIPPI BUSINESS JOURNAL, THE. **VFOAT** Business Journal. Vol. 1 (July 1979)-. Periodical. English. Fifty-two times a year. $30.00. Ventures Publications Inc., PO Box 23607, Jackson MS 39225. **Tel** (601)352-9035. **ED** Kevin D. Jones. **Bk Rev. Ad Acc. Circ:** 13,000 (ctrl). available on an online database (files 635,648/Full-Text) from DIALOG; available via Internet (http://www.inst.com/mbj/). Documents available from UMI Article Clearinghouse.
Desc: A magazine published for the statewide business community. issues include regular columns, features, business news, and a special industry focus.
Ind/Abst Acad. Search; Bus. Dateline; Bus. Index (Jan. 1985-Dec. 1985); Bus. Source Plus; Bus. Source; EP Collect.; Gen. BusinessFile (Jan. 1985-Dec. 1985); Gen. Period. Index (Jan. 1985-Dec. 1985); Homework Help.; INFO-SOUTH Abstr.; MasterFile FullTEXT 1000; MasterFile FullTEXT 350; MasterFile FullTEXT 650; MasterFile FullTEXT (July 1993-); OCLC; PROMT; Telebase; Trade Ind. ASAP [Full Txt.]; Trade Ind. Index [Full Txt.].

LC WMLC L 83/3999 **ISSN** 0544-4969
US

MISSISSIPPI'S BUSINESS POPULATION. Added/Corp Mississippi Employment Security Commission. Research and Statistics Dept. Mississippi Employment Security Commission. Labor Market Information Dept. 2nd Edition (1962-1963)-. English. One time a year. Mississippi Employment Security Commission, PO Box 1699, Jackson MS 39205. **Tel** (601)354-8711. **Continues** Mississippi Employment Security Commission. Business Births, Business Deaths, and Changes in Ownership in Mississippi.

US

MIT PRESS SERIES ON THE REGULATION OF ECONOMIC ACTIVITY. **VFOAT** Series on the Regulation of Economic Activity; Massachusetts Institute of Technology Press Series on the Regulation of Economic Activity. (1981)-. Monographic series. English. Irregular. Price varies per volume. Massachusetts Institute of Technology (MIT) Press, 55 Hayward Street, Cambridge MA 02142. **Tel** (617)253-2889, (617)625-8481, FAX (617)258-6779. **ED** Richard Schmalensee and Nancy Ross.

LC HB9 .M56 **ISSN** 0026-6760
JA

MITA GAKKAI ZASSHI. Added/Corp Keio Gijuku Keizai Gakkai. **VFOAT** Mita Journal of Economics. (19??)-. Periodical. Japanese.
Ind/Abst Am. Hist. Life (1966-1973).

ISSN 0957-4980
DD 621.38 UK

MOBILE BUSINESS. [Mob. bus.]. (1989)-. English. Twelve times a year. $75.29. Fennite Publication Ltd, 134 Petherton Road, Highbury London 52RT United Kingdom. **Tel** 011 44 181 3590493.

ISSN 0734-3108
US

MOBIUS (ALEXANDRIA, VA.). (MOBIUS : THE JOURNAL OF THE SOCIETY OF CONSUMER AFFAIRS PROFESSIONALS IN BUSINESS.). Added/Corp Society of Consumer Affairs Professionals in Business (U.S.). Vol. 1, No. 1 (Oct. 1982)-. Periodical. English. Four times a year. Comes with Society of Consumer Affairs membership. Society of Consumer Affairs, 801 North Fairfax Street, Suite 404, Alexandria VA 22314. **Tel** (703)519-3700, FAX (703)549-4886.

LC HC

US

MOCCASIN TELEGRAPH. Main/Corp Grand Portage Reservation Business Committee. English. Irregular. Moccasin Telegraph, Grand Portage MN 55605.

ISSN 1120-7388
NE
CCC

MOCT-MOST: ECONOMIC POLICY IN TRANSITIONAL ECONOMIES. Added/Corp Nomisma (Firm). **VFOAT** Most. (19??)-. Periodical. English. Four times a year. $242.00. Kluwer Academic Publishers, Postbus 322, 3300 AH Dordrecht The Netherlands. **Tel** 011 31 78 524400, FAX 011 31 78 183273, telex 20083.

Business and Economics

MOD CONTRACTS BULLETIN. [MOD contracts bull.]. **VFOAT** Ministry of Defence Contracts Bulletin. (1986)-. Bulletin. English. Twenty-six times a year. $253.25. Cequel Publishing Limited, PO Box 1335, Lewes East Sussex BN7 3ZF United Kingdom. **Tel** 011 44 171 9317766, FAX 011 44 171 9318377. **Ad Acc. Circ:** 3,000 (ctrl). available on microfilm and microfiche from University Microfilms International (UMI).

ISSN 0269-0365
UK
CCC

MODELIROVANIE EKONOMICHESKIKH SISTEM. **Added/Corp** Lietuvos TSR Mokslu Akademija, Vilna. Ekonomikos Institutas. (1???)-. Russian. Mintis / Idea, Z Sierauausko 15, Vilnius 2600 Lithuania. **Tel** 011 7 3702 632943.

LC HC501 .M64
DD 330.9/6/03

LI

MODERN AFRICA. [Mod. Afr.]. (1977). Periodical. English. Six times a year. $95.00 US and Canada. Johnston International Publishing, Vine House Fairgreen, Reach Cambridge CB50JD United Kingdom. **Tel** 011 44 1638 743688. **ED** Richard Synge. **Ad Acc**, **Adv Mgr:** C. Herriman. **Circ:** 10,000 (ctrl)
  Desc: A business to business magazine with concentration on Africa's major industries: oil, agriculture, construction, power, telecommunications, mining and finance.
  Ind/Abst PAIS Int. Print.

ISSN 0264-8067
UK

MOLISE ECONOMICO. (1978)-(19??). Italian. Six times a year. L24000. Camera Comm Ind Art Agr/Campob, Piazza Vittoria 1, 86100 Campobasso Italy. **Tel** 011 39 874 415741.

ISSN 0392-6427
IT
SUSPENDED

MOMENTO PRATICO CONTABILE. (19??)-. Italian. One time a year. L89930. IPSOA Francis Lefebvre, Cas Postale 12055, 20120 Milan Italy. **Tel** 011 39 2 82476794.

IT

LC HC

ISSN 0029-9898
AU

Pr Rev.
MONATSBERICHTE - OESTERREICHISCHES INSTITUT FUER WIRTSCHAFTSFORSCHUNG. **Main/Corp** Oesterreichisches Institut fuer Wirtschaftsforschung. Vol. 1 (June 17, 1927)-. Periodical. German (English). Twelve times a year. $283.66. Oesterreichisches Institut fuer Wirtschaftsforschung, Postfach 91, A-1103 Vienna Austria. **Tel** 011 43 222 798 26010, FAX 011 43 222 798 9386. **ED** Franz Hahn. Index Bound in First Issue. **Ad Acc. Circ:** 2,500.
  Desc: Provides analyses and forecasts of the Austrian business cycle, regular assessments of the international business cycle, periodical analyses of regional economic trends, as well as medium term projections of the national and the international economy.

DD 071/.1134

ISSN 0832-4719
CN

MONDAY MAGAZINE (1983). (MONDAY MAGAZINE.). [Monday mag.]. Vol. 9, No. 36 (Sept. 2/8, 1983)-. Periodical. English. One time a week (Wednesdays). 56.02Can$. Monday Publications Ltd, 1609 Blanshard Street, Victoria BC Canada V8W 2J5. **Tel** (604)382-6188, FAX (604)381-2662. **ED** Sid Tafler. **Bk Rev**, (Qty: 10). **Ad Acc**, **Adv Mgr:** Craig Maxwell, **Tel** (604)382-6188. **Circ:** 41,000. **Continues** Monday (Victoria, B.C. : 1978)., 0832-4700.
  Desc: Business magazine that covers on real estate and business reports.

LC HB9 .M6

ISSN 0026-959X
SP

MONEDA Y CREDITO. [Moneda credito]. (June 1942)-. Periodical. Spanish. Two times a year. 4000ptas Canary Islands; 4240ptas Spain; 5500ptas other. Recoletos Cia Editorial, Recoletos 1, 28001 Madrid Spain. **Tel** 011 34 1 3373802, 3370512. Index available. cum. index.
  Ind/Abst Am. Hist. Life (1956-1974, 1987-).

LC HG201 .M74
DD 332.4/98

MX

Pr Rev.
MONEY AFFAIRS / CEMLA, CENTRE FOR LATIN AMERICAN MONETARY STUDIES. **Added/Corp** Centro de Estudios Monetarios Latinoamericanos. Vol. 1, No. 1 (Jan./June 1988)-. Periodical. English. Two times a year. $20.00. Centro Estudios Monetarios Latinoamericanos (CEMLA), Durango 54, 06700 Mexico DF Mexico. **Tel** 011 52 5 5330300, FAX 011 52 5 2072847, telex 1771229. Index available. **Bk Rev. Ad Acc.**

US

●**MONEY CARD COLLECTOR.** **VFOAT** Moneycard Collector. Vol. 1, No. 1 (Sept. 1994)-. Periodical. English. Twelve times a year. $19.95. Amos Press, PO Box 29, Sidney OH 45365. **Tel** (513)498-0802, (800)448-7293, FAX (513)498-0812. (**Subscription address:** Moneycard Collector, PO Box 783, Sidney OH 45365. **Tel** (513)498-0879.)

DD 332.05

ISSN 0951-4767
UK
CEASED

MONEY WEEK. [Money week]. (1987)-(Apr. 1994). Newspaper. English. EMAP Business Publishing Ltd., 260 Field End Road, Audit House, Ruislip Middlesex HA4 9LT United Kingdom. **Tel** 011 44 181 9563000, FAX 011 44 181 4293117.
  Ind/Abst Infomat Int. Bus.

ISSN 0745-9858
US

MONEYPAPER, THE. **VFOAT** Money Paper. (198?)-. Periodical. English. Twelve times a year. $63.00. Moneypaper, 930 Mamaroneck Avenue, Mamaroneck NY 10543. **Tel** (914)381-5400.

MONITOR ECONOMIA. Italian. Three times a year. L800000. Monitor, Via Clisio 9, 00199 Rome Italy. **Tel** 011 39 2 862534.

IT

ISSN 0738-3207
US

MONOGRAPH (MAXWELL GRADUATE SCHOOL OF CITIZENSHIP AND PUBLIC AFFAIRS. METROPOLITAN STUDIES PROGRAM). **See** Public Administration.

LC HC

ISSN 0572-6972
CN

MONOGRAPH SERIES - FACULTY OF COMMERCE AND BUSINESS ADMINISTRATION, UNIVERSITY OF BRITISH COLUMBIA. **Main/Corp** University of British Columbia. Faculty of Commerce and Business Administration. No. 1, 196 (196?)-. Monographic series. English. Irregular. Price varies per volume. University of British Columbia Faculty Commerce Business Administration, 1924 West Mall, Room 100, Vancouver British Columbia V6T 1Z2 Canada. **Tel** (604)822-4977, FAX (604)822-8521. **ED** Peter N. Nemetz. **Bk Rev**. **Ad Acc. Circ:** 500.
  Desc: An international journal of business and administrative inquiry.

LC HC
DD 330

UK

MONOGRAPH / UNIVERSITY OF CAMBRIDGE, DEPT. OF APPLIED ECONOMICS. **Added/Corp** University of Cambridge. Dept. of Applied Economics. No. 1 (1948)-. Monographic series. English. Irregular. Price varies per volume. Cambridge University Press / New York, 40 West 20th Street, New York NY 10011-4211. **Tel** (212)924-3900, (800)221-4512, FAX (212)691-3239. (**Subscription address:** Cambridge University Press / Outside of North America, United Kingdom. **Tel** 011 44 223 312 393, FAX 011 44 223 325 959.)

LC S
DD 630

ET

MONOGRAPHS IN ETHIOPIAN LAND TENURE. **See** Agriculture.

LC HC107.M9 M586
DD 330.9786

ISSN 0026-9921
US
CODEN MBQUA9

Pr Rev.
MONTANA BUSINESS QUARTERLY. [Mont. bus. q.]. **Added/Corp** University of Montana (Missoula). Bureau of Business and Economic Research. University of Montana (Missoula). School of Business Administration. Montana State University (Missoula). Bureau of Business and Economic Research. Vol. 1 (Fall 1962)-. Periodical. English. Four times a year (Mar., June, Sept., Dec.). $30.00. Bureau of Business & Economic Research / Montana, University of Montana, Missoula MT 59812. **Tel** (406)243-5113, FAX (406)243-2086. **ED** Marlene Nesary. Index available ($7.00). cum. index. **Circ:** 1,900 (ctrl). available on microfilm from University Microfilms International (UMI). Documents available from UMI Article Clearinghouse. **Supersedes** Montana Business Review.
  Desc: Publication of results of Bureau research and some reports based on major research projects.
  Ind/Abst ABI/INFORM Glob. Ed.; ABI/INFORM [Computer File] (Summer 1971-); Acad. Search; Bus. Index (1985-); Bus. Source Plus; Bus. Source; EP Collect.; Gen. BusinessFile (1985-); Gen. Period. Index (1985-); Homework Help.; INFO-SOUTH Abstr.; MasterFile FullTEXT 1000; MasterFile FullTEXT 350; MasterFile FullTEXT 650; MasterFile FullTEXT (July 1993-); OCLC; PAIS Int. Print (1991-); Telebase; Trade Ind. ASAP [Full Txt.]; Trade Ind. Index [Full Txt.]; UMI ABI/Inform--Bus. Period. Ondisc (Winter 1987-) [Full Txt.].

DD 330

ISSN 0889-4442
US
CEASED

MONTGOMERY BUSINESS. [Montgomery bus.]. **Added/Corp** Montgomery Area Chamber of Commerce (Ala.). (July 1986)-(Jan./Feb. 1995). Periodical. English. Montgomery Area Chamber of Commerce, PO Box 79, Montgomery AL 36101. **Tel** (334)834-5200. **Ad Acc. Circ:** 2,000 (ctrl).

LC HC
DD 330

ISSN 0047-8024
CN

MONTHLY BUSINESS ANALYSIS. (July 1960)-. Periodical. English. Twelve times a year. $46.43. Currie Coopers & Lybrand, 145 King Street West 4th FL, Toronto Ontario M5C 1V8 Canada. **Tel** (416)869-1130.

LC HC
DD 330

US

MONTHLY BUSINESS FAILURES. **Added/Corp** Dun & Bradstreet Corporation. Economic Analysis Dept. **VFOAT** U.S. Monthly Business Failures. Vol. 34, No. 1 (Jan. 1992)-. Periodical. English. Twelve times a year. $30.00. Dun & Bradstreet / New York, 299 Park Avenue, 24th Floor, New York NY 10171. **Tel** (212)593-4173. **Continues** Dun & Bradstreet Record of Business Closings. Monthly Business Failures.

LC HC107.A165 A2
DD 330.5

US

MONTHLY BUSINESS REVIEW - FEDERAL RESERVE BANK OF DALLAS. **Main/Corp** Federal Reserve Bank of Dallas. Periodical. English. Federal Reserve Bank of Dallas, Station K, Dallas TX 75222. **Tel** (214)922-6000, (800)333-4460.

LC HC111
DD 330.971/064

ISSN 0712-4791
CN

MONTHLY ECONOMIC REVIEW (OTTAWA). (MONTHLY ECONOMIC REVIEW.). [Mon. econ. rev.]. **Added/Corp** Informetrica Limited. **VFOAT** National Forecast; Provincial Forecast. Vol. 1, No. 1 (June 1982)-. Periodical. English. Twelve times a year. 300.13Can$. Informetrica Limited, PO Box 828 Station B, Ottawa Ontario K1P 5P9 Canada. **Tel** (613)238-4831, FAX (613)238-7698. **ED** Martha Justus.

LC HC430.5.A1 M66
DD 330.951/249/005

ISSN 1013-9893
CH

MONTHLY ECONOMIC SURVEY - INTERNATIONAL COMMERCIAL BANK OF CHINA. (MONTHLY ECONOMIC SURVEY / YING WEN CHING CHI YUEH HSUN / INTERNATIONAL COMMERCIAL BANK OF CHINA, HEAD OFFICE.). [Mon. econ. surv. - Int. Commer. Bank China]. **Added/Corp** Chung-kuo Kuo Chi Shang Yeh Yin Hang. ead Office. **VFOAT** Ying Wen Ching Chi Yueh Hsun. No. 1 (Oct. 1973)-. Periodical. English. Twelve times a year. Free on request. International Commercial Bank of China, Head Office, 100 Chi Lin Road, Taipei Taiwan. **Tel** 011 886 2 5633156. **ED** S. Y. Chu. **Circ:** 2,300.
  Desc: A newsletter focusing on the current economic situation of Taiwan, the Republic of China.
  Ind/Abst Predicasts.

ISSN 0265-4237
UK

MONTHLY INDEX TO THE FINANCIAL TIMES. **Added/Corp** Financial Times Business Information Ltd. (1981)-. Periodical. English. Twelve times a year. Financial Times / UK, Maple House, 149 Tottenham Court Road, London W1P 9LL United Kingdom. **Tel** 011 44 171 8962276, FAX 011 44 171 8962275, 011 44 171 8962399.

ISSN 0744-9208
US

MONTHLY NEWS LETTER - MAINE MERCHANTS ASSOCIATION. (MONTHLY NEWS LETTER.). **Added/Corp** Maine Merchants Association. **VFOAT** Maine Merchants Association Newsletter; Maine Merchants Association Monthly Newsletter. (19??)-. Periodical. English. Twelve times a year. Maine Merchants Association, 124 Sewall Street, Augusta ME 04330.

LC HX1 .M66
DD 335.05

ISSN 0027-0520
US

Pr Rev.
MONTHLY REVIEW (NEW YORK. 1949). See Political Science-Socialism, Communism, Anarchism, Utopianism.

LC HG4961 .M66
DD 332.6/7

ISSN 0147-3093
US

MOODY'S COMPLETE CORPORATE INDEX. **Added/Corp** Moody's Investors Service. (Feb./May 1977)-. Periodical. English. Three times a year. Moody's Investors Service, 99 Church Street, New York NY 10007. **Tel** (212)553-0547, (212)553-0435, FAX (212)553-4700.
  Desc: Includes all corporations listed in the editions of Moody's manuals.

Business and Economics

DD 332   **ISSN** 1061-1886 US
CEASED

MORNINGSTAR JAPAN. [Morningstar Jpn.]. **Added/Corp** Morningstar, Inc. Vol. 1, No. 1 (Feb. 28, 1992)-(199?). Periodical. English. Morningstar Inc., 225 West Wacker Drive, Chicago IL 60606. **Tel** (312)696-6000, (800)876-5005.

RU

MOSCOW BUSINESS TODAY. **VFOAT** Sincor. (19??)-. English (Russian). One time a week. Kursor, 109 Minna Street Suite 306, San Francisco CA 94105. **Tel** (415)861-2252, FAX (415)418-1160.
Desc: Unique publication which helps foreign businessmen invest money most profitably in Russia and throughout the Commonwealth of Independent States. Offers you the most precise and concise information about the state of affairs in different industries and the economy as a whole.

DD 382   **ISSN** 1046-9621 US
CEASED

MOSCOW INTERNATIONAL BUSINESS. [Mosc. int. bus.]. **VFOAT** Moskva, Interbiznes. Vol. 1, No. 1 (1990)-Vol. 1 No. 2 (1993). Periodical. English. Kompass Publishing Inc., 418 Commonwealth Avenue, Boston MA 02215. **Tel** (617)266-1214.

LC HC106.8 .M47   **ISSN** 1043-8629
DD 330   US

MSA PROFILE. [MSA profile]. **Added/Corp** Woods & Poole Economics. **VAT** Metropolitan Statistical Areas Profile. (1987)-. English. One time a year (Oct.). $301.50. Woods & Poole Economics Inc., 1794 Columbia Road Northwest, Suite 4, Washington DC 20009. **Tel** (202)332-7111, FAX (202)332-6466. available on CD-ROM from the publisher.
Desc: A volume of economic and demographic data for all Metropolitan Statistical Areas and states in the United States. A resource for planners, marketers, demographers and economists.

UK

MULTIMEDIA BUSINESS AND LAW INTERNATIONAL. (199?)-. Periodical. English. Six times a year. £245.00 UK; $380.00 other. Euromoney Publications PLC, Nestor House, Playhouse Yard, London EC4Z 5EX United Kingdom. **Tel** 011 44 171 7798888, FAX 011 44 171 7798630, telex 290700 EUROMON G.
Desc: Briefing for in-house counsel, law firm practitioners and analysts in global media, entertainment, telecommunications and computing.

DD 338   **ISSN** 1065-8300 US
CCC

MULTIMEDIA BUSINESS REPORT. See Communications.

MX
Pr Rev.
MUNDO EJECUTIVO. (19??)-. Periodical. Spanish. Twelve times a year. $40.00. Grupo Internacional Editorial., Rio Tiber 63CP 06500, Mexico DF Mexico. **Tel** 011 52 5 5118875 or, 51188177. **ED** Walter Coratella. Index available. **Bk Rev** (Qty: 36). **Ad Acc.** ctrl circ.
Desc: General financial information directed at CEO's.

US

MY LITTLE SALESMAN - HEAVY EQUIPMENT CATALOG. (1993)-. Catalog. English. Twelve times a year. $18.00. My Little Salesman Inc, PO Box 70208, Eugene OR 97401. **Tel** (503)342-1201, FAX (503)342-3307. **ED** Peter Powell. **Ad Acc, Adv Mgr:** Cathy Redwine.

ISSN 0742-8170
US

N.Y. JOURNAL JAPAN. See Political Science-International Relations.

ISSN 0168-4094
NE
UDC 339.564

NAAMLIJSTEN VOOR DE STATISTIEK VAN DE BUITENLANDSE HANDEL. [Naaml. stat. buitenl. handel]. **VFOAT** Naamlijsten Voor de Statistieken van de Buitenlandse Handel. (19??)-. Periodical. Dutch. Irregular. SDU Uitgeverij, Postbus 20014, Christoffel Plantijnstraat, 2500 EA Den Haag Netherlands. **Tel** 011 31 70 3789911.

NE

NAAMLOOZE VENNOOTSCHAP, DE. (1922)-. Periodical. Dutch. Eleven times a year. $139.78. W. E. J. Tjeenk Willink, Box 25, 8000 AA Zwolle Netherlands. **Tel** 011 31 38 228819, 011 31 38 211444. **(Subscription address:** Libresso BV, Postbus 23, 7400 GA Deventer Netherlands. **Tel** 011 30 5700 47333, 011 31 5700 33155.)

ISSN 0745-3205
US

NABE NEWS (CLEVELAND, OHIO). (NABE NEWS.). [NABE news]. **Added/Corp** National Association of Business Economists (U.S.). **VFOAT** N.A.B.E. News. **VAT** National Association of Business Economists News. (19??)-. Periodical. English. Six times a year. $300.00 (institutions), $55.00 (individuals) membership. NABE / National Association of Business Economists, 1233 20th Street NW, Suite 505, Washington DC 20036. **Tel** (202)463-6223. **ED** Grace Wickershain. **Bk Rev. Ad Acc. Circ:** 3,650 (ctrl).
Desc: Contains timely feature articles, news of local chapters and roundtables, reviews of seminars and meetings, personal notes and advertisements of interest to the business economist.

LC HF1101 .N23a   **ISSN** 0148-5784
DD 658.4/007/1073   US

NABTE REVIEW. Main/Corp National Association for Business Teacher Education. **Added/Corp** National Association for Business Teacher Education. Review. **VAT** National Association for Business Teacher Education Review. (19??)-. Periodical. English. One time a year (Sept.). $15.00. National Association for Business Teacher Education, 1914 Association Drive, Reston VA 22091-1596. **Tel** (703)860-8300, FAX (703)620-4483.
Ind/Abst Bus. Educ. Index.

LC F1401 .N58   **ISSN** 1071-4839
DD 309   US

●**NACLA REPORT ON THE AMERICAS (1993).** (NACLA REPORT ON THE AMERICAS.). [NACLA rep. Am.]. **Added/Corp** North American Congress on Latin America. **VAT** Report on the Americas. **VAT** North American Congress on Latin America Report on the Americas. Vol. 26, No. 5 (May 1993)-. Periodical. English. Six times a year. $50.00. North American Congress on Latin America, 475 Riverside Drive, Room 454, New York NY 10115. **Tel** (212)870-3146. **(Subscription address:** NACLA, PO Box 77, Hopewell PA 16650.) **Continues** Report on the Americas, 1058-5397.

DD 332   **ISSN** 1079-3100 US

●**NAFTA FOCUS ON MEXICO.** [NAFTA focus Mex.]. (1994)-. Periodical. English. Twelve times a year. $188.00. Wheeler's Desert Letter, PO Box 1297, Rancho Mirage CA 92270. **Tel** (619)341-1144, FAX (619)773-9505.

LC HB9 .N23

JA

NAGOYA SHOKA DAIGAKU RONSHU. **Added/Corp** Nagoya Shoka Daigaku. Nagoya Shoka Daigaku. Shogakkai. Nagoya Shoka Daigaku. Shogakubu. **VFOAT** Bulletin of Faculty of Commerce, Nagoya Commercial University. (1956)-. Bulletin. Japanese (English). Two times a year. Free. Nagoya Shoka Daigaku Shogakkai Aichi-gun Aichi-ken, Nagoya-shi Japan. **Tel** 011 81 52 561732111, FAX 011 81 52 561740341. **Circ:** 1,000.

LC DT701 .N36
DD 016.9688   ZA

NAMIBIA ABSTRACTS. See Political Science-Abstracting, Bibliographies and Statistics.

LC DT1501 .N36
SX

NAMIBIA DEVELOPMENT BRIEFING / NAMIBIA SUPPORT COMMITTEE. **Added/Corp** Namibia Support Committee. Namibia Non-Governmental Organisation Forum. Vol. 1, No. 1 (July 1991)-. Periodical. English. Twelve times a year. $60.00. Bricks Community Project, PO Box 20642, Windhoek 9000 Namibia.

LC HF5001
DD 650   RU

NARODNOE KHOZIAISTVO SOTSIALISTICHESKIKH STRAN V ... GODU : SOOBSHCHENIIA TSSU. See Business and Economics-Abstracting, Bibliographies and Statistics.

LC HG4057 .A38   **ISSN** 1058-2886
DD 338.7/4/02573   US
CCC
CEASED

NASDAQ YELLOW BOOK. (NASDAQ YELLOW BOOK: WHO'S WHO AT THE LEADING YOUNGER GROWTH COMPANIES IN THE U.S.). [NASDAQ yellow book]. **Added/Corp** National Association of Securities Dealers. **VFOAT** Yellow Book. **VAT** National Association of Securities Dealers Automated Quotations Yellow Book. Vol. 4, No. 1 (1992)-(Summer 1994). English. Leadership Directories, Inc., 104 Fifth Avenue, Second Floor, New York NY 10011. **Tel** (212)627-4140, FAX (212)645-0931. **Continues** Over-the-Counter 1000 Yellow Book, 1049-7927.
Desc: Lists over 27,000 executives who direct and manage the younger growth companies in America.

Provides names, titles, telephone and facsimile numbers and complete mailing addresses of small innovative companies

LC HB   **ISSN** 0889-2873
DD 330   US
CCC
Pr Rev.
NASHVILLE BUSINESS JOURNAL. [Nashv. bus. j.]. (198?)-. Periodical. English. Fifty-two times a year. $45.00. Nashville Business Journal Inc, 1 Church Street, Nashville TN 37201. **Tel** (615)254-9154, FAX (615)256-9080. **ED** Roger Shirley. cum. index. **Bk Rev**, (Qty: 10). **Ad Acc. Circ:** 11,500 (ctrl). available on an online database (file 635/Full-Text) from DIALOG; available via Internet (http://www.infi.net/nc5/nbj). Documents available from UMI Article Clearinghouse.
Ind/Abst Bus. Dateline; Bus. Source Plus; Bus. Source; EP Collect.; Homework Help.; MasterFile FullTEXT 1000; MasterFile FullTEXT 350; MasterFile FullTEXT 650; MasterFile FullTEXT; OCLC; Telebase.

US

NASHVILLE RECORD, THE. Vol. 1, No. 1 (Jan. 31, 1936)-. Newspaper. English. One time a week. $30.00 Davidson County; $35.00 other. Nashville Record, 198 Stahlman Building, Nashville TN 37201. **Tel** (615)256-8288. **ED** Barbara M. Caskill. **Ad Acc, Adv Mgr:** H. Hayward. **Circ:** 2,300.
Desc: Devoted to Nashville's business, financial, and legal news.

PH

NATIONAL ACCOUNTS OF THE PHILIPPINES, THE. (1988)-. English. Four times a year. $188.00. National Statistical Information Center, 403 Gil Puyat Avenue, Ground Floor, Makati Metro Manila Phillipines. **Tel** 011 63 2 862469. **Continues** National Income Accounts of the Philippines.

LC HC79.I5 N387
DD 339.3   US

NATIONAL ACCOUNTS STATISTICS. ANALYSIS OF MAIN AGGREGATES. **Added/Corp** United Nations. Statistical Office. **VFOAT** Analysis of Main Aggregates. (1982)-. Government Publication. English. Irregular. Price varies per volume. United Nations Publications, 2 United Nations Plaza, Room DC2 0853, Department 007C, New York NY 10017. **Tel** (212)963-8303, (800)253-9646. **Continues in part** Yearbook of National Accounts Statistics, 0084-3881.
Desc: Presents a summary of main national accounts aggregates. Analyses gross domestic product or net material product by type of expenditure, economic activity and cost components, and current and constant prices.

LC HC79.I5 N388
DD 339.3/021   US

NATIONAL ACCOUNTS STATISTICS. MAIN AGGREGATES AND DETAILED TABLES. See Business and Economics-Abstracting, Bibliographies and Statistics.

LC HF5035 .N28A   **ISSN** 0191-5223
DD 338/.0025/73   US

NATIONAL BUSINESS ASSOCIATION. See Industry and Production-Trade and Industrial Directories.

LC HF1101 .N272   **ISSN** 1049-0256
DD 650/.071/073   US
Pr Rev.
NATIONAL BUSINESS EDUCATION YEARBOOK (1987). (NATIONAL BUSINESS EDUCATION YEARBOOK.). [Natl. bus. educ. yearb.]. **Added/Corp** National Business Education Association. No. 25 (1987)-. English. One time a year (May). $16.00. National Business Education Association, 1914 Association Drive, Reston VA 22091-1596. **Tel** (703)860-8300, FAX (703)620-4483. **Continues in part** Business Education Forum, 0007-6678.
Desc: Explores topics on business education. May concentrate on such topics as the global economy, leadership, new directions in teaching, strategic planning, or business education for a changing world.
Ind/Abst Educ. Index.

LC HF   **ISSN** 0110-6813
DD 380   NZ
UDC 38

NATIONAL BUSINESS REVIEW. [Natl. bus. rev.]. (1970)-. Periodical. English. Forty-eight times a year. $335.87. Fourth Estate Holdings Ltd., PO Box 1734, Auckland 1000 New Zealand. **Tel** 011 64 9 3071629, FAX 011 64 09 379060. **ED** Francis O'Sullivan. **Bk Rev. Ad Acc. Circ:** 125,000. available on an online database from DIALOG. **Continues** Admark.
Ind/Abst Bus. Source Plus; Bus. Source; EP Collect.; Homework Help.; MasterFile FullTEXT 1000; MasterFile FullTEXT 350; MasterFile FullTEXT 650; MasterFile FullTEXT; Telebase; World Mag. Bank.

LC HB
DD 330 NZ
NATIONAL BUSINESS REVIEW.
Newspaper. English. Forty-nine times a year (weekly except last two weeks in Dec. and first week in Jan.). 310.00NZ$ New Zealand; 385.00NZ$ Australia and South Pacific; 455.00NZ$ other. Fourth Estate Holdings Ltd., PO Box 1734, Auckland 1000 New Zealand. **Tel** 011 64 9 3071629, FAX 011 64 09 379060. **ED** Francis O'Sullivan. Index available (bound in all issues). **Ad Acc**, **Adv Mgr:** Amanda Harrison-Kyle. **Circ:** 19,000.

LC HD6050 .N3 **ISSN** 0027-8831
DD 331 US
NATIONAL BUSINESS WOMAN.
(NATIONAL BUSINESS WOMAN : THE MAGAZINE OF THE NATIONAL FEDERATION OF BUSINESS AND PROFESSIONAL WOMEN'S CLUBS.). [Natl. bus. woman]. **Added/Corp** National Federation of Business and Professional Women's Clubs. Vol. 35, No. 11 (Nov. 1956)-. Periodical. English. Four times a year. $10.00. National Federation of Business & Professional Women, 2012 Massachusetts Avenue NW, Washington DC 20036. **Tel** (202)293-1100. **ED** Maryanne Sugarman Costa. **Ad Acc**. **Circ:** 75,000 (ctrl). ***Continues*** *Independent Woman.*
Desc: Important to working women with an emphasis on policy, legislative affairs and workplace activity.
Ind/Abst Work Relat. Abstr.

LC HC
US
NATIONAL CORPORATION REPORTER, THE. **Added/Corp** United States Corporation Bureau, Inc. (Sept. 13, 1890)-. Periodical. English. One time a week. $5.00. National Corporation Reporter, 415 North State Street, Chicago IL 60610.

LC HC412 .N35 **ISSN** 0738-3037
DD 338.95/005 US
NATIONAL DEVELOPMENT. ASIA. [Natl. dev., Asia]. **VFOAT** Asia. (19??)-. Periodical. English. Six times a year. $40.00 US, Canada and Mexico; $50.00 (surface mail), $75.00 (airmail) other. Intercontinental Media, Box 5017, Westport CT 06880. **Tel** (203)226-7463, FAX (203)222-8793. ***Continues in part*** *National Development (Westport, Conn.), 0730-0123.*
Ind/Abst J. Ferrocement.

LC HC59.7 .N316 **ISSN** 0730-0123
DD 338.9/005 US
TITLE CHANGE
NATIONAL DEVELOPMENT (WESTPORT, CONN.). (NATIONAL DEVELOPMENT.). [Natl. dev.]. (19??)-(19??). Periodical. English. Intercontinental Media, PO Box 3410, Milford CT 06460. **Tel** (203)226-7463. **ED** Virginia Fairweather. ***Split into*** *National Development. Middle East/Africa, 0738-1670* ***and*** *National Development. Asia, 0738-3037.*

US
NATIONAL DIRECTORY OF ASIAN-AMERICAN ORGANIZATIONS.
(19??)-. English. $25.00 North America; $30.00 other. USPAACC, 1329 18th Street Northwest, Washington DC 20036.

ISSN 0813-9474
AT
CODEN NECREY
NATIONAL ECONOMIC REVIEW. [Natl. econ. rev.]. **Added/Corp** National Institute of Economic and Industry Research (Australia). (1984)-. Periodical. English. Four times a year (Apr., July, Sept., Dec.). 64.13Aus$. National Institute of Economic Industry Research, 416 Queens Parade, Clifton Hill Victoria 3068 Australia. **Tel** 011 61 3 4888444, FAX 011 61 3 4823262.
Ind/Abst AESIS Q.; APAIS, Aust. Public Aff. Inf. Ser.; PAIS Int. Print (1991-).

LC HC101 .N3117 **ISSN** 0430-1986
DD 330 US
NATIONAL ECONOMIC TRENDS. [Natl. econ. trends]. **Main/Corp** Federal Reserve Bank of St. Louis. (19??)-. Periodical. English. Twelve times a year. Free on request. Federal Reserve Bank of St. Louis, PO Box 66953, Research and Publication Information, St. Louis MO 63166. **Tel** (314)444-8444, (314)444-8660, FAX (314)444-8731. **ED** Daniel P Brennan. available on microfilm and microfiche from University Microfilms International (UMI). Documents available from Documents on Demand.
Desc: Charts and tables of various data on national business developments with brief analysis of current conditions.
Ind/Abst Am. Stat. Index.

US
NATIONAL GAMING SUMMARY. **VFOAT** Casino Journal's National Gaming Summary. (19??)-. Newsletter. English. One time a week. $298.00. Las Vegas Casino Journal, 3100 West Sahara Avenue, Suite 207, Las Vegas NV 89102. **Tel** (705)253-6230, (800)394-2467, FAX (702)253-6804.
Desc: Each issue recaps the past week's news and developments throughout the United States, Canada, the Caribbean, Europe and the Pacific Rim. Also includes a chronology of stock activity for 60 major public corporations whose stock trades on NYSE, AMEX or NASDAQ.

LC HC **ISSN** 0315-2286
DD 340/.06/271 CN
NATIONAL (OTTAWA). **See** Law.

AT
NATIONAL REMUNERATION CENTRE REPORT ON SALARIES AND EXECUTIVE REMUNERATION. (19??)-. English. Two times a year. 2250.00Aus$. National Remuneration Centre, GPO Box 5455CC, Melbourne Victoria 3001 Australia. **Tel** 011 61 3 2886081, FAX 011 61 3 2886155.

LC HC **ISSN** 0097-6202
US
NATIONAL REVIEW OF CORPORATE ACQUISITIONS, THE. **VFOAT** Corporate Acquisitions. (19??)-. Periodical. English. Fifty times a year (published on Mon.). $295.00. Tweed Publishing Company, 49 Main Street, Tiburon CA 94920. **Tel** (415)435-2175. **ED** Sonja Mahoney. Index available. cum. index. **Ad Acc**, **Adv Mgr:** Tish Stanny.

ISSN 1188-0945
DD 333.7 CN
NATIONAL ROUND TABLE REVIEW, THE. [Natl. round table rev.]. **Main/Corp** National Round Table on the Environment and the Economy (Canada). **VFOAT** La Revue de la Table Ronde Nationale. (Summer 1991)-. Periodical. English (French). Four times a year.

LC HB9 .N4 **ISSN** 0028-0453
DD 330.0 DK
Pr Rev.
NATIONALKONOMISK TIDSSKRIFT.
(NATIONALKONOMISK TIDSSKRIFT : MAANEDSKRIFT FOR SAMFUNDSSPRGSMAAL, KONOMI OG HANDEL.). [Nationalkon. tidsskr.]. **Added/Corp** Nationalkonomisk Forening. **VFOAT** Nationalkonomisk Tidsskrift for Samfundssprgsmaal, Konomi og handel; Nationalkonomisk Tidsskrift for Samfundspgsmal, Konomi og Handel. Vol. 1 (1873)-. Periodical. Danish. Three times a year. $61.73. Nationalokonomisk Forening, c/o Unibank A/S Economics Department, 1786 Copenhagen V Denmark. **Tel** 011 45 33 333124, FAX 011 45 33 333602. cum. index. **Ad Acc**. available on microfilm from University Microfilms International (UMI). Documents available from The Genuine Article.
Ind/Abst Am. Hist. Life (1959-1988);(1959-); Econ. Lit. Index (1959-); J. Econ. Lit.; Res. Alert [Full Cov.]; Soc. Sci. Cit. Index [Full Cov.].

LC HC380.I5 S74
DD 339.3485 SW
NATIONALRAKENSKAPER. **VFOAT** National Accounts. (19??)-. English (Swedish). Tilastokeskus, PL 504, Annankatu 44, 00101 Helsinki Finland. **Tel** 011 358 0 17341, FAX 011 358 0 17342474, telex 1002111 TILASTO SF.

LC HF1 .N4 **ISSN** 0028-047X
US
CCC
CODEN NBUSAY
Pr Rev.
NATION'S BUSINESS. [Nation's bus.]. **Added/Corp** Chamber of Commerce of the United States of America. Vol. 1 (Sept. 1912)-. Periodical. English. Twelve times a year. $22.00 (one-year), $35.00 (two-year); $46.00 (three-year). Nation's Business, 1615 H Street Northwest, Washington DC 20062. **Tel** (202)463-5650. **(Subscription address:** Neodata / Colorado, PO Box 2606, Boulder CO 80322. **)** **ED** Robert T. Gray. Index available. **Bk Rev**. **Ad Acc**. **Circ:** 850,000. available on microfilm from University Microfilms International (UMI); available on an online database (files 15,647,648/Full-Text) from DIALOG. Documents available from UMI Article Clearinghouse.
Desc: Designed to provide information on health, finance, business trends and management techniques for owners and managers of small to mid-size businesses.
Ind/Abst ABI/INFORM Glob. Ed.; ABI/INFORM Ondisc: Expr. Ed.; ABI/INFORM [Computer File] (Sept. 1971-); Acad. Abstr. Full Text Elite; Acad. Abstr.; Acad. Ind. [Computer File] (1984-); Acad. Search; Am. Bibliogr. Slavic East Europ. Stud.; BioBusiness (1986-); Biogr. Index; Bus. ASAP (1990-) [Full Txt.]; Bus. Index (1985-); Bus. Period. Index; Bus. Source Plus; Bus. Source; Coal Abstr.; Curr. Cit.; Energy Res. Abstr. (June 1978-); EP Collect.; Expand. Acad. Index (1984-); F&S Index Plus Text, Int. [Select. Cov.]; Gen. BusinessFile (1985-); Gen. Period. Index (1985-); Health Plan. Adminis.; Homework Help.; Index Period. Artic. Relat. Law; INFO-SOUTH Abstr.; Mag. Artic. Summar. Elite; Mag. Artic. Summar. Select; Mag. Artic. Summar. CD-ROM; Mag. ASAP Plus [Full Txt.]; Mag. ASAP Sel. [Full Txt.]; Mag. Express (1986-) [Full Txt.]; Mag. Index Plus (1989-); Mag. Index Sel. Microfiche (1986-) [Full Txt.]; Mag. Index. Sel. (1986-); Mag. Search; Manage. Contents (1974-); MasterFile FullTEXT 1000; MasterFile FullTEXT 350; MasterFile FullTEXT 650; MasterFile FullTEXT (July 1984-); Middle East Abstr. Index; Newsp. Period. Abstr. (1986-); OCLC; Pop. Mag. Rev. (1984-1987); Predicasts; PROMT; Pub. Lib. FullTEXT; Read. Guide Abstr. Select Ed.; Read. Guide Period. Lit.; Resource/One Ondisc; Telebase; Mag. Index (1977-);; TOM Gen. Index (1985-) [Full Txt.]; Trade Ind. ASAP [Full Txt.]; Trade Ind. Index (1981-) [Full Txt.]; UMI ABI/Inform--Bus. Period. Ondisc (Jan. 1988-) [Full Txt.]; Vocat. Search; Wilson Bus. Abstr.; Work Relat. Abstr.

LC HD2709
DD 338.74 US
NATO RECOMMENDED PRODUCTS LIST. **Added/Corp** United States. Dept. of Defense. North Atlantic Treaty Organization. Security and Evaluation Agency. Control U.S. COSMIC Registry. **VAT** North Atlantic Treaty Organization Recommended Products List. (19??)-. Government Publication. English. Four times a year. $40.00. US Department of Defense, The Pentagon, Washington DC 20301. **Tel** (703)545-6700. **(Subscription address:** Superintendent of Documents, US Government Printing Office, Washington DC 20402. **)**

US
NATURAL CONNECTION, THE. **See** Environmental Issues-Ecology.

LC HC **ISSN** 0888-949X
DD 330 US
NBER DIGEST, THE. [NBER dig.]. **Added/Corp** National Bureau of Economic Research. (19??)-. Periodical. English. Twelve times a year. Free on request. National Bureau of Economic Research, 1050 Massachusetts Avenue, Cambridge MA 02138. **Tel** (617)868-3900, FAX (617)441-3895. **ED** Donna L. Zerwitz. **Circ:** 13,000.
Desc: Summarizes selected working papers recently produced by the National Bureau. It is issued for informational purposes and has not been reviewed by the Board of Directors of NBER.
Ind/Abst Urban Aff. Abstr.

LC HB172.5 .N39 **ISSN** 0889-3365
DD 339/.05 US
CCC
Pr Rev.
NBER MACROECONOMICS ANNUAL.
Added/Corp National Bureau of Economic Research. **VFOAT** Macroeconomics Annual. **VAT** National Bureau of Economic Research Macroeconomics Annual. Vol. 1 (1986)-. Periodical. English. One time a year. $40.00. Massachusetts Institute of Technology (MIT) Press, 55 Hayward Street, Cambridge MA 02142. **Tel** (617)253-2889, (617)625-8481, FAX (617)258-6779. **ED** Stanley Fischer and Julio J. Rotemberg. Documents available from The Genuine Article.
Desc: Links theoretical and empirical macroeconomic developments with specific real-world examples and problems.
Ind/Abst Econ. Lit. Index; J. Econ. Lit.; Res. Alert [Full Cov.].

LC HC **ISSN** 0276-119X
DD 330 US
NBER REPORTER. [NBER rep.]. **Main/Corp** National Bureau of Economic Research. **Added/Corp** National Bureau of Economic Research. Reporter. **VFOAT** National Bureau Reporter. **VAT** National Bureau of Economic Research Reporter. (April 1977)-. Periodical. English. Four times a year. Free on request. National Bureau of Economic Research, 1050 Massachusetts Avenue, Cambridge MA 02138. **Tel** (617)868-3900, FAX (617)441-3895. **ED** Donna L. Zerwitz. **Circ:** 12,000. available on an online database (file 648/Full-Text) from DIALOG. ***Continues*** *National Bureau of Economic Research. National Bureau Report, 0547-4701.*
Desc: Journal summarizing research and publications of NBER over a three-month period.
Ind/Abst Acad. Search; Bus. ASAP (1990-) [Full Txt.]; Bus. Index (1986-); EP Collect.; Gen. BusinessFile (1986-); Gen. Period. Index (1985-); Homework Help.; Index Period. Artic. Relat. Law; INFO-SOUTH Abstr.; Mag. Search; MasterFile FullTEXT 1000; MasterFile FullTEXT 350; MasterFile FullTEXT 650; MasterFile FullTEXT (July 1993-); OCLC; Telebase; Urban Aff. Abstr.

LC HC **ISSN** 0898-2937
DD 330 US
NBER WORKING PAPER SERIES.
(WORKING PAPER SERIES.). [NBER work. pap. ser.]. **Main/Corp** National Bureau of Economic Research. **Added/Corp** National Bureau of Economic Research. **VFOAT** NBER Working Paper Series. (19??)-. English. Irregular (approx. 400 papers per year). $725.00. National Bureau of Economic Research, 1050 Massachusetts Avenue, Cambridge MA 02138. **Tel** (617)868-3900, FAX (617)441-3895. **ED** Anne Spillane.
Desc: Studies on the U.S. economy intended for discussion before final publication.
Ind/Abst Curr. Cit.; Leis., Rec., Tour. Abstr.; World Agric. Econ. Rural Sociol. Abstr.

LC HD2951 .N32 **ISSN** 1065-7207
DD 334 US
NCBA COOPERATIVE BUSINESS JOURNAL. [NCBA coop. bus. j.]. **Added/Corp** National Cooperative Business Association (U.S.). **VFOAT** National Cooperative Business Association

Business and Economics

Cooperative Business journal; Cooperative Business Journal. (19??)-. Periodical. English. Ten times a year (monthly with combined Jan./Feb. and June/July). $15.00. National Cooperative Business Association, 1401 New York Avenue Northwest, Washington DC 20005. **Tel** (202)638-6222. **ED** Leta M. Mach. **Bk Rev**. **Ad Acc**. **Circ**: 5,000. **Continues** Cooperative Business Journal, 0893-3391.

ISSN 1071-0612
DD 330 US
NEAL SPELCE AUSTIN LETTER, THE.
[Neal Spelce Austin lett.]. Vol. 1, No. 1 (March 30, 1979). Periodical. English. One time a week (fifty issues - not published last two weeks of December). $150.00. Neal Spelce Austin Letter, PO Box 1905, Austin TX 78767. **Tel** (512)288-7595, FAX (512)288-7521. **ED** Neal Spelce. **Circ**: 500.
Desc: Newsletter of developments in economic and public affairs for Austin, Texas.

LC G155.U6 N2A **ISSN** 0149-9165
DD 338.4/7/91782043 US
NEBRASKA VISITOR SURVEY. See Travel and Tourism.

LC HC905.A1 .G844 **ISSN** 0258-6754
DD 330 SA
TITLE CHANGE
NEDBANK QUARTERLY GUIDE TO THE ECONOMY. Added/Corp Nedbank Group.
Economic Unit. **VFOAT** Nedbank Guide to the Economy; Guide to the Economy. (Nov. 1992)-(199?). Periodical. English. NEDBANK Economic Unit, PO Box 9828, Johannesburg South Africa. **Tel** 011 27 11 6309111, FAX 011 27 11 8386580. **ED** E. Osborn. **Continues** Guide to the Economy, 0258-6754. **Continued by** Nedcor Guide to the Economy.

LC HC905.A1 .G844 **ISSN** 0258-6754
DD 330 SA
NEDCOR GUIDE TO THE ECONOMY.
Added/Corp Nedcor Economic Unit. **VFOAT** Guide to the Economy. (199?)-. Periodical. English. Four times a year. Free on request. NEDBANK Economic Unit, PO Box 9828, Johannesburg South Africa. **Tel** 011 27 11 6309111, FAX 011 27 11 8386580. **ED** E. Osborn. **Circ**: 20,000 (ctrl). **Continues** Nedbank Quarterly Guide to the Economy.

US
NEEDED RESEARCH IN BUSINESS EDUCATION. Main/Corp Delta Pi Epsilon. English.
$2.50. Delta Pi Epsilon National Office, PO Box 4340, Little Rock AR 72214. **Tel** (501)562-1233, FAX (501)562-1293.
Desc: Includes research questions in the form of generic questions that could be applied to any business education subject matter area.

ISSN 0960-8710
DD 338 UK
NEGOCIOS AL DIA. [Neg. al dia]. (1990)-.
Periodical. English. Twelve times a year. $188.00. Lettres UK Ltd, 61 Old Street, London EC1V 9HX United Kingdom. **Tel** 011 44 171 2510012, FAX 011 44 171 2538193. **ED** Miquel Angel Diez.
Desc: Confidential newsletter in Spanish dealing with business and management issues on the international scene. Launched as sister to the publication "Al Dia".

ISSN 1042-5063
DD 332 US
NERA ENERGY OUTLOOK. [NERA energy outlook]. Added/Corp National Economic Research Associates. VAT National Economic Research Associates Energy Outlook. (19??)-. Periodical. English.
Ten times a year (monthly except Jan. and July). $450.00. Nera Energy Outlook, 123 Main Street, White Plains NY 10601. **Tel** (914)681-7200, FAX (914)681-7925. **ED** Marion B. Stewart.

US
NEVADA BUSINESS JOURNAL. Vol. 1, No. 1 (Mar. 1986)-. Periodical. English. Twelve times a year.
$36.00. Nevada Business Journal, 2127 Paradise Road, Las Vegas NV 89104. **Tel** (702)735-7003. **Ad Acc**. **Circ**: 15,000 (ctrl).

HK
NEW ASIAN MARKET ATLAS, THE.
(1988)-. English. $385.00. Business Traveller / Hong Kong, 200 Lockhart Road, 13th Floor, Hong Kong Hong Kong. **Tel** 011 852 5 25119317, FAX 011 852 5 25196846, telex 62107.

LC HC **ISSN** 0828-7821
DD 330.9715/04 CN
NEW BRUNSWICK BRANCH NEWS. [N.B. Branch news]. (1982)-. Periodical. English. Twelve times a year. Canadian Manufacturers Association, 75 International Boulevard, 4th Floor, Etobicoke Ontario M9W 6L9 Canada. **Tel** (905)798-8000 ext. 245.

ISSN 0342-4006
GW
NEW BUSINESS. [New bus.]. (197?)-. Periodical.
German. One time a week. Erwin Koch Verlag, Postfach 730720, D 22127 Hamburg Germany. **Tel** 011 49 40 6774055.
Ind/Abst Mark. Advert. Ref. Serv.

US
NEW BUSINESS INCORPORATIONS.
Added/Corp Dun and Bradstreet, Inc. Economic Analysis Dept. **VFOAT** Business Incorporations. (1985)-. Periodical. English. Dun & Bradstreet / New York, 299 Park Avenue, 24th Floor, New York NY 10171. **Tel** (212)593-4173. **Continues** News from Dun & Bradstreet, Inc., Business Economics Division. Monthly New Incorporations.

LC WMLC 93/2822 **ISSN** 1041-3707
DD 338 US
TITLE CHANGE
NEW BUSINESS OPPORTUNITIES (IRVINE, CALIF.). (NEW BUSINESS OPPORTUNITIES.). [New bus. oppor.]. VFOAT New Business Opportunities from Entrepreneur Magazine. Vol. 1, No. 1 (Feb./Mar. 1989)-(1993). Trade Publication.
English. Entrepreneur Inc., 2392 Morse Avenue, Irvine CA 92714. **Tel** (714)261-2393. **ED** Gary Hooks. **Ad Acc**. **Circ**: 250,000. **Continued by** Business Start-Ups, 1069-5818.
Desc: Geared toward Americans who are interested in pursuing their own businesses, but lack the organization or creative resources to do so.

US
NEW BUSINESS REGISTER. English. $79.00.
Telex Communications Inc., PO Box 1986, Toledo OH 43603. **Tel** (419)244-8200.

ISSN 1082-149X
US
●NEW CASTLE BUSINESS LEDGER. VFOAT
Ledger. (1994)-. Periodical. English. Twelve times a year. $15.00. New Castle Business Ledger, 153 East Chestnut Hill Road, Newark DE 19713. **Tel** (302)737-0923.

LC HC426.A1 N43
DD 330.951/005 HK
CEASED
NEW CHINA QUARTERLY. No. 1 (July 1986)-No. 30. Periodical. English. N C N Ltd, 5 Sharp Street West, Wanchai Hong Kong. **Tel** 011 852 5 28313526. **Continues** PRC Quarterly.

US
NEW ECONOMY. (19??)-. Periodical. English.
Irregular. $20.00. Economic Conversion Disarmament, 1828 Jefferson Place Northwest, Washington DC 20036. **Tel** (202)728-0815, FAX (202)728-0826. **ED** Anna D. Darwin (Production Editor). **Circ**: 2,000 (ctrl).

ISSN 1070-3535
UK
●NEW ECONOMY (LONDON, ENGLAND).
(NEW ECONOMY.). (1993)-. Academic Scholarly Publication. English. Four times a year. $179.67. Academic Press Ltd., A Division of Harcourt Brace & Company Ltd., 24-28 Oval Road, London NW1 7DX United Kingdom. **Tel** 011 44 171 2674466, FAX 011 44 171 4822293, 011 44 171 4854752, telex 25775 ACPRES G. (**Subscription address**: Harcourt Brace and Company, Ltd., Foots Cray High Street, Sidcup Kent DA14 5HP United Kingdom. **Tel** 011 44 181 3003322, FAX 011 44 181 3090807, telex 896 377 ACADEM.)

LC WMLC L 83/5925 **ISSN** 0545-106X
US
NEW ENGLAND ECONOMIC ALMANAC.
Added/Corp Federal Reserve Bank of Boston. (1957)-. Periodical. Irregular (every 5 years). Federal Reserve Bank of Boston, 600 Atlantic Avenue, Research Library D, Boston MA 02106. **Tel** (617)973-3397, (617)973-3403.

LC HC
DD 330 US
NEW FIRMS LISTING SERVICES. (19??)-.
Periodical. English. Twelve times a year. $25.00 (nonmembers), $9.00 (members). Long Island Builders Institute, 425 Broad Hollow Road, Suite 425, Melville NY 11747. **Tel** (516)752-9600.

ISSN 0164-8152
US
NEW HAMPSHIRE BUSINESS REVIEW.
Vol. 1, No. 7 (Oct. 1978)-. Newspaper. English. Twenty-four times a year. $24.00. New Hampshire Business Review, 150 Dow Street, Manchester NH 03101. **Tel** (603)624-1442. **ED** Donald B. Madden Jr. **Ad Acc**. ctrl circ. available on an online database (file 635/Full-Text) from DIALOG. Documents available from UMI Article Clearinghouse. **Continues** New Hampshire Business World.
Ind/Abst Acad. Search; Bus. Dateline; Bus. Index (Jan. 1985-Dec. 1985); Bus. Source Plus; Bus. Source; EP Collect.; Gen. BusinessFile (Jan. 1985-Dec. 1985); Gen. Period. Index (Jan. 1985-Dec. 1985); Homework Help.;

INFO-SOUTH Abstr.; MasterFile FullTEXT 1000; MasterFile FullTEXT 350; MasterFile FullTEXT 650; MasterFile FullTEXT (July 1993-); OCLC; PROMT; Telebase.

LC HC107.N5 N38 **ISSN** 0028-5560
DD 330 US
NEW JERSEY BUSINESS. [N.J. bus.].
Added/Corp New Jersey Business & Industry Association. New Jersey Manufacturers Association. Vol. 1, (Sept. 1954)-. Periodical. English. Twelve times a year. $20.00. New Jersey Business & Industry Association, 310 Pasaic Avenue, Fairfield NJ 07006. **Tel** (201)882-5004, FAX (201)882-4648. **ED** James T. Prior. **Ad Acc**. **Circ**: 17,500 (ctrl). available on an online database (file 635/Full-Text) from DIALOG. Documents available from UMI Article Clearinghouse.
Ind/Abst Bus. Dateline (Dec. 1990-) [Full Txt.]; PAIS Int. Print.

LC HF5065.N5 N43 **ISSN** 1049-2879
DD 061/.49 US
Pr Rev.
NEW JERSEY BUSINESS SOURCE BOOK, THE. [N. J. bus. source book]. Added/Corp
Zinn, Graves & Field. **VFOAT** Business Source Book. (1987)-. English. Irregular (once every one to two years). $94.95. Resource Communications Group, 3011 North Lamar Boulevard, Austin TX 78705. **Tel** (512)458-2021, FAX (512)458-2059. **ED** Jeanne Graves. Index available. **Bk Rev**. **Circ**: 700. available on labels.
Desc: A compilation of current top 470 employers in the state, all chambers of commerce, economic development agencies, business publications, labor unions and professional and and trade organizations, services offered to small, women and minority-owned and regular businesses.

UK
TITLE CHANGE
NEW MATERIALS WORLD. (19??)-(19??).
English. World Business Publications Ltd., 960 High Road, Britannia 4th Floor, London N12 9RY United Kingdom. **Tel** 011 44 181 4465141, FAX 011 44 181 4463659, telex 9419208. **Continued by** Performance Materials Technology.

LC HF3161.N6 N65 **ISSN** 0889-5937
DD 330.9789/005 US
NEW MEXICO BUSINESS CURRENT ECONOMIC REPORT. See Business and Economics-Abstracting, Bibliographies and Statistics.

ISSN 0164-6796
US
NEW MEXICO BUSINESS JOURNAL. [N. M. bus. j.]. Added/Corp Association of Commerce and Industry of New Mexico. (1978)-. Trade Publication.
English. Twelve times a year. $24.00. New Mexico Business Journal, PO Box 30550, Albuquerque NM 87190. **Tel** (505)889-2911, FAX (505)889-0822. **ED** Jack Hartsfield. **Ad Acc**, **Adv Mgr Tel** (505)889-2911. **Circ**: 18,000. available on an online database (files 635,648/Full-Text) from DIALOG. Documents available from UMI Article Clearinghouse, Documents on Demand. **Continues** Business Journal.
Desc: Serves the state's business community by providing in-depth coverage of relevant events and issues. New Mexico angle required for all stories.
Ind/Abst Acad. Search; Bus. Dateline; Bus. Index (1985-); Bus. Source Plus; Bus. Source; Coal Abstr.; Energy Inf. Abstr.; Environ. Abstr.; EP Collect.; Gen. BusinessFile (1985-); Gen. Period. Index (1985-); Homework Help.; INFO-SOUTH Abstr.; MasterFile FullTEXT 1000; MasterFile FullTEXT 350; MasterFile FullTEXT 650; MasterFile FullTEXT (July 1993-); OCLC; Telebase; Trade Ind. ASAP [Full Txt.]; Trade Ind. Index [Full Txt.].

US
NEW MEXICO BUSINESS WEEKLY.
(19??)-. English. One time a week. $19.50. Starlight Publications, Po Box 928, Albuquerque NM 87103. **Tel** (505)255-4648. **Continues** New Mexico Business News.

ISSN 1059-4140
DD 051 US
NEW MIAMI. (NEW MIAMI : THE BUSINESS OF SOUTH FLORIDA.). [New Miami]. (1988)-. Periodical.
English. Twelve times a year. $18.00 US; $30.00 Canada; $40.00 Europe; $60.00 other. New Miami The Business of South Florida, 444 Brickell Avenue, Suite 250, Miami FL 33131. **Tel** (305)372-5000. available on an online database (file 635/Full-Text) from DIALOG. Documents available from UMI Article Clearinghouse.
Ind/Abst Bus. Dateline (June 1991-) [Full Txt.].

ISSN 0279-4527
US
NEW ORLEANS CITIBUSINESS. VFOAT
New Orleans CityBusiness; New Orleans City Business; Citibusiness; City Business. (198?)-. Periodical. English. One time a week. $45.00. New Orleans Group, 111 Veterans Memorial Boulevard, Suite 1810, Metairie LA 70005. **Tel** (504)834-9292, FAX (504)837-2258. **ED**

Business and Economics

Kathy Finn. **Ad Acc, Adv Mgr:** Lisa Blossman. **Circ:** 15,000. available on an online database from DIALOG. Documents available from UMI Article Clearinghouse. **Ind/Abst** Acad. Search; Bus. Dateline; Bus. Index (Jan. 1985-July 1985); Bus. Source Plus; Bus. Source; EP Collect.; Gen. BusinessFile (Jan. 1985-Dec. 1985); Gen. Period. Index (Jan. 1985-Dec. 1985); Homework Help.; INFO-SOUTH Abstr.; MasterFile FullTEXT 1000; MasterFile FullTEXT 350; MasterFile FullTEXT 650; MasterFile FullTEXT (Jan. 1994-); OCLC; Telebase.

LC HB71
DD 330
UK

● **NEW POLITICAL ECONOMY.** See Political Science.

US

NEW PRODUCT NEWS. (199?)-. Trade Publication. English. Twelve times a year. $359.00 US and US possessions; $432.00 other. Trend Publishing Inc., 625 North Michigan Avenue, Suite 2500, Chicago IL 60611-3109. **Tel** (312)654-2300, FAX (312)654-2323. **Continues** Gorman's New Product News.

ISSN 0264-2603
DD 338.476292
UK

NEW SERVICE STATION AND PARTS BUYER. [New Serv. Stn. parts buy.]. (1982)-. Periodical. English. Twelve times a year. £30.00 UK; £35.00 other. Datapass Ltd, Overcliffe House, 55 New Road/Suite 3, Gravensend Kent DA11 0AD United Kingdom. **Tel** 011 44 1474 564390. **Continues** Service Station, 0037-265X.

UK

NEW SOURCES OF GRANTS AND AID FOR BUSINESS IN THE UK. (19??)-. English. £37.00. WEKA Publishing, The Forum, 74-80 Camden Street, London NW1 0EG United Kingdom. **Tel** 01 388 8400.

LC HC
DD 330
US
Pr Rev.

NEW YORK ECONOMIC REVIEW : JOURNAL OF THE NEW YORK STATE ECONOMICS ASSOCIATION. Added/Corp New York State Economics Association. Vol. 14 (1984)-. Periodical. English. Four times a year. $40.00. New York State Economics Association, State Univeristy of New York, Oneonta NY 13820. **Tel** (607)436-2127, FAX (607)436-2107. **ED** William P. O'Dea. **Ad Acc. Circ:** 300-500. **Continues** New York State Economics Association. Journal of the New York State Economics Association.

LC HB235.U6 N48
ISSN 0749-6311
DD 338.5/28/09747
US

NEW YORK MODEL. Added/Corp Wharton Econometric Forecasting Associates. WEFA Group. **VFOAT** Wharton New York Model C.P.I. Forecast; Wharton New York Model CPI Forecast. (1984)-. Periodical. English. Two times a year. $10500.00. WEFA / Philadelphia, PO Box 8500, Suite 1995, Philadelphia PA 19178. **Tel** (215)667-6000, telex 710 6700575. **Formed by the union of** Wharton New York Model, 0749-6303 **and** Wharton CPIModel, 0749-632X.

LC HC107.N7 N373a
DD 338/.09747
US

NEW YORK STATE BUSINESS FACT BOOK. Added/Corp New York (State). Dept. of Economic Development. (1990)-. English. New York State Department of Commerce, 99 Washington Avenue, Albany NY 12245. **Tel** (518)474-6950, (518)474-5027. **Continues** New York State Business Fact Book. Supplement, 0545-4662.

LC HC
DD 330
US

NEW YORK STATE ECONOMIC AND REVENUE FORECASTS. Added/Corp New York (State). Legislature. Assembly. Committee on Ways and Means. (1989/90 & 1990/91)-. English. New York State Assembly, Albany Office, Room 844/Legislative Office Building, Albany NY 12248. **Continues** New York State Economic and Revenue Projections.

LC HC621 .N4
ISSN 0071-9571
DD 338
NZ

NEW ZEALAND BUSINESS WHO'S WHO, THE. See Biographies.

LC HG4274.6 .N48
ISSN 0549-0200
DD 338.7/4/09931
NZ

NEW ZEALAND COMPANY REGISTER, THE. [N.Z. co. register]. **Added/Corp** Headliner Publishing Co. (1963)-. English. One time a year. $27.07. Mercantile Gazette of N Z, GPO Box 20-034, Christchurch New Zealand. **Tel** 011 64 006433583 219, FAX 011 64 33584 490.

LC HB9 .N53
ISSN 0077-9954
NZ

NEW ZEALAND ECONOMIC PAPERS. [N. Z. econ. pap.]. **Added/Corp** New Zealand Association of Economics. Vol. 1 (Spring 1966)-. Periodical. English. Two times a year (June and December). $63.99. New Zealand Association of Economists, PO Box 568, Wellington New Zealand. **ED** L. Evans. **Bk Rev. Circ:** 700 (ctrl).
Desc: Economic articles by authors whose views are not necessarily shared by the association or editor. Notes, comments, replies, book reviews, books received, discussion and working papers.
Ind/Abst Contents Recent Econ. J.; Econ. Lit. Index (19??-); Int. Labour Doc.; J. Econ. Lit.; LABORDOC.

ISSN 0113-8138
DD 382.609931
NZ

NEW ZEALAND INTERNATIONAL BUSINESS. [N.Z. int. bus.]. **VFOAT** International Business. (1988)-. Periodical. English. Six times a year. 76.00NZ$ Australia and South Pacific; 113.00NZ$ other. Minty's Media, 22 Heather Street, Private Bag 93218, Parnell Auckland New Zealand. **Tel** 011 64 9 3794233, FAX 011 64 9 3093575. **ED** Eion Scott. **Bk Rev. Ad Acc, Adv Mgr:** Linda Brickland. **Continues** Export Business, 0113-6208.
Desc: Articles and information on many issues such as fishing industry, manufacturing trends, market profiles, air travel options, and legal issues.

LC HF4030.5 .A28
ISSN 0110-9596
DD 650/.09931
NZ

NEW ZEALAND JOURNAL OF BUSINESS. Added/Corp Victoria University of Wellington. Dept. of Business Administration. Vol. 1 (1979)-. English. One time a year (December). Price varies per volume. University of Auckland, Private Bag 92019, Auckland New Zealand. **Tel** 011 64 9 3737999, telex NZ 21480.

ISSN 1052-7338
DD 338
US

... NEWCOMER'S GUIDE TO FLORIDA BUSINESS, THE. [Newcom. guide Fla. bus.]. **VFOAT** Newcomer's Guide; Florida Trend, Newcomer's Guide. (1991)-. English. $9.95 (single issue). The Newcomer's Guide to Florida Business, PO Box 611, St. Petersburg FL 33731.

LC HC117.N4 N456
ISSN 1197-1738
DD 330.9718/005
CN
TITLE CHANGE

NEWFOUNDLAND & LABRADOR ECONOMIC REVIEW. [Nfld. Labrador econ. rev.]. **Added/Corp** Newfoundland. Executive Council. Economic Research & Analysis Division. Newfoundland. Cabinet Secretariat. **VFOAT** Newfoundland and Labrador Economic Review. 1st Quarter (1987)-(1994). Periodical. English. Executive Council Newfoundland and Labrador, 10th Floor East Block, Confederation Building, PO Box 8700, St Johns Newfoundland A1B 4J6 Canada. **Tel** (709)729-3255, (709)729-3649, FAX (709)729-6944. **Continued by** The Economic Review.

ISSN 1186-0413
DD 330.9713
CN

NEWMARKET BUSINESS REPORT. [Newmark. bus. rep.]. **Added/Corp** Newmarket Chamber of Commerce. (1990)-. Periodical. English. Twelve times a year. Limited free distribution. Newmarket Chamber of Commerce, Unit 1, 171 Main Street, Newmarket Ontario L3Y 3Y9 Canada.

LC HX1 .N685
ISSN 0028-8969
DD 335/.005
US

NEWS & LETTERS. [News lett.]. **VFOAT** News and Letters; News Theory/Practice & Letters; News Theory Practice and Letters. **VAT** News and Letters. (June 1955)-. Periodical. English. Ten times a year. $2.50. News & Letters, 59 East van Buren Street/Suite 707, Chicago IL 60605. **Tel** (312)663-0839. **ED** Eugene Walker. **Bk Rev. Circ:** 7,000 (ctrl). available on microfilm and microfiche from University Microfilms International (UMI).
Desc: Labor, women's liberation, civil rights and peace news, with analysis of world events from Marxist-Humanist perspective.

LC HF5001
ISSN 0026-2048
DD 650
US

NEWS BULLETIN. Main/Corp Michigan Business Education Association. (19??)-. Bulletin. English. Five times a year (Jan., Mar., May, Sep., Nov.). $25.00. Michigan Business Education Association, 2552 Oakview Drive SW, Wyoming MI 49509. **Tel** (313)932-5800. cum. index. **Bk Rev,** (Qty: 5). **Ad Acc, Adv Mgr Tel** (616)531-0608. **Circ:** 1,500 (ctrl).
Desc: Official publication of Michigan Business Education Association.

ISSN 1064-6973
DD 338
US

NEWS FOR ENTREPRENEURIAL MOTHERS. [News entrep. mothers]. **Added/Corp** Gabella Secretarial Service. (May 1992)-. Periodical. English. Twelve times a year. $12.00. News for Entrepreneurial Mothers, 1137 Erin Drive, Kent OH 44240.

ISSN 0273-1622
US

NEWS FROM DUN & BRADSTREET, INC. BUSINESS ECONOMICS DIVISION. WEEKLY FAILURES. Main/Corp Dun and Bradstreet, Inc. Business Economics Division. **VFOAT** Weekly Failures. **VAT** News from Dun and Bradstreet, Incorporated. Business Economics Division. Weekly Failures. English. One time a week. $30.00. Dun & Bradstreet / New York, 299 Park Avenue, 24th Floor, New York NY 10171. **Tel** (212)593-4173.

LC HF5001
ISSN 0360-697X
DD 650
US

NEWSLINE. Added/Corp American Assembly of Collegiate Schools of Business. Vol. 22, No. 1 (Fall 1991)-. Periodical. English. Four times a year. $150.00 (professional societies); $750.00 (educational institute); $625.00 (other) US; $1,350.00 (level one), $2,050.00 (level two) Accredited Institute; $1,000 small corporations and large professional organization; $2,000.00 large corporations. American Assembly of Collegiate Schools of Business, 600 Emerson Road, Suite 300, St Louis MO 63141-6762. **Tel** (314)872-8481, FAX (314)872-8495. **ED** Sharon Barber. **Ad Acc. Circ:** 8,000. **Continues** AACSB Newsline.

ISSN 0111-0608
DD 380.016
NZ

NEWZINDEX. See Business and Economics-Abstracting, Bibliographies and Statistics.

LC HB9 .N5
DD 330.1
VM

NGHIEN CU KINH TE. Added/Corp Vien Kinh Te (Vietnam). (1961)-. Periodical. Vietnamese. Six times a year. Xunhasaba Exports and Imports, 7 Nguyen Thi Minh Khai Str, Dit 1 Ho Chi Minh City Vietnam. **Tel** 011 84 8 294893, telex 278 XUNHASABA. **Circ:** 6,000.

LC HC146.A1 N53
DD 330
US

NICARAGUA ECONOMIC REPORT. Added/Corp Banco Central de Nicaragua. Vol. 1, Issue 1 (Mar. 1991)-. Periodical. English. Twelve times a year.
Ind/Abst Int. Labour Doc.

ISSN 0048-038X
NR

NIGERIAN BUSINESS DIGEST. Vol. 1 (Jan. 1971)-. Periodical. English. Twelve times a year. Universal Publications Ltd, 115 Griffith Street, Ebute-Metta Box 1959, Lagos Nigeria. **Tel** LAGOS 47132. available on microfilm from University Microfilms International (UMI).

LC HC517.N48 N5
ISSN 0029-0092
DD 300/.5
NR
CCC

NIGERIAN JOURNAL OF ECONOMIC AND SOCIAL STUDIES, THE. [Niger. j. econ. soc. stud.]. **Added/Corp** Nigerian Economic Society. Vol. 1 (May 1959)-. Academic Scholarly Publication. English. Three times a year. $100.00. Nigerian Economic Society, University of Ibadan, PO Box 22004, Ibadan Nigeria. **ED** Eyitayo Lambo. Index available. cum. index. **Bk Rev. Ad Acc. Circ:** 1,000 (ctrl).
Desc: Highly academic and scholarly journal embracing all aspects of economics and the social sciences.
Ind/Abst Contents Recent Econ. J.; Geogr. Abstr. Human Geogr.; Int. Bibliogr. Sociol.; Int. Dev. Abstr.; Int. Labour Doc.; Popul. Index.

LC HD70.J3 N486
JA

NIHON KEIEI SHINDAN GAKKAI NENPO. VFOAT Annual Report of Society of Business Diagnosis (Japan). (19??)-. Japanese. One time a year. Nihon Keiei Shindan Gakkai, c/o Doyukan, 32-6 Hongo 5 Bunkyo-ku, Tokyo-to Japan.

LC HB9 .N52
DD 330
JA

NIHON KEIZAI KENKYU. Added/Corp Nihon Keizai Kenkyu Senta. **VFOAT** Journal of Japan Economic Research. (19??)-. Multiple languages (Japanese and English). Nihon Keizai Shimbun Inc., 9-5 Otemachi 1 Chome, Chiyoda-ku Tokyo 100 Japan. **Tel** 011 81 3 32700251, 011 81 3 52108502 (Nikkei Business Publications Inc.), FAX 011 81 3 52552661, 011 81 3 52108119 (Nikkei Business Publications Inc.).

LC HC462.9.N48655
DD 330
JA

NIHON KEIZAI NI TSUYOKUNARU HON. (1981)-. Japanese. ¥1180. Eru Shuppansha, 51 Kanda Jinbo-cho 1, Chiyoda-ku, Tokyo-to Japan.

Business and Economics

LC HC461.5.A2 N433
DD 330   JA
NIHON NO KEIEISHA. 1-BU, ZEN JOJO KAISHA, SHACHO NO KEIEI SENRYAKU TO JINBUTSUZO. (1977)-. Japanese. Every 2 years. ¥50000. Jihyosa, c/o Ozawa Building, 21-18 Toranomon 1 Minato-ku, Tokyo Japan.

ISSN 0029-0491
DD 338.952   JA
NIKKEI BIJINESU. **VFOAT** Nikkei Business. (1969)-. Trade Publication. Japanese. Twenty-six times a year. $634.40. Nihon Keizai Shimbun Inc., 9-5 Otemachi 1 Chome, Chiyoda-ku Tokyo 100 Japan. **Tel** 011 81 3 32700251, 011 81 3 52108502 (Nikkei Business Publications Inc.), **FAX** 011 81 3 52552661, 011 81 3 52108119 (Nikkei Business Publications Inc.). **(Subscription address:** OCS / Overseas Courier Service of America Inc., 5 East 44th Street, New York NY 10017. **Tel** (212)599-4517.) **Bk Rev. Ad Acc. Circ:** 290,000.

LC HB
DD 330   JA
NIKKEI : BIMONTHLY FORUM FOR IDEAS AND NEWS FROM NIHON KEIZAI SHIMBUN, INC. Added/Corp Nihon Keizai Shimbun. (19??)-. Periodical. English. Six times a year. Nihon Keizai Shimbun Inc., 9-5 Otemachi 1 Chome, Chiyoda-ku Tokyo 100 Japan. **Tel** 011 81 3 32700251, 011 81 3 52108502 (Nikkei Business Publications Inc.), **FAX** 011 81 3 52552661, 011 81 3 52108119 (Nikkei Business Publications Inc.).

LC HC462.9 .N5339
DD 330   JA
NIKKEI SANGYO SHINBUN. Added/Corp Nihon Keizai Shinbunsha. (19??)-. Newspaper. Japanese. Six times a week (daily except Sun.). Nihon Keizai Shimbun Inc., 9-5 Otemachi 1 Chome, Chiyoda-ku Tokyo 100 Japan. **Tel** 011 81 3 32700251, 011 81 3 52108502 (Nikkei Business Publications Inc.), **FAX** 011 81 3 52552661, 011 81 3 52108119 (Nikkei Business Publications Inc.). **ED** Tomio Sato. Index available. **Ad Acc, Adv Mgr:** Kazuo Imazeki. **Circ:** 255,000. available on an online database (files 772,799/Full-Text) from DIALOG.
Desc: Newspaper covering economic and business developments, industry, etc.
Ind/Abst Infomat Int. Bus.

ISSN 1063-2816
US
NONPROFIT BOARD REPORT, THE. (199?)-. Periodical. English. Twelve times a year. $249.00. Progressive Business Publications, 370 Technology Drive, PO Box 3019, Malvern PA 19355. **Tel** (617)527-8600, (800)220-5000, **FAX** (617)647-8089.

LC TN1 .N75   **ISSN** 0961-1444
DD 553/.05   US
   CCC
NONRENEWABLE RESOURCES. See Environmental Issues-Conservation and Natural Resources.

ISSN 1237-8488
FI
UDC 336.7
●**NORDBALT M&A REPORT.** (1994-)-. Periodical. English. Twelve times a year. Lochlann Publishing, BioCity, Tykistokatu 6A 5 fl., FIN-20520 Turku Finland. **Tel** 011 358 21 2410447, **FAX** 011 358 21 2410449. **ED** Gerard O'Dwyer. available with charts.
Desc: Offers professionals a comprehensive listing of all major deals, including domestic and cross-border takeovers, mergers, MBO's and minority buy-ins in the Nordic and Baltic states. Also tracks cross-border investment by native and foreign groups.

LC HC   **ISSN** 0549-6233
DD 330   DK
NORDISK HANDELSKALENDER : SKANDINAVIASK ADRESSEBOG. (19??)-. Danish. Irregular. Nordisk Handelskalender, Sydvestvej 49, 2600 Glostrup Denmark.

IT
NORMATIVA GENERALE. (19??)-. Periodical. Italian. Four times a year. IPSOA Editore SRL, Casella Postale 12055, Mastrangelo, 20120 Milan Italy. **Tel** 011 39 2 82476248.

IT
NORME DI COMPORTAMENTO IN MATERIA TRIBUTARIA. (19??)-. Periodical. Italian. Two times a year. IPSOA Editore SRL, Casella Postale 12055, Mastrangelo, 20120 Milan Italy. **Tel** 011 39 2 82476248. Index available (Included).

LC HD2346.U5 N67   **ISSN** 0883-3583
DD 338.7/089914073   US
NORTH AMERICAN DIRECTORY & REFERENCE GUIDE OF ASIAN INDIAN BUSINESSES AND INDEPENDENT PROFESSIONAL PRACTITIONERS ALONG WITH COMMUNITY REFERENCE GUIDE & TRAVEL INFORMATION. [North Am. dir. ref. guide Asian Indian bus. indep. prof. pract. community ref. guide travel infor.]. **VFOAT** North American Directory and Reference Guide of Asian Indian Businesses and Independent Professional Practitioners. 1st Ed. -. Directory. English. $22.95. India Enterprises of the West Inc, PO Box 462 Wakefield Station, Bronx NY 10466. **Tel** (203)329-8010. **ED** Thomas Abraham. **Ad Acc. Circ:** 10,000.
Desc: Gives a listing of Asian Indian businesses, professional practitioners, and India associations. Also provides information on religious places and travel. Serves as a reference guide on business and investment opportunities in US and India.

LC F251 .W4
DD 975.6/005   US
NORTH CAROLINA. Added/Corp North Carolina Citizens for Business and Industry. (Jan. 1990)-. Periodical. English. Twelve times a year. $21.20. North Carolina Citizens Business & Industry, PO Box 2508, Raleigh NC 27602. **Tel** (919)828-0758, **FAX** (919)821-4992. **ED** Steve Tuttle. **Ad Acc, Adv Mgr:** C. Couch, P. deLuca. **Circ:** 13,200. Continues We the People of North Carolina (Raleigh, N.C. : 1968).
Desc: Serves businesses in North Carolina. Also includes information of interest to state and local government.

US
NORTHEAST PENNSYLVANIA BUSINESS JOURNAL. English. Twelve times a year. available on an online database (file 635/Full-Text) from DIALOG. Documents available from UMI Article Clearinghouse.
Ind/Abst Bus. Dateline.

LC HC107.C7 U54a
DD 330.9/788/6803   US
NORTHERN COLORADO BUSINESS INFORMATION FACTBOOK. Main/Corp University of Northern Colorado. Bureau of Business and Public Research. (19??)-. English. One time a year. Bureau of Business and Public Research, University of Colorado, Greeley CO 80639.

US
NORTHERN COLORADO BUSINESS REVIEW. Added/Corp University of Northern Colorado. Bureau of Business and Public Research. (1977)-. Periodical. English. Four times a year. Bureau of Business and Public Research, University of Colorado, Greeley CO 80639.

ISSN 0710-2755
DD 380.1/09713/1   CN
NORTHERN ONTARIO BUSINESS. [North. Ont. bus.]. **VFOAT** Design North. Vol. 1, No. 1 (Oct. 1980)-. Periodical. English. Twelve times a year. 16.01Can$. Northern Ontario Business, 158 Elgin Street South, Sudbury Ontario P3E 3N5 Canada. **Tel** (705)673-5705, **FAX** (705)673-9542. **ED** Wendy Parker. **Bk Rev. Ad Acc. Circ:** 16,000 (ctrl). available on microfilm from Micromedia Limited; available on an online database (files 635,648/Full-Text) from DIALOG. Documents available from UMI Article Clearinghouse.
Desc: A regional business publication serving Northern Ontario. Deals with mining, logging, pulp and paper, manufacturing, and service industries.
Ind/Abst Acad. Search; Bus. Dateline; Bus. Index (Jan. 1984-Dec. 1985); Bus. Source Plus; Bus. Source; EP Collect.; Gen. BusinessFile (Jan. 1985-Dec. 1985); Gen. Period. Index (Jan. 1985-Dec. 1985); Homework Help.; INFO-SOUTH Abstr.; MasterFile FullTEXT 1000; MasterFile FullTEXT 350; MasterFile FullTEXT 650; MasterFile FullTEXT (July 1993-); OCLC; PROMT; Telebase; Trade Ind. ASAP [Full Txt.]; Trade Ind. Index [Full Txt.].

LC HB
DD 330   CN
●**NORTHWEST BUSINESS.** (1994)-. English. Four times a year. 11.00Can$. Sylvester Publications Ltd., 101-10118-101 Avenue, Grande Prarie Alberta T8V 0Y4 Canada. **Tel** (403)538-0539. **ED** Donald C. Sylvester. Full Page (B&W) 1,550.00Can$. Full Page (Color) 1,995.00Can$. **Pub. Size:** Standard. **Circ:** 10,000.

LC HB1 .N6   **ISSN** 0029-3474
DD 330.0   US
NORTHWEST TECHNOCRAT, THE. Vol. 4 (June/July 1939)-. Periodical. English. Four times a year. $5.00 U.S. and Canada; $6.00 other. Technocracy Inc, 7513 Greenwood Avenue North, Seattle WA 98103. **Tel** (206)784-2111. **ED** John L Berge. Continues Section

Post.
Desc: Preparing the people of this continent for social change.

ISSN 1078-3865
US
●**NOTABLE CORPORATE CHRONOLOGIES.** (1994)-. English. Every 2 years. $95.00 (each volume). Gale Research Inc., 835 Penobscot Building, 645 Griswold Street, Detroit MI 48226. **Tel** (800)877-GALE, (313)961-2242, **FAX** (313)961-6083, (800)414-5043, telex TWX 810-221-7086. **ED** Susan Boyles Martin.
Desc: The publication presents concise chronologies for 1,500 significant corporations currently operating in the United States and abroad.

CL
NOTAS EJECUTIVAS SOBRE MEDIO AMBIENTE Y DESARROLLO: BOLETIN INFORMATIVO PREPARADO CONJUNTAMENTE POR LA DIVISION DE MEDIO AMBIENTE Y ASENTAMIENTOS HUMANOS Y LOS SERVICIOS DE INFORMACION DE LA COMISION ECONOMICA PARA AMERICA LATINA Y EL CARIBE, CEPAL. Added/Corp United Nations. Economic Commission for Latin America and the Caribbean. Division de Medio Ambiente y Asentamientos Humanos. United Nations. Economic Commission for Latin America and the Caribbean. Information Service. **VFOAT** Medio Ambiente y Desarrollo. (1992)-. Periodical. Spanish.

LC HB7 .N68   **ISSN** 0391-8289
DD 330/.05   IT
NOTE ECONOMICHE - MONTE DEI PASCHI DI SIENA. (NOTE ECONOMICHE : RIVISTA ECONOMICA DEL MONTE DEI PASCHI DI SIENA). [Note econ. - Monte paschi Siena]. **Added/Corp** Monte dei Paschi di Siena. (19??)-. Periodical. Italian. Three times a year. Free on request. Monte dei Paschi di Siena, Piazza Salimbeni 3, 53100 Siena Italy. **Tel** 011 39 577 294401, **FAX** 011 39 577 294084. **ED** Lorenzo Maccari. Index available. cum. index. **Bk Rev. Circ:** 3,300 (ctrl).
Desc: Journal providing information on economic theory, the history of economic thought and economic methodology.

FR
NOTES D'INFORMATION ECONOMIQUE. French. Twenty-three times a year. 843.17F. Comite Professionnel du Petrol CPDP, BP 282, 92505 Rueil Malmaison France. **Tel** 011 3 1 47169460. Index available. *Separated from Bulletin Analytique Petrolier et SES, 0249-0420.*

ISSN 0291-8897
FR
UDC 69
NOTES VERTES ECONOMIQUE. SERIE INFORMATIONS RAPIDES. [Notes vertes econ., . Ser. inf. rapides]. **VFOAT** Notes Vertes Economiques, Serie Informations Rapides - Ministere de l'Equipement du Logement et des Transports, Direction des Affaires Economiques internationales; Notes Vertes Economiques, Serie Informations Rapides - Ministere de l'Environnement et du Cadre de Vie, Direction des Affaires Economiques et internationales; Notes Vertes Economiques, Serie Informations Rapides - Ministere de l'Equipement du Logement et des Transports, Direction des Affaires Economiques et Internationales. (1980)-. Periodical. French. Irregular (25 to 35 times per year). 509.30F. Documentation Francaise, 29 quai Voltaire, 75344 Paris Cedex 7 France. **Tel** 011 33 1 40157000, **FAX** 011 33 1 40157230, telex 204 826 DOCFRAN.

ISSN 0291-8900
FR
UDC 69
NOTES VERTES ECONOMIQUES. SERIE CONJONCTURE. [Notes vertes econ., Ser. conjonct.]. (1980)-. Periodical. French. Six times a year. Documentation Francaise, 29 quai Voltaire, 75344 Paris Cedex 7 France. **Tel** 011 33 1 40157000, **FAX** 011 33 1 40157230, telex 204 826 DOCFRAN.

IT
CEASED
NOTIZIARIO ISTAT. SERIE 1 : ATTIVITA PRODUTTIVA. FOGLLIO 14 : STATISTICA DEL COMMERCIO CON L'ESTERO. See Business and Economics-Abstracting, Bibliographies and Statistics.

ISSN 0711-8287
DD 330.9714/005   CN
NOTRE ECONOMIE. [Notre econ.]. Oct. 1981-. French. One time a year. Hebdos Regionaux, 3E Etage, 81 rue St Pierre, Quebec G1K 4A3 Canada. *Continues Economie Regionale et l'Hebdo, 0820-9634.*

Business and Economics

LC HC271 .N58
DD 330.9/44/083   FR
NOUVEL ECONOMISTE, LE. **VFOAT** Entreprise/Les Informations. No. 1 (10 Oct. 1975)-. Periodical. French. One time a week. $150.92. Leader International Press, 10 rue Guymener, 92136 Issy L Moulineaux France. **Tel** 011 33 1 41093000, 011 33 1 41093198. **ED** Jean Marie Vendroux. **Ad Acc. Circ:** 116,041 (ctrl).
 Desc: Concerns business round up, economics and industry, studies, opinion, leisure, and finance.
 Ind/Abst Contents Pages Manage.; PAIS Int. Print (1991-).

ISSN 0820-2737
DD 330.9716/04   CN
NOVA SCOTIA BUSINESS JOURNAL. [N.S. bus. j.]. Vol. 1, No. 1 (May 1986)-. Periodical. English. Twelve times a year. 19.20Can$. Bilby Holdings Ltd., 6029 Cunard Street, Halifax Nova Scotia B3K 1E5 Canada. **Tel** (920)420-0437, FAX (920)423-8212. **ED** Bette Tetreault. **Ad Acc. Circ:** 30,420 (ctrl).
 Desc: Covers business news and stories relating to Nova Scotia.

LC Z7165.R9 N6
   RU
●**NOVAIA LITERATURA PO SOTSIALNYM I GUMANITARNYM NAUKAM. EKONOMIKA / ROSSIISKAIA AKADEMIIA NAUK, INSTITUT NAUCHNOI INFORMATSII PO OBSHCHESTVENNYM NAUKAM.** **Added/Corp** Institut Nauchnoi Informatsii po Obshchestvennym Naukam (Rossiiskaia Akademiia Nauk). (1993)-. Periodical. Russian. Twelve times a year. Izdatelstvo Nauka / Akademiia Nauk, (Publishing House of the Russian Academy of Sciences), Leninskii Porspekt 14, 117901 Moscow Russia. **Tel** 011 95 9542153, FAX 011 95 9382144, telex 411964. **(Subscription address:** East View Publications Inc., 3020 Harbor Lane North, Suite 110, Minneapolis MN 55447. **Tel** (800)477-1005, (612)550-0961, FAX (612)559-2931.) **Formed by the union of** Novaia Otechestvennaia Literatura po Obshchestvennym Naukam. Ekonomika **and** Novaia Inostrannaia Literatura po Obshchestvennym Naukam: Ekonomika.

   IT
NOVARA. **Main/Corp** Novara, Italy (Province). Camera di Commercio, Industria, Artigianato e Agricoltura. (1968)-. Periodical. Italian. Six times a year. L17710. Camera Commercio Industria Artigianato e Agricoltura, Via Degli Avogadro 4, 28100 Novara Italy. **Tel** 011 39 321 20671, FAX 0321-390309, telex 200662 CAMNO I. **Ad Acc. Circ:** 2,200. **Continues** Novara, Italy (Province). Camera di Commercio, Industria e Agricoltura. Notiziario Economico.

LC F2501 .N68   **ISSN** 0101-3300
DD 981/.005   BL
NOVOS ESTUDOS CEBRAP. **See** Political Science.

LC HF5001   **ISSN** 1189-010X
DD 650/.05   CN
NOWOCZESNY BIZNESMEN. [Nowocz. biznesmen]. **Added/Corp** Centre de Recherche International du Canada. No. 1 (1991)-. Periodical. Polish. Twelve times a year. $90.00 per year. Centre de Recherche du Canada, 211 place Pinkerton, Rosemere Quebec J7A 4I6 Canada.

LC HB   **ISSN** 1074-1674
DD 330   US
NTIS ALERT. BUSINESS & ECONOMICS. [NTIS alert, Bus. econ.]. **Added/Corp** United States. National Technical Information Service. **VFOAT** Business & Economics; Business and Economics; National Technical Information Service Alert. Business & Economics. Vol. 92, No. 01 (Jan. 7, 1992)-. Periodical. English. Twenty-four times a year. $155.00. National Technical Information Service - NTIS, Room 2027S, 5285 Port Royal Road, Springfield VA 22161. **Tel** (703)487-4630, (703)487-4660, (703)487-4650, FAX (703)321-8547, telex 89-9405. **Continues** Business & Economics (Springfield, Va.), 0364-7978.
 Desc: Provides information on banking and finance, consumer affairs, domestic commerce, marketing, minority enterprises, and more.

ISSN 1133-9535
   SP
NUEVO LUNES, EL. **VFOAT** El Nuevo Lunes de la Economia y la Sociedad. (1981)-. Periodical. Spanish. One time a week. 1000.00ptas North and South America; 4500.00ptas Spain; 7500.00ptas Europe. Punto y Seguido, Esp Torre Madrid Pl 32 Ofic 4, 28008 Madrid Spain. **Tel** 011 34 91 5423748.

LC HC301.A1 N85   **ISSN** 0029-4670
DD 330   IT
NUOVO MEZZOGIORNO. Vol. 1, (Jan. 1958)-. Periodical. Italian. Twelve times a year. L61310. Vittorio Ciampi, Corso Vitt Emanuele 154, 00186 Rome Italy. **Tel** 011 39 6 68806288. **ED** Vittorio Ciampi. **Bk Rev. Ad**

Acc. Circ: 6,000.
 Desc: Politics, economics, society and culture. Dedicated to problems of development in Southern Italy.

   IT
NUOVO OSSERVATORE, IL. (19??)-. Italian. Twelve times a year. L50000.00 Italy; L80000.00 other. Nuovo Osservatore, Via del Pozzetto 105, 00187 Rome Italy. **Tel** 011 39 6 6787583, FAX 011 39 6 6785813. **Bk Rev. Ad Acc, Adv Mgr:** Antonella Massaroni. ctrl circ.

LC HC
DD 330   SI
NUS ECONOMIC JOURNAL, THE. **Added/Corp** National University of Singapore. Economics & Statistics Society. **VFOAT** National University of Singapore Economic Journal. Vol. 27 (1991)-. English. **Continues** Suara Ekonomi, 0585-8127.

LC HD659.L68 N86
DD 333.73/13/094359021   GW
NUTZUNGSARTEN DER BODENFLACHEN. (1979)-. German. Irregular (every four years). DM8.70. Niedersaechsisches Landesamt fuer Statistik, Postfach 4460, D-30044 Hannover Germany. **Tel** 011 49 511 9898321, FAX 011 49 511 9898400. **Bk Rev. Circ:** 250.
 Desc: Covers the exploitation of acreage and the results of surface inquiries, available for communities in Lower Saxony.

ISSN 0113-4957
DD 658.02205   NZ
   CCC
NZ BUSINESS. [NZ bus.]. **VFOAT** New Zealand Business. (1987)-. Periodical. English. Eleven times a year. $84.08. Minty's Media, 22 Heather Street, Private Bag 93218, Parnell Auckland New Zealand. **Tel** 011 64 9 3794233, FAX 011 64 9 3093575. **ED** Ena Hutchinson. Index available. cum. index. **Ad Acc. Circ:** 1,000 (ctrl).
 Continues Better Business (Auckland), 0110-7100.
 Ind/Abst Bus. Source Plus; Bus. Source; EP Collect.; Homework Help.; MasterFile FullTEXT 1000; MasterFile FullTEXT 350; MasterFile FullTEXT 650; MasterFile FullTEXT; Telebase; World Mag. Bank.

   UK
OAG FLIGHT PLANNER EUROPE, MIDDLE EAST & AFRICA. **See** Travel and Tourism.

   UY
OBSERVADOR ECONOMICO, EL. VFOAT Observador. Vol. 1, No. 1 (Oct. 1991)-. Periodical. Spanish. Microcosmos S.A., Ituzaingo 1389, Montevideo Uruguay. **Tel** 011 598 963138, FAX 011 598 963278. **ED** Felix O. Carreras. **Ad Acc.**

LC HC271 .O23   **ISSN** 0751-6614
DD 330.944/005   FR
   CCC
OBSERVATIONS ET DIAGNOSTICS ECONOMIQUES. (OBSERVATIONS ET DIAGNOSTICS ECONOMIQUES. REVUE DE L'OFCE.). [Obs. diagn. econ.]. **Added/Corp** Observatoire Francais des Conjonctures Economiques. **VFOAT** Revue de l'OFCE. No. 1 (June 1982)-. Periodical. French (summaries and/or abstracts in English). Four times a year. $119.20. Presses de la Fondation, Nationale des Sciences Politiques, 44 rue du Four, 75006 Paris France. **Tel** 011 33 1 44393960, FAX 011 33 1 45480441.
 Ind/Abst Int. Labour Doc.; LABORDOC; PAIS Int. Print.

   FR
OBSERVATIONS ET DIAGNOSTICS ECONOMIQUES. LETTRE DE L'OFCE. **Added/Corp** Observatoire Francais des Conjonctures Economiques. **VFOAT** Lettre de l'OFCE. (198?)-. Periodical. French. Twelve times a year. 225.00F (institutions), 122.00F (individuals) France; 255.00F (institutions), 153.00F (individuals) other. Presses de la Fondation, Nationale des Sciences Politiques, 44 rue du Four, 75006 Paris France. **Tel** 011 33 1 44393960, FAX 011 33 1 45480441.

LC HF   **ISSN** 1032-0539
DD 380.50994   AT
OCCASIONAL PAPER - BUREAU OF TRANSPORT AND COMMUNICATIONS ECONOMICS. (OCCASIONAL PAPER.). [Occas. pap. - Bur. Transp. Commun. Econ.]. **Added/Corp** Australia. Bureau of Transport and Communications Economics. (1988)-. Monographic series. English. Irregular. Price varies per volume. Australian Bureau of Statistics, PO Box 2796Y, Melbourne 3001 Australia. **Tel** 011 61 3 6157843. **Continues** Occasional Paper - Bureau of Transport Economics, 0157-7085.
 Ind/Abst Geogr. Abstr. Human Geogr.

   II
OCCASIONAL PAPER - ECONOMICS PROGRAM. **See** Agriculture-Agricultural Economics.

ISSN 0814-7973
DD 380.141099   AT
OCCASIONAL PAPER - SOUTH PACIFIC SMALLHOLDER PROJECT, UNIVERSITY OF NEW ENGLAND. [Occas. pap. - S. Pac. Smallhold. Proj. Univ. N. Engl.]. (1986)-. Monographic series. English. Irregular. South Pacific Smallholder Project, University of New England, Department of Agricultural and Resource Economics, Armidale NSW 2351 Australia. **Tel** 011 61 67 732232, FAX 011 61 67 711531. **ED** J.B. Hardaker.
 Ind/Abst World Agric. Econ. Rural Sociol. Abstr.

   AT
OCCASIONAL PAPER (TRANSNATIONAL CORPORATIONS RESEARCH PROJECT (UNIVERSITY OF SYDNEY)). (OCCASIONAL PAPER.). **Added/Corp** Transnational Corporations Research Project (University of Sydney). No. 1 (1977)-. Monographic series. English. Irregular. Price varies per volume. University of Sydney, 116 Darlington Road / H42, Sydney NSW 2006 Australia. **Tel** 011 61 2 6922666, FAX 011 61 2 6922666.

LC HC   **ISSN** 0077-4928
DD 330   UK
OCCASIONAL PAPERS / NATIONAL INSTITUTE OF ECONOMIC AND SOCIAL RESEARCH. **Added/Corp** National Institute of Economic and Social Research. No. 1 (1942)-. Monographic series. English. Irregular. Price varies per volume. Cambridge University Press, The Edinburgh Building, Shaftesbury Road, Cambridge CB2 2RU United Kingdom. **Tel** 011 44 1223 312393, FAX 011 44 1223 315052, telex 851-817256. **(Subscription address:** Cambridge University Press / North America, 110 Midland Avenue, Port Chester NY 10573. **Tel** (800)431-1580, (914)937-9600.)

ISSN 0741-9929
   US
OCEAN STATE BUSINESS. (1983)-. Periodical. English. Twelve times a year. $12.00. Ocean State Business, 4 Davol Square, Providence RI 02903. available on an online database (file 635/Full-Text) from DIALOG. Documents available from UMI Article Clearinghouse.
 Ind/Abst Bus. Dateline; Bus. Index (Jan. 1985-Dec. 1985); Gen. BusinessFile (Jan. 1985-Dec. 1985); Gen. Period. Index (Jan. 1985-Dec. 1985); INFO-SOUTH Abstr.

ISSN 1080-9872
DD 338   US
●**OCTANE WEEK'S REFINING ECONOMICS REPORT.** **See** Petroleum and Natural Gas.

   TU
ODTU : GELISME DERGISI. **Main/Corp** Ankara. Orta Dogu Teknik Universitesi. Idari Ilimler Fakultesi. **VFOAT** Metu : Studies in Development. 1-Autumn 1970-. Periodical. Turkish (English). Four times a year. 8,000TL Turkey; $20.00 US. Middle East Technical University, Faculty of Economic and Administrative Sciences, Ankara 06531 Turkey. **Tel** 011 91 41 2101000 ext. 2006. **ED** Nur Keyder. Index available. **Bk Rev. Circ:** 1,500 (ctrl).
 Desc: Economics, public administration, business administration, social sciences.
 Ind/Abst Middle East J.

DD 332   US
●**O'DWYER'S WASHINGTON REPORT.** [O'Dwyer's F A R A rep.]. **VAT** O'Dwyer's Foreign Agents Registration Act Report. (1992)-. Periodical. English. Twenty-five times a year. $75.00. Jack O'Dwyer Company Inc., 271 Madison Avenue, New York NY 10016. **Tel** (212)679-2471, FAX (212)683-2750.
 Continues O'Dwyer's FARA Report, 1055-3304.
 Desc: Covers public affairs relations of Washington, D.C., along with filers under the Foreign Agents Registration Act.

   FR
OECD COUNTRY REPORT. English. Irregular. OECD Publications and Information Center, 2 rue Andre-Pascal, 75775 Paris Cedex 16 France. **Tel** 011 33 1 49104262, US:(202)785-6323, FAX 011 33 1 45248500, 011 33 1 45248176, telex 620 160 OCDE. **(Subscription address:** OECD Publications Center, 2001 L Street, Suite 700, Washington DC 20036. **Tel** (202)822-3873, (202)785-6323.)

LC HC10 .O18   **ISSN** 0474-5574
DD 330   FR
   CODEN OEEOA8
OECD. ECONOMIC OUTLOOK. (OECD ECONOMIC OUTLOOK.). [OECD. Econ. outlook]. **Main/Corp** Organisation for Economic Co-Operation and Development. **Added/Corp** Organisation for Economic Co-Operation and Development. Organisation for Economic Co-Operation and Development. Dept. of Economics and Statistics. **VFOAT** Economic Outlook. **VAT** Organization for Economic Cooperation and Development Economic Outlook. Vol. 1 (July 1967)-.

Periodical. English. Two times a year (magnetic tape has monthly frequency). $60.00. OECD Publications and Information Center, 2 rue Andre-Pascal, 75775 Paris Cedex 16 France. **Tel** 011 33 1 49104262, US:(202)785-6323, FAX 011 33 1 45248500, 011 33 1 45248176, telex 620 160 OCDE. **(Subscription address:** OECD Publications Center, 2001 L Street, Suite 700, Washington DC 20036. **Tel** (202)822-3873, (202)785-6323.**)** available on diskette; available on microfilm and microfiche from University Microfilms International (UMI); available on magnetic tape; available on an online database (file 648/Full-Text) from DIALOG. Documents available from UMI Article Clearinghouse.
Desc: Facts and recommended solutions regarding economic growth, employment and unemployment, energy, multinational enterprises, financial markets, environment, science and technology, aid and trade to developing worlds.
Ind/Abst ABI/INFORM Glob. Ed.; ABI/INFORM [Computer File] (July 1980-); Acad. Search; Bus. ASAP (1990-) [Full Txt.]; Bus. Index (1986-); Bus. Source Plus; Bus. Source; EP Collect.; F&S Index Plus Text, Int. [Select. Cov.]; Gen. BusinessFile (1986-); Gen. Period. Index (1986-); Homework Help.; INFO-SOUTH Abstr.; Leadscan; Manage. Contents (1974-); MasterFile FullTEXT 1000; MasterFile FullTEXT 350; MasterFile FullTEXT 650; MasterFile FullTEXT (Jan. 1994-); OCLC; Predicasts; Predicasts Forecasts; Selec. Coop. Index Manage. Period.; Ship Abstr.; Telebase; Trade Ind. ASAP [Full Txt.]; Trade Ind. Index [Full Txt.].

ISSN 0376-6438
FR

OECD ECONOMIC SURVEYS. [OECD, econ. surv.]. **Main/Corp** Organisation for Economic Co-Operation and Development. **VFOAT** O.E.C.D. Economic Surveys. (1968)-. English. Twenty times a year. $240.00. OECD Publications and Information Center, 2 rue Andre-Pascal, 75775 Paris Cedex 16 France. **Tel** 011 33 1 49104262, US:(202)785-6323, FAX 011 33 1 45248500, 011 33 1 45248176, telex 620 160 OCDE. **(Subscription address:** OECD Publications Center, 2001 L Street, Suite 700, Washington DC 20036. **Tel** (202)822-3873, (202)785-6323.**)** available on an online database (file 648/Full-Text) from DIALOG.
Desc: OECD's reviews of its member countries economics.
Ind/Abst Predicasts.

LC HC261 .O89 **ISSN** 0474-5124
DD 330 FR
OECD ECONOMIC SURVEYS: AUSTRIA. **Main/Corp** Organisation for Economic Co-Operation and Development. **VAT** Organisation for Economic Co-Operation and Development Economic Surveys: Austria. (1968)-. English. Twenty times a year. $240.00. OECD Publications and Information Center, 2 rue Andre-Pascal, 75775 Paris Cedex 16 France. **Tel** 011 33 1 49104262, US:(202)785-6323, FAX 011 33 1 45248500, 011 33 1 45248176, telex 620 160 OCDE. **(Subscription address:** OECD Publications Center, 2001 L Street, Suite 700, Washington DC 20036. **Tel** (202)822-3873, (202)785-6323.**)** ***Continues*** *Economic Surveys by the OECD. Austria.*
Ind/Abst Trade Ind. ASAP [Full Txt.]; Trade Ind. Index [Full Txt.].

LC HC315 .O73
DD 330.9/493/04 FR
OECD ECONOMIC SURVEYS: BELGIUM-LUXEMBOURG. **Main/Corp** Organisation for Economic Co-Operation and Development. **VAT** Organisation for Economic Co-operation and Development Economic Surveys: Belgium-Luxembourg. (1976)-. English. Twenty times a year. $240.00. OECD Publications and Information Center, 2 rue Andre-Pascal, 75775 Paris Cedex 16 France. **Tel** 011 33 1 49104262, US:(202)785-6323, FAX 011 33 1 45248500, 011 33 1 45248176, telex 620 160 OCDE. **(Subscription address:** OECD Publications Center, 2001 L Street, Suite 700, Washington DC 20036. **Tel** (202)822-3873, (202)785-6323.**)** ***Continues*** *Organisation for Economic Co-Operation and Development. OECD Economic Surveys: BLEU.*
Ind/Abst Trade Ind. ASAP [Full Txt.]; Trade Ind. Index [Full Txt.].

LC HC111 .O7 **ISSN** 0474-5140
DD 330.9/71/064 FR
OECD ECONOMIC SURVEYS: CANADA. [OECD econ. surv., Can.]. **Main/Corp** Organisation for Economic Co-Operation and Development. **Added/Corp** Organisation for Economic Co-Operation and Development. **VAT** Organization for Economic Cooperation and Development Economic Surveys: Canada. (Feb. 1968)-. English. Twenty times a year. $240.00. OECD Publications and Information Center, 2 rue Andre-Pascal, 75775 Paris Cedex 16 France. **Tel** 011 33 1 49104262, US:(202)785-6323, FAX 011 33 1 45248500, 011 33 1 45248176, telex 620 160 OCDE. **(Subscription address:** Renouf Publishing Company Ltd., 1294 Algoma Road, Ottawa Ontario K1B 3WB Canada. **Tel** (613)741-4333.**)** ***Continues*** *Economic Surveys by the OECD. Canada.*
Ind/Abst Trade Ind. ASAP [Full Txt.]; Trade Ind. Index [Full Txt.].

LC HC351 .O72 **ISSN** 0474-5159
DD 330.9/489/05 FR
OECD ECONOMIC SURVEYS: DENMARK. **Main/Corp** Organisation for Economic Co-Operation and Development. **VAT** Organisation for Economic Co-Operation and Development Economic Surveys: Denmark. (1968)-. English. Twenty times a year. $240.00. OECD Publications and Information Center, 2 rue Andre-Pascal, 75775 Paris Cedex 16 France. **Tel** 011 33 1 49104262, US:(202)785-6323, FAX 011 33 1 45248500, 011 33 1 45248176, telex 620 160 OCDE. **(Subscription address:** OECD Publications Center, 2001 L Street, Suite 700, Washington DC 20036. **Tel** (202)822-3873, (202)785-6323.**)** ***Continues*** *Economic Surveys by the OECD: Denmark.*
Ind/Abst Trade Ind. ASAP [Full Txt.]; Trade Ind. Index [Full Txt.].

LC HC286.6 .O73a
DD 330.9/43/087 FR
OECD ECONOMIC SURVEYS: GERMANY. **Main/Corp** Organisation for Economic Co-Operation and Development. (1969)-. English. Twenty times a year. $240.00. OECD Publications and Information Center, 2 rue Andre-Pascal, 75775 Paris Cedex 16 France. **Tel** 011 33 1 49104262, US:(202)785-6323, FAX 011 33 1 45248500, 011 33 1 45248176, telex 620 160 OCDE. **(Subscription address:** OECD Publications Center, 2001 L Street, Suite 700, Washington DC 20036. **Tel** (202)822-3873, (202)785-6323.**)** available on microfiche. ***Continues*** *Economic Surveys by the OCED. Germany.*
Desc: Reviews of member country economies. Analyzes in detail the subject country's economy. Presents extensive, timely statistics and makes short-term forecasts.
Ind/Abst Trade Ind. ASAP [Full Txt.]; Trade Ind. Index [Full Txt.].

LC HC291 .O72a
DD 330.9/495/07 FR
OECD ECONOMIC SURVEYS: GREECE. **Main/Corp** Organisation for Economic Co-Operation and Development. **VAT** Organization for Economic Cooperation and Development Economic Surveys: Greece. (Feb. 1968)-. English. Twenty times a year. $240.00. OECD Publications and Information Center, 2 rue Andre-Pascal, 75775 Paris Cedex 16 France. **Tel** 011 33 1 49104262, US:(202)785-6323, FAX 011 33 1 45248500, 011 33 1 45248176, telex 620 160 OCDE. **(Subscription address:** OECD Publications Center, 2001 L Street, Suite 700, Washington DC 20036. **Tel** (202)822-3873, (202)785-6323.**)** ***Continues*** *Economic Surveys by the OECD. Greece.*
Ind/Abst Trade Ind. ASAP [Full Txt.]; Trade Ind. Index [Full Txt.].

LC HC300.2 .O33
DD 330.9439/005 FR
OECD ECONOMIC SURVEYS. HUNGARY: CENTRE FOR CO-OPERATION WITH EUROPEAN ECONOMIES IN TRANSITION. **Added/Corp** Organisation for Economic Co-Operation and Development. Centre for Co-Operation with European Economies in Transition. **VFOAT** Hungary; Organisation for Economic Co-Operation and Development Economic Surveys. Hungary. (1991)-. Periodical. English. Twenty times a year. $240.00. OECD Publications and Information Center, 2 rue Andre-Pascal, 75775 Paris Cedex 16 France. **Tel** 011 33 1 49104262, US:(202)785-6323, FAX 011 33 1 45248500, 011 33 1 45248176, telex 620 160 OCDE. **(Subscription address:** OECD Publications Center, 2001 L Street, Suite 700, Washington DC 20036. **Tel** (202)822-3873, (202)785-6323.**)**

LC HC360.5 .O7 **ISSN** 0474-5191
DD 330.9/491/204 FR
OECD ECONOMIC SURVEYS: ICELAND. **Main/Corp** Organisation for Economic Co-Operation and Development. (1968)-. English. Twenty times a year. $240.00. OECD Publications and Information Center, 2 rue Andre-Pascal, 75775 Paris Cedex 16 France. **Tel** 011 33 1 49104262, US:(202)785-6323, FAX 011 33 1 45248500, 011 33 1 45248176, telex 620 160 OCDE. **(Subscription address:** OECD Publications Center, 2001 L Street, Suite 700, Washington DC 20036. **Tel** (202)822-3873, (202)785-6323.**)** ***Continues*** *Economic Surveys by the OECD. Iceland.*
Ind/Abst Trade Ind. ASAP [Full Txt.]; Trade Ind. Index [Full Txt.].

FR
OECD ECONOMIC SURVEYS: JAPAN. **Added/Corp** Organisation for Economic Co-Operation and Development. **VFOAT** Japan. **VAT** Organisation for Economic Co-Operation and Development Economic Surveys. Japan. (19??)-. Periodical. English. Twenty times a year. $240.00. OECD Publications and Information Center, 2 rue Andre-Pascal, 75775 Paris Cedex 16 France. **Tel** 011 33 1 49104262, US:(202)785-6323, FAX 011 33 1 45248500, 011 33 1 45248176, telex 620 160 OCDE. **(Subscription address:** OECD Publications Center, 2001 L Street, Suite 700, Washington DC 20036. **Tel** (202)822-3873, (202)785-6323.**)** ***Continues*** *Economic Surveys by the OECD. Japan.*
Ind/Abst Trade Ind. ASAP [Full Txt.]; Trade Ind. Index [Full Txt.].

LC HC662 .O73a
DD 330.9/931/03 FR
OECD ECONOMIC SURVEYS: NEW ZEALAND. **Main/Corp** Organisation for Economic Co-Operation and Development. **VFOAT** New Zealand. **VAT** Organisation for Economic Co-Operation and Development Economic Survey: New Zealand. (1975)-. English. Two times a year. $240.00. OECD Publications and Information Center, 2 rue Andre-Pascal, 75775 Paris Cedex 16 France. **Tel** 011 33 1 49104262, US:(202)785-6323, FAX 011 33 1 45248500, 011 33 1 45248176, telex 620 160 OCDE. **(Subscription address:** OECD Publications Center, 2001 L Street, Suite 700, Washington DC 20036. **Tel** (202)822-3873, (202)785-6323.**)** ***Continues*** *Economic Survey: New Zealand.*
Ind/Abst Trade Ind. ASAP [Full Txt.]; Trade Ind. Index [Full Txt.].

LC HC365 .O74a
DD 330/.9481/04 FR
OECD ECONOMIC SURVEYS: NORWAY. **Main/Corp** Organisation for Economic Co-Operation and Development. **VAT** Organisation for Economic Co-Operation and Development Economic Surveys: Norway. (1968)-. English. Twenty times a year. $240.00. OECD Publications and Information Center, 2 rue Andre-Pascal, 75775 Paris Cedex 16 France. **Tel** 011 33 1 49104262, US:(202)785-6323, FAX 011 33 1 45248500, 011 33 1 45248176, telex 620 160 OCDE. **(Subscription address:** OECD Publications Center, 2001 L Street, Suite 700, Washington DC 20036. **Tel** (202)822-3873, (202)785-6323.**)** ***Continues*** *Economic Surveys by the OECD. Norway.*
Ind/Abst Trade Ind. ASAP [Full Txt.]; Trade Ind. Index [Full Txt.].

LC HC340.3.A1 O323 **ISSN** 0376-6438
DD 330 FR
OECD ECONOMIC SURVEYS: POLAND. **Added/Corp** Organisation for Economic Co-Operation and Development. Centre for Co-Operation with European Economies in Transition. **VFOAT** Organisation for Economic Co-Operation and Development Economic Surveys. Poland; Poland. (1992)-. English. Twenty times a year. $240.00. OECD Publications and Information Center, 2 rue Andre-Pascal, 75775 Paris Cedex 16 France. **Tel** 011 33 1 49104262, US:(202)785-6323, FAX 011 33 1 45248500, 011 33 1 45248176, telex 620 160 OCDE. **(Subscription address:** OECD Publications Center, 2001 L Street, Suite 700, Washington DC 20036. **Tel** (202)822-3873, (202)785-6323.**)**

LC HC381 .O7
DD 330.9/46/083 FR
OECD ECONOMIC SURVEYS: SPAIN. **Main/Corp** Organisation for Economic Co-Operation and Development. **VFOAT** Spain. **VAT** Organisation For Economic Co-Operation and Development Economic Surveys: Spain. (1969)-. English. Twenty times a year. $240.00. OECD Publications and Information Center, 2 rue Andre-Pascal, 75775 Paris Cedex 16 France. **Tel** 011 33 1 49104262, US:(202)785-6323, FAX 011 33 1 45248500, 011 33 1 45248176, telex 620 160 OCDE. **(Subscription address:** OECD Publications Center, 2001 L Street, Suite 700, Washington DC 20036. **Tel** (202)822-3873, (202)785-6323.**)** ***Continues*** *Economic Surveys by the OECD. Spain.*
Ind/Abst Trade Ind. ASAP [Full Txt.]; Trade Ind. Index [Full Txt.].

LC HC371 .O7
DD 330.9/485/05 FR
OECD ECONOMIC SURVEYS: SWEDEN. **Main/Corp** Organisation for Economic Co-Operation and Development. **VFOAT** Sweden. **VAT** Organisation for Economic Co-Operation and Development Surveys: Sweden. (1968)-. English. Twenty times a year. $240.00. OECD Publications and Information Center, 2 rue Andre-Pascal, 75775 Paris Cedex 16 France. **Tel** 011 33 1 49104262, US:(202)785-6323, FAX 011 33 1 45248500, 011 33 1 45248176, telex 620 160 OCDE. **(Subscription address:** OECD Publications Center, 2001 L Street, Suite 700, Washington DC 20036. **Tel** (202)822-3873, (202)785-6323.**)** ***Continues*** *Economic Surveys by the OECD. Sweden.*
Ind/Abst Trade Ind. ASAP [Full Txt.]; Trade Ind. Index [Full Txt.].

LC HC395 .O7
DD 330 FR
OECD ECONOMIC SURVEYS: SWITZERLAND. **Added/Corp** Organisation for Economic Co-Operation and Development. **VFOAT** Switzerland. **VAT** Organisation for Economic Co-Operation and Development Economic Surveys. Switzerland. (1968)-. English. Twenty times a year. $240.00. OECD Publications and Information Center, 2 rue Andre-Pascal, 75775 Paris Cedex 16 France. **Tel** 011 33 1 49104262, US:(202)785-6323, FAX 011 33 1 45248500, 011 33 1 45248176, telex 620 160 OCDE. **(Subscription address:** OECD Publications Center,

2001 L Street, Suite 700, Washington DC 20036. **Tel** (202)822-3873, (202)785-6323.) **ED** Tamad Foldi. ***Continues*** *Economic Surveys by the OECD. Switzerland.*
Ind/Abst Trade Ind. ASAP [Full Txt.]; Trade Ind. Index [Full Txt.].

LC HG176.5 .O38 **ISSN** 0304-3371
DD 332/.05 FR
OECD FINANCIAL STATISTICS. METHODOLOGICAL SUPPLEMENT / STATISTIQUES FINANCIERES DE L'OCDE. SUPPLEMENT METHODOLOGIQUE. **Added/Corp** Organisation for Economic Co-operation and Development. **VFOAT** Statistiques Financieres de l'O.C.D.E.; O.E.C.D. Financial Statistics. Methodological Supplement; Methodological Supplement; Supplement Methodologique; Statistiques Financieres de l'OCDE. Supplement Methodologique. (1981)-. English (French). One time a year. 320.00F (parts 1, 2 and 3, includes supplements). OECD Publications and Information Center, 2 rue Andre-Pascal, 75775 Paris Cedex 16 France. **Tel** 011 33 1 49104262, US:(202)785-6323, FAX 011 33 1 45248500, 011 33 1 45248176, telex 620 160 OCDE. **(Subscription address:** OECD Publications Center, 2001 L Street, Suite 700, Washington DC 20036. **Tel** (202)822-3873, (202)785-6323.) Index available. cum. index. ***Continues in part*** *OECD Financial Statistics, 0048-2188.*
Desc: Facilitates the interpretation of statistics published by explaining methods of calculation of their institutional context.

LC HC240.A1 O2 **ISSN** 0029-7054
DD 330 FR
OECD OBSERVER. (THE OECD OBSERVER.). [OECD obs.]. **Main/Corp** Organisation for Economic Co-Operation and Development. **VFOAT** Observer. **VAT** Organisation for Economic Cooperation and Development Observer. No. 1 (Nov. 1962)-. Periodical. English. Six times a year. $30.00. OECD Publications and Information Center, 2 rue Andre-Pascal, 75775 Paris Cedex 16 France. **Tel** 011 33 1 49104262, US:(202)785-6323, FAX 011 33 1 45248500, 011 33 1 45248176, telex 620 160 OCDE. **(Subscription address:** OECD Publications Center, 2001 L Street, Suite 700, Washington DC 20036. **Tel** (202)822-3873, (202)785-6323.) Index available (free). cum. index. available on microfilm and microfiche from University Microfilms International (UMI); available on an online database (files 15,648/Full-Text) from DIALOG. Documents available from UMI Article Clearinghouse, Documents on Demand.
Desc: Includes articles on economic affairs, energy, social affairs, the environment, multinational enterprises, science and technology, financial markets, and development cooperation.
Ind/Abst Acad. Search; Account. Art.; AgBiotech News Inf.; Aquat. Sci. Fish. Abstr. [CD-ROM Ed.]; Bus. ASAP (1990-) [Full Txt.]; Bus. Index (1985-); Bus. Period. Index; Bus. Source Plus; Bus. Source; Coal Abstr.; Curr. Cit.; Curr. Index J. Educ.; Educ. Adm. Abstr. (?-?); Electron. Commun. Abstr. J.; EMBASE; Energy Inf. Abstr.; Environ. Abstr.; EP Collect.; Expand. Acad. Index (1992-); F&S Index Plus Text, Int. [Select. Cov.]; Gen. BusinessFile (1985-); Gen. Period. Index (1985-); Geogr. Abstr. Human Geogr.; Health Saf. Sci. Abstr.; Homework Help.; Hum. Resour. Abstr. (?-?); Index Period. Artic. Relat. Law; INFO-SOUTH Abstr.; Int. Dev. Abstr.; Int. Labour Doc.; ISMEC Bull.; LABORDOC; Leadscan; Manage. Contents (1974-); MasterFile FullTEXT 1000; MasterFile FullTEXT 350; MasterFile FullTEXT 650; MasterFile FullTEXT (July 1993-); Middle East Abstr. Index; Multicult. Educ. Abstr.; Newsp. Period. Abstr. (1992-); OCLC; PAIS Int. Print (1991-); Pollut. Abstr. Indexes; Predicasts; Predicasts Forecasts; Public Aff. Inf. Serv. Bull.; Saf. Sci. Abstr. J.; Sage Public Adm. Abstr.; Sociol. Educ. Abstr.; Stud. Women Abstr.; Tech. Educ. Train. Abstr.; Telebase; Trade Ind. Index (1981-?);; UMI ABI/Inform--Bus. Period. Ondisc (Dec. 1990-) [Full Txt.]; Wilson Bus. Abstr.; Work Relat. Abstr.; World Text. Abstr.

ISSN 0294-0787
FR
UDC 69.003.13
OFFICE DES PRIX DU BATIMENT. TOUS CORPS D'ETAT. [Off. prix batim., Tous corps etat]. (1975)-. French. Four times a year. 1273.26F. Office des Prix du Batiment, 468 rue Croix Verte, F-34000 Montpellier France. **Tel** 011 33 67 410152.

LC HF5520 .O39 **ISSN** 1056-859X
DD 621.38 US
OFFICE EQUIPMENT. [Off. equip.]. **Added/Corp** Orion Research Corporation. (1991)-. English. $99.99. Orion Research Corp., 1315 Main Avenue, #230, Durango CO 81301.

UK
OFFICE HEALTH AND SAFETY. **See** Industrial Health and Safety.

US
OFFICE HOURS. (19??)-. Newsletter. English. Twenty-six times a year. $53.04. Economics Press Inc, 12 Daniel Road, Fairfield NJ 07004. **Tel** (201)227-1224, (800)526-2554, FAX (201)227-9742.
Desc: Promotes proper work attitudes and builds office skills. Emphasizes the personal benefits of improving employee habits.

ISSN 1068-5170
US
•**OFFICE LAB REPORTS.** (1996)-. Periodical. English. Twelve times a year. $69.00. Office Lab Reports, 3003 W. 11th Avenue, Suite 234, Eugene OR 97402.

ISSN 0737-8122
US
OFFICE MANAGEMENT. (OFFICEMATION MANAGEMENT.). Periodical. English. Twelve times a year. $445.00. Management Information Corporation, 1111 Marlkress Road, Cherry Hill NJ 08003. **Tel** (609)424-1100. **ED** L Feidelman.
Desc: Subscription service covering technical and administrating overviews affecting office automation.
Ind/Abst PROMT.

US
OFFICE SKILLS PROGRAM. (19??)-. English. $51.96 (US); $63.12 (Canada) Includes: Office Guide and Office Skills Workshop. Bureau of Business Practice, 24 Rope Ferry Road, Waterford CT 06386. **Tel** (800)243-0876, (203)442-4365, (800)876-9105, FAX (203)443-1123.

LC HF5547.5.A1 O34 **ISSN** 0737-8998
DD 651.8/4/05 US
Pr Rev.
OFFICE SYSTEMS RESEARCH JOURNAL. (OFFICE SYSTEMS RESEARCH JOURNAL : THE JOURNAL OF THE OFFICE SYSTEMS RESEARCH ASSOCIATION.). [Off. sys. res. j.]. **Added/Corp** Office Systems Research Association (Cleveland, Ohio). Vol. 1, No. 1 (Fall 1982)-. Periodical. English. Two times a year (Spring and Fall). $35.00. Computer Information Systems, Southwest Missouri State University, 901 South National Avenue, Springfield MO 65804. **Tel** (417)836-6319, FAX (417)836-6337. **ED** Carol Lundgren. **Bk Rev**, (Qty: 2-4). **Ad Acc. Circ:** 550 (ctrl). available on microfilm and CD-ROM from University Microfilms International (UMI). Documents available from Ask*IEEE.
Desc: Contains articles on significant research and projects in areas of office and end-user computing. Includes a practical application section of interest to systems professionals and educators.
Ind/Abst Abstr. Hum. Comput. Interact.; Bus. Educ. Index; Curr. Cit.; HILITES; INSPEC (1985-).

ISSN 0269-2430
DD 651.2 UK
OFFICE TRADE NEWS. [Off. trade news]. (1982)-. Periodical. English. Eleven times a year. $109.00 US and Canada; £37.00 UK. Wilmington Publishing Ltd., PO Box 200, Field End Road, Ruislip Middlesex HA4 OSY United Kingdom. **Tel** 011 44 181 8413970, FAX 011 44 181 8419676.

LC HF1118 .O332
US
OFFICIAL SOFTWARE FOR GMAT REVIEW [COMPUTER FILE], THE. **Added/Corp** Graduate Management Admission Council. Educational Testing Service. (198?)-. English. Every 2 years. Educational Testing Service, 1440 Lower Ferry Road, Trenton NJ 08618. **Tel** (609)771-7243, FAX (609)771-7385.
Desc: Available on 5 1/4" or 3 1/2" diskettes. System requirements: IBM PC, XT, AT, PS/2, or compatible computer. 256K RAM, PC-DOS 2.0 through 4.0, at least two disk drives (3 1/2" or 5 1/4") or one disk drive and a hard disk with at least 2MB of free space, IBM Color Graphics adapter, Enhanced Graphics adapter, Video Graphics array, Hercules Graphics, or compatible adapter cards and monitor.

ISSN 0755-1460
FR
UDC 341.18
OFFICIEL DES CONGRES ET DU TOURISME D'AFFAIRES, L'. [Off. congr. tour. aff]. **VFOAT** Officiel du Tourisme d'Affaires et des Congres. (1969)-. Periodical. French. Eleven times a year. $91.86. Edns Communications Industries, 85 rue La Fayette, F 75009 Paris France. **Tel** 011 33 1 42801219.

ISSN 1078-117X
DD 332 US
Pr Rev.
OFFSHORE OUTLOOK. [Offshore outlook]. (199?)-. Periodical. English. Twelve times a year. $325.00. GinsGlobe Communications Inc., 2716 Ocean Park Boulevard # 3075, Santa Monica CA 90405. **Tel** (310)392-2298.

LC HF3161.O3 O36a **ISSN** 0362-9716
DD 338/.09771 US
OHIO INVENTORY OF BUSINESS AND INDUSTRIAL CHANGE. **Main/Corp** Ohio. Bureau of Business Research. (19??)-. Periodical. English. Irregular. Ohio Dept of Economic and Community Development, Economic Division, Bureau of Business Research, 65 South Front Street, Columbus OH 43215.

LC SB298
DD 633.85 GW
OIL WORLD ANNUAL. **See** Agriculture.

ISSN 0849-0872
DD 381/.09711/505 CN
OKANAGAN LIFE PROGRESS. [Okanagan life prog.]. **VFOAT** Progress. (March 1990)-. English. Byrne Publishing Group Inc., PO Box 1479, Kelowana BC V1Y 7V8 Canada. **Tel** (604)861-5399, FAX (604)868-3040. ***Continues*** *Okanagan Life Presents Progress, 0841-2081.*

LC HF3161.O5 O43 **ISSN** 0192-9593
DD 330.9766/005 US
OKLAHOMA BUSINESS. [Okla. bus.]. (Jan. 1976)-. Periodical. English. Twelve times a year. $18.00. Oklahoma Business Magazine, PO Box 12823, Oklahoma City OK 73157. **Tel** (405)948-7788. **ED** J. Ulman. **Ad Acc. Circ:** 11,000 (ctrl). ***Continues*** *Pulse of Oklahoma Business.*
Desc: The business in Oklahoma banking, insurance, architecture, real estate, etc.

LC HC107.O5 A13 **ISSN** 0030-1671
DD 330.9766 US
OKLAHOMA BUSINESS BULLETIN. **Added/Corp** University of Oklahoma. Center for Economic and Management Research. University of Oklahoma. College of Business Administration. University of Oklahoma. Bureau of Business Research. University of Oklahoma. Bureau for Business and Economic Research. Vol. 1 (Jan. 15, 1928)-. Bulletin. English. Twelve times a year. $10.00. University of Oklahoma College of Business Administration, 307 West Brooks Street, Room 4, Norman OK 73019. **Tel** (405)325-2931, FAX (405)325-7688. **ED** John McCraw and Pat Wickham. **Circ:** 700 (ctrl). available on microfilm and microfiche from University Microfilms International (UMI). Documents available from UMI Article Clearinghouse.
Desc: Update of business conditions throughout the state; statistical data, regional articles.
Ind/Abst ABI/INFORM Glob. Ed.; ABI/INFORM [Computer File] (March 1987-); Stat. Ref. Index.

LC HC107.O5 O63 **ISSN** 0734-404X
DD 338.5/443/09766 US
OKLAHOMA ECONOMIC OUTLOOK. **Added/Corp** Oklahoma State University. Office of Business and Economic Research. (1980)-. Periodical. English. One time a year. Oklahoma State University / Nord College of Business, Stillwater OK 74078. **Tel** (405)624-5000.

LC HC361 .O39 **ISSN** 0332-5555
DD 330 NO
OKONOMISK RAPPORT. [økon. rapp.]. (1975)-. Periodical. Norwegian. Twenty-two times a year. $175.72. Okonomisk Rapport, PB 5462 Majorst, 0305 Oslo 1 Norway. **Tel** 011 47 22941241. ***Continues*** *Bedriftskonomisk Informasjon, 0045-1606.*

ISSN 0197-9361
US
CEASED
OLSEN'S AGRIBUSINESS REPORT. **See** Agriculture-Agricultural Economics.

IT
OMEGA GENERATION. BIBLIOGRAFIA ECONOMICA. Italian. Omega Generation, Via Murri 39, 40137 Bologna Italy. **Tel** 011 39 51 306644. available on diskette.

US
ON GUARD. (19??)-. English. Twelve times a year. $19.68 (US); $30.96 (Canada). Bureau of Business Practice, 24 Rope Ferry Road, Waterford CT 06386. **Tel** (800)243-0876, (203)442-4365, (800)876-9105, FAX (203)443-1123.

US
ON THE SAFE SIDE. (19??)-. English. Twelve times a year. $53.28 (US); $65.04 (Canada). Bureau of Business Practice, 24 Rope Ferry Road, Waterford CT 06386. **Tel** (800)243-0876, (203)442-4365, (800)876-9105, FAX (203)443-1123.

ISSN 0267-9515
UK
CODEN OBINE8
ONLINE BUSINESS INFORMATION. [Online bus. inf.]. (1985)-. Periodical. English. Eleven times a year (monthly with Jul./Aug. issue combined). $424.00. Headland Business Information, 1 Henry Smiths Terrace, Headland Cleveland, TS24 0PD United Kingdom. **Tel** 011 44 429 231902, FAX 011 44 429 861403. Documents available from Ask*IEEE.
Ind/Abst INSPEC (Jan. 1987-).

LC HC **ISSN** 0316-6031
DD 346/.713/09202633 CN
ONTARIO SECURITIES LEGISLATION. **Main/Corp** Ontario. **Added/Corp** CCH Canadian Limited. Ontario Securities Commission. 1st Ed. (1966/67)-. Periodical. English. One time a year. Price varies per volume. CCH Canadian Ltd., 6 Garamond Court, Don Mills Ontario M3C 1Z5 Canada. **Tel** (416)441-2992, FAX

(416)441-3418.
Desc: Contains the full text of the Ontario Securities Act and Regulations, as amended to date of publication (August, 1985).

LC HC466 .O633
DD 330 KO
OPCHONGBYOL KYONGGI TONGHYANG.
Added/Corp Chonguk Kyongjein Yonhaphoe. Sanop Chongbo Chosa Wiwonhoe. (19??)-. Korean. Chonguk Yonhaphoe Sanop Chongbo, Chosa Wiwonhoe, Seoul South Korea.

LC HC59.8 .O58
DD 338.91/177 AU
OPEC FUND NEWSLETTER.
VFOAT Newsletter. **VAT** Organization of Petroleum Exporting Countries Fund Newsletter. Vol. 1, No. 1 (March 1983)-. Newsletter. English. Three times a year (Apr., Aug., Dec.). Free on request. OPEC Fund for International Development, PO Box 995 Parkring 8, 1011 Vienna Austria. **Tel** 011 43 1 515640, FAX 011 43 1 2149827. **Circ:** 1,500.

LC HB1 .O68 **ISSN** 0923-7992
DD 330/.05 NE
CCC
CODEN OEREED
OPEN ECONOMIES REVIEW.
Added/Corp Italian International Economic Center. Vol. 1, No. 1 (1990)-. Periodical. English. Four times a year. $268.00. Kluwer Academic Publishers, Postbus 322, 3300 AH Dordrecht The Netherlands. **Tel** 011 31 78 524400, FAX 011 31 78 183273, telex 20083. **ED** Paolo Savona and Michele Fratianni. **Acid Free.** available on microfilm and microfiche from University Microfilms International (UMI). Documents available from UMI Article Clearinghouse.
Desc: Publishes either theoretical or empirical original articles treating international economic issues or national economic issues that have transnational relevance. Topics covered include models and applications of trade flows, commercial policy, adjustment mechanism to external imbalances, exchange rate movements, alternative monetary regimes, real and financial integration, monetary union, economic development and external debt.
Ind/Abst ABI/INFORM Glob. Ed.; Econ. Lit. Index.

ISSN 1071-6394
DD 004 US
CCC
CODEN OSELEX
•OPEN SYSTEMS ECONOMICS LETTER.
[Open syst. econ. lett.]. **Added/Corp** Computer Economics, Inc. **VFOAT** Open Systems Economics. Vol. 1, No. 1 (Jan. 1994)-. Periodical. English. Twelve times a year. $295.00. Computer Economics Inc., 5841 Edison Place, Carlsbad CA 92008. **Tel** (800)326-8100, (619)438-8100, FAX (619)431-1126.

ISSN 0922-0895
NE
UDC 339
OPLEIDING & ONTWIKKELING.
See Education.

LC HF5438 .A32 **ISSN** 0741-3750
DD 650.1/05 US
OPPORTUNITY (CHICAGO, ILL. : 1983).
(OPPORTUNITY.). [Opportunity]. Vol. 122, No. 2 (July 1983)-. Periodical. English. Twelve times a year. $19.95. Opportunity Associates, 73 Spring Street, New York NY 10012. **Tel** (212)925-3180. **(Subscription address:** Palm Coast Data, PO Box 420163, Agency Department, Palm Coast FL 32142. **Tel** (904)445-4662 ext. 669, (800)829-5475.**)** **ED** Jack Weissman. **Bk Rev. Ad Acc. Circ:** 185,000 (ctrl). available on microfilm and microfiche from University Microfilms International (UMI). ***Continues*** *Salesman's Opportunity, 0036-3510.*
Desc: Provides sales, marketing, product and company data relating to opportunities in direct selling.

LC HD28 .O65 **ISSN** 0475-1906
CN
OPTIMUM (OTTAWA).
(OPTIMUM.). [Optimum]. **Added/Corp** Canada. Bureau of Management Consulting. Consulting and Audit Canada. Government Consulting Group. Vol. 1 (Winter 1970)-. Periodical. English (French). Four times a year. 24.01Can$. Canada Communication Group Publishers, Order Processing, Ottawa Ontario K1A 0S9 Canada. **Tel** (819)956-4800, (819)956-4802. available on microfilm and microfiche from University Microfilms International (UMI). Documents available from UMI Article Clearinghouse, Ask*IEEE.
Ind/Abst ABI/INFORM Glob. Ed.; ABI/INFORM [Computer File] (Jan. 1973-); Acad. Search; Anbar Account. Finan. Abstr. [Full Txt.]; Anbar Mark. Distr. Abstr. [Full Txt.]; Anbar Top Manage. Abstr. [Full Txt.]; Bus. ASAP (1992-) [Full Txt.]; Bus. Index (1985-); Can. Period. Index; Curr. Cit.; EP Collect.; Gen. BusinessFile (1985-); Gen. Period. Index (1985-); Homework Help.; INFO-SOUTH Abstr.; INSPEC (1982-); Int. Polit. Sci. Abstr.; Mag. Search; Manage. Bibliogr. Rev.; MasterFile FullTEXT 1000; MasterFile FullTEXT 350; MasterFile FullTEXT 650; MasterFile FullTEXT (July 1993-); OCLC; Oper. Prod. Manage. Abstr. [Full Txt.]; PAIS Int. Print; Person. Train. Abstr. [Full Txt.]; Person. Manage. Abstr.; Telebase; Trade Ind. ASAP [Full Txt.]; Trade Ind. Index [Full Txt.]; Women Manage. Rev. [Full Txt.]; Work Relat. Abstr.

ISSN 1154-5658
FR
UDC 331.885(44)
OPTIONS MONTREUIL.
(OPTIONS.). [Options Montreuil]. (1990)-. Periodical. French. Twenty-four times a year. Journal Options, Case 431, 263 rue de Paris, 93514 Montreuil France. **Tel** 011 33 1 48518433. ***Continues*** *Options Quinzaine (Paris), 0183-875X.*

US
ORANGE COUNTY BUSINESS FIRST.
English. One time a week. Orange County Business First, 17712 Mitchell North, Irvine CA 92714. ***Continues*** *Orange County Businessweek, 0892-6107.*

ISSN 1051-7480
DD 330 US
ORANGE COUNTY BUSINESS JOURNAL (NEWPORT BEACH, CALIF.).
(ORANGE COUNTY BUSINESS JOURNAL.). [Orange Cty. bus. j.]. **VFOAT** Business Journal. (197?)-. Periodical. English. Fifty-one times per year. $53.00. Orange County Business Journal, 4590 MacArthur Boulevard, Suite 100, Newport Beach CA 92660. **Tel** (714)833-8373. **ED** Rick Reiff. **Ad Acc, Adv Mgr:** Roger Kranz. **Circ:** 21,000. available on CD-ROM and an online database from University Microfilms International (UMI). Documents available from UMI Article Clearinghouse.
Ind/Abst Bus. Dateline (Jan. 1985-) [Full Txt.]; Bus. Index (Jan. 1985-Dec. 1985); Gen. BusinessFile (Jan. 1985-Dec. 1985); Gen. Period. Index (Jan. 1985-Dec. 1985); Trade Ind. ASAP [Full Txt.]; Trade Ind. Index [Full Txt.].

ISSN 0890-6432
US
ORBUS.
(ORBUS : THE OFFICIAL BUSINESS MAGAZINE OF THE GREATER ORLANDO CHAMBER OF COMMERCE.). **Added/Corp** Greater Orlando Chamber of Commerce. Vol. 1 No. 1 (July/Aug. 1986)-. Periodical. English. Twelve times a year. $23.95. Zink Media Group Ltd., 701 East Washington Street, Orlando FL 32801. **Tel** (407)628-3880, (407)426-9446. **ED** Michael Candelaria. **Ad Acc. Circ:** 13,000 (ctrl).
Desc: The official business publication of the greater Orlando Chamber of Commerce. Aimed at people conducting business in Central Florida.

LC HB5 .O7 **ISSN** 0048-2129
GW
CCC
ORDO.
(ORDO; JAHRBUCH FUER DIE ORDNUNG VON WIRTSCHAFT UND GESELLSCHAFT.). **VFOAT** Jahrbuch fuer die Ordnung von Wirtschaft und Gesellschaft. Vol. 1 (1948)-. German (English and French; summaries and/or abstracts in English). One time a year. DM118.00. Gustav Fischer Verlag Stuttgart, Postfach 720143, D-70577 Stuttgart Germany. **Tel** 011 49 711 458030, FAX 011 49 711 4580334, telex 2627-7111488. cum. index.
Ind/Abst Int. Bibliogr. Sociol.

ISSN 0279-8190
US
OREGON BUSINESS.
(Feb. 1981)-. Periodical. English. Twelve times a year. $19.95. Oregon Business Magazine, 921 Southwest Morrison Street, Suite 407, Portland OR 97205-2722. **Tel** (503)223-0304. **ED** Robert Hill. **Ad Acc. Circ:** 20,000 (ctrl). available on an online database (files 635,648/Full-Text) from DIALOG. Documents available from UMI Article Clearinghouse. ***Continues*** *Business Success News, 0194-8164.*
Desc: Local business publication.
Ind/Abst Acad. Search; Bus. Dateline; Bus. Index (1985-); Bus. Source Plus; Bus. Source; EP Collect.; Gen. BusinessFile (1985-); Gen. Period. Index (1985-); Homework Help.; MasterFile FullTEXT 1000; MasterFile FullTEXT 350; MasterFile FullTEXT 650; MasterFile FullTEXT (July 1993-); OCLC; PROMT; Telebase; Trade Ind. ASAP [Full Txt.]; Trade Ind. Index [Full Txt.].

FR
ORGANISATION & METHODES.
(19??)-. French. Irregular. 40.00F. Imprimerie Nationale / France, BP 514, 59505 Douai Cedex France. **Tel** 011 33 27 937090.

US
ORGANIZATIONS IN TRANSITION.
(19??)-. Newsletter. English. Four times a year (seasonally). $35.00. William Bridges and Associates, 38 Miller Avenue, Suite 12, Mill Valley CA 94941. **Tel** (415)381-9663, FAX (415)381-8124.
Desc: Deals with organization aspects of transition in business.

LC HC
US
ORGANIZING CORPORATE AND OTHER ENTERPRISES.
(19??)-. English. One time a year. $78.00. Matthew Bender & Company Inc., 1275 Broadway, Albany NY 12204. **Tel** (800)833-9844, (518)487-3000.

ISSN 1065-027X
US
ORIGINAL WNC BUSINESS JOURNAL, THE.
VFOAT WNC Business Journal. **VAT** Original Western North Carolina Business Journal. (199?)-. Periodical. English. Twelve times a year. $35.00. Nason and Associates, Box 8204, Asheville NC 28814. **Tel** (704)258-1322, FAX (704)253-3726. **ED** Steve Nasou (Editor's telephone: (704)258-1323). **Bk Rev,** (Qty: 4-6). **Ad Acc, Adv Mgr:** Michelle Ramsey, **Tel** (704)258-1341. **Circ:** 19,000 (ctrl). ***Continues*** *WNC Business Journal, 1049-7145.*
Desc: Regional business publication for 28 western North Carolina counties.

ISSN 8750-8656
US
CCC
ORLANDO BUSINESS JOURNAL.
(1984)-. Periodical. English. One time a week. $50.00. Orlando Business Journal, 315 East Robinson Street, Suite 250, Orlando FL 32801. **Tel** (407)649-8470, FAX (407)649-8469. **ED** Kent Hoover. **Ad Acc, Adv Mgr:** Joan Watts. ctrl circ. available on microfilm from University Microfilms International (UMI); available on an online database (files 635,648/Full-Text) from DIALOG. Documents available from UMI Article Clearinghouse.
Ind/Abst Acad. Search; Bus. Dateline (Jan. 1992-) [Full Txt.]; Bus. Index (1985-1990); Bus. Source Plus; Bus. Source; EP Collect.; Gen. BusinessFile (1985-1990); Gen. Period. Index (1985-1990); Homework Help.; INFO-SOUTH Abstr.; MasterFile FullTEXT 1000; MasterFile FullTEXT 350; MasterFile FullTEXT 650; MasterFile FullTEXT (July 1993-); OCLC; PROMT; Telebase; Trade Ind. ASAP [Full Txt.]; Trade Ind. Index [Full Txt.].

LC HB9 .O78a
JA
OSAKA DAIGAKU KEIZAIGAKU.
Main/Corp Osaka Daigaku. Keizai Gakubu. **Added/Corp** Osaka Daigaku. Keizai Gakubu. Economic Review of Osaka University. **VFOAT** Economic Review of Osaka University ; Osaka Economic Papers. (19??)-. Periodical. English (Japanese). Four times a year. $132.50. **(Subscription address:** Japan Publications Trading Company Ltd., PO Box 5030, Tokyo International, Tokyo 100-31 Japan. **Tel** 011 81 3 3292 3753.**)** ***Absorbed*** *Osaka Economic Papers, 0030-610X.*
Ind/Abst AGRICOLA; J. Econ. Lit.

LC HG4245.5.O82 O82
DD 658.1509 JA
OSAKA-FU- KOJO BENRAN.
Added/Corp Osaka (Japan : Prefecture) Osaka-fu Kogyo Kyokai. (19??)-. Japanese. Osaka-Fu Kohty Kyokai, c/o Osaka Shoko Kaikan 16, Minami Honcho 5, Higashi-ku Osaka Japan.

LC HC244 .O74 **ISSN** 0030-6460
DD 330.947/0005 GW
CCC
OSTEUROPA WIRTSCHAFT.
[Osteur.-Wirtsch.]. (Aug. 1956)-. Trade Publication. German (English). Four times a year. DM43.60 Germany; $24.30 US. Zenit Pressevertrieb GmbH, Postfach 810640, 7000 Stuttgart 80 Germany. **Tel** 089-773007. Index available. cum. index. **Bk Rev. Ad Acc. Circ:** 700 (ctrl).
Ind/Abst ABC POL SCI; Am. Hist. Life (1979-); Int. Labour Doc.; LABORDOC; PAIS Int. Print (1991-); Risk Abstr.

LC HD7795
DD 331 XO
OTAZKY PRACE.
Added/Corp Czechoslovakia. Federalni Ministerstvo Prace a Socialnich Veci. Vyskumny Ustav Socialneho Rozvoja a Prace (Bratislava). (1990)-. Periodical. Slovak (Czech). Six times a year. $60.00. VUSRP, Bratislava, Mierova 23 PS0C 82748 Slovakia. **(Subscription address:** Slovart GTG Ltd., Krupinska 4, 852 99 Bratislava Slovakia. **Tel** 011 42 7 839471 2.**)**
Ind/Abst Ergon. Abstr.

ISSN 1355-2449
DD 338.476151 UK
•OTC BUSINESS NEWS.
[OTC bus. news]. **VFOAT** Over the Counter Business News. (1994)-. Newsletter. English. Twenty-four times a year. $847.05. Financial Times Magazines, Greystoke Place, Fetter Lane, London EC4A 1ND United Kingdom. **Tel** 011 44 171 8316577.

ISSN 1193-1485
DD 380.1097138405 CN
OTTAWA BUSINESS QUARTERLY.
[Ott. bus. q.]. (1992)-. Periodical. English. Four times a year. 9.61Can$. Ottawa Magazine, 192 Bank Street, Ottawa Ontario K2P 1W8 Canada. **Tel** (613)234-7751, FAX (613)234-9226. **ED** Rick Boychuk. **Circ:** 25,000. ***Continues*** *Ottawa Business Magazine, 0849-1836.*

ISSN 1199-7834
DD 380 CN
OTTAWA BUSINESS SHOPPER, THE. [Ott. bus. shopp.]. (June 1992)-. Periodical. English. Twelve times a year. Ottawa Business Shopper, 48 Colonnade Road, Nepean, Ontario K2E 7J6 Canada.

UK
OUTLOOK CONCENTRATED PHOSPHATES. See Chemistry and Chemicals-Organic Chemistry.

UK
OUTLOOK SULPHUR. See Chemistry and Chemicals-Inorganic Chemistry.

LC HC106.6 .I43a
DD 330.9/773/04 US
OUTLOOK, THE REVENUE PICTURE FOR ... . **Added/Corp** Illinois Economic and Fiscal Commission. **VFOAT** Revenue Estimate Update and Analysis. (1992)-. English. Illinois Economic and Fiscal Commission, 703 Stratton Building, Springfield IL 62706. ***Continues*** *Revenue Estimate and Economic Outlook, 0093-299X.*

LC HC **ISSN** 1063-1798
DD 330 US
OUTREACH (WASHINGTON, D.C. 1992). (OUTREACH.). (1992)-. Periodical. English. Six times a year. $24.00. Minority Business Women's Exchange, 1500 Massachusetts Avenue NW, Suite 831-A, Washington DC 20005.

LC HC107.M5 O94 **ISSN** 1064-3621
DD 338.09774/05 US
OUTSTATE BUSINESS. (OUTSTATE BUSINESS : THE MAGAZINE OF MICHIGAN BUSINESS & INDUSTRY.). [Outstate bus.]. Vol. 5, No. 3 (June-Aug. 1992)-. Periodical. English. Four times a year (published seasonally). $10.00. Harbor House Publishers, 221 Water Street, Boyne City MI 49712. **Tel** (616)582-2814, FAX (615)582-3392. **ED** David Knight. **Ad Acc. Circ:** 10,000 (ctrl). available on microfilm, microfiche, and CD-ROM from University Microfilms International (UMI). ***Continues*** *North Force Magazine.*
Desc: Devoted to outstate Michigan's business and industrial community, covering commercial interests in the entire state outside of metropolitan Detroit.

LC HD38.25.U6 O94 **ISSN** 1056-3326
DD 338.7/025/73 US
CEASED
OWNERS & OFFICERS OF PRIVATE COMPANIES. [Own. off. priv. co.]. **Added/Corp** Taft Group (Rockville, Md.). **VFOAT** Owners and Oofficers of Private Companies; OOPC. 1st Ed. (1991)-(1995). English. Taft Group, 835 Penobscott Building, Customer Service, Detroit MI 48226. **Tel** (800)877-8238, FAX (313)961-6083. available on magnetic tape; available on diskette.
Desc: Presents a geographical arrangement of US private business leaders.

LC HB31 .O77 **ISSN** 0030-7653
DD 330/.05 UK
CCC
Pr Rev.
OXFORD ECONOMIC PAPERS. [Oxf. econ. pap.]. **Added/Corp** University of Oxford. Institute of Statistics. No. 1 (Oct. 1938)-. Periodical. English. Four times a year. $150.00. Oxford University Press / UK, Walton Street, Oxford OX2 6DP United Kingdom. **Tel** 011 44 1865 56767, FAX 011 44 1865 267773, telex 851/837330 OXPRES G. **(Subscription address:** Oxford University Press / USA, Journals Marketing Department, Oxford University Press, 2001 Evans Road, Cary NC 27513. **Tel** (800)451-7556, (919)677-0977, FAX (919)677-1714.**)** **ED** N. H. Dimsdale, C. L. Gilbert, P. J. N. Sinclair. cum. index. **Ad Acc. Circ:** 2,400. available on microfilm and microfiche from University Microfilms International (UMI). Documents available from The Genuine Article, UMI Article Clearinghouse.
Desc: Covers theoretical and applied economics, economic history, public administration and scientific methods. Problems of the international economy and developing countries are also studied and discussed.
Ind/Abst ABI/INFORM Glob. Ed.; ABI/INFORM [Computer File] (Nov. 1984-); Acad. Search; Am. Hist. Life (1955-1990); Br. Humanit. Index; Contents Recent Econ. J.; Contents Pages Manage.; Curr. Cit.; Econ. Lit. Index; EP Collect.; Expand. Acad. Index (1989-); Geogr. Abstr. Human Geogr.; Homework Help.; INFO-SOUTH Abstr.; Int. Dev. Abstr.; Int. Labour Doc.; J. Econ. Lit.; Mag. Search; MasterFile FullTEXT 1000; MasterFile FullTEXT 350; MasterFile FullTEXT 650; MasterFile FullTEXT (Jan. 1993-); Middle East Abstr. Index; Newsp. Period. Abstr. (1991-); OCLC; Res. Alert [Full Cov.]; Rice Abstr.; Selec. Coop. Index Manage. Period.; Soc. Sci. Source; Soc. Sci. Cit. Index [Full Cov.]; Soc. Sci. Index; Soc. Sci. Index Fulltext (Sept. 1988-) [Full Txt.]; Stat. Theory Method Abstr. (1959-1963, 1970); Telebase; UMI ABI/Inform--Bus. Period. Ondisc (Dec. 1987-) [Full Txt.]; World Agric. Econ. Rural Sociol. Abstr.

LC HC251 .O95 **ISSN** 0266-903X
DD 338.941/005 UK
CCC
OXFORD REVIEW OF ECONOMIC POLICY. [Oxf. rev. econ. policy]. Vol. 1, No. 1 (Spring 1985)-. Periodical. English. Four times a year. $195.00. Oxford University Press / UK, Walton Street, Oxford OX2 6DP United Kingdom. **Tel** 011 44 1865 56767, FAX 011 44 1865 267773, telex 851/837330 OXPRES G. **(Subscription address:** Oxford University Press / USA, Journals Marketing Department, Oxford University Press, 2001 Evans Road, Cary NC 27513. **Tel** (800)451-7556, (919)677-0977, FAX (919)677-1714.**)** **ED** Christopher Allsopp. **Ad Acc.** available on microfilm and microfiche from University Microfilms International (UMI). Documents available from The Genuine Article.
Desc: Commentary, forecasts and articles on economic policy in the UK and world economy.
Ind/Abst Br. Humanit. Index; Contents Pages Manage.; Curr. Cit.; Curr. Contents Soc. Behav. Sci.; Econ. Lit. Index; Geogr. Abstr. Human Geogr.; J. Econ. Lit.; PAIS Int. Print (1991-); Res. Alert [Full Cov.]; Soc. Sci. Cit. Index [Full Cov.]; World Agric. Econ. Rural Sociol. Abstr.

AT
P SERIES - COMMITTEE FOR ECONOMIC DEVELOPMENT OF AUSTRALIA. **Main/Corp** Committee for Economic Development of Australia. **Added/Corp** Committee for Economic Development of Australia. Major Research Projects. P Series. **VFOAT** P Series; Major Research Projects. (19??)-. Monographic series. English. Price varies per volume. Committee for Economic Development of Australia, 123 Lonsdale Street, GPO Box 2117T, Melbourne Victoria 3000 Australia. **Tel** 011 61 03 6623544, FAX 011 61 03 6637271. Index available. **Circ:** 2,000 (ctrl).

ISSN 1061-8619
US
SUSPENDED
PACIFIC ASIAN BUSINESS REVIEW. **Added/Corp** University of Hawaii. Pacific Asian Management Institute. (1992)-. Periodical. English. Pacific Asian Management Institute, University of Hawaii, 2404 Maile Way C202, Honolulu HI 96822. **Tel** (808)956-8041, FAX (808)956-9685.

LC HC681.A1 P33 **ISSN** 0817-8038
DD 330.99 AT
PACIFIC ECONOMIC BULLETIN. **Added/Corp** Australian National University. National Centre for Development Studies. Vol. 1, No. 1 (July 1986)-. Bulletin. English. Two times a year (June, Dec.). 28.78Aus$. Anutech Pty. Limited, GPO Box 4, Canberra ACT 2601 Australia. **Tel** 011 61 6 2492479, FAX 011 61 6 2575088.
Ind/Abst For. Prod. Abstr. (1991-); For. Abstr.; Int. Bibliogr. Sociol.; Rural Dev. Abstr.; Sug. Indus. Abstr.; World Agric. Econ. Rural Sociol. Abstr.

ISSN 0898-7904
DD 337 US
PACIFIC ECONOMIC COOPERATION. (PACIFIC ECONOMIC COOPERATION : A NEWSLETTER OF THE UNITED STATES NATIONAL COMMITTEE FOR PACIFIC ECONOMIC COOPERATION.). [Pac. econ. coop.]. **Added/Corp** United States National Committee for Pacific Economic Cooperation. **VFOAT** PEC Newsletter. **VAT** Pacific Economic Cooperation Newsletter. (198?)-. Newsletter. English. Four times a year. $30.00. Pacific Economic Cooperation Council, 1755 Massachusetts Avenue Northwest, Washington DC 20036. **Tel** (202)745-7444.
Ind/Abst Hum. Rights Intern. Rep.

UK
•**PACIFIC ECONOMIC REVIEW.** (1995)-. English. Three times a year. Basil Blackwell Publishers Ltd., 108 Cowley Road, Oxford 0X4 1JF United Kingdom. **Tel** 011 44 1235 465500, FAX 011 44 1235 465556, telex 837022 OXBOOK G. ***Continues*** *Hong Kong Economic Papers.*

ISSN 1031-6981
DD 990.05 AT
PACIFIC REPORT (RED HILL). [Pac. rep. Red Hill]. (1988)-. English. Irregular (24 issues). 201.43Aus$. Pacific Report Pty Ltd., PO Box 25, Monaro Cres PO ACT 2603 Australia. **Tel** 011 61 6 2850142, FAX 011 61 6 2850144. **ED** Helen Fraser. **Bk Rev**, (Qty: 12). **Ad Acc. Circ:** 500.
Desc: Reports on business, politics and development in the region.

US
PAINE WEBBER WORKING PAPER SERIES IN MONEY, ECONOMICS, AND FINANCE. (19??)-. Periodical. English. Four times a year. $240.00 (academic and nonprofit organizations); $260.00 other. Columbia University Graduate School of Business, J. Glazener Hall / 6N Uris Hall, New York NY 10027. **Tel** (212)854-8346.

ISSN 1067-1110
DD 338 US
PAINT DEALER, THE. [Paint deal.]. (1992)-. Periodical. English. Twelve times a year. $25.00. Mugler Publications, 13850 Manchester Road, St. Louis MO 63122. **Tel** (800)984-0801, (314)984-0800.

LC Z7163 Z7163 .P35 **ISSN** 1064-4660
DD 350 US
PAIS INTERNATIONAL. (PAIS INTERNATIONAL [COMPUTER FILE].). [PAIS int.]. **Added/Corp** SilverPlatter Information, Inc. Public Affairs Information Service. **VFOAT** PAIS International on SilverPlatter; PAIS on SilverPlatter. (19??)-. English. Four times a year. $1995.00. Silverplatter Information Inc., 100 River Ridge Drive, Norwood MA 02062. **Tel** (800)343-0064, (617)769-2599, FAX (617)769-8763. available in print; available on magnetic tape from PAIS; available on an online database from OCLC; DIALOG; and DATA-STAR.
Desc: An electronic database incorporating a compilation of material from the printed indexes of the Public Affairs Information Service (PAIS), Inc. Covers the spectrum of public affairs information, highlighting subjects such as business, government, economic and social issues, international trade and relations, banking, environment, health, demographics, law and legislation, public administration and finance.

LC HC415.15.A1 P34
DD 330.956/005 PK
PAKISTAN & GULF ECONOMIST. **VFOAT** Pakistan and Gulf Economist. Vol. 1, No. 1 (March 17-April 2, 1982)-. Periodical. English. One time a week. $170.00. Economist Publications Ltd, Shafi Court, Mereweather Road, PO Box 10449, Karachi-4 Pakistan. **Tel** 011 44 322 289194. **ED** Muzaffar Hasan. **Bk Rev. Ad Acc. Circ:** 20,000. ***Continues*** *Pakistan Economist (Karachi, Pakistan : 1969).*
Desc: Journal specialising in interpretative articles on political and socio-economic subjects.

PK
PAKISTAN BUDGETS. **Main/Corp** Pakistan. Economic Advisor's Wing. English. One time a year. NGM Communication, 3-D-1 Gulberg III, Near TP Exchange, Lahore 54660 Pakistan. **Tel** 011 92 21 428625, FAX 011 92 21 613854.

LC HB1 .P34 **ISSN** 0254-9204
DD 330/.05 PK
PAKISTAN JOURNAL OF APPLIED ECONOMICS. [Pak. j. appl. econ.]. **Added/Corp** University of Karachi. Applied Economics Research Centre. Vol. 1, No. 1 (Summer 1982)-. Periodical. English. Two times a year (June & Dec.). $25.00. University of Karachi Applied Economics Research Center, PO 8403, Karachi 75270 Pakistan. **Tel** 011 92 21 474749 or 474384. **ED** Salim Chishti. Index available. **Bk Rev. Ad Acc. Circ:** 1,500.
Desc: Publication covering applied and policy-oriented research on rural, agricultural, urban, regional, trade, financial and other development issues of Pakistan and other developing economies.
Ind/Abst Econ. Lit. Index (199?-); J. Econ. Lit.

US
PALM BEACH DAILY BUSINESS REVIEW. (19??)-. Newspaper. English. Five times a week (Mon. thru Fri.). Price varies. American Lawyer Media, L.P., 600 3rd Avenue, New York NY 10016. **Tel** (212)973-2800. **(Subscription address:** Palm Beach Review, 100 South Dixie Highway, West Palm Beach FL 33401. **Tel** (407)820-2060.**)** ***Continues*** *Palm Beach Review, 0884-8785.*

ISSN 0538-8759
US
PAMPHLET SERIES - INTERNATIONAL MONETARY FUND. (PAMPHLET SERIES.). [Pam. ser. - Int. Monet. Fund]. **Main/Corp** International Monetary Fund. **VFOAT** IMF Pamphlet Series. (1964)-. Monographic series. English. Irregular. Free on request. International Monetary Fund, 700 19th Street Northwest, Publishing Unit, Washington DC 20431. **Tel** (202)623-7430, FAX (202)623-7201.

ISSN 1060-4952
DD 330 US
PANEL STUDY OF INCOME DYNAMICS. (PANEL STUDY OF INCOME DYNAMICS [COMPUTER FILE].). [Panel study income dyn.]. **Added/Corp** Inter-University Consortium for Political and Social Research. University of Michigan. Survey Research Center. **VFOAT** PSID. (1968-1987)-. English. University of Michigan Survey Research Center, PO Box 1248, Ann Arbor MI 48106. **Tel** (313)936-0099. available on magnetic tape.
Desc: CD is ISO 9660 standard; raw data is uncompressed ASCII format. System requirements: CD-ROM reader, computer system with SAS or SPSS Software.

CU
PANORAMA ECONOMICO LATINOAMERICANO (HAVANA, CUBA : 1977). (PANORAMA ECONOMICO LATINOAMERICANO : PEL.). **VFOAT** PEL. Vol. 1, No. 1

(Jan. 1977)-. Periodical. Spanish. Twenty-four times a year. $100.00. Ediciones Cubanas, Obispo 527 Altos ESQ Bernaza, CP 10100 Havana Cuba. ***Continues*** *Panorama Economico Latinoamericano (Havana, Cuba : 1961).*
Desc: Offers information of the principal political, economic and social questions, and multiple notations of general interest on and in the national and international sphere.

LC HD72 .P36 **ISSN** 0951-8819
DD 338.9/005 UK
CEASED
PANOSCOPE. **Added/Corp** Panos Institute. Netherlands. Ministerie van Buitenlandse Zaken. No. 1 (June 1987)-(Mar. 1995). Periodical. English. Panos London, 9 White Lion Street, London N1 9PD United Kingdom. **Tel** 011 44 171 2781111, telex 9419293.
Ind/Abst Environ. Period. Bibliogr.

LC HD1483 **ISSN** 0956-5280
DD 338.109416 UK
PAPERS IN AGRICULTURAL AND FOOD ECONOMICS NORTHERN IRELAND. **See** Agriculture.

US
PAPERTRONIX. (19??)-. Periodical. English. Four times a year. $73.00. International Business Forms Industries Inc, 2111 Wilson Boulevard, Suite 350, Arlington VA 22201-3008. **Tel** (703)841-9191, FAX (703)522-5750. ***Continues*** *Formsmfg.*
Desc: Contains articles for the manufacturer of business forms, labels, direct mail and information systems on technology, marketing, planning and production.

ISSN 1067-8050
DD 338 US
•**PAPUA NEW GUINEA (SYRACUSE, N.Y.).** (PAPUA NEW GUINEA : AN EXECUTIVE REPORT.). [Papua New Guinea]. **Added/Corp** Political Risk Services (IBC USA (Publications) Inc.). (1993)-. English. $110.00. Political Risk Services, 6320 Fly Road, Suite 102, PO Box 248, East Syracuse NY 13057-0248. **Tel** (315)431-0511, FAX (315)431-0200.
Desc: Focuses on the long-term outlook for business. Includes a brief review of recent events and current circumstances, background intelligence including geography, history, economics and social conditions, as well as the key political and economic forecasts.

LC HC221 .P28
DD 330.9892/005 PY
PARAGUAY ECONOMICO : PUBLICACION MENSUAL DEL BANCO PARAGUAYO DE DATOS. **Added/Corp** Banco Paraguayo de Datos. Vol. 1, No. 1 (May 1979)-. Periodical. Spanish. Twelve times a year. Banco Paraguayo de Datos, Casilla Postal 1140, Asuncion Paraguay.

ISSN 1067-8069
DD 338 US
•**PARAGUAY (SYRACUSE, N.Y.).** (PARAGUAY : AN EXECUTIVE REPORT.). [Paraguay]. **Added/Corp** Political Risk Services (IBC USA (Publications) Inc.). (1993)-. English. $110.00. Political Risk Services, 6320 Fly Road, Suite 102, PO Box 248, East Syracuse NY 13057-0248. **Tel** (315)431-0511, FAX (315)431-0200.
Desc: Focuses on the long-term outlook for business. Includes a brief review of recent events and current circumstances, background intelligence including geography, history, economics and social conditions, as well as the key political and economic forecasts.

ISSN 1186-1274
DD 338.09714 CN
PARLONS AFFAIRES, BEAUCE-ETCHEMINS. [Parlons aff. Beauce-Etchemins]. Vol. 1, No 10 (June 1990)-. Periodical. French. Twelve times a year. Parlons Affaires Beauce-Etchemins, 12625 1re rue, St-Georges Quebec G5Y 2E4 Canada. ***Continues*** *Parlons Affaires en Beauce., 1186-1266.*

ISSN 1184-1117
DD 338.09714/4/05 CN
TITLE CHANGE
PARLONS AFFAIRES DANS LES LAURENTIDES. [Parlons aff. Laurent.]. **Added/Corp** Corporation de Developpement des Laurentides. **VFOAT** Parlons Affaires; Decideur. Vol. 6, No 7 (1990)-(1993). Periodical. French. Publications Laurentiennes, 300 rue Labelle, Saint-Jerome Quebec J7Z 5L1 Canada. ***Continues*** *Decideur (St-Jerome, Quebec)., 0831-7704.* ***Continued by*** *Parlons Affaires Laval/Basses Laurentides, 1195-9738.*

ISSN 0838-0058
DD 658.3/2 CN
PAY EQUITY GUIDE. [Pay equity guide]. Vol. 1, No. 1 (Jan. 1988)-. Periodical. English. Twelve times a year. 316.13Can$. Concord Publishing Ltd., 14 Prince Arthur Avenue, Suite 209, Toronto Ontario M5R 2A9 Canada. **Tel** (416)964-2758, FAX (416)964-0659. Index available ((Dec-Feb) iss.). cum. index.
Desc: Providing a wide range of services in areas such as the protection and well-being of children, and provision for the elderly.

ISSN 0895-7975
DD 658 US
PAYROLL MANAGER'S LETTER. [Payr. manager's lett.]. **VFOAT** ERC Payroll Manager's Letter; PHPN Payroll Manager's Letter. (198?)-. Periodical. English. Twenty-six times a year. $159.36 (US); $192.48 (Canada). Bureau of Business Practice, 24 Rope Ferry Road, Waterford CT 06386. **Tel** (800)243-0876, (203)442-4365, (800)876-9105, FAX (203)443-1123.

ISSN 1059-2075
US
•**PBC BUSINESS GUIDE.** **VFOAT** Business Guide. **VAT** Publishing and Business Consultants Business Guide. (1993)-. Newsletter. English. Four times a year. Publishing & Business Consultants, PO Box 75392, Los Angeles CA 90075. **Tel** (213)732-3477, FAX (213)732-9123.

ISSN 1059-1982
US
PBC SENIOR NEWSLETTER. **VFOAT** Senior Newsletter. **VAT** Publishing and Business Consultants Senior Newsletter. (1992)-. Newsletter. English. Four times a year. Publishing & Business Consultants, PO Box 75392, Los Angeles CA 90075. **Tel** (213)732-3477, FAX (213)732-9123.

ISSN 1059-1966
US
PBC TRAVEL NEWSLETTER. **VFOAT** Travel Newsletter. **VAT** Publishing and Business Consultants Travel Newsletter. (1992)-. Newsletter. English. Four times a year. Publishing & Business Consultants, PO Box 75392, Los Angeles CA 90075. **Tel** (213)732-3477, FAX (213)732-9123.

LC HC321 .S6
DD 330 NE
PBO-BLAD. **Added/Corp** Sociaal-Economische Raad. **VFOAT** PBO Blad. (198?)-. Periodical. Dutch. One time a week. Fl150.00 Netherlands; $50.00 US. SER - Sociaal Economische Raad, Bezuidenhoutseweg 60, Postbus 90405, 2509 LK The Hague Netherlands. **Tel** 011 31 70 3499499, FAX 011 31 70 3832535, telex 41.146. Index available. **Circ:** 450 (ctrl). ***Continues*** *Mededelingen- en Verordeningenblad Bedrijfsorganisatie.*
Desc: Contains information regarding the execution of the Dutch Industrial Organization Act.

US
PC PLUS GLOBAL VANTAGE [COMPUTER FILE]. **Added/Corp** Standard & Poor's Compustat Services. **VFOAT** Global Vantage; Compustat PC Plus Global Vantage. (19??)-. English. Standard & Poor's Corporation, (A Division of McGraw-Hill, Inc.), 25 Broadway, New York NY 10004. **Tel** (212)208-8775, (800)221-5277. **(Subscription address:** Standard & Poor's Compustat, 7400 South Alton Court, Englewood CO 80112. **Tel** (212)208-8467, (800)523-4534.**)**

ISSN 1060-5436
US
PENNSYLVANIA BUSINESS MAGAZINE. (1992)-. Periodical. English. Twelve times a year. Pennsylvania Publishing Company, PO Box 170, Coalport PA 16627.

LC HC107.P4 P44 **ISSN** 0031-4382
DD 330 US
CEASED
PENNSYLVANIA BUSINESS SURVEY. [Pa. bus. surv.]. **Added/Corp** Pennsylvania State University. College of Business Administration. Center for Research. Pennsylvania State College. Dept. of Economics. Pennsylvania State College. Bureau of Business Research. Pennsylvania State University. Bureau of Business Research. (July 1938)-(Dec. 1993). Periodical. English. Pennsylvania State University / College of Business Administration / Center of Research, 108 Business Administration Bldg. 11, University Park PA 16802. **Tel** (814)865-7669, FAX (814)863-2753. **ED** William Anderson. available on microfilm and microfiche from University Microfilms International (UMI).
Desc: Each issue highlights current trends in the Pennsylvania economy in textual, tabular, and graphical format. Each quarter economic conditions in the 15 metropolitan areas are also analyzed. Forecasting is qualitative, as opposed to quantitative, in nature, designed to keep readers informed of the scenarios most likely to unfold.
Ind/Abst Public Aff. Inf. Serv. Bull.; Stat. Ref. Index.

LC HC121 .P46 **ISSN** 0212-0208
DD 361.6/098 SP
PENSAMIENTO IBEROAMERICANO. [Pensam. iberoam.]. No. 1 (Jan./June 1982)-. Periodical. Portuguese (Spanish). Two times a year. $132.00. Institute de Cooperacion Iberoamerica, Avda de Reyes 4 Catolics 4, Madrid 3 Spain. **Tel** 244 06 00. **Bk Rev. Ad Acc. Circ:** 3,500.
Desc: Main objective is to express the particular way of thinking of Latin American political economy.
Ind/Abst Econ. Lit. Index; Hisp. Am. Period. Index, HAPI; Int. Bibliogr. Sociol.; Int. Labour Doc.; Int. Polit. Sci. Abstr.; J. Econ. Lit.; LABORDOC; PAIS Int. Print (1991-).

LC HC146.A1 P46
DD 330 NQ
SUSPENDED
PENSAMIENTO PROPIO : BOLETIN DE INFORMACION Y ANALISIS. **Added/Corp** Instituto de Investigaciones Economicas y Sociales (Managua, Nicaragua) Coordinadora Regional de Investigaciones Economicas y Sociales. Vol. 1, No. 1 (1983)- Suspended (March 1994). Periodical. Spanish. Four times a year. $15.00. Cries, Apartado 3516, Managua Nicaragua. **Tel** 011 505 2 622162. **ED** Enrique Ortego. Index available. cum. index. **Ad Acc, Adv Mgr:** Walter Hernandez. **Circ:** 6,000.
Desc: Contains detailed reviews of the economy and culture of Central America.

IT
PENSIERO ECONOMICO MODERNO. (19??)-. Italian. Four times a year. L46000.00 Italy; L80000.00 other. Il Pensiero Economico Moderno, Via della Fortezza 1, 56100 Pisa Italy. **Tel** 011 39 50 571198, 011 39 50 571181.

ISSN 0742-7085
US
PENSION AND PROFIT SHARING PLANS FOR SMALL & MEDIUM SIZE BUSINESS. [Pension profit shar. plans small medium size bus.]. **Added/Corp** Scudere, Carmine V. Pension and Profit Sharing Plans for Small & Medium Size Businesses. **VAT** Pension and Profit Sharing Plans for Small and Medium Size Businesses. Vol. 1, No. 1 (1984)-. Periodical. English. Four times a year. $191.50. Panel Publishers, A Division of Aspen Publishers Inc., 7201 McKinney Circle, PO Box 990, Frederick MD 21705-9727. **Tel** (800)638-8437. **(Subscription address:** Aspen Publishers Inc., PO Box 990, Frederick MD 21701. **Tel** (800)901-9074, (301)698-7100.**)**
Desc: Analysis on structuring retirement plans, dealing with the IRS, DOL and PBGC, tax treatment of distributions, funding plans, employee stock benefit plans and more.

US
PENSION DIGEST. (19??)-. English. Twelve times a year. $65.00. Collin Fritz & Associates, PO Box 426, Brainerd MN 56401. **Tel** (218)828-0249. **ED** Michael Rahn. cum. index. **Circ:** 1,500.

LC HD891.A1 P46
DD 333.7309598 IO
PENYULUH LANDREFORM & AGRARIA. **See** Agriculture.

LC HD251 .P446 **ISSN** 1058-5664
DD 333.33/8/02573 US
PEOPLE, PROPERTY, PROSPECTS. (PEOPLE, PROPERTY, PROSPECTS : WHO'S LIVING IN AMERICA'S HIGH INCOME NEIGHBORHOODS.). [People prop. prospects]. **Added/Corp** Taft Group (Rockville, Md.). (1992)-. English. Taft Group, 835 Penobscott Building, Customer Service, Detroit MI 48226. **Tel** (800)877-8238, FAX (313)961-6083.

ISSN 1181-9626
DD 333.79/32 CN
TITLE CHANGE
PEOPLE (VANCOUVER). (PEOPLE.). [People]. **Main/Corp** B.C. Hydro. Vol. 1, No. 1 (May 1990)-Vol. 4, No. 4 (Apr. 1993). Periodical. English. ***Continues in part*** *News (B.C. Hydro), 0825-0634.* ***Merged with*** *B.C. Hydro. Issues, 1181-6430* ***and*** *B.C. Hydro. Directions, 1181-9367* ***to form*** *B.C. Hydro. Access Magazine, 1195-0889.*

ISSN 0898-5952
DD 658 US
PERFORMANCE IMPROVEMENT QUARTERLY. [Perform. improv. q.]. **Added/Corp** Florida State University. Learning Systems Institute. National Society for Performance and Instruction. **VFOAT** PIQ. Vol. 1, No. 1 (1988)-. Periodical. English. Four times a year. $64.00. National Society for Performance & Instruction, 1300 L Street Northwest, Suite 1250, Washington DC 20005. **Tel** (202)408-7969, FAX (202)408-7972. **ED** William C. Coscarelli. **Circ:** 1,000.
Desc: Articles on the theoretical and practical issues of the improvement of human performance of individuals and organizations.
Ind/Abst Curr. Cit.; Curr. Index J. Educ. (March 1990); Educ. Index (1992-); Ergon. Abstr.; Person. Manage. Abstr.; Psychol. Abstr. (1988-); PsycINFO (1990-); PsycLit; Work Relat. Abstr.

US
PERRYMAN ECONOMIC FORECAST. (19??)-. Periodical. English. Three times a year (April, July, Nov.). $900.00. Texas Economic Publishers, 510 North Valley Mills Drive, Suite 300, Waco TX 76710. **Tel** (800)949-9049, (817)751-7411, FAX (817)751-7855. **ED** Ray Perryman (editor's phone: (817)751-9595). ***Continues*** *Texas Economic Forecast.*

Desc: Key economic indicators and major industrial sectors for Texas, US, 10 Ty regions, major metros of Texas.

ISSN 1047-8280
DD 338 US
PERRYMAN REPORT, THE. [Perryman rep.]. **Added/Corp** Baylor University. Forecasting Service. (1985)-. Periodical. English. Twelve times a year. $149.00. Texas Economic Publishers, 510 North Valley Mills Drive, Suite 300, Waco TX 76710. **Tel** (800)949-9049, (817)751-7411, FAX (817)751-7855. **ED** Nancy Cunningham.
Desc: Focuses on international, national, and Texas economic issues.

LC HG **ISSN** 1044-503X
DD 332 US
CEASED
PERSONAL ADVANTAGE / FINANCIAL. [Pers. advant./financ.]. **Added/Corp** Boardroom Reports, Inc. **VFOAT** Personal Financial Advantage; Personal Advantage, Financial. Vol. 1, No. 1 (May 1989)-(1995). Periodical. English. Boardroom Reports Inc., 330 West 42nd Street, 14th Floor, New York NY 10036. **Tel** (212)239-9000.
Desc: Shrewd advice on how to manage your money and deal from a position of strength. Tells how to protect your assets from your bankers, insurance agents, and credit card companies. Also covers how to handle bureaucracies and seize investment opportunities. Includes the a collection of freebie information.

ISSN 0883-5608
DD 651 US
PERSONAL IDENTIFICATION NEWS. See Computers-Computer Crimes and Security.

US
PERSONAL INCOME BY MAJOR SOURCE AND EARNINGS BY MAJOR INDUSTRY, COUNTIES [COMPUTER FILE]. **Added/Corp** United States. Bureau of Economic Analysis. (1959)-. English. Economic and Statistical Analysis, Bureau of Economic Affairs, PO Box 100606, 222 Mitchell Street, Atlanta GA 30384.

ISSN 0893-2549
DD 651 US
PERSONAL REPORT FOR THE PROFESSIONAL SECRETARY. [Pers. rep. prof. secr.]. **Added/Corp** National Institute of Business Management (U.S.). (198?)-. Newsletter. English. Twelve times a year. $42.72. National Institute of Business Management, Inc., 1101 King Street, Alexandria VA 22133. **Tel** (800)543-2052, (703)548-3885, (800)543-2049, FAX (703)549-0182. **(Subscription address:** National Institute of Business Management, PO Box 25337, Alexandria VA 22313. **Tel** (800)543-2053.) **ED** Barry Lenson. ***Continues*** *Research Institute Personal Report for the Professional Secretary, 0276-6035.*
Desc: The professional secretary's guide to accelerated career advancement. Covers the changing duties of secretaries and administrative assistants in a streamlined business environment.

ISSN 0946-7505
GW
UDC 33
●**PERSONALPOTENTIAL (STUTTGART).** [Personalpotential Stuttg.]. (1994)-. Periodical. German. Six times a year (Feb., Apr., Jun., Aug., Oct., Dec.). $107.47. Dr. Josef Raabe Verlags GmbH, Postfach 103922, D-70034 Stuttgart Germany. **Tel** 011 49 711 6290093, telex 722232. ***Continues*** *Lernfeld Betrieb, 0930-4460.*

LC HC329.5.I5 P49
DD 330 NE
PERSONELE INKOMENSVERDELING ... WERKENDE GEHUWDE VROUWEN, DE. **VFOAT** Distribution of Personal Income ... Working Married Women. (19??)-. Dutch.

LC HD2851 .P4
DD 338.70 AU
PERSONEN-COMPASS. **VAT** Personen Compass. (1951)-. German. One time a year. S900.00. Compass Verlag, Wipplingerstrabe 32, 1013 Vienna Austria. ***Continues in part*** *Compass (Vienna, Austria).*

LC HC107.T4 P47 **ISSN** 0898-8420
DD 330.9764/005 US
PERSPECTIVE (AUSTIN, TEX.). (PERSPECTIVE.). [Perspective]. **VFOAT** Texas Perspective. (1988)-. English. Twelve times a year. $175.00. Texas Perspectives Inc., 612 Brazos Street, Suite 210, Austin TX 78701. **Tel** (800)365-6581, FAX (512)472-6537. **ED** Jon E. Hockenyos (editor's telephone: (512)328-8300). **Circ:** 200.
Desc: Economic trends that affect Texas and its major urban areas.

LC HC **ISSN** 0831-3571
DD 330.971/0646 CN
PERSPECTIVES ECONOMIQUES (TORONTO). (PERSPECTIVES ECONOMIQUES : INTERNATIONALES, NATIONALES, REGIONALES, INDUSTRIELLES.). [Perspect. econ.]. **Added/Corp** Banque de Nouvelle-Ecosse. Service des Etudes Economiques. (Mar. 1983)-. Periodical. French. Two times a year. Limited free distribution. Banque de Nouvelle-Ecosse, 44 King Street West, Toronto Ontario M5H 1H1 Canada.
Ind/Abst Can. Period. Index (19??-); Repere (1979-1986).

UK
Pr Rev.
PERSPECTIVES ON THE HISTORY OF ECONOMIC THOUGHT. (1989)-. Monographic series. English. One time a year. Price varies per volume. Edward Elgar, 8 Lansdown Place, Cheltenham, Gloucestershire GL50 2HU United Kingdom. **Tel** 011 44 1242 226934, FAX 011 44 1242 262111. **(Subscription address:** Ashgate Publishing Company / US, Old Post Road, Brookfield VT 05036-9704. **Tel** (800)535-9544, (802)276-3162, FAX (802)276-3837.)

LC HC226 .P427
DD 330.985/005 PE
PERUVIAN QUARTERLY REPORT. **Added/Corp** Banco de Credito de Peru. New York Branch. **VFOAT** PQR; P.Q.R. (19??)-. Periodical. English. Four times a year. Free on request. Banco de Credito del Peru, Av Centenario 156, La Molina Lima Peru.

LC HC186 .P47 **ISSN** 0100-0551
DD 338.9 BL
PESQUISA E PLANEJAMENTO ECONOMICO (RIO DE JANEIRO). (PESQUISA E PLANEJAMENTO ECONOMICO.). [Pesqui. planej. econ.]. **Added/Corp** Instituto de Planejamento Economico e Social. Vol. 2 No. 1 (June 1972)-. Periodical. Portuguese. Three times a year (Apr., Aug., Dec.). $25.00 (surface mail), $40.00 (airmail). IPEA Servicio Editorial / Instituto de Pesquisa Economica y Aplicada, Avenue P Antonio Carlos 51-14 Andar, CP 2672, 20020 010 Rio de Janeiro Brazil. **Tel** 011 55 21 2925141 ext. 1118, FAX 011 55 21 2401920. **ED** Lauro Albrecht Ramos. Index available. **Bk Rev. Ad Acc.** ***Continues*** *Pesquisa e Planejamento.*
Desc: Articles on research and studies in economic and social planning.
Ind/Abst Econ. Lit. Index (19??-); Hisp. Am. Period. Index, HAPI; Int. Bibliogr. Sociol.; J. Econ. Lit.; LABORDOC; PAIS Int. Print (1991-).

US
PETER PAUL, INC. ANNUAL REPORT. **Main/Corp** Peter Paul, Inc. (19??)-. English. One time a year. Peter Paul Inc, New Haven Road, Naugatuck CT 06770.

LC HF5001 **ISSN** 1048-3411
DD 650 US
TITLE CHANGE
PETERSON'S JOB OPPORTUNITIES FOR BUSINESS AND LIBERAL ARTS GRADUATES. [Peterson's job oppor. bus. lib. arts grad.]. **Added/Corp** Peterson's Guides, Inc. **VFOAT** Job Opportunities for Business and Liberal Arts Graduates. 7th Ed. (1991)-(1993). Periodical. English. Peterson's Guides, 202 Carnegie Center, Department 2342, PO Box 2123, Princeton NJ 08543-2123. **Tel** (609)243-9111, (800)338-3282, FAX (609)243-9150, (609)452-0966. ***Continues*** *Peterson's Business and Management Jobs, 0894-9433.* ***Continued by*** *Peterson's Job Opportunities in Business.*

ISSN 0956-0661
UK
CODEN PBNEEH
PHARMACEUTICAL BUSINESS NEWS. See Pharmacy and Pharmacology.

ISSN 0744-3587
US
CCC
PHILADELPHIA BUSINESS JOURNAL. [Philadelphia bus. j.]. Vol. 1, No. 1 (Mar. 29-Apr. 4, 1982)-. Periodical. English. One time a week. $62.00. Philadelphia Business Journal, 400 Market Street, Suite 300, Philadelphia PA 19106. **Tel** (215)238-5103. **ED** Brian P. Sullivan. **Circ:** 11,500. available on an online database (files 635,648/Full-Text) from DIALOG. Documents available from UMI Article Clearinghouse.
Desc: Serves the general business information needs or qualified recipients in Philadelphia and it's surrounding countries.
Ind/Abst Acad. Search; Bus. Dateline; Bus. Index (1985-1990); Bus. Source Plus; EP Collect.; Gen. BusinessFile (1985-1990); Gen. Period. Index (1985-); Homework Help.; INFO-SOUTH Abstr.; Mag. Search; MasterFile FullTEXT 1000; MasterFile FullTEXT 350; MasterFile FullTEXT 650; MasterFile FullTEXT (July 1993-); OCLC; PROMT; Telebase; Trade Ind. ASAP [Full Txt.]; Trade Ind. Index [Full Txt.].

LC HC451 .P53316 **ISSN** 0031-7500
DD 330 PH
PHILIPPINE ECONOMIC JOURNAL, THE. [Philipp. econ. j.]. **Added/Corp** Philippine Economic Society. Vol. 1 (1962)-. Periodical. English. Four times a year. $35.00. PSSC Central Subscription Service, PO Box 205 UP Diliman, Quezon City 1101 Philippines. **Tel** 011 63 2 9229621. **ED** Mahar K. Mangahas. **Bk Rev. Ad Acc. Circ:** 1,000.
Desc: Prints articles and original studies by economists in relation to the Philippines.
Ind/Abst Contents Recent Econ. J.; Econ. Lit. Index (-199?); Index Philip. Period. (-199?); J. Econ. Lit.

ISSN 0379-2870
US
PHILIPPINE LETTER, THE. No. 1, (May 1978)-. Periodical. English. Twenty-six times a year. $120.00. Asia Letter Group, GPO Box 10874, Central Hong Kong. **Tel** 011 852 25262950, FAX 011 852 25267131, telex 61166. **ED** Charles R Smith. **Bk Rev.** ctrl circ.
Desc: An analysis of political and economical developments in the Philippines. Published for those doing business in the Philippines.

LC HC451 .P564 **ISSN** 0115-9011
DD 330.9599/005 PH
PHILIPPINE REVIEW OF ECONOMICS & BUSINESS, THE. [Philipp. rev. econ. bus.]. **VFOAT** Philippine Review of Economics and Business. (19??)-. Periodical. English. Two times a year (June & Dec.). $20.00. College of Business Administration / University of the Philippines, Quezon City D55 Philippines. ***Continues*** *Philippine Review of Business and Economics, 0031-7780.*
Ind/Abst Econ. Lit. Index; J. Econ. Lit.

LC HA1821 .N37a
DD 315.99 PH
PHILIPPINE STATISTICAL YEARBOOK. **Added/Corp** Philippines. National Economic and Development Authority. Philippines. National Statistical Coordination Board. (1977)-. Statistical Publication. English. One time a year. $52.00. National Economic and Development Authority, PO Box 419, Greenhills Metro Manila Philippines. **Tel** 011 63 2 6313281. **Circ:** 1,000. ***Continues*** *NEDA Statistical Yearbook of the Philippines.*
Desc: Complies with major economic and social statistical information produced by the government agencies and international organizations.

LC PN
DD 070.4 US
PIERCE COUNTY BUSINESS EXAMINER. See Newspapers.

ISSN 0883-7910
US
CCC
CODEN PBTJES
PITTSBURGH BUSINESS TIMES-JOURNAL. **VFOAT** Pittsburgh Business Times Journal. Vol. 4, No. 32 (April 1-7, 1985)-. Periodical. English. One time a week. $60.00. Pittsburgh Business Weekly Co., 2313 East Carson Street, Suite 200, Pittsburgh PA 15203. **Tel** (412)481-6397, FAX (412)481-9956. **ED** Paul Furiga. **Ad Acc, Adv Mgr:** Rick Linder, **Tel** (412)481-6397. **Circ:** 12,250. available on an online database (file 635/Full-Text) from DIALOG; available on CD-ROM from Business Dateline. Documents available from UMI Article Clearinghouse. ***Formed by the union of*** *Pittsburgh Business Times, 0279-330X* ***and*** *Pittsburgh Business Journal, 0279-2915.*
Desc: The main source of local and regional business news and information. It provides coverage of events, developments and trends of the Greater Pittsburgh market.
Ind/Abst Bus. Dateline; Bus. Index (1985-1986); Gen. BusinessFile (1985-1986); Gen. Period. Index (1985-1986); MasterFile FullTEXT (July 1993-).

LC HC79.D5 P53 **ISSN** 0191-2933
DD 330 US
CCC
PLANTS, SITES & PARKS. **VFOAT** Plants, Sites, and Parks. (1974)-. Trade Publication. English. Six times a year. $30.00. Billboard Publications Inc., 1515 Broadway Billboard, New York NY 10036. **Tel** (212)764-7300, FAX (305)755-7048, telex WU TWX 710-581-6279. **ED** Kathleen Dempsey. **Ad Acc. Circ:** 31,000 (ctrl). available on microfilm and microfiche from University Microfilms International (UMI); available on an online database (files 16/Full-Text) from DIALOG.
Desc: Serves the field of site and office location, facility planning, plant expansion for manufacturers, corporations, wholesalers, distributors and service organizations of all kinds.

ISSN 0882-8768
US
PLAY IT SAFE. **Added/Corp** National Foremen's Institute. (1???)-. Periodical. English. Twelve times a year. $12.36. Bureau of Business Practice, 24 Rope Ferry Road, Waterford CT 06386. **Tel** (800)243-0876, (203)442-4365, (800)876-9105, FAX (203)443-1123.

Business and Economics

DD 332
ISSN 1063-679X
US
POLAND BUSINESS REPORT. [Pol.bus. rep.]. (1992)-. Periodical. English. Twelve times a year. $330.00. Double Eagle Publishing, 200 West 858th Street, Suite 12-I, New York NY 10024-3371.

LC TA4 .O2
ISSN 0032-3004
PL
CODEN PTEAAE
POLISH TECHNICAL AND ECONOMIC ABSTRACTS. [Pol. tech. econ. abstr.]. **Added/Corp** Centralny Instytut Informacji Naukowo-Technicznej i Ekonomicznej (Poland). No. 1 (1968)-. Periodical. English. Four times a year. $40.00. (**Subscription address:** Ars Polona-Ruch, PO Box 1001, Krakowskie Przedmiescie 7, 00-068 Warsaw Poland. **Tel** 011 48 22 261201.) Index available in last issue of volume--attached. *Formed by the union of* Obzor Polskoi Ekonomicheskoi Literatury *and* Obzor Polskoi Tekhnicheskoi Literatury.
Desc: Covers engineering, economics and technology.
Ind/Abst Ceram. Abstr.; Coal Abstr.; Concr. Abstr.; Fluid Abstr., Civil Eng.; Fluid Abstr. Proc. Eng.; FLUIDEX (1973-); World Surf. Coat. Abstr.

LC HB7 .P6
IT
POLITICA ECONOMICA. Vol. 1, No. 1 (April 1985)-. Periodical. Italian (summaries and/or abstracts in English). Three times a year. L77660. Societa Editrice il Mulino, Strada Maggiore 37, 40125 Bologna Italy. **Tel** 011 39 51 256011, FAX 011 39 51 256034.
Ind/Abst Econ. Lit. Index; J. Econ. Lit. (1985-); PAIS Int. Print.

LC HC431 .P6
ISSN 0971-2097
DD 330
II
POLITICAL ECONOMY JOURNAL OF INDIA : A QUARTERLY JOURNAL OF THE CENTRE FOR INDIAN DEVELOPMENT STUDIES. **Added/Corp** Centre for Indian Development Studies. Vol. 1, Issues 1 & 2 (Jan.-June 1992)-. Periodical. English. Four times a year. $30.00. Centre for Indian Development Studies, Chandigarh India. (**Subscription address:** Prints India, 11 Darya Ganj, New Delhi 110002 India. **Tel** 011 91 11 3268645, FAX 011 91 11 3275542, telex 31-61087 PRIN-IN.)

DD 330
ISSN 0887-7629
US
CCC
POLITICAL RISK SERVICES LETTER. [Polit. risk serv. lett.]. **Added/Corp** Frost & Sullivan. Political Risk Services. (198?)-. Newsletter. English. Twelve times a year. $395.00. Political Risk Services, 6320 Fly Road, Suite 102, PO Box 248, East Syracuse NY 13057-0248. **Tel** (315)431-0511, FAX (315)431-0200. **ED** William D. Coplin and Michael K. O'Leary. *Continues* F & S Political Risk Letter.
Desc: Summary of economic and political developments. Covers world events and how they impact international business in specific countries.
Ind/Abst PTS Newsl. Database [Full Txt.].

LC HB9 .P57
ISSN 0032-3233
XR
Pr Rev.
POLITIKA EKONOMIE. **Added/Corp** Ekonomicky Ustav CSAV. Vol. 1 (1953)-. Periodical. Czech (summaries and/or abstracts in English, French and Russian; table of contents in English and Russian). Six times a year. DM222.00. Academia, Publishing House of the Czechoslovak Academy of Sciences, Vodickova 40, PO Box 896, 112 29 Prague 1, Czech Republic. **Tel** 011 42 2 245117. (**Subscription address:** Kubon & Sagner, ABT Zeitschriftenimport, D 80328 Munich Germany. **Tel** 011 49 89 54218130.) **ED** Jiri Dvorak. Index available. **Bk Rev**. **Circ:** 4,200. Documents available from The Genuine Article.
Desc: A theoretical journal publishing results of and discussions in the field of economics science.
Ind/Abst Res. Alert [Full Cov.]; Soc. Sci. Cit. Index [Full Cov.].

LC HD9993.S953 U55
ISSN 0194-5351
DD 338.4/769089
US
POOL & SPA NEWS. **VAT** Pool and Spa News. Vol. 18, No. 6 (Mar. 19, 1979)-. Trade Publication. English. Twenty-four times a year. $17.97. Leisure Publishing Company, 3923 West 6th Street, Los Angeles CA 90020. **Tel** (213)385-3926, FAX (213)383-1152. **ED** Jules Field. **Bk Rev**. **Ad Acc**. **Circ:** 12,453. *Continues* Pool News.
Desc: Magazine for the pool and spa industry.

US
POOR'S FISCAL VOLUME : GOVERNMENTS, MUNICIPALS, BANKS, INSURANCE COMPANIES, REAL ESTATE, MORTGAGE AND FINANCE COMPANIES, INVESTMENT TRUSTS. (1936)-. English. Standard & Poor's Corporation, (A Division of McGraw-Hill, Inc.), 25 Broadway, New York NY 10004. **Tel** (212)208-8775, (800)221-5277. *Continues* Poor's Bank, Government and Municipal Volume.

LC HD
ISSN 1064-6337
DD 338
US
●**PORTABLE MBA EXECUTIVE SERVICE, THE.** [Portable MBA exec. serv.]. Vol. 1, Issue 1 (Winter 1992/1993)-. Periodical. English. Four times a year. $39.95. John Wiley & Sons, Inc., 605 Third Avenue, New York NY 10158-0012. **Tel** (212)850-6000, (212)850-6645, FAX (212)850-6088, telex 12-7063. (**Subscription address:** John Wiley & Sons / UK, Baffins Lane, Chichester, West Sussex PO19 1UD United Kingdom. **Tel** 011 44 1243 779777, FAX 011 44 243 776128, telex 86290 WIBOOKG.)

LC HD2346.S63 P67
SA
PORTFOLIO OF BLACK BUSINESS IN SOUTH AFRICA. **VFOAT** Portfolio of Black Business. (1990)-. English. One time a year. $18.64. Portfolio of Black Businesses in South Africa, PO Box 7485, Johannesburg 2000 South Africa. **Tel** 011 27 11 8868002, FAX 011 27 11 8869933.

LC HC79.D4 P6
ISSN 1065-0075
DD 330
US
POSITIVE ALTERNATIVES. (POSITIVE ALTERNATIVES : A PUBLICATION OF THE CENTER FOR ECONOMIC CONVERSION.). [Posit. altern.]. **Added/Corp** Center for Economic Conversion (Calif.). Vol. 1, No. 1 (Fall 1990)-. Periodical. English. Four times a year (Jan., Apr., July, Oct.). $35.00. Center Economic Conversion, 222 View Street, Suite C, Mountain View CA 94041-1344. **Tel** (415)968-8798. *Continues* Plowshare Press.
Desc: The voice of the conversion movement, our publication covers current activities, news analysis, commentaries, interviews on a wide range of conversion related topics.

US
POSITIVE IMPACT. (19??)-. Periodical. English. Twelve times a year. $132.00. Resort Impression Ltd., PO Box 4018, Evergreen CO 80439. **Tel** (303)670-1001. **ED** John Harris. **Bk Rev**, (Qty: 12). **Circ:** 1,200. available on diskette.
Desc: Collection of articles on customer services and customer satisfaction.

UK
POST NEWS. English. Twelve times a year. $398.00. Post News, Stoke Sub Hamdon, Somerset TA14 6BR United Kingdom. **Tel** 0935 88 1245, FAX 0935 88 1860.
Ind/Abst Comput. Bus. (19??-).

LC HC335 .S588
ISSN 1060-586X
DD 330.947/005
US
CCC
POST-SOVIET AFFAIRS. [Post-Sov. aff.]. **Added/Corp** Joint Committee on Soviet Studies (U.S.). **VAT** Post Soviet affairs. (1992)-. Periodical. English. Four times a year. $209.00. V. H. Winston & Sons Inc., 7961 Eastern Avenue, Suite 202A, Silver Spring MD 20910. **Tel** (301)587-3356. (**Subscription address:** Bellwether Publishing, Ltd, 8640 Guilford Road, Suite 200, Columbia MD 21046. **Tel** (410)290-3870.) **ED** George Breslauer, Center for Slavic and East European Studies, University of California, Berkeley, CA 94720. Index available (bound in Oct/Dec issue). **Circ:** 550. *Continues* Soviet Economy (Silver Spring, Md.), 0882-6994.
Desc: Economic and political transitions of the independent states of the former Soviet Union.
Ind/Abst Curr. Contents Soc. Behav. Sci.; J. Econ. Lit.; Soc. Sci. Cit. Index [Full Cov.].

DD 338
ISSN 0883-3036
US
PRACTICE BUILDER, THE. [Prac. build.]. (Aug. 1985)-. Periodical. English. Eleven times a year. $89.00 (one-year); $149.00 (two-year). Evergreen Group, 2755 Bristol Street, Suite 100, Costa Mesa CA 92626-5909. **Tel** (714)545-8900, FAX (714)662-1002. **ED** Alan Bernstein. **Circ:** 11,000 (ctrl).
Desc: News and information on professional practice marketing of medical, dentists, attorneys, CPA's and MD's.

DD 332
ISSN 1061-2084
US
PRACTITIONERS 1120S DESKBOOK. [Pract. 1120S deskb.]. **VFOAT** Practitioners Eleven Twenty S Deskbook. 1st ed. (1992)-. Periodical. English. Practitioners Publishing Company, PO Box 966, Fort Worth TX 76101-0966. **Tel** (800)332-3709.

LC HC
ISSN 1210-0455
DD 330
XR
PRAGUE ECONOMIC PAPERS. **Added/Corp** Ekonomicky Ustav CSAV. **VFOAT** PEP. (Mar. 1992)-. Periodical. English. Four times a year. $116.68. (**Subscription address:** Kubon & Sagner, ABT Zeitschriftenimport, D 80328 Munich Germany. **Tel** 011 49 89 54218130.) *Continues* Czechoslovak Economic Papers.

DD 330.9712
ISSN 1188-2255
CN
CEASED
PRAIRIE PROGRESS NEWSLETTER. [Prairie prog. newsl.]. **VFOAT** Progress Newsletter. (1991)-Vol. 3 No. 2 (19??). Periodical. English. Westarc Group Inc., Brandon University, 247 18th Street, Brandon Manitoba R7A 5A6 Canada. **Tel** (204)729-3440, FAX (204)729-9090. **Circ:** 2,000 (ctrl).

LC HF5001 .P66
IT
PRATICA AZIENDALE. Vol. 1, (Sept. 1978)-. Periodical. Italian. Twelve times a year. L135570. Pirola Editore, CP 10444, Via Parabiago 19, 20151 Milan Italy. **Tel** 011 39 2 3022888. **ED** Aldo Lanza. **Ad Acc**, **Adv Mgr Tel** 02 3022.1. **Circ:** 3,500.

ISSN 0270-4536
US
CCC
TITLE CHANGE
PREDICASTS F & S INDEX EUROPE. [Predicasts F&S index Eur.]. **Added/Corp** Predicasts, Inc. **VFOAT** Predicasts F and S Index Europe; F & S Index Europe; F&S Index Europe. Vol. 3, No. 4 (June 1980)-(1993). English. Predicasts Inc., A Ziff Communications Company, 11001 Cedar Avenue, Cleveland OH 44106. **Tel** (800)321-6388, (216)795-3000, FAX (216)229-9944, telex 985 604. *Continues in part* F & S Index Europe, 0199-5219. *Continued by* F&S Index Europe.

ISSN 0270-4528
US
CCC
TITLE CHANGE
PREDICASTS F & S INDEX INTERNATIONAL. See Business and Economics-Abstracting, Bibliographies and Statistics.

ISSN 0270-4544
US
CCC
TITLE CHANGE
PREDICASTS F & S INDEX UNITED STATES. [Predicasts F&S index U. S.]. **Added/Corp** Predicasts, Inc. **VFOAT** Predicasts F and S Index United States; Predicasts Funk and Scott Index United States; F & S Index United States. **VAT** Predicasts Funk and Scott Index United States. (198?)-(19??). Periodical. English. Predicasts Inc., A Ziff Communications Company, 11001 Cedar Avenue, Cleveland OH 44106. **Tel** (800)321-6388, (216)795-3000, FAX (216)229-9944, telex 985 604. *Continues* Predicasts F & S Index of Corporations and Industries, 0270-4560. *Continued by* F&S Index United States.
Desc: Covers broad business and economic data, product, industry, company and market activities reported in business publications.

LC HA1320.B2 A32 HD7029
DD 314.3
GW
PREISE, LOEHNE, WIRTSCHAFTSRECHNUNGEN. See Business and Economics-Abstracting, Bibliographies and Statistics.

LC HB235.G3 G47a
GW
PREISE. REIHE 3, PREISINDEX FUER DEN WARENEINGANG DES PRODUZIERENDEN GEWERBES / STATISTISCHES BUNDESAMT. **Added/Corp** Germany. Statistisches Bundesamt. **VFOAT** Preisindex fuer den Wareneingang des Produzierenden Gewerbes; Fachserie 17. (1990)-. German. Metzler Poeschel Verlag Veroeffen, Statist Bundesamt Kernerstr 43, D-70182 Stuttgart Germany. **Tel** 011 49 7071 935350. (**Subscription address:** Metzler Poeschel H Leins GmbH, Postfach 1152, D 72125 Kusterdingen Germany. **Tel** 011 49 7071 935350.) *Continues* Germany (West). Statistisches Bundesamt. Preise. Reihe 3: Index der Grundstoffpreise.

DD 658
ISSN 1041-9780
US
CCC
TITLE CHANGE
PRESENTATION PRODUCTS MAGAZINE. [Present. prod. mag.]. (1988)-(199?)-. Periodical. English. Presentation Products Magazine, 23410 Civic Center Way / E-10, Malibu CA 90265. **Tel** (310)456-2283, FAX (310)456-8686. **ED** Larry Tuck. Index available. **Ad Acc**, **Adv Mgr:** Bill Slapin, **Tel** (310)456-2283. **Circ:** 56,000 (ctrl). *Continued by* Presentation Products, 1070-6089.
Desc: Targeted toward professionals who create and deliver presentations.

IT
PREVISIONI DELL ECONOMIA ITALIANA. Italian. Servizio Italiano Pubblicazioni International, Viale Pasteur 6, 00144 Rome Italy. **Tel** 011 39 6 5920509, telex 614567 SIPIRM I.

Business and Economics

LC HD2845 .P7   **ISSN** 1352-8157
UK
● **PRICE WATERHOUSE CORPORATE REGISTER. Added/Corp** Price Waterhouse (Firm). **VFOAT** Corporate Register. (March 1995)-. Periodical. English. Six times a year. $393.57. Hemmington Scott Publishing Ltd, 25-31 Whiskin Street, City Innovation Centre, London EC1R 0BP United Kingdom. **Tel** 011 44 171 2787769, FAX 011 44 171 2789808. **Continues** Arthur Andersen Corporate Register.

ISSN 1078-4489
US
● **PRICING STATISTICS SOURCEBOOK.** (1994)-. Statistical Publication. English. One time a year. $242.00. PennWell Publishing Company, 1421 South Sheridan, PO Box 1260, Tulsa OK 74101. **Tel** (918)835-3161, (800)331-4463, FAX (918)831-9497.

LC HC   **ISSN** 0079-5240
US
PRINCETON STUDIES IN MATHEMATICAL ECONOMICS. No. 1 (1964)-. Monographic series. English. Irregular. Price varies per volume. Princeton University Press, 41 William Street, Princeton NJ 08540. **Tel** (609)258-4900.
Ind/Abst Math. Rev.

LC HC446 .P73
DD 300/.9598   IO
PRISMA. Added/Corp Lembaga Penelitian, Pendidikan dan Penerangan Ekonomi dan Sosial. Vol. 1 (May 1975)-. Periodical. English (summaries and/or abstracts in French and German). Four times a year. Rp7,000 Indonesia; $26.00 US; $18.00 Asia and Australia; $22.00 Europe. Institute for Economic and Social Research Education and Information (LP3ES), Jalan S Parman 81, PO Box 75, Jakarta 11420 Indonesia. **Tel** 011 62 21 5663525. **ED** Ismid Hadad, Aswab Mahasin. Index available. **Bk Rev. Ad Acc. Circ:** 3,000.
Desc: Contains popularly presented scientific articles, summaries of research and survey reports, or original ideas on social and economic problems.

ISSN 1070-0536
US
● **PRIVACY & AMERICAN BUSINESS. Added/Corp** Center for Sociological Research. **VFOAT** Privacy and American Business. (1993)-. Periodical. English. Six times a year (plus special supplements). $375.00. Privacy & American Business, Center for Social and Legal Research, Two University Plaza, Suite 414, Hackensack NJ 07601. **Tel** (201)996-1154, FAX (201)996-1883. **ED** Alan. F. Westin, Robert R. Belair and Lorrie Sherwood (managing editor). **Bk Rev.**
Desc: Resource to help cope with the privacy challenges ahead. Features surveys, articles, reviews, columns, legislative information, industry-association news, interviews, model codes and policies, and how-to insights. New consumer privacy codes are, also, a regular feature.

ISSN 0953-6795
DD 342.2858   UK
PRIVACY LAWS & BUSINESS. See Law.

UK
Pr Rev.
PRIVATE COMPANY SECRETARY'S MANUAL. See Occupations and Careers.

US
PRIVATE PLACEMENT REPORTER. (19??)-. English. Irregular (48 issues). $705.00. American Banker, Concourse Level, 1 State Street Plaza, New York NY 10004. **Tel** (212)803-8200, (800)221-1809, FAX (212)943-6256, (212)843-9598. **(Subscription address:** American Banker / Newletter Division, PO Box 28315, Washington DC 20038. **Tel** (800)733-4371, (202)347-2665.) available on an online database (files 16,636/Full-Text) from DIALOG.
Ind/Abst PTS Newsl. Database [Full Txt.].

IT
Pr Rev.
PROBLEMI DI GESTIONE. Italian. Six times a year. free. Formez, Mostra Oltremare Pal Congressi, 80125 Naples Italy. **Tel** FAX 081 7256111, telex 615467. **Bk Rev. Ad Acc. Circ:** 6,600.
Desc: Selection and translation in italian language from foreign reviews in management science.

UK
PROBLEMS OF COMMUNISM (AND CAPITALISM). See Political Science-Socialism, Communism, Anarchism, Utopianism.

LC HC10 .P753
DD 330.9/47/085   **ISSN** 1061-1991
US
CCC
PROBLEMS OF ECONOMIC TRANSITION. [Probl. econ. transit.]. Vol. 35, No. 1 (May 1992)-. Periodical. English (translations available in Russian). Twelve times a year. $725.00. M. E. Sharpe Inc., 80 Business Park Drive, Armonk NY 10504. **Tel** (914)273-1800, (800)541-6563, FAX (914)273-2106. Documents available from The Genuine Article.

Continues Problems of Economics, 0032-9436.
Ind/Abst Curr. Cit.; Curr. Contents Soc. Behav. Sci.; Econ. Lit. Index; PAIS Int. Print; Res. Alert [Full Cov.]; Soc. Sci. Cit. Index [Full Cov.].

LC HB9 .P74   **ISSN** 0079-578X
PL
PROBLEMY EKONOMICZNE. Added/Corp Polskie Towarzystwo Ekonomiczne. Akademia Ekonomiczna w Krakowie. (19??)-. Periodical. Polish (summaries and/or abstracts in English, German and Russian). Four times a year. $40.00. **(Subscription address:** Ars Polona-Ruch, PO Box 1001, Krakowskie Przedmiescie 7, 00-068 Warsaw Poland. **Tel** 011 48 22 261201.)

LC HF5548.8 .P688
RU
PROBLEMY INDUSTRIALNOI PSIKHOLOGII. Added/Corp Yaroslavl, Russia (City). Universitet. Vol.4 (1972)-. Periodical. Russian. Yaroslav State University / Iaroslav, Ulitsa Sovetskaia 14, Iaroslavl Russia. **Tel** 0852 22 24 56, FAX 0852 22 52 32, telex 217271.

US
PROCEEDINGS, ... INTERNATIONAL SYMPOSIUM ON PACIFIC ASIAN BUSINESS ... . (1991)-. Proceedings. English. One time a year. $10.00. Pacific Asian Management Institute, University of Hawaii, 2404 Maile Way C202, Honolulu HI 96822. **Tel** (808)956-8041, FAX (808)956-9685.

ISSN 0711-0235
DD 658.5/7   CN
PROCEEDINGS OF INNOVATION CANADA INC. [Proc. Innov. Can. Inc.]. **Added/Corp** Innovation Canada. (1979)-. Proceedings. English. One time a year. 52.02Can$. Innovation Canada Inc, 533 Arbor Road, Mississauga Ontario L5G 2J6 Canada. **Tel** (416)244-0311, (416)278-8848, FAX (514)244-0311. **ED** W. O. Munns and W. F. M. Brown. Index Bound in First Issue. cum. index. **Ad Acc. Circ:** 100. **Continues** Innovation Canada Seminar. Proceedings of the Innovation Canada Seminar., 0708-3416.

ISSN 0278-2375
US
PROCEEDINGS OF THE ... ANNUAL CONFERENCE OF THE ASSOCIATION FOR BUSINESS SIMULATION AND EXPERIENTIAL LEARNING. [Proc. annu. conf. Assoc. Bus. Simul. Exp. Learn.]. **Main/Conf** Association for Business Simulation and Experiential Learning. Conference. **Main/Corp** Association for Business Simulation and Experiential Learning. Conference. **Added/Corp** Association for Business Simulation and Experiential Learning. **VFOAT** Developments in Business Simulation and Experiential Exercises. 4th (1977)-. Proceedings. English. One time a year. University of Louisville School of Business, Louisville KY 40208. **Continues** Proceedings of the International ABSEL Conference.

US
PROCEEDINGS OF THE ... ANNUAL INTERNATIONAL SYMPOSIUM ON PACIFIC ASIAN BUSINESS -- DEVELOPMENTS IN PACIFIC ASIAN BUSINESS: EDUCATION AND RESEARCH. (1989)-. Proceedings. English. One time a year. $10.00. Pacific Asian Management Institute, University of Hawaii, 2404 Maile Way C202, Honolulu HI 96822. **Tel** (808)956-8041, FAX (808)956-9685.

US
PROCEEDINGS OF THE NATIONAL CONFERENCE ON BUSINESS ETHICS. Main/Conf National Conference on Business Ethics. **Added/Corp** Bentley College of Accounting and Finance, Boston. Center for Business Ethics. 1st (1977)-. Proceedings. English. Irregular (Publishes every 1 1/2 years). $59.95. Center for Business Ethics, Beaver & Forest Street, Bentley College, Waltham MA 02154. **Tel** (617)891-2981.

LC HC415.15.A1 P76 K1 .N475   **ISSN** 0254-9379
DD 330   LE
PROCHE-ORIENT, ETUDES ECONOMIQUES. [P.-O. etud. econ.]. **Added/Corp** Universite Saint-Joseph (Beirut, Lebanon). Faculte de Droit et des Sciences Economiques. Universite Saint-Joseph (Beirut, Lebanon). Faculte de Sciences Economiques et de Gestion des Entreprises. Universite Saint-Joseph (Beirut, Lebanon). Faculte de Sciences Economiques. **VFOAT** Sharq al-Adna, Dirasat fi al-Iqtisad; Sharq al-Adna, Dirasat fi al-Qanun. (1967)-. Periodical. French. Four times a year. Faculte de Sciences Economiques de l'Universite Saint-Joseph, Rue Huvelin, BP 293, Beirut Lebanon.
Ind/Abst Int. Labour Doc.

ISSN 0306-1922
UK
PROCUREMENT WEEKLY. [Procure. Wkly.]. (1973)-. Trade Publication. English. One time a week. $102.67. Chartered Institute of Purchasing and Supply, Easton House, Easton on the Hill, Stamford Lincolnshire PE9 3NZ United Kingdom. **Tel** 011 44 1780 56777, FAX 011 44 1780 51610, telex 33251. **Continues** Purchasing Bulletin, 0033-4456.

ISSN 1048-1877
DD 791   US
PRODUCCION Y DISTRIBUCION. (PRODUCCION Y DISTRIBUCION : THE HISPANIC ENTERTAINMENT BUSINESS MAGAZINE.). [Prod. distrib.]. Vol. 1, No. 3 (Mar.-Apr. 1990)-. Periodical. Spanish (English). Six times a year. $15.00 US and Canada. Produccion Editorial, 13300 Southwest 95th Avenue, Miami FL 33176. **Tel** (305)595-3134. **Continues** Produccion (Miami, Fla.), 1048-1869.

UK
PRODUCER PRICE INDICES. MM22. Trade Publication. English. Twelve times a year. £100.00. Her Majesty's Stationery Office, 51 Nine Elms Lane, London SW8 5DR United Kingdom. **Tel** 011 44 171 8738459, 011 44 171 8738499, FAX 011 44 171 8738499, 011 44 171 8738456, telex 297138. **(Subscription address:** Her Majesty's Stationery Office, PO Box 276, Public Centre, London SW8 5DT United Kingdom. **Tel** 011 44 171 8738499, 011 44 171 8738456.)

LC WMLC 93/412   **ISSN** 0217-0205
SI
PRODUCTIVITY DIGEST. Added/Corp Singapore. National Productivity Board. National Productivity Association (Singapore). (198?)-. Periodical. English. Twelve times a year. $55.00. National Productivity Board, 2 Bukit Merah Central, NPB Building, Singapore 0315 Singapore. **Tel** 011 65 2793600. **ED** Ms Lily Chang, (phone: 011 65 2793625). **Ad Acc, Adv Mgr:** JM Publishing Consultants, **Tel** 7431058. **Circ:** 7,500.

II
PRODUCTIVITY NEWS. Added/Corp National Productivity Council of India. Vol. 1 (1959)-. Periodical. English. Twelve times a year. $24.00. National Productivity Council, Productivity House, Lodi Road, New Delhi 110003 India. **(Subscription address:** Prints India, 11 Darya Ganj, New Delhi 110002 India. **Tel** 011 91 11 3268645, FAX 011 91 11 3275542, telex 31-61087 PRIN-IN.)

LC BJ1725 .P75   **ISSN** 1063-6579
DD 174/.05   US
PROFESSIONAL ETHICS (GAINESVILLE, FLA.). See Ethics.

ISSN 1064-2668
US
PROFESSIONAL VCR REPAIR TRAINING MANUAL AND BUSINESS PLAN, THE. See Home Economics-Household Appliances.

ISSN 0162-5241
US
PROFILE (OMAHA). (PROFILE.). **Added/Corp** Greater Omaha Chamber of Commerce. (19??)-. Periodical. English. Twenty-four times a year. Omaha Chamber of Commerce, 1301 Harney, Omaha NE 68102. **Tel** (402)346-5000, FAX (402)346-7050. **ED** Vicki Krecek. **Ad Acc. Circ:** 4,000 (ctrl).
Desc: General business news concentrating on information of interest to or about businesses in the Omaha area.

ISSN 1071-3808
DD 330   US
PROFILE (SOUTH PORTLAND, ME.). (PROFILE : SOUTHERN MAINE'S BUSINESS MAGAZINE.). [Profile]. (1992)-. Periodical. English. Twelve times a year. $24.00. Profile Magazine, 704 Broadway, South Portland ME 04106. **Tel** (207)761-7006. **ED** Catherine & Mark Girr. **Ad Acc. Circ:** 7,000 (ctrl).
Desc: Covers a wide range of business issues.

ISSN 0229-348X
DD 338.7/09714   CN
PROFILS D'ENTREPRISES QUEBECOISES. [Profils entrep. que.]. 1st. Ed. (1980)-. French. One time a year. Editions L'Informateur, C P 124, Succursdale Beaubien, Montreal Quebec H2G 3C8 Canada.

ISSN 1061-9194
DD 330   US
SUSPENDED
PROFIT (ARMONK, N.Y.). (PROFIT: INFORMATION TECHNOLOGY FOR ENTREPRENEURS.). [Profit]. **Added/Corp** International Business Machines Corporation. (1992)-Suspended with Vol. 3, No. 6 (Dec. 1994). Periodical. English. Six times a

Business and Economics

year (Jan., Mar., May, July, Sept., Nov.). $17.00. IBM Magazines, 590 Madison Avenue, 32nd Floor, New York NY 10022. **Tel** (212)745-6429, FAX (212)745-7984. **ED** Timothy Nolan. **Ad Acc, Adv Mgr:** M. Feinberg. **Circ:** 200,000 (ctrl).

DD 658

ISSN 0889-9967
US
CCC
CEASED

PROFIT-BUILDING STRATEGIES FOR BUSINESS OWNERS. [Profit-build. strateg. bus. own.]. **VFOAT** Profit Building Strategies for Business Owners; PBS. Vol. 16, No. 8 (Aug. 1986)-(May 1993). Periodical. English. The Professional Report, 81 Montgomery Street, Scarsdale NY 10583. **Tel** (914)472-0366. available on microfilm and microfiche from University Microfilms International (UMI); available on an online database (files 15,648/Full-Text) from DIALOG. **Continues** Professional Report (Scarsdale, N.Y.), 0890-9288.
Ind/Abst Account. Tax Datab. (Nov. 1987-); Bus. ASAP (1990-) [Full Txt.]; Bus. Index (1986-); F&S Index Plus Text, Int. [Select. Cov.]; Gen. BusinessFile (1986-); Gen. Period. Index (1986-); Mag. Search; PROMT.

US
TITLE CHANGE

PROGRAM TRENDS FOR BUSINESS AND INDUSTRY. (19??)-(19??). English. Learning Resources Network, 1554 Hayes Drive, Manhattan KS 66502. **Tel** (913)539-5376, FAX (913)539-7766. **Continues** Dean and Director. **Merged into** Course Trends.

DD 381

ISSN 8750-6106
US

PROGRESSIVE RENTALS. (PROGRESSIVE RENTALS.). [Prog. rent.]. **Added/Corp** Association of Progressive Rental Organizations (U.S.). (198?)-. Trade Publication. English. Six times a year (Feb., Apr., June, Aug., Oct., Dec.). $30.00. Association of Progressive Rentals Organization, 6300 Bridgeport, Suite 305, Austin TX 78730. **Tel** (512)794-0095. **ED** John Gormley. **Ad Acc. Circ:** 4,000. **Continues** Aproach, 0736-1874.
Desc: The magazine of the home entertainment, appliance, and furniture rental industry. It is published by the Association of Progressive Rental Organizations (APRO), the national trade association of the rental-purchase industry.

LC HF
DD 658
US

PROJECT MANAGEMENT. (19??)-. English. Twelve times a year. $184.00. Practice Management Associates Ltd., 10 Midland Avenue, Newton MA 02158. **Tel** (617)965-0055, FAX (617)965-5152. **Continues** Details-Plus.

ISSN 0767-8320
FR

UDC 656
PROMOTION TRANSPORTS. [Promot. transp.]. (1961)-. Periodical. French. Ten times a year. $98.43. Association pour le Developpement de la Formation Professionnelle dans les Transports / AFT, 46 Avenue de Villiers, 75017 Paris France. **Tel** 011 33 1 42125050.

IT

PRONTUARIO COSTO VITA. Italian. Camera Com Ind Art Agr, Firenze, Piazza Giudici 3, 50122 Florence Italy.

FR

PROPOS, A. Added/Corp France. Documentation Francaise. No. 1 (March 1990)-. French. Irregular (9 or 10 per year). Free on request. Documentation Francaise, 29 quai Voltaire, 75344 Paris Cedex 7 France. **Tel** 011 33 1 40157000, FAX 011 33 1 40157230, telex 204 826 DOCFRAN. **(Subscription address:** Documentation Francaise, 124 rue Henri Barbusse, 93308 Aubervilliers Cedex France. **Tel** 011 33 1 48395600.) **Continues** DF Actualites.

DD 333.91

ISSN 1187-9947
CN

PROPOSITION TARIFAIRE. (PROPOSITION TARIFAIRE POUR ..). [Propos. tarif.]. **Main/Corp** Hydro-Quebec. (1992). French. **Continues** Hydro-Quebec.; Memoire sur la Tarification Proposee Pour ..., 1184-9045.

US

PROSPECT RESEARCHER'S GUIDE TO BIOGRAPHICAL COLLECTIONS. English. One time a year. $79.00. Taft Group, 835 Penobscott Building, Customer Service, Detroit MI 48226. **Tel** (800)877-8238, FAX (313)961-6083.

LC HC446 .P769
DD 330

ISSN 0853-0785
IO

PROSPEK. No. 1 (Sept. 1990)-. Periodical. Indonesian. One time a week.

LC HD
DD 338

ISSN 0887-8226
US

PROVIDENCE BUSINESS NEWS. [Provid. bus. news]. Vol. 1, No. 1 (May 5, 1986)-. Newspaper. English. Fifty-two times a year. $64.00. Providence Business News, 300 Richmond Street, Providence RI 02903. **Tel** (401)273-2201, (800)825-5766, FAX (401)274-0670, (401)274-0270. **ED** Frank Prosnitz, Donald DeMaio (Managing Editor). Index available. **Bk Rev,** (Qty: 12). **Photos. Ad Acc, Adv Mgr:** John Lamp. Full Page (B&W) $3086.00. Half Page (B&W) $1667.00. Full Page (Color) $3686.00. Half Page (Color) $2267.00. **Pub. Size:** Tabloid. **Wire Svcs.:** AP. **Circ:** 11,000 (ctrl). available on an online database (file 635/Full-Text) from DIALOG; available via Internet (http://pbn.com). Documents available from UMI Article Clearinghouse.
Ind/Abst Bus. Dateline (Sept. 16, 1991-) [Full Txt.].

DD 330.9716/04

ISSN 0226-0425
CN

PROVINCE OF NOVA SCOTIA, CANADA, THE. [Prov. N.S., Can.]. **Added/Corp** Nova Scotia Communications and Information Centre. (1972)-. Periodical. English. Nova Scotia Communications and Information Centre, Box 2206, Halifax Nova Scotia B3J 3C4 Canada.

DD 330.971

ISSN 0832-3542
CN

PROVINCIAL OUTLOOK. EXECUTIVE SUMMARY. [Prov. outlook, exec. summ.]. **Added/Corp** Conference Board of Canada. (Feb. 1986)-. Periodical. English. Every 2 years. Conference Board of Canada, 255 Smyth Road, Ottawa Ontario K1H 8M7 Canada. **Tel** (613)526-3280, FAX (613)526-4857, telex 053-3034. **Continues** Quarterly Provincial Forecast. Executive Summary, 0829-111X.

LC HD9735.P68 P73

PL

PRZEMYS DROBNY I USUGI. Added/Corp Naczelna Organizacja Techniczna (Poland). (April 1979)-. Periodical. Polish. Twelve times a year. **(Subscription address:** Ars Polona-Ruch, PO Box 1001, Krakowskie Przedmiescie 7, 00-068 Warsaw Poland. **Tel** 011 48 22 261201.) **Supersedes** Rynek, Usugi.

DD 692.8

ISSN 0955-1204
UK

PSA CONTRACTS BULLETIN. [PSA contract. bull.]. (1989)-. Periodical. English. Twenty-six times a year. $500.00. Longman Group Ltd., Fourth Avenue, Longman House, Harlow Essex CM19 5SR United Kingdom. **Tel** 011 44 1279 429655, FAX 011 44 1279 431067, telex 81259. **ED** Martin Gillate. Index available.
Desc: Contains notices of PSA contracts which are being offered for tender.

LC HF5548.8 .P772
NLM W1 PS66

ISSN 0033-300X
XR
CODEN PSVPB2

PSYCHOLOGIE V EKONOMICKE PRAXI. [Psychol. ekon. praxi]. **Added/Corp** Universita Karlova. (1966)-. Periodical. Czech (summaries and/or abstracts in English). Four times a year. DM59.00. Charles University / Univerzita Karlova, Ovocnytrh 5, 116 36 Prague 1 Czech Republic. **Tel** 228441. **(Subscription address:** Kubon & Sagner, ABT Zeitschriftenimport, D 80328 Munich Germany. **Tel** 011 49 89 54218130.)
Ind/Abst Psychol. Abstr. (1966-); PsycINFO (1966-); PsycLit; Saf. Health Work.

DD 338.47915

ISSN 0957-0071
UK

PTN EUROPE. [PTN Eur.]. (1988)-. Periodical. English. Eight times a year. £25.00 UK and Northern Ireland; $45.00 other. Morgan Grampian, 40 Beresford Street Woolwich, London SE18 6BQ United Kingdom. **Tel** 011 44 181 8557777, FAX 011 44 181 8555548, telex 896238.
Ind/Abst EP Collect.; Homework Help.; MasterFile FullTEXT 1000; MasterFile FullTEXT 350; MasterFile FullTEXT 650; MasterFile FullTEXT; OCLC; Telebase.

US

PTS NEWSLETTER DATABASE [ONLINE DATABASE]. See Business and Economics-Abstracting, Bibliographies and Statistics.

IT

PUBBLICAZIONI CERES. (19??)-. Italian. Twelve times a year. L50000.00 Italy; L60000.00 other. Centro Ricerche Econ E Social, Via Nomentana 201, 00161 Rome Italy. **Tel** 011 39 6 8541016. **Circ:** 1,000 (ctrl).

LC JA1 .P77

ISSN 0048-5829
NE
CCC

Pr Rev.
PUBLIC CHOICE. [Public choice]. **Added/Corp** Virginia Polytechnic Institute and State University. Center for Study of Public Choice. Thomas Jefferson Center for Political Economy. Virginia Polytechnic Institute. Center for Study of Public Choice. Vol. 4 (Spring 1968)-. Periodical. English. Sixteen times a year. $789.00. Kluwer Academic Publishers, Postbus 322, 3300 AH Dordrecht The Netherlands. **Tel** 011 31 78 524400, FAX 011 31 78 183273, telex 20083. **ED** Gordon Tullock, Charles Rowley, and Robert Tollison. **Acid Free.** available on microfilm and microfiche from University Microfilms International (UMI). Documents available from The Genuine Article. **Continues** Papers on Non-Market Decision Making.
Desc: Deals with the intersection between economics and political science. Founded at a time when economists and political scientists became interested in the application of essentially economic methods to problems normally dealt with by political scientists. It has always retained strong traces of economic methodology, but new and fruitful techniques have been developed which are not recognizable by economists. Remains central in its chosen role of introducing the two groups to each other, and allowing them to explain themselves through the medium of its pages.
Ind/Abst ABC POL SCI; Curr. Cit.; Curr. Contents Soc. Behav. Sci.; Econ. Lit. Index; Index Period. Artic. Relat. Law (19??-19??); Int. Bibliogr. Sociol.; Int. Polit. Sci. Abstr.; J. Econ. Lit.; J. Plan. Lit.; PAIS Int. Print (1991-); Res. Alert [Full Cov.]; Sage Public Adm. Abstr.; Soc. Plann. Policy Dev. Abstr.; Soc. Sci. Cit. Index [Full Cov.]; Sociol. Abstr.; U.S. Polit. Sci. Doc.

UK
TITLE CHANGE

PUBLIC LEDGER, THE. (July 3, 1837)-(May 1995). Newspaper. English. UK Publications, 10 Little College Street, London SW1P 3SH United Kingdom. **Tel** 011 44 171 9767772, FAX 011 44 171 9760775. **Ad Acc. Continues** Constitutional and Public Ledger. **Merged into** The Public Ledger & Commodity Week, 0966-4696.

ISSN 0966-4696
UK

PUBLIC LEDGER & COMMODITY WEEK, THE. [Public ledger commod. week]. **VFOAT** Public Ledger and Commodity Week. (1988)-. Newspaper. English. One time a week. $496.25. UK Publications, 10 Little College Street, London SW1P 3SH United Kingdom. **Tel** 011 44 171 9767772, FAX 011 44 171 9760775. **Continues** Public Ledger Commodity Year Book, 0144-8307; **Absorbed** The Public Ledger and Commodity Week.

ISSN 0267-4858
UK
TITLE CHANGE

PUBLIC LEDGER'S COMMODITY WEEK. [Public ledger's commod. week]. (1979)-(May 1995). Newspaper. English. UK Publications, 10 Little College Street, London SW1P 3SH United Kingdom. **Tel** 011 44 171 9767772, FAX 011 44 171 9760775. **Merged into** The Public Ledger & Commodity Week, 0966-4696.

ISSN 0963-5084
UK

PUBLIC NETWORK EUROPE. [Public netw. Eur.]. (1990)-. Periodical. English. Ten times a year. $136.89. Economist Intelligence Unit / Essex, PO Box 14 Harold Hill, Romford RM3 8EQ, Essex United Kingdom. **Tel** 011 44 1322 289194, FAX 011 44 1322 223803. **(Subscription address:** Economist Newspaper Ltd., PO Box 14, Harold Hill Business Center, Romford RM3 8EQ United Kingdom. **Tel** 011 44 708 381555.)

DD 332

ISSN 0891-7183
US

PUBLIC RISK. [Public risk]. **Added/Corp** Public Risk and Insurance Management Association (U.S.). Vol. 1, No. 1 (Nov./Dec. 1986)-. Trade Publication. English. Ten times a year (monthly with May/Jun. and Nov./Dec. issues combined). $125.00. Public Risk Management Association, 1117 North 19th Street, Suite 900, Arlington VA 22209. **Tel** (703)528-7701, FAX (703)528-7966. **ED** Kathleen Rakestraw. cum. index. **Bk Rev. Ad Acc.**

LC HF5489.C2 A37
DD 381

ISSN 0704-5387
CN

PUBLIC WAREHOUSING. Main/Corp Statistics Canada. Surface Transport Section. **VFOAT** Entreposage Public. 1975-. English (French). One time a year. $0.70. Publishing Centre, Supply and Services Canada, Ottawa Ontario K1A 0S9 Canada. **Continues** Warehousing.

LC HC
DD 330

ISSN 0577-8468
CL

PUBLICACIONES. Main/Corp Chile. Universidad, Santiago. Instituto de Economia y Planificacion. (19??)-. Monographic series. Spanish. Irregular. Price varies per volume. Universidad de Chile / Departamento de Economia, Casilla Postal 3861, Santiago Chile. **Tel** 011 56 2 228521.

Business and Economics

LC Z7165.N4 P83 HC321
DD 016.3389492 NE
PUBLICATION BULLETIN (NETHERLANDS. CENTRAAL PLANBUREAU). (PUBLICATION BULLETIN.). **Added/Corp** Netherlands. Centraal Planbureau. (1986)-. Bulletin. English.

UK
PUBLICATIONS REVIEW, INNOVATION & MANAGEMENT. **VFOAT** Publications Review, Innovation and Management. Vol. 5, No. 1 (Jan./March 1982)-. Periodical. English. Four times a year. $55.17. **Continues** Publications Review.

US
PUBLICATIONS UPDATE. Main/Corp International Bank for Reconstruction and Development. **VFOAT** World Bank Publications; World Bank Publications Update. (19??)-. Bulletin. English. Six times a year. Free on request. World Bank Publications, 1818 H Street Northwest, Washington DC 20043. **Tel** (202)473-1155, (202)473-1155, FAX (202)522-3224, telex WUI 64145 WORLDBANK. **(Subscription address:** World Bank Publications, PO Box 7247-8619, Books Department, Philadelphia PA 19170. **) Bk Rev**.
Desc: Brief descriptions of various business and economic publications.

LC HC321 .S63
DD 330 NE
PUBLIKATIE. Added/Corp Sociaal-Economische Raad. (Feb. 12, 1982)-. Monographic series. Dutch. Irregular. Price varies per volume. SER - Sociaal Economische Raad, Bezuidenhoutseweg 60, Postbus 90405, 2509 LK The Hague Netherlands. **Tel** 011 31 70 3499499, FAX 011 31 70 3832535, telex 41.146. ctrl circ. **Continues** Sociaal-Economische Raad. Publicaties.

LC Discard
DD 330 US
PUBLISHED SEARCH BIBLIOGRAPHIES FROM THE NTIS BIBLIOGRAPHIC DATA BASE. BUSINESS AND MANAGEMENT. See Business and Economics-Abstracting, Bibliographies and Statistics.

LC HC154.5.A1 P84 **ISSN** 0270-126X
DD 330.97295/005 US
PUERTO RICO BUSINESS REVIEW. [P. R. bus. rev.]. **Added/Corp** Government Development Bank for Puerto Rico. **VFOAT** Business Review. Vol. 1 (July 1976)-. Periodical. English. Four times a year (March, June, Sept., Dec.). Free on request. Government Development Bank for Puerto Rico, PO Box 42001, San Juan PR 00940. **Tel** (809)722-2525, FAX (809)268-5496. **ED** Eunice A. Pagan-Vega. Index available. cum. index. **Circ:** 11,000.
Desc: Contains articles of interest to the business community.

ISSN 8750-7757
DD 330 US
CCC
PUGET SOUND BUSINESS JOURNAL. [Puget Sound bus. j.]. Vol. 5, No. 35 (Jan. 14, 1985)-. Periodical. English. One time a week. $53.00. Puget Sound Business Journal, 720 Third Avenue, Suite 800, Seattle WA 98104-2552. **Tel** (206)583-0701, FAX (206)447-8510. **ED** Al Hoopek. **Ad Acc. Circ:** 20,000. available on microfilm from University Microfilms International (UMI); available on an online database (files 635,648/Full-Text) from DIALOG. Documents available from UMI Article Clearinghouse. **Continues** Seattle Business Journal, 0274-5453.
Desc: Business feature stories and listings.
Ind/Abst Acad. Search; Bus. Dateline; Bus. Index (1985-1990); Bus. Source Plus; Bus. Source; EP Collect.; Gen. BusinessFile (1985-1990); Homework Help.; INFO-SOUTH Abstr.; Mag. Search; MasterFile FullTEXT 1000; MasterFile FullTEXT 350; MasterFile FullTEXT 650; MasterFile FullTEXT (July 1993-); OCLC; PROMT; Telebase; Trade Ind. ASAP [Full Txt.]; Trade Ind. Index [Full Txt.].

IT
PULCE. Italian. Three times a week. L364000.00. La Pulce, Via da Settimello 5/7, 50135 Florence Italy. **Tel** 011 39 55 65560, FAX 011 39 55 666161. cum. index. **Ad Acc.** ctrl circ.

MX
PUNTO CRITICO. No. 1 (Jan. 1972)-. Periodical. Spanish. Six times a year. $15.00. Punto Critico, Zacatecas 229 314, Mexico 7 DF Mexico. **Tel** 011 52 5 745982. **ED** Raul Alvarez Garin. **Bk Rev. Ad Acc. Circ:** 5,000.
Desc: Mexican economics, political social/labor movement, international politics analysis, Latin American liberation movement, regional analysis debates.
Ind/Abst Hum. Rights Intern. Rep.

NE
PW PERSONEELSMANAGEMENT. (19??)-. Trade Publication. Dutch. Twenty-six times a year. Fl165.00. VNU Business Publications BV, Postbus 9194, 1006 AC Amsterdam Netherlands. **Tel** 011 31 20 4875879. Index available. cum. index. **Bk Rev. Ad Acc. Circ:** 16,000 (ctrl).
Desc: Professional information for personnel management written by journalists on commission by the editorial staff.

ISSN 1067-8077
US
●**QATAR (SYRACUSE, N.Y.).** (QATAR : AN EXECUTIVE REPORT.). **Added/Corp** Political Risk Services (IBC USA (Publications) Inc.). **VFOAT** Executive Report. (1993)-. English. $110.00. Political Risk Services, 6320 Fly Road, Suite 102, PO Box 248, East Syracuse NY 13057-0248. **Tel** (315)431-0511, FAX (315)431-0200.
Desc: Focuses on the long-term outlook for business. Includes a brief review of recent events and current circumstances, background intelligence including geography, history, economics and social conditions, as well as the key political and economic forecasts.

ISSN 1064-2986
US
QUAD CITY REPORTER, THE. (THE QUAD CITY REPORTER : OFFICIAL RECORDS AND NEWS OF BUSINESS, COMMERCE AND FINANCE IN THE IOWA-ILLINOIS QUAD CITY AREA). **VFOAT** Quad-City Reporter. Vol. 92, No. 1 (Jan. 7, 1992)-. Periodical. English. One time a week. D-C Franchising, 5117 Jersey Ridge Road, Davenport IA 52807. **Continues** Quad City Daily Reporter.

IT
QUADERNI DI RICERCA E DOCUMENTAZIONE. (19??)-. Periodical. Italian. Irregular. L18000. Bancaria Editrice SPA, Piazza del Gesu 49, 00186 Rome Italy. **Tel** 011 39 6 6767220.

LC HC
GW
QUAESTIONSA OECONOMICAE. (19??)-. Monographic series. German. Irregular. Price varies per volume. Duncker und Humblot Verlag, Postfach 410329, D-12113 Berlin Germany. **Tel** 011 49 30 79000612, 011 49 30 79000613.

ISSN 0391-6146
IT
UDC 3
QUALE IMPRESA. [Quale impresa]. (1973)-. Periodical. Italian. Ten times a year. L40880. Servizio Italiano Pubblicazioni International, Viale Pasteur 6, 00144 Rome Italy. **Tel** 011 39 6 5920509, telex 614567 SIPIRM I.

ISSN 1042-072X
DD 658 US
QUALITY AND PRODUCTIVITY PLUS. [Qual. prod. plus]. **Added/Corp** National Foremen's Institute. (19??)-. Periodical. English. Twelve times a year. $12.36 US; $15.24 Canada. Bureau of Business Practice, 24 Rope Ferry Road, Waterford CT 06386. **Tel** (800)243-0876, (203)442-4365, (800)876-9105, FAX (203)443-1123. **Continues** Productivity Plus, 0882-8776.

LC TS156.6 .Q33 **ISSN** 1052-9411
DD 658.5/62 CCC
NLM W1; QU158KD CODEN QUASE2
QUALITY ASSURANCE (SAN DIEGO, CALIF.). See Science and Technology.

US
QUALITY BANNER POSTER. (19??)-. English. Twelve times a year. $102.96. Bureau of Business Practice, 24 Rope Ferry Road, Waterford CT 06386. **Tel** (800)243-0876, (203)442-4365, (800)876-9105, FAX (203)443-1123.

US
QUALITY POSTINGS. (19??)-. English. Twelve times a year. $53.28. Bureau of Business Practice, 24 Rope Ferry Road, Waterford CT 06386. **Tel** (800)243-0876, (203)442-4365, (800)876-9105, FAX (203)443-1123. **Continues** High Standards.

HK
QUARTERLY BUSINESS SURVEY REPORT. See Business and Economics-Abstracting, Bibliographies and Statistics.

HK
QUARTERLY COUNTRY RISK REPORTS. English. Four times a year. $495.00 (one country). Political & Economic Risk Consultancy Ltd, GPO 1342, Hong Kong Hong Kong. **Tel** 011 852 25414088, FAX 011 852 28155032, telex 46926.

LC QA76.8.D43 Q37 **ISSN** 1063-1216
DD 004.16 US
Pr Rev. CEASED
QUARTERLY DEC JOURNAL. [Q. DEC j.]. **VAT** Quarterly Digital Equipment Corporation Journal. (Summer 1992)-(Sept. 1994). Periodical. English. Computer Economics Inc., 5841 Edison Place, Carlsbad CA 92008. **Tel** (800)326-8100, (619)438-8100, FAX (619)431-1126. **ED** Anne Zalatan. **Bk Rev**, (Qty: 4/yr). **Ad Acc; Adv Mgr:** Kate Davis.
Desc: A professional journal which publishes and analyses perspectives for users and managers of Digital Equipment Corporations, Systems, and Software.

LC HA1117.M3 A28
DD 314.58/5 MM
QUARTERLY DIGEST OF STATISTICS. See Business and Economics-Abstracting, Bibliographies and Statistics.

US
QUARTERLY DOMESTIC & GLOBAL FORECASTS OF KEY ECONOMIC INDICATORS. (19??)-. English. Four times a year (seasonally). $105.00. Graceway Publishing Company, PO Box 159 Station C, Flushing NY 11367. **Tel** (718)463-3914, FAX (718)544-9086. **Circ:** 500. **Continues** Quarterly Concensus Forecast of Key Economic Indicators, 0888-787X.
Desc: Gives forecasts of key economic indicators of 47 different countries plus industry forecasts of the USA.

LC HC910.A1 Q36
DD 330.96894/005 RH
QUARTERLY ECONOMIC AND STATISTICAL REVIEW / RESERVE BANK OF ZIMBABWE. See Business and Economics-Abstracting, Bibliographies and Statistics.

LC HC
DD 330 UK
QUARTERLY ECONOMIC BULLETIN. **Added/Corp** Liverpool Research Group in Macroeconomics. (October 1981)-. Bulletin. English. Four times a year. $342.24. Liverpool Macroeconomic Res, PO Box 147, Dept of Economics, Liverpool L69 3BX United Kingdom. **Tel** 011 44 151 7943032, FAX 011 44 151 7943028. ctrl circ. **Continues** Liverpool Occasional Papers.

LC HC257.I6 E33 **ISSN** 0376-7191
DD 330.9/415/09 IE
QUARTERLY ECONOMIC COMMENTARY. [Q. econ. comment.]. **Added/Corp** Economic and Social Research Institute. (1968)-. Periodical. English. Four times a year. $192.29. Economic & Social Research Institute / Dublin, 4 Burlington Road, Dublin 4 Ireland. **Tel** 011 353 1 6760115 Ext. 427. **ED** T. J. Baker and S. Scott. **Bk Rev. Circ:** 1,000 (ctrl). **Formed by the union of** Joint Quarterly Industrial Survey **and** Statistics of Economic Level and Trend.
Desc: The scope is to continually improve and widen to include (1) the international economy; (2) the domestic economy; and (3) appraisal.

LC HC157.T8 **ISSN** 0041-3046
DD 330 TR
QUARTERLY ECONOMIC REPORT.
Main/Corp Trinidad and Tobago. Central Statistical Office. 3rd Quarter, (1962)-. Government Publication. English. Four times a year. $2.28. Government Printery / Trinidad, Central Statistical Office, 35 41 Queen Street, Port of Spain Trinidad. **Tel** (809)625-4970, FAX (809)625-3802. **Circ:** 600 (ctrl). available with charts. **Continues** Quarterly Economic Report.
Desc: Contains information on overseas trade, wages, prices, retail sales, agriculture and fishing, industrial production, employment petroleum production, transport communication, finance and banking, population and vital statistics.

HK
QUARTERLY ESTIMATES OF GROSS DOMESTIC PRODUCT. Added/Corp Hong Kong. Census and Statistics Dept. (19??)-. Government Publication. English. Four times a year. HK$4.50. Hong Kong Government Information Service, Beaconsfield House, 4 Queens Road, Hong Kong Hong Kong. **Tel** 011 852 284288014, 011 852 259881947, FAX 011 852 28459078, 011 852 25987482, telex 61190 HKGIS.

LC HG4090 .A357 **ISSN** 1180-3169
DD 338.7/4/0971021 CN
QUARTERLY FINANCIAL STATISTICS FOR ENTERPRISES. See Business and Economics-Abstracting, Bibliographies and Statistics.

LC HC462.9 .N4864a **ISSN** 0910-075X
DD 338.5/44/0952 JA
Pr Rev.
QUARTERLY FORECAST OF JAPAN'S ECONOMY. [Q. forecast Jpn. econ.]. **Main/Corp** Nihon Keizai Kenkyu Senta. (19??)-. English. Three times a year (January, April and July). $189.17. Japan Center of Economic Research, 6 1 Nihombashi Kayabacho 2 Cho, Chuoku Tokyo 103 Japan. **Tel** FAX 011 81 3 36392839. **Continues** Nihon Keizai Kenkyu Senta. Japan's Economy.
Desc: Short-term forecast of Japan's economy.
Ind/Abst F&S Index Plus Text, Int. [Select. Cov.]; Predicasts Forecasts.

LC HC
DD 330 RH

QUARTERLY GUIDE TO THE ECONOMY. **Added/Corp** RAL Merchant Bank. First Merchant Bank of Zimbabwe. (198?)-. Periodical. English. Four times a year. $20.00. First Merchant Bank Ltd., Box 2786, Harare Zimbabwe. **Tel** 703071, FAX 26025, telex 738810. Index available ($20.00). **Bk Rev**, (Qty: 4). ***Continues** Executive Guide to the Economy.*

LC HB1 .N4 **ISSN** 0747-5535
DD 330/.05 US
CCC

QUARTERLY JOURNAL OF BUSINESS AND ECONOMICS. (QUARTERLY JOURNAL OF BUSINESS AND ECONOMICS : QJBE.). [Q. j. bus. econ.]. **Added/Corp** University of Nebraska--Lincoln. College of Business Administration. **VFOAT** QJBE. Vol. 22, No. 4 (Autumn 1983)-. Academic Scholarly Publication. English. Four times a year (Feb., May, Aug., Nov.). $25.00. University of Nebraska / Bureau of Business Research, 200 College Business Administration Building, Lincoln NE 68588-0407. **Tel** (402)472-2334, FAX (402)472-3878. **ED** George McCabe. **Circ:** 500 (ctrl). available on microfilm and microfiche from University Microfilms International (UMI); available on an online database (file 648/Full-Text) from DIALOG. Documents available from UMI Article Clearinghouse. ***Continues** Nebraska Journal of Economics and Business, 0160-6557.*
Desc: Features scholarly articles that empirically test various theories in the fields of finance, accounting, economics, marketing and management.
Ind/Abst ABI/INFORM Glob. Ed.; ABI/INFORM [Computer File] (Autumn 1983-); Acad. Search; Bus. ASAP (1990-) [Full Txt.]; Bus. Index (1985-); Bus. Source Plus; Bus. Source; Contents Recent Econ. J.; Curr. Cit.; Econ. Lit. Index; EP Collect.; Gen. BusinessFile (1985-); Gen. Period. Index (1985-); Homework Help.; INFO-SOUTH Abstr.; J. Econ. Lit. (Autumn 1983-); Mag. Search; MasterFile FullTEXT 1000; MasterFile FullTEXT 350; MasterFile FullTEXT 650; MasterFile FullTEXT (July 1993-); OCLC; Telebase; UMI ABI/Inform--Bus. Period. Ondisc (Spring 1988-) [Full Txt.].

LC HB1 .Q3 **ISSN** 0033-5533
DD 330 US
CCC
CODEN QJECAT

Pr Rev.
QUARTERLY JOURNAL OF ECONOMICS, THE. [Q. j. econ.]. **Added/Corp** Harvard University. **VFOAT** QJE. Vol. 1 (Oct. 1886)-. Periodical. English. Four times a year. $106.00. Massachusetts Institute of Technology (MIT) Press, 55 Hayward Street, Cambridge MA 02142. **Tel** (617)253-2889, (617)625-8481, FAX (617)258-6779. **ED** Olivier J. Blanchard, Lawarence F. Katz, Andrei Shleifer. cum. index. available on microfilm and microfiche from University Microfilms International (UMI). Documents available from The Genuine Article, UMI Article Clearinghouse.
Desc: Covers all aspects of the field. Traditional emphasis on microtheory has been expanded to include both empirical and theoretical macroeconomics.
Ind/Abst ABI/INFORM Glob. Ed.; ABI/INFORM [Computer File] (Feb. 1983-); Acad. Abstr.; Acad. Ind. [Computer File] (1984-); Acad. Search; Am. Hist. Life (1960-); Bus. Index (1985-); Bus. Period. Index; Coal Abstr.; Contents Recent Econ. J.; Contents Pages Manage.; Curr. Cit.; Curr. Contents Soc. Behav. Sci.; Econ. Lit. Index; Energy Res. Abstr. (Dec. 1975-); EP Collect.; Expand. Acad. Index (1984-); Gen. BusinessFile (1985-); Gen. Period. Index (1985-); Geogr. Abstr. Human Geogr. (1974-); Homework Help.; Hum. Resour. Abstr.; Index Period. Artic. Relat. Law; INFO-SOUTH Abstr.; Int. Dev. Abstr. (Feb. 1983-); J. Econ. Lit.; Mag. Search; MasterFile FullTEXT 1000; MasterFile FullTEXT 350; MasterFile FullTEXT 650; MasterFile FullTEXT (July 1990-); Math. Rev.; Middle East Abstr. Index (1960-); Newsp. Period. Abstr. (1991-); OCLC; Oper. Res./Manage. Sci.; Peace Res. Abstr. J. (1972); Qual. Control Appl. Stat.; Res. Alert [Full Cov.]; Risk Abstr.; Sage Fam. Stud. Abstr. (?-?); Sage Public Adm. Abstr.; Sage Urban Stud. Abstr (?-?); Selec. Coop. Index Manage. Period.; Soc. Sci. Source; Soc. Sci. Cit. Index [Full Cov.]; Soc. Sci. Index; Soc. Sci. Index Fulltext (Nov. 1988-) [Full Txt.]; Soc. Work Abstr. [Select. Cov.]; Stat. Theory Method Abstr. (1959-1963); Telebase; UMI ABI/Inform--Bus. Period. Ondisc (Nov. 1987-) [Full Txt.]; Wilson Bus. Abstr.; Work Relat. Abstr.; Zentralbl. Math. Ihre Grenzgeb. (1960-).

LC HC79.I5 O7c **ISSN** 0257-7801
DD 339.3/021 FR

QUARTERLY NATIONAL ACCOUNTS (PARIS, FRANCE : 1983). (QUARTERLY NATIONAL ACCOUNTS.). [Q. natl. acc. - OECD Dep. Econ. Stat.]. **Added/Corp** Organisation for Economic Co-Operation and Development. Dept. of Economics and Statistics. **VFOAT** Comptes Nationaux Trimestriels; Quarterly National Accounts Bulletin. Vol. 1 (1983)-. Bulletin. English (French). Four times a year. $1570.00. OECD Publications and Information Center, 2 rue Andre-Pascal, 75775 Paris Cedex 16 France. **Tel** 011 33 1 49104262, US:(202)785-6323, FAX 011 33 1 45248500, 011 33 1 45248176, telex 620 160 OCDE. **(Subscription address:** OECD Publications Center, 2001 L Street, Suite 700, Washington DC 20036. **Tel** (202)822-3873, (202)785-6323.**)** available on magnetic tape; available on diskette. ***Formed by the union of** Organisation for Economic Co-Operation and Development. Quarterly National Accounts Bulletin, 0304-3738 **and** Organisation for Economic Co-Operation and Development. Quarterly National Accounts. Historical Statistics.*
Desc: Brings together the latest national income statistics from the United States and 11 other OECD countries (Austria, Canada, Japan, Australia, Finland, Germany, Greece, Italy, Sweden and the United Kingdom). Three standard tables are shown for each country: GDP in purchase values, financing and composition of gross capital formation and private consumption expenditure.
Ind/Abst Predicasts.

DD 330.972 MX

QUARTERLY SURVEY OF THE MEXICAN ECONOMY. **Added/Corp** Canada. Embassy (Mexico). Commercial Division. (1978)-. Periodical. English. Canadian Embassy / Mexico, Melchor Ocampo 463-7, Mexico 5 DF Mexico.

NE

QUINTESSENCE. (19??)-. English. Six times a year. Brinkman Business Persgroep, Postbus 155, 6500 AD Nijmegen Netherlands. **Tel** 011 31 080 787444.

LC S
DD 630 US

●**R.B.** **See** Agriculture.

ISSN 0197-6060
DD 658 US

RAGAN REPORT, THE. [Ragan rep.]. **Added/Corp** Lawrence Ragan Communications, Inc. (197?)-. Newsletter. English. One time a week. $287.00. Ragan Communications Inc., 212 West Superior Street, Suite 200, Chicago IL 60610. **Tel** (312)335-0037, (800)878-5331, FAX (312)335-9583. **ED** Janine Ragan. **Bk Rev. Circ:** 5,000 (ctrl).
Desc: Designed for those who are communication executives. It surveys the latest trends in the field of corporate communications, public relations and marketing.

LC HC437.R3 R285
DD 330.9/54/405 II

RAJASTHAN ECONOMIC JOURNAL. **Added/Corp** Rajasthan Economic Association. Vol. 1 (Jan. 1977)-. Periodical. English. Two times a year. $15.00. Rajasthan Economic Association, Jaipur 302004 India. **(Subscription address:** Prints India, 11 Darya Ganj, New Delhi 110002 India. **Tel** 011 91 11 3268645, FAX 011 91 11 3275542, telex 31-61087 PRIN-IN.**)**
Ind/Abst Rice Abstr.

LC HD2763.A2 B4 **ISSN** 0741-6261
DD 338.4/73636/05 US
CODEN RJECEA

Pr Rev.
RAND JOURNAL OF ECONOMICS, THE. [Rand j. econ.]. **Added/Corp** Rand Corporation. Vol. 15, No. 1 (Spring 1984)-. Periodical. English. Four times a year (published within the seasons). $152.00. Rand Corporation, 1700 Main Street, Santa Monica CA 90406. **Tel** (310)393-0411, FAX (310)393-4818, (310)396-6217. **(Subscription address:** Rand Journal of Economics, PO Box 1897, Lawrence KS 66044-8897. **)** **ED** Stanley M. Besen and Alvin K. Klevorick. cum. index. **Bk Rev. Circ:** 5,000. available on microfilm and microfiche from University Microfilms International (UMI). Documents available from Article Express International, The Genuine Article, UMI Article Clearinghouse, Ask*IEEE. ***Continues** Bell Journal of Economics, 0361-915X.*
Desc: Research in the behavior of regulated industries, the economic analysis of organizations, and applied microeconomics. Theoretical and empirical research in economics and law.
Ind/Abst ABI/INFORM Glob. Ed.; ABI/INFORM [Computer File] (Spring 1984-); Acad. Search; Bioeng. Abstr.; Bus. Index (1979-?); Bus. Period. Index; Bus. Source Plus; Bus. Source; Curr. Cit.; Curr. Contents Soc. Behav. Sci.; Econ. Lit. Index (Spring 1984-); Ei Page One; Energy Res. Abstr. (1984-); Eng. Index Annu.; EP Collect.; Gen. BusinessFile (1992-); Health Plan. Adminis.; Highw. Res. Abstr.; Homework Help.; INFO-SOUTH Abstr.; INSPEC (Spring 1984-); Int. Bibliogr. Sociol.; J. Econ. Lit.; J. Plan. Lit.; Mag. Search; MasterFile FullTEXT 1000; MasterFile FullTEXT 350; MasterFile FullTEXT 650; MasterFile FullTEXT (July 1993-); Math. Rev. (?-199?); Middle East Abstr. Index (1991-); OCLC; Oper. Res./Manage. Sci. (1984-); Res. Alert [Full Cov.]; Soc. Sci. Cit. Index [Full Cov.]; Telebase; UMI ABI/Inform--Bus. Period. Ondisc (Spring 1987-) [Full Txt.]; Wilson Bus. Abstr.; World Agric. Econ. Rural Sociol. Abstr.

ISSN 0740-9281
US

RAND RESEARCH REVIEW. **Added/Corp** Rand Corporation. **VFOAT** Research Review. (1977)-. Periodical. English. Four times a year. Free on request. Rand Corporation, 1700 Main Street, Santa Monica CA 90406. **Tel** (310)393-0411, FAX (310)393-4818, (310)396-6217.

CN

RAPPORT DE LA DIRECTION DES RECHERCHES SUR LA CONSOMMATION. **Main/Corp** Canada. Direction de la Recherche sur la Consommation. No. 1 (1972)-. Monographic series. French (English). Irregular. Price varies per volume. Canada Communication Group Publishers, Order Processing, Ottawa Ontario K1A 0S9 Canada. **Tel** (819)956-4800, (819)956-4802.

LC HC **ISSN** 0709-986X
DD 330 CN

RAPPORT DE RECHERCHE - ECOLE DES HAUTES ETUDES COMMERCIALES (MONTREAL). (RAPPORT DE RECHERCHE.). [Rapp. rech. - Ec. hautes etud. commer.]. Monographic series. English (French). Price varies per volume. Ecole des Hautes Etudes Commerciales, 5255 Decelles Avenue, Montreal Quebec H3T 1V6 Canada. **Tel** (514)340-6437, FAX (514)340-6469. **Circ:** 125.
Desc: This is a series of working papers or research papers on the following subjects: management, management sciences, operations research, economics, accounting, management information systems.

ISSN 0347-982X
SW

RAPPORT - SVERIGES LANTBRUKSUNIVERSITET, INSTITUTIONEN FOR EKONOMI OCH STATISTIK. REPORT - DEPARTMENT OF ECONOMICS AND STATISTICS. **See** Business and Economics-Abstracting, Bibliographies and Statistics.

IT

RAPPORTI CER. Italian. Six times a year. CER/Centro Europa Ricerche, Via L Luciani 1, 00197 Rome Italy. **Tel** 011 39 6 3224449.

IT

RAPPORTO CONGIUNTURA. Italian. Lettera Finanziaria Srl, Via de Alessandri 11, 20144 Milan Italy.

IT

RASSEGNA DELL ECONOMIA LUCANA. **Added/Corp** Potenza, Italy (Province). Camera di Commercio, Industria, Artigianato e Agricoltura. Potenza, Italy (Province). Camera di Commercio, Industria, Artigianato e Agricoltura. Prezzi l'Ingrosso Praticati di Fatto in Provincia. Vol. 8 (Jan./Feb. 1970)-. Italian. Six times a year. L68130. Camera Comm Ind Art Agr / Abbon, Abbon Corso XVIII Agosto 34, 85100 Potenza Italy. **Tel** 011 39 971 411346, or 411484. ***Continues** Lucania Economica.*

LC HB7 .R35 **ISSN** 0033-944X
DD 330/.05 IT

RASSEGNA DELLA LETTERATURA SUI CICLI ECONOMICI / ISTITUTO NAZIONALE PER LO STUDIO DELLA CONGIUNTURA. **Added/Corp** Istituto Nazionale per lo Studio della Congiuntura (Italy). (19??)-. Periodical. Italian. L1500000 regular membership. Istituto Nazio Studio Congiuntura, Piazza Indipendenza 4, 00185 Rome Italy. **Tel** 011 39 6 444821, FAX 011 39 6 44482619.

IT
CEASED

RASSEGNA DI FISCO E FINANZA. (19??)-(Dec. 1993). Italian. Bollettino Contributi Tasse, Via Capecelatro 12, 20148 Milan Italy. **Tel** 011 39 2 4036746.

LC HC301 .R33 **ISSN** 0390-010X
DD 330 IT

Pr Rev.
RASSEGNA ECONOMICA. [Rass. econ.]. **Added/Corp** Banco di Napoli. (1955)-. Periodical. Italian. Four times a year. Free on request. IBM Italia Spa, Direzione Studi Economici, 20090 Segrate Italy. ***Continues** Rassegna Economico-Finanziaria.*
Ind/Abst GeoRef; Int. Bibliogr. Sociol.; J. Econ. Lit.; PAIS Int. Print.

IT

RASSEGNA ECONOMICA: TERNI. **Main/Corp** Camera di Commercio, Industria e Agricoltura di Terni. Vol. 1-9, (1954-63); New Series (1965)-. Periodical. Italian. Four times a year. L40880. Camera Comm Ind Agr Art/Terni, Largo Don Minzoni 6, 05100 Terni Italy. **Tel** 011 39 744 4891. **(Subscription address:** Italia Srl, C SO Brescia 75, 10152 Turin, Italy. **Tel** 011 39 11 2480870.**)**

ISSN 1057-090X
DD 333 US

REA REPORT, THE. (REA REPORT: ECONOMIC ANALYSIS AND FORECASTS FOR THE NON-ECONOMIST.). [REA rep.]. **Added/Corp** Regional

Business and Economics

Econometric Associates. **VAT** Regional Econometric Associates Report. (May 1991)-. Periodical. English. Twelve times a year. $285.00. REA Report, 318 East Sycamore Street, Columbus OH 43206-2242.

LC HC101 .R33   **ISSN** 1056-1781
DD 339/.0973   US
READINGS IN INTRODUCTORY MACROECONOMICS. [Read. introd. macroecon.]. (1987/1988)-. English. One time a year. $12.03. McGraw Hill Publishing Company, Inc., 1221 Avenue of the Americas, New York NY 10020. **Tel** (212)512-6410, (800)525-5003, FAX (212)512-6111. **(Subscription address:** McGraw Hill Book Company, Princeton Road, Hightstown NJ 08520. **Tel** (717)794-5461.) *Continues* Introduction to Macroeconomics, 1052-052X.

ISSN 1064-1491
DD 333   US
REAL ESTATE CAPITAL MARKETS REPORT. [Real estate cap. mark. rep.]. **VFOAT** Capital Markets. Vol. 1, No. 1 (1991)-. Periodical. English. Four times a year (Jan., Apr., July, Oct.). $295.00. Institute Real Estate letter, 2211 Olympic Boulevard, Walnut Creek CA 94595. **Tel** (510)933-4040. **ED** Larry Gray. **Ad Acc. Circ:** 1,100 (ctrl).

LC HF5549.5.R44 R4   **ISSN** 0034-1827
    US
RECRUITING TRENDS. (19??)-. Periodical. English. Twelve times a year. $155.00. Remy Publishing Company, 350 Hubbard Street, Suite 440, Chicago IL 60610. **Tel** (312)464-0300, FAX (312)464-0166. **ED** Regina Ann Ludes. Index available (published separately). cum. index. **Bk Rev. ctrl circ.**
Desc: Published for the recruiting executive.

    UK
RED ALERT. (19??)-. English. One time a week (51 issues). £225.00. Red Alert, 15 Monckton Avenue, Lowestoft NR32 3EB United Kingdom. **Tel** FAX 011 44 1502 565900. **ED** Jane Clayton. **Circ:** 117.
Desc: Providing a comprehensive information service listing companies in England and Wales which are in financial difficulties.

ISSN 0730-6563
    US
REED-DUNN'S BUSINESS REVIEW. **VAT** Reed Dunn's Business Review. Vol. 1, No. 1 (Apr. 16, 1982)-. Periodical. English. Four times a year. $12.00. Reed-Dunn, 1 Grand Center Building, 1 Grand Avenue, Sherman TX 75090.

ISSN 0890-9954
DD 330   US
REEDER'S ECONOMIC DIGEST. [Reeder's econ. dig.]. **Added/Corp** Charles Reeder Associates. **VFOAT** Economic Digest. (19??)-. Periodical. English. Twelve times a year. $95.00. Charles Reeder Associates, PO Box 638, Merrit Island FL 32952. **Tel** (407)459-1558. **ED** Charles B. Reeder. **Circ:** 400 (ctrl).
Desc: Review of current economic trends, together with outlook for near-term future.

LC HC111   **ISSN** 0712-4236
DD 330.9714/2704   CN
REFERENCE (COMMUNAUTE URBAINE DE MONTREAL. OFFICE DE L'EXPANSION ECONOMIQUE). (REFERENCE / COMMUNAUTE URBAINE DE MONTREAL, OFFICE D'EXPANSION ECONOMIQUE.). [Reference]. (1974)-. French. Every 3 years. Free. Communaute Urbaine De Montreal, CP 55, Montreal Quebec H4Z 1A8.

LC HC111   **ISSN** 0712-4244
DD 330.9714/2704   CN
REFERENCE (COMMUNAUTE URBAINE DE MONTREAL. OFFICE D'EXPANSION ECONOMIQUE. ENGLISH EDITION). (REFERENCE / COMMUNAUTE URBAINE DE MONTREAL, OFFICE DE L'EXPANSION ECONOMIQUE.). [Reference]. (1974)-. English. Every 3 years. Free. Economic Development Office, Suite 4130 PO Box 55, Tour De La Bourse, Montreal Quebec H4Z 1A8.

ISSN 0395-904X
    FR
REFLETS DE L'ECONOMIE FRANC-COMTOISE. (May 1971)-. Periodical. French. Six times a year. CNGP INSEE - Institut National de la Statistique et des Estudes Economiques, BP 2718, 1 rue V Auriol, F 80027 Amiens Cedex 1 France. **Tel** 011 33 22 927322. Index available. **Circ:** 700. *Supersedes in part* Bulletin de Statistique: Bourgogne (Cote-Dor, Nievre, Saone-et-Loire, Yonne), Franche-Comte (Doubs, Jura, Haute-Saone, Territoire de Belfort).

ISSN 1058-7632
DD 330   US
REFORMA ECONOMICA HOY. **Added/Corp** Center for International Private Enterprise. Vol. 1, No. 1 (Summer 1991)-. Periodical. Spanish. Four times a year. Free. Center for Internaitonal Private Enterprise, 1615 H Street NW, Washington DC 20062. **Tel** (202)463-5901.

LC HC108.W3 R43   **ISSN** 0279-5965
DD 330.9753/005   US
    CEASED
REGARDIE'S. See Real Estate.

LC E41   **ISSN** 0315-212X
DD 917.124/4   CN
REGINA. **VAT** Regina Magazine. Visitor Information Guide. (1972)-. English. One time a year. Regina Chamber of Commerce, 2145 Albert Street, Regina Saskatchewan S4P 2V1 Canada. **Tel** (306)757-4658. **ED** Mack McColl. **Bk Rev. Ad Acc. Circ:** 6,500 (ctrl).
Desc: Paid advertising tabloid providing news and information pertinent to the business community of Regina, Saskatchewan.

    IT
REGIO. Italian. L1284000.00. Office for Official Publications of the European Communities, 2 rue Mercier, 2985 Luxembourg Luxembourg. **Tel** 011 352 499281, FAX 011 352 292942763. **(Subscription address:** Licosa s.p.a., PO Box 552, 50125 Florence Italy. **Tel** 011 39 55 645415.)

LC HC101 .N36   **ISSN** 0090-9262
DD 330.9/73/092   US
REGIONAL ECONOMIC PROJECTIONS SERIES. **Added/Corp** National Planning Association. Center for Economic Studies. (1962)-. English. Three times a year. $1600.00. National Planning Association, 1424 16th Street Northwest, Suite 700, Washington DC 20036. **Tel** (202)265-7685. **ED** Nestor E. Terleckyj. **Circ:** 500 (ctrl). available on an online database; available on magnetic tape; available on diskette; available in print. *Continues* Regional Economic Projections Series, 0090-9262.
Desc: Basic reference source for US Regional economies. Annual data for 155 demographic and 52 economic indicators, 1967-2010, for each state, MSA and county region, economic area.

LC HC   **ISSN** 0896-2537
DD 330   US
    CCC
REGIONAL ECONOMIES AND MARKETS. [Reg. econ. mark.]. **Added/Corp** Economic Analysis Program (Conference Board). Vol. 1, No. 1 (Fall 1986)-. Periodical. English. Four times a year. $295.00. Conference Board, 845 Third Avenue, New York NY 10022. **Tel** (212)759-0900 ext. 582, (800)872-6273, FAX (212)980-7014.

    UK
REGIONAL PAPERS - NATIONAL INSTITUTE OF ECONOMIC AND SOCIAL RESEARCH. **Main/Corp** National Institute of Economic and Social Research. (1970)-. Monographic series. English. Irregular. Price varies per volume. Cambridge University Press, The Edinburgh Building, Shaftesbury Road, Cambridge CB2 2RU United Kingdom. **Tel** 011 44 1223 312393, FAX 011 44 1223 315052, telex 851-817256.

ISSN 0250-7315
    US
    CEASED
REGLEMENTATION GENERALE, REGLES ET REGLEMENTS. [Reglem. gen. regles et reglem., Fonds monet. int.]. **Main/Corp** International Monetary Fund. (19??)-(19??). French. International Monetary Fund, 700 19th Street Northwest, Publishing Unit, Washington DC 20431. **Tel** (202)623-7430, FAX (202)623-7201.

ISSN 1064-1548
DD 368   US
REIMBURSEMENT UPDATE SALT LAKE CITY, UTAH. [Reimburse. update Salt Lake City Utah]. **VFOAT** Update. (19??)-. Periodical. English. Four times a year (Mar., June, Sept., Dec.). $105.00 (one-year); $190.00 (two-year). Reimbursement Update, C/O Dr. Fred Curtiss, 355 Oak Park, Double Oak TX 75067. **Tel** (817)491-3593, FAX (817)491-3593. **ED** Dr. Fred Curtiss. ctrl circ.

    US
REIS [COMPUTER FILE] : REGIONAL ECONOMIC INFORMATION SYSTEM. **Added/Corp** United States. Bureau of Economic Analysis. Regional Economic Measurement Division. **VFOAT** Regional Economic Information System. (July 1990)-. English. Bureau of Economic Analysis, US Department of Commerce, 1401 K Street Northwest, Washington DC 20230. **Tel** (202)523-0777.
Desc: System requirements: computer system capable of using CD-ROM drive; 640K; if IBM compatible personal computer, requires CD-ROM software such as Microsoft CD-ROM extensions version 3.1 or higher; CD-ROM drive and hard disk.

LC AP95.I5 R44
    IO
REKAMAN PERISTIWA ... . See Sociology.

LC WMLC L 83/7957
    IT
RELAZIONE SULLA SITUAZIONE ECONOMICA DELLA CALABRIA NEL / CENTRO DI STUDI E DI RICERCHE ECONOMICO-SOCIALI DELLA CALABRIA. (1967)-. Italian.

LC WMLC L 83/7950
    IT
RELAZIONE SULL'ATTIVITA SVOLTA NEL ... . **Main/Corp** Universita di Genova. Istituto Geofisico e Geodetico. (19??)-. Italian. One time a year. Universita di Genova, Instituto Geofisico e Geodetico, Con Annessi Osservatori Geofisici di Genova, Genova Italy.

ISSN 1070-8081
DD 338   US
RELOCATABLE BUSINESS. [Relocat. bus.]. Vol. 6, No. 7 (1991)-. Periodical. English. Twenty-four times a year. $150.00. Business Listing Services Inc., PO Box 549, Highland Park IL 60035. **Tel** (800)927-1310, FAX (708)433-4711. **ED** Richard J. Carmel. **Bk Rev,** (Qty: 1 or 2). **Circ:** 1,000. *Continues* Business Listing Services.
Desc: News and reports describing the pricing of relocating a business that is currently up for sale.

    US
RELOCATION FACT BOOK. See Real Estate.

ISSN 0275-7613
    US
    CCC
RELOCATION REPORT, THE. See Real Estate.

ISSN 1070-3411
DD 616   US
REMINGTON REPORT, THE. [Remington rep.]. (1992)-. Periodical. English. Six times a year. $99.00. Remington Advisory Group, 28202 Cabot Road, Suite 150, Laguna Niguel CA 92677. **Tel** (800)247-4781. **Circ:** 25,000 (ctrl).
Desc: A business intelligence resource for the healthcare and homecare industries.

    US
RENDEZ VOUS CANADA. (19??)-. English. One time a year. Free on request. Baxter Publishing Company, 310 Dupont Street, Toronto Ontario M5R 1V9 Canada. **Tel** (416)968-7252, FAX (416)968-2377.

LC HB3654.A3 J468   **ISSN** 1000-4149
DD 304.6/0951   CC
RENKOU YU JINGJI. See Population Studies.

ISSN 0721-4588
    GW
UDC 34:377.3 (07)   CCC
RENO. (1981)-. Trade Publication. German. Twelve times a year. $75.23. Gabler Verlag, Postfach 1546, D-65005 Wiesbaden Germany. **Tel** 011 49 611 534129, FAX 011 49 611 534430.

ISSN 0898-7106
DD 333   US
    TITLE CHANGE
RENTAL (FORT ATKINSON, WIS.). (RENTAL.). Vol. 10, No. 4 (April 1988)-(1992). Periodical. English. Johnson Hill Press Inc., (A Division of PTN Publishing Co.), 1233 Janesville Avenue, PO Box 803, Fort Atkinson WI 53538-0803. **Tel** (414)563-6388, FAX (414)563-1704. *Continues* Rental Product News, 0163-3112. *Continued by* Rental Product News (Fort Atkinson, Wis. : 1992), 1067-0904.

LC HD9999.L438 U56   **ISSN** 1042-9085
DD 381/.45   US
RENTAL MANAGEMENT. (RENTAL MANAGEMENT : THE OFFICIAL MAGAZINE OF THE AMERICAN RENTAL MANAGEMENT.). [Rent. manage.]. **Added/Corp** American Rental Association. (198?)-. Periodical. English. Twelve times a year. $24.00. American Rental Association, 1900 19th Street, Moline IL 61265-4179. **Tel** (309)764-2475. *Continues* Rental Age, 0098-8529.

ISSN 1067-0904
DD 338   US
RENTAL PRODUCT NEWS (1992). (RENTAL PRODUCT NEWS.). [Rental prod. news]. (1992)-. Trade Publication. English. Seven times a year. $40.00. Johnson Hill Press Inc., (A Division of PTN Publishing Co.), 1233 Janesville Avenue, PO Box 803, Fort Atkinson WI 53538-0803. **Tel** (414)563-6388, FAX (414)563-1704. **ED** Cynthia Ehrke. **Ad Acc.** Full Page

Business and Economics

(B&W) $2475.00. Full Page (Color) $3435.00 (4-color). **Circ:** 20,095. **Continues** Rental, 1067-0904.
Desc: Serves owners and managers of equipment rental businesses; also provides information on how to profitably rent products.

LC HD9999.L4363 U67
DD 338.7/61 US
RENTAL PRODUCT NEWS SHOWCASE. (1980)-. English. One time a year. $20.00. Johnson Hill Press Inc., (A Division of PTN Publishing Co.), 1233 Janesville Avenue, PO Box 803, Fort Atkinson WI 53538-0803. **Tel** (414)563-6388, FAX (414)563-1704.

ISSN 0395-9031
FR
REPERES (MONTPELLIER). See Business and Economics-Abstracting, Bibliographies and Statistics.

LC HD2321 **ISSN** 0824-0507
DD 338/.0025/714271 CN
REPERTOIRE DES ETABLISSEMENTS. [Repert. etabl. - Serv. rech. stat., Ville Laval]. (1976)-. French. One time a year. Service des Recherches et de la Statistique, 1 place du Souvenir Chomedey, Ville de Laval Quebec H7V 1W7 Canada.

ISSN 0849-0694
DD 338.7/6/02571554 CN
REPERTOIRE DES INDUSTRIES MANUFACTURIERES DU NORD-OUOUEST. (REPERTOIRE DES INDUSTRIES MANUFACTURIERES DU NORD-OUEST.). [Repert. ind. manuf. Nord-Ouest]. **Added/Corp** Commission Industrielle du Nord-Ouest (N.-B.). French. Northwest Industrial Commission, PO Box 490, Edmundston New Brunswick E3V 3L2 Canada. **Continues** Repertoire (Commission Industrielle du Nord-Ouest (N.-B.))., 0822-7454.

IT
CEASED
REPERTORIO COMMERCIALE. (19??)-(1995). Italian. Repertorio Commerciale, Viale Monte Rosa 51, 20149 Milan Italy. **Tel** 011 39 2 48001936, 011 39 2 48001491. **Continues** Europa Management.

LC H62.A1 A6 **ISSN** 0065-6216
DD 330.973 US
NLM W1 AL3175
REPORT - ALFRED P. SLOAN FOUNDATION. **Main/Corp** Alfred P. Sloan Foundation. (1938)-. English. One time a year. Free on request. Alfred P. Sloan Foundation, 630 Fifth Avenue, New York NY 10020. **Tel** (212)582-0450.

LC HC241.25.I7 I74a
DD 330 IE
REPORT / JOINT COMMITTEE ON THE SECONDARY LEGISLATION OF THE EUROPEAN COMMUNITIES. **Main/Corp** Ireland. Oireachtas. Joint Committee on the Secondary Legislation of the European Communities. (198?)-. English. Government Publications, 4 5 Harcourt Road, Dublin 2 Ireland. **Tel** 011 353 1 6613111 ext.4005. **Continues** Ireland. Oireachtas. Joint Committee on the Secondary Legislation of the European Communities. Tuairisc Oifigiuil - An Comhchoiste ar Reachtaiocht Tanaisteach na Comhphobal Eorpach.

LC Z7164.C81 G36 HF5351
DD 016.6584 US
REPORT OF PUBLICATION AND RESEARCH. **Main/Corp** Georgia State University. College of Business Administration. (19??)-. Periodical. English. Georgia State University College of Business Administration, Box 695 University Plaza, Atlanta GA 30303. **Continues** Georgia State University. School of Business Administration. Report of Publication by the Faculty of the School of Business Administration, Georgia State University.

LC HD9066.A1 F58B
DD 338.1/7318/05 IT
REPORT OF THE ... SESSION OF THE CONSULTATIVE SUB-COMMITTEE ON THE ECONOMIC ASPECTS OF RICE TO THE COMMITTEE ON COMMODITY PROBLEMS. **Main/Corp** Food and Agriculture Organization of the United Nations. Consultative Sub-Committee on the Economic Aspects of Rice. **VFOAT** Rice. English. One time a year. Food Agriculture Organization (FAO) / Italy, GIPCI66 via Terme di Caracalla, 00100 Rome Italy. **Tel** 011 39 6 52252925, FAX 011 39 6 52253152.

LC HF3221 **ISSN** 1196-6688
DD 380.1/09711 CN
REPORT ON B.C. [Rep. B.C.]. **VAT** Report on British Columbia. (199?)-. Periodical. English. Twelve times a year. Provincial Newsletters, 1609 Blanchard Street, Victoria BC V8W 2J5 Canada. **Continues** John Twigg's Report on B.C., 0838-1542.

ISSN 0847-2831
DD 338.7/4/0971 CN
CCC
REPORT ON BUSINESS, CANADA COMPANY HANDBOOK. [Rep. bus. Can. co. handb.]. **Added/Corp** Info Globe. (Fall 1989)-. Periodical. English. One time a year. 49.95Can$. Globe & Mail, 444 Front Street West, Toronto Ontario M5V 2S9 Canada. **Tel** (416)585-5000, FAX (416)585-5085. **ED** Alan Husdal. Index available. **Ad Acc.**
Desc: Gives current news, quarterly and annual financial information, ratios and stock price charts for 395 Canadian publicly owned companies.

LC HD2807 .R46 **ISSN** 0827-7680
DD 380.1/0971 CN
CCC
REPORT ON BUSINESS MAGAZINE. [Rep. bus. mag.]. **VFOAT** Investment and Tax Guide; 1000; Report on Business 1000. Vol. 1, No. 3 (Mar. 1985)-. Periodical. English. Twelve times a year. Globe & Mail, 444 Front Street West, Toronto Ontario M5V 2S9 Canada. **Tel** (416)585-5000, FAX (416)585-5085. **Continues** Report on Business (Globe and Mail (Firm)), 0827-7672.
Ind/Abst Can. Period. Index (19??-).

PH
REPORT ON THE ... PDCP SURVEY OF BUSINESS PERFORMANCE FOR MANILA, A. English. One time a year. P3,200 Philippines; $20.00 other. PO Box 757 Makati, Metro Manila 3117 Philippines. **Tel** 810-02-31, telex RCA 22080 RCPI 2131. **ED** Dante M Liwanes. **Ad Acc. Circ:** 150 (ctrl).

UK
REPORT : REVIEW BODY OF TOP SALARIES. (19??)-. English. One time a year. £17.70. Her Majesty's Stationery Office, 51 Nine Elms Lane, London SW8 5DR United Kingdom. **Tel** 011 44 171 8738459, 011 44 171 8738499, FAX 011 44 171 8738499, 011 44 171 8738456, telex 297138. **(Subscription address:** Her Majesty's Stationery Office, PO Box 276, Public Centre, London SW8 5DT United Kingdom. **Tel** 011 44 171 8738499, 011 44 171 8738456.**)**

US
REPORT TO MEMBERS. (19??)-. English. Irregular. Free. Securities Industry Association, 120 Broadway/35th Floor, New York NY 10271. **Tel** (212)608-1500, FAX (212)608-1604.
Desc: For managing executives with information and commentary on matters of particular importance to members.

US
REPORTING CASH PAYMENTS OF OVER $10,000 (RECEIVED IN A TRADE OR BUSINESS). **Added/Corp** United States. Internal Revenue Service. **VFOAT** Reporting Cash Payments of Over Ten Thousand Dollars (Received in a Trade or Business). (Apr. 1991)-. English. Department of the Treasury / Eastern Area Distribution Center, Internal Revenue Service, PO Box 85074, Richmond VA 23261-5074.

LC HC **ISSN** 0414-0508
DD 338.9 UK
REPORTS: E. See Education.

LC DK266.A2 R37 **ISSN** 0034-4931
DD 914.7/03/05 US
UDC 908.47
SUSPENDED
REPRINTS FROM THE SOVIET PRESS. See Political Science.

UK
RESEARCH AT LSE. **Main/Corp** London School of Economics and Political Science. Periodical. English. London School of Economics and Political Science, Tieto Ltd, Bank House, 8A Hill Road, Clevedon Avon BS21 7HH United Kingdom.

ISSN 1185-1902
DD 332.63 CN
RESEARCH BIWEEKLY. [Res. biwkly.]. **Added/Corp** Midland Walwyn Capital.Research Dept. Feb. 15, (1991)-. Periodical. English. Twenty-six times a year. Limited free distribution. Midland Walwyn Capital, Suite 1600, 121 King Street West, Toronto Ontario M5H 3W6 Canada.

LC HC1055.A1 R47 **ISSN** 0189-0085
DD 338.9669/005 NR
RESEARCH FOR DEVELOPMENT : THE JOURNAL OF THE NIGERIAN INSTITUTE OF SOCIAL & ECONOMIC RESEARCH. **Added/Corp** Nigerian Institute of Social and Economic Research. Vol. 1, No. 1 (Jan. 1981)-. Periodical. English. Two times a year. $70.00. Secretary of the Editorial Board / Nigeria, Research for Development, NISER/PMB 5, University of Ibadan, Ibadan Nigeria. **Tel** 011 234 22 40050014, telex 31119 NISER NG. **ED** T. O. Fadayomi. **Bk Rev. Ad Acc.**
Desc: Issued mainly for social science research.

LC HD9000.1 .R49 **ISSN** 0276-1653
DD 338.1/072 US
RESEARCH IN DOMESTIC AND INTERNATIONAL AGRIBUSINESS MANAGEMENT. [Res. domest. int. agribus. manage.]. Vol. 1 (1980)-. Monographic series. English. One time a year. $73.25. JAI Press Inc., 55 Old Post Road, Suite 2, PO Box 1678, Greenwich CT 06836-1678. **Tel** (203)661-7602, FAX (203)661-0792. **ED** Ray A. Goldberg.
Ind/Abst AGRICOLA [Full Cov.].

LC HB1 .R36 **ISSN** 0193-2306
DD 330/.05 US
CCC
RESEARCH IN EXPERIMENTAL ECONOMICS. [Res. exp. econ.]. Vol. 1 (1979)-. Monographic series. English. Irregular. $73.25. JAI Press Inc., 55 Old Post Road, Suite 2, PO Box 1678, Greenwich CT 06836-1678. **Tel** (203)661-7602, FAX (203)661-0792. **ED** Vernon L. Smith.
Ind/Abst AGRICOLA.

LC K18 .E835 **ISSN** 0193-5895
DD 330/.05 US
CCC
RESEARCH IN LAW AND ECONOMICS. See Law.

LC HB75 .R447 **ISSN** 0743-4154
DD 330/.09 US
RESEARCH IN THE HISTORY OF ECONOMIC THOUGHT AND METHODOLOGY. [Res. hist. econ. thought methodol.]. Vol. 1 (1983)-. Periodical. English. One time a year. $73.25. JAI Press Inc., 55 Old Post Road, Suite 2, PO Box 1678, Greenwich CT 06836-1678. **Tel** (203)661-7602, FAX (203)661-0792. **ED** Warren J. Samuels and Jeff Biddle.
Ind/Abst Am. Hist. Life (1989-).

LC HT321 .R47 **ISSN** 0277-0121
DD 330.9173/2 US
RESEARCH IN URBAN ECONOMICS. [Res. urban econ.]. Vol. 1 (1981)-. English. Irregular. $73.25. JAI Press Inc., 55 Old Post Road, Suite 2, PO Box 1678, Greenwich CT 06836-1678. **Tel** (203)661-7602, FAX (203)661-0792. **ED** Robert D. Ebel.

LC Z7164.C81 R397 **ISSN** 0034-5296
DD 016.65 UK
RESEARCH INDEX. See Business and Economics-Abstracting, Bibliographies and Statistics.

US
CEASED
RESEARCH MONOGRAPH. **Main/Corp** Georgia State University. School of Business Administration. (1973)-(June 1995). Periodical. English. Georgia State University College of Business Administration, Box 695 University Plaza, Atlanta GA 30303. **Continues** Georgia State University. Bureau of Business and Economic Research. Research Paper.

US
RESEARCH MONOGRAPH - UNIVERSITY OF TEXAS AT AUSTIN. BUREAU OF BUSINESS RESEARCH. **Main/Corp** University of Texas at Austin. Bureau of Business Research. No. 33 (1971)-. English. Irregular. University of Texas at Austin Institute of Public Affairs, Austin TX 78712. **Continues** Texas. University. Bureau of Business Research. Research Monograph.

LC HC79.I5 R45 **ISSN** 1049-2585
DD 339.2/05 US
RESEARCH ON ECONOMIC INEQUALITY. [Res. econ. inequal.]. Vol. 1 (1989)-. English. Irregular. $73.25. JAI Press Inc., 55 Old Post Road, Suite 2, PO Box 1678, Greenwich CT 06836-1678. **Tel** (203)661-7602, FAX (203)661-0792. **ED** Daniel J. Slottje.

LC HD42 .R47 **ISSN** 1040-9556
DD 658.4 US
CCC
RESEARCH ON NEGOTIATION IN ORGANIZATIONS. See Business and Economics-Management.

ISSN 0819-2642
AT

RESEARCH PAPER - UNIVERSITY OF MELBOURNE, DEPARTMENT OF ECONOMICS. (1973)-. Monographic series. English. Irregular.
Ind/Abst Leis., Rec., Tour. Abstr.; World Agric. Econ. Rural Sociol. Abstr.

ISSN 0893-4347
DD 330 US

RESEARCH RECOMMENDATIONS. [Res. recomm.]. **Added/Corp** National Institute of Business Management. (19??)-. Newsletter. English. One time a week. $128.72. National Institute of Business Management, Inc., 1101 King Street, Alexandria VA 22133. **Tel** (800)543-2052, (703)548-3885, (800)543-2049, FAX (703)549-0182. **ED** Hiram Reisner. ***Continues*** *Research Institute of America, Inc. Research Institute Recommendations, 0048-7317.*
Desc: Serves the specialized information needs of top executives and business owners.

LC HC231 .A63a
DD 338.987 UY

RESENA DE LA ACTIVIDAD DURANTE EL EJERCICIO. **Main/Corp** Academia Nacional de Economia (Uruguay). (19??)-. Spanish.

NE

RESOURCES AND ENERGY ECONOMICS. Academic Scholarly Publication. English. Fl479.00 (includes postage). Elsevier Science Publishers BV, PO Box 211, 1000 AE Amsterdam Netherlands. **Tel** 011 31 20 4853641, 011 31 20 4853642, FAX 011 31 20 4853598. ***Continues*** *Resources and Energy, 0165-0572.*

ISSN 1048-1311
DD 658 US

RESULTS ... ANNUAL SURVEY OF CORPORATE RELOCATION POLICIES. [Results annu. surv. corp. relocat. policies]. 21st (1988)-. Corporate Report. English. One time a year. Atlas Van Lines, PO Box 509, Evansville IN 47703. **Tel** (812)424-2222, telex (800)457-3705. **ED** James E Huth II. **Circ:** 15,000. ***Continues*** *Results, Atlas Van Lines ... Annual Survey of Corporate Moving Practices, 8755-0156.*

ISSN 0263-1377
DD 658.87002853 UK

RETAIL AUTOMATION. [Retail autom.]. (1981)-. Trade Publication. English. Six times a year (Jan., Mar., May, July, Sept., Nov.). £80.00 UK; £84.00 Europe; £92.00 other. RMDP, The Hideway Furze Hill Hove, East Sussec BN3 1PA United Kingdom. **Tel** 011 44 1273 722687, FAX 011 44 1273 821463, telex 67323. **ED** Penny Ody. ctrl circ.

UK

RETHINKING CORPORATE STRATEGY FOR AFRICA : OPPORTUNITIES AND RISKS IN A FAST-CHANGING ENVIRONMENT. (19??)-. English. One time a year. $375.00 (schools and educational libraries), $500.00 (other) North America. The Economist Intelligence Unit, 40 Duke Street, London W1A 1DW United Kingdom. **Tel** 011 44 171 8301000. **(Subscription address:** Economist Intelligence Unit / North America Subscriptions, 111 West 57th Street, New York NY 10019. **Tel** 800 938-4685, (212)554-0600, FAX (212)586-1181, (212)586-1182.)
Desc: Helps you to identify the opportunities starting to appear in sub-Saharan Africa, while developing a corporate strategy that fits the African business environment of the 1990s. It includes the effects of policy changes on business, African growth industries in the 1990s, prospects for privatization, and forecasts of key African economies.

LC HX1 .R52 ISSN 0893-5696
DD 335.43/05 US
CCC

Pr Rev.

RETHINKING MARXISM. **Added/Corp** Association for Economic and Social Analysis. **VFOAT** RM. Vol. 1 No. 1 (Spring 1988)-. Periodical. English. Four times a year. $75.00. Guilford Publications Inc., 72 Spring Street, New York NY 10012. **Tel** (212)431-9800, (800)365-7006, FAX (212)966-6708. **(Subscription address:** Turpin Distribution Services Limited, Blackhorse Road, Letchworth, Hertfordshire SH6 1HN United Kingdom. **Tel** 011 44 1462 672555, FAX 011 44 1462 480947.) **ED** Jack Amariglio. Index available. **Bk Rev. Ad Acc. Circ:** 750.
Desc: Provides a forum for discussing new advances in Marxism taking place across all disciplines and within diverse struggles for social change.
Ind/Abst Altern. Press Index (199?-); Am. Hist. Life (1988-1989); Film Lit. Index (19??-); Hum. Resour. Abstr. (?-?); Left Index; Sage Public Adm. Abstr. (?-?); Soc. Plann. Policy Dev. Abstr.

LC HB9 .A83a
AG

REUNION ANUAL - AAEP. **Main/Corp** Asociacion Argentina de Economia Politica. **Added/Corp** Universidad Nacional de Cuyo. Facultad de Ciencias Economicas. (19??)-. Spanish. One time a year. Universidad Nacional de Cuyo, Facultad de Ciencias Economicas, Mendoza Argentina.

ISSN 0034-6403
MY

REVIEW OF AGRICULTURAL ECONOMICS MALAYSIA. See Agriculture-Agricultural Economics.

LC HB98 .R4 ISSN 0889-3047
DD 330.15/7 US
CCC

REVIEW OF AUSTRIAN ECONOMICS, THE. [Rev. Austrian econ.]. **Added/Corp** Ludwig Von Mises Institute. Vol. 1 (1987)-. Periodical. English. Two times a year. $289.00. Kluwer Academic Publishers / Massachusetts, PO Box 358, Accord Station, Hingham MA 02018. **Tel** (617)871-6600. **ED** Murray Rothbard and Walter Block. **Acid Free.**
Desc: To promote the development and extension of Austrian economics and the analysis of contemporary issues in the mainstream of economics from an Austrian perspective.

LC E185.5 .R45 ISSN 0034-6446
DD 330.9 US
CCC

Pr Rev.

REVIEW OF BLACK POLITICAL ECONOMY, THE. [Rev. Black polit. econ.]. **Added/Corp** National Economic Association (U.S.) Black Economic Research Center. Atlanta University Center (Ga.). Vol. 1 (Spring/Summer 1970)-. Periodical. English. Four times a year. $96.00. Transaction Publishers / Rutgers State University, Department 3091 or 3092, New Brunswick NJ 08903. **Tel** (908)932-2280 ext. 105, FAX (908)932-3138. **ED** James Stewart. cum. index. **Bk Rev. Ad Acc. Circ:** 1,100. available on labels; available on microfilm and microfiche from University Microfilms International (UMI). Documents available from The Genuine Article, UMI Article Clearinghouse.
Desc: Examines issues related to the economic status of black and third world peoples. Identifies and analyzes policy prescriptions designed to reduce racial economic inequality. A publication of the National Economic Association and the Southern Center for Studies in Public Policy of Clark College.
Ind/Abst Acad. Search; Am. Hist. Life (1983-); Bus. ASAP (1990-) [Full Txt.]; Bus. Index (1985-); Curr. Contents Soc. Behav. Sci.; Econ. Lit. Index; EP Collect.; Expand. Acad. Index (1984-); Gen. BusinessFile (1985-); Gen. Period. Index (1985-); Homework Help.; Hum. Resour. Abstr. (?-?); INFO-SOUTH Abstr.; Int. Bibliogr. Sociol.; J. Econ. Lit.; MasterFile FullTEXT 1000; MasterFile FullTEXT 350; MasterFile FullTEXT 650; MasterFile FullTEXT (July 1993-); Newsp. Period. Abstr. (1991-); OCLC; PAIS Int. Print; Res. Alert [Full Cov.]; Sage Fam. Stud. Abstr.; Soc. Sci. Source; Soc. Sci. Cit. Index [Full Cov.]; Soc. Sci. Index; Soc. Sci. Index Fulltext (Sprint 1988-) [Full Txt.]; Telebase; Trade Ind. Index (?-?); U.S. Polit. Sci. Doc.; Work Relat. Abstr.

LC WMLC 93/2913 ISSN 0034-6454
US

Pr Rev.

REVIEW OF BUSINESS. [Rev. bus.]. **Added/Corp** St. John's University (New York, N.Y.). Business Research Institute. (19??)-. Periodical. English. Three times a year. $10.00. St. Johns University / Review of Business, Business Research Institute, 8000 Utopia Parkway, Jamaica NY 11439. **Tel** (718)990-6161, (718)990-6768, FAX (718)380-3803. **ED** Christine Rider. **Bk Rev**, (Qty: 3-4). **Circ:** 6,500. available on microfilm and microfiche from University Microfilms International (UMI).
Desc: Articles presenting the results of original research and analysis are given priority, also invite contributions on new and innovative business techniques and practices, commentaries on contemporary issues and new ideas.
Ind/Abst Bus. ASAP (1990-) [Full Txt.]; Bus. Index (1985-); Bus. Source Plus; Curr. Cit.; EP Collect.; Gen. BusinessFile (1985-); Gen. Period. Index (1985-); Homework Help.; Mag. Search; MasterFile FullTEXT 1000; MasterFile FullTEXT 350; MasterFile FullTEXT 650; MasterFile FullTEXT; OCLC; PAIS Int. Print; Telebase; UMI ABI/Inform--Bus. Period. Ondisc (Summer 1987-) [Full Txt.].

LC HF5001 .R48 ISSN 1047-4595
DD 650/.05 US
TITLE CHANGE

REVIEW OF BUSINESS STUDIES, THE. [Rev. bus. stud.]. **Added/Corp** California State University, Fresno. School of Business. Vol. 1, No. 1 (1992)-(1995). Trade Publication. English. JAI Press Inc., 55 Old Post Road, Suite 2, PO Box 1678, Greenwich CT 06836-1678. **Tel** (203)661-7602, FAX (203)661-0792. ***Continued by*** *International Journal of Business.*

LC HB1 .R4 ISSN 0034-6527
DD 330.5 UK
CCC

Pr Rev.

REVIEW OF ECONOMIC STUDIES, THE. [Rev. econ. stud.]. Vol. 1 (Oct. 1933)-. Academic Scholarly Publication. English. Four times a year. $140.00. Basil Blackwell Publishers Ltd., 108 Cowley Road, Oxford 0X4 1JF United Kingdom. **Tel** 011 44 1235 465500, FAX 011 44 1235 465556, telex 837022 OXBOOK G. **(Subscription address:** Blackwell Publishers / UK, 108 Cowley Road, Oxford OX4 1JF United Kingdom. **Tel** 011 44 1865 791100, FAX 011 44 1865 791347.) **ED** C R Bean and K W S Roberts. Index available. cum. index. **Ad Acc. Circ:** 3,000. available on microfilm and microfiche from University Microfilms International (UMI). Documents available from The Genuine Article, UMI Article Clearinghouse.
Desc: Publishes papers in theoretical and applied econometrics and economic theory.
Ind/Abst ABI/INFORM Glob. Ed.; ABI/INFORM [Computer File] (Oct. 1972-July 1973); Acad. Search; Bus. Source Plus; Bus. Source; Contents Recent Econ. J.; Contents Pages Manage.; Curr. Cit.; Curr. Contents Soc. Behav. Sci.; Econ. Lit. Index; EP Collect.; Expand. Acad. Index (1989-); Homework Help.; INFO-SOUTH Abstr.; Int. Labour Doc.; J. Econ. Lit.; J. Plan. Lit.; Mag. Search; MasterFile FullTEXT 1000; MasterFile FullTEXT 350; MasterFile FullTEXT 650; MasterFile FullTEXT (Jan. 1994-); Math. Rev.; Newsp. Period. Abstr. (1991-); OCLC; Res. Alert [Full Cov.]; Selec. Coop. Index Manage. Period.; Soc. Sci. Source; Soc. Sci. Cit. Index [Full Cov.]; Soc. Sci. Index; Soc. Sci. Index Fulltext (Oct. 1988-) [Full Txt.]; Stat. Theory Method Abstr. (1959-1963, 1969-1973); Telebase; Zentralbl. Math. Ihre Grenzgeb.

LC HA1 .R35
DD 330 NE
CODEN RECSA9

Pr Rev.

REVIEW OF ECONOMICS AND STATISTICS, THE. See Business and Economics-Abstracting, Bibliographies and Statistics.

LC HF5001 .M59 ISSN 1058-3300
DD 330/.05 US

Pr Rev.

REVIEW OF FINANCIAL ECONOMICS. (REVIEW OF FINANCIAL ECONOMICS : RFE.). [Rev. financ. econ.]. **Added/Corp** University of New Orleans. Division of Business and Economic Research. **VFOAT** RFE. Vol. 1, No. 1 (Fall 1991)-. Periodical. English. Two times a year. $140.00. JAI Press Inc., 55 Old Post Road, Suite 2, PO Box 1678, Greenwich CT 06836-1678. **Tel** (203)661-7602, FAX (203)661-0792. **ED** Walton T. Wilford. **Circ:** 1,000. Documents available from UMI Article Clearinghouse. ***Continues*** *RBER, Review of Business and Economic Research, 0362-7985.*
Desc: Publishes theoretical and empirical manuscripts in financial economics.
Ind/Abst ABI/INFORM Glob. Ed.; ABI/INFORM [Computer File]; Acad. Search; Bus. Period. Index; Bus. Source Plus; Bus. Source; EP Collect.; Homework Help.; INFO-SOUTH Abstr.; MasterFile FullTEXT 1000; MasterFile FullTEXT 350; MasterFile FullTEXT 650; MasterFile FullTEXT (July 1993-); OCLC; Telebase; UMI ABI/Inform--Bus. Period. Ondisc (Fall 1987-) [Full Txt.]; Wilson Bus. Abstr.

SZ

REVIEW OF INTERNATIONAL COOPERATION. (19??)-. English. 72.00F combined subscription with ICA News. International Cooperative Alliance, Route des Morillons 15, CH-1218 Geneva Switzerland. **Tel** 011 41 22 7984121, FAX 011 41 22 7984122, telex 845 27935. **ED** Mary Treacy.
Ind/Abst Dairy Sci. Abstr.; Poult. Abstr.; Rural Dev. Abstr.; World Agric. Econ. Rural Sociol. Abstr.

LC HD9018.A7 R4 ISSN 0034-6616
AT

REVIEW OF MARKETING AND AGRICULTURAL ECONOMICS. See Agriculture-Agricultural Economics.

LC HB1 .R46 ISSN 0953-8259
UK
CODEN RPECEI

REVIEW OF POLITICAL ECONOMY. See Political Science.

LC HC101 .R43 ISSN 0486-6134
DD 330.973 US
CCC

REVIEW OF RADICAL POLITICAL ECONOMICS, THE. [Rev. radic. polit. econ.]. **Added/Corp** Union for Radical Political Economics. **VFOAT** RRPE. Vol. 1, (May 1969)-. Periodical. English. Four times a year. $107.00. Blackwell Publishers, 238 Main Street, Cambridge MA 02142. **Tel** (617)547-7110, (800)835-6770, FAX (617)547-0789. **ED** David Houston. **Bk Rev. Ad Acc. Circ:** 2,700 (ctrl). available on microfilm and microfiche from University Microfilms International (UMI). Documents available from UMI Article Clearinghouse.
Desc: Articles and reviews on economic theory and applied analysis from a wide range of perspectives in

Business and Economics

radical political economics. Special issues on topical themes.
Ind/Abst Acad. Abstr.; Acad. Ind. [Computer File] (1987-); Acad. Search; AGRICOLA [Select. Cov.]; Altern. Press Index; Am. Hist. Life (1971-); Am. Bibliogr. Slavic East Europ. Stud.; Econ. Lit. Index; EP Collect.; Expand. Acad. Index (1987-); Geogr. Abstr. Human Geogr.; Homework Help.; Hum. Resour. Abstr.; Index Period. Artic. Relat. Law (19??-19??); INFO-SOUTH Abstr.; Int. Bibliogr. Sociol.; Int. Dev. Abstr.; J. Econ. Lit.; Left Index; Mag. Search; MasterFile FullTEXT 1000; MasterFile FullTEXT 350; MasterFile FullTEXT 650; MasterFile FullTEXT (July 1990-); Middle East Abstr. Index; Newsp. Period. Abstr. (1989-); OCLC; PAIS Int. Print; Sage Public Adm. Abstr.; Soc. Sci. Source; Telebase.

LC HC131 .B324   **ISSN** 0187-3407
DD 330.972   MX
REVIEW OF THE ECONOMIC SITUATION OF MEXICO. [Rev. econ. situat. Mex.]. **Main/Corp** Banco Nacional de Mexico. **Added/Corp** Banco Nacional de Mexico. (19??)-. Periodical. English. Twelve times a year. Free on request. Banco Nacional de Mexico, Avenida Isabel La Catolica 44, Mexico DF Mexico. **ED** Fernando Quiroz. **Circ:** 21,000 (ctrl).
Desc: Covers monetary policy, finance, farming, industry, hydrocarbons, foreign trade, the retail trade, tourism, economic indicators, etc. of Mexico.
Ind/Abst Int. Bibliogr. Sociol.; Predicasts F&S Index, U. S. Annu. Ed.

LC HC106.6 .D37   **ISSN** 0743-7323
DD 330.973/005   US
REVIEW OF THE U.S. ECONOMY. [Rev. U. S. econ.]. **Added/Corp** Data Resources, Inc. **VFOAT** Review of the US Economy. (19??)-. Periodical. English. Twelve times a year. DRI McGraw Hill, 24 Hartwell Avenue, Lexington MA 02173. **Tel** (617)863-5100, FAX (617)860-6464, (617)860-6416. **Continues** Data Resources Review of the U.S. Economy., 0197-9966; **Absorbed** U.S Long Term Review., 0734-4449.

ISSN 0121-0017
DD 330   CK
Pr Rev.
REVISTA ANTIOGUENA DE ECONOMIA Y DESARROLLO. [Rev. antiog. econ. desarro.]. (1988)-. Periodical. Spanish. Three times a year. 15.00Col$. Camara de Comercio de Medellin, Apartado Aereo No. 1894, Medellin Colombia. **Tel** 5116111, FAX 2318648, telex 66768. Index available. cum. index. **Ad Acc. Circ:** 1,500 (ctrl). **Continues** Revista Antioque fna de Economia, 0120-3010.
Desc: Articles on economic studies related to Antioquena and its economy.

LC HC141.A1 R47   **ISSN** 0254-4210
DD 330.9728/005   HO
REVISTA CENTROAMERICANA DE ECONOMIA. [Rev. centroam. econ.]. Yearly Vol. 1, No. 1 (Sept. 1979)-. Periodical. Spanish. Three times a year. $18.00. Programa de Postgrado Centroamericano en Economia y Planificacion del Desarrollo, Ap Postal 1748, Tegucigalpa Honduras. **Tel** 33-16-87. **Circ:** 1,000.
Desc: Treats issues in methodology of economics with additional emphasis on analysis of economic and related political problems in contemporary Latin America, especially Central America.
Ind/Abst Int. Labour Doc.; Int. Polit. Sci. Abstr.; LABORDOC; PAIS Int. Print.

PR
REVISTA COOPERTIVA PUERTORRIQUENA. (19??)-. Spanish.
Ind/Abst LABORDOC.

LC HC152.5.A1 R49
DD 330.97291/005   CU
    SUSPENDED
REVISTA CUBA ECONOMICA. **VFOAT** Cuba Economica. Vol. 1, No. 1 (Apr./May/Jun. 1991)-(19??). Periodical. Spanish (table of contents in English). Four times a year. Ediciones Cubanas, Obispo 527 Altos ESQ Bernaza, CP 10100 Havana Cuba. **(Subscription address:** The Center for Cuban Studies, 124 West 23nd Street, New York NY 10011. **Tel** (212)242-0559.)
Ind/Abst Int. Labour Doc.

LC HB1.A1 R4   **ISSN** 0716-5927
DD 330.0(5/6)   CL
REVISTA DE ANALISIS ECONOMICO.
Added/Corp Programa de Postgrado en Economia. (198?)-. Periodical. English (Spanish). Two times a year. $40.00. ILADES, Casilla 51970, Santiago 1 Chile.

CL
REVISTA DE DERECHO ECONOMICO.
Added/Corp Chile. Universidad, Santiago. Seminario de Ciencias Economicas y Sociales. (1963)-. Periodical. Spanish. Irregular. Editorial Juridica de Chile / Santiago, Casilla Postal 4256, Santiago Chile. **Tel** 011 56 2 2049900.
Ind/Abst Index Foreign Leg. Per.

LC HC186 .R415   **ISSN** 0101-3157
DD 330.981/06   BL
REVISTA DE ECONOMIA POLITICA (CENTRO DE ECONOMIA POLITICA (SAO PAULO, BRAZIL). (REVISTA DE ECONOMIA POLITICA.). [Rev. econ. polit.]. Vol. 1, No. 1 (Jan./March 1981)-. Periodical. Portuguese. Four times a year. $75.00. Centro de Economia Polotica, Av Jorge Saad 104, 05618 Sao Paulo SP, Brazil. **Tel** 11 55 11 8443196, 8429974.
Ind/Abst Am. Hist. Life (1981-1983); Hisp. Am. Period. Index, HAPI; PAIS Int. Print.

ISSN 1130-9121
SP
UDC 334
REVISTA DE LA ECONOMIA SOCIAL Y DE LA EMPRESA. (1991)-. Periodical. Multiple languages. Four times a year.

LC HB9 .M4
AG
REVISTA DE LA FACULTAD DE CIENCIAS ECONOMICAS. **Main/Corp** Mendoza, Argentine Republic (City). Universidad Nacional de Cuyo. Facultad de Ciencias Economicas. Vol. 1, No. 1 (Jan./Apr. 1949)-. Periodical. Spanish. Three times a year.

LC HC141.A1 R48   **ISSN** 0252-8762
DD 330   HO
REVISTA DE LA INTEGRACION Y EL DESARROLLO DE CENTROAMERICA.
[Rev. integr. desarro. Centroam.]. (1976)-. Periodical. Spanish. Two times a year. Free on request. Banco Centroamericano de Integracion Economica, Apartado Postal 772, Tegucigalpa Honduras. **Tel** 011 504 372230 39, telex BANCADIE 1103. Index available. **Bk Rev. Circ:** 2,500 (ctrl). **Continues** Revista de la Integracion Centroamericana.
Ind/Abst PAIS Int. Print.

SP
REVISTA DEL INSTITUTO DE ESTUDIOS ECONOMICOS. **Added/Corp** Instituto de Estudios Economicos (Spain). No. 1 (1980)-. Periodical. Spanish. Four times a year. $75.46. Instituto Estudios Economicos, Castello 128 6TA Planta, 28006 Madrid Spain. **Tel** 011 34 1 5617500, FAX 011 34 1 5623613.
Ind/Abst PAIS Int. Print.

LC HC201 .E25
DD 330   EC
REVISTA ECONOMIA. **Added/Corp** Universidad Central del Ecuador. Instituto de Investigaciones Economicas. (199?)-. Spanish. $10.00. Institut Investigaciones Economica, Apartado 1088, Quito Ecuador. **Tel** 011 593 2 529129. **Continues** Economia, 0012-9704.

LC HB9 .R46
DD 330.05/6   SP
REVISTA ESPANOLA DE ECONOMIA.
Added/Corp Escuela Nacional de Administracion Publica (Spain). Instituto de Desarrollo Economico. No. 1 (Jan./April 1971)-. Periodical. Spanish. Two times a year. $28.50. Servicio de Publicaciones del Min de Economia y Hacienda, Plaza Campillo, Mundo Nuevo 3, 28005 Madrid Spain. **Tel** 011 34 1 5271437, 011 34 1 5835665. **Bk Rev. Circ:** 2,000. Documents available from SWETS.
Ind/Abst Econ. Lit. Index (1985-); J. Econ. Lit.

NE
    TITLE CHANGE
REVUE BENELUX. (19??)-(199?). Multiple languages. SDU Uitgeverij, Postbus 20014, Christoffel Plantijnstraat, 2500 EA Den Haag Netherlands. **Tel** 011 31 70 3789911. **Continued by** Dossiers Benelux.

FR
REVUE DE L'ECONOMIE MERIDIONALE : REM. **Added/Corp** Universite de Montpellier I. Centre Regional de la Productivite et des Etudes Economiques. **VFOAT** REM; R.E.M. Vol. 35, No. 137 (1987)-. Periodical. French (summaries and/or abstracts in English). Four times a year. 50.00F (single issue). Centre Regional de la Productivite et des Etudes Economiques, Faculty Sciences Economics, 39 rue de Universite, 34060 Montpellier France. **Tel** 011 33 67 615430. **Continues** Economie Meridionale, 0035-1369.
Ind/Abst PAIS Int. Print.

LC HC271 .N57   **ISSN** 1145-1378
DD 330.944/005   FR
REVUE DE L'IRES, LA. **Added/Corp** Institut de Recherches Economiques et Sociales (France). **VAT** Revue de l'Institut de Recherches Economiques et Sociales. (1989)-. Periodical. French. Three times a year. $92.96. Institut de Recherches Economiques & Sociales, 16 Bld du Mont d'Est, 93192 Noisy Grand Cdx France. **Tel** 011 33 1 48151890. **Ad Acc**. **Continues** Note de l'IRES, 0762-7238.

LC HC595.55.A1 R49
DD 330   MG
REVUE DE L'OCEAN INDIEN, ECONOMIE. Vol. 1, No. 23, 1st Quarter (Mar. 1982)-. Periodical. French. Four times a year. $29.00. Communication et Media-Ocean Indien, rue H Rabesahala, BP 46, Antsakaviro 101 Antannarivo Malagasy Republic. **Tel** 22536, telex 22350 MALAKY MG. **ED** Georges Ranaivosoa. **Bk Rev. Ad Acc. Circ:** 3,000.
Desc: Covers the general economy in the Indian Ocean region.

ISSN 0980-2282
FR
UDC 380.15
REVUE DE PRESSE CHAMPAGNE-ARDENNE ACTUALITES.
(REVUE DE PRESSE.). (1986)-. Periodical. French. One time a week. $115.68. Chambre Regionale Comm Indust, BP 537, 51011 Chalons SM Cedex France. **Tel** 011 33 16 26705498, FAX 011 33 16 262103330. **Continues** Revue de Presse - Reseau Documentaire inter-consulaire Champagne-Ardenne, 0241-0966.

FR
REVUE D'ECONOMIE DU DEVELOPPEMENT. (19??)-. Periodical. French. Four times a year. 360.00F France; 415.00F other. Presses Universitaires de France, Department des Revues, 17 Rue Souflot, 75005 Paris France. **Tel** 011 33 1 43267741, telex PUF 600 474 F.

FR
REVUE D'ECONOMIE DU DEVELOPPEMENT. French. Four times a year. 350.00F France; 400.00F other. Presses Universitaires de France, Department des Revues, 17 Rue Souflot, 75005 Paris France. **Tel** 011 33 1 43267741, telex PUF 600 474 F.

ISSN 0987-3368
FR
UDC 33
REVUE D'ECONOMIE FINANCIERE. [Rev. econ. financ.]. (1987)-. Periodical. French. Four times a year. $218.73. Association d' Economie Financiere, 56 rue de Lille, 75007 Paris France. **Tel** 011 33 1 45440411.

LC HB3 .R4   **ISSN** 0373-2630
FR
    CCC
REVUE D'ECONOMIE POLITIQUE. [Rev. econ. polit.]. Vol. 1 (1887)-. Periodical. French. Six times a year. 780.00F (France), 875.00F (other) institutions; 540.00F (France) , 680.00F (other) individuals. Dalloz, 35 rue Tournefort, 75240 Paris Cedex 05 France. **Tel** 011 33 1 40515434, 011 33 1 40515454, FAX 011 33 1 45873748, telex 206 446 F. **ED** Bernard Lassudrie-Duchene.
Desc: Covers the branch of economics dealing with the study of production and the distribution of wealth.
Ind/Abst Am. Hist. Life (1954-1958, 1964-); Econ. Lit. Index; Int. Labour Doc.; J. Econ. Lit.; PAIS Int. Print; Repere (1980-1981).

ISSN 0703-6337
DD 341.24/2/05   CN
Pr Rev.
REVUE D'INTEGRATION EUROPEENNE.
See Political Science.

LC HD9014.C2   **ISSN** 0709-5856
DD 388.1/9/71   CN
REVUE DU MARCHE ALIMENTAIRE.
Added/Corp Canada. Ministere de l'Agriculture. Direction des Politiques, de la Planification et de l'Economie. Canada. Agriculture Canada. Marketing and Economics Branch. Vol. 1, No. 1 (1979)-. Government Publication. French. Free on request. Agriculture Canada, Communications Branch, Ottawa Ontario K1A 0C7 Canada.

LC HB3 .R415   **ISSN** 0035-2764
DD 330.5   FR
    CCC
Pr Rev.
REVUE ECONOMIQUE. [Rev. econ.].
Added/Corp Fondation Nationale des Sciences Politiques. Centre Nationale de la Recherche Scientifique (France) Ecole des Hautes Etudes en Sciences Sociales. Vol. 1 (May 1950)-. Periodical. French (summaries and/or abstracts in English). Six times a year (Jan., Mar., May, July, Sept., Nov.). $168.42. Presses de la Fondation, Nationale des Sciences Politiques, 44 rue du Four, 75006 Paris France. **Tel** 011 33 1 44393960, FAX 011 33 1 45480441. **ED** Jeanne-Marie Parly. Index available (Bound in last issue). cum. index. **Bk Rev. Ad Acc. Circ:** 2,000 (ctrl). Documents available from The Genuine Article.
Desc: Articles in all fields of economics, with emphasis on theory and economic policy.
Ind/Abst Am. Hist. Life (1972-); Econ. Lit. Index (199?-); Int. Labour Doc.; Int. Polit. Sci. Abstr. (1972-); J. Econ. Lit.; MLA Int. Bibl. Books Artic. Mod. Lang. Lit.; Res. Alert [Full Cov.]; Saf. Health Work; Soc. Sci. Cit. Index [Full Cov.]; Stat. Theory Method Abstr. (1959-1963).

ISSN 0825-0707
DD 330.9714/271 CN
REVUE ECONOMIQUE - CHAMBRE DE COMMERCE DE LAVAL. (LA REVUE ECONOMIQUE.). [Rev. econ. - Chamb. commerc. Laval]. Vol. 1, No. 1 (April 1984)-. Periodical. French. Four times a year. Chambre De Commerce De Laval, Suite 600, 1435 Ouest rue St-Martin, Laval Quebec H7S 2C6 Canada. **Ad Acc. Circ:** 20,000 (ctrl).
Desc: Economics and business subjects of interests to business people in general and to Laval residents in particular.

LC HB3 .R47 **ISSN** 0035-2772
DD 330.5 SZ
REVUE ECONOMIQUE ET SOCIALE (LAUSANNE). (REVUE ECONOMIQUE ET SOCIALE.). [Rev. econ. soc.]. (1943)-. Periodical. French. Four times a year (Mar., June, Sept., Dec.). $75.40. Societe d'Etudes Economique et Sociale, BFSH 1 Dorigny, CH-1015 Lausanne Switzerland. **Tel** 011 41 21 6915347, FAX 011 41 21 6323385. **ED** Dr. Kaj Noschis. cum. index. **Bk Rev. Ad Acc.**
Ind/Abst Int. Bibliogr. Sociol.; Int. Labour Doc.; Int. Polit. Sci. Abstr.

ISSN 0223-470X
FR
UDC 336
REVUE FIDUCIAIRE. SUPPLEMENT, LA. **See** Finance-Taxation.

LC HD1401 **ISSN** 0035-354X
DD 650 SZ
REVUE INTERNATIONALE POUR L'ENSEIGNEMENT COMMERCIAL = INTERNATIONAL REVIEW FOR BUSINESS EDUCATION = INTERNATIONAL ZEITSCHRIFT FUR KAUFMANNISCHES BILDUNGSWESEN = RIVISTA INTERNAZIONALE PER LA CULTURA COMMERCIALE = REVISTA INTERNACIONAL PARA LA ENSENANZA COMMERCIAL. **Added/Corp** Internatinal Society for Business Education. **VFOAT** International Review for Business Education; International Zeitschrift fur Kaufmannisched Bildungswesen; Rivista Internazionale per la Cultura Commerciale; Revista Internacional para la Ensenanza Comercial. (1901)-. Academic Scholarly Publication. English (French, German, Italian and Spanish). Two times a year (Apr., & Nov.). kr43.00. SIEC, Hunderupvej 122A/DK-5230, Dk-5230 Odense M Denmark. **Tel** (011)45-66-121966, FAX 011 45 66 145794. **ED** Erik Lange. **Ad Acc. Circ:** 2,300. available with charts.

LC HC1025.A1 R49
DD 330.96682/005 IV
REVUE IVOIRIENNE DE DROIT ECONOMIQUE ET COMPTABLE = RIDEC. **VFOAT** RIDEC. (1987)-. Periodical. French. Twelve times a year. Centre Ivoirienne d'Etude et de Recherche Juridique, BP 3811, Abidjan Ivory Coast.
Ind/Abst Int. Labour Doc.; LABORDOC.

LC HF **ISSN** 1192-4551
DD 658.8/708/09714 CN
•**REVUE OCCASIONS D'AFFAIRES (QUEBEC).** (LA REVUE OCCASIONS D'AFFAIRES.). [Rev. occas. aff.]. Vol. 1, No 1 (1993)-. Periodical. French. Six times a year (Jan., Mar., May, Aug., Sept., Nov.). 15.97Can$. Revue Occasions d'Affairs, 1687 Que In, 425 St. Amable Street, Suite 145, Quebec G1R 5E4 Canada. **Tel** (418)640-1686, FAX (418)640-1687. **ED** Pierre Bherer. **Ad Acc, Adv Mgr:** Roger Robitaille, **Tel** (800)361-1686. **Circ:** 50,000.
Desc: Contains information on franchise business opportunities.

SZ
REVUE SCHWEIZ. (19??)-. German (French, English and Italian). Twelve times a year. 71.00SZ$. Rothus Verlag, Postfach, CH-4501 Solothurn Switzerland. **(Subscription address:** Revue Suisse Basler Zeitung, Postfach Publikationen, CH 4002 Basel Switzerland. **Tel** 011 41 61 6616314.) **Bk Rev**, (Qty: 10). **Ad Acc. Circ:** 15,000 (ctrl).

LC HC **ISSN** 0035-5054
DD 330 IT
Pr Rev.
RICERCHE ECONOMICHE. (RICERCHE ECONOMICHE : RIVISTA DEL SERVIZIO STUDI ECONOMICI "DE PIETRI-TONELLI".). [Ric. econ.]. **Added/Corp** Servizio Studi Economici "A. de Pietri-Tonelli." Servizio di Studi Economici "A. de Pietri-Tonelli." Istituto Universitario di Economia e Commercio (Venice, Italy). Laboratoio di Economia Politica. Universita Degli Studi di Venezia. Laboratorio di Economia Politica. Universita Degli Studi di Venezia. Dipartimento di Scienze Economiche. Vol. 9, No. 1 (Jan/Feb. 1955)-. Academic Scholarly Publication. Italian (English). Four times a year. L205350. Academic Press Ltd., A Division of Harcourt Brace & Company Ltd., 24-28 Oval Road, London NW1 7DX United Kingdom. **Tel** 011 44 171 2674466, FAX 011 44 171 4822293, 011 44 171 4854752, telex 25775 ACPRES G. **(Subscription address:** Harcourt Brace & Company, Ltd., Foots Cray High Street, Sidcup Kent DA14 5HP United Kingdom. **Tel** 011 44 181 3003322, FAX 011 44 181 3090807, telex 896 377 ACADEM.) **ED** Medio Alfredo. Index available. cum. index. **Bk Rev. Circ:** 1,000 (ctrl). available on microfilm and microfiche from University Microfilms International (UMI). ***Continues** Bollettino del Servizio Studi Economici "A. de Pietri-Tonelli".*
Desc: Publishes high quality, original research in all fields of economics with no restrictions on school of thought, methodological approach or choice of topic.
Ind/Abst Econ. Lit. Index (19??-); J. Econ. Lit. (1985-); PAIS Int. Print; Stat. Theory Method Abstr.; Zentralbl. Math. Ihre Grenzgeb.

ISSN 0895-1306
DD 332 US
CCC
RICHARD C YOUNG'S INTERNATIONAL GOLD REPORT. [Richard C. Young's int. gold rep.]. **VFOAT** International Gold Report; Gold Report. Vol. 11, No. 3 (Sept. 1987)-. Periodical. English. Twelve times a year. $145.00. Young Research & Publishing Co., 366 Thames Street, Federal Building, Suite 352, Newport RI 02840. **Tel** (401)849-2131. **ED** Richard Young. ***Continues** Young's International Gold Reports.*
Desc: Covers gold and gold-sphere investments.

LC HC **ISSN** 0035-5356
DD 330 JA
RIKKYO KEIZAIGAKU KENKYU. **Added/Corp** Rikkyo Daigaku, Tokyo. Keizaigaku Kenkyukai. **VFOAT** St. Paul's Economic Review. Vol. 1 (1938)-. Academic Scholarly Publication. Japanese. Four times a year. $20.00. Rikkyo Daigaku, Rikkyo Keizaigaku Kenkyukai, Rikkyo University. **ED** Editorial Board. **Bk Rev. Circ:** 4,000. Documents available from BLDSC.
Ind/Abst Am. Hist. Life (1964-1968).

IT
RISORSA UOMO. (19??)-. Italian. Three times a year. L60000 Italy; L90000 other. Franco Angeli Riviste SRL, Viale Monza 106, 20127 Milan Italy. **Tel** 011 39 2 2827651, 011 39 2 289562, FAX 011 39 2 258004, telex 051-511650.

FR
Pr Rev.
RISQUE PAYS. (19??)-. Periodical. French. Two times a year. Dialeco, 4 place Vendome, 75001 Paris France. **Tel** 011 33 1 42980093, FAX 011 33 1 42981992. Index available. **Circ:** 100 (ctrl).
Desc: Contains a country risk analysis in the developing countries. Includes political, economic, and financial criteria.

LC HC **ISSN** 0391-6170
DD 330 IT
RIVISTA DI POLITICA ECONOMICA. [Riv. polit. econ.]. (1921)-. Periodical. Italian (English). Eleven times a year. L156690. Servizio Italiano Pubblicazioni International, Viale Pasteur 6, 00144 Rome Italy. **Tel** 011 39 6 5920509, telex 614567 SIPIRM I. **ED** Mario Baldassarri. Index available. cum. index. **Bk Rev. Ad Acc. Circ:** 1,400. ***Continues** Rivista delle Societa Commerciali.*
Desc: Covers theoretical and research topics of Italian and international economics, current financial and political problems.
Ind/Abst J. Econ. Lit.; PAIS Int. Print; Stat. Theory Method Abstr. (1959-1963).

LC HC
DD 330 IT
RIVISTA DI STORIA ECONOMICA. INTERNATIONAL ISSUE. **VFOAT** Rivista di Storia Economica. Vol. 1 (1984)-. English (translations available in Italian). One time a year. Rivista di Storia Economica, Giulio Einaudi Editore Spa, Via u Biancamanox 1, CP 245, 10100 Turin Italy.

LC K22 .I795
IT
RIVISTA GIURIDICA DEL MEZZOGIORNO : TRIMESTRALE DELLA SVIMEZ, ASSOCIAZIONE PER LO SVILUPPO DELL'INDUSTRIA NEL MEZZOGIORNO. **Added/Corp** Associazione per lo Sviluppo dell'Industria nel Mezzogiorno. Vol. 1 (1987)-. Periodical. Italian. Four times a year. L100000.00 Italy; L140000.00 (surface mail), L170000.00 (airmail) other. Societa Editrice il Mulino, Strada Maggiore 37, 40125 Bologna Italy. **Tel** 011 39 51 256011, FAX 011 39 51 256034.

LC HE7 .R54 **ISSN** 0303-5247
DD 388.05 IT
RIVISTA INTERNAZIONALE DI ECONOMIA DEI TRASPORTI. **See** Transportation.

LC H7 .R57 **ISSN** 0035-6751
DD 330/.05 IT
RIVISTA INTERNAZIONALE DI SCIENZE ECONOMICHE E COMMERCIALI. (RIVISTA INTERNAZIONALE DI SCIENZE ECONOMICHE E COMMERCIALI. INTERNATIONAL REVIEW OF ECONOMICS AND BUSINESS.). [Riv. int. sci. econ. commer.]. **VFOAT** International Review of Economics and Business. (Sept./Oct. 1954)-. Periodical. Italian. Twelve times a year. L200000 Italy; L300000 other. Cedam Spa, Via Jappelli 5 6, 35121 Padua Italy. **Tel** 011 39 49 65667.
Ind/Abst Contents Recent Econ. J.; Curr. Cit.; Econ. Lit. Index (19??-); Int. Bibliogr. Sociol.; J. Econ. Lit.; Leis., Rec., Tour. Abstr.; PAIS Int. Print.

LC HD39.4 .R58
IT
CEASED
RIVISTA ITALIANA DEL LEASING E DELL INTERMEDIAZIONE FINANZIARIA. **Added/Corp** ASSILEA (Association). Vol. 4, No. 1 (April 1988)-(Dec. 1994). Periodical. Italian. Giuffre Editore SPA, Via Busto Arsizio 40, 20151 Milan Italy. **Tel** 011 398 2 38089200. **ED** Renato Clarizia. ***Continues** Rivista Italiana del Leasing.*
Desc: Offers documentation and information for those involved in financial intermediation.

LC HB3599 .R58 **ISSN** 0035-6832
IT
RIVISTA ITALIANA DI ECONOMIA, DEMOGRAFIA E STATISTICA. [Riv. ital. econ., demogr. stat.]. **Added/Corp** Societa Italiana di Economia, Demografia e Statistica. Vol. 4, No. 3/4 (July-Aug. 1950)-. Periodical. Italian. Four times a year. L250000. Sieds Dip Teoria EC Demogr Sta, Universite of La Sapienza, P Le A Moro 5, 00185 Rome Itlay. **Tel** 011 39 6 4462991. **Bk Rev. Circ:** 850 (ctrl). ***Continues** Rivista Italiana di Demografia e Statistica.*
Desc: Problems on economics, demography, statistics, sociology, book reviews and other scientific information.
Ind/Abst Stat. Theory Method Abstr. (1959-1966).

US
RMA ANNUAL STATEMENT STUDIES. **Added/Corp** Robert Morris Associates. (1977)-. English. Robert Morris Associates, One Liberty Plaza, 1650 Market Street, Philadelphia PA 19103. **Tel** (215)851-9118, (215)851-0585, FAX (215)851-9206. ***Continues** Robert Morris Associates. Annual Statement Studies, 0080-3340.*

ISSN 0896-3274
DD 330 US
ROCHESTER BUSINESS JOURNAL (ROCHESTER, N.Y. : 1987). (ROCHESTER BUSINESS JOURNAL.). [Rochester bus. j.]. Vol. 2, No. 21 (Feb. 9-22, 1987)-. Periodical. English. One time a week (53 issues per year). $54.95. Rochester Business Journal Inc., 55 Saint Paul Street, Rochester NY 14604. **Tel** (716)546-8303, FAX (716)546-3398. **ED** Paul Ericson. **Ad Acc. Circ:** 10,000. available on an online database (file 635/Full-Text) from DIALOG. Documents available from UMI Article Clearinghouse. ***Continues** Rochester Business Journal and Chamber of Commerce News, 0884-0199.*
Desc: Provides local business coverage to business executives and owners.
Ind/Abst Bus. Dateline.

GW
ROHSTOFFPREISINDEX. (19??)-. German. DM275.00. HWWA Institut fuer Wirtschaftsforschung, Neuer Jungfernstieg 21, W 2000 Hamburg 36 Germany. **Tel** 011 49 40 3562405, FAX 011 49 40 351900. **ED** Heinz Kolbe. **Ad Acc, Adv Mgr:** G. Mantwill.
Desc: Raw material price index.

ISSN 1060-8893
DD 338 US
ROLLING VENTURES. (ROLLING VENTURES: THE RVER'S INFORMATION SOURCE FOR PROFITING FROM AN ON-THE-ROAD HOBBY OR BUSINESS.). [Roll. ventures]. Vol. 1, No. 1 (winter 1992)-. Periodical. English. Four times a year. $18.00. Page One Press, Inc., 9330-D Bridgeport Way SW #40, Tacoma WA 98499.

LC HC10 .R8
DD 330.05/6 RU
ROSSIISKII EKONOMICHESKII ZHURNAL. **Added/Corp** Gosudarstvennaia Akademiia Upravleniia (Russia (Federation)) Russia (Federation). Ministerstvo Nauki, Vysshei Shkoly i Tekhnicheskoi Politiki. Russia (Federation). Vysshii Ecnomicheskii Sovet. (1992)-. Periodical. Russian. Twelve times a year. $99.95. Izdatelstvo Finansy I Statistika, Ulitsa Chernyshvskogo 7 K-142, 101000 Moscow Russia. **(Subscription address:** East View Publications Inc., 3020 Harbor Lane North, Suite 110, Minneapolis MN 55447. **Tel** (800)477-1005, (612)550-0961, FAX (612)559-2931.) ***Continues** Ekonomicheskie Nauki.*

Business and Economics

DD 917.15
ISSN 1188-9926
CN
ROULANT MA BOSSE, EN. [En roulant ma bosse]. **Added/Corp** Nouveau-Brunswick. Ministere du Developpement Economique et du Tourisme. (1992)-. French.

DD 333.7/2/09711
ISSN 1186-0308
CN
ROUND TABLE NEWS. [Round table news]. **Added/Corp** British Columbia Round Table on the Environment and the Economy. **VFOAT** Round Table. (Nov. 1990)-. Periodical. English. Twelve times a year. British Columbia Round Table on the Environment and the Economy, 229-560 Johnson Street, Victoria British Columbia V8W 3C6 Canada.

US
RUNDT'S WORLD BUSINESS INTELLIGENCE. (19??)-. English. Forty-eight times a year. $675.00 US; $767.00 other. S J Rundt & Associates Inc, 130 East 63rd Street, New York NY 10121. **Tel** (201)783-5206, (201)838-0141, FAX (201)744-3073. Index available. **Bk Rev**. ctrl circ. available on diskette. **Continues** Rundt's Weekly Intelligence.

ISSN 0731-9150
US
CCC
RUNZHEIMER REPORTS ON RELOCATION. See Real Estate.

ISSN 0730-8663
US
CCC
RUNZHEIMER REPORTS ON TRAVEL MANAGEMENT. See Travel and Tourism.

UK
RUSSIA & REPUBLICS NUCLEAR INDUSTRY. (19??)-. Newsletter. English. Twelve times a year. £395.00. Arguments & Facts International, PO Box 35, Hastings East Sussex, TN34 2UX United Kingdom. **Tel** 011 44 1424 444142, FAX 011 44 1424 717498.
Desc: Current news, events, business developments and the many challenges now facing the world's largest nuclear industry.

ISSN 1351-9263
UK
●**RUSSIA BRIEFING.** See Political Science.

LC HC340.12.A1 R87
DD 330
RU
RUSSIA ... : ECONOMIC SITUATION. **Added/Corp** Centre of Economic Analysis and Forecasting (Russia). **VFOAT** Russia, Economic Situation. (1992)-. English. Four times a year. $79.95. (**Subscription address:** East View Publications Inc., 3020 Harbor Lane North, Suite 110, Minneapolis MN 55447. **Tel** (800)477-1005, (612)550-0961, FAX (612)559-2931.)

LC HB
DD 330
US
●**RUSSIAN BUSINESS NEWS UPDATE.** (1994)-. Newsletter. English. Twelve times a year. Josh Zander Financial and Management Consulting Services, 4286 Redwood Highway, Suite 376, San Rafael CA 94903. **Tel** (415)492-3382, FAX (415)472-5709. **ED** Josh Zander. **Ad Acc. Circ:** 500.
Desc: Dedicated to business, economics and finance in Russia.

ISSN 1060-569X
DD 338
US
RUSSIAN BUSINESS REPORTS. [Russ. bus. rep.]. **Added/Corp** Russian Infomation Services. (1992)-. Periodical. English. One time a week. $396.00 US; $500.00 other. Russian Information Services / RIS, 89 Main Street, Box 2, Montpelier VT 05602. **Tel** (802)223-4955, FAX (802)223-6105. **ED** Paul Richardson. **Circ:** 100.
Desc: Includes independent reporting from Moscow by Western and Russian journalists, abstracts of Russian new articles and observer graphs.

ISSN 1060-5894
US
RUSSIAN ECONOMY AND BUSINESS DIGEST. (1992)-. Periodical. English. Twelve times a year. $60.00. Russian Information Services / RIS, 89 Main Street, Box 2, Montpelier VT 05602. **Tel** (802)223-4955, FAX (802)223-6105.

ISSN 1061-5679
DD 947
US
RUSSIAN FAR EAST UPDATE. (RUSSIAN FAR EAST UPDATE: A MONTHLY BUSINESS BRIEFING ON TRADE AND ECONOMIC DEVELOPMENTS IN THE RUSSIAN FAR EAST.). [Russian Far East update]. Vol. 2, No. 1 (Jan. 1992)-. Periodical. English. Twelve times a year. $210.00. Soviet Far East Publishing, PO Box 22126, Seattle WA 98122.

Tel (206)447-2668, FAX (206)583-0345. **ED** Dr. Elisa Miller. Index available. cum. index. **Ad Acc**. **Circ:** 500. **Continues** Soviet Far East Update.

ISSN 0933-0089
GW
UDC 330
RWI-MITTEILUNGEN. [RWI-Mitt.]. **VFOAT** Rheinisch-Westfalisches Institut-Mitteilungen; Rheinisch-Westfalisches Institut feur Wirtschaftsforschung-Mitteilungen. (1987)-. Periodical. German. Four times a year. Duncker and Humblot Verlag, Postfach 410329, D-12113 Berlin Germany. **Tel** 011 49 30 79000612, 011 49 30 79000613. **Continues** Mitteilungen - Rheinisch-Westfalisches Institut feur Wirtschaftsforschung Essen, 0035-4465.

ISSN 0036-052X
PL
UDC 339.5
RYNKI ZAGRANICZNE. [Rynki Zagr.]. (1957)-. Periodical. Polish. Three times a week (156 issues). $234.00. (**Subscription address:** Ars Polona-Ruch, PO Box 1001, Krakowskie Przedmiescie 7, 00-068 Warsaw Poland. **Tel** 011 48 22 261201.)

LC HC
ISSN 0038-7282
FR
S.P.E.L.D - INFORMATION. See Law.

ISSN 0381-548X
DD 658/.91/62928605
CN
S S G M. SERVICE STATION & GARAGE MANAGEMENT. See Transportation-Automobiles.

LC S
ISSN 0953-4148
DD 630
UK
SAC ECONOMIC REPORT. See Agriculture.

CN
SAINT JOHN BUSINESS TODAY. (1991)-. English. Saint John Today, Saint John Board of Trade, Admiral Beatty Hotel, King Square South, Saint John New Brunswick E2L 4W3 Canada.

ISSN 1062-9130
DD 338
US
SAL-NEWS (ROCKVILLE, MD.). (SAL-NEWS: A PUBLICATION OF THE OFFICE OF SUPPORT AND AID TO LATVIA, AMERICAN LATVIAN ASSOCIATION IN THE UNITED STATES, INC.). [SAL-news]. **Added/Corp** American Latvian Association in the United States. Office of Support and Aid to Latvia. **VFOAT** SAL News. Vol. 2, No. 1 (Spring 1992)-. Periodical. English. Four times a year. American Latvian Association of America, PO Box 4578, Rockville MD 20849-4578. **Tel** (301)340-8174, FAX (301)340-8732.

AT
SALES AND LEASING MONITOR. (19??)-. English. Twelve times a year. 1500.00Aus$. Commercial Property Monitor, PO Box 668, Bondi Junction NSW 2022 Australia. **Tel** 011 61 2 2818766, FAX 011 61 2 2819096. ctrl circ.

ISSN 1063-1445
US
SALES IMPROVEMENT FOR PROFESSIONALS. (SALES IMPROVEMENT FOR PROFESSIONALS: A BI-MONTHLY PUBLICATION OF SALES IMPROVEMENT CONSULTANTS.). **Added/Corp** Sales Improvement Consultants. (1992)-. Periodical. English. Six times a year. $95.00. Sales Improvement Consultants, 622 Eagle Rock Avenue, West Orange NJ 07052.

ISSN 0889-4779
DD 658
US
SALES LEADS (RIVIERA BEACH, FLA.). (SALES LEADS.). (19??)-. English. Twenty-four times a year. $995.00. Sales Leads, 705 Park Avenue, Lake Park FL 33403. **Tel** (800)231-7876, (407)845-0133.
Desc: Material comes from many sources known to be reliable, and is published after study for accuracy.

GW
SALES PROFI. (19??)-. Trade Publication. German. Twelve times a year. DM145.00. Gabler Verlag, Postfach 1546, D-65005 Wiesbaden Germany. **Tel** 011 49 611 534129, FAX 011 49 611 534430.

ISSN 0891-1622
DD 659
US
SALES PROMOTION MONITOR. [Sales promot. monit.]. Vol. 1 (May 1983)-. Periodical. English. Twelve times a year. $135.00. Commerce Communications Inc, 5247 Washburn Avenue S, Minneapolis MN 55410. **Tel** (612)924-0957. **ED** Kathryn Sederberg. Index available.
Desc: Interpretation/analysis of what's happening in sales promotion - including planning, budgeting, execution, and result analysis.

ISSN 0889-3209
US
SALES UPBEAT. (1986)-. Periodical. English. Thirteen times a year. $16.22. Economics Press Inc, 12 Daniel Road, Fairfield NJ 07004. **Tel** (201)227-1224,

(800)526-2554, FAX (201)227-9742. **Continues** On the Upbeat, 0192-7868.
Desc: Strives to help people who sell for a living maintain their skills and enthusiasm.

ISSN 1071-0450
DD 330
US
SAM NAGAGAMA'S ECONOMIC PERSPECTIVES. [Sam Nakagama's econ. perspect.]. **VFOAT** Economic Perspectives. (19??)-. Periodical. English. One time a week (50 issues per year). $500.00. Nakagama & Wallace Inc, 74 Trinity Place, Suite 500, New York NY 10006. **Tel** (212)962-4100, FAX (212)962-4297. ctrl circ.

LC HF5230.5.S26 S26
TU
SAMSUN SANAYI REHBERI. (1980)-. Turkish.

ISSN 0895-1551
DD 330
US
SAN ANTONIO BUSINESS JOURNAL. [San Antonio bus. j.]. Vol. 1, No. 1 (Jan. 26, 1987)-. Periodical. English. Fifty-two times a year (Fridays). $48.50. San Antonio Business Journal, 8200 IH West, Suite 300, San Antonio TX 78230. **Tel** (512)341-3202, FAX (512)341-3031. **ED** Scott Rodrian. **Ad Acc, Adv Mgr:** Mary Jonas. **Circ:** 12,000. available on microfilm from University Microfilms International (UMI); available on an online database (files 635,648/Full-Text) from DIALOG. Documents available from UMI Article Clearinghouse.
Desc: Covers the business news and information about the San Antonio and Central South Texas areas. An number of special supplement focusing on specific industries.
Ind/Abst Acad. Search; Bus. Dateline; Bus. Source Plus; Bus. Source; EP Collect.; Homework Help.; MasterFile FullTEXT 1000; MasterFile FullTEXT 350; MasterFile FullTEXT 650; MasterFile FullTEXT (July 1993-); OCLC; PROMT; Telebase; Trade Ind. ASAP [Full Txt.]; Trade Ind. Index [Full Txt.].

US
SAN ANTONIO EXECUTIVE. (19??)-. English. Irregular. San Antonio Business Journal, 8200 IH West, Suite 300, San Antonio TX 78230. **Tel** (512)341-3202, FAX (512)341-3031. available on an online database (file 635/Full-Text) from DIALOG. Documents available from UMI Article Clearinghouse.
Ind/Abst Bus. Dateline (Oct. 28, 1985-Jan. 19, 1987) [Full Txt.]; Bus. Index (Jan. 1985-Dec. 1985); Gen. BusinessFile (Jan. 1985-Dec. 1985); Gen. Period. Index (Jan. 1985-Dec. 1985).

ISSN 0895-6898
DD 338
US
SAN ANTONIO PERSPECTIVE. [San Antonio perspect.]. Vol. 1, No. 1 (Sept. 1987)-. Periodical. English. Texas Perspectives Inc., 612 Brazos Street, Suite 210, Austin TX 78701. **Tel** (800)365-6581, FAX (512)472-6537. **ED** Jon E. Hockenyos. **Circ:** 1,000.
Desc: Economic trends that affect Texas and its major urban areas.

ISSN 8750-6890
DD 330
US
SAN DIEGO BUSINESS JOURNAL. [S. Diego bus. j.]. (198?)-. Periodical. English. One time a week. $58.00. San Diego Business Journal, 4909 Murphy Canyon Road, Suite 20, San Diego CA 92123. **Tel** (619)277-6359. **ED** Dick Gentry. **Bk Rev. Ad Acc. Circ:** 23,500 (ctrl). available on microfilm from University Microfilms International (UMI); available on an online database (files 635,638/Full-Text) from DIALOG. Documents available from UMI Article Clearinghouse.
Ind/Abst Acad. Search; AGRICOLA [Select. Cov.]; Bus. Dateline; Bus. Index (1985-1990); Bus. Source Plus; Bus. Source; EP Collect.; Gen. BusinessFile (1985-1990); Gen. Period. Index (1985-1990); Homework Help.; INFO-SOUTH Abstr.; MasterFile FullTEXT 1000; MasterFile FullTEXT 350; MasterFile FullTEXT 650; MasterFile FullTEXT (July 1993-); OCLC; PROMT; Telebase; Trade Ind. ASAP [Full Txt.]; Trade Ind. Index [Full Txt.].

ISSN 1068-7319
DD 330
US
TITLE CHANGE
SAN DIEGO ECONOMIC BULLETIN. [S.-Diego econ. bull.]. **Added/Corp** San Diego Chamber of Commerce. Greater San Diego Chamber of Commerce. **VFOAT** Economic Bulletin; San Diego Bulletin. (19??)-(199?). Bulletin. English. Greater San Diego Chamber of Commerce, 402 West Broadway, Suite 1000, San Diego CA 92101. **Tel** (619)544-1342. **Circ:** 4,500. **Continues** San Diego Bulletin. **Continued by** Greater San Diego Chamber of Commerce Economic Bulletin, 1075-8631.

ISSN 1067-6384
DD 651
US
Pr Rev.
SAN DIEGO EXECUTIVE. [S. Diego exec.]. (19??)-. Periodical. English. Twelve times a year. $24.00. San Diego Executive, 9449 Balboa Avenue, Suite 111, San Diego CA 92123. **Tel** (619)467-1050, FAX

835

(619)467-1154. **ED** David E. Whiteside. **Ad Acc. Circ:** 19,000 (ctrl).
Desc: The magazine for business leaders.

ISSN 0036-410X
DD 338 US
CEASED

SAN FRANCISCO BUSINESS.

[San Francisco bus.]. **Added/Corp** San Francisco Chamber of Commerce. (1920)-(June 1994). Periodical. English. San Francisco Business Journal, 465 California Street, Ninth Floor, San Francisco CA 94104. **Tel** (415)392-5420, FAX (415)392-0485. **ED** Carol Piasente. **Ad Acc, Adv Mgr:** Carol Haynosch and Joann Serafini, **Tel** (415)392-4511 ext. 806 or ext. 831. **Circ:** 15,000. Documents available from UMI Article Clearinghouse.
Desc: Covers the San Francisco business community and its concerns. Includes profiles and regular in-depth reports on local industries.
Ind/Abst Bus. Dateline (May 1985-) [Full Txt.]; Chicano Index; PAIS Int. Print (?-?); Public Aff. Inf. Serv. Bull.

ISSN 0890-0337
DD 330 US
CCC

SAN FRANCISCO BUSINESS TIMES.

[San Franc. bus. times]. Vol. 1, No. 1 (Sept. 8, 1986)-. Newspaper. English. One time a week. $57.00. San Francisco Business Times, 275 Battery Street, Suite 940, San Francisco CA 94111. **Tel** (415)989-2522. **Ad Acc.** available on microfilm from University Microfilms International (UMI); available on an online database (files 635,648/Full-Text) from DIALOG. Documents available from UMI Article Clearinghouse.
Ind/Abst Acad. Search; Bus. Dateline; Bus. Index (1987-1990); Bus. Source Plus; Bus. Source; EP Collect.; Gen. BusinessFile (1987-1990); Gen. Period. Index (1987-1990); Homework Help.; INFO-SOUTH Abstr.; MasterFile FullTEXT 1000; MasterFile FullTEXT 350; MasterFile FullTEXT 650; MasterFile FullTEXT (July 1993-); OCLC; PROMT; Telebase; Trade Ind. ASAP [Full Txt.]; Trade Ind. Index [Full Txt.].

ISSN 0830-0143
DD 330.97124/005 CN

SASK-TRENDS MONITOR.

[Sask-trends monit.]. (1984)-. English. Twelve times a year. 156.07Can$. Sask Trends Monitor, 444 19th Avenue, Regina Saskatchewan S4N 1H1 Canada. **Tel** (306)522-5515, FAX (306)522-5838. **ED** Douglas H. Elliott. Index available (published in Dec., free). cum. index. **Circ:** 200.
Desc: Tracking economic, social, and demographic trends in Saskatchewan, Canada.

ISSN 0709-0854
DD 381/.097124 CN

SASKATCHEWAN BUSINESS.

[Sask. bus.]. (May/June 1979)-. Periodical. English. Four times a year. 8.79Can$. Sunrise Publication Ltd., 2207 Hanselman Court, Saskatoon Sask S7L 6A8 Canada. **Tel** (306)244-5668, FAX (305)653-4515. **ED** William R. Wilson, (phone: (306)781-2424). **Ad Acc, Adv Mgr:** Mark Reis. **Circ:** 5200. available on an online database (files 635,648/Full-Text) from DIALOG. Documents available from UMI Article Clearinghouse.
Desc: Business news of relevance to people in any kind of business.
Ind/Abst Bus. Dateline; Bus. Index (1985-); Can. Index; Can. Period. Index (19??-); Gen. BusinessFile (1985-); Gen. Period. Index (1987-); INFO-SOUTH Abstr.; PROMT; Trade Ind. Index.

LC HC117.S3 E28 **ISSN** 0558-6976
DD 330.97124/005 CN

SASKATCHEWAN ECONOMIC REVIEW.

(ECONOMIC REVIEW ...). [Sask. econ. rev.]. **Added/Corp** Saskatchewan. Bureau of Statistics. **VAT** Economic Review (Regina). No. 32 (1978)-. English. One time a year (November). 10.00Can$. Saskatchewan Bureau of Statistics, 2350 Albert Street/5th Floor, Regina Saskatchewan S4P 4A6 Canada. **Tel** (613)951-7276, (800)267-6677, telex 053-3585. ***Continues*** *Saskatchewan Economic Review, 0558-6976.*
Desc: Annual analysis of the provincial economy and an historical presentation of economic and social data.

LC HC517.N48 S29 **ISSN** 0331-0523
DD 966.9 NR
CCC

SAVANNA.

[Savanna]. **Added/Corp** Ahmadu Bello University. Vol. 1, No. 1 (June 1972)-. Academic Scholarly Publication. English. Two times a year. $30.80. Ahmadu Bello University Press Ltd, Ahmed Talis Building, PMB 1094 Zaria Nigeria. **Tel** 011 234 50064. **ED** Audee T. Giwa. Index available. **Bk Rev. Ad Acc. Circ:** 1,000. available with illustrations; available with charts. Documents available from BLDSC, The UnCover Company.
Ind/Abst Agrofor. Abstr.; Anthropol. Index; For. Abstr.; Int. Bibliogr. Sociol.; Nutr. Abstr. Rev., Ser. A, Hum. Exp.; Soils Fert.

US
CEASED

SAVVY BUSINESS TRAVELER.

(19??)-(Nov. 1994). Newsletter. English. Ragan Communications Inc., 212 West Superior Street, Suite 200, Chicago IL 60610. **Tel** (312)335-0037, (800)878-5331, FAX (312)335-9583.

ISSN 8750-3158
US

SBANE ENTERPRISE.

(SBANE ENTERPRISE : A MONTHLY PUBLICATION OF THE SMALLER BUSINESS ASSOCIATION OF NEW ENGLAND.). **Added/Corp** Smaller Business Association of New England. **VAT** Smaller Business Association of New England Enterprise. Vol. 1, No. 1 (Sept. 1984)-. Periodical. English. Eleven times a year. $49.00. Smaller Business Association of New England, 204 2nd Avenue, Waltham MA 02154. **Tel** (617)890-9070. **ED** Kerry Stackpole. **Bk Rev**, (Qty: 50). **Ad Acc. Circ:** 4,000. ***Continues*** *Small Business News (Smaller Business Association of New England).*

ISSN 0106-0848
DD 330.948 DK
CODEN 33.18

SCANDINAVIAN ECONOMIES, THE.

[Scand. econ.]. (1971)-. Periodical. English. Twelve times a year. $553.22. Scandinavian Economies, Vimmelskaftet 42 A 5, DK 1161 Copenhagen K Denmark. **Tel** 011 45 3 3142127, FAX 011 45 3 39380032. **ED** Hilary Barnes.

ISSN 0355-032X
FI

SCANDINAVIAN FOREST ECONOMICS.

See Forests and Forestry.

LC HB9 .E6 **ISSN** 0347-0520
DD 330/.05 UK
CCC

Pr Rev.

SCANDINAVIAN JOURNAL OF ECONOMICS, THE.

[Scand. j. econ.]. Vol. 78 (1976)-. Academic Scholarly Publication. English. Four times a year (Mar., June, Sept., Dec.). $193.00. Basil Blackwell Publishers Ltd., 108 Cowley Road, Oxford 0X4 1JF United Kingdom. **Tel** 011 44 1235 465500, FAX 011 44 1235 465556, telex 837022 OXBOOK G. **(Subscription address:** Blackwell Publishers / UK, 108 Cowley Road, Oxford OX4 1JF United Kingdom. **Tel** 011 44 1865 791100, FAX 011 44 1865 791347.**) ED** Lennart Hjalmarsson and Mats Persson. Index available. **Bk Rev. Ad Acc. Circ:** 1,400. available on microfilm and microfiche from University Microfilms International (UMI). Documents available from The Genuine Article, UMI Article Clearinghouse. ***Continues*** *Swedish Journal of Economics, 0039-7318.*
Desc: Aims to make known, to an international readership, original economic research in the Nordic countries.
Ind/Abst ABI/INFORM Glob. Ed.; ABI/INFORM [Computer File] (1982-); Contents Recent Econ. J.; Curr. Cit.; Curr. Contents Soc. Behav. Sci.; Econ. Lit. Index; Gen. BusinessFile (1992-); Int. Labour Doc.; J. Econ. Lit.; Res. Alert [Full Cov.]; Selec. Coop. Index Manage. Period.; Soc. Sci. Cit. Index [Full Cov.]; World Agric. Econ. Rural Sociol. Abstr.; Zentralbl. Math. Ihre Grenzgeb.

LC Z7164.E2 S3 HB1.A1
DD 016.32 FI

SCANDINAVIAN PERIODICALS INDEX IN ECONOMICS AND BUSINESS : SCANP.

See Business and Economics-Abstracting, Bibliographies and Statistics.

ISSN 0346-7775
SW
UDC 380.8

SCANORAMA.

[Scanorama]. (1972)-. Periodical. English. Ten times a year (Dec/Jan. & July/Aug. issues combined). $70.00. Scanorama, Gavlegatan 18 O G, 11330 Stockholm Sweden. **Tel** 46 8 729 7500, FAX 46 8 34 664 61, telex 10619. **ED** Lars Bringert, Jeanne Rudbeck and Alan Wilson. **Circ:** 160,000 regular issue, 260.00 double issue. ***Continues*** *Scandinavian Times, 0105-0664.*
Desc: The Scandinavian magazine for businesspeople.

GW

SCHRIFTEN DES ZENTRALINSTITUTS FUER WIRTSCHAFTWISSENSCHAFTEN BEI AKADEMIE DER WISSENSCHAFT.

(19??)-. Monographic series. German. Irregular. Price varies per volume. LKG Leipziger Kommissions & Grossbuchhandel, Postfach 520, D-04005 Leipzig Germany. **Tel** 011 49 341 71370.

ISSN 0582-0243
GW

SCHRIFTEN ZUM VERGLEICH VON WIRTSCHAFTSORDNUNGEN.

No. 1- 1954-. Monographic series. German. Irregular. Price varies per volume. VCH Publishers Inc, 220 East 23rd Street, New York NY 10010. **Tel** (212)683-8333, FAX (212)481-0897. **(Subscription address:** VCH Publishers Inc., 303 Northwest 12th Avenue, Journals Department, Deerfield FL 33442. **Tel** (800)367-8249, (305)428-5566.**)**

LC HC
GW

SCHRIFTEN ZUM WIRTSCHAFTSRECHT.

(19??)-. Monographic series. German. Irregular. Price varies per volume. Duncker und Humblot Verlag, Postfach 410329, D-12113 Berlin Germany. **Tel** 011 49 30 79000612, 011 49 30 79000613.
Desc: Contributions to German and European law of economics.

GW

SCHRIFTEN ZUR QUANTITATIVEN WIRTSCHAFTSFORSCHUNG.

1980-. Monographic series. German. Price varies per volume. Gustav Fischer Verlag Stuttgart, Postfach 720143, D-70577 Stuttgart Germany. **Tel** 011 49 711 458030, FAX 011 49 711 4580334, telex 2627-7111488.
Ind/Abst Zentralbl. Math. Ihre Grenzgeb.

UK

SCOTLAND'S TOP 1000 COMPANIES.

(19??)-. English. One time a year. £125.00. Jordon & Sons Ltd, 21 St Thomas Street, Bristol BS1 6JS United Kingdom. **Tel** 0272 230600, FAX 0272 230063, telex 0272 449119.

ISSN 0952-1488
DD 338.709411 UK

SCOTTISH BUSINESS INSIDER.

[Scott. bus. insid.]. (1984)-. Periodical. English. Twelve times a year. $80.42. Insider Publications Ltd, 43 Queensferry Street, Edinburgh EH2 4PF United Kingdom. **Tel** 011 44 31 2258323, FAX 011 44 31 2201203. **ED** Chris Baur. **Ad Acc, Adv Mgr:** Grant Johnstone, **Tel** 011 44 31 459 5500. **Circ:** 19,135 (ctrl).
Ind/Abst Museum Abstr.

LC HB1 .S3 **ISSN** 0036-9292
DD 330.9411/005 UK
CCC

Pr Rev.

SCOTTISH JOURNAL OF POLITICAL ECONOMY.

[Scott. j. polit. econ.]. **Added/Corp** Scottish Economic Society. Vol. 1 (March 1954)-. Academic Scholarly Publication. English. Five times a year. $144.00. Basil Blackwell Publishers Ltd., 108 Cowley Road, Oxford 0X4 1JF United Kingdom. **Tel** 011 44 1235 465500, FAX 011 44 1235 465556, telex 837022 OXBOOK G. **(Subscription address:** Blackwell Publishers / UK, 108 Cowley Road, Oxford OX4 1JF United Kingdom. **Tel** 011 44 1865 791100, FAX 011 44 1865 791347.**) ED** R. A. Clarke. **Bk Rev. Ad Acc. Circ:** 2,000. available on microfilm from University Microfilms International (UMI). Documents available from The Genuine Article, UMI Article Clearinghouse.
Desc: Devoted to the political, economic and social affairs of the former Soviet Union and the communist countries of Eastern Europe.
Ind/Abst ABI/INFORM Glob. Ed.; Acad. Search; Am. Hist. Life (1955-1961, 1964-); Br. Humanit. Index; Contents Recent Econ. J.; Contents Pages Manage.; Curr. Cit.; Curr. Contents Arts Humanit.; Econ. Lit. Index; EP Collect.; Geogr. Abstr. Human Geogr.; Homework Help.; INFO-SOUTH Abstr.; Int. Dev. Abstr. (?-?); Int. Labour Doc.; J. Econ. Lit.; Leis., Rec., Tour. Abstr.; Mag. Search; MasterFile FullTEXT 1000; MasterFile FullTEXT 350; MasterFile FullTEXT 650; MasterFile FullTEXT (July 1993-); OCLC; PAIS Int. Print (?-?); Res. Alert [Full Cov.]; Soc. Sci. Cit. Index [Full Cov.]; SportSearch; Stat. Theory Method Abstr. (1959-1963); Telebase; Work Relat. Abstr.

LC HC **ISSN** 1065-6286
DD 330 US

SDB/PRIMES.

(SDB/PRIMES : NEWSLETTER TARGETED TO SMALL DISADVANTAGED BUSINESSES, 8(A)S, AND PRIME CONTRACTERS; NEWS TRENDS & OPPORTUNITIES.). **VAT** Small Disadvantaged Businesses Primes. (1992)-. Newsletter. English. Twelve times a year. $90.00. Global Research, 12008 Twig Court, North Potomac MD 20878-2346.

ISSN 0739-0645
US

SEARCH (FAIRFIELD, CONN.).

(SEARCH. THE SOURCE OF BUSINESS OPPORTUNITIES.). **Added/Corp** Cromwell Group Inc. (19??)-. Periodical. English. Six times a year. $206.70 Connecticut; $195.00 US and Canada; $225.00 other. Cromwell Group Inc, 251 Danbury Road, Wilton CT 06897-3001. **Tel** (203)834-7372.

LC HB3755 .S4
DD 330.971/005 CN

SEASONAL VARIATIONS IN THE CANADIAN ECONOMY.

Added/Corp Statistics Canada. Time Series Research and Analysis. **VFOAT** Variations Saisonnieres dans l'Economie Canadienne. (1982)-. English (French). Statistics Canada Publications Sales and Services, R.H. Coats Building 6th Floor, Ottawa Ontario K1A 0T6 Canada. **Tel** (613)951-5078, (800)267-6677, FAX (613)951-1584, telex 053-3585.

LC HC154.A1 S42
DD 330.97292/005
JM
SECIN ABSTRACTS / SPONSORED BY INTERNATIONAL DEVELOPMENT RESEARCH CENTRE.
Added/Corp International Development Research Centre (Canada) Jamaica. National Planning Agency. Documentation Centre. **VFOAT** S.E.C.I.N. Abstracts. Vol. 1, No. 1 (March 1982)-. English. Two times a year. Planning Institute of Jamaica, 39-41 Barbados Avenue, Kingston 5 Jamaica. **Tel** (809)929-5221, (809)926-1480. **ED** A. Ononaiwu, P. Reid and Y. Griffiths.

LC HD
DD 338
UDC 651
ISSN 1163-2747
FR
TITLE CHANGE
SECRET (PARIS).
(SECRET.). (198?)-(1993). Periodical. French. Six times a year. Secret Magazine, 31 rue Victor Masse, F-75009 Paris France. **Tel** 011 33 1 45265470. **ED** Lalu Jacqueline. **Bk Rev**, (Qty: 6). **Ad Acc**. ctrl circ. *Continued by Secretaires et Assistantes Magazine, 1252-2228.*

FR
SECRETAIRE INFO.
French. Irregular. 654.03F France; 690.00F other. Editions Pratiques, BP 148, F-74941 Annecy Le Vieux France. **Tel** 011 33 16 50640439, FAX 011 33 16 50640320, telex 385060. Index available.

DD 651.3/741
ISSN 0842-1935
CN
TITLE CHANGE
SECRETAIRE MODERNE (1988).
(SECRETAIRE MODERNE.). [Secret. mod.]. Vol. 2, No 9 (1988)-(19??). Periodical. French. Editions Ultima Inc., 655 Jean Paul Vincent, Bureau 18, Longueuil Quebec J4G 1R3 Canada. **Tel** (514) 646-9011. *Continues Magazine Secretaire Moderne., 0838-8180. Continued by Tandem.*
Ind/Abst Repere (1989-).

LC HD
DD 338
UDC 651:681.3(44)
ISSN 1252-2228
FR
SECRETAIRES ET ASSISTANTES MAGAZINE.
VFOAT Secretaires et Assistantes. (199?)-. Periodical. French. Twelve times a year. 293.83F France; 350.00F other. Secret Magazine, 31 rue Victor Masse, F-75009 Paris France. **Tel** 011 33 1 45265470. *Continues Secret (Paris), 1163-2747.*

DD 651
ISSN 1040-4708
US
SECRETARY'S LETTER (ENGLEWOOD, N.J.).
See Occupations and Careers.

LC HC1015.A1 S43
DD 330
TG
SECTEUR PRIVE : MENSUEL D'INFORMATIONS ECONOMIQUES DE LA CHAMBRE DE COMMERCE, D'AGRICULTURE ET D'INDUSTRIE DU TOGO, LE.
Added/Corp Chambre de Commerce, d'Agriculture et d'Industrie de la Republique Togolaise. (19??)-. Periodical. French. Twelve times a year. Chambre de Commerce, d'Agriculture et d'Industrie du Togo, Angle Avenue de la Presidence, Avenue Georges Pompidou, BP 360 Lome, Togo.

LC HG4621 .S43
US
SECURITIES INDUSTRY FACT BOOK.
Added/Corp Securities Industry Association. (19??)-. English. One time a year. $75.00. Securities Industry Association, 120 Broadway/35th Floor, New York NY 10271. **Tel** (212)608-1500, FAX (212)608-1604.

US
SECURITIES : PUBLIC AND PRIVATE OFFERINGS.
English. Clark Boardman Callaghan, 155 Pfingsten Road, Deerfield IL 60015. **Tel** (800)323-8067.

ISSN 0746-2921
US
SECURITY CLINIC.
(19??)-. Periodical. English. Twelve times a year. $45.72 US; $56.04 Canada. Bureau of Business Practice, 24 Rope Ferry Road, Waterford CT 06386. **Tel** (800)243-0876, (203)442-4365, (800)876-9105, FAX (203)443-1123.

US
SECURITY REPORTER.
(19??)-. English. Fulcon Communications, 8879 West Colonial Drive, Suite 138, Ocoee FL 34761. **Tel** (407)294-6750.

DD 332
ISSN 0885-2693
US
SECURITY TRADERS HANDBOOK.
[Secur. traders handb.]. (19??)-. Periodical. English. Twelve times a year. $36.00. Security Traders Handbook, Route 198, Woodstock Valley CT 06282. **Tel** (203)974-2223, (800)4-ANNUAL. **ED** Vickie Michael. Index available. cum. index. **Bk Rev**. **Ad Acc**. **Circ**: 9,000.
Desc: Provides corporate financial reports and news on publicly traded companies, research reports, NASDAQ and NAOTIC news and listings, SEC Civil and legal proceedings, global market news, directory of financial newsletters and advisories, insider/outsider reports, new issues, pending issues, blind pools, public companies' annual reports, etc.

LC HF5001 .S43
KO
SEGYE KYONGJE CHUBO.
VFOAT World Business Week. Periodical. Korean (Korean). Not for Sale. Hanguk Muyok Hyophoe, 10-1 2-ka Hoehyon-dong Chung-ku, Seoul Korea.

LC HB9 .S37
JA
SEIJO DAIGAKU KEIZAI KENKYU.
VFOAT Seijo University Economic Papers. (19??)-. Periodical. Japanese. Seijo Daigaku Keizaigakki, 1-20 Seijo 6, Setagaya-ku Tokyo Japan.

LC HB9 .S38a
JA
SEIKEI DAIGAKU KEIZAIGAKUBU RONSHU.
Main/Corp Seikei Baigaku, Tokyo. Keizaigakubu. **Added/Corp** Seikei Daigaku, Tokyo. Keizaigakubu. Journal of the Faculty of Economics. Seikei Daigaku, Tokyo. Kezai-Gakubu Ronsyu. Seikei Daigaku. Keizai - Gakubu Ronsyu. **VFOAT** Journal of the Faculty of Economics. Seikei University Keizai-Gakubu Ronsyu. (19??)-. Multiple languages (Japanese and English). Seikei Daigaku Keizaigakubu Cakkai, 3-1 Kichijoji, Kitamachi 1, Musashino Japan.

LC HB9 .S4a
DD 330
JA
SEINAN DAIGAKU KEIZAIGAKU RON SHU.
Main/Corp Seinan Gakuin Daigaku. Gakujutsu Kenkyujo. **Added/Corp** Seinan Gakuin Daigaku. Keizaigaku Ron Shu. Seinan Gakuin Daigaku. Economic Review. **VFOAT** Economic Review of Seinan Gakuin University. (Aug. 1966)-. Periodical. Multiple languages (Japanese and English). Seinan Gakuin Daigaku Gakujutsu Kenkyujo, 2-92 Nishijin 6-chome Nishi-ku 814, Fukuoka Japan.

LC HD9502.J3 E534
ISSN 0285-4031
JA
SEKIYU TO SHOHI DOTAI TOKEI GEPPO. SHO-KO-KOGYO / [HENSHU] TSUSHO SANGYO DAIJIN KANBO CHOSA TOKEIBU.
Added/Corp Japan. Tsusho Sangyosho. Chosa Tokeibu. (198?)-. Periodical. Japanese. Twelve times a year. Tsusan Tokei Kyokai, (International Trade & Industry Statistics Assoc.), 8-9 Ginza 2 Chome, Chuoku Tokyo 104 Japan. *Continues Enerugi Shohi Dotai Tokei Geppo.*

ISSN 0171-4937
GW
UDC 651
SEKRETARIAT.
[Sekretariat]. (1979)-. Trade Publication. German. Twelve times a year. $122.82. Gabler Verlag, Postfach 1546, D-65005 Wiesbaden Germany. **Tel** 011 49 611 534129, FAX 011 49 611 534430. *Continues Gabriele, 0016-3708.*
Desc: Magazine for secretaries in middle and high positions.

DD 016.33
ISSN 0383-2392
CN
SELECTION OF RECENT ACQUISITIONS - CANADIAN IMPERIAL BANK OF COMMERCE, INFORMATION CENTRE, A.
See Business and Economics-Abstracting, Bibliographies and Statistics.

ISSN 0736-1912
US
SELF EMPLOYMENT UPDATE.
(1992)-. English. Two times a year. $10.95 US; $12.95 Canada; $15.95 other. Prosperity & Profit Unlimited, PO Box 416, Denver CO 80201-0416. **Tel** (303)575-5676. **ED** A. Doyle. **Circ**: 2500.
Desc: Business idea letters for various types of businesses.

US
SELF-STORAGE ALMANAC.
(1992)-. Trade Publication. English. One time a year. $35.00. Minico Inc., 2531 West Dunlap Avenue, Phoenix AZ 85021. **Tel** (800)824-6864.
Desc: Statistical reference for self-storage operators.

ISSN 1065-3066
US
SELLING EDGE, THE.
(1992)-. Periodical. English. Six times a year. $89.00. The Selling Edge, PO Box 2730, Champlain NY 12919.

PE
Pr Rev.
SEMANA ECONOMICA.
Added/Corp Centro de Informacion, Estudios y Documentacion (Lima, Peru). Vol. 1, No. 1, (March 11, 1982)-. Periodical. Spanish. Fifty times a year. $590.00. Apoyo SA, Apartado 671, Lima 100 Peru. **Tel** 011 51 14 445555, FAX 011 51 14 450536. **ED** Augusto Alvarez-Rodrich. **Ad Acc**, **Adv Mgr**: Roberto. ctrl circ.

LC HC
DD 330
UK
SEMINAR PAPERS (LONDON, 1972-).
(SEMINAR PAPERS.). **Main/Corp** Foundation for Business Responsiblities. (1972)-. Monographic series. English. Irregular. Price varies per volume. Foundation for Business Responsiblities, 40 Doughty Street, London WC1N 2LF, United Kingdom. *Continues Industrial Educational and Research Foundation. Seminar Papers.*

ISSN 0161-4282
US
SUSPENDED
SEMINARS.
(19??)-. English. One time a year (Oct.). Creative Communications Inc., 1402 East Skyline Drive, Madison WI 53705. **Tel** (608)231-3070. **ED** Howard C. Nelson. Index available. **Ad Acc**. **Circ**: 5,000. available on diskette.

FR
SEMPEX.
(19??)-. Periodical. French. Irregular. 1104.55F France; 1310.00F other (includes one basic work and supplements). SEMP / France, 26 rue le Brun, 75013 Paris France. **Tel** 011 33 1 43378350.

US
SENIOR ECONOMIST.
(19??)-. Periodical. English. Four times a year. $14.95 (new); $16.95 (renewal). National Council on Economic Education, 432 Park Ave South, New York NY 10016. **Tel** (212)685-5499, (800)338-1192, FAX (212)213-2872.

LC HB
DD 330
ISSN 1079-1132
US
●SENSOR BUSINESS NEWS. (1994-).
Newsletter. English. Twenty-five times a year. $397.00. Phillips Business Information Inc., 1201 Seven Locks Road, PO Box 61130, Potomac MD 20854. **Tel** (301)424-3338, (301)340-1520, (800)777-5005, FAX (301)424-4297, telex 358149. **ED** Charlie Hartley. Index available.
Desc: Topics include financial developments and marketing and investment news.

LC HC
DD 330
KO
SEOUL JOURNAL OF ECONOMICS.
Added/Corp Soul Taehakkyo. Vol. 1, No. 1 (March 1988)-. Periodical. English. Four times a year. $50.00. Institute of Economic Research / South Korea, Seoul National University, Seoul 151 742 Korea. **Tel** 011 82 2 880 5434, FAX 011 82 2 888 4454. **ED** Cae-One Kim. Index available. cum. index. **Ad Acc**. **Circ**: 250 (ctrl).
Desc: Purported to carry both theoretical and empirical articles in all fields of economics.
Ind/Abst Econ. Lit. Index.

SP
SERIE CIENCIAS ECONOMICAS Y EMPRESARIALES.
VFOAT Ciencias Economicas y Empresariales. No. 1- 1976-. Monographic series. Spanish (Italian). Price varies per volume. Servicio de Publicaciones University of Sevilla, san Fernando 4, 41004 Seville Spain.

ISSN 0252-2993
US
CEASED
SERIE DE FOLLETOS - FONDO MONETARIO INTERNACIONAL.
(SERIE DE FOLLETOS.). [Ser. foll. - Fondo Monet. Int.]. **Added/Corp** International Monetary Fund. **VFOAT** Serie de Folletos del FMI. (1964)-(19??). Monographic series. Spanish. International Monetary Fund, 700 19th Street Northwest, Publishing Unit, Washington DC 20431. **Tel** (202)623-7430, FAX (202)623-7201.

DD 658
ISSN 1068-2902
US
●SERVICE & SUPPORT MANAGEMENT.
[Serv. support manage.]. **VFOAT** Service and Support Management. Vol. 9, No. 1 (Jan. 1993)-. Trade Publication. English. Twelve times a year. $30.00. Publications & Communications, 12416 Hymeadow Drive, Austin TX 78750. **Tel** (512)250-9023, (800)678-9724, FAX (512)331-3900, telex 384303. **Circ**: 32,000. *Continues MSM, 0898-5499.*

DD 330
ISSN 1048-3462
US
SERVICE INDUSTRY NEWSLETTER.
[Serv. ind. newsl.]. **VFOAT** Vol. 9, Issue 8 (Sept. 1989)-. Newsletter. English. Twelve times a year. $245.00. The Ledgeway Dataquest, 550 Cochituate Road, Framingham MA 01701. **Tel** (508)370-5555. ctrl circ. *Continues Field Service Newsletter, 0889-3624.*
Desc: Digest of key events and trends in the service and support segment of the high-tech industry.

Business and Economics

LC HD
DD 338
UDC 659
Pr Rev.
ISSN 1144-2433
FR
SERVICE NEWS (PARIS). (SERVICE NEWS.). **VFOAT** Service Plus (Paris). (1990)-. Periodical. French. Eleven times a year (monthly except Aug.). $360.88. Shamrock Publications, 20 Avenue de Wagram, 75008 Paris France. **Tel** 011 33 1 42675522, **FAX** 011 33 1 42675521. **ED** Philippe Bloch and Ralph Hababou. **Bk Rev. Ad Acc. Circ:** 9,500.
 Desc: Service news focusing on customer service policies, innovations and ideas in Europe, the US and Japan.

LC HB9 .S445
JA
SHINSHU DAIGAKU KEIZAIGAKUBU RONSHU. Main/Corp Shinshu Daigaku (Japan). Keizaigakubu. **Added/Corp** Shinshu Daigaku (Japan). Shinshu Daigaku (Japan). Keizaigakubu. Economic Review, Shinshu University. **VFOAT** Economic Review, Shinshu University. (19??)-. Japanese. Shinshu Daigaku Keizaigakubu, 1-1 Asahi 3-chome, Matsumoto 390 Japan. **Continues** Shinshu Daigaku Keizaigakubu Ronshu.

LC HB9 .S46
DD 330
JA
SHO-KEI RONSO. VFOAT Review of Economics and Commerce. (19??)-. Periodical. Japanese. Kanagawa Daigaku Keizaigakkai, 27-1 Rokkakugashi 3 Kanagawa-ku 221, Yokohama Japan.
 Ind/Abst Am. Hist. Life (1969-1971).

LC HF5126.S25 S5
BL
SHOPPING : OPCOES DE COMPRA PARA A GRANDE SAO PAULO. VFOAT Opcoes de Compra Para a Grande Sao Paulo. 1- 1975-. Portuguese (Portugese). Editora de Guias, PO Box 4724, 01310 Sao Paulo Brazil. **Tel** 288-7667.

US
SHORELINE BUSINESS MONTHLY. (19??)-. English. Twelve times a year. $20.00. Shoreline Business Monthly, 716 Nims Street #16, Muskegon MI 49442. **Tel** (616)726-4375, **FAX** (616)728-8204.

LC HC244.A1 S563
DD 330.947/005
ISSN 1019-9829
FR
●**SHORT-TERM ECONOMIC INDICATORS, TRANSITION ECONOMIES / CENTRE FOR CO-OPERATION WITH THE ECONOMIES IN TRANSITION / INDICATEURS ECONOMIQUES A COURT TERME, ECONOMIES EN TRANSITION / CENTRE POUR LA COOPERATION AVEC LES ECONOMIES EN TRANSITION. Added/Corp** Centre for Co-operation with European Economies in Transition. Organisation for Economic Co-operation and Development. **VFOAT** Short Term Economic Indicators, Transitions Economies; Indicateurs Economiques a Court Terme, Economies en Transition. (1993)-. Periodical (French). Four times a year. $70.00. OECD Publications and Information Center, 2 rue Andre-Pascal, 75775 Paris Cedex 16 France. **Tel** 011 33 1 49104262, US:(202)785-6323, **FAX** 011 33 1 45248500, 011 33 1 45248176, telex 620 160 OCDE. **(Subscription address:** OECD Publications Center, 2001 L Street, Suite 700, Washington DC 20036. **Tel** (202)822-3873, (202)785-6323.) **Continues** Short-Term Economic Indicators, Central and Eastern Europe.

LC HC107.T4 S53
DD 338.7/4/09764
ISSN 0278-3266
US
SIBBALD GUIDE TO THE TEXAS TOP TWO-FIFTY, THE. [Sibbald guide Tex. top two-fifty]. **Added/Corp** John Sibbald Associates. **VFOAT** Texas Top Two-Fifty; Texas Top 250. **VAT** Sibbald Guide to the Texas Top Two Hundred Fifty. (1982)-. English. One time a year. $107.50. Acorn Press Inc, 28 Durham Drive, Dix Hills NY 11746. **Tel** (516)254-4840, **FAX** (201)540-9283. **ED** Deirdre Taub. **Bk Rev. Ad Acc. Circ:** 2,000 (ctrl).
 Desc: Assembles, in one handy reference, pertinent and timely information on 250 of the largest public and private companies.

NE
SIGMA. Dutch. Six times a year. Fl99.00. Kwaliteitsdienst KDI, PO Box 84031, 3009 CA Rotterdam Netherlands. **Tel** 011 31 10 4554700.

ISSN 0893-9888
US
SIGN BUSINESS. [Sign bus.]. (198?)-. Trade Publication. English. Thirteen times a year (June/July iss. combined). $38.00. National Business Media Inc, PO Box 1416, Broomfield CO 80020. **Tel** (303)469-0424, **FAX** (303)469-5730. **ED** Terrance Wike. **Ad Acc, Adv Mgr:** Ken Higgins. ctrl circ.

NE
SIGNAAL ABONNEMENT. Dutch. Irregular. Staatsuitgeverij / Aalsmeer, PO Box 204, 1430 AE Aalsmeer Netherlands.

LC HD58 .I48
DD 338/.0973/05
ISSN 1041-3073
US
TITLE CHANGE
SITE SELECTION & INDUSTRIAL DEVELOPMENT. See Real Estate.

LC HC351 .S58
DD 338.9489
DK
CEASED
SITUATION. (19??)-(19??). Danish. Forlaget Brsen, Postbox 2103, 1014 K Copenhagen Denmark.

LC HC895.A1 S58
DD 338.9691
MG
SITUATION ECONOMIQUE AU DEBUT DE ... . (19??)-. French.

DD 338
ISSN 1050-7078
US
SKYBOX (CINCINNATI, OHIO). (SKYBOX : INSIDE THE SPORTS BUSINESS.). [Skybox]. **VFOAT** Sky Box. Vol. 1, No. 1 (1990)-. Periodical. English. Four times a year (Jan., March, July, Oct.). $19.95 (one-year), $34.95 (two-year), $45.95 (three-year) US; $28.95 (one-year), $52.95 (two-year), $72.95 (three-year) Canada. Dorsey Publishing, 1328 Elam Avenue, Cincinnati OH 45225. **Tel** (513)541-0269, **FAX** (513)541-0057.

IT
SL RIVISTA DI ORGANIZZAZIONE. (19??)-. Italian. Four times a year. L40000.00 Italy; L50000.00 other. AISL Assoc Ital Studio Lavoro, Via Emilio Cornalia 19, 20124 Milan Italy. **Tel** 011 39 2 6692908. **Bk Rev. Ad Acc. Circ:** 1,300.

LC HF3737 .A33
DD 330.9497/3/005
XV
●**SLOVENIAN BUSINESS REPORT.** (Jan. 1993)-. Periodical. English. Twelve times a year. $69.86. Gospodarski Vestnik, Dunajska 5, 61000 Ljubljana Slovenia.

DD 338.64209941
ISSN 0817-5764
AT
SMALL BUSINESS IN WESTERN AUSTRALIA. [Small bus. West. Aust.]. (1985)-. Periodical. English. One time a year (July). 12.33Aus$. Small Business Development Corporation, GPO Box C111, Perth 6001 Australia. **Tel** 11 61 9 2200222, **FAX** 11 61 9 3253981. **ED** M. Pedeler and J. Connell. **Bk Rev, (Qty:** 8). **Circ:** 300.
 Desc: Keeps you up to date on the latest trends and issues affecting this dynamic business sector.

LC HG179 .S537
DD 332
ISSN 1069-2851
US
SMARTMONEY (NEW YORK, N.Y.). (SMARTMONEY.). [SmartMoney]. **Added/Corp** Hearst Corporation. Dow Jones & Co. **VFOAT** Smart Money. Vol. 1, No. 1 (Apr. 15, 1992)-. Periodical. English. Twelve times a year. $24.00. The Hearst Corporation, 250 West 55th Street, New York NY 10019. **Tel** (212)649-4014, (800)925-0485. **(Subscription address:** CDS Agency Hard Copy, PO Box 4966, Des Moines IA 50340. **Tel** (515)247-7569.)
 Desc: Magazine covering personal finance and consumer education.

DD 338
ISSN 0146-9266
US
SMOKESHOP. [Smokeshop]. (19??)-. Periodical. English. Twelve times a year. $32.00. BMT Publications Inc, Seven Penn Plaza, New York NY 10001. **Tel** (800)223-9638, (212)594-4120. **ED** Patrick Doran. **Ad Acc.**
 Desc: Smokeshop is edited for retail tobacco dealers including tobacco shop owners and tobacco department managers. Presents original articles on management, merchandising, display, design, promotion, etc.

DD 332
ISSN 1075-4652
US
SNL REIT WEEKLY, THE. [SNL REIT wkly.]. **Added/Corp** SNL Securities. (19??)-. Periodical. English. One time a week. $299.00. SNL Securities Inc., 410 East Main Street, Charlottesville VA 22902. **Tel** (804)977-1600, (804)977-5877. **(Subscription address:** SNL Securities LP, PO Box 2124, Charlottesville VA 22902. **Tel** (804)977-1600.)

US
SNOW COUNTRY BUSINESS. (19??)-. Trade Publication. English. Six times a year. $30.00. NYT Sports Leisure Magazine, 5520 Park Avenue, Trumball CT 06611. **Tel** (203)373-7249. **Continues** Ski Business, 0037-6191.

LC H1 .S523
DD 300/.5
Pr Rev.
ISSN 0737-7762
US
CEASED
SOCIAL CONCEPT. See Social Sciences.

LC HC
NE
SOCIAL, ECONOMIC AND POLITICAL STUDIES OF THE MIDDLE EAST. See History-History of the Near East.

LC HB9 .S7
DD 330
ISSN 0303-9609
BE
SOCIETE ROYALE D'ECONOMIE POLITIQUE DE BELGIQUE (SERIES). (SOCIETE ROYALE D'ECONOMIE POLITIQUE DE BELGIQUE.). [Soc. r. econ. polit. Belg.]. No. 307 (Feb. 1965)-. Monographic series. French. Irregular (three to four issues per year). Price varies per volume. Societe Royale d'Economie Politique de Belgique, Avenue General Michel 1B, 6000 Charleroi Belgium. **Tel** 32 71 32 73 94, **FAX** 32 71 32 86 76. Index available. ctrl circ. **Continues** Comptes Rendus des Travaux de la Societe Royale d'Economie Politique de Belgique.

FR
SOCIO-ECONOMIC STUDIES. Added/Corp UNESCO. (1980)-. Monographic series. English. Irregular. Price varies per volume. UNESCO / United Nations Educational Scientific and Cultural Organization, 7 place de Fontenoy, 75700 Paris France. **Tel** 011 33 1 456610000.

DD 331.25
ISSN 1195-9681
CN
CEASED
SOHO (MONTREAL). (SOHO.). [Soho]. (Mar. 15 1994)-(Dec. 1994). Consumer Publication. French. JDL Publications, CP 67, Westmount Quebec H32 2T1 Canada. **Tel** (514)933-3985.

JA
CODEN SOKEEO
SOKEIZAI. [Sokeizai]. **Added/Corp** Sokeizai Senta (Japan). Vol. 25, No. 7 (1984)-. Academic Scholarly Publication. Japanese. Twelve times a year. $136.00. Sokeizai, Senta Tokyo-to Minato-ku Shiba Koen 3-chome 5-ban 8-go, Japan 105. Documents available from CASDDS. **Continues** Sogo Imono, 0389-0349.
 Ind/Abst Chem. Abstr. (1984-).

LC TS989
DD 685.31
US
●**SOLE SOURCE.** See Clothing Industry and Fashion.

LC HC
DD 330
ISSN 0536-1613
GW
SONDERSCHRIFT DES IFO-INSTITUTS FUER WIRTSCHAFTSFORSCHUNG. Main/Corp IFO-Institut fur Wirtschaftsforschung. (19??)-. Monographic series. German. Irregular. Price varies per volume. Duncker und Humblot Verlag, Postfach 410329, D-12113 Berlin Germany. **Tel** 011 49 30 79000612, 011 49 30 79000613.

ISSN 0191-6327
US
SONOMA BUSINESS. (1???)-. Periodical. English. Lesher Communications Inc, 2640 Shadelands Drive, Walnut Creek CA 94598.

DD 338
ISSN 1055-906X
US
SORKIN'S DIRECTORY OF BUSINESS & GOVERNMENT (WICHITA/KANSAS ED.). (SORKINS' DIRECTORY OF BUSINESS & GOVERNMENT.). **VFOAT** Sorkin's Directory of Business and Government. (19??)-. Directory. English. One time a year. $395.00. Sorkin's Directories Inc., 1350 Elbridge Payne Road, Suite 101A, Chesterfield MO 63017. **Tel** (800)758-3228, (314)537-2665, **FAX** (314)537-1247, (800)721-5478. available on diskette; available on CD-ROM.
 Desc: A business reference source that profiles all significant companies from every industry and profession in the region and beyond.

LC HF5065.M8 S67
DD 338.7/4/02577
ISSN 1057-9346
US
SORKINS' MAGAZINE. [Sorkins' mag.]. **Added/Corp** Sorkins' Directories, Inc. Summer (1991)-. Periodical. English. Two times a year. $15.00 (single issue). Sorkins' Directories, Inc., PO Box 31549, St, Louis MO 63131.

LC HC361 .S64
DD 330
NO
SOSIALKONOMEN. Added/Corp Sosialkonomisk Samfunn. (1946)-. Periodical. Norwegian. Eleven times a year. Kr40.00. Sosialkonomnes Forening, Storgatan 26, 0184 Oslo 1 Norway. **Tel** 011 47 2 170035, **FAX** 011 47 2 173155. **ED** T. J. Hanisch, E. S. Jansen, I. Korsbakken, A. Rodseth, and J. Aasness. **Bk Rev. Ad Acc. Circ:** 2,000 (ctrl).

Supersedes *Stimulator.*
Desc: Application of economic theory on the Norwegian economy, discussion of economic policy issues for Norway.
Ind/Abst Selec. Coop. Index Manage. Period.

LC HC331 .A13a
DD 330 RU
SOTSIALNYE I GUMANITARNYE NAUKI. SERIIA 2, EKONOMIKA : OTECHESTVENNAIA I ZARUBEZHNAIA LITERATURA.
Added/Corp Institut Nauchnoi Informatsii po Obshchestvennym Naukam (Rossiiskaia Akademiia Nauk). **VFOAT** Ekonomika; Otechestvennaia i Zarubezhnaia Literatura. **VAT** Sotsialnye i Gumanitarnye Nauki. Seriia Dva, Ekonomika. (1992)-. Academic Scholarly Publication. Russian. Four times a year. Izdatelstvo Nauka / Akademiia Nauk, (Publishing House of the Russian Academy of Sciences), Leninskii Porspekt 14, 117901 Moscow Russia. **Tel** 011 95 9542153, FAX 011 95 9382144, telex 411964. ***Formed by the union of*** *Obshchestvennye Nauki za Rubezhom. Seriia 2, Ekonomika Obshchestvennye Nauki* ***and*** *Obshchestvennye Nauki v Rossii. Seriia 2, Ekonomika.*

US
SOUNDINGS (NOTRE DAME).
(SOUNDINGS.). **VFOAT** Soundings: A Series of Books on Ethics, Economics, and Business. 1987-. English. Irregular. University of Notre Dame Press, PO Box 635, South Bend IN 46624. **Tel** (219)239-6349, (800)677-3232, FAX (219)239-8148. **ED** Thomas Donaldson (editor's address: Georgetown University, Washington DC 20057).
Desc: A series of books on ethics, economics, and business.

ISSN 0747-2196
US
CODEN SEBSEJ
SOUNDVIEW EXECUTIVE BOOK SUMMARIES.
VFOAT Executive Book Summaries. (198?)-. Periodical. English. Twelve times a year. $89.50. Soundview, 5 Main Street, Bristol VT 05443. **Tel** (802)453-4062, (800)521-1227, FAX (802)453-5062. Index available (included in subscription). ***Continues*** *Soundview Summaries, 0195-1718.*

ISSN 0898-8811
DD 658 US
TITLE CHANGE
SOURCE (WINTER PARK, FLA.).
(SOURCE: THE NEWS MAGAZINE OF THE FLORIDA SOCIETY OF ASSOCIATION EXECUTIVES.). [Source]. **Added/Corp** Florida Society of Association Executives. **VFOAT** FSAE Source. (198?)-(199?). Periodical. English. Florida Society of Association Executives, 1211 Semoran Boulevard, Suite 165, Casselbery FL 32707. **Tel** (407)678-9344, FAX (407)678-7635. **ED** N Jane Graziani. Index available. **Bk Rev**, (Qty: (varies)). **Ad Acc**, **Adv Mgr:** Janie Graziani. **Circ:** 1500. ***Continued by*** *Association Source, 1066-8691.*

LC HA203 .S65
DD 339.4/1/0973021 US
SOURCEBOOK OF COUNTY DEMOGRAPHICS, THE.
See Business and Economics-Abstracting, Bibliographies and Statistics.

ISSN 1054-8890
DD 330 US
SOURCEMEX (ALBUQUERQUE, N.M.).
(SOURCEMEX [COMPUTER FILE].). [SourceMex]. **Added/Corp** University of New Mexico. Latin America Database. **VFOAT** Source Mex. **VAT** Source Mexico. Vol. 1, No. 1 (Nov. 7, 1990)-. Periodical. English. Two times a week. $175.00 (institutions). Latin American Institute, University of New Mexico, 801 Yale Northeast, Albuquerque NM 87131. **Tel** (505)277-5985, FAX (505)277-5989. available on an online database.
Ind/Abst PROMT [Full Txt.]; PTS Newsl. Database [Full Txt.].

ISSN 1054-8890
US
SOURCEMEX [COMPUTER FILE].
Added/Corp University of New Mexico. Latin America Data Base. Centro de Informaciones Cientificas y Humanisticas (Mexico City, Mexico). **VFOAT** Source Mex. Vol. 1, No. 1 (Nov. 7, 1990)-. Academic Scholarly Publication. English. Twenty-four times a year. $225.00 (institutions). Latin American Institute, University of New Mexico, 801 Yale Northeast, Albuquerque NM 87131. **Tel** (505)277-5985, FAX (505)277-5989. **ED** C. Navarro. available on diskette; available on an online database from NEWSNET; Predicasts, Inc.; and BITNET.
Desc: Provides information on the changing economic environment in Mexico.

LC HB9 .E452 **ISSN** 0038-2280
DD 330.5 SA
Pr Rev.
SOUTH AFRICAN JOURNAL OF ECONOMICS, THE.
[S. Afr. j. econ.]. **Added/Corp** Economic Society of South Africa. **VFOAT** Suid-Afrikaanse Tydskrif vir Ekonomie. Vol. 1 (March 1933)-. Periodical. English (Afrikaans). Four times a year. $38.00. South African Journal of Economics, 4 44 EBW Building University of Pretoria, Pretoria 0002 South Africa. **Tel** 11 27 12 4203525. **ED** D J Botha. Index available. **Bk Rev. Ad Acc. Circ:** 1,500. Documents available from The Genuine Article. ***Supersedes*** *Journal of the Economic Society of South Africa.*
Desc: The promotion of discussion of economic issues at home and abroad. It subscribes to no ideology.
Ind/Abst Abstr. Anthropol.; Coal Abstr.; Contents Recent Econ. J.; Curr. Cit.; Curr. Contents Soc. Behav. Sci.; Econ. Lit. Index; EP Collect.; Homework Help.; Int. Bibliogr. Sociol.; Int. Labour Doc.; J. Econ. Lit.; LABORDOC; Maize Abstr.; MasterFile FullTEXT 1000; MasterFile FullTEXT 350; MasterFile FullTEXT 650; MasterFile FullTEXT; OCLC; PAIS Int. Print; Res. Alert [Full Cov.]; Soc. Sci. Cit. Index [Full Cov.]; Stat. Theory Method Abstr. (1959-1963); Telebase; Work Relat. Abstr.; World Agric. Econ. Rural Sociol. Abstr.; World Mag. Bank.

LC F1401 .S68 **ISSN** 0268-0661
DD 980 UK
CCC
NLM F 1406.5; S726
SOUTH AMERICA, CENTRAL AMERICA, AND THE CARIBBEAN.
See History-History of North and South America.

ISSN 1050-7698
DD 650 US
SOUTH CAROLINA BUSINESS.
[S. C. bus.]. **Added/Corp** South Carolina Chamber of Commerce. Vol. 1, No. 1 (1980/1981)-. Periodical. English. One time a year. $10.00. South Carolina Chamber of Commerce, 1201 Main Street, Suite 1810, AT & T Building, Columbia SC 29201. **Tel** (803)799-4601, FAX (803)779-6043. **ED** Preston McLaurin. **Ad Acc.**
Ind/Abst Acad. Search; Bus. Index (Jan. 1985-Dec. 1985); Bus. Source Plus; Bus. Source; EP Collect.; Gen. BusinessFile (Jan. 1985-Dec. 1985); Gen. Period. Index (Jan. 1985-Dec. 1985); Homework Help.; MasterFile FullTEXT 1000; MasterFile FullTEXT 350; MasterFile FullTEXT 650; MasterFile FullTEXT (July 1993-); OCLC; Telebase.

ISSN 0745-4473
DD 330 US
SOUTH CAROLINA BUSINESS JOURNAL.
[S. C. bus. j.]. Vol. 1, No. 1; Jan. 1983-. Periodical. English. Twelve times a year. $12.00. South Carolina Chamber of Commerce, 1201 Main Street, Suite 1810, AT & T Building, Columbia SC 29201. **Tel** (803)799-4601, FAX (803)779-6043. **ED** Bert Lynan. **Bk Rev. Ad Acc. Circ:** 7,500 (ctrl). available on an online database (files 635,648/Full-Text) from DIALOG. Documents available from UMI Article Clearinghouse. ***Continues*** *Alert.*
Ind/Abst Bus. Dateline; Bus. Index (Jan. 1985-Dec. 1985); Bus. Source Plus; EP Collect.; Gen. BusinessFile (Jan. 1985-Dec. 1985); Gen. Period. Index (Jan. 1985-Dec. 1985); Homework Help.; MasterFile FullTEXT 1000; MasterFile FullTEXT 350; MasterFile FullTEXT 650; MasterFile FullTEXT; OCLC; Telebase.

LC HA621 .S68 **ISSN** 0739-9308
DD 317.57 US
SOUTH CAROLINA STATISTICAL ABSTRACT.
See Population Studies-Abstracting, Bibliographies and Statistics.

ISSN 0746-2271
DD 330 US
CCC
SOUTH FLORIDA BUSINESS JOURNAL.
[South Fla. bus. j.]. Vol. 4, No. 1 (Sept. 12, 1983)-. Periodical. English. One time a week. $55.00. South Florida Business Journal, 1050 Lee Wagner Boulevard, Suite 302, Ft. Lauderdale FL 33315. **Tel** (305)359-2100, FAX (305)359-2135. **ED** Martin Donsky. **Photos. Ad Acc, Adv Mgr:** Karen Van Der Eems. Full Page (B&W) $3303.00. Half Page (B&W) $2215.00. Full Page (Color) $3903.00. Half Page (Color) $2815.00. **Pub. Size:** Tabloid. **Circ:** 21,160. available on microfilm from University Microfilms International (UMI); available on an online database (files 635,648/Full-Text) from DIALOG. Documents available from UMI Article Clearinghouse. ***Continues*** *Miami Business Journal, 0274-9521.*
Desc: Serves Miami, Ft. Lauderdale, and West Palm Beach metropolitan area executives, managers and professionals with local business-to-business news coverage about companies engaging manufacturing, wholesale and retail trade, retail and industrial services, transportation, ranking and finance, insurance, real estate, utilities, construction, agriculture, energy, communications, government, institutions and professional services.
Ind/Abst Acad. Search; Bus. Dateline; Bus. Index (1985-1990); Bus. Source Plus; Bus. Source; EP Collect.; Gen. BusinessFile (1985-1990); Gen. Period. Index (1985-1990); Homework Help.; INFO-SOUTH Abstr.; MasterFile FullTEXT 1000; MasterFile FullTEXT 350; MasterFile FullTEXT 650; MasterFile FullTEXT (July 1993-); OCLC; PROMT; Telebase; Trade Ind. ASAP [Full Txt.]; Trade Ind. Index [Full Txt.].

US
SOUTH GEORGIA BUSINESS JOURNAL.
(19??)-. Periodical. English. Six times a year. $20.00 (one-year), $37.50 (two-year). South Georgia Chamber of Commerce, Box 2036, Thomasville GA 31799. **Tel** (912)228-1299, FAX (912)228-7033. **ED** Ray Willett. **Ad Acc.**

ISSN 1040-5380
US
SOUTHEASTERN MASSACHUSETTS BUSINESS DIGEST.
VFOAT Business Digest. Periodical. English. Twelve times a year. $22.00. Southeastern Massachusetts Business Digest Inc, 5 Dover Street/Suite 101, New Bedford MA 02740. available on an online database (file 635/Full-Text) from DIALOG. Documents available from UMI Article Clearinghouse.
Ind/Abst Bus. Dateline.

LC DT1155 .S68
DD 968/.005 RH
SOUTHERN AFRICA POLITICAL & ECONOMIC MONTHLY.
Added/Corp SAPES Trust. **VFOAT** Southern Africa Political and Economic Monthly; Southern Africa; SAPEM. No. 1 (Oct. 1987)-. Periodical. English. Twelve times a year. $100.00. SAPES Trust, PO Box MP 111 Mount Pleasant, Harare Zimbabwe. **Tel** 011 263 0 727875.
Ind/Abst LABORDOC.

LC HC900.A1 S67
DD 330.968/005 RH
SOUTHERN AFRICAN ECONOMIST.
Added/Corp SADCC Press Trust. Vol. 1, No. 1 (Feb./March 1988)-. Periodical. English. Six times a year. $80.00. SADC Press Trust, PO Box 6290, Harare Zimbabwe. **Tel** 011 2634 738891, FAX 011 2634 795412, telex 26367 SAECON ZW. **ED** Leonard Maveneka. **Ad Acc.**

LC HC101 .A4125 **ISSN** 0743-779X
DD 330.975/005 US
Pr Rev.
SOUTHERN BUSINESS & ECONOMIC JOURNAL, THE.
[Sou. bus. econ. j.]. **Added/Corp** Auburn University at Montgomery. School of Business. **VFOAT** Southern Business and Economic Journal. Vol. 10, No. 2 (Jan. 1987)-. Periodical. English. Four times a year (Jan., Apr., July, Oct.). $20.00. The Southern Business & Economic Journal, Auburn University at Montgomery, 7300 University Drive, Montgomery AL 36117-3596. **Tel** (334)244-3523, FAX (334)244-3762. **ED** Dean Moberly. cum. index. **Bk Rev**, (Qty: 10-12). **Ad Acc.** Full Page (B&W) $300.00. Half Page (B&W) $225.00. **Circ:** 1,600 (ctrl). ***Continues*** *Alabama Business & Economic Journal, 0743-779X.*
Desc: Emphasis is placed on the publication of applied academic studies with a preference for data-based research with practical application.
Ind/Abst PAIS Int. Print.

LC HC107.A13 A67 **ISSN** 0038-4038
DD 330.975/005 US
CODEN SECJAR
Pr Rev.
SOUTHERN ECONOMIC JOURNAL.
[South. econ. j.]. **Added/Corp** Southern Economic Association. University of North Carolina at Chapel Hill. University of North Carolina (1793-1962). Vol. 1 (Oct. 1933)-. Periodical. English. Four times a year. $80.00. Southern Economic Association, 300 Hanes Hall, Campus Box 3540, University of North Carolina, Chapel Hill NC 27599-3540. **Tel** (919)966-5261. **ED** Vincent J. Tarascio. Index available (bound in April issue). cum. index. **Bk Rev. Ad Acc. Circ:** 3,500. available on microfilm and microfiche from University Microfilms International (UMI). Documents available from The Genuine Article, UMI Article Clearinghouse.
Desc: Technical journal dealing with theoretical and empirical research in economics. Addressed primarily to teachers, researchers, and other professionals in business, economics and related fields.
Ind/Abst ABI/INFORM Glob. Ed.; ABI/INFORM [Computer File] (Jan. 1975-); Acad. Abstr.; Acad. Search; Am. Hist. Life (1954-); Am. Bibliogr. Slavic East Europ. Stud.; Arts Humanit. Citation Index [Select. Cov.]; Bus. ASAP (1992-) [Full Txt.]; Bus. Index (1985-); Bus. Period. Index; Bus. Source Plus; Bus. Source; Coal Abstr.; Contents Recent Econ. J.; Curr. Cit.; Curr. Contents Soc. Behav. Sci.; Econ. Lit. Index; Energy Res. Abstr. (Dec. 1975-); EP Collect.; Expand. Acad. Index (1984-); Gen. BusinessFile (1985-); Gen. Period. Index (1985-); Geogr. Abstr. Human Geogr.; Homework Help.; Hum. Resour. Abstr.; INFO-SOUTH Abstr.; Int. Bibliogr. Sociol.; Int. Dev. Abstr.; Int. Index Period.; Int. Labour Doc.; J. Econ. Lit.; Mag. Search; Manage. Contents (1974-); MasterFile FullTEXT 1000; MasterFile FullTEXT 350; MasterFile FullTEXT 650; MasterFile FullTEXT (Jan. 1992-); Newsp. Period. Abstr. (1991-); OCLC; PAIS Int. Print; Popul.

Business and Economics

Index; Public Aff. Inf. Serv. Bull.; Pub. Lib. FullTEXT; Res. Alert [Full Cov.]; Risk Abstr.; Soc. Sci. Source; Soc. Sci. Cit. Index [Full Cov.]; Soc. Sci. Index; Soc. Sci. Index Fulltext (Oct. 1988-) [Full Txt.]; SportSearch; Telebase; Trade Ind. ASAP [Full Txt.]; Trade Ind. Index [Full Txt.]; UMI ABI/Inform--Bus. Period. Ondisc (Jan. 1988-) [Full Txt.]; Wilson Bus. Abstr.; Women Stud. Abstr.; Work Relat. Abstr.

LC HC431 .S6 **ISSN** 0038-4046
DD 330 II

SOUTHERN ECONOMIST. [South. econ.]. Vol. 1 (1962/63)-. Periodical. English. Twenty-six times a year. $40.00. Southern Economist, Infantry Road 106-108, Bangalore 1 India. **Tel** 572330. **(Subscription address:** Prints India, 11 Darya Ganj, New Delhi 110002 India. **Tel** 011 91 11 3268645, FAX 011 91 11 3275542, telex 31-61087 PRIN-IN.) **ED** Susheela Subrahmanya. **Bk Rev. Ad Acc. Circ:** 7,000.
Desc: The publication follows an independent editorial policy. Regular and special features are - editorial, notes and comments, special articles, book reviews, banking, company notes, company meetings, personalities, investments.
Ind/Abst Int. Labour Doc.

LC HC107.A13 S688a
DD 330 US

SOUTHERN GROWTH ALERT. **Added/Corp** Southern Growth Policies Board. **VFOAT** Alert. No. 36 (October 1991)-. English. Southern Growth Policies Board, PO Box 12293, Research Triangle NC 27709. **Tel** (919)941-5145, FAX (919)941-5594. **Continues** SGPB Alert.
Desc: Covers regional planning.

ISSN 0892-8835
DD 650 US

SOUTHERN NEW JERSEY BUSINESS DIGEST. [South. N. J. bus. dig.]. **VFOAT** Business Digest; Business Digest of Southern New Jersey. (198?)-. Periodical. English. Twelve times a year. Southern New Jersey Business Digest, 2449 Golf Road, Philadelphia PA 19131. available on an online database (file 635/Full-Text) from DIALOG. Documents available from UMI Article Clearinghouse.
Ind/Abst Bus. Dateline (Jan. 1985-Feb. 1989) [Full Txt.].

US

SOUTHWEST ECONOMY & SOCIETY NEWSLETTER. Vol. 1 No. 1 (Oct./Nov. 1975)-. Newsletter. English. Irregular. Southwest Economy & Society, Box 4482, Albuquerque NM 87106.

LC HF5001 .S683 **ISSN** 8750-4294
DD 650/.05 US
CEASED

SOUTHWEST JOURNAL OF BUSINESS AND ECONOMICS. [Southwest j. bus. econ.]. Vol. 1, No. 1 (Fall 1983)-(1993). Periodical. English. Southwest Journal of Business and Economics, Bureau of Business and Economic Research El Paso, El Paso TX 79968-0541. **Tel** (915)747-5122. **ED** Gary L Sullivan and Florence Petrofes. Index available. **Circ:** 2,000. available on microfilm and microfiche from University Microfilms International (UMI); available on an online database (file 648/Full-Text) from DIALOG. Documents available from UMI Article Clearinghouse. **Continues in part** Southwest Business and Economic Review, 0195-198X.
Desc: Contains, research on economic development, regional and urban economics, business policy, management (behavioral, quantitative and human capital), finance, accounting and marketing analysis.
Ind/Abst ABI/INFORM Glob. Ed.; ABI/INFORM [Computer File] (Fall 1983-); Bus. ASAP (1990-) [Full Txt.]; Bus. Index (1986-); Gen. BusinessFile (1986-); Gen. Period. Index (1986-); INFO-SOUTH Abstr.; Mag. Search; Trade Ind. ASAP [Full Txt.]; Trade Ind. Index [Full Txt.]; UMI ABI/Inform--Bus. Period. Ondisc (Summer 1987-) [Full Txt.].

LC HB21 .S675 **ISSN** 8756-2278
DD 330/.05 US

SOUTHWESTERN JOURNAL OF ECONOMIC ABSTRACTS. (SOUTHWESTERN JOURNAL OF ECONOMIC ABSTRACTS / A SELECTION OF THE ABSTRACTS OF THE PROCEEDINGS OF THE SOUTHWESTERN ECONOMIC ASSOCIATION). [Southwest. j. econ. abstr.]. **Added/Corp** Southwestern Economic Association. Vol. 1, No. 1 (1980)-. Proceedings. English. One time a year. $12.00. Perryman and Associates, PO Box 6028, Waco TX 76706. **Tel** (817)755-8705. **ED** W. Robert Brazelton. **Ad Acc. Circ:** 100.
Desc: Abstracts of submitted representations of the annual meeting of Southwestern Economics Association and submitted discussants.

ISSN 1057-7467
DD 947 US

SOVIET BUSINESS REPORT, THE. [Sov. bus. rep.]. Vol. 1, No. 1 (July 1991)-. Periodical. English. Twelve times a year. $180.00. Madison South International, 2455 East Sunrise Boulevard, Suite 815, Ft. Lauderdale FL 33304.

SP

SPANISH ECONOMIC NEWS SERVICE. (19??)-. Periodical. English. Forty-six times a year. Spanish Economic News, C/Gran Via 70-9, Madrid Spain. **Tel** 2474812-2410837.

IT

SPECCHIO ECONOMICO. Italian. Twelve times a year. L50000. Ciuffa Editore Srl, Via Rasella 139, 00187 Rome Italy. **Tel** 011 39 6 4821150, FAX 011 39 6 485964. **Bk Rev. Ad Acc. Adv Mgr:** Paola Nardella.

ISSN 1066-1417
DD 338 US
TITLE CHANGE

SPECIAL EVENTS NEWS. (SPECIAL EVENTS NEWS : OFFICIAL PUBLICATION OF THE AMERICAN VENDORS ASSOCIATION.). [Spec. events news]. **Added/Corp** American Vendors Association. **VFOAT** Fair Times Special Events News. (1992)-(199?). Periodical. English. 21st Century Marketing, 523 Route 38, Suite 207, Cherryhill NJ 08002. **Tel** (609)488-5255. **Continues** Fair Times, 0889-0714. **Continued by** Events Business News.

LC HD9710.3.U5 S67 **ISSN** 0193-7278
DD 380.1/456292/05 US

SPECIALTY & CUSTOM DEALER. See Transportation-Automobiles.

ISSN 1044-1247
DD 972 US

SPOTLIGHT (BROOKLYN, N.Y.). (SPOTLIGHT.). [Spotlight]. **Added/Corp** Caribbean American Trade Connection. **VFOAT** CATC Spotlight; CATC-Spotlight. **VAT** Caribbean American Trade Connection Spotlight. (April/June 1989-). Periodical. English. Four times a year. $10.00. Caribbean American Trade Connection, 1601 Nostrand Avenue, Brooklyn NY 11226. **ED** Austin Tuitt. cum. index. **Ad Acc.**
Desc: A business consumer directory.

ISSN 0271-6453
US
CCC

ST. LOUIS BUSINESS JOURNAL. **VAT** Saint Louis Business Journal. Vol. 1 (Jan. 1980)-. Periodical. English. One time a week. $57.70. St Louis Business Journal, 612 North 2nd Street, PO Box 647, St Louis MO 63188. **Tel** (314)421-6200. **ED** Ellen Sherberg. **Bk Rev. Ad Acc. Facs Circ:** 19,000 (ctrl). available on microfilm from University Microfilms International (UMI); available on an online database (files 635,648/Full-Text) from DIALOG. Documents available from UMI Article Clearinghouse.
Desc: Weekly business newspaper.
Ind/Abst Acad. Search; Bus. Dateline; Bus. Index (1985-1990); Bus. Source Plus; Bus. Source; EP Collect.; Gen. BusinessFile (1985-1990); Gen. Period. Index (1985-1990); Homework Help.; MasterFile FullTEXT 1000; MasterFile FullTEXT 350; MasterFile FullTEXT 650; MasterFile FullTEXT (July 1993-); OCLC; PROMT; Telebase; Trade Ind. ASAP [Full Txt.]; Trade Ind. Index [Full Txt.].

UK

ST. PETERSBURG BUSINESS GUIDE. (1991)-. English. Irregular. £27.00 UK and Eire; £30.00 other; $60.00 US and Canada. Arguments & Facts International, PO Box 35, Hastings East Sussex, TN34 2UX United Kingdom. **Tel** 011 44 1424 444142, FAX 011 44 1424 717498.
Desc: A source of facts on business life and legislation in Russia's northern capital government and professional bodies, municipal authorities, commercial organisations, manufacturers, distributors and service companies.

LC HB **ISSN** 1102-9722
DD 338 SW
UDC 338.48

ST. PETERSBURG NEWS. **VFOAT** Saint Petersburg News; Leningrad News. (1990)-. Periodical. English (Russian). Four times a year (Mar., June, Sept., Dec.). $35.00 Europe; $40.00 other. St. Petersburg Media, Nybrogatan 21, S 114 39 Stockholm Sweden. **Tel** 011 46 8 6631970.

LC HG4057 .A44
US

●STANDARD & POOR'S 500 GUIDE / STANDARD & POOR'S. **Added/Corp** Standard and Poor's Corporation. **VFOAT** Standard & Poor's Five Hundred Guide; Standard and Poor's 500 Guide; Standard and Poor's Five Hundred Guide. (1994)-. Directory. English. One time a year. $23.95. Standard & Poor's Corporation, (A Division of McGraw-Hill, Inc.), 25 Broadway, New York NY 10004. **Tel** (212)208-8775, (800)221-5277. **Continues** S & P 500 ... Directory.

LC HG4651 .S19 **ISSN** 1072-1290
DD 338 US

●STANDARD AND POOR'S HIGH YIELD DIRECTIONS. [Standard Poor's high yield dir.]. **Added/Corp** Standard and Poor's Corporation. **VFOAT** High Yield Directions. (1994)-. Periodical. English. Twelve times a year. $1,150.00. Standard & Poor's Corporation, (A Division of McGraw-Hill, Inc.), 25 Broadway, New York NY 10004. **Tel** (212)208-8775, (800)221-5277.
Continues Standard and Poor's High Yield Quarterly, 1049-3263.

LC HC106.6 .S74 **ISSN** 0196-4666
DD 332.6/7 US

STANDARD & POOR'S INDUSTRY SURVEYS. **Main/Corp** Standard and Poor's Corporation. **Added/Corp** Standard and Poor's Corporation. Industry Surveys. **VFOAT** Industry Surveys. **VAT** Standard and Poor's Industry Surveys. (Jan. 1973)-. Periodical. English. Irregular. $1615.00. Standard & Poor's Corporation, (A Division of McGraw-Hill, Inc.), 25 Broadway, New York NY 10004. **Tel** (212)208-8775, (800)221-5277.
Desc: Provides continuous economic and business information on all major U.S. industries and numerous related industries. Financial data on more than 1,300 companies is included in the 22 individual surveys.
Ind/Abst Bus. Index (1991-); Gen. BusinessFile (1991-).

LC HG4057 .A4 **ISSN** 0361-3623
DD 332.6/7 US
NLM HG 4057 S785

STANDARD & POOR'S REGISTER OF CORPORATIONS, DIRECTORS AND EXECUTIVES. See Industry and Production-Trade and Industrial Directories.

LC HC290.5.D5 S73
DD 338.6/042/0943 GW

STANDORTWAHL DER BETRIEBE IN DER BUNDESREPUBLIK DEUTSCHLAND UND BERLIN (WEST) / BUNDESMINISTER FUR ARBEIT UND SOZIALORDNUNG, DIE. 1978 and 1979-. German. Bundesministerium fur Arbeit und Sozialordnung, Postfach 14 02 80, 5300 Bonn 1 Germany. Index available. cum. index. **Bk Rev. Ad Acc. Continues** Standortwahl von Industriebetrieben.

LC HF1134 .S69 **ISSN** 0883-265X
DD 658/.007/1179473 US
Pr Rev.

STANFORD BUSINESS SCHOOL MAGAZINE. [Stanf. Bus. Sch. mag.]. **Main/Corp** Stanford Business School Alumni Association. Vol. 53, No. 3 (Spring 1985)-. Periodical. English. Four times a year (Mar., June, Sept., Dec.). $10.00. Stanford Business School Magazine, Graduate School of Business/Room 34, Stanford University, Stanford CA 94305-5015. **Tel** (415)723-3157, FAX (415)725-1668. **ED** Cathy Castillo. **Bk Rev. Circ:** 24,000 (ctrl). **Continues** Stanford Business School Alumni Association. Stanford GSB, 0164-6605.
Desc: Articles reporting on Stanford Graduate School of Business - students, faculty, curriculum and alumni.

ISSN 1078-8794
DD 340 US

●STANFORD JOURNAL OF LAW, BUSINESS & FINANCE. See Law.

LC HD2425 .S68 **ISSN** 1044-324X
DD 380.1/02573 US

STATE AND REGIONAL ASSOCIATIONS OF THE UNITED STATES. [State reg. assoc. U. S.]. **VFOAT** SRA. 1st Annual Ed. (1989)-. English. One time a year. $65.00. Columbia Books Inc, 1212 New York Avenue NW/Suite 330, Washington DC 20005. **Tel** (202)898-0662, FAX (202)898-0775. **ED** John J Russell. Index available. **Circ:** 1,600 (ctrl).
Desc: Annual directory of the 7,300 principle state and regional trade associations, professional societies and labor unions. Includes address, phone number, facsimile number, name and title of paid executive, membership size, paid staff, annual budget, serial publications, annual meetings, historical and descriptive precis. Has subject, budget, acronym and executive personnel indexes.

LC HA343 .A3 **ISSN** 0737-1543
DD 330.9773/005 US

STATE AND REGIONAL ECONOMIC ILLINOIS DATA BOOK. See Business and Economics-Abstracting, Bibliographies and Statistics.

●STATE CAPITALS. ECONOMIC DEVELOPMENT. (1995)-. English. One time a week. $220.50. Wakeman Walworth Inc., 300 North

Washington Street #204, Alexandria VA 22314. **Tel** (703)549-8606. **Continues** From the State Capitals. Economic Development.

US

●**STATE CAPITALS. EMPLOYEE POLICY FOR THE PRIVATE AND PUBLIC SECTORS.** (1995)-. English. One time a week. $220.50. Wakeman Walworth Inc., 300 North Washington Street #204, Alexandria VA 22314. **Tel** (703)549-8606. **Continues** From the State Capitals. Employee Policy for the Private and Public Sectors.

US

STATE JOURNAL, THE. Vol. 1, No. 1 (Oct. 22, 1984)-. Newspaper. English. Twelve times a year. $40.00. The State Journal / West Virginia, PO Box 28, Charleston WV 25321. **Tel** (304)344-1630, FAX (304)345-2721. **ED** Abbey L. Zink (editor's address: 904 Virginia Street East, Charleston, WV 25301 USA). **Ad Acc, Adv Mgr:** LoreNelle White. **Circ:** 33,000 (ctrl).

LC HC107.W2 E265 HC107.W2 W43a
DD 330.9797/005
US
TITLE CHANGE

STATE OF WASHINGTON ECONOMIC AND REVENUE FORECAST. Added/Corp Economic and Revenue Forecast Council (Washington). Office of the Forecast Council. **VFOAT** Economic and Revenue Forecast; Washington Economic and Revenues Forecast. Vol. 11, No. 2 (June 1988)-Vol. 17, No. 4 (Nov. 1994). Periodical. English. Washington State Forecast Council, 711 South Capitol Way, Suite 300, Olympia WA 98504-0912. **Tel** (206)753-7022. **Continues** Economic and Revenue Forecast for Washington State. **Continued by** Washington Economic and Revenue Forecast.

US

STATEMENT OF THE LAWS OF ARGENTINA IN MATTERS AFFECTING BUSINESS. See Law.

US

STATEMENT OF THE LAWS OF MEXICO IN MATTERS AFFECTING BUSINESS. See Law.

LC HD4295.W4 A3
DD 354.54/14007231
ISSN 0511-5299
II

STATEMENT SHOWING FINANCIAL RESULTS OF IMPORTANT SCHEMES OF GOVERNMENT INVOLVING TRANSACTIONS OF A COMMERCIAL OR SEMI-COMMERCIAL NATURE. Main/Corp West Bengal (India). Finance Dept. (19??)-. English. West Bengal Government Press / Finance Department, Alipore West Bengal India.

DD 651.2
ISSN 1033-758X
AT

STATIONERY NEWS. [Stationery news]. (1989)-. Periodical. English. Twelve times a year. 37.00Aus$. Merrick Publishing Group, PO Box 305, Balgowlah NSW 2093 Australia. **Tel** 011 61 2 9070366, FAX 011 61 2 9079460. **ED** Deborah Carroll Hunter. **Ad Acc, Adv Mgr:** M. Merrick, **Tel** 02 9070366. **Circ:** 6,000 (ctrl).

LC HA661 .S72
DD 317
ISSN 0898-3879
US

STATISTICAL ABSTRACT OF UTAH (SALT LAKE CITY, UTAH. 1987). See Business and Economics-Abstracting, Bibliographies and Statistics.

LC HA1107 .S65a
DD 314.7
UK

STATISTICAL YEARBOOK OF MEMBER STATES OF THE COUNCIL FOR MUTUAL ECONOMIC ASSISTANCE. See Business and Economics-Abstracting, Bibliographies and Statistics.

LC HB235.I5 S77
DD 338.5/28/095984
IO

STATISTIK HARGA ... SULAWESI SELATAN. See Business and Economics-Abstracting, Bibliographies and Statistics.

ISSN 0395-8973
FR

STATISTIQUES POUR L'ECONOMIE NORMANDE. See Business and Economics-Abstracting, Bibliographies and Statistics.

LC HA1320.N6 A337
ISSN 0934-6767
GW

STATISTISCHE RUNDSCHAU NORDRHEIN-WESTFALEN. Added/Corp Landesamt fuer Datenverarbeitung und Statistik Nordrhein-Westfalen. German. Twelve times a year. Landesamt fuer Datenverarbeitung und Statistik Nordrhein-Westfalen, Postfach 101105, 40002 Duesseldorf Germany. **Tel** (0211)944901, FAX (0211)442006, telex 8586654 LDST D. **Continues** Statistische Rundschau fur das Land Nordrhein-Westfalen, 0177-6363.

GW

STATISTISCHES JAHRBUCH DER INDUSTRIE- UND HANDELSKAMMER ZU DORTMUND. See Business and Economics-Abstracting, Bibliographies and Statistics.

LC HC351 .A284a
DD 330.9489
ISSN 0108-5603
DK

STATISTISK MANEDSOVERSIGT. See Business and Economics-Abstracting, Bibliographies and Statistics.

LC HB235.S8 S8
DD 338.5/28/09485
SW

STATISTISKA MEDDELANDEN. P. See Business and Economics-Abstracting, Bibliographies and Statistics.

LC HC360.I5 S73
DD 338.9489
ISSN 0108-5565
DK

STATISTISKE EFTERRETNINGER. INDKOMST, FORBRUG OG PRISER. See Business and Economics-Abstracting, Bibliographies and Statistics.

LC HA
DD 310
ISSN 0039-0690
HU

STATISZTIKAI SZEMLE. See Business and Economics-Abstracting, Bibliographies and Statistics.

SA

STATS. See Business and Economics-Abstracting, Bibliographies and Statistics.

LC HB1435 .N47A

NE

STERFTETAFELS VOOR NEDERLAND AFGELEID UIT WAARNEMINGEN OVER DE PERIODE ... . VFOAT Life Tables for the Netherlands. (1976/1980)-. Dutch (summaries and/or abstracts in English). Irregular. Fl17.50. Centraal Bureau voor de Statistiek, AFD ALG Zaken, Postbus 959, 2270 AZ Voorburg Netherlands. **Tel** 011 31 70 3373800, FAX 011 31 70 0387429, telex 32692 CBS NL. **Continues** Netherlands. Centraal Bureau voor de Statistiek. Sterftetafels voor Nederland.

LC KKW3546.3 .S74
ISSN 0254-8992
SZ

STEUERENTSCHEID : STE / HERAUSGEBER, PRAXIS IN DER WISSENSCHAFT, DER. VFOAT STE. (19??)-. Periodical. French (German). Twelve times a year. Helbing & Lichtenhahn Verlag, Freie Strasse 84, CH-4051 Basel Switzerland. **Tel** 011 41 61 2721116.

US

STOCK WORKBOOK. (19??)-. English. One time a year (Sept.). $45.00. Scott and Daughters Publishing, 940 North Highland Avenue, Los Angeles CA 90038. **Tel** (213)856-0008.

LC HF5485 .S75

UK

STORAGE, HANDLING, DISTRIBUTION. VFOAT SHD, Storage, Handling, Distribution. Vol. 6, No. 6 (Sept. 1962)-. Periodical. English. Twelve times a year. $157.43. Turret Group, 177 Hagden Lane, Watford Hertfordshire WD1 8LN United Kingdom. **Tel** 011 44 1923 228577, FAX 011 44 1923 221346. **Continues** Storage.
Ind/Abst Curr. Cit.; Fluid Abstr., Civil Eng.; Fluid Abstr. Proc. Eng.; FLUIDEX (19??)-; Infomat Int. Bus.; Int. Packag. Abstr.; Pollut. Abstr. Indexes; World Ceram. Abstr.

DD 330
ISSN 1051-9521
US

STRAIGHTTALK -- FROM THE DESK OF THE CHIEF ECONOMIST .... . [Straighttalk desk Chief Econ.]. **Added/Corp** Conference Board. **VFOAT** Straight Talk; Straight Talk--From the Desk of the Chief Economist ....; Straight Talk From the Desk of the Chief Economist .... . (1990)-. Periodical. English. Ten times a year. $395.00. Conference Board, 845 Third Avenue, New York NY 10022. **Tel** (212)759-0900 ext. 582, (800)872-6273, FAX (212)980-7014.

LC HD30.28 .S72924
DD 658.4/012/05
ISSN 0258-0543
UK

STRATEGIC DIRECTION. (Jan. 1992)-. Periodical. English. Twelve times a year. $949.00. MCB University Press, 60 62 Toller Lane, Bradford, West Yorkshire BD8 9BY United Kingdom. **Tel** 011 44 1274 785280, FAX 011 44 1274 785200, telex 51317-MCBUNI-G. **(Subscription address:** MCB University Press / US and Canada Subscriptions, PO Box 10812, Birmingham AL 35201-0812. **Tel** (205)995-1567, (800)633-4931, FAX (205)995-1588.) **Absorbed** Marketing Strategy Letter.

ISSN 0968-0829
UK

STRATEGIC INSIGHTS INTO QUALITY. (19??)-. English. Four times a year. $659.00. MCB University Press, 60 62 Toller Lane, Bradford, West Yorkshire BD8 9BY United Kingdom. **Tel** 011 44 1274 785280, FAX 011 44 1274 785200, telex 51317-MCBUNI-G. **(Subscription address:** MCB University Press / US and Canada Subscriptions, PO Box 10812, Birmingham AL 35201-0812. **Tel** (205)995-1567, (800)633-4931, FAX (205)995-1588.)

LC HF5001
DD 650/.07/11714465
ISSN 0712-9130
CN

STRATEGIE +. ($TRATEGIE +.). [Strateg. +]. **VAT** Strategie Plus. Vol. 1, No. 1 (5 Oct. 1981)-. Periodical. French. Six times a year. Free. Universite du Quebec a Trois-Rivieres, CP 500, Des Forges Trois-Rivieres, Quebec G9A 5H7 Canada. **Tel** (819)376-5085, FAX (819)376-5092.

ISSN 1083-706X
US

●**STRATEGY & BUSINESS. Added/Corp** Booz, Allen & Hamilton. **VFOAT** Strategy and Business. (1995)-. Periodical. English. Four times a year. $38.00. Booz Allen and Hamilton, 101 Park Avenue, New York NY 10178. **Tel** (212)880-9561.

LC HB135 .S77
DD 330/.01/51
ISSN 0954-349X
UK
CCC

STRUCTURAL CHANGE AND ECONOMIC DYNAMICS. VFOAT SC and ED; SCED; SC + ED. Vol. 1, No. 1 (June 1990)-. Academic Scholarly Publication. English. Four times a year (1 volume). $244.00. Elsevier Science Publishers BV, PO Box 211, 1000 AE Amsterdam Netherlands. **Tel** 011 31 20 4853641, 011 31 20 4853642, FAX 011 31 20 4853598. **(Subscription address:** Oxford University Press / UK, PO Box 417, Oxford OX2 6YS United Kingdom. **Tel** 011 44 1865 56767.) **ED** Faye Duchin. available on microfilm and microfiche from University Microfilms International (UMI); available on an online database from Elsevier Electronic Subscriptions (EES).
Desc: Provides a forum to bring together and assess different perspectives for a better understanding of structural change and dynamics in actual economies.
Ind/Abst Econ. Lit. Index.

LC HC
DD 330
ISSN 0039-2928
IT

STUDI ECONOMICI. [Studi econ.]. **Added/Corp** Universita di Napoli. Facolta di Economia e Commercio. (1950)-. Periodical. Italian. Three times a year. L74860. Franco Angeli Riviste SRL, Viale Monza 106, 20127 Milan Italy. **Tel** 011 39 2 2827651, 011 39 2 289562, FAX 011 39 2 258004, telex 051-511650. **Continues** Studi Economici ed Aziendali.
Ind/Abst Econ. Lit. Index; Foreign Lang. Index; Index Econ. Artic. J. Collect. Vol. (1968-); J. Econ. Lit. (1968-); PAIS Int. Print.

LC HC
ISSN 0344-824X
AU

STUDIEN UEBER WIRTSCHAFTS- UND SYSTEMVERGLEICHE. Added/Corp Osterreichisches Institut fuer Wirtschaftsforschung. Osterreichisches Institut fuer Wirtschaftsforschung. Abteilung Internationale Wirtschaftsvergleiche. Vol. 1 (1971)-. Monographic series. German. Irregular. Price varies per volume. Springer-Verlag Vienna, Sachsenplatz 4 6, PO Box 89, A-1201 Vienna Austria. **Tel** 011 43 1 33024150, FAX 011 43 1 330242665. **(Subscription address:** Springer-Verlag New York Inc. / North America, PO Box 2485, Journal Fulfillment, Secaucus NJ 07096. **Tel** (201)348-4033, (800)777-4643, FAX (201)348-4505.)
Desc: Studies in comparative economic systems.

DD 338
ISSN 0081-7635
US

STUDIES IN BUSINESS CYCLES. [Stud. bus. cycles]. **Added/Corp** National Bureau of Economic Research. (19??)-. Monographic series. English. National Bureau of Economic Research, 1050 Massachusetts Avenue, Cambridge MA 02138. **Tel** (617)868-3900, FAX (617)441-3895.

LC HC
US

STUDIES IN BUSINESS EXPECTATIONS AND PLANNING. No. 1 (1953)-. English. Irregular. University of Illinois / Gregory Hall, 309B Gregory Hall, Urbana IL 61801.

ISSN 1062-046X
US

STUDIES IN DEFENCE ECONOMICS. (1992)-. Periodical. English. Four times a year. Harwood Academic Publishers / New York, PO Box 786, Cooper Station, New York NY 10276. **Tel** (212)206-8900, (201)643-7500.

Business and Economics

Business and Economics

Pr Rev.
STUDIES IN ECONOMICS AND FINANCE. (19??)-. English. Two times a year. $20.50 (institutions), $10.50 (individuals). University of North Carolina / Economics, Economics Department, Charlotte NC 28223. **Tel** (704)547-2185. **Continues** Studies in Economic Analysis.

ISSN 0148-6535
US

STUDIES IN ECONOMICS (MENLO PARK). (STUDIES IN ECONOMICS.). No. 1-. Monographic series. English. Price varies per volume. Institute for Humane Studies Inc, 4400 University Drive, Fairfax VA 22030-4444.
Ind/Abst Rice Abstr.; World Agric. Econ. Rural Sociol. Abstr.

LC HC
DD 330/.05
ISSN 0707-8552
CN
CCC

Pr Rev.
STUDIES IN POLITICAL ECONOMY. See Political Science.

ISSN 1062-8916
US

STUDIES ON DEFENCE ECONOMICS. [Stud. def. econ.]. (1992)-. English. Price varies. Harwood Academic Publishers, PO Box 90, Reading RG1 8JL United Kingdom. **Tel** 011 44 1734 560080, FAX 011 44 1734 568211.

LC S560
DD 338.1
UK

STUDY/ UNIVERSITY OF READING, DEPARTMENT OF AGRICULTURAL ECONOMICS & MANAGEMEMT. See Agriculture-Agricultural Economics.

ISSN 1055-1123
DD 333
US

SUBSEA-DATA-BASE (HOUSTON, TEX.). (SUBSEA-DATA-BASE [COMPUTER FILE].). [Subsea-data-base]. **VFOAT** Subsea Data Base; Subsea Database. (198?)-. English. Irregular (two to four times per year). $3400.00. Subsea Data Services, PO Box 270897, Houston TX 77277. **Tel** (713)840-8098.
Desc: Available on 5 1/4" diskettes. System requirements: IBM PC or compatible, 512K RAM, MS-DOS 2.0 or higher.

ISSN 0923-8492
NE

UDC 336.574
SUBSIDIEMEMO DEVENTER. (SUBSIDIEMEMO.). (1980)-. Periodical. Dutch. One time a year. Fl21.46. Kluwer BV, Postbus 23, 7400 GA Deventer Netherlands. **Tel** 011 31 5700 33155, 011 31 5700 47421, FAX 011 31 5700 11504, telex 42829.

LC HF5001
DD 650
ISSN 0745-2489
US
CCC
CODEN SUCSEY

SUCCESS (CHICAGO, ILL.). (SUCCESS.). [Success]. Vol. 28, No. 3 (March 1981)-. Periodical. English. Ten times a year. $15.97. Lang Communications, 230 Park Avenue, New York NY 10169. **Tel** (212)551-9500, FAX (212)599-4597. **(Subscription address:** CDS Agency Hard Copy, PO Box 4966, Des Moines IA 50340. **Tel** (515)247-7569.) **Bk Rev. Ad Acc. Circ:** 475,000. available on microfilm and microfiche from University Microfilms International (UMI); available with charts; available with illustrations. Documents available from UMI Article Clearinghouse, Ask*IEEE. **Continues** Success Unlimited, 0039-4424.
Desc: Appeals to achievement oriented people. Gives practical ideas and positive strategies for career advancement, time management tools, confidence-building strategies to face business strategies and opportunities.
Ind/Abst ABI/INFORM Glob. Ed.; ABI/INFORM [Computer File] (Oct. 1987-); Acad. Abstr. Full Text Elite; Acad. Abstr.; Acad. Search; Bus. Source Plus; Bus. Source; EP Collect.; Homework Help.; INFO-SOUTH Abstr.; INSPEC (Feb. 1990-); Mag. Artic. Summar. Elite; Mag. Artic. Summar. Select; Mag. Artic. Summar. CD-ROM; Mag. Search; MasterFile FullTEXT 1000; MasterFile FullTEXT 350; MasterFile FullTEXT 650; MasterFile FullTEXT (Apr. 1990-); Newsp. Period. Abstr. (1992-); OCLC; Pub. Lib. FullTEXT; Telebase; UMI ABI/Inform--Bus. Period. Ondisc (Dec. 1987-) [Full Txt.]; Vocat. Search; Work Relat. Abstr.

US
SUCCESSFUL BENEFITS COMMUNICATOR. (19??)-. Newsletter. English. Twelve times a year. $179.00. Ragan Communications Inc., 212 West Superior Street, Suite 200, Chicago IL 60610. **Tel** (312)335-0037, (800)878-5331, FAX (312)335-9583. **Continues** Techniques for the Benefits Communicator.
Desc: This publication is used by those whose job it is to communicate the benefits story to the employees of their company. It covers the latest in benefits, pensions, profit sharing and retirement plans.

ISSN 0736-5926
US

SUCCESSFUL CASH FLOW STRATEGIES. [Success. cash flow strategies]. Vol. 1, No. 1 (Feb. 15, 1983)-. Periodical. English. Twelve times a year. $72.00. Belvoir Publications, Subscription Department, Department M, Box 3000, Denville NJ 07834.

LC HF5438 .A317
DD 658.4/56/05
ISSN 0148-4052
US
CCC
CODEN SUMTEJ

SUCCESSFUL MEETINGS : SM. [Success. meet.]. **VFOAT** SM. Vol. 23, No. 11 (Nov. 1974)-. Periodical. English. Twelve times a year. $48.00. Bill Communications Inc., 355 Park Avenue South, New York NY 10010-1789. **Tel** (800)360-5200, (212)592-6200, FAX (212)592-6209. available on microfilm and microfiche from University Microfilms International (UMI). Documents available from UMI Article Clearinghouse. **Continues** Sales Meetings (Philadelphia, Pa. : 1972), 0048-8917.
Ind/Abst ABI/INFORM Glob. Ed.; ABI/INFORM [Computer File] (Nov. 1974-Sept. 1975); Acad. Search; Anbar Account. Finan. Abstr. [Full Txt.]; Anbar Mark. Distr. Abstr. [Full Txt.]; Anbar Top Manage. Abstr. [Full Txt.]; Bus. Index (Jan. 1985-Dec. 1985); Bus. Source Plus; Bus. Source; Curr. Cit.; Curr. Lit. Fam. Plan. (19??-199?); EP Collect.; Gen. BusinessFile (Jan. 1985-Dec. 1985); Gen. Period. Index (Jan. 1985-Dec. 1985); Homework Help.; INFO-SOUTH Abstr.; Mag. Search; Manage. Bibliogr. Rev.; MasterFile FullTEXT 1000; MasterFile FullTEXT 350; MasterFile FullTEXT 650; MasterFile FullTEXT (Jan. 1994-); OCLC; Oper. Prod. Manage. Abstr. [Full Txt.]; Person. Train. Abstr. [Full Txt.]; Telebase; UMI ABI/Inform--Bus. Period. Ondisc (Dec. 1987-) [Full Txt.].

LC HF5001
DD 658
ISSN 0886-1498
US

SUCCESSFUL SALESWOMAN.
Added/Corp National Association for Professional Saleswomen (U.S.). (19??)-. Periodical. English. Twelve times a year. $36.00. National Association for Professional Saleswomen, PO Box 2606, Novato CA 94948. **Tel** (916)484-1234. **ED** Mareella Leaton. **Circ:** 5,000.
Desc: Information useful to professional saleswomen.

US
SUCCESSGUIDE: THE GUIDE TO BLACK RESOURCES. **VFOAT** Success Guide. Chicago; Chicago; SuccessGuide, the Guide to Black Resources. (1989)-. English. One time a year. $14.95 one copy; $99.95 seven-copy set. Successource Inc., 1949 East 10th St. 100, Cleveland OH 44106. **Tel** (216)791-9330.
Desc: Lists thousands of black professionals and entrepreneurs; reference book used by major corporations, libraries, colleges and universities and government offices.

LC WMLC 93/2520
ISSN 1011-7547
SA
CEASED

SUID-AFRIKAAN, DIE. **VFOAT** Suid Afrikaan. (19??)-(1995). Periodical. Afrikaans. Suid-Afrikaan, 215 Bree Street, Cape Town 8000 South Africa. **Tel** 011 27 21 261308, FAX 011 27 21 222033. **ED** A. du Toit, Chris Louw. **Bk Rev. Ad Acc.**

US
SUMMARY DATA FROM THE CONSUMER PRICE INDEX NEWS RELEASE. **Added/Corp** United States. Bureau of Labor Statistics. (Jan. 1991)-. Government Publication. English. Twelve times a year. US Department of Labor / Bureau of Labor Statistics, 441 G Street Northwest, Washington DC 20212. **Tel** (202)606-7800, FAX (202)606-7797. **Continues** Summary of CPI News Release for ... .

LC HG3881.5.I58 I58
ISSN 0074-7025
US

SUMMARY PROCEEDINGS OF THE ANNUAL MEETING OF THE BOARD OF GOVERNORS. INTERNATIONAL MONETARY FUND. (SUMMARY PROCEEDINGS ... ANNUAL MEETING OF THE BOARD OF GOVERNORS / INTERNATIONAL MONETARY FUND.). [Summ. proc. annu. meet. Board of Gov., Int. Monet. Fund]. **Main/Corp** International Monetary Fund. **VFOAT** Summary Proceedings of the ... Annual Meeting of the Board of Governors; Summary Proceedings, Annual Meeting. (1947)-. English. One time a year. Free on request. International Monetary Fund, 700 19th Street Northwest, Publishing Unit, Washington DC 20431. **Tel** (202)623-7430, FAX (202)623-7201. available on microfilm and microfiche from University Microfilms International (UMI). **Continues in part** Annual Meeting of the Board of Governors.

FI
SUOMEN 1500 I.E. VIISITOISTASATAA SUURINTA YRITYSTA. **VFOAT** Finlands 1500 Storsta Foretag; The 1500 Largest Companies in Finland. Periodical. Multiple languages (Finnish, Swedish and English). One time a year.

US
CEASED
SUPERMARKET HQ QUARTERLY. **VFOAT** Supermarket Headquarters Quarterly; HQ Quarterly; SHQ. (Winter 1991)-(Fall 1993). Periodical. English. Lebhar Friedman Inc., PO Box 31203, Tampa FL 33633. **Tel** (800)944-4676, (813)664-6707.

ISSN 1054-3511
US

SUPERVISOR'S QUALITY CLINIC.
Added/Corp National Foremen's Institute. (1990)-. Periodical. English. Twenty-four times a year. $45.72 US; $60.60 Canada. Bureau of Business Practice, 24 Rope Ferry Road, Waterford CT 06386. **Tel** (800)243-0876, (203)442-4365, (800)876-9105, FAX (203)443-1123. **Continues** Quality Clinic, 0746-2913.

LC K23 .U65
DD 343.73/07 347.3037
ISSN 0736-9921
US

SUPREME COURT ECONOMIC REVIEW. [Supreme Court econ. rev.]. **Added/Corp** Emory University. Law and Economics Center. George Mason University. Vol. 1 (1980)-. Monographic series. English. One time a year. Price varies per volume. George Mason University School of Law, 3401 North Fairfax Drive, Room 321B, Arlington VA 22201. **Tel** (703)993-8161, FAX (703)993-8080. **(Subscription address:** University Press of America Inc., 4720 Boston Way, Suite A, Lanham MD 20706. **Tel** (800)462-6420, (301)459-3366.)

ISSN 1067-8085
US

●**SURINAME (SYRACUSE, N.Y.).** (SURINAME : AN EXECUTIVE REPORT.). **Added/Corp** Political Risk Services (IBC USA (Publications) Inc.). **VFOAT** Executive Report. (1993)-. English. $110.00. Political Risk Services, 6320 Fly Road, Suite 102, PO Box 248, East Syracuse NY 13057-0248. **Tel** (315)431-0511, FAX (315)431-0200.
Desc: Focuses on the long-term outlook for business. Includes a brief review of recent events and current circumstances, background intelligence including geography, history, economics and social conditions, as well as the key political and economic forecasts.

LC HE5613 .S93
DD 658.2
ISSN 0278-422X
US

SURVEY AND ANALYSIS OF BUSINESS CAR POLICIES & COSTS. See Transportation-Automobiles.

LC HD28 .S87
DD 658.3/83
ISSN 0735-0376
US

SURVEY AND ANALYSIS OF BUSINESS TRAVEL POLICIES & COSTS. See Travel and Tourism.

US
SURVEY AND ANALYSIS OF EMPLOYEE RELOCATION POLICIES & COST. (19??)-. Periodical. English. Every 2 years. $345.00. Runzheimer International / Wisconsin, Runzheimer Park, Rochester WI 53167. **Tel** (414)767-2200, FAX (414)767-2254, (800)558-1702.

US
SURVEY OF CURRENT BUSINESS.
Added/Corp American Furniture Manufacturers Association. (Mar. 7, 1984)-. Periodical. English. Twelve times a year. American Furniture Manfacturers Association, PO Box HP-7, High Point NC 27261. **Tel** (919)884-5000, FAX (919)884-5303. **Continues** Monthly Business Report (National Association of Furniture Manufacturers), 0735-1380.
Ind/Abst Acad. Ind. [Computer File] (1984-); Bus. ASAP (1990-) [Full Txt.]; Expand. Acad. Index (1992-); F&S Index Plus Text, Int. [Select. Cov.]; Gen. Period. Index (1985-); PAIS Int. Print; Predicasts Forecasts; Trade Ind. ASAP [Full Txt.]; Trade Ind. Index [Full Txt.].

LC HC101 .A13
DD 330.5
ISSN 0039-6222
US
CODEN SVCBAK

SURVEY OF CURRENT BUSINESS. (SURVEY OF CURRENT BUSINESS / UNITED STATES DEPARTMENT OF COMMERCE; COMPILED BY BUREAU OF THE CENSUS, BUREAU OF FOREIGN AND DOMESTIC COMMERCE, BUREAU OF STANDARDS.). [Surv. curr. bus.]. **Added/Corp** United States. Bureau of the Census. United States. Bureau of Foreign and Domestic Commerce. United States. Office of Business Economics. United States. Bureau of Economic Analysis. No. 1 (Aug. 1, 1921)-. Government Publication. English. Twelve times a year. $34.00 US; $42.50 other. Superintendent of Documents, US Government Printing Office, Washington DC 20402. **Tel**

(202)275-3328, FAX (202)786-2377. available on microfilm and microfiche from University Microfilms International (UMI); available on an online database (files 15,648/Full-Text) from DIALOG. Documents available from UMI Article Clearinghouse, Documents on Demand. ***Absorbed in part*** *Business Conditions Digest, 0146-7735.*
Desc: Gives information on trends in industry, the business situation, outlook, and other points pertinent to the business world.
Ind/Abst ABI/INFORM Glob. Ed.; ABI/INFORM Ondisc: Expr. Ed.; ABI/INFORM [Computer File] (Oct. 1983-); Acad. Abstr.; Acad. Search; Am. Stat. Index; Bus. Index (1985-); Bus. Period. Index; Bus. Source Plus; Bus. Source; Econ. Lit. Index; EP Collect.; Gen. BusinessFile (1985-); Homework Help.; INFO-SOUTH Abstr.; J. Econ. Lit.; Mag. Search; MasterFile FullTEXT 1000; MasterFile FullTEXT 350; MasterFile FullTEXT 650; MasterFile FullTEXT (July 1991-); Newsp. Period. Abstr. (1986-); OCLC; Pub. Lib. FullTEXT; Telebase; UMI ABI/Inform--Bus. Period. Ondisc (Oct. 1987-) [Full Txt.]; Wilson Bus. Abstr.

LC HC470.3.A1 C46
DD 338.4/7/00095125021 HK
SURVEY OF STORAGE, COMMUNICATIONS, FINANCING, INSURANCE, AND BUSINESS SERVICES. **Added/Corp** Hong Kong. Census and Statistics Dept. Transport and Services Statistics Section. **VFOAT** Report of the ... Survey of Storage, Communications, Financing, Insurance, and Business Services. (19??)-. Government Publication. English. Irregular. HK$24.00. Hong Kong Government Information Service, Beaconsfield House, 4 Queens Road, Hong Kong Hong Kong. **Tel** 011 852 284288014, 011 852 259881947, FAX 011 852 28459078, 011 852 25987482, telex 61190 HKGIS. ***Continues*** *Census of Storage, Communications, Financing, Insurance, and Business Services.*

LC HF3851 .S96
DD 380.1/0951/25 HK
SURVEY OF WHOLESALE, RETAIL, AND IMPORT/EXPORT TRADES, RESTAURANTS AND HOTELS. **Added/Corp** Hong Kong. Census and Statistics Dept. Wholesale/Retail Trade Statistics Section. (19??)-. English. Irregular. HK$22.00. Hong Kong Government Information Service, Beaconsfield House, 4 Queens Road, Hong Kong Hong Kong. **Tel** 011 852 284288014, 011 852 259881947, FAX 011 852 28459078, 011 852 25987482, telex 61190 HKGIS.

ISSN 0322-7987
CS
UDC 338
SVET HOSPODARSTVI. [Svet hospod.]. (1960)-. Periodical. Czech. One time a week. DM140.00. **(Subscription address:** Kubon & Sagner, ABT Zeitschriftenimport, D 80328 Munich Germany. **Tel** 011 49 89 54218130.**)**
Ind/Abst PROMT.

US
SVOBODAS HOME AND SMALL BUSINESS. (19??)-. English. Twelve times a year. $18.00. American Business Communicator, 1440 West Pratt Boulevard #1, Chicago IL 60626. **Tel** (312)764-1274.

ISSN 1101-4989
SW
UDC 339(485)
SWEDEN INTERNATIONAL. [Swed. int.]. **VFOAT** Quarterly Sweden International Magazine. (1990)-. Periodical. English. Four times a year. $51.30. Sweden International, Reprovagen 6, S-183 64 Tabt Sweden. **Tel** 011 46 8 6301060, FAX 011 46 8 7565740. **ED** Tommy Encandsson. **Ad Acc, Adv Mgr:** Robin Courtenay. **Acid Free. Circ:** 20,000. ***Continues*** *Marketplace Sweden, 0349-3326.*
Desc: Provides information on business events and market developments within Sweden, and is aimed at important decision makers in that European business community.

LC HC371 .S94 **ISSN** 1400-1829
DD 330 SW
●**SWEDISH ECONOMIC POLICY REVIEW.** **Added/Corp** Ekonomiska Radet (Sweden). Vol. 1, No. 1-2 (Autumn 1994)-. Periodical. English. Two times a year. Kr200.00. Ekonomiska Radet, Box 3116, S 103 62 Stockholm Sweden. **Tel** 011 46 8 4535939. **(Subscription address:** STK Distribution, Sorterargatan 2, S 162 26 Vallingsby Sweden. **)**

LC HC371 .S86 **ISSN** 0039-7296
DD 330.9485/005 SW
SWEDISH ECONOMY (STOCKHOLM. 1961), THE. (THE SWEDISH ECONOMY.). [Swed. econ.]. **Added/Corp** Konjunkturinstitutet (Sweden). (Feb. 1961)-. Periodical. English. One time a year. CE Fritzes AB, Kundhhanst, 10647 Stockholm Sweden. **Tel** 011 46 8 6909090. ***Continues in part*** *Meddelanden (Konjunkturinstitutet (Sweden)).*

Ind/Abst F&S Index Plus Text, Int. [Select. Cov.]; Predicasts Forecasts; Trade Ind. ASAP [Full Txt.]; Trade Ind. Index [Full Txt.].

LC HB3732 **ISSN** 1104-9197
DD 339.948 SW
●**SWEDISH EXAMPLE, THE.** **See** Sociology.

US
SWFL BUSINESS VIEWS. (1991)-. Periodical. English. Writers Inferno, 2180 Harbor Road, Naples FL 33942. **Tel** (813)6858.

LC HF3701 .S9
DD 338.09494 SZ
SWISS BUSINESS. **VFOAT** SwissBusiness. Vol. 1, No. 1 (June 1987)-. Periodical. English. Six times a year. $61.29. Handelszeitung Fachverlag AG, Seestrasse 37, CH-8027 Zurich Switzerland. **Tel** 011 41 1 2883545, FAX 011 41 1 2883577. **Ad Acc. Circ:** 50,000. Documents available from UMI Article Clearinghouse.
Ind/Abst ABI/INFORM Glob. Ed.; F&S Index Plus Text, Int. [Select. Cov.]; Infomat Int. Bus.; PROMT.

ISSN 1019-1127
SW
SWISS ECONOMIC NEWS. [Swiss econ. news]. **Added/Corp** Schweizerische Zentrale fur Handelsforderung. No. 6, June (1980)-. Periodical. English. Twelve times a year. Swiss Office for Trade Promotion, PO Box 1128, CH-1001 Lausanne Switzerland. **Tel** 011 41 21 203231. ***Continues*** *Nouvelles Economiques de Suisse.*

ISSN 1067-8093
DD 338 US
●**SWITZERLAND (SYRACUSE, N.Y.).** (SWITZERLAND : AN EXECUTIVE REPORT.). [Switzerland]. **Added/Corp** Political Risk Services (IBC USA (Publications) Inc.). (1993)-. English. $110.00. Political Risk Services, 6320 Fly Road, Suite 102, PO Box 248, East Syracuse NY 13057-0248. **Tel** (315)431-0511, FAX (315)431-0200.
Desc: Focuses on the long-term outlook for business. Includes a brief review of recent events and current circumstances, background intelligence including geography, history, economics and social conditions, as well as the key political and economic forecasts.

US
SYRACUSE BUSINESS. (19??)-. English. Twelve times a year. $15.95. Schueler Communications Inc., 208 North Townsend Street, Syracuse NY 13203. **Tel** (315)472-6911. available on an online database (file 635/Full-Text) from DIALOG. Documents available from UMI Article Clearinghouse.
Ind/Abst Bus. Dateline (Jan. 1985-) [Full Txt.].

LC HC497.S8 S9 **ISSN** 0039-7962
DD 330 SY
SYRIE & MONDE ARABE. [Syrie]. **Added/Corp** Office Arabe de Presse et de Documentation. **VFOAT** Syrie et Monde Arabe. **VAT** Syrie et Monde Arabe. No. 1 (1955)-. Periodical. French (English). Twelve times a year. $300.00. Office Arabe de Presse et de Documentation, 67 Place Chahbandar, BP 3550, Damascus Syria. **Tel** 011 963 11 459166 (operator assisted requested), telex 411613 OFA SY. **ED** A. Khani. Index available. cum. index. **Circ:** 1,000 (ctrl). ***Continues*** *Etudes Economiques sur la Syrie et les Pays Arabe.*
Desc: General survey of economics, politics and statistics of Syria and Arab world.
Ind/Abst Foreign Lang. Index; Public Aff. Inf. Serv. Bull.

ISSN 1074-732X
DD 338 US
CCC
●**SYSTEMS REENGINEERING ECONOMICS.** **See** Computers-Computer Systems.

LC HA1228.C5 T32
DD 314.4/3 FR
TABLEAUX DE L'ECONOMIE CHAMPENOISE. **See** Business and Economics-Abstracting, Bibliographies and Statistics.

ISSN 1056-2206
DD 305 US
TAFT'S WEALTHWATCHER. [Taft's wealthWatcher]. **Added/Corp** Taft Group (Rockville, Md.). **VFOAT** Taft's Wealth Watcher; Wealthwatcher. Vol. 1, No. 1 (May/June 1991)-. Periodical. English. Six times a year. $198.00. Taft Group, 835 Penobscott Building, Customer Service, Detroit MI 48226. **Tel** (800)877-8238, FAX (313)961-6083.

ISSN 1072-5539
DD 650 UK
●**TALKING BUSINESS.** [Talk. bus.]. Vol. 1, No. 1 (Feb. 1994)-. Periodical. English. Five times a year (includes audio cassette). $200.00. John Wiley & Sons Ltd., Baffins Lane, Chichester, West Sussex PO19 1UD United Kingdom. **Tel** 011 44 1243 779777, FAX 011 44 1243 776128 BTG:JWP001, telex 86290 WIBOOKG. ***Continues*** *Talking Medicine.*
Desc: A self-study English language training audio journal designed for professionals for whom English is a second language.

LC E184.K6 T34 **ISSN** 0742-7352
DD 973.04 US
TALLASU HANIN CHUSO MIT OPSOROK. **Added/Corp** Hanguk Chilsong Inswae. **VFOAT** Korean Directory of Dallas. (19??)-. English (Korean). One time a year. Hanguk Chilsong Inswae, 1701 North Greenville Avenue 1001, Richardson TX 75081.

ISSN 0896-467X
US
CCC
Pr Rev.
TAMPA BAY BUSINESS JOURNAL. **VFOAT** Tampa Bay Business. (198?)-. Periodical. English. One time a week. $45.00 (one-year); $78.00 (two-year); $110.00 (three-year). Tampa Bay Business Journal, 405 Reo Street/ Suite 210, Tampa FL 33609. **Tel** (813)289-8225, FAX (813)289-4518. **ED** Martin Donsky. **Ad Acc. Circ:** 13,000 (ctrl). available on microfilm from University Microfilms International (UMI); available on an online database (files 635,648/Full-Text) from DIALOG. Documents available from UMI Article Clearinghouse. ***Continues*** *Tampa Bay Business, 0273-5830.*
Ind/Abst Acad. Search; Bus. Dateline (March 6, 1992-) [Full Txt.]; Bus. Index (1985-1990); Bus. Source Plus; Bus. Source; EP Collect.; Gen. BusinessFile (1985-1990); Gen. Period. Index (1985-1990); Homework Help.; INFO-SOUTH Abstr.; MasterFile FullTEXT 1000; MasterFile FullTEXT 350; MasterFile FullTEXT 650; MasterFile FullTEXT (July 1993-); OCLC; PROMT; Telebase; Trade Ind. ASAP [Full Txt.]; Trade Ind. Index [Full Txt.].

CN
TANDEM. (19??)-. French. Six times a year. 23.95Can$. Editions Ultima Inc., 655 Jean Paul Vincent, Bureau 18, Longueuil Quebec J4G 1R3 Canada. **Tel** (514) 646-9011. ***Continues*** *Secretaire Moderne.*

FR
TARIF DES COLIS POSTAUX. French. One time a year. 40.00F France; 70.00F other. Indicateur Universel des PTT, 6 rue le Goff, 75005 Paris France. **Tel** 011 33 1 43267942.

IT
TARIFFARIO DOGANALE TARIC. (19??)-. Italian. Irregular (two basic volumes with irregular updates). L675000. Edizioni Doganali, Via Nizza 3/2, 16145 Genoa Italy. **Tel** 011 39 10 301514, 011 39 10 301926. ***Continues*** *Nuovo Tariffario Doganale.*

ISSN 1050-5369
US
TARIK (CHICAGO, ILL.). (TARIK.). **Added/Corp** Middle East and North Africa Economic Research Center. (1990)-. Periodical. English. Twelve times a year. $20.00. Middle East and North Africa Economic Research Center, 3528 West 59th Street, Chicago IL 60629.

LC J335 .H26
HU
●**TARSADALOM ES GAZDASAG KOZEP-ES KELET-EUROPABAN.** **Added/Corp** Budapesti Kozgazdasagtudomanyi Egyetem. **VFOAT** Society and Economy in Central and Eastern Europe; Tarsadalom es Gazdasag; Society and Economy. (1994)-. Periodical. Hungarian (English). Four times a year. Budapesti Kozgazdasagtudomanyi Egyetem, Budapest University of Economic Sciences, Management Development Instituk, Vezetesi es Szervezesi lanszek, 1828 Budapest 5. PF 489. Hungary. **Tel** 361 210 0200, FAX 261 210 0228. ***Continues*** *Aula (Budapest, Hungary), 0866-6865.*

ISSN 1042-9557
DD 658 US
$TARTING $MART. [$tart. $mart]. **VFOAT** Starting Smart. (198?)-. Periodical. English. Six times a year. $55.00. Network of Small Businesses, 230 Clay Street, Kane PA 16735. **Tel** (814)837-1096, (800)837-8885, FAX (814)837-6664. **Bk Rev. Circ:** 1,000.

LC HJ10.3 .T39 **ISSN** 0892-8649
DD 336.2/00973 US
CCC
TAX POLICY AND THE ECONOMY. [Tax policy econ.]. **Added/Corp** National Bureau of Economic Research. M.I.T. Press. Vol. 1 (1987)-. Monographic series. English. One time a year. $28.95 (hardcover); $14.95 (paperback). Massachusetts Institute of Technology (MIT) Press, 55 Hayward Street, Cambridge MA 02142. **Tel** (617)253-2889, (617)625-8481, FAX (617)258-6779. **(Subscription address:** MIT Press Books, 55 Hayward Street, Cambridge MA 02142. **)**
Desc: Focusing on the economic effects of tax policies, written in a nontechnical style accessible to policymakers, corporate manages, lawyers and economists, each article demonstrates how economic research can make an important contribution to tax policy debates.
Ind/Abst Econ. Lit. Index.

Business and Economics

LC WMLC L 83/1798
AT

TECHNICAL AND FURTHER EDUCATION. MANAGEMENT, BUSINESS AND COMMERCIAL STUDIES. **Main/Corp** Western Australia. Technical Education Division. **VFOAT** Management, Business and Commercial Studies. (19??)-. Periodical. English. Irregular. Nelson Wadsworth, PO Box 4725, Melbourne Victoria, 3001 Australia. **Tel** 03 329-5199.

ISSN 0318-918X
DD 309.2
CN

TECHNICAL PAPER SERIES - INSTITUTE FOR THE QUANTITATIVE ANALYSIS OF SOCIAL AND ECONOMIC POLICY, UNIVERSITY OF TORONTO. **Main/Corp** University of Toronto. Institute for Policy Analysis. No. 1, (1969)-. Monographic series. English. Irregular. Price varies per volume. University of Toronto Institute for Policy Analysis, Front Campus, Toronto Ontario M5S 7A6 Canada.

ISSN 0267-5307
UK

TECHNICAL REVIEW MIDDLE EAST. See Science and Technology.

FR

TECHNIQUES ET MANAGEMENT DES PROJETS INFORMATIQUES. (19??)-. French. Ten times a year. 1950.00F France; 2150.00F other. Bouhot & Le Gendre Publishers, 75 Bis rue de Bellevue, F 92100 Boulogne France. **Tel** 011 33 1 46040708. **(Subscription address:** Centrale des Revues, 11 rue Gossin, 92543 Montrouge Cedex France. **Tel** 011 33 1 46565266.) **Continues** L'Encyclopedie du Chef de Projet Informatique.

LC TS155 **ISSN** 1165-8568
DD 658.5 FR
UDC 658.5

●**TECHNOLOGIES INTERNATIONALES STRASBOURG.** (1993). Periodical. French. Ten times a year. 1200.00F France; 1466.00F other. ADIT, 2 rue Brulee, 67000 Strasbourg France. **Tel** 011 16 1 88214242.

ISSN 0895-903X
DD 650 US

TECHNOLOGY BUSINESS. See Science and Technology.

ISSN 0739-7208
US

TELE CONFERENCE. See Communications-Telecommunication.

LC HE8700 .T45 **ISSN** 0953-6841
UK

TELEVISION BUSINESS INTERNATIONAL : TBI. See Communications-Television and Cable.

IT

TEMPO ECONOMICO. (19??)-. Italian. Ten times a year. L58000. Fratelli Pini Editori Srl, Via Vitt Emanuele 99, 22100 Como Italy. **Tel** 011 39 31 264584.

AT

TENDERS AUSTRALIA. (19??)-. English. Forty-nine times a year. 269.00Aus$ Australia; 306.00Aus$ New Zealand, Papua New Guinea; 315.00Aus$ Malaysia, Indonesia, Fiji; 318.00Aus$ Japan, India, Hong Kong; 335.00Aus$ US, Canada, Lebanon; 349.00Aus$ Europe, Africa, former USSR. Thomson Publications / Australia, 47 Chippen Street, Chippendale New South Wales 2008 Australia. **Tel** 011 61 2 6992411, FAX 011 61 2 6991184, telex 122226. **(Subscription address:** Thomson Publications Australia, PO Box 815, Strawberry Hills, New South Wales, 2012 Australia. **Tel** 011 61 2 6992411.) **Ad Acc.**

ISSN 0745-1474
US

TENNESSEE BUSINESS (NASHVILLE, TENN.). (TENNESSEE BUSINESS.). Vol. 1, No. 1 (Oct. 1982)-. Periodical. English. Six times a year. $23.00. Tennessee Business, 1200 Fidelity Federal Building, Nashville TN 37219.
Ind/Abst Bus. Index (1984).

ISSN 0194-1240
US

TENNESSEE JOURNAL, THE. See Political Science.

LC HC107.T3 T46 **ISSN** 0735-1135
DD 330.9768/005 US

TENNESSEE'S BUSINESS (MURFREESBORO, TENN.). (TENNESSEE'S BUSINESS.). [Tenn. bus.]. Periodical. English. Three times a year. Business and Economic Research Center, Middle Tennessee State University, PO Box 102, Murfreesboro TN 37132. **Tel** (615)898-2610. **ED** Horace E Johns. cum. index. **Circ:** 2,500 (ctrl).
Ind/Abst PAIS Int. Print.

IT

TERZIARIA. (1985)-. Italian. Four times a year. L50000.00. Gedip SRL, V I Nievo 61, 00153 Rome Italy. **Tel** 011 39 6 5809084, FAX 011 39 6 5806396. **Bk Rev,** (Qty: 30). **Ad Acc.**

IT

TESTO UNICO IVA. (19??)-. Periodical. Italian. Two times a year. IPSOA Editore SRL, Casella Postale 12055, Mastrangelo, 20120 Milan Italy. **Tel** 011 39 2 82476248. Index available (Included).

LC HF1101 .T49A **ISSN** 0196-3198
DD 658/.007/0764 US

TEXAS BUSINESS EDUCATION ASSOCIATION YEARBOOK. Main/Corp Texas Business Education Association. English. One time a year. Texas Business Education Association, 6534 Lindy Ann Lane, Houston TX 77008.

LC HC107.T4 T46 **ISSN** 0040-4209
DD 330.9764 CCC
CODEN TXBRAK

TEXAS BUSINESS REVIEW. [Texas bus. rev.]. **Added/Corp** University of Texas at Austin. Bureau of Business Research. University of Texas. Bureau of Business Research. Vol. 1 (Apr. 25, 1927)-. Trade Publication. English. Six times a year. Free on request. Bureau of Business Research / Texas, University of Texas at Austin, Box 7459, Austin TX 78713. **Tel** (512)471-1616. **ED** Lois Glenn Shrout. **Circ:** 7,000 (ctrl). available on microfilm and microfiche from University Microfilms International (UMI); available on an online database (file 648/Full-Text) from DIALOG. Documents available from UMI Article Clearinghouse.
Desc: Features articles on various aspects of the economic climate in Texas.
Ind/Abst ABI/INFORM Glob. Ed.; ABI/INFORM [Computer File] (Jan. 1980-Dec. 1983); Bus. ASAP (1990-) [Full Txt.]; Bus. Index (1986-); Gen. BusinessFile (1986-); Gen. Period. Index (1985-); MasterFile FullTEXT (July 1993-); PAIS Int. Print; Trade Ind. ASAP [Full Txt.]; Trade Ind. Index [Full Txt.].

LC HC107.T4 T493
DD 330.9764/005 US

TEXAS ECONOMIC QUARTERLY / COMPTROLLER OF PUBLIC ACCOUNTS. Added/Corp Texas. Comptroller's Office. (May 1991)-. Periodical. English. Four times a year. Free on request. Comptroller State of Texas, PO Box 13528, Austin TX 78711. **Tel** (800)531-5441.

ISSN 0563-2978
DD 371 US

TEXAS SCHOOL BUSINESS. See Education-School Management and Organization.

LC HD2428.T4 T48 **ISSN** 0362-7519
DD 338/.006/2764 US

TEXAS TRADE AND PROFESSIONAL ASSOCIATIONS AND OTHER SELECTED ORGANIZATIONS. Added/Corp University of Texas at Austin. Bureau of Business Research. (1972)-. English. One time a year (Nov.). $14.00. Bureau of Business Research / Texas, University of Texas at Austin, Box 7459, Austin TX 78713. **Tel** (512)471-1616. **ED** Rita Wright. **Circ:** 800. **Continues** Selected Trade and Professional Associations of Texas, 0080-8644.
Desc: Lists business and professional associations in Texas. Includes Texas chapters of national associations and titles of association publications.

US

TEXASBUSINESS. (19??)-. English. Twelve times a year. $18.00. Texasbusiness, 2200 North Lamar, Suite 200, Dallas TX 75202. **Tel** (800)483-9267.

LC HF41 .T52
DD 330.9/593/04 TH

THAILAND BUSINESS. Vol. 1 (Nov. 1977)-. Periodical. English. Twelve times a year. $30.00. Business Publications Company Ltd., PO Box 2729, Bangkok 10501 Thailand. **Tel** 011 66 2 2150926.

LC HD3542.55.A4 T47
DD 338.7/4/025593 TH

THAILAND PROFILES. (1984)-. English. One time a year. 980.00B. Thailand Profiles / Media Research, Panavongs Building, 104 Surawong Road, 6th Floor, Bangkok 10500 Thailand.

LC PN1993 .T45
DD 384/.83/0973 US

THEATER FINANCIAL RECORD, THE. See Motion Picture.

US

THIRD WAVE DEVELOPMENT AWARDS, THE. Added/Corp Corporation for Enterprise Development. **VFOAT** CFED's Third Wave Development Awards. 1st Ed. (1992)-. English. CFED, National Office, 777 North Capitol Street NE, Suite 801, Washington DC 20002.

LC HC59.69 .T47 **ISSN** 0128-4134
DD 330.9172/4 MY

THIRD WORLD ECONOMICS. Added/Corp Third World Network. Issue No. 1 (Sept. 15, 1990)-. Periodical. English (Spanish). Twenty-six times a year (First and middle of every month). $60.00. Third World Network, 228 Macalister Road, 10400 Penang Malaysia. **Tel** 011 60 4 2293511, 011 60 4 2293713, FAX 011 60 4 364505, telex MA40989. **(Subscription address:** Michelle Syverson & Associates, PO Box 680, Manzanita OR 97130.) **ED** Martin Khor. **Bk Rev.**
Desc: This journal is edited and published in the South by economists and researchers to give you the news and anaylses that reflect the grassroots interests of people in the Third World.

UK

THIRD WORLD HANDBOOK. (19??)-. English. Irregular. $59.95. St. James Press, An Imprint of Gale Research Inc., PO Box 33477, Detroit MI 48232-5477. **Tel** (800)345-0392. **ED** Stuart Sinclair.
Desc: Provides compact analysis, statistics, and forecasts. Provides a comprehensive economic overview, an analysis showing how the region compares to the rest of the world, and individual chapters on each country of the region with data on trends in economic performance, demographics, government, and society.

LC S **ISSN** 0788-5199
DD 630 FI

TIEDONANTOJA - MAATALOUDEN TALOUDELLINEN TUTKIMUSLAITOS. See Agriculture.

LC AP95.C4 T486
DD 951.24/9005 CH

TIEN HSIA TSA CHIH. VFOAT Tien Hsia; Common Wealth; CommonWealth. (June 1981)-. Periodical. Chinese. Fourteen times a year (Monthly plus 2 special issue per year). $155.00. Commonwealth / Taiwan, Sung Chian Road, Lane 93 1st Floor 1, Taipei Taiwan. **Tel** 011 886 2 5064618, FAX 011 886 2 5056062. **ED** Diane Ying (phone: (02)507 8627). Index available. **Ad Acc. Circ:** 84,000.

LC HB9 .T44 **ISSN** 0772-7674
DD 330 BE

TIJDSCHRIFT VOOR ECONOMIE EN MANAGEMENT. [Tijdschr. econ. manage.]. **Added/Corp** Katholieke Universiteit te Leuven (1970-). Faculteit der Economische en Toegepaste Economische Wetenschappen. Vol. 20 (1975)-. Academic Scholarly Publication. Multiple languages (Dutch and English). Four times a year (Mar., June, Sept., Nov.). $55.98. Tijdschrift voor Economie, Naamsestraat 69, B-3000 Louvain Belgium. **Tel** 011 32 16 326688, FAX 011 32 16 285799. **ED** P. Sercu. Index available. cum. index. **Bk Rev. Ad Acc. Circ:** 2,000 (ctrl). available with charts. Documents available from BLDSC. **Continues** Tijdschrift voor Economie.
Ind/Abst Contents Recent Econ. J.; Econ. Lit. Index; J. Econ. Lit.

LC HC10 .T55 **ISSN** 0040-747X
DD 330.9 NE
CCC

TIJDSCHRIFT VOOR ECONOMISCHE EN SOCIALE GEOGRAFIE : TESG. [Tijdschr. econ. soc. geogr.]. **Added/Corp** Nederlandse Vereniging voor Economische en Sociale Geografie. Koninklijk Nederlands Aardrijkskundig Genootschap. **VFOAT** TESG; Journal of Economic and Social Geography; T.E.S.G. (1948)-. Academic Scholarly Publication. English (Dutch). Five times a year. $147.32. K N A G, PO Box 80123, 3508 TC Utrecht Netherlands. **Tel** 011 31 30 534056, FAX 011 31 30 535523. **ED** H. Reitsma. **Bk Rev. Ad Acc. Circ:** 1,300 (ctrl). Documents available from The Genuine Article. **Continues** Tijdschrift voor Economische Geographie.
Desc: An international journal on all aspects of human geography.
Ind/Abst Bibliogr. Carto.; Contents Recent Econ. J.; Curr. Cit.; Curr. Contents Soc. Behav. Sci.; EMBASE; Geogr. Abstr. Phys. Geogr. (?-?); Geogr. Abstr. Human Geogr.; Highw. Res. Abstr.; Int. Bibliogr. Sociol.; Int. Dev. Abstr.; PAIS Int. Print; Popul. Index; Res. Alert [Full Cov.]; Rural Dev. Abstr.; Soc. Sci. Cit. Index [Full Cov.]; World Agric. Econ. Rural Sociol. Abstr.

LC S **ISSN** 0921-481X
DD 630 NE
UDC 631 :303
Pr Rev.

TIJDSCHRIFT VOOR SOCIAAL WETENSCHAPPELIJK ONDERZOEK VAN DE LANDBOUW. See Agriculture.

ISSN 1041-2891
DD 509 US

TIME TABLE OF HISTORY. SCIENCE AND INNOVATION. (TIME TABLE OF HISTORY. SCIENCE AND INNOVATION [COMPUTER FILE].).

Business and Economics

[Time table hist., Sci. innov.]. **Added/Corp** Xiphias (Firm). **VFOAT** Timetable of History. Science and Innovation; Science and Innovation; Computing & Broadcasting; Time Table of History. Science and Innovation Computing & Broadcasting; Time Line of History; Time Tables of History; Xiphias Time Table. (Spring 1988)-. English. One time a year. $75.00. **Bk Rev. Ad Acc.** Circ: 12,000. **(Subscription address:** New Media Source, 3830 Valley Centre Drive, Suite 215, San Diego CA 92130. **Tel** 800 344-2621.)
Desc: A CD-ROM designed for the growing base of Macintosh business users to help them get the most from their ever-increasing use of voice, data and facsimile communications. System requirements: Apple Hypercard software.

LC HG4135 .T54
DD 338.7/4/0942
UK
TIMES 1000, THE. **VAT** Times One Thousand.
(19??)-. English. One time a year. £25.00 (retail), £16.25 (trade), add £6.00 for postage. The Times / Printing House Square, London EC4P 4DE United Kingdom. **ED** Margaret Allen. **Bk Rev. Ad Acc.** Circ: 12,000. **Supersedes** Times 500.
Desc: Lists industrial and financial companies in the UK and around the world.

LC HC
DD 330
NE
TINBERGEN INSTITUTE RESEARCH BULLETIN. **Added/Corp** Tinbergen Institute. Vol. 1, No. 1 (May 1989)-. Bulletin. English. Three times a year.
Ind/Abst World Agric. Econ. Rural Sociol. Abstr.

ISSN 1064-4598
DD 338
US
TODAY'S BUSINESS OWNER. (TODAY'S BUSINESS OWNER : BUSINESSES FOR SALE NATIONWIDE.). [Today's bus. owner]. Vol. 1, No. 2 (Autumn 1992)-. Periodical. English. Four times a year. VR Business Brokers, 1151 Dove Street, Suite 100, Newport Beach CA 92660. **Continues** Business Owner *(Newport Beach, Calif.).*
Ind/Abst Acad. Search; Bus. Source Plus; Bus. Source; EP Collect.; Homework Help.; MasterFile FullTEXT 1000; MasterFile FullTEXT 350; MasterFile FullTEXT 650; MasterFile FullTEXT (July 1993-); OCLC; Telebase.

ISSN 0898-5561
DD 338
US
TODAY'S DISTRIBUTOR. [Today's distrib.].
Vol. 1, No. 1 (May/June 1988)-. Trade Publication. English. Seven times a year. $40.00. Johnson Hill Press Inc., (A Division of PTN Publishing Co.), 1233 Janesville Avenue, PO Box 803, Fort Atkinson WI 53538-0803. **Tel** (414)563-6388, FAX (414)563-1704. **ED** Greg Udelhofen. **Ad Acc.** Full Page (B&W) $6300.00. Full Page (Color) $7875.00 (4-color). Circ: 42,024 (ctrl).
Desc: Targeted to industrial and construction distributors. Profiles successful distributors, suppliers, sales managers, marketing executives, economist and customers.

ISSN 1043-2671
DD 330
US
TODAY'S ECONOMY (DENVER, COLO.). (TODAY'S ECONOMY.). [Today's econ.].
(Jan. 1989)-. Periodical. English. Eleven times a year (monthly except Dec.). $160.00. Executive Direction Inc., 12501 County Road 74, Eaton CO 80615. **Tel** (303)654-0094, FAX (303)377-4865. **Continues** Economic Viewpoint.
Desc: Provides economic analysis of Colorado and the Mountain West.

LC HC411 .O7 **ISSN** 0911-7008
DD 330.952/005 JA
CEASED
TOKYO BUSINESS TODAY. [Tokyo bus. today]. **Added/Corp** Toyo Keizai Shinposha. (Jan. 1986)-(Feb. 1996). Periodical. English. 1-4 Nihonbashi Hongokucho Chuo-ku, Tokyo 103 Japan. **(Subscription address:** Maruzen Company Ltd., PO Box 5050, Import & Export Department, Tokyo 100 31 Japan. **Tel** 011 81 3 32789224.) Documents available from UMI Article Clearinghouse. **Continues** Oriental Economist, 0030-5294.
Desc: Presents analysis and commentary on business in Japan from an insider's perspective. Provides you with the same information Japanese executives rely on.
Ind/Abst ABI/INFORM Glob. Ed.; ABI/INFORM [Computer File] (May 1988-); Chem. Bus. Bull.; Chem. Bus. NewsBase (1986-); Chem. Bus. Update; Contents Pages Manage.; Curr. Cit.; F&S Index Plus Text, Int. [Select. Cov.]; PAIS Int. Print.; PROMT.

LC HF5475.J32 T66b
DD 381.18
JA
TOKYO-TO CHUO OROSHIURI SHIJO GAIYO. **Main/Corp** Tokyo-to Chuo Oroshiuri Shijo. (19??)-. Japanese. Tokyo-to Chuo Oroshiuri Shijo Gaiyo, 1-go Tsukiji 5-chome Chuo-ku, Tokyo Japan.

US
TOLEDO BUSINESS JOURNAL. (19??)-.
English. Twelve times a year. $15.00 (one-year), $25.00 (two-year), $35.00 (three-year). Telex Communications Inc., PO Box 1986, Toledo OH 43603. **Tel** (419)244-8200. available on an online database (file 635/Full-Text) from DIALOG. Documents available from UMI Article Clearinghouse.
Ind/Abst Bus. Dateline (May 1987-) [Full Txt.].

UK
TOLLEY'S COMPANIES HANDBOOK.
VFOAT Companies Handbook. 1st Ed. (1992)-. English. £27.95. Tolley Publishing Company Ltd., Tolley House, 2 Addiscombe Road, Croydon, Surrey CR9 5AF United Kingdom. **Tel** 011 44 181 6869141, FAX 011 44 181 6863155.
Desc: Concise and comprehensive guide to the Companies Acts, supporting legislation and case law, providing a first source of reference for those wanting a clear understanding of the law as it affects company administration.

US
TOMORROW'S JOBS, TOMORROW'S WORKERS. CAPITAL REGION. **Added/Corp** New York (State) Dept. of Labor. Division of Research and Statistics. New York (State). Bureau of Labor Market Information. **VFOAT** Capital Region. (1991)-. English. New York State Department of Labor / Rochester, Division of Research and Statistics, 155 West Main Street, Rochester NY 14614. **Continues** Labor Market Assessment, Occupational Supply and Demand. Albany-Schenectady-Troy Area.

LC HF5465.K64 T667
DD 381.1
KO
TONGA PAEKHWAJOM SABO.
Added/Corp Hwasong Sanop (Chu). (19??)-. Periodical. Korean. Six times a year. Not for sale. Hwasong Sanop (Chu), 20-11 Tongmun-dong, Chung-ku Taegu Korea.

ISSN 0967-6368
UK
TOP 100 BUSINESS LIBRARIES. See
Library and Information Sciences.

LC HD4965.5.U6 C67a
DD 331.2/81/658420973
US
TOP EXECUTIVE COMPENSATION.
Main/Corp Conference Board. (1970)-. English. One time a year. $120.00. Conference Board, 845 Third Avenue, New York NY 10022. **Tel** (212)759-0900 ext. 582, (800)872-6273, FAX (212)980-7014. **ED** Elizabeth Arreglado. ctrl circ. **Continues** Top Executive Compensation.

ISSN 0996-8067
UDC 65 FR
TOP VENTES BOULOGNE-BILLANCOURT. (TOP VENTES.). (1989)-. Periodical. French. Twelve times a year. 360.00F. Top Ventes Publications, 5 Av du Marechal Juin, BP 139, F-92106 Blgne Blnct Cedex France. **Tel** 011 33 1 48254740.

ISSN 0889-6992
US
TOPEKA BUSINESS REPORT, THE.
VFOAT Business Report. Vol. 94, No. 3 (Jan. 6, 1986)-. Periodical. English. One time a week. Hall Directory Inc, PO Box 8348, Topeka KS 66608. **Continues in part** Topeka Daily Legal News.

LC HA1911 .A3L HB235.T9
DD 310
TU
TOPTAN FIYAT ISTATISTIKLERI.
Main/Corp Devlet Istatistik Enstitusu (Turkey). **Added/Corp** Devlet Istatistik Enstitusu (Turkey). Wholesale Price Statistics. **VFOAT** Wholesale Price Statistics. (19??)-. Statistical Publication. Turkish (English). One time a year. $40.00. Turkish State Institute of Statistics, Necatibey Cadessi 114, Ankara 016100 Turkey. **Tel** 011 90 4 1188719, FAX 011 90 4 1253387, telex 46347 DIETR. **ED** Gianrocco Tucci. Index available. cum. index. Circ: 1,000 (ctrl). Documents available from BLDSC, SWETS.

LC HD9866.K64 T668
KO
TOPURON SOSIK. **Added/Corp** Tongyang Nairon Chusik Hoesa. **VFOAT** The Toplon News; Toplon News. (19??)-. Periodical. Korean (English and Chinese). Twelve times a year. Tongyang Nylon Company Ltd, 21-1 Sosomun-dong chung-ku, Seoul Korea. **Tel** 011 82 2 7450001, FAX 011 82 2 540089, telex K23400 TOPSTAR. **ED** Lee Sang Cheol. Circ: 5,300 (ctrl).
Desc: News, monthly special volumes, management journal, office automation, mental revolution, information lecture, activities of informal groups, and application of quality control.

LC G155 **ISSN** 1354-8166
DD 338.4791 UK
Pr Rev.
●TOURISM ECONOMICS. [Tour. econ.]. (1995)-.
Academic Scholarly Publication. English. Four times a year. $213.90. In Print Publishing Ltd., Distribution Center, Blackhorse Road, Letchworth SG6 1HN United Kingdom. **Tel** 011 44 1462 672555. **(Subscription address:** Turpin Distribution Services Limited, Blackhorse Road, Letchworth, Hertfordshire SH6 1HN United Kingdom. **Tel** 011 44 1462 672555, FAX 011 44 1462 480947.) **ED** Stephen Wanhill.
Desc: Devoted to the economics of the world's tourist business, the journal is a reference work for academic departments of tourism, economics and geography, as well as for researchers and planners in national and local government.

ISSN 0988-8233
FR
UDC 33 (4)
TOUT EN CARTES. (FORMAT EUROPE.).
(1988)-. Periodical. French. Four times a year. $67.81. Prodiges, 51 rue de Prony, F 75017 Paris France. **Tel** 011 33 1 40540308.

ISSN 0310-4664
DD 658.31240994 AT
Pr Rev.
TRAINING AND DEVELOPMENT IN AUSTRALIA. [Train. dev. Aust.]. (1972)-. Trade Publication. English. Four times a year (Mar., July, Sept., Nov.). 41.11Aus$. Australian Institute of Training and Development, PO Box 1011, Lalor Victoria 3075 Australia. **Tel** 011 61 3 4651107, FAX 011 61 3 4658054. **ED** Daryl Douglas (editor's address: Level 1, 2-4 Thomas Street, Chatswood New South Wales, 2067 Australia, phone: 011 61 2 419 4966). **Bk Rev. Ad Acc. Adv Mgr:** C. Felle, **Tel** 03 465 1107. Circ: 5,000 (ctrl).
Ind/Abst Aust. Educ. Index.

UK
TITLE CHANGE
TRAINING DIGEST EUROPE. (19??)-(1994).
English. MCB University Press, 60 62 Toller Lane, Bradford, West Yorkshire BD8 9BY United Kingdom. **Tel** 011 44 1274 785280, FAX 011 44 1274 785200, telex 51317-MCBUNI-G. **Merged into** European Business & Economic Digest.

ISSN 0267-8950
UK
CEASED
TRANSITION (LONDON, ENGLAND). See
Education-Vocational Education.

LC HD2755.5 .T674 **ISSN** 1014-9562
DD 338.8/8/05 US
TRANSNATIONAL CORPORATIONS.
Added/Corp Centre on Transnational Corporations (United Nations). Vol. 1, No. 1 (Feb. 1992)-. Government Publication. English. Three times a year (Twice and year plus special supplement.). $35.00. United Nations Publications, 2 United Nations Plaza, Room DC2 0853, Department 007C, New York NY 10017. **Tel** (212)963-8303, (800)253-9646. **(Subscription address:** United Nations Publications, Subscription Office, PO Box 361, Birmingham AL 35201-0361. **Tel** (800)633-4931, (205)995-1567 (outside US and Canada), FAX (205)995-1588.) **Continues** CTC Reporter, 0255-4216.
Desc: Provides a new focus on major issues about TNC be they legal, sectoral, regional or environmental.
Ind/Abst PAIS Int. Print.

ISSN 0165-330X
UDC 656.073 NE
TRANSPORT + OPSLAG. (1977)-. Periodical.
Dutch. Twelve times a year. $174.89. Misset Uitgeverij BV / Doetinchem, Postbus 4, 7000 BA Doetinchem Netherlands. **Tel** 011 31 8340 49911, 011 31 8340 49562, FAX 011 31 8340 43839, 011 31 8340 40515. **Absorbed** Logistiek Signaal, 0927-0590.

ISSN 1011-7768
HK
UDC 38
TRAVEL BUSINESS ANALYST ASIA ED. See Travel and Tourism.

ISSN 0256-419X
HK
UDC 38
TRAVEL BUSINESS ANALYST EUROPE ED. See Travel and Tourism.

ISSN 0886-6147
DD 658 US
TITLE CHANGE
TRAVEL BUSINESS MANAGER, THE.
See Travel and Tourism.

ISSN 0741-5818
US
TITLE CHANGE
TRAVEL SMART FOR BUSINESS. See
Travel and Tourism.

ISSN 0264-0937
DD 658.150941 UK
TREASURER. [Treasurer]. (1979)-. Periodical.
English. Eleven times a year (monthly with July-Aug. combined). Association of Corporate Treasurers, 12 Devereux Court, London WC25 3JJ United Kingdom. **Tel** 011 44 181 9362354, FAX 011 44 181 9364685.
Ind/Abst Curr. Cit.

LC HG4028.C45 T73 ISSN 1067-0432
DD 658.15/05 US
TREASURY AND RISK MANAGEMENT. [Treas. risk manag.]. **VFOAT** Treasury & Risk Management; Treasury. (1991)-. Periodical. English. Six times a year. $19.00. CFO Publishing Corporation, 253 Summer Street, Boston MA 02210. **Tel** (617)345-9700. ***Continues** Treasury (Boston, Mass.).*
Ind/Abst Acad. Search; Bus. Source Plus; Bus. Source; EP Collect.; Homework Help.; MasterFile FullTEXT 1000; MasterFile FullTEXT 350; MasterFile FullTEXT 650; MasterFile FullTEXT (Jan. 1994-); OCLC; Telebase.

LC HC270.2 .T73
DD 330 XO
TREND. (1991)-. Periodical. Slovak (summaries and/or abstracts in English). One time a week. $188.07. Slovart GTG LTD, Krupinska 4, 852 99 Bratislava, Slovakia. **Tel** 011 42 7 839471, 011 42 7 839472, 011 42 7 839473.

AT
TRENDEX NEWSLETTER. (19??)-. Newsletter. English. Twenty-four times a year. 164.44Aus$. Business Review Weekly, 469 La Trobe Street, Melbourne Victoria 3000 Australia. **Tel** 011 61 3 6033888, FAX 011 61 3 6704328.

GW
TRENDLETTER MEGATRENDS AKTUELL. (1991)-. German. Twelve times a year. DM297.60. Verlag Norman Rentrop, Theodor Heuss Strasse 4, D-53177 Bonn Germany. **Tel** 011 49 228 82050, FAX 011 49 228 364411, telex 17228309 TTX D. ***Formed by the union of** Trendletter **and** Megatrends Aktuell.*

ISSN 1065-2094
DD 338 US
TRENDS, THE. [Trends j.]. **Added/Corp** Socio-Economic Research Institute (Rhinebeck, N.Y.). (1992)-. Periodical. English. Four times a year (March, June, Sept., Dec.). $185.00. Trends Research Institute, PO Box 660, Rhineback NY 12572. **Tel** (914)876-6700, FAX (914)758-5252. **ED** Gerald Celente.
Desc: The inside track on trends affecting your business, your profession, your life. Forecasts on over 300 trend catagories,-consumer, social, economic, political, media, health, family, and other domestic and international trends.

LC HD4140.7 .A48 ISSN 1021-3287
DD 338.947/005 FR
•TRENDS AND POLICIES IN PRIVATISATION. **Added/Corp** Centre for Co-Operation with European Economies in Transition. **VFOAT** Tendances et Politiques des Privatisations. (1993)-. Periodical. English (French). Two times a year. $40.00. OECD Publications and Information Center, 2 rue Andre-Pascal, 75775 Paris Cedex 16 France. **Tel** 011 33 1 49104262, US:(202)785-6323, FAX 011 33 1 45248500, 011 33 1 45248176, telex 620 160 OCDE. **(Subscription address:** OECD Publications Center, 2001 L Street, Suite 700, Washington DC 20036. **Tel** (202)822-3873, (202)785-6323.**)**

ISSN 1183-1855
DD 070.1/75 CN
TRENDS (SCARBOROUGH). **See** Publishing.

ISSN 0897-0408
US
TRIAD BUSINESS. (1986)-. Periodical. English. One time a week. $22.00 North Carolina; $48.00 others. Spectator Publishers Inc. / Triad Business, 5601 Roanne Way, Suite 113, Greensboro NC 27409. **Tel** (910)854-3001, FAX (910)854-3013. **ED** Dick Barron. **Ad Acc, Adv Mgr:** Sarah Paffe, **Tel** (910)854-3001. ctrl circ. available on an online database from America Online.
Ind/Abst AGRICOLA [Select. Cov.].

ISSN 1060-5096
US
TRIANGLE BUSINESS JOURNAL. (19??)-. Periodical. English. Fifty-one times per year. $40.00. Triangle Business, PO Box 91453, Raleigh NC 27625. ***Continues** Triangle Business, 0891-0022.*
Ind/Abst Bus. Source Plus; Bus. Source; EP Collect.; Homework Help.; MasterFile FullTEXT 1000; MasterFile FullTEXT 350; MasterFile FullTEXT 650; MasterFile FullTEXT (Jan. 1995-); OCLC; Telebase.

SP
TITLE CHANGE
TRIBUNA INFORMATICA. (19??)-(19??). Spanish. VNU Business Publications / Spain, Cinca 13, 28002 Madrid Spain. **Tel** 011 34 1 563-8100, FAX 011 34 1 563-7572. ***Continued by** Computing Espana.*
Ind/Abst Infomat Int. Bus.

ISSN 1051-7367
DD 330 US
TRIBUNE BUSINESS WEEKLY. [Trib. bus. wkly.]. Vol. 1, No. 1 (April 1990)-. Periodical. English. One time a week. $36.00. South Bend Tribune Corporation, 225 West Colfax Avenue, South Bend IN 46626. **Tel** (219)233-6161, FAX (219)239-2642. **Ad Acc, Adv Mgr:** Smith, **Tel** (219)235-6161. **Circ:** 9,200 (ctrl). available on an online database (file 635/Full-Text) from DIALOG. Documents available from UMI Article Clearinghouse.
Desc: Covers regional business news.
Ind/Abst Bus. Dateline (March 11, 1992-) [Full Txt.].

IT
TRIESTE ECONOMICA. Italian. Four times a year. Free. Trieste Consult Srl, Piazza Scorcola 1, 34132 Trieste Italy. **Tel** 011 39 40 364580.

ISSN 1067-8107
DD 338 US
•TRINIDAD AND TOBAGO (SYRACUSE, N.Y.). (TRINIDAD AND TOBAGO : AN EXECUTIVE REPORT.). [Trinidad Tobago]. **Added/Corp** Political Risk Services (IBC USA (Publications) Inc.). (1993)-. English. $110.00. Political Risk Services, 6320 Fly Road, Suite 102, PO Box 248, East Syracuse NY 13057-0248. **Tel** (315)431-0511, FAX (315)431-0200.
Desc: Focuses on the long-term outlook for business. Includes a brief review of recent events and current circumstances, background intelligence including geography, history, economics and social conditions, as well as the key political and economic forecasts.

SI
TRIPLE I. English. Six times a year. Free to qualified readers; $50.00 Asia; $60.00 other. Asian Business Press Pte Limited / Singapore, 100 Beach Road, 26-00 Shaw Towers, Singapore 0718 Singapore. **Tel** 65-2943366, FAX 65-2985534, telex RS 25280 ABPSIN. **ED** Andren Yeo. **Ad Acc. Circ:** 6,500 (ctrl).
Desc: A magazine for the business community in South-Asia.

ISSN 1062-2330
DD 332 US
TROUBLED COMPANY PROSPECTOR, THE. [Troubl. co. prospect.]. (Apr. 1992)-. Periodical. English. One time a week. $1,150.00. Beard Group, PO Box 9867, Washington DC 20016. **Tel** (301)951-6400.

LC HD2346.U5 N34 ISSN 0191-6106
DD 338/.0025/73 US
TRY US. **See** Ethnic Interests.

LC Z7166 .J35B HB180.J3
DD 016.3 JA
TSUSHO SANGYOSHO TOSHOKAN TOSHO MOKUROKU. **Main/Corp** Japan. Tsusho Sangyosho Toshokan. (19??)-. Multiple languages (Japanese and English). Tsusho Sangyosho Toshokan, 3-1 Kasumigaseki 1 Chiyoda-ku, Tokyo 100 Japan.

ISSN 0564-4291
GW
TUBINGER WIRTSCHAFTSWISENSCHAFTLICHE ABHANDLUNGEN. **Added/Corp** Tubingen. Universitat. Rechts- und Wirtschaftswissenschaftliche Fakultat. Rechtswissenschaftliche Abteilung. Vol. 1 (1967)-. Monographic series. German. Irregular. Price varies per volume. JCB Mohr / Paul Siebeck, Postfach 2040, D-72010 Tuebingen Germany. **Tel** 011 49 7071 9230, FAX 011 49 7071 51104, telex 7/262872 mohr d.

ISSN 0950-3234
DD 330.9561038 UK
TITLE CHANGE
TURKEY MONITOR. [Turk. monit.]. (1986)-(1993). Periodical. English. The Economist Intelligence Unit, 40 Duke Street, London W1A 1DW United Kingdom. **Tel** 011 44 171 8301000. **ED** Stephen Harris. **Bk Rev. Circ:** 400 (ctrl). ***Absorbed by** Business Middle East.*
Desc: Provides guidance and analysis on the meaning and practical effects of the UK financial services regulatory system. Contains news on official announcements and procedures by every SRO and all the main RPBs. Clarifies compliance regulations and includes international aspects.

ISSN 0274-8894
DD 330 US
TURNING POINTS (CHESHIRE). (TURNING POINTS.). [Turn. points]. **Added/Corp** Micrometrics, Inc. (19??)-. Periodical. English. Eleven times a year (monthly, not published in July). $183.00. Micrometrics Press, Box 28317, Temple AZ 85285. **Tel** (602)966-3809. **ED** John V. Crosby. **Bk Rev. Circ:** 500.
Desc: Practical approach to short, medium and long term business cycle forecasting. Simple, unique methods can be adapted to small and large businesses. High accuracy record.

ISSN 0342-7951
GW
UDC 061.3/.4
TW. TAGUNGS-WIRTSCHAFT TW, TAG.-WIRTSCH. [TW, Tag.-Wirtsch.]. **VFOAT** Convention Industry; Tagungs-Wirtschaft. (1977)-. Periodical. English (German). Eight times a year. DM86.00. M + A Verlag fuer Messen, Ausstellungen und Kongresse GmbH, Postfach 101528, D-60015 Frankfurt Germany. **Tel** 011 49 69 759502, FAX 011 49 69 75951280, telex 841-411699.
Ind/Abst Leis., Rec., Tour. Abstr.

ISSN 1072-673X
DD 338 US
•TWIN CITIES BUSINESS MONTHLY. [Twin Cities bus. mon.]. **VFOAT** Twin Cities. Vol. 1, No. 1 (Sept. 1993)-. Periodical. English. Twelve times a year. $22.00. M.S.P. Communications, 220 south Sixth Street, Suite 500, Minneapolis MN 55402. **Tel** (612) 339-7571, FAX (612) 339-5806. **(Subscription address:** Kable Publishers Aide / Illinois, 308 East Hitt Street, Subscription Department, Mt. Morris IL 61054-1473. **Tel** (815)734-1261.**)**

US
TWR'S INSIDER REPORT. **See** Women's Interests.

LC HB9 .T94 ISSN 0379-6205
SA
TYDSKRIF VIR STUDIES IN EKONOMIE EN EKONOMETRIE. (TYDSKRIF VIR STUDIES IN EKONOMIE EN EKONOMETRIE = JOURNAL FOR STUDIES IN ECONOMICS AND ECONOMETRICS.). [Tydskr. stud. ekon. ekon.]. **Added/Corp** University of Stellenbosch. Bureau for Economic Research. University of Stellenbosch. Business School. **VFOAT** Journal for Studies in Economics and Econometrics; S.E.E.; SEE. No. 6 (Dec. 1979)-. Periodical. Afrikaans (English). Three times a year. $34.29. Bureau for Economic Research, Private BAG 5050, University of Stellenbosch, 7599 Stellenbosch South Africa. **Tel** 011 27 21 8872810, FAX 011 27 21 8839225. ***Continues** Tydskryf vir Studies in Ekonomie en Ekonometrie.*
Ind/Abst Econ. Lit. Index; J. Econ. Lit.

LC KF6419.Z9 U17 ISSN 1066-1778
DD 343.7305/248 347.3035248 US
U.S. CORPORATIONS DOING BUSINESS ABROAD. [U.S. corp. doing bus. abroad]. **Added/Corp** Price, Waterhouse & Co. Price Waterhouse (Firm). **VFOAT** US Corporations Doing Business Abroad. **VAT** United States Corporations Doing Business Abroad. (1972)-. English. One time a year. Free on request. Price Waterhouse & Company, 1177 Avenue of the Americas, New York NY 10020. **Tel** (212)596-7000. ***Continues** Price, Waterhouse & Co. Information Guide for United States Corporations Doing Business Abroad.*

LC HC101 .D36a ISSN 0734-4449
DD 338.5/443/0973 US
U.S. LONG-TERM REVIEW. **See** Business and Economics-Abstracting, Bibliographies and Statistics.

LC HC101 .B962 ISSN 0740-851X
DD 330 US
UCLA BUSINESS FORECAST FOR CALIFORNIA, THE. [UCLA bus. forecast Calif.]. **Added/Corp** UCLA Business Forecasting Project. **VFOAT** U.C.L.A. Business Forecast for California; Business Forecast for California. **VAT** University of California, Los Angeles Business Forecast for California. (19??)-. Periodical. English. One time a year. $600.00. UCLA / Business Forecasting, Dodd Hall Room 50, 405 Hilgard Avenue, Los Angeles CA 90024-1463. **Tel** (310)825-1623, FAX (310)206-9940. ***Continues in part** Business Forecasting Conference. UCLA Business Forecast for the Nation and California in ...; **Continues** Proceedings of the...Annual Business Forecasting Conference Held at UCLA. Volume II, The UCLA Business Forecast for California.*

LC HC101 .U353
DD 330 US
UCLA BUSINESS FORECAST FOR THE NATION AND CALIFORNIA, THE. **Added/Corp** UCLA Business Forecasting Project. John E. Anderson Graduate School of Management at UCLA. (Dec. 1991)-. English. One time a year. $750.00. UCLA / Business Forecasting, Dodd Hall Room 50, 405 Hilgard Avenue, Los Angeles CA 90024-1463. **Tel** (310)825-1623, FAX (310)206-9940.
Ind/Abst F&S Index Plus Text, Int. [Select. Cov.]; Predicasts Forecasts.

NE
UIT EUROPOORTKRINGEN. **See** Transportation-Ships and Shipping.

LC HF1040 ISSN 1356-6369
DD 338.025 UK
•UK WEALTH DIRECTORY, THE. [UK wealth dir.]. **VFOAT** United Kingdom Wealth Directory. (1994)-. Directory. English. Every 2 years. £81.00 UK; £86.00 other. Rowland Lybrand of London, 28 Wheatley Court, Mixenden, Halifax, West Yorkshire HX2 8QL United Kingdom. **Tel** 011 44 1422 241197.
Desc: Lists information on the multi-millionaires of the U.K.; includes assets, names and addresses.

ISSN 0969-3483
UK
•UKRAINE BUSINESS REVIEW. **Main/Corp** London Ukrainian Business Agency. (1992)-. English. Twenty-four times a year. $295.00. Ukraine Business Agency, Vigilant House 120, Wilton Road, London SW1V 1JZ United Kingdom. **Tel** 011 44 171 9310665. ***Absorbed** Ukrainian Reporter.*

Business and Economics

LC HF3629.U7 U38   **ISSN** 1053-4237
DD 330.947/71/005   US
UKRAINIAN BUSINESS DIGEST. [Ukr. bus. dig.]. Vol. 1, No. 1 (Dec. 15, 1990)-. Periodical. English. Twelve times a year. $245.00. International Information Systems, PO Box 3127, Westport CT 06880. **Tel** (203)221-7450, FAX (203)221-7414.

    UK
UK'S ... LARGEST COMPANIES.
Added/Corp Environment Liaison Centre (International). **VFOAT** United Kingdom's ... Largest Companies. 1st Editon (1986)-. English. One time a year. $290.91. ELC Publishing, 109 Uxbridge Road Ealing, London W5 5TL United Kingdom. **Tel** 011 44 181 5662288, FAX 011 44 181 5664931.

    PP
UMBEN. See Sociology.

LC Z7164.C81   **ISSN** 1064-5381
DD 330   US
UMI ABI/INFORM--BUSINESS PERIODICALS ONDISC. See Business and Economics-Abstracting, Bibliographies and Statistics.

    US
●**UNIDOS : JOURNAL OF OPPORTUNITY.** (1993)-. English. Twelve times a year. $30.00. Unidos, 378 Ballena Drive, Diamond Bar CA 91765. **Tel** (909)396-5935. **ED** Leah Sanchez (editor's phone: (909)396-5939). **Bk Rev. Ad Acc. Adv Mgr:** Irma Rey. ctrl circ. available on CD-ROM; available on microfilm.
Desc: Aimed at women in business.

    ISSN 0750-3555
UDC 392 (44)   FR
UNION (PARIS. 1972). (UNION.). (1972)-. Periodical. French. Twelve times a year. 200.00F France; 248.00 other. Publications Filipacchi, 149 rue Anatole, 92534 Levallois Perret France. **Tel** 011 33 1 41346456, telex 651-294.

LC HC260.I5 A3   **ISSN** 0267-8691
DD 339.341   UK
UNITED KINGDOM NATIONAL ACCOUNTS. (UNITED KINGDOM NATIONAL ACCOUNTS.). [U.K. natl. acc.]. **Added/Corp** Great Britain. Central Statistical Office. **VFOAT** CSO Blue Book. (1984)-. Statistical Publication. English. One time a year (September). £10.00. Her Majesty's Stationery Office, 51 Nine Elms Lane, London SW8 5DR United Kingdom. **Tel** 011 44 171 8738459, 011 44 171 8738499, FAX 011 44 171 8738499, 011 44 171 8738456, telex 297138. **(Subscription address:** Her Majesty's Stationery Office, PO Box 276, Public Centre, London SW8 5DT United Kingdom. **Tel** 011 44 171 87384998456.) **Continues** National Income and Expenditures (London, England).

LC HD2346.U5 U58   **ISSN** 0731-5643
DD 338.6/422   US
UNITED STATES DIRECTORIES OF MINORITY CONTRACTORS, YELLOW PAGES, THE. **VFOAT** US Directories of Minority Contractors; U.S. Directories of Minority Contractors. (1981)-. English. One time a year. US Directories of Minority Contractors, PO Box 82, Brentwood TN 37027.

LC HF3099 .G38A   **ISSN** 1044-4351
    US
UNITED STATES-GERMAN ECONOMIC YEARBOOK. [U. S.-Ger. econ. yearb.]. **VFOAT** Deutsch-Amerikanisches Wirtschaftsjahrbuch. 13th Ed. (1987)-. Periodical. (German). One time a year. $22.00. German American Chamber of Commerce Inc, 666 Fifth Avenue, New York NY 10103. **Tel** (914)271-5194. **(Subscription address:** Manhattan Publishing Company, PO Box 650, Croton-on-Hudson NY 10022. **) ED** Richard C Jacob. **Ad Acc. Circ:** 5,000. **Continues** United States-German Economic Survey, 0147-4421.
Desc: Articles by American/German business and government leaders; statistics and corporate directory.

LC HC
DD 330   US
UNIVERSITY OF MICHIGAN OCCASIONAL PAPERS. **VFOAT** Occasional Papers. Vol. 1, No. 1 (Apr. 1980)-. Periodical. English. University of Michigan Graduate School of Business Administration, Ann Arbor MI 48109.

LC Z7165.U5 A8 HB171   **ISSN** 0736-8968
DD 016.33   US
    CEASED
UNIVERSITY RESEARCH IN BUSINESS AND ECONOMICS. See Business and Economics-Abstracting, Bibliographies and Statistics.

    ISSN 0738-7032
    US
UNLIMITED TIMES, THE. **Main/Corp** Joel H. Weldon & Associates. (1982)-. Periodical. English. Twelve times a year. $27.00. Joel H. Weldon & Associates Inc., 7975 North Hayden Road, Suite D 261, Scottsdale AZ 85258. **Tel** (602)948-5633. **ED** Judy Weldon. **Circ:** 2,000 (ctrl).
Desc: Dedicated to helping you tap your unlimited potential. Ideas on attitude, goals, creativity, sales, marketing, management and personal growth.

    IT
UOMINI E BUSINESS. (19??)-. Italian. Eleven times a year. L61000 Italy; L97900 other. ESTE, Via Giorgio Vasari 15, 20135 Milan Italy. **Tel** 011 39 2 55018039.

LC S900   **ISSN** 1185-3999
DD 333.7/2/09712405   CN
UPDATE / SASKATCHEWAN ROUND TABLE ON ENVIRONMENT AND ECONOMY. See Environmental Issues.

    ISSN 0810-3011
DD 330.05   AT
UPDATED ECONOMICS. [Updat. econ.]. (1982)-. Periodical. English. Three times a year. 30.34Aus$. J. Bulmer & J. R. Chapman, PO Box 59, Westmead NSW 2145 Australia. **Tel** 02 688 1869, FAX 02 896 2775. **ED** J. Bulmer and J. R. Chapman.
Desc: Introductory treatment of a blend of theory and current economic updates in Australia.

    ISSN 0732-3115
    US
UPPER MIDWEST REPORT. (UPPER MIDWEST REPORT : A PUBLICATION OF THE UPPER MIDWEST COUNCIL.). **Added/Corp** Upper Midwest Council. (Nov. 1979)-. Periodical. English. Six times a year. Free. Upper Midwest Council, Federal Reserve Bank Building, 250 Marquette Avenue, Minneapolis MN 55480. **Tel** (612)340-9666. **Continues** Upper Midwest Council, 0731-7921.

LC HC110.H53 U67   **ISSN** 1052-0341
DD 338.4/762/00097305   US
UPSIDE (U.S. ED.). See Computers-Computer Industry and Industry Directories.

    ISSN 1068-9095
DD 330   US
    SUSPENDED
URBAN BUSINESS MAGAZINE. [Urban bus. mag.]. **VFOAT** Urban Business. (1989)-Suspended (19??). Periodical. English. Twelve times a year. $10.00. Urban Business Magazine, PO Box 26792, Tampa FL 33623. **Tel** (813)289-9093. **Continues** Minority Business Advertiser.

LC HC   **ISSN** 0743-1694
DD 330   US
URPE. (URPE : NEWSLETTER OF THE UNION FOR RADICAL POLITICAL ECONOMICS.). [URPE]. **Added/Corp** Union for Radical Political Economics. **VFOAT** URPE Newsletter. **VAT** Union for Radical Political Economics. Vol. 5, No. 3 (June 1973)-. Newsletter. English. Four times a year. $15.00. Union for Radical Political Economics / URPE, University of California, Department of Economics, Riverside CA 92521. **Tel** (909)787-5037 ext. 1580, FAX (714)787-5685. **Bk Rev. Ad Acc. Adv Mgr:** D. Olsen. **Circ:** 2,000. **Continues** Newsletter of the Union for Radical Political Economics, 0891-8201.
Desc: Provides information on organization activities and other events to URPE members, and subscribers to Review of Radical Political Economics.
Ind/Abst Public Aff. Inf. Serv. Bull.

LC HC   **ISSN** 1081-1249
DD 330   US
●**USA/FRANCE BUSINESS & CULTURE UPDATE.** [USA/France bus. culture update]. **VFOAT** USA/France Business and Culture Update; USA/France. (Nov. 1994)-. Periodical. English. Twelve times a year. $190.00. Integrated Information Technologies, Inc, 3 Church Circle, Suite 211, Annapolis MD 21401.

LC HF1040   **ISSN** 1356-6377
DD 338.025   UK
●**USA WEALTH DIRECTORY.** (1994)-. Directory. English. Every 2 years. £47.00, £52.00 other. Rowland Lybrand of London, 28 Wheatley Court, Mixenden, Halifax, West Yorkshire HX2 8QL United Kingdom. **Tel** 011 44 1422 241197.
Desc: Lists information on the multi-millionaires of the U.S.; includes assets, names and addresses.

    US
UTAH BUSINESS MAGAZINE. English. Six times a year. Free on qualified request in Utah; $39.00 other US. Utah Business Magazine, 5 Triad Center #470, Salt Lake City UT 84180. **Tel** (801)328-8200, FAX (801)328-8249. **ED** Craig Hickman. **Bk Rev.** (Qty: 8-12/year). **Ad Acc. Adv Mgr:** Karen. **Circ:** 49,000 (ctrl).

LC HC107.U8 A17   **ISSN** 0042-1405
DD 330.9792   US
UTAH ECONOMIC AND BUSINESS REVIEW. [Utah econ. bus. rev.]. **Added/Corp** University of Utah. Bureau of Economic and Business Research. Vol. 1 (Dec. 1941)-. Periodical. English. Nine times a year. Free on request. Bureau of Economic & Business Research / Utah, University of Utah, 401 Kendall G Draff, Salt Lake City UT 84112. **Tel** (801)581-6333, FAX (801)581-3354. **ED** Mari Lou Wood. **Circ:** 3,900.
Desc: Articles pertinent to the economy of Utah.
Ind/Abst PAIS Int. Print; Stat. Ref. Index.

    ISSN 1065-6480
DD 333   US
    CCC
UTILITY SPOTLIGHT. [Util. spotlight]. (19??)-. Periodical. English. One time a week. $595.00. Utility Spotlight, PO Box 819, McLean VA 22101. **Tel** (703)847-6344, FAX (703)847-0544. **ED** Gene Smith (phone: (914)359-1972).

LC T4 .T16
    ER
UURIMUSI. **Main/Corp** Tallinna Polutehniline Instituut. Poliitilise Okonoomia Kateeder. Estonian.

LC HC
    US
V B E A NEWSLETTER. (19??)-. Newsletter. English. Irregular. $10.00. Virginia Business Education Association, 3727 Parliament Rd, Apt. 10, Roanoke VA 24014. **Tel** (703)387-6452.

LC HB3608.3.H44 V33
    FI
VAESTONMUUTOKSET HELSINGISSA VUOSINA ... . **VFOAT** Vaestonmuutokset Helsingissa; Befolkningsrorelsen in Helsingfors Aren ... . (1975)-. Finnish (summaries and/or abstracts in Swedish). Helsingin Kaupungin Tilastokeskus, Toolontorink 2B, 00260 Helsinki 26 Finland.

LC S
DD 630   SP
VALENCIA FRUITS. See Agriculture.

LC HC   **ISSN** 0733-8538
    US
VALUATION CONSULTANT, THE. **Added/Corp** Marshall and Stevens Incorporated. (1964)-. Periodical. English. Four times a year. Marshall & Stevens Company, 1645 Beverly Boulevard, Los Angeles CA 90026.

    US
VALUATION JOURNAL. **Added/Corp** American Appraisal Associates. (Summer 1984)-. Periodical. English. Four times a year. Free. E.H. Boeckh Company, 2885 South Calhoun Road, New Berlin WI 53151. **Tel** (800)285-1288, (414)780-2800. **ED** Laura Kapp. **Formed by the union of** Boeckh Factor; SRC Quarter Reports and Clients' Service Bulletin.
Desc: Regular reports, tax laws relying on business evaluations.

    ISSN 1064-6310
    US
VALUE LINE EARNINGS FORECASTS. (1992)-. Periodical. English. Twenty-six times a year. $225.00. Value Line Publishing, 711 3rd Avenue, New York NY 10017-4064.

    US
VALUE WORLD. **Added/Corp** Society of American Value Engineers. (1978)-. Periodical. English. Three times a year (Jan., May, Sept.). $75.00. Society American Value Engineers, 60 Revere Drive, Suite 500, Northbrook IL 60602. **Tel** (708)480-9080. **ED** O. James Voge. **Ad Acc. Circ:** 2,000 (ctrl).

LC HB71
DD 330   US
●**VANCOUVER BUSINESS JOURNAL.** (1994)-. English. Twelve times a year. $14.00. Vancouver Business Journal, Box 1586, 2200 Broadway, Suite D, Vancouver WA 98668. **Tel** (206)695-2442, FAX (206)695-3056. **ED** Al Raines.

    ISSN 0823-0153
DD 971.4/47/005   CN
VANIEROIS, LE. See Housing and Urban Development.

    NE
VBA JOURNAAL. Dutch. Four times a year. FI95.00. Kluwer Berdijfswetenschappen, Postbus 4, 2400 Alphen Rijn Netherlands. **Tel** 011 31 01720 66855.

    ISSN 0506-4406
    SW
VECKANS AFFARER. [Veckans affarer]. (1965)-. Periodical. Swedish. Irregular. $193.79. Affars Forlaget, PO Box 3188, S 10363 Stockholm Sweden. **Tel** 011 46 8 7365600. available on one national database (files 771,772,799/Full-Text) from DIALOG.
Ind/Abst Chem. Bus. Bull. (19??-); Chem. Bus. NewsBase (1985-); Chem. Bus. Update (19??-); Infomat Int. Bus. (19??-); PROMT (19??-).

Business and Economics

LC HB LC1031
DD 330 371.3
ISSN 1357-1044
UK
●**VENTURE.** (1995)-. Academic Scholarly Publication. English. Four times a year. £13.95 UK; £23.00 Europe; £28.50 other. Philip Allan Publishers Ltd., Market Place, Deddington, Oxfordshire OX15 0SE United Kingdom. **Tel** 011 44 1869 338652, FAX 011 44 1869 338803.

DD 971.23/005
ISSN 0843-7904
CN
VENTURE (EDMONTON). (VENTURE.). [Venture]. **Added/Corp** Alberta. Alberta Economic Development and Trade. Vol. 3, No. 1 (Winter 1989)-. Periodical. English. Four times a year. Free on request. Communications & Information, 9940 106th Street 12th Floor, Sterling, Edmonton Alberta T5K 2P6 Canada. **Tel** (403)422-5334, FAX (403)422-9107. **Continues** Alberta Venture, 0828-3206.

LC HF
DD 650
UDC 651.93
ISSN 0246-0882
FR
VERITE STENOGRAPHIQUE, LA. [Verite stenogr.]. (1918)-. Periodical. French. Four times a year. $40.46. IISD - Institut International de Stenographie Duploye, 47 rue Rabat, F-75018 Paris France. **Tel** 011 33 1 42647361. **Absorbed** Bulletin de l'Institut International de Stenographie Duploye, 0246-1315.

UDC 65.012.4
ISSN 0178-5893
GW
VERKAUFSLEITER-SERVICE. [Verkaufsleit.-Serv.]. (19??)-. Newsletter. German. Twenty-four times a year. DM44.80. Verlag Norbert Mueller AG & Co. KG, Postfach 450632, Munich 80906 Germany. **Tel** 011 44 89 35093-02, FAX 011 44 89 35093-218. **ED** Andrea Krukow. Index available. cum. index. **Bk Rev. Circ:** 4,500 (ctrl).
Desc: Consultative newsletter for sales managers and sales executives.

DD 330
ISSN 0897-7925
US
VERMONT BUSINESS MAGAZINE. [Vt. bus. mag.]. **VFOAT** VT Business. (Jan. 1988)-. Periodical. English. Twelve times a year. $12.00 (out of state and nonbusiness residents); Free (business and government agencies) Vermont. Manning Inc., PO Box 6120, Battleboro VT 05301. **Tel** (802)257-4100. available on an online database (file 635/Full-Text) from DIALOG. Documents available from UMI Article Clearinghouse. **Continues** Vermont Business, 0746-4436.
Ind/Abst Bus. Dateline (Jan. 1986-) [Full Txt.]; PROMT.

LC JK3030 .V4
ISSN 0083-5781
US
VERMONT YEAR BOOK. [Vt. year book]. **Added/Corp** National Survey (Firm). **VFOAT** Vermont Yearbook. (193?)-. Directory. English. One time a year. $31.65. The National Survey, School Street Drawer D, Chester VT 05143. **Tel** (802)875-2121, FAX (802)875-2123. **ED** Cecil Waldo. Index available ($27.00). **Ad Acc. Circ:** 2,000 (ctrl). **Continues** Vermont Year-Book & Guide.
Desc: Business directory covering the entire state of Vermont. It is a source for general Vermont information, directory of Vermont products and manufacturers, local information and business directory.

DD 338.4/7/0002571352
ISSN 1183-5494
CN
VERNON'S BUSINESS SOURCES, HAMILTON & NIAGARA AREA EDITION FOR SELECTED COMMUNITIES. [Vernon's bus. sources Hamilt. Niagara area ed. sel. commun.]. **Added/Corp** Vernon Directories. **VFOAT** Hamilton & Niagara Area Edition for Selected Communities. **VAT** Vernon's Business Sources, Hamilton and Niagara Area Edition for Selected Communities. (1991)-. English. $150.00 per volume. Vernon Directories Ltd., 111 Fried Street, Hamilton Ontario L8P 4M3 Canada. **Tel** (416)522-5066.

LC HB97.5 .M615a
ISSN 0130-0105
RU
VESTNIK MOSKOVSKOGO UNIVERSITETA. SERIIA VI, EKONOMIKA. **Added/Corp** Moskovskii Gosudarstvennyi Universitet im. M.V. Lomonosova. **VFOAT** Ekonomika. (1977)-. Periodical. Russian. Six times a year. $109.95. Izdatelstvo Moskovskogo Universiteta, Ul-9 Ulitsa Gertsena 5/7, 103009 Moscow Russia. **Tel** (301)881-5973. **(Subscription address:** East View Publications Inc., 3020 Harbor Lane North, Suite 110, Minneapolis MN 55447. **Tel** (800)477-1005, (612)550-0961, FAX (612)559-2931.) Index available. **Bk Rev. Continues** Vestnik Moskovskogo Universiteta. Seriia VII, Ekonomika, 0579-9430.
Ind/Abst Int. Bibliogr. Sociol.; Int. Labour Doc.; LABORDOC.

LC HC
DD 330
RU
CODEN VSUEEX
VESTNIK SANKT-PETERBURGSKOGO UNIVERSITETA. SERIIA 5, EKONOMIKA. **Added/Corp** Sankt-Peterburgskii Universitet. **VFOAT** Ekonomika. (1992)-. Periodical. Russian (summaries and/or abstracts in English). Four times a year. $119.95. St. Petersburg State University / Izdatelstvo Leningradskogo Universiteta, Universitetskaia Nab 7/9, 199034 St. Petersburg Russia. **Tel** 011 7 812 2189788, FAX 011 7 812 2185152, telex 121481. **(Subscription address:** East View Publications Inc., 3020 Harbor Lane North, Suite 110, Minneapolis MN 55447. **Tel** (800)477-1005, (612)550-0961, FAX (612)559-2931.) **Continues** Vestnik Leningradskogo Universiteta. Seriia 5, Ekonomika, 0233-755X.

ISSN 0209-0554
PL
UDC 05 + 07
VETO WARSZAWA. [Veto Warsz.]. (1982)-. Periodical. Polish. One time a week. $52.00. **(Subscription address:** Ars Polona-Ruch, PO Box 1001, Krakowskie Przedmiescie 7, 00-068 Warsaw Poland. **Tel** 011 48 22 261201.)

LC PN1992 .V53
DD 384.55/4/05
ISSN 0278-5013
US
VIDEO AGE INTERNATIONAL. See Communications-Television and Cable.

DD 384
ISSN 1042-7694
VIDEO INVESTOR. See Communications-Video.

UDC 65(597)
ISSN 1023-6252
HK
VIET NAM NGAY NAY. (1992)-. Periodical. English. Twenty-four times a year. Pearson Professional Hong Kong, Suite 1808 Asian House, 1 Hennessy Road, Wan Chai Hong Kong. **Tel** 852 2863 2600, FAX 852 2520 6646.
Desc: Monitor of business and economic news and information about Vietnam.

DD 330.9597
ISSN 1351-9425
UK
●**VIETNAM BUSINESS REPORT.** [Vietnam bus. rep.]. (1993)-. Periodical. English. Twelve times a year. $290.91. IBC Publishing, 57-61 Mortimer St., London W1N 7TD United Kingdom. **Tel** 011 44 171 6374383, FAX 011 44 171 6366314. **ED** Malcolm Nixon.

DD 959
ISSN 1077-5749
●**VIETNAM BUSINESS YELLOW PAGES, THE.** [Vietnam bus. yellow pages]. (1993)-. Directory. English. One time a year. $100.00. VIAM Communications Group, 381 Park Avenue South, Suite 919, New York NY 10016. **Tel** (212)725-1717, FAX (212)725-8160.

DD 338
ISSN 1071-7900
US
●**VIETNAM MARKET WATCH.** [Vietnam mark. watch]. **Added/Corp** Rialto Ventures International, Inc. **VFOAT** Vietnam. Vol. 1, No. 1 (Oct. 1993)-. Newsletter. English. Twelve times a year. $295.00. Vietnam Market Resources Inc., 1616 Post Road, Fairfield CT 06430. **Tel** (203)256-0370, (800)999-8438, FAX (203)256-9790. available on an online database from NEWSNET.
Desc: The latest business news from Vietnam.

DD 331
ISSN 1070-1362
US
CEASED
VIEW (BEDFORD, N.H.). See Business and Economics-Abstracting, Bibliographies and Statistics.

DD 330.9/71/064
ISSN 0702-8547
CN
VIEWPOINT (TORONTO. 1961). (VIEWPOINT.). (Jan. 1961)-. Periodical. English. Four times a year. Creditel of Canada Ltd, 931 Yonge Street, Toronto Ontario M4W 2H2 Canada.

LC AP20 .E927
DD 054/.1
BE
VIF EXPRESS, LE. **VFOAT** Vif, l'Express; Pourquoi Pas?/l'Express; Weekend/l'Express. (198?)-. Periodical. French. One time a week. $300.00F. Le VIF SA, place Jamblinne de Meux 33, B-1040 Brussels Belgium. **Tel** 011 32 2 7366018. **Formed by the union of** Vif **and** Pourquoi Pas?.

LC HC107.V8V437
DD 338.09755/05
ISSN 0888-1340
US
VIRGINIA BUSINESS. [Va. bus.]. Vol. 1 No. 1 (March 1986)-. Periodical. English. Twelve times a year. $30.00. Virginia Business Magazine, PO Box 85333, Richmond VA 23293. **Tel** (804)649-6999, FAX (804)649-6311. **ED** James A. Bacon. **Ad Acc. Circ:** 40,500 (ctrl). **Continues** Tidewater Virginian.
Desc: Business publication about Virginia businesses and people.
Ind/Abst PROMT; Text. Technol. Dig.

LC HC107.V8 V438
DD 338/.0029/4755
ISSN 1047-2711
US
VIRGINIA BUSINESS DIRECTORY. [Va. bus. dir.]. **Added/Corp** American Directory Publishing Co. (1989)-. English. American Business Directory, 5711 South 86th Circle, PO Box 27347, Omaha NE 68127. **Tel** (402)593-4600, FAX (402)331-5481.

LC GV188.3.U6 V57
DD 338.4/7790/01350973
ISSN 0277-5204
VISIONS IN LEISURE AND BUSINESS. **See** Leisure and Recreation.

LC HC10 .V53
DD 303.49/05
ISSN 1075-0576
US
VITAL SIGNS (NEW YORK, N.Y.). (VITAL SIGNS : THE TRENDS THAT ARE SHAPING OUR FUTURE.). [Vital signs]. **Added/Corp** Worldwatch Institute. (1992)-. Periodical. English. One time a year. $10.95. Worldwatch Institute, 1776 Massachusetts Avenue Northwest, Washington DC 20036-1904. **Tel** (202)452-1999, (800)825-0061. **(Subscription address:** Worldwatch Institute, PO Box 6991, Syracuse NY 13217.)

ISSN 0042-8108
US
VOICE OF BUSINESS. **Added/Corp** Chamber of Commerce of Hawaii. (19??-). Newsletter. English. Twenty-six times a year. Comes with Chamber of Commerce of Hawaii membership. Chamber of Commerce of Hawaii, 735 Bishop Street, Suite 220, Honolulu HI 96813. **Tel** (808)522-8813, FAX (808)522-8836.

LC HC
ISSN 0505-9372
GW
VOLKSWIRTSCHAFTLICHE SCHRIFTEN. No. 1 (1952)-. Monographic series. German. Irregular. Price varies per volume. Duncker und Humblot Verlag, Postfach 410329, D-12113 Berlin Germany. **Tel** 011 49 30 79000612, 011 49 30 79000613. **Ind/Abst** Math. Rev.

RU
VOPROSY EKONOMIKI I KONVERSII. **Added/Corp** Nauchnyi Sovet Mezhotraslevoi Ekonomiki i Konversii. (1989)-. Periodical. Russian. Four times a year. $219.95. **(Subscription address:** East View Publications Inc., 3020 Harbor Lane North, Suite 110, Minneapolis MN 55447. **Tel** (800)477-1005, (612)550-0961, FAX (612)559-2931.)

LC HB41
DD 330
ISSN 0509-6065
GW
VORTRAGE UND AUFSATZE. Main/Corp Walter Eucken Institut. Vol. 1 (1958)-. Monographic series. German. Irregular. Price varies per volume. JCB Mohr / Paul Siebeck, Postfach 2040, D-72010 Tuebingen Germany. **Tel** 011 49 7071 9230, FAX 011 49 7071 51104, telex 7/262872 mohr d.

LC G155
DD 338.4/7917104/05
ISSN 1202-6883
CN
VOYAGE EXPRESS. [Voyage express]. **Added/Corp** Institut Canadien de Recherche sur le Tourisme. Conference Board du Canada. (199?)-. Periodical. French. Irregular. Price varies per volume. Institut Canadien de Recherche sur le Tourisme, A/S le Conference Board du Canada, 255 CH Smyth, Ottawa Ontario, K1H 8M7 Canada. **Continues** Exclusif (Institut Canadien de Recherche sur le Tourisme), 1187-3175.

UDC 910.4
ISSN 0995-4228
FR
VOYAGES D'AFFAIRES PARIS. (VOYAGES D'AFFAIRES.). (1988)-. Periodical. French. Six times a year. $98.43. Voyages d Affaires, BP 463 07, 75327 Paris Cedex 07 France, 011 33 1 42946001.

UDC 696
ISSN 1101-5764
SW
VVS' NYHETER. [VVS' nyheter]. (1988)-. Periodical. Swedish. Twenty times a year. Kr1950.00. SBR Affarsvarlden, PO Box 26036, S 10041 Stockholm Sweden. **Tel** 011 46 8 6110525. Index available (Free). **Continues** Sweden Business, 0348-6508.

LC HC101 .W23
DD 339.5
ISSN 0361-6665
US
WAGE-PRICE LAW & ECONOMICS REVIEW. [Wage-price law econ. rev.]. **VAT** Wage-Price Law and Economics Review. (1975)-. Periodical. English. Four times a year. $98.50. Antitrust Law and Economic Review Inc., PO Box 3532, Vero Beach FL 32964. **Tel** FAX (407)461-6007. **Bk Rev. Desc:** Economic analysis of antitrust, industrial organization, and related macroeconomic issues.

DD 332
ISSN 0894-153X
US
SUSPENDED
WALKER'S MANUAL OF WESTERN CORPORATIONS. [Walker's man. West. corp.]. 67th Ed. (1975)-Suspended (1995). English. Five times a year. Walker's Western Research, 1650 Borel Place,

Business and Economics

Suite 130, San Mateo CA 94402. **Tel** (800)258-5737, (415)341-1110, FAX (415)341-2351. Index available (bound in issue). *Continues* Walker's Manual of Western Corporations & Securities, 0092-749X.
 Desc: A business tool for sales and marketing and a financial and investment resource.

US

WALL STREET JOURNAL ONDISC COMPUTER FILE, THE. **Added/Corp** University Microfilms International. **VFOAT** ProQuest, The Wall Street Journal Ondisc. Vol. WSJ 89 (Jan. 1989)-. Periodical. English. Twelve times a year. $2,295.00. University Microfilms International, 300 North Zeeb Road, Ann Arbor MI 48106-1346. **Tel** (313)761-4700, (800)521-0600 Exts. 2490, 2491, FAX (313)973-1540.
 Desc: Provides full-text access to printed articles. Excludes advertisements, dividend tables, digests of earnings tables, future prices, and stock tables and other free-standing tabular material. Articles printed in, or after, 1990 include section and page numbers. System requirements: IBM PC or compatible; 640K hard disk; DOS 3.0 or higher; monochrome monitor; CD-ROM player.

LC HG4009   **ISSN** 1071-9555
DD 330   US

●WARD'S PRIVATE COMPANY PROFILES. **VFOAT** Private Company Profiles. (1993)-. Directory. English. One time a year. $139.00. Gale Research Inc., 835 Penobscot Building, 645 Griswold Street, Detroit MI 48226. **Tel** (800)877-GALE, (313)961-2242, FAX (313)961-6083, (800)414-5043, telex TWX 810-221-7086. **ED** Jennifer Mast.
 Desc: Provides researchers with textual information on private companies.

LC HF5487.A295   **ISSN** 0738-0348
DD 381/.41/02573   US

WAREHOUSES LICENSED UNDER U.S. WAREHOUSE ACT. (WAREHOUSES LICENSED UNDER U.S. WAREHOUSE ACT AS OF ...). **VFOAT** Warehouses Licensed Under US Warehouse Act as of ... . (19??)-. Government Publication. English. US Department of Agriculture / Agricultural Marketing Service / Washington, DC, Market News Branch, Fruit and Vegetable Division, Washington DC 20250. **Tel** (202)720-2745, (202)720-3343, FAX (202)720-7502.

ISSN 0744-8864
US

WAREHOUSING SUPERVISOR'S BULLETIN. (19??)-. Bulletin. English. Twenty-four times a year. $155.16 Canada; $118.68 US. Bureau of Business Practice, 24 Rope Ferry Road, Waterford CT 06386. **Tel** (800)243-0876, (203)442-4365, (800)876-9105, FAX (203)443-1123. **ED** Isabel Will Becker.

GW

WARENVERZEICHNIS FUER DIE AUSSENHANDELSSTATISTIK. See Encyclopedias and General Reference Books.

ISSN 0043-0331
GW

UDC 347.772

TITLE CHANGE

WARENZEICHENBLATT. TEIL 1, (ANGEMELDETE ZEICHEN) *AUSGABE A. See Encyclopedias and General Reference Books.

ISSN 0043-034X
GW

UDC 347.772

TITLE CHANGE

WARENZEICHENBLATT. TEIL 2, (EINGETRAGENE ZEICHEN). AUSGABE A. See Encyclopedias and General Reference Books.

ISSN 1061-1622
US

WARFIELD'S BUSINESS RECORD. **VFOAT** Business Record. (Jan. 10, 1992)-. Periodical. English. Fifty-two times a year. $45.00 (one-year), $79.00 (two-years), $99.00 (three-years). Baltimore Daily Record, 11 East Saratoga Street, Baltimore MD 21202. **Tel** (410)752-3849, FAX (410)752-2894. **ED** Keith Girard. Circ: 5,000. Documents available from UMI Article Clearinghouse. *Continues* Warfield's, 0892-7243.
 Desc: Provides Maryland with insightful business news.
 Ind/Abst Bus. Dateline (Dec. 1990-) [Full Txt.]; PROMT (19??-).

LC HF41 .W33   **ISSN** 0388-1008
DD 330.9/52/04   JA

WASEDA BUSINESS & ECONOMIC STUDIES. [Waseda bus. econ. stud.]. **VFOAT** Waseda Business and Economic Studies. No. 1- 1965-. English. One time a year. Waseda University, Institute of Comparative Law-647 Totsuka, Shinjuku-ku Tokyo 16 Japan. **Tel** 011 81 3 203 2034141.

LC HB9 .W38   **ISSN** 0511-1943
DD 330   JA

WASEDA ECONOMIC PAPERS.
Added/Corp Waseda Daigaku, Tokyo. Daigakuin. Keizaigaku Kenkyuka. (1955)-. Periodical. English (French). Irregular. **(Subscription address:** Japan Publications Trading Company Ltd., PO Box 5030, Tokyo International, Tokyo 100-31 Japan. **Tel** 011 81 3 3292 3753.)

LC F192.5 .W3   **ISSN** 0083-7393
DD X800 917.53/0025 S 975.3   US
NLM F 192.3 W318

WASHINGTON. **Added/Corp** Columbia Books, Inc. (Washington, D.C.). Vol. 1 (1966)-. English. One time a year. $79.50 Washington, DC; $75.00 other. Columbia Books Inc, 1212 New York Avenue NW/Suite 330, Washington DC 20005. **Tel** (202)898-0662, FAX (202)898-0775. **ED** John J Russell. Index available. **Circ:** 3,400.
 Desc: Lists 4,200 key public and private institutions of Washington, DC area and their 20,000 leaders. Arranged by subject businesses, associations, interest groups, educational and cultural institutions, media. Combined index of individuals and organizations shows multiple affiliations and responsibilities of leaders.

ISSN 0737-3147
DD 330   US
CCC

WASHINGTON BUSINESS JOURNAL.
[Wash. bus. j.]. Vol. 1, No. 1 (May 17, 1982)-. Periodical. English. One time a week. $54.60. Washington Business Journal, 2000 14th Street, Suite 500, Arlington VA 22201. **Tel** (703)875-2200. **ED** Dave Yochum (editor's phone: (703)816-0330). **Bk Rev**, (Qty: 56). **Ad Acc, Adv Mgr:** Lisa Bormaster, **Tel** (703)816-0307. **Circ:** 20,000. available on microfilm from University Microfilms International (UMI). Documents available from UMI Article Clearinghouse.
 Ind/Abst Acad. Search; Bus. Dateline; Bus. Index (1985-1990); Bus. Source; Bus. Source; EP Collect.; Gen. BusinessFile (1985-1990); Gen. Period. Index (1985-1990); Homework Help.; INFO-SOUTH Abstr.; Mag. Search; MasterFile FullTEXT 1000; MasterFile FullTEXT 350; MasterFile FullTEXT 650; MasterFile FullTEXT (July 1993-); OCLC; PROMT; Telebase; Trade Ind. Index.

LC HD38.25.U6 W36   **ISSN** 1048-4981
DD 338   US

WASHINGTON CEO. [Wash. CEO]. **VAT** Washington Chief Executive Officer. (Dec. 1989)-. Periodical. English. Twelve times a year. $19.95. Washington CEO Inc., 2505 Second Avenue, Suite 602, Seattle WA 98121. **Tel** (206)441-8415, FAX (206)441-8325. **ED** Kevin Dwyer (editor's address: 2505 Second Avenue, Suite 602, Seattle, WA 98121). **Ad Acc, Adv Mgr:** June Ford. **Circ:** 20,000.
 Desc: Statewide business magazine covering the personalities, events, trends and ideas which shape the business characters of the state. Focus on the economy, business trends, marketing, management, and international trade.

LC HC107.W2 E265
DD 330.9797/005   US

●WASHINGTON ECONOMIC AND REVENUE FORECAST. **Added/Corp** Economic and Revenue Forecast Council (Washington). Office of the Forecast Council. **VFOAT** Economic and Revenue Forecast. Vol. 18, No. 1 (March 1995)-. English. Four times a year. Washington State Forecast Council, 711 South Capitol Way, Suite 300, Olympia WA 98504-0912. **Tel** (206)753-7022. *Continues* State of Washington Economic and Revenue Forecast.

ISSN 1060-5665
DD 333   US

WASHINGTON GREEN. (WASHINGTON GREEN : A PUBLICATION OF THE GREENS OF WASHINGTON STATE.). [Wash. Green]. Vol. 1, No. 1 (Spring 1992)-. Periodical. English. Twelve times a year. $15.00. Washington Greens, PO Box 1123, Enumclaw WA 98022.

LC J   **ISSN** 0749-1050
DD 320   US

WASHINGTON INQUIRER. See Political Science-International Relations.

LC HC121 .W37
DD 338.98/005   US
CEASED

WASHINGTON REPORT (COUNCIL OF THE AMERICAS). (WASHINGTON REPORT.). **Added/Corp** Council of the Americas. (19??)-(Winter/Spring 1994). Periodical. English. Council of the Americas, 1625 K Street Northwest, Suite 1200, Washington DC 20006. **Tel** (202)639-0724.
 Desc: This magazine covers Washington events and interests to companies that is doing business in Latin American and the Caribbean. Includes segments of the US government, Congress and international banks.

LC HC107.W2 E25
DD 330   US

●WASHINGTON STATE ALMANAC. See Population Studies.

LC TD257 .W4   **ISSN** 0262-9909
DD 363.6/1/0941   UK

WATERBULLETIN. See Water Resources.

US

WATERSPORTS BUSINESS. See Sports and Games.

ISSN 0957-1124
UK

WATFORD BUSINESS DIRECTORY.
(1989)-. English. One time a year. £9.00. Holcot Press Ltd, Station House, Station Road, Newport Pognell, Milton Keynes MK16 0AG United Kingdom. **Tel** 011 44 1908 614477, FAX 011 44 1908 217425. **Ad Acc**.

LC HB71
DD 330   US

●WD. **VFOAT** Workforce Diversity. (1994)-. Trade Publication. English. One time a year. Equal Opportunity Publications Inc, 150 Motor Parkway, Suite 420, Hauppauge NY 11788. **Tel** (516)273-0066, FAX (516)273-8936.

ISSN 1066-7903
US

●WEALTH RANKINGS. **Added/Corp** Taft Group (Rockville, Md.). (1993)-. English. One time a year. $99.00. Taft Group, 835 Penobscott Building, Customer Service, Detroit MI 48226. **Tel** (800)877-8238, FAX (313)961-6083.
 Desc: Reprints over 80 lists, providing information on over 6,000 business leaders, entrepreneurs, entertainers, athletes, nonprofit executives, public administrators, and more.

LC DD290 .W44
US

WEEK IN GERMANY, THE. **Added/Corp** German Information Center (New York, N.Y.). **VFOAT** Relay From Bonn. (197?)-. Periodical. English. One time a week. Free on request. German Information Center, 950 Third Avenue, New York NY 10022. **Tel** (212)888-9840, FAX (212)752-6691. available on an online database (file 636/Full-Text) from DIALOG.
 Ind/Abst PTS Newsl. Database [Full Txt.].

ISSN 0252-2659
EC

WEEKLY ANALYSIS OF ECUADOREAN ISSUES. [Wkly anal. Ecuad. issues]. **VFOAT** Weekly Analysis. (197?)-. Periodical. English (Spanish). One time a week. $400.00. Weekly Analysis of Ecuadorean Issues, PO Box 4925, Elizalde 119 70C, Guayaquil Ecuador. **Tel** 011 593 4 325712, 011 593 4 514472. **ED** Walter Spurier. Index available (Free). **Circ:** 1,000 (ctrl).
 Desc: Report on Ecuadorean affairs, including stress on economic and political issues, and statistics.

AT

WEEKLY BUSINESS BRIEF. (19??)-. English. Forty-eight times a year. 406.98Aus$. Syntec Economic Services Pty, GPO Box 2455V, Melbourne VIC 3001 Australia. **Tel** 011 61 3 96621911.

ISSN 0888-0670
US

WEEKLY COMMERCIAL NEWS (LOS ANGELES, CALIF.). (WEEKLY COMMERCIAL NEWS : FEATURING BUSINESS AND TRANSPORTATION NEWS.). **VFOAT** Commercial News; Los Angeles Weekly Commercial News; L.A. Commercial News. Vol. 74, No. 37 (Sept. 16-20, 1985)-. Periodical. English. One time a week (Published on Mondays). $95.00 (one-year), $165.00 (two-year). CA Page Publishing Company, 3820 El Amo Blvd, Suite 334, Torrance CA 90503. *Continues* WCN.

ISSN 1060-2259
DD 330   US

WEEKLY JAPAN DIGEST, THE. See Political Science.

ISSN 1055-8535
US

WEEKLY SALE & DISCOUNT MAGAZINE (LOS ANGELES ED.).
(WEEKLY SALE & DISCOUNT MAGAZINE.). **VFOAT** Weekly Sale Dnd Miscount Magazine; Weekly Sale & Discount. (1991)-. Periodical. English. One time a week. Free. Weekly Sale & Discount Publishing, 7507 Sunset Boulevard, #213, Hollywood CA 90046.

UK

WEINBURG & BLACK ON TAKE-OVERS AND MERGERS. (1989)-. English. Irregular. £250.00 (main work). Sweet & Maxwell Ltd., South Quay Plaza, 183 Marsh Wall 7th Floor, London E14 9FT United Kingdom. **Tel** 011 44 171 5388686, FAX 011 44 171 5389508, telex 929089 ITPINF G.

Business and Economics

DD 380.1   **ISSN** 1189-069X   CN
WELLAND & PELHAM BUSINESS BOOK, THE. [Welland Pelham bus. book].
Added/Corp Greater Welland Chamber of Commerce. **VFOAT** Welland and Pelham Business Book. (1991)-. English. $5.00. Greater Welland Chamber of Commerce, 55 East Main Street, Welland Ontario L3B 3W4 Canada.

LC HA1161 .W44a
DD 330.9/429/085   UK
WELSH ECONOMIC TRENDS. Added/Corp
Great Britain. Welsh Office. **VFOAT** Tueddiadau'r Economi. (19??)-. Multiple languages (English and Welsh). One time a year. $17.11. Welsh Office Publications Unit, Crown Building, Cathay's Park, Cardiff CF1 3NQ United Kingdom. **Tel** 011 44 1222 825111, FAX 011 44 1222 823036.

LC HN398.W26 W45   **ISSN** 0140-9018   UK
WELSH SOCIAL TRENDS = TUEDDIADAU CYMDEITHASOL.
Added/Corp Great Britain. Welsh Office. **VFOAT** Tueddiadau Cymdeithasol. No. 1 (1977)-. Periodical. English. Every 2 years. Welsh Office Publications Unit, Crown Building, Cathay's Park, Cardiff CF1 3NQ United Kingdom. **Tel** 011 44 1222 825111, FAX 011 44 1222 823036.

AU
WEST OST JOURNAL. See Political Science.

LC HC107.W5 W35   **ISSN** 0195-4644
DD 330.9754   US
WEST VIRGINIA BUSINESS INDEX.
Added/Corp West Virginia Chamber of Commerce. (May 1938)-. Trade Publication. English. Twelve times a year. $60.00. West Virginia Chamber of Commerce, PO Box 2789, Charleston WV 25330. **Tel** (304)342-1115. **ED** Maggie Poling. cum. index. **Ad Acc**. ctrl circ.

ISSN 1057-686X
DD 330   US
WESTCHESTER COUNTY BUSINESS JOURNAL. [Westchest. Cty. bus. j.]. Vol. 20, No. 24 (Apr. 25, 1988)-. Trade Publication. English. One time a week (Monday). $52.00. Westfair Communications Inc., 22 Sawmill River Road, Hawthorne NY 10532. **Tel** (914)347-5200, FAX (914)327-5576. **ED** Mills Kortk. **Circ**: 12,500. available on microfilm and microfiche from University Microfilms International (UMI); available on an online database (files 635,648/Full-Text) from DIALOG. Documents available from UMI Article Clearinghouse. **Continues** Westchester Business Journal, 0889-5317.
Desc: Provides information on local business news and features.
Ind/Abst Acad. Search; Bus. Dateline (Nov. 16, 1987-) [Full Txt.]; Bus. Source Plus; Bus. Source; EP Collect.; Gen. Period. Index (Jan. 1985-Dec. 1985); Homework Help.; INFO-SOUTH Abstr.; MasterFile FullTEXT 1000; MasterFile FullTEXT 350; MasterFile FullTEXT 650; MasterFile FullTEXT (July 1993-); OCLC; Telebase; Trade Ind. ASAP [Full Txt.]; Trade Ind. Index [Full Txt.].

LC HC651 .W47
DD 330.9/941/06   AT
WESTERN AUSTRALIAN ECONOMY, THE. Added/Corp Western Australia. Treasury. (19??)-. English.
Ind/Abst AESIS Q.

ISSN 1042-6795
DD 330   US
WESTERN BLUE CHIP ECONOMIC FORECAST. [West. blue chip econ. forecast].
Added/Corp Arizona State University. Economic Outlook Center. **VFOAT** Western Blue Chip. Vol. 1, No. 1 (Oct. 1987)-. Periodical. English. Ten times a year. $99.00. Economic Outlook Center, PO Box 874406, College of Business, Arizona State University, Tempe AZ 85287-4406. **Tel** (602)965-5543, 800 448-9432, FAX (602)965-5458. **ED** Lee R. McPheters, Tracy Clark and Robert J. Eggert Sr. **Circ**: 200.
Desc: Economic forecast for the current year and the next for 9 western states based upon a consensus of opinions by economists in each state.

CN
WESTERN COMMERCE & INDUSTRY MAGAZINE. See Food and Food Industry.

AT
WESTPAC MELBOURNE INSTITUTE OF INDEXES OF ECONOMIC ACTIVITY.
English. Twelve times a year. 450.00Aus$. Institute of Applied Economic and Social Research / Australia, University of Melbourne, Economics Building, Parkville Victoria 3052 Australia. **Tel** 011 61 3 3445330, FAX 011 61 3 3445630, telex 35185.

LC KF6455.Z9 W47   **ISSN** 1054-1918
DD 346   US
WEST'S FEDERAL TAXATION. CORPORATION, S CORPORATION, AND PARTNERSHIP PRACTICE SETS.
[West's. Fed. tax., Corp. S corp. partnersh. pract. sets].
Added/Corp West Publishing Co. **VFOAT** Corporation, S Corporation, and Partnership Practice Sets. (1990/91)-. English. West Publishing Company, 620 Opperman Drive, PO Box 64526, Eagan MN 55123-1308. **Tel** (612)687-8000, (800)328-9352, FAX (612)687-7602. **Continues in part** West's Federal Taxation. Practice Sets, 0749-1476.

AT
WETTANK. WOMENS ECONOMIC THINK TANK. (19??)-. English. Irregular (Published 2 or 3 times a year). $10.00Aus$ Australia; 15.00Aus$ other. Wettank, PO Box 303, Camperdown NSW 2050 Australia. **Tel** 011 61 2 5571955, FAX 011 61 2 5172400.
Desc: Different views on current issues and different issues for the political agenda.

LC HC101 .W54223   **ISSN** 0749-6494
DD 338.5/443/0973   US
WHARTON LONG-TERM FORECAST EXTENSION TO THE YEAR ... . [Wharton long-term forecast ext.]. **VFOAT** Wharton Long Term Forecast Extension to the Year ... . English. WEFA / Philadelphia, PO Box 8500, Suite 1995, Philadelphia PA 19178. **Tel** (215)667-6000, telex 710 6700575.

ISSN 0950-1800
DD 651   UK
WHARTON REPORT. See Computers.

US
WHAT'S NEW FOR FAMILY FUN CENTERS. (19??)-. Trade Publication. English. Six times a year. $24.00 US; $27.00 Canada; $50.00 other. Lakewood Publications, 50 South Ninth Street, Minneapolis MN 55402. **Tel** (612)333-0471, (800)328-4329, FAX (612)333-6526.
Desc: Directed toward the professional interests of the owners, managers and operators of family entertainment centers. Designed to provide information on products and services that can enhance the growth and profitability of these facilities.

ISSN 0952-7001
UK
WHAT'S NEW IN BUSINESS INFORMATION. [What's new bus. inf.]. (1987)-. Periodical. English. Twenty times a year. $424.00. Headland Business Information, 1 Henry Smiths Terrace, Headland Cleveland, TS24 0PD United Kingdom. **Tel** 011 44 429 231902, FAX 011 44 429 861403.

US
WHAT'S WORKING. (19??)-. Periodical. English. Twenty-five times a year. $242.00. United Communications Group, 11300 Rockville Pike, Suite 1100, Rockville MD 20852. **Tel** (301)816-8950 ext. 313, FAX (301)816-8945. **Continues** Fulfill.
Desc: Helps you position yourself for profit under restrictive new postal regulations, rate increases, use taxes, and state and federal laws that affect the way you do business.

ISSN 0164-629X
DD 330   US
WHEELER'S DESERT LETTER. [Wheeler's desert lett.]. **VFOAT** Desert Letter. (19??)-. Periodical. English. Twenty-four times a year. $105.00. Wheeler's Desert Letter, PO Box 1297, Rancho Mirage CA 92270. **Tel** (619)341-1144, FAX (619)773-9505. **ED** Hans P. Dubach. **Circ**: 1,500.
Desc: Covers all business related activities in Coachella Valley. Tracks population, retail sales, building valuations, housing starts, real estate closings, hotel room tax, and airport traffic.

ISSN 1064-1610
DD 330   US
WHEELER'S INLAND EMPIRE.
(WHEELER'S INLAND EMPIRE : WIE.). [Wheeler's inland emp.]. **VFOAT** WIE. Vol. 1, No. 1 (Jan. 1992)-. Periodical. English. Twelve times a year. $95.00. Wheeler's Desert Letter, PO Box 1297, Rancho Mirage CA 92270. **Tel** (619)341-1144, FAX (619)773-9505. **ED** Hans P. Dubach.
Desc: Economic/business newsletter on the western Riverside County and San Bernardino County area.

ISSN 0967-6406
UK
WHERE TO BUY BUSINESS INFORMATION. [where buy bus. inf.]. (1990)-. English. One time a year. $174.00. Headland Business Information, 1 Henry Smiths Terrace, Headland Cleveland, TS24 0PD United Kingdom. **Tel** 011 44 429 231902, FAX 011 44 429 861403.

LC JK6 .W37a   **ISSN** 0894-8801
DD 353.04/025   US
NLM JK 6; R432
TITLE CHANGE
WHO KNOWS, A GUIDE TO WASHINGTON EXPERTS. See Public Administration.

US
WHO KNOWS WHO. English. One time a year. $150.00. Taft Group, 835 Penobscot Building, Customer Service, Detroit MI 48226. **Tel** (800)877-8238, FAX (313)961-6083.

LC HG4009 .W46
UK
●WHO OWNS WHOM. (1993)-. English. Irregular. Dun & Bradstreet, Holmer's Farm Way, High Wycombe, Buckingham HP12 4UL United Kingdom. **Tel** 011 44 1494 422000, FAX 011 44 1494 422260. **(Subscription address**: Dun & Bradstreet Information Service, Business Reference Service, 3 Sylvan Way, Parsippany NJ 07054. **Tel** 800 526-0651.**)** *Formed by the union of Who Owns Whom. Australasia and Far East, 0302-4091; Who Owns Whom. Continental Europe, 0140-6582; Who Owns Whom. North America, 0308-8502 and Who Owns Whom. United Kingdom and Republic of Ireland.*

LC E154.7 .W45   **ISSN** 1048-809X
DD 973/.025   US
WHO'S WEALTHY IN AMERICA. [Who's wealthy Am.]. **VFOAT** Who is Wealthy in America. 1st Ed. (1990). English. Two times a year. $415.00. Taft Group, 835 Penobscot Building, Customer Service, Detroit MI 48226. **Tel** (800)877-8238, FAX (313)961-6083.
Desc: Gives information on the 50,000 richest people in America. Information includes names, phone numbers, and addresses, plus important information on political contributions, stock ownership, educational background, and lifestyles.

LC HC252.5.A2 W48   **ISSN** 1068-2260
DD 338.7/092/241   US
WHO'S WHO IN BUSINESS AND INDUSTRY IN THE UK. See Biographies.

LC D1060 .W46
GW
WHO'S WHO IN EUROPEAN INTEGRATION STUDIES. VFOAT Who's Who dans les Etudes sur l'Integration Europeenne. (1989)-. Periodical. English. Irregular. Nomos Verlagsgesellschaft, Postfach 610, D-76484 Baden Baden Germany. **Tel** 011 49 7221 210439.

LC HF3023.A2 W5   **ISSN** 0083-9523
DD 338/.00922 B   US
CCC
WHO'S WHO IN FINANCE AND INDUSTRY. See Biographies.

ISSN 1056-6147
DD 338   US
WHO'S WHO OF AMERICAN BUSINESS LEADERS. [Who's who Am. bus. lead.]. (1991)-. English. Who's Who Worldwide Registry, Inc., 1983 Marcus Avenue, Suite C120, Lake Success NY 11042.

LC HB K237   **ISSN** 0945-2346
DD 330 340   GW
UDC 33
●WIB. WIRTSCHAFTSRECHTLICHE BERATUNG. VFOAT Wirtschaftsrechtliche Beratung. (1994)-. Bulletin. German. Twenty-four times a year. DM380.00. CH Beck'sche Verlagsbuchhandlung, Wilhelmstrasse 9, 80801 Munich Germany. **Tel** 011 49 89 38189338, FAX 011 49 89 38189398. **ED** Board. **Bk Rev**. **Ad Acc**. Full Page (B&W) DM2600.00. Full Page (Color) DM4550.00. **Circ**: 4,000.

GW
WIENER WIRTSCHAFTS- UND FINANZWISSENSCHAFTLICHE UNTERSUCHUNGEN. Vol. 1 (1968)-.
Monographic series. German. Irregular. Price varies per volume. Duncker und Humblot Verlag, Postfach 410329, D-12113 Berlin Germany. **Tel** 011 49 30 79000612, 011 49 30 79000613.

ISSN 0935-5758
GW
UDC 343.53
WIK. ZEITSCHRIFT FUER WIRTSCHAFT, KRIMINALITAT UND SICHERHEIT. See Security Systems and Alarms.

ISSN 1073-3213
UK
●WILEY BUSINESS INTELLIGENCE REPORTS. ALGERIA. VFOAT Algeria. (1994)-. English. Two times a year. $125.00. John Wiley & Sons Ltd., Baffins Lane, Chichester, West Sussex PO19 1UD United Kingdom. **Tel** 011 44 1243 779777, FAX 011 44 1243 776128 BTG:JWP001, telex 86290 WIBOOKG.
(Subscription address: John Wiley & Sons, Inc. /

Business and Economics

Philadelphia, PO Box 7247, Philadelphia PA 19170. **Tel** (212)850-6645, (800)225-5945.)
Desc: Provides comprehensive and precise information, hard-to-get statistics, and incisive analysis of world events and markets.

ISSN 1073-3221
UK

●**WILEY BUSINESS INTELLIGENCE REPORTS. ANGOLA.** VFOAT Angola. (1994)-. English. Two times a year. $125.00. John Wiley & Sons Ltd., Baffins Lane, Chichester, West Sussex PO19 1UD United Kingdom. **Tel** 011 44 1243 779777, FAX 011 44 1243 776128 BTG:JWP001, telex 86290 WIBOOKG. **(Subscription address:** John Wiley & Sons, Inc. / Philadelphia, PO Box 7247, Philadelphia PA 19170. **Tel** (212)850-6645, (800)225-5945.)

ISSN 1073-323X
UK

●**WILEY BUSINESS INTELLIGENCE REPORTS. ARGENTINA.** VFOAT Argentina. (1994)-. English. Two times a year. $125.00. John Wiley & Sons Ltd., Baffins Lane, Chichester, West Sussex PO19 1UD United Kingdom. **Tel** 011 44 1243 779777, FAX 011 44 1243 776128 BTG:JWP001, telex 86290 WIBOOKG. **(Subscription address:** John Wiley & Sons, Inc. / Philadelphia, PO Box 7247, Philadelphia PA 19170. **Tel** (212)850-6645, (800)225-5945.)

ISSN 1073-3256
UK

●**WILEY BUSINESS INTELLIGENCE REPORTS. AUSTRALIA.** VFOAT Australia. (1994)-. English. Two times a year. $125.00. John Wiley & Sons Ltd., Baffins Lane, Chichester, West Sussex PO19 1UD United Kingdom. **Tel** 011 44 1243 779777, FAX 011 44 1243 776128 BTG:JWP001, telex 86290 WIBOOKG. **(Subscription address:** John Wiley & Sons, Inc. / Philadelphia, PO Box 7247, Philadelphia PA 19170. **Tel** (212)850-6645, (800)225-5945.)

ISSN 1073-3248
UK

●**WILEY BUSINESS INTELLIGENCE REPORTS. AUSTRIA.** VFOAT Austria. (1994)-. English. Two times a year. $125.00. John Wiley & Sons Ltd., Baffins Lane, Chichester, West Sussex PO19 1UD United Kingdom. **Tel** 011 44 1243 779777, FAX 011 44 1243 776128 BTG:JWP001, telex 86290 WIBOOKG. **(Subscription address:** John Wiley & Sons, Inc. / Philadelphia, PO Box 7247, Philadelphia PA 19170. **Tel** (212)850-6645, (800)225-5945.)

ISSN 1073-3264
UK

●**WILEY BUSINESS INTELLIGENCE REPORTS. AZERBAIJAN.** VFOAT Azerbaijan. (1994)-. English. Two times a year. $125.00. John Wiley & Sons Ltd., Baffins Lane, Chichester, West Sussex PO19 1UD United Kingdom. **Tel** 011 44 1243 779777, FAX 011 44 1243 776128 BTG:JWP001, telex 86290 WIBOOKG. **(Subscription address:** John Wiley & Sons, Inc. / Philadelphia, PO Box 7247, Philadelphia PA 19170. **Tel** (212)850-6645, (800)225-5945.)

ISSN 1073-3272
UK

●**WILEY BUSINESS INTELLIGENCE REPORTS. BAHAMAS.** VFOAT Bahamas. (1994)-. English. Two times a year. $125.00. John Wiley & Sons Ltd., Baffins Lane, Chichester, West Sussex PO19 1UD United Kingdom. **Tel** 011 44 1243 779777, FAX 011 44 1243 776128 BTG:JWP001, telex 86290 WIBOOKG. **(Subscription address:** John Wiley & Sons, Inc. / Philadelphia, PO Box 7247, Philadelphia PA 19170. **Tel** (212)850-6645, (800)225-5945.)

ISSN 1073-3299
UK

●**WILEY BUSINESS INTELLIGENCE REPORTS. BAHRAIN.** VFOAT Bahrain. (1994)-. English. Two times a year. $125.00. John Wiley & Sons Ltd., Baffins Lane, Chichester, West Sussex PO19 1UD United Kingdom. **Tel** 011 44 1243 779777, FAX 011 44 1243 776128 BTG:JWP001, telex 86290 WIBOOKG. **(Subscription address:** John Wiley & Sons, Inc. / Philadelphia, PO Box 7247, Philadelphia PA 19170. **Tel** (212)850-6645, (800)225-5945.)

ISSN 1073-3302
UK

●**WILEY BUSINESS INTELLIGENCE REPORTS. BANGLADESH.** VFOAT Bangladesh. (1994)-. English. Two times a year. $125.00. John Wiley & Sons Ltd., Baffins Lane, Chichester, West Sussex PO19 1UD United Kingdom. **Tel** 011 44 1243 779777, FAX 011 44 1243 776128 BTG:JWP001, telex 86290 WIBOOKG. **(Subscription address:** John Wiley & Sons, Inc. / Philadelphia, PO Box 7247, Philadelphia PA 19170. **Tel** (212)850-6645, (800)225-5945.)

ISSN 1073-3280
UK

●**WILEY BUSINESS INTELLIGENCE REPORTS. BELGIUM.** VFOAT Belgium. (1994)-. English. Two times a year. $125.00. John Wiley & Sons Ltd., Baffins Lane, Chichester, West Sussex PO19 1UD United Kingdom. **Tel** 011 44 1243 779777, FAX 011 44 1243 776128 BTG:JWP001, telex 86290 WIBOOKG. **(Subscription address:** John Wiley & Sons, Inc. / Philadelphia, PO Box 7247, Philadelphia PA 19170. **Tel** (212)850-6645, (800)225-5945.)

ISSN 1073-3310
UK

●**WILEY BUSINESS INTELLIGENCE REPORTS. BOLIVIA.** VFOAT Bolivia. (1994)-. English. Two times a year. $125.00. John Wiley & Sons Ltd., Baffins Lane, Chichester, West Sussex PO19 1UD United Kingdom. **Tel** 011 44 1243 779777, FAX 011 44 1243 776128 BTG:JWP001, telex 86290 WIBOOKG. **(Subscription address:** John Wiley & Sons, Inc. / Philadelphia, PO Box 7247, Philadelphia PA 19170. **Tel** (212)850-6645, (800)225-5945.)

ISSN 1073-3329
UK

●**WILEY BUSINESS INTELLIGENCE REPORTS. BOTSWANA.** VFOAT Botswana. (1994)-. English. Two times a year. $125.00. John Wiley & Sons Ltd., Baffins Lane, Chichester, West Sussex PO19 1UD United Kingdom. **Tel** 011 44 1243 779777, FAX 011 44 1243 776128 BTG:JWP001, telex 86290 WIBOOKG. **(Subscription address:** John Wiley & Sons, Inc. / Philadelphia, PO Box 7247, Philadelphia PA 19170. **Tel** (212)850-6645, (800)225-5945.)

ISSN 1073-3345
UK

●**WILEY BUSINESS INTELLIGENCE REPORTS. BRAZIL.** VFOAT Brazil. (1994)-. English. Two times a year. $125.00. John Wiley & Sons Ltd., Baffins Lane, Chichester, West Sussex PO19 1UD United Kingdom. **Tel** 011 44 1243 779777, FAX 011 44 1243 776128 BTG:JWP001, telex 86290 WIBOOKG. **(Subscription address:** John Wiley & Sons, Inc. / Philadelphia, PO Box 7247, Philadelphia PA 19170. **Tel** (212)850-6645, (800)225-5945.)

ISSN 1073-3337
UK

●**WILEY BUSINESS INTELLIGENCE REPORTS. BRUNEI.** VFOAT Brunei. (1994)-. English. Two times a year. $125.00. John Wiley & Sons Ltd., Baffins Lane, Chichester, West Sussex PO19 1UD United Kingdom. **Tel** 011 44 1243 779777, FAX 011 44 1243 776128 BTG:JWP001, telex 86290 WIBOOKG. **(Subscription address:** John Wiley & Sons, Inc. / Philadelphia, PO Box 7247, Philadelphia PA 19170. **Tel** (212)850-6645, (800)225-5945.)

LC HB241 ISSN 1073-3353
DD 338 UK

●**WILEY BUSINESS INTELLIGENCE REPORTS. BULGARIA.** [Wiley bus. intell. rep., Bulg.]. VFOAT Bulgaria. (1994)-. English. Two times a year. $125.00. John Wiley & Sons Ltd., Baffins Lane, Chichester, West Sussex PO19 1UD United Kingdom. **Tel** 011 44 1243 779777, FAX 011 44 1243 776128 BTG:JWP001, telex 86290 WIBOOKG.

ISSN 1073-337X
UK

●**WILEY BUSINESS INTELLIGENCE REPORTS. CAMEROON.** VFOAT Cameroon. (1994)-. English. Two times a year. $125.00. John Wiley & Sons Ltd., Baffins Lane, Chichester, West Sussex PO19 1UD United Kingdom. **Tel** 011 44 1243 779777, FAX 011 44 1243 776128 BTG:JWP001, telex 86290 WIBOOKG. **(Subscription address:** John Wiley & Sons, Inc. / Philadelphia, PO Box 7247, Philadelphia PA 19170. **Tel** (212)850-6645, (800)225-5945.)

ISSN 1073-3361
UK

●**WILEY BUSINESS INTELLIGENCE REPORTS. CANADA.** VFOAT Canada. (1994)-. English. Two times a year. $125.00. John Wiley & Sons Ltd., Baffins Lane, Chichester, West Sussex PO19 1UD United Kingdom. **Tel** 011 44 1243 779777, FAX 011 44 1243 776128 BTG:JWP001, telex 86290 WIBOOKG. **(Subscription address:** John Wiley & Sons, Inc. / Philadelphia, PO Box 7247, Philadelphia PA 19170. **Tel** (212)850-6645, (800)225-5945.)

ISSN 1073-3388
DD 338 UK

●**WILEY BUSINESS INTELLIGENCE REPORTS. CHILE.** [Wiley bus. intell. rep., Chile]. VFOAT Chile. (1994)-. English. Two times a year. $125.00. John Wiley & Sons Ltd., Baffins Lane, Chichester, West Sussex PO19 1UD United Kingdom. **Tel** 011 44 1243 779777, FAX 011 44 1243 776128 BTG:JWP001, telex 86290 WIBOOKG.

ISSN 1073-3396
UK

●**WILEY BUSINESS INTELLIGENCE REPORTS. CHINA.** VFOAT China. (1994)-. English. Two times a year. $125.00. John Wiley & Sons Ltd., Baffins Lane, Chichester, West Sussex PO19 1UD United Kingdom. **Tel** 011 44 1243 779777, FAX 011 44 1243 776128 BTG:JWP001, telex 86290 WIBOOKG. **(Subscription address:** John Wiley & Sons, Inc. / Philadelphia, PO Box 7247, Philadelphia PA 19170. **Tel** (212)850-6645, (800)225-5945.)

ISSN 1073-340X
UK

●**WILEY BUSINESS INTELLIGENCE REPORTS. COLOMBIA.** VFOAT Colombia. (1994)-. English. Two times a year. $125.00. John Wiley & Sons Ltd., Baffins Lane, Chichester, West Sussex PO19 1UD United Kingdom. **Tel** 011 44 1243 779777, FAX 011 44 1243 776128 BTG:JWP001, telex 86290 WIBOOKG. **(Subscription address:** John Wiley & Sons, Inc. / Philadelphia, PO Box 7247, Philadelphia PA 19170. **Tel** (212)850-6645, (800)225-5945.)

LC HC ISSN 1073-3418
DD 338 UK

●**WILEY BUSINESS INTELLIGENCE REPORTS. COSTA RICA.** [Wiley bus. intell. rep., Costa Rica]. VFOAT Costa Rica. Issue 1 (1994)-. Periodical. English. Two times a year. $125.00. John Wiley & Sons Ltd., Baffins Lane, Chichester, West Sussex PO19 1UD United Kingdom. **Tel** 011 44 1243 779777, FAX 011 44 1243 776128 BTG:JWP001, telex 86290 WIBOOKG. **(Subscription address:** John Wiley & Sons, Inc. / Philadelphia, PO Box 7247, Philadelphia PA 19170. **Tel** (212)850-6645, (800)225-5945.)

ISSN 1073-368X
DD 338 UK

●**WILEY BUSINESS INTELLIGENCE REPORTS. COTE D'IVOIRE.** [Wiley bus. intell. rep., Cote-d'Iv.]. VFOAT Cote d'Ivoire. (1994)-. English. Two times a year. $125.00. John Wiley & Sons Ltd., Baffins Lane, Chichester, West Sussex PO19 1UD United Kingdom. **Tel** 011 44 1243 779777, FAX 011 44 1243 776128 BTG:JWP001, telex 86290 WIBOOKG.

ISSN 1073-3426
UK

●**WILEY BUSINESS INTELLIGENCE REPORTS. CUBA.** VFOAT Cuba. (1994)-. English. Two times a year. $125.00. John Wiley & Sons Ltd., Baffins Lane, Chichester, West Sussex PO19 1UD United Kingdom. **Tel** 011 44 1243 779777, FAX 011 44 1243 776128 BTG:JWP001, telex 86290 WIBOOKG. **(Subscription address:** John Wiley & Sons, Inc. / Philadelphia, PO Box 7247, Philadelphia PA 19170. **Tel** (212)850-6645, (800)225-5945.)

ISSN 1073-3434
UK

●**WILEY BUSINESS INTELLIGENCE REPORTS. CZECH REPUBLIC.** VFOAT Czech Republic. (1994)-. English. Two times a year. $125.00. John Wiley & Sons Ltd., Baffins Lane, Chichester, West Sussex PO19 1UD United Kingdom. **Tel** 011 44 1243 779777, FAX 011 44 1243 776128 BTG:JWP001, telex 86290 WIBOOKG. **(Subscription address:** John Wiley & Sons, Inc. / Philadelphia, PO Box 7247, Philadelphia PA 19170. **Tel** (212)850-6645, (800)225-5945.)

ISSN 1073-3442
DD 338 UK

●**WILEY BUSINESS INTELLIGENCE REPORTS. DENMARK.** [Wiley bus. intell. rep., Den.]. VFOAT Denmark. (1994)-. English. Two times a year. $125.00. John Wiley & Sons Ltd., Baffins Lane, Chichester, West Sussex PO19 1UD United Kingdom. **Tel** 011 44 1243 779777, FAX 011 44 1243 776128 BTG:JWP001, telex 86290 WIBOOKG.

ISSN 1073-3450
UK

●**WILEY BUSINESS INTELLIGENCE REPORTS. ECUADOR.** VFOAT Ecuador. (1994)-. English. Two times a year. $125.00. John Wiley & Sons Ltd., Baffins Lane, Chichester, West Sussex PO19 1UD United Kingdom. **Tel** 011 44 1243 779777, FAX 011 44 1243 776128 BTG:JWP001, telex 86290 WIBOOKG. **(Subscription address:** John Wiley & Sons, Inc. / Philadelphia, PO Box 7247, Philadelphia PA 19170. **Tel** (212)850-6645, (800)225-5945.)

ISSN 1073-3469
UK

●**WILEY BUSINESS INTELLIGENCE REPORTS. EGYPT.** VFOAT Egypt. (1994)-. English. Two times a year. $125.00. John Wiley & Sons Ltd., Baffins Lane, Chichester, West Sussex PO19 1UD United Kingdom. **Tel** 011 44 1243 779777, FAX 011 44 1243 776128 BTG:JWP001, telex 86290 WIBOOKG. **(Subscription address:** John Wiley & Sons, Inc. / Philadelphia, PO Box 7247, Philadelphia PA 19170. **Tel** (212)850-6645, (800)225-5945.)

Business and Economics

LC HG
DD 332

ISSN 1073-3477
UK

●WILEY BUSINESS INTELLIGENCE REPORTS. EL SALVADOR. VFOAT El Salvador. (1994)-. English. Two times a year. $125.00. John Wiley & Sons Ltd., Baffins Lane, Chichester, West Sussex PO19 1UD United Kingdom. Tel 011 44 1243 779777, FAX 011 44 1243 776128 BTG:JWP001, telex 86290 WIBOOKG. (Subscription address: John Wiley & Sons, Inc. / Philadelphia, PO Box 7247, Philadelphia PA 19170. Tel (212)850-6645, (800)225-5945.)

ISSN 1073-3485
UK

●WILEY BUSINESS INTELLIGENCE REPORTS. ESTONIA. VFOAT Estonia. (1994)-. English. Two times a year. $125.00. John Wiley & Sons Ltd., Baffins Lane, Chichester, West Sussex PO19 1UD United Kingdom. Tel 011 44 1243 779777, FAX 011 44 1243 776128 BTG:JWP001, telex 86290 WIBOOKG. (Subscription address: John Wiley & Sons, Inc. / Philadelphia, PO Box 7247, Philadelphia PA 19170. Tel (212)850-6645, (800)225-5945.)

ISSN 1073-3493
UK

●WILEY BUSINESS INTELLIGENCE REPORTS. FINLAND. VFOAT Finland. (1994)-. English. Two times a year. $125.00. John Wiley & Sons Ltd., Baffins Lane, Chichester, West Sussex PO19 1UD United Kingdom. Tel 011 44 1243 779777, FAX 011 44 1243 776128 BTG:JWP001, telex 86290 WIBOOKG. (Subscription address: John Wiley & Sons, Inc. / Philadelphia, PO Box 7247, Philadelphia PA 19170. Tel (212)850-6645, (800)225-5945.)

ISSN 1073-3507
UK

●WILEY BUSINESS INTELLIGENCE REPORTS. FRANCE. VFOAT France. (1994)-. English. Two times a year. $125.00. John Wiley & Sons Ltd., Baffins Lane, Chichester, West Sussex PO19 1UD United Kingdom. Tel 011 44 1243 779777, FAX 011 44 1243 776128 BTG:JWP001, telex 86290 WIBOOKG. (Subscription address: John Wiley & Sons, Inc. / Philadelphia, PO Box 7247, Philadelphia PA 19170. Tel (212)850-6645, (800)225-5945.)

ISSN 1073-3515
UK

●WILEY BUSINESS INTELLIGENCE REPORTS. GABON. VFOAT Gabon. (1994)-. English. Two times a year. $125.00. John Wiley & Sons Ltd., Baffins Lane, Chichester, West Sussex PO19 1UD United Kingdom. Tel 011 44 1243 779777, FAX 011 44 1243 776128 BTG:JWP001, telex 86290 WIBOOKG. (Subscription address: John Wiley & Sons, Inc. / Philadelphia, PO Box 7247, Philadelphia PA 19170. Tel (212)850-6645, (800)225-5945.)

ISSN 1073-3523
UK

●WILEY BUSINESS INTELLIGENCE REPORTS. GERMANY. VFOAT Germany. (1994)-. English. Two times a year. $125.00. John Wiley & Sons Ltd., Baffins Lane, Chichester, West Sussex PO19 1UD United Kingdom. Tel 011 44 1243 779777, FAX 011 44 1243 776128 BTG:JWP001, telex 86290 WIBOOKG. (Subscription address: John Wiley & Sons, Inc. / Philadelphia, PO Box 7247, Philadelphia PA 19170. Tel (212)850-6645, (800)225-5945.)

ISSN 1073-3531
UK

●WILEY BUSINESS INTELLIGENCE REPORTS. GHANA. VFOAT Ghana. (1994)-. English. Two times a year. $125.00. John Wiley & Sons Ltd., Baffins Lane, Chichester, West Sussex PO19 1UD United Kingdom. Tel 011 44 1243 779777, FAX 011 44 1243 776128 BTG:JWP001, telex 86290 WIBOOKG. (Subscription address: John Wiley & Sons, Inc. / Philadelphia, PO Box 7247, Philadelphia PA 19170. Tel (212)850-6645, (800)225-5945.)

ISSN 1073-354X
UK

●WILEY BUSINESS INTELLIGENCE REPORTS. GREECE. VFOAT Greece. (1994)-. English. Two times a year. $125.00. John Wiley & Sons Ltd., Baffins Lane, Chichester, West Sussex PO19 1UD United Kingdom. Tel 011 44 1243 779777, FAX 011 44 1243 776128 BTG:JWP001, telex 86290 WIBOOKG. (Subscription address: John Wiley & Sons, Inc. / Philadelphia, PO Box 7247, Philadelphia PA 19170. Tel (212)850-6645, (800)225-5945.)

ISSN 1073-3558
UK

●WILEY BUSINESS INTELLIGENCE REPORTS. GUATEMALA. VFOAT Guatemala. (1994)-. English. Two times a year. $125.00. John Wiley & Sons Ltd., Baffins Lane, Chichester, West Sussex PO19 1UD United Kingdom. Tel 011 44 1243 779777, FAX 011 44 1243 776128 BTG:JWP001, telex 86290 WIBOOKG. (Subscription address: John Wiley & Sons, Inc. / Philadelphia, PO Box 7247, Philadelphia PA 19170. Tel (212)850-6645, (800)225-5945.)

ISSN 1073-3566
UK

●WILEY BUSINESS INTELLIGENCE REPORTS. GUYANA. VFOAT Guyana. (1994)-. English. Two times a year. $125.00. John Wiley & Sons Ltd., Baffins Lane, Chichester, West Sussex PO19 1UD United Kingdom. Tel 011 44 1243 779777, FAX 011 44 1243 776128 BTG:JWP001, telex 86290 WIBOOKG. (Subscription address: John Wiley & Sons, Inc. / Philadelphia, PO Box 7247, Philadelphia PA 19170. Tel (212)850-6645, (800)225-5945.)

ISSN 1073-3574
UK

●WILEY BUSINESS INTELLIGENCE REPORTS. HAITI. VFOAT Haiti. (1994)-. English. Two times a year. $125.00. John Wiley & Sons Ltd., Baffins Lane, Chichester, West Sussex PO19 1UD United Kingdom. Tel 011 44 1243 779777, FAX 011 44 1243 776128 BTG:JWP001, telex 86290 WIBOOKG. (Subscription address: John Wiley & Sons, Inc. / Philadelphia, PO Box 7247, Philadelphia PA 19170. Tel (212)850-6645, (800)225-5945.)

ISSN 1073-3604
UK

●WILEY BUSINESS INTELLIGENCE REPORTS. HONDURAS. VFOAT Honduras. (1994)-. English. Two times a year. $125.00. John Wiley & Sons Ltd., Baffins Lane, Chichester, West Sussex PO19 1UD United Kingdom. Tel 011 44 1243 779777, FAX 011 44 1243 776128 BTG:JWP001, telex 86290 WIBOOKG. (Subscription address: John Wiley & Sons, Inc. / Philadelphia, PO Box 7247, Philadelphia PA 19170. Tel (212)850-6645, (800)225-5945.)

ISSN 1073-3590
UK

●WILEY BUSINESS INTELLIGENCE REPORTS. HONG KONG. VFOAT Hong Kong. (1994)-. English. Two times a year. $125.00. John Wiley & Sons Ltd., Baffins Lane, Chichester, West Sussex PO19 1UD United Kingdom. Tel 011 44 1243 779777, FAX 011 44 1243 776128 BTG:JWP001, telex 86290 WIBOOKG. (Subscription address: John Wiley & Sons, Inc. / Philadelphia, PO Box 7247, Philadelphia PA 19170. Tel (212)850-6645, (800)225-5945.)

ISSN 1073-3582
UK

●WILEY BUSINESS INTELLIGENCE REPORTS. HUNGARY. VFOAT Hungary. (1994)-. English. Two times a year. $125.00. John Wiley & Sons Ltd., Baffins Lane, Chichester, West Sussex PO19 1UD United Kingdom. Tel 011 44 1243 779777, FAX 011 44 1243 776128 BTG:JWP001, telex 86290 WIBOOKG. (Subscription address: John Wiley & Sons, Inc. / Philadelphia, PO Box 7247, Philadelphia PA 19170. Tel (212)850-6645, (800)225-5945.)

ISSN 1073-3620
UK

●WILEY BUSINESS INTELLIGENCE REPORTS. INDIA. VFOAT India. (1994)-. English. Two times a year. $125.00. John Wiley & Sons Ltd., Baffins Lane, Chichester, West Sussex PO19 1UD United Kingdom. Tel 011 44 1243 779777, FAX 011 44 1243 776128 BTG:JWP001, telex 86290 WIBOOKG. (Subscription address: John Wiley & Sons, Inc. / Philadelphia, PO Box 7247, Philadelphia PA 19170. Tel (212)850-6645, (800)225-5945.)

ISSN 1073-3612
UK

●WILEY BUSINESS INTELLIGENCE REPORTS. INDONESIA. VFOAT Indonesia. (1994)-. English. Two times a year. $125.00. John Wiley & Sons Ltd., Baffins Lane, Chichester, West Sussex PO19 1UD United Kingdom. Tel 011 44 1243 779777, FAX 011 44 1243 776128 BTG:JWP001, telex 86290 WIBOOKG. (Subscription address: John Wiley & Sons, Inc. / Philadelphia, PO Box 7247, Philadelphia PA 19170. Tel (212)850-6645, (800)225-5945.)

ISSN 1073-3647
UK

●WILEY BUSINESS INTELLIGENCE REPORTS. IRAN. VFOAT Iran. (1994)-. English. Two times a year. $125.00. John Wiley & Sons Ltd., Baffins Lane, Chichester, West Sussex PO19 1UD United Kingdom. Tel 011 44 1243 779777, FAX 011 44 1243 776128 BTG:JWP001, telex 86290 WIBOOKG. (Subscription address: John Wiley & Sons, Inc. / Philadelphia, PO Box 7247, Philadelphia PA 19170. Tel (212)850-6645, (800)225-5945.)

ISSN 1073-3655
UK

●WILEY BUSINESS INTELLIGENCE REPORTS. IRAQ. VFOAT Iraq. (1994)-. English. Two times a year. $125.00. John Wiley & Sons Ltd., Baffins Lane, Chichester, West Sussex PO19 1UD United Kingdom. Tel 011 44 1243 779777, FAX 011 44 1243 776128 BTG:JWP001, telex 86290 WIBOOKG. (Subscription address: John Wiley & Sons, Inc. / Philadelphia, PO Box 7247, Philadelphia PA 19170. Tel (212)850-6645, (800)225-5945.)

ISSN 1073-3639
UK

●WILEY BUSINESS INTELLIGENCE REPORTS. IRELAND. VFOAT Ireland. (1994)-. English. Two times a year. $125.00. John Wiley & Sons Ltd., Baffins Lane, Chichester, West Sussex PO19 1UD United Kingdom. Tel 011 44 1243 779777, FAX 011 44 1243 776128 BTG:JWP001, telex 86290 WIBOOKG. (Subscription address: John Wiley & Sons, Inc. / Philadelphia, PO Box 7247, Philadelphia PA 19170. Tel (212)850-6645, (800)225-5945.)

ISSN 1073-3663
UK

●WILEY BUSINESS INTELLIGENCE REPORTS. ISRAEL. VFOAT Israel. (1994)-. English. Two times a year. $125.00. John Wiley & Sons Ltd., Baffins Lane, Chichester, West Sussex PO19 1UD United Kingdom. Tel 011 44 1243 779777, FAX 011 44 1243 776128 BTG:JWP001, telex 86290 WIBOOKG. (Subscription address: John Wiley & Sons, Inc. / Philadelphia, PO Box 7247, Philadelphia PA 19170. Tel (212)850-6645, (800)225-5945.)

ISSN 1073-3671
UK

●WILEY BUSINESS INTELLIGENCE REPORTS. ITALY. VFOAT Italy. (1994)-. English. Two times a year. $125.00. John Wiley & Sons Ltd., Baffins Lane, Chichester, West Sussex PO19 1UD United Kingdom. Tel 011 44 1243 779777, FAX 011 44 1243 776128 BTG:JWP001, telex 86290 WIBOOKG. (Subscription address: John Wiley & Sons, Inc. / Philadelphia, PO Box 7247, Philadelphia PA 19170. Tel (212)850-6645, (800)225-5945.)

ISSN 1073-3698
UK

●WILEY BUSINESS INTELLIGENCE REPORTS. JAMAICA. VFOAT Jamaica. (1994)-. English. Two times a year. $125.00. John Wiley & Sons Ltd., Baffins Lane, Chichester, West Sussex PO19 1UD United Kingdom. Tel 011 44 1243 779777, FAX 011 44 1243 776128 BTG:JWP001, telex 86290 WIBOOKG. (Subscription address: John Wiley & Sons, Inc. / Philadelphia, PO Box 7247, Philadelphia PA 19170. Tel (212)850-6645, (800)225-5945.)

ISSN 1073-3701
UK

●WILEY BUSINESS INTELLIGENCE REPORTS. JAPAN. VFOAT Japan. (1994)-. English. Two times a year. $125.00. John Wiley & Sons Ltd., Baffins Lane, Chichester, West Sussex PO19 1UD United Kingdom. Tel 011 44 1243 779777, FAX 011 44 1243 776128 BTG:JWP001, telex 86290 WIBOOKG. (Subscription address: John Wiley & Sons, Inc. / Philadelphia, PO Box 7247, Philadelphia PA 19170. Tel (212)850-6645, (800)225-5945.)

ISSN 1073-371X
UK

●WILEY BUSINESS INTELLIGENCE REPORTS. JORDAN. VFOAT Jordan. (1994)-. English. Two times a year. $125.00. John Wiley & Sons Ltd., Baffins Lane, Chichester, West Sussex PO19 1UD United Kingdom. Tel 011 44 1243 779777, FAX 011 44 1243 776128 BTG:JWP001, telex 86290 WIBOOKG. (Subscription address: John Wiley & Sons, Inc. / Philadelphia, PO Box 7247, Philadelphia PA 19170. Tel (212)850-6645, (800)225-5945.)

ISSN 1073-3728
UK

●WILEY BUSINESS INTELLIGENCE REPORTS. KAZAKHSTAN. VFOAT Kazakhstan. (1994)-. English. Two times a year. $125.00. John Wiley & Sons Ltd., Baffins Lane, Chichester, West Sussex PO19 1UD United Kingdom. Tel 011 44 1243 779777, FAX 011 44 1243 776128 BTG:JWP001, telex 86290 WIBOOKG. (Subscription address: John Wiley & Sons, Inc. / Philadelphia, PO Box 7247, Philadelphia PA 19170. Tel (212)850-6645, (800)225-5945.)

ISSN 1073-3736
UK

●WILEY BUSINESS INTELLIGENCE REPORTS. KENYA. VFOAT Kenya. (1994)-. English. Two times a year. $125.00. John Wiley & Sons Ltd., Baffins Lane, Chichester, West Sussex PO19 1UD United Kingdom. Tel 011 44 1243 779777, FAX 011 44 1243 776128 BTG:JWP001, telex 86290 WIBOOKG. (Subscription address: John Wiley & Sons, Inc. / Philadelphia, PO Box 7247, Philadelphia PA 19170. Tel (212)850-6645, (800)225-5945.)

ISSN 1073-3744
UK

●WILEY BUSINESS INTELLIGENCE REPORTS. KOREA. VFOAT Korea. (1994)-. English. Two times a year. $125.00. John Wiley & Sons Ltd., Baffins Lane, Chichester, West Sussex PO19 1UD

Business and Economics

United Kingdom. **Tel** 011 44 1243 779777, FAX 011 44 1243 776128 BTG:JWP001, telex 86290 WIBOOKG. **(Subscription address:** John Wiley & Sons, Inc. / Philadelphia, PO Box 7247, Philadelphia PA 19170. **Tel** (212)850-6645, (800)225-5945.**)**

ISSN 1073-3752
UK

● **WILEY BUSINESS INTELLIGENCE REPORTS. KUWAIT. VFOAT** Kuwait. (1994)-. English. Two times a year. $125.00. John Wiley & Sons Ltd., Baffins Lane, Chichester, West Sussex PO19 1UD United Kingdom. **Tel** 011 44 1243 779777, FAX 011 44 1243 776128 BTG:JWP001, telex 86290 WIBOOKG. **(Subscription address:** John Wiley & Sons, Inc. / Philadelphia, PO Box 7247, Philadelphia PA 19170. **Tel** (212)850-6645, (800)225-5945.**)**

ISSN 1073-3760
UK

● **WILEY BUSINESS INTELLIGENCE REPORTS. LEBANON. VFOAT** Lebanon. (1994)-. English. Two times a year. $125.00. John Wiley & Sons Ltd., Baffins Lane, Chichester, West Sussex PO19 1UD United Kingdom. **Tel** 011 44 1243 779777, FAX 011 44 1243 776128 BTG:JWP001, telex 86290 WIBOOKG. **(Subscription address:** John Wiley & Sons, Inc. / Philadelphia, PO Box 7247, Philadelphia PA 19170. **Tel** (212)850-6645, (800)225-5945.**)**

ISSN 1073-3779
UK

● **WILEY BUSINESS INTELLIGENCE REPORTS. LIBYA. VFOAT** Libya. (1994)-. English. Two times a year. $125.00. John Wiley & Sons Ltd., Baffins Lane, Chichester, West Sussex PO19 1UD United Kingdom. **Tel** 011 44 1243 779777, FAX 011 44 1243 776128 BTG:JWP001, telex 86290 WIBOOKG. **(Subscription address:** John Wiley & Sons, Inc. / Philadelphia, PO Box 7247, Philadelphia PA 19170. **Tel** (212)850-6645, (800)225-5945.**)**

ISSN 1073-3787
UK

● **WILEY BUSINESS INTELLIGENCE REPORTS. LUXEMBOURG. VFOAT** Luxembourg. (1994)-. English. Two times a year. $125.00. John Wiley & Sons Ltd., Baffins Lane, Chichester, West Sussex PO19 1UD United Kingdom. **Tel** 011 44 1243 779777, FAX 011 44 1243 776128 BTG:JWP001, telex 86290 WIBOOKG. **(Subscription address:** John Wiley & Sons, Inc. / Philadelphia, PO Box 7247, Philadelphia PA 19170. **Tel** (212)850-6645, (800)225-5945.**)**

ISSN 1073-3795
UK

● **WILEY BUSINESS INTELLIGENCE REPORTS. MALAYSIA. VFOAT** Malaysia. (1994)-. English. Two times a year. $125.00. John Wiley & Sons Ltd., Baffins Lane, Chichester, West Sussex PO19 1UD United Kingdom. **Tel** 011 44 1243 779777, FAX 011 44 1243 776128 BTG:JWP001, telex 86290 WIBOOKG. **(Subscription address:** John Wiley & Sons, Inc. / Philadelphia, PO Box 7247, Philadelphia PA 19170. **Tel** (212)850-6645, (800)225-5945.**)**

ISSN 1073-4236
UK

● **WILEY BUSINESS INTELLIGENCE REPORTS. MEXICO. VFOAT** Mexico. (1994)-. English. Two times a year. $125.00. John Wiley & Sons Ltd., Baffins Lane, Chichester, West Sussex PO19 1UD United Kingdom. **Tel** 011 44 1243 779777, FAX 011 44 1243 776128 BTG:JWP001, telex 86290 WIBOOKG. **(Subscription address:** John Wiley & Sons, Inc. / Philadelphia, PO Box 7247, Philadelphia PA 19170. **Tel** (212)850-6645, (800)225-5945.**)**

ISSN 1073-3809
UK

● **WILEY BUSINESS INTELLIGENCE REPORTS. MOROCCO. VFOAT** Morocco. (1994)-. English. Two times a year. $125.00. John Wiley & Sons Ltd., Baffins Lane, Chichester, West Sussex PO19 1UD United Kingdom. **Tel** 011 44 1243 779777, FAX 011 44 1243 776128 BTG:JWP001, telex 86290 WIBOOKG. **(Subscription address:** John Wiley & Sons, Inc. / Philadelphia, PO Box 7247, Philadelphia PA 19170. **Tel** (212)850-6645, (800)225-5945.**)**

ISSN 1073-3817
UK

● **WILEY BUSINESS INTELLIGENCE REPORTS. MOZAMBIQUE. VFOAT** Mozambique. (1994)-. English. Two times a year. $125.00. John Wiley & Sons Ltd., Baffins Lane, Chichester, West Sussex PO19 1UD United Kingdom. **Tel** 011 44 1243 779777, FAX 011 44 1243 776128 BTG:JWP001, telex 86290 WIBOOKG. **(Subscription address:** John Wiley & Sons, Inc. / Philadelphia, PO Box 7247, Philadelphia PA 19170. **Tel** (212)850-6645, (800)225-5945.**)**

ISSN 1073-3841
UK

● **WILEY BUSINESS INTELLIGENCE REPORTS. NETHERLANDS. VFOAT** Netherlands. (1994)-. English. Two times a year. $125.00. John Wiley & Sons Ltd., Baffins Lane, Chichester, West Sussex PO19 1UD United Kingdom. **Tel** 011 44 1243 779777, FAX 011 44 1243 776128 BTG:JWP001, telex 86290 WIBOOKG. **(Subscription address:** John Wiley & Sons, Inc. / Philadelphia, PO Box 7247, Philadelphia PA 19170. **Tel** (212)850-6645, (800)225-5945.**)**

ISSN 1073-3868
UK

● **WILEY BUSINESS INTELLIGENCE REPORTS. NEW ZEALAND. VFOAT** New Zealand. (1994)-. English. Two times a year. $125.00. John Wiley & Sons Ltd., Baffins Lane, Chichester, West Sussex PO19 1UD United Kingdom. **Tel** 011 44 1243 779777, FAX 011 44 1243 776128 BTG:JWP001, telex 86290 WIBOOKG. **(Subscription address:** John Wiley & Sons, Inc. / Philadelphia, PO Box 7247, Philadelphia PA 19170. **Tel** (212)850-6645, (800)225-5945.**)**

ISSN 1073-3833
UK

● **WILEY BUSINESS INTELLIGENCE REPORTS. NICARAGUE. VFOAT** Nicarague. (1994)-. English. Two times a year. $125.00. John Wiley & Sons Ltd., Baffins Lane, Chichester, West Sussex PO19 1UD United Kingdom. **Tel** 011 44 1243 779777, FAX 011 44 1243 776128 BTG:JWP001, telex 86290 WIBOOKG. **(Subscription address:** John Wiley & Sons, Inc. / Philadelphia, PO Box 7247, Philadelphia PA 19170. **Tel** (212)850-6645, (800)225-5945.**)**

ISSN 1073-3825
UK

● **WILEY BUSINESS INTELLIGENCE REPORTS. NIGERIA. VFOAT** Nigeria. (1994)-. English. Two times a year. $125.00. John Wiley & Sons Ltd., Baffins Lane, Chichester, West Sussex PO19 1UD United Kingdom. **Tel** 011 44 1243 779777, FAX 011 44 1243 776128 BTG:JWP001, telex 86290 WIBOOKG. **(Subscription address:** John Wiley & Sons, Inc. / Philadelphia, PO Box 7247, Philadelphia PA 19170. **Tel** (212)850-6645, (800)225-5945.**)**

ISSN 1073-385X
UK

● **WILEY BUSINESS INTELLIGENCE REPORTS. NORWAY. VFOAT** Norway. (1994)-. English. Two times a year. $125.00. John Wiley & Sons Ltd., Baffins Lane, Chichester, West Sussex PO19 1UD United Kingdom. **Tel** 011 44 1243 779777, FAX 011 44 1243 776128 BTG:JWP001, telex 86290 WIBOOKG. **(Subscription address:** John Wiley & Sons, Inc. / Philadelphia, PO Box 7247, Philadelphia PA 19170. **Tel** (212)850-6645, (800)225-5945.**)**

ISSN 1073-3876
UK

● **WILEY BUSINESS INTELLIGENCE REPORTS. OMAN. VFOAT** Oman. (1994)-. English. Two times a year. $125.00. John Wiley & Sons Ltd., Baffins Lane, Chichester, West Sussex PO19 1UD United Kingdom. **Tel** 011 44 1243 779777, FAX 011 44 1243 776128 BTG:JWP001, telex 86290 WIBOOKG. **(Subscription address:** John Wiley & Sons, Inc. / Philadelphia, PO Box 7247, Philadelphia PA 19170. **Tel** (212)850-6645, (800)225-5945.**)**

ISSN 1073-3884
UK

● **WILEY BUSINESS INTELLIGENCE REPORTS. PAKISTAN. VFOAT** Pakistan. (1994)-. English. Two times a year. $125.00. John Wiley & Sons Ltd., Baffins Lane, Chichester, West Sussex PO19 1UD United Kingdom. **Tel** 011 44 1243 779777, FAX 011 44 1243 776128 BTG:JWP001, telex 86290 WIBOOKG. **(Subscription address:** John Wiley & Sons, Inc. / Philadelphia, PO Box 7247, Philadelphia PA 19170. **Tel** (212)850-6645, (800)225-5945.**)**

ISSN 1073-3892
DD 338 UK

● **WILEY BUSINESS INTELLIGENCE REPORTS. PANAMA.** [Wiley bus. intell. rep., Panama]. **VFOAT** Panama. (1994)-. English. Two times a year. $125.00. John Wiley & Sons Ltd., Baffins Lane, Chichester, West Sussex PO19 1UD United Kingdom. **Tel** 011 44 1243 779777, FAX 011 44 1243 776128 BTG:JWP001, telex 86290 WIBOOKG.

ISSN 1073-3906
DD 338 UK

● **WILEY BUSINESS INTELLIGENCE REPORTS. PAPUA NEW GUINEA.** [Wiley bus. intell. rep., P.N.G.]. **VFOAT** Papua New Guinea. (1994)-. English. Two times a year. $125.00. John Wiley & Sons Ltd., Baffins Lane, Chichester, West Sussex PO19 1UD United Kingdom. **Tel** 011 44 1243 779777, FAX 011 44 1243 776128 BTG:JWP001, telex 86290 WIBOOKG.

ISSN 1073-3914
UK

● **WILEY BUSINESS INTELLIGENCE REPORTS. PARAGUAY. VFOAT** Paraguay. (1994)-. English. Two times a year. $125.00. John Wiley & Sons Ltd., Baffins Lane, Chichester, West Sussex PO19 1UD United Kingdom. **Tel** 011 44 1243 779777, FAX 011 44 1243 776128 BTG:JWP001, telex 86290 WIBOOKG. **(Subscription address:** John Wiley & Sons, Inc. / Philadelphia, PO Box 7247, Philadelphia PA 19170. **Tel** (212)850-6645, (800)225-5945.**)**

ISSN 1073-3957
UK

● **WILEY BUSINESS INTELLIGENCE REPORTS. PERU. VFOAT** Peru. (1994)-. English. Two times a year. $125.00. John Wiley & Sons Ltd., Baffins Lane, Chichester, West Sussex PO19 1UD United Kingdom. **Tel** 011 44 1243 779777, FAX 011 44 1243 776128 BTG:JWP001, telex 86290 WIBOOKG. **(Subscription address:** John Wiley & Sons, Inc. / Philadelphia, PO Box 7247, Philadelphia PA 19170. **Tel** (212)850-6645, (800)225-5945.**)**

ISSN 1073-3922
UK

● **WILEY BUSINESS INTELLIGENCE REPORTS. PHILIPPINES. VFOAT** Philippines. (1994)-. English. Two times a year. $125.00. John Wiley & Sons Ltd., Baffins Lane, Chichester, West Sussex PO19 1UD United Kingdom. **Tel** 011 44 1243 779777, FAX 011 44 1243 776128 BTG:JWP001, telex 86290 WIBOOKG. **(Subscription address:** John Wiley & Sons, Inc. / Philadelphia, PO Box 7247, Philadelphia PA 19170. **Tel** (212)850-6645, (800)225-5945.**)**

ISSN 1073-3930
UK

● **WILEY BUSINESS INTELLIGENCE REPORTS. POLAND. VFOAT** Poland. (1994)-. English. Two times a year. $125.00. John Wiley & Sons Ltd., Baffins Lane, Chichester, West Sussex PO19 1UD United Kingdom. **Tel** 011 44 1243 779777, FAX 011 44 1243 776128 BTG:JWP001, telex 86290 WIBOOKG. **(Subscription address:** John Wiley & Sons, Inc. / Philadelphia, PO Box 7247, Philadelphia PA 19170. **Tel** (212)850-6645, (800)225-5945.**)**

ISSN 1073-3949
UK

● **WILEY BUSINESS INTELLIGENCE REPORTS. PORTUGAL. VFOAT** Portugal. (1994)-. English. Two times a year. $125.00. John Wiley & Sons Ltd., Baffins Lane, Chichester, West Sussex PO19 1UD United Kingdom. **Tel** 011 44 1243 779777, FAX 011 44 1243 776128 BTG:JWP001, telex 86290 WIBOOKG. **(Subscription address:** John Wiley & Sons, Inc. / Philadelphia, PO Box 7247, Philadelphia PA 19170. **Tel** (212)850-6645, (800)225-5945.**)**

ISSN 1073-3965
UK

● **WILEY BUSINESS INTELLIGENCE REPORTS. PUERTO RICO. VFOAT** Puerto Rico. (1994)-. English. Two times a year. $125.00. John Wiley & Sons Ltd., Baffins Lane, Chichester, West Sussex PO19 1UD United Kingdom. **Tel** 011 44 1243 779777, FAX 011 44 1243 776128 BTG:JWP001, telex 86290 WIBOOKG. **(Subscription address:** John Wiley & Sons, Inc. / Philadelphia, PO Box 7247, Philadelphia PA 19170. **Tel** (212)850-6645, (800)225-5945.**)**

ISSN 1073-3973
UK

● **WILEY BUSINESS INTELLIGENCE REPORTS. RUSSIA. VFOAT** Russia. (1994)-. English. Two times a year. $125.00. John Wiley & Sons Ltd., Baffins Lane, Chichester, West Sussex PO19 1UD United Kingdom. **Tel** 011 44 1243 779777, FAX 011 44 1243 776128 BTG:JWP001, telex 86290 WIBOOKG. **(Subscription address:** John Wiley & Sons, Inc. / Philadelphia, PO Box 7247, Philadelphia PA 19170. **Tel** (212)850-6645, (800)225-5945.**)**

ISSN 1073-399X
UK

● **WILEY BUSINESS INTELLIGENCE REPORTS. SAUDI ARABIA. VFOAT** Saudi Arabia. (1994)-. English. Two times a year. $125.00. John Wiley & Sons Ltd., Baffins Lane, Chichester, West Sussex PO19 1UD United Kingdom. **Tel** 011 44 1243 779777, FAX 011 44 1243 776128 BTG:JWP001, telex 86290 WIBOOKG. **(Subscription address:** John Wiley & Sons, Inc. / Philadelphia, PO Box 7247, Philadelphia PA 19170. **Tel** (212)850-6645, (800)225-5945.**)**

ISSN 1073-4007
UK

● **WILEY BUSINESS INTELLIGENCE REPORTS. SENEGAL. VFOAT** Senegal. (1994)-. English. Two times a year. $125.00. John Wiley & Sons Ltd., Baffins Lane, Chichester, West Sussex PO19 1UD United Kingdom. **Tel** 011 44 1243 779777, FAX 011 44 1243 776128 BTG:JWP001, telex 86290

Business and Economics

WIBOOKG. **(Subscription address:** John Wiley & Sons, Inc. / Philadelphia, PO Box 7247, Philadelphia PA 19170. **Tel** (212)850-6645, (800)225-5945.)

ISSN 1073-4023
UK

●**WILEY BUSINESS INTELLIGENCE REPORTS. SINGAPORE.** **VFOAT** Singapore. (1994)-. English. Two times a year. $125.00. John Wiley & Sons Ltd., Baffins Lane, Chichester, West Sussex PO19 1UD United Kingdom. **Tel** 011 44 1243 779777, FAX 011 44 1243 776128 BTG:JWP001, telex 86290 WIBOOKG. **(Subscription address:** John Wiley & Sons, Inc. / Philadelphia, PO Box 7247, Philadelphia PA 19170. **Tel** (212)850-6645, (800)225-5945.)

ISSN 1073-4015
UK

●**WILEY BUSINESS INTELLIGENCE REPORTS. SLOVAK REPUBLIC.** **VFOAT** Slovak Republic. (1994)-. English. Two times a year. $125.00. John Wiley & Sons Ltd., Baffins Lane, Chichester, West Sussex PO19 1UD United Kingdom. **Tel** 011 44 1243 779777, FAX 011 44 1243 776128 BTG:JWP001, telex 86290 WIBOOKG. **(Subscription address:** John Wiley & Sons, Inc. / Philadelphia, PO Box 7247, Philadelphia PA 19170. **Tel** (212)850-6645, (800)225-5945.)

ISSN 1073-3981
UK

●**WILEY BUSINESS INTELLIGENCE REPORTS. SOUTH AFRICA.** **VFOAT** South Africa. (1994)-. English. Two times a year. $125.00. John Wiley & Sons Ltd., Baffins Lane, Chichester, West Sussex PO19 1UD United Kingdom. **Tel** 011 44 1243 779777, FAX 011 44 1243 776128 BTG:JWP001, telex 86290 WIBOOKG. **(Subscription address:** John Wiley & Sons, Inc. / Philadelphia, PO Box 7247, Philadelphia PA 19170. **Tel** (212)850-6645, (800)225-5945.)

ISSN 1073-4031
UK

●**WILEY BUSINESS INTELLIGENCE REPORTS. SPAIN.** **VFOAT** Spain. (1994)-. English. Two times a year. $125.00. John Wiley & Sons Ltd., Baffins Lane, Chichester, West Sussex PO19 1UD United Kingdom. **Tel** 011 44 1243 779777, FAX 011 44 1243 776128 BTG:JWP001, telex 86290 WIBOOKG. **(Subscription address:** John Wiley & Sons, Inc. / Philadelphia, PO Box 7247, Philadelphia PA 19170. **Tel** (212)850-6645, (800)225-5945.)

ISSN 1073-404X
UK

●**WILEY BUSINESS INTELLIGENCE REPORTS. SRI LANKA.** **VFOAT** Sri Lanka. (1994)-. English. Two times a year. $125.00. John Wiley & Sons Ltd., Baffins Lane, Chichester, West Sussex PO19 1UD United Kingdom. **Tel** 011 44 1243 779777, FAX 011 44 1243 776128 BTG:JWP001, telex 86290 WIBOOKG. **(Subscription address:** John Wiley & Sons, Inc. / Philadelphia, PO Box 7247, Philadelphia PA 19170. **Tel** (212)850-6645, (800)225-5945.)

ISSN 1073-4058
UK

●**WILEY BUSINESS INTELLIGENCE REPORTS. SUDAN.** **VFOAT** Sudan. (1994)-. English. Two times a year. $125.00. John Wiley & Sons Ltd., Baffins Lane, Chichester, West Sussex PO19 1UD United Kingdom. **Tel** 011 44 1243 779777, FAX 011 44 1243 776128 BTG:JWP001, telex 86290 WIBOOKG. **(Subscription address:** John Wiley & Sons, Inc. / Philadelphia, PO Box 7247, Philadelphia PA 19170. **Tel** (212)850-6645, (800)225-5945.)

ISSN 1073-4260
UK

●**WILEY BUSINESS INTELLIGENCE REPORTS. SWEDEN.** **VFOAT** Sweden. (1994)-. English. Two times a year. $125.00. John Wiley & Sons Ltd., Baffins Lane, Chichester, West Sussex PO19 1UD United Kingdom. **Tel** 011 44 1243 779777, FAX 011 44 1243 776128 BTG:JWP001, telex 86290 WIBOOKG. **(Subscription address:** John Wiley & Sons, Inc. / Philadelphia, PO Box 7247, Philadelphia PA 19170. **Tel** (212)850-6645, (800)225-5945.)

ISSN 1073-4066
UK

●**WILEY BUSINESS INTELLIGENCE REPORTS. SWITZERLAND.** **VFOAT** Switzerland. (1994)-. English. Two times a year. $125.00. John Wiley & Sons Ltd., Baffins Lane, Chichester, West Sussex PO19 1UD United Kingdom. **Tel** 011 44 1243 779777, FAX 011 44 1243 776128 BTG:JWP001, telex 86290 WIBOOKG. **(Subscription address:** John Wiley & Sons, Inc. / Philadelphia, PO Box 7247, Philadelphia PA 19170. **Tel** (212)850-6645, (800)225-5945.)

ISSN 1073-4074
UK

●**WILEY BUSINESS INTELLIGENCE REPORTS. SYRIA.** **VFOAT** Syria. (1994)-. English. Two times a year. $125.00. John Wiley & Sons Ltd., Baffins Lane, Chichester, West Sussex PO19 1UD United Kingdom. **Tel** 011 44 1243 779777, FAX 011 44 1243 776128 BTG:JWP001, telex 86290 WIBOOKG. **(Subscription address:** John Wiley & Sons, Inc. / Philadelphia, PO Box 7247, Philadelphia PA 19170. **Tel** (212)850-6645, (800)225-5945.)

ISSN 1073-4082
UK

●**WILEY BUSINESS INTELLIGENCE REPORTS. TAIWAN.** **VFOAT** Taiwan. (1994)-. English. Two times a year. $125.00. John Wiley & Sons Ltd., Baffins Lane, Chichester, West Sussex PO19 1UD United Kingdom. **Tel** 011 44 1243 779777, FAX 011 44 1243 776128 BTG:JWP001, telex 86290 WIBOOKG. **(Subscription address:** John Wiley & Sons, Inc. / Philadelphia, PO Box 7247, Philadelphia PA 19170. **Tel** (212)850-6645, (800)225-5945.)

ISSN 1073-4090
UK

●**WILEY BUSINESS INTELLIGENCE REPORTS. TAJIKISTAN.** **VFOAT** Tajikistan. (1994)-. English. Two times a year. $125.00. John Wiley & Sons Ltd., Baffins Lane, Chichester, West Sussex PO19 1UD United Kingdom. **Tel** 011 44 1243 779777, FAX 011 44 1243 776128 BTG:JWP001, telex 86290 WIBOOKG. **(Subscription address:** John Wiley & Sons, Inc. / Philadelphia, PO Box 7247, Philadelphia PA 19170. **Tel** (212)850-6645, (800)225-5945.)

ISSN 1073-4112
UK

●**WILEY BUSINESS INTELLIGENCE REPORTS. TANZANIA.** **VFOAT** Tanzania. (1994)-. English. Two times a year. $125.00. John Wiley & Sons Ltd., Baffins Lane, Chichester, West Sussex PO19 1UD United Kingdom. **Tel** 011 44 1243 779777, FAX 011 44 1243 776128 BTG:JWP001, telex 86290 WIBOOKG. **(Subscription address:** John Wiley & Sons, Inc. / Philadelphia, PO Box 7247, Philadelphia PA 19170. **Tel** (212)850-6645, (800)225-5945.)

ISSN 1073-4104
UK

●**WILEY BUSINESS INTELLIGENCE REPORTS. THAILAND.** **VFOAT** Thailand. (1994)-. English. Two times a year. $125.00. John Wiley & Sons Ltd., Baffins Lane, Chichester, West Sussex PO19 1UD United Kingdom. **Tel** 011 44 1243 779777, FAX 011 44 1243 776128 BTG:JWP001, telex 86290 WIBOOKG. **(Subscription address:** John Wiley & Sons, Inc. / Philadelphia, PO Box 7247, Philadelphia PA 19170. **Tel** (212)850-6645, (800)225-5945.)

ISSN 1073-4120
UK

●**WILEY BUSINESS INTELLIGENCE REPORTS. TUNISIA.** **VFOAT** Tunisia. (1994)-. English. Two times a year. $125.00. John Wiley & Sons Ltd., Baffins Lane, Chichester, West Sussex PO19 1UD United Kingdom. **Tel** 011 44 1243 779777, FAX 011 44 1243 776128 BTG:JWP001, telex 86290 WIBOOKG. **(Subscription address:** John Wiley & Sons, Inc. / Philadelphia, PO Box 7247, Philadelphia PA 19170. **Tel** (212)850-6645, (800)225-5945.)

ISSN 1073-4139
UK

●**WILEY BUSINESS INTELLIGENCE REPORTS. TURKEY.** **VFOAT** Turkey. (1994)-. English. Two times a year. $125.00. John Wiley & Sons Ltd., Baffins Lane, Chichester, West Sussex PO19 1UD United Kingdom. **Tel** 011 44 1243 779777, FAX 011 44 1243 776128 BTG:JWP001, telex 86290 WIBOOKG. **(Subscription address:** John Wiley & Sons, Inc. / Philadelphia, PO Box 7247, Philadelphia PA 19170. **Tel** (212)850-6645, (800)225-5945.)

ISSN 1073-4155
DD 338　UK

●**WILEY BUSINESS INTELLIGENCE REPORTS. UGANDA.** [Wiley bus. intell. rep., Uganda]. **VFOAT** Uganda. (1994)-. English. Two times a year. $125.00. John Wiley & Sons Ltd., Baffins Lane, Chichester, West Sussex PO19 1UD United Kingdom. **Tel** 011 44 1243 779777, FAX 011 44 1243 776128 BTG:JWP001, telex 86290 WIBOOKG. **Desc:** Provides comprehensive and precise information, hard-to-get statistics, and incisive analysis of world events and markets.

ISSN 1073-4147
DD 338　UK

●**WILEY BUSINESS INTELLIGENCE REPORTS. UNITED ARAB EMIRATES.** [Wiley bus. intell. rep., United Arab Emir.]. **VFOAT** United Arab Emirates. (1994)-. English. Two times a year. $125.00. John Wiley & Sons Ltd., Baffins Lane, Chichester, West Sussex PO19 1UD United Kingdom. **Tel** 011 44 1243 779777, FAX 011 44 1243 776128 BTG:JWP001, telex 86290 WIBOOKG. **Desc:** Provides comprehensive and precise information, hard-to-get statistics, and incisive analysis of world events and markets.

ISSN 1073-418X
DD 338　UK

●**WILEY BUSINESS INTELLIGENCE REPORTS. UNITED KINGDOM.** [Wiley bus. intell. rep., U.K.]. **VFOAT** United Kingdom. (1994)-. English. Two times a year. $125.00. John Wiley & Sons Ltd., Baffins Lane, Chichester, West Sussex PO19 1UD United Kingdom. **Tel** 011 44 1243 779777, FAX 011 44 1243 776128 BTG:JWP001, telex 86290 WIBOOKG. **Desc:** Provides comprehensive and precise information, hard-to-get statistics, and incisive analysis of world events and markets.

ISSN 1073-4171
DD 338　UK

●**WILEY BUSINESS INTELLIGENCE REPORTS. UNITED STATES OF AMERICA.** [Wiley bus. intell. rep., U.S.A.]. **VFOAT** United States of America. (1994)-. English. Two times a year. $125.00. John Wiley & Sons Ltd., Baffins Lane, Chichester, West Sussex PO19 1UD United Kingdom. **Tel** 011 44 1243 779777, FAX 011 44 1243 776128 BTG:JWP001, telex 86290 WIBOOKG. **Desc:** Provides comprehensive and precise information, hard-to-get statistics, and incisive analysis of world events and markets.

ISSN 1073-4163
DD 338　UK

●**WILEY BUSINESS INTELLIGENCE REPORTS. URUGUAY.** [Wiley bus. intell. rep., Urug.]. **VFOAT** Uruguay. (1994)-. English. Two times a year. $125.00. John Wiley & Sons Ltd., Baffins Lane, Chichester, West Sussex PO19 1UD United Kingdom. **Tel** 011 44 1243 779777, FAX 011 44 1243 776128 BTG:JWP001, telex 86290 WIBOOKG. **Desc:** Provides comprehensive and precise information, hard-to-get statistics, and incisive analysis of world events and markets.

ISSN 1073-4198
DD 338　UK

●**WILEY BUSINESS INTELLIGENCE REPORTS. UZBEKISTAN.** [Wiley bus. intell. rep., Uzbek.]. **VFOAT** Uzbekistan. (1994)-. English. Two times a year. $125.00. John Wiley & Sons Ltd., Baffins Lane, Chichester, West Sussex PO19 1UD United Kingdom. **Tel** 011 44 1243 779777, FAX 011 44 1243 776128 BTG:JWP001, telex 86290 WIBOOKG. **Desc:** Provides comprehensive and precise information, hard-to-get statistics, and incisive analysis of world events and markets.

ISSN 1073-4201
DD 338　UK

●**WILEY BUSINESS INTELLIGENCE REPORTS. VENEZUELA.** [Wiley bus. intell. rep., Venez.]. **VFOAT** Venezuela. (1994)-. English. Two times a year. $125.00. John Wiley & Sons Ltd., Baffins Lane, Chichester, West Sussex PO19 1UD United Kingdom. **Tel** 011 44 1243 779777, FAX 011 44 1243 776128 BTG:JWP001, telex 86290 WIBOOKG. **Desc:** Provides comprehensive and precise information, hard-to-get statistics, and incisive analysis of world events and markets.

ISSN 1073-421X
DD 338　UK

●**WILEY BUSINESS INTELLIGENCE REPORTS. ZAIRE.** [Wiley bus. intell. rep., Zaire]. **VFOAT** Zaire. (1994)-. English. Two times a year. $125.00. John Wiley & Sons Ltd., Baffins Lane, Chichester, West Sussex PO19 1UD United Kingdom. **Tel** 011 44 1243 779777, FAX 011 44 1243 776128 BTG:JWP001, telex 86290 WIBOOKG. **Desc:** Provides comprehensive and precise information, hard-to-get statistics, and incisive analysis of world events and markets.

ISSN 1073-4228
DD 338　UK

●**WILEY BUSINESS INTELLIGENCE REPORTS. ZAMBIA.** [Wiley bus. intell. rep., Zamb.]. **VFOAT** Zambia. (1994)-. English. Two times a year. $125.00. John Wiley & Sons Ltd., Baffins Lane, Chichester, West Sussex PO19 1UD United Kingdom. **Tel** 011 44 1243 779777, FAX 011 44 1243 776128 BTG:JWP001, telex 86290 WIBOOKG. **Desc:** Provides comprehensive and precise information, hard-to-get statistics, and incisive analysis of world events and markets.

ISSN 0890-2674
US

WILHELM REPORT, THE. (19??)-. Periodical. English. Four times a year. $95.00. Wilhelm Report, PO Box 55902, Birmingham AL 35255. **Tel** (205)991-1501.

LC HF5001 .W53　　ISSN 0160-5232
DD 330.9/73/092　　US

WILLIAM AND MARY BUSINESS REVIEW. [William Mary bus. rev.]. **VFOAT** William & Mary Business Review. Vol. 1 (1975)-. Periodical. English. Congressional Education Associates, 302 East Capital Street NE, Washington DC 20002.

Business and Economics

LC Z7164.C81
DD 650
ISSN 1057-6533
US
WILSON BUSINESS ABSTRACTS. See Business and Economics-Abstracting, Bibliographies and Statistics.

US
WIRELESS BUSINESS & FINANCE. See Communications-Telecommunication.

LC HC281
DD 330
ISSN 0508-8550
GW
WIRTSCHAFT, DIE. 1.- Yearly volume; April 1946-. Periodical. German. Irregular. Osterreich Wirtschaftsverlag, Nikolsdorfergasse 7-11, A-1501 Vienna Austria. **Tel** 0222/55-55-85.
Ind/Abst Saf. Health Work.

GW
WIRTSCHAFT UDSSR INTERN. (19??)-. German. Twelve times a year. DM600.00. Institut Ost Marktforschung, Postfach 760602, W2000 Hamburg 76 Germany.

LC HC287.B3 W57
DD 330.943/3/021
GW
WIRTSCHAFTSRUCKBLICK IN ZAHLEN / BAYERISCHES STAATSMINISTERIUM FUER WIRTSCHAFT UND VERKEHR. **Added/Corp** Bavaria (Germany). Staatsministerium fur Wirtschaft und Verkehr. German.

LC HC
DD 330
GW
WIRTSCHAFTSWISSENSCHAFTLICHE UND WIRTSCHAFTSRECHTLICHE UNTERSUCHUNGEN. (1962)-. Monographic series. German. Irregular. Price varies per volume. JCB Mohr / Paul Siebeck, Postfach 2040, D-72010 Tuebingen Germany. **Tel** 011 49 7071 9230, **FAX** 011 49 7071 51104, telex 7/262872 mohr d.

ISSN 0067-5938
DD 330 380
GW
WIRTSCHAFTSWISSENSCHAFTLICHE VEROFFENTLICHUNGEN. **Main/Corp** Berlin. Freie Universitat. Osteuropa-Institut. (1954)-. Monographic series. German. One time a year. Price varies per volume. Duncker und Humblot Verlag, Postfach 410329, D-12113 Berlin Germany. **Tel** 011 49 30 79000612, 011 49 30 79000613.

ISSN 0508-9921
US
WISCONSIN BUSINESS WOMAN, THE. **Added/Corp** Wisconsin Federation of Business and Professional Women's Clubs. (Oct. 1928)-. Periodical. English. Four times a year. $3.00. Wisconsin Federation of Business and Professional Women's Club, 4512 Grandview Road, Larsen WI 54947. **Tel** (414)836-3112.

LC HC
DD 330
ISSN 0435-7523
GW
WISSENSCHAFTLICHE SCHRIFTENREIHE. **Main/Corp** Germany (Federal Republic, 1949-). Bundesministerium fur Wirtschaftliche Zusammenarbeit. Vol. 1 (1965)-. Monographic series. German. Irregular. Price varies per volume. Bouvier GmbH & Co. KG ABT Verlag, Am HOF 28, D-53113 Bonn Germany. **Tel** 011 49 228 7290141, **FAX** 011 49 228 7290179.

ISSN 0067-5954
GW
WISSENSCHAFTLICHE ZEITSCHRIFT DER HOCHSCHULE FUER OEKONOMIE. **Main/Corp** Berlin. Hochschule fuer Oekonomie. (1956)-. Periodical. German (summaries and/or abstracts in English and Russian). Four times a year. LKG Leipziger Kommissions & Grossbuchhandel, Postfach 520, D-04005 Leipzig Germany. **Tel** 011 49 341 71370.

ISSN 0340-1650
GW
UDC 658
WIST. WIRTSCHAFTSWISSENSCHAFTLICHES STUDIUM. (1972)-. Periodical. German. Twelve times a year. DM172.00. CH Beck Verlagsbuchhandlung, D-80791 Munich Germany. **Tel** 011 49 89 381891. **ED** Mannheim Dichtl and Wurzburg Norbert.
Desc: Contains scientific articles which have not been published thus far. It contains explanations on economic laws and theories, current economical keywords, latest news on data processing, studies and job conditions.
Ind/Abst PAIS Int. Print.

LC HF5500.2 .W65
DD 331.4/8165/00973
ISSN 0043-7441
US
WOMEN IN BUSINESS (KANSAS CITY, MO.). (WOMEN IN BUSINESS.). [Women bus.]. **Added/Corp** American Business Women's Association. (1949)-. Periodical. English. Six times a year (Jan., Mar., May, July, Sept., Nov.). $16.00. American Business Women's Association, 9100 Ward Parkway, PO Box 8728, Kansas City MO 64114-0728. **Tel** (816)361-6621. **ED** Wendy S. Myers. **Bk Rev,** (Qty: 6). **Ad Acc, Adv Mgr:** Lynn Weddle-Judkins. **Circ:** 90,000 (ctrl). Documents available from UMI Article Clearinghouse.
Desc: Articles on business trends, small-business ownership, self-improvement and retirement issues. Development for women in all levels of business and should reflect a how-to-format with bulleted information that makes it easy to take action.
Ind/Abst Acad. Abstr. Full Text Elite; Acad. Abstr.; Acad. Search; Bus. Index (1985-); Bus. Source Plus; Bus. Source; EP Collect.; Gen. BusinessFile (1985-); Gen. Period. Index (1985-); Homework Help.; INFO-SOUTH Abstr.; Mag. Artic. Summar. Elite; Mag. Artic. Summar. Select; Mag. Artic. Summar. CD-ROM; Mag. Search; MasterFile FullTEXT 1000; MasterFile FullTEXT 350; MasterFile FullTEXT 650; MasterFile FullTEXT (July 1990-) [Full Txt.]; Newsp. Period. Abstr. (1992-); OCLC; Pub. Lib. FullTEXT; Telebase; Vocat. Search.

ISSN 1063-6595
DD 338
US
WORCESTER BUSINESS JOURNAL. [Worcester bus. j.]. (1990)-. Periodical. English. Twenty-six times a year. $30.00. Worcester Business Journal, 172 Shrewsbury Street, Worcester MA 01604. **Tel** (508)755-8004. **ED** Steve Jones-D'Agostino. **Ad Acc, Adv Mgr:** Donna Rickoff. **Circ:** 15,000 (ctrl).

ISSN 0736-9166
US
WORK TIMES. [Work times]. **Added/Corp** New Ways to Work (Firm). Vol. 1, No. 1 (Summer 1982)-. Periodical. English. Four times a year. $75.00 (institutions), $35.00 (individuals). New Ways to Work, 149 9th Street, San Francisco CA 94103-2016. **Tel** (415)995-9860, **FAX** (415)995-9867. **ED** Barney Olmsted and Darcy Fink. **Bk Rev. Circ:** 500.
Desc: Conducts research and provides information on work time options and other workplace issues.

LC HC
DD 330
ISSN 1011-4971
SZ
WORKING PAPER / MULTINATIONAL ENTERPRISES PROGRAMME. **Added/Corp** Multinational Enterprises Programme. No. 1 (1979)-. Monographic series. English. Irregular. $12.00 (£7.20) per paper. International Labour Office - ILO, Publications Sales Service, CH-1211 Geneva 22 Switzerland. **Tel** 011 41 22 7996111, **FAX** 011 41 22 7986253, telex 415 647 ilo ch.
Ind/Abst Geogr. Abstr. Human Geogr.

ISSN 0714-7228
DD 380.1
CN
WORKING PAPER SERIES - DEPARTMENT OF BUSINESS, SCHOOL OF BUSINESS AND ECONOMICS, WILFRID LAURIER UNIVERSITY. (WORKING PAPER SERIES.). [Work. pap. ser. - Dep. Bus., Sch. Bus. Econ., Wilfrid Laurier Univ.]. **Added/Corp** Wilfrid Laurier University. Dept. of Business. Wilfrid Laurier University. School of Business and Economics. **VFOAT** Research Paper Series. No. 3582 (1982)-. Monographic series. English. Irregular. Price varies per volume. Wilfrid Laurier University School of Business & Economics, 75 University Avenue, Waterloo Ontario N2L 3C5 Canada. ctrl circ. **Continues** Research Paper Series (Wilfrid Laurier University. Dept. of Business), 0229-9607.

US
WORKING PAPERS. (19??)-. English. Twelve times a year. $200.00. International Monetary Fund, 700 19th Street Northwest, Publishing Unit, Washington DC 20431. **Tel** (202)623-7430, **FAX** (202)623-7201.

LC HD72 .W66
DD 338.9/005
FR
WORKING PAPERS / ECONOMICS DEPARTMENT, OECD. **Added/Corp** Organisation for Economic Co-Operation and Development. Economics Dept. **VFOAT** Working Papers; Economics Department Workings Papers. No. 108 (1992)-. Monographic series. English. Irregular. Price varies per volume. OECD Publications and Information Center, 2 rue Andre-Pascal, 75775 Paris Cedex 16 France. **Tel** 011 33 1 49104262, US/(202)785-6323, FAX 011 33 1 45248500, 011 33 1 45248176, telex 620 160 OCDE. (**Subscription address:** OECD Publications Center, 2001 L Street, Suite 700, Washington DC 20036. **Tel** (202)822-3873, (202)785-6323.) **Continues** Working Papers (Organisation for Economic Co-Operation and Development. Dept. of Economics and Statistics).

ISSN 0112-8191
NZ
DD 330
WORKING PAPERS IN ECONOMICS HAMILTON. [Work. pap. econ. Hamilt.]. (1985)-. Monographic series. English. Irregular.
Ind/Abst World Agric. Econ. Rural Sociol. Abstr.

LC HC
DD 330
US
WORKING PAPERS / ROCHESTER CENTER FOR ECONOMIC RESEARCH. (19??)-. English. $50.00. Rochester Center for Economic Research, University of Rochester, Rochester NY 14627. **Tel** (716)275-8396.
Ind/Abst Curr. Cit.

LC HC
DD 330
US
WORKING PAPERS / RODNEY L. WHITE CENTER FOR FINANCIAL RESEARCH. (19??)-. English. Irregular (approximately 40 times per year). $395.00. University of Pennsylvania / Wharton Account, 3254 Steinberg Dietrich Hall, Philadelphia PA 19104. **Tel** (215)898-7616.

US
WORKSHOP PROCEEDINGS OF THE PACIFIC ASIAN CONSORTIUM FOR INTERNATIONAL BUSINESS EDUCATION AND RESEARCH (PACIBER). (1992)-. Proceedings. English. One time a year. $10.00 per issue. Pacific Asian Consortium for International Business Education and Research, College of Business Administration, University of Hawaii at Manoa, 2404 Maile Way C202, Honolulu HI 96822.

ISSN 0259-210X
US
WORLD BANK DISCUSSION PAPERS. [World Bank discuss. pap.]. **Added/Corp** International Bank for Reconstruction and Development. (1986)-. Monographic series. English. Irregular. Price varies per volume. World Bank Publications, 1818 H Street Northwest, Washington DC 20043. **Tel** (202)473-1155, (202)473-1155, **FAX** (202)522-3224, telex WUI 64145 WORLDBANK.
Ind/Abst Curr. Cit.; For. Abstr.; Geogr. Abstr. Human Geogr.; Int. Dev. Abstr.; Nutr. Abstr. Rev., Ser. A, Hum. Exp.; World Agric. Econ. Rural Sociol. Abstr.

LC HD28 .W63
DD 650/.05
ISSN 1061-9917
US
WORLD BUSINESS ACADEMY PERSPECTIVES. [World Bus. Acad. perspect.]. **Added/Corp** World Business Academy. **VFOAT** Perspectives. (1987)-. Periodical. English. Four times a year (Feb., May, Aug., Nov.). $96.00. Berrett-Koehler Publishers, 155 Montgomery Street, San Francisco CA 94104-4109. **Tel** (415)288-0260, **FAX** (415)362-2512. **ED** Alis Valen, (editor's address: 6433 Westover Drive, Oakland, CA 94611, phone: (510)530-4000). **Circ:** 750. **Continues** WBA Perspectives.

LC HF5001 .W67
DD 650
ISSN 1351-4725
UK
●**WORLD BUSINESS & ECONOMIC REVIEW.** **Added/Corp** Walden Publishing. Kogan Page (Firm) World of Information (Firm). **VFOAT** World Business and Economic Review. (1994)-. English. One time a year. $240.00. Kogan Page Ltd., 120 Pentonville Road, London N1 9BR United Kingdom. **Tel** 011 44 171 2780433, **FAX** 011 44 171 8376348, telex 263088 KOGAN G. (**Subscription address:** Kogan Page / North America Subscriptions, PO Box 830430, Birmingham AL 35283-0430. **Tel** (800)633-4931, **FAX** (205)995-1588.) **Continues** World Economic & Business Review, 0957-8099.

LC HF5001
DD 650
ISSN 0731-003X
US
WORLD BUSINESS DIGEST. [World bus. dig.]. **Added/Corp** Alexander Hamilton Institute (U.S.). (198?)-. Periodical. English. Twelve times a year. Alexander Hamilton Institute, 70 Hilltop Road, Ramsey NJ 07446-1119. **Tel** (201)825-8161, (800)879-2441, FAX (201)825-8696.

LC HF5001
DD 650/.05
ISSN 1182-0993
CN
WORLD BUSINESS (OTTAWA). (WORLD BUSINESS.). [World bus.]. (May 1, 1990)-. Periodical. English. Twelve times a year. 40.00Can$ Canada; 50.00Can$ US; 60.00Can$ other. World Business, 14 - 5480 Canotek Road, Suite 14, Ottawa Ontario K1J 9H6 Canada. **Tel** (613)747-2732, **FAX** (613)747-2735. **ED** Douglas MacArthur. **Ad Acc, Adv Mgr:** Tom Eyres. **Circ:** 5,000.
Desc: This magazine deals with Canada's international trade and investment activities.

ISSN 1081-3284
US
DD 330
WORLD BUSINESS REVIEW (BALTIMORE, MD.). (WORLD BUSINESS REVIEW.). [World bus. rev.]. (1991)-. Periodical. English.

Business and Economics

Six times a year. $20.95. World Business Research Center, PO Box 11437, Baltimore MD 21239. **Tel** (410)685-5104.

UK

WORLD COMMODITY FORECASTS. INDUSTRIAL RAW MATERIALS. (199?)-. Trade Publication. English. Six times a year. $416.25 (schools and educational libraries), $555.00 (other) North America. The Economist Intelligence Unit, 40 Duke Street, London W1A 1DW United Kingdom. **Tel** 011 44 171 8301000. *Separated from* World Commodity Forecasts, 0267-6303.

LC HF1051 .W68
DD 333.7
ISSN 1351-8976
UK

●**WORLD COMMODITY FORECASTS. INDUSTRIAL RAW MATERIALS.** **Added/Corp** Economist Intelligence Unit (Great Britain). **VFOAT** Industrial Raw Materials; WCF: Industrial Raw Materials. (June 1993)-. Periodical. English. Six times a year. $575.00. The Economist Intelligence Unit, 40 Duke Street, London W1A 1DW United Kingdom. **Tel** 011 44 171 8301000. **(Subscription address:** Economist Intelligence Unit / North America Subscriptions, 111 West 57th Street, New York NY 10019. **Tel** 800 938-4685, (212)554-0600, FAX (212)586-1181, (212)586-1182.**)** *Continues in part* World Commodity Forecasts, 0267-6303.

ISSN 0966-467X
UK

WORLD COMMODITY REPORT. [World commod. rep.]. **VFOAT** WCR. (19??)-. Newspaper. English. Twenty-four times a year. $925.00. UK Publications, 10 Little College Street, London SW1P 3SH United Kingdom. **Tel** 011 44 171 9767772, FAX 011 44 171 9760775.

LC HC10 .W7975
DD 330.9/005
US
TITLE CHANGE

WORLD ECONOMIC AND BUSINESS REVIEW. (19??)-(19??). English. Kogan Page Ltd., 120 Pentonville Road, London N1 9BR United Kingdom. **Tel** 011 44 171 2780433, FAX 011 44 171 8376348, telex 263088 KOGAN G. *Continued by* World Economic & Business Review.

LC HC10 .W7978
DD 310
ISSN 0891-4125
US

WORLD ECONOMIC DATA. [World econ. data]. (1987)-. English. Irregular. $35.00. ABC Clio Inc, PO Box 1911, 130 Cremona, Santa Barbara CA 93116. **Tel** (805)968-1911, (800)422-2546, FAX (805)685-9685.

HK

WORLD EXECUTIVES DIGEST. (19??)-. English. Twelve times a year. $45.00 Asia; $60.00 other. World Executives Digest, 3 F Garden Square Building, Greenbelt Drive, Makati Manila Philippines. **Tel** 011 63 2 8173191.

LC HF5410 .W67
DD 380
ISSN 1078-6783
US

●**WORLD MARKET SHARE REPORTER.** [World mark. share rep.]. **Added/Corp** Gale Research Inc. **VFOAT** A.WMSR. (1995/1996)-. Periodical. English. Every 2 years. $295.00. Gale Research Inc., 835 Penobscot Building, 645 Griswold Street, Detroit MI 48226. **Tel** (800)877-GALE, (313)961-2242, FAX (313)961-6083, (800)414-5043, telex TWX 810-221-7086.

HK

WORLD MONEY ANALYST. (19??)-. English. Ten times a year. $189.00. WMA Publishing Co. Ltd., 45 Lyndhurst Ter, 5th Floor Center, Hong Kong Hong Kong. **Tel** 011 852 25416110, FAX 011 852 5411124.

UK

WORLD NEWS. (19??)-. English. Twenty-four times a year. £199.00. World News, PO Box 600, Oxford OX2 6FT United Kingdom. **Tel** 011 44 1865 511738, FAX 011 44 1865 310730. **ED** David Jefferibs. Index available (published separately). **Bk Rev**, (Qty: varies). **Ad Acc, Adv Mgr:** M. Mathews. **Circ:** 150,000 (ctrl). *Continues* World Countertrade and Barter News. **Desc:** Joint ventures, offset and technology transfer.

ISSN 0824-5533
CN

WORLD OIL MARKET ANALYSIS. See Petroleum and Natural Gas.

LC HF5601 .W65
DD 658
ISSN 0512-2295
US
TITLE CHANGE

WORLD (PEAT, MARWICK, MITCHELL & CO.). (WORLD.). [World]. **Added/Corp** Peat, Marwick, Mitchell & Co. Vol. 1 (Autumn 1967)-(1994). Periodical. English. Peat, Marwick, Mitchell & Company / New York, 345 Park Avenue, New York NY 10154. **Tel** (212)758-9700. Documents available from Ask*IEEE. *Absorbed* Management Focus, 0193-8266. *Continued by* Worldbusiness, 1081-5724. **Ind/Abst** Acad. Search; Account. Tax Datab. (1974-19??); Bus. Source Plus; Bus. Source; EP Collect.;

Homework Help.; INFO-SOUTH Abstr.; INSPEC (July-Aug. 1985-19??); Mag. Search; MasterFile FullTEXT 1000; MasterFile FullTEXT 350; MasterFile FullTEXT 650; MasterFile FullTEXT (July 1993-); OCLC; Telebase.

ISSN 0730-1537
US
SUSPENDED

WORLD PRODUCTIVITY NEWS. [World prod. news]. Vol. 1, No. 1 (Jan. 4, 1982)-. Periodical. English. Twenty-four times a year. Technical Insights Inc., PO Box 1304, Fort Lee NJ 07024-9967. **Tel** (201)568-4744, FAX (201)568-4722, telex 425900 SWIFT UI.

ISSN 0896-0615
DD 363
US
CODEN WOWAEE

WORLD WATCH (WASHINGTON, D.C.). (WORLD WATCH.). [World watch]. **Added/Corp** Worldwatch Institute. **VFOAT** Worldwatch. Vol. 1, No. 1 (Jan./Feb. 1988)-. Periodical. English. Six times a year. $15.00. Worldwatch Institute, 1776 Massachusetts Avenue Northwest, Washington DC 20036-1904. **Tel** (202)452-1999, (800)825-0061. **(Subscription address:** Small Publishing Fulfillment Service, 202 Twin Oaks Drive, Syracuse NY 13206. **Tel** 800 825-0061, (315)437-5972.**)** Documents available from The Genuine Article, UMI Article Clearinghouse, Documents on Demand. **Ind/Abst** Acad. Search; BioBusiness (1990-); Environ. Abstr.; Environ. Period. Bibliogr.; EP Collect.; Expand. Acad. Index (1992-); Gen. Sci. Index (1992-); Gen. Sci. Source; Geogr. Abstr. Human Geogr.; Homework Help.; INFO-SOUTH Abstr.; Int. Dev. Abstr.; Mag. Search; MasterFile FullTEXT 1000; MasterFile FullTEXT 350; MasterFile FullTEXT 650; MasterFile FullTEXT (July 1993-); Newsp. Period. Abstr. (1992-); OCLC; PAIS Int. Print; Res. Alert [Select. Cov.]; Soc. Sci. Index [Select. Cov.]; Telebase.

UK

WORLD'S NEW PRODUCTS. (19??)-. Trade Publication. English. £254.00 UK; $445.00 other. World Business Publications Ltd., 960 High Road, Britannia 4th Floor, London N12 9RY United Kingdom. **Tel** 011 44 181 4465141, FAX 011 44 181 4463659, telex 9419208.

US

WORLDWIDE BRANCH LOCATIONS OF MULTINATIONAL COMPANIES. 1st Edition (1993)-. Directory. English. $200.00. Gale Research Inc., 835 Penobscot Building, 645 Griswold Street, Detroit MI 48226. **Tel** (800)877-GALE, (313)961-2242, FAX (313)961-6083, (800)414-5043, telex TWX 810-221-7086. **ED** David S. Hoopes. available on magnetic tape; available on diskette. **Desc:** Guide to 26,000 plants, branches, sales offices and subsidiaries around the world.

LC HD
DD 338
ISSN 1069-4447
US

●**WORLDWIDE BUSINESS PRACTICES REPORT.** [Worldw. bus. pract. rep.]. **Added/Corp** International Cultural Enterprises Inc. Vol. 1, No. 1 (Sept. 1993)-. Periodical. English. Twelve times a year. $195.00. International Cultural Enterprises Inc., 1241 Dartmouth Lane, Deerfield IL 60015. **Tel** (800)626-2772, FAX (708)945-9614. **ED** Yuri Kovalenko. Index available. cum. index. **Bk Rev**. available via Internet. **Desc:** Covers international business.

ISSN 0192-5512
DD 338
US

●**WORLDWIDE PROJECTS. See** Engineering.

ISSN 0821-1248
DD 331/.0971
CN

WRF COMMENT. [WRF comment]. **Added/Corp** Work Research Foundation. **VAT** Work Research Foundation Comment. Vol. 1, No. 1 (Jan. 1983)-. Periodical. English. Four times a year. Free. Work Research Foundation, PO Box 78, Weston Ontario M9N 3M6 Canada. **Tel** (416)744-2144. **ED** Harry Antonides. **Bk Rev**. 500 (ctrl). **Desc:** A newsletter reporting on trends and developments in economics and industrial relations from a christian perspective.

ISSN 0886-1447
DD 333
US

WRI PAPER. [WRI pap.]. **Added/Corp** World Resources Institute. **VFOAT** WRI Papers. **VAT** World Resources Institute Paper. No. 1 (1985)-. Monographic series. English. WRI Publications, PO Box 4852, Baltimore MD 21211. **Tel** (800)822-0504.

LC WMLC L 83/6746
GW

WURZBURG HEUTE : ZEITSCHRIFT FUER KULTUR UND WIRTSCHAFT. **Added/Corp** Universitatsbund Wurzburg. 1970-. Periodical. German. Two times a year. *Continues* Wurzburg.

LC HC107.W9 W947
DD 330
ISSN 0512-4611
US

WYOMING TRADE WINDS. Added/Corp Wyoming. University. Division of Business and Economic Reseach. (1955)-. Periodical. English. Four times a year. College of Commerce and Industry, University of Wyoming, Laramie WY 82070.

LC HC
DD 330
ISSN 0439-8017
CH
CEASED

XUESHU JIKAN. (HSUEH SHU CHI KAN.). [Xueshu jikan]. **VFOAT** Academic Review Quarterly. (1952)-(19??). Periodical. Chinese. **Ind/Abst** Am. Hist. Life (1955-1956).

LC HJ4965.5.J3 S44d
JA

YAKUIN NO HOSHU SHOYO NENSHU. See Finance-Taxation.

LC HD4946.5.J3 S44c
DD 331.2813
JA

YAKUIN NO HOSHU SHOYO TO KIMEKATA. Main/Corp Seikei Kenkyujo. (19??)-. Japanese. Seikei Kenkyu, 1-4 Nihonbashi Honcho, Chuo-ku Tokyo 103 Japan. *Continues* Yakuin no Hoshu Shoyo Chosa Hokokokusho.

JA

YASASHII BUSINESS EIGO. English. Twelve times a year. $77.00. **(Subscription address:** Kinokuniya Company Ltd., 38-1 Sakuragaoka 5, chome Setagaya-ku, Tokyo 156 Japan. **Tel** FAX 011 03 3439 0136.**)**

LC HB221
DD 338.52
KU

YEARLY BULLETIN OF PRICE STATISTICS. WHOLESALE. Added/Corp Kuwait. Idarah al-Markaziyah lil-Ihsa. (1981)-. Bulletin. English. Central Statistical Office / Kuwait, Box 26188, Kuwait 13122 Kuwait. **Tel** 011 965 5628231, 011 965 2428200. *Continues in part* Kuwait. Idarah al-Markaziyah lil-Ihsa. Yearly Bulletin of Price Statistics.

ISSN 1067-8115
US

●**YEMEN (SYRACUSE, N.Y.).** (YEMEN : AN EXECUTIVE REPORT.). **Added/Corp** Political Risk Services (IBC USA (Publications) Inc.) **VFOAT** Executive Report. (1993)-. English. $110.00. Political Risk Services, 6320 Fly Road, Suite 102, PO Box 248, East Syracuse NY 13057-0248. **Tel** (315)431-0511, FAX (315)431-0200. **Desc:** Focuses on the long-term outlook for business. Includes a brief review of recent events and current circumstances, background intelligence including geography, history, economics and social conditions, as well as the key political and economic forecasts.

LC HC
ISSN 0049-836X
II

YOUNG ALLIANCE. Vol. 3, No. 1 (Jan. 1971)-. Periodical. English. available on microfilm from University Microfilms International (UMI).

LC HC
DD 330
ISSN 1047-8582
US

YOUNGSTOWN/WARREN BUSINESS JOURNAL. VFOAT Y/WBJ; Youngstown, Warren Business Journal. (1986)-. Periodical. English. Twenty-four times a year. $18.00. Youngstown Publications, 57 South Champion Street, PO Box 714, Youngstown OH 44501. available on microfilm and microfiche from University Microfilms International (UMI). *Continues* Youngstown Business Journal.

ISSN 0832-1647
DD 380.1/09713/82
CN

YOUR BUSINESS (SMITHS FALLS). (YOUR BUSINESS.). [Your bus.]. Vol. 1, No. 1 (Nov./Dec. 1984)-. Periodical. English. Irregular. Free. Your Business, PO Box 158, Smiths Falls Ontario K7A 4T1 Canada.

ISSN 1198-046X
CN

●**YOUR GUIDE TO GOVERNMENT FINANCIAL ASSISTANCE FOR BUSINESS IN ALBERTA. VFOAT** Your Guide to Government Financial Assistance for Business; Government Financial Assistance for Business. (1993)-. English. One time a year. $39.95. Productive Publications, PO Box 7200, Station A, Toronto Ontario M5W 1X8 Canada. **Tel** (416)483-0634. *Continues in part* Your Guide to Financial Assistance for Business in Western Canada, 1191-050X. **Desc:** Provides details of every government business assistance program in the province of Alberta.

ISSN 1198-0478
DD 658.15
CN

●**YOUR GUIDE TO GOVERNMENT FINANCIAL ASSISTANCE FOR BUSINESS IN BRITISH COLUMBIA.** [Your guide gov. financ. assist. bus. B.C.]. **VFOAT** Your Guide

to Government Financial Assistance for Business; Government Financial Assistance for Business. (1993)-. English. One time a year. $39.95. Productive Publications, PO Box 7200, Station A, Toronto Ontario M5W 1X8 Canada. **Tel** (416)483-0634. ***Continues in part*** *Williamson, Iain. Your Guide to Financial Assistance for Business in Western Canada., 1191-050X.*
Desc: Provides details of every government business assistance program in the province of British Columbia.

ISSN 1198-0486
CN

●**YOUR GUIDE TO GOVERNMENT FINANCIAL ASSISTANCE FOR BUSINESS IN MANITOBA. VFOAT** Your Guide to Government Financial Assistance for Business; Government Financial Assistance for Business. (1993)-. English. One time a year. $39.95. Productive Publications, PO Box 7200, Station A, Toronto Ontario M5W 1X8 Canada. **Tel** (416)483-0634. ***Continues in part*** *Your Guide to Financial Assistance for Business in Western Canada, 1191-050X.*
Desc: Provides details of every government business assistance program in the province of Manitoba.

ISSN 1198-0494
DD 354.710082/048045/097151 CN

●**YOUR GUIDE TO GOVERNMENT FINANCIAL ASSISTANCE FOR BUSINESS IN NEW BRUNSWICK.** [Your guide gov. financ. assist. bus. N.B.]. **VFOAT** Your Guide to Government Financial Assistance for Business; Government Financial Assistance for Business. (1993)-. English. One time a year. $39.95. Productive Publications, PO Box 7200, Station A, Toronto Ontario M5W 1X8 Canada. **Tel** (416)483-0634. ***Continues in part*** *Williamson, Iain. Your Guide to Financial Assistance for Business in Atlantic Canada., 1191-0356.*
Desc: Provides details of every government business assistance program in the province of New Brunswick.

LC HG4001 **ISSN** 1198-0508
DD 658.15 CN

●**YOUR GUIDE TO GOVERNMENT FINANCIAL ASSISTANCE FOR BUSINESS IN NEWFOUNDLAND & LABRADOR. VFOAT** Your Guide to Government Financial Assistance for Business; Government Financial Assistance for Business. (1993)-. English. One time a year. $39.95. Productive Publications, PO Box 7200, Station A, Toronto Ontario M5W 1X8 Canada. **Tel** (416)483-0634. ***Continues in part*** *Your Guide to Financial Assistance for Business in Atlantic Canada, 1191-0356.*
Desc: Provides details of every government business assistance program for the province.

LC HG4001 **ISSN** 1198-0516
DD 658.15 CN

●**YOUR GUIDE TO GOVERNMENT FINANCIAL ASSISTANCE FOR BUSINESS IN NOVA SCOTIA. VFOAT** Your Guide to Government Financial Assistance for Business; Government Financial Assistance for Business. (1993)-. English. One time a year. $39.95. Productive Publications, PO Box 7200, Station A, Toronto Ontario M5W 1X8 Canada. **Tel** (416)483-0634. ***Continues*** *Your Guide to Financial Assistance for Business in Atlantic Canada, 1191-0356.*
Desc: Provides details of every government business assistance program in the province of Nova Scotia.

LC HG4001 **ISSN** 1198-0524
DD 658.15 CN

●**YOUR GUIDE TO GOVERNMENT FINANCIAL ASSISTANCE FOR BUSINESS IN ONTARIO. VFOAT** Your Guide to Government Financial Assistance for Business; Government Financial Assistance for Business. (1993)-. English. One time a year. $39.95. Productive Publications, PO Box 7200, Station A, Toronto Ontario M5W 1X8 Canada. **Tel** (416)483-0634. ***Continues*** *Your Guide to Financial Assistance for Business in Ontario, 1191-0348.*
Desc: Provides details of every government business assistance program in the province of Ontario.

ISSN 1198-0532
DD 354.710082/048045/09717 CN

●**YOUR GUIDE TO GOVERNMENT FINANCIAL ASSISTANCE FOR BUSINESS IN PRINCE EDWARD ISLAND.** (YOUR GUIDE TO GOVERNMENT FINANCIAL ASSISTANCE FOR BUSINESS IN PRINCE EDWARD ISLAND.). [Your guide gov. financ. assist. bus. P.E.I.]. **VFOAT** Your Guide to Government Financial Assistance for Business; Government Financial Assistance for Business. (1993)-. English. One time a year. $39.95. Productive Publications, PO Box 7200, Station A, Toronto Ontario M5W 1X8 Canada. **Tel** (416)483-0634. ***Continues in part*** *Williamson, Iain. Your Guide to Financial Assistance for Business in Atlantic Canada., 1191-0356.*
Desc: Provides details of every government business assistance program in the province.

ISSN 1198-0540
DD 354.71032048/045/09714 CN

●**YOUR GUIDE TO GOVERNMENT FINANCIAL ASSISTANCE FOR BUSINESS IN QUEBEC.** [Your guide gov. financ. assist. bus. Que.]. **VFOAT** Your Guide to Government Financial Assistance for Business; Government Financial Assistance for Business. (1993)-. Government Publication. English. One time a year. $39.95. Productive Publications, PO Box 7200, Station A, Toronto Ontario M5W 1X8 Canada. **Tel** (416)483-0634. ***Continues*** *Your Guide to Financial Assistance for Business in Quebec, 1191-0526.*
Desc: Provides details of every government business assistance program in the province of Quebec.

ISSN 1198-0559
DD 658.15 CN

●**YOUR GUIDE TO GOVERNMENT FINANCIAL ASSISTANCE FOR BUSINESS IN SASKATCHEWAN.** [Your guide gov. financ. assist. bus. Sask.]. **VFOAT** Your Guide to Government Financial Assistance for Business; Government Financial Assistance for Business. (1993)-. English. One time a year. $39.95. Productive Publications, PO Box 7200, Station A, Toronto Ontario M5W 1X8 Canada. **Tel** (416)483-0634. ***Continues in part*** *Your Guide to Financial Assistance for Business in Western Canada, 1191-050X.*
Desc: Provides details of every government business assistance program in the province of Saskatchewan.

ISSN 1198-0567
DD 658.15 CN

●**YOUR GUIDE TO GOVERNMENT FINANCIAL ASSISTANCE FOR BUSINESS IN THE NORTHWEST TERRITORIES.** [Your guide gov. financ. assist. bus. N.W.T.]. **VFOAT** Your Guide to Government Financial Assistance for Business; Government Financial Assistance for Business. (1993)-. English. One time a year. $39.95. Productive Publications, PO Box 7200, Station A, Toronto Ontario M5W 1X8 Canada. **Tel** (416)483-0634. ***Continues in part*** *Williamson, Iain. Your Guide to Financial Assistance for Business in Western Canada., 1191-050X.*
Desc: Provides details of every government business assistance program in the territory.

LC HG4001 **ISSN** 1198-0575
DD 658.15 CN

●**YOUR GUIDE TO GOVERNMENT FINANCIAL ASSISTANCE FOR BUSINESS IN THE YUKON.** [Your guide gov. financ. assist. bus. Yukon]. **VFOAT** Your Guide to Government Financial Assistance for Business; Government Financial Assistance for Business. (1993)-. English. One time a year. $39.95. Productive Publications, PO Box 7200, Station A, Toronto Ontario M5W 1X8 Canada. **Tel** (416)483-0634. ***Continues in part*** *Williamson, Iain. Your Guide to Financial Assistance for Business in Western Canada., 1191-050X.*
Desc: Provides details of every government business assistance program in the territory.

LC HD **ISSN** 1191-0496
DD 658.4/012 CN

YOUR GUIDE TO PREPARING A PLAN TO RAISE MONEY FOR YOUR OWN BUSINESS. [Your guide prep. plan raise money your own bus.]. **VFOAT** Preparing a Plan to Raise Money. (1991)-. English. One time a year. 23.17Can$. Productive Publications, PO Box 7200, Station A, Toronto Ontario M5W 1X8 Canada. **Tel** (416)483-0634. **ED** Iain Williamson.
Desc: Step-by-step guide on how to create a plan to raise money for your own business. Contains tips on how to structure the plan for the best results and a sample plan as an example.

ISSN 1191-0534
DD 658.15/22 CN

YOUR GUIDE TO RAISING VENTURE CAPITAL FOR YOUR OWN BUSINESS IN CANADA. (YOUR GUIDE TO RAISING VENTURE CAPITAL FOR YOUR OWN BUSINESS IN CANADA.). [Your guide rais. venture cap. your own bus. Can.]. **VFOAT** Raising Venture Capital. (1991)-. English. One time a year. 27.17Can$. Productive Publications, PO Box 7200, Station A, Toronto Ontario M5W 1X8 Canada. **Tel** (416)483-0634. **ED** Iain Williamson.
Desc: Helps readers find out how to contact formal and informal venture capitalists in Canada.

ISSN 1191-0518
DD 658.15 CN

YOUR GUIDE TO STARTING & SELF-FINANCING YOUR OWN BUSINESS IN CANADA. [Your guide start. self-financ. your own bus. Can.]. **VFOAT** Starting and Self-Financing Your Own Business in Canada; Starting & Self-Financing Your Own Business. **VAT** Your Guide to Starting and Self-Financing Your Own Business in Canada. (1991)-. English. One time a year. 23.17Can$. Productive Publications, PO Box 7200, Station A, Toronto Ontario M5W 1X8 Canada. **Tel** (416)483-0634. **ED** Iain Williamson.
Desc: Provides information on establishing a marketing strategy, obtaining the latest marketing information, and self-financing your own business.

US

YOUR TELEPHONE PERSONALITY. (19??)-. English. Twenty-six times a year. $.69 per copy (3 copy minimum required). Economics Press Inc, 12 Daniel Road, Fairfield NJ 07004. **Tel** (201)227-1224, (800)526-2554, FAX (201)227-9742.
Desc: Deals with topics related to the skillful handling of phone calls, both incoming and outgoing.

LC HC407.A1 Y843 **ISSN** 0352-3543
DD 330 YU
CODEN YEREEL
SUSPENDED

YUGOSLAV ECONOMIC REVIEW. (1984)-(19??). Periodical. English. Twelve times a year. $89.00. Yugoslav Economic Review, Privredni Pregled M Birjuzova 3, Belgrad Yugoslavia.

LC HF3731 .Y88
DD 338/.09497 XV

YUGOSLAVIA ECHO : ECONOMY, FINANCE, TRADE. Periodical. English (summaries and/or abstracts in Russian and Spanish). Six times a year. **(Subscription address:** Jugoslovenska Knjiga, PO Box 36, YU 11001 Belgrade Yugoslovia. **Tel** 011 38 11 621055, FAX 011 38 11 325970.) ***Continues*** *Economic Echo from Yugoslavia, 0012-916X.*
Ind/Abst PROMT.

ISSN 1060-6092
US

ZA ZAGOLOVKAMI. See Law.

JA

ZAIKAI KANSOKU. FINANCIAL WORLD OBSERVING. Japanese. Twelve times a year. $90.00. **(Subscription address:** Maruzen Company Ltd., PO Box 5050, Import & Export Department, Tokyo 100 31 Japan. **Tel** 011 81 3 32789224.)

LC HC591.C6 Z34 **ISSN** 0377-810X
DD 330.9/675/103 CG

ZAIRE BUSINESS. No. 1- Nov. 24/Dec. 1, 1973-. Periodical. French (French). 3986 rue Ex-Belgika-Building Amasco, B P 9839, 1 Kinshasa Congo Zaire.

LC HC **ISSN** 0084-537X
AU

ZEITSCHRIFT FUER NATIONALOKONOMIE. SUPPLEMENTUM. See Mathematics.

GW

ZEITSCHRIFT FUER POLITISCHE, OEKONOMIE UND SOZIALISTISCHE POLITIK. See Political Science.

LC HC281 .T7 **ISSN** 0342-2852
DD 330 GW
CCC

ZEITSCHRIFT FUER UNTERNEHMENSGESCHICHTE. [Z. Unternehm.gesch.]. **Added/Corp** Gesellschaft fuer Unternehmensgeschichte. (1977)-. Periodical. German. Two times a year. DM58.00. Franz Steiner Verlag GmbH, Postfach 101061, D-70009 Stuttgart Germany. **Tel** 011 49 711 2582372, FAX 011 49 711 2582290, telex 723636 daz d. **ED** Hans Pohl. **Bk Rev**. **Ad Acc**. **Circ:** 700. ***Continues*** *Tradition.*
Desc: Articles and reviews about business history.
Ind/Abst Am. Hist. Life (1962-);(1977-); Int. Bibliogr. Sociol.

LC HB5 .Z55 **ISSN** 0342-1783
DD 330/.05 GW
CCC

ZEITSCHRIFT FUER WIRTSCHAFTS- UND SOZIALWISSENSCHAFTEN. [Z. Wirtsch.- Sozialwiss.]. Vol. 92 (1972)-. Periodical. German (summaries and/or abstracts in English). Four times a year. DM158.30 Germany; DM162.40 other. Duncker und Humblot Verlag, Postfach 410329, D-12113 Berlin Germany. **Tel** 011 49 30 79000612, 011 49 30 79000613. **ED** A. Woll, Gruber, and Bosshann. Index Available, published separately, free-automatically sent. **Bk Rev**. **Ad Acc**. **Circ:** 850. ***Continues*** *Schmollers Jahrbuch fuer Wirtschafts- und Sozialwissenschaften.*
Desc: Economics and Social Sciences.
Ind/Abst ABC POL SCI; Econ. Lit. Index; Int. Bibliogr. Sociol.; Int. Polit. Sci. Abstr.; J. Econ. Lit.; PAIS Int. Print (?-?).

LC HB5 .C633 **ISSN** 0721-3808
DD 330 GW
CODEN ZEWIEZ

ZEITSCHRIFT FUER WIRTSCHAFTSPOLITIK. (ZEITSCHRIFT FUER WIRTSCHAFTSPOLITIK.). [Z. Wirtsch.polit.]. **Added/Corp** Universitaet zu Koeln. Institut fuer

Wirtschaftspolitik. (1981)-. Periodical. German. Three times a year. DM82.00 Germany; DM88.00 other. Institut fuer Wirtschaftspolitik an der Universitaet zu Koeln, Pohligstrasse 1, D-50969 Cologne Germany. **Tel** 011 49 221 3671147, 011 49 221 3671149. ***Continues*** *Wirtschaftspolitische Chronik, 0043-6305.*
Ind/Abst Int. Bibliogr. Sociol.; PAIS Int. Print.

LC HB54 .P6 **ISSN** 0208-4902
DD 330 PL
CODEN ZNASDH
ZESZYTY NAUKOWE. SERIA I. No. 1 (1961)-. Academic Scholarly Publication. Polish (summaries and/or abstracts in English and Russian). Irregular. Price varies per volume. Wydawnictwo Akademia Ekonomicznej w Poznaniu, Ul. Marchlewskiego 146/150, 60-967 Poznan Poland. Documents available from CASDDS, BLDSC. ***Continues in part*** *Zezsyty Naukowe (Wyzsza Szkoa Ekonomiczna w Poznaniu).*
Ind/Abst Chem. Abstr.; Zentralbl. Math. Ihre Grenzgeb.

SZ
ZUERCHER WIRTSCHAFTSBRIEF. German. Two times a week (104 per year). 415.80F. Gesellschaft F Unternehmerberatung mbH, Zuercher Wirtschaftsbrief, Postfach 8700 Kusnacht Switzerland. **Tel** 011 41 1 9103100, FAX 011 41 1 9103353.

US
ZWEIG FORECAST. English. $265.00 (one-year), $445.00 (two-year). Zweig Securities, PO Box 2900, Wantagh NY 11793. **Tel** (516)785-1300.

ABSTRACTING, BIBLIOGRAPHIES AND STATISTICS

LC Z7164.U5 U54A HC59.7 **ISSN** 0362-644X
DD 016.3015/4/091724 US
A.I.D. BIBLIOGRAPHY SERIES : DEVELOPMENT ADMINISTRATION. **Main/Corp** United States. Agency for International Development. **VAT** Agency for International Development Bibliography Series: Development Administration. Bibliography. English.

LC HB **ISSN** 0503-4922
DD 330 US
A.I.D. ECONOMIC DATA BOOK, NEAR EAST AND SOUTH ASIA. **Main/Corp** United States. Agency for International Development. Statistics and Reports Division. No. 243 (April 1967)-. Bulletin. English. Irregular. National Technical Information Service - NTIS, Room 2027S, 5285 Port Royal Road, Springfield VA 22161. **Tel** (703)487-4630, (703)487-4660, (703)487-4650, FAX (703)321-8547, telex 89-9405. **Circ:** 18,500 (ctrl).
Desc: Bulletin listing a sampling of reports contained in the NTIS database in five categories: manufacturing processing industry, agriculture and food, construction, and management and economic development.

LC HD82 .U535a **ISSN** 0096-1507
DD 016.33891/172/4073 US
A.I.D. RESEARCH AND DEVELOPMENT ABSTRACTS. **Added/Corp** United States. Agency for International Development. Division of Documentation and Information. United States. Agency for International Development. Bureau for Technical Assistance. LTS Corporation. **VFOAT** AID Research and Development Abstracts; ARDA; A.R.D.A. **VAT** Agency for International Development Research and Development Abstracts. Vol. 1, No. 4 (1974)-. Abstracting/Indexing Service. English. Four times a year. $10.00. ARDA / Agency for International Development US, 1500 Wilson Boulevard, Suite 1010, Arlington VA 22209-2404. **Tel** (703)351-4006, FAX (703)351-4039, telex 3730100 LTSCORP. **ED** Roger A. Reynolds. Index available. **Circ:** 4,000 (ctrl). ***Continues*** *A.I.D. Reference Center. A.I.D. Research Abstracts, 0094-4599.*
Desc: Provides annotative abstracts of AID-produced reports on a wide variety of topics related to international development - agriculture, health, private enterprise, housing, environment, and economics.

US
ABI/INFORM GLOBAL EDITION [COMPUTER FILE]. (19??)-. Abstracting/Indexing Service. English. One time a year. University Microfilms International, 300 North Zeeb Road, Ann Arbor MI 48106-1346. **Tel** (313)761-4700, (800)521-0600 Exts. 2490, 2491, FAX (313)973-1540. available on microfilm; available on magnetic tape; available in print; available on an online database from ORBIT; Mead Data Central; HRIN file (ABI); ESA-IRS; DIALOG; DATA-STAR; and BRS.
Desc: Covers business conditions, trends, corporate strategies and tactics, management techniques, competitive and product information, and a wide variety of other topics. Most publications in ABI/INFORM are indexed virtually cover to cover. Records include 150-word abstracts and full bibliographic citations.

US
ABI/INFORM ONDISC: EXPRESS EDITION [COMPUTER FILE]. (19??)-. Abstracting/Indexing Service. English. Irregular. $1950.00 per year. University Microfilms International, 300 North Zeeb Road, Ann Arbor MI 48106-1346. **Tel** (313)761-4700, (800)521-0600 Exts. 2490, 2491, FAX (313)973-1540. available on an online database from ORBIT; ESA-ISA; HRIN file (ABI); DIALOG; BRS; and DATA-STAR; available on magnetic tape; available on microfilm; available in print.
Desc: Covers business conditions, trends, corporate strategies and tactics, management techniques, competitive and product information, and a wide variety of other topics. Most publications in ABI/INFORM are indexed virtually cover to cover. Records include 150-word abstracts and full bibliographic citations.

LC HF5635 .A224
DD 657 US
•**ACCOUNTING & TAX DATABASE [COMPUTER FILE].** **VFOAT** Accounting and Tax Database; Proquest Accounting and Tax Database. (1993)-. Abstracting/Indexing Service. English. One time a year. University Microfilms International, 300 North Zeeb Road, Ann Arbor MI 48106-1346. **Tel** (313)761-4700, (800)521-0600 Exts. 2490, 2491, FAX (313)973-1540. available on magnetic tape and CD-ROM from DIALOG.
Desc: Online service containing thorough indexing and abstracts of articles about accounting, taxation and related financial information from more than 240 key journals, newspapers and newsletters. Selected records are available from hundreds of other serial publications, dissertations, books and pamphlets. Over 100 key sources are available online in full text form. Coverage dates from 1971.

LC Z7164.C81 A224 HF5635 **ISSN** 1063-0287
DD 016.657 US
ACCOUNTING AND TAX INDEX. [Account. tax index]. **VFOAT** Accounting and Tax Index. Vol. 1, 1st Quarter (1992)-. Abstracting/Indexing Service. English. Four times a year (3 issues plus annual index). $286.00. University Microfilms International, 300 North Zeeb Road, Ann Arbor MI 48106-1346. **Tel** (313)761-4700, (800)521-0600 Exts. 2490, 2491, FAX (313)973-1540. available on magnetic tape; available on CD-ROM; available on an online database from DIALOG. ***Continues*** *Accountants' Index. Supplement, 0748-7975.*
Desc: A journal about virtually every trend and event in accounting and taxation; (FASB statements, AICPA policies, and personal financial planning); Also cites important information in thousands of journals, books, pamphlets, conference proceedings and industry newsletters.

LC Z7164.C81 C782a HF563
DD 016.657 US
ACCOUNTING ARTICLES. **Main/Corp** Commerce Clearing House. **VFOAT** CCH Accounting Articles. (1963/1966)-. Abstracting/Indexing Service. English. Irregular. Commerce Clearing House Inc., 4025 West Peterson Avenue, Chicago IL 60646-6085. **Tel** (312)583-8500, FAX (708)940-4600. cum. index.
Desc: Highlights current articles published in accounting, business and other publications covering the many phases of accounting, including budgeting, auditing, management services, education, training programs and professional development.

LC HC59.69 .A26 **ISSN** 1015-213X
DD 330.9172/4 LU
ACP BASIC STATISTICS. [ACP, Basic stat.]. **Added/Corp** Statistical Office of the European Communities. **VFOAT** ACP, Statistiques de Base. **VAT** A C P Basic Statistics. (198?)-. English (French). One time a year. £6.80 UK; 7.40p Ireland. Office for Official Publications of the European Communities, 2 rue Mercier, 2985 Luxembourg Luxembourg. **Tel** 011 352 499281, FAX 011 352 292942763. ***Continues*** *ACP : Statistical Yearbook.*

NE
ADVANCED STUDIES IN THEORETICAL AND APPLIED ECONOMETRICS. Vol. 1 (1982)-. Monographic series. English. Irregular. Price varies per volume. Kluwer Academic Publishers, Postbus 322, 3300 AH Dordrecht The Netherlands. **Tel** 011 31 78 524400, FAX 011 31 78 183273, telex 20083.
Ind/Abst Math. Rev. (1988-); Zentralbl. Math. Ihre Grenzgeb.

LC HD5726.O49 A33
DD 331.11/43 US
AFFIRMATIVE ACTION INFORMATION. OLYMPIA MSA, METROPOLITAN STATISTICAL AREA (THURSTON COUNTY). **Added/Corp** Washington (State). Employment Security Dept. Research & Analysis Branch. **VFOAT** Olympia MSA, Metropolitan Statistical Area (Thurston County); Affirmative Action Information ... Olympia MSA; Affirmative Action Information ... Olympia MSA. (1984)-. Statistical Publication. English. One time a year. Price varies. Research and Analysis Branch, Washington State Employment Security Department, Box 9046, Olympia WA 98507. **Tel** (206)438-4800, FAX (206)438-4846. ***Continues*** *Affirmative Action Information, Olympia Standard Metropolitan Statistical Area.*

LC HG2051.U5 A13 **ISSN** 0091-3502
DD 332.7/1/0973 US
AGRICULTURAL FINANCE STATISTICS. **Main/Corp** United States. Dept. of Agriculture. Economic Research Service. Vol. 1 (1973)-. English. Cornell University / S Allen, 155 Warren Hall, Ithaca NY 14853-7801. **Tel** (607)255-1587, FAX (607)255-9984. ***Continues in part*** *Agricultural Finance Review.*

LC Z7164.S66 I5 1970 Suppl HN8 **ISSN** 0099-0779
DD 019/.1 US
ALPHABETICAL CATALOG OF THE BOOKS AND PAMPHLETS OF THE INTERNATIONAL INSTITUTE OF SOCIAL HISTORY, AMSTERDAM. SUPPLEMENT. **Main/Corp** International Institute for Social History. **Added/Corp** International Institute for Social History. Alfabetische Catalogus van de Boeken en Brochures van het Internationaal Instituut voor Sociale Geschiedenis, Amsterdam. Supplement. **VFOAT** Alfabetische Catalogus Van de Boeken en Brochures Van Het Internationaal Instituut voor Sociale Geschiedenis, Amsterdam. Supplement. (1975)-. Catalog. Multiple languages (Dutch, French, German, Polish and Russian). GK Hall & Co., 100 Front Street, Riverside NJ 08075. **Tel** (800)257-5755 ext. 2223.

LC HG1501.A52 B44A **ISSN** 0893-2468
DD 332.1/0973/05 US
AMERICAN BANKER INDEX (ANN ARBOR, MICH.). (AMERICAN BANKER INDEX.). [Am. bank. index]. (Jan. 1987)-. Abstracting/Indexing Service. English. Twelve times a year. University Microfilms International, 300 North Zeeb Road, Ann Arbor MI 48106-1346. **Tel** (313)761-4700, (800)521-0600 Exts. 2490, 2491, FAX (313)973-1540. Index available. cum. index. available in microform from University Microfilms International (UMI); available on CD-ROM; available on an online database from Orbit Search Service. ***Continues*** *Bell & Howell's Index to American Banker, 0195-6426.*

LC HB
DD 330 UK
•**AMERICAN COMPANIES: GUIDE TO SOURCES OF INFORMATION.** (1995)-. Directory. English. Irregular. £78.00. CBD Research Ltd., 15 Wickham Road, Beckenham Kent BR3 2JS United Kingdom. **Tel** 011 44 181 6507745, FAX 011 44 181 6500768.

LC HD5777 .A67 **ISSN** 0170-2696
DD 331.1/0943/021 GW
AMTLICHE NACHRICHTEN DER BUNDESANSTALT FUER ARBEIT. ARBEITSSTATISTIK ... JAHRESZAHLEN. **VFOAT** Arbeitsstatistik ... Jahreszahlen. Statistical Publication. German. DM100.00. Bundesanstalt fuer Arbeit, Regensburger Strasse 104, 8500 Nuernberg Germany. ***Continues*** *Bundesanstalt fur Arbeit (Germany). Jahreszahlen, Arbeitsstatistik.*

LC HF5635 .A665 **ISSN** 0961-2742
DD 657/.05 UK
ANBAR ACCOUNTING & FINANCE ABSTRACTS. **Added/Corp** Anbar Abstracts (Firm) Institute of Chartered Accountants in England and Wales. **VFOAT** Anbar Accounting and Finance Abstracts; Accounting & Finance Abstracts; Accounting & Finance. Vol. 1, No. 1 (Jan. 1991)-. Abstracting/Indexing Service. English. Twelve times a year. $2999.00. MCB University Press, 60 62 Toller Lane, Bradford, West Yorkshire BD8 9BY United Kingdom. **Tel** 011 44 1274 785280, FAX 011 44 1274 785200, telex 51317-MCBUNI-G. **(Subscription address:** MCB University Press / US and Canada Subscriptions, PO Box 10812, Birmingham AL 35201-0812. **Tel** (205)995-1567, (800)633-4931, FAX (205)995-1588.**)** available on CD-ROM; available on diskette. ***Continues*** *Accounting + Data Processing Abstracts.*

LC HB **ISSN** 1351-3044
DD 330 UK
•**ANBAR MANAGEMENT OF QUALITY ABSTRACTS.** **VFOAT** Management of Quality Abstracts; Management of Quality ANBAR Abstracts. (1994)-. Abstracting/Indexing Service. English. Four times a year. $359.00. MCB University Press, 60 62 Toller Lane, Bradford, West Yorkshire BD8 9BY United Kingdom. **Tel** 011 44 1274 785280, FAX 011 44 1274 785200, telex 51317-MCBUNI-G. **(Subscription address:** MCB University Press / US and Canada Subscriptions, PO Box 10812, Birmingham AL 35201-0812. **Tel** (205)995-1567, (800)633-4931, FAX (205)995-1588.**)** ***Absorbed*** *Quality Abstracts, 1071-1945.*

Business and Economics —Abstracting, Bibliographies and Statistics

LC HF5415 .A613   **ISSN** 0305-0661
DD 016.6588   UK
ANBAR MARKETING & DISTRIBUTION ABSTRACTS. **Added/Corp** Anbar Abstracts (Firm) Chartered Institute of Marketing. **VFOAT** Anbar Marketing and Distribution Abstracts. (199?)-. Abstracting/Indexing Service. English. Twelve times a year. $2999.00. MCB University Press, 60 62 Toller Lane, Bradford, West Yorkshire BD8 9BY United Kingdom. **Tel** 011 44 1274 785280, FAX 011 44 1274 785200, telex 51317-MCBUNI-G. (**Subscription address:** MCB University Press / US and Canada Subscriptions, PO Box 10812, Birmingham AL 35201-0812. **Tel** (205)995-1567, (800)633-4931, FAX (205)995-1588.) **ED** Andrew Ede. Index available. cum. index. **Circ:** 1,000. available on CD-ROM; available on diskette. **Continues** Marketing + Distribution Abstracts.
Desc: Contains abstracts of articles appearing in international management journals. Articles selected are on topics such as: market planning; the retail trade; advertising; new product development; logistics; direct marketing; design and stock control.

LC TS155.A1 A55   **ISSN** 1353-5498
DD 658.5/05   UK
ANBAR OPERATIONS & PRODUCTION MANAGEMENT ABSTRACTS. **Added/Corp** Anbar Abstracts (Firm) Institute of Management Services (Great Britain). **VFOAT** Anbar Operations and Production Management Abstracts; Operations & Production Management; Operations and Production Management. (19??)-. English. Twelve times a year. $1531.53. MCB University Press, 60 62 Toller Lane, Bradford, West Yorkshire BD8 9BY United Kingdom. **Tel** 011 44 1274 785280, FAX 011 44 1274 785200, telex 51317-MCBUNI-G. **Continues** Anbar Management Services + Production Abstracts, 0952-4614.

LC HD28 .T66
DD 658.4/005   UK
ANBAR TOP MANAGEMENT ABSTRACTS. **Added/Corp** ANBAR Abstracts (Firm) British Institute of Management. **VFOAT** Top Management Abstracts. Vol. 17, No. 1 (Mid-Oct. 1987)-. Abstracting/Indexing Service. English. Twelve times a year. $3999.00. MCB University Press, 60 62 Toller Lane, Bradford, West Yorkshire BD8 9BY United Kingdom. **Tel** 011 44 1274 785280, FAX 011 44 1274 785200, telex 51317-MCBUNI-G. (**Subscription address:** MCB University Press / US and Canada Subscriptions, PO Box 10812, Birmingham AL 35201-0812. **Tel** (205)995-1567, (800)633-4931, FAX (205)995-1588.) available on CD-ROM; available on diskette. **Continues** Top Management Abstracts.
Desc: Includes literature on all subjects of interest to senior and strategic managers.

ISSN 0720-8227
GW
ANGEWANDTE STATISTIK UND OKONOMETRIE. (ANGEWANDTE STATISTIK UND OKONOMETRIE. APPLIED STATISTICS AND ECONOMETRICS. STATISTIQUE APPLIQUEE ET ECONOMETRIE.). [Angew. Stat. Okon.]. **VFOAT** Applied Statistics and Econometrics; Statistique Appliquee et Econometrie. (1975)-. Monographic series. English. Irregular. Vandenhoeck & Ruprecht, Robert Bosch Breite 6, D-3709 Goettingen Germany. **Tel** 011 49 551 695911, FAX 011 49 551 695917, telex 965226 VAN d.
Ind/Abst Math. Rev.; Zentralbl. Math. Ihre Grenzgeb.

LC HA1631 .A33 HD8631
DD 317.971   YU
ANKETA O OSTVARIVANJU PRAVA RADNIKA IZ RADNOG ODNOSA. **Main/Corp** Savezni Zavod Za Statistiku (Yugoslavia). Serbo-Croatian (Roman). 4.00 Din. Savezni Zavod za Statistiku, Kneza Milosa 20, Belgrad Yugoslavia.

LC HA1631 .A33 HD7045.5   **ISSN** 0300-2543
DD 314.971   YU
ANKETA O PORODICNIM BUDZETIMA RADNICKIH DOMACINSTAVA. **Main/Corp** Savezni Zavod Za Statistiku (Yugoslavia). Serbo-Croatian (Roman). 4.00 Din per issue. Savezni Zavod za Statistiku, Kneza Milosa 20, Belgrad Yugoslavia.

LC HA1631 .A33 HC407.Z9
DD 314.971   YU
ANKETA O PRIHODIMA, RASHEDIMA I POTRESNJI DOMACINSTAVA. **Main/Corp** Savezni Zavod Za Statistiku (Yugoslavia). (1963)-. Serbo-Croatian (Roman). 10.00. Savezni Zavod za Statistiku, Kneza Milosa 20, Belgrad Yugoslavia.

LC HF270.5 .A5   **ISSN** 0304-5692
DD 382/.09675/1   CG
ANNUAIRE DES STATISTIQUES DU COMMERCE EXTERIEUR (KINSHASA). (ANNUAIRE DES STATISTIQUES DU COMMERCE EXTERIEUR.). [Annu. stat. commer. exter.]. (19??)-. Statistical Publication. French. Twelve times a year. Free. Institut National de la Statistique / Zaire, Kinshasa Zaire. **Tel** 33313-33313. **Bk Rev**. **Ad Acc**.

LC HC
DD 330   BD
ANNUAIRE STATISTIQUE. (1989)-. French. One time a year. $45.00. Institut de Statistiques et d'Etudes Economiques du Burundi, Service Naitonal des Etudes Statistiques, BP 1156, Bujumbura Republique du Burundi. **Tel** 22 6729. **Ad Acc**, **Adv Mgr:** Jean Paul Nimpagaritse. **Continues** Annuaire Statistique du Burundi.

LC HA1213 .A4   **ISSN** 0066-3654
DD 314.4   FR
NLM W2 GF7 I5A
ANNUAIRE STATISTIQUE DE LA FRANCE (PARIS, FRANCE : 1952). (ANNUAIRE STATISTIQUE DE LA FRANCE.). **Added/Corp** Institut National de la Statistique et des Etudes Economiques pour la Metropole et la France d'Outre-mer. Institut National de la Statistique et des Etudes Economiques (France). Vol. 59 (1952)-. French. One time a year (Nov.). $150.92. CNGP INSEE - Institut National de la Statistique et des Esdudes Economiques, BP 2718, 1 rue V Auriol, F 80027 Amiens Cedex 1 France. **Tel** 011 33 22 927322. (**Subscription address:** CDL Hachette Consignation, Avenue Gutenberg ZA de Coignieres, 78316 Maurepas France.) available on microfiche. **Continues** Annuaire Statistique (Paris, France : 1900).
Desc: Gives a picture of the economic movement in France through detailed statistical data on economy and demography. Includes sources of data and bibliography.

LC HA4007.G5 A25
DD 330.9967   GU
ANNUAL ECONOMIC REVIEW AND STATISTICAL ABSTRACT, GUAM. See Business and Economics-Economic History, Conditions.

FR
ANNUAL FOREIGN TRADE STATISTICS BY COMMODITIES. SERIES C. (19??)-. English (French). Irregular. $365.00 (microfiche). OECD Publications and Information Center, 2 rue Andre-Pascal, 75775 Paris Cedex 16 France. **Tel** 011 33 1 49104262, US:(202)785-6323, FAX 011 33 1 45248500, 011 33 1 45248176, telex 620 160 OCDE. (**Subscription address:** OECD Publications Center, 2001 L Street, Suite 700, Washington DC 20036. **Tel** (202)822-3873, (202)785-6323.) available on microfiche.
Desc: Annual data on trade of OECD countries at the 2-digit SITC commodity classification level.

TU
ANNUAL FOREIGN TRADE STATISTICS TURKEY. (19??)-. English. One time a year. Turkish State Institute of Statistics, Necatibey Cadessi 114, Ankara 016100 Turkey. **Tel** 011 90 4 1188719, FAX 011 90 4 1253387, telex 46347 DIETR.

LC HD5726.C37 W48A
DD 331.12/09754/38   US
ANNUAL PLANNING INFORMATION. CHARLESTON, WEST VIRGINIA STANDARD METROPOLITAN STATISTICAL AREA. **VFOAT** Charleston, West Virginia Standard Metropolitan Statistical Area; Charleston Standard Metropolitan Statistical Area for ...; Charleston Metropolitan Statistical Area and Kanawha County; Vice Delivery Area for ... . Fiscal Year 1983-. Statistical Publication. English. One time a year. Free. West Virginia Employment Programs Bureau, 112 California Avenue, Charleston WV 25305. **Tel** (304)558-2630, FAX (304)348-0301. **Circ:** 250 (ctrl). **Continues** Charleston, West Virginia Standard Metropolitan Statistical Area, Annual Planning Information.
Desc: Provides comprehensive information relating to projected estimates of manpower statistics based upon previous labor market conditions and current indicators. Updated data provided.

LC HD5725.M5 M49A
DD 331.1/09774   US
ANNUAL PLANNING INFORMATION, FISCAL YEAR ... - MICHIGAN EMPLOYMENT SECURITY COMMISSION, BUREAU OF RESEARCH AND STATISTICS. (19??)-. English. One time a year. Detroit Labor Market Analysis Unit, 7310 Woodward Avenue, Detroit MI 48202. **Continues** Michigan Employment Security Commission. Detroit Labor Market Analysis Unit. Annual Planning Report, State of Michigan.

LC HD5726.C68 M57A
DD 331.12/09778/29   US
ANNUAL PLANNING INFORMATION FOR COLUMBIA SMSA. **Main/Corp** Missouri. Division of Employment Security. English. One time a year. Division of Employment Security / Columbia Missouri, 2101 Whitegate Drive, PO Box 898, Columbia MO 65205.

LC HD5726.H9 A55
DD 331.12/09754/42   US
ANNUAL PLANNING INFORMATION. HUNTINGTON-ASHLAND-IRONTON STANDARD METROPOLITAN STATISTICAL AREA. **Added/Corp** West Virginia. Dept. of Employment Security. Labor and Economic Research Section. **VFOAT** Huntington-Ashland-Ironton Standard Metropolitan Statistical Area. (19??)-. Statistical Publication. English. One time a year. Free. West Virginia Employment Programs Bureau, 112 California Avenue, Charleston WV 25305. **Tel** (304)558-2630, FAX (304)348-0301. **Circ:** 300.
Desc: Provides comprehensive information relating to projected estimates of manpower statistics based upon previous labor market conditions and current indicators. Updated data provided.

LC HD5726.B42 T48A
DD 331.12/09764/145   US
ANNUAL PLANNING INFORMATION REPORT : BEAUMONT-PORT ARTHUR-ORANGE SMSA. **Main/Corp** Texas. Employment Commission. **VFOAT** Beaumont-Port Arthur-Orange SMSA. (19??)-. English. One time a year. Texas Employment Commission, 101 East 15th Street, Room 208T, Austin TX 78778. **Tel** (512)463-2619.

LC HD5726.S48 A56
DD 331.1/09758/724   US
ANNUAL PLANNING INFORMATION REPORT FOR FISCAL YEAR ... SAVANNAH SMSA SAVANNAH/CHATHAM CONSORTIUM. **VFOAT** Annual Planning Information for Fiscal Year ... Savannah. English. One time a year. Georgia Department of Labor, CES Unit, 148 International Boulevard, Atlanta GA 30303. **Tel** (404)656-2994.

LC HD5726.O7 F57A
DD 331.12/09759/24   US
ANNUAL PLANNING INFORMATION REPORT. ORLANDO SMSA AND ORANGE COUNTY, ORLANDO CITY, SEMINOLE COUNTY CETA PRIME SPONSOR AREAS. **Main/Corp** Florida. Division of Employment Security. **VFOAT** Orlando S.M.S.A. Annual Planning Information; Orlando SMSA Annual Planning Information. 1981-. English. One time a year. Florida State Employment Service / Winter Park, State Office Building, 941 Morse Boulevard, Winter Park FL 32789. **Continues** Annual Planning Information Report ... Orlando SMSA, and Orange, and Seminole Counties CETA Prime Sponsor Areas.
Desc: Includes supplementary material for the CETA prime sponsor area.

LC HD5726.P44 F57a
DD 331.12/09759/982   US
ANNUAL PLANNING INFORMATION REPORT ... PENSACOLA SMSA AND OKALOOSA COUNTY. **Main/Corp** Florida State Employment Service. **VFOAT** Pensacola S.M.S.A. Annual Planning Information; Pensacola SMSA Annual Planning Information. (19??)-. English. One time a year. Florida State Employment Service / Pensacola, PO Box 1393, 236 West Garden Street, Pensacola FL 32596.
Desc: Includes supplementary material for the CETA prime sponsor area.

LC HD5726.S56 A66
DD 331.1/09777/41   US
ANNUAL PLANNING INFORMATION, SIOUX CITY SMSA. **Added/Corp** Job Service of Iowa. (1979)-. English. One time a year. Free. Job Service of Iowa / Sioux City, 2508 4th Street, Sioux City IA 51101. **Continues** Annual Planning Report, Sioux City SMSA and Woodbury County.
Desc: Statistical and analytical presentation of labor market data.

LC HD5726.C36 I44A
DD 331.1/09773/6   US
ANNUAL PLANNING REPORT, FISCAL YEAR ... CHAMPAIGN SMSA. **Main/Corp** Illinois. Bureau of Employment Security. Research and Analysis Division. English. One time a year. Bureau of Employment Security Research and Analysis, 402 North Randolph, Champaign IL 61820.

LC HD5725.W2 W35H
DD 331.1/09797/79   US
ANNUAL PLANNING REPORT. OLYMPIA SMSA. **VFOAT** Olympia SMSA. VAT Annual Planning Report. Olympia Standard Metropolitan Statistical Area. (1982)-. English. One time a year. **Continues** Washington (State). Employment Security Dept. Labor Market Information. Annual Planning Report, Thurston County.

LC HA742 .A35 **ISSN** 0703-2633
DD 354.710081/9 CN
CEASED

ANNUAL REPORT - STATISTICS CANADA. See Social Sciences-Abstracting, Bibliographies and Statistics.

LC HD7103.65.U6 A56
DD 368.4/1/00973 US

ANNUAL STATISTICAL BULLETIN. **Added/Corp** National Council on Compensation Insurance. **VFOAT** Statistical Bulletin. 1st Ed. (1981)-. Bulletin. English. One time a year. $225.00. National Council on Compensation Insurance, 777 Ymatto Road, Suite 200, Boca Raton FL 33431. **Tel** (800)622-4123.

LC HG8555.A4 E87 **ISSN** 0067-3234
DD 332/.097284/021 ES

ANUARIO ESTADISTICO. **Added/Corp** El Salvador. Superintendencia del Sistema Financiero. Asesoria Actuarial y Estadistica. No. 21 (1983)-. Statistical Publication. Spanish. One time a year. Free. Superintendencia del Sistema Financiero, Postal 2942, San Salvador El Salvador. **Circ:** 500. ***Continues*** *Estadisticas: Seguros, Fianzas, Bancos.*

LC HA1320.N6 A32 HD5030.N6 **ISSN** 0722-2432
DD 314.3 GW

ARBEITSKOSTEN IM PRODUZIERENDEN GEWERBE UND IM DIENSTLEISTUNGSBEREICH. **Added/Corp** Landesamt fuer Datenverarbeitung und Statistik Nordrhein-Westfalen. (19??)-. Statistical Publication. German. Irregular. Landesamt fuer Datenverarbeitung und Statistik Nordrhein-Westfalen, Postfach 101105, 40002 Duesseldorf Germany. **Tel** (0211)944901, FAX (0211)442006, telex 8586654 LDST D. **Circ:** 250.
Desc: Statistical returns about costs and wages concerning banks and insurance companies.

LC HD5780.B23 B23a
DD 331.12/0943/46 GW

ARBEITSMARKT IN BADEN-WURTTEMBERG; JAHRESBERICHT, DER. **Main/Corp** Baden-Wurttemberg. Landesarbeitsamt. (19??)-. Statistical Publication. German. One time a year. Landesarbeitsamt Baden-Wurttemberg, Postfach 10 29 52, 70025 Stuttgart Germany. **Acid Free. Circ:** 900 (ctrl).
Desc: Statistics reports on unemployment figures in Baden-Wurtemberg.

LC HA1320 .R453 HF3569.R55
DD 314.3/43 381/.2/094343021 GW

ARBEITSSTATTEN DES GROSSHANDELS UND DER HANDELSVERMITTLUNG IN RHEINLAND-PFALZ, DIE. **Added/Corp** Statistisches Landesamt Rheinland-Pfalz. (19??)-. Periodical. German. Statistisches Landesamt Rheinland-Pfalz, Postfach Mainzer Strasse 15/16, 5427 Bad Ems Germany.

LC HD5715.5.D4 A74 **ISSN** 0106-9896
DD 331.2592 DK

ARBEJDSMARKEDSUDDANNELSERNE STATISTIK. TABELMATERIALE VEDRRENDE OMSKOLING OG ERHVERVSINTRODUKTION. **VFOAT** Tabelmateriale Vedrrende Omskoling OG Erhvervsintroduktion; Omskoling Og Erhvervsintroduktion, Tabelmateriale. (19??)-. Danish. AMU-Direktoratet for Arbejdsmarkedsuddannelserne, Hejrevej 43, 2400 Kobenhavn NV Denmark. **Tel** 01 33 22 00.

LC HD5801 .A33
DD 331 SW

ARBETSKRAFTSUNDERSOKNINGEN : AKU. **Added/Corp** Sweden. Statistiska Centralbyran. Avdelningen for Arbetsmarknadsstatistik. **VFOAT** Aku. (19??)-. Swedish. Twelve times a year (with quarterly and annual cumulations). SCB Statistiska Centralbyran, 11581 Stockholm Sweden.

LC CD1040 .A73 **ISSN** 0955-1034
DD 027.542 UK

ARCHIVE SERVICES STATISTICS ... ESTIMATES. **Added/Corp** Chartered Institute of Public Finance and Accountancy. Statistical Information Service. (19??)-. Statistical Publication. English. One time a year. £34.00. Chartered Institute of Public Finance and Accountancy, 2 3 Robert Street, London WC2N 6BH United Kingdom. **Tel** 011 44 171 8958823, FAX 011 44 171 8958825.

LC HD4976.G7 U53A **ISSN** 0361-655X
DD 331.2/9757/2 US

AREA WAGE SURVEY. GREENVILLE-SPARTANBURG, SOUTH CAROLINA, METROPOLITAN AREA. **Added/Corp** United States. Bureau of Labor Statistics. **VFOAT** Greenville-Spartanburg, South Carolina, Metropolitan Area. (June 1975)-. English. One time a year. US Department of Labor, 200 Constitution Avenue NW, Washington DC 20210. **Tel** (202)219-7316, FAX (202)219-7312. available on microfiche (Vols. for (1984-) distributed to depository libraries). ***Continues*** *Area Wage Survey. The Greenville, South Carolina, Metropolitan Area;* ***Continues in part*** *Occupational Wage Survey. Greenville-Spartanburg, South Carolina.*

DD 331.2975912 US

AREA WAGE SURVEY. JACKSONVILLE, FLORIDA, METROPOLITAN AREA. (AREA WAGE SURVEY. JACKSONVILLE, FLORIDA, METROPOLITAN AREA.). **Added/Corp** United States. Bureau of Labor Statistics. **VFOAT** Jacksonville, Florida, Metropolitan Area. (1966)-. English. One time a year. US Department of Labor, 200 Constitution Avenue NW, Washington DC 20210. **Tel** (202)219-7316, FAX (202)219-7312. available on microfiche (Vols. for (1983-) distributed to depository libraries). ***Continues in part*** *Occupational Wage Survey. Jacksonville, Florida.*

LC HA251 .A74
DD 317.67 US

ARKANSAS STATISTICAL ABSTRACT. **Added/Corp** University of Arkansas at Little Rock. State Data Center. (1986)-. Statistical Publication. English. One time a year (Every two years). $25.00. Arkansas State Data Center, University of Arkansas, 2801 South University, Little Rock AR 72204. **Tel** (501)569-8530, FAX (501)569-8538. **ED** Jerry Bell. **Circ:** 400.
Desc: A comprehensive single source reference volume of economic and demographic data pertaining to the state. its basic goal is to bring together data in a format that will be useful to government agencies, business firms, organizations, and individuals.

LC HC411 .A733 **ISSN** 0818-9935
DD 330.95/005 UK
CODEN AELIEB

Pr Rev.

ASIAN-PACIFIC ECONOMIC LITERATURE. [Asia.-Pac. econ. lit.]. **Added/Corp** Australian National University. National Centre for Development Studies. **VFOAT** Asian Pacific Economic Literature. Vol. 1, No. 1 (May 1987)-. Abstracting/Indexing Service. English. Two times a year (May & Nov.). 82.22Aus$. Asian Pacific Economic Literature - APEL Bibliotech, Anutech Court, Australian National University, Canberra ACT 2601 Australia. **Tel** 011 61 6 2490407, FAX 011 61 6 2493700. **ED** Professor H. W. Arnde, Australian National University. Index available (bound in each issue). **Bk Rev**, (Qty: 60 year). **Ad Acc, Adv Mgr:** W. Hacker. **Circ:** 3,000.
Desc: Contains literature survey papers, 20-30 book reviews, 50-60 book summaries, plus abstracts of journal articles, indexes, etc.
Ind/Abst Econ. Lit. Index (199?-); Geogr. Abstr. Human Geogr.; Int. Dev. Abstr.; J. Econ. Lit.

LC HD2425 .A88 **ISSN** 1054-4070
DD 061/.3/025 US
CCC

ASSOCIATIONS YELLOW BOOK. (ASSOCIATIONS YELLOW BOOK : A PUBLICATION OF MONITOR PUBLISHING COMPANY.). [Assoc. yellow book]. Vol. 1, No. 1 (Summer 1991)-. Directory. English. Two times a year. $180.00 first subscription, $126.00 each additional subscription. Leadership Directories, Inc., 104 Fifth Avenue, Second Floor, New York NY 10011. **Tel** (212)627-4140, FAX (212)645-0931. **ED** Christiane Muntone. Index available (included in each issue). **Acid Free.** available on CD-ROM from Chadwyck-Healey, Inc.
Desc: Lists over 42,000 officers, managers, professional staff and directors at over 1,170 leading U.S. trade and professional associations with budgets over one million dollars. Provides the names, titles, addresses, telephone and facsimile numbers. Includes year founded/accreditation, number of employees, annual meetings, mailing list contacts, publications and advertising information. Indexed by association name, individual's name, location, budget, industry, PAC and acronym.

LC HA1320.B2 A32 HF196.B28
DD 314.3/46 S 382/.0943/46 GW

AUSSENHANDEL, DER. **Main/Corp** Statistisches Landesamt Baden-Wurttemberg. (19??)-. German. Statistisches Landesamt Baden-Wuerttemberg, Postfach 10 60 33, 70049 Stuttgart Germany. **Tel** 011 49 771 6410, FAX 011 49 711 6412440.

ISSN 1035-865X
DD 330.0994 AT

AUSTRALIAN ECONOMIC INDICATORS. See Business and Economics.

ISSN 0727-1476
DD 339.230994 AT

AUSTRALIAN NATIONAL ACCOUNTS, INPUT-OUTPUT TABLES, COMMODITY DETAILS. [Aust. natl. acc. input-output tables commod. details]. **Added/Corp** Australian Bureau of Statistics. (1975)-. English. Three times a year. 50.00Aus$. Australian Bureau of Statistics, PO Box 2796Y, Melbourne 3001 Australia. **Tel** 011 61 3 6157843.
Desc: Provides detailed information about the Input-Output Commodity Classification. Also shows the value of Australian production, imports and exports for over 1,000 commodities classified to the industry of origin.

ISSN 0817-3192
DD 338.702594 AT

AUSTRALIA'S TOP 500 COMPANIES. (AUSTRALIA'S TOP 500 COMPANIES.). [Aust. top 500 co.]. **VFOAT** Australia's Top Five Hundred Companies. (1986/87)-. English. One time a year. 265.00Aus$. Riddell Information Services Pty Limited, PO Box 3942, Sydney New South Wales 2001 Australia. **Tel** 11 61 23682100, FAX 11 61 23682150, telex 126736. **ED** Fran DeBiasi. **Bk Rev**, (Qty: 1/year). **Ad Acc, Adv Mgr:** Max Cunningham.

LC LB1043 .A86 **ISSN** 1044-0445
DD 011 001 US
NLM LB 1043; A912

AV MARKET PLACE. [AV mark. place]. **VFOAT** AV Marketplace; AVMP; AV Market Place with Industry Yellow Pages. **VAT** Audio Visual Market Place. (1989)-. English. One time a year. $144.95. R.R. Bowker, A Reed Reference Publishing Company, Part of Reed International PLC, PO Box 31, 121 Chanlon Drive, New Providence NJ 07974. **Tel** (908)464-6800, (800)521-8110, FAX (908)665-6688, telex 138-755. ***Continues*** *Audio Video Market Place, 0000-1112.*
Desc: Contains information on more than 6,500 companies that create, supply, or distribute an extraordinary range of A/V equipment and services for business, education, science, and government.

LC Z7165.I9 I94A HC547.I8
DD 016.3309/666/805 IC

B.D.I.-INFORMATIONS. **Main/Corp** Ivory Coast. Bureau de Developpement Industriel. Service de Documentation. **VAT** Bureau de Developpement Industriel-Informations. No. 1- April 1974-. Multiple languages (English and French). Cote d"Ivoire Bureau de Developpement Industriel, BP 4196, Abidjan Ivory Coast.

LC HG3882 .B34 **ISSN** 0252-3035
DD 382.1/7/0212 US

BALANCE OF PAYMENTS STATISTICS. YEARBOOK. [Balance paym. stat. yearb. - Int. Monet. Fund]. **Added/Corp** International Monetary Fund. Balance of Payments Division. International Monetary Fund. Balance of Payments and External Debt Division. Vol. 32, Pt. 1 (1981)-. Periodical. English. One time a year. $64.00. International Monetary Fund, 700 19th Street Northwest, Publishing Unit, Washington DC 20431. **Tel** (202)623-7430, FAX (202)623-7201. available on magnetic tape; available on microfilm and microfiche from University Microfilms International (UMI). ***Continues in part*** *Balance of Payments Yearbook, 0378-2662.*
Desc: Includes aggregates as well as detailed presentations and explanatory notes. Includes tables of data, featuring area and world totals of balance of payments, components and aggregates.

LC HF3790.6.A45 B36a
DD 382/.095492/00212 BG

BANGLADESH EXPORT STATISTICS. **Main/Corp** Bangladesh. Raptani Unnayana Byuro. (1978)-. English (Bengali). One time a year. Free. Export Promotion Bureau Bangladesh, 122-124 Montijheel Commercial Area, Dacca Bangladesh. **Tel** 232245-49, telex 642204 EPBBBJ. **Circ:** 4,000 (ctrl).

LC HG1501 **ISSN** 0333-1504
DD 332.1 NO

BANK- OG KREDITTSTATISTIKK: AKTUELLE TALL. **Added/Corp** Norway. Statstisk Sentralbyra. No. 1 (March 30, 1981)-. Statistical Publication. Norwegian. Irregular. Kr440.00. Central Bureau of Statistics / Norway, PO Box 8131 DEP, N-0033 Oslo 1 Norway. **Tel** 011 47 2 2864964, FAX 011 47 2 864973. ***Continues in part*** *Kvartalshefte for Private OG Offentlige Banker.*

LC HG3051 .D48 **ISSN** 0943-8750
DD 332.1 GW

●**BANKENSTATISTIK.** **Added/Corp** Deutsche Bundesbank. (Jan. 1993)-. German (English). Twelve times a year. Deutsche Bundesbank Presse, Information Wilh Epsteinstrasse 14, D-60431 Frankfurt Germany. **Tel** 011 49 69 1583509 or 1583455, telex 41 227 OR 414 431. ***Continues*** *Statistische Beihefte zu den Monatsberichten der Deutschen Bundesbank. Reihe 1, Bankenstatistik nach Bankengruppen, 0419-9014.*

LC Z7164.F5 A53 HG1501 **ISSN** 1075-282X
DD 016.3321 US

●**BANKING INFORMATION INDEX.** [Bank. inf. index]. **Added/Corp** American Bankers Association. Vol. 1, 1st Quarter (1994)-. Periodical. English. Four times a year. $203.00. University Microfilms International, 300 North Zeeb Road, Ann Arbor MI 48106-1346. **Tel** (313)761-4700, (800)521-0600 Exts. 2490, 2491, FAX (313)973-1540. ***Continues*** *American Bankers Association Banking Literature Index, 0736-5659.*

LC HG3290.5.S8 A326 **ISSN** 0067-3811
DD 332 PK

BANKING STATISTICS OF PAKISTAN. **Main/Corp** State Bank of Pakistan. Dept. of Statistics. (1948/1957)-. English. One time a year. $6.00. State

Bank of Pakistan - Public Relation Department, PO Box 4456, Central Directorate, Karachi Pakistan. **Tel** 011 92 21 2414141310, telex 2754 SBP. **Circ:** 485.
Desc: Covers banking and finance.

LC HA1320.N6 A32 HD5780.N
DD 314.3 GW
BESCHAFTIGTENENTWICKLUNG IN NORDRHEIN-WESTFALEN. ERGEBNISSE EINER REGIONAL DISAGGREGIERTEN ANALYSE, DIE.
VFOAT Ergebnisse Einer Regional Disaggregierten Analyse. (1983)-. German. Landesamt fuer Datenverarbeitung und Statistik Nordrhein-Westfalen, Postfach 101105, 40002 Duesseldorf Germany. **Tel** (0211)944901, FAX (0211)442006, telex 8586654 LDST D.

LC Z7165.B7 B53 HC186 **ISSN** 0103-2038
DD 016.338981 BL
BIBLIOGRAFIA DE POLITICA INDUSTRIAL. **Added/Corp** Confederacao Nacional da Industria. Divisao de Documentacao e Informacao Bibliografica. Vol. 1, No. 1 (1987)-. Portuguese. One time a year. Confederacao Nacional da Industria / Brazil, Av Nilo Pecanha 50 GR 2608, 20044 Rio de Janeiro Brazil. **Tel** 011 55 21 5320330, 011 55 21 2927766.

ISSN 0067-6764
PO
BIBLIOGRAFIA SOBRE A ECONOMIA PORTUGUESA. Portuguese. One time a year. Instituto Nacional de Estatistica, Avenida Antonio Jose de Almeida, 1078 Lisbon Codex Portugal. **Tel** 011 351 1 8470050.

LC Z7164.C81 N353a **ISSN** 0360-2702
DD 016.3 US
BIBLIOGRAPHIC GUIDE TO BUSINESS AND ECONOMICS. **Main/Corp** New York Public Library. Research Libraries. (1975)-. English. One time a year. $575.00. GK Hall & Co., 100 Front Street, Riverside NJ 08075. **Tel** (800)257-5755 ext. 2223.
Desc: Lists materials cataloged during the past year by the New York Public Library with additional entries from LC MARC tapes. All aspects of business and economics covered: industry, labor, finance, demography, etc.

LC Z7164.E2 B5185 HC54 **ISSN** 0006-1417
DD 016.33 GW
CCC
BIBLIOGRAPHIE DER WIRTSCHAFTSPRESSE. [Bibliogr. Wirtschaftspr.]. **Added/Corp** Hamburgisches Welt-Wirtschafts-Archiv. HWWA-Institut fuer Wirtschaftsforschung-Hamburg. (1949)-. Periodical. German (French, English and Italian). Twelve times a year. $161.20. Verlag Weltarchiv GmBH, Neuer Jungfernstieg 21, D-20354 Hamburg Germany. **Tel** 011 49 40 3562500. **Circ:** 400.

LC Z1605 .B46 F1401 **ISSN** 0752-4080
DD 016.98 FR
BIBLIOGRAPHIE LATINOAMERICAINE D'ARTICLES. No. 10 (May 1981)-. Bibliography. English (Portuguese, Spanish and Dutch). Two times a year. 80.00F (individuals), 100.00F (institutions) France; $19.00 (individuals), $24.00 (institutions) US. 28 rue Saint Guillaume, 75007 Paris France. **Tel** 42 22 35-93. **Circ:** 250 (ctrl). ***Continues*** *Bibliographie d'Articles de Revues.*
Desc: Covers the economic, social and political aspects of Latin American development studies, as well as history, education and geography. Also covers Latin American, American, English and German journals.

LC Z7164.L1 B53 HD8448 **ISSN** 0343-4117
DD 016.3 GW
CCC
BIBLIOGRAPHIE ZUR GESCHICHTE DER DEUTSCHEN ARBEITERBEWEGUNG. [Bibliogr. Gesch. dtsch. Arb. beweg.]. Vol. 1 (1976)-. Periodical. German (Multiple languages). One time a year. DM68.00 (add DM4.00 postage) Germany; add DM6.00 (postage) other. Verlag Neue Gesellschaft GmbH, Godesberger Allee 143, W-5300 Bonn 2 Germany. **Tel** 0288/37 80 21. **ED** Friedrich-Ebert-Sfiftung. Index Available, published separately, free-automatically sent. **Circ:** 500.
Desc: Labour movement, working class problems, socialism, communism, anarchism and social history.

ISSN 0749-1786
DD 330 US
BIBLIOGRAPHIES AND INDEXES IN ECONOMICS AND ECONOMIC HISTORY. [Bibliogr. indexes econ. econ. hist.]. No. 1-. English. Irregular. Greenwood Press Inc., PO Box 5007, Westport CT 06881-5007. **Tel** (203)226-3571, FAX (203)222-1502.

LC Z7164.C83 B52 HG6046
DD 016.33264/4 US
BIBLIOGRAPHY & INFORMATION SOURCE LIST. **VFOAT** Bibliography and Information Source List; Information Source List; Bibliography. (19??)-. Bibliography. English. Chicago Mercantile Exchange, 30 South Wacker Drive, Chicago IL 60606. **Tel** (312)930-8210.

LC Z7165.T3 B5 HC557.T3
DD 016.3309/678 TZ
BIBLIOGRAPHY OF ECONOMIC AND STATISTICAL PUBLICATIONS ON TANZANIA, A. 1967-. Statistical Publication. English. Bureau of Statistics / Tanzania, PO Box 796, Dar es Salaam Tanzania.

LC Z7164.C8 B55
DD 016.382/6/0954 II
BIBLIOGRAPHY ON OVERSEAS MARKET SURVEYS OF INDIAN PRODUCTS. **Added/Corp** Indian Institute of Foreign Trade. (19??)-. Bibliography. English. Indian Institute of Foreign Trade, H 24 Green Park Ext., New Delhi India.

US
BIOBUSINESS. (19??)-. Abstracting/Indexing Service. English. Irregular. BioSciences Information Service, Biological Abstracts / BIOSIS, 2100 Arch Street, Philadelphia PA 19103. **Tel** (800)523-4806, (215)587-4847, FAX (215)587-2016, telex 831739.
Desc: Monitors the business applications and economic implications of biological and biomedical research. Monitors both technical and business literature for developments that affect the life science marketplace.

ISSN 0898-5227
DD 660 US
BIOBUSINESS SEARCH GUIDE. [Biobusiness search guide]. **Added/Corp** BioSciences Information Service of Biological Abstracts. (1986)-. English. Irregular. $75.00. BioSciences Information Service, Biological Abstracts / BIOSIS, 2100 Arch Street, Philadelphia PA 19103. **Tel** (800)523-4806, (215)587-4847, FAX (215)587-2016, telex 831739.
Desc: Designed to support users of the BioBusiness database. Provides a list of indexing codes, vocabulary words, and more.

LC TP HB **ISSN** 1354-280X
DD 660 330 UK
BIOCOMMERCE FINANCIAL ABSTRACTS. **See** Biology-Abstracting, Bibliographies and Statistics.

LC HA1025 .B36A
DD 318.66 EC
BOLETIN ANUARIO - BANCO CENTRAL DEL ECUADOR. **Main/Corp** Banco Central del Ecuador. No. 1- 1978-. Bulletin. Spanish. One time a year. Museo Antropologico, Banco Central de Ecuador, Secretaria General, PO Box 1331, Guayaquil Ecuador. **Tel** 011 593 4 517717, telex 043257 BCOCNG ED MUSEO. Index available. **Bk Rev**. **Ad Acc**. ctrl circ.

LC HD8581 .B65 **ISSN** 0212-7180
DD 331.0946 SP
BOLETIN DE ESTADISTICAS LABORALES. **Added/Corp** Spain. Ministerio de Trabajo y Seguridad Social. Subdirecion General Estadistica e Informatica. Spain. Ministerio de Trabajo y Seguridad Social. Subdireccion General de Estadistica. **VFOAT** Estadisticas Laborales. (19??)-. Statistical Publication. Spanish. Twelve times a year. $106.58. Centro de Publicaciones Min Trabajo, Augustin de Bethencourt 11, 28071 Madrid Spain. **Tel** 011 34 1 5543400, 5330106.

LC HA943 .B3
DD 318.2 AG
BOLETIN ESTADISTICO. **Added/Corp** Banco Central de la Republica Argentina. Gerencia de Investigaciones y Estadisticas Economicas. Vol. 23, No. 1 (Jan. 1980)-. Statistical Publication. Spanish. Twelve times a year. $180.00. Banco Central de la Republica Argentina, Reconquista 266, 1003 Buenos Aires Argentina. ***Continues*** *Boletin Estadistico (Banco Central de la Republica Argentina).*

LC HC60 .G693 **ISSN** 0068-1210
DD 338.91/172/4041 UK
CCC
BRITISH AID STATISTICS. **Main/Corp** Great Britain. Ministry of Overseas Development. **Added/Corp** Great Britain. Ministry of Overseas Development. Great Britain. Overseas Development Administration. (1966)-. English. One time a year. £8.00. Overseas Development Administration / Glasgow, Abercombie House, Eaglesham Road, Glasgow G75 8EA United Kingdom. **Tel** 011 44 141 355843599, FAX 011 44 141 355844099. ***Continues*** *British Aid Statistics, 0068-1210.*
Desc: Annual publication showing flows of UK overseas aid for economic and social development. Gives information for year in question and previous years for comparison.

UG
BROCHURE FOR ... / INSTITUTE OF STATISTICS AND APPLIED ECONOMICS. **Main/Corp** Institute of Statistics and Applied Economics (Uganda). (1990)-. English. Institute of Statistics and Applied Economics, Makerere University, PO Box 7062, Kampala Uganda.

LC Z7165.A4 P36A HC800
DD 016.33096 UV
BULLETIN BIBLIOGRAPHIQUE DU FONDS DOCUMENTAIRE DU CENTRE DE DOCUMENTATION DE L'IPD-AOS.
Main/Corp Centre de Documentation de l'IPD-AOS. (19??)-. Bulletin. French. IPD/AOS, BP 1756, Ouagadougou Burkina Faso.

LC Z7164.U5 B85 HC59.7 .B837 **ISSN** 0020-2398
DD 016.33/09172/4 FR
BULLETIN BIBLIOGRAPHIQUE - INSTITUT NATIONALE DE LA STATISTIQUE ET DES ETUDES ECONOMIQUES. (BULLETIN BIBLIOGRAPHIQUE.). [Bull. bibliogr. - Inst. nat. stat. etud. econ.]. (1983)-. Bulletin. French. Three times a year. 51.00F France; 63.00F other. CNGP INSEE - Institut National de la Statistique et des Estudes Economiques, BP 2718, 1 rue V Auriol, F 80027 Amiens Cedex 1 France. **Tel** 011 33 22 927322. Index available. cum. index. **Bk Rev**. **Ad Acc**. **Circ:** 800.
Desc: Analyses periodical articles and books dealing with the statistical methodology applicable or currently being applied to developing countries.

LC HC330. A456 **ISSN** 0076-1583
DD 330 LU
BULLETIN DU STATEC. [Bull. Statec]. **Main/Corp** Luxembourg. Service Central de la Statistique et des Etudes Economiques. **Added/Corp** Luxembourg. Service Central de la Statistique et des Etudes Economiques. Vol. 9, No. 7/8 (July/Aug. 1963)-. Bulletin. French. Eight times a year. 680.00F. Statistique et Etudes Economiques Statec, PO Box 304, 2013 Luxembourg Luxembourg. **Tel** 011 352 4784268, FAX 011 352 464289, telex 3464 ECOLU. Index available. cum. index. **Bk Rev**. **Circ:** 950. Documents available from BLDSC. ***Formed by the union of*** *Bulletin Statistique (Luxembourg. Service Central de la Statistique et des Etudes Economiques)* ***and*** *Bulletin Economique (Luxembourg, Luxembourg).*
Desc: Economic studies of statistical series and inquiries.
Ind/Abst Foreign Lang. Index; PAIS Int. Print (1991-); World Agric. Econ. Rural Sociol. Abstr.

LC HA2126 .M55A
DD 310 TG
BULLETIN MENSUEL DE STATISTIQUE (LOME, TOGO). (BULLETIN MENSUEL DE STATISTIQUE.). (19??)-. Bulletin. French. Twelve times a year. 2,000CFAF. Ministere du Plan, BP 118, Lome Togo.

LC HD5773 .A369 Suppl.
DD 331/.0944 FR
BULLETIN MENSUEL DES STATISTIQUES DU TRAVAIL. SUPPLEMENT (PARIS, FRANCE : 1982). (BULLETIN MENSUEL DES STATISTIQUES DU TRAVAIL. SUPPLEMENT.). **Added/Corp** France. Ministere du Travail. Service des Etudes et de la Statistique. France. Ministere de l'Emploi. France. Ministere des Affaires Sociales et de la Solidarite Nationale. Service des Etudes et de la Statistique. **VFOAT** Supplement au Bulletin Mensuel des Statistiques du Travail. No. 99 (1982)-. Bulletin. French. Twelve times a year. Ministere du Travail et Service d'Etudes, Statistique place Fontenoy, 75007 Paris France. ***Continues*** *Statistiques du Travail. Supplement au Bulletin Mensuel.*

LC HD4826 .I53 **ISSN** 0007-4950
DD 331/.0212 SZ
CCC
BULLETIN OF LABOUR STATISTICS. (BULLETIN OF LABOUR STATISTICS / INTERNATIONAL LABOUR OFFICE.). [Bull. labour stat.]. **Added/Corp** International Labour Office. **VFOAT** Bulletin des Statistiques du Travail; Boletin de Estadisticas del Trabajo. 1st Quarter (1965)-. Bulletin. English (French and Spanish). Nine times a year. $95.00. International Labour Office - ILO, Publications Sales Service, CH-1211 Geneva 22 Switzerland. **Tel** 011 41 22 7996111, FAX 011 41 22 7986253, telex 415 647 ilo ch. **(Subscription address:** International Labour Office / Washington, DC, 1828 L Street Northwest, Suite 801, Washington DC 20036. **Tel** (202)653-7652.) ***Continues in part*** *International Labour Review, 0020-7780.* ***Continued in part by*** *Bulletin of Labour Statistics. October Inquiry Results.*
Desc: Articles on methodology and special topics. Trilingual tables of current statistics on employment,

unemployment, wages, hours of work, consumer prices, (with updated supplements for intervening months). A separate issue gives results of ILO October Inquiry on wages and hours of work by occupation and retail food prices.
Ind/Abst Int. Labour Doc.; LABORDOC.

LC HA2090 .A15a
DD 316.7/21 GO
BULLETIN TRIMESTRIEL DE STATISTIQUE. **Added/Corp** Gabon. Direction Generale de la Statistique et des Etudes Economiques. **VFOAT** Bulletin Mensuel de Statistique. (198?)-. French. Four times a year. Direction de la Statistique et des Etudes Economiques, BP 2081, Libreville Gabon. ***Continues*** *Bulletin Mensuel de Statistique de la Republique Gabonaise, 0304-9485.*

US
BUSINESS ASAP [COMPUTER FILE]. (19??)-. Abstracting/Indexing Service. English. Twelve times a year. $11,500.00 (one workstation), $15,000.00 (two to four workstations) academic libraries. Information Access Company, 362 Lakeside Drive, Foster City CA 94404. **Tel** (800)227-8431, (800)458-1565.
Desc: Provides full text of over 340 titles indexed in the Business Index, Business & Company Profile, and General BusinessFile databases.

US
BUSINESS DATELINE. (BUSINESS DATELINE ONDISC [COMPUTER FILE].). Abstracting/Indexing Service. English. One time a year. Price varies per vendor for online service (Vendors: BRS, DIALOG Information Services, Dow Jones News/Retrieval, HRIN, Mead Data Central's Nexis, OCLC, VU/TEXT); $3150.00 (CD-ROM format). University Microfilms International, 300 North Zeeb Road, Ann Arbor MI 48106-1346. **Tel** (313)761-4700, (800)521-0600 Exts. 2490, 2491, FAX (313)973-1540. available on magnetic tape from University Microfilms International (UMI); available on microfilm from University Microfilms International (UMI); available on an online database from University Microfilms International (UMI).
Desc: Features over 200,000 articles from more than 300 regional business journals, daily newspapers, and business wire services. Records contain bibliographic and indexing information, plus the entire text of articles in ASCII format. Coverage begins with 1985 material.

LC Z5814.C7 B85 **ISSN** 0068-4414
DD 016.6507 US
BUSINESS EDUCATION INDEX. **Added/Corp** Delta Pi Epsilon. Business Education World. (1940)-. Abstracting/Indexing Service. English. One time a year. $25.00. Delta Pi Epsilon National Office, PO Box 4340, Little Rock AR 72214. **Tel** (501)562-1233, FAX (501)562-1293. **ED** Pat R Graves. **Circ:** 10,000 (ctrl). available on diskette; available on microfilm and microfiche from University Microfilms International (UMI).
Desc: Index of business education articles, research studies, and textbooks for year.

LC HB **ISSN** 0273-3684
DD 016.330 US
BUSINESS INDEX. (BUSINESS INDEX MICROFORM.). **Added/Corp** Information Access Corporation. (Sept. 1980)-. Abstracting/Indexing Service. English. Twelve times a year. $3500.00. Information Access Company, 362 Lakeside Drive, Foster City CA 94404. **Tel** (800)227-8431, (800)458-1565. **(Subscription address:** Information Access Company, PO Box 61000, Department 1851, San Francisco CA 94161. **Tel** (800)321-6388.**)** available on CD-ROM; available on an online database from Lexis-Nexis; DIALOG; and BRS.
Desc: Provides complete, cover-to-cover indexing and abstracting to over 930 business, management and trade journals.

LC HF1371 **ISSN** 1353-0208
DD 382.094104 UK
•**BUSINESS MONITOR MQ20. OVERSEAS TRADE STATISTICS OF THE UNITED KINGDOM WITH COUNTRIES WITHIN THE EUROPEAN COMMUNITY.** [Bus. monit. MQ20, Overseas trade stat. U.K. ctries Eur. Community]. (1993)-. Periodical. English. Four times a year. Her Majesty's Stationery Office, 51 Nine Elms Lane, London SW8 5DR United Kingdom. **Tel** 011 44 171 8738459, 011 44 171 8738499, FAX 011 44 171 8738499, 011 44 171 8738456, telex 297138. **(Subscription address:** Her Majesty's Stationery Office, PO Box 276, Public Centre, London SW8 5DT United Kingdom. **Tel** 011 44 171 8738499, 011 44 171 8738456.**)**

ISSN 0007-6961
US
NLM Z 7164.C81 B979
Pr Rev.
BUSINESS PERIODICALS INDEX. [Bus. period. index]. **Added/Corp** H.W. Wilson Company. Vol. 1 (Jan. 1958)-. Abstracting/Indexing Service. English. Eleven times a year (monthly except Aug.). $1,495.00 CD-ROM; Print edition sold on the service basis. H W Wilson Company, 950 University Avenue, Bronx NY 10452. **Tel** (800)367-6770, (718)588-8400 ext. 2245, FAX (718)681-1511, telex 4990003 HWILSON. **ED** Walter Webb. Index available. cum. index. ctrl circ. available on CD-ROM from WILSONDISC; available on diskette from WILSONSEARCH; available on magnetic tape from WILSONTAPE; available on an online database from WILSONLINE; and BRS. Documents available from BLDSC. ***Continues in part*** *Industrial Arts Index, 0275-1682.*
Desc: Provides thorough, accurate, and timely indexing of every article in over 400 important business magazines. Coverage provides access to information as varied and wide-ranging as the business world itself.

ISSN 0007-6961
US
NLM Z 7164.C81 B979
Pr Rev.
BUSINESS PERIODICALS INDEX. **See** Business and Economics-Abstracting, Bibliographies and Statistics.

LC HD **ISSN** 1076-7053
DD 338 US
BUSINESS PERIODICALS INDEX (CD-ROM). (BUSINESS PERIODICALS INDEX [COMPUTER FILE].). [Bus. period. index]. **Added/Corp** H.W. Wilson Company. **VFOAT** Wilsondisc Business Periodicals Index. (1987)-. Periodical. English. Twelve times a year. $1515.00. H W Wilson Company, 950 University Avenue, Bronx NY 10452. **Tel** (800)367-6770, (718)588-8400 ext. 2245, FAX (718)681-1511, telex 4990003 HWILSON. available in print; available on an online database.
Desc: Provides indexing of 345 of the key international business periodicals. Covers accounting, foreign trade, management, communications, and more.

LC HF **ISSN** 1073-1946
DD 650 US
•**BUSINESS SOURCE (PEABODY, MASS.).** (BUSINESS SOURCE [COMPUTER FILE] : EBSCO CD-ROM.). [Bus. source]. **Added/Corp** EBSCO Publishing (Firm). (1993)-. Abstracting/Indexing Service. English. Twelve times a year. $1,495.00. EBSCO Publishing / Boston, 83 Pine Street, Peabody MA 01960. **Tel** (800)653-2726 North America, (508)535-8500, FAX (508)535-8545. **ED** Melissa Kummerer.
Desc: Business Source provides access to abstracts and indexing coverage of over 500 journals in international business, finance, management, and corporate organization. The business titles selected cover all areas of the country, and have the highest subscriber volume in corporate and college/university libraries.

LC HF **ISSN** 1083-4508
DD 650 US
•**BUSINESS SOURCE PLUS [COMPUTER FILE].** (1995)-. Abstracting/Indexing Service. English. Twelve times a year. $2,995.00. EBSCO Publishing / Boston, 83 Pine Street, Peabody MA 01960. **Tel** (800)653-2726 North America, (508)535-8500, FAX (508)535-8545.

LC HC101 .A13122 **ISSN** 0083-2545
DD 338.9 US
BUSINESS STATISTICS (BIENNIAL). (BUSINESS STATISTICS.). **Added/Corp** United States. Bureau of Economic Analysis. United States. Office of Business Economics. (1951)-. Statistical Publication. English. Every 2 years. $30.00. Superintendent of Documents, US Government Printing Office, Washington DC 20402. **Tel** (202)275-3328, FAX (202)786-2377. available on microfilm and microfiche from University Microfilms International (UMI). ***Continues*** *Statistical Supplement to the Survey of Current Business.*
Ind/Abst Predicasts Forecasts.

ISSN 0967-6392
UK
BUSINESS STATISTICS LONDON. [Bus. stat.Lond.]. (1990)-. English. Irregular (every 2 years). $204.00. Headland Business Information, 1 Henry Smiths Terrace, Headland Cleveland, TS24 0PD United Kingdom. **Tel** 011 44 429 231902, FAX 011 44 429 861403.

US
BUSINESS STATISTICS, NEW YORK STATE. **Main/Corp** New York (State). Bureau of Business Research. Jan./Mar. 1977-. English. Irregular. New York Economic Development Department, 1 Commerce Plaza, Room 900, Albany NY 12245. **Tel** (518)474-4100, FAX (518)474-1512. ***Continues*** *Quarterly Summary of Business Statistics, New York State.*

ISSN 1031-1343
DD 338.0029494 AT
BUSINESS WHO'S WHO PRODUCTS AND TRADENAMES GUIDE. [Bus. who's who prod. traden. guide]. **VFOAT** Products and Tradenames Guide. (1989)-. English. One time a year. 287.76Aus$. Riddell Information Services Pty Limited, PO Box 3942, Sydney New South Wales 2001 Australia. **Tel** 11 61 23682100, FAX 11 61 23682150, telex 126736. **ED** Sue Francis. Index available. **Bk Rev**, (Qty: 1/year). **Ad Acc, Adv Mgr:** Max Cunningham. **Circ:** 2,500. ***Continues*** *Australian Buying Reference, 0311-5070.*
Desc: Industrial purchasing reference guide listing products and services provided by over 11,000 large companies throughout Australia.

LC HG4651 **ISSN** 0046-9777
DD 332.63/2/0973 US
C.F.A. DIGEST, THE. **Main/Corp** Institute of Chartered Financial Analysts. **VAT** Chartered Financial Analyst Digest. Vol. 1 (Summer 1971)-. Periodical. English. Four times a year. $40.00. Association for Investment Management Research, 5 Boar's Head Lane, Charlottesville VA 22903. **Tel** (804)980-9712, (804)977-6600. **ED** John W. Peavy. **Circ:** 12,000 (ctrl).
Desc: Presents abstracts of articles on subjects such as equity securities analysis, fixed-income securities analysis, portfolio management, financial accounting, economics, and ethics. Articles are taken from publications in the industry of finance, and the Journal of Portfolio Management.

LC HD5727 .C395 **ISSN** 0835-8478
DD 331.11/0971/021 CN
CANADA'S MEN. (CANADA'S MEN = LES HOMMES AU CANADA.). [Can. men]. **Added/Corp** Statistics Canada. Labour and Household Surveys Analysis Division. Canada. Employment and Immigration Canada (Dept.). **VFOAT** Hommes au Canada. (1986)-. English (French). One time a year. 12.00Can$ Canada; $14.00 US; $17.00 other. Statistics Canada Publications Sales and Services, R.H. Coats Building 6th Floor, Ottawa Ontario K1A 0T6 Canada. **Tel** (613)951-5078, (800)267-6677, FAX (613)951-1584, telex 053-3585.

LC HD6283.C2 .C37 **ISSN** 0835-8494
DD 331.3/98/0971021 CN
CANADA'S OLDER WORKERS. (CANADA'S OLDER WORKERS.). [Can. older work.]. **Added/Corp** Statistics Canada. Labour and Household Surveys Analysis Division. Canada. Employment and Immigration Canada (Dept.). **VFOAT** Travailleurs Plus Ages au Canada; Travailleurs Ages au Canada. (1986)-. English (French). One time a year. 9.61Can$. Statistics Canada Publications Sales and Services, R.H. Coats Building 6th Floor, Ottawa Ontario K1A 0T6 Canada. **Tel** (613)951-5078, (800)267-6677, FAX (613)951-1584, telex 053-3585.

LC WMLC L 83/9245 **ISSN** 0835-8559
DD 331.88/0971 CN
CANADA'S UNIONIZED WORKERS. (CANADA'S UNIONIZED WORKERS.). [Can. union. work.]. **Added/Corp** Statistics Canada. Labour and Household Surveys Analysis Division. Canada. Employment and Immigration Canada (Dept.). **VFOAT** Travailleurs Syndiques au Canada. (1986)-. English (French). One time a year. 12.00Can$ Canada; $14.00 US; $17.00 other. Statistics Canada Publications Sales and Services, R.H. Coats Building 6th Floor, Ottawa Ontario K1A 0T6 Canada. **Tel** (613)951-5078, (800)267-6677, FAX (613)951-1584, telex 053-3585.

LC HD6097 .C37 **ISSN** 0835-846X
DD 331.4/0971/021 CN
CANADA'S WOMEN. (CANADA'S WOMEN = LES FEMMES AU CANADA.). [Can. women]. **Added/Corp** Statistics Canada. Labour and Household Surveys Analysis Division. Canada. Employment and Immigration Canada (Dept.). **VFOAT** Femmes au Canada. (1986)-. English (French). One time a year. 12.00Can$ Canada; $14.00 US; $17.00 other. Statistics Canada Publications Sales and Services, R.H. Coats Building 6th Floor, Ottawa Ontario K1A 0T6 Canada. **Tel** (613)951-5078, (800)267-6677, FAX (613)951-1584, telex 053-3585.
Desc: This report looks at the annual patterns of employment and unemployment of women and the characteristics of jobs they hold.

LC HD6276.C29 C36 **ISSN** 0835-8486
DD 331.3/4/0971021 CN
CANADA'S YOUTH. (CANADA'S YOUTH.). [Can. youth]. **Added/Corp** Statistics Canada. Labour and Household Surveys Analysis Division. Canada. Employment and Immigration Canada (Dept.). **VFOAT** Jeunes au Canada. (1986)-. English (French). One time a year. 9.61Can$. Statistics Canada Publications Sales and Services, R.H. Coats Building 6th Floor, Ottawa Ontario K1A 0T6 Canada. **Tel** (613)951-5078, (800)267-6677, FAX (613)951-1584, telex 053-3585.

LC HC111 .B8 **ISSN** 0832-2503
DD 330.971/0021 CN
CANADIAN MARKETS (1986). (CANADIAN MARKETS.). [Can. mark.]. **Added/Corp** Financial Post Information Service. **VFOAT** Financial Post Canadian Markets. 61st Ed. (1986)-. English. One time a year. 96.00Can$. Financial Post DataGroup, 333 King Street East, Toronto Ontario M5A 4N2 Canada. **Tel** (800)661-7678, FAX (416)350-6501. ***Continues*** *Financial Post Canadian Markets, 0227-6038.*
Desc: Contains complete demographic summaries on over 500 Canadian urban markets; features comparative rankings of urban centers by population, retail sales, and individual income.

LC HC151.A1 C376
DD 016.3309182/1 /2 19 TR
CARISPLAN ABSTRACTS / CARIBBEAN DEVELOPMENT AND COOPERATION COMMITTEE.
Added/Corp United Nations. Caribbean Development and Co-operation Committee. United Nations. Economic Commission for Latin America. Office for the Caribbean. Caribbean Documentation Centre (United Nations). **VFOAT** C.A.R.I.S.P.L.A.N. Abstracts. **VAT** Caribbean Information System for Economic and Social Planning Abstracts. No. 1 (1980)-. English (Spanish and French). Four times a year. Free. CEPAL / United Nations Economic Commission for Latin America / Trinidad and Tobago, Subregional Headquarters for the Caribbean, Caribbean Documentation Centre, PO Box 1113, Port of Spain Trinidad Tobago. **Tel** 62-35595, telex 22394 ECLAC WG. **ED** Wilma Primus. **Circ:** 600. available on microfilm.
Desc: Disseminates bibliographic information (generated by information units in a regional network, CARISPLAN) on Caribbean socio-economic planning and development literature, with special emphasis on locally-produced, unpublished documents.

LC HG1616.E7 Z55 **ISSN** 0148-5423
DD 658.89/332120973 US
CASH DISPENSERS AND AUTOMATED TELLERS.
(CASH DISPENSERS AND AUTOMATED TELLERS : STATISTICAL DATA AND ANALYSIS WITH SELECTED CASE HISTORIES.). (1972)-. Statistical Publication. English. One time a year. Payment Services Correspondent, 80 Lawn Street, Park Ridge NJ 07656.

LC HG4530 **ISSN** 0813-1139
DD 332.63270994 AT
CASH MANAGEMENT TRUSTS, AUSTRALIA.
[Cash manage. trusts Aust.]. **Added/Corp** Australian Bureau of Statistics. (1983)-. Periodical. English. Twelve times a year. 6.10Aus$. Australian Bureau of Statistics, PO Box 2796Y, Melbourne 3001 Australia. **Tel** 011 61 3 6157843.
Desc: Covers financial operations, net yield to unit holders, assets and maturity dissection of assets.

LC Z1413 .F6
DD 016 MX
CATALOGO GENERAL - FONDO DE CULTURA ECONOMICA, MEXICO.
Main/Corp Fondo de Cultura Economica, Mexico. Spanish. One time a year. Avenida Universidad 975, Mexico 12 DF Mexico. **Tel** 660-14-61, telex 775866. **Bk Rev**.

LC HC307.A4 C4
DD 330.945/14/005 IT
CE.D.R.E.S. DOCUMENTI.
Added/Corp Alessandria (Italy : Province). Centro Documentazione e Richerche Economico-Sociali. **VFOAT** CeDRES Documenti. (19??)-. Periodical. Italian. Four times a year. Ce.D.R.E.S., Via Galimberti 2/A, 15100 Alessandria Italy. **Bk Rev**. **Circ:** 1,500.

LC QD **ISSN** 0009-2258
DD 540 US
CODEN CHABA8
CHEMICAL ABSTRACTS.
(CHEMICAL ABSTRACTS [MICROFORM].). **Added/Corp** American Chemical Society. American Chemical Society. Chemical Abstracts Service. Vol. 1, No. 1 (Jan. 1, 1907)-. Periodical. English. $17,400.00 (full service). Chemical Abstracts Service, (Subsidiary of The American Chemical Society), 2540 Olentangy River Road, PO Box 3012, Columbus OH 43210-0012. **Tel** (614)447-3731, (800)753-4227, FAX (614)447-3751. **(Subscription address:** Chemical Abstracts Service, Customer Service Department, PO Box 3012, Columbus OH 43210. **Tel** (800)848-6538, (614)447-3600.) cum. index. available in print. ***Continues*** *Review of American Chemical Research.*

ISSN 0278-1832
US
CODEN CAISDJ
CHEMICAL ABSTRACTS. PHYSICAL, INORGANIC, AND ANALYTICAL CHEMISTRY SECTIONS.
[Chem. abstr., Phys., inorg., anal. chem. sect.]. **Added/Corp** American Chemical Society. Chemical Abstracts Service. Vol. 97, No. 1 (July 12, 1982)-. Academic Scholarly Publication. English. Twenty-six times a year. $2240.00. Chemical Abstracts Service, (Subsidiary of The American Chemical Society), 2540 Olentangy River Road, PO Box 3012, Columbus OH 43210-0012. **Tel** (614)447-3731, (800)753-4227, FAX (614)447-3751. **(Subscription address:** Chemical Abstracts Service, Customer Service Department, PO Box 3012, Columbus OH 43210. **Tel** (800)848-6538, (614)447-3600.) available on an online database from STN International. Documents available from CASDDS. ***Continues*** *Chemical Abstracts. Physical and Analytical Chemistry Sections, 0009-2290.*
Ind/Abst Chem. Abstr.

UK
CHEMICAL BUSINESS BULLETINS.
(19??)-. Bulletin. English. One time a week (50 issues per year). £285.00 EC; $630.00 US; $£315.00 other. Royal Society of Chemistry, Thomas Graham House, Science Park, Cambridge CB4 4WF United Kingdom. **Tel** 011 44 1223 420066, FAX 011 44 1223 423623, telex 818293 ROYAL. **(Subscription address:** Royal Society of Chemistry, Turpin Distribution Services Ltd., Blackhorse Road, Letchworth, Hertfordshire SG6 1HN United Kingdom. **Tel** 011 44 1462 672555, FAX 011 44 1462 480947.) **ED** Kate Pearce. Index available. available on an online database from Textline; DIALOG; and DATA-STAR.
Desc: Weekly current awareness alerts reporting on the latest business news concerning specific industry sectors or business topics.

UK
•CHEMICAL BUSINESS NEWSBASE [ONLINE DATABASE].
(1993)-. Abstracting/Indexing Service. English. One time a year. Royal Society of Chemistry, Thomas Graham House, Science Park, Cambridge CB4 4WF United Kingdom. **Tel** 011 44 1223 420066, FAX 011 44 1223 423623, telex 818293 ROYAL. **(Subscription address:** Royal Society of Chemistry, Turpin Distribution Services Ltd., Blackhorse Road, Letchworth, Hertfordshire SG6 1HN United Kingdom. **Tel** 011 44 1462 672555, FAX 011 44 1462 480947.) available on an online database from Textline; STI International; DATA-STAR; and DIALOG.
Desc: CBNB, introduced in January 1985, is a major business information database containing entries drawn from worldwide business journals, newspapers and company literature. Updated weekly, CBNB covers the latest news, including facts and figures on companies, products, markets, sales and trends. Over 70% of the sources are published in Europe.

ISSN 0395-8191
FR
CHIFFRES POUR L'ALSACE.
(1971)-. Periodical. French. Four times a year. 120.00F. CNGP INSEE - Institut National de la Statistique et des Estudes Economiques, BP 2718, 1 rue V Auriol, F 80027 Amiens Cedex 1 France. **Tel** 011 33 22 927322. ***Supersedes*** *France. Institut National de la Statistique et des Etudes Economiques. Bulletin Regional de Statistique: Alsace (Bas-Rhin, Haut-Rhin).*
Desc: Publishes socio-economic information on the Strasbourg region of France in an accessible format with concise analysis of statistics.

LC HF3831.5 .C483 **ISSN** 0739-3512
DD 382/.0951/00212 US
CHINA : INTERNATIONAL TRADE. ANNUAL STATISTICAL SUPPLEMENT.
(CHINA, INTERNATIONAL TRADE. ANNUAL STATISTICAL SUPPLEMENT.). [China: int. trade., Annu. stat. suppl.]. **Added/Corp** United States. Central Intelligence Agency. Directorate of Intelligence. (19??)-. Statistical Publication. English. One time a year. National Technical Information Service - NTIS, Room 2027S, 5285 Port Royal Road, Springfield VA 22161. **Tel** (703)487-4630, (703)487-4660, (703)487-4650, FAX (703)321-8547, telex 89-9405. available on microfiche (Vols. for (1983-) distributed to depository libraries).

LC HC463.C48 J36a
DD 330 JA
CHUGOKU CHIIKI TSUSHO SANGYO TOKEI NEMPO.
Added/Corp Japan. Hiroshima Tsusho Sangyokyoku. Somubu. Chosaka. (19??)-. Statistical Publication. Japanese. One time a year. Tsusho Sangyosho Hiroshima Tsusho Sangyokyoku, (Hiroshima Regional Bureau of International Trade and Industry, Ministry of International Trade and Industry), 6-30 Kamihatchobori, Nakaku Hiroshimashi Hiroshimaken 730 Japan. ***Continues*** *Chugoku Tsusan Tokei Nempo.*

LC HF3831.5 .C584
DD 380.1/0951/021 HK
CHUNG-KUO HAI KUAN TUNG CHI.
Added/Corp China. Hai Kuan Tsung Shu. Ching Chi Tao Pao She. **VFOAT** China's Customs Statistics. (June 1983)-. Periodical. English (Chinese). Twelve times a year. $130.00. Economic Information & Agency, 342 Hennessy Road, 10-16th Floor, Hong Kong Hong Kong. **Tel** 011 852 25738217, FAX 011 852 8388304, telex 60647 EICC HX. **Circ:** 2,000. ***Continued in part by*** *China's Customs Statistics Yearbook.*
Desc: Provides statistical information on import and export commodities of China. Import and export value by commodities, and country.

LC HG3691 **ISSN** 1031-0193
DD 332.70994 AT
COMMERCIAL FINANCE AUSTRALIA.
[Commer. finance Aust.]. **Added/Corp** Australian Bureau of Statistics. (1985)-. Periodical. English. Twelve times a year. 6.10Aus$. Australian Bureau of Statistics, PO Box 2796Y, Melbourne 3001 Australia. **Tel** 011 61 3 6157843.
Desc: Finance commitments to businesses under fixed loan and revolving credit facilities by type of major lender; fixed loan commitments are classified by purpose and by industry of borrower.

LC K3550
DD 344.063635 UK
•COMPENDIUM OF HOUSING FINANCE STATISTICS.
See Housing and Urban Development-Abstracting, Bibliographies and Statistics.

LC HA1 .C57
DD 310/.5 US
COMPENDIUM OF SOCIAL STATISTICS AND INDICATORS = RECUEIL DE STATISTIQUES ET D'INDICATEURS SOCIAUX.
Added/Corp United Nations. Statistical Office. **VFOAT** Recueil de Statistiques et d'Indicateurs Sociaux. (1988)-. Government Publication. English (French). Twelve times a year. $75.00. United Nations Publications, 2 United Nations Plaza, Room DC2 0853, Department 007C, New York NY 10017. **Tel** (212)963-8303, (800)253-9646. ***Continues*** *Compendium of Social Statistics.*
Desc: A compilation of principle series and indicators which describe important social and related economic conditions and changes.

LC HC107.C8 C564a **ISSN** 0573-665X
DD 330.9746/005 US
CONNECTICUT MARKET DATA.
(CONNECTICUT MARKET DATA / PREPARED BY CONNECTICUT DEVELOPMENT COMMISSION.). [Conn. mark. data]. **Added/Corp** Connecticut Development Commission. Connecticut Development Commission. Economic Research Division. Connecticut Development Division. Business and Industrial Development Division. Connecticut. Dept. of Commerce. Connecticut. Dept. of Economic Development. (1958)-. English. One time a year. Free on request. Connecticut Department of Economic Development & Administration, 865 Brook Street, Rocky Hill CT 06067. **Tel** (203)258-4200, FAX (203)721-7650. **Circ:** 5,000 (ctrl).
Desc: Statistics dealing with Connecticut sales and trade markets, transportation systems, population, income, retail sales, economy and employment, housing and utilities.
Ind/Abst Stat. Ref. Index.

LC HB235.A8 A93a
DD 339.4/2/0994 AT
CONSUMER PRICE INDEX.
Main/Corp Australian Bureau of Statistics. (Dec. 1973)-. English. Four times a year. 42.76Aus$. Australian Bureau of Statistics, PO Box 2796Y, Melbourne 3001 Australia. **Tel** 011 61 3 6157843. ***Continues*** *Consumer Price Index.*
Desc: Covers movements in retail prices of goods and services commonly purchased by metropolitan wage and salary earner households.

LC Z
DD 016.64 US
CONSUMER PRICE INDEX (NEWS).
(NEWS. THE CONSUMER PRICE INDEX.). **Added/Corp** United States. Bureau of Labor Statistics. **VFOAT** Consumer Price Index. (197?)-. Government Publication. English. Twelve times a year. Free. US Department of Labor / Bureau of Labor Statistics, 441 G Street Northwest, Washington DC 20212. **Tel** (202)606-7800, FAX (202)606-7797. Documents available from Documents on Demand.
Ind/Abst Am. Stat. Index.

UK
CONTENTS OF CURRENT JOURNALS.
English. Twelve times a year. £300.00. London Business School Library, Sussex Place Regents Park, London NW1 4SA United Kingdom. **Tel** 011 44 171 2625050 ext. 444, FAX 011 44 171 7247875, telex 27461.
Desc: A monthly bulletin of contents pages from a selection of periodicals to which the London Business School Library subscribes.

UK
CEASED
CONTENTS OF RECENT ECONOMICS JOURNALS.
Added/Corp Gt. Brit., Dept. of Trade and Industry, Library Services, Economics Division. (199?)-(June 1994). Abstracting/Indexing Service. English. Her Majesty's Stationery Office, 51 Nine Elms Lane, London SW8 5DR United Kingdom. **Tel** 011 44 171 8738459, 011 44 171 8738499, FAX 011 44 171 8738499, 011 44 171 8738456, telex 297138. **Circ:** 600.

ISSN 0306-3224
UK
CONTENTS PAGES IN MANAGEMENT.
[Contents pages manage.]. (1974)-. Abstracting/Indexing Service. English. Twenty-six times a year. $212.19. Manchester Business School, Booth Street West, Manchester M15 6PB United Kingdom. **Tel** 011 44 161 2756333, FAX 011 44 161 2737732, telex 668354. **ED** Dorothy Ross. **Circ:** 250. ***Continues*** *Current Contents in Management.*
Desc: Consists of contents pages from over 250 major journals relating to management, economics and the social sciences.

LC WMLC L 83/1129
IT
CONTI DEGLI ITALIANI : COMPENDIO DELLA VITA ECONOMICA NAZIONALE / ISTITUTO CENTRALE DI STATISTICA, I.
Added/Corp Istituto Centrale di Statistica (Italy). (196?)-. Italian. One time a year. L19000. Istituto Nazionale Statistica, GBP SEZ4 Via Cesare Balbo 16, 00184 Rome Italy. **Tel** 011 39 6 46735118.

LC HG1501
DD 332.1 US
COSTS AND MARGINS IN BANKING. STATISTICAL SUPPLEMENTS.
Statistical Publication. English (French). Irregular. Price varies per volume. OECD Publications and Information Center, 2 rue Andre-Pascal, 75775 Paris Cedex 16 France. **Tel** 011 33 1 49104262, US:(202)785-6323, FAX 011 33 1 45248500, 011 33 1 45248176, telex 620 160 OCDE. available on microfiche.
Desc: Data on costs and margins in the banking industry in OECD countries.

LC HC687.F5 A23
DD 330.9/96/11 FJ
CURRENT ECONOMIC STATISTICS.
Main/Corp Fiji. Bureau of Statistics. (19??)-. English. Four times a year. $33.00. Fiji Government Printing & Statistics Department, PO Box 98, Suva Fiji Islands. **Tel** 011 679 385999.

LC Z7164.E2 D58a HB87
DD 016.32 IO
DAFTAR TAMBAHAN KOLEKSI PERPUSTAKAAN LEKNAS.
Main/Corp Lembaga Ekonomi Dan Kemasyarakatan Nasional. Perpustakaan. **Added/Corp** Lembaga Ekonomi Dan Kemasyarakatan Nasional. **VFOAT** Daftar Tambahan Koleksi Perpustakaan LEKNAS. **VAT** Daftar Tambahan Koleksi Perpustakaan Lembaga Ekonomi Dan Kemasyarakatan Nasional. No. 1 (Oct.-Dec. 1983/1984)-?. Indonesian (Indonesian, English and Dutch). Lembaga Ekonomi Dan Kemasyarakatan Nasional, Jalan Gondangdia Lama 39, Jakarta Indonesia. ***Continues*** *Daftar Tambahan Koleksi Perpustakaan Leknas.* ***Continued in part by*** *Berita Majalah.*

FR
DECIMAL.
No. 1 (1979)-. Periodical. French. Ten times a year. Price varies. CNGP INSEE - Institut National de la Statistique et des Estudes Economiques, BP 2718, 1 rue V Auriol, F 80027 Amiens Cedex 1 France. **Tel** 011 33 22 927322. ***Supersedes in part*** *Resultats Statistiques du Poitou Charentes.*
Desc: Publishes socio-economic information on the Poitiers region of France in an accessible format with concise analysis of statistics.

LC HC188.P4 .D47
DD 338.981 BL
DESEMPENHO DA ECONOMIA DE PERNAMBUCO.
No. 1- 1976-. Portuguese. Instituto de Desenvolvimento de Pernambuco (CONDEPE), Caixa Postal 3344, Recife Pernambuco Brazil. **Tel** 231-5005. **Circ:** 100.
Desc: Analysis of the economy of Pernambuco, showing total production and production by sector comparing performance for the year against that of the last two years. Also covers production activities on the levels of employment and cost of living and solvency levels of individuals and corporate bodies.

ISSN 0417-0164
DK
DETAILPRISER.
Main/Corp Denmark. Danmarks Statistik. **Added/Corp** Denmark. Statistiske Departement. Detailpriser. (19??)-. Statistical Publication. Dutch. Four times a year. Danmarks Statistik, Sejrgade 11, DK-2100 Copenhagen Denmark. **Tel** 011 45 3 9173917, FAX 011 45 31 18 48 01, telex 1 62 36. **Circ:** 775. ***Continues*** *Denmark. Statistiske Departement. Detailpriser.*
Desc: Average prices for 41 local municipalities collected for 81 items of the Danish consumer price indices.

ISSN 0955-0569
UK
DEVELOPMENT BIBLIOGRAPHIES.
[Dev. bibliogr.]. **VFOAT** Development Bibliography Series. (1988)-. Bibliography. English. Irregular. Institute of Development Studies SS, University of Sussex, Brighton BN1 9RE United Kingdom. **Tel** 011 44 1273 606261, FAX 011 44 1273 621202, 011 44 1273 691647. **ED** Katherine Orme.
Desc: Deals with subjects within the development field. Devoted to a key theme in development studies. Contains articles on agriculture, family, food, women and also bibliographies.
Ind/Abst Rural Dev. Abstr.; World Agric. Econ. Rural Sociol. Abstr.

LC HA1161 .A3
DD 318.5 UK
DIGEST OF WELSH STATISTICS.
Added/Corp Great Britain. Welsh Office. Great Britain. Ministry of Housing and Local Government. Great Britain. Home Office. **VFOAT** Crynhoad o Ystadegau Cymru. No. 1 (1954)-. Statistical Publication. English. One time a year. Welsh Office Publications Unit, Crown Building, Cathay's Park, Cardiff CF1 3NQ United Kingdom. **Tel** 011 44 1222 825111, FAX 011 44 1222 823036.

LC HD4141 .D57
DD 338.909 UK
DIRECT LABOUR ORGANISATIONS STATISTICS ... ACTUALS.
1981-82-. Statistical Publication. English. One time a year. £15.00. Chartered Institute of Public Finance and Accountancy, 2 3 Robert Street, London WC2N 6BH United Kingdom. **Tel** 011 44 171 8958823, FAX 011 44 171 8958825.

LC HF5415.1 .D57 **ISSN** 0192-3137
DD 381 US
DIRECT MARKETING MARKET PLACE, THE.
VFOAT Direct Marketing Marketplace; DMMP. (1980)-. English. One time a year (Mar.). $201.57. National Register Publishing Company Inc., PO Box 31, 121 Chanlon Road, New Providence NJ 07974. **Tel** (800)521-8110, (800)323-6772, FAX (908)665-6688. **ED** Edward L. Stern. **Ad Acc. Circ:** 5,000 (ctrl).
Desc: A networking source of the direct marketing industry including over 9,500 companies and 22,000 individuals in the various facets of direct marketing. Lists name and address; telephone and fax numbers; key executives; product/service description; sales and billings, etc.

LC HF1016 .I652a **ISSN** 0252-306X
DD 382/.0212 US
TITLE CHANGE
DIRECTION OF TRADE STATISTICS - INTERNATIONAL MONETARY FUND (MONTHLY EDITION).
(DIRECTION OF TRADE STATISTICS.). [Dir. trade stat. - Int. Monet. Fund]. **Added/Corp** International Monetary Fund. (1981)-(1994). Periodical. English. Four times a year. International Monetary Fund, 700 19th Street Northwest, Publishing Unit, Washington DC 20431. **Tel** (202)623-7430, FAX (202)623-7201. available on magnetic tape; available on microfilm and microfiche from University Microfilms International (UMI). ***Continues*** *Direction of Trade (International Monetary Fund. Bureau of Statistics), 0012-3226.* ***Continued by*** *Direction of Trade Statistics Quarterly.*
Desc: Provides data on the country and area distribution of the country's exports and imports as reported by themselves or their partners. Covers data for recent periods for about 135 countries.

LC HF1016 .I652a
DD 382/.0212 US
•DIRECTION OF TRADE STATISTICS QUARTERLY.
Added/Corp International Monetary Fund. Real Sector Division. **VFOAT** DOTS; Direction of Trade Statistics. (June 1994)-. Academic Scholarly Publication. English. Four times a year (plus yearbook). $104.00. International Monetary Fund, 700 19th Street Northwest, Publishing Unit, Washington DC 20431. **Tel** (202)623-7430, FAX (202)623-7201. **ED** John B. McLenaghan. **Circ:** 6,000. available on microfilm from University Microfilms International (UMI); available on microfiche from CIS / Congressional Information Service, Inc.; available on magnetic tape; available in reprints from University Microfilms International (UMI); available on an online database. Documents available from BLDSC, UMI Article Clearinghouse. ***Continues*** *Direction of Trade Statistics, 0252-306X.*
Desc: Presents import and export data as reported by the country or their partners.

LC HF91 .I65 **ISSN** 0252-3019
DD 382/.0212 US
DIRECTION OF TRADE STATISTICS. YEARBOOK - INTERNATIONAL MONETARY FUND.
(DIRECTION OF TRADE STATISTICS. YEARBOOK.). [Dir. trade stat., Yearb. - Int. Monet. Fund]. **Added/Corp** International Monetary Fund. (1981)-. Periodical. English. One time a year. $34.00. International Monetary Fund, 700 19th Street Northwest, Publishing Unit, Washington DC 20431. **Tel** (202)623-7430, FAX (202)623-7201. available on magnetic tape. ***Continues*** *Direction of Trade Yearbook, 0250-7358.*
Desc: Provides data on the country and area of distribution of the country's exports and imports as reported by themselves or their partners. Provides seven years of data for about 160 countries and two sets of world and area summaries: world and area trade as seen by the reporting countries and as seen by the partner countries to those transactions.

LC HA37 .A318
DD 310/.25/6 ET
DIRECTORY OF AFRICAN STATISTICIANS.
Added/Corp United Nations. Economic Commission for Africa. **VFOAT** Repertoire des Statisticiens Africains. (19??)-. Directory. English (French). Every 2 years. Free. United Nations Economic Commission for Africa, PO Box 3001, Addis Ababa Ethiopia. **Tel** (212)754-8302, telex 21029 VNECA ET. **Circ:** 1,800. ***Continues*** *African Directory of Statisticians.*

LC Z7165.U5 D59 HC101 **ISSN** 0278-0119
DD 016.3380973 016.3380971 US
DIRECTORY OF INDUSTRY DATA SOURCES. THE UNITED STATES OF AMERICA AND CANADA.
[Dir. ind. data sources]. Vol. 1 (1981)-. Directory. English. Irregular. Ballinger Publishing Company, 10 East 53rd Street, New York NY 10022-5244.

ISSN 0715-1055
DD 331.11/0971 CN
DONNEES SUR LA POPULATION ACTIVE : QUEBEC, ONTARIO ET CANADA.
[Donnees popul. act.: Que. Ont. Can.]. (1979)-. Periodical. French. Twelve times a year (also quarterly). 99.46Can$ (monthly), 43.82Can$ (quarterly). Bureau of Statistics / Quebec, Publications, 117 rue Saint Andre, Quebec Quebec G1K 3Y3 Canada. **Tel** (418)691-2401, (800)463-4090. **Circ:** 125 (ctrl).
Desc: Statistics on manpower.

LC HG181 .D35a **ISSN** 0271-1931
DD 332/.0973 US
DRI-FACS, FINANCIAL AND CREDIT STATISTICS INFORMATION SERVICE: APPLIED REPORTS AND GRAPHICS LIBRARY.
Main/Corp Data Resources, Inc. **Added/Corp** Data Resources, Inc. Applied Reports and Graphics Library. (19??)-. English. DRI McGraw Hill, 24 Hartwell Avenue, Lexington MA 02173. **Tel** (617)863-5100, FAX (617)860-6464, (617)860-6416.

LC HA1631 .A33 HD2346.Y8
DD 314.971 YU
DRUSTVENE ZANATSKE ORGANIZACIJE.
Main/Corp Savezni Zavod Za Statistiku (Yugoslavia). Serbo-Croatian (Roman). 4.00 Din. Savezni Zavod za Statistiku, Kneza Milosa 20, Belgrad Yugoslavia.

TU
DS TICARET ISTATISTIKLERI.
Added/Corp Devlet Istatistik Enstitusu (Turkey). **VFOAT** Foreign Trade Statistics. (19??)-. Statistical Publication. Turkish. Turkish State Institute of Statistics, Necatibey Cadessi 114, Ankara 016100 Turkey. **Tel** 011 90 4 1188719, FAX 011 90 4 1253387, telex 46347 DIETR. ***Continues*** *Ds Ticaret Yllk Istastistik.*

LC HF5343 .D8a **ISSN** 0196-8610
DD 338.0973 US
DUN'S CENSUS OF AMERICAN BUSINESS.
[Dun's census Am. bus.]. **Main/Corp** Dun and Bradstreet, Inc. **Added/Corp** Dun and Bradstreet, Inc. Census of American Business. **VFOAT** Census of American Business. (1979)-. English. One time a year. $325.00 libraries, $395.00 other. Dun & Bradstreet Information Services, 3 Sylvan Way, Parsippany NJ 07054. **Tel** (201)605-6000, (800)526-0651. **Bk Rev.**
Desc: Statistical resource covering more than 5 million US businesses. Provides a count of establishments in all industrial and commercial classifications, at the national, state and county levels.

LC HD4977 .E37 **ISSN** 0829-6235
DD 331.2/971021 CN
EARNINGS OF MEN AND WOMEN.
(EARNINGS OF MEN AND WOMEN = GAINS DES HOMMES ET DES FEMMES.). [Earn. men women]. **Added/Corp** Statistics Canada. Consumer Income and Expenditure Division. Statistics Canada. Labour and Household Surveys Analysis Division. Statistics Canada. Household Surveys Division. **VFOAT** Gains des Hommes et des Femmes. (1967/1969)-. English (French). One time a year. 27.00Can$ Canada; $33.00 North America; $38.00 other. Statistics Canada Publications Sales and Services, R.H. Coats Building 6th Floor, Ottawa Ontario K1A 0T6 Canada. **Tel** (613)951-5078, (800)267-6677, FAX (613)951-1584, telex 053-3585. **Circ:** 700.
Desc: Based on 1984 income data from the 1985 Survey of Consumer Finances, this publication is the latest report showing annual earnings by sex. Earnings distributions are shown for men and women by province, age, education, occupation and work experience; includes data on the earnings contributions of husbands and wives to family income.

LC HC244.A1 E28a
DD 330.947/0005 BE
EAST EUROPEAN STATISTICS SERVICE.
Main/Corp East-West S.P.R.L. (19??)-. English (French). Twelve times a year. $410.42. East West Publications, 10 boulevard Saint Lazare, B 1210 Brussels Belgium. **Tel** 011 32 2 2184349, FAX 011 32 2 2181985, telex 21 108 EUROPE B. **ED** Jan Zoubek. Index available. **Bk Rev. Circ:** 500 (ctrl).

LC HC
DD 330 US
ECON/STATS I. [CD-ROM].
(19??)-. English. $69.00 Minnesota residents; $65.00 US and Canada; $150.00 Africa, Russia, and Eastern Europe; $130.00 India; $115.00 other. Hopkins Technology, 421 Hazel Lane, Suite 120, Hopkins MN 55343. **Tel** (612)931-9376, FAX (612)931-9377.
Desc: Eight economic databases including: Consumer Price Index, Producer Price Index, Export-Import Price Index, Industrial Production Index, Money Stock, Selected Interest Rates, Industry Employment Hours & Earnings by State and Areas and Capacity Utilization.

LC Z7164.E2 E266
DD 016.3 US
ECONLIT [COMPUTER FILE]. **Added/Corp** American Economic Association. SilverPlatter Information. **VFOAT** Econ Lit; Economics Literature. (1969)-. Abstracting/Indexing Service. English. Four times a year. Price varies. Silverplatter Information Inc., 100 River Ridge Drive, Norwood MA 02062. **Tel** (800)343-0064, (617)769-2599, FAX (617)769-8763. available on an online database (Economic Literature Index) from DIALOG.
Desc: Comprehensive indexed bibliography with selected abstracts of the world's economic literature compiled from the American Economic Association's Journal of Economic Literature; and, the Index of Economic Articles in Journals and Collective Volumes. Over 90% of the articles are in English or include English summaries.

LC HC157.B35 C46A **ISSN** 0378-178X
DD 330.9/729/81 BB
ECONOMIC AND FINANCIAL STATISTICS. **Main/Corp** Central Bank of Barbados. Research Dept. **VFOAT** Economic and Financial Statements. English. Twelve times a year. Central Bank of Barbados, PO Box 1016, Treasury Building, Bridgetown Barbados. **Tel** (809)436-6870, FAX (809)427-9559, telex 2251 CENBANK WB. ctrl circ.

US
ECONOMIC LITERATURE INDEX. (19??)-. Abstracting/Indexing Service. English. One time a year. $78.00 ($1.30/minute). American Economic Association / Pennsylvania, PO Box 7320, Oakland Station, Pittsburgh PA 15213. **Tel** (412)268-3869, FAX (412)268-6810.
Desc: Online service containing bibliographic citations of journal articles on economics from the journals indexed in the Journal of Economic Literature. Contains over 200,000 citations from over 400 journals in economics and related fields from 1969 to present.

LC HG1501 **ISSN** 0440-2588
DD 332.1 KO
ECONOMIC STATISTICS YEARBOOK. **Main/Corp** Hanguk Unhaeng. Chosabu. **Added/Corp** Choson Unhaeng. (1960)-. English (Korean). One time a year. Bank of Korea, 110 3 Ka Namdaemun Ro, Seoul Korea. **Tel** 011 82 2 7594340. ***Supersedes*** *Choson Unhaeng. Economic Review.*
Desc: Major sections are devoted to money and banking, producer prices, balance of payments, flow of funds accounts, national accounts, financial statements analysis and an input-output table.

ISSN 0336-1454
FR
ECONOMIE ET STATISTIQUE. (E & S. ECONOMIE ET STATISTIQUE.). [Econ. stat.]. **Added/Corp** Institut National de la Statistique et des Etudes Economiques (France). **VFOAT** Economie et Statistique. No. 97 (Feb. 1978)-. Statistical Publication. French (summaries and/or abstracts in English and Spanish). Ten times a year (10 issues). 414.00F France; 518.00F other. CNGP INSEE - Institut National de la Statistique et des Estudes Economiques, BP 2718, 1 rue V Auriol, F 80027 Amiens Cedex 1 France. **Tel** 011 33 22 927322. **Bk Rev. Ad Acc.** available on microfiche. ***Continues*** *Economie et Statistique.*
Desc: Publishes original articles covering the current French socio-economic picture through applied statistics. Statistical data gathering methodology is fully explained.
Ind/Abst Int. Labour Doc.; LABORDOC; PAIS Int. Print; Popul. Index.

UK
ECONOMIST QUARTERLY INDEX, THE. (19??)-. English. Four times a year (3 indexes plus 1 annual index). £40.00. Economist Intelligence Unit / Essex, PO Box 14 Harold Hill, Romford RM3 8EQ, Essex United Kingdom. **Tel** 011 44 1322 289194, FAX 011 44 1322 223803. Index available. **Circ:** 2,500. ***Continues*** *Economist Annual Index.*
Desc: An index to articles published in The Economist.

LC HA1320 .H529 H3569.H4
DD 314.3 GW
EINFUHR NACH HESSEN, DIE. German. One time a year. DM7.50. Hessisches Statistisches Landesamt, Rheinstrasse 35/37, D-65185 Wiesbaden Germany. **Tel** 011 49 611 38020, FAX 011 49 611 3802990.
Desc: Detailed materials by countries of production and goods.

ISSN 0380-6936
CN
EMPLOYMENT, EARNINGS AND HOURS. **Main/Corp** Canada. Statistique Canada. Section des Statistiques de l'Emploi et de la Remuneration. **VFOAT** Emploi, Gains et Duree du Travail. (Jan. 1978)-. Periodical. French (English). Twelve times a year. 372.00Can$. Statistics Canada Publications Sales and Services, R.H. Coats Building 6th Floor, Ottawa Ontario K1A 0T6 Canada. **Tel** (613)951-5078, (800)267-6677, FAX (613)951-1584, telex 053-3585. ***Continues*** *Canada. Statistique Canada. Section des Statistiques Mensuelles de l'Emploi, de la Remuneration et du Revenu de Travail. Employment, Earnings and Hours., 0380-6936.*

LC HD7096.U6 A3 **ISSN** 0735-3286
DD 368.4/4/009761 US
EMPLOYMENT SECURITY STATISTICAL BULLETIN. **Added/Corp** Alabama. Dept. of Industrial Relations. Research and Statistics Division. **VFOAT** Statistical Bulletin. Aug.(1979)-. Bulletin. English. Twelve times a year. free. Alabama Department of Industrial Relations, Industrial Relations Building, 649 Monroe Street, Montgomery AL 36131. **Tel** (334)261-5465. ***Continues*** *Statistical Bulletin (Alabama. Division of Employment Security), 0731-3977.*

LC Z7164.C81 E93 HF5351 **ISSN** 0071-0210
DD 016.33 US
NLM HF 5353 E56
ENCYCLOPEDIA OF BUSINESS INFORMATION SOURCES. [Encycl. bus. inf. sources]. **Added/Corp** Gale Research Company. **VFOAT** EBIS. 1st Ed. (1970)-. English. Every 2 years. $245.00. Gale Research Inc., 835 Penobscot Building, 645 Griswold Street, Detroit MI 48226. **Tel** (800)877-GALE, (313)961-2242, FAX (313)961-6083, (800)414-5043, telex TWX 810-221-7086. **ED** James Woy. available on diskette; available on magnetic tape. ***Continues*** *Executive's Guide to Information Sources, 0531-5271.*
Desc: Comprehensive guide to sources of information on highly specific topics. Arranged by subject, the new edition contains entries on 1,100 specific subjects.

LC HC337.F5 F4245a **ISSN** 0785-4218
DD 330 FI
ENNAKKOTIETOJA TEOLLISUUDESTA / TILASTOKESKUS. **Added/Corp** Finland. Tilastokeskus. **VFOAT** Forhandsuppgifter Over Industrin. (1988)-. Finnish (Swedish; summaries and/or abstracts in English). One time a year. Fmk169.00. Tilastokeskus, PL 504, Annankatu 44, 00101 Helsinki Finland. **Tel** 011 358 0 17341, FAX 011 358 0 17342474, telex 1002111 TILASTO SF. **ED** Mr. Heikki Pihlaja. ***Continues*** *Finland. Tilastokeskus. Ennakkotietoja Suomen Teollisuudesta.*

LC HC271 .E484
DD 338.0944 FR
TITLE CHANGE
ENQUETE ANNUELLE D'ENTREPRISE. TEXTILES, HABILLEMENT, CUIR, PAPIER, BOIS, INDUSTRIES DIVERSES / MINISTERE DE L'INDUSTRIE, STISI, DIRECTION GENERALE DES STRATEGIES INDUSTRIELLES, SERVICE DU TRAITEMENT DE L'INFORMATION ET DES STATISTIQUES INDUSTRIELLES, CENTRE D'ENQUETES STATISTIQUES DE CAEN. **Added/Corp** Centre d'Enquetes Statistiques de Caen. **VFOAT** Textiles, Habillement, Cuir, Papier, Bois, Industries Diverses. (1979)-(198?). French. Documentation Francaise, 29 quai Voltaire, 75344 Paris Cedex 7 France. **Tel** 011 33 1 40157000, FAX 011 33 1 40157230, telex 204 826 DOCFRAN. available in microform. ***Continues*** *Centre d'Enquetes Statistiques de Caen. Enquete Annuelle d'Entreprise. Textiles, Habillement, Cuir.* ***Continued by*** *Industrie en ... Textiles, Habillement, Cuir, Papier, Bois, Industries Diverses.*

LC HA1173 .A27 HD1536.A93 A93
DD 314.36 331.7/63/09436 AU
ERHEBUNG DER LAND- UND FORSTWIRTSCHAFTLICHEN ARBEITSKRAFTE. **Main/Corp** Osterreichisches Statistisches Zentralamt. German. Kommissionsverlag Osterreichische Staatsdruckerei, Rennweg 12A, 1037 Vienna Austria.

PN
ESTADISTICA PANAMENA. SITUACION ECONOMICA, SECCION 331 : ANUARIO DE COMERCIO EXTERIOR. **Main/Corp** Panama. Direccion de Estadistica y Censo. **VFOAT** Situacion Economica: Comercio Exterior; Anuario de Comercio Exterior. (1975)-. Statistical Publication. Spanish. One time a year. $7.00 (latest edition). Direccion de Estadistica y Censo, Contraloria General, Apartado 5213, Panama 5 Panama. **Tel** 011 507 640777 Ext. 269 or 203. **ED** Amilcar Villarreal L. Index available. ***Supersedes*** *Estadistica Panamena. Serie K: Anuario de Comercio Exterior.*
Desc: Presents revised and more detailed figures of imports, exports, re-exports and the movement of merchandise in the free zone of Colon, Panama.

ISSN 0186-0496
MX
ESTADISTICAS DEL COMERCIO EXTERIOR DE MEXICO. INFORMACION PRELIMINAR. **Added/Corp** Instituto Nacional de Estadistica, Geografia e Informatica (Mexico) Banco de Mexico (1925-). **VFOAT** Informacion Preliminar del Comercio Exterior de Mexico. Vol. 9, No. 4 (1986)-. Statistical Publication. Spanish. Twelve times a year. Free on request. INEGI / Instituto Nacional de Estadistica, Geografia e Informatica, Avenida Patriotismo 711 Segundo Piso, 03730 Mexico DF Mexico. **Tel** 011 52 5 5639935, 011 52 5 5988935, FAX 011 52 55987941. **(Subscription address:** INEGI / Instituto Nacional de Estadistica, Geografia e Informatica, Avenida Heroe de Nacozari 2301 Sur, Fracc. Jardines del Parque, CP 20270, Aguascalientes Mexico. **Tel** 011 52 49 182998.**)** available with charts. ***Continues*** *Comercio Exterior de Mexico. Informacion Preliminar.*

VE
ESTADISTICAS DEL COMERCIO EXTERIOR DE VENEZUELA; IMPORTACION: ARTICULO Y PAIS. **Main/Corp** Venezuela. Direccion General de Estadistica y Censos Nacionales. (19??)-. Statistical Publication. Spanish. Irregular. Bs900.00. Instituto Comercio Exterior, Bibl Ctr Comerical Cedros, Av Libertador, Carcas Venezuela.

LC HG1501 **ISSN** 0252-3078
DD 332.1 US
ESTADISTICAS FINANCIERAS INTERNACIONALES. [Estad. financ. int. - Fondo Monet. Int.]. **Added/Corp** International Monetary Fund. Bureau of Statistics. (1981)-. Statistical Publication. Spanish. Twelve times a year (plus yearbook). $109.00 (individual, academic); $218.00 (ther. International Monetary Fund, 700 19th Street Northwest, Publishing Unit, Washington DC 20431. **Tel** (202)623-7430, FAX (202)623-7201. available on magnetic tape; available on microfilm from University Microfilms International (UMI). ***Continues*** *International Financial Statistics. Ed. Espanol, 0250-734X.*
Desc: International statistics on all aspects of international and domestic finance. Reports current data needed in the analysis of problems of international payments and of inflation and deflation; data on exchange rates, international liquidity, money and banking, international transactions, prices, production, government finance, interest rates and other items.
Ind/Abst Predicasts F&S Index, U. S. Annu. Ed.

LC HC391 .E7 **ISSN** 0079-418X
DD 338 PO
ESTATISTICA INDUSTRIAL (LISBOA). (ESTATISTICA INDUSTRIAL.). **Added/Corp** Portugal. Instituto Nacional de Estatistica. **VFOAT** Statistique Industrielle. (1943?)-. Periodical. Multiple languages (Portuguese and French). Instituto Nacional de Estatistica, Avenida Antonio Jose de Almeida, 1078 Lisbon Codex Portugal. **Tel** 011 351 1 8470050.

LC HF272.A6 E85
DD 380.1 AO
ESTATISTICAS DO COMERCIO EXTERNO. **VFOAT** Statistiques du Commerce Exterieur. Portuguese (Portuguese). Direccao Provincial dos Servicos de Estatistica, Caixa Postal 1215, Luanda Angola. ***Continues*** *Comercio Externo.*

LC HD5728 .B85a **ISSN** 0702-0961
DD 331.1/1/0971 CN
ESTIMATES OF EMPLOYEES BY PROVINCE AND INDUSTRY (CUMULATED EDITION). (ESTIMATES OF EMPLOYEES BY PROVINCE AND INDUSTRY.). **Main/Corp** tatistics Canada. Monthly Employment, Payrolls and Labour Income Section. **Added/Corp** Statistics Canada. Monthly Employment, Payrolls and Labour Income Section. Estimations du Nombre de Salaries par Province et par Industrie. **VFOAT** Estimations du Nombre de Salaries par Province et par Industrie. **VAT** Estimations du Nombre de Salaries par Province et par Industrie (Edition Cumulative). (1961/1972)-. Statistical Publication. English (French). Irregular. 1.40Can$ Canada; $1.70 other. Statistics Canada Publications Sales and Services, R.H. Coats Building 6th Floor, Ottawa Ontario K1A 0T6 Canada. **Tel** (613)951-5078, (800)267-6677, FAX (613)951-1584, telex 053-3585. ***Continues*** *Canada. Dominion Bureau of Statistics. Employment. Estimates of Employees by Province and Industry, 0702-0961.*
Desc: Presents monthly estimates of total employees by industry and province in the non-agricultural sector.

LC HD4977 .A24 **ISSN** 0318-9007
DD 331.2/971 CN
Pr Rev.
ESTIMATES OF LABOUR INCOME (OTTAWA). (ESTIMATES OF LABOUR INCOME.). [Estim. labour income]. **Main/Corp** Statistics Canada. Labor Income Section. **Added/Corp** Canada. Dominion Bureau of Statistics. Labour and Prices Division. Canada. Dominion Bureau of Statistics. Canada. Dominion Bureau of Statistics. Labour Division. Canada. Dominion Bureau of Statistics. Labour Division. Research and Analysis Section. Canada. Dominion Bureau of Statistics. Employment Section. Statistics Canada. Employment Section. Statistics Canada. Monthly Employment, Payroll and Labour Income Section. Statistics Canada. Labour Income Section. **VFOAT** Estimations du Revenu du Travail. Vol. 3, No. 10 (Oct. 1949)-. English (French). Four times a year. 96.00Can$ Canada; $116.00 North America; $135.00 other. Statistics Canada Publications

Sales and Services, R.H. Coats Building 6th Floor, Ottawa Ontario K1A 0T6 Canada. **Tel** (613)951-5078, (800)267-6677, FAX (613)951-1584, telex 053-3585. **ED** Ed Banko. **Ad Acc. Circ:** 1,000. ***Continues** Monthly Estimates of Labour Income in Canada.*
Desc: Estimates of wages and salaries and supplementary labor income on an unadjusted and seasonally adjusted basis by industry for Canada and the provinces, with annual totals for the last five years.

LC Z7165.E74 E87 HC845.A1
DD 016.338963 ET
ETHIOPIA'S DEVELOPMENT CURRENT ABSTRACTS. Added/Corp Ethiopia. Service of Documentation and Communication or Development. (19??)-. Abstracting/Indexing Service. English. Twelve times a year. $40.00. SEDEC-Ethiopia, PO Box 5788, Addis Ababa Ethiopia. **Circ:** 200.

LC HG3409.E65 B33 **ISSN** 0014-2069
DD 330.9/67 CM
ETUDES ET STATISTIQUES - BANQUE DES ETATS DE L'AFRIQUE CENTRALE. (ETUDES ET STATISTIQUES; BULLETIN MENSUEL.). [Etud. stat. - Banque etats Afr. cent.]. **Main/Corp** Banque des Etats de l'Afrique Centrale. No. 1 (April 1973)-. Bulletin. French. Twelve times a year. $72.18. Banque Etats l'Afrique Central Yaoundi Cameroun, Bolte Postale 1917, Younde Cameroon. **Tel** 011 237 222505. cum. index. **Bk Rev. Ad Acc. Circ:** 1,500. ***Continues** Banque Centrale des Etats de l'Afrique Equatoriale et du Cameroun. Etudes et Statistiques.*
Ind/Abst PAIS Int. Print; World Agric. Econ. Rural Sociol. Abstr.

LC HA1107.5 .A14
DD 309.1/4/055 UK
EUROPEAN COMMUNITY : FACTS AND FIGURES, THE. (19??)-. English.

LC HA1107 .E87 **ISSN** 0071-2930
DD 338.09/4 UK
EUROPEAN MARKETING DATA AND STATISTICS. VFOAT EMDAS. Vol. 1 (1962)-. English. One time a year (May). $310.00. Gale Research Inc., 835 Penobscot Building, 645 Griswold Street, Detroit MI 48226. **Tel** (800)877-GALE, (313)961-2242, FAX (313)961-6083, (800)414-5043, telex TWX 810-221-7086.
Desc: More than 240 statistical tables compare essential market data for 31 countries of Europe. Fifteen major sections cover such broad areas as population, employment, production, trade, economy, standard of living, consumer expenditures, consumption, etc.

LC Z **ISSN** 0252-8266
DD 330 LU
EUROSTATISTIK, DATEN ZUR KONJUNKTURANALYSE. Added/Corp Statistical Office of the European Communities. **VFOAT** Eurostatistics, Data for Short-Term Economic Analysis. (1982)-. Periodical. German (English and French). Eleven times a year. £71.00 UK; 77.00p Ireland. Office for Official Publications of the European Communities, 2 rue Mercier, 2985 Luxembourg Luxembourg. **Tel** 011 352 499281, FAX 011 352 292942763. ***Formed by the union of** Eurostatistik, Data til Konjunkturanalyse **and** Eurostatistiken, Daten zur Konjunkturanalyse.*
Desc: Includes statistics on unemployment, consumer price index, industrial production, steel, energy, extra community trade, intra-community trade, exchange rates, and public finance.

LC HJ8899 .E963 **ISSN** 1015-4159
DD 336.3/435/091724021 FR
EXTERNAL DEBT STATISTICS. [Extern. debt stat.]. **Added/Corp** Organisation for Economic Co-Operation and Development. (19??)-. English. One time a year. $26.00. OECD Publications and Information Center, 2 rue Andre-Pascal, 75775 Paris Cedex 16 France. **Tel** 011 33 1 49104262, US:(202)785-6323, FAX 011 33 1 45248500, 011 33 1 45248176, telex 620 160 OCDE. **(Subscription address:** OECD Publications Center, 2001 L Street, Suite 700, Washington DC 20036. **Tel** (202)822-3873, (202)785-6323.**)**

LC HF3500.5 .A189
DD 382/.094/0021 LU
TITLE CHANGE
EXTERNAL TRADE AND BALANCE OF PAYMENTS. Added/Corp Statistical Office of the European Communities. **VFOAT** Comercio Exterior y Balanza de Pagos. Glossarium. (1992)-(1993). Periodical. English. Office for Official Publications of the European Communities, 2 rue Mercier, 2985 Luxembourg Luxembourg. **Tel** 011 352 499281, FAX 011 352 292942763. ***Formed by the union of** External Trade (Luxembourg, Luxembourg), 1017-6004 **and** Balance of Payments. Quarterly Data. **Continued by** External Trade (Luxembourg, Luxembourg : 1994).*
Desc: Statistics on Community external trade, its development by country and product, trade of the main non-member countries and the balance of payments.

LC HF3770.8 .A33
DD 382/.095493/00212 CE
EXTERNAL TRADE STATISTICS, SRI LANKA. Added/Corp Sri Lanka. Regu Departamentuva. (19??)-. English. Two times a year. Sri Lanka Government Publ Bureau, The Superintendent, Colombo Sri Lanka Colombia. **Tel** 93527.

US
FACT BOOK : TABLES AND CHARTS ON THE NEW YORK METROPOLITAN REGION. Main/Corp New York City Council on Economic Education. (1970)-. English. Every 2 years. $19.95. New York City Council on Economic Education, 17 Lexington Avenue, Box 405 Baruch College, New York NY 10010. **Tel** (212)725-4431. **ED** Albert Alexander. **Bk Rev. Circ:** 1,000 (ctrl).
Desc: A concise one-volume unique collection of selected economic and related statistics about New York City and the surrounding region.

LC HG4596 .T64a
DD 332.63/2/0952 JA
FACT BOOK - TOKYO SHOKEN TORIHIKIJO. Main/Corp Tokyo Shoken Torihikijo. **VFOAT** TSE ... Fact Book. (1982)-. Statistical Publication. English. One time a year. ¥1,030. Tokyo Stock Exchange, 2-1-1 Kayabacho Nihonbashi, Choku Tokyo 103 Japan. **Tel** 011 81 3 6660141, FAX 011 81 3 6395016, telex 2522759 TKOSE. **(Subscription address:** Oversea Courier Service Company, 9-Shibaura 2-chome, Minatuku Tokyo 108 Japan. **)**
Desc: A variety of statistical information on the Tokyo stock exchange.

LC HD2321
DD 338 US
•**F&S INDEX INTERNATIONAL. Added/Corp** Information Access Company. **VFOAT** F and S Index International. Vol. 26, No. 5 (May 1993)-. Abstracting/Indexing Service. English. Seventeen times a year. $1075.00. Predicasts Inc., A Ziff Communications Company, 11001 Cedar Avenue, Cleveland OH 44106. **Tel** (800)321-6388, (216)795-3000, FAX (216)229-9944, telex 985 604. **(Subscription address:** Information Access Company, PO Box 61000, Department 1851, San Francisco CA 94161. **Tel** (800)321-6388.**)** ***Continues** Predicasts F&S Index International, 0277-4528.*
Desc: Provides comprehensive reference indexes of business and economic information. Covers worldwide company, product, and industry information. One- and two-line article summaries offer access to information on international companies, business and financial activities, demographics, government regulations, and economic trends.

LC Z7164.C81 F132 **ISSN** 1065-5956
DD 382 US
F&S INDEX PLUS TEXT. INTERNATIONAL. (F&S INDEX PLUS TEXT. INTERNATIONAL [COMPUTER FILE] / PREDICASTS.). [F&S index plus text, Int.]. **Added/Corp** Predicasts, Inc. **VFOAT** Predicasts' F&S Index Plus Text. International; F&S Index Plus Text. International with Europe. **VAT** F & S Index Plus Text International. (19??)-. Abstracting/Indexing Service. English. Twelve times a year. $3500.00. Predicasts Inc., A Ziff Communications Company, 11001 Cedar Avenue, Cleveland OH 44106. **Tel** (800)321-6388, (216)795-3000, FAX (216)229-9944, telex 985 604. **(Subscription address:** Information Access Company, PO Box 61000, Department 1851, San Francisco CA 94161. **Tel** (800)321-6388.**)** available in print.
Desc: Contains facts and figures about companies, products, markets, and applied technology in all manufacturing and service industries worldwide.

LC Z7165.U5 F232 **ISSN** 1065-5964
DD 381 US
F&S INDEX PLUS TEXT. UNITED STATES. (F&S INDEX PLUS TEXT. UNITED STATES [COMPUTER FILE].). [F&S index plus text, U.S.]. **Added/Corp** Predicasts, Inc. **VFOAT** Predicasts' F&S Index Plus Text. United States. **VAT** F & S Index Plus Text United States. (1991)-. Abstracting/Indexing Service. English. Twelve times a year. $2500.00. Predicasts Inc., A Ziff Communications Company, 11001 Cedar Avenue, Cleveland OH 44106. **Tel** (800)321-6388, (216)795-3000, FAX (216)229-9944, telex 985 604. **(Subscription address:** Information Access Company, PO Box 61000, Department 1851, San Francisco CA 94161. **Tel** (800)321-6388.**)** available in print.
Desc: Contains facts and figures about companies, products, markets, and applied technology in all manufacturing and service industries worldwide.

LC HD9000.4 .T7 **ISSN** 1014-7632
DD 380.1/41/021 IT
FAO YEARBOOK, TRADE. (FAO YEARBOOK. TRADE = FAO ANNUAIRE. COMMERCE = FAO ANUARIO. COMERCIO.). [FAO yearb. Trade]. **Added/Corp** Food and Agriculture Organization of the United Nations. **VFOAT** Trade; FAO Annuaire. Commerce; FAO Anuario. Comercio; Commerce; Comercio. Vol. 41 (1987)-. Statistical Publication. English (French and Spanish). $45.00. Food Agriculture Organization (FAO) / Italy, GIPCI66 via Terme di Caracalla, 00100 Rome Italy. **Tel** 011 39 6 52252925, FAX 011 39 6 52253152. **(Subscription address:** UNIPUB, 4611 F Assembly Drive, Lanham MD 20706. **Tel** (800)274-4888, (301)459-7666.**)** ***Continues** FAO Trade Yearbook, 0071-7126.*
Desc: Gives the latest trade figures for imports and exports of more than 100 agricultural, fishery and forestry products worldwide. Tables provide both the production volume and value of all agricultural commodities by both product and country.

LC HD1491.U5 C619 **ISSN** 0742-9495
DD 334/subser.683/0973 S 334/.683/0973 US
FARMER COOPERATIVE STATISTICS. [Farmer coop. stat.]. 1976-77-. English. One time a year. Agricultural Cooperative Service, US Department of Agriculture, 14th Street and Independence Avenue SW, Washington DC 20250. **Tel** (202)653-6973, FAX (202)653-7033. available on microfiche (Vols. for (1984-) distributed to depository libraries). ***Continues** Statistics of Farmer Cooperatives.*
Desc: Reports aggregate national statistics for marketing, farm supply, and related service cooperatives. Figures are carried on memberships, number of cooperatives, and business volume by commodity and state. Trends are indicated, particularly for the past 10 years.

LC Z7164.C81 F43
DD 016.32 US
FED IN PRINT: ECONOMICS AND BANKING TOPICS. Added/Corp Federal Reserve Bank of Philadelphia. **VFOAT** Economics and Banking Topics. (1990)-. Abstracting/Indexing Service. English. Two times a year (Aug. and Feb.). Free on request. Federal Reserve Bank of Philadelphia, Research Department, 100 North 6th Street, Philadelphia PA 19105-1574. **Tel** (215)574-6448. **ED** Deborah Naulty, (215)574-6543. Index available (published separately). **Bk Rev**, (Qty: 8). **Circ:** 2,600 (ctrl). available on diskette from National Technical Information Service. ***Continues** Fed in Print: Business and Banking Topics, 0891-2769.*
Desc: An index to all the publications of the Federal Reserve research departments. This includes the twelve Federal Reserve Banks and the Federal Reserve Board.

ISSN 0163-8270
DD 353.001 US
FEDERAL CIVILIAN WORK FORCE STATISTICS. Added/Corp United States Civil Service Commission. Bureau of Manpower Information Systems. United States Civil Service Commission. Bureau of Personnel Management Information Systems. **VFOAT** Federal Civilian Workforce Statistics. (Jan. 1977)-. Government Publication. English. Twelve times a year. $21.00. Office of Personnel Management, 1900 East Street Northwest, OELR Room 7429, Washington DC 20415. **Tel** (202)632-6256. **(Subscription address:** Superintendent of Documents, US Government Printing Office, Washington DC 20402. **)** ***Continues** Federal Civilian Manpower Statistics, 0090-7227.*
Desc: Presents employment information on civilians in the Federal work force based on reports received from each department and agency in the Federal government.

LC HG4551 .I532b
DD 332.6/42 FR
FIBV STATISTICAL DATA. Main/Corp International Federation of Stock Exchanges. **Added/Corp** International Federation of Stock Exchanges. Statistical Data. (1976)-. Statistical Publication. English (French). Federation Internationale des Bourses de Valeurs, 22 boulevard de Courcelles, 75017 Paris France. **Tel** 011 33 1 47631760, telex FIBV 642720 F.

LC HD9259.P73 U545 **ISSN** 0737-4852
DD 380.1/4566480421 US
FINAL STATISTICAL REPORT - CALIFORNIA. PRUNE MARKETING COMMITTEE. (FINAL STATISTICAL REPORT / PRUNE MARKETING COMMITTEE.). **Added/Corp** California. Prune Marketing Committee. (19??)-. Statistical Publication. English. Prune Marketing Committee, 103 World Trade Center, San Francisco CA 94111-4293.

LC HG1501 **ISSN** 1038-7609
DD 332.1 AT
•**FINANCIAL ESTIMATES OF COMMONWEALTH PUBLIC TRADING ENTERPRISES, AUSTRALIA.** (1993)-. English. One time a year. 5.00Aus$. Australian Bureau of Statistics, PO Box 2796Y, Melbourne 3001 Australia. **Tel** 011 61 3 6157843.
Desc: Contains a table showing current and capital outlays, revenue and financing transactions for the Commonwealth public trading sector for the last five years, and estimates of these transactions for the budget year.

FR
FINANCIAL STATISTICS. Main/Corp Trinidad and Tobago. Central Statistical Office. (1966)-. English. Irregular (28 issues, includes supplements). $340.00. OECD Publications and Information Center, 2 rue Andre-Pascal, 75775 Paris Cedex 16 France. **Tel** 011 33

1 49104262, US:(202)785-6323, FAX 011 33 1 45248500, 011 33 1 45248176, telex 620 160 OCDE. **(Subscription address:** OECD Publications Center, 2001 L Street, Suite 700, Washington DC 20036. **Tel** (202)822-3873, (202)785-6323.)

ISSN 0015-203X
UK
CCC

FINANCIAL STATISTICS LONDON. [Financ. stat. Lond.]. (1962)-. English. Twelve times a year. £120.00. Her Majesty's Stationery Office, 51 Nine Elms Lane, London SW8 5DR United Kingdom. **Tel** 011 44 171 8738459, 011 44 171 8738499, FAX 011 44 171 8738499, 011 44 171 8738456, telex 297138. **(Subscription address:** Her Majesty's Stationery Office, PO Box 276, Public Centre, London SW8 5DT United Kingdom. **Tel** 011 44 171 8738499, 011 44 171 8738456.)
Desc: Provides data on a wide variety of financial topics including financial accounts for sectors of the economy, government income and expenditure, public sector borrowing, banking statistics, monetary aggregates, institutional investment, company finance and liquidity, security prices and exchange and interest rates.

LC HG176 .F56
DD 336/.021 FR
FINANCIAL STATISTICS MONTHLY. SECTION 2, DOMESTIC MARKETS, INTEREST RATES. Added/Corp Organisation for Economic Co-Operation and Development. **VFOAT** Domestic Markets, Interest Rates; Marches Domestiques, Taux d'Interet; Statistiques Financieres Mensuelles. Section 2, Marches Domestiques, Taux d'Interet; OECD Financial Statistics. Part 1, Financial Statistics Monthly. Domestic Markets, Interest Rates; Statistiques Financieres de l'OCDE. 1 Partie, Statistiques Financieres Mensuelles. Marches Domestiques, Taux d'Interet. (Jan. 1984)-. English (French). Twelve times a year. OECD Publications and Information Center, 2 rue Andre-Pascal, 75775 Paris Cedex 16 France. **Tel** 011 33 1 49104262, US:(202)785-6323, FAX 011 33 1 45248500, 011 33 1 45248176, telex 620 160 OCDE. **(Subscription address:** OECD Publications Center, 2001 L Street, Suite 700, Washington DC 20036. **Tel** (202)822-3873, (202)785-6323.) ***Continues in part*** *OECD Financial Statistics. Part 1, Financial Statistics Monthly.*

LC HF3941 .E85 **ISSN** 1036-9449
DD 380.1099 AT
FOREIGN TRADE, AUSTRALIA. MERCHANDISE EXPORTS. Added/Corp Australian Bureau of Statistics. **VFOAT** Merchandise Exports. (May 1991)-. Periodical. English. Twelve times a year. 9.70Aus$. Australian Bureau of Statistics, PO Box 2796Y, Melbourne 3001 Australia. **Tel** 011 61 3 6157843. ***Continues*** *Exports, Australia. Monthly Summary Tables, 0819-0933.*
Desc: Contains merchandise exports information for the latest three years and selected major commodities classified at the 5-digit level of the Standard International Trade Classification.

ISSN 1037-888X
DD 382.60994 AT
FOREIGN TRADE, AUSTRALIA, MERCHANDISE EXPORTS, DETAILED COMMODITY TABLES. [Foreign trade Aust. merch. exports detail. commod. tables]. **Added/Corp** Australian Bureau of Statistics. (1991)-. Statistical Publication. English. One time a year. 64.30Aus$. Australian Bureau of Statistics, PO Box 2796Y, Melbourne 3001 Australia. **Tel** 011 61 3 6157843. ***Continues*** *Foreign Trade, Australia, Exports, 0819-4688.*
Desc: Contains the quantity and value of merchandise exports cross-classified by detailed commodity by country.

LC HF3941 .I44 **ISSN** 1036-904X
DD 380.1 AT
FOREIGN TRADE, AUSTRALIA. MERCHANDISE IMPORTS / AUSTRALIAN BUREAU OF STATISTICS. Added/Corp Australian Bureau of Statistics. (May 1991)-. Periodical. English. Twelve times a year. 9.70Aus$. Australian Bureau of Statistics, PO Box 2796Y, Melbourne 3001 Australia. **Tel** 011 61 3 6157843. ***Continues*** *Imports, Australia. Monthly Summary Tables, 0819-2839.*
Desc: Contains merchandise imports of selected major commodities from selected countries, imports classified by broad commodity grouping, imports classified by State, imports by industry of origin, imports by Broad Economic Category and imports by country.

LC HF275 .A92
DD 380.1 AT
FOREIGN TRADE, AUSTRALIA. MERCHANDISE IMPORTS. DETAILED COMMODITY TABLES. Added/Corp Australian Bureau of Statistics. **VFOAT** Merchandise Imports. (1991)-. English. One time a year. 96.90Aus$. Australian Bureau of Statistics, PO Box 2796Y, Melbourne 3001 Australia. **Tel** 011 61 3 6157843. ***Continues*** *Froeign Trade, Australia. Imports.*
Desc: Contains the quantity and value of merchandise imports cross-classified by detailed commodity Harmonised Tariff Item Statistical Code and by country for the latest year.

US
FOREIGN TRADE STATISTICS FOR AFRICA. SERIES A: DIRECTION OF TRADE. STATISTIQUES AFRICAINES DU COMMERCE EXTERIEUR. SERIE. ECHANGES PAR PAYS. Main/Corp United Nations. Economic Commission for Africa. **VFOAT** Statistiques Africaines du Commerce Exterieur. Series A : Echanges par Pays; Direction of Trade; Echanges par Pays. (1968)-. Government Publication. English (French). Irregular. $35.00. United Nations Publications, 2 United Nations Plaza, Room DC2 0853, Department 007C, New York NY 10017. **Tel** (212)963-8303, (800)253-9646. ***Continues*** *United Nations. Economic Commission for Africa. Foreign Trade Statistics of Africa. Series A: Direction of Trade,, 0071-7398.*
Desc: Focuses on trade issues by country.

LC HF3871 .U58
DD 380.1 US
FOREIGN TRADE STATISTICS FOR AFRICA. SERIES B. TRADE BY COMMODITY. STATISTIQUES AFRICAINES DU COMMERCE EXTERIEUR. SERIE ECHANGES PAR PRODUITS. Added/Corp United Nations. Economic Commission for Africa. **VFOAT** Statistiques Africaines du Commerce Exterieur. Serie B. Echanges par Produits; Trade by Commodity; Echanges par Produits. (1969)-. Government Publication. English (French). Irregular. $35.00. United Nations Publications, 2 United Nations Plaza, Room DC2 0853, Department 007C, New York NY 10017. **Tel** (212)963-8303, (800)253-9646. ***Continues*** *Foreign Trade Statistics of Africa. Series B: Trade by Ccommodity.*
Desc: Focuses on African trade issues, by commodity.

PH
FOREIGN TRADE STATISTICS OF THE PHILIPPINES. Added/Corp Philippines. Bureau of the Census and Statistics. Philippines. National Census and Statistics Office. (19??)-. Statistical Publication. English. One time a year (Aug.). $237.60. National Statistics Office of Manila, PO Box 779, Manila Philippines. **Tel** 011 63 613645.

ISSN 0071-9277
DD 338/.4/02571 CN
FRASER'S CANADIAN TRADE DIRECTORY. VFOAT Canadian Trade Directory. (1913)-. Directory. English. One time a year. 156.07Can$. Maclean Hunter Canada / Montreal, 1001 bvd. de Maisonneuve W., Montreal Quebec H3A 3E1 Canada. **Tel** (514)845-5141, FAX (514)845-4302, telex 055-60604. **(Subscription address:** Frasers Trade Directories, 777 Bay Street, Toronto Ontario M5W 1A7 Canada. **Tel** (416)596-5086.) **Ad Acc. Circ:** 10,000.
Desc: Contains over 20,000 product classifications and over 500,000 listings. Also contains over 12,500 trade names and lists in excess of 11,000 foreign companies who have Canadian representatives.

LC HM24 .F84 **ISSN** 0190-3241
DD 301.01 US
FUTURE SURVEY. Added/Corp World Future Society. Vol. 1, No. 1 (Jan. 1979)-. Abstracting/Indexing Service. English. Thirteen times a year (published monthly with an annual volume). $119.00. World Future Society, 7910 Woodmont Avenue, Suite 450, Bethesda MD 20814. **Tel** (301)656-8274, FAX (301)951-0394. **ED** Michael Marien. Index available (bound in every issue). **Bk Rev. Circ:** 2,500. ***Continues*** *Public Policy Book Forecast, 0197-9035.*
Desc: Each month provides about 50 abstracts of recent books, reports, and articles on trends, forecasts, and proposals in all areas of national and global concerns: world futures, the global economy, regions and nations, defense and disarmament, energy, environment and resources, food and agriculture, general societal directions, government, the US economy, urban affairs, health, education, communications, science and technology and methods to shape the future.

LC Z7164.T2 C6 **ISSN** 0589-5634
DD 337 380 SZ
GATT BIBLIOGRAPHY, 1947-1953; THE TEXT OF THE GATT, SELECTED GATT PUBLICATIONS, A CHRONOLOGICAL LIST OF REFERENCES TO THE GATT. SUPPLEMENT. Main/Corp Contracting Parties to the General Agreement on Tariffs and Trade. No. 1 (1954)-. Bibliography. English. GATT Secretariat, rue de Lausanne 154, 1211 Geneva Lausanne Switzerland.

US
GENERAL BUSINESSFILE [COMPUTER FILE]. (19??)-. Abstracting/Indexing Service. English. Twelve times a year. $12300.00 (with one workstation), $17600.00 (with two workstations), $19400.00 (with three workstations), $21200.00 (with four workstations) basic subscription with InfoTrac Enhanced Workstation; $10500.00 (with one workstation), $14000.00 (with two to four workstations) basic subscription. Information Access Company, 362 Lakeside Drive, Foster City CA 94404. **Tel** (800)227-8431, (800)458-1565.
Desc: Covers all aspects of management, business, company and industry information. Consolidates investment reports, corporate profiles of public and private companies and wide-ranging, current business news from trade, management, and industry journals and newspapers.

LC HG293 .G64 **ISSN** 0736-1777
DD 338.2/741/05 US
GOLD STATISTICS AND ANALYSIS. English. J Aron & Company, 160 Water Street, New York NY 10038.

LC HC120.I5 A35 **ISSN** 0711-852X
DD 339.371 CN
Pr Rev.
GROSS DOMESTIC PRODUCT BY INDUSTRY (MONTHLY EDITION). (GROSS DOMESTIC PRODUCT BY INDUSTRY.). [Gross domest. prod. ind.]. **Added/Corp** Statistics Canada. Industry Product Division. Monthly Measures Section. Statistics Canada. Industry Measures and Analysis Division. Monthly Measures Section. **VFOAT** Produit Interieur Brut par Industrie. **VAT** Produit Interieur Brut par Industrie (Edition Mensuelle). Vol. 21, No. 7/8 (July/Aug. 1981)-. Periodical. English (French). Twelve times a year. 168.00Can$. Statistics Canada Publications Sales and Services, R.H. Coats Building 6th Floor, Ottawa Ontario K1A 0T6 Canada. **Tel** (613)951-5078, (800)267-6677, FAX (613)951-1584, telex 053-3585. **ED** D. W. Rhoades and Lyle Sager. **Circ:** 500. ***Continues*** *Indexes of Real Domestic Products by Industry, Including the Index of Industrial Production, 0317-3453.*
Desc: Contains industry real output measures. Monthly quantities produced revalued using base year prices for Canada. Approximately 150 seasonally adjusted and unadjusted industries and aggregates constant dollars and indexes are shown as well as special groupings.

LC HD8103 .G84
DD 331.1/077 CN
GUIDE TO FEDERAL GOVERNMENT LABOUR STATISTICS. VFOAT Guide de la Statistique du Travail du Gouvernement Federal. Multiple languages (English and French). $1.00. Information Canada, 171 Slater Street, Ottawa Ontario K1A 0S9 Canada. **Tel** (819)997-1095.
Desc: Provides researchers and others using federal government labour statistics with a reference document to 92 different surveys and administrative data sources plus reference to about 500 publications.

LC HF105 .B73a **ISSN** 0565-0933
DD 382/.0973 US
GUIDE TO FOREIGN TRADE STATISTICS. Added/Corp United States. Bureau of the Census. (1967)-. English. Irregular. Superintendent of Documents, US Government Printing Office, Washington DC 20402. **Tel** (202)275-3328, FAX (202)786-2377.
Desc: The Foreign Trade Statistics program involves the compilation and dissemination of thousands of facts relating to imports and exports of the United States.

ISSN 0709-8065
DD 016.65/005 CN
GUIDE TO SERIAL PUBLICATIONS - MANAGEMENT STUDIES LIBRARY, UNIVERSITY OF TORONTO. [Guide ser. publ. - Manage. Stud. Libr., Univ. Toronto]. **Main/Corp** University of Toronto. Management Studies Library. (1972)-. English. One time a year. Free to faculty and other libraries. Faculty of Management Studies University of Toronto, 246 Bloor Street West, Toronto Ontario M5S 1V4 Canada.

LC HD7096.U6 O514 **ISSN** 0361-2902
DD 368.4/4/009766 US
HANDBOOK OF EMPLOYMENT SECURITY PROGRAM STATISTICS. Main/Corp Oklahoma. State Employment Service. (19??)-. English. Irregular. Oklahoma Employment Security Commission, Will Rogers Building, Room 310, Oklahoma City OK 73105. **Tel** (405)521-3735. ***Continues*** *Oklahoma. Employment Security Commission. Research and Planning Division. Handbook of Employment Security Program Statistics.*

LC HF1016 .U54a
DD 382/.021 US
HANDBOOK OF INTERNATIONAL TRADE AND DEVELOPMENT STATISTICS. Main/Corp United Nations Conference on Trade and Development. **VFOAT** Manuel de Statistiques du Commerce International et du Developpement. (1969)-. Government Publication. English (French). One time a year. $80.00. United Nations Publications, 2 United Nations Plaza, Room DC2 0853, Department 007C, New York NY 10017. **Tel** (212)963-8303, (800)253-9646.
Desc: Complete basic collection of statistical data relevant to the analysis of world trade and development.

LC HD8051 .A62 **ISSN** 0082-9056
DD 331/.0973 331/.0973 US
HANDBOOK OF LABOR STATISTICS / U.S. DEPARTMENT OF LABOR, BUREAU OF LABOR STATISTICS. [Handb. labor stat.]. (1924-26)-. English. Irregular. Price varies. US Department of Labor, 200 Constitution Avenue NW, Washington DC 20210. **Tel** (202)219-7316, FAX (202)219-7312. available on microfiche (Vols. for (1983-) distributed to depository libraries).
Ind/Abst Predicasts Forecasts.

LC Z7164.C81 H265 HF5351 **ISSN** 1044-2111
DD 338 US
HARVARD BUSINESS SCHOOL CORE COLLECTION. (HARVARD BUSINESS SCHOOL CORE COLLECTION : AUTHOR, TITLE, AND SUBJECT GUIDE.). [Harv. Bus. Sch. core collect.]. **Main/Corp** Baker Library. (1990)-. English. One time a year (May). $69.00. Harvard Business School Publishing Division, Operations Department, 60 Harvard Way, Boston MA 02163. **Tel** (617)495-6192, (617)495-8948, FAX (617)495-6891, telex 6817229.
Desc: An index to Baker Library's reading room collection of over 3,000 books, updated with recent titles.

ISSN 0891-5016
DD 658 US
CCC
HEALTHCARE MARKETING ABSTRACTS. [Healthc. mark. abstr.]. **VFOAT** Health Care Marketing Abstracts. Vol. 1, No. 1 (Nov. 1986)-. Abstracting/Indexing Service. English. Eleven times a year (monthly except July). $96.00. COR Healthcare Resources, (A Division of COR Research Inc.), PO Box 40959, Santa Barbara CA 93140. **Tel** (805)564-2177, FAX (805)564-2146. **ED** Dean H. Anderson. **Bk Rev**.
Desc: Abstracts of articles selected from more than 120 periodicals in the field of healthcare marketing.

LC HA1320 .H529 HF3569.H4
DD 314.3 GW
HESSISCHE AUSFUHR, DIE. Added/Corp Hessisches Statistisches Landesamt. (19??)-. Statistical Publication. German. One time a year. DM12.00. Hessisches Statistisches Landesamt, Rheinstrasse 35/37, D-65185 Wiesbaden Germany. **Tel** 011 49 611 38020, FAX 011 49 611 3802990.
Desc: Detailed materials by countries of consumption and goods.

LC HD5727 .H58 **ISSN** 1181-957X
DD 331.11/0971 CN
HISTORICAL LABOUR FORCE STATISTICS. (HISTORICAL LABOUR FORCE STATISTICS.). [Hist. lab. force stat.]. **Added/Corp** Statistics Canada. Household Surveys Division. **VFOAT** Statistiques Chronologiques sur la Population Active. (1990)-. English (French). One time a year. 74.00Can$ Canada; $89.00 US; $104.00 other. Statistics Canada Publications Sales and Services, R.H. Coats Building 6th Floor, Ottawa Ontario K1A 0T6 Canada. **Tel** (613)951-5078, (800)267-6677, FAX (613)951-1584, telex 053-3585. ***Continues** Historical Labour Force Statistics, Actual Data, Seasonal Factors, Seasonally Adjusted Data., 0703-2684.*

LC HF1016 .H57
DD 382/.0212 FR
HISTORICAL STATISTICS OF FOREIGN TRADE / ORGANISATION FOR ECONOMIC CO-OPERATION AND DEVELOPMENT. Added/Corp Organisation for Economic Co-Operation and Development. **VFOAT** Statistiques Retrospectives du Commerce Exterieur. (19??)-. English (French). One time a year. OECD Publications and Information Center, 2 rue Andre-Pascal, 75775 Paris Cedex 16 France. **Tel** 011 33 1 49104262, US:(202)785-6323, FAX 011 33 1 45248500, 011 33 1 45248176, telex 620 160 OCDE. **(Subscription address:** OECD Publications Center, 2001 L Street, Suite 700, Washington DC 20036. **Tel** (202)822-3873, (202)785-6323.**)**

LC HA4651 .H66a
DD 330.951/2500212 HK
HONG KONG SOCIAL & ECONOMIC TRENDS. Main/Corp Hong Kong. Census and Statistics Dept. **VFOAT** Hong Kong Social and Economic Trends. (1968/1972)-. English. Irregular (Publishes every three years). HK$46.00 Hong Kong; $8.50 (surface mail) other. Hong Kong Government Information Service, Beaconsfield House, 4 Queens Road, Hong Kong Hong Kong. **Tel** 011 852 284288014, 011 852 259881947, FAX 011 852 28459078, 011 852 25987482, telex 61190 HKGIS. **Circ:** 1,100 (ctrl).
Desc: Containing the main statistics series that are descriptive of the social and economic developments in Hong Kong over the past decade.

LC HF259.H6 H64A
DD 382/.0951/25 HK
HONG KONG TRADE STATISTICS. Main/Corp Hong Kong. Census and Statistics Dept. English. Twelve times a year. HK$1,920 Hong Kong; $331.50 (surface mail) other. Census and Statistics Department / Hong Kong, Beaconsfield House/6th Floor, Queens Road, Central Victoria Hong Kong. **Tel** 5-8428801-4, telex 61190 HKGIS. **Circ:** 750 (ctrl). available on microfiche (from Census & Statistics Department). ***Continues** Hong Kong Trade Statistic.*
Desc: Statistical tables listing major changes in the direction and content of trade, trade figures for commodity groups, and country statistics by principal divisions.

LC Z7165.U5 P2 **ISSN** 0099-2453
DD 331/.05 US
CCC
NLM Z 7164.C4 P115
HUMAN RESOURCES ABSTRACTS. [Hum. resour. abstr.]. **Added/Corp** Institute of Labor and Industrial Relations (University of Michigan--Wayne State University). Vol. 10 (March 1975)-. Abstracting/Indexing Service. English. Four times a year. $330.00. SAGE Periodical Press, 2455 Teller Road, Thousand Oaks CA 91320. **Tel** (805)499-0721, FAX (805)499-0871, telex 100799. **Bk Rev. Acid Free. Circ:** 750. available on microfilm and microfiche from University Microfilms International (UMI). ***Continues** Poverty and Human Resources Abstracts, 0094-4394.*
Desc: Contains abstracts of the most important recent literature for the professional who needs easy reference to current and changing ideas in the diverse area of manpower and human resources development, and related social/governmental policy questions.

LC HF1371 **ISSN** 1024-7475
DD 382 IC
•**ICELANDIC EXTERNAL TRADE.** (1995)-. Government Publication. English. One time a year. Hagstofa Islands, Statistics Iceland, Skuggasund 3, IS-150 Reykjavik Iceland. **Tel** 011 354 5609800, FAX 011 354 5628865. **ED** Hallgrimur Snorrason.

LC HB1 .I347
DD 330/.05 II
ICSSR JOURNAL OF ABSTRACTS AND REVIEWS : ECONOMICS. Main/Corp Indian Council of Social Science Research. **Added/Corp** Indian Council of Social Science Research. Journal of Abstracts and Reviews: Economics. **VFOAT** Journal of Abstracts and Reviews: Economics. **VAT** Indian Council of Social Science Research Journal of Abstracts and Reviews: Economics. (19??)-. Periodical. English. Four times a year (Jan., Apr., July, Oct.). $8.00. Indian Council of Social Science Research, 35 Ferozshah Road, New Delhi 110 001 India. **Tel** 011 91 11 38959, 011 91 11 381571. **ED** N. K. Singh. **Bk Rev. Ad Acc. Circ:** 550.
Desc: Publishes abstracts of articles and reviews in political science published in Indian journals, and a list of reviews published in political science journals.

ISSN 1180-0410
DD 016.3389/1 CN
IDRC ACQUIRES. [IDRC acquir.]. **Main/Corp** International Development Research Centre (Canada). **VFOAT** CRDI Acquiert. **VAT** International Development Research Centre Acquires. Vol. 1, No. 1 (1990)-. Periodical. English (French and Spanish). Four times a year. International Development Research Center, PO Box 117, Richmond Hill Ontario L4C 4X9 Canada. **Tel** (905)475-4145, FAX (416)940-3606.

LC HC281 .I26a **ISSN** 0170-3617
DD 330.9/43/087 GW
CEASED
IFO SPIEGEL DER WIRTSCHAFT. Main/Corp IFO-Institut fuer Wirtschaftsforschung. (19??)-(1995). Statistical Publication. German (English). IFO-Institut fuer Wirtschaftsforschung, Postfach 860460, D-81631 Munich Germany. **Tel** 011 49 89 92241, telex 5-22269. Index available. **Circ:** 700 (ctrl).
Desc: Provides a comprehensive survey of economic development in West Germany and adds a series of international overviews, using statistics of international and German authorities.

LC HF259.C9 A3 **ISSN** 0253-858X
DD 382/.095645/0021 CY
IMPORTS AND EXPORTS STATISTICS. Added/Corp Cyprus. Tmema Statistikes kai Ereunon. **VFOAT** Imports & Exports Statistics. (19??)-. English. One time a year. Department of Statistics and Research / Cyprus, 13 Lord Byron Avenue, Nicosia 162 Cyprus. **Tel** 011 357 2 303286. **Circ:** 550. ***Continues** Statistics of Imports and Exports, 0253-858X.*

LC HA1363 .A27 HD5264.I8
DD 314.5 IT
INDAGINE SPECIALE SULLE VACANZE DEGLI ITALIANI. Main/Corp Istituto Centrale di Statistica (Italy). (1959)-. Italian. L2.500. Istituto Nazionale Statistica, GBP SEZ4 Via Cesare Balbo 16, 00184 Rome Italy. **Tel** 011 39 6 46735118.

LC HC171 .I523
DD 330 AG
INDEX ESTADISTICO. ANALISIS DE COYUNTURA. VFOAT Analisis de Coyuntura. Vol. 1, No. 1 (April 16, 1990)-. Periodical. Spanish.

LC HD2930.4 .I5
DD 338.7/4/09931 NZ
INDEX OF COMPANIES REGISTERED IN NEW ZEALAND. Added/Corp New Zealand. Office of the Registrar of Companies. (19??)-. English. Irregular. 90.00NZ$ (address index), 45.00NZ$ (nominal index). Government Printing Office / New Zealand, 10 Mulgrave Street, Wellington New Zealand. **Tel** 011 64 4 4737211, FAX 011 64 4 734943, telex GOVPRINT NZ 31320. **(Subscription address:** Government Printing Office / New Zealand, PO Box 12052, Wellington New Zealand. **Tel** 011 64 4 4737211.**) Circ:** 200. available on microfiche.
Desc: Official register of companies, incorporated societies and charitable trusts.

LC Z7164.E2 I4812 HB1 **ISSN** 0536-647X
DD 016.33 US
INDEX OF ECONOMIC ARTICLES IN JOURNALS AND COLLECTIVE VOLUMES. [Index econ. artic. j. collect. vol.]. **Added/Corp** American Economic Association. **VFOAT** Index of Economic Articles. Vol. 8 (1966)-. Abstracting/Indexing Service. English. One time a year. $110.00. American Economic Association / Tennessee, 2014 Broadway, Suite 305, Nashville TN 37203-2418. **Tel** (615)322-2595, FAX (615)343-7590. available on CD-ROM (EconLit) from SilverPlatter (US); available on an online database (Economic Literature Index) from DIALOG. ***Formed by the union of** Index of Economic Journals, 0893-9527 **and** Index of Economic Articles in Collective Volumes.*
Desc: Contains bibliographic citations of journal articles, collected essays, and conference proceedings on economics from publications listed in the Journal of Economic Literature from 1969 to present. Contains over 10,000 citations of articles from over 400 publications in economics and related fields.

LC Z7165.D44 I57b HC59.7
DD 016.332/532 US
INDEX OF PUBLICATIONS & GUIDE TO INFORMATION PRODUCTS AND SERVICES. Main/Corp International Bank for Reconstruction and Development. **VFOAT** Index of Publications and Guide to Information Products and Services; Index of Publications; World Bank Index of Publications and Guide to Information Products and Services. (19??)-. Bibliography. English. One time a year. Free on request. World Bank Publications, 1818 H Street Northwest, Washington DC 20043. **Tel** (202)473-1155, (202)473-1155, FAX (202)522-3224, telex WUI 64145 WORLDBANK. ***Continues** International Bank for Reconstruction and Development. Index of Publications.*

UK
INDEX TO BUSINESS REPORTS. (1982)-. Abstracting/Indexing Service. English. Four times a year. £29.95 UK. Headland Business Information, 1 Henry Smiths Terrace, Headland Cleveland, TS24 0PD United Kingdom. **Tel** 011 44 429 231902, FAX 011 44 429 861403. **ED** N. R. Hunter. **Circ:** 400. ***Continues** Index to Special Reports in UK Newspapers and Selected Periodicals.*
Desc: Provides information from 800 Special Reports on industrial, commercial, financial and economic topics, and include industry studies and market research data.

ISSN 0963-5572
UK
INDEX TO MEED. MIDDLE EAST ECONOMIC DIGEST. [Index MEED, Middle East Econ. Dig.]. (1957)-. English. Irregular. £45.00. MEED Limited, MEED House, 21 John Street, London WC1N 2BP United Kingdom. **Tel** 011 44 171 4045513, FAX 011 44 171 2421450, telex 266872 MEEDAR G.

LC HA361 .I59 **ISSN** 0886-330X
DD 317.72 US
INDIANA FACTBOOK (BLOOMINGTON, IND.). (INDIANA FACTBOOK / INDIANA UNIVERSITY, SCHOOL OF BUSINESS, INDIANA BUSINESS RESEARCH CENTER.). [Indiana factbook]. **Added/Corp** Indiana University. Indiana Business Research Center. Indiana Economic Forum. **VFOAT** Indiana Fact Book. (1985)-. Periodical. English. Irregular (approximately every 4 years). $44.95. Indiana University Press, 601 North Morton Street, Bloomington IN 47404. **Tel** (812)855-3830, (800)842-6796.

LC HC171 .I53 **ISSN** 0537-3468
DD 330.982/005 AG
INDICADORES DE COYUNTURA (BUENOS AIRES, ARGENTINA). (INDICADORES DE COYUNTURA.). [Indic. coyunt.]. **Added/Corp** Fundacion de Investigaciones Economicas Latinoamericanas (Buenos Aires, Argentina). (Mar. 1966)-. Spanish. Twelve times a year. $318.00. Fundacion de Investigaciones Economicas Latinoamericanas, Maipu 757 Piso 7, 1006 Buenos Aires Argentina. **Tel** 011 54 1 3937154, 011 54 1 3937189, 011 54 1 3937206. **Bk Rev. Ad Acc. Circ:** 2,000 (ctrl).
Desc: The publication includes a short term analysis, a market labor analysis and more or less 1,500 economic statistics.

LC HC131 .B28a
DD 330.972 MX
INDICADORES ECONOMICOS (BANCOO DE MEXICO (1925-). SUBDIRECCION DE INVESTIGACION ECONOMICA). (INDICADORES ECONOMICOS.). **Added/Corp** Banco de Mexico (1925-). Subdireccion de Investigacion Economica. (19??)-. Spanish. Twelve times a year. $240.00. Banco de Mexico SA, Av. Juarez 90 Col. Centro, Delegacion Cuauhtemoc, 06050 Mexico D F Mexico. **Tel** 52 5 7618588 Ext. 4027 or 4028. Index available. **Circ:** 2,200. available on diskette. ***Continues*** *Serie Informacion Economica. Indicadores Economicos.*
Desc: Statistics of foreign trade, of industry production, of the financial sector and of prices to the national consumer.

BL
INDICADORES IBGE. ESTATISTICA DA PRODUCAO AGRICOLA ANUAL. **Added/Corp** Fundacao Instituto Brasileiro de Geografia e Estatistica. **VFOAT** Estatistica da Producao Agricola Anual. (Jan. 1991)-. Portuguese. Twelve times a year. IBGE/CDDI/GEMAR/SERCOM, Av Beira Mar/436 CEP 20021, Rio de Janeiro RJ Brasil. **Tel** (021)533.30.94, telex 021.30939 IBGE BR. ***Continues in part*** *Indicadores IBGE.*

BL
INDICADORES IBGE. INDICES DE PRECOS AO CONSUMIDOR, INPC, IPCA. **Added/Corp** Fundacao Instituto Brasileiro de Geografia e Estatistica. **VFOAT** Indices de Precos ao Consumidor, INPC, IPCA. (1991)-. Portuguese. Twelve times a year. IBGE/CDDI/GEMAR/SERCOM, Av Beira Mar/436 CEP 20021, Rio de Janeiro RJ Brasil. **Tel** (021)533.30.94, telex 021.30939 IBGE BR. ***Continues in part*** *Indicadores IBGE.*

ISSN 0121-2613
DD 330 CK
INDICE COLOMBIANO DE ECONOMIA Y NEGOCIOS. [Indice colomb. econ. neg.]. Vol. 1, No. 1 (1990)-. Abstracting/Indexing Service. Spanish. Four times a year (Jan., Apr., July, Oct.). $41.97. Rojas Eberhard Editores Ltda, Carrera 6A 51-21, Apartado Aereo 34270, Bogota DE Colombia. **Tel** 011 57 2851779, FAX 011 57 2744460. **ED** Rojas Eberhard. Index available. cum. index. **Ad Acc. Circ:** 2,000.
Desc: An indexing service to business and economics literature published in Colombia.

LC HA1815 .F55A **ISSN** 0376-9984
DD 315.98 IO
INDONESIA STATISTICS. **Main/Corp** First National City Bank (New York, N.Y.). (19??)-. English. First National City Bank, PO Box 2463, Jakarta Indonesia. ***Continues*** *Indonesia: Economic Statistics.*

ISSN 0791-329X
DD 331.809417 331.80212 IE
INDUSTRIAL DISPUTES (DUBLIN). (INDUSTRIAL DISPUTES.). [Ind. disput.Dublin]. (1987)-. Government Publication. English. Four times a year. 8.00p. Central Statistics Office / Ireland, Ardee Road, Dublin 6 Ireland. **Tel** 011 353 1 4977144.
Desc: Industrial disputes reported during the quarter.

ISSN 0791-2927
DD 331.209417 IE
INDUSTRIAL EMPLOYMENT, EARNINGS AND HOURS WORKED, DETAILS FOR SUPPLEMENTARY NACE SUB-SECTORS. [Ind. employ. earn. hours work. details suppl. NACE sub-sect.]. (1987)-. Government Publication. English. Four times a year. 8.00p. Central Statistics Office / Ireland, Ardee Road, Dublin 6 Ireland. **Tel** 011 353 1 4977144. ***Continues*** *Industrial Employment, Earnings and Hours Worked, Details for Supplementary NACE Sub-Groups, 0790-1003.*
Desc: Industrial earnings and hours worked.

LC HC10 .I614
DD 338/.0021 FR
INDUSTRIAL STRUCTURE STATISTICS / STATISTIQUES DES STRUCTURES INDUSTRIELLES. **Added/Corp** Organisation for Economic Co-Operation and Development. Directorate for Science, Technology, and Industry. **VFOAT** Statistiques des Structures Industrielles. (19??)-. English (French). One time a year. $55.00. OECD Publications and Information Center, 2 rue Andre-Pascal, 75775 Paris Cedex 16 France. **Tel** 011 33 1 49104262, US:(202)785-6323, FAX 011 33 1 45248500, 011 33 1 45248176, telex 620 160 OCDE. **(Subscription address:** OECD Publications Center, 2001 L Street, Suite 700, Washington DC 20036. **Tel** (202)822-3873, (202)785-6323.)
Desc: Provides detailed statistics on production, value added, employment, exports, imports, investments, wages and salaries, and supplements to wages and salaries for over 60 industries in 20 OECD countries.

LC HA1320.N6 A32 HC287.N6 N6
DD 330 GW
INDUSTRIE IN NORDHEIN-WESTFALEN, DIE. **Main/Corp** North Rhine-Westphalia (Germany). Landesamt fur Datenverarbeitung und Statistik. (19??)-. Statistical Publication. German. 9.50. Landesamt fuer Datenverarbeitung und Statistik Nordrhein-Westfalen, Postfach 101105, 40002 Duesseldorf Germany. **Tel** (0211)944901, FAX (0211)442006, telex 8586654 LDST D.

LC HA1631 .A33 HF1040.9.Y8 Y8
DD 317.971 YU
INDUSTRIJSKI PROIZVODI. **Main/Corp** Savenzi Zavod Za Statistiku (Yugoslavia). Serbo-Croatian (Roman). 5.00 Din. Savezni Zavod za Statistiku, Kneza Milosa 20, Belgrad Yugoslavia.

LC HA1501 HC361 **ISSN** 0078-1886
DD 314.81 S 338.4/767/09481021 NO
INDUSTRISTATISTIKK. HEFTE 1, NRINGSTALL. **VFOAT** Industrial Figures; Manufacturing Statistics. Volume 1, Industrial Figures. (1982)-. Norwegian (English). One time a year. Kr24.00. Central Bureau of Statistics / Norway, PO Box 8131 DEP, N-0033 Oslo 1 Norway. **Tel** 011 47 2 2864964, FAX 011 47 2 864973. ***Continues in part*** *Industristatistikk.*

LC Z1601 .I56 **ISSN** 1059-5910
US
CEASED
INFO-SOUTH ABSTRACTS. (INFO-SOUTH ABSTRACTS : LATIN AMERICAN INFORMATION SYSTEM.). [Info-south abstr.]. **Added/Corp** Transaction Periodicals Consortium. University of Miami. North-South Center. **VFOAT** Info South Abstracts. Vol. 1, No. 1 (Spring 1992)-(19??). Abstracting/Indexing Service. English. Transaction Publishers / Rutgers State University, Department 3091 or 3092, New Brunswick NJ 08903. **Tel** (908)932-2280 ext. 105, FAX (908)932-3138. **(Subscription address:** Maruzen Company Ltd., PO Box 5050, Import & Export Department, Tokyo 100 31 Japan. **Tel** 011 81 3 32789224.) **ED** Deborah R. Farrell. Index available. cum. index. **Ad Acc.** available in microform from University Microfilms International (UMI).
Desc: A comprehensive abstracting service for contemporary social, political, and economic information on Latin America drawn from the INFO-SOUTH on-line database. Abstracts are selected from journals, news magazines, newspapers, and newsletters from all Latin American countries, as well as those in the US and Europe.

LC HG201 .I48
DD 332.4 IO
INFOBANK. **Added/Corp** Bank Duta Ekonomi (Jakarta, Indonesia). (19??)-. Abstracting/Indexing Service. Indonesian (Indonesian). Twelve times a year. Rp4.00 per issue. Jakarta Selatan, Bank Duta Ekonomi, Bank Duta Ekonomi, Jl Hanglekir VIII/5 Kebayoran Baru Indonesia.

US
INFOMAT INTERNATIONAL BUSINESS [ONLINE DATABASE]. (19??)-. Abstracting/Indexing Service. English. Predicasts Inc., A Ziff Communications Company, 11001 Cedar Avenue, Cleveland OH 44106. **Tel** (800)321-6388, (216)795-3000, FAX (216)229-9944, telex 985 604. **(Subscription address:** Information Access Company, PO Box 61000, Department 1851, San Francisco CA 94161. **Tel** (800)321-6388.)
Desc: Offers extended coverage of business events and conditions in all areas of the world, with a focus on Europe. Provides access to publications covering market information, technology, industry trends, regulatory activities, and the economic environment.

NL
INFORMATIONS STATISTIQUES RAPIDES, NOUVELLE CALEDONIE / INSTITUT TERRITORIAL DE LA STATISTIQUE ET DES ETUDES ECONOMIQUES. **Added/Corp** Institut Territorial de la Statistique et des etudes Economiques (New Caledonia). (1986)-. French. Twelve times a year. Direction Territoriale de la Statistique et des Études Economiques, BP 823, Noumea Nouvelle-Caledonie. ***Continues*** *Informations Statistiques Rapides (New Caledonia. Direction Territoriale de la Statistique et des etudes Economiques).*

LC JX1977
DD 016.3392/3 US
INPUT-OUTPUT BIBLIOGRAPHY. 1955/60-. Bibliography. English. $6.50. ***Continues*** *V. Riley's Interindustry Economic Studies.*

ISSN 0998-4844
FR
INSEE. CADRAGE ET INSEE RESULTATS EMPLOIS REVENUS. French. Institut National de la Statistique et des Etudes Economiques, 18 Bd Adolphe Pinard, 75675 Paris 14 France.

ISSN 0998-4836
FR
INSEE. CADRAGE ET INSEE RESULTATS SYSTEME PRODUCTIF. (19??)-. French. Irregular. Institut National de la Statistique et des Etudes Economiques, 18 Bd Adolphe Pinard, 75675 Paris 14 France.

LC HD7096.U6 W444
DD 331.12/5/09754 US
INSURED WORKERS IN WEST VIRGINIA / PREPARED BY WEST VIRGINIA DEPARTMENT OF EMPLOYMENT SECURITY, LABOR AND ECONOMIC RESEARCH SECTION. **Added/Corp** West Virginia. Dept. of Employment Security. Labor and Economic Research Section. (19??)-. English. One time a year. Free. West Virginia Employment Programs Bureau, 112 California Avenue, Charleston WV 25305. **Tel** (304)558-2630, FAX (304)348-0301. **Circ:** 250.
Desc: Updated study of workers insured under state's unemployment insurance law and claimants receiving UI benefits. Provides data by industry in a five-year sequence.

LC HC661 .A23
DD 339.2/3/09931 NZ
INTER-INDUSTRY STUDY OF THE NEW ZEALAND ECONOMY. **Main/Corp** New Zealand. Dept. of Statistics. (1960)-. Statistical Publication. English. Irregular. Government Printing Office / New Zealand, 10 Mulgrave Street, Wellington New Zealand. **Tel** 011 64 4 4737211, FAX 011 64 4 734943, telex GOVPRINT NZ 31320. **(Subscription address:** GP Legislation Services, PO Box 12418, Wellington New Zealand. **Tel** 011 64 4 4965655.) ***Continues*** *Report on the Inter-Industry Study of the New Zealand Economy.*
Desc: Presents a statistical model of the New Zealand economy.

LC Z7164.E2 I58 **ISSN** 0085-204X
DD 016.33 US
INTERNATIONAL BIBLIOGRAPHY OF ECONOMICS. (INTERNATIONAL BIBLIOGRAPHY OF ECONOMICS / PREPARED BY THE FONDATION NATIONALE DES SCIENCES POLITIQUES (PARIS) WITH THE ASSISTANCE OF THE INTERNATIONAL ECONOMIC ASSOCIATION AND THE INTERNATIONAL COMMITTEE FOR SOCIAL SCIENCE DOCUMENTATION.). **Added/Corp** Fondation Nationale des Sciences Politiques. International Economic Association. International Committee for Social Sciences Documentation. Unesco. International Committee for Social Science Information and Documentation. **VFOAT** Bibliographie Internationale de Science Economique. Vol. 1 (1952)-. Abstracting/Indexing Service. English (French). Irregular. Price varies per volume. UNESCO / France, 31 rue Francois Bonvin, 75732 Paris Cedex 15 France. **Tel** 011 33 1 45684564, 011 33 1 45684565, FAX 011 33 1 45669270, telex 204461 Paris. available on an online database from QL Systems Ltd.

US
INTERNATIONAL BIBLIOGRAPHY OF SOCIAL SCIENCES: ECONOMICS. Bibliography. English. Irregular. $150.00 US; $187.50 Canada. Routledge Chapman & Hall Inc., 29 West 35th Street, New York NY 10001. **Tel** (212)244-3336, (212)244-6412. Index available.
Desc: Covers over 1,500 journals published throughout the world in 30 languages and stands as the long-term reference resource in the social sciences.

LC HC59.69 .I57 **ISSN** 0262-0855
DD 909/09724 UK
CCC
Pr Rev.
INTERNATIONAL DEVELOPMENT ABSTRACTS. [Int. dev. abstr.]. **Added/Corp** University College of Swansea. Centre for Development Studies. Vol. 1 (1982)-. Abstracting/Indexing Service. English. Six times a year. $557.00. Elsevier Geo Abstracts, An Imprint of Elsevier Science Ltd., The Boulevard, Langford Lane, Kidlington, Oxford OX5 1GB United Kingdom. **Tel** 011 44 1865 843000, 011 44 1865 843699, FAX 011 44 1865 843010. **(Subscription address:** Elsevier Science Ltd. / Oxford Fulfillment Centre, PO Box 800, Kidlington OX5 1DX United Kingdom. **Tel** 011 44 865 843355.) **ED** Marion Amos. Index available. **Bk Rev. Ad Acc. Circ:** 350. available on microfilm and microfiche from University Microfilms International (UMI); available on an online database from Elsevier Electronic Subscriptions (EES); Orbit Search Service; and (File no. 292) DIALOG. Documents available from BLDSC. ***Absorbed*** *International Development Index, 0262-0862.*
Desc: Provides an information service designed to assist researchers, fieldworkers, teachers and students in identifying recent material.

UK
INTERNATIONAL DIRECTORY OF NON-OFFICIAL STATISTICAL SOURCES, THE. **Added/Corp** Euromonitor Publications Limited. Business Information Associates.

VFOAT Directory of Non-Official Statistical Sources; IDNoss. (1990)-. Statistical Publication. English. $270.00. Euromonitor Publications Ltd., 60-61 Britton Street, London EC1M 5NA United Kingdom. **Tel** 011 44 171 2518024, FAX 011 44 171 6083149, telex 21120.
Desc: Provides brief descriptions of more than 1,000 key business periodicals, trade association publications, economic research journals, university newspapers, statistical database newsletters, company magazines, and other non-government publications.

LC HG3881 .I626 **ISSN** 0020-6725
DD 332.05 US

INTERNATIONAL FINANCIAL STATISTICS. [Int. financ. stat.]. **Main/Corp** International Monetary Fund. Vol. 1 (Jan. 1948)-. Periodical. English (French and Spanish). Twelve times a year (plus a yearbook issue). $230.00. International Monetary Fund, 700 19th Street Northwest, Publishing Unit, Washington DC 20431. **Tel** (202)623-7430, FAX (202)623-7201. available on magnetic tape; available on microfilm and microfiche from University Microfilms International (UMI).
Desc: Standard source of international statistics on all aspects of international and domestic finance. Contains current data needed in the analysis of problems of international payments and of inflation and deflation.
Ind/Abst Leadscan.

LC HG1501 **ISSN** 0250-7471
DD 332.1 US
CEASED

INTERNATIONAL FINANCIAL STATISTICS ANUARIO. [Int. financ. stat. anu.]. (1979)-(19??). Spanish (English and French). International Monetary Fund, 700 19th Street Northwest, Publishing Unit, Washington DC 20431. **Tel** (202)623-7430, FAX (202)623-7201. ***Continues in part*** *International Financial Statistics.*
Desc: Contains available annual data for up to 35 years for countries appearing in the monthly issues of IFS. Some additional time series in country tables and some additional tables of area and world aggregates.
Ind/Abst Predicasts F&S Index, U. S. Annu. Ed.

LC HG61 .I57 **ISSN** 0250-7463
DD 332/.02/12 US

INTERNATIONAL FINANCIAL STATISTICS YEARBOOK - INTERNATIONAL MONETARY FUND. (INTERNATIONAL FINANCIAL STATISTICS YEARBOOK.). [Int. financ. stat. yearb. - Int. Monet. Fund]. **Added/Corp** International Monetary Fund. (1979)-. Periodical. English (French and Spanish). One time a year. $60.00. International Monetary Fund, 700 19th Street Northwest, Publishing Unit, Washington DC 20431. **Tel** (202)623-7430, FAX (202)623-7201.
Desc: Contains annual data for up to 35 years for countries appearing in the monthly issue of IFS.
Ind/Abst Predicasts F&S Index, U. S. Annu. Ed.

LC Z7164.L1 I646 HD4811 **ISSN** 0020-7756
DD 016.331 SZ
CCC

INTERNATIONAL LABOUR DOCUMENTATION. [Int. labour doc.]. **Main/Corp** International Labour Office. Central Library and Documentation Branch. Vol. 1, No. 1 (Jan. 4, 1965)-. Abstracting/Indexing Service. English (French and Spanish). Ten times a year. $80.00. International Labour Office - ILO, Publications Sales Service, CH-1211 Geneva 22 Switzerland. **Tel** 011 41 22 7996111, FAX 011 41 22 7986253, telex 415 647 ilo ch. **(Subscription address:** International Labour Office / Washington, DC, 1828 L Street Northwest, Suite 801, Washington DC 20036. **Tel** (202)653-7652.**)** **Circ:** 1,300. available on an online database from Orbit Search Service; Human Resources Information Network; and European Space Agency. Documents available from BLDSC. ***Continues*** *International Labour Office. Library. International Labour Documentation.*
Desc: A bibliographical record based on current acquisitions in the ILO Central Library. Covers the fields of industrial relations, management, manpower planning, vocational training, project evaluation, labour-related aspects of rural development, and technological change of economics and social development.
Ind/Abst Hum. Rights Intern. Rep.; Popul. Index.

LC HA42 .I56 **ISSN** 0308-2938
DD 382/.09 UK

INTERNATIONAL MARKETING DATA AND STATISTICS. [Int. mark. data stat.]. 1st Ed. (1975/1976)-. English. $310.00. Euromonitor Publications Ltd., 60-61 Britton Street, London EC1M 5NA United Kingdom. **Tel** 011 44 171 2518024, FAX 011 44 171 6083149, telex 21120. **(Subscription address:** Gale Research Co., 835 Penobscot Building, Detroit MI 48226. **Tel** (800)347-4253.**)**
Desc: Provides comparative statistical data from 15 regional groups. Sections cover population, employment, production, trade, economy, standard of living, consumption, communications, and more.

LC HA154 .I58 **ISSN** 1059-3810
DD 310/.5 US

INTERNATIONAL REFERENCE. [Int. ref.]. **Added/Corp** BTA Economic Research Institute. (1991)-. English. Economic Research Institute, 16770 Northeast 79th Street, Suite 104, Redmond WA 98052. **Tel** (800)627-3697, (206)627-3697, FAX (206)885-5091.

LC HA42 .I57a **ISSN** 0098-5643
DD 310/.8 US

INTERNATIONAL RESEARCH DOCUMENT. [Int. res. doc.]. **Added/Corp** United States. Bureau of the Census. International Statistical Programs Center (U.S.). No. 1 (1975)-. Government Publication. English. US Department of Commerce / Bureau of the Census, Data User Services Division, Customer Services, Washington DC 20233-0800. **Tel** (301)763-4100. **(Subscription address:** Superintendent of Documents, US Government Printing Office, Washington DC 20402. **)**
Ind/Abst Popul. Index (?-?).

ISSN 1034-0505
DD 382.170994 AT

INTERNATIONAL TRADE IN SERVICES, AUSTRALIA. [Intern. trade serv. Aust.]. **Added/Corp** Australian Bureau of Statistics. (1989)-. English. Two times a year. 20.40Aus$. Australian Bureau of Statistics, PO Box 2796Y, Melbourne 3001 Australia. **Tel** 011 61 3 6157843.
Desc: Presents detailed estimates of Australia's international trade in services and related royalties transactions, within the context of the balance of payments accounts.

LC HF91 .U473
DD 382/.021 US

INTERNATIONAL TRADE STATISTICS YEARBOOK. **Added/Corp** United Nations. Statistical Office. **VFOAT** Annuaire Statistique du Commerce International. (1983)-. Government Publication. English (French). One time a year. Price varies per volume. United Nations Publications, 2 United Nations Plaza, Room DC2 0853, Department 007C, New York NY 10017. **Tel** (212)963-8303, (800)253-9646. ***Continues*** *Yearbook of International Trade Statistics, 0498-0204.*
Desc: Provides data on world economy, its structure, major trends and current performance, as well as on issues such as world population, employment, inflation, production of energy, supply of food, external debt of developing countries, education, availability of dwellings, production of energy, development of new energy sources and environmental pollution and management.

LC HA1651 .A334 HC407.Z7S4 Z7S46
DD 314 CI

INVESTICIJE SR SRBIJE / SOCIJALISTICKA REPUBLIKA SRBIJA, REPUBLICKI ZAVOD ZA STATISTIKU. (1966)-(1970). Serbo-Croatian (Roman). 100.00 Din. Republicki Zavod za Statistiku, Central Bureau of Statistics of the Republic of Croatia, Ilica 3, Zagreb Croatia. **Tel** 011 385 41 45 44 22, FAX 011 385 41 42 94 13, 011 385 41 42 37 11, telex 21130 DZSTAT RH.

LC HA1138.M3 M35a
DD 314.27/9 UK

ISLE OF MAN DIGEST OF ECONOMIC AND SOCIAL STATISTICS. **Main/Corp** Isle of Man. Treasury. Economics Section. (19??)-. English. Every 2 years. Central Government Offices, Buckinghamshire Road, Douglas Isle of Man United Kingdom. **Tel** 011 44 1624 26262, FAX 011 44 1624 26288. **ED** MD Kelly. **Circ:** 750 (ctrl).
Desc: Digest of economic and social statistics of the Isle of Man.

NE

JAARSTATISTIEK VAN DE BUITENLANDSE HANDEL PER LAND EN GOEDERENSOORT. (19??)-. Dutch. One time a year. Fl125.00. SDU Uitgeverij, Postbus 20014, Christoffel Plantijnstraat, 2500 EA Den Haag Netherlands. **Tel** 011 31 70 3789911.

SZ

JAHRESSTATISTIK DES AUSSENHANDELS DER SCHWEIZ. STATISTIQUE ANNUELLE DU COMMERCE EXTERIEUR DE LA SUISSE. **Main/Corp** Switzerland Edigenossische Oberzolldirektion. **Added/Corp** Switzerland. Obersolldirektion. Switzerland. Obersolldirektion. Jahresstatistik des Aussenhandels der Schweiz. Switzerland. Obersolldirektion. Statistique Annuelle du Commerce Exterieur de la Suisse. (1885)-. Statistical Publication. Multiple languages. One time a year. 190.00F Switzerland; 217.00F other. Eidg Oberzolldirektion Abt Aussenhandelsstatistik, Monbijoustrasse 40, CH-3003 Bern Switzerland. **Tel** 011 41 31 3226610, FAX 011 41 31 3227872, telex 911100 OZD CH. **Bk Rev.** **Circ:** 1,000 (ctrl).
Desc: Foreign trade statistics: imports and exports by quantity, value and countries.

LC Z7165.J3 J34 HC462
DD 016.330952 JA

JAPAN PERIODICALS. **Added/Corp** Keizai Koho Senta (Tokyo, Japan). (1982). English. $5.00. Keizai Koho Center, Otemachi Building, 6-1 Otemachi 1-chome Chiyoda-ku, Tokyo 100 Japan. **Tel** (03)201-1415, telex 222-5452 KKCTOK J.

LC HF1371 .J13
DD 380.1 JA

JETRO WHITE PAPER ON INTERNATIONAL TRADE. **Added/Corp** Nihon Boeki Shinkokai. **VFOAT** World and Japanese Trade. (1990)-. Statistical Publication. English. One time a year (May). $143.00. Japan External Trade Organization, 2 5 2 Chome Toranomon, Minato-ku Tokyo 107, Japan. **Tel** 011 81 3 3582 5521, FAX 011 81 3 3582 0504, telex J24378. ***Continues*** *Japan. Tsusho Sangyosho. Tsusho Hakusho. English.* ***and*** *White Paper on International Trade: Japan.*
Desc: Contains trade statistics.

LC HB137 .J68 **ISSN** 0735-0015
DD 330/.072 US
CCC
Pr Rev.

JOURNAL OF BUSINESS & ECONOMIC STATISTICS. (JOURNAL OF BUSINESS & ECONOMIC STATISTICS : A PUBLICATION OF THE AMERICAN STATISTICAL ASSOCIATION.). [J. bus. econ. stat.]. **Added/Corp** American Statistical Association. **VFOAT** Journal of Business and Economic Statistics; J.B.E.S.; JBES. Vol. 1, No. 1 (Jan. 1983)-. Statistical Publication. English. Four times a year (Jan., Apr., July, Oct.). $72.00. American Statistical Association, 1429 Duke Street, Alexandria VA 22314. **Tel** (703)684-1221, (202)393-3253, FAX (703)684-2037 (orders). available on microfilm and microfiche from University Microfilms International (UMI). Documents available from The Genuine Article, UMI Article Clearinghouse, Ask*IEEE.
Ind/Abst ABI/INFORM Glob. Ed.; ABI/INFORM [Computer File] (Jan. 1988-); Bus. Source Plus; Bus. Source; Contents Pages Manage.; Curr. Cit.; Curr. Contents Soc. Behav. Sci.; Curr. Index Stat.; Econ. Lit. Index (1985-1989, 19??-); EP Collect.; Homework Help.; INSPEC (Jan. 1985-Oct. 1989); Int. Bibliogr. Sociol.; J. Econ. Lit.; MasterFile FullTEXT 1000; MasterFile FullTEXT 350; MasterFile FullTEXT 650; MasterFile FullTEXT; OCLC; Oper. Res./Manage. Sci. (1985-1989); Qual. Control Appl. Stat. (1985-1989); Res. Alert [Full Cov.]; Soc. Sci. Cit. Index [Full Cov.]; Soc. Res. Methodol. Abstr. (1987-); Stat. Theory Method Abstr. (1983-1984, 1986-1987); Telebase.

LC H62.A1 R47 **ISSN** 0747-9662
DD 300/.72073 US
CCC
CODEN JEMEEZ

JOURNAL OF ECONOMIC AND SOCIAL MEASUREMENT. [J. econ. soc. meas.]. Vol. 13, No. 1 (Apr. 1985)-. Periodical. English. Four times a year. $260.37. IOS Press, Van Diemenstraat 94, 1013 CN Amsterdam Netherlands. **Tel** 011 31 20 6382189, FAX 011 31 20 6203419. **ED** Charles Renfro. Documents available from UMI Article Clearinghouse. ***Continues*** *Review of Public Data Use, 0092-2846.*
Desc: A unique guide to the production, distribution and use of publicly available statistical data. It publishes original articles and information on quantitative research and methodology using publicly available data bases.
Ind/Abst Appl. Soc. Sci. Index Abstr.; Curr. Contents Soc. Behav. Sci.; Econ. Lit. Index (-1986); Expand. Acad. Index (1992-); Health Plan. Adminis.; Hosp. Health Admin. Index (1985-); Hum. Resour. Abstr. (?-?); Int. Bibliogr. Sociol.; J. Econ. Lit. (1985-); Newsp. Period. Abstr. (1992-); PAIS Int. Print (1991-); Life Sci. Collect.; Popul. Index (1985-); Soc. Plann. Policy Dev. Abstr.; Sociol. Abstr. (1985-); Urban Aff. Abstr.; Women Stud. Abstr. (1985-).

LC HB1 .J6 **ISSN** 0022-0515
DD 330 US
CODEN JECLB3
Pr Rev.

JOURNAL OF ECONOMIC LITERATURE. [J. econ. lit.]. **Added/Corp** American Economic Association. Vol. 7 (March 1969)-. Abstracting/Indexing Service. English. Irregular. $49.00 membership. American Economic Association / Tennessee, 2014 Broadway, Suite 305, Nashville TN 37203-2418. **Tel** (615)322-2595, FAX (615)343-7590. Index available. cum. index. **Bk Rev.** **Ad Acc.** **Circ:** 25,000. available on CD-ROM (Econ Lit) from SilverPlatter (US); available on microfilm and microfiche from University Microfilms International (UMI); available on an online database from DIALOG. Documents available from The Genuine Article, UMI Article Clearinghouse. ***Continues*** *Journal of Economic Abstracts, 0364-281X.*
Desc: Subject indexing and abstracts of articles in over 390 journals; subject indexing of articles in collective volumes; subject indexing and abstracts of books; and subject indexing of dissertation titles. Records contain basic bibliographic data plus descriptor codes corresponding descriptor the 4-digit subject headings in the Index of Economic Articles, geographic descriptors and author affiliations.

Ind/Abst ABI/INFORM Glob. Ed.; ABI/INFORM [Computer File] (Sept. 1973-); Acad. Abstr.; Acad. Ind. [Computer File] (1984-); Acad. Search; Am. Hist. Life (1969-); Am. Bibliogr. Slavic East Europ. Stud.; Book Rev. Digest; Book Rev. Index; Bus. Index (1985-); Bus. Source Plus; Bus. Source; Contents Recent Econ. J.; Curr. Cit.; Curr. Contents Soc. Behav. Sci.; Econ. Lit. Index; Energy Res. Abstr. (April 1976-); EP Collect.; Expand. Acad. Index (1984-); Gen. BusinessFile (1985-); Gen. Period. Index (1985-); Hist. Source (July 1990-); Homework Help.; INFO-SOUTH Abstr.; Int. Bibliogr. Sociol.; Int. Dev. Abstr. (?-?); Int. Labour Doc.; J. Econ. Lit.; J. Plan. Lit.; Leis., Rec., Tour. Abstr.; Mag. Search; MasterFile FullTEXT 1000; MasterFile FullTEXT 350; MasterFile FullTEXT 650; MasterFile FullTEXT (July 1990-); Middle East Abstr. Index; Newsp. Period. Abstr. (1990-); OCLC; Oper. Res./Manage. Sci.; PAIS Int. Print (1991-); Popul. Index; Qual. Control Appl. Stat.; Res. Alert [Full Cov.]; Rural Dev. Abstr.; Selec. Coop. Index Manage. Period.; Soc. Sci. Source; Soc. Sci. Cit. Index [Full Cov.]; Soc. Sci. Index; Soc. Sci. Index Fulltext (Dec. 1988-) [Full Txt.]; Telebase; UMI ABI/Inform--Bus. Period. Ondisc (Mar. 1987-) [Full Txt.]; Women Stud. Abstr.; World Agric. Econ. Rural Sociol. Abstr.

LC HG5491 .D47 **ISSN** 0943-8769
DD 332.609 GW
●**KAPITALMARKTSTATISTIK. Added/Corp** Deutsche Bundesbank. (Jan. 1993)-. Bulletin. German (English). Twelve times a year. Deutsche Bundesbank Presse, Information Wilh Epsteinstrasse 14, D-60431 Frankfurt Germany. **Tel** 011 49 69 1583509 or 1583455, telex 41 227 OR 414 431. ***Continues*** *Statistische Beihefte zu den Monatsberichten der Deutschen Bundesbank. Reihe 2, Wertpapierstatistik, 0418-8314.*

LC HC461 .H65
DD 330 JA
KEIZAI TOKEI NEMPO. Added/Corp Nihon Ginko. Tokeikyoku. **VFOAT** Economic Statistics Annual. (1967)-. Statistical Publication. Japanese (English). One time a year. $63.00. **(Subscription address:** Japan Publications Trading Company Ltd., PO Box 5030, Tokyo International, Tokyo 100-31 Japan. **Tel** 011 81 3 3292 3753.) ***Continues*** *Hompo Keizai Tokei.*

LC HC461 .K4593
DD 338.95 JA
KEIZAI TOKEI NENKAN. VFOAT Economic Statistics Year Book; Year Book of Economic Statistics. 1952-. Japanese. One time a year. Tokyo Keizai Shimpo Sha, 1-4 Nihonbashi Hongokucho Chuo-ku 103, Tokyo Japan.

LC HC602 .K65
DD 338/.025/94 AT
KOMPASS; AUSTRALIA. Added/Corp Australian Chamber of Commerce. Associated Chambers of Manufacturers of Australia. Metal Trades Industry Association of Australia. (1970)-. English (French, German, Italian and Spanish). One time a year. 415.20Aus$. Peter Isaacson Publications, 46-50 Porter Street, Prahran Victoria, 3181 Australia. **Tel** 011 61 3 2457777, FAX 011 61 3 2457606. **ED** John Ross. **Bk Rev. Ad Acc. Circ:** 4,000.
Desc: A guide to who's who in Australian industry and business, where they are located, what products and services they provide, key personnel, and other information.

LC HC365 .A35 **ISSN** 0078-1924
DD 330 NO
KONOMISK UTSYN. Added/Corp Norway. Statistisk Sentralbyra. **VFOAT** Economic Survey. Periodical. Norwegian (Norwegian; summaries and/or abstracts in English). One time a year. Kr45.00. Central Bureau of Statistics / Norway, PO Box 8131 DEP, N-0033 Oslo 1 Norway. **Tel** 011 47 2 2864964, FAX 011 47 2 864973. **ED** Olav Bjerkholt. **Circ:** 3,000. ***Continues*** *Statistisk Konomisk Oversikt.*
Desc: Presents reviews on the Norwegian economy covering quarterly and annual national accounts, with results from the research activity on economics from the Central Bureau of Statistics.

LC JK2403 .A35 HD8008.A1 **ISSN** 0272-3689
DD 300/.973 S 331/.04135/0000973 US
LABOR-MANAGEMENT RELATIONS IN STATE AND LOCAL GOVERNMENTS. Added/Corp United States. Bureau of the Census. United States. Labor-Management Services Administration. **VAT** Labor Management Relations in State and Local Governments. (1974)-. Government Publication. English. One time a year. $3.00. US Department of Commerce / Bureau of the Census, Data User Services Division, Customer Services, Washington DC 20233-0800. **Tel** (301)763-4100. **(Subscription address:** Superintendent of Documents, US Government Printing Office, Washington DC 20402. **)**
Desc: Provides statistics on the nature and characteristics of state and local government labor-management relations.

SZ
LABORDOC [ONLINE DATABASE]. (19??)-. Abstracting/Indexing Service. English. International Labour Office - ILO, Publications Sales Service, CH-1211 Geneva 22 Switzerland. **Tel** 011 41 22 7996111, FAX 011 41 22 7986253, telex 415 647 ilo ch.
Desc: Contains bibliographical references, with English-language abstracts and descriptors, to recent acquisitions in ILO's Central Library and specialized departmental units. Provides world-wide coverage of labour relations, labour law, employment, working conditions, vocational training, management project evaluation, and labour-related aspects of economics, social development, rural development, technological change and more. Available through ESA-IRS, HRIN, and ORBIT.

AT
LABOUR FORCE. (19??)-. English. Four times a year. $66.00. Australian Bureau of Statistics, PO Box 2796Y, Melbourne 3001 Australia. **Tel** 011 61 3 6157843.

ISSN 1181-6627
DD 331.12/5/0971021 CN
LABOUR FORCE ANNUAL AVERAGES. (LABOUR FORCE ANNUAL AVERAGES.). [Labour force annu. aver.]. **Added/Corp** Statistics Canada. Household Surveys Division. **VFOAT** Moyennes Annuelles de la Population Active. (1990)-. English (French). One time a year. 47.22Can$. Statistics Canada Publications Sales and Services, R.H. Coats Building 6th Floor, Ottawa Ontario K1A 0T6 Canada. **Tel** (613)951-5078, (800)267-6677, FAX (613)951-1584, telex 053-3585.

LC HA867 .A385 HD5745.T72
DD 317.29/83 S 331./1/0972983 TR
LABOUR FORCE BY SEX. Main/Corp Trinidad and Tobago. Central Statistical Office. (19??)-. Statistical Publication. English. Six times a year. TT$6.00. Government Printery / Trinidad, Central Statistical Office, 35 41 Queen Street, Port of Spain Trinidad. **Tel** (809)625-4970, FAX (809)625-3802. **Circ:** 400 (ctrl).
Desc: Gives a description of the labour in Trinidad and Tobago.

ISSN 0708-3157
DD 331.11/0971 CN
LABOUR FORCE INFORMATION. [Labour force inf.]. **Main/Corp** Canada. Statistics Canada. **Added/Corp** Statistics Canada. **VFOAT** Information Population Active. (Oct. 16, 1976)-. Statistical Publication. English (French). Twelve times a year. 120.00Can$. Statistics Canada Publications Sales and Services, R.H. Coats Building 6th Floor, Ottawa Ontario K1A 0T6 Canada. **Tel** (613)951-5078, (800)267-6677, FAX (613)951-1584, telex 053-3585.

LC HD5727 .A33 **ISSN** 0380-6804
DD 331.1/1/0971 CN
LABOUR FORCE (MONTHLY ED.). (THE LABOUR FORCE.). [Labour force]. **Added/Corp** Canada. Dominion Bureau of Statistics. Special Surveys Division. Canada. Dominion Bureau of Statistics. Labour Division. Statistics Canada. Labour Force Survey Section. Statistics Canada. Labour Force Survey Group. Statistics Canada. Labour Force Survey Division. Processing and Data Dissemination Section. Statistics Canada. Labour Force Survey Division. Statistics Canada. Household Surveys Division. **VFOAT** Population Active; Main-d'Oeuvre. Vol. 16, No. 9 (Sept. 1960)-. English (French). Twelve times a year. 276.00Can$. Statistics Canada Publications Sales and Services, R.H. Coats Building 6th Floor, Ottawa Ontario K1A 0T6 Canada. **Tel** (613)951-5078, (800)267-6677, FAX (613)951-1584, telex 053-3585. ***Absorbed*** *Main-d'Oeuvre (Ottawa, Ont. : 1964);* ***Continues*** *Labour Force, Monthly Survey, 0837-8827.*
Desc: Presents seasonally adjusted and unadjusted estimates of labor force, employment and unemployment, with unemployment and participation rates analyzed by selected geographic, demographic and occupational variables. Includes occasional special analyses and sample questionnaires.

LC HD5850 .A56
DD 312/.9 AT
LABOUR FORCE STATUS AND OTHER CHARACTERISTICS OF FAMILIES / AUSTRALIAN BUREAU OF STATISTICS. Added/Corp Australian Bureau of Statistics. (19??)-. English. One time a year. 12.70Aus$. Australian Bureau of Statistics, PO Box 2796Y, Melbourne 3001 Australia. **Tel** 011 61 3 6157843.
Desc: Family type, classified by family size, number of employed and unemployed family members, labour force status of husband/wife/head, birthplace of head, number of dependent children, age of wife/head/dependent children, status of worker.

LC HD8841 .A32a **ISSN** 0314-2779
DD 331/.0994/021 AT
LABOUR STATISTICS ... AUSTRALIA. Added/Corp Australian Bureau of Statistics. **VFOAT** Labour Statistics, Australia. (1979)-. English. One time a year. 32.06Aus$. Australian Bureau of Statistics, PO Box 2796Y, Melbourne 3001 Australia. **Tel** 011 61 3 6157843. ***Continues*** *Labor Statistics.*
Desc: Presents a wide range of information, including time series statistics, on the Australian labour market in tabular and graphical forms.

LC HD5091.Z9 S673A
DD 331.2/968 SA
LABOUR STATISTICS : WAGE RATES, EARNINGS AND AVERAGE HOURS WORKED IN THE PRINTING AND NEWSPAPER INDUSTRY, ENGINEERING INDUSTRY, BUILDING INDUSTRY AND COMMERCE. Main/Corp South Africa. Dept. of Statistics. **VFOAT** Arbeidstatistieke Loontariewe, Verdienste en Gemiddelde ure Gewerk in die Druk- en Nuusbladnywerheid, Ingenieursbedryf, Bounywerheid en die Handel. (19??)-. Multiple languages (Afrikaans and English). R3.75. Government Printer / South Africa, Bosman Street, Private Bag X85, Pretoria 0001 South Africa. **Tel** 011 27 12 3239731 ext. 262.

LC HC415.38.A1 S73
DD 330.953/65/005 GW
LAENDERBERICHT. BAHRAIN. Added/Corp Germany. Statistisches Bundesamt. (1991)-. German (table of contents in English). Hermann Leins GmbH & Co., Verlags-KG, Holzwiesenstrasse 2, Postfach 11 52, D-7408 Kusterdingen Germany. ***Continues*** *Statistik des Auslandes. Laenderbericht. Bahrein, 0176-3075.*

LC HD5824 .A32f
DD 331.12 IO
LAPORAN STATISTIK BULANAN - BAGIAN PENGUMPULAN DAN PENGOLAHAN DATA, BIRO PERENCANAAN, DEPARTEMEN TENAGA KERJA, TRANSMIGRASI DAN KOPERASI. Main/Corp Indonesia. Departmen Tenaga Kerja, Transmigrasi dan Koperasi. Biro Perencanaan. Bagian Pengumpulan dan Pengolahan Data. (June 1975)-. Indonesian. Bagian Pengumpulan dan Pengolahan Data, Biro Perencanaan, Jl Let Jen Haryono Mt, Jakarta Indonesia. ***Continues*** *Indonesia. Departmen Tenaga Kerja, Transmigrasi dan Koperasi. Biro Perencanaan. Bagian Penelitian dan Statistik. Laporan Statistik Bulanan - Bagian Penelitian dan Statistik, Departemen Tenaga Kerja, Transmigrasi dan Koperas.*

LC HC448.S782 I54A
DD 330 IO
LAPORAN TAHUNAN - KANTOR WILAYAH DEPARTEMEN PERINDUSTRIAN PROPINSI SULAWESI TENGAH. Main/Corp Indonesia. Departemen Perindustrian. Kantor Wilayah Propinsi Sulawesi Tengah. (19??)-. Indonesian.

LC HA1631 .A33 HC407.Y6 **ISSN** 0300-2535
DD 314.971 YU
LICNI DOHOCI. Main/Corp Savezni Zavod za Statistiku (Yugoslavia). Serbo-Croatian (Roman). One time a year. 5.00 Din single issue. Savezni Zavod za Statistiku, Kneza Milosa 20, Belgrad Yugoslavia.

LC HC **ISSN** 0005-8521
DD 330 BE
LISTE MENSUELLE. Main/Corp Belgium. Ministere des Affaires Economiques. Direction Generale des ,Etudes et de la Documentation. Biblioth·eque Centrale Accroisements. (19??)-. Periodical. French. Irregular. 250F Belgium, 375F other. Direction Generales des Etudes et de la Documentation, 6 rue de l'Industrie, 1040 Brussels Belgium. **Tel** 02 506.51.11, 02 506.63.07, FAX 02 513.46.57.

ISSN 0791-3206
DD 331.119417 331.110212 IE
LIVE REGISTER, MONTHLY AREA ANALYSIS (DUBLIN). [Live regist. mon. area anal. Dublin]. (1989)-. Government Publication. English. Twelve times a year. 24.00p. Central Statistics Office / Ireland, Ardee Road, Dublin 6 Ireland. **Tel** 011 353 1 4977144. ***Continues*** *Live Register, Quarterly Area of Residence Analysis (Dublin), 0791-3214.*
Desc: Unemployment data classified by area.

ISSN 0791-3222
DD 331.119417 331.110212 IE
LIVE REGISTER STATEMENT (DUBLIN). [Live regist. statement Dublin]. (1989)-. Government Publication. English. Twelve times a year. 24.00p. Central Statistics Office / Ireland, Ardee Road, Dublin 6 Ireland. **Tel** 011 353 1 4977144. ***Continues*** *Live Register, Monthly Statement (Dublin), 0791-3230.*
Desc: Monthly updates on the number of males and females registered at local unemployment offices.

LC HA1501 HD5050
DD 314.81 NO
LNNINGER OG INNTEKTER. VFOAT Wages, Salaries, and Income. 1980-. English (Norwegian). 15.00.

LC HA1501 HD8039.M4N77
DD 314.81 S 331.2/9481 NO
LNNSSTATISTIKK FOR ANSATTE I FORRETNINGSMESSIG TJENESTEYTING OG I INTERESSEORGANISASJONER. **VFOAT** Wage Statistics for Employees in Business Services and in Business, Professional and Labour Associations; Lnnsstatistikk, Forretningsmessig Tjenesteyting og Interesseorganisasjoner. Norwegian (English). One time a year. Kr40.00 Norway; $6.00 US. Central Bureau of Statistics / Norway, PO Box 8131 DEP, N-0033 Oslo 1 Norway. **Tel** 011 47 2 2864964, FAX 011 47 2 864973.

LC HA1501
DD 381/.09481 NO
LNNSSTATISTIKK FOR ANSATTE I VAREHANDEL. **Main/Corp** Norway. Statistisk Sentralbyra. **VFOAT** Wage Statistics for Employees in Wholesale and Retail Trade; Lnnsstatistikk: Varehandel. (1960)-. English (Norwegian).

LC HC
DD 330 US
•**LOTUS NOTES.** (LOTUS NOTES [COMPUTER FILE].). (1995)-. Abstracting/Indexing Service. English. EBSCO Publishing / Boston, 83 Pine Street, Peabody MA 01960. **Tel** (800)653-2726 North America, (508)535-8500, FAX (508)535-8545.

LC HF265 .A42
DD 380.1 SA
MAANDELIKSE UITTREKSEL VAN HANDELSTATISTIEKE : STATISTIEKE VRYGESTEL DEUT DIE KOMMISSARIS VAN DOEANE EN AKSYNS VAN DIE REPUBLIEK VAN SUID-AFRIKA TEN OPSIGTE VAN BUITELANDSE HANDEL VAN DIE TOLUNIEGEBIED BOTSWANA, LESOTHO, NAMIBIE, SUID-AFRIKA EN SWAZILAND / MONTHLY ABSTRACT OF TRADE STATISTICS : STATISTICS RELEASED BY THE COMMISSIONER FOR CUSTOMS AND EXCISE OF THE REPUBLIC OF SOUTH AFRICA IN RESPECT OF THE FOREIGN TRADE OF THE CUSTOMS UNION AREA OF BOTSWANA, LESOTHO, NAMIBIA, SOUTH AFRICA, AND SWAZILAND. **Added/Corp** South Africa. Dept. of Customs and Excise. **VFOAT** Monthly Abstract of Trade Statistics. (Jan./Apr. 1992)-. Government Publication. Afrikaans (English). Twelve times a year. R540.00 South Africa; R592.08 other. Staatsdrukkery Government Printing Works, Bosmanstraat/Bosman Street, Private Bag X85, Pretoria 0001 South Africa. **Tel** 011 27 12 3239731, FAX 011 27 12 3230009. ***Continues*** *Maandelikse Bulletin van Handelstatistieke.*

LC HB235.N2 N47a
DD 338.52 NE
MAANDSTATISTIEK VAN DE PRIJZEN. **Main/Corp** Netherlands. Centraal Bureau Voor de Statistiek. Vol. 1 (Jan. 1976)-. Dutch. Twelve times a year. $63.38. SDU Uitgeverij, Postbus 20014, Christoffel Plantijnstraat, 2500 EA Den Haag Netherlands. **Tel** 011 31 70 3789911.

LC HD28 .M3217 **ISSN** 0308-2172
DD 658/.005 UK
CCC
Pr Rev.
MANAGEMENT & MARKETING ABSTRACTS. [Manage. market. abstr.]. **Added/Corp** Pira (Association). **VFOAT** Management and Marketing Abstracts. (1976)-. Abstracting/Indexing Service. English. Twelve times a year. £548.00, $877.00. Pira International, Randalls Road Leatherhead, Surrey KT22 7RU United Kingdom. **Tel** 011 44 1372 802050, FAX 011 44 1372 802239, telex 929810. **ED** Marie Rushton, Diana Deavin, and Kathy Young (editor's address: PIRA, Research Association for the Paper and Board, Printing and Packaging Industries, Randalls Road, Leatherhead Surrey KT22 7RU UK). **Bk Rev.** available on CD-ROM; available on microfilm and microfiche from University Microfilms International (UMI); available on an online database from DATA-STAR; and Pergamon Financial Data Services. Documents available from BLDSC.
Desc: Provides coverage of business and management information for decision makers. Covers company products and industries.

LC HD28 .M3417 **ISSN** 0309-0582
DD 658/.005 UK
MANAGEMENT BIBLIOGRAPHIES & REVIEWS. [Manage. bibliogr. rev.]. **VFOAT** Management Bibliographies & Reviews. Vol. 1 (1975)-. Abstracting/Indexing Service. English. Eight times a year. $4999.00. MCB University Press, 60 62 Toller Lane, Bradford, West Yorkshire BD8 9BY United Kingdom. **Tel** 011 44 1274 785280, FAX 011 44 1274 785200, telex 51317-MCBUNI-G. **(Subscription address:** MCB University Press / US and Canada Subscriptions, PO Box 10812, Birmingham AL 35201-0812. **Tel** (205)995-1567, (800)633-4931, FAX (205)995-1588.) **ED** Andrew Ede. ***Continues*** *Business Education, 0144-2813.*
Desc: Designed to help teachers, researchers, and students of management gain access to information on their particular specialization. Aims to help librarians manage their books more accurately, and to choose new books to buy and recommend to others.
Ind/Abst Int. Labour Doc.

US
MANAGEMENT CONTENTS [ONLINE DATABASE]. (19??)-. Abstracting/Indexing Service. English. Information Access Company, 362 Lakeside Drive, Foster City CA 94404. **Tel** (800)227-8431, (800)458-1565.
Desc: Offers indexing and abstracting of more than 100 key management journals. Four broad management disciplines are covered including banking, finance, and accounting; human resources, training and benefits; sales, marketing and advertising; and general management.

LC HF215 .A4 **ISSN** 0332-6403
DD 380.1 NO
MANEDSSTATISTIKK OVER UTENRIKSHANDELEN. **Main/Corp** Norway. Statistisk Sentralbyra. **Added/Corp** Norway. Statistisk Sentralbyra. **VFOAT** Monthly Bulletin of External Trade. Vol. 48 (1960)-. Bulletin. Norwegian (summaries and/or abstracts in English). Twelve times a year. $75.35. Central Bureau of Statistics / Norway, PO Box 8131 DEP, N-0033 Oslo 1 Norway. **Tel** 011 47 2 2864964, FAX 011 47 2 864973. **Bk Rev. Ad Acc. Circ:** 1,300 (ctrl). ***Continues*** *Manedsoppgaver Over Vareomsetningen Med Utlandet.*
Desc: Contains detailed data on imports and exports.

ISSN 0700-2971
CN
MANITOBA STATISTICAL REVIEW. **Main/Corp** Manitoba Bureau of Statistics. Vol. 1, No. 3 (1976)-. Statistical Publication. English. Four times a year (June, Sept., Dec., March). 44.02Can$. Manitoba Bureau of Statistics, 333 260 St. Mary Avenue, Winnipeg Manitoba R3C OM6 Canada. **Tel** (204)945-2995, FAX (204)945-0695. **Circ:** 200 (ctrl). ***Supersedes*** *Manitoba Bureau of Statistics. Manitoba Digest of Statistics., 0700-298X;* ***Supersedes in part*** *Manitoba Price Statistics., 0317-7475.*
Desc: Compendium of socio-economic statistics on Manitoba with comparisons with other provinces.

LC HF5415.2 .M328 **ISSN** 0025-3596
DD 658.8/3/05 UK
MARKET RESEARCH ABSTRACTS. **Added/Corp** Market Research Society. (1963)-. Abstracting/Indexing Service. English. Two times a year. $179.67. NTC Publications Ltd., PO Box 69, Henley-on-Thames, Oxfordshire RG9 1GB United Kingdom. **Tel** 011 44 1491 574671, FAX 011 44 1491 571188. **Circ:** 700. available on microfilm and microfiche from University Microfilms International (UMI); available on an online database from DIALOG. Documents available from BLDSC, UMI Article Clearinghouse.
Desc: Synopses of articles related to market research and related fields in statistics, psychology, economics, and sociology.

LC HF5410 **ISSN** 0308-3446
DD 658.83 UK
MARKET RESEARCH EUROPE. [Mark. res. Eur.]. Vol. 8 (1976)-. Statistical Publication. English. Twelve times a year. $895.00 North America; £445.00 other. Euromonitor Publications Ltd., 60-61 Britton Street, London EC1M 5NA United Kingdom. **Tel** 011 44 171 2518024, FAX 011 44 171 6083149, telex 21120. **ED** Robert Hill. cum. index. **Circ:** 500 (ctrl). available on diskette; available on an online database from Lexis-Nexis; and (file 648/Full-Text) DIALOG. Documents available from BLDSC, SWETS. ***Continues*** *Euromonitor Review.*
Desc: A statistical analysis of specialized European markets, i.e. snack foods, alcoholic beverages retailing concentrating in France, Spain, Italy and Germany.
Ind/Abst F&S Index Plus Text, Int. [Select. Cov.]; Int. Packag. Abstr.; PROMT; Selec. Coop. Index Manage. Period.; Trade Ind. ASAP [Full Txt.]; Trade Ind. Index [Full Txt.].

US
MARKETING AND ADVERTISING REFERENCE SERVICE [ONLINE DATABASE]. **VFOAT** MARS. Abstracting/Indexing Service. English. Predicasts Inc., A Ziff Communications Company, 11001 Cedar Avenue, Cleveland OH 44106. **Tel** (800)321-6388, (216)795-3000, FAX (216)229-9944, telex 985 604. **(Subscription address:** Information Access Company, PO Box 61000, Department 1851, San Francisco CA 94161. **Tel** (800)321-6388.)
Desc: Offers information on the advertising and marketing of consumer products and services, including: advertising campaigns and budgets, new products, market size and share, marketing strategies, ad agency activities, consumer research, regulation and more.

LC HF5415.2 .E96 **ISSN** 0923-5957
DD 658.8/394/05 NE
CCC
MARKETING AND RESEARCH TODAY : THE JOURNAL OF THE EUROPEAN SOCIETY FOR OPINION AND MARKETING RESEARCH. **Added/Corp** Esomar. Vol. 17, No. 1 (Feb. 1989)-. Abstracting/Indexing Service. English (summaries and/or abstracts in French and German). Four times a year (1 volume). $170.00. ESOMAR Central Secretariat, J J Viottastraat 29, 1071 JP Amsterdam Netherlands. **Tel** 011 31 20 6642141, FAX 011 31 20 6642922. available on microfilm and microfiche from University Microfilms International (UMI). ***Continues*** *European Research, 0304-4297.*
Ind/Abst Curr. Cit.; Manage. Market. Abstr.; Selec. Coop. Index Manage. Period.; Soc. Res. Methodol. Abstr. (1990-).

LC HF5410
DD 658.83 UK
CODEN MRKEED
MARKETSEARCH. **Added/Corp** Arlington Management Publications (London, England) British Overseas Trade Board. **VFOAT** International Directory of Published Market Research; Market Search. 10th Edition (1986)-. English. One time a year (Apr.). $245.00. Arlington Management Publications, 1 Hay Hill Berkeley Square, London W1X 7LF United Kingdom. **Tel** 011 44 171 4951940, FAX 011 44 171 4092557, telex 917835. **ED** Kathleen Mann (phone: 011 44 81 874 7633). Index available. ***Continues*** *International Directory of Published Market Research.*
Desc: Contains over 18,000 abstracts of market research reports and surveys on industrial and consumer goods and services in the US and abroad. Each listing includes title, a brief summary, countries covered, page count, price and date of publication.

II
MASIKA ANKARA SARA. MONTHLY ABSTRACT OF STATISTICS. **Main/Corp** India. Central Statistical Organisation. **VFOAT** Monthly Abstract of Statistics. Vol. 30, No. 1/2 (Jan./Feb. 1977)-. Periodical. English (Hindi). Twelve times a year. Rs720.00 India; $259.20 US. Deputy Director, Government of India, Ministry of Planning, Department of Statistics, Central Statistical Organisation, Industrial Statistics Wing 1, Council House Street, Calcutta-700001 India. **Tel** 23-6534. Index available. **Circ:** 700 (ctrl). ***Continues*** *India. Central Statistical Organisation. Monthly Abstract of Statistics.*
Desc: Presents statistical data pertaining to various facets of the Indian economy. Subject coverage is periodically reviewed and attempts made to improve it, keeping in view comparability and continuity.

LC HG3066 .A44 **ISSN** 1105-0519
DD 332 GR
MENIAIO STATISTIKO DELTIO - TRAPEZA TES HELLADOS. (MENIAION STATISTIKON DELTION.). [Men. Stat. Delt. - Trapeza Ell.]. **Added/Corp** Trapeza Tes Hellados. Dieuthynsis Oikonomikon Meleton. **VFOAT** Meniaio Statistiko Deltio; Monthly Statistical Bulletin. (1956)-. Bulletin. Greek, Modern (English). Twelve times a year. $55.00. Bank of Greece/ Economic Research, 21 Panepistimiou Street, Athens Greece. **Tel** 3202392, 3202391, FAX 3232239. **Circ:** 3,000 (ctrl). ***Continues*** *Meniaion Deltion (Trapeza tes Hellados : 1934).*
Desc: Statistical data on money and banking, public finance, balance of payments, production and prices.

US
MERCHANDISING ... STATISTICAL AND MARKETING REPORT. **VFOAT** Merchandising Statistical Issue and Marketing Report. 56th (1978)-. Statistical Publication. English. One time a year. ***Continues*** *Statistical Issues and Marketing Report. Forecast.*

ISSN 0959-7441
UK
MERGERS & ACQUISITIONS ABSTRACTS. **Added/Corp** Anbar Abstracts (Firm). **VFOAT** Mergers and Acquisitions Abstracts; Mergers & Acquisitions; Mergers and Acquisitions; MAA. (1990)-. English. Three times a year. MCB University Press, 60 62 Toller Lane, Bradford, West Yorkshire BD8 9BY United Kingdom. **Tel** 011 44 1274 785280, FAX 011 44 1274 785200, telex 51317-MCBUNI-G.

LC HV86 .M536
DD 361/.9774 S 362.8/5 US
MIGRANT SERVICES STATISTICAL REPORT. **Main/Corp** Michigan. Dept. of Social Services. Statistical Publication. English. Department of Social Services / South Carolina, Columbia SC 29201. **Tel** (803)758-5749. ***Continues*** *Migrant Services Report, 0360-9359.*

LC HC57 .U66 **ISSN** 0041-7432
DD 330.9/0021 US
MONTHLY BULLETIN OF STATISTICS - UNITED NATIONS. (MONTHLY BULLETIN OF STATISTICS.). [Mon. bull. stat. - U. N.]. **Added/Corp**

United Nations. Statistical Office. **VFOAT** Bulletin Mensuel de Statistique. Vol. 1, No. 1 (Jan. 1947)-. Bulletin. English (French). Twelve times a year. $450.00. United Nations Publications, 2 United Nations Plaza, Room DC2 0853, Department 007C, New York NY 10017. **Tel** (212)963-8303, (800)253-9646. **(Subscription address:** United Nations Publications, Subscription Office, PO Box 361, Birmingham AL 35201-0361. **Tel** (800)633-4931, (205)995-1567 (outside US and Canada), FAX (205)995-1588.**)** available on microfilm and microfiche from University Microfilms International (UMI). ***Continues*** *Monthly Bulletin of Statistics (United Nations. Statistical Office : 1946).*
Desc: Provides statistics from over 200 countries and territories on more than 70 subjects such as population, food, trade, production, finance and national income.

LC HC251 .A32 **ISSN** 0017-3622
DD 330.942 UK

MONTHLY DIGEST OF STATISTICS.
Main/Corp Great Britain. Central Statistical Office. No. 1 (Jan. 1946)-. Periodical. English. Twelve times a year. £85.00. Her Majesty's Stationery Office, 51 Nine Elms Lane, London SW8 5DR United Kingdom. **Tel** 011 44 171 8738459, 011 44 171 8738499, FAX 011 44 171 8738499, 011 44 171 8738456, telex 297138. **(Subscription address:** Her Majesty's Stationery Office, PO Box 276, Public Centre, London SW8 5DT United Kingdom. **Tel** 011 44 171 8738499, 011 44 171 8738456.**)**

LC HF3790.5 .A32 **ISSN** 0552-8267
DD 380.1095 PK

MONTHLY FOREIGN TRADE STATISTICS OF PAKISTAN.
Main/Corp Pakistan. Central Statistical Office. **Added/Corp** Pakistan. Central Statistical Office. (1965)-. Periodical. English. Twelve times a year. $600.00. Readers Associates, PO Box 7485, Victoria Chambers 1, Karachi 3 Pakistan. **Tel** 011 92 21 514068, telex 23108 MNJ PK. **Circ:** 1,000 (ctrl).
Desc: Deals with import and export statistical data of Pakistan.

LC HG450
DD 332.6 HK

MONTHLY MARKET STATISTICS.
Chinese. Twelve times a year. HK$120.00 Hong Kong; HK$204.00 Asia; HK$216.00 other. Stock Exchange Hong Kong Ltd., Exchange Square, Box 8888, Hong Kong Hong Kong. **Tel** 011 852 25221122, FAX 011 852 28453554.

LC HF91 .O672a
DD 382/.0212 FR

MONTHLY STATISTICS OF FOREIGN TRADE / OECD DEPARTMENT OF ECONOMICS AND STATISTICS.
Added/Corp Organisation for Economic Co-Operation and Development. Dept. of Economics and Statistics. **VFOAT** Statistiques Mensuelles du Commerce Exterieur. (Jan. 1983)-. Periodical. English (French). Twelve times a year. $190.00. OECD Publications and Information Center, 2 rue Andre-Pascal, 75775 Paris Cedex 16 France. **Tel** 011 33 1 49104262, US:(202)785-6323, FAX 011 33 1 45248500, 011 33 1 45248176, telex 620 160 OCDE. **(Subscription address:** OECD Publications Center, 2001 L Street, Suite 700, Washington DC 20036. **Tel** (202)822-3873, (202)785-6323.**)** available on microfiche. ***Continues*** *Statistics of Foreign Trade. Monthly Bulletin. Series A, 0377-1547.*
Desc: Presents an overall picture of trade of OECD countries including analysis by flows with countries and country groupings of origin and destination, seasonally adjusted foreign trade indicators and summary tables showing trade by commodity categories.

LC HC601 .A32
DD 330.994/005 AT

MONTHLY SUMMARY OF STATISTICS, AUSTRALIA.
Main/Corp Australian Bureau of Statistics. (July 1979)-. English. Twelve times a year. 217.05Aus$. Australian Bureau of Statistics, PO Box 2796Y, Melbourne 3001 Australia. **Tel** 011 61 3 6157843. ***Continues*** *Monthly Review of Business Statistics, 0311-9025.*
Desc: Data on a range of items classified in varying degree of details for population and vital statistics, employment and unemployment, internal and overseas trade, etc.

LC HF266.U4 A33
DD 382/.09676/1 UG

MONTHLY TRADE BULLETIN - MINISTRY OF FINANCE, PLANNING AND ECONOMIC DEVELOPMENT, STATISTICS DIVISION.
Main/Corp Uganda. Ministry of Finance, Planning and Economic Development. Statistics Division. (19??)-. Bulletin. English. Twelve times a year. Ministry of Finance, Planning and Economics Development/ Statistics Division, PO Box 13, Entebbe Uganda. ***Continues*** *Uganda. Ministry of Planning and Economic Development. Statistics Division. Monthly Trade Bulletin.*

LC HA1448.L3 N37
DD 314.7 LV

NARODNOE KHOZIAISTVO LATVIISKOI SSR.
Added/Corp Latvian S. S. R. Centrala Statistikas Parvalde. (19??)-. Russian. One time a year. 1.47rub. Liesma / Flame Publishing House, Aspazijas Bulv 24, Riga Latvia 1455. **Tel** 3712 223 063.

LC HF5001
DD 650 RU

NARODNOE KHOZIAISTVO SOTSIALISTICHESKIKH STRAN V ... GODU : SOOBSHCHENIIA TSSU.
Added/Corp Institut Ekonomiki Mirovoi Sotsialisticheskoi Sistemy (Akademiia Nauk SSSR). Sektor Statistiki. Institut Ekonomiki Mirovoi Sotsialisticheskoi Sistemy (Akademiia Nauk SSSR). (1961)-. Russian. One time a year. Izdatelstvo Ekonomika, Berezhkovskaia Nab. 6, 121864 Moscow Russia.

LC HC79.I5 N388
DD 339.3/021 US

NATIONAL ACCOUNTS STATISTICS. MAIN AGGREGATES AND DETAILED TABLES.
Added/Corp United Nations. Statistical Office. **VFOAT** Main Aggregates and Detailed Tables. (1982)-. Government Publication. English. Irregular. United Nations Publications, 2 United Nations Plaza, Room DC2 0853, Department 007C, New York NY 10017. **Tel** (212)963-8303, (800)253-9646. ***Continues in part*** *United Nations. Yearbook of National Accounts Statistics, 0084-3881.*

ISSN 0448-1933
JM

NATIONAL INCOME AND PRODUCT.
Main/Corp Jamaica. Dept. of Statistics. (1959)-. English. One time a year. $15.00 (preliminary), $40.00 (provisional). Statistical Institute of Jamaica, 9 Swallowfield Road, PO Box 643, Kingston 5 Jamaica. **Tel** 011 809 92621756, FAX 011 809 9264859.

ISSN 1184-6313
DD 001.4/071/071 CN

NATIONAL INVENTORY OF ACADEMIC & TRAINING COURSES IN PROGRAM & PROJECT EVALUATION.
[Natl. inventory acad. train. courses program proj. eval.]. **Added/Corp** Canadian Evaluation Society. **VFOAT** Inventaire des Cours Universitaires et des Cours de Formation en Evaluation. (Dec. 1990)-. English (French). $10.00. Canadian Evaluation Society, 309 James Street, Ottawa Ontario K1R 5M8 Canada. **Tel** (613)230-1007, FAX (613)237-9900.

ISSN 0282-3489
SW

NATIONALRAKENSKAPER = NATIONAL ACCOUNTS.
Added/Corp Sweden. Statistiska Centralbyran. **VFOAT** National Accounts; Nationalrakenskaper Arsrapport. (19??)-. Swedish (summaries and/or abstracts in English). Irregular. Kr500.00. Statistiska Centralbyran Publishing Unit, S-701 89, Orebo Sweden.

LC HA218 .N53 **ISSN** 0548-4448
DD 330.974 US

NEW ENGLAND ECONOMIC INDICATORS.
[New Engl. econ. indic.]. **Added/Corp** Federal Reserve Bank of Boston. **VFOAT** Economic Indicators. (Sept. 1969)-. Periodical. English. Four times a year. Free on Request. Federal Reserve Bank of Boston, 600 Atlantic Avenue, Research Library D, Boston MA 02106. **Tel** (617)973-3397, (617)973-3403. **ED** Tom Miles. Index available. available on an online database; available on microfilm and microfiche from University Microfilms International (UMI).
Desc: Economic indicators for New England and the United States.
Ind/Abst Fed. Print Econ. Bank. Top.

LC HD5725.N4 N45d **ISSN** 0149-9211
DD 331.1/33 US

NEW HAMPSHIRE AFFIRMATIVE ACTION DATA.
Main/Corp New Hampshire. Dept. of Employment Security. (19??)-. English. New Hampshire Department of Unemployment Security, 32 South Main Street, Concord NH 03301. **Tel** (603)224-3311. **ED** Wesley S. Noyes Jr. **Circ:** 1,000.
Desc: An average data on population, labor force, applicants and employment by occupation and industry by sex and minority status.

LC HC107.N5 N423 **ISSN** 1064-5942
DD 330.9749/005 US

NEW JERSEY ECONOMIC INDICATORS (1976).
(NEW JERSEY ECONOMIC INDICATORS.). [N.J. econ. indic.]. **Added/Corp** New Jersey. Dept. of Labor. Division of Planning and Research. New Jersey. Division of Labor Market and Demographic Research. New Jersey. Dept. of Labor and Industry. No. 150 (Feb. 1976)-. Periodical. English. Eleven times a year (Jan./Feb. issues combined). Free on request. New Jersey Department of Labor & Industry, Labor Market & Demographic, CN 388, Trenton NJ 08625. **Tel** (609)984-2595. **ED** Mary Ann Unger. **Circ:** 2,000. ***Continues*** *New Jersey. Dept. of Labor and Industry. Bulletin & Economic Indicators, 0098-227X.*
Desc: Set of current statistics on various time series related to New Jersey's economy.

LC HF3161.N6 N65 **ISSN** 0889-5937
DD 330.9789/005 US

NEW MEXICO BUSINESS CURRENT ECONOMIC REPORT.
[N.M. bus. curr. econ. rep.]. **Added/Corp** University of New Mexico. Bureau of Business & Economic Research. **VFOAT** New Mexico Business. Vol. 1, No. 7-12 (July-Dec. 1980)-. Periodical. English. Eleven times a year (Jan./Feb. combined). $22.00. University of New Mexico / Bureau of Business and Economic Research, 1920 Lomas, Albuquerque NM 87131. **Tel** (505)277-2216, 277-2217, FAX (505)277-7066. **ED** Kevin Kargacin. **Circ:** 550 (ctrl). available on microfilm from University Microfilms International (UMI). ***Continues*** *New Mexico Business, 0028-6168.*
Desc: Contains a variety of statistical tables, which present economic trends and current economic conditions in the state of New Mexico in selected cities and counties.
Ind/Abst Stat. Ref. Index.

LC HA531 .N48 **ISSN** 0077-8575
DD 317.89 US
SUSPENDED

NEW MEXICO STATISTICAL ABSTRACT.
Added/Corp University of New Mexico. Bureau of Business & Economic Research. University of New Mexico. Bureau of Business Research. (1970)-Suspended. Statistical Publication. English. Irregular. $22.50. University of New Mexico Bureau of Business Research / Lomas Avenue, 1920 Lomas Avenue, Albuquerque NM 87131. **Tel** (505)277-2216. **ED** Kevin Kargacin. **Circ:** 450 (ctrl).
Desc: Contains historical information on economic sectors, education, population, taxation, vital statistics, etc., concerning the state of New Mexico, its cities and counties.

US

NEW YORK STATE BUSINESS STATISTICS. QUARTERLY SUMMARY.
Added/Corp New York (State). Bureau of Business Research. (Jan.-Mar. 1989)-. Periodical. English. Four times a year. New York Department of Commerce, 99 Washington Avenue, Albany NY 12245. **Tel** (518)474-6950, (518)474-5027. ***Continues*** *Business Statistics, New York State. Quarterly Summary.*

DD 016.33 US

NEWS. AVERAGE ANNUAL PAY BY STATE AND INDUSTRY.
Added/Corp United States. Bureau of Labor Statistics. **VFOAT** Average Annual Pay by State and Industry. (19??)-. Government Publication. English. One time a year. Free on request. US Department of Labor / Bureau of Labor Statistics, 441 G Street Northwest, Washington DC 20212. **Tel** (202)606-7800, FAX (202)606-7797.

US

NEWS - BUREAU OF LABOR STATISTICS.
Main/Corp United States. Bureau of Labor Statistics. (19??)-. English. Irregular. Free. US Department of Labor Labor Statistics, Postal Square Building, 2 Massachusetts Avenue Northeast, Washington DC 20212. **Tel** (202)606-6392.

LC HD4928 .N49
DD 331.216 US

NEWS. EMPLOYMENT COST INDEX.
Added/Corp United States. Bureau of Labor Statistics. **VFOAT** Employment Cost Index. (19??)-. English. Four times a year. $20.00. Superintendent of Documents, US Government Printing Office, Washington DC 20402. **Tel** (202)275-3328, FAX (202)786-2377.

ISSN 0111-0608
DD 380.016 NZ

NEWZINDEX.
[Newzindex]. (1979)-. Abstracting/Indexing Service. English. Twelve times a year. $423.42. Information Opportunities Ltd., PO Box 26 254, Auckland New Zealand. **Tel** 011 64 9 5252181, FAX 011 64 9 5250876.
Desc: Index to New Zealand's business press. Covers more than 60 of New Zealand's weekly & daily newspapers, trade journals and business magazines.

FR

NORTH/SOUTH ISSUES : BIBLIOGRAPHY OF THEORETICAL AND CURRENT EVENT ANALYSIS.
Bibliography. French (Spanish and English). Four times a year. 1300F Belgium; 240.00F France; $45.00 other. Centre Tricontinental, Avenue Saint Gertrude 5, B-1348 Louvain La Neuve Belgium. **Tel** 011 32 10 450822. Index available. **Ad Acc.** ***Continues*** *Tricontinental Bibliographical Review.*
Desc: A bibliography of theoretical and current event analysis selected on third world subjects including: economic, social, political, religious and cultural problems.

IT
CEASED

NOTIZIARIO ISTAT. SERIE 1 : ATTIVITA PRODUTTIVA. FOGLLIO 14 : STATISTICA DEL COMMERCIO CON L'ESTERO. **Main/Corp** Istituto Centrale di Statistica (Italy). (19??)-(Dec. 1993). Italian. Istituto Nazionale Statistica, GBP SEZ4 Via Cesare Balbo 16, 00184 Rome Italy. **Tel** 011 39 6 46735118.

IT
CEASED

NOTIZIARIO ISTAT. SERIE 2: STATISTICHE DELL ATTIVITA PRODUTTIVA. (19??)-(Dec. 1993). Italian. Istituto Nazionale Statistica, GBP SEZ4 Via Cesare Balbo 16, 00184 Rome Italy. **Tel** 011 39 6 46735118.

LC HG1501 **ISSN** 0080-178X
DD 332.1 AT

OCCASIONAL PAPER - RESERVE BANK OF AUSTRALIA. **Main/Corp** Reserve Bank of Australia. No. 1 (1968)-. Monographic series. English. Irregular. Price varies per volume. Reserve Bank of Australia / Secretary Department, GPO Box 3947, Sydney New South Wales 2001 Australia. **Tel** 11 61 2 5519724, 011 61 2 5518841, FAX 011 61 2 234900, telex 20106. **ED** P. J. Kennedy. ctrl circ.
Desc: Issues include economic performance statistics and other Australian finance and monetary matters.

LC HB549.O6 O64a
DD 332/.8/021/2 FR

OECD FINANCIAL STATISTICS. MONTHLY SUPPLEMENT: INTEREST RATES. STATISTIQUES FINANCIERES DE L'OCDE. SUPPLEMENT MENSUEL: TAUX D'INTERET. **Main/Corp** Organization for Economic Co-Operation and Development. **Added/Corp** Organisation for Economic Co-Operation and Development. Statistiques Financieres de l'OCDE. Supplement Mensuel: Taux d'Interet. Organisation for Economic Co-Operation and Development. Financial Statistics. Monthly Supplement: Interest Rates. **VFOAT** Statistiques Financieres de l'OCDE. Supplement Mensuel : Taux d'Interet. **VAT** Organization for Economic Cooperation and Development Financial Statistics. Monthly Supplement: Interest Rates. (19??)-. Periodical. English (French). Twelve times a year. OECD Publications and Information Center, 2 rue Andre-Pascal, 75775 Paris Cedex 16 France. **Tel** 011 33 1 49104262, US:(202)785-6323, FAX 011 33 1 45248500, 011 33 1 45248176, telex 620 160 OCDE.

LC HG186.S6 O37
DD 336.416/021 FR

OECD FINANCIAL STATISTICS. PART 2, FINANCIAL ACCOUNTS OF OECD COUNTRIES. SPAIN = STATISTIQUES FINANCIERES DE L'OCDE. 2. PARTIE, COMPTES FINANCIERS DES PAYS DE L'OCDE. ESPAGNE. **Added/Corp** Organisation for Economic Co-Operation and Development. **VFOAT** Spain; Financial Accounts of OECD Countries. Spain; Comptes Financiers des Pays de l'OCDE. Espagne; Statistiques Financieres de l'OCDE. 2. Partie, Espagne. **VAT** Organisation for Economic Co-Operation and Development Financial Statistics. Part 2, Financial Accounts of Organisation for Economic Co-Operation and Development Countries. Spain; Financial Accounts of Organisation for Economic Co-Operation and Development Countries. Spain. (1988)-. Statistical Publication. English (French). Two times a year. OECD Publications and Information Center, 2 rue Andre-Pascal, 75775 Paris Cedex 16 France. **Tel** 011 33 1 49104262, US:(202)785-6323, FAX 011 33 1 45248500, 011 33 1 45248176, telex 620 160 OCDE. **(Subscription address:** OECD Publications Center, 2001 L Street, Suite 700, Washington DC 20036. **Tel** (202)822-3873, (202)785-6323.**)** ***Continues in part*** *OECD Financial Statistics Part 2, Financial Accounts of OECD Countries, 0255-6979.*

LC HG4001 .O35
DD 338.7/4/05 FR

OECD FINANCIAL STATISTICS. PART 3, NON-FINANCIAL ENTERPRISES FINANCIAL STATEMENTS. **Added/Corp** Organisation for Economic Co-Operation and Development. **VFOAT** Non-Financial Enterprises Financial Statements; Comptes des Entreprises Non Financieres; O.E.C.D. Financial Statistics. Part 3, Non-Financial Enterprises Financial Statements; Statistiques Financieres de l'O.C.D.E. 3E Partie, Comptes des Entreprises Non Financieres; Statistiques Financieres de l'OCDE. 3E Parite, Comptes. (1981)-. English (French). One time a year. Comes with membership. OECD Publications and Information Center, 2 rue Andre-Pascal, 75775 Paris Cedex 16 France. **Tel** 011 33 1 49104262, US:(202)785-6323, FAX 011 33 1 45248500, 011 33 1 45248176, telex 620 160 OCDE. **(Subscription address:** OECD Publications Center, 2001 L Street, Suite 700, Washington DC 20036. **Tel** (202)822-3873, (202)785-6323.**)** ***Continues in part*** *OECD Financial Statistics.*
Desc: Gives balance-sheets, statements of income and sources and uses of funds for a representative sample of companies in 12 countries.

LC HD5725.O35 O54 **ISSN** 0147-8052
DD 331.12/51/09766 US

OKLAHOMA OCCUPATIONAL EMPLOYMENT STATISTICS. (OKLAHOMA OCCUPATIONAL EMPLOYMENT STATISTICS; BULLETIN.). **Added/Corp** Oklahoma Employment Security Commission. **VFOAT** OOES. Oklahoma Occupational Employment Statistics. (Sept. 1975)-. Bulletin. English. Oklahoma Employment Security Commission, Will Rogers Building, Room 310, Oklahoma City OK 73105. **Tel** (405)521-3735.

LC HA1631 .A33 HF5549.5.T7 T7
DD 317.971 YU

OSTRUCAVANJE RADNIKA U RADNIM ORGANIZACIJAMA. **Main/Corp** Savezni Zavod Za Statistiku (Yugoslavia). Serbo-Croatian (Roman). 4.00 Din. Savezni Zavod za Statistiku, Kneza Milosa 20, Belgrad Yugoslavia.

LC HF3501 .O94
DD 380.10941 UK

●**OVERSEAS TRADE STATISTICS OF THE UNITED KINGDOM WITH COUNTRIES OUTSIDE THE EUROPEAN COMMUNITY (EXTRA-EC TRADE).** **Added/Corp** Great Britain. Central Statistical Office. (Jan. 1993)-. English. Twelve times a year. Her Majesty's Stationery Office, 51 Nine Elms Lane, London SW8 5DR United Kingdom. **Tel** 011 44 171 8738459, 011 44 171 8738499, FAX 011 44 171 8738499, 011 44 171 8738456, telex 297138. **(Subscription address:** Her Majesty's Stationery Office, PO Box 276, Public Centre, London SW8 5DT United Kingdom. **Tel** 011 44 171 8738499, 011 44 171 8738456.**)** ***Continues*** *Overseas Trade Statistics of the United Kingdom, 0436-3574.*

LC HC10 .O78 **ISSN** 0305-9049
DD 330.9/005 UK
CCC
Pr Rev.

OXFORD BULLETIN OF ECONOMICS AND STATISTICS. [Oxf. bull. econ. stat.]. Vol. 35, No. 1 (Feb. 1973)-. Bulletin. English. Four times a year. $167.00. Basil Blackwell Publishers Ltd., 108 Cowley Road, Oxford OX4 1JF United Kingdom. **Tel** 011 44 1235 465500, FAX 011 44 1235 465556, telex 837022 OXBOOK G. **(Subscription address:** Blackwell Publishers / UK, 108 Cowley Road, Oxford OX4 1JF United Kingdom. **Tel** 011 44 1865 791100, FAX 011 44 1865 791347.**)** **ED** David F Hendry. **Bk Rev. Ad Acc. Circ:** 1,300 (ctrl). available on microfilm and microfiche from University Microfilms International (UMI); available on an online database (file 648/Full-Text) from DIALOG. Documents available from The Genuine Article, UMI Article Clearinghouse. ***Continues*** *Bulletin of the Oxford University Institute of Economics and Statistics.*
Desc: This is largely devoted to applied economics, but articles on statistical and econometric methodology are also included. It features a regular practitioner's corner.
Ind/Abst ABI/INFORM Glob. Ed.; ABI/INFORM [Computer File] (Feb. 1981-); Bus. ASAP (1992-) [Full Txt.]; Bus. Index (1985-); Coal Abstr.; CompuMath Cit. Index [Full Cov.]; Contents Recent Econ. J.; Contents Pages Manage.; Curr. Cit.; Curr. Contents Soc. Behav. Sci.; Econ. Lit. Index; Gen. BusinessFile (1985-); Int. Labour Doc.; J. Econ. Lit.; LABORDOC; Middle East Abstr. Index; Res. Alert [Full Cov.]; Rural Dev. Abstr.; Soc. Sci. Cit. Index [Full Cov.]; World Agric. Econ. Rural Sociol. Abstr.

LC HG2889.G8 S55a
DD 332.1/0981/5 BL

PANORAMA ESTATISTICO DO SETOR BANCARIO. **Main/Corp** Sindicato dos Bancos do Estado da Guanabara. No. 1 (Dec. 1971)-. Periodical. Portuguese. Four times a year. Sindicato dos Bancos do Estado da Guanabara, Av Rio Branco 81, Rio de Janeiro Brazil.

LC HD7127 .P46 **ISSN** 0835-8583
DD 331.25/2/097105 CN

PENSION PLAN COVERAGE IN CANADA. [Pension plan cover. Can.]. **Added/Corp** Statistics Canada. Labour and Household Surveys Analysis Division. **VFOAT** Participants aux Regimes de Retraite au Canada. (1986)-. English (French). One time a year. 12.00Can$ Canada; $14.00 US; $17.00 other. Statistics Canada Publications Sales and Services, R.H. Coats Building 6th Floor, Ottawa Ontario K1A 0T6 Canada. **Tel** (613)951-5078, (800)267-6677, FAX (613)951-1584, telex 053-3585.

CN

PENSION PLANS IN CANADA : STATISTICAL HIGHLIGHTS AND KEY TABLES. (19??)-. Statistical Publication. English (French). Irregular. 39.00Can$ Canada; $47.00 US; $55.00 other. Statistics Canada Publications Sales and Services, R.H. Coats Building 6th Floor, Ottawa Ontario K1A 0T6 Canada. **Tel** (613)951-5078, (800)267-6677, FAX (613)951-1584, telex 053-3585. **Circ:** 500. ***Continues*** *Pension Plans in Canada.*
Desc: Provides information on the terms and conditions of employee pension plans. Labor force coverage figures are also provided.

LC HG450 **ISSN** 0275-0333
DD 332.6 US

PENSIONS & INVESTMENT AGE. EDITORIAL INDEX. [Pensions investm. age, Ed. index]. **Added/Corp** Crain Communications Inc. Bell & Howell Co. Indexing Center. **VFOAT** Editorial Index. **VAT** Pensions and Investment Age. Editorial Index. 1st Quarter (1981)-. Periodical. English. Four times a year (3 issues & cumlative index). $100.00. Crain Communications Inc., 1400 Woodbridge, Detroit MI 48207-3187. **Tel** (313)446-6000, (800)992-9970. Index available. cum. index. **Ad Acc.** available on microfiche.

LC HF5549 .P452 **ISSN** 0031-577X
DD 658.3082 US

PERSONNEL MANAGEMENT ABSTRACTS. [Person. manage. abstr.]. **Added/Corp** University of Michigan. Graduate School of Business Administration. **VFOAT** Personnel & Management Abstracts. Vol. 1, No. 1 (Jan./Feb. 1955)-. Abstracting/Indexing Service. English. Four times a year (fourth issue is annual cumulative index). $120.00. Personnel Management Abstracts, 704 Island Lake Road, Chelsea MI 48118. **Tel** (313)475-1979. **ED** Gloria Reo. Index available. cum. index. **Bk Rev. Ad Acc. Circ:** 1,100 (ctrl). available on microfilm and microfiche from University Microfilms International (UMI).
Desc: A quick reference tool for managers and human resources staff. Journals are annotated and indexed by author and subject matter. Seventy-two subject areas range from absenteeism to turnover.

LC HF5549.A2 A545 **ISSN** 0305-067X
DD 016.6583 UK

PERSONNEL + TRAINING ABSTRACTS. **Added/Corp** Anbar Management Services. Anbar Management Publications. Anbar Abstracts (Firm) Institute of Personnel Management. **VFOAT** Personnel & Training Abstracts; Personnel and Training Abstracts; Personnel & Training; Personnel and Training; Anbar Personnel and Training Abstracts; Anbar Personnel & Training Abstracts; PTA. Vol. 1 (Oct. 1971)-. Abstracting/Indexing Service. English. Twelve times a year. $2999.00. MCB University Press, 60 62 Toller Lane, Bradford, West Yorkshire BD8 9BY United Kingdom. **Tel** 011 44 1274 785280, FAX 011 44 1274 785200, telex 51317-MCBUNI-G. **(Subscription address:** MCB University Press / US and Canada Subscriptions, PO Box 10812, Birmingham AL 35201-0812. **Tel** (205)995-1567, (800)633-4931, FAX (205)995-1588.**)** **ED** Andrew Ede. cum. index. available on CD-ROM; available on diskette. ***Continues in part*** *Anbar Management Services Abstracts.*
Desc: Contains abstracts of articles appearing in international management journals. Covers such topics as: health and safety; management development; industrial relations; the role of women in employment; internal communications; training techniques; pay; appraisal; working hours; and manpower planning.

LC HD5850 .A34d
DD 331.1/37994 AT

PERSONS NOT IN THE LABOUR FORCE. **Main/Corp** Australian Bureau of Statistics. (19??)-. English. One time a year. 12.70Aus$. Australian Bureau of Statistics, PO Box 2796Y, Melbourne 3001 Australia. **Tel** 011 61 3 6157843.
Desc: Covers persons who were not in the labour force, whether they intended to look for work, whether they would prefer full-time or part-time work, time since they left their last job, persons who wanted a job, etc.

LC HD5727 .P47 **ISSN** 0840-8750
DD 331.12/5/097105 CN
CODEN PLAIEY

PERSPECTIVES ON LABOUR AND INCOME. [Perspect. labour income]. **Added/Corp** Statistics Canada. **VFOAT** Perspectives. (Summer 1989)-. Periodical. English (French). Four times a year. 68.00Can$. Statistics Canada Publications Sales and Services, R.H. Coats Building 6th Floor, Ottawa Ontario K1A 0T6 Canada. **Tel** (613)951-5078, (800)267-6677, FAX (613)951-1584, telex 053-3585.
Ind/Abst PAIS Int. Print.

LC HA1821 .N37a
DD 315.99 PH

PHILIPPINE STATISTICAL YEARBOOK. **See** Business and Economics.

US

PLANT AND EQUIPMENT EXPENDITURES: UNPUBLISHED DATA. (1947)-. Government Publication. English. Four times a year. $50.00 (detailed data set). US Department of Commerce / Bureau of the Census, Data User Services Division, Customer Services, Washington DC 20233-0800. **Tel** (301)763-4100. **(Subscription address:** Superintendent of Documents, US Government Printing Office, Washington DC 20402. **)** available on diskette; available in print; available on magnetic tape.

Desc: Provides statistics on expenditures for new plant and equipment in current dollars for private-nonfarm (SIC) groups 10 through 80 on an industry-enterprise basis.

LC HA891 .P6
DD 317.292 JM
POCKETBOOK OF STATISTICS: JAMAICA. **Added/Corp** Jamaica. Dept. of Statistics. Statistical Institute of Jamaica. **VFOAT** Pocketbook of Statistics. (19??)-. English. One time a year. $20.50. Statistical Institute of Jamaica, 9 Swallowfield Road, PO Box 643, Kingston 5 Jamaica. **Tel** 011 809 92621756, FAX 011 809 9264859. **Circ:** 1,500 (ctrl).
Desc: The publication deals with population, migration, health, education, housing, labor and employment transport and communication, external trade consumer price indexes among other economic topics.

LC HA1228.A9 A32
DD 314.4 FR
POINT ECONOMIQUE DE L'AUVERGNE, LE. **Main/Corp** Institut National de la Statistique et des Etudes Economiques (France). (May 1971)-. Periodical. French. Six times a year. 96.00F US. CNGP INSEE - Institut National de la Statistique et des Etudes Economiques, BP 2718, 1 rue V Auriol, F 80027 Amiens Cedex 1 France. **Tel** 011 33 22 927322. ***Continues*** *Bulletin de Statistique: Auvergne (Allier, Cantal, Haute-Loire, Puy-de-Dome).*
Desc: Publishes socio-economic information on the Clermontferrand region of France in an accessible format with concise analysis of statistics.

ISSN 0270-4528
US
CCC
TITLE CHANGE
PREDICASTS F & S INDEX INTERNATIONAL. **Added/Corp** Predicasts, Inc. **VFOAT** F&S Index International. (198?)-(19??). Abstracting/Indexing Service. English. Predicasts Inc., A Ziff Communications Company, 11001 Cedar Avenue, Cleveland OH 44106. **Tel** (800)321-6388, (216)795-3000, FAX (216)229-9944, telex 985 604. ***Continues in part*** *F & S Index International, 0014-5661.* ***Continued by*** *F&S Index International (Foster City, Calif.).*
Desc: Provides comprehensive reference indexes of business and economic information. Covers worldwide company, product, and industry information. One- and two-line article summaries offer access to information on international companies, business and financial activities, demographics, government regulations, and economic trends.

LC HC101 .P7 **ISSN** 0278-0135
DD 338.5/443/0973 US
CCC
PREDICASTS FORECASTS. [Predicasts forecasts]. **Added/Corp** Predicasts, Inc. Vol. 1 (July 24, 1980)-. Abstracting/Indexing Service. English. Five times a year. $1050.00. Predicasts Inc., A Ziff Communications Company, 11001 Cedar Avenue, Cleveland OH 44106. **Tel** (800)321-6388, (216)795-3000, FAX (216)229-9944, telex 985 604. **(Subscription address:** Information Access Company, PO Box 61000, Department 1851, San Francisco CA 94161. **Tel** (800)321-6388.) cum. index. ***Continues*** *Predicasts, 0032-7166.*
Desc: Nearly 50,000 short- and long-range projections for products, markets, industries and the United States economy are abstracted each year from more than 500 worldwide business, trade and economic sources.

LC HA1320.B2 A32 HD7029
DD 314.3 GW
PREISE, LOEHNE, WIRTSCHAFTSRECHNUNGEN. **Added/Corp** Statistisches Landesamt Baden-Wuerttemberg. (19??)-. German. One time a year. DM9.00. Statistisches Landesami, Baden-Wuerttemberg, Postfach 10 60 33, W-7000 Stuttgart 10 Germany. **Tel** 011 49 711 64651, FAX 011 49 711 6465440, telex 722 815 STALA D. **ED** Max Wingen. **Circ:** 450. ***Continues*** *Statistisches Landesamt Baden-Wuerttemberg. Preise und Loehne.*

LC HF6146.P7 D57
DD 658.8/2 US
PREMIUM, INCENTIVE, & TRAVEL BUYERS. **Added/Corp** Salesman's Guide, Inc. **VFOAT** Premium, Incentive, and Travel Buyers; Nationwide Directory, Premium, Incentive, and Travel Buyers; Nationwide Directory, Premium, Incentive, & Travel Buyers. (1986)-. Trade Publication. English. One time a year (Feb.). $217.00 (includes a mid-year supplemental update). Salesman's Guide, A Reed Reference Publishing Company, Part of Reed International PLC, 121 Chanlon Road, New Providence NJ 07974. **Tel** (800)223-1797, (908)464-6800, FAX (908)665-3560, telex 138755. Index available (free on request). available on magnetic tape. ***Continues*** *Directory of Premium, Incentive, and Travel Buyers, 0196-8262.*
Desc: Profiles 22,000 buyers of premiums, incentives and travel programs in over 11,000 companies, providing hard-to-find information on premium usage and expenditures.

LC HA1 .A663 **ISSN** 0066-0736
DD 310.6273 US
PROCEEDINGS OF THE BUSINESS AND ECONOMIC STATISTICS SECTION. (PROCEEDINGS OF THE BUSINESS AND ECONOMIC STATISTICS SECTION / AMERICAN STATISTICAL ASSOCIATION.). [Proc. Bus. Econ. Stat. Sect.]. **Main/Corp** American Statistical Association. Business and Economic Statistics Section. 114th (1954)-. Proceedings. English. One time a year. $58.50. American Statistical Association, 1429 Duke Street, Alexandria VA 22314. **Tel** (703)684-1221, (202)393-3253, FAX (703)684-2037 (orders). **Circ:** 1,000. available on microfilm and microfiche from University Microfilms International (UMI).
Ind/Abst Curr. Index Stat.

LC HD9650.1 .P16 **ISSN** 0161-8032
DD 338.4/05 US
CCC
PROMT / PREDICASTS OVERVIEW OF MARKETS AND TECHNOLOGY. **Added/Corp** Predicasts, inc. **VFOAT** Predicasts Overview of Markets and Technology. (1977)-. Abstracting/Indexing Service. English. Seventeen times a year. $1100.00. Predicasts Inc., A Ziff Communications Company, 11001 Cedar Avenue, Cleveland OH 44106. **Tel** (800)321-6388, (216)795-3000, FAX (216)229-9944, telex 985 604. **(Subscription address:** Information Access Company, PO Box 61000, Department 1851, San Francisco CA 94161. **Tel** (800)321-6388.) Index available. cum. index. ***Formed by the union of*** *Chemical Market Abstracts, 0009-2606* ***and*** *EMA, Equipment Market Abstracts, 0098-4779.*
Desc: Multi-industry reference work provides more than 4,000 abstracts of industrial activities as reported in the world's major business and trade literature.

LC Z7164.E2 P95 **ISSN** 0032-8138
DD 016.3 PL
PRZEGLAD BIBLIOGRAFICZNY PISMIENNICTWA EKONOMICZNEGO. **Added/Corp** Polskie Wydawnictwa Gospodarcze, Warsaw. Panstwowe Wydawnictwo Ekonomiczne. Vol. 1 (1947)-. Periodical. Polish. Six times a year. **(Subscription address:** Ars Polona-Ruch, PO Box 1001, Krakowskie Przedmiescie 7, 00-068 Warsaw Poland. **Tel** 011 48 22 261201.)

US
PTS NEWSLETTER DATABASE [ONLINE DATABASE]. (19??)-. Newsletter. English. Predicasts Inc., A Ziff Communications Company, 11001 Cedar Avenue, Cleveland OH 44106. **Tel** (800)321-6388, (216)795-3000, FAX (216)229-9944, telex 985 604. **(Subscription address:** Information Access Company, PO Box 61000, Department 1851, San Francisco CA 94161. **Tel** (800)321-6388.)
Desc: Ideal for keeping abreast of industry developments and searching for information on company activities, new products and applied technologies, market and industry trends, national and world business events, government regulatory action and its impact on business, and international trade opportunities.

ISSN 1067-4489
DD 658 US
•**PUBLIC SECTOR QUALITY REPORT.** [Public sect. qual. rep.]. **Added/Corp** Benchmark Communications. (1993)-. Newsletter. English. Twelve times a year. $78.00. Benchmark Communications, 17733 Kingsway Path, Lakeville MN 55044-5209. **Tel** (612)898-5058, FAX (612)892-7710. **ED** Vince Giorgi. **Bk Rev**, (Qty: 6-8). **Ad Acc. Circ:** 600.
Desc: A newsletter for people working on total quality management and other organizational improvement strategies in government. Each issue includes news, case studies, and a calendar of upcoming training opportunities.

LC Z7165.E8 P8 HC241.2
DD 015.4 LU
PUBLICATIONS OF THE EUROPEAN COMMUNITIES. CATALOGUE. English (English, French, German, Italian, Spanish, Portuguese, Dutch, Danish and Greek, Modern). One time a year. Free. Publications Department of the European Communities, PO Box 1003, Luxembourg 2985 Luxembourg.
Desc: Comprises the monographs and series published by the Institutions of the Community during the reference period, as well as the periodicals.

LC Discard
DD 330 US
PUBLISHED SEARCH BIBLIOGRAPHIES FROM THE NTIS BIBLIOGRAPHIC DATA BASE. BUSINESS AND MANAGEMENT. **Added/Corp** United States. National Technical Information Service. **VFOAT** Published Search Bibliographies from the N.T.I.S. Bibliographic Data Base. Business and Management; Business and Management. (19??)-. English. Irregular. Free on request. National Technical Information Service - NTIS, Room 2027S, 5285 Port Royal Road, Springfield VA 22161. **Tel** (703)487-4630, (703)487-4660, (703)487-4650, FAX (703)321-8547, telex 89-9405.

HK
QUARTERLY BUSINESS SURVEY REPORT. **Added/Corp** Hong Kong. Census and Statistics Dept. **VFOAT** Business Survey Report. (19??)-. Periodical. English. Four times a year. $7.62. Hong Kong Government Information Service, Beaconsfield House, 4 Queens Road, Hong Kong Hong Kong. **Tel** 011 852 284288014, 011 852 259881947, FAX 011 852 28459078, 011 852 25987482, telex 61190 HKGIS. **(Subscription address:** Government Information Service, Publications Office, 1 Battery Path, Hong Kong Hong Kong. **) Circ:** 800.
Desc: A survey of views on Hong Kong's business performance during the reference quarter and expectations for the following quarter.

LC HD9016.M3 L44a
DD 338.1/7 MY
QUARTERLY COMMODITY STATISTICS. **Main/Corp** Lembaga Pemasaran Pertanian Persekutuan. (19??)-. Statistical Publication. English. Four times a year. 4th & 5th Floors/Bangkok Bank Building, Kuala Lumpur Malaysia.

LC HA1117.M3 A28
DD 314.58/5 MM
QUARTERLY DIGEST OF STATISTICS. **Main/Corp** Malta. Office of Statistics. No. 1 (Mar. 1960)-. English. Four times a year. £M80.0. Central Office of Statistics / Malta, Auberge d' Italie, Merchants Street, Valletta Malta CMR 02. **Tel** 011 356 224597, FAX 011 356 248483.
Desc: Records changes in the main sector of the economy. Statistical information in respect of previous periods for analysis and comparative purposes.

LC HC910.A1 Q36
DD 330.96894/005 RH
QUARTERLY ECONOMIC AND STATISTICAL REVIEW / RESERVE BANK OF ZIMBABWE. **Added/Corp** Reserve Bank of Zimbabwe. Vol. 1, No. 1 (Sept. 1980)-. Statistical Publication. English. Four times a year (Mar., Jun., Sept., Dec.). Free on request. Reserve Bank of Zimbabwe, Economic Research Department, PO Box 1283, Harare Zimbabwe. **Circ:** 2,500 (ctrl).

LC HG4090 .A357 **ISSN** 1180-3169
DD 338.7/4/0971021 CN
QUARTERLY FINANCIAL STATISTICS FOR ENTERPRISES. (QUARTERLY FINANCIAL STATISTICS FOR ENTERPRISES.). [Q. financ. stat. enterp.]. **Added/Corp** Statistics Canada. Industrial Organization and Finance Division. **VFOAT** Statistiques Financieres Trimestrielles des Enterprises. Vol. 1, No. 4 (4th Quarter 1990)-. Periodical. English (French). Four times a year. 132.00Can$. Statistics Canada Publications Sales and Services, R.H. Coats Building 6th Floor, Ottawa Ontario K1A 0T6 Canada. **Tel** (613)951-5078, (800)267-6677, FAX (613)951-1584, telex 053-3585. ***Formed by the union of*** *Financial Institutions, Financial Statistics, 0380-075X* ***and*** *Industrial Corporations, Financial Statistics, 0380-7525.*

LC HD5701 .Q38 **ISSN** 0255-3627
DD 331.11/021 FR
QUARTERLY LABOUR FORCE STATISTICS. [Q. labour force stat.]. **Added/Corp** Organisation for Economic Co-Operation and Development. Dept. of Economics and Statistics. **VFOAT** Statistiques Trimestrielles de la Population Active. No. 1 (1983)-. English (French). Four times a year. $60.00. OECD Publications and Information Center, 2 rue Andre-Pascal, 75775 Paris Cedex 16 France. **Tel** 011 33 1 49104262, US:(202)785-6323, FAX 011 33 1 45248500, 011 33 1 45248176, telex 620 160 OCDE. **(Subscription address:** OECD Publications Center, 2001 L Street, Suite 700, Washington DC 20036. **Tel** (202)822-3873, (202)785-6323.) ***Continues*** *Organisation for Economic Co-Operation and Development. Labour Force Statistics, Quarterly Supplement to the Yearbook, 0304-3312.*
Desc: Provides statistics on the short-term development of the major components of the labor force in the United States and 12 other OECD countries. Includes total labor force, civilian labor force; unemployment, civilian labor force in industry, agriculture and other activities.
Ind/Abst Predicasts.

ISSN 0347-982X
SW
RAPPORT - SVERIGES LANTBRUKSUNIVERSITET, INSTITUTIONEN FOR EKONOMI OCH STATISTIK. REPORT - DEPARTMENT OF ECONOMICS AND STATISTICS. **Main/Corp** Sveriges Lantbruksuniversitet. Institutionen for Ekonomi Och Statistik. **VFOAT** Report - Department of Economics and Statistics.; Rapport fran Institutionen for Ekonomi och Statistik. (August 1977)-. Monographic series. Swedish (English; summaries and/or abstracts in English). Price varies per volume. Swedish University of

Agricultural Sciences / Ekonomi & Statistik, Sveriges Lantruksuniversitet, Institutionen for Ekonomi och Statistik, S-75007 Uppsala Sweden. **Tel** 011 46 18 671000, telex 003939. ***Continues*** *Rapport Fran Institutionen for Ekonomi Och Statistik.*
Ind/Abst Field Crop Abstr.

LC HD4826 .R37 **ISSN** 0033-961X
DD 331 IT
CEASED
RASSEGNA DI STATISTICHE DEL LAVORO. [Rass. stat. lav.]. Year 1 (Jan./Feb. 1949)-(Dec. 1993). Periodical. Italian. Servizio Italiano Pubblicazioni International, Viale Pasteur 6, 00144 Rome Italy. **Tel** 011 39 6 5920509, telex 614567 SIPIRM I. Index available. cum. index. **Bk Rev**. **Ad Acc**.
Desc: Offers articles by specialists and statistics on Italian labor topics, such as employment and unemployment, salaries, social security, cost of living and international comparisons.

FR
RECUEIL STATISTIQUES. Monographic series. French. Irregular. Price varies per volume. SESSI Ministere de l'Industrie, 85 boulevard du Montparnasse, 75270 Paris Cedex 06 France. **Tel** 011 33 1 43194118, FAX 011 33 1 43194173, telex 202624.

ISSN 0395-9031
FR
REPERES (MONTPELLIER). (REPERES.). [Reperes]. **Added/Corp** Institut National de la Statistique et des Etudes Economiques (France). (April 1972)-. Periodical. French. Four times a year. 65.00F France; 75.00F other. CNGP INSEE - Institut National de la Statistique et des Estudes Economiques, BP 2718, 1 rue V Auriol, F 80027 Amiens Cedex 1 France. **Tel** 011 33 22 927322. ***Continues in part*** *Sud (Marseille, France : 1971), 0150-729X.*
Ind/Abst ARTbibliogr. Mod.

LC Z7164.C81 R397 **ISSN** 0034-5296
DD 016.65 UK
RESEARCH INDEX. **Added/Corp** Business Surveys, Ltd. (Aug. 1965)-. Periodical. English. Twenty-six times a year. $581.81. Business Surveys Ltd, Broadmayne House Farm, Osmington Drove Broadmayne, Dorset DT2 8EP United Kingdom. **Tel** 011 44 1305 853704, FAX 011 44 1305 854162. **ED** Samantha Denman. Index available. cum. index. **Circ:** 370. available on an online database from Orbit Search Service. Documents available from BLDSC.
Desc: An index for business and trade taken from all daily papers and trade magazines.

LC HC188.R4 R49 **ISSN** 0102-0226
DD 318.1/65 BL
RESENHA ESTATISTICA DO RIO GRANDE DO SUL / SECRETARIA DE COORDENACAO E PLANEJAMENTO, FUNDACAO DE ECONOMIA E ESTATISTICA. **Added/Corp** Rio Grande do Sul (Brazil). Fundacao de Economia e Estatistica. (19??)-. Portuguese. Fundacao de Economia e Estatistica, Rua Duque de Caixias 1691, 90010 Porto Alegre, Rio Grande do Sul Brazil. **Tel** 0512-259455, FAX 0512-25006, telex 0515042.

LC HA1 .R35
DD 330 NE
CODEN RECSA9
Pr Rev.
REVIEW OF ECONOMICS AND STATISTICS, THE. [Rev. econ. stat.]. **Added/Corp** Harvard University. Dept. of Economics. Harvard Economic Society. Vol. 30, No. 1 (Feb. 1948)-. Academic Scholarly Publication. English. Four times a year (1 volume). $165.00. Elsevier Science Publishers BV, PO Box 211, 1000 AE Amsterdam Netherlands. **Tel** 011 31 20 4853641, 011 31 20 4853642, FAX 011 31 20 4853598. **ED** Richard E. Caves, Robert A. Moffitt, James H. Stock, C. Peter Timmer. available on microfilm and microfiche from University Microfilms International (UMI); available on an online database from Elsevier Electronic Subscriptions (EES). Documents available from UMI Article Clearinghouse, The Genuine Article. ***Continues*** *Review of Economic Statistics.*
Desc: Its articles and notes exemplify the combination of theoretical, empirical and statistical analysis that characterizes modern economics.
Ind/Abst ABI/INFORM Glob. Ed.; ABI/INFORM [Computer File] (Nov. 1971-); AGRICOLA [Select. Cov.]; Am. Hist. Life (1967-1974); Bus. Index (1985-); Bus. Period. Index; Contents Recent Econ. J.; Contents Pages Manage.; Curr. Cit.; Curr. Contents Soc. Behav. Sci.; Econ. Lit. Index (19??-); Energy Res. Abstr. (1975-); Gen. BusinessFile (1985-); Gen. Period. Index (1985-); Geogr. Abstr. Human Geogr.; Hum. Resour. Abstr. (?-?); INFO-SOUTH Abstr.; Int. Aerosp. Abstr.; Int. Bibliogr. Sociol.; Int. Dev. Abstr.; Int. Labour Doc.; Int. Polit. Sci. Abstr.; J. Econ. Lit.; LABORDOC; Mag. Index Plus (1989-); Mag. Search; MasterFile FullTEXT (Jan. 1993-); Math. Rev.; Middle East Abstr. Index; Newsp. Period. Abstr. (1989-); PAIS Int. Print; Popul. Index; Res. Alert [Full Cov.]; Selec. Coop. Index Manage. Period.; Soc. Sci. Cit. Index [Full Cov.]; Soc. Sci. Index; Stat. Theory Method Abstr. (1959-1963); Mag. Index (1977-); Trade Ind. Index (1981-?); Wilson Bus. Abstr.; Women Stud. Abstr.; Work Relat. Abstr.

LC HA984 .R4 **ISSN** 0034-7175
DD 330.981 BL
NLM W1 RE317
REVISTA BRASILEIRA DE ESTATISTICA. [Rev. bras. estat.]. **Added/Corp** Fundacao Instituto Brasileiro de Geografia e Estatistica. Departamento de Divulgacao Estatistica. Conselho Nacional de Estatistica (Brazil) Sociedade Brasileira de Estatistica. No. 1 (Jan./Mar. 1940)-. Periodical. Portuguese. Four times a year. $120.00. Instituto Brasileiro de Geografia e Estatistica, Rua General Canabarro 666 AN2, 20271 Rio de Janeiro RJ Brazil. **Tel** 011 55 21 2847690, 011 55 21 2342043. ***Supersedes*** *Revista de Economia e Estatistica.*
Ind/Abst Popul. Index.

ISSN 1245-3927
FR
UDC 31(442.1/.5-14)
CODEN 312(442.1/.5-14)
●**REVUE - INSEE BASSE-NORMANDIE, LA.** (LA REVUE.). **VFOAT** Revue - Institut National de la Statistique et des Etudes Economiques Basse-Normandie; Revue de l'INSEE de Basse-Normandie. (1993)-. Periodical. French. Four times a year. $12.03. Observatoire Economique, 93 95 rue de Geole, 14051 Caen Cedex France. **Tel** 011 33 31 853311. ***Continues*** *Medial Caen.*

PL
●**ROCZNIK STATYSTYCZNY HANDLU ZAGRANICZNEGO.** **Added/Corp** Poland. Glowny Urzad Statystyczny. (1993)-. Government Publication. Polish. Irregular. Zaklad Wydawnictw Statystycznych, Al. Niepodleglosci 208, 00-925 Warsaw Poland. **Tel** 011 48 22 250345, telex 814581 A GUS PL. **(Subscription address:** Ars Polona-Ruch, PO Box 1001, Krakowskie Przedmiescie 7, 00-068 Warsaw Poland. **Tel** 011 48 22 261201.) ***Continues*** *Roczniki Statystyczne. Handel Zagraniczny.*
Desc: Yearbook of the Polish foreign trade.

LC Z7165.J3 R96 HF3821
DD 016.3 JA
RYUTSU SHISUTEMU JOHO GAIDOBUKKU / RYUTSU SHISUTEMU KAIHATSU SENTA HEN. **Added/Corp** Ryutsu Shisutemu Kaihatsu Senta. (19??)-. Japanese. One time a year. ¥2300. Ryutsu Shisutemu Kaihatsu Senta Dai, 3Toc Building Nai 23-1 Nishi Gotanda 7 Shinagawa-ku, Tokyo-to 141 Japan.

LC HC290.5.I5 D43 **ISSN** 0943-8785
DD 330 GW
●**SAISONBEREINIGTE WIRTSCHAFTSZAHLEN.** **Added/Corp** Deutsche Bundesbank. (Jan. 1993)-. Statistical Publication. German (English). Twelve times a year (statistical supplement to the Monthly Report of the Deutsche Bundesbank). Free on request. Deutsche Bundesbank Presse, Information Wilh Epsteinstrasse 14, D-60431 Frankfurt Germany. **Tel** 011 49 69 1583509 or 1583455, telex 41 227 OR 414 431. ***Continues*** *Statistische Beihefte zu den Monatsberichten der Deutschen Bundesbank. Reihe 4, Saisonbereinigte Wirtschaftszahlen, 0418-8330.*

LC JS451.O57 S24 **ISSN** 0147-7080
DD 331.28/1/35200809766 US
SALARIES, WAGES AND FRINGE BENEFITS OF OKLAHOMA CITIES AND TOWNS. **Added/Corp** Oklahoma Municipal League. (1973)-. English. One time a year. Oklahoma Municipal League, 201 NE 23rd Street, Oklahoma City OK 73105. **Tel** (405)528-7560.

LC HA1631 .A33 HG3232
DD 314.971 YU
SAMOUPRAVLJANJE U BANKAMA I ZAJEDNICAMA OSIGURANJA. **VFOAT** Self-Management in Banks and Communities of Insurance. 1979-. Serbo-Croatian (Roman). 5.00. Savezni Zavod za Statistiku, Kneza Milosa 20, Belgrad Yugoslavia.

LC HA1631 .A33 HD5660.Y8
DD 314.971 YU
SAMOUPRAVLJANJE U PRIVREDI. **Main/Corp** Savezni Zavod Za Statistiku (Yugoslavia). Serbo-Croatian (Roman). 5.00 Din. Savezni Zavod za Statistiku, Kneza Milosa 20, Belgrad Yugoslavia.

LC HA1631 .A33 HD5660.Y8
DD 314.971 YU
SAMOUPRAVLJANJE U USTANOVAMA DRUSTVENIH SLUZBI. **Main/Corp** Savezni Zavod Za Statistiku (Yugoslavia). (19??)-. Statistical Publication. Serbo-Croatian (Roman). 10.00. Savezni Zavod za Statistiku, Kneza Milosa 20, Belgrad Yugoslavia.

LC Z7164.E2 S3 HB1.A1
DD 016.32 FI
SCANDINAVIAN PERIODICALS INDEX IN ECONOMICS AND BUSINESS : SCANP. **Added/Corp** Helsingin Kauppakorkeakoulu. Kirjasto. Helsingin Kauppakorkeakoulu. Laskentakeskus. **VFOAT** SCANP. (19??)-. English (English and German). Irregular (4 issues a year). $163.75. Helsinki School of Economics Library, Uneberginkatu 22-24 Scimp, 00100 Helsinki Finland. **Tel** 011 358 0 43131, telex 122220 ECON SF. Index available. cum. index. **Circ:** 200. available on an online database.
Desc: Bibliographic references to Scandinavian journal articles and research reports.

LC HF1414.5
DD 382.6 US
SCHEDULE B, STATISTICAL CLASSIFICATION OF DOMESTIC AND FOREIGN COMMODITIES EXPORTED FROM THE UNITED STATES. **Main/Corp** United States. Bureau of the Census. **VFOAT** Statistical Classification of Domestic and Foreign Commodities Exported from the United States. (Nov. 1941)-. Statistical Publication. English. Irregular. $77.00 domestic; $96.25 other. Superintendent of Documents, US Government Printing Office, Washington DC 20402. **Tel** (202)275-3328, FAX (202)786-2377. ***Continues*** *Schedule B, Statistical Classification of Domestic and Foreign Commodities Exported from the United States.*
Desc: Contains approximately 40,000 digit commodity classifications, based on the organization framework of the Tariff Schedules of the United States. Annotated, to be used by shippers in reporting export shipments from the United States and for use in compiling official statistics on exports of merchandise from the United States.

LC HC **ISSN** 0303-9692
DD 330 SZ
SCHWEIZERISCHE ZEITSCHRIFT FUER VOLKSWIRTSCHAFT UND STATISTIK. [Schweiz. z. volkswirtsch. stat.]. **Added/Corp** Schweizerische Gesellschaft fuer Statistik und Volkswirtschaft. **VFOAT** Revue Suisse d'Economie Politique et de Statistique. (1945)-. Periodical. German (French and English). Four times a year. $124.46. Staempfli & Cie SA, Postfach 8326, CH-3001 Bern Switzerland. **Tel** 011 41 31 3006666, telex 031 911 515 EDMZ CH. **ED** Ernst Baltensperger. Index available. cum. index. **Bk Rev**. **Ad Acc**. **Circ:** 1,450. available on an online database from Knight-Ridder Information, Inc.; available on CD-ROM from SilverPlatter (UK). Documents available from BLDSC. ***Continues*** *Zeitschrift fuer Schweizerische Statistik und Volkswirtschaft.*
Desc: Covers economic policy, economic history, fiscal policy, labor economics, income distribution, financial flows and assets, economic forecasts, energy problems, index numbers, and prices.
Ind/Abst Econ. Lit. Index; Int. Polit. Sci. Abstr.; J. Econ. Lit.; PAIS Int. Print; Popul. Index (?-?); Selec. Coop. Index Manage. Period.; Stat. Theory Method Abstr. (1959-1963).

ISSN 0782-2979
FI
CEASED
SCIMP SELECTIVE CO-OPERATIVE INDEX OF MANAGEMENT PERIODICALS. **Added/Corp** European Business School Libraries Group. **VFOAT** Selective Co-Operative Index of Management Periodicals. Vol. 1 (April 1978)-(Dec. 1993). Abstracting/Indexing Service. English (French and German). Helsinki School of Economics, Runeberginkatu 22 24 SCIMP, 00100 Helsinki Finland. **Tel** 358 0 43131. Index available. cum. index. **Ad Acc**. **Circ:** 250. available on CD-ROM and an online database from Helsinki School of Economics Library.
Desc: Over 260 journals in management and business studies are indexed. Articles are listed in broad subject groups. Subject and author index exists.

LC HA1931 .A354 **ISSN** 0075-1421
DD 382 IS
SEHAR HUTS SHEL YISRAEL. **Added/Corp** Israel. ha-Lishkah ha-Merkazit le-Statistikah. **VFOAT** Israel's Foreign Trade. (1951)-. Periodical. Multiple languages (English and Hebrew). $39.50. Central Bureau of Statistics / Israel, PO Box 13015, 91 130 Hakirya Jerusalem Israel. **Tel** 011-972-2-553553.
Desc: Detailed classified statistics of Israel's imports and exports, by country, commodity, value (partly also quantity).

LC Z7164.T4 N27 **ISSN** 0077-4014
DD 016.3 US
SELECTED AND ANNOTATED BIBLIOGRAPHY OF REFERENCE MATERIAL IN CONSUMER FINANCE. **Main/Corp** National Consumer Finance Association. Educational Services Division. **VFOAT** Consumer Finance. Bibliography. English. National Consumer Finance Association, 1000 16th Street NW, Washington DC 20036. **Tel** (202)638-1340.

LC Z7164.L1 P83 ISSN 0037-1351
DD 016.3311 US
SELECTED REFERENCES - INDUSTRIAL RELATIONS SECTION, PRINCETON UNIVERSITY. Main/Corp Princeton University. Industrial Relations Section. **Added/Corp** Princeton University. Industrial Relations Section. No. 1 (Jan. 1945)-. Monographic series. English. Five times a year. Price varies per volume. Firestone Library Industrial Relations Section, Princeton University, Princeton NJ 08544. **Tel** (609)452-4041. Index available. ctrl circ.

ISSN 0383-2392
DD 016.33 CN
SELECTION OF RECENT ACQUISITIONS - CANADIAN IMPERIAL BANK OF COMMERCE, INFORMATION CENTRE, A. Main/Corp Canadian Imperial Bank of Commerce. Information Centre. Vol. 1 (1972)-. Periodical. English. Twelve times a year. Canadian Imperial Bank of Commerce Economic Division, Commerce Court North, 7th Floor, Toronto Ontario M5L 1A2 Canada. **Tel** (416)980-2211, (416)980-3721. ctrl circ. ***Continues*** *Canadian Imperial Bank of Commerce. Economics Dept. Selection of Recent Acquisitions.*

LC HG450
DD 332.6 US
SIA FACT BOOK. (19??)-. Statistical Publication. English. One time a year. $40.00 (members); $75.00 (nonmembers). Securities Industry Association, 120 Broadway/35th Floor, New York NY 10271. **Tel** (212)608-1500, FAX (212)608-1604.
Desc: Statistical guide offering a decade of data covering global and domestic capital markets and the securities industry in general. Provides tables, charts, and editorial on various aspects of the securities industry.

LC HF3128 .S573 ISSN 0196-4607
DD 382/.0951/073 US
SINO-US TRADE STATISTICS. VAT Sino-United States Trade Statistics. English. One time a year. $25.00. National Council for US-China Trade, 1050 17th Street NW, Suite 350, Washington DC 20036. **ED** Marianna Graham. **Circ:** 5,000 (ctrl).
Desc: Publication of US-China trade statistics, including information on imports and exports in both value and volume terms for the past five years.

LC Z7164.E2 S68 HB180.J3
DD 016.3 JA
SOGO TOSHO MOKUROKU. Japanese. Toyo Keizai Shimpo Sha, 1-2-1 Nihombashi Hongoku-cho, Chuo-ku Tokyo 103 Japan. **Tel** (03)3246-5470.

LC Z7164.C81 P68a ISSN 0092-7767
DD 016.338 US
CEASED
SOURCE DIRECTORY OF PREDICASTS, INC, THE. Main/Corp Predicasts, Inc. Vol. 1 (June 1973)-(1993). Directory. English. Predicasts Inc., A Ziff Communications Company, 11001 Cedar Avenue, Cleveland OH 44106. **Tel** (800)321-6388, (216)795-3000, FAX (216)229-9944, telex 985 604.
Desc: Names and addresses of publications abstracted and indexed in Predicasts' hardcopy publications and online databases.

LC HA203 .S65
DD 339.4/1/0973021 US
SOURCEBOOK OF COUNTY DEMOGRAPHICS, THE. Added/Corp CACI, Inc. - Federal. 5th Ed. (1990)-. English. $295.00. CACI Market Systems, 1100 North Glebe Road, Arlington VA 22201. **Tel** (703)841-8841, (800)292-2224. **(Subscription address:** Gale Research Co., 835 Penobscot Building, Detroit MI 48226. **Tel** (800)347-4253.) ***Continues*** *Sourcebook of Demographics and Buying Power for Every County in the USA.*
Desc: Provides consumer and business data in a county arrangement.

LC HD4925
DD 331.21 US
SOURCEBOOK OF ZIP CODE DEMOGRAPHICS, THE. Added/Corp CACI, Inc. Federal. 7th Ed. (1990)-. English. One time a year (July). $295.00. CACI Market Systems, 1100 North Glebe Road, Arlington VA 22201. **Tel** (703)841-8841, (800)292-2224. **(Subscription address:** Gale Research Co., 835 Penobscot Building, Detroit MI 48226. **Tel** (800)347-4253.) Index available. available on diskette; available on magnetic tape. ***Continues*** *Sourcebook of Demographics and Buying Power for Every Zip Code in the USA.*
Desc: Provides demographic information for more than 34,000 ZIP codes and contains more than 3 million data items. Over 80 different characteristics are available for residential ZIP codes, key demographic variables, census information, market potential, key housing variables, business statistics, establishments, and SIC code rankings by employment.

LC HG4651
DD 332.632 US
STANDARD & POOR'S STATISTICAL SERVICE. Main/Corp Standard and Poor's Corporation. **Added/Corp** Standard and Poor's Corporation. Current Statistics Standard and Poor's Corporation. Basic Statistics Standard and Poor's Corporation. Security Price Index Record. **VFOAT** Statistical Service. (1977)-. Statistical Publication. English. Twelve times a year. $640.00. Standard & Poor's Corporation, (A Division of McGraw-Hill, Inc.), 25 Broadway, New York NY 10004. **Tel** (212)208-8775, (800)221-5277. ***Continues*** *Standard and Poor's Corporation. Standard & Poor's Trade and Securities Statistics.*
Desc: Comprehensive collection of economic and financial statistics published in three sections. Widely used by business planners in analyzing and forecasting, economists, research departments, and individual investors.

LC HC101 .S74a ISSN 0147-636X
DD 330.9/73/092 US
STANDARD & POOR'S STATISTICAL SERVICE CURRENT STATISTICS. [Stand. Poor's stat. serv., Curr. stat.]. **Main/Corp** Standard and Poor's Corporation. **Added/Corp** Standard and Poor's Corporation. Statistical Service Current Statistics. **VAT** Standard and Poor's Statistical Service. Current Statistics. (19??)-. Statistical Publication. English. Twelve times a year. $545.00. Standard & Poor's Corporation, (A Division of McGraw-Hill, Inc.), 25 Broadway, New York NY 10004. **Tel** (212)208-8775, (800)221-5277.

LC HF5805 .S714
DD 659.1/025/73 US
STANDARD DIRECTORY OF ADVERTISERS. TRADENAME INDEX. Added/Corp National Register Publishing Company (Wilmette, Ill.). **VFOAT** Standard Directory of Advertisers. Trade Name Index; Tradename Index; Trade Name Index; Advertising Red Book; Standard Industrial Classification Index; Who's Where in Corporate Advertising; Standard Directory of Advertisers. Indexes; Tradename List. (1992)-. Directory. English. One time a year. Included with Standard Directory of Advertisers (Business Classifications Ed. or the Geographic Ed.). National Register Publishing Company Inc., PO Box 31, 121 Chanlon Road, New Providence NJ 07974. **Tel** (800)521-8110, (800)323-6772, FAX (908)665-6688. ***Continues in part*** *Standard Directory of Advertisers (Classified Ed.), 1048-2415; Standard Directory of Advertisers (Geographical Ed.), 0081-4229.*

LC HA343 .A3 ISSN 0737-1543
DD 330.9773/005 US
STATE AND REGIONAL ECONOMIC ILLINOIS DATA BOOK. Added/Corp Illinois. Dept. of Business and Economic Development. Illinois. Dept. of Commerce and Community Affairs. **VFOAT** Illinois Data Book. (1976)-. Periodical. English. Every 2 years. Free on request. Illinois Department of Commerce & Community Affairs, 620 East Adams Street, Springfield IL 62701. **Tel** (217)782-7500, FAX (217)785-6454. **ED** Wallace Biermann. **Circ:** 4,000 (ctrl). ***Continues*** *Illinois State and Regional Economic Data Book, 0093-9552.*
Desc: General reference for those interested in business or industrial planning and investment in Illinois.

LC HA37.U7 N717
DD 310/.6/0747 US
STATE DATA CENTER DATA DEVELOPMENTS BULLETIN. No. 1 (Jan. 1983)-. Bulletin. English. Twelve times a year. Free. New York Department of Commerce, 99 Washington Avenue, Albany NY 12245. **Tel** (518)474-6950, (518)474-5027. **ED** Leonard M Gaines. **Circ:** 1,200.
Desc: Newsletter containing news about the release of data and reports from the US Census Bureau or other sources regarding New York state.

ISSN 0390-6566
IT
UDC 382
STATISTICA ANNUALE DEL COMMERCIO CON L'ESTERO. TOMO 2. MERCI PER PAESI. [Stat. annu. commer. estero Tomo 2]. (1964)-. Periodical. Italian. One time a year. L124000.00. Istituto Nazionale Statistica, GBP SEZ4 Via Cesare Balbo 16, 00184 Rome Italy. **Tel** 011 39 6 46735118. ***Continues*** *Statistica Annuale del Commercio con l'Estero, 0075-1871.*

LC HA661 .S72 ISSN 0898-3879
DD 317 US
STATISTICAL ABSTRACT OF UTAH (SALT LAKE CITY, UTAH. 1987). (STATISTICAL ABSTRACT OF UTAH.). [Stat. abstr. Utah]. **Added/Corp** University of Utah. Bureau of Economic and Business Research. (1987)-. Statistical Publication. English. Irregular. University of Utah College of Business, 401 Buo, Salt Lake City UT 84112. **Tel** (801)581-6333. ***Continues*** *Utah Statistical Abstract, 0278-3770.*

LC HD8053.R4 A26
DD 331.0973 US
STATISTICAL AND FISCAL DIGEST - RHODE ISLAND. DEPT. OF EMPLOYMENT SECURITY. Main/Corp Rhode Island. Dept. of Employment Security. 29th- 1964-. Statistical Publication. English. One time a year. ***Continues*** *Annual Report - Rhode Island Department of Employment Security.*

JM
STATISTICAL BULLETIN: PRODUCTION STATISTICS. Main/Corp Jamaica. Dept. of Statistics. (19??)-. Bulletin. English. One time a year. $30.00. Statistical Institute of Jamaica, 9 Swallowfield Road, PO Box 643, Kingston 5 Jamaica. **Tel** 011 809 92621756, FAX 011 809 9264859.

LC HC411 .S73
DD 330.95/0021 TH
STATISTICAL INDICATORS FOR ASIA AND THE PACIFIC. Added/Corp United Nations. Economic and Social Commission for Asia and the Pacific. United Nations. Economic and Social Commission for Asia and the Pacific. Statistics Division. Vol. 7, No. 2 (June 1977)-. Statistical Publication. English. Four times a year. $15.00. United Nations Publications, 2 United Nations Plaza, Room DC2 0853, Department 007C, New York NY 10017. **Tel** (212)963-8303, (800)253-9646. ***Continues*** *Statistical Indicators in ESCAP Countries.*
Desc: Provides current data for assessing demographic and economic trends in the region.

LC HG181 .S794
DD 332.1/0973/021 US
STATISTICAL INFORMATION ON THE FINANCIAL SERVICES INDUSTRY. (1981)-. Statistical Publication. English. American Bankers Association, 1120 Connecticut Avenue Northwest, Washington DC 20036. **Tel** (202)663-5221, (202)663-5000, FAX (202)828-4544.

LC HC431 .S79 ISSN 0496-9464
DD 330.954/0021 II
STATISTICAL OUTLINE OF INDIA. Added/Corp Tata Industries Limited. Dept. of Economics & Statistics. Tata Industries Private Limited. Dept. of Economics and Statistics. Tata Economic Consultancy Services. Tata Services Limited. Dept. of Economics and Statistics. (1953)-. Statistical Publication. English. One time a year. $5.00. Tata Services Ltd., Department of Economics and Statistics, Bombay House, Bombay 400023 India. **Tel** 204-5928. **(Subscription address:** Prints India, 11 Darya Ganj, New Delhi 110002 India. **Tel** 011 91 11 3268645, FAX 011 91 11 3275542, telex 31-61087 PRIN-IN.) **Circ:** 18,000.
Desc: Covers latest statistics on various aspects of Indian economy and also contains tables showing international comparisons.

LC HF1 .C84 ISSN 0010-3233
DD 382/.021 US
STATISTICAL PAPERS - UNITED NATIONS. SERIES D. COMMODITY TRADE STATISTICS. (COMMODITY TRADE STATISTICS.). [Stat. pap. - U. N., Ser. D, Commod. trade stat.]. **Added/Corp** United Nations. Statistical Office. (Jan./Mar. 1951)-. Government Publication. English. Twenty-eight times a year. $225.00. United Nations Publications, 2 United Nations Plaza, Room DC2 0853, Department 007C, New York NY 10017. **Tel** (212)963-8303, (800)253-9646. **(Subscription address:** United Nations Publications, Subscription Office, PO Box 361, Birmingham AL 35201-0361. **Tel** (800)633-4931, (205)995-1567 (outside US and Canada), FAX (205)995-1588.) ***Continues*** *Summary of World Trade Statistics.*
Desc: Analyzes more than 150 groups of commodities exported or imported by the world's principal trading nations.

LC HA1631 .A33 HC407.Y63
DD 314.971 YU
STATISTICAL REPORT. Main/Corp Savezni Zavod Za Statistiku (Yugoslavia). (1966)-. Statistical Publication. Serbo-Croatian (Roman). 20.00 Din. Savezni Zavod za Statistiku, Kneza Milosa 20, Belgrad Yugoslavia.

LC HD2775 .F92c ISSN 0731-0692
DD 338.8/3/0973 US
STATISTICAL REPORT ON MERGERS AND ACQUISITIONS. Added/Corp United States. Federal Trade Commission. Bureau of Economics. (19??)-. Statistical Publication. English. One time a year. F T C Bureau of Economics, Washington DC 20850. ***Continues*** *F.T.C. Statistical Report on Mergers and Acquisitions, 0094-1662.*

LC HD3537 .R4
DD 334/.0954 II
STATISTICAL STATEMENTS RELATING TO THE CO-OPERATIVE MOVEMENT IN INDIA, FOR THE YEAR ...
. VFOAT Bharata Mem Sahakari Andolana Se

Sambandhita Sankhyikiya Vivarana. Statistical Publication. English (Hindi). One time a year. ***Continues*** *Statements Showing Progress of the Co-Operative Movement in India.*

LC HG **ISSN** 1046-820X
DD 332 US
STATISTICAL YEARBOOK / CHICAGO MERCANTILE EXCHANGE. [Stat. yearb. - Chic. Merc. Exch.]. **Added/Corp** Chicago Mercantile Exchange. Chicago Mercantile Exchange. International Monetary Market Division. **VFOAT** Yearbook; Chicago Mercantile Exchange Yearbook. (1984)-. Statistical Publication. English. One time a year. Chicago Mercantile Exchange, 30 South Wacker Drive, Chicago IL 60606. **Tel** (312)930-8210. ***Formed by the union of*** *Chicago Mercantile Exchange. Year Book - Chicago Mercantile Exchange, 0577-7259; International Monetary Market Year Book, 0195-9980* ***and*** *Yearbook (Chicago Mercantile Exchange. Index and Option Market), 0884-3686.*

LC HA1107 .S65a
DD 314.7 UK
STATISTICAL YEARBOOK OF MEMBER STATES OF THE COUNCIL FOR MUTUAL ECONOMIC ASSISTANCE. **Main/Corp** Sovet Ekonomicheskoi Vzaimopomoshchi. **Added/Corp** Council for Mutual Economic Assistance. Secretariat. (19??)-. Statistical Publication. English (Russian). One time a year. $38.31. Reed Business Publishing / West Sussex, England, Perrymount Road, Haywards Heath, West Sussex RH16 3DH United Kingdom. **Tel** 011 44 1444 441212, FAX 011 44 1444 445447.

LC HC301 .A683
DD 330 IT
CEASED
STATISTICHE INDUSTRIALI. **Added/Corp** Istituto Centrale di Statistica (Italy). Vol. 27 (Ed. 1987)-Series complete. Italian (English). Istituto Nazionale Statistica, GBP SEZ4 Via Cesare Balbo 16, 00184 Rome Italy. **Tel** 011 39 6 46735118. ***Continues*** *Annuario di Statistiche Industriali, 0075-1723.*

LC JS7025.W4 A3 **ISSN** 0511-5507
DD 331.7/61/331795095414 II
STATISTICS OF EMPLOYMENT IN LOCAL BODIES IN WEST BENGAL. **Main/Corp** West Bengal. Bureau of Applied Economics and Statistics. (19??)-. English. West Bengal Government Press / Duplicating Section, Alipore India. ***Supersedes*** *Statistics of Employment in Local Bodies in West Bengal.*

LC HF91 .O66
DD 382 FR
STATISTICS OF FOREIGN TRADE. STATISTIQUES DU COMMERCE EXTERIER. SERIES B. TRADE BY COMMODITIES: COUNTRY SUMMARIES. ECHANGES PAR PRODUITS: RESUME PAR PAYS. **Main/Corp** Organization for Economic Cooperation and Development. **Added/Corp** Organization for Economic Cooperation and Development. Statistiques du Commerce Exterieur. Series B. **VFOAT** Statistiques du Commerce Exterieur. Echanges par Produits : Resume par Pays. (19??)-. Periodical. English (French). Four times a year. OECD Publications and Information Center, 2 rue Andre-Pascal, 75775 Paris Cedex 16 France. **Tel** 011 33 1 49104262, US:(202)785-6323, FAX 011 33 1 45248500, 011 33 1 45248176, telex 620 160 OCDE. **(Subscription address:** OECD Publications Center, 2001 L Street, Suite 700, Washington DC 20036. **Tel** (202)822-3873, (202)785-6323.**)** ***Continues*** *Organization for Economic Cooperation and Development. Statistics of Foreign Trade. Statistiques du Commerce Exterieur. Series B. Trade by Commodities: Analytical Abstracts. Exchanges par Produits: Tableaux Analytiques.*

LC HC431 .A3272A
DD 338.0954 II
STATISTICS RELATING TO DGTD UNITS. **Main/Corp** India Directorate General of Technical Development. **VAT** Statistics Relating to Directorate General of Technical Development Units. 1977-. English. One time a year. Rs15.00 India; Rs45.40 other. Government of India / Director of Public Relations & Publications, Directorate General of Technical Development, Udyog Bhevan Maulana Ozad Road, New Delhi 110011 India. ***Supersedes in part*** *Annual Report - Directorate General of Technical Development.*

ISSN 1033-8640
DD 319.94 AT
STATISTICS WEEKLY. [Stat. w.]. **Added/Corp** Australian Bureau of Statistics. (1989)-. Periodical. English. One time a week. 4.20Aus$. Australian Bureau of Statistics, PO Box 2796Y, Melbourne 3001 Australia. **Tel** 011 61 3 6157843.
Desc: Presents statistical feature articles for each of the week's major releases, together with reference tables containing figures for major national and State economic indicators.

LC HC280
DD 330/338.943 GW
STATISTIK DES AUSLANDES. LAENDERBERICHT. KATAR. **Added/Corp** Germany (West). Statistisches Bundesamt. **VFOAT** Laenderbericht. Katar. (19??)-. Periodical. German. W. Kohlhammer Verlag GmbH, Postfach 800430, D-70549 Stuttgart Germany. **Tel** 011 49 711 78630, FAX 011 49 711 7863430, telex 7-255820.

LC HC446 .S74
DD 330.9598/021 IO
STATISTIK EKONOMI DAN KEUANGAN INDONESIA. **VFOAT** Economic and Financial Statistics of Indonesia. English (Indonesian). One time a year. Jalan Imam Bonjol No. 61, Jakarta 10310 Kotak Pos, PO Box 106, Jakarta 10002 Indonesia.

LC HB235.I5 S77
DD 338.5/28/095984 IO
STATISTIK HARGA ... SULAWESI SELATAN. **VFOAT** Price Statistics ... Sulawesi Selatan. 1980-. English (Indonesian). One time a year. Kantor Statistik Propinsi Sulawesi Selatan, Jl Haji Bau No 6, Ujung Pandang Indonesia.

LC HA1 .S77 **ISSN** 0585-2013
DD 310 XR
STATISTIKA. **Added/Corp** Czechoslovakia. Federalni Statisticky Urad. Czechoslovakia. Ustredni Komise Lidove Kontroly a Statistiky. Czechoslovakia. Statni Statisticky Urad. (1964)-. Periodical. Czech (summaries and/or abstracts in English and Russian). Twelve times a year. $86.00. **(Subscription address:** Kubon & Sagner, ABT Zeitschriftenimport, D 80328 Munich Germany. **Tel** 011 49 89 54218130.**)** ***Continues in part*** *Statistika a Kontrola.*

LC HD7106.B3 S73
DD 331.252 BE
STATISTIQUES DES BENEFICIAIRES DE PRESTATIONS DE RETRAITE ET DE SURVIE. **VFOAT** Statistiek van de Personen die Een Rust- en Overlevingsprestatie Genieten. 1970-. Multiple languages (Dutch and French). Place Jean Jacobs 6, 1000 Brussels Belgium.

LC HD7352.A3 P67B
DD 363 PO
STATISTIQUES DU BATIMENT ET DE L'HABITATION : CONTINENT, AZORES ET MADERE. **Main/Corp** Portugal. Instituto Nacional de Estatistica. Servicos Centrais. **VFOAT** Estatisticas da Construcao e da Habitacao : Continente, Acores e Madeira. Periodical. Portuguese (French). One time a year. Instituto Nacional de Estatistica, Avenida Antonio Jose de Almeida, 1078 Lisbon Codex Portugal. **Tel** 011 351 1 8470050. **Circ:** 900.

LC HF3601 .S74
DD 380/.09493/021 BE
STATISTIQUES DU COMMERCE INTERIEUR ET DES TRANSPORTS / ROYAUME DE BELGIQUE, MINISTERE DES AFFAIRES ECONOMIQUES, INSTITUT NATIONAL DE STATISTIQUE. **Added/Corp** Institut National de Statistique (Belgium). No. 1-2 (Jan./Feb. 1985)-. Periodical. French. Eight times a year. $82.08. Institut National de Statistique / Belgium, rue de Louvain 44, 1000 Brussels Belgium. **Tel** 011 32 2 5486211, FAX 011 32 2 5486367. **Bk Rev. Ad Acc. Circ:** 500 (ctrl). ***Formed by the union of*** *Institut National de Statistique (Belgium). Statistiques des Transports, 0772-7755* ***and*** *Institut National de Statistique (Belgium). Statistiques du Commerce, 0772-7747.*
Desc: Statistics about inland trade and transportation.

LC HC271 .A218 HC280.Z6
DD 330/.08 S 309.2/5/0944 FR
STATISTIQUES ET INDICATEURS DES REGIONS FRANCAISES. **Main/Corp** Institut National de la Statistique et des Etudes Economiques (France). French (summaries and/or abstracts in English and Spanish). One time a year. 140.00F, 51.00F (microfiche). CNGP INSEE - Institut National de la Statistique et des Etudes Economiques, BP 2718, 1 rue V Auriol, F 80027 Amiens Cedex 1 France. **Tel** 011 33 22 927322. available on microfiche. ***Continues*** *Statistiques et Indicateurs des Regions Francaises.*
Desc: Records the most recent statistical data for each of the 22 regions of France on their economic, demographic and social situation, and their differences and developments.

LC HG21 .A27
DD 332 BE
STATISTIQUES FINANCIERES. **Main/Corp** Belgium. Institut National de Statistique. No. 1 (1972)-. French. Three times a year. 580F Belgium; 730F other. Institut National de Statistique / Belgium, rue de Louvain 44, 1000 Brussels Belgium. **Tel** 011 32 2 5486211, FAX 011 32 2 5486367. **Bk Rev. Ad Acc. Circ:** 600 (ctrl).
Desc: Covers income statistics and sales of real estate.

LC HG188.T77 B35A
DD 332/.0961/1 TI
STATISTIQUES FINANCIERES. **Main/Corp** Al-Bank Al-Markazi-Al-Tunisi. No. 1- Sept. 1972-. French. Twelve times a year. ***Supersedes in part*** *Al-Bank Al-Markazi-Al-Tunisia Bulletin.*

LC HD7105.35.C2 S8 **ISSN** 0846-8001
DD 331.25/2/09714 CN
STATISTIQUES FINANCIERES EN ..., LES. [Regimes retraite Que. stat. financ.]. (1974)-. French. Regie des Rentes du Quebec, Case Postale 5200, Quebec Quebec G1K 7S9 Canada. **Tel** (418)643-8309.

ISSN 0395-8973
FR
STATISTIQUES POUR L'ECONOMIE NORMANDE. **Added/Corp** Institut National de la Statistique et des Etudes Economiques (France). (June 1971)-. Periodical. French. Six times a year. 70.00F Europe; 85.00F other. CNGP INSEE - Institut National de la Statistique et des Etudes Economiques, BP 2718, 1 rue V Auriol, F 80027 Amiens Cedex 1 France. **Tel** 011 33 22 927322. ***Supersedes*** *Bulletin de Statistique: Basse-Normandie (Calvados, Manche, Orne), Haute-Normandie (Eure, Seine-Maritime).*

LC HA1107 **ISSN** 0067-5563
DD 314 BE
NLM W2 GB4 I5SK
STATISTIQUES SOCIALES. [Stat. soc.]. (1970)-. Periodical. French (Dutch). Three times a year. $21.45. Institut National de Statistique / Belgium, rue de Louvain 44, 1000 Brussels Belgium. **Tel** 011 32 2 5486211, FAX 011 32 2 5486367. **Circ:** 700 (ctrl). ***Continues in part*** *Institut National de Statistique (Belgium). Bulletin de Statistique.*
Desc: Social statistics: employment, unemployment, earnings, working accidents, and prices.

GW
STATISTISCHES JAHRBUCH DER INDUSTRIE- UND HANDELSKAMMER ZU DORTMUND. (1954)-. Statistical Publication. German. One time a year. DM39.50. Industrie- und Handelskammer zu Dortmund, Markische Strasse 120, 44141 Dortmund Germany. **Tel** 0231/54 17 230, FAX 0231 54 17 195, telex 969017. **ED** Reinhard Schulz and Jurgen Skupin. Index available. **Circ:** 1,000 (ctrl).

LC HC351 .A284a **ISSN** 0108-5603
DD 330.9489 DK
STATISTISK MANEDSOVERSIGT. (STATISTISK MANEDSOVERSIGT = MONTHLY REVIEW OF STATISTICS.). [Stat. manedsovers.]. **Added/Corp** Danmarks statistik. **VFOAT** Monthly Review of Statistics. Vol. 1 (1983)-. Statistical Publication. Danish (English). Twelve times a year. $179.80. Danmarks Statistik, Sejrgade 11, DK-2100 Copenhagen Denmark. **Tel** 011 45 3 9173917, FAX 011 45 31 18 48 01, telex 1 62 36. ***Continues*** *Danmarks Statistik. Konjunkturoversigt, 0106-2417.*
Desc: Provides an overall view of essential short-term statistics. Contains some of the most frequently used statistical indicators of economic trends in Denmark, with a separate chapter on international statistics, including main economic indicators. Primarily intended for those who wish to follow some key items of important monthly and quarterly statistics.

LC HB235.S8 S8
DD 338.5/28/09485 SW
STATISTISKA MEDDELANDEN. P. **Added/Corp** Sweden. Statistiska Centralbyran. **VFOAT** Statistiska Meddelanden. Serie P. (19??)-. English (Swedish).

LC HD5799 .A4 **ISSN** 0108-5514
DD 331.11 DK
STATISTISKE EFTERRETNINGER. ARBEJDSMARKED. **VFOAT** Arbejdsmarket. Vol. 1 (1983)-. Monographic series. Danish. Price varies per volume. Danmarks Statistik, Sejrgade 11, DK-2100 Copenhagen Denmark. **Tel** 011 45 3 9173917, FAX 011 45 31 18 48 01, telex 1 62 36. ***Continues in part*** *Danmarks Statistik. Statistiske Efterretninger.*
Desc: Statistics on employment and unemployment, notified employee vacancies, industrial accidents, commuting and government employees.

LC HF3649.F3 S72 **ISSN** 0108-5557
DD 380.1 DK
STATISTISKE EFTERRETNINGER. FRERNE OG GRNLAND. **VFOAT** Frerne og Grnland. Vol. 1 (1983)-. Monographic series. Danish. Price varies per volume. Danmarks Statistik, Sejrgade 11, DK-2100 Copenhagen Denmark. **Tel** 011 45 3 9173917, FAX 011 45 31 18 48 01, telex 1 62 36. ***Continues in part*** *Danmarks Statistik. Statistiske Efterretninger.*
Desc: Statistics on population size and changes, external trade, prices and incomes for the Faroe Islands and Greenland.

LC HF3641 .S72 ISSN 0108-5573
DD 380.1 DK
STATISTISKE EFTERRETNINGER. GENEREL ERHVERVSSTATISTIK OG HANDEL. **VFOAT** Generel Erhvervsstatistik og Handel. Vol. 1 (1983)-. Monographic series. Danish. Price varies per volume. Danmarks Statistik, Sejrgade 11, DK-2100 Copenhagen Denmark. **Tel** 011 45 3 9173917, FAX 011 45 31 18 48 01, telex 1 62 36. ***Continues in part*** *Danmarks Statistik. Statistiske Efterretninger.*
Desc: Statistics on accounts, joint-stock companies and business units registered by VAT settlement, with register-based workplace statistics, sales by non-agricultural industries and an index of retail sales.

LC HC360.I5 S73 ISSN 0108-5565
DD 338.9489 DK
STATISTISKE EFTERRETNINGER. INDKOMST, FORBRUG OG PRISER. **VFOAT** Indkomst, Forbrug og Priser. Vol. 1 (Feb. 7, 1983)-. Periodical. Danish. kr122.95, (add kr123.00 for postage); kr9.02 (4-24 pages), kr13.93 (28-48 pages) single copies. Danmarks Statistik, Sejrgade 11, DK-2100 Copenhagen Denmark. **Tel** 011 45 3 9173917, FAX 011 45 31 18 48 01, telex 1 62 36. ***Continues in part*** *Denmark. Danmarks Statistik. Statistiske Efterretninger.*
Desc: Statistics on income, earnings and wealth, with consumer expectation surveys, household budget surveys, a consumer price index, an index of net retail prices, a wage regulating price index, a wholesale price index and a price index for imported raw materials.

LC HG27 .S72 ISSN 0108-5476
DD 332.05/6 DK
STATISTISKE EFTERRETNINGER. PENGE- OG KAPITALMARKED. **VFOAT** Penge- og Kapitalmarked. Vol. 1 (1983)-. Monographic series. Danish. Price varies per volume. Danmarks Statistik, Sejrgade 11, DK-2100 Copenhagen Denmark. **Tel** 011 45 3 9173917, FAX 011 45 31 18 48 01, telex 1 62 36. ***Continues in part*** *Danmarks Statistik. Statistiske Efterretninger.*
Desc: Statistics on liquidity, bank balances, mortgage registrations, bond issues, insolvencies, insurance, pension funds, fire damages, forced sales of real property, etc.

LC HF3641 .S73 ISSN 0108-5506
DD 380.1 DK
STATISTISKE EFTERRETNINGER. UDENRIGSHANDEL. **Added/Corp** Danmarks Statistik. **VFOAT** Udenrigshandel. Vol. 1 (1983)-. Monographic series. Danish. Irregular. $118.55. Danmarks Statistik, Sejrgade 11, DK-2100 Copenhagen Denmark. **Tel** 011 45 3 9173917, FAX 011 45 31 18 48 01, telex 1 62 36. ***Continues in part*** *Danmarks Statistik. Statistiske Efterretninger;* ***Formed by the union of*** *Danmarks Statistik. Manedsstatistik Over Udenrigshandelen.*
Desc: Statistics on imports and exports, with quantity indexes; the terms of trade; distributions by countries, commodity groups and modes of transport; and EAGGF subsidies.

LC HA ISSN 0039-0690
DD 310 HU
STATISZTIKAI SZEMLE. (STATISZTIKAI SZEMLE = STATISTICHESKOE OBOZRENIE = STATISTICAL REVIEW.). [Stat. szle.]. **Main/Corp** Hungary. Kozponti Statisztikai Hivatal. **Added/Corp** Hungary. Kozponti Statisztikai Hivatal. **VFOAT** Statisticheskoe Obozrenie; Statistical Review. (1949)-. Statistical Publication. Hungarian (summaries and/or abstracts in English, Russian and Hungarian). Twelve times a year. $46.00. Hungarian Central Statistical Office, Keleti Karoly Utca, PO Box 51, H-1525 Budapest Hungary. **Tel** 011 36 1 2024011. **(Subscription address:** Kultura, PO Box 143, H-1300 Budapest 3 Hungary. **Tel** 011 36 1 2500194.) **ED** Marie Visi-Lakatos. **Bk Rev. Ad Acc. Circ:** 1,500 (ctrl). ***Continues*** *Magyar Statisztikai Szemle.*
Desc: Covers all fields of social and economic life, giving comprehensive information to statisticians and economists. Reviews regularly the newest examination methods, the news of statistical organizations and of special literature.
Ind/Abst Popul. Index.

SA
STATS. (May 30, 1964)-. English. Twelve times a year. $59.64. George Warman Publications Pty, PO Box 704, Cape Town 8000 South Africa. **Tel** 011 27 21 245320, FAX 011 27 21 261332, telex 5-21849. **ED** R.E. Pretorius. cum. index.
Desc: Supplies updated economic trend indicators; also statistics from a wide range of sources on a variety of subjects.

RU
STRANY CHLENY SODRUZHESTVA NEZAVISIMYHK GOSUDARSTV. (19??)-. Russian. Eighteen times a year. $69.95 US and Canada; $79.95 Europe; $94.95 other. **(Subscription address:** East View Publications Inc., 3020 Harbor Lane North, Suite 110, Minneapolis MN 55447. **Tel** (800)477-1005, (612)550-0961, FAX (612)559-2931.) ***Continues*** *Narodnoe Khoziaistvo SSSR V.*

AT
SUCCESSFUL AND UNSUCCESSFUL JOB SEARCH EXPERIENCE, AUSTRALIA. **Added/Corp** Australian Bureau of Statistics. (June 1986)-. English. Two times a year. 12.50Aus$. Australian Bureau of Statistics, PO Box 2796Y, Melbourne 3001 Australia. **Tel** 011 61 3 6157843.
Desc: Provides information on persons who began work during the previous 12 months, method of job attainment, and details of the job.

LC HG4090.Z65 S87 ISSN 0833-9597
DD 338.7/4/02571 CN
SURVEY OF INDUSTRIALS (TORONTO. 1985). (SURVEY OF INDUSTRIALS.). [Surv. ind.]. **Added/Corp** Financial Post Information Service. **VFOAT** Financial Post Survey of Industrials. 59th (1985)-. English. One time a year. 79.19Can$. Financial Post DataGroup, 333 King Street East, Toronto Ontario M5A 4N2 Canada. **Tel** (800)661-7678, FAX (416)350-6501. ***Continues*** *Financial Post Survey of Industrials, 0071-5050.*
Desc: Gives details on all Canadian publicly-owned companies engaged in the manufacturing, sales and service industries with details on their operations, management and financial status.

ISSN 0832-0772
DD 338.7/4/02571 CN
SURVEY OF PREDECESSOR AND DEFUNCT COMPANIES (1985). (SURVEY OF PREDECESSOR AND DEFUNCT COMPANIES.). [Surv. predecess. defunct co.]. **Added/Corp** Financial Post Corporation Service Group. **VFOAT** Financial Post Survey of Predecessor and Defunct Companies. 3rd. Ed. (1985)-. English. Every 2 years (every 2 years). 57.59Can$. Financial Post DataGroup, 333 King Street East, Toronto Ontario M5A 4N2 Canada. **Tel** (800)661-7678, FAX (416)350-6501. ***Continues*** *Financial Post Survey of Predecessor and Defunct Companies, 0712-3256.*
Desc: A history of changes affecting Canadian public corporations with details of name changes, amalgamations and acquisitions covering some 12,000 corporate entities.

LC HA4015 .A35
DD 319.597 NL
TABLEAUX DE L'ECONOMIE CALEDONIENNE. French. Three times a year. 1800CFPF Caledonia; 2500CFPF other. Institut Territorial de la Statistique et des Etudes Economiques, BP 823, Noumea Nouvelle-Caledonie. **Tel** (27 54 81. cum. index. **Bk Rev. Circ:** 2,000.
Desc: The principal reference work of the ITSEE, with condensed information about government, demography, health, building, education, employment, agriculture, mining, overseas transactions, tourism, etc.

LC HA1228.C5 T32
DD 314.4/3 FR
TABLEAUX DE L'ECONOMIE CHAMPENOISE. **VFOAT** T.E.C.; TEC. (19??)-. French. 32. Direction Regionale de Reims, 1 rue de l'Arbalete, 51079 Reims Ce France. **Tel** 26882412. **Circ:** 1,000.
Desc: Our main subjects are local studies about population, industry, education, housing and urban development in Champagne Ardenne.

ISSN 0496-7046
DD 332 CH
TAIWAN FINANCIAL STATISTICS MONTHLY. **Main/Corp** China (Republic). Economic Research Department. **Added/Corp** Chung Yang Yin Hang. Ching Chi Yen Chiu Ch'u. **VFOAT** Republic of China Taiwan Financial Statistics Monthly; Tai-Wan Chin Jung T'ung Chi Yueh Pao. (1951)-. Statistical Publication. English (Chinese). Twelve times a year. $60.00. Central Bank of China, 2 Roosevelt Road, Economic Research Department, Taipei 107 Taiwan. **Tel** 011 886 2 3936161.

LC HG4190 .A44 ISSN 0784-9079
DD 658.1509 FI
TEOLLISUUSYRITYSTEN TILINPAEAETOESTILASTO. **Added/Corp** Finland. Tilastokeskus. **VFOAT** Bokslutsstatistik Oever Industrifoeretag; Financial Statements Statistics of Industrial Enterprises; Financial Statements Statistics of Industry. (1986)-. Finnish (Swedish; summaries and/or abstracts in English). One time a year. Central Statistical Office, PO Box 504, SF-00101 Helsinki Finland. **Tel** 011 358 0 17347, FAX 011 358 0 17342279. ***Continues in part*** *Tilastotiedotus. YR, 0355-2373.*

ISSN 1133-0686
SP
UDC 311
TEST (MADRID). (1992)-. Statistical Publication. Spanish. Irregular (2-3 issues per year). $106.53. Sociedad de Estadistica e Investigacion Operativa, Hortaleza 104-2 IZDA, 28004 Madrid Spain. **Tel** 011 34 1 3082474. ***Continues in part*** *Trabajos de Estadistica (Madrid. 1986), 0213-8190.*

LC HB3608.3.A3 T56 ISSN 0358-6243
DD 304.6094897 FI
TILASTOTIEDOTUS. VL. **VFOAT** VL; Statistisk Rapport. VL. **VAT** Tilastotiedotus. Vaesto- Ja Asuntolaskenta. Monographic series. Finnish (Swedish). Irregular. Price varies per volume. Central Statistical Office, PO Box 504, SF-00101 Helsinki Finland. **Tel** 011 358 0 17347, FAX 011 358 0 17342279.

LC HG5160.T6 T68a ISSN 0049-4216
DD 332.6/42/09713541 CN
TORONTO STOCK EXCHANGE REVIEW, THE. [Tor. Stock Exch. rev.]. **Main/Corp** Toronto Stock Exchange. **Added/Corp** Toronto Stock Exchange. Review. (19??)-. Statistical Publication. English. Twelve times a year. 208.00Can$. Toronto Stock Exchange, The Exchange Tower, 2 First Canadian Place, Toronto Ontario M5X 1J2 Canada. **Tel** (416)947-4681. **ED** David Marcus-Roland. **Circ:** 3,000. available on microfiche from Micromedia Limited; available on microfilm and microfiche from University Microfilms International (UMI). Documents available from UMI Article Clearinghouse.
Desc: Trading statistics on equities, options, futures traded on the Toronto Stock and Futures Exchanges plus a wealth of related information.
Ind/Abst ABI/INFORM Glob. Ed.; Can. Period. Index (19??-).

US
TRADE & INDUSTRY ASAP [ONLINE DATABASE]. (19??)-. Abstracting/Indexing Service. English. Information Access Company, 362 Lakeside Drive, Foster City CA 94404. **Tel** (800)227-8431, (800)458-1565.
Desc: Provides current and comprehensive coverage of over 550 business and industry publications, including specialized trade journals, regional business publications, international periodicals, and newspapers and newswires.

US
TRADE & INDUSTRY INDEX [ONLINE DATABASE]. (19??)-. Abstracting/Indexing Service. English. Twelve times a year. Information Access Company, 362 Lakeside Drive, Foster City CA 94404. **Tel** (800)227-8431, (800)458-1565.
Desc: A computer-readable database that provides indexing of trade and industry journals, as well as selective coverage of additional publications. Coverage includes business and trade-related books and government documents, as well as full-text news releases gathered by PR Newswire.

LC HF189.A532 ISSN 0790-5122
DD 382/.09417/0021 IE
TRADE STATISTICS OF IRELAND. **Added/Corp** Irish Free State. Dept. of Industry and Commerce. Ireland. Dept. of Industry and Commerce. Ireland. Central Statistics Office. Ireland. Office of the Revenue Commissioners. **VFOAT** Trade Statistics of Ireland. (19??)-. Periodical. English. Twelve times a year. $148.59. Government Publications, 4 5 Harcourt Road, Dublin 2 Ireland. **Tel** 011 353 1 6613111 ext.4005. **Circ:** 1,000.

LC HD6891 .A23
DD 331.88/0994 AT
TRADE UNION STATISTICS: AUSTRALIA. **Main/Corp** Australian Bureau of Statistics. (19??)-. English. One time a year. 10.70Aus$. Australian Bureau of Statistics, PO Box 2796Y, Melbourne 3001 Australia. **Tel** 011 61 3 6157843. ***Continues*** *Australia. Commonwealth Bureau of Census and Statistics. Trade Union Statistics: Australia.*
Desc: Number of separate trade unions; financial and total members classified by state, territory and sex; proportion of employed wage and salary earners who were union members.

LC T394 .T725 ISSN 0000-1023
DD 607/.3473 US
TRADESHOW WEEK DATA BOOK, THE. [Tradeshow week data book]. **Added/Corp** Trade Show Bureau (U.S.). **VFOAT** Trade Show Week Data Book. (1985)-. English. One time a year. $315.00. R.R. Bowker, A Reed Reference Publishing Company, Part of Reed International PLC, PO Box 31, 121 Chanlon Drive, New Providence NJ 07974. **Tel** (908)464-6800, (800)521-8110, FAX (908)665-6688, telex 138-755.
Desc: Provides detailed contact information for each show's manager, sponsor, and general contractor, plus details on exhibitors, attendees, registration fees, exhibit space cost, last show statistics, and more. Updated annually.

ISSN 0192-0596
DD 658 US
CCC
SUSPENDED
TRAINING AND DEVELOPMENT ALERT. [Train. dev. alert]. (1979)-Suspended Vol. 16 No. 5 (19??). Periodical. English. Six times a year (Feb., Apr.,

June, Aug., Oct., Dec.). $100.00 US; $112.00 Canada; $110.00 Pan-American nations; $118.00 other. Advanced Personnel Systems, PO Box 1438, Roseville CA 95678. **Tel** (916)781-2900, FAX (916)781-2901. **ED** Richard B. Frantzreb. **Bk Rev. Circ:** 300. available on an online database.
Desc: A abstract publication covering industrial training, management, and career development.

LC HF5549.5.T7 T6653 **ISSN** 1049-3875
DD 658.3/124/05 US
TRAINING AND DEVELOPMENT YEARBOOK. [Train. dev. yearb.]. **VFOAT** TDY. (1990)-. English. One time a year. $79.95. Arco Publishing Company, 200 Old Tappan Road, Old Tappan NJ 07675. **Tel** (800)223-2348, (201)767-5937. **ED** Richard B. Frantzreb.
Desc: Contains reprint articles and abstracts from training literature of the previous year. Case studies and research summaries are highlighted.

LC HC461 .T78
DD 330 JA
TSUSAN TOKEI. INDUSTRIAL STATISTICS MONTHLY. Added/Corp Japan. Tsusho Sangyosho. Chosa Tokeibu. **VFOAT** Industrial Statistics Monthly. (1963)-. Periodical. Multiple languages (Japanese and English). Twelve times a year. $495.00. Government Publications Service Center, 2-1 Kasumigaseki 1-Chome, Chiyoda-Ku Tokyo 100 Japan. **Tel** 011 81 3 3504 3885. **(Subscription address:** Maruzen Company Ltd., PO Box 5050, Import & Export Department, Tokyo 100 31 Japan. **Tel** 011 81 3 32789224.) ***Continues*** *Tsusan Ttokei Geppo.*

US
U.S. EXPORT AND IMPORT PRICE INDEXES. Main/Corp United States. Bureau of Labor Statistics. **VAT** United States Export and Import Price Indexes. (19??)-. Government Publication. English. Four times a year. Free on request. US Department of Labor / Bureau of Labor Statistics, 441 G Street Northwest, Washington DC 20212. **Tel** (202)606-7800, FAX (202)606-7797. **(Subscription address:** Superintendent of Documents, US Government Printing Office, Washington DC 20402.)

LC HF1042 .U54a **ISSN** 0193-1687
DD 382/.0973 US
U.S. FOREIGN TRADE: CONCORDANCE OF STATISTICAL CLASSIFICATIONS OF DOMESTIC AND FOREIGN COMMODITIES EXPORTED FROM THE UNITED STATES. Main/Corp United States. Bureau of the Census. **Added/Corp** United States. Bureau of the Census. Concordance of Statistical Classifications of Domestic and Foreign Commodities Exported from the United States. United States. Bureau of the Census. Statistical Classifications of Domestic and Foreign Commodities Exported from the United States. United States. Bureau of the Census. U.S. Exports Commodity Classifications Concordance. **VFOAT** Concordance of Statistical Classifications of Domestic and Foreign Commodities Exported from the United States; Statistical Classifications of Domestic and Foreign Commodities Exported from the United States; U.S. Exports Commodity Classifications Concordance. **VAT** United States Foreign Trade. Concordance of Statistical Classifications of Domestic and Foreign Commodities Exported from the United States. (1978)-. Statistical Publication. English. One time a year. OECD Publications and Information Center, 2 rue Andre-Pascal, 75775 Paris Cedex 16 France. **Tel** 011 33 1 49104262, US:(202)785-6323, FAX 011 33 1 45248500, 011 33 1 45248176, telex 620 160 OCDE. **(Subscription address:** OECD Publications Center, 2001 L Street, Suite 700, Washington DC 20036. **Tel** (202)822-3873, (202)785-6323.)

LC HC101 .D36a **ISSN** 0734-4449
DD 338.5/443/0973 US
U.S. LONG-TERM REVIEW. [U.S. long-term rev.]. **Added/Corp** Data Resources, Inc. **VFOAT** US Long-Term Review; Data Resources US Long-Term Review; Data Resources U.S. Long-Term Review. (19??)-. Periodical. English. Irregular. $275.00. DRI McGraw Hill, 24 Hartwell Avenue, Lexington MA 02173. **Tel** (617)863-5100, FAX (617)860-6464, (617)860-6416. **(Subscription address:** Data Resources, PO Box 5 0210, Woburn MA 01815.) **ED** Christopher Caton. **Circ:** 400 (ctrl). ***Continues*** *Data Resources U.S. Long-Term Review, 0734-4430;* ***Absorbed*** *U.S. Business Outlook, Long-Term.*
Desc: Presents and discusses long-term projections of the U.S. economy.

LC Z7164.C81 **ISSN** 1064-5381
DD 330 US
UMI ABI/INFORM--BUSINESS PERIODICALS ONDISC. (UMI ABI/INFORM--BUSINESS PERIODICALS ONDISC [COMPUTER FILE].). [UMI ABI/Inform--Bus. period. ondisc]. **Added/Corp** University Microfilms International. **VFOAT** UMI ABI/Inform Business Periodicals Ondisc; ABI/Inform--Business Periodicals Ondisc; Business Periodicals On Disc; ProQuest Business Periodicals Ondisc; Business Periodicals Ondisc; BPO. (199?)-. Abstracting/Indexing Service. English. One time a year. $15,000.00. University Microfilms International, 300 North Zeeb Road, Ann Arbor MI 48106-1346. **Tel** (313)761-4700, (800)521-0600 Exts. 2490, 2491, FAX (313)973-1540.

LC Z7165.U5 A8 HB171 **ISSN** 0736-8968
DD 016.33 US
CEASED
UNIVERSITY RESEARCH IN BUSINESS AND ECONOMICS. [Univ. res. bus. econ.]. **Added/Corp** West Virginia University. Bureau of Business Research. Association for University Business and Economic Research. Vol. 26 (1981)-vOL. 34 (19??). English. West Virginia University Fnd Inc., Bureau of Business Research, PO Box 26506, Morgantown WV 26506. **Tel** (304)293-7534, FAX (304)293-7061. **ED** Janice B. Ward. **Circ:** 700 (ctrl). ***Continues*** *AUBER Bibliography, 0738-3215.*
Desc: Lists publications of college and university research units in areas of business and economics.

LC HA1631 .A33 HF3732.3 **ISSN** 0300-2462
DD 314.971 YU
UNUTRASNJA TRGOVINA. Main/Corp Yugoslavia. Savezni Zavod za Statistiku. Statistical Publication. Serbo-Croatian (Roman). 10.00 Din each issue. Savezni Zavod za Statistiku, Kneza Milosa 20, Belgrad Yugoslavia.

LC HF3128 .U8 **ISSN** 0732-8478
DD 382/.0951/0730212 US
US-CHINA TRADE STATISTICS. [US-China trade stat.]. **Added/Corp** National Council for United States-China Trade. **VFOAT** US China Trade Statistics; U.S. China Trade Statistics; U.S.-China Trade Statistics. **VAT** United States-China Trade Statistics. (1981)-. English. One time a year. $25.00. National Council for US-China Trade, 1050 17th Street NW, Suite 350, Washington DC 20036. **ED** Marianna Graham. **Circ:** 5,000 (ctrl). ***Continues*** *US-Sino Trade Statistics.*
Desc: Publication of US-China trade statistics, including imports and exports in both value and volume terms for the past five years.

LC HF1371 **ISSN** 1024-7467
DD 382 IC
●**UTANRIKISVERSLUN EFTIR TOLLSKRARNUMERUM = EXTERNAL TRADE BY HS-NUMBERS.** (1995)-. Government Publication. Icelandic (English). One time a year. Hagstofa Islands, Statistics Iceland, Skuggasund 3, IS-150 Reykjavik Iceland. **Tel** 011 354 5609800, FAX 011 354 5628865. **ED** Hallgrimur Snorrason.

LC HF1371 **ISSN** 1024-7483
DD 382 IC
●**UTANRIKISVERSLUN = EXTERNAL TRADE.** (1995)-. Government Publication. English. One time a year. Hagstofa Islands, Statistics Iceland, Skuggasund 3, IS-150 Reykjavik Iceland. **Tel** 011 354 5609800, FAX 011 354 5628865. **ED** Hallgrimur Snorrason.

ISSN 1070-1362
DD 331 US
CEASED
VIEW (BEDFORD, N.H.). (VIEW : THE MONTHLY NEWSLETTER OF BUSINESS AND TRAINING VIDEOS.). [View]. (1992)-(June 1995). Newsletter. English. View, PO Box 10624, Bedford NH 03110. **Tel** (800)225-8439, FAX (603)472-8860. **ED** Michael Weber. Index available ($15.00). cum. index. **Circ:** 250. available on an online database from HRIN.
Desc: Reviews business and training videos and surveys categories of videos each month and covers multimedia trends.

LC HD5701 **ISSN** 1024-0020
DD 331.12 IC
●**VINNUMARKAUR = LABOUR MARKET STATISTICS. Added/Corp** Iceland. Hagstofa. **VFOAT** Labour Market Statistics. (1994)-. Icelandic (English). One time a year. $20.00. Hagstofa Islands, Statistics Iceland, Skuggasund 3, IS-150 Reykjavik Iceland. **Tel** 011 354 5609800, FAX 011 354 5628865. **ED** Hallgrimur Snorrason.

LC HA1228.A75 A332 **ISSN** 0395-9473
DD 314.4 FR
VUES SUR L'ECONOMIE D'AQUITAINE. [Vues econ. Aquitaine]. **Added/Corp** Institut National de la Statistique et des Etudes Economiques (France). (May 1971)-. Periodical. French. Six times a year. 70.00F. CNGP INSEE - Institut National de la Statistique et des Estudes Economiques, BP 2718, 1 rue V Auriol, F 80027 Amiens Cedex 1 France. **Tel** 011 33 22 927322. ***Supersedes*** *Bulletin de Statistique: Aquitaine (Dordogne, Gironde, Landes, Lot-et-Garonne, Pyrnees-Atlantiques), 0150-8369.*
Desc: Publishes socio-economic information on the Bordeaux region of France in an accessible format with concise analysis of statistics.

LC HD4801 **ISSN** 1081-0846
DD 331 US
●**WAGES AND COST OF LIVING.** (WAGES AND COST OF LIVING : 508 COUNTY INDEXES.). [Wages cost living]. **Added/Corp** Research Associates of Washington (D.C.). (May 1995)-. Academic Scholarly Publication. English. Every 2 years. $50.00. Research Associates of Washington, 2605 Klingle Road Northwest, Washington DC 20008. **Tel** (202)966-3326, FAX (202)966-0309. available on diskette.

LC HD5725.W4 A464A **ISSN** 0097-7837
DD 331.1/1/09754 US
WEST VIRGINIA LABOR FORCE ANNUAL AVERAGES HOURS & EARNINGS : WEST VIRGINIA STANDARD METROPOLITAN STATISTICAL AREAS. Main/Corp West Virginia. Dept. of Employment Security. Research and Statistics Division. Statistical Publication. English. One time a year. West Virginia Employment Programs Bureau, 112 California Avenue, Charleston WV 25305. **Tel** (304)558-2630, FAX (304)348-0301.

LC HF251 .J35a
DD 382/.0952 JA
TITLE CHANGE
WHITE PAPER ON INTERNATIONAL TRADE : JAPAN. Main/Corp Japan. Tsusho Sangyosho. **Added/Corp** Nihon Boeki Shinkokai. Vol. 24 (1972)-(19??). Statistical Publication. English (Japanese). Japan External Trade Organization, 2 5 2 Chome Toranomon, Minato-ku Tokyo 107, Japan. **Tel** 011 81 3 3582 5521, FAX 011 81 3 3582 0504, telex J24378. ***Continues*** *Foreign Trade of Japan.* ***Continued by*** *JETRO White Paper on International Trade Japan.*
Desc: Contains trade statistics.

LC Z7164.C81 **ISSN** 1057-6533
DD 650 US
WILSON BUSINESS ABSTRACTS. (WILSON BUSINESS ABSTRACTS [COMPUTER FILE].). [Wilson bus. abstr.]. **VFOAT** Business Abstracts. (1991)-. Abstracting/Indexing Service. English. Twelve times a year. $2515.00. H W Wilson Company, 950 University Avenue, Bronx NY 10452. **Tel** (800)367-6770, (718)588-8400 ext. 2245, FAX (718)681-1511, telex 4990003 HWILSON. available on magnetic tape, an online database, and CD-ROM from H W Wilson; available on diskette from WILSONSEARCH; available on an online database from WILSONLINE.
Desc: Presents abstracts, ranging from 50 to 150 words each, that provide precise descriptions of the content and scope of the article. Provides cover-to-cover abstracting of 330 core business journals.

LC HD5725.M3 M34b **ISSN** 0149-8959
DD 331.4/09741 US
WOMEN AND MINORITY MANPOWER STATISTICS. Main/Corp Maine. Manpower Research Division. (19??)-. English. One time a year. Manpower Research Division, 20 Union Street, Augusta ME 04330.

LC HD **ISSN** 0964-9425
DD 658 UK
CCC
WOMEN IN MANAGEMENT REVIEW. Added/Corp Great Britain. Equal Opportunities Commission. Vol. 7, No. 1 (1992)-. Abstracting/Indexing Service. English. Eight times a year. $1729.00. MCB University Press, 60 62 Toller Lane, Bradford, West Yorkshire BD8 9BY United Kingdom. **Tel** 011 44 1274 785280, FAX 011 44 1274 785200, telex 51317-MCBUNI-G. **(Subscription address:** MCB University Press / US and Canada Subscriptions, PO Box 10812, Birmingham AL 35201-0812. **Tel** (205)995-1567, (800)633-4931, FAX (205)995-1588.) **ED** Marilyn Davidson. available on CD-ROM; available on diskette. ***Continues*** *Women in Management Review & Abstracts, 0955-8357.*
Desc: Aims to foster and encourage the flow of ideas and information amongst those committed to the advancement of women in managerial positions in industry, business, commerce, the professions, and the public sector aid, in a practical way, the day-to-day functioning of women managers examine the organizational opportunities created through the contributions of women in management.

LC Z7164.L1 W68 HD4901 **ISSN** 0273-3234
DD 016.331 US
WORK RELATED ABSTRACTS. [Work relat. abstr.]. (1973)-. Abstracting/Indexing Service. English. Twelve times a year. $470.00. Harmonie Park Press, 23630 Pinewood, Warren MI 48091. **Tel** (313)755-3080, (800)886-3080, FAX (313)755-4213. **ED** Sonja Hempseed. **Bk Rev. Circ:** 300. ***Continues*** *Employment Relations Abstracts.*
Desc: Concerned with behavior at work, labor-management relations, personnel management, employee representation, negotiation process and dispute settlement, current labor contracts, compensation and fringe benefits, safety and health, education and training, industry engineering, socioeconomic and political issues, economics, labor force and labor market, occupations, and labor unions.

LC Z7164.F5 I555A HC59.7 **ISSN** 0253-7389
DD 016.3321/532 US

WORLD BANK CATALOG OF PUBLICATIONS, THE. [World Bank cat. publ.]. **Main/Corp** International Bank for Reconstruction and Development. Catalog. English. One time a year. World Bank Publications, 1818 H Street Northwest, Washington DC 20043. **Tel** (202)473-1155, (202)473-1155, FAX (202)522-3224, telex WUI 64145 WORLDBANK. ***Continues*** *Catalog. World Bank Publications.*

LC HD2757 **ISSN** 0258-3143
DD 338.9 US

WORLD BANK RESEARCH PROGRAM (1986), THE. (THE WORLD BANK RESEARCH PROGRAM : ABSTRACTS OF CURRENT STUDIES.). [World Bank res. program]. **Added/Corp** International Bank for Reconstruction and Development. **VFOAT** Abstracts of Current Studies. (1985)-. English. One time a year. $12.00. World Bank Publications, 1818 H Street Northwest, Washington DC 20043. **Tel** (202)473-1155, (202)473-1155, FAX (202)522-3224, telex WUI 64145 WORLDBANK. ***Continues*** *Abstracts of Current Studies, 0253-9535.*
Desc: Information on economic and technical assistance.

LC HG1505 .W67 **ISSN** 0265-9484
DD 332.1/05 UK
CCC

WORLD BANKING ABSTRACTS. [World bank. abstr.]. **Added/Corp** University College of North Wales. Institute of European Finance. Bank Administration Institute. (19??)-. Academic Scholarly Publication. English. Six times a year. $540.00. Basil Blackwell Publishers Ltd., 108 Cowley Road, Oxford 0X4 1JF United Kingdom. **Tel** 011 44 1235 465500, FAX 011 44 1235 465556, telex 837022 OXBOOK G. **(Subscription address:** Blackwell Publishers / UK, 108 Cowley Road, Oxford OX4 1JF United Kingdom. **Tel** 011 44 1865 791100, FAX 011 44 1865 791347.**) ED** Professor E.P.M Gardener and Philip Molyneux. Index available (December). available in microform from University Microfilms International (UMI).
Desc: Provides access to articles published in over 400 banking and finance publications internationally.

LC HJ8899 .W672 **ISSN** 0253-2859
DD 336.3/435/091724 US

WORLD DEBT TABLES. [World debt tables]. **Added/Corp** World Bank. (19??)-. English. One time a year. $125.00. World Bank Publications, 1818 H Street Northwest, Washington DC 20043. **Tel** (202)473-1155, (202)473-1155, FAX (202)522-3224, telex WUI 64145 WORLDBANK. available on an online database from GSI-ECO. Documents available from BLDSC. ***Continues*** *External Public Debt.*
Desc: Provides data on the external debt of developing countries. Shows statistical tables by country outlines and characteristics of debt situation.
Ind/Abst Curr. Cit.

ISSN 0952-5734
UK

WORLD TRADE STEEL. (1970)-. Abstracting/Indexing Service. English. Four times a year. £300.00 UK and Europe; £320.00 other. United Kingdom Iron & Steel Statistics Bureau, Canterbury House, 2 Sydenham Road, Croydon CR9 2LZ United Kingdom. **Tel** 011 44 181 6869050, FAX 011 44 181 6808616, telex 932575. **ED** Averil Kovacs. **Circ:** 200. available in print.
Desc: Details the export trade of 16 major steel producing countries collectively accounting for over 80% of world exports.

LC HD4826 .I63 **ISSN** 0084-3857
DD 331 SZ
CCC

YEAR-BOOK OF LABOUR STATISTICS. **Added/Corp** International Labour Office. **VFOAT** Yearbook of Labour Statistics; Annuaire des Statistiques du Travail; Anuario de Estadisticas del Trabajo. **VAT** Year Book of Labour Statistics. Issue 1 (1935/1936)-. English (French and Spanish). One time a year (two volumes). $189.00. International Labour Office - ILO, Publications Sales Service, CH-1211 Geneva 22 Switzerland. **Tel** 011 41 22 7996111, FAX 011 41 22 7986253, telex 415 647 ilo ch. **(Subscription address:** International Labour Office / Washington, DC, 1828 L Street Northwest, Suite 801, Washington DC 20036. **Tel** (202)653-7652.**)** available on microfiche from University Microfilms International (UMI).
Desc: A comprehensive survey of annual data from all parts of the world relating to economically active population, employment, unemployment, hours of work, wages, labour cost, industrial disputes, occupational injuries (most tables by major division of economic activity) and consumer prices.

LC HG5470.5.A2 Y42 **ISSN** 0230-418X
DD 332.6/09439 HU

YEARBOOK OF INVESTMENT STATISTICS. **VFOAT** Ezhegodnik Po Kapitalnym Vlozheniiam; Beruhazasi Evkonyv. Hungarian (English and Russian). One time a year. Hungarian Central Statistical Office, Keleti Karoly Utca, PO Box 51, H-1525 Budapest Hungary. **Tel** 011 36 1 2024011.

LC HF1044.J3 N54C
DD 380 JA

YUNYU TOKEI HIMMOKU HYO. **Main/Corp** Nihon Kanzei Kyokai. **VFOAT** Import Statistical Schedule, Japan. Multiple languages (English and Japanese). One time a year. $48.50. OCS America Inc, 14th & F Street NW, Washington DC 20045. **Tel** (202)347-4233.

LC HF1044.J3 N54b
DD 338.02 JA

YUSHUTSU TOKEI HIMMOKU HYO = EXPORT STATISTICAL SCHEDULE, JAPAN. **Main/Corp** Nihon Kanzei Kyokai. **Added/Corp** Nihon Kanzei Kyokai. Export Statistical Schedule: Japan. **VFOAT** Export Statistical Schedule: Japan. (19??)-. Statistical Publication. Japanese (English). $36.06 Europe; $20.06 Japan; $32.06 other. Japan Tariff Association Ed, 4-7-8 Kojimachi Chiyoda ku, Tokyo Japan. **Tel** 011 81 3 3263 7221.

LC HB235.P6 Z6 **ISSN** 1230-5782
DD 338.52 PL

ZMIANY CEN W GOSPODARCE NARODOWEJ W ... . **Added/Corp** Poland. Glowny Urzad Statystyczny. Departament Cen. (1989)-. Government Publication. Polish. Irregular. Zaklad Wydawnictw Statystycznych, Al. Niepodleglosci 208, 00-925 Warsaw Poland. **Tel** 011 48 22 250345, telex 814581 A GUS PL. ctrl circ.

ACCOUNTING

LC HF5601 .A136 **ISSN** 0001-3072
DD 657/.05 AT
CCC
CODEN ABACAF

ABACUS (SYDNEY). (ABACUS.). [Abacus]. Vol. 1, No. 1 (Sept. 1965)-. Academic Scholarly Publication. English. Two times a year. $111.00. Basil Blackwell Publishers Ltd., 108 Cowley Road, Oxford 0X4 1JF United Kingdom. **Tel** 011 44 1235 465500, FAX 011 44 1235 465556, telex 837022 OXBOOK G. **(Subscription address:** Blackwell Publishers / UK, 108 Cowley Road, Oxford OX4 1JF United Kingdom. **Tel** 011 44 1865 791100, FAX 011 44 1865 791347.**) ED** M C Wells. Index available. **Ad Acc. Circ:** 1,000 (ctrl). available on microfilm and microfiche from University Microfilms International (UMI); available on an online database from OCLC EPIC; ORBIT; ESA-IRS; DIALOG; and (INFO) BRS. Documents available from The Genuine Article, BIOSIS Document Express, UMI Article Clearinghouse.
Desc: Publishes exploratory, constructive and critical articles on accounting and the administration of organizations, particularly related to accounting and finance.
Ind/Abst ABI/INFORM Glob. Ed. (June 1976-); ABI/INFORM [Computer File] (June 1976-); Account. Tax Datab. (1974-); Account. Art.; Anbar Account. Finan. Abstr. [Full Txt.]; Anbar Mark. Distr. Abstr. [Full Txt.]; Anbar Top Manage. Abstr. [Full Txt.]; APAIS, Aust. Public Aff. Inf. Ser. (1972-); Curr. Contents Soc. Behav. Sci.; Gen. BusinessFile (1992-); Manage. Market. Abstr.; Manage. Bibliogr. Rev.; Oper. Prod. Manage. Abstr. [Full Txt.]; PAIS Int. Print; Person. Train. Abstr. [Full Txt.]; Res. Alert [Full Cov.]; Selec. Coop. Index Manage. Period.; UMI ABI/Inform--Bus. Period. Ondisc (March 1988-) [Full Txt.]; Women Manage. Rev. [Full Txt.].

LC HF5601 **ISSN** 0001-4672
DD 657 UK
CODEN AAGEEE

ACCOUNTANCY AGE. [Acc. age]. (19??)-. Trade Publication. English. One time a week. $205.35. VNU Business Publications BV, 32-34 Broadwick Street, London W1A 2HG United Kingdom. **Tel** 011 44 171 4394242 ext. 2222, FAX 011 44 171 4379638, telex 23918 VNU G, 8952440. available on microfilm and microfiche from University Microfilms International (UMI); available on an online database from DIALOG.
Ind/Abst Account. Tax Datab. (Sept. 17, 1992-); Anbar Account. Finan. Abstr. [Full Txt.]; Anbar Mark. Distr. Abstr. [Full Txt.]; Anbar Top Manage. Abstr. [Full Txt.]; Manage. Bibliogr. Rev.; Oper. Prod. Manage. Abstr. [Full Txt.]; Person. Train. Abstr. [Full Txt.]; Women Manage. Rev. [Full Txt.].

LC HF5601 **ISSN** 0001-4699
DD 657 IE

ACCOUNTANCY IRELAND. [Accountancy Irel.]. **Added/Corp** Institute of Chartered Accountants in Ireland. Vol. 1 (1969)-. Periodical. English. Six times a year. $40.00. Institute of Chartered Accountants in Ireland, Chartered Accountants House, 87-89 Pembroke Road, Dublin 4 Ireland. **Tel** 6680400, FAX 6680842, telex 30567. **ED** Charles O'Rourke. Index available. cum. index. **Bk Rev**, (Qty: 12-20). **Ad Acc. Circ:** 17,000. available on an online database; available on microfilm and microfiche from University Microfilms International (UMI). Documents available from UMI Article Clearinghouse.
Ind/Abst ABI/INFORM Glob. Ed.; Account. Tax Datab. (1974-); Anbar Account. Finan. Abstr. [Full Txt.]; Anbar Mark. Distr. Abstr. [Full Txt.]; Anbar Top Manage. Abstr. [Full Txt.]; Manage. Bibliogr. Rev.; Oper. Prod. Manage. Abstr. [Full Txt.]; Person. Train. Abstr. [Full Txt.]; Women Manage. Rev. [Full Txt.].

LC HF5601 .S6 **ISSN** 0001-4664
DD 657/.05 UK
CODEN ACTYAD

ACCOUNTANCY (LONDON). (ACCOUNTANCY.). [Accountancy]. **Added/Corp** Society of Incorporated Accountants and Auditors (Great Britain) Society of Incorporated Accountants (Great Britain) Institute of Chartered Accountants in England and Wales. Vol. 50, No. 542 (1938)-. Trade Publication. English. Twelve times a year. $107.81. Institute of Chartered Accountants, 399 Silbury Boulevard, Central Milton, Keynes Buckinghamshire MK9 2HL United Kingdom. **Tel** 011 44 1908 248100, FAX 011 44 1908 248001, telex 727530. **ED** Brian Singleton-Green. Index available. cum. index. **Bk Rev. Ad Acc. Circ:** 74,500. available on microfilm and microfiche from University Microfilms International (UMI); available on an online database from DIALOG. Documents available from Ask*IEEE, UMI Article Clearinghouse. ***Continues*** *Incorporated Accountants' Journal;* ***Absorbed*** *Accounting Research.*
Desc: News and features on accounting, tax, finance, law, auditing and management.
Ind/Abst ABI/INFORM Glob. Ed. (Nov. 1972-); ABI/INFORM [Computer File] (Nov. 1972-); Acad. Search; Account. Tax Datab. (Nov. 1972-) [Full Txt.]; Account. Art.; Anbar Account. Finan. Abstr. [Full Txt.]; Anbar Mark. Distr. Abstr. [Full Txt.]; Bus. Index (1985-); Bus. Period. Index; Bus. Source Plus; Bus. Source; Contents Pages Manage.; Curr. Cit.; EP Collect.; Gen. BusinessFile (1985-); Gen. Period. Index (1985-); Homework Help.; INFO-SOUTH Abstr.; INSPEC (July 1983-); Mag. Search; Manage. Market. Abstr.; Manage. Bibliogr. Rev.; Manage. Contents; MasterFile FullTEXT 1000; MasterFile FullTEXT 350; MasterFile FullTEXT 650; MasterFile FullTEXT (July 1993-); OCLC; Oper. Prod. Manage. Abstr. [Full Txt.]; Person. Train. Abstr. [Full Txt.]; Selec. Coop. Index Manage. Period.; Telebase; Trade Ind. Index; Wilson Bus. Abstr.; Women Manage. Rev. [Full Txt.].

LC HF5601 **ISSN** 0258-7254
DD 657 SA

ACCOUNTANCY SA. [Account. SA]. **VFOAT** Rekeningkunde SA. **VAT** Accountancy S.A. Vol. 1, No. 1 (Sept. 1983)-. Trade Publication. English (Afrikaans). Twelve times a year. $29.52. South African Chartered Accountants, PO Box 59875, Kengray 2100 South Africa. **Tel** 011 27 11 6226655, FAX 011 27 11) 8343071, telex 489529SA. **ED** Laraine Flood. Index available. **Bk Rev. Ad Acc. Circ:** 18,000 (ctrl). available in microform. ***Continues*** *South African Chartered Accountant.*
Desc: Covers anything of interest to chartered accountants in public practice of commerce and industry. Articles on accounting, auditing, general business, computers, legal matters, etc.

LC HF5601 **ISSN** 0001-4729
DD 657 NE

ACCOUNTANT (AMSTERDAM). (DE ACCOUNTANT.). [Accountant]. **Added/Corp** Nederlandsch Instituut van Accountants. Vol. 1 (1895)-. Periodical. Dutch. Eleven times a year. $51.39. Nederlands Inst Van Reg Accountant, PO Box 7984, 1008 AD Amsterdam Netherlands. **Tel** 011 31 20 6464046. available on an online database. Documents available from UMI Article Clearinghouse.
Ind/Abst ABI/INFORM [Computer File] (July 1981-).

LC HF5601 .A14 **ISSN** 0001-4710
DD 657 UK
CCC

ACCOUNTANT (LONDON). (THE ACCOUNTANT.). [Account.]. Vol. 1 (Oct. 1874)-. Trade Publication. English. Twenty-six times a year. $449.00. Lafferty Publications Ltd., Tower Ida Centre Pearse Street, Dublin 2 Ireland. **Tel** 011 353 1 6718022, FAX 011 353 1 718520. available on microfilm and microfiche from University Microfilms International (UMI); available on an online database. Documents available from Ask*IEEE. ***Absorbed*** *UK Accounting Bulletin.*
Desc: Directed at senior accountants in countries which share the Anglo-Saxon accounting tradition. Covers financial reporting, the accountancy profession, corporate finance, corporate recovery and insolvency, tax, personal financial planning, information technology, legislation, and business.
Ind/Abst Anbar Account. Finan. Abstr. [Full Txt.]; Anbar Mark. Distr. Abstr. [Full Txt.]; Anbar Top Manage. Abstr. [Full Txt.]; Contents Pages Manage.; INSPEC (Aug. 1983-Oct. 1988); Manage. Bibliogr. Rev.; Oper. Prod. Manage. Abstr. [Full Txt.]; Person. Train. Abstr. [Full Txt.]; Trade Ind. Index; Women Manage. Rev. [Full Txt.].

LC HF5601 **ISSN** 1010-4135
DD 657 KE

ACCOUNTANT (NAIROBI), THE. (THE ACCOUNTANT : THE JOURNAL OF THE INSTITUTE OF CERTIFIED PUBLIC ACCOUNTANTS OF KENYA.). [Accountant]. **Added/Corp** Institute of Certified Public Accountants of Kenya. (1980)-. Trade Publication. English. Four times a year. Institute of Certified Public Accountants of Kenya, PO Box 59963, Nairobi Kenya. **Tel** 011 254 2 224629, FAX 011 254 2 211563. **ED** Board. **Bk Rev. Ad Acc. Circ:** 14,000 (ctrl).
Ind/Abst Account. Index Suppl.

LC HF5601 ISSN 0307-0336
DD 657 UK

ACCOUNTANTS DIGEST (LONDON, ENGLAND). (ACCOUNTANTS DIGEST.). [Account. dig.]. **Added/Corp** Institute of Chartered Accountants in England and Wales. Technical Services Dept. (19??)-. Periodical. English. Eighteen times a year. $461.17. Institute of Chartered Accountants, 399 Silbury Boulevard, Central Milton, Keynes Buckinghamshire MK9 2HL United Kingdom. **Tel** 011 44 1908 248100, FAX 011 44 1908 248001, telex 727530.
Desc: Provides an overview of the latest legislation, regulations, standards, and practice and financial management issues.
Ind/Abst Contents Pages Manage. (19??-); Curr. Cit.

LC HF5601 .P5333 ISSN 0001-4753
DD 657.05 PH

ACCOUNTANTS' JOURNAL. (THE ACCOUNTANTS' JOURNAL.). [Account. j.]. **Added/Corp** Philippine Institute of Certified Public Accountants. Philippine Institute of Accountants. (1952)-. Trade Publication. English. Two times a year. $22.00. Philippines Institute of Accountants, PO Box 1440, Manila Philippines. **Bk Rev. Ad Acc.** ctrl circ. available on an online database.
Desc: Accounting issues and developments in the Philippines.
Ind/Abst Account. Art.; Index Philip. Period.

LC HF5601 .A19 ISSN 0001-4745
DD 657.05 NZ
CCC
TITLE CHANGE

ACCOUNTANTS' JOURNAL (WELLINGTON). (THE ACCOUNTANTS' JOURNAL.). [Account. j.]. **Added/Corp** New Zealand Society of Accountants. Vol. 1 (1922)-(19??). Trade Publication. English. New Zealand Society of Accountants, PO Box 11342, Wellington New Zealand. **Tel** 011 64 4 4738544, FAX 011 64 4 726282. **ED** A. McLeod. Index available. **Bk Rev. Ad Acc. Circ:** 13,214. available on an online database. Documents available from UMI Article Clearinghouse. ***Continued by*** *Chartered Accountants Journal of New Zealand, 1172-9929.*
Ind/Abst ABI/INFORM Glob. Ed.; Account. Tax Datab. (1974-); Anbar Account. Finan. Abstr. [Full Txt.]; Anbar Mark. Distr. Abstr. [Full Txt.]; Anbar Top Manage. Abstr. [Full Txt.]; Curr. Cit.; Manage. Bibliogr. Rev.; Oper. Prod. Manage. Abstr. [Full Txt.]; Person. Train. Abstr. [Full Txt.]; Women Manage. Rev. [Full Txt.].

LC KF2920.3.Z9 A25 ISSN 8756-4262
DD 346.7303/3 347.30633 US

ACCOUNTANTS' LIABILITY. [Account. liabil.]. **Added/Corp** Practising Law Institute. (19??)-. English. One time a year (July or Aug.). $70.00. Practising Law Institute, 810 Seventh Avenue, New York NY 10019-5818. **Tel** (212)765-5700, FAX (212)581-4670 general correspondence, (212)265-4742 orders and billing inquiries. available on an online database.

LC HF5601 .A22 ISSN 0001-4761
DD 657/.05 UK
TITLE CHANGE

ACCOUNTANT'S MAGAZINE, THE. [Account. mag.]. Vol. 1 (1897)-(19??). Periodical. English (Japanese). Institute of Chartered Accountants, 399 Silbury Boulevard, Central Milton, Keynes Buckinghamshire MK9 2HL United Kingdom. **Tel** 011 44 1908 248100, FAX 011 44 1908 248001, telex 727530. **ED** Winifred Elliott. Index available in last issue of volume--attached. **Bk Rev. Ad Acc. Circ:** 13,500 (ctrl). available on an online database; available on microfilm and microfiche from University Microfilms International (UMI). Documents available from Ask*IEEE. ***Merged into*** *CA Magazine.*
Desc: Authoritative articles on topics of interest to accountants in practice and industry. Covers areas such as: business, finance, marketing, management and information technology as well as accounting and auditing. Features tax cases, developments in legislation, technical updates and book reviews, and profiles of interesting people in business.
Ind/Abst Acad. Search; Account. Art.; Anbar Account. Finan. Abstr. [Full Txt.]; Anbar Mark. Distr. Abstr. [Full Txt.]; Anbar Top Manage. Abstr. [Full Txt.]; Bus. Index (1985-); Bus. Source Plus; Bus. Source; Contents Pages Manage.; EP Collect.; Gen. BusinessFile (1985-); Gen. Period. Index (1985-); Homework Help.; INSPEC (1983-); Mag. Search; Manage. Bibliogr. Rev.; Manage. Contents; MasterFile FullTEXT 1000; MasterFile FullTEXT 350; MasterFile FullTEXT 650; MasterFile FullTEXT; OCLC; Oper. Prod. Manage. Abstr. [Full Txt.]; Person. Train. Abstr. [Full Txt.]; Telebase; Trade Ind. Index; Women Manage. Rev. [Full Txt.].

LC HF5601 ISSN 1059-7654
DD 657 US

ACCOUNTANT'S TAX WEEKLY. [Account. tax wkly.]. (19??)-. Periodical. English. One time a week. $223.32. Bureau of Business Practice, 24 Rope Ferry Road, Waterford CT 06386. **Tel** (800)243-0876, (203)442-4365, (800)876-9105, FAX (203)443-1123. ***Continues*** *Accountant's Weekly Tax Report, 1049-1139.*

LC HF5601 ISSN 1049-1139
DD 657 US
TITLE CHANGE

ACCOUNTANT'S WEEKLY TAX REPORT. [Account. wkly. tax rep.]. (198?)-(19??). Periodical. English. ***Continues*** *Accountant's Weekly Report.* ***Continued by*** *Accountant's Tax Weekly, 1059-7654.*

LC HF5601 ISSN 1037-1869
DD 657.099405 AT

ACCOUNTING & ASC COMPLIANCE. [Account. ASC compliance]. **VFOAT** Accounting and Australian Securities Commission Compliance.; Accountant's & Corporate Affairs Alert. (1991)-. Periodical. English. Eleven times a year. 152.11Aus$. Centre for Professional Development, 100 Albert Road, South Melbourne Victoria 3205 Australia. **Tel** 011 61 3 6903933, FAX 011 61 3 6962757. ***Continues*** *Accountant's and ASC Alert, 1036-1510.*
Desc: This publication provides news on the TPC, FIRB, AASB, AARF, along with illustrated examples, changes to ASC requirements, plus relevant court decisions and new corporate legislation.

LC HF5658 .A23 ISSN 0737-3325
DD 657 US

ACCOUNTING AND AUDITING DISCLOSURE MANUAL. [Account. audit. discl. man.]. **Added/Corp** Warren, Gorham & Lamont, inc. (1983)-. English. One time a year. $130.00. Warren Gorham & Lamont Inc., Park Square Building, 31 St. James Avenue, Boston MA 02116-4112. **Tel** (617)423-2020, (800)950-1207, FAX (617)423-2026.

LC HG ISSN 1045-1447
DD 332 US
CCC

ACCOUNTING & AUDITING UPDATE SERVICE. (ACCOUNTING & AUDITING UPDATE SERVICE.). [Account. audit. update serv.]. **VFOAT** Accounting and Auditing Update Service. (19??)-. Periodical. English. Forty-eight times a year. $284.25. Warren Gorham & Lamont Inc., Park Square Building, 31 St. James Avenue, Boston MA 02116-4112. **Tel** (617)423-2020, (800)950-1207, FAX (617)423-2026. **ED** Paul Wendell. **Circ:** 1400.
Desc: Provides straight forward analysis and interpretation of all new FASB pronouncements as they are issued.

LC HF5601 ISSN 0001-4788
DD 657 UK
Pr Rev.

ACCOUNTING AND BUSINESS RESEARCH. [Account. bus. res.]. **Added/Corp** Institute of Chartered Accountants in England and Wales. Vol. 1 (Winter 1970)-. Academic Scholarly Publication. English. Four times a year. $150.59. Institute of Chartered Accountants, 399 Silbury Boulevard, Central Milton, Keynes Buckinghamshire MK9 2HL United Kingdom. **Tel** 011 44 1908 248100, FAX 011 44 1908 248001, telex 727530. **ED** Bob Parker. Index available (free). **Ad Acc. Circ:** 1,500. available on an online database; available on microfilm and microfiche from University Microfilms International (UMI). Documents available from Ask*IEEE, FAXON Xpress, The UnCover Company, SWETS, UMI Article Clearinghouse.
Desc: Academic accounting research papers.
Ind/Abst ABI/INFORM Glob. Ed.; ABI/INFORM [Computer File] (Winter 1982-); Acad. Search; Account. Tax Datab. (1974-); Anbar Account. Finan. Abstr. [Full Txt.]; Anbar Mark. Distr. Abstr. [Full Txt.]; Anbar Top Manage. Abstr. [Full Txt.]; Bus. Index (Jan. 1985-Dec. 1985); Bus. Period. Index; Bus. Source Plus; Bus. Source; Coal Abstr.; Contents Recent Econ. J.; Contents Pages Manage.; Curr. Cit.; EP Collect.; Gen. BusinessFile (Jan. 1985-Dec. 1985); Gen. Period. Index (Jan. 1985-Dec. 1985); Homework Help.; INFO-SOUTH Abstr.; INSPEC (1984-1985); Mag. Search; Manage. Market. Abstr.; MasterFile FullTEXT 1000; MasterFile FullTEXT 350; MasterFile FullTEXT 650; MasterFile FullTEXT (July 1993-); OCLC; Oper. Prod. Manage. Abstr. [Full Txt.]; Person. Train. Abstr. [Full Txt.]; Selec. Coop. Index Manage. Period.; Telebase; UMI ABI/Inform--Bus. Period. Ondisc (Fall 1987-) [Full Txt.]; Wilson Bus. Abstr.; Women Manage. Rev. [Full Txt.].

LC HF5601 ISSN 0218-5563
DD 657 SI
Pr Rev.

●**ACCOUNTING AND BUSINESS REVIEW.** **Added/Corp** Nanyang Technological University. School of Accountancy & Business. Vol. 1, No. 1 (Jan. 1994)-. Periodical. English. Two times a year. $60.00. World Scientific Publishing Company, PO Box 128, Farrer Road, Singapore 9128 Singapore. **Tel** 011 65 3825663, FAX 011 65 3825919, telex RS 28561 WSPC. **(Subscription address:** World Scientific Publishing Company, Inc., 1060 Main Street, Suite 1 B, River Edge NJ 07661. **Tel** (800)227-7562, (201)487-9655.**)** **ED** Pang Yang Hoong.
Desc: Provides a forum between practitioners and academics and features issues on contemporary business practices and theories.

LC HF5601 ISSN 0110-5159
DD 657 AT
Pr Rev.

ACCOUNTING AND FINANCE. (ACCOUNTING AND FINANCE : JOURNAL OF THE ACCOUNTING ASSOCIATION OF AUSTRALIA AND NEW ZEALAND.). [Account. finance]. **Added/Corp** Accounting Association of Australia and New Zealand. Vol. 19, No. 1 (May 1979)-. Periodical. English. Two times a year (May & Nov.). 82.22Aus$. Accounting Association of Australia and New Zealand, c/o Department of Accounting and Finance, Faculty of Economics and Commerce, University of Melbourne, Parkville Victoria 3052 Australia. **Tel** 011 61 3 3471727, FAX 011 61 3 3471727, telex AA40315. **ED** Professor Peter Brownell. Index available. **Bk Rev**, (Qty: varies). **Ad Acc, Adv Mgr:** Effie Margiolis. **Circ:** 1,200 (ctrl). available on microfilm and microfiche from University Microfilms International (UMI); available on CD-ROM. Documents available from UMI Article Clearinghouse. ***Continues*** *Accounting Education.*
Desc: Includes articles in accounting, finance, information systems and commercial law.
Ind/Abst ABI/INFORM Glob. Ed.; ABI/INFORM [Computer File] (Nov. 1984-); Account. Tax Datab. (1979-); Account. Art.; Bus. ASAP (1992-) [Full Txt.]; Bus. Index (1985-); Curr. Cit.; Gen. BusinessFile (1985-); Gen. Period. Index (1985-); INFO-SOUTH Abstr.; Mag. Search; Manage. Contents; Res. High. Educ. Abstr.; Trade Ind. Index; UMI ABI/Inform--Bus. Period. Ondisc (May 1988-) [Full Txt.].

LC HF5604 ISSN 0810-5391
DD 657 AT

ACCOUNTING AND FINANCE PARKVILLE. (1979)-. Periodical. English. Two times a year (May, Nov.). 60.00Aus$ (institutions); 35.00Aus$ (individuals). Accounting Association of Australia and New Zealand, Melbourne University, Accounting & Finance Department, Parkville VIC 3052 Australia. **Tel** 011 61 3 3471727, FAX 011 61 3 3471727, telex AA40315. **ED** Professor Peter Brownell. **Bk Rev**, (Qty: varies). **Ad Acc. Circ:** 1,300 (ctrl). available on an online database. Documents available from The UnCover Company.
Ind/Abst Acad. Search; Bus. Source Plus; Bus. Source; EP Collect.; Homework Help.; MasterFile FullTEXT 1000; MasterFile FullTEXT 350; MasterFile FullTEXT 650; MasterFile FullTEXT (Jan. 1993-); OCLC; Telebase.

LC HF5635 .A224
DD 657 US

●**ACCOUNTING & TAX DATABASE [COMPUTER FILE].** See Business and Economics-Abstracting, Bibliographies and Statistics.

LC Z7164.C81 A224 HF5635 ISSN 1063-0287
DD 016.657 US

ACCOUNTING AND TAX INDEX. See Business and Economics-Abstracting, Bibliographies and Statistics.

LC Z7164.C81 C782a HF563
DD 016.657 US

ACCOUNTING ARTICLES. See Business and Economics-Abstracting, Bibliographies and Statistics.

LC HF5601
DD 657 UK

ACCOUNTING, AUDITING & ACCOUNTABILITY JOURNAL. **VFOAT** Accounting, Auditing and Accountability Journal; AAAJ. Vol. 2, No. 1 (1989)-. Periodical. English. Four times a year. $499.00. MCB University Press, 60 62 Toller Lane, Bradford, West Yorkshire BD8 9BY United Kingdom. **Tel** 011 44 1274 785280, FAX 011 44 1274 785200, telex 51317-MCBUNI-G. **(Subscription address:** MCB University Press / US and Canada Subscriptions, PO Box 10812, Birmingham AL 35201-0812. **Tel** (205)995-1567, (800)633-4931, FAX (205)995-1588.**)** ***Continues*** *Accounting, Auditing, & Accountability.*
Desc: Aims to publish research that examines accounting and auditing practice and policy from critical, interdisciplinary and historical perspectives. Encourages consideration of the philosophies and traditions that underpin thought and practice - and of the impacts of accountancy upon the socioeconomic and political environment.
Ind/Abst Account. Tax Datab. (1992-) [Full Txt.]; Curr. Cit.

LC HF5341 .A33 ISSN 0958-5206
DD 657 UK
CCC

ACCOUNTING BUSINESS AND FINANCIAL HISTORY. **VFOAT** Accounting, Business and Financial History. Vol. 1, No. 1 (Oct. 1990)-. Periodical. English. Three times a year. $148.00. Routledge, 11 New Fetter Lane, London EC4P 4EE United Kingdom. **Tel** 011 44 171 5839855, FAX 011 44 171 5830701. **(Subscription address:** Kinokuniya Company Ltd., 38-1 Sakuragaoka 5, chome Setagaya-ku, Tokyo 156 Japan. **Tel** FAX 011 03 3439 0136.**)**

LC HD28 ISSN 1042-928X
DD 658 US
CCC

ACCOUNTING DEPARTMENT MANAGEMENT & ADMINISTRATION REPORT.
[Account. dep. manage. adm. rep.]. **Added/Corp** Institute of Management & Administration. **VFOAT** Accounting Department Management and Administration Report. (1989)-. Periodical. English. Twelve times a year. $245.00. Institute of Management and Administration, 29 West 35th Street, 5th Floor, New York NY 10001-2299. **Tel** (212)244-0360, FAX (212)564-0465.

LC HF5601 ISSN 0963-9284
DD 657 UK
CCC

ACCOUNTING EDUCATION.
Added/Corp Chartered Association of Certified Accountants (Great Britain) Chartered Institute of Management Accountants. Consultative Committee of Accountancy Bodies. Vol. 1, No. 1 (Mar. 1992)-. Periodical. English. Four times a year. $232.00. Chapman & Hall, 2-6 Boundary Row, London SE1 8HN United Kingdom. **Tel** 011 44 171 8650066, FAX 011 44 171 5229623, telex 290164 CHAPMA G.
Desc: Devoted to publishing research-based papers and information on key aspects of accounting education and training. Provides a unique forum for the exchange of ideas, experiences, opinions and research results relating to the educational base of accounting practice. Publishes innovative teaching resource material that can be used by readers in their own institutions.

LC HF5601
DD 657.07 US

•ACCOUNTING EDUCATION.
(1996)-. Academic Scholarly Publication. English. Two times a year. $125.00. JAI Press Inc., 55 Old Post Road, Suite 2, PO Box 1678, Greenwich CT 06836-1678. **Tel** (203)661-7602, FAX (203)661-0792. **ED** Bill N. Schwartz and David E. Stout.

LC HD28 ISSN 0882-956X
DD 658 US

ACCOUNTING EDUCATION NEWS.
[Account. educ. news]. **Added/Corp** American Accounting Association. (197?)-. Periodical. English. Irregular (6 times a year). $30.00. American Accounting Association, 5717 Bessie Drive, Sarasota FL 34223. **Tel** (813)921-7747. **ED** Paul L. Gerhardt. **Ad Acc.**
Desc: News and information for accountants and accounting educators about events and programs of the American Accounting Association.
Ind/Abst Account. Tax Datab. (1981-).

LC WMLC 93/1768 HF5630 .A32 ISSN 1041-0392
DD 657 US
Pr Rev.

ACCOUNTING EDUCATORS' JOURNAL, THE.
[Account. educ. j.]. **Added/Corp** American Accounting Association. University of Nevada, Las Vegas. Vol. 1, No. 1 (Spring 1988)-. Periodical. English. Two times a year (Spring & Fall). $40.00. Accounting Educators Journal / Department of Accounting, University of Idaho, Moscow ID 83843. **Tel** (208)885-7602, FAX (208)885-8939. **ED** Jeff Harkins (phone: (208)882-9170). cum. index. **Ad Acc. Circ:** 450 (ctrl).
Desc: Primary purpose is to provide a means for accounting educators to communicate about matters relevant to the design, delivery, and assessment of the educational process.
Ind/Abst Account. Art.

LC HF5601 ISSN 1183-904X
DD 657/.05 CN

ACCOUNTING ENQUIRIES.
[Acc. enq.]. Vol. 1, No. 1 (Aug. 1991)-. Periodical. English. Two times a year. 80.00Can$. Stanversal Publishing, Business Manager, 117 Courtlands Drive, Scarborough Ontario M1B 4N1 Canada.

LC KF320.A2 A27 ISSN 0898-8102
DD 657 US

ACCOUNTING FOR LAW FIRMS.
[Account. law firms]. **VFOAT** Accounting. Vol. 1, No. 1 (Jan. 1988)-. Periodical. English. Twelve times a year. $110.00. Leader Publications, 345 Park Avenue South, New York NY 10010. **Tel** (800)888-8300 ext. 6170, (212)545-6170, FAX (212)696-1848. **ED** Mark Hopkins. Index available. cum. index.
Desc: Collection of information, techniques and strategies developed by legal accounting experts.

LC HF5601 ISSN 0155-9982
DD 657 AT
Pr Rev.

ACCOUNTING FORUM (ADELAIDE, S. AUST.).
(ACCOUNTING FORUM.). [Account. forum]. **VFOAT** AF. (19??)-. Periodical. English. Four times a year (Mar., June., Sept., Dec.). 49.34Aus$. South Australia Institute of Technology, School of Accountancy, PO Box 2471, GPO Adelaide, South Australia 5001 Australia. **Tel** 011 61 8 3022309, FAX 011 61 8 2235060, telex 82565. **ED** R. W. Peacock. **Ad Acc.** Documents available from UMI Article Clearinghouse.
Desc: Items of interest to accountants, academics and students and others interested in accounting. A bridge between accounting education and practice.
Ind/Abst ABI/INFORM Glob. Ed.; APAIS, Aust. Public Aff. Inf. Ser. (1982-).

LC HF5601 .A34 ISSN 0148-4184
DD 657/.09 US
Pr Rev.

ACCOUNTING HISTORIANS JOURNAL, THE.
[Account. hist. j.]. **Added/Corp** Academy of Accounting Historians. Vol. 4 (Spring 1977)-. Periodical. English. Two times a year. $44.00 (institutions), $34.00 (individuals) 1993; $46.00 (institutions), $36.00 (individuals). Academy Accounting Historian, University of Arkansas, Building 204, Fayetteville AR 72701. **Tel** (501)575-6125. Index available. cum. index. **Bk Rev. Circ:** 850 (ctrl). available on an online database. ***Continues** Accounting Historian.*
Desc: Refereed papers on accounting history and accounting history research.
Ind/Abst Account. Tax Datab. (1977-); Account. Art.; Am. Hist. Life (1989-).

LC HF5601 .A344 ISSN 1075-1416
DD 657/.09 US

ACCOUNTING HISTORIANS NOTEBOOK, THE.
[Account. hist. noteb.]. **Added/Corp** Academy of Accounting Historians. **VFOAT** Notebook. Vol. 1, No. 1 (Spring 1978)-. Periodical. English. Two times a year (Spring & Fall). $4.00. Academy of Accounting Historians, University Arkansas, Building 204, Fayetteville AR 72701. **Tel** (501)575-6125. **ED** Elliott L. Slocum (editor's address: School of Accountancy, Georgia State University, University Plaza, Atlanta, GA 30303). **Bk Rev. Circ:** 1,000 (ctrl).
Desc: History of accounting, taxation and accountants.

LC HF5616.U5 A33 ISSN 0888-7993
DD 657/.0973 US

ACCOUNTING HORIZONS.
[Account. horiz.]. **Added/Corp** American Accounting Association. Vol. 1, No. 1 (March 1987)-. Periodical. English. Four times a year. $60.00. American Accounting Association, 5717 Bessie Drive, Sarasota FL 34233-2399. **Tel** (813)921-7747, FAX (813)923-4093. available on microfilm and microfiche from University Microfilms International (UMI); available on an online database from DIALOG. Documents available from UMI Article Clearinghouse.
Desc: A forum for the exchange of ideas and views surrounding the practice of public accounting, management accounting, and the development of accounting policies and procedures.
Ind/Abst ABI/INFORM Glob. Ed.; ABI/INFORM [Computer File] (Dec. 1987-); Acad. Search; Account. Tax Datab. (Dec. 1987-) [Full Txt.]; Account. Art.; Bus. Period. Index; Bus. Source Plus; Bus. Source; Curr. Cit.; EP Collect.; Fed. Tax Artic.; Homework Help.; INFO-SOUTH Abstr.; Mag. Search; MasterFile FullTEXT 1000; MasterFile FullTEXT 350; MasterFile FullTEXT 650; MasterFile FullTEXT (July 1993-); OCLC; Telebase; UMI ABI/Inform--Bus. Period. Ondisc (Dec. 1987-) [Full Txt.]; Wilson Bus. Abstr.

LC HD28 ISSN 0882-9551
DD 658 US

ACCOUNTING ISSUES.
[Account. issues]. **Main/Corp** Bear, Stearns & Co. Periodical. English. One time a week. Bear Stearns & Company, Investment Research, 55 Water Street, New York NY 10041. **Tel** (212)272-2000. available on an online database.

LC HF5601 .A36 ISSN 0126-625X
DD 657 MY

ACCOUNTING JOURNAL, THE.
[Account. j.]. Vol. 1 (1970/71)-. Multiple languages (English and Malay). Irregular. University of Maylaya Accounting Club, Faculty of Economics and Administration, Kuala Lumpur 22-11 Malaysia.

LC HF5601 ISSN 0198-7283
DD 657 US

ACCOUNTING JOURNAL (NEW YORK), THE.
(THE ACCOUNTING JOURNAL.). **VFOAT** Accounting Journal of the Northeast Region. Vol. 1 (Spring 1977)-. Periodical. English. Two times a year. $20.00 institutions, $7.00 individuals, $5.00 students. Northeast Regional Group of the American Accounting Association, PO Box 1761 Grand Central Station, New York NY 10017. available on an online database from Federal Document Retrieval.

LC HF5679 .A342 ISSN 0959-8022
DD 658.15/11/05 US
CCC

ACCOUNTING, MANAGEMENT, AND INFORMATION TECHNOLOGIES.
Vol. 1, No. 1 (1991)-. Periodical. English. Four times a year (1 volume). $342.00. Pergamon Press, An Imprint of Elsevier Science Ltd., The Boulevard, Langford Lane, Kidlington, Oxford OX5 1GB United Kingdom. **Tel** 011 44 1865 843000, 011 44 1865 843699, FAX 011 44 1865 843010. **(Subscription address:** Elsevier Science Ltd. / Oxford Fulfillment Centre, PO Box 800, Kidlington OX5 1DX United Kingdom. **Tel** 011 44 865 843355.**) ED** Richard Boland, Jr. and Ted O'Leary. available on microfilm and microfiche from University Microfilms International (UMI); available on an online database from Elsevier Electronic Subscriptions (EES).
Desc: An international journal offering a forum for research on the interrelations of information technologies with accounting and control systems and with management practices and policies. The journal invites a broad range of analyses of these interrelated technologies as well as a critical questioning of them from such fields as philosophy, anthropology, law, and social and political theory. Of special concern is the design, deployment and use of information technologies in the practice of accounting or management, including, but not limited to, expert systems, integrated manufacturing, individual and group decision support, performance monitoring and collaborative work.

LC HF5601 ISSN 0749-2928
DD 657 US
CCC

ACCOUNTING OFFICE MANAGEMENT & ADMINISTRATION REPORT.
[Account. off. manage. adm. rep.]. **Added/Corp** Institute for Office Management and Administration (U.S.). **VFOAT** Accounting Office Management and Administration Report. (19??)-. Periodical. English. Twelve times a year. $245.00. Institute of Management and Administration, 29 West 35th Street, 5th Floor, New York NY 10001-2299. **Tel** (212)244-0360, FAX (212)564-0465. **ED** David L. Foster. Index available.
Desc: Newsletter on all aspects of managing an accounting firm including personnel, financial management, professional news, automation, insurance, and more.

LC HF5601 .A365 ISSN 0361-3682
DD 657/.05 UK
CCC
CODEN AOSOPB
Pr Rev.

ACCOUNTING, ORGANIZATIONS AND SOCIETY.
[Account. organ. soc.]. (1976)-. Periodical. English. Eight times a year (1 volume). $897.00. Pergamon Press, An Imprint of Elsevier Science Ltd., The Boulevard, Langford Lane, Kidlington, Oxford OX5 1GB United Kingdom. **Tel** 011 44 1865 843000, 011 44 1865 843699, FAX 011 44 1865 843010. **(Subscription address:** Elsevier Science Ltd. / Oxford Fulfillment Centre, PO Box 800, Kidlington OX5 1DX United Kingdom. **Tel** 011 44 865 843355.**) ED** Anthony G. Hopwood (editor's address: Department of Accounting and Finance, London School of Economics and Political Science, Houghton Street, London WC2A United Kingdom). available on microfilm and microfiche from University Microfilms International (UMI); available on an online database from Elsevier Electronic Subscriptions (EES); and Federal Document Retrieval. Documents available from The Genuine Article, UMI Article Clearinghouse.
Desc: Concerned with all aspects of the relationship between accounting and human behavior, organizational structures and processes, and the changing social and political environment of the enterprise. Its focus covers such topics as the social role of accounting, social accounting, social audit and accounting for scarce resources and more.
Ind/Abst ABI/INFORM Glob. Ed.; ABI/INFORM [Computer File] (Spring 1980-); Acad. Search; Account. Tax Datab. (1976-); Anbar Account. Finan. Abstr. [Full Txt.]; Anbar Mark. Distr. Abstr. [Full Txt.]; Anbar Top Manage. Abstr. [Full Txt.]; Bus. Source Plus; Bus. Source; Contents Pages Manage.; Curr. Cit.; Curr. Contents Soc. Behav. Sci.; EP Collect.; Gen. BusinessFile (1992-); Gen. Period. Index (1985-); Homework Help.; Mag. Search; Manage. Bibliogr. Rev.; Manage. Contents; MasterFile FullTEXT 1000; MasterFile FullTEXT 350; MasterFile FullTEXT 650; MasterFile FullTEXT (July 1993-); Middle East Abstr. Index; OCLC; Oper. Prod. Manage. Abstr. [Full Txt.]; Person. Train. Abstr. [Full Txt.]; Res. Alert [Full Cov.]; Selec. Coop. Index Manage. Period.; Soc. Sci. Cit. Index [Full Cov.]; Telebase; Women Manage. Rev. [Full Txt.].

LC HF5601 ISSN 0824-300X
DD 657 CN

ACCOUNTING PRINCIPLES AND PRACTICES IN CANADA AND THE UNITED STATES OF AMERICA.
[Account. princ. pract. Can. U.S.A.]. **Added/Corp** Price, Waterhouse (Firm). (1981)-. English. One time a year. Free to Clients. Price Waterhouse Company, PO Box 190, Toronto Ontario M5X 1H7 Canada. **Tel** (416)863-1133. **Bk Rev. Circ:** 5,000.
Desc: Comparison of significant accounting differences between US and Canada.

LC HF5601 ISSN 1030-9616
DD 657 AT

ACCOUNTING RESEARCH JOURNAL.
[Account. res. j.]. (1988)-. English. Two times a year (May & Oct.). 20.00Aus$. Queensland University of Technology / School of Accountancy, GPO Box 2434, Brisbane 4001 Australia. **Tel** 011 61 7 8642663. ***Continues** QIT Accounting Research Journal.*
Ind/Abst APAIS, Aust. Public Aff. Inf. Ser. (1989-).

Business and Economics — Accounting

LC HF5601 **ISSN** 0146-9800
DD 657 US
ACCOUNTING RESEARCH MONOGRAPH.
Added/Corp American Institute of Certified Public Accountants. Technical Research Division. (1975)-. Monographic series. English. Irregular. Price varies per volume. American Institute of Certified Public Accountants, Harborside Financial Center, #201 Plaza 3, Jersey City NJ 07311. **Tel** (201)938-3333, (800)862-4272, FAX (201)938-3329.

LC HF5601 .A6 **ISSN** 0001-4826
DD 657 US
CODEN ACRVAS
Pr Rev.
ACCOUNTING REVIEW, THE. [Account. rev.].
Added/Corp American Accounting Association. American Association of University Instructors in Accounting. Vol. 1 (March 1926)-. Periodical. English. Four times a year (Jan., Mar., July, Oct.). $90.00. American Accounting Association, 5717 Bessie Drive, Sarasota FL 34233-2399. **Tel** (813)921-7747, FAX (813)923-4093. **ED** William R. Kinney, Jr. (bound in Oct. issue). cum. index. **Circ:** 17,000. available on microfilm and microfiche from University Microfilms International (UMI); available on an online database. Documents available from The Genuine Article, UMI Article Clearinghouse. **Supersedes** American Association of University Instructors in Accounting. Papers and Proceedings of the Annual Meeting.
Desc: Provides accounting theory and research, business problems, and the teaching of business and accounting subjects.
Ind/Abst ABI/INFORM Glob. Ed.; ABI/INFORM [Computer File] (Oct. 1971-); Acad. Search; Account. Tax Datab. (1989-); Account. Art.; Anbar Account. Finan. Abstr. [Full Txt.]; Anbar Mark. Distr. Abstr. [Full Txt.]; Anbar Top Manage. Abstr. [Full Txt.]; Book Rev. Index; Bus. Index (1985-); Bus. Period. Index; Bus. Source Plus; Bus. Source; Comput. Lit. Index; Contents Recent Econ. J.; Contents Pages Manage.; Curr. Cit.; Curr. Contents Soc. Behav. Sci.; Econ. Lit. Index; EP Collect.; Fed. Tax Artic.; Gen. BusinessFile (1985-); Gen. Period. Index (1985-); Homework Help.; Index Period. Artic. Relat. Law; INFO-SOUTH Abstr.; J. Econ. Lit.; Mag. Search; Manage. Market. Abstr.; Manage. Bibliogr. Rev.; Manage. Contents; MasterFile FullTEXT 1000; MasterFile FullTEXT 350; MasterFile FullTEXT 650; MasterFile FullTEXT (July 1993-); Middle East Abstr. Index; OCLC; Oper. Prod. Manage. Abstr. (Oct. 1971-) [Full Txt.]; Person. Train. Abstr. [Full Txt.]; Res. Alert [Full Cov.]; Selec. Coop. Index Manage. Period.; Soc. Sci. Cit. Index [Full Cov.]; Telebase; UMI ABI/Inform—Bus. Period. Ondisc (Jan. 1988-) [Full Txt.]; Wilson Bus. Abstr.; Women Manage. Rev. (1974-) [Full Txt.].

LC HF5603 .A28a
DD 657 US
ACCOUNTING SERVICES CONFERENCE.
Main/Conf Acccounting Services Conference. (1982)-. English. California Certified Public Accountants Foundation for Education and Research, 275 Shoreline Drive, Redwood City CA 94065. **Continues** Accounting and Auditing Conference.; Accounting and Auditing Conference, 0164-2898.

LC HF5601
DD 657 UK
ACCOUNTING STANDARDS BOARD AND INTERNATIONAL ACCOUNTING STANDARDS.
(19??)-. English. Irregular. £85.00. Institute of Chartered Accountants, 399 Silbury Boulevard, Central Milton, Keynes Buckinghamshire MK9 2HL United Kingdom. **Tel** 011 44 1908 248100, FAX 011 44 1908 248001, telex 727530.

LC HF5601
DD 657 UK
ACCOUNTING STANDARDS BOARD PAPERS.
(19??)-. English. Irregular. £65.00. Institute of Chartered Accountants, 399 Silbury Boulevard, Central Milton, Keynes Buckinghamshire MK9 2HL United Kingdom. **Tel** 011 44 1908 248100, FAX 011 44 1908 248001, telex 727530.
Desc: Provides all statements produced by the ASB as published.

LC HF5601 **ISSN** 0745-886X
DD 657 US
ACCOUNTING STANDARDS. CURRENT TEXT.
(ACCOUNTING STANDARDS. CURRENT TEXT AS OF ... / [Account. stand., Curr. text].
Added/Corp Financial Accounting Standards Board. **VFOAT** Current Text. (June 1, 1982)-. English. One time a year. $251.00. Financial Accounting Standards Board, PO Box 5116, Norwalk CT 06856. **Tel** (203)847-0700, FAX (203)849-9714. **Continues in part** AICPA Professional Standards.

LC HF5616.U5 A35 **ISSN** 0745-886X
DD 657/.0218 US
ACCOUNTING STANDARDS. CURRENT TEXT AS OF JUNE 1 ... / FINANCIAL ACCOUNTING STANDARDS BOARD.
[Account. stand., Curr. text]. (1982)-. English. One time a year. FASB, 401 Merritt 7, POB 5116, Norwalk CT 06856-5116. **Continues in part** AICPA Professional Standards.

LC HF5601
DD 657 UK
ACCOUNTING STANDARDS. GUIDELINES AND EXPOSURE DRAFTS.
(19??)-. English. £65.00. Institute of Chartered Accountants, 399 Silbury Boulevard, Central Milton, Keynes Buckinghamshire MK9 2HL United Kingdom. **Tel** 011 44 1908 248100, FAX 011 44 1908 248001, telex 727530.

LC HF5679 .C587 **ISSN** 1068-6452
DD 657 US
CCC
●ACCOUNTING TECHNOLOGY. [Account. technol.].
Vol. 9, No. 2 (Feb./Mar. 1993)-. Trade Publication. English. Eleven times a year. $65.95. Faulkner & Gray Inc., 11 Penn Plaza, 17th Floor, New York NY 10001. **Tel** (212)967-7000, (800)535-8403. **Continues** Computers in Accounting.
Ind/Abst Curr. Cit.

LC HG **ISSN** 1044-5714
DD 332 US
CCC
ACCOUNTING TODAY. [Account. today].
(1987)-. Periodical. English. Twenty-two times a year. $82.95. Faulkner & Gray Inc., 11 Penn Plaza, 17th Floor, New York NY 10001. **Tel** (212)967-7000, (800)535-8403. available in microform from University Microfilms International (UMI); available on an online database (full text) from DIALOG. **Absorbed** Practical Accountant Alert.
Desc: Chronicles changes & records impacting the accounting industry. Coverage of people, companies, issues, rules, regulations and new technologies.
Ind/Abst Account. Tax Datab. (May 1992-) [Full Txt.]; Trade Ind. ASAP [Full Txt.]; Trade Ind. Index [Full Txt.].

LC HF5681.B2 A35
DD 657 US
ACCOUNTING TRENDS & TECHNIQUES.
Added/Corp American Institute of Certified Public Accountants. **VFOAT** Accounting Trends and Techniques. 16th Ed. (1962)-. English. One time a year (Oct.). $84.25. American Institute of Certified Public Accountants, Harborside Financial Center, #201 Plaza 3, Jersey City NJ 07311. **Tel** (201)938-3333, (800)862-4272, FAX (201)938-3329. **Continues** Accounting Trends and Techniques in Published Annual Reports.
Desc: Covers financial statements and corporate reports.

LC HF5601 **ISSN** 0953-2579
DD 657.0941 UK
ACCOUNTING WORLD. [Account. world].
(1987)-. Trade Publication. English. Six times a year. $34.23. Institution of Financial Accountants, 11 St. Marks Road, Windsor SL4 3BD ngland. **Tel** 011 44 171 753830909. **ED** Garry Carter. Bk Rev, (Qty: 60). Ad Acc. Circ: 13,500. **Continues** Administrative Accountant.
Desc: News and features on tax, insurance, accountancy and technology for accountants.

LC HF5601
DD 657 US
ACTION PAYROLL INSERTS. (1993)-.
English. Twenty-four times a year. $14.00 (US), $17.64 (Canada). Bureau of Business Practice, 24 Rope Ferry Road, Waterford CT 06386. **Tel** (800)243-0876, (203)442-4365, (800)876-9105, FAX (203)443-1123.

LC HF5601 **ISSN** 0888-5400
DD 657 US
CEASED
ADMINISTRATIVE AND ACCOUNTING GUIDE FOR GOVERNMENT CONTRACTS.
[Adm. account. guide gov. contracts]. (19??)-(March 1994). Periodical. English. Admin Acct Guide Govt Contract, 121 Monmouth Parkway, West Long Branch NJ 07764. **Tel** (908)229-8000. **Continues** Administrative and Accounting Guide for Defense Contracts.

LC HF5601 .A62 **ISSN** 0882-6110
DD 657/.05 US
CCC
ADVANCES IN ACCOUNTING.
[Adv. account.]. Vol. 1 (1984)-. English. One time a year. $73.25. JAI Press Inc., 55 Old Post Road, Suite 2, PO Box 1678, Greenwich CT 06836-1678. **Tel** (203)661-7602, FAX (203)661-0792. **ED** Bill Schwartz.
Desc: Aims to bridge the gap by meeting the information needs of both academicians and practitioners. Includes articles that address contemporary issues and/or problems in financial or managerial accounting, accounting education, or auditing, and display sound analyses.

LC HF5679 .A328
DD 657/.0285 US
ADVANCES IN ACCOUNTING INFORMATION SYSTEMS.
VFOAT Accounting Information Systems. Vol. 1 (1992)-. Periodical. English. $73.25. JAI Press Inc., 55 Old Post Road, Suite 2, PO Box 1678, Greenwich CT 06836-1678. **Tel** (203)661-7602, FAX (203)661-0792. **ED** Steven G. Sutton.

LC HF5601 .A625 **ISSN** 0897-3660
DD 657/.05 CCC
ADVANCES IN INTERNATIONAL ACCOUNTING.
[Adv. int. account.]. **VFOAT** International Accounting. Vol. 1 (1987)-. Periodical. English. One time a year. $73.25. JAI Press Inc., 55 Old Post Road, Suite 2, PO Box 1678, Greenwich CT 06836-1678. **Tel** (203)661-7602, FAX (203)661-0792. **ED** Kenneth Most.

LC HF5657.4 .A38
DD 658.15/11 US
ADVANCES IN MANAGEMENT ACCOUNTING.
VFOAT Management Accounting. Vol. 1 (1992)-. English. Irregular. $73.25. JAI Press Inc., 55 Old Post Road, Suite 2, PO Box 1678, Greenwich CT 06836-1678. **Tel** (203)661-7602, FAX (203)661-0792. **ED** Marc Epstein.

LC HD60 .A34 **ISSN** 1041-7060
DD 306/.05 US
ADVANCES IN PUBLIC INTEREST ACCOUNTING.
[Adv. public interest account.]. Vol. 1 (1986)-. English. One time a year. $73.25. JAI Press Inc., 55 Old Post Road, Suite 2, PO Box 1678, Greenwich CT 06836-1678. **Tel** (203)661-7602, FAX (203)661-0792. **ED** Cheryl Lehman. Documents available from UMI Article Clearinghouse.
Ind/Abst ABI/INFORM Glob. Ed.; Int. Bibliogr. Sociol.

LC HG174 .A38 **ISSN** 1061-8910
DD 332 US
ADVANCES IN QUANTITATIVE ANALYSIS OF FINANCE AND ACCOUNTING.
[Adv. quant. anal. finance account.]. Vol. 1 (1991)-. English. $146.50 (2 volume set). JAI Press Inc., 55 Old Post Road, Suite 2, PO Box 1678, Greenwich CT 06836-1678. **Tel** (203)661-7602, FAX (203)661-0792. **ED** Cheng-Few Lee.

LC HF5667 .A43
DD 657/.0218 US
AICPA PROFESSIONAL STANDARDS.
Added/Corp American Institute of Certified Public Accountants. **VFOAT** Professional Standards. **VAT** American Institute of Certified Public Accountants Professional Standards. (19??)-. English. One time a year (Aug.). $92.00. Commerce Clearing House Inc., 4025 West Peterson Avenue, Chicago IL 60646-6085. **Tel** (312)583-8500, FAX (708)940-4600. **ED** A. E. Schechter. **Continued in part by** Accounting Standards. Current Text as of June 1 ..., 0745-886X.
Desc: This report presents pronouncements of AICPA, and includes various AICPA statements.

LC HF5601
DD 657 US
AICPA TECHNICAL PRACTICE AIDS.
Added/Corp American Institute of Certified Public Accountants. **VFOAT** Technical Practice Aids. **VAT** American Institute of Certified Public Accountants Technical Practice Aids. (19??)-. English. Irregular. 104.00Aus$. CCH Australia Ltd., PO Box 230, North Ryde NSW 2113 Australia. **Tel** 011 61 2 8571300, 011 61 2 8571555.

LC HF5661 .A55a **ISSN** 1047-5079
DD 657/.076 US
AICPA'S UNIFORM CPA EXAM, THE.
[AICPA's unif. CPA exam]. **Main/Corp** American Institute of Certified Public Accountants. Added/Corp American Institute of Certified Public Accountants. Board of Examiners. American Institute of Certified Public Accountants. Examinations Division. **VFOAT** Uniform CPA Exam. (1988)-. English. Irregular. $8.50. American Institute of Certified Public Accountants, Harborside Financial Center, #201 Plaza 3, Jersey City NJ 07311. **Tel** (201)938-3333, (800)862-4272, FAX (201)938-3329.

LC HF5601
DD 657 US
ALABAMA CPA NEWSLETTER. (19??)-.
Newsletter. English. Twelve times a year. Alabama Society of CPAs, PO Box 4187, Montgomery AL 36101.
Ind/Abst Account. Art.

LC HF5635 .A665 **ISSN** 0961-2742
DD 657/.05 UK
ANBAR ACCOUNTING & FINANCE ABSTRACTS.
See Business and Economics-Abstracting, Bibliographies and Statistics.

LC HF5601 **ISSN** 0307-0409
DD 657 UK
ANBAR YEARBOOK.
See Business and Economics-Management.

LC HF5601 **ISSN** 0820-0386
DD 657/.076 CN
ANNALES DE L'EXAMEN FINAL UNIFORME. [Annu. examen final unif. - Ordres comptab. agrees Can. Bermud.]. **Main/Corp** Ordres des Comptables Agrees du Canada et des Bermudes. 1981-. French. One time a year. $12.00 per vol. Institut Canadien des Comptables Agrees, 250 Est rue Bloor, Toronto Ontario M4W 1G5 Canada. ***Continues*** *Annales de l'Examen Final Uniforme, 0226-0255.*

LC HF5616.U6 W83
DD 657/.025/787 US
ANNUAL REGISTER, CERTIFIED PUBLIC ACCOUNTANTS. **Added/Corp** Wyoming Board of Certified Public Accountants. (19??)-. English. One time a year (July). $50.00. Wyoming Board of Certified Public Accountants, Equality State Building, 2nd Floor, Cheyenne WY 82002. **Circ:** 700. ***Continues*** *Register of Certified Public Accountants and Rules and Regulations.*

LC HF5601
DD 657 US
ANNUAL REGISTER OF CERTIFIED PUBLIC ACCOUNTANTS, PUBLIC ACCOUNTANTS, ACCOUNTING PRACTITIONERS. **Added/Corp** Iowa. Board of Accountancy. (1976)-. English. One time a year. ***Continues*** *Iowa. Board of Accountancy. Annual Register of Certified Public Accountants and Public Accountants.*
Desc: Registered certified public accountants, public accountants, and accounting practitioners in Iowa; and the rules used by the board in its administration of the Public Accountancy Act.

LC HF5601
DD 657 US
ANNUAL REPORT / FINANCIAL ACCOUNTING STANDARDS BOARD. **Main/Corp** Financial Accounting Standards Board. (1983)-. English. One time a year. Free on request. Financial Accounting Standards Board, PO Box 5116, Norwalk CT 06856. **Tel** (203)847-0700, FAX (203)849-9714. ***Continues*** *Annual Report of the Financial Accounting Standards Board.*
Desc: Annual report of the Financial Accounts Standards Board.

LC HF5657 .A64X **ISSN** 0883-2102
DD 657 US
API ACCOUNT, THE. [API acc.]. **Added/Corp** Accountants for the Public Interest. **VAT** Accountants for the Public Interest Account. Vol. 5, No. 1 (Jan./Feb. 1978)-. Periodical. English. Four times a year. $35.00 Comes with Accountants for the Public Interest membership. Accountants Public Interest, 1012 14th Street Northwest, Suite 906, Washington DC 20005. **Tel** (202)347-1668. **ED** Desmond D. Ross. **Circ:** 2,500 (ctrl). ***Continues*** *NAAPI Account.*
Ind/Abst Account. Tax Datab. (1978-).

LC HF5601
DD 657 UK
APPLICATION OF FINANCIAL REPORTING STANDARDS. (19??)-. English. Irregular. £40.00.
Desc: Guides to the ASB's financial reporting standards, giving practical examples of how to apply the standards.

LC KF4288.A15 A78 **ISSN** 0886-1013
DD 344.73/097 347.30497 US
Pr Rev.
ART LAW AND ACCOUNTING REPORTER. **See** Law-Entertainment Law.

LC HF5601
DD 657 UK
ASC REPORT. (19??)-. English. Three times a year. Free on request. Accounting Standards Committee, PO Box 433 Moorgate Place, London EC2P 2BJ United Kingdom. **Tel** 011 44 171 6287060.

LC HF5601
DD 657 HK
ASIA PACIFIC JOURNAL OF ACCOUNTING. (1995)-. English. One time a year. $50.00. City Polytechnic HK Department of Accounting, 83 Tat Chee Avenue, Kowloon Hong Kong. **Tel** 011 852 27887945.

LC HF5601
DD 657 NE
ASIA-PACIFIC TAX BULLETIN. **See** Finance-Taxation.

LC HF5601 **ISSN** 1321-7348
DD 657 AT
ASIAN REVIEW OF ACCOUNTING. (1992)-. English. Four times a year. Curtin University of Technology, GPO Box U 1987, Perth Western Australia 6001 Australia. **Tel** 011 61 9 3517702, FAX 011 61 9 3513554, telex 92983. **ED** Gabriel D. Donleavy and Dennis W. Taylor. **Bk Rev**.

LC HF5601 .A88 **ISSN** 0883-7384
DD 332 US
ASSET (ST. LOUIS, MO.), THE. (THE ASSET.). [Asset]. **Added/Corp** Missouri Society of Certified Public Accountants. (19??)-. Periodical. English. Six times a year. $15.00. Missouri Society of Certified Public Accountants, PO Box 27342, St Louis MO 63141-1742. **Tel** (314)997-7966, FAX (314)997-2592. **ED** Ronald W. Wilson. **Ad Acc. Circ:** 7,300 (ctrl).
Desc: Member newsletter for members of Missouri Society of CPA's and other interested parties.
Ind/Abst Account. Tax Datab. (1974-); Account. Art.

LC KF297.A1 A86 **ISSN** 0571-8279
DD 349.73 347.3 US
ATTORNEY-CPA, THE. **See** Law.

LC HF5601 **ISSN** 0958-367X
DD 657.450941 UK
AUDIT BRIEFING. [Audit brief]. (1989)-. Trade Publication. English. Twelve times a year. £77.00. Tolley Publishing Company Ltd., Tolley House, 2 Addiscombe Road, Croydon, Surrey CR9 5AF United Kingdom. **Tel** 011 44 181 6869141, FAX 011 44 181 6863155.
Desc: Provides news and guidance on standards, regulatory and ethical issues for auditors.

LC F1405.5 1959 .O7 F1402
DD 341.24/5 S 341.24/5 US
CEASED
AUDIT OF ACCOUNTS AND FINANCIAL STATEMENTS ; REPORT TO THE GENERAL ASSEMBLY OF THE ORGANIZATION OF AMERICAN STATES BY THE BOARD OF EXTERNAL AUDITORS. **Main/Corp** Organization of American States. Board of External Auditors. (19??)-Series complete. English. Organization of American States, 19th Street & Constitution Avenue NW, Suite 300, Washington DC 20006. **Tel** (202)458-6256.

LC HV9305.N3 N45c **ISSN** 0149-2144
DD 353.9/793/00849 US
AUDIT REPORT, STATE OF NEVADA DEPARTMENT OF PAROLE AND PROBATION, RESTITUTION TRUST FUND. **Main/Corp** Nevada. Legislature. Legislative Auditor. (19??)-. English. Legislative Auditor / Nevada, Legislative Building, Capitol Complex, Carson City NV 89710.

LC HF5681.B2 A94 **ISSN** 1067-5418
DD 657/.95/097305 US
AUDIT RISK ALERT. [Audit risk alert]. **Added/Corp** American Institute of Certified Public Accountants. Auditing Standards Division. (1990)-. English. One time a year. $8.25. American Institute of Certified Public Accountants, Harborside Financial Center, #201 Plaza 3, Jersey City NJ 07311. **Tel** (201)938-3333, (800)862-4272, FAX (201)938-3329.
Desc: Covers financial statements and internal auditing.

LC HF5667 .A79 **ISSN** 0278-0380
DD 657 US
Pr Rev.
AUDITING. [Auditing]. **Added/Corp** American Accounting Association. Auditing Section. Vol. 1, No. 1 (Summer 1981)-. Periodical. English. Two times a year. $25.00. American Accounting Association, 5717 Bessie Drive, Sarasota FL 34233-2399. **Tel** (813)921-7747, FAX (813)923-4093. **ED** Andrew D. Bailey, Jr. and Kurt Pany. **Ad Acc. Circ:** 1,700. available on microfilm and microfiche from University Microfilms International (UMI). Documents available from The Genuine Article.
Ind/Abst Account. Art.; Bus. Source Plus; Curr. Cit.; Curr. Contents Soc. Behav. Sci.; EP Collect.; Homework Help.; MasterFile FullTEXT 1000; MasterFile FullTEXT 350; MasterFile FullTEXT 650; MasterFile FullTEXT; OCLC; Res. Alert [Full Cov.]; Soc. Sci. Cit. Index [Full Cov.]; Telebase.

LC HF5601
DD 657 UK
AUDITING AND REPORTING. **Main/Corp** Institute of Chartered Accountants in England and Wales. (1980)-. English. One time a year. $44.49. Institute of Chartered Accountants, 399 Silbury Boulevard, Central Milton, Keynes Buckinghamshire MK9 2HL United Kingdom. **Tel** 011 44 1908 248100, FAX 011 44 1908 248001, telex 727530.

LC HF5601
DD 657 UK
AUDITING PRACTICES BOARD AND INTERNATIONAL FEDERATION OF ACCOUNTANTS. (19??)-. English. Irregular. £65.00. Institute of Chartered Accountants, 399 Silbury Boulevard, Central Milton, Keynes Buckinghamshire MK9 2HL United Kingdom. **Tel** 011 44 1908 248100, FAX 011 44 1908 248001, telex 727530.
Desc: Provides all statements produced by the APB and IFA as published.

LC HF5601
DD 657 UK
AUDITING PRACTICES BOARD PAPERS. (19??)-. English. Irregular. £45.00. Institute of Chartered Accountants, 399 Silbury Boulevard, Central Milton, Keynes Buckinghamshire MK9 2HL United Kingdom. **Tel** 011 44 1908 248100, FAX 011 44 1908 248001, telex 727530.

LC HF5601 **ISSN** 0146-9819
DD 657 US
AUDITING RESEARCH MONOGRAPH. [Audit. res. monogr.]. **Added/Corp** American Institute of Certified Public Accountants. Technical Research Division. (19??)-. Monographic series. English. Irregular. Price varies per volume. American Institute of Certified Public Accountants, Harborside Financial Center, #201 Plaza 3, Jersey City NJ 07311. **Tel** (201)938-3333, (800)862-4272, FAX (201)938-3329.

LC HF5686.C7 A799 **ISSN** 1063-4053
DD 657/.45/097305 US
AUDITOR-TRAK (ATLANTA, GA.). (AUDITOR-TRAK : THE COMPREHENSIVE REPORT AND ANALYSIS OF AUDITOR CHANGES.). [Auditor-trak]. **Added/Corp** Strafford Publications. **VFOAT** Auditor Trak. 1st Quarter (1992)-. Trade Publication. English. Four times a year. $492.00. Strafford Publications Inc., 590 Dutch Valley Road Northeast, Atlanta GA 30324. **Tel** (404)881-1141, (800)926-7926, FAX (404)881-0074.

LC HF5601
DD 657 UK
AUDITORS FACT BOOK. (19??)-. English. Twenty-four times a year. Gee & Company Limited, 183 Marsh Wall, South Quay Plaza, London E14 9FS United Kingdom. **Tel** 011 44 171 5385386, FAX 011 44 171 5388623.

LC HF5601 **ISSN** 0746-7265
DD 657 US
CCC
AUERBACH EDP AUDITING. [Auerbach EDP audit.]. (1983)-. Trade Publication. English. Six times a year. $395.00 US; $514.00 other. Auerbach Publishers Inc., Park Square Building, 31 St. James Avenue, Boston MA 02116. **Tel** (800)950-1207. **ED** William E Perry and Rich Mansfield. ***Continues*** *EDP Auditing, 0736-3656.*
Desc: A reference service dealing with all aspects of the discipline in 80+ articles. Contains figures, charts, and checklists.

LC HF5601 .A94 **ISSN** 0004-8631
DD 657.05 AT
CCC
CODEN AUACAC
Pr Rev.
AUSTRALIAN ACCOUNTANT, THE. [Aust. account.]. (Feb. 1936)-. Periodical. English. Eleven times a year (monthly except Jan.). 61.66Aus$. Australian Society of Certified Practising Accountants, 170 Queen Street, Melbourne Victoria 3000 Australia. **Tel** 011 61 3 6069606, FAX 011 61 3 6708901, telex 32283-ASAML. **ED** Anna Ivanon. Index available (Feb. iss.). cum. index. **Bk Rev**, (Qty: 1-2). **Ad Acc. Circ:** 79,000. available on microfilm and microfiche from University Microfilms International (UMI); available on an online database (files 15,485/Full-Text) from DIALOG. Documents available from UMI Article Clearinghouse. ***Supersedes*** *Commonwealth Journal of Accountancy.*
Desc: Covers finance, investment, taxation, company law, computers, business systems, financial reporting, auditing, professional development, information technology and general subjects relating to these topics.
Ind/Abst ABI/INFORM Glob. Ed.; ABI/INFORM [Computer File] (Jan. 1984-); Account. Tax Datab. (1974-) [Full Txt.]; Account. Art.; Anbar Account. Finan. Abstr. [Full Txt.]; Anbar Mark. Distr. Abstr. [Full Txt.]; Anbar Top Manage. Abstr. [Full Txt.]; APAIS, Aust. Public Aff. Inf. Ser. (1963-); Aust. Leg. Mon. Dig.; Bus. Source Plus; Bus. Source; Curr. Cit.; EP Collect.; Homework Help.; Manage. Bibliogr. Rev.; MasterFile FullTEXT 1000; MasterFile FullTEXT 350; MasterFile FullTEXT 650; MasterFile FullTEXT; OCLC; Oper. Prod. Manage. Abstr. [Full Txt.]; Person. Train. Abstr. [Full Txt.]; Telebase; UMI ABI/Inform--Bus. Period. Ondisc (Dec. 1987-) [Full Txt.]; Women Manage. Rev. [Full Txt.]; World Mag. Bank.

LC HF
DD 657 AT
AUSTRALIAN ACCOUNTING REVIEW. (19??)-. English. Two times a year (Feb., & Aug.). 25.00Aus$ (members and students), 35.00Aus$ (nonmembers) 40.00Aus$ (institutions and libraries) Australia; 75.00Aus$ other. Australian Society of Certified Practising Accountants, 170 Queen Street, Melbourne Victoria 3000 Australia. **Tel** 011 61 3 6069606, FAX 011 61 3 6708901, telex 32283-ASAML. **ED** Linda English and David Anderson. **Ad Acc. Circ:** 1,000.

LC HF5601
DD 657 US
AUTOMATED MEDICAL PAYMENTS DIRECTORY. **See** Medical Sciences-Health Services Administration.

LC HF5601
DD 657 UK
BALANCE SHEETS AND THE LENDING BANKER.
(19??)-. English. $18.00. Europa Publications Ltd., 18 Bedford Square, London WC1B 3JN United Kingdom. **Tel** 011 44 171 5808236, telex 21540 EUROPA G. **(Subscription address:** Gale Research Co., 835 Penobscot Building, Detroit MI 48226. **Tel** (800)347-4253.)
Desc: An assessment of accounting statements and their interpretation in relation to bank advances.

LC HF5601 **ISSN** 0522-2478
DD 657 US
CCC
BANK AUDITING AND ACCOUNTING REPORT.
See Business and Economics-Banks and Banking.

LC HF5601 .B42 **ISSN** 1050-4753
DD 657/.05 US
BEHAVIORAL RESEARCH IN ACCOUNTING.
[Behav. res. account.]. **Added/Corp** American Accounting Association. Accounting, Behavior, and Organizations Section. **VFOAT** BRIA. Vol. 1 (1989)-. English. One time a year (Spring). $20.00. American Accounting Association, 5717 Bessie Drive, Sarasota FL 34233-2399. **Tel** (813)921-7747, FAX (813)923-4093.
Ind/Abst Account. Tax Datab. (1989-); Bus. Source Plus; Bus. Source; EP Collect.; Homework Help.; MasterFile FullTEXT 1000; MasterFile FullTEXT 350; MasterFile FullTEXT 650; MasterFile FullTEXT; OCLC; Telebase.

LC HF5601
DD 657 IT
BILANCIO E CONTABILITA DI ESERCIZIO.
(19??)-. Periodical. Italian. Three times a year. IPSOA Editore SRL, Casella Postale 12055, Mastrangelo, 20120 Milan Italy. **Tel** 011 39 2 82476248. Index available.

LC HF5601 **ISSN** 0930-0597
DD 657 GW
UDC 657.372
BILANZ & BUCHHALTUNG.
[Bilauz Buchhalt.]. **VFOAT** Bilanz und Buchhaltung. (1986)-. Trade Publication. German. Eleven times a year. $118.22. Gabler Verlag, Postfach 1546, D-65005 Wiesbaden Germany. **Tel** 011 49 611 534129, FAX 011 49 611 534430. ***Continues*** *Bilanz- und Buchhaltungs-Praxis, 0006-2359.*

LC HF5601
DD 657 BE
BNB NBB COMPTES ANNUELS DES ENTERPRISES BELGES. CD-ROM.
(19??)-. Dutch (French and English). Four times a year. $4000.00. Banque National de Belgique, boulevard de Berlaimont 14-B, 1000 Brussels Belgium. **Tel** 011 32 2 2212033, FAX 011 32 2 2213163. **Ad Acc. Circ:** 160 (ctrl). available on microfilm; available on diskette; available in print.
Desc: Annual accounts of 160,000 Belgian firms over three years.

LC HF5616.S7 I68a
DD 657 SP
BOLETIN / ICAC, INSTITUTO DE CONTABILIDAD Y AUDITORIA DE CUENTAS.
Main/Corp Instituto de Contabilidad y Auditoria de Cuentas (Spain). **VFOAT** Boletin Oficial del Instituto de Contabilidad y Auditoria de Cuentas.; BOICAC. No. 1 (1990)-. Bulletin. Spanish. Four times a year. Institut Contabilidad y Auditoria de Cuentas, Huertas 26, 28014 Madrid Spain. **Tel** 011 34 1 4290960.

LC HF5601
DD 657 MX
BOLETIN INTERAMERICANO DE CONTABILIDAD.
Added/Corp Instituto Mexicano de Contadores Publicos. Conferencia Interamericana de Contabilidad. (19??)-. Periodical. Spanish. Four times a year. $10.00. Boletin Interamericano de Uruguay, 824-1 P, 1015 Buenos Aires Argentina.

LC HF5601 **ISSN** 0279-1889
DD 657 US
Pr Rev.
BOTTOM LINE (CHARLESTON, S.C.), THE.
(THE BOTTOM LINE.). **Added/Corp** International Association of Hospitality Accountants. **VFOAT** Bottomline. (19??)-. Periodical. English. Six times a year. $50.00. International Association of Hospitality Accountants, PO Box 203008, Austin TX 78720. **Tel** (512)346-5680. **ED** Carla Jo Schaefer. **Bk Rev. Ad Acc, Adv Mgr:** Linda Timmons. **Circ:** 3,600 (ctrl).
Desc: Focuses on issues related to hospitality financial management, technology, human resource management, accounting, and club/casino issues.

LC HF5601
DD 657 US
BOTTOM LINE FOR KENTUCKY CPA'S, THE.
Added/Corp Kentucky Society of Certified Public Accountants. **VFOAT** Bottom Line. Vol. 1 (Aug. 1979)-. Periodical. English. Twelve times a year. Kentucky Society of Certified Public Accountants, 310 West Liberty, Louisville KY 40202. ***Supersedes*** *Kentucky Accountant.*
Ind/Abst Account. Art.; Fed. Tax Artic.

LC HF5601 **ISSN** 0831-5477
DD 657/.0971 CN
BOTTOM LINE (MARKHAM).
(THE BOTTOM LINE.). [Bottom line]. Vol. 1 No. 1 (Sept. 1985)-. Trade Publication. English. Twelve times a year. 65.00Can$. Butterworth & Company Ltd. / Canada, 75 Clegg Road, Markham Ontario L6G 1A1 Canada. **Tel** (905)479-2665, (800)668-6481, FAX (905)479-2826. available on microfilm from University Microfilms International (UMI).
Ind/Abst Can. Period. Index.

LC HF5601 **ISSN** 0897-3482
DD 657 US
Pr Rev.
BOWMAN'S ACCOUNTING REPORT.
[Bowman's account. rep.]. (198?)-. Periodical. English. Twelve times a year. $215.00. Hudson Sawer Proessional Services Marketing Inc, 950 East Paces Ferry Road, Suite 2425, Atlanta GA 30326. **Tel** (404)264-9977, FAX (404)264-9968. **ED** Arthur W. Bowman. **Bk Rev**, (Qty: 5). available on microfiche (University Microfilms).
Desc: Reporting and analyzing the news, trends, strategies, and politics that affect accountants and their firms.
Ind/Abst Account. Tax Datab. (1987-).

LC HF5601 .B77 **ISSN** 0890-8389
DD 657 UK
CCC
BRITISH ACCOUNTING REVIEW, THE.
[Br. account. rev.]. (19??)-. Academic Scholarly Publication. English. Four times a year. $231.02. Academic Press Ltd., A Division of Harcourt Brace & Company Ltd., 24-28 Oval Road, London NW1 7DX United Kingdom. **Tel** 011 44 171 2674466, FAX 011 44 171 4822293, 011 44 171 4854752, telex 25775 ACPRES G. **(Subscription address:** Harcourt Brace & Company, Ltd., Foots Cray High Street, Sidcup Kent DA14 5HP United Kingdom. **Tel** 011 44 181 3003322, FAX 011 44 181 3090807, telex 896 377 ACADEM.) **ED** R. H. Gray. **Bk Rev.**
Desc: A forum for communication throughout the world between members of the academic and professional community concerned with the research and teaching, at degree level and above, of accounting, finance, and cognate disciplines.
Ind/Abst Account. Tax Datab. (1987-); Contents Pages Manage.; Curr. Cit.

LC HF5616.G7 B734
DD 657/.025/41 UK
BRITISH ACCOUNTING REVIEW RESEARCH REGISTER, THE.
Added/Corp British Accounting Association. Institute of Chartered Accountants in England and Wales. **VFOAT** BAR Research Register. **VAT** British Accounting Association Research Register. (1984)-. English. Irregular. Price varies per volume. Harcourt Brace & Company Ltd., Foots Cray High Street, Sidcup Kent DA14 5HP United Kingdom. **Tel** 011 44 181 3003322, FAX 011 44 181 3090807. **(Subscription address:** W. B. Saunders Company / North America Subscriptions, c/o Periodicals, 6277 Sea Harbour Drive, 4th Floor, Orlando FL 32887. **Tel** (800)654-2452, (407)345-3668.)

LC HF5601 **ISSN** 0867-7204
DD 657 PL
UDC 657
BUCHALTER SZCZECIN.
(BUCHALTER.). [Buchalter Szczec.]. (1991)-. Periodical. Polish. Twelve times a year. **(Subscription address:** Ars Polona-Ruch, PO Box 1001, Krakowskie Przedmiescie 7, 00-068 Warsaw Poland. **Tel** 011 48 22 261201.)

LC HF5601 **ISSN** 0007-3776
DD 657 RU
BUKHGALTERSKII UCHET.
Added/Corp Russia (1923-U.S.S.R). Ministerstvo Finansov. (1938)-. Periodical. Russian. Twelve times a year. $99.95. Izdatelstvo Finansy I Statistika, Ulitsa Chernyshvskogo 7 K-142, 101000 Moscow Russia. **(Subscription address:** East View Publications Inc., 3020 Harbor Lane North, Suite 110, Minneapolis MN 55447. **Tel** (800)477-1005, (612)550-0961, FAX (612)559-2931.) Index available.

LC HF5601 **ISSN** 0229-9461
DD 657/.06/0714 CN
BULLETIN DES C.G.A.
(LE BULLETIN DES C.G.A.). [Bull. C.G.A.]. **Added/Corp** Corporation Professionnelle des Comptables Generaux Licencies du Quebec. Vol. 5, No. 2 (Nov./Dec. 1980)-. Bulletin. French. Six times a year. Corporation Professionelle Des Comptables Generaux Licencies, du Quebec 152 Est rue Notre-Dame, Montreal Quebec H2Y 3P6 Canada. ***Continues*** *Corporation Professionnelle des Comptables Generaux Licencies du Quebec. Bulletin, 0701-8975.*

LC HF5601
DD 657 UK
BUSINESS BRIEFING LOOSELEAF.
(19??)-. English. Three times a year. £150.00. Institute of Chartered Accountants, 399 Silbury Boulevard, Central Milton, Keynes Buckinghamshire MK9 2HL United Kingdom. **Tel** 011 44 1908 248100, FAX 011 44 1908 248001, telex 727530.
Desc: An information resource for industry-specific accounting procedures.

LC HF5601 **ISSN** 0703-1939
DD 657/.73 CN
BUSINESS VALUATOR, THE.
Added/Corp Canadian Association of Business Valuators. **VFOAT** Valuator. (1977)-. Periodical. English. Six times a year. Canadian Association of Business Valuators, Suite 401/8 Colborne Street, Toronto Ontario M5E 1E1 Canada.

LC HF5601
DD 657 UK
CA MAGAZINE.
Added/Corp Institute of Chartered Accountants of Scotland. **VFOAT** Accountant's Magazine, Nov.1990-Feb.1991. (1990)-. English. Twelve times a year. $94.11. Institute of Chartered Accountants / Edinburgh, 27 Queen's Street, Edinburgh EH2 1LA United Kingdom. **Tel** 011 44 131 12255673, FAX 011 44 31 12253813. ***Absorbed*** *Accountant's Magazine, 0001-4761.*
Ind/Abst Account. Index Suppl.; INSPEC (1983-); Manage. Contents (1974-); MasterFile FullTEXT (July 1993-); Ref. Sources.

LC HF5601 .C3 **ISSN** 0317-6878
DD 657/.05 CN
CCC
CODEN CAMADJ
CA MAGAZINE (TORONTO).
(CA MAGAZINE.). [CA mag.]. **Added/Corp** Canadian Institute of Chartered Accountants. Vol. 104 (Jan. 1974)-. Periodical. English (French). Ten times a year (monthly with Jan./Feb. and Jun./Jul. issues combined). 37.61Can$. Canadian Institute of Chartered Accountants, 277 Wellington Street West, Toronto Ontario M5V 3H2 Canada. **Tel** (416)977-3222, FAX (416)204-3415. **ED** Nelson Luscombe. **Bk Rev. Ad Acc.** available on microfilm and microfiche from University Microfilms International (UMI). Documents available from UMI Article Clearinghouse, Ask*IEEE. ***Continues*** *CA, 0703-685X.*
Desc: Provides readers, both CA's and others, with a range of articles, departments and news coverage on accounting, auditing and financial management and related topics.
Ind/Abst ABI/INFORM Glob. Ed. (Aug. 1971-); ABI/INFORM Ondisc: Expr. Ed.; ABI/INFORM [Computer File] (Jan. 1974-); Acad. Search; Account. Tax Datab. (Aug. 1971-) [Full Txt.]; Account. Art.; Anbar Account. Finan. Abstr. [Full Txt.]; Anbar Mark. Distr. Abstr. [Full Txt.]; Anbar Top Manage. Abstr. [Full Txt.]; Bus. Index (1985-); Bus. Period. Index; Bus. Source Plus; Bus. Source; Can. Legal Lit.; Can. Period. Index; Curr. Cit.; EP Collect.; Fed. Tax Artic.; Gen. BusinessFile (1985-); Homework Help.; Index Can. Leg. Period. Lit.; INFO-SOUTH Abstr.; INSPEC (Aug. 1974-); Mag. Search; Manage. Market. Abstr.; Manage. Bibliogr. Rev.; MasterFile FullTEXT 1000; MasterFile FullTEXT 350; MasterFile FullTEXT 650; MasterFile FullTEXT (July 1993-); OCLC; Oper. Prod. Manage. Abstr. [Full Txt.]; PAIS Int. Print (1991-); Person. Train. Abstr. [Full Txt.]; Telebase; Trade Ind. Index; UMI ABI/Inform--Bus. Period. Ondisc [Full Txt.]; Wilson Bus. Abstr.; Women Manage. Rev. [Full Txt.].

LC HF5601 **ISSN** 0832-9117
DD 657/.05 CN
CA MAGAZINE (TORONTO. ED. FRANCAISE).
(CA MAGAZINE.). [CA mag.]. **Added/Corp** Institut Canadien des Comptables Agrees. **VAT** Chartered Accountant Magazine (Toronto. Ed. Francaise). Vol. 119, No. 10 (Oct. 1986)-. Periodical. French. Twelve times a year. 47.00Can$. Canadian Institute of Chartered Accountants, 277 Wellington Street West, Toronto Ontario M5V 3H2 Canada. **Tel** (416)977-3222, FAX (416)204-3415.
Ind/Abst Can. Legal Lit.; Can. Period. Index; Gen. Period. Index (1985-).

LC HF5601
DD 657 FR
CAHIERS DE L'IFEC.
(19??)-. Monographic series. French. Irregular. Price varies per volume. IFEC / Institut Francais des Experts Comptables, 139 rue Faubourg Saint Honore, 75008 Paris France. **Tel** 011 33 1 42564967. **(Subscription address:** Editions Comptables Malesherbe, 88 rue de Courcelles, 75008 Paris France. **Tel** 011 33 1 44159595.)

LC HF5616.U6 C3 **ISSN** 0095-6147
DD 657/.025/794 US
CALIFORNIA ACCOUNTANCY ACT WITH RULES AND REGULATIONS.
(CALIFORNIA ACCOUNTANCY ACT WITH RULES AND REGULATIONS; REGISTER.). **Added/Corp** California. State Board of Accountancy. Register. (19??)-. English. Irregular (every two years). $4.50. California State Board Accountancy, 2135 Butano Drive, Suite 112, Sacramento CA 95825. **Tel** (916)574-2175, FAX (916)574-2289. **ED** Tuan Lai. cum. index. **Circ:** 50,000. ***Continues*** *California. State Board of Accountancy. Register.*

LC HF5601 .C4 **ISSN** 0306-2406
DD 657/.05 IE
CERTIFIED ACCOUNTANT. [Certif. account.]. **Added/Corp** Association of Certified Accountants. Chartered Association of Certified Accountants (Great Britain). Vol. 64, No. 1 (Jan. 1972)-. Trade Publication. English. Twelve times a year. $128.34. Cork Publishing Ltd., Granary House, Rutland Street, Cork Ireland. **Tel** 011-353-21-313855, FAX 011-353-21-313496. **ED** Brian O'Kane. Index available. **Bk Rev**, (Qty: 15-20). **Ad Acc, Adv Mgr Tel** 44-420-477381. **Circ:** 55,000. available in microform. ***Continues*** *Certified Accountants Journal (London, England : 1966), 0009-0417.*
Desc: Magazine primarily for members of the Chartered Association of Certified Accountants; includes news of the association and its members, technical updates and features.
Ind/Abst Account. Index Suppl.; Account. Tax Datab. (1974-); Anbar Account. Finan. Abstr. [Full Txt.]; Anbar Mark. Distr. Abstr. [Full Txt.]; Anbar Top Manage. Abstr. [Full Txt.]; Manage. Bibliogr. Rev.; Oper. Prod. Manage. Abstr. [Full Txt.]; Person. Train. Abstr. [Full Txt.]; Women Manage. Rev. [Full Txt.].

LC HF5661 .C39 **ISSN** 1041-7222
DD 658.15/11/076 US
CERTIFIED MANAGEMENT ACCOUNTANT EXAMINATION. QUESTIONS AND UNOFFICIAL ANSWERS (MONTVALE, N.J.). (CERTIFIED MANAGEMENT ACCOUNTANT EXAMINATION. QUESTIONS AND UNOFFICIAL ANSWERS.). [Certif. manage. account. exam., Quest. unoff. answ.]. **Added/Corp** Institute of Certified Management Accountants (U.S.). **VFOAT** Questions and Unofficial Answers; CMA Examination. (June 1986)-. English. Irregular. $6.00. Institute of Management Accountants, 10 Paragon Drive, Montvale NJ 07645. **Tel** (201)573-9000, (800)638-4427, FAX (201)573-8185, telex 9102509487. ***Continues*** *Certificate in Management Accounting Examination. Questions and Unofficial Answers, 0277-7614.*

LC HF5616.C2 C43 **ISSN** 0318-742X
DD 657/.0971 CN
CGA MAGAZINE. [CGA mag.]. **Added/Corp** Canadian Certified General Accountants' Association. (Aug. 1975)-. Periodical. English (French). Twelve times a year. 24.01Can$. Canadian Certified General Accountant's Association, 1188 West Georgia Street, Suite 700, Vancouver British Columbia V6E 4A2 Canada. **Tel** (604)669-3555, (800)663-1529. **ED** Tony Toth. **Bk Rev. Ad Acc. Circ:** 40,000 (ctrl). ***Continues*** *CGA, 0009-0425.*
Desc: The official publication of the Certified General Accountants' Association, it covers the topics of accounting, finance and business.
Ind/Abst Account. Tax Datab. (1974-); Can. Period. Index (19??-).

LC HF5601 **ISSN** 1037-6267
DD 657 AT
CHARTAC ACCOUNTANCY NEWS. (1991)-. Periodical. English. Eleven times a year (monthly except Jan.). 326.41Aus$. Professional Information Pty., 196 Drummond Street, Carlton VIC 3053 Australia. **Tel** 011 61 3 6622822, FAX 011 61 3 6623191. **ED** Ashley McKeon. **Ad Acc.** ***Continues*** *Chartac Accounting Report, 0814-8074.*

LC HF5601
DD 657 AT
CHARTAC TAX PLANNING NEWS. (19??)-. English. Eleven times a year (monthly except Jan.). 326.41Aus$. Professional Information Pty., 196 Drummond Street, Carlton VIC 3053 Australia. **Tel** 011 61 3 6622822, FAX 011 61 3 6623191. ***Continues*** *Chartac Taxation Report.*

LC HF5601
DD 657 AT
TITLE CHANGE
CHARTAC TAX PRACTICE IDEAS. (1993)-(199?). English. Professional Information Pty., 196 Drummond Street, Carlton VIC 3053 Australia. **Tel** 011 61 3 6622822, FAX 011 61 3 6623191. ***Continued by*** *Chartac Tax Planning News.*

LC HF5601 .C5
DD 657 AT
Pr Rev.
CHARTER (SYDNEY, AUSTRALIA). (CHARTER.). **Added/Corp** Institute of Chartered Accountants in Austalia. **VFOAT** Journal of the Institute of Chartered Accountants in Australia. Vol. 61, No. 1 (Feb. 1990)-. Periodical. English. Eleven times a year. 49.34Aus$. Institute of Chartered Accountants in Australia, GPO Box 3921, Sydney New South Wales, 2001 Australia. **Tel** 011 61 2 290 1344, FAX 011 61 2 262 3953. **ED** Ian Hay. Index available. **Bk Rev**, (Qty: 6). **Ad Acc, Adv Mgr:** Chris St. John, **Tel** (02)290-1344. **Circ:** 33,000 (ctrl). available on microfilm and microfiche from University Microfilms International (UMI). ***Continues*** *Chartered Accountant.*
Desc: Focuses on Australian business and keeps professionals up to date.
Ind/Abst Account. Tax Datab. (1974-) [Full Txt.].

LC HF5601 .C48 **ISSN** 0009-188X
DD 657 II
CHARTERED ACCOUNTANT, THE. [Chart. account.]. **Added/Corp** Institute of Chartered Accountants of India. (1952)-. Periodical. English. Twelve times a year. $30.00. Institute Chartered Accountant India, Box 268 Indraprastha Marg, New Delhi India. **Tel** 3312055, telex 31-62236 CICA IN. **(Subscription address:** Prints India, 11 Darya Ganj, New Delhi 110002 India. **Tel** 011 91 11 3268645, FAX 011 91 11 3275542, telex 31-61087 PRIN-IN.) **ED** K G Somani and A H Dalal. Index available. cum. index. **Bk Rev. Ad Acc. Circ:** 65,000 (ctrl). available in microform from University Microfilms International (UMI).
Desc: Contains articles on accounting, auditing, taxation, laws, computers, etc. Book reviews, news from regions, accounting abroad, legal decisions, institute news, student section, etc.

LC HF5601 .A19 **ISSN** 1172-9929
DD 657.05 NZ
•**CHARTERED ACCOUNTANTS JOURNAL OF NEW ZEALAND.** **Added/Corp** New Zealand Society of Accountants. **VFOAT** Chartered Accountants Journal. Vol. 73, No. 4 (May 1994)-. Periodical. English. Twelve times a year. New Zealand Society of Accountants, PO Box 11342, Wellington New Zealand. **Tel** 011 64 4 4738544, FAX 011 64 4 726282. **ED** A. McLeod. Index available. **Bk Rev. Ad Acc. Circ:** 13,214. available on an online database. ***Continues*** *Accountants' Journal, 0001-4745.*
Ind/Abst ABI/INFORM Glob. Ed.; Account. Tax Datab.; Anbar Account. Finan. Abstr. [Full Txt.]; Anbar Mark. Distr. Abstr. [Full Txt.]; Anbar Top Manage. Abstr. [Full Txt.]; Curr. Cit.; Manage. Bibliogr. Rev.; Oper. Prod. Manage. Abstr. [Full Txt.]; Person. Train. Abstr. [Full Txt.]; Women Manage. Rev. [Full Txt.].

LC HF5601
DD 657 UK
•**CHARTERED INSTITUTE OF MANAGEMENT ACCOUNTANTS. FINANCIAL SKILLS SERIES.** (1994)-. Monographic series. English. Irregular. Price varies. Kogan Page Ltd., 120 Pentonville Road, London N1 9BR United Kingdom. **Tel** 011 44 171 2780433, FAX 011 44 171 8376348, telex 263088 KOGAN G. **(Subscription address:** C.I.M.A., Publishing Sales Department, 63 Portland Place, London W1N 4AB United Kingdom. **Tel** 011 44 171 9179229, FAX 011 44 171 6315309.)

LC HF5681.N65 C54
DD 657 US
CHECKLISTS AND ILLUSTRATIVE FINANCIAL STATEMENTS FOR EMPLOYEE HEALTH AND WELFARE BENEFIT PLANS. **Added/Corp** American Institute of Certified Public Accountants. Technical Information Division. (July 1991)-. Periodical. English. Irregular. $25.00. American Institute of Certified Public Accountants, Harborside Financial Center, #201 Plaza 3, Jersey City NJ 07311. **Tel** (201)938-3333, (800)862-4272, FAX (201)938-3329.

LC HF5686.H7 C454
DD 657 US
CHECKLISTS AND ILLUSTRATIVE FINANCIAL STATEMENTS FOR HEALTH CARE PROVIDERS. **Added/Corp** American Institute of Certified Public Accountants. Technical Information Division. (July 1991)-. Periodical. English. Irregular. $25.00 (latest edition). American Institute of Certified Public Accountants, Harborside Financial Center, #201 Plaza 3, Jersey City NJ 07311. **Tel** (201)938-3333, (800)862-4272, FAX (201)938-3329.

LC HF5601
DD 657 US
CLIENTS MONTHLY ALERT. (19??)-. Periodical. English. Twelve times a year. $390.00. Faulkner & Gray Inc., 11 Penn Plaza, 17th Floor, New York NY 10001. **Tel** (212)967-7000, (800)535-8403.

LC HF5601
DD 657 UK
•**CLINICAL AUDIT.** (1995)-. Periodical. English. Four times a year. £102.00. Churchill Livingstone, 1-3 Baxter's Place, Leith Walk, Edinburgh EH1 3AF United Kingdom. **Tel** 011 44 131 5562424, FAX 011 44 131 5581278, telex 727511. ***Continues*** *Medical Audit News.*

LC HF5601
DD 657 CN
•**CMA MAGAZINE.** (1995)-. English. Ten times a year. Society of Management Accountants of Canada, 120 King Street West, Suite 850, Hamilton Ontario L8N 3C3 Canada. **Tel** (416)525-4100, FAX (416)525-4533. **(Subscription address:** Society of Management Accountants Canada, PO Box 176, Hamilton Ontario L8N 3C3 Canada. **Tel** (905)525-4100.) ***Continues*** *CMA : The Management Accounting Magazine, 0831-3881.*

LC HF5601 .C66 **ISSN** 0831-3881
DD 658.1/511/05 657/.42/0971 CN
CCC
CODEN CMAAEA
TITLE CHANGE
CMA : THE MANAGEMENT ACCOUNTING MAGAZINE. [CMA, Certif. manage. account.]. **Added/Corp** Society of Management Accountants of Canada. **VFOAT** Management Accounting Magazine; Revue de la Comptabilite de Management; Directory of Services; CMA Dimensions; CMA. **VAT** Certified Management Accountant. Vol. 59, No. 5 (Sept./Oct. 1985)-(1995). Periodical. English (French). Society of Management Accountants of Canada, 120 King Street West, Suite 850, Hamilton Ontario L8N 3C3 Canada. **Tel** (416)525-4100, FAX (416)525-4533. **(Subscription address:** Society of Management Accountants Canada, PO Box 176, Hamilton Ontario L8N 3C3 Canada. **Tel** (905)525-4100.) available on microfilm and microfiche from University Microfilms International (UMI); available on an online database (files 15,485,648/Full-Text) from DIALOG. Documents available from UMI Article Clearinghouse, Ask*IEEE. ***Continues*** *Cost and Management, 0010-9592.* ***Continued by*** *CMA Magazine.*
Ind/Abst ABI/INFORM Glob. Ed.; ABI/INFORM [Computer File]; Acad. Search; Account. Tax Datab. (Nov. 1972-) [Full Txt.]; Account. Art.; Bus. ASAP (1992-) [Full Txt.]; Bus. Index (1985-); Bus. Source Plus; Can. Period. Index (19??-); Curr. Cit.; EP Collect.; Gen. BusinessFile (1985-); Gen. Period. Index (1985-); Homework Help.; INFO-SOUTH Abstr.; INSPEC (1985-); Mag. Search; Manage. Contents; MasterFile FullTEXT 1000; MasterFile FullTEXT 350; MasterFile FullTEXT 650; MasterFile FullTEXT (Jan. 1993-); OCLC; Person. Manage. Abstr.; Telebase; UMI ABI/Inform--Bus. Period. Ondisc [Full Txt.]; Work Relat. Abstr.

LC HF5601
DD 657 IT
CODICE ANALISI DI BILANCIO E CONTABILI. (19??)-. Periodical. Italian. Two times a year. IPSOA Editore SRL, Casella Postale 12055, Mastrangelo, 20120 Milan Italy. **Tel** 011 39 2 82476248. Index available (Included).

LC HF5601
DD 657 IT
CODICE BILANCIO E CONTABILITA D'ESERCIZIO. (19??)-. Periodical. Italian. Two times a year. IPSOA Editore SRL, Casella Postale 12055, Mastrangelo, 20120 Milan Italy. **Tel** 011 39 2 82476248. Index available (Included).

LC HF5601
DD 657 IT
CODICE DI PROCEDURA E CONTENZIOSO TRIBUTARIO : 4 RIFORMA TRIBUTARIA. (19??)-. Periodical. Italian. Six times a year. IPSOA Editore SRL, Casella Postale 12055, Mastrangelo, 20120 Milan Italy. **Tel** 011 39 2 82476248.

LC HF5601
DD 657 IT
CODICE IMPOSTE DIRETTE : 4 CODICI RIFORMA TRIBUTARIA. (19??)-. Periodical. Italian. Six times a year. IPSOA Editore SRL, Casella Postale 12055, Mastrangelo, 20120 Milan Italy. **Tel** 011 39 2 82476248. Index available.

LC HF5601
DD 657 IT
CODICE IVA : 4 CODICI RIFORMA TRIBUTARIA. (19??)-. Periodical. Italian. Six times a year. IPSOA Editore SRL, Casella Postale 12055, Mastrangelo, 20120 Milan Italy. **Tel** 011 39 2 82476248. Index available (Included).

LC HF5601
DD 657 US
COLORADO CPA NEWSACCOUNT. (19??)-. English. Eight times a year. Colorado Society of Certified Public Accountants, 7720 East Bellview Avenue 46B, Englewood CO 80111.
Ind/Abst Account. Art.; Fed. Tax Artic.

LC HF5601
DD 657 US
COMBINED ROSTERS OF CERTIFIED PUBLIC ACCOUNTS, PUBLIC ACCOUNTANTS, AND ACCOUNTANTS AUTHORIZED TO CONDUCT MUNICIPAL AUDITS LICENSED OREGON AS OF ... . English. Rosters of Certified Public Accountants, 325 13th Street NE, Suite 604, Salem OR 97310.

LC HF5601
DD 657 IT
COMMISSIONE TRIBUTARIA CENTRALE. Italian. Casa Editrice Italedi, Piazza Cavour 19, 00193 Rome Italy. **Tel** 011 39 6 3210803.

LC HF5601 .A782 **ISSN** 0147-5673
DD 657/.61/06273 US
COMMITTEE HANDBOOK - AICPA.
(COMMITTEE HANDBOOK.). **Main/Corp** American Institute of Certified Public Accountants. **VAT** Committee Handbook - American Institute of Certified Public Accountants. (19??)-. English. One time a year. Free on request. American Institute of Certified Public Accountants, Harborside Financial Center, #201 Plaza 3, Jersey City NJ 07311. **Tel** (201)938-3333, (800)862-4272, FAX (201)938-3329.

LC HF5601 **ISSN** 0834-0188
DD 657/.06/0711 CN
COMMUNICATION - INSTITUTE OF CHARTERED ACCOUNTANTS OF BRITISH COLUMBIA. (COMMUNICATION : A PUBLICATION OF THE INSTITUTE OF CHARTERED ACCOUNTANTS OF BRITISH COLUMBIA.). [Commun. - Inst. Chart. Account. B.C.]. **Added/Corp** Institute of Chartered Accountants of British Columbia. No. 246 (July 1986)-. Periodical. English. Eleven times a year. 17.61Can$. Institute of Chartered Accountants of British Columbia, 1133 Melville Street, Sixth Floor, Vancouver BC V6E 4E5 Canada. **Tel** (604)681-3264. ***Continues*** *Institute of Chartered Accountants of British Columbia. News and Views - Institute of Chartered Accountants of British Columbia., 0380-4011.*

LC HF5601 **ISSN** 0954-8106
DD 657 UK
COMPANY ACCOUNTANT. Added/Corp Institute of Company Accountants. Issue No. 98 (Oct. 1990)-. Periodical. English. Six times a year (Feb., Apr., June, Aug., Oct., Dec.). $37.64. Soc Company & Commercial Accn, 40 Tyndalls Park Road, Clifton Bristol BS81PL United Kingdom. ***Continues*** *Accountants Record, 0305-8239.*

LC HF5601
DD 657 NE
COMPENDIUM VOOR DE JAARREKENING. (19??)-. Dutch. Irregular. Kluwer BV, Postbus 23, 7400 GA Deventer Netherlands. **Tel** 011 31 5700 33155, 011 31 5700 47421, FAX 011 31 5700 11504, telex 42829. Index available. cum. index. **Circ:** 2,500.
Desc: Business book for the accounting professional and accounting advisor.

LC HF5601
DD 657 US
COMPREHENSIVE MANAGEMENT REPORT. **See** Business and Economics-Management.

LC HF5601 .C67 **ISSN** 0884-2817
DD 657 US
CEASED
CONNECTICUT CPA QUARTERLY. [Conn. CPA q.]. **Added/Corp** Connecticut Society of Certified Public Accountants. **VAT** Connecticut Certified Public Accountant Quarterly. Vol. 45, No. 2 (Dec. 1981)-Vol. 56, No. 4 (June 1993). Periodical. English. Connecticut Society of Certified Public Accountants, 179 Allyn Street, Hartford CT 06103. **Tel** (203)525-1153. **ED** Andrea Massa. available on microfilm from University Microfilms International (UMI); available on an online database (file 485/Full-Text) from DIALOG. ***Continues*** *Connecticut CPA.*
Ind/Abst Account. Tax Datab. (1974-) [Full Txt.]; Account. Art.; Fed. Tax Artic.

LC HF5601
DD 657 IT
CONTABILITA DI MAGAZZINO. (19??)-. Periodical. Italian. Two times a year. IPSOA Editore SRL, Casella Postale 12055, Mastrangelo, 20120 Milan Italy. **Tel** 011 39 2 82476248. Index available (Included).

LC HF5616.C7 C66 **ISSN** 0120-4203
DD 657/.09861 CK
CONTADURIA UNIVERSIDAD DE ANTIOQUIA. Added/Corp Universidad de Antioquia. Departamento de Contaduria. **VFOAT** Contaduria. (19??)-. Periodical. Spanish. Two times a year. 1500Col$ Colombia; $40.00 other. Facultad de Ciencias Economicas / Medillin, Universidad de Antioquia, Apartado Aereo 1226, Medillin Columbia. **Tel** 244-97-27, FAX 263-82-82. **ED** Luis Alberto Cadavid Arango. Index available. cum. index. **Bk Rev. Ad Acc. Circ:** 1,000 (ctrl).
Desc: Articles of academic, technical and professional character relative to the discipline of accounting.

LC HF5601 **ISSN** 0823-9150
DD 657/.05 CN
CCC
Pr Rev.
CONTEMPORARY ACCOUNTING RESEARCH. [Contemp. account. res.]. **Added/Corp** Canadian Academic Accounting Association. **VFOAT** Recherche Comptable Contemporaine. Vol. 1, No. 1 (Fall 1984)-. Periodical. English (French). Two times a year (May, Dec.). 60.00Can$. Canadian Academic Accounting Association, 2-32C Business Building, University of Alberta, Edmonton Alberta T6G 2R6 Canada. **Tel** (403)492-7513, FAX (403)492-3325. **ED** Lane A. Daley (editor's phone number: (403)492-2517). **Bk Rev**, (Qty: 1-6). **Ad Acc, Adv Mgr:** Jane E. A. Flower. **Circ:** 1,200. available on microfilm and microfiche from University Microfilms International (UMI).
Desc: Reaches Canada's academic accountants. For those responsible for the selection of textbooks and reference materials for business schools of Canadian universities and colleges.
Ind/Abst Account. Tax Datab. (1984-); Curr. Cit.

LC HF5601 **ISSN** 0010-8391
DD 657 US
Pr Rev.
COOPERATIVE ACCOUNTANT, THE. [Coop. account.]. Vol. 1 (Winter 1945)-. Periodical. English. Four times a year. $40.00 US; $50.00 other. National Society of Accounts Co-Ops, 6320 Augusta Drive/Suite 800, Springfield VA 22150. **Tel** (703)569-3088, FAX (703)569-0235. **ED** Allen Ludlow. **Bk Rev. Circ:** 2,500 (ctrl).
Desc: Accounting tax and legal issues of agricultural cooperatives for use by co-op management, CPAs and auditors.
Ind/Abst Account. Tax Datab. (1974-); Account. Art.; Fed. Tax Artic.

LC HF5686.C7 C67 **ISSN** 0791-2471
DD 657 US
CORPORATE ACCOUNTING INTERNATIONAL. [Corp. account. int.]. Issue No. 1 (Nov. 1989)-. Corporate Report. English. Ten times a year. $749.00. Lafferty Publications Ltd., Tower Ida Centre Pearse Street, Dublin 2 Ireland. **Tel** 011 353 1 6718022, FAX 011 353 1 718520.
Desc: Provides a briefing on developments and trends in corporate reporting standard requirements and practices worldwide.

LC HF5668 .C67 **ISSN** 0743-4774
DD 338.4/365745/0973 US
CORPORATE AUDIT COSTS AND STAFFING. English. Institute of Internal Auditors / Orlando, Florida, PO Box 140099, Orlando FL 32889. **Tel** (407)830-7600, FAX (407)831-5171, telex 567443. **ED** Richard Holman. **Bk Rev. Circ:** 29,000.
Desc: More than 100 tables provide information on scope and methods of the study, cost and staff trends, audit cost comparisons for various industry groups, and audit staff qualifications and positions.

LC HF5601
DD 657 IT
CORRIERE TRIBUTARIO, IL. (19??)-. Periodical. Italian. One time a week. L430000 Italy; L860000 other. IPSOA Editore SRL, Casella Postale 12055, Mastrangelo, 20120 Milan Italy. **Tel** 011 39 2 82476248.

LC HF5661 .C7248
DD 657 US
CPA COMPREHENSIVE EXAM REVIEW. Added/Corp National Institute of Accountants (U.S.). **VAT** Certified Public Accountant Comprehensive Exam Review. (1991)-. English.

LC HF5601 **ISSN** 1047-5796
DD 657 US
CPA CONSTRUCTION NICHE BUILDER. [CPA constr. niche build.]. **VAT** Certified Public Accountant Construction Niche Builder. (1989)-. Periodical. English. Twelve times a year. $167.00. Harcourt Brace Professional Publishing, 525 B Street, Suite 1900, San Diego CA 92101-4495. **Tel** (619)699-6716, FAX (619)699-6593.

LC HF5601 **ISSN** 0741-3610
DD 657 US
Pr Rev.
CPA DIGEST. [CPA dig.]. **VFOAT** C.P.A. Digest. **VAT** Certified Public Accountant Digest. (1980)-. Periodical. English. Twelve times a year. $192.00. Harcourt Brace Professional Publishing, 525 B Street, Suite 1900, San Diego CA 92101-4495. **Tel** (619)699-6716, FAX (619)699-6593. **(Subscription address:** Harcourt Brace Jovanovich, 6277 Sea Harbor Drive, Orlando FL 32887-4600. **Tel** (800)543-9534, (800)831-7799, FAX (407)363-9661.) **ED** John R. Brandt. Index available. **Bk Rev.** ***Absorbed*** *Accounting Practices & Regulation, 8756-3061.*

LC HF5661 .C7234 **ISSN** 0743-815X
DD 657/.076 US
CPA EXAMINATION REVIEW. VFOAT C.P.A. Examination Review; Wiley CPA Examination Review. **VAT** Certified Public Accountant Examination Review. (1975)-. English. One time a year. $102.00. John Wiley & Sons, Inc., 605 Third Avenue, New York NY 10158-0012. **Tel** (212)850-6000, (212)850-6645, FAX (212)850-6088, telex 12-7063. **(Subscription address:** John Wiley & Sons / UK, Baffins Lane, Chichester, West Sussex PO19 1UD United Kingdom. **Tel** 011 44 1243 779777, FAX 011 44 243 776128, telex 86290 WIBOOKG.) ***Continues*** *CPA Examination Review Outlines and Study Guides, 0743-8567.*

LC HF5601 .N53 **ISSN** 0732-8435
DD 657.05 US
CODEN CPAABS
Pr Rev.
CPA JOURNAL (1975), THE. (THE CPA JOURNAL.). [CPA j.]. **Added/Corp** New York State Society of Certified Public Accountants. **VFOAT** C.P.A. Journal. **VAT** Certified Public Accountant Journal (1975). Vol. 45, No. 12 (Dec. 1975)-. Periodical. English. Twelve times a year. $48.00. CPA Journal, 530 Fifth Avenue, 5th Floor, New York NY 10036. **Tel** (212)719-8336, FAX (212)719-3365. Index available (Dec. iss.). **Ad Acc, Adv Mgr:** David Boniface, **Tel** (212)719-8313. **Circ:** 50,000. available on microfilm and microfiche from University Microfilms International (UMI); available on an online database from DIALOG. Documents available from BLDSC, FAXON Xpress, SWETS, The UnCover Company, UMI Article Clearinghouse. ***Continues*** *CPA (New York, N.Y. : 1975), 0732-8443.*
Desc: Features in-depth analysis and expert advice on latest developments in accounting.
Ind/Abst ABI/INFORM Glob. Ed.; ABI/INFORM [Computer File] (Dec. 1975-); Acad. Search; Account. Index Suppl.; Account. Tax Datab. (Sept. 1971-) [Full Txt.]; Account. Art.; Anbar Account. Finan. Abstr. [Full Txt.]; Anbar Mark. Distr. Abstr. [Full Txt.]; Anbar Top Manage. Abstr. [Full Txt.]; Bus. ASAP (1990-) [Full Txt.]; Bus. Index (1985-); Bus. Period. Index; Bus. Source Plus; Bus. Source; Curr. Cit.; EP Collect.; Fed. Tax Artic.; Gen. BusinessFile (1985-); Gen. Period. Index (1985-); Homework Help.; INFO-SOUTH Abstr.; Mag. Search; Manage. Bibliogr. Rev.; Manage. Contents (1975-); Manage. Contents; MasterFile FullTEXT 1000; MasterFile FullTEXT 350; MasterFile FullTEXT 650; MasterFile FullTEXT (July 1993-); OCLC; Oper. Prod. Manage. Abstr. [Full Txt.]; Person. Train. Abstr. [Full Txt.]; Telebase; Trade Ind. ASAP [Full Txt.]; Trade Ind. Index [Full Txt.]; UMI ABI/Inform--Bus. Period. Ondisc [Full Txt.]; Wilson Bus. Abstr.; Women Manage. Rev. [Full Txt.].

LC HF5601 .C18 **ISSN** 0094-792X
DD 657/.61 US
CPA LETTER, THE. [CPA lett.]. **Added/Corp** American Institute of Certified Public Accountants. **VAT** Certified Public Accountants Letter. (19??)-. Trade Publication. English. Twelve times a year. $40.00. American Institute of Certified Public Accountants, Harborside Financial Center, #201 Plaza 3, Jersey City NJ 07311. **Tel** (201)938-3333, (800)862-4272, FAX (201)938-3329. available on microfilm from University Microfilms International (UMI). ***Continues*** *C.P.A., 0007-8867.*
Ind/Abst Account. Tax Datab. (Jun. 1992-) [Full Txt.].

LC HF5601 **ISSN** 0894-1815
DD 657 US
CPA MANAGING PARTNER REPORT. [CPA manag. partn. rep.]. **VFOAT** Managing Partner Report. **VAT** Certified Public Accountant Managing Partner Report. (198?)-. Trade Publication. English. Twelve times a year. $257.00. Strafford Publications Inc., 590 Dutch Valley Road Northeast, Atlanta GA 30324. **Tel** (404)881-1141, (800)926-7926, FAX (404)881-0074.

LC HF5601 **ISSN** 0279-1021
DD 657 US
CPA MARKETING REPORT. **See** Business and Economics-Marketing and Purchasing.

LC HF5601 **ISSN** 0745-0877
DD 657 US
CPA PERSONNEL REPORT. **See** Business and Economics-Personnel Management.

LC HF5601 **ISSN** 1047-5834
DD 657 US
CPA PROFIT REPORT. [CPA profit rep.]. **VAT** Certified Public Accountant Profit Report. (1986)-. Periodical. English. Twelve times a year. $204.00. Harcourt Brace Professional Publishing, 525 B Street, Suite 1900, San Diego CA 92101-4495. **Tel** (619)699-6716, FAX (619)699-6593. **Bk Rev.** ctrl circ.

LC HF560L .C75 **ISSN** 1045-2354
DD 657/.05 UK
CCC
CRITICAL PERSPECTIVES ON ACCOUNTING. [Crit. perspect. account.]. (1990)-. Academic Scholarly Publication. English. Six times a year. $338.81. Academic Press Ltd., A Division of Harcourt Brace & Company Ltd., 24-28 Oval Road, London NW1 7DX United Kingdom. **Tel** 011 44 171 2674466, FAX 011 44 171 4822293, 011 44 171 4854752, telex 25775 ACPRES G. **(Subscription address:** Harcourt Brace & Company, Ltd., Foots Cray High Street, Sidcup Kent DA14 5HP United Kingdom. **Tel** 011 44 181 3003322, FAX 011 44 181 3090807, telex 896 377 ACADEM.) **ED** Tony Tinker and David Cooper.
Desc: Provides a forum for the emerging literature that connects accounting practices and corporate behavior to the broader environment of corporate, social, and political activity and the many related allocative, distributive, social, and ecological issues.
Ind/Abst Int. Bibliogr. Sociol.

Business and Economics —Accounting

LC HF5601 ISSN 1130-6254
DD 657 SP
UDC 657
CUADERNOS DE INVESTIGACION CONTABLE. [Cuad. investig. contab.]. (1987)-. Periodical. Spanish. One time a year. Free on request. Universidad Sevilla Dept. Economy Finance Contable, Avenida Ramon y Cajal 1, 41015 Sevilla Spain. **Tel** 011 34 5 4557616.

LC KD2042 .W55
DD 346/.41/0664 UK
CURRENT ACCOUNTING LAW & PRACTICE. (1976)-. English. One time a year. $487.70. Sweet & Maxwell Ltd., South Quay Plaza, 183 Marsh Wall 7th Floor, London E14 9FT United Kingdom. **Tel** 011 44 171 5388686, FAX 011 44 171 5389508, telex 929089 ITPINF G.

LC Z7164.C81 I43a HF5635
DD 016.657 UK
CURRENT ACCOUNTING LITERATURE. **Main/Corp** Institute of Chartered Accountants in England and Wales. London. Library. (1971)-. English. $42.00. Institute of Chartered Accountants, 399 Silbury Boulevard, Central Milton, Keynes Buckinghamshire MK9 2HL United Kingdom. **Tel** 011 44 1908 248100, FAX 011 44 1908 248001, telex 727530.
Desc: Covers areas of historical library publications.

LC HF5601
DD 657 UK
CURRENT ACCOUNTING LITERATURE; A SUPPLEMENT. **Added/Corp** Institute of Chartered Accountants in England and Wales, London. Library. **VFOAT** Current Accounting Literature 1972-. (1972)-. English. Irregular. Institute of Chartered Accountants, 399 Silbury Boulevard, Central Milton, Keynes Buckinghamshire MK9 2HL United Kingdom. **Tel** 011 44 1908 248100, FAX 011 44 1908 248001, telex 727530.

LC HF5611 .A318 ISSN 1054-3619
DD 657/.09 US
DIRECTORY - ACADEMY OF ACCOUNTING HISTORIANS. (DIRECTORY / THE ACADEMY OF ACCOUNTING HISTORIANS.). [Dir. - Acad. Account. Hist.]. **Main/Corp** Academy of Accounting Historians. (1990)-. Periodical. English. One time a year. $46.00 institutional membership; $36.00 individual membership. University of Arkansas / Academy of Accounting Historians, Building 204, Fayetteville AR 72701. **Tel** (501)575-6125. **Continues** Academy of Accounting Historians. Membership Roster.
Desc: Membership directory for the Academy of Accounting Historians.

LC HF5686.P3 C62a
DD 657/.862 US
DIRECTORY / COUNCIL OF PETROLEUM ACCOUNTANTS SOCIETIES. **Main/Corp** Council of Petroleum Accountants Societies (U.S.). **Added/Corp** North Texas State University. College of Business Administration. Professional Development Institute. **VFOAT** C.O.P.A.S. Directory; COPAS Directory. (19??)-. Directory. English. Irregular. $8.95 (per copy). Kraftbilt, PO Box 800, Tulsa OK 74101. **Tel** (800)331-7290.

LC HF5616.C2 C23 ISSN 0527-9275
DD 657/.025/71 CN
DIRECTORY OF CANADIAN CHARTERED ACCOUNTANTS. (DIRECTORY OF CANADIAN CHARTERED ACCOUNTANTS. ANNUAIRE DES COMPTABLES AGREES CANADIENS.). **Added/Corp** Canadian Institute of Chartered Accountants. **VFOAT** Bottin des Comptables Agrees Canadiens; Annuaire des Comptables Agrees Canadiens; Repertoire des Comptables Agrees Canadiens. (1958)-. Directory. English (French). One time a year. Canadian Institute of Chartered Accountants, 277 Wellington Street West, Toronto Ontario M5V 3H2 Canada. **Tel** (416)977-3222, FAX (416)204-3415. **Circ:** 4,000. **Continues** Directory of Chartered Accountants in Canada, 0703-4490.
Desc: Contains addresses and council for Canadian and Provincial institutes, alphabetical list of members with addresses, geographical list of CA firms and sole practitioners listed alphabetically by city and a list of firm partners.

LC HF5616.U5 T42a ISSN 0731-2415
DD 657/.025/764 US
DIRECTORY OF LICENSEES / TEXAS STATE BOARD OF PUBLIC ACCOUNTANCY. **Main/Corp** Texas State Board of Public Accountancy. (19??)-. Directory. English. One time a year. Texas State Board of Public Accountancy, 333 Guadalupe Tower 111, Suite 900, Austin TX 78701. **Tel** (512)505-5500, FAX (512)505-5575. **Continues** Texas State Board of Public Accountancy. Permit Holders.

LC HF5686.P3 C62b
DD 657 US
DIRECTORY OF LIMITED MEMBERS / COUNCIL OF PETROLEUM ACCOUNTANTS SOCIETIES. **Main/Corp** Council of Petroleum Accountants Societies (U.S.). **Added/Corp** North Texas State University. College of Business Administration. Professional Development Institute. (19??)-. Directory. English. One time a year. Council of Petroleum Accountants Societies, PO Box 3244, Englewood CO 80155-3244.

LC HF5601
DD 657 IT
DIRITTO E PRATICA TRIBUTARIA. (19??)-. Italian. Six times a year. L480000 Italy; L650000 other. Cedam Spa, Via Jappelli 5 6, 35121 Padua Italy. **Tel** 011 39 49 65667.

LC HF5616.U5 F36a ISSN 1055-3746
DD 657 US
EITF ABSTRACTS. [EITF abstr.]. **Main/Corp** FASB Emerging Issues Task Force. **Added/Corp** Financial Accounting Standards Board. **VAT** Emerging Issues Task Force Abstracts. Issue No. 84-1 (1984)-. English. Irregular. $578.00. Financial Accounting Standards Board, PO Box 5116, Norwalk CT 06856. **Tel** (203)847-0700, FAX (203)849-9714.

LC HF5601
DD 657 LV
EKONOMIKAS INFORMACIJAS APSTRADES MEHANIZACIJA. See Computers-Electronic Data Processing.

LC HF5601 ISSN 0847-1568
DD 657/.06/0714 CN
ELITE CMA. [Elite CMA]. **Added/Corp** Corporation Professionnelle des Comptables en Management Accredites du Quebec. **VFOAT** Elite CMA. **VAT** Elite Corporation Professionnelle des Comptables en Management Accredites du Quebec. Vol. 1, No 1 (Sept. 1989)-. Periodical. English (French). Six times a year. Free to members. Corporation Professionnelle Des Comptables En Management, Bureau 724, 555 Ouest boulevard Dorchester, Montreal Quebec H2Z 1B1 Canada. **Continues** Conte Rendu., 0713-5491.

LC HF5601 ISSN 1060-8168
DD 657 US
CEASED
EMERSON'S AUDITOR CHANGE REPORT. (EMERSON'S AUDITOR CHANGE REPORT: ACR.). [Emerson's audit. change rep.]. **VFOAT** ACR; Auditor Change Report. (1991)-(Sept. 1994). Periodical. English. Emerson Company, 12356 Northup Way, #103, Bellevue WA 98005. **Tel** (206)869-0655, FAX (206)869-0746. **ED** James C. Emerson.
Desc: Analysis of auditor charges at publicly held companies. Auditors serving P.O's.

LC HF5616.U5 E47
DD 657 US
●**EMERSON'S DIRECTORY OF LEADING ACCOUNTING FIRMS WORLDWIDE.** **VFOAT** Directory of Leading Accounting Firms Worldwide; Leading Accounting Firms Worldwide. 4th Ed. (1994/1995)-. Directory. English. Every 2 years. Emerson Company, 12356 Northup Way, #103, Bellevue WA 98005. **Tel** (206)869-0655, FAX (206)869-0746. **Continues** Emerson's Directory of Leading U.S. Accounting Firms.

LC HF5601 ISSN 1060-8729
DD 657 US
EMERSON'S PROFESSIONAL SERVICES REVIEW : PSR. [Emerson's prof. serv. rev.]. **VFOAT** Emerson's PSR; PSR; Professional Services Review. (Jan./Feb. 1990)-. Trade Publication. English. Six times a year. $295.00. Emerson Company, 12356 Northup Way, #103, Bellevue WA 98005. **Tel** (206)869-0655, FAX (206)869-0746. **ED** James C. Emerson. **Continues** Big Eight Review, 0748-4763.
Desc: Summary of significant events impacting professional services firms which provide information and business solutions for the world's largest companies. A special report that investigates the success of a major firm is included.
Ind/Abst Account. Tax Datab. (Jan. 1992-).

LC HJ9921 .Z33a
DD 354.710072/32 CN
ESTIMATES. PART III, TREASURY BOARD OF CANADA, COMPTROLLER GENERAL. **Main/Corp** Canada. **VFOAT** Budget des Depenses. Partie III, Conseil du Tresor du Canada, Controleur General. (19??)-. English (French). $3.00 Canada; $3.60 other. Canada Communication Group Publishers, Order Processing, Ottawa Ontario K1A 0S9 Canada. **Tel** (819)956-4800, (819)956-4802.

LC HF5616.E8 E97 ISSN 0963-0538
DD 338.7/61657/0254 UK
EUROPEAN ACCOUNTANCY YEARBOOK. (1992/1993)-. English. $235.00. Graham & Trotman Ltd., Sterling House, 66 Wilton Road, London SW1V 1DE United Kingdom. **Tel** 011 44 171 8211123, FAX 011 44 171 8288935. **(Subscription address:** Gale Research Co., 835 Penobscot Building, Detroit MI 48226. **Tel** (800)347-4253.)
Desc: Includes articles by industry figures, a directory, corporate tax data, national accounting qualifications, national institutes and associations.

LC HF5601 ISSN 0791-3664
DD 657 IE
EUROPEAN ACCOUNTANT DUBLIN. (EUROPEAN ACCOUNTANT.). [Eur. account.Dublin]. (1990)-. Periodical. English. Ten times a year. $799.00. Lafferty Publications Ltd., Tower Ida Centre Pearse Street, Dublin 2 Ireland. **Tel** 011 353 1 6718022, FAX 011 353 1 718520. **ED** Niahl Brady.
Desc: Looks at the accounting marketplace in Europe's major cities and provides detailed surveys of the profession in all European countries (not just the EC), with league tables showing trends and revenue and staff growth.

LC HF5601
DD 657 BE
EUROPEAN ACCOUNTING : A PUBLICATION OF THE EUROPEAN ACCOUNTING ASSOCIATION. **Added/Corp** European Accounting Association. **VFOAT** European Accounting News. (19??)-. Periodical. English. Four times a year. Comes with European Accounting Association membership. European Accounting Association, rue d'Egmont Straat 13, EIASM, B-1050 Brussels Belgium. **Tel** 011 32 2 511 9116.

LC HF5601 ISSN 0955-4882
DD 657.094 UK
EUROPEAN ACCOUNTING FOCUS. [Eur. account. focus]. (1989)-. Trade Publication. English. Ten times a year. $602.00. Intellectual Property Publishing, 3rd Floor Brigade House, Parsons GRN, London SW6 7NE United Kingdom. **Tel** 011 44 171 7367111.

LC HF5601 ISSN 0963-8180
DD 657 UK
CCC
Pr Rev.
EUROPEAN ACCOUNTING REVIEW. **Added/Corp** European Accounting Association. **VFOAT** EAR. Vol. 1, No. 1 (May 1992)-. Periodical. English. Three times a year (May, Sept., Dec.). $188.00. Routledge, 11 New Fetter Lane, London EC4P 4EE United Kingdom. **Tel** 011 44 171 5839855, FAX 011 44 171 5830701. **(Subscription address:** Kinokuniya Company Ltd., 38-1 Sakuragaoka 5, chome Setagaya-ku, Tokyo 156 Japan. **Tel** FAX 011 03 3439 0136.) **ED** Anne Loft and Anne Jorissen. Index available (December). **Bk Rev. Ad Acc, Adv Mgr:** David Polley.
Desc: Published for the European Accounting Association of Brussels.

LC HC125 .U588c ISSN 0094-5609
DD 658.1/5 US
EXAMINATION OF FINANCIAL STATEMENTS INTER-AMERICAN FOUNDATION. (EXAMINATION OF FINANCIAL STATEMENTS, INTER-AMERICAN FOUNDATION; REPORT TO THE CONGRESS BY THE COMPTROLLER GENERAL OF THE UNITED STATES.). **Main/Corp** United States. General Accounting Office. (19??)-. Government Publication. English. US General Accounting Office / District of Columbia, 441 G Street Northwest, Room 4528, Washington DC 20548. **Tel** (202)275-2812.

LC HF5601
DD 657 US
EXAMINATION OF THE PANAMA CANAL COMMISSION'S FISCAL YEAR ... FINANCIAL STATEMENTS AND TREATY-RELATED ISSUES. SUMMARY. **Added/Corp** United States. General Accounting Office. (1980)-. Government Publication. English. One time a year. US General Accounting Office / District of Columbia, 441 G Street Northwest, Room 4528, Washington DC 20548. **Tel** (202)275-2812. **Continues** Examination of Fiscal Year ... Financial Statements of the Panama Canal Organization and Treaty-Related Issues. Summary.

LC HE8803 .G45a ISSN 0096-9893
DD 353.007/232 US
EXAMINATION OF THE RURAL TELEPHONE BANK'S FINANCIAL STATEMENTS. (EXAMINATION OF THE RURAL TELEPHONE BANK'S FINANCIAL STATEMENTS; REPORT TO THE CONGRESS BY THE COMPTROLLER GENERAL OF THE UNITED STATES.). **Main/Corp** United States. General Accounting Office. (19??)-. Government Publication. English. One time a year. US General Accounting Office / District of Columbia, 441 G Street Northwest, Room 4528, Washington DC 20548. **Tel** (202)275-2812. **Continues** United States. General Accounting Office. Audit of the Rural Telephone Bank, Department of Agriculture; Report to the Congress by the Comptroller General of the United States.

Business and Economics — Accounting

LC HF5601
DD 657 UK
EXECUTIVE ACCOUNTANT. (19??)-. English. Four times a year. £12.00 UK; £15.00 other. Association of Cost & Executive Accounts, 141 149 Fonthill Road/Tower House, London N4 3HF United Kingdom. **Tel** 011 44 181 2723925, telex 21610. available on microfilm and microfiche from University Microfilms International (UMI); available on an online database (file 485/Full-Text) from DIALOG.
Ind/Abst Account. Tax Datab. (1986-) [Full Txt.].

LC HF5601
DD 657 US
EXECUTIVE'S TAX REPORT. (19??)-. Periodical. English. One time a week. $213.96. Harcourt Brace Professional Publishing, 525 B Street, Suite 1900, San Diego CA 92101-4495. **Tel** (619)699-6716, FAX (619)699-6593. **(Subscription address:** Harcourt Brace Jovanovich, 6277 Sea Harbor Drive, Orlando FL 32887-4600. **Tel** (800)543-9534, (800)831-7799, FAX (407)363-9661.) **Continues** Executive's Tax Report & What's Happening in Taxation, 0423-8990.

LC HF5601 **ISSN** 0885-9116
DD 657 US
EXPOSURE DRAFT (STAMFORD, CONN. 1974). (EXPOSURE DRAFT : PROPOSED STATEMENT OF FINANCIAL ACCOUNTING STANDARDS.). [Expo. draft]. **Main/Corp** Financial Accounting Standards Board. **Added/Corp** Financial Accounting Standards Board. (1974?)-. Monographic series. English. Irregular. Comes with Financial Accounting Standards'Board Financial Accounting Series (comprehensive). Financial Accounting Standards Board, PO Box 5116, Norwalk CT 06856. **Tel** (203)847-0700, FAX (203)849-9714.
Desc: Preliminary document, part of comprehensive subscription plan, and various subject matter.

LC HF5601
DD 657 US
FASB ACTION ALERT. Added/Corp Financial Accounting Standards Board. **VFOAT** Action Alert. **VAT** Financial Accounting Standards Board Action Alert. (19??)-. Periodical. English. One time a week. $66.00. Financial Accounting Standards Board, PO Box 5116, Norwalk CT 06856. **Tel** (203)847-0700, FAX (203)849-9714.

LC HF5601
DD 657 US
FASB DISCUSSION MEMORANDUM. Main/Corp Financial Accounting Standards Board. **VFOAT** Financial Accounting Standards Board Discussion Memoranda. (19??)-. Monographic series. English. Irregular. Price varies per volume. Financial Accounting Standards Board, PO Box 5116, Norwalk CT 06856. **Tel** (203)847-0700, FAX (203)849-9714.

LC HF5601 **ISSN** 0193-7855
DD 657 US
FASB INTERPRETATION. Main/Corp Financial Accounting Standards Board. **Added/Corp** Financial Accounting Standards Board. Interpretation. **VAT** Financial Accounting Standards Board Interpretation. (1974)-. Monographic series. English. Irregular. $9.50 (nonmembers) North America; $11.50 (nonmembers) other. Financial Accounting Standards Board, PO Box 5116, Norwalk CT 06856. **Tel** (203)847-0700, FAX (203)849-9714.
Desc: Part of FASB subscription plans.

LC HF5616.U5 F518 **ISSN** 0886-4535
DD 657 US
FASB TECHNICAL BULLETIN. [FASB tech. bull.]. **Main/Corp** Financial Accounting Standards Board. **Added/Corp** Financial Accounting Standards Board. **VFOAT** Technical Bulletin. No. 79-1 (1979)-. Bulletin. English. Irregular. $6.00 (nonmembers) North America; $9.00 (nonmembers) other. Financial Accounting Standards Board, PO Box 5116, Norwalk CT 06856. **Tel** (203)847-0700, FAX (203)849-9714.

LC HD4965.5.U6 F56
DD 331.281331714 US
FINANCE, ACCOUNTING & LEGAL COMPENSATION SURVEY RESULTS. Added/Corp William M. Mercer-Meidinger-Hansen, Inc. **VFOAT** Finance, Accounting, and Legal Compensation Survey Results. (19??)-. English. One time a year. price varies. National Survey Group, 1417 Lake Cook Road, Deerfield IL 60015. **Tel** (800)333-3070.

LC HG **ISSN** 0260-1176
DD 332.05 UK
FINANCE DIRECTOR'S REVIEW CROYDON. [Finance dir. rev. Croydon]. (1980)-. English. Twelve times a year. $282.35. Tolley Publishing Company Ltd., Tolley House, 2 Addiscombe Road, Croydon, Surrey CR9 5AF United Kingdom. **Tel** 011 44 181 6869141, FAX 011 44 181 6863155.
Desc: Deals with all aspects of accounting, financial management and regulatory issues.

LC HF5601 **ISSN** 0267-4424
DD 657 UK
  CCC
FINANCIAL ACCOUNTABILITY & MANAGEMENT IN GOVERNMENTS, PUBLIC SERVICES, AND CHARITIES. See Finance-Public Finance.

LC HC60.U4 F55
DD 354.1 US
FINANCIAL REPORT AND AUDITED FINANCIAL STATEMENTS FOR THE YEAR ENDED 31 DECEMBER ... AND REPORT OF THE BOARD OF AUDITORS. Main/Corp United Nations Development Programme. **Added/Corp** United Nations. Board of Auditors. **VFOAT** Report of the Board of Auditors. (1979)-. Government Publication. English. One time a year. United Nations Publications, 2 United Nations Plaza, Room DC2 0853, Department 007C, New York NY 10017. **Tel** (212)963-8303, (800)253-9646. **Continues** United Nations Development Programme. Financial Report and Accounts and Report of the Board of Auditors.

LC HF5601
DD 657 UK
FINANCIAL REPORTING... A SURVEY OF UK PUBLISHED ACCOUNTS. Added/Corp Institute of Chartered Accountants in England and Wales. (1982)-. Periodical. English. One time a year (March). $100.97. Institute of Chartered Accountants, 399 Silbury Boulevard, Central Milton, Keynes Buckinghamshire MK9 2HL United Kingdom. **Tel** 011 44 1908 248100, FAX 011 44 1908 248001, telex 727530. **Continues** Survey of Published Accounts (London, England), 0308-1761.

LC HF5601 **ISSN** 0071-5115
DD 657/.3/0971 CN
FINANCIAL REPORTING IN CANADA. Added/Corp Canadian Institute of Chartered Accountants. (1953/54)-. Periodical. English. Every 2 years. 27.61Can$. Canadian Institute of Chartered Accountants, 277 Wellington Street West, Toronto Ontario M5V 3H2 Canada. **Tel** (416)977-3222, FAX (416)204-3415. **ED** G. Lew. **Circ:** 3,000.
Desc: Comparison of the financial statements of 325 Canadian companies with CICA handbook recommendations.

LC HF5601
DD 657 IT
FISCO, IL. (19??)-. Periodical. Italian. Irregular (59 issues). L286130. Editoriale Tributaria Italiana, Viale Mazzini 25, 00195 Rome Italy. **Tel** 011 39 6 87130300. Index available (bound in issue).

LC HF5601
DD 657 US
FLORIDA CPA TODAY : A PUBLICATION OF THE FLORIDA INSTITUTE OF CERTIFIED PUBLIC ACCOUNTANTS. Added/Corp Florida Institute of Certified Public Accountants. **VFOAT** CPA Today. Vol. 1, No. 1 (Jan. 1985)-. Periodical. English. Twelve times a year. Free on request. Florida Institute of CPA, PO Box 5437, Tallahassee FL 32314. **Tel** (904)224-2727, FAX (904)222-8190. cum. index. **Ad Acc. Circ:** 18,500 (ctrl). **Continues** Florida Certified Public Accountant News Notes.
Ind/Abst Account. Index Suppl. (1986-); Account. Tax Datab. (1986-).

LC HF5616.U5 G33 **ISSN** 0883-4245
DD 657/.0218 US
GAAP. [GAAP]. **Added/Corp** Financial Accounting Standards Board. **VAT** Generally Accepted Accounting Principles. 1985 Edition (1985)-. English. One time a year. $33.60. John Wiley & Sons Inc / New Jersey, 1 Wiley Drive, Somerset NJ 08875. **Tel** (800)225-5945, (908)469-4400. **ED** Patrick R. Delaney.

LC HF5601 **ISSN** 1046-2910
DD 657 US
GENERAL LEDGER, THE. (THE GENERAL LEDGER : THE COMPLETE NEWSLETTER FOR PROFESSIONAL BOOKKEEPERS.). [Gen. ledger]. **Added/Corp** American Institute of Professional Bookkeepers. (198?)-. Newsletter. English. Twelve times a year. $39.00. American Institute of Professional Bookkeepers, 6001 Montrose Road, Suite 207, Rockville MD 20852. **Tel** (301)770-7300.

LC QH426 **ISSN** 0272-9032
DD 575.1 CCC
NLM W1; GE285 **CODEN** GTNEEA
GENETIC TECHNOLOGY NEWS. See Biology-Genetics.

LC HF5601 **ISSN** 1055-3940
DD 657 US
GLOBAL COMMUNIQUE. [Glob. commun.]. **Added/Corp** EDP Auditors Association. Sept. 1990-. Periodical. English. Four times a year. EDP Auditors Association Inc, PO Box 74171, Chicago IL 60690. **Tel** (708)253-1545, FAX (708)253-1443. **Continues** EDP Auditor Update, 0885-9450.

LC HJ9801 **ISSN** 0883-1483
DD 657/.835/05 US
GOVERNMENT ACCOUNTANTS JOURNAL, THE. [Gov. account. j.]. Vol. 25 (1976)-. Government Publication. English. Four times a year. $60.00. Association of Government Accountants, 2200 Mount Vernon Avenue, Alexandria VA 22301. **Tel** (703)684-6931. Index available. **Bk Rev.** available on microfilm and microfiche from University Microfilms International (UMI). Documents available from UMI Article Clearinghouse. **Continues** Federal Accountant.
Ind/Abst ABI/INFORM Glob. Ed.; ABI/INFORM [Computer File] (1976-); Acad. Search; Account. Tax Datab. (Sept. 1972-) [Full Txt.]; Account. Art.; Bus. Source Plus; Bus. Source; Curr. Cit.; EP Collect.; Gen. BusinessFile (1992-); Gen. Period. Index (1985-); Homework Help.; INFO-SOUTH Abstr.; Mag. Search; Manage. Contents; MasterFile FullTEXT 1000; MasterFile FullTEXT 350; MasterFile FullTEXT 650; MasterFile FullTEXT (July 1993-); OCLC; Telebase.

LC JF201 **ISSN** 1048-1389
DD 351 US
GOVERNMENT ACCOUNTING AND AUDITING UPDATE. See Public Administration.

LC JK404 **ISSN** 1052-5777
DD 353 US
GOVERNMENT CONTRACT, COSTS, PRICING & ACCOUNTING REPORT. See Public Administration.

LC HF5601
DD 657 US
GOVERNMENTAL ACCOUNTING STANDARDS BOARD (SUBSCRIPTION SERVICE). (19??)-. Government Publication. English. Irregular. $84.80. Government Finance Officers Association, 180 North Michigan Avenue, Suite 800, Chicago IL 60601-7476. **Tel** (312)977-9700, FAX (312)977-4806. **(Subscription address:** GASB, PO Box 5116, 401 Merritt 7, Norwalk CT 06856. **Tel** (203)847-0700 ext. 200.)

LC HF5635 .G94 Suppl. **ISSN** 0734-8525
DD 658.1/511 US
  SUSPENDED
GUIDE TO ACCOUNTING CONTROLS. SUPPLEMENT. [Guide account. controls, Suppl.]. (1981)-Suspended (1982). English. One time a year. Warren Gorham & Lamont Inc., Park Square Building, 31 St. James Avenue, Boston MA 02116-4112. **Tel** (617)423-2020, (800)950-1207, FAX (617)423-2026. **ED** Joseph E Conner and Burnell H de Vos Jr.

LC HF5601 **ISSN** 1060-2933
DD 657 US
GUIDE TO AUDITS OF EMPLOYEE BENEFIT PLANS. [Guide audits empl. benefit plans]. **Added/Corp** Practitioners Publishing Company. 1st Ed. (1991)-. Directory. English. One time a year. Practitioners Publishing Company, PO Box 966, Fort Worth TX 76101-0966. **Tel** (800)332-3709.

LC HF5601 **ISSN** 1046-3534
DD 657 US
  CCC
HANDBOOK OF SEC ACCOUNTING AND DISCLOSURE. [Handb. SEC account. discl.]. **VAT** Handbook of Securities and Exchange Commission Accounting and Disclosure. (1988)-. English. One time a year (published in May). $160.00. Warren Gorham & Lamont Inc., Park Square Building, 31 St. James Avenue, Boston MA 02116-4112. **Tel** (617)423-2020, (800)950-1207, FAX (617)423-2026.

LC HF5601 **ISSN** 1058-952X
DD 657 US
HBJ MILLER COMPREHENSIVE COMPILATION AND REVIEW GUIDE. [HBJ Miller compil. rev. guide]. **VFOAT** Compilation and Review Guide. (1992)-. English. $75.00. HBJ Professional Publications, 6277 Sea Harbor Drive, Orlando FL 32821. **Tel** (800)543-9534.

LC HF5601 **ISSN** 1080-4994
DD 657 US
  TITLE CHANGE
HBJ MILLER COMPREHENSIVE GOVERNMENTAL GAAP GUIDE. See Finance-Public Finance.

LC HF5601 **ISSN** 1064-7163
DD 657 US
●**HBJ MILLER COMPREHENSIVE LOCAL AUDIT GUIDE. VFOAT** Comprehensive Local Audit Guide. **VAT** Harcourt Brace Jovanovich Miller Comprehensive Local Audit Guide. (1993)-. English. $115.00. HBJ Professional Publications, 6277 Sea Harbor Drive, Orlando FL 32821. **Tel** (800)543-9534.

LC HF5601 .H63
DD 657 KO
HOEGYE WA SEMU. **VFOAT** Accounting and Taxation. Periodical. Korean (Korean). W800 single issue. Taehan Semu Hyophoe, 158-5 Cho-dong, Chung-ku, Seoul South Korea.

LC HF5601
DD 657 US
IN OUR OPINION. Vol. 1, No. 1 (April 1985)-. Periodical. English. Four times a year. Auditing Standards Division, American Institute of CPA's, 1211 Avenue of the Americas, New York NY 10036-8775.
Ind/Abst Account. Tax Datab. (Mar. 1992-) [Full Txt.].

LC Z7164.C81 I285 HF5635 **ISSN** 0163-7150
DD 016.657 US
INDEX TO ACCOUNTING AND AUDITING TECHNICAL PRONOUNCEMENTS. **Added/Corp** American Institute of Certified Public Accountants. (19??)-. English. Irregular. $46.00. American Institute of Certified Public Accountants, Harborside Financial Center, #201 Plaza 3, Jersey City NJ 07311. **Tel** (201)938-3333, (800)862-4272, FAX (201)938-3329.

LC HD47 .I63 **ISSN** 0019-7793
DD 338.51 PK
TITLE CHANGE
INDUSTRIAL ACCOUNTANT. [Ind. account.]. **Added/Corp** Pakistan Institute of Industrial Accountants. Vol. 1 (Sept. 1960)-(19??). Periodical. English. Institute of Cost Management Accountants, PO Box 7284, Karachi 3 Pakistan. **Tel** 011 92 21 460900. available on microfilm and microfiche from University Microfilms International (UMI). ***Continued by*** *Management Accountant.*
Ind/Abst Account. Index Suppl. (?-?).

LC HF5601 **ISSN** 1053-8542
DD 657 US
INSIGHT (CHICAGO, ILL.). (INSIGHT.). [Insight]. **Added/Corp** Illinois CPA Society. Vol. 40, No. 4 (Sept. 1990)-. Trade Publication. English. Ten times a year. $20.00. Illinois CPA Society, 511 West Capitol, Suite 101, Springfield IL 62704. **Tel** (312)993-0393, FAX (312)993-7713. ***Continues*** *Newsjournal (Chicago, Ill.), 1043-7215.*

LC HF5601
DD 657 AT
INSTITUTE OF CHARTERED ACCOUNTANTS IN AUSTRALIA MEMBERS HANDBOOK. (19??)-. English. Two times a year. 90.00Aus$ (handbook), 10.00Aus$ (updates). Institute of Chartered Accountants in Australia, GPO Box 3921, Sydney New South Wales, 2001 Australia. **Tel** 011 61 2 290 1344, FAX 011 61 2 262 3953. **Circ:** 25,000.

LC HF5601 **ISSN** 0384-8639
DD 657/.076 CN
INSTITUTS DE COMPTABLES AGREES DU CANADA. EXAMENS FINAL. (EXAMENS FINAL SIC.). **Main/Corp** Institutes of Chartered Accountants in Canada. 1969-. French. One time a year. $1.00 per number. Instituts de Comptables Agrees du Canada, 250 East rue Bloor, Toronto Ontario M4W 1E6 Canada. ***Supersedes*** *Examens Intermediaire et Final, 0384-8620.*

LC HF5601 **ISSN** 0744-2947
DD 657 US
CCC
INTERNAL AUDITING ALERT. [Intern. audit. alert]. **Added/Corp** Warren, Gorham & Lamont. Vol. 1, No. 1 (Feb. 1981)-. Newsletter. English. Twelve times a year. $146.75. Warren Gorham & Lamont Inc., Park Square Building, 31 St. James Avenue, Boston MA 02116-4112. **Tel** (617)423-2020, (800)950-1207, FAX (617)423-2026. **ED** Paul J. Wendell.
Desc: Designed to keep the reader current on key developments in operational, control, and managerial areas. It supplies hints, ideas, and suggestions for administering operations and improving the usefulness of the internal audit function.

LC HF5668 .I58 **ISSN** 0897-0378
DD 657/.458/05 US
CCC
INTERNAL AUDITING (BOSTON, MASS.). (INTERNAL AUDITING.). [Intern. audit.]. Vol. 1, No. 1 (1985)-. Trade Publication. English. Four times a year. $115.98. Warren Gorham & Lamont Inc., Park Square Building, 31 St. James Avenue, Boston MA 02116-4112. **Tel** (617)423-2020, (800)950-1207, FAX (617)423-2026. available on microfilm and microfiche from University Microfilms International (UMI).
Ind/Abst Account. Tax Datab. (1985-); Curr. Cit.; Gen. BusinessFile (1992-).

LC HF5667 .I52 **ISSN** 0020-5745
DD 657.6062* US
CCC
CODEN ITAUA
INTERNAL AUDITOR, THE. (THE INTERNAL AUDITOR : JOURNAL OF THE INSTITUTE OF INTERNAL AUDITORS.). [Intern. aud.]. **Added/Corp** Institute of Internal Auditors. Vol. 1 (Sept. 1944)-. Trade Publication. English. Six times a year. $60.00. Institute of Internal Auditors / Orlando, Florida, PO Box 140099, Orlando FL 32889. **Tel** (407)830-7600, FAX (407)831-5171, telex 567443. **ED** Anne Graham. Index available. cum. index. **Bk Rev. Ad Acc. Circ:** 31,000. available on CD-ROM; available on microfilm and microfiche from University Microfilms International (UMI); available on an online database (files 15,485,648/Full-Text) from DIALOG. Documents available from Ask*IEEE, UMI Article Clearinghouse. ***Continues*** *IIA Today.*
Desc: Covers all phases of internal auditing, from ethics and standards to specific techniques. Explores risks, internal control, informative systems, other operational audits and cost-saving case studies.
Ind/Abst ABI/INFORM Glob. Ed.; ABI/INFORM Ondisc: Expr. Ed.; ABI/INFORM [Computer File] (Jan. 1972-); Acad. Search; Account. Tax Datab. (Jan. 1972-) [Full Txt.]; Anbar Account. Finan. Abstr. [Full Txt.]; Anbar Mark. Distr. Abstr. [Full Txt.]; Anbar Top Manage. Abstr. [Full Txt.]; Bus. ASAP (1990-) [Full Txt.]; Bus. Index (1985-); Bus. Period. Index; Bus. Source Plus; Bus. Source; Comput. Lit. Index; Curr. Cit.; EP Collect.; Gen. BusinessFile (1985-); Gen. Period. Index (1985-); Homework Help.; INFO-SOUTH Abstr.; INSPEC (Dec. 1983-); Mag. Search; Manage. Bibliogr. Rev.; Manage. Contents; MasterFile FullTEXT 1000; MasterFile FullTEXT 350; MasterFile FullTEXT 650; MasterFile FullTEXT (July 1993-); OCLC; Oper. Prod. Manage. Abstr. [Full Txt.]; Person. Train. Abstr. (Jan. 1972-) [Full Txt.]; Telebase; Trade Ind. ASAP [Full Txt.]; Trade Ind. Index [Full Txt.]; UMI ABI/Inform--Bus. Period. Ondisc (Dec. 1987-) [Full Txt.]; Vocat. Search; Wilson Bus. Abstr.; Women Manage. Rev. (1974-) [Full Txt.].

LC HF5601 **ISSN** 0265-0223
DD 657 UK
INTERNATIONAL ACCOUNTING BULLETIN. [Int. account. bull.]. (19??)-. Bulletin. English. Six times a year (23 issues). $799.00. Lafferty Publications Ltd., Tower Ida Centre Pearse Street, Dublin 2 Ireland. **Tel** 011 353 1 6718022, FAX 011 353 1 718520. **ED** Michael Lafferty. **Bk Rev.**
Desc: Provides a briefing on developments in the accounting and financial advisory business worldwide.
Ind/Abst Account. Tax Datab. (1983-).

LC HF5601 .I78 **ISSN** 1056-2583
DD 657/.05 US
INTERNATIONAL ACCOUNTING SUMMARIES. (INTERNATIONAL ACCOUNTING SUMMARIES : A GUIDE FOR INTERPRETATION AND COMPARISON.). [Int. account. summ.]. **Added/Corp** Coopers & Lybrand. (1991)-. English. Irregular. $95.00 (per copy). John Wiley & Sons, Inc., 605 Third Avenue, New York NY 10158-0012. **Tel** (212)850-6000, (212)850-6645, FAX (212)850-6088, telex 12-7063. **(Subscription address:** John Wiley & Sons, Inc. / Philadelphia, PO Box 7247, Philadelphia PA 19170. **Tel** (212)850-6645, (800)225-5945.**)**

LC HF5601 .I613
DD 657 UK
INTERNATIONAL JOURNAL OF ACCOUNTING, THE. Vol. 24, No. 1 (1989)-. Periodical. English. Four times a year. £88.00. Springer-Verlag London Ltd., Springer House, 8 Alexandra Road Wimbledon, London SW19 7JZ United Kingdom. **Tel** 011 44 181 9471280, 011 44 181 9475885, FAX 011 44 181 9474651, telex 21531 SPRGB G. **(Subscription address:** Springer-Verlag New York Inc. / North America, PO Box 2485, Journal Fulfillment, Secaucus NJ 07096. **Tel** (201)348-4033, (800)777-4643, FAX (201)348-4505.**)** ***Continues*** *International Journal of Accounting Education and Research, 0020-7063.*
Ind/Abst Contents Pages Manage.

LC HF5601 **ISSN** 0746-6579
DD 657 US
IOWA IIA AUDIT UPDATE. **Added/Corp** Institute of Internal Auditors. Iowa Chapter. **VFOAT** Iowa I.I.A. Audit Update; Iowa Audit Update; Audit Update. **VAT** Iowa Institute of Internal Auditors Audit Update. (19??)-. Periodical. English. Twelve times a year. $5.00. Audit Update, 711 High Street, Des Moines IA 50307. **Tel** (515)246-7000. **ED** Lee Flint. **Circ:** 200 (ctrl).
Desc: Monthly membership newsletter of the Iowa Chapter of the Internal Auditors.

LC HF5601
DD 657 US
IOWA TAX RULES. (19??)-. English. Twelve times a year. $195.00. Iowa Tax Publishing Inc., 712 West Main, Manchester IA 52057. **Tel** (800)472-2664, (319)927-2385.

LC HF5601
DD 657 UK
IRR RACE AUDIT BULLETIN. (19??)-. English. Six times a year. $17.11. Institute of Race Relations, 2-6 Leeke Street, Kings Crossroad, London WC1X 9HS United Kingdom. **Tel** 011 44 171 8370041, FAX 011 44 171 2780623.

LC HF5630 .I77 **ISSN** 0739-3172
DD 657/.07/1173 US
ISSUES IN ACCOUNTING EDUCATION. [Issues account. educ.]. **Added/Corp** American Accounting Association. Vol. 1, No. 1 (Spring 1983)-. Periodical. English. Two times a year (Spring and Fall). $30.00. American Accounting Association, 5717 Bessie Drive, Sarasota FL 34233-2399. **Tel** (813)921-7747, FAX (813)923-4093. **ED** Robert W. Ingram. available in microform from University Microfilms International (UMI).
Desc: Information and studies by and for accounting educators. Contains ideas and techniques for teaching undergraduate and graduate accounting courses.
Ind/Abst Account. Tax Datab. (1986-) [Full Txt.]; Bus. Source Plus; Bus. Source; EP Collect.; Fed. Tax Artic.; Homework Help.; MasterFile FullTEXT 1000; MasterFile FullTEXT 350; MasterFile FullTEXT 650; MasterFile FullTEXT; OCLC; Telebase.

LC HF5601 .J7 **ISSN** 0021-8448
DD 657.05 US
CCC
CODEN JACYAD
Pr Rev.
JOURNAL OF ACCOUNTANCY. [J. account.]. **Added/Corp** American Association of Public Accountants. American Institute of Certified Public Accountants. Vol. 1 (Nov. 1905)-. Trade Publication. English. Fourteen times a year. $56.00. American Institute of Certified Public Accountants, Harborside Financial Center, #201 Plaza 3, Jersey City NJ 07311. **Tel** (201)938-3333, (800)862-4272, FAX (201)938-3329. **ED** Colleen Katz. Index available. cum. index. **Bk Rev. Ad Acc. Circ:** 325,000. available on microfilm and microfiche from University Microfilms International (UMI). Documents available from The Genuine Article, UMI Article Clearinghouse.
Desc: Covers new developments and practical techniques in accounting, auditing, taxation, practice management, management advisory services and related business and professional subjects.
Ind/Abst ABI/INFORM Glob. Ed.; ABI/INFORM Ondisc: Expr. Ed.; ABI/INFORM [Computer File] (Sept. 1971-); Acad. Search; Account. Tax Datab. (Sept. 1971-) [Full Txt.]; Account. Art.; ACM Guide Comput. Lit.; Anbar Account. Finan. Abstr. [Full Txt.]; Anbar Mark. Distr. Abstr. [Full Txt.]; Anbar Top Manage. Abstr. [Full Txt.]; Bus. ASAP (1990-) [Full Txt.]; Bus. Educ. Index; Bus. Index (1985-); Bus. Period. Index; Bus. Source Plus; Bus. Source; Comput. Lit. Index; Comput. Rev.; Contents Pages Manage.; Curr. Cit.; Curr. Contents Soc. Behav. Sci.; Curr. Law Index (1980-); EP Collect.; Fed. Tax Artic.; Gen. BusinessFile (1985-); Gen. Period. Index (1985-); Homework Help.; INFO-SOUTH Abstr.; Law Office Inf. Serv.; Leg. Resour. Index (1980-); LegalTrac (1980-); Mag. Search; Manage. Market. Abstr.; Manage. Bibliogr. Rev.; MasterFile FullTEXT 1000; MasterFile FullTEXT 350; MasterFile FullTEXT 650; MasterFile FullTEXT (July 1993-) [Full Txt.]; Newsp. Period. Abstr. (1988-); OCLC; Oper. Prod. Manage. Abstr. [Full Txt.]; PAIS Int. Print (1991-); Person. Train. Abstr. [Full Txt.]; Res. Alert [Full Cov.]; Selec. Coop. Index Manage. Period.; Soc. Sci. Cit. Index [Full Cov.]; Telebase; Trade Ind. ASAP [Full Txt.]; Trade Ind. Index (1981-) [Full Txt.]; UMI ABI/Inform--Bus. Period. Ondisc (Jan. 1987-) [Full Txt.]; Wilson Bus. Abstr.; Women Manage. Rev. [Full Txt.].

LC HF5601 **ISSN** 0165-4101
DD 657 NE
CCC
CODEN JAECDS
Pr Rev.
JOURNAL OF ACCOUNTING & ECONOMICS. [J. account. & econ.]. **VFOAT** Journal of Accounting and Economics. Vol. 1 (Mar. 1979)-. Academic Scholarly Publication. English. Six times a year (2 volumes). $588.00. Elsevier Science Publishers BV, PO Box 211, 1000 AE Amsterdam Netherlands. **Tel** 011 31 20 4853641, 011 31 20 4853642, FAX 011 31 20 4853598. **ED** Ross L. Watts, Jerold L. Zimmerman, and Robert S. Kaplan. **Bk Rev. Ad Acc.** available on microfilm and microfiche from University Microfilms International (UMI); available on an online database from Elsevier Electronic Subscriptions (EES). Documents available from The Genuine Article, UMI Article Clearinghouse.
Desc: Encourages the application of economic theory to the explanation of accounting phenomena.
Ind/Abst ABI/INFORM Glob. Ed.; ABI/INFORM [Computer File] (March 1981-); Acad. Search; Account. Tax Datab. (1979-); Account. Art.; Bus. Index (1985-); Bus. Source Plus; Bus. Source; Contents Recent Econ. J.; Curr. Cit.; Curr. Contents Soc. Behav. Sci.; Econ. Lit. Index (19??-); EP Collect.; Gen. BusinessFile (1985-); Gen. Period. Index (1985-); Homework Help.; INFO-SOUTH Abstr.; J. Econ. Lit.; Mag. Search; MasterFile FullTEXT 1000; MasterFile FullTEXT 350; MasterFile FullTEXT 650; MasterFile FullTEXT (Jan. 1993-); OCLC; Res. Alert [Full Cov.]; Soc. Sci. Cit. Index [Full Cov.]; Telebase.

LC H97 .J66 **ISSN** 0278-4254
DD 361.6/1/05 US
CCC
CODEN JACPDN
Pr Rev.
JOURNAL OF ACCOUNTING AND PUBLIC POLICY. [J. account. public policy]. Vol. 1, No. 1 (Fall 1982)-. Academic Scholarly Publication.

English. Four times a year (1 volume). $278.00. Elsevier Science Publishing Company Inc, Madison Square Station, PO Box 882, New York NY 10159-0882. **Tel** (212)633-3950, FAX (212)633-3990. **ED** Lawrence A Gordon and Stephen E Loeb. **Ad Acc.** available on microfilm and microfiche from University Microfilms International (UMI); available on an online database from Elsevier Electronic Subscriptions (EES). Documents available from The Genuine Article, UMI Article Clearinghouse.
Desc: Publishes essential articles exploring the interaction of accounting with a wide range of professional disciplines including economics, public administration, political science, social psychology, policy science and the law.
Ind/Abst ABI/INFORM Glob. Ed.; ABI/INFORM [Computer File] (Spring 1983-); Account. Tax Datab. (Spring 1983-) [Full Txt.]; Account. Art.; Contents Pages Manage.; Curr. Cit.; Curr. Contents Soc. Behav. Sci.; Gen. BusinessFile (1992-); PAIS Int. Print (1991-); Res. Alert [Full Cov.]; Sage Public Adm. Abstr.; Sage Urban Stud. Abstr; Soc. Sci. Cit. Index [Full Cov.].

LC HF5601 .J73 **ISSN** 0148-558X
DD 657/.05 US
CCC

JOURNAL OF ACCOUNTING AUDITING & FINANCE. [J. account. audit. financ.]. **Added/Corp** Vincent C. Ross Institute of Accounting Research. **VAT** Journal of Accounting, Auditing and Finance. Vol. 1, No. 1 (Fall 1977)-. Periodical. English. Four times a year. $105.00. Greenwood Press Inc., PO Box 5007, Westport CT 06881-5007. **Tel** (203)226-3571, FAX (203)222-1502. **ED** Joshua Ronen. Documents available from UMI Article Clearinghouse.
Desc: One forum where both practitioners and academics are brought together on the common ground of intelligent and thorough anaylsis of accounting and auditing principles.
Ind/Abst ABI/INFORM Glob. Ed.; ABI/INFORM [Computer File] (Fall 1977-); Acad. Search; Account. Tax Datab. (Fall 1977-); Account. Art.; Bus. Period. Index; Bus. Source Plus; Bus. Source; Curr. Cit.; EP Collect.; Gen. Period. Index (Jan. 1985-Oct. 1985); Homework Help.; INFO-SOUTH Abstr.; Mag. Search; MasterFile FullTEXT 1000; MasterFile FullTEXT 350; MasterFile FullTEXT 650; MasterFile FullTEXT (July 1993-); OCLC; Telebase; Wilson Bus. Abstr.

LC HF5601 **ISSN** 1192-2621
DD 657 CN
Pr Rev.

JOURNAL OF ACCOUNTING CASE RESEARCH, THE. [J. account. case res.]. **Added/Corp** University of Lethbridge. Accounting Education Resource Centre. **VFOAT** Accounting Case Research. Vol. 1, No. 1 (Fall 1992)-. Periodical. English. Three times a year. 60.00Can$. Captus Press Inc., 4700 Keele Street, York University Campus, North York Ontario M3J 1P3 Canada. **Tel** (416)736-5537, FAX (416)736-5793. **ED** Eldon Gardner (editor's address: Faculty of Management, University of Lethbridge, Lethbridge, Alberta Canada, (403)329-2726). ctrl circ.
Desc: Publishes cases on accounting and related topics of interest to the world community of academic accountants. Aim is to encourage the development of cases in accounting education by making them readily available to faculty and students.

LC HF5630 .J68 **ISSN** 0748-5751
DD 657/.07/1073 US
CCC
Pr Rev.

JOURNAL OF ACCOUNTING EDUCATION. [J. account. educ.]. **Added/Corp** James Madison University. Center for Research in Accounting Education. Vol. 1, No. 1 (Spring 1983)-. Periodical. English. Four times a year. $255.00. Pergamon Press, An Imprint of Elsevier Science Ltd., The Boulevard, Langford Lane, Kidlington, Oxford OX5 1GB United Kingdom. **Tel** 011 44 1865 843000, 011 44 1865 843699, FAX 011 44 1865 843010. **(Subscription address:** Elsevier Science Ltd. / Oxford Fulfillment Centre, PO Box 800, Kidlington OX5 1DX United Kingdom. **Tel** 011 44 865 843355.**) ED** Kent St Pierre. **Bk Rev. Ad Acc. Circ:** 1,500 (ctrl). available on microfilm and microfiche from University Microfilms International (UMI); available on an online database from Elsevier Electronic Subscriptions (EES).
Desc: Dedicated to promoting excellence in teaching and stimulating research in all areas of accounting education. Particular emphasis is given to educational methods and educating accounting students.
Ind/Abst Account. Tax Datab. (1983-); Account. Art.

LC HF5601 .J74 **ISSN** 0737-4607
DD 657/.05 US
Pr Rev.

JOURNAL OF ACCOUNTING LITERATURE. [J. account. lit.]. **Added/Corp** University of Florida. Accounting Research Center. Society of Accounting Research Digest (U.S.). Vol. 1 (Spring 1982)-. English. One time a year (Dec.). $32.00. University of Florida, 255 New Business Building, Gainesville FL 32611. **Tel** (904)392-0155. **ED** Bipin B. Ajinkya and William F. Messier. **Circ:** 700. available on microfilm and microfiche from University Microfilms International (UMI).
Desc: State-of-the-art review articles and research on accounting and auditing standards.
Ind/Abst Account. Tax Datab. (Jan. 1991-).

LC HF5601 .J75 **ISSN** 0021-8456
DD 657/.05 US
CODEN JACRBR
Pr Rev.

JOURNAL OF ACCOUNTING RESEARCH. [J. acc. res.]. **Added/Corp** London School of Economics and Political Science. University of Chicago. Institute of Professional Accounting. Vol. 1, No. 1 (Spring 1963)-. Periodical. English. Three times a year. $86.00. Journal of Accounting Research, Graduate School of Business, University of Chicago, 1101 East 58th Street, Chicago IL 60637. **Tel** (312)702-7460. **ED** N. Dopuch and K. Schipper. **Circ:** 2,850 (ctrl). available on microfilm and microfiche from University Microfilms International (UMI). Documents available from The Genuine Article, UMI Article Clearinghouse.
Desc: Reports new developments in accounting occasioned by similarly new developments in economic, operations research, behavioral sciences, and other related fields.
Ind/Abst ABI/INFORM Glob. Ed.; ABI/INFORM [Computer File] (Fall 1972-); Acad. Search; Account. Tax Datab. (Fall 1972-); Account. Art.; Anbar Account. Finan. Abstr. [Full Txt.]; Anbar Mark. Distr. Abstr. [Full Txt.]; Anbar Top Manage. Abstr. [Full Txt.]; APAIS, Aust. Public Aff. Inf. Ser.; Bus. Index (1986-); Bus. Period. Index; Bus. Source Plus; Bus. Source; Contents Recent Econ. J.; Contents Pages Manage.; Curr. Cit.; Curr. Contents Soc. Behav. Sci.; Econ. Lit. Index; EP Collect.; Gen. BusinessFile (1986-); Gen. Period. Index (1986-); Homework Help.; INFO-SOUTH Abstr.; J. Econ. Lit.; Mag. Search; Manage. Bibliogr. Rev.; Manage. Contents; MasterFile FullTEXT 1000; MasterFile FullTEXT 350; MasterFile FullTEXT 650; MasterFile FullTEXT (Jan. 1993-); OCLC; Oper. Prod. Manage. Abstr. [Full Txt.]; Person. Train. Abstr. [Full Txt.]; Res. Alert [Full Cov.]; Selec. Coop. Index Manage. Period.; Soc. Sci. Cit. Index [Full Cov.]; Telebase; UMI ABI/Inform--Bus. Period. Ondisc (Fall 1987-) [Full Txt.]; Wilson Bus. Abstr.; Women Manage. Rev. [Full Txt.].

LC HF5601 **ISSN** 1078-0726
DD 657 US

•**JOURNAL OF ACCOUNTING, TAXATION AND FINANCE FOR BUSINESS, THE.** [J. account. tax. finance bus.]. **Added/Corp** American Institute of Professional Bookkeepers. Vol. 4, No. 1 (Summer 1994)-. Periodical. English. Four times a year. $69.00. American Institute of Professional Bookkeepers, 6001 Montrose Road, Suite 207, Rockville MD 20852. **Tel** (301)770-7300. ***Continues** Journal of Professional Bookkeeping and Management, 1056-8662.*
Desc: Covers bookkeeping, accounting, tax, financial, legal and management developments. Translates the needed accounting and tax techniques into easy-to-understand "how-to" segments with clear, illustrative examples.

LC HF5601 **ISSN** 1070-941X
DD 657 US
Pr Rev.

JOURNAL OF BANK COST & MANAGEMENT ACCOUNTING, THE. [J. bank cost manag. account.]. **Added/Corp** National Association for Bank Cost & Management Accounting (U.S.). **VFOAT** Journal of Bank Cost and Management Accounting. Vol. 1, No. 1 (1985)-. Periodical. English. Three times a year (Mar., July, Nov.). $90.00. NABCA - National Association of Bank Cost and Management Accounting, PO Box 458, Northbrook IL 60065-0458. **Tel** (708)272-4233, FAX (708)272-6445. **ED** Al Schneider. Index available. **Circ:** 600. available on microfilm and microfiche from University Microfilms International (UMI); available on an online database (file 485/Full-Text) from DIALOG; and University Microfilms International (UMI).
Desc: Information on banks, banking, cost accounting, and bank management.
Ind/Abst Account. Tax Datab. (1985-).

LC HG11 .J66 **ISSN** 0306-686X
DD 332/.05 UK
CCC

JOURNAL OF BUSINESS FINANCE & ACCOUNTING. [J. bus. finance account.]. **VFOAT** Journal of Business Finance and Accounting. (Spring 1974)-. Academic Scholarly Publication. English. Ten times a year. $417.00. Basil Blackwell Publishers Ltd., 108 Cowley Road, Oxford 0X4 1JF United Kingdom. **Tel** 011 44 1235 465500, FAX 011 44 1235 465556, telex 837022 OXBOOK G. **(Subscription address:** Blackwell Publishers / UK, 108 Cowley Road, Oxford OX4 1JF United Kingdom. **Tel** 011 44 1865 791100, FAX 011 44 1865 791347.**) ED** Richard Briston. **Ad Acc. Circ:** 1,300. available on microfilm and microfiche from University Microfilms International (UMI). Documents available from UMI Article Clearinghouse.
Desc: This international journal publishes research based and serious polemical articles on all aspects of accountancy and the financial administration of business.
Ind/Abst ABI/INFORM Glob. Ed.; ABI/INFORM [Computer File] (Spring 1979-); Acad. Search; Account. Tax Datab. (1974-); Anbar Account. Finan. Abstr. [Full Txt.]; Anbar Mark. Distr. Abstr. [Full Txt.]; Anbar Top Manage. Abstr. [Full Txt.]; Bus. Index (1985-); Bus. Source Plus; Bus. Source; Contents Recent Econ. J.; Contents Pages Manage.; Curr. Cit.; EP Collect.; Gen. BusinessFile (1985-); Gen. Period. Index (1985-); Homework Help.; INFO-SOUTH Abstr.; Mag. Search; Manage. Market. Abstr.; Manage. Bibliogr. Rev.; MasterFile FullTEXT 1000; MasterFile FullTEXT 350; MasterFile FullTEXT 650; MasterFile FullTEXT (July 1993-); OCLC; Oper. Prod. Manage. Abstr. [Full Txt.]; Person. Train. Abstr. [Full Txt.]; Pollut. Abstr. Indexes; Selec. Coop. Index Manage. Period.; Telebase; UMI ABI/Inform--Bus. Period. Ondisc (Winter 1987-) [Full Txt.]; Women Manage. Rev. [Full Txt.].

LC HF5686.B7 J66 **ISSN** 1054-3007
DD 657/.869/0097305 US
CCC
Pr Rev.

JOURNAL OF CONSTRUCTION ACCOUNTING & TAXATION. See Building and Construction.

LC HF5601 .J667 **ISSN** 1044-8136
DD 657 US
CCC

JOURNAL OF CORPORATE ACCOUNTING AND FINANCE. [J. corp. account. finance]. **VFOAT** Journal of Corporate Accounting and Finance; Corporate Accounting and Finance. Vol. 1, No. 1 (Autumn 1989)-. Periodical. English. Four times a year. $188.00. John Wiley & Sons, Inc., 605 Third Avenue, New York NY 10158-0012. **Tel** (212)850-6000, (212)850-6645, FAX (212)850-6088, telex 12-7063. **(Subscription address:** John Wiley & Sons Inc / New Jersey, PO Box 2575, Secaucus NJ 07096-2575. **) ED** Jane G. Bensahely. Index available. **Ad Acc.** available on microfilm and microfiche from University Microfilms International (UMI). ***Continues** Financial Accounting Reporter, 0890-3484.*
Desc: Offers advice on how to deal with current issues affecting corporate accounting practices and policies. Analysis of rulings, statements and tax code changes currently being considered or revised.
Ind/Abst Account. Tax Datab. (1989-) [Full Txt.].

LC HF5686.C8 J59 **ISSN** 0882-3871
DD 658.15/52/05 US
Pr Rev.

JOURNAL OF COST ANALYSIS, THE. **Added/Corp** Institute of Cost Analysis. Vol. 1, No. 1 (Spring 1984)-. Periodical. English. Two times a year (Mar. & Sept.). $40.00. Society Cost Estimating and Analysis, 101 South Whiting Street, Suite 201, Alexandria VA 22304. **Tel** (703)751-8069, FAX (703)461-7328. **ED** Roland Kankey (phone: (513)255-7777 ext. 3382). **Circ:** 3,000.
Ind/Abst Account. Index Suppl. (1984-).

LC HF5601 **ISSN** 1061-9518
DD 657 US
CCC

JOURNAL OF INTERNATIONAL ACCOUNTING AUDITING & TAXATION. [J. int. account. audit. tax.]. Vol. 1, No. 1 (1992)-. Trade Publication. English. Two times a year. $155.00. JAI Press Inc., 55 Old Post Road, Suite 2, PO Box 1678, Greenwich CT 06836-1678. **Tel** (203)661-7602, FAX (203)661-0792. **ED** James Schweikart.
Desc: Publishes articles in all areas of international accounting including auditing, taxation, management advisory services, and internal reporting.
Ind/Abst Account. Tax Datab. (1992-).

LC HG4027.5 .J67 **ISSN** 0954-1314
DD 658.15/99/05 UK
CCC

JOURNAL OF INTERNATIONAL FINANCIAL MANAGEMENT & ACCOUNTING. **VFOAT** Journal of International Financial Management and Accounting. Vol. 1, No. 1 (Spring 1989)-. Academic Scholarly Publication. English. Three times a year. $142.00. Basil Blackwell Publishers Ltd., 108 Cowley Road, Oxford 0X4 1JF United Kingdom. **Tel** 011 44 1235 465500, FAX 011 44 1235 465556, telex 837022 OXBOOK G. **(Subscription address:** Blackwell Publishers / UK, 108 Cowley Road, Oxford OX4 1JF United Kingdom. **Tel** 011 44 1865 791100, FAX 011 44 1865 791347.**)** available on microfilm and microfiche from University Microfilms International (UMI). Documents available from UMI Article Clearinghouse.
Ind/Abst ABI/INFORM Glob. Ed.

LC HF5657.4 .J68 **ISSN** 1049-2127
DD 658.15/11/05 US

JOURNAL OF MANAGEMENT ACCOUNTING RESEARCH. [J. manage. account. res.]. **Added/Corp** American Accounting Association. Management Accounting Section. **VFOAT** JMAR. Vol. 1 (Fall 1989)-. English. One time a year (July). $15.00. American Accounting Association, 5717 Bessie Drive, Sarasota FL 34233-2399. **Tel** (813)921-7747, FAX (813)923-4093.
Ind/Abst Account. Tax Datab. (Fall 1992-); Bus. Source Plus; EP Collect.; Homework Help.; MasterFile FullTEXT 1000; MasterFile FullTEXT 350; MasterFile FullTEXT 650; MasterFile FullTEXT; OCLC; Telebase.

LC HF5601 ISSN 1015-7891
DD 657 US
Pr Rev.

JOURNAL OF PARAMETRICS. (JOURNAL OF PARAMETRICS : A PUBLICATION OF THE INTERNATIONAL SOCIETY OF PARAMETRIC ANALYSTS.). [J. parametr.]. **Added/Corp** International Society of Parametric Analysts. (1981)-. Trade Publication. English. Four times a year. Comes with International Society of Parametric Analysts membership: $45.00 regular; $23.00 student; $450.00 life. International Society of Parametric Analysts, PO Box 1056, Germantown MD 20875-1056. **Tel** (301)670-8925, FAX (301)670-1942. **ED** Arlene Cooper and Arlene Wusterbath. **Bk Rev**. **Ad Acc**, **Adv Mgr:** Amy Johnson. **Circ:** 500 (ctrl).
Desc: Deals with cost estimation.

LC HF5601 .J76 ISSN 1056-8662
DD 657/.0973/05 US
TITLE CHANGE

JOURNAL OF PROFESSIONAL BOOKKEEPING AND MANAGEMENT, THE. [J. prof. bookkeep. manag.]. **Added/Corp** American Institute of Professional Bookkeepers. Vol. 1, No. 1 (Summer 1991)-(199?). Periodical. English. American Institute of Professional Bookkeepers, 6001 Montrose Road, Suite 207, Rockville MD 20852. **Tel** (301)770-7300. ***Continued by*** *Journal of Accounting, Taxation and Finance for Business, 1078-0726.*
Desc: Covers bookkeeping, accounting, tax, financial, legal and management developments as they affect small-company bookkeepers and accountants. Translates the needed accounting and tax techniques into easy-to-understand "how-to" with clear, illustrative examples. A practical reference for small-company bookkeepers and accountants, freelance practitioners and students.

LC HF5601 .J77 ISSN 1015-0005
DD 657/.09549/3 CE

JOURNAL OF THE INSTITUTE OF CHARTERED ACCOUNTANTS OF SRI LANKA. [J. Inst. Chart. Account. Sri Lanka]. **Added/Corp** Institute of Chartered Accountants of Sri Lanka. **VFOAT** Institute of Chartered Accountants of Sri Lanka Journal. (Sept. 1978)-. Periodical. English (Sinhalese and Tamil). Two times a year. Institute of Chartered Accountants of Sri Lanka, 30A Malalasekera Mawatha, Colombo 7 Sri Lanka. **Bk Rev**. **Ad Acc**. **Circ:** 1,000. ***Continues*** *Ganakadhikari.*
Ind/Abst Account. Index Suppl.

LC K
DD 343 JA

KIGYO KAIKEI KISOKUSHU. See Law-Corporation Law.

LC HF5601 ISSN 0823-6313
DD 657/.01/4 CN

LEXICOM. (LEXICOM : BULLETIN TERMINOLOGIQUE DE LA SOCIETE DES COMPTABLES EN MANAGEMENT AU CANADA.). [Lexicom]. **Added/Corp** Society of Management Accountants of Canada. (Jan. 1983)-. Bulletin. French. Three times a year. 12.00Can$. Society of Management Accountants of Canada, 120 King Street West, Suite 850, Hamilton Ontario L8N 3C3 Canada. **Tel** (416)525-4100, FAX (416)525-4533.

LC HF5601
DD 657 US

LIFO LOOKOUT. (19??)-. English. Four times a year. $325.00. LIFO Lookout, 317 West Prospect Avenue, Mt. Prospect IL 60056. **Tel** (708)577-3977.

LC HF5601 .I77
DD 657/.025/41 UK

LIST OF MEMBERS AND FIRMS.
Main/Corp Institute of Chartered Accountants in England and Wales. **Added/Corp** Institute of Chartered Accountants in England and Wales Directories. (19??)-. Directory. English. One time a year. $65.03. Institute of Chartered Accountants, 399 Silbury Boulevard, Central Milton, Keynes Buckinghamshire MK9 2HL United Kingdom. **Tel** 011 44 1908 248100, FAX 011 44 1908 248001, telex 727530. ***Continues*** *Institute of Chartered Accountants in England and Wales. List of Members.*
Desc: Lists members of ICAEW, both alphabetically and geographically, with partner's names and addresses.

LC HF5616.G7 C45a
DD 657/.025/41 UK

LIST OF MEMBERS / CHARTERED ASSOCIATION OF CERTIFIED ACCOUNTANTS. **Main/Corp** Chartered Association of Certified Accountants (Great Britain). (1987)-. English. One time a year. £20.00. Chartered Association of Certified Accountants, 29 Lincolns Inn Fields, London WC2A 3EE United Kingdom. **Tel** 011 44 171 2426855, telex CERTAC 24381. ***Continues*** *List of Members in Practice.*

LC HG1706 ISSN 0924-6304
DD 657 NE
UDC 657

MAB 'S-GRAVENHAGE. (MAB.). **VFOAT** Maandblad voor Accountancy en Bedrijfseconomie ('s-Gravenhage). (1989)-. Periodical. Dutch. Ten times a year. Fl180.00. Delwel Uitgeverij BV, Postbus 19110, 2500 CC Den Haag Netherlands. **Tel** 011 31 70 3624800, FAX 011 31 70 3605606. Index available. **Bk Rev**. **Ad Acc**. **Circ:** 5,000.
Desc: Includes issues of interest to those involved in the accounting profession.

LC HF5601
DD 657 PK

MANAGEMENT ACCOUNTANT. (19??)-. Periodical. English. Four times a year. $20.20. Institute of Cost Management Accountants, PO Box 7284, Karachi 3 Pakistan. **Tel** 011 92 21 460900. ***Continues*** *Industrial Accountant.*

LC HF5686.C8 M26 ISSN 0025-1674
DD 657.4/2/0954 II

MANAGEMENT ACCOUNTANT, THE. [Manage. account.]. **Added/Corp** Institute of Cost & Works Accountants of India. (1966)-. Periodical. English. Twelve times a year. $30.00. The Institute of Cost and Works Accountants of India, 12 Sudder Street, Calcutta 16, W Bengal India. **Tel** 24-1031. **(Subscription address:** Prints India, 11 Darya Ganj, New Delhi 110002 India. **Tel** 011 91 11 3268645, FAX 011 91 11 3275542, telex 31-61087 PRIN-IN.) **ED** A N Dutta. **Bk Rev**. **Ad Acc**. **Circ:** 21,000. available on microfilm and microfiche from University Microfilms International (UMI).
Ind/Abst Bus. Index (1979-?).

LC HF5686.C8 C684 ISSN 0025-1682
DD 657 UK
CODEN MATGBA

MANAGEMENT ACCOUNTING (LONDON). (MANAGEMENT ACCOUNTING : JOURNAL OF THE INSTITUTE OF COST AND WORKS ACCOUNTANTS.). [Manage. account.]. **Added/Corp** Institute of Cost and Works Accountants (Great Britain) Institute of Cost and Management Accountants. Vol. 43, No. 1 (Jan. 1965)-. Trade Publication. English. Eleven times a year. £30.00. Chartered Institute of Management Accountants, 63 Portland Place, London W1N 4AB United Kingdom. **Tel** 011 44 171 6372311. **ED** John Hillary. Index available (free). cum. index. **Bk Rev**. **Ad Acc**. ctrl circ. available on microfilm and microfiche from University Microfilms International (UMI). Documents available from UMI Article Clearinghouse. ***Continues*** *Cost Accountant.*
Ind/Abst ABI/INFORM Glob. Ed.; ABI/INFORM [Computer File] (Sept. 1971-); Acad. Search; Account. Tax Datab. (Sept. 1971-) [Full Txt.]; Bus. Source Plus; Bus. Source; Contents Pages Manage.; Curr. Cit.; EP Collect.; Homework Help.; MasterFile FullTEXT 1000; MasterFile FullTEXT 350; MasterFile FullTEXT 650; MasterFile FullTEXT (July 1993-); OCLC; Selec. Coop. Index Manage. Period.; Telebase; UMI ABI/Inform--Bus. Period. Ondisc (Oct. 1987-) [Full Txt.]; World Mag. Bank.

LC HF5686.C8 A27 ISSN 0025-1690
DD 658.1/552 US
CCC
CODEN MGACBD

MANAGEMENT ACCOUNTING (NEW YORK, N.Y.). (MANAGEMENT ACCOUNTING.). [Manage. account.]. **Added/Corp** National Association of Accountants. Vol. 50, No. 1 (Sept. 1968)-. Periodical. English. Twelve times a year. $65.00. Institute of Management Accountants, 10 Paragon Drive, Montvale NJ 07645. **Tel** (201)573-9000, (800)638-4427, FAX (201)573-8185, telex 9102509487. **ED** Bob Randall. Index available. **Bk Rev**. **Ad Acc**. **Circ:** 93,290. available on microfilm and microfiche from University Microfilms International (UMI). Documents available from Ask*IEEE, UMI Article Clearinghouse. ***Continues*** *NAA Management Accounting.*
Desc: Finance and accounting management topics for corporate accountants, chief financial officers, controllers, treasurers.
Ind/Abst ABI/INFORM Glob. Ed.; ABI/INFORM [Computer File] (Oct. 1971-); Account. Tax Datab. (Oct. 1971-) [Full Txt.]; Account. Art.; Anbar Account. Finan. Abstr. [Full Txt.]; Anbar Mark. Distr. Abstr. (1974-) [Full Txt.]; Anbar Top Manage. Abstr. [Full Txt.]; Bus. ASAP (1992-) [Full Txt.]; Bus. Index (1985-); Bus. Period. Index; Comput. Lit. Index; Contents Pages Manage.; Curr. Cit.; Data Process. Dig.; Fed. Tax Artic.; Gen. BusinessFile (1985-); Gen. Period. Index (1985-); INFO-SOUTH Abstr.; INSPEC (Oct. 1983-); J. Econ. Lit.; Mag. Search; Manage. Market. Abstr.; Manage. Bibliogr. Rev.; Manage. Contents; Oper. Prod. Manage. Abstr. [Full Txt.]; Person. Train. Abstr. (Oct. 1971-) [Full Txt.]; Selec. Coop. Index Manage. Period.; UMI ABI/Inform--Bus. Period. Ondisc (Jan. 1987-) [Full Txt.]; Wilson Bus. Abstr.; Women Manage. Rev. (1974-) [Full Txt.].

LC HF5657.4 .M34 ISSN 1044-5005
DD 658.15/11/05 UK
CCC

MANAGEMENT ACCOUNTING RESEARCH. [Manage. account. res.]. (1990)-. Academic Scholarly Publication. English. Four times a year. $205.35. Academic Press Ltd., A Division of Harcourt Brace & Company Ltd., 24-28 Oval Road, London NW1 7DX United Kingdom. **Tel** 011 44 171 2674466, FAX 011 44 171 4822293, 011 44 171 4854752, telex 25775 ACPRES G. **(Subscription address:** Harcourt Brace & Company, Ltd., Foots Cray High Street, Sidcup Kent DA14 5HP United Kingdom. **Tel** 011 44 181 3003322, FAX 011 44 181 3090807, telex 896 377 ACADEM.) **ED** M. Bromwich, R. W. Scapens and R. Dixon. Documents available from UMI Article Clearinghouse.
Desc: A vehicle for original research in the field of management accounting. The journal also provides access to current literature on this topic via abstracts of journal articles and books.
Ind/Abst ABI/INFORM Glob. Ed.; Account. Tax Datab. (Mar. 1992-); Curr. Cit.

LC HF5657 .M23 ISSN 0065-8766
DD 657.6 US

MANAGEMENT ADVISORY SERVICES: GUIDELINE SERIES. See Business and Economics-Management.

LC HF5601
DD 657 US

MANAGERIAL ACCOUNTING. (19??)-. Periodical. English. Irregular. $19.95. Gleim Publications Inc., PO Box 12848, University Station, Gainesville FL 32604. **Tel** (904)375-0722.

LC HF5601 ISSN 0268-6902
DD 657.45 UK

MANAGERIAL AUDITING JOURNAL. (1986)-. Periodical. English. Eight times a year. $1299.00. MCB University Press, 60 62 Toller Lane, Bradford, West Yorkshire BD8 9BY United Kingdom. **Tel** 011 44 1274 785280, FAX 011 44 1274 785200, telex 51317-MCBUNI-G. **(Subscription address:** MCB University Press / US and Canada Subscriptions, PO Box 10812, Birmingham AL 35201-0812. **Tel** (205)995-1567, (800)633-4931, FAX (205)995-1588.) **ED** Mei Whei Lin and Morris Brodie. **Ad Acc**. **Circ:** 1,000. Documents available from UMI Article Clearinghouse.
Desc: Reflects the modern practice, allowing readers to assess the work of others in relation to their own situation. Its wide-ranging coverage takes you beyond the traditional approach of auditing to describe ways in which auditors are improving managerial and organisational performance.
Ind/Abst ABI/INFORM Glob. Ed.; Account. Tax Datab. (1992-) [Full Txt.]; Curr. Cit.; Manage. Market. Abstr.

LC HF5601 ISSN 0025-4770
DD 657 US

MASSACHUSETTS CPA REVIEW. [Mass. CPA rev.]. **VAT** Massachusetts Certified Public Accountant Review. Vol. 1- 1928-. Periodical. English. Three times a year. $20.00. MSCPA: Massachusettes Society of Certified Public Accountants, 105 Chauncy Street/10th Floor, Boston MA 02111-1742. **Tel** (617)556-4000, (800)392-6145, FAX (617)556-4126. **ED** Cheryl McCloud. cum. index. **Ad Acc**. **Circ:** 8,000 (ctrl). available on microfilm and microfiche from University Microfilms International (UMI); available on an online database (files 15,485/Full-Text) from DIALOG. Documents available from UMI Article Clearinghouse.
Desc: Covers accounting, taxation, business, computers, financial planning, management advisory services and related topics.
Ind/Abst ABI/INFORM Glob. Ed.; ABI/INFORM [Computer File] (May 1979-); Account. Tax Datab. (1974-) [Full Txt.]; Account. Art.; EP Collect.; Fed. Tax Artic.; Homework Help.; MasterFile FullTEXT 1000; MasterFile FullTEXT 350; MasterFile FullTEXT 650; MasterFile FullTEXT; OCLC; Telebase; UMI ABI/Inform--Bus. Period. Ondisc (Winter 1987-) [Full Txt.].

LC HF5601
DD 657 US

MASTER TAX FORM FILE. (19??)-. English. One time a year. $109.50. National Tax Training School, PO Box 382, Monsey NY 10952. **Tel** (914)352-3634.

LC HV ISSN 0959-2903
DD 362.1068 UK
Pr Rev. TITLE CHANGE

MEDICAL AUDIT NEWS. [Med. audit news]. (1991)-(1995). Periodical. English. Churchill Livingstone, 1-3 Baxter's Place, Leith Walk, Edinburgh EH1 3AF United Kingdom. **Tel** 011 44 131 5562424, FAX 011 44 131 5581278, telex 727511. **(Subscription address:** Maruzen Company Ltd., PO Box 5050, Import & Export Department, Tokyo 100 31 Japan. **Tel** 011 81 3 32789224.) **Bk Rev**. **Ad Acc**. **Circ:** 750. ***Continued by*** *Clinical Audit.*

LC R ISSN 1078-1285
DD 610 US

•**MEDICAL OFFICE BILLER, THE.** See Medical Sciences-Health Services Administration.

LC NOT IN LC ISSN 0026-2064
DD 657 US
Pr Rev.

MICHIGAN CPA, THE. [Mich. CPA]. **Added/Corp** Michigan Association of Certified Public Accountants. **VAT** Michigan Certified Public Accountant. (1950)-. Trade Publication. English. Four times a year (Jan., Apr., July, Oct.). $6.00. Michigan Association of Certified Public Accountants, PO Box 9054, Farmington Hills MI 48333.

Tel (313)855-2288, FAX (313)855-9122. ED Deborah C. Wilk and Susan Humes. Ad Acc, Adv Mgr: Sara Bocketti. Circ: 15,000 (ctrl). available on microfilm and microfiche from University Microfilms International (UMI); available on an online database (files 485,648/Full-Text) from DIALOG.
Ind/Abst Acad. Search; Account. Tax Datab. (1974-) [Full Txt.]; Account. Art.; Bus. ASAP (1992-) [Full Txt.]; Bus. Index (1985-); Bus. Source Plus; Bus. Source; EP Collect.; Fed. Tax Artic.; Gen. BusinessFile (1985-); Gen. Period. Index (1985-); Homework Help.; INFO-SOUTH Abstr.; MasterFile FullTEXT 1000; MasterFile FullTEXT 350; MasterFile FullTEXT 650; MasterFile FullTEXT (July 1993-); OCLC; Telebase.

LC HF5601
DD 657 US
•MILLER EUROPEAN ACCOUNTING GUIDE. (1995)-. English. Miller Accounting Publications Inc., 1250 6th Avenue, San Diego CA 92101. Tel (619)699-6726. *Continues European Accounting Guide.*

LC HF5667 .M54
DD 657 US
•MILLER GAAS GUIDE. VFOAT GAAS Guide. (1994)-. English. One time a year. Miller Accounting Publications Inc., 1250 6th Avenue, San Diego CA 92101. Tel (619)699-6726. (Subscription address: Harcourt Brace Jovanovich, 6277 Sea Harbor Drive, Orlando FL 32887-4600. Tel (800)543-9534, (800)831-7799, FAX (407)363-9661.) *Continues HBJ Miller Comprehensive GAAS Guide.*

LC HF5601 ISSN 0736-8577
DD 657 US
MILLER'S COMPREHENSIVE GAAP GUIDE. STUDENT EDITION. (MILLER'S COMPREHENSIVE GAAP GUIDE.). [Miller's Compr. GAAP guide, Stud. ed.]. VFOAT Miller's Comprehensive G.A.A.P. Guide; Comprehensive GAAP Guide; Comprehensive G.A.A.P. Guide. (1983)-. English. One time a year (Dec.). $55.00 (softbound), $75.00 (hardbound). Miller Accounting Publications Inc., 1250 6th Avenue, San Diego CA 92101. Tel (619)699-6726. (Subscription address: Harcourt Brace & Company, Ltd., Foots Cray High Street, Sidcup Kent DA14 5HP United Kingdom. Tel 011 44 181 3003322, FAX 011 44 181 3090807, telex 896 377 ACADEM.)

LC HF5601
DD 657 US
MILLER'S COMPREHENSIVE GAAP GUIDE UPDATE. Added/Corp Financial Accounting Standards Board. VFOAT Comprehensive GAAP Guide Update; GAAP Guide Update. (198?)-. Periodical. English. Irregular. Price varies per volume. Miller Accounting Publications Inc., 1250 6th Avenue, San Diego CA 92101. Tel (619)699-6726. ED David M. Pierce. cum. index. Bk Rev. Circ: 2,000.
Desc: Up-to-the-minute technical analyses of newly issued GAAP throughout the year.

LC HF5661 .M49 ISSN 0736-8542
DD 657/.076 US
MILLER'S SOLUTIONS TO THE UNIFORM CPA EXAM. [Miller's Solut. unif. CPA exam]. (19??)-. English. Two times a year. $9.95. Miller Accounting Publications Inc., 1250 6th Avenue, San Diego CA 92101. Tel (619)699-6726.

LC HF5601
DD 657 US
MISSISSIPPI CERTIFIED PUBLIC ACCOUNTANT : YEARBOOK, THE. Main/Corp Mississippi Society of Certified Public Accountants. (19??)-. English.
Ind/Abst Fed. Tax Artic.

LC HF5601
DD 657 US
MONTANA CPA. (19??)-. English. Six times a year. University of Montana / School of Business Administration, Missoula MT 59801.
Ind/Abst Account. Art.; Fed. Tax Artic.

LC HF5601
DD 657 US
MONTHLY STATEMENT. Added/Corp California Society of Certified Public Accountants. (19??)-. Periodical. English. Twelve times a year. $20.00. California Society of CPA's, 275 Shoreline Drive, Redwood City CA 94065. Tel (415)802-2600. available in microform from University Microfilms International (UMI).
Desc: Contains information on accountants and accounting.
Ind/Abst Account. Art.

LC HF5601 ISSN 0316-6546
DD 657/.06/27123 CN
MONTHLY STATEMENT - INSTITUTE OF CHARTERED ACCOUNTANTS OF ALBERTA, A. Main/Corp Institute of Chartered Accountants of Alberta. Vol. 12 No. 2 (Sept. 1974)-. Periodical. English. Twelve times a year. Free on request. Institute of Chartered Accountants of Alberta, 10180 101 Street, Edmonton Alberta T5J 4R2 Canada. Tel (403)424-7391. *Continues Institute of Chartered Accountants of Alberta. C.A. Newsletter., 0316-6538.*

LC HD2753.U6 M85 ISSN 1051-1555
DD 343.7305/267/05 347.303526705 US
MULTISTATE CORPORATE TAX GUIDE. See Finance-Taxation.

LC KF2920.Z95 N3 ISSN 0161-4290
DD 344/.73/01761657 US
NASBA DIGEST OF STATE ACCOUNTANCY LAWS AND STATE BOARD REGULATIONS. See Law.

LC HF5601 ISSN 0271-9150
DD 657 US
NATIONAL CONSULTOR. Added/Corp National Association of Tax Consultors. (1978)-. Periodical. English. Four times a year (Jan., Apr., Jul., Oct.). $60.00. National Association of Tax Consultors, 454 North 13th Street, San Jose CA 95112. Tel (408)298-1458. ED Ken Valentine. Circ: 2,300.
Desc: Tax planning information relevant to a tax practitioner.

LC HF5601 ISSN 1188-6153
DD 657/.025/71 CN
NATIONAL DIRECTORY OF PUBLIC PRACTITIONERS. [Natl. dir. public. pract.]. Main/Corp Association des Comptables Generaux Agrees du Canada. VFOAT Repertoire National des Membres Exercant en Cabinet Prive. (1992)-. Directory. French (English). Association des Comptables Generaux Agrees du Canada, 700-1188 West Georgia Street, Vancouver British Columbia V6E 4A2 Canada.

LC HF5601 ISSN 1188-6153
DD 657/.025/71 CN
NATIONAL DIRECTORY OF PUBLIC PRACTITIONERS. [Natl. dir. public. pract.]. Main/Corp Certified General Accountants' Association of Canada. VFOAT Repertoire National des Membres Exercant en Cabinet Prive. (1992)-. Directory. English (French). $15.00 to members who subscribe. Certified General Accountants' Association of Canada, 700-1188 West Georgia Street, Vancouver British Columbia V6E 4A2 Canada.

LC HF5601 ISSN 1193-8765
DD 657 CN
CEASED
NATIONAL INTERNAL AUDITING LETTER, THE. [Natl. intern. audit. lett.]. Vol. 5, No. 12 (Oct. 1992)-(March 1994). Periodical. English. Four times a year. Free on request. National Internal Auditing Letter, 55 University Avenue, Suite 300, Toronto Ontario M5J 2H7 Canada. Tel (416)234-2779, FAX (416)234-8057. ED John G. Sayers. *Continues The Bottom Line's Canadian Internal Auditing Letter., 1193-8757.*

LC HF5601 .N335 ISSN 0027-9978
DD 657.605 US
CODEN NPACAI
NATIONAL PUBLIC ACCOUNTANT (1957), THE. (THE NATIONAL PUBLIC ACCOUNTANT.). [Natl. public account.]. Added/Corp National Society of Public Accountants. VFOAT Public Accountant. (1957)-. Periodical. English. Twelve times a year. $18.00. National Society of Public Accountants, 1010 North Fairfax Street, Alexandria VA 22314. Tel (703)549-6400. ED Stanley H. Stearman and Susan Cappitelli. Index available. Bk Rev. Ad Acc. Circ: 20,000. available on microfilm from University Microfilms International (UMI); available on an online database (files 15,485,648/Full-Text) from DIALOG. Documents available from UMI Article Clearinghouse. *Continues National Public Accountant and the PA.*
Desc: Articles of interest to the independent accountant, including taxes, accounting for small business, practice management, computers, marketing professional services and professional liability.
Ind/Abst ABI/INFORM Glob. Ed.; ABI/INFORM [Computer File] (Sept. 1971-); Acad. Search; Account. Tax Datab. (Sept. 1971-) [Full Txt.]; Account. Art.; Bus. ASAP (1990-) [Full Txt.]; Bus. Index (1985-); Bus. Period. Index; Bus. Source Plus; Bus. Source; Curr. Cit.; EP Collect.; Fed. Tax Artic.; Gen. BusinessFile (1985-); Gen. Period. Index (1985-); Homework Help.; INFO-SOUTH Abstr.; Mag. Search; MasterFile FullTEXT 1000; MasterFile FullTEXT 350; MasterFile FullTEXT 650; MasterFile FullTEXT (July 1993-); OCLC; PAIS Int. Print; Telebase; Trade Ind. ASAP [Full Txt.]; Trade Ind. Index [Full Txt.]; UMI ABI/Inform--Bus. Period. Ondisc (Jan. 1987-) [Full Txt.]; Wilson Bus. Abstr.

LC HF5601
DD 657 US
NEBRASKA CPA. (19??)-. English. Twelve times a year. Nebraska Society of Certified Public Accountants, 635 South 14th Street, Suite 330, Lincoln NE 68508.
Ind/Abst Account. Art.; Fed. Tax Artic.

LC HF5601
DD 657 NE
NEDERLANDSE JURISPRUDENTIE INZAKE INTERNATIONAAL BELASTINGRECHT: DIRECTE BELASTINGEN VAN INTERNATIONAAL OPERERENDE ONDERNEMINGEN. See Finance-Taxation.

LC WMLC 93/1990 ISSN 0882-8067
DD 657 US
NEW ACCOUNTANT. [New account.]. Vol. 1, No. 1 (Sept. 1985)-. Trade Publication. English. Eight times a year. $31.00. Real Estate News Corp, 3525 West Peterson, Suite 103, Chicago IL 60659. Tel (312)866-9900. ED Louise Dratler Haberman. Index available. Bk Rev. Ad Acc. Circ: 64,000 (ctrl). available on an online database (files 485,771,772,799/Full-Text) from DIALOG.
Desc: For business-oriented accountants with practical articles, features and columns on careers, style and strategy, computer software and hardware, entrepreneurship and management.
Ind/Abst Account. Index Suppl. (1985-); Account. Tax Datab. (1985-); Account. Art.

LC KFN5860.A15 N485 ISSN 1056-4829
DD 343.74704/05 347.4703405 US
Pr Rev.
NEW YORK TAX UPDATE. [N. Y. tax update]. Vol. 1, No. 1 (Oct. 1988)-. Periodical. English. Six times a year. $140.00. William S. Hein & Company Inc., 1285 Main Street, Buffalo NY 14209. Tel (716)882-2600, (800)828-7571, FAX (716)883-8100, telex 91-209 WM S HEIN BUF. ED Mark S Klein and Robert D Plattner, Hodgson, Russ, Andrews, Woods & Goodyear.
Desc: A timely source for important new cases, new legislation, administrative trends and new regulations. Every article gives you complete citations to target or expand your research. To save time and effort each new development is categorized by the type of tax involved allowing you to quickly find your area of interest.

LC HF5601 .P5335
DD 657/.05 PH
NEWSETTE - PHILIPPINE INSTITUTE OF CERTIFIED PUBLIC ACCOUNTANTS. Main/Corp Philippine Institute of Certified Public Accountants. VFOAT PICPA Newsette. (19??)-. Periodical. English. Twelve times a year. $7.00. Philippine Institute of Certified Public Accountants, PICPA House, 700 Shaw Boulevard, Mandaluyong Rizal Philippines. *Continues Philippine Institute of Accountants. Newsette.*

LC HF5601 ISSN 1196-5991
DD 657 CN
•NEWSLETTER - CANADIAN ACADEMIC ACCOUNTING ASSOCIATION. (BULLETIN : INFORMATION, RECHERCHE, ET FORMATION EN COMPTABILITE AU CANADA.). [Newsl. - Can. Acad. Account. Assoc.]. Added/Corp Association Canadienne des Professeurs de Comptabilite. VFOAT Newsletter; Information, Recherche, et Formation en Comptabilite au Canada. (1993)-. Newsletter. French (English). Irregular. Canadian Academic Accounting Association, 2-32C Business Building, University of Alberta, Edmonton Alberta T6G 2R6 Canada. Tel (403)492-7513, FAX (403)492-3325. *Continues Information, Recherche et Formation en Comptabilite au Canada, 0834-7921.*

LC HF5601 ISSN 1196-5991
DD 657 CN
•NEWSLETTER : CANADIAN ACCOUNTING EDUCATION AND RESEARCH NEWS. [Newsl. - Can. Acad. Account. Assoc.]. Added/Corp Canadian Academic Accounting Association. VFOAT Bulletin; Canadian Accounting Education and Research News. VAT Bulletin - Association Canadienne des Professeurs de Comptabilite. (1993)-. Periodical. English (French). Irregular. Canadian Academic Accounting Association, 2-32C Business Building, University of Alberta, Edmonton Alberta T6G 2R6 Canada. Tel (403)492-7513, FAX (403)492-3325. *Continues Canadian Accounting Education and Research News, 0834-7921.*

LC HF5601 ISSN 0048-0371
DD 657 NR
NIGERIAN ACCOUNTANT, THE. [Niger. account.]. Added/Corp Institute of Chartered Accountants of Nigeria. (1965)-. Periodical. English. Four times a year (Jan., Apr., July, Oct.). $30.73. Institute of Chartered Accountants Nigeria Plot, 16 Idowu Taylor Street, St. Vict. Isle, Lagos Nigeria. Tel 011 234 1 614235, FAX 011 234 1 610304.

LC HF5681.V3 J36a
DD 657 JA
NO-CHIKUSANGYOYO KOTEI SHISAN HYOKA HYOJUN. Main/Corp Japan. Norin Suisansho. Keizaikyoku. Tokei Johobu. (1978)-. Japanese. Norin Tokei Kyokai, (Association of Agriculture & Forestry Statistics), 11-14 Meguro 2 Chome, Meguroku Tokyo 153 Japan. *Continues Norin Chikusangyo yo Kotei Shisan Hyoka Hyojun.*

LC HD28 ISSN 1056-5094
DD 658 US
NONPROFIT REPORT (BOSTON, MASS.), THE. (THE NONPROFIT REPORT.). [Nonprofit rep.]. Vol. 1, No. 1 (July 1991)-. Periodical. English. Twelve times a year. $108.48 US and Canada; $151.40 other. Warren Gorham & Lamont Inc., Park Square Building, 31 St. James Avenue, Boston MA 02116-4112. **Tel** (617)423-2020, (800)950-1207, FAX (617)423-2026. **ED** Steve Collins. **Circ:** 1,100.
Desc: Delivers articles on the latest auditing, accounting, management and taxation development that affect your work.

LC HF5601 .O44 ISSN 0749-8284
DD 657/.05 US
CODEN OCPAA7
Pr Rev.
OHIO CPA JOURNAL, THE. [Ohio CPA j.]. **Added/Corp** Ohio Society of Certified Public Accountants. **VFOAT** Ohio C.P.A. Journal. Vol. 39, No. 1 (Winter 1980)-. Periodical. English. Six times a year (Feb., Apr., June, Aug., Oct., Dec.). $20.00. Ohio Society of Certified Public Accountants, PO Box 1810, Dublin OH 43017. **Tel** (614)764-2727, FAX (614)764-5880. **ED** James Raybali. Index available. **Bk Rev**. **Photos**. **Ad Acc**. **Circ:** 18,000 (ctrl). available on microfilm and microfiche from University Microfilms International (UMI); available on an online database (files 15,485/Full-Text) from DIALOG. Documents available from UMI Article Clearinghouse, Ask*IEEE. ***Continues*** *Ohio CPA, 0737-7371.*
Desc: Technical and educational articles for the accounting and business professionals.
Ind/Abst ABI/INFORM Glob. Ed.; ABI/INFORM [Computer File] (1980-); Acad. Search; Account. Tax Datab. (Fall 1972-) [Full Txt.]; Account. Art.; Anbar Account. Finan. Abstr. [Full Txt.]; Anbar Mark. Distr. Abstr. [Full Txt.]; Anbar Top Manage. Abstr. [Full Txt.]; Bus. Index (1985-); Bus. Source Plus; Bus. Source; Curr. Cit.; EP Collect.; Fed. Tax Artic.; Gen. BusinessFile (1985-); Gen. Period. Index (1985-); Homework Help.; INFO-SOUTH Abstr.; INSPEC (Summer 1984-); Manage. Bibliogr. Rev.; Manage. Contents; MasterFile FullTEXT 1000; MasterFile FullTEXT 350; MasterFile FullTEXT 650; MasterFile FullTEXT (July 1993-); OCLC; Oper. Prod. Manage. Abstr. [Full Txt.]; Person. Train. Abstr. [Full Txt.]; Telebase; UMI ABI/Inform--Bus. Period. Ondisc (Fall 1987-) [Full Txt.]; Women Manage. Rev. [Full Txt.].

LC HD ISSN 0962-3752
DD 338.2328 UK
OIL & GAS FINANCE AND ACCOUNTING. [Oil gas financ. account.]. **VFOAT** Oil and Gas Finance and Accounting. (198?)-. Trade Publication. English. Four times a year. $196.79. Langham Publishing Ltd, 21 Pointers Close Isle of Dogs, London E14 3AP United Kingdom. **Tel** 011 44 171 9878631. **ED** Tudor David. Index available. **Bk Rev**, (Qty: 8-9). **Ad Acc**. **Circ:** 200. ***Continues*** *Journal of Oil and Gas Accountancy, 0267-4920.*
Desc: Aimed chiefly at controllers or accountants in oil and gas companies and relevant accounting firms.

LC HF5616.U5 O38a
DD 657/.61/025766 US
OKLAHOMA ACCOUNTANCY ACT ; AND TITLE 10 OF THE OKLAHOMA ADMINISTRATIVE CODE. DIRECTORY OF REGISTRANTS. **Added/Corp** Oklahoma Accountancy Board. **VFOAT** Directory of Registrants. (19??)-. English. Oklahoma State Board of Public Accountancy, 265 West Court 4545 Lincoln Boulevard, Oklahoma City OK 73105. **Tel** (405)521-2397. ***Continues*** *Oklahoma State Board of Public Accountancy. Directory of Certified Public Accountants and Public Accountants of Oklahoma Registered in Accordance with Oklahoma Statutes and Rules of the Oklahoma State Board of Public Accountancy, 0361-4115.*

LC HF5601 .C293 ISSN 0273-835X
DD 657/.05 US
OUTLOOK (PALO ALTO). (OUTLOOK.). [Outlook]. (Sept. 1980)-. Trade Publication. English. Four times a year. $26.00. California Society of CPA's, 275 Shoreline Drive, Redwood City CA 94065. **Tel** (415)321-9545. **ED** Linda Fresques. **Ad Acc. Circ:** 27,000 (ctrl). available on microfilm and microfiche from University Microfilms International (UMI). ***Continues*** *California CPA Quarterly, 0008-0934.*
Desc: Articles reporting issues of interest to the CPA profession, with emphasis placed on the human side of the profession.
Ind/Abst Acad. Search; Account. Tax Datab. (Winter 1992-) [Full Txt.]; Account. Art.; EP Collect.; Homework Help.; MasterFile FullTEXT 1000; MasterFile FullTEXT 350; MasterFile FullTEXT 650; MasterFile FullTEXT (July 1993-); OCLC; Telebase.

LC HF5601
DD 657 PK
PAKISTAN ACCOUNTANT, THE. (1961)-. Periodical. English. Four times a year. $10.00. Institute of Chartered S Pakis Accountants, Pakis G-3 1/8 Kehkashan Clifton, Karachi 6 Pakistan. **ED** Ebrahin S-H-Dahodwala. **Ad Acc.**

LC HF5601 ISSN 0885-6311
DD 657 US
PANORAMA (HOUSTON, TEX.). (PANORAMA.). [Panorama]. **Added/Corp** Pannell, Kerr, Forster & Company. **VFOAT** PKF Panorama. No. 12 (2nd Quarter 1981)-. English. Two times a year. Free on request. Pannell Kerr Forster, 262 North Belt/Suite 300, Houston TX 77060. **Tel** (713)999-5134. ***Continues*** *HFK/PKF Panorama.*

LC HF5601 ISSN 1061-3854
DD 657 US
PAPERMASTER'S DIRECTORY OF PREMIER U.S. ACCOUNTING FIRMS. [Papermaster's dir. prem. U.S. account. firms]. **VFOAT** Directory of Premier U.S. Accounting Firms. (1992 ed.)-. Directory. English. $69.00. Papermaster Accounting Publications, PO Box 1046, Milwaukee WI 53201-1046.

LC HF5601 ISSN 0195-7775
DD 657 US
CCC
NLM W1 PA963M
PATIENT ACCOUNTS. **See** Medical Sciences-Health Services Administration.

LC HJ5623.A6 P4 ISSN 0277-5840
DD 657/.74 US
PAYROLL ACCOUNTING. (19??)-. English. One time a year. South-Western Publishing Company, 5101 Madison Road, College University Department, Cincinnati OH 45227. **Tel** (513)271-8811. ***Continues*** *Payroll Records and Accounting.*

LC HF5601
DD 657 UK
PAYROLL HANDBOOK. (19??)-. Periodical. English. Irregular (updates published quarterly). $526.03. Croner Publ Ltd., Croner House London Road, Kingston Upon Thames, Surrey KT2 6SR United Kingdom. **Tel** 011 44 181 5473333, FAX 011 44 181 5472637.

LC HF5601
DD 657 US
PAYROLL SOURCE. (19??)-. English. One time a year. $145.00. API Fund for Payroll Education, 30 East 33rd Street, 5th Floor, New York NY 10016. **Tel** (212)686-2030, FAX (212)686-2789.

LC HF5601 ISSN 1063-9047
DD 657 US
PAYTECH (NEW YORK, N.Y.). (PAYTECH : THE OFFICIAL PUBLICATION OF THE AMERICAN PAYROLL ASSOCIATION.). [Paytech]. **Added/Corp** American Payroll Association. Vol. 1, Issue 1 (Sept./Oct. 1992)-. Periodical. English. Six times a year. $125.00. American Payroll Association, PO Box 2344 Grand Central Station, New York NY 10163. **Tel** (212)661-9145, FAX (212)686-2789. **ED** Eileen Anderson. **Ad Acc. Circ:** 9,000.
Desc: Provides current information on tax legislation and payroll systems.

LC HF5601 ISSN 0746-1062
DD 657 US
PENNSYLVANIA CPA JOURNAL. [Pa. CPA j.]. **Added/Corp** Pennsylvania Institute of Certified Public Accountants. **VFOAT** Pennsylvania C.P.A. Journal. **VAT** Pennsylvania Certified Public Accountant Journal. Vol. 54, No. 1 (June 1983)-. Periodical. English. Four times a year. $3.00. Pennsylvania Institute of Certified Public Accountants, 1608 Walnut Street/3rd Floor, Philadelphia PA 19103. **Tel** (215)735-2635, FAX (215)735-3694. **ED** Bernadette E Smedile. Index available. cum. index. **Ad Acc**. ctrl circ. available on microfilm and microfiche from University Microfilms International (UMI); available on an online database (files 15,485/Full-Text) from DIALOG. Documents available from UMI Article Clearinghouse. ***Continues*** *Pennsylvania CPA Spokesman, 0031-4390.*
Desc: Theme oriented journal for certified public accountants.
Ind/Abst ABI/INFORM Glob. Ed.; ABI/INFORM [Computer File] (Fall 1987-); Account. Tax Datab. (1974-) [Full Txt.]; Account. Art.; Fed. Tax Artic.

LC HF5601 ISSN 1065-3643
DD 657 US
PPC ACCOUNTING AND AUDITING UPDATE, THE. [PPC account. audit. update]. Vol. 1, No. 1 (Sept. 1992)-. Periodical. English. Twelve times a year. $96.00. Practitioners Publishing Company, PO Box 966, Fort Worth TX 76101-0966. **Tel** (800)332-3709.

LC HF5601 ISSN 1075-9190
DD 657 US
●**PPC NONPROFIT UPDATE, THE.** [PPC nonprofit update]. **Added/Corp** Practitioners Publishing Company. Vol. 1, No. 1 (Apr. 1994)-. Periodical. English. Twelve times a year. $89.00. Practitioners Publishing Company, PO Box 966, Fort Worth TX 76101-0966. **Tel** (800)332-3709.

LC HF5601 .P65 ISSN 0032-6321
DD 657 US
CCC
CODEN PACNBD
PRACTICAL ACCOUNTANT, THE. [Pract. account.]. **Added/Corp** Warren, Gorham & Lamont, Inc. Institute for Continuing Professional Development. Vol. 1 (Jan./Feb. 1968)-. Periodical. English. Twelve times a year. $69.95. Faulkner & Gray Inc., 11 Penn Plaza, 17th Floor, New York NY 10001. **Tel** (212)967-7000, (800)535-8403. **ED** Alex Cohen. **Bk Rev**. **Ad Acc**. **Circ:** 45,000. available on microfilm and microfiche from University Microfilms International (UMI). Documents available from UMI Article Clearinghouse.
Desc: The how-to magazine covering every facet of accounting and taxes.
Ind/Abst ABI/INFORM Glob. Ed.; ABI/INFORM [Computer File] (Sept. 1971-); Acad. Search; Account. Index Suppl.; Account. Tax Datab. (Sept. 1971-); Account. Art.; Bus. Index (1988-); Bus. Period. Index; Bus. Source Plus; Bus. Source; Curr. Cit.; EP Collect.; Fed. Tax Artic.; Gen. BusinessFile (1988-); Gen. Period. Index (1988-); Homework Help.; INFO-SOUTH Abstr.; Law Office Inf. Serv. (Sept. 1971-); Mag. Search; Manage. Contents (1974-); MasterFile FullTEXT 1000; MasterFile FullTEXT 350; MasterFile FullTEXT 650; MasterFile FullTEXT (Jan. 1994-); OCLC; Predicasts; Ref. Sources; Telebase; Wilson Bus. Abstr.

LC HF5601 ISSN 0885-6931
DD 657 US
PRACTICING CPA, THE. [Pract. CPA]. **Added/Corp** American Institute of Certified Public Accountants. (197?)-. Periodical. English. Twelve times a year. American Institute of Certified Public Accountants, Harborside Financial Center, #201 Plaza 3, Jersey City NJ 07311. **Tel** (201)938-3333, (800)862-4272, FAX (201)938-3329.
Ind/Abst Account. Tax Datab. (1978-) [Full Txt.].

LC HF5601
DD 657 IT
SUSPENDED
PRATICA AMMINISTRATIVA. (19??)-Suspended (1992). Italian. Six times a year. Tipogr Tappini Editrice, Via Morandi 19, 06012 Citta Castello PG Italy. **Tel** 011 39 75 8558194.

LC HF5630 .P73 ISSN 0277-6618
DD 657/.025/73 US
PRENTICE-HALL ACCOUNTING FACULTY DIRECTORY. **Added/Corp** Prentice-Hall, Inc. **VFOAT** Accounting Faculty Directory. **VAT** Prentice Hall Accounting Faculty Directory. (1978-79)-. Directory. English. One time a year. Prentice-Hall Law and Business, 270 Sylvan Avenue, Englewood Cliffs NJ 07632. **Tel** (800)223-0231, (201)894-8538, FAX (201)894-8666. ***Continues*** *Accounting Faculty.*

LC HF5601
DD 657 US
PRENTICE-HALL PAYROLL GUIDE. **Main/Corp** Prentice-Hall, Inc. (1970)-. English. One time a year. Research Institute of America, 117 East Stevens Avenue, Valhalla NY 10595. **Tel** (800)431-9025, FAX (800)820-3135 (914)749-5300.

LC HF5601
DD 657 IT
PRINCIPI CONTABILI. (19??)-. Periodical. Italian. Irregular. IPSOA Editore SRL, Casella Postale 12055, Mastrangelo, 20120 Milan Italy. **Tel** 011 39 2 82476248. Index available.

LC HF5601
DD 657 IT
PRINCIPI REVISIONE. (19??)-. Periodical. Italian. Irregular. IPSOA Editore SRL, Casella Postale 12055, Mastrangelo, 20120 Milan Italy. **Tel** 011 39 2 82476248. Index available (Included).

LC HF5601
DD 657 IT
PROCEDURE REVISIONE FISCALE ADEMPIMENTI SOSTITUTO IMPOSTA. (19??)-. Periodical. Italian. Two times a year. IPSOA Editore SRL, Casella Postale 12055, Mastrangelo, 20120 Milan Italy. **Tel** 011 39 2 82476248. Index available.

LC HF5601 ISSN 0711-3730
DD 657 CN
PROCEEDINGS. ANNUAL CONFERENCE - CANADIAN ACADEMIC ACCOUNTING ASSOCIATION. (COMPTE RENDU, CONGRES ANNUEL DE.). [Proc., Annu. conf. - Can. Acad. Account. Assoc.]. **Main/Corp** Canadian Academic Accounting Association. Conference. **Added/Corp** Canadian Academic Accounting Association. **VFOAT** Proceedings, ... Annual Conference. (June 1982)-. Proceedings. English (French; summaries and/or abstracts in French). One time a year (Oct., or Nov.). 25.00Can$. Canadian Academic Accounting Association, 2-32C Business Building, University of Alberta, Edmonton Alberta T6G 2R6 Canada. **Tel** (403)492-7513, FAX (403)492-3325. **Circ:** 150 (ctrl). ***Continues*** *Canadian Academic Accounting Association.*

Business and Economics — Accounting

Conference. Proceedings, 0711-3730.
 Desc: These are papers given at the annual conference of the association.
LC HF5601   ISSN 0766-9208
DD 657   FR
UDC 657
PROFESSION COMPTABLE, LA. (1984)-. Newspaper. French. Twelve times a year. 890.00F. Communication Profession Comptable Sarl, Chemin des Pres - Z. I. R. S. T, BP 137, 38243 Meylan Cedex France. **Tel** 011 33 76 41 33 00, FAX 011 33 76 41 14 72, telex Siret 331 290 841 00013. **ED** Jean Burner. Index available. cum. index. **Bk Rev**. **Ad Acc**, **Adv Mgr:** Pascale Borjolami. Full Page (B&W) 4828.00F. Half Page (B&W) 2873.00F. **Circ:** 2,000. **Continues** Aujourd'hui et Demain, 0762-6347.

LC HF5681.B2 C5914
DD 657/.3/05   US
PUBLIC ACCOUNTING PRACTICE MANUAL. [Pub. acctg. pract. man.]. **Added/Corp** Warren, Gorham & Lamont, Inc. (1992)-. Periodical. English. One time a year. $149.95. Warren Gorham & Lamont Inc., Park Square Building, 31 St. James Avenue, Boston MA 02116-4112. **Tel** (617)423-2020, (800)950-1207, FAX (617)423-2026. **(Subscription address:** Warren Gorham & Lamont, PO Box 4966, Chicago IL 60680. **) Continues** CPA Firm Practice Manual, 1052-7362.

LC HF5601   ISSN 0161-309X
DD 657   US
PUBLIC ACCOUNTING REPORT. [Public account. rep.]. (1978)-. Newsletter. English. Twenty-four times a year. $247.00. Strafford Publications Inc., 590 Dutch Valley Road Northeast, Atlanta GA 30324. **Tel** (404)881-1141, (800)926-7926, FAX (404)881-0074. **ED** Kari Berman and Molly Miller. Index available (extra at cost of $15.00). **Bk Rev**.
 Desc: Independent newsletter of the accounting profession. Reports news, trends, features and auditor changes by public companies. Also ranks firms and schools.
 Ind/Abst Account. Index Suppl.; Account. Tax Datab. (1981-).

LC HJ9701 .P8   ISSN 0305-9014
DD 657/.835/00941   UK
     TITLE CHANGE
PUBLIC FINANCE AND ACCOUNTANCY. See Finance-Public Finance.

LC HF5601
DD 657   AT
     TITLE CHANGE
QIT ACCOUNTING RESEARCH JOURNAL. (1???)-(19??). English. Queensland University of Technology / School of Accountancy, GPO Box 2434, Brisbane 4001 Australia. **Tel** 011 61 7 8642663. **Continued by** QUT Accounting Research Journal.

LC HF5601
DD 657   IT
RASSEGNA MENSILE DELLE IMPOSTE. Italian. Centro Studi d'Impresa, Via Quintino Sella 5, 20052 Monza Italy.

LC HF5601
DD 657   UK
RECORD KEEPING BOOK FOR COSHH. (19??)-. English. Irregular. £107.45. Croner Publ Ltd., Croner House London Road, Kingston Upon Thames, Surrey KT2 6SR United Kingdom. **Tel** 011 44 181 5473333, FAX 011 44 181 5472637.

LC HF5616.U6 N8
DD 657/.025/756   US
REGISTER / NORTH CAROLINA STATE BOARD OF CERTIFIED PUBLIC ACCOUNTANT EXAMINERS. Added/Corp North Carolina State Board of Certified Public Accountant Examiners. (Mar. 15, 1959)-. English. One time a year. North Carolina State Board of Public Accountant Examiners, PO Box 2248, 209 Lennox Bulding, Chapel Hill NC 27514. **Continues** Certified Public Accountants.

LC HF5616.U5 C64a
DD 657/.61/09746   US
REGISTER OF CERTIFIED PUBLIC ACCOUNTANTS AND PUBLIC ACCOUNTANTS REGISTERED TO PRACTICE IN CONNECTICUT. Added/Corp Connecticut. State Board of Accountancy. (19??)-. English. One time a year. Connecticut State Board of Accountancy, 30 Trinity Street, Hartford CT 06115. **Continues** Certified Public Accountants and Public Accountants Registered to Practice in Connecticut, 0149-3736.

LC HF5616.U5 W37a
DD 657/.025/797   US
REGISTER - WASHINGTON STATE BOARD OF ACCOUNTANCY. Main/Corp Washington (State). Board of Accountancy. (19??)-. English. Washington State Board of Accountancy, 210 East Union, Olympia WA 98504.

LC HJ9929.Z35 Z33B
DD 354.68940072/32   ZA
REPORT OF THE AUDITOR-GENERAL FOR ... ON THE ACCOUNTS OF PARASTATAL BODIES. See Finance-Public Finance.

LC HD9284.A45 A3
DD 354.680082/336   SA
REPORT OF THE AUDITOR-GENERAL ON THE ACCOUNTS OF THE EGG BOARD FOR THE FINANCIAL YEAR ... / VERSLAG VAN DIE OUDITEUR-GENERAAL OOR DIE REKENINGS VAN DIE EIERRAAD VIR DIE BOEKJAAR ... . See Business and Economics-Commerce.

LC JK3353.L5 C66a
DD 353.974603/18   US
REPORT ON OFFICE OF THE LIEUTENANT GOVERNOR. See Finance-Public Finance.

LC HF5601
DD 657   II
RESEARCH BULLETIN OF THE INSTITUTE OF COST AND WORKS ACCOUNTANTS OF INDIA. Added/Corp Institute of Cost & Works Accountants of India. Vol. 1, No. 1 (Jan. 1982)-. Bulletin. English. One time a year. $15.00 (two-year). The Institute of Cost and Works Accountants of India, 12 Sudder Street, Calcutta 16, W Bengal India. **Tel** 24-1031.

LC HF5601
DD 657   US
●**RESEARCH IN ACCOUNTING IN EMERGING ECONOMICS.** (1995)-. English. Twelve times a year. $80.42. JAI Press Inc., 55 Old Post Road, Suite 2, PO Box 1678, Greenwich CT 06836-1678. **Tel** (203)661-7602, FAX (203)661-0792. **(Subscription address:** Jai Press Ltd. / United Kingdom, 28 High Street, Hampton Hill, Middx TW12 1PD United Kingdom. **)** **Continues** Research in Third World Accounting.
 Desc: Concerned with the theoretical, empirical and applied research into the macro and micro accounting issues of developing countries. Concerned with the relevance to the third world of international accounting standards.

LC K18 .E833   ISSN 1052-0457
DD 346.73/063 347.30663   US
RESEARCH IN ACCOUNTING REGULATION. [Res. account. regul.]. Vol. 1 (1987)-. English. One time a year. $73.25. JAI Press Inc., 55 Old Post Road, Suite 2, PO Box 1678, Greenwich CT 06836-1678. **Tel** (203)661-7602, FAX (203)661-0792. **ED** Gary John Previts.

LC HF5616.D44 R47   ISSN 1058-1995
DD 657/.091724/05   US
Pr Rev.   **TITLE CHANGE**
RESEARCH IN THIRD WORLD ACCOUNTING. [Res. third world account.]. Vol. 1 (1990)-(1995). English. JAI Press Inc., 55 Old Post Road, Suite 2, PO Box 1678, Greenwich CT 06836-1678. **Tel** (203)661-7602, FAX (203)661-0792. **ED** R.S.O. Wallace. **Continued by** Research in Accounting in Emerging Economies.
 Desc: Concerned with the theoretical, empirical and applied research into the macro and micro accounting issues of developing countries. Concerned with the relevance to the third world of international accounting standards.

LC HF5601
DD 657   US
RESEARCH REPORT - INSTITUTE OF INTERNAL AUDITORS. Main/Corp Institute of Internal Auditors. **Added/Corp** Institute of Internal Auditors. No. 19 (1975)-. Monographic series. English. Irregular. Price varies per volume. Institute of Internal Auditors / Orlando, Florida, PO Box 140099, Orlando FL 32889. **Tel** (407)830-7600, FAX (407)831-5171, telex 567443. **Circ:** 28,000 (ctrl). **Continues** Institute of Internal Auditors. Research Committee Report.

LC HF5601   ISSN 1380-6653
DD 657   NE
     CCC
Pr Rev.
●**REVIEW OF ACCOUNTING STUDIES.** Vol. 1 (1996)-. Academic Scholarly Publication. English. Four times a year. $267.00. Kluwer Academic Publishers / Massachusetts, PO Box 358, Accord Station, Hingham MA 02018. **Tel** (617)871-6600. **(Subscription address:** Kluwer Academic Publishers / Netherlands, PO Box 322, 3300 AH Dordrecht Netherlands. **Tel** 011 31 78 392392, FAX 011 31 78 546474.**) ED** John S. Hughes.
 Desc: Publishes significant academic research in accounting, including theoretical, empirical and experimental work.

LC HG173 .R48   ISSN 0924-865X
DD 332/.05   US
     CCC
     CODEN RQFAEO
REVIEW OF QUANTITATIVE FINANCE AND ACCOUNTING. Vol. 1, No. 1 (Jan. 1991)-. Periodical. English. Six times a year. $435.00. Kluwer Academic Publishers / Massachusetts, PO Box 358, Accord Station, Hingham MA 02018. **Tel** (617)871-6600. **ED** Cheng-few Lee. available on microfilm and microfiche from University Microfilms International (UMI).
 Desc: Deals with research involving the interaction of finance with accounting, economics, and quantitative methods.

LC HF5601
DD 657   SP
UDC 33
REVISTA ESPANOLA DE FINANCIACION Y CONTABILIDAD. Spanish. Four times a year. 8962.00ptas Spain; 11000.00ptas other. Edersa Editoriales de Derecho, Reunidas SA Valverde 32 i, 28004 Madrid Spain. **Tel** 011 34 1 5210246, 011 34 1 5229849.

LC HF5601
DD 657   BE
REVUE BELGE DE LA COMPTABILITE. Added/Corp Ordre des Experts Comptables et Comptables Brevetes de Belgique. (1960)-. Periodical. French. Four times a year. 2,400F. Ordre des Experts Comptables et Comptables Brevetes de Belgique, rue Mutualite 13A, B-1180 Brussels Belgium. **Tel** 011 32 2 3430212.

LC HF5601   ISSN 0035-2713
DD 657   FR
REVUE DU TRESOR, LA. See Finance-Taxation.

LC HF5601 .R48   ISSN 0484-8764
DD 657   FR
REVUE FRANCAISE DE COMPTABILITE. Added/Corp Ordre des Experts Comptables et des Comptables Agrees (France). Conseil Superieur. **VFOAT** Comptabilite. No. 1. (1955)-. Periodical. French. Eleven times a year. $120.30. Ed Comptables Malesherbes, 153 rue de Courcelles, 75817 Paris Cedex France. **Tel** 011 33 1 44156000, FAX 011 33 1 44159005, telex 640994. **ED** Gerard Nicol.
 Ind/Abst Selec. Coop. Index Manage. Period.

LC HF5601
DD 657   FR
REVUE FRANCAISE DE L'AUDIT INTERNE. (19??)-. French. Five times a year. 473.93F France. Institut Francais des Auditeurs et Consultants Internes, 8 rue Jean Goujon, F-75008 Paris France.
 Desc: Promotion of internal auditing.

LC HF5601
DD 657   IT
RIFORMA TRIBUTARIA : CASI E QUESTIONI. (19??)-. Periodical. Italian. Six times a year. IPSOA Editore SRL, Casella Postale 12055, Mastrangelo, 20120 Milan Italy. **Tel** 011 39 2 82476248. Index available (Included).

LC HF5601
DD 657   IT
RIVISTA DI RAGIONERIA E TECNICA COMMERCIALE. (19??)-. Periodical. Italian. Irregular. L14990. Tramontana Spa, Via A Mario 65, 20149 Milan Italy. **Tel** 011 39 2 4984451, FAX 011 39 2 4818916.

LC HF5601
DD 657   IT
RIVISTA ITALIANA DI RAGIONERIA E DI ECONOMIA AZIENDALE. (19??)-. Periodical. Italian. Six times a year (Feb., Apr., Jun., Aug., Oct., Dec.). L102190. Rivista Italiana di Ragioneria, Via delle Isole 30, 0018 Rome Italy. **Tel** 011 39 6 8845732.

LC HF5616.U5 A74A   ISSN 0363-2954
DD 657/.025/791   US
ROSTER - ARIZONA STATE BOARD OF ACCOUNTANCY. Main/Corp Arizona. State Board of Accountancy. English. Arizona State Board of Accounting, 222 West Osborn Road, Suite 410, Roster AZ 85013.

LC HF5601
DD 657   UK
SCAS & VSCAS COMPANIES' ACCOUNTS DISCLOSURE CHECKLIST. (19??)-. English. Four times a year. £99.00. Institute of

Chartered Accountants, 399 Silbury Boulevard, Central Milton, Keynes Buckinghamshire MK9 2HL United Kingdom. **Tel** 011 44 1908 248100, FAX 011 44 1908 248001, telex 727530.
Desc: A checklist with all the disclosure requirements of company law and accounting and financial reporting standards.

LC HG **ISSN** 1045-1439
DD 332 US
CCC

SEC ACCOUNTING & REPORTING UPDATE SERVICE. [SEC account. report. update serv.]. **VFOAT** SEC Accounting and Reporting Update Service; Accounting & Reporting Update Service. **VAT** Securities Exchange Commission Accounting & Reporting Update Service. (1985)-. Periodical. English. Irregular (1-6 issues per month). $363.95. Warren Gorham & Lamont Inc., Park Square Building, 31 St. James Avenue, Boston MA 02116-4112. **Tel** (617)423-2020, (800)950-1207, FAX (617)423-2026. **ED** Paul Wendell. Index available. **Circ:** 1700.
Desc: This service brings updates in all SEC accounting pronouncements within 12 days of their release. They provide examples and illustrations of the pronouncements' impact and includes a synopsis of its major features.

LC KF1446.A15 S14 **ISSN** 0146-485X
DD 346/.73/0664 US
CCC

SEC ACCOUNTING REPORT. [SEC account. rep.]. **Added/Corp** United States. Securities and Exchange Commission. Warren, Gorham & Lamont, Inc. **VAT** Securities and Exchange Commission Accounting Report. (19??)-. Periodical. English. Twelve times a year. $239.25. Warren Gorham & Lamont Inc., Park Square Building, 31 St. James Avenue, Boston MA 02116-4112. **Tel** (617)423-2020, (800)950-1207, FAX (617)423-2026. **ED** Paul J. Wendell.
Desc: A newsletter devoted to coverage of SEC, FASB and related financial reporting matters. Offers information on new SEC developments and federal regulations.
Ind/Abst Account. Tax Datab. (1975-).

LC KF1446 .A88
DD 353.0082/58 US

SECURITIES AND EXCHANGE COMMISSION REPORT TO CONGRESS ON THE ACCOUNTING PROFESSION AND THE COMMISSION'S OVERSIGHT ROLE. **Main/Corp** United States. Securities and Exchange Commission. **Added/Corp** United States. Congress. Senate. Committee on Governmental Affairs. Subcommittee on Governmental Efficiency and the District of Columbia. **VFOAT** Report to Congress on the Accounting Profession and the Commission's Oversight Role. (19??)-. Government Publication. English. One time a year. $15.00 US; $16.25 other. Superintendent of Documents, US Government Printing Office, Washington DC 20402. **Tel** (202)275-3328, FAX (202)786-2377. **(Subscription address:** US Government Bookstore, O'Neil Building, 2023 3rd Avenue North, Birmingham AL 35203. **)**

LC HF5601 .S52
DD 657 CC

SHANG-HAI KUAI CHI. **Added/Corp** Shang-Hai Shih Kuai Chi Hsueh Hui. **VFOAT** Shanghai Kuaiji. (19??)-. Chinese. Post Office / China, People's Republic of China.

LC HF5601 **ISSN** 0080-9640
DD 657 SI

SINGAPORE ACCOUNTANT, THE. [Singap. account.]. **Added/Corp** Singapore Society of Accountants. Singapore Polytechnic Society of Commerce. Vol. 1 (1966)-. English. Twelve times a year. $65.61. Institute of Certified Public Accountants of Singapore, 116 Middle Road 09 01, Singapore 0718 Singapore. **Tel** 011 65 3367020, FAX 011 65 3394150, telex 29208. Documents available from UMI Article Clearinghouse. ***Supersedes*** *Calculator Annual.*
Ind/Abst ABI/INFORM Glob. Ed.; Anbar Account. Finan. Abstr. [Full Txt.]; Anbar Mark. Distr. Abstr. [Full Txt.]; Anbar Top Manage. Abstr. [Full Txt.]; Manage. Bibliogr. Rev.; Oper. Prod. Manage. Abstr. [Full Txt.]; Person. Train. Abstr. [Full Txt.]; Women Manage. Rev. [Full Txt.].

LC HF5601 **ISSN** 8756-3886
DD 657 US

SINGLE AUDIT INFORMATION SERVICE. [Single audit inf. serv.]. (1985)-. Periodical. English. Twelve times a year. $298.00. Thompson Publishing Group, 7711 Anderson Road, Tampa FL 33634. **Tel** (800)677-3789, (813)282-8607. Index available (free).

LC HF5601 **ISSN** 0394-3631
DD 657 IT
UDC 658

SOCIETA BILANCIO E CONTABILITA. [Soc. bilan. contab.]. (1979)-. Periodical. Italian. Twelve times a year. L129440. De Lillo Editore Srl, Via Mecenate 76/3, 20138 Milan Italy. **Tel** 011 39 2 58013112. **Circ:** 14,500.

LC HF5601 **ISSN** 0741-336X
DD 657 US

STANDARD FOR AUDITING COMPUTER APPLICATIONS, A. **See** Business and Economics-Computer Applications.

LC HF5601 **ISSN** 0746-7486
DD 657 US

STATEMENT OF FINANCIAL ACCOUNTING STANDARDS. [Statement financ. account. stand.]. **Added/Corp** Financial Accounting Standards Board. No. 1, (1973)-. Periodical. English. Irregular. Price varies. Financial Accounting Standards Board, PO Box 5116, Norwalk CT 06856. **Tel** (203)847-0700, FAX (203)849-9714.

LC HF5601
DD 657 US

STATEMENTS OF POSITION OF THE ACCOUNTING STANDARDS DIVISION AS OF JANUARY 1 ... . **Main/Corp** American Institute of Certified Public Accountants. Accounting Standards Division. **Added/Corp** Commerce Clearing House. **VFOAT** AICPA Statements of Position of the Accounting Standards Divisional; Statements of Position. (19??)-. English. Irregular. $6.00. American Institute of Certified Public Accountants, Harborside Financial Center, #201 Plaza 3, Jersey City NJ 07311. **Tel** (201)938-3333, (800)862-4272, FAX (201)938-3329. Each issue contains an index to its own contents (no volume index)--loose.

LC HF5601 **ISSN** 0149-8452
DD 657 US

STATUS REPORT - FINANCIAL ACCOUNTING STANDARDS BOARD. [Status rep. - Financ. Account. Stand. Board]. **Main/Corp** Financial Accounting Standards Board. No. 1 (1973)-. Periodical. English. Twelve times a year (with extra editions as developments warrant). Comes with Financial Accounting Standards Board Financial Accounting Series and membership. Financial Accounting Standards Board, PO Box 5116, Norwalk CT 06856. **Tel** (203)847-0700, FAX (203)849-9714. ***Absorbed*** *FASB Viewpoints.*
Ind/Abst Account. Tax Datab. (1986-).

LC HF5601
DD 657 US

STUDIES IN MANAGERIAL AND FINANCIAL ACCOUNTING. (19??)-. Monographic series. English. $73.25. JAI Press Inc., 55 Old Post Road, Suite 2, PO Box 1678, Greenwich CT 06836-1678. **Tel** (203)661-7602, FAX (203)661-0792. **ED** Mark J. Epstein.

LC HF5601 **ISSN** 0826-2926
DD 657 CN

STUDY PAPER SERIES. [Study pap. ser. - Can. Certif. Gen. Account. Res. Found.]. **Added/Corp** Canadian Certified General Accountants' Research Foundation. **VFOAT** La Fondation de Recherche de l'Association des Comptables Generaux Licencies du Canada. Vol. 1 (1983)-. Monographic series. English (French). Irregular. Price varies per volume. Canadian Certified General Accountant Research Foundation Street, Vancouver British Columbia V6E 4A2 Canada. **Tel** (604)669-3555.
Desc: Pure and applied research in accounting and related topics.

LC HF5601 **ISSN** 1382-3167
DD 657 NE

●**SUBSIDIEWIJZER ALPHEN A/D RIJN.** (SUBSIDIEWIJZER.). (1995)-. Periodical. Dutch. Twelve times a year. Samsom Bedrijfsinformatie BV, Postbus 4, 2400 MA Alphen Rij Netherlands. **Tel** 011 31 1720 66633. **(Subscription address:** Intermedia BV, Postbus 4, 2400 MA Alphen AD Rijn Netherlands. **Tel** 011 31 1720 66481.**)** ***Absorbed in part*** *Nieuwsbrief Nationale Subsidie Wijzer, 0927-4162* ***and*** *Terzake (Amsterdam), 1382-1237.*

LC HF5616.U62 S83 **ISSN** 1078-0106
DD 657 US
TITLE CHANGE

SUCCESSFUL CALIFORNIA ACCOUNTANT, THE. [Success. Calif. account.]. **Added/Corp** Society of California Accountants. (199?)-(1995). Trade Publication. English. Four times a year (plus eight supplements). $20.00. Society of California Accountants, 2131 Capitol Avenue, Suite 305, Sacramento CA 95816. **Tel** (916)443-2057, FAX (916)443-0486. **Ad Acc, Adv Mgr:** Diana Granger, **Tel** (916)427-0227. **Circ:** 2,500 (ctrl). ***Continues*** *California Accountant, 0744-9895.* ***Continued by*** *Successful California Accountant Update, 1084-9688.*

LC HF5616.U62 S83 **ISSN** 1084-9688
DD 657 US

●**SUCCESSFUL CALIFORNIA ACCOUNTANT UPDATE, THE.** [Success. Calif. account. update]. **Added/Corp** Society of California Accountants. (1995)-. Periodical. English. Twelve times a year. Society of California Accountants, 2131 Capitol Avenue, Suite 305, Sacramento CA 95816. **Tel** (916)443-2057, FAX (916)443-0486. ***Continues*** *Successful California Accountant, 1078-0106.*

LC HF5601
DD 657 US

SURVEY OF FINANCIAL REPORTING AND ACCOUNTING DEVELOPMENTS IN THE PUBLIC UTILITY INDUSTRY, A. **Added/Corp** Price, Waterhouse & Co. (19??)-. English. Price Waterhouse & Company, 1177 Avenue of the Americas, New York NY 10020. **Tel** (212)596-7000.

LC HF5601
DD 657 UK

TAX BRIEFINGS LOOSELEAF. (19??)-. English. Two times a year. £170.00. Institute of Chartered Accountants, 399 Silbury Boulevard, Central Milton, Keynes Buckinghamshire MK9 2HL United Kingdom. **Tel** 011 44 1908 248100, FAX 011 44 1908 248001, telex 727530.
Desc: Covers the major tax aspects of one industry or business type in each briefing.

LC HF5601
DD 657 UK

TAX CLAIMS AND ELECTIONS. (19??)-. English. One time a year. £95.00. Institute of Chartered Accountants, 399 Silbury Boulevard, Central Milton, Keynes Buckinghamshire MK9 2HL United Kingdom. **Tel** 011 44 1908 248100, FAX 011 44 1908 248001, telex 727530.
Desc: A manual designed for day-to-day use, containing 73 tried and tested standard claims and elections.

LC KF6450 .T39 **ISSN** 8756-5137
DD 343.7306/8 347.30368 US

TAX PLANNING FOR THE TROUBLED BUSINESS. (1983)-. Periodical. English. One time a year. John Wiley & Sons, Inc., 605 Third Avenue, New York NY 10158-0012. **Tel** (212)850-6000, (212)850-6645, FAX (212)850-6088, telex 12-7063. **(Subscription address:** John Wiley & Sons / UK, Baffins Lane, Chichester, West Sussex PO19 1UD United Kingdom. **Tel** 011 44 1243 779777, FAX 011 44 243 776128, telex 86290 WIBOOKG.**)** **ED** Jeff Brown.

LC HF5681.T3 T35 **ISSN** 0040-0165
DD 657.6 US
CCC

TAXATION FOR ACCOUNTANTS. [Tax. account.]. Vol. 1 (Mar. 1966)-. Trade Publication. English. Twelve times a year. $120.98. Warren Gorham & Lamont Inc., Park Square Building, 31 St. James Avenue, Boston MA 02116-4112. **Tel** (617)423-2020, (800)950-1207, FAX (617)423-2026. available on microfilm and microfiche from University Microfilms International (UMI). Documents available from UMI Article Clearinghouse.
Desc: Provides coverage of current tax developments and their implications, as well as offering solutions to tax problems that arise frequently in general accounting practice.
Ind/Abst ABI/INFORM Glob. Ed.; ABI/INFORM [Computer File] (Aug. 1971-); Account. Tax Datab. (1974-); Account. Art.; Bus. Period. Index; Fed. Tax Artic.; Gen. BusinessFile (1992-); Gen. Period. Index (1985-); Law Office Inf. Serv.; Mag. Search; Manage. Contents; MasterFile FullTEXT (Jan. 1994-); PAIS Int. Print; Wilson Bus. Abstr.

LC HF5601
DD 657 UK

TAXLINE. (19??)-. English. Six times a year. £40.00. Institute of Chartered Accountants, 399 Silbury Boulevard, Central Milton, Keynes Buckinghamshire MK9 2HL United Kingdom. **Tel** 011 44 1908 248100, FAX 011 44 1908 248001, telex 727530.

LC HF5601
DD 657 UK

TECHNICAL RELEASE. (1972)-. Bulletin. English. Irregular. £60.00. Institute of Chartered Accountants, 399 Silbury Boulevard, Central Milton, Keynes Buckinghamshire MK9 2HL United Kingdom. **Tel** 011 44 1908 248100, FAX 011 44 1908 248001, telex 727530. Index available (on request).

LC HF5601 **ISSN** 0210-2129
DD 657 SP
UDC 657

TECNICA CONTABLE. [Tec. contab.]. (1949)-. Periodical. Spanish. Twelve times a year. $150.99. Institute de Contabilidad, Glorieta de Quevedo 7, 28015 Madrid Spain. **Tel** 011 34 1 4466336.

LC HF5601 **ISSN** 0896-386X
DD 657 US

TEMPO. [Tempo]. Vol. 16 (1970)-. Periodical. English. Irregular. Touche Ross, 1900 M Street Northwest, Washington DC 20036. **Tel** (202)955-4238. Documents available from UMI Article Clearinghouse. ***Continues*** *Touche Ross Tempo, 0563-9670.*
Ind/Abst ABI/INFORM Glob. Ed.; ABI/INFORM [Computer File] (Fall 1972-Jan. 1976).

Business and Economics —Accounting

LC HF5601   **ISSN** 0705-3673
DD 657/.01/4   CN
TERMINOLOGIE COMPTABLE. Main/Corp
Ordre des Comptables Agrees du Quebec. Comite de Terminologie Francaise. (1974)-. Periodical. French. Four times a year. 7.49Can$. Ordre Comptables Agrees Quebec, 680 Sherbrooke Quest, Montreal Quebec H3A 2S3 Canada. **Tel** (514)288-3256. **Continues** Terminologie Comptable, 0705-3673.
Desc: French terminology for accountants.

LC HF5601   **ISSN** 1382-1237
DD 657   NE
TITLE CHANGE
TERZAKE (AMSTERDAM). (TERZAKE.).
(1984)-(1994). Periodical. Dutch. Samsom Bedrijfsinformatie BV, Postbus 4, 2400 MA Alphen Rij Netherlands. **Tel** 011 31 1720 66633. **(Subscription address:** Intermedia BV, Postbus 4, 2400 MA Alphen AD Rijn Netherlands. **Tel** 011 31 1720 66481.**) Continues** Terzake. Subsidies, 0167-4722. **Merged with** Nieuwsbrief Nationale Subsidie Wijzer, 0927-4162 **to form** Subsidiewijzer, 1382-3167.

LC HF5601   **ISSN** 1382-1237
DD 657   NE
TITLE CHANGE
TERZAKE (AMSTERDAM). (TERZAKE.).
(1984)-(1994). Periodical. Dutch. Samsom Bedrijfsinformatie BV, Postbus 4, 2400 MA Alphen Rij Netherlands. **Tel** 011 31 1720 66633. **(Subscription address:** Intermedia BV, Postbus 4, 2400 MA Alphen AD Rijn Netherlands. **Tel** 011 31 1720 66481.**) Continues** Terzake. Subsidies, 0167-4722. **Merged with** Nieuwsbrief Nationale Subsidie Wijzer, 0927-4162 **to form** Subsidiewijzer, 1382-3167.

LC HF5601
DD 657   NE
TIJDSCHRIFT VOOR ADMINISTRATEURS EN CONTROLLERS.
(19??)-. Periodical. Dutch. Ten times a year (monthly with Jan./Feb. and Jul./Aug. issues combined). Fl182.50. Intermedia BV, Postbus 4, 2400 MA Alphen AD Rijn Netherlands. **Tel** 011 31 1720 66855, FAX 011 31 1720 94714.

LC HF5601   **ISSN** 0889-4337
DD 657   US
Pr Rev.
TODAY'S CPA. [Today's CPA]. Added/Corp
Texas Society of Certified Public Accountants. Vol. 12, No. 1 (June/July 1986)-. Trade Publication. English. Six times a year (Feb., Apr., June, Aug., Oct., Dec.). $28.00. Texas Society of Certified Public Accountants, 1421 West Mockingbird Lane, Suite 100, Dallas TX 75247. **Tel** (214)689-6000, FAX (214)689-6046. **ED** Brux Austin (phone: (214)689-6073). **Ad Acc, Adv Mgr:** J. Ourcton, **Tel** (214)689-6036. **Circ:** 31,000. **Continues** CPA, 0164-5099.
Ind/Abst Account. Tax Datab. (1983-); Account. Art.; Fed. Tax Artic.

LC HF5601   **ISSN** 1056-9782
DD 657   US
TRACKKER (FORT WORTH, TEX.).
(TRACKKER.). [Trackker]. (Nov. 1990)-. Periodical. English. Practitioners Publishing Company, PO Box 966, Fort Worth TX 76101-0966. **Tel** (800)332-3709.

LC HG4001   **ISSN** 0961-5261
DD 658.15   UK
TREASURY TODAY. [Treas. today]. (1991)-.
Periodical. English. Twelve times a year. $301.17. Chartac Books, PO Box 620 Central Milton, Keynes MK9 2JX United Kingdom. **Tel** 011 44 1908 668833.

LC HF5601
DD 657   UK
TREASURY TODAY. (19??)-. English. Twelve
times a year. £160.00. Institute of Chartered Accountants, 399 Silbury Boulevard, Central Milton, Keynes Buckinghamshire MK9 2HL United Kingdom. **Tel** 011 44 1908 248100, FAX 011 44 1908 248001, telex 727530.
Desc: Gives guidance to anyone involved in treasury and financial management, particularly those who are relatively inexperienced in the field.

LC HF5601
DD 657   UK
TRUE & FAIR. VFOAT True and Fair. No. 1 (Aug.
1976)-. Periodical. English. Twelve times a year. £200.00 (medium to large firms/3 copies); £150.00 (small firms, 3 partnews or less/1 copy). KATO Communications Ltd.,, Paul Osborne, FREEPOST, 16 Apollo Studios, Charlton Kings Road, London NW5 2YP United Kingdom. **Tel** 011 44 171 4826242, FAX 011 44 171 4826309.
Desc: Publication geared to audit firms and practices carrying on investment business.

LC HG41 .T75
DD 332/.05   CC
TSAI WU YU KUAI CHI = CAIWU YUKUAIJI. VFOAT
Caiwu Yukuaiji. (1978)-. Periodical. Chinese. Twelve times a year. RMBY0.25. Zhongguo Caizheng Zazhishe, No. C-27 Wanshou Lu, Beijing 100036, People's Republic of China. **ED** Qian Duling.

LC HF5601   **ISSN** 1183-3297
DD 657/.023/714   CN
UNIVERSITY GUIDE ACCOUNTANCY.
[Univ. guide account.]. VFOAT University Guide for Accounting. Vol. 2, No. 2 (1991)-. English (summaries and/or abstracts in French). $2.95 per issue. University Guide for Accounting, 9942 St-Hubert Street, Montreal Quebec H2C 2H4 Canada.

LC HF5661 .A44
DD 657   US
     CEASED
UNOFFICIAL ANSWERS TO THE UNIFORM CERTIFIED PUBLIC ACCOUNTANT EXAMINATIONS OF THE AMERICAN INSTITUTE OF CERTIFIED PUBLIC ACCOUNTANTS.
Main/Corp American Institute of Certified Public Accountants. Board of Examiners. (1927)-(1994). English. American Institute of Certified Public Accountants, Harborside Financial Center, #201 Plaza 3, Jersey City NJ 07311. **Tel** (201)938-3333, (800)862-4272, FAX (201)938-3329.

LC HF5601   **ISSN** 0266-7053
DD 657.0941   UK
UPDATE (LONDON. 1984). [Update Lond.,
1984]. (1984)-. Newsletter. English. Twelve times a year. $145.45. Institute of Chartered Accountants, 399 Silbury Boulevard, Central Milton, Keynes Buckinghamshire MK9 2HL United Kingdom. **Tel** 011 44 1908 248100, FAX 011 44 1908 248001, telex 727530. Index available.

LC HD9235.C52 A4
DD 331.7   SA
VERSLAG VAN DIE OUDITEUR-GENERAAL OOR DIE REKENINGS VAN DIE SIGOREIRAAD. REPORT OF THE AUDITOR-GENERAL ON THE AACCOUNTS OF THE CHICORY BOARD. Main/Corp
South Africa. Chicory Board. **Added/Corp** South Africa. Dept. of the Auditor-General. VFOAT Report of the Auditor-General on the Accounts of the Chicory Board. (1978)-. Government Publication. Afrikaans (English). One time a year. Government Printer / South Africa, Bosman Street, Private Bag X85, Pretoria 0001 South Africa. **Tel** 011 27 12 3239731 ext. 262. **Continues** South Africa. Chicory Control Board. Verslag van die Ouditeur-Generaal oor die Rekeninge van die Sigoreibeheerraad vir die Boekjaar ... .

LC HF5601
DD 657   UK
VERY SMALL COMPANY AUDIT SYSTEM.
(19??)-. English. Four times a year. £99.00. Institute of Chartered Accountants, 399 Silbury Boulevard, Central Milton, Keynes Buckinghamshire MK9 2HL United Kingdom. **Tel** 011 44 1908 248100, FAX 011 44 1908 248001, telex 727530.
Desc: Offers a practical and profitable way to audit the very smallest of clients.

LC HF5601
DD 657   US
WEST VIRGINIA CPA. (19??)-. English. Four
times a year. West Virginia Society of CPAs, Box 1257, Bluefield WV 24701.
Ind/Abst Account. Art.

LC HF5601   **ISSN** 0826-094X
DD 657/.0971   CN
WHAT'S NEW IN ACCOUNTING CANADA. [What's new account. Can.]. 1982-.
Periodical. English. One time a year. Free. Touche Ross, 1900 M Street Northwest, Washington DC 20036. **Tel** (202)955-4238. ctrl circ. **Continues** What's New in Accounting, 0826-0931.

LC HF5616.U5 W5   **ISSN** 0149-0281
DD 657/.45/02573   US
WHO AUDITS AMERICA. 1st Ed. (1976)-.
English. Two times a year. $142.00. Data Financial Press, PO Box 801, Menlo Park CA 94025. **Tel** (415)321-4553, FAX (415)321-4427. **Circ:** 3,000.
Desc: A directory of 10,000 companies with financial information and auditors.

LC HF5601   **ISSN** 1035-2015
DD 657.450994   AT
WHO AUDITS AUSTRALIA? (1987). [Who
audits Aust.? 1987]. (1987)-. English. One time a year. 123.33Aus$. University of Sydney / Accounting Research Center, Department of Accounting HO4, Sydney NSW 2006 Australia. **Tel** 011 61 2 6923901, FAX 011 61 2 5524183.

LC HJ9101 .W5   **ISSN** 1062-2209
DD 657   US
WI CPA. [WI CPA]. Added/Corp Wisconsin Institute of
Certified Public Accountants. VFOAT Wisconsin CPA.; Wisconsin Certified Public Accountant; WICPA. Vol. 1, No. 158 (Winter 1991)-. Periodical. English. Three times a year. $9.00 (US); $12.00 (Canada and Mexico); $20.00 (other). Wisconsin Institute of Certified Public Accountants, PO Box 1010, Brookfield WI 53008. **Tel** (414)785-0445, (800)772-6939, FAX (414)785-0838. **ED** Amy E. Gaeth. **Ad Acc. Circ:** 7,400 (ctrl). **Continues** Wisconsin CPA, 0043-6402.
Desc: Accounting updates, regulatory news, tax (state and federal), personal financial planning, continuing ed. public, industry, government and education accounting news.
Ind/Abst Account. Index Suppl.

LC HF5601   **ISSN** 0821-4069
DD 657/.06/071344   CN
WORKING PAPER (UNIVERSITY OF WATERLOO. ACCOUNTING GROUP).
(THE WORKING PAPER : A PERIODIC PUBLICATION OF THE ACCOUNTING GROUP, UNIVERSITY OF WATERLOO.). [Work. pap. - Account. Group Univ. Waterloo]. **Added/Corp** University of Waterloo. Accounting Group. Vol. 1, No. 1 (1982)-. Periodical. English. Irregular. University of Waterloo Accounting Group, Waterloo Ontario N2L 3G1 Canada.

LC HF5601
DD 657   UK
WORLD ACCOUNTING REPORT; A MONTHLY BULLETIN ON DEVELOPMENTS IN INTERNATIONAL ACCOUNTING. VFOAT WAR. (19??)-. Bulletin.
English. Twelve times a year. $710.15. Financial Times / UK, Maple House, 149 Tottenham Court Road, London W1P 9LL United Kingdom. **Tel** 011 44 171 8962276, FAX 011 44 171 8962275, 011 44 171 8962399. **ED** Leon Hopkins. **Bk Rev.** ctrl circ. available on an online database (files 16,636/Full-Text) from DIALOG.
Desc: Bulletin on developments in international accounting.
Ind/Abst Account. Tax Datab. (1981-); PROMT [Full Txt.]; PTS Newsl. Database [Full Txt.].

LC HF5601   **ISSN** 1055-2103
DD 657   US
WORLDWIDE ACCOUNTING, BUSINESS, AND EDUCATION JOURNAL, THE. [Worldw. account. bus. educ. j.].
VFOAT TWABE. Vol. 1, No. 1 (Summer 1991)-. Periodical. English. Four times a year. $40.00. Worldwide Publishers, PO Box 1018, State University, Jonesboro AR 72467.

LC HF5601   **ISSN** 0340-9031
DD 657   GW
UDC 657.6
WPG. DIE WIRTSCHAFTSPRUEFUNG.
[WPg. Wirtschaftspruef.]. VFOAT Wirtschaftspruefung (1970). (1970)-. Periodical. German. Twenty-four times a year. DM309.43 Germany; DM357.00 other. IDW Verlag GmbH, Postfach 320580, D-40420 Duesseldorf Germany. **Tel** 011 49 211 45610119. Index available. cum. index. **Circ:** 10,500 (ctrl). **Continues** Die Wirtschaftspruefung, 0043-6313.
Ind/Abst ABI/INFORM Glob. Ed.; ABI/INFORM [Computer File] (Feb. 1982-).

LC LB2826.W8 W93A LC144.W9 W9
DD 379.1/52/09787, 379.1/3/09787   US
WYOMING PUBLIC SCHOOLS FUND ACCOUNTING AND REPORTING.
Main/Corp Wyoming. State Dept. of Education. Division of Administrative Services. English. One time a year. Division of Administrative Services, State Department of Education, Cheyenne WY 82002. **Continues** Wyoming Public Schools Fund Accounting and Reporting, 0146-793X.

LC HF5601 .N342   **ISSN** 0547-9193
DD 657.6/062/73   US
YEARBOOK - NATIONAL SOCIETY OF PUBLIC ACCOUNTANTS. Main/Corp National
Society of Public Accountants. (19??)-. English. One time a year. National Society of Public Accountants, 1010 North Fairfax Street, Alexandria VA 22314. **Tel** (703)549-6400.
Desc: Includes membership directory.

LC HF5667 .Z4   **ISSN** 0044-3816
DD 657.4/5/05   GW
     CCC
     CODEN ZIREAM
ZEITSCHRIFT INTERNE REVISION. [Z.
interne Revis.]. **Added/Corp** Institut fuer Interne Revision. VFOAT Interne Revision; ZIR. Vol. 1 (1966)-. Periodical. German. Six times a year. $73.70. Erich Schmidt Verlag GmbH, Postfach 304240, D-10724 Berlin Germany. **Tel** 011 49 30 25008525. **Bk Rev. Ad Acc.** ctrl circ. Documents available from UMI Article Clearinghouse.
Desc: Internal audition.
Ind/Abst ABI/INFORM Glob. Ed.; ABI/INFORM [Computer File] (1983-).

Business and Economics—Advertising and Public Relations

ADVERTISING AND PUBLIC RELATIONS

ISSN 0001-8066
US
AC. THE ADCRAFTER. **Added/Corp** Adcraft Club of Detroit, Inc. **VFOAT** Adcrafter. (19??)-. Periodical. English. One time a week. $25.00. Adcrafter, 2630 Book Tower, Detroit MI 48226. **Tel** (313)962-7225. **ED** Lee H. Wilson. **Ad Acc. Circ:** 4,000 (ctrl).
 Desc: Advertising marketing news of the Detroit area.

ISSN 0193-4457
US
ACT. ADVERTISING/COMMUNICATIONS TIMES. **VFOAT** Advertising Communications Times; Advertising and Communications Times. (197?)-. Trade Publication. English. Twelve times a year. $39.00. ACT-Advertising/Communications Times, 121 Chestnut Street, Philadelphia PA 19106. **Tel** (215)629-1666, FAX (215)923-8358. **ED** Carole Morganti. **Ad Acc. Circ:** 40,000 (ctrl).
 Desc: General business newspaper for the advertising industry.
 Ind/Abst Mark. Advert. Ref. Serv.

ISSN 1071-3654
US
•**AD AGENCEO, THE.** (1993)-. Periodical. English. Twelve times a year. $372.00. Corporate Marketing Consulting Group, PO Box 500491, Atlanta GA 31150.

ISSN 1061-1371
DD 658 US
AD BUSINESS REPORT. [Ad bus. rep.]. (1978)- Vol. 15 (Dec. 1992)- Vol. 16 (Dec. 1993)-. Periodical. English. Twelve times a year. $75.00. Executive Communications, 185 East 85th Street, Suite 11 C, New York NY 10028. **Tel** (212)831-3147. **ED** Sue Sutton. **Bk Rev.** available via fax. **Continues** New Business Report.
 Desc: Covers advertising agency management, growth strategies and business developments, as well as studies of consumer product and service markets.

US
CEASED
AD CHANGE; THE STANDARD DIRECTORY OF ADVERTISERS BULLETIN. (Jan. 3, 1977)-(19??). Bulletin. English. National Register Publishing Company Inc., PO Box 31, 121 Chanlon Road, New Providence NJ 07974. **Tel** (800)521-8110, (800)323-6772, FAX (908)665-6688.

LC HF5801 **ISSN** 0112-6997
DD 659.1 NZ
AD/MEDIA. [AD/Media]. (1985)-. Periodical. English. Eleven times a year. Minty's Media, 22 Heather Street, Private Bag 93218, Parnell Auckland New Zealand. **Tel** 011 64 9 3794233, FAX 011 64 9 3093575.

LC HF5801 **ISSN** 0112-8876
DD 659.112509931 NZ
AD/MEDIA'S AGENCIES AND CLIENTS. [Ad/Media's agencies clients]. **VFOAT** Agencies and Clients. (1985)-. English. One time a year. Minty's Media, 22 Heather Street, Private Bag 93218, Parnell Auckland New Zealand. **Tel** 011 64 9 3794233, FAX 011 64 9 3093575. **ED** Kevin Lawrence.

AT
AD NEWS HANDBOOK. (19??)-. English. Two times a year. 65.78Aus$. Yaffa Publishing Group Pty Ltd., GPO Box 606, Sydney New South Wales 2001 Australia. **Tel** 011 61 2 2812333, FAX 011 61 2 2812750.

ISSN 0814-6942
DD 659.1 AT
AD NEWS SURRY HILLS. [Ad news Surry Hills]. (1984)-. Trade Publication. English. Twenty-six times a year. 73.99Aus$. Yaffa Publishing Group Pty Ltd., GPO Box 606, Sydney New South Wales 2001 Australia. **Tel** 011 61 2 2812333, FAX 011 61 2 2812750. **Continues** Advertising News, 0814-6934.

ISSN 0190-7166
DD 659 US
AD $ SUMMARY. [Ad $ summ.]. **Added/Corp** Leading National Advertisers, Inc. **VFOAT** Bar LNA Multi-Media Service; Bar/LNA Multi-Media Service; LNA Ad $ Summary. **VAT** Ad Dollar Summary. (1973)-. English. Four times a year. $790.00. Competitive Media Reporting, 11 West 42nd Street, New York NY 10036. **Tel** (212)789-1400.

ISSN 0886-6813
DD 659 US
AD VANTAGE (CANOGA PARK, CALIF.). (AD VANTAGE.). **VFOAT** AdVantage. (1985)-. Periodical. English. Twelve times a year. Reid Publishing, 8429 Sales Avenue, Canoga Park CA 91304. **Tel** (818)347-9799. **ED** Gerene Reid. Index available. **Bk Rev.**
 Desc: Resource newsletter for advertising managers and others involved in the planning and implementation of promotion programs.

ISSN 0311-2225
DD 659.10994 AT
CCC
ADBRIEF. [Adbrief]. (1974)-. Periodical. English. One time a week. 337.10Aus$. Newsletter Information Service, PO Box 693, Manly New South Wales 2095 Australia. **Tel** 011 61 2 9777500, FAX 011 61 2 9773310. **Continues** Inside Advertising & Media, 0310-7124.

ISSN 0819-6648
DD 659.102594 AT
ADBRIEF REGISTER. [Adbrief regist.]. (1986)-. English. Three times a year. 283.65Aus$. Newsletter Information Service, PO Box 693, Manly New South Wales 2095 Australia. **Tel** 011 61 2 9777500, FAX 011 61 2 9773310.

ISSN 0847-9097
DD 659.1/042 CN
CCC
ADBUSTERS (VANCOUVER). (ADBUSTERS.). [Adbusters]. **Added/Corp** Media Foundation (Organization). **VFOAT** Ad Busters. Vol. 1, No. 1 (Summer 1989)-. Periodical. English. Four times a year. 32.00Can$. Media Foundation, 1243 West 7th Avenue, Vancouver BC V6H 1B7 Canada. **Tel** (604)736-9401. **ED** Kalle Lasn. **Bk Rev. Circ:** 20,000.
 Desc: Welcomes articles, illustrations, cartoons and advertising concepts. Instigates a media revolution through media literacy and artistic activism.
 Ind/Abst Can. Period. Index (1990-).

LC HF **ISSN** 1061-3242
DD 659 US
ADCOM (BOSTON, MASS.). (ADCOM : NEW ENGLAND'S OWN ADVERTISING AND MARKETING MAGAZINE.). [Adcom]. (1991)-. Trade Publication. English. Twelve times a year. $24.00. Publitech Inc., PO Box 840, Sherborn MA 01770. **Tel** (617)423-1122. available on diskette.
 Desc: Available only online.

LC HF5801
DD 659.1 US
ADCOM. [DISKETTE]. (19??)-. Trade Publication. English. Publitech Inc., PO Box 840, Sherborn MA 01770. **Tel** (617)423-1122.

UK
ADMAP : THE JOURNAL OF ADVERTISING MEDIA ANALYSIS AND PLANNING. (19??)-. Periodical. English. Eleven times a year (July/Aug. issues combined). £180.00 UK; £195.00 Europe; £240.00 other. NTC Publications Ltd., PO Box 69, Henley-on-Thames, Oxfordshire RG9 1GB United Kingdom. **Tel** 011 44 1491 574671, FAX 011 44 1491 571188. **ED** Nicholas Staveley. **Bk Rev.** (Qty: not fixed). **Ad Acc, Adv Mgr:** T. Clifton, **Tel** 0491 411000. **Circ:** 1,300.
 Desc: Forum for world-wide views, news and opinions on advertising, marketing and related research.
 Ind/Abst Curr. Cit.; Index Bus. Reports; Women Manage. Rev. [Full Txt.].

ISSN 0712-9041
DD 659.1/0971 CN
Pr Rev. CEASED
ADNEWS (OCT. 13, 1981). (ADNEWS.). [Adnews]. **VFOAT** Adnews & Information; Stimulus Adnews. **VAT** Adnews and Information; Stimulur Adnews (Oct. 13, 1981). Vol. 1, No. 33 (Oct. 13, 1981)-(19??)-. Periodical. English. Bale Communications, 2 Lansing Square Suite 801, Willowdale Ontario M2J 4P8 Canada. **Tel** (416)498-5164, FAX (416)498-6845. **ED** Mike Deibert. Index available. **Ad Acc, Adv Mgr:** Rob Bale. **Circ:** 6,500 (ctrl). **Continues** Stimulus Adnews, 0711-2297.
 Desc: Tightly edited news covering ad campaigns, new products, media schedules, account shifts, and people profiles.

ISSN 1350-1402
UK
•**ADS INTERNATIONAL.** (1993)-. Trade Publication. English. $35.00. Creative Magazines Ltd., 35 Britannia Row, London N1 8QH United Kingdom. **Tel** 011 44 171 2261739, FAX 011 44 171 2261540. **Continues** Hotads International.

US
ADVANCING PHILANTHROPY. (19??)-. English. Four times a year (Jan., Apr., June, Oct.). $50.00 all. National Society of Fund Raising, 1101 King Street, Suite 3000, Alexandria VA 22314. **Tel** (703)684-0410, FAX (703)684-0540. **Continues** NSFRE Journal, 1056-2443.

LC HV42 **ISSN** 1022-6982
DD 659.3 SA
UDC 659.3(68)
•**ADVANTAGE SANDTON.** [ADvantage Sandton]. (1994)-. Trade Publication. English. Twelve times a year. Platinum Publications Pty., PO Box 784698, Sandton 2146 South Africa. **Tel** 011 27 11 3582090, FAX 011 27 11 7268430. **Ad Acc.**

LC HF5802 .A23
DD 338.7/616591/025171241 UK
ADVERTISER'S ANNUAL. **VFOAT** AA. (1975)-. English. One time a year. $320.43. Reed Information Services Ltd., Windsor Court, East Grinstead House, East Grinstead RH19 1BR United Kingdom. **Tel** 011 44 1342 326972, FAX 011 44 1342 335977, telex 95127 INFSER G. **ED** Joyce Lewis. Each issue contains an index to its own contents (no volume index)--loose. **Ad Acc. Circ:** 4,000. **Continues** Advertiser's Annual with Overseas Sections.
 Desc: Gives the answer to any question about the world of advertising, marketing, and sales promotion in the famous 'Blue Book'.

LC HF5801 .A276 **ISSN** 0001-8899
DD 659.105 US
CCC
CODEN ADVAAQ
ADVERTISING AGE. [Advert. age]. **Added/Corp** Advertising Publications, Inc. Crain Communications Inc. (1930)-. Trade Publication. English. One time a week. $99.00. Crain Communications Inc., 1400 Woodbridge, Detroit MI 48207-3187. **Tel** (313)446-6000, (800)992-9970. **ED** Fred Danzig. **Bk Rev**. **Ad Acc. Circ:** 93,000. available on microfilm and microfiche from University Microfilms International (UMI); available on an online database (files 16,570/Full-Text) from DIALOG; and Mead Data Central. Documents available from UMI Article Clearinghouse. **Absorbed** Advertising Agency (Bristol, Conn. : 1958).
 Desc: International newspaper on advertising and marketing.
 Ind/Abst ABI/INFORM Glob. Ed.; ABI/INFORM Ondisc: Expr. Ed. (Jan. 1987-); ABI/INFORM [Computer File] (Oct. 1971-); Acad. Abstr. Full Text Elite; Acad. Abstr.; Acad. Ind. [Computer File] (1985-); Acad. Search; BioBusiness (1986-); Biogr. Index; Bus. Index (1985-); Bus. Period. Index; Bus. Source Plus; Bus. Source; Chicano Index; Curr. Lit. Fam. Plan.; EP Collect.; Expand. Acad. Index (1985-); F&S Index Plus Text, Int. [Full Txt.] [Select. Cov.]; Foods Adlibra; GATFWORLD (1984-); Gen. BusinessFile (1985-); Gen. Period. Index (1985-); Health Plan. Adminis.; Healthcare Leader. Rev.; Homework Help.; INFO-SOUTH Abstr.; Infobank (1969-); Mag. Artic. Summar. Elite; Mag. Artic. Summar. Select; Mag. Artic. Summar. CD-ROM; Mag. Search; Manage. Market. Abstr.; Mark. Advert. Ref. Serv. [Full Txt.]; MasterFile FullTEXT 1000; MasterFile FullTEXT 350; MasterFile FullTEXT 650; MasterFile FullTEXT (July 1990-); Newsp. Period. Abstr. (1986-); OCLC; PROMT [Full Txt.]; Pub. Lib. FullTEXT; Stat. Ref. Index; Telebase; Topicator; Trade Ind. Index (1981-); UMI ABI/Inform--Bus. Period. Ondisc (Nov. 1987-) [Full Txt.]; Vocat. Search; Wilson Bus. Abstr.

LC HF5805 .A4
DD 659.1025 US
ADVERTISING AGE. 100 LEADING NATIONAL ADVERTISERS. **VFOAT** 100 Leading National Advertisers; One Hundred Leading National Advertisers; Leading National Advertisers. (19??)-. English. One time a year. Crain Communications Inc., 1400 Woodbridge, Detroit MI 48207-3187. **Tel** (313)446-6000, (800)992-9970.

UK
ADVERTISING AGENCY REVIEW. (19??)-. Periodical. English. Four times a year. £450.00. ELC Publishing, 109 Uxbridge Road Ealing, London W5 5TL United Kingdom. **Tel** 011 44 181 5662288, FAX 011 44 181 5664931.

ISSN 1072-9119
DD 659 US
•**ADVERTISING AGE'S CREATIVITY.** [Advert. age's creat.]. **VFOAT** Creativity. (1993)-. Periodical. English. Ten times a year. $39.00. Crain Communications Inc., 1400 Woodbridge, Detroit MI 48207-3187. **Tel** (313)446-6000, (800)992-9970. **(Subscription address:** Crain Communications, 965 East Jefferson Avenue, Detroit MI 48207. **Tel** (800)678-9595, (313)446-1616.)

ISSN 0277-9943
DD 343 US
ADVERTISING COMPLIANCE SERVICE. [Advert. compliance serv.]. (1981)-. Periodical. English. Twenty-four times a year. $695.00. Greenwood Press Inc., PO Box 5007, Westport CT 06881-5007. **Tel** (203)226-3571, FAX (203)222-1502. **ED** John Lichtenberger. available on an online database from NEXIS.
 Desc: A comprehensive cumulation of significant developments in advertising regulation; includes information on changes in federal, state, and international laws and regulations, industry guideline revisions, landmark court decisions, consent decrees, private civil litigation, and industry trends.

ISSN 0161-6889
US
ADVERTISING DIGEST. CLASSIFIED EDITION. (ADVERTISING DIGEST.). (1978)-. English. Six times a year. $15.00. Scout Weygandt, 323 South Franklin #804, Chicago IL 60606.

ISSN 0263-8118
UK
ADVERTISING FORECAST, THE. [Forecast Advert. Expend.]. (1978)-. Periodical. English. Four times a year (Apr., July, Oct., Dec.). £825.00. NTC Publications Ltd., PO Box 69, Henley-on-Thames, Oxfordshire RG9 1GB United Kingdom. **Tel** 011 44 1491 574671, FAX 011 44 1491 571188.

LC KF1614.A73 A925 **ISSN** 0093-1985
DD 343/.73/082 US
ADVERTISING LAW ANTHOLOGY. **See** Law.

ISSN 1066-0178
DD 659 US
ADVERTISING NEWS DIGEST (SOUTHEAST ED., NEWSPAPER ED.). (ADVERTISING NEWS DIGEST.). [Advert. news dig.]. Vol. 1, No. 1 (Sept. 15, 1992)-. Periodical. English. Twenty-four times a year. $84.00. Advertising News Digest, PO Box 921222, Norcross GA 30092. **Tel** (404)394-4571.

ISSN 1067-1226
DD 659 US
ADVERTISING NEWS DIGEST (SOUTHERN ED., TELEVISION ED.). (ADVERTISING NEWS DIGEST.). [Advert. news dig.]. **VFOAT** Flash Sales Report for Advertising Executives. (1992)-. Periodical. English. Twenty-four times a year. $84.00 US; $94.00 Canada. Advertising News Digest, PO Box 921222, Norcross GA 30092. **Tel** (404)394-4571.

ISSN 1058-2592
DD 659 US
TITLE CHANGE
ADVERTISING OPTIONS PLUS. (ADVERTISING OPTIONS PLUS : SRDS DIRECTORY OF OUT-OF-HOME MEDIA.). [Advert. options plus]. **Added/Corp** Standard Rate & Data Service. **VFOAT** SRDS Advertising Options Plus. Vol. 1, No. 1 (1990-91)-(1994). Trade Publication. English. SRDS / Standard Rate & Data Service, 3004 Glenview Road, Wilmette IL 60091. **Tel** (708)375-5049, (800)851-7737, FAX (708)375-5003. **(Subscription address:** Neodata / Colorado, PO Box 2606, Boulder CO 80322. **)** ***Continued by*** *Out of Home Advertising Source, 1078-7887.*
Desc: Advertising rates and data for out-of-home media. Tool for corporate marketers and advertising agencies.

LC HF5801 .A2446
US
ADVERTISING RATIOS AND BUDGETS. **Added/Corp** Schonfeld & Associates. **VFOAT** A.Advertising ratios and budgets. (19??)-. English. One time a year. $325.00. Schonfeld & Associates, Inc., 1 Sherwood Drive, Lincolnshire IL 60069. **Tel** (708)948-8080, FAX (708)948-8096. Index available. available on diskette.
Desc: An annual study covering 5,700+ companies and 390+ industries with historical advertising budgets, ad-to-sales ratios and ad-to-gross margin ratios, along with budget forecasts. Also included are average annual compound growth rates in ad spending and net sales.

ISSN 1046-3755
DD 659 US
ADVERTISING RESEARCH DIRECTORY. (ADVERTISING RESEARCH DIRECTORY / ARF.). [Advert. res. dir.]. **Main/Corp** Advertising Research Foundation. (198?)-. Directory. English. One time a year. Free on request. Advertising Research Foundation, 641 Lexington Avenue, New York NY 10022. **Tel** (212)751-5656, FAX (212)319-5265. ***Continues*** *Advertising Research Foundation. Membership Roster.*

LC HF6146 .N7A415 **ISSN** 0740-2716
DD 602/.9/473 US
ADVERTISING SPECIALTY REGISTER (1983). (ADVERTISING SPECIALTY REGISTER.). [Advert. spec. reg.]. **Added/Corp** Advertising Specialty Institute. (1983/1984)-. English. One time a year. Advertising Specialty Institute, 1120 Wheeler Way, Langhorne PA 19047. **Tel** (215)752-4200. ***Formed by the union of*** *Advertising Specialty Register. Micro Master File of Catalogs of Specialty Advertising, 0363-9533; Advertising Specialty Register. Product Research and Source Data, 0364-0221; Advertising Specialty Register. Supplier Facts, Policies and Performance Data, 0363-9541* ***and*** *Advertising Specialty Register. Price Index & Source and Resource File, 0736-6167.*

ISSN 0892-3892
DD 650 US
ADVISOR (NOROTON, CONN.). (THE ADVISOR.). (198?)-. Periodical. English. Twelve times a year. $109.00. Mitchell Advertising Services Inc, Box 3127, Noroton CT 06820. **Tel** (203)655-4788.
Ind/Abst Ei Page One.

LC HF5801 .A273
DD 659.1/05 UK
ADWEEK. (19??)-. Periodical. English. One time a week. £10.00. Mercury House Business Publications, Waterloo Road, London SE1 8W United Kingdom. ***Continues*** *Advertiser's Weekly.*

ISSN 0898-2228
DD 338 US
ADWEEK AGENCY DIRECTORY (EASTERN ED. 1986). (ADWEEK AGENCY DIRECTORY.). [Adweek agency dir.]. (1986)-. English. One time a year. $287.00. Billboard Publications Inc., 1515 Broadway Billboard, New York NY 10036. **Tel** (212)764-7300, FAX (305)755-7048, telex WU TWX 710-581-6279. **(Subscription address:** Adweek Directories / New Jersey, PO Box 2006, Lakewood NJ 08701. **Tel** (800)468-2395.**)** ***Continues*** *Adweek ... Directory of Advertising (Eastern Edition).*
Desc: Contains detailed information on US advertising agencies, public relations firms, and media buying services.
Ind/Abst Bus. ASAP (1990-) [Full Txt.].

ISSN 1054-0555
DD 659 US
ADWEEK AGENCY DIRECTORY (MIDWESTERN EDITION). (ADWEEK AGENCY DIRECTORY.). [Adweek agency dir.]. (1986)-. Directory. English. One time a year. $250.00. Billboard Publications Inc., 1515 Broadway Billboard, New York NY 10036. **Tel** (212)764-7300, FAX (305)755-7048, telex WU TWX 710-581-6279. **(Subscription address:** Adweek Directories / New Jersey, PO Box 2006, Lakewood NJ 08701. **Tel** (800)468-2395.**)** ***Continues*** *Adweek ... Directory of Advertising (Midwestern Edition), 1047-9910.*
Desc: Contains detailed information on US advertising agencies, public relations firms, and media buying services.

LC HF5805 .A394 **ISSN** 1055-8950
DD 659 US
ADWEEK AGENCY DIRECTORY (NATIONAL ED.). (ADWEEK AGENCY DIRECTORY.). [Adweek agency dir.]. **VFOAT** Agency Directory. (1983)-. Directory. English. One time a year. $250.00. Billboard Publications Inc., 1515 Broadway Billboard, New York NY 10036. **Tel** (212)764-7300, FAX (305)755-7048, telex WU TWX 710-581-6279. **(Subscription address:** Adweek Directories / New Jersey, PO Box 2006, Lakewood NJ 08701. **Tel** (800)468-2395.**)** ***Continues*** *Adweek ... Directory of Advertising (National Agency Ed.).*

US
ADWEEK AGENCY DIRECTORY NATIONAL EDITION SOUTHWEST. (19??)-. English. Two times a year. $397.00. Billboard Publications Inc., 1515 Broadway Billboard, New York NY 10036. **Tel** (212)764-7300, FAX (305)755-7048, telex WU TWX 710-581-6279. **(Subscription address:** Adweek / Connecticut, PO Box 1973, Danbury CT 06813. **Tel** (800)722-6658.**)** ***Continues*** *Adweek Agency Directory.*

US
ADWEEK CLIENT/BRAND DIRECTORY. (1989)-. Directory. English. One time a year. $247.00 (includes shipping). Billboard Publications Inc., 1515 Broadway Billboard, New York NY 10036. **Tel** (212)764-7300, FAX (305)755-7048, telex WU TWX 710-581-6279.

LC HF6182.U5 A39 **ISSN** 1049-7064
DD 338.7/616591/02573 US
ADWEEK CLIENT/BRAND DIRECTORY (NATIONAL ED.). (ADWEEK CLIENT/BRAND DIRECTORY.). [Adweek client/brand dir.]. **VFOAT** Adweek Client Brand Directory; Client/Brand Directory. (1989)-. Directory. English. One time a year. $287.00. Billboard Publications Inc., 1515 Broadway Billboard, New York NY 10036. **Tel** (212)764-7300, FAX (305)755-7048, telex WU TWX 710-581-6279. **(Subscription address:** Adweek Directories / New Jersey, PO Box 2006, Lakewood NJ 08701. **Tel** (800)468-2395.**)** ***Continues*** *Adweek ... National Directory of Advertising. Clients.*
Desc: Includes full details on lead advertising agencies, media expenditures, and the companies which produce or market the brands.

ISSN 0199-2864
US
CCC
CODEN AWEEEM
ADWEEK (EASTERN ED.). (ADWEEK.). [Adweek]. Vol. 20, No. 47 (Nov. 19, 1979)-. Trade Publication. English. One time a week. $105.00. Billboard Publications Inc., 1515 Broadway Billboard, New York NY 10036. **Tel** (212)764-7300, FAX (305)755-7048, telex WU TWX 710-581-6279. **(Subscription address:** Adweek, PO Box 1973, Danbury CT 06813. **Tel** (800)722-6658.**)** **ED** Greg Farrell. **Bk Rev. Ad Acc. Circ:** 84,000. available on microfilm and microfiche from University Microfilms International (UMI); available on an online database from Mead Data Central; DIALOG; and BRS. ***Continues*** *Advertising News of New York, 0001-2041.*
Desc: Focuses on national and local advertising news. Offers coverage of ad/marketing trends, creative work, direct mail, print, TV and radio. Provides an insider's view on the world of advertising.
Ind/Abst BioBusiness (1988-); Bus. Index (1989-); F&S Index Plus Text, Int. [Full Txt.] [Select. Cov.]; Gen. BusinessFile (1989-); Gen. Period. Index (1989-); Infobank (Jan. 1979-); Mark. Advert. Ref. Serv. [Full Txt.]; PROMT [Full Txt.]; Trade Ind. ASAP [Full Txt.]; Trade Ind. Index [Full Txt.].

US
●ADWEEK MAJOR MEDIA DIRECTORY. (1995)-. Directory. English. One time a year. $287.00. Billboard Publications Inc., 1515 Broadway Billboard, New York NY 10036. **Tel** (212)764-7300, FAX (305)755-7048, telex WU TWX 710-581-6279. **(Subscription address:** Adweek Directories / New Jersey, PO Box 2006, Lakewood NJ 08701. **Tel** (800)468-2395.**)**

ISSN 0276-6612
DD 659 US
ADWEEK (MIDWEST ED.). (ADWEEK.). [Adweek]. Vol. 19, No. 2 (Jan. 12, 1981)-. Periodical. English. One time a week (with 5 special issues). $105.00. Billboard Publications Inc., 1515 Broadway Billboard, New York NY 10036. **Tel** (212)764-7300, FAX (305)755-7048, telex WU TWX 710-581-6279. **(Subscription address:** Adweek / Connecticut, PO Box 1973, Danbury CT 06813. **Tel** (800)722-6658.**)** ***Continues*** *Adweek. Midwest Advertising News, 0199-8188.*
Desc: Focuses on national and local advertising news. Offers unrivalled coverage of ad/marketing trends, creative work, direct mail, print, TV and radio. Provides an insider's view on the world of advertising.
Ind/Abst F&S Index Plus Text, Int. [Full Txt.] [Select. Cov.]; Foods Adlibra; Infobank (1980-); Mark. Advert. Ref. Serv. [Full Txt.]; PROMT [Full Txt.]; Trade Ind. Index.

LC HE5806.A11 A39 **ISSN** 0888-0840
DD 659.1/0974 US
ADWEEK (NEW ENGLAND ED.). (ADWEEK : NEW ENGLAND ADVERTISING WEEK.). [Adweek]. **VFOAT** Adweek, New England; Ad Week. Vol. 23, No. 6 (Feb. 3, 1986)-. Trade Publication. English. One time a week (Plus 5 special issues). $105.00. Billboard Publications Inc., 1515 Broadway Billboard, New York NY 10036. **Tel** (212)764-7300, FAX (305)755-7048, telex WU TWX 710-581-6279. **(Subscription address:** Adweek / Connecticut, PO Box 1973, Danbury CT 06813. **Tel** (800)722-6658.**)** available on an online database (files 16,570/Full-Text) from DIALOG. ***Continues*** *New England Advertising Week, 0028-4653;* ***Absorbed*** *Ad East, 0192-7922.*
Ind/Abst F&S Index Plus Text, Int. [Full Txt.] [Select. Cov.]; Mark. Advert. Ref. Serv. [Full Txt.]; PROMT [Full Txt.]; Trade Ind. Index.

LC HF5801 .A42 **ISSN** 8756-6389
DD 659.1/0975/05 US
ADWEEK (SOUTHEAST EDITION). (ADWEEK.). [Adweek]. (198?)-. Periodical. English. One time a week (with 5 special issues). $105.00. Billboard Publications Inc., 1515 Broadway Billboard, New York NY 10036. **Tel** (212)764-7300, FAX (305)755-7048, telex WU TWX 710-581-6279. **(Subscription address:** Adweek / Connecticut, PO Box 1973, Danbury CT 06813. **Tel** (800)722-6658.**)** available on an online database from Mead Data Central. ***Continues*** *Adweek/Southeast Advertising News, 0270-8302.*
Desc: Focuses on national and local advertising news. Offers unrivalled coverage of ad/marketing trends, creative work, direct mail, print, TV and radio. Provides an insider's view on the world of advertising.
Ind/Abst F&S Index Plus Text, Int. [Full Txt.] [Select. Cov.]; Mark. Advert. Ref. Serv. [Full Txt.]; PROMT [Full Txt.]; Trade Ind. Index.

ISSN 0746-892X
DD 659 US
ADWEEK (SOUTHWEST ED.). (ADWEEK.). [Adweek]. (198?)-. Trade Publication. English. One time a week (with 5 special issues). $105.00. Billboard Publications Inc., 1515 Broadway Billboard, New York NY 10036. **Tel** (212)764-7300, FAX (305)755-7048, telex WU TWX 710-581-6279. **(Subscription address:** Adweek / Connecticut, PO Box 1973, Danbury CT 06813. **Tel** (800)722-6658.**)** ***Continues*** *Adweek. Southwest Advertising News, 0194-3553.*
Desc: Focuses on national and local advertising news. Offers unrivalled coverage of ad/marketing trends, creative work, direct mail, print, TV and radio. Provides an insider's view on the world of advertising.
Ind/Abst F&S Index Plus Text, Int. [Full Txt.] [Select. Cov.]; Infobank (1980-); Mark. Advert. Ref. Serv. [Full Txt.]; PROMT [Full Txt.]; Trade Ind. Index.

LC HF5801 .A425 **ISSN** 0895-3848
DD 659.1/0973/05 US
ADWEEK SPECIAL REPORT. [Adweek spec. rep.]. **VFOAT** Ad Week Special Report; Special Report. (Aug. 3, 1987)-. Periodical. English. Twelve times a year. Billboard Publications Inc., 1515 Broadway Billboard, New York NY 10036. **Tel** (212)764-7300, FAX (305)755-7048, telex WU TWX 710-581-6279. available on an online database (files 16,570/Full-Text) from DIALOG.

Ind/Abst F&S Index Plus Text, Int. [Full Txt.] [Select. Cov.]; Mark. Advert. Ref. Serv. [Full Txt.]; PROMT [Full Txt.].

ISSN 0199-4743
DD 659 US
ADWEEK. WESTERN ADVERTISING NEWS. [Adweek, West. advert. news]. **VFOAT** Adweek. MAC/Western Advertising News; Adweek/West. (1980)-. Trade Publication. English. Fifty-one times per year. $105.00. Billboard Publications Inc., 1515 Broadway Billboard, New York NY 10036. **Tel** (212)764-7300, FAX (305)755-7048, telex WU TWX 710-581-6279. **(Subscription address:** Adweek, PO Box 1973, Danbury CT 06813. **Tel** (800)722-6658.**) Bk Rev. Ad Acc. Circ:** 98,000. available on an online database (File 648,16,570/Full-Text) from DIALOG; and BRS. ***Continues** MAC/Western Advertising News, 0194-4789.*
Desc: Focuses on national and local advertising news. Offers coverage of ad/marketing trends, creative work, direct mail, print, TV and radio. Provides an insider's view on the world of advertising.
Ind/Abst Acad. Search; Bus. ASAP (1990-) [Full Txt.]; Bus. Index (1989-); Bus. Source Plus; Bus. Source; EP Collect.; F&S Index Plus Text, Int. [Full Txt.] [Select. Cov.]; Foods Adlibra (1980-); Gen. BusinessFile (1989-); Gen. Period. Index (1989-); Homework Help.; Infobank (1980-); Mag. Search; MasterFile FullTEXT 1000; MasterFile FullTEXT 350; MasterFile FullTEXT 650; MasterFile FullTEXT (July 1993-); OCLC; Telebase; Trade Ind. ASAP [Full Txt.]; Trade Ind. Index [Full Txt.].

US
ADWEEK'S GUIDE TO NEW ENGLAND ADVERTISING, DIRECT MARKETING & PUBLIC RELATIONS AGENCIES. VFOAT Advertising, Direct Marketing & Public Relations Agencies; Advertising, Direct Marketing and Public Relations Agencies. (1991/1992)-. English. Billboard Publications Inc., 1515 Broadway Billboard, New York NY 10036. **Tel** (212)764-7300, FAX (305)755-7048, telex WU TWX 710-581-6279. ***Continues** Adweek's Guide to New England Advertising & Public Relations Agencies, 1050-3072.*

ISSN 1145-8488
FR
UDC 070.485 (442.5)
AFFICHES DE NORMANDIE, LES. (1949)-. Periodical. French. One time a week. 35.00F France; 200.00F other. Affiches de Normandie, 86 94 BD des Belges/BP550, F-76006 Paris Cedex France. **Tel** 011 33 1 35713336. ***Continues** Les Petites Affiches de Normandie et le Bulletin Economique Reunis, 1145-847X.*

LC HF6146.T42 A45 **ISSN** 0889-2717
DD 659.14/3/02573 US
ALL TV PUBLICITY OUTLETS, NATIONWIDE. See Communications-Television and Cable.

IT
ALLESTIRE. (19??)-. Trade Publication. Italian. Four times a year. L70000.00 Italy; L95000.00 other. Editoriale Galfa, Viale Monza 57, 20125 Milan Italy. **Tel** 011 39 2 2891452, FAX 011 39 2 2840574, telex 315614. **ED** Laura Fagotti. **Ad Acc, Adv Mgr:** Giorgio Dell'Orto. **Circ:** 8,000 (ctrl).
Desc: Covers the politics, technology, and economics of exhibition, fairs and displays.

LC PN5650 .A47 **ISSN** 1041-0139
DD 302.23/089924073 US
... AMERICAN-JEWISH MEDIA DIRECTORY, THE. [Am.-Jew. media dir.]. **VFOAT** American Jewish Media Directory. (1989)-. Directory. English. Every 2 years. $50.00. R K Associates, PO Box 18, Rego Park NY 11374. **Tel** (718)275-2546. **ED** Ray Kestenbaum and Jeffrey Haveson. Index available. **Ad Acc.**
Desc: A compilation of editorial and advertising data for 760 Jewish media; useful to marketing, advertising and editorial specialists.

LC TR690 .A453 **ISSN** 0278-8683
DD 770/.25/73 US
AMERICAN SHOWCASE OF ILLUSTRATION AND PHOTOGRAPHY. See Photography.

ISSN 1194-3386
DD 658.8/4 CN
ANNUAL FACT BOOK / CANADIAN DIRECT MARKETING ASSOCIATION. [Annu. fact book - Can. Direct Mark. Assoc.]. **Added/Corp** Canadian Direct Marketing Association. **VFOAT** Current Information About Direct Maketing in Canada; Canadian Direct Marketing Association's Annual Fact Book. (Sept. 1992)-. Trade Publication. English. One time a year. 158.47Can$. Canadian Direct Marketing Association, 1 Concorde Gate #607, Don Mills Ontario M3C 3N6 Canada. **Tel** (416)391-2262, FAX (416)441-4062. **ED** Scott McClellan.

ISSN 0895-7150
DD 659 US
ANNUAL REPORT - ADVERTISING RESEARCH FOUNDATION. 1986. (ANNUAL REPORT / ADVERTISING RESEARCH FOUNDATION.). [Annu. rep. - Advert. Res. Found., 1986]. **Main/Corp** Advertising Research Foundation. (1986)-. Periodical. English. One time a year. comes with Advertising Research Foundation membership. Advertising Research Foundation, 641 Lexington Avenue, New York NY 10022. **Tel** (212)751-5656, FAX (212)319-5265. ***Continues** Advertising Research Foundation. Report to the Membership.*

LC HF5813.B8 A57
BL
ANUNCIO. (19??)-. Portuguese. Irregular. Anuncio, Caixa Postal 1148, Porto Alegre 90000 Brazil.

NE
APPEL, DE. (19??)-. Dutch (English). Stichting de Appel, Neiuwe Spiegelstraat 10, 1017 DE Amsterdam Netherlands. **Tel** 011 31 20 6255651. **ED** Edna Van Duyn. cum. index. **Circ:** 750 (ctrl).
Desc: Magazine with articles on activities.

LC HF5801 .A77
NE
ARIADNE : REVUE DER RECLAME. VFOAT Revue der Reclame. (Jan. 1946)-. Periodical. Dutch. Twelve times a year. Eska Tijdschriften B V, Lijmarkt 43, Utrecht Netherlands.
Ind/Abst Annu. Bibliogr. Engl. Lang. Lit.

LC NC997.A1 A684 **ISSN** 0004-3109
DD 741.6/05 US
CCC
ART DIRECTION. See The Arts-Graphic Arts.

LC HF6161.H75 A77 **ISSN** 0735-9233
DD 659.1/96479473 US
ART OF HOTEL ADVERTISING, THE. [Art hotel advert.]. (1982)-. English. One time a year. Hotel Sales Management Association, 1235 Jesserson Davis Highway, Suite 610, Arlington VA 22202.

LC HF **ISSN** 0257-893X
DD 658.8 HK
ASIAN ADVERTISING & MARKETING. [Asian advert. mark.]. **VFOAT** Asian Advertising and Marketing; A & M; A & M. Asian Advertising and Marketing. (1986)-. Periodical. English. Twenty-four times a year. $99.00. A & M Publishing Ltd., 32 Hollywood Road, 9 Fl Kinwick Court, Central Hong Kong. **Tel** 011 852 25818960.
Ind/Abst Mark. Advert. Ref. Serv.

LC HF5808.A7 A8 **ISSN** 0115-2254
DD 070/.025/5 FR
ASIAN PRESS AND MEDIA DIRECTORY. (THE ASIAN PRESS AND MEDIA DIRECTORY.). **Added/Corp** Press Foundation of Asia. (1974)-. Directory. English (French). One time a year. Publiworld, 5 rue Rude, F 75116 Paris France. **Tel** 011 33 1 45018070.

LC AS6 .A82 **ISSN** 1042-3141
DD 658.4/56 US
CCC
ASSOCIATION MEETINGS. [Assoc. meet.]. Vol. 1, No. 1 (Apr. 1989)-. Periodical. English. Six times a year (Feb., Apr., June, Aug., Oct., Dec.). $42.00. Laux Company Inc, 63 Great Road, Maynard MA 01754. **Tel** (508)897-5552, FAX (508)897-6824. **ED** Terry Brown. **Ad Acc. Circ:** 21,000 (ctrl). ***Continues** Convention World, 8750-1686.*

LC NA6815 .A9
US
•AUDARENA STADIUM ... INTERNATIONAL GUIDE & FACILITY BUYERS GUIDE. VFOAT AudArena Stadium ... International Guide and Facility Buyers Guide; Aud Arena Stadium ... International Guide & Facility Buyers Guide; AudArena Stadium Guide; AudArena stadium Guide & Facility Buyers Guide. (1994)-. English. One time a year (Oct.). $75.00. Amusement Business, PO Box 24970, Nashville TN 37202. **Tel** (615)321-4250, FAX (615)327-1575. ***Continues** AudArena Stadium ... International Guide to Facilities, Supplies & Services.*
Desc: Complete data on over 5,500 arenas, auditoriums, stadiums, exhibit halls and amphitheatres in the U.S., Canada, and most European countries, as well as listings of companies offering services and supplies to the industry.

LC NA6815 .A9
DD 725 US
TITLE CHANGE
AUDARENA STADIUM ... INTERNATIONAL GUIDE TO FACILITIES, SUPPLIES & SERVICES. VFOAT AudArena Stadium ... International Guide to Facilities, Supplies, and Services; Aud Arena Stadium ... International Guide to Facilities, Supplies & Services; AudArena Stadium Guide. (1991)-(1993). English. Billboard Publications Inc., 1515 Broadway Billboard, New York NY 10036. **Tel** (212)764-7300, FAX (305)755-7048, telex WU TWX 710-581-6279. ***Continues** Audarena Stadium ... International Guide. **Continued by** AudArena Stadium ... International Guide & Facility Buyers Guide.*
Desc: Complete data on venues worldwide. Plus complete listings of companies providing entertainment facility supplies and services.

ISSN 0885-8292
DD 659 US
AUTO ADVERTISING REPORT. [Auto advert. rep.]. (198?)-. Newsletter. English. Twenty-six times a year. $225.00. Auto Advertising Report, PO Box 565, Phoenix AZ 85001. **Tel** (602)234-0444, FAX (602)265-6372. **ED** William H. Sauro. **Circ:** 1,000 (ctrl).
Desc: Newsletter of advertising and marketing for retail automobile dealerships.

LC PN1560 **ISSN** 1055-9825
DD 792 US
TITLE CHANGE
BACK STAGE SHOOT. [Back stage shoot]. **VFOAT** Back Stage/Shoot. Vol. 31, No. 27 (July 6, 1990)-Vol. 34, No. 51 (Dec. 17, 1993). Trade Publication. English. Billboard Publications Inc., 1515 Broadway Billboard, New York NY 10036. **Tel** (212)764-7300, FAX (305)755-7048, telex WU TWX 710-581-6279. **(Subscription address:** Back Stage Shoot, PO Box 5023, Brentwood TN 37024. **Tel** (800)999-3322.**)** ***Continues in part** Back Stage, 0005-3635. **Continued by** Shoot, 1074-5297.*
Desc: Covers commercial production and the industry, from creation through production to post-production.
Ind/Abst Bus. Index (1985-199?); EP Collect.; Gen. BusinessFile (1985-19??); Gen. Period. Index (1990-199?); Homework Help.; Mag. Search; MasterFile FullTEXT 1000; MasterFile FullTEXT 350; MasterFile FullTEXT 650; MasterFile FullTEXT (Sept. 1993-Dec. 1993); OCLC; Pub. Lib. FullTEXT; Telebase; Vocat. Search.

LC HF5813.E79 B3a **ISSN** 0161-4363
DD 659.2/025/4 US
TITLE CHANGE
BACON'S INTERNATIONAL PUBLICITY CHECKER. Main/Corp Bacon's Information International Ltd. **Added/Corp** Media Information Group of London. Bacon's Information International Ltd. International Publicity Checker. (19??)-. English. Bacons Information Inc., 332 South Michigan Avenue, Chicago IL 60604. **Tel** (312)922-2400, (800)624-0561, FAX (312)922-3127. ***Continued by** Bacons International Media Directory.*

US
BACON'S MEDIA CALENDAR DIRECTORY. (19??)-. English. One time a year. $250.00 US. Bacons Information Inc., 332 South Michigan Avenue, Chicago IL 60604. **Tel** (312)922-2400, (800)624-0561, FAX (312)922-3127. Index available (free, published in Dec.). ***Continues** Bacon's Media Alert, 0736-4644.*
Desc: A one volume compilation of editorial calendars and profiles of major magazines; used in planning advertising placements and researching editorial placement opportunities; includes editorial lead times, closing dates, convention/trade show index. Free phone updating and midyear revisions provided.

LC HE8699.A8 B7
DD 384.54/0994 AT
B&T YEAR BOOK. See Communications-Television and Cable.

CN
•BC AD NETWORK. See Business and Economics-Marketing and Purchasing.

LC HF5801 .B45 **ISSN** 1046-8242
DD 659.1/13/05 US
BEST IN ADVERTISING, THE. [Best advert.]. **VFOAT** Advertising. 2nd Ed. (1977)-. Trade Publication. English. Every 2 years. $79.50. RC Publications Inc., 3200 Tower Oaks Boulevard, Rockville MD 20852. **Tel** (800)222-2654, (301)770-2900, FAX (301)984-3203. ***Continues** Best in Advertising Campaigns, 0360-8263.*

LC T391 .B47 **ISSN** 1048-2644
DD 069.5 US
BEST IN EXHIBITION DESIGN, THE. [Best exhib. des.]. 2nd Annual Ed. (1977)-. Trade Publication. English. Every 2 years. $14.95. RC Publications Inc., 3200 Tower Oaks Boulevard, Rockville MD 20852. **Tel** (800)222-2654, (301)770-2900, FAX (301)984-3203.

LC TR12 .B58 **ISSN** 1054-464X
DD 026/.779/02573 US
BLACK BOOK STOCK. See Photography.

LC HF5806.A11 B65 **ISSN** 0094-1255
DD 380.1/025/74 US
BOOK OF NAMES, THE. English. $7.50. New England Marketing Publications, 62 Northgate Road, Wellesley MA 02181.

ISSN 0144-6126
DD 659.10941 UK
BRAD ADVERTISER & AGENCY LIST.
[BRAD advert. agency list]. **VFOAT** British Rate and Data Advertiser and Agency List; Advertiser & Agency List. (1971)-. English. Four times a year (Jan., Apr., July, Oct.). £175.00 UK; £436.50 other. Maclean Hunter Ltd. / UK, Chalk Lane Cockfosters Road, Barnet Hertfordshire EN4 0BU United Kingdom. **Tel** 011 44 181 2423000, FAX 011 44 181 9759753, telex 299072.

ISSN 0165-4675
NE
UDC 614.84
BRAND & BRANDWEER. [Brand brandweer]. (1977)-. Periodical. Dutch. Eleven times a year. Fl46.23. Koninklijke Vermande, Postbus 20, 8200 AA Lelystad Netherlands. **Tel** 011 31 3200 22944, FAX 011 31 3200 26334. Index available. ***Formed by the union of** Brand **and** Brandweer.*
Ind/Abst Infomat Int. Bus.

LC HF5801 .A43 ISSN 1064-4318
DD 659.1/0973 US
CCC
CODEN BANDEN
BRANDWEEK (NEW YORK, N.Y.).
(BRANDWEEK.). [Brandweek]. **VFOAT** Brand Week. Vol. 33, No. 27 (July 13, 1992)-. Trade Publication. English. Forty-seven times a year. $105.00. Billboard Publications Inc., 1515 Broadway Billboard, New York NY 10036. **Tel** (212)764-7300, FAX (305)755-7048, telex WU TWX 710-581-6279. **(Subscription address:** Adweek, PO Box 1973, Danbury CT 06813. **Tel** (800)722-6658.) **ED** Buck Rinker. **Bk Rev**. **Ad Acc**. **Circ:** 32,000. available on microfilm and microfiche from University Microfilms International (UMI); available on an online database (File # 648) from DIALOG; and BRS. Documents available from UMI Article Clearinghouse. ***Continues** Adweek's Marketing Week, 0892-8274.*
Desc: Gives fast-track marketing executives indepth reports on national and international marketing, new case studies of successes and failures, brand strategies and new product news.
Ind/Abst ABI/INFORM Glob. Ed.; ABI/INFORM [Computer File] (1992-); BioBusiness (1992-); Bus. Period. Index (1992-); Foods Adlibra; INFO-SOUTH Abstr.; MasterFile FullTEXT (July 1993-); Newsp. Period. Abstr. (1992-); Wilson Bus. Abstr.

ISSN 0744-1797
US
TITLE CHANGE
BULLDOG (LOS ANGELES, CALIF.).
(BULLDOG.). (1979)-(19??). Newsletter. English. Intercom Group, 1250 45th Street, Suite 200, Emeryville CA 94608. **Tel** (800)959-1059, (510)596-9337, FAX (510)596-9331. Index available (free on request). **Circ:** 880 (ctrl). ***Continued by** Bulldog Reporter.*
Desc: The media placement newsletter for PR professionals.

US
BULLDOG REPORTER. (19??)-. Newsletter. English. Twenty-four times a year. $349.00. Intercom Group, 1250 45th Street, Suite 200, Emeryville CA 94608. **Tel** (800)959-1059, (510)596-9337, FAX (510)596-9331. ***Continues** Bulldog.*
Desc: The media placement newsletter for PR professionals.

US
BULLDOG REPORTER'S WESTERN MEDIA CONTACTS. (19??)-. Periodical. English. One time a year. $397.00. Intercom Group, 1250 45th Street, Suite 200, Emeryville CA 94608. **Tel** (800)959-1059, (510)596-9337, FAX (510)596-9331.

LC HF5863 .B84 ISSN 1067-1641
DD 659.13/3 US
CODEN BULLE7
BULLET (WILMETTE, ILL.), THE. (THE BULLET.). [Bullet]. **Added/Corp** Standard Rate & Data Service. Vol. 1, No. 1 (Feb. 16, 1991)-. Trade Publication. English. Six times a year. SRDS / Standard Rate & Data Service, 3004 Glenview Road, Wilmette IL 60091. **Tel** (708)375-5049, (800)851-7737, FAX (708)375-5003. **(Subscription address:** Neodata / Colorado, PO Box 2606, Boulder CO 80322. **)**

LC Z673 .S8222
US
BULLETIN / ADVERTISING AND MARKETING DIVISION, SPECIAL LIBRARIES ASSOCIATION. **Main/Corp** Special Libraries Association. Advertising and Marketing Division. Vol. 22, No. 3 (Jan. 1965)-. Bulletin. English. Irregular. Special Libraries Association, 1700 18th Street Northwest, Washington DC 20009. **Tel** (202)234-4700, FAX (202)265-9317. **ED** David Mullan (editor's telephone: (212)399-8015). **Ad Acc**, **Adv Mgr:** Gretchen Reed, **Tel** (212)886-4326. ***Continues** Special Libraries Association. Advertising Division. Bulletin.*

ISSN 0714-2080
DD 659.2/09714 CN
BULLETIN DE LIAISON - ASSOCIATION DES RELATIONNISTES DU QUEBEC.
(BULLETIN DE LIAISON.). [Bull. liaison - Assoc. relat. Que.]. **Added/Corp** Association des Relationnistes du Quebec. (1975)-. Bulletin. French. Irregular. Free to members. Association des Relationnistes du Quebec, Bureau 5427/Pavillon Casault, Universite Laval, Quebec Quebec Canada.

ISSN 0521-8136
RU
BURENIE (MOSKVA). (BURENIE.). [Burenie]. **Added/Corp** Vsesoiuznyi Nauchno-Issledovatelskii Institut Organizatsii, Upravleniia i Ekonomiki Neftegazovoi Promyshlennosti (Soviet Union). (1963)-. Periodical. Russian. Twelve times a year. $29.70. **(Subscription address:** Victor Kamkin, 4956 Boiling Brook Parkway, Rockville MD 20852. **Tel** (301)881-5973.)
Ind/Abst Energy Res. Abstr. (Sept. 1982-).

LC HF3000 .P53 ISSN 1064-430X
DD 658.8/2/05 US
CEASED
BUSINESS AND INCENTIVE STRATEGIES. (BUSINESS AND INCENTIVE STRATEGIES : B + I.). [Bus. incent. strateg.]. **VFOAT** B Plus I Strategies; Business and Incentive Strategies Magazine; Business + Incentive Strategies. (199?)-(Dec. 1993). Trade Publication. English. Miller Freeman Inc., 600 Harrison Street, San Francisco CA 94107. **Tel** (415)905-2337, (415)905-2200, FAX (415)905-2240, telex 278273. **(Subscription address:** B + I Strategies, PO Box 1791, Riverton NJ 08077. **)** ***Continues** PIB's Business & Incentives, 1056-5442.*
Ind/Abst PAIS Int. Print (?-?).

ISSN 1071-4642
US
•BUSINESS PUBLICATION ADVERTISING SOURCE. (1993)-. Trade Publication. English. Twelve times a year. $571.56. SRDS / Standard Rate & Data Service, 3004 Glenview Road, Wilmette IL 60091. **Tel** (708)375-5049, (800)851-7737, FAX (708)375-5003. **(Subscription address:** Neodata / Colorado, PO Box 2606, Boulder CO 80322. **)**

LC HF5843 .O82 ISSN 0095-5531
DD 659.13/42/02573 US
BUYERS GUIDE TO OUTDOOR ADVERTISING, THE. (19??)-. Consumer Publication. English. Two times a year. $340.00. Leading National Advertisers Inc., 11 West 42nd Street, New York NY 10036. **Tel** (212)789-1418. **Ad Acc**. ***Continues** Outdoor Buyers Guide.*
Desc: Rate and market reference source for outdoor advertising opportunities across the country. Contains over 700 outdoor companies and their market information.

LC GV742.3 .C33 ISSN 1049-6009
DD 070.4/49796/0973 US
CABLE MEDIA ADVERTISING. (CABLE MEDIA ADVERTISING : CMA.). [Cable media advert.]. **VFOAT** CMA. Vol. 1, Issue 1 (Apr. 1990)-. Periodical. English. Four times a year. $30.00. QV Publishing Inc., 647 US Route One, PO Box 3000, York ME 03909. **Tel** (207)363-6222, FAX (207)363-6182.

ISSN 0270-885X
DD 659 US
CABLE TV ADVERTISING. (CABLE TV ADVERTISING / PAUL KAGAN ASSOCIATES, INC.). [Cable TV advert.]. **Added/Corp** Paul Kagan Associates. **VFOAT** Cable T.V. Advertising. **VAT** Cable Television Advertising. (19??)-. Newsletter. English. Twelve times a year. $650.00. Paul Kagan Associates Inc., 126 Clock Tower Place, Carmel CA 93923-8734. **Tel** (408)624-1536, FAX (408)625-3225, telex ITT 4938124 PKA UI. Index available. ctrl circ. available via fax.
Desc: Newsletter on the sale of commercial time by cable television systems and networks, with local ad sales, national ad sales, case studies and projections.
Ind/Abst Predicasts.

US
CABLE TV ADVERTISING REPORT.
Added/Corp Paul Kagan Associates. **VAT** Cable Television Advertising Report. (19??)-. English. One time a year. $495.00. Paul Kagan Associates Inc., 126 Clock Tower Place, Carmel CA 93923-8734. **Tel** (408)624-1536, FAX (408)625-3225, telex ITT 4938124 PKA UI.
Desc: Analysis of cable advertising sales and the revenues of interconnects and standalone operations.

ISSN 1054-8955
US
CALIFORNIA TRADESHOW & EXHIBIT CALENDAR. **VFOAT** California Tradeshow and Exhibit Calendar. (Dec./Jan. 1991)-. English. Four times a year. $45.00. Pacific Publications / California, PO Box 4500, Laguna Beach CA 92652. **Tel** (714)497-7108.

LC PN4701 .W62 ISSN 0008-2309
DD 659 070 UK
CCC
CODEN CMPGBW
CAMPAIGN (LONDON. 1968).
(CAMPAIGN.). [Campaign]. (Sept. 12, 1968)-. Trade Publication. English. One time a week (50 issues - published on Thursdays). $277.21. Haymarket Publishing Ltd., 12 14 Ansdell Street, London W8 5TR United Kingdom. **Tel** 011 44 171 9380705, 011 44 171 2786686, FAX 011 44 171 9380772. **(Subscription address:** Haymarket Magazines Ltd., PO Box 219, Subscription Department, Woking Surrey GU21 1ZW United Kingdom. **Tel** 011 44 1483 776345.) **ED** Christine Barker. **Ad Acc**. available on an online database from VU-TEXT. Documents available from BLDSC. ***Continues** WPN, Advertisers' Review.*
Desc: Influential publications for advertising, marketing and media personnel. Essential medium for the communication of advertising information.
Ind/Abst Anbar Account. Finan. Abstr. [Full Txt.]; Anbar Mark. Distr. Abstr. [Full Txt.]; Anbar Top Manage. Abstr. [Full Txt.]; BioBusiness; Index Bus. Reports; Infomat Int. Bus.; Manage. Market. Abstr.; Manage. Bibliogr. Rev.; Mark. Advert. Ref. Serv.; Oper. Prod. Manage. Abstr. [Full Txt.]; Person. Train. Abstr. [Full Txt.]; Print. Abstr.; Women Manage. Rev. [Full Txt.].

LC HF5816 .C35
DD 659.1/079 UK
CAMPAIGN PRESS ADVERTISING AWARDS. (19??)-. English. One time a year. Haymarket Publishing Ltd., 12 14 Ansdell Street, London W8 5TR United Kingdom. **Tel** 011 44 171 9380705, 011 44 171 2786686, FAX 011 44 171 9380772.

LC HF5801 .C27 ISSN 0038-9498
DD 338.7/616591/02571 CN
CCC
CANADIAN ADVERTISING RATES & DATA. **Added/Corp** Maclean-Hunter Research Bureau. Standard Rate & Data Service. **VFOAT** Canadian Advertising Rates and Data. Vol. 39, No. 6 (Nov. 1966)-. English. Twelve times a year. 495.00Can$. MacLean Hunter Ltd. Business Publishers / Canada, Box 9100, Station A, Toronto Ontario M5W 1A5 Canada. **Tel** (416)596-5000, , FAX (416)596-5552. **(Subscription address:** Standard Rate & Data Service, 3004 Glenview Road, Wilmette IL 60091. **Tel** (708)256-6067, (800)323-4588.) **ED** Irvine A. Brace. ***Continues** Canadian Advertising; **Absorbed** Canadian Media Rates and Data.*
Desc: Information on over 4,000 Canadian media by more than 30 categories.

LC HF5861 .C28 ISSN 1071-4626
DD 381/.45659133 US
CEASED
CARD DECK ADVERTISING SOURCE.
[Card deck advert. source]. **Added/Corp** Standard Rate & Data Service. **VFOAT** SRDS Card Deck Advertising Source. (1993)-(19??). Periodical. English. SRDS / Standard Rate & Data Service, 3004 Glenview Road, Wilmette IL 60091. **Tel** (708)375-5049, (800)851-7737, FAX (708)375-5003. **(Subscription address:** Neodata / Colorado, PO Box 2606, Boulder CO 80322. **)**
***Continues** Card Deck Rates and Data, 1067-1579.*

LC HF5861 .C35 ISSN 0740-3119
DD 658.8/72/05 US
CATALOG AGE. [Cat. age]. Vol. 1 No 1 (March 1984)-. Trade Publication. English. Twelve times a year. $74.00. Cowles Business Media Inc. / Connecticut, 6 River Bend Center, 911 Hope Street, Stamford CT 06907. **Tel** (203)358-9900, (800)775-3777, FAX (203)357-9014. **(Subscription address:** Catalog Age, PO Box 1017, Skokie IL 60076. **) ED** Scot Finnie. **Ad Acc**. **Circ:** 13,500 (ctrl). available on microfilm and microfiche from University Microfilms International (UMI); available on an online database (file 648/Full-Text) from DIALOG. Documents available from UMI Article Clearinghouse. ***Continues** Catalog Product News, 1048-0633.*
Desc: For catalog executives who make strategic business and buying decisions.
Ind/Abst ABI/INFORM Glob. Ed.; ABI/INFORM [Computer File] (May 1988); Curr. Cit.; F&S Index Plus Text, Int. [Select. Cov.]; Mark. Advert. Ref. Serv.; PROMT; Trade Ind. ASAP [Full Txt.]; Trade Ind. Index [Full Txt.]; UMI ABI/Inform--Bus. Period. Ondisc [Full Txt.].

LC HF5806.A14 C46 ISSN 1063-1984
DD 338.7/616591/02577 US
CENTRAL CITIES SOURCEBOOK, THE.
[Cent. cities sourceb.]. **VFOAT** Central Cities Source Book. (1991)-. English.

LC HF5807.C4 M43 ISSN 1069-2355
DD 659.1/025/77311 US
•CHICAGO ... MEDIA SOURCEBOOK. [Chic. media sourceb.]. **Added/Corp** Standard Rate & Data Service. **VFOAT** Chicago ... Media Source Book. (1993)-. English. SRDS / Standard Rate & Data Service, 3004 Glenview Road, Wilmette IL 60091. **Tel** (708)375-5049, (800)851-7737, FAX (708)375-5003. ***Continues** MediaScope. Chicago Market & Media Planner, 1064-5764.*

Business and Economics — Advertising and Public Relations

LC HF5068.C4 C63 **ISSN** 0145-4714
DD 338/.0025/7732 US
CEASED
CHICAGO METRO BOOK, THE.
(19??)-(19??). English. National Register Publishing Company Inc., PO Box 31, 121 Chanlon Road, New Providence NJ 07974. **Tel** (800)521-8110, (800)323-6772, FAX (908)665-6688.

DD 659 **ISSN** 1078-5949
US
CHICAGO SOURCEBOOK. [Chic. sourceb.].
(199?)-. English. One time a year. Black Book Marketing Group, 10 Astor Place, 6th Floor, New York NY 10003. **Tel** (212)539-9800, FAX (212)539-9801. **Bk Rev. Ad Acc. Circ:** 12,000 (ctrl). **Continues** Chicago Talent Sourcebook, 0734-6662.
Desc: Reference for the Chicago area covering creative talent and graphic services available.

US
CLIP ART QUARTERLY.
English. Four times a year. Artmaster, 500 North Claremont Boulevard, Claremont CA 91711. **Tel** (714)626-8065.

CN
CMC MEMBERSHIP DIRECTORY.
(19??)-. Directory. English. One time a year. 32.95Can$. Canadian Community Newspapers Association, 90 Eglanton Avenue E, Suite 206, Toronto Ontario M4P 2Y3 Canada. **Tel** (416)482-1090. **Continues** Community Markets Canada, 0229-1630.

LC HF5827.4 .C66 **ISSN** 0736-0878
DD 659.1/025/73 US
CO-OP SOURCE DIRECTORY. (CO-OP
SOURCE DIRECTORY : A PUBLICATION OF STANDARD RATE & DATA SERVICE, INC.). [Co-op source dir.]. **Added/Corp** Standard Rate & Data Service. Vol. 1 (1981)-. Periodical. English. Two times a year. $446.86. National Register Publishing Company Inc., PO Box 31, 121 Chanlon Road, New Providence NJ 07974. **Tel** (800)521-8110, (800)323-6772, FAX (908)665-6688. available on magnetic tape.
Desc: Aimed to help readers find manufacturers' co-op programs that retailers and wholesalers use to fund advertising and promotional campaigns.

LC NK1125 .A363 **ISSN** 0091-0473
DD 659.1/075 US
COLLECTABLE OLD ADVERTISING.
[Collect. old advert.]. (19??)-. English. Jim Cope, PO Box 1417, Orange TX 77630.

ISSN 0010-3497
GW
CCC
COMMUNICATIO SOCIALIS. See Religions
and Theology-Catholicism.

ISSN 0730-7799
DD 658 US
COMMUNICATION BRIEFINGS. See
Communications.
LC HF5905 .C66
US
COMMUNITY PUBLICATION
ADVERTISING SOURCE. **Added/Corp**
Standard Rate & Data Service. (199?)-. Consumer Publication. English. Two times a year (May and Nov.). $90.00. SRDS / Standard Rate & Data Service, 3004 Glenview Road, Wilmette IL 60091. **Tel** (708)375-5049, (800)851-7737, FAX (708)375-5003. **(Subscription address:** Neodata / Colorado, PO Box 2606, Boulder CO 80322.) **Continues** Community Publication Source, 1071-4650.

LC HF5905 .S72 **ISSN** 0162-8887
DD 338.4/3 US
TITLE CHANGE
COMMUNITY PUBLICATION RATES
AND DATA. [Community publ. rates data].
Added/Corp Standard Rate & Data Service. Vol. 60 (March 1978)-(1993). Periodical. English. SRDS / Standard Rate & Data Service, 3004 Glenview Road, Wilmette IL 60091. **Tel** (708)375-5049, (800)851-7737, FAX (708)375-5003. **ED** Howard Friedman. Index available. **Ad Acc. Circ:** 2,000 (ctrl). **Continues** Weekly Newspaper and Shopping Guide Rates and Data, 0162-8895. **Continued by** Community Publication Advertising Source, 1071-4650.
Desc: Profiles over 2,200 weekly newspapers and shopping guides.

LC HF5905 .S72 **ISSN** 1071-4650
DD 659 US
TITLE CHANGE
COMMUNITY PUBLICATION SOURCE.
[Community publ. source]. **Added/Corp** Standard Rate & Data Service; SRDS Community Publication Advertising Source. Vol. 75, No. 2 (Nov. 1993)-(199?). Trade Publication. English. SRDS / Standard Rate & Data Service, 3004 Glenview Road, Wilmette IL 60091. **Tel** (708)375-5049, (800)851-7737, FAX (708)375-5003. **(Subscription address:** Neodata / Colorado, PO Box 2606, Boulder CO 80322.) **Continues** Community Publications Rates and Data, 0162-8887. **Continued by** Community Publication Advertising Source.

ISSN 0736-7147
US
Pr Rev.
COMMUNITY RELATIONS REPORT
(BARTLESVILLE, OKLA.), THE. (THE
COMMUNITY RELATIONS REPORT.). (198?)-. Periodical. English. Twelve times a year. $139.00. Joe Williams Communication Inc., PO Box 924, Bartlesville OK 74005. **Tel** (918)336-2267, FAX (918)336-2733. **ED** Reba Payne. **Bk Rev**, (Qty: 4/yr). **Circ:** 500 (ctrl).
Desc: Corporate community relations.

ISSN 0886-1994
DD 659 US
COMPETITIVE ADVANTAGE, THE. Vol. 1,
No. 1 (1986)-. Periodical. English. Twelve times a year. $99.00. The Competitive Advantage, 1901 Northwest 23rd Avenue, PO Box 10091, Portland OR 97210. **Tel** (503)274-2953, FAX (503)274-4349. **ED** Deirdre Hackett. Index available (Feb. iss.). **Circ:** 11,000.
Desc: Marketing, sales, and general management strategies, techniques, and ideas for business owners, presidents, and sales/marketing managers.

LC HF5813.U6 C72 **ISSN** 0010-4272
DD 659.1/0973 US
COMPETITIVE BRAND CUMULATIVE.
Added/Corp Leading National Advertisers, inc. **VFOAT** LNA Competitive Brand Cumulative. (19??)-. English. Irregular. $100.00. Leading National Advertisers Inc, 11 West 42nd Street, 11th Floor, New York NY 10016. **Tel** (212)725-2700, (800)562-3282.

●COMPUTER ADVERTISING AND
MARKETING STRATEGIES REVIEW
TRENDS AND FORECAST. See Business and
Economics-Computer Applications.

LC HF6161.C55 C64
DD 659.1/9004/0973 US
TITLE CHANGE
COMPUTER INDUSTRY ADVERTISING &
MARKETING FORECAST. See Business and
Economics-Computer Applications.

ISSN 0276-9972
US
CEASED
COMPUTER PUBLICITY NEWS.
Added/Corp Hi-Tech Publicity Consultants. (June 1981)-(Dec. 1993). Periodical. English. Hi-Tech Public Relations Inc, 101 Howard Street, 2nd Floor, San Francisco CA 94105. **Tel** (415) 904-7000 ext 249, FAX (415)904-7025. **ED** Tony Reveaux. **Bk Rev. Circ:** 600 (ctrl).
Desc: Newsletter for advertising, marketing and public relations professionals in the computer and electronics fields.

ISSN 0740-6231
US
CCC
COMPUTER PUBLISHING &
ADVERTISING REPORT. See Business and
Economics-Computer Applications.

IT
COMUNICARE. (19??)-. Italian. Eleven times a
year. Editoriale Comunicare SRL, Via Stefanardo da Vimercate 19, 20128 Milan Italy. **Tel** 011 39 2 27002670.

ISSN 0761-5779
FR
UDC 64.06
CONFORT MENAGER. (1983)-. Periodical.
French. Twelve times a year. $104.98. Societe d'Edition et de Presse, 106 BD Malesherbes, 75017 Paris France. **Tel** 011 33 1 47660460, FAX 011 33 47229879.

US
●CONSUMER MAGAZINE ADVERTISING
SOURCE. See Consumer Education and Protection.

LC HF5905 .S725 **ISSN** 0746-2522
DD 659.1/025/73 US
TITLE CHANGE
CONSUMER MAGAZINE AND
AGRI-MEDIA RATES AND DATA / SRDS.
[Consum. mag. agri-media rates data]. **Added/Corp** Standard Rate & Data Service. **VFOAT** Consumer Magazine and Agri-Media Rates. (19??)-(1993). Periodical. English. SRDS / Standard Rate & Data Service, 3004 Glenview Road, Wilmette IL 60091. **Tel** (708)375-5049, (800)851-7737, FAX (708)375-5003. **ED** Sarah Hirshman. **Ad Acc. Continues** Consumer Magazine and Farm Publication Rates and Data, 0038-9595. **Continued by** Consumer Magazine & Agri-Media Source, 1071-4537.
Desc: Over 2,000 listings of consumer and farm magazines giving advertising rates, circulation, mechanics, etc. Also includes radio and tv stations with farm programming.

LC HF5905 .S725 **ISSN** 1071-4537
DD 659.1/025/73 US
TITLE CHANGE
CONSUMER MAGAZINE & AGRI-MEDIA
SOURCE. [Consum. mag. agri-media source].
Added/Corp Standard Rate & Data Service. **VFOAT** Consumer Magazine and Agri Media Source. (1993)-(1995). Trade Publication. English. SRDS / Standard Rate & Data Service, 3004 Glenview Road, Wilmette IL 60091. **Tel** (708)375-5049, (800)851-7737, FAX (708)375-5003. **(Subscription address:** Neodata / Colorado, PO Box 2606, Boulder CO 80322.) **Continues** Consumer Magazine and Agri-Media Rates and Data, 0746-2522. **Continued by** Consumer Magazine Advertising Source.

ISSN 0038-9595
US
CONSUMER MAGAZINE AND FARM
PUBLICATION RATES AND DATA.
Main/Corp Standard Rate & Data Service. Vol. 33 (Jan. 1951)-. Periodical. English. Twelve times a year. SRDS / Standard Rate & Data Service, 3004 Glenview Road, Wilmette IL 60091. **Tel** (708)375-5049, (800)851-7737, FAX (708)375-5003. **Continues in part** Standard Rate and Data Service.

ISSN 0894-0207
DD 795 US
CONTEST NEWS-LETTER. [Contest news-l.].
(19??)-. Periodical. English. Twelve times a year. $15.97. Contest News-Letter, 49 Richmondville Avenue, c/o CSI Inc., Westport CT 06880. **Tel** (203)454-0344, FAX (203)454-8871. **ED** Deni Hamilton and Les Whiteley (phone: (502)222-9051). **Circ:** 325,000.
Desc: How to enter and how to win big price sweepstakes. Up-to-date information for contest and sweepstakes hobbyists.

ISSN 0011-0027
US
COUNSELOR. Periodical. English. Twelve times a
year. Advertising Specialty Institute, 1120 Wheeler Way, Langhorne PA 19047. **Tel** (215)752-4200.

ISSN 0765-9911
FR
UDC 659.1
CEASED
CREATION MAGAZINE. [Creat. mag.]. VFOAT
Creation (Paris.1985). (1985)-(1994). Periodical. French. Groupe Strategie, 15 bis rue Ernest Renan, 92133 Issy Mlineaux Cdx France. **Tel** 011 33 (1) 40930102, FAX (1)40 93 05 06, telex 202 003. **ED** Sylvie Delevle. **Bk Rev. Ad Acc. Circ:** 14,132 (ctrl).
Desc: About creativity and the technical aspects of advertising.

ISSN 0737-5883
US
CREATIVE. [Creative]. (1968)-. Periodical. English.
Six times a year. $30.00. Magazines Creative Inc., 37 West 39th Street, New York NY 10018. **Tel** (212)840-0160. **ED** David Flasterstein. **Bk Rev. Ad Acc. Circ:** 12,800 (ctrl). available on microfilm from University Microfilms International (UMI). **Continues** Creative Signs & Displays.
Desc: Covers all aspects of sales promotion, including point of purchase displays, exhibits, premiums, sweepstakes, coupon directed marketing, and meetings.
Ind/Abst Mark. Advert. Ref. Serv.

LC HF6146.T42 C67 **ISSN** 0738-9000
DD 338.7/61659143/0257 US
CREATIVE BLACK BOOK, THE. [Creat.
black book]. **VFOAT** Black Book. (1970)-. English. One time a year. $96.95. Black Book Marketing Group, 10 Astor Place, 6th Floor, New York NY 10003. **Tel** (212)539-9800, FAX (212)539-9801. **Bk Rev. Circ:** 30,000 (ctrl).
Desc: Creative annual sourcebook of photography and illustration film for today's advertising professionals.

LC TR690.4 .C74 **ISSN** 0740-283X
DD 741.6/025/73 US
CREATIVE BLACK BOOK (PORTFOLIO
ED.), THE. (THE CREATIVE BLACK BOOK.). [Creat. black book.]. **VFOAT** Portfolio; Creative Black Book. Portfolio. (1984)-. English. One time a year. $150.00. Black Book Marketing Group, 10 Astor Place, 6th Floor, New York NY 10003. **Tel** (212)539-9800, FAX (212)539-9801. **Bk Rev. Circ:** 10,000 (ctrl).
Desc: Creative annual sourcebook of photography and illustrated film for today's advertising professionals.

LC PN1992.75 .C7 **ISSN** 0889-6372
DD 791.45/0232/0257 US
CREATIVE BLACK BOOK
(PRODUCER'S ED.), THE. (THE CREATIVE
BLACK BOOK.). [Creat. black book.]. **VFOAT** Black Book, Producer's Edition. (1987)-. Directory. English. One time a year (Dec.). $120.00. Black Book Marketing Group, 10 Astor Place, 6th Floor, New York NY 10003. **Tel** (212)539-9800, FAX (212)539-9801. **Bk Rev. Circ:** 30,000 (ctrl).
Desc: A directory of all creative talent used by the

Business and Economics —Advertising and Public Relations

production, film, video and post-production industry. Includes a listing of names, addresses and telephone numbers of creative suppliers.

DD 659
ISSN 1070-826X
US
TITLE CHANGE
CREATIVE EXHIBITING TECHNIQUES. (CREATIVE EXHIBITING TECHNIQUES : THE NEWSLETTER OF TIPS, TACTICS AND HOW-TOS FOR EFFECTIVE TRADE SHOW MARKETING.). [Creat. exhib. tech.]. (May 1992)-(1995). Newsletter. English. Exhibitor Publications Inc, PO Box 368, Rochester MN 55904. **Tel** (507)289-6556, FAX (507)289-5253. **ED** Paulo Marlow. **Circ:** 1,500. **Merged into** Exhibitor Magazine.

IT
CREATIVI E FORNITORI. (19??)-. Italian. One time a year. L300000. Bragadin Editore Srl, Via Stradella 3, 20123 Milan Italy. **Tel** 011 39 2 29400554.

LC NC997 .A682 NC998
ISSN 0097-6075
DD 659.13 741.6/0973
US
CREATIVITY. Added/Corp Art Direction Book Co. (1971)-. Trade Publication. English. One time a year. $62.95. Art Direction Book Company, 10 East 39th Street, 6th Floor, New York NY 10016. **Tel** (212)889-6500. **ED** Don Barron. available on an online database (files 16,570/Full-Text) from DIALOG.
Desc: Covers current advertising.
Ind/Abst F&S Index Plus Text, Int. [Full Txt.] [Select. Cov.]; Mark. Advert. Ref. Serv. [Full Txt.]; PROMT [Full Txt.].

DD 659
ISSN 0893-5947
US
CYCON COMMUNICATIONS' COMPUTER PR UPDATE. [Cycon Commun. comput. PR update]. **Added/Corp** Cycon Communications Inc. **VFOAT** Computer PR Update. **VAT** Cycon Communications' Computer Public Relations Update. (198?)-. Periodical. English. Twelve times a year. $68.00. Cycon Communications Inc, 1315 West 22nd Street, Suite 250, Oak Brook IL 60521. **Tel** (312)571-7075.

IT
DATI E TARIFFE PUBBLICITARIE. (1991)-. Italian. Six times a year. L806.00. Maclean Hunter SRL / Italy, P le a Cantore 12, 20123 Milan Italy. **Tel** 011 39 2 89401365, 011 39 2 58188204, FAX 011 39 2 8378590. **Ad Acc. Circ:** 10,700 (ctrl).
Desc: Supplies the advertising industry with relevent facts on national consumer and local press, business publications, exhibitions and postersites.

LC HF5861 .D54
ISSN 0419-182X
DD 659.13/3 658.8
US
CODEN DMLRAL
TITLE CHANGE
DIRECT MAIL LIST RATES AND DATA. [Dir. mail list rates data]. **Added/Corp** Standard Rate & Data Service. Vol. 1, No. 1 (July 1967)-(1993). Periodical. English. SRDS / Standard Rate & Data Service, 3004 Glenview Road, Wilmette IL 60091. **Tel** (708)375-5049, (800)851-7737, FAX (708)375-5003. **(Subscription address:** Neodata / Colorado, PO Box 2606, Boulder CO 80322. **) Continued by** Direct Marketing List Source, 1071-4561.

US
●**DIRECT RESPONSE DONOR.** (1995)-. English. The National Copy Clinic Inc, PO Box 127, West Newton MA 02165. **Continues** Techniques for Success.

US
CEASED
DIRECTORY OF ADVERTISING & MARKETING SERVICES, THE. VFOAT Directory of Advertising and Marketing Services. (1994)-(1995). Directory. English. Executive Communications, 185 East 85th Street, Suite 11 C, New York NY 10028. **Tel** (212)-831-3147. **Continues** Handbook of Advertising & Marketing Services, 0749-2243.

LC HE8689.9.C3 D57
ISSN 0419-2273
DD 384.54/025/71
CN
DIRECTORY OF BROADCAST EXECUTIVES (TORONTO). See Communications-Television and Cable.

ISSN 1076-7878
US
●**DIRECTORY OF CONVENTIONS. NORTHEAST & MID-ATLANTIC CONVENTION GUIDE. VFOAT** Directory of Conventions. Northeast and Mid-Atlantic Convention guide; Northeast and Mid-Atlantic Convention Guide; Northeast and Mid-Atlantic Convention Guide. (1994)-. English. Irregular. $140.00. Successful Meetings, 633 Third Avenue, New York NY 10017. **Continues in part** Directory of Conventions, 0417-5751.

ISSN 1076-7843
US
●**DIRECTORY OF CONVENTIONS. SOUTHEAST CONVENTION GUIDE. VFOAT** Southeast Convention Guide. (1995)-. English. One time a year. $140.00. Successful Meetings, 633 Third Avenue, New York NY 10017. **Continues in part** Directory of Conventions, 0417-5751.

ISSN 1076-7851
US
●**DIRECTORY OF CONVENTIONS. WEST CONVENTION GUIDE. VFOAT** West Convention Guide. (1995)-. English. Irregular. $140.00. Successful Meetings, 633 Third Avenue, New York NY 10017. **Continues in part** Directory of Conventions, 0417-5751.

UK
DIRECTORY OF EUROPEAN MEDIA REGULATION. See Communications-Television and Cable.

US
DIRECTORY OF MAILING LISTS COMPANIES. (19??)-. English. Irregular. $59.00 (two-year). B. Klein Publications, PO Box 8503, Coral Springs FL 33065. **Tel** (305)752-1708, FAX (305)752-2547. **Continues** Directory of Mailing List Houses.

LC HD59 .D58
ISSN 0163-6537
DD 659.2/025/73
US
DIRECTORY OF PERSONAL IMAGE CONSULTANTS. (19??)-. Directory. English. One time a year. $27.50. Editorial Services Co., 1140 Avenue of the Americas, New York NY 10036.

ISSN 0012-3323
IT
UDC 658
DIRETTORE COMMERCIALE, IL. [Dir. commer.]. (1957)-. Periodical. Italian. Eleven times a year. L54500. Finedit, Residenza I Portici Milan 2, 20090 Segrate Italy. **Tel** 011 39 2 26415312, FAX 011 39 2 2365238. **Continues** Il Direttore Commerciale.

ISSN 1049-9172
DD 659
US
CCC
DISPLAY & DESIGN IDEAS. [Disp. des. ideas]. **VFOAT** Display and Design Ideas. (1989)-. Trade Publication. English. Ten times a year. $60.00. Shore Communications Inc., 6255 Barfield Road, Suite 200, Atlanta GA 30328. **Tel** (404)252-8831, (800)241-9034, FAX (404)252-4436. **ED** Karen Benning. **Bk Rev. Ad Acc. Circ:** 18,000 (ctrl).
Desc: Emphasis on store design and visual merchandising techniques, with heavy emphasis on products.

US
DO'S AND DON'TS IN ADVERTISING. (19??)-. English. Twelve times a year. $350.00. Council of Better Business Bureaus, 4200 Wilson Boulevard, Suite 800, Arlington VA 22203. **Tel** (703)276-0100, FAX (703)525-8277.

ISSN 0363-2830
US
DOWNTOWN PROMOTION REPORTER. **Added/Corp** Downtown Research and Development Center. Vol. 1 (Aug. 1976)-. Periodical. English. Twelve times a year. $120.00. Alexander Research & Communications, Inc, 215 Park Avenue South, Suite 1301, New York NY 10003. **Tel** (212)228-0246, FAX (212)228-0376. **ED** Laurence A. Alexander. **Ad Acc.**
Desc: The illustrated source of plans, programs and techniques for promoting the central business district.

ISSN 1061-9402
US
Pr Rev.
●**EASY MONEY. See** Business and Economics-Management.

US
ECONOMICS OF BASIC CABLE NETWORKS, THE. See Communications-Television and Cable.

ISSN 0749-2316
DD 659
US
EFFECTIVE ADVERTISING. [Eff. advert.]. (June 1984)-. Periodical. English. Twelve times a year. $35.00. Effective Advertising, PO Box 1173, Rockford IL 61105-1173. **ED** Ann Hunt.
Desc: A practical and concise guide that demonstrates how a modest advertising budget can be stretched to build sales, oil the marketing machinery and aid expansion.

LC HF6182.F8 E46
DD 338.4/76591/0944
FR
ENQUETE ANNUELLE D'ENTREPRISE. LES ENTREPRISES DE PUBLICITE EN ... . VFOAT Enterprise de Publicite en ... . (1980)-. French. One time a year. **Circ:** 500. **Continues** Enquete Annuelle d'Entreprise. Les Entreprises de Publicite en ... .
Desc: Survey of advertising firms in France. Number of employees, sales, purchases, account balances, etc.

LC NC997
DD 741.6
SZ
EPICA BOOK, ... EUROPEAN ADVERTISING ANNUAL. See The Arts-Graphic Arts.

ISSN 0823-7107
DD 659.1/0971
CN
ETHNIC CLOUT. (ETHNIC CLOUT : THE CANADIAN ETHNIC MARKET REPORT.). [Ethn. clout]. Oct. 82-. Periodical. English. Twelve times a year. $110.00. Canadian Ethnic Market Report, Suite 41 1390 Sherbrooke Street West, Montreal Quebec H3G 1J9 Canada.

ISSN 0952-3820
UK
EUROMARKETING : THE WEEKLY EUROPEAN NEWS BULLETIN FROM ADVERTISING AGE. Issue 01 (Sept. 22, 1987)-. Bulletin. English. One time a week (49 issues per year). $395.00. Crain Communications Ltd., 75-77 Cowcross Street, Cowcross Court, London EC1M 6BP United Kingdom. **Tel** 011 44 171 6082774, FAX 011 44 171 6081173. **ED** Bill Britt. **Ad Acc, Adv Mgr:** J. Palley. **Circ:** 1,000. available on an online database (files 16,570,636,771,772,799/Full-Text) from DIALOG.
Ind/Abst F&S Index Plus Text, Int. [Select. Cov.]; Manage. Market. Abstr.; Mark. Advert. Ref. Serv. [Full Txt.]; PROMT [Full Txt.]; PTS Newsl. Database [Full Txt.].

LC HF5808.E85 E9
DD 659.1/025/4
GW
EUROPA HANDBUCH. German. One time a year. Team-Fachverlag GmbH & Company, Auwanne 19, D-63791 Karlstein Germany. **Tel** 011 49 6188 603132. **Continues** Europa Handbuch der Werbegesellschaften.

ISSN 0951-7758
DD 659.13094
UK
EUROPEAN ADVERTISING & MEDIA FORECAST, THE. [Eur. advert. media forecast]. **VFOAT** European Advertising and Media Forecast. (1986)-. English. Four times a year (Jan., Apr., July, Oct.). $2036.33. NTC Publications Ltd., PO Box 69, Henley-on-Thames, Oxfordshire RG9 1GB United Kingdom. **Tel** 011 44 1491 574671, FAX 011 44 1491 571188.

UK
EUROPEAN ADVERTISING REPORT. (19??)-. English. One time a year. $395.00. Kagan World Media Inc., 126 Clock Tower Place, Carmel CA 93923-8734. **Tel** (408)624-1536, FAX (408)625-3225. **(Subscription address:** Kagan World Media Ltd., 524 Fulham Road, London SW6 5NR United Kingdom. **Tel** 011 44 171 3718880, FAX 011 44 171 3718715.**)**
Desc: Guide to European advertising with comprehensive statistics of advertising and media markets divided by Western European country and by medium. Reviews advertising agencies and media buyers.

ISSN 0276-3842
US
EVA'S AD SHEET. (19??)-. Periodical. English. Twelve times a year. Eva Lee, 6916-18th Avenue, Brooklyn NY 11204.

US
EXECUTIVE SPEECHWRITER NEWSLETTER. VFOAT Executive Speechwriter. (19??)-. Newsletter. English. Six times a year. $83.00. Words Inc., Emerson Falls, Business Park, St Johnsbury VT 05819. **Tel** (802)748-4472, FAX (802)748-1939. **ED** Joe Taylor Ford. Index available ($5.00 at the end of each volume). **Circ:** 6,500. Documents available.
Desc: Anecdotal material for speech writers and speech makers.

ISSN 1046-2872
DD 658
US
CEASED
EXHIBIT REVIEW, THE. [Exhib. rev.]. (Summer 1989)-(May 1995). English. Phoenix Communications Inc., 3800 Southwest Cedar Hills Boulevard, Suite 251, Beaverton OR 97005. **Tel** (503)643-2783, FAX (503)643-7101. **ED** Deborah M. King. **Bk Rev,** (Qty: 10-12). **Ad Acc, Adv Mgr:** Cameron Perry, **Tel** (503)643-2783. **Circ:** 11,500.
Desc: Provides complete information for thousands of domestic and international trade and consumer shows.

ISSN 0014-4649
UK
EXHIBITION BULLETIN. [Exhib. bull.]. (1948)-. English. Twelve times a year. $109.52. London Bureau, 266-272 Kirkdale, Sydenham, London SE26 4RZ United Kingdom. **Tel** 011 44 181 7782288, FAX 011 44 181 6598495. **ED** P. B. H. Colls. **Ad Acc, Adv Mgr:** L. Colls.

Circ: 5,000.
Desc: World listing of international exhibition and trade fairs.

ISSN 0965-3457
DD 659.152 UK
EXHIBITION MANAGEMENT. [Exhib. manag.]. (1992)-. Periodical. English. Six times a year. $57.40. Argus Press Group, Queensway House, 2 Queensway Redhill, Surrey RH1 1QS United Kingdom. **Tel** 011 44 1737 768611, 011 44 1737 761685, FAX 011 44 1737 760510, telex 948669 TOPJNL G. **(Subscription address:** FMJ International Publications Ltd., Queensway House 2 Queensway, Redhill Surrey RH1 1QS United Kingdom. **Tel** 011 44 1737 768611, FAX 011 44 1737 773993, telex 948669 TOPJNL G.)
Desc: Reviews products, techniques and skills for professional exhibition organizers of events ranging from 400 to 750,000 visitors.

CH
EXHIBITIONS 'ROUND THE WORLD.
Added/Corp Trade Winds. **VFOAT** Exhibitions Around the World. (19??)-. English. One time a year. $80.00. Trade Winds Inc., PO Box 7-179, #7 Lane 75 Yungkang Street, Taipei Taiwan. **Tel** 011 886 2 3932718, FAX 011 886 2 3964022. **(Subscription address:** Trade Winds Inc., PO Box 820654, Dallas TX 75382.) **Ad Acc.**

LC T391 .E88 **ISSN** 0739-6821
DD 659.1/52/05 US
CODEN EXHIDV
EXHIBITOR (ROCHESTER, MINN.).
(EXHIBITOR.). [Exhibitor]. (1982)-. Periodical. English. Twelve times a year. $98.00. Exhibitor Publications Inc, PO Box 368, Rochester MN 55904. **Tel** (507)289-6556, FAX (507)289-5253. ***Absorbed*** *Creative Exhibiting Techniques.*

ISSN 1078-6198
DD 381 US
●**EXHIBITOR TIMES.** [Exhib. times]. (1993)-. Periodical. English. Twelve times a year. $65.00. Virgo Publishing Inc., 4141 North Scottsdale Road, Suite 316, Scottsdale AZ 85251. **Tel** (602)483-0014, (602)990-1101, FAX (602)990-0819.

LC HF5470 .E93 **ISSN** 0927-7420
DD 381.18 NE
TITLE CHANGE
EXPO/CONGRESVISIE. Added/Corp Vereniging Nederlandse Congresbelangen. **VFOAT** Expovisie. (1992)-(1994). Trade Publication. Dutch. Twelve times a year. Langford's Publications BV, Postbus 10099, 1001 EB Amsterdam Netherlands. **Tel** 011 31 20 6260151. ***Continues*** *Expovisie (Amsterdam, Netherlands).* ***Continued in part by*** *Congresvisie;* ***Continued by*** *Expovisie (Wormerveer, Netherlands), 1381-3587.*

LC HF5470 .E93 **ISSN** 1381-3587
DD 381.18 NE
●**EXPOVISIE.** (1995)-. Trade Publication. Dutch. Six times a year. Langford's Publications BV, Postbus 10099, 1001 EB Amsterdam Netherlands. **Tel** 011 31 20 6260151. **ED** H. Klompenhouwer. **Ad Acc. Circ:** 5,000. available with illustrations. Documents available from SWETS. ***Continues*** *Expo/Congresvisie, 0927-7420.*

ISSN 1059-4035
DD 363 US
FACILITY FAST FACTS. [Facil. fast facts]. **VFOAT** Fast Facts. (1991)-. Periodical. English. Ten times a year. $125.00. Cash-Callahan & Co., PO Box 859, Norwalk CT 06856. **Tel** (203)849-1940, FAX (203)847-6120. **ED** Connacht Cash. ***Continues*** *Inform (Norwalk, Conn.).*

ISSN 0748-1845
DD 659 US
CCC
FINANCIAL ADVERTISING REVIEW.
[Financ. advert. rev.]. (197?)-. Trade Publication. English. Twelve times a year. $239.00. Wentworth Publishing Company, 1866 Colonial Village Lane, Lancaster PA 17605. **Tel** (800)331-5196, (717)393-1000, FAX (717)393-5752. **(Subscription address:** Wentworth Publishing Co., PO Box 10488, Lancaster PA 17605.) Index available (bound in all issues).

ISSN 0276-2153
US
FINDER BINDER. DALLAS/FORT WORTH METROPLEX AREA NEWS MEDIA. VAT Finderbinder. Dallas Fort Worth Metroplex Area News Media. 1st Ed. (1980)-. English. Irregular. Liz Oliphant and Associates, 3627 Howell/Suite 240, Dallas TX 75204. **Tel** (214)521-2432.

ISSN 0276-2196
US
FINDER BINDER. DETROIT AREA UPDATED MEDIA DIRECTORY. (FINDER BINDER.). **VAT** Finderbinder. Detroit Area Updated Media Directory. (1980)-. Directory. English. One time a year. $109.00. Tom McPhail Associates Inc, 3233 Schoolcradt, Suite 108, Livonia MI 48150. **Tel** (313)522-2233. **ED** Tom McPhail. ctrl circ.
Desc: Detroit area media directory and updating service. Details key people, deadlines, interview shows, and PSA's.

LC P88.8 .F56 **ISSN** 0739-8190
DD 001.51/025/763 US
FINDER BINDER, (NEW ORLEANS, LA.).
(FINDER BINDER. LOUISIANA'S UPDATED MEDIA DIRECTORY.). **Added/Corp** Robert H. Mehaffey & Assoc. Premier Edition (1980)-. Directory. English. Twelve times a year. $77.60. Robert H. Mehaffey and Associates, 6001 Winchester Park Drive, New Orleans LA 70128. **Tel** (504)241-9515.

ISSN 0196-8726
US
FINDER BINDER. NORTHEAST OHIO/GREATER CLEVELAND. VAT Finderbinder. Northeast Ohio/Greater Cleveland. 1st Ed. (1980)-. English. Twelve times a year. $50.00. Beals Advertising, 8546 Chevy Chase Drive, San Diego CA 91941. **Tel** (619)463-5050, FAX (619)463-5097. **ED** Ann Nolan. Index available. **Circ:** 300 (ctrl).
Desc: Comprehensive media directory covering a 7 county area in northeast Ohio including all newspapers, radio, TV, cable TV and magazines.

ISSN 0196-8734
US
FINDER BINDER. OKLAHOMA CITY METROPOLITAN UPDATED MEDIA DIRECTORY. VAT Finderbinder. Oklahoma City Metropolitan Updated Media Directory. 1st Ed. (1980)-. Directory. English. Twelve times a year. $85.00. Finderbinder of Oklahoma, PO Box 3093, Edmond OK 63083. **Tel** (405)348-1779. **ED** Joe Park.

ISSN 0196-853X
US
FINDER BINDER. SAN DIEGO COUNTY'S UPDATED MEDIA DIRECTORY. (FINDERBINDER.). **VAT** Finderbinder. (1974)-. Directory. English. One time a year. $95.00. Beals Advertising, 8546 Chevy Chase Drive, San Diego CA 91941. **Tel** (619)463-5050, FAX (619)463-5097. **ED** Barabara Beals. Index available. cum. index. **Circ:** 500 (ctrl).
Desc: Media directory plus six detailed updating newsletters.

ISSN 0196-8513
US
FINDER BINDER. WILLAMETTE VALLEY'S UPDATED MEDIA DIRECTORY. VAT Finderbinder. Willamette Valley's Updated Media Directory. 1st. Ed. (1979)-. Directory. English. Twelve times a year. Hauser Webb Wykoff, 30 Northwest 23rd Place, Portland OR 97210. **Tel** (503)221-0284. Index available (free).

ISSN 0279-6058
US
FORMAT (MINNETONKA, MINN.).
(FORMAT.). **Added/Corp** Advertising Federation of Minnesota. (19??)-. Trade Publication. English. Twelve times a year. $39.00. Format, Inc., 275 Market Street, Minneapolis MN 55405. **Tel** (612)339-5470. **Ad Acc, Adv Mgr:** M.Johnson.
Desc: Trade journal for the advertising industry.

US
CEASED
FRASER SEITEL'S WHAT'S WORKING IN PR AND CORPORATE COMMUNICATIONS. (19??)-(Oct. 1995). English. Ragan Communications Inc., 212 West Superior Street, Suite 200, Chicago IL 60610. **Tel** (312)335-0037, (800)878-5331, FAX (312)335-9583.

ISSN 1056-8743
US
FREE PUBLICITY GUIDE. (1992)-. Periodical. English. $30.00. Mediarite Publications, PO Box 191832, Sacramento CA 95819.

US
FRIDAY REPORT. Added/Corp Hoke Communications Inc. (Apr. 28, 1961)-. Periodical. English. One time a week. $165.00. Hoke Communications Inc, 224 7th Street, Garden City NY 11530. **Tel** (516)746-6700, (800)229-6700.
Desc: Brings direct response marketing professionals news and information on industrial happenings.
Ind/Abst Mark. Advert. Ref. Serv.

LC HF5905 .G66 **ISSN** 1058-2355
DD 659.13/2 US
GOODALE'S DIRECTORY OF CLASSIFIED ADVERTISING. [Goodale's dir. classif. advert.]. **VFOAT** Directory of Classified Advertising. Issue 1 (1991)-. Directory. English. $42.50. Focal Point Ltd, PO Box 11742, Milwaukee WI 53211.

LC NC998.5.A1 G67
DD 741.6/0973 US
CODEN GDUSE9
GRAPHIC DESIGN, USA. **See** The Arts-Graphic Arts.

ISSN 0432-658X
DD 658.8 US
GREY MATTER. RETAIL EDITION.
Added/Corp Grey Advertising Agency, Inc. Vol. 1, No. 1 (1955)-. Periodical. English. Irregular. Grey Advertising Inc., Third Avenue, New York NY 10017. ***Supersedes*** *Grey Matter.*

LC LB3223.3 .G83 **ISSN** 1066-7679
DD 378.1/9625/02573 US
GUIDE TO CAMPUS & NON-PROFIT MEETING FACILITIES, THE. [Guide campus non-profit meet. facil.]. **VFOAT** Guide to Campus and Non-Profit Meeting Facilities; Guide. (198?)-. English. One time a year. $29.95. Amarc Inc., PO Box 279, Minturn CO 81645. **Tel** (303)827-5500.

ISSN 0749-2243
US
TITLE CHANGE
HANDBOOK OF ADVERTISING & MARKETING SERVICES. [Handb. advert. mark. serv.]. **VFOAT** Handbook of Advertising and Marketing Services. (1984/85)-(1993 Ed.). English. Executive Communications, 185 East 85th Street, Suite 11 C, New York NY 10028. **Tel** (212)-831-3147. **ED** Susan Fulton and Leslie Moreno. **Circ:** 1,000 (ctrl). ***Continues*** *Handbook of Independent Advertising & Marketing Services, 0734-6212.* ***Continued by*** *Directory of Advertising and Marketing Services.*
Desc: Contains 12 categories of hard to find services useful to marketing directories. The entries (400) are each described in 200-300 words.

US
HEALTH CARE PR GRAPHICS. English. Twelve times a year. $358.87 New York residents; $335.40 US; add $48.00 postage to other. Solution Resources, 1121 Oswego Street, Suite 1, Liverpool NY 13088-0686. **Tel** (315)451-9339, (800)962-1353, FAX (315)453-3950. **ED** Mary De Santis. **Circ:** 300.
Desc: Topical Healthcare related clip art.

ISSN 8756-4513
DD 659 US
CCC
NLM W1; HE298P
HEALTHCARE ADVERTISING REVIEW.
[Healthc. advert. rev.]. **VFOAT** Health Care Advertising Review. Vol. 1, No. 1 (May/June 1985)-. Trade Publication. English. Six times a year (Jan., Mar., May, July, Sept., Nov.). $239.00. Business Word Inc., 5350 South Roslyn Street, Suite 400, Englewood CA 80111-2125. **Tel** (303)290-8500, FAX (303)290-9025. **ED** Sandra Bridges. Index available ($20.00). **Ad Acc. Circ:** 1,500.
Desc: Features nearly 100 healthcare ads showing the latest trends in print, radio, TV, outdoor, and direct mail nationwide.
Ind/Abst Healthcare Leader. Rev.; Mark. Advert. Ref. Serv.

ISSN 1072-3684
DD 659 US
CCC
●**HEALTHCARE PR & MARKETING NEWS.** **See** Medical Sciences-Health Services Administration.

ISSN 1068-0403
DD 659 US
TITLE CHANGE
HEALTHCARE PR NEWS. **See** Medical Sciences-Health Services Administration.

ISSN 0889-9606
DD 659 US
HI-TECH AD PLACEMENT REPORT.
[Hi-tech ad place. rep.]. **Added/Corp** C Systems, Ltd. **VFOAT** High Tech Ad Placement Report; HITAP Report; HITAP; C Systems' High-Tech Ad Placement Report. (198?)-. English. Two times a year. $790.00. C Systems Ltd, PO Box 708, Winnsboro TX 75494-0708. **Tel** (903)342-5284.

US
●**HIGH TECH HOT SHEET AND HIGH TECH HOT WIRE.** (1995)-. English. Irregular. $395.00. High Tech Hot Sheet, 114 Sansome Street, Suite 1224, San Francisco CA 94104. **Tel** (415)421-6220, (800)842-4307. ***Absorbed*** *High Tech Hot Sheet* ***and*** *High Tech Hot Wire.*

ISSN 1075-007X
DD 659 US
TITLE CHANGE
HIGH-TECH HOT WIRE. [High-tech hot wire]. **VFOAT** High Tech Hot Wire. (1994)-(1995). Periodical. English. High Tech Hot Sheet, 114 Sansome Street, Suite 1224, San Francisco CA 94104. **Tel** (415)421-6220, (800)842-4307. **(Subscription address:** Hot Sheet Publishing, PO Box 2507, Martinez CA 94553.) ***Merged into*** *High Tech Hot Sheet and High Tech Hot Wire.*

ISSN 0773-1922
BE

UDC 659

HINTERLAND ENGLISH ED. See Transportation-Ships and Shipping.

ISSN 0962-3590
DD 338.476592094 UK

HOLLIS (EUROPE). [Hollis Eur.]. (1990)-. Directory. English. One time a year. £135.00. Hollis Directories Ltd., L Hampton Road, Sunbury on Thames, Middlesex TW16 5HG United Kingdom. **Tel** 011 44 1932 784781, FAX 011 44 1932 787844. **ED** Rosemary Sarginson. Index available. cum. index. **Ad Acc, Adv Mgr:** Richard Bagnall. **Circ:** 1,000 (ctrl).
Desc: Comprehensive reference guide to public relations in 30 countries of Europe.

LC HM263 .H58 ISSN 0073-3059
DD 659.2/0925 UK

HOLLIS PRESS & PUBLIC RELATIONS ANNUAL. **VFOAT** Hollis Press and Public Relations Annual. (196?)-. English. Four times a year. £95.00 UK; £98.00 Europe; £105.00 other. Hollis Directories Ltd., L Hampton Road, Sunbury on Thames, Middlesex TW16 5HG United Kingdom. **Tel** 011 44 1932 784781, FAX 011 44 1932 787844. **ED** Nesta Hollis. Index available. **Ad Acc. Circ:** 5,000 (ctrl).
Desc: The classified guide to UK press contacts, public relations departments, news and information sources, services to communicators, plus worldwide register of public relations counselling firms.

LC HF5801 ISSN 1354-2397
DD 659.14 UK

•HOLLIS SPONSORSHIP NEWSLETTER, THE. [Hollis spons. newsl.]. (1994)-. Newsletter. English. Ten times a year. £195.00. Hollis Directories Ltd., L Hampton Road, Sunbury on Thames, Middlesex TW16 5HG United Kingdom. **Tel** 011 44 1932 784781, FAX 011 44 1932 787844.
Desc: Covers developments in the sponsorship industry.

ISSN 1074-0236
US

HUSTLER, THE. (19??)-. English. One time a week. Free on request. The Hustler, 43 Mount Evans Boulevard, Pine CO 80470. **Tel** (303)838-5830, (303)674-6290, FAX (303)838-6007. **Ad Acc. Circ:** 12,400 (ctrl).
Desc: Providing mountain & foothill businesses & residents a timely link to each other's ads.

US

•IAA WORLD NEWS. (1995)-. Newsletter. English. Six times a year. $80.00. International Advertising Association, 521 Fifth Avenue, Suite 1807, New York NY 10175. **Tel** (212)557-1133, FAX (212)983-0455, telex 237969. **ED** Ellen Corey. **Circ:** 3,800 (ctrl). ***Continues*** *International Advertiser, 0885-3363.*
Desc: Newsletter focusing on activities and events of the IAA worldwide.
Ind/Abst INFO-SOUTH Abstr.; Mag. Search; MasterFile FullTEXT (Jan. 1995-).

LC HF6146.P7 I49
DD 658.8/2/0941 UK

INCENTIVE MARKETING AND SALES PROMOTION: ANNUAL REVIEW AND BUYERS' GUIDE. Consumer Publication. English. One time a year. £0.80. EMAP Readerlink, Audit House, 260 Field End Road, Ruislip Middlesex HA4 9LT United Kingdom. **Tel** 011 44 1773 63100, FAX 011 44 1733 87367. **ED** Max Cuff. **Ad Acc. Circ:** 11,500 (ctrl).
Desc: Contains listings detailing products and services used for below the line promotions and incentives.

LC HF6146.N7 N7 ISSN 1042-5195
DD 658.8/2/05 US
CCC
CODEN INCNEU

INCENTIVE (NEW YORK, N.Y. 1988). (INCENTIVE.). [Incentive]. Vol. 162, No. 5 (May 1988)-. Periodical. English. Twelve times a year. $48.00. Bill Communications Inc., 355 Park Avenue South, New York NY 10010-1789. **Tel** (800)360-5200, (212)592-6200, FAX (212)592-6209. **(Subscription address:** Bill Communications, PDS Distribution Center, PO Box 231, Hopkinton MA 01748.) available on microfilm and microfiche from University Microfilms International (UMI). Documents available from UMI Article Clearinghouse. ***Continues*** *Incentive Marketing, 0019-3364.*
Ind/Abst ABI/INFORM Glob. Ed.; ABI/INFORM [Computer File] (Jan. 1982-); Mark. Advert. Ref. Serv.; MasterFile FullTEXT (Jan. 1995-); UMI ABI/Inform--Bus. Period. Ondisc (Nov. 1987-) [Full Txt.].

ISSN 0967-2613
DD 659 UK

INCENTIVE TODAY. [Incent. today]. (1986)-. Periodical. English. Twelve times a year. Langfords Publications Ltd., Ridgeland House, 165 Dyke Road, Hove East Sussex BN3 ITL United Kingdom.

IT

INDICITALIA COMUNICAZIONI. (19??)-. Italian. Irregular. 300000L. Indicitalia SRL, Via G A Resti 36, 00143 Rome Italy. **Tel** 011 39 6 5193544.

IT

INFORMAZIONE. Italian. Six times a year. Ordine Ingegneri Prov Cagliari, Via Tasso 25, 09100 Cagliari Italy. **Tel** 011 39 70 45703.

LC HF5801 .M14 ISSN 1046-5316
DD 659.13/2/05 US

INSIDE MEDIA (STAMFORD, CONN.). (INSIDE MEDIA.). [Inside media]. (Sept. 14, 1989)-. Trade Publication. English. Twenty-four times a year. $79.00. Cowles Business Media Inc. / Connecticut, 6 River Bend Center, 911 Hope Street, Stamford CT 06907. **Tel** (203)358-9900, (800)775-3777, FAX (203)357-9014. **(Subscription address:** Inside Media, PO Box 1017, Skokie IL 60076. **Tel** (708)647-0771.**)** **ED** Gene Ely and Candy Port. **Ad Acc.** ctrl circ. available on an online database (file 648/Full-Text) from DIALOG. ***Continues*** *Inside Print, 0886-9928.*
Desc: News magazine written exclusively for and about the media department.
Ind/Abst Mark. Advert. Ref. Serv.; Trade Ind. ASAP [Full Txt.]; Trade Ind. Index [Full Txt.].

LC HF5410 .I56 ISSN 1053-8828
DD 659 US
CODEN IPUBEU
TITLE CHANGE

INSIDE PR. [Inside PR]. **Added/Corp** Editorial Media Marketing International, Inc. **VFOAT** Inside Public Relations; Inside P.R. **VAT** Inside Public Relations. Vol. 1, No. 1 (May 1990)-(19??). Periodical. English. EMMI Inc., 235 West 48th Street, Suite 34A, New York NY 10036. **Tel** (212)245-8680. **(Subscription address:** Unique Data, PO Box 314, Streamwood IL 60107. **Tel** (708)289-3075.**)** ***Split into*** *Reputation Management Magazine* ***and*** *Inside PR Newsletter.*

US

•INSIDE PR NEWSLETTER. (1995)-. Newsletter. English. One time a week. $250.00. EMMI Inc., 235 West 48th Street, Suite 34A, New York NY 10036. **Tel** (212)245-8680. **(Subscription address:** Unique Data, PO Box 314, Streamwood IL 60107. **Tel** (708)289-3075.**)** ***Separated from*** *Inside PR, 1053-8828.*

LC HF5465.5 .I57 ISSN 0743-2895
DD 381/14/02573 US

INSIDE THE LEADING MAIL ORDER HOUSES. [Inside lead. mail order houses]. (1982)-. English. Every 2 years. $89.95. National Textbook Company, 4255 West Touhy Avenue, Lincolnwood IL 60646. **Tel** (708)679-5500, (800)323-4900, FAX (708)679-2494, telex TWX 9102230736. **Bk Rev. Ad Acc.** ctrl circ.
Desc: An inside look 250 of the nation's mail order houses. Contains information such as; who owns them, who runs them, and their history and financial data.

US

INSTANT BACKGROUND. See Communications-Radio.

LC HM263.A1 P85
UK

•INSTITUTE OF PUBLIC RELATIONS JOURNAL, THE. **Added/Corp** Institute of Public Relations (Great Britain). **VFOAT** IPR Journal. Vol. 12, No. 1 (June 1993)-. Periodical. English. Six times a year. £78.00 institutions; £55.00 individuals. Institute of Public Relations, Old Trading House, 15 Northburgh, London EC1V 0PR United Kingdom. **Tel** 011 44 171 2535151, FAX 011 44 171 4900588. ***Continues*** *Public Relations (Harlow, England), 0263-6166.*

LC HF5410
DD 658.8 US

INTERACTIVE MARKETING NEWSLETTER. (19??)-. Newsletter. English. Twelve times a year. $395.00. Interactive Marketing, inc, 34700 Coast Highway, Ste. 200, Capistrano Beach CA 92624. **Tel** (714)489-8649, FAX (714)489-8752. **ED** Laura Dalton. **Circ:** 500 (ctrl).
Desc: Publication for advertising, marketing, and promotion executives. Covers interactive television, telephone & fax, online services, site based marketing as well as video and PC games.

US

INTERACTIVE PR. (19??)-. English. $199.00. Interactive PR Group, 12021 Wilshire Boulevard, Suite 861, Los Angeles CA 90025. **Tel** (310)442-9149.

ISSN 0885-3363
DD 659 US
TITLE CHANGE

INTERNATIONAL ADVERTISER (NEW YORK, N.Y. 1985). (INTERNATIONAL ADVERTISER.). [Int. advert.]. Vol. 12, No. 4 (Sept. 1985)-Vol. 7, No. 2 (1995). Newsletter. English. International Advertising Association, 521 Fifth Avenue, Suite 1807, New York NY 10175. **Tel** (212)557-1133, FAX (212)983-0455, telex 237969. **ED** Ellen Corey. **Circ:** 3,800 (ctrl). ***Continues*** *Advertising World (Evanston, Ill. : 1978), 0163-9412;* ***Absorbed*** *International Advertiser, 0198-6228.* ***Continued by*** *IAA World News.*
Desc: Newsletter focusing on activities and events of the IAA worldwide.
Ind/Abst Acad. Search; Bus. Source Plus; Bus. Source; EP Collect.; Homework Help.; INFO-SOUTH Abstr.; Mag. Search; MasterFile FullTEXT 1000; MasterFile FullTEXT 350; MasterFile FullTEXT 650; MasterFile FullTEXT (July 1993-Feb. 1995); OCLC; Telebase.

LC HD9999.M64 I67
DD 659.1/52 US

INTERNATIONAL DIRECTORY OF MODEL & TALENT AGENCIES & SCHOOLS. **Added/Corp** Peter Glenn Publications. **VFOAT** International Directory of Model and Talent Agencies and Schools. (1986)-. Directory. English. One time a year (Dec.). $29.95. Peter Glenn Publications, 42nd West 38th Street, Suite 802, New York NY 10018. **Tel** (800)223-1254, (212)869-2020, FAX (212)869-3287. **ED** David Vando and Gregory James. **Ad Acc, Adv Mgr:** Greg James, **Tel** (212)869-2020. ctrl circ. ***Continues*** *Directory of Talent & Modeling Agencies & Schools International, 0742-5570.*
Desc: A detailed listing of model and talent agencies and modeling schools worldwide.

ISSN 0265-0487
UK
CCC

INTERNATIONAL JOURNAL OF ADVERTISING. [Int. j. advert.]. Vol. 2, No. 1 (Jan./Mar. 1983)-. Trade Publication. English. Four times a year. $229.00. Basil Blackwell Publishers Ltd., 108 Cowley Road, Oxford 0X4 1JF United Kingdom. **Tel** 011 44 1235 465500, FAX 011 44 1235 465556, telex 837022 OXBOOK G. **(Subscription address:** Blackwell Publishers / UK, 108 Cowley Road, Oxford OX4 1JF United Kingdom. **Tel** 011 44 1865 791100, FAX 011 44 1865 791347.**)** **ED** Alan Wolfe. **Bk Rev. Ad Acc. Circ:** 2,000. available on microfilm from University Microfilms International (UMI). Documents available from UMI Article Clearinghouse. ***Continues*** *Journal of Advertising (Advertising Association of Great Britain), 0261-9903.*
Desc: Covers all aspects of marketing communications from the academic practitioner and public policy perspectives; includes law, statistics, consumer interests and broadcasting.
Ind/Abst ABI/INFORM Glob. Ed.; ABI/INFORM [Computer File] (Jan. 1983-); Acad. Search; Anbar Account. Finan. Abstr. [Full Txt.]; Anbar Mark. Distr. Abstr. [Full Txt.]; Anbar Top Manage. Abstr. [Full Txt.]; Bus. ASAP (1990-) [Full Txt.]; Bus. Index (1985-); Contents Pages Manage.; Curr. Cit.; EP Collect.; Expand. Acad. Index (1992-); Gen. BusinessFile (1985-); Gen. Period. Index (1985-); Homework Help.; INFO-SOUTH Abstr.; Mag. Search; Manage. Market. Abstr.; Manage. Bibliogr. Rev.; MasterFile FullTEXT 1000; MasterFile FullTEXT 350; MasterFile FullTEXT 650; MasterFile FullTEXT (July 1993-); Newsp. Period. Abstr. (1992-); OCLC; Oper. Prod. Manage. Abstr. [Full Txt.]; PAIS Int. Print; Person. Train. Abstr. [Full Txt.]; Telebase; Trade Ind. ASAP [Full Txt.]; Trade Ind. Index [Full Txt.].

LC HF5826.5 .I575 ISSN 1073-8002
DD 015.6034 US

INTERNATIONAL MEDIA GUIDE. BUSINESS/PROFESSIONAL, ASIA/PACIFIC, MIDDLE EAST/AFICA. [Int. media guide, Bus./prof. Asia/Pac. Middle East/Afr.]. **VFOAT** Business/Professional, Asia/Pacific, Middle East/Africa; Asia/Pacific, Middle East/Africa; International Media Guide. Edition, Business/Professional Publications, Asia/Pacific, Middle East/Afica; Media Guide International; IMG. Business/Professional Publications, Asia/Pacific, Middle East/Africa; International Media Guide. Asia/Pacific, Middle East/Africa. (1991)-. English. $150.00. IMG Inc., 85 Perimeter Road, Nashua NH 03063. **Tel** (603)882-9576, FAX (603)595-0437. ***Formed by the union of*** *International Media Guide. Business/Professional, Asia/Pacific, 1073-8010* ***and*** *International Media Guide. Business/Professional, Middle East/Africa, 1073-7995.*

ISSN 0730-5257
US

INTERNATIONAL MEDIA GUIDE. BUSINESS/PROFESSIONAL, EUROPE. **VFOAT** Business/Professional, Europe; International Media Guide. Edition, Business/Professional Publications, Europe. (198?)-. English. $150.00. IMG Inc., 85 Perimeter Road, Nashua NH 03063. **Tel** (603)882-9576, FAX (603)595-0437. ***Continues*** *International Media Guide. Edition, Business/Professional Publications, Europe.*

LC HF5826.5 .I57 **ISSN** 1069-4277
DD 015.7/034 US

INTERNATIONAL MEDIA GUIDE. BUSINESS/PROFESSIONAL THE AMERICAS. (INTERNATIONAL MEDIA GUIDE. BUSINESS/PROFESSIONAL, THE AMERICAS : IMG.). [Int. media guide, Bus./prof. Am.]. **Added/Corp** International Media Enterprises. **VFOAT** Business/Professional, The Americas; IMG. Business Professional, The Americas; IMG. Business/Professional, The Americas. (1989)-. English. $150.00. IMG Inc., 85 Perimeter Road, Nashua NH 03063. **Tel** (603)882-9576, FAX (603)595-0437. ***Continues** International Media Guide. Business/Professional, Latin America, 1069-4269.*

LC HF6121.A5 M4 **ISSN** 0730-5257
DD 050/.25 US

INTERNATIONAL MEDIA GUIDE. CONSUMER MAGAZINES WORLDWIDE : IMG. Added/Corp International Media Enterprises. **VFOAT** IMG; Consumer Magazines Worldwide; IMG. Consumer Magazine Worldwide. (198?)-. English. One time a year. $150.00. IMG Inc., 85 Perimeter Road, Nashua NH 03063. **Tel** (603)882-9576, FAX (603)595-0437. ***Continues** International Media Guide. Edition, Consumer Magazines (Selected Classifications) Worldwide.*

ISSN 0730-5273
US
TITLE CHANGE

INTERNATIONAL MEDIA GUIDE. EDITION, BUSINESS/PROFESSIONAL PUBLICATIONS, EUROPE. Added/Corp Directories International, Inc. **VFOAT** Business/Professional Publications, Europe; IMG. Business/Professional Publications, Europe; Media Guide International. (1983)-(198?). English. Directories International Inc, 118 21 Queens Boulevard, Room 417, Forest Hills NY 11375-7201. **Tel** (203)853-7880, FAX (203)853-7370. **Bk Rev**. **Ad Acc**. **Circ:** 950 (ctrl). ***Continues** Media Guide International. Edition, Business/Professional Publications, Europe. **Continued by** International Media Guide. Business/Professional, Europe.*
Desc: Covers over 50 professional categories. Lists publisher, personnel, advertising rates, US representatives, mechanical specifications, advertisement closings and circulation.

ISSN 0269-0357
UK
CCC
CODEN IPRRET

INTERNATIONAL PUBLIC RELATIONS REVIEW. [Int. public relat. rev.]. **Added/Corp** International Public Relations Association. **VFOAT** Review. Vol. 10, No. 1 (Feb. 1986)-. Periodical. English. Four times a year. $56.58. Wordsworth, 18 West Church Street, Frederick MD 21701. **Tel** (301)695-8240, FAX (301)845-2991. **ED** John M. Reed. Index available. **Bk Rev**, (Qty: 10). **Ad Acc**, **Adv Mgr:** V.Glenn. **Circ:** 1,500. ***Continues** IPRA Review, 0142-7067.*
Desc: The forum for senior-level international public relations practitioners; how they cope successfully with the international challenge of communications.
Ind/Abst Curr. Cit.; Int. Bibliogr. Sociol.; Soc. Plann. Policy Dev. Abstr.

ISSN 1195-9622
CN

INTERNET ADVERTISING REVIEW ONLINE. (INTERNET ADVERTISING REVIEW.). (1993)-. Periodical. English. Twelve times a year. Free. Strangelove Press, 208 Somerset Street East, Suite A, Ottawa Ontario K1N 6V2 Canada. **Tel** (613)565-0982. available via Internet (gopher.fonorola.net).
Desc: Covers advertising on the Internet. Strives to explain techniques, trends and responsible use of online advertising.

US

•IT STARTS ON THE FRONTLINE. Added/Corp National School Public Relations Association. (Sept. 1993)-. Periodical. English. Ten times a year. $75.00. National School Public Relations Association, 1501 Lee Highway, Suite 201, Arlington VA 22209. **Tel** (703)528-5840. ***Continues** It Starts in the Classroom.*

ISSN 0047-1690
DD 659 US

JACK O'DWYER'S NEWSLETTER. [Jack O'Dwyer's newsl.]. **Added/Corp** J.R. O'Dwyer Co. Vol. 1 (1968)-. Newsletter. English. One time a week (50 per year). $225.00. Jack O'Dwyer Company Inc., 271 Madison Avenue, New York NY 10016. **Tel** (212)679-2471, FAX (212)683-2750. **ED** Jack O'Dwyer.

US

JACK O'DWYER'S NEWSLETTER INDEX. (19??)-. Newsletter. English. One time a year. $50.00. Jack O'Dwyer Company Inc., 271 Madison Avenue, New York NY 10016. **Tel** (212)679-2471, FAX (212)683-2750. **ED** Jack O'Dwyer.

LC HF5802 .W4 **ISSN** 0932-6251
GW

JAHRBUCH DER WERBUNG IN DEUTSCHLAND, OESTERREICH UND DER SCHWEIZ. VFOAT Advertiser's Annual for Germany, Austria, and Switzerland; Jahrbuch Jahrbuch der Werbung. (198?)-. German. One time a year. $126.74. Econ Verlag GmbH, Kaiserwerther Str 282, W 4000 Duesseldorf, 30 Germany. **Tel** 011 49 211 439-0674. ***Continues** Jahrbuch der Werbung, Marketingkommunikation in Deutschland, Osttereich und der Schweiz.*

LC HF5415.12.J3 D45 **ISSN** 0918-4406
DD 658.8/00952 JA

JAPAN ... MARKETING AND ADVERTISING YEARBOOK. Added/Corp Dentsu. (1991)-. English. One time a year. $83.00. Dentsu Inc, 111 Chome Tsukiji, Chuo-ku, Tokyo Japan. **Tel** (212)869-8318. **(Subscription address:** Kinokuniya Book Store, 10 West 49th Street, New York NY 10020. **Tel** (212)765-1461.) Index available. ***Continues** Dentsu Japan Marketing/Advertising Yearbook.*

ISSN 0883-7929
DD 659 US
TITLE CHANGE

JEWELRY AD REVIEW. [Jewel. ad rev.]. (198?)-(19??). Trade Publication. English. Retail Reporting Corporation, 302 Fifth Avenue, New York NY 10001. **Tel** (212)279-7000, (800)251-4545, FAX (221)279-7014. ***Continues** Fashion Jewelry Review. **Continued by** Jewelry Marketing Review, 1075-8143.*
Desc: A report of costume and fine jewelry advertising with columns analyzing store promotions and market trends.

ISSN 1056-2443
DD 658 US
TITLE CHANGE

JOURNAL / NATIONAL SOCIETY OF FUND RAISING EXECUTIVES, THE. [J. - Natl. Soc. Fund Rais. Exec.]. **Added/Corp** National Society of Fund Raising Executives. **VFOAT** NSFRE Journal. (19??)-(19??). Periodical. English. National Society of Fund Raising, 1101 King Street, Suite 3000, Alexandria VA 22314. **Tel** (703)684-0410, FAX (703)684-0540. ***Continues** NSFRE Journal, 0196-3295. **Continued by** Advancing Philanthropy.*

LC HF5801 .J59 **ISSN** 0091-3367
DD 659.1/05 US
CCC
Pr Rev.

JOURNAL OF ADVERTISING. [J. advert.]. **Added/Corp** American Academy of Advertising. (1972)-. Periodical. English. Four times a year. $40.00. University of Houston / Journal of Advertising, College of Business, Houston TX 77204. **Tel** (713)749-6671, FAX (713)749-6895. **(Subscription address:** CTC Press, PO Box 1826, Clemson SC 29633. **Tel** (803)654-0510.) **ED** Anthony F. McGann. **Bk Rev**. **Ad Acc**. **Circ:** 1,300. available on microfilm and microfiche from University Microfilms International (UMI); available on CD-ROM. Documents available from The Genuine Article, UMI Article Clearinghouse.
Desc: Publishes articles of an empirical or theoretical nature concerning the psychological and philosophical aspects of advertising and communication.
Ind/Abst ABI/INFORM Glob. Ed.; ABI/INFORM Ondisc: Expr. Ed.; ABI/INFORM [Computer File] (1975-); Acad. Abstr.; Acad. Ind. [Computer File] (1984-); Acad. Search; Anbar Account. Finan. Abstr. [Full Txt.]; Anbar Mark. Distr. Abstr. [Full Txt.]; Anbar Top Manage. Abstr. [Full Txt.]; Bus. ASAP (1990-) [Full Txt.]; Bus. Index (1985-); Bus. Period. Index; Bus. Source Plus; Bus. Source; Commun. Abstr. (?-?); Curr. Cit.; Curr. Contents Soc. Behav. Sci.; EP Collect.; Expand. Acad. Index (1984-); Gen. BusinessFile (1985-); Gen. Period. Index (1985-); Homework Help.; INFO-SOUTH Abstr.; Infobank (1979-); Mag. Search; Manage. Bibliogr. Rev.; Manage. Contents; Mark. Advert. Ref. Serv.; MasterFile FullTEXT 1000; MasterFile FullTEXT 350; MasterFile FullTEXT 650; MasterFile FullTEXT (Jan. 1991-); Newsp. Period. Abstr. (1989-); OCLC; Oper. Prod. Manage. Abstr. [Full Txt.]; PAIS Int. Print (1991-); Person. Train. Abstr. [Full Txt.]; Psychol. Abstr. (1982-); PsycINFO; PsycLit; Pub. Lib. FullTEXT; Res. Alert [Full Cov.]; Soc. Plann. Policy Dev. Abstr.; Soc. Sci. Cit. Index [Full Cov.]; Sociol. Abstr.; Telebase; Topicator; Trade Ind. ASAP [Full Txt.]; Trade Ind. Index [Full Txt.]; UMI ABI/Inform--Bus. Period. Ondisc (1987-) [Full Txt.]; Wilson Bus. Abstr.; Women Manage. Rev. [Full Txt.].

LC HF5801 .J6 **ISSN** 0021-8499
DD 659.1/07/2 US
CODEN JADRAV
Pr Rev.

JOURNAL OF ADVERTISING RESEARCH. [J. advert. res.]. **Added/Corp** Advertising Research Foundation. Vol. 1 (Sept. 1960)-. Trade Publication. English. Six times a year. $100.00. Advertising Research Foundation, 641 Lexington Avenue, New York NY 10022. **Tel** (212)751-5656, FAX (212)319-5265. **(Subscription address:** Journal of Advertising Research, PO Box 208, Pearl River NY 10965.) **ED** Edward M. Tauber. Index available (bound in Dec. issue). **Ad Acc**. **Circ:** 4,800. available on microfilm and microfiche from University Microfilms International (UMI). Documents available from The Genuine Article, UMI Article Clearinghouse.
Desc: Original reports of findings in the advertising and marketing research fields published for practitioners and users of advertising and marketing research.
Ind/Abst ABI/INFORM Glob. Ed.; ABI/INFORM Ondisc: Expr. Ed.; ABI/INFORM [Computer File] (Oct. 1971-); Acad. Abstr.; Acad. Ind. [Computer File] (1984-); Acad. Search; Anbar Account. Finan. Abstr. [Full Txt.]; Anbar Mark. Distr. Abstr. [Full Txt.]; Anbar Top Manage. Abstr. [Full Txt.]; BioBusiness (1990); Bus. Index (1985-); Bus. Period. Index; Bus. Source Plus; Bus. Source; Commun. Abstr.; Contents Pages Manage.; Curr. Cit.; Curr. Contents Soc. Behav. Sci.; EP Collect.; Expand. Acad. Index (1984-); Gen. BusinessFile (1985-); Gen. Period. Index (1985-); Homework Help.; INFO-SOUTH Abstr.; Infobank (1979-); Mag. Search; Manage. Market. Abstr.; Manage. Bibliogr. Rev.; Manage. Contents; MasterFile FullTEXT 1000; MasterFile FullTEXT 350; MasterFile FullTEXT 650; MasterFile FullTEXT (July 1990-); Newsp. Period. Abstr. (1990-); OCLC; Oper. Prod. Manage. Abstr. [Full Txt.]; Person. Train. Abstr. [Full Txt.]; Psychol. Abstr. (1960-); PsycINFO; PsycLit; PsycScan: Appl. Psych.; Pub. Lib. FullTEXT; Res. Alert [Full Cov.]; Selec. Coop. Index Manage. Period.; Soc. Plann. Policy Dev. Abstr.; Soc. Sci. Cit. Index [Full Cov.]; Sociol. Abstr. (?-?); Soc. Res. Methodol. Abstr. (1984-); Telebase; Trade Ind. Index; UMI ABI/Inform--Bus. Period. Ondisc (Dec. 1987-) [Full Txt.]; Wilson Bus. Abstr.; Women Manage. Rev. [Full Txt.].

LC HF5415.32 .J677 **ISSN** 1057-7408
DD 658.8/342/05 US

JOURNAL OF CONSUMER PSYCHOLOGY: OFFICIAL JOURNAL OF THE SOCIETY FOR CONSUMER PSYCHOLOGY. [J. consum. psychol.]. **Added/Corp** Society for Consumer Psychology. Vol. 1, No. 1 (1992)-. Periodical. English. Four times a year. $150.00. Lawrence Erlbaum Associates, Inc., 10 Industrial Avenue, Mahwah NJ 07430. **Tel** (201)236-9500, (800)926-6579, FAX (201)666-2394. **ED** Dipankar Chakravarti. **Ad Acc**. Full Page (B&W) $225.00. Half Page (B&W) $150.00.
Desc: Information on advertising in consumer psychology.
Ind/Abst Commun. Abstr.

LC HF5801 .C84 **ISSN** 1064-1734
DD 659 US

JOURNAL OF CURRENT ISSUES AND RESEARCH IN ADVERTISING. [J. curr. issues res. advert.]. **VFOAT** JCIRA; J.C.I.R.A. Vol. 14, No. 1 (Spring 1992)-. Trade Publication. English. Two times a year (Spring and Fall). $24.00. CTC Press, PO Box 1826, Clemson SC 29633-1826. **Tel** (803)654-0510, FAX (803)654-7438. ***Continues** Current Issues and Research in Advertising, 0163-3392.*

ISSN 0741-3653
US
TITLE CHANGE

JOURNAL OF EDUCATIONAL PUBLIC RELATIONS. Added/Corp Educational Communication Center. Vol. 7, No. 1 (March 1984)-(1995). Periodical. English. Journal of Educational Public Relations, PO Box 657, Camphill PA 17011. **Tel** (717)761-6620. **ED** Albert E. Holliday. Index available. cum. index. **Bk Rev**, (Qty: 30-40). **Circ:** 1,000 (ctrl). available on microfiche from University Microfilms International (UMI). ***Continues** Journal of Educational Communication, 0745-4058. **Continued by** Journal of Educational Relations.*
Desc: Contains information about successful practices related to internal and external communications, media relations, parent and community involvements.
Ind/Abst Contents Pages Educ.; Curr. Index J. Educ.; Educ. Adm. Abstr.; Sage Fam. Stud. Abstr.

LC HF5415.153 .J675 **ISSN** 1061-0421
DD 658.5/75/05 UK

JOURNAL OF PRODUCT & BRAND MANAGEMENT, THE. [J. prod. brand manag.]. **VFOAT** Journal of Product and Brand Management. (1992)-. Periodical. English. Four times a year. $199.00. MCB University Press, 60 62 Toller Lane, Bradford, West Yorkshire BD8 9BY United Kingdom. **Tel** 011 44 1274 785280, FAX 011 44 1274 785200, telex 51317-MCBUNI-G. **(Subscription address:** MCB University Press / US and Canada Subscriptions, PO Box 10812, Birmingham AL 35201-0812. **Tel** (205)995-1567, (800)633-4931, FAX (205)995-1588.) **ED** Kenneth Traynor.

LC HM263 .J65 **ISSN** 1062-726X
DD 659.2/072 US

JOURNAL OF PUBLIC RELATIONS RESEARCH. [J. public relat. res.]. **Added/Corp** Association for Education in Journalism and Mass Communication. Public Relations Division. Vol. 4, No. 1 (1992)-. Periodical. English. Four times a year. $175.00. Lawrence Erlbaum Associates, Inc., 10 Industrial Avenue, Mahwah NJ 07430. **Tel** (201)236-9500, (800)926-6579, FAX (201)666-2394. **ED** Elizabeth Toth. **Ad Acc**. Full Page (B&W) $175.00. Half Page (B&W) $375.00.

Business and Economics —Advertising and Public Relations

Continues Public Relations Research Annual, 1042-1408.
Desc: Examines understanding of why organizations practice public relations as they do and ways to conduct public relations more effectively, as well as providing scholarly criticism and developing the history, ethics, and philosophy of public relations.

ISSN 0160-8932
US

KEY (GOREVILLE). See Business and Economics-Marketing and Purchasing.

LC HD9680 ISSN 1357-0463
DD 338.47 UK
●**KEY NOTE MARKET REVIEW. CORPORATE SERVICES IN THE UK.** [Key note Mark. rev., Corp. serv. UK]. **VFOAT** Key Note Market Review. Corporate Services in the United Kingdom. (1994)-. Trade Publication. English. Key Note Publications Ltd., Field House, 72 Oldfield Road, Hampton Middlesex TW12 2HQ United Kingdom. **Tel** 011 0181 7830755, FAX 011 0181 7831940.

LC HD9680 ISSN 1357-1370
DD 338.4762138 UK
●**KEY NOTE MARKET REVIEW. MULTIMEDIA IN THE UK.** [Key note mark. rev., Multimed. UK]. **VFOAT** Key Note Market Review. Multimedia in the United Kingdom; Multimedia in the UK. (1994)-. Trade Publication. English. Key Note Publications Ltd., Field House, 72 Oldfield Road, Hampton Middlesex TW12 2HQ United Kingdom. **Tel** 011 0181 7830755, FAX 011 0181 7831940.

LC HD9502 ISSN 1357-8901
DD 333.790941 UK
●**KEY NOTE MARKET REVIEW. THE ENERGY INDUSTRY IN THE UK.** [Key note mark. rev., Energy ind. UK]. **VFOAT** Key Note Market Review. The Energy Industry in the United Kingdom. (1994)-. Trade Publication. English. Key Note Publications Ltd., Field House, 72 Oldfield Road, Hampton Middlesex TW12 2HQ United Kingdom. **Tel** 011 0181 7830755, FAX 011 0181 7831940.

LC HF5081 ISSN 1356-6105
DD 659.1 UK
●**KEY NOTE MARKET REVIEW. THE YOUTH MARKET IN THE UK.** [Key note Mark. rev., Youth mark. UK]. **VFOAT** Key Note Market Review. The Youth Market in the United Kingdom. (1994)-. Trade Publication. English. Irregular. Key Note Publications Ltd., Field House, 72 Oldfield Road, Hampton Middlesex TW12 2HQ United Kingdom. **Tel** 011 0181 7830755, FAX 011 0181 7831940.

LC HF5081 ISSN 1356-6113
DD 659.1 UK
●**KEY NOTE MARKET REVIEW. UK HEALTHCARE.** [Key note mark. rev., UK healthc.]. **VFOAT** Key Note Market Review. United Kingdom Healthcare. (1994)-. English. One time a year. Key Note Publications Ltd., Field House, 72 Oldfield Road, Hampton Middlesex TW12 2HQ United Kingdom. **Tel** 011 0181 7830755, FAX 011 0181 7831940.

LC HF4519 ISSN 1356-6210
DD 381.20941 UK
●**KEY NOTE MARKET REVIEW. WHOLESALING IN THE UK.** [Key note mark. rev., Wholes. UK]. **VFOAT** Key Note Market Review. Wholesaling in the United Kingdom. (1994)-. English. Key Note Publications Ltd., Field House, 72 Oldfield Road, Hampton Middlesex TW12 2HQ United Kingdom. **Tel** 011 0181 7830755, FAX 011 0181 7831940.

LC HF5801 .K64
DD 659.1 JA
KOKOKU KAGAKU. Added/Corp Nihon Kokoku Gakkai. (19??)-. Japanese. Nihon Kokoku Gakkai, c/o Waseda Daigaku Sangyo Keiei Kenkyujo, 6-1 Nishi Waseda 1, Shinjuku-ku, Tokyo-to Japan.

ISSN 0164-9566
US

LIBRARY PR NEWS. See Library and Information Sciences.

ISSN 1045-9723
DD 659 US
LINK (TROY, MICH.). (LINK : THE MAGAZINE OF THE YELLOW PAGES MEDIUM.). [Link]. **Added/Corp** Yellow Pages Publishers Association. Vol. 1, No. 1 (Nov./Dec. 1989)-. Periodical. English. Ten times a year. $60.00. Yellow Pages Publishers Association, PO Box 77000, Department 77382, Detroit MI 48277. **Tel** (810)244-6202, (810)244-0743, FAX (810)244-6230. **ED** Dawn Williams (editor's address: Suite 2000, The Merchandise Mart, 200 World Trade Center, Chicago, IL 60654-1003; telephone: (312)527-7412). **Ad Acc. Circ:** 12,000.
Desc: Target audiences include yellow page directory publishers, ASR'S, large yellow page advertisers, university advertising educators, and others.

ISSN 0893-0260
DD 659 US
LURZER'S INT'L ARCHIVE. [Lurzer's int. arch.]. **VFOAT** Lurzer's International Archive; Archive. (1985)-. Trade Publication. English. Six times a year (Jan., Mar., May, July, Sep., Nov.). $48.00. Luerzer GmbH, Hamburger Allee 45, D-60486 Frankfurt Germany. **Tel** 011 49 69 2477170. **(Subscription address:** American Showcase, PO Box 6338, Syracuse NY 13217.) **ED** Walter Lurzer and Ann Middlebrook. **Ad Acc. Circ:** 23,000 international/8,000 US.
Desc: Collection of worldwide advertising campaigns, print, poster & TV.

GW
M + A MESSEPLANER. VFOAT M+A Messeplanner. German (English). Two times a year. DM115.00. M + A Verlag fuer Messen, Ausstellungen und Kongresse GmbH, Postfach 101528, D-60015 Frankfurt Germany. **Tel** 011 49 69 759502, FAX 011 49 69 75951280, telex 841-411699. **ED** Dorit Vogel Seib, Ellen Maass, Gabriele Buhting Uhle. **Ad Acc. Circ:** 8,600 (ctrl). *Continues* M + A Kalender.
Desc: Covers trade fairs and exhibitions worldwide, event dates and basic information on each event.

LC HD ISSN 0390-2692
DD 338 IT
UDC 380
M & C. MEETING & CONGRESSI. [M & C Meet. congr.]. **VFOAT** Meeting & Congressi. (1973)-. Periodical. Italian. Eleven times a year. L170310. Ediman Srl, C So San Gottardo 39, 20136 Milan Italy. **Tel** 011 39 2 58103791, 011 39 2 58100139, FAX 011 39 2 58103789. **ED** Rossella Giovannini. **Ad Acc. Circ:** 12,000 (ctrl).

ISSN 1058-7411
DD 659 US
MACINTOSH ADVERTISING REPORT. [Macintosh advert. rep.]. **VFOAT** Macintosh Advertising Quarterly Review; Macintosh Market Advertising Report; MAdreport. (1991)-. Periodical. English. Four times a year. $265.00. Irvine Resource Group, 91 Summerstone, Irvine CA 92714. **Tel** (714)756-1319.

LC [HF5805] ISSN 0076-2148
DD 338.7/616591/02573 US
MADISON AVENUE HANDBOOK, THE. [Madison Ave. hand b.]. (1956)-. English. One time a year (Jan.). $50.00. Peter Glenn Publications, 42nd West 38th Street, Suite 802, New York NY 10018. **Tel** (800)223-1254, (212)869-2020, FAX (212)869-3287. **ED** Peter Glenn. Index available. **Bk Rev. Ad Acc. Circ:** 20,000.
Desc: Complete guide to the advertising, film and fashion centers of New York, Chicago, Boston, Florida, Detroit, Atlanta and Canada. It features a list of advertising agencies, design studios, radio and TV producers, photographers, beauty services, agents, sources of supply and more in the fields of art, media and fashion.

LC PN4888.C59 M33 ISSN 1044-6079
DD 051/.068/8 US
MAGAZINE TREND REPORT. [Mag. trend rep.]. **Added/Corp** Audit Bureau of Circulations. **VFOAT** ABC Magazine Trend Report. **VAT** Audit Bureau of Circulations Magazine Trend Report. Issue 1 (1978)-. Trade Publication. English. One time a year (July). $55.00 (members). Audit Bureau of Circulations / Illinois, 900 North Meacham Road, Schaumburg IL 60173. **Tel** (708)605-0909, FAX (708)605-0483. ctrl circ. *Continues* Association of National Advertisers. Magazine Committee. Magazine Circulation and Rate Trends.
Desc: Contains 4-color and black and white ad rates, advertising cost per thousand and other calculations.

LC HM263.A1 M365 ISSN 0277-7398
US
MANAGING THE HUMAN CLIMATE. VFOAT Philip Lesly's Managing the Human Climate. (19??)-. Periodical. English. Six times a year. $30.00. Philip Lesly Company, 155 North Harbor Drive, Suite 2201, Chicago IL 60601. **Tel** (312)819-3590, FAX (312)819-3592. **ED** Philip Lesly. **Circ:** 1,800 (ctrl).
Desc: Guidelines on public relations and public affairs.

LC HF5415 .M2967 ISSN 0306-3615
DD 658.8/005 UK
SUSPENDED
MARKETING AND ADVERTISING NEWS.
See Business and Economics-Marketing and Purchasing.

US
MARKETING AND ADVERTISING REFERENCE SERVICE [ONLINE DATABASE]. See Business and Economics-Abstracting, Bibliographies and Statistics.

US
MARKETING COMMUNICATIONS. (19??)-. English. Twelve times a year. $12.00. Meridian Media Group Inc., 3420 Via Oporto, Suite 201, Newport Beach CA 92663. **Tel** (714)261-0707. *Continues* California Ad News.

ISSN 1067-1234
DD 658 US
MARKETING FACT BOOK, THE. [Mark. fact book]. **Added/Corp** Information Resources Inc. (19??)-. English. One time a year. $500.00. Information Resources, 150 North Clinton Street, Chicago IL 60603. **Tel** (312)726-1221.

LC HD59
DD 659 UK
●**MARKETING MEDIA MAP.** (1995)-. Directory. English. One time a year. Communications and Information Technology Research Ltd., 3 Colleton Crescent, Exeter Devon EX2 4DG United Kingdom. **Tel** 011 01392 493444, FAX 011 01392 493626.

ISSN 0394-9575
UDC 339.13 IT
MEDIA FORUM. [Media forum Media forum]. (1970)-. Periodical. Italian. Twenty times a year. L109000. Ediforum Srl, Via Trebbia 5, 20135 Milan Italy. **Tel** 11 39 2 58300548, 58300341, FAX 11 39 2 58300870. **Bk Rev. Ad Acc, Adv Mgr:** Piero Silvesvri. **Circ:** 6,000 (ctrl).

US
MEDIA INC. See The Arts.

LC HF5801 ISSN 0024-9793
DD 659.1 US
CCC
MEDIA INDUSTRY NEWSLETTER. (MEDIA INDUSTRY NEWSLETTER : MIN.). [Media ind. newsl.]. **VFOAT** MIN. Vol. 23, No. 39 (Oct. 1, 1970)-. Newsletter. English. One time a week (50 issues). $395.00. Phillips Business Information Inc., 1201 Seven Locks Road, PO Box 61130, Potomac MD 20854. **Tel** (301)424-3338, (301)340-1520, (800)777-5005, FAX (301)424-4297, telex 358149. Index available. **Bk Rev. Circ:** 2,100. available on an online database (file 636/Full-Text) from DIALOG; available with charts. *Continues* Magazine Industry Newsletter.
Desc: Provides current news and information on advertising and marketing trends in the media industry.
Ind/Abst Infobank (1979-); PTS Newsl. Database [Full Txt.]; Trade Ind. Index.

LC HF5801- HF5802 ISSN 0266-8688
DD 659.1 UK
MEDIA INTERNATIONAL. [Media int.]. (1973)-. Trade Publication. English. Twelve times a year. $95.00. Reed Business Publishing / West Sussex, England, Perrymount Road, Haywards Heath, West Sussex RH16 3DH United Kingdom. **Tel** 011 44 1444 441212, FAX 011 44 1444 445447.
Ind/Abst Manage. Market. Abstr.; Mark. Advert. Ref. Serv.

UK
MEDIA MAP : THE EUROPEAN MEDIA YEARBOOK. (19??)-. English. One time a year. £95.00. CIT Research Ltd, 1 Harewood, Placehanover Square, London W1R 9HA United Kingdom. **Tel** 011 44 171 4939247.

LC HF5826.5 .M43
DD 659.13/0973 US
MEDIA MARKET GUIDE (NEW YORK, N.Y.). (MEDIA MARKET GUIDE : TOP 100 MARKETING AREAS PLUS MARKETS 101 DOWN.). **VFOAT** M.M. Guide; MM Guide. 4th Quarter (1980)-. English. Four times a year. $500.00. Bethlehem Publishing Inc, Box 119, Bethlehem NH 03574. **Tel** (212)832-7170. **ED** Mala E Herbst and Martin Herbst. **Ad Acc. Circ:** 3,000. Formed by the union of Media Market Guide, 0149-7626 and Media Market Guide. Markets 101 Down, 0149-7138.
Desc: Realistic cost-per-point ratios for spot tv and radio for all U.S. market.

LC HD59
DD 659 BL
●**MEM INFORME REGIONAL.** (1995)-. Portuguese. Irregular. Editora Meio e Mensagem Ltda., Avenue Caetes 139, 05016-080 Sao Paolo SP Brazil. **Tel** 011 55 11 8729477, FAX 011 55 11 2635400. **Ad Acc.**

DD 659.13/2/02573 US
MEMBERSHIP ROSTER - AUDIT BUREAU OF CIRCULATIONS. Main/Corp Audit Bureau of Circulations. (1958)-. English. One time a year. Audit Bureau of Circulations / Illinois, Audit Bureau of Circulations / Illinois, 900 North Meacham Road, 900 North Meacham Road, Schaumburg Schaumburg IL IL 60173 60173. **Tel** (708)605-0909, (708)605-0909, FAX (708)605-0483, (708)605-0483, telex .
Desc: Lists all publisher and non-publisher members of ABC in the United States and Canada.

ISSN 0279-8999
US
MEN'S AD REVIEW. Added/Corp Retail Reporting Bureau (New York, N.Y.). Vol. 45, No. 6 (2nd March 1981)-. Periodical. English. Twelve times a year. $234.00. Retail Reporting Corporation, 302 Fifth Avenue, New York NY 10001. **Tel** (212)279-7000, (800)251-4545, FAX (221)279-7014. *Continues* Menswear Advertising.
Desc: A report on the advertising of menswear by

Business and Economics —Advertising and Public Relations

department and specialty stores throughout the U.S. and Canada. Ads are selected to show advertising ideas and marketing trends.

IT
MI MENSILE : IL MERCATO DELL INFORMAZIONE. Italian. Medianet Srl, Via Carlo B Piazza 24, 00161 Rome Italy.
LC HF5813.B8 M53
DD 659.109

BL
MIDIA & MERCADO. VFOAT Midia e Mercado. (1987?)-. Trade Publication. Portuguese. Twelve times a year. Editora Meio e Mensagem Ltda., Avenue Caetes 139, 05016-080 Sao Paolo SP Brazil. **Tel** 011 55 11 8729477, **FAX** 011 55 11 2635400. **Ad Acc.**
Desc: Information on marketing and the media.

ISSN 0898-4980
DD 646 US
MODEL (NEW YORK, N.Y.). (MODEL.). [Model]. Vol. 1, No. 1 (July/Aug. 1988)-. Periodical. English. Ten times a year. $24.00. Family Media Inc., 3 Park Avenue, New York NY 10016. **Tel** (212)340-9200. **(Subscription address:** Palm Coast Data, PO Box 420163, Agency Department, Palm Coast FL 32142. **Tel** (904)445-4662 ext. 669, (800)829-5475.)

ISSN 0890-9512
DD 659 CCC
TITLE CHANGE
MORGAN REPORT ON DIRECTORY PUBLISHING. See Publishing.

US
MOTORSPORTS MARKETING NEWS. English. Twelve times a year. $80.00 (one-year), $140.00 (two-year), $200.00 (three-year), $90.00 (one-year), $150.00 (two-year), $210.00 (three-year) Canada and Mexico. Ernie Saxton Communications, 1448 Hollywood Avenue, Langhorne PA 19047. **Tel** (215)752-2392, (215)752-7797, **FAX** (215)752-1518. **ED** Marilyn Saxton. **Bk Rev**, (Qty: 12). **Ad Acc**, **Adv Mgr:** Ernie Saxton.
Desc: Monthly newsletter covering marketing, sponsorship and promotion in motor sports.

ISSN 0271-9517
US
NACADA JOURNAL. English. Two times a year (March and October). $40.00. National Academic Advertising Association, 2323 Anderson Avenue, Suite 225, Manhattan KS 66502. **Tel** (913)532-5717, **FAX** (913)532-7732.

US
NAD CASE REPORT. Main/Corp Council of Better Business Bureaus. National Advertising Division. Vol. 12, No. 1 (Feb. 15, 1982)-. Periodical. English. Twelve times a year. $1000.00. Council of Better Business Bureaus, 4200 Wilson Boulevard, Suite 800, Arlington VA 22203. **Tel** (703)276-0100, **FAX** (703)525-8277.
LC HF6105.U5 N37
DD 659.13/2

ISSN 0732-541X
US
NATIONAL ADVERTISING INVESTMENTS IN NEWSPAPERS. (19??)-. English. Media Records, 370 Seventh Avenue, New York NY 10001. **Continues** National Advertising Investments on Media Records Newspapers.
LC HD59 .N24
DD 659.2/85/02573

ISSN 0749-9736
US
NATIONAL DIRECTORY OF CORPORATE PUBLIC AFFAIRS. [Natl. dir. corp. public aff.]. **VFOAT** Corporate Public Affairs. 1st Ed. (1983)-. Directory. English. One time a year. $95.00. Columbia Books Inc, 1212 New York Avenue NW/Suite 330, Washington DC 20005. **Tel** (202)898-0662, **FAX** (202)898-0775. **ED** Arthur C Close, and Michael Buckner. Index available. **Circ:** 2,000.
Desc: Annual directory of 13,000 public affairs professional in over 1,750 companies. Provides addresses of headquarters, Washington office, PAC and foundation - data on PAC publication, PAC receipts and expenditures and foundation grant levels - and names, titles, addresses of public affairs personnel, identifying those registered as lobbyists at national and state levels.
LC HF5808.C2 N3
DD 659.1/025/71

ISSN 0077-5175
CN
NATIONAL LIST OF ADVERTISERS (TORONTO). (THE NATIONAL LIST OF ADVERTISERS.). Vol. 14, (1954)-. English. One time a year. 87.64Can$. MacLean Hunter Ltd. Business Publishers / Canada, Box 9100, Station A, Toronto Ontario M5W 1A5 Canada. **Tel** (416)596-5000, , **FAX** (416)596-5552. **(Subscription address:** Indas Customer Service, 35 Riviera Drive, Building 17, Markham Ontario L3R 8N4 Canada. **Tel** (905)946-0406.) **Continues** National List, 0315-9485.

Desc: Lists over 3,000 national advertisers in Canada, including names of key personnel, addresses, telephone numbers, advertising budget, and media used.

US
NATIONAL PR PITCH BOOK. (19??)-. Periodical. English. One time a year. $345.00. Intercom Group, 1250 45th Street, Suite 200, Emeryville CA 94608. **Tel** (800)959-1059, (510)596-9337, **FAX** (510)596-9331.

ISSN 0276-4520
US
NATIONAL RADIO PUBLICITY DIRECTORY. See Communications-Radio.
LC HE8664 .N38
DD 384.54/53/02573

ISSN 0889-2784
US
NATIONAL RADIO PUBLICITY OUTLETS. See Communications-Radio.
LC TR690.4 .N43
DD 779/.974167/095205

JA
NENKAN NIHON NO KOKOKU SHASHIN. See Photography.

ISSN 0077-9024
DD 659 US
NEW YORK PUBLICITY OUTLETS. [N. Y. public. outlets]. (19??)-. Periodical. English. Two times a year (July & Dec.). $165.00. Public Relations Plus Inc., PO Drawer 1197, New Milford CT 06776. **Tel** (800)-999-8448, **FAX** (203)355-8048. **ED** Harold D. Hansen (phone: (203)354-9361). Index available (Free). cum. index.
Desc: Comprehensive directory covering all 50 states.
Ind/Abst Curr. Lit. Fam. Plan. (19??-199?).
LC HF5905 .S73
DD 338.4/30713

ISSN 1071-4529
US
●**NEWSPAPER ADVERTISING SOURCE.** [Newsp. advert. source]. **Added/Corp** Standard Rate & Data Service. **VFOAT** SRDS Newspaper Advertising Source. (1993)-. Trade Publication. English. Twelve times a year. $550.99. SRDS / Standard Rate & Data Service, 3004 Glenview Road, Wilmette IL 60091. **Tel** (708)375-5049, (800)851-7737, **FAX** (708)375-5003. **(Subscription address:** Neodata / Colorado, PO Box 2606, Boulder CO 80322.) **Continues** Newspaper Rates and Data, 0038-9544.
LC HF5905 .S73
DD 338.4/30713

ISSN 0038-9544
US
TITLE CHANGE
NEWSPAPER RATES AND DATA. [Newsp. rates data]. **Added/Corp** Standard Rate & Data Service. Vol. 34 (Mar. 1952)-. Periodical. English. SRDS / Standard Rate & Data Service, 3004 Glenview Road, Wilmette IL 60091. **Tel** (708)375-5049, (800)851-7737, **FAX** (708)375-5003. **ED** Howard Friedman. **Ad Acc**. **Circ:** 6,400 (ctrl). **Continues** Newspaper Advertising Rates and Data. **Continued by** Newspaper Advertising Source, 1071-4529.
Desc: Profiles over 1,600 U.S. newspapers, distributed magazines, comics, and weekly specialized newspapers.
LC HD59 .N54

JA
NIHON PR NENKAN. Added/Corp Nihon Paburikku Rireshonzu Kyokai. (1983)-. Japanese. One time a year. ¥25000. Nihon Paburikku Rireshonzu Kyokai, c/o Kosan Dai, 3 Building 16-7 Ginza 2 chuo-ku, Tokyo-to 104 Japan.

ISSN 0913-3437
DD 659.152 JA
NIKKEI IBENTO. [Nikkei ibento]. **VFOAT** Nikkei Events. (1987)-. Periodical. Japanese. Twelve times a year. ¥19300. Nihon Keizai Shimbun Inc., 9-5 Otemachi 1 Chome, Chiyoda-ku Tokyo 100 Japan. **Tel** 011 81 3 32700251, 011 81 3 52108502 (Nikkei Business Publications Inc.), **FAX** 011 81 3 52552661, 011 81 3 52108119 (Nikkei Business Publications Inc.). **ED** Kimiaki Sudo.
Desc: Aimed at those who plan events, meetings, conventions, etc.

ISSN 0748-8327
DD 659 US
NRMA AD/PRO. [NRMA ad/pro]. **VFOAT** AD/PRO; N.R.M.A. AD/PRO; NRMA ADPRO. **VAT** National Retail Merchants Association AD/PRO. Periodical. English. Twelve times a year. $50.00 members, $75.00 nonmembers. NRMA, 100 West 31st Street, New York NY 10001. **Tel** (212)244-8780, telex 220 883 TAUR. **ED** Joan Bergmann. **Ad Acc**. **Circ:** 2,000.
Desc: Covers what retail advertising professionals are doing and thinking about planning, budgeting, positioning, media selection, market research and more.

ISSN 0890-2828
DD 361 US
NSFRE NEWS. [NSFRE news]. **Added/Corp** National Society of Fund Raising Executives. **VAT** National Society of Fund Raising Executives News. (19??)-. Periodical. English. Twelve times a year. $25.00. National Society of Fund Raising, 1101 King Street, Suite 3000, Alexandria VA 22314. **Tel** (703)684-0410, **FAX** (703)684-0540.

LC HD59 .O35a
DD 338.7/61/659202573

ISSN 0149-1091
US
O'DWYER'S DIRECTORY OF CORPORATE COMMUNICATIONS. **Main/Corp** O'Dwyer (J.R.) Company. **Added/Corp** J.R. O'Dwyer Company. **VFOAT** Directory of Corporate Communications. (1976)-. Directory. English. One time a year. $119.08. Jack O'Dwyer Company Inc., 271 Madison Avenue, New York NY 10016. **Tel** (212)679-2471, **FAX** (212)683-2750. **ED** Jack O'Dwyer. **Ad Acc**. **Circ:** 2,000 (ctrl).
Desc: Listings of 5,400 corporate public relations departments and 500 association public relations departments including names and titles of public relations executives and staff members, direct dial phone numbers for many addresses and phones of corporate headquarters and divisional offices.

LC HD59 .O353
DD 659.2/025/73

ISSN 0191-0051
US
O'DWYER'S DIRECTORY OF PUBLIC RELATIONS EXECUTIVES. Added/Corp J.R. O'Dwyer Co. (1979)-. Directory. English. One time a year. $97.43. Jack O'Dwyer Company Inc., 271 Madison Avenue, New York NY 10016. **Tel** (212)679-2471, **FAX** (212)683-2750. **ED** Jack O'Dwyer. **Ad Acc**. ctrl circ.
Desc: Biographical data on more than 5,000 public relations executives.

LC HM263 .O37
DD 338.7/61659202573

ISSN 0078-3374
US
O'DWYER'S DIRECTORY OF PUBLIC RELATIONS FIRMS. Added/Corp J.R. O'Dwyer Co. **VFOAT** Directory of Public Relations Firms. (19??)-. Directory. English. One time a year. $135.31. Jack O'Dwyer Company Inc., 271 Madison Avenue, New York NY 10016. **Tel** (212)679-2471, **FAX** (212)683-2750. **ED** Jack O'Dwyer. **Bk Rev**. **Ad Acc**. ctrl circ.
Desc: Listings on more than 1,600 public relations firms throughout the US accounts, executives, branch offices.

US
O'DWYER'S PR MARKET PLACE NEWSLETTER. (19??)-. Newsletter. English. Twenty-six times a year. $24.00. Jack O'Dwyer Company Inc., 271 Madison Avenue, New York NY 10016. **Tel** (212)679-2471, **FAX** (212)683-2750.

ISSN 1043-2957
DD 659 US
O'DWYER'S PR SERVICES REPORT. [O'Dwyer's public relat. serv. rep.]. **VAT** O'Dwyer's Public Relations Services Report. (198?)-. Trade Publication. English. Twelve times a year. $40.00. Jack O'Dwyer Company Inc., 271 Madison Avenue, New York NY 10016. **Tel** (212)679-2471, **FAX** (212)683-2750. **ED** Jack O'Dwyer and Kevin McCauley. **Ad Acc**. **Circ:** 5,000.
Desc: Contains public relations, news, features, and how-to articles.
Ind/Abst Mark. Advert. Ref. Serv.

ISSN 0228-0213
DD 659.1/09714 CN
OFFICIEL DE LA PUBLICITE AU QUEBEC, L'. [Off. public. Que.]. Vol. 1, No. 1 (1981)-. French. One time a year. $60.00. AGEP, 2355 rue Morin, Brossard Quebec, J4Y 1K7 Canada.

LC NC1001.5 .O53
DD 741.6/0973

ISSN 0273-2033
SZ
ONE SHOW - ONE CLUB FOR ART & COPY (NEW YORK, N.Y.), THE. (THE ONE SHOW.). **Added/Corp** One Club for Art & Copy (New York, N.Y.). Vol. 1 (1977/78)-. English. One time a year. $68.00. Rotovision SA, Route Suisse 9, CH1295 Mies Switzerland. **Tel** 011 41 22 7553055, **FAX** 011 41 22 7554072, telex 419246. **(Subscription address:** RC Publications, 3200 Tower Oaks Boulevard, Rockville MD 20852-9799. **Tel** (800)222-2654, (301)770-2900, **FAX** (301)984-3203.)
Desc: Includes advertising's best from the current year compiled from newspapers, magazines, billboards, posters, and brochures.

LC HF5801 .O75
DD 659.1 IS
OTOT. Added/Corp Igud Ha-Mefarsemim Be-Yisrael. No. 17 (April 1978)-. Periodical. Hebrew. Igud Ha-Mefarsemim Be-Yisrael, Shederot Rotshild 107, Tel Aviv Israel.

ISSN 1078-7887
US
●**OUT OF HOME ADVERTISING SOURCE.** **VFOAT** SRDS Out-of-Home Advertising Source. (1995)-. Trade Publication. English. One time a year. $99.00. SRDS / Standard Rate & Data Service, 3004 Glenview Road, Wilmette IL 60091. **Tel** (708)375-5049, (800)851-7737, **FAX** (708)375-5003. **(Subscription address:** Real Time Publications Service, PO Box 1962, Danbury CT 06813.) **Continues** Advertising Options Plus, 1058-2592.
Desc: Advertising rates and data for out-of-home media. Tool for corporate marketers and advertising agencies.

Business and Economics —Advertising and Public Relations

DD 659   **ISSN** 1040-8169   US
P-O-P TIMES. [P-O-P times]. **VFOAT** POP Times. **VAT** Point-of-Purchase Times; Point of Purchase Times. Vol. 1, No. 1 (Sept./Oct. 1988)-. Periodical. English. Ten times a year. $72.00. Hoyt Publishing Company, 2000 North Racine Avenue, Chicago IL 60614. **Tel** (312)281-3400. **ED** Ted Isaacman. **Bk Rev**. **Ad Acc**. **Circ**: 16,000 (ctrl).
  Desc: Reports on corporate developments, point-of-purchase campaigns, research, new technologies and personnel to consumer marketers who use point-of-purchase ads and displays.

LC HF5905 .P4958   **ISSN** 0749-0992
DD 659.13/2   US
PIB MAGAZINE ADVERTISING ANALYSIS. ADVERTISING PAGE INDEX. **Added/Corp** Publishers Information Bureau, Inc. Publishers Advertising Reports (Firm). **VFOAT** Advertising Page Index. **VAT** Publishers Information Bureau Magazine Advertising Analysis. Advertising Page Index. (198?)-. English. Twelve times a year. PAR, 136 Madison Avenue, New York NY 10016. **Tel** (212)725-2700 OR (800)562-3282 (OUTSIDE NY).

DD 070.02541   **ISSN** 0261-5169   UK
PIMS MEDIA DIRECTORY. See Communications.

LC HF6146.P7 P67
DD 670/.29/473   US
    TITLE CHANGE
POTENTIALS MART. (1984)-(19??). English. Lakewood Publications, 50 South Ninth Street, Minneapolis MN 55402. **Tel** (612)333-0471, (800)328-4329, FAX (612)333-6526. **Absorbed by** Potentials in Marketing, 0032-5619.

ISSN 0927-619X   NE
UDC 659
PR & V. [PR V]. **VFOAT** Public Relations en Voorlichting. (1991)-. Periodical. Dutch. Twelve times a year. NGPR Bureau, Koninginnegracht 22, 2514 AB Hague Netherlands. **Tel** 011 31 70 3467049, FAX 011 31 70 3615896. **Continues** PR en Voorlichting, 0165-7232.

ISSN 0275-3677   US
PR CASEBOOK. [PR casebook]. **VFOAT** P.R. Casebook. **VAT** Public Relations Casebook. Vol. 1 (Sept. 1980)-. Periodical. English. Twelve times a year. $90.00. P R Casebook, PO Box 431, Cohasset MA 02025-0003. Documents available from UMI Article Clearinghouse. **Ind/Abst** ABI/INFORM Glob. Ed.; ABI/INFORM [Computer File] (Aug. 1983-); Bibliogr. Mission. (Aug. 1983-).

ISSN 0342-8702   GW   CCC
PR-MAGAZIN. [PR-Mag.]. **VFOAT** Public-Relation-Magazin. (1975)-. Periodical. German. Twelve times a year. $212.64. Verlag Rommerskirchen GmbH & Co, Rolandshof, W 5480 Remagen Germany. **Tel** 011 49 2228 600140. **Continues** PR (Remagen), 0342-913X; **Absorbed** PR-Magazin Aktuell, 0170-4567; Format (Rheinzabern), 0015-7759.

LC HM263.A1 P84
DD 301.154   US
PR NEWS. (19??)-. Periodical. English. One time a week (50 issues). $297.00 US; $360.00 other. Phillips Business Information Inc., 1201 Seven Locks Road, PO Box 61130, Potomac MD 20854. **Tel** (301)424-3338, (301)340-1520, (800)777-5005, FAX (301)424-4297, telex 358149. available on an online database (file 636/Full-Text) from DIALOG. **Continues** Public Relations News, 0033-3697.

LC Discard   **ISSN** 0048-2609   US
PR REPORTER (EXETER, N.H.). (PR REPORTER.). **VAT** Public Relations Reporter (Exeter, N.H.). (1958)-. Periodical. English. One time a week. $185.00. PR Publishing Company Inc, PO Box 600, Exeter NH 03833. **Tel** (603)778-0514. **ED** Patrick Jackson. Index available. **Bk Rev**.
  Desc: Analysis of trends, issues, research and case studies in public relations, public affairs and communications.

UK
PR WEEK. VFOAT PRWeek; P R Week. (1984)-. English. One time a week. Rangenine Ltd, 100 Fleet Street, London EC4Y 1DE United Kingdom. **Tel** 011 44 181 35399804, FAX 011 44 181 5830146. available on an online database (files 771,772,799/Full-Text) from DIALOG.

ISSN 0267-6087
DD 659.205   UK
PR WEEK. [PR week]. **VFOAT** Public Relations Week. (1984)-. English. One time a week (47 issues). $213.90. Haymarket Publishing Ltd., 12 14 Ansdell Street, London W8 5TR United Kingdom. **Tel** 011 44 171 9380705, 011 44 171 2786686, FAX 011 44 171 9380772. **(Subscription address:** Haymarket Magazines Ltd., PO Box 219, Subscription Department, Woking Surrey GU21 1ZW United Kingdom. **Tel** 011 44 1483 776345.**)**

ISSN 0951-7693
DD 338.476592   UK
PR WORLD. [PR world]. **VFOAT** Public Relations World. (1987)-. Periodical. English. Twelve times a year. Rangenine Ltd, 100 Fleet Street, London EC4Y 1DE United Kingdom. **Tel** 011 44 181 35399804, FAX 011 44 181 5830146.

LC PN4709 .I2
DD 079/.54   II
PRESS AND ADVERTISERS YEAR BOOK. **Added/Corp** India News and Feature Alliance. **VFOAT** INFA. (19??)-. English. Twelve times a year. $95.00. INFA Publications, Parliament Street-Jeevandeep, New Delhi India. **Tel** 343330. **(Subscription address:** Prints India, 11 Darya Ganj, New Delhi 110002 India. **Tel** 011 91 11 3268645, FAX 011 91 11 3275542, telex 31-61087 PRIN-IN.**)** **ED** Inder Jit. **Ad Acc**. **Circ**: 3,000 (ctrl). **Continues** INFA ... Press and Advertisers Year Book.
  Desc: Complete information on media for advertisers, advertising agencies and communication managers.

LC HF5905 .P7   **ISSN** 0555-1633
DD 659.13/24/02573   US
    TITLE CHANGE
PRINT MEDIA PRODUCTION DATA. [Print media prod. data]. **Added/Corp** Standard Rate & Data Service. Vol. 1 (Dec. 1968)-(1993). Periodical. English. SRDS / Standard Rate & Data Service, 3004 Glenview Road, Wilmette IL 60091. **Tel** (708)375-5049, (800)851-7737, FAX (708)375-5003. **ED** Otis Kirchhoefer. **Ad Acc**. **Circ**: 5,400. **Continued by** Print Media Production Source, 1071-4545.
  Desc: Production profiles of business, consumer and farm publications and daily newspapers.

LC HF5905 .P7   **ISSN** 1071-4545
DD 659.13/24/02573   US
●**PRINT MEDIA PRODUCTION SOURCE.** [Print media prod. source]. **Added/Corp** Standard Rate & Data Service. (1993)-. Periodical. English. Four times a year. $329.08. SRDS / Standard Rate & Data Service, 3004 Glenview Road, Wilmette IL 60091. **Tel** (708)375-5049, (800)851-7737, FAX (708)375-5003. **(Subscription address:** Neodata / Colorado, PO Box 2606, Boulder CO 80322. **)** **Continues** Print Media Production Data, 0555-1633.

LC Z119 .P8985   **ISSN** 0032-8510
DD 070.5/068   US
PRINT (NEW YORK). See The Arts-Graphic Arts.

LC P92.I8 P76
DD 301.16/1/0945   IT
PROBLEMI DELL'INFORMAZIONE. Vol. 1 (Jan./Mar. 1976)-. Periodical. Italian. Four times a year. L61310. Societa Editrice il Mulino, Strada Maggiore 37, 40125 Bologna Italy. **Tel** 011 39 51 256011, FAX 011 39 51 256034. cum. index.
  Ind/Abst PAIS Int. Print.

ISSN 0883-2404
DD 659   US
Pr Rev.
PROCEEDINGS OF THE CONFERENCE OF THE AMERICAN ACADEMY OF ADVERTISING (1985). (PROCEEDINGS OF THE ... CONFERENCE OF THE AMERICAN ACADEMY OF ADVERTISING.). **Main/Corp** American Academy of Advertising. Conference. (1985)-. English. One time a year (Mid-year). $25.00. American Academy Advertising, University of Richmond/School Business, Richmond VA 23173. **Tel** (804)289-8902, FAX (804)289-8878. **Circ**: 1,000. **Continues** American Academy of Advertising. Convention. Proceedings of the ... American Academy of Advertising, 0883-8666.
  Desc: Papers on all aspects of advertising, presented at the annual conference.

US
PROFESSIONAL MEETING MANAGEMENT. English. Eleven times a year (monthly except Jan.). $50.00. Professional Convention Management Association, 100 Vestavia Office Park #220, Birmingham AL 35216. **Tel** (205)823-7262, FAX (205)823-7271. **ED** Amy Cates Lyle. **Ad Acc**. **Circ**: 20,000 (ctrl).
  Desc: Publication targets meeting/convention planners and suppliers for nonprofit associations.

LC Z6959 .A65 HF5808.S57
DD 659.1/025/68   SA
PROMADATA, PROMOTION, MARKETING & ADVERTISING DATA. (1981)-. English. Irregular. R50.00 South Africa; £28.85 UK; $67.72 US. Clarion Communications Media Pty Ltd, 1134/5 Maritime House at Main & Loveday Streets, Johannesburg 2001 South Africa. **Continues** Advertising & Press Annual of Southern Africa.

ISSN 1072-3293
DD 338   US
PROMOTIONAL PRODUCTS BUSINESS. [Promot. prod. bus.]. **Added/Corp** Specialty Advertising Association International. (19??)-. Periodical. English. Twelve times a year. $54.00. Specialty Advertising, 3125 Skyway Circle North, Irving TX 75038. **Tel** (214)580-0404, FAX (214)550-8331. **ED** Tina Berres Filipski (phone: (214)252-0404 ext. 112). **Photos**. **Ad Acc**. Full Page (B&W) $1,244.00. Half Page (B&W) $953.00. **Circ**: 6,500 (ctrl). **Continues** Specialty Advertising Business, 0195-0495.
  Desc: Covers industry and associated news, legislative issues from Washington, product news, educational articles and selling marketing news.

IT
    TITLE CHANGE
PROMOZIONE. (19??)-(199?). Italian. Maclean Hunter SRL / Italy, P le a Cantore 12, 20123 Milan Italy. **Tel** 011 39 2 89401365, 011 39 2 58188204, FAX 011 39 2 8378590. **Merged into** Strategia.

LC HM263 .P76   **ISSN** 1047-0239
DD 303   US
    CODEN PORVE9
    SUSPENDED
PROPAGANDA REVIEW. [Propag. rev.]. **Added/Corp** Media Alliance (San Francisco, Calif.). **VFOAT** Propaganda. No. 1 (Winter 1987/88)-Suspended (Aug. 1994). Periodical. English. Irregular. Media Alliance, 814 Mission Street, Suite 205, San Francisco CA 94103. **Tel** (415)546-6334. **Continues** Propaganda Analysis Review.
  Ind/Abst Altern. Press Index (199?-); PAIS Int. Print.

US
PRSA DIRECTORY / PUBLIC RELATIONS SOCIETY OF AMERICA. **Main/Corp** Public Relations Society of America. **VFOAT** P.R.S.A. Directory. **VAT** Public Relations Society of America Directory. (1981)-. Directory. English. One time a year. $131.00 (institutions), $125.00 (individuals). Public Relations Society of America, 33 Irving Place, New York NY 10003. **Tel** (212)460-1426, (212)460-1413, FAX (212)995-0757. **Continues in part** Public Relations Society of America. Public Relations Handbook and Register.

BE
PUB NEWSLETTER. See Publishing.

IT
PUBBLICITA DOMANI. Trade Publication. Italian. New International Media, Via Lovanio 6, 20121 Milan Italy. **Tel** 011 39 2 29005329.

LC HF5813.I8 P8
DD 659.1/0945   US
    SUSPENDED
PUBBLICITA IN ITALIA. VFOAT Advertising in Italy; Publicite en Italie. (1953/54)-Suspended (1986). Italian. Irregular. $57.50. Marketing Finanza Italia, Via Stradella 3, 20129 Milan Italy. **Tel** 011 39 2 29400554, FAX 011 39 2 29401816. **ED** Lorea Bliss. **Bk Rev**. **Ad Acc**.
  Desc: Current advertising in Italy.

LC HF5813.I8 P815
IT
PUBBLICITA ITALIA. (19??)-. Periodical. Italian. Forty-Five times a year. L295000. Marketing Finanza Italia, Via Stradella 3, 20129 Milan Italy. **Tel** 011 39 2 29400554, FAX 011 39 2 29401816. **Ad Acc**, **Adv Mgr:** Danieue Monai.

IT
PUBBLICITA SUCCESSO. Italian. One time a year. L90000. New International Media, Via Lovanio 6, 20121 Milan Italy. **Tel** 011 39 2 29005329.

ISSN 0751-5464
    FR
UDC 659.1   CCC
PUBLI 10. VFOAT Publi Dix. (1973)-. Periodical. French. Twelve times a year. $65.61. Nouvelles Editions de la Publicite, 9 rue Leo Delibes, 75016 Paris France. **Tel** 011 33 1 47277749, FAX 011 33 1 455538501, telex 620243. **Ad Acc**. **Continues** Publi Hebdo (Paris), 1141-3921.
  Desc: News of the advertising world.

ISSN 0712-8193
DD 659.1/06/071   CN
PUBLI-NORMES. (PUBLI-NORMES : LE BULLETIN DU CONSEIL DES NORMES DE LA PUBLICITE). [Publi-normes]. Vol. 1, No. 1 Jan. 1982-. Bulletin. French. Four times a year. Free. Conseil Des Normes De La Publicite, Bureau 200, 1499 rue De Bleury, Montreal Quebec H3A 2H5 Canada.

UK
PUBLIC RELATIONS. VFOAT IPR Public Relations. Vol. 5 (Oct. 1952)-. Periodical. English. Twelve times a year. **Bk Rev**. **Ad Acc**. **Absorbed** IPR News; **Continues** Journal of the Institute of Public Relations.
  Desc: Journal of public relations.

LC LB2847 .P8 ISSN 0273-3757
DD 659.2/9371/00973 US
PUBLIC RELATIONS ALMANAC FOR EDUCATORS, THE. [Public relat. alm. educ.]. Vol. 1 (1980)-. Periodical. English. Four times a year. $24.00 US; $28.00 other. Journal of Educational Public Relations, PO Box 657, Camphill PA 17011. **Tel** (717)761-6620. **ED** Albert E Holliday, Joan M Holliday. Index available. **Bk Rev.** available on microfiche.
Desc: Contains articles about school, community relations, media relations, internal relations, writing and editing, speaking, and human relations.

LC HM263 .P7654 ISSN 0882-8288
DD 659.2/023/73 US
CEASED
PUBLIC RELATIONS CAREER DIRECTORY. [Public relat. career dir.]. **Added/Corp** Career Publishing Corp. (New York, N.Y.) Career Press Inc. Visible Ink Press. (1986)-(1993). Directory. English. Every 2 years. Gale Research Inc., 835 Penobscot Building, 645 Griswold Street, Detroit MI 48226. **Tel** (800)877-GALE, (313)961-2242, FAX (313)961-6083, (800)414-5043, telex TWX 810-221-7086. **Bk Rev. Ad Acc.**
Desc: Covers opportunities in corporate communications, international public relations, community affairs, media relations, finanical and sports organizations and what it's like to work at a small PR firm.

ISSN 0263-6166
UK
CCC
TITLE CHANGE
PUBLIC RELATIONS (HARLOW, ESSEX). (PUBLIC RELATIONS : THE INTERNATIONAL JOURNAL OF THE INSTITUTE OF PUBLIC RELATIONS.). **Added/Corp** Institute of Public Relations (Great Britain). Vol. 1, No. 1 (Autumn 1982)-Vol. 11, No. 6 (Apr. 1993). Periodical. English. Institute of Public Relations, Old Trading House, 15 Northburgh, London EC1V 0PR United Kingdom. **Tel** 011 44 171 2535151, FAX 011 44 171 4900588. ***Continued by*** *Institute of Public Relations Journal.*

LC HM263.A1 P83 ISSN 0033-3670
DD 301.154 US
CODEN PREJAR
PUBLIC RELATIONS JOURNAL, THE. [Publ. relat. j.]. **Added/Corp** American Council on Public Relations. Public Relations Society of America. Vol. 1 (Oct. 1945)-. Periodical. English. Three times a year. $55.00. Public Relations Society of America, 33 Irving Place, New York NY 10003. **Tel** (212)460-1426, (212)460-1413, FAX (212)995-0757. **ED** Michael Winkleman. **Bk Rev. Ad Acc. Circ:** 16,000. available on microfilm and microfiche from University Microfilms International (UMI); available on an online database from NEXIS. Documents available from UMI Article Clearinghouse.
Desc: Covers trends, developments and techniques in the practice of public relations.
Ind/Abst ABI/INFORM Glob. Ed.; ABI/INFORM Ondisc: Expr. Ed.; ABI/INFORM [Computer File] (Apr. 1972-); Acad. Search; Anbar Account. Finan. Abstr. [Full Txt.]; Anbar Mark. Distr. Abstr. [Full Txt.]; Anbar Top Manage. Abstr. [Full Txt.]; Bus. ASAP (1990-) [Full Txt.]; Bus. Index (1979-?); Bus. Period. Index; Bus. Source Plus; Bus. Source; Commun. Abstr. (?-?); Curr. Cit.; EP Collect.; Expand. Acad. Index (1992-); Gen. BusinessFile (1985-); Gen. Period. Index (1985-); Homework Help.; Hosp. Health Admin. Index (1978-1989); INFO-SOUTH Abstr.; Infobank (1979-); Mag. Search; Manage. Market. Abstr.; Manage. Bibliogr. Rev.; Manage. Contents; Mark. Advert. Ref. Serv.; MasterFile FullTEXT 1000; MasterFile FullTEXT 350; MasterFile FullTEXT 650; MasterFile FullTEXT (Jan. 1993-Dec. 1994); Newsp. Period. Abstr. (1988-); OCLC; Oper. Prod. Manage. Abstr. [Full Txt.]; Person. Train. Abstr. [Full Txt.]; Stat. Ref. Index; Telebase; Trade Ind. Index [Full Txt.]; UMI ABI/Inform--Bus. Period. Ondisc (Dec. 1987-) [Full Txt.]; Vocat. Search; Wilson Bus. Abstr.; Women Manage. Rev. [Full Txt.].

US
PUBLIC RELATIONS JOURNAL. PRSA REGISTER ISSUE. Main/Corp Public Relations Society of America. **VFOAT** PRSA Register Issue. (1985/86)-. English. One time a year. $120.00. Public Relations Society of America, 33 Irving Place, New York NY 10003. **Tel** (212)460-1426, (212)460-1413, FAX (212)995-0757. **Ad Acc. Circ:** 14,265. ***Continues*** *PRSA Register.*
Desc: Contains names, addresses, and telephone numbers of all PRSA members.

LC HV42 ISSN 0033-3700
DD 659.2/05 US
CCC
CODEN PREUEU
PUBLIC RELATIONS QUARTERLY. [Public relat. q.]. **VFOAT** PRQ. Vol. 8, No. 2 (July 1963)-. Periodical. English. Four times a year (March, June, Sept., Dec.). $49.00. Public Relations Quarterly, PO Box 311, 44 West Market Street, Rhinebeck NY 12572. **Tel** (914)876-2081, FAX (914)876-2561. **ED** Paul Swift. Index Available published separately, bound from publisher, free-automatically sent. cum. index. **Bk Rev** (Qty: 8-10). **Ad Acc, Adv Mgr:** EW Hopper, **Tel** (212)673-5220. **Circ:** 5,000 (ctrl). available on microfilm and microfiche from University Microfilms International (UMI); available on an online database (file15/Full-Text) from DIALOG. Documents available from UMI Article Clearinghouse. ***Continues*** *Quarterly Review of Public Relations;* ***Absorbed*** *International Public Relations Review.*
Desc: Articles on and about professional public relations by professionals.
Ind/Abst ABI/INFORM Glob. Ed.; ABI/INFORM [Computer File] (Winter 1972-); Acad. Search; Anbar Account. Finan. Abstr. [Full Txt.]; Anbar Mark. Distr. Abstr. [Full Txt.]; Anbar Top Manage. Abstr. [Full Txt.]; Bus. ASAP (1992-) [Full Txt.]; Bus. Index (1985-); Bus. Period. Index; Bus. Source Plus; Bus. Source; Curr. Cit.; EP Collect.; Expand. Acad. Index (1992-); Gen. BusinessFile (1985-); Gen. Period. Index (1985-); Homework Help.; INFO-SOUTH Abstr.; Lotus Notes; Mag. Search; Manage. Bibliogr. Rev.; Manage. Contents; Mark. Advert. Ref. Serv.; MasterFile FullTEXT 1000; MasterFile FullTEXT 350; MasterFile FullTEXT 650; MasterFile FullTEXT (Jan. 1993-); Newsp. Period. Abstr. (1992-); OCLC; Oper. Prod. Manage. Abstr. [Full Txt.]; Person. Train. Abstr. [Full Txt.]; Telebase; UMI ABI/Inform--Bus. Period. Ondisc (Fall 1987-) [Full Txt.]; Vocat. Search; Wilson Bus. Abstr.; Women Manage. Rev. [Full Txt.].

LC HM263 .P767 ISSN 0363-8111
DD 659.2/05 US
CCC
CODEN PREREL
Pr Rev.
PUBLIC RELATIONS REVIEW (RIVERDALE, N.Y.). (PUBLIC RELATIONS REVIEW.). **Added/Corp** Foundation for Public Relations Research and Education (U.S.). Vol. 1 (Summer 1975)-. Trade Publication. English. Five times a year. $215.00. JAI Press Inc., 55 Old Post Road, Suite 2, PO Box 1678, Greenwich CT 06836-1678. **Tel** (203)661-7602, FAX (203)661-0792. **ED** Ray E. Hiebert. Index available. **Bk Rev. Ad Acc. Circ:** 2,000. available on microfilm and microfiche from University Microfilms International (UMI). Documents available from The Genuine Article, UMI Article Clearinghouse.
Desc: Provides research and analysis of P.R. techniques, theories, research, plans, policies and procedures.
Ind/Abst ABI/INFORM Glob. Ed. (1979-); ABI/INFORM [Computer File] (Spring 1981-); Acad. Search; Bus. ASAP (1990-) [Full Txt.]; Bus. Index (1985-); Bus. Period. Index; Bus. Source Plus; Bus. Source; Commun. Abstr. (Spring 1981-); Curr. Cit.; Curr. Contents Soc. Behav. Sci.; Curr. Index J. Educ. (1975-); EP Collect.; Expand. Acad. Index (1984-); Gen. BusinessFile (1985-); Gen. Period. Index (1985-); Homework Help.; INFO-SOUTH Abstr.; Infobank (1979-); Mag. Search; Manage. Contents; Mark. Advert. Ref. Serv.; MasterFile FullTEXT 1000; MasterFile FullTEXT 350; MasterFile FullTEXT 650; MasterFile FullTEXT (Jan. 1993-); Newsp. Period. Abstr. (1989-); OCLC; PAIS Int. Print (1991-); Res. Alert [Full Cov.]; Soc. Plann. Policy Dev. Abstr.; Soc. Sci. Cit. Index [Full Cov.]; Telebase; Trade Ind. ASAP [Full Txt.]; Trade Ind. Index [Full Txt.]; Vocat. Search; Wilson Bus. Abstr.

ISSN 1082-9113
DD 659 US
•**PUBLIC RELATIONS STRATEGIST, THE.** [Public relat. strateg.]. **Added/Corp** Public Relations Society of America. **VFOAT** Strategist. Vol. 1, No. 1 (Spring 1995)-. Periodical. English. Four times a year (Apr., Jun., Sept., Dec.). $48.00 (comes also with Public Relations Tactics). Public Relations Society of America, 33 Irving Place, New York NY 10003. **Tel** (212)460-1426, (212)460-1413, FAX (212)995-0757.
Ind/Abst MasterFile FullTEXT (Jan. 1995-).

LC HM263.A1 .P838 ISSN 1080-6792
DD 659 US
•**PUBLIC RELATIONS TACTICS.** [Public relat. tactics]. **Added/Corp** Public Relations Society of America. **VFOAT** Tactics. (1994)-. Periodical. English. Twelve times a year. $40.00. Public Relations Society of America, 33 Irving Place, New York NY 10003. **Tel** (212)460-1426, (212)460-1413, FAX (212)995-0757.
Pub. Size: Tabloid.
Ind/Abst Bus. Source Plus; EP Collect.; Homework Help.; MasterFile FullTEXT 1000; MasterFile FullTEXT 350; MasterFile FullTEXT 650; MasterFile FullTEXT; OCLC; Telebase.

ISSN 0262-9534
DD 338.7616592025 UK
PUBLIC RELATIONS YEAR BOOK. [Public relat. year book]. (1980)-. English. One time a year. $77.01. Public Relations Consultants Association, Willow House, Willow Place, London SW1P 1JH United Kingdom. **Tel** 011 44 171 2336026, FAX 011 44 171 8284797. ***Continues*** *Register of Members - Public Relations Consultants Association, 0140-8739.*

LC HF3221 .C37
DD 015.71/034/05 CN
PUBLICATION PROFILES. VFOAT Canadian Advertising Rates and Data. Publication Profiles; Canadian Advertising Rates & Data. Publication Profiles. Vol. 9 (1990)-. English. One time a year. 86.03Can$. MacLean Hunter Ltd. Business Publishers / Canada, Box 9100, Station A, Toronto Ontario M5W 1A5 Canada. **Tel** (416)596-5000, , FAX (416)596-5552. **(Subscription address:** Indas Customer Service, 35 Riviera Drive, Building 17, Markham Ontario L3R 8N4 Canada. **Tel** (905)946-0406.) ***Continues*** *Canadian Advertising Rates & Data. Publication Profiles, 0836-5024.*

LC HF5813.S8 P8 ISSN 0377-2624
SP
PUBLICOTEC. (19??)-. Spanish. Coetec, Pocafort 39-41 Edificio Avenida, 15 Barcelona Spain.

ISSN 1184-8782
DD 659.2/09714/05 CN
PUBLICS (MONTREAL). (PUBLICS.). [Publics]. **Added/Corp** Societe des Relationnistes du Quebec. Vol. 17, No 1 (Jan. 1991)-. Periodical. French. Six times a year. Free for members. ***Continues*** *Bulletin (Societe des Relationnistes du Quebec : 1985). Francais., 0829-7908.*

ISSN 0951-7766
UK
QUARTERLY SURVEY OF ADVERTISING EXPENDITURE. [Q. surv. advert. expend.]. (1987)-. English. Four times a year (Apr., July, Oct., Dec.). £350.00. NTC Publications Ltd., PO Box 69, Henley-on-Thames, Oxfordshire RG9 1GB United Kingdom. **Tel** 011 44 1491 574671, FAX 011 44 1491 571188. ***Continues*** *Quarterly Review of Advertising Statistics, 0266-5646.*

ISSN 0211-3333
SP
UDC 659.4 CCC
R.P. INTERNACIONAL DE RELACIONES PUBLICAS. [R.P. Int. Relac. Publicas]. **VFOAT** Relaciones Publicas. Internacional de Relaciones Publicas; R.P. Relaciones Publicas; Relaciones Publicas (Madrid); Revista Internacional de Relaciones Publicas. (1962)-. Periodical. Spanish. Six times a year. $60.00. Internacional de Relaciones Publicas, Jose Ortega y Gasset 50, Madrid 28006 Spain. **Tel** 011 34 1 4022609, 011 94 1 3091954.

ISSN 1071-4669
US
TITLE CHANGE
RADIO LOCAL MARKETS SOURCE. See Communications-Radio.

ISSN 1044-985X
DD 659 US
Pr Rev.
RADIO PROMOTION BULLETIN. See Communications-Radio.

LC HF5801
DD 659.1 US
•**RAGAN'S INTERACTIVE PUBLIC RELATIONS.** (1995)-. Newsletter. English. Twenty-six times a year. $279.00. Ragan Communications Inc., 212 West Superior Street, Suite 200, Chicago IL 60610. **Tel** (312)335-0037, (800)878-5331, FAX (312)335-9583. **ED** Steve Crescenzo.
Desc: Computer aid for those in the public relations industry.

LC HF6125.5 .R43 ISSN 1058-2118
DD 658.3/111/05 US
RECRUITMENT SOLUTION, THE. [Recruit. solut.]. **Added/Corp** Standard Rate & Data Service. (1991)-. Trade Publication. English. SRDS / Standard Rate & Data Service, 3004 Glenview Road, Wilmette IL 60091. **Tel** (708)375-5049, (800)851-7737, FAX (708)375-5003.

LC LB2847 .J68 ISSN 1080-1235
DD 370 US
•**RELATIONS (CAMP HILL, PA.).** (RELATIONS.). [Relations]. **Added/Corp** Educational Communication Center. **VFOAT** Journal of Educational Public Relations. Vol. 15, No. 2 (Dec. 1993)-. Periodical. English. Four times a year. $36.00. Journal of Educational Public Relations, PO Box 657, Camphill PA 17011. **Tel** (717)761-6620. ***Continues*** *Journal of Educational Public Relations, 0741-3653.*

ISSN 0034-3811
FR
RELATIONS PUBLIQUES INFORMATIONS. (19??)-. French. Forty-eight times a year. 1,700.00F France; 1,900.00F other. EPCI C O Iserp, 87 Bis rue Carnot, 92300 Levallois Perret France. **Tel** 011 33 47481515.

LC HF5801 .W75a
DD 659.1/06/01 BE
REPORT & REVIEW / WORLD FEDERATION OF ADVERTISERS, WFA. Main/Corp World Federation of Advertisers. **VFOAT** Report and Review. (1988)-. Newsletter. English. One time a year. Free. World Federation of Advertisers, rue des Colonies 18-24, Box 6, B-1000 Brussels Belgium. **Tel** 32 2 502 5740, FAX 32 2 502 5666. **ED** Paul P. de Win. **Ad Acc.** available on diskette. ***Continues*** *World Federation of Advertisers. Annual Report.*

Business and Economics —Advertising and Public Relations

Desc: Representing advertisers in the international arena on all Commerical Communication related issues. Its role to defend and, where possible, to extend the freedom of advertising and commerical speech in all countries of the world.

ISSN 0227-6747
DD 659.1/0971
CN

REPORT ON COUNCIL ACTIVITY - CANADIAN ADVERTISING ADVISORY BOARD. ADVERTISING STANDARDS COUNCIL. (REPORT ON COUNCIL ACTIVITY.). [Rep. Counc. act. - Can. Advert. Advis. Board. Advert. Stand. Counc.]. **Main/Corp** Canadian Advertising Advisory Board. Advertising Standards Council. Periodical. English. Two times a year. Free. Canadian Advertising Advisory Board, Suite 302, 1240 Bay Street, Toronto Ontario M5R 2A7. ctrl circ.

ISSN 1071-4197
DD 384
US
CCC
TITLE CHANGE

REPORT ON TELECOM ADVERTISING & PUBLISHING, TA. See Communications-Telecommunication.

US

●**REPUTATION MANAGEMENT MAGAZINE.** **VFOAT** Inside Public Relations; Inside P.R. (1995)-. Periodical. English. Six times a year. $50.00. EMMI Inc., 235 West 48th Street, Suite 34A, New York NY 10036. **Tel** (212)245-6680. **(Subscription address:** Unique Data, PO Box 314, Streamwood IL 60107. **Tel** (708)289-3075.**) Separated from** Inside PR, 1053-8828.

ISSN 0735-7087
DD 659
US

RETAIL AD WEEK. [Retail ad week]. **Added/Corp** Retail Reporting Bureau (New York, N.Y.). **VFOAT** Retail Ad-week. **VAT** Retail Advertising Week. (Dec. 1971)-. Periodical. English. One time a week (except last week in Dec.). $383.40 US and Canada; $385.00 other. Retail Reporting Corporation, 302 Fifth Avenue, New York NY 10001. **Tel** (212)279-7000, (800)251-4545, FAX (221)279-7014. available on microfilm. **Continues** Retail Advertising Week.

LC HD59
DD 659
BL

●**REVISTA DE CRIACAO.** (1995)-. Portuguese. Twelve times a year. Editora Meio e Mensagem Ltda., Avenue Caetes 139, 05016-080 Sao Paolo SP Brazil. **Tel** 011 55 11 8729477, FAX 011 55 11 2635400. **Ad Acc.** **Desc:** Covers creation and production in advertising.

LC HG1616.M3 S25
ISSN 1060-2860
DD 332.1/0973/021
US

SALES & MARKETING SURVEY / SHESHUNOFF. See Business and Economics-Marketing and Purchasing.

GW

SCHEBEN NEWS. **VFOAT** News. (19??)-. German. Six times a year. Scheben PR GmbH, Zum Biotop 11, 5010 Bergheim Germany. **Tel** 02271-6050. **ED** Mathias Scheben. **Circ:** 600.

ISSN 1069-210X
DD 384
US

●**SE HABLA ESPANOL.** [Se habla esp.]. Vol. 1, No. 1 (Winter 1993)-. Trade Publication. English. Four times a year. $25.00. Hispanic Business, 360 South Hope Avenue, Suite 300 C, Santa Barbara CA 93105. **Tel** (805)682-5843, FAX (805)563-1239, (805)687-4546. **Desc:** Hispanic communications, media, marketing and advertising industry newsletter.

ISSN 1188-2980
DD 659/.05
CN

SELF-STARTER (MARKHAM). (SELF-STARTER.). [Self-start.]. Vol. 1, No. 1 (Jan. 1992)-. Periodical. English. Twelve times a year. $20.00. FCS/PUB Division, 3 Arrowflight Drive, Markham Ontario L3P 1R9.

LC PN1560
ISSN 1074-5297
DD 792
US

●**SHOOT (NEW YORK, N.Y.).** (SHOOT.). [Shoot]. (1994)-. Periodical. English. One time a week (51 issues). $79.00. Billboard Publications Inc., 1515 Broadway Billboard, New York NY 10036. **Tel** (212)764-7300, FAX (305)755-7048, telex WU TWX 710-581-6279. **(Subscription address:** Back Stage Shoot, PO Box 5023, Brentwood TN 37024. **Tel** (800)999-3322.**) ED** Peter Caranicas. **Circ:** 15,000. Documents available from UMI Article Clearinghouse. **Continues** Back Stage/Shoot, 1055-9825.
Desc: Covers commercial production and the industry, from creation through production to post-production.
Ind/Abst Bus. Index; Gen. BusinessFile; Gen. Period. Index; Mag. Search; MasterFile FullTEXT (Jan. 1994-).

ISSN 0845-8448
DD 607/.34/71
CN

SHOWS & EXHIBITIONS. [Shows exhib.]. **VFOAT** Shows and Exhibitions. (March/April 1989)-. Directory. English. Five times a year. 87.64Can$. MacLean Hunter Ltd. Business Publishers / Canada, Box 9100, Station A, Toronto Ontario M5W 1A5 Canada. **Tel** (416)596-5000, , FAX (416)596-5552. **(Subscription address:** Indas Customer Service, 35 Riviera Drive, Building 17, Markham Ontario L3R 8N4 Canada. **Tel** (905)946-0406.**) Continues** Canadian Industry Shows and Exhibitions, 0068-8967.

ISSN 0929-1431
UDC 659.1
NE

SIGN & DISPLAY. [Sign display]. **VFOAT** Sign and Display. (1989)-. Periodical. Dutch. Eight times a year. $86.95. Misset Uitgeverij BV / Doetinchem, Postbus 4, 7000 BA Doetinchem Netherlands. **Tel** 011 31 8340 49911, 011 31 8340 49562, FAX 011 31 8340 43839, 011 31 8340 40515. **(Subscription address:** Misset Uitgeverij BV, Postbus 9000, 6800 DA Arnhem Netherlands. **Tel** 011 31 85 209830.**)**

ISSN 0964-7740
DD 338.476591340941
UK

SIGN INDUSTRY NEWS. [Sign ind. news]. (1991)-. Periodical. English. Eight times a year. $82.13. Argus Press Group, Queensway House, 2 Queensway Redhill, Surrey RH1 1QS United Kingdom. **Tel** 011 44 1737 768611, 011 44 1737 761685, FAX 011 44 1737 760510, telex 948669 TOPJNL G. **(Subscription address:** FMJ International Publications Ltd., Queensway House 2 Queensway, Redhill Surrey RH1 1QS United Kingdom. **Tel** 011 44 1737 768611, FAX 011 44 1737 773993, telex 948669 TOPJNL G.**) Bk Rev.** **Ad Acc, Adv Mgr:** Simon Law. **Circ:** 4000 (ctrl).
Desc: Providing analysis of this field of business. Includes product profiles, reviews of new equipment and software; reports on major sign exhibitions; and news and views from the industry.

ISSN 0049-0466
UK

SIGN WORLD. (1964)-. Trade Publication. English (French). Twelve times a year. $39.35. A E Morgan Publications Ltd, Stanley House, 9 West Street, Epsom Surrey KT18 7RL United Kingdom. **Tel** 011 44 1372 741411, FAX 011 44 1372 744493, telex 291561 VIA SOS G. **ED** Mike Connolly. **Bk Rev.** **Ad Acc.** **Circ:** 2,500. available with illustrations.
Desc: Articles on recent developments in the field of signs.

LC TT360.A4 S6
ISSN 0037-5063
US
CCC

SIGNS OF THE TIMES (CINCINNATI). (SIGNS OF THE TIMES; THE NATIONAL JOURNAL OF ADVERTISING DISPLAYS). (1906)-. Trade Publication. English. Twelve times a year (Buyer's Guide published in Nov.). $48.00. Signs of the Times Publishing Company, 407 Gilbert Avenue, Cincinnati OH 45202. **Tel** (513)421-2050, (800)925-1110, FAX (513)421-5144. **ED** Tod Swormstedt. Index available (bound in Jan. issue). **Bk Rev.** **Ad Acc.** **Circ:** 18,000. available on microfilm and microfiche from University Microfilms International (UMI).
Desc: The trade journal for the out-of-home, environmental graphics and sign industries.

US

SIMBA REPORT ON DIRECTORY PUBLISHING. See Publishing.

US

SOURCES: THE SECURITIES EXECUTIVE'S GUIDE TO PRODUCTS AND SERVICES. (19??)-. Directory. English. One time a year. $5.00 (per copy). Securities Industry Association, 120 Broadway/35th Floor, New York NY 10271. **Tel** (212)608-1500, FAX (212)608-1604. **Circ:** 15,000 (ctrl).
Desc: A comprehensive buyer's guide expressly designed to assist securities firm executives in their search for sources of products/services. Consists of listings and display ads covering over 70 different categories from accounting forms and clearing houses to training institutions and video production.

LC HF5805 .S63
ISSN 1057-6185
DD 659.1/029/473
US

... SOUTHEAST SOURCEBOOK, THE. [Southeast sourceb.]. (1992)-. English. $45.00. Black Book Marketing Group, 10 Astor Place, 6th Floor, New York NY 10003. **Tel** (212)539-9800, FAX (212)539-9801. **Continues** Florida Creative Directory, 1054-237X.

LC HF5826.5 .S68
ISSN 1071-4685
DD 659.1/025/7949
US

●**SOUTHERN CALIFORNIA MEDIA SOURCEBOOK.** (SOUTHERN CALIFORNIA ... MEDIA SOURCEBOOK.). [South. Calif. media sourceb.]. **Added/Corp** Standard Rate & Data Service. **VFOAT** Media Sourcebook. (1993)-. English. Irregular. SRDS / Standard Rate & Data Service, 3004 Glenview Road, Wilmette IL 60091. **Tel** (708)375-5049, (800)851-7737, FAX (708)375-5003. **(Subscription address:** Neodata / Colorado, PO Box 2606, Boulder CO 80322. **) Continues** MediaScope. Southern California Market & Media Planner, 1064-5772.

LC HF6182.U5 S66
ISSN 0361-3593
DD 338.7/61/659102576
US

SOUTHWEST DIRECTORY OF ADVERTISING AND PUBLIC RELATIONS AGENCIES. (1976)-. Directory. English. Houston Business Journal, One West Loop South, Suite 650, Houston TX 77027. **Tel** (713)688-8811, FAX (713)963-0482. **Continues** Southwest Directory of Ad & PR Agencies, 0360-1854.

LC TR690.4 .S66
SP

SPAFOTO. See Photography.

ISSN 0195-0495
US

SPECIALTY ADVERTISING BUSINESS. **Added/Corp** Specialty Advertising Association International. (19??)-. Periodical. English. Twelve times a year. $48.00. Specialty Advertising, 3125 Skyway Circle North, Irving TX 75038. **Tel** (214)580-0404, FAX (214)550-8331. **ED** Leonard J Strub. **Ad Acc.** **Circ:** 6,000.

NE

SPONSERING. (19??)-. Dutch. Ten times a year. Fl150.00. Sponsering Int Bv Tav Adf Abon, Postbut 75506, 1070 AM Amsterdam Netherlands. **Tel** 011 31 20 6645576.

LC GV716 .S645
ISSN 1064-573X
DD 338.4/7796
US
CEASED

SPORTS ADVANTAGE. [Sports advant.]. **Added/Corp** Standard Rate & Data Service. Vol. 1, No. 1 (1991)-(Fall 1993). Trade Publication. English. SRDS / Standard Rate & Data Service, 3004 Glenview Road, Wilmette IL 60091. **Tel** (708)375-5049, (800)851-7737, FAX (708)375-5003. **(Subscription address:** Neodata / Colorado, PO Box 2606, Boulder CO 80322. **)**
Desc: Source for sports marketing opportunities; current sports media rates and data; national, international, and regional sports marketing information.

LC HF5905 .S74
ISSN 0038-9560
DD 659.1/42/02573
US
TITLE CHANGE

SPOT RADIO RATES AND DATA. [Spot radio rates data]. **Added/Corp** Standard Rate & Data Service. Vol. 36-75, No. 9 (Oct. 1954-Sept. 1993). Periodical. English. SRDS / Standard Rate & Data Service, 3004 Glenview Road, Wilmette IL 60091. **Tel** (708)375-5049, (800)851-7737, FAX (708)375-5003. **ED** Otis Kirchhoefer. **Ad Acc.** **Circ:** 4,400 (ctrl). **Continues** Radio Rates and Data. **Continued by** Radio Advertising Source, 1071-4707.
Desc: Profiles 8,200 commercial US radio stations. Lists planning and buying information for advertising agencies: call letters, addresses, reps, programming, rates, etc. Arranged geographically.

LC HF5905 .S745
ISSN 0038-9552
DD 384.55/43
US
TITLE CHANGE

SPOT TELEVISION RATES AND DATA. [Spot televr. rates data]. **Added/Corp** Standard Rate & Data Service. Vol. 36 (Oct. 1954)-(1993). Periodical. English. SRDS / Standard Rate & Data Service, 3004 Glenview Road, Wilmette IL 60091. **Tel** (708)375-5049, (800)851-7737, FAX (708)375-5003. **ED** Otis Kirchhoefer. **Ad Acc.** **Circ:** 4,500. **Continues** Television Rates and Data. **Continued by** Spot TV & Cable Source, 1071-4596.
Desc: Contains individual profiles for 1,000 commercial TV stations, national/regional networks and statistics groups. Also includes state, county, city, metro area, ADI and DMA market data.

LC HF5905 .S745
ISSN 1071-4596
DD 384.55/43
US
TITLE CHANGE

SPOT TV & CABLE SOURCE. See Communications-Television and Cable.

ISSN 1047-0433
DD 338
US
CEASED

SRDS REPORT, THE. [SRDS rep.]. **Added/Corp** Standard Rate & Data Service. **VAT** Standard Rate and Data Service Report; Standard Rate & Data Service Report. (198?)-(September 1993). Periodical. English. SRDS / Standard Rate & Data Service, 3004 Glenview Road, Wilmette IL 60091. **Tel** (708)375-5049, (800)851-7737, FAX (708)375-5003.
Ind/Abst F&S Index Plus Text, Int. (Select. Cov.); Mark. Advert. Ref. Serv.; PROMT.

US

STANDARD DIRECTORY OF ADVERTISERS (BUSINESS CLASSIFICATIONS ED.). (STANDARD DIRECTORY OF ADVERTISERS.). (1916)-. Directory.

Business and Economics —Advertising and Public Relations

English. One time a year (with quarterly updates). $617.50. National Register Publishing Company Inc., PO Box 31, 121 Chanlon Road, New Providence NJ 07974. **Tel** (800)521-8110, (800)323-6772, FAX (908)665-6688. Index available. *Continues* McKittrick Directory of Advertisers.
 Desc: Information on over 26,000 companies that spend over $75,000 annually to advertise their products and services. Arranged by business classifications.

LC HF5805 .S7 **ISSN** 0081-4229
DD 659 US

STANDARD DIRECTORY OF ADVERTISERS (GEOGRAPHICAL ED.).
(STANDARD DIRECTORY OF ADVERTISERS.). [Stand. dir. advert.]. (1964)-. Directory. English. One time a year (with quarterly updates). $958.78. National Register Publishing Company Inc., PO Box 31, 121 Chanlon Road, New Providence NJ 07974. **Tel** (800)521-8110, (800)323-6772, FAX (908)665-6688. available on magnetic tape and CD-ROM. *Formed by the union of* Standard Advertising Register *and* McKittrick Directory of Advertisers. *Continued in part by* Standard Directory of Advertisers. Tradename Index (Wilmette, Ill. : 1992).
 Desc: Information on over 26,000 companies that spend over $75,000 annually to advertise their products and services. Arranged geographically.

LC HF5805 .S714
DD 659.1/025/73 US

STANDARD DIRECTORY OF ADVERTISERS. TRADENAME INDEX.
See Business and Economics-Abstracting, Bibliographies and Statistics.

 ISSN 0085-6614
DD 659 US
 CCC

STANDARD DIRECTORY OF ADVERTISING AGENCIES.
[Stand. dir. advert. agencies]. (1964)-. Directory. English. Two times a year (includes supplements). $510.85. National Register Publishing Company Inc., PO Box 31, 121 Chanlon Road, New Providence NJ 07974. **Tel** (800)521-8110, (800)323-6772, FAX (908)665-6688. available on magnetic tape and CD-ROM. *Formed by the union of* Agency List of the Standard Advertising Register *and* McKittrick Agency List.
 Desc: Covers full service agencies, public relations firms, services and suppliers. Includes over 9,000 agency profiles.

LC HF5804 .S73
 US

STANDARD DIRECTORY OF INTERNATIONAL ADVERTISERS & AGENCIES.
Added/Corp National Register Publishing Company (Wilmette, Ill.). (1992)-. Directory. English. One time a year. $404.20. National Register Publishing Company Inc., PO Box 31, 121 Chanlon Road, New Providence NJ 07974. **Tel** (800)521-8110, (800)323-6772, FAX (908)665-6688. available on magnetic tape and CD-ROM. *Continues* Macmillan Directory of International Advertisers and Agencies, 1056-0947.
 Desc: Covers the advertising industry in over 127 countries. More than 1,700 companies and 2,000 top agencies worldwide are organized in this directory.

 ISSN 1055-1026
DD 659 US

STARCH TESTED COPY.
[Starch tested copy]. **Added/Corp** Starch INRA Hooper (Firm). **VFOAT** Tested Copy. Vol. 1, No. 1 (Feb. 1989)-. Periodical. English. Twelve times a year. $250.00. Starch INRA Hooper, 566 East Boston Post Road, Mamaroneck NY 10543. **Tel** (914)698-0800, FAX (914)698-0485. **ED** Philip W. Sawyer. Index available. cum. index. **Circ:** 800.
 Desc: Displayed to demonstrate what works in print advertising and what does not and to offer principles of effective to advertising. This data is based on and uses real life samples.

 IT

STRATEGIA.
(199?)-. Trade Publication. Italian. Ten times a year. L96740. Maclean Hunter SRL / Italy, P le a Cantore 12, 20123 Milan Italy. **Tel** 011 39 2 89401365, 011 39 2 58188204, FAX 011 39 2 8378590. *Absorbed* Promozione.
 Desc: Covers Italian and international current events.

 ISSN 0180-6424
 FR

UDC 65

STRATEGIES PARIS.
VFOAT Strategies (Issy-les-Moulineaux). (1971)-. Trade Publication. French. Forty-Four times a year. $413.39. Groupe Strategies, 15 Bis rue Ernest Renan, 92133 Issy Moulineaux Cedex France. **Tel** 011 33 1 40930102.

LC HF5801 .S77
DD 659.1/0973/05 US

SUPERBRANDS.
VFOAT America's Top 2,000 Brands. (1990)-. English. Billboard Publications Inc., 1515 Broadway Billboard, New York NY 10036. **Tel** (212)764-7300, FAX (305)755-7048, telex WU TWX 710-581-6279.
 Ind/Abst Mark. Advert. Ref. Serv. [Full Txt.]; PROMT.

 ISSN 0899-1898
DD 659 US

SUPERMARKET ADVERTISING NEWSLETTER.
[Supermark. advert. newsl.]. (1980)-. Newsletter. English. Twelve times a year. $150.00. Supermarket Associates, 5901 Shamrock Road, Durham NC 27713. **Tel** (919)544-0950. **ED** Sheldon B. Sosna.

LC HF5801 .S8
 SW

SVENSKA MARKNADEN, KNOW HOW, DEN.
VFOAT Marknaden, Know How; Know How; DSM och Know How; Svenska Marknaden Med Know How; DSM Med Know How; DSM & Know How. (June 1991)-. Periodical. Swedish. Six times a year. Svenska Marknaden, PO Box 5150, 102 43 Stockholm Sweden. *Formed by the union of* Svenska Marknaden *and* Know How (Djursholm, Sweden).
 Ind/Abst Selec. Coop. Index Manage. Period.

 ISSN 0038-9579
 FR

UDC 659.1

TARIF MEDIA.
[Tarif media]. (1961)-. Periodical. French. Six times a year. $1115.48. Tarif Media, 5 rue la Boetie, 75008 Paris France. **Tel** 011 33 1 44563156. Index available (free).

 FR

TARIF MEDIA MEDICAL.
(19??)-. French. Irregular. 607.08F France; 720.00F other. Tarif Media, 5 rue la Boetie, 75008 Paris France. **Tel** 011 33 1 44563156.

LC HF6111 .T37
 MX

TARIFAS Y DATOS: MEDIOS IMPRESOS.
VFOAT Medios Impresos; Directorio MPM: Informacion y Tarifas de Medios Impresos. (19??)-. Spanish. Four times a year (February, May, August, November). $60,000 Mexico; $120.00 other. Medios Publicitarios Mexicanos, Av Mexico 99-303, Col. Hipodromo-Condesa, 06170 Mexico City DF Mexico. **Tel** 011 52 5 5742858, FAX 011 52 5 5742668. **ED** Fernando Villamil Avila. **Ad Acc. Circ:** 1,200 (ctrl). *Continues* Medicos Impresos.
 Desc: Rates and data of newspapers, consumer magazines, business publications, outdoor advertising.

 ISSN 0738-9612
 US
 TITLE CHANGE

TECHNIQUES FOR SUCCESS IN FUND-RAISING, MARKETING, AND PUBLIC RELATIONS FOR NONPROFIT ORGANIZATIONS.
VFOAT Techniques for Success. (1982)-(19??). Periodical. English. The National Copy Clinic Inc, PO Box 127, West Newton MA 02165. *Continued by* Direct Response Donor.

LC HE **ISSN** 1082-5908
DD 384 US

●**TELECOM ADVERTISING REPORT.** *See* Communications-Telecommunication.

LC HF **ISSN** 0736-167X
DD 658 US
 CCC

TELEMARKETING UPDATE.
[Telemark. update]. (198?)-. English. Twelve times a year. Update Publishing Co., PO Box 570122, Houston TX 77527. **Tel** (713)867-3438. **ED** A Doyle. available on microfiche.
 Desc: References on telemarketing. Contains excerpts from publications, bibliographies, etc.

LC HE8700.8 .T915 **ISSN** 1056-0963
DD 384.55/025/73 US

TELEVISION DATATRAK. *See*
Communications-Television and Cable.

LC T394 .T72 **ISSN** 0743-9709
DD 380.1/025/7 US

TRADE SHOW & CONVENTION GUIDE.
[Trade show conv. guide]. **VFOAT** Trade Show and Convention Guide; Tradeshow and Convention Guide; Tradeshow & Convention Guide. (19??)-. Trade Publication. English. One time a year (June). $95.00. Amusement Business, PO Box 24970, Nashville TN 37202. **Tel** (615)321-4250, FAX (615)327-1575. *Continues* Trade Show Convention Guide, 0278-6443.
 Desc: Sourcebook for those planning trade shows and conventions, corporate or association meetings and exhibits. Includes dates and data for conventions and trade shows for up to the next 5 years. Also lists hotels, auditoriums, convention centers and facilities servicing the industry. Data on locations, expected attendance, cost, size, number of booths, products displayed, contact names and addresses.

LC T394 .T723 **ISSN** 1046-4395
DD 381/.1 US

TRADE SHOWS WORLDWIDE.
[Trade shows worldw.]. **Added/Corp** Gale Research Inc. 4th Ed. (1989)-. Directory. English. One time a year. $220.00. Gale Research Inc., 835 Penobscot Building, 645 Griswold Street, Detroit MI 48226. **Tel** (800)877-GALE, (313)961-2242, FAX (313)961-6083, (800)414-5043, telex TWX 810-221-7086. **ED** Valerie Webster. available on magnetic tape; available on diskette. *Continues* Trade Shows and Professional Exhibits Directory, 0886-1439.
 Desc: Contains detailed entries for more than 6,300 scheduled exhibitions, trade shows, association conventions, and similar events.

LC T391 .T715 **ISSN** 0893-2662
DD 659.1/52 US

TRADESHOW & EXHIBIT MANAGER.
[Tradeshow exhib. manager]. **VFOAT** Tradeshow and Exhibit Manager; Trade Show and Exhibit Manager. Vol. 1, No. 1 (Feb. 1986)-. Trade Publication. English. Six times a year (includes annual Buyers Guide). $80.00. Goldstein and Associates, 1150 Yale Street, Suite 12, Santa Monica CA 90403. **Tel** (310)828-1309, FAX (310)829-1169. **ED** Les Plesko. Index available. **Bk Rev**. **Ad Acc. Circ:** 13,000 (ctrl).
 Desc: For corporate exhibit managers, association trade show and exposition managers and independent show producers. Covers issues, trends, products, services and facilities.

LC T391 .T72 **ISSN** 0145-5559
DD 659.1/52 US

TRADESHOW (LOS ANGELES, CALIF.).
(TRADESHOW ...). [Tradeshow]. **VFOAT** Annual Edition of the Tradeshow ...; Tradeshow Week ... . (19??)-. Trade Publication. English. One time a year. $15.00. Tradeshow Week Inc., 12233 West Olympic Boulevard, Suite 236, Los Angeles CA 90064. **Tel** (310)826-5696, FAX (310)826-2039.

 ISSN 0733-0170
 US

TRADESHOW WEEK.
[Tradeshow week]. (19??)-. Trade Publication. English. Forty-nine times a year. $319.00. R.R. Bowker, A Reed Reference Publishing Company, Part of Reed International PLC, PO Box 31, 121 Chanlon Drive, New Providence NJ 07974. **Tel** (908)464-6800, (800)521-8110, FAX (908)665-6688, telex 138-755. **ED** Darlene Gudea. **Ad Acc**.
 Desc: Features news on tradeshows, surveys of costs, statistical profiles, calendar of shows, etc.

LC NA6750.A2 A55
DD 725/.91/02573 US

TRADESHOW WEEK'S MAJOR EXHIBIT HALL DIRECTORY.
VFOAT Major Exhibit Hall Directory. (19??)-. Trade Publication. English. One time a year. $50.00. Tradeshow Week Inc., 12233 West Olympic Boulevard, Suite 236, Los Angeles CA 90064. **Tel** (310)826-5696, FAX (310)826-2039. **ED** Darlene Gudea. **Ad Acc.** ctrl circ. *Continues* Annual Major Exhibit Hall Directory, 0160-8630.
 Desc: Gives facts about every exhibit hall in the US and Canada with over 25,000 square feet of exhibit space. Statistics cover square footage, number of floors, size of meeting rooms, and more.

LC AS6 .T69
 US

TRADESHOW WEEK'S ... TRADESHOW SERVICES DIRECTORY.
(1988)-. Trade Publication. English. One time a year. $95.00. Tradeshow Week Inc., 12233 West Olympic Boulevard, Suite 236, Los Angeles CA 90064. **Tel** (310)826-5696, FAX (310)826-2039. **ED** Darlene Gudea. **Ad Acc.** ctrl circ. *Continues* Tradeshow Week's National Tradeshow Services Directory.
 Desc: A yellow pages directory of suppliers to the trade show industry. Indexed by industry category and city. Includes company name, address, phone and contact.

LC HF5438.8.M4 E94
DD 607/.34 US

... TRADESHOWS & EXHIBITS SCHEDULE, THE.
VFOAT Tradeshows and Exhibits Schedule. (198?)-. English. One time a year. $105.00. Successful Meetings, 633 Third Avenue, New York NY 10017. *Continues* Exhibits Schedule, 0531-5360.

LC HF5905 .S745 **ISSN** 1076-3988
DD 384.55/43 US

●**TV & CABLE SOURCE.** *See*
Communications-Television and Cable.

 GW

WERBUNG IN DEUTSCHLAND.
Added/Corp Zentralausschuss der Werbewirtschaft (Germany). (1989)-. German. Zentralausschus der Werbewirtschaft, Postfach 20 14 14, Villichgasse 17, D-5300 Bonn 2 Germany. *Continues* Werbung.

ISSN 0043-4558
DD 026 US

WHAT'S NEW IN ADVERTISING AND MARKETING. (WHAT'S NEW IN ADVERTISING AND MARKETING / PREPARED BY THE ADVERTISING AND MARKETING DIVISION, SPECIAL LIBRARIES ASSOCIATION.). [What's new advert. mark.]. **Added/Corp** Special Libraries Association. National Advertising Group. Special Libraries Association. Advertising and Marketing Division. (1946)-. Periodical. English. Ten times a year (Dec./Jan. and July/Aug. issues combined). $30.00. Advertising and Marketing Division Special Library, 627 North Sunrise Service Road, Bellport NY 11713. **Tel** (516)286-1600. **ED** Julie-Ann Zilavy. **Circ:** 650. ***Continues*** *What's New.*
Desc: Complete listing of books and materials in advertising and marketing.
Ind/Abst Public Aff. Inf. Serv. Bull.

LC HF5801
DD 659.1 US

•**WHAT'S WORKING IN P.R.** (1995)-. Newsletter. English. Twelve times a year. $189.00. Ragan Communications Inc., 212 West Superior Street, Suite 200, Chicago IL 60610. **Tel** (312)335-0037, (800)878-5331, FAX (312)335-9583. **ED** Mike Michaelson.

ISSN 1049-0116
US

WHOLESALE-BY-MAIL CATALOG, THE. [Wholes.-by-mail cat.]. **Added/Corp** Print Project. **VAT** Wholesale By Mail Catalog. (1991)-. Catalog. English. One time a year. $15.00. Harper Collins Publishers, Keystone Industrial Park, Scranton PA 18512. **Tel** (800)242-7737, (800)233-4727, FAX (800)822-4090.

LC HD59 **ISSN** 8755-2671
DD 659 US

WHO'S MAILING WHAT!. **VAT** Who Is Mailing What. (Oct. 1984)-. Newsletter. English. Ten times a year. $295.00. North American Publishing Company, 401 North Broad Street, Philadelphia PA 19108. **Tel** (215)238-5300, (800)777-8074, FAX (215)238-5283. **ED** Denison Hatch. Index available. **Bk Rev. Ad Acc. Circ:** 1500.
Desc: Newsletter on direct mail advertising. Subscribers can access the Direct Marketing Archive, a source of direct mail packages, with 8,000 mailings in 175 categories.

LC HF6178 .W48 **ISSN** 1049-1201
DD 659.1/092/2 [B] US

WHO'S WHO IN ADVERTISING (WILMETTE, ILL.). (WHO'S WHO IN ADVERTISING.). [Who's who advert.]. 1st Ed. (1990/1991)-. English. Irregular. $210.00. Marquis Who's Who Marquis Who's Who, A Reed Reference Publishing Company, Part of Reed International PLC, 121 Chanlon Road, A Reed Reference Publishing Company, Part of Reed International PLC, 121 Chanlon Road, New Providence New Providence NJ NJ 07974 07974. **Tel** (908)464-6800, (800)521-8110, (908)464-6800, (800)521-8110, FAX (908)665-6688, (908)665-6688, telex 138 755, 138 755.

LC Z6956.E5 W5 **ISSN** 0000-0213
UK
NLM Z 6956.E5 W733

WILLING'S PRESS GUIDE. [Willing's press guide]. 54th Ed. (1928)-. English. One time a year. $310.00 US; $330.00 Canada and Mexico; $350.00 other. Reed Information Services Ltd., Windsor Court, East Grinstead House, East Grinstead RH19 1BR United Kingdom. **Tel** 011 44 1342 326972, FAX 011 44 1342 335977, telex 95127 INFSER G. **(Subscription address:** Reed Reference Publishing Company / New Jersey, 131 Chanlon Road, PO Box 31, New Providence NJ 07974. **Tel** 800 223-1797, (908)464-6802.**)** ***Continues*** *Willing's Press Guide and Advertisers' Directory and Handbook.*
Desc: Details on the news and periodical industry.

ISSN 0934-585X
GW
UDC 659

WORKSHOP DARMSTADT. [Workshop Darmst.]. (1988)-. Periodical. German. Six times a year. $64.48. GIT Verlag GmbH, Roblerstrabe 90, Postfach 110564, D-64220 Darmstadt Germany. **Tel** 011 49 6151 80900, FAX 011 49 6151 809045.

ISSN 0950-4540
UK

WORLD ADVERTISING REVIEW. [World advert. rev.]. (1985)-. English. One time a year. £45.00 UK; $90.00 other. Holt Saunders Ltd, High Street, Foots Cray Sidcup, Kent DA14 5HP United Kingdom. **Tel** 011 44 181 3003322. **ED** P Kleinman. ***Continues*** *Modern Publicity.*
Desc: A selection of print advertisements from around the world, with a commentary by Philip Kleinman.

LC TX907 .W69
DD 647/.969 US

WORLD CONVENTION DATES. EVENT PLANNER'S GUIDE. **VFOAT** Event Planner's Guide. (19??)-. English. One time a year. World Convent Dates, 500 Summer Street, Stamford CT 06901-1384.

UK

•**WORLD DIRECTORY OF ADVERTISING AGENCIES.** (1993)-. Directory. English. $500.00. Euromonitor Publications Ltd., 60-61 Britton Street, London EC1M 5NA United Kingdom. **Tel** 011 44 171 2518024, FAX 011 44 171 6083149, telex 21120. **(Subscription address:** Gale Research Co., 835 Penobscot Building, Detroit MI 48226. **Tel** (800)347-4253.**)**
Desc: Contains full contact details and background information for more than 2,000 advertising agencies around the world with full company profiles for the top 10% in each country.

US

WORLDBOOK OF IABC. (19??)-. English. One time a year. $100.00. International Association of Business Communicators / IABC, One Hallidie Plaza, Suite 600, San Francisco CA 94102. **Tel** (415)433-3400, FAX (415)362-8762.
Desc: Directory of all IABC members, officers and award winners in the P.R. community.

BANKS AND BANKING

LC HG1501 **ISSN** 0885-4777
DD 332.1 US

100 HIGHEST YIELDS. **VFOAT** One Hundred Highest Yields. (1984)-. Periodical. English. One time a week (publihed Mondays). $124.00. Financial Rates Inc., 11811 US Highway 1, Suite 200, North Palm Beach FL 33408-8888. **Tel** (407)627-7330, FAX (407)627-7335. **(Subscription address:** Financial Rates Inc., PO Box 088888, North Palm Beach FL 33408. **Tel** (407)627-7330.**)** **ED** Hugo Ottolenghi.
Desc: Top yielding Federally insured banks and thrifts. Money-market accounts and CD's.

LC HG1501
DD 332.1 FR

200 PREMIERES BANQUES DU MONDE ARABE : A34. (19??)-. French. Irregular. 990.00F. IC Publications Ediafric, 10 rue Vineuse, 75116 Paris France. **Tel** 011 33 1 44308100.

LC HG2150 .A56
DD 332.3/2/0973021 US

1000 LARGEST SAVINGS & LOANS. **Added/Corp** Sheshunoff & Company. **VFOAT** 1000 Largest Savings and Loans; One Thousand Largest Savings and Loans. (19??)-. English. Two times a year. Sheshunoff Information Services Inc., PO Box 13203, Capitol Station, Austin TX 78711. **Tel** (800)456-2340, (512)472-2244.

LC HG2441 .O52 **ISSN** 0361-4727
DD 332.1/0973 US

1000 LARGEST U.S. BANKS. **Added/Corp** Sheshunoff & Company. **VAT** One Thousand Largest United States Banks. (19??)-. English. Sheshunoff Information Services Inc., PO Box 13203, Capitol Station, Austin TX 78711. **Tel** (800)456-2340, (512)472-2244.

LC HG **ISSN** 0883-0827
DD 332 US

AAEL NEWS BULLETIN. [AAEL news bull.]. **Added/Corp** American Association of Equipment Lessors. **VFOAT** AEL News Bulletin; AAEL. (198?)-. Bulletin. English. Ten times a year. $40.00. American Association of Equipment Lessors, 1300 North 17th Street, Suite 1010, Arlington VA 22209-3801. **Tel** (703)527-8655, FAX (703)527-8649.

LC KF967 .B36 **ISSN** 0887-0187
DD 346.73/082/05 347.3068205 US

ABA BANK COMPLIANCE. [ABA bank compliance]. **Added/Corp** American Bankers Association. **VAT** American Bankers Association Bank Compliance. (198?)-. Trade Publication. English. Sixteen times a year. $295.00. American Bankers Association, 1120 Connecticut Avenue Northwest, Washington DC 20036. **Tel** (202)663-5221, (202)663-5000, FAX (202)828-4544. **(Subscription address:** American Bankers Association / Maryland, PO Box 630544, Order Processing Department, Baltimore MD 21263. **)** Index available (Free). Documents available from UMI Article Clearinghouse. ***Continues*** *Bank Compliance, 0276-4253.*
Ind/Abst ABI/INFORM Glob. Ed.; ABI/INFORM [Computer File] (Fall 1984-); Account. Tax Datab. (Fall 1984-).

LC HG1501 **ISSN** 0889-7662
DD 332 US
TITLE CHANGE

ABA BANKERS WEEKLY. (ABA BANKERS WEEKLY : THE NEWSPAPER OF THE AMERICAN BANKERS ASSOCIATION.). [ABA bank. wkly.]. **Added/Corp** American Bankers Association. **VAT** American Bankers Association Bankers Weekly. Vol. 5, No. 35 (Sept. 2, 1986)-(1993). Periodical. English. American Bankers Association, 1120 Connecticut Avenue Northwest, Washington DC 20036. **Tel** (202)663-5221, (202)663-5000, FAX (202)828-4544. **ED** Laura Keefe. ***Continues*** *ABA Bankers News Weekly, 0746-3367.* ***Continued by*** *Bankers News, 1069-5907.*
Desc: Written by ABA's veteran reporters and experts on banking law.

LC HG1501 .B6 **ISSN** 0194-5947
DD 332.1/0973 US
CCC
CODEN ABAJD5

ABA BANKING JOURNAL. [ABA bank. j.]. **Main/Corp** American Bankers Association. **VFOAT** Banking Journal. **VAT** American Bankers Association Banking Journal. Vol. 71, No. 4 (April 1979)-. Periodical. English. Twelve times a year. $25.00. Simmons Boardman Publishing Corporation / New York, 345 Hudson Street, New York NY 10014. **Tel** (212)620-7200. **(Subscription address:** Simmons Boardman Publishing Corporation, PO Box 986, Omaha NE 68101. **Tel** (402)346-4740.**)** Index Available Published separately--free--upon request. available on microfilm and microfiche from University Microfilms International (UMI); available on an online database from NEXIS; and DIALOG. Documents available from UMI Article Clearinghouse, Ask*IEEE. ***Continues*** *Banking, 0005-5492.*
Desc: Covers a wide variety of subjects bearing on commercial bank and trust company activities - operations, automation, correspondent services, business conditions, investments, trust services, lending, legislation, marketing, protection, agriculture, and bank construction. Also news articles, Q and A interviews, case histories, and articles by authorities in several fields.
Ind/Abst ABI/INFORM Glob. Ed. (Aug. 1971-); ABI/INFORM Ondisc: Expr. Ed. (Aug. 1971-); ABI/INFORM [Computer File] (Aug. 1971-); Acad. Search; Account. Tax Datab. (Aug. 1971-) [Full Txt.]; Bus. ASAP (1990-) [Full Txt.]; Bus. Index (1985-); Bus. Period. Index; Bus. Source Plus; Bus. Source; Chicano Index; Curr. Cit.; EP Collect.; Fed. Tax Artic.; Gen. BusinessFile (1985-); Gen. Period. Index (1985-); Homework Help.; INFO-SOUTH Abstr.; INSPEC (April 1982-); Mag. Search; Mark. Advert. Ref. Serv.; MasterFile FullTEXT 1000; MasterFile FullTEXT 350; MasterFile FullTEXT 650; MasterFile FullTEXT (July 1993-); Middle East Abstr. Index; OCLC; PAIS Int. Print; Telebase; Trade Ind. ASAP [Full Txt.]; Trade Ind. Index (1981-) [Full Txt.]; UMI ABI/Inform--Bus. Period. Ondisc (Jan. 1987-) [Full Txt.]; Wilson Bus. Abstr.

LC HG1501 **ISSN** 0169-5363
DD 332.1 NE

ABN ECONOMIC REVIEW. [ABN econ. rev.]. **Added/Corp** Algemene Bank Nederland. Economic Research Dept. No. 95 (Feb. 1983)-. Periodical. English. Six times a year. Free. Algemene Bank Nederland NV, PO Box 669, Econ Res Dept 2D 40, 1000 EG Amsterdam Netherlands. **Tel** 011 31 20 299111. available on an online database from BRS. ***Continues*** *Economic Review (Amsterdam, Netherlands).*
Ind/Abst PAIS Int. Print.

LC HG1501
DD 332.1 US

ACTIONS OF THE BOARD, APPLICATIONS AND REPORTS RECEIVED DURING THE WEEK ENDING ... : ANNOUNCEMENT. **Main/Corp** Board of Governors of the Federal Reserve System (U.S.). (1977)-. Periodical. English. One time a week (Fri.). $55.00. Board of Governors of the Federal Reserve System, Mail Stop 127, Washington DC 20551. **Tel** (202)452-3244, (202)452-3245. ***Continues*** *Board of Governors of the Federal Reserve System (U.S.). Applications and Report Received or Acted on and All Other Actions of the Board, 0364-5428.*

LC HG1501 **ISSN** 0319-5112
DD 332.1/2/0971 CN

ACTIVITES : LES BANQUES A CHARTE DU CANADA. **VFOAT** Banques a Charte du Canada. **VAT** Association des Banquiers Canadiens. Activites. First issue in 1970?. French. One time a year. Institut Des Banquiers Canadiens, 1801 Av. Du College McGill, Bureau 720, Montreal Quebec H3A 2N4 Canada.

LC HF1410 .B3 **ISSN** 0183-5017
DD 382/.3/05 FR
SUSPENDED

ACTUALITES (PARIS). (ACTUALITES.). [Actualites]. **Added/Corp** Banque Francaise du Commerce Exterieur. Departement des Etudes Economiques et de Developpement, Relations Exterieures. (1977)-Suspended (19??). French. Ten times a year. 700.00F France; 850.00F other. Banque Francaise Commerce Ext, 21 boulevard Haussmann, 75427 Paris Cedex 09 France. **Tel** 011 33 42852485.

Index available. **Bk Rev. Circ:** 3,000 (ctrl). ***Continues*** *Actualites du Commerce Exterieur.*
Desc: Economic and banking review presenting regulations of international transactions, financial and economic figures and comments about other countries.
Ind/Abst GeoRef.

LC HG1501 **ISSN** 0015-6209
DD 332.1 PH
ADB BUSINESS OPPORTUNITIES : PROPOSED PROJECTS, PROCUREMENT NOTICES AND CONTRACT AWARDS. (1990)-. English. Twelve times a year. $100.00. Asian Development Bank / Information Office, PO Box 789, 1099 Manila Philippines. **Tel** 011 63 2 8344444, 011 63 2 7113851, FAX 011 63 2 7417961, 011 63 2 6326816, telex 63587 ADB PN ETPI, 42205 ADB PM ITT, 29066 ADB PH RCA. ***Continues*** *Proposed Projects, Procurement Notices and Contracts Awarded.*

LC HG4517 .A83 **ISSN** 0115-074X
DD 332.1/53 PH
TITLE CHANGE
ADB QUARTERLY REVIEW. [ADB q. rev.]. **Main/Corp** Asian Development Bank. **Added/Corp** Asian Development Bank. Quarterly Review. **VAT** Asian Development Bank Quarterly Review. (Jan. 1976)-(May 1994). Periodical. English (French, German and Japanese). Asian Development Bank / Information Office, PO Box 789, 1099 Manila Philippines. **Tel** 011 63 2 8344444, 011 63 2 7113851, FAX 011 63 2 7417961, 011 63 2 6326816, telex 63587 ADB PN ETPI, 42205 ADB PM ITT, 29066 ADB PH RCA. **Bk Rev. Circ:** 10,000 (ctrl). ***Continues*** *Asian Development Bank. ABD Quarterly Newsletter.* ***Continued by*** *Asian Development Bank. ADB Review.*
Desc: Contains reviews of all approved loans during each quarter and other bank activities, such as annual meetings, new publications, seminars, etc.
Ind/Abst AESIS Q.; Index Philip. Period.; Leis., Rec., Tour. Abstr.; Rural Dev. Abstr.; World Agric. Econ. Rural Sociol. Abstr.

LC HG4517 .A83 HG3318 .A83
DD 332 PH
●**ADB REVIEW. Main/Corp** Asian Development Bank. **VFOAT** Asian Development Bank Review. (July/Aug. 1994)-. Periodical. English. Six times a year. Free on request. Asian Development Bank / Information Office, PO Box 789, 1099 Manila Philippines. **Tel** 011 63 2 8344444, 011 63 2 7113851, FAX 011 63 2 7417961, 011 63 2 6326816, telex 63587 ADB PN ETPI, 42205 ADB PM ITT, 29066 ADB PH RCA. **Bk Rev. Circ:** 10,000 (ctrl). ***Continues*** *Asian Development Bank. ADB Quarterly Review.*
Desc: Contains reviews of all approved loans during each quarter and other bank activities, such as annual meetings, new publications, seminars, etc.
Ind/Abst AESIS Q.; Index Philip. Period.; Leis., Rec., Tour. Abstr.; Rural Dev. Abstr.; World Agric. Econ. Rural Sociol. Abstr.

LC HG3691 **ISSN** 0226-5575
DD 332.7/06/0714281 CN
ADC DU CREDIT. (L'A D C DU CREDIT.). [ADC credit]. **Main/Corp** Association des Directeurs de Credit de Montreal. **VFOAT** Bulletin d'Information Destine aux Directeurs de Credit. **VAT** Association des Directeurs de Credit du Credit. Vol. 1 (Jan. 1980)-. Bulletin. French. Association des Directeurs de Credit de Montreal, 4875 East boulevard Metropolitain, Montreal Quebec H1R 3J2 Canada.

LC HF5559.U5 A6 **ISSN** 0148-5350
DD 332.7 US
ADCA, AMERICAN DIRECTORY OF COLLECTION AGENCIES AND ATTORNEYS. VFOAT American Directory of Collection Agencies and Attorneys. (1918)-. English. One time a year (Jan.). $30.95. Service Publishing Company, Park Lane Building, 2025 I Street Northwest, Washington DC 20006. **Tel** (202)872-0082. **Ad Acc.** ctrl circ. ***Continues*** *ADCA, American Directory of Collection Agencies, 0360-3806.*
Desc: A directory of firms and individuals throughout the United States, Canada and some European countries whose profession or business is to collect delinquent accounts.

LC HG4001 .A38
DD 658.1/5/05 US
ADVANCES IN FINANCIAL PLANNING AND FORECASTING. VFOAT Financial Planning and Forecasting. Vol. 1 (1985)-. Periodical. English. One time a year. $157.50. JAI Press Inc., 55 Old Post Road, Suite 2, PO Box 1678, Greenwich CT 06836-1678. **Tel** (203)661-7602, FAX (203)661-0792. **ED** Cheng-Few Lee.
Desc: Theoretical and empirical research in financial analysis, planning and forecasting.

LC HG6001 .A35 **ISSN** 1048-1559
DD 332.64/5/05 US
CCC
ADVANCES IN FUTURES AND OPTIONS RESEARCH. [Adv. futures options res.]. Vol. 1 (1986)-. English. $73.25. JAI Press Inc., 55 Old Post Road, Suite 2, PO Box 1678, Greenwich CT 06836-1678. **Tel** (203)661-7602, FAX (203)661-0792. **ED** Don Chance and Robert Trippi.

LC HG **ISSN** 1076-464X
DD 332 US
AFCPE NEWSLETTER. [AFCPE newsl.]. **Added/Corp** Association for Financial Counseling and Planning Education (U.S.). **VFOAT** Newsletter; AFCPE; Association for Financial Counseling and Planning Education Newsletter. (Jan. 1984)-. Newsletter. English. Irregular. $60.00 Comes with Association for Financial Counseling and Planning Education. Association Finance Counsel Planning Education, 1787 Neil Avenue, Columbus OH 43210. **Tel** (614)292-3741, FAX (614)292-7536.
Desc: Guide to resources, publications and trends in the field.

LC HG1501
DD 332.1 IT
AFFARI E FINANZA. (19??)-. Italian. One time a week. L130000 Africa; L144000 Western Hemisphere and Asia; L79000 Europe; L194000 other. La Repubblica Editoriale Spa, Piazza Indipendenza 11 B, 00185 Rome Italy. **Tel** 011 39 6 49823247.

LC HC800.A1 A355 **ISSN** 1017-6772
DD 338.96/005 IV
AFRICAN DEVELOPMENT REVIEW. Added/Corp African Development Bank. **VFOAT** Revue Africaine de Developpement. Vol. 1, No. 1 (June 1989)-. Periodical. English (French). Two times a year. $20.00. African Development Bank, BP 1387, Abidjan 01 Ivory Coast. **Tel** 011 255 320711.
Ind/Abst Geogr. Abstr. Human Geogr.; Int. Dev. Abstr.; LABORDOC; World Agric. Econ. Rural Sociol. Abstr.

LC HG1501 **ISSN** 0755-1940
DD 332.1 FR
UDC 33
AGENCE ECONOMIQUE ET FINANCIERE. [Agence econ. financ.]. **VFOAT** AGEFI. (1911)-. Newspaper. French. Irregular. 1150.00F. Societe de l'AGEFI, 5 7 rue Saint Augustin, 75002 Paris Cedex 02 France. **Tel** 011 33 1 42861200.
Ind/Abst F&S Index Plus Text, Int. [Select. Cov.]; PROMT.

LC HG1501
DD 332.1 IT
AGEVOLAZIONI FINANZIARIE TESTO UNICO. (19??)-. Italian. Two times a year. IPSOA Editore SRL, Casella Postale 12055, Mastrangelo, 20120 Milan Italy. **Tel** 011 39 2 82476248.

LC HG **ISSN** 0749-9035
DD 332 US
AGGREGATE RESERVES OF DEPOSITORY INSTITUTIONS AND MONETARY BASE. [Aggreg. reserves depos. inst. monet. base]. **Added/Corp** Board of Governors of the Federal Reserve System (U.S.). (19??)-. Periodical. English. Fifty-two times a year. Free on request. Board of Governors of the Federal Reserve System, Mail Stop 127, Washington DC 20551. **Tel** (202)452-3244, (202)452-3245.

LC HG2051.U5 A5968 **ISSN** 0002-1164
DD 332.7/1/097305 US
AGRI FINANCE. [Agri finance]. Vol. 10, No. 5 (Sept./Oct. 1968)-. Trade Publication. English. Nine times a year. $45.00. Century Communications Inc., 6201 Howard Street, Niles IL 60714-3435. **Tel** (708)647-1200, FAX (708)647-7055. **ED** David Pelzer. **Bk Rev. Ad Acc. Circ:** 22,000 (ctrl). available on microfilm from University Microfilms International (UMI). ***Continues*** *Agricultural Banking and Finance.*
Desc: Written for agricultural bankers and farm managers.

LC HG1501 **ISSN** 0737-948X
DD 332.1 US
AGRICULTURAL CREDIT CONDITIONS SURVEY. See Agriculture-Agricultural Economics.

LC HG1501
DD 332.1 PK
AGRICULTURAL CREDIT INDICATORS. See Agriculture-Agricultural Economics.

LC HG2051.U5 A13 **ISSN** 0091-3502
DD 332.7/1/0973 US
AGRICULTURAL FINANCE STATISTICS. See Business and Economics-Abstracting, Bibliographies and Statistics.

LC HE9782 .A37 **ISSN** 0143-2257
DD 387.7/1 UK
AIRFINANCE JOURNAL. See Aeronautics, Astronautics.

LC HG3387.A8 B362
DD 332.1/1/09624 SJ
AL-TAQRIR AL-SANAWI - BANK AL-NILAYN. Main/Corp Bank Al-Nilayn. **Added/Corp** Bank Al-Nilayn. Annual Report. **VFOAT** Annual Report - El Nilein Bank. (1975)-. Multiple languages (Arabic and English). Bank Al-Nilayn, PO Box 466, Al-Khartum Sudan. ***Continues*** *Bank Al-Nilayn. Annual Report - El Nilein Bank.*

LC HG3266.A7 U53A
DD 354/.53/500822 TS
AL-TAQRIR AL-SANAWI - MAJLIS AL-NAQD. Main/Corp United Arab Emirates. Majlis Al-Naqd. **VFOAT** Annual Report - Currency Board. 1974-. Arabic (English). PO Box 854, Abuzaby Trucial States.

LC HG187.A65 A72B
DD 332 TS
AL-TAQRIR AL-SANAWI WA-AL-BAYANT AL-HISABIYAH AL-KHITAMIY AH LIL-SANAH AL-MUNTAHIYAH FI ... . Main/Corp Arab Monetary Fund. **VFOAT** Taqrir Al-Sanawi. Arabic (English). One time a year. Free. Sunduq Al-Naqd Al-Arabi, Arab Monetary Fund, S B 2818 Abu Zaby, PO Box ABU Dhabi 2818, Dawlat Al-Imarat Al-Arabiyah Al-Muttahidah Egypt. **Tel** 971(2)21500, FAX 332089, telex 22989 AMEEM. **Circ:** 2,000. ***Continues*** *Arab Monetary Fund. Annual Report. Arabic. Taqrir Al-Sanawi.*

ISSN 1079-1191
DD 658 US
●**ALLIANCE ANALYST, THE.** (THE ALLIANCE ANALYST : FORTNIGHTLY REPORT TO SENIOR EXECUTIVES AND ALLIANCE MANAGERS.). [Alliance anal.]. **Added/Corp** Strategic Alliance Group (Philadelphia, Pa.). (Sept. 16, 1994)-. Periodical. English. Twenty-four times a year. $590.00. Strategic Alliance Group, 415 South Van Pelt Street, Suite B 3, Philadelphia PA 19146. **Tel** (215)546-2441.

LC HG1501
DD 332.1 US
AMERICAN BANK DIRECTORY. SINGLE STATE EDITION. (19??)-. English. One time a year (Spring or Fall). $26.00. Thomson Financial Publishing, PO Box 65, 4709 West Golf Road, Skokie IL 60076-0065. **Tel** (800)321-3373, (708)933-8031. ***Absorbed*** *American Bank Directory.*

LC HG1501
DD 332.1 US
AMERICAN BANK DIRECTORY. US EDITION. (19??)-. English. Two times a year (June & Dec.). Price varies. Thomson Financial Publishing, PO Box 65, 4709 West Golf Road, Skokie IL 60076-0065. **Tel** (800)321-3373, (708)933-8031. ***Absorbed*** *American Bank Directory.*

LC HG1501
DD 332.1 US
AMERICAN BANKER. VFOAT Banking Week for Financial Services Executives. (19??)-. Periodical. English. One time a week. $495.00 (non-subscribers), $170.00 (subscribers) US; $585.00 (non-subscribers), $297.00 (subscribers) other. American Banker, Concourse Level, 1 State Street Plaza, New York NY 10004. **Tel** (212)803-8200, (800)221-1809, FAX (212)943-6256, (212)843-9598. ***Continues*** *Banking Week.*

LC HG1501 .A5 **ISSN** 0002-7561
DD 332 US
CCC
AMERICAN BANKER. [Am. bank.]. Vol. 52 (Jan. 29, 1887)-. Periodical. English. Five times a week (Mon.-Fri.). $750.00. American Banker, Concourse Level, 1 State Street Plaza, New York NY 10004. **Tel** (212)803-8200, (800)221-1809, FAX (212)943-6256, (212)843-9598. **ED** Fred Bleakley. **Bk Rev. Ad Acc. Circ:** 24,000. available on microfilm and microfiche from University Microfilms International (UMI); available on an online database from NEXIS; NEWSNET; Mead Data Central; DATA-STAR; BRS; and DIALOG. Documents available from UMI Article Clearinghouse. ***Continues*** *Thompson's Bank Note and Commercial Reporter.*
Desc: Reports on all levels and in all areas of banking and financial services. Provides coverage on: investment products and services, including mutual funds, commercial banking, community banking, operation and technology, mortgage companies, mergers and acquisitions, and regulations.
Ind/Abst Acad. Search; Account. Tax Datab. (Jan. 1989-); Bus. Index (1985-); Bus. Source Plus; Bus. Source; EP Collect.; F&S Index Plus Text, Int. [Select. Cov.]; Gen. BusinessFile (1985-); Gen. Period. Index (1985-); Homework Help.; INFO-SOUTH Abstr.; Infobank (Jan. 1969-); Mag. Search; MasterFile FullTEXT 1000; MasterFile FullTEXT 350; MasterFile FullTEXT 650; MasterFile FullTEXT (July 1993-); Newsp. Abstr.; OCLC; PROMT; Stat. Ref. Index; Telebase; Trade Ind. ASAP [Full Txt.]; Trade Ind. Index (1981-) [Full Txt.].

LC HG1616.C87 C66 **ISSN** 1055-1077
DD 332.1/0973/05 US
AMERICAN BANKER. CONSUMER SURVEY. [Am. bank., Consum. surv.]. **VFOAT** Consumer Survey; American Banker Consumer Survey. (1990)-. English. $57.50. American Banker, Concourse Level, 1 State Street Plaza, New York NY 10004. **Tel** (212)803-8200, (800)221-1809, FAX (212)943-6256,

Business and Economics —Banks and Banking

(212)843-9598. **Continues** Voice of the ... Consumer, 1044-1778.
Ind/Abst PROMT.

LC HG4050 .C67   ISSN 1043-724X
DD 658.1/5/0973   US
     CEASED
AMERICAN BANKER CORPORATE SURVEY. [Am. bank. corp. surv.]. **VFOAT** Corporate Survey; Corporate America Survey. (1988)-(19??). English. American Banker, Concourse Level, 1 State Street Plaza, New York NY 10004. **Tel** (212)803-8200, (800)221-1809, FAX (212)943-6256, (212)843-9598.
Ind/Abst PROMT.

LC HG1501.A52 B44A   ISSN 0893-2468
DD 332.1/0973/05   US
AMERICAN BANKER INDEX (ANN ARBOR, MICH.). See Business and Economics-Abstracting, Bibliographies and Statistics.

LC HG   ISSN 1076-3082
DD 332   US
     CCC
●**AMERICAN BANKER'S BANK MUTUAL FUND REPORT.** [Am. Bank. bank mutual fund rep.]. **Added/Corp** American Banker, Inc. **VFOAT** Bank Mutual Fund Report. (Jan. 1994)-. Newsletter. English. Fifty-two times a year. $795.00. American Banker, Concourse Level, 1 State Street Plaza, New York NY 10004. **Tel** (212)803-8200, (800)221-1809, FAX (212)943-6256, (212)843-9598. **(Subscription address:** American Banker / Newletter Division, PO Box 28315, Washington DC 20038. **Tel** (800)733-4371, (202)347-2665.**)** **ED** John Jedlicka. **Ad Acc.**
Desc: Provides information on products and people of the banking industry.

LC HG1501
DD 332.1   US
AMERICAN BANKER'S WASHINGTON WATCH. (19??)-. Newsletter. English. Irregular (48 issues). $625.00. American Banker, Concourse Level, 1 State Street Plaza, New York NY 10004. **Tel** (212)803-8200, (800)221-1809, FAX (212)943-6256, (212)843-9598. **(Subscription address:** American Banker / Newletter Division, PO Box 28315, Washington DC 20038. **Tel** (800)733-4371, (202)347-2665.**)** **ED** Miles Maguire. **Ad Acc.** available on an online database from NEWSNET; Mead Data Central; and DIALOG.
Continues FDIC Watch.

LC HG1501   ISSN 0743-2348
DD 332.1   US
AMERICAN BUSINESS REVIEW. See Business and Economics-Management.

LC HG2441 .A58   ISSN 1047-9759
DD 332.1/025/73   US
AMERICAN FINANCIAL DIRECTORY. (MCFADDEN AMERICAN FINANCIAL DIRECTORY.). [McFadden Am. financ. dir.]. **Added/Corp** McFadden Business Publications. **VFOAT** American Financial Directory. (198?)-. English. Two times a year. $375.00. Thomson Financial Publishing, PO Box 65, 4709 West Golf Road, Skokie IL 60076-0065. **Tel** (800)321-3373, (708)933-8031. available on diskette; available on magnetic tape. **Continues** American Financial Institutions Directory.
Desc: For all US financial institutions, banks, S&L's, credit unions and non-banks.

LC HG2150 .A66
DD 332.3/2/02573   US
AMERICAN SAVINGS DIRECTORY.
Added/Corp McFadden Business Publications. (1982)-. Directory. English. One time a year. $165.58. McFadden Business Publications / Norcross, GA, 6195 Crooked Creek Road, Norcross GA 30092. **Tel** (404)448-1011, (800)247-7376, FAX (404)446-6421.

LC HG2150 .S285   ISSN 1082-7919
DD 332   US
●**AMERICA'S COMMUNITY BANKER.** [Am. community bank.]. **Added/Corp** America's Community Bankers. **VFOAT** Community Banker. Vol. 4, No. 4 (Apr. 1995)-. Periodical. English. Twelve times a year. Savings and Community Bankers of America, 1101 15th Street Northwest, Suite 400, Washington DC 20005. **Tel** (202)857-3100, FAX (202)659-4816. **Continues** Savings & Community Banker, 1067-1757.

     ISSN 1062-8118
DD 380   US
     TITLE CHANGE
AMERICAS TRADE & FINANCE. [Am. trade finance]. **Added/Corp** Latin American Information Services, Inc. **VFOAT** Americas Trade and Finance. (April 1992)-(1995). Corporate Report. English. Latin American Information Services Inc., 159 West 53rd Street, Suite 28B, New York NY 10019-6050. **Tel** (212)765-5520, FAX (212)765-2927. **ED** Rosemary Werrett. cum. index. available on an online database from Mead Data Central. **Continued by** Lagniappe Monthly on Latin American Projects and Finance.
Desc: Tracks new business developments arising in Latin America as a result of sub-regional trade liberation and market integration. Focuses on government policy

measures, cross border deals among companies and banks, industry developments and innovations in trade and project finance.

LC HG1501
DD 332.1   IT
AMMINISTRAZIONE & FINANZA. (19??)-. Periodical. Italian. Twenty-six times a year. L285000 Italy; L570000 other. IPSOA Editore SRL, Casella Postale 12055, Mastrangelo, 20120 Milan Italy. **Tel** 011 39 2 82476248.

LC HG1501   ISSN 1121-2438
DD 332.1   IT
UDC 650
AMMINISTRAZIONE & FINANZA ORO.
[Ammin. finanza oro]. **VFOAT** Amministrazione e Finanza Oro. (1990)-. Periodical. Italian. Twenty-six times a year. L204280. IPSOA Editore SRL, Casella Postale 12055, Mastrangelo, 20120 Milan Italy. **Tel** 011 39 2 82476248. Index available (Included).

LC HG1501
DD 332.1   IT
ANALISI FINANZIARIA. (19??)-. Italian. Four times a year. L90000. Editrice IFAF, Largo Schuster 1, 20122 Milan Italy. **Tel** 011 39 2 72002170.

LC HG1501   ISSN 0153-9841
DD 332.1   FR
UDC 658.15
ANALYSE FINANCIERE. [Anal. financ.]. (1969)-. Periodical. French. Four times a year. Soc Francaise des Analystes Financieres, 11 rue St. Augustin, 75002 Paris France. **Tel** 011 33 1 42619079.
Ind/Abst Selec. Coop. Index Manage. Period.

LC HG1501   ISSN 1167-5128
DD 332.1   FR
UDC 336.71(44)
ANALYSES COMPARATIVES - COMMISSION BANCAIRE PARIS.
(ANALYSES COMPARATIVES.). [Anal. comp. -Comm. banc. Paris]. **VFOAT** Resultats des Etablissements de Credit (Paris. 1992); Activite des Etablissements de Credit (Paris). (1992)-. Periodical. French. Two times a year. $43.74. Commission Bancaire Secretary Generale, 4 rue Des Colonnes, F 75002 Paris France. **Tel** 011 33 1 42925931, FAX 011 33 1 42925940. **Continues** Resultats des Etablissements de Credit, 1155-4029.

LC HG1501
DD 332.1   US
ANALYSIS AND SUMMARY OF CONDITION AND PERFORMANCE OF THE FARM CREDIT BANKS AND ASSOCIATIONS. See Agriculture-Agricultural Economics.

LC HG1501   ISSN 0172-7419
DD 332.1   GW
UDC 336.76   CCC
ANLAGEPRAXIS. [Anlagepraxis]. (1979)-. Trade Publication. German. Six times a year. $152.00. Gabler Verlag, Postfach 1546, D-65005 Wiesbaden Germany. **Tel** 011 49 611 534129, FAX 011 49 611 534430.
Continues Bankwirtschaftliche Wertpapierpraxis + Vermogensberatung, 0342-5738.

LC WMLC L 83/3598   ISSN 0081-2528
DD 332.1   SA
ANNUAL ECONOMIC REPORT / SOUTH AFRICAN RESERVE BANK. (19??)-. Corporate Report. English. One time a year. South African Reserve Bank, PO Box 7433, Pretoria 0001 South Africa. **Tel** 011 27 12 3133675, FAX 011 27 12 3134013.
Ind/Abst F&S Index Plus Text, Int. [Select. Cov.].

LC HG3308.B85 B36a
DD 332.1/1/09598   IO
ANNUAL REPORT. Main/Corp Bank Bumi Daya (Indonesia). **VFOAT** Laporan Tahunan Bank Bumi Daya. (19??)-. Periodical. English. One time a year. Bank Bumi Daya, Jalan Imam Bonjol No. 61, PO Box No. 1106, Jakarta 10011 Indonesia. **Tel** 021 2300300, FAX 021 2301848, 2301852, telex 61277, 61400, 61355, 61876, 61896, BDPST IA. available with charts.
Desc: Provides financial and operational highlights from the previous year and also provides projections for the upcoming year. Information on the organization and management of Bank Bumi Daya.

LC HG3269.A7 B36a
DD 330.953/67/005   KU
ANNUAL REPORT. Main/Corp Bank Al-Kuwayt Al-Watani. (19??)-. English. One time a year. National Bank of Kuwait, Abdullah Al Salem Street, PO Box 95, Safat Kuwait.

LC HG3729.M28 I53a
DD 332.2   MW
ANNUAL REPORT AND ACCOUNTS / INDEFUND LIMITED. Main/Corp Indefund Limited. (1982)-. English. One time a year. Indefund Ltd, PO Box 2339, Blantyre Malawi.

LC HG3729.K42 I5a   ISSN 0304-6486
DD 332.1   KE
ANNUAL REPORT AND ACCOUNTS - INDUSTRIAL DEVELOPMENT BANK LIMITED. Main/Corp Industrial Development Bank Limited. (19??)-. English. Industrial Development Bank, Bima House, PO Box 44036, Nairobi Kenya.

LC HG3729.I4 M9   ISSN 0304-6710
DD 354.54/8700825/06   II
ANNUAL REPORT AND ACCOUNTS - KARNATAKA STATE FINANCIAL CORPORATION. Main/Corp Karnataka State Financial Corporation. 15th- 1973/74-. English. Karnataka State Financial Corporation, 1/1 Second Main Road, Malleswaram Bangalore 560-003 India. **Continues** Mysore State Financial Corporations. Annual Report and Accounts.

LC HG3450.S94 .B363A
DD 332.1/23/09944   AT
ANNUAL REPORT AND NOTICE OF ORDINARY GENERAL MEETING / BANK OF NEW SOUTH WALES. Main/Corp Bank of New South Wales. 1981-. English. One time a year. Bank of New South Wales Annual, GPO Box 1, Sydney New South Wales 2001 Australia. **Continues** Bank of New South Wales. Annual Report.

LC HG1501
DD 332.1   SO
ANNUAL REPORT AND STATEMENT OF ACCOUNTS. Main/Corp Banca Nazionale Somala. (1969)-. English. Somali National Bank, Mogadiscio Somalia. **Continues** Banca Nazionale Somala. Relazione e Bilancio. Report and Balance Sheet.

LC HG746 .M65a
DD 354/.729/600822   BF
ANNUAL REPORT AND STATEMENT OF ACCOUNTS. Main/Corp Bahamas. Monetary Authority. (19??)-. Statistical Publication. English. One time a year. Free. Central Bank of the Bahamas, PO Box N-4868, Nassau Bahamas. **Tel** 809-322- 2193, FAX (809)322-4321, telex 20115. Index available. cum. index. **Circ:** 1,200.
Desc: Analysis of domestic, monetary and fiscal trends covering the past twelve months. Additionally, audited accounts of the Central Bank of the Bahamas and an overview of internal operations during the previous year are included.

LC HG3090.5.A7 C45a
DD 330.945/85/005   MM
ANNUAL REPORT AND STATEMENT OF ACCOUNTS - CENTRAL BANK OF MALTA. Main/Corp Central Bank of Malta. (1968)-. English. One time a year. Free on request. Central Bank of Malta, Castille Place, Valletta Malta. **Tel** 011 356 247480. **Circ:** 1,600 (ctrl).

LC HG1501
DD 332.1   DQ
ANNUAL REPORT AND STATEMENT OF ACCOUNTS FOR THE YEAR ENDED 30TH JUNE ... / NATIONAL COMMERCIAL BANK OF DOMINICA.
Main/Corp National Commercial Bank of Dominica. (1982)-. English. **Continues in part** National Commercial and Development Bank of Dominica. Annual Report and Statement of Accounts for the Year Ended 30th June ... .

LC HG187.A65 A72a
DD 332   TS
ANNUAL REPORT / ARAB MONETARY FUND. Main/Corp Arab Monetary Fund. (1992)-. English. One time a year. Free on request. Arab Monetary Fund, PO Box 2818, Abu Dhabi United Arab Emirates. **Tel** 971(2)215000, telex 2989 AMF EM. **Continues** Arab Monetary Fund. Annual Report and Financial Statements for the Year Ended ... .

LC HG4517 .A8   ISSN 0066-8370
DD 332.1/53/095   PH
ANNUAL REPORT - ASIAN DEVELOPMENT BANK. (ANNUAL REPORT FOR ... / ASIAN DEVELOPMENT BANK.). **Main/Corp** Asian Development Bank. **VFOAT** Annual Report. (1966/67)-. English. One time a year. Free on request. Asian Development Bank / Information Office, PO Box 789, 1099 Manila Philippines. **Tel** 011 63 2 8344444, 011 63 2 7113581, FAX 011 63 2 7417961, 011 63 2 6326816, telex 63587 ADB PN ETPI, 42205 ADB PM ITT, 29066 ADB PH RCA. **ED** Ian Gill. **Circ:** 15,000 (ctrl).
Desc: Publishes accounts of the bank's principal activities during the year.
Ind/Abst AESIS Q.

Business and Economics — Banks and Banking

LC HG2799.B33 B332A
DD 332.2   BF
ANNUAL REPORT ... / BAHAMAS DEVELOPMENT BANK. Main/Corp Bahamas Development Bank. 1979-. English. One time a year. Bahamas Development Bank, Bay Street at Rawson Square, PO Box N-3034, Nassau Bahamas.

LC HG1501
DD 332.1   PH
●**ANNUAL REPORT / BANGKO SENTRAL NG PILIPINAS. Main/Corp** Bangko Sentral ng Pilipinas. 1st (1993)-. Periodical. English. Central Bank of Philippines Corporate Affairs Office, Room 412, Manila Philippines. **Continues** Central Bank of the Philippines. Annual Report.

LC HG3290.6.A7 B26a
DD 332.1/1/095492   BG
ANNUAL REPORT - BANGLADESH BANK. Main/Corp Bangladesh Bank. **Added/Corp** Bangladesh Bank. Dept. of Public Relations and Publications. (19??)-. English. One time a year. Bangladesh Bank, Motijheel Commercial Area, Dhaka 2 Bangladesh.

LC HG3310.J34 E3522A   **ISSN** 0302-6795
DD 330.9/598/03   IO
ANNUAL REPORT - BANK EKSPOR IMPOR INDONESIA. Main/Corp Bank Ekspor Impor Indonesia. **VFOAT** Laporan Tahunan. Multiple languages (English and Indonesian). Bank Ekspor Impor Indonesia, Jl Lapagan Setasium No 1, PO Box 32, Jakarta Indonesia.

LC HG1997.I6   **ISSN** 0067-3560
DD 332.1   SZ
ANNUAL REPORT - BANK FOR INTERNATIONAL SETTLEMENTS. Main/Corp Bank for International Settlements. 1st-1930/31-. English (French and German). Bank for International Settlements, Cent Bahn Strasse, CH-4002 Basel Switzerland. cum. index.

LC HG3406.A7 B36a   **ISSN** 0255-9684
DD 332.1   BS
ANNUAL REPORT / BANK OF BOTSWANA. [Annu. rep. - Bank Botsw.]. **Main/Corp** Bank of Botswana. (1976)-. English. One time a year. $5.00. Bank of Botswana, Library, PO Box 712, Gaborone Botswana. **Tel** 351911 5.

LC HG3769.A84 A97   **ISSN** 0811-4498
DD 332   AT
ANNUAL REPORT BY THE INSPECTOR-GENERAL IN BANKRUPTCY ON THE OPERATION OF THE BANKRUPTCY ACT 1966. See Law-Judicial Process.

LC HG1501
DD 332.1   CN
ANNUAL REPORT - CAISSE DE DEPOT ET PLACEMENT DU QUEBEC. Main/Corp Quebec Deposit and Investment Fund. **VFOAT** Rapport Annuel de Gestion. No. 1; 1966-?. English (French). One time a year. **Continued in part by** Financial Statements & Financial Statistics, 0825-7043.

LC HG4517 .C35
DD 332.1   BB
ANNUAL REPORT / CARIBBEAN DEVELOPMENT BANK. Main/Corp Caribbean Development Bank. (1970)-. Periodical. English. One time a year. Caribbean Development Bank, PO Box 408, Wildey St. Michael Barbados. **Tel** 011 809 4311600, FAX 011 809 4267269, telex WB2287.

LC HG2846.B3 C45A   **ISSN** 0304-6796
DD 330.9/729/81   BB
ANNUAL REPORT - CENTRAL BANK OF BARBADOS. Main/Corp Central Bank of Barbados. 1st (1972)-. Corporate Report. English. One time a year. Free on request. Central Bank of Barbados, PO Box 1016, Treasury Building, Bridgetown Barbados. **Tel** (809)436-6870, FAX (809)427-9559, telex 2251 CENBANK WB. **Circ:** 2,400 (ctrl).
Desc: Provides a review of economic conditions during the year and summarizes the bank administrative and operational activity and the bank's balance sheet.

LC HG3386.A7 B35a
DD 332.1/1/0962   UA
ANNUAL REPORT - CENTRAL BANK OF EGYPT. Main/Corp Bank al-Markazi al-Misri. (19??)-. English. Central Bank of Egypt, 31 Sharia Kasr El Nil, Cairo Egypt. **Tel** 751513, FAX 3926361, telex 22386 CBECR UN. **Continues** Bank al-Markazi al-Misri. Report of the Board of Directors for the Year.
Ind/Abst F&S Index Plus Text, Int. [Select. Cov.].

LC HC920.A1 C46A
DD 330.9681/6/005   LO
ANNUAL REPORT ... / CENTRAL BANK OF LESOTHO. Main/Corp Central Bank of Lesotho. English. One time a year. Central Bank of Lesotho, PO Box 1184, Maseru 100 Lesotho. **Tel** 011 9266 324281, 011 9266 314281, FAX 011 9266 310051.

LC HG3439.9 .A35A
DD 354.69/600822/06   SE
ANNUAL REPORT / CENTRAL BANK OF SEYCHELLES. Main/Corp Central Bank of Seychelles. 1983-. English. One time a year. R30.00 Seychelles; $9.50, $16.00 (for back issues). Central Bank of Seychelles, PO Box 701, Liberty House, Victoria Seychelles. **Tel** 011 25200, telex 2301 CENBNK SZ. **Continues** Annual Report / Sychelles Monetary Authority.

LC HC157.T8 C4A   **ISSN** 0069-1593
DD 330.9/729/8304   TR
ANNUAL REPORT - CENTRAL BANK OF TRINIDAD AND TOBAGO. Main/Corp Central Bank of Trinidad and Tobago. ?-(1985). English. One time a year. Central Bank of Trinidad and Tobago, PO Box 1250, Port of Spain Trinidad. **Tel** (809)625-4835, (809)625-5028. **Continued in part by** Annual Economic Survey.

LC HG3170.O82 N62
DD 332.1/2/09481   NO
ANNUAL REPORT / DEN NORSKE CREDITBANK. Main/Corp Norske Credit Bank. (1981)-. English. Den Norske Creditbank, PO Box 1171, Sentrum Oslo 1 Norway. **Continues** Norske Creditbank. Annual Report for ... .

LC HG3881 .E73   **ISSN** 0071-2868
DD 332.1/534/05   BE
ANNUAL REPORT - EUROPEAN INVESTMENT BANK. See Business and Economics-Investments.

LC HD1491   **ISSN** 0382-1501
DD 338.1   CN
ANNUAL REPORT - FARM CREDIT CORPORATION. Main/Corp Farm Credit Corporation. **VFOAT** Rapport Annuel - Societe du Credit Agricole. (1966/1967)-. Government Publication. English (French). One time a year. Free on request. Agriculture Canada, Communications Branch, Ottawa Ontario K1A 0C7 Canada. **Continues** Farm Credit Corporation. Annual Report and Financial Statements.
Desc: Dedicated to serving the financial needs of Canadian farmers.

LC HG1707.5 .F43A
DD 332.1/0973   US
ANNUAL REPORT / FEDERAL FINANCIAL INSTITUTIONS EXAMINATION COUNCIL (U.S.). Main/Corp Federal Financial Institutions Examination Council (U.S.). (1979)-. English. One time a year. Federal Financial Institutions Examination Council, 1776 G Street NW/Suite 701, Washington DC 20006. **Tel** (202)357-0177. available on microfiche (Vols. for (1985-) distributed to depository libraries).
Desc: A chronological record of the examination council of federal regulations which pertain to banking and regulations set by the Federal Reserve System.

LC HG2613.C64 F42   **ISSN** 0361-798X
DD 332.1/1/0977132   US
ANNUAL REPORT - FEDERAL RESERVE BANK OF CLEVELAND. Main/Corp Federal Reserve Bank of Cleveland. (1916)-. English. One time a year. Free on request. Federal Reserve Bank of Cleveland, PO Box 6387, Cleveland OH 44101. **Tel** (216)579-3079, FAX (216)579-2477. **ED** Bill Murmann. **Circ:** 15,000.
Desc: Report for the Federal Reserve Bank of Cleveland.

LC HG2613.N54 F42   **ISSN** 0361-7998
DD 332.1/1/09747   US
ANNUAL REPORT - FEDERAL RESERVE BANK OF NEW YORK. [Annu. rep. - Fed. Reserve Bank N. Y.]. **Main/Corp** Federal Reserve Bank of New York. 1st- 1914/15-. English. One time a year. Federal Reserve Bank of New York, 33 Liberty Street, New York NY 10045. **Tel** (212)720-5000. available on microfilm and microfiche from University Microfilms International (UMI).

LC HG4949 .M35A
DD 338.9741/005   US
ANNUAL REPORT / FINANCE AUTHORITY OF MAINE. Main/Corp Finance Authority of Maine. 1983-. English. One time a year. Finance Authority of Maine, PO Box 949, 83 Western Avenue, August ME 04330. **Continues** Maine Guarantee Authority. Annual Report, 0098-9320.

   ISSN 1192-0254
DD 354.7110082/5/05   CN
ANNUAL REPORT / FINANCIAL INSTITUTIONS COMMISSION. Main/Corp British Columbia. Financial Institutions Commission. **Added/Corp** Credit Union Deposit Insurance Corporation of British Columbia. Audited Financial Statements. (1992)-. English.

LC HG3361.P25 T453A
DD 332.3/2/095694   IS
ANNUAL REPORT FOR ... / LEUMI MORTGAGE BANK LTD. Main/Corp Leumi Mortgage Bank. 1980-. English. One time a year. Leumi Mortgage Bank Ltd, 13 Ahad Ha'Am Street, Tel Aviv Israel. **Continues** Bank Apotekai Kelali. Annual Report and Accounts.

LC HG2956 .B27B
DD 332.1/1/09895   UY
ANNUAL REPORT FOR THE ... FISCAL YEAR / BANCO DE LA REPUBLICA ORIENTAL DEL URUGUAY. Main/Corp Banco de la Republica Oriental del Uruguay. English. One time a year. Banco de la Republica Oriental del Urugual Head Office, Cerrito and Zabala Streets, Montevideo Uruguay.

LC HG3387.A7 B363A
DD 330.9624/005   SJ
ANNUAL REPORT FOR THE YEAR ENDING 31ST DECEMBER ... / BANK OF SUDAN. Main/Corp Bank Al-Sudan. English. One time a year. Bank of Sudan, Statistics Department, PO Box 313, Khartoum Sudan. **Tel** 78064, telex 22352 ELBNK SD.
Ind/Abst Numis. Lit. (?-?).

LC HG3879 .G76A   **ISSN** 0735-2034
DD 332/.042/0601   US
ANNUAL REPORT / GROUP OF THIRTY. [Annu. rep. - Group Thirty]. **Main/Corp** Group of Thirty. English. One time a year. Two World Trade Center, Suite 9630, New York NY 10048.

LC HG1501
DD 332.1   KO
ANNUAL REPORT / INDUSTRIAL BANK OF KOREA. Main/Corp Industrial Bank of Korea. (1987)-. English. Medium Industry Bank, 36-1 2-ka Ulchiro Choong-ku, Seoul Korea. **Continues** Annual Report - Medium Industry Bank (Korea).

LC HG3368.A8 I844
DD 332.1/53   SU
ANNUAL REPORT : ISLAMIC DEVELOPMENT BANK. Main/Corp Islamic Development Bank. 1st (1975/76)-. English. One time a year. Free on request. Islamic Development Bank, Box 5925, Jeddah 21432 Saudi Arabia. **Tel** 011 966 2 6301400.

LC HG3110.B84 K725
DD 332.1/2/094933   BE
ANNUAL REPORT - KREDIETBANK, N. V., BRUSSELS. Main/Corp Kredietbank (Brussels, Belgium). Dutch (French, English and German). One time a year. Free. Kredietbank NV, Arenbergstraat 7, 1000 Brussels Belgium. **Tel** 011 32 2 4272700.
Desc: Report of Kredietbank N.V. of Belgium with a survey of activities and balance of the past financial year.

LC HG3318.L3 A3
DD 354/.599/00825   PH
ANNUAL REPORT - LAND BANK OF THE PHILIPPINES. Main/Corp Land Bank of the Philippines. (19??)-. English. Land Bank of the Philippines, PO Box 163, Manila Philippines.

LC HG1501
DD 332.1   UK
ANNUAL REPORT - LLOYD'S REGISTER OF SHIPPING. (19??)-. Periodical. English. Lloyd's Register of Shipping / London, 71 Senchurch Street, London EC3 M4BS United Kingdom. **Tel** 011 44 171 7099166. **(Subscription address:** Lloyd's Register of Shipping, 17 Battery Place, New York NY 10004. **Tel** (212)425-8050.)

LC HG2040.5.U6 M46A   **ISSN** 0271-1621
DD 353.97440086/5045   US
ANNUAL REPORT - MASSACHUSETTS HOME MORTGAGE FINANCE AGENCY. Main/Corp Massachusetts Home Mortgage Finance Agency. 1st- 1978/79-. English. One time a year. Massachusetts Home Mortgage Finance Agency, Old City Hall, 45 School Street, Boston MA 02108.
Desc: Contain the Agency's certified financial statements.

Business and Economics — Banks and Banking

LC HG3729.U49 M38a
DD 353.97440082
US
ANNUAL REPORT - MASSACHUSETTS INDUSTRIAL FINANCE AGENCY.
Main/Corp Massachusetts Industrial Finance Agency. (1979)-. English. One time a year.

LC HG1501
DD 332.1
AT
ANNUAL REPORT / NATIONAL AUSTRALIA BANK LIMITED. Main/Corp
National Australia Bank. (19??)-. English. One time a year. National Australia Bank Ltd, PO Box 84A, Melbourne Victoria 3001 Australia. **Tel** 61346053269.
Desc: Reports the important news and information for the National Australia Bank for the previous year, including a detailed discussion of financial performance.

LC HG3389.A7 Y34
DD 332.1
ET
ANNUAL REPORT / NATIONAL BANK OF ETHIOPIA. Main/Corp Yaltyopya Beherawi
Bank. 1st (1964)-. Government Publication. English. One time a year. $2.50. National Bank of Ethiopia, PO Box 5550, Addis Ababa Ethiopia. **Continues** Yaltyopya Mangest Bank. Annual Report.

LC HG3691 .N38a
DD 332/.06/073
ISSN 8755-7754
US
ANNUAL REPORT - NATIONAL COMMERCIAL FINANCE ASSOCIATION (U.S.). (ANNUAL REPORT / NATIONAL
COMMERCIAL FINANCE ASSOCIATION.). [Annu. rep. - Natl. Comm. Financ. Assoc. (U.S.)]. **Main/Corp** National Commercial Finance Association (U.S.). (19??)-. English. One time a year. $24.00 (members); $48.00 (nonmembers). Commercial Finance Association, 225 West 34th Street, New York NY 10122. **Tel** (212)594-3490, FAX (212)564-6053.

LC HG2038.I5 A33
DD 334/.22/09773
US
ANNUAL REPORT OF ILLINOIS STATE CHARTERED CREDIT UNIONS. Main/Corp
Illinois. Division of Credit Unions. English. One time a year. **Continues** Annual Report of Illinois Credit Unions.

LC HG2611.V8 B87A
DD 353.97550082/52
US
ANNUAL REPORT OF THE BUREAU OF FINANCIAL INSTITUTIONS, STATE CORPORATION COMMISSION, COMMONWEALTH OF VIRGINIA.
Main/Corp Virginia. Bureau of Financial Institutions. (1978)-. English. One time a year. **Continues** Bureau of Banking. Annual Report of the Bureau of Banking, State Corporation Commission, Commonwealth of Virginia, Showing the Condition of Banks, Savings and Loan Associations, Industrial Loan Associations, Credit Unions Operating in Virginia.

LC HG2038.M4 M37a
DD 334/.22/09744021
US
ANNUAL REPORT OF THE COMMISSION OF BANKS RELATING TO CREDIT UNIONS FOR THE YEAR ENDED ... FINANICIAL STATEMENT.
Main/Corp Massachusetts. Office of the Commissioner of Banks. English. **Continues in part** Annual Credit Union Call Report.

LC HG2038.M4 M37b
DD 334/.22/025744
US
ANNUAL REPORT OF THE COMMISSIONER OF BANKS RELATING TO CREDIT UNIONS FOR THE YEAR ENDED ... OFFICERS. Main/Corp
Massachusetts. Office of the Commissioner of Banks. English. **Continues in part** Annual Credit Union Call Report.

LC HG3881 .I634
DD 332.1/52
ISSN 0250-7498
US
ANNUAL REPORT OF THE EXECUTIVE BOARD - INTERNATIONAL MONETARY FUND. (ANNUAL REPORT OF THE EXECUTIVE
BOARD FOR THE FINANCIAL YEAR ENDED APRIL 30 ...). [Annu. rep. exec. board - Int. Monet. Fund]. **Main/Corp** International Monetary Fund. **VFOAT** Annual Report. (1978)-. Periodical. English (German, Spanish and French). One time a year. Free on request. International Monetary Fund, 700 19th Street Northwest, Publishing Unit, Washington DC 20431. **Tel** (202)623-7430, FAX (202)623-7201. available on microfilm and microfiche from University Microfilms International (UMI). **Continues** International Monetary Fund. Annual Report of the Executive Directors for the Fiscal Year, 0085-2171.
Desc: Reviews IMF's activities, policies, organization and administration and surveys the world economy, with special emphasis on balance of payments problems, exchange rates, world trade, international liquidity and developments in the international monetary system.

LC HG2037 .U55b
DD 353.008/25
ISSN 0146-6046
US
ANNUAL REPORT OF THE NATIONAL CREDIT UNION ADMINISTRATION.
Main/Corp United States. National Credit Union Administration. (1970)-. English. One time a year. NCAU Agency, 1775 G Street NW/Room 7670, Washington DC 20456. **Tel** (202)254-9809. available on microfiche (Vols. for (1985-) distributed to depository libraries). **Continues** United States. National Credit Union Administration. Annual Report of the Federal Credit Union Program.

LC HG2411 .W6
DD 353.9/775/00825
ISSN 0146-8871
US
ANNUAL REPORT OF THE OFFICE OF COMMISSIONER OF BANKING. (ANNUAL
REPORT OF THE OFFICE OF COMMISSIONER OF BANKING (WISCONSIN).). **Main/Corp** Wisconsin. Office of Commissioner of Banking. English. One time a year. Wisconsin Office of Commission on Banking, 30 West Mifflin Street, Madison WI 53703. **Continues** Wisconsin. Banking Dept. Annual Report.

LC HG3351 .H65a
DD 354.5125008/52043/06
HK
ANNUAL REPORT OF THE OFFICE OF THE COMMISSIONER OF BANKING.
Main/Corp Hong Kong. Office of Commissioner of Banking. **VFOAT** Annual Report of the Commissioner of Banking for ... . (19??)-. Government Publication. English. One time a year. HK$30.00. Hong Kong Government Information Service, Beaconsfield House, 4 Queens Road, Hong Kong Hong Kong. **Tel** 011 852 284288014, 011 852 259881947, FAX 011 852 28459078, 011 852 25987482, telex 61190 HKGIS.

LC HG3403 .A32A
DD 332.1/096894/021
ZA
ANNUAL REPORT OF THE REGISTRAR OF BANKS AND FINANCIAL INSTITUTIONS FOR THE YEAR ENDED 31ST DEC. .... 1976-. English. 30. Continues
Annual Report of the Registrar of Banks for the Year ... .

LC HG3401 .A27A
DD 332/.68/00825
SA
ANNUAL REPORT OF THE REGISTRAR OF BANKS (SOUTH AFRICA). Main/Corp
South Africa. Financial Institutions Office. **VFOAT** Jaarverslag van die Registrateur van Banke. Multiple languages (Afrikaans and English). R3.10. Financial Institutions Office, The Government Printer, Bosman Street, Private Bag X85, Pretoria 0001 South Africa.

LC HG5160.S27 S27A
DD 354/.7124/0082
ISSN 0702-3316
CN
ANNUAL REPORT OF THE SASKATCHEWAN DEVELOPMENT FUND CORPORATION OF THE PROVINCE OF SASKATCHEWAN.
(ANNUAL REPORT OF THE SASKATCHEWAN DEVELOPMENT FUND CORPORATION.). **Main/Corp** Saskatchewan Development Fund Corporation. 1974-. English. One time a year. Saskatchewan Development Fund Corporation, 2151 Scarth Street, Regina Saskatchewan S4P 3V7 Canada. **Tel** (306)787-2664.

LC HG2411.S6 A25
DD 353.97570082/52/06
US
ANNUAL REPORT OF THE STATE BOARD OF FINANCIAL INSTITUTIONS OF THE STATE OF SOUTH CAROLINA.
Main/Corp South Carolina. Board of Financial Institutions. 74th (1980)-. English. One time a year. **Continues** Annual Report of the State Banking Department of the State of South Carolina.
Desc: Includes the annual reports of the Consumer Finance Division and the Examining Division, 1980.

LC HG2150 .I3
DD 332.3/2/09773
US
ANNUAL REPORT / OFFICE OF THE COMMISSIONER OF SAVINGS AND RESIDENTIAL FINANCE, STATE OF ILLINOIS. Added/Corp Illinois. Office of the
Commissioner of Savings and Residential Finance. 99th (1990)-. English. Office of the Commissioner of Savings and Residential Finance, 500 East Monroe Street, Suite 800, Springfield IL 62701-1509. **Continues** Illinois. Office of the Commissioner of Savings and Loan Associations. Annual Report.

LC HG2039.C2 O58A
DD 354.7130082/52045
ISSN 0227-5864
CN
ANNUAL REPORT / ONTARIO SHARE AND DEPOSIT INSURANCE CORPORATION. [Annu. rep. - Ont. Share Depos.
Insur. Corp.]. **Main/Corp** Ontario Share and Deposit Insurance Corporation. **VFOAT** Rapport Annuel. (1978)-. English (French). One time a year. Free.

LC HG3290.D44 P83
DD 332.1/223/0954552
ISSN 0304-8101
II
ANNUAL REPORT - PUNJAB NATIONAL BANK. Main/Corp Punjab National Bank, Ltd. (19??)-.
Corporate Report. English. One time a year. Punjab National Bank, 5 Parliament Street, New Delhi 10001 India. **Continues** Punjab National Bank. Directors' Report and Statement of Accounts.

LC HC685.5.A1 R47
DD 332.1/1/09961105
FJ
ANNUAL REPORT / RESERVE BANK OF FIJI. Main/Corp Reserve Bank of Fiji. (1988)-. English.
One time a year. $9.00. Reserve Bank of Fiji, Suva Fiji Islands. **Tel** 011 679 313611, telex 2164. **Continues** Reserve Bank of Fiji. Operations and Annual Accounts for Fiscal Year.

LC HG1501
DD 332.1
NZ
ANNUAL REPORT / RURAL BANK LIMITED. Main/Corp Rural Bank Limited. (1991)-.
English. **Continues** Rural Bank, 0114-6475.

LC HG2611.N5 N48a
DD 353.9/749/00825
US
ANNUAL REPORT - STATE OF NEW JERSEY, DEPARTMENT OF BANKING, COMMISSIONER OF BANKING. Main/Corp
New Jersey. Dept. of Banking. (1977)-. Government Publication. English. One time a year. $10.00. New Jersey Department of Banking, State House of Annex, Trenton NJ 08625. **Tel** (609)292-3723. **Continues** New Jersey. Division of Banking. Annual Report - New Jersey, Division of Banking.

LC HG3280.5.A7 C49
DD 332
CH
ANNUAL REPORT / THE CENTRAL BANK OF CHINA. Main/Corp Chung Yang Yin
Hang. (1962)-. English. One time a year (June). Free on request. Central Bank of China, 2 Roosevelt Road, Economic Research Department, Taipei 107 Taiwan. **Tel** 011 886 2 3936161.

LC HG2994 .A3
DD 332
UK
ANNUAL REPORT UNDER THE BANKING ACT FOR ... . Main/Corp Bank of
England. **Added/Corp** Great Britain. Banking Act 1987. **VFOAT** Bank of England Banking Act Report for ... . (1988)-. English. One time a year. Free on request. Bank of England Bulletin Group, Threadneedle Street, London EC2R 8AH United Kingdom. **Tel** 011 44 171 6014139, FAX 011 44 171 6015288. **Continues in part** Bank of England. and Report and Accounts for the Year Ended ..., 0308-5279.

LC HG3881 .I5
DD 332.1/532/05
ISSN 0252-2942
US
ANNUAL REPORT - WORLD BANK. See
Business and Economics-Economic Assistance and Development.

LC HG3439.9.A8 D483a
DD 332.2
SE
ANNUAL REPORT [DEVELOPMENT BANK OF SEYCHELLES]. Main/Corp
Development Bank of Seychelles. (1982)-. Corporate Report. English. One time a year. Development Bank of Seychelles, PO Box 217, Victoria Seychelles. **Tel** 224471, FAX 224274, telex 2348 DEVBAN S2. **Circ:** 100 (ctrl).
Desc: Reports and descriptions of bank activities during the year.

LC HG1501
DD 332.1
AT
ANNUAL REPORTS OF THE BOARD OF MANAGEMENT AND OF THE CLOSER SETTLEMENT BOARD FOR THE YEAR ENDED 30TH JUNE ... TO WHICH ARE APPENDED FINANCIAL STATEMENTS AND OTHER INFORMATION. Main/Corp
Agricultural Bank of Tasmania. Board of Management. (19??)-. English.

LC HG181.A1 U55a
DD 332/.0973
ISSN 0148-4338
US
ANNUAL STATISTICAL DIGEST - BOARD OF GOVERNORS OF THE FEDERAL RESERVE SYSTEM. (ANNUAL
STATISTICAL DIGEST.). **Main/Corp** Board of Governors of the Federal Reserve System (U.S.). (1975)-. Statistical Publication. English. Irregular. Free on request. Board of Governors of the Federal Reserve System, Mail Stop 127, Washington DC 20551. **Tel** (202)452-3244, (202)452-3245.

LC HG1501
DD 332.1 IT
ANNUARIO DELLE AZIENDE DI CREDITO E FINANZIARE.
Main/Corp Associazione Bancaria Italiana. (19??)-. Periodical. Italian. One time a year (Dec.). Bancaria Editrice SPA, Piazza del Gesu 49, 00186 Rome Italy. **Tel** 011 39 6 6767220.

LC HG4109 .A58
DD 332 BL
ANUARIO : EMPRESAS JAPONESAS NO BRASIL.
VFOAT Empresas Japonesas No Brasil; Burajiru Nikkei Kigyo Nenkan. 1979-. Multiple languages (Japanese and Portuguese). ***Continues*** *Almanaque, Empresas Japonesas No Brasil.*

LC HG8555.A4 E87 **ISSN** 0067-3234
DD 332/.097284/021 ES
ANUARIO ESTADISTICO.
See Business and Economics-Abstracting, Bibliographies and Statistics.

LC HG69.M6 A6
DD 332.0972 MX
ANUARIO FINANCIERO DE MEXICO.
Added/Corp Asociacion de Banqueros de Mexico. Vol. 1 (1940)-. Spanish. One time a year. Asociacion Mexicana de Bancos, Mexico DF Mexico. **Tel** 521 40 80 AL 84, telex 1774510 ABAMME. Index available. **Ad Acc. Circ:** 2,500.

ISSN 1075-4636
DD 333 US
APARTMENT ADVISOR, THE.
[Apartm. advis.]. **Added/Corp** Cain and Scott, Inc. (199?)-. Periodical. English. Twelve times a year. $60.00. Dupre and Scott Apt. Advisors Inc., 6041 CA Avenue Southwest, # 104, Seattle WA 98136. **Tel** (206)935-3458. ***Continues*** *Apartment Letter, 1067-1498.*

ISSN 1067-1498
DD 333 US
TITLE CHANGE
APARTMENT LETTER, THE.
[Apartm. lett.]. **Added/Corp** Cain and Scott, Inc. Vol. 15, No. 2 (1992)-(199?). Periodical. English. Dupre and Scott Apt. Advisors Inc., 6041 CA Avenue Southwest, # 104, Seattle WA 98136. **Tel** (206)935-3458. ***Continues*** *Cain and Scott Market Summary, 1043-3678.* ***Continued by*** *Apartment Advisor, 1075-4636.*

LC HG11 .A77 **ISSN** 0960-3107
DD 332/.05 UK
CCC
APPLIED FINANCIAL ECONOMICS.
Vol. 1, No. 1 (Mar. 1991)-. Periodical. English. Six times a year. $322.00. Chapman & Hall, 2-6 Boundary Row, London SE1 8HN United Kingdom. **Tel** 011 44 171 8650066, FAX 011 44 171 5229623, telex 290164 CHAPMA G. Documents available from UMI Article Clearinghouse.
Desc: Companion to Applied Economics. Publishes research papers, short articles, notes and comments on financial economics, banking and monetary economics with a particular bias towards practical aspects and applied topics. Special attention is paid to the actual operations of financial institutions and financial markets.
Ind/Abst ABI/INFORM Glob. Ed.; Acad. Search; Bus. Source Plus; Bus. Source; Econ. Lit. Index; EP Collect.; Homework Help.; MasterFile FullTEXT 1000; MasterFile FullTEXT 350; MasterFile FullTEXT 650; MasterFile FullTEXT (Jan. 1994-); OCLC; Telebase.

LC HB QA276 **ISSN** 1350-486X
DD 330 519.5 UK
CCC
•APPLIED MATHEMATICAL FINANCE.
(1994)-. Academic Scholarly Publication. English. Four times a year. $246.00. Chapman & Hall, 2-6 Boundary Row, London SE1 8HN United Kingdom. **Tel** 011 44 171 8650066, FAX 011 44 171 5229623, telex 290164 CHAPMA G. **(Subscription address:** International Thomson Publishing Services Ltd., North Way Andover, Hampshire SP10 5BE United Kingdom. **Tel** 011 44 1264 332424.**)** **ED** Board. Documents available from BLDSC.
Desc: Aimed at finance practitioners, academics and applied mathematicians.

LC HG1501 **ISSN** 0261-2925
DD 332.1 UK
ARAB BANKER.
[Arab bank.]. **Added/Corp** Arab Bankers Association. (1981)-. Periodical. English. Six times a year. Arab Bankers Association, 1/2 Hanover Street, London W1R 8WB United Kingdom. **Tel** 011 44 171 6295423, FAX 011 44 171 6298631.
Ind/Abst Infomat Int. Bus.

LC HG3366.A5 A7
DD 332.1/089927 FR
ARABANKS MIDYEAR SURVEY FOR ... .
VFOAT Arabanks. (19??)-. English.

LC HG1501 **ISSN** 0004-1726
DD 332.1 US
ARKANSAS BANKER, THE.
Vol. 1, (1917)-. Trade Publication. English. Twelve times a year. $19.95. Arkansas Bankers Association, 221 West 2nd Street/Suite 1027, Little Rock AR 72201. **Tel** (501)376-3741. **ED** H Carvill. **Bk Rev. Ad Acc. Circ:** 2,400.
Desc: Official publication of the Arkansas Bankers Association.

LC HG4234.85 .A84
DD 330.95/005 HK
ASIA ... MEASURES & MAGNITUDES.
VFOAT Asia ... Measures and Magnitudes. (1980)-. English. One time a year. Asian Finance Publications Ltd., 3 Floor Hollywood Centre, 233 Hollywood Road, Hong Kong. **Tel** 011 852 28155221, FAX 011 852 28542794, telex HX83013. **ED** Barun Roy. **Ad Acc. Circ:** 10,000. ***Continues*** *Asia Corporate Profile and National Finance.*
Desc: Local and national budgets, GNP's, import and export statistics plus Asia's top 1,000 companies with summarised balance sheet figures, names of CEO's, etc.

LC HG41 .A82
DD 332/.095/05 HK
TITLE CHANGE
ASIA MONEY & FINANCE.
VFOAT Asia Money and Finance. No. 1 (Nov. 1991)-(199?). Periodical. English. Euromoney Publications PLC, Nestor House, Playhouse Yard, London EC4Z 5EX United Kingdom. **Tel** 011 44 171 7798888, FAX 011 44 171 7798630, telex 290700 EUROMON G. Documents available from UMI Article Clearinghouse. ***Formed by the union of*** *Asian Finance, 1010-4143* ***and*** *Asiamoney (London, England), 0958-9309.* ***Continued by*** *Asiamoney (London, England : 1993), 0958-9309.*
Desc: Information on corporate finance, capital markets and investments in Asia. Tracks activity in mergers and acquisitions, project financing, equity offerings, loans and trade financing in Asia, and provides profiles of Asian companies, and policymakers.
Ind/Abst ABI/INFORM Glob. Ed.; Predicasts Forecasts.

LC HG **ISSN** 0739-6244
DD 332 US
ASIA/PACIFIC CURRENCY REPORT.
[Asia/Pac. curr. rep.]. **Added/Corp** International Business Information Inc. **VAT** Asia Pacific Currency Report. (19??)-. Periodical. English. Twenty-four times a year. $437.00. Asia Pacific Currency Report, 700 Walnut Street, Suite 202, Cincinnati OH 45202. **Tel** (513)421-5447. **ED** Kevin Horsley.

LC HG1501 **ISSN** 1010-416X
DD 332.1 HK
ASIAN MONETARY MONITOR.
[Asian monet. monit.]. (Sept./Oct. 1977)-. Periodical. English. Six times a year. $300.00. Asian Monetary Monitor, GPO Box 12964, Hong Kong Hong Kong. **Tel** 011 852 5 28427200.
Ind/Abst Contents Recent Econ. J.; Curr. Cit.; World Agric. Econ. Rural Sociol. Abstr.

LC HG1501
DD 332.1 BE
Pr Rev.
ASPECTS & DOCUMENTS.
(19??)-. English (French and Dutch). Irregular (published 15-20 times per year). 1000F. Association Belge des Banques, rue Ravenstein 36 Boite 5, 1000 Brussels Belgium. **Tel** 011 32 2 5076811. **Circ:** 6,000.

LC HG1923.N5 A84
DD 332.2/1/09749 US
ASSET RATIO REPORT FOR ... .
Added/Corp New Jersey. Dept. of Banking. (Dec. 31, 1981)-. English. One time a year. New Jersey Department of Banking, State House of Annex, Trenton NJ 08625. **Tel** (609)292-3723.

LC HG **ISSN** 0894-6175
DD 332 US
ASSET SALES REPORT.
[Asset sales rep.]. (1987)-. Periodical. English. One time a week. $1125.00. American Banker, Concourse Level, 1 State Street Plaza, New York NY 10004. **Tel** (212)803-8200, (800)221-1809, FAX (212)943-6256, (212)843-9598. available on an online database from NEWSNET; Mead Data Central; DIALOG; and DATA-STAR. ***Absorbed*** *Global Guaranty.*
Ind/Abst PROMT [Full Txt.]; PTS Newsl. Database [Full Txt.].

LC HG1501
DD 332.1 US
•ASSETS AND LIABILITIES OF COMMERCIAL BANKS IN THE UNITED STATES.
Added/Corp Board of Governors of the Federal Reserve System (U.S.). (Mar. 18, 1994)-. Periodical. English. Fifty-two times a year (published on Fridays). $30.00. Board of Governors of the Federal Reserve System, Mail Stop 127, Washington DC 20551. **Tel** (202)452-3244, (202)452-3245. ***Formed by the union of*** *Assets and Liabilities of Insured Domestically Chartered and Foreign Related Banking Institutions (Partly Estimated, in Millions of Dollars), 0895-1217; Major Nondeposit Funds of Commercials Banks* ***and*** *Loans and Securities of Commercial Banks.*

LC HG1501 **ISSN** 0895-1217
DD 332 US
TITLE CHANGE
ASSETS AND LIABILITIES OF INSURED DOMESTICALLY CHARTERED AND FOREIGN RELATED BANKING INSTITUTIONS (PARTLY ESTIMATED, IN MILLIONS OF DOLLARS).
[Assets liabil. insur. domest. chart. foreign relat. bank. inst.]. **Added/Corp** Board of Governors of the Federal Reserve System (U.S.). **VFOAT** Assets and Liabilities of Commercial Banking Institutions. (Jan. 30, 1985)-(1994). Periodical. English. Board of Governors of the Federal Reserve System, Mail Stop 127, Washington DC 20551. **Tel** (202)452-3244, (202)452-3245. ***Continues*** *Assets and Liabilities of Domestically Chartered and Foreign Related Banking Institutions (Partly Estimated, in Millions of Dollars).* ***Merged with*** *Loans and Securities at Commerical Banks; Major Nondeposit Funds of Commerical Banks* ***to form*** *Assets and Liabilities of Commerical Banks in the United States.*

LC HG1503 .B43 **ISSN** 0814-2912
DD 332.1/0994 AT
AUSTRALIAN BANKER.
(THE AUSTRALIAN BANKER : JOURNAL OF THE AUSTRALIAN INSTITUTE OF BANKERS.). [Aust. bank.]. Vol. 98, No. 1 (Feb. 1984)-. Periodical. English. Six times a year. $50.00. Australian Institute of Bankers, 385 Bourke Street, State Bank Center / 19, Melbourne Victoria 3000 Australia. **Tel** 011-61-3-6025811, FAX 011-61-3-6023923. **ED** Leanne Byrne. Index available. cum. index. **Bk Rev. Ad Acc. Circ:** 21,000 (ctrl). Documents available from UMI Article Clearinghouse. ***Continues*** *Banker's Magazine (Melbourne, Vic.), 0811-6423.*
Desc: Aimed at those within the banking industry.
Ind/Abst ABI/INFORM Glob. Ed.; APAIS, Aust. Public Aff. Inf. Ser. (1984-).

LC HG1501 **ISSN** 1034-9685
DD 332.10994 AT
AUSTRALIAN BANKING STATISTICS - RESERVE BANK OF AUSTRALIA.
(AUSTRALIAN BANKING STATISTICS.). [Aust. bank. stat. - Reserve Bank Aust.]. (1990)-. Periodical. English. Twelve times a year. 12.33Aus$. Reserve Bank of Australia / Secretary Department, GPO Box 3947, Sydney New South Wales 2001 Australia. **Tel** 11 61 2 5519724, 011 61 2 5518841, FAX 011 61 2 234900, telex 20106.

LC HG51 .A87
DD 332/.0994 AT
AUSTRALIAN FINANCIAL REVIEW, THE.
(Aug. 16, 1951)-. Periodical. English. Five times a week (260 per year). 554.97Aus$. John Fairfax & Sons Ltd, GPO Box 506, Sydney NSW 2001 Australia. **Tel** 011 61 2 2822833, FAX 011 61 2 2822424, telex 23425. **ED** Alan Kohler. **Bk Rev. Ad Acc. Circ:** 69,000. available on an online database (files 771,772,799/Full-Text) from DIALOG. Documents available from UMI Article Clearinghouse.
Desc: Australia's financial daily newspaper. Provides coverage of all Australian markets.
Ind/Abst ABI/INFORM Glob. Ed.; F&S Index Plus Text, Int. [Select. Cov.]; Infomat Int. Bus.; PROMT.

ISSN 0819-341X
DD 331.2520994 AT
AUSTRALIAN SUPER REVIEW.
[Aust. super rev.]. (1986)-. Periodical. English. Eleven times a year. 89.00Aus$ (Australia); 119.00Aus$ (New Zealand, Papua, New Guinea, and Southeast Asia); 139.00Aus$ (other). Reed Business Publishing Pty Ltd. / Australia, PO Box 5487, W Chatswood New South Wales 2057, Australia. **Tel** 011 61 2 3725222, FAX 011 61 2 4197533. **ED** Jennifer Fletcher. **Ad Acc. Circ:** 3,000.
Desc: Magazine servicing the superannuation industry from fund management to administration.

LC HG2151. .F56a **ISSN** 0160-6441
DD 332.3/2/02573 US
AUTOMATION SURVEY.
Main/Corp Financial Managers Society For Savings Institutions. Systems Automation Division. (19??)-. English. Financial Managers Society Inc., 8 South Michigan Avenue, Suite 500, Chicago IL 60603. **Tel** (312)578-1300, FAX (312)578-1308.

LC HG **ISSN** 1355-7793
DD 332 UK
•BACK OFFICE FOCUS.
(1994)-. Newsletter. English. Twelve times a year. £395.00. Armstrong Information Ltd., 3rd Floor Brigade House, Parsons Green, London SW6 4TH United Kingdom. **Tel** 011 44 171 7367111, FAX 011 44 171 3717806. **ED** Graeme Austin.
Desc: Covers global issues regarding post-trade activity in the securities industry.

LC HG1692 .B35a
DD 332.76 US
BAI SURVEY OF THE CHECK COLLECTION SYSTEM.
Added/Corp Bank Administration Institute. **VFOAT** Survey of the Check Collection System. (1986)-. English. Bank Administration Institute / Chicago, One North Franklin, Chicago IL 60606.

Business and Economics —Banks and Banking

Tel (312)553-4600, (800)323-8552, FAX (312)683-2373. **Continues** Bank Administration Institute. Survey of the Check Collection System.

LC HG1501 ISSN 0549-317X
DD 332.1 JA
BALANCE OF PAYMENTS MONTHLY.
Main/Corp Nihon Ginko Gaikoku-Kyoku. (Apr./May 1966)-. Periodical. English (Japanese). Twelve times a year. $192.00. Bank of Japan / Public Relations Department, C.P.O. Box 203, Tokyo 100-91 Japan. **Tel** 81 3 3279 1111, FAX 81 3 5200 2256, 81 3 3664-4348. **(Subscription address:** Maruzen Company Ltd., PO Box 5050, Import & Export Department, Tokyo 100 31 Japan. **Tel** 011 81 3 32789224.)

LC HG3883.J2 B34a ISSN 0259-6776
DD 382.1/7/097292 JM
BALANCE OF PAYMENTS OF JAMAICA.
Main/Corp Bank of Jamaica. Research Dept. **Added/Corp** Bank of Jamaica. Research Dept. Bank of Jamaica. Balance of Payments and Foreign Exchange Management Division. (19??)-. English. Irregular. Free on request. Bank of Jamaica, Research Department, PO Box 621, Kingston Jamaica. **Tel** (809)922-0750, FAX (809)922-0854, telex 2165.

LC HG3882 .B34 ISSN 0252-3035
DD 382.1/7/0212 US
BALANCE OF PAYMENTS STATISTICS. YEARBOOK. See Business and Economics-Abstracting, Bibliographies and Statistics.

LC HG3883.T28 T34a
DD 382.1/7/0951249 CH
BALANCE OF PAYMENTS / TAIWAN DISTRICT, THE REPUBLIC OF CHINA.
Main/Corp Taiwan. **Added/Corp** Chung Yang Yin Hang. (19??)-. English (English). Four times a year. $5.00. Central Bank of China, 2 Roosevelt Road Section 1, Taipei 107 Taiwan. **Tel** 0231 36161, FAX 02 3173768.

LC HF5601
DD 657 UK
BALANCE SHEETS AND THE LENDING BANKER. See Business and Economics-Accounting.

LC HG3882 .B344
DD 382.1/7/021 FR
BALANCES OF PAYMENTS OF OECD COUNTRIES.
Added/Corp Organisation for Economic Co-Operation and Development. Dept. of Economics and Statistics. **VFOAT** Balances des Paiements des Pays de l'OCDE. (19??)-. English (French). Irregular. $32.00. OECD Publications and Information Center, 2 rue Andre-Pascal, 75775 Paris Cedex 16 France. **Tel** 011 33 1 49104262, US:(202)785-6323, FAX 011 33 1 45248500, 011 33 1 45248176, telex 620 160 OCDE. **(Subscription address:** OECD Publications Center, 2001 L Street, Suite 700, Washington DC 20036. **Tel** (202)822-3873, (202)785-6323.)

LC HG1501
DD 332.1 SP
BALANCES Y ESTADISTICAS DE LA BANCA PRIVADA. (19??)-. Statistical Publication. Spanish. Twelve times a year. 11150ptas. Consejo Superior Bancario, Jose Abascal 57 1, 28003 Madrid Spain. **Tel** 011 34 1 4412720.

LC HC186 .B27 ISSN 0005-4585
DD 330.981/005 BL
BANAS. (Oct. 13, 1979)-. Periodical. Portuguese. Twelve times a year. CR$400.00. Editora Banas SA, Av Presidente Castelo Branco 6241, CEP 05038, Sao Paulo Brazil. **ED** Elizabeth Banas. **Bk Rev. Ad Acc. Circ:** 34,000. available with charts; available with illustrations. **Continues** Banas Informa.

LC HG1501
DD 332.1 IT
BANCA & LAVORO. (19??)-. Italian. Six times a year. L50000.00 Italy; L60000.00 other. Assn Sindacale Aziende Credito, Via Paisiello 5, 00198 Rome Italy. **Tel** 011 39 6 854591.

LC HG1501
DD 332.1 IT
BANCA, BORSA E TITOLI DI CREDITO. (19??)-. Periodical. Italian. Six times a year. L153120. Giuffre Editore SPA, Via Busto Arsizio 40, 20151 Milan Italy. **Tel** 011 398 2 38089200. **ED** Federico Martorano. **Bk Rev. Ad Acc. Circ:** 3,500. **Desc:** Deals with the problems of banking, the stock exchange, and credit instruments from a strictly juridical standpoint.

LC HG1501 ISSN 0210-1688
DD 332.1 SP
UDC 336
BANCA ESPANOLA. [Banca esp.]. (1970)-. Periodical. Spanish. Eleven times a year. $48.85. Banca Espanola, Avda Alfonso XIII 15, Bajo B, 28002 Madrid Spain. **Tel** 011 31 1 5191799.

LC HG3071 .B36
DD 332.1 IT
BANCA, IMPRESA, SOCIETA. Added/Corp Federazione delle Casse di Risparmio dell'Emilia e Romagna. Federazione delle Casse di Risparmio delle Banche del Monte dell'Emilia e Romagna. Vol. 1 (1982)-. Periodical. Italian (English). Three times a year. L73580. Societa Editrice il Mulino, Strada Maggiore 37, 40125 Bologna Italy. **Tel** 011 39 51 256011, FAX 011 39 51 256034.

LC HG1501 ISSN 0005-4615
DD 332.1 MX
BANCA Y COMERCIO. Vol. 1 (Jan. 1962)-. Periodical. Spanish. Four times a year (Jan., Apr., July, Oct.). Escuela Bancaria Y Comercial, Paseo de la Reforma 202, Mexico 6 DF Mexico. **Supersedes** Revista Credito.

LC HG185.C6 A86a ISSN 0120-7040
DD 332 CK
Pr Rev.
BANCA Y FINANZAS. Added/Corp Asociacion Bancaria de Colombia. No. 152 (1976)-. Periodical. Spanish. Six times a year (Jan., Mar., May, July, Sept., Nov.). $57.00. Asociacion Bancaria Colombia, Apartado Aereo 13994, Bogota de 1 Colombia. **Tel** 011 57 1 2813501, FAX 281-3017, telex 44300 ABC CO. **ED** Santiago Gutierrez Viana. Index available. **Circ:** 1,000 (ctrl). **Continues** Asociacion Bancaria de Colombia. Informacion Financiera. **Desc:** Contains technical economic articles and notes.

LC HG1501 ISSN 0393-7062
DD 332.1 IT
UDC 621.38
BANCAMATICA. (1984)-. Periodical. Italian. Ten times a year. L122630. EPC Spa, Via dell'Acqua Traversa 187/189, 00135 Rome Italy. **Tel** 011 39 6 3313000, FAX 011 39 6 3313212. **ED** Pier Roberdo Pais. Index available. **Bk Rev. Ad Acc, Adv Mgr:** Nicolo de Nicolo. **Circ:** 5,000. **Desc:** Contains monthly electronic and safety information for banking and finance.

LC HG19 .B33 ISSN 0005-4623
DD 332.1/05 IT
BANCARIA. [Bancaria]. Added/Corp Associazione Bancaria Italiana. (1945)-. Periodical. Italian. Eleven times a year (publishes monthly except August with two supplements). L88560. Bancaria Editrice SPA, Piazza del Gesu 49, 00186 Rome Italy. **Tel** 011 39 6 6767220. cum. index.
Ind/Abst J. Econ. Lit.; PAIS Int. Print (1991-).

LC HG1501 ISSN 0766-821X
DD 332.1 FR
UDC 681.3 : 336.71
TITLE CHANGE
BANCATIQUE. (1984)-(1993). Periodical. French. Groupe Banque, 18 rue La Fayette, 75009 Paris France. **Tel** 011 33 1 42463787. **Absorbed by** Banque, 0005-5581.

LC HG1501 ISSN 0390-1378
DD 332.1 IT
UDC 332
Pr Rev.
BANCHE E BANCHIERI. [Banche e banchieri]. (1974)-. Periodical. Italian. Twelve times a year. L68130. ICEB, Via Mose Bianchi 71, 20149 Milan Italy. **Tel** 011 39 2 48013830. **ED** Tancredi Bianchi. Index available. cum. index. **Bk Rev. Ad Acc. Circ:** 3,000. **Desc:** Covers banking and finance.

LC HG2889.P47 B35
DD 332 BL
BANDEPE RELATORIO. Main/Corp Banco do Estado de Pernambuco. Portuguese (summaries and/or abstracts in English). One time a year. Cais do Apolo 222, Recife Brazil.

LC HG1501
DD 332.1 PH
●BANGKO SENTRAL REVIEW : A MONTHLY PUBLICATION OF THE BANGKO SENTRAL NG PILIPINAS.
Added/Corp Bangko Sentral ng Pilipinas. **VFOAT** Review. Vol. 1, No. 1 (July 1993)-. Periodical. English. Twelve times a year. $90.00. Central Bank of the Philippines, 5-Storey Building, Mabini Street Room 410, Malate Manila Philippines. **ED** Mercedes B. Suleik. **Circ:** 4,500 (ctrl). **Continues** CB Review. **Desc:** Articles on monetary policies, external debt, industry, banking and finance.

LC HG1501 ISSN 0342-3182
DD 332.1 GW
BANK, DIE. [Bank]. (1977)-. Periodical. German. Twelve times a year. DM120.20. Bank Verlag GmbH, Postfach 300149, Melat 113-115, 50771 Cologne Germany. **Tel** 49 221 54900, FAX 49 221 5490120. **Supersedes** Bank - Betrieb.
Ind/Abst PAIS Int. Print.

LC HG1707 .B361 ISSN 0894-3958
DD 332 US
BANK ACCOUNTING & FINANCE. [Bank account. finance]. VFOAT Bank Accounting and Finance. Vol. 1, No. 1 (Fall 1987)-. Periodical. English. Four times a year. $155.00. Institutional Investor Inc., 488 Madison Avenue, New York NY 10022. **Tel** (212)303-3234, (212)303-3233, FAX (212)303-3353. **ED** Claire Greene. Index available. cum. index. **Bk Rev. Ad Acc. Circ:** 3,000. available on microfilm from University Microfilms International (UMI).
Desc: Designed to keep banking professionals and investors updated on accounting rulings and strategies for risk management and other financial reporting issues.
Ind/Abst Account. Index Suppl. (1987-); Account. Tax Datab. (1987-) [Full Txt.].

LC HG1616.M3 B21 ISSN 0274-7111
DD 332 US
BANK ADVERTISING NEWS. [Bank advert. news]. (19??)-. Periodical. English. Twenty-six times a year (published every other Monday). $398.00. Financial Rates Inc., 11811 US Highway 1, Suite 200, North Palm Beach FL 33408-8888. **Tel** (407)627-7330, FAX (407)627-7335. **(Subscription address:** Financial Rates Inc., PO Box 088888, North Palm Beach FL 33408. **Tel** (407)627-7330.) **ED** Linda Green.
Desc: Provides coverage of bank, thrift and credit union promotions, marketing efforts and advertising campaigns in the nation's top 100 markets as well as financial marketing related conferences.
Ind/Abst F&S Index Plus Text, Int. [Select. Cov.]; Mark. Advert. Ref. Serv.; PROMT.

LC HG4501 .B15 ISSN 0005-5026
DD 332.05 US
BANK AND QUOTATION RECORD. [Bank quota. rec.]. Vol. 1- March 9, 1928-. Periodical. English. Twelve times a year. $130.00. William B. Dana Company, PO Box 1839, Daytona Beach FL 32115. **ED** John Dunne. **Ad Acc. Circ:** 612. **Continues** Commercial and Financial Chronicle. Bank and Quotation Section.
Desc: A compendium of market activity on principal national exchanges. Stocks, bonds, and over-the-counter securities. Plus additional statistical information including call loan rates, certificates of deposit, commercial paper, exchange seats, federal funds, foreign exchange rates, prime bankers acceptance rates, volume of exchange business, and much more.

LC HG13 .O43
DD 332.1/09436 AU
BANK-ARCHIV. VFOAT Bank Archiv. Vol. 36, No. 2 (Feb. 1988)-. Periodical. German. Twelve times a year. S1240.00 Austria; S1149.82 other. Verlag Orac GmbH and Company, Graben 17, A-1014 Vienna Austria. **Tel** 011 43 222 534520, FAX 011 43 222 55162178, telex 136365. **Continues** Osterreichisches Bank-Archiv.
Ind/Abst PAIS Int. Print (1991-).

LC HG1615.25 .B35 ISSN 0896-6230
DD 332.1 US
CCC
BANK ASSET/LIABILITY MANAGEMENT. [Bank asset/liabil. manage.]. VFOAT Bank Asset, Liability Management. Vol. 1, No. 1 (Jan. 1985)-. Periodical. English. Twelve times a year. $204.25. Warren Gorham & Lamont Inc., Park Square Building, 31 St. James Avenue, Boston MA 02116-4112. **Tel** (617)423-2020, (800)950-1207, FAX (617)423-2026. **ED** Peter A. Milhaltian and J. Rubinson, (212)971-5000. **Circ:** 1000.
Desc: Offers practical ways to reduce exposure to interest rate risks, whether it's from the asset or liability side of the balance sheet.

LC HF5601 ISSN 0522-2478
DD 657 US
CCC
BANK AUDITING AND ACCOUNTING REPORT. Vol. 1 (Nov. 1967)-. Periodical. English. Twelve times a year. $173.25. Warren Gorham & Lamont Inc., Park Square Building, 31 St. James Avenue, Boston MA 02116-4112. **Tel** (617)423-2020, (800)950-1207, FAX (617)423-2026. **ED** K. Gary Gibbs and Brent E. Olney.
Desc: Gives up-to-date information on developments in regard to government regulations, practices and techniques in bank accounting and financial controls surrounding the industry.

LC KF967 .B35 ISSN 1047-5133
DD 346.73/0821 347.306821 US
CCC
BANK BAILOUT LITIGATION NEWS. [Bank bailout litig. news]. Vol. 1, No. 1 (Dec. 20, 1989)-. Periodical. English. Twenty-six times a year. $645.00. LRP Publications, 747 Dresher Road, Suite 500, Horsham PA 19044. **Tel** (800)341-7874, (215)784-0941, FAX (215)784-9639, (215)784-0870.

LC HG1501 ISSN 1070-7611
DD 332 US
BANK DIRECTOR (BRENTWOOD, TENN.). (BANK DIRECTOR). [Bank dir.]. Vol. 1, No. 1 (1st Quarter 1991)-. Trade Publication. English. Four times a year. $85.00. Private Business Inc, PO Box 1603,

Brentwood TN 37024. **Tel** (615)371-9095, FAX (615)371-6193. **ED** Deborah Scally. **Ad Acc. Circ:** 40,000.

LC HG1501
DD 332.1 NE
BANK- EN EFFECTENBEDRIJF. **Added/Corp** Nederlands Instituut voor het Bank- en Effectenbedrijf. Vol. 1 (1952)-. Periodical. Dutch. Ten times a year. $102.13. Tibe TAV, Herengracht 205, 1016 BE Amsterdam Netherlands. **Tel** 011 31 20 5208520.

LC HG1501 **ISSN** 0711-6497
DD 332.1/2/0971 CN
BANK FACTS. [Bank facts]. **Added/Corp** Canadian Bankers' Association. **VFOAT** CBA Bank Facts; C.B.A. Bank Facts. **VAT** Canadian Bankers' Association Bank Facts. (1981)-. Trade Publication. English (French). One time a year. Free. Canadian Bankers' Association, Box 348, Commerce Court West, 30th Floor, Toronto Ontario M5L 1G2 Canada. **Tel** (416)362-6092, FAX (416)362-5658, telex 0623402. **Circ:** 55,000 English, 12,000 French. ***Continues*** *Factbook: Chartered Banks of Canada, 0317-4751.*
Desc: A compilation of facts and figures on Canadian chartered banks.

LC HG2401 .B3
DD 332.1/0973/021 US
BANK FINANCIAL QUARTERLY. Vol. 1 (Oct. 1985)-. Corporate Report. English. Four times a year. $369.00. IDC Financial Publishing Inc, PO Box 140, Hartland WI 53029.

LC HG1501 **ISSN** 1065-8165
DD 332 US
BANK FRAUD. [Bank fraud]. **Added/Corp** Bank Administration Institute. Bank Administration Institute Foundation. (1986)-. Periodical. English. Twelve times a year. $174.00. Bank Administration Institute / Chicago, One North Franklin, Chicago IL 60606. **Tel** (312)553-4600, (800)323-8552, FAX (312)683-2373.
Desc: Profiles typical fraud cases, telling what happened, how it was handled, and the final outcome. This is followed by details on preventive measures.

LC HG2481 .A84a **ISSN** 0519-1572
DD 332.1/6 US
BANK HOLDING COMPANY FACTS. **Main/Corp** Association of Bank Holding Companies. (1976)-. English. One time a year. Free on request. Banker's Roundtable, 805 15th Street Nortwest, Suite 600, Washington DC 20002. **Tel** (202)289-4322, FAX (202)785-2605. ***Continues*** *Banking Holding Company Facts.*

LC HG1615.5 .B21
DD 332.1 US
CEASED
BANK HR : BANK HUMAN RESOURCES REPORT. **VFOAT** Bank Human Resources Report. Vol. 24, No. 8 (Oct. 1991)-(1993). Periodical. English. Warren Gorham & Lamont Inc., Park Square Building, 31 St. James Avenue, Boston MA 02116-4112. **Tel** (617)423-2020, (800)950-1207, FAX (617)423-2026. ***Continues*** *Bank Personnel Report, 0162-7449.*

LC HG3137 .B3
DD 332.1 PL
BANK I KREDYT. Vol. 1 (1970)-. Periodical. Polish. Twelve times a year. Price on request. **(Subscription address:** Ars Polona-Ruch, PO Box 1001, Krakowskie Przedmiescie 7, 00-068 Warsaw Poland. **Tel** 011 48 22 261201.) ***Supersedes*** *Narodowy Bank Polski. Wiadomosci.*

LC KF6495.B2 B18 **ISSN** 0734-8037
DD 343.7305/267 347.3035267 US
BANK INCOME TAX RETURN MANUAL, THE. (THE BANK INCOME TAX RETURN MANUAL, WITH SPECIMEN FILLED-IN ... RETURNS.). [Bank income tax return man.]. (1977)-. Trade Publication. English. One time a year. $186.45. Warren Gorham & Lamont Inc., Park Square Building, 31 St. James Avenue, Boston MA 02116-4112. **Tel** (617)423-2020, (800)950-1207, FAX (617)423-2026.

LC HG8011 HG1501
DD 368 332.1 US
•**BANK INSURANCE AND RISK MANAGEMENT.** **See** Insurance.

LC HG9974.3 .B36 **ISSN** 1068-025X
DD 368.8 US
BANK INSURANCE SURVEY REPORT. **See** Insurance.

LC HG1501 **ISSN** 1055-3193
DD 332.1 US
BANK INVESTMENT REPRESENTATIVE. (BANK INVESTMENT REPRESENTATIVE : THE MAGAZINE OF INVESTMENT MARKETING IN FINANCIAL INSTITUTIONS.). (1991)-. Trade Publication. English. Four times a year. Free on request. Quantum Communications Inc., PO Box 4364, Logan UT 84321.
Ind/Abst F&S Index Plus Text, Int. [Select. Cov.].

LC HG1501
DD 332.1 US
BANK LETTER. (19??)-. Newsletter. English. One time a week (51 issues). $1395.00 (one-year), $2495.00 (two-year). Institutional Investor Inc., 488 Madison Avenue, New York NY 10022. **Tel** (212)303-3234, (212)303-3233, FAX (212)303-3353. available on CD-ROM.
Desc: Key information resource for senior banking officials. Coverage includes corporate lending, retail banking, marketing plans, technology and governmental regulations.

LC HG1501
DD 332.1 US
BANK LOAN REPORT. (19??)-. Periodical. English. One time a week. $2700.00. Investment Dealers Digest Inc., Two World Trade Center, 18th Floor, New York NY 10048. **Tel** (212)227-1200, FAX (212)432-1039. available in microform from University Microfilms International (UMI); available on an online database (files 16,485,636/Full-Text) from DIALOG.
Ind/Abst Account. Tax Datab. (Dec. 1991-) [Full Txt.]; PROMT [Full Txt.]; PTS Newsl. Database [Full Txt.].

LC HG1501
DD 332.1 GW
BANK MAGAZIN. (19??)-. German. Twelve times a year. DM160.00. Gabler Verlag, Postfach 1546, D-65005 Wiesbaden Germany. **Tel** 011 49 611 534129, FAX 011 49 611 534430. ***Continues*** *Bankkaufmann.*

LC HG1501 .A87 **ISSN** 1049-1775
DD 332.1/068 US
CODEN BAMAE9
BANK MANAGEMENT (ROLLING MEADOWS, ILL.). (BANK MANAGEMENT.). [Bank manage.]. **Added/Corp** Bank Administration Institute. Vol. 66, No. 1 (Jan. 1990)-. Periodical. English. Six times a year. $59.00. Bank Administration Institute / Chicago, One North Franklin, Chicago IL 60606. **Tel** (312)553-4600, (800)323-8552, FAX (312)683-2373. available on microfilm and microfiche from University Microfilms International (UMI); available on an online database from Lexis-Nexis. Documents available from Ask*IEEE. ***Continues*** *Bank Administration, 1046-1264;* ***Absorbed*** *Bankers Monthly, 0005-5476.*
Ind/Abst Acad. Search; Bus. ASAP (1990-) [Full Txt.]; Bus. Index (1990-); Bus. Source Plus; Bus. Source; Comput. Lit. Index; Curr. Cit.; EP Collect.; Gen. BusinessFile (1990-); Gen. Period. Index (1990-); Homework Help.; INFO-SOUTH Abstr.; INSPEC (Jan. 1990-); Manage. Contents; MasterFile FullTEXT 1000; MasterFile FullTEXT 350; MasterFile FullTEXT 650; MasterFile FullTEXT (July 1993-); OCLC; Telebase; Trade Ind. ASAP [Full Txt.]; Trade Ind. Index [Full Txt.]; UMI ABI/Inform--Bus. Period. Ondisc (Jan. 1987-) [Full Txt.]; Wilson Bus. Abstr.

LC HG1501 .B157 **ISSN** 0888-3149
DD 332 US
BANK MARKETING. [Bank mark.]. Trade Publication. English. Twelve times a year. $98.00. Bank Marketing Association, 309 W Washington Street, Chicago IL 60606. **Tel** (312)782-1442. **ED** James Rubinstein. Index available. cum. index. **Bk Rev. Ad Acc.** available on microfilm and microfiche from University Microfilms International (UMI). Documents available from UMI Article Clearinghouse. ***Continues*** *Bank Marketing Management.*
Ind/Abst ABI/INFORM Glob. Ed.; ABI/INFORM [Computer File] (April 1979-); Acad. Search; Bus. ASAP (1990-) [Full Txt.]; Bus. Index (1985-); Bus. Period. Index; Bus. Source Plus; Bus. Source; Curr. Cit.; EP Collect.; Gen. BusinessFile (1985-); Gen. Period. Index (1985-); Homework Help.; INFO-SOUTH Abstr.; Mag. Search; Manage. Contents; Mark. Advert. Ref. Serv.; MasterFile FullTEXT 1000; MasterFile FullTEXT 350; MasterFile FullTEXT 650; MasterFile FullTEXT (July 1993-); OCLC; PROMT; Telebase; Trade Ind. ASAP [Full Txt.]; Trade Ind. Index [Full Txt.]; UMI ABI/Inform--Bus. Period. Ondisc (Dec. 1987-) [Full Txt.]; Wilson Bus. Abstr.

LC HG1501 **ISSN** 0791-2765
DD 332.1 IE
BANK MARKETING INTERNATIONAL (DUBLIN). **See** Business and Economics-Marketing and Purchasing.

LC HG **ISSN** 1074-6684
DD 332 US
BANK MERGERFAX. [Bank mergerFax]. **Added/Corp** SNL Securities. **VFOAT** Bank Merger Fax; SNL MergerFax. (199?)-. Periodical. English. One time a week. $1700.00. SNL Securities Inc., 410 East Main Street, Charlottesville VA 22902. **Tel** (804)977-1600, (804)977-5877. ***Continues*** *SNL Bank MergerFax.*

LC HG1722 .B35 **ISSN** 1074-6706
DD 332 US
BANK MERGERS & ACQUISITIONS. [Bank mergers acquis.]. **Added/Corp** SNL Securities. **VFOAT** Bank Mergers and Acquisitions. (Aug. 1986)-. Periodical. English. Twelve times a year. $795.00. SNL Securities Inc., 410 East Main Street, Charlottesville VA 22902. **Tel** (804)977-1600, (804)977-5877. available on an online database from NEWSNET.
Desc: In-depth analysis, and national news coverage of mergers and acquisitions in commercial banking and thrift banking in the United States.

LC HG2611.T4 B27 **ISSN** 1056-0777
DD 332.1/09764/021 US
BANK MIDYEAR REVIEW. TEXAS. [Bank midyear rev., Tex.]. **Added/Corp** Sheshunoff Information Services. (19??)-. English. Sheshunoff Information Services Inc., PO Box 13203, Capitol Station, Austin TX 78711. **Tel** (800)456-2340, (512)472-2244. ***Separated from*** *Banks of Texas, 0096-3488.*

LC HG1710 .B36
DD 332.10285 US
BANK NETWORK NEWS. (1982)-. Periodical. English. Twenty-four times a year. $469.95. Faulkner & Gray Inc., 11 Penn Plaza, 17th Floor, New York NY 10001. **Tel** (212)967-7000, (800)535-8403. available on an online database from NEWSNET. ***Absorbed*** *Payment Systems Newsletter (Tampa, Fla.).*
Ind/Abst Account. Tax Datab. (Jan. 1991-) [Full Txt.]; PROMT [Full Txt.]; PTS Newsl. Database [Full Txt.].

LC HG1501 .B158 **ISSN** 0005-5123
DD 332 US
BANK NEWS. [Bank news]. **VFOAT** Bank News Combining Mountain States Banking. 1901-. Trade Publication. English. Twelve times a year. $35.14. Bank News, 912 Baltimore Avenue, Suite 900, Kansas City MO 64105-1784. **Tel** (816)421-7941, FAX (816)472-0397. **ED** Sharon Smith. **Bk Rev. Ad Acc. Circ:** 10,000. ***Absorbed*** *Mountain States Banker, 0027-2590; Mid-Continent Banker (Northern Edition); Mid-Continent Banker (Southern Edition), 0749-7911.*

LC HG4001 .C68
DD 658.15 US
•**BANK OF AMERICA JOURNAL OF APPLIED CORPORATE FINANCE, THE.** **Added/Corp** Bank of America. **VFOAT** Journal of Applied Corporate Finance. Vol. 7, No. 3 (Fall 1994)-. Periodical. English. Four times a year. $125.00. Stern Stewart Management Services Inc, 40 West 57th Street, New York NY 10019. **Tel** (212)261-0600, FAX (212)581-6420. ***Continues*** *BankAmerica Journal of Applied Corporate Finance, 1078-1196.*

LC HG2706 .B35A **ISSN** 0067-3587
DD 332.1/1/0971 CN
BANK OF CANADA. ANNUAL REPORT OF THE GOVERNOR TO THE MINISTER OF FINANCE AND STATEMENT OF ACCOUNTS. (ANNUAL REPORT OF THE GOVERNOR TO THE MINISTER OF FINANCE AND STATEMENT OF ACCOUNTS.). **Main/Corp** Bank of Canada. **VFOAT** Rapport Annuel du Gouverneur au Ministre des Finances et Releve de Comptes. (1955)-. English (French). One time a year. Free. Bank of Canada, 234 Wellington Street, Secretariat Department, Ottawa Ontario K1A 0G9 Canada. **Tel** (613)782-8248, , FAX (613)782-8655, telex 053-4241. ***Supersedes*** *Annual Report to Minister of Finance and Statement of Accounts, 0319-065X.*

LC HC111 .B26 **ISSN** 0045-1460
DD 330.971/005 CN
BANK OF CANADA REVIEW. (BANK OF CANADA REVIEW. REVUE DE LA BANQUE DU CANADA.). [Bank Can. rev.]. **Main/Corp** Bank of Canada. **VFOAT** Revue de la Banque du Canada. (Dec. 1971)-. Periodical. English (French). Four times a year (plus eight supplements). 24.01Can$. Bank of Canada, 234 Wellington Street, Secretariat Department, Ottawa Ontario K1A 0G9 Canada. **Tel** (613)782-8248, , FAX (613)782-8655, telex 053-4241. **ED** Maura Giuliani. Index available. cum. index. ctrl circ. available on an online database from University Microfilms International (UMI). Documents available from UMI Article Clearinghouse. ***Continues*** *Bank of Canada. Statistical Summary, 0005-514X.*
Desc: Wide range of Canadian financial and economic statistics. There are articles in financial and economic topics.
Ind/Abst ABI/INFORM Glob. Ed.; Can. Period. Index (19??-); EP Collect.; Homework Help.; MasterFile FullTEXT 1000; MasterFile FullTEXT 350; MasterFile FullTEXT 650; MasterFile FullTEXT; OCLC; PAIS Int. Print (1991-?); Repere (1983-19??); Telebase.

LC HG2994 .A17 **ISSN** 0005-5166
DD 332/.0941 UK
BANK OF ENGLAND QUARTERLY BULLETIN. [Bank Engl. q. bull.]. Vol. 7, No. 1 (March 1967)-. Bulletin. English. Four times a year. $51.33. Bank of England Bulletin Group, Threadneedle Street, London EC2R 8AH United Kingdom. **Tel** 011 44 171 6014139, FAX 011 44 171 6015288. Index available. cum. index. available on microfilm and microfiche from University Microfilms International (UMI). Documents available from UMI Article Clearinghouse. ***Continues*** *Quarterly Bulletin (Bank of England).*
Ind/Abst ABI/INFORM Glob. Ed.; Contents Recent Econ. J.; Contents Pages Manage.; Curr. Cit.; Manage. Market. Abstr.; PAIS Int. Print.

Business and Economics — Banks and Banking

LC HG41 .B35 ISSN 0288-8432
DD 332/.05 JA
BANK OF JAPAN MONETARY AND ECONOMIC STUDIES. [Bank Jpn. monet. econ. stud.]. Added/Corp Nihon Ginko. Kinyu Kenkyukyoku. VFOAT Monetary and Economic Studies. Vol. 1 No. 1 (June 1983)-. Periodical. English. Two times a year. Institute for Monetary and Economic Studies, Research Division 1, Bank of Japan, CPO Box 203, Tokyo 100-91 Japan.
 Ind/Abst Econ. Lit. Index (1989-); J. Econ. Lit.

LC HG1501 ISSN 0919-1380
DD 332.1 JA
●BANK OF JAPAN QUARTERLY BULLETIN. [Bank Jpn. q. bull.]. Added/Corp Nihon Ginko. VFOAT Quarterly Bulletin. Vol. 1, No. 1 (Feb. 1993)-. Bulletin. English. Four times a year. $51.86. Bank of Japan / Research and Statistics Department, Nihon Ginko, CPO Box 203, Tokyo 100 91 Japan. Tel FAX 011 81 3 6644342. (Subscription address: OCS / Overseas Courier Service Company Ltd. / Japan, 9 2 Shibaura Minato-ku, Tokyo 108 Japan. Tel 011 81 3 4538311.) Continues in part Special Paper (Nihon Ginko. Chosa Tokeikyoku), 0067-3692.

LC HG1501 ISSN 0333-1504
DD 332.1 NO
BANK- OG KREDITTSTATISTIKK: AKTUELLE TALL. See Business and Economics-Abstracting, Bibliographies and Statistics.

LC HG1501 US
DD 332.1
BANK OPERATIONS BULLETIN. 1987-. Bulletin. English. Twelve times a year. $49.00 (one-year) $88.00 (two-year) ASA members, $61.00 (one-year), $112.00 (two-year) other. American Bankers Association, 1120 Connecticut Avenue Northwest, Washington DC 20036. Tel (202)663-5221, (202)663-5000, FAX (202)828-4544. Bk Rev. Ad Acc. Circ: 3,000 (ctrl).
 Desc: Informs bank operations and data processing personnel of the multitude of industry developments and changes in regulations, operational techniques, systems, procedures and standards.

LC HG1501 ISSN 0272-3271
DD 332.1 US
BANK PERSONNEL NEWS. [Bank pers. news]. Added/Corp American Bankers Association. Bank Personnel Division. (19??)-. Trade Publication. English. Twelve times a year. $150.00. American Bankers Association, 1120 Connecticut Avenue Northwest, Washington DC 20036. Tel (202)663-5221, (202)663-5000, FAX (202)828-4544. Bk Rev. Ad Acc. Circ: 2,600 (ctrl).
 Desc: Developments in the human resource area of banking and private industry.

LC HG1507 .A5147 ISSN 0091-0392
DD 332.1/7 US
BANK PROTECTION BULLETIN. Added/Corp American Bankers Association. (19??)-. Bulletin. English. Twelve times a year. $24.00. American Bankers Association, 1120 Connecticut Avenue Northwest, Washington DC 20036. Tel (202)663-5221, (202)663-5000, FAX (202)828-4544. Bk Rev. Ad Acc. Circ: 14,000 (ctrl). Continues American Bankers Association. Protective Bulletin; Issued by the Protective Department of the American Bankers Association.
 Desc: Contains current reports on trends in risk management, and insurance and security topics affecting financial institutions.

LC HG2401 .B34 US
DD 332.1/0973/021
BANK QUARTERLY (AUSTIN, TEX.). (BANK QUARTERLY.). Added/Corp Sheshunoff Rating Services, Inc. VFOAT Bank Quarterly Ratings and Analysis; Bank Quarterly Ratings & Analysis. (19??)-. English. Eight times a year. $225.00. Sheshunoff Information Services, Inc., PO Box 13203, Capitol Station, Austin TX 78711. Tel (800)456-2340, (512)472-2244.
 Desc: Analysis of every bank in the United States. Lists the Sheshunoff rating for each bank, and contains tables and graphs illustrating industry trends.

LC HG1501 US
DD 332.1
BANK RATE MONITOR. Vol. 1, No. 1 (Dec. 20, 1982)-. Periodical. English. One time a week (published on Mondays). $695.00. Financial Rates Inc., 11811 US Highway 1, Suite 200, North Palm Beach FL 33408-8888. Tel (407)627-7330, FAX (407)627-5775. (Subscription address: Financial Rates Inc., PO Box 088888, North Palm Beach FL 33408. Tel (407)627-7330.) ED Gail Liberman.
 Desc: Geared for banking industry - top 100 Federally insured institutions - CD, mortgage, and loan rates. Pricing details on current accounts.

LC HG ISSN 1056-7232
DD 332 US
 TITLE CHANGE
BANK RESOLUTION REPORTER. (BANK RESOLUTION REPORTER.). [Bank resolut. report.]. Added/Corp Dorset Group. Vol. 1, No. 1 (June 24, 1991)-(19??). Periodical. English. Dorset Group Inc., 212 West 35th Street, 13th Floor, New York NY 10001. Tel (212)563-4405, FAX (212)564-8879. Ad Acc, Adv Mgr: Jim Hallander. Merged with Resolution Trust Reporter, 1045-0130 to form Problem Asset Reporter, 1071-4960.

LC HG1501 ISSN 0861-671X
DD 332.1 BU
BANK REVIEW : QUARTERLY JOURNAL. English. Added/Corp Bulgarska Narodna Banka. (19??)-. Periodical. English. Four times a year. $50.00. (Subscription address: Hemus Foreign Trade Organization, 1B Raiko Daskalov Sq Books, 1000 Sofia Bulgaria. Tel 011 359 2 882544, 011 359 2 801575.)

LC HG2441 .B23 ISSN 1049-5673
DD 332.1/025/73 US
... BANK SAFETY DIRECTORY, THE. [Bank saf. dir.]. Added/Corp T.J. Holt & Co. (19??)-. Directory. English. Four times a year. $438.00. Weiss Research Inc., PO Box 109665, Palm Beach Gardens FL 33410. Tel (407)627-3300, FAX (407)625-6685. (Subscription address: Weiss Ratings Inc., PO Box 109665, Palm Beach Garden FL 33410. Tel (407)627-3330 ext. 7.)

LC HG1660.U5 B35 US
DD 332.1/75
BANK, SAVINGS & LOAN CD RATINGS. Added/Corp Standard and Poor's Corporation. VFOAT Bank, Savings and Loan CD Ratings; CD Ratings. (198?)-. Periodical. English. Four times a year. Standard & Poor's Corporation, (A Division of McGraw-Hill, Inc.), 25 Broadway, New York NY 10004. Tel (212)208-8775, (800)221-5277.

LC HG ISSN 1079-1558
DD 332 US
●BANK SECURITIES AND INVESTMENT SERVICES ALERT. [Bank secur. invest. serv. alert]. Added/Corp Warren, Gorham & Lamont, inc. Vol. 1, No. 1 (Oct. 1994)-. Periodical. English. Twelve times a year. $234.75. Warren Gorham & Lamont Inc., Park Square Building, 31 St. James Avenue, Boston MA 02116-4112. Tel (617)423-2020, (800)950-1207, FAX (617)423-2026. (Subscription address: Warren Gorham & Lamont, PO Box 4966, Chicago IL 60680.)

LC HG ISSN 1071-2038
DD 332 US
 CCC
 TITLE CHANGE
BANK SECURITIES REPORT. [Bank secur. rep.]. Added/Corp Phillips Business Information, Inc. Vol. 1, No. 13 (Aug. 27, 1993)-(1994). Corporate Report. English. Phillips Business Information Inc., 1201 Seven Locks Road, PO Box 61130, Potomac MD 20854. Tel (301)424-3338, (301)340-1520, (800)777-5005, FAX (301)424-4297, telex 358149. Continues Bank Securities News, 1068-3763. Continued by Securities Marketing News, 1074-8385.

LC HG1501 ISSN 0162-7457
DD 332.1 US
 CCC
BANK SECURITY REPORT. (19??)-. Periodical. English. Twelve times a year. $167.25. Warren Gorham & Lamont Inc., Park Square Building, 31 St. James Avenue, Boston MA 02116-4112. Tel (617)423-2020, (800)950-1207, FAX (617)423-2026. ED Richard F. Cross.
 Desc: Designed to keep the security/ operations officer informed of the latest developments and newest strategies in both physical and data bank security systems design and equipment, risk analysis, ATM liability and security guard services.

 ISSN 1045-9472
DD 004 US
 CCC
 CODEN BSYTEE
BANK SYSTEMS + TECHNOLOGY. [Bank syst. + technol.]. VFOAT Bank Systems Plus Technology; Bank Systems and Technology. Vol. 26 No. 10 (Oct. 1989)-. Periodical. English. Twelve times a year. $65.00. Miller Freeman Inc., 600 Harrison Street, San Francisco CA 94107. Tel (415)905-2337, (415)905-2200, FAX (415)905-2240, telex 278273. (Subscription address: Bank Systems & Technology, PO Box 1052, Skokie IL 60076. Tel 800-255-2825.) available on microfilm and microfiche from University Microfilms International (UMI); available on an online database (file 15/Full-Text) from DIALOG. Documents available from Ask*IEEE. Continues Bank Systems & Equipment, 0146-0900.
 Ind/Abst Curr. Cit.; F&S Index Plus Text, Int. (19??-) [Select. Cov.]; INSPEC (Oct. 1989-); PROMT (19??-); UMI ABI/Inform--Bus. Period. Ondisc (Feb. 1988-) [Full Txt.].

LC HG ISSN 1060-3506
DD 332 US
 CCC
BANK TECHNOLOGY NEWS. [Bank technol. news]. (Nov./Dec. 1991)-. Periodical. English. Twelve times a year. $63.95. Faulkner & Gray Inc., 11 Penn Plaza, 17th Floor, New York NY 10001. Tel (212)967-7000, (800)535-8403. available on an online database from DIALOG; and NEWSNET. Continues Bank New Product News, 0895-9293.
 Ind/Abst PROMT [Full Txt.].

LC HG ISSN 1061-5555
DD 332 US
 CCC
 CEASED
BANK TECHNOLOGY REPORT. [Bank technol. rep.]. (1992)-(Feb. 1993). Periodical. English. Warren Gorham & Lamont Inc., Park Square Building, 31 St. James Avenue, Boston MA 02116-4112. Tel (617)423-2020, (800)950-1207, FAX (617)423-2026. Continues Bank Operations Report, 0045-1487.

LC HG1501 ISSN 0162-7473
DD 332.1 US
 CCC
BANK TELLER'S REPORT. Added/Corp Warren, Gorham and Lamont, inc. (19??)-. Periodical. English. Twelve times a year. $115.98. Warren Gorham & Lamont Inc., Park Square Building, 31 St. James Avenue, Boston MA 02116-4112. Tel (617)423-2020, (800)950-1207, FAX (617)423-2026. ED Joan German.
 Desc: A timely training tool for bank's tellers. Each issue provides tellers with practical pointers on all phases of banking.

LC HG4001 .C68 ISSN 1078-1196
DD 332 US
 TITLE CHANGE
BANKAMERICA JOURNAL OF APPLIED CORPORATE FINANCE, THE. [BankAm. j. appl. corp. finance]. Added/Corp BankAmerica. VFOAT Journal of Applied Corporate Finance; Bank America Journal of Applied Corporate Finance. (1994)-(1994). Periodical. English. Stern Stewart Management Services Inc, 40 West 57th Street, New York NY 10019. Tel (212)261-0600, FAX (212)581-6420. Continues Continental Bank Journal of Applied Corporate Finance, 0898-4484. Continued by Bank of America Journal of Applied Corporate Finance.

LC HG3051 .D48 ISSN 0943-8750
DD 332.1 GW
●BANKENSTATISTIK. See Business and Economics-Abstracting, Bibliographies and Statistics.

LC HG1505 .B32 ISSN 0522-2931
DD 332.1 II
BANKER, THE. Periodical. English.
 Ind/Abst Bus. Index (1985-); Bus. Period. Index; Contents Recent Econ. J.; Gen. BusinessFile (1985-).

LC HG3290.6.A5 B35
DD 332.1/09549/1 PK
BANKER & BUSINESSMAN. Vol. 1 (Oct. 1971)-. English. $4.00. National Publications Service, PO Box 3431, Karachi 5 Pakistan.

 ISSN 0005-5409
DD 657.833 3 US
BANKER & TRADESMAN. See Real Estate.

LC HG1501 ISSN 0005-5395
DD 332.1 UK
 CODEN BNKRB2
BANKER (LONDON). (THE BANKER.). [Banker]. No. 1 (Jan. 1926)-. Periodical. English. Twelve times a year. $180.00. Financial Times Business Information Ltd, Greystoke Place, Fetter Lane, London EC4A 1ND United Kingdom. Tel 011 44 171 4056969, FAX 011 44 171 2420347. available on microfilm and microfiche from University Microfilms International (UMI). Documents available from UMI Article Clearinghouse.
 Ind/Abst ABI/INFORM Glob. Ed. (19??-); ABI/INFORM [Computer File] (Aug. 1971-); Acad. Search; Br. Humanit. Index (19??-); Bus. Period. Index (19??-); Bus. Source Plus; Bus. Source; Contents Pages Manage. (19??-); EP Collect.; Gen. Period. Index (19??-); Homework Help.; Index Bus. Reports (19??-); INFO-SOUTH Abstr. (19??-); Infomat Int. Bus. (19??-); Mag. Search (19??-); Manage. Market. Abstr. (19??-); MasterFile FullTEXT 1000; MasterFile FullTEXT 350; MasterFile FullTEXT 650; MasterFile FullTEXT (July 1993-); OCLC; Selec. Coop. Index Manage. Period. (19??-); Telebase; Trade Ind. Index (1981-); UMI ABI/Inform--Bus. Period. Ondisc (Nov. 1987-) [Full Txt.]; Wilson Bus. Abstr. (19??-); World Mag. Bank.

LC HG1503 .B18
DD 332.1/05 UK
BANKERS' ALMANAC WORLD RANKING, THE. VFOAT World Ranking. 1st Ed. (1985)-. English. One time a year. $239.00. Reed Information Services Ltd., Windsor Court, East Grinstead House, East Grinstead RH19 1BR United Kingdom. Tel 011 44 1342 326972, FAX 011 44 1342 335977, telex 95127 INFSER G.
 Desc: Provides a listing of the world's leading 3000 international banks arranged according to their world ranking. Ranked by total assets in US dollars, each bank's entry also shows paid-up capital in US dollars and percentage growth in assets.

LC HG1501 ISSN 0005-5425
DD 332.1 US
BANKERS DIGEST (DALLAS, TEX.). (BANKERS DIGEST.). Vol. 1, (June 15, 1942)-. Trade Publication. English. Twenty-six times a year. $24.00. Banker Digest, 7515 Greenville Avenue, Suite 901, Dallas TX 75231. **Tel** (214)373-4544. **ED** Bonnie J. Blackman. cum. index (Legal Phases.). **Bk Rev**, (Qty: varies). **Ad Acc**, **Adv Mgr:** B.J.B. **Circ:** 3,200. available on diskette.
Desc: This magazine is about the financial institution in the Southwest USA.

LC HG3251 .B36
DD 332.1/095 HK
BANKERS HANDBOOK FOR ASIA. (1976)-. English. One time a year. $165.00. Dataline Asia Pacific Limited, 233 Hollywood Road, 3 F Hollywood, Hong Kong Hong Kong. **Tel** 011 852 258155221, FAX 011 852 258542794. **ED** Barun Roy. **Ad Acc**.
Desc: Listing of finance institutions in Asia plus Middle East, information includes summarised balance sheets, names of CEO'S, and addresses of head-office.

LC HG1501 ISSN 0005-545X
DD 332.1 US
CCC
CODEN BNMGBD
BANKERS MAGAZINE (BOSTON), THE. (THE BANKERS MAGAZINE.). [Bank. mag.]. Vol. 147 (1964)-. Trade Publication. English. Six times a year. $141.75. Warren Gorham & Lamont Inc., Park Square Building, 31 St. James Avenue, Boston MA 02116-4112. **Tel** (617)423-2020, (800)950-1207, FAX (617)423-2026. **ED** Philip Ruppel. cum. index. **Ad Acc. Circ:** 6,000. available on microfilm from University Microfilms International (UMI). Documents available from UMI Article Clearinghouse. ***Continues in part** Banking Law Journal, 0005-5506.*
Desc: Features regular columns in key industry areas, such as operations and technology, marketing, international banking, corporate banking, and human resources. Includes analysis of successful strategies and case studies in all areas of the banking and financial services industry.
Ind/Abst ABI/INFORM Glob. Ed.; ABI/INFORM [Computer File] (Fall 1971-); Acad. Search; Account. Art.; Bus. Index (1985-); Bus. Period. Index; Bus. Source Plus; Bus. Source; Comput. Lit. Index; Contents Pages Manage.; Curr. Cit.; EP Collect.; Fed. Tax Artic.; Gen. BusinessFile (1985-); Gen. Period. Index (1985-); Homework Help.; INFO-SOUTH Abstr.; Mag. Search; MasterFile FullTEXT 1000; MasterFile FullTEXT 350; MasterFile FullTEXT 650; MasterFile FullTEXT (July 1993-); OCLC; PAIS Int. Print (1991-); Telebase; Trade Ind. Index (1981-); Wilson Bus. Abstr.

LC HG ISSN 1046-1620
DD 332 US
BANKERS MIDDLE MARKET LENDING LETTER. [Bank. middle mark. lend. lett.]. Vol. 1, No. 1 (Aug. 1989)-. Periodical. English. Twelve times a year. $98.00. Faulkner & Gray Inc., 11 Penn Plaza, 17th Floor, New York NY 10001. **Tel** (212)967-7000, (800)535-8403. ***Continues** Bankers Lending Letter, 8755-271X.*

LC HG1501 ISSN 0005-5476
DD 332.1 US
CODEN BNKMAK
TITLE CHANGE
BANKERS MONTHLY. [Bank. mon.]. (1917)-(1993). Periodical. English. Bankers Monthly Inc, 200 West 57th Street, New York NY 10019. **Tel** (212)399-1084. **ED** Robert Bruce Slater. Index available. **Bk Rev**. **Ad Acc. Circ:** 25,000 (ctrl). available on microfilm and microfiche from University Microfilms International (UMI). Documents available from UMI Article Clearinghouse. ***Absorbed** Bankers Service Bulletin; **Continues** Rand McNally Bankers Monthly. **Absorbed by** Bank Management, 1049-1775.*
Desc: Written to meet the information needs of bank and financial executives. Areas include banking and financial news, trends, and developments.
Ind/Abst ABI/INFORM Glob. Ed.; ABI/INFORM [Computer File] (Aug. 1971-); Bus. ASAP (1992-) [Full Txt.]; Bus. Index (1985-); Bus. Period. Index; Gen. BusinessFile (1985-); Gen. Period. Index (1985-); Mag. Search; Trade Ind. ASAP [Full Txt.]; Trade Ind. Index (1981-) [Full Txt.]; UMI ABI/Inform--Bus. Period. Ondisc (Jan. 1987-) [Full Txt.]; Wilson Bus. Abstr.

LC HG1501 ISSN 1069-5907
DD 332 US
●**BANKERS NEWS.** (BANKERS NEWS : THE BIWEEKLY NEWSPAPER OF THE AMERICAN BANKERS ASSOCIATION.). [Bank. news]. **Added/Corp** American Bankers Association. Vol. 1, Issue 1 (Apr. 27, 1993)-. Trade Publication. English. Irregular (25 issues). $96.00. American Bankers Association, 1120 Connecticut Avenue Northwest, Washington DC 20036. **Tel** (202)663-5221, (202)663-5000, FAX (202)828-4544. ***Continues** ABA Bankers Weekly, 0889-7662.*
Desc: Information concerning banks and banking.

LC HG1581 .B34 ISSN 0145-5850
DD 332.1/07/1173 US
BANKERS SCHOOLS DIRECTORY. Directory. English. Every 2 years. $9.00. American Bankers Association, 1120 Connecticut Avenue Northwest, Washington DC 20036. **Tel** (202)663-5221, (202)663-5000, FAX (202)828-4544.

LC HG1536 .B33 ISSN 0376-6616
DD 332.1/025 BE
BANKER'S WORLD DIRECTORY, THE. Directory. Multiple languages (English, French, German and Spanish).

LC HG1501 ISSN 0170-6659
DD 332.1 GW
UDC 336.7 (075) CCC
BANKFACHKLASSE, DIE. [Bankfachklasse]. (1978)-. Periodical. German. Twelve times a year. DM98.00. Gabler Verlag, Postfach 1546, D-65005 Wiesbaden Germany. **Tel** 011 49 611 534129, FAX 011 49 611 534430.

LC HG1551 .Z44
DD 332.1 GW
BANKHISTORISCHES ARCHIV. **Added/Corp** Institut fuer Bankhistorisches Forschung. (19??)-. Periodical. German. Two times a year. $66.79. Fritz Knapp Verlag, Postfach 111151, D-60046 Frankfurt Germany. **Tel** 011 49 69 9708330, FAX 011 49 69 7078400. ***Continues** Archiv des Instituts fuer Bankhistorische Forschung.*
Desc: Publication providing information on money, banks and banking.
Ind/Abst Am. Hist. Life (1990-).

LC HG1501
DD 332.1 IT
Pr Rev.
BANKING ABSTRACTS. (19??)-. Italian. Eleven times a year. L160000 Italy; L200000 other. ICEB, Via Mose Bianchi 71, 20149 Milan Italy. **Tel** 011 39 2 48013830. **ED** Laura Pirovano. **Bk Rev. Circ:** 1,500.

LC HG1501
DD 332.1 US
BANKING & FINANCE. **Added/Corp** Federal Reserve Bank of St. Louis. **VFOAT** Banking and Finance. (19??)-. Periodical. English. Four times a year. Free. Research and Public Information Department, Federal Reserve Bank of St. Louis, PO Box 442, St Louis MO 63166. **Tel** (314)444-8660. **ED** Daniel P. Brennan. **Circ:** 5,000.
Desc: A regionally oriented publication devoted to the developments in banking in the Eighth Federal Reserve District.

LC HG1501 ISSN 0265-7988
DD 332.107 UK
BANKING & FINANCIAL TRAINING. [Bank. financ. train.]. **VFOAT** Banking and Financial Training; Banking & Financial Training International Newsletter. (1983)-. Trade Publication. English. Ten times a year. $419.25. Armstrong Information Ltd., 3rd Floor Brigade House, Parsons Green, London SW6 4TH United Kingdom. **Tel** 011 44 171 7367111, FAX 011 44 171 3717806. **ED** Richard Warren. **Ad Acc. Circ:** 4,000 (ctrl).
Desc: Information and opinions on training in the financial sector worldwide.

LC HG1501 ISSN 1351-5543
DD 332.1 UK
BANKING AUTOMATION BULLETIN FOR EUROPE. **VFOAT** BABE. (1991)-. Newsletter. English. Ten times a year. $480.00. Retail Banking Research Ltd., 15 Hanover Square, London W1R 9AJ United Kingdom. **Tel** 011 44 171 495 8871, FAX 011 44 171 493 0539. **ED** P. Hirsch. Index available. cum. index. **Bk Rev**, (Qty: 10). **Acid Free. Circ:** 1,000. ***Continues** Battelle on Automated Banking in Europe.*
Desc: Issues are written by industry specialists and provides you with information and analysis with a Pan-European perspective.

LC HG1501
DD 332.1 US
BANKING COMPANY REPORT. (19??)-. English. Four times a year. $200.00. Swords Associates Inc., 1600 h Creek, Genessee Suite 828, Kansas City MO 64102. **Tel** (816)283-3377, FAX (816)283-3366. **ED** Michael Swords. **Circ:** 200.

LC HG1501 ISSN 1356-6431
DD 332.1 UK
BANKING GUIDE TO THE FORMER SOVIET UNION, THE. (19??)-. English. Two times a year. £470.00. The CIS Technical Publishing Institute, 11-13 Charterhouse Buildings, London EC1M 7AN United Kingdom. **Tel** 011 44 171 4903774, FAX 011 44 171 4905371.

LC Z7164.F5 A53 HG1501 ISSN 1075-282X
DD 016.3321 US
●**BANKING INFORMATION INDEX. See** Business and Economics-Abstracting, Bibliographies and Statistics.

LC HG1501 ISSN 0791-1386
DD 332.1 IE
BANKING IRELAND. **Added/Corp** Institute of Bankers in Ireland. Vol. 1, No. 1 (Spring 1989)-. Trade Publication. English. Four times a year. $43.71. Institute of Bankers in Ireland, Nassau House, Nassau Street, Dublin 2 Ireland. **Tel** 011 353 1 793311, FAX 011 353 1 793504. **ED** Sean McQuaid. Index available. ***Continues** Journal of the Institute of Bankers in Ireland, 0020-272X.*

LC HG1501
DD 332.1 US
CEASED
BANKING SAFETY DIGEST. (19??)-(1994). English. Veribanc Inc., PO Box 461, Wakefield MA 01880. **Tel** (617)245-8370, (800)442-2657, FAX (617)246-5291. **ED** Warren G. Heller. **Bk Rev**, (Qty: 2).
Desc: Contains financial information.

LC HG1501 ISSN 0266-0865
DD 332.1 UK
CODEN BATEEM
BANKING TECHNOLOGY. [Bank. technol.]. Trade Publication. English. Twelve times a year. $220.00. World Wide Subscription Services, Unit 4, Gibbs Reed Farm, East Sussex TN5 7HE United Kingdom. **Tel** 011 44 1580 200657, FAX 011 44 1580 200616. **(Subscription address:** IBC Subscription Services, IBC House, Vickers Drive, Weybridge, Surrey KT13 OXS United Kingdom. **Tel** 011 44 1932 354020.) Documents available from Ask*IEEE.
Ind/Abst Contents Pages Manage.; Curr. Cit.; HILITES; Infomat Int. Bus.; INSPEC (1987-).

LC HG1709 .B353 ISSN 1054-3317
DD 004/.029/473 US
TITLE CHANGE
... BANKING TECHNOLOGY DIRECTORY, THE. [Bank. technol. dir.]. 3rd Ed. (1991)-(1993). Directory. English. Phillips Business Information Inc., 1201 Seven Locks Road, PO Box 61130, Potomac MD 20854. **Tel** (301)424-3338, (301)340-1520, (800)777-5005, FAX (301)424-4297, telex 358149. ***Continues** EFT Sourcebook. **Continued by** Retail Banking Sourcebook.*
Desc: Directory and buyer's guide for electronic banking operations. It covers key areas of banking technology--automation teller machines, branch automation, bank card terminals, computers, ATM/POS support products, networking, communications, item processing equipment, imaging, etc.

LC HG ISSN 0893-8873
DD 332 US
CCC
TITLE CHANGE
BANKING WEEK. [Bank. week]. **VFOAT** Banking Week for Financial Services Executives. (198?)-(19??). Periodical. English. American Banker, Concourse Level, 1 State Street Plaza, New York NY 10004. **Tel** (212)803-8200, (800)221-1809, FAX (212)943-6256, (212)843-9598. ***Continues** Practical Banker. **Continued by** American Banker.*

LC HG1503 .B44 ISSN 0737-6413
DD 332.1/05 UK
CCC
CEASED
BANKING WORLD. **Added/Corp** Institute of Bankers (Great Britain). Vol. 1, No. 1 (July 1983)-(June 1995). Trade Publication. English. Headway Home and Law Publ Ltd., Haymarket House, 1 Oxendon Street, London SW1Y 4EE United Kingdom. **Tel** 011 44 171 9761515. **ED** Garth Hewitt. Index available. **Bk Rev. Ad Acc. Circ:** 125,000. available on microfilm and microfiche from University Microfilms International (UMI). Documents available from UMI Article Clearinghouse, Ask*IEEE. ***Formed by the union of** Bankers Magazine, 0005-5441 **and** Institute of Bankers (Great Britain). Journal of the Institute of Bankers, 0020-2738.*
Desc: Banking and finance periodical, for bankers at all levels; a means of communication between members of the institute.
Ind/Abst ABI/INFORM Glob. Ed.; ABI/INFORM [Computer File] (October 1987); Comput. Lit. Index; Contents Pages Manage.; Curr. Cit.; Infomat Int. Bus.; INSPEC (July 1983-); PAIS Int. Print (1991-); Public Aff. Inf. Serv. Bull.

LC HG3221 .B36 ISSN 0861-6701
DD 332.1 BU
BANKOV PREGLED / BULGARSKA NARODNA BANKA. **Added/Corp** Bulgarska Narodna Banka. Vol. 1, No. 1 (1992)-. Periodical. Bulgarian. Four times a year. DM98.00. Bulgarska Narodna Banka, Sofiia Bulgaria. **(Subscription address:** Kubon & Sagner, ABT Zeitschriftenimport, D 80328 Munich Germany. **Tel** 011 49 89 54218130.)

LC HD61 .B345 ISSN 1056-8115
DD 332 US
Pr Rev. CEASED
BANKRISK (STAMFORD, CONN.). (BANKRISK : THE BANK RISK MANAGEMENT QUARTERLY.). [Bankrisk]. **Added/Corp** Tillinghast (Firm). **VFOAT** Bank Risk. (1983)-(Dec. 1995). Periodical. English. Tillinghast Publications, 695 East Main Street, Suite 600, Stamford CT 06901. **Tel** (203)326-5400, FAX

(203)326-5498. **ED** Edith Lichota. **Circ:** 800.
Desc: A quarterly publication dedicated to effective bank and financial institution risk management. The bank officer's guide to challenge and change, from risk assessment and control to risk assessment and control to risk financing and administration.

LC KF1507.5 .B36 **ISSN** 1054-9463
DD 346/.078/05 342.67805 US
BANKRUPTCY YEARBOOK AND ALMANAC, THE. [Bankruptcy yearb. alm.]. **Added/Corp** New Generation Research. **VFOAT** Bankruptcy Yearbook & Almanac. 1st Ed. (1991)-. English. One time a year. $175.00. New Generation Research Inc / Boston, 225 Friend Street, Suite 801, Box 6721, Boston MA 02114. **Tel** (800)468-3810.

LC HG2611.A7 B35 **ISSN** 0360-232X
DD 332.1/09767 US
BANKS OF ARKANSAS, THE. [Banks Ark.]. **Added/Corp** Sheshunoff & Company. (19??)-?. English. Two times a year. Sheshunoff Information Services Inc., PO Box 13203, Capitol Station, Austin TX 78711. **Tel** (800)456-2340, (512)472-2244. ***Continued in part by*** *Bank Midyear Review. Arkansas.*

LC HG2611.C6 B35 **ISSN** 0360-425X
DD 332.1/09788 US
BANKS OF COLORADO, THE. [Banks Colo.]. **Added/Corp** Sheshunoff & Company. (19??)-?. English. Two times a year. Sheshunoff Information Services Inc., PO Box 13203, Capitol Station, Austin TX 78711. **Tel** (800)456-2340, (512)472-2244. ***Continued in part by*** *Bank Midyear Review. Colorado, 1056-117X.*

LC HG2611.G42 B35 **ISSN** 0361-4808
DD 332.1/09758 US
BANKS OF GEORGIA, THE. [Banks Ga.]. **Added/Corp** Sheshunoff & Company. (19??)-?. English. Two times a year. Sheshunoff Information Services Inc., PO Box 13203, Capitol Station, Austin TX 78711. **Tel** (800)456-2340, (512)472-2244. ***Continued in part by*** *Bank Midyear Review. Georgia, 1056-0645.*

LC HG2611.I3 B35 **ISSN** 0360-4268
DD 332.1/09773 US
BANKS OF ILLINOIS, THE. [Banks Ill.]. **Added/Corp** Sheshunoff & Company. (19??)-?. English. Two times a year. Sheshunoff Information Services Inc., PO Box 13203, Capitol Station, Austin TX 78711. **Tel** (800)456-2340, (512)472-2244. ***Continued in part by*** *Bank Midyear Review. Illinois, 1056-1188.*

LC HG2611.I4 B35 **ISSN** 0360-4276
DD 332.1/09772 US
BANKS OF INDIANA, THE. [Banks Ind.]. **Added/Corp** Sheshunoff & Company. Sheshunoff Information Services. (19??)-?. English. Two times a year. Sheshunoff Information Services Inc., PO Box 13203, Capitol Station, Austin TX 78711. **Tel** (800)456-2340, (512)472-2244. ***Continued in part by*** *Bank Midyear Review. Indiana, 1056-0653.*

LC HG2611.I8 B35 **ISSN** 0360-4284
DD 332.1/09777 US
BANKS OF IOWA, THE. [Banks Iowa]. **Added/Corp** Sheshunoff & Company. (19??)-?. English. Two times a year. Sheshunoff Information Services Inc., PO Box 13203, Capitol Station, Austin TX 78711. **Tel** (800)456-2340, (512)472-2244. ***Continued in part by*** *Bank Midyear Review. Iowa, 1056-0661.*

LC HG2611.K22 B35 **ISSN** 0361-4816
DD 332.1/09781 US
BANKS OF KANSAS. [Banks Kans.]. **Added/Corp** Sheshunoff & Company. (19??)-?. English. Two times a year. Sheshunoff Information Services Inc., PO Box 13203, Capitol Station, Austin TX 78711. **Tel** (800)456-2340, (512)472-2244. ***Continued in part by*** *Bank Midyear Review. Kansas, 1056-067X.*

LC HG2611.K42 B35 **ISSN** 0361-4824
DD 332.1/09769 US
BANKS OF KENTUCKY, THE. [Banks Ky.]. **Added/Corp** Sheshunoff & Company. (19??)-. English. Two times a year. Sheshunoff Information Services Inc., PO Box 13203, Capitol Station, Austin TX 78711. **Tel** (800)456-2340, (512)472-2244. ***Continued in part by*** *Bank Midyear Review. Kentucky, 1056-0688.*

LC HG2611.L6 B35 **ISSN** 0360-4292
DD 332.1/09763 US
BANKS OF LOUISIANA. [Banks La.]. **Added/Corp** Sheshunoff & Company. (19??)-?. English. Two times a year. Sheshunoff Information Services Inc., PO Box 13203, Capitol Station, Austin TX 78711. **Tel** (800)456-2340, (512)472-2244. ***Continued in part by*** *Bank Midyear Review. Louisiana, 1056-0696.*

LC HG2611.M5 B35 **ISSN** 0360-2338
DD 332.1/09774 US
BANKS OF MICHIGAN, THE. [Banks Mich.]. **Added/Corp** Sheshunoff & Company. (19??)-?. English. Two times a year. Sheshunoff Information Services Inc., PO Box 13203, Capitol Station, Austin TX 78711. **Tel** (800)456-2340, (512)472-2244. ***Continued in part by*** *Bank Midyear Review. Michigan, 1056-070X.*

LC HG2611.M6 B35 **ISSN** 0360-4306
DD 332.1/09776 US
BANKS OF MINNESOTA. [Banks Minn.]. **Added/Corp** Sheshunoff & Company. (19??)-?. English. Two times a year. Sheshunoff Information Services Inc., PO Box 13203, Capitol Station, Austin TX 78711. **Tel** (800)456-2340, (512)472-2244. ***Continued in part by*** *Bank Midyear Review. Minnesota, 1056-1277.*

LC HG2611.M72 B35 **ISSN** 0361-4832
DD 332.1/09762 US
BANKS OF MISSISSIPPI, THE. [Banks Miss.]. **Added/Corp** Sheshunoff & Company. (19??)-?. English. Two times a year. Sheshunoff Information Services Inc., PO Box 13203, Capitol Station, Austin TX 78711. **Tel** (800)456-2340, (512)472-2244. ***Continued in part by*** *Bank Midyear Review. Mississippi, 1056-0718.*

LC HG2611.M8 B35 **ISSN** 0360-4314
DD 332.1/09778 US
BANKS OF MISSOURI, THE. [Banks Mo.]. **Added/Corp** Sheshunoff & Company. (19??)-?. English. Sheshunoff Information Services Inc., PO Box 13203, Capitol Station, Austin TX 78711. **Tel** (800)456-2340, (512)472-2244. ***Continued in part by*** *Bank Midyear Review. Missouri, 1061-5075.*

LC HG2611.N22 B35 **ISSN** 0361-4840
DD 332.1/09782 US
BANKS OF NEBRASKA. [Banks Neb.]. **Added/Corp** Sheshunoff & Company. (19??)-?. English. Sheshunoff Information Services Inc., PO Box 13203, Capitol Station, Austin TX 78711. **Tel** (800)456-2340, (512)472-2244. ***Continued in part by*** *Bank Midyear Review. Nebraska, 1056-0726.*

LC HG2601 .B35 **ISSN** 0361-4859
DD 332.1/0974 US
BANKS OF NEW ENGLAND. Added/Corp Sheshunoff & Company. (19??)-. English. Sheshunoff Information Services Inc., PO Box 13203, Capitol Station, Austin TX 78711. **Tel** (800)456-2340, (512)472-2244. ***Continued in part by*** *Bank Midyear Review. New England, 1056-0734.*

LC HG2611.O3 B35 **ISSN** 0360-2362
DD 332.1/09771 US
BANKS OF OHIO, THE. [Banks Ohio]. (19??)-. English. One time a year. Sheshunoff Information Services Inc., PO Box 13203, Capitol Station, Austin TX 78711. **Tel** (800)456-2340, (512)472-2244. ***Continued in part by*** *Bank Midyear Review. Ohio.*

LC HG2611.O5 B35 **ISSN** 0360-2354
DD 332.1/09766 US
BANKS OF OKLAHOMA. [Banks Okla.]. **Added/Corp** Sheshunoff & Company. (19??)-?. English. Two times a year. Sheshunoff Information Services Inc., PO Box 13203, Capitol Station, Austin TX 78711. **Tel** (800)456-2340, (512)472-2244. ***Continued in part by*** *Bank Midyear Review. Oklahoma, 1056-0769.*

LC HG2611.P4 B35 **ISSN** 0360-2346
DD 332.1/09748 US
BANKS OF PENNSYLVANIA. [Banks Pa.]. **Added/Corp** Sheshunoff & Company. (19??)-?. English. Two times a year. Sheshunoff Information Services Inc., PO Box 13203, Capitol Station, Austin TX 78711. **Tel** (800)456-2340, (512)472-2244. ***Continued in part by*** *Bank Midyear Review. Pennsylvania, 1056-5205.*

LC HG2611.T22 B35 **ISSN** 0361-4867
DD 332.1/09768 US
BANKS OF TENNESSEE. [Bank Tenn.]. **Added/Corp** Sheshunoff & Company. (19??)-?. English. Two times a year. Sheshunoff Information Services Inc., PO Box 13203, Capitol Station, Austin TX 78711. **Tel** (800)456-2340, (512)472-2244. ***Continued in part by*** *Bank Midyear Review. Tennessee.*

LC HG2611.T4 B28 **ISSN** 0096-3488
DD 332.1/09764 US
BANKS OF TEXAS, THE. [Banks Tex.]. **Added/Corp** Sheshunoff & Company. (19??)-?. English. Sheshunoff Information Services Inc., PO Box 13203, Capitol Station, Austin TX 78711. **Tel** (800)456-2340, (512)472-2244. ***Continued in part by*** *Bank Midyear Review. Texas, 1056-0777.*

LC HG2611.N82 B35 **ISSN** 0361-4875
DD 332.1/09756 US
BANKS OF THE CAROLINAS, THE. [Banks Carol.]. **Added/Corp** Sheshunoff & Company. (19??)-?. English. Sheshunoff Information Services Inc., PO Box 13203, Capitol Station, Austin TX 78711. **Tel** (800)456-2340, (512)472-2244. ***Continued in part by*** *Bank Midyear Review. Carolinas, 1061-6195.*

LC HG2609 .B35 **ISSN** 0361-4883
DD 332.1/0978 US
BANKS OF THE WEST. [Banks west]. **Added/Corp** Sheshunoff & Company. (19??)-?. English. Two times a year. Sheshunoff Information Services Inc., PO Box 13203, Capitol Station, Austin TX 78711. **Tel** (800)456-2340, (512)472-2244. ***Continued in part by*** *Bank Midyear Review. West, 1056-1315.*

LC HG2611.W6 B35 **ISSN** 0360-4322
DD 332.1/09775 US
BANKS OF WISCONSIN. [Banks Wis.]. **Added/Corp** Sheshunoff & Company. (19??)-?. English. Two times a year. Sheshunoff Information Services Inc., PO Box 13203, Capitol Station, Austin TX 78711. **Tel** (800)456-2340, (512)472-2244. ***Continued in part by*** *Bank Midyear Review. Wisconsin, 1056-0785.*

LC HG1501
DD 332.1 HU
BANKSZEMLE. [Bankszemle]. (1957)-. Hungarian. Twelve times a year.
Ind/Abst Numis. Lit.; World Agric. Econ. Rural Sociol. Abstr.

LC HG1501 **ISSN** 0184-9719
DD 332.1 FR
UDC 38
BANQUE AFRIQUE PARIS. (BANQUE AFRIQUE.). (1975)-. Periodical. French. Six times a year. $874.88. IC Publications Ediafric, 10 rue Vineuse, 75116 Paris France. **Tel** 011 33 1 44308100.

LC HG1501 **ISSN** 0992-3233
DD 332.1 FR
UDC 347.734(44)
BANQUE & DROIT PARIS. (BANQUE & DROIT.). **VFOAT** Banque et Droit (Paris). (1988)-. Periodical. French. Six times a year. $240.60. Groupe Banque, 18 rue La Fayette, 75009 Paris France. **Tel** 011 33 1 42463787.

LC HG3038.B3 B36A
DD 332.1/5/094 FR
BANQUE COMMERCIALE POUR L'EUROPE DU NORD (EUROBANK) : RAPPORT. Main/Corp Banque Commerciale pour l'Europe du Nord. (19??)-. English (French). 79-81 Boulevard Haussmann, 75382 Paris Cedex 08 France.

LC HG1501
DD 332.1 FR
BANQUE ET INFORMATIQUE. [Banque inform.]. **VFOAT** B.I. Magazine. Banque et Informatique. (1981)-. French. Seven times a year. $131.23. Groupe Bi Magazines, 14 rue du Champ de Mars, 75007 Paris France. **Tel** 011 33 1 45517534, FAX 011 33 1 45561576. cum. index. **Ad Acc.**

LC HG1505 .B4 **ISSN** 0005-5581
DD 332.1 FR
CCC
BANQUE (PARIS. 1926). (BANQUE.). [Banque]. (1926)-. Periodical. French. Eleven times a year. $166.22. Banque, 18 rue La Fayette, 75009 Paris France. **Tel** 42 47 17 80, FAX 48 24 12 97. ***Absorbed*** *Bancatique, 0766-821X.*
Ind/Abst PAIS Int. Print (1991-); Selec. Coop. Index Manage. Period.

LC HG1501 **ISSN** 0822-6849
DD 331.1/0971 CN
BANQUIER (MONTREAL). (LE BANQUIER.). [Banquier]. (Aug. 1983)-. Periodical. French. Six times a year. 35.00Can$. Canadian Bankers' Association, Box 348, Commerce Court West, 30th Floor, Toronto Ontario M5L 1G2 Canada. **Tel** (416)362-6092, FAX (416)362-5658, telex 0623402. **ED** Jacques Hebert. **Bk Rev. Ad Acc. Circ:** 7,700 (ctrl). ***Continues*** *Banquier et Revue IBC, 0315-6281.*
Desc: Articles of interest to those in the banking industry, other financial institutions and business, on Canadian and international banking and economics; interviews with senior bankers; nostalgic and opinion articles.
Ind/Abst Can. Legal Lit.; Can. Period. Index (19??-); Repere (1983-).

LC HG3000.L84 B294 **ISSN** 0956-5574
DD 332/.05 UK
BARCLAYS ECONOMIC REVIEW. **Added/Corp** Barclays Bank. (May 1989)-. Periodical. English. Four times a year. $51.33. Barclays Bank Ltd, PO Box 12, 1 Wimborne Road, Poole Dorset BH15 2BB United Kingdom. **Tel** 011 44 1202 671212, telex 887591. available on an online database from DIALOG; and DATA-STAR. ***Continues*** *Barclays Review, 0269-7009.*
Ind/Abst Gen. BusinessFile (1992-); Selec. Coop. Index Manage. Period.

LC HG1 .B3 **ISSN** 1077-8039
DD 332 US
CCC
●**BARRON'S (CHICOPEE, MASS.). See** Business and Economics-Investments.

LC HG1 .B3 **ISSN** 0005-6073
DD 332 US
CCC
CODEN BRNSAD
TITLE CHANGE
BARRON'S NATIONAL BUSINESS AND FINANCIAL WEEKLY. [Barron's natl. bus. financ. wkly.]. **VFOAT** Barron's. Vol. 22, No. 32 (Aug. 10, 1942)-Vol. 74, No. 9 (Feb. 28, 1994). Periodical. English. Dow Jones and Company Inc., 200 Burnett Road, Chicopee MA 01021. **Tel** (413)592-7761, (800)568-7625. **Bk Rev. Ad Acc. Circ:** 280,000. available on microfilm

Business and Economics —Banks and Banking

from University Microfilms International (UMI). Documents available from UMI Article Clearinghouse, Documents on Demand. **Continues** Barron's. **Continued by** Barron's (Chicopee, Mass.), 1077-8039.
  Ind/Abst ABI/INFORM Glob. Ed.; ABI/INFORM Ondisc: Expr. Ed.; ABI/INFORM [Computer File]; Abstr. BioCommer.; AGRICOLA; BioBusiness; Bus. Index; Bus. Period. Index; Energy Inf. Abstr.; Environ. Abstr.; F&S Index Plus Text, Int.; Foods Adlibra; Gen. BusinessFile; Gen. Period. Index; INFO-SOUTH Abstr.; Infobank; Mag. Index Plus; Mag. Index. Sel.; Mag. Search; MasterFile FullTEXT (Jan. 1994-); Newsp. Period. Abstr.; PROMT; Mag. Index; Trade Ind. Index; UMI ABI/Inform--Bus. Period. Ondisc; Wilson Bus. Abstr.

LC HG1501
DD 332.1 US
BAUER FINANCIAL REPORTS OF ALL BANKS & THRIFTS. (19??)-. English. Four times a year. $117.00 (Illinois and Texas); $87.00 (other). Bauer Financial Reports Inc, PO Drawer 145510, Coral Gables FL 33114. **Tel** (305)441-2062.

LC HG1501
DD 332.1 CN
BCA FORETRENDS. (19??)-. English. $6000.00 (full service). BCA Publications Ltd., 1002 Sherbrooke Street West, Suite 1600, Montreal Quebec H3A 3L6 Canada. **Tel** (514)499-9706, FAX (514)499-9709.

LC HG226 .B36 ISSN 0849-1364
DD 332.63/23 CN
CODEN BIRFE3
BCA INTEREST RATE FORECAST. [BCA interest rate forecast]. **VFOAT** Interest Rate Forecast. **VAT** Bank Credit Analyst Interest Rate Forecast. Vol. 12, No. 2 (Feb. 1990)-. Periodical. English. Twelve times a year. 695.00Can$. BCA Publications Ltd., 1002 Sherbrooke Street West, Suite 1600, Montreal Quebec H3A 3L6 Canada. **Tel** (514)499-9706, FAX (514)499-9709. **Continues** Bank Credit Analyst. Interest Rate Forecast., 0821-7858.

LC HG1501 ISSN 0005-8343
DD 332.1 NE
UDC 336.76
BELEGGERS BELANGEN. [Beleggers belangen]. **VFOAT** Financieel Economisch Weekblad. (1956)-. Periodical. Dutch. One time a week. Fl215.20. BV Uitgeversmaatschappij Bonaventura, PO Box 2158, 1000 CD Amsterdam Netherlands. **Tel** 011 31 20 6914111, 011 31 20 5674911. **Continues** Bericht - Vereniging Effectenbescherming; **Absorbed** Financiele Koerier.

LC HG1501
DD 332.1 US
BELL & HOWELL NEWSPAPER INDEX TO THE AMERICAN BANKER. **Added/Corp** Bell & Howell Co. Indexing Center. **VFOAT** Bell and Howell Newspaper Index to the American Banker; Newspaper Index to the American Banker. (Jan. 1984)-. English. Twelve times a year. University Microfilms International, 300 North Zeeb Road, Ann Arbor MI 48106-1346. **Tel** (313)761-4700, (800)521-0600 Exts. 2490, 2491, FAX (313)973-1540. **Continues** Bell & Howell's Index to American Banker.

LC HG2121 .B4 ISSN 0522-8670
DD 332.3/2/08 UK
BELLMAN LECTURE, THE. (19??)-. English. Abbey National Building Society, Abbey House, Baker Street, London NW1 United Kingdom. **Continues** Bellman Memorial Lecture.

LC HG3754.D4 E47A
DD 332 DK
BERETNING FOR FINANSARET .... **Main/Corp** Eksportkreditradet (Denmark). **VFOAT** Arsberetning. Vol. 1 (Dec. 1979)-. Danish (English). One time a year. Eksportkreditradet, GL Kongevej 60, 1850 Frederiksberg C Denmark. **Tel** 01 31 38 25, FAX 01 31 24 25, telex 22910 DEFDK. **Continues** Eksportkreditradet (Denmark). Eksportkreditradets Beretning.

LC HG8655 .D45A ISSN 0905-0965
DD 332 DK
BERETNING FRA FINANSTILSYNET. See Insurance.

LC HG1501
DD 332.1 AU
BERICHT / OSTERREICHISCHER RAIFFEISENVERBAND. **Main/Corp** Oesterreichischer Raiffeisenverband. **VFOAT** OERV-Bericht. (198?)-. German (summaries and/or abstracts in English and French). One time a year. Oesterreichische Agrarverlag, Inkustr 1 7 Bueropark Donau, A 3400 Klosterneuberg Austria. **Tel** 011 43 2243 33300. **Continues** Oesterreichischer Raiffeisenverband. Jahresbericht.

ISSN 0893-9519
DD 333 US
TITLE CHANGE
BERNARD ZICK'S REAL ESTATE FINANCING & MORTGAGE REPORT. See Real Estate.

LC HJ1150.A2 S63 ISSN 0939-415X
DD 336.43 GW
BETRIEB UND WIRTSCHAFT : ZEITSCHRIFT FUER RECHNUNGSWESEN, STEUERN, WIRTSCHAFTS-, ARBEITS- UND SOZIALRECHT IM BETRIEB. (1991)-. Periodical. German. Twelve times a year. $149.23. Verlag die Wirtschaft Berlin, Am Friedrichshain 22, D-10407 Berlin Germany. **Tel** 011 49 30 42151421. **Continues** Finanzwirtschaft.

LC HG1501
DD 332.1 US
BEYOND THE BOTTOM LINE. (19??)-. Newsletter. English. Thirty-six times a year. $3.35 per copy. Economics Press Inc, 12 Daniel Road, Fairfield NJ 07004. **Tel** (201)227-1224, (800)526-2554, FAX (201)227-9742.
  Desc: Brings managers information on dealing with financial aspects of their company and do their jobs better. Strives to avoid jargon and sticks to the basic financial and accounting concepts that underlie all managerial responsibility.

LC Z7164.F5 W3
DD 330 US
BIBLIO LIST UPDATES IN PRINT. **Added/Corp** Joint Bank-Fund Library. **VFOAT** BLU Print; Blue List. (Jan. 1991)-. Periodical. English. Twelve times a year. Free on request. International Monetary Fund, 700 19th Street Northwest, Publishing Unit, Washington DC 20431. **Tel** (202)623-7430, FAX (202)623-7201. **Continues** Joint Bank-Fund Library. List of Recent Periodical Articles, 0885-4408.

LC HG2411 .L7 ISSN 0097-8582
DD 353.9/763/00825 US
BIENNIAL REPORT OF THE COMMISSIONER OF FINANCIAL INSTITUTIONS AND SUPERVISOR OF HOMESTEAD AND BUILDING AND LOAN ASSOCIATIONS. (BIENNIAL REPORT OF THE COMMISSIONER OF FINANCIAL INSTITUTIONS AND SUPERVISOR OF HOMESTEAD AND BUILDING AND LOAN ASSOCIATIONS RELATING TO STATE BANKS, SAVINGS BANKS AND TRUST COMPANIES, HOMESTEAD AND BUILDING AND LOAN ASSOCIATIONS, CREDIT UNIONS, LOUISIANA CONSUMER CREDIT LAW, LOUISIANA CONSUMER CREDIT LAW, SALE OF CHECKS DIVISION.). **Main/Corp** Louisiana. State Banking Dept. **VFOAT** Biennial Report - State of Louisiana, State Banking Department / Louisiana, State Capitol Building, Baton Rouge LA 70801. **Continues** Report of the State Bank Commissioner and Supervisor of Homestead and Building and Loan Associations Relative to State Banks, Savings, Banks and Trust Companies, Homestead and Building and Loan Associations, Credit Unions and Licensees Under "Louisiana Small Loan Law".

LC HG3259.A5 J34a
DD 332.1/095692 LE
BILANS DES BANQUES. **Main/Corp** Jamiyat Masarif Lubnan. (19??)-. French. Jamiyat Masarif Lubnan, rue de l'Armee Boite Postale 976, Beyrouth Lebanon.

LC HG1501 ISSN 0741-8345
DD 332.1 US
CCC
BLUE CHIP FINANCIAL FORECASTS. [Blue chip financ. forecasts]. **Added/Corp** Capitol Publications, Inc. **VFOAT** Financial Forecasts. (198?)-. Periodical. English. Twelve times a year. $439.00. Capitol Publications, 1101 King Street, Suite 444, Alexandria VA 22314. **Tel** (703)683-4100, (800)655-5597, FAX (703)739-6517, (800)645-4104. **(Subscription address:** Capitol Publications, PO Box 1455, Alexandria VA 22313. **Tel** (800)655-5597, FAX (703)739-6517.**)**
  Desc: Timely interest rate forecasts and analysis for corporate planners, portfolio and investment managers, pension plan managers, and pension fund advisors. Monthly forecasts from 50 financial experts.

LC HG
DD 332 US
BLUE RIBBON BANK REPORT. (19??)-. English. Four times a year. $108.00. Veribanc Inc., PO Box 461, Wakefield MA 01880. **Tel** (617)245-8370, (800)442-2657, FAX (617)246-5291. **ED** Warren G. Heller.
  Desc: Bank financial reports.

LC HG1501
DD 332.1 BL
BOAVISTA NEWSLETTER. **Added/Corp** Banco Boavista. No. 1 (Nov. 1991)-. Newsletter. Portuguese. **Continues** Economic Newsletter (Rio de Janeiro, Brazil).

LC HG1501 ISSN 0870-1008
DD 332.1 PO
UDC 33
BOLETIM DE LEGISLACAO ECONOMICA. (1985)-. Periodical. Portuguese. Twelve times a year. 430$00. Livraria Barata, Av de Roma 11-A, 1000 Lisbon Portugal. **Tel** 52 35 59, FAX 52 38 41, telex 165540 BAGAL P.

LC HG1501 ISSN 0102-5171
DD 332.1 BL
BOLETIM MENSAL / BANCO CENTRAL DO BRASIL. [Bol. mens. - Banco Cent. Bras.]. Vol. 17, No. 6 (June 1981)-. Bulletin. Portuguese (English). Twelve times a year. $801.11. Banco Central do Brazil, Demap Disvp Secre Sbs Ed Sede, 20 SS Brasilia 70074 DF Brazil. **Continues** Boletim do Banco Central do Brasil (1971).

LC HG186.P8 B65 ISSN 0870-0095
DD 330.9469/005 PO
CEASED
BOLETIM TRIMESTRAL - BANCO DE PORTUGAL. See Business and Economics-Economic History, Conditions.

LC HA1025 .B36A
DD 318.66 EC
BOLETIN ANUARIO - BANCO CENTRAL DEL ECUADOR. See Business and Economics-Abstracting, Bibliographies and Statistics.

LC HG6 .C43
DD 332/.05 MX
Pr Rev.
BOLETIN / CENTRO DE ESTUDIOS MONETARIOS LATINOAMERICANOS. **Added/Corp** Centro de Estudios Monetarios Latinoamericanos. Vol. 23, No. 1 (Jan./Feb. 1977)-. Periodical. Spanish. Six times a year. $70.00. Centro Estudios Monetarios Latinoamericanos (CEMLA), Durango 54, 06700 Mexico DF Mexico. **Tel** 011 52 5 5330300, FAX 011 52 5 2072847, telex 1771229. **ED** Juan Manuel Rodriguez. Index available in last issue of volume-attached. cum. index. **Bk Rev**. **Ad Acc**. **Circ:** 700. **Continues** Boletin Mensual.

LC HG1501 ISSN 0250-7420
DD 332.1 US
BOLETIN DEL FMI. [Bol. FMI]. **Added/Corp** International Monetary Fund. **VAT** Boletin del Fondo Monetario Internacional. (1972)-. Periodical. Spanish (English and French). Twenty-three times a year. Free on request. International Monetary Fund, 700 19th Street Northwest, Publishing Unit, Washington DC 20431. **Tel** (202)623-7430, FAX (202)623-7201. **ED** Alexander Mountford. Index available.
  Desc: Topical report of the Fund's activities presented in the broader context of developments in the world economy, economic research and policy, national economies and international finance.

LC HA1045 .B33 ISSN 0408-330X
DD 330.9892/00212 PY
BOLETIN ESTADISTICO. [Bol. estad. - Banco Cent. Parag.]. **Added/Corp** Banco Central del Paraguay. Departamento de Estudios Economicos. No. 216 (May 1976)-. Periodical. Spanish. Twelve times a year. **Continues** Boletin Estadistico Mensual (Banco Central del Paraguay. Departamento de Estudios Economicos), 0522-1161.

LC HA943 .B3
DD 318.2 AG
BOLETIN ESTADISTICO. See Business and Economics-Abstracting, Bibliographies and Statistics.

LC HG2746 .A557 ISSN 0005-481X
DD 332 GT
BOLETIN ESTADISTICO - BANCO DE GUATEMALA. (BOLETIN ESTADISTICO.). [Bol. estad. - Banco Guatem.]. **Main/Corp** Banco de Guatemala (1945-). (195?)-. Spanish. Twelve times a year (includes supplements and annual report). Banco de Espana, Alcala 50, 28014 Madrid Spain. **Tel** 011 34 1 4469055, 011 34 1 3385072. available on microfilm. **Continues** Banco de Guatemala (1945-). Boletin.

LC HG1501
DD 332.1 CK
BOLETIN ESTADISTICO / BANCOS CENTRALES DE LOS PAISES MIEMBROS DEL FLAR. **Added/Corp** Bancos Centrales de los Paises Miembros del FLAR. Latin American Reserve Fund. Ser. 2, No. 27 (First Quarter 1991)-. Spanish. Four times a year. **Continues** Boletin Estadistico.

LC HG3186 .B29A
DD 332 SP
BOLETIN ESTADISTICO. INDICADORES ECONOMICOS. **Main/Corp** Banco de Espana, Madrid. **Added/Corp** Banco de Espana. Indicadores Economicos. (1974)-. Spanish.

Business and Economics — Banks and Banking

Banco de Espana, Alcala 50, 28014 Madrid Spain. **Tel** 011 34 1 4469055, 011 34 1 3385072. **Continues** Boletin Estadistico. Suplemento.

LC HC381 .B332
DD 330
SP
BOLETIN INFORMATIVO / CENTRAL HISPANO. Added/Corp Central Hispano (Bank). No. 485 (Apr. 1992)-. Periodical. Spanish. **Continues** Boletin Informativo (Banco Central Hispanoamericano), 0211-7142.

LC HG2900.S3 B33 **ISSN** 0716-2367
DD 332
CL
BOLETIN MENSUAL - BANCO CENTRAL DE CHILE. [Bol. mens. - Banco Cent. Chile]. **Main/Corp** Banco Central de Chile. **Added/Corp** Banco Central de Chile. Vol. 1 No. 1 (Jan. 1928)-. Periodical. Spanish. Twelve times a year. $300.00. Banco Central de Chile, Casilla 967, 1180 Santiago Chile. **Tel** 011 56 2 6962281, FAX 011 56 2 6984847, telex 40569 CENBC CL. Index Available, published separately, free-automatically sent. cum. index. **Circ:** 1,300 (ctrl). available on diskette. Documents available.
 Ind/Abst PAIS Int. Print (1991-).

LC HG2966 .B25 **ISSN** 0252-8991
DD 332
VE
BOLETIN MENSUAL - BANCO CENTRAL DE VENEZUELA. [Bol. mens. - Banco Cent. Venez.]. **Main/Corp** Banco Central de Venezuela. No. 372- Jan. 1975-. Periodical. Spanish. Twelve times a year. $220.00. Banco Central de Venezuela, Apartado 2017, Caracas Venezuela. **Tel** 011 58 2 8629811, 8629821, 8629831, telex 22875.
Continues Boletin Mensual - Banco Central de Venezuela, Departamento de Investigaciones Economicas.

LC HG2156.V42 B36a
DD 332
VE
BOLETIN MENSUAL - BANCO NACIONAL DE AHORRO Y PRESTAMO, GERENCIA DE ESTUDIOS E INVESTIGACIONES. Main/Corp Banco Nacional de Ahorro y Prestamo. Gerencia de Estudios e Investigaciones. (19??)-. Spanish. Banco Nacional de Ahorro y Prestamo, Gerencia de Estudios e Investigaciones, Cale Real de Sabana Grande, Esquina Los Jabillos Edif Continental, Caracus Venezuela.

LC HG1501 **ISSN** 1120-2998
DD 332.1
IT
UDC 616-053.2
BOLLETINO - CONSOB. [Boll. - Consob]. **VFOAT** Bollettino - Commissione Nazionale per le Societa e la Borsa. (1984)-. Periodical. Italian. Twelve times a year. L136100. Istituto Poligrafico Zecca Stato, Piazza Verdi 10, 00198 Rome Italy. **Tel** 011 39 6 85082307, 011 39 6 85082221.

LC HG1501 **ISSN** 0393-2400
DD 332.1
IT
BOLLETTINO ECONOMICO (ROME, ITALY). (BOLLETTINO ECONOMICO.). **Added/Corp** Banca D'italia. Servizio Studi. **VFOAT** Bollettino Economico del Servizio Studi. Vol. 1, No. 1, Oct. (1983)-. Periodical. Italian. Two times a year. Banca Italia Servizio Studi Bollettino, Via Nazionale 91, 00184 Rome Italy.

LC HC301.A1 B65 **ISSN** 0393-604X
DD 330
IT
BOLLETTINO STATISTICO (ROME, ITALY). (BOLLETTINO STATISTICO.). **Added/Corp** Banca d'Italia. Servizio Studi. Banca d'Italia. Vol. 38, No. 3-4, July/Dec. (1983). Italian. Four times a year. Banca Italia Servizio Studi Bollettino, Via Nazionale 91, 00184 Rome Italy. **Continues** Banca d'Italia. Bollettino, 0393-6090.

LC HG4501 .D3 **ISSN** 0732-0469
DD 332.63/233/0973
US
CCC
BOND BUYER (NEW YORK, N.Y. 1982), THE. See Business and Economics-Investments.

LC HG **ISSN** 0738-5579
DD 332
US
BOND FUND SURVEY. [Bond fund sur.]. (1983)-. Periodical. English. Twelve times a year. $450.00. Survey Publications, PO Box 4180, Grand Central Station, New York NY 10163. **Tel** (212)988-2498. **ED** Judith C. Lack (editor's address: PO Box 1702, Wall St. Station, NY, NY 10268 phone: (212)988-2416).
 Desc: Performance reports on bond funds--corporate, municipal, government, closed-end funds plus unit investment trusts. Includes encyclopedic reports on bond funds.

LC HG4502 .B6 **ISSN** 0961-8171
DD 332.63/23/05
UK
BONDHOLDER, THE. VFOAT Bond Holder. (1990)-. English. One time a week. £2750.00. Valorinform, 103 New Oxford Street, Centre Point, London WC1A 1DD United Kingdom. **Tel** 011 44 171 9171553. **ED** Colette Young. Index available. cum. index.

Ad Acc. ctrl circ. **Continues** Bondholder's Register.
 Desc: A weekly publication of redemptions, rights, dividends, etc. pertaining to bearer securities.

LC HG3891.5 .B67
DD 336.3/435/05
US
BORROWING IN INTERNATIONAL CAPITAL MARKETS. Added/Corp World Bank. International Finance Division. World Bank. Financial Studies Division. (19??)-. Periodical. English. Four times a year. Free on request. International Bank for Reconstruction and Development / Washington, DC, 1818 H Street Northwest, Washington DC 20433.

LC HG1501
DD 332.1
US
BRANCH DEPOSIT REPORT OF FLORIDA BANK AND THRIFT INSTITUTIONS. Added/Corp Florida Bankers Association. Florida League of Financial Institutions. (19??)-. English. Four times a year. $200.00. Florida Bankers Association, PO Box 531126, Orlando FL 32853-6847. **Tel** (407)896-6511, FAX (407)896-9720. **Continues** Office Level Report on Florida Bank Deposits.

LC HG2444.N6 B7 **ISSN** 0147-3131
DD 332.1/752/09747
US
BRANCH DIRECTORY AND SUMMARY OF DEPOSITS FOR THE STATE OF NEW YORK. Added/Corp Decision Research Sciences, Inc. (19??)-. Directory. English. One time a year. $175.00. Denco Data Equipment, 2550 Industry Lane, Norristown PA 19403-3988.

LC HG2444.P4 B7 **ISSN** 0148-3021
DD 332.1/752/09748
US
BRANCH DIRECTORY AND SUMMARY OF DEPOSITS FOR THE STATE OF PENNSYLVANIA. [Branch dir. summ. depos. State Pa.]. **Added/Corp** Decision Research Sciences, inc. (19??)-. English. One time a year. $290.00 (latest edition). Decision Research Sciences Inc., 800 Penllyn Blue Bell Pike, Blue Bell PA 19422. **Tel** (610)542-9550. available on diskette; available on magnetic tape.

LC HG2441 .B68 **ISSN** 0147-3115
DD 332.1/752/09789
US
BRANCH DIRECTORY AND SUMMARY OF DEPOSITS FOR THE STATES OF CALIFORNIA, NEW MEXICO, ARIZONA. (19??)-. Directory. English. One time a year. $480.00. Decision Research Sciences Inc., 800 Penllyn Blue Bell Pike, Blue Bell PA 19422. **Tel** (610)542-9550. available on diskette; available on magnetic tape.

LC HG2441 .B7 **ISSN** 0147-5002
DD 332.1/752/0974
US
BRANCH DIRECTORY AND SUMMARY OF DEPOSITS FOR THE STATES OF CONNECTICUT, MAINE, MASSACHUSETTS, NEW HAMPSHIRE, RHODE ISLAND, VERMONT. Added/Corp Decision Research Sciences, Inc. (19??)-. Directory. English. One time a year. $480.00. Decision Research Sciences Inc., 800 Penllyn Blue Bell Pike, Blue Bell PA 19422. **Tel** (610)542-9550. available on diskette; available on magnetic tape.

LC HG2444.N5 B72 **ISSN** 0147-3778
DD 332.1/752/09749
US
BRANCH DIRECTORY AND SUMMARY OF DEPOSITS FOR THE STATES OF NEW JERSEY, DELAWARE. (19??)-. Directory. English. One time a year. Decision Research Sciences Inc., 800 Penllyn Blue Bell Pike, Blue Bell PA 19422. **Tel** (610)542-9550. available on diskette; available on magnetic tape.

ISSN 0889-2644
DD 384
US
BROADCAST BANKER/BROKER. [Broadcast bank./brok.]. **Added/Corp** Paul Kagan Associates. **VFOAT** Broadcast Banker Broker. No. 26 (June 25, 1986)-. Newsletter. English. Twelve times a year. $625.00. Paul Kagan Associates Inc., 126 Clock Tower Place, Carmel CA 93923-8734. **Tel** (408)624-1536, FAX (408)625-3225, telex ITT 4938124 PKA UI. available via fax. **Continues** Broadcast Banking, 0749-677X.
 Desc: Newsletter on equity and debt financing for radio and TV. Analysis of interest rates and cash flow.

LC HJ70.8 .A23A **ISSN** 0129-4679
DD 354.595/70072252/05
SI
BUDGET FOR THE FINANCIAL YEAR / REPUBLIC OF SINGAPORE, THE. Main/Corp Singapore. 1978/79-. English. One time a year. Singapore National Printers, 303 Upper Serangoon Road, Singapore 1334 Singapore. **Tel** 011 65 2820611. **Formed by the union of** Singapore. Maine and Development Estimates **and** Establishment List - Singapore, 0376-8937.

LC HC440.8.A1 B28a **ISSN** 0304-9345
DD 330.9/549/205
BG
BULLETIN - BANGLADESH BANK.
Main/Corp Bangladesh Bank. (19??)-. Bulletin. English. Twelve times a year. $36.00. Bangladesh Bank, Motijheel Commercial Area, Dhaka 2 Bangladesh.

LC HG1501 **ISSN** 0220-2352
DD 332.1
FR
UDC 65
BULLETIN COMPTABLE & FINANCIER.
VFOAT Bulletin Comptable et Financier. (1978)-. Bulletin. French. Four times a year. Editions Lefebvre, 5 Rue Jacques Bingen, 75854 Paris Cedex 17 France. **Tel** 011 33 1 47631260, 011 33 1 41052200, FAX 011 33 1 46227266, telex 649 470 F.

LC HC395 .C7 **ISSN** 1016-1570
DD 330
SZ
BULLETIN - CREDIT SUISSE (ENGLISH ED.). (BULLETIN / CREDIT SUISSE.). [Bull. - Credit suisse]. **Main/Corp** Credit Suisse. Vol. 77 (Oct. 1971)-. Bulletin. English. Four times a year. Free on request. Credit Suisse, Service Marketing Publicite, CH-1211 Geneva Switzerland. **Tel** 011 41 22 222111.

LC HG3026 .B84
DD 332.1
FR
●**BULLETIN DE LA BANQUE DE FRANCE.**
Added/Corp Banque de France. No. 1 (Jan. 1994)-. Bulletin. French. Twenty times a year (Publishes monthly plus supplements). 489.72F France; 500.00F Europe; 1400.00F other. Banque de France, BP 140 01, 75049 Paris Cedex 01 France. **Tel** 011 33 1 42922954. **Formed by the union of** Banque de France. Bulletin Trimestriel, 0150-7583; Bulletin Mensuel (Banque de France) **and** Situation Economique a l'Etranger et les Statistiques Monetaires et Financieres Trimestrielles.

LC HC311 .B312 **ISSN** 0005-5611
DD 330
BE
CEASED
BULLETIN DE LA BANQUE NATIONALE DE BELGIQUE. Main/Corp Banque Nationale de Belgique. Vol. 1 (Jan. 1971)-(Dec. 1995). Bulletin. French. Banque Nationale de Belgique, boulevard de Berlaimont 14-B, 1000 Brussels Belgium. **Tel** 011 32 2 2212033, FAX 011 32 2 2213163. Index available (published separately). cum. index. **Bk Rev**.
 Ad Acc. Continues Banque Nationale de Belgique. Departement d'Etudes et de Documentation. Bulletin d'Information et de Documentation.

ISSN 0227-5961
DD 054/.1
CN
BULLETIN DE LA BANQUE ROYALE.
[Bull. Banque r.]. **Added/Corp** Royal Bank of Canada. Vol. 61, No. 6 (July 1980)-. Bulletin. French. Six times a year. Free on request. Royal Bank of Canada, 200 Bay Street, 18th Floor South Tower, Toronto Ontario M5J 2J5 Canada. **Tel** (416)974-7242. **Continues** Banque Royale du Canada. Bulletin Mensuel, 0382-4594.
 Ind/Abst Can. Period. Index.

LC HG1501 **ISSN** 1142-2858
DD 332.1
FR
UDC 336.71(44)
BULLETIN DE LA COMMISSION BANCAIRE. (1989)-. Bulletin. French. Two times a year (Apr., & Nov.). $43.74. Commission Bancaire Secretary Generale, 4 rue Des Colonnes, F 75002 Paris France. **Tel** 011 33 1 42925931, FAX 011 33 1 42925940.

LC HC311 .S63a
DD 330
BE
BULLETIN DE LA GENERALE DE BANQUE. Added/Corp Generale de Banque. (198?)-. Bulletin. French. Twelve times a year. $26.12. Generale de Banque, 23 M 3 Montagne du Parc, 1000 Brussels Belgium. **Tel** 011 32 2 5164867. **Continues** Bulletin de la Societe Generale de Banque.

LC HG4150 .F7a
DD 338.7/6/0944
FR
BULLETIN DES ANNONCES LEGALES OBLIGATOIRES. Main/Corp France. **Added/Corp** France. Journal Officiel. (1907)-. Bulletin. French. Irregular (Publishes at least twice weekly). 487.00F France; 1227.00F other. Direction des Journaux Officiels, 26 rue Desaix, 75727 Paris Cedex 15 France. **Tel** 011 33 1 40587500.

LC HG1501 **ISSN** 0250-7412
DD 332.1
US
BULLETIN DU FMI. [Bull. FMI]. **Added/Corp** International Monetary Fund. **VAT** Bulletin du Fonds Monetaire International. (1972)-. Bulletin. French. Twenty-three times a year. Free on request. International Monetary Fund, 700 19th Street Northwest, Publishing Unit, Washington DC 20431. **Tel** (202)623-7430, FAX (202)623-7201.

LC HG1501 ISSN 0771-6273
DD 332.1 BE
UDC 336.76
BULLETIN FINANCIER - BANQUE BRUXELLES LAMBERT. [Bull. Financ. - Banq. Brux. Lambert]. **VFOAT** Bulletin Financier - BBL. (1975)-. Bulletin. French. One time a week. Banque Bruxelles Lambert, Av. Marnix 24, 1050 Brussels Belgium. ***Continues*** *Bulletin Financier - Banque de Bruxelles, 0771-6281.*
Ind/Abst PAIS Int. Print.

LC HC167.A5 B85
DD 330 CK
BULLETIN / LARF, LATIN AMERICAN RESERVE FUND. **Added/Corp** Latin American Reserve Fund. **VFOAT** LARF Bulletin. No. 35 (Jan./Mar. 1991)-. Bulletin. English. Four times a year. Free. Latin American Reserve Fund, Apdo. Aereo 241523, Bogota Columbia. ***Continues*** *Bulletin (Andean Reserve Fund).*

LC HC880.A1 B84 ISSN 1013-5332
DD 330.967/572/005 BD
BULLETIN MENSUEL - BANQUE DE LA REPUBLIQUE DU BURUNDI. (BULLETIN MENSUEL / BANQUE DE LA REPUBLIQUE DU BURUNDI, SERVICE DES ETUDES.). [Bull. mens. - Banque Repub. Burundi]. **Added/Corp** Banque de la Republique du Burundi. Direction des Etudes. No. 1 (Jan. 1978)-. Bulletin. French. Twelve times a year. $75.00. Banque de la Republique du Burundi, Service des Etudes, BP 705, Bujumbura-Burundi. **Tel** 011 257 22 5142, telex (2)5142. **Circ:** 280. ***Continues*** *Bulletin Mensuel de la Banque de la Republique du Burundi.*
Desc: Prepared and offered by the bank's research section, the bulletin is composed of statistical tables divided into five groups: 1) production and consumption of various products, 2) currency and credit, 3) public finance, 4) foreign commerce/balance of payments, 5) miscellaneous. End-of-quarter bulletins include notes that analyze various aspects of the economic life of Burundi.
Ind/Abst Foreign Lang. Index.

LC HG189 .B84 ISSN 0725-0320
DD 332/.0994 AT
BULLETIN / RESERVE BANK OF AUSTRALIA. [Bull. - Reserve Bank Aust.]. **Added/Corp** Reserve Bank of Australia. (19??)-. Bulletin. English. Twelve times a year. 20.55Aus$. Reserve Bank of Australia / Secretary Department, GPO Box 3947, Sydney New South Wales 2001 Australia. **Tel** 11 61 2 5519724, 011 61 2 5518841, FAX 011 61 2 234900, telex 20106. Index available. **Circ:** 4,500 (ctrl). available on microfiche; available on magnetic tape. Documents available from UMI Article Clearinghouse. ***Continues*** *Reserve Bank of Australia. Statistical Bulletin - Reserve Bank of Australia.*
Ind/Abst ABI/INFORM Glob. Ed.; PAIS Int. Print.

LC HC621 .R4 ISSN 0034-5539
DD 330.9931 NZ
CCC
BULLETIN - RESERVE BANK OF NEW ZEALAND. **Main/Corp** Reserve Bank of New Zealand. Vol. 1, No. 1 (June 1938)-. Bulletin. English. Four times a year. $83.79. Reserve Bank of New Zealand, PO Box 2498, Wellington 6000 New Zealand. **Tel** 64 4 722029, telex N2 3368. Index available. **Circ:** 1,550. available on microfilm from University Microfilms International (UMI).
Desc: Contains articles on general economics, monetary policy external economy, etc. Tables on trading banks, saving banks, financial statistics liquidity and interest rates.
Ind/Abst PAIS Int. Print.

LC HC440.5 .S83 ISSN 0039-0011
DD 330.9547 PK
TITLE CHANGE
BULLETIN - STATE BANK OF PAKISTAN. **Main/Corp** State Bank of Pakistan. (May 1951)-(Oct. 1993). Bulletin. English. State Bank of Pakistan - Public Relation Department, PO Box 4456, Central Directorate, Karachi Pakistan. **Tel** 011 92 21 2414141310, telex 2754 SBP. **ED** Ashraf Janjua, Muhammad Huusain and Sabiha Hasan. **Bk Rev. Circ:** 727. ***Supersedes*** *State Bank of Pakistan. Statistical Summary.* ***Continued by*** *Statistical Bulletin (State Bank of Pakistan).*

LC HC337.F5 A15 ISSN 0784-6509
DD 332.1/1/09489705 FI
BULLETIN (SUOMEN PANKKI). (BULLETIN / BANK OF FINLAND.). **Added/Corp** Suomen Pankki. **VFOAT** Bank of Finland Bulletin. Vol. 62, No. 1 (Jan. 1988)-. Bulletin. English. Eleven times a year (June/July issues combined). Free on request. Bank of Finland, PO Box 160, SF-00101 Helsinki Finland. **Tel** 011 358 0 1832629, FAX 011 358 0 174872, telex 121224. **ED** Antero Arimo and Marja Hirvensalo-Niim. cum. index. **Circ:** 6,700. available on microfilm. ***Continues*** *Monthly Bulletin (Suomen Pankki), 0005-5174.*
Desc: Central bank publication which explores banking industry, financial markets, monetary policy; includes statistics and charts.
Ind/Abst PAIS Int. Print (1991-).

LC HG1501
DD 332.1 LU
BULLETIN TRIMESTRIEL / INSTITUT MONETAIRE LUXEMBOURGEOIS. **Added/Corp** Institut Monetaire Luxembourgeois. **VFOAT** Quarterly Bulletin; Rapport Annuel de l'Institut Monetaire Luxembourgeois pour l'Annee ...; Annual Report of the IML for the Year ... . (Apr. 1985)-. Bulletin. French (summaries and/or abstracts in English). Four times a year. $35.53. L'Institut Monetaire Luxembourgeois, BP 1501, 2983 Luxembourg Luxembourg. **Tel** 011 352 402929. ***Continued in part by*** *Institut Monetaire Luxembourgeois. Rapport Annuel de l'Institut Monetaire Luxembourgeois pour l'Annee ... .*

LC HG2153.I65 F4a
DD 332.3/2/0977252 US
BULLETIN - [ECONOMICS DEPARTMENT, FEDERAL HOME LOAN BANK OF INDIANAPOLIS]. **Main/Corp** Federal Home Loan Bank of Indianapolis. Economics Dept. (19??)-. Bulletin. English. Federal Home Loan Bank of Indianapolis, 2900 Indiana Tower, Indianapolis IN 46204.

LC HG1501
DD 332.1 IR
BULLETIN / [PREPARED BY ECONOMIC RESEARCH DEPARTMENT, THE CENTRAL BANK OF THE ISLAMIC REPUBLIC OF IRAN]. **Added/Corp** Bank-i Markazi-i Jumhuri-i Islami-i Iran. Bank-i Markazi-i Jumhuri-i Islami-i Iran. Idarah-i Bar'rasiha-yi Iqtisadi. (1982)-. Bulletin. English (Persian). Two times a year. Free on request. Central Bank of Iran / Economic Research Department, Gharani & Somaye Aves, Tehran Iran. **Tel** 830061-9 Ext. 275, telex 3965-8 MKZBANK TEHRAN. ***Continues*** *Majallah-i Bank-i Markazi-i Iran. English. Bulletin, 0256-5323.*

LC HG1501
DD 332.1 IT
BUSARL : LIGURIA. Italian. Camera Comm Ind Art Agr Genova, Via Garibaldi 4, 16124 Genoa Italy.

LC HF5001 .B765 ISSN 0007-6473
DD 650 IE
BUSINESS AND FINANCE. [Bus. finance]. **VFOAT** Business & Finance. (1964)-. Trade Publication. English. One time a week. $533.17. Business & Finance, 50 Fitzwilliam Square West, Dublin 2 Ireland. **Tel** 011 353 1 760869, 011 353 1 764587, FAX 011 353 1 619781, telex 93374. **ED** William Ambrose, Jim Dunne, Aileen O'Toole and Gerald Luke. **Bk Rev. Ad Acc. Circ:** 11,374. Documents available from UMI Article Clearinghouse.
Desc: Magazine which covers the Irish economy, financial and business news, and various aspects of Irish industry.
Ind/Abst ABI/INFORM Glob. Ed.; Infomat Int. Bus.; PAIS Int. Print (1991-); Predicasts.

LC HG181 .B87 ISSN 1064-8127
DD 332.1/023/73 US
CEASED
BUSINESS & FINANCE CAREER DIRECTORY. [Bus. finance career dir.]. **Added/Corp** Career Press Inc. **VFOAT** Business and Finance Career Directory. 1st Ed. (1989)-(199?). Directory. English. Gale Research Inc., 835 Penobscot Building, 645 Griswold Street, Detroit MI 48226. **Tel** (800)877-GALE, (313)961-2242, FAX (313)961-6083, (800)414-5043, telex TWX 810-221-7086.
Desc: Covers such topics as working as a certified public accountant, what it's like to be a securities analyst or trader, becoming a financial planner, management information consulting as a career, and the facts about banking and insurance.

LC HG1501 ISSN 0146-4744
DD 332.1 US
BUSINESS ASSISTANCE MONOGRAPH SERIES, THE. **See** Business and Economics.

LC HF5565 .N3 ISSN 0897-0181
DD 658.8/8/05 US
BUSINESS CREDIT. (BUSINESS CREDIT : PUBLICATION OF NATIONAL ASSOCIATION OF CREDIT MANAGEMENT.). [Bus. credit]. **Added/Corp** National Association of Credit Management. Vol. 89, No. 11 (Dec. 1987)-. Trade Publication. English. Ten times a year (monthly with July/Aub. and Nov./Dec. issues combined). $44.00. National Association of Credit Management, 8815 Centre Park Drive, Suite 200, Columbia MD 21045-2158. **Tel** (410)740-5560, FAX (410)740-5574. **ED** Cindy Tursman. Index available (bound in tenth issue). cum. index. **Ad Acc, Adv Mgr:** Diane Wade. **Circ:** 35,000 (ctrl). available on microfilm from University Microfilms International (UMI); available on an online database (files 15,485,648/Full-Text) from DIALOG. Documents available from UMI Article Clearinghouse. ***Continues*** *Credit and Financial Management, 0011-0973.*
Desc: Deals with credit and financial management.
Ind/Abst ABI/INFORM Glob. Ed.; ABI/INFORM [Computer File] (Dec. 1987-); Acad. Search; Account. Index Suppl. (Dec. 1987-); Account. Tax Datab. (Sept. 1971-) [Full Txt.]; Bus. ASAP (1992-) [Full Txt.]; Bus. Index (1987-); Bus. Period. Index (Dec. 1987-); Bus. Source Plus; Bus. Source; Curr. Cit.; EP Collect.; Gen. BusinessFile (1987-); Gen. Period. Index (1985-); Homework Help.; INFO-SOUTH Abstr.; Mag. Search; Manage. Contents (Dec. 1987-); MasterFile FullTEXT 1000; MasterFile FullTEXT 350; MasterFile FullTEXT 650; MasterFile FullTEXT (July 1993-); OCLC; Telebase; Trade Ind. ASAP [Full Txt.]; Trade Ind. Index (Dec. 1987-) [Full Txt.]; UMI ABI/Inform--Bus. Period. Ondisc (Dec. 1987-) [Full Txt.]; Wilson Bus. Abstr.

LC HF5001 .B846 ISSN 0190-4914
DD 650.05 US
BUSINESS OWNER (HICKSVILLE, N.Y.), THE. (THE BUSINESS OWNER.). [Bus. own.]. Vol. 1, (Jan./Feb. 1977)-. Trade Publication. English. Six times a year. $96.00. Thomar Publications Inc, 383 South Broadway, Hicksville NY 11801. **Tel** (516)681-2111. **ED** Thomas J. Martin. Documents available from UMI Article Clearinghouse.
Desc: Financial publication geared to the owners and their advisers in the small to medium-sized business (i.e. taxes, insurance, valuing a business, selling a business).
Ind/Abst ABI/INFORM Glob. Ed.; ABI/INFORM [Computer File] (Jan. 1981-); Account. Tax Datab. (Jan. 1981-); Bus. Index (1985-); Gen. BusinessFile (1985-); Gen. Period. Index (1985-); Mag. Search; Trade Ind. Index.

LC K2 .U85 ISSN 0269-2694
DD 341.7/51 UK
CCC
BUTTERWORTHS JOURNAL OF INTERNATIONAL BANKING AND FINANCIAL LAW. [Butterworths j. int. bank. fianc. law]. **Added/Corp** Butterworths (Firm). **VFOAT** Journal of International Banking and Financial Law. Vol. 1, No. 1 (June 1986)-. Trade Publication. English. Twelve times a year. 1270.00Aus$. Butterworth & Co. Ltd. / UK, Halsbury House, 35 Chancery Lane, London WC2A 1EL United Kingdom. **Tel** 011 44 171 4002500. **ED** Josephine McAfee. Index available. **Ad Acc.**
Desc: A journal of news and comment from major financial centres around the world. Contributors are knowledgeable of the international banking system and financial markets.
Ind/Abst Curr. Cit.

LC HC451 .C38 ISSN 0115-1401
DD 330.9/599/04 PH
TITLE CHANGE
C. B. REVIEW. (CB REVIEW.). [CB rev.]. **Added/Corp** Central Bank of the Philippines. Dept. of Economic Research. Vol. 26, No. 14- 2, (April 1974)-(1993). Periodical. English. Central Bank of the Philippines, 5-Storey Building, Mabini Street Room 410, Malate Manila Philippines. **ED** Mercedes B. Suleik. **Circ:** 4,500 (ctrl). ***Continues*** *Central Bank News Digest.* ***Continued by*** *Bangko Sentral Review.*
Desc: Articles on monetary policies, external debt, industry, banking and finance.
Ind/Abst Index Philip. Period. (?-?); PAIS Int. Print (?-?).

ISSN 8755-3732
DD 336 US
CAAS NEWS. **See** Real Estate.

LC WMLC 93/2814 ISSN 0257-7755
DD 332.042 LU
CAHIERS BEI = EIB PAPERS. **See** Business and Economics-Investments.

LC HG1501 ISSN 1152-8427
DD 332.1 FR
UDC 336.7
CAHIERS DU CRABB MONT-SAINT-AIGNAN, LES. (CAHIERS DU CRABB.). [Cah. CRABB Mt. St. Aignan]. **VFOAT** Cahiers du Centre de Recherche et d'Analyses Bancaires et Boursieres. (1990)-. Periodical. French. Four times a year. $107.18. Center Recherches & Analyses Bancaires, Fac de Droit de Rouen, BP 158, 76135 Mt St. Aignan CDX France. **Tel** 011 33 35 146124.

LC HG1501 ISSN 0395-8175
DD 332.1 FR
UDC 36
CAHIERS DU CREDIT MUTUEL. [Cah. Credit mutuel]. (1963)-. Periodical. French. Five times a year. 171.40F France; 195.00F other. Cahiers du Credit Mutuel, 34 rue du Wacken, F 67000 Strasbourg France. **Tel** 011 33 88 359111, FAX 011 33 88 352570. **Bk Rev. Ad Acc. Circ:** 15.000 (ctrl).

LC HC271 .C32 ISSN 0396-4701
DD 330.944 FR
CEASED
CAHIERS ECONOMIQUES ET MONETAIRES. [Cah. econ. monet.]. No. 1-(1995). Periodical. French (summaries and/or abstracts in English). Irregular. Banque de France, BP 140 01, 75049 Paris Cedex 01 France. **Tel** 011 33 1 42922954. **ED** M Raymond. Index available. cum. index. **Bk Rev. Ad Acc. Circ:** 2,500 (ctrl).

Desc: Studies performed by the Bank of France in monetary economics.
Ind/Abst PAIS Int. Print (1991-?).

LC K3 .A425 **ISSN** 1047-0743
DD 346.794/07805 347.94067805 US
CALIFORNIA BANKRUPTCY JOURNAL. (CALIFORNIA BANKRUPTCY JOURNAL : A QUARTERLY JOURNAL OF THE CALIFORNIA BANKRUPTCY FORUM.). [Calif. bankruptcy j.]. **Added/Corp** California Bankruptcy Forum. (19??)-. Periodical. English. Four times a year. $50.00. California Bankruptcy Forum, 1278 Glenneyre 101, Laguna Beach CA 92651. **Tel** (714)363-6643. **ED** Janet Shapiro. Index available. **Ad Acc. Circ:** 2,500. available on CD-ROM and an online database from WESTLAW. ***Continues*** *Bankruptcy Study Group Journal.*
Ind/Abst Index Leg. Period. (1992-).

LC HD2746.5 .C34 **ISSN** 0273-6357
DD 338.8/3/0973 US
CCC
CAMBRIDGE REPORT ON CORPORATE MERGERS AND CORPORATE POLICY, THE. [Camb. rep. corp. mergers corp. policy]. **VFOAT** Mergers and Corporate Policy. (1977)-. Corporate Report. English. One time a week. $895.00. Securities Data Company, 40 West 57th Street, 11th Floor, New York NY 10019. **Tel** (212)765-5311. **ED** Jaye Rasmussen. Index available. **Bk Rev.** ***Continues*** *Mergers and Federal Policy, 0164-6052;* ***Absorbed*** *Capital Markets Analyst.*
Desc: Reports mergers and acquisitions by industry with prices. Includes articles, special reports, book reviews and editorials, for corporate executives and investment banking professionals.

LC HG1507 .C4 **ISSN** 0822-6830
DD 332.1/0971 CN
CANADIAN BANKER (1983). (CANADIAN BANKER.). [Can. bank.]. **Added/Corp** Canadian Bankers' Association. Vol. 90, No. 4 (Aug. 1983)-. Periodical. English (French). Six times a year. 35.00Can$. Canadian Bankers' Association, Box 348, Commerce Court West, 30th Floor, Toronto Ontario M5L 1G2 Canada. **Tel** (416)362-6092, FAX (416)362-5658, telex 0623402. **ED** Simon Hally. Index available. **Bk Rev. Ad Acc, Adv Mgr:** Sally Longfield. **Circ:** 36,384 (ctrl). available on microfilm from Micromedia Limited; available on microfilm and microfiche from University Microfilms International (UMI); available on an online database (file 648/Full-Text) from DIALOG. Documents available from UMI Article Clearinghouse. ***Continues*** *Canadian Banker & ICB Review, 0315-6230.*
Desc: Articles of interest to those in the banking industry. Covers financial institutions and business, Canadian and international banking and economics. Also includes interviews with senior bankers, as well as opinion articles.
Ind/Abst ABI/INFORM Glob. Ed.; ABI/INFORM [Computer File] (Aug. 1983-); Acad. Search; Bus. ASAP (1992-) [Full Txt.]; Bus. Index (1985-); Bus. Period. Index; Bus. Source Plus; Bus. Source; Can. Bus. Index; Can. Legal Lit.; Can. Period. Index; Curr. Cit.; EP Collect.; Gen. BusinessFile (1985-); Gen. Period. Index (1985-); Homework Help.; Index Can. Leg. Period. Lit.; INFO-SOUTH Abstr.; Mag. Search; Manage. Contents (1983-); MasterFile FullTEXT 1000; MasterFile FullTEXT 350; MasterFile FullTEXT 650; MasterFile FullTEXT (July 1993-); OCLC; PAIS Int. Print (1991-); Telebase; UMI ABI/Inform--Bus. Period. Ondisc [Full Txt.]; Wilson Bus. Abstr.

LC HG4001 **ISSN** 0829-4003
DD 658.1/5244 CN
CEASED
CANADIAN TREASURY MANAGEMENT REVIEW. (CANADIAN TREASURY MANAGEMENT REVIEW. THE ROYAL BANK OF CANADA.). [Can. treas. manage. rev.]. **Added/Corp** Royal Bank of Canada. Vol. 1, No. 1 (Sept./Oct. 1984)-(1995). Periodical. English. Royal Bank of Canada, Royal Bank Plaza 9th Floor, South Tower, Toronto Ontario M5J 2J5 Canada. **Tel** (416)974-2274, (416)974-8114, FAX (416)974-3733, (416)974-3361. **ED** Colleen Killeavy. **Circ:** 3,500. ***Continues*** *Canadian Cash Management Review., 0229-1657.*
Desc: Leading Canadian journal for cash and treasury managers.

LC HG1616.C87 C36 **ISSN** 0883-0622
DD 332.1/7/0971 US
CANADIAN TREASURY SERVICES. [Can. treas. serv.]. **Added/Corp** Greenwich Research Associates. (19??)-. English. One time a year. Greenwich Research Associates Inc, Office Park 8, Greenwich CT 06830.

LC HC431 .C3
DD 330 II
CAPITAL. Vol. 1 (1888)-. Periodical. English. Capital / India, 1-2 Old Court House Center, PO Box 14, Calcutta 700001 India. ***Absorbed*** *Indian Financial Review.*
Ind/Abst Indian Geosci. Abstr.

LC HG1501 **ISSN** 0952-7486
DD 332.1 UK
•**CAPITAL MARKET STRATEGIES.** (1994)-. Periodical. English. Four times a year. $443.00. IFR Publishing Ltd., Aldgate House, 33 Aldgate High Street, London EC3N 1DL United Kingdom. **Tel** 011 44 171 369 7536, FAX 011 44 171 369 7395, telex 889365/8953051 IFRPUBG. **(Subscription address:** IFR Publishing, 90 Broad Street, 2nd Floor, New York NY 10004. **Tel** (212)952-7060.) ***Continues*** *Journal of International Securities Markets.*

LC HG1501 **ISSN** 1358-1619
DD 332.1 UK
•**CAPITAL MARKETS GUIDE TO THE FORMER SOVIET UNION, THE.** (July 1995)-. English. Two times a year. £470.00. The CIS Technical Publishing Institute, 11-13 Charterhouse Buildings, London EC1M 7AN United Kingdom. **Tel** 011 44 171 4903774, FAX 011 44 171 4905371.
Desc: Covers areas such as corporate finance, debt/bond markets, money markets, equity markets, stock exchanges, and information vendors.

LC HG1501 **ISSN** 1024-5499
DD 332.1 UK
CAPITAL MARKETS REPORT. (19??)-. Newsletter. English. One time a week. £996.00. The CIS Technical Publishing Institute, 11-13 Charterhouse Buildings, London EC1M 7AN United Kingdom. **Tel** 011 44 171 4903774, FAX 011 44 171 4905371.
Desc: Analysis of developments within the Russian capital markets as well as major developments as they occur in the other markets. Provides stock prices, company news, foreign exchange trading, etc.

LC HG1501
DD 332.1 UK
CAPITAL MARKETS STRATEGIES. (19??)-. Periodical. English. Four times a year. $443.00. IFR Publishing Ltd., Aldgate House, 33 Aldgate High Street, London EC3N 1DL United Kingdom. **Tel** 011 44 171 369 7536, FAX 011 44 171 369 7395, telex 889365/8953051 IFRPUBG. **(Subscription address:** IFR Publishing, 90 Broad Street, Second Floor, New York NY 10004.) ***Continues*** *The Journal of International Securities Markets.*

LC HG1 .C37 **ISSN** 1072-6594
DD 332/.0973/05 US
CAPITALIST'S COMPANION, THE. (THE CAPITALIST'S COMPANION : JOURNAL OF POLITICS AND THE FINANCIAL MARKETS.). [Capital. companion]. (199?)-. Periodical. English. Irregular. $130.00. Capitalists Companion, 175 5th Avenue, Suite 1503, New York NY 10010.

LC HG3756.U54 C395 **ISSN** 1051-6778
DD 332.1/78 US
CARD INDUSTRY DIRECTORY. [Card ind. dir.]. (1990)-. Directory. English. One time a year. $369.95. Faulkner & Gray Inc., 11 Penn Plaza, 17th Floor, New York NY 10001. **Tel** (212)967-7000, (800)535-8403. **(Subscription address:** Faulkner & Gray, Inc., 118 South Clinton St., Suite 700, Chicago IL 60661. **Tel** 800 826-3115, (312)648-0261.)

LC HG **ISSN** 0894-0797
DD 332 US
CCC
CARD NEWS. [Card news]. Vol. 2, No. 6 (June 12, 1987)-. Periodical. English. Twenty-five times a year. $595.00. Phillips Business Information Inc., 1201 Seven Locks Road, PO Box 61130, Potomac MD 20854. **Tel** (301)424-3338, (301)340-1520, (800)777-5005, FAX (301)424-4297, telex 358149. available on an online database from NEWSNET; (files 636,648/Full-Text) DIALOG; and DATA-STAR. ***Continues*** *Money Card News, 0885-9515;* ***Absorbed*** *Credit Card Insider.*
Ind/Abst F&S Index Plus Text, Int. [Select. Cov.]; PTS Newsl. Database [Full Txt.]; Trade Ind. ASAP [Full Txt.]; Trade Ind. Index [Full Txt.].

LC HG1616.E7 Z55 **ISSN** 0148-5423
DD 658.89/332120973 US
CASH DISPENSERS AND AUTOMATED TELLERS. **See** Business and Economics-Abstracting, Bibliographies and Statistics.

LC HG1501
DD 332.1 NE
CASH FLOW. CASH- EN CREDITMANAGEMENT. (1981)-. English. Four times a year. Free on request. Graydon Nederland Bv, Postbus 16991, 2500 BZ Den-Haag Netherlands. **Tel** 011 31 70 3810495.

LC HG1501 **ISSN** 0197-2987
DD 332.1 US
CASH MANAGEMENT FORUM. [Cash manage. forum]. **Added/Corp** First National Bank of Atlanta. Vol. 1 (Jan. 1975)-. Periodical. English. Four times a year. Free on request. First National Bank of Atlanta, 2 Peachtree Street, Mail Code 204, Atlanta GA 30383. **Tel** (404)588-5000.

LC HG4530 **ISSN** 0813-1139
DD 332.63270994 AT
CASH MANAGEMENT TRUSTS, AUSTRALIA. **See** Business and Economics-Abstracting, Bibliographies and Statistics.

LC HG **ISSN** 1054-9994
DD 332 US
CASH RICH COS. [Cash rich co.]. **VFOAT** Cash Rich Companies. Vol. 1, No. 1 (Jan. 1991)-. English. Twelve times a year. $24.00. Cash Rich Cos, Route 3, Box 310-D, Kingston TN 37763.

LC HG1616.I5 S63
DD 332 US
CDA/SPECTRUM. 13(F) INSTITUTIONAL STOCK HOLDINGS. **See** Business and Economics-Investments.

LC HG2794.C38 C37
DD 332.1/53 BB
CDB NEWS. **Added/Corp** Caribbean Development Bank. **VFOAT** C.D.B. News; News. **VAT** Caribbean Development Bank News. Vol. 1, No. 1 (Jan./March 1983)-. Periodical. English. Four times a year. Free. Caribbean Development Bank, PO Box 408, Wildey St. Michael Barbados. **Tel** 011 809 4311600, FAX 011 809 4267269, telex WB2287. **ED** Hubert S. Williams. cum. index. **Circ:** 4,000 (ctrl). available on diskette. Documents available from Documents on Demand.
Desc: Contents focus on the operations and activities of the Caribbean Development Bank (CDB) as bank and development agency and in promoting regional integration in the Commonwealth Caribbean. The contents often include other matters related to the economic and social development of CDB's Borrowing Member Countries.

LC HG65 .C36 **ISSN** 0197-0313
DD 332.1/0973 US
CDE STOCK OWNERSHIP DIRECTORY : BANKING & FINANCE. [CDE stock ownersh. dir., Bank. financ.]. **VFOAT** C.D.E. Stock Ownership Directory. Banking & Finance; Stock Ownership Directory. Banking & Finance. **VAT** Corporate Data Exchange Stock Ownership Directory. Banking and Finance. 1980-. Directory. English. Every 2 years. $250.00 profit institutions, $75.00 nonprofit institutions. Corporate Data Exchange Inc., 198 Broadway, Room 707, New York NY 10038.

LC HG4057 .A1564 **ISSN** 0276-7775
DD 338.7/4/0973 US
CDE STOCK OWNERSHIP DIRECTORY : FORTUNE 500. [CDE stock ownersh. dir., Fortune 500]. **VFOAT** Fortune 500; C.D.E. Stock Ownership Directory. Fortune 500; Stock Ownership Directory. Fortune 500. **VAT** Corporate Data Exchange Stock Ownership Directory. Fortune Five Hundred. (1981)-. Directory. English. Every 2 years. Corporate Data Exchange Inc., 198 Broadway, Room 707, New York NY 10038.

LC HG3881 .C4
DD 332.1 UK
•**CEDEL EUROMONEY DIRECTORY, THE.** **Added/Corp** Cedel (Firm). (1993)-. Directory. English. One time a year. $421.00. Euromoney Publications PLC, Nestor House, Playhouse Yard, London EC4Z 5EX United Kingdom. **Tel** 011 44 171 7798888, FAX 011 44 171 7798630, telex 290700 EUROMON G. ***Continues*** *Merrill Lynch Euromoney Directory.*

LC HG4471.S7 S68A **ISSN** 0303-9226
DD 332.2/6/0968 SP
CENSUS OF BOARDS OF EXECUTORS AND TRUST COMPANIES. (CENSUS OF BOARDS OF EXECUTORS AND TRUST COMPANIES (SOUTH AFRICA).). **Main/Corp** South Africa. Dept. of Statistics. **VFOAT** Sensus van Eksekuteurskamers en Trustmaatskappye. (19??)-. Multiple languages (Afrikaans and English). 3.75. ***Continues*** *Sensus van Eksekuteurskamers en Trustmaatskappye.*

LC HG1811 .C457 **ISSN** 0960-6319
DD 332.1/1/05 UK
CENTRAL BANKING. No. 1 (Summer 1990)-. Periodical. English. Four times a year. $290.00. Central Banking Publ Ltd., 27 Chancery Lane, London WC2A 1PA United Kingdom. **Tel** 011 44 171 4046435, FAX 011 44 171 4046436. **ED** Robert Pringle (editor's phone number: 011 44 171 4046435). **Bk Rev**, (Qty: 20). **Ad Acc. Circ:** 500.
Desc: Banking anaylsis for Bank of England, Bank of Japan, and Bank of Sweden.
Ind/Abst PAIS Int. Print (1991-).

LC HG4026 .C43 **ISSN** 8756-7113
DD 658.15/05 US
CCC
CODEN CFOMEX
CFO. (CFO : THE MAGAZINE FOR CHIEF FINANCIAL OFFICERS.). [CFO]. **VAT** Chief Financial Officer. Vol. 1, No. 1 (Feb. 1985)-. Periodical. English. Twelve times a year. $19.00. CFO Publishing Corporation, 253 Summer Street, Boston MA 02210. **Tel** (617)345-9700. available on microfilm and microfiche from University Microfilms International (UMI). Documents available from UMI Article Clearinghouse.
Ind/Abst ABI/INFORM Glob. Ed. (March 1987-); ABI/INFORM [Computer File] (March 1987-); Acad. Search; Account. Tax Datab. (Mar. 1987-) [Full Txt.]; Bus.

Source Plus; Bus. Source; Curr. Cit.; EP Collect.; Gen. BusinessFile (1992-); Homework Help.; MasterFile FullTEXT 1000; MasterFile FullTEXT 350; MasterFile FullTEXT 650; MasterFile FullTEXT (July 1994-); OCLC; Telebase.

LC HG **ISSN** 0894-4822
DD 332 US
TITLE CHANGE

CFO ALERT. [CFO alert]. **Added/Corp** Warren, Gorham & Lamont, Inc. **VAT** Corporate Financial Officer Alert. Vol. 8, No. 9 (Feb. 1987)-(19??). Periodical. English. Warren Gorham & Lamont Inc., Park Square Building, 31 St. James Avenue, Boston MA 02116-4112. **Tel** (617)423-2020, (800)950-1207, FAX (617)423-2026. **ED** Paul Wendell. **Circ:** 1000. ***Continues*** *Corporate Controller's Report, 0745-3078; International Bank Accountant.* ***Continued by*** *Wendell's Report for Controllers, 1067-7313.*
Desc: Delivers hard news and practical guidance for top-level financial executives on new accounting rules, corporate financing, merges and acquisitions, case management techniques and much more.

LC HG **ISSN** 1081-9525
DD 332 US

●**CFO & CONTROLLER ALERT.** [CFO control. alert]. **VFOAT** Chief Financial Officer and Controller Alert; CFO and Controller Alert. (1995)-. Periodical. English. Twenty-three times a year. $299.00. Progressive Business Publications, 370 Technology Drive, PO Box 3019, Malvern PA 19355. **Tel** (617)527-8600, (800)220-5000, FAX (617)647-8089.

LC HG **ISSN** 1058-4455
DD 332 US
CEASED

CFP TODAY. [CFP today]. **Added/Corp** Institute of Certified Financial Planners (U.S.). **VAT** Certified Financial Planners Today. (19??)-(Dec. 1995). Trade Publication. English. Institute of Certified Financial Planners, 7600 East Eastman Avenue, Suite 301, Denver CO 80231. **Tel** (303)751-7600, (800)322-ICFP, FAX (303)751-1037. **Ad Acc.** Full Page (B&W) $2,400.00. Half Page (B&W) $1,750.00. ***Continues*** *Institute Today, 0897-4527.*
Desc: Designed to provide readers with information, from asset management to the needs of the elderly. All of the aspects of the finanical planning process are explored.

LC HC340.12 .R87
DD 330 US

●**CHAMBER WORLD REPORTS. RUSSIA.** **Added/Corp** Chamber World Network. **VFOAT** Russia; Political & Economic Analysis & Business Directory, Russia; Russia ... Political and Economic Analysis & Business Directory; Political and Economic Analysis and Business Directory; Russia ... Political & Economic Analysis & Business Directory. (1994)-. English. One time a year. $65.00. Chamber World Network, New York NY 10003. **Tel** (212)645-2464. **(Subscription address:** SCB Distributors, 15612 South New Centennial, Gardenia CA 90248. **)** ***Continues*** *Russia (New York, N.Y. : 1993).*

ISSN 1055-9477
DD 346 US

CHAPTER 11 UPDATE. [Chapter 11 update]. **VFOAT** Chapter Eleven Update. Vol. 1, No. 1 (Apr. 29, 1991)-. Periodical. English. Twenty-four times a year. $450.00. Andrews Publications Inc., 1646 West Chester Pike, PO Box 1000, Westtown PA 19395. **Tel** (610)399-6600, (800)345-1101, FAX (610)399-6610.
Desc: It allows attorneys and other interested parties to track developments in the country's largest and most significant business bankruptcies.

LC HG1501
DD 332.1 UK

CHART LIBRARIES. CURRENCY AND FINANCIAL FUTURES WEEKLY. (19??)-. English. One time a week. £950.00 UK; £1025.00 Europe and Ireland; £1175.00 North Africa and Middle East; £1220.00 other. Chart Analysis Ltd, 7 Swallow Street, London W1R 7HD United Kingdom. **Tel** 011 44 1439 4961.

LC HG4001 .C47 **ISSN** 0730-0360
DD 658.1/5/05 US

CHASE FINANCIAL QUARTERLY. **Added/Corp** Chase Financial Policy (Chase Manhattan Bank, N.A.). Vol. 1, No. 1 (Fall 1981)-. Trade Publication. English. Four times a year. $5,000.00. Chase Financial Policy, 1 Chase Manhattan Plaza, New York NY 10031.

LC HG **ISSN** 1046-4956
DD 332 US

CHECKS & CHECKING. **VFOAT** Checks and Checking. (1990)-. Periodical. English. Twelve times a year. $349.95. Faulkner & Gray Inc., 11 Penn Plaza, 17th Floor, New York NY 10001. **Tel** (212)967-7000, (800)535-8403.

LC HG2613.C4 C47 **ISSN** 0361-7661
DD 332.1/025/77311 US

CHICAGO BANKS. (19??)-. English. Two times a year. $7.30. Chicago Lawyer, 415 North State Street, Chicago IL 60610. **Tel** (312)644-7800, FAX (312)644-4255. **ED** Alan Bergner. **Circ:** 4,700.
Desc: Lists of officers and directors of approximately 300 Cook county banks, plus financial statements for more than half of them.

LC HG1501 **ISSN** 0895-0164
DD 332 US

CHICAGO FED LETTER. [Chic. fed lett.]. **Added/Corp** Federal Reserve Bank of Chicago. Research Dept. No. 1 (Sept. 1987)-. Periodical. English. Twelve times a year. Free. Federal Reserve Bank of Chicago, 230 South LaSalle, PO Box 834, Chicago IL 60690. **Tel** (312)322-5111, FAX (312)322-5700. **ED** Edward G. Nash. **Circ:** 40,000. available on microfilm and microfiche from University Microfilms International (UMI). Documents available from UMI Article Clearinghouse.
Ind/Abst ABI/INFORM Glob. Ed.; ABI/INFORM [Computer File] (September 1987); EP Collect.; Gen. BusinessFile (1992-); Homework Help.; MasterFile FullTEXT 1000; MasterFile FullTEXT 350; MasterFile FullTEXT 650; MasterFile FullTEXT; OCLC; Telebase; UMI ABI/Inform--Bus. Period. Ondisc [Full Txt.]; Urban Aff. Abstr.

LC HG41 .C48
DD 332 HK

CHIN YIN CHENG CHUAN YUEH PAO. **VFOAT** Kam Ngan Monthly Bulletin. (Sept. 1973)-. Bulletin. Chinese.

ISSN 1189-7090
DD 330.951/005 CN

●**CHINA ANALYST, THE.** [China anal.]. **Added/Corp** Bank Credit Analyst Research Group. **VFOAT** China Analyst From the Bank Credit Analyst Research Group. Vol. 1, No. 1 (Sept. 1993)-. Periodical. English. Twelve times a year. 595.00Can$. BCA Publications Ltd., 1002 Sherbrooke Street West, Suite 1600, Montreal Quebec H3A 3L6 Canada. **Tel** (514)499-9706, FAX (514)499-9709.

LC HG **ISSN** 1060-3239
DD 332 US

CHOICE$ (RESEARCH TRIANGLE PARK, N.C.). (CHOICE$: YOUR GUIDE TO MAKING INFORMED FINANCIAL DECISIONS.). [Choice$]. **Added/Corp** Financial Research Services. **VFOAT** Research Triangle Park, NC. Vol. 1, Issue 1 (Dec. 1991)-. Periodical. English. Twelve times a year. $30.00. Financial Research Services, PO Box 13662, Research Triangle Park NC 27709.

LC HC466 .C4736
DD 330.9519/5043 KO

CHOSA WOLBO (KUNGMIN UNHAENG). **See** Business and Economics-Small Business.

LC HG2040 **ISSN** 0712-2756
DD 332.7/2/0971 CN

CHRONIQUE HYPOTHECAIRE. [Chron. hypothec.]. Sept. 1981-. Periodical. French. Four times a year. Chronique Hypothecaire CAHC, CP 14, Suite 1200/401 rue Bay, Toronto Ontario M5H 2Y4 Canada. ***Continues*** *Nouvelles dans le Domaine d'Hypotheque, 0710-6483.*

LC HG201 .C48
DD 332/.0951 CC

CHUNG-KUO CHIN JUNG. **Added/Corp** Chung-kuo Jen Min Yin Hang. **VFOAT** Zhongguo Jinrong. (19??)-. Periodical. Chinese. Twelve times a year. $36.40. Chung-Kuo Kuo Chi Shu Tien, PO Box 2820, Beijing China. **(Subscription address:** China International Book Trading Corporation, PO Box 399, Library Service Department, Beijing 100044 People's Republic of China. **Tel** 011 86 1 8414284, FAX 011 86 1 8412023, telex 22496 CIBTC CN.**)**

LC HG3331 .C48
DD 332.1/0951 CC

CHUNG-KUO CHIN JUNG NIEN CHIEN = ALMANAC OF CHINA'S FINANCE AND BANKING. **Added/Corp** Chung-kuo Chin Jung Hsueh Hui. **VFOAT** Almanac of China's Finance and Banking. (1986)-. Chinese. One time a year (Dec.). $25.00. China National Publishing Import & Export Corporation, 16 Gongti E Rd., Chaoyang Dist., Beijing 100704, People's Republic of China. **Tel** 011 8601 50630169, 5066688, FAX 011 8601 5063101, 5063010, telex 22313.

LC HG **ISSN** 1063-2220
DD 332 US
CCC

CLARK'S BANK DEPOSITS AND PAYMENTS MONTHLY. [Clark's bank depos. paym. mon.]. **Added/Corp** Warren, Gorham & Lamont, Inc. **VFOAT** Bank Deposits and Payments Monthly. (1992)-. Periodical. English. Twelve times a year. $173.25. Warren Gorham & Lamont Inc., Park Square Building, 31 St. James Avenue, Boston MA 02116-4112. **Tel** (617)423-2020, (800)950-1207, FAX (617)423-2026. **ED** Barbara Clark & Barkley Clark.

LC HG **ISSN** 1076-0571
DD 332 US

●**CLOSED-END FUNDS ONFLOPPY.** (CLOSED-END FUNDS ONFLOPPY [COMPUTER FILE].). [Closed-end funds onfloppy]. **Added/Corp** Morningstar, Inc. **VFOAT** Closed End Funds on Floppy. (1993)-. Periodical. English. Twelve times a year. $200.00. Morningstar Inc., 225 West Wacker Drive, Chicago IL 60606. **Tel** (312)696-6000, (800)876-5005.

LC HG2040 **ISSN** 1188-4215
DD 332.7/2/097105 CN

CMHC MORTGAGE MARKET TRENDS. [CMHC mortg. mark. trends]. **Added/Corp** Canada Mortgage and Housing Corporation. Market Analysis Centre. **VAT** Canada Mortgage and Housing Corporation Mortgage Market Trends. (Oct. 1988)-. Periodical. English. Four times a year. 35.21Can$. Canada Mortgage and Housing Corporation / Canadian Housing Information Centre, 700 Montreal Road, Ottawa Ontario K1A 0P7 Canada. **Tel** (613)748-2550, (613)748-2367, FAX (613)748-4069, (613)748-7855.

LC HG1501
DD 332.1 US

CODE OF FEDERAL REGULATIONS. 13, BUSINESS CREDIT AND ASSISTANCE. **Added/Corp** United States. Office of the Federal Register. **VFOAT** CFR. 13, Business Credit and Assistance; Business Credit and Assistance. (19??)-. Government Publication. English. One time a year. $42.00. Superintendent of Documents, US Government Printing Office, Washington DC 20402. **Tel** (202)275-3328, FAX (202)786-2377. **(Subscription address:** US Government Bookstore, O'Neil Building, 2023 3rd Avenue North, Birmingham AL 35203. **)** available on microfiche (Vols. for (1984-) distributed to some depository libraries).
Desc: Special edition of the Federal Register, containing a codification of documents.

LC HG1501
DD 332.1 IT

CODICE DEI TRIBUTI LOCALI. (19??)-. Periodical. Italian. Two times a year. IPSOA Editore SRL, Casella Postale 12055, Mastrangelo, 20120 Milan Italy. **Tel** 011 39 2 82476248. Index available (Included).

LC HG3729.E82 C63A
DD 332 EC

COFIEC INFORME ANUAL. **Main/Corp** COFIEC. **VFOAT** COFIEC Annual Report. (19??)-. Spanish. One time a year. COFIEC, Av 10 de Agosto No 1546, Apartado No 411, Quito Ecuador. **Tel** 546177, FAX 564224, telex COFIEC 22131 ED. **Circ:** 2,000.

ISSN 1052-4029
DD 338 US

COLLECTION AGENCY REPORT. [Collect. agency rep.]. (1990)-. Periodical. English. Twelve times a year. $420.00. Collection Agency Report, PO Box 5025, Warren MI 48090. **Tel** (800)366-5995. **ED** Albert W Scale (editors telephone: (313) 573-0045). **Bk Rev**, (Qty: 4 /yr). **Circ:** 400.
Desc: News and advisory service for collection executives and managers.

LC HG **ISSN** 0010-082X
DD 332 US

COLLECTOR (MINNEAPOLIS, MINN.). (COLLECTOR.). [Collector]. **Added/Corp** American Collectors Association. Vol. 1 (Oct. 1934)-. Periodical. English. Twelve times a year. $60.00. American Collectors Association, PO Box 35106, Minneapolis MN 55435. **Tel** (612)926-6547.

LC HG1501
DD 332.1 US

COMMENTS. **Main/Corp** Philadelphia National Bank. (19??)-. Periodical. English. Free on request. Philadelphia National Bank, Broad and Chestnut Streets, Philadelphia PA 19101. **Tel** (215)629-3100. available on microfilm from KTO Microform.

LC HG1501 **ISSN** 1038-6505
DD 332.1 AT

COMMERCIAL BANKING PRODUCTS SURVEY. BUSINESS CHEQUE ACCOUNTS. (19??)-. Trade Publication. English. Twelve times a year. 1730.00Aus$. Horan Wall & Walker Pty Ltd, 15-19 Prospect Street, POB 8, Surry Hills New South Wales 2010 Australia. **Tel** 02 331 6600, FAX 02 380 5533. **ED** Jayson Forrest. available on an online database; available on diskette.

LC HG1501 **ISSN** 1038-6491
DD 332.1 AT

COMMERCIAL BANKING PRODUCTS SURVEY. COMMERCIAL LOANS. (19??)-. Trade Publication. English. Twelve times a year. 1730.00Aus$. Horan Wall & Walker Pty Ltd, 15-19 Prospect Street, POB 8, Surry Hills New South Wales 2010 Australia. **Tel** 02 331 6600, FAX 02 380 5533. **ED** Jayson Forrest. available on an online database; available on diskette.

Business and Economics —Banks and Banking

LC HG3691
DD 332.70994   **ISSN** 1031-0193
                                 AT
COMMERCIAL FINANCE AUSTRALIA.
See Business and Economics-Abstracting, Bibliographies and Statistics.

LC HG1501
DD 332.1   US
COMMERCIAL LENDING NEWSLETTER.
Added/Corp Robert Morris Associates. **VFOAT** RMA Commercial Lending Newsletter. Vol. 9, No. 4 (April 1977)-. Newsletter. English. Twelve times a year. $30.00. Robert Morris Associates, One Liberty Plaza, 1650 Market Street, Philadelphia PA 19103. **Tel** (215)851-9118, (215)851-0585, FAX (215)851-9206. **ED** Carol McGinn. Index available. **Bk Rev**. **Circ**: 19,000 (ctrl). available on an online database (LEXIS-NEXIS) from Mead Data Central; (file FINI) BRS; and (on FINIS) DIALOG. *Continues* RMA News.
Desc: Articles of interest to commercial lenders.

LC HG1641 .C59
DD 332.1/753/05   **ISSN** 0886-8204
                                 US
COMMERCIAL LENDING REVIEW.
[Commer. lend. rev.]. Vol. 1, No. 1 (Winter 1985)-. Periodical. English. Four times a year. $105.00 US; $125.00 other. Institutional Investor Inc., 488 Madison Avenue, New York NY 10022. **Tel** (212)303-3234, (212)303-3233, FAX (212)303-3353. Index available (extra for $25.00). cum. index. **Bk Rev**. **Circ**: 3,000. available on microfilm and microfiche from University Microfilms International (UMI); available on an online database (files 15,485/Full-Text) from DIALOG. Documents available from UMI Article Clearinghouse.
Desc: Provides commercial lending guidance and how-to techniques in credit and financial analysis. Contains regular coverage of issues like asset-based lending and lending law and leasing.
Ind/Abst ABI/INFORM Glob. Ed.; ABI/INFORM [Computer File] (Winter 1985-1986); Account. Tax Datab. (Winter 1985-1986) [Full Txt.]; Curr. Cit.; Gen. BusinessFile (1992-); UMI ABI/Inform--Bus. Period. Ondisc [Full Txt.].

LC HG2613.S54 B282
DD 332.1/0973   **ISSN** 0162-363X
                                 US
COMMUNITY AND THE BANK. **Main/Corp** Bank of America. (19??)-. English. One time a year. San Francisco Bank of America, PO Box 37140, San Francisco CA 94137.

LC HG1501
DD 332.1   **ISSN** 1055-4947
             US
COMMUNITY BANK MARKETING.
Added/Corp Bank Marketing Association (U.S.). (1991)-. Periodical. English. Six times a year. $48.00 (membership). Bank Marketing Association, 309 W Washington Street, Chicago IL 60606. **Tel** (312)782-1442. *Continues* Community Bank Marketing Newsletter.

LC HG1501
DD 332.1   **ISSN** 0276-0908
            US
COMMUNITY BANK PRESIDENT, THE.
Added/Corp Center for Management Systems. (19??)-. Newsletter. English. Twenty-four times a year. $319.00. Siefer Consultants Inc., PO Box 1384, 525 Cayuga Street, Sioux Center IA 50588. **Tel** (712)732-7340, (712)747-7342, FAX (712)732-7906. **ED** Joe Sheller. Index available. ctrl circ.

LC HG1501
DD 332.1   **ISSN** 1077-9728
            US
●**COMMUNITY BANKER, THE. VFOAT** Community Banker, A Management Advisory on Today's Critical Issues, Strategies & Trends. (1994)-. Periodical. English. Four times a year (Feb., May, Aug., Nov.). $225.00. Probus Publishing Company, 1925 North Clybourn Avenue, Chicago IL 60614. **Tel** (800)776-2871, (312)868-1100.

LC HG2611.A4 C65
DD 332.1/09798   US
COMPARATIVE STATEMENT OF ASSETS, LIABILITIES, AND CAPITAL ACCOUNTS OF ALASKA BANKS AS OF
... . Added/Corp Alaska. Division of Banking, Securities, Small Loans, and Corporations. (19??)-. English. Four times a year. $10.00. Alaska Department of Commerce and Economic Development, PO Box D, Juneau AK 99811. **Tel** (907)465-2521, FAX (907)463-3841.

LC HG2611.P42 C65
DD 332.1/09748   **ISSN** 0361-4786
            US
COMPETITIVE ANALYSIS: PENNSYLVANIA. [Compet. anal., Pa.].
Added/Corp Sheshunoff & Company. (19??)-. English. Sheshunoff Information Services Inc., PO Box 13203, Capitol Station, Austin TX 78711. **Tel** (800)456-2340, (512)472-2244.

LC HG3024 .A88a
DD 332.1/0944   FR
COMPTE RENDU - ASSOCIATION PROFESSIONNELLE DES BANQUES, COMITE D'ETUDES TECHNIQUES ET DE NORMALISATION BANCAIRE.
Main/Corp Association Professionnelle des Banques. Comite d'Etudes Techniques et de Normalisation Bancaire. (19??)-. French. Secretariat du Comite Monetaire de la Zone Franc, 39 rue Croix-des-Petit-Champs, 75049 Paris France.

LC HC111 .A353b
DD 330.9/71/0644   CN
COMPTE RENDU DE LA SITUATION ECONOMIQUE. Main/Corp Canada. Dept. of Finance. (19??)-. French. One time a year. Information Canada, 171 Slater Street, Ottawa Ontario K1A 0S9 Canada. **Tel** (819)997-1095.

LC HG186.F8 C55
DD 332   FR
COMPTES ANNUELS DES ETABLISSEMENTS DE CREDIT.
Added/Corp France. Commission Bancaire. (19??)-. French. One time a year. $87.49. Commission Bancaire Secretary Generale, 4 rue Des Colonnes, F 75002 Paris France. **Tel** 011 33 1 42925931, FAX 011 33 1 42925940.

LC HG3729.C18 S65c
DD 354.67/110072254   CM
COMPTES DE RESULTATS D'EXECUTION DU BUDGET. Main/Corp Societe de Developpement du Nkam. (19??)-. French. Societe de Developpement du Nkam, Boite Postale 02, Nkondjock Cameroon.

LC HG1501
DD 332.1   US
COMPTROLLER'S MANUAL FOR REPRESENTATIVES IN TRUSTS : REGULATIONS, INSTRUCTIONS, OPINIONS. Main/Corp United States. Office of the Comptroller of the Currency. English.

LC HG1501
DD 332.1   US
COMPUTER LETTER. See Science and Technology.

LC HG1501
DD 332.1   **ISSN** 0361-8714
            US
CONFERENCE SERIES - FEDERAL RESERVE BANK OF BOSTON.
(CONFERENCE SERIES.). **Main/Corp** Federal Reserve Bank of Boston. **VFOAT** Monetary Conference Series. No. 1 (1969)-. Monographic series. English. One time a year. Price varies per volume. Federal Reserve Bank of Boston, 600 Atlantic Avenue, Research Library D, Boston MA 02106. **Tel** (617)973-3397, (617)973-3403.
Ind/Abst Fed. Print Econ. Bank. Top.

DD 330.971/005   **ISSN** 0834-3152
            CN
CONJONCTURE CANADIENNE. (LA CONJONCTURE CANADIENNE.). [Conjonct. can.]. **Added/Corp** Banque de Commerce Canadienne Imperiale. Division Economique. (197?)-. Periodical. French. Limited free distribution.
Ind/Abst Can. Period. Index (19??-).

LC HG1501
DD 332.1   **ISSN** 0746-9233
            US
CONNECTION (ATLANTA, GA. 1983), THE. (THE CONNECTION.). (1983)-. Periodical. English. Twenty-six times a year. Georgia Credit Union Affiliates, PO Box 29884, Atlanta GA 30359. *Continues* Georgian.

LC HG2611.M6 M56A
DD 332.3/2/09776   US
CONSOLIDATED ANNUAL REPORT FOR THE YEAR ENDING DECEMBER 31 ... / DEPARTMENT OF COMMERCE, BANKING DIVISION. Main/Corp Minnesota. Banking Division. English. One time a year.

LC HG2038.I5 A33
DD 334/.22/09773   US
CONSOLIDATED ANNUAL REPORT OF ILLINOIS STATE CHARTERED CREDIT UNIONS. Main/Corp Illinois. Credit Union Division. **VFOAT** Illinois Chartered Credit Unions Annual Report. (1975)-. English. One time a year. Illinois State Chartered Credit Unions, Illinois Credit Union Division, 500 Iles Park Place, Suite 500, Springfield IL 62718. *Continues* Illinois. Credit Union Division. Annual Report of Illinois State Chartered Credit Unions.

LC HG1501
DD 332.1   US
CONSULTANT COMPENDIUM. (19??)-. Periodical. English. Irregular (3 or 4 per year). $695.00. Money Market Directories Inc., 320 East Main Street, PO Box 1608, Charlottesville VA 22902. **Tel** (800)446-2810, (804)977-1450. Index available.

LC HG1501
DD 640.73   US
CONSUMER AND COMMUNITY AFFAIRS HANDBOOK. Added/Corp Board of Governors of the Federal Reserve System (U.S.). (19??)-. Periodical. English. One time a year. $75.00. Board of Governors of the Federal Reserve System, Mail Stop 127, Washington DC 20551. **Tel** (202)452-3244, (202)452-3245.

LC HG179 .C667
DD 332.024   US
CONSUMER FINANCE NEWSLETTER.
Added/Corp California. Dept. of Corporations. No. 1 (Aug. 1970)-. Newsletter. English. Twelve times a year. $24.50. Financial Publishing Company, 82 Brookline Avenue, Boston MA 02215. **Tel** (617)262-4040. **ED** Dorothy B. Walter. **Circ**: 1,300.
Desc: Reports effective and pending legislative changes affecting the consumer finance industry in each of the 50 states and the nation as a whole.

LC HG1501
DD 332.1   **ISSN** 0364-2844
            US
CONSUMER INSTALLMENT CREDIT.
Added/Corp Board of Governors of the Federal Reserve System (U.S.). (19??)-. English. Twelve times a year. $5.00. Board of Governors of the Federal Reserve System, Mail Stop 127, Washington DC 20551. **Tel** (202)452-3244, (202)452-3245. *Continues* Consumer Credit (Board of Governors of the Federal Reserve System), 0196-5379; *Absorbed* Automobile Credit.

LC HG1501
DD 332.1   US
CONSUMER TRENDS. (196?)-. Periodical. English. Twelve times a year. $100.00. International Credit Association, PO Box 27357, St Louis MO 63141. **Tel** (314)991-3030, FAX (314)991-3029. **ED** Janet Lipkind. **Circ**: 1,150 (ctrl). *Continues* Report on Consumer Trends.
Desc: An independent newsletter on credit and financial affairs, forecasts and statistics, legislative, litigative and regulatory developments plus more.

LC HG4001 .C68
DD 658.1/5/05   **ISSN** 0898-4484
            CCC
            TITLE CHANGE
CONTINENTAL BANK JOURNAL OF APPLIED CORPORATE FINANCE. [Cont. Bank j. appl. corp. finance]. **Added/Corp** Continental Illinois National Bank and Trust Company of Chicago. **VFOAT** Journal of Applied Corporate Finance. (1988)-(1994). Periodical. English. Stern Stewart Management Services Inc, 40 West 57th Street, New York NY 10019. **Tel** (212)261-0600, FAX (212)581-6420. cum. index. available on microfilm and microfiche from University Microfilms International (UMI). *Continued by* BankAmerica Journal of Applied Corporate Finance, 1078-1196.
Ind/Abst Account. Tax Datab. (1988-); Anbar Account. Finan. Abstr.; Curr. Cit.

LC HG
DD 332   **ISSN** 1081-9215
            US
●**CONTROLLER'S COST REPORT.** [Control. cost rep.]. **Added/Corp** Warren, Gorham & Lamont, Inc. Vol. 1, No. 1 (Mar. 1995)-. Periodical. English. Twelve times a year. $141.75. Warren Gorham & Lamont Inc., Park Square Building, 31 St. James Avenue, Boston MA 02116-4112. **Tel** (617)423-2020, (800)950-1207, FAX (617)423-2026. **(Subscription address:** Warren Gorham & Lamont, PO Box 4966, Chicago IL 60680. **)** *Continues* Wendell's Report for Controllers, 1067-7313.

LC HG1501
DD 332.1   **ISSN** 0926-7158
            NE
UDC 657.6
Pr Rev.
CONTROLLERS MAGAZINE. [Control. mag.]. (1987)-. Periodical. Dutch. Six times a year (Feb., May, Jul., Sept., Oct., Dec.). $81.54. Sim Publishers BV, Postbus 10281, 2501 HG The Hague Netherlands. **Tel** 011 31 70 3640054. **ED** Joyce Martinus. Index available. cum. index. **Bk Rev**. **Ad Acc**. **Circ**: 8,500.
Desc: A professional magazine for controllers, treasurers, credit managers and other financial managers.

LC HG
DD 332   **ISSN** 8756-5676
            US
            CCC
CONTROLLERS' UPDATE, THE. [Control. update]. **Added/Corp** Controllers' Council (U.S.). Issue No. 1 (Jan. 1985)-. Periodical. English. Twelve times a year. Comes with Controllers Council membership - $75.00. Institute of Management Accountants, 10 Paragon Drive, Montvale NJ 07645. **Tel** (201)573-9000, (800)638-4427, FAX (201)573-8185, telex 9102509487.
Ind/Abst Account. Tax Datab. (Jan. 1992-) [Full Txt.].

LC HG4028.C45 C37 ISSN 1040-0311
DD 658.1/5244 US
CCC
CODEN CCASES

CORPORATE CASHFLOW. **VFOAT** Corporate Cash Flow; Cash Flow; Cash Flow Magazine; Cashflow Magazine; Cashflow. Vol. 9, No. 5 (May 1988)-. Corporate Report. English. Twelve times a year. $78.00. Argus Business, 6151 Powers Ferry Road Northwest, Atlanta GA 30339. **Tel** (404)995-2500, FAX (404)995-0400. **(Subscription address:** Sunbelt Fulfillment Services / Nashville, PO Box 41369, Nashville TN 37204. **Tel** (615)377-3322, (800)888-5139.**)** Index available (free). available on microfilm and microfiche from University Microfilms International (UMI). Documents available from UMI Article Clearinghouse. ***Continues*** *Cashflow, 0196-6227.*
Ind/Abst ABI/INFORM Glob. Ed. (Jan. 1981-); ABI/INFORM Ondisc: Expr. Ed. (Jan. 1987-); ABI/INFORM [Computer File] (Jan. 1981-); Acad. Search; Account. Tax Datab. (Jan. 1981-) [Full Txt.]; Bus. ASAP (1990-) [Full Txt.]; Bus. Index (1988-); Bus. Source Plus; Bus. Source; Curr. Cit.; EP Collect.; F&S Index Plus Text, Int. [Select. Cov.]; Gen. BusinessFile (1988-); Gen. Period. Index (1988-); Homework Help.; INFO-SOUTH Abstr.; Mag. Search; Manage. Contents; MasterFile FullTEXT 1000; MasterFile FullTEXT 350; MasterFile FullTEXT 650; MasterFile FullTEXT (Jan. 1994-); OCLC; PAIS Int. Print (1991-); PROMT; Telebase; Trade Ind. ASAP [Full Txt.]; Trade Ind. Index [Full Txt.].

LC HG1501 ISSN 0272-0299
DD 332.1 US
CCC

CORPORATE EFT REPORT. **VAT** Corporate Electronic Funds Transfer Report. Vol. 1 (Oct. 8, 1980)-. Corporate Report. English. Twenty-five times a year. $595.00. Phillips Business Information Inc., 1201 Seven Locks Road, PO Box 61130, Potomac MD 20854. **Tel** (301)424-3338, (301)340-1520, (800)777-5005, FAX (301)424-4297, telex 358149. **ED** Patricia A. Murphy. available on an online database from NEWSNET; Lexis-Nexis; and (files 636,648/Full-Text) DIALOG. ***Absorbed*** *Treasury Manager, 0896-2987; Treasury Watch.*
Desc: Information for those in cash management and money transfer. Opportunities, interest-bearing corporate checking accounts, security methods, securities processing, etc.
Ind/Abst F&S Index Plus Text, Int. [Select. Cov.]; PTS Newsl. Database [Full Txt.].

LC HG4050 .C68 ISSN 0894-6817
DD 658.1/5/0973 US
CCC
TITLE CHANGE

CORPORATE FINANCE. [Corp. finance]. Vol. 1, No. 1 (Nov. 1986)-(199?). Periodical. English. Corporate Finance, 415 Madison Avenue, New York NY 10017. **Tel** (212)754-0850, FAX (212)754-0151. ***Continued by*** *Financial World's Corporate Finance.*
Desc: Magazine for the financing strategist.

LC HG4057 .A15647 ISSN 0740-2546
DD 338.7/4/02573 US
TITLE CHANGE

CORPORATE FINANCE BLUEBOOK, THE. [Corp. financ. blueb.]. (1983)-(19??). English. National Register Publishing Company Inc., PO Box 31, 121 Chanlon Road, New Providence NJ 07974. **Tel** (800)521-8110, (800)323-6772, FAX (908)665-6688. **ED** Cathy Patruno. Index available. cum. index. **Bk Rev. Ad Acc.** ctrl circ. available on magnetic tape and CD-ROM. ***Continued by*** *America's Corporate Finance Directory.*
Desc: Contains over 5,200 companies and 20,000 subsidiaries of America's financial executives. Each entry lists up to 23 financial service firms, including insurance brokers, insurers, pension managers, auditors and master trustees.

LC HG ISSN 0882-3073
DD 332 US

CORPORATE FINANCE LETTER. **Added/Corp** National Council of Savings Institutions (U.S.). (19??)-. Periodical. English. Twelve times a year. Savings and Community Bankers of America, 1101 15th Street Northwest, Suite 400, Washington DC 20005. **Tel** (202)857-3100, FAX (202)659-4816. **ED** Harding de C. Williams. **Circ:** 1,000.
Desc: A newsletter reporting in-depth research on new financing and management techniques in the savings industry.

LC HG3810 .C67 ISSN 0958-2053
DD 658.1/5/05 UK

CORPORATE FINANCE (LONDON). (CORPORATE FINANCE.). [Corp. finance]. No. 34 (Sept. 1987)-. Trade Publication. English. Twelve times a year. $450.00. Euromoney Publications PLC, Nestor House, Playhouse Yard, London EC4Z 5EX United Kingdom. **Tel** 011 44 171 7798888, FAX 011 44 171 7798630, telex 290700 EUROMON G. ***Continues*** *Euromoney Corporate Finance, 0266-7002.*
Desc: Leading international journal of financing techniques, M&A and risk management for corporate treasury and financial executives, and their advisers. Reports, analyses and explains all the latest techniques and practices in international corporate finance.
Ind/Abst Curr. Cit.

LC HG4057 .A2194 ISSN 1057-8056
DD 332.6/6 US
CEASED

CORPORATE FINANCE (NEW YORK, N.Y. 1991). (CORPORATE FINANCE : THE IDD REVIEW OF INVESTMENT BANKING.). [Corp. finance]. **Added/Corp** Investment Dealers' Digest, Inc. **VFOAT** IDD Review of Investment Banking. (Spring 1991)-(Fall 1995). Periodical. English. Investment Dealers Digest Inc., Two World Trade Center, 18th Floor, New York NY 10048. **Tel** (212)227-1200, FAX (212)432-1039. ***Continues*** *Directory of Corporate Financing, 0882-7591.*

LC HG4057 .A1565 ISSN 0163-3031
DD 332/.025/73 US
CCC

CORPORATE FINANCE SOURCEBOOK, THE. (1979)-. English. One time a year (Apr.). $510.85. National Register Publishing Company Inc., PO Box 31, 121 Chanlon Road, New Providence NJ 07974. **Tel** (800)521-8110, (800)323-6772, FAX (908)665-6688. **ED** Cathy Patruno. Index available (free). cum. index. **Bk Rev. Ad Acc. Circ:** 5,000 (ctrl).
Desc: Lists names, addresses, services offered, specialities, lending requirements, clients handled, and direct phone numbers for 3,700 firms and over 15,000 financial specialists in 17 different categories.

LC HG4050 .C683 ISSN 1064-1912
DD 338.7/0973/05 US

CORPORATE FINANCING WEEK - INSTITUTIONAL INVESTOR (FIRM). (CORPORATE FINANCING WEEK : A PUBLICATION OF INSTITUTIONAL INVESTOR.). [Corp. financ. week - Inst. invest. (Firm)]. **Added/Corp** Institutional Investor (Firm). Vol. 1 (1974)-. Newsletter. English. One time a week. $1495.00. Institutional Investor Inc., 488 Madison Avenue, New York NY 10022. **Tel** (212)303-3234, (212)303-3233, FAX (212)303-3353. available on CD-ROM. ***Supersedes*** *Corporation Finance and New Issue Weekly, 0090-919X.*
Desc: Reports on financing strategies--corporations explain what they are doing and why. Coverage includes investment banking news, financing techniques, regulatory developments and financing trends.

LC HG1501 ISSN 0951-3639
DD 332.05 UK

CORPORATE MONEY. [Corp. money]. (1987)-. Newsletter. English. Twenty-four times a year. $487.70. Centaur Communications Ltd., St. Giles House, 50 Poland Street, London W1V 4AX United Kingdom. **Tel** 011 44 171 4394222, FAX 011 44 171 7346748, telex 261352. **ED** Gill Baker. **Ad Acc, Adv Mgr:** Phil Dwyer.
Desc: Information on corporate financing and transactions.

LC KF6455.A15 C67 ISSN 0898-798X
DD 343.7306/7/05 347.3036705 US
CEASED

CORPORATE TAXATION. [Corp. tax.]. Vol. 1, No. 1 (May/June 1988)-(199?). Periodical. English. Faulkner & Gray Inc., 11 Penn Plaza, 17th Floor, New York NY 10001. **Tel** (212)967-7000, (800)535-8403. **ED** L Nick Deane. **Ad Acc. Circ:** 3,000. available on microfilm and microfiche from University Microfilms International (UMI); available on an online database (files 15,485/Full-Text) from DIALOG.
Ind/Abst Account. Tax Datab. (1988-) [Full Txt.]; Account. Art.; Fed. Tax Artic.

LC HG ISSN 1353-1700
DD 332 UK

•**CORPORATE TREASURY INTERNATIONAL.** [Corp. treas. int.]. (1994)-. Periodical. English. Irregular. $4.00. Twickenham J & W Communications, 10 Fieldend, Twickenham Middlesex TW1 4TF United Kingdom. **Tel** 011 44 181 8922444. ***Continues*** *Corporate Treasury Grapevine, 0960-7757.*

LC HG1616.C55 C67 ISSN 0277-1454
DD 332.1/7 US

CORRESPONDENT BANKING. **Added/Corp** Greenwich Research Associates. (19??)-. English. Greenwich Research Associates Inc, Office Park 8, Greenwich CT 06830.

LC HG1501
DD 332.1 US

COSTS AND MARGINS IN BANKING. STATISTICAL SUPPLEMENTS. **See** Business and Economics-Abstracting, Bibliographies and Statistics.

LC HG3311 .C85 ISSN 0115-0693
DD 332.1 PH

COUNTRYSIDE BANKING. **Added/Corp** Central Bank of the Philippines. Vol. 1 (Sept. 1975)-. Periodical. English. Twelve times a year. Central Banking of the Philippines, A Mabini Corner, Vito Cruz Streets, Malate Manila Philippines. **ED** Celine Quinio. **Circ:** 4,000.
Ind/Abst Philip. Sci. Technol. Abstr.

LC HG1501
DD 332.1 UK

CRAWFORD DIRECTORY OF CITY CONNECTIONS. (19??)-. English. One time a year. £185.00. Miller Freeman Technical Ltd., Riverbank House, Angel Lane, Tonbridge Kent TN9 1SE United Kingdom. **Tel** 011 44 1732 362666, FAX 011 44 1732 770483, telex 95454 BBIS. **ED** Adria Kinloch.

ISSN 0262-1037
DD 659.105 UK

CREATIVE REVIEW (LONDON. 1980). **See** Business and Economics-Marketing and Purchasing.

LC HG3691 ISSN 0746-293X
DD 332.6 US

CREDIT & COLLECTION CLINIC. **VFOAT** Credit and Collection Clinic. (19??)-. Periodical. English. Twelve times a year. $45.72. Bureau of Business Practice, 24 Rope Ferry Road, Waterford CT 06386. **Tel** (800)243-0876, (203)442-4365, (800)876-9105, FAX (203)443-1123. **ED** Candee Mordello.
Desc: Easy-to-read clinic aimed at consumer-credit clerks, tellers, and collectors which strives to stimulate thinking and give suggestions to help employees achieve peak efficiency.

ISSN 1060-2739
DD 658 US

CREDIT & COLLECTION MANAGERS' LETTER. [Credit collect. managers' lett.]. **VFOAT** Credit and Collection Managers' Letter. (199?)-. Periodical. English. Twenty-four times a year. $154.87. Bureau of Business Practice, 24 Rope Ferry Road, Waterford CT 06386. **Tel** (800)243-0876, (203)442-4365, (800)876-9105, FAX (203)443-1123. ***Continues*** *Credit & Collection Management Bulletin, 1048-275X.*

LC WMLC 93/976 HG3756.U6 C73 ISSN 0896-9329
DD 332 US

CREDIT CARD MANAGEMENT. [Credit card manage.]. Vol. 1, No. 1 (March/April 1988)-. Periodical. English. Twelve times a year. $102.95. Faulkner & Gray Inc., 11 Penn Plaza, 17th Floor, New York NY 10001. **Tel** (212)967-7000, (800)535-8403. **ED** John Stewart. **Bk Rev. Ad Acc. Circ:** 4,500 (ctrl). available on microfilm and microfiche from University Microfilms International (UMI); available on an online database (files 15,16,485,570/Full-Text) from DIALOG.
Ind/Abst Account. Tax Datab. (Jan. 1992-) [Full Txt.]; Curr. Cit.; Mark. Advert. Ref. Serv. [Full Txt.]; PROMT [Full Txt.].

LC HG1501
DD 332.1 US

CREDIT CARD NEWS. (1993)-. English. Twenty-four times a year. $449.95. Faulkner & Gray Inc., 11 Penn Plaza, 17th Floor, New York NY 10001. **Tel** (212)967-7000, (800)535-8403. **(Subscription address:** Faulkner & Gray, Inc., 118 South Clinton St., Suite 700, Chicago IL 60661. **Tel** 800 826-3115, (312)648-0261.**)** available on microfilm and microfiche from University Microfilms International (UMI); available on an online database (files 485,636/Full-Text) from DIALOG.
Ind/Abst Account. Tax Datab. (Jan. 1991-) [Full Txt.]; PROMT [Full Txt.]; PTS Newsl. Database [Full Txt.].

LC HG1501 ISSN 0738-6877
DD 332.1 US

CREDIT CODE LETTER, THE. **See** Consumer Education and Protection.

LC HG1501 ISSN 0143-5329
DD 332.1 UK

CREDIT CONTROL. [Credit control]. (1979)-. Periodical. English. Irregular (13 issues). $443.21. House of Words Ltd., 7 Greding Walk, Hutton Brentwood Essex, CM13 2UF United Kingdom. **Tel** 011 44 277 225402, FAX 011 44 277 201554. **Ad Acc.**
Desc: Specifically designed to support all credit controllers with solid advice, information and encouragement. Covers all major credit control issues, especially the latest developments in training.

LC HG4501 .C7 ISSN 0748-6030
DD 332 US
TITLE CHANGE

CREDIT DECISIONS. [Credit decis.]. **Added/Corp** Duff & Phelps Corp. Duff & Phelps Credit Rating Co. (1964)-(19??). Periodical. English. Duff & Phelps Inc, 55 East Monroe Street/Suite 3600, Chicago Il 60603. **Tel** (312)263-2610. **ED** K Renee Kinzie. Index available. ***Continued by*** *Rating Guide Subsciption.*
Desc: Contains a feature article dealing with the most pressing concerns in fixed income analysis. Provides a summary of the past week's most significant rating actions and a column devoted to current economic trends. Every other issue contains the Duff & Phelps watch list in a pull-out section. Once a month an update on ratings of commercial paper and certificates of deposit is included, etc.

LC HG1501 ISSN 0265-2099
DD 332.1 UK

CREDIT MANAGEMENT. (CREDIT MANAGEMENT : JOURNAL OF THE INSTITUTE OF CREDIT MANAGEMENT.). [Credit manage.]. **Added/Corp** Institute of Credit Management. (1948)-.

Business and Economics —Banks and Banking

Trade Publication. English. Twelve times a year. $85.56. Inst Credit Management, Water Mill Station Road, South Luffenham, Oakam Leicestershire, LE15 8NB United Kingdom. **Tel** 011 44 780 721888, FAX 011 44 780 721333, telex 32251. **ED** Ron Aldridge. Index available. **Bk Rev**, (Qty: 6). **Ad Acc. Circ:** 8,500.
Desc: Covers all aspects of credit management and its auxillary services.
Ind/Abst Curr. Cit.

LC HG1501
DD 332.1 UK
CREDIT MANAGEMENT. (19??)-. Periodical. English. £183.60. Croner Publ Ltd., Croner House London Road, Kingston Upon Thames, Surrey KT2 6SR United Kingdom. **Tel** 011 44 181 5473333, FAX 011 44 181 5472637.

ISSN 1079-3720
DD 658 US
•**CREDIT MANAGEMENT AND MARKETPLACE NEWS.** [Credit manag. mark.pl. news]. Vol. 1, No. 1 (Oct. 17, 1994)-. Periodical. English. Seventeen times a year (approximately every 3 weeks). $398.00. Business Development Publishing Inc., PO Box 5531, Arlington VA 22205. **Tel** (703)536-2209.

LC HG **ISSN** 1054-5069
DD 332 US
CCC
CREDIT RISK MANAGEMENT REPORT. [Credit risk manage. rep.]. (1991)-. Periodical. English. Twenty-five times a year. $595.00. Phillips Business Information Inc., 1201 Seven Locks Road, PO Box 61130, Potomac MD 20854. **Tel** (301)424-3338, (301)340-1520, (800)777-5005, FAX (301)424-4297, telex 358149. available on an online database (file 636/Full-Text) from DIALOG. ***Continues*** *Retail Banking Strategist.*
Ind/Abst PTS Newsl. Database [Full Txt.].

LC HG2037 .C6 **ISSN** 1061-3676
DD 334/.22/0973021 US
CREDIT UNION $50 MILLION YEARBOOK. [Credit union $50 million yearb.]. **Added/Corp** Callahan & Associates. **VFOAT** Credit Union Fifty Million Dollar Yearbook; Credit Union Fifty to One Hundred Million Dollar Yearbook; Credit Union $50-$100 Million Yearbook. (1991)-. English. Callahan & Associates, 1001 Connecticut Avenue NW, Suite 728, Washington DC 20036.

LC HG **ISSN** 1040-9246
DD 332 US
CREDIT UNION DIRECTOR. [Credit union dir.]. **Added/Corp** Credit Union Executives Society. (198?)-. Trade Publication. English. Four times a year. $42.00. Credit Union Executives Society, PO Box 14167, Madison WI 53714. **Tel** (608)271-2664, FAX (608)271-2303.

ISSN 1058-1561
DD 658 US
CCC
CREDIT UNION DIRECTORS NEWSLETTER. [Credit union dir. newsl.]. (19??)-. Newsletter. English. Twelve times a year. $65.00. Credit Union National Association, PO Box 431, Madison WI 53701. **Tel** (608)231-4088, (800)356-9655, FAX (608)231-4370. **ED** James Hanson. **Circ:** 7,000.

LC HG2037 .C65 **ISSN** 0092-4954
DD 334/.2 US
CREDIT UNION DIRECTORY AND BUYERS' GUIDE. **Added/Corp** Credit Union Information Service. Vol. 1 (1973)-. Consumer Publication. English. One time a year. $77.00. United Communications Group, 11300 Rockville Pike, Suite 1100, Rockville MD 20852. **Tel** (301)816-8950 ext. 313, FAX (301)816-8945.

LC HG2035 .C69 **ISSN** 1053-6744
DD 334/.22/068 US
CCC
CREDIT UNION EXECUTIVE (MADISON, WIS. 1989). (CREDIT UNION EXECUTIVE.). [Credit union exec.]. **Added/Corp** Credit Union National Association. **VFOAT** Executive. Vol. 29, No. 4 (Winter 1989/90)-. Periodical. English. Six times a year. $99.00. Credit Union National Association, PO Box 431, Madison WI 53701. **Tel** (608)231-4088, (800)356-9655, FAX (608)231-4370. **ED** James Hanson (editor's phone: (608)231-4080). **Ad Acc, Adv Mgr:** Phyllis Peterson, **Tel** (608)231-4077. **Circ:** 3,000. available on an online database (file 648/Full-Text) from DIALOG. ***Continues*** *Executive (Madison, Wis.), 8756-0194.*
Desc: Management journal for credit union CEOs and senior staff.
Ind/Abst Acad. Search; Bus. ASAP (1992-) [Full Txt.]; Bus. Index (1985-); Bus. Source Plus; Bus. Source; EP Collect.; Gen. BusinessFile (1985-); Homework Help.; MasterFile FullTEXT 1000; MasterFile FullTEXT 350; MasterFile FullTEXT 650; MasterFile FullTEXT; OCLC; Telebase.

LC HG2037 .C6524 **ISSN** 1043-1888
DD 334/.22/0973021 US
CREDIT UNION FINANCIAL PROFILES. [Credit union financ. profiles]. (19??)-. Trade Publication. English. Two times a year. United Communications Group, 11300 Rockville Pike, Suite 1100, Rockville MD 20852. **Tel** (301)816-8950 ext. 313, FAX (301)816-8945.

LC HG2033 .B7 **ISSN** 0011-1066
DD 334/.2/0973 US
CCC
CREDIT UNION MAGAZINE. [Credit union mag.]. **Added/Corp** Credit Union National Association. Vol. 28, No. 6, (June 1963)-. Trade Publication. English. Twelve times a year. $33.00. Credit Union National Association, PO Box 431, Madison WI 53701. **Tel** (608)231-4088, (800)356-9655, FAX (608)231-4370. **ED** James Hanson (editor's phone: (608)231-4080). Index available. **Ad Acc, Adv Mgr:** Phyllis Peterson, **Tel** (608)231-4077. **Circ:** 45,000. available on diskette; available on microfilm and microfiche from University Microfilms International (UMI). Documents available from UMI Article Clearinghouse. ***Continues*** *Credit Union Bridge.*
Desc: News and educational articles for credit union officers and managers on operations, legislation, regulation, marketing, and public relations.
Ind/Abst ABI/INFORM Glob. Ed. (July 1980-); ABI/INFORM [Computer File] (July 1980-); PAIS Int. Print.

LC HG1501 **ISSN** 0273-9267
DD 332.1 US
CREDIT UNION MANAGEMENT. **Added/Corp** Credit Union Executives Society. (19??)-. Trade Publication. English. Twelve times a year. $69.00. Credit Union Executives Society, PO Box 14167, Madison WI 53714. **Tel** (608)271-2664, FAX (608)271-2303. **ED** Mary Anestad Arnold, Paula Symons, Kelly Radloff. Index available. **Bk Rev. Ad Acc. Circ:** 5,900. available on microfilm and microfiche from University Microfilms International (UMI). Documents available from UMI Article Clearinghouse.
Desc: Articles for credit union executives in the US and other countries, including topics like investments, personnel, equipment and technology; facilities, planning, marketing, and regulatory information.
Ind/Abst ABI/INFORM Glob. Ed.; ABI/INFORM [Computer File] (Jan. 1985-); Curr. Cit.; PAIS Int. Print; UMI ABI/Inform--Bus. Period. Ondisc [Full Txt.].

LC HG1501 **ISSN** 1068-2120
DD 332.1 US
CCC
CREDIT UNION MANAGER NEWSLETTER. (19??)-. Newsletter. English. Twenty-six times a year. $145.00. Credit Union National Association, PO Box 431, Madison WI 53701. **Tel** (608)231-4088, (800)356-9655, FAX (608)231-4370. **ED** James Hanson. **Circ:** 2,500.

ISSN 0199-9311
DD 334 US
CREDIT UNION NEWS. [Credit union news]. Vol. 1 (May 8, 1980)-. Periodical. English. Twenty-four times a year. $95.00. BKB Publications Inc., 150 Nassau Street, Suite 2030, New York NY 10038. **Tel** (212)267-7707, FAX (212)267-7726. **ED** Charlene Komar Storey. **Ad Acc, Adv Mgr:** Brian K. Burkart. **Circ:** 7,000. available on microfilm from University Microfilms International (UMI).

LC HG **ISSN** 0889-5597
DD 332 US
CREDIT UNION NEWSWATCH. [Credit union newswatch]. **Added/Corp** Credit Union National Association. **VFOAT** Credit Union News Watch; Newswatch. (19??)-. Periodical. English. One time a week. $100.00. Credit Union National Association, PO Box 431, Madison WI 53701. **Tel** (608)231-4088, (800)356-9655, FAX (608)231-4370. **ED** Jake Blake. **Circ:** 24,000 (ctrl).
Desc: Weekly news publication of the US credit union system.

LC HG2037 .C65 **ISSN** 0894-752X
DD 332 US
CREDIT UNION REPORT. [Credit union rep.]. **Added/Corp** Credit Union National Association. (1981)-. English. Irregular. $15.00. Credit Union National Association, PO Box 431, Madison WI 53701. **Tel** (608)231-4088, (800)356-9655, FAX (608)231-4370. **ED** Lucy Harr. **Bk Rev. Ad Acc. Circ:** 5,000 (ctrl). ***Continues*** *Credit Union Statistical Report.*
Desc: Statistical reports on U.S. credit unions by state.

ISSN 1054-7304
DD 334 US
CREDIT UNION TECHNOLOGY. [Cred. union technol.]. (Jan./Feb. 1991)-. Trade Publication. English. Six times a year. Credit Union Technology, Inc., 156 5th Avenue, Suite 1218, New York NY 10010-7002.

LC HG2037 .C658 **ISSN** 1058-7764
DD 334/.22/097305 US
CREDIT UNION TIMES. [Credit union times]. (1990)-. Trade Publication. English. One time a week. $112.00. Credit Union Times, PO Box 3828, West Palm Beach FL 33409. **Tel** (800)345-9936, (407)683-8515, FAX (407)683-8514. **ED** Frank Diekmann. **Ad Acc, Adv Mgr:** Tim O'Hara. **Circ:** 11,000 (ctrl).

LC HG1501 **ISSN** 0829-2175
DD 332.1 CN
CREDIT UNION WAY. [Credit union way]. **Added/Corp** Credit Union Central (Sask.). (1948)-. Trade Publication. English. Six times a year. 20.81Can$. Credit Union Central, 2055 Albert Street, Box 3030, Regina Saskatchewan S4P 3G8 Canada. **Tel** (306)566-1360, FAX (306)566-1770. **ED** Eric Eggertson (editor's phone: (306)566-1263). **Ad Acc, Adv Mgr:** Kelly Lee, **Tel** (306)566-1260. **Circ:** 5,300 (ctrl). available on microfilm and microfiche from University Microfilms International (UMI).
Desc: Issues-oriented magazine for decision makers in the Canadian credit union system.
Ind/Abst AGRICOLA.

LC HF5565 .C87 **ISSN** 0011-1074
DD 650 US
CREDIT WORLD, THE. (THE CREDIT WORLD : THE OFFICIAL ORGAN OF THE RETAIL CREDIT MEN'S NATIONAL ASSOCIATION.). [Credit world]. **Added/Corp** International Credit Association International Consumer Credit Association. National Retail Credit Association (U.S.) Retail Credit Men's National Association (U.S.). Vol. 1 (1912)-. Trade Publication. English. Six times a year. $50.00. International Credit Association, PO Box 27357, St Louis MO 63141. **Tel** (314)991-3030, FAX (314)991-3029. **ED** Janet Lipkind. Index available. **Bk Rev**, (Qty: 6). **Ad Acc, Adv Mgr:** Bill Murray. **Circ:** 9,000 (ctrl). available on microfilm and microfiche from University Microfilms International (UMI); available on an online database (files 15,485/Full-Text) from DIALOG. Documents available from UMI Article Clearinghouse.
Desc: Covers credit reporting, federal and state legislative and regulatory news, new technology and trends in credit, business trends affecting credit, and association activities.
Ind/Abst ABI/INFORM Glob. Ed.; ABI/INFORM [Computer File] (June 1973-); Acad. Search; Account. Tax Datab. (Jun. 1973-) [Full Txt.]; Bus. Period. Index; Bus. Source Plus; Bus. Source; EP Collect.; Gen. Period. Index (1985-); Homework Help.; INFO-SOUTH Abstr.; Mag. Search; Manage. Contents; MasterFile FullTEXT 1000; MasterFile FullTEXT 350; MasterFile FullTEXT 650; MasterFile FullTEXT (July 1993-); OCLC; Telebase; UMI ABI/Inform--Bus. Period. Ondisc [Full Txt.]; Wilson Bus. Abstr.

LC HG1501
DD 332.1 IT
CREDITO E COOPERAZIONE : RIVISTA DELLE CASSE RURALI ED ARTIGIANE. **Added/Corp** Federazione Italiana delle Casse Rurali ed Artigiane. (198?)-. Periodical. Italian. Four times a year. L54500. ECRA, Via M d'Azeglio #33, 00184 Rome Italy. **Tel** 011 39 6 4741157.

LC HG1501 **ISSN** 0747-5543
DD 332.1 US
CROSS SECTIONS (RICHMOND, VA.). (CROSS SECTIONS.). [Cross sect.]. **Added/Corp** Federal Reserve Bank of Richmond. Vol. 1, No. 1 (Apr. 1984)-. Periodical. English. Four times a year. Free on request. Federal Reserve Bank of Richmond, PO Box 27622, Public Services, Richmond VA 23261. **Tel** (804)697-8000.
Ind/Abst Fed. Print Econ. Bank. Top.

LC HG **ISSN** 1354-0904
DD 332 UK
•**CROSS-SHAREHOLDINGS IN EUROPE.** (1994)-. Academic Scholarly Publication. English. Irregular. £195.00. OXERA Press, Blue Boar Court, Alfred Street, Oxford OX1 4HE United Kingdom. **Tel** 011 44 865 251142, FAX 011 44 865 251172.
Desc: Provides an evaluation of the use of cross-shareholdings, particularly as a form of proactive takeover defense.

LC HG2734 .B35a
DD 332.1/097286 CR
TITLE CHANGE
CUENTAS MONETARIAS. **Added/Corp** Banco Central de Costa Rica. Departamento Monetario. (198?)-(19??). Spanish. Banco Central de Costa Rica, Av. Central y la, Calle 2 San Jose Costa Rica. ***Continues*** *Banco Central de Costa Rica. Departamento Monetario. Credito y Cuentas Monetarias.* ***Continued by*** *Cuentas Monetarias del Sistema Bancario Nacional.*

LC HG2734 .B35a
DD 332.1/097286 CR
CUENTAS MONETARIAS DEL SISTEMA BANCARIO NACIONAL. **Added/Corp** Banco Central de Costa Rica. (19??)-. Spanish. Banco Central de Costa Rica, Av. Central y la, Calle 2 San Jose Costa Rica. ***Continues*** *Cuentas Monetarias.*

LC HG2037 .C653a **ISSN** 0195-8674
DD 334/.22/0973 US
CUNA NATIONAL MEMBER SURVEY. **Main/Corp** Credit Union National Association. **VAT** Credit Union National Association National Member Survey.

Business and Economics —Banks and Banking

(19??)-. English. Irregular. Credit Union National Association, PO Box 431, Madison WI 53701. **Tel** (608)231-4088, (800)356-9655, FAX (608)231-4370.

LC HG1501
DD 332.1 GW
CURRENCIES & CREDIT MARKETS.
English. Twelve times a year. $400.00. Dr. Kurt Richebacher, Mendelssohn Strasse 51, W 6000 Frankfurt 1 Germany. **Tel** 011 49 69 746908, FAX 011 49 69 752883. **ED** Kurt Richebacher. **Circ:** 1,500.

LC HG1501 **ISSN** 0731-3551
DD 332.1 US
CURRENCY COMPETITION. Added/Corp U.S. Choice in Currency Commission. No. 1 (Jan. 1982)-. English. Twelve times a year. $10.00. US Choice in Currency Commission, 325 Pennsylvania Avenue SE, Washington DC 20003.

LC HG1501 **ISSN** 0141-1047
DD 332.1 UK
CEASED
CURRENCY CONFIDENTIAL. (19??)-(19??).
English. IBC Publishing, 57-61 Mortimer St., London W1N 7TD United Kingdom. **Tel** 011 44 171 6374383, FAX 011 44 171 6366314. available on an online database (file 636/Full-Text) from DIALOG.

LC HG1501 **ISSN** 0143-0769
DD 332.1 UK
CURRENCY PROFILES. [Curr. profiles].
Added/Corp Henley Centre for Forecasting. Manufacturers Hanover Trust Co. Foreign Exchange Advisory Service. **VFOAT** Foreign Exchange Advisory Service. (1979)-. Periodical. English. Twelve times a year. $1350.00. Henley Centre for Forecasting, 9 Bridewell Place, Blackfriars, London EC4V 6AY United Kingdom. **Tel** 011 44 171 3539961. **ED** Jon Shepheard. **Circ:** 200. **Supersedes** Forecasts of Exchange Rate Movements. Dollar Edition.

LC HG1501
DD 332.1 UK
CEASED
CURRENCY QUARTERLY. (19??)-(19??).
English. IBC Publishing, 57-61 Mortimer St., London W1N 7TD United Kingdom. **Tel** 011 44 171 6374383, FAX 011 44 171 6366314. available on an online database (file 636/Full-Text) from DIALOG.
Desc: Provides reference data on forecasts on the world's smaller currencies.
Ind/Abst PTS Newsl. Database [Full Txt.].

LC HG1501
DD 332.1 US
CURRENT ISSUES IN BANK AUDITING.
English. Twelve times a year. $68.00. Bank Research Associates, 6712 Ashland Drive, Boise ID 83707. **Tel** (208)322-3508. **ED** D. L. Raymond.
Desc: Information on guidelines for audit findings and reviews.

LC HG4651 **ISSN** 1187-7367
DD 332.63 CN
CYCLES THEN AND NOW. [Cycles then now].
Added/Corp RBC Dominion Securities Inc. RBC Dominion Securities Inc. Quantitative Research. (June 1991)-. Periodical. English. Twelve times a year. RBC Dominion Securities, PO Box 21, Commerce Ct. South, Toronto Ontario M5L 1A7 Canada.

LC HG1501
DD 332.1 US
DAILY GRAPHS OPTION GUIDE WEEKLY. See Business and Economics-Investments.

LC HG1501
DD 332.1 AT
DAILY RATES UPDATE. (19??)-. Trade Publication. English. Seven times a week. 2320.00Aus$. Horan Wall & Walker Pty Ltd, 15-19 Prospect Street, POB 8, Surry Hills New South Wales 2010 Australia. **Tel** 02 331 6600, FAX 02 380 5533. **ED** Jayson Forrest. available on an online database; available on diskette.

ISSN 0145-0239
DD 336 US
DAILY TREASURY STATEMENT. [Daily Treas. statement]. **Added/Corp** United States. Dept. of the Treasury. Financial Management Service. United States. Dept. of the Treasury. (19??)-. Government Publication. English. Five times a week (except Sat. and Sun.). $581.00. US Department of the Treasury, Office of Public Affairs, 1500 Pennsylvania Avenue, Washington DC 20220. **Tel** (202)566-2041. **(Subscription address:** Superintendent of Documents, US Government Printing Office, Washington DC 20402.) Documents available from Documents on Demand. **Continues** Daily Statement of the United States Treasury.
Desc: Cash and debt operations of the United States Treasury.
Ind/Abst Am. Stat. Index.

LC HC107.A165 D33 **ISSN** 0739-7720
DD 330.976/005 US
DALLASFED DISTRICT HIGHLIGHTS.
[Dallasfed dist. highlights]. **Added/Corp** Federal Reserve Bank of Dallas. **VFOAT** District Highlights. (Sept. 1982)-. Periodical. English. Four times a year. Free on request. Federal Reserve Bank of Dallas, Station K, Dallas TX 75222. **Tel** (214)922-6000, (800)333-4460. **Continues in part** Voice of the Federal Reserve Bank of Dallas, 0161-9527.
Ind/Abst Energy Res. Abstr. (Jan. 1983-); Index Period. Artic. Relat. Law (19??-).

LC HG4651 **ISSN** 0909-0487
DD 332.632 320 948 9 DK
● **DANISH GOVERNMENT SECURITIES.**
[Dan. gov. secur.]. (1994)-. English. One time a year. Free. Danmarks Nationalbank, Havnegade 5, DK-1093 Copenhagen K Denmark. **Tel** FAX 011 45 33 141404. **Circ:** 2,000.

LC HG1501
DD 332.1 US
DEBIT CARD DIRECTORY. (19??)-. Directory. English. One time a year. $275.00. Faulkner & Gray Inc., 11 Penn Plaza, 17th Floor, New York NY 10001. **Tel** (212)967-7000, (800)535-8403.

LC HG1660.U5 D43 **ISSN** 0731-0536
DD 332 US
DEBITS AND DEPOSIT TURNOVER AT COMMERCIAL BANKS. Added/Corp Board of Governors of the Federal Reserve System (U.S.). (Oct. 1977)-. Periodical. English. Twelve times a year. $5.00. Board of Governors of the Federal Reserve System, Mail Stop 127, Washington DC 20551. **Tel** (202)452-3244, (202)452-3245. Documents available from Documents on Demand. **Continues** Bank Debits, Deposits and Deposit Turnover, 0730-4900.
Ind/Abst Am. Stat. Index.

LC HG1501
DD 332.1 US
DEBT-EQUITY SWAP HANDBOOK.
(19??)-. English. One time a year. $725.00 Middle East and Africa. Business International Corp, 215 Park Avenue South, New York NY 10003. **Tel** (212)460-0600. **ED** Anna Szterenfeld. **Circ:** 100.
Desc: A corporate guide to debt-equity swaps worldwide, providing information on activity and innovations in the market. Features executive summary of latest developments, legal and accounting issues, overview of debt swaps, country programs, etc.

LC HG **ISSN** 1076-9676
DD 332 US
DEBT FREE & PROSPEROUS LIVING.
Added/Corp Financial Independence Network. **VFOAT** Debt Free and Prosperous Living. (1992)-. Periodical. English. Twelve times a year. $74.00. Financial Independent Network Ltd., 824 South Main Street, Crystal Lake IL 60014. **Tel** (800)321-3465.

LC HF3621 .B87
DD 650 FR
DELOVIE LYUDI. VFOAT Business in the Ex-USSR. No. 20 (Feb. 1992)-. Periodical. English (Russian). Twelve times a year. $85.00. Soc Commun & D Innovation Intl, 4 rue Brunel, 75017 Paris France. **Tel** 011 33 1 43809000. **(Subscription address:** Delovie Lyundi, 1560 Broadway, Suite 511, New York NY 10036. **Tel** (212)221-6700.) **Continues** Business in the Ex-USSR.
Ind/Abst Int. Labour Doc.

LC HG1501
DD 332.1 US
DEPOSIT HISTORY AND PROJECTIONS. Main/Corp Decision Research Sciences. **Added/Corp** Federal Deposit Insurance Corporation. United States. Federal Home Loan Bank Board. (1978/79)-. Periodical. English. Irregular. $225.00. Decision Research Sciences Inc., 800 Penllyn Blue Bell Pike, Blue Bell PA 19422. **Tel** (610)542-9550.

LC HG1501
DD 332.1 UK
DERIVATIVES IN FUND MANAGEMENT.
(19??)-. Periodical. English. Ten times a year. £125.00 UK; $261.00 US, Canada and South America. Metal Bulletin PLC, PO Box 28E, Worcester Park, Surrey KT4 7HY United Kingdom. **Tel** 011 44 171 8279977, FAX 011 44 171 3378943.

LC HG1501
DD 332.1 US
TITLE CHANGE
DERIVATIVES REVIEW. (19??)-(19??). Periodical. English. Institutional Investor Inc., 488 Madison Avenue, New York NY 10022. **Tel** (212)303-2324, (212)303-3233, FAX (212)303-3353. **Continued by** Derivatives Quarterly.

LC HG **ISSN** 1075-2412
DD 332 US
DERIVATIVES WEEK. [Deriv. week].
Added/Corp Institutional Investor (Firm). Vol. 1, No. 1 (April 6, 1992)-. Newsletter. English. One time a week.

$1495.00. Institutional Investor Inc., 488 Madison Avenue, New York NY 10022. **Tel** (212)303-3234, (212)303-3233, FAX (212)303-3353.
Desc: Delivers the information needed to keep abreast of what CFOs, treasurers and portfolio managers are doing with derivatives. Innovative new products and their applications are highlighted. Coverage includes interest rate, currency, equity and commodity derivatives.

LC HG1501
DD 332.1 US
DESKTOP BANK DIRECTORY, THE.
(1985)-. English. One time a year. Rand McNally & Company, PO Box 32, Skokie IL 60076. **Tel** (708)673-0813, (800)444-4062.

LC HG2039.G4 D46A
DD 332.1/0943 GW
DG BANK MITTEILUNGEN. Main/Corp DG Bank. **VAT** Deutsche Genossenschaftsbank Bank Mitteilungen. Vol. 25 (1976)-. Periodical. German. Deutsche Genossenschaftsbank der Mitteilungen, W-6000 Frankfurt AM Main Germany. **Continues** DGK Mitteilungen.

LC HG1501
DD 332.1 RU
DIEN'GI I KREDIT. (19??)-. Russian. Twelve times a year. $129.95. Libreria Italia URSS, Via E Raggio 1/10, 16124 Genoa Italy. **Tel** 011 39 10 295446.

LC HG1501 **ISSN** 0822-7152
DD 332.1/025/71 CN
Pr Rev.
DIRECTORY - CANADIAN PAYMENTS ASSOCIATION. (DIRECTORY / CANADIAN PAYMENTS ASSOCIATION = REPERTOIRE / ASSOCIATION CANADIENNE DES PAIEMENTS.). [Dir. - Can. Paym. Assoc.]. **Main/Corp** Canadian Payments Association. **VFOAT** Repertoire. (1983)-. English. One time a year. Price varies. Bowne of Canada Ltd., 60 Gervais Drive, Toronto Ontario M3C 1Z3 Canada. **Tel** (416)449-6400. **Formed by the union of** Bank Directory of Canada, 0045-1436 **and** Routing Numbers of Deposit-Taking Institutions in Canada Other than Chartered Banks, 0708-9988.

LC HG1501
DD 332.1 US
DIRECTORY OF BANK ECONOMISTS.
Added/Corp American Bankers Association. Economic and Financial Research Division. (19??)-. Directory. English. One time a year. Free on request. American Bankers Association, 1120 Connecticut Avenue Northwest, Washington DC 20036. **Tel** (202)663-5221, (202)663-5000, FAX (202)828-4544.

LC HG1581 .D57 **ISSN** 0092-4717
DD 332.1/07/1073 US
DIRECTORY OF BANKING INSTRUCTORS. Added/Corp American Bankers Association. (1973)-. Directory. English. American Bankers Association, 1120 Connecticut Avenue Northwest, Washington DC 20036. **Tel** (202)663-5221, (202)663-5000, FAX (202)828-4544.

LC HG65 .D568 **ISSN** 1066-9736
DD 332.1/025/73 US
DIRECTORY OF BUYOUT FINANCING SOURCES. [Dir. buyout financ. sources]. (1992)-. Directory. English. One time a year. $249.00. Securities Data Company, 40 West 57th Street, 11th Floor, New York NY 10019. **Tel** (212)765-5311. **Continues** Buyouts Directory of LBO Financing Sources, 1050-4915.

LC HG2153.F6 F56
DD 332 US
DIRECTORY OF FLORIDA SAVINGS ASSOCIATIONS. Added/Corp Florida League of Financial Institutions. (1990)-. Directory. English. **Continues** Florida League of Financial Institutions. Directory.

LC HG1643 .D57 **ISSN** 1061-3358
DD 332.1/78 US
DIRECTORY OF MASTERCARD AND VISA CREDIT CARD SOURCES, THE. [Dir. MasterCard VISA credit card sources]. **VFOAT** Directory of Master Card and VISA Credit Card Sources. (1991)-. Directory. English. Todd Publications, 18 North Greenbush Road, West Nyack NY 10994. **Tel** (914)358-6213, FAX (914)358-6213.

LC HG4347.A1 D56 **ISSN** 0093-951X
DD 332.1/78 US
DIRECTORY OF TRUST INSTITUTIONS.
(1969/1970)-. English. One time a year (Dec.). $64.95. Argus Business, 6151 Powers Ferry Road Northwest, Atlanta GA 30339. **Tel** (404)995-2500, FAX (404)995-0400. **Continues** Directory of Trust Institutions of United States and Canada.

LC HG1501
DD 332.1 IT
DIRIGENZA BANCARIA. (19??)-. Italian. Six times a year. L60000. Dirigenza Bancaria, Via Torino 150, 00184 Rome Italy. **Tel** 011 39 6 4746219.

LC HG1501
DD 332.1 IT
DIRITTO DELLA BANCA E MERCATO FINANZIARIO. (19??)-. Italian. Four times a year. L155000 Italy; L200000. Cedam Spa, Via Jappelli 5 6, 35121 Padua Italy. **Tel** 011 39 49 65667.

LC HG4905 .D58 **ISSN** 0094-2561
DD 332.6/32/0973 US
DISCLOSURE RECORD. (19??)-. Periodical. English. One time a week. Disclosure Record, PO Box 639, Floral Park NY 11001. **Tel** (718)347-1100. **ED** Jack Lotto. **Bk Rev. Ad Acc. Circ:** 10,000 (ctrl).
Desc: Official transcripts of corporate reports.

LC HG1501
DD 332.1 US
DOCTOR'S FINANCIAL REPORT. English. Twelve times a year. $217.32 US; $262.80 Canada. Bureau of Business Practice, 24 Rope Ferry Road, Waterford CT 06386. **Tel** (800)243-0876, (203)442-4365, (800)876-9105, FAX (203)443-1123.

ISSN 1186-8635
DD 336.2 CN
DOFASCO (TORONTO). (DOFASCO.). [Dofasco]. **Added/Corp** Midland Walwyn Capital. Research Dept. Midland Walwyn Capital. (Apr. 29, 1991)-. Periodical. English. Limited free distribution to selected clients of Midland Walwyn Capital. Midland Walwyn Capital, Suite 1600, 121 King Street West, Toronto Ontario M5H 3W6 Canada.

LC HG1642.U5 D65 **ISSN** 0192-7639
DD 332.1/753/0973 US
DOMESTIC AND INTERNATIONAL COMMERCIAL LOAN CHARGE-OFFS. (19??)-. English. One time a year. Price varies per volume. Robert Morris Associates, One Liberty Plaza, 1650 Market Street, Philadelphia PA 19103. **Tel** (215)851-9118, (215)851-0585, FAX (215)851-9206. **ED** Paul Freeman. **Circ:** 4,000 (ctrl).
Desc: This report contains the results of charge-off experience of RMA's member banks of the year ending December 31, 1984.

LC HG1501 **ISSN** 0197-7083
DD 332.1 US
TITLE CHANGE
DONOGHUE'S MONEYLETTER. See Business and Economics-Investments.

LC HG1536 .D6
DD 332.1 UK
•**DOW JONES TELERATE BANK REGISTER. Added/Corp** Dow Jones Telerate Ltd. **VFOAT** Dow Jones Telerate; Bank Register. 9th Ed. (1994/95)-. English. One time a year (4 volume set). $300.00. Euromoney Publications PLC, Nestor House, Playhouse Yard, London EC4Z 5EX United Kingdom. **Tel** 011 44 171 7798888, FAX 011 44 171 7798630, telex 290700 EUROMON G. **(Subscription address:** Plymbridge Distributors Ltd., Estover Road, Plymouth PL6 7PZ United Kingdom. **Tel** 011 44 1752 695745.) ***Continues*** *Telerate Bank Register.*

LC HG181 .D35a **ISSN** 0271-1931
DD 332/.0973 US
DRI-FACS, FINANCIAL AND CREDIT STATISTICS INFORMATION SERVICE: APPLIED REPORTS AND GRAPHICS LIBRARY. See Business and Economics-Abstracting, Bibliographies and Statistics.

LC HG4001 .D37a **ISSN** 0197-1654
DD 332.6/72/0973 US
DRI INDUSTRY FINANCIAL SERVICE. [DRI ind. financ. serv.]. **Main/Corp** Data Resources, Inc. **Added/Corp** Data Resources, Inc. Industry Financial Service. **VAT** Data Resources Incorporated Industry Financial Service. (19??)-. English. Four times a year. DRI McGraw Hill, 24 Hartwell Avenue, Lexington MA 02173. **Tel** (617)863-5100, FAX (617)860-6464, (617)860-6416. **(Subscription address:** Data Resources, PO Box 5 0210, Woburn MA 01815.)

LC HG4050 .D37a **ISSN** 0271-4868
DD 338.7/4/0973 US
DRI INDUSTRY FINANCIAL SERVICES: ANNUAL LONG-TERM REVIEW. [DRI ind. financ. serv., Annu. long-term rev.]. **Main/Corp** Data Resources, Inc. **Added/Corp** Data Resources, Inc. Annual Long-Term Review. **VAT** Data Resources Inc. Industry Financial Services. Annual Long-Term Review. (19??)-. English. One time a year. DRI McGraw Hill, 24 Hartwell Avenue, Lexington MA 02173. **Tel** (617)863-5100, FAX (617)860-6464, (617)860-6416.

LC HG6255.I8 M53B
DD 332 IS
DUAH HA-DIREKTORYON U-MAAZAN. Main/Corp Mifal Ha-Payis. **VFOAT** Annual Report. Hebrew (summaries and/or abstracts in English). Mifal Ha-Payis, 3 Heftman Street, Tel Aviv Israel.

LC HG1501 **ISSN** 0739-554X
DD 332.1 US
E-Z TELEPHONE DIRECTORY OF BROKERS AND BANKS, THE. VFOAT Easy Telephone Directory of Brokers and Banks; EZ Telephone Directory of Brokers and Banks; E-Z Telephone Directory. (19??)-. Directory. English. Two times a year. $75.00. EZ Telephone Directory, 106 7th Street, Gareden City NY 11530. **Tel** (212)422-9492, (516)294-0350, FAX (516)294-0356.

LC HG2156.F8 E16
DD 332 FR
EAE SERVICES, RESULTATS DETAILLEES. PROMOTION, LOCATION, SOCIETES IMMOBILIERES EN ... . VFOAT Promotion, Location, Societes Imobilieres en ...; Enquete Annuelle d'Entreprise dans les Services. **VAT** Enquete Annuelle d'Entreprise Services, Resultats Detaillees. Promotion, Location, Societes Immobilieres en ... . (198?)-. French. One time a year. Institut National de la Statistique et des Etudes Economiques, 18 Bd Adolphe Pinard, 75675 Paris 14 France.

LC HG1501
DD 332.1 MF
EAGLEVIEW : THE STAFF MAGAZINE OF BARCLAYS BANK PLC MAURITIUS. Main/Corp Barclays Bank PLC Mauritius. 1st issue (Jan. 1990)-. Periodical. English (French).

LC HG1501 **ISSN** 0791-3931
DD 332.1 IE
EAST EUROPEAN BANKER DUBLIN. (EAST EUROPEAN BANKER.). [East Euro. bank. Dublin]. (1990)-. Periodical. English. Ten times a year. $749.00. Lafferty Publications Ltd., Tower Ida Centre Pearse Street, Dublin 2 Ireland. **Tel** 011 353 1 6718022, FAX 011 353 1 718520. **ED** Gerard Lysaghk, Lisa Jaffe and Nessa O'Mahony.
Desc: Provides insight into major developments across the complete spectrum of financial services in East and Central Europe.

LC HG1501 **ISSN** 0161-6110
DD 332.1 US
EASTERN FINANCIAL TIMES. (1978)-. Periodical. English. Twelve times a year. $14.00. Eastern Financial Times Inc., 935 South 53rd Street, Philadelphia PA 19143. **Tel** (215)471-3000.

LC HG1501 **ISSN** 0987-2507
DD 332.1 FR
UDC 336
Pr Rev.
EBA NEWSLETTER. [EBA newslet.]. **Added/Corp** Association Bancaire pour l'ECU. **VFOAT** ECU Banking Association Newsletter. (1987)-. Newsletter. English (French). Six times a year. Free on request. Association Bancaire pour ECU, 4 rue de la Paix, F 75002 Paris France. **Tel** 011 33 1 44860420, FAX 011 33 1 44860425. **Ad Acc. Circ:** 1,500.
Desc: Articles on the ECU, its use and its development. Information on the European monetary union by politicians, bankers and academics.

LC HG1501 **ISSN** 0956-3261
DD 332.1 IE
EC FINANCIAL INDUSTRY MONITOR. [EC financ. ind. monit.]. (1989)-. Periodical. English. Ten times a year. $449.00. Lafferty Publications Ltd., Tower Ida Centre Pearse Street, Dublin 2 Ireland. **Tel** 011 353 1 6718022, FAX 011 353 1 718520. ***Absorbed in part by*** *European Banker, 0953-8399.*

LC HG1501 **ISSN** 0393-9243
DD 332.1 IT
UDC 330
Pr Rev.
ECONOMIA E BANCA. (1986)-. Periodical. Italian. Three times a year. L68130. Manfrini Editori, Via Brennero #2, 38060 Calliano Italy. **Tel** 011 39 464 84156, FAX 011 39 464 85086. cum. index. **Ad Acc, Adv Mgr:** Dr. Sergio Costa. ctrl circ.

LC HB143.5 .E36 **ISSN** 0962-2780
DD 330.01 UK
CCC
ECONOMIC AND FINANCIAL COMPUTING. Added/Corp European Economics and Financial Centre. **VFOAT** Economic and Financial Computing. Vol. 1, No. 1 (Spring 1991)-. Periodical. English. Four times a year. $350.79. European Economics & Finance Center, PO Box 2498, London W2 4LE United Kingdom. **Tel** 011 44 171 2290402, FAX 011 44 171 2215118. **Ad Acc. Acid Free.**
Desc: Provides a forum to present recent advances on the measurement aspects of economic and financial problems. The journal focuses on both the methodological and practical facets of quantitative and computational techniques as applied to economic and financial issues.

LC HG1501 **ISSN** 0256-3525
DD 332.1 SZ
ECONOMIC AND FINANCIAL PROSPECTS. [Econ. financ. prospects]. **Added/Corp** Swiss Bank Corporation. Swiss Bank Corporation. Economics Division. **VFOAT** Prospects. No. 1 (Feb. 1983)-. Periodical. English. Six times a year. Free. Swiss Bank Corporation, PO Box 3767, Aeschenvorstadt 1, CH-4002 Basel Switzerland. **Tel** 011 41 6 202020. **ED** Wolfgang Fautz. **Circ:** 55,000. ***Continues*** *Prospects, 0552-3648.*
Desc: Covers economic forecasting, international monetary system, international capital markets, foreign exchange rates, interest rates, international debt, and basic financial statistics.
Ind/Abst PAIS Int. Print.

LC HC157.B35 C46A **ISSN** 0378-178X
DD 330.9/729/81 BB
ECONOMIC AND FINANCIAL STATISTICS. See Business and Economics-Abstracting, Bibliographies and Statistics.

LC HG1501
DD 332.1 JM
ECONOMIC BULLETIN / BANK OF JAMAICA. Added/Corp Bank of Jamaica. Research & Development Division. Vol. 1, No. 1 (1986)-. Bulletin. English. Twelve times a year. Free on request. Bank of Jamaica, Research Department, PO Box 621, Kingston Jamaica. **Tel** (809)922-0750, FAX (809)922-0854, telex 2165.

LC HC531 .B3 **ISSN** 0304-274X
DD 330.962 UA
ECONOMIC BULLETIN - NATIONAL BANK OF EGYPT. (ECONOMIC BULLETIN.). [Econ. bull. - Natl. Bank Egypt]. **Main/Corp** Bank al-Ahli al-Misri. Vol. 1 (Apr. 1948)-. Bulletin. English. Four times a year. Free on request. National Bank of Egypt, Head Office, Research Department, Cairo Egypt.
Ind/Abst PAIS Int. Print.

LC HG179 .A53 **ISSN** 0424-2769
DD 332.024/005 US
ECONOMIC EDUCATION BULLETIN (GREAT BARRINGTON). (ECONOMIC EDUCATION BULLETIN.). [Econ. educ. bull.]. **Added/Corp** American Institute for Economic Research. Vol. 1 (Dec. 1960)-. Bulletin. English. Twelve times a year. $25.00. American Institute for Economic Research, Division Street, Great Barrington MA 01230. **Tel** (413)528-1216, FAX (413)528-0103. **ED** Robert Gilmour. cum. index. **Bk Rev. Circ:** 1,000.
Desc: Research on different problems of the world, such as energy crisis, health care reform and other issues.
Ind/Abst PAIS Int. Print (1991-).

LC HC135 .E25
DD 330.972/005 MX
ECONOMIC PANORAMA BANCOMER. Added/Corp Bancomer. (Nov./Dec. 1977)-. English. Six times a year. Free. Bancomer, Sociedad Natioanal Crdito, Groupo Investigaciones Economicas, Universidad Avenue 1200, C.P. 03339 Mexico 12 D.F. Mexico. **Tel** 534 00 34 ext. 5245. ***Continues*** *Economic Panorama.*
Ind/Abst Public Aff. Inf. Serv. Bull.

LC HG1501 **ISSN** 1048-115X
DD 330 US
ECONOMIC PERSPECTIVES (1989). (ECONOMIC PERSPECTIVES : A REVIEW FROM THE FEDERAL RESERVE BANK OF CHICAGO.). [Econ. perspect.]. **Added/Corp** Federal Reserve Bank of Chicago. Research Dept. Vol. 13, Issue 1 (Jan./Feb. 1989)-. Periodical. English. Six times a year. Free on request. Economic Perspectives, Federal Reserve Bank of Chicago, 230 South LaSalle, PO Box 834, Chicago IL 60690-0834. **Tel** (312)322-5111, FAX (312)325-5700. **Circ:** 29,000. available on microfilm and microfiche from University Microfilms International (UMI). Documents available from UMI Article Clearinghouse. ***Continues*** *FRB Chicago Economic Perspectives, 0884-7576.*
Ind/Abst ABI/INFORM Glob. Ed.; ABI/INFORM [Computer File] (Sept. 1980-); Gen. BusinessFile (1992-); Newsp. Period. Abstr. (1992-); PAIS Int. Print.

LC HC101 .F43
DD 330 US
•**ECONOMIC POLICY REVIEW. Added/Corp** Federal Reserve Bank of New York. **VFOAT** Federal Reserve Bank of New York Economic Policy Review. Vol. 1, No. 1 (Jan. 1995)-. Periodical. English. Four times a year. Free on request (first copy); $12.00 each additional subscription. Federal Reserve Bank of New York, 33 Liberty Street, New York NY 10045. **Tel** (212)720-5000. **Circ:** 45,000. available on microfilm and microfiche from University Microfilms International (UMI). Documents available from UMI Article Clearinghouse. ***Continues*** *Federal Reserve Bank of New York. Quarterly Review - Federal Reserve Bank of New York, 0147-6580.*
Desc: Reports on business activity, money and bond markets. Discusses selected subjects in economics and usually reprints of major speeches of top bank officials.
Ind/Abst ABI/INFORM Glob. Ed.; ABI/INFORM [Computer File]; Bus. ASAP [Full Txt.]; Bus. Index; Econ. Lit. Index; Expand. Acad. Index; F&S Index Plus Text, Int.

[Select. Cov.]; Fed. Print Econ. Bank. Top.; Gen. BusinessFile; Gen. Period. Index; INFO-SOUTH Abstr.; J. Econ. Lit.; Mat. Fact; Middle East Abstr. Index; Newsp. Period. Abstr.; PAIS Int. Print; UMI ABI/Inform--Bus. Period. Ondisc [Full Txt.]; Wilson Bus. Abstr.

LC HG1501
DD 332.1 KU
ECONOMIC REPORT - CENTRAL BANK OF KUWAIT. **Main/Corp** Bank Al-Kuwayt Al-Markazi. (19??)-. English. One time a year. Free on request. Central Bank of Kuwait, PO Box 526, Kuwait. **Tel** (449)200-449219.

LC HC107.A13 E186 **ISSN** 0732-1813
DD 332.1/1/0973 US
CODEN ECRWDA
ECONOMIC REVIEW (ATLANTA, GA.). (ECONOMIC REVIEW.). [Econ. rev.]. **Added/Corp** Federal Reserve Bank of Atlanta. (May/June 1977)-. Periodical. English. Six times a year. $15.00. Federal Reserve Bank of Atlanta, 104 Marietta Street Northwest, Atlanta GA 30303. **Tel** (404)521-8788. available on microfilm and microfiche from University Microfilms International (UMI). Documents available from UMI Article Clearinghouse, Ask*IEEE. ***Continues** Federal Reserve Bank of Atlanta. Monthly Review - Federal Reserve Bank of Atlanta, 0014-9144; **Absorbed** Caribbean Basin Economic Survey.*
Ind/Abst ABI/INFORM Glob. Ed.; ABI/INFORM [Computer File] (March 1980-); AGRICOLA [Select. Cov.]; BioBusiness (19??-); Curr. Cit.; Econ. Lit. Index; EP Collect.; Expand. Acad. Index (1992-); Fed. Print Econ. Bank. Top.; Gen. BusinessFile (1992-); Homework Help.; INSPEC (1983-1989); J. Econ. Lit.; MasterFile FullTEXT 1000; MasterFile FullTEXT 350; MasterFile FullTEXT 650; MasterFile FullTEXT; Newsp. Period. Abstr. (1992-); OCLC; PAIS Int. Print (1991-); Telebase; UMI ABI/Inform--Bus. Period. Ondisc (Jan. 1987-) [Full Txt.].

LC HC157.B35 C46B **ISSN** 0255-7460
DD 330.97298/1 BB
ECONOMIC REVIEW (BRIDGETOWN, BARBADOS). (ECONOMIC REVIEW / CENTRAL BANK OF BARBADOS.). [Econ. rev. - Cent. Bank Barbados]. Vol. 9, No. 1 (June 1982)-. Periodical. English. Three times a year. Central Bank of Barbados, PO Box 1016, Treasury Building, Bridgetown Barbados. **Tel** (809)436-6870, FAX (809)427-9559, telex 2251 CENBANK WB. **Circ:** 1,500 (ctrl). ***Continues** Quarterly Report Central Bank of Barbados.*

LC HF46 .B3 **ISSN** 0008-9249
DD 330 UA
ECONOMIC REVIEW - CENTRAL BANK OF EGYPT. [Econ. rev. - Cent. Bank Egypt]. **Main/Corp** Bank al-Markazai al-Misri. Vol. 1 (1961)-. Periodical. English (Arabic). Irregular. Free. Central Bank of Egypt, 31 Sharia Kasr El Nil, Cairo Egypt. **Tel** 751513, FAX 3926361, telex 22386 CBECR UN. **(Subscription address:** Central Bank of Egypt, Economic Research Department, 44 Ramsis Street, Cairo Egypt. **)** Index available. cum. index. **Circ:** 2,500. available on microfilm.
Desc: Analysis of national economic developments: state budget, development plans, monetary and credit developments, balance of payments, cotton, merchandise transactions, etc., plus a statistical section.
Ind/Abst Middle East J. (?-?).

LC HC101 .E437 **ISSN** 0732-1414
DD 330.973.005 US
ECONOMIC REVIEW (DALLAS, TEX.). (ECONOMIC REVIEW.). [Econ. rev.]. **Added/Corp** Federal Reserve Bank of Dallas. (Mar. 1982)-. Periodical. English. Irregular. Free. Federal Reserve Bank of Dallas, Station K, Dallas TX 75222. **Tel** (214)922-6000, (800)333-4460. available on microfilm and microfiche from University Microfilms International (UMI). Documents available from UMI Article Clearinghouse. ***Continues in part** Voice of the Federal Reserve Bank of Dallas, 0161-9527.*
Ind/Abst ABI/INFORM Glob. Ed. (19??-); ABI/INFORM [Computer File] (March 1982-); Econ. Lit. Index (19??-); Energy Res. Abstr. (June 1982-); Expand. Acad. Index (1992-); Index Period. Artic. Relat. Law (19??-19??); J. Econ. Lit. (19??-); Maize Abstr. (19??-); Newsp. Period. Abstr. (1992-); PAIS Int. Print (19??-); UMI ABI/Inform--Bus. Period. Ondisc (Jan. 1987-) [Full Txt.].

LC HC107.03
DD 332 US
ECONOMIC REVIEW / FEDERAL RESERVE BANK OF SAN FRANCISCO. (1991)-. Periodical. English. Irregular. Federal Reserve Bank of San Francisco, PO Box 7702, San Francisco CA 94120. **Tel** (415)974-2163, FAX (415)974-3429.
Ind/Abst Econ. Lit. Index; Expand. Acad. Index (1992-); UMI ABI/Inform--Bus. Period. Ondisc (Fall 1987-) [Full Txt.].

LC HG1501 **ISSN** 0440-2588
DD 332.1 KO
ECONOMIC STATISTICS YEARBOOK. **See** Business and Economics-Abstracting, Bibliographies and Statistics.

LC HG1501 **ISSN** 0882-3081
DD 332 US
ECONOMIC UPDATE (WASHINGTON, D.C.). (ECONOMIC UPDATE.). **Added/Corp** National Council of Savings Institutions (U.S.). (19??)-. Periodical. English. Twelve times a year. Savings and Community Bankers of America, 1101 15th Street Northwest, Suite 400, Washington DC 20005. **Tel** (202)857-3100, FAX (202)659-4816.

LC HG **ISSN** 1011-0844
DD 332 LU
TITLE CHANGE
ECU-EMS INFORMATION. **Added/Corp** Statistical Office of the European Communities. Vol. 1/4 (1987)-(1994). Periodical. English. Office for Official Publications of the European Communities, 2 rue Mercier, 2985 Luxembourg Luxembourg. **Tel** 011 352 499281, FAX 011 352 292942763. ***Continued by** ECU EMS Information and Central Bank Interest Rates.*

LC HG
DD 332 LU
•**ECU-EMS INFORMATION AND CENTRAL BANK INTEREST RATES.** **Added/Corp** Statistical Office of the European Communities. (1995)-. Periodical. English. Twelve times a year. Office for Official Publications of the European Communities, 2 rue Mercier, 2985 Luxembourg Luxembourg. **Tel** 011 352 499281, FAX 011 352 292942763. ***Continues** ECU EMS Information.*

LC HG1501
DD 332.1 IT
EFFEBI-BANCA DOMANI. Italian. Four times a year. L50000. Assn Formatori Bancari B Toscana, V Pian Carpini 136, 50100 Florence Italy. **Tel** 011 39 55 4391783.

LC HG1501 **ISSN** 0195-7287
DD 332.1 US
CCC
EFT REPORT. [EFT rep.]. **VAT** Electronic Funds Transfer Report. (1979)-. Periodical. English. Twenty-five times a year. $595.00. Phillips Business Information Inc., 1201 Seven Locks Road, PO Box 61130, Potomac MD 20854. **Tel** (301)424-3338, (301)340-1520, (800)777-5005, FAX (301)424-4297, telex 358149. **ED** Patti Murphy. available on an online database from NEXIS; and (files 636,648/Full-Text) DIALOG.
Desc: Get the behind-the-scenes reports in electronic funds transfer. ATMs, debit cards, industry leaders, emerging trends, interchange programs, and EFT-retail services.
Ind/Abst F&S Index Plus Text, Int. [Select. Cov.]; Predicasts; PTS Newsl. Database [Full Txt.]; Trade Ind. ASAP [Full Txt.]; Trade Ind. Index [Full Txt.].

LC HG1501 **ISSN** 0250-3891
DD 332.1 LU
EIB-INFORMATION. **See** Business and Economics-Investments.

LC HG1501
DD 332.1 VE
EKARE. **Added/Corp** Banco del Libro, Caracas. No. 1 (Jan./Feb. 1976)-. Periodical. Spanish. Four times a year. $8.00. Ekare, Apartado 5893, Caracas 1010 A Venezuela.
Ind/Abst Libr. Inf. Sci. Abstr.

LC HG **ISSN** 1065-8750
DD 332 US
CEASED
ELECTRONIC COMMERCE BULLETIN, THE. [Electron. commer. bull.]. Vol. 1, No. 1 (Oct. 1992)-(Dec. 1993). Bulletin. English. Little Brown & Company, 34 Beacon Street, Boston MA 02108. **Tel** (617)227-0730, (800)759-0190.

LC HG1501
DD 332.1 US
ELLIOT SHARPS FINANCIAL NEWSLETTER. (19??)-. Newsletter. English. Seven times a week. $4979.50 New York; $4600.00 other. Investment Dealers Digest Inc., Two World Trade Center, 18th Floor, New York NY 10048. **Tel** (212)227-1200, FAX (212)432-1039.

ISSN 1199-0597
DD 658.8/3 CN
EMERGING MARKETS ANALYST. [Emerg. mark. anal.]. **Added/Corp** Bank Credit Analyst (Firm). BCA Publications (Firm). (1992)-. Periodical. English. Twelve times a year. 795.00Can$. BCA Publications Ltd., 1002 Sherbrooke Street West, Suite 1600, Montreal Quebec H3A 3L6 Canada. **Tel** (514)499-9706, FAX (514)499-9709.

LC HG1501
DD 332.1 US
EMERGING MARKETS DEBT REPORT. (19??)-. English. Forty-eight times a year. $850.00. American Banker, Concourse Level, 1 State Street Plaza, New York NY 10004. **Tel** (212)803-8200, (800)221-1809, FAX (212)943-6256, (212)843-9598. **(Subscription address:** American Banker / Newletter Division, PO Box 28315, Washington DC 20038. **Tel** (800)733-4371, (202)347-2665.**)** ***Continues** LDC Debt Report.*

LC HG1501
DD 332.1 US
ENCYCLOPEDIA OF BANKING AND FINANCE. **See** Finance.

LC HG185.A7 E58 **ISSN** 0325-3937
DD 332 AG
ENSAYOS ECONOMICOS. **See** Finance.

LC HG1501 **ISSN** 0319-8626
DD 332.1 CN
ENTERPRISE (VANCOUVER). (ENTERPRISE.). **Added/Corp** B.C. Central Credit Union. B.C. Credit Union League. Vol. 27, No. 1 (Jan. 1967)-. Periodical. English. Six times a year. 20.01Can$. BC Central Credit Union, 1441 Creekside Drive, Vancouver British Columbia V6J 4S7 Canada. **Tel** (604)734-2511, FAX (604)737-5055, telex 0455291. **ED** Gayle Stevenson. **Bk Rev. Ad Acc. Circ:** 2,500. ***Continues** B.C. Credit Unionist, 0319-8634.*
Desc: Focuses on western Canadian financial issues of special interest to directors, managers, staff and members of British Columbia's credit unions. Explores security and risk management, financial competition and economic development. Delivers advice on credit union operations and practical solutions to problems shared by financial decision-makers.

LC HG2032 **ISSN** 0704-6146
DD 334/.2/09714 CN
ENTRE GENS. **See** Business and Economics-Cooperatives.

LC HG **ISSN** 1076-5735
DD 332 US
EPS CALENDAR. (EPS CALENDAR : EXPECTED EARNINGS REPORT DATES.). [EPS cal.]. **Added/Corp** Zacks Investment Research (Firm). (19??)-. Periodical. English. One time a week. $1500.00. Zacks Investment Research, 155 North Wacker Drive, 3rd Floor, Chicago IL 60606-1719. **Tel** (312)630-9880 ext. 149, FAX (312)630-9617.

LC HG2037 .U55D **ISSN** 0360-6694
DD 331.2 US
EQUAL EMPLOYMENT OPPORTUNITY AFFIRMATIVE ACTION PLAN. **Main/Corp** United States. National Credit Union Administration. English. National Credit Union Administration, 1775 G Street NW, Washington DC 20456. **Tel** (202)357-1100.

LC HG **ISSN** 0889-7093
DD 332 US
EQUIPMENT FINANCING JOURNAL. [Equip. financ. j.]. (19??)-. Periodical. English. Six times a year (Feb., Apr., June, Aug., Oct., Dec.). $50.00. Equipment Financing Journal, 110 Oakland Place, Buffalo NY 14222. **Tel** (716)885-0444, FAX (716)885-0454. **ED** Ron Caruso. **Bk Rev. Ad Acc, Adv Mgr:** Denise Breissinger. **Circ:** 30,000.

LC WMLC 93/2051 **ISSN** 1046-6665
DD 658 US
EQUIPMENT LEASING TODAY. [Equip. leas. today]. **Added/Corp** American Association of Equipment Lessors. Vol. 1, No. 1 (Nov./Dec. 1989)-. Periodical. English. Ten times a year (monthly except July/Aug. and Nov./Dec.). $100.00. American Association of Equipment Lessors, 1300 North 17th Street, Suite 1010, Arlington VA 22209-3801. **Tel** (703)527-8655, FAX (703)527-8649. **ED** Eileen Griffiths. Index available. cum. index. **Ad Acc, Adv Mgr:** Nick Larich, **Tel** (216)247-1060. **Circ:** 4,000.

LC HG136 .P7 **ISSN** 0071-142X
DD 332.15082 US
ESSAYS IN INTERNATIONAL FINANCE. [Essays int. finance]. **Added/Corp** Princeton University. International Finance Section. No. 1 (1943)-. Monographic series. English. Irregular. $40.00. International Finance Section, Princeton University, Department of Economics, Princeton NJ 08544. **Tel** (609)258-4051, FAX (609)258-6419, telex 499-1258 TIGER. **ED** Peter B. Kenen, Ellen V. Seiler. **Bk Rev. Circ:** 2,000. available on microfilm and microfiche from University Microfilms International (UMI).
Desc: Discussion of current subjects in international finance accessible to professional economists and other interested readers.

LC HG1642.S7 E84
DD 332 SP
ESTADISTICA DE CREDITOS BANCARIOS. **Added/Corp** Consejo Superior Bancario (Spain). (19??)-. Statistical Publication. Spanish. One time a year.

LC HG1501 **ISSN** 0252-3078
DD 332.1 US
ESTADISTICAS FINANCIERAS INTERNACIONALES. **See** Business and Economics-Abstracting, Bibliographies and Statistics.

Business and Economics —Banks and Banking

LC HG1501   **ISSN** 0252-3043
DD 332.1   US
  CEASED
ESTADISTICAS FINANCIERAS INTERNACIONALES ANUARIO - FONDO MONETARIO INTERNACIONAL.
(ESTADISTICAS FINANCIERAS INTERNACIONALES ANUARIO.). [Estad. financ. int. anu. - Fondo Monet. Int.]. **Added/Corp** International Monetary Fund. (1981)-(19??). Statistical Publication. Spanish. International Monetary Fund, 700 19th Street Northwest, Publishing Unit, Washington DC 20431. **Tel** (202)623-7430, FAX (202)623-7201. **Continues** International Financial Statistics Anuario, 0250-7471.

LC HG185.C2 C32a
DD 354.710082/55043/06   CN
ESTIMATES. PART III, OFFICE OF THE SUPERINTENDENT OF FINANCIAL INSTITUTIONS CANADA. **Main/Corp** Canada.
VFOAT Estimates. Part 3, Office of the Superintendent of Financial Institutions Canada; Budget des Depenses. Partie III, Bureau du Surintendant des Institutions Financieres Canada. (198?)-. English (French). One time a year. Canada Communication Group Publishers, Order Processing, Ottawa Ontario K1A 0S9 Canada. **Tel** (819)956-4800, (819)956-4802. **Continues in part** Canada. Estimates. Part III, Department of Insurance Canada.

LC HC196 .E78   **ISSN** 0121-4802
DD 330   CK
Pr Rev.
ESTRATEGIA ECONOMICA Y FINANCIERA. No. 1 (June 1977)-. Periodical.
Spanish. Twenty-four times a year. $145.00. Servicios de Information SA, C 53120 Calle 18 3 82 Piso 3, Bogota Columbia. **Bk Rev. Ad Acc. Adv Mgr:** Graciela Gonzalez Sanguino, **Tel** 243 7911 1213. **Circ:** 10,000.

LC HG3250.5.A8 H444A
DD 332   GR
ETESIA EKTHESE. **Main/Corp** Hellenike Trapeza Viomechanikes Anaptyxeos (Greece). (19??)-. Greek, Modern. One time a year.

LC HG3409.E65 B33   **ISSN** 0014-2069
DD 330.9/67   CM
ETUDES ET STATISTIQUES - BANQUE DES ETATS DE L'AFRIQUE CENTRALE.
See Business and Economics-Abstracting, Bibliographies and Statistics.

LC HG1811   **ISSN** 1356-9147
DD 332.1   UK
●EU BANKING AND FINANCE LAW. (1995)-.
Trade Publication. English. £375.00. Agra Europe London Limited, 25 Frant Road, Tunbridge Wells, Kent TN2 5JT United Kingdom. **Tel** 011 44 1892 533813, FAX 011 44 1892 544895, telex 95114 AGRATW G.

  ISSN 1070-3233
DD 338   UK
  TITLE CHANGE
EUROMEDIA FINANCE. [Euromedia finance].
No. 1 (May 5, 1993)-(June 1995). Newsletter. English. Kagan World Media Inc., 126 Clock Tower Place, Carmel CA 93923-8734. **Tel** (408)624-1536, FAX (408)625-3225. **(Subscription address:** Kagan World Media Ltd., 524 Fulham Road, London SW6 5NR United Kingdom. **Tel** 011 44 171 3718880, FAX 011 44 171 3718715.) available via fax. **Merged into** European Acquisitions and Finance.
Desc: Comprehensive analysis of single-country and cross-border media financing throughout Europe. Information on financing activity, sources of capital, capital markets and financing structures.

LC HG3879   **ISSN** 0014-2433
DD 332.1/5   UK
EUROMONEY. [Euromoney]. (June 1969)-. Trade Publication. English (Japanese). Twelve times a year.
$380.00. Euromoney Publications PLC, Nestor House, Playhouse Yard, London EC4Z 5EX United Kingdom. **Tel** 011 44 171 7798888, FAX 011 44 171 7798630, telex 290700 EUROMON G. **ED** Garry Evans. Index available. cum. index. **Ad Acc. Circ:** 28,000. available on microfilm and microfiche from University Microfilms International (UMI); available on an online database (files 648,771,572,799/Full-Text) from DIALOG. Documents available from UMI Article Clearinghouse.
Desc: Covers capital markets and international finance.
Ind/Abst ABI/INFORM Glob. Ed. (Apr. 1979-); ABI/INFORM [Computer File] (April 1979-); Acad. Search; Bus. Index (1985-); Bus. Period. Index; Bus. Source Plus; Bus. Source; Contents Recent Econ. J.; Curr. Cit.; EP Collect.; F&S Index Plus Text, Int. [Select. Cov.]; Gen. BusinessFile (1985-); Gen. Period. Index (1985-); Homework Help.; Index Bus. Reports (1974-); Index Period. Artic. Relat. Law; INFO-SOUTH Abstr.; Informat Int. Bus.; Leis., Rec., Tour. Abstr.; Manage. Contents 1000; MasterFile FullTEXT 1000; MasterFile FullTEXT 350; MasterFile FullTEXT 650; MasterFile FullTEXT (July 1993-); OCLC; PAIS Int. Print; Selec. Coop. Index Manage. Period.; Telebase; Trade Ind. Index; Wilson Bus. Abstr.; World Mag. Bank.

LC HG1501
DD 332.1   UK
EUROMONEY JAPANESE DIGEST.
(19??)-. Trade Publication. Japanese. Four times a year. $225.00. Euromoney Publications PLC, Nestor House, Playhouse Yard, London EC4Z 5EX United Kingdom. **Tel** 011 44 171 7798888, FAX 011 44 171 7798630, telex 290700 EUROMON G. **(Subscription address:** Euromoney Publications PLC, Perrymount Road Haywards Heath, West Sussex RH16 3DH United Kingdom. **Tel** 011 44 1444 440421.)
Desc: A selection of articles from Euromoney magazine and its sister publications, translated into Japanese.

LC HF3581 .E9   **ISSN** 0390-2102
DD 382/.0945/005   IT
EUROPA DOMANI. **See** Business and Economics-Commerce.

LC HG1501   **ISSN** 0953-8399
DD 332.1   IE
EUROPEAN BANKER. [Eur. bank.]. (1988)-.
Periodical. English. Ten times a year. $995.00. Lafferty Publications Ltd., Tower Ida Centre Pearse Street, Dublin 2 Ireland. **Tel** 011 353 1 6718022, FAX 011 353 1 718522. **ED** Isadore Ryan, Peter Kinahan and Ciara Linnane. **Absorbed** EC Financial Industry Monitor, 0956-3261.
Desc: News and market intelligence on national and cross-border developments in European banking, insurance and finance.

LC HG1501
DD 332.1   UK
EUROPEAN EQUITIES. (19??)-. English.
Twelve times a year. £430.00 UK; £465.00 Europe and EIRE; £520.00 other. Chart Analysis Limited, 7 Swallow Street, London W1R 7HD United Kingdom. **Tel** 011 44 171 4394961.

LC HG1501
DD 332.1   UK
EUROPEAN FINANCIAL DIGEST. English.
One time a week. £295.00. European Business Digest Ltd, Glen House, 200-208 Tottenhamrd, London W1P 9LA United Kingdom. **Tel** (071) 323-4700, FAX (071)323-3710. **ED** James Wootten and Mike Hockings. Index available.
Desc: Weekly summary of financial news from European press.

LC HG1501   **ISSN** 1354-7798
DD 332.1   UK
  CCC
●EUROPEAN FINANCIAL MANAGEMENT.
(1994)-. English. Three times a year. $192.00. Basil Blackwell Publishers Ltd., 108 Cowley Road, Oxford OX4 1JF United Kingdom. **Tel** 011 44 1235 465500, FAX 011 44 1235 465556, telex 837022 OXBOOK G. **(Subscription address:** Blackwell Publishers / UK, 108 Cowley Road, Oxford OX4 1JF United Kingdom. **Tel** 011 44 1865 791100, FAX 011 44 1865 791347.)

LC HG   **ISSN** 1351-847X
DD 332   UK
  CCC
Pr Rev.
●EUROPEAN JOURNAL OF FINANCE.
(1995)-. Academic Scholarly Publication. English. Four times a year. $225.00 US and Canada; £130.00 Europe; £145.00 other. Chapman & Hall, 2-6 Boundary Row, London SE1 8HN United Kingdom. **Tel** 011 44 171 8650066, FAX 011 44 171 5229623, telex 290164 CHAPMA G. **(Subscription address:** International Thomson Publishing Services Ltd., North Way Andover, Hampshire SP10 5BE United Kingdom. **Tel** 011 44 1264 332424.) **ED** Christopher Adcock and Eve Hicks. **Ad Acc.**
Desc: Covers all areas of finance, whether theoretical, practical, or empirical.

LC HG930.5 .M65   **ISSN** 0255-6510
DD 332/.094/021   LU
EUROSTAT, MONEY AND FINANCE.
(MONEY AND FINANCE.). [EUROSTAT, Money and finance]. **Added/Corp** Statistical Office of the European Communities. **VFOAT** Monnaie & Finances. (1984)-. Periodical. English (French). Four times a year. $90.00. Office for Official Publications of the European Communities, 2 rue Mercier, 2985 Luxembourg Luxembourg. **Tel** 011 352 499281, FAX 011 352 292942763.

LC HG1501
DD 332.1   UK
EUROWEEK : THE EUROMARKETS FIRST NEWSPAPER. English. One time a week.
£1650.00 UK; $2,890.00 US; £130.00 other. Euromoney Publications PLC, Nestor House, Playhouse Yard, London EC4Z 5EX United Kingdom. **Tel** 011 44 171 7798888, FAX 011 44 171 7798630, telex 290700 EUROMON G. **ED** Nick Evans. **Ad Acc.** available on an online database (files 771,772,799/Full-Text) from DIALOG.
Desc: The latest news and exclusives through detailed coverage and analysis of new financings, trends and developments. Captures the week's activities in the markets.

LC HG1501   **ISSN** 1038-5398
DD 332.1   AT
EVALUATION PAPERS CANBERRA.
(1992)-. Monographic series. English. Ten times a year. 65.00Aus$. Australian Government Publishing Service, GPO Box 84, Canberra ACT 2601 Australia. **Tel** 011 61 6 2954411, FAX 011 61 6 2954455.

LC HG1501   **ISSN** 0423-8710
DD 332.1   US
  CCC
EVERYBODY'S MONEY. **See** Consumer Education and Protection.

LC HG1501
DD 332.1   US
EXAMINATION OF THE NATIONAL CONSUMER COOPERATIVE BANK'S FINANCIAL STATEMENTS FOR THE FISCAL YEAR ENDED ..., AND THE QUARTER ENDED ... - COMPTROLLER GENERAL OF THE UNITED STATES.
(19??)-. English. One time a year. US General Accounting Office / Maryland, Document Handling and Information Services Facility, PO Box 6015, Gaithersburg MD 20877. **Tel** (202)275-6241. available on microfiche (Vols. for 1981- distributed to depository libraries).

LC HG1501   **ISSN** 0190-2733
DD 332.1   US
EXAMINER (DAYTON), THE. (THE EXAMINER.). **Added/Corp** Society of Financial Examiners. (197?)-. Periodical. English. Four times a year. $65.00. Society of Financial Examiners, 4101 Lake Boone Trail, Suite 201, Raleigh NC 27607. **Tel** (919)787-5181, (800)962-2384, FAX (919)787-4916. **ED** Nancy Weatherly. **Circ:** 2,500.

LC HG1501
DD 332.1   UK
  CEASED
EXCHANGE RATE OUTLOOK. (19??)-(Dec. 1993). English. Gower Publishing Co. Ltd., Gower House Croft Road Aldershot, Hampshire GU11 3HR United Kingdom. **Tel** 011 44 1252 331551, FAX 011 44 1252 344405, telex 858001.

LC HF5601   **ISSN** 0885-9116
DD 657   US
EXPOSURE DRAFT (STAMFORD, CONN. 1974). **See** Business and Economics-Accounting.

LC HG1501   **ISSN** 0014-5289
DD 332.1   FR
EXPRESS DOCUMENTS. (19??)-. French.
Forty-seven times a year. 2200.00F. Express Documents, 1 Bis Avenue de la Republique, 75011 Paris France. **Tel** 011 33 1 49293000. **(Subscription address:** Express Documents, B 522, 60732 Sainte Genevieve France. **Tel** 011 33 1 44034419.) **ED** Robert Monteux. **Ad Acc. Circ:** 15,000. available with charts; available with illustrations.

LC HG3311 .F3
DD 332.1/09599   PH
FACT BOOK. PHILIPPINE FINANCIAL SYSTEM. SUPPLEMENT. **VFOAT** Regional Profile of the Philippine Banking System. English. Two times a year.

LC HG   **ISSN** 8755-1624
DD 332   US
FACTORS AFFECTING RESERVES OF DEPOSITORY INSTITUTIONS AND CONDITION STATEMENT OF F.R. BANKS. [Factors affect. reserv. depos. inst. cond. statement F.R. banks]. **Added/Corp** Board of Governors of the Federal Reserve System (U.S.). (1980)-. English. One time a week. $20.00. Board of Governors of the Federal Reserve System, Mail Stop 127, Washington DC 20551. **Tel** (202)452-3244, (202)452-3245. **Continues** Factors Affecting Bank Reserves and Condition Statement of F.R. Banks, 0364-961X.

LC HG3810
DD 332.4/5   UK
  CEASED
FAR EAST FOREIGN EXCHANGE DEALERS DIRECTORY, THE. (19??)-(19??).
Directory. English. IBC Publishing, 57-61 Mortimer St., London W1N 7TD United Kingdom. **Tel** 011 44 171 6374383, FAX 011 44 171 6366314.
Desc: Fast and accurate dealing room tool this directory covers 600 banks in 26 countries (both listed in alphabetical order) and provides information on over 3,000 FX dealers by name, specifying the currency traded by each dealer.

LC Z7164.C81 F43
DD 016.32   US
FED IN PRINT: ECONOMICS AND BANKING TOPICS. **See** Business and Economics-Abstracting, Bibliographies and Statistics.

LC HG1501
DD 332.1 US
FEDERAL AND STATE AUDIT GUIDE FOR THE REVIEW OF PROJECT CLAIMS PRESENTED UNDER THE FEDERAL DISASTER ASSISTANCE PROGRAMS. **Added/Corp** United States. Dept. of Housing and Urban Development. Office of Inspector General. (19??)-. Government Publication. English. US Department of Housing and Urban Development, 451 Seventh Street SW, Washington DC 20401. **Tel** (202)708-0980, FAX (202)708-0299.

LC HG1501 **ISSN** 0744-8791
DD 332.1 US
FEDERAL BANKING LAW REPORT (ARLINGTON, VA.). (FEDERAL BANKING LAW REPORT.). [Fed. bank. law rep.]. (19??)-. Periodical. English. Thirty-five times a year. $288.00. A. S. Pratt and Sons Inc., 1911 Fort Myer Drive, Arlington VA 22209. **Tel** (703)528-0145. **ED** David Stemler. cum. index.

LC HG2613.M64 F42 **ISSN** 0361-8013
DD 332.1/1/09776579 US
FEDERAL RESERVE BANK OF MINNEAPOLIS ANNUAL REPORT. **Main/Corp** Federal Reserve Bank of Minneapolis. **Added/Corp** Federal Reserve Bank of Minneapolis. Annual Report. (19??)-. English. One time a year (May). Free on request. Federal Reserve Bank of Minneapolis, 250 Marquette Avenue, Publ Affairs, Minneapolis MN 55480. **Tel** (612)340-2356.

LC HG2401 .A5 **ISSN** 0014-9209
DD 332.1/1/0973 US
CODEN FDRBAU
FEDERAL RESERVE BULLETIN. [Fed. reserve bull.]. **Added/Corp** United States. Federal Reserve Board. Board of Governors of the Federal Reserve System (U.S.). Vol. 1, No. 1 (May 1, 1915)-. Bulletin. English. Twelve times a year. $25.00. Board of Governors of the Federal Reserve System, Mail Stop 127, Washington DC 20551. **Tel** (202)452-3244, (202)452-3245. Index available in last issue of volume--attached. available on microfilm and microfiche from University Microfilms International (UMI); available on an online database (file 648/Full-Text) from DIALOG. Documents available from UMI Article Clearinghouse, Documents on Demand.
Ind/Abst ABI/INFORM Glob. Ed.; ABI/INFORM [Computer File] (Jan. 1983-); Acad. Abstr. Full Text Elite; Acad. Abstr.; Acad. Ind. [Computer File] (1984-); Acad. Search; Am. Stat. Index; Bus. ASAP (1990-) [Full Txt.]; Bus. Index (1985-); Bus. Period. Index; Bus. Source Plus; Bus. Source; Contents Recent Econ. J.; Econ. Lit. Index; EP Collect.; Expand. Acad. Index (1984-); Fed. Print Econ. Bank. Top.; Gen. BusinessFile (1985-); Gen. Period. Index (1985-); Homework Help.; INFO-SOUTH Abstr.; J. Econ. Lit.; MasterFile FullTEXT 1000; MasterFile FullTEXT 350; MasterFile FullTEXT 650; MasterFile FullTEXT (July 1990-); Middle East Abstr. Index; Newsp. Period. Abstr. (1988-); OCLC; PAIS Int. Print (1991-); Predicasts Forecasts; Telebase; UMI ABI/Inform--Bus. Period. Ondisc [Full Txt.]; Wilson Bus. Abstr.

LC HG1501 **ISSN** 0734-7863
DD 332.1 US
FEDERAL RESERVE PRESS RELEASE. [Fed. Reserve press release]. **Main/Corp** Board of Governors of the Federal Reserve System (U.S.). (19??)-. English. Four times a year. Free on request. Federal Reserve Bank of Minneapolis, 250 Marquette Avenue, Publ Affairs, Minneapolis MN 55480. **Tel** (612)340-2356.

LC HG1501 **ISSN** 0892-7383
DD 332.1 US
FEE INCOME REPORT. [Fee income rep.]. **Added/Corp** Siefer Consultants (Storm Lake, Iowa). **VFOAT** Fee Income Report for Financial Institutions. (198?)-. Periodical. English. Twenty-four times a year. $319.00. Siefer Consultants Inc., PO Box 1384, 525 Cayuga Street, Storm Lake IA 50588. **Tel** (712)732-7340, (712)747-7342, FAX (712)732-7906. **ED** Steve Herron. Index available (Dec. issue). cum. index (Only yearly index).
Desc: Ideas to increase fee income and non-interest income.

LC HB **ISSN** 0165-5655
DD 332.1 NE
UDC 33
FEM. FINANCIEEL-ECONOMISCH MAGAZINE. (FEM.). [FEM, Financ.-econ. mag.]. **VFOAT** Financieel-Economisch Magazine. (1970)-. Periodical. Dutch. Twenty-six times a year. Fl315.00. BV Uitgeversmaatschappij Bonaventura, PO Box 2158, 1000 CD Amsterdam Netherlands. **Tel** 011 31 20 6914111, 011 31 20 5674911.

LC HG1501 **ISSN** 1150-7608
DD 332.1 FR
UDC 336.71(6)
FICHIER BANQUE AFRIQUE PARIS. (FICHIER BANQUE AFRIQUE.). (1990)-. Periodical. French. Twelve times a year. IC Publications Ediafric, 10 rue Vineuse, 75116 Paris France. **Tel** 011 33 1 44308100.

LC HG37.G9 F5 **ISSN** 0015-1920
DD 332.05/6 XR
FINANCE A UVER. **Added/Corp** Czechoslovak Republic. Ministerstvo Financi. Statni Banka Ceskoslovenska. Czechoslovak Republic. Federalni Cenovy Urad. (19??)-. Periodical. Czech (German and Russian; table of contents in Russian and German). Twelve times a year. DM148.00. **(Subscription address:** Kubon & Sagner, ABT Zeitschriftenimport, D 80328 Munich Germany. **Tel** 011 49 89 54218130.**)**

LC HG3881 .F85 **ISSN** 0015-1947
DD 332.1/5/05 US
CODEN FNDVAM
FINANCE & DEVELOPMENT. [Finance dev.]. **Added/Corp** International Monetary Fund. World Bank Group. World Bank. International Bank for Reconstruction and Development. **VAT** Finance and Development. Vol. 5 (March 1968)-. Periodical. English (French, Spanish, Arabic, Chinese, German and Portuguese). Four times a year. $20.00. International Monetary Fund, 700 19th Street Northwest, Publishing Unit, Washington DC 20431. **Tel** (202)623-7430, FAX (202)623-7201. **ED** Claire Liuksila. Index available. cum. index. **Bk Rev. Circ:** 140,000 (ctrl). available on microfilm and microfiche from University Microfilms International (UMI). Documents available from UMI Article Clearinghouse. ***Continues*** *Fund and Bank Review.*
Desc: Nontechnical pieces on issues in international finance and economic development and the work of the International Monetary Fund and World Bank.
Ind/Abst ABI/INFORM Glob. Ed.; ABI/INFORM [Computer File] (Sept. 1971-); Acad. Abstr.; Acad. Search; Bus. ASAP (1990-) [Full Txt.]; Bus. Index (1985-); Bus. Period. Index; Bus. Source Plus; Bus. Source; Curr. Cit.; EP Collect.; Expand. Acad. Index (1984-); Gen. BusinessFile (1985-); Homework Help.; Index Period. Artic. Relat. Law; INFO-SOUTH Abstr.; Int. Dev. Abstr.; Int. Labour Doc.; J. Econ. Lit.; Leis., Rec., Tour. Abstr.; Mag. Search; MasterFile FullTEXT 1000; MasterFile FullTEXT 350; MasterFile FullTEXT 650; MasterFile FullTEXT (Jan. 1991-); Mat. Fact; Newsp. Period. Abstr. (1990-); OCLC; PAIS Int. Print (1991-); Rice Abstr.; Rural Dev. Abstr.; Sage Public Adm. Abstr.; Soc. Sci. Source; Soc. Sci. Index; Soc. Sci. Index Fulltext (Dec. 1988-) [Full Txt.]; Telebase; UMI ABI/Inform--Bus. Period. Ondisc [Full Txt.]; Wilson Bus. Abstr.; World Agric. Econ. Rural Sociol. Abstr.

LC HG1501
DD 332.1 US
FINANCE AND ECONOMICS DISCUSSION SERIES. **Added/Corp** Board of Governors of the Federal Reserve System (U.S.) Division of Research and Statistics. (1987)-. Monographic series. English. Irregular. Free on request. Federal Reserve System, 20th & C Street Northwest, Mail Stop 138, Washington DC 20551. **Tel** (202)452-3000. ***Continues*** *Board of Governors of the Federal Reserve System (U.S.) Special Studies Paper - [Division of Research and Statistics, Federal Reserve Board]* ***and*** *Financial Studies Papers.*

LC HG1 .B96a **ISSN** 1070-9215
DD 332/.05 US
FINANCE & TREASURY. [Finance treas.]. **Added/Corp** Economist Intelligence Unit (New York, N.Y.). **VFOAT** Finance and Treasury. Dec. 14, (1992)-. Periodical. English. One time a week. $995.00. WorldTrade Executive Incorporated, PO Box 761, Concord MA 01742. **Tel** (508)287-0301, FAX (508)287-0302. available on an online database (file 627/Full-Text) from DIALOG. ***Continues*** *Business International Corporation. Business International Money Report, 0161-0384.*
Desc: Information on international finance, business enterprises and risk management.

LC HG **ISSN** 1059-1354
DD 332 US
FINANCE AT A GLANCE. [Financ. glance]. **VFOAT** Finance. Vol. 3, No. 10 (Oct. 1991)-. Periodical. English. Twelve times a year. $199.00. Finance at a Glance, 5678 Scripps Street, San Diego CA 92122.

LC HG65 .F56 **ISSN** 1070-9193
DD 332 US
•**FINANCE (BOSTON, MASS.).** (FINANCE.). [Finance]. **Added/Corp** Harvard University. Graduate School of Business Administration. Harvard University. Finance Club. (1993)-. English. One time a year. $25.00. Harvard Business School Publishing Division, Operations Department, 60 Harvard Way, Boston MA 02163. **Tel** (617)495-6192, (617)495-8948, FAX (617)495-6891, telex 6817229. ***Continues*** *Investment Banking (Boston, Mass.), 0899-7098.*
Desc: Provides in-depth profiles of a wide range of firms that offer financial services career opportunities, including new descriptions of commercial banks, Fortune 500 companies, and regional firms that actively recruit MBAs for positions in finance.

LC HG1501 **ISSN** 0965-9560
DD 332.1 UK
FINANCE EAST EUROPE. [Financ. East Eur.]. (1991)-. Periodical. English. Twenty-six times a year. £411.00 UK; £452.00 other. Financial Times Magazines, Greystoke Place, Fetter Lane, London EC4A 1ND United Kingdom. **Tel** 011 44 171 8316577.
Ind/Abst PROMT [Full Txt.]; PTS Newsl. Database [Full Txt.].

LC HG181 .F56 **ISSN** 1066-7350
DD 332.1/0973/021 US
•**FINANCE, INSURANCE & REAL ESTATE USA.** [Finance insur. real estate USA]. **Added/Corp** Gale Research Inc. **VFOAT** Finance, Insurance, and Real Estate USA; FIRE USA. 1st Ed. (1993)-. Trade Publication. English. $169.00. Gale Research Inc., 835 Penobscot Building, 645 Griswold Street, Detroit MI 48226. **Tel** (800)877-GALE, (313)961-2242, FAX (313)961-6083, (800)414-5043, telex TWX 810-221-7086. **ED** Arsen J. Darnay.
Desc: Provides economic and statistical data on this sector of American business.

LC HG46 .F48 **ISSN** 0256-0321
DD 332/.0968 SA
FINANCE WEEK. [Finance week]. Vol. 1 (Jan. 19, 1979)-. Periodical. English. One time a week. $62.63. Finance Week, Private Bag 78816, Sandton 2146 South Africa. **Tel** 011 27 11 4440555. **ED** A. Greenblo. **Bk Rev. Ad Acc. Circ:** 17,500.
Ind/Abst Energy Res. Abstr. (July 1979-).

LC HG3881 **ISSN** 0430-473X
DD 332.1 US
FINANCES & DEVELOPPEMENT. (FINANCES ET DEVELOPPEMENT.). [Financ. dev.]. **Added/Corp** International Monetary Fund. World Bank Group. World Bank. International Bank for Reconstruction and Development. (Mar. 1968)-. Periodical. French. Four times a year. Free. World Bank Publications, 1818 H Street Northwest, Washington DC 20043. **Tel** (202)473-1155, (202)473-1155, FAX (202)522-3224, telex WUI 64145 WORLDBANK. available on microfilm from University Microfilms International (UMI).
Ind/Abst LABORDOC.

LC HG1501
DD 332.1 US
FINANCIAL AD TRENDS. English. Twelve times a year. $350.00. National System Inc, 56 Worthington Drive, Maryland Heights MD 63043. **Tel** 800-231-8179, (314)205-1995, FAX (314)205-1996. **ED** Jane Mason. **Ad Acc. Circ:** 10,000.
Desc: Contains collections of newspaper ads from reader's choice of industry category. Also, provides features by industry professionals and guest editors.

ISSN 0748-1845
DD 659 US
CCC
FINANCIAL ADVERTISING REVIEW. **See** Business and Economics-Advertising and Public Relations.

LC HG1501
DD 332.1 UK
FINANCIAL ADVISER. (19??)-. Trade Publication. English. One time a week. Free (trade), £50.00 (non-trade). Financial Times Magazines, Greystoke Place, Fetter Lane, London EC4A 1ND United Kingdom. **Tel** 011 44 171 8316577.
Ind/Abst Infomat Int. Bus.

LC HG2150 .N84a **ISSN** 0098-6704
DD 332.3/2/09756 US
FINANCIAL CONDITION OF SAVINGS AND LOAN ASSOCIATIONS DOING BUSINESS IN NORTH CAROLINA. **Main/Corp** North Carolina. Dept. of Commerce. Savings and Loan Division. (1972)-. English. North Carolina Department of Commerce, 430 North Salisbury Street, Raleigh NC 27611. **Tel** (919)733-4151.

LC HG4028.B6 F55 **ISSN** 0360-5825
DD 332.6/323 US
FINANCIAL CORPORATE BOND TRANSFER SERVICE. **Added/Corp** Financial Information, Inc. (1972)-. English. One time a year. Financial Information Inc., 30 Montgomery Street, Jersey City NJ 07302. **Tel** (201)332-5400.
Desc: Corporate-municipal guide listing transfer agents, paying agents, and registrars with complete mailing addresses.

LC HG179 .F459 **ISSN** 1052-3073
DD 332.024/005 US
FINANCIAL COUNSELING AND PLANNING. (FINANCIAL COUNSELING AND PLANNING : THE JOURNAL OF THE ASSOCIATION FOR FINANCIAL COUNSELING AND PLANNING EDUCATION.). [Financ. couns. plan.]. **Added/Corp** Association for Financial Counseling and Planning

Education (U.S.). Vol. 1 (1990)-. Periodical. English. One time a year (May). $60.00 Comes with Association for Financial Counseling and Planning Education membership. Association Finance Counsel Planning Education, 1787 Neil Avenue, Columbus OH 43210. **Tel** (614)292-3741, FAX (614)292-7536. **ED** Sherman Hanna. Index available (Bound in every 5th year.). cum. index. **Bk Rev**, (Qty: 1-3). **Ad Acc**, **Adv Mgr:** Tahara. **Circ:** 400.
Desc: Journal publishes scholarly research related to financial counseling and planning.

LC HG4905 .F45 **ISSN** 0093-4070
DD 332.6/7/0973 US
FINANCIAL DAILY CARD SERVICE, CUMULATIVE. (19??)-. English. Irregular. $340.00 US; $410.00 Canada; $675.00 other. Financial Information Inc., 30 Montgomery Street, Jersey City NJ 07302. **Tel** (201)332-5400. **Ad Acc.**
Desc: Daily alerting card system for publicly traded securities.

LC HG1501 **ISSN** 0961-2556
DD 332.1 UK
FINANCIAL DIRECTOR. [Financ. dir.]. (1989)-. Periodical. English. Twelve times a year. £45.00 UK; £65.00 (airmail) Europe; £55.00 (surface mail) other. VNU Business Publications BV, 32-34 Broadwick Street, London W1A 2HG United Kingdom. **Tel** 011 44 171 4394242 ext. 2222, FAX 011 44 171 4379638, telex 23918 VNU G, 8952440. available on an online database from DIALOG. Documents available from Ask*IEEE. ***Continues** Financial Decisions, 0267-4785.*
Ind/Abst Anbar Account. Finan. Abstr.; Curr. Cit.; INSPEC (Feb. 1990-).

LC HG1501 **ISSN** 1380-2011
DD 332.1 NE
CCC
•FINANCIAL ENGINEERING AND THE JAPANESE MARKETS. (1994)-. Periodical. English. Four times a year. Free on request. New Concepts in Publishing Ltd., 20 Queens Road Buckhurst Hill, Essex IG9 5BY United Kingdom. **Tel** 011 44 181 5058640.

LC HG1501 **ISSN** 1038-7609
DD 332.1 AT
•FINANCIAL ESTIMATES OF COMMONWEALTH PUBLIC TRADING ENTERPRISES, AUSTRALIA. See Business and Economics-Abstracting, Bibliographies and Statistics.

LC HG1501
DD 332.1 US
FINANCIAL EXCHANGE, THE. Added/Corp Chicago Board of Trade. (19??)-. Periodical. English. Four times a year (Mar., June, Sept., Dec.). Free on request. Chicago Board of Trade, 141 West Jackson, #2210 Education / Marketing, Chicago IL 60604. **Tel** (312)435-7208, FAX (312)341-3027.

LC HF5001 .F514 **ISSN** 0895-4186
DD 658.1/5/05 US
CCC
CODEN FIEXAW
FINANCIAL EXECUTIVE (1987). See Business and Economics-Management.

LC HG1501
DD 332.1 US
FINANCIAL EXECUTIVE'S COUNTRY RISK ALERT, THE. English. Three times a year. $450.00. S J Rundt & Associates Inc, 130 East 63rd Street, New York NY 10121. **Tel** (201)783-5206, (201)838-0141, FAX (201)744-3073. Index available. **Bk Rev**. ctrl circ.

LC HG1501
DD 332.1 UK
FINANCIAL FACTBOOK. English. Irregular. £65.00 UK; £75.00 other. Gee & Company Limited, 183 Marsh Wall, South Quay Plaza, London E14 9FS United Kingdom. **Tel** 011 44 171 5385386, FAX 011 44 171 5388623.

LC HG1501
DD 332.1 US
FINANCIAL FORUM, THE. Added/Corp National Consumer Finance Association. **VFOAT** Financial Forum of the National Consumer Finance Association. Vol. 1 (July 1963)-. Trade Publication. English. Two times a year. American Financial Services Association, 919 18th Street Norhtwest, Washington DC 20006. **Tel** (202)296-5544.
Ind/Abst Account. Tax Datab. (Aug. 1992-).

LC HG **ISSN** 1065-5816
DD 332 US
FINANCIAL FREEDOM REPORT QUARTERLY. [Financ. freedom rep. q.]. **VFOAT** Financial Freedom Report; Financial Freedom Quarterly Report. Vol. 16, No. 1 (Summer 1992)-. Periodical. English. Four times a year. $120.00. Mark O Haroldsen Inc, 2450 East Fort Union Boulevard, Salt Lake City UT 84121. **Tel** (801)943-1280, FAX (801)942-7489. **ED** Carolyn Tice; Telephone: (801)944-2489. **Circ:** 5,000. ***Continues** Financial Freedom Report, 0196-514X.*

LC HG1501
DD 332.1 RH
FINANCIAL GAZETTE (ZIMBABWE). (FINANCIAL GAZETTE.). English. One time a week. 160.00Zin$. Financial Gazette, PO Box 1819, Harare Zimbabwe.

LC HF5550 .F5
DD 658 US
FINANCIAL HANDBOOK. 1st Ed. (1925)-. Monographic series. English. Irregular. Price varies per volume. John Wiley & Sons, Inc., 605 Third Avenue, New York NY 10158-0012. **Tel** (212)850-6000, (212)850-6645, FAX (212)850-6088, telex 12-7063. **(Subscription address:** John Wiley & Sons / UK, Baffins Lane, Chichester, West Sussex PO19 1UD United Kingdom. **Tel** 011 44 1243 779777, FAX 011 44 243 776128, telex 86290 WIBOOKG.) **ED** R H Montgomery and J I Bogen.

LC HG171 .F56 **ISSN** 0968-5650
DD 332 US
CCC
Pr Rev.
•FINANCIAL HISTORY REVIEW. Added/Corp European Association for Banking History. Vol. 1, Pt. 1 (Apr. 1994)-. Academic Scholarly Publication. English (summaries and/or abstracts in French, German and Spanish). Two times a year. $84.00. Cambridge University Press / New York, 40 West 20th Street, New York NY 10011-4211. **Tel** (212)924-3900, (800)221-4512, FAX (212)691-3239. **(Subscription address:** Cambridge University Press / Outside of North America, United Kingdom. **Tel** 011 44 223 312 393, FAX 011 44 223 325 959.) **ED** Youssef Cassis and Philip Cottrell. **Bk Rev. Ad Acc.** Documents available from BLDSC, SWETS, UMI Article Clearinghouse.
Desc: Designed as the international forum for all scholars with interests in the development of banking, finance, and monetary matters.
Ind/Abst Am. Hist. Life (1995-); Hist. Abstr. (1995-).

LC HG **ISSN** 1051-5453
DD 332 US
TITLE CHANGE
FINANCIAL IMAGING NEWS. [Financ. imaging news]. Vol. 1, No. 1 (Jan./Feb. 1991)-(19??). Periodical. English. Faulkner & Gray Inc., 11 Penn Plaza, 17th Floor, New York NY 10001. **Tel** (212)967-7000, (800)535-8403. ***Merged into** Checks & Checking, 1046-4956.*

LC HG1501 **ISSN** 0889-9452
DD 332.1 US
FINANCIAL INDEPENDENCE. [Financ. indep.]. **Added/Corp** Capitol Planning Corporation. Communications Division. **VFOAT** Financial Independence Money Management Magazine. (198?)-. Periodical. English. Six times a year. $24.00. available on an online database (file 485/Full-Text) from DIALOG.
Ind/Abst Account. Tax Datab. (1990-).

LC HG2613.K34 F55 **ISSN** 1072-0049
DD 332.1/0973/05 US
FINANCIAL INDUSTRY PERSPECTIVES. [Financ. ind. perspect.]. **Added/Corp** Federal Reserve Bank of Kansas City. Division of Bank Supervision and Structure. (Dec. 1992)-. English. Three times a year. Free on request. Federal Reserve Bank of Kansas City, 925 Grand Avenue, Kansas City MO 64198. **Tel** (816)881-2683. ***Continues in part** Banking Studies, 0743-6351.*

LC HG2609 .F5
DD 332.1 US
FINANCIAL INDUSTRY TRENDS. Added/Corp Federal Reserve Bank of Kansas City. Division of Bank Supervision and Structure. (1992)-. English. Three times a year. Free on request. Federal Reserve Bank of Kansas City, 925 Grand Avenue, Kansas City MO 64198. **Tel** (816)881-2683. ***Continues in part** Banking Studies, 0743-6351.*

LC HG187.T5 F55
DD 332.1/09593 TH
FINANCIAL INSTITUTIONS IN THAILAND (MICROFORM). Periodical. English. One time a year. Free. Bangkok Bank Ltd, Economic Research Division, Economic and Marketing Research Center, 9 Suapa Road, Bangkok Thailand. **Tel** 234-3333. **ED** Viraphong Vachratith. ctrl circ.
Desc: Statistics on financial institutions in Thailand.

LC HG46 .S6 **ISSN** 0015-2013
DD 332/.0968 SA
FINANCIAL MAIL. [Financ. mail]. Vol. 1 (March 1959)-. Periodical. English. One time a week. $94.13. Times Media Ltd., PO Box 1138, Johannesburg 2000 South Africa. **Tel** 011 27 11 4972602. **(Subscription address:** National Circulation Services, PO Box 91080, Auckland Park 2006 South Africa. **Tel** 011 27 11 3582000.) Index available. ***Continues** Southern Africa Financial Mail; **Absorbed** Property Mail.*
Ind/Abst PAIS Int. Print; Predicasts F&S Index, U. S. Annu. Ed.

LC HG4001 .F55 **ISSN** 0046-3892
DD 658.1/5/08 US
CCC
CODEN FINMEE
Pr Rev.
FINANCIAL MANAGEMENT. [Financ. manage.]. **Added/Corp** Financial Management Association. **VFOAT** FM. Vol. 1 (Spring 1972)-. Periodical. English. Four times a year. $100.00 (institutions), $65.00 (individuals) US; $108.00 (institutions), $80.00 (individuals) Canada and Mexico; $110.00 (institutions), $85.00 (individuals) others Comes with Finanical Management Associaton membership. Financial Management Association International, College of Business Administration, University of South Florida, Tampa FL 33620-5500. **Tel** (813)974-2084, FAX (813)974-3318. **ED** James Ang. Index available. cum. index. **Ad Acc. Circ:** 12,500 (ctrl). available on microfilm and microfiche from University Microfilms International (UMI). Documents available from The Genuine Article, UMI Article Clearinghouse.
Desc: Articles appearing in financial management provide readers with a unique blend of financial practice and theory. In addition to exploring the latest frontiers of finance, journal authors examine and report on current practices used by executives. Topics covered include - capital budgeting, financial institutions, captial structure, mergers, financial analysis and planning, portfolio theory.
Ind/Abst ABI/INFORM Glob. Ed.; ABI/INFORM [Computer File] (Spring 1974-); Acad. Search; Account. Tax Datab. (Spring 1974-) [Full Txt.]; Anbar Account. Finan. Abstr. [Full Txt.]; Anbar Mark. Distr. Abstr. [Full Txt.]; Anbar Top Manage. Abstr. [Full Txt.]; Bus. ASAP (1992-) [Full Txt.]; Bus. Index (1985-); Bus. Period. Index; Bus. Source Plus; Bus. Source; Contents Pages Manage.; Curr. Cit.; Curr. Contents Soc. Behav. Sci.; EP Collect.; Gen. BusinessFile (1985-); Gen. Period. Index (1985-); Homework Help.; INFO-SOUTH Abstr.; Law Office Inf. Serv.; Mag. Search; Manage. Market. Abstr.; Manage. Bibliogr. Rev.; Manage. Contents; MasterFile FullTEXT 1000; MasterFile FullTEXT 350; MasterFile FullTEXT 650; MasterFile FullTEXT (July 1993-); Middle East Abstr. Index; OCLC; Oper. Prod. Manage. Abstr. [Full Txt.]; Oper. Res./Manage. Sci.; PAIS Int. Print (1991-); Person. Train. Abstr. [Full Txt.]; Res. Alert [Full Cov.]; Selec. Coop. Index Manage. Period.; Soc. Sci. Cit. Index [Full Cov.]; Telebase; Trade Ind. ASAP [Full Txt.]; Trade Ind. Index [Full Txt.]; UMI ABI/Inform--Bus. Period. Ondisc [Full Txt.]; Wilson Bus. Abstr.; Women Manage. Rev. [Full Txt.].

LC HG1501 **ISSN** 0731-0021
DD 332.1 US
FINANCIAL MANAGEMENT LETTER (SPANISH ED.), THE. (THE FINANCIAL MANAGEMENT LETTER.). [Financ. manage lett.]. **Added/Corp** Alexander Hamilton Institute (U.S.). (19??)-. Periodical. Spanish. Twenty-four times a year. Alexander Hamilton Institute, 70 Hilltop Road, Ramsey NJ 07446-1119. **Tel** (201)825-8161, (800)879-2441, FAX (201)825-8696.

LC HG136 .F56 **ISSN** 0378-651X
DD 332/.042/05 FR
CODEN FMTRDI
FINANCIAL MARKET TRENDS. [Finan. mark. trends]. **Added/Corp** Organisation for Economic Co-Operation and Development. **VFOAT** Tendances des Marches des Capitaux. No. 1 (Oct. 1977)-. Periodical. English (French). Three times a year. $67.00. OECD Publications and Information Center, 2 rue Andre-Pascal, 75775 Paris Cedex 16 France. **Tel** 011 33 1 49104262, US:(202)785-6323, FAX 011 33 1 45248500, 011 33 1 45248176, telex 620 160 OCDE. **(Subscription address:** OECD Publications Center, 2001 L Street, Suite 700, Washington DC 20036. **Tel** (202)822-3873, (202)785-6323.) available on microfilm and microfiche from University Microfilms International (UMI); available on an online database (file 648/Full-Text) from DIALOG. Documents available from UMI Article Clearinghouse.
Desc: An assessment of trends and prospects in the international and major domestic financial markets of the OECD area.
Ind/Abst ABI/INFORM Glob. Ed.; ABI/INFORM [Computer File] (Feb. 1980-); Acad. Search; Bus. ASAP (1990-) [Full Txt.]; Bus. Index (1986-); Bus. Source Plus; Bus. Source; EP Collect.; Gen. BusinessFile (1986-); Gen. Period. Index (1986-); Homework Help.; INFO-SOUTH Abstr.; Mag. Search; Manage. Contents (1977-); MasterFile FullTEXT 1000; MasterFile FullTEXT 350; MasterFile FullTEXT 650; MasterFile FullTEXT (Jan. 1993-); OCLC; PAIS Int. Print (1991-); Public Aff. Inf. Serv. Bull.; Telebase; Trade Ind. ASAP [Full Txt.]; Trade Ind. Index [Full Txt.].

LC HG1501 **ISSN** 0963-8008
DD 332 US
CCC
FINANCIAL MARKETS, INSTITUTIONS & INSTRUMENTS. [Financ. mark. inst. instrum.]. **Added/Corp** New York University. Salomon Center. **VFOAT** Financial Markets, Institutions and Instruments. Vol. 1 No. 1 (1992)-. Monographic series. English. Five times a year. $140.00. Blackwell Publishers, 238 Main Street, Cambridge MA 02142. **Tel** (617)547-7110, (800)835-6770, FAX (617)547-0789. ***Continues** Monograph Series in Finance and Economics, 0276-2021.*

ISSN 1065-6456
DD 658 US
CODEN FOTREX
FINANCIAL OFFICER'S TAX & MANAGEMENT REPORT. [Financ. off. tax manag. rep.]. **VFOAT** Financial Officer's Tax and Management Report. Vol. 32, No. 9 (May 7, 1992)-. Periodical. English. Twenty-four times a year. $183.92. Bureau of Business Practice, 24 Rope Ferry Road, Waterford CT 06386. **Tel** (800)243-0876, (203)442-4365, (800)876-9105, FAX (203)443-1123. ***Continues*** *CFO's Report for Treasurers, Financial Officers & Business Managers, 1056-5469; Controller's Tax Report.*

LC HG1 .F474 **ISSN** 0746-7915
DD 332.024/005 US
CCC
FINANCIAL PLANNING (ATLANTA, GA.). (FINANCIAL PLANNING.). [Financ. plan.]. **Added/Corp** International Association for Financial Planning. Vol. 13, No. 1 (Jan. 1984)-. Periodical. English. Twelve times a year. $79.00. Securities Data Company, 40 West 57th Street, 11th Floor, New York NY 10019. **Tel** (212)765-5311. **ED** Robert Veres. Index available. **Bk Rev. Ad Acc. Circ:** 73,000 (ctrl). Documents available from UMI Article Clearinghouse. ***Continues*** *Financial Planner, 0363-7441.*
Desc: Serves the field of the financial services industry.
Ind/Abst ABI/INFORM Glob. Ed.; ABI/INFORM [Computer File] (Jan. 1984-); Account. Art.

ISSN 0829-1640
DD 338.7/4/02571 CN
FINANCIAL POST 500, THE. [Financ. post 500]. **Added/Corp** Financial Post Corporation Service. **VFOAT** Financial Post 500 Address List. **VAT** Financial Post Five Hundred. (June 1979)-. English. One time a year. Financial Post DataGroup, 333 King Street East, Toronto Ontario M5A 4N2 Canada. **Tel** (800)661-7678, FAX (416)350-6501. **Ad Acc.** ***Continues*** *Financial Post 300, 0829-1632.*
Desc: The ranking of Canada's largest corporations, with listings of top subsidiaries, exporters, etc.
Ind/Abst Can. Index (?-?); Can. Period. Index (19??-).

LC HG4001 .F57
DD 332 US
FINANCIAL PRACTICE AND EDUCATION : FPE : JOURNAL OF THE FINANCIAL MANAGEMENT ASSOCIATION. **Added/Corp** Financial Management Association. **VFOAT** FPE. Vol. 1, No. 1 (Spring 1991)-. Periodical. English. Two times a year (May & Oct.). $40.00. Financial Management Association International, College of Business Administration, University of South Florida, Tampa FL 33620-5500. **Tel** (813)974-2084, FAX (813)974-3318.
Ind/Abst MasterFile FullTEXT (Jan. 1995-).

LC HG **ISSN** 1059-0013
DD 332 US
FINANCIAL PRIVACY REPORT, THE. [Financ. priv. rep.]. Vol. 1, No. 1 (1991)-. Periodical. English. Twelve times a year. $96.00. The Financial Privacy Report, PO Box 1277, Burnsville MN 55337. **Tel** (612)895-8757, FAX (612)895-5536. **ED** Michael Ketcher.
Desc: Designed to provide accurate information regarding the subject matter covered. It is sold with the understanding that the publisher is not engaged in rendering legal, accounting, or other professional services.

ISSN 0950-592X
DD 362.1720681 UK
FINANCIAL PULSE. [Financ. pulse]. Periodical. English. Twenty-four times a year. £57.00 UK and Northern Ireland; $124.00 other. Morgan Grampian, 40 Beresford Street Woolwich, London SE18 6BQ United Kingdom. **Tel** 011 44 181 8557777, FAX 011 44 181 8555548, telex 896238.

LC HG1501
DD 332.1 US
FINANCIAL QUARTERLY REVIEW / AMERICAN GAS ASSOCIATION. **VFOAT** AGA Financial Quarterly Review. (195?)-. Periodical. English. Four times a year. $20.00 (nonmembers), $16.00 (members). American Gas Association / Virginia, 1515 Wilson Boulevard, Arlington VA 22209. **Tel** (703)841-8400, (703)841-8559, FAX (703)841-8697. Documents available from Documents on Demand.
Ind/Abst Environ. Abstr.

LC HG1501
DD 332.1 US
FINANCIAL REPORT ON COLORADO STATE CHARTERED SAVINGS AND LOAN ASSOCIATIONS AND CREDIT UNIONS. **Main/Corp** Colorado. Division of Financial Services. **VFOAT** Financial Report on Colorado State Chartered Savings and Loan Associations and State Chartered Credit Unions. (1989)-. English. Division of Financial Services, Department of Regulatory Agencies, 1560 Broadway/Suite 705, Denver CO 80202. **Tel** (303)894-2336. ***Continues*** *Financial Report on Colorado State Chartered Savings and Loan Associations, 0364-3212.*
Desc: Year-end financial statement of state-chartered institutions regulated by the Colorado Division of Financial Services.

LC HG1501
DD 332.1 UK
FINANCIAL REPORTING FOR CHARITIES. (19??)-. Periodical. English. £90.95. Croner Publ Ltd., Croner House London Road, Kingston Upon Thames, Surrey KT2 6SR United Kingdom. **Tel** 011 44 181 5473333, FAX 011 44 181 5472637.

LC HG181 .A67 **ISSN** 0732-8516
DD 332/.0974 US
Pr Rev.
FINANCIAL REVIEW (BUFFALO, N.Y.), THE. (THE FINANCIAL REVIEW : THE OFFICIAL PUBLICATION OF THE EASTERN FINANCE ASSOCIATION.). [Financ. rev.]. **Added/Corp** Eastern Finance Association (U.S.). (1972)-. Academic Scholarly Publication. English. Four times a year. Comes with Eastern Finance Association membership. The Eastern Finance Association, Florida State University, Finacne Department, Tallahassee FL 32306. **Tel** (904)644-4220, FAX (904)644-4225. **ED** Joseph Finnerty and Cheng Feux Lee. **Bk Rev. Ad Acc. Circ:** 2,100 (ctrl). available on microfilm and microfiche from University Microfilms International (UMI). Documents available from UMI Article Clearinghouse. ***Continues*** *Appalachian Financial Review.*
Desc: Scholarly articles in finance.
Ind/Abst ABI/INFORM Glob. Ed.; ABI/INFORM [Computer File] (Feb. 1983-); Acad. Search; Account. Tax Datab. (Feb. 1983-); Bus. ASAP (1990-) [Full Txt.]; Bus. Index (1985-); Bus. Source Plus; Bus. Source; Curr. Cit.; Econ. Lit. Index; EP Collect.; Gen. BusinessFile (1985-); Gen. Period. Index (1985-); Homework Help.; INFO-SOUTH Abstr.; J. Econ. Lit.; Mag. Search; Manage. Contents; MasterFile FullTEXT 1000; MasterFile FullTEXT 350; MasterFile FullTEXT 650; MasterFile FullTEXT (July 1993-); Middle East Abstr. Index; OCLC; Telebase; UMI ABI/Inform--Bus. Period. Ondisc [Full Txt.].

LC HG46 .F49
DD 332/.09676/2 KE
FINANCIAL REVIEW (NAIROBI, KENYA). (FINANCIAL REVIEW.). (Feb. 1985)-. Periodical. English. Twelve times a year. Nation Newspapers Limited, PO Box 49010, Nairobi Kenya. **Tel** 011 254 2 228831.

LC HG **ISSN** 8756-4106
DD 332 US
FINANCIAL SECURITY ALERT. (1984)-. Periodical. English. Twelve times a year. $78.00. Financial Security Alert, 700 Shelard Plaza North, Golden Valley MN 55426. **Tel** (800)328-7413.

LC HG1501
DD 332.1 UK
FINANCIAL SERVICES BRIEF. (1992)-. English. Ten times a year. £145.00 Europe; £152.00 other. Sweet & Maxwell Ltd., South Quay Plaza, 183 Marsh Wall 7th Floor, London E14 9FT United Kingdom. **Tel** 011 44 171 5388686, FAX 011 44 171 5389508, telex 929089 ITPINF G.

LC HG1501
DD 332.1 UK
FINANCIAL SERVICES LAW LETTER. English. Twelve times a year. £107.00 UK; £122.00 other. Monitor Press, Rectory Road, Great Waldingfield, Sudbury Suffolk CO10 0TL United Kingdom. **Tel** 011 44 1787 378607, FAX 011 44 1787 880201.

LC HG **ISSN** 0894-7260
DD 332 US
CCC
FINANCIAL SERVICES REPORT (POTOMAC, MD.). (FINANCIAL SERVICES REPORT.). [Financ. serv. rep.]. Vol. 4, No. 27 (July 20, 1987)-. Periodical. English. Twenty-five times a year. $795.00. Phillips Business Information Inc., 1201 Seven Locks Road, PO Box 61130, Potomac MD 20854. **Tel** (301)424-3338, (301)340-1520, (800)777-5005, FAX (301)424-4297, telex 358149. ***Continues*** *Financial Services Week, 0895-0288;* ***Absorbed*** *Securities Marketing Report, 1074-8385.*
Ind/Abst F&S Index Plus Text, Int. [Select. Cov.]; PTS Newsl. Database [Full Txt.]; Trade Ind. ASAP [Full Txt.]; Trade Ind. Index [Full Txt.].

LC HG179 .F474a **ISSN** 1057-0810
DD 332.024/005 US
CCC
FINANCIAL SERVICES REVIEW (GREENWICH, CONN.). (FINANCIAL SERVICES REVIEW : THE JOURNAL OF INDIVIDUAL FINANCIAL MANAGEMENT.). [Financ. serv. rev.]. Vol. 1, No. 1 (1991)-. Trade Publication. English. Two times a year. $170.00. JAI Press Inc., 55 Old Post Road, Suite 2, PO Box 1678, Greenwich CT 06836-1678. **Tel** (203)661-7602, FAX (203)661-0792.

LC HG **ISSN** 0747-8305
DD 332 US
FINANCIAL SERVICES STRATEGIST, THE. (THE FINANCIAL SERVICES STRATEGIST : A PUBLICATION OF THE BUREAU FOR ECONOMIC INFORMATION, LTD.). [Financ. serv. strateg.]. Vol. 1, No. 1 (Aug. 15, 1984)-. Periodical. English. Twenty-four times a year. $527.00 or $2,000 in securities commissions. Bureau for Economic Information, 888 Seventh Avenue, 16th Floor, New York NY 10106.

LC HG1615.7.T7 F56 **ISSN** 0967-4969
DD 332.1/068/3 UK
●**FINANCIAL SERVICES TRAINING JOURNAL.** Vol. 1, No. 1 (1993)-. Periodical. English. Three times a year. $499.00. MCB University Press, 60 62 Toller Lane, Bradford, West Yorkshire BD8 9BY United Kingdom. **Tel** 011 44 1274 785280, FAX 011 44 1274 785200, telex 51317-MCBUNI-G. **(Subscription address:** MCB University Press / US and Canada Subscriptions, PO Box 10812, Birmingham AL 35201. **Tel** (205)995-1567, (800)633-4931, FAX (205)995-1588.**)**

LC HG **ISSN** 0895-8440
DD 332 US
CCC
CEASED
FINANCIAL SERVICES WEEK (FAIRCHILD PUBLICATIONS). (FINANCIAL SERVICES WEEK.). [Financ. serv. week]. Vol. 1, No. 1 (Oct. 5, 1987)-Vol. 6 (Oct. 10, 1993). Periodical. English. Phillips Business Information Inc., 1201 Seven Locks Road, PO Box 61130, Potomac MD 20854. **Tel** (301)424-3338, (301)340-1520, (800)777-5005, FAX (301)424-4297, telex 358149. available on microfilm and microfiche from University Microfilms International (UMI); available on an online database from NEXIS; and (files 16,485/Full-Text) DIALOG. ***Continues*** *Financial Services Times, 0890-0469.*
Ind/Abst Account. Tax Datab. (Dec. 1991-) [Full Txt.]; F&S Index Plus Text, Int. [Full Txt.] [Select. Cov.]; PROMT [Full Txt.].

LC HG1501 **ISSN** 0892-7812
DD 332.1 US
FINANCIAL SOURCEBOOKS' SOURCES. **VFOAT** Sources. (1989)-. Directory. English. Every 2 years (1 issues). $165.00. Financial Sourcebooks, PO Box 313, Naperville IL 60566. **Tel** (708)961-2161.

LC HG1501
DD 332.1 US
FINANCIAL STATEMENTS FOR THE FISCAL YEAR ENDED ... / TENNESSEE VALLEY AUTHORITY. **Main/Corp** Tennessee Valley Authority. (1953)-. English. One time a year. US Tennessee Valley Authority, W12D140 C K, 400 Commerce Avenue, Knoxville TN 37902. available on microfiche (Vols. for (1982-) distributed to depository libraries). ***Continues*** *Tennessee Valley Authority. Financial Statements, 0362-093X.*

LC HG3881 .I5764 **ISSN** 0149-6050
DD 332 US
FINANCIAL STATEMENTS OF THE GENERAL ACCOUNT AND SPECIAL DRAWING ACCOUNT. **Main/Corp** International Monetary Fund. (19??)-. English. Four times a year. Free on request. International Monetary Fund, 700 19th Street Northwest, Publishing Unit, Washington DC 20431. **Tel** (202)623-7430, FAX (202)623-7201. ***Continues*** *International Monetary Fund. Financial Statements.*

LC HG3879 .I57a
DD 332.1/52 US
FINANCIAL STATEMENTS OF THE GENERAL DEPARTMENT, GENERAL RESOURCES ACCOUNT, AND THE SPECIAL DRAWING RIGHTS DEPARTMENT, AND ACCOUNTS ADMINISTERED BY THE INTERNATIONAL MONETARY FUND: SUBSIDY ACCOUNT, TRUST FUND. **Main/Corp** International Monetary Fund. (April 1978)-. English. Four times a year. Free on request. International Monetary Fund, 700 19th Street Northwest, Publishing Unit, Washington DC 20431. **Tel** (202)623-7430, FAX (202)623-7201. ***Continues*** *International Monetary Fund. Financial Statements of the General Account and Special Drawing Account, and Accounts Administered by the International Monetary Fund: Subsidy Account, Trust Fund.*

LC HD2346.U5 F55a **ISSN** 0363-8987
DD 658.1/5904 US
FINANCIAL STUDIES OF THE SMALL BUSINESS. **Main/Corp** Financial Research Associates. (1976)-. Periodical. English. One time a year (Oct.). $89.00. Financial Research Association, 510 Avenue J Southeast, Winter Haven FL 33880. **Tel** (813)299-3969, FAX (813)299-2131. Index available (free).

Business and Economics — Banks and Banking

LC HG1709 .F567
DD 332.1 UK
CODEN FTINEZ
TITLE CHANGE
FINANCIAL TECHNOLOGY INSIGHT.
VFOAT Insight. (Dec. 1990)-(19??). Newsletter. English. Eurostudy Publishing Co. Ltd., 36 38 Willesden Lane, London N26 7SW United Kingdom. **Tel** 011 44 171 6374383, FAX 011 44 171 6256223. **(Subscription address:** IBC Subscription Services, IBC House, Vickers Drive, Weybridge, Surrey KT13 0XS United Kingdom. **Tel** 011 44 1932 354020.) available on an online database (file 636/Full-Text) from DIALOG. Documents available from Ask*IEEE. **Formed by the union of** Electronic Banking & Finance **and** Online Finance. **Merged into** Financial Technology International Bulletin.
Desc: A newsletter giving analysis of applications in the financial marketplace as it moves towards globalization, highlighting areas such as dealing roams and back office technology, information feeds and online assistance, modem banking techniques and international electronic trading.
Ind/Abst INSPEC (Dec. 1990-); PTS Newsl. Database [Full Txt.].

LC HG1501 ISSN 0956-554X
DD 332.1 US
FINANCIAL TECHNOLOGY MARKETS.
[Financ. technol. mark.]. (1989)-. Periodical. English. Twelve times a year. $630.00. Lafferty Publications Ltd., Tower Ida Centre Pearse Street, Dublin 2 Ireland. **Tel** 011 353 1 6718022, FAX 011 353 1 718520.

LC HG1501
DD 332.1 US
FINANCIAL TIMES INDUSTRIAL COMPANIES. VOLUME I, ELECTRONICS. **VFOAT** Financial Times Industrial Companies; Industrial Companies. Volume I, Electronics. (1987)-. English. One time a year. £95.00. Longman Group Ltd., Fourth Avenue, Longman House, Harlow Essex CM19 5SR United Kingdom. **Tel** 011 44 1279 429655, FAX 011 44 1279 431067, telex 81259. available on diskette. **Continues in part** Financial Times Industrial Companies Year Book, 0141-321X.

LC HG ISSN 1070-1826
DD 332 US
CCC
●**FINANCIAL TRADER.** [Financ. trader]. Vol. 1, Issue 1 (June 1993)-. Periodical. English. Six times a year. $79.97. Miller Freeman Inc., 600 Harrison Street, San Francisco CA 94107. **Tel** (415)905-2337, (415)905-2200, FAX (415)905-2240, telex 278273.

LC HG1501 ISSN 1059-3950
DD 332 US
FINANCIAL WOMAN TODAY. [Financ. woman today]. **Added/Corp** Financial Women International. (1990)-. Periodical. English. Seven times a year. $24.00. Financial Women International, 200 North Glebe Road, Arlington VA 22203. **Tel** (703)807-2007. **ED** Lora Engdahl. **Bk Rev. Ad Acc. Circ:** 22,000. **Continues** Executive Financial Woman, 0886-540X.
Desc: Reports and analyzes key competitive issues affecting banks and other financial institutions and is a source of information on the financial services job market with special emphasis on work force issues. Dedicated to providing information readers need to excel in their jobs and advance in the financial services industry.

LC HG4501 .F5 ISSN 0015-2064
DD 332/.05 US
CCC
CODEN FIWOAR
TITLE CHANGE
FINANCIAL WORLD. See Business and Economics-Investments.

LC HG65 .F52 ISSN 1058-2878
DD 332 US
CCC
FINANCIAL YELLOW BOOK. [Financ. yellow book]. **Added/Corp** Monitor Publishing Company. **VFOAT** Yellow Book. Vol. 5, No. 1 (Winter 1992)-. Directory. English. Two times a year. $190.00. Leadership Directories, Inc., 104 Fifth Avenue, Second Floor, New York NY 10011. **Tel** (212)627-4140, FAX (212)645-0931. **ED** James Marcus. Index available. **Acid Free.** available on CD-ROM from Chadwyck-Healey, Inc. **Continues** Financial 1000 Yellow Book, 1049-7935.
Desc: Provides listings of names, titles, addresses, facsimile and telephone numbers of over 42,000 key financial executives who manage and direct the leading U.S. financial institutions. Includes assets and business descriptions. Also lists government financial institutions, their officers and directors. Five indexes organize data by institution, executive's name, state, service segment and parent company.

LC HG1501
DD 332.1 NE
FINANCIEEL MANAGEMENT. (19??)-. Dutch. One time a year. Fl196.23. Bocaal Business Press BV, Stolbergstraat 14, 2012 EP Haarlem Netherlands. **Tel** 011 31 23 319014.

LC Newspaper
DD 332 NE
FINANCIEELE DAGBLAD [MICROFORM], HET. (1943)-. Newspaper. Dutch (English). Seven times a week. Fl410.40. H Sijthoffs Financiele Dagblad, PO Box 216, 1000 AE Amsterdam Netherlands. **Tel** 011 31 20 5574511.
Ind/Abst Infomat Int. Bus.

LC HG37.P6 F5 ISSN 0430-4896
DD 332 PL
FINANSE. **Added/Corp** Panstwowe Wydawnictwo Ekonomiczne. Vol. 1- (Nov. 1950)-. Periodical. Polish. Twelve times a year. **(Subscription address:** Ars Polona-Ruch, PO Box 1001, Krakowskie Przedmiescie 7, 00-068 Warsaw Poland. **Tel** 011 48 22 261201.)

LC HA1501 HG3161
DD 332 NO
FINANSINSTITUSJONER. Main/Corp Norway. Statistisk Sentralbyra. **VFOAT** Financial Institutions. Multiple languages (English and Norwegian). One time a year. Kr9.00.

LC HG1501 ISSN 0015-220X
DD 332.1 SZ
FINANZ UND WIRTSCHAFT. (19??)-. Periodical. Swedish. Twenty-six times a year. $446.01. Finanz und Wirtschaft AG, Weberstrasse 8-10, Postfach 913, CH-8021 Zurich Switzerland. **Tel** 011 41 1 2411134, FAX 011 41 1 2426397, telex 812 386.

LC HG1501 ISSN 0394-8307
DD 332 IT
UDC 336.12
FINANZA LOCALE, LA. [Finanza locale]. (1981)-. Periodical. Italian. Twelve times a year. L164860. Maggioli Editore, Casella Postale 290, 47037 Rimini Italy. **Tel** 011 39 541 628666, FAX 011 39 541 742217.

LC HG ISSN 0094-0240
DD 332 US
FIRST FRIDAY (MADISON, WIS.). (FIRST FRIDAY.). [First Friday]. **Added/Corp** Association of State Colleges and Universities. (1973)-. Periodical. English. Twelve times a year. $35.00. Walter Polner ASCU, PO Box 5488, Madison WI 53705. **Tel** (608)238-2646. **ED** Walter Polner. **Bk Rev. Circ:** 1,300.
Desc: Current trends in financial intermediaries. New products and procedures for market store.

ISSN 1185-9024
DD 354.710072 SZ
FIS BULLETIN. [FIS bull.]. **Added/Corp** Canada. Office of the Comptroller General. Canada. Supply and Services Canada. **VFOAT** Bulletin de la SIF. **VAT** Financial Information Strategy Bulletin. (Sept. 1991)-. Bulletin. German. Three times a year. $49.02. Hallwag AG, Nordring 4, CH-3001 Bern Switzerland. **Tel** 011 41 31 3323131, FAX 011 41 31 414133, telex 912661 HAWA CH.
Ind/Abst SPORT Discus.

ISSN 1185-9024
DD 354.710072 CN
FIS BULLETIN. (BULLETIN DE LA SIF.). [FIS bull.]. **Added/Corp** Canada. Bureau du controleur General. Canada. Approvisionnements et Services Canada. **VFOAT** FIS Bulletin. **VAT** Bulletin de la Strategie d'Information Financiere. (Sept 1991)-. Bulletin. French (English). Four times a year.

LC HG1501 ISSN 1064-0673
DD 332 US
FLORIDA BANKING. (FLORIDA BANKING : MAGAZINE OF THE FLORIDA BANKERS ASSOCIATION.). [Fla. bank.]. **Added/Corp** Florida Bankers Association. Vol. 1, No. 1 (Aug. 1987)-. Periodical. English. Twelve times a year. TCI, PO Box 12338, Tallahassee FL 32301. **Tel** (904)681-9405. **ED** Catherine Haagenson. **Bk Rev. Ad Acc. Circ:** 7,000. **Continues** Banking Today, 1052-0562.
Desc: Banking and financial for Florida.

LC HG1501
DD 332.1 US
FLORIDA FINANCIAL INSTITUTIONS DIRECTORY. **Added/Corp** Florida Bankers Association. (19??)-. Directory. English. One time a year (May, Nov.). $30.00 (members); $40.00 (nonmembers). Florida Bankers Association, PO Box 531126, Orlando FL 32853-6847. **Tel** (407)896-6511, FAX (407)896-9720.

LC HG1501
DD 332.1 US
FMS UPDATE. (19??)-. English. Twenty-four times a year. $195.00 (nonmembers); $325.00 (members), $375.00 (affiliate members) Comes with Financial Managers Society Membership. Financial Managers Society Inc., 8 South Michigan Avenue, Suite 500, Chicago IL 60603. **Tel** (312)578-1300, FAX (312)578-1308.

LC HG1501
DD 332.1 US
FOR BROKERS ONLY FBO NEWS BY FAX. **VFOAT** For Brokers Only. (19??)-. English. Eighteen times a year. $89.00. Hostetler Communications, PO Box 97035, Raleigh NC 27624. **Tel** (919)870-8295. **Continues** Hostetler Memo for Brokers Only, 1052-7575.

LC HJ2052 .U57b
DD 332.4/5 US
FOREIGN CURRENCIES HELD BY THE U.S. GOVERNMENT. Added/Corp United States. Dept. of the Treasury. Financial Management Service. **VFOAT** Foreign Currencies Held by the US Government. (1991)-. Periodical. English. Four times a year. Department of the Treasury Fiscal Service, Bureau of Government, Fifteenth Street and Pennsylvania Avenue Northwest, Washington DC 20220. **Continues** Report on Foreign Currencies Held by the United States Government, 0098-3896.

LC HG1501 ISSN 0196-352X
DD 332.1 US
FOREIGN EXCHANGE (NEW YORK, N.Y.). (FOREIGN EXCHANGE.). [Foreign exch.]. (198?)-. Periodical. English. Ten times a year. $950.00. World Reports Ltd, 280 Madison Avenue/Suite 1206, New York NY 10016. **Tel** (212)689-7442, FAX (212)481-0915.

LC HG3810 ISSN 0704-7304
DD 332.4/5/0212 CN
FOREIGN EXCHANGE QUOTATIONS.
Main/Corp Royal Bank of Canada. Foreign Exchange Dept. (Jan. 14, 1959)-. Periodical. English. Twelve times a year. Free on request. Royal Bank of Canada, Royal Bank Plaza 9th Floor, South Tower, Toronto Ontario M5J 2J5 Canada. **Tel** (416)974-2274, (416)974-8114, FAX (416)974-3733, (416)974-3361. ctrl circ.

LC HG3810 .W47 ISSN 0749-6397
DD 332.4/56/05 US
FOREIGN EXCHANGE RATE OUTLOOK.
[Foreign exch. rate outlook]. **Added/Corp** Wharton Econometric Forecasting Associates. (June 1984)-. English. Twelve times a year. $12,700 limited service; $18,750 full service. WEFA / Philadelphia, Inc Box 8500, Suite 1995, Philadelphia PA 19178. **Tel** (215)667-6000, telex 710 6700575. ctrl circ. **Continues** Wharton Foreign Exchange Rate Outlook, 0749-6389.
Desc: Contains forecasts of exchange rates and interest rates with summary economic and financial analysis. Includes two monthly publications, and two in house consulting visits.

LC HG1501 ISSN 0364-1341
DD 332.1 US
FOREIGN EXCHANGE RATES. Added/Corp Board of Governors of the Federal Reserve System (U.S.). (1???)-. Periodical. English. Twelve times a year. $5.00 (monthly fax service). Board of Governors of the Federal Reserve System, Mail Stop 127, Washington DC 20551. **Tel** (202)452-3244, (202)452-3245.

LC HG1501 ISSN 0364-1333
DD 332.1 US
FOREIGN EXCHANGE RATES FOR THE WEEK. (FOREIGN EXCHANGE RATES FOR THE WEEK ENDING ...). **Added/Corp** Board of Governors of the Federal Reserve System (U.S.). (1???)-. English. Fifty-two times a year. $20.00. Board of Governors of the Federal Reserve System, Mail Stop 127, Washington DC 20551. **Tel** (202)452-3244, (202)452-3245. Documents available from Documents on Demand.
Ind/Abst Am. Stat. Index.

LC HG ISSN 0897-473X
DD 332 US
FOREIGN EXCHANGE SOURCEBOOK, THE. [Foreign exch. sourceb.]. (1988)-. Periodical. English. One time a year. £139.00, $236.00. Forex Analytics, 4350 La Jolla Village Drive, Third Floor, San Diego CA 92122.
Desc: Provides information, including the companies' services, staff, branch and representative locations, clients and contacts. Offers a guide to firms serving the global foreign exchange markets.

LC HG3810 ISSN 0849-4940
DD 332.4/5/05 CN
FOREXCAST (MONTREAL). (FOREXCAST.). [Forexcast]. **VFOAT** Focus Report. No. 89.33 (Sept. 5, 1989)-. Periodical. English. Three times a year. 4500.00Can$. BCA Publications Ltd., 1002 Sherbrooke Street West, Suite 1600, Montreal Quebec H3A 3L6 Canada. **Tel** (514)499-9706, FAX (514)499-9707.

LC HG ISSN 1067-7704
DD 332 US
CEASED
FRASER'S EXIMBANK, AID INTELLIGENCE WEEKLY. [Fraser's Eximbank AID intell. wkly.]. **VFOAT** Fraser's Barter, Countertrade and Offset Intelligence Weekly. (19??)-(1995). Periodical. English. R H Publishers, 1701 North Kent Street, Suite 708, Arlington VA 22209-2107. **Tel** (703)524-4226, FAX (703)524-4226. **ED** Robert D. Fraser. Index available. cum. index. **Bk Rev.**
Desc: Covers all US government loans, guarantees, insurance, grants for American exports, foreign investments aid, bid opportunities and awards up to $1

Business and Economics —Banks and Banking

million for feasibility studies. Actual transaction for intelligence information of potential customers, competitors, and other related issues.

LC HG **ISSN** 1067-7682
DD 332 US
FRASER'S INTERNATIONAL BANKING & FINANCE BIWEEKLY. (FRASER'S INTERNATIONAL BANKING & FINANCE BIWEEKLY : DOMESTIC & FOREIGN.). [Fraser's int. bank. finance biwkly.]. **VFOAT** Fraser's International Banking and Finance Biweekly. (19??)-. Periodical. English. Twenty-six times a year. $165.00. R H Publishers, 1701 North Kent Street, Suite 708, Arlington VA 22209-2107. **Tel** (703)524-4226, FAX (703)524-4226. **ED** Robert D. Fraser. Index available. cum. index. **Bk Rev**.

LC HG1501 **ISSN** 0964-4105
DD 332.1 UK
FUNDING DIGEST. [Funding dig.]. (1987)-. Periodical. English. Six times a year.
Ind/Abst Museum Abstr.

LC HG6024.A3 F874
DD 332.64/5/05 US
FUTURES AND OPTIONS FACT BOOK. **Added/Corp** Futures Industry Institute. (19??)-. English. Irregular. $145.00. Futures Industry Association, 2001 Pennsylvania Avenue Northwest, Washington DC 20006. **Tel** (202)466-5460, FAX (202)296-3184.

LC HG1501
DD 332.1 UK
FUTURES & OPTIONS PLUS. (19??)-. Periodical. English. Irregular (23 issues). £299.00 UK; $634.00 US, Canada and South America. Metal Bulletin PLC, PO Box 28E, Worcester Park, Surrey KT4 7HY United Kingdom. **Tel** 011 44 171 8279977, FAX 011 44 171 3378943.

LC HG1501
DD 332.1 US
FUTURES CHART SERVICE. FINANCIAL. **Added/Corp** Commodity Research Bureau (U.S.). **VFOAT** Commodity Research Bureau Futures Chart Service; CRB Futures Chart Service. Vol. 35, No. 31 (Aug. 3, 1990)-. Periodical. English. Twenty-six times a year. $205.00. Commodity Trend Service, PO Box 32309, Palm Beach Gardens FL 33420. **Tel** (407)694-0960, (800)331-1069, FAX (407)622-7623. **(Subscription address:** Knight Ridder Financial Publications, PO Box 94513, Chicago IL 60690. **) ED** Nick Van Nice. **Continues in part** Futures Chart Service.

LC HG6024.A3 F876
DD 332 US
FUTURES CHART SERVICE. LONG RANGE CHARTS. **Added/Corp** Commodity Research Bureau (New York, N.Y.). **VFOAT** Long Range Charts. (Apr. 12, 1991)-. Periodical. English. Four times a year. Commodity Research Bureau, 75 Wall Street, 22nd Floor, New York NY 10005.

LC HG **ISSN** 1065-6855
DD 332 US
FUTURES INDUSTRY (WASHINGTON, D.C.). (FUTURES INDUSTRY : THE MAGAZINE OF THE FUTURES INDUSTRY ASSOCIATION.). [Futur. ind.]. **Added/Corp** Futures Industry Association. (1991)-. Periodical. English. Six times a year. Free on request. Futures Industry Association, 2001 Pennsylvania Avenue Northwest, Washington DC 20006. **Tel** (202)466-5460, FAX (202)296-3184. **Continues** FIA Review.

LC HG1501
DD 332.1 US
FW / FINANCIAL WORLD. See Business and Economics-Investments.

LC HG1501
DD 332.1 US
GAIN. (19??)-. English. Irregular. $995.00. Institute of Internal Auditors / Orlando, Florida, PO Box 140099, Orlando FL 32889. **Tel** (407)830-7600, FAX (407)831-5171, telex 567443.

LC HG3136 .G39 **ISSN** 0860-7613
DD 332 PL
GAZETA BANKOWA. (19??)-. Periodical. Polish. One time a week. $143.00. Gazeta Bankowa, 00-696 Warsaw, Pankiewicza 3 Poland. **Tel** (22)6287272, FAX (22)212653. **(Subscription address:** Ars Polona-Ruch, PO Box 1001, Krakowskie Przedmiescie 7, 00-068 Warsaw Poland. **Tel** 011 48 22 261201.) **ED** Andrzej Bankowa. **Circ:** 40,000.
Desc: Information on banking, business and finance.

LC HG3879 .G44
DD 332.4/9494 SZ
GELD, WAHRUNG UND KONJUNKTUR. MONNAIE ET CONJONCTURE. **Added/Corp** Schweizerische Nationalbank. **VFOAT** Monnaie et Conjuncture. (1983)-. Periodical. French (German). Four times a year. 30.00F Europe; 55.00F others. Zuerichsee Zeitschriftenverlag, Seestrasse 86, CH-8712 Staefa Switzerland. **Tel** 011 41 1 9285611.

LC HG231 .G44 **ISSN** 0435-1835
DD 332.4/9 GW
GELDGESCHICHTLICHE NACHRICHTEN. **Added/Corp** Gesellschaft Fur Internationale Geldgeschichte (Frankfurt am Main, Germany) Museum Fur Internationale Geldgeschichte (Frankfurt am Main, Germany). Vol. 1, No. 1 (Jan. 1966)-. Periodical. German. Six times a year. $65.25. Gesellschaft fuer Internationale Geldgeschichte, Postfach 140, W 6082 Walldorf F R Germany. **Tel** 011 49 6105 6505.
Ind/Abst BHA : Biblio. Hist. Art.

LC HB **ISSN** 0393-7925
DD 330 IT
UDC 336.7
GENTE MONEY. [Gente money]. (1984)-. Periodical. Italian. Twelve times a year. L67200 Italy; L115000 other. Rusconi Editore Spa, Servicio Abbonements, Viale Le Sarca 235, 20126 Milan Italy. **Tel** 011 39 2 66192634, FAX 011 39 2 66192206. **ED** E. Cisnetto. **Circ:** 115,000.
Ind/Abst Infomat Int. Bus.

LC HG186.I8 G4
DD 332/.0945 IT
GENTEMONEY. **VFOAT** Gente Money. Vol. 1, No. 1 (Oct. 1984)-. Periodical. Italian (Italian). Twelve times a year. L45780. Rusconi Editore Spa, Servicio Abbonements, Viale Le Sarca 235, 20126 Milan Italy. **Tel** 011 39 2 66192634, FAX 011 39 2 66192206.

LC HG3054 .D38 **ISSN** 0070-394X
DD 332.1 GW
GESCHAFTSBERICHT DER DEUTSCHEN BUNDESBANK FUER DAS JAHR. **Main/Corp** Deutsche Bundesbank. (1957)-. German (English). Free on request. Deutsche Bundesbank, Wilhelm Epsteinstrasse 14, 6000 Frankfurt am Main Germany. **Tel** 069 95 66 35 15, FAX 069 95 66 30 77. **Bk Rev**. **Ad Acc**. ctrl circ. **Continues** Bank Deutscher Lander Geschaftsbericht.

LC HG3208.L38 L38A
DD 332.1/5/094945 SZ
GESCHAFTSBERICHT FUR DAS JAHR ... / LAVORO BANK AG. **Main/Corp** Lavoro Bank (Zurich, Switzerland). **VFOAT** Annual Report for the Year .... English (German). One time a year. Lavoro Bank AG, Talacker 21, Postfach 8039, 8001 Zurich Switzerland.

LC HG1501
DD 332.1 IT
GIORNALE D'BANCA, IL. (19??)-. Italian. L77000 Italy; L90150 other. Arnoldo Mondadori Editore, UFF Cont Abbonamenti, 20090 Segrate MI Italy. **Tel** 011 39 2 75422015, telex 320457 MONDMI I.

LC HG4027.5 .G55 **ISSN** 0896-4181
DD 332/.042/05 CCC
GLOBAL FINANCE. [Glob. finance]. (Oct. 1987)-. Trade Publication. English (Japanese; summaries or abstracts in Japanese). Twelve times a year. $255.00. Global Finance Joint Venture, 11 West 19th Street, Second Floor, New York NY 10011. **Tel** (212)337-5900, FAX (212)337-5055. **ED** Carl G. Bergen. **Ad Acc, Adv Mgr:** J. Brooks. **Circ:** 55,000 (ctrl). available on microfilm and microfiche from University Microfilms International (UMI).
Ind/Abst Curr. Cit.; PAIS Int. Print (1991-).

LC HG3879 .G58 **ISSN** 1044-0283
DD 332/.042/05 US
GLOBAL FINANCE JOURNAL. [Glob. financ. j.]. **Added/Corp** California State University, Fresno. School of Business. Vol. 1, No. 1 (Fall 1989)-. Trade Publication. English. Two times a year. $165.00. JAI Press Inc., 55 Old Post Road, Suite 2, PO Box 1678, Greenwich CT 06836-1678. **Tel** (203)661-7602, FAX (203)661-0792.

LC HG1501 **ISSN** 1069-9899
DD 332.1 US
●**GLOBAL FINANCIAL REPORT ON TELECOMMUNICATIONS AND COMPUTER COMPANIES.** **Added/Corp** Center for International Financial Analysis and Research (Princeton, N.J.). (1993)-. Periodical. English. Twelve times a year. $330.00. CIFAR, 3490 US Route 1, Princeton NJ 08540. **Tel** (609)520-9333, FAX (609)520-0905.

LC HG1501
DD 332.1 US
●**GLOBAL M AND A.** (Sept. 1994)-. Periodical. English. Four times a year. $170.00. Euromoney Publications PLC, Nestor House, Playhouse Yard, London EC4Z 5EX United Kingdom. **Tel** 011 44 171 7798888, FAX 011 44 171 7798630, telex 290700 EUROMON G. **(Subscription address:** Euromoney Publications PLC, Perrymount Road Haywards Heath, West Sussex RH16 3DH United Kingdom. **Tel** 011 44 1444 440421.**)**

LC HG1501
DD 332.1 US
GLOBAL MONEY MANAGEMENT. (19??)-. Newsletter. English. Twenty-six times a year. $1495.00 (one-year), $2695.00 (two-year). Institutional Investor Inc., 488 Madison Avenue, New York NY 10022. **Tel** (212)303-3234, (212)303-3233, FAX (212)303-3353. available on an online database (files 772,799/Full-Text) from DIALOG.
Desc: Devoted to international fund management. Reports on investment strategies, pension fund searches and market news. Also includes performance measurement data for more than 25 countries.

LC HG1501
DD 332.1 UK
GLOBAL PRIVATE POWER. (19??)-. English. Twelve times a year. $1060.95. Financial Times / UK, Maple House, 149 Tottenham Court Road, London W1P 9LL United Kingdom. **Tel** 011 44 171 8962276, FAX 011 44 171 8962275, 011 44 171 8962399.

LC HG1501 **ISSN** 1060-8702
DD 332.1 US
GLOBAL STOCK GUIDE. **Added/Corp** Center for International Financial Analysis and Research (Princeton, N.J.). (1992)-. Periodical. English. Twelve times a year. $481.00. CIFAR, 3490 US Route 1, Princeton NJ 08540. **Tel** (609)520-9333, FAX (609)520-0905.

LC HG4050 .G64 **ISSN** 0278-0038
DD 338.7/4/0973 US
  CCC
GOING PUBLIC, THE IPO REPORTER. **Added/Corp** Howard & Company. **VFOAT** IPO Reporter. **VAT** Going Public, The Initial Public Offering Reporter. (1977)-. Periodical. English. One time a week (51 issues). $1195.00. Investment Dealers Digest Inc., Two World Trade Center, 18th Floor, New York NY 10048. **Tel** (212)227-1200, FAX (212)432-1039. **ED** Clint Winstead. available on microfilm and microfiche from University Microfilms International (UMI). **Continues** Going Public, 0882-9489.
Desc: Reports on companies filing with the SEC.
Ind/Abst Account. Tax Datab. (Sept. 1991-) [Full Txt.]; PROMT [Full Txt.]; PTS Newsl. Database [Full Txt.].

LC HG **ISSN** 0195-0398
DD 332 US
GOLD BUG, THE. [Gold bug]. **Added/Corp** Committee to Establish the Gold Standard. (19??)-. Periodical. English. Twelve times a year. $36.00. Committee to Establish the Gold Standard, 2151 Center Avenue, Fort Lee NJ 07024. **Tel** (201)461-2887.

LC TN760 .G67
DD 669/.22/05 SZ
GOLD BULLETIN & GOLD PATENT DIGEST. **Added/Corp** World Gold Council. **VFOAT** Gold Bulletin and Gold Patent Digest; Gold Bull. Vol. 21, No. 1 (1988)-. Bulletin. English. Four times a year (Mar., June, Oct., Dec.). Free on request. World Gold Council, 1 rue de la Rotisserie, CH-1204 Geneva Switzerland. **Tel** 011 41 22 219666. Documents available from Article Express International, CASDDS. **Formed by the union of** Gold Bulletin, 0017-1557 **and** Gold Patent Digest.
Ind/Abst Alum. Ind. Abstr.; Art Archaeol. Tech. Abstr.; Bioeng. Abstr.; Chem. Abstr.; Corros. Abstr. (199?-); Ei Page One; Eng. Index Annu.; Met. Abstr.; MINPROC; Mintec, Min. Technol. Abstr.; World Text. Abstr.

LC HG293 .G64 **ISSN** 0736-1777
DD 338.2/741/05 US
GOLD STATISTICS AND ANALYSIS. See Business and Economics-Abstracting, Bibliographies and Statistics.

LC HG1501
DD 332.1 US
GOLEMBE REPORTS. (19??)-. English. Irregular (approximately 10 per year). $340.00. CHG Consulting, PO Box 1119, Delray Beach FL 33447-1119. **Tel** (407)243-1205, FAX (407)243-0635. **ED** Carter H. Golembe.
Desc: Covers major public policy issues affecting financial institutions.

LC HG1501 **ISSN** 0743-5185
DD 332.1 US
GOURGUES REPORT, THE. See Business and Economics-Investments.

LC HG1501 **ISSN** 0436-2233
DD 332.1 PR
GOVBANK TECHNICAL PAPERS. **Main/Corp** Government Development Bank for Puerto Rico. No. 1 (1964)-. English. Government Development Bank for Puerto Rico, PO Box 42001, San Juan PR 00940. **Tel** (809)722-2525, FAX (809)268-5496.

LC HG4651 **ISSN** 0833-9430
DD 332.63/232/0971 CN
GOVERNMENT BOND RECORD. [Gov. bond rec.]. **Added/Corp** Financial Post Corporation Service Group. (1985 Edition)-. English. One time a year. 39.98Can$. Financial Post Company Ltd., 333 King Street East, Toronto Ontario M5A 4N2, Canada. **Tel**

Business and Economics — Banks and Banking

(416)350-6500, FAX (416)350-6601. **Continues** The Bond Record, 0317-607X.
Desc: Complete description of Canadian federal and provincial debt issues.

LC HG2051.U5 A2763 **ISSN** 0360-6279
DD 353.008/25 US
GOVERNMENT NATIONAL MORTGAGE ASSOCIATION EXAMINATION OF FINANCIAL STATEMENTS. **Main/Corp** United States. General Accounting Office. **Added/Corp** Government National Mortgage Association. (19??)-. English. Irregular. Comptroller General of the US, 490 l'Enfant Plaza SW, Washington DC 20219. **Continues** Examination of Financial Statements, the Government National Mortgage Association, the Federal National Mortgage Association.

LC HC291 .G753
DD 330 GR
GREECE'S WEEKLY : GREECE'S INTERNATIONAL NEWS MAGAZINE. (19??)-. Periodical. English. One time a week. Coronakis Press Ltd., 10 Fokidos Street, Athens 115 26 Greece. **Tel** 011 30 1 7706922. **Continues** Greece's Weekly for Business & Finance.

LC HG185.E2 G85
DD 332.1 EC
GUIA DEL SECTOR FINANCIERO ECUATORIANO. **VFOAT** Guia Financiera del Ecuador. No. 1 (1991)-. Spanish. Dinediciones S.A., 12 de Octubre y Lizardo Garcia, Quito Ecuardo. **Tel** 565-477.

LC HG3025 .G84
DD 332.1 FR
GUIDE DU BANQUIER, LE. **Added/Corp** Centre de Competence Bancaire (Paris, France). 1st Ed. (1987)-. French. One time a year. 200.00F. Guide du Banquier, 14 rue Champ-de-Mars, 75007 Paris France. **Tel** 011 33 1 45517534.

LC HF5415.12.F7 G84
DD 650 FR
GUIDE MARKETING MIX, LE. (1986)-. French. Ten times a year. 390.00F France, $480.00 other. Groupe Strategie, 15 bis rue Ernest Renan, 92133 Issy Mlineaux Cdx France. **Tel** 011 33 (1) 40930102, FAX (1)40 93 05 06, telex 202 003.

LC JN5060.A1 G84
DD 354/.495/002 GR
GUIDE. PUBLIC SERVICES, ORGANISATION OF PUBLIC AND PRIVATE LAW, BANKS, DIPLOMATIC CORPS, AIR COMPANIES, CONCISE GUIDE TO THESSALONIKI. English. .500 Each. Horizon / Greece, Public Relations Organization, 50A Nikis Str, Athens Greece 119.

LC HG1501
DD 332.1 UK
GUIDE TO CORPORATION TAX. (19??)-. Periodical. English. Four times a year. $398.80. Croner Publ Ltd., Croner House London Road, Kingston Upon Thames, Surrey KT2 6SR United Kingdom. **Tel** 011 44 181 5473333, FAX 011 44 181 5472637.

ISSN 0848-7855
DD 657/.32 CN
GUIDE TO PREPARING FINANCIAL STATEMENTS. [Guide prep. financ. statements]. **Added/Corp** Richard De Boo Publishers. **VFOAT** Preparing Financial Statements. (1990)-. English. $135.00 per set of 2 vols. Practitioners Publishing Company, PO Box 966, Fort Worth TX 76101-0966. **Tel** (800)332-3709.

LC HG1501 **ISSN** 0827-0864
DD 332.1/025/71 CN
GUIDE TO THE CANADIAN FINANCIAL SERVICES INDUSTRY. [Guide Can. financ. serv. ind.]. (1986)-. English. One time a year. $299.95. Financial Times of Canada, 444 Front Street West, Toronto Ontario M5V 3E6 Canada. **Tel** (416)585-5265, telex 06-218681. **Bk Rev**. **Ad Acc**. **Circ:** 1,000.
Desc: Profiles financial services industry in Canada including banks; trust, insurance and venture capital companies. Also profiles executives of these companies, government regulators, associations as well as twenty top accounting firms in Canada.

LC HG3330.T64 N623
DD 332 JA
GYOMU BENRAN. **Added/Corp** Nihon YushutsunyÂu Ginko. Nihon Yushutsunyu Ginko, Tokyo. Kaigai Toshi Kenkyujo. (19??)-. Japanese. One time a year. Nihon Yushutsunyo Ginko, 9-1 Otemachi 1-chome, Chiyoda-ku 100 Tokyo Japan.

LC HG3326 .N54a
DD 332.1 JA
GYOMU HOKOKUSHO - NIHON KAIHATSU GINKO. **Main/Corp** Nihon Kaihatsu Ginko. (19??)-. Periodical. Japanese. Nihon Kaihatsu Ginko Joho Senta, (Information Services Japan Development Bank), 9-1 Otemachi 1-chome Chiyoda-ku, Tokyo 100 Japan.

LC HG3330.T64 N625
DD 332 JA
GYOMU HOKOKUSHO - NIHON YUSHUTSUNYU GINKO. **Main/Corp** Nihon Yushutsunyu Ginko. (19??)-. Periodical. Japanese. One time a year. Nihon Yushutsunyo Ginko, 9-1 Otemachi 1-chome, Chiyoda-ku 100 Tokyo Japan.

LC HG2051.J4 A26
DD 332.31 JA
GYOMU TOKEI NEMPO - NORIN GYOGYO KINYU KOKO. **Main/Corp** Norin Gyogyo Kinyu Koko. (19??)-. Periodical. Japanese. Norin Gyogyo Kinyu Koko, 9-3 Otemachi 1-chome, Tokyo 100 Japan.

LC HG1501 **ISSN** 0018-473X
DD 332.1 US
HB. HOOSIER BANKER. (HOOSIER BANKER.). **Added/Corp** Indiana Bankers Association. (1916)-. Trade Publication. English. Twelve times a year. $27.00. Indiana Bankers Association, 1 North Capital/Suite 315, Indianapolis IN 46204. **Tel** (317)632-9533, FAX (317)236-0754. **ED** Laura Wilson. **Bk Rev**. **Ad Acc**. **Circ:** 4,000 (ctrl).
Desc: Official publication of Indiana Bankers Association serving Indiana's banking industry.

LC HG **ISSN** 1041-1860
DD 332 US
HENINGER/NOELL WEEKLY M&A "GREEN SHEET", THE. (M&A GREEN SHEET.). [Heninger/Noell wkly. M A "green sheet"]. **VFOAT** M and A Green Sheet. **VAT** Merger and Acquisitions Green Sheet. (Nov. 1986)-. Periodical. English. One time a week. $397.50. Sales Action of California, PO Box 352, Lancaster CA 93534. **Tel** (805)948-3799. **ED** June Heninger.
Desc: Charts merger and acquisition activity by SIC number, separating public, private, Canada, and foreign sellers.

LC HG **ISSN** 1052-7575
DD 332 US
TITLE CHANGE
HOSTETLER MEMO FOR BROKERS ONLY, THE. [Hostetler memo brok. only]. **VFOAT** For Brokers Only. (1989)-(19??). Periodical. English. Hostetler Communications, PO Box 97035, Raleigh NC 27624. **Tel** (919)870-8295. **Continued by** Brokers Only FBO News by Fax.

LC HG **ISSN** 0899-9791
DD 332 US
HVAC PROFITMAKER. **See** Heating, Plumbing, and Refrigeration.

LC HG353 .I57a
DD 769/.55/05 UK
I.B.N.S. JOURNAL. **Main/Corp** International Bank Note Society. **Added/Corp** International Bank Note Society. Journal. **VAT** International Bank Note Society Journal. Vol. 12, No. 6 (1973)-. Periodical. English. Four times a year. $10.20. **Continues** Quarterly Journal - International Bank Note Society.
Ind/Abst Numis. Lit. (199?-).

LC HG201 .D66
DD 332 US
TITLE CHANGE
IBC/DONOGHUE'S MONEY FUND REPORT. **Added/Corp** International Business Communications, Inc. **VFOAT** Money Fund Report; Donoghue's Money Fund Report; International Business Communications Donoghue's Money Fund Report. (May 1989)-(1993). Periodical. English. IBC Donoghue Organization, 290 Eliot Street, Ashland MA 01721. **Tel** (800)343-5413, (508)881-2800. **Continues** Donoghue's Money Fund Report, 0197-7091. **Continued by** Money Fund Report.

LC HG1501
DD 332.1 US
●**IBC'S MONEYLETTER**. **See** Business and Economics-Investments.

LC HG1501
DD 332.1 US
IBC'S QUARTERLY REPORT ON MONEY FUNDS PERFORMANCE. (19??)-. Periodical. English. Four times a year. $446.25 Massachusetts; $460.06 New York; $425.00 other. IBC Donoghue Organization, 290 Eliot Street, Ashland MA 01721. **Tel** (800)343-5413, (508)881-2800.

LC HG3881 .I486d
DD 332.1/538/05 US
IDB : MONTHLY NEWS FROM THE INTER-AMERICAN DEVELOPMENT BANK, THE. **Added/Corp** Inter-American Development Bank. **VFOAT** I.D.B. **VAT** Inter-American Development Bank. (April/May 1987)-. Periodical. English. Twelve times a year. Inter-American Development Bank, 1300 New York Avenue Northwest, Suite E 0105, Washington DC 20577. **Tel** (202)623-1381. **Continues** Inter-American Development Bank. IDB News, 0145-2274.

LC HG1501 **ISSN** 0018-9073
DD 332.1 US
IDB NEWSLETTER. **Main/Corp** Inter-American Development Bank. **VFOAT** I.D.B. Newsletter. Vol. 1, No. 1 (July 1963)-. Newsletter. English. Four times a year. Inter-American Development Bank, 1300 New York Avenue Northwest, Suite E 0105, Washington DC 20577. **Tel** (202)623-1381. Documents available from Documents on Demand.
Ind/Abst Environ. Abstr.

LC HG1501 **ISSN** 1076-8424
DD 332.1 US
●**IDB PROJECTS**. **VAT** Inter-American Development Bank projects. (1994)-. Periodical. English (Spanish). Ten times a year. $150.00. Inter-American Development Bank, 1300 New York Avenue Northwest, Suite E 0105, Washington DC 20577. **Tel** (202)623-1381.

LC HG1501 **ISSN** 0160-9238
DD 332.1 US
IFC GENERAL POLICIES. **Main/Corp** International Finance Corporation. **Added/Corp** International Finance Corporation. General Policies. **VAT** International Finance Corporation General Policies. (1962)-. English. International Finance Corporation, 1818 H Street NW, Washington DC 20433. **Tel** (202)473-8979, (202)473-8981.

LC HG1501
DD 332.1 UK
IFR GLOBAL FINANCING DIRECTORY, THE. (1987)-. Directory. English. One time a year. $333.69. IFR Publishing Ltd., Aldgate House, 33 Aldgate High Street, London EC3N 1DL United Kingdom. **Tel** 011 44 171 369 7536, FAX 011 44 171 369 7395, telex 889365/8953051 IFRPUBG. (**Subscription address:** IFR Publishing, 90 Broad Street, Second Floor, New York NY 10004.)

LC HG1501 **ISSN** 0019-185X
DD 332.1 US
ILLINOIS BANKER. [Ill. bank.]. (19??)-. Periodical. English. Twelve times a year. $60.00. Illinois Bankers Association, 111 North Canal Street, Suite 1111, Chicago IL 60606. **Tel** (312)876-9900, FAX (312)876-3826. **ED** Meg Bullock. **Ad Acc**. **Circ:** 2,500.
Desc: Informs readers on public policy issues affecting banking, also ideas on operations, management, banking and business trends in the Midwest.

LC HG3881 .I6197 HG3879 .I57 **ISSN** 0047-083X
DD 332.1/52 US
IMF SURVEY. [IMF surv.]. **Main/Corp** International Monetary Fund. **VAT** International Monetary Fund Survey. Vol. 1 (Aug. 14, 1972)-. Periodical. English (French and Spanish). Twenty-three times a year (plus one supplement). Free on request. International Monetary Fund, 700 19th Street Northwest, Publishing Unit, Washington DC 20431. **Tel** (202)623-7430, FAX (202)623-7201. **ED** Alexander Mountford. Index available. available on microfilm and microfiche from University Microfilms International (UMI); available on an online database (file 648/Full-Text) from DIALOG.
Desc: Topical report of the Fund's activities; press releases, texts of communiques and major statements, SCR valuations and exchange rates presented in broader context of developments in the world economy, economic research and policy, national economies and international finance.
Ind/Abst F&S Index Plus Text, Int. [Select. Cov.]; Index Period. Artic. Relat. Law; Leis., Rec., Tour. Abstr.; Predicasts Forecasts; Rural Dev. Abstr.; Trade Ind. Index (1981-?); World Agric. Econ. Rural Sociol. Abstr.

LC HG3810 .I45
DD 332/.042/05 US
IMF WORKING PAPER. **Added/Corp** International Monetary Fund. **VAT** International Monetary Fund Working Paper. (1988)-. Monographic series. English. Irregular. $210.00. International Monetary Fund, 700 19th Street Northwest, Publishing Unit, Washington DC 20431. **Tel** (202)623-7430, FAX (202)623-7201.
Ind/Abst Soyabean Abstr.; World Agric. Econ. Rural Sociol. Abstr.

LC HG **ISSN** 1061-3536
DD 332 US
IN RE, EAGLE-PICHER INDUSTRIES, INC., ET AL. (IN RE, EAGLE-PICHER INDUSTRIES, INC., ET AL. : THE NEWSLETTER DEVOTED TO COVERAGE OF THE CHAPTER 11 PROCEEDINGS UNDER THE BANKRUPTCY REFORM ACT.). [In re, Eagle-Picher Ind. Inc. et al.]. **Added/Corp** Bankruptcy Creditors' Service. Bankruptcy Report No. 1 (1991)-. Newsletter. English. One time a week. $40.00(single issue). Bankruptcy Creditors' Service, Inc., 6326 Graceland Avenue, Cincinnati OH 45237-4808.

LC HG ISSN 0749-8543
DD 332 US
INCOME PER SHARE BEFORE SECURITIES GAINS OR LOSSES. [Income per share before secur. gains losses]. Trade Publication. English. Four times a year. Salomon Brothers Center / Finance, 7 World Trade Center, 36th Floor, New York NY 10048. **Tel** (212)747-7000.

LC HG1501
DD 332.1 US
INDEBTEDNESS. Main/Corp Wisconsin. Bureau of Local Financial Assistance. 1976-. English. One time a year. Department of Revenue / Wisconsin, PO Box 8933, 125 South Webster Street, Madison WI 53708. **Tel** (608)266-8661. ***Continues** Indebtedness.*

LC HG1501 ISSN 0019-3674
DD 332.1 US
INDEPENDENT BANKER. [Indep. bank.]. **Added/Corp** Independent Bankers Association of America. (195?)-. Trade Publication. English. Twelve times a year. $35.00. The Independent Bankers Association of America, PO Box 267, Sauk Centre MN 56378. **Tel** (612)352-6546. **ED** Dave Bordewyk, Elmer Ramos. **Ad Acc, Adv Mgr:** F Moeckel, **Tel** (301)469-0800. **Circ:** 10,000 (ctrl). available on microfilm and microfiche from University Microfilms International (UMI).
Desc: Trade journal for officers of small banks. Content features bank administration, credit, personnel development, marketing, auditing and operations.
Ind/Abst PAIS Int. Print (1991-).

LC HG1501
DD 332.1 US
INDEX TO BANK LETTERS, BULLETINS, AND REVIEWS : SOURCES. Vol. 1 (1976)-. Bulletin. English. KTO Press, Route 100, Millwood NY 10546.

LC HG41 .I6 ISSN 0019-4794
DD 332.1/0954 II
INDIAN FINANCE. (1928)-. Periodical. English. One time a week. K.K. Roy Private Ltd., PO Box 10210, 55 Gariahat Road, Calcutta 700019 India. **Tel** 011 91 33 4754872, 011 91 33 4755069.

LC HG4751 .P44 ISSN 1049-4596
DD 332.63/22 US
INDIVIDUAL INVESTOR (NEW YORK, N.Y.). (INDIVIDUAL INVESTOR.). [Individ. investor]. Vol. 9, No. 101 (April 1990)-. Periodical. English. Twelve times a year. $36.00. Individual Investor Group Inc, 333 7th Avenue, 5th Floor, New York NY 10001. **Tel** (212)843-2777. **(Subscription address:** Kable Publishers Aide / Illinois, 308 East Hitt Street, Subscription Department, Mt. Morris IL 61054-1473. **Tel** (815)734-1261.**)** ***Continues** Penny Stock Journal, 0745-4457.*

LC HG1501 ISSN 0744-6268
DD 332.1 US
INDIVIDUAL RETIREMENT PLANS GUIDE : IRA, SEP, KEOGH. Added/Corp Commerce Clearing House. (1982)-. Periodical. English. Twelve times a year. $240.00. Commerce Clearing House Inc., 4025 West Peterson Avenue, Chicago IL 60646-6085. **Tel** (312)583-8500, FAX (708)940-4600. **ED** A. E. Schechter.
Desc: Keeps subscribers informed on changes in the tax, contribution, reporting and disclosure, qualification, prohibited transactions, withdrawal, distribution, rollover and other rules that apply to these plans.

LC HF5681.R25 I533
DD 650 US
INDUSTRY NORMS & RATIOS, ONE YEAR. FINANCE, REAL ESTATE, SERVICES. Added/Corp Dun & Bradstreet Information Services. **VFOAT** Industry Norms and Ratios, One Year. Finance, Real Estate, Services; Industry Norms & Key Business Ratios, One Year Edition. Finance, Real Estate, Services; Norms & Ratios, One Year. Finance, Real Estate, Services. (1989/1990)-. English. Dun & Bradstreet Information Services, 3 Sylvan Way, Parsippany NJ 07054. **Tel** (201)605-6000, (800)526-0651. ***Continues** Industry Norms & Ratios, One Year. Finance, Insurance, Real Estate, Services.*

LC WMLC 91/3395 ISSN 0019-946X
DD 338.951/249 CH
INDUSTRY OF FREE CHINA. (TZU YU CHUNG-KUO CHIH KUNG YEH.). [Ind. free China]. **Added/Corp** Hsing Cheng Yuan Ching chi she chi wei Yuan hui (China) China (Republic : 1949-). Industrial Development Commission. **VFOAT** Industry of Free China. (1954)-. Periodical. Chinese (English). Twelve times a year. Free on request. Council for Economic Planning and Development, Nanjing E Road Sec 2 9th Floor 87, Taipei 10408 Taiwan. **Tel** 02 522 5403. **ED** W. P. Chang.
Ind/Abst Asia.-Pac. Econ. Lit.; PAIS Int. Print.

LC HD49.5 ISSN 0229-3234
DD 332.4/1/0971 CN
CEASED
INFLATION IN CANADA. (INFLATION IN CANADA : A MONETARIST INTERPRETATION & FORECAST.). (Spring 1978)-(19??). English. Friedberg Commodity Management Co., 347 Bay Street/Suite 1100, Toronto Ontario M5H 2P7 Canada. **Tel** (416)364-1171, FAX (416)364-0572, telex 065-24674. **ED** Albert D. Friedberg.

LC HG201 .I48
DD 332.4 IO
INFOBANK. See Business and Economics-Abstracting, Bibliographies and Statistics.

LC HG2911 .I54
DD 332 EC
INFORMACION ESTADISTICA MENSUAL. Added/Corp Banco Central del Ecuador. No. 1,687 (Sept. 30 1992)-. Statistical Publication. Spanish. Twelve times a year. Free on request. Banco Central Ecuador Libreria, Casilla 339, Quito Ecuador. **Tel** 011 593 2 516932. ***Continues** Informacion Estadistica Quincenal.*

LC HG185.C5 I53
DD 332.1/025/83 CL
INFORMACION FINANCIERA (SANTIAGO, CHILE). (INFORMACION FINANCIERA.). **Added/Corp** Chile. Superintendencia de Bancos e Instituciones Financieras. Chile. Superintendencia de Bancos e Instituciones Financieras. Departamento de Procesamiento e Informacion. (Oct. 1978)-. Spanish. Sixteen times a year. $300.00. Superintendencia de Bancos, Casilla 15 D, Santiago Chile. **Tel** 011 56 2 6990072.

ISSN 0713-3804
DD 657/.3/0971 CN
INFORMATION FINANCIERE ET LES FLUCTUATIONS DES PRIX, L'. Added/Corp Clarkson, Gordon & Co. (197?)-. Periodical. French. Irregular. Free. Clarkson Gordon, 630 Ouest boulevard Dorchester, Bureau 2000, Montreal Quebec H3B 1T9 Canada.

LC HG
DD 332 UK
●**INFORMATION SOURCES IN FINANCE AND BANKING.** (1994)-. Directory. English. Irregular. £55.00. Bowker - Saur Ltd., A Reed Reference Publishing Company, Part of the Reed Elsevier Group, Maypole House, Maypole Road, East Grinstead, West Sussex RH19 1HH United Kingdom. **Tel** 011 44 342 330100, FAX 011 44 342 330191. **(Subscription address:** Butterworths Service Co., Borough Green, Sevenoaks, Kent TN15 8PH United Kingdom. **Tel** 011 44 732 884567.**) ED** R.G. Lester.
Desc: Includes information on both computerized and traditional sources of the financial system.

LC HG1501
DD 332.1 SP
INFORME ANUAL. Main/Corp Instituto de Credito Oficial (Spain). (1990)-. Spanish. Instituto de Credito Oficial, Paseo del Prado 4, 28014 Madrid Spain. **Tel** 4474700, FAX 5311915. ***Continues** Instituto de Credito Oficial (Spain). Memoria del Grupo ICO.*

LC HG2766 .A145 ISSN 0067-3226
DD 332.1 NQ
INFORME ANUAL / BANCO CENTRAL DE NICARAGUA. Main/Corp Banco Central de Nicaragua. 1st- 1961-. Spanish. One time a year. Banco Central de Nicaragua, APDO 2252, Managua Niger.

LC HC79.C3 I52 ISSN 1063-0260
DD 338.4/3363/05 US
INFRASTRUCTURE FINANCE. [Infrastruct. finance]. **Added/Corp** Institutional Investor, Inc. (1992)-. Trade Publication. English. Six times a year. $200.00. Institutional Investor Inc., 488 Madison Avenue, New York NY 10022. **Tel** (212)303-3234, (212)303-3233, FAX (212)303-3353.

LC HG1501
DD 332.1 US
CEASED
INSIDE FINANCIAL SERVICES MARKETING. (19??)-(Jan. 9, 1995). Newsletter. English. Hoke Communications Inc, 224 7th Street, Garden City NY 11530. **Tel** (516)746-6700, (800)229-6700.
Desc: Directed to marketing executives in the insurance, banking, investments and credit card areas with emphasis on databased marketing.

LC HG1501
DD 332.1 US
INSIDE MORTGAGE CAPITAL MARKETS. (1985)-. Periodical. English. One time a week (48 times a year). $535.00. Inside Mortgage Finance Inc., PO Box 42387, Washington DC 20015. **Tel** (301)951-1240, FAX (301)656-1709.
Desc: Complete coverage of the mortgage related securities market and secondary mortgage market including regulatory and market developments of derivative products. Includes exclusive data on all mortgage related securities broken down by type, issuer, collateral, rating, underwriter, etc. as well as rankings of issuers and underwriters. Complete coverage of private label MBS market.

LC HG ISSN 8756-0003
DD 332 US
INSIDE MORTGAGE FINANCE. [Insid. mortg. finance]. **Added/Corp** Financial World Publications. (1984)-. Periodical. English. Forty-eight times a year. $595.00. Inside Mortgage Finance Inc., PO Box 42387, Washington DC 20015. **Tel** (301)951-1240, FAX (301)656-1709. **ED** Guy D. Cecola. Index available (free on request).
Desc: Complete coverage and analysis of market trends and developments affecting residential mortgage finance. Emphasis on legislative and regulatory changes impacting mortgage lending and mortgage servicing as well as mortgage products. Regular analysis on mortgage banking and thrift business, and underwriting change.

ISSN 1059-1400
DD 333 US
INSIDE MORTGAGE FINANCE'S CRA/HMDA UPDATE. [Inside mort. financ. CRA/HMDA update]. **VFOAT** CRA/HMDA Update; CRA, HMDA Update. **VAT** Inside Mortgage Finance's Community Reinvestment Act, Mortgage Disclosure Act Update; Community Reinvestment Act, Mortgage Disclosure Act Update. (1990)-. Periodical. English. Twelve times a year. $395.00. Inside Mortgage Finance Inc., PO Box 42387, Washington DC 20015. **Tel** (301)951-1240, FAX (301)656-1709.
Desc: Coverage and analysis of regulatory compliance issues and legislative developments. Focus on CRA protests, fair lending issues, lender and agency affordable housing programs, including the Federal Home Loan Banks' popular Affordable Housing Program.

LC HG1501 ISSN 1065-6413
DD 332.1 US
INSIGHTS & STRATEGIES. (INSIGHTS & STRATEGIES : FINANCIAL AND ESTATE PLANNING.). **VFOAT** Insights and Srategies. (1992)-. Periodical. English. Twenty-four times a year. $95.00. Insights and Strategies Inc., 390 Plandome Road, Manhasset NY 11030.

LC HG ISSN 0959-5791
DD 332 UK
INSOLVENCY (LONDON). (INSOLVENCY.). [Insolvency Lond.]. (1989)-. English. One time a year. $427.80. Longman Group Ltd., Fourth Avenue, Longman House, Harlow Essex CM19 5SR United Kingdom. **Tel** 011 44 1279 429655, FAX 011 44 1279 431067, telex 81259. ***Continues** Bankruptcy (London), 0267-0933.*

LC HG1642.U5 R48 ISSN 1041-6390
DD 332.7/42/0973021 US
INSTALLMENT CREDIT REPORT. [Install. credit rep.]. **Added/Corp** American Bankers Association. **VFOAT** Consumer Installment Credit Report; Installment Credit Report. (1988)-. English. One time a year. $264.00 (nonmembers), $164.00 (members). American Bankers Association, 1120 Connecticut Avenue Northwest, Washington DC 20036. **Tel** (202)663-5221, (202)663-5000, FAX (202)828-4544. **(Subscription address:** American Bankers Association / Maryland, PO Box 630544, Order Processing Department, Baltimore MD 21263.**)** ***Continues in part** Retail Bank Credit Report, 0276-9093.*

LC HG ISSN 0897-4527
DD 332 US
INSTITUTE TODAY. [Inst. today]. Vol. 88, Issue 1 (Jan./Feb. 1988)-. Periodical. English. Six times a year. $30.00. Institute of Certified Financial Planners, 7600 East Eastman Avenue, Suite 301, Denver CO 80231. **Tel** (303)751-7600, (800)322-ICFP, FAX (303)751-1037. **ED** Leslie S Emerson. **Ad Acc. Circ:** 10,000 (ctrl). ***Continues** Newsworthy, 0883-7120.*
Desc: Membership newsletter featuring institute and professional information.

LC HG1505 .A8 ISSN 0311-0192
DD 332/.09931 AT
INSURANCE & BANKING RECORD, THE. VAT Insurance and Banking Record. (1973)-. Periodical. English. Eleven times a year (monthly except Jan.). 55.00Aus$. Craftsman Publishing Pty. Ltd., 125 Highway Road, Burwood Victoria 3165 Australia. **Tel** 011 61 03 808 9622, FAX 011 61 03 808 0317. **ED** Edward Morgan. **Bk Rev. Ad Acc. Circ:** 1,200. ***Continues** Australasian Insurance & Banking Record, 0004-8372.*

LC HG1501 ISSN 0816-1224
DD 332.15 AT
INTERDATA FINANCIAL HANDBOOK. [Interdata financ. handb.]. 5th Ed. (Oct. 1989)-. English. One time a year. 100.72Aus$. IDP Interdata Pty Ltd, Suite 5 9 Natier Street, North Sydney New South Wales, 2060 Australia. **Tel** 11 61 2 957 2881.

LC HG1501 ISSN 0308-9002
DD 332 US
INTEREST RATE SERVICE. [Interest rate serv.]. **Added/Corp** International Currency Review, Ltd. Vol. 1 (June 20, 1977)-. Periodical. English. Four times a year. $950.00. World Reports Ltd., 108 Horse Ferry Road, Westminster, London SW1P 2EF United Kingdom. **Tel** 011 44 171 2223836, FAX 11 44 171 2330185.
Desc: Consists of interest rate/country reports, global monetary analysis, extensive interest rate and monetary data and charts, comprehensive interest rate statistics, and a separate section of global interest rate charts.

LC HG1501
DD 332.1 UK
INTERNATIONAL, THE. Added/Corp Financial Times Business Information Ltd. Issue No. 1 (Mar. 1988)-. Periodical. English. Twelve times a year. £60.00. FT Business Information Ltd., Fetter Lane, Greystoke Pl Kirkland, London EC4A 1ND United Kingdom. **Tel** 011 44 171 4056969, FAX 011 44 171 8312181, telex 883694. **ED** David Turner. **Ad Acc, Adv Mgr:** R. Symondon. **Circ:** 40,000 (ctrl).
Desc: International financial advice for the global investor and saver.

LC HG1501
DD 332.1 UK
INTERNATIONAL BANK ACCOUNTING. (19??)-. Periodical. English. Irregular. Euromoney Publications PLC, Nestor House, Playhouse Yard, London EC4Z 5EX United Kingdom. **Tel** 011 44 171 7798888, FAX 011 44 171 7798630, telex 290700 EUROMON G.

LC HG1501 ISSN 1042-3370
DD 332 US
INTERNATIONAL BANKING FOCUS. [Int. bank. focus]. **Added/Corp** Institute of International Bankers (U.S.). (19??)-. Periodical. English (Japanese). Twelve times a year. $190.00. Institute of International Bankers, 299 Park Avenue, 38th Floor, New York NY 10017. **Tel** (212)421-1611. **ED** Larry Uhlick. cum. index. **Circ:** 1,500 (ctrl). ***Continues** Foreign Bank Focus, 0748-9366.*

LC HG3810 .I47
DD 332.4/5/05 SA
INTERNATIONAL BUSINESS REPORT. Added/Corp Standard Bank of South Africa Limited (1962-). International Division. (1973)-. English. Twenty-six times a year. Standard Bank Centre, 15th Floor, 78 Fox Street, Johannesburg 2001 South Africa. ***Continues** Standard Bank International Business Report.*

LC HG3881 .I5756 ISSN 0020-6490
DD 332.1/5/05 UK
INTERNATIONAL CURRENCY REVIEW. [Int. curr. rev.]. (Feb. 1969)-. Periodical. English. Four times a year. Including Occasional Papers: £225.00 UK and Ireland; $465.00 US. World Reports Ltd., 108 Horse Ferry Road, Westminster, London SW1P 2EF United Kingdom. **Tel** 011 44 171 2223836, FAX 11 44 171 2330185. **ED** Christopher Story.
Desc: Independent review of global financial and economic affairs with specific relevance to the foreign exchange markets.
Ind/Abst Contents Recent Econ. J.; PAIS Int. Print (1991-).

LC HG1501 ISSN 0823-1362
DD 332.1/5/025 CN
INTERNATIONAL DIRECTORY - ROYAL BANK OF CANADA. (INTERNATIONAL DIRECTORY.). [Int. dir. - Roy. Bank Can.]. **Main/Corp** Royal Bank of Canada. (19??)-. Directory. English. One time a year. Royal Bank of Canada, 200 Bay Street, 18th Floor South Tower, Toronto Ontario M5J 2J5 Canada. **Tel** (416)974-7242.

LC HG1501
DD 332.1 UK
INTERNATIONAL FINANCIAL PRODUCTS. (19??)-. English. $1,295.00. IFR Publishing Ltd., Aldgate House, 33 Aldgate High Street, London EC3N 1DL United Kingdom. **Tel** 011 44 171 369 7536, FAX 011 44 171 369 7395, telex 889365/8953051 IFRPUBG. **(Subscription address:** IFR Publishing, 90 Broad Street, Second Floor, New York NY 10004. **)**

LC HG1501 ISSN 0250-7471
DD 332.1 US
CEASED
INTERNATIONAL FINANCIAL STATISTICS ANUARIO. See Business and Economics-Abstracting, Bibliographies and Statistics.

LC HG61 .I57 ISSN 0250-7463
DD 332/.02/12 US
INTERNATIONAL FINANCIAL STATISTICS YEARBOOK - INTERNATIONAL MONETARY FUND. See Business and Economics-Abstracting, Bibliographies and Statistics.

LC HG3879 .I567 ISSN 0953-0223
DD 332/.042/05 UK
INTERNATIONAL FINANCING REVIEW. (INTERNATIONAL FINANCING REVIEW : IFR.). [Int. financ. rev.]. **VFOAT** IFR. (1984)-. Periodical. English. Fifty-one times per year (Sat. except Christmas). $4095.00. IFR Publishing Ltd., Aldgate House, 33 Aldgate High Street, London EC3N 1DL United Kingdom. **Tel** 011 44 171 369 7536, FAX 011 44 171 369 7395, telex 889365/8953051 IFRPUBG. **(Subscription address:** IFR Publishing, 90 Broad Street, 2nd Floor, New York NY 10004. **Tel** (212)952-7060.**)** ***Continues** AGEFI International Financing Review.*

LC HG1501
DD 332.1 UK
INTERNATIONAL FUTURES DATABOOK. (19??)-. Periodical. English. Four times a year. £149.00 UK; $320.00 US, Canada and South America. Metal Bulletin PLC, PO Box 28E, Worcester Park, Surrey KT4 7HY United Kingdom. **Tel** 011 44 171 8279977, FAX 011 44 171 3378943.

LC HG1501 ISSN 0265-2323
DD 332.1 UK
CCC
CODEN IJBMES
INTERNATIONAL JOURNAL OF BANK MARKETING. [Int. j. bank mark.]. **VFOAT** Bank Marketing. Vol. 1, No. 1 (1983)-. Periodical. English. Eight times a year. $3739.00. MCB University Press, 60 62 Toller Lane, Bradford, West Yorkshire BD8 9BY United Kingdom. **Tel** 011 44 1274 785280, FAX 011 44 1274 785200, telex 51317-MCBUNI-G. **(Subscription address:** MCB University Press / US and Canada Subscriptions, PO Box 10812, Birmingham AL 35201-0812. **Tel** (205)995-1567, (800)633-4931, FAX (205)995-1588.**) ED** Trevor Watkins and John Gwin. **Ad Acc.** available on an online database (file 15/Full-Text) from DIALOG. Documents available from UMI Article Clearinghouse, Ask*IEEE.
Desc: Aims to present the latest innovations and research findings on all the issues of concern for bank marketers. Focuses attention on the adoption and implementation of marketing planning and management in personal, corporate and international banking.
Ind/Abst ABI/INFORM Glob. Ed.; ABI/INFORM [Computer File] (1983-); Anbar Account. Finan. Abstr. [Full Txt.]; Anbar Mark. Distr. Abstr. [Full Txt.]; Anbar Top Manage. Abstr. [Full Txt.]; Contents Pages Manage.; Curr. Cit.; Gen. BusinessFile (1992-); INSPEC (1986-); Manage. Bibliogr. Rev.; Oper. Prod. Manage. Abstr. [Full Txt.]; Person. Train. Abstr. [Full Txt.].

LC HG1505 .I52
DD 332.1/53/05 II
INTERNATIONAL JOURNAL OF DEVELOPMENT BANKING : IJDB. Added/Corp Industrial Credit and Investment Corporation of India. **VFOAT** IJDB. Vol. 1, No. 1 (Jan. 1983)-. Periodical. English. Two times a year. $40.00. Industrial Credit and Investment Corporation of India Ltd, 163 Backbay Reclamation, Bombay 400 020 India. **Tel** 2022535, FAX 2046582, telex 11 3062 ICIC IN. **(Subscription address:** Prints India, 11 Darya Ganj, New Delhi 110002 India. **Tel** 011 91 11 3268645, FAX 011 91 11 3275542, telex 31-61087 PRIN-IN.**) ED** N Jhaveri and Nita Mukherjee. **Bk Rev. Ad Acc. Circ:** 300.
Desc: Concerned with development banking; provides a medium for exchange of information and views among development bankers and contributes to the growth of literature on the subject.

LC HG3901 ISSN 0711-5644
DD 332.4/56/05 CN
INTERNATIONAL MONEY MARKETS (TORONTO). (INTERNATIONAL MONEY MARKETS.). [Int. money mark.]. **Added/Corp** Royal Bank of Canada. International Money Markets. (1981)-. Periodical. English. Six times a year. Free on request. Royal Bank of Canada Economics Group, Royal Bank Plaza, South Tower, 18th Floor, Toronto Ontario M5J 2J5 Canada. **Tel** (416)974-2274. ***Continues** Foreign Exchange (Montreal, Quebec), 0227-1648.*

LC HG ISSN 0020-8507
DD 332 US
CCC
INTERNATIONAL REPORTS. [Int. rep.]. **VFOAT** Financial Times International Reports; IR. (194?)-. Periodical. English. One time a week (51 issues). $645.00. United Communications Group, 11300 Rockville Pike, Suite 1100, Rockville MD 20852. **Tel** (301)816-8950 ext. 313, FAX (301)816-8945. **ED** Brooke Unger. available on an online database from Lexis-Nexis; and DATA-STAR.
Desc: Authoritative summary of trends and developments in foreign exchange, interest rates, international debt, and the economic and investment environment in important markets worldwide.
Ind/Abst PTS Newsl. Database [Full Txt.].

LC HB1 .I47 ISSN 1059-0560
DD 330/.05 US
INTERNATIONAL REVIEW OF ECONOMICS & FINANCE. (INTERNATIONAL REVIEW OF ECONOMICS & FINANCE : IREF.). [Int. rev. econ. finance]. **VFOAT** IREF; International Review of Economics and Finance. Vol. 1, No. 1 (1992)-. Trade Publication. English. Four times a year. $165.00. JAI Press Inc., 55 Old Post Road, Suite 2, PO Box 1678, Greenwich CT 06836-1678. **Tel** (203)661-7602, FAX (203)661-0792.

LC HG1 .I48 ISSN 1057-5219
DD 332/.05 US
INTERNATIONAL REVIEW OF FINANCIAL ANALYSIS. [Int. rev. financ. analy.]. Vol. 1, No. 1 (1992)-. Trade Publication. English. Three times a year. $160.00. JAI Press Inc., 55 Old Post Road, Suite 2, PO Box 1678, Greenwich CT 06836-1678. **Tel** (203)661-7602, FAX (203)661-0792.

LC HG1501
DD 332.1 UK
INTERNATIONAL RISK MANAGEMENT. (19??)-. Periodical. English. Four times a year. £38.50 UK; £55.00 Europe; £66.00 other. EMAP Readerlink, Audit House, 260 Field End Road, Ruislip Middlesex HA4 9LT United Kingdom. **Tel** 011 44 1773 63100, FAX 011 44 1733 87367. **(Subscription address:** EMAP Business Publishing, 4 Admiral House Cardinal Way, Middlesex HA3 5SQ United Kingdom. **Tel** 011 44 181 8684499.**)**

LC HG1501 ISSN 0964-9301
DD 332.1 UK
INTERNATIONAL SECURITIES LENDING. VFOAT Securities Lending. (19??)-. Periodical. English. Four times a year. $220.00. Euromoney Publications PLC, Nestor House, Playhouse Yard, London EC4Z 5EX United Kingdom. **Tel** 011 44 171 7798888, FAX 011 44 171 7798630, telex 290700 EUROMON G. Documents available from UMI Article Clearinghouse.
Desc: Profiles the activities of lenders and borrowers, providing coverage of the international securities lending and repo markets.
Ind/Abst ABI/INFORM Glob. Ed.

LC HG4027.5 .I583 ISSN 0883-4601
DD 658.1/599/05 US
INTERNATIONAL TREASURY SERVICES. See Finance-Public Finance.

LC HG1501
DD 332.1 MX
INVERSIONISTA MEXICANO, EL. (19??)-. Periodical. Spanish (English). Twenty-two times a year. $370.00. El Inversionista Mexicano, Felix Cuevas 301-204, Col Valle, 03100 Mexico D F Mexico. **Tel** 011 52 5 5349297, 011 52 5 5245396. **ED** Evangelina Astorsa. **Circ:** 4,000.

LC HG1501 ISSN 0759-7673
DD 332.1 FR
INVESTIR (PARIS). (INVESTIR.). (1974)-. Periodical. French. One time a week. $187.01. Investir, 16 rue de la Banque, 75002 Paris France. **Tel** 33 1 44584800, FAX 33 1 44584801.

LC HG4501 .I732 ISSN 0021-0080
DD 332 US
CCC
INVESTMENT DEALERS' DIGEST, THE. [Investm. deal. dig.]. **VFOAT** Dealer's Digest. (1935)-. Periodical. English. Fifty-one times per year. $495.00. Investment Dealers Digest Inc., Two World Trade Center, 18th Floor, New York NY 10048. **Tel** (212)227-1200, FAX (212)432-1039. **ED** Derek Drew. **Bk Rev. Ad Acc. Circ:** 5,000. available on microfilm and microfiche from University Microfilms International (UMI).
Desc: Covers the debt and equity markets, issues in registration, investment banking, and corporate finance.
Ind/Abst Account. Tax Datab. (Jul. 1991-) [Full Txt.]; F&S Index Plus Text, Int. [Full Txt.] [Select. Cov.]; Predicasts; PROMT [Full Txt.]; Public Aff. Inf. Serv. Bull.; Trade Ind. Index.

LC HG1501
DD 332.1 US
INVESTOR'S DAILY. See Business and Economics-Investments.

LC HG1 .I62 ISSN 1076-3805
DD 332.6/05 US
●**INVESTOR'S WORLD.** [Invest. world]. (1993)-. Periodical. English. Twelve times a year. $99.00. Investor's World, 7811 Montrose Road, Potomac MD 20854. **Tel** (800)777-5005, FAX (310)340-2647. ***Continues** John Dessauer's Investor's World.*

LC HG1501 ISSN 1074-8903
DD 332.1 US
CCC
●**IOMA'S REPORT ON MANAGING CREDIT, RECEIVABLES & COLLECTIONS. Added/Corp** Institute of Management and Administration. **VFOAT** IOMA's Report on Managing Credit, Receivables and Collections. (1994)-. Periodical. English. Twelve times a year. $195.00. Institute of Management and Administration, 29 West 35th Street, 5th Floor, New York NY 10001-2299. **Tel** (212)244-0360, FAX (212)564-0465.

LC HC257.I6 I7 ISSN 0021-1060
DD 338.941 IE
IRISH BANKING REVIEW, THE. [Ir. bank. rev.]. (Nov. 1957)-. Periodical. English. Four times a year. $6.00. Irish Banking Review, Nassau House, Nassau Street, Dublin 2 Ireland. **Tel** 353 1 715311, FAX 353 1 796880, telex 93957. **ED** Stewart Mackinnon. Index available. cum. index. **Circ:** 5,000 (ctrl).
Desc: The aim of the review is to stimulate independent economic thought and discussion.
Ind/Abst Contents Recent Econ. J.; Curr. Cit.; Dairy Sci. Abstr.; J. Econ. Lit.; Leis., Rec., Tour. Abstr.; PAIS Int. Print; Rural Dev. Abstr.; World Agric. Econ. Rural Sociol. Abstr.

LC HG1501
DD 332.1 SZ
ISSA NEWSLETTER. **Added/Corp** International Society of Securities Administrators. (19??)-. Newsletter. English. Two times a year. Union Bank of Switzerland / UBS, Economic Research Department, PO Box 8021, Zurich Switzerland. **Tel** 011 41 1 2344243.
Ind/Abst Chem. Hazards Ind.; Lab. Hazards Bull.

LC HG ISSN 1048-5120
DD 332 US
CCC
ITEM PROCESSING REPORT. (ITEM PROCESSING REPORT : NEW TECHNOLOGIES AND STRATEGIES FOR REMITTANCE AND CHECK PROCESSING EXECUTIVES.). [Item process. rep.]. **VFOAT** New Technologies and Strategies for Remittance and Check Processing Executives. (1990)-. Periodical. English. Twenty-five times a year. $495.00. Phillips Business Information Inc., 1201 Seven Locks Road, PO Box 61130, Potomac MD 20854. **Tel** (301)424-3338, (301)340-1520, (800)777-5005, FAX (301)424-4297, telex 358149. available on an online database (file 636/Full-Text) from DIALOG. ***Absorbed** The Powell Report.*
Ind/Abst PTS Newsl. Database [Full Txt.].

LC HG3111 .J32
DD 332.1 NE
JAARVERSLAG (NEDERLANDSCHE BANK (AMSTERDAM, NETHERLANDS)). (JAARVERSLAG.). **Added/Corp** Nederlandsche Bank (Amsterdam, Netherlands). (19??)-. Dutch. One time a year. Free. De Nederlandsche Bank NV, Postbus 98, 1000 AB Amsterdam Netherlands. **Tel** 011 31 20 5249111. ***Continues** Nederlandsche Bank (Amsterdam, Netherlands). Verslag Van Den President en Verslag Van de Commissarissen.*

LC HG1939.A8 H3
DD 332.2/1/09436 AU
JAHRESBERICHT - HAUPTVERBAND DER OSTERREICHISCHEN SPARKASSEN. **Main/Corp** Hauptverband der Osterreichischen Sparkassen. German. Grimmelshausengasse 1, Vienna Austria. ***Continues** Tatigkeitsbericht / Hauptverband der Osterreichischen Sparkassen.*

LC HG1501 ISSN 0448-8520
DD 332.1 JA
JAPAN BANKING BRIEFS. (196?)-. Periodical. English. Twelve times a year. The Fuji Bank Ltd, 1-chome Otemachi Chiyoda-ku, Tokyo Japan.
Ind/Abst Predicasts F&S Index, U. S. Annu. Ed.

LC HG ISSN 1049-4383
DD 332 US
TITLE CHANGE
JAPAN M&A REPORTER. (JAPAN M & A REPORTER.). [Jpn. M&A report.]. **Added/Corp** Ulmer Brothers, Inc. **VFOAT** Japan M & A Reporter; Japan M and A Reporter. **VAT** Japan Merger & Acquisition Reporter; Japan Merger and Acquisition Reporter. Vol. 1, No. 1 (Jan./Feb. 1987)-(199?). Periodical. English. Ulmer Brothers Inc., 80 Maiden Lane, 22nd Floor, New York NY 10038. **Tel** (212)344-4411, FAX (212)344-8074. **ED** Rebecca Fannin. **Ad Acc, Adv Mgr:** Dan Schwartz. **Circ:** 250. ***Merged with** China M&A and Investment Reporter, 1074-0619 **and** Pacific M&A Reporter, 1049-4367 **to form** Asian M&A and Investment Reporter, 1076-3708.*

LC HG41 .S8 ISSN 0385-2369
DD 338/.0952 JA
JAPANESE FINANCE AND INDUSTRY : QUARTERLY SURVEY. [Jpn. finance ind., q. surv.]. No. 27, Jan./March 1975-. Periodical. English. Four times a year. IBJ Reference and Stat Center, 123 Marunouchi, Chiyoda-ku Tokyo Japan. ***Continues** Quarterly Survey of Japanese Finance & Industry.*
Ind/Abst PAIS Int. Print (1991-?).

LC HG1271 .Z64b
DD 332 JA
JIGYO ANNAI - ZOHEIKYOKU. **Main/Corp** Japan. Zoheikyoku. (19??)-. Periodical. Japanese. Okurasho Zoheikyoku, 1 Shin Kawasakichoo, Kita-ku 530 Osaka Japan.

ISSN 0714-3117
DD 330.9714/604 CN
J'INVESTRIE. [J'investrie]. Vol. 1, No. 1 (June 1982)-. Periodical. French. Twelve times a year. Free. Communications J'Investrie, Bureau 01, 2355 Ouest rue King, Sherbrooke Quebec J1J 2O6 Canada. ctrl circ.

LC HG1501 ISSN 1057-283X
DD 332.1 US
JOURNAL - ILLINOIS. OFFICE OF THE COMMISSIONER OF SAVINGS AND RESIDENTIAL FINANCE, THE. (THE JOURNAL.). **Added/Corp** Illinois. Office of the Commissioner of Savings and Residential Finance. (1991)-. Periodical. English. Office of the Commissioner of Savings and Loan Associations, 500 East Monroe, Suite 800, Springfield IL 62701-1509. ***Continues** Journal (Illinois. Office of the Commissioner of Savings and Loan Associations), 1056-6031.*

LC HG1501
DD 332.1 US
JOURNAL OF AGRICULTURAL LENDING. **See** Agriculture-Agricultural Economics.

LC KF6495.B2 A135 ISSN 0895-4720
DD 343.7306/7 347.30367 US
CCC
JOURNAL OF BANK TAXATION, THE. [J. bank tax.]. Vol. 1, No. 1 (Fall 1987)-. Trade Publication. English. Four times a year. $167.25. Warren Gorham & Lamont Inc., Park Square Building, 31 St. James Avenue, Boston MA 02116-4112. **Tel** (617)423-2020, (800)950-1207, FAX (617)423-2026. **ED** L. Nicholas Deane. **Bk Rev. Ad Acc. Circ:** 1,500 (ctrl). available on microfilm and microfiche from University Microfilms International (UMI); available on an online database (files 15,485/Full-Text) from DIALOG.
Ind/Abst Account. Tax Datab. (Winter 1991-) [Full Txt.].

LC HG23 .J68 ISSN 0378-4266
DD 332.1/05 NE
CCC
CODEN JBFIDO
Pr Rev.
JOURNAL OF BANKING & FINANCE. [J. bank. financ.]. **VFOAT** Journal of Banking and Finance. Vol. 1 (June 1977)-. Academic Scholarly Publication. English. Eight times a year (1 volume). $1006.00. Elsevier Science Publishers BV, PO Box 211, 1000 AE Amsterdam Netherlands. **Tel** 011 31 20 4853641, 011 31 20 4853642, FAX 011 31 20 4853598. **ED** E.I. Altman, B. Jacquillat, M. Sarnat, and G.P. Szego. **Ad Acc.** available on microfilm and microfiche from University Microfilms International (UMI); available on an online database from Elsevier Electronic Subscriptions (EES). Documents available from The Genuine Article, UMI Article Clearinghouse.
Desc: Provides an outlet for the increasing flow of scholarly research concerning financial institutions and the money and capital markets within which they function. Emphasis is primarily on applied and policy oriented research.
Ind/Abst ABI/INFORM Glob. Ed.; ABI/INFORM [Computer File] (March 1981); Acad. Search; Account. Tax Datab. (Mar. 1981-); Bus. Index (1985-); Bus. Period. Index; Bus. Source Plus; Bus. Source; Contents Recent Econ. J.; Contents Pages Manage.; Curr. Cit.; Curr. Contents Soc. Behav. Sci.; Econ. Lit. Index; EP Collect.; Gen. BusinessFile (1985-); Gen. Period. Index (1985-); Homework Help.; INFO-SOUTH Abstr.; J. Econ. Lit. (1983-); Mag. Search; MasterFile FullTEXT 1000; MasterFile FullTEXT 350; MasterFile FullTEXT 650; MasterFile FullTEXT (July 1993-); OCLC; PAIS Int. Print (1991-); Res. Alert [Full Cov.]; Soc. Sci. Cit. Index [Full Cov.]; Telebase; Trade Ind. Index; Wilson Bus. Abstr.

LC K10 .O846 ISSN 1059-048X
DD 346.73/078/05 347.3067805 US
JOURNAL OF BANKRUPTCY, LAW, AND PRACTICE. **VFOAT** Journal of Bankruptcy; Bankruptcy Law and Practice. Vol. 1, No. 1 (Nov./Dec. 1991)-. Trade Publication. English. Six times a year. $157.25. Warren Gorham & Lamont Inc., Park Square Building, 31 St. James Avenue, Boston MA 02116-4112. **Tel** (617)423-2020, (800)950-1207, FAX (617)423-2026.
Ind/Abst Index Leg. Period. (1993-).

LC HG11 .J66 ISSN 0306-686X
DD 332/.05 UK
CCC
JOURNAL OF BUSINESS FINANCE & ACCOUNTING. **See** Business and Economics-Accounting.

LC HG1507 .R57 ISSN 1062-6271
DD 332.1/753/05 US
JOURNAL OF COMMERCIAL LENDING, THE. [J. commer. lend.]. **Added/Corp** Robert Morris Associates. Vol. 74, No. 5 (Jan. 1992)-. Periodical. English. Twelve times a year. $49.50. Robert Morris Associates, One Liberty Plaza, 1650 Market Street, Philadelphia PA 19103. **Tel** (215)851-9118, (215)851-0585, FAX (215)851-9206. available on an online database (file 15/Full-Text) from DIALOG. Documents available from UMI Article Clearinghouse. ***Continues** Journal of Commercial Bank Lending, 0021-986X.*
Ind/Abst ABI/INFORM Glob. Ed.; ABI/INFORM [Computer File] (Jan. 1992-); Bus. ASAP (1992-) [Full Txt.]; Bus. Index (1992-); Bus. Period. Index (Jan. 1992-); Gen. BusinessFile (1992-); Gen. Period. Index (1985-); INFO-SOUTH Abstr.; Mag. Search; MasterFile FullTEXT (July 1993-); PAIS Int. Print; Stat. Ref. Index; Wilson Bus. Abstr.

LC HB1 .J6454 ISSN 1055-0925
DD 330/.05 US
Pr Rev.
JOURNAL OF ECONOMICS AND FINANCE. [J. econ. finance]. **Added/Corp** Midsouth Academy of Economics and Finance. Midsouth Academy of Economics and Finance. Meeting. Memphis State University. Dept. of Economics. Mississippi State University. Dept. of Economics, Finance and Applied Legal Studies. **VFOAT** Papers and Proceedings of the ... Annual Meeting of the Midsouth Academy of Economics and Finance. Vol. 13, No. 2 (Summer 1989)-. Proceedings. English. Three times a year. $35.00. University of Southern Mississippi / Journal of Economics and Finance, Box 5076, Hattiesburg MS 39406. **Tel** (601)266-4637, (601)266-4691, FAX (601)266-4639. **ED** James T. Lindley. **Circ:** 350. ***Continues** Midsouth Journal of Economics and Finance, 0892-5682. **Continued in part by** Midsouth Academy of Economics and Finance. Meeting.; **Continued by** Papers and proceedings, 1068-9125.*
Desc: Scholarly research in economics and finance with both empirical and applied research articles.
Ind/Abst Econ. Lit. Index.

LC HG1 .J6 ISSN 0022-1082
DD 332.05 US
CCC
CODEN JLFIAN
Pr Rev.
JOURNAL OF FINANCE (NEW YORK), THE. (THE JOURNAL OF FINANCE.). [J. financ.]. **Added/Corp** American Finance Association. Vol. 1 (Aug. 1946)-. Periodical. English. Five times a year. $64.00 (institutions), $48.00 (individuals) surface mail; Also comes with American Finance Association membership. American Finance Association, New York University, 44 West 4th Street, New York NY 10012. **Tel** (212)998-0355. **(Subscription address:** Fulco, 30 Broad Street, Denville NJ 07834. **Tel** (800)783-4903, (201)627-2427.) Index available (bound in Dec. issue). available on microfilm and microfiche from University Microfilms International (UMI). Documents available from The Genuine Article, UMI Article Clearinghouse.
Ind/Abst ABI/INFORM Glob. Ed.; ABI/INFORM [Computer File] (Sept. 1971-); Acad. Search; Account. Tax Datab. (Sept. 1971-); Account. Art.; Bus. ASAP (1992-) [Full Txt.]; Bus. Index (1985-); Bus. Period. Index; Contents Recent Econ. J.; Contents Pages Manage.; Curr. Cit.; Econ. Lit. Index (1976-1982); EP Collect.; Fed. Tax Artic.; Gen. BusinessFile (1985-); Gen. Period. Index (1985-); Homework Help.; INFO-SOUTH Abstr.; Int. Bibliogr. Sociol.; Int. Exec.; J. Econ. Lit.; Mag. Search; Manage. Market. Abstr.; Manage. Contents; MasterFile FullTEXT 1000; MasterFile FullTEXT 350; MasterFile FullTEXT 650; MasterFile FullTEXT (July 1993-); Math. Rev. (?-199?); OCLC; PAIS Int. Print; Res. Alert [Full Cov.]; Selec. Coop. Index Manage. Period.; Soc. Sci. Cit. Index [Full Cov.]; Telebase; UMI ABI/Inform--Bus. Period. Ondisc (Dec. 1987-) [Full Txt.]; Wilson Bus. Abstr.

LC HG1501
DD 332.1 US
•**JOURNAL OF FINANCIAL ABSTRACTS.** (1993)-. English. Two times a week. Financial Economics Network, A Division of Social Science Electronic Publishing Inc., 8430 Southwest 55th Place, Gainesville FL 32608. **Tel** (904)336-3853, FAX (904)336-3858. **Ad Acc. Circ:** 5,000.
Desc: Publishes abstracts of working papers from around the world and forthcoming articles in major finance and economics journals.

LC HG1 .J65 ISSN 0022-1090
DD 332/.05 US
CODEN JFQAAC
Pr Rev.
JOURNAL OF FINANCIAL AND QUANTITATIVE ANALYSIS. [J. financ. quant. anal.]. **Added/Corp** University of Washington. Graduate School of Business Administration. Western Finance Association (U.S.). **VFOAT** J.F.Q.A.; JFQA. (March 1966)-. Periodical. English. Four times a year. $85.00. JFQA Office - University of Washington, School of Business, Box 353200, Seattle WA 98195-3200. **Tel** (206)543-4598, FAX (206)543-6872. **ED** Paul Malatesta and Jonathan Karpoff. Index available. cum. index. **Ad Acc. Circ:** 3,000. available on microfilm and microfiche from University Microfilms International (UMI). Documents available from The Genuine Article, UMI Article Clearinghouse.
Desc: Covers development of new theories, empirical tests of theories and issues in public and financial affairs of individuals, firms and institutions.
Ind/Abst ABI/INFORM Glob. Ed.; ABI/INFORM [Computer File] (Sept. 1971-); Acad. Search; Account. Tax Datab. (Sept. 1971-); Bus. Index (1985-); Bus. Period. Index; Contents Pages Manage.; Curr. Cit.; Curr. Contents Soc. Behav. Sci.; Econ. Lit. Index; EP Collect.;

For. Abstr.; Gen. BusinessFile (1985-); Gen. Period. Index (1985-); Homework Help.; INFO-SOUTH Abstr.; J. Econ. Lit.; Mag. Search; MasterFile FullTEXT 1000; MasterFile FullTEXT 350; MasterFile FullTEXT 650; MasterFile FullTEXT (July 1993-); OCLC; Oper. Res./Manage. Sci.; Res. Alert [Full Cov.]; Risk Abstr. (19??-19??); Selec. Coop. Index Manage. Period.; Soc. Sci. Cit. Index [Full Cov.]; Telebase; UMI ABI/Inform--Bus. Period. Ondisc (Mar. 1987-) [Full Txt.]; Wilson Bus. Abstr.

LC HG4501 .J678 **ISSN** 0304-405X
DD 332/.05 NE
CCC
CODEN JFECDT
Pr Rev.
JOURNAL OF FINANCIAL ECONOMICS. [J. financ. econ.]. **Added/Corp** University of Rochester. Graduate School of Management. William E. Simon Graduate School of Business Administration. Harvard University. Graduate School of Business Administration. (May 1974)-. Periodical. English. Nine times a year (3 vols.). $873.00. Elsevier Sequoia SA, PO Box 564, CH-1001 Lausanne 1 Switzerland. **Tel** 011 41 21 3207381, FAX 011 41 21 3235444. **ED** M.C. Jensen, J.B. Long Jr., G.W. Schwert, C.W. Smith Jr, R.M. Stulz, and E.F. Fama. available on microfilm and microfiche from University Microfilms International (UMI); available on an online database from Elsevier Electronic Subscriptions (EES). Documents available from The Genuine Article, UMI Article Clearinghouse.
Desc: Intends to provide a specialized forum for the publication of research in the general area of financial emphasis on the highest analytical, mathematical and empirical contributions.
Ind/Abst ABI/INFORM Glob. Ed.; ABI/INFORM [Computer File] (March 1978-); Acad. Search; Account. Tax Datab. (Mar. 1978-); Bowne Dig. Corp. Sec. Lawyers; Bus. Index (1985-); Bus. Source Plus; Bus. Source; Contents Recent Econ. J.; Contents Pages Manage.; Curr. Cit.; Curr. Contents Soc. Behav. Sci.; Econ. Lit. Index; EP Collect.; Gen. BusinessFile (1985-); Gen. Period. Index (1985-); Homework Help.; INFO-SOUTH Abstr.; J. Econ. Lit.; Mag. Search; MasterFile FullTEXT 1000; MasterFile FullTEXT 350; MasterFile FullTEXT 650; MasterFile FullTEXT (July 1993-); OCLC; Res. Alert [Full Cov.]; Risk Abstr. (19??-19??); Selec. Coop. Index Manage. Period.; Soc. Sci. Cit. Index [Full Cov.]; Telebase.

LC HG174 .J65 **ISSN** 0093-3961
DD 332/.07 US
JOURNAL OF FINANCIAL EDUCATION. **Added/Corp** California State University, San Jose. School of Business. Illinois State University. College of Business. DePaul University. College of Commerce. Vol. 1, No. 2 (Fall 1973)-. English. Two times a year. $25.00. Journal of Financial Education, Villanova University, College of Commerce and Finance, Villanova PA 19085. **ED** Dan McCarty. cum. index. **Circ:** 450. ***Continues*** *Financial Education, 0190-7654.*
Desc: The journal provides a forum for the exchange of ideas, information and experience related to the process of educating students of finance.

LC HG176.7 .J68 **ISSN** 1062-8924
DD 658.15/224/05 US
JOURNAL OF FINANCIAL ENGINEERING, THE. [J. financ. eng.]. **Added/Corp** American Association of Financial Engineers. International Association of Financial Engineers. Vol. 1, No. 1 (June 1992)-. Periodical. English. Four times a year (Mar., June, Sept., Dec.). $180.00. International Association of Financial Engineers, St. John's University, Department of Finance, Jamaica NY 11439. **Tel** (718)990-6161 ext. 7381, FAX (718)990-1868. **Bk Rev. Ad Acc, Adv Mgr:** Joe Inzeritto, **Tel** (718)260-3984. **Circ:** 1,500 (ctrl).
Desc: A scholarly yet readable journal devoted to the study of the many aspects of financial engineering.

LC HG4515.2 .J68 **ISSN** 1042-9573
DD 332.1/05 US
CCC
Pr Rev.
JOURNAL OF FINANCIAL INTERMEDIATION. **See** Business and Economics-Investments.

LC HG4001 .J68 **ISSN** 0970-4205
DD 658.15/05 II
Pr Rev.
JOURNAL OF FINANCIAL MANAGEMENT AND ANALYSIS. **Added/Corp** Om Sai Ram Centre for Financial Management Research and Training. **VFOAT** JFMA. Vol. 1, No. 1 (Jan. 1988)-. Periodical. English. Two times a year. $85.00. Om Sai Ram Center for Financial Management Research and Training, 15 Prakash Co-Op Housing Society, Bombay 400 054 India. **Tel** 11 91 22 6121715. **(Subscription address:** Prints India, 11 Darya Ganj, New Delhi 110002 India. **Tel** 011 91 11 3268645, FAX 011 91 11 3275542, telex 31-61087 PRIN-IN.) **ED** Prof (Dr.) M.R.K. Swamy. Index available. cum. index. **Bk Rev. Ad Acc. Circ:** 5,000. available on CD-ROM and an online database from R.R. Bowker; available on microfiche.
Desc: Application of financial management theory to practice with special reference to developing countries, especially in the context of techno-capital flow from capital rich countries to capital deficit countries.
Ind/Abst Geogr. Abstr. Human Geogr.; Int. Dev. Abstr.; Maize Abstr.; Rev. Agric. Entomol.; Rice Abstr.; Rural Dev. Abstr.; World Agric. Econ. Rural Sociol. Abstr.

LC HG179 .J65 **ISSN** 1040-3981
DD 332.6/7253/05 US
Pr Rev.
JOURNAL OF FINANCIAL PLANNING (DENVER, COLO.). (JOURNAL OF FINANCIAL PLANNING.). [J. financ. plan.]. **Added/Corp** Institute of Certified Financial Planners (U.S.). Vol. 1 No. 1 (July 1988)-. Periodical. English. Four times a year. $60.00. Institute of Certified Financial Planners, 7600 East Eastman Avenue, Suite 301, Denver CO 80231. **Tel** (303)751-7600, (800)322-ICFP, FAX (303)751-1037. **ED** Bruce W. Most, (303)755-1030. Index available (yearly). cum. index. **Ad Acc, Adv Mgr:** Farley Associates, Greenwich, CT, **Tel** (203)629-3400. **Circ:** 6,000. available on microfilm and microfiche from University Microfilms International (UMI). ***Continues*** *Journal (Institute of Certified Financial Planners (U.S.)), 0746-1984.*
Desc: Articles on all aspects of the financial planning process.
Ind/Abst Account. Tax Datab. (1979-).

LC HG1 .J66 **ISSN** 0920-8550
DD 332.1/0973 US
CCC
CODEN JFSRE9
JOURNAL OF FINANCIAL SERVICES RESEARCH. [J. financ. serv. res.]. Vol. 1, No. 1 (Sept. 1987)-. Periodical. English. Four times a year. $293.00. Kluwer Academic Publishers / Massachusetts, PO Box 358, Accord Station, Hingham MA 02018. **Tel** (617)871-6600. **ED** George Benston, Robert Eisenbeis, Paul Horvitz, George Kaufman, and Franklin Edwards. **Acid Free.** available on microfilm and microfiche from University Microfilms International (UMI). Documents available from UMI Article Clearinghouse.
Desc: Provides a comprehensive forum for rigorous theoretical and applied microeconomic analysis of financial services institutions, instruments and markets. The focus is on private and public policy issues common to firms in the US and abroad.
Ind/Abst ABI/INFORM Glob. Ed.; Curr. Cit.; Econ. Lit. Index (1987-); J. Econ. Lit. (1987-).

LC HG3810 .J68
DD 332.4/5/05 II
JOURNAL OF FOREIGN EXCHANGE AND INTERNATIONAL FINANCE. **Added/Corp** National Institute of Bank Management (India). **VFOAT** JFEIF. Vol. 1, No. 1 (Jan. 1987)-. Periodical. English. Four times a year (Jan., Apr., July, Oct.). $50.00. National Institute of Bank Management, Post Bag 1/Kondhwe Khurd, Pune 411-022 India. **Tel** 011 44 673 08087, telex 145 256 NIBM IN. **(Subscription address:** Prints India, 11 Darya Ganj, New Delhi 110002 India. **Tel** 011 91 11 3268645, FAX 011 91 11 3275542, telex 31-61087 PRIN-IN.) **ED** Ganti Subrahmanyan. Index available. **Bk Rev. Ad Acc. Circ:** 500.
Desc: Foreign exchange and international finance.

LC HC79.I5 J68
DD 339.2/0954 II
JOURNAL OF INCOME AND WEALTH, THE. **Added/Corp** Indian Association for Research in National Income and Wealth. Vol. 1 (Oct. 1976)-. Periodical. English. Two times a year. $40.00. Indian Association for Research in NationalIncome and Wealth, New Delhi India. **(Subscription address:** Prints India, 11 Darya Ganj, New Delhi 110002 India. **Tel** 011 91 11 3268645, FAX 011 91 11 3275542, telex 31-61087 PRIN-IN.)

LC HG1501
DD 332.1 UK
JOURNAL OF INCOME DISTRIBUTION. English. Two times a year. $140.00 (institutions), $65.00 (individuals) UK; $150.00 (institutions), $75.00 (individuals) (surface mail), $160.00 (institutions), $85.00 (individuals) (airmail) other. JAI Press Ltd., The Courtyard, 28 High Street, Hampton Hill Middlesex TW12 1PD United Kingdom. **Tel** 011 44 181 9439296, FAX 011 44 181 9439317.

LC HG1501 **ISSN** 0911-1247
DD 332.1 JA
JOURNAL OF INTERNATIONAL ECONOMIC STUDIES. [J. int. eco. Stud.]. **Added/Corp** Hosei Daigaku. Hikaku Keizai Kenkyujo. No. 1 (Mar. 1985)-. English. Every 2 years. Free. H K Lewis & Company Ltd, 136 Gower Street, London WC1E 6BS United Kingdom.

LC HG3879 .J678 **ISSN** 1042-4431
DD 332/.042/05 US
Pr Rev.
JOURNAL OF INTERNATIONAL FINANCIAL MARKETS, INSTITUTIONS & MONEY. [J. int. financ. mark. inst. money]. **VFOAT** Journal of International Financial Markets, Institutions and Money. (1991)-. Periodical. English. Four times a year (Mar., June, Sept., Dec.). $85.00. Mercado International Press, PO Box 371, Carbondale IL 62903. **Tel** (618)453-2459, FAX (618)453-1431. **ED** Ike Mathur (editor's address: Chairman Department of Finance, College of Business and Administration, Southern Illinois University at Carbondale, Carbondale, IL 62901). **Bk Rev. Ad Acc. Acid Free.** available on microfilm and microfiche. Documents available from Haworth Document Delivery Service.
Desc: Gives attention to scholarship on international financial systems, international securities, markets, euromarkets, options, futures and other derivative instruments, exchange rates, forward rates, interest rates, swaps, international payment mechanisms, international commercial and investment banking, central bank interventions, balance of payments, and international monetary systems.
Ind/Abst Bus. Period. Index; Econ. Lit. Index; Index Period. Artic. Relat. Law.

LC HG3879 .J68 **ISSN** 0261-5606
DD 332/.042/05 UK
CCC
Pr Rev.
JOURNAL OF INTERNATIONAL MONEY AND FINANCE. [J. int. money financ.]. (1982)-. Periodical. English. Six times a year. $533.00. Butterworth Heinemann Publishers, Linacre House Jordan Hill, Oxford OX2 8DP United Kingdom. **Tel** 011 44 1865 310366, FAX 011 44 1865 310898. **(Subscription address:** Elsevier Science Ltd. / Oxford Fulfillment Centre, PO Box 800, Kidlington OX5 1DX United Kingdom. **Tel** 011 44 865 843355.) **ED** James R. Lothian. Index available. available on microfilm and microfiche from University Microfilms International (UMI); available on an online database from Elsevier Electronic Subscriptions (EES). Documents available from The Genuine Article, UMI Article Clearinghouse.
Desc: Major papers appear on foreign exchange markets, international monetary arrangements, international interactions of prices, income and money, finance of multinational corporations, and international economic institutions.
Ind/Abst ABI/INFORM Glob. Ed.; ABI/INFORM [Computer File] (Dec. 1984-); Contents Pages Manage.; Curr. Cit.; Curr. Contents Soc. Behav. Sci.; Econ. Lit. Index; Expand. Acad. Index (1992-); Gen. BusinessFile (1992-); J. Econ. Lit.; Newsp. Period. Abstr. (1992-); PAIS Int. Print; Res. Alert [Full Cov.]; Soc. Sci. Cit. Index [Full Cov.].

LC HG3368 .A25
DD 332.1/0917/671 PK
JOURNAL OF ISLAMIC BANKING & FINANCE : QUARTERLY PUBLICATION OF THE INTERNATIONAL ASSOCIATION OF ISLAMIC BANKS, KARACHI (ASIAN REGION). **Added/Corp** International Association of Islamic Banks. Asian Region. **VFOAT** Islamic Banking & Finance; Journal of Islamic Banking and Finance. Vol. 1, No. 1 (Winter 1984)-. Periodical. English. Four times a year. $46.00. International Association of Islamic Banks, 5 B 1st Floor, Blk 7 Kehkashan Apt, Karachi Pakistan. **Tel** 011 92 1 537315. **ED** Mukhtar Zaman. **Bk Rev. Ad Acc. Circ:** 600 (ctrl).
Desc: Attempts to put forward the point of view of Islamic principles relating to banking, finance and economics. Carries reports about financial institutions and banks in Middle East and other Islamic countries.
Ind/Abst Index Islam. Lit.; PAIS Int. Print.

LC HG201 .J6 **ISSN** 0022-2879
DD 332/.05 US
CCC
CODEN JMCBBT
Pr Rev.
JOURNAL OF MONEY, CREDIT, AND BANKING. [J. money, credit bank.]. Vol. 1 (Feb. 1969)-. Periodical. English. Four times a year (Feb., May, Aug., Nov.). $100.00. Ohio State University Press, 1070 Carmack Road, Columbus OH 43210. **Tel** (614)292-6930, (614)292-1407, FAX (614)292-2065. **ED** Stephen Cecchetti, Paul D. Evans (Dept. of Economics, Ohio State University). Index available (published in Nov. issue). cum. index. **Bk Rev. Ad Acc. Circ:** 3,500. available on microfilm and microfiche from University Microfilms International (UMI); available on an online database (file 648/Full-Text) from DIALOG; available on CD-ROM from University Microfilms International (UMI). Documents available from The Genuine Article, UMI Article Clearinghouse.
Desc: A primary economics journal reporting major findings in the study of monetary and fiscal policy, credit markets, money and banking, portfolio management, and related subjects.
Ind/Abst ABI/INFORM Glob. Ed.; ABI/INFORM [Computer File] (Aug. 1972-); Acad. Search; Account. Tax Datab. (Aug. 1972-); Account. Art.; Bus. ASAP (1990-) [Full Txt.]; Bus. Index (1985-); Bus. Period. Index; Contents Recent Econ. J.; Contents Pages Manage.; Curr. Cit.; Curr. Contents Soc. Behav. Sci.; Econ. Lit. Index; EP Collect.; Expand. Acad. Index (1992-); Fed. Tax Artic.; Gen. BusinessFile (1985-); Gen. Period. Index (1985-); Homework Help.; INFO-SOUTH Abstr.; J. Econ. Lit.; Mag. Search; Manage. Contents; MasterFile FullTEXT 1000; MasterFile FullTEXT 350; MasterFile

Business and Economics —Banks and Banking

FullTEXT 650; MasterFile FullTEXT (July 1993-); Newsp. Period. Abstr. (1992-); OCLC; PAIS Int. Print; Res. Alert [Full Cov.]; Risk Abstr.; Soc. Sci. Cit. Index [Full Cov.]; Soc. Sci. Index; Telebase; UMI ABI/Inform--Bus. Period. Ondisc (Feb. 1988-) [Full Txt.]; Wilson Bus. Abstr.

LC HG2040 .J66 ISSN 0895-5638
DD 332.7/2/05 US
CCC
CODEN JREEEI
JOURNAL OF REAL ESTATE FINANCE AND ECONOMICS, THE. See Real Estate.

LC HG1501 .J63 ISSN 0195-2064
DD 332.1/0973 US
CCC
TITLE CHANGE
JOURNAL OF RETAIL BANKING. [J. retail bank.]. Added/Corp Consumer Bankers Association. McIntire School of Commerce. (June 1979)-(1995). Periodical. English. American Banker, Concourse Level, 1 State Street Plaza, New York NY 10004. Tel (212)803-8200, (800)221-1809, FAX (212)943-6256, (212)843-9598. ED Diana Roberts. Index available. cum. index. Ad Acc. Circ: 2,500. available on microfilm and microfiche from University Microfilms International (UMI); available on an online database (files 15,485/Full-Text) from DIALOG. Documents available from UMI Article Clearinghouse. Continued by Journal of Retail Banking Services.
  Desc: Featuring the latest research, thought and innovations in retail banking, including marketing, product development, credit, technology, consumer behavior, competition, planning.
  Ind/Abst ABI/INFORM Glob. Ed.; ABI/INFORM [Computer File] (June 1979-); Acad. Search; Account. Tax Datab. (Jun. 1979-) [Full Txt.]; Bus. Index (1985-); Bus. Period. Index; Bus. Source Plus; Bus. Source; Curr. Cit.; EP Collect.; Gen. BusinessFile (1985-); Gen. Period. Index (1985-); Homework Help.; INFO-SOUTH Abstr.; Mag. Search; MasterFile FullTEXT 1000; MasterFile FullTEXT 350; MasterFile FullTEXT 650; MasterFile FullTEXT (July 1993-); OCLC; PAIS Int. Print (1991-); Telebase; Trade Ind. ASAP [Full Txt.]; Trade Ind. Index [Full Txt.]; UMI ABI/Inform--Bus. Period. Ondisc (Winter 1987-) [Full Txt.]; Wilson Bus. Abstr.

LC HG1501 US
●DD 332.1
JOURNAL OF RETAIL BANKING SERVICES. (1995-). English. Four times a year. $125.00. American Banker, Concourse Level, 1 State Street Plaza, New York NY 10004. Tel (212)803-8200, (800)221-1809, FAX (212)943-6256, (212)843-9598. Continues Journal of Retail Banking.

LC HG4027.7 .J68 ISSN 1057-2287
DD 658.15/92/05 US
CCC
JOURNAL OF SMALL BUSINESS FINANCE, THE. See Business and Economics-Small Business.

LC KF6491.A15 J68 ISSN 1040-502X
DD 343.7306/7/05 347.3036705 US
CEASED
JOURNAL OF TAXATION OF S CORPORATIONS, THE. [J. tax. S corp.]. Vol. 1, No. 1 (Fall 1988)-(199?). Periodical. English. Faulkner & Gray Inc., 11 Penn Plaza, 17th Floor, New York NY 10001. Tel (212)967-7000, (800)535-8403. ED Alice V Benson. Bk Rev. Ad Acc. Circ: 1,500 (ctrl). available in microform from University Microfilms International (UMI); available on an online database (file 485/Full-Text) from DIALOG.
  Ind/Abst Account. Tax Datab. (1989-1992) [Full Txt.]; Account. Art.; Fed. Tax Artic.; Index Leg. Period.

LC HG8751 .A53 ISSN 1052-2875
DD 368.3/2/00973 US
JOURNAL OF THE AMERICAN SOCIETY OF CLU & CHFC. See Insurance.

LC HG1505 .I46 ISSN 0019-4921
DD 332.1 II
JOURNAL OF THE INDIAN INSTITUTE OF BANKERS. [J. Indian Inst. Bank.]. Main/Corp Indian Institute of Bankers. (Jan. 1930)-. Periodical. English. Irregular. K.K. Roy Private Ltd., PO Box 10210, 55 Gariahat Road, Calcutta 700019 India. Tel 011 91 33 4754872, 011 91 33 4755069.
  Ind/Abst Curr. Lit. Sci. Sci.

LC HG1501 US
DD 332.1
JUMBO FLASH REPORTS. See Business and Economics-Marketing and Purchasing.

LC HG2040.5.J3 A2b
DD 333.722 JA
JUTAKU KINYU KOKO NEMPO. Main/Corp Jutaku Kinyu Koko. (1953)-. Japanese. Jutaku Kinyu Koko, 4-1 Koraku 1-chome, Bunkyo-ku 112, Tokyo Japan. Supersedes Jutaku Kinyu Koko. Jutaku Kinyu Koko no Genkyo.

LC HG1501 ISSN 0022-8478
DD 332.1 US
KANSAS BANKER, THE. Added/Corp Kansas Bankers Association. (1910)-. Periodical. English. Twelve times a year. $12.00. Kansas Bankers Association, 1500 Merchants National Building, Topeka KS 66612. Tel (913)232-3444, FAX (913)232-3484. ED Gary Reser. Ad Acc. Circ: 1,300 (ctrl).

LC HG5491 .D47 ISSN 0943-8769
DD 332.609 GW
●### KAPITALMARKTSTATISTIK. See Business and Economics-Abstracting, Bibliographies and Statistics.

LC HG1501 ISSN 0937-597X
DD 332.1 GW
UDC 33
KARTEN. [Karten]. VFOAT Cards; Cartes. (1990)-. Periodical. Multiple languages. Four times a year. DM103.00. Fritz Knapp Verlag, Postfach 111151, D-60046 Frankfurt Germany. Tel 011 49 69 9708330, FAX 011 49 69 7078400. ED Klaus-Friedrich Otto, Juergen Meissner, Juergen Fischer, Berthold Morschhaeuser, Roland Fischer.
  Desc: Journal providing information on the credit card industry.

LC HG4246 .S55
DD 658.1509 JA
KEIEI SHISU HAND BUKKU : SANGYOBETSU HEN. VFOAT Handbook of Financial Data of Industries. 1973-. Japanese. Chiyoda Eijenshi, 9-1 Otemachi 1, Chioda-Ku 100, Tokyo Japan. Continues Shuyo Sangyo Keiei Shihyo Benran.

LC HG2441 .R4 ISSN 1064-5349
DD 332.1/025/73 US
KEY TO ROUTING NUMBERS. [Key routing numbers]. Added/Corp American Bankers Association. (1983)-. English. One time a year. $85.00. Thomson Financial Publishing, PO Box 65, 4709 West Golf Road, Skokie IL 60076-0065. Tel (800)321-3373, (708)933-8031. Continues American Bankers Association Key to Routing Numbers.
  Desc: The official source for all current and recently retired financial institution routing numbers.

LC HG4245.Z5 K48
DD 332 JA
KIGYOBETSU GAISHI DONYU SORAN : JOJO KIGYO HEN. Added/Corp Keizai Chosa Kyokai. (19??)-. Periodical. Japanese. ¥38000. Keizai Chosa Kyokai, c/o Toranomon Ogura Building, 2 Shiba Kotohiracho Minato-ku, Tokyo 105 Japan.

LC HG1778.I5 P47
DD 332.1 IO
KINERJA BANK-BANK UMUM PERSERO DI INDONESIA = THE PERFORMANCE OF PERSERO COMMERCIAL BANKS IN INDONESIA. Added/Corp Bank Bumi Daya (Indonesia). VFOAT Performance of Persero Commercial Banks in Indonesia. (1992)-. Indonesian (English). Two times a year. Bank Bumi Daya, Jalan Imam Bonjol No. 61, PO Box No. 1106, Jakarta 10011 Indonesia. Tel 021 2300300, FAX 021 2301848, 2301852, telex 61277, 66110, 61355, 61876, 61896, BDPST IA. Continues Perkembangan Bank-Bank Umum Pemerintah di Indonesia.

LC HC101 .C47 ISSN 1056-697X
DD 330.973/005 US
CODEN KPFMEA
KIPLINGER'S PERSONAL FINANCE MAGAZINE. [Kiplinger's pers. financ. mag.]. Added/Corp Kiplinger Washington Editors, Inc. Vol. 45, No. 7 (July 1991)-. Periodical. English. Twelve times a year. $19.95. Kiplinger Washington Editors, 1729 H Street Northwest, Washington DC 20006. Tel (202)887-6400, (800)544-0155, FAX (202)331-1206. (Subscription address: Kiplinger Washington Editors, 3401 East West Highway, c/o Rick Topolski, Editors Park MD 20782. Tel (800)544-0155, (301)853-6600.) ED T. J. Miller. Index available (bound in Dec. issue). Bk Rev. Circ: 1,150,000. available on microfilm and microfiche from University Microfilms International (UMI); available on an online database (file 647/Full-Text) from DIALOG. Documents available from UMI Article Clearinghouse. Continues Changing Times, 0009-143X.
  Desc: Contains advice on all aspects of finance.
  Ind/Abst Abr. Read. Guide Period. Lit.; Acad. Abstr.; Acad. Ind. [Computer File] (1991-); Acad. Search; Account. Tax Datab. (Jan. 1986-); BioBusiness (1991-); Book Rev. Index; Bus. Source Plus; Bus. Source; EP Collect.; Expand. Acad. Index (1991-); Foods Adlibra; Gen. Period. Index (1991-); Homework Help.; INFO-SOUTH Abstr.; Lotus Notes; Mag. Artic. Summar. Elite; Mag. Artic. Summar. Select; Mag. Artic. Summar. CD-ROM; Mag. ASAP Plus [Full Txt.]; Mag. ASAP Sel. [Full Txt.]; Mag. Express (1991-) [Full Txt.]; Mag. Index Plus (1991-); Mag. Index Sel. Microfiche (1991-) [Full Txt.]; Mag. Index. Sel. (1991-); Mag. Search; MasterFile FullTEXT 1000; MasterFile FullTEXT 350; MasterFile FullTEXT 650; MasterFile FullTEXT (July 1991-) [Full Txt.]; Newsp. Period. Abstr. (1986-); OCLC; Pub. Lib. FullTEXT; Read. Guide Abstr. Select Ed.; Read. Guide

Period. Lit.; Resource/One Ondisc; Telebase; Mag. Index; TOM Gen. Index (1991-) [Full Txt.]; Vocat. Search; World Mag. Bank.

LC HG2040.5.J3 A24
DD 332 JA
KOJIN JUTAKU, IPPAN KASHITSUKE, KENSETSU SHIKIN RIYOSHA CHOSA HOKOKU. Added/Corp Jutaku Kinyu Koko. (19??)-. Japanese. One time a year. Jutaku Kinyu Koko, 4-1 Koraku 1-chome, Bunkyo-ku 112, Tokyo Japan.

LC HG2032 ISSN 0384-8566
DD 334/.2/0971 CN
KOORDINATOR VISTI UKRAJINSKOJ KREDYTOVOJ KOOPERACIJI. (KOORDYNATOR VISTI UKRAINS KOI KREDYTOVOI KOOPERATSII KANADY.). VFOAT Coordinator of the Ukrainian Credit Unions in Canada. (1971)-. Periodical. Ukrainian (English). Four times a year. Free. Coordinator of the Ukrainian Credit Unions, 297 College Street, Toronto Ontario M5T 1S2 Canada. Continues Koordynator Ukrainskykh Kredytovykh Spilok u Toronto-Ont., 0384-8558.

LC HG1501 KO
DD 332.1
KOREAN FINANCIAL REVIEW. Added/Corp Korea Institute of Finance. Financial Outlook Team. (1991)-. Periodical. English. Four times a year (Mar.,June, Sept., Dec.). $50.00. Korea Institue of Finance, 33 Sedren Dong, Building 8 9th Floor, Jongro-ku Seoul 110-110 Korea.

LC HG999.5 .K7 ISSN 0023-4591
DD 332 GW
CCC
KREDIT UND KAPITAL. [Kredit Kap.]. Vol. 1 (1968)-. Periodical. German (English; summaries and/or abstracts in English, French and German). Four times a year. $105.02. Duncker und Humblot Verlag, Postfach 410329, D-12113 Berlin Germany. Tel 011 49 30 79000612, 011 49 30 79000613. ED W. Ehrlicher and H. Lipfert.
  Ind/Abst Contents Recent Econ. J.; Econ. Lit. Index; Int. Bibliogr. Sociol.; J. Econ. Lit.; PAIS Int. Print; World Agric. Econ. Rural Sociol. Abstr.

LC HG1501 ISSN 0172-7400
DD 332.1 GW
UDC 336.77 CCC
KREDITPRAXIS (1979). [Kreditpraxis 1979]. (1979)-. Trade Publication. German. Six times a year. DM144.00. Gabler Verlag, Postfach 1546, D-65005 Wiesbaden Germany. Tel 011 49 611 534129, FAX 011 49 611 534430. Continues Bankwirtschaftliche Kreditpraxis + Finanzberatung, 0342-4928.

ISSN 0380-2159
DD 334/.2/09713541 CN
KREDYTOVA KOOPERATYVA BUDUCHNIST'. Main/Corp Kredytova Kooperatyva Buduchnist'. (1973)-. Ukrainian. One time a year. Buduchnist Credit Union Ltd., 140 Bathurst Street, Toronto Ontario M5V 2R3 Canada. Supersedes Oshchadnist, Udily, 0380-2167.

LC HG1501 US
DD 332.1
LACE QUARTERLY FINANCIAL INSTITUTION RATINGS. VFOAT Quarterly Bank and Savings and Loan Rating Service; Bank and Savings & Loan Rating Service; Bank and Savings and Loan Rating Service; LACE Bank and Savings and Loan Rating Service; LACE Bank and Savings & Loan Rating Service. (19??)-. Trade Publication. English. Four times a year. $324.95. LACE Financial Corporation, 118 North Court Street, Frederick MD 21701. Tel (301)662-1011. Continues Quarterly Bank and Savings and Loan Rating Service.

LC HG ISSN 0890-8079
DD 332 US
LALOGGIA'S SPECIAL SITUATION REPORT AND STOCK MARKET FORECAST. [LaLoggia's spec. situat. rep. stock mark. forecast]. VFOAT Special Situation Report; Special Situation Report and Stock Market Forecast; Charles M. LaLoggia's Special Situation Report. (19??)-. Periodical. English. Irregular (issued every three weeks). $230.00. CML Market Letter, PO Box 167, Rochester NY 14601. Tel (716)232-1240. ED Charles M Laloggia. Circ: 3,000.

LC HG1501 ISSN 1062-8932
DD 332.1 US
LANE GUIDE (WESTERN ED.). (LANE GUIDE.). (1992)-. Periodical. English. Six times a year. $75.00. Lane Guide, 1055 South Wells Avenue #150, Reno NV 89502-2550. Tel (800)LANE-GUIDE, FAX (702)333-9024. ED John M Lane, Richard Lane and Melanie Mabrey, (702)333-9374. Continues Lane Guide, 1045-1307.
  Desc: A complete guide to financial institutions in western states. Listings include loan and account information, for ratings and inquiries, mortgage service

Business and Economics —Banks and Banking

departments, hours, fees, payoff and assumption information. All listings are verified prior to publication. Update issues are circulated as a periodical.

LC HG3308.B85 B36b
DD 332.1   IO
LAPORAN TAHUNAN. **Main/Corp** Bank Bumi Daya (Indonesia). (19??)-. Indonesian. One time a year. Bank Bumi Daya, Jalan Imam Bonjol No. 61, PO Box No. 1106, Jakarta 10011 Indonesia. **Tel** 021 2300300, FAX 021 2301848, 2301852, telex 61277, 61400, 61355, 61876, 61896, BDPST IA. **Desc:** Provides financial and operational highlights for the previous year and projections for the upcoming year. Information on the organization and management of Bank Bumi Daya.

LC HG2431 .G73a   **ISSN** 0197-4181
DD 332.1/0973   US
LARGE CORPORATE BANKING. [Large corp. bank.]. **Main/Corp** Greenwich Research Associates. **Added/Corp** Greenwich Research Associates. Greenwich Associates (Firm). (1973)-. English. One time a year. Greenwich Associates, 135 East Putnam Avenue, Greenwich CT 06830.

   ISSN 0887-882X
DD 338   US
LATIN AMERICA FINANCE. **VFOAT** Finance. (198?)-. Periodical. Spanish. Eight times a year (6 issues plus 2 special issues). $50.00 (one-year), $90.00 (two-year), $120.00 (three-year). Timberman Media Corporation, 520 West 17th Street, Suite 1079, New York NY 10011. **Tel** (212)505-6670.

LC HG1501
DD 332.1   US
LBA BANKER NEWSLETTER, THE. (19??)-. Newsletter. English. Twenty-four times a year. $15.00. Louisiana Bankers Association, 666 North Street, Baton Rouge LA 70821. **Tel** (504)387-3282, FAX (504)343-3159. **Continues** The Louisiana Banker, 1050-379X.

LC K1110   **ISSN** 1189-3257
DD 346.71/092   CN
LEGAL FOR LIFE. (LEGAL FOR LIFE : INSTITUTIONAL INVESTMENT RULES IN CANADA.). [Leg. life]. **Added/Corp** Stikeman, Elliott (Firm) Richard De Boo Limited. (1989)-. Periodical. English. Irregular (2 volume basic set with irregular updates). 345.00Can$. Carswell / Canada, 2075 Kennedy Road, Scarborough Ontario M1T 3V4 Canada. **Tel** (416)298-5092, (800)387-5164, FAX (416)298-5094.

LC JK1430.B3 A35   **ISSN** 0190-5473
DD 328.73/07/65   US
LEGISLATIVE CALENDAR / UNITED STATES HOUSE OF REPRESENTATIVES, COMMITTEE ON BANKING, FINANCE, AND URBAN AFFAIRS. See Public Administration.

LC HG   **ISSN** 0883-0487
DD 332   US
    CCC
LETTER OF CREDIT UPDATE. (LETTER OF CREDIT UPDATE : LCU.). [Lett. credit update]. **VFOAT** LCU. Vol. 1, No. 1 (Aug. 1985)-. Periodical. English. Twelve times a year. $495.00. Government Information Services / Virginia, 4301 North Fairfax Drive, Suite 875, Arlington VA 22203. **Tel** (703)528-1082, FAX (703)528-6060, telex RCA 263591 GIS UR. **ED** James E. Byrne. **Desc:** Each issue covers legislative and judicial developments concerning letter of credit practices of special interest to businessmen, bankers and lawyers. Every issue features regulatory alerts, a case study, drafting tips, innovative uses of L/C's, interviews with L/C experts, L/C basics, behind-the-scenes coverage of banking and trade organizations and schedules of activities of interest.

LC HG1501   **ISSN** 0391-7711
DD 332.1   IT
UDC 070 (443)
    CEASED
LETTERA FINANZIARIA. [Lett. finanz.]. (19??)-No. 28, (July 1993). Periodical. Italian. Lettera Finanziaria Srl, Via de Alessandri 11, 20144 Milan Italy.

LC HG   **ISSN** 0886-0459
DD 332   US
    CCC
LETTERS OF CREDIT REPORT. [Lett. credit rep.]. **Added/Corp** Executive Enterprises (New York, N.Y.). (1986)-. Periodical. English. Six times a year. $248.00. John Wiley & Sons, Inc., 605 Third Avenue, New York NY 10158-0012. **Tel** (212)850-6000, (212)850-6645, FAX (212)850-6088, telex 12-7063. **(Subscription address:** John Wiley & Sons Inc / New Jersey, PO Box 2575, Secaucus NJ 07096-2575. **) ED** Jane G. Bensahel. Index available. **Ad Acc**. available on microfilm; available on microfiche; available in microform. **Continues** Foreign and Domestic Update. **Desc:** Covers latest legal and financial developments affecting letters of credit, bank acceptances and bank guaranties, domestic and international. Contains case information for bankers and lawyers.

LC HG3269 .A32
DD 332.1/0953/67   KU
LIBRARY MONITOR, THE. **VFOAT** Dawriyat Al-Maktabah. (1984)-. Periodical. English (English). One time a year. National Bank of Kuwait / The Library, Economics & Planning Division, PO Box 95, Safat Kuwait.

LC HG1616.I5 C66A   **ISSN** 0098-0005
DD 332.6/725   US
LIST OF LEGAL INVESTMENTS FOR SAVINGS BANKS IN CONNECTICUT. See Business and Economics-Investments.

LC HG1616.I5 L57
DD 332.63/09742   US
LIST OF LEGAL INVESTMENTS FOR SAVINGS BANKS, SAVINGS DEPOSITS OF TRUST COMPANIES AND COOPERATIVE BANKS. See Business and Economics-Investments.

LC HG1662.U5 F42b   **ISSN** 0428-1365
DD 368.8/54/01673   US
LIST OF MEMBER INSTITUTIONS - FEDERAL SAVINGS AND LOAN INSURANCE CORPORATION. See Insurance.

LC HG1501   **ISSN** 0261-0175
DD 332.1   UK
LLOYD'S BANK ECONOMIC BULLETIN. [Lloyds Bank econ bull.]. (1979)-. Periodical. English. Twelve times a year. $61.60. Lloyd's Bank International Ltd., PO Box 215, 71 Lombard Street, London EC3 3BS United Kingdom. **Tel** 011 44 171 6261500, FAX 011 44 171 9291571. **(Subscription address:** Lloyd's of London Press Inc. / North America, 611 Broadway, Suite 308, New York NY 10012. **Tel** (212)529-9500.**) Desc:** Covers topics of current interest, setting out some of the economic principles involved in a manner understandable to the non-economist.

   ISSN 1030-0724
DD 336.014945   AT
LOCAL GOVERNMENT FINANCE, VICTORIA. See Public Administration.

LC HG   **ISSN** 1354-8689
DD 332   UK
●**LOCAL GOVERNMENT REORGANISATION.** [Local gov. reorgan.]. **Added/Corp** Audit Commission for Local Authorities and the National Health Service in England and Wales. (1994)-. Government Publication. English. Irregular. £6.00 per no. Audit Commission for Local Authorities and the National Health Service in England and Wales, 1 Vincent Square, London SW1P 2PN United Kingdom. **(Subscription address:** H.M.S.O., PO Box 276, London SW1E 5HE United Kingdom. **Tel** 011 44 171 8739090, FAX 011 44 171 8738200.**)**

LC HG1501   **ISSN** 0307-0360
DD 332.1   UK
LONDON CURRENCY REPORT. **Added/Corp** International Currency Review. (19??)-. Periodical. English. Four times a year. $950.00. World Reports Ltd., 108 Horse Ferry Road, Westminster, London SW1P 2EF United Kingdom. **Tel** 011 44 171 2223836, FAX 11 44 171 2330185. **Desc:** Consists of currency/country reports, global analysis, currency forecasts, economic data bank, comprehensive currency rate coverage, and international currency charts.

LC HG1501
DD 332.1   US
LOWRY'S POWER AND VELOCITY RATINGS REPORT. See Business and Economics-Investments.

LC HG1501
DD 332.1   US
LOWRY'S WEEKLY MARKET TREND ANALYSIS. See Business and Economics-Investments.

LC HG1501   **ISSN** 0287-2404
DD 332.1   JA
LTCB RESEARCH. [LTCB res.]. **Added/Corp** Nihon Choki Shinyo Ginko. Nihon Choki Shinyo Ginko. Chosabu. Nihon Choki Shinyo Ginko. Economics Division. **VFOAT** Monthly Economic Review. **VAT** Long-Term Credit Bank Research. No. 12 (July 1973)-. Periodical. English. Twelve times a year. Free on request. The Long-Term Credit Bank of Japan Ltd, Economics Division, 2-4 Ohtemachi 1-chome Chiyoda-ku, Tokyo 100 Japan. **Tel** 03-211-5111, telex J24308. **Circ:** 5,500. **Continues** Chogin Research. **Ind/Abst** Public Aff. Inf. Serv. Bull.

LC HG1501
DD 332.1   UK
M & A JAPAN. English. Ten times a year. £125.00 UK, $225.00 North America, ¥35,000 Japan (institutions); £250.00 UK; $450.00 North America; ¥69,000 Japan (other). M & A Japan, South Park Office Penshurst, Tonbrige Kent TN11 8JX United Kingdom. **Tel** 011 44 1892 870059, FAX 011 44 1892 870160. **ED** David Lough. **Bk Rev**. **Ad Acc**. **Circ:** 1,000. **Desc:** International Japanese mergers and acquisitions.

LC HG2032   **ISSN** 0704-0881
DD 334/.09714   CN
MA CAISSE D'ECONOMIE. **Added/Corp** Federation des Caisses d'Economie du Quebec. (Fall 1976)-. Periodical. French. Irregular. Editions Du Jour, 5705 Est rue Sherbrooke, Montreal Quebec H1N 1A7 Canada. **Supersedes** Choix du Jour, 0383-6533.

   ISSN 1187-0176
DD 650/.09714/05   CN
MAGAZINE AFFAIRES PLUS. [Mag. aff. plus]. **VFOAT** Affaires Plus; Magazine Affaires +. Vol. 14, No 1 (Feb. 1991)-. Periodical. French. Ten times a year. 9.47Can$. Publications Transcontinental Inc, 1100 Rene-Levesque, 24Fl boulevard West, Montreal Quebec H3B 4X9 Canada. **Tel** (514)392-9000, FAX (514)392-4724. **Continues** A+, 0836-6942. **Ind/Abst** Repere (1991)-.

LC HG1501   **ISSN** 1012-3326
DD 332.1   HT
MAGAZINE / BANQUE DE LA REPUBLIQUE D'HAITI. **Added/Corp** Banque de la Republique d'Haiti. **VFOAT** Revue Trimestrielle. (19??)-. French. Four times a year. Direction des Etudes Economiques, Banque de la Republique d'Haiti, BP 1570, Port-au-Prince Haiti. **Ind/Abst** PAIS Int. Print.

LC HG3310.J34 N432A
DD 332.1   IO
MAJALAH BANK NEGARA INDONESIA 1946. **Main/Corp** Bank Negara Indonesia 1946. **VAT** Majalah Bank Negara Indonesia Sembilan-Belas Empat-Puluh Enam. Indonesian. Bank Negara Indonesia, Jl Lada No 1, Jakarta Indonesia. **Continues** Bank Negara Indonesia 1946.

LC HG186.A2 M34   **ISSN** 0268-232X
DD 332.1/025/4   UK
MAJOR FINANCIAL INSTITUTIONS OF EUROPE. **VFOAT** Major Financial Institutions of Continental Europe. (19??)-. Directory. English. One time a year. £195.00. Graham & Trotman Ltd., Sterling House, 66 Wilton Road, London SW1V 1DE United Kingdom. **Tel** 011 44 171 8211123, FAX 011 44 171 8288935. **(Subscription address:** Kluwer Academic Publishers / Netherlands, PO Box 322, 3300 AH Dordrecht Netherlands. **Tel** 011 31 78 392392, FAX 011 31 78 546474.**) ED** Ruth Whiteside. **Continues** Major Financial Institutions of Continental Europe.

LC HG1501
DD 332.1   US
    TITLE CHANGE
MAJOR NONDEPOSIT FUNDS OF COMMERCIAL BANKS. **Added/Corp** Board of Governors of the Federal Reserve System (U.S.). (19??)-(1994). English. Board of Governors of the Federal Reserve System, Mail Stop 127, Washington DC 20551. **Tel** (202)452-3244, (202)452-3245. **Merged with** Loans and Securities at Commerical Banks **to form** Assets and Liabilities of Commerical Banks in the United States.

LC HG1501
DD 332.1   UK
MANAGED ACCOUNT REPORTS. (19??)-. Periodical. English. Twelve times a year. $425.00 UK; $345.00 US, Canada and South America. Metal Bulletin PLC, PO Box 28E, Worcester Park, Surrey KT4 7HY United Kingdom. **Tel** 011 44 171 8279977, FAX 011 44 171 3378943.

LC HG   **ISSN** 0383-7874
DD 658/.91/33210971   CN
MANAGEMENT COMPENSATION IN CANADIAN BANKING & FINANCE. See Business and Economics-Management.

LC HG4001 .M36   **ISSN** 0307-4358
DD 658.15/05   UK
    CCC
MANAGERIAL FINANCE. [Manage. finance]. VOL. 1 (1975)-. Periodical. English. Eight times a year. $2056.00. MCB University Press, 60 62 Toller Lane, Bradford, West Yorkshire BD8 9BY United Kingdom. **Tel** 011 44 1274 785280, FAX 011 44 1274 785200, telex 51317-MCBUNI-G. **(Subscription address:** MCB University Press / US and Canada Subscriptions, PO Box 10812, Birmingham AL 35201-0812. **Tel** (205)995-1567, (800)633-4931, FAX (205)995-1588.**) ED** Richard Dobbins. Documents available from UMI Article Clearinghouse. **Desc:** An important worldwide management publication devoted to the dissemination of financial management

practice. In both economic booms and crises, the financial aspects of corporate management are extremely relevant to all those involved in ensuring the survival and prosperity of enterprises today.
Ind/Abst ABI/INFORM Glob. Ed.; ABI/INFORM [Computer File] (Jan. 1980-); Anbar Account. Finan. Abstr. [Full Txt.]; Anbar Mark. Distr. Abstr. [Full Txt.]; Anbar Top Manage. Abstr. [Full Txt.]; Bus. Index (1985-); Contents Pages Manage.; Curr. Cit.; Gen. BusinessFile (1985-); Gen. Period. Index (1985-); INFO-SOUTH Abstr.; Mag. Search; Manage. Market. Abstr.; Manage. Bibliogr. Rev.; MasterFile FullTEXT (Jan. 1994-); Oper. Prod. Manage. Abstr. [Full Txt.]; Person. Train. Abstr. [Full Txt.]; Selec. Coop. Index Manage. Period.; Women Manage. Rev. [Full Txt.].

LC HG179 .M342   **ISSN** 8755-1586
DD 332.024/005   US
     TITLE CHANGE
MARSHALL LOEB'S MONEY GUIDE.
[Marshall Loeb's money guide]. **VFOAT** Money Guide. (1984-)-(199?). English. Little Brown & Company, 34 Beacon Street, Boston MA 02108. **Tel** (617)227-0730, (800)759-0190. **Continued by** Your Money Guide.

LC HG1501
DD 332.1   IT
MASTER : AMMINISTRAZIONE E FINANZA.
(19??)-. Italian. Irregular. Gemma SRL, Cas Postale 12055, 20120 Milan Italy. **Tel** 011 39 2 82476619.

LC HG19 .M37
DD 332/.0945   IT
MATECON.
Added/Corp Centro di Ricerche Economiche Finanziarie (Rome, Italy). (Jan./Feb. 1982)-. Periodical. Italian. Twelve times a year. L102190. Liocorno Editori SRL, Via Collina 48, 00187 Rome Italy. **Tel** 11 39 6 4821226, 4821101, FAX 11 39 6 4743768. Index available. cum. index. **Bk Rev**, (Qty: 30). **Ad Acc**. **Circ:** 3,000.
Desc: Research on financial economics and business enterprises.
Ind/Abst PAIS Int. Print.

LC HF5691 .M27   **ISSN** 0960-1627
DD 650   UK
     CCC
MATHEMATICAL FINANCE : AN INTERNATIONAL JOURNAL OF MATHEMATICS, STATISTICS AND FINANCIAL THEORY.
See Mathematics.

LC HG6024.A3 M34
DD 332   UK
MCGRAW-HILL WORLD FUTURES AND OPTIONS DIRECTORY.
VFOAT World Futures and Options Directory; McGraw-Hill World Futures & Options Directory. (1992)-. Directory. English. McGraw Hill Book Company, Shoppenhangers Road, Maidenhead Berkshire SL6 2QL United Kingdom. **Tel** 011 44 1628 23432.

LC HG1501   **ISSN** 0197-7229
DD 332.1   US
MCGREGOR FUND REPORT. Main/Corp
McGregor Fund. English. McGregor Fund, 2026 Commonwealth Building, Detroit MI 48226.

LC HG2559 .F425A   **ISSN** 0091-2549
DD 332.1/09781/39   US
MEMBER BANK CONDITION, TENTH FEDERAL RESERVE DISTRICT. Main/Corp
Federal Reserve Bank of Kansas City. **VFOAT** Summary and Analysis of Yearend Condition Reports. English. Federal Reserve Bank of Kansas City, 925 Grand Avenue, Kansas City MO 64198. **Tel** (816)881-2683.

LC HG1501
DD 332.1   US
MEMBER BANK OPERATING RATIOS, FOURTH FEDERAL RESERVE DISTRICT. Main/Corp
Federal Reserve Bank of Cleveland. (1968)-. Periodical. English. Federal Reserve Bank of Cleveland, PO Box 6387, Cleveland OH 44101. **Tel** (216)579-3079, FAX (216)579-2477.

LC HG1507 .R572   **ISSN** 0195-5985
DD 332.1/753/06073   US
MEMBER ROSTER - ROBERT MORRIS ASSOCIATES. Main/Corp
Robert Morris Associates. English. Robert Morris Associates, One Liberty Plaza, 1650 Market Street, Philadelphia PA 19103. **Tel** (215)851-9118, (215)851-0585, FAX (215)851-9206. ctrl circ. available on microfilm from University Microfilms International (UMI).

LC HG177 .N37a   **ISSN** 0195-6795
DD 361.7/025/73   US
MEMBERSHIP DIRECTORY - NATIONAL SOCIETY OF FUND RAISING EXECUTIVES. Main/Corp
National Society of Fund Raising Executives. (19??)-. Directory. English. One time a year. Comes with National Society of Fund Raising Executives membership. National Society of Fund Raising, 1101 King Street, Suite 3000, Alexandria VA 22314. **Tel** (703)684-0410, FAX (703)684-0540.

LC HG1501
DD 332.1   DR
MEMORIA / BANCO CENTRAL DE LA REPUBLICA DOMINICA. Main/Corp
Banco Central de la Republica Dominicana. (19??)-. Spanish. Three times a year. $48.00. Biblioteca Banco Central Republic Dominica, Calle Pedro Urena, Santo Domingo Dominican Republic. **Tel** (809)685-1487, FAX (809)687-1163, telex ITT: 346-0052 BANCEN, RCA:326-4186 BANCENT. Index available ($48.00 US). **Circ:** 550 (ctrl). **Continues** Banco Central de la Republica Dominicana. Memoria Anual.
Desc: This bulletin contains the principal macroeconomic statistics of the country in a detailed form.

LC HG1501
DD 332.1   SP
MEMORIA / BANCO DE CREDITO AGRICOLA (MICROFORM). Main/Corp
Banco de Credito Agricola. (19??)-. Spanish. One time a year. **Continues** Banco de Credito Agricola, Madrid. Memoria de Actividades.

LC HG1501
DD 332.1   VE
MEMORIA / CORPORACION ANDINA DE FOMENTO. Main/Corp
Corporacion Andina de Fomento. Spanish. One time a year. Corporacion Andina de Fomento Centro Comercial Av Libertador, Esq Negrin Piso 2 Apdo de Correos 8086, Caracas Venezuela. **Continues** Memoria y Estados Financieros.

LC HG2916   **ISSN** 0067-3277
DD 332.1   EC
MEMORIA DEL GERENTE GENERAL DEL BANCO CENTRAL DEL ECUADOR. Main/Corp
Banco Central del Ecuador. **VFOAT** Memoria del Gerente General - Banco Central del Ecuador. (1928)-. Spanish. Secretaria General / Ecuador, Quito Ecuador.

LC HG1501   **ISSN** 0428-4119
DD 332.1   CU
MEMORIA - FINANCIERA NACIONAL DE CUBA. Main/Corp
Financiera Nacional de Cuba. (1953)-. Periodical. Spanish.

LC HG3066 .A44   **ISSN** 1105-0519
DD 332   GR
MENIAIO STATISTIKO DELTIO - TRAPEZA TES HELLADOS.
See Business and Economics-Abstracting, Bibliographies and Statistics.

LC HG4503 .M37   **ISSN** 0025-9756
DD 332.63/2/0972   MX
Pr Rev.
MERCADO DE VALORES, EL. Added/Corp
Nacional Financiera (Corporation : Mexico). (1941)-. Periodical. Spanish. One time a week. Free on request. Nacional Financiera SNC, Venostiano Caranza 25 / 1er Piso, 06000 Mexico DF Mexico. **Tel** 011 52 5 5100560. **ED** Dauno Totoro Nieto. Index available. cum. index. **Circ:** 12,000.

LC HG1501
DD 332.1   US
     CEASED
MERGERS + ACQUISITIONS INTERNATIONAL.
[Mergers + accquisit. int.]. **Added/Corp** Investment Dealers' Digest, Inc. **VFOAT** Mergers and Acquisitions International; Mergers Plus Acquisitions International. (1992)-(Nov. 1995). Periodical. English. Investment Dealers Digest Inc., Two World Trade Center, 18th Floor, New York NY 10048. **Tel** (212)227-1200, FAX (212)432-1039. **Absorbed** M & A Europe.

LC HG4028.M4 M45   **ISSN** 0026-0010
DD 338.805   US
     CCC
     CODEN AMACDR
MERGERS & ACQUISITIONS.
[Mergers acquis.]. **VAT** Mergers and Acquisitions. Vol. 1, No. 1 (Fall 1965)-. Periodical. English. Six times a year. $325.00. Investment Dealers Digest Inc., Two World Trade Center, 18th Floor, New York NY 10048. **Tel** (212)227-1200, FAX (212)432-1039. **ED** Martin Sikora. Index available. **Ad Acc**. **Circ:** 5,000. available on microfilm and microfiche from University Microfilms International (UMI). Documents available from UMI Article Clearinghouse. **Absorbed** Mergers and Acquisitions Monthly, 0543-5137.
Desc: Features articles and research reports on the merger/acquisition/divestiture field. Features articles on new merger techniques, case studies of recent deals, roundtable discussions with M&A experts, and reports analyzing deal successes and failures, and rosters of mergers, acquisitions and divestitures.
Ind/Abst ABI/INFORM Glob. Ed.; ABI/INFORM Ondisc: Expr. Ed.; ABI/INFORM [Computer File] (Summer 1980-); Acad. Search; Account. Index Suppl.; Anbar Account. Finan. Abstr. [Full Txt.]; Anbar Mark. Distr. Abstr. [Full Txt.]; Anbar Top Manage. Abstr. [Full Txt.]; Bus. Index (1985-); Bus. Period. Index; Bus. Source Plus; Bus. Source; Curr. Cit.; Curr. Law Index (1980-); EP Collect.; F&S Index Plus Text, Int. [Select. Cov.]; Fed. Tax Artic.; Gen. BusinessFile (1985-); Gen. Period. Index (1985-); Homework Help.; INFO-SOUTH Abstr.; Leg. Resour. Index (1980-?);; LegalTrac (1980-1985); Mag. Search; Manage. Bibliogr. Rev.; Manage. Contents (1974-); MasterFile FullTEXT 1000; MasterFile FullTEXT 350; MasterFile FullTEXT 650; MasterFile FullTEXT (July 1993-); OCLC; Oper. Prod. Manage. Abstr. [Full Txt.]; PAIS Int. Print; Person. Train. Abstr. [Full Txt.]; Predicasts; PROMT; Stat. Ref. Index; Telebase; Trade Ind. ASAP [Full Txt.]; Trade Ind. Index (1981-) [Full Txt.]; Wilson Bus. Abstr.; Women Manage. Rev. [Full Txt.].

LC HC131 .M28
DD 330.972/005   MX
Pr Rev.
MEXICAN ECONOMY : ECONOMIC AND FINANCIAL DEVELOPMENTS IN ... POLICIES FOR ... / BANCO DE MEXICO, THE.
Added/Corp Banco de Mexico (1925-). (19??)-. English. One time a year. Nacional Financiera SNC, Venostiano Caranza 25 / 1er Piso, 06000 Mexico DF Mexico. **Tel** 011 52 5 5100560. **ED** Dauno Totoro Nieto. **Circ:** 2,000.

LC HG1501
DD 332.1   MX
MEXICAN FORECAST.
Vol. 1, No. 1 (July 10, 1992)-. Periodical. English. Twenty-four times a year. $595.00. Grupo Editorial Expansion, Sinaloa 149 P9, Col Roma, 06700 Mexico DF Mexico. **Tel** 011 52 5 2072066, 2072619, FAX 011 52 5 5116351. **ED** Lindajoy Fenley. Index available ($24.79 per issue). cum. index. **Circ:** 1,200 (ctrl).

LC HC131 .M578
DD 330.972/005   MX
MEXICO DATA BANK = MEXICO, BANCO DE DATOS.
VFOAT Mexico, Banco de Datos. (198?)-. Statistical Publication. English (Spanish). One time a year. $298.00. El Inversionista Mexicano, Felix Cuevas 301-204, Col Valle, 03100 Mexico D F Mexico. **Tel** 011 52 5 5349297, 011 52 5 5245396.
Desc: A useful tool for marketing, investment research, business statistics, projects and academic investigation on Mexico.

LC HG1501
DD 332.1   US
MIC/TECH-RETAIL AND BANKING. See
Computers-Computer Systems.

LC HG1501
DD 332.1   US
MICHIE ON BANKS AND BANKING.
Main/Corp Michie Company, Charlottesville, Virginia. English. One time a year. Shroyer Michie Co, PO Box 346, Wilsonville AL 35186. **Tel** (205)295-6171.

LC HG1501   **ISSN** 1044-1948
DD 332.1   US
MICHIGAN BANKER (LANSING, MICH.).
(MICHIGAN BANKER.). (Jan. 1989)-. Trade Publication. English. Twelve times a year. $92.50. Michigan Banker, PO Box 12236, Lansing MI 48901. **Tel** (517)484-0775. **ED** Jerome H. O'Neal.

LC HG1501   **ISSN** 0738-7156
DD 332.1   US
     TITLE CHANGE
MICROBANKER.
[Microbanker]. **VFOAT** Micro Banker. (1981)-(1995). Periodical. English. Microbanker Inc., PO Box 708, Lake George NY 12845. **Tel** (518)745-7071. **Continued by** Microbanker's High-Tech Banking Strategies.

LC HG1709 .M47
DD 332.1/028/5536   US
MICROBANKER SOFTWARE BUYER'S GUIDE, THE. Added/Corp
Microbanker (Firm). (19??)-. English. One time a year (Jan.). $195.00. Microbanker Inc., PO Box 708, Lake George NY 12845. **Tel** (518)745-7071.

LC HG1501
DD 332.1   US
MICROBANKER'S HIGH-TECH BANKING STRATEGIES.
(1995)-. Periodical. English. Twenty-four times a year. $395.00. Microbanker Inc., PO Box 708, Lake George NY 12845. **Tel** (518)745-7071. **Continues** Microbanker Research Newsletter.

LC HG1501
DD 332.1   TU
MIDDLE EAST BUSINESS & BANKING.
See Business and Economics-International Economic Relations.

LC HD9576.N36 M47   **ISSN** 0544-0424
DD 331.7   CY
MIDDLE EAST ECONOMIC SURVEY. See
Petroleum and Natural Gas.

Business and Economics — Banks and Banking

LC HG3729.M35 S53
DD 332
MY
MIDF MELAPURKAN. Main/Corp Syarikat Permodalan Kemajuan Perusahaan Malaysia Berhad. **Added/Corp** Syarikat Permodalan Kemajuan Perusahaan Malaysia Berhad. MIDF Reports. **VFOAT** MIDF Reports. Vol. 1, No. 12 (Aug. 1972)-. Multiple languages (English and Malay). Four times a year. Jalan Ampang, Bangunan Midf, Kuala Lumpur Malaysia. **Tel** 2610066, FAX 2615973, telex MA30534. cum. index. ctrl circ. available on microfilm; available on videocassette. *Continues* Sharikat Permodalan Kemajuan Perusahaan Malaysia Berhad. MIDF Melaporkan.

LC HG2037 .U55g
DD 334/.22/0973021
US
MIDYEAR STATISTICS FOR FEDERALLY INSURED CREDIT UNIONS. Added/Corp United States. National Credit Union Administration. (1987)-. English. National Credit Union Administration, 1775 G Street NW, Washington DC 20456. **Tel** (202)357-1100. *Continues* Mid-year ... Statistics of the National Credit Union Administration.

LC HG1501
DD 332.1
JA
●**MIKUNI'S CREDIT RATINGS.** (1995)-. English. Irregular. $5000.00. Mikuni and Company Limited, Toranomon 45 Mori Building, 1-5 Toranomon 5-chome, Minato-ku Tokyo 105 Japan. **Tel** 011 81 3 5472 6631, FAX 011 81 3 5472 6635.

LC HG19 .M55
DD 332
IT
MILANO FINANZA : MF. VFOAT MF. (1986)-. Periodical. Italian. One time a week. L115810. Milano Finanza Spa, Corso Italia 22, 20122 Milan Italy. Index available. cum. index. **Bk Rev. Ad Acc. Circ:** 25,000 (ctrl).
Desc: The Italian weekly of financial markets.
Ind/Abst PAIS Int. Print.

LC KE991 **ISSN** 1187-452X
DD 346.71/08/0262
CN
MINUTES OF PROCEEDINGS AND EVIDENCE OF THE SUB-COMMITTEE ON FINANCIAL INSTITUTIONS LEGISLATION OF THE STANDING COMMITTEE ON FINANCE. See Law-Banking Law.

LC HG3879 .C36a **ISSN** 1193-2643
DD 332.1/5/05
CN
MINUTES OF PROCEEDINGS AND EVIDENCE OF THE SUB-COMMITTEE ON INTERNATIONAL FINANCIAL INSTITUTIONS OF THE STANDING COMMITTEE ON FINANCE. (MINUTES OF PROCEEDINGS AND EVIDENCE OF THE SUB-COMMITTEE ON INTERNATIONAL FINANCIAL INSTITUTIONS OF THE STANDING COMMITTEE ON FINANCE.). [Minutes proc. evid. Sub-Comm. Int. Financ. Inst. Standing Comm. Finance]. **Main/Corp** Canada. Parliament. House of Commons. Sub-Committee on International Financial Institutions. **VFOAT** International Financial Institutions; Proces-Verbaux et Temoignages du Sous-Comite sur les Institutions Financieres Internationales du Comite Permanent des Finances. 34th Parliament, 3rd Session, Issue No. 1 (May 11, 1992)-. Proceedings. English (French).

LC HG1501 **ISSN** 1193-2643
DD 332.1/5/05
CN
MINUTES OF PROCEEDINGS AND EVIDENCE OF THE SUB-COMMITTEE ON INTERNATIONAL FINANCIAL INSTITUTIONS OF THE STANDING COMMITTEE ON FINANCE (ENGLISH EDITION). [Minutes proc. evid. Sub-Comm. Int. Financ. Inst. Standing Comm. Finance]. **Main/Corp** Canada. Parlement. Chambre des Communes. Sous-Comite sur les Institutions Financieres Internationales. **VFOAT** Les Institutions Financieres Internationales; Proces-Verbaux et Temoignages du Sous-Comite sur les Institutions Financieres Internationales du Comite Permanent des Finances. (1992)-. Proceedings. English (French and English).

LC HG1501 **ISSN** 1187-6506
DD 332.1/1/0971
CN
MINUTES OF PROCEEDINGS AND EVIDENCE OF THE SUB-COMMITTEE ON THE BANK OF CANADA OF THE STANDING COMMITTEE ON FINANCE. (MINUTES OF PROCEEDINGS AND EVIDENCE OF THE SUB-COMMITTEE ON THE BANK OF CANADA OF THE STANDING COMMITTEE ON FINANCE = PROCES-VERBAUX ET TEMOIGNAGES DU SOUS-COMITE DE LA BANQUE DU CANADA DU COMITE PERMANENT DES FINANCES.). [Minutes proc. evid. Sub-Comm. Bank Can. Standing Comm. Finance]. **Main/Corp** Canada. Parlement. Chambre des Communes. Sous-Comite de la Banque du Canada. **VFOAT** Proces-Verbaux et Temoignages du Sous-Comite de la Banque du Canada et du Comite Permanent des Finances. 34th Parliament, 3rd Session, Issue No. 1 (Nov. 19, 1991)-. Proceedings. French (English). Bank of Canada, 234 Wellington Street, Secretariat Department, Ottawa Ontario K1A 0G9 Canada. **Tel** (613)782-8248, , FAX (613)782-8655, telex 053-4241.

LC HG1501
DD 332.1
US
MISSISSIPPI BANK DIRECTORY. (19??)-. Directory. English. $20.00. Mississippi Bankers Association, PO Box 37, Jackson MS 39505. **Tel** (601)948-6366.

LC HG1501 **ISSN** 0026-6159
DD 332.1
US
MISSISSIPPI BANKER, THE. Added/Corp Mississippi Bankers Association. (19??)-. Trade Publication. English. Twelve times a year. $25.00. Mississippi Bankers Association, PO Box 37, Jackson MS 39505. **Tel** (601)948-6366. **ED** J. Ben Woods. **Bk Rev. Ad Acc. Circ:** 1,329.
Desc: News about Mississippi banks and bankers.

LC HG4509 .M63 **ISSN** 0883-0495
DD 332.6/7254
US
MMD 1,000, THE. See Business and Economics-Marketing and Purchasing.

LC HG185.B7 M63
DD 332
BL
MOEDA E FINANCAS. Portuguese. Rua 24 de Maio, 35 - 50 Andar Conj. 506, Sao Paulo Brazil.

LC HG35 .M63 **ISSN** 0304-2162
DD 332/.09494
SZ
MOIS, LE. [Mois econ. financ.]. **VFOAT** Mois Economique et Financier. 1974-. German (French and Italian). Ten times a year. Societe de Banque Suisse, 1 Aeschenvorstadt, Bale 4002 Switzerland. **Tel** 061 20 20 20, FAX 061 20 37 08, telex 061 20 67. **Circ:** 220,000. *Formed by the union of* Mois *and* Swiss Bank Corporation. Bulletin.
Ind/Abst Int. Polit. Sci. Abstr.

LC HG1501 **ISSN** 0026-9506
DD 332.1
IT
MONDO BANCARIO. [Mondo banc.]. **VFOAT** World Banking. (1959)-. Periodical. Italian. Six times a year. L51100. Futura 2000 Srl, V J Sanazzaro 6-8, 00141 Rome Italy. **Tel** 011 39 6 4746240, 8260326, FAX 011 39 6 4820552, 8260338. cum. index. **Bk Rev. Ad Acc.** ctrl circ.
Ind/Abst PAIS Int. Print.

LC HG1501
DD 332.1
PE
MONEDA : REVISTA DEL BANCO CENTRAL DE RESERVA DEL PERU. Added/Corp Banco Central de Reserva del Peru. Vol. 1, No. 1 (July 1988)-. Periodical. Spanish. Banco Central de Reserva del Peru, Jiron A, Miro Quesada 441-445, Lima 1 Peru.
Ind/Abst PAIS Int. Print.

LC HG19 .M66 **ISSN** 0026-9611
DD 332
IT
MONETA E CREDITO. [Moneta credito]. **Added/Corp** Banca Nazionale del Lavoro. Vol. 1, No. 1 (1948)-. Periodical. Italian. Four times a year. L54500. Editoriale Lavoro Srl, Via Lucullo 39, 00187 Rome Italy. **Tel** 011 39 6 4826050.

LC HG185.L3 M66 **ISSN** 0185-1136
DD 332
MX
Pr Rev.
MONETARIA. [Monetaria]. **Added/Corp** Centro de Estudios Monetarios Latinoamericanos. (1978)-. Periodical. Spanish. Four times a year. $60.00. Centro Estudios Monetarios Latinoamericanos (CEMLA), Durango 54, 06700 Mexico DF Mexico. **Tel** 011 52 5 5330300, FAX 011 52 5 2072847, telex 1771229. Index available (bound in Dec. issue). **Bk Rev. Ad Acc. Adv Mgr:** Claudio Antonovich M. **Circ:** 600.
Ind/Abst PAIS Int. Print.

LC HG1501
DD 332.1
NE
MONETARY MONOGRAPHS. Added/Corp Nederlandsche Bank (Amsterdam, Netherlands). (1984)-. Monographic series. English. Irregular. Price varies per volume.

LC HG1501
DD 332.1
US
MONETARY POLICY OBJECTIVES FOR ... . Added/Corp Board of Governors of the Federal Reserve System (U.S.). **VFOAT** Monetary Policy Objectives; Summary Report of the Federal Reserve Board; Midyear Review of the Federal Reserve Board; Tentative Monetary Growth Ranges for ... (19??)-. English. Two times a year. Free on request. Board of Governors of the Federal Reserve System, Mail Stop 127, Washington DC 20551. **Tel** (202)452-3244, (202)452-3245.

LC HG540 .U54A **ISSN** 0270-4005
DD 332.4/973
US
MONETARY POLICY REPORT FROM THE COMMITTEE ON BANKING, HOUSING, AND URBAN AFFAIRS, UNITED STATES SENATE. (MONETARY POLICY REPORT FOR ... FROM THE COMMITTEE ON BANKING, HOUSING, AND URBAN AFFAIRS, UNITED STATES SENATE : A REPORT TOGETHER WITH ADDITIONAL VIEWS SUBMITTED PURSUANT TO PUBLIC LAW 95-523.). [Monet. policy rep. Comm. Bank. Hous. Urban Aff., U.S. Senate]. **Main/Corp** United States. Congress. Senate. Committee on Banking, Housing, and Urban Affairs. English. available on microfiche (Vols. for (1983-) distributed to some libraries). *Continues* Report on the Conduct of Monetary Policy from the Committee on Banking, Housing, and Urban Affairs, United States Senate.

LC HG1501 **ISSN** 0277-5751
DD 332.1
US
MONETARY POLICY REPORT TO CONGRESS PURSUANT TO THE FULL EMPLOYMENT AND BALANCED GROWTH ACT OF L978. Added/Corp Board of Governors of the Federal Reserve System (U.S.). (Feb. 20, 1979)-. English. Two times a year. Free on request. Board of Governors of the Federal Reserve System, Mail Stop 127, Washington DC 20551. **Tel** (202)452-3244, (202)452-3245.

LC HG2563 .F457 **ISSN** 0430-1978
DD 332.1/F
US
MONETARY TRENDS. See Finance.

LC HG1501- HG3550
DD 332.1
US
MONEY AND BANKING (GUILFORD, CONN.). (MONEY AND BANKING). (1990/91)-. English. One time a year. $10.95. Dushkin Publishing Group Inc., Sluice Dock, Guilford CT 06437. **Tel** (203)453-4351, (800)243-6532, FAX (203)453-6000. **ED** James P Egan.
Desc: Focuses on current issues, trends, and practices in financial markets, financial institutions, monetary theory and policy, and international finance.

LC HG1501 **ISSN** 0273-8015
DD 332.1
US
MONEY FINDER. (19??)-. Periodical. English. Twelve times a year. $12.00. Money Finder Reports, 18 Lois Street, Norwalk CT 06851. *Continues* Money-Finder Reports, 0164-7407.

LC HG201 .D66
DD 332.4
US
●**MONEY FUND REPORT. See** Business and Economics-Investments.

LC HG1501
DD 332.1
UK
MONEY MANAGEMENT. English. Twelve times a year. £59.00 (surface mail); £103.00 (airmail). Financial Times Business Information Ltd, Greystoke Place, Fetter Lane, London EC4A 1ND United Kingdom. **Tel** 011 44 171 4056969, FAX 011 44 171 2420347.
Ind/Abst Infomat Int. Bus. (19??)-.

LC HG4501 .M49
DD 332.63/2/0973
US
MONEY MANAGER INTERVIEWS. (199?)-. Periodical. English. One time a week. Wall Street Transcript, 100 Wall Street, New York NY 10005. **Tel** (212)747-9500. *Continues* Money Manager Previews, 0895-3635.

LC HG4501 .M49 **ISSN** 0895-3635
DD 332.63/2/0973
US
TITLE CHANGE
MONEY MANAGER PREVIEWS. [Money manager previews]. Vol. 1, No. 1 (Sept. 28, 1987)-(199?). Periodical. English. Wall Street Transcript, 100 Wall Street, New York NY 10005. **Tel** (212)747-9500. *Continued by* Money Manager Interviews.

LC HG1501
DD 332.1
US
MONEY STOCK, LIQUID ASSETS, AND DEBT MEASURES. Added/Corp Board of Governors of the Federal Reserve System (U.S.). (Feb. 16, 1984)-. Periodical. English. Fifty-two times a year. Free on request. Board of Governors of the Federal Reserve System, Mail Stop 127, Washington DC 20551. **Tel** (202)452-3244, (202)452-3245. *Continues* Money Stock Measures and Liquid Assets.

LC HG **ISSN** 0898-1671
DD 332
US
SUSPENDED
MONEY WATCH (WASHINGTON, D.C.). (MONEY WATCH.). [Money watch]. Vol. 1, No. 1 (Nov./Dec. 1987)-Suspended. Periodical. English. Six times a year. Money Watch, PO Box 23558, Washington DC 20026.

Business and Economics —Banks and Banking

DD 330   **ISSN** 1055-9787   US
MONEYPLU$ NEWS. [Moneyplu$ news]. **VFOAT** Money Plus News; Moneyplus; Moneyplus News. Issue No. 1001 (April 1991)-. Periodical. English. Twelve times a year. $60.00. First Estate, PO Box 5879, Riverside CA 92517.

LC HG201
DD 332.4/07   **ISSN** 0734-0486   US
MONOGRAPH / COMMITTEE FOR MONETARY RESEARCH AND EDUCATION. [Monogr. - Comm. Monet. Res. Educ.]. **Added/Corp** Committee for Monetary Research and Education. **VFOAT** CMRE Monographs; C.M.R.E. Monographs. No. 30 (1981)-. Monographic series. English. Price varies per volume. Committee for Monetary Research & Education Inc, PO Box 1630, Greenwich CT 06830. **Tel** (203)661-2533. **Continues** Monetary Tract.

LC HG186.B4 M65
DD 332.64/2493   BE
MONTHLY BULLETIN (KREDIETBANK (BRUSSELS, BELGIUM)). (MONTHLY BULLETIN / KREDIETBANK.). (Jan. 1988)-. Bulletin. English (Dutch and French). Twelve times a year. 100.00F Belgium; 350.00 Europe; 375.00F other. Kredietbank NV, Arenbergstraat 7, 1000 Brussels Belgium. **Tel** 011 32 2 4272700. Index available. **Circ:** 30,000. **Continues** Weekly Bulletin.
Desc: Economic, financial, industrial articles concerning Belgium and abroad.
Ind/Abst PAIS Int. Print (1991-).

LC HC107.A165 A2
DD 330.5   US
MONTHLY BUSINESS REVIEW - FEDERAL RESERVE BANK OF DALLAS. See Business and Economics.

LC HG41 .P75A
DD 330.9/599/04   PH
MONTHLY ECONOMIC LETTER - PRIVATE DEVELOPMENT CORPORATION OF THE PHILIPPINES. **Main/Corp** Private Development Corporation of the Philippines. Periodical. English. Private Development Corporation of the Philippines, Ayala Avenue Makati Metro, Manila 3117 Philippines.

LC HC462.9 .M65
DD 330.952   **ISSN** 0005-5255   JA
MONTHLY ECONOMIC REVIEW. **Added/Corp** Nihon Ginko. Chosakyoku. Nihon Ginko. Chosa Tokeikyoku. Nihon Ginko. (Jan. 1953)-. Periodical. English. Twelve times a year. Free on request. Bank of Japan / Research and Statistics Department, Nihon Ginko, CPO Box 203, Tokyo 100 91 Japan. **Tel** FAX 011 81 3 6644342. **Continues** Monthly Review (Tokyo, Japan).
Ind/Abst Asia.-Pac. Econ. Lit.

LC HC435.2 .I573a
DD 330.9/54/05   **ISSN** 0019-4999   II
MONTHLY NEWSLETTER - INDIAN INVESTMENT CENTRE. See Business and Economics-Investments.

LC HG3881.5.W57 W65b
DD 332   **ISSN** 0379-8674   US
MONTHLY OPERATIONAL SUMMARY. See Business and Economics-Economic Assistance and Development.

LC HG1501
DD 332.1   HU
MONTHLY REPORT / NATIONAL BANK OF HUNGARY. **Added/Corp** Magyar Nemzeti Bank. (Jan. 1992)-. Periodical. English. Twelve times a year. National Bank of Hungary, Foreign Exchange, Szabadsag Ter 8-9, H-1850 Budapest Hungary. **Tel** 011 36 1 1532326, FAX 011 36 1 1324179. **Formed by the union of** Quarterly Review (Magyar Nemzeti Bank), 0231-3456 **and** Market Letter (Budapest, Hungary).

LC HC281 .B3
DD 332   **ISSN** 0418-8292   GW   CCC
MONTHLY REPORT OF THE DEUTSCHE BUNDESBANK. [Mon. rep. Dtsch. Bundesbank]. **Added/Corp** Deutsche Bundesbank. (Aug. 1957)-. Periodical. English (German, Spanish and French; translations available in German). Twelve times a year. Free on request. Deutsche Bundesbank Presse, Information Wilh Epsteinstrasse 14, D-60431 Frankfurt Germany. **Tel** 011 49 69 1583509 or 1583455, telex 41 227 OR 414 431. Index available. cum. index. **Circ:** 52,000 (ctrl).
Continues Monatsberichte der Bank Deutscher Laender. **English.** Monthly Reports of the Bank Deutscher Laender.
Ind/Abst PAIS Int. Print (1991-).

LC HC497.S5 A2
DD 330.9593/005   TH
MONTHLY REVIEW. (BANGKOK BANK). **Added/Corp** Bangkok Bank. **VFOAT** Bangkok Bank Monthly Review. 1984 Vol. 25, No. 9 (Sept. 1984)-. Periodical. English. Twelve times a year. Bangkok Bank, Research Office, 333 Silom Road, Bangkok Thailand. **Continues** Bangkok Bank Monthly Review (1971).

DD 336   **ISSN** 0364-1007   US
MONTHLY TREASURY STATEMENT OF RECEIPTS AND OUTLAYS OF THE UNITED STATES GOVERNMENT FOR PERIOD FROM ... . [Mon. Treas. statement receipts outlays U. S. gov.]. **Added/Corp** United States. Dept. of the Treasury. United States. Dept. of the Treasury. Financial Management Service. (July/Nov. 1974)-. Government Publication. English. Twelve times a year. $46.00. US Department of the Treasury, Office of Public Affairs, 1500 Pennsylvania Avenue, Washington DC 20220. **Tel** (202)566-2041. (**Subscription address:** Superintendent of Documents, US Government Printing Office, Washington DC 20402.) Documents available from Documents on Demand. **Continues** Monthly Statement of Receipts and Outlays of the United States Government.
Ind/Abst Am. Stat. Index.

LC HG4961 .M65
DD 332/.0973   **ISSN** 0545-0152   US   CCC
MOODY'S BANK AND FINANCE MANUAL. **Added/Corp** Moody's Investors Service. (1955)-. Periodical. English. One time a year. $1995.00 (with Weekly News Report). Moody's Investors Service, 99 Church Street, New York NY 10007. **Tel** (212)553-0547, (212)553-0435, FAX (212)553-4700. **Continues in part** Moody's Manual of Investments.

LC HG5123.B3 M6
DD 332   **ISSN** 0027-0814   US   CCC
MOODY'S BANK & FINANCE NEWS REPORTS. **Added/Corp** Moody's Investors Service. **VAT** Moody's Bank and Finance. News Reports. (19??)-. English. Irregular (53 issues per year). $1995.00. Moody's Investors Service, 99 Church Street, New York NY 10007. **Tel** (212)553-0547, (212)553-0435, FAX (212)553-4700. **Supersedes in part** Moody's Analyses of Investments. Bank and Finance Section. Monthly Reports.

LC HG176 .M66
DD 332.1/0973   US
MOODY'S CREDIT OPTIONS. FINANCIAL INSTITUTIONS/SOVEREIGNS. **Added/Corp** Moody's Investors Service. **VFOAT** Credit Opinions; Financial Institutions Sovereigns; Financial Institutions/Sovereigns. (19??)-. English. Twelve times a year. Moody's Investors Service, 99 Church Street, New York NY 10007. **Tel** (212)553-0547, (212)553-0435, FAX (212)553-4700.

LC HG4538 .M598
DD 338.7/4/05   **ISSN** 1076-2744   US
●**MORNINGSTAR AMERICAN DEPOSITARY RECEIPTS.** See Business and Economics-Investments.

LC HG1501
DD 332.1   US   CEASED
MORNINGSTAR CLOSED END FUND SOURCEBOOK. (19??)-(19??). Periodical. English. Morningstar Inc., 225 West Wacker Drive, Chicago IL 60606. **Tel** (312)696-6000, (800)876-5005.

LC HG1501
DD 332.1   US
MORNINGSTAR NO LOAD. (19??)-. English. $145.00 US; $190.00 Canada and Mexico; $290.00 other. Morningstar Inc., 225 West Wacker Drive, Chicago IL 60606. **Tel** (312)696-6000, (800)876-5005.

LC HG1501
DD 332.1   US
MORTGAGE AND HOME IMPROVEMENT LENDING IN MICHICGAN PURSUANT TO THE ANTI-REDLINING ACT, ANNUAL REPORT. **Main/Corp** Michigan. Financial Institutions Bureau. **VFOAT** Annual Report ... Data Analysis, Enforcement Activity. (1983)-. English. Financial Institutions Bureau, PO Box 30224, Lansing MI 48909. **Tel** (517)373-8674. **Continues** Mortgage Anti-Redlining Annual Report.

LC HG1501
DD 332.1   US
MORTGAGE BACKED SECURITIES LETTER. (19??)-. Periodical. English. One time a week. $1395.00. Investment Dealers Digest Inc., Two World Trade Center, 18th Floor, New York NY 10048. **Tel** (212)227-1200, FAX (212)432-1039. available on microfilm and microfiche from University Microfilms International (UMI); available on an online database (files 16,485,636/Full-Text) from DIALOG.
Ind/Abst Account. Tax Datab. (Dec. 1991-) [Full Txt.]; PROMT [Full Txt.]; PTS Newsl. Database [Full Txt.].

LC HG2051.U5 M8
DD 332.3/2/0973   **ISSN** 0730-0212   US   CCC   CODEN MOBAAX
MORTGAGE BANKING. [Mortg. bank.]. Vol. 41, No. 10 (July 1981)-. Periodical. English. Twelve times a year. $40.00. Mortgage Bankers Association of America, Department 0021, Washington DC 20073-0021. **Tel** (202)861-6992. **ED** Janet Hewitt, Deborah Scally, LaDonna Curzon. Index available. cum. index. **Bk Rev**. **Ad Acc**. **Circ:** 15,600 (ctrl). available on microfilm and microfiche from University Microfilms International (UMI); available on an online database (files 15,648/Full-Text) from DIALOG. Documents available from UMI Article Clearinghouse. **Continues** Mortgage Banker, 0027-1241.
Desc: Real estate finance.
Ind/Abst ABI/INFORM Glob. Ed.; ABI/INFORM Ondisc: Expr. Ed.; ABI/INFORM [Computer File] (July 1981-); Acad. Search; Account. Art.; Bus. ASAP (1990-) [Full Txt.]; Bus. Index (1985-); Bus. Period. Index; Bus. Source Plus; Bus. Source; EP Collect.; Fed. Tax Artic.; Gen. BusinessFile (1985-); Gen. Period. Index (1985-); Homework Help.; INFO-SOUTH Abstr.; Mag. Search; MasterFile FullTEXT 1000; MasterFile FullTEXT 350; MasterFile FullTEXT 650; MasterFile FullTEXT (July 1993-); OCLC; Stat. Ref. Index; Telebase; Trade Ind. ASAP [Full Txt.]; Trade Ind. Index (1981-) [Full Txt.]; UMI ABI/Inform--Bus. Period. Ondisc (Dec. 1987-) [Full Txt.]; Wilson Bus. Abstr.

LC HG2040
DD 332.72   **ISSN** 0957-1388   UK
MORTGAGE FINANCE MONTHLY. [Mort. finance mon.]. (1989)-. English. Twelve times a year. **Continues** Savings and Loan News, 0955-5870.
Ind/Abst Infomat Int. Bus.

LC HG1501
DD 332.1   **ISSN** 0744-3927   US   CCC
MORTGAGE MARKETPLACE, THE. (19??)-. English. One time a week. $675.00. American Banker, Concourse Level, 1 State Street Plaza, New York NY 10004. **Tel** (212)803-8200, (800)221-1809, FAX (212)943-6256, (212)843-9598. **ED** Andrew R Mandala. **Ad Acc**. available on an online database (files 636,648/Full-Text) from DIALOG. **Formed by the union of** MBS Reports **and** Secondary Market Reporter.
Ind/Abst PTS Newsl. Database [Full Txt.]; Trade Ind. ASAP [Full Txt.]; Trade Ind. Index [Full Txt.].

LC HG1501
DD 332.1   US
MORTGAGE SERVICING DIRECTORY, THE. (1990)-. Directory. English. One time a year. $125.00. Inside Mortgage Finance Inc., PO Box 42387, Washington DC 20015. **Tel** (301)951-1240, FAX (301)656-1709.
Desc: Contains over 600 telephone numbers, addresses, listings, and names of individuals and firms needed in dealing with the servicing market. Includes: annual estimates of total servicing transfers, ranking of top servicers, as well as listings of servicers and brokers.

LC HG1501
DD 332.1   US
MOUNTAIN STATES BANK DIRECTORY. (19??)-. Directory. English. One time a year (May). $24.00. Bank News, 912 Baltimore Avenue, Suite 900, Kansas City MO 64105-1784. **Tel** (816)421-7941, FAX (816)472-0397. **ED** Sharon Smith. **Ad Acc**, **Adv Mgr:** Beth Wilson.
Desc: List the names of officers & directors, addresses, telephone numbers and finanical information for all banks and savings and loan offices located in Colorado, Montana, New Mexico, Utah and Wyoming.

LC HG2032
DD 334/.2/09713   **ISSN** 0705-6532   CN
MOUVEMENT (OTTAWA). See Business and Economics-Cooperatives.

LC HG
DD 332   **ISSN** 1055-3851   US
MRI BANKERS' GUIDE TO FOREIGN CURRENCY. [MRI bank. guide foreign curr.]. **Added/Corp** Monetary Research International. **VFOAT** Bankers' Guide to Foreign Currency. **VAT** Monetary Research International Bankers' Guide to Foreign Currency. Vol. 1, No. 1 (Jan.-Mar. 1991)-. Periodical. English (German, Portuguese and Spanish). Four times a year. $160.00. Monetary Research International, PO Box 3174, Houston TX 77253. **Tel** (713)827-1796.

LC HC381 .M8
DD 330   **ISSN** 0300-3884   SP
MUNDO FINANCIERO. (EL MUNDO FINANCIERO.). (March 1946)-. Periodical. Spanish (French). Eleven times a year. $13.32. Mundo Financiero, Apartado 6119, Hermosilla 93 1RA IZ, 28080 Madrid Spain. **Tel** 011 34 1 5773376, 8580080, FAX 011 34 1

5778981. **ED** Jose L. Barcelo. **Bk Rev**. **Ad Acc**. **Circ:** 15,700 (ctrl).
Desc: Dedicated to publishing information on the subject of economics, finances and commercialism through sections on banks, securities, exterior commerce, communications, industry and agriculture.

LC HG **ISSN** 1064-0843
DD 332 US
MUTUAL FUND MONTHLY. [Mutual fund m.]. **Added/Corp** Prentice Hall Legal & Financial Services. (1985)-. Periodical. English. Twelve times a year. $495.00. Prentice-Hall Press Legal & Financial Services, 15 Columbus Circle, Third Floor, New York NY 10023. **Tel** (212)373-7500. ***Continues** Simon's Mutual Fund Monthly.*

LC HG1501
DD 332.1 US
MUTUAL FUND PORTFOLIO DEVELOPER. (19??)-. Periodical. English. Four times a year. comes with Morningstar Mutual Funds floppy disk. Morningstar Inc., 225 West Wacker Drive, Chicago IL 60606. **Tel** (312)696-6000, (800)876-5005.

LC HG **ISSN** 8755-8319
DD 332 US
MUTUAL FUND REPORTER (MONTHLY ED.). (MUTUAL FUND REPORTER.). [Mutual fund report.]. Vol. 1, Issue M-7 (July 1984)-. Periodical. English. Twelve times a year. $60.00. Investors Reporting Service, Suite 234/2465 Grand Avenue, Ventura CA 93003.

LC HG4651 **ISSN** 1186-091X
DD 332.63 CN
MW-Q. (THE MW-Q.). [MW-Q]. **Added/Corp** Midland Walwyn Capital. Research Dept. Midland Walwyn Capital. **VFOAT** Midland Walwyn Quantitative Analyis. (Jan. 1991)-. Periodical. English. Four times a year. Limited free distribution to clients of Midland Walwyn Capital. Midland Walwyn Capital, Suite 1600, 121 King Street West, Toronto Ontario M5H 3W6 Canada.

LC HG1501 **ISSN** 1055-8381
DD 332.1 US
NACM BANKRUPTCY REORGANIZATION GUIDE. **Added/Corp** National Association of Credit Management. **VAT** National Association of Credit Management Bankruptcy Reorganization Guide. (1991)-. English. Every 2 years. $27.50 (nonmembers), $36.50 (members). National Association of Credit Management, 8815 Centre Park Drive, Suite 200, Columbia MD 21045-2158. **Tel** (410)740-5560, FAX (410)740-5574.

LC HA1448.L3 N37
DD 314.7 LV
NARODNOE KHOZIAISTVO LATVIISKOI SSR. **See** Business and Economics-Abstracting, Bibliographies and Statistics.

LC HG1501
DD 332.1 US
NATIONAL AVERAGE REPORT, COMMERCIAL BANKS. **VFOAT** Functional Cost Analysis. (1987)-. English. Fed Reserve Bank of New York, 33 Liberty Street, New York NY 10045. **Tel** (212)720-5000. ***Continues** Functional Cost Analysis.*

LC HG3250.5.A7 N38
DD 332.1 GR
NATIONAL BANK OF GREECE REPORT. **Main/Corp** Ethnike Trapeza tes Hellados. **VFOAT** National Bank of Greece Annual Report. (19??)-. English. National Bank of Greece, Economic Research Department, Pub 8-4, Athens Greece.
Ind/Abst F&S Index Plus Text, Int. [Select. Cov.].

LC HG1501 **ISSN** 1172-3300
DD 332.1 NZ
NATIONAL BUSINESS OUTLOOK. **VFOAT** Business Outlook. (1993)-. English. Eleven times a year. Free on request. National Bank of New Zealand Ltd., Economics Department, PO Box 540, Wellington New Zealand. **Tel** 011 64 4 725175, FAX 011 64 4 734928. ***Continues** Business Outlook (Wellington), 1170-4268.*

LC HG641 .A45
DD 332.905 US
NATIONAL COUNTERFEIT DETECTOR, THE. (19??)-. Periodical. English. Twelve times a year. Grant Bushnell Company, PO Box 249, Pawling NY 12564.

LC HG1501
DD 332.1 US
NATIONAL CREDIT UNION ADMINISTRATION RULES AND REGULATIONS. **Main/Corp** United States. National Credit Union Administration. 1980-. English. Irregular. $44.00 US; $55.00 other. National Credit Union Administration, 1775 G Street NW, Washington DC 20456. **Tel** (202)357-1100. ***Continues** Rules and Regulations - National Credit Union Administration.*
Desc: Consists of a basic manual and changes for an indeterminate period.

LC HG1501 **ISSN** 0197-7938
DD 332.1 US
NATIONAL DELINQUENCY SURVEY. [Natl. delinq. surv.]. **Main/Corp** Mortgage Bankers Association of America. Economics and Research Dept. **VFOAT** MBA'S National Delinquency Survey. **VAT** Mortgage Bankers Association of America's National Delinquency Survey. (19??)-. Periodical. English. Four times a year. $60.00. Mortgage Bankers Association of America, Department 0021, Washington DC 20073-0021. **Tel** (202)861-6992. **Circ:** 4,500.

LC HG2040.5.U5 A145
DD 332.3/2/097305 US
NATIONAL MORTGAGE BROKER : A MONTHLY PUBLICATION OF THE NATIONAL ASSOCIATION OF MORTGAGE BROKERS. **Added/Corp** National Association of Mortgage Brokers. (19??)-. Periodical. English. Twelve times a year. $39.95. National Association of Mortgage Brokers, 706 East Bell Road, Suite 101, Phoenix AZ 85022. **Tel** (602)992-6181.

LC HG **ISSN** 1050-3331
DD 332 US
CCC
NATIONAL MORTGAGE NEWS. [Natl. mort. news]. Vol. 14, No. 24 (April 30, 1990)-. Periodical. English. One time a week. $208.00. National Thrift News Inc , 212 West 35th Street, 13th Floor, New York NY 10001. **Tel** (212)563-4008, FAX (212)564-8879. **(Subscription address:** National Mortgage News, PO Box 1738, Riverton NJ 08077. **Tel** (800)765-6700.) **Ad Acc**, **Adv Mgr:** Jim Hollander, **Tel** (212)563-4008. **Circ:** 15,000. available on microfilm and microfiche from University Microfilms International (UMI); available on an online database from NEXIS. ***Continues** National Thrift & Mortgage News, 1045-9766.*
Desc: News of mortgage/real estate industry.

LC HG1709 .N37a **ISSN** 0095-5396
DD 332.1/028/54 US
NATIONAL OPERATIONS AND AUTOMATION CONFERENCE PROCEEDINGS, THE. **Added/Corp** American Bankers Association. Operations and Automation Division. (19??)-. Proceedings. English. Irregular. American Bankers Association, 1120 Connecticut Avenue Northwest, Washington DC 20036. **Tel** (202)663-5221, (202)663-5000, FAX (202)828-4544. ***Continues** National Automation Conference. Proceedings.*

LC HG1709 .A47a HG1709 .N4a **ISSN** 1081-7336
DD 332.1/028/54 US
NATIONAL RETAIL OPERATIONS & AUTOMATION SURVEY. [Natl. retail oper. autom. surv.]. **Added/Corp** American Bankers Association. **VFOAT** National Retail Operations and Automation Survey; National Retail Operations & Automation Survey Report. (1992)-. English. Every 2 years. American Bankers Association, 1120 Connecticut Avenue Northwest, Washington DC 20036. **Tel** (202)663-5221, (202)663-5000, FAX (202)828-4544. ***Continues** National Operations/Automation Survey, 0735-0058.*

LC HG1501
DD 332.1 US
NCUA WATCH NEWSLETTER, THE. (19??)-. Newsletter. English. One time a week. $595.00. American Banker, Concourse Level, 1 State Street Plaza, New York NY 10004. **Tel** (212)803-8200, (800)221-1809, FAX (212)943-6256, (212)843-9598. **(Subscription address:** American Banker / Newletter Division, PO Box 28315, Washington DC 20038. **Tel** (800)733-4371, (202)347-2665.)
Ind/Abst PTS Newsl. Database [Full Txt.].

LC HG1501 **ISSN** 0028-2456
DD 332.1 MX
NEGOCIOS Y BANCOS : REVISTA PARA EL EJECUTIVO. **VFOAT** Nego Bancos. (19??)-. Periodical. Spanish (English). Twenty-four times a year. $60.00. Publicaciones Importantes SA, Bolivar 8-601 Apdopostal 1907, 06000 Mexico City D F Mexico. **Tel** 011 52 5 5101884. **ED** Alfredo Fdrrugia Reed. **Ad Acc**. **Circ:** 50,000 (ctrl). ***Continues** Bancos : La Revista del Mundo Financiero.*
Desc: Economy, finance, statistics and public finance politics.

LC HG **ISSN** 1049-3344
DD 332 US
NELSON'S EARNINGS OUTLOOK. [Nelson's earn. outlook]. **Added/Corp** Nelson Publicaitons (Firm). **VFOAT** Earnings Outlook. Vol. 1, No. 1 (May 1990)-. Trade Publication. English. Twelve times a year. $249.75. Nelson Publications, One Gateway Plaza, PO Box 591, Port Chester NY 10573. **Tel** (914)937-8400, (800)333-6357, FAX (914)937-8908.
Desc: An investment information service providing estimated earnings per share for over 3,000 companies-NYSE, AMEX and NASDAQ.

LC HG1501 **ISSN** 1081-2539
DD 332.1 US
●**NELSON'S THE WORLD'S BEST MONEY MANAGERS.** **VFOAT** World's Best Money Managers. (1995)-. English. One time a year. $125.00. Nelson Publications, One Gateway Plaza, PO Box 591, Port Chester NY 10573. **Tel** (914)937-8400, (800)333-6357, FAX (914)937-8908. ***Continues** Nelson's America's Best Money Managers.*

LC WMLC 93/3944 **ISSN** 1074-5637
DD 332 US
●**NEUROVEST JOURNAL.** [Neurovest j.]. **VFOAT** Neurove$t Journal. Vol. 1, No. 1 (Sept./Oct. 1993)-. Periodical. English. Six times a year. $200.00. Neurovest Journal, PO Box 764, Haymarket VA 22069. **Tel** (703)754-0696.

LC HC107.A11 N342 **ISSN** 0028-4726
DD 330.974/005 US
CODEN NWEEAP
NEW ENGLAND ECONOMIC REVIEW. [New Engl. econ. rev.]. **Added/Corp** Federal Reserve Bank of Boston. Research Dept. (Jan./Feb. 1969)-. Periodical. English. Six times a year. Free on request. Federal Reserve Bank of Boston, 600 Atlantic Avenue, Research Library D, Boston MA 02106. **Tel** (617)973-3397, (617)973-3403. **ED** Joan Poskanzer. Index Available, published separately, free-automatically sent. **Circ:** 15,000. available on microfilm and microfiche from University Microfilms International (UMI). Documents available from The Genuine Article, UMI Article Clearinghouse. ***Continues** New England Business Review, 0548-4405.*
Desc: Articles on economics and business of current particular interest to bankers, academics, financial service research organizations and government.
Ind/Abst ABI/INFORM Glob. Ed.; ABI/INFORM [Computer File] (Sept. 1980-); Acad. Search; Bus. Period. Index; Bus. Source Plus; Bus. Source; Curr. Cit.; Curr. Contents Soc. Behav. Sci.; Econ. Lit. Index; Energy Res. Abstr. (Oct. 1977-); EP Collect.; Expand. Acad. Index (1992-); Fed. Print Econ. Bank. Top.; Gen. BusinessFile (1992-); Homework Help.; INFO-SOUTH Abstr.; J. Econ. Lit.; J. Plan. Lit.; Mag. Search; MasterFile FullTEXT 1000; MasterFile FullTEXT 350; MasterFile FullTEXT 650; MasterFile FullTEXT (July 1993-) [Full Txt.]; Newsp. Period. Abstr. (1992-); OCLC; PAIS Int. Print; Res. Alert [Full Cov.]; Soc. Sci. Cit. Index [Full Cov.]; Telebase; Wilson Bus. Abstr.

LC HG1501
DD 332.1 US
NEW ENGLAND FINANCIAL DIGEST. (1982)-. Periodical. English. Twelve times a year. Free on request. New England Real Estate, PO Box 55, Accord MA 02018. **Tel** (617)878-4540. ***Continues** Real Estate Mortgage/Finance Journal.*

LC HC110.W4 N49 **ISSN** 1066-789X
DD 330 US
●**NEW FORTUNES.** [New fortunes]. **Added/Corp** Taft Group (Rockville, Md.). (1994)-. English. $155.00. Taft Group, 835 Penobscott Building, Customer Service, Detroit MI 48226. **Tel** (800)877-8238, FAX (313)961-6083.

LC HG1501 **ISSN** 0028-7539
DD 332.1 US
NEW YORK STATE BANKER, THE. **Added/Corp** New York State Bankers Association. (19??)-. Periodical. English. Twenty-six times a year. $24.00. New York State Bankers Association, 485 Lexington Avenue, New York NY 10017. **Tel** (212)949-1155. **ED** Gwen Williams. **Bk Rev**. **Circ:** 2,600.
Desc: Legislative and educational issues of special interest to New York state commercial bankers.

ISSN 1064-0762
DD 351 US
NEW YORK STATE GFOA NEWSLETTER. [N.Y. State GFOA newsl.]. **Added/Corp** GFOA (Association). **VFOAT** GFOA Newsletter. **VAT** Government Finance Officers' Association Newsletter; New York State Government Finance Officers' Association Newsletter. (19??)-. Newsletter. English. Four times a year. $65.00 (governmental), $165.00 (non-governmental). Government Finance Officers Association / New York, 119 Washington Avenue, 1st Floor, Albany NY 12210. **Tel** (518)465-1512, FAX (518)434-1303. **ED** J. Dwight Hadley. **Bk Rev**, (Qty: 2). **Ad Acc**. **Circ:** 3,000 (ctrl).

LC HG1501 **ISSN** 0710-5924
DD 332.1/2/0971 CN
NEWSLETTER AND INTERIM REPORT. [Newsl. interim rep. - R. Bank Can.]. **Added/Corp** Royal Bank of Canada. (1976)-. Newsletter. English. Four times a year. Free on request. Royal Bank of Canada, 200 Bay Street, 18th Floor South Tower, Toronto Ontario M5J 2J5 Canada. **Tel** (416)974-7242. ***Continues** Royal Bank of Canada. Interim Report.*

LC HC415.2.A1 N49 **ISSN** 0254-3214
DD 330.95645/005 CY
NEWSLETTER (CYPRUS POPULAR BANK). (NEWSLETTER / THE CYPRUS POPULAR BANK LTD.). **Added/Corp** Cyprus Popular Bank. (19??)-.

Business and Economics —Banks and Banking

Newsletter. English. Six times a year. Cyprus Popular Bank Ltd, PO Box 2032, Nicosia Cyprus. **Tel** 2-450000, FAX 2-450631, telex 2494.

LC HG4245 .T34
DD 332   JA
NIHON NO YURYO KAISHA HACHIJUHASSHA. (1979)-. Japanese. ¥950.
Nihon Horei Yoshiki Hambaisho, 20-15-101 Shinbashi 2-chome Minato-ku, Tokyo 105 Japan. **Continues** Seicho Kaisha Hachijuhassha.

LC HG1501
DD 332.1   JA
NIKKEI KINYU SHINBUN. VFOAT Nikkei
Financial Daily. (19??)-. Newspaper. Japanese. Six times a week (312 per year). $1399.20 US. Nihon Keizai Shimbun Inc., 9-5 Otemachi 1 Chome, Chiyoda-ku Tokyo 100 Japan. **Tel** 011 81 3 32700251, 011 81 3 52108502 (Nikkei Business Publications Inc.), FAX 011 81 3 52552661, 011 81 3 52108119 (Nikkei Business Publications Inc.). **(Subscription address:** OCS / Overseas Courier Service of America Inc., 5 East 44th Street, New York NY 10017. **Tel** (212)599-4517.**)**

LC HG1501
DD 332.1   US
NILSON REPORT, THE. (19??)-. Periodical.
English. Twenty-four times a year. $695.00. The Nilson Report, 300 Esplanade Drive, Suite 1790, Oxnard CA 93030. **Tel** (805)983-0448, FAX (805)983-0792.

LC HG1501
DD 332.1   NE
NMB BANKBLAD. Dutch. Four times a year. Free.
NMB Bankblad, Tav Dhr H Wessels, Postbus 1800, 1000 BV Amsterdam Netherlands. **Tel** 011 020 5634478.

ISSN 1074-6331
DD 658   US
●**NONPROFIT FINANCIAL ADVISOR.**
[Nonprofit financ. advis.]. Vol. 1, Issue 1 (June 1994)-. Periodical. English. Twelve times a year. $135.00. Aspen Publishers Inc., 7201 McKinney Circle, Frederick MD 21701. **Tel** (800)234-1660, (301)698-7100, FAX (301)251-5784, telex 5106014543. **(Subscription address:** Aspen Publishers Inc., PO Box 990, Frederick MD 21701. **Tel** (800)901-9074, (301)698-7100.**)**

ISSN 1062-9408
DD 330   US
NORTH AMERICAN JOURNAL OF ECONOMICS AND FINANCE. [N. Am. j. econ. finance]. Added/Corp North American Economics and Finance Association. (1992)-. Periodical. English. Two times a year. $150.00 (institutions), $60.00 (individuals) US; $160.00 (institutions), $70.00 (individuals) (surface mail), $170.00 (institutions), $80.00 (individuals) (airmail) other. JAI Press Inc., 55 Old Post Road, Suite 2, PO Box 1678, Greenwich CT 06836-1678. **Tel** (203)661-7602, FAX (203)661-0792. **Continues** North American Review of Economics and Finance, 1042-752X.

LC HG1501
DD 332.1   US
NORTHWEST CORPORATION ANNUAL REPORT. English. Northwest Corporation, Northwest Center, Sixth and Marquette, Minneapolis MN 55479.

LC HF1 .N75   **ISSN** 1042-1254
DD 332.1/0977/05   US
NORTHWESTERN FINANCIAL REVIEW.
[Northwest. financ. rev.]. **VFOAT** Update; Northwestern Financial Review Update. Vol. 173, No. 45 (Nov. 5, 1988)-. Trade Publication. English. One time a week. $65.00. NFR Communications, 2850 Metro Drive #524, Minneapolis MN 55425. **Tel** (612)854-2177, FAX (612)854-2627. **Formed by the union of** Commercial West, 0010-3144; Michigan Investor, 1040-0389 **and** Northwestern Banker.

LC HG1501   **ISSN** 0399-1636
DD 332.1   FR
UDC 331.881:35.08
NOUVELLES FISCALES (PARIS), LES.
(LES NOUVELLES FISCALES.). (1973)-. Periodical. French. Thirty times a year (semimonthly with 6 special issues). 1714.01F. Liaisons Sociales, 1 Avenue Edouard Belin, F 92856 Rueil Malmaison France. **Tel** 011 33 1 41299878, 011 33 1 41299879. **ED** A. Bouron. Index available (published separately). **Bk Rev**, (Qty: 7). **Ad Acc, Ad Mgr:** JB Monier. **Circ:** 13,000. **Continues** Aide-Memoire Fiscal (Paris), 0995-9106.

LC HG   **ISSN** 0251-6365
DD 332   US
OCCASIONAL PAPER / INTERNATIONAL MONETARY FUND.
[Occas. pap. - Int. Monet. Fund]. **Added/Corp** International Monetary Fund. No. 1 (1980)-. Monographic series. English. Irregular (5 to 6 per year). Price varies per volume. International Monetary Fund, 700 19th Street Northwest, Publishing Unit, Washington DC 20431. **Tel** (202)623-7430, FAX (202)623-7201. available in microform.
Desc: Contains studies on a variety of economic and financial subjects of long-term interest.
Ind/Abst Curr. Cit.

LC HG1501   **ISSN** 0080-178X
DD 332.1   AT
OCCASIONAL PAPER - RESERVE BANK OF AUSTRALIA. See Business and Economics-Abstracting, Bibliographies and Statistics.

LC HG1501
DD 332.1   SW
OCCASIONAL PAPER / SVERIGES RIKSBANK. Monographic series. English. Price varies per volume. Sveriges Riksbank, PO Box 16283, S 103 25 Stockholm Sweden. **Tel** 011 46 8 7870000, FAX 011 46 8 210531.

LC HG1501   **ISSN** 0278-1468
DD 332.1   US
OCCASIONAL PAPERS (GROUP OF THIRTY). (OCCASIONAL PAPERS.). Added/Corp
Group of Thirty. **VFOAT** Occasional Paper. No. 1, (1980)-. Monographic series. English. Ten times a year. $125.00. Group of Thirty, 1990 M Street Northwest, Suite 450, Washington DC 20036. **Tel** (202)331-2472 CGIUR, FAX (202)785-9423. **ED** David Holland.
Desc: International monetary issues.

LC HG1501
DD 332.1   NE
●**ODE.** See Finance.

LC HB549.O6 O64a
DD 332/.8/021/2   FR
OECD FINANCIAL STATISTICS. MONTHLY SUPPLEMENT: INTEREST RATES. STATISTIQUES FINANCIERES DE L'OCDE. SUPPLEMENT MENSUEL: TAUX D'INTERET. See Business and Economics-Abstracting, Bibliographies and Statistics.

LC HG186.S6 O37
DD 336.416/021   FR
OECD FINANCIAL STATISTICS. PART 2, FINANCIAL ACCOUNTS OF OECD COUNTRIES. SPAIN = STATISTIQUES FINANCIERES DE L'OCDE. 2. PARTIE, COMPTES FINANCIERS DES PAYS DE L'OCDE. ESPAGNE. See Business and Economics-Abstracting, Bibliographies and Statistics.

LC HG1507 .V5716   **ISSN** 0160-5267
DD 332.1/22/062755   US
OFFICIAL DIRECTORY - VIRGINIA BANKERS ASSOCIATION. Main/Corp Virginia
Bankers' Association. (19??)-. English. Virginia Bankers Association, 700 East Main Street, Suite 1411, Richmond VA 23203.

LC HG3752.7.U6 T55a   **ISSN** 0732-2798
DD 332.7   US
OFFICIAL GUIDE - TIME FINANCE ADJUSTERS (FIRM). (OFFICIAL GUIDE / TIME
FINANCE ADJUSTERS.). [Off. guide - Time Financ. Adjust. (Firm)]. **Main/Corp** Time Finance Adjusters (Firm). (1982)-. English. One time a year. Free. Time Finance Adjusters, PO Box 2225, Daytona Beach FL 32015. **Tel** (904)253-0992. **ED** Margaret Squires. **Ad Acc. Circ:** 30,000 (ctrl).
Desc: Distribution of service companies of financing firms.

LC HG1501   **ISSN** 0030-0802
DD 332.1   US
           CCC
OHIO BANKER, THE. Added/Corp Ohio Bankers
Association. (19??)-. Periodical. English. Twelve times a year. $25.00. OBA Service Corporation, 17 South High Street, Suite 670, Columbus OH 43215. **Tel** (614)221-5121. **ED** Melea Wachtman. **Ad Acc, Adv Mgr Tel** (614)222-0106. **Circ:** 3,200 (ctrl).
Desc: Banking news and trends which impact Ohio commercial banks. News about the state's banks and bankers themselves, and general management tips are also published.

LC HG1501   **ISSN** 0030-1647
DD 332.1   US
OKLAHOMA BANKER. Added/Corp Oklahoma
Bankers Association. **VFOAT** OBA. (1909)-. Newspaper. English. Twenty-six times a year. $30.00. Oklahoma Bankers Association, 643 NE 41st, PO Box 18246, Oklahoma City OK 73154. **Tel** (405)424-5252. **ED** D.J. Morrow. **Bk Rev. Ad Acc, Adv Mgr:** Beth Payne. **Circ:** 3,000.
Desc: Financial news, regulatory and legal issues, and new trends of interest to the Oklahoma Banking Industry.

LC HG1501   **ISSN** 1062-9777
DD 332.1   US
OLYMPIA & YORK BANKRUPTCY NEWS. VFOAT Olympia and York Bankruptcy News.
(1992)-. Periodical. English. One time a week. $30.00 (single issue) (available only via facsimile). Bankruptcy Creditors' Service, Inc., 6326 Graceland Avenue, Cincinnati OH 45237-4808.

LC HG   **ISSN** 0749-3401
DD 332   US
O'NEIL DATABASE. [O'Neil database]. (Nov. 4, 1983)-. Periodical. English. One time a week. William O'Neil & Company Inc., PO Box 66919, Los Angeles CA 90066. **Tel** (310)448-6843. **Formed by the union of** O'Neil Database. Finance, Insurance, Utilities, Food & Transportation Edition, 0740-8455 **and** O'Neil Database. Industrials, 0749-873X.

LC HG2559 .F43a   **ISSN** 0091-2565
DD 332.1/09747   US
OPERATING RATIOS OF SECOND DISTRICT MEMBER BANKS. Main/Corp
Federal Reserve Bank of New York. (19??)-. English. One time a year. Free. New York Federal Reserve Bank, 33 Liberty Street, Bank Studies Department, New York NY 10045. **Tel** (212)720-5000.

LC HG
DD 332   II
●**OPTIONS.** See Finance.

LC HG835 .O7
DD 332.4/981   BL
ORCAMENTO MONETARIO PARA ... .
Portuguese. One time a year.

LC HG1501
DD 332.1   CN
ORIENTATION A LA GESTION FINANCIERE. Main/Corp Canada. Conseil du
Tesor. **VFOAT** Orientation to Financial Management. Monographic series. French (English). Irregular. Price varies per volume. Orientation a la Gestion Financiere, Conseil du Tesor, Ottawa Ontario K1A 0R5 Canada. **Tel** (418)656-5106.

LC HG3 .O88   **ISSN** 0849-1348
DD 330.973/001/12   CN
OUTLOOK - BANK CREDIT ANALYST RESEARCH GROUP. (OUTLOOK.). [Outlook -
Bank Credit Anal. Res. Group]. **Added/Corp** Bank Credit Analyst Research Group. (1990)-. English. One time a year. Free supplement to BCA Foretrends. BCA Publications Ltd., 1002 Sherbrooke Street West, Suite 1600, Montreal Quebec H3A 3L6 Canada. **Tel** (514)499-9706, FAX (514)499-9709.

LC HG5980.7.A2 P334   **ISSN** 0927-538X
DD 336.9/05   NE
           CCC
           CODEN PBFJEQ
Pr Rev.
●**PACIFIC-BASIN FINANCE JOURNAL.**
Added/Corp Pacific-Basin Capital Markets Research Center. **VFOAT** Pacific Basin Finance Journal; PBFJ. Vol. 1, No. 1 (Mar. 1993)-. Academic Scholarly Publication. English. Four times a year (1 volume). $244.00. Elsevier Science Publishers BV, PO Box 211, 1000 AE Amsterdam Netherlands. **Tel** 011 31 20 4853641, 011 31 20 4853642, FAX 011 31 20 4853598. **ED** S. Ghon Rhee. available on an online database from Elsevier Electronic Subscriptions (EES).
Desc: Provides a forum for the publication of academic research on capital markets of the Asian and Pacific region. Emphasizes empirical and theoretical research in the area of finance.

LC HF3790.5 .S78   **ISSN** 0078-852X
DD 650   PK
PAKISTAN'S BALANCE OF PAYMENTS. Main/Corp State Bank of Pakistan.
Dept. of Statistics. (1948/1950)-. English. One time a year. $2.00. State Bank of Pakistan - Public Relation Department, PO Box 4456, Central Directorate, Karachi Pakistan. **Tel** 011 92 21 2414141310, telex 2754 SBP.

LC HG1501   **ISSN** 0164-5773
DD 332.1   US
PALMETTO BANKER. Added/Corp South
Carolina Bankers Association. Vol. 1 (1966)-. Periodical. English. Four times a year. $20.00. South Carolina Bankers Association, PO Box 1483, Columbia SC 29202. **Tel** (803)779-0850, FAX (803)256-8150. **ED** Sally E. Tibshrany. **Ad Acc, Adv Mgr:** Linda Vazquez, **Tel** same as publisher. **Circ:** 1,600 (ctrl).
Desc: Covers the events, during a six month period, of the South Carolina Bankers Association. Also highlights crucial legislation to the organization during that period.

LC HG2889.G8 S55a
DD 332.1/0981/5   BL
PANORAMA ESTATISTICO DO SETOR BANCARIO. See Business and Economics-Abstracting, Bibliographies and Statistics.

LC HG1501
DD 332.1   IT
           CEASED
PARABANCARIA. (19??)-(1994). Italian.
Editoriale Lavoro Srl, Via Lucullo 39, 00187 Rome Italy. **Tel** 011 39 6 4826050.

ISSN 1018-5089
DD 337 US
PAS RESEARCH PAPER SERIES. [PAS res. paper ser.]. **Added/Corp** Policy and Advisory Services. **VFOAT** Policy and Advisory Services Research Paper Series. **VAT** Policy and Advisory Services Research Paper Series. (1991)-. English. World Bank Publications, 1818 H Street Northwest, Washington DC 20043. **Tel** (202)473-1155, (202)473-1155, FAX (202)522-3224, telex WUI 64145 WORLDBANK.

LC HG1501 ISSN 1051-7359
DD 332 US
PAYMENT SYSTEMS WORLDWIDE. [Paym. syst. worldw.]. **VFOAT** Payment Systems. Vol. 1, No. 1 (Spring 1990)-. Periodical. English. Four times a year. $98.00. World of Banking Publishing Company, 582 Oakwood Avenue, Suite 203, Lake Forest IL 60045. **Tel** (708)615-0405, FAX (708)615-0416.

LC HG1501 ISSN 1059-2059
DD 332.1 US
•**PBC CREDIT BRIEFS.** **VFOAT** Credit Briefs. **VAT** Publishing and Business Consultants Credit Briefs. (1993)-. Newsletter. English. Four times a year. Publishing & Business Consultants, PO Box 75392, Los Angeles CA 90075. **Tel** (213)732-3477, FAX (213)732-9123.

LC HG1501
DD 332.1 NE
PENSIOEN BULLETIN. (19??)-. Bulletin. Dutch. Six times a year. Fl92.50. Consultass, Postbus 70, 8000 AB Zwolle Netherlands. **Tel** 011 31 038 550400.

LC HG1501
DD 332.1 IO
PERFORMANCE OF PERSERO COMMERCIAL BANKS IN INDONESIA, THE. **VFOAT** Kinerja Bank-Bank Umum Persero di Indonesia. Indonesian (English). Bank Bumi Daya, Jalan Imam Bonjol No. 61, PO Box No. 1106, Jakarta 10011 Indonesia. **Tel** 021 2300300, FAX 021 2301848, 2301852, telex 61277, 61400, 61355, 61876, 61896, BDPST IA.

LC HG1501
DD 332.1 UK
CEASED
PERFORMANCE RANKING GUIDE. (19??)-(1994). English. Hemmington Scott Publishing Ltd, 25-31 Whiskin Street, City Innovation Centre, London EC1R OBP United Kingdom. **Tel** 011 44 171 2787769, FAX 011 44 171 2789808. **Ad Acc**, **Adv Mgr:** Andy Parson.
Desc: Evaluates the financial performance of over 2000 UK fully listed companies. Performance ranked on 22 different counts, plus comparative league performance trades based on 27 different criteria.

LC HG ISSN 0164-7768
DD 332 US
PERSONAL FINANCE (ARLINGTON, VA.). (PERSONAL FINANCE.). [Pers. finance]. (1978)-. Periodical. English. Twenty-six times a year. $59.00. KCI Communications Inc, 1101 King Street, Suite 400, Alexandria VA 22314. **Tel** (703)548-2400, (800)832-2330, FAX (703)683-6974. **ED** Richard E Band, Leon Rubis. **Circ:** 100,000. ***Continues*** *Inflation Survival Letter.*
Desc: Covers stocks, bonds, real estate, precious metals, mutual funds, investing, tax shelters, and a number of others.
Ind/Abst Can. Index (?-?).

LC HG1501
DD 332.1 UK
PERSONAL FINANCIAL MANAGEMENT. (19??)-. English. £201.85. Croner Publ Ltd., Croner House London Road, Kingston Upon Thames, Surrey KT2 6SR United Kingdom. **Tel** 011 44 181 5473333, FAX 011 44 181 5472637.

LC HG179 .P378 ISSN 1044-4343
DD 332.024/005 US
CCC
PERSONAL FINANCIAL PLANNING (BOSTON, MASS.). (PERSONAL FINANCIAL PLANNING.). [Pers. financ. plan.]. **Added/Corp** Warren, Gorham & Lamont, Inc. (Nov./Dec. 1988)-. Trade Publication. English. Six times a year. $120.98. Warren Gorham & Lamont Inc., Park Square Building, 31 St. James Avenue, Boston MA 02116-4112. **Tel** (617)423-2020, (800)950-1207, FAX (617)423-2026.
Desc: Comprehensive, in-depth advisors and financial planners.
Ind/Abst Acad. Search; Bus. Source Plus; Bus. Source; EP Collect.; Homework Help.; INFO-SOUTH Abstr.; Mag. Search; MasterFile FullTEXT 1000; MasterFile FullTEXT 350; MasterFile FullTEXT 650; MasterFile FullTEXT (July 1993-); OCLC; Telebase.

LC HG1501
DD 332.1 BE
PERSPECTIVES BELGIUM. (19??)-. Periodical. English (French). Free on request. Perspectives Communications DEP, avenue de la Renaissance 12, B 1040 Brussels Belgium. **Tel** 011 32 2 7391611. **ED** P. Lehner. ***Continues*** *Savings Banks International Monde des Caisses d Epargne.*
Desc: Articles concerning various aspects of savings banking.

LC HG2941 .P47
DD 332.1/0985 PE
PERU BANKING PORTFOLIO. **VFOAT** Andean Report Peru Banking Portfolio. (19??)-. English. Irregular. $135.00. Peru Banking Portfolio, Casilla 531, Lima 100 Peru. **Tel** (5114)46-7888.

LC HE7677.B2 P45 ISSN 0882-8296
DD 332.1/025 US
PETERSON DIRECTORY. **See** Communications-Telecommunication.

LC HG1501
DD 332.1 US
Pr Rev. **TITLE CHANGE**
PIECES OF EIGHT. **Added/Corp** Federal Reserve Bank of St. Louis. (Mar. 1989)-(19??). Periodical. English. Federal Reserve Bank of St. Louis, PO Box 66953, Research and Publication Information, St. Louis MO 63166. **Tel** (314)444-8444, (314)444-8660, FAX (314)444-8731. **Circ:** 3,140 (ctrl). ***Formed by the union of*** *Agriculture (Saint Louis, Mo.); Banking & finance* ***and*** *Business (Saint Louis, Mo.).* ***Continued by*** *Regional Economist.*
Desc: A regionally oriented publication devoted to the developments in banking, business and agriculture in the Eighth Federal Reserve District.

LC HG1501 ISSN 0746-746X
DD 332.1 US
TITLE CHANGE
PINELLAS COUNTY REVIEW. (198?)-(1995). Periodical. English. Pinellas Review Inc., 14100 US 19 #105, Clearwater FL 34624. **Tel** (813)538-2100. **ED** John J. Tischner (Editor's address: PO Box 14446, St. Petersburg, FL 33733). **Bk Rev**, (Qty: 4-6 per year). **Ad Acc. Circ:** 4,000 (ctrl). available on microfilm. ***Continues*** *Pinellas Review.* ***Continued by*** *Warfield's Tampa Bay Review, 1084-5399.*
Desc: Financial, banking, real estate legal newspaper. All deeds, mortages, judgements, new business, law matters and politics.

LC HG1501
DD 332.1 CN
PLAN FINANCIER - COMMISSION DE L'ENSEIGNEMENT SUPERIEUR DES PROVINCES MARITIMES. **Main/Corp** Commission de l'Enseignement Superieur des Provinces Maritimes. **VFOAT** Financial Plan. 1978/79-. French (English and English). One time a year. Commission de l'Enseignement Superieur des Provinces, Maritimes Kings Place, CP 6000, Fredericton New Brunswick E3B 5H1 Canada.

LC HG ISSN 0032-0668
DD 332 UK
UDC 33
PLANNED SAVINGS. [Planned sav.]. (1968)-. Periodical. English. Twelve times a year. $112.00. EMAP Business & Computer Publishing Ltd., 1 Lincoln Court 1 Lincoln Road, Peterborough PE1 2RP United Kingdom. **Tel** 011 44 1733 68900, FAX 011 44 1733 349290. available on an online database (files 771,772,799/Full-Text) from DIALOG.

LC HG2889.M55 B37A
DD 332 BL
PLANO DE ACAO - BANCO DE DESENVOLVIMENTO DE MINAS GERAIS. **Main/Corp** Banco de Desenvolvimento de Minas Gerais. Portuguese. Banco de Desenvolvimento de Minas Gerias, rua da Bahia 1600 - 40 Andar, 30.000 Belo Horizonte Brazil.

LC HG1501 ISSN 1034-9952
DD 332.1 AT
POLICY ORGANISATION & SOCIETY. (19??)-. Periodical. English. Two times a year. 15.00Aus$. Policy Organisation & Society, Flinders University, GPO Box 2100, Adelaide 5001 Australia. **Tel** 011 61 8 2013516. **ED** Dr. Haydon Manning. **Ad Acc. Circ:** 250.

LC HG1536 .P635
DD 332.1/0257 US
•**POLK FINANCIAL INSTITUTIONS DIRECTORY.** **VFOAT** Financial Institutions Directory; Polk's Financial Institutions Directory. 197th Iss. (Spring 1993)-. Directory. English. Two times a year. $627.42. R. L. Polk & Company, 2001 Elm Hill Pike, PO Box 305100, Nashville TN 37230-5100. **Tel** (615)889-3350, FAX (615)885-3081, telex 554344 ENCYCOBANK NAS. ***Continues*** *Polk's Bank Directory (North American Ed.), 1058-0611.*

LC HG1536 .P633 ISSN 1058-0603
DD 332 US
POLK'S BANK DIRECTORY (INTERNATIONAL ED.). (POLK'S BANK DIRECTORY.). [Polk's bank dir.]. **VFOAT** Bank Directory; Polk Bank Directory; A.Polk's international edition. (1986)-. Directory. English. One time a year. $276.69 US; $302.65 other. R. L. Polk & Company, 2001 Elm Hill Pike, PO Box 305100, Nashville TN 37230-5100. **Tel** (615)889-3350, FAX (615)885-3081, telex 554344 ENCYCOBANK NAS. ***Continues*** *Polk's World Bank Directory (International Edition).*

LC HG4651 ISSN 0711-7965
DD 332.63/22/0973 CN
POLYMETRIC REPORT (N.Y.S.E. ED.). (THE POLYMETRIC REPORT.). [Polymetric rep.]. **Added/Corp** Polymetric Consultants. **VAT** Polymetric Report (New York Stock Exchange Ed.). (1981)-. Periodical. English. Twelve times a year. 239.36Can$. Polymetric Consultants, 84 Valentine Drive, Toronto Ontario M3A 3J8 Canada. **Tel** 275.00CAN$. **ED** Picton Davies. ***Continues*** *Polymetric Report. N.Y.S.E. Stocks, 0822-6989.*

LC HG1501 ISSN 0957-1973
DD 332.15 UK
PORTFOLIO INTERNATIONAL. **See** Business and Economics-International Economic Relations.

LC HG1501
DD 332.1 US
POS NEWS. (19??)-. English. Twelve times a year. $295.00. Faulkner & Gray Inc., 11 Penn Plaza, 17th Floor, New York NY 10001. **Tel** (212)967-7000, (800)535-8403. available on microfilm and microfiche from University Microfilms International (UMI); available on an online database (files 16,485,636/Full-Text) from DIALOG.
Ind/Abst Account. Tax Datab. (Jan. 1991-) [Full Txt.]; PROMT [Full Txt.]; PTS Newsl. Database [Full Txt.].

LC HG1501 ISSN 0198-9936
DD 332.1 US
POWELL ALERT, THE. **See** Consumer Education and Protection.

LC HG1505 .P7 ISSN 0032-6690
DD 332.1/0954 II
PRAJNAN. **Added/Corp** National Institute of Bank Management (India). Vol. 1 (Jan./March 1972)-. Periodical. English. Four times a year (Jan., Apr., July, Oct.). $30.00. National Institute of Bank Management, Post Bag 1/Kondhwe Khurd, Pune 411-022 India. **Tel** 011 44 673 08087, telex 145 256 NIBM IN. **ED** G. L. Karkal. Index available. cum. index. **Bk Rev**. **Ad Acc. Circ:** 1,500.

ISSN 1186-1363
DD 331.89 CN
PRECIS DE CONCORDANCE DE LA CONVENTION COLLECTIVE U.Q.I.I. ... EN VIGUEUR DANS LES CENTRES D'ACCUEIL MEMBRES DE L'ASSOCIATION DES CENTRES D'ACCUEIL DU QUEBEC. [Precis concord. conven. collect. U.Q.I.E.(C.E.Q.) vigueur centr. acceuil memb. Assoc. centr. accueil Que.]. **Added/Corp** Association des Centres d'Accueil du Quebec. Service-Conseil en Gestion des Ressources Humaines. Union Quebecoise des Infirmieres et Infirmiers. (1990/1991)-. French. Every 3 years. Limited free distribution; 20.00Can$ per volume other. Service-Conseil en Gestion des Ressources Humaines, Association des Centres D'Accueil du Quebec, 1001 Est boulevard de Maisonneuve, Montreal Quebec H2L 4P9 Canada.

LC HG4951 .M76 ISSN 0737-9595
DD 332.63/233/0973 US
PREREFUNDED BOND SERVICE. [Prerefund. bond serv.]. **VFOAT** KIS Prerefunded Bond Service. (1983)-. Periodical. English. One time a year (with 3 quarterly updates). $1100.00. Kenny Information Systems, 65 Broadway 17th FL, New York NY 10006. **Tel** (212) 770-4500. **ED** Maryrose Kelly. Index available. cum. index. **Ad Acc. Circ:** 300 (ctrl). available on an online database. ***Continues*** *MSES Prerefunded Bond Service, 0737-4348.*
Desc: Identifies and describes the refunding features of all prerefunded and escrowed bonds.

LC HG1501
DD 332.1 IT
PREVISIONE DEI BILANCI BANCARI. (19??)-. Italian. Two times a year. Prometeia Calcolo Srl, Via San Vitale 15, 40125 Bologna Italy. **Tel** 011 39 51 268883.

LC HG ISSN 0889-9894
DD 332 US
PRICING STRATEGY. [Pricing strategy]. (19??)-. Periodical. English. Twelve times a year. $192.00. Moebs Services, PO Box 306, Wabsworth IL 60083. **Tel** (800)237-3317.

LC HG1501 **ISSN** 1047-112X
DD 332.1 US
PRIME RATE UPDATE SERVICE. (1991)-. Periodical. English. Irregular. $95.00. Mecklermedia Corporation, 11 Ferry Lane West, Westport CT 06880. **Tel** (203)226-6967, (800)632-5537, FAX (203)454-5840.

LC HG1501
DD 332.1 FR
PRINCIPALES PROCEDURES DE FINANCEMENT DES BESOINS DES ENTREPRISES ET DES MENAGES.
Added/Corp Banque de France. French. Service de l'Information / Paris, 43 rue de Valois, Paris 1ER France. **Tel** 42.92.29.29, telex 220932B. ***Continues*** *Principaux Mecanismes de Distribution du Credit.*

LC HG1501 .P42a **ISSN** 0195-6264
DD 657/.833 US
PRINCIPLES AND PRESENTATION : BANKING. **Main/Corp** Peat, Marwick, Mitchell & Co. 6th Ed. (1976)-. English. One time a year. $50.00. Peat Marwick Main & Company / New Jersey, PO Box 23331, Newark NJ 07189. **Tel** (212)758-9700. ***Continues*** *Principles and Presentation.*

LC HG **ISSN** 0892-189X
DD 332 US
PRING MARKET REVIEW. [Pring mark. rev.]. **Added/Corp** International Institute for Economic Research. (198?)-. Periodical. English. Twelve times a year. $395.00 US; $415.00 other. International Institute of Economic Research, PO Box 624, Gloucester VA 23061. **Tel** (804)694-0415, FAX (804)694-0028. **ED** Martin J Pring.
Desc: Review of the technical position of the world's major financial markets with special emphasis on US debt and equities. Standard features are a glossary of technical terms and an interpretive explanation of all the principal charts.

LC HG1501 **ISSN** 0953-7031
DD 332.1 IE
PRIVATE BANKER INTERNATIONAL. [Priv. bank. int.]. (198?)-. Trade Publication. English. Ten times a year. $749.00. Lafferty Publications Ltd., Tower Ida Centre Pearse Street, Dublin 2 Ireland. **Tel** 011 353 1 6718022, FAX 011 353 1 718520.
Desc: Designed to meet the needs of all who service the private or upscale banking customer. It is a mix of news, comment, analysis, case studies, interviews, country surveys and statistics. Strives to provide answers to the questions faced when starting or running a profitable private banking operation.

LC HG1501
DD 332.1 US
PRIVATE PLACEMENT LETTER. (19??)-. Periodical. English. Twenty-four times a year. $796.00. Investment Dealers Digest Inc., Two World Trade Center, 18th Floor, New York NY 10048. **Tel** (212)227-1200, FAX (212)432-1039. **ED** Ted Weissberg. ***Continues*** *Private Placements, 0735-9950.*

LC HG **ISSN** 1071-4960
DD 332 US
CCC
●**PROBLEM ASSET REPORTER.** [Probl. asset report.]. Vol. 4, #26 (Sept. 7, 1993)-. Periodical. English. Twenty-six times a year. $398.00. Dorset Group Inc., 212 West 35th Street, 13th Floor, New York NY 10001. **Tel** (212)563-4405, FAX (212)564-8879. ***Formed by the union of*** *Resolution Trust Reporter, 1045-0130* ***and*** *Bank Resolution Reporter, 1056-7232.*

LC HG2461 .C65 **ISSN** 0084-9146
DD 332.1/0973 US
PROCEEDINGS OF A CONFERENCE ON BANK STRUCTURE AND COMPETITION. [Proc. Conf. Bank Struct. Compet.]. **Main/Conf** Conference on Bank Structure and Competition. **Added/Corp** Federal Reserve Bank of Chicago. Research Dept. **VFOAT** Proceedings, A Conference on Bank Structure and Competition. (1963)-. English. One time a year (Dec.). $10.00. Federal Reserve Bank of Chicago, 230 South LaSalle, PO Box 834, Chicago IL 60690. **Tel** (312)322-5111, FAX (312)322-5700. **ED** Harvey Rosenblum and Edward G. Nash. **Circ:** 2,000 (ctrl).
Desc: A compilation of working papers from practitioners, academies and regulators in the financial industry.

LC HG2146 .F4
DD 332.11 US
PROCEEDINGS OF THE MEETING. - FEDERAL RESERVE RELATIONS COMMITTEE. **Main/Corp** Federal Reserve Relations Committee. Proceedings. English. Federal Reserve Relations Committee, Philadelphia PA 19105.

LC HG2051.I4 R432 **ISSN** 0377-2861
DD 332.7/1/0954 II
PROCEEDINGS OF THE ... MEETING OF THE AGRICULTURAL CREDIT BOARD. **Main/Corp** Reserve Bank of India. Agricultural Credit Board. **VFOAT** Meeting of the Agricultural Credit Board. (1970)-. Proceedings. English. Irregular. Reserve Bank of India, Economic Department, PO Box 1036, Bombay 400001 India. ***Continues*** *Reserve Bank of India. Standing Advisory Committee on Rural and Co-Operative Credit. Proceedings of the Meeting.*

LC HG1501 **ISSN** 0829-7460
DD 332.1 CN
PROCEEDINGS OF THE STANDING SENATE COMMITTEE ON BANKING, TRADE AND COMMERCE. **See** Business and Economics-Commerce.

LC HG2573 .P76 **ISSN** 0734-6638
DD 353.9/38252043/05 US
PROFILE OF STATE-CHARTERED BANKING, A. [Profile state-chart. bank.]. **Added/Corp** Conference of State Bank Supervisors. National Association of Supervisors of State Banks. **VAT** Profile of State Chartered Banking. (1965)-. English. Every 2 years. $48.00. Conference of State Bank Supervisors, 1015 18th Street Northwest, Washington DC 20036. **Tel** (202)296-2840. **ED** Donna James. Index available.
Desc: Deals with banking statistics and laws regarding banking.

ISSN 0711-0316
DD 658/.022/0971 CN
PROFITS. [Profits - Fed. Bus. Dev. Bank]. **Added/Corp** Federal Business Development Bank (Canada). **VFOAT** Profits. Vol. 1, No. 1 (July 1981)-. Periodical. English (French). Four times a year. Free on request. Federal Business Development Bank, Public Affairs Department, 800 Victoria Square, 11th Floor, Montreal Quebec H4Z 4L4 Canada. **Tel** (514)283-0406.
Ind/Abst Can. Period. Index (19??-).

LC HG1501 **ISSN** 0821-607X
DD 332.1/07/1171 CN
PROGRAMS REGULATIONS - INSTITUTE OF CANADIAN BANKERS. (PROGRAM REGULATIONS.). [Program regul. - Inst. Can. Bankers]. **Main/Corp** Institute of Canadian Bankers. 1982/1983-. English. One time a year. Free. Institute of Canadian Bankers, Suite 720 1801 McGill College Avenue, Montreal Quebec H3A 2N4 Canada. ctrl circ. ***Continues*** *Institute of Canadian Bankers. Calendar, 0229-995X.*

LC HGG3753 .T74
DD 332.1/5/05 UK
●**PROJECT AND TRADE FINANCE.** **Added/Corp** Euromoney Publications Ltd. **VFOAT** Project and Trade Finance. (1993)-. Periodical. English. Twelve times a year. $580.00. Euromoney Publications PLC, Nestor House, Playhouse Yard, London EC4Z 5EX United Kingdom. **Tel** 011 44 171 7798888, FAX 011 44 171 7798630, telex 290700 EUROMON G. **(Subscription address:** Euromoney Publications PLC, Perrymount Road Haywards Heath, West Sussex RH16 3DH United Kingdom. **Tel** 011 44 1444 440421.**)** ***Continues*** *Trade Finance.*

LC HG1501 **ISSN** 0967-5914
DD 332.1753 UK
PROJECT FINANCE INTERNATIONAL. [Proj. financ. int.]. (1992)-. Periodical. English. Twenty-six times a year. $925.00. IFR Publishing Ltd., Aldgate House, 33 Aldgate High Street, London EC3N 1DL United Kingdom. **Tel** 011 44 171 369 7536, FAX 011 44 171 369 7395, telex 889365/8953051 IFRPUBG. **(Subscription address:** IFR Publishing, 90 Broad Street, Second Floor, New York NY 10004. **)** ***Absorbed*** *Project Finance. Asia Briefing, 0963-9535; Project Finance Europe, 0964-413X* ***and*** *Project Finance, 0961-818X.*

LC HG1501
DD 332.1 UK
PROJECT FINANCING. (19??)-. Periodical. English. Irregular. $95.00. Euromoney Publications PLC, Nestor House, Playhouse Yard, London EC4Z 5EX United Kingdom. **Tel** 011 44 171 7798888, FAX 011 44 171 7798630, telex 290700 EUROMON G.

LC HG1501
DD 332.1 BL
PROJETO DE LEI ORCAMENTARIA ANUAL - COORDENACAO DO SISTEMA DE ORCAMENTO. **Main/Corp** Distrito Federal (Brazil). Coordenacao do Sistema de Orcamento. Portuguese.

LC HG4651 **ISSN** 0955-8659
DD 332.63240941 UK
TITLE CHANGE
PROPERTY FINANCE. [Prop. Financ.]. (1989)-(1993). English. Legan Studies and Services Publishing Ltd., 1st Floor, 9-13 St. Andrew Street, London EL4H 3AE United Kingdom. **Tel** 011 44 181 9362016, FAX 011 44 181 9362303. **ED** Kerry Stephenson, (Editors Phone: (071)936-2016). Index available. **Bk Rev. Ad Acc. Acid Free.** ctrl circ. ***Continued by*** *Property Finance & Development, 1353-6745.*
Desc: Regular newsletter providing practical information to professionals involved in funding, borrowing and lending in the UK property market.

LC HG1501 **ISSN** 1353-6745
DD 332.13240941 UK
●**PROPERTY FINANCE & DEVELOPMENT.** [Prop. Financ. Dev.]. **VFOAT** PF & D. Property Finance Development; Property Finance and Development; PF & D. (1994)-. Periodical. English. Twelve times a year. $325.00. Legan Studies and Services Publishing Ltd., 1st Floor, 9-13 St. Andrew Street, London EL4H 3AE United Kingdom. **Tel** 011 44 181 9362016, FAX 011 44 181 9362303. **(Subscription address:** IBC Subscription Services, IBC House Vickers, Surrey KT13 0XS United Kingdom. **Tel** 011 44 1932 354020.**)** ***Continues*** *Property Finance, 0955-8659.*

LC HG1501 **ISSN** 0740-137X
DD 332.1 US
PROTECTION OF ASSETS BULLETIN. [Prot. assets bull.]. (19??)-. Bulletin. English. Twenty-four times a year. Comes with Protection of Assets Manual. Merritt Company, 1661 Ninth Street, PO Box 955, Santa Monica CA 90406. **Tel** (310)450-7234, (800)638-7597, FAX (310)396-4563. **ED** Timothy J. Walsh. **Circ:** 3,500.
Desc: Testing program for security managers and staff for use in association with Protection of Assets Reference Manual and continuing update service. Updated monthly.

LC HG1501
DD 332.1 US
PROTECTION OF ASSETS MANUAL. (19??)-. English. Twenty-four times a year (bulletins, briefings, and revisions published monthly). $424.79 US; $469.79 other. Merritt Company, 1661 Ninth Street, PO Box 955, Santa Monica CA 90406. **Tel** (310)450-7234, (800)638-7597, FAX (310)396-4563.

LC HG1501
DD 332.1 US
PROTECTION OF ASSETS MANUAL TESTING PROGRAM. (19??)-. English. One time a year. $253.59. Merritt Company, 1661 Ninth Street, PO Box 955, Santa Monica CA 90406. **Tel** (310)450-7234, (800)638-7597, FAX (310)396-4563.

LC HG1501
DD 332.1 IT
PUBBLICAZIONI UFFICIO STUDI BNL. (19??)-. Italian. Editoriale Lavoro Srl, Via Lucullo 39, 00187 Rome Italy. **Tel** 011 39 6 4826050.

LC HG **ISSN** 1065-3619
DD 332 US
PYRAMID (BURKE, VA.). (PYRAMID : FINANCIAL NEWSLETTER.). [Pyramid]. **VFOAT** Pyramid Financial Newsletter. (1992)-. Newsletter. English. Six times a year. $45.00. Valjean Enterprises, 10524 Reeds Landing Circle, Burke VA 22015-2512.

LC HG2401 .Q37 **ISSN** 1051-8010
DD 332.1/0973/021 US
TITLE CHANGE
QUARTERLY BANK AND SAVINGS & LOAN RATING SERVICE. [Q. bank sav. loan rat. serv.]. **Added/Corp** LACE Financial Corporation. **VFOAT** Quarterly Bank and Savings and Loan Rating Service; Bank and Savings & Loan Rating Service; Bank and Savings and Loan Rating Service; LACE Bank and Savings and Loan Rating Service; LACE Bank and Savings & Loan Rating Service. (March 1989)-(19??). Trade Publication. English. LACE Financial Corporation, 118 North Court Street, Frederick MD 21701. **Tel** (301)662-1011. ***Continues*** *Bank Rating Service for Fund Managers and Investors.* ***Continued by*** *Lace Quarterly Financial Institution Ratings.*

LC HG3300.55 .A33 **ISSN** 0125-605X
DD 330.9593/005 TH
QUARTERLY BULLETIN - BANK OF THAILAND. (QUARTERLY BULLETIN.). [Q. bull. - Bank Thail.]. **Added/Corp** Thanakhan Hng Prathet Thai. Fai Wichakan. **VFOAT** Bank of Thailand Quarterly Bulletin. Vol. 21, No. 1 (March 1981)-. Bulletin. English. Four times a year (Mar., June, Sept., Dec.). $20.00. Bank of Thailand, GPO Box 154, Department of Economics, Bangkok 10000 Thailand. **Tel** 11 66 2 2823322 Ext. 2617, FAX 011 66 2 2800449, telex 20139 BNKCHAT TH. **ED** Chitrapa Udomsab (editor's address: Publications Section, Economic Research Department, Bank of Thailand, phone: 011 66 2 28356179). **Circ:** 2,500 (ctrl). ***Continues*** *Monthly Bulletin (Thanackhan HNG Prathet Thai. Fai Wichakan).*
Desc: Covers economic conditions, articles, laws and regulations, and statistical tables.
Ind/Abst PAIS Int. Print.

LC HC321 .N383a **ISSN** 0167-3998
DD 330.9692/005 NE
QUARTERLY BULLETIN / DE NEDERLANDSCHE BANK N.V. **Main/Corp** Nederlandsche Bank (Amsterdam, Netherlands). (19??)-. Bulletin. English. Four times a year. Free on request. Kluwer Academic Publishers, Postbus 322, 3300 AH Dordrecht The Netherlands. **Tel** 011 31 78 524400, FAX 011 31 78 183273, telex 20083. **Acid Free.** ***Continues*** *Nederlandsche Bank (Amsterdam, Netherlands). Quarterly Statistics, 0922-6184.*

LC HG3399.S7 S63 **ISSN** 0038-2620
DD 332.1/1/0968 SA
QUARTERLY BULLETIN - SOUTH AFRICAN RESERVE BANK. (QUARTERLY BULLETIN.). [Q. bull. - S. Afr. Reserve Bank]. **Main/Corp** South African Reserve Bank. **Added/Corp** South African Reserve Bank. Kwartaalblad. **VFOAT** Kwartaalblad. (1966)-. Bulletin. English (Afrikaans). Four times a year. $21.47. South African Reserve Bank, PO Box 7433, Pretoria 0001 South Africa. **Tel** 011 27 12 3133675, FAX 011 27 12 3134013. **Circ:** 4,100 (ctrl). ***Continues*** *South African Reserve Bank. Quarterly Bulletin of Statistics.*

LC HG1501
DD 332.1 GY
QUARTERLY ECONOMIC AND FINANCIAL REVIEW. **Added/Corp** Bank of Guyana. Research Dept. Vol. 1, No. 1 (Mar. 1990)-. Corporate Report. English. Four times a year.

LC HG2798 .Q36
DD 330.97296 BF
QUARTERLY ECONOMIC REVIEW. **Added/Corp** Central Bank of the Bahamas. Central Bank of the Bahamas. Research Dept. Vol. 1, No. 2 (June 1992)-. Periodical. English. Four times a year. Free. Central Bank of the Bahamas, PO Box N-4868, Nassau Bahamas. **Tel** 809-322- 2193, FAX (809)322-4321, telex 20115. ***Continues in part*** *Quarterly Review (Central Bank of the Bahamas).*
Desc: Quarterly analysis of domestic, monetary and fiscal activities including an overview of international economic conditions.

LC HC870.A1 Q37
DD 330.9676/1/005 UG
QUARTERLY ECONOMIC REVIEW. **Added/Corp** Uganda Commercial Bank. **VFOAT** UCB Quarterly Economic Review. Vol. 1, No. 1 (Jan./Mar. 1983)-. Periodical. English. Four times a year. $5.00. Uganda Commercial Bank, 12 Kampala Road, PO Box 973, Kampala Uganda. **Tel** 011 256 41 234710. cum. index. **Bk Rev. Ad Acc. Circ:** 2,000.
Desc: Intended to educate and promote public consciousness of the factors that influence the economy.

LC HG2543 .U56a **ISSN** 0738-2146
DD 353.0082/52043/05 US
QUARTERLY JOURNAL / OFFICE OF THE COMPTROLLER OF THE CURRENCY. [Q. j. - U. S., Off. Comptrol. Curr.]. **Main/Corp** United States. Office of the Comptroller of the Currency. **Added/Corp** United States. Office of the Comptroller of the Currency. Multinational Banking Division. Vol. 1, No. 1 (1982)-. Periodical. English. Four times a year. Free on request. Comptroller of the Currency, 490 l'EnfantPlaza East SW, Washington DC 20219. **Tel** (202)874-4700. **ED** Patricia B. Boyd. Index available. cum. index. **Circ:** 7,500 (ctrl). Documents available from Documents on Demand. ***Continues*** *United States. Office of the Comptroller of the Currency. Annual Report.*
Desc: Journal of record for actions and policies of the office of the comptroller of the currency. Contains speeches and testimony, bank merger information, statistical data system and articles covering policies or research conducted by agency staff members.
Ind/Abst Am. Stat. Index.

LC HG1501
DD 332.1 UK
QUARTERLY PERFORMANCE REPORT. (19??)-. Periodical. English. Four times a year. $495.00 UK; $345.00 US, Canada and South America. Metal Bulletin Inc., 220 5th Avenue, 10th Floor, New York NY 10001. **Tel** (800)638-2525, (212)213-6202.

LC HG **ISSN** 0897-2044
DD 332 US
CCC
QUARTERLY REPORT ON MONEY FUND EXPENSE RATIOS. [Q. rep. money fund expens. ratios]. **VFOAT** Donoghue's Quarterly/Money Fund Expense Ratios; Money Fund Expense Ratios. Vol. 1, No. 1 (4th Quarter 1987)-. Periodical. English. Four times a year. $446.25 Massachusetts; $460.06 New York; $425.00 other. IBC Donoghue Organization, 290 Eliot Street, Ashland MA 01721. **Tel** (800)343-5413, (508)881-2800.
Desc: Statistical summary on over 500 taxable and tax-free money funds, identifying top performing funds with similar investment strategies and allowing comparison between trends in different industry segments. Representation on how one fund's performance compares either to another fund or to all funds in a specific category.

LC HG2726 .Q37
DD 332.1/097282 BH
QUARTERLY REVIEW (CENTRAL BANK OF BELIZE. RESEARCH DEPT.). (QUARTERLY REVIEW / PREPARED BY THE RESEARCH DEPARTMENT OF THE CENTRAL BANK OF BELIZE.). **Added/Corp** Central Bank of Belize. Research Dept. Vol. 6, No. 3 (Sept. 1982)-. Periodical. English. Four times a year. $1.00 per copy. Central Bank of Belize, PO Box 852, Belize City Belize. ***Continues*** *Quarterly Review (Monetary Authority of Belize. Research Dept.).*

LC WMLC 93/1699
DD 332.1 LO
QUARTERLY REVIEW / CENTRAL BANK OF LESOTHO. **Added/Corp** Central Bank of Lesotho. Vol. 1, No. 1 (June 1982)-. Periodical. English. Four times a year. $16.00. Central Bank of Lesotho, PO Box 1184, Maseru 100 Lesotho. **Tel** 011 9266 324281, 011 9266 314281, FAX 011 9266 310051.

LC HG3090.5.A7 Q37
DD 330.945/85/005 MM
QUARTERLY REVIEW - CENTRAL BANK OF MALTA. RESEARCH DIVISION. **Added/Corp** Central Bank of Malta. Research Division. Vol. 8, No. 2 (June 1975)-. Periodical. English. Four times a year. Free on request. Central Bank of Malta, Castille Place, Valletta Malta. **Tel** 011 356 247480. ***Continues*** *Quarterly Review (Central Bank of Malta. Research Dept.).*

LC HG1501
DD 332.1 SA
QUARTERLY REVIEW / CENTRAL BANK OF SOLOMON ISLANDS. **Added/Corp** Central Bank of Solomon Islands. Vol. 1, No. 1 (March 1990)-. Periodical. English. Four times a year.

LC HG2559 .F427a **ISSN** 0271-5287
DD 330.977/005 US
QUARTERLY REVIEW - FEDERAL RESERVE BANK OF MINNEAPOLIS. [Q. rev. - Fed. Reserve Bank Minneapolis]. **Main/Corp** Federal Reserve Bank of Minneapolis. **VFOAT** Federal Reserve Bank of Minneapolis Quarterly Review. Vol. 1 (Summer 1977)-. Periodical. English. Four times a year. Free on request. Federal Reserve Bank of Minneapolis, 250 Marquette Avenue, Publ Affairs, Minneapolis MN 55480. **Tel** (612)340-2356. **ED** Kathleen Rolfe, (phone: (612)340-2355). cum. index. **Circ:** 17,000. available on microfilm and microfiche from University Microfilms International (UMI). Documents available from UMI Article Clearinghouse. ***Supersedes*** *Federal Reserve Bank of Minneapolis. Ninth District Quarterly, 0364-4529.*
Desc: Primarily presents economic research aimed at improving policymaking by the Federal Reserve System and other governmental authorities.
Ind/Abst ABI/INFORM Glob. Ed.; ABI/INFORM [Computer File] (Summer 1980-); Acad. Search; Bus. Source Plus; Bus. Source; Econ. Lit. Index; EP Collect.; Expand. Acad. Index (1992-); Fed. Print Econ. Bank. Top.; Gen. BusinessFile; Homework Help.; INFO-SOUTH Abstr.; J. Econ. Lit.; MasterFile FullTEXT 1000; MasterFile FullTEXT 350; MasterFile FullTEXT 650; MasterFile FullTEXT (July 1993-) [Full Txt.]; Newsp. Period. Abstr. (1992-); OCLC; Telebase; UMI ABI/Inform--Bus. Period. Ondisc [Full Txt.]; Wilson Bus. Abstr.

LC HC101 .F42b **ISSN** 0147-6580
DD 330.9/73/092 US
CODEN FRYMAQ
TITLE CHANGE
QUARTERLY REVIEW - FEDERAL RESERVE BANK OF NEW YORK. [Q. rev. - Fed. Reserve Bank New York]. **Main/Corp** Federal Reserve Bank of New York. **Added/Corp** Federal Reserve Bank of New York. FRBNY Quarterly Review. **VFOAT** FRBNY Quarterly Review. Vol. 1 (Winter 1976)-(1994). Periodical. English. Federal Reserve Bank of New York, 33 Liberty Street, New York NY 10045. **Tel** (212)720-5000. **Circ:** 45,000. available on microfilm and microfiche from University Microfilms International (UMI). Documents available from UMI Article Clearinghouse. ***Supersedes*** *Monthly Review - Federal Reserve Bank of New York, 0014-9160.* ***Continued by*** *Economic Policy Review.*
Desc: Reports on business activity, money and bond markets. Discusses selected subjects in economics and usually reprints major speeches of top bank officials.
Ind/Abst ABI/INFORM Glob. Ed.; ABI/INFORM [Computer File] (1990-) [Full Txt.]; Acad. Search (1985-); Bus. ASAP; Bus. Index; Bus. Source Plus; Bus. Source; Curr. Cit.; Econ. Lit. Index (1992-); EP Collect. [Select. Cov.]; Expand. Acad. Index; F&S Index Plus Text, Int. (1985-); Fed. Print Econ. Bank. Top. (1985-); Gen. BusinessFile; Gen. Period. Index; Homework Help.; INFO-SOUTH Abstr.; J. Econ. Lit.; MasterFile FullTEXT 1000; MasterFile FullTEXT 350 (July 1993-Dec. 1994) [Full Txt.]; MasterFile FullTEXT 650; MasterFile FullTEXT; Mat. Fact (1992-); Middle East Abstr. Index; Newsp. Period. Abstr. (1991-); OCLC; PAIS Int. Print [Full Txt.]; Telebase; UMI ABI/Inform--Bus. Period. Ondisc; Wilson Bus. Abstr.

LC HC251.A1 N36 **ISSN** 0028-0399
DD 330.942 UK
Pr Rev.
QUARTERLY REVIEW - NATIONAL WESTMINSTER BANK. (QUARTERLY REVIEW.). [Natl. Westminster Bank - Q. rev.]. **Added/Corp** National Westminster Bank. (Nov. 1968)-. Periodical. English. Four times a year. Free on request. National Westminster Bank PLC, 41 Lothbury, London EC2P 2BP United Kingdom. **Tel** 011 44 171 7261864. available on microfilm and microfiche from University Microfilms International (UMI). Documents available from The Genuine Article. ***Formed by the union of*** *Westminster Bank Review; National Provincial Bank Review* ***and*** *District Bank Review.*
Ind/Abst AGRICOLA; Coal Abstr.; Contents Pages Manage.; Curr. Contents Soc. Behav. Sci.; Econ. Lit. Index (19??-); Gen. BusinessFile (1992-); Geogr. Abstr. Human Geogr.; Int. Dev. Abstr.; J. Econ. Lit.; Manage. Market. Abstr.; Middle East Abstr. Index; Res. Alert [Full Cov.]; Selec. Coop. Index Manage. Period.; Soc. Sci. Cit. Index [Select. Cov.].

LC HC10 .Q33 **ISSN** 1062-9769
DD 330 US
CCC
QUARTERLY REVIEW OF ECONOMICS AND FINANCE, THE. (THE QUARTERLY REVIEW OF ECONOMICS AND FINANCE: JOURNAL OF THE MIDWEST ECONOMICS ASSOCIATION.). [Q. rev. econ. finance]. **Added/Corp** Midwest Economics Association. University of Illinois at Urbana-Champaign. Bureau of Economic and Business Research. Vol. 32, No. 1 (Spring 1992)-. Periodical. English. Four times a year (plus one special issue). $215.00. JAI Press Inc., 55 Old Post Road, Suite 2, PO Box 1678, Greenwich CT 06836-1678. **Tel** (203)661-7602, FAX (203)661-0792. **ED** Richard J. Arnould and Joseph E. Finnerty. Documents available from The Genuine Article, UMI Article Clearinghouse. ***Continues*** *Quarterly Review of Economics and Business, 0033-5797.*
Desc: Articles on economics, financial economics, and finance issues.
Ind/Abst ABI/INFORM Glob. Ed.; ABI/INFORM [Computer File] (Apr. 1976-); Am. Hist. Life; Bus. Period. Index (1966-); Curr. Contents Soc. Behav. Sci.; Energy Res. Abstr. (Apr. 1976-); Hosp. Health Admin. Index; INFO-SOUTH Abstr.; J. Econ. Lit.; Mag. Search; MasterFile FullTEXT (Jan. 1994-); Newsp. Period. Abstr. (1989-); Res. Alert [Full Cov.]; Soc. Sci. Cit. Index [Full Cov.]; UMI ABI/Inform--Bus. Period. Ondisc (Fall 1987-) [Full Txt.]; Wilson Bus. Abstr.

LC HG1501
DD 332.1 FJ
QUARTERLY REVIEW / RESERVE BANK OF FIJI. **Added/Corp** Reserve Bank of Fiji. (June 1985)-. Periodical. English. Four times a year. $41.00. Reserve Bank of Fiji, Suva Fiji Islands. **Tel** 011 679 313611, telex 2164. ***Continues*** *Quarterly Review (Central Monetary Authority of Fiji).*
Desc: Contains quarterly analysis of the Fiji economy and data on economic indicators.

LC HG1121 .Q36 **ISSN** 0346-6583
DD 332.4/9485 SW
QUARTERLY REVIEW / SVERIGES RIKSBANK. [Q. rev. - Sver. riksbank]. **Added/Corp** Sveriges Riksbank. (1979)-. Corporate Report. English. Four times a year. Free on request. Sveriges Riksbank, PO Box 16283, S 103 25 Stockholm Sweden. **Tel** 011 46 8 7870000, FAX 011 46 8 210531. **ED** Kerstin Wallmark.
Desc: News and information from the Swedish Central Bank.
Ind/Abst PAIS Int. Print.

LC HG2798 .Q37
DD 330.97296 BF
QUARTERLY STATISTICAL DIGEST. **Added/Corp** Central Bank of the Bahamas. Central Bank of the Bahamas. Research Dept. Vol. 1, No. 3 (Aug. 1992)-. Statistical Publication. English. Four times a year. Free. Central Bank of the Bahamas, PO Box N-4868, Nassau Bahamas. **Tel** 809-322- 2193, FAX (809)322-4321, telex 20115. ***Continues in part*** *Quarterly Review (Central Bank of the Bahamas).*
Desc: Quarterly publication of selected domestic monetary and fiscal statistics including annual, quarterly, and monthly data.

LC HG1501 **ISSN** 1031-332X
DD 332.1 AT
CEASED
QUARTERLY SUMMARY / NATIONAL AUSTRALIA BANK. [Q. summ. - Natl. Aust. Bank]. **Added/Corp** National Australia Bank. (1988)-(1994). Periodical. English. National Australia Bank Ltd, PO Box 84A, Melbourne Victoria 3001 Australia. **Tel** 61346053269. ***Continues*** *Monthly Summary (National Commercial Banking Corporation of Australia), 0314-755X.*
Ind/Abst APAIS, Aust. Public Aff. Inf. Ser.; F&S Index Plus Text, Int. [Select. Cov.].

LC HG **ISSN** 1061-317X
DD 332 US
R.H. MACY & CO. BANKRUPTCY NEWS. [R.H. Macy Co. bankruptcy news]. **Added/Corp** Bankruptcy Creditors' Service. **VFOAT** Bankruptcy News. Issue No. 1 (Jan. 28, 1992)-. Periodical. English. One time a week. $30.00 (single issue). Bankruptcy Creditors' Service, Inc., 6326 Graceland Avenue, Cincinnati OH 45237-4808.

Business and Economics — Banks and Banking

LC HG1501 **ISSN** 1065-724X
DD 332.1 US
RACZ' FINANCIAL DIRECTORY. (1992)-.
Directory. English. $195.00. Racz Publishing, 6000 South Eastern Avenue, Building 7, Suite D, Las Vegas NV 89119.

LC HG3131 .R33
DD 332.1 FI
RAHOITUSMARKKINATILASTOA. VFOAT
Financial Market Statistics; Finansieringsmarknadsstatistik. Multiple languages (Finnish and Swedish). One time a year. Tilastokeskus, PL 504, Annankatu 44, 00101 Helsinki Finland. **Tel** 011 358 0 17341, **FAX** 011 358 0 17342474, telex 1002111 TILASTO SF.
 Desc: Some vols. include revised statistics for the previous year.

LC HG **ISSN** 1040-8959
DD 332 US
RAM RESEARCH BANKCARD UPDATE.
Added/Corp RAM Research/Publishing Co. **VFOAT** RAM Research's Bankcard Update. (198?)-. Trade Publication. English. Twelve times a year. $995.00. RAM Research Corporation, PO Box 1700 (College Estates), Frederick MD 21701. **Tel** (301)695-4660, (301)662-6640, **FAX** (301)695-0160. **ED** Robert McKinley (editor's address: PO Box 1916, Frederick, MD 21702; phone: (301)662-6640). **Circ:** 1,500. **Continues** RAM Bankcard Update, 0894-2390.
 Desc: Focuses on bank credit card trends, pricing and marketing strategies, presents current research on different industry sectors.

LC HG **ISSN** 1053-9719
DD 332 US
Pr Rev.
RAM RESEARCH'S CARDTRAK. See
Consumer Education and Protection.

LC HG1501 **ISSN** 1057-8854
DD 332 US
RANKING THE BANKS. [Rank. banks]. VFOAT
American Banker Ranking the Banks. (1991)-. English. $138.00. American Banker, Concourse Level, 1 State Street Plaza, New York NY 10004. **Tel** (212)803-8200, (800)221-1809, **FAX** (212)943-6256, (212)843-9598. **Continues** Top Numbers, 1042-5349.

LC HG1501
DD 332.1 CM
RAPPORT ANNUEL. Main/Corp BICIC (Bank).
French. Editions Cape, 20 rue Molitor, Paris France. **Continues** Rapport General / BICIC (Bank).

LC HG1501
DD 332.1 BE
RAPPORT ANNUEL. Main/Corp Belgium.
Commission Bancaire et Financiere. 55th (1991)-. French. **Continues** Rapport Annuel.

LC HG1501
DD 332.1 SZ
RAPPORT ANNUEL : BANQUE NATIONALE SUISSE. (19??)-. French (English and German). One time a year. Free. Banque Nationale Suisse, Secretariat General, Bundesplatz 1, CH-3003 Bern Switzerland. **Tel** 011 41 31 210211.

LC HG3396.A7 B36a
DD 332.1/1/0967572 BD
RAPPORT ANNUEL DE LA BANQUE DE LA REPUBLIQUE DU BURUNDI. Main/Corp
Banque de la Republique du Burundi. (19??)-. French. One time a year. Banque de la Republique du Burundi, Service des Etudes, BP 705, Bujumbura-Burundi. **Tel** 011 257 22 5142, telex (2)5142. **Ad Acc. Circ:** 400.
 Desc: Composed of four parts and statistical tables. Parts are: 1) economic and financial change (production, employment, price changes and public finance), 2) currency and credit (fiscal policy, bank liquidity, resources and exploration of the banking system, liquidity of the economy and risks of the fiscal system), 3) balance of payments and changes in the rate of exchange, and 4) bank activities and budget.

LC HG1501
DD 332.1 BE
RAPPORT ANNUEL DE LA BANQUE NATIONALE DE BELGIQUE. (19??)-. French (English and Dutch). One time a year. Free. Banque Nationale de Belgique, rue de Berlaimont 14, B 1000 Brussels Belgium. **Tel** 011 32 2 2212033, **FAX** 011 32 2 2213101, telex 21355 BNKLE B.

LC HG1501
DD 332.1 LU
RAPPORT ANNUEL DE L'INSTITUTE MONETAIRE LUXEMBOURGEOIS POUR L'ANNEE ... = ANNUAL REPORT OF THE IML FOR THE YEAR ... INSTITUT MONETAIRE LUXEMBOURGEOIS.
Main/Corp Institut Monetaire Luxembourgeois. **VFOAT** Annual Report of the IML for the Year ... . (1991)-. French (summaries and/or abstracts in English). L'Institut Monetaire Luxembourgeois, BP 1501, 2983 Luxembourg Luxembourg. **Tel** 011 352 402929. **Continues in part** Bulletin Trimestriel (Institut Monetaire Luxembourgeois).

LC HG4581 .F7a
DD 354/.44/0072 FR
RAPPORT AU PRESIDENT DE LA REPUBLIQUE. Main/Corp France. Commission
des Operations de Bourse. (19??)-. French. One time a year. 135.00F (latest issue). Cob Service Abonnement, 39-40 Quai A Citroen, 75739 Paris Cedex 15 France. **Tel** 011 33 1 40586565. **(Subscription address:** Agent Comptable de la Cob, 39 43 Quai a Citroen, 75739 Paris Cedex 15 France. **Tel** 011 33 1 40586532.) **ED** Jean Farge.
 Desc: This series constitutes the periodic report to the President of the French Republic on the state, development, and data organization of the French Stock Exchange. Ramifications such as social security, international finance, bonds, and salaries/markets are discussed.

LC HG3021 .F73A
DD 332.1/0946 FR
RAPPORT - COMMISSION BANCAIRE.
Main/Corp France. Commission Bancaire. (1984)-. French. Commission Bancaire Secretary Generale, 4 rue Des Colonnes, F 75002 Paris France. **Tel** 011 33 1 42925931, **FAX** 011 33 1 42925940. **Continues** Rapport (France. Commission de Controle des Banques).

LC HG2051.C39 Q46a **ISSN** 0711-1835
DD 332.3/1 CN
RAPPORT DE L'OFFICE DU CREDIT AGRICOLE DU QUEBEC CONCERNANT L'ADMINISTRATION DE LA LOI SUR LE CREDIT FORESTIER. Main/Corp Office du
Credit Agricole du Quebec. (19??)-. French. One time a year.

LC HG1501
DD 332.1 FR
RAPPORT DU CONSEIL NATIONAL DU CREDIT. French. One time a year. 200.00F. Banque
de France, BP 140 01, 75049 Paris Cedex 01 France. **Tel** 011 33 1 42922954.

LC HG3420.A8 B353
DD 332.1/5 FR
RAPPORT ET RESOLUTIONS DU CONSEIL D'ADMINISTRATION, RAPPORT DES COMMISSAIRES AUX COMPTES. Main/Corp Banque Internationale pour
l'Afrique Occidentale. **Added/Corp** Banque Internationale pour l'Afrique Occidentale. Conseil d'Administration. Banque Internationale pour l'Afrique Occidentale. Conseil d'Administration. Assemblee Generale Ordinaire. (19??)-. French. Irregular. Banque International pour l'Afrique Occidentale, 9 Ave de Messine, 75008 Paris France.

LC HG1501
DD 332.1 US
 CEASED
RATE TREND ANALYSIS. (19??)-(Fall 1994).
English. Financial Rates Inc., 11811 US Highway 1, Suite 200, North Palm Beach FL 33408-8888. **Tel** (407)627-7330, **FAX** (407)627-7335. **(Subscription address:** Financial Rates Inc., PO Box 088888, North Palm Beach FL 33408. **Tel** (407)627-7330.)

LC HG1501 **ISSN** 0430-1994
DD 332.1 US
RATES OF CHANGE IN ECONOMIC DATA FOR TEN INDUSTRIAL COUNTRIES. Main/Corp Federal Reserve Bank of
St. Louis. (19??)-. English. Four times a year. Federal Reserve Bank of St. Louis, PO Box 66953, Research and Publication Information, St. Louis MO 63166. **Tel** (314)444-8444, (314)444-8660, **FAX** (314)444-8731.

LC HC186 .R37 **ISSN** 0034-706X
DD 338.981 BL
RBB, REVISTA BANCARIA BRASILEIRA. (REVISTA BANCARIA
BRASILEIRA.). [RBB Rev. banc. bras.]. (19??)-. Periodical. Portuguese. Twelve times a year. $150.00. Revista Bancaria Brasileira, BP Teixeira / Caixa Postal 2291, ZC 00 Rio de Janeiro Brazil. **Tel** 011 55 21 2404175, 011 55 21 2407275, **FAX** 011 55 21 2400747. **ED** Oyama Pereira Teixeria. **Ad Acc, Adv Mgr:** Ronaldo Boucas. Full Page (B&W) $500.00. **Circ:** 15,000.
 Ind/Abst Foreign Lang. Index.

LC HG **ISSN** 0430-1862
DD 332 US
READINGS IN SOUTHERN FINANCE.
Main/Corp Federal Reserve Bank of Atlanta. Research Dept. No. 1 (Jan. 1960)-. English. Federal Reserve Bank of Atlanta, 104 Marietta Street Northwest, Atlanta GA 30303. **Tel** (404)521-8788.

LC KF1501.Z9 R4 **ISSN** 0734-9653
DD 346.73/077 347.30677 US
REAL ESTATE: DEBTORS' AND CREDITOR'S RIGHTS. (REAL ESTATE,
DEBTORS' AND CREDITORS' RIGHTS : ALI-ABA COURSE OF STUDY, MATERIALS.). **Added/Corp** American Law Institute-American Bar Association Committee on Continuing Professional Education. **VFOAT** ALI-ABA Course of Study, Materials; A.L.I.-A.B.A. Course of Study, Materials. (19??)-. Periodical. English. One time a year. American Law Institute, 4025 Chestnut Street, Philadelphia PA 19104-3099. **Tel** (215)243-1661, (800)253-6397, **FAX** (215)243-1664.

LC HG **ISSN** 1056-506X
DD 332 US
 TITLE CHANGE
REDEMPTION DIGEST AND CORPORATE ACTIONS. [Redempt. dig. corp.
actions]. **VFOAT** Redemption Digest. (198?)-(1995). Periodical. English. Redemption Digest, PO Box 2055, Canal Street Station, New York NY 10013. **Tel** (800)879-2663, (212)219-1550, **FAX** (212)925-0262. **ED** Chris Kentouris. cum. index. **Bk Rev. Ad Acc, Adv Mgr:** Rafi Reguer, **Tel** (212)966-9031. available on an online database; available via fax. **Continued by** Redemption Digest and Securities Industry Daily.
 Desc: Covers the municipal and corporate bond market with emphasis on redemptions, restructurings, bankruptcies, tender offers, consent solicitations, and etc.

LC HG1501 **ISSN** 1045-3369
DD 332 US
REGION (MINNEAPOLIS, MINN.), THE.
(THE REGION.). [Region]. **Added/Corp** Federal Reserve Bank of Minneapolis. (Aug. 1987)-. Periodical. English. Four times a year (Mar., June, Sept., Dec.). Free on request. Federal Reserve Bank of Minneapolis, 250 Marquette Avenue, Publ Affairs, Minneapolis MN 55480. **Tel** (612)340-2356.
 Ind/Abst EP Collect.; Homework Help.; MasterFile FullTEXT 1000; MasterFile FullTEXT 350; MasterFile FullTEXT 650; MasterFile FullTEXT; OCLC; Telebase.

LC HC107.A165 R44 **ISSN** 1049-5339
DD 330.978/005 US
REGIONAL ECONOMIC DIGEST. [Reg.
econ. dig.]. **Added/Corp** Federal Reserve Bank of Kansas City. Economic Research Dept. 1st Quarter (1990)-. Periodical. English. Four times a year. Free on request. Federal Reserve Bank of Kansas City, 925 Grand Avenue, Kansas City MO 64198. **Tel** (816)881-2683. **Continues** Financial Letter, 0739-5299.
 Ind/Abst Fed. Print Econ. Bank. Top.

LC HG1501
DD 332.1 US
●REGIONAL ECONOMIST, THE. Added/Corp
Federal Reserve Bank of Saint Louis. (Jan. 1993)-. Periodical. English. Four times a year. Free on request. Federal Reserve Bank of St. Louis, PO Box 66953, Research and Publication Information, St. Louis MO 63166. **Tel** (314)444-8444, (314)444-8660, **FAX** (314)444-8731. **Continues** Pieces of Eight.
 Desc: A regional economics publication addressing national and regional economic issues as they affect the Eighth Federal Reserve District.

LC HG1501 **ISSN** 1062-1865
DD 330 US
REGIONAL REVIEW (BOSTON, MASS.).
(REGIONAL REVIEW / THE FEDERAL RESERVE BANK OF BOSTON.). [Reg. rev.]. **Added/Corp** Federal Reserve Bank of Boston. **VFOAT** Federal Reserve Bank of Boston Regional Review. Vol. 1, No. 1 (Winter 1991)-. Periodical. English. Four times a year. Free on request. Federal Reserve Bank of Boston, 600 Atlantic Avenue, Research Library D, Boston MA 02106. **Tel** (617)973-3397, (617)973-3403.
 Ind/Abst EP Collect.; Fed. Print Econ. Bank. Top.; Homework Help.; MasterFile FullTEXT 1000; MasterFile FullTEXT 350; MasterFile FullTEXT 650; MasterFile FullTEXT; OCLC; Telebase.

LC HG1501 **ISSN** 0821-6088
DD 332.1/07/1171 CN
REGLEMENTS RELATIFS AUX PROGRAMMES - INSTITUT DES BANQUIERS CANADIENS. (REGLEMENTS
RELATIFS AUX PROGRAMMES.). [Reglem. relat. programmes - Inst. banq. can.]. **Main/Corp** Institut des Banquiers Canadiens. 1982/1983-. French. One time a year. Free. Institut Des Banquiers Canadiens, 1801 Av. Du College McGill, Bureau 720, Montreal Quebec H3A 2N4 Canada. ctrl circ. **Continues** Institut des Banquiers Canadiens. Annuaires, 0229-9941.

LC HG **ISSN** 1064-4342
DD 332 US
REGULATORY COMPLIANCE WATCH.
(REGULATORY COMPLIANCE WATCH : A WEEKLY POLICY REPORT ON ENFORCEMENT AND SUPERVISION BY FINANCIAL REGULATORS.). [Regul.

Business and Economics — Banks and Banking

compliance watch]. (Oct. 27, 1989)-. Periodical. English. One time a week. Mortgage Commentary Publications, 4829 Fairmont Avenue, Bethesda MD 20814-0240. **Tel** (301)654-5580.
Ind/Abst PTS Newsl. Database [Full Txt.].

LC HG2889.A25 B35A
DD 332.1/2/098112 BL
RELATORIO DE ATIVIDADES / BANCO DO ESTADO DO ACRE, S.A. Main/Corp
Banco do Estado do Acre. 1979-. Portuguese. One time a year. **Continues** Banco do Estado do Acre. Relatorio.

LC HG5720.8.A2 N37a
DD 332.2 CE
REPORT & ACCOUNTS. Main/Corp National Development Bank of Sri Lanka. **VFOAT** Report and Accounts. (1980)-. English (Tamil and Sinhalese). One time a year. free. National Development Bank of Sri Lanka, PO Box 1825, No. 40 Nawam Mawatha, Colombo 02, Sri Lanka. **Tel** 011 94 1 4373503, 437701-10, FAX 011 94 1 440262, telex 21399 NDB CE. **Circ:** 1,500 (ctrl).

LC HG2998.B34 B37A
DD 332.1/0941 UK
REPORT & ACCOUNTS. Main/Corp Barclays Bank. **VFOAT** Report and Accounts. English. One time a year. Barclays Bank Ltd, PO Box 12, 1 Wimborne Road, Poole Dorset BH15 2BB United Kingdom. **Tel** 011 44 1202 671212, telex 887591. **Formed by the union of** Barclays Bank. Report & Accounts **and** Barclays Bank International. Report and Accounts.

LC HG2994 .A2 ISSN 0308-5279
DD 332.1/1/0941 UK
REPORT AND ACCOUNTS - BANK OF ENGLAND. [Rep. acc. - Bank Engl.]. **Main/Corp** Bank of England. (1970/71)-?. English. One time a year. Free on request. Bank of England Bulletin Group, Threadneedle Street, London EC2R 8AH United Kingdom. **Tel** 011 44 171 6014139, FAX 011 44 171 6015288. **Continues** Bank of England. Report, 0067-3625. **Continued in part by** Annual Report Under the Banking Act for ... .

LC HG185.B47 B475a
DD 354.72990082/2/06 BM
REPORT & ACCOUNTS - BERMUDA MONETARY AUTHORITY. Main/Corp
Bermuda Monetary Authority. (1978)-. Corporate Report. English. One time a year. Free on request. Bermuda Monetary Authority, PO Box HM 2447, Hamilton HMJX Bermuda. **Tel** 809 295 5278, FAX 809 292 7471, telex 029 3567 BEEMA BA. **Continues** Bermuda Monetary Authority. Final Accounts and Annual Report - Bermuda Monetary Authority.

LC HG3440.3.P574 M385C
DD 332.1/2/096982 MF
REPORT & ACCOUNTS FOR THE YEAR ENDED 30TH APRIL ... / THE MAURITIUS COMMERCIAL BANK LIMITED. Main/Corp Mauritius Commercial Bank Limited. **VFOAT** Report and Accounts for the Year Ended 30th April ... . English.

LC HG3399.S53 N34
DD 332.2 SL
REPORT AND ACCOUNTS - NATIONAL DEVELOPMENT BANK, SIERRA LEONE.
Main/Corp National Development Bank, Sierra Leone. English. National Development Bank / Sierra Leone, Leone House, 21/23 Staka Stevens Street, Sierra Leone.

LC HG3446 .R4 ISSN 0484-5412
DD 330.994/005 AT
REPORT AND FINANCIAL STATEMENTS - RESERVE BANK OF AUSTRALIA. Main/Corp Reserve Bank of Australia. 1959/60-. English. One time a year. Reserve Bank of Australia / Secretary Department, GPO Box 3947, Sydney New South Wales 2001 Australia. **Tel** 11 61 2 5519724, 011 61 2 5518841, FAX 011 61 2 234900, telex 20106.

LC HG2411 .N4
DD 332.109 US
REPORT - NEW HAMPSHIRE. BANK COMMISSIONER'S OFFICE. Main/Corp New Hampshire. Bank Commissioner's Office. (1844)-. English.

LC HG1581 .A56A ISSN 0735-7982
DD 332.1/06/073 US
REPORT OF AIB CHAPTER PROGRAMS & ... ACTIVITIES. Main/Corp American Institute of Banking. **VFOAT** Report of A.I.B. Chapter Programs and ... Activities. English. One time a year. American Bankers Association, 1120 Connecticut Avenue Northwest, Washington DC 20036. **Tel** (202)663-5221, (202)663-5000, FAX (202)828-4541.

LC HG1501
DD 332.1 US
REPORT OF FINANCIAL CONDITION AND OPERATIONS OF THE COMMODITY CREDIT CORPORATION / UNITED STATES DEPARTMENT OF AGRICULTURE, COMMODITY CREDIT CORPORATION. Main/Corp Commodity Credit Corporation. Government Publication. English. One time a year. US Department of Agriculture / Commodity Credit Corporation, 14th Street & Independence Avenue SW, Room 200-A, Washington DC 20250. **Tel** (202)720-3631, FAX (202)205-2883. available on microfiche (Vols. for (1981-) distributed to depository libraries). **Continues** Commodity Credit Corporation. Report of Financial Condition and Operations.

LC HG2038.A2 A4a
DD 334/.22/09761 US
REPORT OF THE CREDIT UNION SUPERVISOR. Main/Corp Alabama. Bureau of Credit Unions. (19??)-. English. One time a year. State Banking Department of Alabama, State Banking Department, 651 Administrative Building, Montgomery AL 36130.

LC HG2040.5.U5 F38A ISSN 0094-7156
DD 353.0086/5045 US
REPORT OF THE FEDERAL HOME LOAN MORTGAGE CORPORATION.
Main/Corp Federal Home Loan Mortgage Corporation. English. One time a year. Federal Home Loan Mortgage Corporation, PO Box 37248, Washington DC 20013.

LC JQ2921.A2 A3 HG3399.R5
DD 354/.689/100825 RH
REPORT OF THE REGISTRAR OF BANKS AND FINANCIAL INSTITUTIONS.
Main/Corp Southern Rhodesia. Ministry of Finance. (19??)-. Government Publication. English. One time a year. $10.00. Ministry of Finance Economic Planning and Development, Munhumutapa Building, Private Bag 7705, Causeway Harare Zimbabwe. **Tel** 7945711, telex 2141 MINFIN.
Desc: Information pertaining to Ministry of Finance, economic planning and development. The Registrar of Banks and Financial institutions, and Registrar of Building societies.

LC HG3402 .A37A
DD 354.68910082/52/06 RH
REPORT OF THE REGISTRAR OF BANKS AND FINANCIAL INSTITUTIONS AND REGISTRAR OF BUILDING SOCIETIES FOR THE YEAR ENDED DECEMBER 31 ... - (ZIMBABWE).
Main/Corp Zimbabwe. Registrar of Banks and Financial Institutions. 1979-. English. One time a year. $0.50. Zimbabwe Government Printing, PO Box 8062, Causeway Harare Zimbabwe. **Tel** 011 263 4 706161. **Continues** Report of the Registrar of Banks and Financial Institutions and Registrar of Building Societies for the Year Ended December 31 ... .

LC HG2156.I2 R43a
DD 332.3/2/09417 IE
REPORT OF THE REGISTRAR OF BUILDING SOCIETIES. Main/Corp Ireland (Eire). Registry of Building Societies. (19??)-. English. Registry of Building Societies Centre, South Frederick Street, Dublin 2 Ireland.

LC HG3286 .A25
DD 332.110954 II
REPORT ON CURRENCY AND FINANCE - RESERVE BANK OF INDIA. (REPORT ON CURRENCY AND FINANCE.). **Main/Corp** Reserve Bank of India. (1936)-. English. Price varies. Reserve Bank of India, Economic Department, PO Box 1036, Bombay 400001 India. **(Subscription address:** Prints India, 11 Darya Ganj, New Delhi 110002 India. **Tel** 011 91 11 3268645, FAX 011 91 11 3275542, telex 31-61087 PRIN-IN.**)**

LC HG3756.U54 K36A ISSN 0360-5663
DD 332.7/43 US
REPORT ON KANSAS UNIFORM CONSUMER CREDIT CODE. Main/Corp
Kansas. Office of Consumer Credit Commissioner. (19??)-. English. One time a year. Kansas Consumer Credit Commissioner, 900 Jackson, Room 352, Topeka KS 66612. **Tel** (913)296-3151.

LC HG1501
DD 332.1 US
REPORT ON PRODUCTION AND EARNINGS OF RRS. (19??)-. English. One time a year. $1,400.00 (nonmembers); $300.00 to $675.00 for SIA members. Securities Industry Association, 120 Broadway/35th Floor, New York NY 10271. **Tel** (212)608-1500, FAX (212)608-1604. **Circ:** 125 (ctrl).
Desc: In addition to information on production and earnings, this survey includes extensive and detailed data on payouts and ticket size. The publication also provides thorough information on production, earnings, and the training costs of newly-registered retail RRs.

LC HG1501
DD 332.1 US
REPORT ON THE CONDITION OF SAVINGS AND LOAN ASSOCIATIONS FOR THE YEAR ENDING ... . Main/Corp Iowa. Savings and Loan Division. **VFOAT** Iowa Building and Loan Associations, Annual Report; Iowa Savings and Loan Associations, Annual Report; Annual Report, Savings and Loan Associations, State of Iowa. English. One time a year.
Desc: Publication of the Iowa Savings and Loan Association. The report provides available economic information on the current status of savings and loan associations.

LC HG3284 .R43
DD 332.1/0954 II
REPORT ON TREND AND PROGRESS OF BANKING IN INDIA. 1976-77-. English. One time a year. **Continues in part** Annual Report (Reserve Bank of India. Central Board of Directors).

LC HG3450.M444 S727B
DD 332.1/224/09945 AT
REPORT, STATEMENTS, RETURNS, ETC., FOR THE YEAR ENDED 30TH JUNE ... . Main/Corp State Bank of Victoria. (198?)-. English. One time a year.

LC HG4050 .R45 ISSN 0883-4644
DD 338.6/44/0973 US
REPORT TO EXECUTIVES ON LARGE COMPANIES' BANKING PRACTICES.
[Rep. exec. large co. bank. pract.]. **Added/Corp** Greenwich Research Associates. (19??)-. English. Greenwich Research Associates Inc, Office Park 8, Greenwich CT 06830.

LC HG4050 .R46 ISSN 0748-7541
DD 332.1/0973 US
REPORT TO EXECUTIVES ON MIDDLE MARKET FINANCIAL MANAGEMENT.
Added/Corp Greenwich Research Associates. (19??)-. Trade Publication. English. One time a year. Greenwich Research Associates Inc, Office Park 8, Greenwich CT 06830.

LC HG2411.N9 D46a
DD 332.1/09784 US
REPORT TO THE STATE BANKING BOARD, STATE CREDIT UNION BOARD, AND TO THE GOVERNOR.
Main/Corp North Dakota. Dept. of Banking and Financial Institutions. **Added/Corp** North Dakota. State Banking Board. North Dakota. State Credit Union Board. (1979)-. English. Every 2 years. **Continues** North Dakota. Dept. of Banking and Financial Institutions. Biennial Report of the Department of Banking and Financial Institutions to the State Banking Board of North Dakota; **Absorbed** Biennial Report for the Years Ending ... .

LC HG3110.B84 B442A
DD 332 BE
REPORTS AND BALANCE SHEET PRESENTED TO THE SHAREHOLDERS AT THEIR GENERAL MEETING. Main/Corp
Belgolaise. **VFOAT** Rapports et Bilan Presentes a l'Assemblee Generale des Actionnaires. 1st- 1961-. Multiple languages (English and French). Belgolaise, 1 Cantersteen, Brussels Belgium.

LC HG187.5 .Z33 R46
DD 354.68940072/31 ZA
REPUBLIC OF ZAMBIA, FINANCIAL REPORT. Added/Corp Bank of Zambia. (19??)-. English. One time a year. Price varies per volume. Zambia Government Printer, PO Box 30136, Lusaka Zambia. **Circ:** 900.
Desc: The report provides information on the accounting system used by the government. The publication also presents relevant facts and figures relating the current condition of accounts used in the estimates of revenue and expenditure.

LC HG1 .R38 ISSN 0196-3821
DD 382/.05 US
RESEARCH IN FINANCE. Vol.1 (1979)-. English. Irregular. $73.25. JAI Press Inc., 55 Old Post Road, Suite 2, PO Box 1678, Greenwich CT 06836-1678. **Tel** (203)661-7602, FAX (203)661-0792. **ED** Andrew H. Chen.

LC HG136 .R47 ISSN 0882-3138
DD 332/.05 US
RESEARCH IN FINANCE. SUPPLEMENT. Vol. 1 (1984)-. Monographic series. English. Irregular. JAI Press Inc., 55 Old Post Road, Suite 2, PO Box 1678, Greenwich CT 06836-1678. **Tel** (203)661-7602, FAX (203)661-0792. **ED** Haim Levy.

LC HG1 .R39 ISSN 1052-7788
DD 332.1/05 US
RESEARCH IN FINANCIAL SERVICES. [Res. financ. serv.]. Vol. 1 (1989)-. English. One time a year. $73.25. JAI Press Inc., 55 Old Post Road, Suite 2, PO Box 1678, Greenwich CT 06836-1678. **Tel** (203)661-7602, FAX (203)661-0792. **ED** George Kaufman.

LC HD2755.5 .R467 ISSN 0275-5319
DD 338.8/8/05 US
RESEARCH IN INTERNATIONAL BUSINESS AND FINANCE. See Business and Economics-International Economic Relations.

LC HG1501 ISSN 0145-0301
DD 332.1 US
RESEARCH LIBRARY, RECENT ACQUISITIONS. **Main/Corp** Board of Governors of the Federal Reserve System (U.S.). No. 1 (June 1980)-. Periodical. English. Twelve times a year. Free on request. Board of Governors of the Federal Reserve System, Mail Stop 127, Washington DC 20551. **Tel** (202)452-3244, (202)452-3245. ***Continues*** *Board of Governors of the Federal Reserve System (U.S.). Research Library, Recent Acquisitions, 0145-0301.*

LC HG1501 ISSN 0269-3933
DD 332.1 UK
RESEARCH PAPERS IN BANKING AND FINANCE. [Res. pap. bank. finance]. **VFOAT** IEF Research Papers in Banking and Finance. (1986)-. Monographic series. English. Irregular. University College of North Wales, Institute for European Finance, Bangor Gwynedd LL572DG United Kingdom. **Tel** 011 44 1248 382277, FAX 011 44 1248 364760. **ED** E. P. M. Gardener and J. R. S. Rewell. **Circ:** 100.
Desc: Research in banking and finance.
Ind/Abst Curr. Cit.

ISSN 0430-1897
DD 330 US
RESEARCH REPORT - FEDERAL RESERVE BANK OF BOSTON. (RESEARCH REPORT TO THE FEDERAL RESERVE BANK OF BOSTON.). **Added/Corp** Federal Reserve Bank of Boston. No. 30 (1965)-. Monographic series. English. Irregular. Price varies per volume. Centre Distribution Reunion Musee Nationale, 1 31 Allee Du 12 Fev 1934, 77186 Noisiel France. **Tel** 11 33 1 60060314. ***Continues*** *Research Report to Federal Reserve Bank of Boston (1962).*

LC HG188.I6 R38 ISSN 0034-5512
DD 332.1/1/0954 II
RESERVE BANK OF INDIA BULLETIN. **Added/Corp** Reserve Bank of India. **VFOAT** Bulletin. (Jan. 1947)-. Bulletin. English. Twelve times a year. $200.00. Reserve Bank of India, Economic Department, PO Box 1036, Bombay 400001 India. **(Subscription address:** Prints India, 11 Darya Ganj, New Delhi 110002 India. **Tel** 011 91 11 3268645, FAX 011 91 11 3275542, telex 31-61087 PRIN-IN.) ***Continues*** *Statistical Summary (Reserve Bank of India).*

LC HG ISSN 1045-0130
DD 332 US
TITLE CHANGE
RESOLUTION TRUST REPORTER. [Resolut. trust report.]. Vol. 1, #1 (Sept. 11, 1989)-(19??). Periodical. English. Dorset Group Inc., 212 West 35th Street, 13th Floor, New York NY 10001. **Tel** (212)563-4405, FAX (212)564-8879. **Ad Acc, Adv Mgr:** Jim Hollander. ***Merged with*** *Bank Resolution Reporter, 1056-7232* ***to form*** *Problem Asset Reporter, 1071-4960.*

LC HG2611.I3 R47
DD 332.1/09773 US
RESOURCES AND LIABILITIES OF ILLINOIS STATE BANKS AT THE CLOSE OF BUSINESS ON ... . **Added/Corp** Illinois. Commissioner of Banks and Trust Companies. (19??)-. English. Four times a year. Illinois Commissioner of Banks & Trust Companies, Resisch Building/Room 400, Springfield IL 62701.

LC HG1501
DD 332.1 US
RESPA SPECIAL REPORT AND OPINION LETTERS. **VAT** Real Estate Settlement Procedures Act Special Report and Opinion Letters. (1987)-. Periodical. English. Irregular. $100.00 (opinion letters), $25.00 (copy of regulations as proposed). Inside Mortgage Finance Inc., PO Box 42387, Washington DC 20015. **Tel** (301)951-1240, FAX (301)656-1709.
Desc: Compilation of proposals, drafts and opinion letters from 1988 to the present of the controversial Real Estate Settlement Procedures Act. Includes letters from lenders, Realtors and others concerning legal and technical issues related to RESPA as well as the response from the Department of Housing and Urban Development.

ISSN 0835-7366
DD 354.7110072/32/05 CN
RESPONSE TO THE ... REPORT OF THE AUDITOR GENERAL - PROVINCE OF BRITISH COLUMBIA. FINANCE AND CORPORATE RELATIONS. (RESPONSE TO THE ... REPORT OF THE AUDITOR GENERAL.). [Response Rep. Audit. Gen. - Prov. B.C., Minist. Finance Corp. Relat.]. **Main/Corp** British Columbia. Ministry of Finance and Corporate Relations. (1987)-. English. Ministry of Finance, 1450 Government Street, Information Service, Victoria British Columbia V8W 3E7 Canada. ***Continues*** *Response to the ... Report of the Auditor General / British Columbia. Ministry of Finance, 0711-9054.*

LC HG2441 .R52 ISSN 0272-0000
DD 332.1/025/73 US
RETAIL BANK CREDIT REFERRAL DIRECTORY. (19??)-. Directory. English. Irregular. $35.00 (per copy). American Bankers Association, 1120 Connecticut Avenue Northwest, Washington DC 20036. **Tel** (202)663-5221, (202)663-5000, FAX (202)828-4544.

LC HG1501 ISSN 0261-1740
DD 332.1 UK
RETAIL BANKER INTERNATIONAL (LONDON EDITION). (RETAIL BANKER INTERNATIONAL.). [Retail banker int.]. **VFOAT** Retail Banker. Issue No. 1 (18 May 1981)-. Trade Publication. English. Six times a year (23 issues). $879.00. Lafferty Publications Ltd., Tower Ida Centre Pearse Street, Dublin 2 Ireland. **Tel** 011 353 1 6718022, FAX 011 353 1 718520. **ED** Patrick A. T. Frazer.
Desc: A worldwide bulletin on the consumer financial services industry.

LC HG1501
DD 332.1 AT
RETAIL BANKING PRODUCTS SURVEY. (19??)-. Trade Publication. English. Twelve times a year. 1730.00Aus$. Horan Wall & Walker Pty Ltd, 15-19 Prospect Street, POB 8, Surry Hills New South Wales 2010 Australia. **Tel** 02 331 6600, FAX 02 380 5533. **ED** Jayson Forrest. available on an online database; available on diskette.
Desc: Detailed surveys of interest rates, terms and conditions, fees and charges for retail products available from Australian banks and building societies.

LC HG1501 ISSN 1032-870X
DD 332.17520994 AT
RETAIL BANKING PRODUCTS SURVEY. AT CALL DEPOSITS. (RETAIL BANKING PRODUCTS SURVEY. AT CALL DEPOSITS.). [Retail bank. prod. surv., Depos.]. **VFOAT** HWW information; At Call Deposits. (1989)-. Trade Publication. English. Twelve times a year. 1730.00Aus$. Horan Wall & Walker Pty Ltd, 15-19 Prospect Street, POB 8, Surry Hills New South Wales 2010 Australia. **Tel** 02 331 6600, FAX 02 380 5533. **ED** Jayson Forrest. available on an online database; available on diskette. ***Continues in part*** *HWW Retail Banking Products Survey, 1031-4148.*

LC HG3691 ISSN 1032-8726
DD 332.740994 AT
RETAIL BANKING PRODUCTS SURVEY. CONTINUING CREDIT. [Retail bank. prod. surv., Contin. credit]. **VFOAT** HWW information; Continuing Credit. (1989)-. Trade Publication. English. Twelve times a year. 1730.00aus$. Horan Wall & Walker Pty Ltd, 15-19 Prospect Street, POB 8, Surry Hills New South Wales 2010 Australia. **Tel** 02 331 6600, FAX 02 380 5533. **ED** Jayson Forrest. available on an online database; available on diskette. ***Continues in part*** *HWW Retail Banking Products Survey, 1031-4148.*

LC HG1685 ISSN 1032-8742
DD 332.760994 AT
RETAIL BANKING PRODUCTS SURVEY. CREDIT CARDS. [Retail bank. prod. surv., Credit cards]. **VFOAT** HWW information; Credit Cards. (1989)-. Trade Publication. English. Twelve times a year. 1730.00Aus$. Horan Wall & Walker Pty Ltd, 15-19 Prospect Street, POB 8, Surry Hills New South Wales 2010 Australia. **Tel** 02 331 6600, FAX 02 380 5533. **ED** Jayson Forrest. available on an online database; available on diskette. ***Continues in part*** *HWW Retail Banking Products Survey, 1031-4148.*

LC HG1501 ISSN 1032-8718
DD 332.17520994 AT
RETAIL BANKING PRODUCTS SURVEY. TERM DEPOSITS. [Retail bank. prod. surv., Term depos.]. **VFOAT** HWW information; Term Deposits. (1989)-. Trade Publication. English. Twelve times a year. 1730.00Aus$. Horan Wall & Walker Pty Ltd, 15-19 Prospect Street, POB 8, Surry Hills New South Wales 2010 Australia. **Tel** 02 331 6600, FAX 02 380 5533. **ED** Jayson Forrest. available on an online database; available on diskette. ***Continues in part*** *HWW Retail Banking Products Survey, 1031-4148.*

LC HG1501 ISSN 1032-8734
DD 332.17530994 AT
RETAIL BANKING PRODUCTS SURVEY. TERM LOANS. [Retail bank. prod. surv., Term loans]. **VFOAT** HWW information; Term Loans. (1989)-. Trade Publication. English. Twelve times a year. 1730.00Aus$. Horan Wall & Walker Pty Ltd, 15-19 Prospect Street, POB 8, Surry Hills New South Wales 2010 Australia. **Tel** 02 331 6600, FAX 02 380 5533. **ED** Jayson Forrest. available on an online database; available on diskette. ***Continues in part*** *HWW Retail Banking Products Survey, 1031-4148.*

LC HG1660.U5 A53a ISSN 1058-885X
DD 332.1/752/0973 US
RETAIL BANKING REPORT. (RETAIL BANKING REPORT : PEER PERFORMANCE SURVEY.). [Retail bank. rep.]. **Added/Corp** American Bankers Association. Branch Administration Division. **VFOAT** Peer Performance Survey. (1990/91)-. English. One time a year. $180.00. American Bankers Association, 1120 Connecticut Avenue Northwest, Washington DC 20036. **Tel** (202)663-5221, (202)663-5000, FAX (202)828-4544. ***Continues*** *American Bankers Association. Retail Deposit Services Report, 0270-2762.*

LC HG1601
DD 332.1/2 UK
RETAIL BANKING REVOLUTION : AN INTERNATIONAL PERSPECTIVE, THE. (19??)-. English. Lafferty Publications Ltd., Tower Ida Centre Pearse Street, Dublin 2 Ireland. **Tel** 011 353 1 6718022, FAX 011 353 1 718520.

LC HG1501
DD 332.1 US
RETAIL BANKING SOURCEBOOK. (19??)-. Directory. English. $247.00. Phillips Business Information Inc., 1201 Seven Locks Road, PO Box 61130, Potomac MD 20854. **Tel** (301)424-3338, (301)340-1520, (800)777-5005, FAX (301)424-4297, telex 358149. ***Continues*** *The ... Banking Technology Directory, 1054-3317.*
Desc: Serves as a guide to technologies, delivery systems and services. Gives key business contacts and profiles suppliers of retail banking products and services, including ATMs, POS terminals, plastic cards, branch automation components, credit scoring, etc.

LC HC107.A15 A33 ISSN 0014-9187
DD 330.973/005 US
CODEN FRBRDV
REVIEW / FEDERAL RESERVE BANK OF ST. LOUIS. [Rev. - Fed. Reserve Bank of St. Louis]. **Added/Corp** Federal Reserve Bank of St. Louis. **VAT** Review - Federal Reserve Bank of Saint Louis. Vol. 44, No. 1 (Jan. 1962)-. Periodical. English. Six times a year. Free on request. Federal Reserve Bank of St. Louis, PO Box 66953, Research and Publication Information, St. Louis MO 63166. **Tel** (314)444-8444, (314)444-8660, FAX (314)444-8731. available on microfilm and microfiche from University Microfilms International (UMI). Documents available from UMI Article Clearinghouse. ***Continues*** *Monthly Review (Federal Reserve Bank of St. Louis), 0362-3491.*
Ind/Abst ABI/INFORM Glob. Ed.; ABI/INFORM [Computer File] (Feb. 1981-); Acad. Search; Bus. ASAP (1992-) [Full Txt.]; Bus. Index (1985-); Bus. Period. Index; Bus. Source Plus; Bus. Source; Curr. Cit.; Econ. Lit. Index (199?-); Energy Res. Abstr. (July 1979-); EP Collect.; Expand. Acad. Index (1992-); Fed. Print Econ. Bank. Top.; Gen. BusinessFile (1988-); Gen. Period. Index (1988-); Homework Help.; INFO-SOUTH Abstr.; J. Econ. Lit.; Leis., Rec., Tour. Abstr.; MasterFile FullTEXT 1000; MasterFile FullTEXT 350; MasterFile FullTEXT 650; MasterFile FullTEXT (Jan. 1993-) [Full Txt.]; Middle East Abstr. Index; Newsp. Period. Abstr. (1992-); OCLC; Rural Dev. Abstr.; Telebase; UMI ABI/Inform--Bus. Period. Ondisc [Full Txt.]; Wilson Bus. Abstr.; World Agric. Econ. Rural Sociol. Abstr.

LC HG1 .R485 ISSN 0893-9454
DD 332.05/6 US
CCC
REVIEW OF FINANCIAL STUDIES, THE. [Rev. financ. stud.]. **Added/Corp** Society for Financial Studies. Vol. 1, No. 1 (Spring 1988)-. Periodical. English. Four times a year. $195.00. Oxford University Press / New York, 200 Madison Avenue, New York NY 10016. **Tel** (212)679-7300, (919)677-0977, (800)451-7556, (800)445-9714, FAX (919)677-1303. **(Subscription address:** Oxford University Press / USA, Journals Marketing Department, Oxford University Press, 2001 Evans Road, Cary NC 27513. **Tel** (800)451-7556,

(919)677-0977, FAX (919)677-1714.) **ED** Stephen Brown, Chester Spatt, Michael Gibbons and Jonathan Ingersoll. available on microfilm and microfiche from University Microfilms International (UMI). Documents available from The Genuine Article.
Desc: Publishes significant new research in financial economics, striving to establish a balance between theoretical and empirical studies. The principal criteria for inclusion is a paper's quality and contribution to the field of finance, without undue regard to its technical difficulties.
Ind/Abst Curr. Cit.; Curr. Contents Soc. Behav. Sci.; Econ. Lit. Index (199?-); J. Econ. Lit.; Res. Alert [Full Cov.]; Soc. Sci. Cit. Index [Full Cov.].

LC HG1501 **ISSN** 1355-6223
DD 332.1 UK
●**REVIEW OF POLICY ISSUES, THE.** [Rev. policy issues]. (1994)-. Academic Scholarly Publication. English. Four times a year. £45.00 (institutions), £20.00 (individuals). Sheffield Hallam University, 113 Arundel Street, Sheffield S1 2NT United Kingdom. **Tel** 011 44 114 2781112, FAX 011 44 114 2753606. **ED** Peter Curwen. Documents available from BLDSC.

LC HG2037 .R4 **ISSN** 0741-529X
DD 353.0082/52 US
REVIEW OF THE AUDIT OF THE NATIONAL CONSUMER COOPERATIVE BANK'S FINANCIAL STATEMENTS. (REVIEW OF THE AUDIT OF THE NATIONAL CONSUMER COOPERATIVE BANK'S FINANCIAL STATEMENTS FOR THE YEAR ENDED DECEMBER 31 ...). English. US General Accounting Office / District of Columbia, 441 G Street Northwest, Room 4528, Washington DC 20548. **Tel** (202)275-2812. available on microfiche (Vols. for 1982- distributed to depository libraries).

LC HG2051.U5 A113A **ISSN** 8756-0763
DD 353.0082/33/045 US
REVIEW OF THE COMMODITY CREDIT CORPORATION'S FINANCIAL STATEMENTS. (REVIEW OF THE COMMODITY CREDIT CORPORATION'S FINANCIAL STATEMENTS FOR THE YEAR ENDED ...). **Main/Corp** Commodity Credit Corporation. English. One time a year. US General Accounting Office / Maryland, Document Handling and Information Services Facility, PO Box 6015, Gaithersburg MD 20877. **Tel** (202)275-6241. available on microfiche (Vols. for 1981- distributed to depository libraries).

LC HG9968 .R48 **ISSN** 0741-4676
DD 353.0082/333045 US
REVIEW OF THE FEDERAL CROP INSURANCE CORPORATION'S FINANCIAL STATEMENTS. (REVIEW OF THE FEDERAL CROP INSURANCE CORPORATION'S FINANCIAL STATEMENTS FOR THE YEAR ENDED SEPTEMBER 30 ...). English. One time a year. US General Accounting Office / District of Columbia, 441 G Street Northwest, Room 4528, Washington DC 20548. **Tel** (202)275-2812. available on microfiche (Vols. for 1981- distributed to depository libraries).

LC HG2906 .A35 **ISSN** 0005-4828
DD 332.10986 CK
REVISTA DEL BANCO DE LA REPUBLICA. [Rev. Banco Repub.]. **Main/Corp** Banco de la Republica (Colombia). Vol. 1 (Nov. 1927)-. Periodical. Spanish. Twelve times a year. $65.00. Banco de la Republica Departamento Editorial, Calle 13 35 51, Bogota de 1 Columbia. **Tel** 011 57 1 2010900, 011 57 1 2776872.
Ind/Abst Foreign Lang. Index (-1984); PAIS Foreign Lang. Index (1985-).

LC HF6 .B33
DD 330.97284 ES
Pr Rev.
REVISTA TRIMESTRAL / BANCO CENTRAL DE RESERVA DE EL SALVADOR. **Added/Corp** Banco Central de Reserva de El Salvador. Departamento de Investigaciones Economicas. Banco Central de Reserva de El Salvador. Gerencia de Politica Economica. **VFOAT** Revista del Banco Central de Reserva de El Salvador. (Apr./June 1985)-. Periodical. Spanish. Four times a year. Free on request. Banco Central Reserva Salvador, Department of Commerce, Apartado Postal 106, San Salvador El Salvador. **Tel** 011 503 225022, 011 503 221144, FAX 011 503 710381, telex 20088. **Circ:** 3,000 (ctrl). ***Continues*** *Banco Central de Reserva de El Salvador. Revista Mensual, 0005-4704.*

LC HG21 .R44
DD 332 BE
REVUE DE LA BANQUE, LA. (19??)-. Periodical. French. Ten times a year. $149.25. Kluwer Editorial, Excelsiorlaan 18, 1930 Zaventem Belgium. **Tel** 011 32 2 7191592. **Bk Rev. Ad Acc. Circ:** 3,000.
Desc: Written by prominent financial specialists anxious to acquire a better knowledge of and to keep informed of the financial evolution in Belgium as well as at an international level.
Ind/Abst Numis. Lit.

LC HG2032 **ISSN** 0714-3559
DD 334/.2/060714 CN
REVUE DE PRESSE. [Rev. presse - Fed. caisses pop. Desjardins Montr. Ouest-du-Quebec]. **Added/Corp** Federation des Caisses Populaires Desjardins de Montreal et de l'Ouest-du-Quebec. (Oct. 1980)-. Periodical. French (English; summaries and/or abstracts in English). Federation des Caisses Populaires Desjardins de Montreal et de l'Ouest-du-Quebec, Service des Communications, CP 35 Succursale Desjardins, Montreal Quebec H5B 1E7 Canada. ***Continues*** *Revue de Presse (Federation de Quebec des Caisses Populaires Desjardins. Union Regionale de Montreal), 0714-2196.*

LC HG15 .R48 **ISSN** 0987-3368
DD 332 FR
REVUE D'ECONOMIE FINANCIERE : REVUE TRIMESTRIELLE DE L'ASSOCIATION D'ECONOMIE FINANCIERE. **Added/Corp** Association d'Economie Financiere. (19??)-. Periodical. French. Four times a year. $218.73. Association d' Economie Financiere, 56 rue de Lille, 75007 Paris France. **Tel** 011 33 1 45440411. **(Subscription address:** BSI REF, 50 route de Longjumeau, 91588 Chilly Mazarin France. **Tel** 011 33 1 69103465.**)**

LC HG4150 .R48
DD 332/.05 FR
REVUE DU FINANCIER, LA. (Feb. March 1979)-. Periodical. French. Five times a year. $240.00. Masson SA, Avenue Beauregard 12, CH-1701 Fribourg Switzerland. **Tel** 011 41 37 249585, FAX 011 41 37 247559, telex 942658 SEMI CH. available on microfilm and microfiche from University Microfilms International (UMI).

ISSN 1192-392X
DD 658.15 CN
●**RFP REPORT, THE.** [RFP rep.]. **Added/Corp** Michael Asner Consulting. **VAT** Request For Proposal report. (May 1993)-. Periodical. English. Four times a year. 59.23Can$. Modern Purchasing Magazine, 777 Bay Street, Toronto Ontario, M5W 1A7 Canada. **Tel** (416)596-5792.

LC HG **ISSN** 0884-3031
DD 332 US
CCC
RICHARD C. YOUNG'S INTELLIGENCE REPORT. [Richard C. Young's intell. rep.]. **VFOAT** Intelligence Report. Vol. 1, No. 1 (Sept. 1985)-. Periodical. English. Twelve times a year. $99.95. Phillips Business Information Inc., 1201 Seven Locks Road, PO Box 61130, Potomac MD 20854. **Tel** (301)424-3338, (301)340-1520, (800)777-5005, FAX (301)424-4297, telex 358149. **(Subscription address:** Phillips Publishing Inc., 7811 Montrose Road, Potomac MD 20854. **Tel** (800)777-5005 ext. 5450.**)**

LC HG4502 .R58 **ISSN** 0952-8776
DD 332.6 UK
RISK (LONDON. 1987). (RISK.). [Risk]. (1987)-. Periodical. English. Ten times a year. $399.00. Risk Magazine Ltd., 104-112 Marylebone Lane, London W1M 5FU United Kingdom. **Tel** 011 44 171 4875326, 011 44 181 4875328, FAX 011 44 171 4860879. **ED** Peter Field. Index available. **Bk Rev. Ad Acc. Circ:** 10,000.
Desc: Deals with financial risk management.

LC HG1881 .A833
DD 332.1 IT
RISPARMIO, IL. **Added/Corp** Associazione fra le Casse di Risparmio Italiane. Vol. 1 (March. 1953)-. Periodical. Italian. Six times a year. L91870. Giuffre Editore SPA, Via Busto Arsizio 40, 20151 Milan Italy. **Tel** 011 398 2 38089200. **ED** Roberto Mazzotta. **Bk Rev. Circ:** 3,000 (ctrl). ***Supersedes*** *Rivista delle Casse di Risparmio.*
Desc: This is the journal of the Association of Italian Saving Banks.
Ind/Abst Foreign Lang. Index.

LC HG1501
DD 332.1 IT
RIVISTA BANCARIA. (RIVISTA BANCARIA. MINERVA BANCARIA.). **Added/Corp** Istituto di Cultura Bancaria, Milan. **VFOAT** Minerva Bancaria. (Mar./Nov. 1920)-. Periodical. Italian. Six times a year. L51100. Editrice Minerva Bancaria, Via Silvio Pellico 12, 20121 Milan Italy. **Tel** 011 39 2 8692700. ***Formed by the union of*** *Minerva Bancaria.*
Ind/Abst PAIS Int. Print.

LC HG **ISSN** 1056-0270
DD 332 US
RON CRAM'S EMERGING PROFIT NEWSLETTER. [Ron Cram's emerg. profit newsl.]. **VFOAT** EPN; Emerging Profit Newsletter. (1990)-. Newsletter. English. Twelve times a year. $40.00. Ron Cram, 26127 Edgemont, Highland CA 92346.

LC HC111 .R6 **ISSN** 0229-0243
DD 330.971/005 CN
ROYAL BANK LETTER, THE. **See** Business and Economics-Economic History, Conditions.

LC HG **ISSN** 0898-1515
DD 332 US
RTFI INDEX, THE. [RTFI index]. **VFOAT** RTFI; Real Time Financial Information Index. **VAT** Real-Time Financial Information Index. Vol. 1, No. 1 (June 20, 1988)-. Periodical. English. Eight times a year (1 index and 7 updates). $2495.00. Waters Information Services, PO Box 2248, Binghamton NY 13902-2248. **Tel** (607)770-8535, FAX (607)798-1692. Index available.

LC HG1501
DD 332.1 US
RULES AND REGULATIONS - NATIONAL CREDIT UNION ADMINISTRATION. **Main/Corp** United States. National Credit Union Administration. (19??)-. Government Publication. English. Four times a year. $56.00 US; $70.00 other. National Credit Union Administration, 1775 G Street NW, Washington DC 20456. **Tel** (202)357-1100. **(Subscription address:** Superintendent of Documents, US Government Printing Office, Washington DC 20402. **)**

LC HG2150 .S25 **ISSN** 1051-9939
DD 332.3/2/0973021 US
S & L- SAVINGS BANK FINANCIAL QUARTERLY. [S&L-sav. bank financ. q.]. **Added/Corp** IDC Financial Publishing. **VFOAT** S and L- Savings Bank Financial Quarterly; Savings Bank Financial Quarterly. **VAT** Savings and Loan, Savings Bank Financial Quarterly. Corporate Report. English. Four times a year. $359.00. IDC Financial Publishing Inc, PO Box 140, Hartland WI 53029. **ED** John E. Rickmeier.
Desc: Summary ranks and financial ratios for US Savings and Loans and Savings Banks.

LC HC290.5.I5 D43 **ISSN** 0943-8785
DD 330 GW
●**SAISONBEREINIGTE WIRTSCHAFTSZAHLEN.** **See** Business and Economics-Abstracting, Bibliographies and Statistics.

LC HA1631 .A33 HG3232
DD 314.971 YU
SAMOUPRAVLJANJE U BANKAMA I ZAJEDNICAMA OSIGURANJA. **See** Business and Economics-Abstracting, Bibliographies and Statistics.

LC HG1503 .S63A
DD 332.1 SA
SASBO NEWS. **Main/Corp** South African Society of Bank Officials. **VFOAT** SASBO Nuus. Periodical. Multiple languages (Afrikaans and English). South African Society of Bank Officials, Johannesburg South Africa. ***Supersedes*** *South African Banking Magazine.*

LC HG2150 .S382 **ISSN** 1067-1757
DD 332 US
TITLE CHANGE
SAVINGS & COMMUNITY BANKER. [Sav. community bank.]. **Added/Corp** Savings & Community Bankers of America. **VFOAT** Savings and Community Banker. (1992)-(1995). Periodical. English. Savings and Community Bankers of America, 1101 15th Street Northwest, Suite 400, Washington DC 20005. **Tel** (202)857-3100, FAX (202)659-4816. ***Formed by the union of*** *Savings Institutions, 0746-1321* ***and*** *Bottomline (Washington, D.C.), 0740-5464.* ***Continued by*** *America's Community Banker, 1082-7919.*

LC HG2150 .A384
DD 332.32 US
SAVINGS & HOME FINANCING SOURCE BOOK. **VAT** Savings and Home Financing Source Book. (1952)-. English. One time a year. Federal Home Loan Bank Board, 1700 G Street Northwest, Washington DC 20552. **Tel** (202)377-6904. ***Continues*** *Statistical Summary (United States. Home Loan Bank Board).*
Ind/Abst Predicasts Forecasts.

LC HG1881 .S27
DD 332.1/5/025 SZ
SAVINGS BANKS FOREIGN BUSINESS DIRECTORY. **Added/Corp** International Savings Banks Institute. (19??)-. Directory. English. International Savings Banks Institute, PO Box 355, 1211 Geneva 25 Switzerland. **Tel** 011 41 22 3477466.

LC HG1881 .W6 **ISSN** 1010-4038
DD 332.2/1/05 SZ
TITLE CHANGE
SAVINGS BANKS INTERNATIONAL. [Sav. Banks Int.]. **Added/Corp** International Savings Banks Institute. (Apr. 1972)-(19??). Periodical. English (French and German). International Savings Banks Institute, PO Box 355, 1211 Geneva 25 Switzerland. **Tel** 011 41 22 3477466. **ED** P. Lehner. Index available. **Ad Acc. Circ:** 5,000. ***Continues*** *World Thrift.* ***Merged into*** *Perspectives.*
Desc: Articles concerning various aspects of savings banking.
Ind/Abst PAIS Int. Print.

Business and Economics —Banks and Banking

LC HG1501
DD 332.1   IT
SCHEDARIO DELLA NORMATIVA CONSOB.
(19??)-. Italian. Giuffre Editore SPA, Via Busto Arsizio 40, 20151 Milan Italy. **Tel** 011 398 2 38089200.

LC HG
DD 332   **ISSN** 1074-6498   US
●SCOR REPORT.
[SCOR rep.]. **VFOAT** Small Corporate Offering Registration Report. Vol. 1, No. 1 (Jan. 15, 1994)-. Periodical. English. Fourteen times a year (additional issues in Feb. and Aug.). $200.00. Stewart-Gordon Associates, Inc., PO Box 781992, Dallas TX 75378-1992. **Tel** (214)406-1838, FAX (214)406-0213. **ED** Tom Stewart-Gordon. Index available. cum. index. **Bk Rev**, (Qty: 3-4). **Circ**: 200.

LC HG1503 .S34
DD 332.1/09411   UK
SCOTTISH BANKER : MAGAZINE OF THE INSTITUTE OF BANKERS IN SCOTLAND, THE.
(1987)-. Trade Publication. English. Four times a year. Free to members, £12.00 other. Institute of Bankers in Scotland, 20 Rutland Square, Edinburgh EHI 2DE United Kingdom. **Continues** Scottish Bankers Magazine.

LC HG2040.25 .S433
DD 332.7/22/097305   **ISSN** 0740-4271   US
SECONDARY MORTGAGE MARKETS.
[Second. mortg. mark.]. **Added/Corp** Federal Home Loan Mortgage Corporation. Economic Research Dept. **VFOAT** SMM. Vol. 1, No. 1 (Feb. 1984)-. Periodical. English. Four times a year. Free on request. Federal Home Loan Mortgage Corporation, 8200 Jones Branch Drive, McLean VA 22102. **Tel** (703)903-2000. Documents available from UMI Article Clearinghouse.
Desc: Provides in-depth analysis of the latest developments in housing, finance and the secondary mortgage markets.
Ind/Abst ABI/INFORM Glob. Ed.; ABI/INFORM [Computer File] (Winter 1987-1988); Account. Tax Datab. (Winter 1987-Winter 1988); Gen. BusinessFile (1985-).

LC HF5565 .C65
DD 332.7/42/0973   **ISSN** 0888-255X   US
SECURED LENDER, THE. Added/Corp
National Commercial Finance Association (U.S.). Vol. 42, No. 1 (Jan./Feb. 1986)-. Trade Publication. English. Six times a year (Jan., March, May, July, Sept., Nov.). $48.00. Commercial Finance Association, 225 West 34th Street, New York NY 10122. **Tel** (212)594-3490, FAX (212)564-6053. **ED** Bruce H Jones. Index available. **Bk Rev**. **Ad Acc**. **Circ**: 5,000. available on microfilm and microfiche from University Microfilms International (UMI); available on an online database (files 15,485/Full-Text) from DIALOG. Documents available from UMI Article Clearinghouse. **Continues** Journal (National Commercial Finance Association (U.S.)), 0278-9353.
Desc: Directed toward practitioners of asset-based financing, including factors, bankers, independent asset-based lenders. Also includes legal and legislative developments.
Ind/Abst ABI/INFORM Glob. Ed.; ABI/INFORM [Computer File] (May 1986-); Account. Tax Datab. (May 1986-) [Full Txt.]; Curr. Cit.; EP Collect.; Homework Help.; MasterFile FullTEXT 1000; MasterFile FullTEXT 350; MasterFile FullTEXT 650; MasterFile FullTEXT; OCLC; Telebase; UMI ABI/Inform--Bus. Period. Ondisc (Jan. 1988-) [Full Txt.].

LC HG1501
DD 332   **ISSN** 0895-5492   US
   CCC
   TITLE CHANGE
SECURED LENDING ALERT.
(SECURED LENDING ALERT : STRATEGIES FOR LENDERS AND COUNSEL.). [Secur. lend. alert]. **Added/Corp** Warren, Gorham & Lamont, Inc. (March 1985)-(19??). Periodical. English. Warren Gorham & Lamont Inc., Park Square Building, 31 St. James Avenue, Boston MA 02116-4112. **Tel** (617)423-2020, (800)950-1207, FAX (617)423-2026. **ED** Barkely Clark and Barbara Brewer Clark. **Continued by** Clark's Secured Transactions Monthly.
Desc: A one-stop source for the most current information in the complex area of secured lending. Brings lenders how-to guidance on drafting airtight lending agreements.

LC HG1501
DD 332.1   US
SECURITIES CREDIT TRANSACTIONS HANDBOOK. TRANSMITTAL. Main/Corp
Board of Governors of the Federal Reserve System (U.S.). (1981)-. Periodical. English. One time a year. $75.00. Board of Governors of the Federal Reserve System, Mail Stop 127, Washington DC 20551. **Tel** (202)452-3244, (202)452-3245.

LC HG1501
DD 332.1   HK
SECURITIES JOURNAL.
(19??)-. English. Twelve times a year. $150.00. Capital Communications Corporation, 7 F Paramount Building, 12 Ka Yip Street, Chai Wan Hong Kong. **Tel** 011 852 25952378, FAX 011 852 28892854. **Ad Acc**, **Adv Mgr**: Ricky Ma, **Tel** 011 852 896 8333.

LC HG
DD 332   **ISSN** 1074-8385   US
   CCC
   TITLE CHANGE
SECURITIES MARKETING NEWS.
[Secur. mark. news]. **Added/Corp** Phillips Business Information, Inc. Vol. 2, No. 1 (Jan. 28, 1994)-(Mar. 1995). Periodical. English. Phillips Business Information Inc., 1201 Seven Locks Road, PO Box 61130, Potomac MD 20854. **Tel** (301)424-3338, (301)340-1520, (800)777-5005, FAX (301)424-4297, telex 358149. **Continues** Bank Securities Report, 1071-2038. **Merged into** Financial Services Report, 0894-7260.

LC HG1501
DD 332.1   US
SECURITIES REGULATION.
English. Little Brown & Company, 34 Beacon Street, Boston MA 02108. **Tel** (617)227-0730, (800)759-0190.

LC HG
DD 332   **ISSN** 1062-5135   US
SECURITIZATION DIRECTORY & HANDBOOK.
[Secur. dir. handb.]. **VFOAT** Securitization Directory and Handbook; Asset Sales Report Securitization Directory. (1992)-. Directory. English. One time a year. $200.00. American Banker, Concourse Level, 1 State Street Plaza, New York NY 10004. **Tel** (212)803-8200, (800)221-1809, FAX (212)943-6256, (212)843-9598. **Continues in part** Securitization Handbook.

LC HG4009 .S39
DD 332.1   JA
SEKAI KIGYO YORAN.
1974-. Japanese. ¥12000. Zaikei Shohosha, 2-14 Higashi Shinbashi 1-chome Minato-ku, Tokyo Japan. **Formed by the union of** Sekai Kigyo Yoran. Sangyohen **and** Sekai Kigyo Yoran. Kinyehen.

LC HG4007 .J35
DD 332   JA
SEKAI NO KIGYO NO KEIEI BUNSEKI: KOKUSAI KEIEI HIKAKU. Main/Corp
Japan. Tsusho Sangyosho. Sangyo Seisakukyoku. (1972)-. Periodical. Japanese. ¥4500. Okurasho Insatsukyoku, (Printing Bureau Ministry of Finance), 2-4 Toranomon 2 chome, Minatoku Tokyo 105 Japan. **Continues** Sekai No Kigyo No Keiei Bunseki: Kokusai Keiei Hikaku.

LC Z7164.T4 N27
DD 016.3   **ISSN** 0077-4014   US
SELECTED AND ANNOTATED BIBLIOGRAPHY OF REFERENCE MATERIAL IN CONSUMER FINANCE. See
Business and Economics-Abstracting, Bibliographies and Statistics.

LC HG1501
DD 332.1   US
SELECTED DECISIONS AND SELECTED DOCUMENTS OF THE INTERNATIONAL MONETARY FUND. Main/Corp
International Monetary Fund. **VFOAT** Selected Decisions; Selected Decisions of the International Monetary Fund. (19??)-. Periodical. English. International Monetary Fund, 700 19th Street Northwest, Publishing Unit, Washington DC 20431. **Tel** (202)623-7430, FAX (202)623-7201. **Continues** International Monetary Fund. Selected Decisions of the International Monetary Fund and Selected Documents, 0094-1735.

LC HG1501
DD 332.1   **ISSN** 0364-8370   US
SELECTED INTEREST & EXCHANGE RATES. Added/Corp
Board of Governors of the Federal Reserve System (U.S.). Division of International Finance. Financial Markets Section. Board of Governors of the Federal Reserve System (U.S.). Division of International Finance. (19??)-. Periodical. English. Fifty-two times a year. Free on request. Board of Governors of the Federal Reserve System, Mail Stop 127, Washington DC 20551. **Tel** (202)452-3244, (202)452-3245. Documents available from Documents on Demand.
Ind/Abst Am. Stat. Index.

LC HG1501
DD 332.1   US
SELECTED INTEREST RATES (MONTHLY).
(SELECTED INTEREST RATES.). **Added/Corp** Board of Governors of the Federal Reserve System (U.S.). (Nov. 1979)-. Periodical. English. Twelve times a year. $5.00. Board of Governors of the Federal Reserve System, Mail Stop 127, Washington DC 20551. **Tel** (202)452-3244, (202)452-3245. Documents available from Documents on Demand. **Continues** Selected Interest Rates and Bond Prices.
Ind/Abst Am. Stat. Index.

LC HG1501
DD 332.1   US
SELECTED INTEREST RATES (WEEKLY).
(SELECTED INTEREST RATES.). **Added/Corp** Board of Governors of the Federal Reserve System (U.S.). (Oct. 13, 1979)-. Periodical. English. Fifty-two times a year. $20.00. Board of Governors of the Federal Reserve System, Mail Stop 127, Washington DC 20551. **Tel** (202)452-3244, (202)452-3245. **Continues** Selected Interest Rates and Bond Prices.

LC HG1501
DD 332.1   US
SELLER/SERVICER UPDATE. VFOAT
Seller Servicer Update. (1988)-. Periodical. English. Twelve times a year. $375.00. Inside Mortgage Finance, PO Box 42387, Washington DC 20015. **Tel** (301)951-1240, FAX (301)656-1709.
Desc: Report on all mortgage seller and servicer announcements put out by major governmental mortgage corporations. Also included are all Federal Register announcements related to mortgage lending. Includes a "Trends" section.

LC HG2150 .S47
DD 332.3./2/02573   **ISSN** 0272-3484   US
SERVICE CORPORATION DIRECTORY.
Added/Corp United States League of Savings Associations. (19??)-. English. United States League of Savings Associations, 111 East Wacker Drive, Chicago IL 60601. **Tel** (312)644-3100.

LC HG1501
DD 332.1   PN
SERVICIOS Y ESTADOS FINANCIEROS.
Main/Corp Banco Interoceanico de Panama. (19??)-. Spanish (English). One time a year. Calle Ricardo Arias, Edificio Banco Interoceanico No 9/Apartado 8437, Panama 7 Republica de Panama.

LC HG1501
DD 332.1
UDC 681.3:336   **ISSN** 0765-0418   FR
SFT. SMARTER FINANCIAL TECHNOLOGIES ENGLISH ED.
(SFT.). **VFOAT** Smarter Financial Technologies (English Ed.). (1984)-. Periodical. English (French). Twenty times a year. 4200.00F. Bernard Perier Consultants, 12 Bis rue Duphot, 75001 Paris France. **Tel** 011 33 1 42618361.

LC HG1501
DD 332.1   **ISSN** 1065-8467   US
●SHERMAN'S COMPLETE GUIDE TO BUSINESS LOAN SOURCES.
(1993)-. English. Twelve times a year. $319.00. Business Finance Publications, 92 State Street, Boston MA 02109.

LC HG1501
DD 332.1   US
SHESHUNOFF BANKS OF CALIFORNIA.
(19??)-. English. One time a year. Sheshunoff Information Services Inc., PO Box 13203, Capitol Station, Austin TX 78711. **Tel** (800)456-2340, (512)472-2244.

LC HG4245.Z5 S56
DD 658.1509   JA
SHOKURYO KEIZAI NENKAN. Added/Corp
ShokuryÂo Keizai Shimbun Sha. (19??)-. Japanese. Irregular. ¥2500. Shokuryo Keizai Shimbun Sha, 35-12 Tshigatsujimachi Tennoji-ku, Osaka 543 Japan.

LC HG1501
DD 332.1   IT
SIAM.
Italian. Four times a year. Consulbank Srl, Via Amedei 15, 20123 Milan Italy. **Tel** 011 39 2 861026.

LC HG4057.M8 S52
DD 338.7/4/09778   **ISSN** 0197-3029   US
SIBBALD GUIDE, THE. Added/Corp
John Sibbald Associates. (1980)-. English. One time a year. Acorn Press Inc, 28 Durham Drive, Dix Hills NY 11746. **Tel** (516)254-4840, FAX (201)540-9283.

LC HG1501
DD 332.1   IT
SISTEMA CASSE.
(19??)-. Italian. Twelve times a year. L60000.00. Ace Acri, Via Lovanio 11, 00198 Rome Italy. **Tel** 011 39 6 85354395. **Continues** Informazioni Acri.

LC HC381 .S573
DD 330.946/005   SP
SITUACION (BILBAO, SPAIN).
(SITUACION.). Periodical. English (English). Three times a year.

LC HG1501
DD 332.1   SP
SITUACION EN EL DIA ... . Main/Corp
Banco de Espana. (19??)-. Periodical. Spanish. Twelve times a year. Banco de Espana, Alcala 50, 28014 Madrid Spain. **Tel** 011 34 1 4469055, 011 34 1 3385072.

LC HG
DD 332   **ISSN** 1058-5044   US
SITUATION (ENCINITAS, CALIF.), THE.
(THE SITUATION.). (Sept. 13, 1991)-. Periodical. English. One time a week. $79.95. The Situation, Inc., PO Box 141, 272 North El Camino Real, Encinitas CA 92024.

Business and Economics —Banks and Banking

LC HG1501
DD 332.1   NO
SKRIFTSERIE. Main/Corp Norges Bank. No. 1 (1973)-. Monographic series. Multiple languages (English and Norwegian). Irregular. Free on request. Norges Bank, Postboks 1179 Sentrum, 0107 Oslo 1 Norway. **Tel** 011 47 2 31600, FAX 011 47 2 413105, telex 71369 N BANK N. **Circ:** 5,000 (ctrl).
Desc: Banking and finance.

LC HG   **ISSN** 1074-6676
DD 332   US
●**SNL MORTGAGE BANK WEEKLY.** [SNL mortg. bank wkly.]. **Added/Corp** SNL Securities. **VFOAT** Mortgage Bank Weekly. (1993)-. Periodical. English. One time a week. $295.00. SNL Securities Inc., 410 East Main Street, Charlottesville VA 22902. **Tel** (804)977-1600, (804)977-5877.

LC HG1501   **ISSN** 1074-5904
DD 332   US
SNL QUARTERLY BANK DIGEST, THE. [SNL q. bank dig.]. **Added/Corp** SNL Securities. **VFOAT** Quarterly Bank Digest. (March 1990)-. Periodical. English. Four times a year. $699.00. SNL Securities Inc., 410 East Main Street, Charlottesville VA 22902. **Tel** (804)977-1600, (804)977-5877.

LC HG   **ISSN** 1074-6641
DD 332   US
SNL WEEKLY BANKFAX (WESTERN ED.). (SNL WEEKLY BANKFAX.). [SNL wkly. BankFax]. **Added/Corp** SNL Securities. **VFOAT** BankFax; SNL Weekly Bank Fax. (19??)-. Periodical. English. One time a week. $220.00. SNL Securities Inc., 410 East Main Street, Charlottesville VA 22902. **Tel** (804)977-1600, (804)977-5877.

LC HG   **ISSN** 1074-665X
DD 332   US
●**SNL WEEKLY COMPLIANCEFAX.** [SNL wkly. complianceFax]. **Added/Corp** SNL Securities. **VFOAT** ComplianceFax; SNL Weekly Compliance Fax. (1993)-. Periodical. English. One time a week. $197.00. SNL Securities Inc., 410 East Main Street, Charlottesville VA 22902. **Tel** (804)977-1600, (804)977-5877.

LC HG1501
DD 332.1   UK
SORTING CODE NUMBERS. (19??)-. English. One time a year. £3.00 (add £1.25 postage). Reed Information Services Ltd., Windsor Court, East Grinstead House, East Grinstead RH19 1BR United Kingdom. **Tel** 011 44 1342 326972, FAX 011 44 1342 335977, telex 95127 INFSER G.
Desc: An alphabetical and numerical listing of sorting code numbers to bank branches and other financial institutions throughout the UK.

   ISSN 1184-602X
DD 658.15/92/0971   CN
SOURCES FOR SUCCESSFUL SMALL BUSINESS FINANCING IN CANADA. See Business and Economics-Small Business.

LC HG1939.G2 S58   **ISSN** 0038-6561
DD 332   GW
   CCC
SPARKASSE. [Sparkasse]. **Added/Corp** Deutscher Sparkassen- und Giroverband. (1971)-. Periodical. German. Twelve times a year. Verlag Otto Schwartz & Company, Annastrasse 7, D-37075 Goettingen Germany. **Tel** 011 49 551 31051, 011 49 551 31052, FAX 011 49 551 372812.
Ind/Abst PAIS Int. Print.

LC HG2121 .S63   **ISSN** 0094-7180
DD 658/.91/332320973   US
SPECIAL MANAGEMENT BULLETIN. [Spec. manage. bull.]. **Added/Corp** United States League of Savings Institutions. United States Savings and Loan League. United States League of Savings Associations. (19??)-. Bulletin. English. Irregular. United States League of Savings Associations, 111 East Wacker Drive, Chicago IL 60601. **Tel** (312)644-3100.

LC HG   **ISSN** 1063-5173
DD 332   US
SRC ORANGE BOOK OF 5-TREND LONG-TERM O-T-C CHARTS, THE. [SRC orange book 5-trend long-term O-T-C charts]. **VFOAT** Orange Book of 5-Trend Long-Term O-T-C Charts; SRC Orange Book of Five-Trend Long-Term O-T-C Charts. **VAT** Securities Research Company Orange Book of Five-Trend Long-Term Over-the-Counter Charts. (Mar. 1992)-. English. Four times a year. Securities Research Co., Babson-United Building, 101 Prescott Street, Wellsley Hills MA 02181-3319.

LC HG1501   **ISSN** 0253-3537
DD 332.1   US
STAFF COMMODITY WORKING PAPER - WORLD BANK. (WORLD BANK STAFF COMMODITY WORKING PAPER.). [World Bank staff commod. work pap.]. **Added/Corp** World Bank. **VFOAT** Staff Commodity Working Paper. (19??)-. Monographic series. English. Price varies per volume. World Bank Publications, 1818 H Street Northwest, Washington DC 20043. **Tel** (202)473-1155, (202)473-1155, FAX (202)522-3224, telex WUI 64145 WORLDBANK.
Ind/Abst Geogr. Abstr. Human Geogr.; World Agric. Econ. Rural Sociol. Abstr.

LC HG3810 .I5   **ISSN** 0020-8027
DD 332.082   US
Pr Rev.
STAFF PAPERS - INTERNATIONAL MONETARY FUND. [Staff pap. - Int. Monet. Fund]. **Main/Corp** International Monetary Fund. Vol. 1 (Feb. 1950)-. Periodical. English (summaries and/or abstracts in French and Spanish). Four times a year. $54.00. International Monetary Fund, 700 19th Street Northwest, Publishing Unit, Washington DC 20431. **Tel** (202)623-7430, FAX (202)623-7201. cum. index. available on microfilm and microfiche from University Microfilms International (UMI); available on an online database (file 648/Full-Text) from DIALOG. Documents available from The Genuine Article, UMI Article Clearinghouse.
Desc: Contains studies on monetary and financial problems. Covers balance of payments and exchange rates, monetary systems and analysis, national monetary and fiscal problems and international liquidity, as well as IMF's Articles of Agreement.
Ind/Abst ABI/INFORM Glob. Ed.; Acad. Search; Am. Hist. Life (1963-1969); Bus. ASAP (1992-) [Full Txt.]; Bus. Index (1985-); Bus. Source Plus; Bus. Source; Contents Recent Econ. J.; Contents Pages Manage.; Curr. Cit.; Curr. Contents Soc. Behav. Sci.; Econ. Lit. Index; EP Collect.; Expand. Acad. Index (1992-); Gen. BusinessFile (1985-); Gen. Period. Index (1985-); Homework Help.; J. Econ. Lit.; J. Plan. Lit.; MasterFile FullTEXT 1000; MasterFile FullTEXT 350; MasterFile FullTEXT 650; MasterFile FullTEXT (July 1993-); Middle East Abstr. Index; Newsp. Period. Abstr. (1992-); OCLC; PAIS Int. Print (1991-); Res. Alert [Full Cov.]; Soc. Sci. Cit. Index [Full Cov.]; Soc. Sci. Index; Telebase; Wilson Bus. Abstr.

LC HG3741 .S73   **ISSN** 1057-3305
DD 332/.55/05   US
STANDARD & POOR'S COMMERCIAL PAPER GUIDE. [Stand. Poor's commer. pap. guide]. **Added/Corp** Standard & Poor's Corporation. **VFOAT** Standard & Poor's Commercial Paper Guide; Commercial Paper Guide. Vol. 1, No. 1 (June 1991)-. English. Twelve times a year. $1600.00. Standard & Poor's Corporation, (A Division of McGraw-Hill, Inc.), 25 Broadway, New York NY 10004. **Tel** (212)208-8775, (800)221-5277. **Continues** S&P's Commercial Paper Ratings Guide.

LC HG4961 .S74   **ISSN** 1047-9341
DD 338.7/4/0973021   US
   TITLE CHANGE
STANDARD & POOR'S CREDITSTATS. [Standard Poor's creditstat.]. **Added/Corp** Standard and Poor's Corporation. **VFOAT** Standard and Poor's Creditstats; Standard & Poor's Credit Stats; Standard and Poor's Credit Stats; Credit Stats. (198?)-(19??). English. Standard & Poor's Corporation, (A Division of McGraw-Hill, Inc.), 25 Broadway, New York NY 10004. **Tel** (212)208-8775, (800)221-5277. **Merged into** Standard & Poor's Global Sector Review, 1076-0423.

LC HG   **ISSN** 1076-0423
DD 332   US
●**STANDARD & POOR'S GLOBAL SECTOR REVIEW.** [Stand. Poor's glob. sect. rev.]. **Added/Corp** Standard and Poor's Ratings Group. **VFOAT** Standard and Poor's Global Sector Review; Global Sector Review. (June 1994)-. Periodical. English. Five times a year. $1695.00. Standard & Poor's Corporation, (A Division of McGraw-Hill, Inc.), 25 Broadway, New York NY 10004. **Tel** (212)208-8775, (800)221-5277. **Absorbed** Standard & Poor's Creditstats, 1047-9341.

LC HG4951 .S78   **ISSN** 1069-0778
DD 332.63/233/097305   US
●**STANDARD & POOR'S MUNICIPAL FINANCE CRITERIA.** [Standard & Poor's munic. finance criteria]. **Added/Corp** Standard and Poor's Ratings Group. **VFOAT** Standard and Poor's Municipal Finance Criteria; Municipal Finance Criteria. (1994)-. English. Every 2 years. Free on request. Standard & Poor's Corporation, (A Division of McGraw-Hill, Inc.), 25 Broadway, New York NY 10004. **Tel** (212)208-8775, (800)221-5277. **Continues** S & P Municipal Finance Criteria.

LC HG4501 .S68
DD 332   US
●**STANDARD & POOR'S NASDAQ AND REGIONAL EXCHANGE STOCK REPORTS.** See Business and Economics-Investments.

LC HG1501
DD 332.1   US
●**STARK REPORT.** (1995)-. English. Four times a year. $495.00. Stark Research Inc., 1020 Prospect Street, Suite 3, La Jolla CA 92037. **Tel** (800)591-5886, (619)459-0818. **Absorbed** Norwood Index Report.

LC HG
DD 332   US
STATE 50 REPORT. (19??)-. English. Four times a year. $240.00. Veribanc Inc., PO Box 461, Wakefield MA 01880. **Tel** (617)245-8370, (800)442-2657, FAX (617)246-5291.

LC HG1505 .S7
DD 332.1   II
STATE BANK OF INDIA MONTHLY REVIEW. **Main/Corp** State Bank of India. Economic and Statistical Research Dept. **Added/Corp** State Bank of India. Economic and Statistical Research Dept. Review. (19??)-. Statistical Publication. English. Twelve times a year.
Ind/Abst World Agric. Econ. Rural Sociol. Abstr.

LC HG1501   **ISSN** 0228-7633
DD 332.1   CN
STATEMENT OF FINANCIAL OPERATIONS. **Added/Corp** Canada. Dept. of Supply and Services. Canada Supply and Services. Canada. Canada. Government of Canada Accounting Branch. Canada. Government of Canada Banking and Accounting Branch. **VFOAT** Etat des Operations Financieres. (1979)-. Periodical. English (French). Twelve times a year. Free on request. Financial Distribution Center, 300 Laurie Avenue West Esplanade Lau, Ottawa Ontario K1A 0R5 Canada. **Tel** (613)995-2855.
Desc: Monthly financial standings for the government of Canada.

LC HG1501
DD 332.1   PK
●**STATISTICAL BULLETIN / STATE BANK OF PAKISTAN.** **Added/Corp** State Bank of Pakistan. State Bank of Pakistan. Dept. of Statistics. (Nov. 1993)-. Bulletin. English. Twelve times a year. State Bank of Pakistan - Public Relation Department, PO Box 4456, Central Directorate, Karachi Pakistan. **Tel** 011 92 21 2414141310, telex 2754 SBP. **Continues** State Bank of Pakistan Bulletin - State Bank of Pakistan, 0039-0011.

LC HG181 .S794
DD 332.1/0973/021   US
STATISTICAL INFORMATION ON THE FINANCIAL SERVICES INDUSTRY. See Business and Economics-Abstracting, Bibliographies and Statistics.

LC HG21 .A27
DD 332   BE
STATISTIQUES FINANCIERES. See Business and Economics-Abstracting, Bibliographies and Statistics.

LC HG188.T77 B35A
DD 332/.0961/1   TI
STATISTIQUES FINANCIERES. See Business and Economics-Abstracting, Bibliographies and Statistics.

LC HA   **ISSN** 0252-2977
DD 310   US
STATISTIQUES FINANCIERES INTERNATIONALES. See Finance-Abstracting, Bibliographies and Statistics.

LC HG1501   **ISSN** 0252-029X
DD 332.1   US
   CEASED
STATISTIQUES FINANCIERES INTERNATIONALES ANNUAIRE - FONDS MONETAIRE INTERNATIONAL. (STATISTIQUES FINANCIERES INTERNATIONALES ANNUAIRE.). [Stat. financ. int. annu. - Fonds monet. int.]. **Added/Corp** International Monetary Fund. (1981)-(19??). French. International Monetary Fund, 700 19th Street Northwest, Publishing Unit, Washington DC 20431. **Tel** (202)623-7430, FAX (202)623-7201. **Continues** International Financial Statistics Annuaire, 0250-748X.

LC HG186.P8 A33
DD 332   PO
STATISTIQUES MONETAIRES ET FINANCIERES : CONTINENT ET REGIONS AUTONOMES DES AZORES ET MADERE. **VFOAT** Estatisticas Monetarias e Financieras: Continente e Regioes Autonomas dos Acores e da Madeira. French (Portuguese). Instituto Nacional de Estatistica, Avenida Antonio Jose de Almeida, 1078 Lisbon Codex Portugal. **Tel** 011 351 1 8470050. **Continues** Statistiques Monetaires et Financieres.

LC HG999.5 .D48a
DD 332.4/5/0212   GW
STATISTISCHE BEIHEFTE ZU DEN MONATSBERICHTEN DER DEUTSCHEN BUNDESBANK. REIHE 5, DIE WAHRUNGEN DER WELT. **Main/Corp** Deutsche Bundesbank. **Added/Corp** Deutsche Bundesbank. Monatsberichte. **VFOAT** Wahrungen der Welt. (19??)-. Periodical. German. Four times a year.

Free on request. Deutsche Bundesbank, Wilhelm Epsteinstrasse 14, 6000 Frankfurt am Main Germany. **Tel** 069 95 66 35 15, FAX 069 95 66 30 77.

LC HG27 .S72 **ISSN** 0108-5476
DD 332.05/6 DK
STATISTISKE EFTERRETNINGER. PENGE- OG KAPITALMARKED. See
Business and Economics-Abstracting, Bibliographies and Statistics.

LC HG4651 **ISSN** 0844-9082
DD 332.63/22/0971 CN
STOCK GUIDE (WILLIAMSTOWN).
(STOCK GUIDE.). [Stock guide]. Vol. 1, No. 5 (May 1988)- . Periodical. English (French). Twelve times a year. 141.00Can$. Stock Guide, PO Box 160, Williamstown Ontario, K0C2J0 Canada. **Tel** (613)931-2897, FAX (613)931-1968. **Continues** Corporate Ratio., 0846-4596.

LC HC301 .S92
DD 330 IT
SUCCESSO.
Vol. 1 (1959)- . Periodical. English. Twelve times a year. L55000. Nuovo Editrice SRL, Via Turati 6 8, 20121 Milan Italy. **Tel** (2)6596181. **Ad Acc**. **Circ:** 30,000.
 Desc: Magazine for entrepreneurs who need information, ideas, and useful services to better run their own firm. Publication contains four sections: close up, financing, survey and the enterprise.
 Ind/Abst Predicasts.

LC HG1 .S85
DD 332 US
SUMMARY OF INSIDER TRANSACTIONS.
[Summ. insid. trans.]. Vol. 1, No. 1 (Mar. 1-Sept. 1, 1983)- . Periodical. English. Four times a year. American Banker, Concourse Level, 1 State Street Plaza, New York NY 10004. **Tel** (212)803-8200, (800)221-1809, FAX (212)943-6256, (212)843-9598. **Continues** Summary of Insider Transactions (Riverside, Conn.), 0277-2450.
 Ind/Abst MasterFile FullTEXT (July 1993-).

LC HG1501
DD 332.1 UK
SUMPTION TAXATION CAPITAL GAINS.
(19??)- . English. Three times a year. £105.00. Hans Zell Publishing / Butterworth Company, Halsbury House, 35 Chance Lane, London WC2A 1ER United Kingdom. **Tel** 011 44 1732 884567, FAX 011 44 1732 884530. **(Subscription address:** Butterworth Heinemann Publishers, 225 Wildwood Avenue, Unit B, Woburn MA 01801. **Tel** (800)366-2665.**)**

LC HG3871.F5 F55A
DD 332.45609 FI
SUOMEN MAKSUTASE. Main/Corp Finland.
Tilastokeskus. **VFOAT** Finlands Betalningsbalans; Finland's Balance of Payments. Multiple languages (English, Finnish and Swedish). 0.50. Tilastokeskus, PL 504, Annankatu 44, 00101 Helsinki Finland. **Tel** 011 358 0 17341, FAX 011 358 0 17342474, telex 1002111 TILASTO SF.

ISSN 1187-5917
DD 354.71270072/2252/05 CN
SUPPLEMENTARY INFORMATION FOR LEGISLATIVE REVIEW, REVENUE ESTIMATES.
[Suppl. inf. legis. rev., revenue estim.]. **Main/Corp** Manitoba. Manitoba Finance. (1991/1992)- . English. Minister of Finance Manitoba, 103 Legislative Building, Winnipeg Manitoba Canada.

ISSN 1187-8266
DD 354.7124001 CN
SUPPLEMENTARY INFORMATION ..., PAYMENTS TO INDIVIDUALS.
[Suppl. inf. paym. individ.]. **Main/Corp** Saskatchewan. **Added/Corp** Saskatchewan. Dept. of Finance. (1991)- . English.

LC HG1501 **ISSN** 0195-5225
DD 332.1 US
SUREPAY UPDATE. VFOAT Nacha Surepay
Update. (1976)- . Periodical. English. Four times a year. $25.00. American Bankers Association, 1120 Connecticut Avenue Northwest, Washington DC 20036. **Tel** (202)663-5221, (202)663-5000, FAX (202)828-4544. **ED** Karen Reed. **Bk Rev**. **Ad Acc**. **Circ:** 2,000 (ctrl).
 Desc: Latest information to automated clearing house events, changes. Informational guide to current happenings for this EFT area.

LC HG1501 **ISSN** 0039-6249
DD 332.1 JA
SURVEY OF JAPANESE FINANCE AND INDUSTRY. Added/Corp Nippon Kogyo Ginko.
Vol. 1 (June, 1949)- . Periodical. English. Four times a year. Industrial Bank of Japan, 1 3 3 Marunouchi, Chiyoda ku Tokyo Japan.

LC HG1501
DD 332.1 US
SURVEY OF TERMS OF BANK LENDING MADE DURING ... . Added/Corp Board of
Governors of the Federal Reserve System (U.S.). (19??)- . Periodical. English. Four times a year. $5.00. Board of Governors of the Federal Reserve System, Mail Stop 127, Washington DC 20551. **Tel** (202)452-3244, (202)452-3245. **Continues** Bank Rates on Short-Term Business Loans, 0364-2852.

LC HG1501 **ISSN** 0985-2174
DD 332.1 FR
UDC 336
SYNTHESE FINANCIERE, LA. [Synth.
financ.]. (19??)- . Periodical. French. One time a week. $1804.44. EDIPHI, 80 82 rue Anatole France, 92592 Levallois Perret France. **Tel** 011 33 1 49644747.

LC HG1501 **ISSN** 0039-9663
DD 332.1 US
CEASED
TARHEEL BANKER, THE. Added/Corp North
Carolina Bankers Association. (19??)-(May 1994). Trade Publication. English. North Carolina Bankers Association, PO Box 30609, Raleigh NC 27612-0609. **Tel** (919)782-6960, FAX (919)782-6701. **ED** William E. Stroupe. **Bk Rev**. **Ad Acc**, **Adv Mgr:** William E. Stroupe. **Circ:** 3,500.
 Desc: News and features about the North Carolina Bankers Association and full service banks in North Carolina.

LC HG1501
DD 332.1 US
CEASED
TAX BRIEFS.
(19??)-(Oct. 1993). Trade Publication. English. Securities Industry Association, 120 Broadway/35th Floor, New York NY 10271. **Tel** (212)608-1500, FAX (212)608-1604.
 Desc: Serves to alert firms to important technical tax issues affecting day-to-day operations.

LC HG1501 **ISSN** 1018-5097
DD 332.1 US
TECHNICAL PAPERS - INTERNATIONAL FINANCE CORPORATION. (TECHNICAL
PAPERS.). **Added/Corp** International Finance Corporation. (1991)- . English. World Bank Publications, 1818 H Street Northwest, Washington DC 20043. **Tel** (202)473-1155, (202)473-1155, FAX (202)522-3224, telex WUI 64145 WORLDBANK.

LC HG1501 **ISSN** 0765-3069
DD 332.1 FR
UDC 336.7
TECHNOLOGIES BANCAIRES. (1984)- .
Periodical. French. Six times a year. $118.11. Publinews, Mme Guignard, 3 rue Gallieni, 92000 Nanterre France. **Tel** 011 33 1 47298811, FAX 011 33 1 47298818. **ED** Ange Galula. **Bk Rev**. **Ad Acc**. **Circ:** 10,000.

LC HG1501
DD 332.1 UK
TITLE CHANGE
TELERATE BANK REGISTER. Added/Corp
Euromoney Publications Ltd. (1988)-(1993). Trade Publication. English. Euromoney Publications PLC, Nestor House, Playhouse Yard, London EC4Z 5EX United Kingdom. **Tel** 011 44 171 7798888, FAX 011 44 171 7798630, telex 290700 EUROMON G. **(Subscription address:** Plymbridge Distributors Ltd., Estover Road, Plymouth PL6 7PZ United Kingdom. **Tel** 011 44 1752 695745.**) Continues** Bank Register. **Continued by** Dow Jones Telerate Bank Register.

LC HG1501
DD 332.1 US
TELLER SENSE. (19??)- . English. Twenty-four
times a year. $43.08 US; $52.20 Canada. Bureau of Business Practice, 24 Rope Ferry Road, Waterford CT 06386. **Tel** (800)243-0876, (203)442-4365, (800)876-9105, FAX (203)443-1123.

LC HG1501 **ISSN** 0895-1039
DD 332.1 US
TELLER VISION. Added/Corp Bureau of Business
Practice. **VFOAT** Tellervision. (198?)- . Periodical. English. Twenty-four times a year. $59.76 US; $73.56 Canada. Bureau of Business Practice, 24 Rope Ferry Road, Waterford CT 06386. **Tel** (800)243-0876, (203)442-4365, (800)876-9105, FAX (203)443-1123.

LC HG1501 **ISSN** 0040-3199
DD 332.1 US
TENNESSEE BANKER, THE. (19??)- . Trade
Publication. English. Twelve times a year. $37.89. Tennessee Bankers Association, 201 Venture Circle, Nashville TN 37228. **Tel** (615)244-4871, FAX (615)244-0995. **ED** Dianne W. Martin. **Ad Acc**, **Adv Mgr:** D. Martin, **Tel** same as publisher. **Circ:** 2,360.
 Desc: News for and about bankers in Tennessee, the Southeast, and of national importance. A regional trade association publication containing issues and news related to financial institution and the banking industry.

LC HG1507 .T4 **ISSN** 0885-6907
DD 332.1/09764 US
TEXAS BANKING. (TEXAS BANKING : OFFICIAL PUBLICATION OF THE TEXAS BANKERS ASSOCIATION).
Vol. 74, No. 9 (Sept. 1985)- . Trade Publication. English. Twelve times a year. $35.00. Texas Bankers Association, 203 West 10th Street, Austin TX 78701. **Tel** (512)472-8388, FAX (512)473-2560. **ED**
Panchita Garrett. Index available. cum. index. **Bk Rev**, (Qty: 3). **Ad Acc**, **Adv Mgr:** L. Cafferty. **Circ:** 5,000. available on an online database (file 15/Full-Text) from DIALOG. Documents available from UMI Article Clearinghouse. **Continues** Texas Bankers Record, 0738-7652.
 Desc: Provides the latest in economic, legislative and regulatory news and technological trends for the Texas banking industry.
 Ind/Abst ABI/INFORM Glob. Ed.; ABI/INFORM [Computer File] (Nov. 1987-).

LC HG1501
DD 332.1 US
TEXAS BANKING REDBOOK. English. Two
times a year (pblished May and Oct.). $24.00 (fall edition), 26.00 (spring edition). Texas Banking Redbook, 912 Baltimore Avenue, Suite 900, Kansas City MO 64105-1784. **Tel** (816)421-7941, 800-336-1120, FAX (816)472-0397. **ED** Sharon Smith. Index available. cum. index. **Ad Acc**, **Adv Mgr:** Beth Wilson.
 Desc: Lists all banks and savings and loans in the state of Texas along with their addresses, phone numbers, directors and financial information.

LC HJ11 .T44423a
DD 353.97640072/31 US
TEXAS COMPREHENSIVE ANNUAL FINANCIAL REPORT. Main/Corp Texas.
Comptroller's Office. **VFOAT** Comprehensive Annual Financial Report. (1990)- . English. **Continues** Texas. Comptroller's Office. Texas Annual Financial Report.

LC HG2153.T4 T42
DD 332.3/2/09764 US
TEXAS SAVINGS & LOAN DIRECTORY.
VFOAT Texas Savings and Loan Directory. Fall/Winter 1983-84- . Directory. English. One time a year. $24.95. Texas State Directory Press, PO Box 12186 Capitol Station, Austin TX 78711. **Tel** (512)477-5698, (800)388-8075, FAX (512)473-2447. **ED** Julie Sayers. **Ad Acc**. **Circ:** 2,500 (ctrl). *Formed by the union of Annual Report of Savings and Loan Associations and Membership Roster / Texas Savings and Loan League.*
 Desc: Listings of all savings and loans in Texas with addresses and phone numbers. Lists all their financial information.

LC HG2441 .R3 **ISSN** 1057-8986
DD 332.1/025/73 US
THOMSON BANK DIRECTORY. [Thomson
bank dir.]. **Added/Corp** Thomson Financial Publishing. 230th Ed. (July-Dec. 1991)- . Periodical. English. Two times a year. $340.00. Thomson Financial Publishing, PO Box 65, 4709 West Golf Road, Skokie IL 60076-0065. **Tel** (800)321-3373, (708)933-8031. **Continues** Rand McNally Bankers Directory (Chicago, Ill. : 1986), 0895-4623.

LC HG2037 .R28 **ISSN** 1061-1681
DD 334/.22/02573 US
THOMSON CREDIT UNION DIRECTORY.
[Thomson credit union dir.]. **Added/Corp** Thomson Financial Information (Firm). (1991)- . Directory. English. One time a year. $99.00. Thomson Financial Publishing, PO Box 65, 4709 West Golf Road, Skokie IL 60076-0065. **Tel** (800)321-3373, (708)933-8031. **Continues** Rand McNally Credit Union Directory.

LC HG1501 **ISSN** 1062-0729
DD 332 US
THOMSON DESKTOP FINANCIAL DIRECTORY : ROUTING NUMBER INDEX. [Thomson deskt. financ. dir.]. Added/Corp
Thomson Financial Publishing. 1st Ed. (July-Dec. 1991)- . Directory. English. Two times a year. Thomson Financial Publishing, PO Box 65, 4709 West Golf Road, Skokie IL 60076-0065. **Tel** (800)321-3373, (708)933-8031.

LC HG2150 .U18 **ISSN** 1062-1717
DD 332.3/2/02573 US
THOMSON SAVINGS DIRECTORY.
[Thomson sav. dir.]. (1991)- . Directory. English. Two times a year (June & Dec.). Price varies. Thomson Financial Publishing, PO Box 65, 4709 West Golf Road, Skokie IL 60076-0065. **Tel** (800)321-3373, (708)933-8031. **Continues** U.S. Savings Institutions Directory, 1045-8883.

LC HG1616.E7 T46 **ISSN** 1070-9452
DD 332.1/0294/73 US
●THOMSON'S BLUE BOOK OF BANK SUPPLIERS. VFOAT Blue Book of Bank Suppliers.
Vol. 1, No. 1 (1993)- . Periodical. English. Four times a year. $20.00. Thomson Financial Publishing, PO Box 65, 4709 West Golf Road, Skokie IL 60076-0065. **Tel** (800)321-3373, (708)933-8031.

LC K1066.A13 T48 **ISSN** 0958-353X
DD 341.7/51 UK
THOMSON'S INTERNATIONAL BANKING REGULATOR. Added/Corp
American Banker, Inc. Mortgage Commentary Publications. **VFOAT** International Banking Regulator. (1990)- . Periodical. English. Forty-eight times a year. $825.00. American Banker, Concourse Level, 1 State Street Plaza, New York NY 10004. **Tel** (212)803-8200,

(800)221-1809, FAX (212)943-6256, (212)843-9598. **(Subscription address:** American Banker / Newletter Division, PO Box 28315, Washington DC 20038. **Tel** (800)733-4371, (202)347-2665.) available on an online database (file 636/Full-Text) from DIALOG. ***Continues*** *International Banking Report, 0307-4889.*
Ind/Abst PTS Newsl. Database [Full Txt.].

LC HG1501
DD 332.1 US
THORNDIKE ENCYCLOPEDIA OF BANKING AND FINANCIAL TABLES, THE. (1973)-. English. One time a year. $150.00 US and Canada; $195.00 other (includes yearbook). Warren Gorham & Lamont Inc., Park Square Building, 31 St. James Avenue, Boston MA 02116-4112. **Tel** (617)423-2020, (800)950-1207, FAX (617)423-2026.

LC HG1626 .T493 **ISSN** 0196-7762
DD 332.8/2/0212 US
THORNDIKE ENCYCLOPEDIA OF BANKING AND FINANCIAL TABLES. YEARBOOK. [Thorndike encycl. bank. financ. tables, Yearb.]. **VFOAT** Encyclopedia of Banking and Financial Tables; Yearbook, Thorndike Encyclopedia. (19??)-. English. One time a year. $10.95 US and Canada; $35.00 other. Warren Gorham & Lamont Inc., Park Square Building, 31 St. James Avenue, Boston MA 02116-4112. **Tel** (617)423-2020, (800)950-1207, FAX (617)423-2026.

LC HG1501
DD 332.1 US
CEASED
THRIFT REGULATOR. (19??)-(Aug. 1995). English. American Banker, Concourse Level, 1 State Street Plaza, New York NY 10004. **Tel** (212)803-8200, (800)221-1809, FAX (212)943-6256, (212)843-9598. **(Subscription address:** American Banker / Newletter Division, PO Box 28315, Washington DC 20038. **Tel** (800)733-4371, (202)347-2665.) available on an online database (file 636/Full-Text) from DIALOG. ***Continues*** *Bank Board Watch.*
Ind/Abst PTS Newsl. Database [Full Txt.].

LC HG1501 **ISSN** 0147-0698
DD 332.1 US
THRUPUT. Vol. 1 (Sept. 1970)-. Periodical. English. Twelve times a year. $88.00. American Bankers Association, 1120 Connecticut Avenue Northwest, Washington DC 20036. **Tel** (202)663-5221, (202)663-5000, FAX (202)828-4544. **Circ:** 3,000 (ctrl).
Desc: Informs bank operations and data processing personnel of the multitude of industry developments and changes in regulations, operational techniques, systems, procedures and standards.

LC HG **ISSN** 0883-5322
DD 332 US
TICKER TAPE PARADE. Vol. 1, No. 1 (Mar. 1985)-. Periodical. English. Four times a year. $48.00. Kathy Bakas, PO Box 440418, Aurora CO 80014.

LC HG1501 **ISSN** 0167-0581
DD 332.1 NE
UDC 658.15
TIJDSCHRIFT FINANCIEEL MANAGEMENT. [Tijdschr. financ. manage.]. (1980)-. Periodical. Dutch. Six times a year. Bocaal Business Press BV, Stolbergstraat 14, 2012 EP Haarlem Netherlands. **Tel** 011 31 23 319014.
Ind/Abst Selec. Coop. Index Manage. Period.

LC HG1501 **ISSN** 0772-2621
DD 332.1 BE
UDC 336.711
TIJDSCHRIFT VAN DE NATIONALE BANK VAN BELGIE. [Tijdschr. Natl. bank Belg.]. (1971)-. Periodical. Dutch (French). Twelve times a year. 530F Belgium; 500F Luxembourg; 750F other. Nationale Bank van Belgie, Abonnmntndnst de Berlaimont 5, 1000 Brussels Belgium. Index available. ***Continues*** *Tijdschrift voor Documentatie en Voorlichting - Nationale Bank van Belgie, 0772-2613.*

ISSN 0216-7050
DD 330 Vol.4, no.1 (1980) IO
TINJAUAN EKONOMI. [Tinjauan ekon.]. (1977)-. Statistical Publication. Indonesian (English). Twelve times a year. PT Bank Bumi Daya (Persero), Planning and Development Division, Jl. Imam Bonjol No. 61, Jakarta 10310. **Tel** 2300300, FAX 2301852.
Desc: Contains Indonesian financial statistics.

LC HG1501
DD 332.1 FI
TOIMINTAKERTOMUS. Main/Corp Finland. Pankkitarkastusvirasto. **VFOAT** Verksamhetsberattelse. Finnish (Finnish). One time a year.

LC HG1501 **ISSN** 0387-6896
DD 332.1 JA
TOKYO FINANCIAL REVIEW. [Tokyo financ. rev.]. **Added/Corp** Tokyo Ginko. Tokyo Ginko. Chosabu. (Aug. 1976)-. Periodical. English. Twelve times a year. Bank of Tokyo Ltd, 3-26 Kanda Nishikiltn, Chiyoda ku Tokyo 101 Japan. **ED** Teruhiko Mano. ***Absorbed*** *Weekly Review (Tokyo Ginko).*

LC HG2037 .T66
DD 334/.22/0973021 US
TOP ... CREDIT UNION INVESTORS IN BANKS AND S&L'S. VFOAT Credit Union Investors in Banks and S&L's. English. One time a year. Advanced Asset Management Inc, 3990 Old Town Avenue/Suite 208A, San Diego CA 92110.

LC HG1501 **ISSN** 0843-221X
DD 332.1/2/025713541 CN
TORONTO FINANCIAL INSTITUTIONS TELEPHONE DIRECTORY, METRO TORONTO AND VICINITY. [Tor. financ. inst. teleph. dir. Metro Tor. vicin.]. **VFOAT** Telephone Directory. (May 1987/88)-. Directory. English. One time a year (June). 10.95Can$. Bowne of Canada, Ltd., 60 Gervais Drive, Toronto Ontario M3C 1Z3 Canada. **Tel** (416)449-6400, FAX (416)449-7114. ***Continues*** *Chartered Banks & Trust Companies (Savings Branches) Telephone Directory, Metro Toronto & Vicinity, 0822-5354.*

LC HG4245.Z5 T64
DD 332 JA
TOSHO SHINYOROKU. KANTO-BAN. Main/Corp Tokyo Shoko Risachi. **VAT** Tokyo Shoko Risachi Shinyoroku. (1974)-. Periodical. Japanese. ¥40000. Tokyo Shoko Risachi, c/o Shinichi Building, 9-6 Shinbashi 1-chome Minato-ku 105, Tokyo Japan. **ED** Yukinbu Takahashi. **Ad Acc. *Continues*** *Tosho Shinyoroku Kanto-Ban.*
Desc: Lists 21 elements of information concerning business transactions such as name of company, address, bankers, purchasers, customers, etc.

LC HG1501
DD 332.1 UK
TITLE CHANGE
TRADE FINANCE. See Business and Economics-Commerce.

LC HG2032 **ISSN** 0822-3521
DD 334/.09715 CN
TRAIT D'UNION - FEDERATION DES CAISSES POPULAIRES ACADIENNES. See Business and Economics-Cooperatives.

LC HG1501 **ISSN** 0967-523X
DD 332.1 UK
Pr Rev.
TREASURY MANAGEMENT INTERNATIONAL. (1992)-. Trade Publication. English. Eleven times a year. £155.00 (institutions), £124.00 (treasurers) UK and Europe; £175.00 (institutions), £140.00 (treasurers) other. Hemmington Scott Publishing Ltd, 25-31 Whiskin Street, City Innovation Centre, London EC1R OBP United Kingdom. **Tel** 011 44 171 2787769, FAX 011 44 171 2789808. **ED** Carol Howland. Index available. cum. index. **Bk Rev**, (Qty: 1 per year). **Ad Acc, Adv Mgr:** Geert Reinders. **Circ:** 6,500.
Desc: Devoted to analysis of two topics of current importance to international corporate treasurers. The practicalities and implications of the subject are explained and discussed through articles written by corporate treasurers from their own experience and by treasury specialists operating in different parts of the world.

LC HG1501
DD 332.1 UK
TREASURY MANAGER. (19??)-. English. Twelve times a year. £485.00 UK; $790.00 US. Euromoney Publications PLC, Nestor House, Playhouse Yard, London EC4Z 5EX United Kingdom. **Tel** 011 44 171 7798888, FAX 011 44 171 7798630, telex 290700 EUROMON G. **(Subscription address:** Euromoney Publications PLC, Perrymount Road Haywards Heath, West Sussex RH16 3DH United Kingdom. **Tel** 011 44 1444 440421.) ***Continues*** *Euromoney Treasury Report, 0953-8798.*
Desc: Risk management newsletter which forecasts currency and interest rate movements in both major and minor markets. Provides recommendations and features on derivative products and compiles concensus forecasts of over 40 analysts' views on exchange and interest rate.

LC HG1501 **ISSN** 1071-8532
DD 332.1 US
CCC
•TREASURY MANAGER'S REPORT. Added/Corp Phillips Business Information, Inc. (1993)-. Periodical. English. Twenty-five times a year. $595.00. Phillips Business Information Inc., 1201 Seven Locks Road, PO Box 61130, Potomac MD 20854. **Tel** (301)424-3338, (301)340-1520, (800)777-5005, FAX (301)424-4297, telex 358149.

LC HG3881 .T655 **ISSN** 0309-8001
DD 332.1/5 UK
TRENDS IN INTERNATIONAL BANKING AND CAPITAL MARKETS. Added/Corp Banker Research Unit. (May 1977)-. Periodical. English. Six times a year. $325.00. Financial Times Magazines, Greystoke Place, Fetter Lane, London EC4A 1ND United Kingdom. **Tel** 011 44 171 8316577.
Desc: A loose-leaf service, of which one issue per year is a detailed annual survey; two issues are revisions to data with commentary, and the remaining issues are monthly data adjustments series.

LC HG1501
DD 332.1 US
TRUST LETTER. Added/Corp American Bankers Association. Trust Division. (Jan. 29, 1971)-. Periodical. English. Twelve times a year. $210.00. American Bankers Association, 1120 Connecticut Avenue Northwest, Washington DC 20036. **Tel** (202)663-5221, (202)663-5000, FAX (202)828-4544. **ED** Allyn Buzzell. **Circ:** 2,000. ***Continues*** *Trust Bulletin.*
Desc: Information on national legislation and regulation that impacts the trust and investment business. Contains reports on on industry happenings, including research, and provides coverage of ABA legislative/regulatory testimony and committee activities.

ISSN 0968-8137
DD 361.76 UK
TRUST MONITOR & GRANT NEWS. [Trust monit. grant news]. **VFOAT** Trust Monitor and Grant News. (1989)-. English. Three times a year.
Ind/Abst Museum Abstr.

LC HB9 .T75 **ISSN** 1000-8306
DD 330.05 CC
TSAI CHING KO HSUEH. Added/Corp Hsi-Nan Tsai Ching ta Hsueh (China). **VFOAT** Finance and Economics. (19??)-. Periodical. Chinese. Six times a year. $14.16. **(Subscription address:** China International Book Trading Corporation, PO Box 399, Library Service Department, Beijing 100044 People's Republic of China. **Tel** 011 86 1 8414284, FAX 011 86 1 8412023, telex 22496 CIBTC CN.)
Desc: Covers finance and economics.

LC HC427.92 .T72
DD 330.951/057 CC
TSAI CHING YEN CHIU. Added/Corp Shang-Hai Tsai Cheng Ching Chi Hsueh Yuan. **VFOAT** Caijing Yanjiu; Study of Finance and Economics. (19??)-. Periodical. Chinese. Twelve times a year. $20.65. Chung-Kuo Chu Pan Tui Wai Mao I Kung SSU, Shing-Hai Fen Kung SSU, 380 Pei Su-Chou Road, Shanghai, People's Republic of China. **(Subscription address:** China International Book Trading Corporation, PO Box 399, Library Service Department, Beijing 100044 People's Republic of China. **Tel** 011 86 1 8414284, FAX 011 86 1 8412023, telex 22496 CIBTC CN.)
Desc: Study of finance and economics.

LC HG **ISSN** 0889-1699
DD 332 US
TURNAROUNDS & WORKOUTS. VFOAT Turnarounds and Workouts. Vol. 1, No. 1 (Feb. 1, 1987)-. Periodical. English. Twenty times a year. $354.00. Beard Group, PO Box 9867, Washington DC 20016. **Tel** (301)951-6400, FAX (301)951-3621.

LC HG **ISSN** 1061-4176
DD 332 US
TURNAROUNDS & WORKOUTS. EUROPE. [Turnarounds workouts, Eur.]. **Added/Corp** Beard Group, Inc. **VFOAT** Turnarounds and Wworkouts. Europe; Europe; Turnarounds & Workouts; Turnarounds and Workouts. (1991)-. Periodical. English. Six times a year. $295.00. Beard Group, PO Box 9867, Washington DC 20016. **Tel** (301)951-6400, FAX (301)951-3621.

LC HG1501
DD 332.1 US
U. S. FINANCIAL DATA. Main/Corp Federal Reserve Bank of St. Louis. (1966)-. Periodical. English. Fifty times a year. $21.00. Federal Reserve Bank of St. Louis, PO Box 66953, Research and Publication Information, St. Louis MO 63166. **Tel** (314)444-8444, (314)444-8660, FAX (314)444-8731. **ED** Daniel P Brennan. **Circ:** 56,000.
Desc: Charts and tables relating to weekly monetary data and selected interest rate data with brief analysis of current conditions.

LC HG4931 .G57 **ISSN** 0272-8427
DD 332.63/232/0973 US
U.S. GOVERNMENT AGENCY SECURITY MARKET REPORT : FORECASTS AND ANALYSES, THE. [U. S. Gov. agency secur. mark. rep.: forecasts anal.]. **Added/Corp** Data Resources, Inc. **VFOAT** Data Resources Agency Yield Service; Agency Security Market Review. **VAT** United States Government Agency Security Market Report: Forecasts and Analyses. (19??)-. English. DRI McGraw Hill, 24 Hartwell Avenue, Lexington MA 02173. **Tel** (617)863-5100, FAX (617)860-6464, (617)860-6416.

LC HG4135.5 .S85
DD 332.1/025/41 UK
UK BUSINESS FINANCE DIRECTORY. VFOAT Business Finance Directory. 4th Ed. (1990/91)-. Directory. English. Graham & Trotman Ltd., Sterling House, 66 Wilton Road, London SW1V 1DE United

Business and Economics —Banks and Banking

Kingdom. **Tel** 011 44 171 8211123, FAX 011 44 171 8288935. **Continues** Sunday Telegraph Business Finance Directory, 0268-2249.

LC HG1501   **ISSN** 0265-8364
DD 332.1   UK
    CCC
UK VENTURE CAPITAL JOURNAL. [UK
venture cap. j.]. **VFOAT** Venture Capital Journal. **VAT** United Kingdom Venture Capital Journal. No. 1 (April 1983)-. Periodical. English. Six times a year. $821.37. Venture Economics Ltd, Quadrange 180, Wardourst Street, London W1A 4YG United Kingdom. **Tel** 011 44 171 4340411, FAX 011 44 171 4343918. **ED** S. Lloyd. Index available. cum. index. ctrl circ. available on an online database (files 16,636/Full-Text) from DIALOG.
  Desc: Covers UK venture capital and related investment activity.
  Ind/Abst PROMT [Full Txt.]; PTS Newsl. Database [Full Txt.].

LC HG4503 .U53
DD 332.6   KO
UNHAENGGYE. (1966)-. Periodical. Korean.
Twelve times a year.

LC HG1501
DD 332.1   US
UNIDEX QUARTERLY. English. Four times a
year. $960.00. Unidex Corporation, PO Box 567566, Atlanta GA 30356. **Tel** (800)528-5342, FAX (404)847-9301. cum. index. ctrl circ.
  Desc: Consumer attitudes, opinions and habits concerning financial services.

LC HG1501
DD 332.1   US
UNIDEX REPORTS. (19??)-. English. Twelve
times a year. $695.00. Unidex Corporation, PO Box 567566, Atlanta GA 30356. **Tel** (800)528-5342, FAX (404)847-9301.
  Desc: Consumer attitudes, opinions and habits concerning financial services.

LC HG1501
DD 332.1   US
UNIFORM PRACTICES FOR THE CLEARANCE AND SETTLEMENT OF MORTGAGE-BACKED SECURITIES.
(19??)-. English. $395.00. Public Securities Association, 40 Broad Street, 12th Floor, New York NY 10004. **Tel** (212)809-7000, (212)440-9430, FAX (212) 797-3895, (212) 742-1549.

LC HG1 .U5   **ISSN** 0148-8848
DD 332/.0973   US
    CCC
    CODEN USBAEH
    TITLE CHANGE
UNITED STATES BANKER (COS COB).
(UNITED STATES BANKER.). [U. S. bank.]. Vol. 88, No. 19 (Sept. 1977)-(19??). Periodical. English. Kalo Communications Inc., 10 Valley Drive, Greenwich CT 06831. **Tel** (212)599-3310. **ED** Raoul D. Edwards. **Ad Acc. Circ:** 22,000 (ctrl). available on microfilm and microfiche from University Microfilms International (UMI); available on an online database from NEXIS; and (files 15,648/Full-Text) DIALOG. Documents available from Ask*IEEE, UMI Article Clearinghouse. **Continues** United States Investor/Eastern Banker, 0362-6741. **Continued by** US Banker.
  Desc: An independent magazine of commentary and analysis for the financial services industry and management.
  Ind/Abst ABI/INFORM Glob. Ed.; ABI/INFORM [Computer File]; Acad. Search; Bus. ASAP (1985-); Bus. Index (1985-); Bus. Period. Index; Bus. Source Plus; Bus. Source (Jan. 1988-); Curr. Cit.; EP Collect.; Gen. BusinessFile; Gen. Period. Index; Homework Help. (July 1993-Feb. 1994); INFO-SOUTH Abstr.; INSPEC; Mag. Search; MasterFile FullTEXT 1000 [Full Txt.]; MasterFile FullTEXT 350 [Full Txt.]; MasterFile FullTEXT 650 (Dec. 1987-) [Full Txt.]; MasterFile FullTEXT; OCLC; PAIS Int. Print; Telebase; Trade Ind. ASAP; Trade Ind. Index; UMI ABI/Inform--Bus. Period. Ondisc; Wilson Bus. Abstr.

LC HG1501
DD 332.1   US
UPDATE - CASH MANAGEMENT INSTITUTE. (19??)-. Periodical. English. One time a
year. $20.00. IBC Donoghue Organization, 290 Eliot Street, Ashland MA 01721. **Tel** (800)343-5413, (508)881-2800.

LC HG1501
DD 332.1   US
UPDATE - FEDERAL RESERVE BANK OF ATLANTA. Main/Corp Federal Reserve Bank of
Atlanta. (19??)-. Periodical. English. Free on request. Federal Reserve Bank of Atlanta, 104 Marietta Street Northwest, Atlanta GA 30303. **Tel** (404)521-8788.
  Ind/Abst Fed. Print Econ. Bank. Top.

LC HG1501
DD 332.1   US
US BANKER. (19??)-. Periodical. English. Twelve
times a year. $59.00. Faulkner & Gray Inc., 11 Penn Plaza, 17th Floor, New York NY 10001. **Tel**

(212)967-7000, (800)535-8403. **Continues** United States Banker.
  Ind/Abst Curr. Cit.; MasterFile FullTEXT (Mar. 1994-).

ISSN 0899-5524
DD 338   US
USA FINANCIAL NEWS. [USA financ. news].
VFOAT USA Financial. **VAT** United States of America Financial News. (1988)-. Periodical. English. Twelve times a year. $48.00. BFG Publishers Inc., 3855 S Valley View 1, Las Vegas NV 89103. **Continues** Capital Opportunities Digest, 0898-0861.

ISSN 0042-238X
DD 338   US
VALUATION (AMERICAN SOCIETY OF APPRAISERS). (VALUATION.). [Valuation].
(196?)-. Trade Publication. English. Irregular. $8.00. American Society of Appraisers / Washington D.C, PO Box 17265, Dulles Airport, Washington DC 20041. **Tel** (703)478-2228. **ED** Shirley Belz. **Circ:** 5,500 (ctrl). **Continues** Technical Valuation.
  Desc: Presents articles concerned with the appraisal of real estate, fine arts, antiques, machinery and equipment, public utilities, aircraft and other properties. Includes business valuations.
  Ind/Abst Account. Tax Datab. (1974-).

LC HG1501   **ISSN** 1061-3870
DD 332.1   US
VANDERWICKEN'S FINANCIAL DIGEST.
Added/Corp Plumstead Group, Inc. (1992)-. Periodical. English. Twelve times a year. $237.00. Plumstead Group Inc., PO Box 545, New Hope PA 18938. **Tel** (800)892-6280, (215)297-8222, FAX (215)297-8222. **ED** Peter Vanderwicken. **Circ:** 1,000.
  Desc: Strives to keep readers well informed about the fast-changing financial industry, to provide a broad information base in a brief digest, and to identify new developments and new strategies that create new business and investment opportunities in the industry.

LC HG   **ISSN** 1056-2338
DD 332   US
VANGUARD ADVISER, THE. [Vanguard
advis.]. (1991)-. Periodical. English. Twelve times a year. $89.00. Fund Family Shareholder Association, 328 Flatbush Avenue, Suite 106, New York NY 11238.

LC HG2611.N5 V37
DD 332.1/2/09749   US
VARIOUS AVERAGES OF NEW JERSEY COMMERCIAL BANKS AS OF DECEMBER 31 ... ARRANGED BY GROUPS ACCORDING TO TOTAL ASSETS IN MILLIONS.
English. One time a year. New Jersey Department of Banking, State House of Annex, Trenton NJ 08625. **Tel** (609)292-3723.

ISSN 0263-9947
DD 336.271405   UK
VAT INTELLIGENCE. [VAT intell.]. VFOAT Value
Added Tax Intelligence. (1983)-. Periodical. English. Twelve times a year. $248.13. GEE Publishing Limited, South Quay Plaza, 18 Marsh Wall, London E14 9FS United Kingdom. **Tel** 011 44 171 5385368. (**Subscription address:** Professional Publishing Ltd., South Quay Plaza, 183 Marsh Wall, London E14 9FS United Kingdom. **Tel** 011 44 181 5385386.) **ED** Victor Durkacz and Denise Owen. Index available (free). **Bk Rev**. ctrl circ.
  Desc: Matters concerning VAT, including planning case law developments, editors comments and letters.

LC HG1501
DD 332.1   NE
VERSLAG OVER HET BOEKJAAR ... .
Main/Corp Bank voor Nederlandsche Gemeenten, N.V. Dutch (English). One time a year. Bank voor Nederlandsche Gemeenten, Koninginnegracht 2, 2514 AA Gravenhage The Netherlands. **Tel** 31.70.483.991, FAX 31.70.454.743, telex 31046 BNG NL.

LC HC271 .V49   **ISSN** 0220-5858
DD 330.944/005   FR
VIE FRANCAISE (PARIS, FRANCE: 1978). See Business and Economics-Economic
History, Conditions.

LC HG1881 .O416a
DD 332   AU
VIERTELJAHRES-SCHRIFTENREIHE - OSTERREICHISCHES FORSCHUNGSINSTITUT FUR SPARKASSENWESEN. Added/Corp
Osterreichisches Forschungsinstitut fur Sparkassenwesen. (19??)-. Periodical. German. S195.00. Verleger, Sparkassenverlag Gesellschaft, A 1030 Vienna Grimmelshausengasse, Vienna Austria. **Tel** 734581-290. **Bk Rev**, (Qty: 4). **Acid Free. Circ:** 1,000.
Supersedes Osterreichisches Forschungsinstitut fur Sparkassenwesen. Schriftenreihe.

LC HG4245 .A33a
DD 332   JA
WAGA KUNI KIGYO NO KEIEI BUNSEKI. KIGYOBETSU TOKEI HEN. Main/Corp Japan.
Tsusho Sangyosho. Sangyo Seisakukyoku. **Added/Corp** Japan. Tsusho Sangyosho. Kigyokyoku. Japan. Periodical. Japanese. Two times a year. ¥4700. Okurasho Insatukyoku, (Printing Bureau Ministry of Finance), 2-4 Toranomon 2 chome, Minatoku Tokyo 105 Japan.
Continues in part Waga Kuni Kigyo No Keiei Bunseki.

LC HG1501   **ISSN** 0193-225X
DD 332.1   US
    CCC
WALL STREET JOURNAL. SOUTHWEST EDITION, THE. (THE WALL STREET JOURNAL.).
Vol. 1, No. 1 (May 3, 1948)-. Newspaper. English. Seven times a week. $149.00. Dow Jones and Company Inc., 200 Burnett Road, Chicopee MA 01021. **Tel** (413)592-7761, (800)568-7625. Documents available from UMI Article Clearinghouse.
  Ind/Abst Account. Tax Datab. (1990-); Infobank; Music Index (-19??); Newsp. Abstr.; Newsp. Abstr.; Predicasts F&S Index, U. S. Annu. Ed.

LC HG1501   **ISSN** 1084-5399
DD 332.1   US
●WARFIELD'S TAMPA BAY REVIEW.
Added/Corp Warfield Media Company. **VFOAT** Tampa Bay Review. Vol. 43, No. 53 (July 7, 1995)-. Newspaper. English. One time a week. Warfield Media Co., 14100 US 19 #105, Clearwater FL 34624. **Tel** (813)538-2100.
Continues Pinellas County Review, 0746-746X.

LC HG   **ISSN** 0882-2247
DD 332   US
WASHINGTON MEMO - NATIONAL COUNCIL OF SAVINGS INSTITUTIONS (U.S.). (WASHINGTON MEMO.). [Wash. memo (Natl.
Counc. Sav. Inst. (U. S.))]. **Added/Corp** National Council of Savings Institutions (U.S.). Vol. 1, No. 1 (Nov. 4, 1983)-. Periodical. English. Irregular. Savings and Community Bankers of America, 1101 15th Street Northwest, Suite 400, Washington DC 20005. **Tel** (202)857-1000, FAX (202)659-4816. **ED** Joe Hutnyan.
  Desc: An interpretive newsletter about Washington actions and events affecting savings institutions. Optional supplements of regulatory and legislative documents.

LC HG   **ISSN** 0899-8396
DD 332   US
    TITLE CHANGE
WEALTH AND RICHES NEWSLETTER.
VFOAT Wealth and Riches. (198?)-(19??). Newsletter. English. The LPS Newsletter, PO Box 67279, Los Angeles CA 90067. **Continues** Low Price Stocks Newsletter, 0745-4597. **Continued by** USA Financial News, 0899-5524.

LC HG1501
DD 332.1   GW
    SUSPENDED
WECHSEL- UND SCHECKRECHT ALLER LANDER, DAS. (19??)-(19??).
Periodical. German. Deutscher Wirtschaftsdienst GmbH, Marienburgerstrasse 22, D-50968 Cologne Germany. **Tel** 011 49 221 376950.

LC HG1501   **ISSN** 1064-5918
DD 332.1   US
WEEKLY BULLETIN - CALIFORNIA. STATE BANKING DEPT. (WEEKLY BULLETIN
- STATE OF CALIFORNIA, STATE BANKING DEPARTMENT.). **Main/Corp** California. State Banking Dept. (Oct. 21, 1955)-. Bulletin. English. One time a week. $30.00. State Banking Department / California, 111 Pine Street, Suite 1100, San Francisco CA 94111-5613. **Tel** (415)557-3232. **ED** Cari Rodriguez. **Circ:** 2,200 (ctrl).
Continues Bulletin - California State Banking Dept.
  Desc: Details the actions of the superintendent of banks regarding filings, approvals, licensings of new banks, branches, etc. as well as other information for bankers.

LC HG1501   **ISSN** 0276-8488
DD 332.1   US
WEEKLY BULLETIN - NEW YORK (STATE). BANKING DEPT. (WEEKLY
BULLETIN - NEW YORK STATE BANKING DEPARTMENT.). **Main/Corp** New York (State). Banking Dept. (19??)-. Bulletin. English. One time a week. $35.00. New York State Banking Department, 2 Rector Street, New York NY 10006. **Tel** (212)618-6440, FAX (212)618-6962. **Circ:** 2,000.
  Desc: Records the filing of applications and notices filed with the New York State (NYS) Banking Department as well as action and activities concerning the NYS Banking Department.

LC HG1501
DD 332.1   US
WEEKLY CONSOLIDATED CONDITION REPORT OF LARGE COMMERCIAL BANKS AND DOMESTIC SUBSIDIARIES. Added/Corp Board of Governors
of the Federal Reserve System (U.S.). (19??)-. Periodical.

Business and Economics — Banks and Banking

English. Fifty-two times a year. Free on request. Board of Governors of the Federal Reserve System, Mail Stop 127, Washington DC 20551. **Tel** (202)452-3244, (202)452-3245. Documents available from Documents on Demand. **Continues** Board of Governors of the Federal Reserve System (U.S.). Weekly Condition Report of Large Commercial Banks and Domestic Subsidiaries, 0364-7331.
Desc: Includes: Weekly consolidated condition report of large commercial banks, by district, and for New York city, H.4.2 (504) A,B.
Ind/Abst Am. Stat. Index.

LC HG1501
DD 332.1 UK

WEEKLY EUROBOND GUIDE. (19??)-.
English. One time a week. £1960.00 UK; $1,707.91 US. International Securities Market Assn Ltd., Seven Limeharbour Docklands, London E14 9NQ United Kingdom. **Tel** 011 44 171 5385656, FAX 011 44 171 5384902. **Circ:** 3,500 copies per week.
Desc: Contains information on bond prices.

LC HG1501
DD 332.1 AT

WEEKLY RATES SUMMARY. (1989)-.
Trade Publication. English. One time a week. 2320.00Aus$. Horan Wall & Walker Pty Ltd, 15-19 Prospect Street, POB 8, Surry Hills New South Wales 2010 Australia. **Tel** 02 331 6600, FAX 02 380 5533. **ED** Jayson Forrest. available on an online database; available on diskette.
Desc: Lists names of retail banking deposit interest rates for products available from Australian banks and building societies and interest rates for each product. Summary presents the weeks changes.

LC HG4001 .C67 ISSN 1067-7313
DD 332 US
TITLE CHANGE

WENDELL'S REPORT FOR CONTROLLERS. [Wendell's rep. control.].
Added/Corp Warren, Gorham & Lamont, Inc. Vol. 14, No. 8 (Jan. 1993)-(199?). Periodical. English. Warren Gorham & Lamont Inc., Park Square Building, 31 St. James Avenue, Boston MA 02116-4112. **Tel** (617)423-2020, (800)950-1207, FAX (617)423-2026. **(Subscription address:** Warren Gorham & Lamont, PO Box 4966, Chicago IL 60680. **) Continues** CFO Alert, 0894-4822. **Continued by** Controller's Cost Report, 1081-9215.

LC HG2609 .W47 ISSN 0272-5371
DD 332.1/025/78 US
TITLE CHANGE

WESTERN BANK DIRECTORY.
(19??)-(19??). Directory. English. McFadden Business Publications / Norcross, GA, 6195 Crooked Creek Road, Norcross GA 30092. **Tel** (404)448-1011, (800)247-7376, FAX (404)446-6421. **Continued by** Western Bankers Directory.

LC HG1501
DD 332.1 US

WESTERN BANKERS DIRECTORY.
(19??)-. Directory. English. Two times a year. $50.00 US; $60.00 other. McFadden Business Publications / Norcross, GA, 6195 Crooked Creek Road, Norcross GA 30092. **Tel** (404)448-1011, (800)247-7376, FAX (404)446-6421. **Continues** Western Bank Directory, 0272-5371.

LC HG1501
DD 332.1 UK

WHO'S WHO IN INTERNATIONAL BANKING. (1984)-.
English. One time a year. $239.18. Bowker Saur Ltd., A Reed Reference Publishing Company, Part of Reed International PLC, 59-60 Grosvenor Street, London WIX 9DA United Kingdom. **Tel** 011 44 171 4935841, FAX 011 44 171 4991590.
Desc: A unique guide to key people in international banking. Detailed biographical information for over 4000 international banks in over 130 countries around the world, plus over 600 major borrowers in the international capital markets, listed by country and listing the name of their senior treasury officer, address and contact number to make up three distinct sections.

LC HG1501
DD 332.1 US

WORKING PAPER SERIES / FEDERAL RESERVE BANK OF ATLANTA.
Added/Corp Federal Reserve Bank of Atlanta. (1986)-. Monographic series. English. Price varies per volume. Federal Reserve Bank of Atlanta, 104 Marietta Street Northwest, Atlanta GA 30303. **Tel** (404)521-8788.
Ind/Abst Fed. Print Econ. Bank. Top.

LC HG1501
DD 332.1 US

WORLD BANK.
English. Free on request. World Bank Publications, 1818 H Street Northwest, Washington DC 20043. **Tel** (202)473-1155, (202)473-1155, FAX (202)522-3224, telex WUI 64145 WORLDBANK.

LC Z7164.F5 I555B HG3881 ISSN 0303-9463
DD 016.3321/53

WORLD BANK CATALOG. ACCESSION LIST. **Main/Corp** International Bank for Reconstruction and Development. Catalog. English. International Bank for Reconstruction and Development / Washington, DC, 1818 H Street Northwest, Washington DC 20433.

LC HG1501 ISSN 0254-6353
DD 332.1 US

WORLD BANK NEWS. [World Bank news].
Added/Corp International Bank for Reconstruction and Development. Vol. 1, No. 1 (Nov. 18, 1982)-. Newsletter. English (French and German). One time a week. Free on request. World Bank Information and Public Affairs, External Affairs Department, Washington DC 20433. **Tel** (202)473-9661. **ED** Michael Prest.

LC HG1501 ISSN 0253-2131
DD 332.1 US

WORLD BANK REPRINT SERIES. [World Bank repr. ser.]. (19??)-. Monographic series. English. Irregular. Price varies per volume. World Bank Publications, 1818 H Street Northwest, Washington DC 20043. **Tel** (202)473-1155, (202)473-1155, FAX (202)522-3224, telex WUI 64145 WORLDBANK.

LC HG1505 .W67 ISSN 0265-9484
DD 332.1/05 UK
CCC

WORLD BANKING ABSTRACTS. See
Business and Economics-Abstracting, Bibliographies and Statistics.

LC HG219 .P5 ISSN 0743-5363
DD 332.4/05 US

WORLD CURRENCY YEARBOOK. [World curr. yearb.].
Added/Corp International Currency Analysis, Inc. **VFOAT** World Currency Year Book. (1984)-. English. Irregular. $250.00. International Currency Analysis Inc, 7239 Avenue North, Brooklyn NY 11234. **Tel** (718)531-3685, (205)991-6925. **ED** Philip Cowitt. Index available. **Bk Rev. Circ:** 1,000. **Continues** Pick's Currency Yearbook, 0079-2063.
Desc: Complete source of monetary information analyses 145 currency units.

ISSN 0258-7440
DD 338 US

WORLD ECONOMIC AND FINANCIAL SURVEYS. **Added/Corp** International Monetary Fund. (April 1986)-. Monographic series. English. Irregular. Price varies per volume. International Monetary Fund, 700 19th Street Northwest, Publishing Unit, Washington DC 20431. **Tel** (202)623-7430, FAX (202)623-7201.

LC HG1501
DD 332.1 UK

WORLD EQUITY. (19??)-.
English. Twelve times a year. $495.00. IFR Publishing Ltd., Aldgate House, 33 Aldgate High Street, London EC3N 1DL United Kingdom. **Tel** 011 44 171 369 7536, FAX 011 44 171 369 7395, telex 889365/8953051 IFRPUBG. **(Subscription address:** IFR Publishing, 90 Broad Street, Second Floor, New York NY 10004. **)**

LC HG1 .W67 ISSN 0190-2083
DD 332/.05 US

WORLD FINANCIAL MARKETS. [World financ. mark.].
Added/Corp Morgan Guaranty Trust Company of New York. (1972)-. Periodical. English. Twelve times a year. Morgan Guaranty Trust, 14 place Vendome, 75001 Paris France. **Tel** 011 33 1 40154500. available on an online database from Lexis-Nexis.

LC HD1393.25 .W67 ISSN 1046-4778
DD 338.8/3/025 US

WORLD M&A NETWORK. [World MA netw.].
VFOAT Network; World M and A Network; M & A; M and A. **VAT** World Merger & Acquisition Network; World Merger and Acquisition Network. (Aug. 1988)-. Periodical. English. Four times a year. $365.70. International Executive Reports, 717 D Street NW/Suite 300, Washington DC 20004-2807. **Tel** (202)628-6900, FAX (202)628 6618, telex 440462 MEER UI.

LC HG1501 .W67 ISSN 0730-8736
DD 332.1/068 US
CODEN WOBADA

WORLD OF BANKING, THE. [World bank.].
Added/Corp Bank Administration Institute. Vol. 1, No. 1 (Jan.-Feb. 1982)-. Periodical. English. Six times a year. $90.00. World of Banking Publishing Company, 582 Oakwood Avenue, Suite 203, Lake Forest IL 60045. **Tel** (708)615-0405, FAX (708)615-0416. **ED** J Christopher Svare. **Bk Rev. Ad Acc. Circ:** 8,000 (ctrl). Documents available from UMI Article Clearinghouse, Ask*IEEE.
Desc: This magazine features information of common interest to the world banking community. Articles deal with operations, internal control, payment systems, auditing, accounting, security, and more.
Ind/Abst ABI/INFORM Glob. Ed.; ABI/INFORM [Computer File] (Sept. 1983-); Curr. Cit.; INSPEC (Sept.-Oct. 1982-); PAIS Bull. (1985-); PAIS Int. Print.

LC HG1501
DD 332.1 US

YEARBOOK - CREDIT UNION NATIONAL ASSOCIATION. **Main/Corp** Credit Union National Association. (1978)-. Periodical. English. One time a year. Free on request. Credit Union National Association, PO Box 431, Madison WI 53701. **Tel** (608)231-4088, (800)356-9655, FAX (608)231-4370. **ED** Lucy Harr. **Bk Rev. Ad Acc. Circ:** 5,000 (ctrl). **Continues** CUNA Yearbook.
Desc: Statistical reports on U.S. credit unions by state.

LC HG2038.I5 I52a ISSN 1046-2996
DD 334/.22/09773 US

YEARBOOK - ILLINOIS CREDIT UNION LEAGUE (1988). (YEARBOOK / ILLINOIS CREDIT UNION LEAGUE.). [Yearbook - Ill. Credit Union Leag.].
Main/Corp Illinois Credit Union League. (198?)-. English. One time a year. Free to public and accredited school libraries; $50.00 other. Illinois Credit Union League, 2011 Swift Drive, Oak Brook IL 60521. **Tel** (312)574-3205, FAX (312)574-3218. **Circ:** 2,000. **Continues** Illinois Credit Union League. Yearbook/Annual Report.
Desc: Operating results for prior year for 90% of credit unions operating in Illinois.

LC HG2033 .W67a ISSN 0147-7803
DD 334/.2 US

YEARBOOK - WORLD COUNCIL OF CREDIT UNIONS. [Yearb. - World Counc. Credit Unions].
Main/Corp World Council of Credit Unions. (19??)-. Periodical. English (French and Spanish). One time a year. Free. World Council of Credit Unions, 5810 Mineral Point Road, PO Box 2982, Madison WI 53701. **Tel** (608)231-7130, telex 467918. **ED** Jim Jerving. **Circ:** 10,000 (ctrl).

ISSN 1191-0542
DD 658.15 CN

YOUR GUIDE TO ARRANGING BANK & DEBT FINANCING FOR YOUR OWN BUSINESS IN CANADA. [Your guide arrange. bank debt financ. your own bus. Can.]. **VFOAT** Arranging Bank and Debt Financing for Your Own Business in Canada; Arranging Bank & Debt Financing. **VAT** Your Guide to Arranging Bank and Debt Financing for Your Own Business in Canada. (1991)-. English. One time a year. 16.77Can$. Productive Publications, PO Box 7200, Station A, Toronto Ontario M5W 1X8 Canada. **Tel** (416)483-0634. **ED** Iain Williamson.
Desc: Helps readers learn the secrets of successful debt financing in Canada.

ISSN 1191-0488
DD 658.15/224 CN

YOUR GUIDE TO FINANCING BUSINESS GROWTH BY SELLING A PIECE OF THE PIE. [Your guide financ. bus. growth sell. piece pie]. **VFOAT** Financing Business Growth. (1991)-. English. One time a year. 18.37Can$. Productive Publications, PO Box 7200, Station A, Toronto Ontario M5W 1X8 Canada. **Tel** (416)483-0634. **ED** Iain Williamson.
Desc: Provides a critical examination of three methods of achieving business growth. Also tells how to sell shares to the public, how to raise money from employees, and how to expand through franchising.

LC HG1501
DD 332.1 US

YOUR MONEY GUIDE. (199?)-. Periodical.
English. One time a year. Little Brown & Company, 34 Beacon Street, Boston MA 02108. **Tel** (617)227-0730, (800)759-0190. **Continues** Marshall Loeb's Money Guide, 8755-1586.

LC HG2040 ISSN 1039-0081
DD 332.7220994 AT

YOUR MORTGAGE MAGAZINE. [Your Mortg. Mag.]. (1993)-. Periodical. English. Three times a year. 5.95Aus$. Horan Wall & Walker Pty Ltd, 15-19 Prospect Street, POB 8, Surry Hills New South Wales 2010 Australia. **Tel** 02 331 6600, FAX 02 380 5533. **ED** Tony Shannon. **Bk Rev,** (Qty: 3). **Ad Acc, Adv Mgr:** Bruce Ewan. Full Page (B&W) 2500.00Aus$. Half Page (B&W) 1500.00Aus$. **Circ:** 40,000 (ctrl).
Desc: Provides homebuyers with advice on areas such as house-hunting, and searching through the myriad of loans currently available. It offers advice on switching loans, and examines at least one non-lending side of retail banking each issue.

LC HG1956.J35 Y82
DD 332.1 JA

YUBIN CHOKIN. (19??)-. Periodical. Japanese.
Twelve times a year. ¥1320. Yubin Chokin Shinkokai Shuppanbu, 6-19 Azabudai, Minato-ku Tokyo 106 Japan.

LC HG1956.J35 Y83
DD 332.1 JA

YUBIN CHOKIN KEIEI SHIRYO. **Added/Corp**
Japan. Chokinkyoku. (1966)-. Periodical. Japanese. Yuseisho Chokinkyoku, 3-2 Kasumigaseki 1 chiyoda-ku (100), Tokyo Japan.

LC HG1956.J35 J38a
DD 334.2   JA
YUBIN CHOKIN TO NI KANSURU SERON CHOSA KEKKA HOKOKUSHO.
Main/Corp Japan. Chokinkyoku. (19??)-. Periodical. Japanese. Yuseisho Chokinkyoku, 3-2 Kasumigaseki 1 chiyoda-ku (100), Tokyo Japan.

LC HG1501
DD 332.1   AU
Z-REPORT.
VFOAT Z Report. (19??)-. English (German). Four times a year. Free on request. Zentralsparkasse und Kommerzialbank Wien, Vordere Zollamtsstrasse 13, A 1030 Vienna Austria. **Tel** 011 43 1 71191 2516.

LC HG41 .Z33
DD 332.05/6   JA
ZAIKAI NAGOYA. See Business and Economics-Management.

LC HG   ISSN 1061-3161
DD 332   US
ZALE CORPORATION BANKRUPTCY NEWS.
[Zale Corp. Bankruptcy News]. **Added/Corp** Bankruptcy Creditors' Service. **VFOAT** Bankruptcy News. (1992)-. Periodical. English. One time a week. $30.00 (single issue). Bankruptcy Creditors' Service, Inc., 6326 Graceland Avenue, Cincinnati OH 45237-4808.

LC HG17 .Z4   ISSN 0340-8485
DD 332.1/05   GW
    CCC
ZEITSCHRIFT FUER DAS GESAMTE KREDITWESEN.
[Z. gesamte Kreditwes.]. Vol. 1 (Aug. 1948)-. Trade Publication. German. Twenty-four times a year. $308.00. Fritz Knapp Verlag, Postfach 111151, D-60046 Frankfurt Germany. **Tel** 011 49 69 9708330, FAX 011 49 69 7078400. **ED** Klaus-Friedrich Otto, Juergen Meissner, Juergen Fischer, Berthold Morschhaeuser. cum. index.
Desc: Detailed reports on problems and topics of national and international economy, including the stock market, banking, law and taxes; includes financial analyses of various credit institutions.
Ind/Abst PAIS Int. Print; Selec. Coop. Index Manage. Period.

LC HG   ISSN 0044-2445
DD 332   GW
ZEITSCHRIFT FUER DAS GESAMTE KREDITWESEN. SCHRIFTENREIHE. Vol. 1
(1950)-. Multiple languages (German). Twenty-four times a year. DM302.16. Fritz Knapp Verlag, Postfach 111151, D-60046 Frankfurt Germany. **Tel** 011 49 69 9708330, FAX 011 49 69 7078400.

LC HG3325 .Z45
DD 332.1   JA
ZENKOKU GINKO SHOKUINROKU.
(1952)-. Periodical. Japanese. ¥38000. Ginko Tsushinsha, 24-2 Hongo 1-chome Bunkyo-ku, Tokyo Japan.

LC HG3321 .Z46
DD 332.1   JA
ZENKOKU GINKO ZAIMU SHOHYO BUNSEKI = ANALYSIS OF FINANCIAL STATEMENTS OF ALL BANKS.
Added/Corp Zenkoku Ginko Kyokai Rengokai. **VFOAT** Analysis of Financial Statements of All Banks. (19??)-. Japanese. Two times a year. Federation Bankers Association of Japan, 3 1 Marunouchi 1 chome, Chiyoda ku Tokyo 100 Japan. **Tel** 011 81 3 2163761.

    ISSN 1065-3600
DD 658   US
ZIMMERMAN CASH FLOW LETTER, THE.
[Zimmerman cash flow lett.]. **VFOAT** Cash Flow Letter. (1991)-. Periodical. English. Twelve times a year. $403.00. Aspen Publishers Inc., 7201 McKinney Circle, Frederick MD 21701. **Tel** (800)234-1660, (301)698-7100, FAX (301)251-5784, telex 5106014543.

LC HG186.F8 A32
DD 332.4/09171/244   FR
ZONE FRANC, LA. Main/Corp France. Comite Monetaire de la Zone Franc. Secretariat. (19??)-. French. Secretariat du Comite Monetaire de la Zone Franc, 39 rue Croix-des-Petit-Champs, 75049 Paris France. **Continues** France. Comite Monetaire de la Zone Franc. Rapport.
Desc: Consists of the annual report of the agency and covers finance and currency questions.

CHAMBER OF COMMERCE

    ISSN 0318-7306
DD 382.0/0971/044   CN
ACTION CANADA FRANCE. [Action Can. Fr.].
(Feb. 1976)-. French. Ten times a year. 12.01Can$. Revue Action Canada France Inc., 360 St. Francois Xavier, 1 Etage, Montreal Quebec H2Y 2S8 Canada. **Tel** (514)281-1246. **Supersedes** Chambre de Commerce Francaise au Canada. Revue, 0045-6306.

LC HF3901 .A13   ISSN 0250-0817
DD 330.968/005   SA
AFRICAN BUSINESS & CHAMBER OF COMMERCE REVIEW. VFOAT African Business and Chamber of Commerce Review; African Business. (19??)-. Trade Publication. English. Twelve times a year. $21.47. African Business, PO Box 2821, Cresta 2118 South Africa. **Tel** 011 27 8868484, FAX 011 27 8868484. **ED** Mr. Rev Ntoula. **Ad Acc**, **Adv Mgr:** J. Kapp. **Circ:** 19,000.

    ISSN 0882-0929
    US
ALERT (SACRAMENTO, CALIF.). (ALERT / CALIFORNIA CHAMBER OF COMMERCE.).
Added/Corp California Chamber of Commerce. (1985)-. Periodical. English. Forty times a year. California Chamber of Commerce, PO Box 1736, Sacramento CA 95812-1736. **Tel** (916)856-5200, (800)331-8877. **ED** Ann Amioka. **Circ:** 9,500 (ctrl). **Continues** Pacific Alert.
Desc: Legislative and regulatory matters of interest to business.

LC HC451 .A452   PH
AMCHAM BUSINESS JOURNAL.
Added/Corp American Chamber of Commerce of the Philippines. **VFOAT** Business Journal; AmCham Journal; Am Cham business Journal; Am Cham Journal. Vol. 66, No. 6 (June 1991)-. Periodical. English. Twelve times a year. $25.00. American Chamber of Commerce in the Philippines, C P O Box 2562, Makati, Metro Manila 1299 Philippines. **Tel** 011 63 2 8187911, telex 45181 AMCHAM PM. **ED** Katherine D. Domingo. **Bk Rev**, (Qty: 12). **Ad Acc**, **Adv Mgr:** L. A. Acejas. **Circ:** 5,000. **Continues** Business Journal, 0116-452X.
Desc: Contains business updates, corporate information, current trends in the different industries and the general business outlook in the Philipines.

LC HF314 .A56   ISSN 0778-2624
DD 382/.09730493/06049332   BE
AMCHAM : THE MAGAZINE OF THE AMERICAN CHAMBER OF COMMERCE IN BELGIUM. Added/Corp American Chamber of Commerce in Belgium. No. 495 (Jan. 1991)-. Periodical. English. Twelve times a year (11 times per year plus annual directory). $194.03. AMCHAM EEC / American Chamber of Commerce / Belgium, 50 Avenue des Artes Boite 5, 1040 Brussels Belgium. **Tel** 011 32 2 5136892. **Continues** Commerce in Belgium.

LC HF331.H6 .A45a
DD 382/.095125/0730255125   HK
AMERICAN CHAMBER OF COMMERCE IN HONG KONG : [DIRECTORY], THE.
Main/Corp American Chamber of Commerce in Hong Kong. **VFOAT** Directory. (19??)-. Directory. English. One time a year (Sept.). $173.00. American Chamber of Commerce in Hong Kong, 1030 Swire House, Hong Kong Hong Kong. **Tel** 011 852 25260165.

LC HF300 .A27
DD 382/.0973/0810258153   BL
ANNUAL DIRECTORY / AMERICAN CHAMBER OF COMMERCE FOR BRAZIL, RIO DE JANEIRO - SALVADOR.
Main/Corp American Chamber of Commerce for Brazil. Rio de Janeiro Chamber. (19??)-. Directory. English. One time a year. American Chamber of Commerce for Brazil, Av Rio Branco 123, 21st Floor/Room 2106 11, Rio de Janeiro Brazil. **Continues** American Chamber of Commerce for Brazil. Rio de Janeiro Chamber. Membership Directory.

LC HF3800.6.Z8 S56
DD 382/.025/5952   SI
ANNUAL REPORT & ACCOUNTS : DIRECTORY OF MEMBERS, PRODUCTS & SERVICES. Main/Corp Singapore Indian Chamber of Commerce & Industry. VFOAT Annual Report and Accounts. (19??)-. Directory. English. One time a year. Singapore Indian Chamber of Commerce, 101 Cecil Street, 23-01 Tong Eng Building, Singapore 0106 Singapore. **Continues** Singapore Indian Chamber of Commerce. Directory - Singapore Indian Chamber of Commerce, 0376-8635.

LC HF336.E8 E83a   ISSN 0376-544X
DD 380.1/06/263   ET
ANNUAL REPORT - ETHIOPIAN CHAMBER OF COMMERCE. Main/Corp
Ethiopian Chamber of Commerce. (19??)-. English. Ethiopian Chamber of Commerce, PO Box 517, Addis Ababa Ethiopia. **Tel** 011 251 1 518240, 011 251 1 448240, FAX 011 251 1 517699, telex 21213.

    SI
ANNUAL REPORT / SINGAPORE INTERNATIONAL CHAMBER OF COMMERCE. Main/Corp Singapore International Chamber of Commerce. (1991)-. English. Singapore International Chamber of Commerce, 50 Raffles PL#03-02, Shell Tower, Singapore 0104 Singapore. **Tel** 011 65 2241255. **Continues** Singapore International Chamber of Commerce. Report, 0377-449X.

    ISSN 0835-426X
DD 330.9715/005   CN
ATLANTIC CHAMBER JOURNAL. [Atl. Chamb. j.]. Added/Corp Atlantic Provinces Chamber of Commerce. Vol. 1, No. 1 (April 1987)-. Periodical. English. Six times a year (Jan., Mar., May, Jul., Sept., Nov.). 20.01Can$. EastCan Publications Inc., 309 rue Amirault Street, Dieppe New Brunswick E1A 1G1 Canada. **Tel** (506)858-8710.

    ISSN 1058-837X
    US
AUSTIN TEXAS MAGAZINE. Added/Corp
Austin Chamber of Commerce. **VFOAT** Austin Texas. (1991)-. Periodical. English. Twelve times a year. Austin Texas Magazine, 3355 Bee Cave Road, #302, Austin TX 78744. **Continues** Austin Magazine, 0890-0574.

    ISSN 0709-0285
DD 380/.06/271   CN
BOARD OF DIRECTORS, COMMITTEE CHAIRMEN - CANADIAN CHAMBER OF COMMERCE. CONSEIL D'ADMINISTRATION, PRESIDENTS DE COMITES - CHAMBRE DE COMMERCE DU CANADA. Main/Corp Canadian Chamber of Commerce. VFOAT Conseil d'Administration, Presidents de Comites - Chambre de Commerce du Canada. (1978/79)-. English (French). One time a year. Free. Canadian Chamber of Commerce, 55 Metcalfe Street, Ottawa Ontario K1P 6N4 Canada. **Tel** (613)238-4000. ctrl circ. **Continues** Canadian Chamber of Commerce. Board of Directors, Executive Council, Committee Chairmen, 0709-0277.

    IT
BOLLETTINO DELLE ESTRAZIONI.
(19??)-. Italian. Twelve times a year. L125000 Italy; L250000 other. Brambilla Fratelli, Via Gaetano Giardino 4, 20123 Milan Italy. **Tel** 011 39 2 72022440.

BOLLETTINO PROTESTI CAMBIARI.
Italian. Camera Comm Ind Art Agr/ Torino, Via S Francesco Da Paola 2, 10100 Turin Italy.

    IT
BOLLETTINO UFFICIALE DEI PROTESTI CAMBIARI. Italian. Twenty-four times a year. L21400. Regione Autonoma Valle Aosta, Piazza della Repubblica 15, 11100 Aosta Italy. **Tel** 011 39 165 303524.

    IT
BOLLETTINO UFFICIALE TASSE E IMPOSTE INDIRETTE SUGLI AFFARI.
Italian. L21000 Italy; L42000 other. Istituto Poligrafico Zecca Stato, Piazza Verdi 10, 00198 Rome Italy. **Tel** 011 39 6 85082307, 011 39 6 85082221.

LC HF336.M29 C48a
ISSN 0302-1343

DD 330.9/66/105   MU
BULLETIN DE LA CHAMBRE DE COMMERCE D'INDUSTRIE ET D'AGRICULTURE DE MAURITANIE.
(BULLETIN.). [Bull. Chamb. commer. ind. agric. Maurit.]. **Main/Corp** Chambre de Commerce, d'Industrie et d'Agriculture de Mauritanie. (19??)-. Bulletin. French. Chambre de Commerce d'Industrie et d'Agriculture, BP 215, Nouakchott Mauritania.

BUSARL : BOLOGNA. (19??)-. Italian.
Twenty-four times a year (24 issues). L248660. Camera Comm Ind Agric Artig Bologna, Piazza Mercanzia 4, 40125 Bologna Italy. **Tel** 011 39 51 6093111.

BUSARL : CAMPOBASSO. (19??)-. Italian.
Twenty-four times a year. L100000. Camera Comm Ind Art Agr Campobasso, Piazza Vittoria 1, 86100 Campobasso Italy. **Tel** 011 39 874 415741.

BUSARL : FIRENZE. Italian. Twenty-four times a
year. L500000. Camera Com Ind Art Agr Firenze, Piazza Giudici 3, 50122 Florence Italy. **Tel** 011 39 55 2795224.

BUSARL : MILAN. (19??)-. Italian. Twenty-six
times a year. L1610000.00. Camera di Commercio

Business and Economics —Chamber of Commerce

Industria Artigianato E Agricoltura di Milano, via Meravigli 9 B, 20123 Milan Italy. **Tel** 011 39 2 85154516.

IT

BUSARL : NAPOLI. Italian. Cam Comm Ind Art Agr Busarl, V Sant Aspreno 2, 80133 Naples Italy. **Tel** 011 39 81 5527575.

US

BUSINESS DIRECTORY & COMMUNITY GUIDE. Directory. English. One time a year (June). $15.00. Pasadena Chamber of Commerce and Civic Association, 117 East Colorado Boulevard, Suite 100, Pasadena CA 91105. **Tel** (818)795-3355, FAX (818)795-5603. **ED** Janet Whaley. **Circ:** 7,500.
Desc: Business directory of Pasedena Chamber of Commerce members; community guide for Pasedena.

HU

BUSINESS DIRECTORY ... OF THE HUNGARIAN CHAMBER OF COMMERCE. Added/Corp Magyar Gazdasagi Kamara. Magyar Gazdasagi Kamara. Information Dept. (1990)-. Directory. English (German and Hungarian). Hungarian Chamber of Commerce, Kossuth Lajos Ter 6-8, 1055 Budapest Hungary. **Continues** *Hungarian Foreign Trade Directory.*

ISSN 0380-3570
CN

CANADA, BELGIUM, LUXEMBOURG. VFOAT Canada, Belgique, Luxembourg. No. 30- March 1967-. Periodical. English (French). Four times a year. Chamber of Commerce for Belguim and Luxembourg in Canada, 4105 1 Place Ville Marie, Montreal Quebec H3B 3R1 Canada. **Continues** *Chamber of Commerce for Belgium and Luxembourg in Canada.*

LC HF296 .L8764
DD 380.1/06/279494

ISSN 0147-2976
US

CATALOG OF MEMBERSHIP PROGRAMS AND SERVICES. Main/Corp Los Angeles Area Chamber of Commerce. (19??)-. Catalog. English. Los Angeles Area Chamber of Commerce, 404 South Bixel Street, Los Angeles CA 90017. **Tel** (213)629-0671, FAX (213)629-0708.

ISSN 1070-2342
US

CHAMBER EXECUTIVE NETWORK, THE. (1984)-. Newsletter. English. Twelve times a year. $98.00. Hakes Publications, PO Box 603, Storm Lake IA 50588. **Tel** (712)732-7718. **ED** Richard L. Hakes. **Circ:** 1,000. **Continues** *Community Development Executive,* 0747-7503.
Desc: Newsletter for Chamber of Commerce managers in U.S. and Canada.

ISSN 1062-905X
US

CHAMBER PROGRESS / DODGE CITY AREA CHAMBER OF COMMERCE, THE. Main/Corp Dodge City Area Chamber of Commerce. Vol. 4, No. 1 (Jan. 1991)-. Periodical. English. Twelve times a year. $1.00. The Chamber Progress, PO Box 939, Dodge City KS 67801-0939. **Continues** *Dodge City Area Chamber of Commerce Digest.*

ISSN 0227-6593
DD 380/.06/071274
CN

CHAMBER (WINNIPEG, MAN.). (THE CHAMBER.). [Chamber]. Periodical. English. Twelve times a year. Free. Winnipeg Chamber of Commerce, 400-177 Lombard Avenue, Winnipeg Manitoba R3B 0W7 Canada.

ISSN 0884-8114
DD 658
US

CHAMBEREXECUTIVE. [Chamb.Exec.].
Added/Corp American Chamber of Commerce Executives. VFOAT Chamber Executive ACCE. Vol. 12, No. 9 (Sept. 1985)-. Trade Publication. English. Eleven times a year. $95.00. American Chamber of Commerce Executives, 4232 King Street, Alexandria VA 22302. **Tel** (703)998-0072, telex 258137 ACCE. **ED** John De Lellis. Index available. **Bk Rev**. **Ad Acc**. **Circ:** 4,500 (ctrl).
Continues *Chamber Executive (American Chamber of Commerce Executives),* 0745-497X.
Desc: Focuses on management and professional development issues for chamber of commerce community organization executives. Includes computerization, staff administration, membership recruiting/retention, economic development and fundraising.

LC HF336.Z54 A88a
DD 380.1/025/6891

RH

CHAMBERS OF COMMERCE DIRECTORY, ZIMBABWE. Main/Corp Associated Chambers of Commerce of Zimbabwe. (1981)-. Directory. English. Twelve times a year. $11.73. Thomson Publications Zimbabwe PVT Ltd., Box 1683, Harare Zimbabwe. **Tel** 011 263 4 736835, FAX 011 263 4 706055.

ISSN 1241-5251
FR

CHAMBRE DE COMMERCE FRANCO-RUSSE. (1992)-. Periodical. French. Twelve times a year. CCFS, 22 Ave F D Roosevelt, F-75008 Paris France. **Tel** 011 33 1 42259710. **Continues** *Flash Informations - Chambre de Commerce Franco-Sovietique,* 1157-8394.

AA
CEASED

COMMERCE EXTERIEUR ALBANAIS. Main/Corp Chamber of Commerce of the P. R. of Albania. (1962)-(19??). Periodical. French. Book Distribution Enterprise, Rruga Kavajes, Tirane Albania. **Tel** 011 355 42 27246.

LC HF55
DD 381/.097123/3

ISSN 0704-8017
CN

COMMERCE NEWS. Added/Corp Edmonton Chamber of Commerce. Vol. 1 (Oct. 1976)-. Periodical. English. Ten times a year. Free on request. Edmonton Chamber of Commerce, 10123 99 Street, Edmonton Alberta T5J 3G9 Canada. **Tel** (403)426-4620, FAX (403)424-7946. **ED** Gretchen Ziegler. **Ad Acc**. **Circ:** 6,500 (ctrl). available on an online database from University Microfilms International (UMI). Documents available from UMI Article Clearinghouse.
Desc: Covers local and national business highlighting Chamber of Commerce news - policy and planning, seminars and events.
Ind/Abst Bus. Dateline (Sept. 1991-) [Full Txt.].

ISSN 0747-7503
US
TITLE CHANGE

COMMUNITY DEVELOPMENT EXECUTIVE, THE. Added/Corp Siefer Consultants, Inc. Vol. 1, No. 1 (June 1984)-. Periodical. English. Hakes Publications, PO Box 603, Storm Lake IA 50588. **Tel** (712)732-7718. **ED** Richard L. Hakes. Index available. **Circ:** 1,000. **Continued by** *Chamber Executive Network,* 1070-2342.
Desc: Management ideas for Chamber of Commerce executives.

ISSN 0011-9709
US

DETROITER, THE. Added/Corp Greater Detroit Chamber of Commerce. (1979)-. Periodical. English. Twelve times a year. $12.00. Greater Detroit Chamber of Commerce, 600 West Lafayette Blouvard, Detroit MI 48226. **Tel** (313)596-0352, FAX (313)964-0531. **ED** Louise P. Thomas. **Bk Rev**. **Ad Acc**. **Adv Mgr:** Barbara Gatton, **Tel** (313)596-0366. **Circ:** 18,000 (ctrl). available on microfilm from University Microfilms International (UMI). Documents available from UMI Article Clearinghouse.
Desc: Guides and articles feature numerous industries and chamber of commerce activities, economic data, local and national business, entrepreneurs, etc.
Ind/Abst Bus. Dateline (Oct. 1991-) [Full Txt.].

ISSN 0702-7877
DD 380/.06/271
CN

DIALOGUE (CANADIAN CHAMBER OF COMMERCE. EDITION FRANCAISE). (DIALOGUE.). **Added/Corp** Chambre de Commerce du Canada. Vol. 1 (Jan./March 1977)-. Periodical. French. Four times a year. La Chambre de Commerce / Montreal, 5 Place Ville Marie Plaze Level, Montreal Quebec H3B 4Y2 Canada. **Tel** (514)871-4000. **Supersedes in part** *Lien: Chambre Nationale, Chambres Locales, Chambres Provinciales,* 0702-7850.

LC HF312 .A697a
DD 382/.0945/0730254521

IT

DIRECTORY / AMERICAN CHAMBER OF COMMERCE IN ITALY. Main/Corp American Chamber of Commerce in Italy. (1983)-. Directory. English (Italian). One time a year. $175.00. American Chamber of Commerce in Italy, Via Cantu 1, 20123 Milan Italy. **Tel** 011 39 2 6890661, FAX 011 39 2 8057737, telex 352128. **(Subscription address:** International Publications Service, A Division of Taylor & Francis, 1900 Frost Road, Suite 101, Bristol PA 19007-1598. **Tel** (800)821-8312.) **Bk Rev**. **Ad Acc**. **Circ:** 5,000 (ctrl). **Continues** *American Chamber of Commerce in Italy. Annual Directory.*
Desc: Source of information regarding American companies in Italy, and Italian companies maintaining close relations with the United States.

LC HD2868 .B36a
DD 338.8/8973/0493

ISSN 0196-7622
US

DIRECTORY - BELGIAN AMERICAN CHAMBER OF COMMERCE IN THE UNITED STATES, INC, THE. (THE DIRECTORY - BELGIAN AMERICAN CHAMBER OF COMMERCE IN THE UNITED STATES.). [Dir. - Belg. Am. Chamb. of Commer. in the U.S.]. **Main/Corp** Belgian American Chamber of Commerce in the United States. (19??)-. Directory. English. Every 2 years. Belgian American Chamber of Commerce, 350 5th Avenue, Suite 703, New York NY 10118. **Tel** (212)967-9898, FAX (212)629-0349, telex 232872. **ED** C. F. Raick. **Ad Acc**.
Circ: 1,500.
Desc: Directory of chamber membership contains information on US/Belgium trade exchanges.

ISSN 0737-5573
US
CEASED

DIRECTORY OF CHAMBERS OF COMMERCE IN TEXAS. Added/Corp East Texas Chamber of Commerce. (19??)-(1993). Directory. English. Texas Chamber of Commerce, 900 Congress, Suite 501, Austin TX 78701. **Tel** (512)472-1594.

LC HF306 .A452a
DD 382/.0944/07302544361

FR

DIRECTORY / THE AMERICAN CHAMBER OF COMMERCE IN FRANCE. Main/Corp American Chamber of Commerce in France. VFOAT Directory of the American Chamber of Commerce in France. (19??)-. Directory. English. Irregular (every two years). 450.00F France; $75.00 North America. American Chamber of Commerce / France, 21 Avenue George V, 75008 Paris France. **Tel** 011 33 1 47238026, FAX 011 33 1 47201862. **ED** Anne Salvan. **Ad Acc**, **Adv Mgr:** A. Salvan, **Tel** 011 33 1 47237028. **Circ:** 3,500.
Desc: Listings of the United States firms in France and includes information on the members of the American Chamber of Commerce.

ISSN 0037-5659
SI

ECONOMIC BULLETIN (SINGAPORE). (ECONOMIC BULLETIN - SINGAPORE INTERNATIONAL CHAMBER OF COMMERCE.). [Econ. bull.]. **Main/Corp** Singapore International Chamber of Commerce. (1963)-. Bulletin. English. Twelve times a year. $44.26. Singapore International Chamber of Commerce, 50 Raffles PL#03-02, Shell Tower, Singapore 0104 Singapore. **Tel** 011 65 2241255. **ED** C.F. Lee. **Ad Acc**. **Circ:** 2,500 (ctrl).
Desc: Digest of regional economic and trade news, Singapore and Malaysian trade statistics, new company registrations, trade inquiries, coming trade fairs and missions, chamber activities, etc.
Ind/Abst PAIS Int. Print.

IT

ELLENCO UFFICIALE PROTESTI CAMBIARI VALLE D AOSTA. Italian. Regione Autonoma Valle Aosta, Piazza della Repubbica 15, 11100 Aosta Italy. **Tel** 011 39 165 303524.

ISSN 0015-6892
XR

FOR YOU FROM CZECHOSLOVAKIA. (1960)-. Periodical. English. Four times a year. DM81.00. **(Subscription address:** Kubon & Sagner, ABT Zeitschriftenimport, D 80328 Munich Germany. **Tel** 011 49 89 54218130.)

LC HF5209.M2 G8
DD 338/.0025/46

SP

GUIA DEL COMERCIO Y DE LA INDUSTRIA. Added/Corp Albacete, Spain (Province). Camara Oficial de Comercio e Industria. (1976)-. Periodical. Spanish. Every 2 years. $31.00. Camara Oficial de Comercio e Industria de Madrid, Huertas 13, 28012 Madrid Spain. **Ad Acc**. **Circ:** 2,100. **Continues** *Guia del Comercio y de la Industria de Madrid.*

LC HF5246.6.S55 S56a
DD 380.1/025/5957

SI

HUI YUAN MING LU = DIRECTORY. Main/Corp Singapore Chinese Chamber of Commerce & Industry. **Added/Corp** Singapore Chinese Chamber of Commerce & Industry. Directory. VFOAT Directory; Hsin-Chia-Po Chung-Hua Tsung Shang Hui Ming Lu. (1978)-. Chinese (English). Singapore Chinese Chamber of Commerce and Industry, 47 Hill Street, Singapore 0617 Singapore. **Tel** FAX 011 65 3390605, telex SCCCI RS33714. **Continues** *Singapore Chinese Chamber of Commerce. Hsin-Chia-po Chung-hua Tsung Shang hui hui Yuan hang yeh Ming tse.*

LC HC267.A2 M37
DD 338.09439/05

HU
SUSPENDED

HUNGARIAN BUSINESS HERALD : HBH : QUARTERLY REVIEW OF THE HUNGARIAN CHAMBER OF COMMERCE. Added/Corp Magyar Kereskedelmi Kamara. VFOAT HBH. Vol. 1 (1985)-Suspended (1994). Periodical. English (summaries and/or abstracts in French and German). Four times a year. $67.00. **(Subscription address:** Kultura, PO Box 143, H-1300 Budapest 3 Hungary. **Tel** 011 36 1 2500194.) **Continues** *Marketing in Hungary,* 0025-3731.
Desc: Review of the Hungarian Chamber of Commerce. Includes detailed information on topical issues and development plans of the Hungarian economy. Under the heading "corporate strategies," managers outline their

Business and Economics — Chamber of Commerce

company's achievements and plans, giving ideas for cooperation possibilities to potential partners abroad. **Ind/Abst** PAIS Int. Print.

FR
ICC BUSINESS WORLD : MAGAZINE OF THE INTERNATIONAL CHAMBER OF COMMERCE. **Added/Corp** International Chamber of Commerce. **VFOAT** Business World. **VAT** International Chamber of Commerce Business World. (198?)-. Periodical. English. Four times a year (Jan., Apr., Jul., Oct.). Free on request. International Chamber of Commerce, 38 Cours Albert 1 ER, 75009 Paris France. **Tel** 011 33 1 49532828, 011 33 1 49532023, FAX 011 33 1 45623456, telex 650770. **ED** Roger Beardwood. **Bk Rev**. **Ad Acc**. ctrl circ.
Desc: International business trade, finance, industry.

LC HF41 .A67 ISSN 0517-2292
US
INFORMATION BULLETIN - AMERICAN INDONESIAN CHAMBER OF COMMERCE, INC. **Main/Corp** American Indonesian Chamber of Commerce. (19??)-. Bulletin. English. Six times a year (Feb., Apr., Jun., Aug., Oct., Dec.). $40.00. American Indonesian Chamber of Commerce, 711 3rd Avenue, 17th Floor, New York NY 10017. **Tel** (212)687-4505.

ISSN 0768-9098
FR
UDC 33(71)
INFORMATIONS CANADIENNES (1969). (INFORMATIONS CANADIENNES.). (1969)-. Periodical. French (English). Eleven times a year (plus annual guide). $50.31. Chambre de Commerce France-Canada, 9-11 Av Franklin D Roosevelt, 75008 Paris France. **Tel** 33 1 43593238, FAX 33 1 42562562. **Ad Acc**. **Circ:** 2,000.
Desc: Economic information for France and Canada.

LC HF41 .A63 ISSN 0002-7847
JA
JOURNAL OF THE AMERICAN CHAMBER OF COMMERCE IN JAPAN / ACCJ, THE. **Added/Corp** American Chamber of Commerce in Japan. **VFOAT** Journal; Janaru; ACCJ Journal; Journal of the ACCJ. (1964)-. Periodical. English. Twelve times a year. ¥8000. P & B International, 18 1 Kamiyama cho, Shibyua ku Toyko 150 Japan. **(Subscription address:** American Chamber of Commerce / Japan, Fukide Building, 2 4 1 21 Toranomo, Minato ku Tokyo 105 Japan. **Tel** 011 33 34335381.) **ED** Henry A. Samson and Terry D. Ragan. Index available. **Bk Rev**. **Ad Acc**. **Circ:** 4,500.
Ind/Abst PAIS Int. Print (1991-).

LC HF331.T5 B36a
DD 380.1/06/052
JA
KAIIN MEIBO - BANKOKU NIHONJIN SHOKO KAIGISHO. / LIST OF MEMBERS - JAPANESE CHAMBER OF COMMERCE, BANGKOK. **Main/Corp** Bankoku Nihonjin Shoko Kaigisho. **Added/Corp** Bankoku Nihonjin Shoko Kaigisho. List of Members - Japanese Chamber of Commerce, Bangkok. **VFOAT** List of Members - Japanese Chamber of Commerce, Bangkok. (19??)-. Directory. Japanese (English). Bankoku Nihonjin Shoko Kaigisho, 4th Floor/Panunee Building, 518/3 Ploenchit Road, Bangkok Thailand.

ISSN 1056-6015
DD 381 US
KANSAS CITY COMMERCE. [Kans. City commer.]. (1990)-. Periodical. English. Twelve times a year. $20.00. EROMDA Publishing Company, 109 West Washington, Milstadt IL 62260. **Tel** (314)621-0176, FAX (618)476-1616.

LC HF5065.K2 K363 ISSN 1042-0355
DD 338.7/6/025781 US
KANSAS DIRECTORY OF COMMERCE, THE. [Kans. dir. commer.]. (1989)-. English. One time a year. $70.00. The Wichita Eagle-Beacon, Box 820, Attention: Mail Desk, Wichita KS 67201. **Tel** (800)825-6397.

ISSN 1046-9257
US
KENTUCKY COMMERCE. **Added/Corp** Kentucky Chamber of Commerce. (Sept./Oct. 1989)-. Periodical. English. Six times a year. $10.00. Kentucky Chamber of Commerce, Box 817, 464 Chenault Road, Frankfort KY 40602. **Tel** (502)695-4700, FAX (502)695-6824. **Continues** Focus (Frankfort, Ky.), 0899-675X.

IT
CEASED
LISTINO BORSA VALORI. (19??)-(1993). Italian. Camera di Commercio Industria Artigianato e Agricoltura di Torino, Via S Francesco da Paolo 24, Turin 10123 Italy. **Tel** 011 39 11 57161. **(Subscription address:** Italia Srl, C SO Brescia 75, 10152 Turin, Italy. **Tel** 011 39 11 2480870.)

IT
LISTINO MENSILE PREZZI INGROSSO SULLA PIAZZA DI SIRACUSA. Italian. Camera Comm Ind Agric Art Siracusa, V Duca Abruzzi 4, 96100 Siracusa Italy.

IT
LISTINO PREZZI ALL INGROSSO. FIRENZE. (19??)-. Italian. Fifty-two times a year. L40880. Camera Com Ind Art Agr Firenze, Piazza Giudici 3, 50122 Florence Italy. **Tel** 011 39 55 2795224.

IT
TITLE CHANGE
LISTINO UFFICIALE BORSA VALORI ROMA. (19??)-(19??). Italian. Tipografia Giovanni Olivieri, via dell Archetto 10 12, 00187 Rome Italy. **Tel** 011 39 6 6792327. **Merged with** Listino Ufficiale Borsa Valori.

IT
LISTINO UFFICIALE DELLE BORSA VALORI DI ITALIANE. (19??)-. Italian. Five times a week (260 issues). L817500. Consiglio di Borsa, Piazza Affari 6, 20123 Milan Italy. **Tel** 011 39 2 72426239.
Absorbed Listino Ufficiale Borsa Valori di Roma; Listino Ufficiale della Borsa Valori de Milano **and** Listino Mercato Ristretto.

ISSN 0723-3361
GW
UDC 339.174
M-+-A-REPORT (1982). **VFOAT** M-und-A-Report (1982). (1982)-. Periodical. German. Eight times a year. $95.96. M & A Verlag fuer Messen Ausstellungen, Postfach 101528, D-60015 Frankfurt Germany. **Tel** 011 49 69 759502, FAX 011 49 69 75951280.

LC HF302 .M28A ISSN 0306-5758
DD 380.1/06/242733 UK
MANCHESTER CHAMBER OF COMMERCE AND INDUSTRY YEARBOOK. [Manch. Chamb. Comm. Ind. yearb.]. **Main/Corp** Manchester Chamber of Commerce and Industry Yearbook. **VFOAT** Annuaire de la Chambre de Commerce et Industrie de Manchester; Jahrbuch der Handels- und Industrie-Kammer Manchester. English (French and German). One time a year. Rex Buildings Wilmslow Cheshire, Manchester SK9 1HZ United Kingdom.

LC HF336.E3 A54A
DD 382/.0962/0730256216 UA
Pr Rev.
MEMBERSHIP DIRECTORY - AMERICAN CHAMBER OF COMMERCE IN EGYPT. **Main/Corp** American Chamber of Commerce in Egypt. (1983/84)-. Directory. English. One time a year. LE40 Egypt; $20.00 other. Cairo Marriott Hotel, Suite 1537, Zamalek Cairo Egypt. **Tel** 3408888, FAX 3409482, telex 20870. **Ad Acc**.
Desc: Includes information about members of the AmCham. Name of company, general member,address, phone,telex, fax, and activity of the company.

LC HF296.T78 T83a
DD 380.1/06/079177 US
MEMBERSHIP DIRECTORY & BUYERS GUIDE. **Main/Corp** Tucson Metropolitan Chamber of Commerce. **VFOAT** Membership Directory and Buyers Guide. (1984)-. Directory. English. One time a year. $10.00. Blake Publishing Company, 365 West Bradley Avenue, Suite D, PO Box 2606, El Cajon CA 92020. **Continues** Tucson Metropolitan Chamber of Commerce. Tucson Buyer's Guide.

LC HF302 .M45a ISSN 0302-4148
DD 380.1/06/2427 UK
MERSEYSIDE CHAMBER OF COMMERCE AND INDUSTRY DIRECTORY. (DIRECTORY.). **Main/Corp** Merseyside Chamber of Commerce and Industry. (19??)-. Directory. English. Guardian Communications Ltd., Albany House, Hurst Street, Birmingham B54 4BD United Kingdom. **Tel** 011 44 171 2487881.

IT
CEASED
MOVIMENTO REGISTRO DITTE E ALBO IMPRESE ARTIGIANE. (19??)-(Jan. 1994). Italian. Camera Com Ind Art Agr Firenze, Piazza Giudici 3, 50122 Florence Italy. **Tel** 011 39 55 2795224.

LC HF5068.N2 N37 ISSN 0278-3223
DD 381/.029/476855 US
NASHVILLE AREA CHAMBER OF COMMERCE BUSINESS DIRECTORY.
See Industry and Production-Trade and Industrial Directories.

LC HF302.5.G7 N37
DD 380.1/06/0411 UK
NATIONAL DIRECTORY / SCOTTISH CHAMBERS OF COMMERCE. **Added/Corp** Association of Scottish Chambers of Commerce. (19??)-. English. Kemps Publishing Ltd., 11 Swan Courtyard Yardley, Birmingham B26 1BU United Kingdom. **Tel** 011 44 121 7654144, FAX 011 44 121 7063941.

NE
NETHERLANDS-AMERICAN TRADE DIRECTORY. **See** Industry and Production-Trade and Industrial Directories.

ISSN 1043-4259
US
OKC ACTION. **Added/Corp** Oklahoma City Chamber of Commerce. **VFOAT** OKC Action Update. **VAT** Oklahoma City Action. No. 1 (Jan. 1989)-. Trade Publication. English. Twenty-four times a year. $25.00. Oklahoma City Chamber of Commerce, One Santa Fe Plaza, Oklahoma City OK 73102. **Tel** (405)278-8900. **ED** Cynthia Kitch. **Ad Acc**. available on microfilm from University Microfilms International (UMI). **Continues** Oklahoma, 0030-1639.

ISSN 1048-2989
US
PROFILE (LOS ANGELES, CALIF. 1989). **See** Societies and Clubs.

ISSN 0705-7334
CN
PROGRAMME DU ... EXERCICE - CHAMBRE DE COMMERCE DU DISTRICT DE MONTREAL. (PROGRAMME DU ... EXERCICE.). [Programme exerc. - Chamb. commer. dist. Montr.]. **Main/Corp** Chambre de Commerce du District de Montreal. Exercice. French. One time a year. Programme de ... Exercice, c/o Commerce Montreal, 1080 Cote de Beaver Hall, Montreal Quebec H2Z 1T1 Canada.

IT
RAPPORTO IRS SUL MERCATO AZIONARIO. Italian. One time a year. L55000 Italy. Sole 24 Ore Libri, Via Parabiago 19, 20151 Milan Italy. **Tel** 011 39 2 66030288.

ISSN 0822-5389
CN
DD 380.1/025/714
REPERTOIRE = DIRECTORY / LA CHAMBRE DE COMMERCE DE LA PROVINCE DE QUEBEC. [Repert. - Chamb. commer. prov. Que.]. **Main/Corp** Province of Quebec Chamber of Commerce. **VFOAT** Directory. English. One time a year. $12.00. Province of Quebec, Chamber of Commerce, 500 St. Francois Xavier, Montreal Quebec H2Y 2T6 Canada.

ISSN 0035-2799
FR
UDC 33(44)
REVUE ECONOMIQUE FRANCO-SUISSE. (1930)-. Periodical. French. Four times a year. 127.33F (members), 190.99F (nonmembers) France; 210.00F other. Chambre de Commerce Suisse, 16 Avenue de l'Opera, 75001 Paris France. **Tel** 011 33 1 42961417.

IT
RIVISTA TRIMESTRALE DEGLI APPALTI. Italian. Maggioli Editore, Casella Postale 290, 47037 Rimini Italy. **Tel** 011 39 541 628666, FAX 011 39 541 742217.

ISSN 1185-3360
CN
DD 380.1
SALMON ARM AND DISTRICT CHAMBER OF COMMERCE BUSINESS DIRECTORY. [Salmon Arm Dist. Chamb. Commer. bus. dir.]. **Added/Corp** Salmon Arm and District Chamber of Commerce. (1991)-. Directory. English. $5.00 per volume. Salmon Arm & District Chamber of Commerce, PO Box 999, Salmon Arm British Columbia V1E 4P2 Canada.

ISSN 0038-3880
DD 330B US
SOUTHERN CALIFORNIA BUSINESS. [South. Calif. bus.]. **Added/Corp** Los Angeles Area Chamber of Commerce. (1903)-. Periodical. English. Twelve times a year. $17.34. Los Angeles Area Chamber of Commerce, 404 South Bixel Street, Los Angeles CA 90017. **Tel** (213)629-0671, FAX (213)629-0170. **ED** Chris Volker. **Bk Rev**, (Qty: 2-3). **Ad Acc**. **Circ:** 7,000 (ctrl). available on an online database (files 635,648/Full-Text) from DIALOG. Documents available from UMI Article

Business and Economics —Chamber of Commerce

Clearinghouse.
Ind/Abst Bus. Dateline; PROMT; Trade Ind. ASAP [Full Txt.]; Trade Ind. Index [Full Txt.].

FR

STATEMENTS AND RESOLUTIONS - INTERNATIONAL CHAMBER OF COMMERCE. CONGRESS. Main/Corp
International Chamber of Commerce. Congress. English. Irregular. International Chamber of Commerce, 38 Cours Albert 1 ER, 75009 Paris France. **Tel** 011 33 1 49532828, 011 33 1 49532023, FAX 011 33 1 45623456, telex 650770.

LC HF1371
DD 382

TH

●THAI-KOREAN CHAMBER OF COMMERCE HANDBOOK AND DIRECTORY. (1995)-. Directory. English. One time a year. Cosmic Group of Companies, 4th Floor Phyathai Building, 31 Phyathai Road, Rajthevi Bangkok Thailand. **Tel** 011 662 2453850, FAX 011 662 2461710.

LC HF294 .W75
DD 380.1/06
ISSN 1048-2849
CODEN WCCDE9

WORLD CHAMBER OF COMMERCE DIRECTORY. [World chamb. commer. dir.]. (1989)-. Directory. English. One time a year (June). $29.00. World Wide Chamber of Commerce Directory, PO Box 1029, Loveland CO 80539. **Tel** (303)663-3231, FAX (303)663-6187. **Continues** World Wide Chamber of Commerce Directory, 0893-326X.

LC HF302 .N66
ISSN 0305-0998

UK

YEAR BOOK. Main/Corp Norske Handelskammer i London. **VFOAT** Year Book and Directory of Members. (19??)-. English. One time a year. £75.00. Norwegian Chamber of Commerce, 21-24 Cockspur Street, London SW1 United Kingdom. **Tel** 011 44 171 9300181, telex 917294. **ED** O. Graham-Flatebo. **Ad Acc. Circ:** 2,000.
Desc: Features information important to all businesses involved in Anglo-Norwegian trade and industry.

LC HF296.A29 V48
DD 380.1/06/287

VE

YEAR BOOK - VENEZUELAN-AMERICAN CHAMBER OF COMMERCE & INDUSTRY. Main/Corp
Venezuelan-American Chamber of Commerce & Industry. **VFOAT** Venamcham Year Book. **VAT** Year Book - Venezuelan-American Chamber of Commerce and Industry. (1975)-. Directory. English (Spanish). One time a year (with bi-annual updates). $80.00. Venezuelan-American Chamber of Commerce and Industry, 2 Avenida Campo Alegre Credival 10, Caracas 1010-A Venezuela. **Tel** 011 58 2 2630833, telex 23627 UACCI UC. **ED** Michael E. Heggie. **Ad Acc. Circ:** 3,000.
Continues Year Book - American Chamber of Commerce of Venezuela.
Desc: Guide to businesses available in Venezuela. Contains the names, addresses, officers, and other data pertaining to 800 member companies.

COMMERCE

LC HF3763 .A64A
DD 380.1/025/5
ISSN 0532-9175

HK

A. A.'S FAR EAST BUSINESSMAN'S DIRECTORY. Main/Corp Artists Associates. **VFOAT** Far East Businessman's Directory. Directory. English. Artists Associates, GPO 1623, Hong Kong.

ISSN 1075-3281
DD 382

US

AAP INSIDE EXPORT. See Business and Economics-International Economic Relations.

LC HF61 .H44

DK

AARBOG - HANDELS- OG SAFARTMUSEET PA KRONBORG. Main/Corp Handels- og Safartmuseet pa Kronborg. (1942)-. Danish. One time a year.
Ind/Abst BHA : Biblio. Hist. Art.

LC HF5601
DD 657
ISSN 0218-5563
Pr Rev.

SI

●ACCOUNTING AND BUSINESS REVIEW. See Business and Economics-Accounting.

FR

ACTUALITE DU DIRIGEANT. (1986)-. French. Six times a year. 710.00F. Centre Perfectionnement aux Affaires Mediatheque, 75838 Paris Cedex 17 France. **ED** Martine le Goues. Index available.

ISSN 1155-4495
UDC 31(44)
CODEN 630(44)

FR

AGRESTE. SERIES, COMMERCE EXTERIEUR BOIS ET DERIVES. See Forests and Forestry-Lumber and Wood.

LC S
DD 630

US

AGRICULTURAL TRADE HIGHLIGHTS. **Added/Corp** United States. Foreign Agricultural Service. (1988)-. Government Publication. English. Twelve times a year. $50.00. Department of Agriculture / Foreign Agricultural Service, 14th Street and Independence Avenue SW, Washington DC 20250-1000. **Tel** (202)720-3935, FAX (202)720-7729.

ISSN 0306-0349

UK

AIRTRADE. [Airtrade]. **VFOAT** Air Trade. (19??)-. Trade Publication. English. Six times a year. $94.11. Maclean Hunter Ltd. / UK, Chalk Lane Cockfosters Road, Barnet Hertfordshire EN4 0BU United Kingdom. **Tel** 011 44 181 2423000, FAX 011 44 181 9759753, telex 299072.

LC HF3886 .A25

UA

AL-DALIL AL-TIJARI. **VFOAT** Trade Directory. Al-Tabah 1.- 1976-. Multiple languages (Arabic and English). Al-Gurfah Al-Tijariyah, 4 Midan el Falaki, Al-Qahirah United Arab Republic Egypt.

LC HF46 .I6

LY

AL-IQTISAD WA-AL-TIJARAH. **VFOAT** Economy & Trade. Periodical. Multiple languages (Arabic and English). 200. Ghurfat Al-Tijarah Wal-Al-Sinaah, Al-Jomhourieh Street, Tarabulus Al-Gharb Libya.

US

ALASKA JOURNAL OF COMMERCE. (1976)-. English. One time a week. $51.00 (one-year), $95.00 (two-year), $133.00 (three-year). Alaska Journal of Commerce Holdings Inc., 3710 Woodland Park Drive, Suite 2100, Anchorage AK 99517. **Tel** (907)249-1900, FAX (907)248-7454. Documents available from UMI Article Clearinghouse.
Ind/Abst Bus. Dateline (Feb. 4, 1985-) [Full Txt.].

ISSN 0271-3276
US

ALASKA JOURNAL OF COMMERCE & PACIFIC RIM REPORTER. **VAT** Alaska Journal of Commerce and Pacific Rim Reporter. (19??)-. Periodical. English. One time a week. $75.00. Alaska Journal of Commerce Holdings Inc., 3710 Woodland Park Drive, Suite 2100, Anchorage AK 99517. **Tel** (907)249-1900, FAX (907)248-7454. **ED** Margaret Bowman. **Ad Acc, Adv Mgr:** Joan Ray, **Tel** (907)249-1942. **Circ:** 5,000. available on an online database from DIALOG.
Desc: Business tabloid covering Alaskan commerce with news briefs, feature stories, industry specials, economic forecasts, people on the move and comprehensive legal notice coverage.

LC HF3803 .A5
DD 382/.025/598

IO

ALMANAK EKUIN. **VFOAT** Almanak E.K.U.I.N. Edition 2 (1983)-. English (Indonesian). Every 2 years.
Continues Almanak Perdagangan Dan Koperasi.

LC HF5421 .A58
DD 318/.2/02573
ISSN 0065-8103
US

AMERICAN DROP-SHIPPERS DIRECTORY. **Added/Corp** World Wide Trade Service. **VFOAT** Drop-Shippers Directory. **VAT** American Drop Shippers Directory. (19??)-. Directory. English. Irregular. $15.00. World Wide Trade Service, Box 283, Medina WA 98039. **ED** Randall Lucas. **Bk Rev. Ad Acc. Circ:** 5,000.
Desc: Most complete wholesale buying guide to U.S. drop-shipment sources of supply published today.

DD 382
ISSN 1079-9133
US

●AMERICAN EXPORT PRODUCTS. (AMERICAN EXPORT PRODUCTS : AEP.). [Am. export prod.]. **VFOAT** AEP. Vol. 9, No. 1 (Winter 1995)-. Periodical. English. Thomas International Publishing Company, American Export Register, 5 Penn Plaza, 7th Floor, New York NY 10001. **Tel** (212)290-7343, FAX (212)967-2150, telex 126266. **Continues** American Literature Review, 0899-1448.

LC HF3010 .A6
DD 382/.6/029473
ISSN 0272-1163
US

AMERICAN EXPORT REGISTER. [Am. export regist.]. (1980)-. English (Arabic, Chinese, French, German, Japanese, Portuguese, Spanish, Italian and Russian). One time a year. $125.00. Thomas International Publishing Company, American Export Register, 5 Penn Plaza, 7th Floor, New York NY 10001. **ED** Barry Klein. **Ad Acc. Adv Mgr Tel** (212)629-1130. **Circ:** 22,000 (ctrl). **Continues** American Register of Exporters and Importers.
Desc: Directory of US manufacturers who export their products and services overseas. Features product listings in more than 4,300 categories, including construction equipment and supplies, machinery, computers and electronics, chemicals, food products, furniture, clothing and many more.

DD 382
ISSN 0899-1448
US
TITLE CHANGE

AMERICAN LITERATURE REVIEW. (AMERICAN LITERATURE REVIEW : ALR.). [Am. lit. rev.]. **VFOAT** ALR. (1988)-(1994). Periodical. English. Todd Publications, 18 North Greenbush Road, West Nyack NY 10994. **Tel** (914)358-6213, FAX (914)358-6213. **Continues** International Literature Review, 0897-1048. **Continued by** American Export Products, 1079-9133.

LC HF1 .F55
DD 387
ISSN 1074-8350
US

AMERICAN SHIPPER (1991). (AMERICAN SHIPPER : THE MONTHLY JOURNAL OF INTERNATIONAL LOGISTICS.). [Am. shipp.]. **VFOAT** American Shipper, International Logistics; American Shipper Magazine. Vol. 33, No. 6 (Aug. 1991)-. Periodical. English. Twelve times a year. $48.00. Howard Publications Inc., PO Box 4728, Jacksonville FL 32201-4728. **Tel** (904)355-2601, FAX (904)791-8836. **ED** David A. Howard. **Ad Acc. ctrl circ. Continues** American Shipper International.

DD 382
ISSN 1056-6287
US

AMERICAS COMMON MARKET NEWS, THE. [Am. common mark. news]. **Added/Corp** Americas Common Market Institute (U.S.). No. 1 (May 1991)-. Periodical. English. Twelve times a year. Americas Comon Market Institute, 1602 Forest Glen Road, Silver Springs MD 20910.

DD 380
ISSN 1062-8118
US
TITLE CHANGE

AMERICAS TRADE & FINANCE. See Business and Economics-Banks and Banking.

LC HF3471 .A75

UY

ANALISIS ESTADISTICO, URUGUAY: IMPORTACION - EXPORTACION. **Added/Corp** Centro de Estadisticas Nacionales y Comercio Internacional del Uruguay. (19??)-. Spanish. One time a year. $115.00. CENCI Centro de Estadisticas Nacionales y Comercio Internacional del Uruguay, Misiones 1381 Casilla 1510, Montevideo Uruguay. **Tel** 011 598 2 95-29-30, 95-45-78. **Bk Rev. Circ:** 2,000 (ctrl).
Desc: Comparative and itemized analysis of annual Uruguayan foreign trade.

LC HF54.G7 .A7
ISSN 0066-1813
UK

ANGLO AMERICAN TRADE DIRECTORY. **Added/Corp** American Chamber of Commerce (United Kingdom). American Chamber of Commerce in London. **VAT** Anglo-American trade directory. (1963)-. Directory. English. One time a year. $192.40. American Chamber of Commerce in United Kingdom, 75 Brook Street, London W1Y 2EB United Kingdom. **Tel** 011 44 171 4930381, FAX 011 44 171 4932394, telex 8954665. **ED** Nina Bird. **Bk Rev,** (Qty: 3): **Ad Acc, Adv Mgr:** Judy Bowyer, **Tel** 44 352 770246. **Circ:** 2,000. **Supersedes** Anglo-American Year Book.
Desc: An annual trade directory which catalogues all the significant business links between the USA and the UK. 18,000 companies listed.

DD 380.1/025/7124
ISSN 0822-9368
CN

ANNUAIRE (CONSEIL DE LA COOPERATION DE LA SASKATCHEWAN). (ANNUAIRE : COMMERCANTS ET PROFESSIONNELS QUI DONNENT UN SERVICE EN FRANCAIS EN SASKATCHEWAN.). [Annu., Commer. prof. donnent serv. fr. Sask.]. **Added/Corp** Conseil de la Cooperation de la Saskatchewan. No. 1 (1983)-. Directory. French. Every 2 years. Free. Conseil De La Cooperation De La Saskatchewan, 2243 rue Lorne, Regina Saskatchewan S4P 2M8 Canada. **ED** N. Lepage. **Ad Acc. Circ:** 3,000.
Desc: Directory of businesses and professionals offering services in French-Saskatchewan.

LC HF3369.A48 A56

MQ

ANNUAIRE DES ENTREPRISES EXPORTATRICES ET EXPEDITRICES. **VFOAT** Annuaire des Entreprises Expeditrices/Exportatrices de la Martinique. (19??)-. French. One time a year. Chambre de Commerce et d'Industrie de la Martinique, 50 rue Ernest Deproge, BP 478, Fort-de-France Martinique.

Business and Economics —Commerce

LC HF270.5 .A5 **ISSN** 0304-5692
DD 382/.09675/1   CG
ANNUAIRE DES STATISTIQUES DU COMMERCE EXTERIEUR (KINSHASA).
See Business and Economics-Abstracting, Bibliographies and Statistics.

LC HF3886.A48 A56
DD 382/.45/00029/462   UA
ANNUAIRE EGYPTIEN DES ENTREPRISES, DES SERVICES, DE L'INDUSTRIE ET DU COMMERCE EXTERIEUR.
Added/Corp International Trade Consulting Co. **VFOAT** Directory of Service, Industrial, and Foreign Trade Companies in Egypt. (19??)-. Directory. English (French and Arabic). One time a year. $156.00. International Trade Consulting Company, 22 E1 Gaber Street From Nasr El Sawra, Auberge Giza Egypt. **Tel** 856958, 5854450. **ED** Abdel Hadi. Index available. cum. index. **Ad Acc**. **Circ:** 5,000 (ctrl).
Desc: Aim is to provide a communication aid that will enable foreign companies to find information on the Egyptian market, and Egyptian companies to introduce themselves to markets abroad.

FR
ANNUAL FOREIGN TRADE STATISTICS BY COMMODITIES. SERIES C.
See Business and Economics-Abstracting, Bibliographies and Statistics.

TU
ANNUAL FOREIGN TRADE STATISTICS TURKEY.
See Business and Economics-Abstracting, Bibliographies and Statistics.

LC HF3790.6 .A2a
DD 382/.5/095492   BG
ANNUAL IMPORT PAYMENTS. Main/Corp
Bangladesh Bank. Statistics Dept. (19??)-. English. Bangladesh Bank, Motijheel Commercial Area, Dhaka 2 Bangladesh.

LC HD9198.N3 S65
DD 354.676/20082333   KE
ANNUAL REPORT AND STATEMENT OF ACCOUNTS. Main/Corp
Kenya Tea Development Authority. (1981)-. English. One time a year. **Continues** Kenya Tea Development Authority. Annual Report and Accounts (1980).

ISSN 1182-3348
DD 382/.6/0711   CN
ANNUAL REPORT - BRITISH COLUMBIA TRADE DEVELOPMENT CORPORATION.
(ANNUAL REPORT.). [Annu. rep. - B.C. Trade Dev. Corp.]. **Main/Corp** British Columbia Trade Development Corporation. (1989/1990)-. English.

LC HF125.A4 D46a **ISSN** 0149-4864
DD 353.9/798/0082   US
ANNUAL REPORT - DEPARTMENT OF COMMERCE AND ECONOMIC DEVELOPMENT. Main/Corp
Alaska. Dept. of Commerce and Economic Development. (1976)-. Government Publication. English. One time a year. Alaska Department of Commerce and Economic Development, PO Box D, Juneau AK 99811. **Tel** (907)465-2521, FAX (907)463-3841. **Formed by the union of** Alaska. Department of Commerce. Annual Report **and** Annual Report - Department of Economic Development, 0092-4121.

LC J905 .L3 JX1162 **ISSN** 1032-2019
DD 382   AT
ANNUAL REPORT / DEPARTMENT OF FOREIGN AFFAIRS AND TRADE.
Main/Corp Australia. Dept. of Foreign Affairs and Trade. **VFOAT** Department of Foreign Affairs and Trade Annual Report. (1988)-. English. One time a year (Dec. or Jan.). 29.95Aus$. Australian Government Publishing Service, GPO Box 84, Canberra ACT 2601 Australia. **Tel** 011 61 6 2954411, FAX 011 61 6 2954455. **Continues** Australia. Dept. of Foreign Affairs. Annual Report.

LC HC453 .P485a
DD 354.95990082/06   PH
ANNUAL REPORT / DEPARTMENT OF TRADE AND INDUSTRY. Main/Corp
Philippines. Dept. of Trade and Industry. English. Ministry of Trade and Industry / Philippines, Trade and Industry Building, 361 Buendia Avenue Extension Makati, Metro Manila Philippines 3117. **Tel** 8185701. **Continues** Annual Report.

LC HF1479 .E9 **ISSN** 0709-1605
DD 354./71/00827   CN
ANNUAL REPORT - EXPORT DEVELOPMENT CORPORATION.
(ANNUAL REPORT - EXPORT DEVELOPMENT CORPORATION. RAPPORT ANNUEL - SOCIETE POUR L'EXPANSION DES EXPORTATIONS.). **Main/Corp** Export Development Corporation (Canada). **VFOAT** Rapport Annuel - Societe pour l'Expansion des Exportations; Rapport Annuel. **VAT** Export Development Corporation Annual Report; Societe pour l'Expansion des Exportations. Rapport Annuel. No. 1 (1969)-. English (French). One time a year. Free on request. Export Development Corporation, 151 O'Conner Street, Box 655, Ottawa Ontario K1A 1K3 Canada. **Tel** (613)598-2784. **Circ:** 5,000. **Continues** Export Credits Insurance Corporation (Canada). Annual Report and Financial Statements. **Continued in part by** Export Development Corporation (Canada). Statistical Review, 0823-3454.
Desc: Covers economic conditions and the financial operations of corporations, including export financing and export insurance.

LC HF3161.M5 M48A
DD 353.97740082/06   US
ANNUAL REPORT FOR THE YEAR ENDING JUNE 30 ... / STATE OF MICHIGAN, DEPARTMENT OF COMMERCE. Main/Corp
Michigan. Dept. of Commerce. (1967)-. English. One time a year. Department of Commerce, PO Box 30004, Lansing MI 48909. **Tel** (517)373-7230, FAX (517)373-3872.

LC HF1589 .I5 **ISSN** 0073-6473
DD 382.0954   II
ANNUAL REPORT - INDIAN INSTITUTE OF FOREIGN TRADE. Main/Corp
Indian Institute of Foreign Trade. (1964/65)-. English. Foreign Trade Library, H-24 Green Park Extension, New Delhi 16 India.

LC HC107.N7 A76 **ISSN** 0731-0560
DD 330.9747   US
ANNUAL REPORT - NEW YORK STATE DEPARTMENT OF COMMERCE.
Main/Corp New York (State). Dept. of Commerce. (19??)-. English. One time a year. New York Department of Commerce, 99 Washington Avenue, Albany NY 12245. **Tel** (518)474-6950, (518)474-5027.

LC HC107.M93 C635A **ISSN** 0093-8246
DD 381/.3   US
ANNUAL REPORT OF THE DEPARTMENT OF BUSINESS REGULATION (HELENA).
(ANNUAL REPORT.). **Main/Corp** Montana. Dept. of Business Regulation. English. One time a year. Montana Department of Business Regulation, 805 North Main, Helena MT 59601.

LC HG8511.T2 T45A
DD 353.97680082/06   US
ANNUAL REPORT OF THE DEPARTMENT OF COMMERCE AND INSURANCE. Main/Corp
Tennessee. Dept. of Commerce and Insurance. **VFOAT** Annual Report of the Commissioner of Commerce and Insurance, State of Tennessee, as of Dec. 31 ... . (1983)-. English. One time a year. Tennessee Department of Commerce and Insurance, Nashville TN 37219. **Continues** Annual Report of the Department of Insurance, 0364-2534.

LC HF1531 .E798 **ISSN** 0531-4127
DD 382   SZ
ANNUAL REPORT OF THE EUROPEAN FREE TRADE ASSOCIATION. Main/Corp
European Free Trade Association. **VFOAT** European Free Trade Association Report; EFTA Report. 1st (1960/61)-. Periodical. English (French and German). One time a year. Free. European Free Trade Association, 9-11 rue de Varembe, CH-1211 Geneva 20 Switzerland. **Tel** 011 41 22 7491111, FAX 011 41 22 339291, telex 22660 EFTA CH. **Circ:** 7,000 (ctrl).
Desc: Review of European Free Trade Association's activities, including external relations.

US
ANNUAL REPORT OF THE FEDERAL TRADE COMMISSION. Main/Corp
United States. Federal Trade Commission. (1914)-. English. One time a year. Free on request. Federal Trade Commission, 6th Street & Pennsylvania Northwest, Washington DC 20590. **Tel** (202)326-2000. (**Subscription address:** Superintendent of Documents, US Government Printing Office, Washington DC 20402.)

LC K4440.A13 I57 **ISSN** 0250-7366
DD 341.7/51   US
ANNUAL REPORT ON EXCHANGE ARRANGEMENTS AND EXCHANGE RESTRICTIONS - INTERNATIONAL MONETARY FUND.
(EXCHANGE ARRANGEMENTS AND EXCHANGE RESTRICTIONS.). [Annu. rep. exch. arrange. exch. restric. - Int. Monet. Fund]. **Added/Corp** International Monetary Fund. **VFOAT** Exchange Arrangements and Exchange Restrictions Annual Report. (1989)-. Periodical. English. One time a year. $70.00. International Monetary Fund, 700 19th Street Northwest, Publishing Unit, Washington DC 20431. **Tel** (202)623-7430, FAX (202)623-7201. available on microfilm and microfiche from University Microfilms International (UMI). **Continues** International Monetary Fund. Annual Report on Exchange Arrangements and Exchange Restrictions, 0250-7366.
Desc: Country-by-country descriptions of the exchange and trade systems and related measures in operation in all IMF member countries and provides a chronological list of the significant changes that have taken place during the year under review.

LC HF3790.6 .A2b
DD 382/.6/095492021   BG
ANNUAL REPORT RECEIPTS. Added/Corp
Bangladesh Bank. Statistics Dept. (1977-78)-. English. Bangladesh Bank, Motijheel Commercial Area, Dhaka 2 Bangladesh. **Continues** Yearly Export Receipts.

LC HF1589 .T7a **ISSN** 0302-4784
DD 354/.54/00827   II
ANNUAL REPORT - TRADE DEVELOPMENT AUTHORITY (NEW DELHI).
(ANNUAL REPORT - TRADE DEVELOPMENT AUTHORITY.). **Main/Corp** Trade Development Authority. (19??)-. English. Irregular. Trade Development Authority, 16 Parliament Street, New Delhi 1 India. (**Subscription address:** Prints India, 11 Darya Ganj, New Delhi 110002 India. **Tel** 011 91 11 3268645, FAX 011 91 11 3275542, telex 31-61087 PRIN-IN.**)**

LC HF1455 .U4664a **ISSN** 0147-5568
DD 353.008/27   US
     CODEN ARUCER
ANNUAL REPORT / UNITED STATES INTERNATIONAL TRADE COMMISSION.
[Annu. rep. - U. S. Int. Trade Comm.]. **Main/Corp** United States International Trade Commission. (1975)-. Periodical. English. One time a year. Free on request. United States International Trade Commission, 500 E Street Southwest, Washington DC 20436. **Tel** (202)205-1806. **Continues** Annual Report of the United States Tariff Commission, 0083-3428.

LC HF259.H6 A28
DD 382/.0951/25   HK
ANNUAL REVIEW OF HONG KONG EXTERNAL TRADE .... . Added/Corp
Hong Kong. Census and Statistics Dept. Trade Analysis Section. (1991)-. English. One time a year. HK$40.00. Hong Kong Government Information Service, Beaconsfield House, 4 Queens Road, Hong Kong Hong Kong. **Tel** 011 852 284288014, 011 852 259881947, FAX 011 852 28459078, 011 852 25987482, telex 61190 HKGIS. (**Subscription address:** Government Information Service, Publications Office, 1 Battery Path, Hong Kong Hong Kong.) **Continues** Hong Kong Review of Overseas Trade.

LC HF300.V3 C36A
VE
ANUARIO - CAMARA VENEZOLANO BRITANICA DE COMERCIO E INDUSTRIA. Main/Corp
Camara Venezolano Britanica de Comercio E Industria. (19??)-. Multiple languages (English and Spanish). Edificio Blandin, Piso 1 Oficina 1 C Chacaito Apartado 5713, Caracas Venezuela.

LC HE8660 TK6001 **ISSN** 1353-0356
DD 384.5 621.38   UK
● APT YEARBOOK. See
Communications-Telecommunication.

LC HF3866.Z5 A73 **ISSN** 0191-9032
DD 346/.07/09174927   US
     CEASED
ARAB MARKETS.
(19??)-(19??). English. Inter-Crescent Publishing Co., 219 East 83rd Street, New York NY 10028.

CL
ARANCEL ADUANERO DE CHILE.
Main/Corp Instituto Coordinador del Comercio Internacional. (197?)-. Spanish. $1309.00. Proman Editores, Paris 823, Santiago Chile. **Tel** 011 53 2 6331107, FAX 011 53 2 381980. Index available. **Bk Rev. Circ:** 1,500 (ctrl).

SP
ARANCEL DE ADUANAS (TARIC) UPDATES.
(19??)-. Spanish. Twenty-four times a year. 64130.00ptas. Editorial Castro Sa, Lira 1, 1RA Derecha, 28007 Madrid Spain. **Tel** 011 34 1 4093190. **Circ:** 2,500 (ctrl). available on an online database from MENSATEX.

LC HA1320 .R453 HF3569.R55
DD 314.3/43 381/.2/094343021   GW
ARBEITSSTATTEN DES GROSSHANDELS UND DER HANDELSVERMITTLUNG IN RHEINLAND-PFALZ, DIE.
See Business and Economics-Abstracting, Bibliographies and Statistics.

IT
ARTI E MERCATURE. Main/Corp
Florence (Provence). Camera di Commercio, Industria e Agricoltura. **Added/Corp** Florence (Province). Camera di Commercio, Industria e Agricoltura. Bollettino Ecomonico. Vol. 1-19 (1946-June 1964)-. Periodical. Italian. Twelve times a year. L30660. Camera Com Ind Art/Firenze, Piazza Giudici 3, 50122 Florence Italy.

Business and Economics —Commerce

LC HF
DD 382.782
ISSN 0957-1817
UK
TITLE CHANGE
ASIA PACIFIC DUTY-FREE. [Asia Pac. duty-free]. (198?)-(1993). Periodical. English. Argus Press Group, Queensway House, 2 Queensway Redhill, Surrey RH1 1QS United Kingdom. **Tel** 011 44 1737 768611, 011 44 1737 761685, FAX 011 44 1737 760510, telex 948669 TOPJNL G. *Continued by Asia Pacific Duty-Free Marketing, 1353-8160.*
Desc: Covers the world's fastest growing duty-free market.

LC HF
DD 382.782
ISSN 1353-8160
UK
●**ASIA PACIFIC DUTY-FREE MARKETING.** [Asia Pac. duty-free mark.]. (1994)-. Periodical. English. Six times a year. Argus Press Group, Queensway House, 2 Queensway Redhill, Surrey RH1 1QS United Kingdom. **Tel** 011 44 1737 768611, 011 44 1737 761685, FAX 011 44 1737 760510, telex 948669 TOPJNL G. **(Subscription address:** International Trade Publishing Ltd., Queensway House 2 Queensway, Redhill Surrey RH1 1QS United Kingdom. **Tel** 011 44 1736 768611.) *Continues Asia Pacific Duty-Free, 0957-1817.*

ISSN 1050-3706
DD 382
US
SUSPENDED
ASIAN LEASING JOURNAL, THE. [Asian leas. j.]. Vol. 1, No. 1 (June/July 1990)-(19??). Periodical. English. Six times a year (Feb., Apr., June, Aug., Oct., Dec.). $125.00. Amembal Halladay & Isom, 4 Triad Center, Suite 850, Salt Lake City UT 84180-1408. **Tel** (801)484-8555, FAX (801)533-8778.

AT
ASIATRADE. (19??)-. English. Irregular. 187.00Aus$. International Business Communications Pty Ltd, Level 11 55 63 Elizabeth Street, Sydney 2000 Australia. **Tel** 011 61 2 2216199, FAX 011 61 2 2215923, telex 72148.

LC HF3790.8 .A15
DD 382/.029/459
SI
ASTRAD : ASEAN TRADE DIRECTORY.
Added/Corp ASEAN. **VFOAT** ASEAN Trade Directory. (1986/1987)-. English. One time a year. 226.50Aus$ (6th edition). Peter Isaacson Publications, 46-50 Porter Street, Prahran Victoria, 3181 Australia. **Tel** 011 61 3 2457777, FAX 011 61 3 2457606.

LC HF296 .A854
DD 330.9758/231/005
ISSN 0004-6701
US
ATLANTA (ATLANTA). (ATLANTA.). [Atlanta]. **Added/Corp** Atlanta Chamber of Commerce. **VFOAT** Atlanta Magazine. Vol. 1 (May 1961)-. Periodical. English. Twelve times a year. $15.00. Atlanta Magazine, 2 Midtown Pl., Peachtree Street 1800, Atlanta GA 30309. **Tel** (404)872-3100, (800)333-7483. **ED** Neil Shister. available on microfilm and microfiche from University Microfilms International (UMI).
Ind/Abst Access (1975-); Urban Aff. Abstr.

ISSN 0828-6213
DD 381/.4591714
CN
ATTRACTION. (1976)-. Periodical. French. Irregular. L'Association Technique Du Tourisme, 1420 rue St.Denis, Montreal Quebec H2X 3J8.

LC HF196.N6 A3
DD 382/.0943/55
GW
AUSFUHR NORDRHEIN-WESTFALENS, DIE. Main/Corp Landesamt fur Datenverarbeitung und Statistik Nordrhein-Westfalen. (19??)-. German. Twelve times a year. DM20.00. Landesamt fuer Datenverarbeitung und Statistik Nordrhein-Westfalen, Postfach 101105, 40002 Duesseldorf Germany. **Tel** (0211)944901, FAX (0211)442202, telex 8586654 LDST D. *Continues North Rhine-Westphalia. Statistisches Landesamt. Ausfuhr Nordrhein-Westfalens im Jahr.*
Desc: Covers exports and imports of the region.

LC HA1320.B2 A32 HF196.B28
DD 314.3/46 S 382/.0943/46
GW
AUSSENHANDEL, DER. See Business and Economics-Abstracting, Bibliographies and Statistics.

LC HF3546.5 .A24
DD 380
AU
TITLE CHANGE
AUSSENHANDEL; LANDER UND WARENGLIEDERUNG. Main/Corp Austria. Bundeskammer der Gewerblichen Wirtschaft, Vienna. Abteilung fur Statistik und Dokumentation. (Dec. 1976)-(1994). Periodical. German. Bundeskammer der Gewerblichen Wirtschaft, Wiedner Hauptstrasse 63, A-1040 Vienna Austria. **Tel** 0222 65 05 DW 4110, telex 111 871 BUKA. *Continues Schnellbericht Aussenhandel. Continued by Aussenhandel Osterreichs.*

LC HF196.N6 N67A
DD 380.1/0943/55
GW
AUSSENHANDEL NORDRHEIN-WESTFALENS : AUS- UND EIN-FUHR. VORLAEUFIGE ERGEBNISSE, DER. Main/Corp North Rhine-Westphalia. Landesamt fur Datenverarbeitung und Statistik. March 1977-. German. Twelve times a year. DM20.00. Landesamt fuer Datenverarbeitung und Statistik Nordrhein-Westfalen, Postfach 101105, 40002 Duesseldorf Germany. **Tel** (0211)944901, FAX (0211)442201, telex 8586654 LDST D. *Formed by the union of Die Einfuhr Nordrhein-Westfalens. Landesamt fuer Datenverarbeitung und Statistik Nordrhein-Westfalen and Die Ausfuhr Nordrhein-Westfalens. Landesamt fuer Datenverarbeitung und Statistik Nordrhein-Westfalen.*
Desc: Statistical returns about commerce of Nordrhein-Westfalen.

LC HF3546.5 .A24
DD 380
AU
●**AUSSENHANDEL OSTERREICHS : LANDER UND WARENGLIEDERUNG, DER. Added/Corp** Bundeskammer der Gewerblichen Wirtschaft (Austria). (1994)-. German. Twelve times a year. Bundeskammer der Gewerblichen Wirtschaft, Wiedner Hauptstrasse 63, A-1040 Vienna Austria. **Tel** 0222 65 05 DW 4110, telex 111 871 BUKA. *Continues Bundeskammer der Gewerblichen Wirtschaft (Austria). Abteilung feur Statistik und Dokumentation. Aussenhandel.*

LC HF195 .A5552
GW
AUSSENHANDEL. REIHE 1: ZUSAMMENFASSENDE UBERSICHTEN FUER DEN AUSSENHANDEL. Main/Corp Germany (West). Statistisches Bundesamt. **Added/Corp** Germany (West). Statistisches Bundesamt. Zusammenfassende Ubersichten fuer den Aussenhandel. (1976)-. German. One time a year. Metzler Poeschel Verlag Veroeffen, Statist Bundesamt Kernerstr 43, D-70182 Stuttgart Germany. **Tel** 011 49 7071 935350. *Continues Aussenhandel. Reihe 1: Zusammenfassende-Ubersichten.*

LC HF195 .A5562
ISSN 0170-2955
GW
AUSSENHANDEL. REIHE 2, AUSSENHANDEL NACH WAREN UND LANDERN, SPEZIALHANDEL.
[Aussenhand., Reihe 2, Aussenhand. Waren Landern Spez.hand.]. **Added/Corp** Germany (West). Statistisches Bundesamt. **VFOAT** Aussenhandel nach Waren und l'Andern, Spezia'handel; Fachserie 7. (Jan. 1971)-. German. Twelve times a year. DM453.60 Germany; DM532.90 Europe; DM803.60 other. Metzler Poeschel Verlag Veroeffen, Statist Bundesamt Kernerstr 43, D-70182 Stuttgart Germany. **Tel** 011 49 7071 935350. **(Subscription address:** Metzler Poeschel H Leins GmbH, Postfach 1152, D 72125 Kusterdingen Germany. **Tel** 011 49 7071 935350.) *Continues Aussenhandel. Reihe 2: Aussenhandel nach Waren und l'Andern.*

LC HF195 .A5572
ISSN 0170-7825
GW
AUSSENHANDEL. REIHE 3: AUSSENHANDEL NACH LAENDERN UND WARENGRUPPEN, SPEZIALHANDEL. [Aussenhandel., Reihe 3, Aussenhandel. LEandern Warengr. (Spez.hand.)]. **Main/Corp** Germany (West). Statistisches Bundesamt. **Added/Corp** Germany (West). Statistisches Bundesamt. Aussenhandel. Reihe drei: Aussenhandel nach Landern und Warengruppen, Spezialhandel. **VFOAT** Fachserie 7. (1977)-. Periodical. German. Four times a year. DM16.10. Metzler Poeschel Verlag Veroeffen, Statist Bundesamt Kernerstr 43, D-70182 Stuttgart Germany. **Tel** 011 49 7071 935350. *Continues Aussenhandel. Reihe 3: Spezialhandel Nach Landern und Warengruppen.*

LC HF35 .A88
ISSN 0004-8216
SZ
AUSSENWIRTSCHAFT.
(AUSSENWIRTSCHAFT : ZEITSCHRIFT FUER INTERNATIONALE WIRTSCHAFTSBEZIEHUNGEN.). [Aussenwirtschaft]. **Added/Corp** Handels-Hochschule St. Gallen. Schweizerisches Institut fuer Aussenwirtschafts- und Marktforschung. Hochschule St. Gallen fuer Wirtschafts- und Sozialwissenschaften. Schweizerisches Institut fuer Aussenwirtschafts- und Marktforschung. Hochschule St. Gallen fuer Wirtschafts- und Sozialwissenschaften. Schweizerisches Institut fuer Aussenwirtschafts-, Struktur- und Marktforschung. **VFOAT** Swiss Review of International Economic Relations. Vol. 1 , No. 1 (Mar. 1946)-. Periodical. German (English and French). Four times a year. $133.85. Verlag Rueggger AG, Kasernenstrasse 1, CH-7007 Chur Switzerland. **Tel** 011 41 81 235111. Index available in last issue of volume--attached. **Bk Rev. Ad Acc. Circ:** 1,600 (ctrl).
Ind/Abst Econ. Lit. Index (199?-); J. Econ. Lit.; PAIS Int. Print; Selec. Coop. Index Manage. Period.

ISSN 0313-623X
DD 347.7
AT
AUSTRALIAN TRADE PRACTICES REPORTER (1975). [Aust. trade pract. rep. 1975]. (1975)-. Periodical. English. Irregular. CCH Australia Ltd., PO Box 230, North Ryde NSW 2113 Australia. **Tel** 011 61 2 8571300, 011 61 2 8571555.
Ind/Abst Aust. Leg. Mon. Dig.

ISSN 0889-9886
DD 380
US
SUSPENDED
AUTHORIZED OA DEALER REPORT, THE. [Auth. Oa dealer rep.]. Suspended. Periodical. English. Twelve times a year. $225.00. Camarro Research, PO Box 691, Fairfield CT 06430.

LC HG4501
DD 332.6
ISSN 0947-3017
GW
●**AW - AUSSENWIRTSCHAFTENLICHE PRAXIS.** (1994)-. Academic Scholarly Publication. German. Twelve times a year. DM420.00. Bundesanzeiger Verlagsges GmbH, Postfach 1320, D-53003 Bonn Germany. **Tel** 011 49 228 3820812.

ISSN 1184-986X
DD 382/.6/09711
CN
B.C. EXPORTER. [B.C. export.]. **Main/Corp** British Columbia Trade Development Corporation. **VAT** British Columbia Exporter. Vol. 2, No. 2 (Mar. 1991)-. Periodical. English. Four times a year. *Continues B.C. Trade., 0846-0159.*

ISSN 0382-8352
DD 382/.0971/073
CN
BACKGROUNDER. Added/Corp
Canadian-American Committee. No. 1 (May 1975)-. Periodical. English. The Heritage Foundation, 214 Massachusetts Avenue NE, Washington DC 20002. **Tel** (202)546-4400, FAX (202)546-8328. available on an online database from Lexis-Nexis.
Ind/Abst INIS Atomindex [Micro.].

LC HF3403 .B35
DD 338.4/025/81
BL
BANAS CLASSIFICADO INDUSTRIAL BRASILEIRO. VFOAT Who Produces What in Brazil. (1974)-. Multiple languages (English, French, German, Portuguese and Spanish). Editora Banas SA, Av Presidente Castelo Branco 6241, CEP 05038, Sao Paulo Brazil.

LC HF3790.6 .A24
DD 380.1/025/5492
II
BANGLADESH DIRECTORY & YEAR BOOK. (19??)-. Directory. English. One time a year (Mar.). $19.00. Associated Book Promoters, 912A Ekbalpur Lane, Calcutta 700023 India.

LC HF3790.6.A45 B36a
DD 382/.095492/00212
BG
BANGLADESH EXPORT STATISTICS. See Business and Economics-Abstracting, Bibliographies and Statistics.

LC HF3790.6.A48 B36
DD 382/.6/02945492
BG
BANGLADESH EXPORTERS' DIRECTORY. Directory. English. One time a year. Free. Export Promotion Bureau Bangladesh, 122-124 Montijheel Commercial Area, Dacca Bangladesh. **Tel** 232245-49, telex 642204 EPBBBJ. **Circ:** 4,000 (ctrl).

LC HF3803 .B16
IO
BANIN, BUKU ALAMAT NIAGA & INDUSTRI SELURUH INDONESIA. VFOAT
Buku Alamat Niaga & Industri Seluruh Indonesia; National Trade & Industry Directory. 1.- 1975-. Multiple languages (English and Indonesian). 6500. Badan Penerbit Alda, Jalan Tambak 11A, Jakarta Indonesia.

LC TN4 .B3
ISSN 0522-3512
HU
CODEN BKLBB6
BANYASZATI ES KOHASZATI LAPOK. BANYASZAT. [Banyasz. kohasz. lapok. Banyasz.]. **VFOAT** Banyaszat; Journal of Mining and Metallurgy. (1968)-. Academic Scholarly Publication. Hungarian. Twelve times a year. **(Subscription address:** Kultura, PO Box 143, H-1300 Budapest 3 Hungary. **Tel** 011 36 1 2500194.) Documents available from CASDDS. *Continues in part Banyaszati Lapok.*
Ind/Abst Chem. Abstr.; Coal Abstr.; GeoRef.; Geotech. Abstr.

ISSN 1060-7722
DD 381
US
BARGAIN HUNTERS GUIDE. ATLANTA/ATHENS AREA. [Bargain hunt. guide, Atlanta/Athens area]. **VFOAT** Atlanta/Athens Area; Atlanta Athens Area. (1992)-. English. $8.95. Firefly Publishing & Production Co., PO Box 1725, Loganville GA 30249.

ISSN 0072-0623
DD 337
SZ
BASIC INSTRUMENTS AND SELECTED DOCUMENTS. SUPPLEMENT / GENERAL AGREEMENTS ON TARIFFS AND TRADE. See Business and Economics-International Economic Relations.

Business and Economics —Commerce

ISSN 0522-6449
DD 910 380   GW
BEITRAEGE ZUR FREMDENVERKEHRSFORSCHUNG. Added/Corp Frankfurt am Main. Institut fur Fremdenverkehrwissenschaft. (1954)-. Monographic series. German. Irregular. Price varies per volume. Duncker und Humblot Verlag, Postfach 410329, D-12113 Berlin Germany. **Tel** 011 49 30 79000612, 011 49 30 79000613.

LC TS1 .B4
DD 338.9493/05   ISSN 0775-1443
BE
TITLE CHANGE
BELGIUM, ECONOMIC AND COMMERCIAL INFORMATION. [Belg. econ. commer. inf.]. Added/Corp Office Belge du Commerce Exterieur. (1982)-(19??). Periodical. English (Dutch, French, German and Spanish). Office Belge du Commerce Exterior, Boulevard Emile Jacqmain 162, 1210 Brussels Belgium. **Tel** 011 32 2 2031886. *Continues* Belgium, Economy and Technique, 0775-1435. *Continued by* Economic and Commercial Information, Belgium.

ISSN 1100-3006
SW
UDC 336
BEST 'N' MOST IN DFS, THE. [Best most DFS]. **VFOAT** Best and Most in Duty-free Shops. (1988)-. English. One time a year. $213.90. Generation Publications, PO Box 234, S-89125 Ornskoldsvik Sweden. **Tel** 011 46 660 10320, FAX 011 46 660 84811, telex 71965. **ED** Yngre Bia. **Ad Acc. Circ:** 6,000 (ctrl). *Continues* Duty & Tax-free Shop World Guide Series, 0349-2737.
Desc: Serving the international duty free trade, documents the scope and importance of international tax free trade in economical terms.

ISSN 0954-9803
DD 745.4   UK
BIG PAPER, THE. [Big pap.]. (1987)-. English. Three times a year. Gillard Welch & Associates, Chester Court, High Street Knowlesolihull, West Midlands B93 0LL United Kingdom. **Tel** 011 44 1564 771772.

LC HF3924 .A35A
DD 354.66/260082/06   FR
BILAN AU 30 SEPTEMBRE ... / SOCIETE NATIONALE DE COMMERCE ET DE PRODUCTION. Main/Corp Societe Nationale de Commerce et de Production (Niger). French. One time a year. Societe Nationale de Commerce et de Production, Niamey Niger.

ISSN 0747-1831
US
BILLINGS COMMERCE. Vol. 1, No. 1 (Jan. 1984)-. Periodical. English. Four times a year. Billings Area Chamber of Commerce, 10 North 27th Street, Billings MT 59101.

FR
BLE CONTACT / LETTRE D'INFORMATION DE L'AGPB. French. Eleven times a year. 68.33F France; 75.00F other. AGPB, 8 Avenue du President Wilson, 75116 Paris France. **Tel** 011 33 1 44311000.

LC HF3800.55 .B63
TH
BOARD OF TRADE OF THAILAND'S TRADE DIRECTORY. Added/Corp Sapha Hokankha hng Prathet Thai. **VFOAT** Trade Directory. (1991)-. Directory. English (Thai). Board of Trade of Thailand, 150 Rajbopit Road, Bangkok Thailand 10200. *Continues* Board of Trade Directory.

LC HF251 .J35d
JA
BOEKI GYOTAI TOKEIHYO. Main/Corp Japan. Tsusho Sangyosho. Tsusho Seisakukyoku. (19??)-. Japanese. Tsusho Sangyo Chosakai, (Research Institute on International Trade and Industry), Kobikikan Ginza Biru, 8-9 Ginza 2 chome Chuoku, Tokyo 104 Japan. *Continues* Japan. Tsusho Sangyosho. Tsushokyoku. Boeki gyotai Tokeihyo.

LC HF164.B25 B27A
BL
BOLETIM DO COMERCIO EXTERIOR DA BAHIA. Main/Corp Bahia (Brazil : State). Departamento Estadual de Estatistica. **VFOAT** Bahia's Foreign Trade Bulletin. Bulletin. Multiple languages (English and Portuguese). Rua Carlos Gomes, 111-20 Andar, Salvador Brazil.

NQ
BOLETIN INFORMATIVO. Added/Corp Corporacion Nicaraguense de Empresas de Comercio Exterior. **VFOAT** Boletin Informativo CONIECE. No. 1 (Jun./Jul. 1990)-. Periodical. Spanish. Six times a year. *Continues* Boletin Informativo (Corporacion Nicaraguense de Empresas de Comercio Exterior).

LC HB235.L25 B64
DD 338   US
BOLETIN TRIMESTRAL DE PRECIOS INTERNACIONALES DE PRODUCTOS BASICOS. Added/Corp Organization of American States. Dept. of Economic Affairs. **VFOAT** International Commodity Quarterly Price Bulletin. (198?)-. Bulletin. Spanish (English). Four times a year. Organization of American States, 19th Street & Constitution Avenue NW, Suite 300, Washington DC 20006. **Tel** (202)458-6256. *Continues* Boletin de Precios Internacionales de Productos Basicos.

IT
BOLLETTINO DEI PREZZI : SETTIMANALE DELLA BORSA MERCI DI BARI. Added/Corp Borsa Merci di Bari. Camera di Commercio, Industria e Agricoltura, Bari. Vol. 17, No. 25 (Aug. 15, 1965)-. Periodical. Italian. One time a week. CCIAA di Modena, Via Ganaceto 134, 41100 Modena Italy. **Tel** 011 39 59 222529. *Continues* Bollettino Settimanale dei Prezzi alla Borsa Merci di Bari.

IT
BOLLETTINO PREZZI INGROSSO MERCATO AGRICOLO ALIMENTARE DI CREMONA. (19??)-. Italian. One time a week. L12000. Camera Commercio di Cremona, Piazza Cavour 5, 26100 Cremona Italy. **Tel** 011 39 372 28301.

ISSN 1121-2861
IT
UDC 655.4
BOLLETTINO QUINDICINALE - AUTORITA GARANTE DELLA CONCORRENZA E DEL MERCATO. (BOLLETTINO QUINDICINALE.). (1991)-. Bulletin. Italian. Twenty-four times a year. Istituto Poligrafico Zecca Stato, Piazza Verdi 10, 00198 Rome Italy. **Tel** 011 39 6 85082307, 011 39 6 85082221.

LC HC301 .A13B
DD 343/.45/07   IT
BOLLETTINO UFFICIALE - MINISTERO DELL'INDUSTRIA DEL COMMERCIO E DELL'ARTIGIANATO. Main/Corp Italy. Ministero dell'Industria, del Commercio e dell'Artigianato. Periodical. Italian. Twelve times a year. Istituto Poligrafico Zecca Stato, Piazza Verdi 10, 00198 Rome Italy. **Tel** 011 39 6 85082307, 011 39 6 85082221. *Continues* Italy. Ministero dell'Industria e del Commercio. Bollettino.

LC HF6. B88
DD 380.1   AG
BOLSA, LA. Added/Corp Bolsa de Comercio de Buenos Aires. (19??)-. Spanish. Bolsa de Comercio de Buenos Aires, Sarmiento 299, Buenos Aires Argentina. *Continues* Bolsa de Comercio de Buenos Aires. Boletin Oficial.

LC HF3503 .B793
DD 382/.094107/0294   UK
BRITISH EXPORTS TO NORTH AMERICA. **VFOAT** British Exports; Exports to North America. Vol. 1 (1990)-. English. One time a year. Kompass Publishers, Windsor Court, East Grinstead House, East Grinstead West Sussex RH19 1XA United Kingdom. **Tel** 011 44 1342 326972, FAX 011 44 1342 317241, telex 95127 INFSERG. **ED** Derek Barley. **Ad Acc. Circ:** 20,000 (ctrl).

LC WMLC 93/4777   ISSN 1380-6564
NE
BUITENLANDSE MARKTEN : BULLETIN VAN DE EVD, ONDERDEEL VAN HET MINISTERIE VAN ECONOMISCHE ZAKEN. Added/Corp Netherlands. Ministerie van Economische Zaken. Netherlands. Exportbevorderings-en Voorlichtingsdienst. (19??)-. Periodical. Dutch. Twenty-six times a year. $219.25. Samsom Bedrijfsinformatie BV, Postbus 4, 2400 MA Alphen Rij Netherlands. **Tel** 011 31 1720 66633. **(Subscription address:** Intermedia BV, Postbus 4, 2400 MA Alphen AD Rijn Netherlands. **Tel** 011 31 1720 66481.)
Desc: International commerce publication with information on export and foreign markets.

ISSN 0007-392X
DD 382   BU
SUSPENDED
BULGARIAN FOREIGN TRADE. Added/Corp Bulgarska Turgovska Palata. (1951)-Suspended (1991). Periodical. English. Six times a year. **(Subscription address:** Hemus Foreign Trade Organization, 1B Raiko Daskalov Sq Books, 1000 Sofia Bulgaria. **Tel** 011 359 2 882544, 011 359 2 801575.)
Ind/Abst Middle East Abstr. Index.

ISSN 0982-8044
FR
UDC 65 : 33
BULLETIN DE GESTION FISCALE DES ENTREPRISES. (1987)-. Periodical. French. Six times a year. $184.24. Editions Fiscalite Europeenne, Formation d'Enterprise, 50 Bis Av de la Grande Armee, F 75017 Paris France. **Tel** 011 33 1 44092424.

ISSN 0399-6174
FR
UDC 66   CODEN 68
BULLETIN DE L'I.N.A.O. **VFOAT** Bulletin de l'Institut National des Appellations d'Origine des Vins et Eaux-de-Vie. (1976)-. Bulletin. French. Four times a year. $40.46. INAO - Institut National des Appellations d'Origine des Vins et Eaux de Vie, 138 Av des Champs Elysees, F 75008 Paris France. **Tel** 011 33 1 45625475.

ISSN 0521-7059
DD 382/.0952   CN
BULLETIN DU JAPON (EDITION CANADIENNE). (BULLETIN DU JAPON.). [Bull. Jpn.]. Added/Corp Japon. Consulat General (Toronto, Ont.). Centre d'Information du Japon. (1972)-. Bulletin. French. Six times a year. Free. Bulletin du Japon, c/o Centre d'Information Consul-General du Japon, Bureau 1806 Toronto Dominion Centre, Toronto Ontario M5K 1A1 Canada.

ISSN 0997-5047
FR
UDC 658(44)
BULLETIN JOLY PARIS. (BULLETIN JOLY.). **VFOAT** Bulletin Joly Mensuel d'Information des Societes. (1988)-. Bulletin. French. Twelve times a year. 900.00F. Juridictionnaires Joly, 1 Av Franklin D. Roosevelt, F 75008 Paris France. **Tel** 011 33 1 42254740, FAX 011 33 1 45638939. *Continues* Bulletin Mensuel d'Information des Societes., 0398-9909.

US
●**BULLETIN OF INTERNATIONAL TRADE ISSUES.** (1994)-. Bulletin. English. Four times a year. $65.00. Nova Science Publishers Inc., 6080 Jericho Turnpike, Suite 207, Commack NY 11725-2808. **Tel** (516)499-3103, (516)499-3106, FAX (516)499-3146.

ISSN 0982-801X
FR
UDC 336.2 : 35.08
BULLETIN OFFICIEL DES IMPOTS. (1987)-. Periodical. French. One time a week. $149.95. Imprimerie Nationale / France, BP 514, 59505 Douai Cedex France. **Tel** 011 33 27 937090.

LC HF1 .B863
DD 330.9/73/092   ISSN 0190-6275
US
CODEN BUAMDM
BUSINESS AMERICA. [Bus. Am.]. Added/Corp United States. Dept. of Commerce. United States. International Trade Administration. Vol. 1, No. 1 (Oct. 23, 1978)-. Government Publication. English. Twelve times a year. $53.00. US Department of Commerce, 14th Street & Constitution Avenue NW, Washington DC 20230. **Tel** (202)482-2000, FAX (202)482-3772. **(Subscription address:** Superintendent of Documents, US Government Printing Office, Washington DC 20402.) available on microfilm and microfiche from University Microfilms International (UMI); available on an online database from Dow Jones News/Retrieval; and (files 15,647,648/Full-Text) DIALOG. Documents available from UMI Article Clearinghouse, CASDDS, Documents on Demand, Magazine Collection. *Continues* Commerce America, 0361-0438.
Desc: Designed to help American exporters penetrate overseas markets by providing them with information on opportunities for trade and methods of doing business in foreign countries.
Ind/Abst ABI/INFORM Glob. Ed. (Oct. 1978-); ABI/INFORM Ondisc: Expr. Ed. (Jan. 1987-); ABI/INFORM [Computer File] (Oct. 1978-); Acad. Search; Am. Bibliogr. Slavic East Europ. Stud.; Am. Stat. Index; Bus. ASAP (1990-) [Full Txt.]; Bus. Index (1985-); Bus. Period. Index; Bus. Source Plus; Bus. Source; Chem. Abstr.; Coal Abstr.; Curr. Cit.; Energy Res. Abstr. (Feb. 1979-); EP Collect.; Gen. BusinessFile (1985-); Gen. Period. Index (1985-); Homework Help.; INFO-SOUTH Abstr.; Mag. ASAP Plus [Full Txt.]; Mag. Index Plus (1989-); Mag. Search; MasterFile FullTEXT 1000; MasterFile FullTEXT 350; MasterFile FullTEXT 650; MasterFile FullTEXT (July 1993-) [Full Txt.]; Newsp. Period. Abstr. (1988-); OCLC; Telebase; Mag. Index (1977-); Trade Ind. ASAP [Full Txt.]; Trade Ind. Index (1981-) [Full Txt.]; UMI ABI/Inform--Bus. Period. Ondisc (Nov. 1987-) [Full Txt.]; Urban Aff. Abstr.; Wilson Bus. Abstr.

LC HF25 .S58
DD 382/.6/094705   ISSN 0235-764X
RU
CODEN BUCOE5
BUSINESS CONTACT. Added/Corp Torgovo-Promyshlennaia Palata SSSR. (Jan.-Feb. 1990)-. Periodical. English (German, Russian and French). Twelve times a year. $139.95. Vneshtorgreklama, 31 Kakhovka Str, 113461 Moscow Russia. **Tel** 331-95-55, FAX 310-70-05, telex 411265

Business and Economics —Commerce

VTR SU. (**Subscription address:** East View Publications Inc., 3020 Harbor Lane North, Suite 110, Minneapolis MN 55447. **Tel** (800)477-1005, (612)550-0961, FAX (612)559-2931.) **ED** N I Petrov and O V Miliukov. **Ad Acc. Circ:** 32,000. **Continues** Soviet Export, 0201-4505.
Desc: Informs Russian businessmen on market economy.

ISSN 0360-7208
US

NLM W1 BU9735
BUSINESS, HEALTH AND EDUCATIONAL DISCIPLINES. Vol. 1 (Apr. 1974)-. Periodical. English. Four times a year. $11.00. WH Green, 10 South Brentwood Blvd., St. Louis MO 63105.

LC HD28   ISSN 0007-6996
DD 658   CN
                    CODEN BUQUAL
BUSINESS QUARTERLY, THE. See Business and Economics-Management.

ISSN 0261-846X
UK
DD 381.45621880941
BUSINESS RATIO REPORT. INDUSTRIAL FASTENER DISTRIBUTORS. [Bus. Ratio Rep., Ind. Fasten. Distrib.]. **VFOAT** Industrial Fastener Distributors; ICC Business Ratio Report. Industrial Fastener Distributors. (1979)-. Trade Publication. English. One time a year. ICC Business Publications Ltd, Field House, Old Field Road, Hampton Middlesex TW12 2HQ United Kingdom. **Tel** 011 44 181 7830755.

LC HD9753 .B88   ISSN 0145-5915
DD 381/.45/68   US
BUYERS' GUIDE & DEALER DIRECTORY: NORTHEASTERN AREA.
[Buy. guide deal. dir., Northeast. area]. **VAT** Buyer's Guide and Dealer Directory. Northeastern Area. No. 1- 1976/77-. Consumer Publication. English. Twelve times a year. $125.00. Lumber Co-Operator, 339 East Avenue, Rochester NY 14604. **Tel** (716)325-1626, FAX (716)325-6179. **ED** Christine Mattke. **Ad Acc. Circ:** 3,400 (ctrl).
Desc: A reference manual containing pertinent information on manufacturers, wholesalers and service organizations serving the lumber and building materials industry. Listing of retail lumber dealers in the Northeast broken down by state and city. Information includes name, address, phone, fax, contact name and branch location.

LC HF5237.5 .B88
DD 381/.025/51249   CH
BUYERS' GUIDE, THE REPUBLIC OF CHINA. VFOAT Chung-Hua Min Kuo Kuo Chi Mao I Cheng Hsin Iu. 1976-. Consumer Publication. English. $30.00. Chiao-Hung Trade & Industry Publishing Center, PO Box 37-22, Taipei Taiwan.

LC KJE6456.A7 C66
DD 343.4/0721 344.03721   UK
C.M.L.R. ANTITRUST REPORTS. See Law-Corporation Law.

ISSN 1199-7982
DD 381.3   CN
●**CAC NEWSLETTER (OTTAWA).** (CAC NEWSLETTER / CONSUMERS' ASSOCIATION OF CANADA.). [CAC newsl.]. **Added/Corp** Consumers' Association of Canada. **VFOAT** Consumers' Association of Canada Newsletter. Vol. 1, Issue 1 (April 1994)-. Newsletter. English. Four times a year. Comes with membership. Consumers Association of Canada, PO Box 9300, Ottawa Ontario K1G 3T9 Canada. **Tel** (613)238-2533, FAX (613)723-9783. **Continues** Bulletin (Consumers' Association of Canada)., 1199-7974.

ISSN 0242-0627
FR
CAHIERS JURIDIQUES ET FISCAUX DE L'EXPORTATION. Added/Corp Centre Francais du Commerce Exterieur. (19??)-. Periodical. French. Six times a year. $284.34. Librairie de Commerce International, 24 boulevard de l'Hopital, 75005 Paris Cedex 05 France. **Tel** 011 33 1 40733000, FAX 011 33 1 43364798, telex 206 811.

ISSN 0242-0627
FR
UDC 382
CAHIERS JURIDIQUES ET FISCAUX DE L'EXPORTATION. [Cah. jurid. fisc. export.]. (1980)-. Periodical. French. Six times a year. $284.34. Librairie du Commerce Intl, 24 boulevard de l' Hopital, 75005 Paris Cedex 05 France. **Tel** 011 33 1 40733000.

ISSN 0707-8064
DD 380/.097123/3   CN
CALGARY COMMERCE. Added/Corp Calgary Chamber of Commerce. (March 1978)-. Periodical. English. Eight times a year. 19.20Can$. Calgary Chamber of Commerce, 273 One Palliser Square, 125 9th Avenue SE, Calgary Alberta T2G 0P6 Canada. **Tel** (403)263-7435. **ED** Jean Andryiszyn. **Ad Acc. Circ:** 15,000. Documents available from UMI Article Clearinghouse. **Supersedes** Calgary Chamber of Commerce. Business News., 0382-7887.
Desc: Reflects on issues relevant to Calgary's business community.
Ind/Abst Bus. Dateline (Nov. 1991-) [Full Txt.].

LC HF1371   ISSN 1064-9670
DD 382   US
CALIFORNIA AGRICULTURAL EXPORTS ANNUAL BULLETIN AND STATISTICAL APPENDIX. See Agriculture.

LC HF5065.C2 C27   ISSN 0270-4862
DD 382/.029/4794   US
CALIFORNIA INTERNATIONAL TRADE REGISTER. [Calif. int. trade regist.]. **Added/Corp** California. Office of International Trade. California State World Trade Commission. (1981)-. English. One time a year (January). $132.00. Database Publishing Company, PO Box 7440, Newport Beach CA 92658. **Tel** (714)646-1623, (800)-888-8434, FAX (714)631-8471. **Ad Acc. Circ:** 1,000 (ctrl). available on diskette.
Desc: Contains 4,500 manufacturing and service companies located in California engaged in international trade. Includes addresses, business descriptions, SIC codes, year established, annual revenues, number of employees, names and titles of officers. Alphabetical, geographical, SIC, and product sections.

ISSN 0241-0257
FR
UDC 330 (671.1)
CAMEROUN SELECTION. [Cameroun sel.]. (1979)-. Periodical. French. Six times a year. $874.88. IC Publications Ediafric, 10 rue Vineuse, 75116 Paris France. **Tel** 011 33 1 44308100.

LC HF3221 .C36
CN
CANADA. VFOAT Canada Facts. (1991)-. English. **Continues** Canada Facts (Ottawa, Ont.).

ISSN 1185-9679
DD 382/.971073   CN
CANADA-U.S. TRADE DISPUTES.
[Can.-U.S. trade disput.]. **Added/Corp** Canada. Library of Parliament. Research Branch. **VAT** Canada-United States Trade Disputes. (January 22, 1991)-. Periodical. English.

ISSN 1190-9684
DD 382   CN
●**CANADA'S EXPORT STRATEGY, THE INTERNATIONAL TRADE BUSINESS PLAN. 1, ADVANCED MANUFACTURING TECHNOLOGIES.**
[Can. export strategy int. trade bus. plan, 1 Adv. manuf. technol.]. **Added/Corp** Canada. **VFOAT** Advanced Manufacturing Technologies. (1996)-. Government Publication. English. **Continues** Canada's International Trade Business Plan. 1, Advanced Manufacturing Technologies, 1200-1066.

LC HF1371   ISSN 1190-9722
DD 382   CN
●**CANADA'S EXPORT STRATEGY, THE INTERNATIONAL TRADE BUSINESS PLAN. 3, AIRCRAFT AND PARTS. See** Aeronautics, Astronautics.

ISSN 1190-9749
DD 382   CN
●**CANADA'S EXPORT STRATEGY, THE INTERNATIONAL TRADE BUSINESS PLAN. 4, AUTOMOTIVE.** [Can. export strategy int. trade bus. plan, 4 Automot.]. **Added/Corp** Canada. **VFOAT** Automotive. (1996)-. Government Publication. English. Irregular. **Continues** Canada's International Trade Business Plan. 5, Automotive, 1200-1147.

ISSN 1190-9765
DD 382   CN
●**CANADA'S EXPORT STRATEGY, THE INTERNATIONAL TRADE BUSINESS PLAN. 5, BIOTECHNOLOGIES. See** Science and Technology.

ISSN 1190-9781
DD 382   CN
●**CANADA'S EXPORT STRATEGY, THE INTERNATIONAL TRADE BUSINESS PLAN. 6, BUSINESS, PROFESSIONAL AND EDUCATIONAL SERVICES.** [Can. export strategy int. trade bus. plan, 6 Bus. prof. educ. serv.]. **Added/Corp** Canada. **VFOAT** Business, Professional and Educational Services. (1996)-. Government Publication. English. Irregular. **Continues** Canada's International Trade Business Plan. 7, Business and Professional Services, 1200-118X.

ISSN 1190-9803
DD 382   CN
●**CANADA'S EXPORT STRATEGY, THE INTERNATIONAL TRADE BUSINESS PLAN. 7, CHEMICALS, PLASTICS AND ADVANCED MATERIALS. See** Plastics.

ISSN 1190-982X
DD 382   CN
●**CANADA'S EXPORT STRATEGY, THE INTERNATIONAL TRADE BUSINESS PLAN. 8, CONSTRUCTION PRODUCTS.**
See Building and Construction.

ISSN 1190-9846
DD 382   CN
●**CANADA'S EXPORT STRATEGY, THE INTERNATIONAL TRADE BUSINESS PLAN. 9, CONSUMER PRODUCTS.** [Can. export strategy int. trade bus. plan, 9 Consum. prod.]. **Added/Corp** Canada. **VFOAT** Consumer Products. (1996)-. Government Publication. English. **Continues** Canada's International Trade Business Plan. 9, Consumer Products, 1200-1228.

ISSN 1190-9862
DD 382   CN
●**CANADA'S EXPORT STRATEGY, THE INTERNATIONAL TRADE BUSINESS PLAN. 10, CULTURAL INDUSTRIES. See** The Arts.

ISSN 1190-9889
DD 382   CN
●**CANADA'S EXPORT STRATEGY, THE INTERNATIONAL TRADE BUSINESS PLAN. 11, DEFENCE PRODUCTS. See** Military and Defense.

ISSN 1190-9900
DD 382   CN
●**CANADA'S EXPORT STRATEGY, THE INTERNATIONAL TRADE BUSINESS PLAN. 12, ENVIRONMENTAL EQUIPMENT AND SERVICES. See** Environmental Issues.

ISSN 1190-9927
DD 382   CN
●**CANADA'S EXPORT STRATEGY, THE INTERNATIONAL TRADE BUSINESS PLAN. 13, FISH AND SEA PRODUCTS.**
See Food and Food Industry.

ISSN 1190-996X
DD 382   CN
●**CANADA'S EXPORT STRATEGY, THE INTERNATIONAL TRADE BUSINESS PLAN. 15, INFORMATION TECHNOLOGIES AND TELECOMMUNICATIONS. See** Communications-Telecommunication.

ISSN 1200-4855
DD 382   CN
●**CANADA'S EXPORT STRATEGY, THE INTERNATIONAL TRADE BUSINESS PLAN. 17, MINERALS AND METALS. See** Metals and Metallurgy.

ISSN 1200-4871
DD 382   CN
●**CANADA'S EXPORT STRATEGY, THE INTERNATIONAL TRADE BUSINESS PLAN. 18, OIL AND GAS PRODUCTS AND ENERGY EQUIPMENT. See** Petroleum and Natural Gas.

ISSN 1200-4898
DD 382   CN
●**CANADA'S EXPORT STRATEGY, THE INTERNATIONAL TRADE BUSINESS PLAN. 19, POWER EQUIPMENT.** [Can. export strategy int. trade bus. plan, 19 Power equip.]. **Added/Corp** Canada. **VFOAT** Power Equipment. (1996)-. Government Publication. English. Irregular. **Continues in part** Canada's International Trade Business Plan. 11, Electrical and Energy Equipment, 1200-1260.

ISSN 1200-491X
DD 382   CN
●**CANADA'S EXPORT STRATEGY, THE INTERNATIONAL TRADE BUSINESS PLAN. 20, PRIMARY/SECONDARY INDUSTRIAL MACHINERY. See** Industry and Production.

ISSN 1200-4936
DD 382 CN
●CANADA'S EXPORT STRATEGY, THE INTERNATIONAL TRADE BUSINESS PLAN. 21, RAIL AND BUS EQUIPMENT. [Can. export strategy int. trade bus. plan, 21 Rail bus equip.]. **Added/Corp** Canada. **VFOAT** Rail and Bus Equipment. (1996)-. Government Publication. English. Irregular. ***Continues*** *Canada's International Trade Business Plan. 21, Urban Transit and Rail, 1200-1465.*

ISSN 1200-4979
DD 382 CN
●CANADA'S EXPORT STRATEGY, THE INTERNATIONAL TRADE BUSINESS PLAN. 23, TOURISM. **See** Travel and Tourism.

ISSN 1190-9668
DD 382 CN
●CANADA'S EXPORT STRATEGY, THE INTERNATIONAL TRADE BUSINESS PLAN. OVERVIEW. [Can. export strategy int. trade bus. plan, Overv.]. **Added/Corp** Canada. (1996)-. Government Publication. English. ***Continues*** *Canada's International Trade Business Plan. Strategic Overview, 1200-104X.*

ISSN 1200-2283
DD 382/.098071/05 CN
●CANADA'S THE LATIN TRADE REPORT. [Can. Lat. trade rep.]. **VFOAT** Latin Trade Report. (1994)-. Periodical. English. Six times a year. 9.61Can$. CDN Ibero American Trade, 35 Thelinks Road, Suite 204, Wilowdale Ontario Canada. **Tel** (416)223-6944. ***Continues*** *The Canadian Trade Report Ibero-American., 1197-1258.*

ISSN 0823-3330
DD 382/.6/0971 CN
CANADEXPORT (ENGLISH ED.). (CANADEXPORT.). [CanadExport]. **Added/Corp** Canada. Dept. of External Affairs. Vol. 1, No. 1 (Sept. 1983)-. Periodical. English (French). Twenty-three times a year. Department of External Affairs, Information Division, Ottawa Ontario, K1A 0G2 Canada. **Tel** (613)996-2225. ***Absorbed*** *Trade News; Food and Agriculture, 0700-2114.*

ISSN 0708-7241
DD 381/.45/6702571 CN
CANADIAN DIRECTORY OF INDUSTRIAL DISTRIBUTORS. (1980)-. Directory. English. One time a year. DM245.00. Clifford Elliot & Associates Ltd, PO Box 358, Oakville Ontario L6J 5A2 Canada. **Tel** (905)842-2884, FAX (905)842-8226. ***Continues*** *Manufacturers' Distributor Directory.*

ISSN 0229-6551
DD 380.1/0971 CN
CANADIAN ENTREPRENEUR MAGAZINE. (THE CANADIAN ENTREPRENEUR.). **VFOAT** Entrepreneur. **VAT** Entrepreneur (Guelph). (Aug./Sept. 1980)-. Periodical. English. Twelve times a year. $1.50 per issue. Bradley and Duncan, PO Box 65, Guelph Ontario N1H 6J6.

ISSN 0226-0263
DD 382/.45 CN
CANADIAN EXPORTER (SCARBORO). (CANADIAN EXPORTER.). [Can. export.]. Vol. 1 (Sept. 1979)-. Periodical. English. One time a year. $12.00. Centre Publications, Suite 3 2000 Ellesmere Road, Scarborough Ontario M1H 2W4.

ISSN 0831-4527
DD 382.7/1/0971 CN
CANADIAN FREE TRADER. [Can. free trader.]. **Added/Corp** CCH Capital Communications. E.L. Littlejohn and Associates. No. 1 (Jan. 1986)-. Periodical. English. Twelve times a year. 100.04Can$. E L Littlejohn and Assoc. Ltd., Minto Pl Pstl Outlet, Box 56067, Ottawa Ontario K1R 7Z1 Canada. **Tel** (613)235-9183, FAX (613)594-3857.

ISSN 0830-0097
DD 382/.5/0971 CN
CANADIAN IMPORTS BY DOMESTIC AND FOREIGN CONTROLLED ENTERPRISES. (CANADIAN IMPORTS BY DOMESTIC AND FOREIGN CONTROLLED ENTERPRISES = IMPORTATIONS AU CANADA DES ENTERPRISES SOUS CONTROLE NATIONAL ET ETRANGER.). [Can. imports domest. foreign control. enterp.]. **Added/Corp** Statistics Canada. Financial Flows and Multinational Enterprises Division. Statistics Canada. International and Financial Economics Division. **VFOAT** Importation au Canada des Entreprises Sous Controle National Etranger. (1978)-. English (French). Every 2 years. 20.01Can$. Statistics Canada Publications Sales and Services, R.H. Coats Building 6th Floor, Ottawa Ontario K1A 0T6 Canada. **Tel** (613)951-5078, (800)267-6677, FAX (613)951-1584, telex 053-3585.

LC HF3221 .C363 ISSN 1198-7391
DD 382/.0971/021 CN
●CANADIAN INTERNATIONAL MERCHANDISE TRADE. [Can. int. merch. trade]. **Added/Corp** Statistics Canada. International Trade Division. **VFOAT** Commerce International de Marchandises du Canada. Vol. 48, No. 5 (May 1994)-. Periodical. English (French). Twelve times a year. 182.00Can$. Statistics Canada Publications Sales and Services, R.H. Coats Building 6th Floor, Ottawa Ontario K1A 0T6 Canada. **Tel** (613)951-5078, (800)267-6677, FAX (613)951-1584, telex 053-3585. ***Formed by the union of*** *Summary of Canadian International Trade, 0828-1556* ***and*** *Preliminary Statement of Canadian International Trade, 0828-1998.*

CN
CANADIAN TRADE & COMMODITY TAX CASES COMBINATIONS. (19??)-. English. Irregular. CCH Canadian Ltd., 6 Garamond Court, Don Mills Ontario M3C 1Z5 Canada. **Tel** (416)441-2992, FAX (416)441-3418.

LC HF
DD 380.1 UK
●CAPITAL BUSINESS MAGAZINE. (1995)-. Trade Publication. English. Twelve times a year. £36.00. **(Subscription address:** Commerce Publications, Station House, Station Road, Newport Pagnell Milton Keynes, Buckinghamshire MK16 0AG United Kingdom. **)** **Ad Acc**. Full Page (B&W) £950.00. Full Page (Color) £1,250.00.
Desc: Features profiles on leading figures in the business world.

LC HF5254.C4 C4
DD 380.1/025/599 PH
CEBU COMMERCIAL GUIDE. (19??)-. English.

US
CENSUS OF WHOLESALE TRADE. **Main/Corp** United States. Bureau of the Census. (1972)-. Government Publication. English. Irregular. US Department of Commerce / Bureau of the Census, Data User Services Division, Customer Services, Washington DC 20233-0800. **Tel** (301)763-4100. **(Subscription address:** Superintendent of Documents, US Government Printing Office, Washington DC 20402. **)** ***Continues*** *United States Census of Business, Wholesale Trade* ***and*** *Census of Business, Wholesale Trade.*
Desc: Provides statistical and brief factual information on the structure and functioning of the industrial establishments that form our Nation's economy in the United States on a whole and in selected States. Statistics cover the number of establishments, employees, production, sales, supply cost, capital expenditures, major commodity line sales, and much more. Written for a wide audience: government, business, industry, and the public.

ISSN 0745-8452
US
CCC
CFTC ADMINISTRATIVE REPORTER. [CFTC admin. report.]. **Added/Corp** United States. Commodity Futures Trading Commission. Washington Service Bureau. **VFOAT** C.F.T.C. Administrative Reporter. **VAT** Commodity Futures Trading Commission Administrative Reporter. (Jan. 1983)-. English. Twelve times a year. $1625.00. Washington Service Bureau Inc., 655 15th Street Northwest, Suite 270, Washington DC 20005. **Tel** (800)955-5219, (202)508-0600. **ED** Peggy Marsilii. Index available (topical index).
Desc: Provides every reparations and enforcement decision from the Commodity Futures Trading Commission; subscriptions include full text of all substantive Administrative Law Judge and Commissions decisions, a detailed listing of default decisions and dismissal orders, a topical index and an alphabetized case table by names of both principal parties.

ISSN 0897-067X
US
CFTC REPORT. [CFTC rep.]. **Added/Corp** United States. Commodity Futures Trading Commission. Office of Communications and Education Services. **VAT** Commodity Futures Trading Commission Report. (Mar. 1987)-. Periodical. English. Commodity Futures Trading Commission, 2033 K Street NW, Washington DC 20581. ***Formed by the union of*** *CFTC AgReport, 0895-1705* ***and*** *Education Quarterly (United States. Commodity Futures Trading Commission. Division of Economics and Education.).*

ISSN 1183-2916
DD 381.3 CN
CHANGEMENTS (MONTREAL). (CHANGEMENTS.). [Changements]. **Added/Corp** Federation des Associations Cooperatives d'Economie Familiale du Quebec. Vol. 1, No 1 (Feb. 1991)-. Periodical. French. Four times a year. 28.01Can$. Federation des ACEF du Quebec, 5225 Berri Bureau 305, Montreal Quebec H2J 2S4 Canada. **Tel** (514)271-7004.

LC HF1040.9.K6 C49
DD 380.1 KO
CHAPHWA CHEPUM PUMJIL PAEKSO. **Added/Corp** Hanguk Chaphwa Pojang Sihom Komsaso. Hanguk Chaphwa Sihom Komsaso. (1982)-. Periodical. Korean. Hanguk Chaphwa Sihom Komsaso, 125 4-ka Myongyun-dong Chongno-ku, Seoul Korea.

ISSN 0956-9286
DD 381.45641300941 UK
CHECKOUT (LONDON). (CHECKOUT.). [Checkout Lond.]. (1989)-. Periodical. English. Twelve times a year. $129.00. Reed Business Publishing / West Sussex, England, Perrymount Road, Haywards Heath, West Sussex RH16 3DH United Kingdom. **Tel** 011 44 1444 441212, FAX 011 44 1444 445447.

ISSN 0952-9756
UK
CHINA-BRITAIN TRADE REVIEW. [China-Bri. trade rev.]. **Added/Corp** Sino-British Trade Council. 48 Group. **VFOAT** Ying-Chung Mao i Yueh Kan. Issue 271 (April 1987)-. Periodical. English. Twelve times a year. $213.90. (China-Britain) Sino-British Trade Group, Abford House/5th Floor, 15 Wilton Road, London SW1V 1LT United Kingdom. **Tel** 011 44 171 8285176, FAX 011 44 171 6305780, telex 24489 SBTC G. **ED** J. Kealey. Index available (Bound in Dec. issue). **Bk Rev**, (Qty: 25). **Ad Acc. Circ:** 6,000. ***Continues*** *Sino-British Trade Review & China Trade and Economic Newsletter, 0952-9969.*
Desc: Provides monthly update on China's economy and trade relations with the West.
Ind/Abst Coal Abstr.

LC HF ISSN 0731-7700
DD 380.1 US
CODEN CHBTD2
CHINA BUSINESS & TRADE. [China bus. trade]. **VFOAT** China Business and Trade. Vol. 3, Issue 14 (Jan. 21, 1982)-. Periodical. English. Twenty-four times a year. $459.00. Welt Publishing Company, 1413 K Street NW, Suite 1400, Washington DC 20005. **Tel** (202)371-0555, FAX (202)408-9369, telex 281409 TAOA UR. **ED** Ma Li Ubois. **Bk Rev**, (Qty: 5 per year). **Ad Acc, Adv Mgr:** Justin Ford. Documents available from CASDDS. ***Continues in part*** *Business & Trade, 0196-8602.*
Desc: A newsletter reporting on recent commercial, economic and legislative developments in trade between the People's Republic of China, Taiwan, Hong Kong and the West.
Ind/Abst Chem. Abstr.; Chem. Ind. Notes.

LC HF3128 .U58 ISSN 0163-7169
DD 330.951/05 US
CCC
CHINA BUSINESS REVIEW, THE. [China bus. rev.]. **Added/Corp** National Council for United States-China Trade. Vol. 4, (Jan./Feb. 1977)-. Periodical. English. Six times a year. $99.00. The China Business Review, 1818 North Street Northwest, Suite 500, Washington DC 20036. **Tel** (202)429-0340. **ED** Pamela Baldinger. Index available. **Bk Rev**, (Qty: 3). **Ad Acc, Adv Mgr:** Pat Jordan. **Circ:** 4,500. available on microfilm and microfiche from University Microfilms International (UMI); available on an online database from WILSONLINE; and (files 15,648/Full-Text) DIALOG. Documents available from UMI Article Clearinghouse, BLDSC, FAXON Xpress, The UnCover Company, SWETS. ***Continues*** *U.S. China Business Review, 0094-0089.*
Desc: Journal on US and China trade which covers economics, finance, industry planning and business practices.
Ind/Abst ABI/INFORM Glob. Ed.; ABI/INFORM [Computer File] (Nov. 1980-); Acad. Search; Bus. ASAP (1990-) [Full Txt.]; Bus. Index (1985-); Bus. Period. Index; Bus. Source Plus; Bus. Source; Contents Pages Manage.; Curr. Cit.; EP Collect.; F&S Index Plus Text, Int. [Select. Cov.]; Gen. BusinessFile (1985-); Gen. Period. Index (1985-); Homework Help.; INFO-SOUTH Abstr.; Int. Labour Doc.; MasterFile FullTEXT 1000; MasterFile FullTEXT 350; MasterFile FullTEXT 650; MasterFile FullTEXT (July 1993-); OCLC; PAIS Int. Print (1991-); PROMT; Stat. Ref. Index; Telebase; Trade Ind. ASAP [Full Txt.]; Trade Ind. Index [Full Txt.]; UMI ABI/Inform--Bus. Period. Ondisc [Full Txt.]; Wilson Bus. Abstr.

HK
●CHINA FAX AND TELEX DIRECTORY. (1993)-. Directory. English (Chinese). One time a year. $52.00. China Phone Book Company Ltd, GPO Box 11581, Hong Kong Hong Kong. **Tel** 011 852 25084448, FAX 011 852 25031526, telex 84958. **ED** K.S. Tang. Index available. **Ad Acc. Circ:** 10,000. ***Continues*** *China Telex and Fax Directory.*

LC HF3831.5 .C483 ISSN 0739-3512
DD 382/.0951/00212 US
CHINA : INTERNATIONAL TRADE. ANNUAL STATISTICAL SUPPLEMENT. **See** Business and Economics-Abstracting, Bibliographies and Statistics.

US
●CHINA MONTHLY CUSTOMS STATISTICS OF SOFT COMMODITIES. (1995)-. Statistical Publication. English. Twelve times a year. $480.00. Noisiel and Appert Ltd., 1 Bridge Plaza,

Business and Economics — Commerce

Suite 400, Fort Lee NJ 07024. **Tel** (800)884-8987, (201)592-5001.

LC HF3838.J3 C46
DD 337.51052
JA
CHINA NEWSLETTER. Added/Corp Nihon Boeki Shinkokai. No. 22 (July 1979)-. Newsletter. English. Six times a year. $144.00. Japan External Trade Organization, 2 5 2 Chome Toranomon, Minato-ku Tokyo 107, Japan. **Tel** 011 81 3 3582 5521, **FAX** 011 81 3 3582 0504, telex J24378. (**Subscription address:** Maruzen Company Ltd., PO Box 5050, Import & Export Department, Tokyo 100 31 Japan. **Tel** 011 81 3 32789224.) **ED** Slozo Sugano and Kimiaki Taira. **Circ:** 3,000. **Continues** Nihon Boeki Shinkokai. JETRO China Newsletter.
 Desc: Analysis, commentary, statistics, on-site report, etc. on China's domestic economy, foreign trade, investment opportunities, politics and international relations.
 Ind/Abst Int. Bibliogr. Sociol.; PAIS Int. Print.

LC HF41 .C48   **ISSN** 0009-448X
DD 382/.0951
HK
CODEN CTRTAR
CHINA TRADE REPORT. [China trade rep.]. Vol. 1 (May 1963)-. English. Twelve times a year. $425.00. Review Publishing Company Ltd., 25 F Citicorp Center, 18 Whitfield Road, GPO Box 160, Hong Kong Hong Kong. **Tel** 011 852 25084337, **FAX** 011 852 25031549, 25031553, telex 66452 REVCD HX. (**Subscription address:** Review Publishing Company Ltd., PO Box 160, Hong Kong Hong Kong. **Tel** 011 852 25084300.) **ED** Louise do Rosario. Index available. **Circ:** 1,000. Documents available from CASDDS.
 Desc: Contains information and statistics, supply trade indicators and assessments of China's fluid trade relations.
 Ind/Abst Chem. Abstr. (-1991); Chem. Ind. Notes.

HK
CHINA'S EXPORTS. English. Six times a year. $21.00. Grossource Ltd., China Resources, Bldg 4102 41 F, 26 Harbor Road, Wanchai Hong Kong. **Tel** 011 852 25727038, **FAX** 011 852 28380701.

LC HF3833 .C48
DD 338/.0025/51
CC
CHINA'S FOREIGN TRADE CORPORATIONS AND ORGANIZATIONS / COMPILED BY DEPARTMENT OF PUBLIC RELATIONS, CHINA COUNCIL FOR THE PROMOTION OF INTERNATIONAL TRADE. Added/Corp Chung-kuo Kuo Chi Mao i Tsu Chin Wei Yuan Hui. Hsuan Chuan Pu. **VFOAT** Chung-kuo Tui Wai Mao i Kung Ssu Ho Yu Kuan Chi Kuo; China's Foreign Trade Corporations & Organizations. (19??)-. Chinese (English). Irregular. $43.00.
(**Subscription address:** China International Book Trading Corporation, PO Box 399, Library Service Department, Beijing 100044 People's Republic of China. **Tel** 011 86 1 8414284, **FAX** 011 86 1 8412013, telex 22496 CIBTC CN.)

LC HF3831.5 .C584
DD 380.1/0951/021
HK
CHUNG-KUO HAI KUAN TUNG CHI. See Business and Economics-Abstracting, Bibliographies and Statistics.

LC HF3831 .C484
DD 380.1/0951
CC
**CHUNG-KUO SHANG YEH NIEN CHIEN.
Added/Corp** "Chung-Kuo Shang Yeh Nien Chien" Pien Chi Wei Yuan Hui. **VFOAT** Almanac of China's Commerce. (1988)-. Chinese. One time a year. $40.00. China National Publishing Import & Export Corporation, 16 Gongti E Rd., Chaoyang Dist., Beijing 100704, People's Republic of China. **Tel** 011 8601 50630169, 5066688, **FAX** 011 8601 5063101, 5063010, telex 22313.

HK
CHUNG-KUO TUI WAI CHING CHI MAO I NIEN CHIEN. VFOAT Almanac of China's Foreign Economic Relations and Trade. (1984)-. Chinese (English). One time a year. $50.00. China National Publishing Import & Export Corporation, 16 Gongti E Rd., Chaoyang Dist., Beijing 100704, People's Republic of China. **Tel** 011 8601 50630169, 5066688, **FAX** 011 8601 5063101, 5063010, telex 22313.

LC HF3831 .C485
DD 0951
HK
CHUNG-KUO TUI WAI CHING CHI MAO I NIEN CHIEN. See Business and Economics-Economic History, Conditions.

LC HF41 .C49 **ISSN** 0009-4498
DD 382/.0951/005
CC
CHUNG-KUO TUI WAI MAO I. (CHINA'S FOREIGN TRADE). [China foreign trade]. **Added/Corp VFOAT** Chung-kuo Kuo Chi Mao I Tsu Chin Wei Yuan Hui. **VFOAT** Chung-kuo Tui Wai Mao I. (1966)-. Periodical. English. Twelve times a year. $63.00. China Council for the Promotion of International Trade - CCPIT, 1 Fuxingmenwai Dajie, Beijing People's Republic of China.

Tel FAX 8011370. (**Subscription address:** China Books & Periodicals Inc., 2929 24th Street, San Francisco CA 94110. **Tel** (415)282-2994.) **ED** Liu Deyu. **Ad Acc. Circ:** 70,000.
 Desc: Reflects the growth of China's foreign trade as the country deepens its reforms and opens its doors to the outside world.

LC HF3762.A48 C48
DD 338/.0025/536
CH
CHUNG TUNG KO KUO MAO I MING LU. English (Chinese). Shu Hsin Chu Pan She 8-2, 165 Lane Third Floor, Hsin Sheng S Road, Section 1, Taipei Taiwan.

LC HF6 .C46
BL
CIFRAO; REVISTA DE ECONOMIA E NEGOCIOS. Vol. 1 (May 19, 1972)-. Periodical. Portuguese. One time a week. Cr$156. Rio Grafica E Editora, rua Itapiru 1209, 20 000 Rio de Janeiro Brazil.

ISSN 1000-9310
DD 951
CC
CINA, LA. [Cina]. **VFOAT** Renmin Huabao. (1964)-. Periodical. Italian. Twelve times a year. L31070. Libreria Marco Polo, Via del Seminario 103, 00186 Rome Italy. **Tel** 011 39 6 6785764.

ISSN 0712-2918
DD 382/.06/0714281
CN
CMI EXPRESS. [CMI express]. **VAT** Commerce Montreal International Express. No. 1 (Oct 1, 1981)-. Periodical. French. Irregular. Free to members of CMI. Chambre de Commerce du District de Montreal, Maison du Commerce, 6E Etage 1080 Cote du Beaver Hall, Montreal Quebec H2Z 1T1 Canada.

ISSN 0272-0205
DD 662
US
CODEN CWIOEQ
COAL WEEK INTERNATIONAL. See Mines and Mining-Mineralogy.

US
CODE OF FEDERAL REGULATIONS. 16, COMMERCIAL PRACTICES. See Law.

ISSN 0950-916X
DD 382
UK
Pr Rev.
COI. COUNTERTRADE AND OFFSET INTELLIGENCE. [COI. Countertr. offset intell.]. **VFOAT** Countertrade and Offset Intelligence. (1986)-. Periodical. English. Twelve times a year. £299.00. Countertrade and Offset Intelligence Ltd., 197 Knightsbridge House, Sixth Floor, London SW7 1RS United Kingdom. **Tel** 011 44 181 63118015, **FAX** 011 44 181 6314879, telex 295117 BGMLG. **ED** Jonathon Bell. **Bk Rev,** (Qty: (3-4)). **Ad Acc, Adv Mgr:** J Wain, **Tel** 071 584 1333. **Circ:** 1,000 (ctrl).
 Desc: Analysis and developments relating to all forms of international reciprocal trade, from barter to offset.

US
COLORADO GUIDE TO GOVERNMENT. English. One time a year. $5.65 members, Colorado Association of Commerce and Industry; $10.65 nonmembers. Colorado Association of Commerce and Industry, 1776 Lincoln Street, Suite 1200, Denver CO 80203. **Tel** (303)831-7411, **FAX** (303)860-1439. **ED** Anne P. Lawshe.

MX
COMERCIO. (19??)-. Periodical. Spanish. Twelve times a year. Paseo de la Reforma, 369-1, Mexico City Mexico. **Continues** Revista Comercio.

LC HF3301 .C65
DD 338.097284
ES
Pr Rev.
COMERCIO E INDUSTRIA (SAN SALVADOR, EL SALVADOR). (COMERCIO E INDUSTRIA). **Added/Corp** Camara de Comercio e Industria de El Salvador. (19??)-. Periodical. Spanish. Irregular. $18.00. Camara de Comercio e Industria, 9A Avenida Norte y 5A Calle Poniente, 01118 San Salvador El Salvador. **Tel** 011 503 712055, 011 503 816622, **FAX** 011 503 714461, telex (0373)20753. **ED** Alfonso Morales. Index available. cum. index. **Ad Acc. Circ:** 3,000 (ctrl).
 Desc: Dedicated to economic subjects, trade, industrial progress and problems in the productive sectors. Publishes interviews, articles about supply and demand, protection of free enterprise, opinions of managers etc.

LC HF6 .B43   **ISSN** 0185-0601
MX
COMERCIO EXTERIOR. [Comer. exter.]. **Main/Corp** Banco Nacional de Comercio Exterior (Mexico). Vol. 1 (Jan. 1951)-. Periodical. Spanish. Twelve times a year. Free (surface mail) $25.00 (airmail) U.S.; $55.00 (airmail) other. Banco Nacional de Comercio Exterior SA, Venustiano Carranza 32, Mexico 1 DF Mexico. **Tel** 688.0688, telex 017-71-070.
 Ind/Abst Chicano Index; Hisp. Am. Period. Index, HAPI; PAIS Int. Print (1991-).

LC WMLC 91/4504
BO
COMERCIO EXTERIOR : IBCE, INSTITUTO BOLIVIANO DE COMERCIO EXTERIOR. Added/Corp Instituto Boliviano de Comercio Exterior. (1991)-. Newsletter. Spanish. Twelve times a year. Free on request. Instituto Boliviano de Comercio Exterior, Santa Cruz de la Sierra Bolivia. **Tel FAX** 5913 321509, telex 4293 IBCE BV. **Ad Acc, Adv Mgr:** Juan Carlos Lijeron, **Tel** 347173. Full Page (B&W) $400.00. Half Page (B&W) $200.00. available on diskette.

LC HF161 .A37   **ISSN** 0520-4712
DD 382
BO
COMERCIO EXTERIOR (LA PAZ). (COMERCIO EXTERIOR; ANUARIO.). **Added/Corp** Bolivia- Nacional de Estadistica Censos. Bolivia- General de Estaistica. Bolivia-Direccion Nacional de Estadistica Censos. (1934/35)-. Periodical. Spanish. One time a year. **Continues** Comercio Exterior de Bolivia.

LC HF3500.5 .A15
DD 382/.094/021
LU
COMERCIO EXTERIOR, SISTEMA DE PREFERENCIAS ARANCELARIAS GENERALIZADAS (SPG). IMPORTACIONES. VFOAT Udenrigshandel, Ordningen Med Generelle Toldprferencer (GSP) Import; External Trade, System of Generalized Tariff Preferences (GSP). Imports; Sistema de Preferencias Arancelarias Generalizadas (SPG); System of Generalized Tariff Preferences (GSP). (1987)-. French.

AG
COMMENTS ON ARGENTINE TRADE (BUENOS AIRES, ARGENTINA : 1985). (COMMENTS ON ARGENTINE TRADE / PUBLISHED BY THE AMERICAN CHAMBER OF COMMERCE IN ARGENTINA.). **Added/Corp** Chamber of Commerce of the United States of America in the Argentine Republic. **VFOAT** Comments. No. 3 (June/July 1985)-. Periodical. English. Six times a year. American Chamber of Commerce in Argentina, Av Roque Saenz Pena 567, 1352 Buenos Aires Argentina. **Tel** 331-5591, 21210, 22550, 18264, BOSBK FOR AMCHAM, telex 21139. **ED** Nicolas Meyer. **Ad Acc. Continues** Comments on Argentine and U.S. Trade, 0010-2660.

LC HC431 .C57   **ISSN** 0010-275X
II
COMMERCE. [Commerce]. Vol. 1 (1910)-. Periodical. English. One time a week. $40.00 (surface mail), $113.00 (airmail). Indian Books & Periodicals Syn, 3341 Chrstn Colony, Pyarey LAL, New Delhi 110005 India. **Tel** 565-444.
 Ind/Abst AGRICOLA; Indian Geosci. Abstr.; Int. Labour Doc.

CN
COMMERCE DU CANADA: EXPORTATIONS PAR MERCHANDISES. Main/Corp Canada. Statistics Canada. External Trade Division. **VFOAT** Commerce du Canada : Exportations par Merchandises. (19??)-. Periodical. Multiple languages (English and French). Twelve times a year. 60.00Can$ Canada; $72.00 US; $84.00 other. Statistics Canada Publications Sales and Services, R.H. Coats Building 6th Floor, Ottawa Ontario K1A 0T6 Canada. **Tel** (613)951-5078, (800)267-6677, **FAX** (613)951-1584, telex 053-3585.

LC HF   **ISSN** 0222-6618
DD 650
UDC 65
FR
TITLE CHANGE
COMMERCE ET COOPERATION (PARIS). (1970)-(1993). Periodical. French. Four times a year. CCFS, 22 Ave F D Roosevelt, F-75008 Paris France. **Tel** 011 33 1 42259710. **Continued by** Carrefours France-Russie, 1245-0820.

LC HF3601 .C65
BE
COMMERCE EXTERIEUR DE L'U.E.B.L. AVEC LES PAYS D'AFRIQUE, LE. VFOAT Buitenlandse Handel van de B.L.E.U. et de Landen van Afrika. Multiple languages (Dutch and French).
 Desc: Includes comparative figures for previous two years.

LC HF3601 .C66
BE
COMMERCE EXTERIEUR DE L'U.E.B.L. AVEC LES PAYS D'AMERIQUE LATINE, LE. VFOAT Buitenlandse Handel van de B.L.E.U Met de Landen van Latijns Amerika. (19??)-. Multiple languages (Dutch and French).
 Desc: Includes comparative figures for previous two years.

LC HF3601 .C665
BE
COMMERCE EXTERIEUR DE L'U.E.B.L. AVEC LES PAYS DE L'A.E.L.E, LE. Added/Corp Office Belge du Commerce Exterieur.

Business and Economics — Commerce

VFOAT Buitenlandse Handel van de B.L.E.U. Met de E.V.A.-Lidstaten. (19??)-. Multiple languages (Dutch and French). Office Belge du Commerce Exterieur, 4 Galerie Ravenstein, 1000 Brussels Belgium.
  Desc: Each issue includes comparative figures for previous two years.
LC HF3601 .C67
DD 382/.09493 BE

COMMERCE EXTERIEUR DE L'U. L'U.E.B.L. AVEC LES PAYS INDUSTRIALISES (AUTRES QUE LES PAYS DE LA C.E.E. ET DE L'A.E.L.E.), LE.
VFOAT Buitenlandse Handel van de B.L.E.U. Met de Industrielanden (Niet E.E.G.-en E.V.A -Lidstaten). Multiple languages (Dutch and French). Office Belge du Commerce Exterieur, 4 Galerie Ravenstein, 1000 Brussels Belgium.
  Desc: Includes comparative figures for previous two years.
LC HF306 .C65
DD 382/.0944/9 FR

COMMERCE EXTERIEUR DES REGIONS PROVENCE, ALPES, COTE D'AZUR ET CORSE, LE.
Added/Corp Chambre de Commerce et d'Industrie de Marseille. France. Service des Statistiques de l'Interregion des Douanes de la Mediterranee. **VFOAT** Commerce Exterieur de la Region Provence, Alpes, Cote d'Azur. (19??)-. French. One time a year. Chambre de Commerce et d'Industrie de Marseille, Palais de la Bourse, BP 826 Bis 13222, Marseille Cedex 1 France.

ISSN 0010-2849 FR

COMMERCE IN FRANCE.
Added/Corp American Chamber of Commerce in France. (19??)-. English (French). Eight times a year. $25.00. American Chamber of Commerce / France, 21 Avenue George V, 75008 Paris France. **Tel** 011 33 1 47238026, FAX 011 33 1 47201862. **ED** John Davidson. **Circ:** 1,300.

ISSN 1192-7933
DD 382 CN

●COMMERCE INTERNATIONAL (MONTREAL. 1993).
(COMMERCE INTERNATIONAL.). [Comm. int.]. Vol. 1, No 1 (1993)-. Periodical. French. Six times a year. 26.41Can$. Nouveau Monde International, CP 163 SUCC Outremeont, Montreal, Quebec H2V 4M8 Canada. **Tel** (514)272-3394.

ISSN 0383-9699
DD 330.9/71/0644 CN

COMMERCE LEADING INDICATOR, THE.
Added/Corp Canadian Imperial Bank of Commerce. Economics Division. **VFOAT** Canadian Business Conditions. (Nov. 1975)-. Periodical. English. Twelve times a year. Free on request. Canadian Imperial Bank of Commerce Economic Division, Commerce Court North, 7th Floor, Toronto Ontario M5L 1A2 Canada. **Tel** (416)980-2211, (416)980-3721.

ISSN 0227-079X
DD 381/.09715/235 CN
TITLE CHANGE

COMMERCE MONCTON (1981).
(COMMERCE MONCTON.). [Commer. Moncton]. **Added/Corp** Greater Moncton Chamber of Commerce. **VAT** Chamber News (Moncton, 1981). (March 1981)-(199?). Periodical. English (summaries and/or abstracts in French). Commerce Moncton, Greater Moncton Chamber of Commerce, PO Box 1009, 236 Saint George Street, Moncton New Brunswick E1C 8P2 Canada. **Continues** Chamber News (Moncton, N.B.), 0711-5989. **Continued by** Commerce (Moncton, N.B.), 0227-079X.

ISSN 1057-9672
DD 353 US
CEASED

COMMERCE PUBLICATIONS UPDATE.
(COMMERCE PUBLICATIONS UPDATE : A BIWEEKLY LISTING OF LATEST TITLES FROM THE U.S. DEPARTMENT OF COMMERCE.). [Commer. publ. update]. **Added/Corp** United States. Dept. of Commerce. Vol. 1, No. 1 (July 4, 1980)-Vol. 14 (July 1993). English. Superintendent of Documents, US Government Printing Office, Washington DC 20402. **Tel** (202)275-3328, FAX (202)786-2377. **Continues** Recent Commerce Department Publications.
  Desc: Contains a listing of all publications and press releases issued by the United States Department of Commerce, highlighting Commerce publications of special interest and providing the latest figures in 19 key areas of business and economic activity.

ISSN 1187-4651
DD 380.1 CN

COMMERCE (RED DEER). (COMMERCE.).
[Commerce]. **Added/Corp** Red Deer Chamber of Commerce. Vol. 1, No. 1 (Summer 1991)-. Periodical. English. Four times a year. Limited free distribution. Sylvester Publications Ltd., 101-10118-101 Avenue, Grande Prarie Alberta T8V 0Y4 Canada. **Tel** (403)538-0539. **Continues** Red Deer Commerce., 0832-8811.

ISSN 0823-6658
DD 380.1/06/07143 CN

COMMERCE RIVE-SUD. [Commer. Rive-Sud].
Added/Corp Chambre de Commerce de la Rive-Sud. (1975)-. Periodical. French. Twelve times a year. Limited free distribution. Commerce Rive-Sud, CP 27 Succursale A, Longueuil Quebec J4H 3W2 Canada.

LC HF1455 .C58 **ISSN** 0161-9772
DD 382/.3/0973 US

COMMERCIAL NEWS USA. [Commer. news USA].
Added/Corp United States. Industry and Trade Administration. United States. International Trade Administration. U. S. and Foreign Commercial Service. **VFOAT CN.** Commercial News United States of America. No. 32 (March/April 1978)-. Government Publication. English. Twelve times a year. US Department of Commerce, 14th Street & Constitution Avenue NW, Washington DC 20230. **Tel** (202)482-2000, FAX (202)482-3772. **Continues** Commercial News for the Foreign Service, 0363-678X.
  Ind/Abst Energy Res. Abstr. (Jan. 1979-).

LC HF1040.8 .C64 **ISSN** 0738-0992
DD 382/.6/029473 US

COMMERCIAL NEWS USA. ANNUAL DIRECTORY.
(COMMERCIAL NEWS USA. ANNUAL DIRECTORY FOR ...). [Commer. news USA, Annu. dir.]. **VFOAT** Commercial News USA; U.S. Products for Export. **VAT** Commercial News United States of America. Annual Directory for .... (1982)-. Government Publication. English. One time a year. US Department of Commerce, 14th Street & Constitution Avenue NW, Washington DC 20230. **Tel** (202)482-2000, FAX (202)482-3772. **Continues** Commercial News USA. U.S. Products for Export, 0732-846X.

COMMERCIO.
Added/Corp Universita Commerciale Luigi Bocconi. Centro di Studi Sul Commercio. (1979)-. Periodical. Italian. Three times a year. L81660. Franco Angeli Riviste SRL, Viale Monza 106, 20127 Milan Italy. **Tel** 011 39 2 2827651, 011 39 2 289562, FAX 011 39 2 258004, telex 051-511650.

IT

COMMERCIO CARTOLERIA E CANCELLERIA.
(19??)-. Italian. Six times a year. L48000.00. Edinova, Piazza Udine 8, 20132 Milan Italy. **Tel** 011 39 2 2158021.

IT

COMMERCIO INTERNAZIONALE.
(19??)-. Periodical. Italian. Twenty-six times a year. L370000 Italy; L740000 other. IPSOA Editore SRL, Casella Postale 12055, Mastrangelo, 20120 Milan Italy. **Tel** 011 39 2 82476248.

US
CEASED

COMMITMENTS OF TRADERS.
(19??)-(Oct. 1993). English. Commodities Futures Trade Commission, 2033 K Street Northwest, 18th Floor, Washington DC 20581. **Tel** (202)254-8630.

ISSN 0279-0939
US

COMMODEX.
(19??)-. Periodical. English. Seven times a week. $375.00. Commodex Systems Inc, 114 Liberty Street, New York NY 10006. **Tel** (212)227-6730.

LC HF1 .C83 **ISSN** 0251-401X
DD 380.1/05 US

COMMODITY TRADE AND PRICE TRENDS. [Commod. trade price trends].
Added/Corp World Bank. Commodities and Export Projections Division. **VFOAT** Tendances du Commerce et des Prix des Produits de Base; Tendencias del Comercio y de los Precios de los Productos Basicos. (19?)-. Monographic series. English (French and Spanish). Irregular. Price varies per volume. World Bank Publications, 1818 H Street Northwest, Washington DC 20043. **Tel** (202)473-1155, (202)473-1155, FAX (202)522-3224, telex WUI 64145 WORLDBANK. **(Subscription address:** World Bank Publications, PO Box 7247-8619, Books Department, Philadelphia PA 19170. **) ED** Peter Muncie. **Circ:** 197. **Continues** Commodity Price Trends.
  Desc: Provides information on the export trade of developing countries, including an overview of the primary commodity market developments during the preceding year. Analyzes 51 commodities, among them foods, non-foods, fuels, metals, and minerals.

ISSN 0813-8389
DD 382.780994 AT

COMMONWEALTH OF AUSTRALIA GAZETTE. TARIFF CONCESSIONS.
[Commonw. Aust. gaz., Tariff concess.]. **Added/Corp** Australia. (1983)-. Government Publication. English. One time a week. 115.00Aus$. Australian Government Publishing Service, GPO Box 84, Canberra ACT 2601 Australia. **Tel** 011 61 6 2954411, FAX 011 61 6 2954455.

US

COMP-TECH FEDERAL REGISTER, THE.
(1989)-. English. Irregular. $240.00 US; $290.00 other. Comp-Tech Export Publications, PO Box 1367, Bethesda MD 20827-1367. **Tel** (301)983-3339, FAX (301)983-9035.

US

COMPARATIVE SUMMARY OF WATER BORNE FOREIGN COMMERCE WITH GRAPHIC CHARTS.
See Transportation-Ships and Shipping.

LC K
DD 343.805/6/05 348.035605 AG

COMPENDIO TEORICO Y PRACTICO - ALALC.
Main/Corp Asociacion Latinoamericana de Libre Comercio. (19??)-. Spanish. One time a year. Asociacion Latinoamericana de Libre Comercio, Peru 707 CAP, Casilla 5051 C. Central Buenos Aires Argentina.

ISSN 1080-420X
DD 337 US

●COMPLETE EUROPEAN TRADE DIGEST, THE.
[Complete Eur. trade dig.]. (1994)-. Periodical. English. Twenty-four times a year. $180.00. SIMCOM, PO Box 420511, Atlanta GA 30342. **Tel** (404)875-3105, FAX (404)872-1620. **Bk Rev,** (Qty: 12). **Formed by the union of** European Report on Industry, 1075-5101 **and** European Marketing Guide, 1075-511X.

US

●COMPLETE EUROPEAN TRADE DIGEST - ELECTRICAL.
(1995)-. English. Twenty-four times a year. SIMCOM, PO Box 420511, Atlanta GA 30342. **Tel** (404)875-3105, FAX (404)872-1620. **Separated from** Complete European Trade Digest.

US

●COMPLETE EUROPEAN TRADE DIGEST - MACHINERY.
(1995)-. English. Twenty-four times a year. SIMCOM, PO Box 420511, Atlanta GA 30342. **Tel** (404)875-3105, FAX (404)872-1620. **Separated from** Complete European Trade Digest.

US

●COMPLETE EUROPEAN TRADE DIGEST - MEDICAL DEVICES.
(1995)-. English. Twenty-four times a year. SIMCOM, PO Box 420511, Atlanta GA 30342. **Tel** (404)875-3105, FAX (404)872-1620. **Separated from** Complete European Trade Digest.

IT

COMPRARE OGGI.
(19??)-. Italian. Ten times a year. L120000 Italy. Soc Editoriale Farmaceutica, Via Ausonio 12, 20123 Milan Italy. **Tel** 011 39 2 89404545.

US

COMPUTERS & SOFTWARE - EXPORT LICENSING CONTROLS.
(1989)-. English. Irregular. $350.00. Comp-Tech Export Publications, PO Box 1367, Bethesda MD 20827-1367. **Tel** (301)983-3339, FAX (301)983-9035.
  Desc: Coverage of software and software controls; technical data and export controls; and full descriptions on exporting computers, software and technology with a validated license.

LC HF5429.6.C3 C66
DD 381/.0971/021 CN

CONCENTRATION AND FOREIGN CONTROL IN RETAIL AND WHOLESALE TRADE IN CANADA.
Added/Corp Statistics Canada. Merchandising and Services Division. **VFOAT** Concentration et Controle Etranger dans les Commerces de Gros et de Detail au Canada. (1979)-. English (French). Irregular. 6.35Can$ Canada; $7.60 other. Statistics Canada Publications Sales and Services, R.H. Coats Building 6th Floor, Ottawa Ontario K1A 0T6 Canada. **Tel** (613)951-5078, (800)267-6677, FAX (613)951-1584, telex 053-3585.
  Desc: Presents enterprise concentration and foreign control in the Canadian wholesale and retail sectors.

ISSN 1052-6838
DD 380 US

CONFERENCE PROCEEDINGS / ANNUAL ADVANCED RESEARCH TECHNIQUES FORUM.
Main/Conf Advanced Research Techniques Forum. **Added/Corp** American Marketing Association. 1st (1991)-. Proceedings. English. $38.50. American Marketing Association, 250 South Wacker Drive, Suite 200, Chicago IL 60606-5819. **Tel** (312)648-0536, FAX (312)993-7542.

ISSN 1071-1783
DD 381 US

CONSUMER ACTION NEWS. [Consum. action news].
Added/Corp Consumer Action (Organization). **VFOAT** CA News. (19??)-. Periodical. English. Six times

Business and Economics —Commerce

a year. $25.00 US; $30.00 Canada; $35.00 other. Consumer Action Inc., 116 New Montgomery Street, Suite 223, San Francisco CA 94105. **Tel** (415)777-9648. **Circ:** 2,500.

UK

●**CONSUMER ASIA.** (May 1993)-. Trade Publication. English. One time a year. $550.00. Euromonitor Publications Ltd., 60-61 Britton Street, London EC1M 5NA United Kingdom. **Tel** 011 44 171 2518024, FAX 011 44 171 6083149, telex 21120. **(Subscription address:** Gale Research Co., 835 Penobscot Building, Detroit MI 48226. **Tel** (800)347-4253.)
  Desc: Includes coverage of volume and value market sizes, key regional and national marketing parameters, detailed assessment of growth areas and extensive country-by-country statistical analysis.

UK

CONSUMER SOUTH AMERICA. (Oct. 1993)-. English. One time a year. $550.00. Euromonitor Publications Ltd., 60-61 Britton Street, London EC1M 5NA United Kingdom. **Tel** 011 44 171 2518024, FAX 011 44 171 6083149, telex 21120. **(Subscription address:** Gale Research Co., 835 Penobscot Building, Detroit MI 48226. **Tel** (800)347-4253.)
  Desc: Allows researchers to plug into the potential of this promising consumer market. Provides a market overview, regional marketing parameters and more.

ISSN 0951-5879
DD 387.5
UK

CONTAINERISATION INTERNATIONAL WORLD DIRECTORY OF LINER SHIPPING AGENTS. [Contain. int. world dir. liner shipp. agents]. **VFOAT** World Directory of Liner Shipping Agents. (19??)-. English. One time a year (May). $95.00. EMAP Response Publishing Ltd., 67 Clerkenwell Road, London EC1R 5BH United Kingdom. **Tel** 011 44 171 4042763, FAX 011 44 171 4042765. **ED** Mark R. Lambert. Index available. **Bk Rev**. **Ad Acc**, **Adv Mgr:** P. G. Owen, **Tel** 71 404 2763 Ext.2161.
  Desc: Information on international shipping contacts. Includes list of the freight contacts.

ISSN 1059-7093
US

CONTRA COSTA COUNTY COMMERCE AND INDUSTRY DIRECTORY. (1992)-. Directory. English. $75.00. Database Publishing Company, PO Box 7440, Newport Beach CA 92658. **Tel** (714)646-1623, (800)-888-8434, FAX (714)631-8471.

LC HD9116.I39 C65
DD 334/.6836/0954
II

COOPERATIVE SUGAR / NATIONAL FEDERATION OF COOPERATIVE SUGAR FACTORIES LTD. See Food and Food Industry.

ISSN 1323-6393
AT

●**COUNTDOWN 2000 : THE INDEPENDENT NEWSLETTER OF SYDNEY OLYMPIC BUSINESS OPPORTUNITIES.** (Feb. 1995)-. Newsletter. English. Ten times a year. 201.43Aus$. International Business Communications Pty Ltd, Level 11 55 63 Elizabeth Street, Sydney 2000 Australia. **Tel** 011 61 2 2216199, FAX 011 61 2 2215923, telex 72148.

ISSN 0743-250X
DD 382
US

COUNTERTRADE & BARTER INTERNATIONAL. Added/Corp World Trade Data Systems, Inc. **VFOAT** Countertrade and Barter International. Vol. 1, No. 1 (Nov. 1993)-. Periodical. English. Four times a year. $125.00. World Trade Data Systems Inc, 159 Main Dunstable Road, Nashua NH 03060. **Tel** (617)268-0724.

ISSN 0743-0396
US

COUNTERTRADE OUTLOOK. (April 1983)-. Periodical. English. Twenty-four times a year. $488.00 North America; $548.00 other. DP Publications Company, PO Box 7188, Fairfax Station VA 22039. **Tel** (703)425-1322, FAX (703)425-7911, telex 263 128 CTOUR. **ED** Michael Morrison.

LC HF4030.5 .A25a
DD 382/.09931
NZ

COUNTRY ANALYSIS OF EXTERNAL TRADE. Main/Corp New Zealand. Dept. of Statistics. (19??)-. English. One time a year. Government Printing Office / New Zealand, 10 Mulgrave Street, Wellington New Zealand. **Tel** 011 64 4 4737211, FAX 011 64 4 734943, telex GOVPRINT NZ 31320. **(Subscription address:** Government Printing Office / New Zealand, PO Box 12052, Wellington New Zealand. **Tel** 011 64 4 4737211.) **Continues** New Zealand. Dept. of Statistics. External Trade of New Zealand; Country Analysis.

ISSN 0828-6345
DD 380.5/24
CN

COURIER NETWORK. [Cour. netw.]. (1984/85)-. English. One time a year. $8.95. Business Network Publications, 209-2951 Tillicum Road, Victoria BC V9A 2A6.

ISSN 0757-8768
FR
UDC 336.747

COURRIER DE LA MONETIQUE ET DE LA CARTE A MEMOIRE, LE. [Courr. monet. carte mem.]. (1983)-. Periodical. French. Six times a year. $853.01. Analyses & Syntheses, 14 Avenue de Corbera, 75102 Paris France. **Tel** 011 33 1 46283210, 011 33 1 43446916, FAX 1 46 28 9563. Index available. **Bk Rev**. **Circ:** 1,000.
  Desc: Electronic fund transfer and small card applications and technology.

ISSN 1143-4325
FR
UDC 339.96

COURRIER EUROPEEN DE L'ENTREPRISE PARIS, LE. (LE COURRIER EUROPEEN DE L'ENTREPRISE.). (1989)-. Periodical. French. Twenty-four times a year. Courrier Europeen de l' Entreprise, 42 Bd de la Bastille, F-75012 Paris France.

LC HF11 .I722
DD 658.8/48/0941
UK

CRONER'S EXPORT DIGEST. (198?)-. Periodical. English. Twelve times a year. £29.00. Croner Publ Ltd., Croner House London Road, Kingston Upon Thames, Surrey KT2 6SR United Kingdom. **Tel** 011 44 181 5473333, FAX 011 44 181 5472637. **Continues** Export Digest (New Malden, London, England).

ISSN 0070-1599
UK

CRONER'S REFERENCE BOOK FOR EXPORTERS. **VFOAT** Reference Book for Exporters. (19??)-. English. Twelve times a year. £198.80. Croner Publ Ltd., Croner House London Road, Kingston Upon Thames, Surrey KT2 6SR United Kingdom. **Tel** 011 44 181 5473333, FAX 011 44 181 5472637. Index available (Free).

ISSN 0070-1602
UK

CRONER'S REFERENCE BOOK FOR IMPORTERS. (19??)-. English. Twelve times a year. £131.35. Croner Publ Ltd., Croner House London Road, Kingston Upon Thames, Surrey KT2 6SR United Kingdom. **Tel** 011 44 181 5473333, FAX 011 44 181 5472637.

LC HF41 .C75
DD 380.1/0954
II

CROSS SECTION. Periodical. English. 24.00. N Berry, 188 Golf Links, New Delhi India. **Absorbed** Trader. **Ind/Abst** Urban Aff. Abstr.

CU

CUBA FOREIGN TRADE. Added/Corp Camara de Comercio de la Republica de Cuba. No. 1 (1964)-. Periodical. English (Spanish and Multiple languages). Four times a year. $16.80. Camara de Comercio de la Rrpublica de Cuba, Calle 21 No. 661 Vedado, La Habana (4) Cuba- Cable, Comercio - Apartado 370. Index available ($20.00 in Cuba). **Ad Acc**, **Adv Mgr:** P. Medero, **Tel** 30-9643. **Circ:** 3,000 (ctrl).

LC HF5114.3.C87 C86
NA

CURACAO BUSINESS INFORMATION GUIDE / CURACAO CHAMBER OF COMMERCE & INDUSTRY. Added/Corp Kamer van Koophandel en Nijverdig op Curacao. (199?)-. English. Curacao Chamber of Commerce & Industry, Pietermaai 21, PO Box 10, Curacao Netherlands Antilles. **Tel** 599-9-613918, FAX 599-9-615652.
  Desc: Trade information guide.

LC HF3368.C8 C86
DD 380.1/025/72986
NA

CURACAO TRADE AND INDUSTRY DIRECTORY. Directory. Multiple languages (Dutch, English and Spanish). One time a year. Citroen-daal, Malmokweg 2, Aruba Netherlands Antilles. **Continues** Curacao Trade Directory.

ISSN 0736-606X
US

CURRENT ANALYSIS. [Curr. anal.].
Added/Corp Institute of Strategic Trade. (19??)-. Monograph series. English. Twelve times a year. Price varies per volume. Institute on Strategic Trade, 499 South Capitol Street/Suite 404 A, Washington DC 20003.

LC HF5421 .C85
DD 381.2/0973021
US

CURRENT BUSINESS REPORTS. COMBINED ANNUAL AND REVISED MONTHLY WHOLESALE TRADE.
Added/Corp United States. Bureau of the Census. **VFOAT** Combined Annual and Revised Monthly Wholesale Trade. (1992)-. English. Irregular. $1.00. US Department of Commerce / Bureau of the Census, Data User Services Division, Customer Services, Washington DC 20233-0800. **Tel** (301)763-4100. **(Subscription address:** Superintendent of Documents, US Government Printing Office, Washington DC 20402.) **Formed by the union of** Current Business Reports. Wholesale Trade, Annual Sales and Year-End Inventories, Purchases, and Gross Margin Estimates of Merchant Wholesalers **and** Current Business Reports. Revised Monthly Wholesale Trade, Sales and Inventories, 0741-7268.
  Desc: Presents revised, seasonally adjusted and unadjusted estimates of monthly merchant wholesalers' sales, inventories on a non-LIFO ("last in - first out") basis, and stock-sale ratios, by kind-of-business groups.

LC HF5421 .C87
DD 381.2
US
TITLE CHANGE

CURRENT BUSINESS REPORTS. WHOLESALE TRADE, ANNUAL SALES AND YEAR-END INVENTORIES, PURCHASES, AND GROSS MARGIN ESTIMATES OF MERCHANT WHOLESALERS. Added/Corp United States. Bureau of the Census. **VFOAT** Wholesale Trade, Annual Sales and Year-End Inventories, Purchases, and Gross Margin Estimates of Merchant Wholesalers. (1983)-(19??). English. US Department of Commerce / Bureau of the Census, Data User Services Division, Customer Services, Washington DC 20233-0800. **Tel** (301)763-4100. **Formed by the union of** Current Business Reports. Wholesale Trade, Annual Sales, and Year-End Inventories of Merchant Wholesalers. **Merged with** Current Business Reports. Revised Monthly Wholesale Trade, Sales and Inventories **to form** Current Business Reports. Combined Annual and Revised Monthly Wholesale Trade, 1073-0079.

ISSN 1019-2530
SA
UDC 38

CURRENT COMMERCIAL CASES. [Curr. commer. cases]. (1992)-. Periodical. English. Six times a year. $87.98. Law Publisher, PO Box 59502, Kengray 2100 South Africa. **Tel** 27 11 3375380, FAX 27 11 3376634. **ED** M Stranex. cum. index.

LC HF37.C9 C93
XR
CODEN CBUTEM

●**CZECH BUSINESS AND TRADE.**
Added/Corp Czech Republic. Ministry of Industry and Trade. **VFOAT** CBT. (1994)-. Trade Publication. English. Twelve times a year. $84.40. Czech Ministry of Industry and Trade, Prague Czech Republic. **(Subscription address:** Artia Pegas Press Ltd., Palac Metro Narodni Trida 25, 11210 Prague 1 Czech Republic. **Tel** 011 42 2 24196265, 011 42 2 24196266.) **ED** Pavla Podskalska. **Continues** Czech Foreign Trade, 1210-5546.

LC Newspaper
ISSN 0279-4195
US

DAILY COMMERCE. (198?)-. Newspaper. English. Five times a week (Mon.-Fri.). $192.00. Daily Journal Corporation, 915 East First Street, Los Angeles CA 90012. **Tel** (213)229-5300, FAX (213)680-3682. **ED** Gerald L. Salzman. Index available. **Bk Rev**. **Ad Acc**. **Circ:** 8,084. available on microfilm. **Continues** Los Angeles Daily Journal of Commerce.

US

DAILY INFORMATION BULLETIN.
Main/Corp Chicago Mercantile Exchange. (19??)-. Bulletin. English. Seven times a week. $140.00. Chicago Mercantile Exchange, 30 South Wacker Drive, Chicago IL 60606. **Tel** (312)930-8210.

NO

DAILY NORWEGIAN PRESS DIGEST. (19??)-. Norwegian. Seven times a week. Kr8700. Translatorservice AS, Strandkaien 2, Postboks 749, N 4001 Stavanger Norway. **ED** Steinar Lone. **Circ:** 60. available via fax; available via electronic mail.
  Desc: Summary of business news from Norway, especially oil industry news.

LC HD9275.A1 M54
DD 338.1/77/021
FR

●**DAIRY SECTOR INDICATORS = INDICATEURS DU SECTEUR LAITIER.** See Agriculture-Dairy Industry.

LC HF3886 .A23
UA

DALIL AL-QITAAT AL-INTAJIYAH WA-AL-SHARIKAT. Arabic. 11 Falaki Circle, Al-Qahirah United Arab Republic.

LC HF3641 .D35
ISSN 0070-2781
DD 382/.09489/00212
DK

DANMARKS VAREINDFRSEL OG -UDFRSEL. Added/Corp Danmarks Statistik. Denmark. Statistiske Departement. **VFOAT** Foreign Trade of Denmark; External Trade of Denmark. (1959)-. Danish (English). One time a year. kr320.20. Danmarks

Statistik, Sejrgade 11, DK-2100 Copenhagen Denmark. **Tel** 011 45 3 9173917, FAX 011 45 31 18 48 01, telex 1 62 36.

DD 381   ISSN 1195-8642   CN
●**DETAIL (MONTREAL).** (DETAIL.). [D,etail]. (1994)-. Periodical. French. Four times a year. 16.01Can$. Editions Info Presse, 4316 boulevard Saint-Laurent, Bureau 400, Montreal Quebec H2W 1Z3 Canada. **Tel** (514)842-5873.

LC HF240.K27 J3a   ISSN 0303-8629
DD 354/.54/60082   II
DETAILED DEMAND FOR GRANTS OF INDUSTRIES & COMMERCE DEPARTMENT. GOVERNMENT OF JAMMU AND KASHMIR. (DETAILED DEMAND FOR GRANTS OF INDUSTRIES AND COMMERCE DEPARTMENT.). **Main/Corp** Jammu and Kashmir (India). Dept. of Industries & Commerce. **VAT** Detailed Demand for Grants of Industries and Commerce Department. Government of Jammu and Kashmir. (19??)-. English. Ranbir Government Press / Industries and Commerce, Jammu and Kashmir, Industries and Commerce Department, Jammu India.

ISSN 0168-0021
UDC 339.3   NE
DETAILHANDEL MAGAZINE. [Detailhand. mag.]. (1982)-. Periodical. Dutch. Twenty-six times a year. $119.91. Hoofdbedrijfschap Detailhandel, AFD Intern Zaken, Postbus 90703, 2509 Lss Den Haag, Netherlands. **Tel** 011 31 70 3529800. *Continues Detailhandelsbulletin, 0167-031X.*

ISSN 1185-9687
DD 382/.971073   CN
DIFFERENDS COMMERCIAUX ENTRE LE CANADA ET LES ETATS-UNIS. [Differ. commer. entre Can. E.-U.]. **Added/Corp** Canada. Bibliotheque du Parlement. Service de Recherche. (Jan 1991)-. Periodical. French.

LC JX1757.B35 B37
DD 351.8/92/0972981   BB
DIPLOMATIC AND CONSULAR LIST. **Main/Corp** Barbados. Ministry of Foreign Affairs and International Trade. English. Ministry of Foreign Affairs Barbados, 3rd Floor, Marine House, Hastings Christ Church, Bridgetown Barbados. *Continues Barbados Diplomatic and Consular List.*

ISSN 0082-5735
UK
DIPLOMATIC PRESS SUDAN TRADE DIRECTORY, THE. **VFOAT** Trade Directory of the Republic of the Sudan; Sudan Trade Directory. 1st Ed. (1957/58)-. Directory. English. One time a year. Arthur H Thrower Ltd, 44-46 South Ealing Road, Ealing London W5 United Kingdom.

ISSN 1017-2734
US
CEASED
DIRECTION OF TRADE STATISTICS (ELECTRONIC ED.). (DIRECTION OF TRADE STATISTICS [COMPUTER FILE].). [Dir. trade stat.]. **Added/Corp** International Monetary Fund. International Monetary Fund. General Statistics Division. **VFOAT** DOTDATA; DOTS. (19??)-(19??). Periodical. English. International Monetary Fund, 700 19th Street Northwest, Publishing Unit, Washington DC 20431. **Tel** (202)623-7430, FAX (202)623-7201.

LC HF1016 .I652a   ISSN 0252-306X
DD 382/.0212
TITLE CHANGE
DIRECTION OF TRADE STATISTICS - INTERNATIONAL MONETARY FUND (MONTHLY EDITION). *See* Business and Economics-Abstracting, Bibliographies and Statistics.

LC HF1016 .I652a
DD 382/.0212   US
●**DIRECTION OF TRADE STATISTICS QUARTERLY.** *See* Business and Economics-Abstracting, Bibliographies and Statistics.

LC HF91 .I65   ISSN 0252-3019
DD 382/.0212   US
DIRECTION OF TRADE STATISTICS. YEARBOOK - INTERNATIONAL MONETARY FUND. *See* Business and Economics-Abstracting, Bibliographies and Statistics.

LC HD2868 .B36a   ISSN 0196-7622
DD 338.8/8973/0493   US
DIRECTORY - BELGIAN AMERICAN CHAMBER OF COMMERCE IN THE UNITED STATES, INC, THE. *See* Business and Economics-Chamber of Commerce.

LC HF3291.8 D57
DD 338.6/025/7287   PN
DIRECTORY DE EXPORTADORES. **Added/Corp** Instituto Panameno de Comercio Exterior. **VFOAT** Export Directory; Exporters Directory. Directory. Spanish (English). *Continues Directorio de Exportadores de Panama.*

LC HF5421.5.L29 D57   ISSN 8755-3821
DD 382/.025   US
DIRECTORY OF DISTRIBUTORS. (DIRECTORY OF DISTRIBUTORS : LATIN AMERICA, AFRICA, ASIA, MIDDLE EAST.). [Dir. distrib.]. Directory. English. One time a year. International Publications Inc, 15 Ketchum Street, Westport CT 06880.

LC HD9666.3 .D573   ISSN 1054-3082
DD 381/.456151/02573   US
DIRECTORY OF HIGH VOLUME INDEPENDENT DRUG STORES. [Dir. high vol. indep. drug stores]. **VFOAT** Chain Store Guide Directory of High Volume Independent Drug Stores. 1st Ed. (1991/92)-. Directory. English. $269.00. Business Guides Inc, 425 Park Avenue, New York NY 10022. **Tel** (212)371-9400, FAX (212)838-9487.

SI
DIRECTORY OF INDONESIAN IMPORTERS & EXPORTERS. **Added/Corp** World-Wide Import-Export Promotion Centre. **VFOAT** Directory of Indonesian Importers and Exporters. (19??)-. Directory. English. Irregular. 300.00Sing$. World Wide Impt Export Prom Ct, PO Box 503, Marine Parade PO, Singapore 9144 Singapore. **Tel** 011 65 2943069, 011 65 2927550, FAX 011 65 2413982.

US
DIRECTORY OF KEY CONTACTS AND SERVICES / COMMERCE DEPARTMENT. **VFOAT** Commerce Department Directory of Key Contacts and Services. 1980-. Government Publication. English. One time a year. US Department of Commerce, 14th Street & Constitution Avenue NW, Washington DC 20230. **Tel** (202)482-2000, FAX (202)482-3772. *Continues Commerce Department Resources and Services for Economic Development.*

LC TD785
DD 628.4   UK
●**DIRECTORY OF LANDFILL TECHNOLOGY AND ORGANIC WASTE.** *See* Environmental Issues-Pollution and Waste Management.

US
DIRECTORY OF LEADING US EXPORT MANAGEMENT COMPANIES. (19??)-. Directory. English. One time a year. $65.00. Todd Publications, 18 North Greenbush Road, West Nyack NY 10994. **Tel** (914)358-6213, FAX (914)358-6213. **Circ:** 5,000.
Desc: Contains information on hundreds of export management companies who annually export billions of dollars worth of products and equipment to every country in the world.

LC HF5421 .D57   ISSN 1049-6076
DD 382/.2/025764   US
CEASED
DIRECTORY OF TEXAS WHOLESALERS. [Dir. Tex. wholes.]. **Added/Corp** University of Texas at Austin. Bureau of Business Research. (1989)-(1994). Directory. English. Every 2 years. $70.00 (two-year). Bureau of Business Research / Texas, University of Texas at Austin, Box 7459, Austin TX 78713. **Tel** (512)471-1616.

LC HF3011 .D63   ISSN 1057-6878
DD 382/.6/029473 382   US
CCC
DIRECTORY OF UNITED STATES EXPORTERS. [Dir. U. S. export.]. (1991)-. Periodical. English. One time a year. $399.00. Journal of Commerce Inc., 445 Marshall Street, Phillipsburg NJ 08865. **Tel** (800)222-0356, (908)859-1300. *Continues in part United States Importers & Exporters Directory, 1057-512X.*
Desc: Lists complete names, address, telephone and fax numbers, names of key executives, country of destination, port and products exported. All products are listed by harmonized commodity codes used by the customs department.

LC HF3012 .D54   ISSN 1057-5111
DD 382/.6/029473   US
DIRECTORY OF UNITED STATES IMPORTERS (1991). (DIRECTORY OF UNITED STATES IMPORTERS.). [Dir. U. S. import.]. (1991)-. Directory. English. One time a year. $399.00. Journal of Commerce Inc., 445 Marshall Street, Phillipsburg NJ 08865. **Tel** (800)222-0356, (908)859-1300. *Continues in part United States Importers & Exporters Directory, 1057-512X.*

LC HF3623 .D56   ISSN 0742-9118
DD 354.470082/7/025   US
DIRECTORY OF USSR FOREIGN TRADE ORGANIZATIONS AND OFFICIALS. [Dir. USSR foreign trade organ. off.]. **Added/Corp** United States. Central Intelligence Agency. National Foreign Assessment Center (U.S.) United States. Central Intelligence Agency. Directorate of Intelligence. **VFOAT** Directory of U.S.S.R. Foreign Trade Organizations and Officials. **VAT** Directory of Union of Soviet Socialist Republics Foreign Trade Organizations and Officials. (19??)-. Directory. English. Irregular. Document Expediting Project, Exchange and Gift Division, Library of Congress, Photoduplication Service, Washington DC 20540. **Tel** (202)287-9527. available on microfiche (Vols. for (Jan. 1984)- distributed to depository libraries). *Continues Directory of USSR Ministry of Foreign Trade Officials.*

LC HF306 .A452a
DD 382/.0944/07302544361   FR
DIRECTORY / THE AMERICAN CHAMBER OF COMMERCE IN FRANCE. *See* Business and Economics-Chamber of Commerce.

IT
CEASED
DISCIPLINA DEL COMMERCIO. (19??)-(Dec. 1993). Italian. Franco Angeli Riviste SRL, Viale Monza 106, 20127 Milan Italy. **Tel** 011 39 2 2827651, 011 39 2 289562, FAX 011 39 2 258004, telex 051-511650.

US
DISTRICT EXPORT COUNCILS MEMBERSHIP DIRECTORY. **Added/Corp** United States. International Trade Administration. **VFOAT** Membership Directory. (19??)-. Directory. English. Every 2 years. US Department of Commerce / International Trade Administration, 14th Street & Constitution Avenue NW, Hoover Building, Room 3850, Washington DC 20230. **Tel** (202)482-2867, FAX (202)482-5933.

LC Z7164.C8 D63
DD 016.382/0954   II
DOCUMENTATION ON FOREIGN TRADE. Vol. 1 (Jan./June 1972)-. English. Two times a year. Foreign Trade Library, H-24 Green Park Extension, New Delhi 16 India.

LC HE563.U5 A376
DD 386/.244/0973   US
DOMESTIC WATERBORNE TRADE OF THE UNITED STATES. (1965/72)-. English. One time a year. Department of Transportation, 400 Seventh Street SW, Washington DC 20590. **Tel** (202)426-4000. *Continues Domestic Oceanborne and Great Lakes Commerce of the United States.*

LC HF   ISSN 1077-3452
DD 380   US
●**DOT.COM (NORWALK, CONN.).** (DOT.COM.). [Dot.COM]. **VFOAT** Dot. COM. (1994)-. Newsletter. English. Twelve times a year. $295.00. Business Communications Inc, 25 Van Zant Street, Suite 13, Norwalk CT 06855. **Tel** (203)853-4266, FAX (203)853-0348. available via Internet.
Desc: Covers online business. Provides information on advertising, billing, and more.

LC K4 .R594   ISSN 0335-5047
DD 343.08/7   US
CCC
DROIT ET PRATIQUE DU COMMERCE INTERNATIONAL. [Droit prat. commer. int.]. **VFOAT** International Trade Law and Practice. Vol. 1 (Jan. 1975)-. Periodical. Multiple languages (English and French; summaries and/or abstracts in English). Four times a year. $324.80. Masson Editeur, BP 22, 41354 Vineuil Cedex France. **Tel** 011 33 54 504612, FAX 011 33 54 504611. **(Subscription address:** Masson SA, 7A Boulevard de Perolles,, CH-1701 Fribourg Switzerland. **Tel** 011 41 37 249585.) available on microfilm and microfiche from University Microfilms International (UMI). **Ind/Abst** Index Foreign Leg. Per.; PAIS Int. Print.

UK
DRY CARGO MARKET REPORT FOR WEEK ENDING NOON. English. One time a week. Free. Galbraiths Ltd, Shackleton House, 4 Battle Bridge Lane, London SE1 2HY United Kingdom. **Tel** 011 071 378-6363.

TU
DS TICARET ISTATISTIKLERI. *See* Business and Economics-Abstracting, Bibliographies and Statistics.

LC HD9651.9.D8 D76   ISSN 0300-7138
DD 338.7/66/00973   US
DU PONT CONTEXT. [Du Pont context]. **Added/Corp** E.I. du Pont de Nemours & Company. Vol. 1 (1972)-. Periodical. English. Three times a year. E I du Pont du Nemours & Company, External Affairs N2400,

Business and Economics — Commerce

Wilmington DE 19898. **Tel** (302)774-2725. *Supersedes Better Living.*
Ind/Abst GeoRef; Text. Technol. Dig.

LC HF3766.Z8 D823
DD 382/.0953/5
UK
DUBAI ANNUAL TRADE REVIEW. English. One time a year. £1.00. External Development Services, 22 Charing Cross Road, London WC2H 0H United Kingdom.

ISSN 0012-7116
US
DULUTHIAN, THE. Added/Corp Duluth. Chamber of Commerce. Duluth Chamber of Commerce. Annual Report. (Sept. 1924)-. Periodical. English. Seven times a year. $5.00 (nonmembers); $3.00 (members). Duluth Chamber of Commerce, 325 Harbor Drive, Duluth MN 55802. Documents available from UMI Article Clearinghouse.
Ind/Abst Bus. Dateline (Sept. 1991-) [Full Txt.].

UK
DUTY-FREE NEWS INTERNATIONAL. (19??)-. Trade Publication. English. Twenty-four times a year. £230.00. Raven Fox Ltd., 12 Lawn Lane Park Place, London SW8 1UD United Kingdom. **Tel** 011 44 171 7350811. Index available (bound in Jan. issue).

LC HF54.S7 E18
DD 382/.025/5
SP
EADI EAST TRADE DIRECTORY. VFOAT East Trade Directory. (1970)-. Directory. Multiple languages (English, French and Spanish). Irregular. Eadi East Trade Directory, Apartado 14-126, Madrid Spain.

LC HF3626.5 .S682
DD 330.947/005
ISSN 1065-6790
US
CODEN EBTREX
EAST/WEST BUSINESS & TRADE. (EAST/WEST BUSINESS & TRADE : WITH NEWS FROM RUSSIA, THE BALTICS, CENTRAL & EASTERN EUROPE.). [East/West bus. trade]. **VFOAT** East West Business and Trade. Vol. 20, No. 14 (Aug. 15, 1992)-. Periodical. English. Twenty-four times a year. $459.00. Welt Publishing Company, 1413 K Street NW, Suite 1400, Washington DC 20005. **Tel** (202)371-0555, FAX (202)408-9369, telex 281409 TAOA UR. **ED** Walter B. Smith. **Bk Rev**, (Qty: 5 per year). **Ad Acc, Adv Mgr:** Justin Ford. *Absorbed Soviet Business & Trade (1982), 0731-7372 and East West Technology Digest, 0145-1421.*
Ind/Abst Chem. Ind. Notes.

LC HF3626.5 .E16
DD 337
ISSN 1081-8421
US
●**EAST/WEST COMMERSANT. See** Business and Economics-International Economic Relations.

LC HF1532.7 .E373
DD 382/.3/094705
ISSN 1067-635X
US
EAST/WEST EXECUTIVE GUIDE. [East/West exec. guide]. **VFOAT** East West Executive Guide. Vol. 2, No. 1 (Jan. 1992)-. Periodical. English. Twelve times a year. $576.00. WorldTrade Executive Incorporated, PO Box 761, Concord MA 01742. **Tel** (508)287-0301, FAX (508)287-0302. *Continues East Europe/Soviet Union Executive Guide; Absorbed East/West Business Report, 1053-7155; Environment Watch- East Europe, Russia & Eurasia, 1063-5955.*

LC HF499 .E19
DD 382/.09171/301717
ISSN 0376-9186
AU
EAST WEST TRADE INFORMATION BULLETIN. (19??)-. Bulletin. English. Irregular. US East-West Trade Center Etc., Prinz Eugen-Strasse 8 1041, Vienna.

LC HF1410 .E213
DD 382/.091713/01717
ISSN 0195-7503
US
EAST-WEST TRADE, WORLD MARKETS. VFOAT World Markets. **VAT** East West Trade, World Markets. Periodical. English. Robin International, 410 Park Avenue, New York NY 10022.

DD 382
ISSN 1060-2518
US
CCC
CEASED
EASTERN EUROPE FINANCE. [East. Eur. finance]. Vol. 2, No. 8 (Apr. 15, 1991)-(1994). Periodical. English. DP Publications Company, PO Box 7188, Fairfax Station VA 22039. **Tel** (703)425-1322, FAX (703)425-7911, telex 263 128 CTOUR. **ED** Michael Morrison. *Formed by the union of Eastern Europe Times and Creative Trade Finance.*

LC HF3496.5 .E96a
SZ
TITLE CHANGE
ECHANGES DE L'A.E.L.E, LES. Main/Corp European Free Trade Association. **VAT** Echanges de l'Association Europeene de Libre-Echange. (19??)-(19??). French. European Free Trade Association, 9-11 rue de Varembe, CH-1211 Geneva 20 Switzerland. **Tel** 011 41 22 7491111, FAX 011 41 22 339291, telex 22660 EFTA CH. *Continued by EFTA Trade Les Echanges de l'AELE.*

ISSN 1148-1757
FR
UDC 382.6
ECHOS DE L'EXPORTATION PARIS, LES. (LES ECHOS DE L'EXPORTATION.). (1991)-. Periodical. French. Fourteen times a year. $686.79. Les Echos, 46 rue de la Boetie, 75381 Paris Cedex 08 France. **Tel** 011 33 1 49536565. *Continues L'Exportation Magazine (Paris), 0761-2818.*

LC HG4057 .A24
DD 338.8/8
ISSN 0163-4682
US
CEASED
ECONOMIC WORLD DIRECTORY OF JAPANESE COMPANIES IN USA. [Econ. world dir. Jpn. co. USA]. **VFOAT** Directory of Japanese Companies in USA. (1978)-(1993). Directory. English. Economic Salon Ltd, 60 East 42nd Street/Room 734, New York NY 10165. **Tel** (212)986-1588, FAX (212)557-7541. **ED** Yoshimasa Takagi. **Ad Acc. Circ:** 5,000 (ctrl).
Desc: A directory of Japanese companies operating in the United States and their parent firms in Japan; provides revenue and income data, executives, locations, and more.

LU
ECU SME INFORMAZIONI. (19??)-. Italian. Twelve times a year. L79000.00. Office for Official Publications of the European Communities, 2 rue Mercier, 2985 Luxembourg Luxembourg. **Tel** 011 352 499281, FAX 011 352 292942763. **(Subscription address:** Licosa s.p.a., PO Box 552, 50125 Florence Italy. **Tel** 011 39 55 645415.)

DD 382/.6/0971
ISSN 0839-9549
CN
EDC TODAY. [EDC today]. **VFOAT** Actualites de la See. **VAT** Export Development Corporation Today. (May 1983)-. Periodical. English (French). Four times a year. Free on request. Export Development Corporation, 151 O'Conner Street, Box 655, Ottawa Ontario K1A 1K3 Canada. **Tel** (613)598-2784. **Circ:** 23,000 (ctrl). *Continues EDC News, 0383-4212.*
Desc: Designed to promote the financial services available to Canadian exporters from EDC; inform companies about market opportunities; provide advice on the successful export formula.

DD 380/.097123/3
ISSN 0702-7435
CN
EDMONTON COMMERCE AND INDUSTRY. Vol. 3, No. 3 (Aug. 1976)-. Periodical. English. Twelve times a year. 4.01Can$. Edmonton Commerce & Industry, 124th & 215th Inglewood Boulevard, Suite 11802, Edmonton Alberta T5L OM3 Canada. **Tel** (403)454-5540. *Continues Edmonton Commerce, 0702-7443.*

LC HF1531 .E2
ISSN 0012-7655
SZ
EFTA BULLETIN. [EFTA bull.]. **VAT** European Free Trade Association Bulletin. Vol. 1 (Oct. 1960)-. Bulletin. English (French and German). Three times a year. Free. European Free Trade Association, 9-11 rue de Varembe, CH-1211 Geneva 20 Switzerland. **Tel** 011 41 22 7491111, FAX 011 41 22 339291, telex 22660 EFTA CH. **ED** Hansjorg Renk. **Circ:** 26,000. available on microfilm and microfiche from University Microfilms International (UMI). Documents available from UMI Article Clearinghouse.
Ind/Abst ABI/INFORM Glob. Ed.; Acad. Search; Bus. ASAP (1992-) [Full Txt.]; Bus. Index (1984-); Bus. Period. Index; Bus. Source Plus; Bus. Source; EP Collect.; Gen. BusinessFile (1984-); Gen. Period. Index (1985-); Geogr. Abstr. Human Geogr.; Homework Help.; INFO-SOUTH Abstr.; Leis., Rec., Tour. Abstr.; Mag. Search; MasterFile FullTEXT 1000; MasterFile FullTEXT 350; MasterFile FullTEXT 650; MasterFile FullTEXT (Jan. 1994-); OCLC; PAIS Int. Print (1991); Rural Dev. Abstr.; Telebase; Wilson Bus. Abstr.; World Agric. Econ. Rural Sociol. Abstr.; World Text. Abstr.

SZ
CEASED
EFTA NEWS / EFTA. Added/Corp European Free Trade Association. (May 1989)-(1994). English (French and German). European Free Trade Association, 9-11 rue de Varembe, CH-1211 Geneva 20 Switzerland. **Tel** 011 41 22 7491111, FAX 011 41 22 339291, telex 22660 EFTA CH. *Absorbed EFTA Bulletin, 0012-7655.*

ISSN 0531-4119
SZ
EFTA TRADE LES ECHANGES DE L'AELE. Main/Corp European Free Trade Association. **Added/Corp** European Free Trade Association. **VFOAT** Echanges de l'AELE; EFTA-Handel. **VAT** European Free Trade Association trade. (1963)-. Trade Publication. English (French and German; summaries and/or abstracts in French and German). One time a year. Free on request. European Free Trade Association, 9-11 rue de Varembe, CH-1211 Geneva 20

Switzerland. **Tel** 011 41 22 7491111, FAX 011 41 22 339291, telex 22660 EFTA CH. **Circ:** 5,500. *Continues Annual Report of the European Free Trade Association.*
Desc: A statistical analysis of EFTA trade, of interest mainly to economists.

ISSN 0171-2713
GW
UDC 351.82 (094)
EICHGESETZ, FERTIGPACKUNGS-VO. KOMMENTAR. See Public Administration.

LC HF197 .A34
GR
EIDIKON PEIRAMATIKON ERGASTERION (SERIES). (EIDIKON PEIRAMATIKON ERGASTERION : MELETAI.). **VFOAT** Hypourgeion Emporiou, Dieuthynsis Chem. Ereunon, Eidikon Peiramatikon Ergasterion; Hypourgeion Emporiou, Eidikon Peiramatikon Ergasterion; Hypourgeion Emporiou, Dieuthynsis 4E Chemikon Kai Technologikonunon, Eidikon Peiramatikon Ergasterion; Hypourgeion Emporiou, Dieuthynsis Tetarte Chemikon Kai Hnologikon Ereunon, Eidikon Peiramatikon Ergasterion. Monographic series. Greek, Modern (Greek, Modern). Price varies per volume.

LC HA1320 .H529 H3569.H4
DD 314.3
GW
EINFUHR NACH HESSEN, DIE. See Business and Economics-Abstracting, Bibliographies and Statistics.

LC HF3563 .E37
DD 380.1/029/443
ISSN 0343-5881
GW
EINKAUFS-1X1 DER DEUTSCHEN INDUSTRIE. VFOAT Einkaufs-Einxeins der Deutschen Industrie; Einkaufs-Einmaleins der Deutschen Industrie. (19??)-. Directory. German (English and French). One time a year. DM138.00. Deutscher Adressbuch-Verlag fur Wirtschaft und Verkehr GmbH, Dav-Verlagshaus, Arheilger Weg 17, D-64380 Rossdorf Germany. **Tel** 06154 699500, FAX 06154 6995490, telex 4191324 DAV D. Index available. **Ad Acc. Acid Free. Circ:** 21,000 (ctrl). available on CD-ROM. *Continues Deutsches Bundes-Adressbuch Bezugsquellenteil.*
Desc: Buyer's guide that includes 200,000 sources of supply for 70,000 products. Also contains a list of German trade associations and organizations with address and telephone numbers, a list of important German fairs with international participation, and detailed indexes.

LC HF37.P6 E38
PL
EKONOMISTA. (1969)-. Periodical. English (English). Six times a year. $96.00. **(Subscription address:** Ars Polona-Ruch, PO Box 1001, Krakowskie Przedmiescie 7, 00-068 Warsaw Poland. **Tel** 011 48 22 261201.) *Continues Polish Exporter, 0477-2245.*
Ind/Abst Am. Hist. Life (1955-).

LC HF29 .E37
ISSN 0800-6733
NO
EKSPORT AKTUELT / FRA NORGES EKSPORTRAD. Added/Corp Norges Eksportrad. **VFOAT** Eksport Aktuelt Fra Norges Eksportrad. (Jan. 11, 1984)-. Periodical. Norwegian. Irregular (twenty issues yearly). $68.00. Norges Eksportrad, Norweigan Trade Council, 0243 Oslo Norway. **Tel** 011 47 22 92 6300, telex 78532. **ED** Jorn Inge Dorum. **Ad Acc. Circ:** 3,000 (ctrl). *Absorbed Norges Utenrikshandel, 0029-1722.*

ISSN 0900-3177
DK
DD 330.904 8
EKSPORT KOEBENHAVN. (EKSPORT.). [Eksport Kbh.]. (1985)-. Periodical. Danish. One time a week. Udenrigsministeriet Handelsafdelingen, Ministry of Foreign Affairs, Commerce Department, Asiatisk Plads 2, DK-1448 Copenhagen K Denmark. **Tel** FAX 011 45 4 315 40533. **ED** Thorkild Borre. Index available. **Ad Acc. Circ:** 3,700. *Formed by the union of Udenrigsministeriets Tidsskrift (1979), 0106-3952 and Sidste Nyt Fra Eksportmarkederne, 0106-4584.*

ISSN 1071-247X
US
CCC
●**ELECTRONIC MARKETPLACE REPORT.** (1993)-. Periodical. English. Twenty-four times a year. $432.00. SIMBA Information Inc., 213 Danbury Road, PO Box 7430, Wilton CT 06897-7430. **Tel** (203)834-0033 ext. 173, FAX (203)884-1771. **(Subscription address:** Simba Information Inc., PO Box 7430, Wilton CT 06897. **Tel** (203)834-0033 ext. 160, FAX (203)834-1771.) *Continues Electronic Directory & Classified Report.*
Desc: News, analysis, and opinion for the business of electronic shopping and commerce. Covers all forms of electronic marketing.

Business and Economics —Commerce

DD 381
ISSN 1062-9068
US
CEASED
EMBASSY'S MARINE MARKETPLACE.
[Embassy's mar. marketpl.]. **VFOAT** Marine Marketplace. Vol. 1, No. 1 (July 1992)-Vol. 2, No. 3 (March 1993). Periodical. English. Embassy's Marine Marketplace, 142 Ferry Road, Suite 16, Old Saybrook CT 06475. **Tel** (203)395-0188, FAX (203)395-0410.

LC HD9502.J3 J35a

JA
ENERUGI TOKEI GEPPO. See Petroleum and Natural Gas.

LC HF314 .B86
DD 380.1/06/04933
BE
ENTREPRENDRE : REVUE MENSUELLE DE LA CHAMBRE DE COMMERCE DE BRUXELLES. Added/Corp Chambre de Commerce de Bruxelles. Chambre de Commerce et d'Industrie de Bruxelles. Vol. 106 No. 3, (Mar 1980)-. Periodical. French. Twelve times a year. Chambre de Commerce de Bruxelles, rue de Treves 112, 1040 Brussels Belgium. **Continues** Chambre de Commerce de Bruxelles. Bulletin Officiel.

IT
ESPRESSIONI IN VETRINA. Italian. Six times a year. L80000.00. G.B.P. Communications, Via Natale Battaglia 19, 20127 Milan Italy. **Tel** 011 39 2 26140708. **Continues** Vetrina, 0391-5840.

DD 381/.4566553827/09714
ISSN 0844-8698
CN
ESSENCE EXPRESS. (ESSENCE EXPRESS : BULLETIN DU BUREAU D'INSPECTION ET D'INFORMATION DU PRIX DE L'ESSENCE.). [Essence express]. **Added/Corp** Quebec (Province). Bureau d'Inspection et d'Information du Prix de l'Essence. **VFOAT** Bulletin du Bureau d'Inspection et d'Information du Prix de l'Essence. Vol. 1, No. 1 (Nov. 1987)-. Bulletin. French. Twelve times a year. Free on request. Ministere Energie & Resources, 1530 boulevard de Entente, Quebec Quebec G1S 4N6 Canada. **Tel** (418)643-1809.

LC HF3553 .R46
DD 338.7/029/444
FR
●**ESSOR FRANCAIS DU COMMERCE INTERNATIONAL. Added/Corp** Union Francaise d'Annuaires Professionnels. (1993/1994)-. French (English, German and Spanish). One time a year. 950.00F. Union Francaise d'Annuaires Professionnels, 13 Avenue Hennequin, BP 36, 78192 Trappes Cedex France. **Tel** 011 33 1 30506148, FAX 011 33 1 30504827. **Continues** Essor Francais du Commerce Exterieur.

PN
ESTADISTICA PANAMENA. SITUACION ECONOMICA, SECCION 331 : ANUARIO DE COMERCIO EXTERIOR. See Business and Economics-Abstracting, Bibliographies and Statistics.

VE
ESTADISTICAS DEL COMERCIO EXTERIOR DE VENEZUELA; IMPORTACION: ARTICULO Y PAIS. See Business and Economics-Abstracting, Bibliographies and Statistics.

LC HF272.A6 E85
DD 380.1
AO
ESTATISTICAS DO COMERCIO EXTERNO. See Business and Economics-Abstracting, Bibliographies and Statistics.

LC HF46 .E8
DD 382/.0963/005
ISSN 0014-1763
ET
ETHIOPIAN TRADE JOURNAL. Added/Corp Addis Ababa Chamber of Commerce. Ethiopian Chamber of Commerce. **VFOAT** ETJ. Vol. 1, No. 1 (Aug. 1960)-. Trade Publication. English. Three times a year. $16.00. Ethiopian Chamber of Commerce, PO Box 517, Addis Ababa Ethiopia. **Tel** 011 251 1 518240, 011 251 1 448240, FAX 011 251 1 517699, telex 21213. **ED** Getachew Zicke. **Ad Acc. Circ:** 3,000 (ctrl).
Desc: Covers Ethiopian export products, trade relations, markets for Ethiopian products and investments in joint ventures.

IT
ETICA DEGLI AFFARI. Italian. Prospecta SRL, Via Tiziano 11, 20145 Milan Italy.

NE
EURO HOLLAND TRADE. Dutch. Six times a year. Uitgeverij Informa, Postbus 85506, 2508 CE Den Haag Netherlands. **Tel** 011 31 070 3505800.

ISSN 0245-8438
FR
UDC 658.85
EURO P.V. [Euro P.V.]. **VFOAT** Euro Promotion des Ventes. (1978)-. Periodical. French. Seven times a year. $131.23. Euro PV, 41 rue des Bergers, 75015 Paris France. **Tel** 011 33 1 45583276, FAX 1 40600451. **ED** Alain Willard. **Ad Acc. Circ:** 10,000 (ctrl). **Continues** Euro P.V. News, 0245-8446.
Desc: Devoted to sales promotion specialty advertising, and point of purchase advertising.

ISSN 0065-003X
GW
EUROP PRODUCTION. VFOAT ABC Edition, Europ Production. (19??)-. Periodical. Multiple languages (English, French, German, Portuguese and Spanish). One time a year. $211.00. ABC Publishing Group, POB 100262, D 64202 Darmstadt Germany. **Tel** 011 49 6151 38920. (**Subscription address:** Western Hemisphere Publishing Group, PO Box 847, Hillsboro OR 97123.)

LC HF3500.5 .A18
DD 382/.094/005
ISSN 1049-9040
US
EUROPA 1992. [Eur. 1992]. **Added/Corp** American European Trade Group. (1989)-. Periodical. English. Twelve times a year. $175.00 (regular) $275.00 (includes weekly updates). Wolfe Publishing Inc, 210 Daniel Webster Highway South, Nashua NH 03060. **Tel** (508)649-9731, FAX (508)649-6926. **ED** Robert J. Wolfgang.
Desc: Features a list of all major trade shows in Western and Eastern Europe.

LC HF3581 .E9
DD 382/.0945/005
ISSN 0390-2102
IT
EUROPA DOMANI. [Eur. domani]. **VFOAT** Europa Domani; Domani Europa. No. 1 (Feb. 1974)-. Periodical. Italian. Eleven times a year (monthly except Aug.). L47690. Stampa Economica Srl, Vle Lombardia 22, 20131 Milan Italy. **Tel** 011 39 2 712424, FAX 011 39 2 7381191. **Bk Rev**, (Qty: 4-5). **Ad Acc, Adv Mgr:** Diana Giani, **Tel** 70635333. **Circ:** 15,000.
Ind/Abst F&S Index Plus Text, Int. [Select. Cov.]; Infomat Int. Bus.

LC HF3493 .E78
DD 380.1/029/44
FR
EUROPAGES. (19??)-. Directory. English. One time a year. Euredit SA, 9 Avenue de Friedland, 75008 Paris France. **Tel** 1 42 89 34 66.

ISSN 1054-8335
US
EUROPE 1992 AND BEYOND (MINNEAPOLIS, MINN.). (EUROPE 1992 AND BEYOND: ACTION PLAN FOR U.S. EXPORTERS.). (1991)-. English. Four times a year. $195.00 (manual), $150 (quarterly updates). Export USA Publications, PO Box 39264, Minneapolis MN 55439-0264. **Tel** (612)943-1505, FAX (612)943-1535.

LC HD9525.A2 E52
DD 382/.9142/05
ISSN 0191-4545
US
CODEN ERPEDH
EUROPE (WASHINGTON, D.C.). (EUROPE.). [Europe]. **Added/Corp** Commission of the European Communities. Delegation (U.S.). No. 211 (Jan./Feb. 1979)-. Periodical. English. Ten times a year. $19.95. Information Office of the European Community, 2100 M Street NW, 7th Floor, Washington DC 20037. **Tel** (202)862-9555. (**Subscription address:** Neodata / Colorado, PO Box 2606, Boulder CO 80322.) **ED** Webster Martin. **Ad Acc. Circ:** 15,000. available on microfilm and microfiche from University Microfilms International (UMI). Documents available from UMI Article Clearinghouse. **Continues** European Community, 0014-2891.
Desc: Devoted exclusively to detailing relations between the United States and the European Community.
Ind/Abst ABI/INFORM Glob. Ed.; ABI/INFORM [Computer File] (Sept. 1980-); Coal Abstr.; Curr. Cit.; Energy Res. Abstr. (1979-); Int. Labour Doc.; Mag. Search; MasterFile FullTEXT (July 1993-); Newsp. Period. Abstr. (1992-); PAIS Int. Print (1991-); Predicasts Forecasts; UMI ABI/Inform--Bus. Period. Ondisc [Full Txt.].

IT
EUROSCAMBI. (19??)-. Italian. Irregular. L120000. Euroitalia Editrice Srl, Via XX Settembre 37/12, 16121 Genoa Italy. **Tel** 011 39 10 593519, 011 39 10 566648.

BE
EUROTAX. (19??)-. German. Eleven times a year. Eurotax Nederlan, Klauwaertslaan 27, B-1050 Brussels Belgium. **Tel** 011 32 2 6481697. (**Subscription address:** Eurotax AG, Oberdorfstrasse 2, Ch 8808 Pfaeffikon Switzerland. **Tel** 011 41 55 482743.)

IT
EUROTAX AUTOVETTURE. (19??)-. Italian. Twelve times a year. L198000. Sanguinetti Editore, Via Hoepli 7, 20121 Milan Italy. **Tel** 011 39 2 86462726.

IT
EUROTAX FUORISTRADA. (19??)-. Italian. Three times a year. L51100. Sanguinetti Editore, Via Hoepli 7, 20121 Milan Italy. **Tel** 011 39 2 86462726.

IT
EUROTAX NAUTICA. Italian. Two times a year. L38000. Sanguinetti Editore, Via Hoepli 7, 20121 Milan Italy. **Tel** 011 39 2 86462726.

DD 381/.09713/44
ISSN 0824-457X
CN
EXCHANGE (KITCHENER). (EXCHANGE : WATERLOO REGION'S MONTHLY BUSINESS PUBLICATION.). Vol. 1, No. 1 (Oct. 1983)-. Periodical. English. Twelve times a year. 20.95Can$. Exchange, 215 Fairway Road, Kitchener Ontario N2G 4E5 Canada. **Tel** (519)886-2831. **ED** Alan Howell and Doug Hallett. **Ad Acc.** ctrl circ.

ISSN 0212-7350
SP
UDC 339.5
TITLE CHANGE
EXPANSION COMERCIAL. [Expans. comer.]. **VFOAT** Expansion (Madrid). (1983)-(1993). Periodical. Spanish. Inst Espanol Comercio Exterior, Paseo de la Castellana 14, 28046 Madrid Spain. **Tel** 011 34 1 3496100. **Continued by** Expansion Internacional, 1133-8075.
Ind/Abst Infomat Int. Bus.; PROMT.

ISSN 1133-8075
SP
UDC 339.5
●**EXPANSION INTERNACIONAL.** [Expans. int.]. (1994)-. Periodical. Spanish. Eleven times a year. $50.00. Inst Espanol Comercio Exterior, Paseo de la Castellana 14, 28046 Madrid Spain. **Tel** 011 34 1 3496100. **Continues** Expansion Comercial, 0212-7350.

BE
EXPLANATORY NOTES TO THE HARMONIZED SYSTEM. (19??)-. Periodical. English. Irregular (supplements issued 2 times per year). Customs Cooperation Council, rue de l'Industrie 26-38, 1040 Brussels Belgium. **Tel** 011 32 2 5084211. (**Subscription address:** McMullin Publishers Ltd., 1 Trans Border Drive, Champlain NY 12919. **Tel** (514)849-1424.) Index available. **Continues** Explanatory Notes of the Brussels Nomenclature.
Desc: Gives list of main products included and excluded, together with technical descriptions of the goods concerned and practical guidance for their identification. Where appropriate, the journal also clarifies the scope of particular subheadings.

ISSN 0757-4223
FR
UDC 061.4
EXPO NEWS. (1983)-. Periodical. French. One time a week (42 issues plus supplement). $349.95. Expo News, WTC-CNIT BP 437, 92053 Paris la Defense France. **Tel** 011 33 1 46921925, FAX 011 33 1 46921950. **ED** Jean Dominique. **Ad Acc.**

LC KF1987.A329 Q45
DD 343.73/0878/05
US
EXPORT ADMINISTRATION REGULATIONS. See Law.

LC HF3223 .E9
DD 382/.6/02571
ISSN 0708-1332
CN
EXPORT CANADA. (1978)-. English. One time a year. CANEX Enterprises Inc., 6199 136 Street, Surrey British Columbia V3W 6E5 Canada.

DD 382
ISSN 1058-2533
US
EXPORT COMMUNICATIONS : EC. [Export commun.]. **VFOAT** EC. Vol. 1, No. 1 (Fall 1991)-. Periodical. English. Four times a year. $48.00. Artisto Marketing Corporation, Weybossett Station, PO Box 23391, Providence RI 02903-0397.

LC HF1455 .E88
DD 382/.64/097305
ISSN 0896-0682
US
EXPORT CONTROL NEWS. [Export control news]. **Added/Corp** MK Technology Associates. **VFOAT** ECN. Vol. 1, No. 1 (May 1987)-. Newsletter. English. Twelve times a year. $350.00 (one-year), $650.00 (two-year) US; $390.00 (one-year), $730.00 (two-year) other. Export Control News, 1920 North Street NW, Suite 600, Washington DC 20036. **Tel** (202)463-1250, FAX (202)429-9812, telex 650 3140 383. **ED** Erik Wemple (editor's phone: (202)463-0904). **Ad Acc. Circ:** 1,000. available on an online database (file 636/Full-Text) from DIALOG.
Desc: Provides reports of all legislative, regulatory and policy developments in US export controls and export licensing.
Ind/Abst PTS Newsl. Database [Full Txt.].

LC HF3643 .K6
DK
●**EXPORT DENMARK : KONGERIGET DANMARKS HANDELS- OG EKSPORTKALENDER. VFOAT** Kongeriget Danmarks Handels- og Eksportkalender. (1994)-. Periodical. Danish (English, French, German and Spanish). Mntergade 19, 1116 Copenhagen Denmark. **Continues** Kongeriget Danmarks Handels-Kalender (Copenhagen, Denmark : 1965), 0302-5403.

CL
Pr Rev.
EXPORT DIRECTORY OF CHILE. GUIA CHILENA DE LA EXPORTACION. **Added/Corp** Instituto de Promocion de Exportaciones de Chile. **VFOAT** Guia Chilena de la Exportacion. (1977)-. Directory. English (French, Spanish and German). One time a year. Free on request. Export Directory of Chile, Baldivia 0193 2nd Floor, Santiago Chile. **Tel** (011 56 2)696-0043, FAX (011 56 2)696-0639. **Ad Acc, Adv Mgr:** ITV, **Tel** 232-4316. **Circ:** 15,000 (ctrl). available on diskette.
Desc: This publication registers export companies that have sold over $30,000 in the previous year.

ISSN 1065-6677
DD 382 US
EXPORT EN ESPANOL. **See** Heating, Plumbing, and Refrigeration.

UK
EXPORT FINANCE. **See** Insurance.

ISSN 0970-6186
II
UDC 382.6
EXPORT GAZETTE. [Export Gaz.]. (1978)-. Periodical. English. Twelve times a year. $40.00. Amalgamated Press / India, Narang House 2nd Floor 41 Ambalal, Bombay 400 023 India. **Tel** 011 91 22 270268, 011 91 22 274184. ***Continues*** *Afrasian Markets, 0001-9712.*
Desc: Publication for trade promotion, facilitating contacts between companies and individuals involved in international trade.

LC HF41 .A35
DD 382/.05 II
EXPORT GAZETTE. Vol. 20 (Jan. 1975)-. Periodical. English. Twelve times a year. $40.00. Amalgamated Press / India, Narang House 2nd Floor 41 Ambalal, Bombay 400 023 India. **Tel** 011 91 22 270268, 011 91 22 274184. **ED** Norman da Silva. **Bk Rev. Ad Acc.** Full Page (B&W) Rs4,000 India; $350.00 US. Half Page (B&W) Rs2,500 India; $225.00 US. **Circ:** 8,000 (ctrl). ***Continues*** *Afrasian Markets.*
Desc: Carries export-import information and inquiries.

LC HF3493 .E86 **ISSN** 0269-7777
DD 382/.025/4 US
CEASED
EXPORT GUIDE TO EUROPE, THE. [Export guide Eur.]. **Added/Corp** World Trade Intelligence (Firm) Gale Research Company. (1986/1987)-1986 Edition. English. Gale Research Inc., 835 Penobscot Building, 645 Griswold Street, Detroit MI 48226. **Tel** (800)877-GALE, (313)961-2242, FAX (313)961-6083, (800)414-5043, telex TWX 810-221-7086.

LC HF3851 .E88
DD 382/.6/0255125 HK
EXPORT HONG KONG. (19??)-. English. Export Hong Kong, PO Box 33458, Cheung Wan Hong Kong.

LC HF3230.5.A48 E95 **ISSN** 0270-5184
DD 382/.029/48 PR
EXPORT-IMPORT MARKETS. **VAT** Export Import Markets. English (Spanish). One time a year. Witcom Group Inc., El Caribe Building/15th Floor, San Juan Puerto Rico 00901. **Tel** (809)725-8075.

LC HF3851 .E9
DD 382/.6/0255125 HK
EXPORT INTERNATIONAL. (19??)-. Periodical. English. Irregular. $35.00. Pearl Publications, PO Box 33749, Southwest Hong Kong.

ISSN 1064-1513
DD 382 US
EXPORT LEADS. [Export leads]. Vol. 1, No. 1 (Aug. 1989)-. English. Twelve times a year. $85.00. Export Leads, 1741 Kekamek Northwest, Poulsbo WA 98370. **Tel** (206)779-1511, FAX (206)697-4696. **Ad Acc, Adv Mgr:** Barbara MacIntyre, **Tel** (206)779-1511. **Circ:** 2,000.
Desc: Provides trade leads for exporters and importers.

ISSN 0014-519X
DD 382 US
EXPORT (NEW YORK, N.Y.). **See** Heating, Plumbing, and Refrigeration.

ISSN 0713-0341
DD 382/.6/0971 CN
EXPORT NEWS (OTTAWA). (EXPORT NEWS / CANADIAN EXPORT ASSOCIATION / ASSOCIATION CANADIENNE D'EXPORTATION.). [Export news]. **Added/Corp** Canadian Export Association. Canadian Exporters' Association. **VFOAT** Export Digest. No. 688/89 (July/Aug. 1981)-. Periodical. English (French). Twenty-four times a year. 92.04Can$. Canadian Export Association, 99 Bank Street, Suite 250, Ottawa Ontario K1P 6B9 Canada. **Tel** (613)238-8888. ***Continues*** *Export News Bulletin, 0316-7631;* ***Absorbed*** *Export U.S.A., 0712-2349; Export Digest, 0713-0376.*

LC HF **ISSN** 0113-1338
DD 382.6099305 NZ
UDC 38
EXPORT NEWS (WELLINGTON). (EXPORT NEWS.). [Export news Wellingt.]. (1957)-. Periodical. English. Twenty-six times a year. $66.22. Headliner, PO Box 3762, Christchurch New Zealand. **Tel** 011 64 3 3650301. ***Absorbed*** *EN. Export News New Zealand, 0112-3408.*

LC HF1717.P18 E95
DD 343.549105/6/05 PK
EXPORT POLICIES, REBATES, PROCEDURES, RULES AND NOTIFICATIONS. 12th Ed. (Feb. 1989)-. English. Irregular. Pioneer Book House, Opp Dow Medical College M A, Jinnah Road, Karachi Pakistan. ***Continues*** *Export Rebates.*

ISSN 0730-5176
US
EXPORT REPORT. **See** Forests and Forestry-Lumber and Wood.

LC HF1416.5 .E9 **ISSN** 1054-8327
DD 658.8/48/05 US
Pr Rev.
EXPORT SALES AND MARKETING MANUAL. [Export sales mark. man.]. 1st Ed. (1987)-. Trade Publication. English. One time a year. $298.50. Export USA Publications, PO Box 39264, Minneapolis MN 55439-0264. **Tel** (612)943-1505, FAX (612)943-1535. **ED** George Donnelly. Index available. **Bk Rev.** ctrl circ.
Desc: Contains special features on North American Free Trade Agreement (NAFTA), ISO 9000 Product Standard Series, European Community (EC) and a step-by-step business plan showing how to become a successful export agent. Contains 100 pages of sources of export information, a glossary of terms and acronyms used in foreign trade and a cross-referenced index. Includes illustrations, flow charts, worksheets, sample contracts and examples of effective international correspondence.

LC HF41 .E9 **ISSN** 0257-8018
DD 382/.0954 II
EXPORT TIMES (NEW DELHI), THE. (THE EXPORT TIMES.). [Export times]. Vol. 1 (Dec. 1973)-. Periodical. English. Rs40.00 India; $20.00 other. S S Gandhi, 221 3 Deendayal Upadhyaya Marg, New Delhi 110002 India. **Tel** 331-7491. **ED** R R Diwakar and Mahendra Agrawal. **Bk Rev. Ad Acc. Circ:** 1,100. available on an online database (files 771,772/Full-Text) from DIALOG. Documents available from UMI Article Clearinghouse.
Desc: A journal of Gandhi Peace Foundation which seeks to probe Gandhian perspectives on the various current, national and international problems and to promote normative approaches to their analyses through free discussion by eminent thinkers and activists in diverse fields of human endeavour all over the world.
Ind/Abst ABI/INFORM Glob. Ed.; Int. Packag. Abstr.; Manage. Market. Abstr.

LC HF1455 .E934 **ISSN** 0882-4711
DD 382/6/097305 US
CCC
EXPORT TODAY. [Export today]. Vol. 1, No. 1 (Spring 1985)-. Trade Publication. English. Twelve times a year. $64.00. Export Today, 733 15th Street Northwest, Suite 1100, Washington DC 20005. **Tel** (202)737-1060, FAX (202)783-5966. **ED** Leah Young; (202)737-3156. **Ad Acc, Adv Mgr:** Pat Steele. **Circ:** 41,000 (ctrl).
Desc: Information for current and potential exporters in all areas of trade: taxes, tariffs, shipping, marketing, insurance, government policy and regulation, financing, etc.

LC HF1589 .A32
DD 382/.6/0954 II
EXPORT TRADE CONTROL HAND-BOOK OF POLICY AND PROCEDURE. **Main/Corp** India. Ministry of Commerce. 3rd Ed. (1974)-. English. ***Continues*** *India (Republic). Ministry of Foreign Trade. Export Trade Control.*

LC Discard **ISSN** 0278-1646
US
EXPORT TRADE REPORTER. (EXPORT TRADE REPORTER : ETR.). [Export trade report.]. **VFOAT** ETR; E.T.R. Vol. 1, No. 1 (Jan. 15, 1982)-. English. Irregular. $147.00. Export Trade Reporter, 1524 31st Street Northwest, Washington DC 20007.

LC HF1416.5 .E9 **ISSN** 1055-8365
DD 382 US
EXPORT YELLOW PAGES, THE. [Export yellow pages]. **Added/Corp** United States. International Trade Administration. Office of Export Trading Company Affairs. US West Communications (Firm). (1991)-. English. Free. Venture Publishing, 600 Watergate NW, Washington DC 20037.

CF
EXPORTATEUR CONGOLAIS : REVUE TRIMESTRIELLE DU CENTRE CONGOLAIS DU COMMERCE EXTERIEUR, L'. **Added/Corp** Centre Congolais du Commerce Exterieur. (1983)-. French. Four times a year. Centre Congolais du Commerce Exterieur, B P 127, Brazzaville R P Congo. ***Continues*** *Centre Congolais du Commerce Exterieur. Bulcomex.*

ISSN 0713-0368
DD 382/.6/0971 CN
EXPORTATIONS NOUVELLES. [Export. nouv.]. No. 688/689 (July/Aug. 1981)-. Periodical. French. Twelve times a year. Exportations Nouvelles, c/o Association Canadienne d'Exportation, Bureau 250/99 rue Bank, Ottawa Ontario K1P 6B9 Canada. ***Continues*** *Bulletin de Nouvelles (Association Canadienne d'Exportation), 0713-035X;* ***Absorbed*** *Exportations Etats-Unis, 0712-2357; Exportations Analyse, 0713-0392.*

ISSN 0736-9239
US
CCC
EXPORTER (NEW YORK, N.Y.), THE. (THE EXPORTER.). [Exporter]. (1980)-. Trade Publication. English. Twelve times a year. $160.00. Trade Data Reports, 34 West 37th Street, New York NY 10018. **Tel** (212)563-2772, FAX (212)563-2798. **ED** Leslie Stroh.

CR
EXPORTERS. **Added/Corp** Centro para la Promocion de las Exportaciones y las Inversiones (Costa Rica). **VFOAT** Costa Rican Export Directory. 9th Ed. (1990)-. English (Spanish). ***Continues*** *Exportadores.*

LC HF3011 .E9 **ISSN** 8755-013X
DD 382/.6/02573 US
EXPORTERS' ENCYCLOPAEDIA, (1982). (EXPORTERS' ENCYCLOPAEDIA.). [Export. encycl.]. **Added/Corp** Dun's Marketing Services. Dun & Bradstreet International. 77th Ed. (1982)-. English. One time a year. $565.00. Dun & Bradstreet Information Services, 3 Sylvan Way, Parsippany NJ 07054. **Tel** (201)605-6000, (800)526-0651. ***Continues*** *Exporters' Encyclopaedia. World Marketing Guide, 0732-0159.*

LC HC121 .E87
DD 382/.6/0972 PR
EXPORTERS GUIDE. 1.- 1977/78-. Multiple languages (English and Spanish).

LC HC121 .E87
PR
EXPORTERS GUIDE & KEY BUSINESS DIRECTORY - CARIBBEAN & LATIN AMERICA. GUIA DEL EXPORTADOR Y DIRECTOR DE EMPRESAS CLAVES - CARIBE Y AMERICA LATINA. **VFOAT** Guia del Exportador y Director de Empresas Claves - Caribe y America Latina. **VAT** Exporters Guide and Key Business Directory - Caribbean and Latin America. 2nd Ed. (1979)-. Periodical. English (Spanish). One time a year. $60.00. Witcom Group Inc., El Caribe Building/15th Floor, San Juan Puerto Rico 00901. **Tel** (809)725-8075. ***Continues*** *Exporters Guide.*

LC HF3011 .E95 **ISSN** 1062-3191
DD 382/.6/029473 US
EXPORTERS RESOURCES DIRECTORY. **See** Industry and Production-Trade and Industrial Directories.

US
EXPORTING COMPUTERS WITHOUT A VALIDATED LICENSE. (1989)-. English. Irregular. $245.00. Comp-Tech Export Publications, PO Box 1367, Bethesda MD 20827-1367. **Tel** (301)983-3339, FAX (301)983-9035.
Desc: Analyzes the Computer Export Regulations. Devotes 60 pages to 25 peripheral devices and decontrolled computers and examines 12 General Licenses applicable to computer export regulations. Provides examples, tables, and clarifications of terms throughout the text and explains how to export computers or computer-related equipment without a license.

LC HF129 .A34 **ISSN** 1181-6724
DD 382/.6/0971021 CN
EXPORTS BY COUNTRIES (OTTAWA). (EXPORTS BY COUNTRIES.). [Exports ctries.]. **Added/Corp** Canada. Dominion Bureau of Statistics. External Trade Division. Statistics Canada. External Trade Division. Statistics Canada. International Trade Division. **VFOAT** Exports by Country; Exportations par Pays; Exports by Country (H.S. Based); Exportations par Pays (Base du S.H.). **VAT** Exportations par Pays (Ottawa). Vol. 19, No. 1 (Jan./March 1962)-. Periodical. English (French). Four times a year. 360.00Can$ Canada; $432.00 US; $504.00 other. Statistics Canada

Business and Economics —Commerce

Publications Sales and Services, R.H. Coats Building 6th Floor, Ottawa Ontario K1A 0T6 Canada. **Tel** (613)951-5078, (800)267-6677, FAX (613)951-1584, telex 053-3585. **Continues** Trade of Canada. Commodities Exported to Each Country, 0703-0541.
 Desc: Contains domestic export data (values only) by countries and commodity categories showing three-year figures of latest and proceeding quarter together with cumulative year-to-date totals.

LC HF1414.5 ISSN 0844-8361
DD 382/.6/0971 CN
EXPORTS, MERCHANDISE TRADE, H.S. BASED.
(EXPORTS, MERCHANDISE TRADE (H.S. BASED).). [Exports merch. trade H.S. based]. **Added/Corp** Statistics Canada. International Trade Division. **VFOAT** Exportations, Commerce de Marchandises (Base du S.H.). (1988)-. English (French). One time a year. 180.00Can$ Canada; $216.00 US; $252.00 other. Statistics Canada Publications Sales and Services, R.H. Coats Building 6th Floor, Ottawa Ontario K1A 0T6 Canada. **Tel** (613)951-5078, (800)267-6677, FAX (613)951-1584, telex 053-3585. **Continues** Exports, Merchandise Trade, 0317-5375.

LC HG4135 .E96a
DD 332.6/7 UK
EXTEL HANDBOOK OF MARKET LEADERS.
Main/Corp Extel Statistical Services. (19??)-. English. Two times a year (Jan. & July). $359.36. Extel Financial Ltd., Fitzroy House, 13-17 Epworth Street, London EC2A 4DL United Kingdom. **Tel** 011 44 171 8258000, FAX 011 44 171 8258328, telex 884319 EXTELX G. **ED** John Hunt. ctrl circ.
 Desc: Handbook provides financial and other information covering a five year period for the 743 companies making up the FT Actuaries All Share Index.

LC HF3500.5 .A189
DD 382/.094/0021 LU
●EXTERNAL TRADE.
Added/Corp Statistical Office of the European Communities. (1994)-. Periodical. English. Twelve times a year. Office for Official Publications of the European Communities, 2 rue Mercier, 2985 Luxembourg Luxembourg. **Tel** 011 352 499281, FAX 011 352 292942763. **(Subscription address:** Renouf Publishing Company Ltd., 1294 Algoma Road, Ottawa Ontario K1B 3WB Canada. **Tel** (613)741-4333.) **Continues** External Trade and Balance of Payments.

LC HF3500.5 .A189
DD 382/.094/0021 LU
TITLE CHANGE
EXTERNAL TRADE AND BALANCE OF PAYMENTS.
See Business and Economics-Abstracting, Bibliographies and Statistics.

PR
EXTERNAL TRADE STATISTICS, PUERTO RICO.
Added/Corp Puerto Rico. Area of Economic and Social Planning. Puerto Rico. Bureau of Economic Analysis. **VFOAT** Estadisticas de Comercio Exterior. (19??)-. English (Spanish). Government Printing Office / New Zealand, 10 Mulgrave Street, Wellington New Zealand. **Tel** 011 64 4 4737211, FAX 011 64 4 734943, telex GOVPRINT NZ 31320. **Continues** Puerto Rico External Trade Statistics.

LC HF3770.8 .A33
DD 382/.095493/00212 CE
EXTERNAL TRADE STATISTICS, SRI LANKA.
See Business and Economics-Abstracting, Bibliographies and Statistics.

LC HF
DD 380.1 CN
EXTERNAL TRADE ... THROUGH BRITISH COLUMBIA CUSTOMS PORTS.
VFOAT External Trade Report. English. One time a year. **Continues** External Trade Through British Columbia Customs Ports.

LC HD9000.4 .T7 ISSN 1014-7632
DD 380.1/41/021 IT
FAO YEARBOOK, TRADE.
See Business and Economics-Abstracting, Bibliographies and Statistics.

ISSN 0144-8218
DD 609.5 UK
TITLE CHANGE
FAR EASTERN TECHNICAL REVIEW.
[Far East. tech. rev.]. (1979)-(1988). Periodical. English. Alain Charles Publishing Ltd., 27 Wilfred Street, London SW1E 6PR United Kingdom. **Tel** 011 44 171 8347676, FAX 011 44 171 9730076, telex 297165. **ED** David Clancy. **Ad Acc. Circ:** 25,000 (ctrl). **Continues** Far Eastern Technical Review. **Continued by** Asian Review of Business and Technology, 0956-3784.
 Desc: General review of commerce trade and technical development in Asia. Includes all aspects of industry, engineering, and business.

ISSN 1184-7549
DD 380.1/09711 CN
FAX BY TWIGG.
[Fax Twigg]. Vol. 1, No. 1 (Jan. 16, 1991)-. Periodical. English. Twenty-four times a year. 120.00Can$ in Victoria Canada; 240.00Can$ other.

Maitland Publications, 7 Cook Street, Victoria BC V8V 3W6 Canada. **Tel** (604)360-4053, FAX (604)360-0548. **(Subscription address:** Monday Publications, 1609 Blanshard Street, Victoria, British Columbia, V8W 2J5 Canada. **Tel** (604)382-6188, (800)661-6335.) **ED** John Twigg. **Continues** John Twigg's Feature Report., 0843-4387.

LC HD9259.P73 U545 ISSN 0737-4852
DD 380.1/4566480421 US
FINAL STATISTICAL REPORT - CALIFORNIA. PRUNE MARKETING COMMITTEE.
See Business and Economics-Abstracting, Bibliographies and Statistics.

ISSN 1120-9461
UDC 658.1 IT
FINANZA IMPRESE E MERCATI.
(1989)-. Periodical. Italian. Three times a year. L64000.00 Italy; L110000.00 (surface mail), L140000.00 (airmail) other. Societa Editrice il Mulino, Strada Maggiore 37, 40125 Bologna Italy. **Tel** 011 39 51 256011, FAX 011 39 51 256034.

LC HF25 .F5 ISSN 0015-2463
DD 382/.094897/005 FI
CEASED
FINNISH TRADE REVIEW.
Added/Corp Suomen Ulkomaankauppaliitto. (March 1930)-(Dec. 1993). Periodical. English (French, Spanish, German, Italian, Hungarian, Chinese, Japanese and Turkish). Finnish Foreign Trade Association, PO Box 908, Arkadiankatu 4-6 BSF, 00101 Helsinki 10 Finland. **Tel** 011 358 0 69591, FAX 011 358 0 694-0028, telex 121696. **ED** Elina Joensuu, Danuta Manninen and Risto Pitkanen. Index available. **Ad Acc. Circ:** 25,000 (ctrl). available on an online database (file 648/Full-Text) from DIALOG. **Supersedes** Finnish Trade.
 Desc: Concerned with different fields of the Finnish export industry.
 Ind/Abst F&S Index Plus Text, Int. [Select. Cov.]; PROMT; Selec. Coop. Index Manage. Period.; Trade Ind. ASAP [Full Txt.]; Trade Ind. Index [Full Txt.].

LC HF1040 ISSN 1358-5754
DD 338.02 UK
●FIS DIRECTORY OF U.K. EXPORTERS, THE.
(1995)-. Directory. English. One time a year. £125.00 UK; £135.00 other. FIS Publications Ltd., 32 Vauxhall Bridge Road, London SW1V 2SS United Kingdom. **Tel** 011 44 171 9736402, FAX 011 44 171 2335056. **ED** David Ricketts.

LC HF1040 ISSN 1358-5762
DD 338.02 UK
●FIS DIRECTORY OF U.K. IMPORTERS, THE.
(1995)-. Directory. English. One time a year. £115.00 UK; £125.00 other. FIS Publications Ltd., 32 Vauxhall Bridge Road, London SW1V 2SS United Kingdom. **Tel** 011 44 171 9736402, FAX 011 44 171 2335056. **ED** David Ricketts.

LC HF5482 .F57 ISSN 0364-023X
DD 381 US
FLEA MARKET TRADER.
(1977)-. English. One time a year. $12.95. Collector Books, PO Box 3009, Paducah KY 42002. **Tel** (502)898-6211, (800)626-5420.

LC HF41 .F56 ISSN 0388-0311
DD 338/.0952 JA
FOCUS. JAPAN.
[Focus Jpn.]. **Added/Corp** Nihon Boeki Shinkokai. Vol. 1 (May 1974)-. Periodical. English (English). Twelve times a year. $31.00. Japan External Trade Organization, 2 5 2 Chome Toranomon, Minato-ku Tokyo 107, Japan. **Tel** 011 81 3 3582 5521, FAX 011 81 3 3582 0504, telex J24378. **ED** Hiroshi Nakano. **Circ:** 9,000 (ctrl). Documents available from UMI Article Clearinghouse. **Supersedes** Trade and Industry of Japan, 0041-0381.
 Desc: Information on Japan's business and trade relations, as well as ready-to-use statistics and interviews with business personalities.
 Ind/Abst ABI/INFORM Glob. Ed.; Energy Inf. Abstr.; Int. Packag. Abstr.; Manage. Market. Abstr.

LC HF41 .F564 ISSN 0388-032X
DD 338/.0952 JA
FOCUS JAPAN. NOW IN JAPAN.
[Now Jpn.]. **Added/Corp** Nihon Boeki Shinkokai. **VFOAT** Now in Japan. (19??)-. Periodical. English. Japan External Trade Organization, 2 5 2 Chome Toranomon, Minato-ku Tokyo 107, Japan. **Tel** 011 81 3 3582 5521, FAX 011 81 3 3582 0504, telex J24378.
 Ind/Abst World Text. Abstr.

ISSN 0225-0888
DD 381/.4163/0097123 CN
FOOT NOTES - BEEF AND SHEEP BRANCH (EDMONTON).
(FOOT NOTES.). [Foot notes - Beef Sheep Branch (Edmonton)]. Vol. 1 (Sept. 1979)-. Periodical. English. Twelve times a year. Alberta Agriculture and Rural Development, Beef and Sheep Branch, 7000 113 Street, Edmonton Alberta T6H 5T6 Canada. **Continues in part** Notes and News, 0709-3047.

LC S
DD 630 US
FOREIGN AGRICULTURAL TRADE OF THE UNITED AND STATES FISCAL YEAR ... SUPPLEMENT.
See Agriculture.

LC HD9001 .F654 ISSN 0046-4546
DD 382/.41/0973 US
FOREIGN AGRICULTURAL TRADE OF THE UNITED STATES.
See Agriculture.

LC Z7164.C8 F7 HF54.U5 ISSN 0732-1384
DD 016.382/025 US
FOREIGN FORUM YEARBOOK INTERNATIONAL.
[Foreign forum yearb. int.]. **VFOAT** Foreign Forum. **VAT** Foreign Forum Year Book International. English. Success Publishing, PO Box 296, Estero FL 33928.

US
FOREIGN PROSPECTS.
English. Twelve times a year. $200.00. Thomae & Associates, Box 1056, Seffner FL 33584. **Tel** (813)681-3105. **Continues** International Round Table.

LC HF3561 .F59
DD 382/.0943/00212 GW
FOREIGN TRADE ACCORDING TO THE STANDARD INTERNATIONAL TRADE CLASSIFICATION (SITC)--SPECIAL TRADE.
Added/Corp Germany (West). Statistisches Bundesamt. Germany. Statistisches Bundesamt. **VFOAT** Foreign Trade According to the SITC (Rev.II)--Special Trade. 1st Quarter (1977)-. Statistical Publication. English. Irregular. DM31.60. Metzler Poeschel Verlag Veroeffen, Statist Bundesamt Kernerstr 43, D-70182 Stuttgart Germany. **Tel** 011 49 7071 935350.
 (Subscription address: Metzler Poeschel H Leins GmbH, Postfach 1152, D 72125 Kusterdingen Germany. **Tel** 011 49 7071 935350.) **Continues** Germany (West). Statistisches Bundesamt. Aussenhandel. Reihe 5: Special Trade According to the Classification for Statistics and Tariffs (CST).

LC HF125.V8 V58A ISSN 0095-3903
DD 382/.09755 US
FOREIGN TRADE ANNUAL REPORT; VIRGINIA PORTS.
Main/Corp Virginia. State Port Authority. Research Dept. English. One time a year. State Port Authority, Research Department, 1600 Maritime Tower, Norfolk VA 23510.

LC HF3941 .E85 ISSN 1036-9449
DD 380.1099 AT
FOREIGN TRADE, AUSTRALIA. MERCHANDISE EXPORTS.
See Business and Economics-Abstracting, Bibliographies and Statistics.

ISSN 1037-888X
DD 382.60994 AT
FOREIGN TRADE, AUSTRALIA, MERCHANDISE EXPORTS, DETAILED COMMODITY TABLES.
See Business and Economics-Abstracting, Bibliographies and Statistics.

LC HF3941 .I44 ISSN 1036-904X
DD 380.1 AT
FOREIGN TRADE, AUSTRALIA. MERCHANDISE IMPORTS / AUSTRALIAN BUREAU OF STATISTICS.
See Business and Economics-Abstracting, Bibliographies and Statistics.

LC HF275 .A92
DD 380.1 AT
FOREIGN TRADE, AUSTRALIA. MERCHANDISE IMPORTS. DETAILED COMMODITY TABLES.
See Business and Economics-Abstracting, Bibliographies and Statistics.

ISSN 0015-7317
II
FOREIGN TRADE BULLETIN.
Added/Corp Indian Institute of Foreign Trade. Vol. 1 (July 1970)-. Bulletin. English. Twelve times a year. $25.00. Indian Institute of Foreign Trade, H-24 Green Park Extension, New Delhi India. **Tel** 615628. **(Subscription address:** Prints India, 11 Darya Ganj, New Delhi 110002 India. **Tel** 011 91 11 3268645, FAX 011 91 11 3275542, telex 31-61087 PRIN-IN.) **ED** Shri Hartirath Singh. **Bk Rev. Ad Acc. Circ:** 1,500.
 Desc: Latest trends in foreign trade and to disseminate the information to policies on foreign trade.

LC HF1016 .F67
DD 382/.0021 FR
FOREIGN TRADE BY COMMODITIES / OECD DEPARTMENT OF ECONOMICS AND STATISTICS.
Added/Corp Organisation for Economic Co-Operation and Development. Dept. of Economics and Statistics. **VFOAT** Commerce Exterieur par Produits. (1981)-. English (French). Five times a year. $490.00. OECD Publications and Information Center, 2

Business and Economics — Commerce

rue Andre-Pascal, 75775 Paris Cedex 16 France. **Tel** 011 33 1 49104262, US:(202)785-6323, **FAX** 011 33 1 45248500, 011 33 1 45248176, telex 620 160 OCDE. **(Subscription address:** OECD Publications Center, 2001 L Street, Suite 700, Washington DC 20036. **Tel** (202)822-3873, (202)785-6323.**)** *Formed by the union of* Organisation for Economic Co-Operation and Development. Statistics of Foreign Trade. Series C: Trade by Commodities; Market Summaries. Exports **and** Organisation for Economic Co-Operation and Development. Statistics of Foreign Trade. Series C: Trade by Commodities; Market Summaries. Imports.
 Desc: Provides trade figures for individual OECD Member Countries (reporting countries) and the main OECD country groupings.

ISSN 0883-4687
DD 382 US
FOREIGN TRADE FAIRS NEW PRODUCTS NEWSLETTER.
[Foreign trade fairs new prod. newsl.]. **Added/Corp** International Intertrade Index (Firm). **VFOAT** New Products Newsletter; Foreign Trade Fairs Newsletter. (198?)-. Newsletter. English. Twelve times a year. $45.00. Printing Consultants, Box 636 Federal Square, Newark NJ 07101. **Tel** (201)686-2382. **ED** John E. Felber.
 Desc: Imported products available to US firms that seek new products. Products are award winners at foreign trade fairs.

ISSN 1055-1468
DD 337 US
FOREIGN TRADE (MCLEAN, VA.).
(FOREIGN TRADE.). [Foreign trade]. (Jan./Feb. 1991)-. Trade Publication. English. Ten times a year (monthly with Jan./Feb. and July/Aug. issues combined) $45.00. Foreign Trade Inc., 6849 Old Dominion Drive, Suite 200, Mclean VA 22101. **Tel** (703)448-1338, FAX (703)448-1841. **ED** Russell Goodman.

LC HF3500.5 .A2
DD 382/.094/0021 LU
FOREIGN TRADE OF THE COMMUNITY.
English. European Communities Commission, Case Postale 1003, Luxembourg Luxembourg. **Tel** (352)48 80 41, FAX (352)48 80 40, telex 2181.

LC HF41 .F63
DD 382/.095193/005 KN
FOREIGN TRADE OF THE DEMOCRATIC PEOPLE'S REPUBLIC OF KOREA.
Added/Corp Choson Kukche Muyok Chokchin Wiwonhoe. **VFOAT** Foreign Trade. (19??)-. Periodical. English (Arabic, Chinese, French, Japanese, Russian and Spanish). Twelve times a year. Foreign Trade Publishing House, Potonggang District, Pyongyang North Korea. **Continues** Korean Foreign Trade.

LC HF3836.5 .S72a
DD 382/.0951 LU
FOREIGN TRADE OF THE PEOPLE'S REPUBLIC OF CHINA. LE COMMERCE EXTERIEUR DE LA REPUBLIQUE POPULAIRE DE CHINE.
Main/Corp Statistical Office of the European Communities. **Added/Corp** Statistical Office of the European Communities. Commerce Exterieur de la Republique Populaire de Chine. **VFOAT** Le Commerce Exterieur de la Republique Populaire de Chine. (19??)-. English (French). Irregular. UNIPUB, 4611-F Assembly Drive, Lanham MD 20706-4391. **Tel** (800)274-4888, FAX (301)459-0056, telex 28787 GATT CH.

LC HF41 .F65
DD 382/.0954/005 **ISSN** 0015-7325
II
FOREIGN TRADE REVIEW.
(FOREIGN TRADE REVIEW : QUARTERLY JOURNAL OF THE INDIAN INSTITUTE OF FOREIGN TRADE.). [Foreign trade rev.]. **Added/Corp** Indian Institute of Foreign Trade. Vol. 1 (April/June 1966)-. Trade Publication. English. Four times a year. $20.00. Indian Institute of Foreign Trade, H-24 Green Park Extension, New Delhi India. **Tel** 615628. **(Subscription address:** Prints India, 11 Darya Ganj, New Delhi 110002 India. **Tel** 011 91 11 3268645, FAX 011 91 11 3275542, telex 31-61087 PRIN-IN.**)**
 Desc: Publishes papers and articles by national and international authors on different topics relating to foreign trade that are of special interest to trade and industry, government, research and academic institutions that are concerned with foreign trade and international marketing.
 Ind/Abst Contents Recent Econ. J.

US
FOREIGN TRADE STATISTICS FOR AFRICA. SERIES A: DIRECTION OF TRADE. STATISTIQUES AFRICAINES DU COMMERCE EXTERIEUR. SERIE. ECHANGES PAR PAYS.
See Business and Economics-Abstracting, Bibliographies and Statistics.

LC HF3871 .U58
DD 380.1 US
FOREIGN TRADE STATISTICS FOR AFRICA. SERIES B. TRADE BY COMMODITY. STATISTIQUES AFRICAINES DU COMMERCE EXTERIEUR. SERIE ECHANGES PAR PRODUITS.
See Business and Economics-Abstracting, Bibliographies and Statistics.

ISSN 1011-4858
US
FOREIGN TRADE STATISTICS OF ASIA AND THE PACIFIC.
Added/Corp United Nations. Economic and Social Commission for Asia and the Pacific. **VFOAT** Statsitiques du Commerce Exterieur de l'Asie et du Pacifique. A.(1981-1985)-. Government Publication. English (French). One time a year. $45.00. United Nations Publications, 2 United Nations Plaza, Room DC2 0853, Department 007C, New York NY 10017. **Tel** (212)963-8303, (800)253-9646. *Formed by the union of* Foreign Trade Statistics of Asia and the Pacific. Series A **and** Foreign Trade Statistics of Asia and the Pacific. Series B.

PH
FOREIGN TRADE STATISTICS OF THE PHILIPPINES.
See Business and Economics-Abstracting, Bibliographies and Statistics.

SZ
FORUM.
Added/Corp International Trade Centre UNCTAD/GATT. **VFOAT** International Trade Forum. (198?)-. Periodical. Spanish. Four times a year. Free to developing countries; $20.00 other. International Trade Centre, UNCTAD/GATT, Palais des Nations, 1211 Geneva 10 Switzerland. **Tel** 011 41 22 7300111. **Continues** International Trade Forum (Geneva, Switzerland).

SZ
FORUM DU COMMERCE INTERNATIONAL.
French. Four times a year. $20.00. Centre Commerce International, Palais des Nations Gatt, 1211 Geneva Switzerland. **Tel** 011 41 22 7300111.

LC HF3921.A48 F73
FR
CEASED
FRANCE AFRIQUE.
VFOAT Annuaire des Societes et Fournisseurs. (1988)-(1993). French. Ediafric la Documentation Africaine, 10 rue Vineuse, 75116 Paris France. **Tel** 011 33 1 44308100, FAX 011 33 1 45208174. *Formed by the union of* Annuaire des Exportateurs; Annuaire de l'Afrique du Nord (Ediafric, La Documentation Africaine (Firm)) **and** Annuaire de l'Afrique Noire.

LC HF3551 .F7
DD 381/.0944 FR
FRANCE DES COMMERCES, LA.
(19??)-. French. One time a year. Free. Direction du Commerce Interieur, Mission Information, A135, 41 Quai Branly, 75700 Paris France. **Tel** (1)45 50 73 84. **Circ:** 100,000.
 Desc: This handbook publishes statistics on all aspects of French commerce. Tables are given for commercial activity, labor and salaries, and commercial establishments.

LC HF3553 .F68 **ISSN** 0244-710X
DD 382.6 FR
FRANCEXPORT.
Added/Corp Centre Francais du Commerce Exterieur. **VFOAT** France Export. (19??)-. English (French, English, German and Spanish). One time a year. Price varies. Addor Associates, 115 Roseville Road, PO Box 2128, Westport CT 06880. **Tel** (203)226-9791. Index available. **Ad Acc. Circ:** 12,000.
 Desc: A directory of French firms that do business abroad.

ISSN 0071-9277
DD 338/.4/02571 CN
FRASER'S CANADIAN TRADE DIRECTORY.
See Business and Economics-Abstracting, Bibliographies and Statistics.

ISSN 1058-5745
DD 338 US
FREE TRADE ADVISORY : THE BIWEEKLY ADVISORY ON HOW THE NORTH AMERICAN FREE TRADE TALKS WILL AFFECT YOUR BUSINESS AND INVESTMENTS IN MEXICO.
[Free trade advis.]. Vol. 1, No. 1 (Sept. 10, 1991)-. Periodical. English. Twenty-six times a year. $535.00. Integrated Reports Inc, 114 East 32nd Street, Suite 602, New York NY 10016-5506. **Tel** (212)685-6900, FAX (212) 685-8566, telex 233139 RPTUR. available on an online database (file 636/Full-Text) from DIALOG.
 Ind/Abst PTS Newsl. Database [Full Txt.].

CN
FREE TRADE LAW REPORTER. See Law.

LC G155.A8 F69
DD 380.1/45914363 AU
FREMDENVERKEHR IM LANDE SALZBURG IM ..., DER.
German. Landesverkehrsamt Salzburg, Mozartplatz 1, 5010 Salzburg Austria.

LC HF1 .F77
DD 382 US
FRENCH-AMERICAN COMMERCE.
Added/Corp Chambre de Commerce Francaise des Etats-Unis. (19??)-. Periodical. English (French). Three times a year. French-American Chamber of Commerce in US Inc, 509 Madison Avenue 1900, New York NY 10022. **Tel** (212)371-4466, telex 6720504 FRENCH UW. **ED** Serge Bellanger. **Ad Acc. Circ:** 4,000 (ctrl).
 Desc: Focuses on topics concerning international business topics, mainly concentrating on French and U.S. trade.

LC HD9241 .F72 **ISSN** 0749-5390
DD 380/.1/414/0973 US
FRESH FRUIT AND VEGETABLE ARRIVAL TOTALS FOR 23 CITIES / UNITED STATES DEPARTMENT OF AGRICULTURE, AGRICULTURAL MARKETING SERVICE, FRUIT AND VEGETABLE DIVISION.
[Fresh fruit veg. arriv. totals 23 cities]. Calendar Year 1982-. Government Publication. English. One time a year. US Department of Agriculture / Agricultural Marketing Service / Washington, DC, Market News Branch, Fruit and Vegetable Division, Washington DC 20250. **Tel** (202)720-2745, (202)720-3343, FAX (202)720-7502. available on microfiche (Vols. for calendar year 1983- distributed to depository libraries). **Continues** Fresh Fruit and Vegetable Unload Totals for 41 Cities.

LC HD9241 .F73 **ISSN** 0738-1786
DD 381/.414/0974 US
FRESH FRUIT AND VEGETABLE ARRIVALS IN EASTERN CITIES BY COMMODITIES, STATES, AND MONTHS.
See Industry and Production.

LC HD 9001 .U53A **ISSN** 0160-2942
DD 381/.41/4097 US
FRESH FRUIT AND VEGETABLE SHIPMENTS BY COMMODITIES, STATES, MONTHS.
See Food and Food Industry.

LC HD9001 .U53A **ISSN** 0565-2065
DD 381/.41/40971 S 381/.41/40971 US
FRESH FRUIT AND VEGETABLE SHIPMENTS BY STATES, COMMODITIES, COUNTIES, STATIONS.
Government Publication. English. US Department of Agriculture / Agricultural Marketing Service / Washington, DC, Market News Branch, Fruit and Vegetable Division, Washington DC 20250. **Tel** (202)720-2745, (202)720-3343, FAX (202)720-7502.

LC HD9001 .U53A HD9007.A3 A3 **ISSN** 0501-462X
DD 381/.41/4097 S 381/.41/40977 US
FRESH FRUIT AND VEGETABLE UNLOADS IN MIDWESTERN CITIES BY COMMODITIES, STATES AND MONTHS.
(FRESH FRUIT AND VEGETABLE UNLOADS IN MIDWESTERN CITIES BY COMMODITIES, STATES AND MONTHS / UNITED STATES DEPARTMENT OF AGRICULTURE, AGRICULTURAL MARKETING SERVICE, FRUIT AND VEGETABLE DIVISION.). [Fresh fruit veg. unloads midwest. cities commod. states months]. English. One time a year. US Department of Agriculture / Agricultural Marketing Service / Washington, DC, Market News Branch, Fruit and Vegetable Division, Washington DC 20250. **Tel** (202)720-2745, (202)720-3343, FAX (202)720-7502.

LC HD9247.A13 F73 **ISSN** 0501-4603
DD 381/.414/0975 US
FRESH FRUIT AND VEGETABLE UNLOADS IN SOUTHERN CITIES BY COMMODITIES, STATES, AND MONTHS.
(19??)-. Government Publication. English. One time a year. US Department of Agriculture / Agricultural Marketing Service / Washington, DC, Market News Branch, Fruit and Vegetable Division, Washington DC 20250. **Tel** (202)720-2745, (202)720-3343, FAX (202)720-7502.

US
FRUIT AND VEGETABLE NATIONAL SHIPPING POINT TRENDS.
(19??)-. English. One time a week. $96.00. US Department of Agriculture /

Business and Economics —Commerce

Agricultural Marketing Service / Washington, DC, Market News Branch, Fruit and Vegetable Division, Washington DC 20250. **Tel** (202)720-2745, (202)720-3343, FAX (202)720-7502.

US
FRUIT AND VEGETABLE TRUCK RATE REPORT / UNITED STATES DEPARTMENT OF AGRICULTURE, AGRICULTURAL MARKETING SERVICE, FRUIT AND VEGETABLE MARKET NEWS SERVICE. Added/Corp United States. Agricultural Marketing Service. Fruit and Vegetable Division. Vol. 1 (1979)-. English. One time a week. US Department of Agriculture / Agricultural Marketing Service / New York, Fruit and Vegetable Market News Branch, 4A New York City Terminal Market, New York NY 10474. **Tel** (212)542-2225. **ED** W.H. Crocker. **Bk Rev**. ctrl circ.
 Desc: Truck rates per load from major shipping areas to six receiving cities and monthly truck cost reports per mile.

ISSN 0161-7036
DD 343
US
CCC
FTC FREEDOM OF INFORMATION LOG. [FTC freedom inf. log]. **Main/Corp** United States. Federal Trade Commission. **Added/Corp** Washington Regulatory Reporting Associates. **VFOAT** FTC Watch, FTC Freedom of Information Log. **VAT** Federal Trade Commission Freedom of Information Log. (1976)-. Periodical. English. Forty-eight times a year. $345.00. Washington Regulatory Reporting Association, PO Box 356, Basye VA 22810. **Tel** (703)856-2216. available on an online database (file 636/Full-Text) from DIALOG.
 Desc: Summaries of Freedom of Information Act and requests received by the US Federal Trade Commission.
 Ind/Abst PTS Newsl. Database [Full Txt.].

US
FTC NEWS NOTES. Added/Corp United States. Federal Trade Commission. United States. Federal Trade Commission. Office of Public Affairs. **VFOAT** F.T.C. News Notes. **VAT** Federal Trade Commission News Notes. Vol. 19-83 (Feb. 4, 1983)-. Periodical. English. One time a week. Free on request. Federal Trade Commission, 6th Street & Pennsylvania Northwest, Washington DC 20590. **Tel** (202)326-2000. **Continues** FTC News Summary.

LC KF1602 .F18 ISSN 0196-0016
DD 343.73/08/05 US
CCC
FTC : WATCH. See Law.

LC S
DD 630 US
FUTURES CHART SERVICE. AGRICULTURAL. See Agriculture.

LC HG6046 .F76 ISSN 1065-9722
DD 332.64/5 US
FUTURES CHARTS. [Futures charts]. **Added/Corp** Commodity Trend Service. (19??)-. Periodical. English. Twelve times a year. $180.00. Commodity Trend Service, PO Box 32309, Palm Beach Gardens FL 33420. **Tel** (407)694-0960, (800)331-1069, FAX (407)622-7623. **ED** Nick Van Nice.
 Desc: Bar charts of financial and agricultural commodity markets.

ISSN 0247-8315
UDC 070.431 FR
GABON SELECTION PARIS. [Gabon sel. Paris]. (1980)-. Periodical. French. Six times a year. $874.88. IC Publications Ediafric, 10 rue Vineuse, 75116 Paris France. **Tel** 011 33 1 44308100.

LC HF41 .J17a
JA
GAIKOKU BOEKI GAIKYO. THE SUMMARY REPORT, TRADE OF JAPAN. Main/Corp Japan. Okurasho. Kanzeikyoku. **VFOAT** Summary Report; Trade of Japan. (19??)-. Multiple languages (Japanese and English). Twelve times a year. $512.00. Gaikoku Boeki Gaikyo, 7-8, Kojimachi 4-chome, Chiyoda-ku Tokyo Japan.

LC HF3689.G3 G35
SP
GALICIA, CATALOGO DE EXPORTADORES/COMERCIO EXTERIOR. VFOAT Catalogo de Exportadores/Comercio Exterior. **VAT** Galicia, Catalogo de Exportadores Comercio Exterior. Periodical. Gallegan (English, French and German). Visecretario General de la Camara de Comercio, Industria y Navegacion de la Coruna.

LC HF1721 .C55
DD 382.7/05 SZ
GATT ACTIVITIES IN ... / GENERAL AGREEMENT ON TARIFFS AND TRADE. Main/Corp General Agreement on Tariffs and Trade (Organization). **VFOAT** GATT Activities; Activities in ...; Activities. (1969/70)-. Monographic series. English. Irregular. Price varies per volume. General Agreement on Tariffs and Trade / GATT, Centre William Rappard, 154 rue de Lausanne, 1211 Geneva 21 Switzerland. **Tel** 011 41 22 7395111, 011 41 22 7395019, FAX 011 41 22 7395458. **(Subscription address:** UNIPUB, 4611 F Assembly Drive, Lanham MD 20706. **Tel** (800)274-4888, (301)459-7666.) **Continues** General Agreement on Tariffs and Trade (Organization). Activities of GATT, 0589-560X.
 Desc: Comprehensive report on every aspect of GATT's work during the previous year.

LC HF1701 .G38 ISSN 0256-0119
DD 382/.92/05 SZ
TITLE CHANGE
GATT FOCUS (ENGLISH ED.). (GATT FOCUS.). [GATT focus]. **Added/Corp** General Agreement on Tariffs and Trade (Organization). **VFOAT** General Agreement on Tariffs and Trade Focus; Focus Newsletter; GATT Newsletter, Focus. (Feb./March 1981)-(1995). Newsletter. English (French and Spanish). General Agreement on Tariffs and Trade / GATT, Centre William Rappard, 154 rue de Lausanne, 1211 Geneva 21 Switzerland. **Tel** 011 41 22 7395111, 011 41 22 7395019, FAX 011 41 22 7395458. **Continued by** WTO Focus.
 Desc: Reports on trade-related matters, including features on economic developments and major trade policy issues. Covers negotiations, dispute settlements and other activities of the member states and the GATT Secretariat.

SZ
GATT STUDIES IN INTERNATIONAL TRADE. VFOAT G.A.T.T. Studies in International Trade; GATT Studies; G.A.T.T. Studies. Vol. 1; 1971-. Monographic series. English. Price varies per volume. UNIPUB, 4611-F Assembly Drive, Lanham MD 20706-4391. **Tel** (800)274-4888, FAX (301)459-0056, telex 28787 GATT CH.

LC HF1601 .G42
JA
GEKKAN BOEKI SEISAKU. Added/Corp Tsusho Seisaku Kenkyukai. **VFOAT** Boeki Seisaku. (19??)-. Periodical. Japanese. ¥3000. Tousan Seisaku Kohosha, c/o Toranomon Kotohira Kaikan Building, 1 Shiba Kotohiracho Minato-ku, Tokyo Japan.

LC HF3099 .G39 ISSN 1182-803X
DD 382/.0943073/05 CN
GERMAN AMERICAN TRADE. (GERMAN AMERICAN TRADE : MAGAZINE OF THE GERMAN AMERICAN CHAMBER OF COMMERCE.). [Ger. Am. trade]. **Added/Corp** German American Chamber of Commerce. Vol. 1, No. 1 (Apr. 1990)-. Periodical. English (German). Ten times a year. $50.00. German American Chamber of Commerce, 40 West 57th Street, 31st Floor, New York NY 10019. **Tel** (212)974-8830, FAX (212)315-2183, telex 234209.
 Ind/Abst PAIS Int. Print.

ISSN 1063-9772
US
GLOBAL GEORGIA. Added/Corp Savannah International Trade Association. **VFOAT** Global Buy. (1992)-. Periodical. English. Twelve times a year. $3.00 (single issue). SITA, Savannah International Trade Association, PO Box 2674, Savannah GA 31402.

LC HF1 .A58 ISSN 1069-2843
DD 658.8/48/0973 US
CCC
CEASED
GLOBAL TRADE & TRANSPORTATION. [Glob. trade transp.]. **VFOAT** Global Trade and Transportation; Global Trade. Vol. 113, No. 1 (Jan. 1993)-Vol. 114 No. 11 (19??). Trade Publication. English. North American Publishing Company, 401 North Broad Street, Philadelphia PA 19108. **Tel** (215)238-5300, (800)777-8074, FAX (215)238-5283. **Continues** Global Trade, 1060-0906.
 Desc: Magazine for the executives involved in international trade. Articles cover sales, marketing, finance, ports, transportation and distribution of products imported to and exported from the United States.
 Ind/Abst Bus. Period. Index; Curr. Cit.; MasterFile FullTEXT (July 1993-Dec. 1994).

LC HJ6622 .A584 ISSN 1056-3857
DD 353.0072/46/05 US
GLOBAL TRADE TALK. (GLOBAL TRADE TALK : THE U.S. CUSTOMS SERVICE JOURNAL FOR THE INTERNATIONAL TRADE COMMUNITY.). [Glob. trade talk]. **Added/Corp** U.S. Customs Service. Vol. 1, No. 1 (Jan./Feb. 1991)-. Government Publication. English. Six times a year. $21.00. US Department of the Treasury, Office of Public Affairs, 1500 Pennsylvania Avenue, Washington DC 20220. **Tel** (202)566-2041. **(Subscription address:** Superintendent of Documents, US Government Printing Office, Washington DC 20402.) **Formed by the union of** Customs Trade Quarterly **and** Customs Trade Topics.
 Desc: Focuses on issues concerning international trade and the role of the United States Customs Service in facilitating international trade.

UK
GMB DIRECT. Added/Corp General, Municipal, Boilermakers, and Allied Trades Union. **VFOAT** Direct. **VAT** General, Municipal, Boilermakers Direct. Issue 1 (Feb. 1992)-. Periodical. English. Twelve times a year. **Continues** GMB Journal.

ISSN 0951-5798
UK
GRAIN (LONDON, ENGLAND). (GRAIN.). **Added/Corp** Drewry Shipping Consultants. (May 1986)-. English. Every 2 years. Drewry Shipping Consultants Ltd, 11 Heron Quay, London E14 4JF United Kingdom. **Tel** 011 44 171 5380191, FAX 011 44 171 9879396, telex 21167 HPDLDG.

ISSN 0711-2947
DD 382/.05 CN
GREY/CLARK TRADE NEWS. Vol. 1, No. 1 (March 1980)-. Periodical. English. Twelve times a year. $120.00. Grey/Clark Trade News, c/o Luper Publications, 141 Laurier Avenue West, Suite 804, Ottawa Ontario K1P 5J3 Canada.

ISSN 1196-0817
DD 381/.456413/009712 CN
●**GROCER TODAY.** [Groc. today]. Vol. 6, No. 10 or Vol. 7, No. 1 (Jan. or Feb. 1993)-. Trade Publication. English. Nine times a year. 21.61Can$. Canada Wide Magazines Ltd., 401-4180 Lougheed Highway, Burnaby British Columbia V5C 6A7 Canada. **Tel** (604)299-7311, FAX (604)299-9188. **ED** Nancy Ryder. **Ad Acc, Adv Mgr:** Pat Sasso. **Continues** British Columbia, Alberta, Saskatchewan and Manitoba Grocer., 1193-3658.

LC HA1173 .A27 HF5421.5A9 5A9
AU
GROSS- UND EINZELHANDELSSTATISTIK. Main/Corp Osterreichisches Statistisches Zentralamt. German. One time a year. S170.00.
 Desc: Publishes results of surveys taken for wholesale and retail businesses. It shows the sales figures broken down into the different branches of business by months and states.

LC HF1622.19.A5 G83
AO
GUIA-ANUARIO DOS EXPORTADORES E IMPORTADORES DE ANGOLA. (19??)-. Portuguese. Sociedade Publicitaria de Angola, rua Tavares de Angola 85-C e 85-D, Luanda Angola.

LC HF3383 .G84
DD 382/.029/482 AG
GUIA DE EXPORTADORES E IMPORTADORES ARGENTINOS. VFOAT Directory of Argentine Exporters & Importers; Directory of Argentine Exporters and Importers. (1983)-. Spanish (English). One time a year. $80.00. Editorial Scott S A, Guemes 3440 PB A, 1425 Buenos Aires Argentina. **Tel** 771-7940. **Ad Acc, Adv Mgr:** Telmo Mirat, **Tel** 011 54 1 771 7940. **Circ:** 5,000 (ctrl). **Continues** Scott Directory of Argentine Exporters & Importers.
 Desc: Trade directory listing names and addresses of Argentine exporters and importers, classified and alphabetically by products.

LC K ISSN 0432-8884
DD 343.82/087/05 348.2038705 AG
GUIA PRACTICA DEL EXPORTADOR E IMPORTADOR Y PARA TODO HOMBRE DE NEGOCIOS. VFOAT Guia Practica del Exportador e Importador. (19??)-. Spanish. Twelve times a year. $1450.00. Guia Practica del Exportador e Importador, Lavalle 1125, P 3 of 8, 1048 Buenos Aires Argentina. **Tel** 011 54 1 358533. **Continues** Guia Practica del Exportador e Importador.

LC K
DD 343.82/087/05 348.2038705 AG
GUIA PRACTICA DEL EXPORTADOR E IMPORTADOR Y PARA TODO HOMBRE DE NEGOCIOS. SUPLEMENTO. VFOAT Guia Practica del Exportador e Importador - Suplemento. (19??)-. Spanish. Guia Practica del Exportador e Importador, Lavalle 1125, P 3 of 8, 1048 Buenos Aires Argentina. **Tel** 011 54 1 358533.

LC K
DD 343.82/087 348.20387 AG
GUIA PRACTICA DEL EXPORTADOR E IMPORTADOR Y PARA TODO HOMBRE DE NEGOCIOS. SUPLEMENTO DE LA SECCION INFORMATIVA. See Law.

LC HF105 .B73a ISSN 0565-0933
DD 382/.0973 US
GUIDE TO FOREIGN TRADE STATISTICS. See Business and Economics-Abstracting, Bibliographies and Statistics.

Business and Economics — Commerce

LC HF3230.5 .A26

AG

GUIPREX, GUIA DE PRODUCTORES Y EXPORTADORES LATINOAMERICANOS. **VFOAT** Guia de Productores y Exportadores Latinoamericanos. (1974/75)-. Multiple languages (English and Spanish).

NE

HAGUE-ZAGREB-GHENT : ESSAYS ON THE LAW OF INTERNATIONAL TRADE. See Law-International Law.

LC HF308 .H388
DD 381/.0943/51505

GW

HAMBURGER WIRTSCHAFT : ZEITSCHRIFT DER HANDELSKAMMER HAMBURG. **VFOAT** Zeitschrift der Handelskammer Hamburg. Periodical. German. Twelve times a year. DM36.00. Handelskammer Hamburg, Postfach 11 14 49, Borse 2000 Hamburg 11 Germany. **Continues** Mitteilungen / Handelskammer Hamburg.

LC HF5001 .D474
DD 650/.05

GW

HANDEL, DER. (1992)-. Periodical. German. Ten times a year. $38.38. Verlagsgruppe Dtsch Fachverlag, Mainzer Landstr 251, 60326 Frankfurt Germany. **Tel** 011 49 69 75951001. **Continues** DFZ Wirtschaftsmagazine, 0341-549X.

LC HF5421.5.G4 H36

GW

HANDEL, GASTGEWERBE, REISEVERKEHR. REIHE 1.1, BESCHAFTIGTE UND UMSATZ IM GROSSHANDEL (MESSZAHLEN). **VFOAT** Beschaftigte und Umsatz im Grosshandel (Messzahlen). Fachserie 6. English. Twelve times a year. W. Kohlhammer Verlag GmbH, Postfach 800430, D-70549 Stuttgart Germany. **Tel** 011 49 711 78630, FAX 011 49 711 7863430, telex 7-255820. **Absorbed** Handel, Gastgewerbe, Reiseverkehr. Reihe 1.1: Beschaftigte und Umsatz im Grosshandel, Messzahlen.

LC HF37.P6. H3

ISSN 0438-5403
PL

HANDEL WEWNETRZNY. **Added/Corp** Polskie Towarzystwo Ekonomiczne. Sekcja Handlu. Instytut Handlu Wewnetrznego (Warsaw, Poland). (1955)-. Periodical. Polish (table of contents in English and Russian). Six times a year. $57.00. **(Subscription address:** Ars Polona-Ruch, PO Box 1001, Krakowskie Przedmiescie 7, 00-068 Warsaw Poland. **Tel** 011 48 22 261201.**)**

LC HF37 .H3

ISSN 0017-7245
PL

HANDEL ZAGRANICZNY. **Added/Corp** Polska Izba Handlu Zagranicznego. (1955)-. Periodical. Polish (summaries and/or abstracts in English, German and Russian; table of contents in Russian and English). Twelve times a year. $105.00. **(Subscription address:** Ars Polona-Ruch, PO Box 1001, Krakowskie Przedmiescie 7, 00-068 Warsaw Poland. **Tel** 011 48 22 261201.**)** available on microfilm from University Microfilms International (UMI).

ISSN 0017-7296
GW

HANDELSBLATT. [Handelsblatt]. **Added/Corp** Rheinisch-Westfalische Borse zu Dusseldorf. Vol. 1 (May 16, 1946)-. Newspaper. German. Seven times a week. $490.00. Handelsblatt GmbH, Postfach 102716, D-40018 Duesseldorf Germany. **Tel** 011 49 211 8871730, FAX 011 49 211 133523, telex 172114489. **(Subscription address:** German Language Publications Inc., 153 South Dean Street, Englewood NJ 07631. **Tel** (201)871-1010, (800)457-4443.**)** available in microform. **Absorbed** Industriekurier.
Ind/Abst Chem. Bus. Bull.; Chem. Bus. NewsBase (1989-); Chem. Bus. Update; F&S Index Plus Text, Int. [Select. Cov.]; Infomat Int. Bus.; PROMT.

ISSN 1061-494X
DD 380
US

HERMES (LANSING, MICH.). (HERMES [COMPUTER FILE] : A CYBERCAST PERIODICAL OF COMMERCE / BY MICHAEL E. MAROTTA.). [Hermes]. Vol. 1, No. 1 (Apr. 20, 1991)-. Periodical. English. **Desc:** Available through BITNET: mercury@well.sf.ca.us.

AU

HEROLD EXPORT-ADRESSBUCH VON OESTERREICH. **Added/Corp** Bundeskammer der Gewerblichen Wirtschaft (Austria). Abteilung fuer Handelspolitik und Aussenhandel. **VFOAT** Austrian Export Directory; Annuaire d'Exportation de l'Autriche; Austria Export. (198?)-. German (English, French and Spanish). One time a year. Herold Business Data GMBH, Schleiergasse 18, A-1100 Vienna Austria. **Tel** 0222 60141 0 0, FAX 0222 60141 8 8. **Continues** Export-Adressbuch von Osterreich.

LC HA1320 .H529 HF3569.H4
DD 314.3

GW

HESSISCHE AUSFUHR, DIE. See Business and Economics-Abstracting, Bibliographies and Statistics.

LC HF41 .H58
DD 380.105/6

ISSN 0018-2796
JA

HITOTSUBASHI JOURNAL OF COMMERCE AND MANAGEMENT. **Added/Corp** Hitotsubashi Daigaku, Tokyo. **VAT** Hitotsubashi Journal of Commerce & Management. (March 1961)-. Periodical. English (German). One time a year. $33.00. **(Subscription address:** Japan Publications Trading Company Ltd., PO Box 5030, Tokyo International, Tokyo 100-31 Japan. **Tel** 011 81 3 3292 3753.**) Supersedes in part** Hitotsubashi Daigaku, Tokyo. Hitotsubashi Gakkai. Annals.
Ind/Abst Econ. Lit. Index.

DD 381

ISSN 0883-0436
US

HOME CENTER PRODUCTS REPORT. [Home cent. prod. rep.]. Vol. 1, No. 1 (Jan./Feb. 1985)-. Periodical. English. Six times a year. $15.00 US; $25.00 other. Irving-Cloud Publishing Company, 417 North Hough Street, Barrington IL 60010. **Tel** (708)382-3405, FAX (708)674-7015.

LC HF5001

HO

HONDURAS ROTARIA. Vol. 1, No. 1 (April 1943)-. Periodical. Spanish. Twelve times a year. L5.00. Honduras Rotaria, Tegucigalpa DC, Honduras Central America. **Tel** 22-08-66. **ED** Jorge Fidel Duron. **Bk Rev. Ad Acc.** Circ: 1,000. available on microfilm from University Microfilms International (UMI).
Desc: The official organ of the Tegucigalpa, Honduras Rotary Club.

LC HF259.H6 H63a
DD 382/.0951/25

HK

HONG KONG EXTERNAL TRADE. **Added/Corp** Hong Kong. Census and Statistics Dept. Hong Kong. Census and Statistics Dept. Trade Research Section. Hong Kong. Census and Statistics Dept. Trade Analysis Section. **VFOAT** Hsiang-Kang Tui Wai Mao I. (19??)-. English. Twelve times a year. HK$822.00 Hong Kong; HK$960.00 other. Hong Kong Government Information Service, Beaconsfield House, 4 Queens Road, Hong Kong Hong Kong. **Tel** 011 852 284288014, 011 852 259881947, FAX 011 852 28459078, 011 852 25987482, telex 61190 HKGIS. **(Subscription address:** Government Information Service, Publications Office, 1 Battery Path, Hong Kong Hong Kong. **)**

UK
SUSPENDED

HONG KONG TRADE DIRECTORY. (19??)-(19??). Directory. English. One time a year. £1.75. Diplomatic Press & Publ Co, 44-46 South Ealing Road, London W.5 United Kingdom. **ED** Harry Richter.

LC HF259.H6 H64A
DD 382/.0951/25

HK

HONG KONG TRADE STATISTICS. See Business and Economics-Abstracting, Bibliographies and Statistics.

LC HF3892.A48 H67
DD 382/.09676/0025

KE

HORIZONS P.T.A. DIRECTORY, THE. **VFOAT** Horizons PTA Directory. **VAT** Horizons Preferential Trade Area Directory. (19??)-. Directory. English. Every 2 years. All Africa Conference of Churches, PO Box 14205, Waiyaki Way, Nairobi Kenya. **Tel** 011 254 2 61166, 011 254 2 60207. **Continues** Horizons.

LC HC267.A2 H785

ISSN 0018-7747
FR

HUNGARIAN FOREIGN TRADE. Year 1- July 1949-. Periodical. Multiple languages (Spanish and French). Four times a year. **(Subscription address:** Kultura, PO Box 143, H-1300 Budapest 3 Hungary. **Tel** 011 36 1 2500194.**)**

US

ICC NEWS. **Main/Corp** United States. Interstate Commerce Commission. (19??)-. English. Irregular. Free on request. Interstate Commerce Commission, 12th Street and Constitution Avenue 4111, Washington DC 20423. **Tel** (202)927-7119.

LC KF2250 .I25
DD 343.73/093/02646 347.3039302646

ISSN 0749-0534
US

ICC REGISTER. See Law.

IO

IMPOR MENURUT JENIS BARANG DAN NEGERI ASAL. **Main/Corp** Indonesia. Biro Pusat Statistik. **VFOAT** Import by Commodity and Country of Origin. (1962)-. Multiple languages (English and Indonesian). One time a year. $12.00. Biro Pusat Statistik / Central Bureau of Statistics, 8 Jalan Dr. Sutomo No. 8, Box 3, Jakarta Pusat 10710 Indonesia. **Tel** 011 62 21 372808, 011 62 21 374908 ext.342. **Bk Rev. Ad Acc.** ctrl circ.

DD 343.9408705

ISSN 1034-7313
AT

IMPORT BANKSTOWN. (IMPORT.). [Import Bankstown]. (1989)-. Periodical. English. Twelve times a year. 295.99Aus$. Import & Publishing Company Pty Ltd, PO Box 688, Riverwood 2210 Australia. **Tel** 011 61 2 5332593, FAX 011 61 2 5331457. **ED** Leon T. Toohey (editor's address: 20 Johnstone Street, Peakhurst 2210 Australia). index available. cum. index. Circ: 200 (ctrl).
Desc: A national journal of Australian import policy law and practice.

US

IMPORT BULLETIN. **Main/Corp** Journal of Commerce and Commercial. (1946)-. Bulletin. English. One time a week. $490.00 US; $615.00 other. Journal of Commerce Inc., 445 Marshall Street, Phillipsburg NJ 08865. **Tel** (800)222-0356, (908)859-1300. **(Subscription address:** Journal of Commerce, PO Box 5570, New York NY 10087. **)**

DD 382/.0971

ISSN 0228-0043
CN

IMPORT EXPORT BULLETIN. [Import export bull.]. **Added/Corp** National Bank of Canada. Vol. 1, No. 1 (Jan./Mar. 1980)-. Bulletin. English. Four times a year. Free on request. Import Export Bulletin, National Bank of Canada, 500 place d'Armes, Montreal Quebec H2Y 1M7 Canada. **Continues** Import/Export Bulletin.

LC HF2570.5 .A25a
DD 382/.54/09931

NZ

IMPORT LICENSING SCHEDULE. **Main/Corp** New Zealand. Dept. of Trade and Industry. (19??)-. English. One time a year. $35.00. Government Printing Office / New Zealand, 10 Mulgrave Street, Wellington New Zealand. **Tel** 011 64 4 4737211, FAX 011 64 4 734943, telex GOVPRINT NZ 31320. **(Subscription address:** Government Printing Office / New Zealand, PO Box 12052, Wellington New Zealand. **Tel** 011 64 4 4737211.**)**

LC HF3035 .I45
DD 658

ISSN 1065-5158
US

●**IMPORTERS MANUAL USA.** [Import. man. USA]. **VFOAT** Importers Manual United States of America. (1993)-. English. One time a year. $96.00. World Trade Press, 1505 Fifth Avenue, San Rafael CA 94901. **Tel** (800)833-8586, (414)454-9934.

LC HF259.C9 A3
DD 382/.095645/0021

ISSN 0253-858X
CY

IMPORTS AND EXPORTS STATISTICS. See Business and Economics-Abstracting, Bibliographies and Statistics.

LC HF1371
DD 382/.5/0971021

ISSN 0844-837X
CN

IMPORTS BY COUNTRY (H.S. BASED). [Imports ctry. H.S. based]. **Added/Corp** Statistics Canada. International Trade Division. **VFOAT** Importations par Pays (Base du S.H.). Vol. 45, No. 1 (Jan./March 1988)-. Periodical. English (French). Four times a year. 360.00Can$ Canada; $432.00 US; $504.00 other. Statistics Canada Publications Sales and Services, R.H. Coats Building 6th Floor, Ottawa Ontario K1A 0T6 Canada. **Tel** (613)951-5078, (800)267-6677, FAX (613)951-1584, telex 053-3585. **Continues** Imports by Countries, 0318-2606.

LC HF3041
DD 382/.5/0971

ISSN 0844-8353
CN

IMPORTS, MERCHANDISE TRADE (H.S. BASED). [Imports merch. trade H.S. based]. **Added/Corp** Statistics Canada. International Trade Division. **VFOAT** Importations, Commerce de Marchandises (Base du S.H.). (1988)-. English (French). One time a year. 180.00Can$ Canada; $216.00 US; $252.00 other. Statistics Canada Publications Sales and Services, R.H. Coats Building 6th Floor, Ottawa Ontario K1A 0T6 Canada. **Tel** (613)951-5078, (800)267-6677, FAX (613)951-1584, telex 053-3585. **Continues** Imports, Merchandise Trade, 0380-1349.

DD 382/.5/0971

ISSN 0702-8385
CN

IMPORTWEEK. **Added/Corp** Canadian Importers Association. Vol. 64, No. 9 (Aug. 31, 1977)-. Periodical. English. One time a week. 80.04Can$. Canadian Importers Association, 210 Dundas Street West, Suite 700, Toronto Ontario M5Q 2E8 Canada. **Tel** (416)595-5333, FAX (416)595-8226. **ED** Catherin Hodgson. Index available. **Bk Rev. Ad Acc.** Circ: 2,000

Business and Economics — Commerce

(ctrl). available on microfilm and microfiche from University Microfilms International (UMI). **Continues** *Importer's Bulletin, 0318-823X.*
Desc: Digest of information, news and features for importing community.

LC HF54   ISSN 0821-7254
DD 380.1/025/714281   CN
INDEX COMMERCIAL DE MONTREAL.
(INDEX COMMERCIAL DE MONTREAL = MONTREAL TRADE INDEX.). [Index commer. Montr.]. **Main/Corp** Montreal Board of Trade. **VFOAT** Montreal Trade Index; Indice Comercial de Montreal Metropolitan. (1978)-. Directory. English (French). One time a year. $25.00 (members), $50.00 (nonmembers). Montreal Board of Trade, 1080 Beaver Hall Hill, Montreal Quebec H2Z 1S9 Canada. **Tel** (514)878-4651, FAX (514)878-2262, telex 055-61944. **ED** Alex Harper, Kevin Saville and Carl Dysthe. cum. index. **Ad Acc. Circ:** 3,000 (ctrl).

LC HF3943 .I48
DD 382/.5/02594   AT
CEASED
INDEX OF AUSTRALIAN IMPORTERS.
VFOAT Australian Importers. (1978-19??). English. Peter Isaacson Publications, 46-50 Porter Street, Prahran Victoria, 3181 Australia. **Tel** 011 61 3 2457777, FAX 011 61 3 2457606.

ISSN 0019-4735
II
INDIAN EXPORT TRADE JOURNAL, THE. See Political Science-International Relations.

LC HF3783 .I45
DD 382/.6/0954   II
INDIAN EXPORT YEAR-BOOK. English. One time a year. $50.00. Sales Overseas, D-20 Green Park, New Delhi 110016 India. **Tel** 666279. **ED** H R Suri. **Ad Acc. Circ:** 10,000.
Desc: Reference on foreign trade of India. Revised and updated every year. Provides comprehensive information to the foreign businessmen for their trade, both export and import, with India. Also covers the surrounding countries - Bangladesh, Bhutan, Maldives, Nepal, Pakistan and Sri Lanka on these lines.

LC HF3783 .I46
DD 382/.029/454   II
INDIAN IMPORT EXPORT DIRECTORY. See Industry and Production-Trade and Industrial Directories.

LC HF41 .I233   ISSN 0019-512x
II
INDIAN JOURNAL OF COMMERCE, THE. (THE INDIAN JOURNAL OF COMMERCE : A QUARTERLY OF THE INDIAN COMMERCE ASSOCIATION.). **Added/Corp** Indian Commerce Association. (1948)-. Periodical. English. Four times a year. $15.00. Mithila University Kameshwar Nagar, c/o Faculty of Commerce, Darbhanga 846004 Bihar India. **(Subscription address:** Prints India, 11 Darya Ganj, New Delhi 110002 India. **Tel** 011 91 11 3268645, FAX 011 91 11 3275542, telex 31-61087 PRIN-IN.**)**

LC HD9210.I5 I55   ISSN 0019-6401
DD 382'.41'383   II
INDIAN SPICES. See Food and Food Industry.

ISSN 0019-6444
II
INDIAN TRADE JOURNAL. **Added/Corp** India. Commercial Intelligence Dept. India (Republic). Dept. of Commercial Intelligence and Statistics. (1906)-. Periodical. English. One time a week. Price varies. Government of India / Ministry of Urban Development, Department of Publication, Civil Lines, Delhi 110054 India. **(Subscription address:** Prints India, 11 Darya Ganj, New Delhi 110002 India. **Tel** 011 91 11 3268645, FAX 011 91 11 3275542, telex 31-61087 PRIN-IN.**)**

ISSN 0716-2405
CL
INDICADORES DE COMERCIO EXTERIOR. **Added/Corp** Banco Central de Chile. Direccion de Comercio Exterior y Cambios. **VFOAT** Foreign Trade Indicators; Foreign Trade. (19??)-. Spanish (English). Twelve times a year. $300.00. Banco Central de Chile, Casilla 967, 1180 Santiago Chile. **Tel** 011 56 2 6962281, FAX 011 56 2 6984847, telex 40569 CENBC CL. Index available. cum. index. **Circ:** 700 (ctrl).

LC HF
DD 380.1   JM
INDICES OF EXTERNAL TRADE.
Added/Corp Jamaica. Dept. of Statistics. Statistical Institute of Jamaica. (19??)-. English. One time a year. $15.50. Statistical Institute of Jamaica, 9 Swallowfield Road, PO Box 643, Kingston 5 Jamaica. **Tel** 011 809 92621756, FAX 011 809 9264859. **Continues** *Trade Indices.*

IT
INDUSTRIA MERCATO. (19??)-. Italian. Twenty-one times a year. L19000 Italy; L98000 other. Eris Spa, Via E Tellini 14, 20155 Milan Italy. **Tel** 011 39 2 33103305.

LC HF3231 .C65
DD 330.972/005   MX
INDUSTRIALIZACION, COMERCIO Y DESARROLLO. Vol. 7, No. 1 & 2 (Jan./June 1984)-. Periodical. Spanish. Irregular. Secretaria de Comerico, Alfonso Reyes 30, Piso 17, Mexico DF Mexico. **Continues** *Comercio y Desarrollo.*

LC HA1631 .A33 HF1040.9.Y8 Y8
DD 317.971   YU
INDUSTRIJSKI PROIZVODI. See Business and Economics-Abstracting, Bibliographies and Statistics.

LC HF3151   ISSN 1187-5321
DD 381/.1/09714/05   CN
INFO-DETAIL (1991 ENGLISH ED.).
(INFO-DETAIL.). [Info-detail]. **Added/Corp** Conseil Quebecois du Commerce de Detail. Vol. 13, No. 1 Dec./Jan. (1991)-. Periodical. English. Four times a year. Conseil Quebecois du Commerce de Detail, 550 Sherbrooke Street W, Suite 1000, Montreal Quebec H3A 1B9. **Continues in part** *Information Bulletin (Conseil Quebecois du Commerce de Detail)., 0714-2099.*

ISSN 1187-5313
DD 381/.1/09714/05   CN
INFO-DETAIL / LE CONSEIL QUEBECOIS DU COMMERCE DE DETAIL. [Info-detail]. **Added/Corp** Conseil Quebecois du Commerce de Detail. Vol. 13, No 1 (Jan 1991)-. Periodical. French. Four times a year. Conseil Quebecois du Commerce de Detail, 550 Sherbrooke Street W, Suite 1000, Montreal Quebec H3A 1B9. **Continues in part** *Bulletin d'Information (Conseil Quebecois du Commerce de Detail)., 0714-2099.*

ISSN 1021-5956
BE
INFO / EUROPEAN TRADE UNION INSTITUTE. [Info - Eur. Trade Union Inst.]. **Added/Corp** European Trade Union Institute. (1978)-. Monographic series. English. Irregular. Price varies per volume. European Trade Union Institut, boulevard Emile Jacqmain 155, B-1210 Brussels Belgium. **Ind/Abst** Int. Labour Doc.

ISSN 0147-5924
US
INFO FRANCHISE NEWSLETTER, THE.
Vol. 1 (Mar. 1977)-. Newsletter. English. Twelve times a year. $96.00. Info Franchise News, 728 Center Street, Box 550, Lewiston NY 14092. **Tel** (716)754-4669, FAX (905)688-7728. **ED** Ted Dixon. **Bk Rev. Circ:** 4,000.
Desc: Deals with business format franchises (McDonalds etc.), present litigation, legislation, and other matters that affect the franchise world.

ISSN 0226-3165
DD 354.710082/76   CN
INFORMATION CIRCULAR - EXPORT DEVELOPMENT CORPORATION. [Inf. circ. - Export Dev. Corp.]. **Main/Corp** Export Development Corporation (Canada). **VFOAT** Circulaire d'Information - Societe pour l'Expansion des Exportations. No. 80/1-. Monographic series. English (French). Irregular. Price varies per volume. Export Development Corporation, 151 O'Conner Street, Box 655, Ottawa Ontario K1A 1K3 Canada. **Tel** (613)598-2784. **Circ:** 20,000 (ctrl).
Desc: Promotes the financial services available to canadian exporters from EDC.

ISSN 1078-4942
DD 384   US
●### INFORMATION FREEWAY REPORT, THE. See Computers-Online Computing and Information.

BE
INFORMATIONS DU COMMERCE EXTERIEUR. **Main/Corp** Belgium. Office Belge du Commerce Exterieur. Vol. 1, (1963)-. Periodical. French. Four times a year. $149.25. Office Belge du Commerce Exterior, Boulevard Emile Jacqmain 162, 1210 Brussels Belgium. **Tel** 011 32 2 2031986.

LC HF6 .B883a   AG
INFORMATIVO MENSUAL. **Main/Corp** Buenos Aires. Camara de Comercio. (19??)-. Periodical. Spanish. Twelve times a year. Informativo Mensual, Florida 1 - 4 Piso, Buenos Aires Argentina.

LC HF1746 .I57   ISSN 1075-5349
DD 382/.917/05   US
●### INSIDE NAFTA. [Inside NAFTA]. **VFOAT** Inside North America Free Trade Agreement. Vol. 1, No. 1 (Jan. 12, 1994)-. Periodical. English. Twenty-six times a year. $595.00. Inside Washington Publishers, PO Box 7167, Benjamin Franklin Station, Washington DC 20044. **Tel** (703)416-8500, (800)424-9068.

LC HF3000 .I57   ISSN 0897-1676
DD 382   US
INSIDE U.S. TRADE. [Inside U. S. trade]. **VFOAT** Inside United States Trade; Inside US Trade. Vol. 1, No. 1 (Oct. 7, 1983)-. Periodical. English. One time a week. $890.00. Inside Washington Publishers, PO Box 7167, Benjamin Franklin Station, Washington DC 20044. **Tel** (703)416-8500, (800)424-9068.

LC JX1162 .A33   ISSN 1038-6726
AT
INSIGHT : AUSTRALIAN FOREIGN AFFAIRS AND TRADE ISSUES. See Political Science-International Relations.

LC HF1410 .I54   ISSN 0020-5346
GW
CCC
INTER ECONOMICS. [Inter econ.]. **VFOAT** Intereconomics. (Jan. 1966)-. Periodical. English. Six times a year. $79.07. Transaction Publishers / Rutgers State University, Department 3091 or 3092, New Brunswick NJ 08903. **Tel** (908)932-2280 ext. 105, FAX (908)932-3138. **ED** Klaus Kwasniewski. **Bk Rev. Ad Acc. Circ:** 2,300. available on labels; available on microfilm and microfiche from University Microfilms International (UMI). **Continues** *Monthly Review of Economic Policy.*
Desc: Provides a European perspective on major issues in international trade and development. Examines the European Economic Community, monetary policy, resource trade, and overall economic trends as they affect the relationship between Europe, America, and the Third World.
Ind/Abst Contents Recent Econ. J.; Curr. Cit.; Energy Res. Abstr. (Mar. 1982-); GeoRef; Int. Labour Doc.; Middle East Abstr. Index; PAIS Int. Print (1991-).

MX
INTERCAMBIO. **Added/Corp** Instituto de Intercambio Nacional e Interamericano. Instituto de Intercambio Nacional e Interamericano. Boletin. (Nov. 1945)-. Bulletin. English (Spanish). Six times a year. Free. Intercambio, c/o British Chamber of Commerce, Tiber 103-6 Piso, 06500 Mexico DF Mexico. **Tel** 011 52 5332453, telex 1771036. **ED** Jennifer Sibley. **Ad Acc. Circ:** 3,000 (ctrl).
Desc: Thematic reports on recent trade, commerce and investment in Mexico and Britain. Articles to promote both countries covering a special theme in each edition.

LC HF1371 .I58   ISSN 0748-4631
DD 382/.05   US
INTERFLO. (INTERFLO : AN EAST-WEST TRADE NEWS MONITOR.). [Interflo]. **VFOAT** East-West Trade News Monitor. **VAT** East West Trade News Monitor. Vol. 1, No. 1 (Nov. 1981)-. Periodical. English. Twelve times a year. $172.00. Interflo, PO Box 42, Paul Surovell, Maplewood NJ 07040. **Tel** (201)763-9493.

LC HD9540.1 .N37a   ISSN 0146-3845
DD 338.2/7/20973   US
INTERNATIONAL COAL. See Mines and Mining-Mineralogy.

LC HF1371   ISSN 1050-5563
DD 382   US
INTERNATIONAL DIRECTORY OF IMPORTERS. MIDDLE EAST, THE. [Int. dir. import., Middle East]. **Added/Corp** Blytmann International. Interdata (Firm : Healdsburg, Calif.). **VFOAT** Middle East. (198?)-. English. Every 2 years. $185.00. US International Marketing Company, 17057 Bellflower Boulevard, PO Box 428, Bellflower CA 90706. **Tel** (310)925-2918, telex 6502978961.

LC HF1419   ISSN 1050-5466
DD 382/.5/02573   US
INTERNATIONAL DIRECTORY OF IMPORTERS. NORTH AMERICA, THE.
[Int. dir. import., North Am.]. **Added/Corp** Blytmann International. Interdata (Firm : Poulsbo, Wash.). **VFOAT** North America. (1982)-. Directory. English. Every 2 years. $185.00. US International Marketing Company, 17057 Bellflower Boulevard, PO Box 428, Bellflower CA 90706. **Tel** (310)925-2918, telex 6502978961.

LC HF3230.5.A48 I57   ISSN 1050-5547
DD 382/.6/02948   US
INTERNATIONAL DIRECTORY OF IMPORTERS. SOUTH/CENTRAL AMERICA, THE. [Int. dir. import., South/Cent. Am.]. **Added/Corp** Blytmann International. Interdata (Firm : Poulsbo, Wash.). **VFOAT** South/Central America; South

Central America; International Directory of Importers. South America. (198?)-. Directory. English. Every 2 years. $185.00. Export Leads, 1741 Kekamek Northwest, Poulsbo WA 98370. **Tel** (206)779-1511, FAX (206)697-4696.
Desc: Designed and compiled for manufacturers, exporters and trading firms who wish to expand overseas sales. Contains over 100,000 entries of importing firms and major wholesalers.

ISSN 0020-7004
DD 382 US
INTERNATIONAL INTERTRADE INDEX. (INTERNATIONAL INTERTRADE INDEX : I.I.I.). **Added/Corp** International Intertrade Index (Firm). **VFOAT** I.I.I.; III. (19??)-. Periodical. English. Twelve times a year. $45.00. Printing Consultants, Box 636 Federal Square, Newark NJ 07101. **Tel** (201)686-2382. **ED** John E Felber. ***Continues*** *International Import Index.*
Desc: Lists new products displayed at foreign trade fairs. They are offered to importers, distributors, dealers, and manufacturer's representatives.

ISSN 1056-9219
DD 658 US
INTERNATIONAL JOURNAL OF COMMERCE AND MANAGEMENT. (INTERNATIONAL JOURNAL OF COMMERCE AND MANAGEMENT : IJCM.). [Int. j. commer. manage.]. **Added/Corp** International Academy of Business Disciplines. Indiana University of Pennsylvania. College of Business. **VFOAT** IJCM. Vol. 1, No. 1 & 2 (Apr. 1991)-. Periodical. English. Four times a year. $40.00. IJCM, PO Box 1659, Indiana PA 15705.

ISSN 1051-8061
DD 330 US
CCC
INTERNATIONAL MARKET ALERT. [Int. mark. alert]. **Added/Corp** International Reports (Firm). (1990)-. Periodical. English. Seven times a week. $3,300.00. International Reports Inc., 11300 Rockville Pike 1100, Rockville MD 20852. **Tel** (212)685-6900, FAX (212)685-8566, telex 233139 RPTUR. available on an online database (file 636/Full-Text) from DIALOG. ***Continues*** *Daily Telex Alert, 1045-957X.*

ISSN 1321-3512
AT
INTERNATIONAL MERCHANDISE TRADE, AUSTRALIA. **Added/Corp** Australian Bureau of Statistics. (19??)-. Periodical. English. Four times a year. 98.66Aus$. Australian Bureau of Statistics, PO Box 2796Y, Melbourne 3001 Australia. **Tel** 011 61 3 6157843. ***Continues*** *Foreign Trade, Australia. Merchandise Exports and Imports by Country, 1037-9061.*

LC HG4501 **ISSN** 0960-0140
DD 332.6 UK
INTERNATIONAL RISK & PAYMENT REVIEW. **VFOAT** International Risk and Payment Review. (19??)-. Periodical. English. Twelve times a year. $675.93. Dun & Bradstreet, Holmer's Farm Way, High Wycombe, Buckinghamshire HP12 4UL United Kingdom. **Tel** 011 44 1494 422000, FAX 011 44 1494 422260.

US
TITLE CHANGE
INTERNATIONAL ROUND TABLE, THE. (1976)-(19??). English. Thomae & Associates, Box 1056, Seffner FL 33584. **Tel** (813)681-3105. **ED** V. J. Thomae. **Bk Rev. Ad Acc. Circ:** 8,000. ***Continued by*** *Foreign Prospects.*
Desc: Articles of interest to U.S. exporters.

ISSN 0538-7094
BE
INTERNATIONAL STANDARD FIL-IDF. **Main/Corp** International Dairy Federation. **VFOAT** Norme Internationale FIL-IDF; IDF Standard; International Standard; Norme Internationale. Vol. 1 (1955)-. Periodical. English (French). International Dairy Federation, 41 Square Vergote, 1040 Brussels Belgium. **Tel** 011 32 2 7339888, FAX 011 32 2 7330413, telex 63818. Documents available from BIOSIS Document Express.
Ind/Abst Agric. Eng. Abstr. (1991-); Biol. Abstr.; Dairy Sci. Abstr.; Rice Abstr.

ISSN 0306-6045
UK
INTERNATIONAL TAX-FREE TRADER & DUTY-FREE WORLD. See Finance-Taxation.

ISSN 0263-5488
DD 380.1025 UK
INTERNATIONAL TAX-FREE TRADER. BUYERS GUIDE & DIRECTORY. [Int. tax-free trader. Buy. guide dir.]. (1982)-. Trade Publication. English. One time a year. $176.26. Argus Press Group, Queensway House, 2 Queensway Redhill, Surrey RH1 1QS United Kingdom. **Tel** 011 44 1737 768611, 011 44 1737 761685, FAX 011 44 1737 760510, telex 948669 TOPJNL G.

ISSN 1055-5587
DD 382 US
INTERNATIONAL TRADE ALERT (BALTIMORE, MD.). (INTERNATIONAL TRADE ALERT.). [Int. trade alert]. Vol. 1, No. 1 (Apr. 1991)-. Periodical. English. Twelve times a year. $72.00. International Trade Alert, PO Box 2011, Baltimore MD 21203-2011.

LC HF1371 **ISSN** 0744-5660
DD 382 US
INTERNATIONAL TRADE ALERT (NEW YORK, N.Y.). (INTERNATIONAL TRADE ALERT.). [Int. trade alert]. **Added/Corp** American Association of Exporters and Importers. **VFOAT** Alert. (198?)-. Periodical. English. One time a week. $475.00. American Association of Exporters and Importers, 11 West 42nd Street, New York NY 10036. **Tel** (212)944-2230. ***Continues*** *Import Alert, 0195-4458.*

LC HF3800.6 .A173 **ISSN** 0377-0176
DD 382/.025/5952 SI
INTERNATIONAL TRADE AND SINGAPORE. **VFOAT** Kuo Chi Mao I Yu Hsin-Chia-Po. 1973/74-. English (English). $36.00. Sima Publishers, 76F/78F Boon Keng Road, Block 4 12 Singapore.

LC HF
DD 380.1 PP
INTERNATIONAL TRADE. EXPORTS. **VFOAT** International Trade; Exports. March Quarter (1980)-. Periodical. English. Four times a year. k6.00 Papua New Guinea; k7.00 (surface mail), k12.00 (airmail) other. National Statistical Office / New Guinea, PO Wards Strip NCO, Papua New Guinea. **Tel** 011 675 27182 271172, FAX 011 657 255057, telex FINANCE NE 22312. ***Continues in part*** *International Trade (Papua New Guinea. Bureau of Statistics).*

LC HG3753 .I645
DD 382/.63 UK
INTERNATIONAL TRADE FINANCE. Issue 1 (Dec. 4, 1985)-. Periodical. English. Twenty-six times a year. $915.50. Financial Times / UK, Maple House, 149 Tottenham Court Road, London W1P 9LL United Kingdom. **Tel** 011 44 171 8962276, FAX 011 44 171 8962275, 011 44 171 8962399. **ED** Alan Spence. available on an online database (files 16,636/Full-Text) from DIALOG. ***Continues*** *Export Finance Service.*
Desc: A guide for today's hard pressed exporter through the latest developments in finance, whether via conventional funding, government assisted credits or less familiar mechanisms.
Ind/Abst PROMT [Full Txt.]; PTS Newsl. Database [Full Txt.].

LC HF1410 .I62 **ISSN** 0020-8957
DD 382/.05 SZ
CODEN ITFREV
INTERNATIONAL TRADE FORUM. See Business and Economics-Marketing and Purchasing.

LC HF499 .C65 **ISSN** 0589-5669
DD 337.91 SZ
TITLE CHANGE
INTERNATIONAL TRADE - GENERAL AGREEMENT ON TARIFFS AND TRADE. (INTERNATIONAL TRADE.). [Int. trade - Gen. Agreem. Tariffs Trade]. **Added/Corp** General Agreement on Tariffs and Trade (Organization). **VFOAT** GATT International Trade. (1952)-(19??). English. General Agreement on Tariffs and Trade / GATT, Centre William Rappard, 154 rue de Lausanne, 1211 Geneva 21 Switzerland. **Tel** 011 41 22 7395111, 011 41 22 7395019, FAX 011 41 22 7395458. ***Continued in part by*** *General Agreement on Tariffs and Trade (Organization). Activities of GATT, 0589-560X;* ***Merged into*** *International Trade : Trends and Statistics.*
Ind/Abst Manage. Contents (1974-).

LC HF4032 .A25
DD 382/.5/09953021 PP
INTERNATIONAL TRADE. IMPORTS. **VFOAT** International Trade; Imports. (March 1980)-. Periodical. English. Four times a year. k6.00 Papua New Guinea; k7.00 (surface mail), k12.00 (airmail) other. National Statistical Office / New Guinea, PO Wards Strip NCO, Papua New Guinea. **Tel** 011 675 27182 271172, FAX 011 657 255057, telex FINANCE NE 22312. ***Continues*** *International Trade (Papua New Guinea. Bureau of Statistics).*

LC HF4032.3 .A26
DD 382/.099681/0021 GB
INTERNATIONAL TRADE, IMPORTS AND EXPORTS / STATISTICS OFFICE, MINISTRY OF FINANCE, REPUBLIC OF KIRIBATI. **Added/Corp** Kiribati. Ministry of Finance. Statistics Office. (1981)-. Trade Publication. English. One time a year. 410.00. Republic of Kiribati, Statistics Office, Ministry of Finance, Tarawa Kiribati. **Tel** 686 21816, FAX 686 21307. available on diskette. ***Continues*** *Trade (Kiribati).*

ISSN 1034-0505
DD 382.170994 AT
INTERNATIONAL TRADE IN SERVICES, AUSTRALIA. See Business and Economics-Abstracting, Bibliographies and Statistics.

ISSN 0885-3908
DD 382 US
CCC
CODEN ITRJEX
Pr Rev.
INTERNATIONAL TRADE JOURNAL, THE. [Int. trade j.]. **Added/Corp** Laredo State University. Institute of International Trade. Vol. 1, No. 1 (Fall 1986)-. Academic Scholarly Publication. English. Four times a year. $140.00. Taylor & Francis Ltd. / UK, Rankine Road, Basingstoke, Hampshire RG24 8PR United Kingdom. **Tel** 011 44 1256 840366, FAX 011 44 1256 479438, telex 858540. **(Subscription address:** Taylor & Francis Inc., 1900 Frost Road, Suite 101, Bristol PA 19007-1598. **Tel** (215)785-5800, (800)821-8312, FAX (215)785-5515.) **ED** Khosrow Fatemi (editor's address: Laredo State University, One West End Washington Street, Laredo, TX 78040-9660). **Bk Rev. Ad Acc.** available on microfilm and microfiche from University Microfilms International (UMI).
Desc: Published for the enhancement of research in international trade. Its editorial objective is to provide a forum for the scholarly exchanges of findings and significant conceptual or theoretical contributions to the field.
Ind/Abst Curr. Cit.; Econ. Lit. Index; Geogr. Abstr. Human Geogr.; Int. Dev. Abstr.

LC HF3000 .I57 **ISSN** 0748-0172
DD 382/.0973/005 US
CCC
INTERNATIONAL TRADE REPORTER. CURRENT REPORTS. [Int. trade report., Curr. rep.]. **VFOAT** International Trade Reporter. Vol. 1, No. 1 (July 4, 1984)-. Periodical. English. One time a week (50 issues). $1035.00. Bureau of National Affairs Inc., 9435 Key West Avenue, Rockville MD 20850. **Tel** (800)372-1033, (301)258-1033, FAX (301)948-5823. **ED** Deanne E. Neuman. ***Formed by the union of*** *International Trade Reporter's U.S. Import Weekly, 0195-7589* ***and*** *International Trade Reporter's U.S. Export Weekly, 0093-9633.*
Desc: A comprehensive source that reports and analyzes legislative and regulatory developments as well as private sector activities affecting international trade (both export and import).

ISSN 0748-0709
DD 343 US
INTERNATIONAL TRADE REPORTER. DECISIONS (1984). (INTERNATIONAL TRADE REPORTER. DECISIONS.). [Int. trade report., Decis.]. **VFOAT** Decisions; I.T.R.D.; ITRD. Vol. 5, No. 20 (July 4, 1984)-. Periodical. English. Twenty-six times a year (except Wednesdays that follow, or fall on Labor Day and Christmas). $1008.00. Bureau of National Affairs Inc., 9435 Key West Avenue, Rockville MD 20850. **Tel** (800)372-1033, (301)258-1033, FAX (301)948-5823. **ED** Deanne E Neuman. ***Continues*** *International Trade Reporter's U.S. Import Weekly. Decisions.*
Desc: Digest and full text of judicial and administrative decisions in major fields of import law; classified and indexed for easy reference.

ISSN 1043-5670
DD 382 US
CCC
INTERNATIONAL TRADE REPORTER. EXPORT REFERENCE MANUAL. [Int. trade report., Export ref. man.]. **VFOAT** Export Reference Manual. No. 1786 (July 5, 1989)-. Periodical. English. One time a week. $662.00. Bureau of National Affairs Inc., 9435 Key West Avenue, Rockville MD 20850. **Tel** (800)372-1033, (301)258-1033, FAX (301)948-5823. **ED** Deanne E Neuman. ***Continues*** *International Trade Reporter. Export Shipping Manual, 0014-5181.*
Desc: A comprehensive source for foreign import regulations. U.S. export controls, and related requirements for preparing U.S. exports for shipment abroad.

ISSN 1043-5662
DD 382 US
INTERNATIONAL TRADE REPORTER. IMPORT REFERENCE MANUAL. [Int. trade report., Import ref. man.]. **VFOAT** Import Reference Manual; Reference File; International Trade Reporter Reference File. No. 78 (July 26, 1989)-. Periodical. English. Six times a year. $1008.00. Bureau of National Affairs Inc., 9435 Key West Avenue, Rockville MD 20850. **Tel** (800)372-1033, (301)258-1033, FAX (301)948-5823. **ED** Deanne E Neuman. ***Continues*** *International Trade Reporter. Reference File, 0748-0695.*
Desc: A guide to the entire import process with analysis and full text of statutes, regulations, and executive orders on subjects such as customhouse brokers, dumping, countervailing duties, escape clauses, and presidential retaliation.

Business and Economics —Commerce

ISSN 0020-8981
II
INTERNATIONAL TRADE REVIEW.
(1969)-. Periodical. English. Twelve times a year. $14.00. United Asia Publishers PVT Ltd., 12 Rampart Row, Bombay 1 India.

LC HF91 .U473
DD 382/.021
US
INTERNATIONAL TRADE STATISTICS YEARBOOK. See Business and Economics-Abstracting, Bibliographies and Statistics.

SZ
INTERNATIONAL TRADE : TRENDS AND STATISTICS. (19??)-. English (French and Spanish). One time a year. 40.00F. General Agreement on Tariffs and Trade / GATT, Centre William Rappard, 154 rue de Lausanne, 1211 Geneva 21 Switzerland. **Tel** 011 41 22 7395111, 011 41 22 7395019, FAX 011 41 22 7395458. **Continues** International Trade.
Desc: Comprehensive review of recent world trade developments, together with 120 pages of statistical tables and charts. Gives a detailed and practical analysis of major trends in world trade and the factors behind changes taking place in the world economy.

SZ
INTERNATIONAL TRADING ENVIRONMENT : REPORT BY THE DIRECTOR-GENERAL, THE. Main/Corp General Agreement on Tariffs and Trade (Organization). (1989/1990)-. English. One time a year. Free. General Agreement on Tariffs and Trade / GATT, Centre William Rappard, 154 rue de Lausanne, 1211 Geneva 21 Switzerland. **Tel** 011 41 22 7395111, 011 41 22 7395019, FAX 011 41 22 7395458.

LC HG4501 .I59
DD 332.6/73/0917561
ISSN 0735-9225
US
INVESTING & TRADING WITH SPANISH SPEAKING COUNTRIES. See Business and Economics-Investments.

ISSN 8750-6645
US
IOWA COMMERCE. Added/Corp Iowa Association of Business & Industry. Vol. 1, No. 1 (Sept./Oct. 1984)-. Periodical. English. Six times a year. $10.00. Iowa Association Business Industry, 431 East Locust Street, Des Moines IA 50309. **Tel** (515)244-6149.

ISSN 0225-1140
DD 382/.0971/045
ITAL COMMERCE. [Ital commer.]. **Added/Corp** Chambre de Commerce Italienne de Montreal. **VFOAT** Italcommerce. No. 70 (June 1979)-. Periodical. French (Italian and English; summaries and/or abstracts in Italian). Three times a year. Italian Chamber of Commerce, 550 Sherbrooke Street West, Suite 680, Montreal Quebec H3A 1B9 Canada. **Tel** (514)844-4249. **Continues** Chambre de Commerce Italienne de Montreal. Italian Chamber of Commerce Bulletin., 0318-7985.

LC HF19 .I8
DD 382.05
IT
ITALIAN-AMERICAN BUSINESS. See Business and Economics-International Economic Relations.

LC HF19 .I82
DD 330.945/092
ISSN 0021-2997
US
ITALIAN TRADE TOPICS. Added/Corp Italy. Ambasciata (U.S.). Ufficio Commerciale. Vol. 1 (June 1957)-. Periodical. English. Three times a year. Commercial Office, 1601 Fuller Street, Washington DC 20009. **Tel** (202)328-35500.

NE
JAARSTATISTIEK VAN DE BUITENLANDSE HANDEL PER LAND EN GOEDERENSOORT. See Business and Economics-Abstracting, Bibliographies and Statistics.

LC HF157.N4 A3
DD 382
ISSN 0077-6645
NE
JAARSTATISTIEK VAN DE IN-EN UITVOER PER LAND VAN DE NEDERLANDSE ANTILLEN. Added/Corp Netherlands Antilles. Statistieken Planbureau. Netherlands Antilles. Bureau voor de Statistiek. Netherlands Antilles. Dienst Economische Zaken en Welvaartszorg. Afdeling Statistiek. Periodical. Dutch. One time a year.

SZ
JAHRESSTATISTIK DES AUSSENHANDELS DER SCHWEIZ. STATISTIQUE ANNUELLE DU COMMERCE EXTERIEUR DE LA SUISSE. See Business and Economics-Abstracting, Bibliographies and Statistics.

LC HF5251.J3 J43
DD 380.1/025/5982
IO
JAKARTA METROPOLITAN BUYERS' GUIDE. (19??)-. Consumer Publication. English. One time a year. C V Taro & Company, Jalan Samanhundi 2B, PO Box 3472, Jakarta Indonesia.

LC HF
DD 380.1
US
JAMES FORD BELL LECTURES, THE.
Added/Corp Associates of the James Ford Bell Library. Associates of the James Ford Bell Collection. No. 1 (1963)-. English. One time a year. Comes with Associates of the James Ford Bell Library membership. Associates of the James Ford Bell Library, 309 19th Avenue South, Minneapolis MN 55455. **Tel** (612)624-1528, FAX (612)626-9353. **ED** Carol Urness, (editor's phone: (612)624-6895). **Circ:** 500.

LC HC461 .J34
DD 382.058
ISSN 0447-5291
JA
CEASED
JAPAN COMMERCE AND INDUSTRY. See Industry and Production.

LC HF3823 .J2517
DD 380.1/025/52
JA
JAPAN DIRECTORY. (19??)-. Directory. English. One time a year. ¥51,500 Japan; ¥68,000 other. Japan Press Ltd, 12-8 Kita Aoyama, 2-chome Minato-ku, Tokyo 107 Japan. **Tel** (03)404-5161, FAX (03)423-2358, telex 242-5374. **ED** Yoshio Wada. **Ad Acc. Circ:** 25,000.
Desc: Complete coverage of all information concerning foreign and Japanese enterprises, along with details of foreign residents and Japanese business executives in Japan.

LC HF41 .J23
JA
JAPAN EXPORTS & IMPORTS. Vol. 1 (Dec. 1949)-. Periodical. English. Twelve times a year. $2940.00. **(Subscription address:** Maruzen Company Ltd., PO Box 5050, Import & Export Department, Tokyo 100 31 Japan. **Tel** 011 81 3 32789224.)

ISSN 1058-8116
US
JAPAN IMPORT-EXPORT TRENDLETTER. VFOAT Japan Import Export Trendletter. (1991)-. Periodical. English. Twenty-six times a year. $297.00. Kammeier-White & Associates, 24 South Quaker Lane, Number 24, Alexandria VA 22314.

LC HF3823 .J343
DD 382/.029/452
JA
JAPAN TRADE DIRECTORY (NIHON BOEKI SHINKOKAI). (JAPAN TRADE DIRECTORY.). **Added/Corp** Nihon Boeki Shinkokai. (1982)-. Directory. English. One time a year. $245.00. JETRO, 2-5 Toranomon 2 chome, Minato-ku Tokyo 105. **Tel** 03-3582-3518. **(Subscription address:** Gale Research Co., 835 Penobscot Building, Detroit MI 48226. **Tel** (800)347-4253.) **Circ:** 10,000.
Desc: Furnishes the latest available information on 3,000 Japanese companies that import or export 24,000 products and services. Detailed company profiles provide financial data, corporate structure, full information on trade contracts, and the company's interests in importing and exporting.

LC HF1371 .J13
DD 380.1
JA
JETRO WHITE PAPER ON INTERNATIONAL TRADE. See Business and Economics-Abstracting, Bibliographies and Statistics.

ISSN 0361-5561
US
CODEN JCOCBM
JOURNAL OF COMMERCE AND COMMERCIAL (NEW YORK, N.Y. : 1927).
(THE JOURNAL OF COMMERCE AND COMMERCIAL.). [J. commer. commer.]. Vol. 134, No. 10,201 (Jan. 24, 1927)-. English. Seven times a week. $349.00. Journal of Commerce Inc., 445 Marshall Street, Phillipsburg NJ 08865. **Tel** (800)222-0356, (908)859-1300. **(Subscription address:** Journal of Commerce, PO Box 5570, New York NY 10087.) Index available. **Ad Acc.** available on microfilm from University Microfilms International (UMI). Documents available from CASDDS. **Continues** Journal of Commerce Commercial Bulletin and Commercial.
Ind/Abst Bus. Index (1985-); Chem. Abstr.; Chem. Ind. Notes; Gen. BusinessFile (1985-); Gen. Period. Index (1985-); INFO-SOUTH Abstr.; Infobank (Jan. 1969-); Mag. Search; Predicasts; Public Aff. Inf. Serv. Bull.; Trade Ind. Index.

US
JOURNAL OF COMMERCE. EXPORT BULLETIN (NEW YORK, N.Y. : 1978).
(THE JOURNAL OF COMMERCE. EXPORT BULLETIN.). **VFOAT** Export Bulletin. (1978)-. Bulletin. English. One time a week. $490.00 US; $564.00 other. Journal of Commerce Inc., 445 Marshall Street, Phillipsburg NJ 08865. **Tel** (800)222-0356, (908)859-1300. **(Subscription address:** Journal of Commerce, PO Box 5570, New York NY 10087.) **Continues** Journal of Commerce. Export Bulletin.

ISSN 0709-1230
DD 330.9/712
CN
JOURNAL OF COMMERCE (VANCOUVER). (JOURNAL OF COMMERCE.). [J. commer.]. 67th Year, No. 1 (Jan. 2, 1978)-. Periodical. English. Two times a week (104 per year). 351.34Can$. Journal of Commerce Ltd., Box 82230, North Burnaby British Columbia V5C 6E7 Canada. **Tel** (604)433-8164, FAX 433-9549. **ED** Brian Martin. **Ad Acc. Circ:** 6,500 (ctrl). **Formed by the union of** Journal of Commerce. B.C.-Yukon Ed., 0318-8345; Journal of Commerce. Wednesday Ed., 0318-837X **and** Journal of Commerce. Western Canada Ed., 0709-1249.
Desc: The latest information on all types of construction projects from preliminary planning through to final completion. Feature editorials highlight projects, people, associations, political events and labor issues.
Ind/Abst F&S Index Plus Text, Int. [Select. Cov.]; PROMT; Trade Ind. Index (1981-?).

LC HF1416.6.E86 J68
DD 382/.6/09405
ISSN 1049-6483
US
CODEN JEMAEN
Pr Rev.
JOURNAL OF EURO MARKETING. See Business and Economics-Marketing and Purchasing.

LC HF1371 .J68
ISSN 0963-8199
UK
Pr Rev.
JOURNAL OF INTERNATIONAL TRADE AND ECONOMIC DEVELOPMENT. See Business and Economics-International Economic Relations.

LC K10 .O8732
DD 346.73/07/05 347.306705
ISSN 0733-2491
US
JOURNAL OF LAW AND COMMERCE, THE. See Law.

LC HD3616.U45 J68
DD 338.973/005
ISSN 0922-680X
US
CCC
CODEN JRECEC
Pr Rev.
JOURNAL OF REGULATORY ECONOMICS. [J. regul. econ.]. Vol. 1 No. 1 (Mar. 1989)-. Periodical. English. Six times a year. $435.00. Kluwer Academic Publishers / Massachusetts, PO Box 358, Accord Station, Hingham MA 02018. **Tel** (617)871-6600. **ED** Michael Crew. **Bk Rev. Ad Acc. Acid Free. Circ:** 250. available on microfilm and microfiche from University Microfilms International (UMI). Documents available from The Genuine Article.
Desc: A forum for the analysis of regulatory theories and institutions by developing the rigorous economic foundations of regulation.
Ind/Abst Curr. Cit.; Curr. Contents Soc. Behav. Sci.; Econ. Lit. Index (199?-); J. Econ. Lit.; Res. Alert [Full Cov.]; Soc. Sci. Index [Full Cov.].

LC HF1 .F53a
DD 382/.05
ISSN 0146-1958
US
JOURNAL OF THE FLAGSTAFF INSTITUTE. Main/Corp Flagstaff Institute. Vol. 1 (Feb. 1977)-. Periodical. English. Two times a year (March and July). $100.00. The Flagstaff Institute, PO Box 986, Flagstaff AZ 86002. **Tel** (602)779-0052, FAX (602)774-8589. **ED** R. L. Bolin. Index available. cum. index. available on diskette (IBM).
Desc: International trade between third world and advanced nations of manufactured goods covering imports of ten countries of Europe, the USA, and Japan. Statistics and interpretive articles.

LC HF41 .I26
DD 330.954
ISSN 0019-5901
II
JOURNAL OF THE INDIAN MERCHANTS' CHAMBER. Main/Corp Indian Merchants' Chamber. (1908)-. Periodical. Multiple languages (English and Gujarati). Six times a year. $15.00. Indian Merchants' Chamber, 76 Veer Nariman Road, Churchgate Bombay, 400020 India. **(Subscription address:** Prints India, 11 Darya Ganj, New Delhi 110002 India. **Tel** 011 91 11 3268645, FAX 011 91 11 3275542, telex 31-61087 PRIN-IN.)

LC G155.A1 J67
DD 338.4/791/05
ISSN 1035-4662
AT
JOURNAL OF TOURISM STUDIES, THE. See Travel and Tourism.

LC K10 .O9
DD 343/.087/05 342.38705
ISSN 1011-6702
SZ
CCC
Pr Rev.
JOURNAL OF WORLD TRADE. [J. world trade]. Vol. 22, No. 1 (Feb. 1988)-. Periodical. English. Six times a year (Feb., Apr., June, Aug., Oct., Dec.). $518.42. Werner Publishing Company Ltd., PO Box 5134, CH-1211 Geneva 11 Switzerland. **Tel** 011 41 22 3103422. Documents available from The Genuine Article,

UMI Article Clearinghouse. ***Continues*** *Journal of World Trade Law, 0022-5444.*
Desc: Research periodical for all those concerned with international trade, whether academics, practitioners, or government officials. Focuses particularly on the multilateral as well as the regional or bilateral trade negotiations, and the various anti-dumping and unfair trade practices legislations and decisions.
Ind/Abst ABI/INFORM Glob. Ed.; Acad. Search; Bus. Index (1988-); Bus. Source Plus; Bus. Source; Contents Pages Manage.; Curr. Cit.; Curr. Contents Soc. Behav. Sci.; Econ. Lit. Index (19??-); EP Collect.; Gen. BusinessFile (1988-); Gen. Period. Index (1988-); Homework Help.; INFO-SOUTH Abstr.; J. Econ. Lit.; Leg. Resour. Index; LegalTrac (1988-); Mag. Search; MasterFile FullTEXT 1000; MasterFile FullTEXT 350; MasterFile FullTEXT 650; MasterFile FullTEXT (July 1993-); OCLC; PAIS Int. Print (1991-); Plant Genet. Resour. Abstr.; Res. Alert [Full Cov.]; Selec. Coop. Index Manage. Period.; Soc. Sci. Cit. Index [Full Cov.]; Telebase; World Agric. Econ. Rural Sociol. Abstr.

LC HF53 .K33
DD 380.10 JA
KAIGAI SHIJO HAKUSHO. DAI 1 BUNSATSU : SEKAI BOEKI NO GENJO. **Added/Corp** Nihon Boeki Shinkokai. **VFOAT** Sekai Boeki No Genjo. (1972)-. Japanese. ¥3000. Nihon Boeki Shinkokai, c/o Okurasho Insatsukuoku, 2-4 Toranomon 2-chome Minato-ku, Tokyo Japan. ***Supersedes in part*** *Kaigai Shi Jo Hakusho; Gaikan, Chiiki, Shohin Hen.*

LC K
DD 340 JA
KANZEI KANKEI KOBETSU TSUTATSU SHU. **Added/Corp** Japan. Okurasho. Japan. Okurasho. Kanzeikyoku. (19??)-. Periodical. Japanese. ¥5000. Nihon Kangei Kyskai, c/o Jibiki Daini Building, 7-8 Kojimachi 4 Chiyoda-ku 102, Tokyo Japan.

LC HF54.G7 K4 **ISSN** 1350-4150
DD 380.1/029/441 UK
•**KELLY'S.** 107th Ed. (1994)-. English. Reed Information Services Ltd., Windsor Court, East Grinstead House, East Grinstead RH19 1BR United Kingdom. **Tel** 011 44 1342 326972, FAX 011 44 1342 335977, telex 95127 INFSER G. available on an online database from Reed Information Services Ltd.; available on CD-ROM. Documents available from BLDSC. ***Continues*** *Kelly's Business Directory, 0269-9265.*

LC HF54.G7 K4 **ISSN** 0269-9265
DD 380.1/029/441 UK
TITLE CHANGE
KELLY'S BUSINESS DIRECTORY. 100th Ed. (1987)-(1993). Directory. English. Kelly's Directories, Windsor Court, East Grinstead House, East Grinstead West Sussex RH19 1XB United Kingdom. **Tel** 011 44 1342 26972, FAX 011 44 1342 315130, telex 95127 INFSER G. **ED** D Lammin and J Foreman. **Ad Acc. Circ:** 11,000. ***Continues*** *Kelly's Manufacturers and Merchants Directory, 0075-5370.* ***Continued by*** *Kelly's, 1350-4150.*
Desc: Contains information on more than 84,000 companies under 10,000 classified trade and professional headings.

UK
CEASED
KELLY'S U.K. EXPORTS. **VFOAT** U.K. Exports. (19??)-(19??). Directory. English (French and German). Reed Information Services Ltd., Windsor Court, East Grinstead House, East Grinstead RH19 1BR United Kingdom. **Tel** 011 44 1342 326972, FAX 011 44 1342 335977, telex 95127 INFSER G. **ED** David Lammin. **Ad Acc. Circ:** 30,000 (ctrl).
Desc: Contains details on more than 16,000 British exporting companies.

ISSN 1102-6650
SW
KEMIVARLDEN. **See** Chemistry and Chemicals-Physical and Theoretical Chemistry.

LC HF **ISSN** 0279-5388
DD 381.0973 US
KENTUCKY JOURNAL OF COMMERCE AND INDUSTRY, THE. **Added/Corp** Associated Industries of Kentucky. (19??)-. Trade Publication. English. Twenty-five times a year. $5.00. Kentucky Journal of Commerce, 2303 Greene Way, Louisville KY 40220. **Tel** (502)587-0769. **ED** Larry A. Maggard. **Bk Rev. Ad Acc. Circ:** 6,000. ***Continues*** *Action in Kentucky.*
Desc: News, features and columns dealing with Kentucky business, tax and labor climate, along with other matters that affect Kentucky employers.

LC HF46 .K43 **ISSN** 0453-6460
DD 382/.6/096762 KE
SUSPENDED
KENYA EXPORT NEWS (1976). (KENYA EXPORT NEWS.). [Kenya export news]. Vol. 1 (July 1967)-(19??). Periodical. English. Twelve times a year. Finlay House, Mfango Street, PO Box 40106, Nairobi Kenya. ***Separated from*** *East African Report on Trade and Industry.*

LC HC252.2 .K48 **ISSN** 0142-5048
DD 338.7/4/02541 UK
KEY BRITISH ENTERPRISES : KBE / COMPILED AND PUBLISHED BY PUBLICATIONS DIVISION, DUN & BRADSTREET LIMITED. **Added/Corp** Dun & Bradstreet, Ltd. **VFOAT** KBE; K.B.E. (19??)-. English. One time a year. $795.00. Dun & Bradstreet Information Services, 3 Sylvan Way, Parsippany NJ 07054. **Tel** (201)605-6000, (800)526-0651. **ED** Steve Birtles. Index available. cum. index. **Bk Rev. Ad Acc. Circ:** 3,000 (ctrl). available on an online database from Pergamon Press. ***Continues*** *Guide to Key British Enterprises.*
Desc: A comprehensive and up-to-date register of 25,000 of the UK's top companies. Each entry gives financial data or turnover and capital, details of trade, trade names, trading styles, a full listing of directors by name and function.

LC HF5415 .K47
JA
KIKAN YUSO TEMBO. **Added/Corp** Nittsu Sogo Kenkyujo. **VFOAT** Quarterly Journal of Distribution; Yuso Tembo. (19??)-. Japanese. Nittsu Sogo Kenkyujo, 12-9 Soto Kanda, 3 Chiyoda-ku Tokyo 101 Japan.

ISSN 1050-169X
DD 382 US
KING'S COALSTATS. GRAIN EXPORT REPORT. (KING'S COALSTATS. GRAIN EXPORT REPORT [COMPUTER FILE].). [King's coalstats, Grain export rep.]. **Added/Corp** King Publishing Company. **VFOAT** Grain Export Report. (198?)-. English. One time a week. King Publishing Company, PO Box 52210, Knoxville TN 37950. **Tel** (615)584-6294, FAX (615)558-6101, telex 705286.
Desc: Available in dBase III+, LOTUS 123, ASCII, and King's Software.

LC HF1051 .K63
JA
KOKUSAI SHIGEN. **Added/Corp** Kokusai Shigen Mondai KenkyÂukai. No. 1 (1974)-. Periodical. Japanese. Twelve times a year. ¥1000. Kokusai Shigen Mondai Kenkyukai, (International Resources Research Council), 14-9 Roppongi, 3-chome Minato-ku Japan. **Tel** (03)470-1958.

RU
KOMMERCHESKII VESTNIK. **Added/Corp** Vsesoiuznyi Nauchno-Issledovatelskii Institut po Izucheniiu Sprosa Naseleniia Na Tovary Narodnogo Potrebleniia It Koniunktury Yorgovii. Mezhduvedomstvennyi Sovet po Izucheniiu Sprosa Naseleniia na Tovary Narodnogo Potreblenia. (1???)-. Periodical. Russian. Twenty-four times a year. $159.95. **(Subscription address:** East View Publications Inc., 3020 Harbor Lane North, Suite 110, Minneapolis MN 55447. **Tel** (800)477-1005, (612)550-0961, FAX (612)559-2931.)

AT
KOMPASS; REGISTER OF SPANISH INDUSTRY AND COMMERCE. **See** Industry and Production.

LC HC430.5.A1 K64
DD 338/.0025/51249 CH
KOMPASS; REGISTER OF TAIWAN INDUSTRY AND COMMERCE. **See** Industry and Production.

ISSN 0217-0604
DD 382 SI
KOMPASS SINGAPORE. [Kompass Singap.]. **VFOAT** Register of Singapore Industry and Commerce. (1971)-. English. One time a year. $370.00. Reed Information Services Ltd., Windsor Court, East Grinstead House, East Grinstead RH19 1BR United Kingdom. **Tel** 011 44 1342 326972, FAX 011 44 1342 335977, telex 95127 INFSER G. **(Subscription address:** Reed Reference Publishing Company / New Jersey, 131 Chanlon Road, PO Box 31, New Providence NJ 07974. **Tel** 800 223-1797, (908)464-6802.)

LC HF1584.5.Z44 E864
GW
KOOPERATION (LIESSEM, WACHTBERG, GERMANY). (KOOPERATION.). **Added/Corp** European Community. Gulf Cooperation Council. **VFOAT** Taawun. (1986)-. Periodical. German (English). Irregular. DM89.00. Vandenhoeck & Ruprecht, Robert Bosch Breite 6, D-37079 Goettingen Germany. **Tel** 011 49 551 695911, FAX 011 49 551 695917, telex 965226 VAN d.
Ind/Abst Postharvest News Inf.

LC G155.K6 K84a
DD 380.1/4591519/504 KO
KOREAN TOURISM ANNUAL REPORT. **Main/Corp** Kukche Kwangwang Kongsa. **VFOAT** Annual Report; Annual Report, Korean Tourism. (19??)-. Trade Publication. English. One time a year.
Desc: Information on the tourist trade in Korea.

LC HF3865 .K6
DD 380.1/025/5195 KO
KOREAN TRADE DIRECTORY. **Added/Corp** Hanguk Muyok Hyophoe. (1959)-. English. One time a year (Jan.). $110.00. Korean Foreign Trade Association, 159-1 Samsund Dong Kangnam-ku, Seoul Korea. **Tel** 011 82 2 5515114, FAX 011 82 2 5515161, 011 82 2 5515100, telex 24265. **ED** Duck-Woo Nam. **Ad Acc. Circ:** 20,000 (ctrl).
Desc: Lists of member firms and their lines of business.

LC HF13 .K6 **ISSN** 0023-4311
XR
KOVOEXPORT : CZECHOSLOVAK EXPORT MAGAZINE. **Added/Corp** Ceskoslovenska Obchodni Komora. Kovo, Prague. (1955)-. Periodical. English. Six times a year. DM72.00. **(Subscription address:** Kubon & Sagner, ABT Zeitschriftenimport, D 80328 Munich Germany. **Tel** 011 49 89 54218130.)
Ind/Abst Text. Technol. Dig.

LC HF37.H8 K84
HU
KUELGAZDASAG. **Added/Corp** Magyar Kereskedelmi Kamara. Konjunktura- es Plackutato Intezet. Vol. 16 (1972)-. Periodical. Hungarian (summaries and/or abstracts in English and Russian). Twelve times a year. $30.00. Kopint Datorg, Dorottya U 6, H-1389 Budapest Hungary. **Tel** 011 36 1 851137. **(Subscription address:** Kultura, PO Box 143, H-1300 Budapest 3 Hungary. **Tel** 011 36 1 2500194.) ***Supersedes*** *Kulkerskedelem.*

LC HD2321
DD 338.025 GW
•**KUENSTLER JAHRBUCH.** (1994)-. Directory. English. One time a year. DM48.00. Verlag Disco Post GmbH, Oststrasse 2, 56424 Staudt Germany. **Tel** 011 49 2602 70044, FAX 011 49 2602 69939. **Ad Acc, Adv Mgr:** Karin Ostrowski. Full Page (B&W) DM1250.00. Full Page (Color) DM1875.00. **Circ:** 10,000.

LC HF41 .K78 **ISSN** 1002-5030
CC
KUO CHI HUO I. (INTERTRADE.). [Intertrade]. **Added/Corp** Kuo Chi Mao I Yen Chiu So (China). **VFOAT** International Trade. (Oct. 1983)-. Periodical. English (summaries and/or abstracts in Chinese; translations available in Chinese). Twelve times a year. $72.00. Ministry of Foreign Economic Trade, Beijing, People's Republic of China. **(Subscription address:** Commercial Marketing Association International, 7515 Topton Street, Suite 100, New Carrollton MD 20784. **Tel** (301)577-9340.) **Ad Acc.** ctrl circ.
Desc: China's official monthly business magazine. It contains information on China's trade and investment policies and provides interpretation of Chinese trade laws.

LC HF3846 .K86
DD 382/.0951/249 CH
KUO CHI MAO I SHIH WU WEN TA TZU LIAO HUI PIEN. Chinese. $500.00. Chung-Hua Chi Yeh Kuan Li Fa Chan Chung Hsin, PO Box 14232, Taipei Taiwan.

LC HC121 .K87
GW
KURZBERICHT UEBER LATEINAMERIKA. **See** Business and Economics-International Economic Relations.

LC HF331.K65 K954
KO
KYONGGI PUKPU SANGUI. Periodical. Korean. Twelve times a year. Not for Sale. Kyonggi Pukpu Sanggong, Hoeuiso 106 Uijongbu 3-dong Uijongbu-si, Kyonggi-do Korea.

LC HB9 .K95
JA
KYUSHU SANGYO DAIGAKU SHOKEI RONSO. **See** Business and Economics.

LC HG1501
DD 332.1 US
•**LAGNIAPPE MONTHLY ON LATIN AMERICAN PROJECTS AND FINANCE.** **See** Finance.

LC HF248.J39 I53A
IO
LAPORAN TAHUNAN / DEPARTEMEN PERDAGANGAN DAN KOPERASI, KANTOR WILAYAH PERDAGANGAN PROPINSI JAWA TIMUR. **Main/Corp** Indonesia. Kantor Wilayah Perdagangan Propinsi Jawa Timur. 1978-. Indonesian. One time a year. JL Kendungdoro No 52, Surabaya Indonesia. ***Continues*** *Indonesia. Departemen Perdagangan. Kantor Wilayah Propinsi Jawa Timur. Laporan Tahunan.*

Business and Economics —Commerce

LC HF1597 .I53A
IO
LAPORAN TAHUNAN - DIREKTORAT JENDERAL HUBUNGAN EKONOMI LUAR NEGERI. Main/Corp Indonesia. Direktorat Jenderal Hubungan Ekonomi Luar Negeri. Indonesian. Direktorat Jenderal Hubungan Ekonomi Luar Negeri, Jl Sisingamangaraja No 73, Jakarta Indonesia.

LC HF248.D5 I54A
IO
LAPORAN TRIWULAN - PERWAKILAN DEPARTEMEN PERDAGANGAN PROPINSI DJAWA-TIMUR. Main/Corp Indonesia. Departemen Perdagangan. Perwakilan Propinsi Jawa Timur. Indonesian. Djalan Kedungdoro Nomor 32, Surabaya Indonesia.

LC WMLC L 83/6521
LO
LESOTHO EXPORT DIRECTORY. Added/Corp Lesotho. Trade Promotion Unit. (19??)-. English. Ministry of Trade, Industry & Tourism, Trade Promotion Unit, Department of Trade and Industry, Maseru Lesotho.

MX
LEY DEL IMPUESTO GENERAL DE IMPORTACION : NUEVO SISTEMA ARMONIZADO. Spanish. Irregular (Includes approximately 7 updates per year). $250.00. Informacion Aduanera de Mexico, Avenido Amores 1544, Col del Valle, 03100 Mexico DF Mexico. **Tel** 011 52 5 5247425, FAX 011 52 5 5249890.
Desc: Includes import and export tariffs, explanation, compensatory fees, and other matters related in to the importation and exportation sectors of Mexico.

NE
LINER TRADE REPORT. (19??)-. Dutch. Irregular. Dynamar BV, PO Box 440, 1800 AK Alkmaar Netherlands.

IT
LISTINO PREZZI PARTI RICAMBIO AUTOVETTURE E VEICOLI COMMERCIALI. (19??)-. Italian. One time a year. L220000. Societa Editoriale Assicurativ, Corso G Matteotti 22, 20121 Milan Italy. **Tel** 011 39 2 7764298.

IT
LISTINO PREZZI PARTI RICAMBIO MOTOVEICOLI E VEICOLI INDUSTRIALI. (19??)-. Italian. L60000. Societa Editoriale Assicurativ, Corso G Matteotti 22, 20121 Milan Italy. **Tel** 011 39 2 7764298.

IT
LISTINO QUINDICINALE DEI PREZZI ALL'INGROSSO PRATICATI SULLA PIAZZA DI ROMA. Added/Corp Camera di Commercio, Industria, Artigianato e Agricoltura (Rome, Italy). (1979)-. Periodical. Italian. Twenty-four times a year. L74940. Camera di Commercio / Rome, Industria e Agricoltura, Via C Columbo 112, 00186 Rome Italy. **Tel** 011 39 6 52082597. **Continues** Rome (City). Camera di Commercio, Industria e Agricoltura. Listino Settimanale dei Prezzi All'Ingrosso Praticati Sulla Piazza di Roma.

ISSN 1043-1039
DD 382
US
LIVE ANIMAL TRADE & TRANSPORT MAGAZINE. [Live anim. trade transp. mag.]. **VFOAT** Live Animal Trade and Transport Magazine. Vol. 1, No. 1 (Apr. 1989)-. Periodical. English. Four times a year. $20.00. Silesia Companies Inc, PO Box 441110, Fort Washington MD 20744. **Tel** (301)292-1970, FAX (301)292-1787, telex 4997385. **ED** D. Anderson (phone: (301)292-1970). Each issue contains an index to its own contents (no volume index)--loose. **Bk Rev**, (Qty: 8 /yr). **Ad Acc. Circ:** 1,700 (ctrl).
Desc: Subject matter is animal transport and the international trade of live animals. Contains stories on shipments, carriers and ports, equipment, markets, regulators, animal welfare, etc. Covers livestock, pets, horses, exotics, lab animals, live fish, birds and biological materials.

LC HF5065.L8 L68
ISSN 0147-4464
DD 382/.025/763
US
LOUISIANA INTERNATIONAL TRADE DIRECTORY. (1973)-. Directory. English. $25.00. International Marketing Institute, University of New Orleans, Lake Front, New Orleans LA 70122. **Tel** (504)286-6963. **ED** Thomas S O'Connor. **Ad Acc. Circ:** 2,500 (ctrl).
Desc: A directory of Louisiana based manufacturers, importers, exporters, and others involved in international trade.

ISSN 0723-3361
GW
UDC 339.174
CCC
M-+-A-REPORT (1982). See Business and Economics-Chamber of Commerce.

LC HF265 .A42
DD 380.1
SA
MAANDELIKSE UITTREKSEL VAN HANDELSTATISTIEKE : STATISTIEKE VRYGESTEL DEUT DIE KOMMISSARIS VAN DOEANE EN AKSYNS VAN DIE REPUBLIEK VAN SUID-AFRIKA TEN OPSIGTE VAN BUITELANDSE HANDEL VAN DIE TOLUNIEGEBIED BOTSWANA, LESOTHO, NAMIBIE, SUID-AFRIKA EN SWAZILAND / MONTHLY ABSTRACT OF TRADE STATISTICS : STATISTICS RELEASED BY THE COMMISSIONER FOR CUSTOMS AND EXCISE OF THE REPUBLIC OF SOUTH AFRICA IN RESPECT OF THE FOREIGN TRADE OF THE CUSTOMS UNION AREA OF BOTSWANA, LESOTHO, NAMIBIA, SOUTH AFRICA, AND SWAZILAND. See Business and Economics-Abstracting, Bibliographies and Statistics.

LC HF5421.5.N4 N48a
NE
MAANDSTATISTIEK VAN DE BINNENLANDSE HANDEL EN DIENSTVERLENING. Main/Corp Netherlands. Centraal Bureau voor de Statistiek. (Jan. 1976)-. Dutch. Twelve times a year. $75.78. SDU Uitgeverij, Postbus 20014, Christoffel Plantijnstraat, 2500 EA Den Haag Netherlands. **Tel** 011 31 70 3789911. **Supersedes** Maandstatistiek van de Binnenlandse Handel.

LC HF3611 .M3
ISSN 0923-1668
NE
MAANDSTATISTIEK VAN DE BUITENLANDSE HANDEL. [Maandstat. buitenl. handel]. **Added/Corp** Netherlands. Centraal Bureau voor de Statistiek. **VFOAT** Monthly Statistical Bulletin of Foreign Trade. (1989)-. Bulletin. Dutch (English). Twelve times a year. $108.25. SDU Uitgeverij, Postbus 20014, Christoffel Plantijnstraat, 2500 EA Den Haag Netherlands. **Tel** 011 31 70 3789911. **Formed by the union of** Maandstatistiek van de Buitenlandse Handel per Goederensoort, 0024-8738 **and** Maandstatistiek van de Buitenlandse Handel per Land, 0024-8746. **Continued in part by** Toelichting op de Statistieken van de Buitenhandel.

NE
MAATSCHAPPIJ BELANGEN. (19??)-. Dutch. Twelve times a year. Fl38.00. Wyt Uitgeefgrouep, Postbus 6438, 3002 AK Rotterdam Netherlands. **Tel** 011 31 10 4762566, 011 31 10 4255944, FAX 011 31 10 4780904.

IT
MADE IN BIELLA. (19??)-. Italian. Two times a year. L14000 Italy; L23000 other. Aemmepi, Via Italia N 50, 13051 Biella VC Italy. **Tel** 011 39 15 31633.

LC HF3031 .M23
ISSN 0160-614X
DD 382/.6/0973
US
SUSPENDED
MADE IN USA. VAT Made in United States of America. Vol. 1 (Jan./Feb. 1979)-Suspended Sept. 1980. Periodical. English. Six times a year. $25.00. World Trade Associates, c/o Circulation Manager, 14842 First Avenue S, Seattle WA 98168.

LC HF1371 .M35
DD 382/.05
FR
●**MAIN DEVELOPMENTS IN TRADE ... ANNUAL REPORT. Added/Corp** Organisation for Economic Co-operation and Development. (1993)-. English. One time a year. $17.50. OECD Publications and Information Center, 2 rue Andre-Pascal, 75775 Paris Cedex 16 France. **Tel** 011 33 1 49104262, US:(202)785-6323, FAX 011 33 1 45248500, 011 33 1 45248176, telex 620 160 OCDE. **(Subscription address:** OECD Publications Center, 2001 L Street, Suite 700, Washington DC 20036. **Tel** (202)822-3873, (202)785-6323.)

US
MAINE REVISED STATUTES ANNOTATED / MAINE LEGISLATIVE SERVICE. Main/Corp Maine. Periodical. English. West Publishing Company, 620 Opperman Drive, PO Box 64526, Eagan MN 55123-1308. **Tel** (612)687-8000, (800)328-9352, FAX (612)687-7602.

LC HF3931 .A25
DD 338.7/4/025669
UK
CEASED
MAJOR COMPANIES OF NIGERIA. (1979)-(19??). English. Graham & Trotman Ltd., Sterling House, 66 Wilton Road, London SW1V 1DE United Kingdom. **Tel** 011 44 171 8211123, FAX 011 44 171 8288935. **ED** M. Lawn and Jennifer Carr. **Bk Rev. Ad Acc.**

ISSN 1355-7939
DD 338.70941
UK
●**MAJOR UK COMPANIES HANDBOOK.** [Major UK Co. handb.]. **VFOAT** Major United Kingdom Companies Handbook. (1994)-. English. Two times a year. £185.00 UK; £210.00 other. Extel Financial Ltd., Fitzroy House, 13-17 Epworth Street, London EC2A 4DL United Kingdom. **Tel** 011 44 171 8258000, FAX 011 44 171 8258328, telex 884319 EXTELX G. **Continues** Extel Financial Handbook of Market Leaders.

LC HF3907.Z6 M34
DD 343.6897/087/05 346.897038705
MW
MALAWI BUYERS GUIDE. See Business and Economics-Marketing and Purchasing.

SZ
MANUAL OF TARIFF COORDINATING CONFERENCES RESOLUTIONS--PASSENGER; TC23/TC123 RESOLUTIONS, EUROPE/MIDDLE EAST-JAPAN/KOREA. Main/Corp International Air Transport Association. **VFOAT** TC23/TC123 Resolutions, Europe/Middle East-Japan/Korea. (19??)-. English. Irregular. 320.00F. International Air Transport Association / Geneva, PO Box 672, CH-1215 Geneva 15 Switzerland. **Tel** 011 41 22 7992525, 011 41 22 7992760. **(Subscription address:** International Air Transport Association, 2000 Peel Street, Room 3050, Montreal, Quebec, H3A 2R4 Canada. **Tel** (514)844-6311.)

UY
MANUAL PRACTICO DEL IMPORTADOR. Added/Corp Centro de Estadisticas Nacionales y Comercio Internacional del Uruguay, Montevideo. Uruguay. Laws, Statutes, etc. (19??)-. Spanish. $650.00. CENCI Centro de Estadisticas Nacionales y Comercio Internacional del Uruguay, Misiones 1361 Casilla 1510, Montevideo Uruguay. **Tel** 011 598 2 95-29-30, 95-45-78.

IT
MANUALE DISCIPLINA ECONOMICA SCAMBI ESTERO. (19??)-. Italian. Irregular. L300000. Edizioni Doganali, Via Nizza 3/2, 16145 Genoa Italy. **Tel** 011 39 10 301514, 011 39 10 301926.

ISSN 0984-9521
UDC 338 (8)
FR
MARCHES AFRICAINS (PARIS. 1988). (MARCHES AFRICAINS.). (1988)-. Periodical. French. One time a week. $1290.45. IC Publications Ediafric, 10 rue Vineuse, 75116 Paris France. **Tel** 011 33 1 44308100. **Continues** Afrique Informations (Paris), 0753-0145.

LC HC10 .M3
ISSN 0025-2859
DD 330.913
FR
MARCHES TROPICAUX ET MEDITERRANEENS. [Marches trop. mediterr.]. No. 674 (Oct. 11, 1958)-. Periodical. French. One time a week. Price varies. Moreux SA, 190 boulevard Haussmann, 75008 Paris France. **Tel** 011 33 1 44959992, FAX 011 33 1 49539016, telex NAVIMAR 290 131 F. **ED** Serge Narpaud. **Bk Rev. Ad Acc. Circ:** 16,000. **Continues** Marches Tropicaux du Monde; **Absorbed** Afrique Industrie.
Desc: African trade review.
Ind/Abst F&S Index Plus Text, Int. [Select. Cov.]; Hum. Rights Intern. Rep.; Int. Dev. Abstr. (?-?); Int. Labour Doc.; LABORDOC; Leis., Rec., Tour. Abstr.; Maize Abstr.; PESTDOC (?-?); PROMT.

LC HE561 .M24
ISSN 1059-2970
DD 387.5/099/05
US
MARINE DIGEST AND TRANSPORTATION NEWS. [Mar. dig. transp. news]. **VFOAT** Marine Digest. Vol. 66, No. 6 (Sept. 19, 1987)-. Trade Publication. English. Twelve times a year. $28.00. Marine Digest, PO Box 3905, Seattle WA 98124. **Tel** (206)682-3607, FAX (206)682-4023. **ED** Alex Fisken. **Bk Rev**, (Qty: 1-2). **Ad Acc, Adv Mgr:** Jim Lengell. **Circ:** 5,000 (ctrl). **Continues** Marine Digest, 0025-3197.
Desc: This magazine serves the maritime and shipping community primarily in California, Oregon, Washington, British Columbia and Alaska.

LC HD9466.I5 M35A
DD 382/.43
IT
MARINE PRODUCTS EXPORT REVIEW. Main/Corp Marine Products Export Development Authority. English. 5.00. M G Road PB 1708, Cochin India.

Business and Economics — Commerce

LC HD9007.V8 V56a
DD 381/.41/09755
ISSN 0507-066X
US
MARKET NEWS (RICHMOND). See Agriculture.

LC HC260.C6 M352
DD 380.1/0941
UK
MARKET RESEARCH GREAT BRITAIN. See Business and Economics-Marketing and Purchasing.

DD 380/.029471
ISSN 1180-4696
CN
MARKETPLACE (TORONTO). (MARKETPLACE / WORLD TRADE CENTRE TORONTO.). [Marketplace]. **Added/Corp** World Trade Centre Toronto. (Apr. 1990)-. Periodical. English. Twelve times a year. Limited free distribution. World Trade Center Toronto, 60 Harbour Street, Toronto Ontario M5J 1B7 Canada.

DD 336.2/65/0971
ISSN 1183-3246
CN
MCGOLDRICK'S CANADIAN CUSTOMS TARIFF HARMONIZED SYSTEM. [McGoldrick's Can. customs tariff "Harmon. Syst."]. **VFOAT** Canadian Customs Tariff "Harmonized System". (198u)-. Trade Publication. English. One time a year. 186.47Can$. McMullin Publishing Ltd, 417 St. Pierre Street, Montreal Quebec H2Y 2M4 Canada. **Tel** (514)849-1424, FAX (514)849-9809. **Continues** McGoldrick's Hand Book of the Canadian Customs Tariff and Excise Duties, 0076-1990.

LC HD9410.4 .O73a
DD 338.4/76649/0021
FR
MEAT BALANCES IN OECD COUNTRIES = BILANS DE LA VIANDE DANS LES PAYS DE L'OCDE. See Agriculture-Livestock.

LC HF3801 .M43
IO
MEDIA KOMUNIKASI & INFORMASI. **Added/Corp** Indonesia. Departemen Perdagangan dan Koperasi. Bagian Hubungan Masyarakat. **VFOAT** Media Komunikasi dan Informasi. Vol. 1, No. 1 (May 1980)-. Periodical. Indonesian. Bagian Humas Depdagkop, Moh. Ridwan Rais No 5A, Jakarta Pusat Indonesia.

GW
MEIER'S ADRESSBUCH INTERNATIONALER EINKAUFSFUHRER. **Added/Corp** Verlag von Meier's Addressbuch der Exporteure und Importure. (1991)-. Periodical. German. **Continues** Meier's Adressbuch der Exporteure und Importeure.

LC HF
DD 380.1
UDC 62(44)
ISSN 1164-1711
FR
MEILLEURES ADRESSES DE LA FONDERIE (PARIS), LES. (LES MEILLEURES ADRESSES DE LA FONDERIE.). (19??)-. French. One time a year. 582.94F France; 790.00F other. Revue Francaise des Metallurgistes, 32 rue Saint Marc, 75002 Paris France. **Tel** 011 31 1 42603151, FAX 011 31 1 42603842.

GT
MEMBERSHIP DIRECTORY. **Main/Corp** Guatemalan-American Chamber of Commerce. Directory. English. Apartado Postal 832 9A Calle 5-54, Zona 1, Guatemala Republica de Guatemala. **Continues** Membership Directory / American Chamber of Commerce of Guatemala.

US
MEMBERSHIP DIRECTORY / AMERICAN ASSOCIATION OF EXPORTERS AND IMPORTERS. **Main/Corp** American Association of Exporters and Importers. (1981/82)-. Periodical. English. One time a year. Price varies per volume. American Association of Exporters and Importers, 11 West 42nd Street, New York NY 10036. **Tel** (212)944-2230. **ED** G. Muller. Index available. **Ad Acc.** ctrl circ. **Continues** Membership Directory (American Importers Association).

LC HF296 .W29a
DD 381/.06/2753
ISSN 0362-3807
US
MEMBERSHIP DIRECTORY - METROPOLITAN WASHINGTON BOARD OF TRADE. **Main/Corp** Metropolitan Washington Board of Trade. (19??)-. Directory. English. One time a year. $25.00. The Greater Washington Board of Trade, 1129 20th Street Northwest, Suite 200, Washington DC 20036. **Tel** (202)857-5944.

LC S
DD 630
FR
MEMOIRES DE LA SOCIETE D'AGRICULTURE, COMMERCE, SCIENCES ET ARTS DU DEPARTEMENT DE LA MARNE. See Agriculture.

LC HF1502 .C46A
DR
MEMORIA ANUAL DEL CENTRO DOMINICANO DE PROMOCION DE EXPORTACIONES. **Main/Corp** Centro Dominicano de Promocion de Exportaciones. Spanish. One time a year. Centro Dominicano de Promocion de Exportaciones, Plaza de la Independencia, Santo Domingo Republica Dominicana. **Continues** Informe de Labores - Centro Dominicano de Promocion de Exportaciones.

SP
MERCADO MUNDIAL. WORLD MARKET. **VFOAT** World Market. No. 1 (March 1962)-. Periodical. Spanish. Twelve times a year. $40.00. Mercado Mundial, Germ Perez Carras 63, Apartado 14440, Madrid 27 Spain.

AT
MERCANTILE AGENT. English. Twelve times a year. 80.00Aus$. Institute of Mercantile Agents Ltd., PO Box 182, Penrith New South Wales, 2750 Australia. **Tel** 047 31 1405, FAX 047 322171. **ED** J. Chesterfield-Evans. **Ad Acc. Circ:** 600 (ctrl).
Desc: Provides professional information for mercantile agents.

LC Z733 .M672 no.1
DD 382
ISSN 0543-5056
US
MERCHANT EXPLORER, THE. (THE MERCHANT EXPLORER; A COMMENTARY ON SELECTED RECENT ACQUISITIONS.). [Merch. explor.]. **Added/Corp** University of Minnesota. Libraries. James Ford Bell Collection. James Ford Bell Library. No. 1 (Apr. 1961)-. English. One time a year. Comes with Associates of the James Ford Bell Library membership. Associates of the James Ford Bell Library, 309 19th Avenue South, Minneapolis MN 55455. **Tel** (612)624-1528, FAX (612)626-9353. **ED** Carol Urness (editor's phone: (612)624-6895). **Circ:** 500.

GW
MEROITICA. **Added/Corp** Berlin. Universitat. Bereich Agyptologie und Sudanarchaeologie. (1973)-. Monographic series. German. Irregular. Price varies per volume. Akademie-Verlag GmbH, Postfach, D-13162 Berlin Germany. **Tel** 011 49 30 47889300, FAX 011 49 30 47889357. **(Subscription address:** VCH Publishers Inc., 303 Northwest 12th Avenue, Journals Department, Deerfield FL 33442. **Tel** (800)367-8249, (305)428-5566.)
Ind/Abst Anthropol. Lit.

LC HC131 .L374
DD 330.972/005
ISSN 0968-2724
UK
●**MEXICO AND NAFTA REPORT.** **VFOAT** Latin American Regional Reports. Mexico Report; Latin American Regional Reports. Mexico and NAFTA Report; Mexico & NAFTA Report. (Jan 14, 1993)-. Periodical. English. Twelve times a year. $265.00. Lettres UK Ltd, 61 Old Street, London EC1V 9HX United Kingdom. **Tel** 011 44 171 2510012, FAX 011 44 171 2538193. **ED** Peter Rodger. available on an online database from Lexis-Nexis. **Continues** Latin America Regional Reports. Mexico & Central America, 0143-5264.
Desc: This has been specially formulated to address the dynamic development of the New Mexican political and economic environment, with expanded coverage of the North American Free Trade Agreement.

DD 341
ISSN 1058-5702
US
MEXICO TRADE AND LAW REPORTER. (MEXICO TRADE AND LAW REPORTER : THE MONTHLY SERVICE COVERING MEXICAN-U.S., MEXICAN-CANADIAN TRADE.). [Mex. trade law report.]. **Added/Corp** International Trade Information Corp. Vol. 1, No. 1 (Oct. 1991)-. Periodical. English. Twelve times a year. $195.00. International Trade Information Corporation, 445 G Street NW Suite 203, Washington DC 20001. **Tel** (202)783-4100.

LC HF1479 .C36d
DD 382/.92/097105
ISSN 1187-6492
CN
MINUTES OF PROCEEDINGS AND EVIDENCE OF THE SUB-COMMITTEE ON INTERNATIONAL TRADE OF THE STANDING COMMITTEE ON EXTERNAL AFFAIRS AND INTERNATIONAL TRADE. [Minutes proc. evid. Sub-Comm. Int. Trade Standing Comm. Extern. Aff. Int. Trade]. **Main/Corp** Canada. Parliament. House of Commons. Sub-Committee on International Trade. **VFOAT** Proces-Verbaux et Temoignages du Sous-Comite du Commerce Exterieur du Comite Permanent des Affaires Etrangeres et du Commerce Exterieur. 34th Parliament, 3rd Session, Issue No. 1 (June 20, 1991/Oct. 10, 1991)-. Proceedings. English (French).

LC UG628
DD 358.4/03/097105
ISSN 0848-7936
CN
MINUTES OF PROCEEDINGS AND EVIDENCE OF THE SUB-COMMITTEE ON NORAD OF THE STANDING COMMITTEE ON EXTERNAL AFFAIRS AND INTERNATIONAL TRADE. [Minutes proc. evid. Sub-Comm. NORAD Standing Comm. Extern. Aff. Int. Trade]. **Main/Corp** Canada. Parlement. Chambre des Communes. Sous-Comite sur le NORAD. **VFOAT** NORAD; Proces-Verbaux et Temoignages du Sous-Comite sur le NORAD du Comite Permanent des Affaires Etrangeres et du Commerce Exterieur. 2nd Session of the 34th Parliament, Issue No. 1 (Oct. 25/Nov. 22, 1990)-. Proceedings. French (English).

UK
SUSPENDED
MOBILE COMMUNICATIONS FOR UK COMMERCE & INDUSTRY. (19??)-Suspended (19??). Periodical. English. Four times a year. EMAP Response Directories, Equity & Law House, 11-19 Priestg, Peterborough PE1 1EL United Kingdom. **Tel** 011 44 1733 63100, FAX 011 44 1733 87367.

DD 343.7105/6/0263
ISSN 1193-1051
CN
TITLE CHANGE
MODIFICATION AU TARIF. [Modif. tarif]. **Main/Corp** Canada. Douanes et accise. (Feb. 27, 1992)-(1993). French. **Continues** Canada. Douanes et Accise., 0849-3839; Tariff Amendment. **Continued by** Canada. Accise, Douanes et Impot. Modification au Tarif, 1193-1051.

SZ
MONATSSTATISTIK DES AUSSENHANDELS DER SCHWEIZ. STATISTIQUE MENSUELLE DU COMMERCE EXTERIEUR DE LA SUISSE. **Main/Corp** Switzerland. Eidgenossische Oberzolldirektion. **VFOAT** Statistique Mensuelle du Commerce Exterieur de la Suisse. (1885)-. Periodical. Multiple languages (French and German). Twelve times a year. $233.85. Directorate General of Swiss Customs, Section Statistics, Monbijoustrasse 40 CH-3003, Bern Switzerland. **Tel** 011 41 31 3226610, FAX 011 41 31 3227872, telex 845 911100.

DD 382/.025
ISSN 0384-6032
CN
MONTHLY EX.-IM. OPPORTUNITIES. (THE MONTHLY EX.-IM. OPPORTUNITIES.). (Feb. 1976)-. Periodical. English. 55.00Can$ US and Canada; 70.00Can$ other. Elic Dass, PO Box 490 Station A, Western Ontario M9N 3N3 Canada. **Tel** (905)438-8266.

LC HF3790.5 .A27
DD 382/.6/095491
PK
MONTHLY EXPORT TRENDS. **VFOAT** Export Trends. Vol. 1, No. 1 (Feb. 1986)-. Periodical. English. Twelve times a year. $30.00. Export Trends/Shareen Chamber, A 4 Commercial Area Block 7 8, K C H S Karachi Pakistan. **Tel** 011 91 21 435804, 011 91 21 443321.

LC HF46 .B35c
DD 382/.0964
ISSN 0851-0202
MR
MONTHLY INFORMATION REVIEW - BANQUE MAROCAINE DU COMMERCE EXTERIEUR. (MONTHLY INFORMATION REVIEW.). [Mon. inf. rev. - Banq. maroc. commer. exter.]. **Main/Corp** Banque Marocaine du Commerce Exterieur. No. 1 (July 1976)-. Periodical. English (French). Twelve times a year. Free on request. Banque Marocaine Commerce Ext, 140 Avenue Hassan II, Casablanca Morocco. **Tel** 011 212 34 272049. Index available. cum. index. **Bk Rev. Circ:** 11,000 (ctrl). **Formed by the union of** Bulletin Bimestriel d'Information - Banque Marocaine du Commerce Exterieur **and** Revue Bimensuelle de la Banque Marocaine du Commerce Exterieur.
Desc: Articles relating to foreign trade, finance and general economy.
Ind/Abst Public Aff. Inf. Serv. Bull.

Business and Economics —Commerce

LC HF266.U4 A33
DD 382/.09676/1 UG
MONTHLY TRADE BULLETIN - MINISTRY OF FINANCE, PLANNING AND ECONOMIC DEVELOPMENT, STATISTICS DIVISION. See Business and Economics-Abstracting, Bibliographies and Statistics.

LC LB2335.86
DD 331.88 UK
MSF : MANUFACTURING, SCIENCE, FINANCE. VFOAT M.S.F.; Manufacturing, Science, Finance. July/Aug. (1988)-. Periodical. English. Six times a year. *Continues in part* ASTMS Journal.

LC HD2755.5 .M8347 **ISSN** 0197-4637
DD 388.8/8/05 US
MULTINATIONAL MONITOR. [Multinatl. monit.]. **Added/Corp** Corporate Accountability Research Group (Washington, D.C.). **VFOAT** Monitor. Vol. 1, No. 1 (Feb. 1980)-. Periodical. English. Ten times a year. $30.00. Corporate Accountability Research, PO Box 19405, Washington DC 20036. **Tel** (202)387-8034. **ED** John Richard. Index available. **Bk Rev. Circ:** 3,700 (ctrl). available on microfilm and microfiche from University Microfilms International (UMI); available via Internet (gopher essential.org). Documents available from UMI Article Clearinghouse.
Desc: Analyzes the impact of multinational corporations on people throughout the world.
Ind/Abst Altern. Press Index; Energy Res. Abstr. (July 1980-); Expand. Acad. Index (1992-); Hum. Rights Intern. Rep.; Left Index; Newsp. Period. Abstr. (1992-); PAIS Int. Print (1991-).

LC HF3041 **ISSN** 1021-4186
DD 382 BE
UDC 38(4)
MULTINATIONAL SERVICE. [Multinatl. serv.]. (1966)-. Periodical. English (French). Twenty-four times a year. 32000.00F Belgium; 32950.00F Rest of Europe; 33150.00F other. Europe Information Service, rue de Geneve 21, 1140 Brussels Belgium. **Tel** 011 32 2 242 6020, FAX 011 32 2 242 9549. available on an online database from DIALOG.
Desc: Reports on multinational corporations and their dealings with the EU.

LC HF5239.M9 M97
DD 338.4/025/5487 II
MYSORE STATE TRADE AND INDUSTRIAL DIRECTORY. (19??)-. Directory. English. Every 2 years. Rs12.00. Allied Business Enterprises, 94 9th Cross Hanumanthanagar, Bangalore 19 India.

ISSN 1075-9050
DD 382/.71/097 US
NAFTA DIGEST / NORTH AMERICAN FREE TRADE AGREEMENT INFORMATION CENTER, THE GRADUATE SCHOOL OF INTERNATIONAL TRADE & BUSINESS ADMINISTRATION, LAREDO STATE UNIVERSITY. [NAFTA dig.]. **Added/Corp** Laredo State University. Office for the Study of U.S.- Mexico Trade Relations. **VFOAT** Digest. Vol. 1, No.1 (Jan. 1992)-. Periodical. English. Twelve times a year. $30.00. Laredo State University, 1 West End Washington Street, Laredo TX 78040. **Tel** (512)722-8001. *Continues* Free-trade Winds.

LC KDZ1100 **ISSN** 1381-4605
DD 341.2 NE
UDC 341.241:339.542
●**NAFTA: LAW AND BUSINESS REVIEW OF THE AMERICAS.** [NAFTA: law bus. rev. Am.]. **Added/Corp** American Bar Association. Section of International Law and Practice. **VFOAT** North American Free Trade Agreement: Law & Business Review of the Americas. (1995)-. Periodical. English. Four times a year. $219.00. Kluwer Law International / Netherlands, PO Box 85889, 2508 CN The Hague Netherlands. **Tel** 011 31 70 3081500, FAX 011 31 70 3081515.

LC HF3811 .N38
DD 381/.025/598 IO
NATIONAL BUYERS' GUIDE TO INDUSTRIAL PRODUCTS AND BUSINESS SERVICES, THE. VFOAT Petunjuk Pembeli di-Indonesia Untuk Produksi Industri dan Bidang Jasa. Consumer Publication. Multiple languages (English and Indonesian).

LC HF5466 N37 **ISSN** 1050-5830
DD 381/.142/029473 US
NATIONAL DIRECTORY OF CATALOGS, THE. VFOAT Oxbridge Directory of Catalogs. (1990)-. Directory. English. One time a year. $245.00. Oxbridge Communications Inc., 150 5th Avenue, Room 302, New York NY 10011. **Tel** (212)741-0231, FAX (212)633-2938. **(Subscription address:** Gale Research Co., 835 Penobscot Building, Detroit MI 48226. **Tel** (800)347-4253.)
Desc: List over 7,000 US & Canadian consumer and business-to-business catalogs.

LC HD9361.7.A3 S35
DD 381/.45/663102541 UK
NATIONAL GUARDIAN DIRECTORY OF THE SCOTTISH LICENSED TRADE, THE. (19??)-. Directory. English. Muro-Barr Publications, 113 St. Vincent Street, Glasgow United Kingdom. *Continues* Scottish Licensed Trade Directory.

ISSN 1079-638X
DD 380 US
NATIONAL HOME CENTER NEWS NEWSFAX. [Natl. home ctr. news newsfax]. VFOAT Newsfax. (1992)-. Periodical. English. One time a week. $150.00. Racher Press, 220 Fifth Avenue, New York NY 10001. **Tel** (212)213-6000, FAX (212)213-6106.

LC HC431 .N27
DD 332.6 II
NATIONAL INVESTMENT AND FINANCE. See Business and Economics-Investments.

LC HF1009.5 HF1416.5 .N38 **ISSN** 1064-9913
DD 382 US
NATIONAL TRADE DATA BANK, THE. (THE NATIONAL TRADE DATA BANK [COMPUTER FILE] : NTDB.). [Natl. trade data bank]. **Added/Corp** United States. Dept. of Commerce. Office of Business Analysis. **VFOAT** NTDB. (Oct. 1990)-. English. Twelve times a year. $370.00. National Technical Information Service - NTIS, Room 2027S, 5285 Port Royal Road, Springfield VA 22161. **Tel** (703)487-4630, (703)487-4660, (703)487-4650, FAX (703)321-8547, telex 89-9405.
Desc: System requirements: IBM PC, XT, AT or compatible, minimum 512K RAM, CD-ROM drive, CD-ROM extensions installed under PC-DOS or MS-DOS version 3.1 or higher (mouse, hard disk, EGA or VGA monitor, and printer are optional).

LC HF3901.A48 N37 **ISSN** 0077-5894
DD 380.1/029/468 SA
NATIONAL TRADE-INDEX OF SOUTH AFRICA. VFOAT National Trade Index of South Africa. (19??)-. English. One time a year. $43.24. Intratex Printing and Publishing Company, PO Box 1405, Pine Town 3600 South Africa. **Tel** 011 27 31 7017021, FAX 011 27 31 7017036, telex 624529. **ED** A Stagg. Index available. ctrl circ. *Absorbed* Afrikaans Handels-Indeks.
Desc: Classified section, trademark and brand-name section, nation-wide phone and address section, government departments, national associations, South African diplomatic missions in other countries, and diplomatic missions in South Africa.

SA
NATIONAL TRADE INDEX OF SOUTH AFRICA AND RHODESIA. (1928)-. English. One time a year. R65.00. AC Braby Pty Ltd, PO Box 1426, Pinetown 3600 South Africa. **Tel** 011 27 31 7017021, FAX 011 27 31 7017036, telex 624529. **ED** Graham Cleveland. **Ad Acc.**
Desc: A reference guide aimed at the businessperson.

US
NATIONAL TRADE POLICY AGENDA : MESSAGE FROM THE PRESIDENT OF THE UNITED STATES TRANSMITTING THE NATIONAL TRADE POLICY AGENDA FOR ... AND AN ADDENDUM TO THE ... ANNUAL REPORT ON THE TRADE AGREEMENTS PROGRAM ... PURSUANT TO PUBLIC LAW 100-418 SEC 1641. **Added/Corp** United States. President. (1989)-. Government Publication. English. One time a year. Superintendent of Documents, US Government Printing Office, Washington DC 20402. **Tel** (202)275-3328, FAX (202)786-2377. available on microfiche

ISSN 1185-5304
DD 380.1 CN
NATURAL GAS MARKET UPDATE. [Nat. gas mark. update]. **Added/Corp** British Columbia. Ministry of Energy, Mines and Petroleum Resources. Vol. 1, No. 1 (Jan. 1991)-. Periodical. English. Twelve times a year. Ministry of Energy, Mines and Petroleum Resources, Petroleum Resources Division, Energy Resources Division, Victoria British Columbia Canada.

II
NEPAL TRADE DIRECTORY. (1967)-. Directory. English. Trade Promotion Centre, PO Box 825, Pulchowk Latipur Nepal. **Tel** 5-24771, 5-24772, telex NP 2302 TPC. **Ad Acc.**
Desc: Lists all exporters and importers of Nepal.

ISSN 1072-3536
DD 384 US
NETFAX NEWS. [Netfax news]. (Apr. 1992)-. Periodical. English. Twelve times a year. $299.00. Davidson Consulting, 530 North Lamer Street, Burbank CA 91506. **Tel** (818)842-5117, FAX (818)842-5488.

LC HF1371
DD 382 UK
●**NEW IN DUTY FREE.** (1995)-. Trade Publication. English. Argus Press Group, Queensway House, 2 Queensway Redhill, Surrey RH1 1QS United Kingdom. **Tel** 011 44 1737 768611, 011 44 1737 761685, FAX 011 44 1737 760510, telex 948669 TOPJNL G.

LC DU421 .N42a **ISSN** 1171-7092
NZ
TITLE CHANGE
NEW ZEALAND EXTERNAL RELATIONS AND TRADE RECORD. Main/Corp New Zealand. **Added/Corp** New Zealand. Ministry of External Relations and Trade. **VFOAT** External Relations and Trade Record; Record. Vol. 1, No. 1 (June 1992)-(1993). Periodical. English. New Zealand Ministry of Foreign Affairs, Private Bag, Wellington 1 New Zealand. **Tel** 011 64 4 728877, FAX 011 64 4 729596, telex NZ 3441. *Continued by* New Zealand. New Zealand Foreign Affairs and Trade Record.

LC DU421 .N42a **ISSN** 1172-7195
NZ
●**NEW ZEALAND FOREIGN AFFAIRS AND TRADE RECORD.** Main/Corp New Zealand. **Added/Corp** New Zealand. Ministry of Foreign Affairs and Trade. **VFOAT** Foreign Affairs and Trade Record; New Zealand External Relations and Trade. Vol. 2, No. 2 (July 1993)-. Periodical. English. Eleven times a year. $59.87. New Zealand Ministry of Foreign Affairs, Private Bag, Wellington 1 New Zealand. **Tel** 011 64 4 728877, FAX 011 64 4 729596, telex NZ 3441. *Continues* New Zealand. New Zealand External Relations and Trade Record, 1171-7092.

JA
NEWS FROM MITI. Main/Corp Japan. Tsusho Sangyosho. **Added/Corp** Japan. Tsusho Sangyosho. Information Office. **VAT** News From Ministry of International Trade and Industry. (19??)-. Periodical. English. Free on request. Ministry of International Trade and Industry Japanese Government, 3 1 1 Chome Kasumigaseki, Chiyoda Ku Tokyo 100 Japan.

ISSN 0738-9485
US
NEWSLETTER / CALIFORNIA COUNCIL FOR INTERNATIONAL TRADE. [Newsl. - Calif. Counc. Int. Trade]. **Added/Corp** California Council for International Trade. (19??)-. Newsletter. English. Four times a year. Price varies. California Council for International Trade, 77 Jack London Square, Oakland CA 94607. **Tel** (510)452-0770. **ED** Niels Erich. ctrl circ.
Desc: Digest of international trade and investment related issues and meetings for the California business community.

LC HF5286.5.A3 N5 **ISSN** 0331-0973
NR
NIGERIAN YELLOW PAGES : AN A TO Z TRADE DIRECTORY. VFOAT A to Z Trade Directory. (1979)-. Directory. English. One time a year. $50.00. ICIC Ltd, Directory House, 28 Taoridi Street PO Box 5736, Opposite Census Office PMB 3204, Suru-Lere Lagos Nigeria. **Tel** 830163, 831909. **Ad Acc. Circ:** 100,000.

LC HF1040.9.J3 N45
JA
NIHON KOGYO SEIHIN SORAN = INDUSTRIAL PRODUCTS INDEX OF JAPAN. VFOAT Industrial Products Index of Japan. (1973)-. Japanese. One time a year. ¥29000. Nihon Kogyo Shimbun, Sankei Building, 7 2 1 Chome Ohtemachi, Chiyoda-Ku Tokyo 100 Japan. **Tel** 11 81 3 231 7111 ext. 3558, FAX 11 81 3 3295-3991.

LC HF3826.5 .N54
JA
NIHON NO PURANTO YUSHUTSU SENRYAKU. **Added/Corp** Jukagaku Kogyo Shimpo. Jukagaku Kogyo Tsushinsha. (19??)-. Periodical. Japanese. ¥5800. Jukagaku Kogyo Tsushinsha, (Heavy and Chemical Industry News Agency), 2-15 Kanda Jinbo-cho Chiyoda-ku, Tokyo 101 Japan.

LC HF1604.Z4 J366
JA
NITCHU KEIZAI KYOKAI KAIHO. Main/Corp Nitchu Keizai Kyokai. (19??)-. Japanese. Twelve times a year. ¥500. Nitchu Keizai Kyokai, c/o Aoyama Building, 2-3 Kita Aoyama 1-chome Minato-ku, Tokyo 107 Japan.

LC HF3828.C6 T62
JA
NITCHU-NISSO BOEKI HANNEMPO. **Added/Corp** Ajia Boeki Tsushiusha. No. 21 (1978)-. Periodical. Japanese. Two times a year. Ajia Boeki

Business and Economics — Commerce

Tsushinsha, c/o Nitchu Yuko Kaikan, 4 Kanda Nishikicho 1-chome Chiyoda-ku, Tokyo 101 Japan. **Continues** *Tozai Boeki Repoto*.

LC HD9787.U45 U55A **ISSN** 0196-4712
DD 338.4/768531/00973 US
NONRUBBER FOOTWEAR: ANNUAL SURVEY OF PRODUCERS AND IMPORTERS. (NONRUBBER FOOTWEAR. ANNUAL SURVEY OF PRODUCERS AND IMPORTERS : REPORT TO THE PRESIDENT ON INVESTIGATION NO. 332-93 UNDER SECTION 332 OF THE TARIFF ACT OF 1930, AS AMENDED.). (1976/1977)-. English. One time a year. United States International Trade Commission, 500 E Street Southwest, Washington DC 20436. **Tel** (202)205-1806.

ISSN 0244-4623
FR
UDC 382(100-77)
NORD SUD EXPORT. [Nord Sud export]. (1981)-. Periodical. French. Twenty-two times a year. $1596.66. Nord Sud Export, 46 rue Provence, 75009 Paris France. **Tel** 011 33 1 48784849.

LC HF1746 .N72 **ISSN** 1071-958X
DD 382/.097/005 US
●**NORTH AMERICAN TRADE GUIDE.** [N. Am. trade guide]. (1994)-. English. One time a year. $385.00. North American Publishing Company, 401 North Broad Street, Philadelphia PA 19108. **Tel** (215)238-5300, (800)777-8074, FAX (215)238-5283.

ISSN 1184-0587
DD 343.71/087/05 CN
NOTICE OF DECISION ON PUBLIC INTEREST REPRESENTATIONS. [Not. decis. public interest represent.]. **Main/Corp** Canadian International Trade Tribunal. (1990)-. English.

ISSN 0225-414X
DD 382/.456853/0971 CN
NOTICE TO IMPORTERS. [Notice import.]. **Main/Corp** Canada. Office of Special Import Policy. **VFOAT** Avis aux Importeurs. No. 101- Nov. 16, 1978-. Periodical. English (French). Free. Office of Special Import Policy, Department of Industry Trade and Commerce, 235 Queen Street, 10th Floor East, Ottawa Ontario K1A 0H5 Canada. ctrl circ.

LC HF19 .M5
DD 380.1/05 IT
NOTIZIARIO COMMERCIALE. **Main/Corp** Camera di Commercio, Industria, Artigianato e Agricoltura di Milano. (19??)-. Italian. Twelve times a year. Free on request. Camera di Commercio Industria Artigianato E Agricoltura di Milano, via Meravigli 9 B, 20123 Milan Italy. **Tel** 011 39 2 85154516. **Continues** *Camera di Commercio, Industria e Agricoltura di Milano. Notiziario Commerciale*.

LC PN1 .N6 **ISSN** 0550-1326
FR
NOUVEAU COMMERCE, LE. (Autumn/Winter 1963)-. Periodical. French. Irregular. $83.11. ACNC Nouveau Commerce, 80 rue des Archives, 75003 Paris France. **ED** Marcelle Fonfrede. Index available ($140.00). **Continues** *Commerce*.

LC HF37 .N6 **ISSN** 0469-0281
YU
NOVA TRGOVINA. **Added/Corp** Sindikat Radnika i Sluzbenika Trgovinskih Preduzeca Jugoslavije. Savez Radnika Namestenika Trgovackih Preduzeca Jugoslavije. Vol. 1 (June 1948)-. Periodical. Serbo-Croatian (Roman). Twelve times a year. $160.00. **(Subscription address:** Jugoslavenska Knjiga, PO Box 36, YU 11001 Belgrade Yugoslavia. **Tel** 011 38 11 621055, FAX 011 38 11 325970.**)**

LC HF25 .N6
RU
NOVYE TOVARY. **Added/Corp** Vsesoiuznaia Torgovaia Palata (Soviet Union). (1957)-. Periodical. Russian. Twelve times a year. $139.95. **(Subscription address:** East View Publications Inc., 3020 Harbor Lane North, Suite 110, Minneapolis MN 55447. **Tel** (800)477-1404, (612)550-0961, FAX (612)559-2931.**)**

IT
NUOVA TARIFFA DOGNALE INTEGRATA. Italian. Euroitalia Editrice Srl, Via XX Settembre 37/12, 16121 Genoa Italy. **Tel** 011 39 10 593519, 011 39 10 566648.

LC HD6935.5.A5 N48
DD 331.88/025/93 NZ
NZCTU DIRECTORY. **Main/Corp** New Zealand Council of Trade Unions. (1991)-. Directory. English. **Continues** *New Zealand Council of Trade Unions. Official ... NZCTU Trade Union Directory, 0114-9296*.

ISSN 0250-6203
US
TITLE CHANGE
OAS CECON TRADE NEWS. **Added/Corp** Organization of American States. External Sector Program. International Trade and Export Development Program (Organization of American States) Organization of American States. Special Committee for Consultation and Negotiation. **VFOAT** CECON Trade News. **VAT** Organization of American States, Special Committee for Consultation and Negotiation Trade News. Vol. 1, No. 2 (Dec. 1976)-Vol. 18, No. 9 (Sept. 1993). Periodical. English. Organization of American States, 19th Street & Constitution Avenue NW, Suite 300, Washington DC 20006. **Tel** (202)458-6256. **Continues** *CECON Trade News*. **Continued by** *Trade News (Washington, D.C.)*.

LC HF37.C9 P7
XR
OBCHOD VE SVETE. **Added/Corp** Vyzkumny Ustav Obchodu (Prague, Czechoslovakia). Vol. 19 (Jan. 1967)-. Czech. Twelve times a year. kcs78.00. Merkur Etc, Gorkeho Nam 36, 115 69 Prague 1, Czech Republic. **Tel** 011 42 2 2362891, FAX 011 42 2 2362873, telex 121648. **Continues** *Dokumentacni Sluzba*.

LC KF1987.A15 O33 **ISSN** 0278-6389
DD 343.73/0878 347.303878 US
OFFICIAL EXPORT GUIDE. [Off. export guid]. (19??)-. Trade Publication. English. One time a year. $399.00. North American Publishing Company, 401 North Broad Street, Philadelphia PA 19108. **Tel** (215)238-5300, (800)777-8074, FAX (215)238-5283.
Desc: Features in-depth market profiles of 197 countries along with the complete Harmonized Schedule B, Export Administration Regulations and country-by-country listing of documentation requirements and port facilities, plus projected needs for US goods and services by market.

LC HF1455 .U4636A **ISSN** 0740-3488
DD 336.24/3/0973 US
OPERATION AND EFFECT OF THE DOMESTIC INTERNATIONAL SALES CORPORATION LEGISLATION ... ANNUAL REPORT, THE. [Operat. eff. domest. int. sales corp. legis. Annu. rep.]. **Main/Corp** United States. Dept. of the Treasury. English. One time a year. Department of the Treasury / Pennsylvania Avenue, Fifteenth Street and Pennsylvania Avenue NW, Washington DC 20220. **Tel** (202)566-2969. **Continues** *Annual Report on the Operation and Effect of the Domestic International Sales Corporation Legislation, 0098-1931*.

LC HF1721 .U47a
DD 382.7/53/05 US
OPERATION AND EFFECTS OF THE GENERALIZED SYSTEM OF PREFERENCES. **Main/Corp** United Nations Conference on Trade and Development. **Added/Corp** United Nations Conference on Trade and Development. Special Committee on Preferences. 1st Review (5th Session, 3-13 Apr. 1973)-. Government Publication. English. Irregular. $12.50. United Nations Publications, 2 United Nations Plaza, Room DC2 0853, Department 007C, New York NY 10017. **Tel** (212)963-8303, (800)253-9646.
Desc: Concentrates on evaluating the effects of the preferential tariff treatment granted to imports from developing countries by developed industrial countries, including special measures in favor of the least-developed countries.

ISSN 1201-3838
CN
OPPORTUNITIES CANADA : FRANCHISE AND DEALERSHIP GUIDE. (19??)-. English. Three times a year. 10.37Can$. Opportunities Canada, 2550 Goldenridge Road, Unit 42, Mississauga Ontario L4X 3S2 Canada. **Tel** (905)277-5600, FAX (905)277-3397. **ED** R.A. Sinclair. Index available. **Ad Acc**. **Circ:** 18,000.

LC HF3161.O7 O76 **ISSN** 0731-9096
DD 382/.025/795 US
OREGON INTERNATIONAL TRADE DIRECTORY. [Oregon int. trade dir.]. **Added/Corp** Oregon. International Trade Division. (1978-79)-. English. One time a year. State of Oregon, 155 Cottage Street Northeast, Salem OR 97310. **ED** Douglas V. Frengle. **Circ:** 3,000 (ctrl).
Desc: Lists Oregon companies engaged in exporting and importing. Information is cross-indexed by company, product, country of activity, and geographic location of the firm.

US
●**ORGANIZATIONAL COMPUTING AND ELECTRONIC COMMERCE.** **See** Business and Economics-Computer Applications.

LC HF91 .U482 **ISSN** 0082-9846
DD 382 US
CEASED
OVERSEAS BUSINESS REPORTS. (1962)-(19??). Monographic series. English. Superintendent of Documents, US Government Printing Office, Washington DC 20402. **Tel** (202)275-3328, FAX (202)786-2377. available on microfilm and microfiche from University Microfilms International (UMI). Documents available from Documents on Demand. **Continues in part** *World Trade Information Service*.
Desc: Information on the economic overlook, industry trends, trade regulations, distribution and sales channels, transportation, credit, and other facets of business in various countries.
Ind/Abst Am. Stat. Index; Predicasts Forecasts.

LC HF1371
DD 382 CN
●**OVERSEAS EXPORTERS.** (1994)-. Newsletter. English. Twelve times a year. $75.00. Global Traders Association, PO Box 797, Station A, Scarborough Ontario M1K 5C8 Canada. **Tel** (416)650-9309, FAX (416)650-9280. **Bk Rev**. **Ad Acc**. **Circ:** 370. available with charts; available with illustrations.

LC J961 .H835 HF4036
DD 300/.996/11 382/.099611/00212 FJ
OVERSEAS TRADE FIJI. English. One time a year. Government of Fiji / Bureau of Statistics, Box 2221, Suva Fiji Islands. **Tel** 011 679 315144. **Circ:** 102.

NZ
OVERSEAS TRADE (WELLINGTON, N.Z.). (OVERSEAS TRADE.). (1987/88)-. English. One time a year. Department of Statistics / New Zealand, PO Box 2922, Wellington New Zealand. **Tel** 011 64 4 4954600. **Formed by the union of** *Report and Analysis of External Trade, 0077-9806*; *Imports (Wellington, N.Z. : 1983)* **and** *Exports (Wellington, N.Z. : 1983)*.

AT
OVERSEAS TRADING. **Added/Corp** Australia. Dept. of Commerce and Agriculture. Australia. Dept. of Trade. Australia. Dept. of Trade and Resources. Vol. 1 (May 1947)-. Periodical. English. Twelve times a year. 45.22Aus$. Minnis Business Press Pty. Ltd., 1 Hobson Street, PO Box 186, South Yarra Victoria 3141 Australia. **Tel** 011 61 3 8266333, FAX 011 61 3 8266284. **ED** M. Wilson. **Ad Acc**, **Adv Mgr:** E. Livingstone. **Circ:** 10,000 (ctrl).
Ind/Abst AESIS Q.

LC HF1371 **ISSN** 1064-9832
DD 382 US
PACIFIC BASIN/ASEAN BUSINESS. [Pac. basin/ASEAN bus.]. Vol. 1, No. 1 (Aug. 1992)-. Periodical. English. Twelve times a year. $350.00. The Lawrence Report, PO Box 215, New Rochelle NY 10804.

US
PACIFIC NORTHWEST TRADE DIRECTORY. (1984)-. English. Every 2 years. $65.00. Times Community Newspapers Inc., 1634 South 312th Street, Federal Way WA 98063. **Tel** (206)839-0700, FAX (206)941-2641. **ED** Howard Hirshman. **Bk Rev**. **Ad Acc**. **Circ:** 20,000 (ctrl).
Desc: International trade - 3,000 importers and exporters. Also trade statistics.

ISSN 1054-8068
DD 382 US
PACIFIC RIM ENTREPRENEUR. ASIAN MARKET UPDATE. [Pac. rim entrep., Asian mark. update]. **VFOAT** Asian Market Update. Vol. 4, No. 1 (1991)-. Periodical. English. Six times a year. $120.00. Pacific Rim Entrepeneur, 1519 3rd Avenue, PO Box 1158, Seattle WA 98111. **Tel** (206)467-0888. **Continues** *Pacific Rim Entrepreneur, 0893-8482*.

LC HF41 .P34 **ISSN** 0030-977X
PK
PAKISTAN EXPORTS. **Added/Corp** Pakistan. Export Promotion Bureau. Vol. 17 (Jan. 1966)-. Periodical. English. Twelve times a year. $325.00. Readers Associates, PO Box 7485, Victoria Chambers 1, Karachi 3 Pakistan. **Tel** 011 92 21 514068, telex 23108 MNJ PK. **Bk Rev**. **Ad Acc**. **Circ:** 5,000. **Continues** *Pakistan Trade*.
Desc: Deals with handicrafts, including onyx, ready made garments, rice, shoes, fertilizer, furniture, etc.

LC HF6 .A75
DD 330.9/82/06 AG
PENSAMIENTO ECONOMICO. **Added/Corp** Argentine Republic. Camara Argentina de Comercio. No. 401 (1975)-. Spanish. Four times a year. Camara Argentina de Comercio, Avda. Leandro N. Alem 36, 1003 Buenos Aires Argentina. **Continues** *Argentine Republic. Camara Argentina de Comercio. Revista Oficial*.

Business and Economics —Commerce

ISSN 0380-6766
DD 381/.45/3333309714 CN
PHOTO COMMERCE EXPRESS. Vol. 1 (May 15, 1974)-. Periodical. Multiple languages (English and French). Irregular. 0.50Can$ per copy. Photo Commerce Express, 407 Street Laurent Blvd., Montreal Quebec H2Y 2Y5 Canada.

US
PLANECON TRADE & FINANCE REVIEWS. (19??)-. English. Two times a year. $7000.00. PlanEcon Inc., 1111 14th Street Northwest, Suite 801, Washington DC 20005. **Tel** (202)898-0471.
Desc: An assessment of key financial and trade indicators for the former Soviet Republics and each East European country.

ISSN 0316-7852
DD 330.9/714 CN
POINT (MONTREAL). (LE POINT COMMERCE.). **VFOAT** Commerce. Vol. 70, No. 2B (Feb. 1968)-. Periodical. French. One time a year. Revue Commerce, 1080 Cote Du Beaver Hall, Montreal Quebec H2X 1T1 Canada.

LC HF3163.N5 N4 **ISSN** 1046-9265
DD 387.1/09763/3505 US
PORT OF NEW ORLEANS RECORD. [Port New Orleans rec.]. **Added/Corp** Louisiana. Board of Commissioners of the Port of New Orleans. Board of Commissioners of the Port of New Orleans. Promotion and Advertising Dept. Vol. 47, No. 1/2 (Jan./Feb. 1989)-. Periodical. English. Twelve times a year. Free on request. Board of Commissioners / Port of New Orleans, PO Box 60046, New Orleans LA 70160. **ED** Paul S. McKelrey. **Ad Acc. Circ:** 16,000 (ctrl). *Continues Port Record, 0194-1836.*
Desc: Features maritime news, coverage of special events and developments that affect shippers. Geared to those who do business in exporting, importing, transportation, manufacturing, freight forwarding and custom house brokerage.
Ind/Abst PAIS Int. Print (1991-?).

US
POSTDOCTORAL RESEARCH ASSOCIATESHIPS : OPPORTUNITIES FOR RESEARCH AT THE U.S. DEPARTMENT OF COMMERCE, NATIONAL BUREAU OF STANDARDS ... IN ASSOCIATION WITH THE NATIONAL RESEARCH COUNCIL ... . VFOAT Postdoctural Research Associateships : Tenable at U.S. Department of Commerce, National Bureau of Standards ... in Association with the National Research Council ... . English. One time a year. US Department of Commerce / National Bureau of Standards / Maryland, Gaithersburg MD 20899.

LC HF3041 **ISSN** 0828-1998
DD 382/.0971/02/1 CN
PRELIMINARY STATEMENT OF CANADIAN INTERNATIONAL TRADE. (PRELIMINARY STATEMENT OF CANADIAN INTERNATIONAL TRADE (S.H. BASED).). [Prelim. statement Can. int. trade]. **Added/Corp** Statistics Canada. International Trade Division. **VFOAT** Communique Preliminaire Sur le Commerce International du Canada (Base du S.H.). Vol. 4, No. 1 (Jan. 1988)-. Periodical. English (French). Twelve times a year. 110.00Can$ Canada; $140.00 US; $160.00 other. Statistics Canada Publications Sales and Services, R.H. Coats Building 6th Floor, Ottawa Ontario K1A 0T6 Canada. **Tel** (613)951-5078, (800)267-6677, FAX (613)951-1584, telex 053-3585. *Continues Preliminary Statement of Canadian International Trade., 0828-1998.*

LC HD9018.A8 T32 **ISSN** 0157-0641
DD 338.1/09946 AT
PRINCIPAL AGRICULTURAL COMMODITIES, TASMANIA / AUSTRALIAN BUREAU OF STATISTICS. See Agriculture.

LC HF54.U5 P74 **ISSN** 0097-6288
DD 380.1/025 US
PRINCIPAL INTERNATIONAL BUSINESSES. **Added/Corp** Dun and Bradstreet, Inc. Dun & Bradstreet International. (1974)-. English. One time a year (Sept.). $655.00. Dun & Bradstreet Information Services, 3 Sylvan Way, Parsippany NJ 07054. **Tel** (201)605-6000, (800)526-0651.
Desc: International marketing directory containing information on the world's top 55,000 firms, covering all types of businesses in 133 countries. Firms cross-referenced by geography and industry.

LC HF
DD 380.1 UK
●**PRINCIPLES OF EXPORT GUIDEBOOKS, THE.** (1994)-. Monographic series. English. Irregular. $34.95. Basil Blackwell Publishers Ltd., 108 Cowley Road, Oxford OX4 1JF United Kingdom. **Tel** 011 44 1235 465500, FAX 011 44 1235 465556, telex 837022 OXBOOK G. **(Subscription address:** Blackwell Publishers / Cambridge, MA, 238 Main Street, Cambridge MA 02142. **Tel** 800-835-6770, (617)876-7000.**) ED** Michael Z. Brooke.

LC HG1501 **ISSN** 0829-7460
DD 332.1 CN
PROCEEDINGS OF THE STANDING SENATE COMMITTEE ON BANKING, TRADE AND COMMERCE. [Proc. Standing Senate Comm. Bank. Trade Commer.]. **Main/Corp** Canada. Parliament. Senate. Standing Committee on Banking and Trade and Commerce. **VFOAT** Deliberations du Comite Senatorial Permanent des Banques et du Commerce. (Jan. 29, 1969)-. Periodical. English. Canada Communication Group Publishers, Order Processing, Ottawa Ontario K1A 0S9 Canada. **Tel** (819)956-4800, (819)956-4802. *Absorbed* Canada. Parliament. Senate. Standing Committee on Banking, Trade and Commerce. Deliberations du Comite Senatorial Permanent des Banques et du Commerce.; *Continues* Canada. Parliament. Senate. Standing Committee on Banking and Commerce. Proceedings of the Standing Senate Committee on Banking and Commerce.

ISSN 0822-8906
DD 382.6/0971 CN
PRODUCT CANADA EXPORT JOURNAL. [Prod. Can. export j.]. Periodical. English (French). Four times a year. $15.00. Product Canada Export Journal, Suite 601/2050 Mansfield, Montreal Quebec H3A 1Z2 Canada. **Tel** (514)842-5263. **ED** Olaf Silva. **Ad Acc. Circ:** 12,000.
Desc: Import-export publication.

LC HD
DD 338 II
PROFODCIL BULLETIN. See Food and Food Industry.

LC HF5410 **ISSN** 0522-9138
DD 380 GW
PROTOKOLL. Main/Corp Bergedorfer Gespraechskreis zu Fragen der Freien Industriellen Gesellschaft. Vol. 1 (March 6, 1961)-. Periodical. German. Bergedorfer Gespraechskreis, Kampchaussee 10, W-2050 Hamburg 80 Germany.

ISSN 0217-4715
SI
PSA NEWS. Added/Corp Port of Singapore Authority. Vol. 1, No. 1 (Jan. 1984)-. Periodical. English. Four times a year.
Ind/Abst Soc. Plann. Policy Dev. Abstr.

LC HF5415.157 .Q348
DD 658.62/09405 IT
QUALITA. (19??)-. Periodical. Italian. Four times a year. L34060. Assn Piemontese Per la Qualita, Via Avogadro 8, 10121 Turin Italy. **Tel** 011 39 11 5627271. **(Subscription address:** AICQ Assn. Ital per la Qualita, Plazza Diaz 2, 20123 Milan, Italy.)

ISSN 0265-0029
DD 387.5448 UK
QUARTERLY DRY BULK MARKET REPORT. [Q. dry bulk mark. rep.]. **VFOAT** Dry Bulk Market Report. (1982)-. Periodical. English. Four times a year. £780.00. Drewry Shipping Consultants Ltd, 11 Heron Quay, London E14 4JF United Kingdom. **Tel** 011 44 171 5380191, FAX 011 44 171 9879396, telex 21167 HPDLDG.

LC HC121 .Q37
DD 330.98/0005 UK
QUARTERLY UPDATE. Added/Corp Latin American Newsletters Ltd. **VFOAT** Latin American Economy and Business. Quarterly Update; Latin American Economy & Business. Quarterly Update. No. 01 (Jan. 1991)-. English. Four times a year. Combined with Latin American Economy and Business: $630.00 (business), $399.00 (academic) US; £485.00 (business), £307.00 (academic) other. Lettres UK Ltd, 61 Old Street, London EC1V 9HX United Kingdom. **Tel** 011 44 171 2510012, FAX 011 44 171 2538193.

LC HF5585.P7 P3 **ISSN** 0190-6070
DD 381/.414/02573 US
RED BOOK (CHICAGO), THE. (THE RED BOOK.). (19??)-. Periodical. English. Four times a year. $575.00. Vance Publishing Corporation, 400 Knightsbridge Parkway, Lincolnshire IL 60069. **Tel** (800)255-5113, (708)634-2600. *Continues Packer Red Book.*

LC VK235 .R4 **ISSN** 0266-3996
DD 627/.34/025 UK
REFERENCE BOOK & BUYERS GUIDE. Added/Corp International Cargo Handling Coordination Association. **VFOAT** Reference Book and Buyers Guide; International Cargo Handling. (1984)-. English. One time a year. $60.00 membership. International Cargo Handling Co-ordination Association, 71 Bondway, London SW8 1SH United Kingdom. **Tel** 011 44 171 7931022.

US
REFERENCE BOOK FOR WORLD TRADERS. VFOAT Croner's Reference Book for World Traders. (1961)-. Periodical. English. Ten times a year. $141.95. Croner Publications Inc., 34 Jericho Turnpike, Jericho NY 11753. **Tel** (516)333-9085. **ED** U. H. E. Croner.
Desc: A comprehensive directory for exporters and importers. Countries listed alphabetically covering general information, consulates, embassies, hotels, ports, etc. Special section covering export documentation required by each country.

ISSN 0820-8522
DD 380.1/025/71523 CN
REPERTOIRE COMMERCIAL DE LA REGION DU SUD-EST. (REPERTOIRE COMMERCIAL DE LA REGION DU SUD-EST / COMMISSION ECONOMIQUE DU SUD-EST / COMMERCIAL DIRECTORY OF THE SOUTH EAST REGION / SOUTH EAST ECONOMIC COMMISSION.). [Repert. commerc. reg. Sud-Est]. **Main/Corp** South East Economic Commission (N.B.). **VFOAT** Commercial Directory of the South East Region. (1982)-. English (French). Every 2 years. Free. Southeast Economic Commission, PO Box 578, Main Street, Shediac New Brunswick E0A 3G0 Canada. ctrl circ.

IT
REPERTORIO DOGANALE CLASSIFICAZIONE MERCI. (19??)-. Italian. Euroitalia Editrice Srl, Via XX Settembre 37/12, 16121 Genoa Italy. **Tel** 011 39 10 593519, 011 39 10 566648.

LC JX1977 .A2
DD 341.23/3 S 382 US
REPORT. Main/Conf United Nations Conference on Trade and Development. Trade and Development Board. **Main/Corp** United Nations Conference on Trade and Development. Trade and Development Board. (1965)-. Government Publication. English. One time a year. $10.00. United Nations Publications, 2 United Nations Plaza, Room DC2 0853, Department 007C, New York NY 10017. **Tel** (212)963-8303, (800)253-9646.

LC HD9284.A45 A3
DD 354.680082/336 SA
REPORT OF THE AUDITOR-GENERAL ON THE ACCOUNTS OF THE EGG BOARD FOR THE FINANCIAL YEAR ... / VERSLAG VAN DIE OUDITEUR-GENERAAL OOR DIE REKENINGS VAN DIE EIERRAAD VIR DIE BOEKJAAR ... . Main/Corp South Africa. Egg Board. **Added/Corp** South Africa. Office of the Auditor-General. **VFOAT** Verslag van die Ouditeur-Generaal oor die Rekenings van die Eierraad vir die Boekjaar ... . (1985)-. Periodical. Afrikaans (English). Government Printer / South Africa, Bosman Street, Private Bag X85, Pretoria 0001 South Africa. **Tel** 011 27 12 3239731 ext. 262. *Continues South Africa. Egg Control Board. Report of the Auditor-General on the Accounts of the Egg Control Board for the Financial Year.*

LC HD6475.A1 I234
BE
REPORT OF THE ... WORLD CONGRESS / INTERNATIONAL CONFEDERATION OF FREE TRADE UNIONS. See Political Science-International Relations.

US
REPORT ON ELECTRIC COMMERCE. See Communications-Telecommunication.

LC JX1977 .A41
DD 341.7/54 US
REPORT ON THE WORK OF ITS SESSIONS - UNITED NATIONS. COMMISSION ON INTERNATIONAL TRADE LAW. See Law-International Law.

LC HF1010 .R47 **ISSN** 1067-0394
DD 380 US
●**RESEARCHING MARKETS, INDUSTRIES, AND BUSINESS OPPORTUNITIES.** [Research. mark., ind., bus. oppor.]. **Added/Corp** Washington Researchers. **VFOAT** Researching Markets, Industries, & Business Opportunities. (1994)-. Directory. English. One time a year. $395.00. Washington Researchers, PO Box 19005, 20th Street Station, Washington DC 20036. **Tel** (202)333-3533, (202)333-3499, FAX (202)625-0656.
Desc: Helps executives, analysts, and researchers assess performance of companies.

Business and Economics —Commerce

DD 380/.06/0713533   **ISSN** 0227-681X   CN
REVIEW / BURLINGTON CHAMBER OF COMMERCE. [Rev. - Burlington Chamb. Commer.]. **Added/Corp** Burlington Chamber of Commerce. Vol. 1 (May 1974)-. Periodical. English. Ten times a year. Burlington Chamber of Commerce PO Box 103, Burlington Ontario L7R 3X8 Canada. **Tel** 639-0174, FAX 333-3956.

LC K19 .D9313
DD 346/.07/05 342.7005   BL
REVISTA DE DIREITO DO COMERCIO DAS RELACOES INTERNACIONAIS. See Law-International Law.

   CN
REVUE COMMERCE 500. (19??)-. French. One time a year. La Revue Commerce 500, 465 rue Saint-Jean, Montreal Quebec H2Y 3R6 Canada. **Ind/Abst** Can. Period. Index (19??-).

DD 338.09714/14/05   **ISSN** 1184-6364   CN
REVUE COMMERCE & INDUSTRIE. [Rev. commer. ind.]. **VFOAT** Revue Commerce et Industrie. Vol. 1, No 1 (Oct. 1990)-. Periodical. French. Twelve times a year. 2.95Can$. VERSA Communication, 2 des Bouleaux Ouest, Quebec Quebec G1L 1L5 Canada. **Continues** Revue Industrie & Commerce., 0836-3404.

DD 381/.09714   **ISSN** 0380-9811   CN
REVUE COMMERCE (MONTREAL. 1975). (REVUE COMMERCE.). [Rev. commer.]. 77th Year, No. 12 (Dec. 1975)-. Periodical. French. Twelve times a year. 19.55Can$. Publications Transcontinental Inc, 1100 Rene-Levesque, 24Fl boulevard West, Montreal Quebec H3B 4X9 Canada. **Tel** (514)392-9000, FAX (514)392-4724. **ED** Michel Lord, Pierre Tourangeau, and Jean-Paul Lejeune. **Ad Acc. Circ:** 34,000 (ctrl). **Continues** Commerce, 0010-2725; **Absorbed** Point, 0316-7852.
Desc: For mid and senior management in both large and small companies throughout Quebec. Presents a special dossier on an important areas of business or the economy, which is of great interest to our business readers. Covers Canada's top 500 companies, economic forecasts, marketing, communications, exports, small business, etc.
Ind/Abst AGRICOLA; Can. Period. Index; Environ.; PAIS Int. Print (?-?); Repere (1983-).

LC HF1531 .R4   FR
REVUE DU MARCHE COMMUN ET DE L'UNION EUROPEENNE. No. 343 (Jan 1991)-. Periodical. French. Ten times a year. 817.83F France; 990.00F other. Les Editions Techniques et Economiques, 3 rue Soufflot, 75005 Paris France. **Tel** 011 33 1 46341030, FAX 011 33 1 46345583, telex 260 717 F. **ED** Daniel Vignes. Index available. cum. index. **Bk Rev**, (Qty: 10). **Ad Acc, Adv Mgr:** Epstein. **Circ:** 2,000. **Continues** Revue du Marche Commun.
Ind/Abst PAIS Int. Print.

LC NK2 .R13
DD 381.1/45/730094   FR
RIA INTERNATIONAL, REVUE DES INDUSTRIES D'ART EXPORT. See The Arts-Art.

   ISSN 0035-5925   IT
UDC 656.61
RIVISTA DEL PORTO DI NAPOLI, LA. [Riv. Porto Napoli]. (1966)-. Periodical. Italian. Three times a year. L12260. Consorzio Porto Napoli, P Le Pisacane, 80133 Naples Italy. **Tel** 011 39 81 266566. **Continues** Bollettino Ufficiale del Porto di Napoli.

   PL
●**ROCZNIK STATYSTYCZNY HANDLU ZAGRANICZNEGO.** See Business and Economics-Abstracting, Bibliographies and Statistics.

LC HF37.R8 R8   RM
   CEASED
ROMANIAN FOREIGN TRADE. **Added/Corp** Camera de Comert a Republicii Socialiste Romania. Camera de Comert si Industrie a Republicii Socialiste Romania. No. 58 (1965)-(19??). Periodical. English. Foreign Trade Publicity AG, BD N Baicescu 22, Bucharest Romania. **Tel** 132379. **Ad Acc. Circ:** 5,000. **Continues** Rumanian Foreign Trade.
Desc: Papers on Romania's trade relations with other countries.

LC HF25 .A65   **ISSN** 1061-2009
DD 382   US
   CCC
RUSSIAN & EAST EUROPEAN FINANCE AND TRADE. [Russ. East Eur. finance trade]. **VFOAT** Russian and East European Finance and Trade. Vol. 28, No. 1 (Spring 1992)-. Periodical. English (translations available in Russian). Six times a year.

$572.00. M. E. Sharpe Inc., 80 Business Park Drive, Armonk NY 10504. **Tel** (914)273-1800, (800)541-6563, FAX (914)273-2106. **Continues** Soviet and Eastern European Foreign Trade, 0038-5263.
Ind/Abst Curr. Contents Soc. Behav. Sci.; J. Econ. Lit.; Soc. Sci. Cit. Index [Full Cov.].

LC HF1371   **ISSN** 1083-3765
DD 338   US
●**S GUIDE, THE.** [S guide]. **Added/Corp** Assist International (Organization). (1993)-. Directory. English. One time a year. $63.45. Assist International, 60 Madison Avenue, 2nd Floor, New York NY 10010. **Tel** (212)725-3311, FAX (212)725-3312. **ED** Peter J. Robinson, Jr.

   ISSN 1063-5513   US
SAN DIEGO COMMERCE. **VFOAT** Commerce. (1991)-. Periodical. English. One time a week. $50.00. Daily Journal Corporation, 915 East First Street, Los Angeles CA 90012. **Tel** (213)229-5300, FAX (213)680-3682. **Continues** San Diego Back Country Trader, 1056-3202.

   ISSN 0925-0530   NE
UDC 343.8
SANCTIES ARNHEM. (SANCTIES). [Sancties Arnhem]. (19??)-. Periodical. Dutch. Six times a year. Uitgeverij Gouda Quint BV, Antwoordnummer 47, 6800 BV Arnhem Netherlands. **Tel** 011 31 85 454762. **Continues** Penitentiaire Informatie, 0166-610X.

LC HF300 .A317
DD 380.1/029/48161   BL
SAO PAULO YEAR BOOK. **VFOAT** Membership Directory. (1980)-. English. One time a year. $175.00. American Chamber of Commerce for Brazil-Sao Paulo, rua Alexandre Dumas 2372, PO Box 12518, 04717 Sao Paulo Brazil. **Tel** (011)246-9199, telex 1136190 AMCH BR. **ED** Elizabeth Mortlock. **Ad Acc. Circ:** 3,000 (ctrl). **Continues** Sao Paulo Yearbook.
Desc: Contains a listing of AMCHAM Sao-Paulo membership, company directors, domestic and export sales, number of employees, products and services.

   IT
SCHEDE DI AGGIORNAMENTO. (19??)-. Periodical. Italian. Irregular. L405.000 Italy; L810.000 other. IPSOA Editore SRL, Casella Postale 12055, Mastrangelo, 20120 Milan Italy. **Tel** 011 39 2 82476248.

LC HF1414.5
DD 382.6   US
SCHEDULE B, STATISTICAL CLASSIFICATION OF DOMESTIC AND FOREIGN COMMODITIES EXPORTED FROM THE UNITED STATES. See Business and Economics-Abstracting, Bibliographies and Statistics.

LC HF17 .Z4   **ISSN** 0341-2687
   GW
   CCC
SCHMALENBACHS ZEITSCHRIFT FUER BETRIEBSWIRTSCHAFTLICHE FORSCHUNG. **Added/Corp** Schmalenbach-Gesellschaft--Deutsche Gesellschaft fuer Betriebswirtschaft. Schmalenbach-Gesellschaft zur Forderung der Betriebswirtschaftlichen Forschung und Praxis. **VFOAT** Zeitschrift fuer betriebswirtschaftliche Forschung; ZfbF. Vol. 16, No. 1 (Jan. 1964)-. Periodical. German. Twelve times a year. DM179.44 Germany; DM192.00 other. Handelsblatt GmbH, Postfach 102716, D-40018 Duesseldorf Germany. **Tel** 011 49 211 8871730, FAX 011 49 211 133523, telex 172114489. available on microfilm. **Continues** Zeitschrift fuer Handelswissenschaftliche Forschung.
Ind/Abst Selec. Coop. Index Manage. Period.

   ISSN 0036-9322
DD 641   UK
SCOTTISH LICENSED TRADE NEWS. [Scott. licens. trade news]. (1964)-. Periodical. English. Twenty-two times a year. Peebles Publishing, Bergius House, Clifton Street, Glasgow G3 7LA United Kingdom. **Tel** 011 41 331 1022.
Ind/Abst Infomat Int. Bus.

LC HE561 .S3175   **ISSN** 0964-8895
DD 387.5/05   UK
SEATRADE REVIEW. See Transportation-Ships and Shipping.

   UK
SECRETARIAT PAPER - INTERNATIONAL WHEAT COUNCIL. See Agriculture-Feed Grain and Milling.

LC HE597.G4 S44   GW
SEEGUTERUMSCHLAG IN SEEHAFEN DER BUNDESREPUBLIK DEUTSCHLAND IM JAHRE ..., DER. German. One time a year.

LC HD1 .S43a   JA
SEINAN GAKUIN DAIGAKU SHOGAKU RON SHU. See Industry and Production.

LC HC244 .U54a   **ISSN** 0160-5968
DD 338/.09171/7   US
SELECTED TRADE AND ECONOMIC DATA OF THE CENTRALLY PLANNED ECONOMIES. **Added/Corp** United States. Office of East-West Trade Policy and Planning. United States. Bureau of East-West Trade. (1975)-. English. One time a year. US Department of Commerce / International Trade Administration, 14th Street & Constitution Avenue NW, Hoover Building, Room 3850, Washington DC 20230. **Tel** (202)482-2867, FAX (202)482-5933. **Continues** United States. Bureau of East-West Trade. Selected U.S.S.R. and Eastern European Foreign Trade and Economic Data.

LC HF1019 .T72   **ISSN** 0745-7170
DD 381   US
$ELF-RELIANT. [$elf-reliant]. **VFOAT** Self-Reliant. **VAT** Self Reliant. Vol. 1, No. 1 (Apr./May 1983)-. Periodical. English. Ten times a year. $12.00. FJL Publishing Company, 817 Stark Circle, Yardley PA 19067-4313. **Continues** Trader's Journal, 0744-7558.

LC HF3503 .S4   **ISSN** 0140-5772
DD 382/.6/02541   UK
   CEASED
SELL'S BRITISH EXPORTERS (1980). (SELL'S BRITISH EXPORTERS). (1980)-(1994). English. Sell's Publications Ltd., 55 High Street, Epsom Surrey KT1 8DW United Kingdom. **Tel** 011 44 1372 726376, FAX 011 44 1372 729241. **Continues** British Exporters.

DD 337   UK
Pr Rev.
●**SERIES IN INTERNATIONAL BUSINESS AND ECONOMICS.** See Business and Economics-Economic History, Conditions.

   ISSN 0822-1839
DD 354.71008276/025   CN
SERVICE COMMERCIAL DU CANADA A L'ETRANGER. [Serv. commer. Can. etrang.]. **Main/Corp** Canada. Industry, Trade and Commerce. (1975)-(19??). Periodical. French. **Supersedes** Commerce Canada, 0315-5722. **Continued in part by** Canada. Industrie et Commerce. Delegations Commeciales du Canada a l'Etranger,, 0822-1847.
Ind/Abst Repere (1978-1987).

   JA
SHIPPING & TRADE NEWS. See Transportation-Ships and Shipping.

LC HE561 .S38
DD 380/.0994   AT
SHIPPING, COMMERCE AND INDUSTRY. See Transportation-Ships and Shipping.

LC HF1040.9.J3 S47   **ISSN** 0286-2212
   JA
SHOHIN KENKYU. **VFOAT** Studies on Commodities. Periodical. Japanese (summaries and/or abstracts in English). Nihon Shohin Gakkai, c/o Hitotsubashi Daigaku, 1 Naka 2 Kunitachi-shi, Tokyo-to 186 Japan.

LC HF5421.5.J3 S439   JA
SHOKIGYO NO KEIEI SHIHYO / KOKUMIN KINYU KOKO CHOSABU HEN. **Added/Corp** Kokumin Kinyu Koko. Chosabu. (1982)-. Periodical. ¥3300. Chusho Kigyo Risachi, Senta 5-11 Uchi Kanda 1 Chiyoda-ku, Tokyo-to Japan. **Continues** Sho-Reisai Kigyo No Keiei Shihyo.

   ISSN 0164-3215
   US
SHOWCASE U.S.A. **Added/Corp** Sell Overseas America. **VAT** Showcase United States of America. Vol. 1 (Winter Quarter 1979)-. Periodical. English. Five times a year. $22.00. Bobit Publishing, 2512 Artesia Boulevard, Redondo Beach CA 90278. **Tel** (310)376-8788, (800)334-8152, FAX (310)376-9043.

   US
SIMPLIFIER, THE. (1989)-. Newsletter. English. Four times a year. $245.00. Comp-Tech Export Publications, PO Box 1367, Bethesda MD 20827-1367. **Tel** (301)983-3339, FAX (301)983-9035.
Desc: Presents a comprehensive, simplified analysis of the technical and regulatory issues and gray areas of the regulations and topics in the exporting fields.

LC HF41 .S58   **ISSN** 0129-2951
DD 338/.09595/2   SI
SINGAPORE BUSINESS. [Singap. bus.]. Vol 1 (Jan. 1977)-. Periodical. English. Twelve times a year. $79.34. Times Periodicals Pte Ltd, 422 Thomson Road, Singapore 1129 Singapore. **Tel** 011 65 2550011. **ED** Mano Sabnani. **Bk Rev**. **Ad Acc. Circ:** 10,000. **Supersedes** Singapore Trade and Industry.
Desc: Update of the stock market, trade and industry, banking, property, company profiles and personalities.
Ind/Abst PAIS Int. Print.

Business and Economics —Commerce

DD 382   ISSN 1060-250X   US
SINGAPORE REPORT ON THE GROWTH TRIANGLE. [Singap. rep. growth triangle]. Vol. 1, No. 1 (Nov. 11, 1991)-. Periodical. English. Twenty-six times a year. $568.00. DP Publications Company, PO Box 7188, Fairfax Station VA 22039. **Tel** (703)425-1322, FAX (703)425-7911, telex 263 128 CTOUR.

LC HF3800.67 .A24
DD 382/.095957/021   SI
SINGAPORE TRADE STATISTICS. IMPORTS AND EXPORTS. **Added/Corp** Trade Development Board (Singapore). Vol. 1, No. 1 (Jan. 1989)-. English. Twelve times a year. $540.14. Singapore National Printers, 303 Upper Serangoon Road, Singapore 1334 Singapore. **Tel** 011 65 2820611. **Continues** Singapore Trade Statistics. Imports and Exports (1980).

LC HF3838.U6 S56   ISSN 1066-1816
DD 382   US
●SINO-U.S. TRADING ALMANAC. **VFOAT** Mei Cung Mao i Nien Chien. (1993)-. Periodical. English. $280.00. Sino-U.S. Information Inc., 81-83 Franklin Street, Suite 3B, New York NY 10013.

LC HF3128 .S573   ISSN 0196-4607
DD 382/.0951/073   US
SINO-US TRADE STATISTICS. See Business and Economics-Abstracting, Bibliographies and Statistics.

LC HD9018.P16 S57
DD 338.1/09182/3021   US
●SITUATION AND OUTLOOK SERIES. ASIA AND PACIFIC RIM INTERNATIONAL AGRICULTURE AND TRADE REPORTS / UNITED STATES DEPARTMENT OF AGRICULTURE, ECONOMIC RESEARCH SERVICE. **Added/Corp** United States. Dept. of Agriculture. Economic Research Service. United States. World Agricultural Outlook Board. **VFOAT** Asia and Pacific Rim; Asia and Pacific Rim International Agriculture and Trade Reports; International Agriculture and Trade Reports. (Sept. 1993)-. English. Four times a year. $20.00. U.S. Department of Agriculture, ERS-NASS, 341 Victory Drive, Herndon VA 22070. **Tel** (800)999-6779, (703)834-0125. **Continues** Situation and Outlook Series. Pacific Rim Agriculture and Trade Report, 1051-869X.

LC K540 HF1371
DD 341 382   US
●SLIP OPINION SERVICES. See Law-International Law.

LC HF5429 .S57   ISSN 0081-0177
DD 658.9   US
SMALL MARKETERS AIDS. **Added/Corp** United States. Small Business Administration. No. 1 (1959)-. English. One time a year. Free. Small Business Administration, 1030 15th Street, Washington DC 20417. **Tel** (202)653-6963.

UK
SMALLER COMPANIES HANDBOOK. (19??)-. Directory. English. One time a year. £165.00 UK; £265.00 other. Extel Financial Ltd., Fitzroy House, 13-17 Epworth Street, London EC2A 4DL United Kingdom. **Tel** 011 44 171 8258000, FAX 011 44 171 8258328, telex 884319 EXTELX G.

IT
SMALTO E SMALTATURA TECNOLOGIE E MERCATI. (19??)-. Italian. Three times a year. Free on request. Cisp Milan, Via Olona 41, 20016 Pero Mi Italy. **Tel** 011 39 2 38103333.

LC HF3621 .S67
JA
SOREN TOO BOEKI CHOSA GEPPO. **Added/Corp** Soren Too Boekikai (Japan). **VFOAT** Monthly Bulletin of Trade with USSR & East Europe. (19??)-. Bulletin. Japanese. Twelve times a year. ¥3000 each issue. Soren Too Boekikai, c/o Kanayama Building 2-12, Shinkawa 1 Chuo-ku, Tokyo-to Japan.

ISSN 0273-4303
US
SOUTHERN EXPORTER, THE. [South. export.]. (19??)-. English. Twelve times a year. $50.00 (one-year), $80.00 (two-year), $100.00 (three-year); $25.00 (one year only) students. The Southern Exporter, PO Box 551, 108 Harpeth Hill Drive, Franklin TN 37064. **Tel** (615)794-7488.

LC HF25 .S65
RU
SOVETSKII EKSPORT. (19??)-. Periodical. Russian. Six times a year. Sovetskii Eksport, 113461 Ul Kakhovka 31, Moscow Russia.

LC HC108.S2 S7   ISSN 0036-293X
DD 330.9778/65/005   US
ST. LOUIS COMMERCE. (ST. LOUIS COMMERCE : OFFICIAL PUBLICATION OF THE ST. LOUIS REGIONAL COMMERCE & GROWTH ASSOCIATION.). [St. Louis commer.]. **Added/Corp** St. Louis Regional Commerce & Growth Association. **VAT** Saint Louis Commerce. Vol. 1, No. 1 (Feb. 1988)-. Periodical. English. Twelve times a year. $36.00. Commerce Magazine, 100 South 4th Street, Suite 500, St. Louis MO 63102. **Tel** (314)231-5555, FAX (317)444-1122. **ED** Laura Barlow (telephone: (314)444-1161) and Alvin Reid (telephone: (314)444-1104). Index available (bound in issue). **Bk Rev. Ad Acc, Adv Mgr:** Karen Clare, **Tel** (314)444-1164; **Circ:** 15,000. available on microfilm and microfiche from University Microfilms International (UMI); available on an online database (file 635/Full-Text) from DIALOG. Documents available from UMI Article Clearinghouse. **Continues** St. Louis Commerce, 0036-293X.
  Desc: Reports on economic and civic progress in metro area. Reflects area's resources and advantages as a place for commerce and industry to grow and prosper.
  Ind/Abst Bus. Dateline (Oct. 1990-) [Full Txt.]; PROMT.

LC HF5035 .S68   ISSN 0147-8486
DD 380.1/025/73   US
STANDARD COMMERCIAL DIRECTORY. Vol. 1 (1976/77)-. Directory. English. Liberty Publications, 11906 Wilshire Boulevard, Suite 8, Los Angeles CA 90025.

LC HF3803 .S73
DD 380.1/025/598   IO
SUSPENDED
STANDARD TRADE & INDUSTRY DIRECTORY OF INDONESIA. **VFOAT** Standard Trade and Industry Directory of Indonesia. 3rd Ed. (1981-1982)-7th Edition (1991). Directory. English (Indonesian). One time a year (Mar.). $200.00 Indonesia; $300.00 North America; $250.00 other. Indonesian Chamber of Commerce & Industry, Jl Hayam Wuruk 4TX, Jakarta PO Box 4556, Jakarta Indonesia. **Tel** 373707, telex 46344 PASSIA IA. **ED** Freddy Sutedi. Index available. **Ad Acc. Circ:** 15,000 (ctrl). available on diskette. **Continues** Standard Trade Directory of Indonesia; **Absorbed** Kompass, 0377-0710.
  Desc: List of companies in Indonesia and other important functionaries and their addresses.

LC HF3803 .S73
DD 380.1/025/598   IO
STANDARD TRADE DIRECTORY OF INDONESIA. 1979-. Directory. English. $100.00. Indonesian Chamber of Commerce & Industry, Jl Hayam Wuruk 4TX, Jakarta PO Box 4556, Jakarta Indonesia. **Tel** 373707, telex 46344 PASSIA IA. **ED** Freddy Sutesi. **Ad Acc. Circ:** 15,000 (ctrl).
  Desc: List of companies in Indonesia and other important functionaries and their addresses.

ISSN 0844-3955
DD 382/.4133   CN
STAT (VANCOUVER). (STAT.). [Stat]. **VFOAT** Grey Book. Vol. 1, No. 1 (Aug. 5, 1988)-. Periodical. English. Fifty times a year (weekly except two weeks during Christmas). 214.49Can$. Stat Publishing, PO Box 8110-361, Blaine WA 98230. **Tel** (604)535-8505, FAX (604)531-8818. **ED** P. B. Clancey. Index available. **Bk Rev. Ad Acc. Circ:** 2,000.
  Desc: International marketing and commodity analysis for pulses, birdseeds and oilseeds.

LC HD9351 .S7   ISSN 0279-2133
DD 381/.45/6630973   US
STATEWAYS. **VAT** State Ways. (Oct. 1972)-. Periodical. English. Six times a year. $20.00. Jobson Publishing Corporation, 100 Avenue of the Americas, New York NY 10013. **Tel** (212)274-7084, (212)274-7000, FAX (212)431-0500. **(Subscription address:** Stateways, PO Box 7649, Riverton NJ 08077. **)**

LC HF3581 .I866
IT
STATISTICA DEL COMMERCIO CON L'ESTERO (ROME, ITALY : 1986). (STATISTICA DEL COMMERCIO CON L'ESTERO.). **Added/Corp** Istituto Centrale di Statistica (Italy). Vol. 52, No. 1 (Jan./March 1986)-. Italian. Four times a year. L85840. Istituto Nazionale Statistica, GBP SEZ4 Via Cesare Balbo 16, 00184 Rome Italy. **Tel** 011 39 6 46735118. **Continues** Statistica Mensile del Commercio Con l'Estero.

LC HF1 .C84   ISSN 0010-3233
DD 382/.021   US
STATISTICAL PAPERS - UNITED NATIONS. SERIES D. COMMODITY TRADE STATISTICS. See Business and Economics-Abstracting, Bibliographies and Statistics.

DD 382/.63/0971   ISSN 0823-3454
CN
STATISTICAL REVIEW - EXPORT DEVELOPMENT CORPORATION. [Stat. rev. - Export Dev. Corp.]. **Main/Corp** Export Development Corporation (Canada). **VFOAT** Statistiques. (1982)-. Statistical Publication. English (French). One time a year. Export Development Corporation, 151 O'Conner Street, Box 655, Ottawa Ontario K1A 1K3 Canada. **Tel** (613)598-2784. **Separated from** Annual Report / Export Development Corporation (Canada), 0709-1605.

LC HF259.P3 I88B
IS
STATISTIKAH SHEL SEHAR HUTS. **Main/Corp** Israel. Ha-Lishkah Ha-Merkazit Li-Statistikah. **VFOAT** Foreign Trade Statistics. Vol. 6 (1974)-. Multiple languages (English and Hebrew). Two times a year. IL220.00. Government Publishing House, Street B/No 29 Hakirya, Tel-Aviv Israel. **Tel** (00-972)2-211400. **Continues** Rivon Li-Statistikah Sehar Huts.

LC HF181 .S784   ISSN 0585-1661
DD 383   LU
STATISTIKEN UEBER DEN AUSSENHANDEL. ANALYTISCHE UBERSICHTEN : AUSFUHR. **Added/Corp** Statistical Office of the European Communities. **VFOAT** Foreign Trade Statistics.; Statistiques du Commerce Exterieur.; Statistiche del Commercio con l'Estero.; Statistiek van de Buitenlandse Handel. (19??)-. Periodical. Dutch (English and French). Twelve times a year. Office for Official Publications of the European Communities, 2 rue Mercier, 2985 Luxembourg Luxembourg. **Tel** 011 352 499281, FAX 011 352 292942763. **(Subscription address:** Licosa s.p.a., PO Box 552, 50125 Florence Italy. **Tel** 011 39 55 645415.**)** **Continues** Jahrbuch des Aussenhandels nach Ursprungs-und Bestimmungslandern,, 0561-9270.

FR
STATISTIQUES DE COMMERCE. EXTERIEUR DE LA FRANCE. (19??)-. Statistical Publication. French. One time a year. 290.00F. Direction Nationale des Statistiques du Commerce Exterieur, 161 Chemin de Lestang, 31057 Toulouse Cedex France. **Tel** 62 11 23 00.

LC HF3551 .S725
DD 382/.0944/021   FR
STATISTIQUES DU COMMERCE EXTERIEUR DE LA FRANCE. IMPORTATIONS, EXPORTATIONS EN N.C.C.D. **VFOAT** Importations, Exportations en N.C.C.D.; Importations, Exportations en NCCD. French. One time a year. 1086.00F. Min de l'Economie des Finances, 139 rue de Bercy, Bat HI 75572 Paris Cedex 12 France. **Tel** 011 33 1 40010201.

LC HF3601 .S74
DD 380/.09493/021   BE
STATISTIQUES DU COMMERCE INTERIEUR ET DES TRANSPORTS / ROYAUME DE BELGIQUE, MINISTERE DES AFFAIRES ECONOMIQUES, INSTITUT NATIONAL DE STATISTIQUE. See Business and Economics-Abstracting, Bibliographies and Statistics.

LC HF3649.F3 S72   ISSN 0108-5557
DD 380.1   DK
STATISTISKE EFTERRETNINGER. FRERNE OG GRNLAND. See Business and Economics-Abstracting, Bibliographies and Statistics.

LC HF3641 .S72   ISSN 0108-5573
DD 380.1   DK
STATISTISKE EFTERRETNINGER. GENEREL ERHVERVSSTATISTIK OG HANDEL. See Business and Economics-Abstracting, Bibliographies and Statistics.

LC HF3641 .S73   ISSN 0108-5506
DD 380.1   DK
STATISTISKE EFTERRETNINGER. UDENRIGSHANDEL. See Business and Economics-Abstracting, Bibliographies and Statistics.

LC HF19 .S82   ISSN 0392-9701
DD 380.1/3/05   IT
STATO E MERCATO. [Stato mercato]. Vol. 1, No. 1 (April 1981)-. Periodical. Italian. Three times a year. L57230. Societa Editrice Il Mulino, Strada Maggiore 37, 40125 Bologna Italy. **Tel** 011 39 51 256011, FAX 011 39 51 256034.
  Ind/Abst Foreign Lang. Index; Int. Bibliogr. Sociol.; Int. Polit. Sci. Abstr.; PAIS Int. Print.

Business and Economics —Commerce

LC HD9510.1 U53
DD 338.4/7/6691
US
●**STEEL MARKET IN ... AND PROSPECTS FOR ... / ECONOMIC COMMISSION FOR EUROPE, THE.** See Metals and Metallurgy.

LC HF1371 ISSN 1076-3406
DD 382 US
●**STRATEGIC ALLIANCE ALERT : JOINT VENTURES & PARTNERSHIPS.** [Strateg. alliance alert]. **VFOAT** Strategic Alert Alliance. (1994)-. Newsletter. English. Twelve times a year. $95.00. Leader Publications, 345 Park Avenue South, New York NY 10010. **Tel** (800)888-8300 ext. 6170, (212)545-6170, FAX (212)696-1848. **ED** Ruthanne Kurtyka.

ISSN 1190-9692
DD 382 CN
●**STRATEGIE D'EXPORTATION DU CANADA, PLAN DE PROMOTION DU COMMERCE EXTERIEUR. 1, TECHNOLOGIES DE FABRICATION DE POINTE.** [Strateg. export. Can. plan promot. commer. exter., 1 Technol. fabr. pointe]. **Added/Corp** Canada. **VFOAT** Technologies de Fabrication de Pointe. (1996)-. Government Publication. French. Irregular. **Continues** Plan de Promotion du Commerce Exterieur du Canada. 1, Technologie de Fabrication de Pointe, 1200-1074.

LC HF1371 ISSN 1190-9730
DD 382 CN
●**STRATEGIE D'EXPORTATION DU CANADA, PLAN DE PROMOTION DU COMMERCE EXTERIEUR. 3, AERONAUTIQUE ET PIECES D'AERONEFS.** See Agriculture.

ISSN 1190-9757
DD 382 CN
●**STRATEGIE D'EXPORTATION DU CANADA, PLAN DE PROMOTION DU COMMERCE EXTERIEUR. 4, AUTOMOBILE.** See Transportation-Automobiles.

ISSN 1190-9773
DD 382 CN
●**STRATEGIE D'EXPORTATION DU CANADA, PLAN DE PROMOTION DU COMMERCE EXTERIEUR. 5, BIOTECHNOLOGIES.** See Science and Technology.

ISSN 1190-9811
DD 382 CN
●**STRATEGIE D'EXPORTATION DU CANADA, PLAN DE PROMOTION DU COMMERCE EXTERIEUR. 7, PRODUITS CHIMIQUES ET PLASTIQUES ET MATERIAUX DE POINTE.** See Plastics.

ISSN 1190-9838
DD 382 CN
●**STRATEGIE D'EXPORTATION DU CANADA, PLAN DE PROMOTION DU COMMERCE EXTERIEUR. 8, PRODUITS DE CONSTRUCTION.** See Metals and Metallurgy.

ISSN 1190-9854
DD 382 CN
●**STRATEGIE D'EXPORTATION DU CANADA, PLAN DE PROMOTION DU COMMERCE EXTERIEUR. 9, BIENS DE CONSOMMATION.** [Strateg. export. Can. plan promot. commer. exter., 9 Biens consomm.]. **Added/Corp** Canada. **VFOAT** Biens de Consommation. (1996)-. Government Publication. French. **Continues** Plan de Promotion du Commerce Exterieur du Canada. 9, Biens de Consommation, 1200-1236.

ISSN 1190-9870
DD 384 CN
●**STRATEGIE D'EXPORTATION DU CANADA, PLAN DE PROMOTION DU COMMERCE EXTERIEUR. 10, INDUSTRIES CULTURELLES.** See The Arts.

ISSN 1190-9897
DD 382 CN
●**STRATEGIE D'EXPORTATION DU CANADA, PLAN DE PROMOTION DU COMMERCE EXTERIEUR. 11, MATERIEL DE DEFENSE.** See Military and Defense.

ISSN 1190-9935
DD 382 CN
●**STRATEGIE D'EXPORTATION DU CANADA, PLAN DE PROMOTION DU COMMERCE EXTERIEUR. 13, POISSONS ET PRODUITS DE LA MER.** See Food and Food Industry.

ISSN 1190-9951
DD 382 CN
●**STRATEGIE D'EXPORTATION DU CANADA, PLAN DE PROMOTION DU COMMERCE EXTERIEUR. 14, INDUSTRIE FORESTIERE.** See Forests and Forestry.

ISSN 1190-9978
DD 382 CN
●**STRATEGIE D'EXPORTATION DU CANADA, PLAN DE PROMOTION DU COMMERCE EXTERIEUR. 15, TECHNOLOGIES DE L'INFORMATION ET TELECOMMUNICATIONS.** See Communications-Telecommunication.

ISSN 1200-4863
DD 382 CN
●**STRATEGIE D'EXPORTATION DU CANADA, PLAN DE PROMOTION DU COMMERCE EXTERIEUR. 17, MINERAUX ET METAUX.** See Metals and Metallurgy.

ISSN 1200-488X
DD 382 CN
●**STRATEGIE D'EXPORTATION DU CANADA, PLAN DE PROMOTION DU COMMERCE EXTERIEUR. 18, PRODUITS PETROLIERS ET GAZIERS ET MATERIEL D'EXPLOITATION DE L'ENERGIE.** See Petroleum and Natural Gas.

ISSN 1200-4901
DD 382 CN
●**STRATEGIE D'EXPORTATION DU CANADA, PLAN DE PROMOTION DU COMMERCE EXTERIEUR. 19, MATERIEL ELECTRIQUE.** [Strateg. export. Can. plan promot. commer. exter., 19 Mater. electr.]. **Added/Corp** Canada. **VFOAT** Materiel Electrique. (1996)-. Government Publication. French. Irregular. **Continues in part** Plan de Promotion du Commerce Exterieur du Canada. 11, Materiel Electrique et biens d'Equipement, 1200-1279.

ISSN 1200-4928
DD 382 CN
●**STRATEGIE D'EXPORTATION DU CANADA, PLAN DE PROMOTION DU COMMERCE EXTERIEUR. 20, MACHINERIE INDUSTRIELLE PRIMAIRE ET SECONDAIRE.** See Industry and Production.

ISSN 1200-4944
DD 382 CN
●**STRATEGIE D'EXPORTATION DU CANADA, PLAN DE PROMOTION DU COMMERCE EXTERIEUR. 21, MATERIEL DE TRANSPORT URBAIN ET FERROVIAIRE.** See Transportation.

ISSN 1200-4960
DD 382 CN
●**STRATEGIE D'EXPORTATION DU CANADA, PLAN DE PROMOTION DU COMMERCE EXTERIEUR. 22, INDUSTRIE SPATIALE.** [Strateg. export. Can. plan promot. commer. exter., 22 Ind. spat.]. **Added/Corp** Canada. **VFOAT** Industrie Spatiale. (1996)-. Government Publication. French. **Continues** Plan de Promotion du Commerce Exterieur du Canada. 19, Industrie Spatiale, 1200-1430.

ISSN 1200-4987
DD 382 CN
●**STRATEGIE D'EXPORTATION DU CANADA, PLAN DE PROMOTION DU COMMERCE EXTERIEUR. 23, TOURISM.** See Travel and Tourism.

ISSN 1190-9676
DD 382 CN
●**STRATEGIE D'EXPORTATION DU CANADA, PLAN DE PROMOTION DU COMMERCE EXTERIEUR. APERCU.** [Strateg. export. Can. plan promot. commer. exter., Apercu]. **Added/Corp** Canada. (1996)-. Government Publication. French. **Continues** Plan de Promotion du Commerce Exterieur du Canada. Apercu Strategique, 1200-1058.

LC HD9100.1 .S84
DD 382/.45641336/0973021 US
●**SUGAR, WORLD MARKETS AND TRADE.** **Added/Corp** United States. Foreign Agricultural Service. United States. World Agricultural Outlook Board. **VFOAT** World Sugar. (1994)-. Periodical. English. Four times a year. $14.00. US Department of Agriculture / Foreign Agricultural Service, 14th Street & Independence Avenue Southwest, Washington DC 20250. **Tel** (202)720-9445, FAX (202)720-7729. **Continues** World Sugar Situation and Outlook, 1075-6442.

LC HF3316 .S86
BF
SUMMARY REPORT OF FOREIGN TRADE STATISTICS. **Added/Corp** Bahamas. Dept. of Statistics. **VFOAT** External Trade Statistics Report. (1989)-. Statistical Publication. English. Four times a year. Department of Statisitics / Bahamas, PO Box 3904, Nassau Bahamas. **Tel** (809)325-6520 ext. 2323. **Continues** Summary Report of External Trade Statistics.

LC VK4 .S852 ISSN 0039-6702
SW
SVENSK SJOFARTSTIDNING. See Naval Science, Navigation.

LC HF3673 .S8
SW
SVERIGES HANDELSKALENDER. (1859)-. Periodical. Swedish. A Bommiero Forlag, Postbox 45054, 104 30 45 Stockholm Sweden.

ISSN 0770-996X
BE
UDC 380.15
SWISS NEWS. [Swiss news]. (1981)-. Periodical. Multiple languages. Ten times a year (Jan./Feb. and July/Aug. issues combined). $75.44. Swiss Scene News and Views on Switzerland, Koeschenruetistr 109, CH-8052 Zurich Switzerland. **Tel** 011 41 1 3027606, FAX 011 41 1 3022022. **Continues** Chambre de Commerce Suisse pour la Belgique et le Grand-Duche de Luxembourg, 0771-0011 **and** Swiss Scene.

LC HD9355 .S94 ISSN 0090-9009
DD 380.1/45/66310973 US
SWIZZLE STICK. [Swizzle stick]. Vol. 1 (Dec. 1972/Jan. 1973)-. Periodical. English. Six times a year. Swizzle Stick, PO Box 370, Vineland NJ 08360.

LC HF192.H8 S95
HU
SZOVOSZ TAJEKOZTATO KERESKEDELMI MELLEKLETE, A. **Main/Corp** Szovetkezetek Orszagos Szovetsege (Hungary). Vol. 9-11 (19??)-. Hungarian. Lapkiado Vallalat, Lenin Korut 9-11, 1073 Budapest 7 Hungary. **Tel** 011 36 1 222408.

UK
T-GUIDE. (1992)-. English. One time a year (with quarterly updates). £500.00. Eurodata Foundation, 175 Piccadilly, Empire House, London W1V 9DB United Kingdom. **Tel** 011 44 171 6291143, FAX 011 44 171 5830516. **ED** Josie Sephton. **Formed by the union of** Voicebook **and** Databook.
Desc: Year round guide to voice and data tariffs.

IT
TABELLA REVISIONE PREZZI. Italian. Ceu Spa, Viale Fulvio Testi 128, 20092 Cinisello Balsamo Italy.

LC HF5237.5 .T34
CH
TAI-WAN MAO I YAO LAN. **VFOAT** Taiwan Trade Directory. (1963)-. Chinese (English). Importers & Exporters Association of Taipei, PO Box 598, Taipei 104 Taiwan.

LC HF3846 .T34
DD 382/.025/51249 CH
TAIWAN EXPORTERS GUIDE. **VFOAT** Tai-Wan Wai Hsiao Chang Shang Ming Lu. (19??)-. Chinese (English, Spanish and Chinese). One time a year. NT$1,200 Taiwan; $35.00 US. Taiwan Exporters Guide, Box 73-4, 25 Foo Shou Street, Taipei 11135 Taiwan. **Tel** (02)8313648, 8313649. Index available. **Bk Rev**. **Ad Acc**. **Circ:** 20,000 (ctrl).
Desc: Information on more than 3,000 manufacturers and exporters of Taiwan's main export products.

LC HF5237.5 .T26
DD 382/.6/0951249 CH
TAIWAN EXPORTS. **VFOAT** Tai-Wan Shu Chu Pin Yao Lan. 1957-. Multiple languages (English). Board of Foreign Trade, Ministry of Economic Affairs, 1 Hu Kou Street, Taipei Taiwan.

Business and Economics — Commerce

LC HF5237.5 .T342
DD 382/.025/51249   CH
TAIWAN TRADE DIRECTORY. VFOAT
Tai-Wan Mao I Yao Lan. (1963)-. Directory. Multiple languages (Chinese and English). Importers & Exporters Association of Taipei, PO Box 598, Taipei 104 Taiwan.

US
TAMRC INTERNATIONAL MARKET RESEARCH REPORT. Added/Corp Texas Agricultural Market Research Center. **VFOAT** U.S.-Mexico Free Trade Issues for Agriculture Series; U.S.-Mexico Free Trade Impacts on Aagriculture Series; TAMRC Report; Texas Agricultural Market Reseach Center Report. (1991)-. Monographic series. English. Six times a year. Price varies per volume. **Continues** Research Report MRC.

LC HF1612.9 .T38   **ISSN** 0856-2105
DD 382/.63/0967805   TZ
TANZANIA TRADE CURRENTS : A JOURNAL OF THE BOARD OF EXTERNAL TRADE. Added/Corp Tanzania. Board of External Trade. **VFOAT** Trade Currents. Vol. 1, No. 1 (July/Aug. 1987)-. Periodical. English.

FR
TARIF DOUANIER ALGERIEN. French. Irregular. 433.00F per copy. Centre Francais du Commerce Exterieur, 10 Avenue d'Iena, 75783 Paris Cedex 16 France. **Tel** 011 33 1 40733415.

IT
TARIFFA DOGANALE D'USO INTEGRATA. Italian. Istituto Poligrafico Zecca Stato, Piazza Verdi 10, 00198 Rome Italy. **Tel** 011 39 6 85082307, 011 39 6 85082221.

UK
TATE'S EXPORT. English. Six times a year. £53.00. Tate Freight Forms, 47 Burners Lane S, Kiln Farm, Milton Keynes MK11 3HD United Kingdom. **Tel** 011 44 1908 221162, FAX 011 44 1908 313800. **ED** H. Massie. Index available. **Bk Rev**. **Ad Acc**. **Circ**: 3,000. available on diskette. **Continues** Tate's Documentation.
Desc: The exporting of goods to countries outside the UK.

ISSN 1056-2699
DD 381   US
TECH MARKET SOUTH. [Tech mark. South]. (1991)-. Periodical. English. Twelve times a year. Free (qualified subscribers); $19.95 (other). Tech Market South, 3200 Professional Parkway, Suite 245, Atlanta GA 30339.

US
TELECOMMUNICATIONS - EXPORT LICENSING CONTROLS. (1989)-. English. Irregular. $350.00. Comp-Tech Export Publications, PO Box 1367, Bethesda MD 20827-1367. **Tel** (301)983-3339, FAX (301)983-9035.
Desc: Examines the regulations for exporting all types of telecommunications equipment, software, and technology, including multiplexers, routers, switches, gateways, terminal interfaces, data switches, protocol converters, front end processors, TDMs, protocols, telecommunications software, network management systems, cluster controllers, T1, T3 and frame relay equipment, etc.

FR
TELEXPORT : LES EXPORTATEURS ET IMPORTATEURS FRANCAIS. Added/Corp Association Telexport. **VFOAT** Exportateurs et Importateurs Francais. (1991)-. Directory. English (French, German and Spanish). One time a year. 700.00F. Chambre de Commerce et Industrie de Paris, CEDIP, 201 avenue Jean Lolive, 93507 Pantin Cedex-France. **Tel** 33 1 47631415, FAX 33 1 42679969. Index available. **Ad Acc**, **Adv Mgr:** Philippe Do. available on CD-ROM from the publisher.

US
TENNESSEE EXPORT / IMPORT TRADE DIRECTORY / EXPORT TRADE PROMOTION OFFICE, DEPARTMENT OF ECONOMIC AND COMMUNITY DEVELOPMENT, STATE OF TENNESSEE. Added/Corp Tennessee. Dept. of Economic and Community Development. Export Trade Promotion Office. Tennessee. Dept. of Agriculture. Foreign Market Section. **VFOAT** Tennessee Export Import Trade Directory. (1979)-. Directory. English. Department of Economic and Community Development / Tennessee, 1018 Andrew Jackson State Office Building, Nashville TN 37219.

IT
TEORIA E PRATICA DEGLI SCAMBI INTERNAZIONALI. Italian. Irregular. L200000. Assoc It Commercio Mondiale, Via G.B. Morgagni 39, 20129 Milan Italy. **Tel** 011 39 2 29400017. ctrl circ.

LC HF3800.55.A48 T47   **ISSN** 1063-3553
DD 338   US
THAILAND PRODUCT GUIDE. [Thail. prod. guide]. **Added/Corp** DePaula Publishing and Services Corp. (1992)-. English. De Paula Publishing and Services Corporation, 421 7th Avenue, Suite 1206, New York NY 10001.

ISSN 1187-0796
DD 380.1/025/71312   CN
THUNDER BAY METRO TRADE INDEX. [Thunder Bay metro trade index]. **Added/Corp** Northwestern Ontario Economic Development Network. Thunder Bay Economic Development Corporation. (1991)-. English. Thunder Bay Economic Development Corp., Suite 203, Royal Bank Building, 620 Victoria Avenue East, Thunder Bay Ontario P7C 1A9. **Continues** Area Trade Index, 0838-6463.

UK
TOLLEY'S TRADING IN EUROPE. (19??)-. English. One time a year. Tolley Publishing Company Ltd., Tolley House, 2 Addiscombe Road, Croydon, Surrey CR9 5AF United Kingdom. **Tel** 011 44 181 6869141, FAX 011 44 181 6863155. **ED** John C. Dixon.
Desc: Provides all the necessary UK and EU information required for planning for, or advising on, a successful expansion into Europe.

CN
TOPICAL LAW REPORTS. See Law.

LC HF1557 .T67

RU
TORGOVLIA. Added/Corp Russia (Federation). Ministerstvo Torgovli i Materialnykh Resursov. (1992)-. Periodical. Russian. Twelve times a year. $109.95. **(Subscription address:** East View Publications Inc., 3020 Harbor Lane North, Suite 110, Minneapolis MN 55447. **Tel** (800)477-1005, (612)550-0961, FAX (612)559-2931.**) Continues** Sovetskaia Torgovlia, 0371-1927.

LC HF3821 .T66

JA
TOSHIBETSU KEIZAI SHIHYO. Added/Corp Chusho Kigyo Shinko Jigyodan. (19??)-. Japanese. ¥2300. 32-6 Hongo 5 chome, Bunkyo-ku 113 Japan.

AT
TRADE-A-BOAT. (19??)-. English. Twelve times a year. 78.93Aus$. Australian Consolidated Press Ltd., Private Bag 92615 Symonds St, Auckland New Zealand. **Tel** 011 64 9 3735408, FAX 011 64 9 3022889.

LC HC111 .C197   **ISSN** 0049-4321

CN
TRADE AND COMMERCE (WINNIPEG). (TRADE AND COMMERCE.). [Trade commer.]. (1955)-. Periodical. English. Five times a year. 24.01Can$. Sanford Evans Communications Ltd., Box 6900, 1700 Church Avenue, Winnipeg Manitoba R3C 3B1 Canada. **Tel** (204)694-2022, FAX (204)694-2347. **(Subscription address:** LW Subscriptions, 60 Renfrew Drive, Suite 260, Markham Ontario L3R 0E1 Canada. **Tel** (905)475-4145.**)** **ED** George Mitchell. **Ad Acc**. **Circ:** 12,400 (ctrl). **Continues** Trade and Commerce in Western Canada, 0380-7207.
Desc: Emphasizes industrial development and points out markets and potential markets for capital investment, commercial development and sales. Reaches key executives in western Canada, including Yukon and Northwest Territories.
Ind/Abst Coal Abstr.; PAIS Int. Print.

LC HF1008 .T7
DD 382/.091724/005   US
TRADE AND DEVELOPMENT REPORT : REPORT BY THE SECRETARIAT OF THE UNITED NATIONS CONFERENCE ON TRADE AND DEVELOPMENT. Added/Corp United Nations Conference on Trade and Development. Secretariat. (1981)-. English. One time a year (Nov., or Dec.). $45.00 (latest edition). United Nations Publications, 2 United Nations Plaza, Room DC2 0853, Department 007C, New York NY 10017. **Tel** (212)963-8303, (800)253-9646.

LC HF3000 .T73   **ISSN** 1057-9702
DD 382./5/0973021   US
TRADE AND EMPLOYMENT. [Trade employ.]. **Added/Corp** United States. Bureau of the Census. United States. Bureau of Labor Statistics. **VFOAT** Trade & Employment. (Nov. 1984)-. Government Publication. English. Four times a year. $25.00. US Department of Commerce / Bureau of the Census, Data User Services Division, Customer Services, Washington DC 20233-0800. **Tel** (301)763-4100. **(Subscription address:** Superintendent of Documents, US Government Printing Office, Washington DC 20402. **)** Documents available from Documents on Demand.
Desc: A comparison of United States imports in terms of commodity classification based on the Standard Industrial Classification Manual.
Ind/Abst Am. Stat. Index.

US
TRADE & INDUSTRY INDEX [ONLINE DATABASE]. See Business and Economics-Abstracting, Bibliographies and Statistics.

US
●**TRADE BETWEEN THE UNITED STATES AND CHINA, THE SUCCESSOR STATES TO THE FORMER SOVIET UNION, AND OTHER TITLE IV COUNTRIES DURING ... [MICROFORM].**
Main/Corp United States International Trade Commission. **VFOAT** Quarterly Report to the Congress and the Trade Policy Committee; Quarterly Report on East-West Trade During ... . 74th (Jan.-Mar. 1993)-. Periodical. English. Four times a year. United States International Trade Commission, 500 E Street Southwest, Washington DC 20436. **Tel** (202)205-1806. **Continues** United States International Trade Commission. Trade Between the United States and China, the Former Soviet Union, Central and Eastern Europe, the Baltic Nations, and Other Selected Countries During ... .

LC Z5771 .C7   **ISSN** 0564-0482
DD 016.38   US
TRADE DIRECTORIES OF THE WORLD. 1st Ed. (1952)-. Directory. English. Ten times a year. $89.90. Croner Publications Inc., 34 Jericho Turnpike, Jericho NY 11753. **Tel** (516)333-9085.
Desc: Directory listing trade, industrial and professional directories. Valuable information for importers and exporters.

LC HG1501
DD 332.1   UK
    TITLE CHANGE
TRADE FINANCE. Added/Corp Euromoney Publications Ltd. **VFOAT** Trade Finance & Banker International. No. 88 (Aug. 1990)-(19??). Periodical. English. Euromoney Publications PLC, Nestor House, Playhouse Yard, London EC4Z 5EX United Kingdom. **Tel** 011 44 171 7798888, FAX 011 44 171 7798630, telex 290700 EUROMON G. **Continues** Trade Finance & Banker International, 0960-1740. **Continued by** Project and Trade Finance.
Desc: Magazine for executives and bankers involved in trade, project and export finance. Contains news, analysis and sound advice.

II
TRADE INTELLIGENCE BULLETIN.
(19??)-. Bulletin. English. Trade Development Authority, 16 Parliament Street, New Delhi 1 India.

US
●**TRADE NEWS / OAS. Added/Corp** Organization of American States. General Secretariat. Vol. 18, No. 10 (Oct. 1993)-. Periodical. English. Twelve times a year. $12.00. Organization of American States, 19th Street & Constitution Avenue NW, Suite 300, Washington DC 20006. **Tel** (202)458-6256. **Continues** OAS CECON Trade News, 0250-6203.

LC HF1455 .T654   **ISSN** 1014-7411
DD 382/.0973/005   SZ
TRADE POLICY REVIEW. (TRADE POLICY REVIEW. THE UNITED STATES OF AMERICA.). [Trade policy rev.]. **Added/Corp** General Agreement on Tariffs and Trade (Organization). **VFOAT** Trade Policy Review. United States. (1989)-. English. Every 2 years. 60.00F. General Agreement on Tariffs and Trade / GATT, Centre William Rappard, 154 rue de Lausanne, 1211 Geneva 21 Switzerland. **Tel** 011 41 22 7395111, 011 41 22 7395019, FAX 011 41 22 7395458.
Desc: Examines the full range of trade policies and practices of individual GATT members. Evaluation is conducted by the GATT Council on the basis of two reports; one presented by the government of the country concerned, and the other presented by the GATT Secretariat.

LC HF1611.7 .T73
DD 382/.3/096205   SZ
TRADE POLICY REVIEW. ARAB REPUBLIC OF EGYPT. Added/Corp General Agreement on Tariffs and Trade (Organization). **VFOAT** Trade Policy Review. Egypt; Arab Republic of Egypt. (1992)-. English. Irregular (every 4 to 6 years). 50.00F. General Agreement on Tariffs and Trade / GATT, Centre William Rappard, 154 rue de Lausanne, 1211 Geneva 21 Switzerland. **Tel** 011 41 22 7395111, 011 41 22 7395019, FAX 011 41 22 7395458.
Desc: Examines the full range of trade policies and practices of individual GATT members. Evaluation is conducted by the GATT Council on the basis of two reports; one presented by the government of the country concerned, and the other presented by the GATT Secretariat.

Business and Economics —Commerce

LC HF1509 .A73
DD 382/.3/0958205 SZ
TRADE POLICY REVIEW. ARGENTINA.
Added/Corp General Agreement on Tariffs and Trade (Organization). **VFOAT** Argentina. (1992)-. English. Irregular (every 4 to 6 years). 50.00F. General Agreement on Tariffs and Trade / GATT, Centre William Rappard, 154 rue de Lausanne, 1211 Geneva 21 Switzerland. **Tel** 011 41 22 7395111, 011 41 22 7395019, FAX 011 41 22 7395458.
Desc: Examines the full range of trade policies and practices of individual GATT members. Evaluation is conducted by the GATT Council on the basis of two reports; one presented by the government of the country concerned, and the other presented by the GATT Secretariat.

LC HF1625 .T7
DD 382/.0994/005 SZ
TRADE POLICY REVIEW. AUSTRALIA.
Added/Corp General Agreement on Tariffs and Trade (Organization). (1989)-. English. Irregular (every 4 to 6 years). 60.00F. General Agreement on Tariffs and Trade / GATT, Centre William Rappard, 154 rue de Lausanne, 1211 Geneva 21 Switzerland. **Tel** 011 41 22 7395111, 011 41 22 7395019, FAX 011 41 22 7395458.
Desc: Examines the full range of trade policies and practices of individual GATT members. Evaluation is conducted by the GATT Council on the basis of two reports; one presented by the government of the country concerned, and the other presented by the GATT Secretariat.

LC HF1541 .T73
DD 382/.3/0943605 SZ
TRADE POLICY REVIEW. AUSTRIA.
Added/Corp General Agreement on Tariffs and Trade (Organization). (1992)-. English. Irregular (every 4 to 6 years). 50.00F. General Agreement on Tariffs and Trade / GATT, Centre William Rappard, 154 rue de Lausanne, 1211 Geneva 21 Switzerland. **Tel** 011 41 22 7395111, 011 41 22 7395019, FAX 011 41 22 7395458.
Desc: Examines the full range of trade policies and practices of individual GATT members. Evaluation is conducted by the GATT Council on the basis of two reports; one presented by the government of the country concerned, and the other presented by the GATT Secretariat.

LC HF1590.6 .T73
SZ
TRADE POLICY REVIEW. BANGLADESH. **Added/Corp** General Agreement on Tariffs and Trade (Organization). **VFOAT** Bangladesh. (1992)-. English. Irregular (every 4 to 6 years). 50.00F. General Agreement on Tariffs and Trade / GATT, Centre William Rappard, 154 rue de Lausanne, 1211 Geneva 21 Switzerland. **Tel** 011 41 22 7395111, 011 41 22 7395019, FAX 011 41 22 7395458.
Desc: Examines the full range of trade policies and practices of individual GATT members. Evaluation is conducted by the GATT Council on the basis of two reports; one presented by the government of the country concerned, and the other presented by the GATT Secretariat.

LC HF1511 .T7
DD 382/.3/098405 SZ
•**TRADE POLICY REVIEW. BOLIVIA.**
Added/Corp General Agreement on Tariffs and Trade (Organization). **VFOAT** Bolivia. (1993)-. English. Irregular (every 4 to 6 years). 50.00F. General Agreement on Tariffs and Trade / GATT, Centre William Rappard, 154 rue de Lausanne, 1211 Geneva 21 Switzerland. **Tel** 011 41 22 7395111, 011 41 22 7395019, FAX 011 41 22 7395458.
Desc: Examines the full range of trade policies and practices of individual GATT members. Evaluation is conducted by the GATT Council on the basis of two reports; one presented by the government of the country concerned, and the other presented by the GATT Secretariat.

LC HF1513 .T73
SZ
TRADE POLICY REVIEW. BRAZIL.
Added/Corp General Agreement on Tariffs and Trade (Organization). **VFOAT** Brazil. (1992)-. English. Irregular (every 4 to 6 years). 50.00F. General Agreement on Tariffs and Trade / GATT, Centre William Rappard, 154 rue de Lausanne, 1211 Geneva 21 Switzerland. **Tel** 011 41 22 7395111, 011 41 22 7395019, FAX 011 41 22 7395458.
Desc: Examines the full range of trade policies and practices of individual GATT members. Evaluation is conducted by the GATT Council on the basis of two reports; one presented by the government of the country concerned, and the other presented by the GATT Secretariat.

LC HF1479 .T73
DD 382/.0971/005 SZ
TRADE POLICY REVIEW. CANADA.
Added/Corp General Agreement on Tariffs and Trade (Organization). (1990)-. English. Every 2 years. 60.00F. General Agreement on Tariffs and Trade / GATT, Centre William Rappard, 154 rue de Lausanne, 1211 Geneva 21 Switzerland. **Tel** 011 41 22 7395111, 011 41 22 7395019, FAX 011 41 22 7395458.
Desc: Examines the full range of trade policies and practices of individual GATT members. Evaluation is conducted by the GATT Council on the basis of two reports; one presented by the government of the country concerned, and the other presented by the GATT Secretariat.

LC HF1515 .T7
DD 382/.3/098305 SZ
TRADE POLICY REVIEW. CHILE.
Added/Corp General Agreement on Tariffs and Trade (Organization). **VFOAT** Chile. (1991)-. English. Irregular (every 4 to 6 years). 50.00F. General Agreement on Tariffs and Trade / GATT, Centre William Rappard, 154 rue de Lausanne, 1211 Geneva 21 Switzerland. **Tel** 011 41 22 7395111, 011 41 22 7395019, FAX 011 41 22 7395458.
Desc: Examines the full range of trade policies and practices of individual GATT members. Evaluation is conducted by the GATT Council on the basis of two reports; one presented by the government of the country concerned, and the other presented by the GATT Secretariat.

LC HF1517 .T7
DD 382/.3/0986105 SZ
TRADE POLICY REVIEW. COLOMBIA.
Added/Corp General Agreement on Tariffs and Trade (Organization). (1990)-. English. Irregular (every 4 to 6 years). 50.00F. General Agreement on Tariffs and Trade / GATT, Centre William Rappard, 154 rue de Lausanne, 1211 Geneva 21 Switzerland. **Tel** 011 41 22 7395111, 011 41 22 7395019, FAX 011 41 22 7395458.
Desc: Examines the full range of trade policies and practices of individual GATT members. Evaluation is conducted by the GATT Council on the basis of two reports; one presented by the government of the country concerned, and the other presented by the GATT Secretariat.

LC HF1558.3 T73
SZ
TRADE POLICY REVIEW. FINLAND.
Added/Corp General Agreement on Tariffs and Trade (Organization). (1992)-. English. Irregular (every 4 to 6 years). 50.00F. General Agreement on Tariffs and Trade / GATT, Centre William Rappard, 154 rue de Lausanne, 1211 Geneva 21 Switzerland. **Tel** 011 41 22 7395111, 011 41 22 7395019, FAX 011 41 22 7395458.
Desc: Examines the full range of trade policies and practices of individual GATT members. Evaluation is conducted by the GATT Council on the basis of two reports; one presented by the government of the country concerned, and the other presented by the GATT Secretariat.

LC HF1616.8 .T72
SZ
TRADE POLICY REVIEW. GHANA.
Added/Corp General Agreement on Tariffs and Trade (Organization). **VFOAT** Ghana. (1992)-. English. Irregular (every 4 to 6 years). 50.00F. General Agreement on Tariffs and Trade / GATT, Centre William Rappard, 154 rue de Lausanne, 1211 Geneva 21 Switzerland. **Tel** 011 41 22 7395111, 011 41 22 7395019, FAX 011 41 22 7395458.
Desc: Examines the full range of trade policies and practices of individual GATT members. Evaluation is conducted by the GATT Council on the basis of two reports; one presented by the government of the country concerned, and the other presented by the GATT Secretariat.

LC HF1607 .T73
DD 382/.095125/005 SZ
TRADE POLICY REVIEW. HONG KONG.
Added/Corp General Agreement on Tariffs and Trade (Organization). (1990)-. English. Irregular (every 4 to 6 years). 60.00F. General Agreement on Tariffs and Trade / GATT, Centre William Rappard, 154 rue de Lausanne, 1211 Geneva 21 Switzerland. **Tel** 011 41 22 7395111, 011 41 22 7395019, FAX 011 41 22 7395458.
Desc: Examines the full range of trade policies and practices of individual GATT members. Evaluation is conducted by the GATT Council on the basis of two reports; one presented by the government of the country concerned, and the other presented by the GATT Secretariat.

LC HF1542.5 .T7
DD 382/.3/0943905 SZ
TRADE POLICY REVIEW. HUNGARY.
Added/Corp General Agreement on Tariffs and Trade (Organization). (1991)-. English. Irregular (every 4 to 6 years). 50.00F. General Agreement on Tariffs and Trade / GATT, Centre William Rappard, 154 rue de Lausanne, 1211 Geneva 21 Switzerland. **Tel** 011 41 22 7395111, 011 41 22 7395019, FAX 011 41 22 7395458.
Desc: Examines the full range of trade policies and practices of individual GATT members. Evaluation is conducted by the GATT Council on the basis of two reports; one presented by the government of the country concerned, and the other presented by the GATT Secretariat.

LC HF1589 .T73
DD 382/3/095405 SZ
•**TRADE POLICY REVIEW. INDIA.**
Added/Corp General Agreement on Tariffs and Trade (Organization). **VFOAT** India. (1993)-. English. Irregular (every 4 to 6 years). 50.00F. General Agreement on Tariffs and Trade / GATT, Centre William Rappard, 154 rue de Lausanne, 1211 Geneva 21 Switzerland. **Tel** 011 41 22 7395111, 011 41 22 7395019, FAX 011 41 22 7395458.
Desc: Examines the full range of trade policies and practices of individual GATT members. Evaluation is conducted by the GATT Council on the basis of two reports; one presented by the government of the country concerned, and the other presented by the GATT Secretariat.

LC HF1597 .T7
DD 382/.3/0959805 SZ
TRADE POLICY REVIEW. INDONESIA.
Added/Corp General Agreement on Tariffs and Trade (Organization). (1991)-. English. Irregular (every 4 to 6 years). 50.00F. General Agreement on Tariffs and Trade / GATT, Centre William Rappard, 154 rue de Lausanne, 1211 Geneva 21 Switzerland. **Tel** 011 41 22 7395111, 011 41 22 7395019, FAX 011 41 22 7395458.
Desc: Examines the full range of trade policies and practices of individual GATT members. Evaluation is conducted by the GATT Council on the basis of two reports; one presented by the government of the country concerned, and the other presented by the GATT Secretariat.

LC HF1601 .T73
DD 382/.00952/05 SZ
TRADE POLICY REVIEW. JAPAN.
Added/Corp General Agreement on Tariffs and Trade (Organization). (1990)-. English. Every 2 years. 60.00F. General Agreement on Tariffs and Trade / GATT, Centre William Rappard, 154 rue de Lausanne, 1211 Geneva 21 Switzerland. **Tel** 011 41 22 7395111, 011 41 22 7395019, FAX 011 41 22 7395458.
Desc: Examines the full range of trade policies and practices of individual GATT members. Evaluation is conducted by the GATT Council on the basis of two reports; one presented by the government of the country concerned, and the other presented by the GATT Secretariat.

LC HF1602.5 .T72
SZ
TRADE POLICY REVIEW. KOREA.
Added/Corp General Agreement on Tariffs and Trade (Organization). **VFOAT** Korea.; Trade Policy Review. Republic of Korea; Republic of Korea, Trade Policy Review. (1992)-. English. Irregular (every 4 to 6 years). 50.00F. General Agreement on Tariffs and Trade / GATT, Centre William Rappard, 154 rue de Lausanne, 1211 Geneva 21 Switzerland. **Tel** 011 41 22 7395111, 011 41 22 7395019, FAX 011 41 22 7395458.
Desc: Examines the full range of trade policies and practices of individual GATT members. Evaluation is conducted by the GATT Council on the basis of two reports; one presented by the government of the country concerned, and the other presented by the GATT Secretariat.

LC HF1594.6 .T73
DD 382/.3/0959505 SZ
•**TRADE POLICY REVIEW. MALAYSIA.**
Added/Corp General Agreement on Tariffs and Trade (Organization). **VFOAT** Malaysia. (1993)-. English. Irregular (every 4 to 6 years). 50.00F. General Agreement on Tariffs and Trade / GATT, Centre William Rappard, 154 rue de Lausanne, 1211 Geneva 21 Switzerland. **Tel** 011 41 22 7395111, 011 41 22 7395019, FAX 011 41 22 7395458.
Desc: Examines the full range of trade policies and practices of individual GATT members. Evaluation is conducted by the GATT Council on the basis of two reports; one presented by the government of the country concerned, and the other presented by the GATT Secretariat.

LC HF1481 .T67
SZ
•**TRADE POLICY REVIEW. MEXICO.**
Added/Corp General Agreement on Tariffs and Trade (Organization). **VFOAT** Mexico. (1993)-. English. Irregular (every 4 to 6 years). 50.00F. General Agreement on Tariffs and Trade / GATT, Centre William Rappard, 154 rue de Lausanne, 1211 Geneva 21 Switzerland. **Tel** 011 41 22 7395111, 011 41 22 7395019, FAX 011 41 22 7395458.
Desc: Examines the full range of trade policies and practices of individual GATT members. Evaluation is conducted by the GATT Council on the basis of two reports; one presented by the government of the country concerned, and the other presented by the GATT Secretariat.

LC HF1642.5 .T73
DD 382/.0993/005 SZ
TRADE POLICY REVIEW. NEW ZEALAND. **Added/Corp** General Agreement on Tariffs and Trade (Organization). (1990)-. English. Irregular (every 4 to 6 years). 60.00F. General Agreement on Tariffs and Trade / GATT, Centre William Rappard, 154 rue de Lausanne, 1211 Geneva 21 Switzerland. **Tel**

Business and Economics —Commerce

011 41 22 7395111, 011 41 22 7395019, FAX 011 41 22 7395458.
Desc: Examines the full range of trade policies and practices of individual GATT members. Evaluation is conducted by the GATT Council on the basis of two reports; one presented by the government of the country concerned, and the other presented by the GATT Secretariat.

LC HF1616.7 .T7
DD 382/.3/0966905 SZ
TRADE POLICY REVIEW. NIGERIA. **Added/Corp** General Agreement on Tariffs and Trade (Organization). **VFOAT** Nigeria. (1991)-. English. Irregular (every 4 to 6 years). 50.00F. General Agreement on Tariffs and Trade / GATT, Centre William Rappard, 154 rue de Lausanne, 1211 Geneva 21 Switzerland. **Tel** 011 41 22 7395111, 011 41 22 7395019, FAX 011 41 22 7395458.
Desc: Examines the full range of trade policies and practices of individual GATT members. Evaluation is conducted by the GATT Council on the basis of two reports; one presented by the government of the country concerned, and the other presented by the GATT Secretariat.

LC HF1565 .T73
DD 382/.3/0948105 SZ
TRADE POLICY REVIEW. NORWAY. **Added/Corp** General Agreement on Tariffs and Trade (Organization). **VFOAT** Norway. (1991)-. English. Irregular (every 4 to 6 years). 50.00F. General Agreement on Tariffs and Trade / GATT, Centre William Rappard, 154 rue de Lausanne, 1211 Geneva 21 Switzerland. **Tel** 011 41 22 7395111, 011 41 22 7395019, FAX 011 41 22 7395458.
Desc: Examines the full range of trade policies and practices of individual GATT members. Evaluation is conducted by the GATT Council on the basis of two reports; one presented by the government of the country concerned, and the other presented by the GATT Secretariat.

LC HF1558.7 .T73
DD 382/.3/0943805 SZ
TRADE POLICY REVIEW. POLAND. **Added/Corp** General Agreement on Tariffs and Trade (Organization). **VFOAT** Poland. (1992)-. English. Irregular (every 4 to 6 years). 50.00F. General Agreement on Tariffs and Trade / GATT, Centre William Rappard, 154 rue de Lausanne, 1211 Geneva 21 Switzerland. **Tel** 011 41 22 7395111, 011 41 22 7395019, FAX 011 41 22 7395458.
Desc: Examines the full range of trade policies and practices of individual GATT members. Evaluation is conducted by the GATT Council on the basis of two reports; one presented by the government of the country concerned, and the other presented by the GATT Secretariat.

LC HF1581 .T7
DD 382/.3/0949805 SZ
TRADE POLICY REVIEW. ROMANIA. **Added/Corp** General Agreement on Tariffs and Trade (Organization). **VFOAT** Romania. (1992)-. English. Irregular (every 4 to 6 years). 50.00F. General Agreement on Tariffs and Trade / GATT, Centre William Rappard, 154 rue de Lausanne, 1211 Geneva 21 Switzerland. **Tel** 011 41 22 7395111, 011 41 22 7395019, FAX 011 41 22 7395458.
Desc: Examines the full range of trade policies and practices of individual GATT members. Evaluation is conducted by the GATT Council on the basis of two reports; one presented by the government of the country concerned, and the other presented by the GATT Secretariat.

LC HF1616.5 .T73
DD 382/.0/0966305 SZ
TRADE POLICY REVIEW. SENEGAL. **Added/Corp** General Agreement on Tariffs and Trade (Organization). **VFOAT** Senegal. (19??)-. English. Irregular (every 4 to 6 years). 50.00F. General Agreement on Tariffs and Trade / GATT, Centre William Rappard, 154 rue de Lausanne, 1211 Geneva 21 Switzerland. **Tel** 011 41 22 7395111, 011 41 22 7395019, FAX 011 41 22 7395458.
Desc: Examines the full range of trade policies and practices of individual GATT members. Evaluation is conducted by the GATT Council on the basis of two reports; one presented by the government of the country concerned, and the other presented by the GATT Secretariat.

LC HF1595 .T72
DD 382/.3/09595705 SZ
TRADE POLICY REVIEW. SINGAPORE. **Added/Corp** General Agreement on Tariffs and Trade (Organization). **VFOAT** Singapore. (1992)-. English. Irregular (every 4 to 6 years). 50.00F. General Agreement on Tariffs and Trade / GATT, Centre William Rappard, 154 rue de Lausanne, 1211 Geneva 21 Switzerland. **Tel** 011 41 22 7395111, 011 41 22 7395019, FAX 011 41 22 7395458.
Desc: Examines the full range of trade policies and practices of individual GATT members. Evaluation is conducted by the GATT Council on the basis of two reports; one presented by the government of the country concerned, and the other presented by the GATT Secretariat.

LC HF1567 .T73
DD 382/.09485/005 SZ
TRADE POLICY REVIEW. SWEDEN. **Added/Corp** General Agreement on Tariffs and Trade (Organization). (1990)-. English. Irregular (every 4 to 6 years). 50.00F. General Agreement on Tariffs and Trade / GATT, Centre William Rappard, 154 rue de Lausanne, 1211 Geneva 21 Switzerland. **Tel** 011 41 22 7395111, 011 41 22 7395019, FAX 011 41 22 7395458.
Desc: Examines the full range of trade policies and practices of individual GATT members. Evaluation is conducted by the GATT Council on the basis of two reports; one presented by the government of the country concerned, and the other presented by the GATT Secretariat.

LC HF1573 .T7
DD 382/.3/0949405 SZ
TRADE POLICY REVIEW. SWITZERLAND. **Added/Corp** General Agreement on Tariffs and Trade (Organization). **VFOAT** Switzerland. (1991)-. English. Irregular (every 4 to 6 years). 50.00F. General Agreement on Tariffs and Trade / GATT, Centre William Rappard, 154 rue de Lausanne, 1211 Geneva 21 Switzerland. **Tel** 011 41 22 7395111, 011 41 22 7395019, FAX 011 41 22 7395458.
Desc: Examines the full range of trade policies and practices of individual GATT members. Evaluation is conducted by the GATT Council on the basis of two reports; one presented by the government of the country concerned, and the other presented by the GATT Secretariat.

LC HF1594.55 .T7
DD 382/.3/0959305 SZ
TRADE POLICY REVIEW. THAILAND. **Added/Corp** General Agreement on Tariffs and Trade (Organization). **VFOAT** Thailand. (1991)-. English. Irregular (every 4 to 6 years). 50.00F. General Agreement on Tariffs and Trade / GATT, Centre William Rappard, 154 rue de Lausanne, 1211 Geneva 21 Switzerland. **Tel** 011 41 22 7395111, 011 41 22 7395019, FAX 011 41 22 7395458.
Desc: Examines the full range of trade policies and practices of individual GATT members. Evaluation is conducted by the GATT Council on the basis of two reports; one presented by the government of the country concerned, and the other presented by the GATT Secretariat.

LC HF1532.92 .T734
DD 382/.3/09405 SZ
TRADE POLICY REVIEW. THE EUROPEAN COMMUNITIES. **Added/Corp** General Agreement on Tariffs and Trade (Organization). **VFOAT** European Communities ... Trade Policy Review. (1991)-. Periodical. English. Every 2 years. 60.00F. General Agreement on Tariffs and Trade / GATT, Centre William Rappard, 154 rue de Lausanne, 1211 Geneva 21 Switzerland. **Tel** 011 41 22 7395111, 011 41 22 7395019, FAX 011 41 22 7395458.
Desc: Examines the full range of trade policies and practices of individual GATT members. Evaluation is conducted by the GATT Council on the basis of two reports; one presented by the government of the country concerned, and the other presented by the GATT Secretariat.

LC HF1611.3 .T7
DD 382/.0964/005 SZ
TRADE POLICY REVIEW. THE KINGDOM OF MOROCCO. **Added/Corp** General Agreement on Tariffs and Trade (Organization). **VFOAT** Trade Policy Review. Morocco. (1989)-. English. Irregular (every 4 to 6 years). 50.00F. General Agreement on Tariffs and Trade / GATT, Centre William Rappard, 154 rue de Lausanne, 1211 Geneva 21 Switzerland. **Tel** 011 41 22 7395111, 011 41 22 7395019, FAX 011 41 22 7395458.
Desc: Examines the full range of trade policies and practices of individual GATT members. Evaluation is conducted by the GATT Council on the basis of two reports; one presented by the government of the country concerned, and the other presented by the GATT Secretariat.

LC HF1599 .T73
DD 382/.3/0959905 SZ
•**TRADE POLICY REVIEW. THE PHILIPPINES.** **Added/Corp** General Agreement on Tariffs and Trade (Organization). **VFOAT** Philippines. (1993)-. English. Irregular (every 4 to 6 years). 50.00F. General Agreement on Tariffs and Trade / GATT, Centre William Rappard, 154 rue de Lausanne, 1211 Geneva 21 Switzerland. **Tel** 011 41 22 7395111, 011 41 22 7395019, FAX 011 41 22 7395458.
Desc: Examines the full range of trade policies and practices of individual GATT members. Evaluation is conducted by the GATT Council on the basis of two reports; one presented by the government of the country concerned, and the other presented by the GATT Secretariat.

LC HF1563 .T73
SZ
•**TRADE POLICY REVIEW. THE REPUBLIC OF ICELAND.** **Added/Corp** General Agreement on Tariffs and Trade (Organization). **VFOAT** Republic of Iceland; Trade Policy Review. Iceland. (1994)-. English. Irregular (every 4 to 6 years). 50.00F. General Agreement on Tariffs and Trade / GATT, Centre William Rappard, 154 rue de Lausanne, 1211 Geneva 21 Switzerland. **Tel** 011 41 22 7395111, 011 41 22 7395019, FAX 011 41 22 7395458.
Desc: Examines the full range of trade policies and practices of individual GATT members. Evaluation is conducted by the GATT Council on the basis of two reports; one presented by the government of the country concerned, and the other presented by the GATT Secretariat.

LC HF1612.5 .T73
DD 382/.3/09676205 SZ
•**TRADE POLICY REVIEW. THE REPUBLIC OF KENYA.** **Added/Corp** General Agreement on Tariffs and Trade (Organization). **VFOAT** Kenya; Republic of Kenya; Trade Policy Review. Kenya. (1994)-. English. Irregular (every 4 to 6 years). 50.00F. General Agreement on Tariffs and Trade / GATT, Centre William Rappard, 154 rue de Lausanne, 1211 Geneva 21 Switzerland. **Tel** 011 41 22 7395111, 011 41 22 7395019, FAX 011 41 22 7395458.
Desc: Examines the full range of trade policies and practices of individual GATT members. Evaluation is conducted by the GATT Council on the basis of two reports; one presented by the government of the country concerned, and the other presented by the GATT Secretariat.

LC HF1525 .T73
DD 382/.3/098505 SZ
TRADE POLICY REVIEW. THE REPUBLIC OF PERU. **Added/Corp** General Agreement on Tariffs and Trade (Organization). **VFOAT** Trade Policy Review. Peru; Peru; Republic of Peru. (19??)-. English. Irregular (every 4 to 6 years). 50.00F. General Agreement on Tariffs and Trade / GATT, Centre William Rappard, 154 rue de Lausanne, 1211 Geneva 21 Switzerland. **Tel** 011 41 22 7395111, 011 41 22 7395019, FAX 011 41 22 7395458.
Desc: Examines the full range of trade policies and practices of individual GATT members. Evaluation is conducted by the GATT Council on the basis of two reports; one presented by the government of the country concerned, and the other presented by the GATT Secretariat.

LC HF1613.4 .T7
DD 382/.3/096805 SZ
•**TRADE POLICY REVIEW. THE REPUBLIC OF SOUTH AFRICA.** **Added/Corp** General Agreement on Tariffs and Trade (Organization). **VFOAT** South Africa; Republic of South Africa; Trade Policy Review. South Africa. (1993)-. English. Irregular (every 4 to 6 years). 50.00F. General Agreement on Tariffs and Trade / GATT, Centre William Rappard, 154 rue de Lausanne, 1211 Geneva 21 Switzerland. **Tel** 011 41 22 7395111, 011 41 22 7395019, FAX 011 41 22 7395458.
Desc: Examines the full range of trade policies and practices of individual GATT members. Evaluation is conducted by the GATT Council on the basis of two reports; one presented by the government of the country concerned, and the other presented by the GATT Secretariat.

LC HF1583.4 .T73
DD 382/.3/0956105 SZ
•**TRADE POLICY REVIEW. THE REPUBLIC OF TURKEY.** **VFOAT** Republic of Turkey. (1994)-. English. Irregular (every 4 to 6 years). 50.00F. General Agreement on Tariffs and Trade / GATT, Centre William Rappard, 154 rue de Lausanne, 1211 Geneva 21 Switzerland. **Tel** 011 41 22 7395111, 011 41 22 7395019, FAX 011 41 22 7395458.
Desc: Examines the full range of trade policies and practices of individual GATT members. Evaluation is conducted by the GATT Council on the basis of two reports; one presented by the government of the country concerned, and the other presented by the GATT Secretariat.

LC HF1527 .T73
SZ
TRADE POLICY REVIEW. URUGUAY. **Added/Corp** General Agreement on Tariffs and Trade (Organization). **VFOAT** Uruguay. (1992)-. English. Irregular (every 4 to 6 years). 50.00F. General Agreement on Tariffs and Trade / GATT, Centre William Rappard, 154 rue de Lausanne, 1211 Geneva 21 Switzerland. **Tel** 011 41 22 7395111, 011 41 22 7395019, FAX 011 41 22 7395458.
Desc: Examines the full range of trade policies and practices of individual GATT members. Evaluation is conducted by the GATT Council on the basis of two reports; one presented by the government of the country concerned, and the other presented by the GATT Secretariat.

Business and Economics —Commerce

LC HF272.A3 S49A
DD 382/.0969/6
SE
TRADE REPORT - SEYCHELLES.
Main/Corp Seychelles. English. One time a year. $14.00. Information Systems Division / Seychelles. Statistics Section, Presidents Office, PO Box 206, Victoria Seychelles. **Tel** 24041, telex 2333 ADMIN S2. **Ad Acc. Circ**: 250.
Desc: Provides detailed statistics on imports and exports of the Seychelles.

LC HF189.A532 **ISSN** 0790-5122
DD 382/.09417/0021
IE
TRADE STATISTICS OF IRELAND. See
Business and Economics-Abstracting, Bibliographies and Statistics.

LC HF41 .T74
JA
TRADE TIMES. Added/Corp Nihon Kikai Yushutsu
Kumiai. (19??)-. Periodical. English. Twelve times a year. $35.00. Trade Times Ltd., 5-16 Nishi-Shimbashi 1-chome, Minatoku, Tokyo Japan.

CH
TRADE WINDS INDUSTRY WEEKLY.
(19??)-. English. One time a week. $110.00 Americas, Africa and Europe; $90.00 other. Trade Winds Inc., PO Box 7-179, #7 Lane 75 Yungkang Street, Taipei Taiwan. **Tel** 011 886 2 3932718, FAX 011 886 2 3964022.
Continues Trade Winds Weekly.
Desc: Export products and industries of Taiwan, including machinery, electronics, auto parts, gift items, etc.

ISSN 0259-9880
CH
TRADE WINDS MONTHLY. [Trade winds
mon.]. **VFOAT** Trade Winds (Taipei). (1980)-. Periodical. English. Twelve times a year. $110.00. Trade Winds Inc., PO Box 7-179, #7 Lane 75 Yungkang Street, Taipei Taiwan. **Tel** 011 886 2 3932718, FAX 011 886 2 3964022.
Desc: Covers economy and exports of Taiwan's industries, as well as economic conditions in other Asian countries.

LC HF37.G7 T7 **ISSN** 0041-0543
GR
TRADE WITH GREECE. [Trade Greece].
Added/Corp Emporikon kai Viomechanikon Epimeleterion Athenon. No. 1 (June 1959)-. Periodical. English (French and German; summaries and/or abstracts in French and German). Four times a year. Free on request. Athens Chamber Commerce Industry, 7 Acadimias Street, Athens 10671 Greece. **Tel** 011 30 1 3618810. **ED** Theodore Vamvakaris.
Ind/Abst Predicasts.

UK
TRADERS DIRECTORY, THE. Added/Corp
Euromoney Publications Ltd. AP-DJ Telerate (Firm). Telerate (Firm). **VFOAT** Traders Directory of Foreign Exchange, Futures and Options Dealers; AP-DJ Telerate/Euromoney Traders Directory; Telerate-Euromoney Traders Directory. (1986)-. Periodical. English. One time a year. $300.00. Euromoney Publications PLC, Nestor House, Playhouse Yard, London EC4Z 5EX United Kingdom. **Tel** 011 44 171 7798888, FAX 011 44 171 7798630, telex 290700 EUROMON G. **Continues** AP-DJ Telerate/Euromoney Worldwide Directory.

ISSN 1060-8249
US
TRADES (NEW ORLEANS, LA.).
(TRADES.). **VFOAT** International Trade Guide. (1992)-. English. Two times a year. $79.99. Cornerstone Company, 5534 Airline Blvd. #7, New Orleans LA 70124.

LC HF.1
DD 380.1
CH
TRADEWEEK. VFOAT Wai Hsiao Hsien Feng Tsa
Chih; Trade Week). Periodical. English. Taiwan Yellow Pages Corp, 57 Tun Hua S Road/2nd Floor, Taipei 10588 Taiwan. **Tel** 886 2 771 5995.

ISSN 1056-8301
DD 382
US
TRADEWEEK (LOS ANGELES, CALIF.).
(TRADEWEEK.). [Tradeweek]. **VFOAT** Trade Week. (Mar. 1991)-. Periodical. English. Fifty times a year (weekly except first week of July & last week of Dec.). $94.00. Newsmedia Research Bureau, 1200 North College Avenue, PO Box 65097, Claremont CA 91711. **Tel** (909)626-5990. **Continues** Import (Los Angeles, Calif.), 1043-9226.

II
TRADO, ASIAN AFRICAN DIRECTORY OF EXPORTERS-IMPORTERS & MANUFACTURERS. (1956)-. Directory. English.
Irregular. $115.00. Trado Publications Pvt Ltd, C-6 Safdarjung, Development Area, Community Center, New Delhi 110016 India. **(Subscription address**: Taylor & Francis Inc., 1900 Frost Road, Suite 101, Bristol PA 19007-1598. **Tel** (215)785-5800, (800)821-8312, FAX (215)785-5515.) **ED** J. K. Chug. Index available. **Ad Acc. Circ**: 10,000. **Continues** Trade Asian Directory of Exporters, Importers & Manufacturers.

ISSN 1171-2961
DD 330.993005
NZ
TRANS TASMAN. [Trans Tasman]. VFOAT
Trans-Tasman. (19??)-. Periodical. English. Forty-seven times a year. $215.00. Trans Tasman News Service Limited, PO Box 377, Wellington New Zealand. **Tel** 011 4 721677 Ext. 846. **ED** I. Templeton. ctrl circ.

ISSN 0842-6546
DD 380.5/068
CN
TRANSPORT CANADA CORPORATE PRIORITIES. [Transp. Can. corp. prior.]. Main/Corp
Canada. Transport Canada. Strategic Planning. **VFOAT** Corporate Priorities; Priorites de Transports Canada. (1985)-. English (French). One time a year. Transport Canada / Strategic Planning Group, Ottawa Ontario K1A 0N5 Canada. **Continues** Strategic Planning Guidelines for the Planning Period, 0842-6538.

ISSN 0041-1515
Pr Rev.
UK
TRANSPORT MANAGEMENT; THE BRITISH JOURNAL OF TRADE AND TRANSPORT. See Transportation.

ISSN 0954-2647
UK
TRANSPORT OF GOODS BY ROAD IN GREAT BRITAIN, THE. See Transportation.

ISSN 0708-3319
DD 386/.242/02571
CN
TRAVERSIERS, PONTS ET CROISIERES. [Traversiers, ponts croisieres].
French. One time a year. Office de Tourisme du Quebec, 235 Queen Street/4th Floor East, Ottawa Ontario K1A 0H6 Canada.

LC HF1 .T74 **ISSN** 0041-2449
DD 380.1/09749/66
US
TRENTON. Periodical. English. Twelve times a year.
$9.00. Mercer County Chamber of Commerce, PO Box 8307, 2550 Kuser Road, Trenton NJ 08650. **Tel** (609)586-2056, FAX (609)586-8052.

ISSN 1168-6944
FR
UDC 338
TRIBUNE (PARIS. 1992), LA. (LA TRIBUNE.).
[Trib. Paris, 1992]. **VFOAT** Tribune Desfosses. (1992)-. Periodical. French. Seven times a week. $808.17. Cote des Fosses SA, 42 rue Notre Dame des Victoire, 75080 Paris Cedex 02 France. **Tel** 011 33 1 44821616.
Continues La Tribune de l'Expansion, 0989-1323 and Cote Desfosses, 0750-0424.

LC HF73.J3 T68
JA
TSUSAN HANDOBUKKU. (19??)-. Periodical.
Japanese. ¥3300. Shoko Kaikan, 4-2 Kasumigaseki 3 Chiyoda-ku, Tokyo 100 Japan.

LC HF3830.N3 T78
JA
TSUSHO NEMPO. Added/Corp Japan. Nagoya
Tsusho Sangyokyoku. Tsushoka. Japan. Nagoya Tsusho Sangyokyoku. Yushutsu Hokenka. (19??)-. Periodical. Japanese. Nagoya Boekikai, c/o Kaigisho Building, 1-10 Sakae 2-chome Naka-ku, Nagoya Japan.

ISSN 0784-9095
FI
TUKKUKAUPAN TILINPAATOSTILASTO. VFOAT Partihandelns
Bokslutsstatistik; Financial Statements Statistics of Wholesale Trade. (1987)-. Finnish (Swedish). One time a year. Tilastokeskus, PL 504, Annankatu 44, 00101 Helsinki Finland. **Tel** 011 358 0 17341, FAX 011 358 0 17342474, telex 1002111 TILASTO SF. **Continues in part** Tilastotiedotus. YR, 0355-2373.

TU
TURKISH EXPORT NEWS. (19??)-. English.
Six times a year. Turkish Export News, PO Box 1277 Karakoy, Istanbul Turkey.

LC HD9734.M43 M498 **ISSN** 1046-9427
DD 338.4/767/09721
US
TWIN PLANT NEWS. (TWIN PLANT NEWS :
TP.). [Twin plant news]. **VFOAT** TP; Twin Plant. Vol. 1, No. 1 (Aug. 1985)-. Periodical. English. Twelve times a year. $65.00. Twin Plant News, PO Box 220082, El Paso TX 79913. **Tel** (800)880-1123, (915)532-1567, FAX (512)734-2204. **ED** Don Nibbe. **Ad Acc, Adv Mgr**: W. Davis, **Tel** (915)532-1567. **Circ**: 10,000 (ctrl).
Desc: Articles feature industries that impact the Mazuiladoras, such as packaging waste management, material handling, transportation, electronics, customs, tax laws and labor laws. Information dedicated to assisting management in all phases of plant operations.

LC HC498 .A7 **ISSN** 0886-3717
DD 382/.0973/0174927
US
U.S.-ARAB COMMERCE. [U.S.-Arab
commer.]. **Added/Corp** U.S.-Arab Chamber of Commerce. **VFOAT** US-Arab Commerce. **VAT** United States-Arab Commerce; U.S. Arab Commerce. Vol. 11, No. 4 (July/Aug. 1978)-. Periodical. English. Ten times a year. US Arab Chamber of Commerce, 1 World Trade Center, Suite 4657, New York NY 10048. **Tel** (212)432-0655. **Continues** Arab Economic Review, 0145-6938.

LC KF6652 .O35
DD 382.7/025/73
US
U.S. CUSTOM HOUSE GUIDE. See
Finance-Taxation.

US
U.S. EXPORT AND IMPORT PRICE INDEXES. See Business and Economics-Abstracting,
Bibliographies and Statistics.

LC HF3003 .U18 **ISSN** 0145-0352
DD 382/.6/0973021
US
U.S. EXPORT SALES. VFOAT US Export Sales.
VAT United States Export Sales. (Oct. 31, 1974)-. Government Publication. English. One time a week. $175.00. US Department of Agriculture / Foreign Agricultural Service, 14th Street & Independence Avenue Southwest, Washington DC 20250. **Tel** (202)720-9445, FAX (202)720-7729. **(Subscription address**: NTIS, 5285 Port Royal Road, Springfield VA 22161. **Tel** (703)487-4630.) available on microfiche (Vols. for (1986)-) distributed to depository libraries. Documents available from Documents on Demand. **Continues** Exports (United States. Crop Reporting Board).
Ind/Abst Am. Stat. Index.

LC HF105 .C137166 **ISSN** 0098-5325
DD 382/.6/0973
US
U.S. EXPORTS. DOMESTIC MERCHANDISE, SIC-BASED PRODUCTS BY WORLD AREA. VFOAT
Domestic Merchandise, SIC-Based Products by World Areas; U.S. Exports SIC-Based Products. **VAT** United States Exports. Domestic Merchandise Standard Industrial Classification-Based Products by World Areas. (1972)-. Government Publication. English. One time a year. US Department of Commerce, 14th Street & Constitution Avenue NW, Washington DC 20230. **Tel** (202)482-2000, FAX (202)482-3772. available on microfiche (Vols. for (1983)-) distributed to depository libraries). **Continues** U.S. Foreign Trade. Exports, SIC-Based Products.

LC HF1701
DD 382.7
US
U.S. EXPORTS. HARMONIED SCHEDULE B COMMODITY BY COUNTRY. English. National Technical Information
Service - NTIS, Room 2027S, 5285 Port Royal Road, Springfield VA 22161. **Tel** (703)487-4630, (703)487-4660, (703)487-4650, FAX (703)321-8547, telex 89-9405.

LC HF1042 .U54a **ISSN** 0193-1687
DD 382/.0973
US
U.S. FOREIGN TRADE: CONCORDANCE OF STATISTICAL CLASSIFICATIONS OF DOMESTIC AND FOREIGN COMMODITIES EXPORTED FROM THE UNITED STATES. See Business and
Economics-Abstracting, Bibliographies and Statistics.

LC HF105 .C137182 **ISSN** 0899-515X
DD 382/.5/0973021
US
U.S. GENERAL IMPORTS. SCHEDULE A, COMMODITY GROUPINGS BY WORLD AREA AND COUNTRY. [U. S. gen.
imports, Sched. A. commod. group. world area ctry.]. **VFOAT** US General Imports. Schedule A, Commodity Groupings by World Area and Country. **VAT** United States General Imports. Schedule A, Commodity Groupings by World Area and Country. 1982-. Government Publication. English. One time a year. US Department of Commerce, 14th Street & Constitution Avenue NW, Washington DC 20230. **Tel** (202)482-2000, FAX (202)482-3772. available on microfiche (Vols. for (1986)-) distributed to depository libraries. **Continues** U.S. General Imports. Schedule A, Commodity Groupings by World Area, 0148-6640.

LC HF105 .C1372 **ISSN** 0095-5485
DD 382/.5/0973
US
U.S. IMPORTS. CONSUMPTION AND GENERAL SIC-BASED PRODUCTS BY WORLD AREAS. VFOAT Consumption and
General SIC-Based Products by World Areas; U.S. Imports SIC-Based Products. **VAT** United States Imports. Consumption and General SIC-Based Products by World Areas. (1972)-. Government Publication. English. One time a year. US Department of Commerce, 14th Street & Constitution Avenue NW, Washington DC 20230. **Tel** (202)482-2000, FAX (202)482-3772. available on

microfiche (Vols. for (1982-) distributed to depository libraries). *Continues* Imports for Consumption & General Imports, SIC-Based Product Classification, by Area.

LC HF1456.5.J3 U55
DD 338.91/73/052
ISSN 0091-407X
US
SUSPENDED

U.S./JAPAN OUTLOOK. Added/Corp Japan Trade Center. (19??)-Suspended (19??). Periodical. English. Irregular. Public Relations Board Inc., 150 East Huron Street, Chicago IL 60611.

LC HF3118.95 .U83

US

... U.S.-KUWAITI TRADE DIRECTORY, THE. (1991)-. Directory. English.

LC HF3230.5 .A35

US
CODEN USLTEM

●**U.S./LATIN TRADE. VFOAT** U.S. Latin Trade; United States/Latin Trade; United States Latin Trade. (1993)-. Periodical. English. Twelve times a year. $36.00. US Latin Trade, PO Box 110640, Miami FL 33131. **Tel** (305)358-8373. **ED** Richard N. Hoffman.

US

U.S. MANUFACTURES TRADE PERFORMANCE. Added/Corp United States. International Trade Administration. United States. International Trade Administration. Office of Trade Information and Analysis. **VFOAT** US Manufactures Trade Performance. **VAT** United States Manufactures Trade Performance. (1991)-. English. US Department of Commerce / International Trade Administration, 14th Street & Constitution Avenue NW, Hoover Building, Room 3850, Washington DC 20230. **Tel** (202)482-2867, **FAX** (202)482-5933. *Continues* U.S. Merchandise Trade Position at Midyear.

US

U.S. MERCHANDISE TRADE, SELECTED HIGHLIGHTS. Added/Corp United States. Bureau of the Census. **VFOAT** US Merchandise Trade, Selected Highlights. (Jan. 1991)-. Government Publication. English. Twelve times a year. $300.00 US; $375.00 other. US Department of Commerce / Bureau of the Census, Data User Services Division, Customer Services, Washington DC 20233-0800. **Tel** (301)763-4100. (**Subscription address:** Superintendent of Documents, US Government Printing Office, Washington DC 20402.)
Desc: Presents data on domestic and foreign exports, general imports, and imports for consumption. Also includes data on US Customs districts and method of transportation, and world area by country of origin and country of destination.

LC HF1750 .U18
DD 382/.0973072/05
ISSN 1064-802X
CCC

U.S.-MEXICO FREE TRADE REPORTER. [U.S. Mex. free trade report.]. **VFOAT** U.S. Mexico Free Trade Reporter. Vol. 1, No. 1 (June 28, 1991)-. Periodical. English. Twenty-two times a year. $597.00. WorldTrade Executive Incorporated, PO Box 761, Concord MA 01742. **Tel** (508)287-0301, **FAX** (508)287-0302.

ISSN 8756-8055
DD 382
US

U.S. TAPE IMPORTS (MANIFEST EDITION). (U.S. TAPE IMPORTS.). **Added/Corp** Werner D. Single Foreign Trade Services. **VAT** United States Tape Imports (Manifest Edition). (1985)-. English. Twelve times a year. Werner C. Single Foreign Trade Services, 6040 Boulevard East, West New York NY 07093.

ISSN 8756-8063
DD 382
US

U.S. TAPE IMPORTS (STATISTICAL ED.). (U.S. TAPE IMPORTS.). [U.S. tape imports]. **Added/Corp** Werner D. Single Foreign Trade Services. **VAT** United States Tape Imports (Statistical Edition). (198?)-. English. Twelve times a year. Werner C. Single Foreign Trade Services, 6040 Boulevard East, West New York NY 07093.

LC HF3000 .U18
DD 382/.0973/00212
ISSN 0736-3397
US

U.S. TRADE SHIFTS IN SELECTED COMMODITY AREAS. [U.S. trade shifts sel. commod. areas]. **VFOAT** US Trade Shifts in Selected Commodity Areas. (1981)-. English. Two times a year. Kenneth R Mason, Secretary to the Commission, United States International Trade Commission, Washington DC 20436. **Tel** (202)523-0235. available on microfiche (Vols. for (1986-) distributed to depository libraries).

Desc: Statistics and information on trade developments in all agricultural and manufactured commodities. Lists effects of trade on domestic industry.

US

U.S. TRADE STATUS WITH SOCIALIST COUNTRIES. 1973-. Government Publication. English. US Department of Commerce, 14th Street & Constitution Avenue NW, Washington DC 20230. **Tel** (202)482-2000, **FAX** (202)482-3772.

LC HF1042 .U55A
DD 382/.0973/0717
ISSN 0196-3953
US

U.S. TRADE WITH THE COMMUNIST COUNTRIES BY SEVEN DIGIT COMMODITY CODE FOR .... VAT United States Trade with the Communist Countries by Seven Digit Commodity Code for .... English. One time a year. US Department of Commerce / International Trade Administration, 14th Street & Constitution Avenue NW, Hoover Building, Room 3850, Washington DC 20230. **Tel** (202)482-2867, **FAX** (202)482-5933.

LC HF105 .A68175
DD 382/.0973
US

U.S. WATERBORNE EXPORTS AND GENERAL IMPORTS. Main/Corp United States. Bureau of the Census. (19??)-. Government Publication. English. Twelve times a year. $120.00 US; $150.00 other. US Department of Commerce / Bureau of the Census, Data User Services Division, Customer Services, Washington DC 20233-0800. **Tel** (301)763-4100. (**Subscription address:** Superintendent of Documents, US Government Printing Office, Washington DC 20402.)
Continues United States. Bureau of the Census. United States Foreign Trade; Waterborne Exports and General Imports.
Desc: Contains data, by vessel, on the shipping weight and value of US domestic and foreign waterborne exports and outbound in-transit merchandise.

ISSN 0041-5707
GW

UBERSEE RUNDSCHAU. 1.- Vol. 1949-. Periodical. German. Four times a year. $12.34. Verlag GmbH, Krahenweg 28B, W-2000 Hamburg 61 Germany. **ED** Irene Reinecke. **Ad Acc. Circ:** 5,000 (ctrl).
Supersedes Ostasiatische Rundschau; Ibero-Amerikanische Rundschau.
Desc: A publication for foreign trade.

LC HF3641 .D48a
DD 380.109
DK

UDENRIGSMINISTERIETS TIDSSKRIFT: NYT FRA EKSPORTMARKEDERNE. Main/Corp Denmark. Udenrigsministeriet. **Added/Corp** Denmark. Udenrigsministeriet. Tidsskrift. Denmark. Udenrigsministeriet. Nyt Fra Eksportmarkederne. (19??)-. Periodical. Danish. Twelve times a year. Udenrigsministeriet, Christiansborg S Lot, DK-1218 Copenhagen K Denmark. **Tel** 212 697 5101, telex 31292.

LC HF3631. .U44
DD 380.1
ISSN 0355-0249
FI

ULKOMAANKAUPPA. VFOAT Utrikeshandel; Foreign Trade. English (English, Finnish and Swedish). One time a year. Valtion Painatuskeskus, PO Box 516, SF 00101 Helsinki Finland. **Tel** 011 358 0 5660266, **FAX** 011 358 0 5660374.

LC HF1410 .M66
DD 337/.05
SZ
CEASED

UNCTAD BULLETIN / UNITED NATIONS CONFERENCE ON TRADE AND DEVELOPMENT. Added/Corp United Nations Conference on Trade and Development. No. 191 (Feb./March 1983)-(199?). Bulletin. English. United Nations Publishers / Department of Humanitarian Affairs, Palais des Nations, CH-1211 Geneva 10 Switzerland. **Tel** 011 41 22 7988400. Documents available from Documents on Demand. *Continues* Monthly Bulletin (United Nations Conference on Trade and Development).
Ind/Abst Environ. Abstr.

LC HF1040 .Y42
DD 382/.021
US

UNCTAD COMMODITY YEARBOOK / UNITED NATIONS CONFERENCE ON TRADE AND DEVELOPMENT. Added/Corp United Nations Conference on Trade and Development. **VFOAT** Commodity Yearbook; UNCTD Commodity Year Book. **VAT** United Nations Conference on Trade and Development Commodity Yearbook. (1986)-. Government Publication. English. One time a year. $70.00. United Nations Publications, 2 United Nations Plaza, Room DC2 0853, Department 007C, New York NY 10017. **Tel** (212)963-8303, (800)253-9646. *Continues* Yearbook of International Commodity Statistics, 0257-1870.

LC HF1371 .U53
DD 337/.05
ISSN 1014-370X
SZ

UNCTAD REVIEW. Added/Corp United Nations Conference on Trade and Development. **VFOAT** U.N.C.T.A.D. Review. **VAT** United Nations Conference on Trade and Development Review. Vol. 1, No. 1 (1989)-.

Government Publication. English. Irregular. Price varies. United Nations Publications, 2 United Nations Plaza, Room DC2 0853, Department 007C, New York NY 10017. **Tel** (212)963-8303, (800)253-9646. *Continues* Trade and Development (United Nations Conference on Trade and Development), 0252-5216.

LC HF3501 .A235
DD 382/.17/094105
UK

UNITED KINGDOM BALANCE OF PAYMENTS. Main/Corp Great Britain. Central Statistical Office. **Added/Corp** Great Britain. Treasury. Great Britain. Central Statistical Office. (1947)-. Government Publication. English. One time a year (Aug.). £13.25. Her Majesty's Stationery Office, 51 Nine Elms Lane, London SW8 5DR United Kingdom. **Tel** 011 44 171 8738459, 011 44 171 8738499, **FAX** 011 44 171 8738499, 011 44 171 8738456, telex 297138. (**Subscription address:** Her Majesty's Stationery Office, PO Box 276, Public Centre, London SW8 5DT United Kingdom. **Tel** 011 44 171 8738499, 011 44 171 8738456.)
Continues United Kingdom Balance of Payments.

LC KF6655.A2 U54
DD 347.73/28 347.30728
ISSN 0740-9540
US

UNITED STATES COURT OF INTERNATIONAL TRADE REPORTS. See Law-International Law.

FR

UNITED STATES. EXPORTS MICROFORM. Added/Corp Organisation for Economic Co-Operation and Development. **VFOAT** Exports; Microtables, Import/Export. (19??)-. English (French). One time a year. OECD Publications and Information Center, 2 rue Andre-Pascal, 75775 Paris Cedex 16 France. **Tel** 011 33 1 49104262, US:(202)785-6323, **FAX** 011 33 1 45248500, 011 33 1 45248176, telex 620 160 OCDE.

US

UNITED STATES FOREIGN TRADE : BUNKER OIL AND COAL LADEN IN THE UNITED STATES ON VESSELS ENGAGED IN FOREIGN TRADE. Main/Corp United States. Bureau of the Census. Government Publication. English. Twelve times a year. US Department of Commerce, 14th Street & Constitution Avenue NW, Washington DC 20230. **Tel** (202)482-2000, **FAX** (202)482-3772.

FR

UNITED STATES. IMPORTS. MICROFORM. Added/Corp Organisation for Economic Co-Operation and Development. **VFOAT** Imports; Microtables, Import/Export. (19??)-. English (French). One time a year. OECD Publications and Information Center, 2 rue Andre-Pascal, 75775 Paris Cedex 16 France. **Tel** 011 33 1 49104262, US:(202)785-6323, **FAX** 011 33 1 45248500, 011 33 1 45248176, telex 620 160 OCDE.

LC HE745 .U48b
DD 387.5/1
ISSN 0161-8830
US

UNITED STATES OCEANBORNE FOREIGN TRADE ROUTES. See Transportation-Ships and Shipping.

ISSN 0072-3975
GW

UNTERNEHMEN UND ARBEITSSTATTEN. REIHE 1 : DIE KOSTENSTRUKTUR IN DER WIRTSCHAFT. V. GROSSHANDEL, HANDELVERTRETER UND HANDELSMAKLER, VERLAGSWESEN. Main/Corp Germany (West). Statistisches Bundesamt. **VFOAT** Kostenstruktur in der Wirtschaft. Grosshandel. Handelvertreter und Handelsmakler, Verlagswesen; Grosshandel, Handelvertreter und Handelsmakler, Verlagswesen. German. W. Kohlhammer Verlag GmbH, Postfach 800430, D-70549 Stuttgart Germany. **Tel** 011 49 711 78630, **FAX** 011 49 711 7863430, telex 7-255820.

ISSN 0042-059X
SZ
CCC

UNTERNEHMUNG. See Business and Economics-Management.

LC HA1631 .A33 HF3732.3
DD 314.971
ISSN 0300-2462
YU

UNUTRASNJA TRGOVINA. See Business and Economics-Abstracting, Bibliographies and Statistics.

LC HF
DD 380.1
US

US CHAMBER WATCH. (19??)-. English. Twelve times a year. 49.50 (members), 65.00 (nonmembers). Chamber of Commerce of the United States of America, 1615 H Street Northwest, Washington DC 20062. **Tel** (800)638-6582.

Business and Economics — Commerce

LC HF3128 .U8
DD 382/.0951/0730212
ISSN 0732-8478
US

US-CHINA TRADE STATISTICS. See Business and Economics-Abstracting, Bibliographies and Statistics.

US

US GLOBAL TRADE OUTLOOK. (19??)-. English. Superintendent of Documents, US Government Printing Office, Washington DC 20402. **Tel** (202)275-3328, FAX (202)786-2377.

LC HA1501
NO

UTENRIKSHANDEL. Added/Corp Norway. Statistisk Sentralbyra. **VFOAT** External Trade. (1961)-. Norwegian (English). One time a year. Kr70.00. Central Bureau of Statistics / Norway, PO Box 8131 DEP, N-0033 Oslo 1 Norway. **Tel** 011 47 2 2864964, FAX 011 47 2 864973. **Circ:** 1,900. **Continues** Norges Handel.

ISSN 0039-7288
SW

UTRIKESHANDEL. MANADSSTATISTIK. See Business and Economics-International Economic Relations.

LC HF
DD 380.1
ISSN 0924-7165
NE

VAKBLAD VOOR DE HANDEL IN AARDAPPELEN, GROENTEN EN FRUIT. See Agriculture-Crop Production and Soils.

ISSN 0391-5840
IT

UDC 67
TITLE CHANGE

VETRINA. (1948)-(1993). Periodical. Italian. Sapil Editrice Srl, Via Pacini 48, 20131 Milan Italy. **Tel** 011 39 2 70600296. **Continued by** Espressioni in Vetrina.

IT

VICENZA ECONOMICA (1984). (VICENZA ECONOMICA : MENSILE DELLA CAMERA DI COMMERCIO INDUSTRIA, ARTIGIANATO E AGRICOLTURA, VICENZA.). **Added/Corp** Camera di Commercio, Industria, Artigianato e Agricoltura, Vicenza. Vol. 10, 3 (March 1984)-. Periodical. Italian. Eleven times a year. L28610. Cam Comm Ind Agr Art Vicenza, C So Fogazzaro 37, 36100 Vicenza Italy. **Tel** 011 39 444 994811. (**Subscription address:** Vicenza Economica, C So Brescia 70, 10152 Turin Italy. **Tel** 011 39 11 2480870.) **Continues** Notiziario Economico.

LC HF239 .I55A
II

VIDESA VYAPARA MANTRALAYA KI ANUDANOM KI MANGEM. Main/Corp India (Republic). Ministry of Foreign Trade. **VFOAT** Demands for Grants of Ministry of Foreign Trade. Multiple languages (English and Hindi). Ministry of Foreign Trade, Minto Road, New Delhi India.

LC HE752.V8 P67
DD 387.1/09755
US

VIRGINIA MARITIMER. See Transportation-Ships and Shipping.

LC HF25 .V871
ISSN 0134-8469
RU

VNESHNIAIA TORGOVLIA. (FOREIGN TRADE.). **Added/Corp** Soviet Union. Ministerstvo Vneshnei Torgovli. (1937)-. Periodical. English (French, Spanish, German and Russian; summaries and/or abstracts in Russian). Twelve times a year. $119.95. (**Subscription address:** East View Publications Inc., 3020 Harbor Lane North, Suite 110, Minneapolis MN 55447. **Tel** (800)477-1005, (612)550-0961, FAX (612)559-2931.) **Continues** Economic Survey (Moscow, R.S.F.S.R. : 1934).
Desc: Journal of the Russian Ministry of Foreign Trade. Contains information on Russia's trade, both domestic and international. Also carries information on foreign relations.
Ind/Abst Middle East Abstr. Index.

ISSN 0321-057X
RU

VNESNJAJA TORGOVLJA. (VNESHNIAIA TORGOVLIA.). [Vnesn. torg.]. **Added/Corp** Soviet Union. Ministerstvo Vneshnei Torgovli. Soviet Union. Narodnyi Komissariat Vneshnei Torgovli. Soviet Union. Ministerstvo Vneshnikh Ekonomicheskikh Sviazei. **VFOAT** Vneshniaia Torgovlia SSSR. (1931)-. Periodical. Russian. Twelve times a year. $109.95. Izdatelstvo Izvestiia, Pl. Pushkina 5, 103798 Moscow Russia. (**Subscription address:** East View Publications Inc., 3020 Harbor Lane North, Suite 110, Minneapolis MN 55447. **Tel** (800)477-1005, (612)559-0961, FAX (612)559-2931.) available on microfilm from University Microfilms International (UMI). **Continues** Nasha Vneshniaia Torgovlia.

ISSN 0249-4914
FR

UDC 656.2

VOIES FERREES. [Voies ferrees]. (1980)-. Periodical. French. Six times a year. $83.11. Presses et Editions Ferroviare, 28 rue Moyrand F, 38100 Grenoble France. **Tel** 76-42-69-22, FAX 76-42-79-55. **ED** Philippe Morel. **Bk Rev. Ad Acc. Circ:** 20,000.

LC HF53 .K34
JA

WAGA KUNI SHOHIN BOEKI NO GENJO: TOKEI; KAIGAI SHIJO HAKUSHO. Added/Corp Nihon Boeki Shinkokai. **VFOAT** Kaigai Shijo Hakusho. (1973)-. Periodical. Japanese. One time a year. ¥2000. JETRO, 2-5 Toranomon 2 chome, Minato-ku Tokyo 105. **Tel** 03-3582-3518. **Continues** Kaigai Shijo Hakusho. Dai 3-Bunsatsu: Waga Kuni Shohin Yushutsu No Genjo, Tokei.

LC HF5415.6 .N37
DD 381/.025/73
ISSN 1075-0282
US

WAREHOUSING / DISTRIBUTION DIRECTORY. (THE WAREHOUSING/DISTRIBUTION DIRECTORY : WDD.]. [Warehous./distrib. dir.]. **VFOAT** Warehousing Distribution Directory; WDD. No. 30 (Fall/Winter 1992)-. Directory. English. Two times a year. K-III Press Inc., 424 West 33rd Street, New York NY 10001. **Tel** (212)714-3100, (800)221-5488. **Continues** MCD Warehousing Distribution Directory, 1075-0517.

IO

WARTA GPEI / GABUNGAN PERUSAHAAN EKSPOR INDONESIA. Added/Corp Gabungan Perusahaan Ekspor Indonesia. (1991)-. Periodical. Indonesian (English). Twenty-six times a year. Rp5000. GPEI/ Gabungan Perusahaan Ekspor Indonesia, Probolinggo No. 5, PO Box 1249, Jakarta 10012 Indonesia. **Continues** Gabungan Perusahaan Ekspor Indonesia IER, Indonesia Export Review.
Desc: Journal concerning the export and trade of commercial products.

LC HF41 .W333
JA

WASEDA SHOGAKU. VFOAT Waseda Commercial Review. (June 1925)-. Periodical. Japanese. Waseda Shogaku Dokokai, 647 Totsukamachi 1-chome, Shinjuku-ku Tokyo Japan.

LC HF1371
DD 382
ISSN 0049-691X
US

WASHINGTON INTERNATIONAL BUSINESS REPORT. [Wash. int. bus. rep.]. **Added/Corp** International Business-Government Counsellors, Inc. (1972)-. Periodical. English. Twelve times a year. $288.00. Washington International Business Report, 818 Connecticut Avenue Northwest, 12th Floor, Washington DC 20006. **Tel** (202)872-8181.

ISSN 0893-1232
US

DD 338

WASHINGTON REPORT ON LATIN AMERICA & THE CARIBBEAN. [Wash. rep. Latin Am. Caribb.]. (198?)-. Periodical. English. Twenty-six times a year. $365.00. Gilston Communications Group, PO Box 467, Washington DC 20044. **Tel** (301)570-4544, FAX (301)570-4545. **ED** Sam Gilston. Index available. cum. index. ctrl circ.
Desc: For businesses, diplomats, and others concerned with Washington's economic and political effect on trade with and investment in Latin America and the Caribbean.

ISSN 0276-8275
US

WASHINGTON TARIFF AND TRADE LETTER. VAT Washington Tariff and Trade Letter. Vol. 1, No. 1 (June 1, 1981)-. Periodical. English. One time a week (except last week of Aug. and Dec.). $487.00. Gilston Communications Group, PO Box 467, Washington DC 20044. **Tel** (301)570-4544, FAX (301)570-4545. **ED** Sam Gilston. ctrl circ.
Desc: For business executives on U.S. international trade policies, legislation, opportunities, and restrictions.

ISSN 0199-4018
US

DD 381

WEAR. [Wear]. Academic Scholarly Publication. English. Twelve times a year. Crow Publishing, Drawer 17F, Denver CO 80217. Documents available from CASDDS.
Ind/Abst Ceram. Abstr.; Chem. Abstr.; Comput. Inf. Syst. Abstr. J. [Full Cov.]; Curr. Contents Eng. Comput. Technol.; For. Prod. Abstr.; Health Saf. Sci. Abstr.

US

WEEKLY ADVISORY / COMMODITY FUTURES TRADING COMMISSION. Added/Corp United States. Commodity Futures Trading Commission. (Mar. 30, 1990)-. Periodical. English. One time a week. $65.00. Commodities Futures Trade Commission, 2033 K Street Northwest, 18th Floor, Washington DC 20581. **Tel** (202)254-8630. **Continues** Advisory (United States. Commodity Futures Trading Commission).

ISSN 0379-4806
SA

UDC 380.15

WEEKLY BULLETIN - CAPE CHAMBER OF INDUSTRIES. [Wkly. bull. - Cape Chamb. Ind.]. (1939)-. Periodical. English. One time a week. $32.81. Cape Chamber of Industries, PO Box 1536, 8000 Cape Town, South Africa. **Tel** 11 27 21 5180. **Continues** Bulletin - Cape Chamber of Industries.

ISSN 1051-807X
US
CCC

DD 330

WEEKLY INTERNATIONAL MARKET ALERT. [Wkly. int. mark. alert]. **Added/Corp** International Reports (Firm). (1990)-. Periodical. English. One time a week. $1,235.00. International Reports Inc., 11300 Rockville Pike 1100, Rockville MD 20852. **Tel** (212)685-6900, FAX (212)685-8566, telex 233139 RPTUR. **Continues** Special Telex Service, 1045-9561.

LC HF54.U5 W45
DD 382/.025
ISSN 0091-9705
US

WENCO INTERNATIONAL TRADE DIRECTORY, THE. 1973/74-. Directory. English. $125.00. Wenco Enterprises, PO Box 4263, Portland OR 97208.

LC HC607.W47 W43
DD 382/.6/09941
AT

WEST AUSTRALIAN TRADE & EXPORT GUIDE. Added/Corp W.A. Chamber of Commerce & Industry. **VFOAT** West Australian Trade and Export Guide; Western Australian Trade and Export Guide; Western Australian Exports. (198?)-. English. One time a year. West Australian Trade & Export Guide, 10 Leura Street, Nedlands Western Australia 6009 Australia.

ISSN 0888-3459
US

WESTCHESTER COMMERCE. (WESTCHESTER COMMERCE / THE OFFICIAL MAGAZINE OF WESTCHESTER'S COUNTY CHAMBER OF COMMERCE.). **Added/Corp** County Chamber of Commerce, Inc. (Westchester County, N.Y.). **VFOAT** Commerce Westchester. Vol. 1, No. 1 (Aug. 1985)-. Periodical. English. Six times a year. $10.00. Suburban Marketing Associates, 201 North Walnut Street, Suite 1204, Wilmington DE 19800. **Tel** (302)656-8440, FAX (302)656-5843. **ED** Carole Haarmann Acunto and Linda Rigano. **Circ:** 5,000.
Desc: Westchester industry news, business briefs, and feature articles.

LC HF251 .J35a
DD 382/.0952
JA
TITLE CHANGE

WHITE PAPER ON INTERNATIONAL TRADE : JAPAN. See Business and Economics-Abstracting, Bibliographies and Statistics.

LC HF3821 .B87a
DD 382/.0952
JA

WHITE PAPER ON JAPANESE TRADE. Main/Corp Business Intercommunications Inc. (19??)-. Periodical. English. Business Intercommunications, 3-21-13 Minamisoyama, Minatoku Tokyo 107 Japan.

LC HF5421.5.C3 C35b
DD 381/.2/0971021
ISSN 0380-7894
CN

WHOLESALE TRADE. [Wholes. trade]. **Added/Corp** Statistics Canada. Merchandising and Services Division. Statistics Canada. Wholesale Trade Section. Statistics Canada. **VFOAT** Commerce de Gros. Vol. 35 No. 1 (Jan. 1972)-. Periodical. English (French). Twelve times a year. 216.00Can$. Statistics Canada Publications Sales and Services, R.H. Coats Building 6th Floor, Ottawa Ontario K1A 0T6 Canada. **Tel** (613)951-5078, (800)267-6677, FAX (613)951-1584, telex 053-3585. **Continues** Wholesale Trade (Canada. Dominion Bureau of Statistics), 0380-7894.
Desc: Estimated dollar sales and inventories (at cost) of wholesale merchants (excluding agents and brokers, manufacturers' sales branches and primary product dealers) for 26 kind-of-business groups; cumulative, current and previous year.

LC HF3946.5 .A95a
DD 382/.6/0994
AT

WINNING EXPORTS. Main/Corp Australia. Dept. of Overseas Trade. (19??)-. English. Irregular. McCarron Bird Pty, 59 Lonsdale Street, Melbourne Australia.

ISSN 0043-6151
GW
CCC

WIRTSCHAFT UND WETTBEWERB. [Wirtsch. Wettbew.]. **VFOAT** Competition and Trade Regulation; Concurrence et Marche. (Nov. 1951)-. Periodical. German (French and English). Twelve times a year. $299.38. Handelsblatt GmbH, Postfach 102716, D-40018 Duesseldorf Germany. **Tel** 011 49 211 8871730, FAX 011 49 211 133523, telex 172114489. **ED** W.

Business and Economics —Computer Applications

Benisch, A. Gaedertz, E. Kantzenbach, W. Kartte and A. Solter. Index available. **Bk Rev**. **Ad Acc**. **Circ**: 1,370 (ctrl).
 Desc: Newspaper for competition and trade regulation.
 Ind/Abst Energy Res. Abstr. (March 1981‑): Index Foreign Leg. Per.; PAIS Int. Print; Selec. Coop. Index Manage. Period.

LC HC281 .V74

GW

WIRTSCHAFTSWOCHE. (March 2, 1973)‑. Trade Publication. German. One time a week. DM355.50. Ges. Wirtschaftspublizistik GWP, MBH Postfach 3752, D‑90018 Nuernberg Germany. **Tel** 011 49 911 5325173.
 Continues Wirtschaftswoche, der Volkswirt, Aktionar; **Absorbed** Karriere; Management Wissen.

LC HD9710.A1 W665
DD 380.1/456292/021

US

WORLD AUTOMOTIVE MARKET REPORT. See Transportation‑Automobiles.

ISSN 0960-0248
DD 382

UK

WORLD COUNTERTRADE & BARTER NEWS. [World countertr. barter news]. **VFOAT** World Countertrade and Barter News. (1990)‑. English. Twenty‑six times a year. World News, PO Box 600, Oxford OX2 6FT United Kingdom. **Tel** 011 44 1865 511738, FAX 011 44 1865 310730. **Continues** Oxford Countertrade & Barter News, 0957-4417.

LC HG3881 .U6228
DD 338.1/05

ISSN 0364-7234
US

WORLD ECONOMIC CONDITIONS IN RELATION TO AGRICULTURAL TRADE. **Main/Corp** United States. Dept. of Agriculture. Economics, Statistics, and Cooperatives Service. WEC 14 (1978)‑. Government Postfach. English. Irregular. Free. US Department of Agriculture / Economic Research Service, 1301 New York Avenue, Room 208, Washington DC 20250. **Tel** (202)447-4111.
 Continues World Economic Conditions in Relation to Agricultural Trade, 0364-7234.

LC SB442
DD 380.1/413/025

ISSN 0846-3212
CN

WORLD GRAIN LIST. See Agriculture.

LC HD2421 .W67
DD 380.1/06/2

ISSN 0094-1611
US

WORLD GUIDE TO TRADE ASSOCIATIONS. [World guide trade assoc.]. **VFOAT** Internationales Verzeichnis der Wirtschaftsverbande. 1st Edition (1973)‑. Trade Publication. Multiple languages (English and German). Irregular. $200.00. R.R. Bowker, A Reed Reference Publishing Company, Part of Reed International PLC, PO Box 31, 121 Chanlon Drive, New Providence NJ 07974. **Tel** (908)464-6800, (800)521-8110, FAX (908)665-6688, telex 138-755. **ED** Barbara Verrell.
 Desc: Provides the names and addresses of more than 31,000 national and international trade associations arranged in almost 400 trade categories, and by country.

LC HD9100.1 .F76
DD 382/.45641336/0973021

ISSN 1075-6442
US
TITLE CHANGE

WORLD SUGAR SITUATION AND OUTLOOK. [World sugar situat. outlook]. **Added/Corp** United States. Foreign Agricultural Service. United States. World Agricultural Outlook Board. **VFOAT** World Honey Situation; World Sugar and Honey Situation and Outlook. (May 1989)‑(1993). Government Publication. English. Irregular. Free. US Department of Agriculture / Foreign Agricultural Service, 14th Street & Independence Avenue Southwest, Washington DC 20250. **Tel** (202)720-9445, FAX (202)720-7729. **Continues** World Sugar and Molasses Situation and Outlook. **Continued by** Sugar, World Markets and Trade.

LC K27 .O78

ISSN 1022-6583
SZ

●**WORLD TRADE AND ARBITRATION MATERIALS.** Vol. 6, No. 1 (Jan. 1994)‑. Periodical. English. Six times a year. $348.75. Werner Publishing Company Ltd., PO Box 5134, CH-1211 Geneva 11 Switzerland. **Tel** 011 41 22 3103422. **Formed by the union of** World Trade Materials, 1013-4514 **and** Arbitration Materials, 1013-7432.
 Desc: Publishes texts of documents relating to international trade.

LC HF53 .W6
DD 382

ISSN 0512-3739
US

WORLD TRADE ANNUAL. Added/Corp United Nations. Statistical Office. (1963)‑. English. Irregular. $985.00 (latest issue). Walker and Company, 435 Hudson Street, New York NY 10014. **Tel** (212)727-8300.

LC HF54.G7 W67
DD 382/.029/4

UK
SUSPENDED

WORLD TRADE INDEX. English. One time a year. $36.78 wholesale, $65.00 retail. Eagle Publishing Company / UK, 185 Angel Place, Fore Street, London N18 LUD United Kingdom. **Tel** 011 44 181 273773174, FAX 011 44 181 18078276, telex 87323. **ED** A M Allen. **Bk Rev**. **Ad Acc**.
 Desc: A comprehensive international trade directory containing listings and advertisements for firms who import and export.

ISSN 1054-8637
DD 382

US
CCC

WORLD TRADE (IRVINE, CALIF.). (WORLD TRADE.). [World trade]. **VFOAT** World Trade Magazine. (1988)‑. Periodical. English. Six times a year. World Trade, 4199 Campus Drive, #230, Irvine CA 92715. **Tel** (714)725-0233, FAX (714)725-0306. available on microfilm and microfiche from University Microfilms International (UMI).
 Ind/Abst F&S Index Plus Text, Int. [Select. Cov.]; PROMT.

UK

WORLD TRADE LINK. English. Twelve times a year. £225.00 UK; $395.00 other. World Business Publications Ltd., 960 High Road, Britannia 4th Floor, London N12 9RY United Kingdom. **Tel** 011 44 181 4465141, FAX 011 44 181 4463659, telex 9419208.
 Continues Import Export Opportunities.

ISSN 1013-4514
SZ
TITLE CHANGE

WORLD TRADE MATERIALS. [World trade mater.]. Vol. 1, No. 1 (Jan. 1989)‑(Jan. 1994). Periodical. English. Werner Publishing Company Ltd., PO Box 5134, CH-1211 Geneva 11 Switzerland. **Tel** 011 41 22 3103422. **Merged with** Arbitration Materials **to form** World Trade and Arbitration Materials.

ISSN 1071-1775
DD 338

US

WORLD TRADE NEWS (CLEVELAND, OHIO). (WORLD TRADE NEWS : A MONTHLY PUBLICATION OF THE CSU WORLD TRADE EDUCATION CENTER.). [World trade news]. **Added/Corp** James J. Nance College of Business Administration. World Trade Education Center. Vol. 4, No. 9 (Sept. 1982)‑. Trade Publication. English. Twelve times a year. $75.00 (regular); $125.00 (institutions). Cleveland State University / World Trade Education Center, World Trade Education Center, Cleveland OH 44115. **Tel** (216)687-3786, FAX (216)687-9354, telex (810)4218252. **ED** Edward G. Thomas. **Continues** CSU World Trade News.

ISSN 0843-4174
DD 382/.05

US

WORLD TRADE NEWSPAPER. [World trade newsp.]. **Added/Corp** International Business Exchange (Organization). (Nov. 1988)‑. Periodical. English. Irregular. 24.00Can$. International Business Exchange, PO Box 726, Waterloo Ontario, N2J 4C2 Canada. **Tel** (519)745-5115. **ED** J. Menkal. **Ad Acc**. ctrl circ. **Continues** International Business Exchange Newsletter., 0828-1688.

LC HF54.U5 W67
DD 382/.025

ISSN 1058-1618
US

WORLD TRADE RESOURCES GUIDE. [World trade resour. guide]. **Added/Corp** Gale Research Inc. 1st Ed. (1992)‑. Periodical. English. Two times a year. $169.00. Gale Research Inc., 835 Penobscot Building, 645 Griswold Street, Detroit MI 48226. **Tel** (800)877-GALE, (313)961-2242, FAX (313)961-6083, (800)414-5043, telex TWX 810-221-7086. **ED** Kenneth Estell. available on magnetic tape; available on diskette.
 Desc: International import/export resource guide for the major trading nations.

ISSN 0952-5742
DD 382.45669142

UK

WORLD TRADE STAINLESS, HIGH SPEED AND OTHER ALLOY STEEL. See Metals and Metallurgy-Abstracting, Bibliographies and Statistics.

ISSN 0952-5734
UK

WORLD TRADE STEEL. See Business and Economics-Abstracting, Bibliographies and Statistics.

JA
CEASED

WORLD TRADERS. (19??)‑(1995). English. World Trade Center of Japan, PO Box 57, 4-1-2 chome, Tokyo 105 Japan. **Tel** 011 81 3 3435 5651.

ISSN 1081-5724
DD 338

US

●**WORLDBUSINESS (NEW YORK, N.Y.).** (WORLDBUSINESS.). [Worldbus.]. **VFOAT** World Business. Issue 1 (Jan. 1995)‑. Periodical. English. Worldbusiness, 767 5th Avenue, 46th Floor, New York NY 10153. **Continues** World, 0512-2295.

LC K4440.A13 W67
DD 343/.032/05

UK

WORLDWIDE FINANCIAL REGULATIONS. **VFOAT** Business International's Financial Regulations Service. (19??)‑. English. Four times a year. $735.00. The Economist Intelligence Unit / New York, 111 West 57th Street, New York NY 10019. **Tel** (800)938-4685, (212)554-0600. available on an online database (file 627/Full-Text) from DIALOG.
 Desc: Provides regulatory information on more than 40 countries, interprets local laws from a business perspective and suggests strategies to deal with them. Monitors restrictions on remittance from overseas subsidiaries; rules on borrowing from abroad to finance local operations; regulations for foreign direct and portfolio investment; hold accounts; leading, lagging and netting guidelines; tax laws; trade controls etc.

SZ

●**WTO FOCUS. Added/Corp** General Agreement on Tariffs and Trade (Organization). **VFOAT** General Agreement on Tariffs and Trade Focus; Focus Newsletter; GATT Newsletter, Focus. (1995)‑. Trade Publication. English (French and Spanish). Ten times a year. Free on request. General Agreement on Tariffs and Trade / GATT, Centre William Rappard, 154 rue de Lausanne, 1211 Geneva 21 Switzerland. **Tel** 011 41 22 7395111, 011 41 22 7395019, FAX 011 41 22 7395458. **Continues** GATT Focus, 0256-0119.
 Desc: Reports on trade-related matters, including features on economic developments and major trade policy issues. Covers negotiations, dispute settlements and other activities of the Member States and the GATT Secretariat.

LC HF1731 .A32

US

YEAR IN TRADE : OPERATION OF THE TRADE AGREEMENTS PROGRAM / UNITED STATES INTERNATIONAL TRADE COMMISSION, THE. Added/Corp United States International Trade Commission. 43rd Report (1991)‑. English. One time a year. Free on request. United States International Trade Commission, 500 E Street Southwest, Washington DC 20436. **Tel** (202)205-1806. **Continues** Operation of the Trade Agreements Program, 0083-3444.

ISSN 1191-047X
DD 382/.63

CN

YOUR GUIDE TO CANADIAN EXPORT FINANCING. [Your guide Can. export financ.]. **VFOAT** Canadian Export Financing. (1991)‑. English. One time a year. 24.77Can$. Productive Publications, PO Box 7200, Station A, Toronto Ontario M5W 1X8 Canada. **Tel** (416)483-0634. **ED** Iain Williamson.
 Desc: Provides information on practical techniques for financing exports, government assistance for exporters, adresses and phone numbers, and more.

ISSN 0044-1368
CI

YUGOSLAVIA EXPORT. [Yugosl. export]. (19??)‑. Periodical. English. Twelve times a year. Yugoslavia Export, Yugoslaviapublic, Knez Mihailova 10, Box 447, 11001 Belgrade Yugoslavia. **Absorbed** Commercial Information.
 Ind/Abst Predicasts.

LC HF1044.J3 N54C
DD 380

JA

YUNYU TOKEI HIMMOKU HYO. See Business and Economics-Abstracting, Bibliographies and Statistics.

LC HF1044.J3 N54b
DD 338.02

JA

YUSHUTSU TOKEI HIMMOKU HYO = EXPORT STATISTICAL SCHEDULE, JAPAN. See Business and Economics-Abstracting, Bibliographies and Statistics.

LC HF1044.J3 N54A

JA

YUSHUTSUNYU TOKEI HIMMOKU HYO. **Main/Corp** Nihon Kanzei Kyokai. **VFOAT** Commodity Classification for Foreign Trade Statistics: Japan. Multiple languages (Japanese and English). ¥3400. Japanese Tariff Association, c/o Jibiki Daini Building, 7-8 Kojimachi 4 Chiyoda-ku, Tokyo Japan.

COMPUTER APPLICATIONS

GW

ABC DER DEUTSCHEN WIRTSCHAFT. CD-ROM. (19??)‑. German (English). Two times a year. $900.00 Western Hemisphere. ABC Publishing

Group, POB 100262, D 64202 Darmstadt Germany. **Tel** 011 49 6151 38920. Index available. **Bk Rev**. **Ad Acc.** **Circ:** 30,000 (ctrl). available in print.

DD 330 US
ABI/INFORM [COMPUTER FILE].
Added/Corp University Microfilms International. **VFOAT** ABI Inform; ABI/Inform Research Edition. (19??)-. Abstracting/Indexing Service. English. Twelve times a year. University Microfilms International, 300 North Zeeb Road, Ann Arbor MI 48106-1346. **Tel** (313)761-4700, (800)521-0600 Exts. 2490, 2491, FAX (313)973-1540. ***Continues*** *ABI/Inform Ondisc, 1062-5127.*
Desc: Covers business conditions, trends, corporate strategies and tactics, management techniques, competitive and product information, and a variety of other topics that meet the needs of researchers.

US
ADVANCES IN ARTIFICIAL INTELLIGENCE IN ECONOMICS, FINANCE, AND MANAGEMENT.
(19??)-. Periodical. English. $73.25. JAI Press Inc., 55 Old Post Road, Suite 2, PO Box 1678, Greenwich CT 06836-1678. **Tel** (203)661-7602, FAX (203)661-0792. **ED** John D. Johnson and Andrew B. Whinston.
Desc: A forum for research in applied artificial intelligence. Goal is to provide researchers in economics, finance, and management with theoretical advances and applications in the field.

ISSN 0957-3224
DD 016.651 UK
AUTOMATED OFFICE ABSTRACTS.
[Autom. off. abstr.]. (1989)-. English. Six times a year. £60.00 UK; £64.00 other Europe; £66.00 other. Techgnosis Ltd., Blade House, Battersea Road, Cheshire SK4 3EA United Kingdom. **Tel** 011 44 161 4422639, FAX 011 44 161 4431162. ***Continues*** *Automated Office Profile, 0265-167X.*

US
BANK AUTOMATION NEWS.
(19??)-. English. Twenty-five times a year. $495.00 US; $530.00 other. Phillips Business Information Inc., 1201 Seven Locks Road, PO Box 61130, Potomac MD 20854. **Tel** (301)424-3338, (301)340-1520, (800)777-5005, FAX (301)424-4297, telex 358149. available on an online database from NEWSNET; DATA-STAR; and (file 636/Full-Text) DIALOG. ***Continues*** *Branch Automation News;* ***Absorbed*** *Bank Automation Contract Watch; Bank Outsourcing Report; Bank Disaster and Contingency Planner.*
Ind/Abst PTS Newsl. Database [Full Txt.].

ISSN 0892-6778
DD 332 US
CCC
CODEN BASREM
CEASED
BANKING SOFTWARE REVIEW.
[Bank. softw. rev.]. **Added/Corp** International Computer Programs, Inc. (198?)-(19??). Periodical. English. International Computer Programs Inc / Barbara Lahiff, 823 East Westfield Boulevard, Indianapolis IN 46220. **Tel** (800)428-6179, (317)251-7727. available on microfilm and microfiche from University Microfilms International (UMI). Documents available from UMI Article Clearinghouse, Ask*IEEE.
Ind/Abst ABI/INFORM Glob. Ed.; ABI/INFORM [Computer File] (Fall 1981); INSPEC (Autumn 1987-).

LC Z7146.C81 B963 HF5548.125 **ISSN** 0741-2363
DD 016.65/002854 US
BUSINESS COMPUTER INDEX, THE.
[Bus. comput. index]. Vol. 1, No. 1 (July/Aug. 1983)-. English. Six times a year. $28.00, $38.00 (with cumulation). BP Publications, 465 Chestnut Tree Hill Road, Southbury CT 06488-1955. **Tel** (203)264-2143. **ED** Beverly A Pajer.

ISSN 0838-438X
DD 004.16/029/4 CN
CEASED
BUSINESS COMPUTER NEWS.
[Bus. comput. news]. Vol. 1, No. 1 (April 15, 1988)-(May 1993). Periodical. English. Moorshead Magazines Ltd., 10 Gateway Boulevard, Suite 490, North York Ontario M3C 3T4 Canada. **Tel** (416)696-5488, FAX (416)696-7395. **ED** Ed Zapletal and Andrew Berthoff. **Ad Acc. Circ:** 16,000 (ctrl).

GW
BUSINESS COMPUTING.
German. Twelve times a year. DM132.00 Germany; DM144.00 other. Vogel Verlag, Postfach 6740, D-97064 Wuerzburg Germany. **Tel** 011 49 931 4182145, 011 49 931 4182483, FAX 011 49 931 4182670, telex 841 680131. **Bk Rev**, (Qty: 20). **Ad Acc. Circ:** 35,000 (ctrl). ***Continues*** *PC Personal Computer, 0930-3200.*

LC HD **ISSN** 1350-5092
DD 658.05 UK
•BUSINESS COMPUTING BRIEF.
[Bus. comput. brief]. **VFOAT** FT Business Computing Brief. (1993)-. Periodical. English. Twenty-four times a year. £199.00. Financial Times / UK, Maple House, 149 Tottenham Court Road, London W1P 9LL United Kingdom. **Tel** 011 44 171 8962276, FAX 011 44 171 8962275, 011 44 171 8962399. ***Continues*** *FinTech. 2, Electronic Office, 0266-7797.*

ISSN 0193-9734
US
BUSINESS DATA PROCESSING: A WILEY SERIES.
VFOAT Business Data Processing. (19??)-. Monographic series. English. Irregular. Price varies per volume. John Wiley & Sons, Inc., 605 Third Avenue, New York NY 10158-0012. **Tel** (212)850-6000, (212)850-6645, FAX (212)850-6088, telex 12-7063. **(Subscription address:** John Wiley & Sons / UK, Baffins Lane, Chichester, West Sussex PO19 1UD United Kingdom. **Tel** 011 44 1243 779777, FAX 011 44 243 776128, telex 86290 WIBOOKG.)

ISSN 8750-2305
US
BUSINESS DIGEST (BURLINGTON, VT.).
(BUSINESS DIGEST.). Vol. 1, No. 1 (June 1984)-. Consumer Publication. English. Twelve times a year. $17.00 (one-year); $30.00 (two-year). Mill Publishing Inc., Lakewood Commons, 1233 Shelburne Road, Suite E5, South Burlington VT 05403-7751. **Tel** (802)862-4109, FAX (802)8562-9322. **ED** Edna Tenney. **Ad Acc, Adv Mgr:** Liz Swain, **Tel** (802)862-4109. Full Page (B&W) $1,300.00. Half Page (B&W) $850.00. **Circ:** 5,500 (ctrl).
Desc: Profiles of business people operating in the Greater Burlington (Vermont) area. Devoted to business applications of interconnected computers with a similar regional focus.

LC HF5548.125 .B884 **ISSN** 0887-9478
DD 650/.028/5536 US
BUSINESS SOFTWARE DIRECTORY.
[Bus. softw. dir.]. **Added/Corp** Information Sources, Inc. 3rd Ed. (1986)-. Directory. English. Irregular. $175.00. Information Sources Inc., 1173 Colusa Avenue, Berkeley CA 94707. **Tel** (510)525-6220. ***Continues*** *Business Mini/Micro Software Directory, 0000-0809.*

LC HD9696.C63 **ISSN** 0885-8055
DD 658/.0553/05 US
CODEN BSREE2
BUSINESS SOFTWARE REVIEW.
[Bus. softw. rev.]. (1985)-. Periodical. English. Twelve times a year. Business Software Review, PO Box 40946, Indianapolis IN 46240. available on microfilm and microfiche from University Microfilms International (UMI). Documents available from UMI Article Clearinghouse, Ask*IEEE. ***Continues*** *ICP Business Software Review, 8750-1368.*
Ind/Abst ABI/INFORM Glob. Ed.; ABI/INFORM [Computer File] (1985-); Comput. Lit. Index; INSPEC (1986-).

LC HD30.2 .C4744 **ISSN** 0899-0182
DD 658.4/038/05 US
CODEN CIOJEB
CEASED
CHIEF INFORMATION OFFICER JOURNAL.
[Chief inf. off. j.]. **VFOAT** CIOJ. Vol. 1, No.1 Summer (1988)-Vol. 5 (Dec. 1993). Periodical. English. Faulkner & Gray Inc., 11 Penn Plaza, 17th Floor, New York NY 10001. **Tel** (212)967-7000, (800)535-8403. **ED** Timothy J Basting. **Bk Rev. Ad Acc. Circ:** 2,000 (ctrl). available on microfilm and microfiche from University Microfilms International (UMI); available on an online database (file 15/Full-Text) from DIALOG.
Ind/Abst Health Plan. Adminis.

ISSN 1071-4138
US
•CLINICAL AND DIAGNOSTIC LABORATORY IMMUNOLOGY (CD-ROM).
(CLINICAL AND DIAGNOSTIC LABORATORY IMMUNOLOGY [COMPUTER FILE].). **Added/Corp** American Society for Microbiology. (1994)-. English. Six times a year. $400.00. American Society for Microbiology / DC, 1325 Massachusetts Avenue Northwest, Washington DC 20005-4171. **Tel** (202)737-3600, FAX (202)737-0367. **(Subscription address:** American Society for Microbiology, Journals Subscription Department, PO Box 11127, Birmingham AL 35201-1127. **Tel** (800)633-4931, FAX (205)995-1588.) available in print from the publisher.

ISSN 0738-4270
US
COM-AND, COMPUTER AUDIT NEWS DEVELOPMENTS.
[COM-and, comput. audit news dev.]. **VFOAT** Computer Audit News Developments; COM-AND; C.O.M.-AND, Computer Audit News and Development; Computer Audit News and Developments. Vol. 1, No. 1 (March 1983)-. Periodical. English. Six times a year. $70.00. Management Advisory Publications, 57 Greylock Road, PO Box 81151, Wellesley Hills MA 02181-0001. **Tel** (617)235-2895, FAX (617)235-5446. **ED** Javier F. Kuong. cum. index. **Bk Rev.** ctrl circ.
Desc: Topics are of interest to auditors, controllers and financial controls personnel. Geared toward the audit, security, and control professions in electronic data processing. Stresses substantive coverage of material, rather than coverage of news announcements. Practical guidelines are included on EDP technology on audit and security.
Ind/Abst Data Process. Dig.

LC HB143.5 .C66 HB143.5 .C65 **ISSN** 0927-7099
DD 658/.05 NE
CCC
CODEN CNOMEL
Pr Rev.
•COMPUTATIONAL ECONOMICS.
Vol. 6, No. 1 (Feb. 1993)-. Monographic series. English. Five times a year. $299.00. Kluwer Academic Publishers, Postbus 322, 3300 AH Dordrecht The Netherlands. **Tel** 011 31 78 524400, FAX 011 31 78 183273, telex 20083. **ED** H.M. Amman. **Acid Free.** ***Continues*** *Computer Science in Economics and Management, 0921-2736.*
Desc: Serves as an interface for work which integrates computer science with economic or management science. Work published in the journal falls in the fields of symbolic information processing, numerical procedures, computational aspects of mathematical programming, hardware developments, operational research, artificial intelligence, user interfaces, database interfaces, and software research.
Ind/Abst Curr. Cit.

US
•COMPUTER ADVERTISING AND MARKETING STRATEGIES REVIEW TRENDS AND FORECAST.
(1995)-. English. One time a year. $1050.00. SIMBA Information Inc., 213 Danbury Road, PO Box 7430, Wilton CT 06897-7430. **Tel** (203)834-0033 ext. 173, FAX (203)884-1771. ***Continues*** *Computer Industry Advertising and Marketing Forecast.*

ISSN 8756-8780
DD 658 US
COMPUTER AIDED SELLING.
[Computer aided sell.]. Vol. 1, No. 1 (Jan. 1985)-. Periodical. English. Ten times a year (not published in Aug. and Dec.). $87.00 (one-year), $128.00 (two-year). Denali Group Inc, 2815 NW Pine Cone Drive/Suite 100, Issaquah WA 98027. **Tel** (206)392-3514, FAX (206)391-7982. **ED** Steven P Pokin. Index available. **Bk Rev**, (Qty: 6-10/yr). **Circ:** 5,000 (ctrl). available on an online database.
Desc: Contains information of how to apply computer technology to sales and sales management applications.

LC HF6161.C55 C64
DD 659.1/9004/0973 US
TITLE CHANGE
COMPUTER INDUSTRY ADVERTISING & MARKETING FORECAST.
Added/Corp Communications Trends, Inc. **VFOAT** Computer Industry Advertising and Marketing Forecast. (1984)-(1995). Trade Publication. English. SIMBA Information Inc., 213 Danbury Road, PO Box 7430, Wilton CT 06897-7430. **Tel** (203)834-0033 ext. 173, FAX (203)884-1771. **(Subscription address:** Simba Information Inc., PO Box 7430, Wilton CT 06897. **Tel** (203)834-0033 ext. 160, FAX (203)834-1771.) ***Continued by*** *Computer Advertising and Marketing Strategies Review Trends and Forecast.*

ISSN 0740-6231
US
CCC
COMPUTER PUBLISHING & ADVERTISING REPORT.
[Comput. publ. advert. rep.]. **Added/Corp** Communications Trends, Inc. **VFOAT** Computer Publishing and Advertising Report. Vol. 1, No. 1 (Aug. 8, 1983)-. Periodical. English. Twenty-four times a year. $498.00. SIMBA Information Inc., 213 Danbury Road, PO Box 7430, Wilton CT 06897-7430. **Tel** (203)834-0033 ext. 173, FAX (203)884-1771. **(Subscription address:** Simba Information Inc., PO Box 7430, Wilton CT 06897. **Tel** (203)834-0033 ext. 160, FAX (203)834-1771.)

LC HF **ISSN** 0896-0402
DD 380.1 US
COMPUTERIZED DIRECTORY OF NEW BUSINESSES.
(COMPUTERIZED DIRECTORY OF NEW BUSINESSES [COMPUTER FILE].). [Comput. dir. new bus.]. (198?)-. Directory. English. The Contractor's Exchange, 2265 Westwood Boulevard, Los Angeles CA 90064-2016.

LC HF5679 .C587 **ISSN** 0883-1866
DD 657/.028/5 US
CCC
CODEN CACCEA
TITLE CHANGE
COMPUTERS IN ACCOUNTING.
[Comput. account.]. **Added/Corp** Warren, Gorham & Lamont, Inc. **VFOAT** CA, Computers in Accounting; CA. Vol. 1, No. 1 (July/Aug. 1984)-Vol. 9, No. 1 (Jan. 1993). Periodical. English. Warren Gorham & Lamont Inc., Park Square Building, 31 St. James Avenue, Boston MA 02116-4112. **Tel** (617)423-2020, (800)950-1207, FAX (617)423-2026. available on microfilm and microfiche from University Microfilms International (UMI). Documents available from UMI Article Clearinghouse, Ask*IEEE. ***Continued by*** *Accounting Technology, 1068-6452.*
Desc: Covers specific accounting oriented questions and problems.
Ind/Abst ABI/INFORM Glob. Ed.; ABI/INFORM [Computer File] (Jan. 1988-); Account. Tax Datab. (1984-); Comput. Lit. Index; Comput. Rev. Index (Sept. 1988-); Data Process. Dig.; Fed. Tax Artic.; INSPEC (Jan./Feb. 1988-).

Business and Economics —Computer Applications

LC HD2771
DD 338.70973 US

CORPORATE DATABASE [COMPUTER FILE]. Added/Corp Datext, Inc. VFOAT Datext Corporate Database. (198?)-. Periodical. English. Twelve times a year. Datext, Inc., 444 Washington Street, Woburn MA 01801.
Desc: Contains information on ca. 10,000 publicly traded U.S. companies (50 industry groups, ca. 1,000 lines of business) and ca. 8,000 corporate executives. The database includes company financial statements, excerpts from annual reports, full-text investment-analyst reports, business literature and trade press abstracts, biographies of corporate officers, and stock price and trading data. The database is menu-driven and can be used to profile a company, review analyst reports, profile key executives, survey the business press, assess financial performance, and prepare competitive analyses. The database may also be used with a variety of commercial software packages to integrate information from it into spreadsheet reports or other business documents.

LC HC101 HC101 .A184c **ISSN** 1064-539X
DD 338 US

COUNTY BUSINESS PATTERNS.
(COUNTY BUSINESS PATTERNS [COMPUTER FILE].). [Cty. bus. patterns]. **Added/Corp** United States. Bureau of the Census. **VFOAT** County Business Patterns ... on CD-ROM. (1987)-. Government Publication. English. $150.00. US Department of Commerce / Bureau of the Census, Data User Services Division, Customer Services, Washington DC 20233-0800. **Tel** (301)763-4100. **(Subscription address:** Superintendent of Documents, US Government Printing Office, Washington DC 20402. **)** available on microfiche; available in print; available on an online database from DIALOG; Compuserve Inc.; and (limited excerpts from this report) CENDATA.
Desc: Provides summary data by standard industrial classification code on total number of establishments, mid-March employment, first quarter and annual payroll.

ISSN 0745-1342
US

CPA COMPUTER REPORT. VFOAT C.P.A.
Computer Report. **VAT** Certified Public Accountant Computer Report. Periodical. English. Twelve times a year. $96.00. Professional Publications Inc, 1201 Peachtree Street Northeast, Atlanta GA 30309. **Tel** (404)455-7600. **ED** Timothy Martin. **Bk Rev**. **Ad Acc**.
Desc: Newsletter dealing exclusively with the operation of computers in CPA firms. Consists of profiles, product reviews and other CPA-specific computer information.

ISSN 1068-8285
DD 005 US
Pr Rev.

CPA SOFTWARE NEWS, THE. [CPA softw. news]. VFOAT Software News. (1991)-. Trade Publication. English. Six times a year (Feb., Apr., June, Aug., Oct., Dec.). $25.00. CPA Software News, 1105 North Beard Street, Suite 200, Shawnee OK 74801. Tel (405)275-3100, FAX (405)275-3101. ED T. Allen Rose. cum. index. Bk Rev, (Qty: 2-6). Ad Acc, Adv Mgr: L. Duncan, Tel (405)275-3100. Circ: 50,000 (ctrl).
Desc: Independent voice for accountants software.

ISSN 1059-4590
DD 657 US
Pr Rev.

CPA'S PC NETWORK ADVISOR. [CPA's PC netw. advis.]. Vol. 1, No. 1 (July 1991)-. Periodical. English. Twelve times a year. $217.00. Harcourt Brace Professional Publishing, 525 B Street, Suite 1900, San Diego CA 92101-4495. Tel (619)699-6716, FAX (619)699-6593. (Subscription address: Harcourt Brace Jovanovich, 6277 Sea Harbor Drive, Orlando FL 32887-4600. Tel (800)543-9534, (800)831-7799, FAX (407)363-9661.) ED Mary and Bruce MacBain. ctrl circ.

ISSN 0730-7497
US
CEASED

DATAPRO BANKNEWS. [Datapro banknews]. Added/Corp Delran Research Corporation. VFOAT Banknews. VAT Datapro Bank News. (19??)-(19??). Periodical. English. Datapro Information Services Group, 600 Delran Parkway, Delran NJ 08075. Tel (609)764-0100, (800)328-2776, FAX (609)764-8953.

UK

DATAPRO CORPORATE SOFTWARE & SOLUTIONS / INTERNATIONAL EDITION. (19??)-. English. Twelve times a year. $1,031.00. Datapro International, McGraw Hill House, Shoppenhangers Road, Maidenhead Berkshire SL6 2QL United Kingdom. Tel 011 44 1628 773277, FAX 011 44 1628 773628.

ISSN 0730-8809
US
CCC

DATAPRO REPORTS ON BANKING AUTOMATION. [Datapro rep. bank. autom.]. Added/Corp Datapro Research Corporation. VFOAT Banking Automation. (19??)-. Periodical. English. Six times a year. $1066.00. Datapro Information Services Group, 600 Delran Parkway, Delran NJ 08075. Tel (609)764-0100, (800)328-2776, FAX (609)764-8953. ED W. J. Muldowney. Index available. cum. index. available on microfilm and microfiche.
Desc: Combines product analysis and user ratings with information for banks, savings and loans and thrift institutions.

US
CEASED

DATAPRO REPORTS ON OFFICE AUTOMATION. Added/Corp Datapro Research Corp. (April 1984)-(19??). Periodical. English. Datapro Information Services Group, 600 Delran Parkway, Delran NJ 08075. Tel (609)764-0100, (800)328-2776, FAX (609)764-8953. ED Margo Downing. Bk Rev. Ad Acc. Continues Datapro Reports on Office Systems.

ISSN 0730-8817
US
CCC
Pr Rev.

DATAPRO REPORTS ON RETAIL AUTOMATION. [Datapro rep. retail autom.]. Added/Corp Datapro Research Corporation. VFOAT Retail Automation. (19??)-. Periodical. English. Six times a year. $1008.00. Datapro Information Services Group, 600 Delran Parkway, Delran NJ 08075. Tel (609)764-0100, (800)328-2776, FAX (609)764-8953. ED W. J. Muldowney. Index available. cum. index. available on microfilm and microfiche.
Desc: Complete information on automated equipment and software for general mechandising, supermarket and major hospital organizations.

LC HB **ISSN** 1350-7419
DD 330.0151 UK
UDC 33
Pr Rev.

●ECONOMIC & FINANCIAL MODELLING. [Econ. financ. model.]. VFOAT Economic and Financial Modelling. (1994)-. Academic Scholarly Publication. English. Four times a year. £190.00 Europe; £295.00 other. European Economics & Finance Center, PO Box 2498, London W2 4LE United Kingdom. Tel 011 44 171 2290402, FAX 011 44 171 2215118. ED H.M. Scobie. Documents available from BLDSC.
Desc: Provides current advances in economic modelling.

ISSN 0740-6886
US

EDUCATIONAL AND BUSINESS SOFTWARE, RELATED PRODUCTS, HOME, SCHOOL, AND OFFICE FOR ATARI. See Education-Computer Applications.

LC L **ISSN** 0740-6894
DD 370 US

EDUCATIONAL AND BUSINESS SOFTWARE, RELATED PRODUCTS - HOME, SCHOOL, AND OFFICE FOR, TRS-80. See Education-Computer Applications.

US

ELECTRONIC RETAILING : IT'S NOT JUST HOME SHOPPING ANYMORE. See Business and Economics-Retail.

LC HG1709 .F53 **ISSN** 0743-0159
DD 332/.028/5 US

FINANCIAL COMPUTING. Vol. 1, No. 1 (Feb./March 1984)-. Periodical. English. Six times a year. $29.00 US / $39.00 other. Cleworth Publishing Company / CT, 1 River Road, Cos Cob CT 06807.

ISSN 1073-4368
DD 006 US

GCA BAR CODE REPORTER, THE. (THE GCA BAR CODE REPORTER : A PUBLICATION OF GRAPHIC COMMUNICATIONS ASSOCIATION.). [GCA bar code report.]. Added/Corp Graphic Communications Association (U.S.). VFOAT Bar Code Reporter. VAT Graphic Communications Association Bar Code Reporter. (1987)-. Periodical. English. Four times a year. $95.00. Graphic Communications Association, 100 Daingerfield Road, Alexandria VA 22314. Tel (703)519-8160.
Ind/Abst Abstr. Bull. Inst. Pap. Sci. Tech.

US

GUIDE TO REAL ESTATE AND MORTGAGE BANKING SOFTWARE. (19??)-. English. One time a year. $49.95. Real Estate Solutions Inc., 2609 Klingle Road Northwest, Washington DC 20008. Tel (202)362-9854, (800)633-1546, FAX (202)363-3925. ED Ina S. Bechhoefer. Index available (Bound in all issues). cum. index. Bk Rev, (Qty: 10).
Desc: Contains descriptions of software products available today for real estate and mortgage banking industries.

ISSN 8750-4928
DD 658 US

HOME COMPUTER & SOFTWARE MERCHANDISING. [Home comput. softw. merch.]. VFOAT Home Computer and Software Merchandising. Vol. 3, No. 10 (Oct. 1984)-. Periodical. English. Twelve times a year. $18.00 US / $70.00 other. Eastman Publishing Company, PO Box 208, Westport CT 06881. Continues Software Merchandising, 0746-147X.

UK

IASB : INTERNATIONAL ACCOUNTANCY SOFTWARE BULLETIN. (19??)-. Bulletin. English. Six times a year. £195.00 UK; £205.00 other. Tate Bramald Ltd, 243-253 Lower Mortlake Road, Richmond Surrey TW92LS United Kingdom. Tel 011 44 181 3322417, FAX 011 44 181 9488948. ED Jyoti Banerjee. Circ: 1,500.
Desc: Information on the accountancy software market, including software reviews. Primarily aimed at accountants and consultants.

ISSN 0747-2102
US

ICP ADMINISTRATIVE & ACCOUNTING SOFTWARE. [ICP adm. acc. softw.]. VFOAT I.C.P. Interface Administrative and Accounting Software; I.C.P. Interface Administrative and Accounting; ICP Interface Administrative & Accounting. VAT International Computer Programs Administrative and Accounting Software. Vol. 9, Issue 1 (Spring 1984)-. Periodical. English. Four times a year. Free to qualified (individuals) residing in the US and employed in one of the industries served by this publication. International Computer Programs Inc / Barbara Lahiff, 823 East Westfield Boulevard, Indianapolis IN 46220. Tel (800)428-6179, (317)251-7727. Documents available from UMI Article Clearinghouse. Continues ICP Interface. Administrative & Accounting, 0744-7108.
Ind/Abst ABI/INFORM Glob. Ed.; ABI/INFORM [Computer File] (Spring 1984-); Comput. Lit. Index.

LC HG1709 .I57A **ISSN** 0094-8020
DD 332.1/028/54 US

ICP SOFTWARE GUIDE : BANKING.
Main/Corp International Computer Programs, Inc. (19??)-. English. Two times a year. $70.00 single issue. International Computer Programs Inc / Barbara Lahiff, 823 East Westfield Boulevard, Indianapolis IN 46220. Tel (800)428-6179, (317)251-7727.

LC T58.6 .J65 **ISSN** 1058-0530
DD 658/.054 658 US
CCC
CODEN ISYME2
Pr Rev.

INFORMATION SYSTEMS MANAGEMENT. [Inf. syst. manage.]. VFOAT Journal of Information Systems Management. Vol. 8, No. 3 (Summer 1991)-. Trade Publication. English. Four times a year. $157.25. Auerbach Publishers Inc., Park Square Building, 31 St. James Avenue, Boston MA 02116. Tel (800)950-1207. ED Karen Brogno, (212)971-5277. Index available. Bk Rev, (Qty: (published in each issue)). Ad Acc, Adv Mgr Tel (212)971-5000. Circ: 5,000. available on microfilm and microfiche from University Microfilms International (UMI). Documents available from Ask*IEEE. Continues Journal of Information Systems Management, 0739-9014.
Desc: Covers all aspects of IS management in organizations whose business goals drive IS development. Articles give guidance on managing the IS department and staff and delivering information systems services.
Ind/Abst Bus. Source Plus; Comput. Lit. Index; Curr. Cit.; EP Collect.; Gen. BusinessFile (1992-); Homework Help.; Inf. Sci. Abstr. [Full Cov.]; INSPEC (Winter 1992-); MasterFile FullTEXT 1000; MasterFile FullTEXT 350; MasterFile FullTEXT 650; MasterFile FullTEXT (Jan. 1995-); OCLC; Telebase.

LC HF5548.2 .J6 **ISSN** 0898-171X
DD 658/.05/05 US
CCC

INSIDE DPMA. [Inside DPMA]. Added/Corp Data Processing Management Association. VAT Inside Data Processing Management Association. Vol. 26, No. 2 (Feb. 1988)-. Periodical. English. Twelve times a year. $45.00. Data Processing Management Association, 505 Busse Highway, Park Ridge IL 60068-3191. Tel (708)825-8124 ext.252, FAX (708)825-1693. ED Paul Zuziak. Ad Acc, Adv Mgr: Mike Wright, Tel (301)577-4030. Circ: 20,000. available on microfilm and microfiche from University Microfilms International (UMI). Documents available from UMI Article Clearinghouse, Ask*IEEE. Continues Data Management (Park Ridge, Ill.), 0148-5431.
Desc: A newspaper for the information processing and computer business.

Ind/Abst ABI/INFORM Glob. Ed.; ABI/INFORM [Computer File] (Sept. 1988-); Bus. Period. Index (Sept. 1988-); Comput. Lit. Index; Cumul. Index Nurs. Allied Health Lit. (1988-); INSPEC; Manage. Market. Abstr. (1988-); Work Relat. Abstr.; World Publ. Monit.

ISSN 1076-8696
DD 004 US
INTERNATIONAL BUSINESS SCHOOLS COMPUTING QUARTERLY. [Int. Bus. Schools Comput. q.]. **Added/Corp** International Business Schools Computing Association. **VFOAT** IBS quarterly. Vol. 4, No. 1 (Spring 1992)-. Periodical. English. Four times a year. International Business School's Computer Users Group, UNC/College of Business Administration, Greeley CO 80639. **Tel** (303) 351-2764, FAX (303) 351-2500. **ED** Steve Teglovic. **Ad Acc. Circ:** 1,000. ***Continues*** *IBSCUG quarterly.*

LC HF5679 .I63 **ISSN** 1055-615X
DD 657/.0285/633 UK
CCC
CODEN IJAMEN
INTERNATIONAL JOURNAL OF INTELLIGENT SYSTEMS IN ACCOUNTING, FINANCE & MANAGEMENT. [Int. j. intell. syst. account. finance manag.]. **VFOAT** International Journal of Intelligent Systems in Accounting, Finance and Management. (1992)-. Periodical. English. Four times a year. $225.00. John Wiley & Sons Ltd., Baffins Lane, Chichester, West Sussex PO19 1UD United Kingdom. **Tel** 011 44 1243 779777, FAX 011 44 1243 776128 BTG:JWP001, telex 86290 WIBOOKG. **(Subscription address:** John Wiley & Sons, Inc. / Philadelphia, PO Box 7247, Philadelphia PA 19170. **Tel** (212)850-6645, (800)225-5945.) **ED** Daniel E. O'Leary. ***Continues*** *Expert Systems Review for Business & Accounting, 1059-3640.*
Desc: Publishes original material concerned with all aspects of intelligent systems in business-based applications. Devoted to the improvement and further development of the theory and practice of intelligent systems design, development and implementation. Provides a communication forum for advancing theory and practice of the application of intelligent systems in business settings. Readership includes academics and practitioners in finance, accounting and taxation; management and accounting information systems; information science; artificial intelligence technologies; and cognitive science.
Ind/Abst Comput. Rev.

LC QA **ISSN** 1078-2176
DD 004 US
●**INTERNET BULLETIN FOR CPAS.** [Internet bull. CPAs]. (Sept. 1994)-. Bulletin. English. Twelve times a year. $105.00. Kent Information Services, 227 East Main, Kent OH 44240. **Tel** (216)673-1300.

LC WMLC 93/1308 **ISSN** 0888-7985
DD 025 US
CODEN JINFE3
JOURNAL OF INFORMATION SYSTEMS, THE. [J. inf. syst.]. **Added/Corp** American Accounting Association. Information Systems/Management Advisory Services Section. Vol. 1, No. 1 (Fall 1986)-. Periodical. English. Two times a year (Spring and Fall). $30.00. American Accounting Association, 5717 Bessie Drive, Sarasota FL 34233-2399. **Tel** (813)921-7747, FAX (813)923-4093. Documents available from Ask*IEEE.
Ind/Abst Ergon. Abstr.; Geogr. Abstr. Phys. Geogr.; INSPEC (Fall 1989-).

LC HF5548.2 .K9
DD 651 KO
KYONGYONG KWA KOMPYUTO. VFOAT The Management & Computer. Periodical. Korean (Korean). Chyoni Pijinesusa, 45-6 Yomchang-dong Kangso-ku, Seoul South Korea.

ISSN 1074-679X
DD 006 US
●**MAGAZINE OF ARTIFICIAL INTELLIGENCE IN FINANCE, THE.** [Mag. artif. intell. financ.]. **VFOAT** Finance; Artificial Intelligence in Finance; AI in Finance. (Spring 1994)-. Periodical. English. Four times a year. $25.00. Miller Freeman Inc., 600 Harrison Street, San Francisco CA 94107. **Tel** (415)905-2337, (415)905-2200, FAX (415)905-2240, telex 278273.

GW
MANAGEMENT & COMPUTER. (19??)-. German. Four times a year. DM188.00. Gabler Verlag, Postfach 1546, D-65005 Wiesbaden Germany. **Tel** 011 49 611 534129, FAX 011 49 611 534430.

LC T58.6 .M55 **ISSN** 0276-7783
DD 658.4/038 US
CCC
CODEN MISQDP
Pr Rev.
MANAGEMENT INFORMATION SYSTEMS QUARTERLY. (MIS QUARTERLY : MANAGEMENT INFORMATION SYSTEMS.). [Manage. inf. syst. q.]. **Added/Corp** Society for Information Management (U.S.) University of Minnesota. Management Information Systems Research Center. Society for Management Information Systems (U.S.). **VFOAT** Management Information Systems Quarterly. Vol. 1, No. 1 (Mar. 1977)-. Periodical. English. Four times a year. $70.00. MIS Quarterly, 271 19th Avenue South, MIS Research Center, Minneapolis MN 55455. **Tel** (612)624-7083, (612)624-2035, FAX (612)626-1316. **ED** Blake Ives. Index available. **Ad Acc, Adv Mgr:** Blake Ives. **Circ:** 4,000 (ctrl). available on microfilm and microfiche from University Microfilms International (UMI); available on an online database (file 15/Full-Text) from DIALOG. Documents available from The Genuine Article, UMI Article Clearinghouse, Ask*IEEE.
Desc: Research in the field of management information systems. Goal is to serve academicians and practitioners.
Ind/Abst ABI/INFORM Glob. Ed.; ABI/INFORM [Computer File] (March 1985-); Acad. Search; ACM Guide Comput. Lit.; Bus. Period. Index; Bus. Source Plus; Bus. Source; CompuMath Cit. Index [Full Cov.]; Comput. Database; Comput. Lit. Index; Comput. Rev.; Contents Pages Manage.; Curr. Cit.; Curr. Contents Soc. Behav. Sci.; EP Collect.; Gen. BusinessFile (1992-); Homework Help.; INFO-SOUTH Abstr.; Inf. Sci. Abstr.; INSPEC (March 1982-); Mag. Search; MasterFile FullTEXT 1000; MasterFile FullTEXT 350; MasterFile FullTEXT 650; MasterFile FullTEXT (July 1993-); OCLC; Res. Alert [Full Cov.]; Soc. Sci. Cit. Index [Full Cov.]; Telebase; UMI ABI/Inform--Bus. Period. Ondisc (Dec. 1987-) [Full Txt.]; Wilson Bus. Abstr.

LC HD30.2 .M3 **ISSN** 0895-3805
DD 650 US
MANAGING AUTOMATION. [Manag. autom.]. Vol. 1, No. 1 (May 1986)-. Periodical. English. Twelve times a year. Free on request. Thomas Publishing Company / Food Industry, 5 Penn Plaza, New York NY 10001. **Tel** (212)290-8700. Documents available from Ask*IEEE.
Ind/Abst Anbar Account. Finan. Abstr. [Full Txt.]; Anbar Mark. Distr. Abstr. [Full Txt.]; Anbar Top Manage. Abstr. [Full Txt.]; Comput. Lit. Index; Curr. Cit.; Graph. Arts Bull. Inst. Pap. Sci. Technol. (March 1989-April 1989); INSPEC (Aug. 1987-); Manage. Bibliogr. Rev.; Oper. Prod. Manage. Abstr. [Full Txt.]; Oper. Res./Manage. Sci.; Person. Train. Abstr. [Full Txt.]; Qual. Control Appl. Stat.; Robotics Abstr.; Text. Technol. Dig.; Women Manage. Rev. [Full Txt.].

ISSN 0891-7973
DD 658 US
MAPICS THE MAGAZINE. [MAPICS mag.]. **VFOAT** MAPICS. Vol. 1, No. 1 (Oct. 1986)-. Trade Publication. English. Eleven times a year (monthly except Dec.). $95.00. Phoenix Publishing Inc. / Georgia, 1000 Holcomb Woods Parkway, Suite 422, Roswell GA 30076. **Tel** (404)992-1757, FAX (404)992-6667. **ED** Jennifer Farwell. Index available (bound in Feb. for previous year). **Bk Rev**, (Qty: 2-3 per year). **Ad Acc, Adv Mgr:** Janet Creel, **Tel** (404)992-1757. **Circ:** 5,000.
Desc: This magazine is dedicated to serving the needs of the MAPICS user. Provides information regarding new product releases, announcements, tips, and techniques and other data vital or effective use of the MAPICS system.

ISSN 0895-5697
DD 658 US
MARKETING COMPUTERS. See Computers-Computer Systems.

ISSN 1061-5458
DD 616 US
MAXWELL COMPACT LIBRARIES. AIDS. (MAXWELL COMPACT LIBRARIES. AIDS [COMPUTER FILE].). [Maxwell compact libr., AIDS]. **VFOAT** AIDS. (1989)-. English. Four times a year. $695.00 (institutions) US. Macmillan New Media, 124 Mt. Auburn Street, Cambridge MA 02138. **Tel** (617)661-2955, (800)342-1338, FAX (617)868-7738. ***Continues*** *Compact Library, AIDS, 0899-997X.*
Desc: A comprehensive collection of databases on the clinical, social, economic and political aspects of AIDS research and treatment. It includes the complete text of 10,000 AIDS-related articles from ten major medical journals.

ISSN 0742-9398
US
MICRO MONEY. See Computers-Microcomputers, Personal Computers.

ISSN 0836-5482
DD 650/.028/5416 CN
MICROVIEW (TORONTO). (MICROVIEW : THE JOURNAL FOR MICRO USERS IN BUSINESS.). [MicroView]. **Added/Corp** Canadian Institute of Chartered Accountants. Vol. 1, Issue 1 (Oct. 1985)-. Periodical. English. Six times a year. 119.25Can$. Canadian Institute of Chartered Accountants, 277 Wellington Street West, Toronto Ontario M5V 3H2 Canada. **Tel** (416)977-3222, FAX (416)204-3415. **Circ:** 1,000.

ISSN 1052-3464
DD 332 US
MONTHLY MASTER/MONTHLY RETURNS [COMPUTER FILE]. [Mon. master/mon. returns]. **Added/Corp** University of Chicago. Center for Research in Security Prices. **VFOAT** Monthly Stock Master File. **VAT** Monthly Master Monthly Returns. (19??)-. English. $600.00. University of Chicago CRSP, 1101 East 58th Street, Graduate School of Business, Chicago IL 60637.

LC HD9696 **ISSN** 1357-0080
DD 338.4762138 UK
●**MULTIMEDIA BUSINESS ANALYST.** [Multimed. bus. anal.]. (1994)-. Newsletter. English. Twenty-six times a year. Financial Times Telecoms & Media Publishing, Maple House, 149 Tottenham Court Road, London W1P 9LL United Kingdom. **Tel** 011 44 171 8962234, FAX 011 44 171 8962256.

LC HD9696
DD 338.4762138 UK
●**MULTIMEDIA NETWORKS NEWSFILE.** (1995)-. Bulletin. English. Twelve times a year. Communications and Information Technology Research Ltd., 3 Colleton Crescent, Exeter Devon EX2 4DG United Kingdom. **Tel** 011 01392 493444, FAX 011 01392 493626.

LC HF5548.125 .S49 **ISSN** 1057-8889
DD 651.8/05 US
CODEN OCREEX
TITLE CHANGE
OFFICE COMPUTING REPORT. [Off. comput. rep.]. **Added/Corp** Patricia Seybold's Office Computing Group. (199?)-(1993). Periodical. English. Patricia Seybolds Office Computing Group, 148 State Street, Suite 700, Boston MA 02109. **Tel** (617)742-5200, (800)826-2424, FAX (617)742-1028. Documents available from Ask*IEEE. ***Continues*** *Patricia Seybold's Office Computing Report, 0894-9921.* ***Continued by*** *Workgroup Computing Report, 1068-9699.*
Ind/Abst INSPEC.

LC HF54.5 .O54 **ISSN** 0953-5055
DD 380.1025 UK
TITLE CHANGE
ONLINE BUSINESS SOURCEBOOK. (Mar. 1988)-(19??). English. Headland Business Information, 1 Henry Smiths Terrace, Headland Cleveland, TS24 0PD United Kingdom. **Tel** 011 44 429 231902, FAX 011 44 429 861403. ***Continued by*** *Online/CD-ROM Business Sourcebook.*

UK
ONLINE/CD-ROM BUSINESS SOURCEBOOK. (19??)-. English. One time a year. £139.00 UK; $279.00 other. Headland Business Information, 1 Henry Smiths Terrace, Headland Cleveland, TS24 0PD United Kingdom. **Tel** 011 44 429 231902, FAX 011 44 429 861403. ***Continues*** *Online Business Sourcebook.*

US
●**ORGANIZATIONAL COMPUTING AND ELECTRONIC COMMERCE.** (1995)-. English. Four times a year. $140.00. Ablex Publishing Corporation, 355 Chestnut Street, Norwood NJ 07648. **Tel** (201)767-8450, (201)767-8455 (Customer Service), FAX (201)767-6717. ***Continues*** *Journal of Organizational Computing.*
Desc: Research articles concerned with the impact of computer and communication technology on organizational design, operations, and performance. It is intended as a forum for stimulating and disseminating research into the implications of these technologies for organizational structure and dynamics, detailing both the technological advances needed to keep pace with organizational changes, and the emerging technological possibilities for improving organizational productivity.

ISSN 0747-9573
DD 001 US
CEASED
PACKAGED SOFTWARE REPORTS / MIC. [Packag. softw. rev.]. **Added/Corp** Management Information Corporation. (19??)-(Feb. 1995). Periodical. English. MIC, 1111 Marlkress Road, Cherry Hill NJ 08003. **Tel** (609)424-1100. Index available.
Desc: Subscription service offering objective evaluations of business applications software packages.

LC QA76.6 .S615 **ISSN** 0954-2833
DD 004 UK
CODEN PBSOE4
TITLE CHANGE
PC BUSINESS SOFTWARE. [PC bus. softw.]. **VFOAT** PC Business Software Incorporating Mini-Micro Software. (Vol. 13, No. 2)-(19??). Periodical. English. A. P. Publications Ltd, 377 Saint Johns Street, London EC1V 4LD United Kingdom. **Tel** 011 44 171 8375921, FAX 011 44 171 8371197, telex 8955107. **ED** E. Patterson. Index available. **Bk Rev. Circ:** 1,000. Documents available from Ask*IEEE. ***Continues*** *Mini-Micro Software, 0265-6760.* ***Merged into*** *Database*

and Network Journal and Software World.
Desc: Records new developments in software for desktop business computer systems. Editorial lists new programs, new language developments and published books.
Ind/Abst Comput. Lit. Index (?-?); INSPEC (1988-?).

ISSN 1069-9228
DD 658 US
TITLE CHANGE
PC MANAGER'S LETTER. [PC manag. lett.]. **Added/Corp** Bureau of Business Practice. (199?)-(199?). Periodical. English. Bureau of Business Practice, 24 Rope Ferry Road, Waterford CT 06386. **Tel** (800)243-0876, (203)442-4365, (800)876-9105, FAX (203)443-1123. ***Continues*** *Data Processing Manager's Bulletin, 1065-7177.* ***Continued by*** *BBP Manager's Letter.*

LC HD9696.C63 U515946 **ISSN** 0746-6773
DD 001.64 US
PC RETAILING. [PC retail.]. **VFOAT** P.C. Retailing. Vol. 1, No. 11 (Nov. 1983)-. Periodical. English. Twelve times a year. Free. Bartex Publishing Group, 115 Second Avenue, Waltham MA 02154-9980. ctrl circ. ***Continues*** *Digital Retailing, 0736-0894.*

LC QA76.5 .P743 **ISSN** 1040-6484
DD 004.16/05 US
CCC
PC TODAY. **See** Computers-Microcomputers, Personal Computers.

LC QA76.8.I2594 P3 **ISSN** 0737-8939
DD 001.64 US
CCC
CODEN PCWDDV
PC WORLD. **See** Computers-Microcomputers, Personal Computers.

ISSN 0142-0232
UK
CODEN PCWODU
PERSONAL COMPUTER WORLD. [Pers. comput. world]. (1978)-. Trade Publication. English. Twelve times a year. $102.67. VNU Business Publications BV, 32-34 Broadwick Street, London W1A 2HG United Kingdom. **Tel** 011 44 171 4394242 ext. 2222, FAX 011 44 171 4379638, telex 23918 VNU G, 8952440. Documents available from Ask*IEEE.
Ind/Abst Comput. Rev.; Curr. Cit.; Curr. Technol. Index; HILITES; Inf. Manage. Technol.; INSPEC (July 1978-); Int. Civil Eng. Abstr.; Microcomput. Abstr. (Jan. 1985-Nov. 1987); Soft. Abstr. Eng.; World Publ. Monit.

LC Z286.D47 P83 **ISSN** 0897-6007
DD 070.5/028/5 US
PUBLISH! (SAN FRANCISCO, CALIF.). **See** Computers-Desktop Publishing.

LC HF5801
DD 659.1 US
•**RAGAN'S INTERACTIVE PUBLIC RELATIONS.** **See** Business and Economics-Advertising and Public Relations.

ISSN 0742-5600
US
REAL ESTATE COMPUTER REVIEW. [Real estate comput. rev.]. Vol. 1, No. 1 (Jan. 1984)-. Periodical. English. Twelve times a year. $97.00. Real Estate Computer Review, 1564 Fitzgerald Drive, Pinole CA 94564.

ISSN 0736-6957
DD 004 US
CODEN SBCNDL
SMALL BUSINESS COMPUTER NEWS. [Small bus. comput. news]. **Added/Corp** Management Information Corporation. (197?)-. Periodical. English. Twelve times a year. $721.00. Management Information Corporation, 1111 Marlkress Road, Cherry Hill NJ 08003. **Tel** (609)424-1100. Documents available from Ask*IEEE.
Ind/Abst Comput. Bus. (19??-19??); Comput. Lit. Index; INSPEC (Sept. 1982-).

US
CEASED
SMARTMEDIA BUSINESS. (19??)-(Jan. 1994). English. Knowledge Industry Publications Inc, 701 Westchester Avenue, White Plains NY 10604. **Tel** (914)328-9157, (800)800-5474, FAX (914)328-9093. ***Continues*** *Interactive Media Business.*

LC HF5601 **ISSN** 0741-336X
DD 657 US
STANDARD FOR AUDITING COMPUTER APPLICATIONS, A. (1984)-. Trade Publication. English. Two times a year. $204.95. Auerbach Publishers Inc., Park Square Building, 31 St. James Avenue, Boston MA 02116. **Tel** (800)950-1207. **ED** William E. Perry.
Desc: A step-by-step instructional guide on how to audit computer applications. Contains a generic audit program as well as programs tailored to audits involving specific technologies and reviews of functional areas.

US
STORE CHECK REPORT. English. Six times a year. $395.00 (6 issues), $695.00 (12 issues) $125.00 (single copy). Re:Launch, 1563 Solano Avenue, Suite 164, Berkeley CA 94707. **Tel** (510)528-9099, FAX (510)528-9067. **ED** Richard Mites and Elizabeth Olech; telephone: (800)875-9099. **Acid Free.**
Desc: The guide to trends in hardware and software retail merchandising. Critical analysis of information gathered from site visits to retail locations. In addition to special topics, regular features cover computer desktop systems, notebook computers, multimedia, consumer software, and business software. Information includes descriptions of merchandising practices and quantitative data on pricing, shelf share and product mix in retail locations.

ISSN 0378-3766
NE
CCC
Pr Rev. **CEASED**
STUDIES IN THE MANAGEMENT SCIENCES. [TIMS stud. manage. sci.]. **VFOAT** Studies in the Management Sciences; North-Holland TIMS Studies in the Management Sciences. Vol. 1 (19??)-Series complete with Vol. 22. Monographic series. English. Elsevier Science Publishers BV, PO Box 211, 1000 AE Amsterdam Netherlands. **Tel** 011 31 20 4853641, 011 31 20 4853642, FAX 011 31 20 4853598. Documents available from Ask*IEEE.
Ind/Abst INSPEC; Zentralbl. Math. Ihre Grenzgeb.

LC HD9801.A1 T43 **ISSN** 8755-4526
DD 001.64 US
TECHNICAL OFFICE, THE. (THE TECHNICAL OFFICE : ANALYSIS & RESEARCH.). [Tech. off.]. Mar. 1978-. Periodical. English. Four times a year. The Yankee Group, 89 Broad Street, 14th Floor, Boston MA 02110.

LC HF3005 **ISSN** 1057-8765
DD 382 US
U.S. IMPORTS OF MERCHANDISE [COMPUTER FILE]. [U. S. imports merch.]. **Added/Corp** United States. Bureau of the Census. Foreign Trade Division. United States. Bureau of the Census. Data User Services Division. **VFOAT** US Imports of Merchandise; Imports of Merchandise; United States Imports of Merchandise. (198?)-. Government Publication. English. Twelve times a year. $1200.00. US Department of Commerce / Bureau of the Census, Data User Services Division, Customer Services, Washington DC 20233-0800. **Tel** (301)763-4100. **(Subscription address:** Superintendent of Documents, US Government Printing Office, Washington DC 20402. **)**
Desc: Provides import data in detail. Includes general imports and imports for consumption.

ISSN 0740-8919
US
CEASED
WALL STREET MICRO INVESTOR. Vol. 3, No. 2 (March/April 1985)-(Jan. 1995). Periodical. English. Wall Street Micro Investor, PO Box 6, Riverdale NY 10471. **Tel** (212)884-5408. ***Continues*** *Financial & Investment Software Review.*

LC QA76.5 .E54 **ISSN** 0937-6429
DD 004 GW
CCC
CODEN WIINE9
WIRTSCHAFTSINFORMATIK. **See** Computers.

COOPERATIVES

LC HD1491.U5 A654 **ISSN** 0277-8025
DD 334/.683/0973 US
ACS SERVICE REPORT. [ACS serv. rep.]. **VFOAT** Service Report. **VAT** Agricultural Cooperative Service Service Report. No. 1-. Monographic series. English. Price varies per volume. Room 550/GHI Building, 500 12th Street SW, Washington DC 20250.

LC HD3540.A3 M272
DD 334/.0954/82 II
ADMINISTRATION REPORTS ON THE WORKING OF CO-OPERATIVE SOCIETIES IN TAMIL NADU / CO-OPERATION DEPARTMENT. **Main/Corp** Tamil Nadu (India). Co-Operation Dept. 30-6-1973-. English. One time a year. ***Continues*** *Report on the Working of Co-Operative Societies in the State of Tamil Nadu.*

LC HE199.U5 A65
DD 334/.681380524/02573 US
AISA GUIDE TO SHIPPING COOPERATIVES. **See** Transportation-Ships and Shipping.

LC HD3559.3 .A35
SJ
AL-TAAWUN. **Added/Corp** Sudan. Wizarat al-Tawun. Vol. 1 No. 1 (Jan. 1976)-. Periodical. Arabic. Twenty-four times a year. Wizarat al-Tawun, PO Box 680, Al-Khartum Sudan.

LC HD3443 .A7 **ISSN** 0065-793X
DD 334 US
AMERICAN COOPERATION. [Am. coop.]. **Main/Corp** American Institute of Cooperation. **Added/Corp** American Institute of Cooperation. Extension and Research Workshop. Land-Grant University Conference on Farmer Cooperatives. Land Grant Conference on Farmer Cooperatives. National Council of Farmer Cooperatives. **VFOAT** Farmer Cooperatives as a Part of the American Economy; Farmers Cooperatives Today and Tomorrow. 1st Session (1925)-. Periodical. English. One time a year (July). $30.00 (softbound); $35.00 (hardbound). National Council Farmers Cooperation, 50 F Street Northwest, Suite 900, Washington DC 20001. **Tel** (202)626-8740. cum. index.
Desc: A collection of papers and discussions comprising the ...session of the American Institute of cooperation at ... in ... (varies).
Ind/Abst AGRICOLA [Select. Cov.].

LC HD **ISSN** 0214-9923
DD 338 SP
UDC 334
TITLE CHANGE
ANDALUCIA COOPERATIVA. [Andal. coop.]. (1982)-(1993). Periodical. Spanish. Federacion Cooperat Andaluzas, Ronda de Capuchinos 4-5, 41003 Seville Spain. **Tel** 011 34 5 4424062. ***Continued by*** *Economia Social Andaluza, 1133-8229.*

LC HD1491.F72 R493a
DD 334/.683/0944582 FR
ANNUAIRE DES ORGANISMES COOPERATIFS, REGION RHONE-ALPES. **Added/Corp** France. Service Regional de Statistique Agricole. Rhone-Alpes. (19??)-. French. Seervice Regional de Statistique Agricole Rhone-Alpes, 55 rue Mazenod, 69426 Lyon Cedex 3 France.

LC HD1483 .A37A **ISSN** 0741-2568
DD 334/.05 US
ANNUAL REPORT / AGRICULTURAL COOPERATIVE DEVELOPMENT INTERNATIONAL. **See** Agriculture.

LC HD3568.A6 E354a
DD 354.669/4 NR
ANNUAL REPORT / EAST-CENTRAL STATE OF NIGERIA, MINISTRY OF CO-OPERATIVES. **Main/Corp** East Central State (Nigeria). Ministry of Co-Operatives. (1974-75)-. English. One time a year.

LC HD3502 .L43a
DD 334.09 IT
ANNUARIO DELLA COOPERAZIONE ITALIANA. **Main/Corp** Lega Nazionale delle Cooperative e delle Mutue. (19??)-. Italian. One time a year.

LC HD3528.A3 P352
SP
ANUARIO DE ESTUDIOS COOPERATIVOS. **Added/Corp** Universidad de Deusto. Instituto de Estudios Cooperativos. **VFOAT** Lankidetzazko Ikaskuntzen Urtekaria. (19??)-. Spanish (English and Italian). One time a year. 1.000ptas. Universidad de Deusto, Departamento de Publicaciones, Ave Universidades s/n, 48007 Bilbao Spain. **Tel** 011 34 94 4453100, FAX 011 34 94 4456817, telex 34221 UDD E. **ED** Dionisio Aranzadi Telleria.
Desc: Socioeconomic and judicial studies on the cooperative movement.

LC HD **ISSN** 0703-5357
DD 334/.09715 CN
ATLANTIC CO-OPERATOR, THE. Vol. 45, No. 1 (Jan. 1977)-. Periodical. English (French). Twelve times a year. 12.81Can$. Atlantic Co-Operative Publishing, PO Box 1386, Antigonish Nova Scotia B2G 2L7 Canada. **Tel** (902)863-2776, FAX (902)863-8077. **ED** Brenda MacKinnon. **Ad Acc. Circ:** 65,000 (ctrl). ***Continues*** *Maritime Co-Operator, 0025-3405.*
Desc: Educational medium for cooperatives and credit unions in Atlantic Canada.

Business and Economics —Cooperatives

B.C. NEWS. Added/Corp St. Paul Bank for Cooperatives. Vol. 21 (Feb. 1976)-. Periodical. English. Six times a year. St. Paul Bank of Cooperatives, 375 Jackson Street, St Paul MN 55101. **Continues** Bank for Cooperatives News.

LC S469.B8 B78
DD 334/.68/3094977 — BU
BULGARIAN CO-OPERATIVE REVIEW.
Added/Corp TSentralen Kooperativen Suiuz. Sofia Press Agency. (19??)-. Periodical. English. Four times a year. $12.00. Central Cooperative Union, 1 Levski Street, 1000 Sofia Bulgaria. **Tel** 011 359 2 716694. **Bk Rev. Ad Acc. Circ:** 5,600 (ctrl).
Desc: Problems and achievements of the Bulgarian cooperative movement, Bulgarian experience in this field and the international activities of the Bulgarian Cooperative Union (cooperative industry, agriculture, social welfare).

LC S
DD 630 — ISSN 0092-9077 US
BULLETIN - COOPERATIVE EXTENSION SERVICE (ATHENS). (BULLETIN - COOPERATIVE EXTENSION SERVICE.). [Bull. Coop. Ext. Serv.]. **Main/Corp** Georgia. Cooperative Extension Service. No. 614 (Jan. 1961)-. Bulletin. English. Price varies per volume. University of Georgia College of Agriculture Extension Service, Athens GA 30602. **Continues** Bulletin - Agricultural Extension Service, 0093-0199.

ISSN 0824-9547 CN
CAHIERS DU GRIDEQ. [Cah. GRIDEQ.].
Main/Corp Universite du Quebec A Rimouski. Groupe de Recherche Interdisciplinaire En Developpement de l'Est du Quebec. **VFOAT** Cahiers du Groupe de Recherche Interdisciplinaire en Developpement de l'Est du Quebec. No. 1 (Nov. 1977)-. Monographic series. French. Irregular. Price varies per volume. Groupe de Recherches Ethos, University of Quebec, 300 Avenue des Ursulines, Rimouski Quebec G5L 3A1 Canada. **Tel** (418)724-1784, (418)724-1440.

ISSN 0226-8655
DD 334/.22/0971466 CN
CAISSE-EXPRESS. [Caisse-express]. Vol. 1 (Jan. 18, 1980)-. Periodical. French. Twelve times a year. Free. Federation des Caisses Populaires Desjardins de l'Estrie, 1845 rue King Ouest, Sherbrooke Quebec J1J 2E4 Canada. **Tel** (819)821-4546. **Circ:** 2,200.

LC HD9904.C2 C34 ISSN 0829-075X
DD 334/.68363145 CN
CANADIAN CO-OPERATIVE WOOLGROWERS MAGAZINE, THE. [Can. Co-op. Woolgrow. mag.]. Spring 1982-. Periodical. English (French). One time a year. 3.00Can$ Canada; $5.00 other. Canadian Co-Operative Wool Growers, PO Box 790, Carleton Place Ontario K0A 1J0 Canada. **Tel** (613)257-2714. **ED** Eric Bjergso and Norman Field. **Circ:** 12,000. **Continues** Canadian Wool Growers Wool Magazine, 0715-8831.
Desc: Informs the sheep and wool farmer of issues and information relative to his industry. Articles cover methods of improving marketability of wool and improving overall production and prevention of specific problems.

ISSN 0008-6746 US
CAROLINA COUNTRY. Added/Corp Tarheel Electric Membership Association. North Carolina Association of Electric Cooperatives. Vol. 1 (Aug. 1969)-. Consumer Publication. English. Twelve times a year. Free on request. North Carolina Association of Electric Cooperatives, PO Box 27306, Raleigh NC 27611. **Tel** (919)872-0800. **ED** Michael Gery. **Bk Rev. Ad Acc. Circ:** 335,000.
Desc: Focuses on issues and developments affecting electric service in North Carolina. Includes articles on history, culture, institutions, and environments.

ISSN 0228-5045
DD 334/.1/0607146 CN
CHAPEAU. (LE CHAPEAU : BULLETIN DE SHAPO.). [Chapeau]. May 1978-. Bulletin. French. Twenty-six times a year. Free. Federation Regionale Des Cantons De L'Est Des Cooperatives, D'Habitation, 2525 Ouest, rue Galt, Sherebrooke Quebec J1K 1L7 Canada. ctrl circ.

LC HD3092 .A24 CH
CHUNG-KUO HO TSO NIEN PAO. CO-OPERATIVE YEARBOOK REPUBLIC OF CHINA. Added/Corp Chung-kuo Ho Tso Shih Yeh Hsieh Hui. **VFOAT** Co-operative Yearbook Republic of China. (197?)-. Statistical Publication. Chinese (English). Irregular. Free. Chung-kuo Ho Tso Shih Yeh Hsieh Hui / The Cooperative League of the Republics of China, No 11-2 Fu-Chow Street, Taipei Taiwan. **Tel** 886 2 3219343, **FAX** 886 2 2517918. **ED** Kao Hsiao-Fen. Index available. **Acid Free. Circ:** 800.

ISSN 0711-1355
DD 334/.1/09713541 CN
CIRCUIT (TORONTO. 1977). (THE CIRCUIT.). [Circuit]. Added/Corp Toronto Non-Profit Co-Operative Housing Federation. Co-Operative Housing Federation of Toronto. Vol. 1, No. 1 (Nov. 1977)-. Periodical. English. Four times a year. Free on request. Co-Op Housing Federation of Canada, 22 Mawat Avenue, Suite 100, Toronto Ontario M6K 3E8 Canada. **Tel** (416)538-7511. **Circ:** 10,000 (ctrl).

LC S ISSN 0099-7676
DD 334 US
CIRCULAR (FLORIDA COOPERATIVE EXTENSION SERVICE). (CIRCULAR.). [Circ. - Fla. Coop. Ext. Serv.]. 343-. Monographic series. English. Price varies per volume. University of Florida, Gainesville FL 32611. **Continues** Circular (University of Florida. Agricultural Extension Service).

ISSN 0822-7438
DD 334/.06/0719 CN
CO-OP NORTH. [Co-op North]. Periodical. English (Eskimo). Four times a year. Free. Canadian Arctic Co-Operative Federation, Box 2039, Yellowknife Northwest Territories X0E 1H0 Canada.

ISSN 0714-3281
DD 334/.09718 CN
CO-OP UPDATE (ST. JOHN'S). (CO-OP UPDATE.). [Co-op update]. Added/Corp Newfoundland Co-Operative Services. Newfoundland-Labrador Federation of Co-Operatives. Vol. 1, No. 1 (Dec. 1980)-. Periodical. English. Irregular. Free on request. Newfoundland & Labrador Federation of Co-Ops, PO Box 13369, Station A, St Johns Newfoundland A1B 4B7 Canada. **Tel** (709)726-9431. **Continues** Newsletter (Newfoundland Co-Operative Services), 0714-3273.

LC HD3450.A3 N75 ISSN 0318-3955
DD 334/.09716 CN
CO-OPERATIVE ASSOCIATIONS IN NOVA SCOTIA. [Co-op. assoc. N.S.]. **Main/Corp** Nova Scotia. Dept. of Agriculture and Marketing. (1951)-. English. One time a year. Department of Agriculture and Marketing, Hollis Building, Halifax Nova Scotia B3J 2M4 Canada. **Tel** (902)895-1571. **ED** Fred Pierce. **Bk Rev. Circ:** 40. **Supersedes** Nova Scotia. Dept. of Agriculture and Marketing. Report of Co-operative Associations of Nova Scotia., 0318-3963.
Desc: Covers cooperative management, guidelines, structures, background, processes, controls, failures and liquidation.

ISSN 0856-2024
DD 334 TZ
CO-OPERATIVE NEWS. [Co-op. news]. (1986)-. Periodical. English. Four times a year. $4.00. Moshi International Cooperative Alliance, Regional Office East, Central and South Africa, PO Box 946, Moshi Tanzania. **Tel** 011 255 51708, 011 255 51706.

ISSN 0226-8531
DD 334/.1/0971 CN
CO-OPSERVATIONS. [CO-OPservations]. Vol. 1, No. 1 (April 1980)-. Periodical. English. Irregular. Free to members and associates. Co-Operative Housing Foundation of Canada, 225 Metcalfe Street, Suite 311, Ottawa Ontario K2P 1P9 Canada. **Tel** (613)230-2201.

ISSN 0226-952X
DD 333.79/16/0971384 CN
COOPERATIVE ENERGY. See Energy.

LC HD1491.U5 C619 ISSN 0742-9487
DD 334/.683/0973 US
COOPERATIVE INFORMATION REPORT. See Agriculture.

LC HD2951 .C6737 ISSN 0302-7767
DD 334/.0954 II
COOPERATIVE PERSPECTIVE. [Coop. perspect.]. Added/Corp Vaikunth Mehta National Institute of Co-Operative Management. Vol. 8 (Feb./April 1973)-. English. Four times a year. $24.00. Vaikunth Mehta Natl Inst Coop Mgmt, University Road, Pune 411 007 India. **Tel** 59445.

ISSN 0227-535X
DD 334/.09714/2 CN
COOPERATIVEMENT VOTRE. [Coop. votre]. Vol. 1, No. 1-. Periodical. French. Three times a year. Free. Conseil Des Cooperatives De L'Outaouais, 131 rue Richer Hull, Quebec J8Y 4T8 Canada.

ISSN 0712-2748
DD 334/.05 CN
CODEN CDEVEU
COOPERATIVES ET DEVELOPPEMENT. [Coop. d,ev.]. Added/Corp Centre Interuniversitaire de Recherche, d'Information et d'Enseignement sur les Cooperatives. **VFOAT** Revue du C.I.R.I.E.C. Vol. 15, No. 1 (1982/83)-. Periodical. French (summaries and/or abstracts in English). Two times a year (Mar. & Oct.). 35.21Can$. Centre Interunivesitaire de Recherche d'Information et d'Enseignement sur les Cooperatives - CIRIEC, 5255 Avenue Decelles, Montreal Quebec, Canada H3T 1V6. **Tel** (514)340-6016. **Continues** Revue du C.I.R.I.E.C., 0831-876X.
Ind/Abst Repere (1990/91-).

IT
COOPERAZIONE ECONOMICA NEI PAESI DEL COMECON. Italian. Twelve times a year. L134400. Libreria Italia Urss, Via E Raggio 1/10, 16124 Genoa Italy. **Tel** 011 39 10 295446.

LC Microfilm 02193 HD HD3502
IT
COOPERAZIONE ITALIANA, LA.
Added/Corp Lega Nazionale delle Cooperative e delle Mutue. (1887)-. Italian. Eleven times a year. L47690. Ed Cooperativa, Via Guattani 13, 00161 Rome Italy. **Tel** 011 39 6 8440507, 011 39 6 8844942, **FAX** 011 39 6 84439216. **Ad Acc, Adv Mgr Tel** (061) 8844942.

ISSN 8755-9099
DD 333 US
COUNTY LINES (ALBERT LEA, MINN.). (COUNTY LINES.). [Cnty. lines]. Periodical. English. Twelve times a year. $0.50. County Lines, PO Box 611, Albert Lea MN 56007. **Tel** (507)373-6421. **ED** Carol DeBoer and Ron Steckman. **Circ:** 5,200 (ctrl). **Continues** Freeborn-Mower Electric Cooperative.
Desc: Newsletter which is designed to keep our electric cooperative member-owners informed on the coop's monthly operations and topics of interest to rural residents.

ISSN 0199-9311
DD 334 US
CREDIT UNION NEWS. See Business and Economics-Banks and Banking.

ISSN 0226-8558
DD 334/.1/02571 CN
DIRECTORY OF HOUSING CO-OPERATIVES. [Dir. hous. coop.]. June 1978-. Directory. English. Two times a year. Free to members. Co-Operative Housing Foundation of Canada, 225 Metcalfe Street, Suite 311, Ottawa Ontario K2P 1P9 Canada. **Tel** (613)230-2201.

LC HD9321.3 .D57 ISSN 0277-1969
DD 381/.456413/002573 US
DIRECTORY OF RETAILER OWNED COOPERATIVES, WHOLESALER SPONSORED VOLUNTARIES, WHOLESALE GROCERS, SERVICES MERCHANDISERS. See Industry and Production-Trade and Industrial Directories.

LC HD ISSN 1133-8229
DD 338 SP
UDC 334.73(460.35)
ECONOMIA SOCIAL ANDALUZA. [Econ. soc. andal.]. (1993)-. Periodical. Spanish. Federacion Cooperat Andaluzas, Ronda de Capuchinos 4-5, 41003 Seville Spain. **Tel** 011 34 5 4424062. **Continues** Andalucia Cooperativa, 0214-9923.

US
●**ELECTRIC CO-OP TODAY.** See Public Administration-Public Utilities.

ISSN 0820-795X
DD 334/.06/0711 CN
ENTRAIDE COOP. [Entraide coop]. Added/Corp Societe d'Entraide du Pacifique. Vol. 1, No. 1 (Spring 1982)-. Periodical. French. Four times a year. Free. Societe d'Entraide du Pacifique, CP 1130-1013 Avenue Brunette, Maillardville British Columbia V3J 6Z4 Canada.

LC HG2032 ISSN 0704-6146
DD 334/.2/09714 CN
ENTRE GENS. (L'ENTRE-GENS.). Added/Corp Federation de Quebec des Caisses Populaires Desjardins. Union Regionale de Montreal. Federation de Caisses Populaires Desjardins de Montreal et de l'Ouest-du-Quebec. Vol. 1 (Mar. 1978)-. Periodical. French. Twelve times a year. Free. Union Regionale de Montreal, C P 35, Montreal Quebec H5B 1E7 Canada. ctrl circ.

Business and Economics —Cooperatives

LC HG1501
DD 332.1   US
EXAMINATION OF THE NATIONAL CONSUMER COOPERATIVE BANK'S FINANCIAL STATEMENTS FOR THE FISCAL YEAR ENDED ..., AND THE QUARTER ENDED ... - COMPTROLLER GENERAL OF THE UNITED STATES. See Business and Economics-Banks and Banking.

US
EXTENSION ENGINEERING IN KANSAS; R. Main/Corp Kansas State University. Cooperative Extension Service. (19??)-. Periodical. English.

LC HD1491.U5 C619   **ISSN** 0742-9495
DD 334/subser.683/0973 S 334/.683/0973   US
FARMER COOPERATIVE STATISTICS. See Business and Economics-Abstracting, Bibliographies and Statistics.

LC S
DD 630   US
FCS SPECIAL REPORT. See Agriculture.

LC S   **ISSN** 0195-3346
DD 630   US
FCX CAROLINA COOPERATOR. See Agriculture.

ISSN 0702-696X
DD 334/.1/0971   CN
FROM THE ROOFTOPS. [From rooftops]. **Added/Corp** Co-operative Housing Foundation of Canada. **VFOAT** Du Haut des Toits. Vol. 1, No. 2 (Apr. 1972)-. Periodical. English. Four times a year. Free on request. Co-Operative Housing Foundation of Canada, 225 Metcalfe Street, Suite 311, Ottawa Ontario K2P 1P9 Canada. **Tel** (613)230-2201. *Continues C H F Newsletter, 0703-5632.*

ISSN 0713-4231
DD 334/.1/09714   CN
HEBDO-COOP. [Hebdo-coop]. No. 1-. Periodical. French. $3.50. Hebdo-Coop, 4302 Ste-Emilie, Montreal Quebec H4C 2A5 Canada.

ISSN 0713-424X
DD 334/.1/09714   CN
HEBDO-COOP. ENGLISH EDITION. (HEBDO-COOP.). [Hebdo-coop. Engl. ed.]. Periodical. English. Irregular. $3.50. Hebdo-Coop, 4302 Ste-Emilie, Montreal Quebec H4C 2A5 Canada.

SZ
ICA NEWS / INTERNATIONAL CO-OPERATIVE ALLIANCE. Added/Corp International Co-Operative Alliance. **VAT** International Co-Operative Alliance News. Issue No 1 (Feb. 1987)-. Periodical. English. 72.00F combined subscription with Review of International Cooperation. International Cooperative Alliance, Route des Morillons 15, CH-1218 Geneva Switzerland. **Tel** 011 41 22 7984121, FAX 011 41 22 7984122, telex 845 27935.

LC S
DD 630   JA
IDACA NEWS: THE INSTITUTE FOR THE DEVELOPMENT OF AGRICULTURAL COOPERATION IN ASIA. See Agriculture.

LC HD3538 .I44   **ISSN** 0376-981X
DD 334/.0954   II
INDIAN CONSUMER COOPERATOR. Added/Corp National Cooperative Consumers' Federation. Vol. 1 (Jan. 1974)-. Periodical. English. Twelve times a year. Rs5.00. National Cooperative Consumers' Federation, 25 Ring Road, Lajpat Nagar-IV, New Delhi 110024 India.

II
INDIAN COOPERATIVE REVIEW. Vol. 1 (Oct. 1963)-. Periodical. English. Four times a year. $10.00. National Cooperative Union of India, 3 Siri Institutional Area, Panchshila Marg New Delhi 110016 India. **ED** M.L. Sharma. **Bk Rev. Ad Acc. Circ:** 2,000. *Continues All India Operative Review.*
Ind/Abst Dairy Sci. Abstr.; Rice Abstr.; Rural Dev. Abstr.; Sorghum Mill. Abstr.; Sug. Indus. Abstr.; World Agric. Econ. Rural Sociol. Abstr.

ISSN 0846-2917
DD 334   CN
INFO CLUB. [Info club]. Vol. 4, No. 2 (Apr. 1991)-. Periodical. English (French). Irregular. Limited free distribution. Info Club, 3010 rue Jacques-Bureau, Laval Quebec H7P 5P8 Canada.

LC S   **ISSN** 0886-5787
DD 630   US
INFORMATION SHEET - MISSISSIPPI STATE UNIVERSITY. COOPERATIVE EXTENSION SERVICE. (INFORMATION SHEET.). [Inf. sheet - Miss. State Univ., Coop. Ext. Serv.]. **Main/Corp** Mississippi State University. Cooperative Extension Service. No. 201. Periodical. English. Association of British Theatre Tech, 4 7 Great Pulteney Street, London WIR 3DF United Kingdom. **Tel** 011 44 171 4343901. available on microfilm.
Ind/Abst AGRICOLA [Select. Cov.].

ISSN 1185-0744
DD 334/.09714/605   CN
INTER COOP. (L'INTER-COOP : LE BULLETIN DE LA COOPERATIVE DE DEVELOPPEMENT DE L'ESTRIE.). [Inter coop]. **Added/Corp** Cooperative de Developpement de l'Estrie. No 1 (May 1990)-. Bulletin. French. Four times a year. Limited free distribution. Cooperative de Developpement de l'Estrie, 2e Etage, 37 rue Brooks, Sherbrooke Quebec J1H 4X7 Canada.

ISSN 0821-6398
DD 334/.07/1171242   CN
INTERCOM. Added/Corp Co-Operative College of Canada. (1973)-. Periodical. English. Four times a year. 20.00Can$. Saskatchewan Teachers Federation, PO Box 1108, Saskatoon Saskatchewan, S7K 3N3 Canada. **Tel** (306)373-1660. *Continues Intercom (Western CoOp College of Canada).*

LC HD1491.A1 J68   **ISSN** 0377-7480
DD 334/.683/05   IS
CODEN JRCOE4
JOURNAL OF RURAL COOPERATION. [J. rural coop.]. **Added/Corp** International Research Centre on Rural Cooperative Communities. Vol. 1 (1973)-. Periodical. English. Two times a year. $25.00. CIRCOM International Research Centre on Rural Cooperative Communities, PO Box 2355, Rehovot 76122 Israel. **Tel** 08-474111, FAX 972-8-475884, telex 381378 STUCE IL. **ED** Yair Levi. Index available. cum. index. **Bk Rev. Circ:** 500 (ctrl)
Desc: Publication of the results of investigation and research on problems relating to rural cooperative communities. Current information on research projects and published works.
Ind/Abst AGRICOLA; Geogr. Abstr. Human Geogr.; Int. Dev. Abstr.; Soc. Plann. Policy Dev. Abstr.; World Agric. Econ. Rural Sociol. Abstr.

ISSN 0380-2159
DD 334/.2/09713541   CN
KREDYTOVA KOOPERATYVA BUDUCHNIST'. See Business and Economics-Banks and Banking.

LC HD101 .L35   **ISSN** 0251-1894
DD 333.3/23/05   IT
LAND REFORM, LAND SETTLEMENT AND COOPERATIVES. [Land reform land settl. coop.]. **Added/Corp** Food and Agriculture Organization of the United Nations. (1972)-. Periodical. English (Spanish and French). One time a year (Sept.). $12.00. **(Subscription address:** UNIPUB, 4611 F Assembly Drive, Lanham MD 20706. **Tel** (800)274-4888, (301)459-7666.} **ED** Hans Meliczek. Index available. cum. index. **Bk Rev. Circ:** 2,000 (ctrl). available on microfiche. *Supersedes Information on Land Reform, Land Settlement and Co-Operatives.*
Desc: Agrarian reform, land settlement, rural cooperatives, land tenure, group farming, and rural development.
Ind/Abst Agrindex; Geogr. Abstr. Human Geogr. (?-?); Int. Dev. Abstr.; Int. Labour Doc.; PAIS Int. Print; Rural Dev. Abstr.; World Agric. Econ. Rural Sociol. Abstr.

ISSN 0823-6828
DD 016.334/05   CN
LIBRARY SERVICES BULLETIN (CO-OPERATIVE COLLEGE OF CANADA). (LIBRARY SERVICES BULLETIN / CO-OPERATIVE COLLEGE OF CANADA.). [Libr. serv. bull.]. Bulletin. English. Four times a year. Free. Co-Operative College of Canada, 141-105 Street West, Saskatoon Sask. S7N 1N3.

LC HG2032   **ISSN** 0704-0881
DD 334/.09714   CN
MA CAISSE D'ECONOMIE. See Business and Economics-Banks and Banking.

LC HG2032   **ISSN** 0705-6532
DD 334/.2/09713   CN
MOUVEMENT (OTTAWA). (LE MOUVEMENT.). [Mouvement]. Vol. 2, No. 7 (Jan./Feb.)-. Periodical. French. Twelve times a year. Federation des Caisses Populaires de l'Ontario, 200 rue Isabella, Ottawa Ontario K1S 1V7 Canada. *Continues Mouvement des Caisses Populaires de l'Ontario, 0825-3420.*

US
NORTH DAKOTA R E C MAGAZINE. (1970)-. Periodical. English. Twelve times a year. $12.00. North Dakota Association of Rural Electric Co-Ops, Box 727, Mandan ND 58554. **Tel** (701)663-6501. **ED** Karl Karlgaard and JoAnn Winistorfer. **Bk Rev. Ad Acc. Circ:** 73,000 (ctrl).
Desc: Helps the state's 72,000 electronic and telephone cooperative consumers understand the issues that affect the rural electric program, their cooperatives, and their quality of life in rural North Dakota.

LC HD3472 .O22
DD 334/.0981   BL
OCB. VFOAT O.C.B. Vol. 1, No. 1 (Jan./Feb. 1978)-. Periodical. Portuguese. Six times a year. Organiza Cao das Cooperativas Brasileiras, Edificio Serra Dourada Sala 110 Setor Commercial sul, Brasilia DF CEP 70309 Brazil.

ISSN 0228-8656
DD 334/.09713/8   CN
OTTAWA CO-OPERATIVE DIRECTORY, THE. Added/Corp Potential Co-op Society. **VFOAT** Repertoire Cooperatif de l'Est de l'Ontario. No. 1 (1981)-. Directory. English (French). One time a year. $0.50 each number. Potential Co-Op Society, PO Box 5, Station B, Ottawa K1P Canada.

LC HD3540.5 .A38 HD3540.5.A4
DD 334/.09549/1   PK
TITLE CHANGE
PAKISTAN COOPERATIVE REVIEW. Added/Corp West Pakistan Cooperative Union. Vol. 6 (July/Sept. 1974)-(19??). Periodical. English. S M Muslim, 11-Masson Road, Lahore Pakistan. *Continues West Pakistan Cooperative Review. Continued by Punjab Cooperative Union. Review.*

ISSN 0701-0230
DD 334/.06/271466   CN
PALABRE. (LA PALABRE.). **Added/Corp** Universite de Sherbrooke. Centre d'Etudes en Economie Cooperative. Vol. 1 (Nov. 1975)-. Periodical. French. Two times a year. Free. Cedec Faculte des Arts, Universite de Sherbrooke, Sherbrooke Quebec J1K 2R1 Canada.

LC HD3542.6 .A26
MY
PELANCAR. Added/Corp Angkatan Kerjasama Kebangsaan Malaysia. (19??)-. Periodical. Malay. Twelve times a year. $1.50 single issue. Angkasa, No 2 & 6, Jalan 222 Malaysia. **Tel** 03-7563200, FAX 03-7569353, telex ANKASA MA 37478. **Ad Acc. Circ:** 5,000.

LC HD3540.A3 G816A
DD 354.54/7500722253   II
PERFORMANCE BUDGET OF AGRICULTURE, FORESTS, AND CO-OPERATION DEPARTMENT. CO-OPERATION. Main/Corp Gujarat (India). Agriculture, Forests, and Co-Operation Department. 1978/79-. English. Agriculture Forests and Co-Operation Department, Gujarat India.

ISSN 0822-2460
DD 334/.1/06071384   CN
PHOENIX (OTTAWA. 1983). (THE PHOENIX.). [Phoenix]. **VFOAT** Le Phenix. No. 1 (1983)-. Periodical. English (French). Twelve times a year. Limited free distribution. Ottawa Federation of Housing Co-Operatives, 303-251 Bank Street, Ottawa Ontario K2P 1X3 Canada. *Continues Co-Oping, 0228-5487.*

ISSN 0143-8484
UK
PLUNKETT DEVELOPMENT SERIES. 1-. Monographic series. English. Irregular. Price varies per volume. Plunkett Foundation, 23 Hanborough Business Park, Long Hanborough, Oxfordshire OX8 8LH United Kingdom. **Tel** 011 44 1993 883636, FAX 011 44 1993 883576. **ED** Elise Bayley. **Circ:** 300.
Desc: Booklets of use to overseas development workers, donor agencies and recipients, for their information on various aspects of rural development through co-operatives.
Ind/Abst World Agric. Econ. Rural Sociol. Abstr.

ISSN 0823-3403
DD 334/.1/09714   CN
PORTE A PORTE. Vol. 1, No. 1 (Fall 1983)-. Periodical. French. Four times a year. Free. SDC-Habitation, 822 Est Sherbrooke, Montreal Quebec H2L 1K4.

ISSN 0130-2507
KZ
POTREBITELSKAIA KOOPERATSIIA KAZAKHSTANA. Added/Corp Profsoiuz Rabotnikov Torgovli, Obshchestvennogo Pitaniia I Potrebkooperatsii (Kazakh S.S.R.). Respublikanskii Komitet. Soiuz Potrebitelskikh Obshchestv Kazakhskoi SSR. (1991)-. Periodical. Russian. Twelve times a year. *Continues Kooperator Kazakhstana.*

LC S
DD 630   US
PUBLICATION (UNIVERSITY OF ALASKA (SYSTEM). COOPERATIVE EXTENSION SERVICE). (PUBLICATION / COOPERATIVE EXTENSION SERVICE, UNIVERSITY

OF ALASKA.). Monographic series. English. Price varies per volume.
Ind/Abst AGRICOLA [Select. Cov.].

PK

PUNJAB COOPERATIVE UNION. REVIEW. (19??)-. English. Four times a year. Rs15.00. Punjab Cooperative Union, 5 Court Street, Lahore Pakistan. **ED** Khalida Saeed. ***Continues*** *Pakistan Cooperative Review.*

LC HD3569.85 .A32A
DD 354.69/820082 MF
REPORT OF THE MINISTRY OF CO-OPERATIVES AND CO-OPERATIVE DEVELOPMENT FOR PERIOD ... . **Main/Corp** Mauritius. Ministry of Cooperatives and Cooperative Development. **VFOAT** Annual Report of the Ministry of Co-Operatives and Co-Operative Development. 1st Mar. 1973 to 28th Feb. 1977-. English. One time a year. Government Printer / Mauritius, Place d'Armes, Government Printing Department, Port Louis Mauritius. ***Continues*** *Mauritius. Ministry of Cooperatives and Cooperative Development. Annual Report.*

DD 338.9 UK
REPORTS: IE. **Main/Conf** Inter-African Conference on Co-Operative Societies. **Added/Corp** Commission for Technical Co-operation for Africa South of the Sahara. (19??)-. Periodical. Multiple languages (English and French). Europa Publications Ltd., 18 Bedford Square, London WC1B 3JN United Kingdom. **Tel** 011 44 171 5808236, telex 21540 EUROPA G.

LC HG2032 **ISSN** 0714-3559
DD 334/.2/060714 CN
REVUE DE PRESSE. **See** Business and Economics-Banks and Banking.

LC HD2951 .R48

FR

REVUE DES ETUDES COOPERATIVES MUTUALISTES ET ASSOCIATIVES. **Added/Corp** Fondation du Credit Cooperatif (France). No. 17 (1986)-. Periodical. French (English). Four times a year (Mar., June, Sept., Dec.). $100.61. Revue des Etudes Cooperatives Mutualistes et Associatives, 33 rue Trois Fontanot, BP 211, 92002 Manterre Cedex France. **Tel** 011 33 1 47248597, FAX 011 33 1 47248838. **ED** Jean-Pievre Dumont. **Bk Rev.** ctrl circ. ***Continues*** *Revue des Etudes Cooperatives, 0035-2020.*
Desc: Information and critical analysis of domestic and foreign cooperative movements, mutual and associative.

ISSN 0747-4784
US
Pr Rev. **TITLE CHANGE**
RURAL ELECTRIC NEWS LETTER. **See** Public Administration-Public Utilities.

LC HD9688.U5 N33 **ISSN** 1054-0474
DD 333.79/32 US
RURAL ELECTRIFICATION MAGAZINE (1987). (RURAL ELECTRIFICATION MAGAZINE.). [Rural electrif. mag.]. **Added/Corp** National Rural Electric Cooperative Association. **VFOAT** Rural Electrification. Vol. 45, No. 5 (Feb. 1987)-. Periodical. English. Twelve times a year. $50.00. National Rural Electric Cooperative Association, 4301 Wilson Boulevard, 10th Floor, Arlington VA 22203. **Tel** (703)907-5578. **ED** Frank K. Gallant (Editor's telephone: (202)857-4888). Index available ($75.00). **Ad Acc**, **Adv Mgr:** Andrea Smith, **Tel** (202)857-9581. **Circ:** 37,000. ***Continues*** *Rural Electrification (Washington, D.C. : 1959).*
Desc: Articles of interest about generation, transmission and distribution of electric power by/for consumer-owned rural electric utilities organized as cooperatives. Tells how co-ops help improve quality of life in rural areas by their involvement in economic development, community-building, education, health care, housing, transportation and other local needs.

LC HD2951 .S293

UA

SAWT AL-TAAWUN (CAIRO, EGYPT). (SAWT AL-TAAWUN.). **Added/Corp** Ittihad al-Taawuni al-Istihlaki lil-Qahirah. **VFOAT** Sawt Al-Taawun Al-Istihlaki. Vol. 1, No. 1 (May 1982)-. Periodical. Arabic. Six times a year. Sawt Al-Taawun, 168 Shari AL-Tahrir, Al-Qahirah Egypt.

ISSN 0823-2040
DD 334/.068 CN
SDC INFORMATIONS. [SDC inf.]. **VAT** Societe de Developpement Cooperatif. Informations. Vol. 1, No. 1 (Summer 1983)-. Periodical. French. Four times a year. Societe de Developpement des Cooperatives, 430 Chemin Sainte-Foy, Quebec Quebec G1S 2J5 Canada. **Tel** (418)687-9221. **ED** Claude Carbonneau. **Circ:** 800.

LC HD3537 .R4
DD 334/.0954 II
STATISTICAL STATEMENTS RELATING TO THE CO-OPERATIVE MOVEMENT IN INDIA, FOR THE YEAR ... . **See** Business and Economics-Abstracting, Bibliographies and Statistics.

LC HD9685.U4 F57a **ISSN** 0197-6877
DD 334/.68136362 US
SURVEY OF GENERATION AND TRANSMISSION COOPERATIVES. [Surv. gener. transm. coop.]. **Main/Corp** First Boston Corporation. Public Finance Dept. (1979)-. English. First Boston Corporation, Park Avenue Plaza, New York NY 10055. **Tel** (212)825-2000.

LC HD3537 .M25 **ISSN** 0377-8002
DD 334/.0954/82 II
TAMIL NADU JOURNAL OF CO-OPERATION, THE. (THE TAMILNADU JOURNAL OF CO-OPERATION : MONTHLY PUBLICATION OF TAMIL NADU CO-OPERATIVE UNION.). **Added/Corp** Tamil Nadu Co-Operative Union. **VFOAT** Tamilnadu Journal of Cooperation; Tamil Nadu Journal of Co-Operation. Vol. 64, No. 5 (Nov. 1972)-. Periodical. English. Twelve times a year. Tamil Nadu Co-Operation Union, 865 Anna Salai, 600 009 Madras India. **(Subscription address:** Prints India, 11 Darya Ganj, New Delhi 110002 India. **Tel** 011 91 11 3268645, FAX 011 91 11 3275542, telex 31-61087 PRIN-IN.**)** ***Continues*** *Madras Journal of Co-Operation.*

LC HD1491.U5 T66
DD 334/.683/0973021 US
TOP 100 COOPERATIVES FINANCIAL PROFILE. **Added/Corp** United States. Agricultural Cooperative Service. **VFOAT** Top One Hundred Cooperatives Financial Profile. **VAT** Top One Hundred Cooperatives Financial Profile. (1980)-. Government Publication. English. One time a year. Agricultural Cooperative Service, US Department of Agriculture, 14th Street and Independence Avenue SW, Washington DC 20250. **Tel** (202)653-6973, FAX (202)653-7033.
Desc: Analyzes changes in sales, assets, financial structure, and sources of debt capital, operating results, and sources and uses of funds.

LC HG2032 **ISSN** 0822-3521
DD 334/.09715 CN
TRAIT D'UNION - FEDERATION DES CAISSES POPULAIRES ACADIENNES. (LE TRAIT D'UNION : LA REVUE DU MOUVEMENT COOPERATIF ACADIEN.). **VAT** Revue le Trait d'Union. Vol. 2, No 2 (March/April 1981)-. Periodical. French. Four times a year. Free. Federation des Caisses Populaires Acadiennes, Place de l'Acadie, CP 920, Caraquet New Brunswick E0B 1K0 Canada. **Tel** (506)727-6565, FAX (506)727-4162. **Ad Acc. Circ:** 2,000 (ctrl). ***Continues*** *Revue du Mouvement Cooperatif Acadien.*

LC HD1491.R95 U58
DD 334/.683/0967571 RW
UMUNYAMUYANGO. **VFOAT** Trafipro; Le Cooperateur. Periodical. French (Ruanda). Republique Rwandaise, Cooperative Trafipro, B P 302, Kigali Rwanda.

ISSN 0745-7200
US
VIRGINIA EXTENSION. (VIRGINIA EXTENSION : THE VIRGINIA COOPERATIVE EXTENSION SERVICE MAGAZINE.). Periodical. English. Four times a year. Distribution Center, Extension Division, 112 Lansdowne Street, Blacksburg VA 24060. ***Continues*** *Virginia Extension News, 0164-3991.*

US

WISCONSIN REC NEWS. Periodical. English. Twelve times a year. $3.50. Wisconsin Electric Cooperative Association, PO Box 686, Madison WI 53701. **Tel** (608)273-0420. **ED** Les Nelson, Lydia Wills, and Perry Baird. **Ad Acc. Circ:** 135,000 (ctrl). ***Continues*** *Wisconsin REA News.*
Desc: Rural living, cooperative rural electrification.

ISSN 0829-576X
DD 334/.6/0971 CN
WORKER CO-OPS (TORONTO. 1980). (WORKER CO-OPS.). [Work. co-ops]. **Added/Corp** University of Saskatchewan. Centre for the Study of Co-Operatives. **VFOAT** Worker Co-Op; Magazine Coop de Travail. **VAT** Worker Co-Ops Newsletter. (Nov. 1980)-. Periodical. English (French). Four times a year. 19.00Can$ (institutions), 17.00Can$ (individuals) Canada; 21.00Can$ (institutions), 19.00Can$ (individuals) US; 25.00Can$ (institutions), 23.00Can$ (individuals) other. Worker Co-Ops Magazine, PO Box 101, Station G, Toronto Ontario M4M 3E8 Canada. **Tel** (416)778-4744. **ED** Jack Quarter. **Bk Rev. Ad Acc. Circ:** 2,500 (ctrl).
Desc: Provides an overview on worker co-operative development in Canada and around the world. It addresses community economic development, workplace democracy, worker self management, union and employee ownership, and job creation strategies. Format includes sections on people, shoptalk, and book reviews as well as features and profiles.
Ind/Abst Altern. Press Index (-199?).

ISSN 0712-1490
DD 334/.05 CN
WORKING PAPER ... / CO-OPERATIVE FUTURE DIRECTIONS PROJECT. [Work. pap. - Co-op. Future Dir. Proj.]. **Added/Corp** Co-Operative Future Directions Project. Co-Operative College of Canada. **VFOAT** Working Papers. **VAT** Working Papers - Co-Operative Future Directions Project. No. 1 (Jan. 1980)-. Monographic series. English. Price varies per volume. Co-Operative College of Canada, 141-105 Street West, Saskatoon Sask. S7N 1N3.

LC HD2951 .Y43
DD 334/05 UK
Pr Rev.
•**WORLD OF CO-OPERATIVE ENTERPRISE, THE.** **Added/Corp** Plunkett Foundation. **VFOAT** World of Cooperative Enterprise. (1994)-. Directory. English. One time a year. $29.01. Plunkett Foundation, 23 Hanborough Business Park, Long Hanborough, Oxfordshire 0X8 8LH United Kingdom. **Tel** 011 44 1993 883636, FAX 011 44 1993 883576. **ED** W. Hurp, K. Targett, E. Parnell. **Bk Rev. Circ:** 1,000. Documents available from BLDSC. ***Continues*** *Yearbook of Co-Operative Enterprise, 0952-5556.*
Desc: Provides common ground for the study of issues of current interest and the exploration of trends in all co-operative sectors.

LC HD2951 .Y43 **ISSN** 0952-5556
DD 334/05 UK
TITLE CHANGE
YEARBOOK OF CO-OPERATIVE ENTERPRISE. **Added/Corp** Plunkett Foundation for Co-operative Studies. **VFOAT** Yearbook of Cooperative Enterprise. (1988)-(1993). English. Plunkett Foundation, 23 Hanborough Business Park, Long Hanborough, Oxfordshire 0X8 8LH United Kingdom. **Tel** 011 44 1993 883636, FAX 011 44 1993 883576. **ED** J. E. Bayley and E. Parnell. **Circ:** 1,000. ***Continues*** *Year Book of Agricultural Co-Operation, 0142-498X.* ***Continued by*** *World of Co-Operative Enterprise.*
Desc: Provides common ground for the study of issues of current interest and the exploration of trends in all co-operative sectors.

LC HG2033 .W67a **ISSN** 0147-7803
DD 334/.2 US
YEARBOOK - WORLD COUNCIL OF CREDIT UNIONS. **See** Business and Economics-Banks and Banking.

LC HD2951 .E723 **ISSN** 0044-2429
DD 334/.0943 GW
CCC
ZEITSCHRIFT FUER DAS GESAMTE GENOSSENSCHAFTSWESEN. [Z. gesamte Genossenschaftswes.]. **Added/Corp** Universitaet Erlangen. Forschungsinstitut fuer Genossenschaftswesen. Friedrich-Alexander-Universitaet Erlangen-Nuernberg. Forschungsinstitut fuer Genossenschaftswesen. Vol. 1 (1950)-. German. Four times a year. $92.12. Vandenhoeck & Ruprecht, Robert Bosch Breite 6, D-37079 Goettingen Germany. **Tel** 011 49 551 695911, FAX 011 49 551 695917, telex 965226 VAN d.
Ind/Abst AGRICOLA; Int. Labour Doc.; LABORDOC.

ECONOMIC ASSISTANCE AND DEVELOPMENT

LC Z7164.U5 U53a **ISSN** 0091-2840
DD 016.3092/233/73 US
A. I. D. MEMORY DOCUMENTS. **Main/Corp** A.I.D. Reference Center. **Added/Corp** United States. National Technical Information Service. Vol. 1 (March 1972)-. English. Four times a year. $23.00 North America; $46.00 other. National Library of Medicine, 8600 Rockville Pike, Bethesda MD 20894. **Tel** (301)496-6308.

LC HD82 .U535a **ISSN** 0096-1507
DD 016.33891/172/4073 US
A.I.D. RESEARCH AND DEVELOPMENT ABSTRACTS. **See** Business and Economics-Abstracting, Bibliographies and Statistics.

US

ADVANCES IN DEVELOPMENTAL POLICY STUDIES. (19??)-. English. One time a year. $73.25. JAI Press Inc., 55 Old Post Road, Suite 2, PO Box 1678, Greenwich CT 06836-1678. **Tel** (203)661-7602, FAX (203)661-0792. **ED** Stuart Nagel.

ISSN 0001-9852
UK

AFRICA RESEARCH BULLETIN : ECONOMIC, FINANCIAL AND TECHNICAL SERIES. Vol. 1 (Jan. 1964)-. Bulletin. English. Twelve times a year. £230.00 UK and Europe; $401.00 North America; £259.00 other. Basil Blackwell Publishers Ltd., 108 Cowley Road, Oxford 0X4 1JF United Kingdom. **Tel** 011 44 1235 465500, FAX 011 44 1235 465556, telex 837022 OXBOOK G. **(Subscription address:** Blackwell Publishers / UK, 108 Cowley Road, Oxford OX4 1JF United Kingdom. **Tel** 011

44 1865 791100, FAX 011 44 1865 791347.) available on microfilm and microfiche from University Microfilms International (UMI).

SA

•**AFRICAN AGENDA.** (1995)-. Periodical. English. Eleven times a year. $16.40. African Agenda, 1 Mayo Centre, Fortesque Road, PO Box 94154, Yeoville 2198, Johannesburg, South Africa. **Tel** 011 27 11 4871596, 011 27 11 4871597, FAX 011 27 11 6480907. **ED** Gwen Ansell.
Desc: Aims to articulate the views of Third World groups on issues related to politics, development, gender and environment, basic needs and culture.

IV

AFRICAN DEVELOPMENT REPORT. (1989)-. English. One time a year. African Development Bank, BP 1387, Abidjan 01 Ivory Coast. **Tel** 011 255 320711.

LC HC501 .A63 **ISSN** 0044-667X
DD 309.1/6/03 NR
AFRISCOPE. [Afriscope]. Vol. 1, No. 1 (June 1971)-. Periodical. English. Twelve times a year. Pan Afriscope Publications, PMB 1119, Yaba Lagos Nigeria. available on microfilm and microfiche from University Microfilms International (UMI).
Ind/Abst Am. Hist. Life (1972-1975); MLA Int. Bibl. Books Artic. Mod. Lang. Lit.

LC HD1417 .B74a **ISSN** 0713-0465
DD 338.1/81/091724 CN
AGRICULTURAL AID TO DEVELOPING COUNTRIES. [Agric. aid dev. ctries.]. **Main/Corp** British Columbia. Ministry of Agriculture and Food. **VFOAT** British Columbia Agricultural Aid to Developing Countries and World Disaster Areas. (1981)-. Periodical. English. One time a year. British Columbia Ministry of Agriculture & Fisheries, Parliament Building, Room 028, Victoria British Columbia V9A 1M9 Canada. **Tel** (604)387-1978. ***Continues*** *British Columbia. Ministry of Agriculture. Agricultural Aid to Developing Countries., 0713-0465.*

ISSN 0002-2942
JA
AJIA KEIZAI. [Ajia keizai]. **Added/Corp** Ajia Keizai Kenkyujo (Tokyo, Japan). Vol. 1 (May 1960)-. Periodical. Japanese (table of contents in English). Twelve times a year. $216.00. Institute of Developing Economies, 42 Ichigaya Hommuracho Shinjuku-ku Tokyo 162 Japan. **Tel** 03-353-4231, FAX 03-226-8475. **(Subscription address:** Japan Publications Trading Company Ltd., PO Box 5030, Tokyo International, Tokyo 100-31 Japan. **Tel** 011 81 3 3292 3753.) cum. index. **Bk Rev. Circ:** 1,800.
Ind/Abst Agric. Eng. Abstr. (1991-); Am. Hist. Life (1969-).

TZ
ANNUAL DEVELOPMENT PLAN FOR ... / PRODUCED BY THE MINISTRY OF FINANCE, ECONOMIC AFFAIRS AND PLANNING. **Main/Corp** Tanzania. Wizara ya Fedha, Uchumi, na Mipango. (19??)-. English. One time a year. Government Printer / Tanzania, PO Box 2483, Dar es Salaam Tanzania. ***Continues*** *Tanzania. Annual Plan.*

LC HC910.A1 W48a
DD 338.9/006/06891 RH
ANNUAL REPORT AND ACCOUNTS / THE WHITSUN FOUNDATION. **Main/Corp** Whitsun Foundation. (19??)-. English. One time a year.

LC HD77.5.G7 U54a
DD 338.9/0072042256 UK
ANNUAL REPORT ... AND ... HANDBOOK / INSTITUTE OF DEVELOPMENT STUDIES. **Main/Corp** University of Sussex. Institute of Development Studies. **Added/Corp** University of Sussex. Institute of Development Studies. Handbook. **VFOAT** Annual Report ... Handbook. (1977)-. English. One time a year. Free upon request. Institute of Development Studies SS, University of Sussex, Brighton BN1 9RE United Kingdom. **Tel** 011 44 1273 606261, FAX 011 44 1273 621202, 011 44 1273 691647. **ED** Katherine Orme. ***Continues*** *University of Sussex. Institute of Development Studies. Annual Report.*

LC HC59.8 .C35 **ISSN** 1240-6538
DD 330.9 FR
ANNUAL REPORT / CAISSE FRANCAISE DE DEVELOPPEMENT. **Main/Corp** Caisse Francaise de Developpement. (1992)-. English. Caisse Centrale de Cooperation Economique, Cite Du Retigo, 35-37 rue Boissy D'Anglas, 75379 Paris Cedex 08 France. **Tel** 1 42 66 93 66, telex 21632 F. ***Continues*** *Caisse Centrale de Cooperation Economique (France). Annual Report.*

LC HC107.C2 C22A **ISSN** 0097-9236
DD 353.7/794/0082 US
ANNUAL REPORT - CALIFORNIA. COMMISSION FOR ECONOMIC DEVELOPMENT. **Main/Corp** California. Commission for Economic Development. English. One time a year. California Commission for Economic Development, 1400 Tenth Street, Room 210, Sacramento CA 95814. **Tel** (916)322-7757.

LC HG3881.I45 A28 **ISSN** 0074-087X
DD 332.1/538/05 US
ANNUAL REPORT / INTER-AMERICAN DEVELOPMENT BANK. **Main/Corp** Inter-American Development Bank. (1960)-. English (Spanish, Portuguese and French). Irregular. Free on request. Inter-American Development Bank, 1300 New York Avenue Northwest, Suite E 0105, Washington DC 20577. **Tel** (202)623-1381. **Circ:** 20,000.

LC HD82 .O92a **ISSN** 0092-7643
DD 338.91 US
ANNUAL REPORT - OVERSEAS DEVELOPMENT COUNCIL. (ANNUAL REPORT.). **Main/Corp** Overseas Development Council. (19??)-. English. Overseas Development Council, 1717 Massachusetts Avenue NW, Washington DC 20036. **Tel** (202)234-8701.

LC HC60 .O58a
DD 338.91/09172/4 AU
Pr Rev.
ANNUAL REPORT / THE OPEC FUND. **Main/Corp** OPEC Fund for International Development. (1979)-. Periodical. English (French, Spanish and Arabic). One time a year. Free on request. OPEC Fund for International Development, PO Box 995 Parkring 8, 1011 Vienna Austria. **Tel** 011 43 1 515640, FAX 011 43 1 2149827. **Circ:** 5,000. ***Continues*** *Opec Special Fund.*

LC HG3881 .I5 **ISSN** 0252-2942
DD 332.1/532/05 US
ANNUAL REPORT - WORLD BANK. (THE WORLD BANK ANNUAL REPORT.). [Annu. rep. - World Bank]. **Main/Corp** International Bank for Reconstruction and Development. **Added/Corp** International Development Association. International Finance Corporation. Multilateral Investment Guarantee Agency. (1982)-. Periodical. English. One time a year (Sept.). Free on request. World Bank Publications, 1818 H Street Northwest, Washington DC 20043. **Tel** (202)473-1155, (202)473-1155, FAX (202)522-3224, telex WUI 64145 WORLDBANK. **(Subscription address:** World Bank Publications, PO Box 7247-8619, Books Department, Philadelphia PA 19170. **)** ***Continues*** *World Bank. World Bank Annual Report, 0252-2942.*
Desc: Information on economic assistance and international banking.

LC HC60 .A459a **ISSN** 0715-240X
DD 338.91/7123/005 CN
ANNUAL REVIEW / ALBERTA AGENCY FOR INTERNATIONAL DEVELOPMENT. [Annu. rev. - Alta. Agency Int. Dev.]. **Main/Corp** Alberta Agency for International Development. **VFOAT** Fiscal Year, Summaries of Projects by Non-Governmental Organizations and by Countries; Summaries of Projects by Non-Governmental Organizations and by Countries. **VAT** Alberta Agency for International Development Summary Review. (1982)-. Periodical. English. One time a year. Alberta Agency for International Development, 14th Floor/CN Tower, 10004-104 Avenue, Edmonton Alberta T5J 0K5 Canada. ***Continues*** *Alberta International Assistance Program. Alberta International Assistance Program Summary Review, 0711-0650.*

ISSN 0003-6595
US
APPALACHIA (WASHINGTON). (APPALACHIA : JOURNAL OF THE APPALACHIAN REGIONAL COMMISSION.). [Appalach.]. **Added/Corp** Appalachian Regional Commission. (Sept. 1967)-. Periodical. English. Four times a year. Free on request. Appalachian Regional Commission, 1666 Connecticut Avenue Northwest, Washington DC 20235. **Tel** (202)673-7968, FAX (202)673-7930. **ED** Jack Russell. **Circ:** 22,500 (ctrl). available on microfilm and microfiche from University Microfilms International (UMI). Documents available from Documents on Demand.
Desc: Economic and social development in Appalachia, especially activities and programs of Appalachia Regional Commission.
Ind/Abst Am. Hist. Life; Curr. Index J. Educ.; Environ. Abstr.; GeoRef; PAIS Int. Print.

LC HC411 .A7545 **ISSN** 0116-1105
DD 330.95/005 PH
ASIAN DEVELOPMENT REVIEW. [Asian dev. rev.]. **Added/Corp** Asian Development Bank. Vol. 1, No. 1, (1983)-. Periodical. English. Two times a year. $8.00. Asian Development Bank / Information Office, PO Box 789, 1099 Manila Philippines. **Tel** 011 63 2 8344444, 011 63 2 7113851, FAX 011 63 2 7417961, 011 63 2 6326816, telex 63587 ADB PN ETPI, 42205 ADB PM ITT, 29066 ADB PH RCA. **ED** Satish C. Jha. **Circ:** 6,000 (ctrl).
Desc: Discussion of recent development issues, results of research by scholars, specialists and bank staff concerned with Asian-Pacific affairs.
Ind/Abst Asia.-Pac. Econ. Lit.; Geogr. Abstr. Human Geogr.; Int. Dev. Abstr.; Int. Labour Doc.; J. Ferrocement; J. Plan. Lit.; LABORDOC; PAIS Int. Print (1991-); Rural Dev. Abstr.

ISSN 0256-7520
HK
UDC 008(5)
ASIAN EXCHANGE. [Asian exch.]. (1983)-. Periodical. English. Two times a year. $40.00 US and Europe; $20.00 other. Asian Regional Exchange for New Alternatives, PO Box 31407, Causeway Bay Post Office, Hong Kong Hong Kong. **Tel** 011 852 28056193.
Desc: Experiences in development, nation building, and livelihood.

LC JF60 .A83 **ISSN** 0066-8508
GW
ASIEN, AFRIKA, LATEINAMERIKA. (ASIEN, AFRIKA, LATEINAMERIKA : ZEITSCHRIFT DES ZENTRALEN RATES FUER ASIEN-, AFRIKA- UND LATEINAMERIKAWISSENSCHAFTEN IN DER DDR.). [Asien, Afr., Lateinam.]. **Added/Corp** Zentraler Rat fur Asien-, Afrika- und Lateinamerikawissenschaften in der DDR. **VFOAT** Zeitschrift des Zentrales Rates fur Asien-, Afrika- und Lateinamerikawissenschaften in der DDR. Vol. 1 (1973)-. Periodical. German. Six times a year. $121.00 (academic institutions), $189.00 (corporate institutions). Harwood Academic Publishers, PO Box 90, Reading RG1 8JL United Kingdom. **Tel** 011 44 1734 560080, FAX 011 44 1734 568211.
Ind/Abst Am. Hist. Life (1987-); Int. Bibliogr. Sociol.; Leis., Rec., Tour. Abstr.; Rural Dev. Abstr.; Middle East J.; World Agric. Econ. Rural Sociol. Abstr.

ISSN 1181-604X
DD 338.9/17101724 CN
AU COURANT - CANADIAN COUNCIL FOR INTERNATIONAL CO-OPERATION. (AU COURANT.). [Au courant - Can. Counc. Int. Co-op.]. **Added/Corp** Canadian Council for International Co-Operation. **VFOAT** Au Courant. **VAT** Au Courant - Conseil Canadien pour la Cooperation Internationale. Vol. 1, No. 1 (July/Aug. 1990)-. Periodical. English (French). Ten times a year. 21.61Can$. Canadian Council for International Cooperation, 1 Nicholas Street, Suite 300, Ottawa Ontario K1N 7B7 Canada. **Tel** (613)241-7007, FAX (613)241-5302, telex 0636700492.
Ind/Abst Bus. ASAP (1992-) [Full Txt.]; Gen. Period. Index (1985-); Manage. Contents.

AT
AUSTRALIAN CAMBODIAN QUARTERLY. **Added/Corp** Australian Cambodian Support Committee. (198?)-. Periodical. English. Four times a year. Australian Cambodian Support Committee, Trades Hall Box 3, 4 Goulburn Street, Sydney NSW 2000 Australia. ***Continues*** *Australian Kampuchean Quarterly.*

AT
AUSTRALIA'S OVERSEAS AID PROGRAM. **Added/Corp** Australia. (1987/88)-. Government Publication. English. One time a year. Australian Government Publishing Service, GPO Box 84, Canberra ACT 2601 Australia. **Tel** 011 61 6 2954411, FAX 011 61 6 2954455. ***Continues*** *Australia's Overseas Development Assistance Program.*

ISSN 1199-1844
DD 361.7 CN
•**BAOBAB INTERNATIONAL.** [Baobab int.]. **Added/Corp** Canadian Crossroads International. Vol. 1, No. 1 (Spring 1993)-. Periodical. English (summaries and/or abstracts in French). Four times a year. Free. Canadian Crossroads International, 31 Madison Avenue, Toronto Ontario M5R 2S2 Canada. **Tel** (416)967-0801, FAX (416)967-9078. ***Continues*** *Crossworld., 0225-3992.*

LC HC107.W6 W652A
DD 353.97750082/06 US
BIENNIAL REPORT / STATE OF WISCONSIN, DEPARTMENT OF DEVELOPMENT. **Main/Corp** Wisconsin. Dept. of Development. 1979-81-. English. Every 2 years. 123 West Washington Avenue, PO Box 7970, Madison WI 53707. **Tel** (608)266-1018, telex 882108 WI DEPT DEV UD. ***Formed by the union of*** *Wisconsin. Dept. of Business Development. Biennial Report* ***and*** *Wisconsin. Dept. of Local Affairs and Development. Biennial Report.*
Desc: Summary of activities and projects of the Wisconsin Department of Development.

LC HC60 .G693 **ISSN** 0068-1210
DD 338.91/172/4041 UK
CCC
BRITISH AID STATISTICS. **See** Business and Economics-Abstracting, Bibliographies and Statistics.

ISSN 0715-4267
DD 338.91/71/01724 CN
BULLETIN - INTER PARES (ENGLISH ED.). (BULLETIN / INTER PARES.). [Bull. - Inter Pares]. **Added/Corp** Inter Pares (Organization). **VAT** Inter Pares Bulletin. (1978)-. Bulletin. English. Inter Pares Bulletin, 205 Pretoria Avenue, Ottawa Ontario K1S 1X1 Canada.

Business and Economics —Economic Assistance and Development

LC HB
DD 330.9410858
Pr Rev.
ISSN 0268-7402
UK
BULLETIN - UK CENTRE FOR ECONOMIC AND ENVIRONMENTAL DEVELOPMENT. [Bull. - UK Cent. Econ. Environ. Dev.]. (1985)-. Periodical. English. Four times a year (Mar., Jun., Sept., Dec.). $41.07. UK Centre for Economic and Environmental Development / UK CEED, 3E King's Parade, Cambridge CB2 1SJ United Kingdom. **Tel** 011 44 1223 67799, **FAX** 011 44 1223 367794. **ED** Justine Harbinson. Index available (published annually). cum. index. **Bk Rev**, (Qty: 4). **Ad Acc; Adv Mgr:** J.R. Harbinson, **Tel** 011 44 1223 367799. **Circ:** 1,500 (ctrl). **Continues** Newsletter - UK Centre for Economic and Environmental Development.
Ind/Abst For. Abstr.; Leis. Rec., Tour. Abstr.; World Agric. Econ. Rural Sociol. Abstr.

DD 338.9/171/005
ISSN 0849-1259
CN
C-FAR NEWSLETTER (1989). (C-FAR NEWSLETTER / CITIZENS FOR FOREIGN AID REFORM.). [C-FAR newsl.]. **Added/Corp** Citizens for Foreign Aid Reform. **VAT** Citizens for Foreign Aid Reform Newsletter (1989). (1989)-. Newsletter. Twenty times a year. Citizens for Foreign Aid Reform, PO Box 332, Rexdale Ontario M9W 5L3 Canada. **Tel** (905)277-1218. **Continues** Newsletter (Citizens for Foreign Aid Reform), 0826-4228.

LC HC110.P63 U53a
DD 338.973
NLM HC 110.P63 C357
ISSN 0097-7799
US
CATALOG OF FEDERAL DOMESTIC ASSISTANCE. **Added/Corp** United States. Office of Management and Budget. United States. Office of Economic Opportunity. United States. General Services Administration. (1971)-. Catalog. English. One time a year (Supplementary material). $50.00 US; $62.50 other. General Services Administration, General Services Building, Eighteenth and F Streets NW, Washington DC 20405. **Tel** (202)655-4000. **(Subscription address:** Superintendent of Documents, US Government Printing Office, Washington DC 20402.) **Continues** Catalog of Federal Domestic Assistance.
Desc: Summary for financial and nonfinancial federal programs, projects, services, and activities that provide assistance or benefits to the American public administered by departments and establishments of the Federal Government. Describes the type of assistance available and the eligibility requirements for the particular assistance being sought, with guidance on how to apply. Intended to improve coordination and communication between Federal, State and local governments.

LC HJ485 .M25a
DD 336.1/85
US
CATALOG OF STATE ASSISTANCE PROGRAMS. (THE RED BOOK : CATALOG OF STATE ASSISTANCE PROGRAMS.). **Added/Corp** Maryland. Office of Planning. **VFOAT** Catalog of State Assistance Programs. (19??)-. Catalog. English. Department of State Planning, State Office Building, Baltimore MD 21201. **Tel** (410)225-4490. **Continues** Maryland. Dept. of State Planning. Catalog of State Assistance Programs, 0097-9309.

FR
CATALOGUE OF SOCIAL AND ECONOMIC DEVELOPMENT INSTITUTES AND PROGRAMMES, TRAINING. **Added/Corp** Organisation for Economic Co-Operation and Development. Development Centre. **VFOAT** Catalogue Training. (19??)-. English. Irregular. OECD Publications and Information Center, 2 rue Andre-Pascal, 75775 Paris Cedex 16 France. **Tel** 011 33 1 49104262, US:(202)785-6323, FAX 011 33 1 45248500, 011 33 1 45248176, telex 620 160 OCDE. **(Subscription address:** OECD Publications Center, 2001 L Street, Suite 700, Washington DC 20036. **Tel** (202)822-3873, (202)785-6323.)

FR
CCIC INFORMATION. English (French). Four times a year. 200.00F France; 220.00F other. SEPIC, 9 rue Cler, 75007 Paris France. **Tel** 11 33 1 47051759, FAX 11 33 1 45569092.

DD 362
ISSN 1061-6691
US
CD-DIS (ARLINGTON, VA.). (CD-DIS [COMPUTER FILE] : A.I.D.'S DEVELOPMENT INFORMATION SYSTEM.). [CD-DIS]. **Added/Corp** United States. Agency for International Development. Center for Development Information and Evaluation (U.S.). **VAT** Compact Disc Development Information System. No. 1 (Mar. 1992)-. English. Four times a year. $130.00. ARDA / Agency for International Development US, 1500 Wilson Boulevard, Suite 1010, Arlington VA 22209-2404. **Tel** (703)351-4006, FAX (703)351-4039, telex 3730100 LTSCORP. **Circ:** 250.
Desc: The CD-DIS, a CD-ROM (compact) disk containing the complete A.I.D. Document and Project Databases, and the full text of selected A.I.D. reports and publications, including the Agency's Congressional Presentation and over 100 project evaluations. The databases currently identify over 8,000 projects initiated since 1974 and 70,000 associated project and technical reports.

LC HC601.A1 C66a
DD 354.940082/06
AT
CEDA ANNUAL REPORT. **Main/Corp** Committee for Economic Development of Australia. **VAT** Committee for Economic Development of Australia Annual Report. (19??)-. Academic Scholarly Publication. English. One time a year. Committee for Economic Development of Australia, 123 Lonsdale Street, GPO Box 2117T, Melbourne Victoria 3000 Australia. **Tel** 011 61 03 6623544, FAX 011 61 03 6637271.

LC HC59.69 .C46a
DD 338.9/006/0489
DK
●**CENTRE FOR DEVELOPMENT RESEARCH : [ANNUAL REPORT].** **Main/Corp** Centret for udviklingsforskning (Denmark). (1995)-. English. Centre for Development Research, Gammel Kongeuej 5, DK-1610 Copenhagen Denmark. **Tel** 011 45 33 251200, FAX 011 45 33 258110. **Continues** Centret for Udviklingsforskning (Denmark). Working Programme ..., Annual Report.

LC HC59.69 .C5
DD 338.9/005
US
SUSPENDED
CHOICES : THE HUMAN DEVELOPMENT MAGAZINE / UNDP. **Added/Corp** United Nations Development Programme. Division of Public Affairs. (1992)-Suspended with Vol. 4 No. 2 (1995). Periodical. English. Four times a year. $16.00 (one-year); $30.00 (two-year). United Nations Development Program, Room DC1, 1900 One UN Plaza, New York NY 10017. **Tel** (212)906-5328, FAX (212)906-5364. **Continues** World Development (New York, N.Y.).
Desc: Highlights international development. Topics include health, education, agriculture, politics, women's issues and more.
Ind/Abst Read. Guide Period. Lit.

LC HC411 .C554
DD 338.95/005
AT
COLOMBO PLAN FOR COOPERATIVE ECONOMIC & SOCIAL DEVELOPMENT IN ASIA & THE PACIFIC : PROCEEDINGS & CONCLUSIONS OF THE CONSULTATIVE COMMITTEE MEETING, THE. **VFOAT** Proceedings & Conclusions of the ... Consultative Committee Meeting; Proceedings and Conclusions of the ... Consultative Committee Meeting. (1977)-. Proceedings. English. One time a year. Colombo Plan Bureau, 12 Melbourne Avenue, Colombo 4 Sri Lanka. **Continues** Colombo Plan for Co-operative Economic Development in South and South-East Asia.

LC HG6051.D44 C66
DD 332.6
ISSN 1020-0967
US
●**COMMODITY MARKETS AND THE DEVELOPING COUNTRIES : A WORLD BANK QUARTERLY.** See Business and Economics-Investments.

LC HF1 .C83
DD 380.1/05
ISSN 0251-401X
US
COMMODITY TRADE AND PRICE TRENDS. See Business and Economics-Commerce.

LC DA10 .C62
DD 909/.09/71241
ISSN 0141-8513
UK
COMMONWEALTH CURRENTS. **Added/Corp** Commonwealth Secretariat. (April 1978)-. Periodical. English. Four times a year. Free on request. Commonwealth Secretariat / London, Marlborough House, Pall Mall, London SW1Y 5HX United Kingdom. **Tel** 011 44 171 8393411, telex 27678. **ED** Dale Gunthorp. **Bk Rev Circ:** 30,000 (ctrl). **Formed by the union of** Commonwealth Record of Recent Events **and** Commonwealth Diary of Coming Events.
Desc: Reports on the work of the Commonwealth Secretariat in effecting international cooperation for development among commonwealth member countries.

LC HJ1753 .V52a
DD 336.1/85
AT
COMMONWEALTH PAYMENTS TO OR FOR VICTORIA. See Finance-Public Finance.

LC HC60 .U4846
DD 338.91/172/401717
ISSN 0148-2998
US
COMMUNIST STATES AND DEVELOPING COUNTRIES, AID AND TRADE. **Main/Corp** United States. Dept. of State. Bureau of Intelligence and Research. (19??)-. English. One time a year. US Department of State / Bureau of Intelligence and Research, 2201 C Street Northwest, Room 6533, Washington DC 20520. **Tel** (202)647-9176.

LC HD72 .C65
DD 338.9/005
IT
CODEN CMSSEI
CEASED
COMPASS (ROME, ITALY). (COMPASS : NEWSLETTER OF THE SOCIETY FOR INTERNATIONAL DEVELOPMENT.). **Added/Corp** Society for International Development. (19??)-(1994). Newsletter. English. Society of International Development, Palazzo Civilta del Lavoro, 00144 Rome Italy. **Tel** 011 39 6 5917897, FAX 011 39 6 5919836, telex 612339.

ISSN 0391-674X
IT
UDC 334
CEASED
COOPERAZIONE. [Cooperazione]. (1972)-(1994). Periodical. Italian (French and English). Editalia Edizioni D Italia, Via di Palla Corda 7, 00186 Rome Italy. **Tel** 011 39 6 6541592, FAX 011 39 6 6869561.

LC HC244 .S59582c
DD 338.91/47
ISSN 0303-8696
RU
COUNCIL FOR MUTUAL ECONOMIC ASSISTANCE. **Main/Corp** Council for Mutual Economic Assistance. (19??)-. English. Novosti Press Agency Publishing House, 4 Zubovski Boulevard, 103786 Moscow GSP K-21 Russia. **Tel** 011 7 95 2015159, FAX 011 7 95 2302170, telex 411323.

LC K
DD 340
UDC 341.178(4)
ISSN 1013-7335
INT
CODEN CE
TITLE CHANGE
COURIER. AFRICA-CARIBBEAN-PACIFIC-EUROPEAN COMMUNITIES, THE. [Cour., Afr.-Caribb.-Pac.-Eur. Communities]. (1975)-(19??). Periodical. English. Commission of the European Communities, Directorate of General Information, Avenue D Auderghem, 45 Breydel boulevard, B 1049 Brussels Belgium. **Tel** 011 32 2 2357639, telex 21877 COMEU B. Index available. **Bk Rev. Circ:** 80,000. **Continued by** The Courier. Africa-Caribbean-Pacific-European Union.
Ind/Abst Curr. Cit.; PAIS Int. Print (1991-199?).

INT
COURIER. AFRICA-CARIBBEAN-PACIFIC-EUROPEAN UNION, THE. (19??)-. Periodical. English (French). Three times a year. Commission of the European Communities, Directorate of General Information, Avenue D Auderghem, 45 Breydel boulevard, B 1049 Brussels Belgium. **Tel** 011 32 2 2357639, telex 21877 COMEU B. **Continues** The Courier. Africa-Caribbean-Pacific-European Communities, 1013-7335.

LC HC59.7 .C664
DD 338.91/6/04
ISSN 0378-3480
BE
COURIER (BRUSSELS). (THE COURIER.). [Courier]. **Added/Corp** Commission of the European Communities. (19??)-. Periodical. English. Six times a year. Free on request. Commission of the European Communities, Directorate of General Information, Avenue D Auderghem, 45 Breydel boulevard, B 1049 Brussels Belgium. **Tel** 011 32 2 2357639, telex 21877 COMEU B.
Ind/Abst AgBiotech News Inf.; Helminthol. Abstr.; Int. Labour Doc.; Protozoolog. Abstr.

UDC 341.16:001
ISSN 0304-3118
FR
CODEN NU053
COURRIER DE L'UNESCO, LE. (COURRIER DE L'UNESCO.). [Courr. Unesco]. **VFOAT** Courrier - Unesco. (1947)-. Periodical. French. Twelve times a year. 132.00F Third World Countries, 211.00F other (surface mail);. UNESCO / France, 31 rue Francois Bonvin, 75732 Paris Cedex 15 France. **Tel** 011 33 1 45684564, 011 33 1 45684565, FAX 011 33 1 45669270, telex 204461 Paris.
Ind/Abst Acad. Abstr. Full Text Elite; Acad. Abstr.; Acad. Search; EP Collect.; Homework Help.; Mag. Artic. Summar. Elite; Mag. Artic. Summar. Select; Mag. Artic. Summar. CD-ROM; MasterFile FullTEXT 1000; MasterFile FullTEXT 350; MasterFile FullTEXT 650; MasterFile FullTEXT (Jan. 1989-) [Full Txt.]; OCLC; Pub. Lib. FullTEXT; Repere (1979-); Soc. Sci. Source; Telebase; Vocat. Search; World Mag. Bank.

ISSN 0380-1438
CN
CRDI EXPLORE, LE. [CRDI explore]. **Main/Corp** Centre de Recherches pour le Developpement International (Canada). **VAT** Cenrre de Recherches pour le Developpement International Informe. Vol. 4 (Mar. 1975)-. Periodical. French. Four times a year. 16.00Can$. International Development Research Center, PO Box 117, Richmond Hill Ontario L4C 4X9 Canada. **Tel** (905)475-4145, FAX (416)940-3606. **ED** Eileen Conway. **Separated from** IDRC Reports, 0315-9981.
Ind/Abst Can. Period. Index (1987-).

ISSN 0823-5740
DD 338.91.71/01724 CN
SUSPENDED
CUSO FORUM (OTTAWA, ONT. : 1980). (CUSO FORUM.). [CUSO forum]. **VAT** Forum (Ottawa. 1980). Vol. 2, No. 3 (Summer 1980)- Vol. 5, No. 1 (Winter 1983)-. Periodical. English. Three times a year. Cuso Forum, 2255 Carling Avenue #400, Ottawa Ontario K2B 1A6 Canada. **Tel** (613)829-7445, FAX (613)829-7445, telex 053 4706. **ED** Maureen Johnson. **Bk Rev. Circ:** 16,000 (ctrl). ***Continues** Forum, 0704-4720.*
Desc: News and views on CUSO and a forum for it's members.

LC HC60 .D4649a
GW
DED BRIEF. Main/Corp Deutscher Entwicklungsdienst. **VAT** Deutscher Entwidklungsdienst Brief. (1964)-. Periodical. German. Four times a year. Free. Deutscher Entwicklungsdienst, Kladower Damm 299, 14089 Berlin Germany. **Tel** 049 030 36509-0, FAX 049 30 365271, telex 182900 DED. **Bk Rev**, (Qty: 6-8). **Acid Free. Circ:** 20,000.
Desc: The work of volunteers and their experiences in personnel development cooperation. Each issue concentrates on a special subject, such as nutrition, water, self-help, women in third world countries and other related topics.

LC HC437.K28 J25a **ISSN** 0303-8637
DD 336.54/6 II
DETAILED DEMAND FOR GRANTS OF LADAKH AFFAIR DEPARTMENT. GOVERNMENT OF JAMMU AND KASHMIR. (DETAILED DEMAND FOR GRANTS OF LADAKH AFFAIR DEPARTMENT.). **Main/Corp** Jammu and Kashmir. Ladakh Affair Dept. (19??)-. English. Ranbir Government Press / Law, Jammu and Kashmir, Law Department, Jammu India.

LC HC431 .D48
DD 338.954/005 II
DEVELOPING INDIA. Added/Corp Centre for Development Research (Hyderabad, India). Vol. 1, No. 1 (Jan./March 1984)-. Periodical. English. Four times a year. $40.00. Centre for Development Research / India, Hyderabad-500 890 India. **Tel** 26 86 45. **(Subscription address:** Prints India, 11 Darya Ganj, New Delhi 110002 India. **Tel** 011 91 11 3268645, FAX 011 91 11 3275542, telex 31-61087 PRIN-IN.**)**

LC HC411 .D48
DD 338.9/931/0505 NZ
DEVELOPMENT. Added/Corp New Zealand. External Aid Division. Vol. 1 (Apr. 1978)-. Periodical. English. Four times a year.
Ind/Abst CSA Neuro. Abstr.; Int. Polit. Sci. Abstr.; J. Ferrocement; Microbiol. Abstr. Sect. C; Middle East Abstr. Index.

XV
DEVELOPMENT & INTERNATIONAL COOPERATION. Added/Corp Center za Proucevanje Sodelovanja z Dezelami v Razvoju--Ljubljana. **VFOAT** Development and International Cooperation. Vol. 7, No. 12 (June 1991)-. Periodical. English. Two times a year. ***Continues** Development & South-South Cooperation, 0352-7670.*
Ind/Abst Middle East J.

LC HC59.7 .D44
DD 330.9/172/4 UA
DEVELOPMENT & SOCIO-ECONOMIC PROGRESS. Added/Corp Permanent Organization for Afro-Asian Peoples' Solidarity. **VFOAT** Development and Socio-Economic Progress. (Nov. 1977)-. Periodical. English. Four times a year. 89 Abdel Aziz Al-Saoud Street, Manial El-Roda, Cairo United Arab Republic Egypt.
Ind/Abst Int. Bibliogr. Sociol.

ISSN 8756-0488
DD 306 US
DEVELOPMENT ANTHROPOLOGY NETWORK. (DEVELOPMENT ANTHROPOLOGY NETWORK : BULLETIN OF THE INSTITUTE FOR DEVELOPMENT ANTHROPOLOGY.). [Dev. anthropol. netw.]. **Added/Corp** Institute for Development Anthropology (Binghamton, N.Y.). **VFOAT** Network. Vol. 1, No. 1 (Dec. 1981)-. Bulletin. English. Two times a year (July & Dec.). $15.00. Institute for Development Anthropology, PO Box 2207, Binghamton NY 13902. **Tel** (607)772-6244. **ED** Michael Horowitz, Peter Little, Muneera Salem Murdock and Michael Painter. Index available. cum. index. **Circ:** 1,900.
Desc: Includes substantive articles on third world development issues by specialists in varied geographic and subject areas.
Ind/Abst Agrofor. Abstr. (1991-); For. Abstr.; Nutr. Abstr. Rev., Ser. A, Hum. Exp.; Rural Dev. Abstr.

ISSN 0955-0569
UK
DEVELOPMENT BIBLIOGRAPHIES. See Business and Economics-Abstracting, Bibliographies and Statistics.

LC HC60 .O688
DD 338.91/172/4 FR
DEVELOPMENT CO-OPERATION EFFORTS AND POLICIES OF THE MEMBERS OF THE DEVELOPMENT ASSISTANCE COMMITTEE; REVIEW. Main/Corp Organisation for Economic Co-Operation and Development. Development Assistance Committee. **VFOAT** Twenty-Five Years of Development Co-Operation; Development Co-Operation in the 1990's; Development Co-Operation. (Dec. 1972)-. English. One time a year. OECD Publications and Information Center, 2 rue Andre-Pascal, 75775 Paris Cedex 16 France. **Tel** 011 33 1 49104262, US:(202)785-6323, FAX 011 33 1 45248500, 011 33 1 45248176, telex 620 160 OCDE. ***Continues** Organisation for Economic Co-Operation and Development. Development Assistance Committee. Development Assistance Efforts and Policies in ... of the Members of the Development Assistance Committee.*
Desc: Includes analysis of the current situation, detailed statistics on financial flows to developing countries, and information on the policies of OECD/DAC members and other donors, including OPEC countries.

LC HN980 .D48 **ISSN** 0192-1312
DD 307 US
CEASED
DEVELOPMENT COMMUNICATION REPORT. See Communications.

LC HD82 .D389 **ISSN** 0345-2328
DD 338.9/005 SW
DEVELOPMENT DIALOGUE. [Dev. dialogue]. **Added/Corp** Dag Hammarskjold Foundation. No. 1 (1972)-. Periodical. English. Irregular. Dag Hammarskjold Centre, Oure Slottsgatan 2, 752 20 Uppsala Sweden. **Tel** 011 46 18 128872.
Ind/Abst AgBiotech News Inf.; Bibliogr. Mission.; Commun. Abstr.; Hum. Rights Intern. Rep.; Int. Dev. Abstr. (?-?); Int. Labour Doc.; J. Plan. Lit.; LABORDOC; Leis., Rec., Tour. Abstr.; Middle East Abstr. Index; Rural Dev. Abstr.; World Agric. Econ. Rural Sociol. Abstr.

US
DEVELOPMENT DISCUSSION PAPER. Added/Corp Harvard Institute for International Development. **VFOAT** Development Discussion Papers. (1974)-. Monographic series. English. Irregular. Price varies per volume. Harvard Institute for International Development, Harvard University, Cambridge MA 02138. cum. index.
Ind/Abst Agrofor. Abstr.

LC HC59.69 .D48
DD 330.9172/4 AT
DEVELOPMENT DOSSIER / ACFOA. Added/Corp Australian Council for Overseas Aid. Vol. 1 (1980)-. Periodical. English. Four times a year. 37.00Aus$. Australian Council for Overseas Aid, Private Bag 3, Deakin ACT 2600 Australia. **Tel** 011 61 6 2851816, FAX 011 61 6 2851720, telex 61643. **Ad Acc. Circ:** 1,000. ***Continues** Development News Digest.*

ISSN 1020-0339
IT
DEVELOPMENT EDUCATION EXCHANGE PAPERS : DEEP. Added/Corp Action for Development. Freedom from Hunger Campaign. Food and Agriculture Organization of the United Nations. **VFOAT** DEEP. (19??)-. Periodical. English (French and Spanish). Six times a year. Free. Food Agriculture Organization (FAO) / Italy, GIPCI66 via Terme di Caracalla, 00100 Rome Italy. **Tel** 011 39 6 52252925, FAX 011 39 6 52253152. **(Subscription address:** UNIPUB, 4611 F Assembly Drive, Lanham MD 20706. **Tel** (800)274-4888, (301)459-7666.**)**

IT
CEASED
DEVELOPMENT HOTLINE. (19??)-(Dec. 1994). English. Society of International Development, Palazzo Civilta del Lavoro, 00144 Rome Italy. **Tel** 011 39 6 5917897, FAX 011 39 6 5919836, telex 612339.

ISSN 0961-4524
UK
CCC
Pr Rev.
DEVELOPMENT IN PRACTICE. Added/Corp Oxfam. Vol. 1, No. 1 (Spring 1991)-. Periodical. English. Three times a year. $198.00. Oxfam Publications, 274 Banbury Road, Oxford OX2 7DZ United Kingdom. **Tel** 011 41 1865 313196, FAX 011 41 1865 313117. **ED** Deborah Eade. Index available (bound in third issue). **Bk Rev**, (Qty: approx. 60 per year). **Ad Acc, Adv Mgr:** T. Milner, **Tel** (0805)313196. **Circ:** 500.
Ind/Abst Rural Dev. Abstr.

LC HC687.S6 A22A
DD 338.993/5 BP
DEVELOPMENT PLAN - BRITISH SOLOMON ISLANDS PROTECTORATE. Main/Corp British Solomon Islands. English. British Solomon Islands Protectorate, Prime Minister, PO Box 718, Honiara British Solomon Islands.
Desc: Vols. for 1971-74 include Annual review and revised project list.

LC HC59.7 .D48 **ISSN** 0950-6764
DD 338.91/09171/4 UK
CCC
CODEN DPORER
DEVELOPMENT POLICY REVIEW. (DEVELOPMENT POLICY REVIEW : THE JOURNAL OF THE OVERSEAS DEVELOPMENT INSTITUTE.). [Dev. policy rev.]. **Added/Corp** Overseas Development Institute (London, England). Vol. 1, No. 1 (May 1983)-. Academic Scholarly Publication. English. Four times a year (Jan., Apr., July, Oct.). $172.00. Basil Blackwell Publishers Ltd., 108 Cowley Road, Oxford 0X4 1JF United Kingdom. **Tel** 011 44 1235 465500, FAX 011 44 1235 465556, telex 837022 OXBOOK G. **(Subscription address:** Blackwell Publishers / UK, 108 Cowley Road, Oxford OX4 1JF United Kingdom. **Tel** 011 44 1865 791100, FAX 011 44 1865 791347.**) ED** Sheila Page. **Bk Rev. Ad Acc.** ***Continues** ODI Review, 0078-7116.*
Desc: Provides a forum for new research and for the exchange of views and information between people directly concerned with development in business, government, and other organizations.
Ind/Abst Agrofor. Abstr. (1991-); Cot. Trop. Fibr. Abstr. Bibliogr.; For. Abstr.; Geogr. Abstr. Human Geogr.; Int. Dev. Abstr.; Int. Labour Doc.; Linguist. Lang. Behav. Abstr.; Middle East Abstr. Index; PAIS Int. Print (1991-); Rural Dev. Abstr.; Soc. Plann. Policy Dev. Abstr.; Sociol. Abstr.; World Agric. Econ. Rural Sociol. Abstr.

LC HC60 .I546 **ISSN** 1011-6370
DD 338.91/05 IT
CCC
DEVELOPMENT (ROME). (DEVELOPMENT.). [Development]. **Added/Corp** Society for International Development. **VFOAT** Developpement; Desarrollo; International Development Review; Revue du Developpement. (1978)-. Academic Scholarly Publication. English (French and Spanish). Four times a year. $60.00. Basil Blackwell Publishers Ltd., 108 Cowley Road, Oxford 0X4 1JF United Kingdom. **Tel** 011 44 1235 465500, FAX 011 44 1235 465556, telex 837022 OXBOOK G. **(Subscription address:** Blackwell Publishers / UK, 108 Cowley Road, Oxford OX4 1JF United Kingdom. **Tel** 011 44 1865 791100, FAX 011 44 1865 791347.**) ED** Maurice Williams. **Circ:** 10,000. available on microfilm and microfiche from University Microfilms International (UMI). Documents available. ***Continues** Revista del Desarrollo Internacional, 0095-7062; **Absorbed** Focus, Technical Cooperation, 0146-8502.*
Desc: Aims beyond the confines of the strictly professional community and intends to catalyse the debate among a broader public.
Ind/Abst ABC POL SCI; AgBiotech News Inf.; Calcium Calcif. Tissue Abstr.; Curr. Cit.; Genet. Abstr.; Hum. Rights Intern. Rep.; Int. Bibliogr. Sociol.; Int. Labour Doc.; LABORDOC; Linguist. Lang. Behav. Abstr.; PAIS Int. Print (1991-); Soc. Plann. Policy Dev. Abstr.; Sociol. Abstr.; U.S. Polit. Sci. Doc. (199?-).

LC HC900.A1 D48
DD 338.9 SA
DEVELOPMENT SOUTHERN AFRICA (SANDTON, SOUTH AFRICA). (DEVELOPMENT SOUTHERN AFRICA.). **Added/Corp** Development Bank of Southern Africa. Vol. 1, No. 1 (May 1984)-. Periodical. English. Four times a year. $30.00. Development Bank of Southern Africa, PO Box 1234, Half Way House, 1685 South Africa. **Tel** 011 313 3911, FAX 011 313 3086, 011 313 3072, telex 4-25546 SA. **ED** R.J.W. van der Kooy. Index available. cum. index. **Bk Rev. Ad Acc. Circ:** 1,800-2,000 (ctrl).
Desc: Promotes research and discussion as well as publishes papers, reviews, notes, on development issues relating to underdeveloped regions and communities in Southern Africa.
Ind/Abst For. Prod. Abstr. (1991-); For. Abstr.; Int. Bibliogr. Sociol.; Irr. Drain. Abstr.; Maize Abstr.; Nutr. Abstr. Rev., Ser. A, Hum. Exp.; Potato Abstr.; Rev. Agric. Entomol.; Rice Abstr.; Rural Dev. Abstr.; Soils Fert.; World Agric. Econ. Rural Sociol. Abstr.

LC HC241.2 .I632a
DD 382/.9142 IE
•**DEVELOPMENTS IN THE EUROPEAN UNION : REPORT COVERING THE PERIOD .... Added/Corp** Ireland. (1993)-. English. Two times a year. Government Publications, 4 5 Harcourt Road, Dublin 2 Ireland. **Tel** 011 353 1 6613111 ext.4005. ***Continues** Ireland. Developments in the European Communities Report.*

LC UA12 .D57
DD 355/.032 US
DISAM JOURNAL OF INTERNATIONAL SECURITY ASSISTANCE MANAGEMENT, THE. Added/Corp Defense Institute of Security Assistance Management (U.S.). **VFOAT** DISAM Journal. **VAT** Defense Institute of Security Assistance Management Journal of International Security Assistance Management. (19??)-. Periodical. English. Four times a year. $12.00. Treasurer of the United States, DISAM, DRP Building 125, 2335 7th Street, Wright-Patterson AFB OH 45433-5000. **Tel** (513)255-2994, (513)255-3669, FAX (513)255-4319. ***Continues** DISAM Newsletter.*
Ind/Abst Air Univ. Libr. Index Mil. Period.

Business and Economics —Economic Assistance and Development

ISSN 0580-6062
US
DISCUSSION PAPER - CENTER FOR RESEARCH ON ECONOMIC DEVELOPMENT, THE UNIVERSITY OF MICHIGAN. **Main/Corp** University of Michigan. Center for Research on Economic Development. No. 1 (Jan. 1968)-. Monographic series. English (French). Irregular. Price varies per volume. Center for Research on Economic Development, University of Michigan, Lorch Hall, Ann Arbor MI 48109-1220. **Tel** (313)764-9490, telex 432-0815. **ED** Robin Barlow and Anne Hudon. **Circ:** 200 (ctrl).
Desc: Preliminary reports on research done by senior research staff; often re-published later in academic journals and books.
Ind/Abst Leis., Rec., Tour. Abstr.; Rural Dev. Abstr.; World Agric. Econ. Rural Sociol. Abstr.

ISSN 1012-8069
US
DISCUSSION PAPER - IFC. (DISCUSSION PAPER / INTERNATIONAL FINANCE CORPORATION.). [Discuss. paper - IFC]. **Added/Corp** International Finance Corporation. No. 1 (1988)-. Monographic series. English. Price varies per volume. World Bank Publications, 1818 H Street Northwest, Washington DC 20043. **Tel** (202)473-1155, (202)473-1155, FAX (202)522-3224, telex WUI 64145 WORLDBANK.
Ind/Abst Geogr. Abstr. Human Geogr.; Int. Dev. Abstr.

LC HC59.69 .D57 ISSN 1012-6511
DD 330.9172/4 SZ
DISCUSSION PAPER / UNITED NATIONS RESEARCH INSTITUTE FOR SOCIAL DEVELOPMENT. **Added/Corp** United Nations Research Institute for Social Development. **VFOAT** DP. No. 1 (1987)-. Monographic series. English. Irregular (published 1-3 times per month). Price varies per volume. United Nations Publishers / Geneva, Palais des Nations, C115 Services Ventes, CH-1211 Geneva 10 Switzerland. **Tel** 011 41 22 7988400, FAX 011 41 22 7332673, telex 415465. **(Subscription address:** United Nations Publications / North America, Sales Section Room DC2 0853, New York NY 10017. **Tel** (212)963-8324.)
Ind/Abst For. Abstr.; Maize Abstr.; Rural Dev. Abstr.; Soils Fert.; World Agric. Econ. Rural Sociol. Abstr.

ISSN 0780-9212
FI
DOCUMENT OF MINISTRY FOR FOREIGN AFFAIRS, FINNISH INTERNATIONAL DEVELOPMENT AGENCY. [Doc. Minist. Foreign Aff., Fin. Int. Dev. Agency]. (1983)-. Monographic series. English. Irregular. Price varies per volume. **Continues** Document of Ministry for Foreign Affairs, Department for International Development Co-Operation, 0359-291X.

LC HC59.7 .D385
GW
DOK. **Main/Corp** Deutsche Stiftung fuer Internationale Entwicklung. **Added/Corp** Deutsche Stiftung fuer Internationale Entwicklung. (1973)-. Monographic series. English (German). Irregular. Price varies per volume. Deutsche Stiftung fuer Internationale EntwicklungEntwicklung, Postfach 30 04 62, 53184 Bonn Germany. **Continues** Dok (Deutsche Stiftung fuer Entwicklungslaender).

CN
EARTHBEAT. English. Ten times a year. 15.00Can$ Canada; 25.00Can$ US. Saskatchewan Council for International Cooperation, 2138 McIntyre Street, Regina Saskatchewan, S4P 2R7 Canada. **Tel** (306)757-4669, FAX (306)757-3226. **ED** Lori Latta. **Circ:** 1,000.

LC HF15 .E315
DD 309.2/2/05 FR
ECHANGES INTERNATIONAUX ET DEVELOPPEMENT. **Added/Corp** Toulouse. Universite. Institut d'Etudes Internationales et des Pays en Voie de Developpement. Association Echanges Internationaux et Developpement. No. 1 (Dec. 1971)-. Periodical. French. Four times a year. 100.00F. Toulouse Universite, Institut d'Etudes Internationales et des Pays en Voie de Developpement, Place Anatole France, 31070 Toulouse Cedex France. **ED** P. Vellas.

LC HC108.C7 F4a ISSN 0428-1276
US
ECONOMIC COMMENTARY (CLEVELAND). (ECONOMIC COMMENTARY.). [Econ. comment.]. **Main/Corp** Federal Reserve Bank of Cleveland. (1967)-. Periodical. English. Twenty-six times a year (1st and 15th of each month). Free on request. Federal Reserve Bank of Cleveland, PO Box 6387, Cleveland OH 44101. **Tel** (216)579-3079, FAX (216)579-2477. **ED** Robin Ratliff and Tess Ferg. Index Bound in First Issue. **Circ:** 15,000. Documents available from UMI Article Clearinghouse. **Continues** Federal Reserve Bank of Cleveland. Research Unit. Business Trends.
Desc: Research articles on current economic developments.
Ind/Abst ABI/INFORM Glob. Ed.; ABI/INFORM [Computer File] (Jan. 1983-); Acad. Search; Bus. Source Plus; Bus. Source; EP Collect.; Fed. Print Econ. Bank. Top.; Gen. BusinessFile (1992-); Homework Help.; MasterFile FullTEXT 1000; MasterFile FullTEXT 350; MasterFile FullTEXT 650; MasterFile FullTEXT (Jan. 1994-) [Full Txt.]; OCLC; Telebase; UMI ABI/Inform--Bus. Period. Ondisc [Full Txt.].

ISSN 1054-0903
DD 338 US
ECONOMIC DEVELOPMENT ABROAD. [Econ. dev. abroad]. (March 1986)-. Periodical. English. Six times a year. CUED, 1730 K Street NW, Washington DC 20006.

LC HC244 .J35 ISSN 0939-3625
GW
ECONOMIC SYSTEMS. **Added/Corp** Osteuropa-Institut Munchen. **VFOAT** Jahrbuch der Wirtschaft Osteuropas. Vol. 15, Issue 1 (Apr. 1991)-. Periodical. English (German). Four times a year. $199.00. Physica-Verlag GmbH & Company, Postfach 105280, D-69042 Heidelberg Germany. **Tel** 011 49 6221 487492, 011 49 6221 345186, FAX 011 49 6221 487177 und 487366, telex 461723 sphdb-d. **(Subscription address:** Springer-Verlag New York Inc. / North America, PO Box 2485, Journal Fulfillment, Secaucus NJ 07096. **Tel** (201)348-4033, (800)777-4643, FAX (201)348-4505.) **ED** R. Frensch. **Continues** Jahrbuch der Wirtschaft Osteuropas, 0449-5225.
Desc: Publishes theoretical contributions and empirical research related to the theory of economic systems in general and its application to the Soviet, East-European, and Chinese economies in particular. Special attention is devoted to the problem of transforming centrally planned economies into market economies.
Ind/Abst Econ. Lit. Index (199?-); J. Econ. Lit.; PAIS Int. Print (1991-?).

LC HC681.A1 E28 ISSN 1038-412X
DD 330.99 AT
ECONOMICS DIVISION WORKING PAPERS. EAST ASIA. **Added/Corp** Australian National University. Research School of Pacific Studies. Economics Division. **VFOAT** East Asia. (19??)-. Monographic series. English. Irregular. Economics Division Working Papers, Research School of Pacific Studies, Australian National University, Canberra ACT 0200 Australia.

ISSN 0824-409X
DD 330.97123/3 CN
EDMONTON REPORT ON ECONOMIC DEVELOPMENT, THE. [Edmont. rep. econ. dev.]. **Added/Corp** Edmonton Economic Development Authority. Vol. 18, No. 2 (Apr. 1983)-. Periodical. English. Four times a year. Free on request. The Edmonton Economic Development Authority, Edmonton Convention Centre, 9797 Jasper Avenue, Edmonton Alberta T5J 1N9 Canada. **Tel** (406)424-7870, FAX (403)426-0535. **ED** Ted Tennison. ctrl circ. **Continues** Edmonton Report on Business and Travel Development, 0707-7580.

BE
ENTREPRISE ET L'HOMME. See Ethics.

LC HD9502 ISSN 1355-770X
DD 333.79 UK
●**ENVIRONMENT AND DEVELOPMENT ECONOMICS.** See Environmental Issues.

LC HC245
DD 338.91 US
●**ENVIRONMENTALLY SUSTAINABLE DEVELOPMENT PROCEEDINGS SERIES.** (1994)-. Proceedings. English (French). Irregular. $47.95. World Bank Publications, 1818 H Street Northwest, Washington DC 20043. **Tel** (202)473-1155, (202)473-1155, FAX (202)522-3224, telex WUI 64145 WORLDBANK.
Desc: Discusses how World Bank policies affect ecologically sustainable development worldwide.

CL
ESTUDIOS E INFORMES DE LA CEPAL. **Added/Corp** United Nations. Economic Commission for Latin America. (1981)-. Monographic series. Spanish. Irregular. Price varies per volume. CEPAL / United Nations Economic Commission for Latin America / Chile, Publications Sales Section, CEPAL Casilla 179-D, Santiago Chile.
Ind/Abst World Agric. Econ. Rural Sociol. Abstr.

LC HC59.69 .E976 ISSN 0957-8811
Pr Rev. UK
EUROPEAN JOURNAL OF DEVELOPMENT RESEARCH, THE. **Added/Corp** European Association of Development Research and Training Institutes. Vol. 1, No. 1 (June 1989)-. Periodical. English. Two times a year. $95.00. Frank Cass & Company Ltd., Newbury House, 890-900 Eastern Avenue, Ilford Essex IG2 7HH United Kingdom. **Tel** 011 44 181 5998866, FAX 011 44 181 5990984, telex 897719. **ED** Helen O'Neill and David Lehmann. Index available. **Bk Rev. Ad Acc, Adv Mgr:** Anne Kidson.
Desc: Covers policy, theory and practice in all aspects of development studies for social scientists, governments and non-government organizations at national regional and international levels.
Ind/Abst Int. Dev. Abstr.; Int. Labour Doc.; LABORDOC.

LC HC245
DD 338.917241 NE
●**EUROPEAN PERSPECTIVES ON RURAL DEVELOPMENT.** (1994)-. Monographic series. English. Irregular. Van Gorcum & Company BV, PO Box 43, NL 9400 AA Assen Netherlands. **Tel** 011 31 5920 46846, FAX 011 31 5920 72064.

LC HG3881.5.W57 E93 ISSN 1019-4363
DD 332.1/532/05 US
EVALUATION RESULTS FOR ... WORLD BANK. See Business and Economics-Economic History, Conditions.

LC HC557.R8 B44A
DD 309.22/33/493067571 RW
EXECUTION DES PROJECTS FINANCES PAR LE PROGRAMME DE COOPERATION BELGO-RWANDAIS. **Main/Corp** Belgium. Ambassade (Rwanda). Section de Cooperation. **VFOAT** Uitvoering Van de Projecten Gefinancierd op Het Belgo-Rwandees Bijstandsprogramma. Multiple languages (Dutch and French).

LC HF1410 .E94 ISSN 0273-6314
DD 337/.05 US
EXECUTIVE INTELLIGENCE REVIEW. [Exec. intell. rev.]. **Added/Corp** New Solidarity International Press Service. **VFOAT** EIR. (19??)-. Periodical. English. Fifty times a year. $396.00. EIR News Service, PO Box 17390, Washington DC 20041. **Tel** (703)777-9451, FAX (703)771-9492. **ED** Nora Hamerman. **Bk Rev.** (Qty: 10). **Ad Acc, Adv Mgr:** Stanley Ezrol, **Tel** (703)777-9451. **Circ:** 10,000 (ctrl). **Continues** New Solidarity International Press Service Weekly News.
Desc: Covers international economics and counter terrorism.

ISSN 0721-2178
GW
E+Z, ENTWICKLUNG UND ZUSAMMENARBEIT. [E+Z, Entwickl. Zs. arb.]. **Added/Corp** Deutsche Stiftung fuer Entwicklungslander. **VFOAT** Entwicklung und Zusammenarbeit. (19??)-. Periodical. German. Twelve times a year. Societats-Druckerei GmbH, Frankenallee 71-81, 6000 Frankfurt/Main 1 Germany.
Ind/Abst PAIS Int. Print.

IT
FAO INVESTMENT CENTRE TECHNICAL PAPER. **VFOAT** F.A.O. Investment Centre Technical Paper; FAO Document Technique du Centre d'Investissement; FAO Documento Tecnico del Centro de Inversiones; Liang Nung Tsu Chih Tou Tzu Chung Hsin Chi Shu Wen Chi. **VAT** Food and Agriculture Organization of the United Nations Investment Centre Technical Paper. (1985)-. Monographic series. English (Arabic, Spanish, Chinese and French). Price varies per volume.

ISSN 1050-3242
DD 351 US
FEDERAL ASSISTANCE MONITOR. See Finance-Public Finance.

US
FEDERAL OUTLAYS IN TERRITORIES AND OTHER AREAS ADMINISTERED BY THE U.S. **Main/Corp** United States. Community Services Administration. 1975-. Periodical. English. One time a year. available on microfiche (Summary V). **Continues** Federal Outlays in Territories and other Areas Administered by the U.S.

LC HG3881 .F85 ISSN 0015-1947
DD 332.1/5/05 US
CODEN FNDVAM
FINANCE & DEVELOPMENT. See Business and Economics-Banks and Banking.

LC HG3881 ISSN 0430-473X
DD 332.1 US
FINANCES & DEVELOPPEMENT. See Business and Economics-Banks and Banking.

LC HG3891 .F56 ISSN 1020-0975
US
●**FINANCIAL FLOWS AND THE DEVELOPING COUNTRIES : A WORLD BANK QUARTERLY.** **Added/Corp** International Bank for Reconstruction and Development. Vol. 1, No. 1 (Nov. 1993)-. English. Four times a year. $150.00. World Bank Publications, 1818 H Street Northwest, Washington DC 20043. **Tel** (202)473-1155, (202)473-1155, FAX (202)522-3224, telex WUI 64145 WORLDBANK.

Business and Economics —Economic Assistance and Development

LC HC60.U4 F55
DD 354.1 US
FINANCIAL REPORT AND AUDITED FINANCIAL STATEMENTS FOR THE YEAR ENDED 31 DECEMBER ... AND REPORT OF THE BOARD OF AUDITORS. See Business and Economics-Accounting.

LC HJ2094.5 .C65B
DD 354.1/0422 LU
FINANCIAL REPORT - COMMISSION OF THE EUROPEAN COMMUNITIES. See Finance-Public Finance.

LC HJ8899 .F545
DD 336.3/435/091724 FR
FINANCING AND EXTERNAL DEBT OF DEVELOPING COUNTRIES. See Finance-Public Finance.

LC HC60 .N4755A ISSN 0110-0424
DD 338.91/172/40931 NZ
FLOW OF RESOURCES FROM NEW ZEALAND TO DEVELOPING COUNTRIES, THE. Main/Corp New Zealand. Ministry of Foreign Affairs. English. New Zealand Ministry of Foreign Affairs, Private Bag, Wellington 1 New Zealand. **Tel** 011 64 4 728877, FAX 011 64 4 729596, telex NZ 3441.

LC HV696.F6 F625 ISSN 0259-4064
DD 363.8/83/021 IT
FOOD AID IN FIGURES. Added/Corp Food and Agriculture Organization of the United Nations. **VFOAT** Aide Alimentaire en Chiffres. Vol. 1 (1983)-. English (French and Spanish). Irregular. Food Agriculture Organization (FAO) / Italy, GIPCI66 via Terme di Caracalla, 00100 Rome Italy. **Tel** 011 39 6 52252925, FAX 011 39 6 52253152. **(Subscription address:** Unipub, 4611 F Assembly Drive, Lanham MD 20706. **Tel** (800)274-4888, (301)459-7666.**)**

LC HD1491
DD 338.19 ET
FOOD AND AGRICULTURE IN AFRICA. Added/Corp Joint ECA/FAO Agriculture Division. United Nations. Economic Commission for Africa. Food and Agriculture Organization of the United Nations. **VFOAT** ECA/FAO Agriculture Division Staff Papers. No. 1 (1991)-. Periodical. English. Two times a year (Jul. and Dec.). Free on request. UN Economic Commission for Africa, PO Box 3001, Agricultural Division, Addis Ababa Ethiopia. **Tel** 011 251 1 510406.

LC TX341 .F8134 ISSN 0379-5721
DD 641.3/05 JA
NLM W1 FO428M CODEN FNBPDV
Pr Rev.
FOOD AND NUTRITION BULLETIN. See Nutrition and Dietetics.

LC TX341 .F662
DD 338 US
FOOD FIRST NEWS & VIEWS. Added/Corp Institute for Food and Development Policy (Oakland, Calif.). **VFOAT** Food First News and Views. Vol. 14, No. 47 (Summer 1992)-. Trade Publication. English. Four times a year. $30.00. Institute for Food and Development Policy, 398 60th Street, Oakland CA 94618. **Tel** (510)654-4400, FAX (510)654-4551. **ED** Kathleen McClung. **Bk Rev**, (Qty: 5-8). **Circ:** 9,000. **Continues** Food First News.
Desc: Hunger and Third World development.
Ind/Abst Hum. Rights Intern. Rep.

US
FOOD FOR PEACE PROGRAM ANNUAL REPORT. Added/Corp United States. President. (19??)-. English. One time a year.

LC HC60 .U472 ISSN 0362-4153
DD 338.91/172/4073 US
FOREIGN ASSISTANCE PROGRAM. Main/Corp United States. Agency for International Development. **VFOAT** Foreign Assistance Programs. (1963)-. English. One time a year. US Department of State Agency for International Development, Office of Public Affairs, Washington DC 20523. **Continues** United States. Agency for International Development. Report to the Congress on the Foreign Assistance Program.

NO
FORUM FOR DEVELOPMENT STUDIES. Added/Corp Norsk Utenrikspolitisk Institutt. Norsk Forening for Utviklingsforskning. **VFOAT** FORUM. No. 1 (1992)-. Periodical. English. Two times a year. $30.00. The Norwegian Institute of International Affairs (NUPI), PO Box 8159 Dep., N-0033 Oslo Norway. **Tel** 011 47 22 177050, FAX 011 47 22 177015. **ED** Olav Stokke. **Continues** Forum for Utviklingsstudier, 0332-8244.
Desc: Presents articles on Third World and development topics, including North-South and aid issues. It also brings discussions on topics within these fields and has a book review section.

LC HC241.2.A1 T37 ISSN 1021-2353
BE
●**FRONTIER-FREE EUROPE / COMMISSION OF THE EUROPEAN COMMUNITIES, DIRECTORATE-GENERAL FOR AUDIOVISUAL MEDIA, INFORMATION, COMMUNICATION AND CULTURE. Added/Corp** Commission of the European Communities. Directorate-General for Audiovisual, Information, Communication, and Culture. **VFOAT** Frontier Free Europe. (Jan. 1993)-. Newsletter. English. Twelve times a year. Free on request. Commission of the European Communities, Directorate of General Information, Avenue D Auderghem, 45 Breydel boulevard, B 1049 Brussels Belgium. **Tel** 011 32 2 2357639, telex 21877 COMEU B. **Continues** Target 92.
Desc: Brief news about developments throughout the European Community towards the creation of a single internal market.

LC HC60 .O73d
DD 338.91/091724/00212 FR
GEOGRAPHICAL DISTRIBUTION OF FINANCIAL FLOWS TO DEVELOPING COUNTRIES. Added/Corp Organisation for Economic Co-Operation and Development. **VFOAT** Repartition Geographique des Ressources Financieres Mises A la Disposition des Pays en Developpement. (1974)-. English (French). One time a year. $66.00. OECD Publications and Information Center, 2 rue Andre-Pascal, 75775 Paris Cedex 16 France. **Tel** 011 33 1 49104262, US:(202)785-6323, FAX 011 33 1 45248500, 011 33 1 45248176, telex 620 160 OCDE. **(Subscription address:** OECD Publications Center, 2001 L Street, Suite 700, Washington DC 20036. **Tel** (202)822-3873, (202)785-6323.**) Continues** Geographical Distribution of Financial Flows to Less Developed Countries.
Desc: The unique source of data on the origin, volume, purpose and terms of the aid and other resource flows channelled to over 130 developing countries.

LC HC60 .O73a
DD 338.91 US
GEOGRAPHICAL DISTRIBUTION OF FINANCIAL FLOWS TO LESS DEVELOPED COUNTRIES (COMMITMENTS). Main/Corp Organisation for Economic Co-operation and Development. Development Assistance Committee. **Added/Corp** Organisation for Economic Co-operation and Development. Development Assistance Committee. Repartition Geographique des Ressources Financieres Mises a la Disposition des Pays Moins Developpes (Engagements). **VFOAT** Repartition Geographique des Ressources Financieres Mises a la Disposition des Pays Moins Developpes (Engagements). (19??)-. Multiple languages (English and French). Three times a year. $32.00. OECD Publications and Information Center, 2 rue Andre-Pascal, 75775 Paris Cedex 16 France. **Tel** 011 33 1 49104262, US:(202)785-6323, FAX 011 33 1 45248500, 011 33 1 45248176, telex 620 160 OCDE. **(Subscription address:** OECD Publications Center, 2001 L Street, Suite 700, Washington DC 20036. **Tel** (202)822-3873, (202)785-6323.**)** available on microfiche; available on magnetic tape.
Desc: Presents data on aid and other resource flows to developing countries and territories from individual, bilateral, and multilateral sources.

ISSN 0882-3251
DD 338 US
GLOBAL DEVELOPMENT REPORT. [Glob. dev. rep.]. **Added/Corp** World Academy of Development and Cooperation. (1984)-. Newsletter. English. Four times a year. World Academy of Development and Cooperation, 4500 College Avenue, College Park MD 20740.

LC HC59.69 .G58 ISSN 1014-8906
DD 330.9172/4 US
GLOBAL ECONOMIC PROSPECTS AND THE DEVELOPING COUNTRIES. [Global econ. prospects dev. ctries.]. **Added/Corp** International Bank for Reconstruction and Development. (May 1991)-. English. One time a year. $10.95. World Bank Publications, 1818 H Street Northwest, Washington DC 20043. **Tel** (202)473-1155, (202)473-1155, FAX (202)522-3224, telex WUI 64145 WORLDBANK. **(Subscription address:** World Bank Publications, PO Box 7247-8619, Books Department, Philadelphia PA 19170. **)**

LC HC110.P63 G69 ISSN 0883-8690
DD 353.0082/025 US
GOVERNMENT ASSISTANCE ALMANAC. [Gov. assist. alm.]. (1986)-. English. One time a year (Mar.). $135.00. Omnigraphics Inc., 2500 Penobscot Building, 25th Floor, Detroit MI 48226. **Tel** (313)961-1340, (800)234-1340, FAX (313)961-1383. **ED** J. Robert Dumouchel. Index available. (bound in all issues.)
Desc: Describes all 1,013 domestic assistance programs available, both financial and non-financial. Contains 3,800 federal addresses and phone numbers. How-to-apply section included in introductory chapter.

LC HC59.8 .G73 ISSN 1056-649X
DD 361.7/632/025 US
GRANTS FOR FOREIGN AND INTERNATIONAL PROGRAMS. [Grants foreign int. prog.]. **Added/Corp** Foundation Center. **VFOAT** Foreign and International Programs. (1991)-. Periodical. English. One time a year. $70.00. Foundation Center, 79 Fifth Avenue, Department EN, New York NY 10003. **Tel** (212)620-4230, (800)424-9836, FAX (212)807-3677. **Continues** Grants for International and Foreign Programs.
Desc: Grants for broad purposes to institutions and organizations in foreign countries, to domestic recipients for international activities, development and relief, peace and security, arms control, policy research, human rights and conferences and research.

LC HC121 .J68 ISSN 0733-6608
DD 338.91/7308/0601 US
GRASSROOTS DEVELOPMENT. (GRASSROOTS DEVELOPMENT : JOURNAL OF THE INTER-AMERICAN FOUNDATION.). [Grassroots dev.]. Vol. 6, No. 1-. Periodical. English (Spanish and Portuguese). Four times a year. Free. Inter-American Foundation / Arlington, 1515 Wilson Boulevard, Arlington VA 22209. **Tel** (703)841-3821, FAX (703)841-0973, telex 247008 IAF. **ED** Kathryn Shaw. Index available. cum. index. **Bk Rev**. **Circ:** 14,000. available on microfilm from University Microfilms International (UMI). **Continues** Journal of the Inter-American Foundation, 0733-6640.
Desc: Reports how the poor in Latin America and the Caribbean organize and work to improve their lives. Its purpose is to explore how development assistance can contribute more effectively to self-help efforts.
Ind/Abst AGRICOLA [Select. Cov.]; Cot. Trop. Fibr. Abstr. Bibliogr.; Dairy Sci. Abstr.; Geogr. Abstr. Human Geogr.; Hisp. Am. Period. Index, HAPI; Int. Dev. Abstr.; Int. Labour Doc.; J. Ferrocement; J. Plan. Lit.; LABORDOC; Mat. Fact; PAIS Int. Print (1991-); Rural Dev. Abstr.

LC HC110.P63 U8 ISSN 0894-4202
DD 351.82/025/73 US
GUIDE TO STATE AND FEDERAL RESOURCES FOR ECONOMIC DEVELOPMENT, THE. See Finance-Public Finance.

LC HD5715.5.D44 G85
DD 331.25/92/0251724 AU
GUIDE TO TRAINING OPPORTUNITIES FOR INDUSTRIAL DEVELOPMENT. Added/Corp United Nations Industrial Development Organization. **VFOAT** Apercu des Moyens de Formation pour le Developpement Industriel; Repertorio de Oportunidades de Capacitacion para el Desarrollo Industrial. 1st Ed. (1972)-. English (French and Spanish). One time a year. Industrial Human Resources Development Branch, Department of Industrial Operations, UNIDO, POB 300, A-1400 Vienna Austria. **Tel** (0222)211310, FAX (0222)237280, telex 135612. **Circ:** 3,000 (ctrl).

LC HC60 .F486A ISSN 0782-7873
FI
HALLITUKSEN KEHITYSYHTEISTYOKERTOMUS EDUSKUNNALLE VUODELTA. Main/Corp Finland. Finnish. One time a year. Valtion Painatuskeskus, PO Box 516, SF 00101 Helsinki Finland. **Tel** 011 358 0 5660266, FAX 011 358 0 5660374.

ISSN 0990-915X
FR
UDC 327 : 338
HISTOIRES DE DEVELOPPEMENT LYON. (HISTOIRES DE DEVELOPPEMENT.). **VFOAT** HDD. Histoires de Developpement. (1988)-. Periodical. French. Four times a year. $20.78. CIEDEL, 30 rue Sainte Helene, 69002 Lyon France. **Tel** 011 33 1 78378324.
Ind/Abst LABORDOC.

ISSN 0740-1116
US
HUNGER NOTES. [Hunger notes]. **Added/Corp** World Hunger Education Service. Vol. 2, No. 8 (Jan. 1977)-. Periodical. English. Twelve times a year. $45.00. World Hunger Education Service, PO Box 29056, Washington DC 20017. **Tel** (202)269-1075. **ED** Patricia L Kutzner. **Bk Rev**. **Ad Acc**. **Circ:** 1,000 (ctrl). **Continues** Hunger Workshop Notes.
Desc: Focuses on the underlying causes of hunger and poverty in developing countries and in the United States. Seeks inter-disciplinary solutions, with guide to further information.
Ind/Abst AGRICOLA; Hum. Rights Intern. Rep.

Business and Economics —Economic Assistance and Development

LC HC59.69 .I37
DD 909/.09724
ISSN 0315-9981
CN
CODEN IDRIDJ
Pr Rev.
I D R C REPORTS. (THE IDRC REPORTS.).
[IDRC rep.]. **Added/Corp** International Development Research Centre (Canada). **VFOAT** I.D.R.C. Reports; C.R.D.I. Informe; CRDI Informe. **VAT** International Development Research Centre Reports. Vol. 1, No. 1 (March 1972)-. Academic Scholarly Publication. English (French). Four times a year. 16.01Can$. International Development Research Center, PO Box 117, Richmond Hill Ontario L4C 4X9 Canada. **Tel** (905)475-4145, FAX (416)940-3606. **ED** Eileen Conway. Index available. **Bk Rev. Circ:** 25,000 (ctrl). available via Internet (order@idrc.ca). Documents available from CASDDS, Documents on Demand. **Continued in part by** International Development Research Centre (Canada). CRDI, 0380-1438.
Desc: Covers third world development issues and particular scientific research made in third world countries.
Ind/Abst Agric. Eng. Abstr.; Biocont. News Inf. (1991-); Can. Index (?-?); Can. Period. Index (19??-);; Chem. Abstr. (1972-1983); Energy Res. Abstr. (1979-); Environ. Abstr.; Environ. Period. Bibliogr.; Food Sci. Technol. Abstr.; For. Abstr.; J. Ferrocement; Nutr. Abstr. Rev., Ser. B, Live Feeds and Feed.; Nutr. Abstr. Rev., Ser. A, Hum. Exp.; Rev. Agric. Entomol.; Rev. Med. Vet. Entomol.; SEA Abstr.; Trop. Dis. Bull.; Weed Abstr.

SZ
ICARA REPORT / INTERNATIONAL CONFERENCE ON ASSISTANCE TO REFUGEES IN AFRICA. Added/Corp International Conference on Assistance to Refugees in Africa. **VFOAT** I.C.A.R.A. Report. No. 1 (Jan. 28, 1981)-. Periodical. English (Arabic, Chinese, French, Spanish and Russian). Irregular. ICARA Secretariat, External Affairs Division, UNHCR Palais des Nations, CH-1211 Geneva 10 Switzerland. **Tel** 011 41 22 398458, telex 415740 HCR CH. ctrl circ.

DD 016.3389/1
ISSN 1180-0410
CN
IDRC ACQUIRES. See Business and Economics-Abstracting, Bibliographies and Statistics.

LC HC59.7 .B69
DD 330.9172/4
UK
Pr Rev.
IDS BULLETIN (UNIVERSITY OF SUSSEX. INSTITUTE OF DEVELOPMENT STUDIES : 1985). (IDS BULLETIN.). **Added/Corp** University of Sussex. Institute of Development Studies. Vol. 16, No. 3 (July 1985)-. Bulletin. English. Four times a year (Jan., Apr., Jul., Oct.). £40.00 surface mail, £52.00 airmail. Institute of Development Studies SS, University of Sussex, Brighton BN1 9RE United Kingdom. **Tel** 011 44 1273 606261, FAX 011 44 1273 621202, 011 44 1273 691647. **Circ:** 2,000 (ctrl). **Continues** Bulletin (University of Sussex. Institute of Development Studies), 0265-5012.
Desc: Publishes brief articles on themes of relevance to all involved in development problems - students, teachers, planners, fieldworkers and administrators of all kinds. Designed to fill the gap between the major professional journals, newspapers and periodicals.
Ind/Abst Appl. Soc. Sci. Index Abstr.; Geogr. Abstr. Human Geogr. (?-?); Int. Dev. Abstr.; Int. Labour Doc.; J. Ferrocement; LABORDOC; PAIS Int. Print (1991-); Rural Dev. Abstr.; Soc. Sci. Cit. Index [Full Cov.]

LC HC121 .I63a

US
IN REVIEW / INTER-AMERICAN FOUNDATION. Main/Corp Inter-American Foundation. (1991)-. English. Inter-American Foundation, Ballston Metro Center, 901 North Stuart Street, 10th Floor, Arlington VA 22203. **Continues** Annual Report.

LC Z7165.D44 I57b HC59.7
DD 016.332/532
US
INDEX OF PUBLICATIONS & GUIDE TO INFORMATION PRODUCTS AND SERVICES. See Business and Economics-Abstracting, Bibliographies and Statistics.

LC DT468
DD 969.05
ISSN 1030-1976
AT
INDIAN OCEAN POLICY PAPERS. [Indian Ocean policy pap.]. **Added/Corp** Australian National University. National Centre for Development Studies Australian National University. Research School of Pacific Studies. (1988)-. Monographic series. English. Irregular. Price varies per volume. Australian National University National Centre for Development Studies, Canberra ACT 0200 Australia. **Tel** 011 61 6 2494705, FAX 011 61 6 2572886. **ED** M Tait.
Ind/Abst Geogr. Abstr. Human Geogr.; Int. Dev. Abstr.; World Agric. Econ. Rural Sociol. Abstr.

LC K9 .N3674
DD 340
ISSN 1080-0727
US
Pr Rev.
●**INDIANA JOURNAL OF GLOBAL LEGAL STUDIES.** See Law-International Law.

AT
INDONESIA ASSESSMENT : PROCEEDINGS OF INDONESIA UPDATE CONFERENCE ... INDONESIA PROJECT, DEPARTMENT OF ECONOMICS AND DEPARTMENT OF POLITICAL AND SOCIAL CHANGE, RESEARCH SCHOOL OF PACIFIC STUDIES, A.N.U. See Business and Economics-International Economic Relations.

LC HV640 .I44
KO
INDOPOP NONCHONG. Added/Corp Taehan Choksipchasa. Indopop Yon'guso. **VFOAT** Korean Journal of Humanitarian Law. Vol. 1 (1977)-. Periodical. English (Korean). Taehan Choksipcha S A, 523-1 Majang-dong Songdong-ku, Seoul Korea.

LC JX1977 .A2 subser HD82
DD 300 S 338.9/005
ISSN 0197-7253
US
CEASED
INDUSTRY AND DEVELOPMENT (NEW YORK. ENGLISH EDITION). (INDUSTRY AND DEVELOPMENT.). [Ind. dev.]. **Added/Corp** United Nations Industrial Development Organization. (1978)-(1993). Government Publication. English. United Nations Publications, 2 United Nations Plaza, Room DC2 0853, Department 007C, New York NY 10017. **Tel** (212)963-8303, (800)253-9646. **Continues** Industrialization and Productivity.
Ind/Abst Asia.-Pac. Econ. Lit.; Contents Recent Econ. J.; Econ. Lit. Index (19??-); J. Econ. Lit.; Rural Dev. Abstr.; World Agric. Econ. Rural Sociol. Abstr.

LC HC601 .C584
DD 330.9/94 S 330.9/94
AT
INFORMATION PAPER - COMMITTEE FOR ECONOMIC DEVELOPMENT OF AUSTRALIA. Added/Corp Committee for Economic Development of Australia. (19??)-. Monographic series. English. Three times a year. Price varies per volume. Committee for Economic Development of Australia, 123 Lonsdale Street, GPO Box 2117T, Melbourne Victoria 3000 Australia. **Tel** 011 61 03 6623544, FAX 011 61 03 6637271. Index available. **Circ:** 2,000 (ctrl).

LC T2 .B87a
FR
INFORMATIONS ET DOCUMENTS - BCEOM. See Science and Technology.

ISSN 0271-1737
US
INFORME SOBRE EL DESARROLLO MUNDIAL. Added/Corp World Bank. (19??)-. Spanish. One time a year (July). $16.95. World Bank Publications, 1818 H Street Northwest, Washington DC 20043. **Tel** (202)473-1155, (202)473-1155, FAX (202)522-3224, telex WUI 64145 WORLDBANK. (**Subscription address:** World Bank Publications, PO Box 7247-8619, Books Department, Philadelphia PA 19170.)

LC HC125 .I545
AG
CEASED
INTEGRACION LATINOAMERICANA. Added/Corp Institute for Latin American Integration. (April 1976)-(1994). Spanish. Institution Integracion America, Latin Casilla de Correos 39, Sucursal 1, Buenos Aires 1401 Argentina. **Tel** (541)394-2059, FAX (541)394-2293, telex 21520 AR BIDBA. **ED** Clara de Ginzburg. cum. index. **Bk Rev. Circ:** 2,500. **Supersedes** Boletin de la Integracion; Revista de la Integracion; **Absorbed** Derecho de la Integracion; BILE, Boletin de Informacion Legal; BIEL : Boletin Sobre Inversiones y Empresas Latinoamericanas.
Desc: Sections include editorial, studies, commentaries and information on Latin American integration and developments.
Ind/Abst Geogr. Abstr. Human Geogr.; Hisp. Am. Period. Index, HAPI; Index Foreign Leg. Per.; Int. Dev. Abstr.; Int. Labour Doc.; LABORDOC; PAIS Int. Print; World Agric. Econ. Rural Sociol. Abstr.

ISSN 0738-1425
US
INTERNATIONAL DEVELOPMENT RESOURCE BOOKS. (INTERNATIONAL DEVELOPMENT RESOURCE BOOKS / PREPARED UNDER THE AUSPICES OF THE CENTER FOR ADVANCED STUDY OF INTERNATIONAL DEVELOPMENT, MICHIGAN STATE UNIVERSITY.). [Int. dev. resour. books]. **Added/Corp** Michigan State University. Center for Advanced Study of International Development. No. 1, (1984)-. Monographic series.

English. Irregular. Price varies per volume. Greenwood Press Inc., PO Box 5007, Westport CT 06881-5007. **Tel** (203)226-3571, FAX (203)222-1502. **ED** Pradip Ghosh.

DD 363
ISSN 1060-815X
US
INTERNATIONAL DRUG PREVENTION QUARTERLY OF THE NAE PROJECT, THE. (THE INTERNATIONAL DRUG PREVENTION QUARTERLY OF THE NAE PROJECT : A PUBLICATION OF DEVELOPMENT ASSOCIATES, INC., FOR THE U.S. AGENCY FOR INTERNATIONAL DEVELOPMENT (A.I.D.).). [Int. drug prev. q. NAE Proj.]. **VFOAT** International Drug Prevention Quarterly. Vol. 1, no. 1 (Fall 1991)-. Periodical. English. Four times a year. International Drug Prevention Quarterly, Development Associates Inc., 1730 North Lynn Street, Arlington VA 22209. **Continues** Asian Drug Prevention Quarterly, 1047-7764.

LC HD72 .I58
DD 338.9/005
II
INTERNATIONAL JOURNAL OF DEVELOPMENT PLANNING LITERATURE. Added/Corp Jan Tinbergen Institute of Development Planning. Vol. 1, No. 1 (Jan./March 1986)-. Periodical. English. Four times a year. $50.00. Jan Tinbergen Institute of Development Planning, PO Box 91, Rohtak 124001 India. (**Subscription address:** Prints India, 11 Darya Ganj, New Delhi 110002 India. **Tel** 011 91 11 3268645, FAX 011 91 11 3275542, telex 31-61087 PRIN-IN.)
Ind/Abst Rural Dev. Abstr.

NE
INTERNATIONALE SAMENWERKING. (198?)-. Government Publication. Dutch. Twelve times a year. The Hague Development Cooperation Information Department, Ministry of Foreign Affairs, PO Box 20061, 2500 EB Den Haag, The Netherlands. **Photos**.
Continues Aspecten van Internationale Samenwerking.

ISSN 0927-5770
NE
UDC 339.96 + 341.232
INZET AMSTERDAM. (INZET.). [Inzet Amst.]. (1992)-. Periodical. Dutch. Six times a year. Secretariaat Veldwerk, Keizersgracht 181, 1016 DR Amsterdam Netherlands. **Tel** 011 31 20 257212. **Formed by the union of** CON-Tekst (Wageningen), 0168-8421 **and** Veldwerk (Amsterdam), 0922-2782 KNV-Kortom (Amsterdam), 0922-355X NIO-Kroniek (Amsterdam), 0927-5657 Stand Van Zaken, 0927-5894.

LC HV580.G3 R42a
GW
JAHRBUCH - DEUTSCHES ROTES KREUZ. See Sociology-Social Services and Welfare.

US
JOINT FORUM FOR PHILIPPINE PROGRESS NEWS. (19??)-. English. One time a year. Free. Carnegie Council on Ethics and International Affairs, 170 East 64th Street, New York NY 10021. **Tel** (212)838-4120, FAX (212)752-2432, telex CRIAPAX NEW YORK. **ED** Christopher J Sigur. **Circ:** 3,000 (ctrl).
Desc: Reports on private sector investments of the US and Japan in the Philippines; progress of the Philippine Assistance Program and the efforts of the US and Japan to work cooperatively to promote growth and development in the Philippines.

LC HC60 .J62
DD 337/.09171/7
ISSN 0258-2384
AU
JOURNAL FUER ENTWICKLUNGSPOLITIK : JEP. Added/Corp Mattersburger Kreis fuer Entwicklungspolitik an den Osterreichischen Universitaten. **VFOAT** JEP. (1985)-. Periodical. English (German). Four times a year.
Ind/Abst Soc. Plann. Policy Dev. Abstr.

LC HC59.7 .J68
ISSN 1012-2591
CY
Pr Rev.
JOURNAL OF BUSINESS AND SOCIETY. Added/Corp Cyprus College. Vol. 1, No. 1 (Spring 1988)-. Periodical. English. Two times a year. $20.00. Cyprus College, PO Box 2006, Nicosia Cyprus. **Tel** 357 2 462258, FAX 357 2 462051, telex 4646 CYCOLEGE. **ED** Andreas G Orphanides, Ph.D. **Circ:** 1,500.

LC HC59.7 .J65
DD 338.91/172/4
ISSN 0022-037X
US
CODEN JDARB4
JOURNAL OF DEVELOPING AREAS, THE. [J. dev. areas]. **Added/Corp** Western Illinois University. Vol. 1 (Oct. 1966)-. Periodical. English. Four times a year. $35.00. Journal of Developing Areas, West Illinois University, 232 Morgan Hall, Macomb IL 61455. **Tel** (309)298-1108, FAX (309)298-2585. **ED** Nicholas C. Pano. Index available (bound in July issue). **Bk Rev.** (Qty: 80). **Ad Acc, Adv Mgr:** Joan Pano. **Circ:** 1,400 (ctrl). Documents available from UMI Article Clearinghouse, Documents on Demand, The Genuine Article.

Desc: Main interest focuses on political, economic, social, cultural, historical, and comparative studies of the third world and the development process.
Ind/Abst ABC POL SCI; ABI/INFORM Glob. Ed.; ABI/INFORM [Computer File] (July 1979-); Abstr. Anthropol.; Acad. Search; AgBiotech News Inf.; AGRICOLA [Select. Cov.]; Am. Hist. Life (1966-); Appl. Soc. Sci. Index Abstr.; Arts Humanit. Citation Index [Select. Cov.]; Asia.-Pac. Econ. Lit.; Bus. Index (1985-); Bus. Period. Index; Curr. Cit.; Curr. Contents Soc. Behav. Sci.; Econ. Lit. Index (19??-); Energy Inf. Abstr.; Environ. Abstr.; EP Collect.; Expand. Acad. Index (1992-); Gen. BusinessFile (1985-); Gen. Period. Index (1985-); Geogr. Abstr. Human Geogr.; Hisp. Am. Period. Index, HAPI; Health Saf. Sci. Abstr.; Homework Help.; Hum. Resour. Abstr.; INFO-SOUTH Abstr.; Int. Bibliogr. Sociol.; Int. Dev. Abstr.; Int. Exec.; Int. Labour Doc.; Int. Polit. Sci. Abstr.; J. Econ. Lit.; J. Plan. Lit.; LABORDOC; Leis., Rec., Tour. Abstr.; Mag. Search; MasterFile FullTEXT 1000; MasterFile FullTEXT 350; MasterFile FullTEXT 650; MasterFile FullTEXT (July 1993-); Middle East Abstr. Index; Newsp. Period. Abstr. (1992-); Nutr. Abstr. Rev., Ser. A, Hum. Exp.; OCLC; PAIS Int. Print (1991-); Pollut. Abstr. Indexes; Res. Alert [Full Cov.]; Rice Abstr.; Rural Dev. Abstr.; Sage Public Adm. Abstr.; Soc. Plann. Policy Dev. Abstr.; Soc. Sci. Cit. Index [Full Cov.]; Sociol. Abstr.; Soils Fert.; Telebase; Middle East J.; Trade Ind. Index (1981-); U.S. Polit. Sci. Doc. (July 1979-); Wilson Bus. Abstr.; Women Stud. Abstr.; World Agric. Econ. Rural Sociol. Abstr.

LC HD82 .J68
NP

JOURNAL OF DEVELOPMENT AND ADMINISTRATIVE STUDIES, THE. **Added/Corp** Centre for Economic Development and Administration. Vol. 1 (Aug. 1978)-. Periodical. English. Four times a year. Rs30.00 Nepal; $6.00 US. Centre for Economic Development and Administration, Publications and Information Services Division, Ceda Post Box No 797, Kirtipur Kathmandu Nepal. **ED** C. B. Khanal. **Ad Acc. Circ:** 1,000.
Desc: Economic, social, cultural, science, technology and current development data. Exchange of ideas, experiences and opinions on all aspects of development on Nepal.

LC HC59 .J633 **ISSN** 0085-2392
DD 338.9/005 US

JOURNAL OF DEVELOPMENT PLANNING. (JOURNAL OF DEVELOPMENT PLANNING / DEPARTMENT OF ECONOMIC AND SOCIAL AFFAIRS.). [J. dev. plann.]. **Added/Corp** United Nations. Dept. of International Economic and Social Affairs. United States. Centre for Development Planning, Projections, and Policies. United Nations. Dept. of Economic and Social Affairs. (1969)-. Government Publication. English. Irregular. $25.00. United Nations Publications, 2 United Nations Plaza, Room DC2 0853, Department 007C, New York NY 10017. **Tel** (212)963-8303, (800)253-9646.
Desc: Focuses on development problems in the North-South agenda that hamper the effective implementation of the international development strategy for the Third United Nations Development Decade.
Ind/Abst Int. Labour Doc.

LC HC10 .J58 **ISSN** 0022-0388
UK
CCC

Pr Rev.

JOURNAL OF DEVELOPMENT STUDIES, THE. [J. dev. stud.]. Vol. 1 (Oct. 1964)-. Periodical. English. Four times a year. $195.00. Frank Cass & Company Ltd., Newbury House, 890-900 Eastern Avenue, Ilford Essex IG2 7HH United Kingdom. **Tel** 011 44 181 5998866, FAX 011 44 181 5990984, telex 897719. **ED** David Booth, Charles Cooper, E. V. K. Fitzgerald, David Lehmann, and Karel Jansen. **Bk Rev. Ad Acc, Adv Mgr:** Anne Kidson. **Circ:** 2,000. available on microfilm and microfiche from University Microfilms International (UMI); available on CD-ROM; available on an online database from Information Access Company. Documents available from The Genuine Article, UMI Article Clearinghouse, BLDSC, FAXON Xpress, The UnCover Company, SWETS.
Desc: A major international forum for the discussion of the fundamental issues of development, interpreting the concept of development in its widest sense.
Ind/Abst ABC POL SCI; ABI/INFORM Glob. Ed.; ABI/INFORM [Computer File] (April 1972-Oct. 1972); Acad. Abstr.; Acad. Search; AGRICOLA; Am. Hist. Life (1968-); Appl. Soc. Sci. Index Abstr.; Asia.-Pac. Econ. Lit.; Br. Humanit. Index; Bus. ASAP (1992-) [Full Txt.]; Bus. Index (1985-); Contents Recent Econ. J.; Curr. Cit.; Curr. Contents Soc. Behav. Sci.; Curr. Lit. Sci. Sci.; Econ. Lit. Index; EP Collect.; Expand. Acad. Index (1984-); Gen. BusinessFile (1985-); Gen. Period. Index (1985-); Geogr. Abstr. Human Geogr.; Homework Help.; Hum. Resour. Abstr.; INFO-SOUTH Abstr.; Int. Bibliogr. Sociol.; Int. Dev. Abstr.; Int. Labour Doc.; Int. Polit. Sci. Abstr.; Irr. Drain. Abstr.; J. Econ. Lit.; J. Plan. Lit.; LABORDOC; Leis., Rec., Tour. Abstr.; Mag. Search; Maize Abstr.; MasterFile FullTEXT 1000; MasterFile FullTEXT 350; MasterFile FullTEXT 650; MasterFile FullTEXT (Jan. 1992-); Newsp. Period. Abstr. (1991-); OCLC; PAIS Int. Print (1991-); Pub. Lib. FullTEXT; Res. Alert [Full Cov.]; Rice Abstr.; Rural Dev. Abstr.; Sage Public Adm. Abstr. (?-?); Soc. Plann. Policy Dev. Abstr.; Soc. Sci. Source; Soc. Sci. Cit. Index [Full Cov.]; Soc. Sci. Index; Soc. Sci. Index Fulltext (Sept. 1988-) [Full Txt.]; Sociol. Abstr.; Telebase; Work Relat. Abstr.; World Agric. Econ. Rural Sociol. Abstr.

ISSN 0254-8372
KO

JOURNAL OF ECONOMIC DEVELOPMENT. [J. econ. dev.]. (July 1976)-. Periodical. English. Two times a year. $46.00. Department of Economics / Richmond, Heuksek Dong Dongjak-ku, Seoul 156 756 Korea. **Tel** 011 82 2 8102598.
Ind/Abst Econ. Lit. Index; J. Econ. Lit.; J. Plan. Lit.

LC HC431 .J69
DD 338.954/005 II

JOURNAL OF NATIONAL DEVELOPMENT. **Added/Corp** Centre for Studies of National Development (Meerut, India). **VFOAT** JND. Vol. 1, No. 1 (Summer 1988)-. Periodical. English. Two times a year. $35.00. Centre for Studies of National Development, Meerut India. **(Subscription address:** Prints India, 11 Darya Ganj, New Delhi 110002 India. **Tel** 011 91 11 3268645, FAX 011 91 11 3275542, telex 31-61087 PRIN-IN.**)**

LC HC440.5.A1 P4 **ISSN** 0047-2751
PK

JOURNAL OF RURAL DEVELOPMENT AND ADMINISTRATION. **Added/Corp** Pakistan Academy for Rural Development, Peshawar. Vol. 4 (1964)-. Periodical. English. Irregular. $20.00. Pakistan Academy of Rural Development, Academy Town Peshawar, Peshawar Pakistan. **Tel** 011 92 42 402967. ***Continues** Academy Quarterly.*
Ind/Abst Cot. Trop. Fibr. Abstr. Bibliogr.; Helminthol. Abstr.; Int. Bibliogr. Sociol.; Poult. Abstr.; Protozoolog. Abstr.; Rice Abstr.; Rural Dev. Abstr.; Sug. Indus. Abstr.; Wheat Barley Trit. Abstr.; World Agric. Econ. Rural Sociol. Abstr.

LC HC60 .K59A
JA

KOKUSAI KYORYOKU JIGYODAN NEMPO. **Main/Corp** Kokusai Kyoryoku Jigyodan. 1975-. Japanese (English, Spanish and French). One time a year. Kokusai Kyoryoku Jigyodan, c/o Shinjuku Mitsui Building, 1 Nishi Shinjuku 2-chome, Shinjuku-ku, Tokyo Japan. **Tel** 03-346-5311, telex J22271. **Circ:** 10,000.
Desc: Report of the Japan International Cooperation Agency.

II

KRISHI SAMEEKSHA. (19??)-. Government Publication. Hindi. Twelve times a year. Rs100.00. Ministry of Agriculture / Directorate of Economics and Statistics, A 2E 3 Kasturba Gandhi Marg Barracks, New Delhi 110 001 India.

ISSN 0715-3023
DD 333 CN

LAND AND HUMAN SETTLEMENTS. (LAND AND HUMAN SETTLEMENTS. OCCASIONAL PAPERS.). [Land hum. settl.]. **Added/Corp** University of British Columbia. Centre for Human Settlements. Vol. 1 (1982)-. Monographic series. English. Irregular. Price varies per volume. Centre for Human Settlements, University of British Columbia V6T 1W5 Canada. **Tel** (604)228-5254. **ED** H. Peter Oberlander. **Bk Rev. Circ:** 1,000.
Desc: Impact of urbanization upon developing countries and their systematic response within national policies and those recommended by UN Centre for Human Settlements.

US

LATIN AMERICA AND THE CARIBBEAN : SELECTED ECONOMIC AND SOCIAL DATA. **Added/Corp** United States. Agency for International Development. (July 1991)-. English. Two times a year. US International Development Cooperation Agency, Agency for International Development, Washington DC 20523.

LC HC59.7 .L328 **ISSN** 0257-7550
DD 330.9172/4 US

LEAST DEVELOPED COUNTRIES ... REPORT, THE. **Added/Corp** United Nations Conference on Trade and Development. Secretariat. (1984)-. English. One time a year. Price varies per voume. United Nations Publications, 2 United Nations Plaza, Room DC2 0853, Department 007C, New York NY 10017. **Tel** (212)963-8303, (800)253-9646.

LC HC60 .L466
DD 330.9172/4 BE

LIBERTE (BRUSSELS, BELGIUM). (LIBERTE.). **Added/Corp** Centre d'Aide au Developpement dans la Liberte et le Progres (Brussels, Belgium). (19??)-. Periodical. French. Four times a year. Centre d'Aide au Developpement dans la Liberte et le Progress, rue de Naples 39, 1050 Brussels Belgium. **ED** Charles Petitjean. **Bk Rev**, (Qty: 4). ctrl circ.

ISSN 0823-1729
DD 016.33891/05 CN

LISTE DES PERIODIQUES / CENTRE D'INFORMATION SUR LE DEVELOPPEMENT. [Liste period. - Cent. inf. dev.]. **Main/Corp** Canadian International Development Agency. Development Information Centre. **VFOAT** Periodicals List. 1982-. English (French, Spanish, Portuguese, German and Chinese). One time a year.

LC HC445.5.A1 M325
DD 338.09595 MY

MALAYSIA SHOWCASE. Vol. 1, No. 1 (1979)-. English (Malay). Tingkat 3 Bangunan Jaya, Jalan Haji Hussein, Kuala Lumpur 03-08 Malaysia.

LC HC445.5.A1 K33
DD 330.9595/005 MY

MALAYSIAN JOURNAL OF ECONOMIC STUDIES : JOURNAL OF THE MALAYSIAN ECONOMIC ASSOCIATION AND THE FACULTY OF ECONOMICS AND ADMINISTRATION, UNIVERSITY OF MALAYA. **Added/Corp** Persatuan Ekonomi Malaysia. Universiti Malaya. Fakulti Ekonomi dan Pentadbiran. Vol. 25, No. 1 (June 1988)-. Periodical. English. Two times a year. $20.00. Malaysian Economic Association, PO Box 1127, Jalan Pantai Baru, Kuala Lumpur Malaysia. ***Continues** Kajian Ekonomi Malaysia, 0126-5350.*

LC HD72 **ISSN** 0826-6433
DD 338.9171 CN

MANUSCRIPT REPORTS - INTERNATIONAL DEVELOPMENT RESEARCH CENTRE. (MANUSCRIPT REPORTS.). [Manuscr. rep. - Int. Dev. Res. Cent.]. **VFOAT** IDRC Manuscript Reports; International Development Research Centre Manuscript Reports. (1978)-. Monographic series. English. Irregular. International Development Research Center, PO Box 117, Richmond Hill Ontario L4C 4X9 Canada. **Tel** (905)475-4145, FAX (416)940-3606.
Ind/Abst Soyabean Abstr.

LC HC244 .S59582d
RU
CODEN MEKSEW

MEZHDUNARODNOE EKONOMICHESKOE SOTRUDNICHESTVO. **Added/Corp** Council for Mutual Economic Assistance. Secretariat. (1991)-. Periodical. Russian. Twelve times a year. Sovet Ekonomicheskoi Vzaimopomoshchi Sekretariat, Prospekt Kalinina 56, Moscow Russia. ***Continues** Ekonomicheskoe Sotrudnichestvo Stran-chlenov SEV.*

LC HC60 .C2876A
DD 338.91/172/4071 CN

MINUTES OF PROCEEDINGS AND EVIDENCE OF THE SUB-COMMITTEE ON INTERNATIONAL DEVELOPMENT OF THE STANDING COMMITTEE ON EXTERNAL AFFAIRS AND NATIONAL DEFENSE. **Main/Corp** Canada. Parliament. House of Commons. Sub-Committee on International Development. **VFOAT** Proces-Verbaux et Temoignages du Sous-Comite sur le Developpement International du Comite Permanent des Affaires Exterieures et de la Permanent des Affaires Exterieures et de la Defense Nationale. (July 22, 1975)-. Proceedings. English (French). Parliament Building, Queen's Park, Toronto Ontario M7A 1B6 Canada.

LC HC59.69 .M57
DD 909.09724 GW

MITTEILUNGEN (IFO-INSTITUT FUR WIRTSCHAFTSFORSCHUNG. ABTEILUNG ENTWICKLUNGSLANDER). (MITTEILUNGEN.). **Added/Corp** Ifo-Institut fur Wirtschaftsforschung. Abteilung Entwicklungslander. (1979)-. Periodical. German. One time a year. Free. IFO-Institut fuer Wirtschaftsforschung, Postfach 860460, D-81631 Munich Germany. **Tel** 011 49 89 92241, telex 5-22269. **Circ:** 350 (ctrl). ***Continues** Ifo-Institut fur Wirtschaftsforschung. Abteilung Entwicklungslander/ Afrikastudienstelle. Mitteilungen.*

LC HD83 .M56 **ISSN** 0302-3052
FR

MONDES EN DEVELOPPEMENT. [Mondes dev.]. **Added/Corp** Centre d'Etudes Internationales pour le Developpement. No. 1 (1973)-. Periodical. Multiple languages (English, French and Spanish). Four times a year. $170.00. Cecoeduc Philippart, Avenue Des Naides 11, B 1170 Brussels Belgium. **Tel** 011 32 2 6478994, FAX 011 32 2 6479274. **Bk Rev. Ad Acc, Adv Mgr:** M. Scohy, **Tel** same as publisher. **Circ:** 1,000.
Desc: Economy, policy, sociology, demography and statistics of developing countries.
Ind/Abst Geogr. Abstr. Human Geogr.; Int. Bibliogr.

Business and Economics —Economic Assistance and Development

Sociol.; Int. Dev. Abstr.; Int. Labour Doc.; Int. Polit. Sci. Abstr.; LABORDOC; PAIS Int. Print (1991-); Rural Dev. Abstr.; World Agric. Econ. Rural Sociol. Abstr.

ISSN 0253-6609
US

MONITORING AND EVALUATION CASE STUDIES SERIES. [Monit. eval. case stud. ser.]. No. 1 (1982)-. Monographic series. English. Irregular. Price varies per volume. World Bank Publications, 1818 H Street Northwest, Washington DC 20043. **Tel** (202)473-1155, (202)473-1155, FAX (202)522-3224, telex WUI 64145 WORLDBANK.

LC HC440.5A1 N37A
DD 330.9/549/105
PK

MONTHLY ECONOMIC REPORT - NATIONAL DEVELOPMENT FINANCE CORPORATION. ECONOMIC RESEARCH & PROJECT DIVISION. **Main/Corp** National Development Finance Corporation. Economic Research & Project Division. Vol. 1 (May 1975)-. Periodical. English. National Development Finance Corporation, MSC Building, Molvi Tamizuddin Khan Road, Karachi Pakistan.

LC HG3881.5.W57 W65b
DD 332
ISSN 0379-8674
US

MONTHLY OPERATIONAL SUMMARY. **Main/Corp** International Bank for Reconstruction and Development. **VFOAT** International Business Opportunities Service Monthly Operational summary; MOS. (198?)-. Periodical. English. Twelve times a year. $131.25 Maryland; $125.00 other. Johns Hopkins University Press, 2715 North Charles Street, Baltimore MD 21218-4319. **Tel** (410)516-6987, FAX (410)516-6968. **(Subscription address:** World Bank Publications, PO Box 7247-8619, Books Department, Philadelphia PA 19170. **)** *Continues* World Bank. Monthly Operational Summary, 0379-8674.

LC HD7293.A1 N238A
DD 350/.865/02573
ISSN 0363-6453
US

NAHRO ROSTER. *See* Housing and Urban Development.

LC HV1 .N36a
DD 362.8
ISSN 0196-9420
US

NEWSLETTER - NATIONAL COUNCIL FOR INTERNATIONAL VISITORS. [Newsl. - Natl. Counc. Int. Visit.]. **Main/Corp** National Council for International Visitors. Vol. 23, No. 4 (Oct. 1979)-. Newsletter. English. Four times a year. Free. National Council for International Visitors, 1420 K Street N.W., Suite 800, Washington DC 20005-2401. **Tel** (202)842-1414, FAX (202)289-4625. **ED** Claire P. Burke. **Bk Rev. Circ:** 8,500. *Continues* Coserv Across the U.S.A.

LC HC60 .N64B
NO

NORGES SAMARBEID MED UTVIKLINGSLANDENE. Main/Corp Norway. Direktoratet for Utviklingshjelp. Norwegian. One time a year. Direktoratet for Utviklingslandene, Bods 8142 Olso-Dep 1, Oslo Norway.

LC HC60 .N64C
NO

NORWAY'S ASSISTANCE TO DEVELOPING COUNTRIES. Main/Corp Norway. Direktoratet for Utviklingshjelp. English. One time a year. Norwegian Agency for International Development, PO Box 8034, 0030 Oslo 1 Norway. **Tel** FAX 011 47 2 314402.

ISSN 0304-3398
FR

OBSERVATEUR DE L'OCDE, L'. [Obs. OCDE]. **Added/Corp** Organization for Economic Co-Operation and Development. (1962)-. Periodical. French. Six times a year. $30.00. OECD Publications and Information Center, 2 rue Andre-Pascal, 75775 Paris Cedex 16 France. **Tel** 011 33 1 49104262, US:(202)785-6323, FAX 011 33 1 45248500, 011 33 1 45248176, telex 620 160 OCDE. **(Subscription address:** OECD Publications Center, 2001 L Street, Suite 700, Washington DC 20036. **Tel** (202)822-3873, (202)785-6323.**)** **Desc:** Includes articles on economic affairs, energy, social affairs, the environment, multinational enterprises, science and technology, financial markets, and development cooperation.
Ind/Abst Int. Labour Doc.; LABORDOC; Repere (1983-).

LC HD72 .O37
DD 338.9/005
Pr Rev.
ISSN 1010-9935
TU

ODTU GELISME DERGISI. (ODTU GELISME DERGISI / METU STUDIES IN DEVELOPMENT.). [ODTU gelis. derg.]. **Added/Corp** Orta Dogu Teknik Universitesi (Ankara, Turkey). Iktisadi ve Idari Bilimler Fakultesi. Orta Dogu Teknik Universitesi (Ankara, Turkey). Idari Ilimler Fakultesi. **VFOAT** METU Studies in Development; Gelisme Dergisi. (1980)-. Periodical. English (Turkish). Four times a year. $40.00. Middle East Technical University, Faculty of Economic and Administrative Sciences, Ankara 06531 Turkey. **Tel** 011 91 41 2101000 ext. 2006. *Continues* Gelisme Dergisi, 1010-9927.
Ind/Abst Math. Rev.; Zentralbl. Math. Ihre Grenzgeb.

FR

OECD DEVELOPMENT COOPERATION REVIEW. (19??)-. English. One time a year. $32.00. OECD Publications and Information Center, 2 rue Andre-Pascal, 75775 Paris Cedex 16 France. **Tel** 011 33 1 49104262, US:(202)785-6323, FAX 011 33 1 45248500, 011 33 1 45248176, telex 620 160 OCDE. **(Subscription address:** OECD Publications Center, 2001 L Street, Suite 700, Washington DC 20036. **Tel** (202)822-3873, (202)785-6323.**)** **Desc:** Annual review of member countries foreign aid programs. Includes statistical information.

LC HC60 .S84
SW

●**OM VARLDEN. Added/Corp** Sweden. Styrelsen for Internationell Utveckling. (1995)-. Periodical. Swedish. Eight times a year. Progek Prospar, Box 31003, S 400-32 Goteborg Sweden. **Tel** 011 46 31 243425. *Continues* SIDA Rapport, 0282-6011.

ISSN 0713-7753
CN

DD 331.1/05
ONE SKY REPORT. [One sky rep.]. **Added/Corp** One Sky Collective. One-Sky Saskatchewan Cross-Cultural Centre. (Nov. 1980)-. Periodical. English. Four times a year (Winter, Spring, Summer, Fall). 28.01Can$. Saskatchewan One Sky Cross Cultural Centre, 136 Avenue F S, Saskatoon Saskatchewan S7M 1S8 Canada. **Tel** (306)652-1571, FAX (306)652-8377. **ED** Bill Robb, Leeanne Hurlburt, Ursula Thoma. **Ad Acc. Circ:** 350.
Desc: Issues of Canadian and international development. Focus of specific Third World countries, native people, women and development.

ISSN 0472-3724
US

ONU CRONICA MENSUAL. *See* Political Science-International Relations.

UK

OVERSEAS DEVELOPMENT. Added/Corp Great Britain. Overseas Development Administration. Great Britain. Ministry of Overseas Development. No. 1 (Nov. 1966)-. Newspaper. English. Irregular. Free on request. Overseas Development Administration / London, Eland House, Stag Place, London SW1 United Kingdom. **ED** David Harris. **Bk Rev. Circ:** 20,000.
Desc: News and illustrated features on Britain's aid program to the Third World, including articles of scientific interest, book reviews and news about voluntary agencies.

ISSN 1031-5969
AT

PACIFECON SURVEY OF DEVELOPMENT ACTIVITY IN NEW ZEALAND. (1984)-. English. Seventeen times a year (Every three weeks). 1050.00Aus$. Pacific Economics Pty. Ltd., PO Box A1450, Sydney New South Wales 2000 Australia. **Tel** 011 61 2 2679882, FAX 011 61 2 2641760.

US

PADF IN ACTION. Main/Corp Pan American Development Foundation. **VFOAT** Action. (19??)-. English (Spanish). One time a year. Pan American Development Foundation, 1889 F Street Northwest, Washington DC 20006. **Tel** (202)789-3000, telex 64128. **ED** Camille Grosdidier.
Desc: Combats poverty in Latin America/Caribbean through vocational training, loans for small businesses, health care, forestry, and agricultural projects. Provides emergency disaster relief and reconstruction assistance.

LC HC440.5 .P27
Pr Rev.
ISSN 0030-9729
PK

PAKISTAN DEVELOPMENT REVIEW. [Pak. dev. rev.]. **Added/Corp** Pakistan Institute of Development Economics. Institute of Development Economics (Pakistan). Vol. 1 (Summer 1961)-. Periodical. English. Four times a year. $100.00. Pakistan Institute of Development Economics, University Campus, PO Box 1091, 44000 Islamabad Pakistan. **Tel** 011 92 51 812440, FAX 011 92 51 811186, telex 5602 PIDE PK. **ED** Syed Nawab Haider Naqvi. Index available. **Bk Rev. Circ:** 1,500. *Supersedes* Economic Digest.
Desc: Carry out fundamental research on development economics in general and on Pakistan's economic problems in particular.
Ind/Abst Econ. Lit. Index; Geogr. Abstr. Human Geogr.; Int. Bibliogr. Sociol.; Int. Dev. Abstr.; Int. Labour Doc.; J. Econ. Lit.; LABORDOC; Popul. Index; Rice Abstr.; Rural Dev. Abstr.; Middle East J.; World Agric. Econ. Rural Sociol. Abstr.

LC HC60.5 .P43
DD 361.2/6/05
ISSN 0884-9196
US

PEACE CORPS TIMES. [Peace Corps times]. Vol. 1, No. 1 (March 1978)-. Periodical. English. Four times a year. Free on request. Peace Corps, Washington DC 20525. **Tel** (202)606-3010, FAX (202)606-3110. **Circ:** 17,500 (ctrl).
Desc: General and technical material published for Peace Corps volunteers serving worldwide.

FR

PERSPECTIVES. French (English and Spanish). Four times a year. 100.00F. UNESCO / France, 31 rue Francois Bonvin, 75732 Paris Cedex 15 France. **Tel** 011 33 1 45684564, 011 33 1 45684565, FAX 011 33 1 45669270, telex 204461 Paris.

LC HC391 .P48
DD 330/338.9469
ISSN 0870-3043
PO

PLANEAMENTO (LISBOA). (PLANEAMENTO.). [Planeamento]. **Added/Corp** Portugal. Departamento Central de Planeamento. Vol. 1, No. 1 (June 1978)-. Periodical. Portuguese (summaries and/or abstracts in English). Three times a year. Index Available in first issue of next volume--attached. *Continues* Planeamento e Integracao Economica.
Ind/Abst LABORDOC.

ISSN 0926-1524
NE

UDC 330.5 :339.3
POVERTY AND DEVELOPMENT. [Poverty dev.]. (1991)-. Monographic series. English. Irregular. Price varies per volume. The Hague Development Cooperation Information Department, Ministry of Foreign Affairs, PO Box 20061, 2500 EB Den Haag, The Netherlands. **ED** Laetitia van Drunen and Fred van der Kraaij.

ISSN 1014-9783
US

POVERTY AND SOCIAL POLICY PAPER. Added/Corp International Bank for Reconstruction and Development. **VFOAT** Poverty and Social Policy Paper Series. (1992)-. Monographic series. English. Price varies per volume. World Bank Publications, 1818 H Street Northwest, Washington DC 20043. **Tel** (202)473-1155, (202)473-1155, FAX (202)522-3224, telex WUI 64145 WORLDBANK.

ISSN 0738-9906
US
CCC

PREDICASTS' BASEBOOK. [Predicasts' basebook]. **Added/Corp** Predicasts, Inc. **VFOAT** Basebook. (1974)-. English. One time a year. $700.00. Predicasts Inc., A Ziff Communications Company, 11001 Cedar Avenue, Cleveland OH 44106. **Tel** (800)321-6388, (216)795-3000, FAX (216)229-9944, telex 985 604. **(Subscription address:** Information Access Company, PO Box 61000, Department 1851, San Francisco CA 94161. **Tel** (800)321-6388.**)** *Continues* Predicasts, Inc. Basebook.
Desc: Provides historical data on United States business and economic activities; more than 26,000 statistical time series in each issue.

DD 330
ISSN 0588-7194
US

PROBLEMS OF UNITED STATES ECONOMIC DEVELOPMENT. Main/Corp Committee for Economic Development. Vol. 1 (1958)-. English. Committee for Economic Development, 477 Madison Avenue, New York NY 10022. **Tel** (212)688-2063.

LC HC59.69 .W66a
DD 330.9172/4
ISSN 1014-7268
US

PROCEEDINGS OF THE WORLD BANK ANNUAL CONFERENCE ON DEVELOPMENT ECONOMICS. [Proc. World Bank Annu. Conf. Dev. Econ.]. **Added/Corp** International Bank for Reconstruction and Development. (1989)-. Proceedings. English. $21.45. World Bank Publications, 1818 H Street Northwest, Washington DC 20043. **Tel** (202)473-1155, (202)473-1155, FAX (202)522-3224, telex WUI 64145 WORLDBANK.

NG

PROGRAMME DES INVESTISSEMENTS DE L'ETAT ... ET BUDGET D'INVESTISSEMENT ... . *See* Finance-Public Finance.

ISSN 1171-2031
NZ

PROGRAMME PROFILES. Main/Corp New Zealand Official Development Assistance. **Added/Corp** New Zealand. Ministry of External Relations and Trade. Development Cooperation Division. **VFOAT** NZ ODA Programme Profiles. (1992)-. Government Publication. English. One time a year. Free. Ministry of Foreign Affairs and Trade / New Zealand, Development Cooperation Division, Private Bag 18 901, Wellington 1 New Zealand. **Tel** 011 64 4 4728877, FAX 011 64 4 4728571. **ED** B. Hallum. *Continues* New Zealand Bilateral Assistance Programme. Programme Profiles.

LC R722 .A24
DD 362.1/0425 362
ISSN 0749-3789
US

PROJECT CONCERN INTERNATIONAL ... ANNUAL REPORT. [Proj. Concern Int. annu. rep.]. **Main/Corp** Project Concern International (Organization). (19??)-. English. One time a year. Project

Business and Economics —Economic Assistance and Development

Concern International, PO Box 85323, San Diego CA 92138. **Tel** (619)279-9690. **Continues** Project Concern, Inc. (U.S.). Project Concern's Annual Report, 0749-3770.

LC HD4420.8 .P82   **ISSN** 0351-3564
DD 351.009/2/05   US
Pr Rev.
PUBLIC ENTERPRISE / INTERNATIONAL CENTER FOR PUBLIC ENTERPRISES IN DEVELOPING COUNTRIES. **Added/Corp** International Center for Public Enterprises in Developing Countries. **VFOAT** PE Journal. Vol. 1, No. 1 (1980)-. Periodical. English. Four times a year (Apr., Jun., Sept., Dec.). $60.00. Kumarian Press Inc., 630 Oakwood Avenue, Suite 119, West Hartford CT 06110. **Tel** (203)953-0214, FAX (203)953-8579. **ED** Edo Pirkmajer (Editor's address: Titova 104, 61109 Ljubljana, PO Box 92, Yugoslavia; telephone: 38 61 182 331). Index available (free on request). cum. index. **Bk Rev.** ctrl circ.
Desc: Discusses the role of the public sector in developing countries.
Ind/Abst Soc. Plann. Policy Dev. Abstr.

    ISSN 0706-6937
DD 909/.09/724082   CN
RAFIKI. (March 1978)-. Periodical. English. Irregular. $5.00. Toronto Miles For Millions, PO Box One Million Station A, Toronto Ontario M5W 1S1.

LC HC60 .C24
DD 338.944   FR
RAPPORT ANNUEL - CAISSE CENTRALE DE COOPERATION ECONOMIQUE. **Main/Corp** Caisse Centrale de Cooperation Economique (France). French. One time a year. Caisse Centrale de Cooperation Economique, Cite Du Retigo, 35-37 rue Boissy D'Anglas, 75379 Paris Cedex 08 France. **Tel** 1 42 66 93 66, telex 21632 F. **Continues** Caisse Centrale de Cooperation Economique. Rapport d'Activite.

    ISSN 0271-1710
    US
RAPPORT SUR LE DEVELOPPEMENT DANS LE MONDE. **Added/Corp** World Bank. (19??)-. French. One time a year. 20.45. World Bank Publications, 1818 H Street Northwest, Washington DC 20043. **Tel** (202)473-1155, (202)473-1155, FAX (202)522-3224, telex WUI 64145 WORLDBANK.

LC HD72 .R42   **ISSN** 0352-8553
    CI
RAZVOJ, DEVELOPMENT INTERNATIONAL. **Added/Corp** Institut za Zemlje u Razvoju (Zagreb, Croatia) Institut za Razvoji Meunarodne Odnose (Zagreb, Croatia). **VFOAT** Development International. Vol. 1, No. 1 (Jan.-June 1986)-. Periodical. Slavic (English). Two times a year. $65.00. Institute of Development & International Relations, PO Box 303, 41000 Zagreb Croatia. **Tel** 011 38 41 444522.
Ind/Abst LABORDOC; Soc. Plann. Policy Dev. Abstr.

LC HD72   **ISSN** 1020-3060
DD 338.9   JA
●**REGIONAL DEVELOPMENT STUDIES :**
RDS. **Added/Corp** United Nations Centre for Regional Development. **VFOAT** RDS. Vol. 1 (Winter 1994/95)-. Academic Scholarly Publication. English. One time a year. United Nations Centre for Regional Development, Nagono 1-47-1 Nakamura-ku, Nagoya 50 Japan. **Tel** 011 52 561 9377, FAX 011 52 5619375.

LC HB9 .R33   **ISSN** 0166-0462
DD 330/.01/51   NE
    CCC
    CODEN RGUEA3
Pr Rev.
REGIONAL SCIENCE AND URBAN ECONOMICS. See Housing and Urban Development.

LC HD1 .R43   **ISSN** 0097-1197
DD 309.2/5/05   US
REGIONAL SCIENCE PERSPECTIVES. [Reg. sci. perspect.]. **Added/Corp** Mid-Continent Regional Science Association. Kansas State University of Agriculture and Applied Science. Dept. of Economics. Vol. 1 (1971)-. English. Two times a year. $45.00. University of Nebraska / Bureau of Business Research, 200 College Business Administration Building, Lincoln NE 68588-0407. **Tel** (402)472-2334, FAX (402)472-3878. **Circ:** 500.
Ind/Abst Econ. Lit. Index (19??-); Geogr. Abstr. Human Geogr.; J. Econ. Lit.

LC RA390.U5 A65a   **ISSN** 0503-485X
DD 353.008/4   US
NLM W2 A A25R
REPORT ON THE HEALTH, POPULATION AND NUTRITION ACTIVITIES OF THE AGENCY FOR INTERNATIONAL DEVELOPMENT, DEPARTMENT OF STATE. (REPORT ON THE HEALTH, POPULATION AND NUTRITION ACTIVITIES.). **Main/Corp** United States. Agency for International Development. (19??)-. English.

LC HD82 .R4   **ISSN** 0194-3960
DD 331.1/1/05   US
NLM W1 RE227FT
RESEARCH IN HUMAN CAPITAL AND DEVELOPMENT. [Res. hum. cap. dev.]. Vol. 1 (1979)-. Monographic series. English. Irregular. $73.25. JAI Press Inc., 55 Old Post Road, Suite 2, PO Box 1678, Greenwich CT 06836-1678. **Tel** (203)661-7602, FAX (203)661-0792. **ED** Ismail Sirageldin.
Ind/Abst Int. Labour Doc.

    SZ
Pr Rev.
REVUE INTERNATIONALE DE LA CROIX-ROUGE. (Jan. 15, 1919)-. Periodical. French. Six times a year. 30.00F. International Committee of the Red Cross, 19 Avenue de la Paix, CH 1202 Geneva Switzerland. **Tel** 011 41 22 7346001. Index available. **Bk Rev,** (Qty: 12/yr). **Circ:** 8000 (ctrl).
Desc: Red Cross principles, humanitarian law in today's world, ICRC activities and subjects of interest to the Red Cross such as environment.

LC HC107.R4 A15
DD 353.9/745/0082   US
RHODE ISLAND DEPARTMENT OF ECONOMIC DEVELOPMENT ANNUAL REPORT. **Main/Corp** Rhode Island. Department of Economic Development. English. One time a year. Rhode Island Department of Economic Development, 7 Jackson Walkway, Providence RI 02903. **Tel** (401)277-2601 ext. 114, FAX (401)277-2102. **Continues** Rhode Island. Development Council. Report.

LC HC60 .S36
DD 338.91/494/017240212   SZ
SCHWEIZERISCHE HILFE FUR ENTWICKLUNGSLANDER / PUBLIE PAR SWISSAID. **VFOAT** Aide Suisse aux pays en Voie de Developpement. (1961)-. French (German). One time a year. 9.00F Switzerland; $5.00 US. Swissaid, Jubilaumsstrasse 60, 3000 Bern 6 Switzerland. **Tel** 011 41 31 449555, telex 912453 SWD CH.
Desc: Statistic containing the public and private foreign beliefs.

    ISSN 1014-739X
DD 960   US
SDA WORKING PAPER SERIES. (SOCIAL DIMENSIONS OF ADJUSTMENT IN SUB-SAHARAN AFRICA.). [SDA working pap. ser.]. **Added/Corp** International Bank for Reconstruction and Development. (1990)-. Monographic series. English. Price varies per volume. World Bank Publications, 1818 H Street Northwest, Washington DC 20043. **Tel** (202)473-1155, (202)473-1155, FAX (202)522-3224, telex WUI 64145 WORLDBANK.
Ind/Abst Int. Dev. Abstr.

    ISSN 0194-4495
    US
Pr Rev.
SEEDS (DECATUR, GA.). (SEEDS.). [Seeds]. **Added/Corp** Oakhurst Baptist Church (Decatur, Ga.). (1977)-. Periodical. English. Four times a year. $40.00. Seeds, PO Box 6170, Waco TX 76706. **Tel** (817)775-7745. **ED** Katherine Cook. **Bk Rev,** (Qty: 15-20). **Ad Acc, Adv Mgr:** Susan Hansen, **Tel** (817)755-7745. **Circ:** 3,000.
Desc: Informs Christian people about the realities of hunger and poverty, and offers a variety of positive ways to respond to the needs of the poor.

    SZ
SERIE DE INFORMES TECNICOS DE LA OMS. (19??)-. Spanish (French, Spanish, Arabic, Chinese and Russian). Irregular (approximately 15 per year). 132.00F. World Health Organization, Distribution and Sales, 20 Avenue Appia, CH-1211 Geneva 27 Switzerland. **Tel** 011 41 22 7912476, FAX 011 41 22 7914857.
Desc: Reports designed to advise scientific and medical communities on ways to tackle selected health or medical problems.

    US
SHIFT IN THE WIND : THE HUNGER PROJECT NEWSPAPER : A PROGRESS REPORT ON THE END OF HUNGER AND STARVATION, A. **VFOAT** Hunger Project Newspaper. No. 1 (May 1978)-. Periodical. English. Four times a year. Free with membership. Hunger Project, 1388 Sutter Street, San Francisco CA 94103. **Tel** (415)928-8700. **ED** Ted Howard. **Circ:** 2,000,000.
Desc: World's largest-circulation publication on hunger. Distributed to Hunger Project participants throughout the world, and to VIP's in media and diplomatic and academic communities.

LC HC60 .S84   **ISSN** 0282-6011
    SW
    TITLE CHANGE
SIDA RAPPORT. **Added/Corp** Sweden. Styrelsen for Internationell Utveckling. (1985)-(1994). Periodical. Swedish. Ord and Bild, Box 2390, 403 16 Goteborg Sweden. **Tel** 011 46 31 7741740, FAX 011 46 31 7742018. **ED** Johan Oberg. Index available. cum. index. **Bk Rev.** **Ad Acc.** **Circ:** 2,500 (ctrl). **Continues** Rapport Fran SIDA. **Continued by** Om Varlden.
Desc: Published by the Swedish International Development Authority as an independent journal for analysis and debate on aid and development. It also contains feature writing on the Third World.

LC HC125 .U588a   **ISSN** 0091-6234
DD 309.2/233/7308   US
SOCIAL DEVELOPMENT ACTIVITIES IN LATIN AMERICA PROMOTED BY THE INTER-AMERICAN FOUNDATION. **Main/Corp** United States. General Accounting Office. (19??)-. English. US General Accounting Office / District of Columbia, 441 G Street Northwest, Room 4528, Washington DC 20548. **Tel** (202)275-2812.

LC HC59.69 .S63   **ISSN** 1012-8026
DD 306/.09172/4   US
SOCIAL INDICATORS OF DEVELOPMENT. [Soc. indic. dev.]. **Added/Corp** International Bank for Reconstruction and Development. Socio-Economic Data Division. **VFOAT** SID. (19??)-. English. One time a year (October). $26.95. World Bank Publications, 1818 H Street Northwest, Washington DC 20043. **Tel** (202)473-1155, (202)473-1155, FAX (202)522-3224, telex WUI 64145 WORLDBANK.
Desc: Information on economic indicators and social indicators.

LC HD82 .S5865   **ISSN** 0038-0121
DD 309.2/05   US
    CCC
Pr Rev.
SOCIO-ECONOMIC PLANNING SCIENCES. See Sociology.

LC HC431 .S78
DD 330.954/005   II
STATE AND SOCIETY : QUARTERLY JOURNAL OF THE INDIAN INSTITUTE FOR REGIONAL DEVELOPMENT STUDIES. **Added/Corp** Indian Institute for Regional Development Studies. Vol. 1, No. 1 (Jan.-March 1980)-. Periodical. English. Four times a year. Rs.30. State and Society Indian Institute for Regional Development Studies, 686 002 Kerala India.

    ISSN 1014-997X
STUDIES OF ECONOMIES IN TRANSFORMATION. (1992)-. English. World Bank Publications, 1818 H Street Northwest, Washington DC 20043. **Tel** (202)473-1155, (202)473-1155, FAX (202)522-3224, telex WUI 64145 WORLDBANK.

    US
SUMMARY OF ONGOING RESEARCH AND TECHNICAL ASSISTANCE PROJECTS IN AGRICULTURE. **Main/Corp** United States. Agency for International Development. English. One time a year. US Department of State, 2201 C Street NW, Room 5819, Washington DC 20520. **Tel** (202)647-9859.

    ISSN 0591-0137
    AT
SUPPLEMENTARY PAPER - COMMITTEE FOR ECONOMIC DEVELOPMENT OF AUSTRALIA. **Main/Corp** Committee for Economic Development of Australia. **Added/Corp** Committee for Economic Development of Australia. Memorandum for Trustees. Supplementary Paper. (19??)-. Monographic series. English. Irregular. Price varies per volume. Committee for Economic Development of Australia, 123 Lonsdale Street, GPO Box 2117T, Melbourne Victoria 3000 Australia. **Tel** 011 61 03 6623544, FAX 011 61 03 6637271. Index available. **Circ:** 2,000 (ctrl).

    ISSN 1058-1286
    US
THIRD WORLD JOURNAL. See Political Science.

LC HC59.7 .T458   **ISSN** 0143-6597
DD 330.9/72/4/005   UK
    CCC
THIRD WORLD QUARTERLY. [Third world q.]. Vol. 1 (Jan. 1979)-. Periodical. English. Five times a year. $298.00. Carfax Publishing Company, PO Box 25, Abingdon, Oxfordshire OX14 3UE United Kingdom. **Tel** 011 44 1235 555335, FAX 011 44 1235 553559, telex 817484. **ED** Shahid Qadir. **Bk Rev.** **Ad Acc.** **Circ:** 4,500. available on microfiche.
Desc: Journal in the field of contemporary social political and economic issues from a Third World perspective.

Business and Economics —Economic Assistance and Development

Ind/Abst ABC POL SCI; Acad. Search; Am. Hist. Life (1990-); Br. Humanit. Index; Curr. Cit.; Curr. Mil. Pol. Lit.; Energy Res. Abstr. (Oct. 1981-); EP Collect.; Geogr. Abstr. Human Geogr. (?-?); Hist. Abstr., Part B, Twent. Century Abstr.; Homework Help.; Hum. Rights Intern. Rep.; Index Islam. Lit.; Int. Bibliogr. Sociol.; Int. Dev. Abstr. (?-?); Int. Labour Doc.; Int. Polit. Sci. Abstr.; Linguist. Lang. Behav. Abstr.; MasterFile FullTEXT 1000; MasterFile FullTEXT 350; MasterFile FullTEXT 650; MasterFile FullTEXT (Jan. 1994-); Middle East Abstr. Index; PAIS Int. Print; Peace Res. Abstr. J. (1980); Sage Public Adm. Abstr.; Soc. Plann. Policy Dev. Abstr.; Soc. Sci. Source; Sociol. Abstr.; Sociol. Educ. Abstr.; Telebase; Middle East J.

LC D880 .C64
DD 909/.09724
UK

THIRD WORLD REPORTS. VFOAT Third World Reports. (19??)-. Periodical. English. One time a week. $220.00. CSI Syndication Service, Wild Acre Plaw Hatch, West Sussex RH19 4JL United Kingdom. **Tel** 011 44 342 810875, FAX 011 44 342 3905400, telex 305 892822. **ED** Colin Legum. cum. index. **Bk Rev**. **Ad Acc.** ctrl circ.
Desc: Reports dealing with political, social and economic matters in the Third World and their relations with the West, Soviet Bloc and China.

ISSN 8755-8831
DD 330
US
TITLE CHANGE

THIRD WORLD RESOURCES. [Third world resour.]. (Spring 1985)-(1995). Periodical. English. Worldviews, 464 19th Street, Oakland CA 94612. **Tel** (510)835-4692 ext. 113, (415)536-1876, FAX (510)835-3017. **ED** Thomas P. Fenton and Mary J. Heffron. Index available. **Bk Rev**. **Ad Acc**. **Circ:** 2,000 (ctrl). available on microfiche. *Continued by* Worldviews.
Desc: Descriptive and evaluative listings of third world-related resources (organizations, books, periodicals, pamphlets, and audiovisuals). Contains pullout of resources on one region.
Ind/Abst Book Rev. Index; Hum. Rights Intern. Rep.

ISSN 1187-0796
DD 380.1/025/71312
CN

THUNDER BAY METRO TRADE INDEX.
See Business and Economics-Commerce.

LC JX
DD 327
ISSN 0742-1524
US

TOGETHER (MONROVIA, CALIF.). (TOGETHER : A JOURNAL OF WORLD VISION INTERNATIONAL.). [Together]. **Added/Corp** World Vision International. No. 1 (Oct./Dec. 1983)-. Periodical. English. Four times a year. $15.00. World Vision, 919 West Huntington Drive, Monrovia CA 91016. **Tel** (818)303-8811, FAX (818)303-7651, telex 275335.

LC HC701 .S6
US
Pr Rev.

TRANSITION : THE NEWSLETTER ABOUT REFORMING ECONOMIES / TRANSITION AND MACRO-ADJUSTMENT, COUNTRY ECONOMICS DEPARTMENT, WORLD BANK. **Added/Corp** International Bank for Reconstruction and Development. Socialist Economies Unit. (1990)-. Newsletter. English. Twelve times a year. World Bank Publications, 1818 H Street Northwest, Washington DC 20043. **Tel** (202)473-1155, (202)473-1155, FAX (202)522-3224, telex WUI 64145 WORLDBANK. **ED** Richard Hirschler. **Bk Rev**. **Circ:** 7000 (ctrl). *Continues* Socialist Economies in Transition.
Desc: Covering economic, social and business changes in transforming economies from the perspective of the World Bank's research arm.

LC HG
DD 332
ISSN 1018-208X
US

TRENDS IN PRIVATE INVESTMENT IN DEVELOPING COUNTRIES. See Business and Economics-Investments.

ISSN 0988-9914
FR

UDC 008

TRIMESTRE DU MONDE, LE. [Trimest. monde]. (1988)-. Periodical. French. Four times a year. $87.49. Revue le Trimestre du Monde, 10 Ave. Pierre Larousse, 92241 Malakoff Cedex France. **Tel** 31 1 42532765, FAX 31 1 46560859.
Ind/Abst PAIS Int. Print; Middle East J.

ISSN 0828-2412
DD 307/.14
CN

U.B.C. PLANNING PAPERS. DISCUSSION PAPERS. [U.B.C. plan. pap., Discuss. pap.]. **Added/Corp** University of British Columbia. School of Community and Regional Planning. DP No. 1 (May 1982)-. Monographic series. English. Price varies per volume.
Ind/Abst Geogr. Abstr. Human Geogr.

LC DT1 .U4
FR

UJAMAA : REVUE DU GROUPE D'ETUDES ET DE RECHERCHES POUR LE DEVELOPPEMENT AFRICAIN.
Added/Corp Groupe d'Etudes et de Recherches pour le Developpement Africain. No. 1 (Apr./June 1987)-. Periodical. French. Four times a year. Nubia Presse, 17 rue du Petit Pont, 75005 Paris France.

LC JX1977 .A2
ISSN 0082-8262
US

UNIDO MONOGRAPHS ON INDUSTRIAL DEVELOPMENT. Main/Corp United Nations. Industrial Development Organization. (1969)-. Government Publication. English. Irregular. United Nations Publications, 2 United Nations Plaza, Room DC2 0853, Department 007C, New York NY 10017. **Tel** (212)963-8303, (800)253-9646.
Desc: Deals with problems and development prospects of various industries.

LC HC60 U468a
DD 361.2/6
SZ

UNVNEWS / THE UNITED NATIONS VOLUNTEERS PROGRAMME. Main/Corp United Nations Volunteers. VFOAT UNV News; News. No. 45 (June 1988)-. Periodical. English (French and Spanish). Four times a year. United Nations Publishers / Geneva, Palais des Nations, C115 Services Ventes, CH-1211 Geneva 10 Switzerland. **Tel** 011 41 22 7988400, FAX 011 41 22 7332673, telex 415465.
Continues UNV Newsletter.

US

URBAN AGE, THE. See Housing and Urban Development.

US

URBAN MANAGEMENT PROGRAM. See Housing and Urban Development.

ISSN 1184-0692
DD 307.1/4/09598
CN

USC COUNTRY PROFILE. INDONESIA. (USC COUNTRY PROFILE. INDONESIA / USC CANADA.). [USC ctry. profile, Indones.]. **Main/Corp** Unitarian Service Committee of Canada. **VAT** Unitarian Service Committee of Canada Country Profile. Indonesia. (1990)-. English. USC Canada, 56 Sparks Street, Ottawa Ontario K1P 5B1 Canada. *Formed by the union of* Unitarian Service Committee of Canada. USC Project Summaries. Indonesia., 0834-1001 *and* Indonesia Fact Sheet., 0826-0060.

ISSN 1184-0757
DD 307.1/4/096885
CN

USC COUNTRY PROFILE. LESOTHO. (USC COUNTRY PROFILE. LESOTHO / USC CANADA.). [USC ctry. profile, Lesotho]. **Main/Corp** Unitarian Service Committee of Canada. **VAT** Unitarian Service Committee of Canada Country Profile. Lesotho. (1990)-. English. USC Canada, 56 Sparks Street, Ottawa Ontario K1P 5B1 Canada. *Formed by the union of* Unitarian Service Committee of Canada. USC Project Summaries. Lesotho., 0834-0986 *and* Lesotho Fact Sheet., 0826-0079.

ISSN 1184-0730
DD 307.1/4/096623
CN

USC COUNTRY PROFILE. MALI. [USC ctry. profile, Mali]. **Main/Corp** Unitarian Service Committee of Canada. **VAT** Unitarian Service Committee of Canada Country Profile. Mali. (1990)-. English. USC Canada, 56 Sparks Street, Ottawa Ontario K1P 5B1 Canada. *Formed by the union of* Unitarian Service Committee of Canada. USC Project Summaries. Mali., 0843-3550.

ISSN 1184-0722
DD 307.1/4/095496
CN

USC COUNTRY PROFILE. NEPAL. [USC ctry. profile, Nepal]. **Main/Corp** Unitarian Service Committee of Canada. **VAT** Unitarian Service Committee of Canada Country Profile. Nepal. (1990)-. English. USC Canada, 56 Sparks Street, Ottawa Ontario K1P 5B1 Canada. *Formed by the union of* Unitarian Service Committee of Canada. USC Project Summaries. Nepal., 0834-096X *and* Nepal Fact Sheet., 0826-0052.

ISSN 1184-0714
DD 307.1/4/096887
CN

USC COUNTRY PROFILE. SWAZILAND. [USC ctry. profile, Swazil.]. **Main/Corp** Unitarian Service Committee of Canada. **VAT** Unitarian Service Committee of Canada Country Profile. Swaziland. (1990)-. English. USC Canada, 56 Sparks Street, Ottawa Ontario K1P 5B1 Canada. *Formed by the union of* Unitarian Service Committee of Canada. USC Project Summaries. Swaziland., 0834-0978 *and* Swaziland Fact Sheet., 0826-0036.

LC HC60 .N58
ISSN 0048-0541
NO

UTVIKLING. **Added/Corp** Norway. Direktoratet for Utviklingshjelp. (198?)-. Periodical. Norwegian. Six times a year. Free on request. Norwegian Agency for International Development, PO Box 8034, 0030 Oslo 1 Norway. **Tel** FAX 011 47 2 314402. *Continues* Sr-Nord Utvikling, 0048-0541.

ISSN 0216-1028
IO

VIBRO. [Vibro]. (1976)-. Periodical. English. Four times a year. $6.50. World Neighbours, 4127 Northwest 122nd Street, Oklahoma City OK 73120-8869. **Tel** (800)242-6387, (405)752-9700, FAX (405)752-9393, telex 5106002674.

ISSN 0506-8894
DD 967.5
CG

VIE DU TIERS-MONDE. **Added/Corp** Congo (Democratic Republic) Institut National d'Etudes Politiques. (1967)-. Periodical. French. Twelve times a year. Institut National d'Etudes Politiques, Kinshasa Congo.

LC DS101 .V59
ISSN 0382-0327
CN

VOICE OF RADOM. **Added/Corp** United Radomer Relief for U.S. and Canada. VFOAT Radomer Shtime. Vol. 1 (Jan. 1957)-. Periodical. English (Yiddish). Twelve times a year. United Radomer Relief for US and Canada, 4415 Bathurst Street, Room 201, Downsview Ontario Canada.

ISSN 0275-5599
US

WASHINGTON REPORT ON THE HEMISPHERE. [Wash. rep. hemisph.].
Added/Corp Council on Hemispheric Affairs (U.S.). VFOAT C.O.H.A.'s Washington Report on the Hemisphere. Vol. 1, No. 4 (Nov. 11, 1980)-. Periodical. English. Twenty-four times a year. Council on Hemisphere Affairs, 724 9th Street Northwest, Suite 401, Washington DC 20001. **Tel** (202)393-3322, FAX (202)393-3423. **ED** Larry Birns. Index available. **Bk Rev**, (Qty: 24). **Circ:** 2,000 (ctrl). *Continues* COHA's Washington Report on the Hemisphere.
Desc: Monitors the full spectrum of U. S.- Latin American as well as U. S.- Canadian-Latin American relations from a Washington perspective. Analysis includes political, economic, trade union, diplomatic, developmental, human rights, and legislative issues through a descriptive and analytical approach.
Ind/Abst Hum. Rights Intern. Rep.

ISSN 1059-4175
DD 327
US

WHO'S DOING WHAT?. (WHO'S DOING WHAT? : A DIRECTORY OF US ORGANIZATIONS & INSTITUTIONS EDUCATING ABOUT DEVELOPMENT & OTHER GLOBAL ISSUES.). [Who's doing what?].
Added/Corp National Clearinghouse on Development Education. American Forum for Global Education. 2nd Ed. (1991)-. Directory. English. Every 2 years. $12.00. National Clearinghouse on Development Education, 45 John Street, Suite 908, New York NY 10038. *Continues* Who's Doing What in Development Education?.

LC HC79.P6 W48
ISSN 1046-7548
DD 363.8/05
US

WHY - WORLD HUNGER YEAR. (WHY.). [Why - World Hung. Year]. **Added/Corp** World Hunger Year. VFOAT Why Magazine. No. 1 (Spring 1989)-. Periodical. English. Four times a year. $18.00. World Hunger Year., 505 Eighth Avenue, 21st Floor, New York NY 10018. **Tel** (212)629-8850, FAX (212)465-9274. available on microfilm and microfiche from University Microfilms International (UMI). *Continues* Food Monitor, 0162-0045.
Desc: Covers articles on how to teach about hunger, food collections, displays and programs to raise public awareness of worldwide hunger and poverty.
Ind/Abst Altern. Press Index (199?-); PAIS Int. Print.

LC HD
ISSN 0804-3639
DD 338.9
NO

WORKING PAPER / CHR. MICHELSEN INSTITUTE, DEVELOPMENT STUDIES AND HUMAN RIGHTS. (19??)-. Periodical. English.
Ind/Abst Geogr. Abstr. Human Geogr.; Int. Dev. Abstr.

US

WORKING PAPER / HELEN KELLOGG INSTITUTE FOR INTERNATIONAL STUDIES, UNIVERSITY OF NOTRE DAME. **Added/Corp** Helen Kellogg Institute for International Studies. (Dec. 1983)-. Monographic series. English (Spanish). Irregular. $50.00. Helen Kellogg Institute for International Studies, University of Notre Dame, Notre Dame IN 46556. **Tel** (219)239-6580, FAX (219)631-6717. **ED** Caroline Domingo.
Ind/Abst Geogr. Abstr. Human Geogr.; Int. Dev. Abstr.

LC HD2329
ISSN 0829-9277
DD 338.9/005
CN

WORKING PAPER / UNIVERSITY OF TORONTO, DEVELOPMENT STUDIES PROGRAMME. [Work. pap. - Univ. Tor., Dev. Stud. Programme.]. **Added/Corp** University of Toronto. Development Studies Programme. (1983)-. Periodical.

English. University of Toronto, Development Studies Programme, Donsview ON M3H 5T8 Canada.
Ind/Abst Hum. Rights Intern. Rep.

LC HC59.69 .W65 **ISSN** 0816-5181
DD 330.9172/4 AT

WORKING PAPERS IN TRADE AND DEVELOPMENT. [Work. pap. trade dev.]. **Added/Corp** Australian National University. Research School of Pacific Studies. Dept. of Economics. Australian National University. National Centre for Development Studies. No. 86/1 (1986)-. Monographic series. English. Price varies per volume. Anutech Pty. Limited, GPO Box 4, Canberra ACT 2601 Australia. **Tel** 011 61 6 2492479, FAX 011 61 6 2575088. **ED** Peter G. Warr. Index available. cum. index. **Acid Free. Circ:** 350 (ctrl).
Ind/Abst Geogr. Abstr. Human Geogr.; Int. Dev. Abstr.; Irr. Drain. Abstr.

LC HC59.69 .C46a
DD 338.9/006/0489 DK
TITLE CHANGE

WORKING PROGRAMME ..., ANNUAL REPORT. **Main/Corp** Centret for Udviklingsforskning (Denmark). **VFOAT** Annual Report. (1992)-(1994). English. Centre for Development Research, Gammel Kongeuej 5, DK-1610 Copenhagen Denmark. **Tel** 011 45 33 251200, FAX 011 45 33 258110. ***Continues*** *Centret for Udviklingsforskning (Denmark). CDR Working Program ... & Annual Report.* ***Continued by*** *Centret for Udviklingsforskning (Denmark). Centre for Development Research : [Annual Report].*

ISSN 0085-8293
US

WORLD BANK ATLAS. **See** Business and Economics-Economic History, Conditions.

LC Z7164.F5 I555A HC59.7 **ISSN** 0253-7389
DD 016.3321/532 US

WORLD BANK CATALOG OF PUBLICATIONS, THE. **See** Business and Economics-Abstracting, Bibliographies and Statistics.

LC HC59.69 .W67 **ISSN** 0258-6770
DD 330.9172/4 US
Pr Rev.

WORLD BANK ECONOMIC REVIEW, THE. [World Bank econ. rev.]. **Added/Corp** International Bank for Reconstruction and Development. Vol. 1, No. 1 (Sept. 1986)-. Periodical. English. Three times a year (Jan., May, Sept.). $45.00. World Bank Publications, 1818 H Street Northwest, Washington DC 20043. **Tel** (202)473-1155, (202)473-1155, FAX (202)522-3224, telex WUI 64145 WORLDBANK. available on microfilm from University Microfilms International (UMI). Documents available from The Genuine Article.
Desc: Information on economic development.
Ind/Abst Curr. Cit.; Curr. Contents Soc. Behav. Sci.; Econ. Lit. Index; Geogr. Abstr. Human Geogr.; Int. Bibliogr. Sociol.; Int. Dev. Abstr. (?-?); Int. Labour Doc.; J. Econ. Lit.; LABORDOC; PAIS Int. Print; Res. Alert [Full Cov.]; Rural Dev. Abstr.; Sage Public Adm. Abstr.; Soc. Sci. Cit. Index [Full Cov.]; World Agric. Econ. Rural Sociol. Abstr.

LC HC60 .I535c **ISSN** 1014-8590
DD 332.1/532/05 US

WORLD BANK POLICY RESEARCH BULLETIN. [World Bank policy res. bull.]. **Main/Corp** International Bank for Reconstruction and Development. **Added/Corp** International Bank for Reconstruction and Development. Office of the Research Administrator. International Bank for Reconstruction and Development. Research Advisory Staff. **VFOAT** Bulletin; Policy Research Bulletin. Vol. 1, No. 1 (Jan./Feb. 1990)-. Bulletin. English. Five times a year. Free on request. World Bank Publications, 1818 H Street Northwest, Washington DC 20043. **Tel** (202)473-1155, (202)473-1155, FAX (202)522-3224, telex WUI 64145 WORLDBANK. ***Continues*** *International Bank for Reconstruction and Development. World Bank Research News.*

LC HD72 .W67 **ISSN** 0257-3032
DD 338.9/009172/4 US

WORLD BANK RESEARCH OBSERVER, THE. [World Bank res. obs.]. **Added/Corp** International Bank for Reconstruction and Development. **VFOAT** Research Observer. Vol. 1, No. 1 (Jan. 1986)-. Periodical. English. Two times a year. $35.00. World Bank Publications, 1818 H Street Northwest, Washington DC 20043. **Tel** (202)473-1155, (202)473-1155, FAX (202)522-3224, telex WUI 64145 WORLDBANK. **(Subscription address:** World Bank Publications, PO Box 7247-8619, Books Department, Philadelphia PA 19170. **)** available on microfilm and microfiche from University Microfilms International (UMI); available on an online database from DIALOG. Documents available from BLDSC, FAXON Xpress, The UnCover Company, SWETS, UMI Article Clearinghouse.
Desc: Information on economic development.
Ind/Abst Curr. Cit.; Econ. Lit. Index; Geogr. Abstr. Human Geogr.; Int. Dev. Abstr.; J. Econ. Lit.; PAIS Int. Print; Rural Dev. Abstr.; Sage Public Adm. Abstr.; Soc. Sci. Cit. Index [Full Cov.]; World Agric. Econ. Rural Sociol. Abstr.

LC HD2757 **ISSN** 0258-3143
DD 338.9 US

WORLD BANK RESEARCH PROGRAM (1986), THE. **See** Business and Economics-Abstracting, Bibliographies and Statistics.

LC S **ISSN** 0253-7494
DD 630 US

WORLD BANK TECHNICAL PAPER. **See** Agriculture.

LC HJ8899 .W672 **ISSN** 0253-2859
DD 336.3/435/091724 US

WORLD DEBT TABLES. **See** Business and Economics-Abstracting, Bibliographies and Statistics.

LC HC4 .W66 **ISSN** 0305-750X
DD 338/.09/04 UK
CCC
CODEN WODEDW
Pr Rev.

WORLD DEVELOPMENT. [World dev.]. Vol. 1 (Feb. 1973)-. Periodical. English. Twelve times a year. $1020.00. Pergamon Press, An Imprint of Elsevier Science Ltd., The Boulevard, Langford Lane, Kidlington, Oxford OX5 1GB United Kingdom. **Tel** 011 44 1865 843000, 011 44 1865 843699, FAX 011 44 1865 843010. **(Subscription address:** Elsevier Science Ltd. / Oxford Fulfillment Centre, PO Box 800, Kidlington OX5 1DX United Kingdom. **Tel** 011 44 865 843355.**) ED** Paul Streeten and Janet Craswell. available on microfilm and microfiche from University Microfilms International (UMI); available on an online database from Elsevier Electronic Subscriptions (EES). Documents available from The Genuine Article, UMI Article Clearinghouse, Documents on Demand. ***Continues*** *New Commonwealth & World Development.*
Desc: A multi-disciplinary journal of development studies. It seeks to explore ways of improving standards of living, and the human condition generally, by examining potential solutions to problems such as: poverty, unemployment, malnutrition, disease, lack of shelter, environmental degradation, inadequate scientific and technological resources, trade and payments imbalances, international debt, gender and ethnic discrimination, militarism and conflict, and lack of popular participation in economic and political life.
Ind/Abst ABC POL SCI; Acad. Search; AGRICOLA [Select. Cov.]; Agrofor. Abstr. (1991-); Br. Humanit. Index; Bus. Index (1985-); Chicano Index; Coal Abstr.; Commun. Abstr. (?-?); Contents Recent Econ. J.; Cot. Trop. Fibr. Abstr. Bibliogr.; Curr. Cit.; Curr. Contents Soc. Behav. Sci.; Curr. Lit. Sci. Sci.; Ecol. Abstr. (?-?); Econ. Lit. Index; Energy Inf. Abstr.; Energy Res. Abstr. (June 1978-); Environ. Abstr.; EP Collect.; Expand. Acad. Index (1984-); For. Prod. Abstr. (19??-19??); For. Abstr.; Gen. BusinessFile (1985-); Gen. Period. Index (1985-); Geogr. Abstr. Human Geogr.; Homework Help.; INFO-SOUTH Abstr.; Int. Bibliogr. Sociol.; Int. Dev. Abstr.; Int. Labour Doc.; J. Econ. Lit.; J. Ferrocement; J. Plan. Lit.; LABORDOC; Mag. Search; Maize Abstr.; MasterFile FullTEXT 1000; MasterFile FullTEXT 350; MasterFile FullTEXT 650; MasterFile FullTEXT (July 1993-); Newsp. Period. Abstr. (1989-); Nutr. Abstr. Rev., Ser. A, Hum. Exp.; OCLC; PAIS Int. Print; Res. Alert [Full Cov.]; Rice Abstr.; Rural Dev. Abstr.; Soc. Plann. Policy Dev. Abstr.; Soc. Sci. Source; Soc. Sci. Cit. Index [Full Cov.]; Soc. Sci. Index; Soc. Sci. Index Fulltext (Sept. 1988-) [Full Txt.]; Sociol. Abstr.; Soils Fert.; Sug. Indus. Abstr.; Telebase; Trade Ind. Index; World Agric. Econ. Rural Sociol. Abstr.

LC HC59.69 .W68
US

WORLD DEVELOPMENT INDICATORS [COMPUTER FILE]. **Added/Corp** International Bank for Reconstruction and Development. (19??)-. Periodical. English. World Bank Publications, 1818 H Street Northwest, Washington DC 20043. **Tel** (202)473-1155, (202)473-1155, FAX (202)522-3224, telex WUI 64145 WORLDBANK.

LC HC59.7 .W659 **ISSN** 0163-5085
DD 330.9/172/4 US

WORLD DEVELOPMENT REPORT. [World dev. rep.]. **Added/Corp** World Bank. (1978)-. English. One time a year (July). $21.43. **(Subscription address:** Oxford University Press / USA, Journals Marketing Department, Oxford University Press, 2001 Evans Road, Cary NC 27513. **Tel** (800)451-7556, (919)677-0977, FAX (919)677-1714.**)**
Ind/Abst Curr. Cit.; F&S Index Plus Text, Int. [Select. Cov.]; Predicasts Forecasts.

LC HV696.F6 W7 **ISSN** 1010-9099
IT
SUSPENDED

WORLD FOOD PROGRAMME JOURNAL. [J. - World Food Programme]. **Added/Corp** World Food Programme. World Food Programme. Public Affairs & Information Branch. **VFOAT** Journal; WFP Journal. (Jan./March 1987)-Suspended (1995). Periodical. English (French and Spanish). Four times a year. Free on request. World Food Programme, Via Cristoforo Colombo 426, 00145 Rome Italy. **Tel** 011 39 6 626675, FAX 52282840, telex 626675 WFP I. **ED** Paul Mitchell. Documents available from Documents on Demand. ***Continues*** *World Food Programme News, 0049-8084.*
Desc: Description of work of World Food Programme (WFP) and various WFP projects that are being undertaken worldwide with help of food aid projects for agricultural development, vulnerable groups, etc.
Ind/Abst Environ. Abstr.; Int. Dev. Abstr.

US

WORLD NEIGHBORS IN ACTION. (19??)-. English (French and Spanish). Two times a year. $10.00 for 4 issues (two-year subscription to a single address or one-year subscription to two addresses) sent to addresses in Northern Hemisphere/industrial nations; Free when sent to addresses in the Southern Hemisphere/developing nations. World Neighbours, 4127 Northwest 122nd Street, Oklahoma City OK 73120-8869. **Tel** (800)242-6387, (405)752-9700, FAX (405)752-9393, telex 5106002674.
Desc: A how-to-do-it newsletter treating a different topic of interest to development workers in each issue. Previous topics have included: caring for the elderly, nutrition, composting, and neighborhood development.

LC HC59 .W669 **ISSN** 1043-5573
DD 330.9/0021 US

WORLD TABLES (BALTIMORE, MD.). **See** Business and Economics-Economic History, Conditions.

LC BV
DD 261 US

WORLD VISION. **Added/Corp** World Vision International. Vol. 16 (Jan. 1972)-. Periodical. English. Six times a year. Free on request. World Vision, 919 West Huntington Drive, Monrovia CA 91016. **Tel** (818)303-8811, FAX (818)303-7651, telex 275335. **ED** Terry Madison. Index available. cum. index. **Bk Rev. Circ:** 200,000 (ctrl). ***Formed by the union of*** *World Vision Magazine* ***and*** *World Vision Heartline.*
Desc: Articles on third world issues (refugees, hunger, famine relief, water, rights of women and children, etc.) that inform, educate, promote action among Christians and the church worldwide to meet these dire human needs.

US

•WORLDVIEWS. (1995)-. English. Four times a year. $50.00. Worldviews, 464 19th Street, Oakland CA 94612. **Tel** (510)835-4692 ext. 113, (415)536-1876, FAX (510)835-3017. ***Continues*** *Third World Resources.*

LC HC107.K23 P633 **ISSN** 0160-0869
DD 338.9781 US

YEAR END REPORT - KANSAS ECONOMIC OPPORTUNITY OFFICE. **Main/Corp** Kansas. Economic Opportunity Office. 1975/1976-. English. Every 2 years. Kansas Economic Opportunity Office, 535 Kansas Avenue, Topeka KS 66603.
Desc: Describes the activities and accomplishments of community programs in the state which receive assistance from the Kansas Office of Economic Opportunity.

ECONOMIC HISTORY, CONDITIONS

LC HC226.A817
PE

1/2 DE CAMBIO. **VFOAT** Medio de Cambio; Mitad de Cambio. **VAT** Mitad de Cambio. (198?)-. Periodical. Spanish. One time a week. $350.00. Editora Libertas SA, Avenue Comandante Espinar 398, Lima 18 Peru. **Tel** 011 54 14 455053.

UK

ABECOR COUNTRY REPORT. BOLIVIA, PARAGUAY, AND URUGUAY. **VFOAT** Bolivia, Paraguay and Uruguay. (March 1989)-. English. One time a year. Barclays Bank Ltd, PO Box 12, 1 Wimborne Road, Poole Dorset BH15 2BB United Kingdom. **Tel** 011 44 1202 671212, telex 887591. ***Formed by the union of*** *ABECOR Country Report. Bolivia; ABECOR Country Report. Paraguay* ***and*** *ABECOR Country Report. Uruguay.*

LC CLASSED SEPARATELY **ISSN** 1054-6944
DD 330 US
TITLE CHANGE

ACADEMIC STUDIES SERIES. [Acad. stud. ser.]. **Added/Corp** Korea Economic Institute (U.S.). **VFOAT** U.S.-Korea Academic Symposium; U.S. Korea Academic Symposium. Vol. 1 (1991)-Vol. 4 (1994). Monographic series. English. Korea Economic Institute of America, 1101 Vermont Avenue NW, Suite 401, Washington DC 20005. ***Continued by*** *Joint U.S.-Korean Academic Studies.*

ISSN 0350-3631
CI

ACTA HISTORICO-OECONOMICA IUGOSLAVIAE. [Acta hist.-oecon. Iugosl.]. Periodical. Serbo-Croatian (Roman) (summaries and/or abstracts in English and French). Komisija za Ekonomsku

Business and Economics —Economic History, Conditions

Historiju Jugoslavije, Zagreb Croatia.
Ind/Abst Am. Hist. Life (1982-); Art Archaeol. Tech. Abstr.

LC HC107.A83 P632   **ISSN** 0363-4337
DD 338.9767   US
ACTION (LITTLE ROCK), THE. (THE ACTION.). Periodical. English. Twelve times a year. Arkansas Division of Human Services, Little Rock AR 72201.

LC HC381.A1 A26   **ISSN** 0001-7655
SP
ACTUALIDAD ECONOMICA. [Actual. Econ.]. **Added/Corp** Sociedad Anonima de Revistas, Periodicos y Ediciones. (1958)-. Periodical. Spanish. One time a week. $450.31. Recoletos Compania Editorial, Recoletos 1 2A Pl, 28001 Madrid Spain. **Tel** 011 34 1 3370518. available on an online database.
Ind/Abst Chem. Bus. Bull.; Chem. Bus. NewsBase (1985-); Chem. Bus. Update; F&S Index Plus Text, Int. [Select. Cov.]; Infomat Int. Bus.; PAIS Int. Print; PROMT.

LC HC226 .A823
DD 330.985/005   PE
ACTUALIDAD ECONOMICA DEL PERU (CENTRO DE ASESORIA LABORAL (LIMA, PERU)). (ACTUALIDAD ECONOMICA DEL PERU.). **VFOAT** Actualidad Economica. Vol. 1, No. 1 (Feb. 1978)-. Periodical. Spanish. Irregular. Av Guzman Blanco 465, Oficina 402, Lima Peru. cum. index.
Ind/Abst LABORDOC.

BE
ACTUALITES EN ANALYSE TRANSACTIONNELLE. Vol. 1 (Jan. 1977)-. French. Four times a year. 1500F. CFIP, 153 Avenue Gribaumont, 1200 Brussels Belgium. **Tel** 011 32 2 7705048.

LC HC271 .A65   **ISSN** 0001-9615
DD 330.9/44/083   FR
AFFAIRES, LES. (Jan. 1962)-. Periodical. French. Twelve times a year. $25.00. Express Documents, 1 Bis Avenue de la Republique, 75011 Paris France. **Tel** 011 33 1 49293000.
Ind/Abst Repere.

LC HC371 .A62   **ISSN** 0345-3766
SW
AFFARSVARLDEN (1974).
(AFFARSVARLDEN.). [Affarsvarlden]. (1974)-. Periodical. Swedish. One time a week. $176.31. Ekonomi och Teknik Foerlag AB, Klara Soedra Kyrkogata 1, 106 12 Stockholm Sweden. **Tel** 011 46 8 796-6652, 796-6661, 796-6500, FAX 46 8 21 76 11. index available. cum. index. **Ad Acc. Circ:** 25,000 (ctrl). available on microfilm and microfiche from University Microfilms International (UMI). **Continues** Affarsvarlden/Finanstidningen.

LC HC501 .A527   **ISSN** 0378-3006
DD 330.9/6/6003   SG
AFRICA DEVELOPMENT. (AFRICA DEVELOPMENT. AFRIQUE ET DEVELOPPEMENT.). [Afr. dev.]. **Added/Corp** Codesria. **VFOAT** Afrique et Developpement. Vol. 1 (May 1976)-. Periodical. English (French). Four times a year. $45.00. CODESRIA, BP 3304, Dakar Senegal. **Tel** 011 221 230211, 011 221 239374, telex 61339. **ED** Tade Akin Aina. Index available. cum. index. **Bk Rev. Ad Acc. Circ:** 1,000 (ctrl).
Desc: A critical analysis of the socio-economic development of Africa.
Ind/Abst Abstr. Anthropol. (19??-); Int. Dev. Abstr. (?-?); Int. Labour Doc.; LABORDOC; Leis., Rec., Tour. Abstr.; Recent. Publ. Artic.; Rural Dev. Abstr.; World Agric. Econ. Rural Sociol. Abstr.

ISSN 0952-4290
UK
AFRICA NEWSFILE. No. 1 (1987)-. English. Twenty-six times a year. Africa Newsfile & Press Services Ltd., 81 103 Euston House, London NW1 2ET United Kingdom. **Tel** 011 44 171 3880537, FAX 011 44 171 3881380, telex 262562.

LC HC800.A1 A35   **ISSN** 0141-3929
DD 330.96/005   UK
CCC
AFRICAN BUSINESS. [Afr. bus.]. (Sept. 1978)-. Trade Publication. English. Twelve times a year. $90.00. IC Publications Ltd., 7 Coldbath Square, London EC1R 4LQ United Kingdom. **Tel** 011 44 171 7137711, FAX 011 44 171 7137898, telex 8811757. **ED** Linda van Buren. **Bk Rev. Ad Acc. Circ:** 15,000. available on an online database from DATA-STAR; BRS; and (file 771,772,799/Full-Text) DIALOG; available on microfilm and microfiche from University Microfilms International (UMI).
Desc: Up-to-date information on African economies, business, industry, markets, commodities, finance, commerce and developments.
Ind/Abst Bus. Index (1992-); F&S Index Plus Text, Int. [Select. Cov.]; Gen. BusinessFile (1992-); PAIS Int. Print; Predicasts Forecasts.

LC HC501 .A54   **ISSN** 0145-2258
DD 330.9/6/03   US
Pr Rev.
AFRICAN ECONOMIC HISTORY. [Afr. econ. hist.]. **Added/Corp** University of Wisconsin--Madison. African Studies Program. Boston University. African Studies Center. No. 1 (Spring 1976)-. Periodical. English (French). One time a year. $33.00. African Studies Program, 1454 Van Hise Hall, University of Wisconsin, Madison WI 53706. **Tel** (608)262-2380, FAX (608)262-6998. **ED** Iris Berger, Margaret Jean Hay, Michael Watts and Richard Roberts. **Bk Rev. Ad Acc. Circ:** 500. Documents available from The Genuine Article. **Continues** African Economic History Review, 0360-6333.
Desc: Focuses on recent economic change in Africa as well as the colonial and precolonial economic history of the continent.
Ind/Abst Am. Hist. Life (1976-1991);; Arts Humanit. Citation Index (19??-19??) [Full Cov.]; Cot. Trop. Fibr. Abstr. Bibliogr.; Curr. Contents Arts Humanit.; Econ. Lit. Index (?-1991); J. Econ. Lit. (1982-); Public Aff. Inf. Serv. Bull.; Res. Alert [Full Cov.]; Soc. Sci. Cit. Index [Select. Cov.]

LC HC970.A1 A36
FR
AFRICASCOPE. **VFOAT** Africa Scope. (19??)-. French. One time a year (June). $21.87. Editions Mermon, 20 rue de Fonparabie, 75020 Paris France. **Tel** 011 33 1 47637080 or 43678700.

ISSN 0721-5088
GW
●**AFRIKA SUD.** See Political Science.

LC HC800.A1 E68   **ISSN** 0221-5772
FR
AFRIQUE ENTREPRISE. (19??)-. Periodical. French. Six times a year. $874.88. IC Publications Ediafric, 10 rue Vineuse, 75116 Paris France. **Tel** 011 33 1 44308100. **Continues** Equip-Afrique.

LC HC10 .A6
UA
SUSPENDED
AFRO-ASIAN ECONOMIC REVIEW.
[Afro-Asian econ. rev.]. **Added/Corp** Afro-Asian Organisation for Economic Co-operation. (19??)-Suspended (19??). Periodical. English. Twelve times a year. Afro-Asian Organisation for Economic Co-operation, Midan Falaki, Chamber of Commerce Building, Cairo Egypt.
Ind/Abst Am. Hist. Life (1973-).

LC HC463.A5 A52A
JA
AICHI REPOTO. **Main/Corp** Aichi, Japan. Dai 3-Ji Chino Keikaku Kenkyujo (Japan). **VFOAT** Aichi Report. (1971)-. Japanese. Daisanji Aichi-Ken Chiho Keikaku Suishin Kaigi, c/o Aichi-Ken Kikubu Kikakuka, Nagoya Japan.

LC HC446 .A58   **ISSN** 0216-8219
DD 338.9   IO
AKADEMIKA (SALA, INDONESIA).
(AKADEMIKA : KAJIAN ISLAM DAN PERKEMBANGAN KEMASYARAKATAN.). **Added/Corp** Universitas Muhammadiyah Surakarta. Lembaga Penelitian dan Studi Kemasyarakatan. Universitas Muhammadiyah Surakarta. Vol. 1, (Jan. 1982)-. Periodical. Indonesian. Four times a year. Kantor Pusat Universitas Muhammadiyah Surakarta, J1. Dr Rajiman 78, Sala Indonesia.

LC HC465.C6 A67
JA
AKUROSU. **VFOAT** Across. (19??)-. Periodical. Japanese. Twelve times a year. Paruko 15-1 Udagawa-cho Minato-ku, Tokyo 150 Japan.

LC HC59.69 .A4
UA
AL-ALAM AL-THALITH. (1991)-. Periodical. Arabic. Four times a year.

LC HC497.S8 D34
DD 330   SY
AL-DALIL AL-SINAI AL-SURI. **Added/Corp** Muassasah al-Arabiyah lil-Ilan. (19??)-. Arabic. Dimashq, 28 Shari Al-Mutanabbi Syria.

LC HC497.J6 F28
JO
AL-FAJR AL-IQTISADI. Periodical. Arabic. 1.5 single issue. PO Box 20060, Amman Jordan.

LC HC415.35.A1 G48
DD 330.953/53/005   MK
AL-GHURFAH. **Added/Corp** Ghurfat Tijarat Wa-Sinaat Uman. **VFOAT** Ghorfa; Chamber. Vol. 1, No. 1 (Nov. 1978)-. Periodical. Arabic (English). Four times a year. 6.000. Ghurfat Tijarat Wa-Sinaat Uman, PO Box 4400, Ruwi Muscat Oman.

LC HC531 .M34
UA
AL-MAL WA-AL-TIJARAH. **Added/Corp** Nadi Al-Tijarah (Cairo, Egypt) Ghurfah Al-Tijariyah Bi-Al-Minufiyah. **VFOAT** Almal Waltegarah. (19??)-. Periodical. Arabic. Twelve times a year. 11 Shiari Marrayn, Al-Qahirah UA Egypt.

LC HC830.A1 S56
UA
AL-SINAAH WA-AL-IQTISAD. **VFOAT** Senaah Wa Al Iktsaad. Periodical. Arabic. Irregular. £0.25 single issue. 5 Shari Muhammad Sidqi Min Huda Sharaw I, Bab Al-Luq, Al-Qahirah Egypt.

LC HC498.A1 S57
UA
AL-SINAI AL-ARABI. **VFOAT** Al Senai Al Arabi; Senai Al Arabi. (1969)-. Periodical. Arabic. £0.20 single issue. Maktab Al-Qahirah, 45 Shari Al-Dunktur Shahin, Al Ajuzah Al-Jizah United Arab Republic.

LC HC415.3.A1 T32
QA
AL-TAAWUN AL-SINAI FI AL-KHALIJ AL-ARABI. **VFOAT** Taawon al Sinae. Periodical. Arabic (English). Four times a year. Munazzamat Al-Khalij Lil-Istisharat Al-Sinaiyah, S B 5114, Al-Dawhah Qatar.

LC HC497.J6 T35
JO
AL-TANMIYAH. Periodical. Arabic. PO Box 8154, Amman Jordan.

LC HC830.A1 T36
UA
AL-TANMIYAH WA-AL-TIJARAH. Vol. 1, No. 1 (October 1982)-. Arabic. £0.15 single issue. Majallat Al-Tanmiyahwa-Al-Tijarah, 339 Shari Al-Sudan, Cairo Egypt.

LC HC498.A1 S94b
KU
AL-TAQRIR AL-SANAWI - AL-SUNDUQ AL-ARABI LIL-INMA AL-IQTISADI WA-AL-IJTIMAI. **Main/Corp** Al-Sunduq Al-Arabi Lil-Inma Al-Iqtisadi Wa-Al-Ijtimia, Periodical. Arabic. Al-Kuwayt Al-Sunduq Al-Arabi Lil-Inma Al-Iqtisadi Wa-al-Ijtimia, PO Box 21923, Ahmed Al Jaber Street, AL-Kuwayt Kuwait.

LC HC497.T82 S487
TS
AL-TIJARAH. (19??)-. Periodical. Arabic (English). Twelve times a year. £E150.00 Arab; £E200.00 other. Sharjah Chamber of Commerce and Industry, PO Box 580, Sharjah, United Arab Emirates. **Tel** 541444, FAX (06)541119, telex 68205 TIJARAH EM. **ED** Sheikh Mohamed, Bin Salem Al Qassimi and Abdul Wahid Al-Embabi. Index available. cum. index. **Bk Rev. Ad Acc. Circ:** 7,000 (ctrl).
Desc: Emphasis is on total economic development and trade and business promotion.

ISSN 0889-7468
DD 330   US
ALABAMA DEVELOPMENT NEWS. [Ala. dev. news]. **Added/Corp** Alabama Development Office. Alabama. Dept. of Economic and Community Affairs. **VFOAT** Alabama Development News ADO. Vol 1 (Feb. 1970)-. Periodical. English. Four times a year. Free on request. Alabama Development Office, 401 Adams Avenue, State Capitol, Montgomery AL 36130. **Tel** (334)242-0400, FAX (334)242-0486. **ED** Gerri Plant Miller. **Circ:** 15,000 (ctrl).

LC HC107.A4 A695
DD 338.5/443/09761   US
ALABAMA ECONOMIC OUTLOOK / DEVELOPED BY CENTER FOR BUSINESS AND ECONOMIC RESEARCH, UNIVERSITY OF ALABAMA. **Added/Corp** University of Alabama. Center for Business and Economic Research. Alabama. Office of State Planning and Federal Programs. (1978)-. Monographic series. English. Irregular. Price varies per volume. Center for Business & Economic Research, PO Box 870221, University of Alabama, Tuscaloosa AL 35487. **Tel** (205)348-6191, FAX (205)248-2951. **Circ:** 600 (ctrl).
Desc: Present and projected economic outlook for the state of Alabama.
Ind/Abst Stat. Ref. Index.

LC HC498 .A66
NE
ALAM AL-ISTITHMAR AL-ARABI. ARAB BUSINESS REPORT. **VFOAT** Arab Business Report. (19??)-. Periodical. Arabic (English). Irregular. Fl150.00 Europe; Fl180.00 other. Arab Group SA, 72 Avenue Franklin Roosevelt, 1050 Brussels Belgium. **Tel** 011 32 2 6405085. **ED** M. A. Saad. **Bk Rev. Ad Acc. Circ:** 25,000 (ctrl)
Desc: Country surveys, tender, contract, petro and

Business and Economics —Economic History, Conditions

economics news, economic and political analysis of relations between Arab countries and the rest of the world, company profiles, interviews.

LC HC107.A45 A5985   **ISSN** 0162-5403
DD 330.9/798/05   US
ALASKA REVIEW OF SOCIAL AND ECONOMIC CONDITIONS. [Alsk. rev. soc. econ. cond.]. **Added/Corp** University of Alaska, Fairbanks. Institute of Social and Economic Research. Vol. 14, No. 3 (Dec. 1977)-. Periodical. English. Irregular. Free to US; $5.00 Canada; $10.00 other. Institute of Social and Economic Research / University of Alaska, University of Alaska, 3211 Providence Drive, Anchorage AK 99508. **Tel** (907)786-7710, FAX (907)786-7739. **ED** Ronald Crowe. **Circ**: 3,000. **Continues** Alaska Review of Business and Economic Conditions, 0034-6462.
 Desc: Primary mission is to study and provide information on the contemporary issues confronting Alaska's economy, population and social and political institutions.
 Ind/Abst Leis., Rec., Tour. Abstr.; PAIS Int. Print; Rural Dev. Abstr.; Stat. Ref. Index; World Agric. Econ. Rural Sociol. Abstr.

    ISSN 1054-5220
DD 965   US
ALGERIA (SYRACUSE, N.Y.). (ALGERIA : A POLITICAL AND ECONOMIC FORECAST.). [Algeria]. **Added/Corp** Political Risk Services (IBC USA (Publications) Inc.). (19??)-. English. $325.00. Political Risk Services, 6320 Fly Road, Suite 102, PO Box 248, East Syracuse NY 13057-0248. **Tel** (315)431-0511, FAX (315)431-0200.
 Desc: Assesses the factors affecting the prospects for business and trade. Each report focuses specifically on business needs such as finding and developing markets, determining currency movements, or making judgements about capital investments or corporate security.

LC HC547.A4   GW
ALGERIEN : WIRTSCHAFTSDATEN UND WIRTSCHAFTSDOKUMENTATION. **Main/Corp** Bundesstelle fur Aussenhandelsinformation (Germany). German. DM2.00. Bundesstelle fuer Aussenhandelsinformation, Agrippastrasse 87 93, D-50676 Cologne Germany. **Tel** 011 49 221 2057316, FAX 011 49 221 2057212.

LC HC815.A1 A43
DD 330.965   GW
ALGERIEN WIRTSCHAFTSSTRUKTUR. **Added/Corp** Bundesstelle fuer Aussenhandelsinformation (Germany). (19??)-. German. DM7.00. Bundesstelle fuer Aussenhandelsinformation, Agrippastrasse 87 93, D-50676 Cologne Germany. **Tel** 011 49 221 2057316, FAX 011 49 221 2057212.

LC HC121 .I62
    US
ALLIANCE FOR PROGRESS : REPORT ON THE PROGRESS OF ECONOMIC AND SOCIAL DEVELOPMENT IN LATIN AMERICA AND PROSPECTS FOR THE FUTURE, THE. **Main/Corp** Inter-American Economic and Social Council. **Added/Corp** Pan American Union. (1961/62)-. English. One time a week. Free on request. Organization of American States, 19th Street & Constitution Avenue NW, Suite 300, Washington DC 20006. **Tel** (202)458-6256.

LC JA   **ISSN** 1077-4521
DD 320   US
●**AMERICA REPORT : A COMMON SENSE ANNUAL REPORT TO THE CITIZENS OF THE UNITED STATES.** [Am. rep.]. **VFOAT** United States of America ... Common Sense Annual Report. (1994)-. Consumer Publication. English. One time a year. $5.95. Blue Heron Press, 5 Starlight Farm Drive, Phoenix MD 21131. **Tel** (410)472-4573, FAX (410)771-4213. **ED** Lyle A. Brecht.
 Desc: Provides information regarding the ways in which taxes are spent each year and what is being accomplished in the government using these taxes.

LC HC186 .A77
DD 330.9/81/06   BL
ANALISE. Portuguese (English). Publicacoes Executivas Brasileiras, rua Dos Ingleses 150, CEP 01329, Caixa Postal 30837, Sao Paulo Brazil.

LC HC226 .A83   **ISSN** 0251-2491
DD 330.98/0005   PE
ANDEAN REPORT, THE. [Andean rep.]. **VFOAT** Andean Air Mail & Peruvian Times's the Andean Report. Vol. 1 (July 1975)-. Periodical. English. One time a week. $520.00. Andean Air Mail and Peruvian Times SA, Apartado Postal 531, Lima 100 Peru. **Tel** 011 51 14 469120. **ED** Nicholas Asheshov. Index available. **Bk Rev. Circ:** 1,500. **Supersedes** Peruvian Times.
 Desc: Covers banking, economy, politics, mining, petroleum, trade and commerce, construction and allied subjects.
 Ind/Abst Predicasts.

LC HA1631 .A33 HD7045.5   **ISSN** 0300-2543
DD 314.971   YU
ANKETA O PORODICNIM BUDZETIMA RADNICKIH DOMACINSTAVA. See Business and Economics-Abstracting, Bibliographies and Statistics.

LC HD3840 .A7   **ISSN** 0770-8548
    BE
    CCC
ANNALS OF PUBLIC AND CO-OPERATIVE ECONOMY. [Ann. public co-op econ.]. **Added/Corp** International Centre of Research and Information on Public and Co-operative Economy. **VFOAT** Annalen der Geineinwirtschaft; Annales de l'Economie, Publique, Sociale et Cooperative; Annals de l'Economie Collective. (Jan./March 1964)-. Academic Scholarly Publication. English (French). Four times a year. $133.00. Basil Blackwell Publishers Ltd., 108 Cowley Road, Oxford 0X4 1JF United Kingdom. **Tel** 011 44 1235 465500, FAX 011 44 1235 465556, telex 837022 OXBOOK G. (**Subscription address:** Blackwell Publishers / UK, 108 Cowley Road, Oxford OX4 1JF United Kingdom. **Tel** 011 44 1865 791100, FAX 011 44 1865 791347.) **Continues** Annals of Collective Economy, 0770-8491.
 Ind/Abst Curr. Cit.; Int. Bibliogr. Sociol.; Int. Labour Doc.; J. Econ. Lit.; Rural Dev. Abstr.

    BE
Pr Rev.
ANNALS OF PUBLIC AND COOPERATIVE ECONOMY. Vol. 1 (1925)-. Periodical. Multiple languages (English, French and German). Four times a year. $32.65. CIRIEC / Belgium, Information Center for Research and Information on Public and Co-operative Economy, Universite de Liege, Batiment B 31, 4000 Liege Belgium. **Tel** 562 746, FAX 56 29 58. Index available. cum. index. **Circ:** 700. **Continues** Annales de la Regie Directe.
 Desc: Articles focus mainly on public economics, management public corporations, public finance, cooperation, self management.
 Ind/Abst Contents Recent Econ. J.; Econ. Lit. Index; Leis., Rec., Tour. Abstr.; Middle East Abstr. Index; Rural Dev. Abstr.; World Agric. Econ. Rural Sociol. Abstr.

LC HC557.C3 A72
DD 330.9/67/11   CM
ANNUAIRE DE L'INDUSTRIE ET DU COMMERCE DE LA REPUBLIQUE UNIE DU CAMEROUN. (19??)-. French. One time a year. Cograca, Angle rue Surcouf-rue de la Gare, BP 1555, Douala Cameroon.

LC HC820.A1 A55
DD 330.961/1/005   TI
ANNUAIRE ECONOMIQUE DE LA TUNISIE. **VFOAT** Economic Yearbook of Tunisia; Dalil Al-Iqtisadi Lil-Jumhuriyah Al-Tunisiyah. Arabic (English and French). One time a year. Union Tunisienne de l'Industrie du Commerce et de l'Artisanat, 32 rue Charles de Gaulle, Tunis Tunisia.

LC HC499.A1 A56
DD 330.917/671   TU
ANNUAL ECONOMIC REPORT. **Main/Corp** Statistical, Economic, and Social Research and Training Centre for Islamic Countries. (19??)-. Statistical Publication. English. One time a year. SESRTCIC Publications Dept, Hemsehri Sokak No 1 GOP, 06700 Ankara Turkey. ctrl circ.

LC HC107.O72 D473
DD 330.9795/87/005   US
ANNUAL ECONOMIC REPORT ... DESCHUTES COUNTY. English. One time a year. Mike Mahan/Labor Economist, PO Box 68, Klamath Falls OR 97601.

LC HC107.O72 D683
DD 330.9795/29/005   US
ANNUAL ECONOMIC REPORT ... DOUGLAS COUNTY. (19??)-. English. One time a year. Oregon Employment Division, 875 Union Street Northeast, Salem OR 97311. **Tel** (503)378-3211.

LC HC107.O72 G715
DD 330.9795/78/05   US
ANNUAL ECONOMIC REPORT ... GRANT COUNTY. English. One time a year. Oregon Employment Division, 875 Union Street Northeast, Salem OR 97311. **Tel** (503)378-3211.

LC HC107.O72 J333
DD 330.9795/27/005   US
ANNUAL ECONOMIC REPORT ... JACKSON COUNTY. 1982-. English. One time a year. Oregon Employment Division / Medford, PO Box 910, Medford OR 97501. **Continues** Jackson County Economic Review.

LC HC107.O72 J433
DD 330.9795/85/005   US
ANNUAL ECONOMIC REPORT ... JEFFERSON COUNTY. English. One time a year. M Mahan Labor Economist, PO Box 68, Klamath Falls OR 97601.

LC HC107.O72 C573
DD 330.9795/4/005   US
ANNUAL ECONOMIC REPORT ... NORTH COAST AREA : CLATSOP COUNTY, COLUMBIA COUNTY, TILLAMOOK COUNTY. 1982-. English. One time a year. Oregon Employment Division, 875 Union Street Northeast, Salem OR 97311. **Tel** (503)378-3211. **Formed by the union of** Annual Economic Report ... Clatsop County; Annual Economic Report ... Columbia County **and** Annual Economic Report ... Tillamook County.

LC HC107.O72 W343
DD 330.9795/73/005   US
ANNUAL ECONOMIC REPORT ... WALLOWA COUNTY. English. One time a year. Oregon Employment Division, 875 Union Street Northeast, Salem OR 97311. **Tel** (503)378-3211.

LC HA4007.G5 A25
DD 330.9967   GU
ANNUAL ECONOMIC REVIEW AND STATISTICAL ABSTRACT, GUAM. **Added/Corp** Guam. Economic Research Center. **VFOAT** Annual Economic Review and Statistical Abstract; Guam Annual Economic Review and Statistical Abstract; Guam Annual Economic Review. (198?)-. Government Publication. English. One time a year. Guam Department of Commerce / Economic Research Center, 590 South Marine Drive, Suite 601, GITC Building, Tamuning, Guam 96911. available with charts. **Continues** Annual Economic Review, Guam.
 Desc: Details current and historical economic and social characteristics of the island of Guam.

LC HC157.A1 A55   **ISSN** 1011-6311
DD 330.97298/3/005   TR
ANNUAL ECONOMIC SURVEY (PORT OF SPAIN, TRINIDAD AND TOBAGO). (ANNUAL ECONOMIC SURVEY / CENTRAL BANK OF TRINIDAD AND TOBAGO.). (1986)-. English. One time a year. $12.00. Central Bank of Trinidad and Tobago, PO Box 1250, Port of Spain Trinidad. **Tel** (809)625-4835, (809)625-5028. **Circ:** 1,200 (ctrl). available on microfilm from University Microfilms International (UMI). **Separated from** Annual Report - Central Bank of Trinidad and Tobago.
 Desc: Analyses economic developments which occurred during the year in Trinidad and Tobago. Also contains appendix tables.

LC HC437.K27 K37B
DD 338.954/87/005   II
ANNUAL PLAN - GOVERNMENT OF KARNATAKA, PLANNING DEPARTMENT. **Main/Corp** Karnataka, India. Planning Dept. English. One time a year. Government Press / Planning Department, Karnataka India. **Continues** Annual Plan - Government of Mysore, Planning Department.

LC HN682.5 .A25
DD 354.540081/8   II
●**ANNUAL REPORT.** **Main/Corp** India. Dept. of Rural Development. (1993)-. English. One time a year. Government of India Ministry of Rural Development, New Delhi, India. **Continues** India. Ministry of Rural Development. Annual Report.

LC HC107.A63 P632   **ISSN** 0090-6182
DD 353.9/791/00845   US
ANNUAL REPORT - ARIZONA STATE ECONOMIC OPPORTUNITY OFFICE. (ANNUAL REPORT.). **Main/Corp** Arizona. State Economic Opportunity Office. (19??)-. English. One time a year. Arizona Economic Opportunity Office, State of Arizona, 3rd Floor/Capital Building, Phoenix AZ 85007.

LC HC107.I3 A33   **ISSN** 0090-1016
DD 353.97730082/06   US
ANNUAL REPORT - ILLINOIS DEPARTMENT OF BUSINESS AND ECONOMIC DEVELOPMENT. (ANNUAL REPORT.). **Main/Corp** Illinois. Dept. of Business and Economic Development. English. One time a year. Department of Business and Economic Development, 222 South College Street, Springfield IL 62706.

LC HC117.M3 M22633a   **ISSN** 1199-3383
DD 354.71270085/6/05   CN
●**ANNUAL REPORT - MANITOBA. ECONOMIC INNOVATION & TECHNOLOGY COUNCIL.** (ANNUAL REPORT.). [Annu. rep. - Manit. Econ. Innov. Technol. Counc.]. **Main/Corp** Manitoba. Economic Innovation &

Business and Economics —Economic History, Conditions

Technology Council. Winnipeg. (1992/93)-. English. *Continues* Manitoba Research Council. Annual Report., 0837-6425.

LC HC607.V53 V49A
DD 354.94507/2/06 AT
ANNUAL REPORT OF THE PLANNING CONSULTATIVE COUNCIL FOR THE YEAR ENDED 30 JUNE ... (VICTORIA). **Main/Corp** Victoria. Planning Consultative Council. 1st (1981)-. English. One time a year. 235 Queen Street, Melbourne 3000 Australia.

LC HC107.O5 O45A ISSN 0364-8257
DD 353.9/766/0082 US
ANNUAL REPORT - STATE OF OKLAHOMA, DEPARTMENT OF ECONOMIC AND COMMUNITY AFFAIRS. **Main/Corp** Oklahoma. Dept. of Economic and Community Affairs. 1975-. English. One time a year. Oklahoma Department of Economic and Community Affairs, 5500 North Western, Oklahoma City OK 73118.

LC HC110.P6 A18 ISSN 0565-4408
DD 353.0082/06 338.9 US
ANNUAL REPORT - UNITED STATES. ECONOMIC DEVELOPMENT ADMINISTRATION (1969). (ANNUAL REPORT / ECONOMIC DEVELOPMENT ADMINISTRATION.). [Annu. rep. - U. S., Econ. Dev. Adm.]. **Main/Corp** United States. Economic Development Administration. (1974)-. English. One time a year. United States Department of Commerce, Economic Development Administration, Washington DC 20044. available on microfiche (Vols. for (1984-) distributed to depository libraries). *Continues* Annual Report of the Economic Development Administration, 0565-4408.

LC HC461 .A136a
DD 330.952/005 JA
ANNUAL REPORTS ON NATIONAL LIFE. **Added/Corp** Japan. Keizai Kikakucho. **VFOAT** Annual Report on National Life; Annual Report on the National Life for Fiscal ... . (1978)-. English. One time a year. Government Publications Service Center, 2-1 Kasumigaseki 1-Chome, Chiyoda-Ku Tokyo 100 Japan. **Tel** 011 81 3 3504 3885. *Continues* Kokumin Seikatsu Hakusho. English. Whitepaper on National Life.

JA
ANNUAL REVIEW BANK OF JAPAN. **Added/Corp** Tokyo Bank of Japan. (1991)-. English. One time a year (Summer). Free. Bank of Japan / Public Relations Department, C.P.O. Box 203, Tokyo 100-91 Japan. **Tel** 81 3 3279 1111, FAX 81 3 5200 2256, 81 3 3664-4348.

LC HC10 .A68 ISSN 1043-6588
DD 330.9/005 US
ANNUAL REVIEW OF NATIONS. [Annu. rev. nations]. (1988)-. English. Irregular. $79.50. Taylor and Francis, 1900 Frost Road, Suite 101, Bristol PA 19007-1598. **Tel** (800)821-8312, (215)785-5800, FAX (215)785-5515.

LC HC437.P57 A2
DD 338.4/767/095486 II
ANNUAL SURVEY OF INDUSTRIES (PONDICHERRY (INDIA : UNION TERRITORY). BUREAU OF ECONOMICS AND STATISTICS). (ANNUAL SURVEY OF INDUSTRIES / UNION TERRITORY OF PONDICHERRY.). **Added/Corp** Pondicherry (India : Union Territory). Bureau of Economics and Statistics. (1975-76)-. English. One time a year. Bureau of Economics and Statistics / Pondicherry India, Pondicherry 605001 India. *Continues* Annual Survey of Industries (Pondicherry (India : Union Territory). Bureau of Statistics and Evaluation).

LC WMLC L 83/8083 ISSN 0066-5088
SP
ANUARIO DE HISTORIA ECONOMICA Y SOCIAL. **Added/Corp** Universidad Complutense de Madrid. Seminario de Historia Social y Economia. Vol. 1, No. 1 (Jan. 1968)-. Spanish. One time a year. **Ind/Abst** Am. Hist. Life.

LC HC171 .A69
DD 330.982/005 AG
ANUARIO PRENSA ECONOMICA. TENDENCIAS ..., ARGENTINA ... . **VFOAT** Tendencias ...; Anuario de Prensa Economica. (1978)-. Spanish. One time a year. Editorial Lourdes, Pte Luis Saenz Pena 747, 1ER Piso, Buenos Aires Argentina. *Continues* Prensa Economica. Tendencias ..., Argentina ... .

LC HC431 .A84
II
ANVESAK. **Added/Corp** Sardar Patel Institute of Economic and Social Research. Vol. 1 (June 1971)-. Periodical. English. Two times a year. $25.00. Institute of Economic and Social Research / India, Box 4062, Navrangpura Ahmedabad India. **(Subscription**

address: Prints India, 11 Darya Ganj, New Delhi 110002 India. **Tel** 011 91 11 3268645, FAX 011 91 11 3275542, telex 31-61087 PRIN-IN.)

LC HC186 .A852 ISSN 0001-2181
DD 330.9/81/06 BL
APEC, ANALISE E PERSPECTIVA ECONOMICA. **VFOAT** Analise e Perspectiva Economica; Brazilian Fortnightly Economic Letter. (19??)-. Periodical. English (Portuguese). Twenty-four times a year. $200.00. APEC - Assoc Promo Estudios Economica, rua Sorocaba 295, 22271 Rio de Janeiro Brazil. **Tel** 011 55 21 2664449, 011 55 21 2664249.

LC HC497.Y4
GW
ARABISCHE REPUBLIK JEMEN : WIRTSCHAFTLICHE ENTWICKLUNG. **Main/Corp** Bundesstelle fur Aussenhandelsinformation (Germany). German. DM2.00. Bundesstelle fuer Aussenhandelsinformation, Agrippastrasse 87 93, D-50676 Cologne Germany. **Tel** 011 49 221 2057316, FAX 011 49 221 2057212.

LC HC415.34.A1
DD 330.953/32/005 GW
ARABISCHE REPUBLIK JEMEN, WIRTSCHAFTSDATEN UND WIRTSCHAFTSDOKUMENTATION / BUNDESSTELLE FUR AUSSENHANDELSINFORMATION. German. One time a year. DM3.00. Bundesstelle fuer Aussenhandelsinformation, Agrippastrasse 87 93, D-50676 Cologne Germany. **Tel** 011 49 221 2057316, FAX 011 49 221 2057212.

LC HC498.A1 T84A
TU
ARAP ULKELERI EKONOMIK RAPORU. **Main/Corp** Turkiye Ticaret Odalar, Sanayi Odalar Ve Ticaret Borsalar Birligi. Turkish. Turkiye Ticaret Odalar, Sanayi Odalar Ve Ticaret, Borsalar Birligi, Turkiye Ticaret Birlogi, Ankara Turkey.

LC HC301 .A686 ISSN 0518-3499
IT
CEASED
ARCHIVIO ECONOMICO DELL'UNIFICAZIONE ITALIANA. SERIE I. (ARCHIVIO ECONOMICO DELL'UNIFICAZIONE ITALIANA.). [Arch. econ. unificazione ital., Ser. I]. **Added/Corp** Istituto per la Ricostruzione Industriale (Italy). Vol. 1 (1956)-(19??). Periodical. Italian. **Ind/Abst** Am. Hist. Life (1956-1967).

ISSN 1054-5239
DD 982 US
ARGENTINA (SYRACUSE, N.Y.). (ARGENTINA : A POLITICAL AND ECONOMIC FORECAST / POLITICAL RISK SERVICES.). [Argentina]. **Added/Corp** Political Risk Services (IBC USA (Publications) Inc.). (19??)-. English. $325.00. Political Risk Services, 6320 Fly Road, Suite 102, PO Box 248, East Syracuse NY 13057-0248. **Tel** (315)431-0511, FAX (315)431-0200.
Desc: Assesses the factors affecting the prospects for business and trade. Each report focuses specifically on business needs such as finding and developing markets, determining currency movements, or making judgements about capital investments or corporate security.

LC HC171 .A717
DD 330.982/005 GW
ARGENTINIEN WIRTSCHAFTSDATEN. **Added/Corp** Bundesstelle fuer Aussenhandelsinformation (Germany). (19??)-. German. DM3.00. Bundesstelle fuer Aussenhandelsinformation, Agrippastrasse 87 93, D-50676 Cologne Germany. **Tel** 011 49 221 2057316, FAX 011 49 221 2057212.

LC HC171 .A718
DD 330.982 GW
ARGENTINIEN WIRTSCHAFTSDATEN UND WIRTSCHAFTSDOKUMENTATION. **Added/Corp** Bundesstelle fur Aussenhandelsinformation (Germany). (19??)-. German. DM3.00. Bundesstelle fuer Aussenhandelsinformation, Agrippastrasse 87 93, D-50676 Cologne Germany. **Tel** 011 49 221 2057316, FAX 011 49 221 2057212.

LC HC171 .A72
DD 330.982 GW
ARGENTINIEN WIRTSCHAFTSSTRUKTUR. **Added/Corp** Bundesstelle fuer Aussenhandelsinformation (Germany). (19??)-. German. Bundesstelle fuer Aussenhandelsinformation, Agrippastrasse 87 93, D-50676 Cologne Germany. **Tel** 011 49 221 2057316, FAX 011 49 221 2057212.

US
ARIZONA ECONOMIC INDICATORS (TUCSON, ARIZ. : 1984). (ARIZONA ECONOMIC INDICATORS.). **Added/Corp** University of

Arizona. Division of Economic and Business Research. Vol. 1, No. 1 (Spring/Summer 1984)-. Periodical. English. Two times a year. $16.00. Economic and Business Research Program, BPA College, McClelland Hall, 204-H, Tucson AZ 85721. **Tel** (602)621-2155, FAX (612)621-2150. **ED** Diana Hunter. **Circ:** 400. available on diskette.
Desc: Presents historical data for measures of economic activity for Arizona and its counties; information for public and private sector professionals.

LC HC107.A6 A78 ISSN 0197-5412
US
ARIZONA PROGRESS. **Added/Corp** Valley National Bank of Arizona. Economic Research Dept. (1946)-. Periodical. English. Nine times a year. Free on request. Valley National Bank Research Department, 241 North Central Avenue, PO Box 71, Phoenix AZ 85001. **Tel** (602)261-2900. available in microform from KTO Microform.

LC HB74.9.D4 R67A
DK
ARSBERETNING. **Main/Corp** Roskilde Universitetscenter. Institut for Samfundskonomi Og Planlgning. Danish. One time a year. Institut for Samfundskonomi Og Planlgning, Roskilde Universitetscenter, Postbox 260, 4000 Roskilde Denmark.

LC HC431 .A87 ISSN 0004-3559
DD 330.954/005 II
ARTHA VIJNANA. (ARTHA VIJNANA : JOURNAL OF THE GOKHALE INSTITUTE OF POLITICS AND ECONOMICS, POONA (INDIA).). [Artha Vijnana]. **Added/Corp** Gokhale Institute of Politics and Economics. **VFOAT** Artha Vijnana : Gokhale Artha Sastra Samstha Dvara Prakasita Traimesika Patrika. Vol. 1 (March 1959)-. Periodical. Indic (Hindi; summaries and/or abstracts in Hindi and English). Four times a year. $65.00. Cokhale Institute of Politics and Economics, Poona 4 India. **Tel** 26 86 45. **(Subscription address:** Prints India, 11 Darya Ganj, New Delhi 110002 India. **Tel** 011 91 11 3268645, FAX 011 91 11 3275542, telex 31-61087 PRIN-IN.)
Ind/Abst Contents Recent Econ. J.; Int. Labour Doc.; Rural Dev. Abstr.; Soils Fert.; Soyabean Abstr.; World Agric. Econ. Rural Sociol. Abstr.

LC HC431 .A88 ISSN 0004-3567
II
ARTHA-VIKAS. [Artha-vikas]. **Added/Corp** Sardar Vallabhbhai Vidyapeeth, Vallabh Vidyanagar, India. Dept. of Economics. **VFOAT** Journal of Economic Development. Vol. 1 (1965)-. Periodical. English (Gujarati). Two times a year (Jan., July). $16.00. Registrar Sardar Patel University, Vallabh Vidyanagar 38 120, Gujarat 388001 India. **Tel** 011 91 2692 388120. **(Subscription address:** UBS Publishers Distributors, 5 Ansari Road, PO Box 7015, New Delhi 110002 India. **Tel** 011 91 11 3273601, 011 91 11 3266645.)
Ind/Abst J. Econ. Lit.; Rural Dev. Abstr.; Sorghum Mill. Abstr.; World Agric. Econ. Rural Sociol. Abstr.

US
ASEAN BRIEFING. **Main/Corp** ASEAN. (1978)-. Periodical. English. Twelve times a year. $60.00. Asia Letter Group, GPO Box 10874, Central Hong Kong. **Tel** 011 852 25262950, FAX 011 852 25267131, telex 61166. **ED** Charles R Smith. **Bk Rev**. ctrl circ.
Desc: An analysis of political and economic developments in the Association of South East Asian nations.
Ind/Abst Asia.-Pac. Econ. Lit.

LC HC411 .F19
DD 330.9/5/042 HK
ASIA YEARBOOK. **VFOAT** Far Eastern Economic Review. (1973)-. English. One time a year (Jan.). $63.00. Review Publishing Company Ltd., 25 F Citicorp Center, 18 Whitfield Road, GPO Box 160, Hong Kong Hong Kong. **Tel** 011 852 25084337, FAX 011 852 25031549, 25031553, telex 66452 REVCD HX. **(Subscription address:** Review Publishing Company Ltd., PO Box 160, Hong Kong Hong Kong. **Tel** 011 852 25084300.) **ED** Mike MacLachlan. **Ad Acc. Circ:** 30,000. *Continues* Far Eastern Economic Review. Yearbook, 0071-3821.
Desc: Covers events of Asian economic, political, social or strategic importance.

LC HC411 .A17 ISSN 0117-0481
DD 330.95/005 PH
ASIAN DEVELOPMENT OUTLOOK : ADO. **Added/Corp** Asian Development Bank. **VFOAT** ADO; A.D.O. (1989)-. English. One time a year. $30.00. Asian Development Bank / Information Office, PO Box 789, 1099 Manila Philippines. **Tel** 011 63 2 8344444, 011 63 2 7113851, FAX 011 63 2 7417961, 011 63 2 6326816, telex 63587 ADB PN ETPI, 42205 ADB PM ITT, 29066 ADB PH RCA.

ISSN 0970-6305
DD 330 II
ASIAN ECONOMIC AND SOCIAL REVIEW, THE. [Asian econ. soc. rev.]. **Added/Corp** Indian Institute of Asian Studies, Bombay. Vol. 1 (Nov. 1976)-. Periodical. English. Four times a year (Jan., Apr., July, Oct.). $75.00. Asian Studies Press, Indian Institute of Asian Studies, 23/354 Azadnagar Jaiprakash Road,

Andheri Bombay 400058 India. **Tel** 011 91 22 6263974. **ED** M. R. Sinha. Index available. cum. index. **Bk Rev. Ad Acc. Circ:** 3,000 (ctrl). ***Formed by the union of*** *Quarterly Journal of Indian Studies in Social Sciences* ***and*** *IFCEP Journal of Modern India.*
Desc: Covers technical transfer and cooperation of the countries of Asia and their social, economic, political and spiritual problems. Includes in-depth studies and research papers.
Ind/Abst Int. Labour Doc.; Leis., Rec., Tour. Abstr.; Rural Dev. Abstr.; World Agric. Econ. Rural Sociol. Abstr.

LC HB9 .A8 **ISSN** 0004-4555
DD 330.05 II
ASIAN ECONOMIC REVIEW, THE. [Asian econ. rev.]. **Added/Corp** Indian Institute of Economics. Vol. 1 (Nov. 1958)-. Periodical. English. Three times a year. $50.00. Indian Institute of Economics, 11-6-841 Red Hills, Hyderabad 500004 India. **Tel** 26 86 45. **(Subscription address:** Prints India, 11 Darya Ganj, New Delhi 110002 India. **Tel** 011 91 11 3268645, FAX 011 91 11 3275542, telex 31-61087 PRIN-IN.**)**
Ind/Abst Contents Recent Econ. J.; Int. Labour Doc.; LABORDOC.

LC HC411 .A755 **ISSN** 0304-260X
DD 330.9/5/042 KO
ASIAN ECONOMIES. [Asian econ.]. **Added/Corp** Asea Kyongje Yonguso. (June 1972)-. Periodical. English. Four times a year (Mar., June, Sept., Dec.). $38.00. Research Institute Asian Economies, KPO Box 1008, Seoul 110 Korea. **Tel** 794 2831. **ED** Taiwhzan Shin. **Ad Acc. Circ:** 1,000.
Desc: Studies on developing economies of North East, South East and West Asia including the Pacific area.
Ind/Abst Asia.-Pac. Econ. Lit.; Contents Recent Econ. J.; Int. Labour Doc.; Leis., Rec., Tour. Abstr.; PAIS Int. Print (1991-); Rice Abstr.; Rural Dev. Abstr.; World Agric. Econ. Rural Sociol. Abstr.

ISSN 0191-0132
US
CCC
ASIAN WALL STREET JOURNAL. WEEKLY, THE. Vol. 1 (April 30, 1979)-. Academic Scholarly Publication. English. One time a week. $245.00. Dow Jones and Company Inc., 200 Burnett Road, Chicopee MA 01021. **Tel** (413)592-7761, (800)568-7625. **ED** Lourdes Lee Valeriano. Index available. **Bk Rev. Ad Acc. Circ:** 6,547. available on an online database from NEXIS. Documents available from CASDDS, Documents on Demand.
Desc: Newspaper reporting on Asian business, political, and economic news in the Asia/Pacific region.
Ind/Abst Bus. Index (1991-); Chem. Abstr.; Energy Inf. Abstr.; Environ. Abstr.; Gen. BusinessFile (1991-); Infomat Int. Bus.

LC HC591.A3
GW
ATHIOPIEN : WIRTSCHAFTLICHE ENTWICKLUNG. Main/Corp Bundesstelle fur Aussenhandelsinformation (Germany). German. DM2.00. Bundesstelle fuer Aussenhandelsinformation, Agrippastrasse 87 93, D-50676 Cologne Germany. **Tel** 011 49 221 2057316, FAX 011 49 221 2057212.

LC HC117.A88 A84 **ISSN** 0004-6841
DD 330.9715/005 CN
CODEN ATRPEV
ATLANTIC REPORT (HALIFAX, N.S.). (ATLANTIC REPORT.). [Atl. rep.]. **Added/Corp** Atlantic Provinces Economic Council. (Jan. 1966)-. Periodical. English. Four times a year (Apr., Jul., Oct., Dec.). 62.50Can$. Atlantic Provinces Economic Council, 5121 Sackville Street, Suite 500, Halifax Nova Scotia B3J 1K1 Canada. **Tel** (902)422-6516, FAX (902)429-6803. **ED** M Mandale. **Bk Rev. Circ:** 1,200 (ctrl). available on microfiche.
Desc: A review of economic conditions in Canada's four eastern provinces with provincial reports, statistics and forecasts.
Ind/Abst Can. Index; Can. Period. Index (19??-).

LC HC59 .A8625
DD 330.9/048/05 FR
ATLASECO DE POCHE. (1985)-. French. Irregular. $131.23. Editions du Serail, 4 rue Comaille, 75007 Paris France. **Tel** 011 33 1 45480314. ***Continues*** *Atlaseco, 0290-036X.*

LC HC186 .A26a
BL
ATUACAO DO MINTER. Main/Corp Brazil. Ministerio do Interior. Secretaria Geral. (19??)-. Portuguese. One time a year. Ministerio do Interior, Gabinete do Ministro Sas, Quadra 1 Bloco A, Lotes 9/10 80 Andar, Brasilia Brazil.

LC HF3000 .A93 **ISSN** 1064-4555
DD 330/.05 US
AUDACITY (NEW YORK, N.Y.). (AUDACITY.). [Audacity]. Vol. 1, No. 1 (Fall 1992)-. Periodical. English. Four times a year. $14.95. American Heritage, Forbes Building, 60 Fifth Avenue, New York NY 10011. **Tel** (212)206-5500, FAX (212)620-2332. **(Subscription address:** Small Publishers Services, PO Box 6606, Syracuse NY 13217. **) ED** John Steele Gordon. **Circ:** 100,000.
Desc: Focuses on understanding how the economic past shapes and provides insight into the economic present. The title targets leaders and aims to entertain as well as offer solutions to today's business problems.

ISSN 1054-5247
DD 994 US
AUSTRALIA (SYRACUSE, N.Y.). (AUSTRALIA : A POLITICAL AND ECONOMIC FORECAST / POLITICAL RISK SERVICES.). [Australia]. **Added/Corp** Political Risk Services (IBC USA (Publications) Inc.). (19??)-. English. $325.00. Political Risk Services, 6320 Fly Road, Suite 102, PO Box 248, East Syracuse NY 13057-0248. **Tel** (315)431-0511, FAX (315)431-0200.
Desc: Assesses the factors affecting the prospects for business and trade. Each report focuses specifically on business needs such as finding and developing markets, determining currency movements, or making judgements about capital investments or corporate security.

LC HC601 .A82 **ISSN** 0004-8992
DD 330.994/005 AT
CCC
Pr Rev.
AUSTRALIAN ECONOMIC HISTORY REVIEW. [Aust. econ. hist. rev.]. **Added/Corp** University of Sydney. Dept. of Economics. University of Sydney. Dept. of Economic History. Economic History Society of Australia and New Zealand. **VFOAT** AEHR; A.E.H.R. Vol. 7, No. 1 (March 1967)-. Periodical. English. Two times a year. 42.76Aus$. Oxford University Press / Australia, GPO Box 2784Y, Melbourne Victoria 3001 Australia. **Tel** 011 61 3 6464200, telex AA 35330. **ED** G. D. Snooks and J. J. Pincus. **Bk Rev. Circ:** 350. available on microfilm and microfiche from University Microfilms International (UMI). Documents available from The Genuine Article. ***Continues*** *Business Archives and History, 0818-3023.*
Desc: Current issues in Australian economic history.
Ind/Abst Acad. Search; Am. Hist. Life (1962-); APAIS, Aust. Public Aff. Inf. Ser. (1967-); Bus. Source Plus; Bus. Source; Curr. Contents Soc. Behav. Sci.; Econ. Lit. Index; EP Collect.; Geogr. Abstr. Human Geogr. (?-?); Homework Help.; INFO-SOUTH Abstr.; J. Econ. Lit.; Mag. Search; MasterFile FullTEXT 1000; MasterFile FullTEXT 350; MasterFile FullTEXT 650; MasterFile FullTEXT (Jan. 1994-); OCLC; Res. Alert [Full Cov.]; Soc. Sci. Cit. Index [Full Cov.]; Telebase; World Mag. Bank.

LC HB1 .A825 **ISSN** 0004-900X
DD 330.994/005 AT
AUSTRALIAN ECONOMIC PAPERS. [Aust. econ. pap.]. **Added/Corp** University of Adelaide. Flinders University of South Australia. Vol. 1 No. (Sept. 1962)-. Periodical. English. Two times a year. 28.78Aus$. University of Adelaide / Economics, Department of Economics, Adelaide SA 5005 Australia. **Tel** 011 61 8 3034499. **ED** M. Burns. Index Available, published separately, free-automatically sent. **Ad Acc. Circ:** 1,000.
Desc: Theoretical and applied economics, economic history and accounting.
Ind/Abst APAIS, Aust. Public Aff. Inf. Ser. (1963-); Contents Recent Econ. J.; Curr. Cit.; Econ. Lit. Index (1963-); Geogr. Abstr. Human Geogr. (?-?); Int. Dev. Abstr. (?-?); Int. Labour Doc.; J. Econ. Lit.; Leis., Rec., Tour. Abstr.; Plant Breed. Abstr.; Rice Abstr.; Rural Dev. Abstr.; World Agric. Econ. Rural Sociol. Abstr.

LC HC601 .A827 **ISSN** 0084-7348
DD 338.5/443/0994 AT
TITLE CHANGE
AUSTRALIAN ECONOMY : BUSINESS FORECASTS, THE. Added/Corp W.D. Scott and Company. (1965)-(19??). English. W D Scott and Company, 100 Pacific Highway, 2060 Sydney Australia. ***Continues*** *Management Guide to the Economy.* ***Continued by*** *Management Reports on the Australian Economy, 0816-2484.*

LC HC601 .A8B
DD 330.994/005 GW
AUSTRALIEN, WIRTSCHAFTLICHE ENTWICKLUNG / BUNDESSTELLE FUR AUSSENHANDELSINFORMATION. German. Bundesstelle fuer Aussenhandelsinformation, Agrippastrasse 87 93, D-50676 Cologne Germany. **Tel** 011 49 221 2057316, FAX 011 49 221 2057212.

ISSN 1054-5255
DD 943 US
AUSTRIA (SYRACUSE, N.Y.). (AUSTRIA : A POLITICAL AND ECONOMIC FORECAST.). [Austria]. **Added/Corp** Political Risk Services (IBC USA (Publications) Inc.). (19??)-. English. $325.00. Political Risk Services, 6320 Fly Road, Suite 102, PO Box 248, East Syracuse NY 13057-0248. **Tel** (315)431-0511, FAX (315)431-0200.
Desc: Assesses the factors affecting the prospects for business and trade. Each report focuses specifically on business needs such as finding and developing markets, determining currency movements, or making judgements about capital investments or corporate security.

LC HD9734.M4 A95 **ISSN** 0187-4977
MX
AVANCE DE INFORMACION ECONOMICA. INDICADORES DEL SECTOR MANUFACTURERO / INEGI. Added/Corp Instituto Nacional de Estadistica, Geografia e Informatica (Mexico). **VFOAT** Indicadores del Sector Manufacturero. (19??)-. Spanish. Twelve times a year. $30.55. INEGI / Instituto Nacional de Estadistica, Geografia e Informatica, Avenida Patriotismo 711 Segundo Piso, 03730 Mexico DF **Mexico. Tel** 011 52 5 5639935, 011 52 5 5988935, FAX 011 52 55987941. **(Subscription address:** INEGI / Instituto Nacional de Estadistica, Geografia e Informatica, Avenida Heroe de Nacozari 2301 Sur, Fracc. Jardines del Parque, CP 20270, Aguascalientes Mexico. **Tel** 011 52 49 182998.**)**

LC HC140.I5 A9
MX
AVANCE DE INFORMACION ECONOMICA. PRODUCTO INTERNO BRUTO TRIMESTRAL. Added/Corp Instituto Nacional de Estadistica, Geografia e Informatica (Mexico). **VFOAT** Producto Interno Bruto Trimestral. (19??)-. Periodical. Spanish. Four times a year. $25.81. INEGI / Instituto Nacional de Estadistica, Geografia e Informatica, Avenida Patriotismo 711 Segundo Piso, 03730 Mexico DF Mexico. **Tel** 011 52 5 5639935, 011 52 5 5988935, FAX 011 52 55987941. **(Subscription address:** INEGI / Instituto Nacional de Estadistica, Geografia e Informatica, Avenida Heroe de Nacozari 2301 Sur, Fracc. Jardines del Parque, CP 20270, Aguascalientes Mexico. **Tel** 011 52 49 182998.**)**

LC HC241.2 .B23
DD 330.9/4/055 UK
BACKGROUND DATA ON THE COMMON MARKET. (1972)-. English. European Data Publishing Company, 32 James Street, SW1 London United Kingdom.

LC HC497.N5 A35
NP
BAITHAKAKO KARYAVAHIKO SANKSHIPTA-VIVARANA. Main/Corp Nepal. Rashtriya Vikasa Parishad. November 2029- 1973-. Nepali. Rs13.20. National Planning Commission Secretariat, Ramshah Path, Kathamadaum India.

LC HC440.8.A1 B3 **ISSN** 0304-095X
DD 330.9/549/205 BG
BANGLADESH DEVELOPMENT STUDIES, THE. [Bangladesh dev. stud.]. **Added/Corp** Bangladesh Institute of Development Studies. Vol. 2, No. 3 (July 1974)-. Periodical. English. Four times a year (Mar., June, Sept., Dec.). $50.00. Bangladesh Institute of Development Studies, E-17 Agargaon, PO Box 3854, Dhaka 7 Bangladesh. **Tel** FAX 880-2-813023. ***Continues*** *Bangladesh Economic Review.*
Ind/Abst Econ. Lit. Index; Int. Bibliogr. Sociol.; Int. Labour Doc.; J. Econ. Lit.; Leis., Rec., Tour. Abstr.; PAIS Int. Print (1991-); Popul. Index; Rural Dev. Abstr.; World Agric. Econ. Rural Sociol. Abstr.

LC HC440.8.A1
GW
BANGLADESH : WIRTSCHAFTLICHE ENTWICKLUNG. Main/Corp Bundesstelle fur Aussenhandelsinformation (Germany). (197?)-. German. DM2.00. Bundesstelle fuer Aussenhandelsinformation, Agrippastrasse 87 93, D-50676 Cologne Germany. **Tel** 011 49 221 2057316, FAX 011 49 221 2057212.

LC HC155.5.Z7
DD 330.97298/1 GW
BARBADOS, WIRTSCHAFTSDATEN / BUNDESSTELLE FUER ASUSENHANDELSINFORMATION. German. DM3.00. Bundesstelle fuer Aussenhandelsinformation, Agrippastrasse 87 93, D-50676 Cologne Germany. **Tel** 011 49 221 2057316, FAX 011 49 221 2057212.

LC HC835 .B37
SJ
BARNAMAJ AL-ISTITHMAR AL-THULATHI LIL-AM ... / JUMHURIYAT AL-SUDAN AL-DIMUQRATIYAH, WIZARAT AL-TAKHTIT AL-QAWMI. 78/1979-80/1981-. Arabic. Every 3 years. Free. PO Box 2092, Khartoum Sudan.

LC HC399.B3 B35 **ISSN** 0303-4380
DD 314.94/3 SZ
BASLER ZAHLENSPIEGEL. [Basl. Zahlenspieg.]. 1974-. German. Twelve times a year. ***Continues*** *Wirtschaft und Verwaltung.*
Ind/Abst Energy Res. Abstr. (Dec. 1979-).

Business and Economics —Economic History, Conditions

LC HC186 .A774
BL
BBT PERSPECTIVAS. (198?)-. Portuguese. One time a week. **Continues** Analise (Sao Paulo, Brazil : 1982).

GW
BEITRAEGE ZU EINER HISTORISCHEN STRUKTURANALYSE BAYERNS IM INDUSTRIEZEITALTER. Vol. 1, (1968)-. Monographic series. German. Irregular. Price varies per volume. Duncker und Humblot Verlag, Postfach 410329, D-12113 Berlin Germany. **Tel** 011 49 30 79000612, 011 49 30 79000613.

ISSN 0522-6376
US
BEITRAEGE ZUR ERFORSCHUNG DER WIRTSCHAFTLICHEN ENTWICKLUNG. (1- 1957)-. Periodical. German. Irregular. VCH Publishers Inc, 220 East 23rd Street, New York NY 10010. **Tel** (212)683-8333, FAX (212)481-0897. **(Subscription address:** VCH Publishers Inc., 303 Northwest 12th Avenue, Journals Department, Deerfield FL 33442. **Tel** (800)367-8249, (305)428-5566.)

LC HC281 B33
GW
BEITRAEGE ZUR STRUKTURFORSCHUNG. Added/Corp Deutsches Institut fuer Wirtschaftsforschung. Vol. 10 (1970)-. Monographic series. German. (summaries and/or abstracts in English). Irregular. Price varies per volume. Duncker und Humblot Verlag, Postfach 410329, D-12113 Berlin Germany. **Tel** 011 49 30 79000612, 011 49 30 79000613. **Continues** DIW-Beitrage zur Strukturforschung.

LC HC311
GW
BELGIEN : WIRTSCHAFT IN ZAHLEN UND WIRTSCHAFTSDOKUMENTATION. Main/Corp Bundesstelle fur Aussenhandelsinformation (Germany). (19??)-. German. DM4.00. Bundesstelle fuer Aussenhandelsinformation, Agrippastrasse 87 93, D-50676 Cologne Germany. **Tel** 011 49 221 2057316, FAX 011 49 221 2057212.

ISSN 1054-5263
DD 949
US
BELGIUM (SYRACUSE, N.Y.). (BELGIUM : A POLITICAL AND ECONOMIC FORECAST.). [Belgium]. **Added/Corp** Political Risk Services (IBC USA (Publications) Inc.). (19??)-. English. $325.00. Political Risk Services, 6320 Fly Road, Suite 102, PO Box 248, East Syracuse NY 13057-0248. **Tel** (315)431-0511, FAX (315)431-0200.
Desc: Assesses the factors affecting the prospects for business and trade. Each report focuses specifically on business needs such as finding and developing markets, determining currency movements, or making judgements about capital investments or corporate security.

GW
BELIZE, WIRTSCHAFTSDATEN / BUNDESSTELLE FUER AUSSENHANDELSINFORMATION. German. Bundesstelle fuer Aussenhandelsinformation, Agrippastrasse 87 93, D-50676 Cologne Germany. **Tel** 011 49 221 2057316, FAX 011 49 221 2057212.

LC HC310.5.A1 B45   **ISSN** 0251-2912
DD 330.9/492/07
BE
BENELUX. [Benelux]. **Added/Corp** Benelux Economic Union. **VFOAT** Benelux Dossier. (1973)-. Periodical. Dutch (French). Irregular. 250F. Benelux Economische Unie Moniteur Belge, Regentschapstr 39 rue Regence, 1000 Brussels Belgium. **Tel** 011 32 2 5193811. **Continues** Benelux; Economisch en Statistisch Kwartaalbericht.
Ind/Abst Int. Bibliogr. Sociol.; PAIS Int. Print.

LC HC267.T9 K29a
GW
BERICHT - KAMMER DER GEWERBLICHEN WIRTSCHAFT FUER TIROL. Main/Corp Kammer der Gewerblichen Wirtschaft fEur Tirol. (19??)-. German. Meinhardstrasse 12-14, A-6010 Innsbruck Austria.

LC HC446 .B37   **ISSN** 0126-1010
IO
BERITA INDUSTRI. [Ber. ind.]. **Added/Corp** Indonesia. Departemen Perindustrian. Vol. 1 (1968)-. Indonesian. Humas, Jalan Gatot Gajah Mada No 1-A Tromol Pos 200, Jakarta Indonesia.

LC HC289.B4 B3815a
DD 330.9/43/1554
GW
BERLINER WIRTSCHAFTSDATEN. Main/Corp Berlin (West Berlin). Senator fur Wirtschaft. (19??)-. German. Twelve times a year. Martin-Luther-Strasse 105, 1 Berlin 62 Schoneberg West Berlin. **Tel** 011 49 30 7838204, 783 8455. Index

available. **Circ:** 350.
Desc: Economic data from Berlin and the German Democratic Republic.

LC HC461 .B47
JA
BESSATSU DAIYAMONDO. No. 1 (1975)-. Periodical. Japanese. Twelve times a year. ¥950. Daiyamondo Sha, (Diamond Inc.), 4-2 1-chome Kasumigaseki, Chiyoda-ku Tokyo 100 Japan.

LC Z1605 .B46 F1401   **ISSN** 0752-4080
DD 016.98
FR
BIBLIOGRAPHIE LATINOAMERICAINE D'ARTICLES. See Business and Economics-Abstracting, Bibliographies and Statistics.

LC HC800.A1 U54a
DD 354.1/82/096
ET
BIENNIAL REPORT OF THE EXECUTIVE SECRETARY. Main/Corp United Nations. Economic Commission for Africa. (1978)-. Government Publication. English (French and Arabic). Every 2 years. Free. United Nations / Economic Commission for Africa, PO Box 3001, Addis Ababa Ethiopia. **Tel** 011 251 1 447200, telex 21029 ECA ADDIS ABABA. **Circ:** 2,000.
Desc: These series were started in 1978 as a vehicle for reporting to African member states on the activities of the commission and its secretariat. Promotes economic growth and development in the region, and assists member states individually and collectively through their intergovernmental organizations, not only to formulate appropriate policies but also to solve problems.

LC HD   **ISSN** 1070-8340
DD 333
US
BIG RIVER. [Big river]. (199?)-. Periodical. English. Twelve times a year. $24.00. Big River, PO Box 741, Winona MN 55987. **Tel** (507)454-6758, FAX (507)454-6758. **ED** Reggie McLeod. **Ad Acc, Adv Mgr:** Molly McGuire. **Circ:** 500.
Desc: Covers anything that has to do with the Mississippi River from St. Cloud, Minnesota to Dubuque, Iowa.

LC HC59 .B54   **ISSN** 1169-7075
FR
BILAN ECONOMIQUE ET SOCIAL. (197?)-. French. One time a year. $15.00. Le Monde / Immeuble Sirius, 1 place Hubert Beuve Mery, 94852 Ivry-sur-Seine CX France. **Tel** 011 33 1 49603000, 011 33 1 49603290, FAX 011 33 1 46716004. **(Subscription address:** International Media Service, 3330 Pacific Avenue Suite 404, Virginia Beach VA 23451. **Tel** (800)428-3003, (804)428-8180.)

LC HC395 .B54
SZ
BILANZ. (19??)-. Periodical. German. Twelve times a year. $142.39. Jean Frey Druck, Edenstrasse 20, CH-8021 Zurich Switzerland. **Tel** 011 41 1 2078257. **ED** Andreas Z'Graggen, Gerd Lohrer. **Bk Rev. Ad Acc.** **Circ:** 50,100 (ctrl). **Supersedes** Wirtschaftsrevue.

LC HC422.A1
DD 330.9591/005
GW
BIRMA, WIRTSCHAFTSDATEN / BUNDESSTELLE FUR AUSSENHANDELSINFORMATION. German. Bundesstelle fuer Aussenhandelsinformation, Agrippastrasse 87 93, D-50676 Cologne Germany. **Tel** 011 49 221 2057316, FAX 011 49 221 2057212.

LC HC422.A1
DD 330.9591
GW
BIRMA WIRTSCHAFTSDATEN UND WIRTSCHAFTSDOKUMENTATION / BUNDESSTELLE FUR AUSSENHANDELSINFORMATION. German. DM2.00. Bundesstelle fuer Aussenhandelsinformation, Agrippastrasse 87 93, D-50676 Cologne Germany. **Tel** 011 49 221 2057316, FAX 011 49 221 2057212.

LC HC59.7 .I535a
DD 309.1/172/4
GW
BLAETTER DES IZ3W. Main/Corp Informationszentrum Dritte Welt. (19??)-. Periodical. German. Twelve times a year. DM18.00. Informationszentrum Dritte Welt, Postfach 5328, D 7800 Freiburg Germany. **Tel** 011 49 761 74003.
Ind/Abst World Agric. Econ. Rural Sociol. Abstr.

ISSN 0193-4600
US
CCC
BLUE CHIP ECONOMIC INDICATORS. [Blue chip econ. indic.]. **Added/Corp** Management Resources, Inc. (197?)-. Periodical. English. Twelve times a year. $498.00. Capitol Publications, 1101 King Street, Suite 444, Alexandria VA 22314. **Tel** (703)683-4100, (800)655-5597, FAX (703)739-6517, (800)645-4104. **(Subscription address:** Capitol Publications, PO Box 1455, Alexandria VA 22313. **Tel** (800)655-5597, FAX (703)739-6517.) **ED** Bob Eggert.
Desc: Economic forecasts for top management, corporate planners, brokers, and investors. Based on

monthly polls of over 50 top economists on 13 key indicators.
Ind/Abst Predicasts.

LC HC188.M6 B65
BL
BOLETIM DE CONJUNTURA. Added/Corp Fundacao Joao Pinheiro. Equipe de Analise da Conjuntura. (19??)-. Bulletin. Portuguese. Four times a year. Analise and Conjuntura, Alameda das Acacias, 70 Pampulha, 31 270 Belo Horizonte MG Brazil. **Tel** 031 441-1133. **ED** Mauricio Andres Ribeiro. Index available. **Bk Rev. Ad Acc. Circ:** 3,000.

LC HG186.P8 B65   **ISSN** 0870-0095
DD 330.9469/005
PO
CEASED
BOLETIM TRIMESTRAL - BANCO DE PORTUGAL. (BOLETIM TRIMESTRAL / BANCO DE PORTUGAL, ESTATISTICS E ESTUDOS ECONOMICOS.). [Bol. trimest. - Banco Port.]. **Added/Corp** Banco de Portugal. Departamento de Estatistica e Estudos Economicos. Vol. 3, No. 1 (March 1981)-(1993). Bulletin. Portuguese (English). Banco de Portugal Departamento de Estatistica e Estudos Economicos, Rua do Comercio, 148-1100 Lisbon Portugal. **Circ:** 3,000. **Continues** Boletim Estadistico (Banco de Portugal. Direccao de Servicos de Estatistica e Estudos Economicos), 0870-0095.
Desc: Covers Portuguese economy, notes on economic and financial issues, statistical data: monetary and financial, exchange rates, external accounts and general statistics.
Ind/Abst Foreign Lang. Index (?-1984); PAIS Foreign Lang. Index (1985-199?).

LC HC121 .O73a   **ISSN** 0250-6092
US
BOLETIN ESTADISTICO DE LA OEA. Added/Corp Organization of American States. Program of Development Programming. Organization of American States. Planning Statistics Program. Organization of American States. Executive Secretariat for Economic and Social Affairs. **VFOAT** Statistical Bulletin of the OAS. **VAT** Boletin Estadistico de la Organizacion de los Estados Americanos. Vol. 1, No. 1 (Jan./March 1979)-. Statistical Publication. Spanish (English). One time a year. $22.50. Organization of American States, 19th Street & Constitution Avenue NW, Suite 200, Washington DC 20006. **Tel** (202)458-6256. **(Subscription address:** Organization of American States, 1889 F Street Northwest, 1st Floor, Washington DC 20006. **Tel** (202)458-3533, (202)458-3535.) **Continues** Organization of American States. Dept. of Statistics. Boletin Estadistico / Organization of American States. Dept. of Statistics; **Absorbed** Organization of American States. Statistical Bulletin of the OAS.

LC HC145.A1 B66
HO
BOLETIN INFORMATIVO HONDURAS / CENTRO DE DOCUMENTACION DE HONDURAS, CEDOH. Added/Corp Centro de Documentacion de Honduras. (July 1982)-. Periodical. Spanish. Twelve times a year. **Continues** Boletin Informativo (Centro de Documentacion de Honduras).
Ind/Abst Hum. Rights Intern. Rep.

ISSN 1054-5271
DD 984
US
BOLIVIA (SYRACUSE, N.Y.). (BOLIVIA : A POLITICAL AND ECONOMIC FORECAST.). [Bolivia]. **Added/Corp** Political Risk Services (IBC USA (Publications) Inc.). (19??)-. English. $325.00. Political Risk Services, 6320 Fly Road, Suite 102, PO Box 248, East Syracuse NY 13057-0248. **Tel** (315)431-0511, FAX (315)431-0200.
Desc: Assesses the factors affecting the prospects for business and trade. Each report focuses specifically on business needs such as finding and developing markets, determining currency movements, or making judgements about capital investments or corporate security.

LC HC181
DD 330.9/84/05
GW
BOLIVIEN, WIRTSCHAFTLICHE ENTWICKLUNG. Main/Corp Germany (West). Bundesstelle fuer Aussenhandelsinformation. German. Bundesstelle fuer Aussenhandelsinformation, Agrippastrasse 87 93, D-50676 Cologne Germany. **Tel** 011 49 221 2057316, FAX 011 49 221 2057212.

LC HC181
DD 330.984/005
GW
BOLIVIEN, WIRTSCHAFTSDATEN UND WIRTSCHAFTSDOKUMENTATION / BUNDESSTELLE FUER AUSSENHANDELSINFORMATION. German. One time a year. DM3.00. Bundesstelle fuer Aussenhandelsinformation, Agrippastrasse 87 93, D-50676 Cologne Germany. **Tel** 011 49 221 2057316, FAX 011 49 221 2057212.

Business and Economics —Economic History, Conditions

LC HC307.V25 V35A
DD 330.945/11/005
IT
BOLLETTINO ECONOMICO (VALLE D'AOSTA (ITALY). ASSESSORATO INDUSTRIA, COMMERCIO, ARTIGIANATO E TRASPORTI DELLA REGIONE. (BOLLETTINO ECONOMICA.). **VFOAT** Bulletin Economique. Bulletin. French (Italian). Twelve times a year. L7400. Regione Autonoma Valle Aosta, Piazza della Repubblica 15, 11100 Aosta Italy. **Tel** 011 39 165 303524. *Continues Valle d'Aosta, Bollettino Economico.*

LC HC181
GW
BOLVIEN : WIRTSCHAFTSDATEN.
Main/Corp Bundesstelle fur Aussenhandelsinformation (Germany). German. Bundesstelle fuer Aussenhandelsinformation, Agrippastrasse 87 93, D-50676 Cologne Germany. **Tel** 011 49 221 2057316, FAX 011 49 221 2057212.

LC HC186 .B672
DD 330.9/81/06
BL
BRASIL. English. One time a year.
Ind/Abst Eng. Mater. Abstr.

LC HC186
GW
BRASILIEN: WIRTSCHAFTLICHE ENTWICKLUNG. Main/Corp Bundesstelle fur Aussenhandelsinformation (Germany). (19??)-. German. DM4.00. Bundesstelle fuer Aussenhandelsinformation, Agrippastrasse 87 93, D-50676 Cologne Germany. **Tel** 011 49 221 2057316, FAX 011 49 221 2057212.

LC HC188.R4
GW
BRASILIEN : WIRTSCHAFTLICHE ENTWICKLUNG DES BUNDESSTATES RIO GRANDE DO SUL. Main/Corp Bundesstelle fur Aussenhandelsinformation (Germany). German. DM2.00. Bundesstelle fuer Aussenhandelsinformation, Agrippastrasse 87 93, D-50676 Cologne Germany. **Tel** 011 49 221 2057316, FAX 011 49 221 2057212.

LC HC186
DD 330.981
GW
BRASILIEN WIRTSCHAFTSDATEN UND WIRTSCHAFTSDOKUMENTATION / BUNDESSTELLE FUR AUSSENHANDELSINFORMATION. German. DM3.00. Bundesstelle fuer Aussenhandelsinformation, Agrippastrasse 87 93, D-50676 Cologne Germany. **Tel** 011 49 221 2057316, FAX 011 49 221 2057212.

LC HC186 .B72813
BL
BRAUDEL PAPERS : DOCUMENT OF THE FERNAND BRAUDEL INSTITUTE OF WORLD ECONOMICS ASSOCIATED WITH THE FUNDACAO ARMANDO ALVARES PENTEADO. Added/Corp Instituto Fernand Braudel de Economia Mundial. (199?)-. Monographic series. English (Portuguese). Six times a year. Editora Instituto Braudel Economia, Rua Ceara 2, 01243 010, Sao Paolo SP Brazil. **Tel** 011 55 11 8249633.

ISSN 0267-9965
UK
BRAZIL (LONDON, ENGLAND). (BRAZIL.).
Added/Corp Latin American Monitor Ltd. (1985)-. English. One time a year (June). $435.00. Business Monitor International, 56 60 St. John Street, London EC1M 4DT United Kingdom. **Tel** 011 44 171 6083646, FAX 011 44 171 6083620.

LC HC186 .B7125 **ISSN** 0143-5272
DD 330.9/81/06
BL
BRAZIL REPORT. (19??)-. English. Ten times a year. $185.00. Lettres UK Ltd, 61 Old Street, London EC1V 9HX United Kingdom. **Tel** 011 44 171 2510012, FAX 011 44 171 2538193. available on an online database from Lexis-Nexis. Documents available from BLDSC. *Continues Latin American Regional Reports. Brazil, 0143-5272.*

ISSN 1054-528X
DD 981
US
BRAZIL (SYRACUSE, N.Y.). (BRAZIL : A POLITICAL AND ECONOMIC FORECAST.). [Brazil].
Added/Corp Political Risk Services (IBC USA (Publications) Inc.). (19??)-. English. $325.00. Political Risk Services, 6320 Fly Road, Suite 102, PO Box 248, East Syracuse NY 13057-0248. **Tel** (315)431-0511, FAX (315)431-0200.
Desc: Assesses the factors affecting the prospects for business and trade. Each report focuses specifically on business needs such as finding and developing markets, determining currency movements, or making judgements about capital investments or corporate security.

LC HC186 .B7128 **ISSN** 0897-3067
DD 330.981/005
US
BRAZIL WATCH (WASHINGTON, D.C. 1985). (BRAZIL WATCH.). [Braz. watch]. Vol. 1, No. 1 (Dec. 10, 1984)-. Periodical. English. Twenty-four times a year. $695.00. Orbis Publications Ltd, 1924 47th Street NW, Washington DC 20007. **Tel** (202)625-2702, FAX (202)333-8740. **ED** Richard W. Foster. *Absorbed Brazil Service.*
Desc: Focuses on business, economic and political events in Brazil. List composed of actives, expires, inquiries, conference and seminar attendees.

LC HC186 .B73 **ISSN** 8755-089X
DD 330.981/005
US
BRAZILIAN ECONOMIC INDICATORS.
[Braz. econ. indic.]. English. Twelve times a year. WEFA / Philadelphia, PO Box 8500, Suite 1995, Philadelphia PA 19178. **Tel** (215)667-6000, telex 710 6700575.

LC HC186 .B735
DD 338.5/443/0981
US
BRAZILIAN ECONOMIC OUTLOOK.
(19??)-. English. WEFA / Philadelphia, PO Box 8500, Suite 1995, Philadelphia PA 19178. **Tel** (215)667-6000, telex 710 6700575.

BL
BRAZILINFORM NEWS LETTER. English.
Twenty-six times a year. $300.00. Brazilinform, Caixa Postal 37584, Rio de Janeiro 22642 Brazil.
Desc: Contains economic and political analyses and projections for Brazil. A source of objective analyses on Brazil.

ISSN 0007-0025
DD 350
US
BRIEFING PAPERS (WASHINGTON, D.C.). (BRIEFING PAPERS.). [Brief. pap.]. (1963)-.
Periodical. English. Thirteen times a year. $703.84. Federal Publications Inc, 1120 20th Street Northwest, Washington DC 20036. **Tel** (202)337-7000, (800)922-4330, FAX (202)659-2233.

LC HC497.H6 H66a
DD 330.9/51/2505
HK
BUDGET : ECONOMIC BACKGROUND.
Main/Corp Hong Kong. Printing Dept. (19??)-. English (Chinese). One time a year. HK$71.00. Hong Kong Government Information Service, Beaconsfield House, 4 Queens Road, Hong Kong Hong Kong. **Tel** 011 852 284288014, 011 852 259881947, FAX 011 852 28459078, 011 852 25987482, telex 61190 HKGIS.
(Subscription address: Government Information Service, Publications Office, 1 Battery Path, Hong Kong Hong Kong. **)**

LC HC311 .A2574c
DD 354.4930072/24/05
BE
BUDGET ECONOMIQUE DE ... VERSION REVISEE / MINISTERE DES AFFAIRES ECONOMIQUES, DIRECTION GENERALE DES ETUDES ET DE LA DOCUMENTATION, CELLULE BUDGET ECONOMIQUE-ETUDES.
Main/Corp Belgium. Ministere des Affaires Economiques. Cellule Budget Economique-etudes. (19??)-. French. One time a year. Ministere des Affaires Economiques Comite de Concertation et du Controle du Petrole, rue de Mot, 1040 Brussels Belgium.

LC HF3611 .B84 **ISSN** 0166-946X
NE
BUITENLANDSE PROJECTEN / EXPORTBEVORDERINGS- EN VOORLICHTINGSDIENST, EVD. Periodical.
Dutch. One time a week. Fl245.00. Exportbevorderings - En Voorlichtingsdienst, Bezuidenhoutseweg 151, 2594 AG 'S-Gravenhage Netherlands.

LC HC445.5.A1 B35 **ISSN** 0127-8428
DD 330.9595/005
MY
BULETIN SUKU TAHUNAN. Added/Corp
Bank Negara Malaysia. **VFOAT** Quarterly Bulletin. (1986)-. Bulletin. English (Malay). Four times a year. *Continues Bank Negara Malaysia. Buletin Ekonomi Suku Tahunan, 0005-5115.*
Ind/Abst Asia.-Pac. Econ. Lit.

ISSN 1054-5298
DD 949
US
BULGARIA (SYRACUSE, N.Y.). (BULGARIA : A POLITICAL AND ECONOMIC FORECAST.).
[Bulgaria]. **Added/Corp** Political Risk Services (IBC USA (Publications) Inc.). (19??)-. English. $325.00. Political Risk Services, 6320 Fly Road, Suite 102, PO Box 248, East Syracuse NY 13057-0248. **Tel** (315)431-0511, FAX (315)431-0200.
Desc: Assesses the factors affecting the prospects for business and trade. Each report focuses specifically on business needs such as finding and developing markets, determining currency movements, or making judgements about capital investments or corporate security.

LC HC403.A1 B85
DD 338.9497/7/005
GW
BULGARIEN VOLKSWIRTSCHAFTSPLAN FUR ... .
(19??)-. German. DM3.00. Bundesstelle fuer Aussenhandelsinformation, Agrippastrasse 87 93, D-50676 Cologne Germany. **Tel** 011 49 221 2057316, FAX 011 49 221 2057212.

LC HC321 .U87A
NE
BULLETIN ALGEMENE SOCIALE GEOGRAFIE. SERIE 1. Main/Corp Utrecht.
Rijksuniversiteit. Geografisch Instituut. Bulletin. Dutch. 2.50 single issue. Geografisch Institute, Heidelberglaan 2, Utrecht Netherlands.

LC HC278.L9 C46a **ISSN** 1241-9257
DD 309.1/44/58
FR
BULLETIN / CENTRE PIERRE LEON D'HISTOIRE ECONOMIQUE ET SOCIALE. Added/Corp Centre Pierre Leon d'Histoire Economique et Sociale. (1992)-. Bulletin. French. Four times a year. $43.74. Centre Pierre Leon d"Histoire Economique et Sociale, Maison Rhone-Alpes des Scieces de l"Homme, 14 Avenue Berthelot, 69363 Lyon Cedex 07 France. **Tel** 011 33 7 72726401, FAX 011 33 7 72800008. **Circ:** 400. *Continues Centre d'Histoire Economique et Sociale de la Region Lyonnaise. Bulletin du Centre d'Histoire Economique et Sociale de la Region Lyonnaise, 0249-5902.*

LC HC311 .C37A
BE
BULLETIN - CHAMBRE DE COMMERCE ET D'INDUSTRIE D'ANVERS. Main/Corp
Chambre de Commerce et d'Industrie d'Anvers. (19??)-. Bulletin. Multiple languages (Dutch and French). Markgracestraat 12, B-2000 Antwerpen Belgium. *Formed by the union of Antwerp. Chambre de Commerce. Bulletin and Antwerp. Chambre d'Industrie. Bulletin.*

LC HC547.N5 A24
DD 330.9/66/2605
NG
BULLETIN DE LA CHAMBRE DE COMMERCE, D'AGRICULTURE, D'INDUSTRIE ET D'ARTISANAT DU NIGER. Main/Corp Chambre de Commerce, d'Agriculture, d'Industrie et d'Artisanat du Niger. Bulletin. French. One time a week. Chambre de Commerce d'Agriculture d'Industrie et d'Artisanat du Niger, B P 209, Niamey Niger. *Continues Chambre de Commerce, d'Agriculture et d'Industrie du Niger. Bulletin.*

LC HC547.S4 S443A
SG
BULLETIN D'INFORMATION SUR L'EXECUTION DU PLAN. VFOAT Bulletin d'Information sur l'Execution du Veme Plan. Bulletin. French. Republique de Senegal, Ministere du Plan et de la Cooperation, Building Administratif, Poste 559 et 717 Dakar Senegal. *Continues Bulletin Semestriel d'Information sur l'Execution du Plan.*

LC HC241.2 .E292d **ISSN** 0256-5846
DD 337.1/42/05
BE
CODEN BSCCEN
BULLETIN / ECONOMIC AND SOCIAL COMMITTEE OF THE EUROPEAN COMMUNITIES. Main/Corp Economic and Social Committee of the European Communities. (Jan./Feb./Mar. 1974)-. Bulletin. English. Twelve times a year. Free on request. Office for Official Publications of the European Communities, 2 rue Mercier, 2985 Luxembourg Luxembourg. **Tel** 011 352 499281, FAX 011 352 292942763. *Continues Economic and Social Committee of the European Communities. Bulletin of the Economic and Social Committee (EEC-EAEC).*
Desc: Account of the activities of the ESC, comprising mainly the opinions delivered at its sessions on proposals for Community legislation.

LC HC431 .M32a
DD 309.1/54/05
II
BULLETIN - MADRAS INSTITUTE OF DEVELOPMENT STUDIES. Main/Corp Madras Institute of Development Studies. (19??)-. Bulletin. English. Twelve times a year. 74 Second Main Road, Gandhinagar Adyar Madras 20 India.

LC HC557.T6 T56A **ISSN** 0303-7460
DD 330.9/66/8104
TG
BULLETIN MENSUEL - CHAMBRE DE COMMERCE, D'AGRICULTURE ET D'INDUSTRIE DE LA REPUBLIQUE TOGOLAISE. Main/Corp Chambre de Commerce, d'Agriculture et d'Industrie de la Republique Togolaise. No. 161- Nov. 1972-. Bulletin. French. Twelve times a year. 100.00CFAF. Hotel de la Chambre de Commerce, Boite Postale No 360, Lome Togo. **Tel** 21-20-65, telex

Business and Economics —Economic History, Conditions

5023 CHAMCOM. **Circ:** 500. **Continues** Chambre de Commerce, d'Agriculture et d'Industrie de la Republique Togolaise. Bulletin Periodique.

US

●**BULLETIN OF ASIAN-PACIFIC ECONOMIC AND POLITICAL ISSUES.** See Political Science.

US

●**BULLETIN OF EUROPEAN POLITICAL AND ECONOMIC ISSUES.** See Political Science.

LC HC440.P6 T74a
DD 301.29/54

II

BULLETIN OF THE TRIBAL RESEARCH AND DEVELOPMENT INSTITUTE BHOPAL. Main/Corp Tribal Research and Development Institute. **Added/Corp** Tribal Research and Development Institute. **VFOAT** Bulletin of the Tribal Research and Development Institute, Bhopal. (196?)-. Bulletin. English. Four times a year. Tribal Research and Development Institute, Chindwara Madhya Prodesa India. **Continues** Bulletin of the Tribal Research and Training Institute, Chhinwara.

LC HC497.T8 U54A
DD 330.9/53/5

TS

BULLETIN - UNITED ARAB EMIRATES CURRENCY BOARD. Main/Corp United Arab Emirates. Majlis Al-Naqd. Vol. 1 (Nov. 1974)-. Bulletin. English. Emirates Medical Association, PO Box 6600, Dubai United Arab Emirates. **Tel** 011 971 4 377377.

LC H67.G46 G46A
DD 330.9

SZ

BULLETIN - UNIVERSITE DE GENEVE, DEPARTEMENT D'HISTOIRE ECONOMIQUE. Main/Corp Geneva. Universite. Departement d'Histoire Economique. Bulletin. French. One time a year. Universite de Geneva, rue de Candolle, 1211 Geneva 4 Switzerland. **Tel** 011 41 22 209333. **Circ:** 300.
Desc: Report of the department of economic history of the University of Geneva: courses, seminars and lectures; research, publications and activities of the teaching staff.

LC HC880.A1 B87
DD 330.967/572

GW

BURUNDI, WIRTSCHAFTDATEN UND WIRTSCHAFTSDOKUMENTATION / BUNDESSTELLE FUR AUSSENHANDELSINFORMATION. German. DM2.00. Bundesstelle fuer Aussenhandelsinformation, Agrippastrasse 87 93, D-50676 Cologne Germany. **Tel** 011 49 221 2057316, FAX 011 49 221 2057212.

US

BUSINESS INDICATORS. CD-ROM. See Energy-Computer Applications.

US

BUSINESS OUTLOOK FOR WEST MICHIGAN. Added/Corp W.E. Upjohn Institute for Employment Research. F.E. Seidman School of Business. Vol. 2, No. 1 (Autumn 1985)-. Periodical. English. Four times a year. $30.00. W.E. Upjohn Institute for Employment Research, 300 South Westnedge Avenue, Kalamazoo MI 49007. **Tel** (616)343-5541, FAX (616)343-7310. **ED** George A. Erickcek. **Circ:** 600 (ctrl). **Continues** Business Outlook (Kalamazoo, Mich.), 0748-4216.
Desc: Economic review and outlook for West Michigan including Battle Creek, Benton Harbor, Grand Rapids, Kalamazoo, and Muskegon.

LC HD
DD 330.9

ISSN 0005-531X
CN
CEASED

BUSINESS REVIEW (MONTREAL). (BUSINESS REVIEW.). [Bus. rev.]. **Main/Corp** Bank of Montreal. **Added/Corp** Bank of Montreal. **VFOAT** Bank of Montreal Business Review. (Apr. 22, 1948)-(19??). Periodical. English (French). Bank of Montreal, PO Box 6002, Montreal Quebec H3C 3B1 Canada. **ED** J. Parish. **Circ:** 12,000 (ctrl). available on microfilm and microfiche from University Microfilms International (UMI); available on an online database (fle 648/Full-Text) from DIALOG. **Supersedes** Bank of Montreal. Business Summary, 0315-4688.
Desc: Articles related to current business and financial conditions and the outlook primarily for Canada and the United States.
Ind/Abst Can. Period. Index.

LC HB9 .B86

UY

BUSQUEDA. Added/Corp Centro Uruguayo de Estudios Economicos y Sociales. (19??)-. Periodical. Spanish. One time a week. $225.00. Editorial Argos SA, Busqueda Avda, Uruguay 1023, 11100 Montevideo Uruguay. **Tel** FAX 2-992036. **ED** Danilo Arbilla Frachia. **Circ:** 18,000.

LC HC1040.A1 C23
DD 330.966/25/005

UV

C.E.D.R.E.S.--ETUDES, REVUE ECONOMIQUE ET SOCIALE VOLTAIQUE. VFOAT CEDRES--Etudes. Periodical. French. Centre d'Etudes de Documentation de Recherches, Universite de Ouagadougou, Economiques et Sociales, BP 7021, Ouagadougou Burkina Faso.

LC HC188.M6 C25

BL

CADASTRO INDUSTRIAL. Portuguese. Departamento de Estatistica do Cici/Mg, Avenida III 746, Contagem Brazil.

LC HC188.D57 C33

BL

CADASTRO INDUSTRIAL DO DISTRITO FEDERAL. 1974-. Portuguese. Companhia do Desenvolvimento, Setor Comercial Sul Quadra 05, Bloco C, Lojas 80/90 Edificio Codeplan, Brasilia Brazil.

LC HC188.E7 A58

BL

CADASTRO INDUSTRIAL DO ESPIRITO SANTO. VFOAT Anuario Industrial do Espirito Santo. Portuguese. One time a year. Federacao das Industries do Estados do Espiritos Santo, Av Princesa Isabel 54-12 Andar, Victoria Brazil. **Continues** Anuario Industrial do Espirito Santo.

LC HC188.P3 C33

BL

CADASTRO INDUSTRIAL DO PARA. Added/Corp Federacao das Industrias do Estado do Para. Instituto Euvaldo Lodi. **VFOAT** Cadastro Industrial do Estado do Para. (19??)-. Portuguese. Federacao das Industrias, Av Nazare 759, Belem Brazil.

LC HC186 .C29

BL
CEASED

CADERNOS DE ESTUDOS BRASILEIROS. Added/Corp Universidade Federal do Rio de Janeiro. Forum de Ciencia e Cultura. (1972)-(19??). Portuguese. Universidade Federal do Rio de Janeiro / Ciencia, Forum de Ciencia e Cultura, Av Pasteur 250 Praia Vermelha, Rio de Janeiro Brazil.

LC HC395 .C33

SW

CAHIERS DE QUESTIONS CONJONCTURELLES. Added/Corp Switzerland. Office Federal des Questions Conjoncturelles. (198?)-. French. Four times a year. Office Federal des Questions Conjoncturelles, Belpstrasse 53, 3003 Bern Switzerland. **Continues** Cahiers de Conjoncture.

LC HC501.A1 C3
DD 330.967

ISSN 0008-0209
CG

CAHIERS ECONOMIQUES ET SOCIAUX (KINSHASA). (CAHIERS ECONOMIQUES ET SOCIAUX.). [Cah. econ. soc.]. **VFOAT** Economic and Social Papers. Vol. 1; Oct. 1962-. Periodical. French. Two times a year. $47.00. University Nationale du Zaire / Department de Philosophie, PO Box 257, Kinshasa 11 Zaire. none available. cum. index. **Bk Rev**. **Ad Acc**. ctrl circ. **Supersedes** Notes et Documents.
Ind/Abst Int. Labour Doc.; Int. Polit. Sci. Abstr.; Rural Dev. Abstr.; World Agric. Econ. Rural Sociol. Abstr.

LC HC10 .C32
DD 330.9

ISSN 1010-3643
SZ

CAHIERS INTERNATIONAUX D'HISTOIRE ECONOMIQUE ET SOCIALE. [Cah. int. hist. econ. soc.]. **VFOAT** Quaderni Internazionali di Storia Economica e Sociali; International Journal of Economic and Social History. (1972)-. Multiple languages (English, French and Italian). Irregular. 80.00F. Librairie Droz SA, 11 rue Massot BP 389, CH-1211 Geneva 12 Switzerland. **Tel** 011 41 22 3466666, FAX 011 41 22 472391. **ED** Demarco. **Bk Rev**. **Circ:** 600.
Desc: Economic history.
Ind/Abst Am. Hist. Life (1972-1973, 1976-).

LC HC591.C6 C34

ISSN 0304-2707
CG

CAHIERS ZAIROIS D'ETUDES POLITIQUES ET SOCIALES. [Cah. zair. etud. polit. soc.]. No. 1- April 1973-. Periodical. French. $4.00. Universite de Lubumbashi / Centre d'Etudes de Recherches, Documentaires sur l'Afrique Centrale, BP 1825, Lubumbashi Zaire.
Ind/Abst Am. Hist. Life (1977-).

LC HC107.C2 C223A
DD 330.9/794/03

ISSN 0364-2895
US

CALIFORNIA ECONOMIC INDICATORS. Main/Corp California. Dept. of Finance. English. Six times a year. $8.00. California Department of Finance, 915 L Street, 8th Floor, Finance-Economic Research, Sacramento CA 95814. **Tel** (916)322-2263. **ED** California Department of Finance. **Circ:** 500 (ctrl). **Continues** California Economic Indicators, 0364-2895.
Desc: A summary of economic trends and data relative to the state of California.

LC HC381 .C33

SP

CAMBIO 16. VFOAT Cambio Dieciseis. No. 1 (Nov. 22, 1971)-. Periodical. Spanish. One time a week. $434.14. Cambio 16, Hermanos Garcia Noblejas 41, 28017 Madrid 17 Spain. **Tel** 011 34 1 4072700, 011 34 1 4074100.
Ind/Abst PAIS Int. Print.

LC HB1 .C28
DD 330/.05

ISSN 0309-166X
UK
CCC

Pr Rev.

CAMBRIDGE JOURNAL OF ECONOMICS. [Camb. j. econ.]. Vol. 1 (March 1977)-. Academic Scholarly Publication. English. Four times a year. $248.13. Academic Press Ltd., A Division of Harcourt Brace & Company Ltd., 24-28 Oval Road, London NW1 7DX United Kingdom. **Tel** 011 44 171 2674466, FAX 011 44 171 4822293, 011 44 171 4854752, telex 25775 ACPRES G. (**Subscription address:** Harcourt Brace & Company, Ltd., Foots Cray High Street, Sidcup Kent DA14 5HP United Kingdom. **Tel** 011 44 181 3003322, FAX 011 44 181 3090807, telex 896 377 ACADEM.) Documents available from The Genuine Article, UMI Article Clearinghouse.
Desc: Provides a forum for non-neoclassical approaches to economics following the tradition of Marx, Kalecki, and Keynes. The journal publishes theoretical and applied articles on major contemporary issues, with strong emphasis on the provision and use of empirical evidence and on the formulation of economic policies.
Ind/Abst ABI/INFORM Glob. Ed.; Acad. Search; Arts Humanit. Citation Index [Select. Cov.]; Bus. Source Plus; Bus. Source; Contents Recent Econ. J.; Curr. Cit.; Curr. Contents Soc. Behav. Sci.; Econ. Lit. Index; EP Collect.; Expand. Acad. Index (1989-); Geogr. Abstr. Human Geogr.; Homework Help.; INFO-SOUTH Abstr.; Int. Dev. Abstr.; Int. Labour Doc.; J. Econ. Lit.; J. Plan. Lit.; LABORDOC; Leis., Rec., Tour. Abstr.; MasterFile FullTEXT 1000; MasterFile FullTEXT 350; MasterFile FullTEXT 650; MasterFile FullTEXT (July 1993-); Newsp. Period. Abstr. (1992-); OCLC; PAIS Int. Print (1991-); Res. Alert [Full Cov.]; Rural Dev. Abstr.; Soc. Sci. Source; Soc. Sci. Cit. Index [Full Cov.]; Soc. Sci. Index; Soc. Sci. Index Fulltext (Sept. 1988-) [Full Txt.]; Telebase; World Agric. Econ. Rural Sociol. Abstr.; World Mag. Bank.

DD 967

ISSN 1054-5301
US

CAMEROON (SYRACUSE, N.Y.). (CAMEROON : A POLITICAL AND ECONOMIC FORECAST / POLITICAL RISK SERVICES.). [Cameroon]. **Added/Corp** Political Risk Services (IBC USA (Publications) Inc.). (19??)-. English. $325.00. Political Risk Services, 6320 Fly Road, Suite 102, PO Box 248, East Syracuse NY 13057-0248. **Tel** (315)431-0511, FAX (315)431-0200.
Desc: Assesses the factors affecting the prospects for business and trade. Each report focuses specifically on business needs such as finding and developing markets, determining currency movements, or making judgements about capital investments or corporate security.

LC HC557.C3 C37
DD 309.1/67/1104

ISSN 0376-7612
CM

CAMEROUN 3E REPUBLIQUE. (CAMEROUN, 3E [I.E. TROISIEME] REPUBLIQUE.). **VAT** Cameroun Troisieme Republique. (19??)-. Periodical. French. Twelve times a year. 4000. Agence Niew S.A.R.L, 26 Avenue King Akwa, BP 2012 Cameroon.

LC HC115 .A425
DD 971/.005

ISSN 0840-6014
CN

CANADA, A PORTRAIT. (CANADA, A PORTRAIT.). [Can. portrait]. **Added/Corp** Statistics Canada. Communications Division. 52nd Ed. (1989)-. English. Every 2 years. 47.95Can$. Statistics Canada Publications Sales and Services, R.H. Coats Building 6th Floor, Ottawa Ontario K1A 0T6 Canada. **Tel** (613)951-5078, (800)267-6677, FAX (613)951-1584, telex 053-3585. **Continues** Canada Handbook, The ... Handbook of Present Conditions and Recent Progress, 0705-5331.

DD 971

ISSN 1054-531X
US

CANADA (SYRACUSE, N.Y.). (CANADA : A POLITICAL AND ECONOMIC FORECAST.). [Canada]. **Added/Corp** Political Risk Services (IBC USA (Publications) Inc.). (19??)-. English. $325.00. Political Risk Services, 6320 Fly Road, Suite 102, PO Box 248, East Syracuse NY 13057-0248. **Tel** (315)431-0511, FAX (315)431-0200.
Desc: Assesses the factors affecting the prospects for business and trade. Each report focuses specifically on business needs such as finding and developing markets, determining currency movements, or making judgements about capital investments or corporate security.

Business and Economics —Economic History, Conditions

DD 330.971/0645   ISSN 0226-1979   CN
CANADIAN PODIUM, THE. [Can. podium]. (Jan. 1980)-. Periodical. English. Twelve times a year. $260.00. Matrix Communications, 120 North Oak Park Avenue, Suite 202, Oak Park IL 60301-1317. **Tel** (312)386-0066.

DD 330.971   ISSN 0715-4542   CN
CANADIAN QUARTERLY ECONOMIC REVIEW. [Can. q. econ. rev.]. (1976)-. Periodical. English. Four times a year. 200.08Can$. Bunting Warburg Inc, 130 Adelaide Street W/Suite 3000, Toronto Ontario M5H 3V4 Canada. **Tel** (416)364-3293.

LC HB5 .C36   ISSN 0008-5847
DD 330.943/005   GW
CAPITAL (HAMBURG). (CAPITAL.). [Capital]. (1962)-. Trade Publication. German. Twelve times a year. DM102.00. Gruner und Jahr Ag & Co, Abonnement Service, D-20080 Hamburg Germany. **Tel** 011 49 40 37030, FAX 011 49 40 37035657. **(Subscription address:** Deutscher Pressevertrieb Buch, POB 101602 Hansa GMBH, D-20010 Hamburg Germany. **Tel** 011 49 40 23711249.) available on microfilm from University Microfilms International (UMI).
Ind/Abst Energy Res. Abstr. (Nov. 1978-).

BB
CARIBBEAN DIGEST. Vol. 1 No. 1 (April/May 1977)-. Periodical. English. Twelve times a year. Horizons Publishing and Publicity House Ltd, PO Box 865 East Saint Michael, Bridgetown Barbados.

LC HC151.A1 C374   ISSN 0185-2426
DD 330.9182/1   MX
SUSPENDED
CARIBE CONTEMPORANEO, EL. No. 1 (March 1980)-. Periodical. Spanish. Three times a year. $2.25 single issue. Centro de Estudios Latinoamericanos, Area del Caribe, Facultad de Ciencias Politicas y Sociales, EDIF C Piso 2 Unam, 04510 Mexico 20 DF Mexico. **Tel** 011 52 5 6656211 ext. 7965.
Ind/Abst Hisp. Am. Period. Index, HAPI; Hum. Rights Intern. Rep.; Int. Bibliogr. Sociol.; Int. Labour Doc.; Int. Polit. Sci. Abstr.; LABORDOC; PAIS Int. Print (1991-?).

LC HC151.A1 C37A
DD 341.24/5   GY
CARICOM BULLETIN. Main/Corp Caribbean Community. Secretariat. No. 1- Aug. 1978-. Bulletin. English. Twelve times a year. $5.00 (single issue), $12.00 (special rate, three issues). Caribbean Community Secretariat, PO Box 10827, Bank of Guyana Building, Georgetown Guyana. **Tel** 011 592 2 69281-9, FAX 011 592 2 67816, 011 592 2 58039, telex 2263 CARISEC GY. **ED** Carol Collins. **Bk Rev. Ad Acc. Circ:** 525 (ctrl).
Desc: Focusses on integration trends and issues in and related to the Caribbean community. Provides in-depth information on the programmes and activities of the CARICOM secretariat.

LC HC151.A1 C376
DD 016.3309182/1 /2 19   TR
CARISPLAN ABSTRACTS / CARIBBEAN DEVELOPMENT AND COOPERATION COMMITTEE. See Business and Economics-Abstracting, Bibliographies and Statistics.

LC HC188.P5 F84B
BL
CARTA CEPRO. Main/Corp Fundacao Centro Regional de Produtividade do Piaui. **VAT** Carta Fundacao Centro Regional de Produtividade do Piaui. Vol. 1 (1974)-. Portuguese. Fundacao Centro Regional de Produtividade do Piaui, Avenida Miguel Rosa 3190 Sul, Teresina Brazil.

LC HC147.A1 B34a
PN
CARTA ECONOMICA. Main/Corp Banco Nacional de Panama. Asesoria Economica y Planificacion. **Added/Corp** Banco Nacional de Panama. Asesoria Economica y Planificacion. (19??)-. Periodical. Spanish. Banco Nacional de Panama, Casilla Postal 5220, Panama 5 Panama.

LC HC387.B2 C36
SP
CATALOGO INDUSTRIAL VASCO-NAVARRO. (1973)-. Spanish. Iparraguirre 66 - Lo Dpto 3, Bilbao Spain.

LC HC107.N33 P634a   ISSN 0091-0694
DD 338.9793   US
CATALOGUE OF STATE PROGRAMS (CARSON CITY). (CATALOGUE OF STATE PROGRAMS.). **Main/Corp** Nevada. State Planning Board. (19??)-. English. Nevada State Planning Board, Carson City NV 89710.

LC HD28 HC26   ISSN 1381-4346
DD 658 330.1   US
Pr Rev.
●**CEMS BUSINESS REVIEW. See** Business and Economics-Management.

LC HC517.R43 A25
DD 338.096891   RH
CENSUS OF PRODUCTION (ZIMBABWE. CENTRAL STATISTICAL OFFICE.). (THE CENSUS OF PRODUCTION.). 1978/79-. English. One time a year. Central Statistical Office / Zimbabwe, PO Box 8063, Causeway Salisbury Harare, Zimbabwe. **Tel** 011 263 0 706681. **Continues** Census of Production (Southern Rhodesia. Central Statistical Office.

LC HC321 .A36
DD 338.9492   NE
CENTRAAL ECONOMISCH PLAN.
Main/Corp Netherlands. Centraal Planbureau. (1947)-. Dutch. One time a year. $25.69. SDU Uitgeverij, Postbus 20014, Christoffel Plantijnstraat, 2500 EA Den Haag Netherlands. **Tel** 011 31 70 3789911.
Desc: Includes the National budget.

LC HC141.A1 C46   ISSN 0254-2471
DD 330.9/728/05   GT
CENTRAL AMERICA REPORT (GUATEMALA CITY). (CENTRAL AMERICA REPORT.). [Cent. Am. rep.]. Vol. 1, (Aug. 23, 1974)-. Periodical. English. One time a week (except for New Year's, Easter, and Christmas). $219.35. Inforpress Centroamericana, 9 Calle 3-19/Zona 1, Guatemala City Guatemala. **Tel** 011 502 2 29432, or 81997, FAX 011 502 2 83859. **Circ:** 500.
Desc: Information and analysis of economic and political developments in the several Central American countries.
Ind/Abst Hum. Rights Intern. Rep.

DD 330.9728   UK
CENTRAL AMERICAN ECONOMIST HANDBOOK. English. Irregular. £90.00 per copy. Euromonitor Publications Ltd., 60-61 Britton Street, London EC1M 5NA United Kingdom. **Tel** 011 44 171 2518024, FAX 011 44 171 6083149, telex 21120.

NE
●**CENTRAL EUROPEAN ECONOMIC REVIEW. VFOAT** Wall Street Journal Europe's Central European Economic Review. Vol. 1, No. 1 (Summer 1993)-. English. Ten times a year. $95.00. Dow Jones and Company Inc., 200 Burnett Road, Chicopee MA 01021. **Tel** (413)592-7761, (800)568-7625. **(Subscription address:** Dow Jones Publishing Company Europe Inc., In de Cramer 37, NL 6411 RS Heerlen Netherlands. **Tel** 011 31 45 761222.)

ISSN 0771-3398
BE
UDC 330
CENTRE DE DOCUMENTATION PAYSANNE DU PARAGUAY. [Cent. doc. paysanne Parag.]. (1975)-. Periodical. French. Six times a year. Centre de Documentation Paysanne du Paraguay, Brussels Belgium.
Ind/Abst Hum. Rights Intern. Rep.

LC HC121 .U55b   ISSN 0251-2920
DD 330.9/8/003   CL
CCC
CEPAL REVIEW. [CEPAL rev.]. **Main/Corp** United Nations. Economic Commission for Latin America. **Added/Corp** United Nations. Economic Commission for Latin America. Review. **VAT** Comision Economica Para America Latina Review. 1st Semester (1976)-. Government Publication. English. Three times a year. $35.00. United Nations Publications, 2 United Nations Plaza, Room DC2 0853, Department 007C, New York NY 10017. **Tel** (212)963-8303, (800)253-9646. **(Subscription address:** United Nations Publications, Subscription Office, PO Box 361, Birmingham AL 35201-0361. **Tel** (800)633-4931, (205)995-1567 (outside US and Canada), FAX (205)995-1588.) **Supersedes** Economic Bulletin for Latin America.
Desc: Focuses on economic trends, industrializations, income distributions, technological development, monetary system and implementation of economic reform and transfer of technology. Contains studies and essays written by prestigious experts or gathered from conference proceedings.
Ind/Abst Contents Recent Econ. J.; Curr. Cit.; Econ. Lit. Index; Hisp. Am. Period. Index, HAPI; Int. Bibliogr. Sociol.; Int. Dev. Abstr. (?-?); Int. Labour Doc.; J. Econ. Lit.; LABORDOC; Leis., Rec., Tour. Abstr.; Middle East Abstr. Index; PAIS Int. Print (1991-?); Peace Res. Abstr. J. (1980-1981); Rice Abstr.; Rural Dev. Abstr.; Soyabean Abstr.; World Agric. Econ. Rural Sociol. Abstr.

LC Z7164.E2 H355A HC21
KO
CHANGSO MONGNOK. Main/Corp Hanguk Muyok Hyophoe. English (Japanese and Korean). Hanguk Muyok Hyophoe, 10-1 2-ka Hoehyon-dong Chung-ku, Seoul Korea.

LC HD9579.C3 C48   ISSN 0577-6406
DD 338.4/7/66005   US
CHEMSPHERE. See Petroleum and Natural Gas.

LC HC191 .C47   ISSN 0884-4488
DD 330   US
CHILE ECOMOMIC REPORT. [Chile econ. rep.]. **Added/Corp** Corporacion de Fomento de la Produccion (Chile). No. 116 (Nov. 1980)-. Periodical. English. Twelve times a year. Free on request. CORFO, One World Trade Center, Suite 5151, New York NY 10048. **Tel** (212)938-0550, FAX (212)938-0568. **ED** Marco A. Vallejo. **Circ:** 7,500 (ctrl). **Continues** Chile Economic News.
Desc: Summaries of business and economic developments in Chile. Includes economic indicators also.

ISSN 1054-5328
DD 983   US
CHILE (SYRACUSE, N.Y.). (CHILE : A POLITICAL AND ECONOMIC FORECAST / POLITICAL RISK SERVICES.). [Chile]. **Added/Corp** Political Risk Services (IBC USA (Publications) Inc.). (19??)-. English. $325.00. Political Risk Services, 6320 Fly Road, Suite 102, PO Box 248, East Syracuse NY 13057-0248. **Tel** (315)431-0511, FAX (315)431-0200.
Desc: Assesses the factors affecting the prospects for business and trade. Each report focuses specifically on business needs such as finding and developing markets, determining currency movements, or making judgements about capital investments or corporate security.

LC HC191 .C45
DD 330.983/005   GW
CHILE WIRTSCHAFTLICHE ENTWICKLUNG / BUNDESSTELLE FUR AUSSENHANDELSINFORMATION.
German. One time a year. DM2.00. Bundesstelle fuer Aussenhandelsinformation, Agrippastrasse 87 93, D-50676 Cologne Germany. **Tel** 011 49 221 2057316, FAX 011 49 221 2057212.

LC HC191
DD 330.983/005   GW
CHILE, WIRTSCHAFTSDATEN UND WIRTSCHAFTSDOKUMENTATION / BUNDESSTELLE FUER AUSSENHANDELSINFORMATION.
German. One time a year. DM3.00. Bundesstelle fuer Aussenhandelsinformation, Agrippastrasse 87 93, D-50676 Cologne Germany. **Tel** 011 49 221 2057316, FAX 011 49 221 2057212.

ISSN 1353-4688
DD 330.951   UK
●**CHINA & NORTH ASIA MONITOR.** [China North Asia monit.]. **VFOAT** China and North Asia Monitor; CNAM. (1994)-. English. Twelve times a year. $420.00. Business Monitor International, 56 60 St. John Street, London EC1M 4DT United Kingdom. **Tel** 011 44 171 6083646, FAX 011 44 171 6083620.

UK
CHINA ECONOMIC REVIEW. (1991)-. Periodical. English. Twelve times a year. $198.00. Alain Charles Publishing Ltd., 27 Wilfred Street, London SW1E 6PR United Kingdom. **Tel** 011 44 171 8347676, FAX 011 44 171 9730076, telex 297165. **ED** David Lammie. **Ad Acc, Adv Mgr:** Cordelia Boyd and Rachel Groves.
Desc: The latest news and developments within China, including projects, contracts, the domestic economic situation, travel, trade statistics, transportation, and reports from the provinces as well as feature articles on important issues affecting business and investment.

ISSN 1054-5336
DD 951   US
CHINA (SYRACUSE, N.Y.). (CHINA : A POLITICAL AND ECONOMIC FORECAST / POLITICAL RISK SERVICES.). [China]. **Added/Corp** Political Risk Services (IBC USA (Publications) Inc.). (19??)-. English. $325.00. Political Risk Services, 6320 Fly Road, Suite 102, PO Box 248, East Syracuse NY 13057-0248. **Tel** (315)431-0511, FAX (315)431-0200.
Desc: Assesses the factors affecting the prospects for business and trade. Each report focuses specifically on business needs such as finding and developing markets, determining currency movements, or making judgements about capital investments or corporate security.

LC HC59 .C52975   ISSN 0013-0265
DD 330.9/047   HK
CHING CHI TAO PAO = ECONOMIC REPORTER. VFOAT Economic Reporter. (1947)-. Periodical. Chinese. Fifty times a year. $170.00. Economic Information & Agency, 342 Hennessy Road, 10-16th Floor, Hong Kong Hong Kong. **Tel** 011 852 25738217, FAX 011 852 8388304, telex 60647 EICC HX.

LC HC466 .C42
KO
CHOHUNG KYONGJE. Periodical. Korean. Twelve times a year. Chohung Unhaeng, 14 1-ka Namdaemun-ro, Chung-ku, Seoul South Korea.

LC HC466 .C47b
KO
CHON'GONGNYON HOEBO. Main/Corp Chon'guk Kyongjein Yonhaphoe. **Added/Corp** Chon'guk Kyongjein Yonhaphoe. FKI Bulletin. **VFOAT** FKI Bulletin.

Business and Economics — Economic History, Conditions

(19??)-. Bulletin. Korean. One time a week. Chonguk Kyongjein Yonhaphel, 10 Kwanchol-dong, Chongno-ku Seoul South Korea.

LC HC466 .C47A
    KO
CHONGYONGNYON. Main/Corp Chonguk Kyongjein Yonhaphoe. Vol. 143- No.; 1976-. Periodical. Korean. 100 single issue. Chonguk Kyongjein Yonhaphoe, 1-124 Youido-dong, Yongdungpo-ku, Seoul South Korea. **Continues** Kyonghyop.

LC HC461 .N462a
    JA
CHOSA GEPPO. Added/Corp Nihon Ginko. Chosa Tokeikyoku. (1981)-. Japanese. Twelve times a year. **(Subscription address:** Japan Publications Trading Company Ltd., PO Box 5030, Tokyo International, Tokyo 100-31 Japan. **Tel** 011 81 3 3292 3753.) **Continues** Chosa Geppo (Nihon Ginko. Chosakyoku : 1950).

LC HC466 .A15
    KO
CHOSA TONGGYE WOLBO. VFOAT Monthly Bulletin. Vol. 36, No. 1 (1982)-. Bulletin. English (Korean). Twelve times a year. W931 (single issue). Hanguk Unhaeng, 110 3-ka Namdaemunro Chung-ku, Seoul Korea. **Tel** 535-5498. Formed by the union of Chosa Wolbo (Hanguk Unhaeng) **and** Tonggye Wolbo (Hanguk Unhaeng), 0300-0850.

LC HC466 .C476
DD 330/338.9519
    KO
CHUGAN KYONGJE. Added/Corp Suwon Sanggong Hoeuiso. (19??)-. Korean. Suwon Sanggong Hoeuiso, 13-3 2-ka Maesan-no, Suwon Korea.

LC HC466 .C478
    KO
CHUGAN MAEGYONG. VFOAT Maegyong. Periodical. Korean. One time a week. W35,000. Maeil Kyongje Sinmunsa, 51 1-ka Pil-dong Chung-ku, Seoul Korea.

LC HC463.C48 J36a
DD 330
    JA
CHUGOKU CHIIKI TSUSHO SANGYO TOKEI NEMPO. See Business and Economics-Abstracting, Bibliographies and Statistics.

LC HC427.9 .C581229
    JA
CHUGOKU KEIZAI KANKEI SHUYO RONSETSU SHU. Japanese. Nitchu Keizai Kyokai, c/o Aoyama Building, 2-3 Kita Aoyama 1-chome Minato-ku, Tokyo 107 Japan.

LC HC427.92 .C495
  ISSN 0285-8282
    JA
CHUGOKU MONDAI. Added/Corp Chugoku Mondai Kenkyujo (Kokusai Zenrin Kyokai) Kokusai Zenrin Kyokai (Japan). (Oct. 1981)-. Japanese. Chugoku Mondai Kenkyujo (Kikusai Zenrin Kyokai), 5-5 Shinbashi 1, Minato-ku, Tokyo-to 105 Japan.

LC HC427.92 .C5484
DD 330.951/057
    HK
CHUNG-KUO CHING CHI NIEN CHIEN. VFOAT Almanac of China's Economy; Annual Economic Report of China. (1981)-. Chinese (English). One time a year. $300.00. Chung-Kuo Ching Chi Nien Chien Yu Hsien Kung Ssu, 2-4 Tung Lo Wan Hsin Ning Tao, Third Floor, Hsiang-kang Hong Kong.

LC HC427.92 .C5485
  ISSN 1000-4181
DD 330.951/05
    CH
CHUNG-KUO CHING CHI WEN TI. [Zhongguo jingji wenti]. **VFOAT** Zhongguo Jingjiwenti; China's Economic Problems; Zhongguojingjiwenti. Periodical. Chinese. Six times a year. Science Press, 16 Donghuangchenggen North Street, Beijing 100707, People's Republic of China. **Tel** 011 86 1 4019821, 011 86 1 4010642, FAX 011 86 1 4012180, 011 86 1 4019810, telex 210147.

LC HC426 .C556
DD 330.951
    CH
CHUNG-KUO SHE HUI CHING CHI SHIH LUN TSUNG / SHAN-HSI SHENG SHE HUI KO HSUEH YEN CHIU SO PIEN.
(1981)-. Periodical. Chinese (table of contents in English). NT$1.86. Hsin Hua Shu Tien / Tai-Yuan, People's Republic of China.

LC HF3831 .C485
DD 382/.0951
    HK
CHUNG-KUO TUI WAI CHING CHI MAO I NIEN CHIEN. (ALMANAC OF CHINA'S FOREIGN ECONOMIC RELATIONS AND TRADE.). **VFOAT** Chung-Kuo Tui Wai Ching Chi Mao I Nien Chien. (1984)-. Periodical. English (Chinese). One time a year. $104.00. China Resources Advertising Company, 40 F High Block, 26 Harbour Road, Wanchai Hong Kong. **Tel** 011 852 25938831, FAX 011 852 258275453, telex 76757. **ED** Mu Defu. **Ad Acc, Adv Mgr Tel** 0852-5938831. **Circ:** 10,000.
Desc: Information on foreign economic relations and trade in China.

LC HC501 .A512a
  ISSN 1011-839X
DD 309.1/6/00305
    IV
CIRES, CAHIERS IVOIRIENS DE RECHERCHE ECONOMIQUE ET SOCIALE. [CIRES, Cah. ivoir. rech. econ. soc.]. **Main/Corp** Abidjan, Ivory Coast. Universite. **VFOAT** Cahiers Ivoiriens de Recherche Economique et Sociale. **VAT** Cahiers Ivoiriens de Recherche Economique et Sociale, Cahiers Ivoiriens de Recherche Economique et Sociale. No. 1 (1970)-. French. Four times a year. Price varies per volume. Univ Nationale Cote Ivoire, Cires BP 1295, Abidjan 08 Ivory Coast. **Tel** 225 440953.
Ind/Abst Int. Labour Doc.

LC JF37 .C53
  ISSN 0145-9686
DD 320.4/03
    US
CLEMENTS' ENCYCLOPEDIA OF WORLD GOVERNMENTS. See Political Science.

DD 382
  ISSN 0587-8160
    MX
COLECCION DE DOCUMENTOS PARA LA HISTORIA DEL COMERCIO EXTERIOR DE MEXICO. Added/Corp Banco Nacional de Comercio Exterior (Mexico). Series 1, No. 1 (1958)- Series 2, No. 1 (1965)-. Periodical. Spanish. Irregular. Banco Nacional de Comercio Exterior SA, Venustiano Carranza 32, Mexico 1 DF Mexico. **Tel** 688.0688, telex 017-71-070. **ED** L. Chavez Orozco.

LC HC121 .C56
  ISSN 0716-0631
DD 330.98/0005
    CL
COLECCION ESTUDIOS CIEPLAN.
[Colecc. estud. CIEPLAN]. **Added/Corp** Corporacion de Investigaciones Economicas para Latinoamerica. **VFOAT** Estudios C.I.E.P.L.A.N.; Coleccion Estudios C.I.E.P.L.A.N. (July 1979)-. Periodical. Spanish. Three times a year. $40.00. Cieplan, Av C Colon 3494, Comuna Condes, Santiago Chile. **Tel** 56 2 2283262. **Bk Rev. Ad Acc. Circ:** 2,500 (ctrl). **Continues** Estudios CIEPLAN, 0716-4963.
Desc: Economic analysis of Chile and Latin America.
Ind/Abst Econ. Lit. Index; Int. Labour Doc.; LABORDOC; PAIS Int. Print (1991-).

DD 986
  ISSN 1054-5344
    US
COLOMBIA (SYRACUSE, N.Y.).
(COLOMBIA : A POLITICAL AND ECONOMIC FORECAST / POLITICAL RISK SERVICES.). [Colombia]. **Added/Corp** Political Risk Services (IBC USA (Publications) Inc.). (19??)-. English. $325.00. Political Risk Services, 6320 Fly Road, Suite 102, PO Box 248, East Syracuse NY 13057-0248. **Tel** (315)431-0511, FAX (315)431-0200.
Desc: Assesses the factors affecting the prospects for business and trade. Each report focuses specifically on business needs such as finding and developing markets, determining currency movements, or making judgements about capital investments or corporate security.

LC HC445.6.A1 N66A
DD 330.9/595/305
    MY
COLONY OF NORTH BORNEO ANNUAL REPORT. Main/Corp North Borneo. **VFOAT** North Borneo Annual Report. English. One time a year. Government Printing Department, Jesselton Malaysia.

LC HC191 .C58
    CL
COMENTARIOS SOBRE LA SITUACION ECONOMICA. VFOAT Situacion Economica. (1971)-. Spanish. Two times a year. 2,500Chil$ Chile; $35.00 US. Universidad de Chile / Departamento de Economia, Casilla Postal 3861, Santiago Chile. **Tel** 011 56 2 228521. **ED** Clemente Torres (editor's address: Dept. de Economie, Universidad de Chile, Casilla 3861 Santiago Chile). **Circ:** 350.
Desc: Semesterly appraisal of the Chilean economy with trend projections; covers employment, growth, the public sector, monetary aggregates and foreign trade.

LC HE
  ISSN 1356-3327
DD 384
    UK
●**COMMUNICATIONS MARKETS ANALYSIS. See** Communications.

LC HC591.C6 C63
DD 382/.09675/1
    BE
COMPAGNIE EUROPEENNE ET D'OUTRE-MER. RAPPORTS. Main/Corp Compagnie Europeenne et d'Outre-Mer. (1971/72)-. French. Compagnie Europeenne et d'Outre-Mer, 13 rue de Brederode, Brussels Belgium. **Continues** Compagnie du Congo pour le Commerce et l'Industrie, Brussels. Assemblee Generale. Rapports.

LC HC101 .C616
  ISSN 1044-2545
DD 330.973/0021
    US
COMPLETE ECONOMIC AND DEMOGRAPHIC DATA SOURCE : CEDDS, THE. [Complet. econ. demogr. data source]. **Added/Corp** Woods & Poole Economics. **VFOAT** CEDDS. (1984)-. English. One time a year. $750.00. Woods & Poole Economics Inc., 1794 Columbia Road Northwest, Suite 4, Washington DC 20009. **Tel** (202)332-7111, FAX (202)332-6466.

LC HC158.5.Z9 I513
DD 339.37297/6
    FR
COMPTES ECONOMIQUES DE LA GUADELOUPE. Added/Corp Institut National de la Statistique et des Etudes Economiques (France). (19??)-. French. 18 Boulevard Adolphe Pinard, 75 675 Paris France.

LC HC875.A1 R85A
DD 330.967/571/00212
    RW
COMPTES ECONOMIQUES NATIONAUX DU RWANDA / REPUBLIQUE RWANDAISE, MINISTERE DU PLAN, DIRECTION GENERALE DE LA STATISTIQUE, BUREAU DE LA COMPTABILITE NATIONALE. No. 1 (1975-1976)-. French. One time a year. 500F. Bureau de la Comptabilite Nationale, BP 46, Kigali Republique Rwandaise.

LC HC131 .C5733
    MX
CONFEDERACION DE CAMARAS INDUSTRIALES. Main/Corp Confederacion de Camaras Industriales de los Estados Unidos Mex. Periodical. Spanish. Twelve times a year. Free. Confederacion de Camaras Industriales, Departamento de Communicaciones, Manuel Maria Contreras 133, Mexico City Mexico. **Tel** 566 78 22 546 90 53, telex CCINME 1773789. **Ad Acc. Circ:** 10,000. **Continues** Publicacion Quincenal.
Desc: Covers the most important activities of the Confederation and affiliated organizations; provides economic and financial information on the industrial sector.

LC HC301.A1 C65
  ISSN 0010-5759
    IT
CONGIUNTURA ITALIANA. [Congiunt. ital.]. **Added/Corp** Istituto Nazionale per lo Studio Della Congiuntura (Italy). (1958)-. Periodical. Italian. Twelve times a year. L238180. Istituto Nazio Studio Congiuntura, Piazza Indipendenza 4, 00185 Rome Italy. **Tel** 011 39 6 444821, FAX 011 39 6 44482619.

    FR
CONJONCTURE. (197?)-. Periodical. French. Six times a year. Documentation Francaise, 29 quai Voltaire, 75344 Paris Cedex 7 France. **Tel** 011 33 1 40157000, FAX 011 33 1 40157230, telex 204 826 DOCFRAN.
Ind/Abst World Agric. Econ. Rural Sociol. Abstr.

LC HC547.T8 C64
DD 330.9/61/105
    TI
CONJONCTURE; BULLETIN D'INFORMATION ECONOMIQUE. VFOAT Conjoncture BIE. Bulletin. French. Irregular. 4.00. Ministere de l'Economie Nationale, CCB U I B Siege, La Kabash 700438 Tunisia.

LC HC271 .C713
  ISSN 1140-5228
    FR
CONJONCTURE ET PREVISION / REPUBLIQUE FRANCAISE, MINISTERE DE L'ECONOMIE, DES FINANCES ET DU BUDGET. Added/Corp France. Ministere de l'Economie, des Finances et du Budget. (1989)-. Periodical. French. Ministere de l'Economie des Finances et du Budget, Service de la Communication et des Relations Avec le Public, 139 rue de Bercy, 75572 Paris Cedex 2-RP-France.

LC HC321 .A356a
  ISSN 0166-9087
DD 330
    NL
CONJUNCTUURTEST. Main/Corp Netherlands. Centraal Bureau voor de Statistiek. (Jan. 1962)-. Dutch. Twelve times a year. $102.91. Centraal Bureau voor de Statistiek, AFD ALG Zaken, Postbus 959, 2270 AZ Voorburg Netherlands. **Tel** 011 31 70 3373800, FAX 011 31 70 0387429, telex 32692 CBS NL.

  ISSN 0381-7385
DD 330.9/71/0644
    CN
CONSENSUS (TORONTO. 1975).
(CONSENSUS.). **Added/Corp** National Citizens' Coalition. Vol. 1 (Oct. 1975)-. English. Six times a year. 28.01Can$. National Citizens Coalition, 100 Adelaide Street West, Suite 907, Toronto Ontario M5H 1S3 Canada. **Tel** (416)869-3838, FAX (416)869-1891.

LC HC110.I5 C64 ISSN 0148-3072
DD 339.4/1/0973 US
CONSUMER BUSINESS REVIEW.
Added/Corp Data Resources, Inc. Consumer Products Service. (19??)-. English. DRI McGraw Hill, 24 Hartwell Avenue, Lexington MA 02173. **Tel** (617)863-5100, FAX (617)860-6464, (617)860-6416.

LC HD6993.V8 M37
DD 338.5/28/09755 US
CONSUMER PRICE INDICATORS FOR VIRGINIA METROPOLITAN AREAS.
Added/Corp Tayloe Murphy Institute. (1978)-. Periodical. English. One time a year. $5.00. Taylor Murphy Institute, Box 6550, Charlottesville VA 22906. ***Continues*** *Relative Price Indices in Virginia Metropolitan Areas.*

ISSN 0892-3981
DD 330 US
CONTEMPORARY ECONOMIC PROBLEMS (1987). (CONTEMPORARY ECONOMIC PROBLEMS.). [Contemp. econ. probl.]. **Added/Corp** American Enterprise Institute for Public Policy Research. (1987)-. English. One time a year. Price varies per volume. American Enterprise Institute, 1150 17th Street Northwest, Department 260, Washington DC 20036. **Tel** (202)862-5800, (800)269-6267. ***Continues*** *Essays in Contemporary Economic Problems, 0732-4308.*

ISSN 0084-9235
US
CONTRIBUTIONS IN ECONOMICS AND ECONOMIC HISTORY. **VFOAT** Greenwood Contributions in Economics and Economic History. No. 1 (1970)-. Monographic series. English. Irregular. Price varies per volume. Greenwood Press Inc., PO Box 5007, Westport CT 06881-5007. **Tel** (203)226-3571, FAX (203)222-1502. **ED** Robert Sobel.
Ind/Abst Curr. Cit.

ISSN 0743-2569
US
COST OF LIVING NEWS. [Cost living news]. **Added/Corp** Cost Comparison Counselors, Inc. (Oct. 1983)-. Periodical. English. Four times a year (Mar., June, Sept., Dec.). $200.00. Cost Comparison Counselors Inc, PO Box 77192, Washington DC 20013. **Tel** (703)893-5355. Index available. ctrl circ.
Desc: Highlights public and private cost of living information. Covers corporate compensation practices and includes a fifty-city cost of living comparison in the last issue of each volume.

ISSN 0276-4644
US
COSTA RICA REPORT. [Costa Rica rep.]. (1981)-. Periodical. English. Twelve times a year. $42.00. US International Marketing Company, 17057 Bellflower Boulevard, PO Box 428, Bellflower CA 90706. **Tel** (310)925-2918, telex 6502978961.

ISSN 1054-5352
DD 972 US
COSTA RICA (SYRACUSE, N.Y.). (COSTA RICA : A POLITICAL AND ECONOMIC FORECAST.). [Costa Rica]. **Added/Corp** Political Risk Services (IBC USA (Publications) Inc.). (19??)-. English. $325.00. Political Risk Services, 6320 Fly Road, Suite 102, PO Box 248, East Syracuse NY 13057-0248. **Tel** (315)431-0511, FAX (315)431-0200.
Desc: Assesses the factors affecting the prospects for business and trade. Each report focuses specifically on business needs such as finding and developing markets, determining currency movements, or making judgements about capital investments or corporate security.

LC HC143.A1
DD 330.97286 GW
COSTA RICA WIRTSCHAFTSDATEN / BUNDESSTELLE FUR AUSSENHANDELSINFORMATION.
German. One time a year. DM2.00. Bundesstelle fuer Aussenhandelsinformation, Agrippastrasse 87 93, D-50676 Cologne Germany. **Tel** 011 49 221 2057316, FAX 011 49 221 2057212.

LC HC547.I8 F73a
DD 330.9/666/805 FR
COTE D'IVOIRE. **Main/Corp** France. Direction de l'Aide au Developpement. Sectour Information Economique et Conjoncture. (19??)-. French. Direction de l'Aide au Developpement, 20 rue Monsieur Viie, Paris France.

ISSN 1054-5670
DD 966 US
COTE D'IVOIRE (SYRACUSE, N.Y.). (COTE D'IVOIRE : A POLITICAL AND ECONOMIC FORECAST / POLITICAL RISK SERVICES.). [Cote d'Iv.]. **Added/Corp** Political Risk Services (IBC USA (Publications) Inc.). (19??)-. English. $325.00. Political Risk Services, 6320 Fly Road, Suite 102, PO Box 248, East Syracuse NY 13057-0248. **Tel** (315)431-0511, FAX (315)431-0200.
Desc: Assesses the factors affecting the prospects for business and trade. Each report focuses specifically on business needs such as finding and developing markets, determining currency movements, or making judgements about capital investments or corporate security.

US
COUNTRY DATA FORECASTS. (19??)-. English. Two times a year. $495.00. Bank of America / World Information Service, PO Box 37000, Department 3015, San Francisco CA 94137. **Tel** (800)645-6667, (415)622-1446.

LC HC815.A1 C678
DD 330.965/005 UK
COUNTRY PROFILE. ALGERIA. **VFOAT** Algeria. (1986/87)-. English. One time a year. Included with Country Reports.. subscription. The Economist Intelligence Unit, 40 Duke Street, London W1A 1DW United Kingdom. **Tel** 011 44 171 8301000. **(Subscription address:** Economist Intelligence Unit / North America Subscriptions, 111 West 57th Street, New York NY 10019. **Tel** 800 938-4685, (212)554-0600, FAX (212)586-1181, (212)586-1182.**)** ***Continues in part*** *Quarterly Economic Review of Algeria, 0142-4130.*

LC HC980.A1 C66 ISSN 1352-0849
UK
•COUNTRY PROFILE. CONGO, SAO TOME AND PRINCIPE, GUINEA-BISSAU, CAPE VERDE. **Added/Corp** Economist Intelligence Unit (Great Britain). **VFOAT** Congo, Sao Tome and Principe, Guinea-Bissau, Cape Verde. (1994)-. English. One time a year. $125.00. The Economist Intelligence Unit, 40 Duke Street, London W1A 1DW United Kingdom. **Tel** 011 44 171 8301000. ***Formed by the union of*** *Country Profile. Congo, 0269-6363; Country Profile. Angola, Sao Tome & Principe, 0269-7092* ***and*** *Country Profile. Gambia, Guinea-Bissau, Cape Verde, 0968-2422.*

LC HC1025.A1 C67
DD 330.96668/005 UK
TITLE CHANGE
COUNTRY PROFILE. COTE D'IVOIRE.
Added/Corp Economist Intelligence Unit (Great Britain). **VFOAT** Cote d'Ivoire. (1989)-(1993). English. The Economist Intelligence Unit, 40 Duke Street, London W1A 1DW United Kingdom. **Tel** 011 44 171 8301000. ***Continues*** *Country Profile. Ivory Coast, 0269-7068.* ***Merged with*** *Country Profile. Guinea, Mali, Mauritania, 0269-4417* ***to form*** *Country Profile. Cote d'Ivoire, Mali.*

LC HC1025.A1 C685
UK
•COUNTRY PROFILE. COTE D'IVOIRE, MALI. **Added/Corp** Economist Intelligence Unit (Great Britain). **VFOAT** Cote d'Ivoire, Mali. (1993/1994)-. English. One time a year. Included with Country Reports.. subscription. The Economist Intelligence Unit, 40 Duke Street, London W1A 1DW United Kingdom. **Tel** 011 44 171 8301000. **(Subscription address:** Economist Intelligence Unit / North America Subscriptions, 111 West 57th Street, New York NY 10019. **Tel** 800 938-4685, (212)554-0600, FAX (212)586-1181, (212)586-1182.**)** ***Formed by the union of*** *Country Profile. Cote d'Ivoire* ***and*** *Country Profile. Guinea, Mali, Mauritania, 0269-4417.*
Desc: Evaluates growth prospects, assesses opportunities, and examines problems. Provides concise and lucid business-oriented analysis of the latest economic and political indicators.

LC HC415.2.A1 C68
UK
•COUNTRY PROFILE. CYPRUS, MALTA.
Added/Corp Economist Intelligence Unit (Great Britain). **VFOAT** Cyprus, Malta; EIU Country Profile. (1994)-. English. The Economist Intelligence Unit, 40 Duke Street, London W1A 1DW United Kingdom. **Tel** 011 44 171 8301000. **(Subscription address:** Economist Intelligence Unit / North America Subscriptions, 111 West 57th Street, New York NY 10019. **Tel** 800 938-4685, (212)554-0600, FAX (212)586-1181, (212)586-1182.**)** ***Formed by the union of*** *Country Profile. Lebanon, Cyprus, 0269-7351* ***and*** *Country Profile. Malta, 0269-8137.*

LC HC351 .C67 ISSN 0269-5138
DD 330.9489/005 UK
COUNTRY PROFILE. DENMARK, ICELAND. [Ctry. profile, Den. Icel.]. **VFOAT** Denmark, Iceland. (1986/87)-. English. One time a year. Included with Country Reports.. subscription. The Economist Intelligence Unit, 40 Duke Street, London W1A 1DW United Kingdom. **Tel** 011 44 171 8301000. **(Subscription address:** Economist Intelligence Unit / North America Subscriptions, 111 West 57th Street, New York NY 10019. **Tel** 800 938-4685, (212)554-0600, FAX (212)586-1181, (212)586-1182.**)** ***Continues in part*** *Quarterly Economic Review of Denmark, Iceland, 0142-4181.*

LC HC281 .C67
DD 330/338.94 UK
COUNTRY PROFILE. GERMANY.
Added/Corp Economist Intelligence Unit (Great Britain). **VFOAT** Germany. (1992)-. English. available on microfilm. ***Formed by the union of*** *Country Profile. East Germany, 0269-7033* ***and*** *Country Profile. West Germany, 0269-8021.*

UK
•COUNTRY PROFILE. GUINEA, SIERRA LEONE, LIBERIA. **Added/Corp** Economist Intelligence Unit (Great Britain). **VFOAT** Guinea, Sierra Leone, Liberia. (1993/1994)-. English. One time a year. Included with Country Reports.. subscription. The Economist Intelligence Unit, 40 Duke Street, London W1A 1DW United Kingdom. **Tel** 011 44 171 8301000. **(Subscription address:** Economist Intelligence Unit / North America Subscriptions, 111 West 57th Street, New York NY 10019. **Tel** 800 938-4685, (212)554-0600, FAX (212)586-1181, (212)586-1182.**)** ***Formed by the union of*** *Country Profile. Guinea, Mali, Mauritania, 0269-4417* ***and*** *Country Profile. Sierra Leone, Liberia, 0269-5057.*
Desc: Evaluates growth prospects, assesses opportunities, and examines problems. Provides concise and lucid business-oriented analysis of the latest economic and political indicators.

LC HC156.A1 C686
UK
•COUNTRY PROFILE. GUYANA, WINDWARD & LEEWARD ISLANDS.
Added/Corp Economist Intelligence Unit (Great Britain). **VFOAT** Guyana, Windward & Leeward Islands. (1993/1994)-. English. One time a year. Included with Country Reports.. subscription. The Economist Intelligence Unit, 40 Duke Street, London W1A 1DW United Kingdom. **Tel** 011 44 171 8301000. **(Subscription address:** Economist Intelligence Unit / North America Subscriptions, 111 West 57th Street, New York NY 10019. **Tel** 800 938-4685, (212)554-0600, FAX (212)586-1181, (212)586-1182.**)** ***Continues in part*** *Country Profile. Guyana, Barbados, Windward & Leeward Islands, 0269-8110.*

LC HC4709.3.A1 C66
DD 330.951/25/005 UK
COUNTRY PROFILE. HONG KONG, MACAU. **VFOAT** Hong Kong, Macau. (1987)-. English. One time a year. Included with Country Reports.. subscription. The Economist Intelligence Unit, 40 Duke Street, London W1A 1DW United Kingdom. **Tel** 011 44 171 8301000. **(Subscription address:** Economist Intelligence Unit / North America Subscriptions, 111 West 57th Street, New York NY 10019. **Tel** 800 938-4685, (212)554-0600, FAX (212)586-1181, (212)586-1182.**)** ***Continues in part*** *Quarterly Economic Review of Hongkong, Macau, 0265-6906.*

LC HC471 .C67 ISSN 0269-5960
DD 330.955/005 UK
COUNTRY PROFILE. IRAN. [Ctry. profile, Iran]. **VFOAT** Iran. 1986-87-. English. One time a year. Included with Country Reports.. subscription. The Economist Intelligence Unit, 40 Duke Street, London W1A 1DW United Kingdom. **Tel** 011 44 171 8301000. **(Subscription address:** Economist Intelligence Unit / North America Subscriptions, 111 West 57th Street, New York NY 10019. **Tel** 800 938-4685, (212)554-0600, FAX (212)586-1181, (212)586-1182.**)** ***Continues in part*** *Quarterly Economic Review of Iran, 0142-3924.*

LC HC415.24.A1 C678
DD 330.95692/005 UK
•COUNTRY PROFILE. LEBANON. [Ctry. profile, Leban.]. **Added/Corp** Economist Intelligence Unit (Great Britain). **VFOAT** Lebanon. (1994)-. English. One time a year. $125.00. The Economist Intelligence Unit, 40 Duke Street, London W1A 1DW United Kingdom. **Tel** 011 44 171 8301000. **(Subscription address:** Economist Intelligence Unit / North America Subscriptions, 111 West 57th Street, New York NY 10019. **Tel** 800 938-4685, (212)554-0600, FAX (212)586-1181, (212)586-1182.**)** ***Continues in part*** *Country Profile. Lebanon, Cyprus, 0269-7351.*

LC HC415.24.A1 C68 ISSN 0269-7351
DD 330.9564/5/005 UK
TITLE CHANGE
COUNTRY PROFILE. LEBANON, CYPRUS. [Ctry. profile, Leban. Cyprus]. **Added/Corp** Economist Intelligence Unit (Great Britain). **VFOAT** Lebanon, Cyprus. (1986/87)-(1993). English. The Economist Intelligence Unit, 40 Duke Street, London W1A 1DW United Kingdom. **Tel** 011 44 171 8301000. **(Subscription address:** Economist Intelligence Unit / North America Subscriptions, 111 West 57th Street, New York NY 10019. **Tel** 800 938-4685, (212)554-0600, FAX (212)586-1181, (212)586-1182.**)** ***Continues in part*** *Quarterly Economic Review of Lebanon, Cyprus, 0142-4106.* ***Continued in part by*** *Country Profile. Cyprus, Malta; Country Profile. Lebanon.*

LC HC895.A1 C679
UK
•COUNTRY PROFILE. MADAGASCAR.
Added/Corp Economist Intelligence Unit (Great Britain). **VFOAT** Madagascar. (1993/1994)-. English. One time a year. Included with Country Reports.. subscription. The Economist Intelligence Unit, 40 Duke Street, London W1A 1DW United Kingdom. **Tel** 011 44 171 8301000. **(Subscription address:** Economist Intelligence Unit / North America Subscriptions, 111 West 57th Street, New

York NY 10019. **Tel** 800 938-4685, (212)554-0600, FAX (212)586-1181, (212)586-1182.**)** ***Continues in part*** *Country Profile. Madagascar, Comoros, 0269-736X.*

LC HC895.A1 C678 **ISSN** 0269-736X
DD 330.969/1/005 UK
TITLE CHANGE

COUNTRY PROFILE. MADAGASCAR, COMOROS. [Ctry. profile, Madag. Comoros]. **Added/Corp** Economist Intelligence Unit (Great Britain). **VFOAT** Madagascar, Comoros. (1986/1987)-(1992/1993). English. The Economist Intelligence Unit, 40 Duke Street, London W1A 1DW United Kingdom. **Tel** 011 44 171 8301000. ***Continues in part*** *Quarterly Economic Review of Madagascar, Mauritius, Seychelles, Comoros, 0141-8092.* ***Split into*** *Country Profile. Madagascar;* ***Merged with*** *Country Profile. Tanzania* ***to form*** *Country Profile. Tanzania, Comoros.*

LC HC445.5.A1 C678 **ISSN** 0269-5588
DD 330.9595/005 UK

COUNTRY PROFILE. MALAYSIA, BRUNEI. [Ctry. profile, Malays. Brunei]. **Added/Corp** Economist Intelligence Unit (Great Britain). **VFOAT** Malaysia, Brunei. (1987)-. English. One time a year. Included with Country Reports.. subscription. The Economist Intelligence Unit, 40 Duke Street, London W1A 1DW United Kingdom. **Tel** 011 44 171 8301000. **(Subscription address:** Economist Intelligence Unit / North America Subscriptions, 111 West 57th Street, New York NY 10019. **Tel** 800 938-4685, (212)554-0600, FAX (212)586-1181, (212)586-1182.**)** ***Continues in part*** *Quarterly Economic Review of Malaysia, Brunei, 0144-8919.*
Desc: Evaluates growth prospects, assesses opportunities, and examines problems. Provides concise and lucid business-oriented analysis of the latest economic and political indicators.

LC HC597.5.A1 C68 **ISSN** 0269-7378
DD 330.969/6 UK

COUNTRY PROFILE. MAURITIUS, SEYCHELLES. [Ctry. profile. Maurit. Seychelles]. **VFOAT** Mauritius, Seychelles. (1986/87)-. English. One time a year. Included with Country Reports.. subscription. The Economist Intelligence Unit, 40 Duke Street, London W1A 1DW United Kingdom. **Tel** 011 44 171 8301000. **(Subscription address:** Economist Intelligence Unit / North America Subscriptions, 111 West 57th Street, New York NY 10019. **Tel** 800 938-4685, (212)554-0600, FAX (212)586-1181, (212)586-1182.**)** ***Continues in part*** *Quarterly Economic Review of Madagascar, Mauritius, Seychelles, Comoros, 0141-8092.*

LC HC890.A1 C68 **ISSN** 0269-7017
DD 330.967/9/005 UK

COUNTRY PROFILE. MOZAMBIQUE. **VFOAT** Mozambique. (1986/87)-. English. One time a year. Included with Country Reports.. subscription. The Economist Intelligence Unit, 40 Duke Street, London W1A 1DW United Kingdom. **Tel** 011 44 171 8301000. **(Subscription address:** Economist Intelligence Unit / North America Subscriptions, 111 West 57th Street, New York NY 10019. **Tel** 800 938-4685, (212)554-0600, FAX (212)586-1181, (212)586-1182.**)** ***Continues in part*** *Quarterly Economic Review of Tanzania, Mozambique, 0142-4505.*

LC HC415.35.A1 C68
UK

COUNTRY PROFILE. OMAN, YEMEN. **Added/Corp** Economist Intelligence Unit (Great Britain). **VFOAT** Oman, Yemen. (1991)-. English. One time a year. Included with Country Reports.. subscription. The Economist Intelligence Unit, 40 Duke Street, London W1A 1DW United Kingdom. **Tel** 011 44 171 8301000. **(Subscription address:** Economist Intelligence Unit / North America Subscriptions, 111 West 57th Street, New York NY 10019. **Tel** 800 938-4685, (212)554-0600, FAX (212)586-1181, (212)586-1182.**)** ***Continues*** *Country Profile. Oman, the Yemens.*
Desc: Evaluates growth prospects, assesses opportunities, and examines problems. Provides concise and lucid business-oriented analysis of the latest economic and political indicators.

LC HC415.33.A1C67 **ISSN** 0269-6355
DD 330.953/8/005 UK

COUNTRY PROFILE. SAUDI ARABIA. [Ctry. profile, Saudi Arab.]. **VFOAT** Saudi Arabi. (1986/87)-. English. One time a year. Included with Country Reports.. subscription. The Economist Intelligence Unit, 40 Duke Street, London W1A 1DW United Kingdom. **Tel** 011 44 171 8301000. **(Subscription address:** Economist Intelligence Unit / North America Subscriptions, 111 West 57th Street, New York NY 10019. **Tel** 800 938-4685, (212)554-0600, FAX (212)586-1181, (212)586-1182.**)** ***Continues in part*** *Quarterly Economic Review of Saudi Arabia, 0142-4491.*

LC HC1045.A1 C658
DD 330.9663/005 UK

COUNTRY PROFILE. SENEGAL. **Added/Corp** Economist Intelligence Unit (Great Britain). **VFOAT** Senegal; EIU Country Profile. Senegal. **VAT** Economist Intelligence Unit Country Profile. Senegal. (1991/1992)-. English. One time a year. Included with Country Reports.. subscription. The Economist Intelligence Unit, 40 Duke Street, London W1A 1DW United Kingdom. **Tel** 011 44 171 8301000. **(Subscription address:** Economist Intelligence Unit / North America Subscriptions, 111 West 57th Street, New York NY 10019. **Tel** 800 938-4685, (212)554-0600, FAX (212)586-1181, (212)586-1182.**)** available on an online database, CD-ROM, magnetic tape, and microfilm. ***Continues in part*** *Country Profile.Senegal, The Gambia, Guinea-Bissau, Cape Verde, 0269-6037.*
Desc: Evaluates growth prospects, assesses opportunities, and examines problems. Provides concise and lucid business-oriented analysis of the latest economic and political indicators.

LC HC445.8.A1 C68 **ISSN** 0269-7041
DD 330.9595/7/005 UK

COUNTRY PROFILE. SINGAPORE. [Ctry. profile, Singap.]. **Added/Corp** Economist Intelligence Unit (Great Britain). **VFOAT** Singapore. (1987)-. English. One time a year. Included with Country Reports.. subscription. The Economist Intelligence Unit, 40 Duke Street, London W1A 1DW United Kingdom. **Tel** 011 44 171 8301000. **(Subscription address:** Economist Intelligence Unit / North America Subscriptions, 111 West 57th Street, New York NY 10019. **Tel** 800 938-4685, (212)554-0600, FAX (212)586-1181, (212)586-1182.**)** ***Continues in part*** *Quarterly Economic Review of Singapore, 0144-8927.*
Desc: Evaluates growth prospects, assesses opportunities, and examines problems. Provides concise and lucid business-oriented analysis of the latest economic and political indicators.

LC HC424.A1 C67 **ISSN** 0269-5073
DD 330.9549/3/005 UK

COUNTRY PROFILE. SRI LANKA. [Ctry. profile, Sri Lanka]. **Added/Corp** Economist Intelligence Unit (Great Britain). **VFOAT** Sri Lanka. (1986)-. English. One time a year. Included with Country Reports.. subscription. The Economist Intelligence Unit, 40 Duke Street, London W1A 1DW United Kingdom. **Tel** 011 44 171 8301000. **(Subscription address:** Economist Intelligence Unit / North America Subscriptions, 111 West 57th Street, New York NY 10019. **Tel** 800 938-4685, (212)554-0600, FAX (212)586-1181, (212)586-1182.**)** ***Continues in part*** *Quarterly Economic Review of Sri Lanka (Ceylon), 0142-3770.*
Desc: Evaluates growth prospects, assesses opportunities, and examines problems. Provides concise and lucid business-oriented analysis of the latest economic and political indicators.

LC HC885.A1 C67 **ISSN** 0269-6630
DD 330.9678/005 UK
TITLE CHANGE

COUNTRY PROFILE. TANZANIA. [Ctry. profile, Tanzan.]. **Added/Corp** Economist Intelligence Unit (Great Britain). **VFOAT** Tanzania. (1986/87)-(1993). English. The Economist Intelligence Unit, 40 Duke Street, London W1A 1DW United Kingdom. **Tel** 011 44 171 8301000. **(Subscription address:** Economist Intelligence Unit / North America Subscriptions, 111 West 57th Street, New York NY 10019. **Tel** 800 938-4685, (212)554-0600, FAX (212)586-1181, (212)586-1182.**)** ***Continues in part*** *Quarterly Economic Review of Tanzania, Mozambique, 0142-4505.* ***Merged with*** *Country Profile. Madagascar, Comoros, 0269-736X* ***to form*** *Country Profile. Tanzania, Comoros.*

LC HC885.A1 C673
DD 330.9678/005 UK

•**COUNTRY PROFILE. TANZANIA, COMOROS.** **Added/Corp** Economist Intelligence Unit (Great Britain). **VFOAT** Tanzania, Comoros. (1993/94)-. English. One time a year. $125.00. The Economist Intelligence Unit, 40 Duke Street, London W1A 1DW United Kingdom. **Tel** 011 44 171 8301000. ***Formed by the union of*** *Country Profile. Tanzania, 0269-6630* ***and*** *Country Profile. Madagascar, Comoros, 0269-736X.*

LC HC1070.A1 C68 **ISSN** 0968-2422
DD 330.9665 UK
TITLE CHANGE

COUNTRY PROFILE. THE GAMBIA, GUINEA-BISSAU, CAPE VERDE. [Ctry. profile, Gamb., Guin.-Bissau, Cape Verde]. **Added/Corp** Economist Intelligence Unit (Great Britain). **VFOAT** Gambia, Guinea-Bissau, Cape Verde; EIU Country Profile .... **VAT** Economist Intelligence Unit Country Profile. (1991/1992)-(1993). English. The Economist Intelligence Unit, 40 Duke Street, London W1A 1DW United Kingdom. **Tel** 011 44 171 8301000. **(Subscription address:** Economist Intelligence Unit / North America Subscriptions, 111 West 57th Street, New York NY 10019. **Tel** 800 938-4685, (212)554-0600, FAX (212)586-1181, (212)586-1182.**)** available on an online database, CD-ROM, magnetic tape, and microfilm. ***Continues in part*** *Country Profile. Senegal, The Gambia, Guinea-Bissau, Cape Verde, 0269-6037.* ***Continued in part by*** *Country Profile. Gambia, Mauritania, 1352-0938* ***and*** *Country Profile. Congo, Sao Tome and Principe, Guinea-Bissau, Cape Verde, 1352-0849.*
Desc: Evaluates growth prospects, assesses opportunities, and examines problems. Provides concise and lucid business-oriented analysis of the latest economic and political indicators.

LC HC1070.A1 C69 **ISSN** 1352-0938
UK

•**COUNTRY PROFILE. THE GAMBIA, MAURITANIA.** **Added/Corp** Economist Intelligence Unit (Great Britain). **VFOAT** Gambia, Mauritania. (1994)-. English. $125.00. The Economist Intelligence Unit, 40 Duke Street, London W1A 1DW United Kingdom. **Tel** 011 44 171 8301000. **(Subscription address:** Economist Intelligence Unit / North America Subscriptions, 111 West 57th Street, New York NY 10019. **Tel** 800 938-4685, (212)554-0600, FAX (212)586-1181, (212)586-1182.**)** ***Continues in part*** *Country Profile. Guinea, Mali, Mauritania, 0269-4417* ***and*** *Country Profile. Gambia, Guinea-Bissau, Cape Verde, 0968-2422.*

LC HC151 .Q333
UK

•**COUNTRY PROFILE. TRINIDAD AND TOBAGO, SURINAME, NETHERLANDS ANTILLES, ARUBA.** [Ctry. profile, Trinidad Tobago Suriname Netherlands Antilles Aruba]. **Added/Corp** Economist Intelligence Unit (Great Britain). **VFOAT** Trinidad and Tobago, Suriname, Netherlands Antilles, Aruba; EIU Country Profile. (1993/1994)-. English. One time a year. Included with Country Reports.. subscription. The Economist Intelligence Unit, 40 Duke Street, London W1A 1DW United Kingdom. **Tel** 011 44 171 8301000. **(Subscription address:** Economist Intelligence Unit / North America Subscriptions, 111 West 57th Street, New York NY 10019. **Tel** 800 938-4685, (212)554-0600, FAX (212)586-1181, (212)586-1182.**)** ***Continues*** *Country Profile. Trinidad & Tobago;* ***Continues in part*** *Country Profile. Venezuela, Suriname, Netherlands Antilles.*

LC HC415.36.A1 C688 **ISSN** 0269-6606
DD 330.953.57/005 UK

COUNTRY PROFILE. UNITED ARAB EMIRATES. [Ctry. profile, United Arab Emir.]. **VFOAT** United Arab Emirates. (1986/87)-. English. One time a year. Included with Country Reports.. subscription. The Economist Intelligence Unit, 40 Duke Street, London W1A 1DW United Kingdom. **Tel** 011 44 171 8301000. **(Subscription address:** Economist Intelligence Unit / North America Subscriptions, 111 West 57th Street, New York NY 10019. **Tel** 800 938-4685, (212)554-0600, FAX (212)586-1181, (212)586-1182.**)** ***Continues in part*** *Quarterly Economic Review of United Arab Emirates, 0141-8416.*

LC HC101 .C686
DD 330.973/005 UK

•**COUNTRY PROFILE. UNITED STATES OF AMERICA.** **Added/Corp** Economist Intelligence Unit (Great Britain). **VFOAT** United States of America. (1994/95)-. English. The Economist Intelligence Unit, 40 Duke Street, London W1A 1DW United Kingdom. **Tel** 011 44 171 8301000. ***Continues*** *Country Profile. USA.*

LC HC101 .C757 **ISSN** 0269-8005
DD 330.973/005 UK
TITLE CHANGE

COUNTRY PROFILE. USA. [Ctry. profile, USA]. **Added/Corp** Economist Intelligence Unit (Great Britain). **VFOAT** USA; U.S.A. (1987)-(1994). English. The Economist Intelligence Unit, 40 Duke Street, London W1A 1DW United Kingdom. **Tel** 011 44 171 8301000. **(Subscription address:** Economist Intelligence Unit / North America Subscriptions, 111 West 57th Street, New York NY 10019. **Tel** 800 938-4685, (212)554-0600, FAX (212)586-1181, (212)586-1182.**)** ***Continues in part*** *Quarterly Economic Review of USA, 0142-4459.* ***Continued by*** *Country Profile. United States of America.*

LC HC815.A1 C68
DD 330.965/005 UK

COUNTRY REPORT. ALGERIA. **VFOAT** Algeria. No. 2, (1986)-. Periodical. English. Four times a year. $335.00 (per country), $100.00 (single issue) North America. The Economist Intelligence Unit, 40 Duke Street, London W1A 1DW United Kingdom. **Tel** 011 44 171 8301000. **(Subscription address:** Economist Intelligence Unit / North America Subscriptions, 111 West 57th Street, New York NY 10019. **Tel** 800 938-4685, (212)554-0600, FAX (212)586-1181, (212)586-1182.**)** ***Continues in part*** *Quarterly Economic Review of Algeria, 0142-4130.*

LC HC101 .C76
DD 330 UK

•**COUNTRY REPORT. UNITED STATES OF AMERICA.** **Added/Corp** Economist Intelligence Unit (Great Britain). **VFOAT** United States of America. 2nd Quarter (1994)-. Periodical. English. Four times a year. The Economist Intelligence Unit, 40 Duke Street, London W1A 1DW United Kingdom. **Tel** 011 44 171 8301000. **(Subscription address:** Economist Intelligence Unit / North America Subscriptions, 111 West 57th Street, New York NY 10019. **Tel** 800 938-4685, (212)554-0600, FAX (212)586-1181, (212)586-1182.**)** ***Continues*** *Country Report. USA.*

Business and Economics — Economic History, Conditions

LC HC101 .C76
DD 330.973/005
ISSN 0269-6185
UK
TITLE CHANGE
COUNTRY REPORT. USA. [Ctry. rep., USA]. **Added/Corp** Economist Intelligence Unit (Great Britain). **VFOAT** USA. (1986)-(1994). Periodical. English. The Economist Intelligence Unit, 40 Duke Street, London W1A 1DW United Kingdom. **Tel** 011 44 171 8301000. **(Subscription address:** Economist Intelligence Unit / North America Subscriptions, 111 West 57th Street, New York NY 10019. **Tel** 800 938-4685, (212)554-0600, FAX (212)586-1181, (212)586-1182.) *Continues in part Quarterly Economic Review of USA, 0142-4459. Continued by Country Report. United States of America.*

LC HC101 HC101 .A184c
DD 338
ISSN 1064-539X
US
COUNTY BUSINESS PATTERNS. See Business and Economics-Computer Applications.

LC HC387.V3 C66
SP
COYUNTURA INDUSTRIAL, REGION VALENCIANA. Added/Corp Camara Oficial de Comercio, Industria y Navegacion de Alicante, (Alicante, Spain). Periodical. Spanish. Twelve times a year. Camara Oficial de Comercio Industria y Navegacion de Valencia, Poeta Querol 15, Valencia Spain.

LC HC131 .C83
DD 330
ISSN 0186-0445
MX
CUADERNO DE INFORMACION OPORTUNA. Added/Corp Instituto Nacional de Estadistica, Geografia e Informatica (Mexico). (19??)-. Statistical Publication. Spanish. Twelve times a year. INEGI / Instituto Nacional de Estadistica, Geografia e Informatica, Avenida Patriotismo 711 Segundo Piso, 03730 Mexico DF Mexico. **Tel** 011 52 5 5639935, 011 52 5 5988935, FAX 011 52 55987941. **(Subscription address:** INEGI / Instituto Nacional de Estadistica, Geografia e Informatica, Avenida Heroe de Nacozari 2301 Sur, Fracc. Jardines del Parque, CP 20270, Aguascalientes Mexico. **Tel** 011 52 49 182998.) available with charts; available with illustrations.

LC HC10 .C68
ISSN 0210-0266
SP
CUADERNOS DE ECONOMIA. [Cuad. econ.]. **Added/Corp** Consejo Superior de Investigaciones Cientificas (Spain). Centro de Estudios Economicos y Sociales. Universidad de Barcelona. Departamento de Teoria Economica. Vol. 1, No. 1 (Jan./June 1973)-. Periodical. Spanish. Ten times a year. 12000.00ptas Spain; 15000.00ptas Europe; 31000.00ptas North American and Africa; 42000.00ptas other. Fundacion Fondo para la Investigacion Economica y Social, Juan Hurtado de Mendoza 14, 28036 Madrid Spain. **Tel** 011 34 1 3504400, FAX 011 34 1 3508040. cum. index. *Supersedes Cuadernos de Informacion Economia, 0590-1979.*
Ind/Abst Econ. Lit. Index; Int. Labour Doc.; J. Econ. Lit.

LC HC387.C77 C8
ISSN 0045-9186
SP
CUADERNOS DE HISTORIA EECONOMICA DE CATALUNA. [Cuad. hist. econ. Catalunya]. **Added/Corp** Universidad de Barcelona. Departamento de Historia Economica. Universidad de Barcelona. Catedra de Historia Economica. Barcelona. Instituto Municipal de Historia. (1969)-. Multiple languages (Catalan, English, French and Spanish). available on microfilm and microfiche from University Microfilms International (UMI).
Ind/Abst Am. Hist. Life (1969-1980).

SP
CUADERNOS DE INFORMACION ECONOMICA. Spanish. Ten times a year. 12,000ptas Spain; 15,000ptas other. Fundacion Fondo para la Investigacion Economica y Social, Juan Hurtado de Mendoza 14, 28036 Madrid Spain. **Tel** 011 34 1 3504400, FAX 011 34 1 3508040. **ED** Padre Damian. **Circ:** 2,000 (ctrl). available on microfiche.
Desc: Focuses on Spanish as well as international economy matters.

LC HC171 .C8
DD 309.1/82/06
AG
CUADERNOS NACIONALES. Added/Corp Universidad de Buenos Aires. Facultad de Derecho y Ciencias Sociales. (1974)-. Periodical. Spanish. Avda Figueroa Alcorta, 2263 Buenos Aires Argentina.

US
●**CURRENT POLITICS AND ECONOMICS OF CHINA. See** Political Science.

LC D2009 .C87
ISSN 1057-2309
US
CURRENT POLITICS AND ECONOMICS OF EUROPE. See Political Science.

LC HC462.9 .C87
DD 338.952/005
ISSN 1056-7593
US
CURRENT POLITICS AND ECONOMICS OF JAPAN. See Political Science.

LC DK510.763 .C87
ISSN 1061-9186
US
CURRENT POLITICS AND ECONOMICS OF RUSSIA. See Political Science.

US
●**CURRENT POLITICS AND ECONOMICS OF THE MIDDLE EAST. See** Political Science.

US
CURRENT POLITICS AND ECONOMICS OF THE UNITED STATES. See Political Science.

LC HN571 .C87
ISSN 1101-6345
SW
CURRENT SWEDEN / THE SWEDISH INSTITUTE. Added/Corp Svenska Institutet. Svenska Institutet for Culturellt Utbyte med Utlandet. (197?)-. Monographic series. English (French, German and Spanish). Irregular. Free on request. Swedish Institute, PO Box 7434, Distribution Section, S-103 91 Stockholm Sweden. **Tel** 011 46 8 7892000, FAX 011 46 8 207248.
Desc: Presents information on issues featured in the Swedish public debate.

LC HC351 .D3
DD 330.9489/005
GW
DANEMARK, FAROER UND GRONLAND, WIRTSCHAFT IN ZAHLEN UND WIRTSCHAFTSDOKUMENTATION / BUNDESSTELLE FUR AUSSENHANDELSINFORMATION. German. DM5.00. Bundesstelle fuer Aussenhandelsinformation, Agrippastrasse 87 93, D-50676 Cologne Germany. **Tel** 011 49 221 2057316, FAX 011 49 221 2057212.

LC HC351
GW
DANEMARK : WIRTSCHAFTLICHE ENTWICKLUNG. Main/Corp Bundesstelle fur Aussenhandelsinformation (Germany). German. DM2.00. Bundesstelle fuer Aussenhandelsinformation, Agrippastrasse 87 93, D-50676 Cologne Germany. **Tel** 011 49 221 2057316, FAX 011 49 221 2057212.

LC HC412 .D18
DD 330.95/005
PH
DATA ASIA. Periodical. English. One time a week. Press Foundation of Asia, PO Box 1843, Manila Philippines. *Continues DA, Data Asia.*

ISSN 0723-6980
GW
D+C. DEVELOPMENT AND COOPERATION (ENGLISH EDITION). (DEVELOPMENT AND COOPERATION : D+C). [D+C, Dev. coop.]. **Added/Corp** Deutsche Stiftung fuer Internationale Entwicklung. **VFOAT** D+C. (1974)-. Academic Scholarly Publication. English. Six times a year. DM19.00. DSE Bonn Deut Stift International, Hans Boeckler Str 5, D-53225 Bonn Germany. **Tel** 011 49 228 40010. **(Subscription address:** Frankfurter Societaetsdruckere, Postfach 100801, D 60008 Frankfurt Germany. **Tel** 011 49 69 75014272.)
Ind/Abst EMBASE; For. Abstr.; Middle East Abstr. Index; Nutr. Abstr. Rev., Ser. A, Hum. Exp.; Rural Dev. Abstr.; Soils Fert.; World Agric. Econ. Rural Sociol. Abstr.

LC HC291 .T44
GR
DELTIO EMPORIKOU KAI VIOMECHANIKOU EPIMELETERIOU THESSALONIKES. VFOAT Deltio Eveth. Periodical. Greek, Modern. Emporikon Kai Viomechanikon Epimeleterion Thessalonikes, Tsimiski 29, Thessaloniki Greece. **Tel** 031/224438, FAX 031/230237, telex 412115. *Continues Meniaio Deltio Emporikou Kai Viomechanikou Epimeleteriou Thessalonikes.*

LC HC415.342.A1 D44
DD 330.953/32
GW
DEMOKRATISCHE VOLKSREPUBLIK JEMEN, WIRTSCHAFTLICHE ENTWICKLUNG / BUNDESSTELLE FUER AUSSENHANDELSINFORMATION. German. Bundesstelle fuer Aussenhandelsinformation, Agrippastrasse 87 93, D-50676 Cologne Germany. **Tel** 011 49 221 2057316, FAX 011 49 221 2057212.

LC HC415.342.A1
DD 330.953/35053
GW
DEMOKRATISCHE VOLKSREPUBLIK JEMEN, WIRTSCHAFTSDATEN. (19??)-. German. DM3.00. Bundesstelle fuer Aussenhandelsinformation, Agrippastrasse 87 93, D-50676 Cologne Germany. **Tel** 011 49 221 2057316, FAX 011 49 221 2057212.

DD 330
ISSN 0011-8427
DK
DENMARK QUARTERLY REVIEW. Added/Corp Kjbenhavns Handelsbank, A/S. Kjbenhavns Handelsbank, A/S. Economics Dept. (1???)-. Danish (German and French). Four times a year. Den Dansk Bank, 2 Holmens Kanal / Economics Department, DK-1092 Copenhagen Denmark. **Tel** 011 45 33 440000, telex 12186 COCO DK. **ED** Per Bendix. **Circ:** 17,000.
Desc: Statistics and comments on the Danish economy and the political scene.
Ind/Abst F&S Index Plus Text, Int. [Select. Cov.]; Trade Ind. Index.

DD 948
ISSN 1054-5379
US
DENMARK (SYRACUSE, N.Y.). (DENMARK : A POLITICAL AND ECONOMIC FORECAST / POLITICAL RISK SERVICES.). [Denmark]. **Added/Corp** Political Risk Services (IBC USA (Publications) Inc.). (19??)-. English. $325.00. Political Risk Services, 6320 Fly Road, Suite 102, PO Box 248, East Syracuse NY 13057-0248. **Tel** (315)431-0511, FAX (315)431-0200.
Desc: Assesses the factors affecting the prospects for business and trade. Each report focuses specifically on business needs such as finding and developing markets, determining currency movements, or making judgements about capital investments or corporate security.

LC HC446 .D46
DD 330
ISSN 0376-8201
IO
DEPTH NEWS INDONESIA. (DEPTH NEWS INDONESIA.). **Added/Corp** Yayasan Pembina Pers Indonesia. (19??)-. Indonesian (English). Fifty-two times a year. $460.00. Press Foundation of Indonesia, Jatinegara Barat III/6, Jakarta 13310 Indonesia. **Tel** 011 62 21 8194994, FAX 011 62 21 8195501. **ED** Sumono Mustoffa.

LC HC177.B8 D48
ISSN 0325-5824
AG
DESARROLLO Y MODERNIZACION. Vol. 1, No. 1 (August 1978)-. Periodical. Spanish. Twelve times a year. Secretaria de Planeamiento Y Desarrollo, Calle 7 No 370, 1900 La Plata Argentina.

LC HC188.P4 .D47
DD 338.981
BL
DESEMPENHO DA ECONOMIA DE PERNAMBUCO. See Business and Economics-Abstracting, Bibliographies and Statistics.

US
DEVELOPING NATIONS MONOGRAPH SERIES. Main/Corp Wake Forest University. Overseas Research Center. (1970)-. Monographic series. English. Irregular. Price varies per volume. Overseas Research Center, PO Box 7805, Wake Forest University, Winston Salem NC 27109.

LC HC106.8 .M318
DD 330
ISSN 1053-3672
US
... DEVELOPMENT REPORT CARD FOR THE STATES, THE. [Dev. rep. card states]. **Added/Corp** Corporation for Enterprise Development. (1989)-. English. One time a year. $75.00. Corporation for Enterprise Development, 777 North Capital Street Northeast, Suite 801, Washington DC 20002. **Tel** (202)408-9788, FAX (202)408-9793. *Continues Making the Grade, 1045-4691.*

LC HC241.2 .I632a
DD 382/.9142
ISSN 0302-7465
IE
TITLE CHANGE
DEVELOPMENTS IN THE EUROPEAN COMMUNITIES (DUBLIN). (DEVELOPMENTS IN THE EUROPEAN COMMUNITIES; REPORT.). [Dev. Eur. Communities (Dublin)]. **Main/Corp** Ireland (EIRE). (May 1973)-(1993). English. Government Publications, 4 5 Harcourt Road, Dublin 2 Ireland. **Tel** 011 353 1 6613111 ext.4005. **Circ:** 1,000. *Continued by Developments in the European Union.*

LC HC188.R4 R56a
DD 338./0981/6
BL
DIARIO OFICIAL: INDUSTRIA & [I.E. E] COMERCIO. Main/Corp Rio Grande do Sul (Brazil). (19??)-. Portuguese. Companhia Riograndense de Artes Graficas, rua Dos Andradas 963, Porto Alegre Brazil.

LC HC131 .D543
DD 338.5/443/0972
ISSN 8755-0113
US
DIEMEX-WHARTON MEXICAN PROJECT, THE. [Diemex-Wharton Mexican proj.]. **VFOAT** Diemex Wharton Mexican Project. Periodical. English. WEFA / Philadelphia, PO Box 8500, Suite 1995, Philadelphia PA 19178. **Tel** (215)667-6000, telex 710 6700575.

LC HC186 .D5
DD 330
BL
DIGESTO ECONOMICO. Added/Corp Associacao Comercial de Sao Paulo. Federacao do Comercio do Estado de Sao Paulo. Vol. 1, No. 1 (Dec. 1944)-. Periodical. Portuguese. Six times a year. $40.00. Associacao Comercial de Sao Paulo, Rua Boa Vista 51, CP 8082, 01014 Sao Paulo SP Brazil. **Tel** 011 234-3322.

Business and Economics — Economic History, Conditions

ED Joao de Scantimburgo. **Bk Rev**. **Ad Acc**. **Circ**: 10,000.
Ind/Abst PAIS Int. Print.

LC HC171 .D57

AG
DISCUSION. (19??)-. Periodical. Spanish. Avenida Chiclana 3374, Buenos Aires Argentina.

LC Z7164.N3 Q43A HC117.Q4 **ISSN** 0824-3689
DD 016.3337/09714

CN
DOCUMENTATION DU MINISTERE DE L'ENERGIE ET DES RESSOURCES, REPERTOIRE. [Doc. Minist. energ. ressour., Repert.]. **Main/Corp** Quebec (Province). Ministere de l'Energie et des Ressources. **VFOAT** Repertoire de la Documentation du MER; Repertoire de la Documentation M.E.R. French. One time a year. Free. 200 Chemin Ste Foy 7E Etage, Quebec Quebec G1R 4X7 Canada. Index available. ctrl circ.

DD 940 330

FR
DOCUMENTS ET RECHERCHES SUR L'ECONOMIE DES PAYS BYZANTINES, ISLAMIQUES ET SLAVES ET LEURS RELATIONS COMMERCIALES AU MOYEN-AGE. **Main/Corp** Paris. Ecole Pratique des Hautes Etudes. Section des Sciences Economiques et Sociales. No. 1 (1958)-. Monographic series. French. Irregular. Price varies per volume. Walter de Gruyter Inc., PO Box 303421, D-10728 Berlin Germany. **Tel** 011 49 30 260050, FAX 011 49 30 26005251, telex 184027.
(**Subscription address:** Walter de Gruyter Inc. / North America, 200 Saw Mill River Road, Hawthorne NY 10532. **Tel** (914)747-0110.)

DD 972 **ISSN** 1054-5387

US
DOMINICAN REPUBLIC (SYRACUSE, N.Y.). (DOMINICAN REPUBLIC : A POLITICAL AND ECONOMIC FORECAST / POLITICAL RISK SERVICES.). [Dominican Republic]. **Added/Corp** Political Risk Services (IBC USA (Publications) Inc.). (19??)-. English. $325.00. Political Risk services, 6320 Fly Road, Suite 102, PO Box 248, East Syracuse NY 13057-0248. **Tel** (315)431-0511, FAX (315)431-0200.
Desc: Assesses the factors affecting the prospects for business and trade. Each report focuses specifically on business needs such as finding and developing markets, determining currency movements, or making judgements about capital investments or corporate security.

LC HC153.5.A1 D65
DD 330.97293/00212

GW
DOMINIKANISCHE REPUBLIK, WIRTSCHAFTSDATEN. **Added/Corp** Bundesstelle fuer Aussenhandelsinformation (Germany). (19??)-. German. One time a year. DM3.00. Bundesstelle fuer Aussenhandelsinformation, Agrippastrasse 87 93, D-50676 Cologne Germany. **Tel** 011 49 221 2057316, FAX 011 49 221 2057212.

LC HC288.S2 C58A
DD 330.943/42/005

GW
DONNEES ECONOMIQUES DES REGIONS FRONTALIEERES SAAR-LOR-LUX. **Main/Corp** Commission Regionale Sarre, Lorraine, Luxembourg, Rhenanie-Palatinat. **VFOAT** Wirtschaftszahlen des Grenzraumes Saar-Lor-Lux. French (German). Kommissionsverlag SDV Saarbrucker Druckerei und Verlag GmbH, Halbergstrasse 3, W-6600 Saarbrucken Germany.

LC HD28 .D63A

JA
DOSHISHA DAIGAKU DAIGAKUIN SHOGAKU RONSHU. **Main/Corp** Doshisha Daigaku. Daigakuin. **VFOAT** Doshisha Business Review of Graduate Students. Japanese. One time a year. Free. Doshisha Daigaku Daigakuin Shogaku Kenkyuka Inseikai, Karasumaru Imadegawa, Kamikyo-ku, Koyto Japan. **Tel** 075-251-3925. **Circ**: 400 (ctrl)

FR
DOSSIERS DE L'ECONOMIE LORRAINE, LES. **Added/Corp** Institut National de la Statistique et des Etudes Economiques (France). No. 1 (May 1971)-. Periodical. French. Twelve times a year. 85.00F France; 100.00F other. CNGP INSEE - Institut National de la Statistique et des CNustes Economiques, BP 2718, 1 rue V Auriol, F 80027 Amiens Cedex 1 France. **Tel** 011 33 22 927322. **Supersedes** Bulletin de Statistique: Lorraine (Meurthe-et-Moselle, Meuse, Moselle, Vosges).

LC HC279 .D67 **ISSN** 0337-4084
DD 330.9171/244

FR
DOSSIERS DE L'OUTRE-MER : BULLETIN D'INFORMATION DU CENADDOM, LES. **Added/Corp** Centre National de Documentation des Departements d'Outre-Mer. (1985)-. Bulletin. French. Four times a year. Bt. du Centre d'Etudes de Geographie Tropicale, Domaine Universitaire, 33405 Talence France. **Bk Rev**. **Circ**: 1,300. **Continues** Bulletin d'Information - Cenaddom.

DD 330.9/713/541

CN
DOWNTOWN ACTION. Vol. 1 (March 1976)-. Periodical. English. Irregular (seven no. a year). $1.50 per no. Downtown Action Inc, Suite 26/165 Spadina Avenue, Toronto Ontario M5T 2C3 Canada.

LC HA1631 .A33 HC407.Y63I5 Y63I5

YU
DRUSTVENI PROIZVOD I NARODNI DOHODAK. **Main/Corp** Savezni Zavod Za Statistiku (Yugoslavia). 1969/70-. Serbo-Croatian (Roman). 10.00 Din. Savezni Zavod za Statistiku, Kneza Milosa 20, Belgrad Yugoslavia.

LC HA1651.A334 HC407.Z7S46 Z7S46

YU
DRUSTVENI RACUNI TERITORIJE REPUBLIKE VAN TERITORIJA AUTONOMNIH POKRAJINA / SOCIJALISTICKA REPUBLIKA SRBIJA, REPUBLICKI ZAVOD ZA STATISTIKU. 1973-1974-. Serbo-Croatian (Cyrillic). One time a year.

LC HC460.5.A1 E25 **ISSN** 0723-8398
DD 330.95/005

GW
EAST ASIA (FRANKFURT AM MAIN, GERMANY). (EAST ASIA.). Vol. 1 (1985)-. English. One time a year. $45.00. Westview Press Inc., 5500 Central Avenue, Boulder CO 80301. **Tel** (303)444-3541, (800)456-1995, FAX (303)449-3356. **ED** Sung-Jo Park. **Bk Rev**. **Circ**: 800.

LC DJK50 .E152 **ISSN** 0267-808X
DD 947/.0005

UK
EAST EUROPEAN REPORTER. [East Eur. report.]. **Added/Corp** East European Cultural Foundation. Vol. 1, No. 1 (Spring 1985)-. Academic Scholarly Publication. English. Six times a year. $70.00. East European Reporter, 6-10 Csalogany Utca III 18, Budapest 1015 Hungary. **Tel** 011 36 1 2011056. **ED** Stephen Saracco. **Bk Rev**. **Ad Acc**. **Circ**: 4,000. available in microform; available in reprints.
Desc: Post-communist political, economic, and social development of central and Eastern European countries.
Ind/Abst Altern. Press Index (199?-); Hum. Rights Intern. Rep.; Left Index (19??-); PAIS Int. Print (1991-).

DD 330.9/71/0644 **ISSN** 0319-1877

CN
ECOINDICATEUR DE LA BANQUE ROYALE. (L'ECOINDICATEUR DE LA BANQUE ROYALE; RAPPORT.). **Main/Corp** Banque Royale du Canada. Vol. 1 (Dec. 1974)-. French. Banque Royale du Canada, CP 6001, Montreal Quebec H3C 3A9 Canada.

LC HC59 .E36 **ISSN** 0151-5055
DD 330.9/04

FR
ECONOMIA. [Economia]. Periodical. French (French). Twelve times a year. 150.00F.

LC HC186 .E274

BL
ECONOMIA BRASILEIRA, A. (A ECONOMIA BRASILEIRA. THE BRAZILIAN ECONOMY.). **VFOAT** The Brazilian Economy. (1969)-. Portuguese (English). One time a year. Free on request. Banco Lar Brasileiro SA, CP 221-ZC-00 rue do Ouvidoe, 98 Rio de Janerio Brazil.
Ind/Abst Predicasts F&S Index, U. S. Annu. Ed.

CK
ECONOMIA COLOMBIANA, LA. Spanish. Asociacion Nacional de Induatriales, Apartado Aereo 997, Medellin Colombia.
Ind/Abst PAIS Int. Print.

LC HC391 .E26

PO
ECONOMIA E SOCIALISMO. (1976)-. Portuguese. Twelve times a year. $10.00 Portugal; $22.00 Europe; $24.00 other. Edit Economia e Socialismo, rue do Borja 57 3, C. V. Esq, 1300 Lisbon Portugal.

LC HC391 .E264 **ISSN** 0390-5330
DD 306/.09469

PO
ECONOMIA E SOCIOLOGIA. [Econ. sociol.]. **Added/Corp** Instituto de Estudos Superiores de Evora. Instituto Superior Economico e Social (Evora, Portugal); Instituto Superior Economico e Social (Evora, Portugal). Gabinete de Investigacao e Accao Social. No. 4 (1968)-. Periodical. Portuguese. Two times a year. $20.00. Revista Economia e Sociologia, Rua Vasco da Gama 15, 7000 Evora Portugal. **Tel** 011 351 23 23327. **Continues** Estudos Eborenses.
Ind/Abst PAIS Int. Print.

IT
ECONOMIA E STORIA. Monographic series. Italian. Price varies per volume.
Ind/Abst Am. Hist. Life (1956-1984); Numis. Lit.

IT
●ECONOMIA EMILIA-ROMAGNA. (1994)-. Trade Publication. Italian. Twelve times a year. Free. Unione Regionale Camere Commercio dell'Emilia-Romagna, Via Montegrappa 4-D, 40121 Bologna Italy. **Tel** 011 39 51 223030, FAX 011 39 51 234945.

LC HC301 .E317
DD 330.945

IT
ECONOMIA ITALIANA (CENTRO STUDI DI POLITICA ECONOMICA (TURIN, ITALY). (L'ECONOMIA ITALIANA.). **Added/Corp** Centro Studi di Politica Economica (Turin, Italy). (19??)-. Italian. One time a year. L16000. Franco Angeli Riviste SRL, Viale Monza 106, 20127 Milan Italy. **Tel** 011 39 2 2827651, 011 39 2 289562, FAX 011 39 2 258004, telex 051-511650.

LC HC307.M27 E3 **ISSN** 0391-5271
DD 330.9/45/67092

IT
ECONOMIA MARCHE. [Econ. Marche]. (1976)-. Periodical. Italian. Three times a year. L49050. Societa Editrice il Mulino, Strada Maggiore 37, 40125 Bologna Italy. **Tel** 011 39 51 256011, FAX 011 39 51 256034. cum. index.
Ind/Abst Foreign Lang. Index; PAIS Int. Print.

LC HC131 .E246
DD 330.972/005

MX
ECONOMIA MEXICANA EN GRAFICAS, LA. (March 1979)-. Spanish. Secretaria de Programacion Y Presupuesto, Dr Ugarte No 7E Integracion, 20 Piso Mexico 7 D F Mexico.

LC HC131 .E244
DD 330.972/005

MX
ECONOMIA MEXICANA (MEXICO CITY, MEXICO). (ECONOMIA MEXICANA.). **Added/Corp** Centro de Investigacion y Docencia Economicas. Departamento de Economia. No. 1 (1979)-. Spanish. Two times a year. $25.00. CIDE / Centro de Invest y Docencia Economicas, AP 116, 114 Dlg Alvaro Obregon, 01130 Mexico DF Mexico. **Tel** 011 52 5 7269004 ext. 289.

DD 330.971 **ISSN** 1186-1053

CN
ECONOMIC ADVISOR (TORONTO). TITLE CHANGE (ECONOMIC ADVISOR.). [Econ. advis.]. **Added/Corp** Midland Walwyn Capital. Research Dept. Midland Walwyn Capital. (Jan. 22, 1991)-(June 27, 1994). Periodical. English. Midland Walwyn Capital, Suite 1600, 121 King Street West, Toronto Ontario M5H 3W6 Canada. **Continued by** On the Margin (Toronto, Ont.), 1196-7005.

LC HC431 .E322
DD 330.9/54/04

II
ECONOMIC AGE. (19??)-. Periodical. English. 0.75. Indian Exchange Place, P-36 2nd Floor/Room No 40, Calcutta 700001 India.

DD 330.971/0644 **ISSN** 0225-5952

CN
ECONOMIC AND FINANCIAL OUTLOOK. [Econ. financ. outlook]. (1972)-. Periodical. English. Two times a year. Economic Department, Royal Bank of Canada, 14th Floor, 1 Place Ville Marie, Montreal Quebec H3C 3A9 Canada.

LC HC995.A1 E28

US
ECONOMIC AND FINANCIAL REPORT OF THE FINANCE LAW FOR THE FINANCIAL YEAR. English.

LC HC157.B35 C46A **ISSN** 0378-178X
DD 330.9/729/81

BB
ECONOMIC AND FINANCIAL STATISTICS. See Business and Economics-Abstracting, Bibliographies and Statistics.

LC HC431 .E326 **ISSN** 0012-9976
DD 330.954
Pr Rev.

II
ECONOMIC AND POLITICAL WEEKLY. [Econ. polit. wkly]. (Aug. 1966)-. Periodical. English. One time a week. $90.00. Economic and Political Weekly, Hitkari House, 284 Shahid Bhagatsingh Road, Bombay 400 038 India. **Tel** 011 91 22 2616072. (**Subscription address:** Prints India, 11 Darya Ganj, New Delhi 110002 India. **Tel** 011 91 11 3268645, FAX 011 91 11 3275542, telex 31-61087 PRIN-IN.) Index Available, published separately, free-automatically sent. Documents available from The Genuine Article. **Continues** Economic Weekly.
Ind/Abst AGRICOLA; Arts Humanit. Citation Index

[Select. Cov.]; Curr. Cit.; Curr. Contents Soc. Behav. Sci.; Curr. Lit. Sci. Sci.; Dairy Sci. Abstr.; For. Abstr.; Int. Dev. Abstr. (?-?); Int. Labour Doc.; Int. Polit. Sci. Abstr.; Nutr. Abstr. Rev., Ser. A, Hum. Exp.; Popul. Index; Res. Alert [Full Cov.]; Rice Abstr.; Rural Dev. Abstr.; Soc. Sci. Cit. Index [Full Cov.]; Wheat Barley Trit. Abstr.; World Agric. Econ. Rural Sociol. Abstr.

LC HC321 .E26 **ISSN** 0925-1669
NE

ECONOMIC AND SOCIAL HISTORY IN THE NETHERLANDS. Added/Corp Nederlandsch Economisch-Historisch Archief. Vol. 1 (1989)-. English. One time a year. $35.00. Nederlandsch Economisch Historisch Archief NEHA, Cruquiusweg 31, 1019 AT Amsterdam Netherlands. **Tel** 011 31 20 6685866.
Ind/Abst Am. Hist. Life (1989-); Int. Bibliogr. Sociol.

LC HC491 .U54A
DD 330.9/561/03 US

ECONOMIC AND SOCIAL INDICATORS-TURKEY. Main/Corp United States. Aid Mission to Turkey. Economic Analysis Staff. English. US Agency for International Development, Economic Data Branch, Washington DC 20523.

LC HC125 .I514 **ISSN** 0095-2850
DD 330.9/8/003 US

ECONOMIC AND SOCIAL PROGRESS IN LATIN AMERICA. (ECONOMIC AND SOCIAL PROGRESS IN LATIN AMERICA; ANNUAL REPORT.). [Econ. soc. prog. Lat. Am.]. **Main/Corp** Inter-American Development Bank. (1972)-. Periodical. English (Spanish, Portuguese and French). One time a year. $19.95. Johns Hopkins University Press, 2715 North Charles Street, Baltimore MD 21218-4319. **Tel** (410)516-6987, FAX (410)516-6968. **Circ:** 20,000. ***Continues*** *Socio-Economic Progress in Latin America, 0160-4902.*

LC HC257.I6 E26 **ISSN** 0012-9984
DD 309.1/415 IE
Pr Rev.

ECONOMIC AND SOCIAL REVIEW, THE. **See** Social Sciences.

LC HC445.5.A1 E26
DD 330.9/595/05 MY

ECONOMIC BULLETIN, THE. Vol. 1 (Sept. 1975)-. Bulletin. English. 25.00. Academic Publishers, Room 1702 86 Jalan Raja Chulan, Kuala Lumpur 05-10 Malaysia.

LC HC10 .B44a **ISSN** 0343-754X
UK

ECONOMIC BULLETIN (BERLIN). (ECONOMIC BULLETIN / DEUTSCHES INSTITUT FUER WIRTSCHAFTSFORSCHUNG, INSTITUT FUER KONJUNKTURFORSCHUNG.). [Econ. bull.]. **Added/Corp** Deutsches Institut fuer Wirtschaftsforschung. Deutsches Institut fuer Wirtschaftsforschung. Wochenbericht. New Series Vol. 1, No. 1 (Jan. 1964)-. Bulletin. English. Twelve times a year. £150.00. Gower Publishing Co. Ltd., Gower House Croft Road Aldershot, Hampshire GU11 3HR United Kingdom. **Tel** 011 44 1252 331551, FAX 011 44 1252 344405, telex 858001. **(Subscription address:** Ashgate Distribution Services / UK, Unite 2-4 Lower Farnham Road, Aldershot GU12 4DY United Kingdom. **Tel** 011 44 1252 331551.)

LC HC101 **ISSN** 0083-0062
US

ECONOMIC COOPERATION SERIES. 1948-. Monographic series. English. Price varies per volume. US Department of State, 2201 C Street NW, Room 5819, Washington DC 20520. **Tel** (202)647-9859.

LC KF5722 .N373 **ISSN** 0731-6941
DD 346.7304/5 347.30645 US

ECONOMIC DEVELOPMENT AND LAW CENTER REPORT. **See** Law.

LC HT123 .E28 **ISSN** 8755-8629
DD 338.9/00973/091732 US

ECONOMIC DEVELOPMENT COMMENTARY. [Econ. dev. comment.]. Vol. 5, No. 2 (Apr. 1981)-. Periodical. English. Four times a year. $45.00. National Council for Urban & Economic Development, 1730 K Street NW, Suite 1009, Washington DC 20006. **Tel** (202)223-4735, FAX (202)223-4745. ***Continues*** *Commentary (Washington, D.C.), 0193-4619.*
Ind/Abst Urban Aff. Abstr.

LC HC491 .E254
DD 330.9561/005 TU

ECONOMIC DIALOGUE TURKEY. **Added/Corp** Diyalog Publishing and Organization (Istanbul, Turkey). **VFOAT** Ekonomide Diyalog. (198?)-. Periodical. English. Four times a year. $10.00. Payas As Abidei Hurriyet Cad, Gokfiliz Ishani Kat 2, Mecidiyekoy Istanbul Turkey.

LC HC461 .E36 **ISSN** 0389-0503
DD 330.952/005 JA
CEASED

ECONOMIC EYE. [Econ. eye]. **Added/Corp** Keizai Koho Senta (Tokyo, Japan). Vol. 1, No. 1 (Sept. 1980)-Vol. 16 (1995). Periodical. English. Keizai Koho Center, Otemachi Building, 6-1 Otemachi 1-chome Chiyoda-ku, Tokyo 100 Japan. **Tel** (03)201-1415, telex 222-5452 KKCTOK J. **ED** Katsura Kuno. **Circ:** 15,500 (ctrl).
Desc: Translations of important Japanese magazine articles dealing with economic topics.
Ind/Abst Int. Labour Doc.; LABORDOC; PAIS Int. Print (1991-).

LC HC10 .E3745 **ISSN** 0169-1767
DD 330.9/001/12 NE
CCC
Pr Rev.

ECONOMIC FORECASTS. Vol. 1, No. 1 (July 1984)-. Periodical. English. Twelve times a year. $851.00. Elsevier Advanced Technology, An Imprint of Elsevier Science Ltd., The Boulevard, Langford Lane, Kidlington, Oxford OX5 1GB United Kingdom. **Tel** 011 44 1865 843000, 011 44 1865 843699, FAX 011 44 1865 843010. **(Subscription address:** Elsevier Science Ltd. / Oxford Fulfillment Centre, PO Box 800, Kidlington OX5 1DX United Kingdom. **Tel** 011 44 865 843355.) available on microfilm and microfiche from University Microfilms International (UMI); available on an online database from Elsevier Electronic Subscriptions (EES).
Desc: Designed to provide a useful service to private and public decisionmakers and their advisers. It addresses a wide and influential audience of corporate managers, business economists, financial analysts, government agencies, research departments and institutions.
Ind/Abst F&S Index Plus Text, Int. [Select. Cov.]; Predicasts Forecasts.

LC HC10 .E4 **ISSN** 0013-0117
UK
CCC
Pr Rev.

ECONOMIC HISTORY REVIEW, THE. [Econ. hist. rev.]. Vol. 1-18, Jan. 1927-48; Ser. 2, Vol. 1 (1948)-. Academic Scholarly Publication. English. Four times a year. $122.00. Basil Blackwell Publishers Ltd., 108 Cowley Road, Oxford 0X4 1JF United Kingdom. **Tel** 011 44 1235 465500, FAX 011 44 1235 465556, telex 837022 OXBOOK G. **(Subscription address:** Blackwell Publishers / UK, 108 Cowley Road, Oxford OX4 1JF United Kingdom. **Tel** 011 44 1865 791100, FAX 011 44 1865 791347.) **ED** R A Church. cum. index. **Bk Rev. Ad Acc. Circ:** 4,500 (ctrl). available on microfilm and microfiche from University Microfilms International (UMI). Documents available from The Genuine Article, UMI Article Clearinghouse.
Desc: Publishes research and reviews on economic and social history.
Ind/Abst Acad. Abstr.; Acad. Search; AGRICOLA; Am. Hist. Life (1954-); Arts Humanit. Citation Index [Full Cov.]; Br. Humanit. Index; Curr. Cit.; Curr. Contents Arts Humanit.; Curr. Contents Soc. Behav. Sci.; Econ. Lit. Index; EP Collect.; Expand. Acad. Index (1989-); Geogr. Abstr. Human Geogr.; Hist. Source (Jan. 1992-); Homework Help.; Humanit. Source; INFO-SOUTH Abstr.; Int. Bibliogr. Sociol.; J. Econ. Lit.; Mag. Search; MasterFile FullTEXT 1000; MasterFile FullTEXT 350; MasterFile FullTEXT 650; MasterFile FullTEXT (Jan. 1992-); Middle East Abstr. Index; Newsp. Period. Abstr. (1991-); Numis. Lit.; OCLC; Popul. Index (?-?); Pub. Lib. FullTEXT; Res. Alert [Full Cov.]; Romant. Move.; Soc. Sci. Source; Soc. Sci. Cit. Index [Full Cov.]; Soc. Sci. Index; Soc. Sci. Index Fulltext (Nov. 1988-) [Full Txt.]; Telebase; West. Hist. Q.; Work Relat. Abstr.

ISSN 0886-8085
DD 330 US
CEASED

ECONOMIC IMPACT (WASHINGTON, D.C.). (ECONOMIC IMPACT.). [Econ. impact]. **Added/Corp** United States Information Agency. (1972)-(19??). Periodical. English. United States Information Agency / Washington, D.C., 301 4th Street SW, Washington DC 20547. Documents available from Documents on Demand.
Ind/Abst Environ. Abstr.; Int. Labour Doc.; Rural Dev. Abstr.

LC HA203 .E27 **ISSN** 0278-8381
DD 330.973/00212 US

ECONOMIC INDICATORS (CHARLESTON, W. VA.). (ECONOMIC INDICATORS.). [Econ. indic.]. **Added/Corp** West Virginia Research League. (May 30, 1981)-. English. Irregular (issued every five years). $25.00, free to West Virginians. West Virginia Research League, 405 Capitol Street, Suite 414, Charleston WV 25301-1727. **Tel** (304)346-9451. **ED** Sarah F. Roach. **Circ:** 4,000.
Desc: Providing comparison information on major public policy functions in all 50 states over a period of 3 1/2 decades.

NR

ECONOMIC INDICATORS; EAST-CENTRAL STATE - (NIGERIA). **Main/Corp** Nigeria, Eastern. Ministry of Economic Development and Reconstruction. Statistics Division. (March 1973)-. Periodical. English. Twelve times a year. Ministry of Economic Development and Reconstruction, Nigeria.
Ind/Abst Mag. Index (?-?).

PP

ECONOMIC INDICATORS / NATIONAL STATISTICAL OFFICE, PAPUA, NEW GUINEA. (Jan. 1982)-. Statistical Publication. English. Twelve times a year. k12.00 Papua New Guinea; k18.00 (airmail) other. National Statistical Office / New Guinea, PO Wards Strip NCO, Papua New Guinea. **Tel** 011 675 27182 271172, FAX 011 657 255057, telex FINANCE NE 22312. ***Continues*** *Economic Indicators (Papua New Guinea. Bureau of Statistics).*

TR

ECONOMIC INDICATORS / REPUBLIC OF TRINIDAD & TOBAGO, CENTRAL STATISTICAL OFFICE. Added/Corp Trinidad and Tobago. Central Statistical Office. (1988/89)-. Statistical Publication. English. Two times a year. Government Printery / Trinidad, Central Statistical Office, 35 41 Queen Street, Port of Spain Trinidad. **Tel** (809)625-4970, FAX (809)625-3802. ***Continues*** *Economic Indicators, 0376-9259.*

LC HC101 .A186 **ISSN** 0013-0125
DD 330.973/005 US
CODEN ECINA3

ECONOMIC INDICATORS (WASHINGTON, D.C.). (ECONOMIC INDICATORS.). [Econ. indic.]. **Added/Corp** United States. Congress. Joint Economic Committee. Council of Economic Advisers (U.S.) United States. Congress. Joint Committee on the Economic Report. (May 1948)-. Government Publication. English. Twelve times a year. $43.00. US Congress, 515 House Annex 2, Washington DC 20515. **(Subscription address:** Superintendent of Documents, US Government Printing Office, Washington DC 20402. **)** available on microfilm and microfiche from University Microfilms International (UMI). Documents available from UMI Article Clearinghouse, Documents on Demand, Magazine Collection.
Desc: Gives pertinent economic information on prices, wages, production, business activity, purchasing power, credit, money and Federal finance.
Ind/Abst Acad. Ind. [Computer File] (1984-); Acad. Search; Am. Stat. Index; Bus. ASAP (1992-) [Full Txt.]; Bus. Index (1985-); Bus. Source Plus; Bus. Source; CIS Index Publ. U.S. Congr.; EP Collect.; Expand. Acad. Index (1984-); Gen. BusinessFile (1985-); Gen. Period. Index (1985-); Homework Help.; Mag. Index Plus (1989-); Mag. Search; MasterFile FullTEXT 1000; MasterFile FullTEXT 350; MasterFile FullTEXT 650; MasterFile FullTEXT (July 1993-); Newsp. Period. Abstr. (1988-); OCLC; Telebase; Mag. Index (1977-); Trade Ind. Index (1981-?).

LC HC425.A1 E28
DD 330.9549/6 NP

ECONOMIC JOURNAL OF NEPAL, THE. Vol. 1, No. 4 (Oct./Dec. 1978)-. Periodical. English. Four times a year. $10.00. Executive Editors, Economics Instruction Committee, Tribhuvan University, Kirtipur Kathmandu Nepal. ***Continues*** *Economic Monthly.*
Ind/Abst Rural Dev. Abstr.; World Agric. Econ. Rural Sociol. Abstr.

ISSN 0849-3391
DD 330.9/005 CN

ECONOMIC JUSTICE REPORT. [Econ. justice rep.]. **Added/Corp** Ecumenical Coalition for Economic Justice. Vol. 1, No. 1 (April 1990)-. Periodical. English. Four times a year. 40.00Can$. Ecumenical Coalition Econo Justice, 11 Madison Avenue, Toronto Ontario M5R 2S2 Canada. **Tel** (416)921-4615. ***Continues*** *GATT-Fly Report., 0228-359X.*

LC HC107.F6 A13
DD 330.9759 US

ECONOMIC LEAFLETS. - FLORIDA. UNIVERSITY, GAINESVILLE. BUREAU OF ECONOMIC AND BUSINESS RESEARCH. Main/Corp Florida. University, Gainesville. Bureau of Economic and Business Research. Vol. 1 (Dec. 1941)-. Periodical. English. Twelve times a year. $10.00. University of Florida / CBA, College of Business Administration, Gainesville FL 32601. **Tel** (904)392-0171, FAX (904)392-6250. **ED** Ann C. Pierce. **Circ:** 1,000.
Desc: Reports, in layman's language, on current Florida-related research in business, population and economic trends, with consumer surveys, etc.
Ind/Abst PAIS Int. Print (1991-).

ISSN 1183-6296
DD 330.9/001/12 CN

ECONOMIC OUTLOOK FOR INDUSTRIAL COUNTRIES. [Econ. outl. ind. ctries]. **Added/Corp** Conference Board of Canada. International Business Research Centre. (Spring 1991)-. Periodical. English. Two times a year. Limited free distribution. International Business Research Centre, Conference Board of Canada, Suite 100 25 Mcarthur Avenue, Ottawa Ontario K1L 6R3.

Business and Economics — Economic History, Conditions

LC HC107.N5 E27
DD 338.5/443/09749 US
ECONOMIC OUTLOOK FOR NEW JERSEY / ECONOMIC POLICY COUNCIL. English. One time a year. Office of Economic Policy, 142 West State Street, Trenton NJ 08625.

LC HC256.6 .G77a   **ISSN** 0262-5067
DD 330.9/41/085 UK
ECONOMIC PROGRESS REPORT. [Econ. prog. rep.]. **Main/Corp** Great Britain. Treasury. Information Division. (1970)-. Periodical. English. Six times a year. Free on request. Treasury Chambers, Parliament Street, London SW1P 3AG United Kingdom. **Tel** 011 44 171 2705251, FAX 011 44 171 2705244.
Ind/Abst Manage. Market. Abstr.; World Text. Abstr.

 ISSN 1017-8929
 KO
●**ECONOMIC REPORT.** Vol. 10, No. 1 (Jan. 1995)-. English. Twelve times a year. $72.00. World Media Inc., Yodio PO Box 963, Seoul 151-609 Korea. **Tel** 011 82 2 7835283, FAX 011 82 2 7801717. **Continues** Korea Economic Report.

LC HC445.5 .A3A
DD 330.9/595/05 MY
ECONOMIC REPORT - MALAYSIA. KEMENTERIAN KEWANGAN. Main/Corp Malaysia. Kementerian Kewangan. Vol. 5 (1976/77)-. English. One time a year. $8.00. Director General of Printing, Peninsular Malaysia, Jalan Chan Sow Lin, Kuala Lumpur 07-03 Malaysia. **Continues** Malaysia. Perbendaharaan. Economic Report.

LC HC107.A6 A757A
DD 330.9791/005 US
ECONOMIC REPORT OF THE GOVERNOR - (ARIZONA). Main/Corp Arizona. Office of the Governor. 1980. English. One time a year. Arizona Office of Economic Planning and Development, Executive Tower, 1700 West Washington, Phoenix AZ 85007.

LC HC107.N5 N375A
DD 330.9749/005 US
ECONOMIC REPORT OF THE GOVERNOR / STATE OF NEW JERSEY, GOVERNOR. Main/Corp New Jersey. Office of the Governor. 1982-. English. One time a year. New Jersey Office of Economic Policy, 142 West State Street, Trenton NJ 08625.

LC HC106.5 .A218
DD 338.973 US
ECONOMIC REPORT OF THE PRESIDENT; HEARINGS BEFORE THE JOINT ECONOMIC COMMITTEE, CONGRESS OF THE UNITED STATES. Main/Corp United States. Congress. Joint Economic Committee. (19??)-. Government Publication. English. One time a year. $17.00. Superintendent of Documents, US Government Printing Office, Washington DC 20402. **Tel** (202)275-3328, FAX (202)786-2377.

LC HC107.S7 S587a   **ISSN** 0145-3637
DD 330.9/757/04 US
ECONOMIC REPORT, THE STATE OF SOUTH CAROLINA. Main/Corp South Carolina. State Budget and Control Board. Division of Research and Statistical Services. **Added/Corp** South Carolina. State Budget and Control Board. Division of Research and Statistical Services. Economic Report for South Carolina. **VFOAT** Economic Report for South Carolina. (19??)-. English. One time a year (Aug.). $5.00. South Carolina Board of Economic Advisors, 1205 Pendleton Street, Suite 535, Columbia SC 29201. **Tel** (803)734-1510, FAX (803)734-1530. **ED** Robert W. Martin. Index available. **Circ:** 250-300.
Desc: A compact compendium of events which shaped the South Carolina economy in the previous year and a source of data on the South Carolina economy.

LC HC491 .T84a   **ISSN** 0376-9275
DD 330.9/561/03 TU
ECONOMIC REPORT - TURKIYE IS BANKAS A.S. (ECONOMIC REPORT.). **Main/Corp** Turkiye is Bankas. (19??)-. Periodical. English (Turkish). One time a year. Free. Turkiye is Bankasi A S, Ataturk Bulvari 191, Kavaklidere Ankara Turkey. **Tel** 011 90 4 188096, FAX 011 90 4 4250750, telex 42082 TAB TR. **Circ:** 2,000 (ctrl).
Desc: Report for the Turkish economy.

LC HC440.8.A1 B26a
DD 330.9/549/205 BG
ECONOMIC REVIEW. Main/Corp Bangladesh. Parikalpana Kamisana. (1974/75)-. English. One time a year. Bangladesh Planning Commission, Adamjee Ct Motisheel Comm, Dacca 2 Bangladesh Pakistan.

LC HC260.5.A1 E33
DD 330.9417/005 IE
ECONOMIC REVIEW AND OUTLOOK. Added/Corp Ireland. Dept. of Finance. (July 1976)-. English. One time a year. 1.57p. Government Publications, 4 5 Harcourt Road, Dublin 2 Ireland. **Tel** 011 353 1 6613111 ext.4005. **Circ:** 1,000. **Continues** Review of ... and Present Outlook.

LC HC446 .E38   **ISSN** 0216-7107
DD 330.9598/005 IO
ECONOMIC REVIEW (JAKARTA, INDONESIA). (ECONOMIC REVIEW / BANK BUMI DAYA.). [Econ. rev.]. **Added/Corp** Bank Bumi Daya (Indonesia). (1977)-. Periodical. English. Twelve times a year. Bank Bumi Daya, Jalan Imam Bonjol No. 61, PO Box No. 1106, Jakarta 10011 Indonesia. **Tel** 021 2300300, FAX 021 2301848, 2301852, telex 61277, 61400, 61355, 61876, 61896, BDPST IA. **ED** F. X. Sutanta.
Desc: Covers economics relative to Indonesia; contains charts and graphs.

LC HC337.F5 K34   **ISSN** 0022-8419
 FI
ECONOMIC REVIEW - KANSALLIS-OSAKE-PANKKI. (ECONOMIC REVIEW.). [Econ. rev. - Kansallis-Osake-Pankki]. **Main/Corp** Kansallis-Osake-Pankki. (19??)-. Periodical. English. Two times a year. $3.93. Kansallis Osake Pankki, PO Box 10, Head Office Room 674, SF-00101 Helsinki 10 Finland. **Tel** 011 358 0 1633572, telex 124702 KOPK. **ED** Jussi Mustonen. **Circ:** 11,000. available on microfilm and microfiche from University Microfilms International (UMI). Documents available from UMI Article Clearinghouse.
Ind/Abst ABI/INFORM Glob. Ed.; ABI/INFORM [Computer File] (1983-); PAIS Int. Print (1991-?); Selec. Coop. Index Manage. Period.; UMI ABI/Inform--Bus. Period. Ondisc (1987-) [Full Txt.].

LC HC440.5.A1 E22   **ISSN** 0531-8955
DD 330.549 PK
ECONOMIC REVIEW (KARACHI). (ECONOMIC REVIEW.). [Econ. rev.]. **VFOAT** Monthly Economic Review. Vol. 1 (Jan. 1970)-. Periodical. English. Twelve times a year. $75.00. Economic and Industrial Publications, PO Box 7843, Karachi 74400 Pakistan. **Tel** 011 92 21 7728434, 011 92 21 7728963. **ED** Iqbal Haidari. **Bk Rev. Ad Acc. Adv Mgr:** Saleem Haidari. **Circ:** 10,000.
Ind/Abst Bus. ASAP (1990-) [Full Txt.]; PAIS Int. Print (1991-).

LC HC101 .E435   **ISSN** 0363-0021
DD 330.9/73/092 US
ECONOMIC REVIEW (SAN FRANCISCO). (ECONOMIC REVIEW.). [Econ. rev.]. **Added/Corp** Federal Reserve Bank of San Francisco. Research Dept. **Added/Corp** Federal Reserve Bank of San Francisco. Research and Public Information Dept. (Dec. 1975)-. Periodical. English. Three times a year. Free. Federal Reserve Bank of San Francisco, PO Box 7702, San Francisco CA 94120. **Tel** (415)974-2163, FAX (415)974-3429. available on microfilm and microfiche from University Microfilms International (UMI). Documents available from UMI Article Clearinghouse. **Continues** Business Review, 0093-8262.
Ind/Abst Red. Print Econ. Bank. Top.; Gen. BusinessFile (1992-); J. Econ. Lit.; Newsp. Period. Abstr. (1992-); PAIS Int. Print.

LC HC437.B43 A53   **ISSN** 0511-5272
DD 330.954/14/005 II
ECONOMIC REVIEW (WEST BENGAL, INDIA). (ECONOMIC REVIEW / [GOVERNMENT OF WEST BENGAL].). **Added/Corp** West Bengal (India) West Bengal (India). Finance Dept. (19??)-. English. One time a year. Rs.8.00. Superintendent of Documents (India).

LC HC10 .E415   **ISSN** 0013-0362
 II
Pr Rev.
ECONOMIC STUDIES (CALCUTTA, INDIA). (THE ECONOMIC STUDIES.). (1960)-. Periodical. English. Four times a year (Mar., June, Sept., Dec.). $60.00. Economic Studies & Journals Publishing Company, PO Box 10868, Calcutta 9 India. **Tel** 51-2288. **ED** D. N. Mukherjee. Index available. **Bk Rev,** (Qty: 12-15/yr). **Circ:** 22,000 (ctrl).
Desc: Covers almost all subjects in the range of economics: econometrics, macro-economics, social sciences, political science, international relations and history, labour relations, taxation, etc.
Ind/Abst Curr. Lit. Sci. Sci.

LC HC437.H29 A29
DD 330.9/54/55804 II
ECONOMIC SURVEY OF HARYANA.
Main/Corp Haryana. Economic and Statistical Organisation. (1970)-. English. Economic & Statistical Organization, Government of Haryan, Chandigarh 160011 India.

LC HC461 .E3   **ISSN** 0021-4833
DD 330.952 JA
ECONOMIC SURVEY OF JAPAN.
Added/Corp Japan. Keizai Kikakucho. Japan. Keizai Kikakucho. Report on Current Economy. Japan. Keizai Antei Hombu. (1949/1950)-. Periodical. English. One time a year. Price varies. **(Subscription address:** Japan Publications Trading Company Ltd., PO Box 5030, Tokyo International, Tokyo 100-31 Japan. **Tel** 011 81 3 3292 3753.)
Ind/Abst F&S Index Plus Text, Int. [Select. Cov.].

LC HC445.8.A1 E26   **ISSN** 0376-8791
DD 330.9/595/205 SI
ECONOMIC SURVEY OF SINGAPORE.
Added/Corp Singapore. Ministry of Finance. (19??)-. Periodical. English. Four times a year (Feb., May, Aug., Nov.). $150.00 (7 issues). Singapore National Printers, 303 Upper Serangoon Road, Singapore 1334 Singapore. **Tel** 011 65 2820611.

LC HC466 .A25   **ISSN** 0454-3653
DD 330.9519/5/005 KO
ECONOMIC SURVEY OF THE ... KOREAN ECONOMY. (1958)-. English. One time a year. Economic Planning Board, Government of the Republic of Korea, Seoul Korea.

LC HC557.T3 A1697   **ISSN** 0300-1741
DD 330.9/678/04 TZ
ECONOMIC SURVEY - UNITED REPUBLIC OF TANZANIA. (THE ECONOMIC SURVEY.). (1971)-. English. One time a year. Government Publishing Agency, PO Box 2483, Dar es Salaam Tanzania. **Continues in part** Tanzania. Economic Survey and Annual Plan.

LC HC431 .E334
DD 330.9/54/05 II
ECONOMIC TIMES ANNUAL, THE. (19??)-. English. One time a year. Rs.5.00. Bennett Coleman & Co., Dr D N Road, Bombay 400 001 India. **Tel** 011 91 22 2620271.
Ind/Abst PROMT.

LC HC440.8.A1 B28b
DD 330.9/549/205 BG
ECONOMIC TRENDS. Main/Corp Bangladesh Bank. Statistics Dept. (19??)-. English. Twelve times a year. Bangladesh Bank, Motijheel Commercial Area, Dhaka 2 Bangladesh.

 ISSN 1216-1829
 HU
UDC 339
ECONOMIC TRENDS IN EASTERN EUROPE. [Econ. trends East. Eur.]. (1992)-. Periodical. English. Three times a year. $157.00. Kopint Datorg, Dorottya U 6, H-1389 Budapest Hungary. **Tel** 011 36 1 851137. **(Subscription address:** Minerva Wissenschaftl Buchhdlg, Sachsenplatz 4 6, Postfach 88, A 1201 Vienna Austria. **Tel** 011 43 1 3302433.)
Continues Economic Trends in Eastern Europe and the World Economy, 0865-8943.

 HU
ECONOMIC TRENDS IN HUNGARY.
(19??)-. English. Four times a year. $200.00. GKI Economic Research Company, Ltd., PO Box 51, 1525 Budapest Hungary. **Tel** 011 36 1 1359713.

LC HC101 .A635
DD 330.973/005 US
ECONOMICS (DUSHKIN PUBLISHING GROUP). (ECONOMICS.). **VFOAT** Annual Editions. Economics. (1981)-. Periodical. English. One time a year. $12.95. Dushkin Publishing Group Inc., Sluice Dock, Guilford CT 06437. **Tel** (203)453-4351, (800)243-6532, FAX (203)453-6000. **ED** Don Cole. **Continues** Annual Editions. Readings in Economics.
Desc: A collection touching on issues of interest in the study of economics. Provides a review of microeconomics, macroeconomics, and the global economy. Contains a number of current charts and graphs, a glossary, and a topic guide.

LC HC10 .E42   **ISSN** 0013-0478
 FR
ECONOMIE, L'. (June 7, 1945)-. Periodical. French. Four times a year. $69.11. IFEC / Institut Francais des Experts Comptables, 139 rue Faubourg Saint Honore, 75008 Paris France. **Tel** 011 33 1 42564967. **Bk Rev. Ad Acc.**
Desc: Professional review about audit, economics and compatibility.

LC HC815.A1 E27
DD 330.965/005 FR
ECONOMIE ALGERIENNE, L'. (1978)-. French. One time a year. 354F. Ediafric la Documentation Africaine, 10 rue Vineuse, 75116 Paris France. **Tel** 011 33 1 44308100, FAX 011 33 1 45208174.

LC HC277.F7 R48 **ISSN** 0153-4459
DD 330.944/4/005 FR
ECONOMIE DU CENTRE-EST, L'. [Econ. Centre-Est]. **Added/Corp** Institut d'Economie Regionale Bourgogne-Franche-Comte. 19th Vol., No. 75-76 (1976-1977)-. Periodical. French. Four times a year. 120.00F France; $25.32 other. Institut D'Economie Regionale Bourgogne, Franche Comte, 4 boulevard Gabriel, 21100 Dijon France. **Tel** 011 33 80653263. **Circ:** 500. ***Continues*** *Revue de l'Economie du Centre-Est.*
Ind/Abst Int. Bibliogr. Sociol.

LC HC547.G3 E28
DD 330.9/67/2104 FR
ECONOMIE GABONAISE, L'. (1976)-. French. Irregular. Ediafric la Documentation Africaine, 10 rue Vineuse, 75116 Paris France. **Tel** 011 33 1 44308100, FAX 011 33 1 45208174.

LC HC271 .E344
DD 330.9/33/083 FR
ECONOMIE, GEOGRAPHIE. Added/Corp Conseil National du Patronat Francais. **VFOAT** Universite, Industrie. (19??)-. Periodical. French. Ten times a year. 78.35F. Institut d Enterprise COM Liai Ensmnt, 6 rue Clement Marot, F 75008 Paris France. **Tel** 011 33 1 47239075. **Circ:** 9,000.

LC HC547.I8 S64A
DD 338/.09666/8 IV
ECONOMIE IVOIRIENNE, L'. Main/Corp Societe Generale de Banques en Cote d'Ivoire. (1977)-. French. One time a year. Ediafric la Documentation Africaine, 10 rue Vineuse, 75116 Paris France. **Tel** 011 33 1 44308100, FAX 011 33 1 45208174.

LC HC547.S4 E26
DD 330.9/66/305 FR
ECONOMIE SENEGALAISE, L'. (1970)-. French. 57 Avenue Diena, XVI Paris France.

LC HC321 .E3 **ISSN** 0167-7942
DD 330/338.9492 NE
TITLE CHANGE
ECONOMISCH- EN SOCIAAL-HISTORISCH JAARBOEK. [Econ. soc.-hist. jaarb.]. **Added/Corp** Nederlandsch Economisch-Historisch Archief. No. 33 (1973)-No. 56 (1993). Dutch. Nederlandsch Economisch Historisch Archief NEHA, Cruquiusweg 31, 1019 AT Amsterdam Netherlands. **Tel** 011 31 20 6685866. ***Continues*** *Economisch-Historisch Jaarboek.* ***Merged with*** *Jaarboek voor de Geschiedenis van Bedrijf en Techniek* ***to form*** *NEHA-Jaarboek voor Economische, Bedrijfs- en Techniekgeschiedenis.*
Ind/Abst Am. Hist. Life.

LC HC157.5.A1 E27
NE
ECONOMISCH PROFIEL NEDERLANDSE ANTILLEN. Periodical. Dutch. Centraal Bureau voor de Statistiek, AFD ALG Zaken, Postbus 959, 2270 AZ Voorburg Netherlands. **Tel** 011 31 70 3373800, FAX 011 31 70 0387429, telex 32692 CBS NL.

ISSN 0013-0583
NE
ECONOMISCH-STATISTISCHE BERICHTEN. [Econ.-stat. ber.]. **Added/Corp** Nederlands Economisch Instituut. Central Commission for the Navigation of the Rhine. Instituut voor Economische Geschriften (Hague, Netherlands). **VFOAT** Economisch Statistische Berichten. (1916)-. Periodical. Dutch. Fifty times a year. $255.32. Stichting Het Neth Econ Inst, Postbus 4224, 3006 AE Rotterdam Netherlands. **Tel** 011 31 10 4538742, FAX 011 31 10 4525840.
Ind/Abst EMBASE; Selec. Coop. Index Manage. Period.; World Agric. Econ. Rural Sociol. Abstr.

LC HB9 .E5 **ISSN** 0013-063X
NE
CCC
Pr Rev.
ECONOMIST, DE. [Economist]. **Added/Corp** Nederlands Economisch Instituut. (1852)-. Periodical. Dutch. Four times a year. $216.00. Kluwer Academic Publishers, Postbus 322, 3300 AH Dordrecht The Netherlands. **Tel** 011 31 78 524400, FAX 011 31 78 183273, telex 20083. cum. index. available on microfilm and microfiche from University Microfilms International (UMI). Documents available from UMI Article Clearinghouse.
Ind/Abst ABI/INFORM Glob. Ed.; ABI/INFORM [Computer File] (1981-); Curr. Cit.; Econ. Lit. Index (19??-); Gen. BusinessFile (1992-); J. Econ. Lit.; PAIS Int. Print (1991-?); UMI ABI/Inform--Bus. Period. Ondisc (1987-) [Full Txt.].

ISSN 0422-3586
UK
ECONOMIST. BRIEF, THE. VFOAT Economist Brief Booklets; Economist Brief Books. 1- 1968-. Monographic series. English. Price varies per volume.

LC HG11 .E2 **ISSN** 0013-0613
DD 330/.05 UK
CCC
CODEN EONOEH
ECONOMIST (LONDON). (THE ECONOMIST.). [Economist]. Vol. 1 (Sept. 2, 1843)-. Periodical. English. One time a week (Saturday). $125.00. Economist Intelligence Unit / Essex, PO Box 14 Harold Hill, Romford RM3 8EQ, Essex United Kingdom. **Tel** 011 44 1322 289194, FAX 011 44 1322 223803. **(Subscription address:** Neodata / Colorado, PO Box 2606, Boulder CO 80322. **)** Index Available, published separately, free-automatically sent. cum. index. **Ad Acc. Circ:** 300,000. available on microfilm and microfiche from University Microfilms International (UMI); available on CD-ROM; available on an online database from VU-TEXT; and Lexis-Nexis. Documents available from The Genuine Article, UMI Article Clearinghouse, Documents on Demand, BLDSC, SWETS, CASDDS.
Desc: A business news publication edited for senior management and policy makers in finance, industry, and governments in the United States and throughout the world. It reports on and analyzes world politics, business economics and finance.
Ind/Abst ABI/INFORM Glob. Ed. (Feb. 1988-); ABI/INFORM Ondisc: Expr. Ed. (Feb. 1988-); ABI/INFORM [Computer File] (Feb. 1988-); Abstr. BioCommer.; Acad. Abstr. Full Text Elite; Acad. Abstr.; Acad. Ind. [Computer File] (1985-); Acad. Search; AESIS Q.; AgBiotech News Inf.; Art Archaeol. Tech. Abstr.; Aviat. Tradescan [Select. Cov.]; Book Rev. Digest; Book Rev. Index; Br. Humanit. Index; Bus. ASAP (1990-) [Full Txt.]; Bus. Index (1985-); Bus. Period. Index; Bus. Source Plus; Bus. Source; Chem. Bus. Bull.; Chem. Bus. NewsBase (1985-); Chem. Bus. Update; Coal Abstr.; Curr. Biotechnol.; Curr. Contents Soc. Behav. Sci.; Eng. Mater. Abstr.; Environ. Abstr.; EP Collect.; Expand. Acad. Index (1985-); F&S Index Plus Text, Int. [Select. Cov.]; Gen. BusinessFile (1985-); Gen. Period. Index (1985-); Glob. Views; Homework Help.; Index Bus. Reports; Index Period. Artic. Relat. Law; INFO-SOUTH Abstr.; Infobank (Jan. 1969-); Infomat Int. Bus.; Leis., Rec., Tour. Abstr.; Mag. Artic. Summar. Elite; Mag. Artic. Summar. Select; Mag. Artic. Summar. CD-ROM; Mag. ASAP Plus [Full Txt.]; Mag. Express (1986-) [Full Txt.]; Mag. Index Plus (1989-); Mag. Search; Manage. Market. Abstr.; MasterFile FullTEXT 1000; MasterFile FullTEXT 350; MasterFile FullTEXT 650; MasterFile FullTEXT (July 1990-) [Full Txt.]; Middle East Abstr. Index; Newsp. Period. Abstr. (1986-); OCLC; PAIS Int. Print (1991-); Peace Res. Abstr. J.; PROMT; Pub. Lib. FullTEXT; Res. Alert [Full Cov.]; Resource/One Ondisc; Rice Abstr.; Rural Dev. Abstr.; Soc. Sci. Source; Soc. Sci. Cit. Index [Full Cov.]; Soc. Sci. Index; Soc. Sci. Index Fulltext (Aug. 1988-) [Full Txt.]; Telebase; Mag. Index (1981-); TOM Gen. Index (1992-) [Full Txt.]; Trade Ind. ASAP [Full Txt.]; Trade Ind. Index (1981-) [Full Txt.]; UMI ABI/Inform--Bus. Period. Ondisc (Feb. 1988-) [Full Txt.]; Vocat. Search; Wilson Bus. Abstr.; World Agric. Econ. Rural Sociol. Abstr.; World Mag. Bank; World Text. Abstr.

LC HC131 .E27
MX
TITLE CHANGE
ECONOMISTA MEXICANO, EL. Added/Corp Colegio Nacional de Economistas, A.C. Colegio de Economistas de Mexico, A.C. Vol. 1, No. 1 (Nov./Dec. 1961)-. Periodical. Spanish. Colegio de Economicticas Mexico, AC Calle Antonio Casa 86-, Mexico 4 DF Mexico. ***Continued by*** *Tematica Economica.*

LC HC59.7 .E315 **ISSN** 0223-5978
DD 330.9/172/4 FR
ECONOMISTE DU TIERS MONDE, L'. [Econ. tiers monde]. Periodical. French. 40.00. Soc Ed Afrique Asie Amer Latin, 3 rue de Metz, F 75010 Paris France. **Tel** 011 33 1 40220672.
Ind/Abst Leis., Rec., Tour. Abstr.; Rural Dev. Abstr.; World Agric. Econ. Rural Sociol. Abstr.

ISSN 0381-0828
DD 330.9/714/04 CN
ECONOMISTE (QUEBEC). (L'ECONOMISTE.). Vol. 1 (Sept. 1976)-. Periodical. French. Four times a year. $10.00, Free (ASDEQ members). l'Economiste, CP 965, Chicoutimi Quebec G7H 5EB Canada.

US
ECONOMY AT A GLANCE. (19??)-. English. Twelve times a year. $24.00. Greater Houston Partnership, 1200 Smith Street, Suite 700, Houston TX 77002. **Tel** (713)651-2100.

ISSN 0193-6468
US
ECONOSCOPE VIEW, THE. Periodical. English. Irregular. Econoscope Group Inc, 2739 West Celeste/Apartment 1, Fresno CA 93711-2223. **Tel** (201)356-6400. **ED** Milton L Godfrey. **Circ:** 400.
Desc: Quarterly forecasts two years ahead. Ten-year annual forecasts of 95 individual industry sectors totaling the US economy. Plus macroeconomic indicators.

LC HC1055.A1 E26
DD 330.9669/005 NR
ECONOTRACK. Periodical. English. Twelve times a year. $50.00. Econotrack (Nigeria) Ltd, 52 Raufu Williams Crescent, PO Box 3061, Surulere Lagos Nigeria. **Tel** 01 832 440, telex 23356 WATOM NG. **ED** Cornelius O Tay and Emmanuel Nwokolo. **Circ:** 18,000.
Desc: Nigeria's economic journal. Featuring analyses, reports, viewpoints and interview on socio-economic issues relating to Nigeria, Africa and the world.

ISSN 1054-5395
DD 986 US
ECUADOR (SYRACUSE, N.Y.). (ECUADOR : A POLITICAL AND ECONOMIC FORECAST / POLITICAL RISK SERVICES.). [Ecuador]. **Added/Corp** Political Risk Services (IBC USA (Publications) Inc.). (19??)-. English. $325.00. Political Risk Services, 6320 Fly Road, Suite 102, PO Box 248, East Syracuse NY 13057-0248. **Tel** (315)431-0511, FAX (315)431-0200.
Desc: Assesses the factors affecting the prospects for business and trade. Each report focuses specifically on business needs such as finding and developing markets, determining currency movements, or making judgements about capital investments or corporate security.

LC HC201
DD 330.9866/005 GW
ECUADOR, WIRTSCHAFTSDATEN UND WIRTSCHAFTSDOKUMENTATION / BUNDESSTELLE FUR AUSSENHANDELSINFORMATION. German. One time a year. DM2.00. Bundesstelle fuer Aussenhandelsinformation, Agrippastrasse 87 93, D-50676 Cologne Germany. **Tel** 011 49 221 2057316, FAX 011 49 221 2057212.

LC HC201 .E28
DD 330.9866/005 GW
ECUADOR, WIRTSCHAFTSSTRUKTUR / BUNDESSTELLE FUR AUSSENHANDELSINFORMATION. German. DM10.00. Bundesstelle fuer Aussenhandelsinformation, Agrippastrasse 87 93, D-50676 Cologne Germany. **Tel** 011 49 221 2057316, FAX 011 49 221 2057212.

ISSN 1054-5484
DD 962 US
EGYPT (SYRACUSE, N.Y.). (EGYPT : A POLITICAL AND ECONOMIC FORECAST / POLITICAL RISK SERVICES.). [Egypt]. **Added/Corp** Political Risk Services (IBC USA (Publications) Inc.). (19??)-. English. $325.00. Political Risk Services, 6320 Fly Road, Suite 102, PO Box 248, East Syracuse NY 13057-0248. **Tel** (315)431-0511, FAX (315)431-0200.
Desc: Assesses the factors affecting the prospects for business and trade. Each report focuses specifically on business needs such as finding and developing markets, determining currency movements, or making judgements about capital investments or corporate security.

UK
EIU SPECIAL REPORT. Added/Corp Economist Intelligence Unit (Great Britain). **VFOAT** Special Report. (19??)-. Monographic series. English. Price varies per volume. The Economist Intelligence Unit, 40 Duke Street, London W1A 1DW United Kingdom. **Tel** 011 44 171 8301000. **(Subscription address:** Economist Intelligence Unit / North America Subscriptions, 111 West 57th Street, New York NY 10019. **Tel** 800 938-4685, (212)554-0600, FAX (212)586-1181, (212)586-1182.**)**
Ind/Abst Curr. Cit.; Leis., Rec., Tour. Abstr.; World Agric. Econ. Rural Sociol. Abstr.

LC HC446 .E443
IO
EKONOMI DAN PEMBANGUNAN. Vol. 1 Apr. 1977-. Periodical. Indonesian. Fakultas Ekonomi Unlam, Jln Lambung Mangkurat 20, Banjarmasin Indonesia. ***Supersedes*** *Bulletin Fakultas Ekonomi Unlam.*

LC HC448.S79 E46 **ISSN** 0377-7162
IO
EKONOMI SUMATERA UTARA. (19??)-. Indonesian. Twenty-four times a year. $1.50 per month. Institute of Economic Research Consultancy, DJL Seram 70, PO Box 653, Medan Indonesia.

LC HC387.P28 E38 **ISSN** 0213-3865
DD 330.946/005 SP
EKONOMIAZ. Added/Corp Pais Vasco (Spain). Direccion de Estudios Economicos y Coyuntura. Pais Vasco (Spain). Departamento de Economia y Planificacion. (1985)-. Periodical. Spanish (summaries and/or abstracts in Basque and English). Three times a year. 2500ptas. Gobierno Vasco, Duque de Wellington 2, 01010 Vitoria Gasteiz Spain. **Tel** 011 34 45 188623, 011 34 45 188647.

LC HC10 .E543 **ISSN** 0868-6955
DD 330.0 UN
EKONOMICHNA TA SOTSIALNA HEOHRAFIIA. Added/Corp Kyivskyi Derzhavnyi Universytet im. T.H. Shevchenka. (1992)-. Periodical. Ukrainian. Vyshcha Shkola, Ulitsa Universitetskaia 16, Kharkov Ukraine. ***Continues*** *Ekonomichna Heohrafiia (Kiev, Ukraine : 1991).*

Business and Economics — Economic History, Conditions

LC HC10 .E523 — **ISSN** 0474-2974
DD 330.9/04 — US
EKONOMIKA. (1965)-. Periodical. Polish (summaries and/or abstracts in English). Twelve times a year. $64.00 airmail. **(Subscription address:** Victor Kamkin, 4956 Boiling Brook Parkway, Rockville MD 20852. **Tel** (301)881-5973.)

LC S
DD 630 — YU
EKONOMIKA PROIZVODNJE HRANE. See Agriculture.

LC F — **ISSN** 1054-5492
DD 972 — US
EL SALVADOR (SYRACUSE, N.Y.). (EL SALVADOR : A POLITICAL AND ECONOMIC FORECAST.). [El Salv.]. **Added/Corp** Political Risk Services (IBC USA (Publications) Inc.). (19??)-. English. $325.00. Political Risk Services, 6320 Fly Road, Suite 102, PO Box 248, East Syracuse NY 13057-0248. **Tel** (315)431-0511, FAX (315)431-0200.
Desc: Assesses the factors affecting the prospects for business and trade. Each report focuses specifically on business needs such as finding and developing markets, determining currency movements, or making judgements about capital investments or corporate security.

LC HC148 .G47a
DD 330.9/7284/05 — GW
EL SALVADOR: WIRTSCHAFTLICHE ENTWICKLUNG. Main/Corp Bundesstelle fuer Aussenhandelsinformation (Germany). (19??)-. German. Bundesstelle fuer Aussenhandelsinformation, Agrippastrasse 87 93, D-50676 Cologne Germany. **Tel** 011 49 221 2057316, FAX 011 49 221 2057212.

LC HC148.A1 E58
DD 330.97284/00212 — GW
EL SALVADOR, WIRTSCHAFTSDATEN / BUNDESSTELLE FUER AUSSENHANDELSINFORMATION. Added/Corp Bundesstelle fuer Aussenhandelsinformation (Germany). (19??)-. German. DM3.00. Bundesstelle fuer Aussenhandelsinformation, Agrippastrasse 87 93, D-50676 Cologne Germany. **Tel** 011 49 221 2057316, FAX 011 49 221 2057212.

LC HC547.I8 — GW
ELFENBEINKUSTE : WIRTSCHAFTLICHE ENTWICKLUNG. Main/Corp Bundesstelle fur Aussenhandelsinformation (Germany). German. DM4.00. Bundesstelle fuer Aussenhandelsinformation, Agrippastrasse 87 93, D-50676 Cologne Germany. **Tel** 011 49 221 2057316, FAX 011 49 221 2057212.

LC HC1025.A1
DD 330.9666/8/00212 — GW
ELFENBEINKUSTE, WIRTSCHAFTSDATEN UND WIRTSCHAFTSDOKUMENTATION / BUNDESSTELLE FUER AUSSENHANDELSINFORMATION. German. Every 2 years. DM3.00. Bundesstelle fuer Aussenhandelsinformation, Agrippastrasse 87 93, D-50676 Cologne Germany. **Tel** 011 49 221 2057316, FAX 011 49 221 2057212.

LC HC578.M6 E16 — **ISSN** 0012-9755
DD 330.9 — MZ
EM; ECONOMIA DE MOCAMBIQUE. [EM, Econ. Mocamb.]. **VFOAT** Economia de Mocambique. Periodical. Portuguese. Twelve times a year. Companhia Editora de Mozambique/Sarl, rua D Joao de Macarenhas, Caixa Postal 81, Beria Mozambique. **ED** Antonia de Almeida. **Ad Acc.**

LC HC186 .E53a
DD 330.981/062 — BL
ENCONTRO NACIONAL DE ECONOMIA. Main/Corp Encontro Nacional de Economia. **Added/Corp** Associacao Nacional dos Centros de Pos-Graduacao em Economia. (19??)-. English (Portuguese). Universidade de Sao Paulo, Cidade Universitaria CP 8191, Sao Paulo Brazil. **Tel** 011 55 11 8150899, FAX 011 55 11 8154272.

LC HC171 .F85a — AG
ENCUESTAS DE COYUNTURA. SERIE 1 : EVOLUCION DE LA ACTIVIDAD INDUSTRIAL. Main/Corp Fundacion de Investigaciones Economicas Latinoamericanas (Buenos Aires, Argentina). **Added/Corp** Union Industrial Argentina. **VFOAT** Evolucion de la Actividad Industrial. (19??)-. Periodical. Spanish. Four times a year. Esmeralda 320 4 Piso, Buenos Aires Argentina.

LC HC271 .E44 — **ISSN** 1167-2196
FR
ENJEUX, LES ECHOS. VFOAT Enjeux; Echos. (19??)-. Periodical. French. Twelve times a year. $58.62. Les Echos, 46 rue de la Boetie, 75381 Paris Cedex 08 France. **Tel** 011 33 1 49536565. **(Subscription address:** Enjeux les Echos Serv Abonn, B 500, 60732 Sainte Gene Cedex 9 France. **Tel** 011 33 44074655.)

LC HC337.F5 F4245a — **ISSN** 0785-4218
DD 330 — FI
ENNAKKOTIETOJA TEOLLISUUDESTA / TILASTOKESKUS. See Business and Economics-Abstracting, Bibliographies and Statistics.

LC HC337.F5 F4243A — FI
ENNAKKOTIETOJA TUTKIMUS- JA KEHIITTAMISTOIMINNASTA SUOMESSA. Main/Corp Finland. Tilastokeskus. **VFOAT** Forhandsuppgifter om Forskinngs- Och Utvecklingsverksamheten I Finland. Multiple languages (Finnish and Swedish). Tilastokeskus, PL 504, Annankatu 44, 00101 Helsinki Finland. **Tel** 011 358 0 17341, FAX 011 358 0 17342474, telex 1002111 TILASTO SF.

LC HC271 .E46
DD 338.0944 — FR
ENQUETE ANNUELLE D'ENTREPRISE. PREMIERS RESULTATS PAR SECTEUR D'ENTREPRISES. French. One time a year. SESSI, 85 bd du Montparnasse, Paris Cedex 06 France.

LC HC271 .E484
DD 338.0944 — FR
TITLE CHANGE
ENQUETE ANNUELLE D'ENTREPRISE. TEXTILES, HABILLEMENT, CUIR, PAPIER, BOIS, INDUSTRIES DIVERSES / MINISTERE DE L'INDUSTRIE, STISI, DIRECTION GENERALE DES STRATEGIES INDUSTRIELLES, SERVICE DU TRAITEMENT DE L'INFORMATION ET DES STATISTIQUES INDUSTRIELLES, CENTRE D'ENQUETES STATISTIQUES DE CAEN. See Business and Economics-Abstracting, Bibliographies and Statistics.

LC HC196 .E57
DD 330.9861/005 — CK
ENSAYOS SOBRE POLITICA ECONOMICA : DOCUMENTOS DE TRABAJO. Added/Corp Banco de la Republica (Colombia). Departamento de Investigaciones Economicas. No. 1 (March 1982)-. Periodical. Spanish. Two times a year. $20.00. Banco de la Republica Departamento Editorial, Calle 13 35 51, Bogota de 1 Columbia. **Tel** 011 57 1 2010900, 011 57 1 2776872. **Circ:** 2,500 (ctrl).
Desc: A collection of macroeconomic studies that analyze the monetary, financial, and trade aspects of the country.
Ind/Abst Econ. Lit. Index; PAIS Int. Print (1991-).

LC HC60 .G465A
DD 338.91/43 — GW
ENTWICKLUNGSPOLITIK; JAHRESBERICHT. Main/Corp Germany (Federal Republic, 1949-). Bundesministerium fur Wirtschaftliche Zusammenarbeit. German. One time a year. Bundesministerium fur Wirtschaftliche Zusammenarbeit, Karl-Marx-Strasse 4-6, 5300 Bonn 1 Germany.

ISSN 1105-2503
GR
UDC 330
EPILOGE : OIKONOMIKE EPITHEORESE. [Epiloge, Oikon. Epitheor.]. (1963)-. Periodical. Greek, Modern. Twelve times a year. $150.00. S Ch Papaioannou, Vas Georgiou 50, Athens Greece. **Tel** 3238427, FAX 3235160, telex 210564. **ED** Christos Papaioannou. **Bk Rev**. **Ad Acc**. **Circ:** 9,000.

LC HD651.A1 E73 — GW
ERGEBNIS DER FORDERUNGSMASSNAHMEN AUF GRUND DES FLUCHTLINGSSIEDLUNGSGESETZES UND DES BUNDESVERTRIEBENENGESEZES ZUGUNSTEN DER VERTRIEBENEN UND GEFLUCHTETEN LANDWIRTE VOM. Added/Corp Germany (West). Bundesministerium fuer Ernahrung, Landwirtschaft und Forsten. (19??)-. German.

LC HC10 .E73 — **ISSN** 0896-226X
DD 330.9/005 — US
ESSAYS IN ECONOMIC AND BUSINESS HISTORY : SELECTED PAPERS FROM THE ECONOMIC AND BUSINESS HISTORICAL SOCIETY. [Essays econ. bus. hist.]. **Added/Corp** Economic and Business Historical Society (U.S.) Michigan State University. Graduate School of Business Administration. Division of Research. University of Southern California. History Dept. (1978)-. English. University of California, Department of History, Los Angeles CA 90089. **Tel** (213)740-1668, FAX (213)740-6999.
Ind/Abst Am. Hist. Life (1989-).

LC HC188.G8 I5 — BL
ESTADO DO RIO DE JANEIRO : INDICADORES ECONOMICOS. Main/Corp Instituto de Desenvolvimento Economico E Gerencial. Portuguese. Instituto de Desenvolvimento Economico E Gerencial, Av Calogeras 15-30 Andar, Rio de Janeiro Brazil. **Continues** Guanabara: Indicadores Economicos.

LC HC497.H6 A317a
DD 339.351/25 — HK
ESTIMATES OF GROSS DOMESTIC PRODUCT. Main/Corp Hong Kong. Census and Statistics Dept. (1971)-. English. One time a year. HK61.00. Hong Kong Government Information Service, Beaconsfield House, 4 Queens Road, Hong Kong Hong Kong. **Tel** 011 852 284288014, 011 852 259881947, FAX 011 852 28459078, 011 852 25987482, telex 61190 HKGIS. **(Subscription address:** Government Information Service, Publications Office, 1 Battery Path, Hong Kong Hong Kong.)

LC HD9698.C2 C32a
DD 354.710082/32 — CN
ESTIMATES. PART III, ATOMIC ENERGY CONTROL BOARD. See Public Administration.

LC HC60 .C2835a
DD 354.710089 — CN
ESTIMATES. PART III, CANADIAN INTERNATIONAL DEVELOPMENT AGENCY. See Public Administration.

LC HC120.C63 C36a
DD 354.9710082/042 — CN
TITLE CHANGE
ESTIMATES. PART III, CONSUMER AND CORPORATE AFFAIRS EXPENDITURE PLAN. See Public Administration.

LC HC120.E5 C28a
DD 354.710082/32/06 — CN
ESTIMATES. PART III, ENVIRONMENT CANADA. See Public Administration.

LC HC111 .C14a
DD 354.710082 — CN
ESTIMATES. PART III, MINISTRY OF STATE, ECONOMIC AND REGIONAL DEVELOPMENT. See Public Administration.

LC HD9581.C3 C219a
DD 354.710087/8 — CN
ESTIMATES. PART III, NORTHERN PIPELINE AGENCY. See Public Administration.

LC HC137.M46 E78 — MX
ESTUDIOS FRONTERIZOS : REVISTA DEL INSTITUTO DE INVESTIGACIONES SOCIALES. Added/Corp Universidad Autonoma de Baja California. Instituto de Investigaciones Sociales. Vol. 1, No. 1 (May/Aug. 1983)-. Periodical. Spanish. Three times a year. $35.00. Inst Invest Oceanologicas UABC, Apartado Postal 423, Ensenada Baja California Mexico. **Tel** 011 52 617 44601, FAX 011 52 617 45303. **(Subscription address:** Univ Autonoma de Baja California, PO Box 3280, Calexico CA 92232.)
Ind/Abst Hisp. Am. Period. Index, HAPI.

LC HC14 .E8
DD 330.9/005 — FR
ETAT DU MONDE, L'. Ed. 1981-. French. One time a year. 120.00F. F Maspero, 1 Place Paul-Painleve, 75005 Paris France. **Tel** 011 33 1 46334116. **ED** Francois Geze, Yves Lacoste, Annie Lennkh, Thierry Paquot, and Alfredo G A Valladao. **Continued in part by** Pour en Savoir Plus sur le Tiers Monde et Letat du Monde.
Desc: An economical and geopolitical yearbook (640 pages, pocket book format), reflecting the situation and developments in the 34 huge states and 33 geopolitical groups in the world. Also includes every year, important articles on particular burning topics.

LC HC241.2 .E76
DD 382/.9142 — FR
EURO COOPERATION; ECONOMIC STUDIES ON EUROPE. Added/Corp Banco di Roma. Commerzbank. Credit Lyonnais. **VFOAT** Economic Studies on Europe. (19??)-. English. 5 Avenue du Coq F, 750009 Paris France.

LC HB **ISSN** 1021-4283
DD 330 BE
UDC 658(4)
EUROPEAN INSIGHT. [Eur. insight]. (1982)-. Periodical. English (French). Forty-eight times a year (irregular). 16200F Belgium; 18500F Rest of Europe; 19200F other. Europe Information Service, rue de Geneve 6, 1140 Brussels Belgium. **Tel** 011 32 2 242 6020, FAX 011 32 2 242 9549. available on an online database from Lexis-Nexis.
Desc: Information package covering the week's EEC-related happenings.

LC HB1 .E93
NE
EUROPEAN JOURNAL OF POLITICAL ECONOMY. **VFOAT** POLECO. Vol. 5, No. 1 (1988)-. Academic Scholarly Publication. English. Four times a year (1 volume). Fl600.00. Elsevier Science Publishers BV, PO Box 211, 1000 AE Amsterdam Netherlands. **Tel** 011 31 20 4853641, 011 31 20 4853642, FAX 011 31 20 4853598. available on an online database from Elsevier Electronic Subscriptions (EES). Documents available from UMI Article Clearinghouse. ***Continues*** *Europaische Zeitschrift fur Politische Okonomie, 0176-2680.*
Ind/Abst ABI/INFORM Glob. Ed.

LC HC240.A1 E875
DD 338.5/443/094 US
EUROPEAN LONG-TERM REVIEW.
Added/Corp Data Resources, Inc. **VFOAT** Data Resources European Long-Term Review. (19??)-. English. Four times a year. DRI McGraw Hill, 24 Hartwell Avenue, Lexington MA 02173. **Tel** (617)863-5100, FAX (617)860-6464, (617)860-6416.

LC HC240.A1 D38a **ISSN** 0276-7430
DD 330.94/005 US
EUROPEAN REVIEW (LEXINGTON, MASS.). (EUROPEAN REVIEW.). [Eur. rev.]. **Added/Corp** Data Resources, inc. **VFOAT** Data Resources European Review. (19??)-. Periodical. English. Four times a year. $6300.00. DRI McGraw Hill, 24 Hartwell Avenue, Lexington MA 02173. **Tel** (617)863-5100, FAX (617)860-6464, (617)860-6416. **(Subscription address:** Data Resources, PO Box 5 0210, Woburn MA 01815. **)** ***Continues*** *DRI European Review, 0362-4730.*
Ind/Abst Am. Hist. Life (1973-1974); Peace Res. Abstr. J. (1964-1966).

ISSN 0531-4631
DD 338.9 BE
EUROPEEN, L'. (L'EUROPEEN. DER EUROPAER.). **VFOAT** Der Europaer; Quest Europa; This Europe. (1959)-. Periodical. French. Four times a year. 400F Belgium; 450F other. L'Europeen, Avenue du Cor Chasse 19, 1170 Brussels Belgium.

LC HF1532.92 .A18
DD 337.1/42/05 US
EUROWATCH: ECONOMICS, POLICY, AND LAW IN THE NEW EUROPE. Vol. 3, No. 21 (Feb. 10, 1992)-. Newspaper. English. Irregular (24 issues). $797.00. Buraff Publications Inc., 714 Church Street, Alexandria VA 22314. **Tel** (800)333-1291, (703)739-8500. ***Continues*** *1992, The External Impact of European Unification, 1043-4380.*

LC HC437.G6 A25
DD 330.954/799/005 II
EVALUATION REPORT / GOA, DAMAN AND DIU (INDIA). DIRECTORATE OF PLANNING, STATISTICS AND EVALUATION. **Added/Corp** Goa, Daman and Diu (India). Directorate of Planning, Statistics & Evaluation. No. 1 (1969)-. English. Government of Goa Daman and Diu, Bureau of Economics Statistics and Evaluation, Panaji India.

LC HG3881.5.W57 E93 **ISSN** 1019-4363
DD 332.1/532/05 US
EVALUATION RESULTS FOR ... WORLD BANK. (EVALUATION RESULTS FOR ...). [Eval. results - World Bank]. **Added/Corp** International Bank for Reconstruction and Development. Operations Evaluation Dept. (1988)-. English. One time a year. Price varies. World Bank Publications, 1818 H Street Northwest, Washington DC 20043. **Tel** (202)473-1155, (202)473-1155, FAX (202)522-3224, telex WUI 64145 WORLDBANK. **(Subscription address:** World Bank Publications, PO Box 7247-8619, Books Department, Philadelphia PA 19170. **)** ***Continues*** *Project Performance Results for ... .*

LC HC497.N5 E8 **ISSN** 0376-9100
DD 338.9549/6 SP
EVEREST REVIEW. Periodical. English. Four times a year. 10.00. Nepalese Association for World Understanding, 21/485 Dilli Bazar, Kathmandu Nepal.

LC HC271 .E96 **ISSN** 0014-4703
DD 330.9/44 FR
CCC
EXPANSION, L'. [Expansion]. (Oct. 1967)-. Periodical. French. Twenty-four times a year (biweekly except Aug.). $132.10. Groupe Expansion, Le Ponant, 25 rue LeBlanc, 75842 Paris Cedex 15 France. **Tel** 011 33 1 40604115. **(Subscription address:** L'Expansion, Service Abonnements B 040, 60732 Suite Genevieve 9 France. **)** **ED** Jean Boissonnat. Index available. **Ad Acc.** ctrl circ. available on microfilm and microfiche from University Microfilms International (UMI).
Ind/Abst F&S Index Plus Text, Int. [Select. Cov.]; Infomat Int. Bus.; Int. Labour Doc.; LABORDOC; PAIS Int. Print.

LC HB615 .E8 **ISSN** 0014-4983
DD 330.9 US
CCC
Pr Rev.
EXPLORATIONS IN ECONOMIC HISTORY. [Explor. econ. hist.]. **VFOAT** EEH. Vol. 7 (Fall 1969)-. Academic Scholarly Publication. English. Four times a year. $225.00. Academic Press Inc., 6277 Sea Harbor Drive, Orlando FL 32887. **Tel** (800)543-9534, (407)345-4100, FAX (407)352-3445. **ED** Larry Neal. Documents available from The Genuine Article, UMI Article Clearinghouse. ***Continues*** *Explorations in Entrepreneurial History, 0884-5425.*
Desc: Publishes original papers that provide broad coverage of the application of economic analysis to historical episodes. The journal has a tradition of innovative application of theory and quantitative technique and is concerned with all aspects of economic change, all historical periods, all geographical locations, and all political and social systems. The journal includes papers by economists, economic historians, demographers, geographers, and sociologists.
Ind/Abst Acad. Search; AGRICOLA [Select. Cov.]; Am. Hist. Life (1955-); Curr. Contents Soc. Behav. Sci.; Econ. Lit. Index; EP Collect.; Expand. Acad. Index (1989-); Geogr. Abstr. Human Geogr.; Hist. Source (July 1993-); Homework Help.; Humanit. Source; INFO-SOUTH Abstr.; J. Econ. Lit.; MasterFile FullTEXT 1000; MasterFile FullTEXT 350; MasterFile FullTEXT 650; MasterFile FullTEXT (Jan. 1994-); Middle East Abstr. Index; Newsp. Period. Abstr. (1992-); OCLC; Popul. Index (?-?); Res. Alert [Full Cov.]; Soc. Plann. Policy Dev. Abstr.; Soc. Sci. Source; Soc. Sci. Cit. Index [Full Cov.]; Soc. Sci. Index; Soc. Sci. Index Fulltext (Oct. 1988-) [Full Txt.]; Sociol. Abstr. (?-?); Telebase; West. Hist. Q.

LC HD1039.W47 F33
DD 333.33/22/0994105 AT
FACTORS AFFECTING ECONOMIC CONDITIONS IN REAL ESTATE.
Added/Corp Western Australia. Valuer General's Office. Research and Development Branch. (19??)-. English. Four times a year (Mar., June, Sept., Dec.). 82.22Aus$. Valuer Generals, PO Box 7201, Cloisters Square, Perth WA 6000 Australia. **Tel** 011 09 3222400, FAX 011 09 3223016. **ED** G. Penner and M. Palandri. Index available. cum. index (Articles only). **Circ:** 100.
Desc: Provide articles studies, research into topics of interest to the real estate industry and general community which is independent & impartial covering facts of valuation and land, and general economic conditions

LC HC431 .F32
DD 330.9/54/05 II
FACTS AND FIGURES. (19??)-. Periodical. English. Twelve times a year. Patel Chambers, 16 Shatisadam Estate Lal Darwaja, Ahmedabad-1 India.

LC HC431 .F33 **ISSN** 0046-3132
DD 330.9/54/05 II
FACTS FILE. [Facts file]. (19??)-. Periodical. English. Twelve times a year. Rs60.00. Southern Publishers, 12 Third Main Road, Madras 20 India.

LC HC431 .F34
DD 330.954/005 II
FACTS FOR YOU. **VFOAT** FFY. Vol. 1 (July/Aug. 1979)-. Periodical. English. Twelve times a year. $15.00. Facts for You, 605 Siddhartha, 96 Nehru Place, New Delhi 110019 India. **Tel** 011 91 11 6415330, 011 91 11 6434799. **ED** S P Chopra. **Bk Rev. Ad Acc. Circ:** 7,000.
Desc: An essay on executive health, taxation tips and labor. Notes are regular features India and the world is a special feature.

LC HC241.2 .F267 **ISSN** 1100-049X
SW
FAKTA EUROPA. Vol. 1 (1988)-. Monographic series. Swedish. Price varies per volume. Utrikesdepartementet, Press Och Informationsenheten, Box 161212, 103 23 Stockholm 16 Sweden.

LC HC411 .F17
DD 330.9/5/042 RU
FAR EASTERN AFFAIRS. **Added/Corp** Institut Dalnego Vostoka (Akademiiia Nauk SSSR). (19??)-. Periodical. English (Japanese, Spanish and Russian). Six times a year. $192.00. **(Subscription address:** East View Publications Inc., 3020 Harbor Lane North, Suite 110, Minneapolis MN 55447. **Tel** (800)477-1005, (612)550-0961, FAX (612)559-2931.**)** **Bk Rev.**
Desc: Considers questions on the ideology, culture, language, foreign policy and international relations of the countries and peoples of the Far East and Southeast Asia.
Ind/Abst Am. Hist. Life (1979-).

LC HC411 .F18 **ISSN** 0014-7591
DD 330.95 HK
CODEN FEERAK
FAR EASTERN ECONOMIC REVIEW. [Far East. econ. rev.]. Vol. 1 (Oct. 16, 1946)-. Periodical. English. Fifty-two times a year (Thurs.). $199.00. Review Publishing Company Ltd., 25 F Citicorp Center, 18 Whitfield Road, GPO Box 160, Hong Kong Hong Kong. **Tel** 011 852 25084337, FAX 011 852 25031549, 25031553, telex 66452 REVCD HX. **(Subscription address:** Review Publishing Company Ltd., PO Box 160, Hong Kong Hong Kong. **Tel** 011 852 25084300.**)** **ED** Derek Davies. **Ad Acc. Circ:** 65,000. available on microfilm and microfiche from University Microfilms International (UMI). Documents available from UMI Article Clearinghouse.
Desc: Reports and interprets the events that make news and influence business in 30 Asian countries.
Ind/Abst ABI/INFORM Glob. Ed.; ABI/INFORM [Computer File] (Oct. 1987-); Acad. Ind. [Computer File] (1987-); Acad. Search; AESIS Q.; BioBusiness (1986-); Bus. Index (1992-); Bus. Source Plus; Bus. Source; Eng. Mater. Abstr.; EP Collect.; Expand. Acad. Index (1987-); Gen. BusinessFile (1992-); Homework Help.; Hum. Rights Intern. Rep.; Index Bus. Reports; INFO-SOUTH Abstr.; Infobank (Jan. 1969-); Leis., Rec., Tour. Abstr.; MasterFile FullTEXT 1000; MasterFile FullTEXT 350; MasterFile FullTEXT 650; MasterFile FullTEXT (July 1993-); Newsp. Period. Abstr. (1989-); OCLC; PAIS Int. Print; Peace Res. Abstr. J. (1965-1979); Rural Dev. Abstr.; Soc. Sci. Source; Soc. Sci. Index; Soc. Sci. Index Fulltext (Sept. 1988-) [Full Txt.]; Telebase; Trade Ind. Index; UMI ABI/Inform--Bus. Period. Ondisc [Full Txt.]; World Agric. Econ. Rural Sociol. Abstr.; World Mag. Bank.

LC HC171 .F53 **ISSN** 0325-5476
DD 330.982/005 AG
FIDE, COYUNTURA Y DESARROLLO.
VFOAT Coyuntura y Desarrollo. **VAT** Fundacion de Investigaciones Para El Desarrollo Coyuntura y Desarrollo. No. 1 (Sept. 1978)-. Periodical. Spanish. Twelve times a year. $225.00. Fundacion de Investigaciones Para el Desarrollo, Santa Fe 1592 Piso 60, 1060 Buenos Aires Argentina.
Ind/Abst PAIS Int. Print (1991-?).

LC HC120.I5 A34 **ISSN** 0380-0938
DD 339.2/6/0971 CN
FINANCIAL FLOW ACCOUNTS (PRELIMINARY DATA). (FINANCIAL FLOW ACCOUNTS = COMPTES DES FLUX FINANCIERS.). [Financ. flow acc.]. **Added/Corp** Statistics Canada. **VFOAT** Comptes des Flux Financiers. (1971)-. Periodical. English (French). Four times a year. 140.00Can$. Statistics Canada Publications Sales and Services, R.H. Coats Building 6th Floor, Ottawa Ontario K1A 0T6 Canada. **Tel** (613)951-5078, (800)267-6677, FAX (613)951-1584, telex 053-3585. ***Continues in part*** *Comptes des Flux Financiers (Preliminary);* ***Absorbed*** *Comptes des Flux Financiers (Preliminary);* ***Continues*** *Financial Flow Accounts (Final), 0380-092X.*

ISSN 1054-5506
DD 948 US
FINLAND (SYRACUSE, N.Y.). (FINLAND : A POLITICAL AND ECONOMIC FORECAST.). [Finland]. **Added/Corp** Political Risk Services (IBC USA (Publications) Inc.). (19??)-. English. $325.00. Political Risk Services, 6320 Fly Road, Suite 102, PO Box 248, East Syracuse NY 13057-0248. **Tel** (315)431-0511, FAX (315)431-0200.
Desc: Assesses the factors affecting the prospects for business and trade. Each report focuses specifically on business needs such as finding and developing markets, determining currency movements, or making judgements about capital investments or corporate security.

LC HC337.F5
GW
FINNLAND : WIRTSCHAFT IN ZAHLEN UND WIRTSCHAFTSDOKUMENTATION.
Main/Corp Bundesstelle fur Aussenhandelsinformation (Germany). German. DM4.00. Bundesstelle fuer Aussenhandelsinformation, Agrippastrasse 87 93, D-50676 Cologne Germany. **Tel** 011 49 221 2057316, FAX 011 49 221 2057212.

LC HC337.F5 G47a
GW
FINNLAND: WIRTSCHAFTLICHE ENTWICKLUNG. **Main/Corp** Bundesstelle fur Aussenhandelsinformation (Germany). (19??)-. German. DM2.00. Bundesstelle fuer Aussenhandelsinformation, Agrippastrasse 87 93, D-50676 Cologne Germany. **Tel** 011 49 221 2057316, FAX 011 49 221 2057212.

US
FLORIDA FACTS AND FIGURES. (19??)-. English. $2.95. Florida Trend, Inc., PO Box 611, St Petersburg FL 33731. **Tel** (813)821-5800, FAX (813)822-5083.

Business and Economics — Economic History, Conditions

LC HF5065.F6 F6 HC107.F6 F4448
DD 338.4/025/759 US
FLORIDA INDUSTRIES GUIDE, THE.
(1971)-. Directory. English. Irregular (every 18 months). $97.00. Industries Guides Inc / Altamonte Springs, PO Box 160158, Altamonte Springs FL 32716. **Tel** (407)682-5600. **ED** Richard J. McHenry. **Ad Acc**. **Circ:** 50,000.
Desc: Directory of manufacturing firms. Listings are alphabetical by cities with S.I.C. Code breakdown.

LC HC107.F6 F446 **ISSN** 0147-7986
DD 330.9/759/06 US
FLORIDA OUTLOOK, THE. Added/Corp
University of Florida. Bureau of Economic and Business Research. (1977)-. Periodical. English. Four times a year (Mar., Jun., Sept., Dec.). $200.00. University of Florida / CBA, College of Business Administration, Gainesville FL 32601. **Tel** (904)392-0171, FAX (904)392-6250. **ED** Carol Taylor West. **Circ:** 400.
Desc: Economic forecasts for Florida and its metropolitan areas.

LC HC107.F6 F47 **ISSN** 0015-4326
US
CCC
FLORIDA TREND. [Fla. trend]. (April 1958)-.
Periodical. English. Twelve times a year. $39.95. Florida Trend, Inc., PO Box 611, St Petersburg FL 33731. **Tel** (813)821-5800, FAX (813)822-5083. **(Subscription address:** Palm Coast Data, PO Box 420163, Agency Department, Palm Coast FL 32142. **Tel** (904)445-4662 ext. 669, (800)829-5475.) **ED** John Berry. **Ad Acc, Adv Mgr:** Deanna Kealor, **Tel** (813)821-5800. **Circ:** 50,000. available on microfilm and microfiche from University Microfilms International (UMI); available on an online database (files 635,648/Full-Text) from DIALOG. Documents available from UMI Article Clearinghouse.
Ind/Abst Acad. Search; Bus. ASAP (1990-) [Full Txt.]; Bus. Dateline; Bus. Index (1985-); EP Collect.; Gen. BusinessFile (1985-); Gen. Period. Index (1985-); Homework Help.; INFO-SOUTH Abstr.; MasterFile FullTEXT 1000; MasterFile FullTEXT 350; MasterFile FullTEXT 650; MasterFile FullTEXT (July 1993-); OCLC; PAIS Int. Print; PROMT; Telebase; Trade Ind. ASAP [Full Txt.]; Trade Ind. Index [Full Txt.].

LC HD7011 .S25b
DD 339.4/2/09821 AG
FLUCTUACIONES MONETARIAS; METODO GENERAL DE ACTUALIZACION. Main/Corp
Santiago del Estero, Argentine Republic (Province). Direccion General de Investigaciones, Estadistica y Censos. Division Economicos y Financieros. (19??)-. Spanish.

LC HC800 **ISSN** 0947-9368
DD 330.96 GW
●FOCUS AFRIKA. (1994)-. German. Irregular. Institut fuer Afrika-Kunde, Neuer Jungfernstieg 21, D-20354 Hamburg Germany. **Tel** 011 49 40 3562523, 011 49 40 3562524.

LC HC79.P6 F62 **ISSN** 0195-5705
DD 339.4/6/05 US
FOCUS (MADISON). (FOCUS.). Added/Corp
University of Wisconsin--Madison. Institute for Research on Poverty. VFOAT IRP Focus. Vol. 1, No. 2 (Winter 1976/77)-. Periodical. English. Four times a year. Free. University of Wisconsin / Institute of Poverty, 1180 Observatory Drive, Madison WI 53706. **Tel** (608)262-6579. **ED** Elizabeth Uhr. Index available. cum. index. **Bk Rev**. **Circ:** 5,000 (ctrl). **Continues** Focus on Poverty Research, 0191-2186.
Desc: Measurements of income poverty and economic inequality, employment strategies and labor market structure, income maintenance programs, status attainment, social mobility methodology and data sets. Primarily short, nontechnical essays disseminating research findings.
Ind/Abst Index Period. Artic. Relat. Law.

LC HC517.S7 F6
DD 330.9/68/06 SA
FOCUS ON KEY ECONOMIC ISSUES.
Periodical. English. Mercabank Ltd, PO Box 62324, Marshalltown 2107 Johannesburg South Africa.

LC HC381 .H6
SP
FOMENTO DEL TRABAJO. Added/Corp
Fomento del Trabajo Nacional (Spain). VFOAT Fomento. (19??)-. Periodical. Spanish. Twelve times a year. Fomento del Trbajo Nacional, Via Layetana 32-34, 08003 Barcelona Spain. **Tel** 93-319-61-00, telex 97826-1831.
Continues Horizonte Empresarial, 0212-0607.

LC HC107.C2 U54A **ISSN** 0071-7282
DD 338.5/443/09794 US
FORECAST (LOS ANGELES). (FORECAST.).
English. One time a year. Research and Planning Division / Los Angeles, 707 Wilshire Boulevard, Los Angeles CA 90017.

ISSN 0095-294X
US
FORECASTER. (THE FORECASTER.). (19??)-.
Periodical. English. Forty times a year (Wednesdays except last Wednesday of each month). $150.00. Forecaster, 19623 Ventura Boulevard, Tarzana CA 91356. **Tel** (818)345-4421, FAX (818)345-0468. **ED** John Kamin. Index available. cum. index. ctrl circ.

LC HC10 .E416 **ISSN** 0090-9467
DD 330.9/04 US
CEASED
FOREIGN ECONOMIC TRENDS AND THEIR IMPLICATIONS FOR THE UNITED STATES. VFOAT FET. ET 69 (1969)-(1993).
Government Publication. English. Superintendent of Documents, US Government Printing Office, Washington DC 20402. **Tel** (202)275-3328, FAX (202)786-2377. available on microfilm and microfiche from University Microfilms International (UMI). Documents available from Documents on Demand. **Continues** Economic Trends and Their Implications for the United States, 0090-9424.
Desc: Includes key economic indicators, a brief summary of the state of the economy of the subject country, the current situation and economic trends, industrial report, agricultural report, foreign trade situation, living costs, monetary situation, and conclusions and implications for the United States.
Ind/Abst Am. Bibliogr. Slavic East Europ. Stud.; Am. Stat. Index; Predicasts Forecasts.

LC HD30.42.A9 A95a
AU
FORSCHUNG UND DOKUMENTATION IN OESTERREICH. Main/Corp Austria.
Bundeskammer der Gewerblichen Wirtschaft, Vienna. Abteilung fur Statistik und Dokumentation. (19??)-. German. Every 3 years. Bundeskammer der Gewerblichen Wirtschaft, Wiedner Hauptstrasse 63, A-1040 Vienna Austria. **Tel** 0222 65 05 DW 4110, telex 111 871 BUKA. **Circ:** 800.

LC HC186 .F67
DD 330.981/005 BL
FORUM GAZETA MERCANTIL. 1 (1981)-.
Periodical. Portuguese. One time a year. Editora Jornalistica Gazeta Mercantil SA, rue Major Quedinho 90, Sao Paulo SP Brazil.

ISSN 1054-5514
DD 944 US
FRANCE (SYRACUSE, N.Y.). (FRANCE : A POLITICAL AND ECONOMIC FORECAST / POLITICAL RISK SERVICES.). [France]. Added/Corp Political Risk Services (IBC USA (Publications) Inc.). (19??)-. English. $325.00. Political Risk Services, 6320 Fly Road, Suite 102, PO Box 248, East Syracuse NY 13057-0248. **Tel** (315)431-0511, FAX (315)431-0200.
Desc: Assesses the factors affecting the prospects for business and trade. Each report focuses specifically on business needs such as finding and developing markets, determining currency movements, or making judgements about capital investments or corporate security.

LC HC271
GW
FRANKREICH : WIRTSCHAFT IN ZAHLEN UND WIRTSCHAFTSDOKUMENTATION.
Main/Corp Bundesstelle fur Aussenhandelsinformation (Germany). German. DM4.00. Bundesstelle fuer Aussenhandelsinformation, Agrippastrasse 87 93, D-50676 Cologne Germany. **Tel** 011 49 221 2057316, FAX 011 49 221 2057212.

LC HC337.P7 F84
PL
FUNDAMENTY. (19??)-. Periodical. Polish.
Centrala Kolportazu Prasy I Wydawnictw RSW Prasa-Ksiazka-Ruch, Ul Towarowa 28, 00-958 Warszawa Poland.

ISSN 1054-5522
DD 967 US
GABON (SYRACUSE, N.Y.). (GABON : A POLITICAL AND ECONOMIC FORECAST / POLITICAL RISK SERVICES.). [Gabon]. Added/Corp Political Risk Services (IBC USA (Publications) Inc.). (19??)-. English. $325.00. Political Risk Services, 6320 Fly Road, Suite 102, PO Box 248, East Syracuse NY 13057-0248. **Tel** (315)431-0511, FAX (315)431-0200.
Desc: Assesses the factors affecting the prospects for business and trade. Each report focuses specifically on business needs such as finding and developing markets, determining currency movements, or making judgements about capital investments or corporate security.

LC HC
DD 330.9 GW
GABUN, WIRTSCHAFTSDATEN UND WIRTSCHAFTSDOKUMENTATION.
Added/Corp Bundesstelle feur Aussenhandelsinformation (Germany). (Aug. 1984)-. German. DM3.00. Bundesstelle fuer Aussenhandelsinformation, Agrippastrasse 87 93, D-50676 Cologne Germany. **Tel** 011 49 221 2057316, FAX 011 49 221 2057212. **Continues** Gabun, Wirtschaftsdaten.

BL
GAZETA MERCANTIL. (1920)-. Periodical.
Portuguese. One time a week. $545.00. Gazeta Mercantil Jornal SA, Rua Major Quedinho 90 5 Andar, 01050 Sao Paulo Brazil. **Tel** 011 55 11 2563133. **(Subscription address:** Ana Magalhaes, PO Box 994, New York NY 10163. **Tel** (914)665-9867, FAX (914)665-9699.) **Ad Acc, Adv Mgr:** M. Fares. **Circ:** 1,500.
Ind/Abst Chem. Bus. Bull.; Chem. Bus. NewsBase (1986-); Chem. Bus. Update.

LC HC186 .G38
DD 330.981/005 US
GAZETA MERCANTIL (NEW YORK WEEKLY EDITION). (GAZETA MERCANTIL.).
(19??)-. Periodical. English (English). One time a week. $185.00. Gazeta Mercantil / New York, SA Editora Jornalistica, Room 930, 220 East 42nd Street, New York NY.
Ind/Abst PROMT.

ISSN 0072-0534
GW
GEGENWARTSFRAGEN DER OST-WIRTSCHAFT. Added/Corp Munich.
Universitat. Seminar fur Wirtschaft und Gesellschaft Osteuropa. Vol. 1 (1966)-. Monographic series. German. Price varies per volume. Gunter Olzog Verlag GmbH, Thierschstrabe 11, 8 Munich 22 Germany.

LC HC107.A43 P634 **ISSN** 0192-3218
DD 336.1/85 US
GEOGRAPHIC DISTRIBUTION OF FEDERAL FUNDS IN ALABAMA.
(1976/77)-. Government Publication. English. One time a year. National Technical Information Service - NTIS, Room 2027S, 5285 Port Royal Road, Springfield VA 22161. **Tel** (703)487-4630, (703)487-4660, (703)487-4650, FAX (703)321-8547, telex 89-9405. available on microfiche. **Continues** Federal Outlays in Alabama, 0362-207X.
Desc: Includes data for the executive branch of the federal government only.

LC HC107.A47 P639 **ISSN** 0162-0576
DD 336.1/85 US
GEOGRAPHIC DISTRIBUTION OF FEDERAL FUNDS IN ALASKA. (1976/77)-.
Government Publication. English. One time a year. National Technical Information Service - NTIS, Room 2027S, 5285 Port Royal Road, Springfield VA 22161. **Tel** (703)487-4630, (703)487-4660, (703)487-4650, FAX (703)321-8547, telex 89-9405. available on microfiche. **Continues** Federal Outlays in Alaska, 0362-2088.
Desc: Includes data for the executive branch of the federal government only.

LC HC107.A63 P6372 **ISSN** 0161-9799
DD 336.1/85 US
GEOGRAPHIC DISTRIBUTION OF FEDERAL FUNDS IN ARIZONA. (1976/77)-.
Government Publication. English. One time a year. National Technical Information Service - NTIS, Room 2027S, 5285 Port Royal Road, Springfield VA 22161. **Tel** (703)487-4630, (703)487-4660, (703)487-4650, FAX (703)321-8547, telex 89-9405. available on microfiche. **Continues** Federal Outlays in Arizona, 0362-2266.
Desc: Includes data for the executive branch of the federal government only.

LC HC107.A83 P634 **ISSN** 0162-0398
DD 336.1/85 US
GEOGRAPHIC DISTRIBUTION OF FEDERAL FUNDS IN ARKANSAS.
(1976/77)-. Government Publication. English. One time a year. National Technical Information Service - NTIS, Room 2027S, 5285 Port Royal Road, Springfield VA 22161. **Tel** (703)487-4630, (703)487-4660, (703)487-4650, FAX (703)321-8547, telex 89-9405. available on microfiche. **Continues** Federal Outlays in Arkansas, 0362-2096.
Desc: Includes data for the executive branch of the federal government only.

LC HC107.C23 P634 **ISSN** 0162-0479
DD 336.1/85 US
GEOGRAPHIC DISTRIBUTION OF FEDERAL FUNDS IN CALIFORNIA.
Added/Corp United States. Community Services Administration. United States. Community Services Administration. Office of the Controller. United States. Executive Office of the President. (1977)-. English. One time a year. National Technical Information Service - NTIS, Room 2027S, 5285 Port Royal Road, Springfield VA 22161. **Tel** (703)487-4630, (703)487-4660, (703)487-4650, FAX (703)321-8547, telex 89-9405. available on microfiche. **Continues** Federal Outlays in California, 0362-2126.
Desc: Includes data for the executive branch of the federal government.

Business and Economics —Economic History, Conditions

LC HC107.C73 P6382 ISSN 0161-8997
DD 338.97 US
GEOGRAPHIC DISTRIBUTION OF FEDERAL FUNDS IN COLORADO. (1976/77)-. Government Publication. English. One time a year. National Technical Information Service - NTIS, Room 2027S, 5285 Port Royal Road, Springfield VA 22161. **Tel** (703)487-4630, (703)487-4660, (703)487-4650, FAX (703)321-8547, telex 89-9405. available on microfiche. ***Continues*** *Federal Outlays in Colorado, 0362-2118.*
Desc: Includes data for the executive branch of the federal government only.

LC HC107.C83 P6362 ISSN 0190-1230
DD 336.1/85 US
GEOGRAPHIC DISTRIBUTION OF FEDERAL FUNDS IN CONNECTICUT. (1976/77)-. Government Publication. English. One time a year. National Technical Information Service - NTIS, Room 2027S, 5285 Port Royal Road, Springfield VA 22161. **Tel** (703)487-4630, (703)487-4660, (703)487-4650, FAX (703)321-8547, telex 89-9405. available on microfiche. ***Continues*** *Federal Outlays in Connecticut, 0362-2134.*
Desc: Includes data for the executive branch of the federal government only.

LC HC107.D33 P637 ISSN 0162-0711
DD 336.1/85 US
GEOGRAPHIC DISTRIBUTION OF FEDERAL FUNDS IN DELAWARE. (1976/77)-. Government Publication. English. One time a year. National Technical Information Service - NTIS, Room 2027S, 5285 Port Royal Road, Springfield VA 22161. **Tel** (703)487-4630, (703)487-4660, (703)487-4650, FAX (703)321-8547, telex 89-9405. available on microfiche. ***Continues*** *Federal Outlays in Delaware, 0362-2703.*
Desc: Includes data for the executive branch of the federal government only.

LC HC108.W3 U67 ISSN 0192-3722
DD 336.1/85 US
GEOGRAPHIC DISTRIBUTION OF FEDERAL FUNDS IN DISTRICT OF COLUMBIA. (1976/77)-. Government Publication. English. One time a year. National Technical Information Service - NTIS, Room 2027S, 5285 Port Royal Road, Springfield VA 22161. **Tel** (703)487-4630, (703)487-4660, (703)487-4650, FAX (703)321-8547, telex 89-9405. available on microfiche. ***Continues*** *Federal Outlays in District of Columbia, 0362-269X.*
Desc: Includes data for the executive branch of the federal government only.

LC HC107.F63 P633 ISSN 0162-0495
DD 336.1/85 US
GEOGRAPHIC DISTRIBUTION OF FEDERAL FUNDS IN FLORIDA. (1976/77)-. Government Publication. English. One time a year. National Technical Information Service - NTIS, Room 2027S, 5285 Port Royal Road, Springfield VA 22161. **Tel** (703)487-4630, (703)487-4660, (703)487-4650, FAX (703)321-8547, telex 89-9405. available on microfiche. ***Continues*** *Federal Outlays in Florida, 0362-2029.*
Desc: Includes data for the executive branch of the federal government only.

LC HC107.G43 P637 ISSN 0162-0754
DD 336.1/85 US
GEOGRAPHIC DISTRIBUTION OF FEDERAL FUNDS IN GEORGIA. (1976/77)-. Government Publication. English. One time a year. National Technical Information Service - NTIS, Room 2027S, 5285 Port Royal Road, Springfield VA 22161. **Tel** (703)487-4630, (703)487-4660, (703)487-4650, FAX (703)321-8547, telex 89-9405. available on microfiche. ***Continues*** *Federal Outlays in Georgia, 0362-2207.*
Desc: Includes data for the executive branch of the federal government only.

LC HC107.H33 P635 ISSN 0161-9012
DD 336.1/85 US
GEOGRAPHIC DISTRIBUTION OF FEDERAL FUNDS IN HAWAII. (1976/77)-. Government Publication. English. One time a year. National Technical Information Service - NTIS, Room 2027S, 5285 Port Royal Road, Springfield VA 22161. **Tel** (703)487-4630, (703)487-4660, (703)487-4650, FAX (703)321-8547, telex 89-9405. available on microfiche. ***Continues*** *Federal Outlays in Hawaii, 0362-2037.*
Desc: Includes data for the executive branch of the federal government only.

LC HC107.I23 P637 ISSN 0192-3803
DD 336.1/85 US
GEOGRAPHIC DISTRIBUTION OF FEDERAL FUNDS IN IDAHO. (1976/77)-. Government Publication. English. One time a year. National Technical Information Service - NTIS, Room 2027S, 5285 Port Royal Road, Springfield VA 22161. **Tel** (703)487-4630, (703)487-4660, (703)487-4650, FAX (703)321-8547, telex 89-9405. available on microfiche. ***Continues*** *Federal Outlays in Idaho, 0362-2002.*
Desc: Includes data for the executive branch of the federal government only.

LC HC107.I33 P635 ISSN 0161-9969
DD 336.1/85 US
GEOGRAPHIC DISTRIBUTION OF FEDERAL FUNDS IN ILLINOIS. (1976/77)-. Government Publication. English. One time a year. National Technical Information Service - NTIS, Room 2027S, 5285 Port Royal Road, Springfield VA 22161. **Tel** (703)487-4630, (703)487-4660, (703)487-4650, FAX (703)321-8547, telex 89-9405. available on microfiche. ***Continues*** *Federal Outlays in Illinois, 0362-2010.*
Desc: Includes data for the executive branch of the federal government only.

LC HC107.I63 P634 ISSN 0161-8989
DD 336.1/85 US
GEOGRAPHIC DISTRIBUTION OF FEDERAL FUNDS IN INDIANA. (1976/77)-. English. One time a year. National Technical Information Service - NTIS, Room 2027S, 5285 Port Royal Road, Springfield VA 22161. **Tel** (703)487-4630, (703)487-4660, (703)487-4650, FAX (703)321-8547, telex 89-9405. available on microfiche. ***Continues*** *Federal Outlays in Indiana, 0362-2681.*

LC HC107.I73 P6362 ISSN 0161-8199
DD 336.1/85 US
GEOGRAPHIC DISTRIBUTION OF FEDERAL FUNDS IN IOWA. (1976/77)-. Government Publication. English. One time a year. National Technical Information Service - NTIS, Room 2027S, 5285 Port Royal Road, Springfield VA 22161. **Tel** (703)487-4630, (703)487-4660, (703)487-4650, FAX (703)321-8547, telex 89-9405. available on microfiche. ***Continues*** *Federal Outlays in Iowa, 0362-2215.*
Desc: Includes data for the executive branch of the federal government only.

LC HC107.K23 P634 ISSN 0162-0487
DD 336.1/85 US
GEOGRAPHIC DISTRIBUTION OF FEDERAL FUNDS IN KANSAS. (1976/77)-. Government Publication. English. One time a year. National Technical Information Service - NTIS, Room 2027S, 5285 Port Royal Road, Springfield VA 22161. **Tel** (703)487-4630, (703)487-4660, (703)487-4650, FAX (703)321-8547, telex 89-9405. available on microfiche. ***Continues*** *Federal Outlays in Kansas, 0362-2223.*
Desc: Includes data for the executive branch of the federal government only.

LC HC107.K43 P6362 ISSN 0192-5024
DD 336.1/85 US
GEOGRAPHIC DISTRIBUTION OF FEDERAL FUNDS IN KENTUCKY. (1976/77)-. Government Publication. English. One time a year. National Technical Information Service - NTIS, Room 2027S, 5285 Port Royal Road, Springfield VA 22161. **Tel** (703)487-4630, (703)487-4660, (703)487-4650, FAX (703)321-8547, telex 89-9405. available on microfiche. ***Continues*** *Federal Outlays in Kentucky, 0362-2045.*
Desc: Includes data for the executive branch of the federal government only.

LC HC107.L83 P634 ISSN 0161-8547
DD 336.1/85 US
GEOGRAPHIC DISTRIBUTION OF FEDERAL FUNDS IN LOUISIANA. (1976/77)-. Government Publication. English. One time a year. National Technical Information Service - NTIS, Room 2027S, 5285 Port Royal Road, Springfield VA 22161. **Tel** (703)487-4630, (703)487-4660, (703)487-4650, FAX (703)321-8547, telex 89-9405. available on microfiche. ***Continues*** *Federal Outlays in Louisiana, 0362-2673.*
Desc: Includes data for the executive branch of the federal government only.

LC HC107.M23 P6362 ISSN 0162-0355
DD 336.1/85 US
GEOGRAPHIC DISTRIBUTION OF FEDERAL FUNDS IN MAINE. (1976/77)-. Government Publication. English. One time a year. National Technical Information Service - NTIS, Room 2027S, 5285 Port Royal Road, Springfield VA 22161. **Tel** (703)487-4630, (703)487-4660, (703)487-4650, FAX (703)321-8547, telex 89-9405. available on microfiche. ***Continues*** *Federal Outlays in Maine, 0362-2053.*
Desc: Includes data for the executive branch of the federal government only.

LC HC107.M33 P6362 ISSN 0162-1688
DD 336.1/85 US
GEOGRAPHIC DISTRIBUTION OF FEDERAL FUNDS IN MARYLAND. (1976/77)-. Government Publication. English. One time a year. National Technical Information Service - NTIS, Room 2027S, 5285 Port Royal Road, Springfield VA 22161. **Tel** (703)487-4630, (703)487-4660, (703)487-4650, FAX (703)321-8547, telex 89-9405. available on microfiche. ***Continues*** *Federal Outlays in Maryland, 0362-2231.*
Desc: Includes data for the executive branch of the federal government only.

LC HC107.M43 P6382 ISSN 0162-0622
DD 336.1/85 US
GEOGRAPHIC DISTRIBUTION OF FEDERAL FUNDS IN MASSACHUSETTS. (1976/77)-. Government Publication. English. One time a year. National Technical Information Service - NTIS, Room 2027S, 5285 Port Royal Road, Springfield VA 22161. **Tel** (703)487-4630, (703)487-4660, (703)487-4650, FAX (703)321-8547, telex 89-9405. available on microfiche. ***Continues*** *Federal Outlays in Massachusetts, 0362-2061.*
Desc: Includes data for the executive branch of the federal government only.

LC HC107.M53 P6362 ISSN 0162-0347
DD 336.1/85 US
GEOGRAPHIC DISTRIBUTION OF FEDERAL FUNDS IN MICHIGAN. (1976/77)-. Government Publication. English. One time a year. National Technical Information Service - NTIS, Room 2027S, 5285 Port Royal Road, Springfield VA 22161. **Tel** (703)487-4630, (703)487-4660, (703)487-4650, FAX (703)321-8547, telex 89-9405. available on microfiche. ***Continues*** *Federal Outlays in Michigan, 0362-224X.*
Desc: Includes data for the executive branch of the federal government only.

LC HC107.M63 P634 ISSN 0161-8539
DD 336.1/85 US
GEOGRAPHIC DISTRIBUTION OF FEDERAL FUNDS IN MINNESOTA. (1976/77)-. Newsletter. English. One time a year. National Technical Information Service - NTIS, Room 2027S, 5285 Port Royal Road, Springfield VA 22161. **Tel** (703)487-4630, (703)487-4660, (703)487-4650, FAX (703)321-8547, telex 89-9405. available on microfiche. ***Continues*** *Federal Outlays in Minnesota, 0362-2274.*
Desc: Includes data for the exectuive branch of the federal government only.

LC HC107.M73 P634 ISSN 0162-1874
DD 336.1/85 US
GEOGRAPHIC DISTRIBUTION OF FEDERAL FUNDS IN MISSISSIPPI. (1976/77)-. Government Publication. English. One time a year. National Technical Information Service - NTIS, Room 2027S, 5285 Port Royal Road, Springfield VA 22161. **Tel** (703)487-4630, (703)487-4660, (703)487-4650, FAX (703)321-8547, telex 89-9405. available on microfiche. ***Continues*** *Federal Outlays in Mississippi, 0362-210X.*
Desc: Includes data for the executive branch of the federal government only.

LC HC107.M83 P6362 ISSN 0161-9985
DD 336.1/85 US
GEOGRAPHIC DISTRIBUTION OF FEDERAL FUNDS IN MISSOURI. (1976/77)-. Government Publication. English. One time a year. National Technical Information Service - NTIS, Room 2027S, 5285 Port Royal Road, Springfield VA 22161. **Tel** (703)487-4630, (703)487-4660, (703)487-4650, FAX (703)321-8547, telex 89-9405. available on microfiche. ***Continues*** *Federal Outlays in Missouri, 0362-2290.*
Desc: Includes data for the executive branch of the federal government only.

LC HC107.M93 P6352 ISSN 0162-0460
DD 336.1/85 US
GEOGRAPHIC DISTRIBUTION OF FEDERAL FUNDS IN MONTANA. (1976/77)-. Government Publication. English. One time a year. National Technical Information Service - NTIS, Room 2027S, 5285 Port Royal Road, Springfield VA 22161. **Tel** (703)487-4630, (703)487-4660, (703)487-4650, FAX (703)321-8547, telex 89-9405. available on microfiche. ***Continues*** *Federal Outlays in Montana, 0362-2282.*
Desc: Includes data for the executive branch of the federal government only.

LC HC107.N23 P6362 ISSN 0161-9128
DD 336.1/85 US
GEOGRAPHIC DISTRIBUTION OF FEDERAL FUNDS IN NEBRASKA. (1976/77)-. Government Publication. English. One time a year. National Technical Information Service - NTIS, Room 2027S, 5285 Port Royal Road, Springfield VA 22161. **Tel** (703)487-4630, (703)487-4660, (703)487-4650, FAX (703)321-8547, telex 89-9405. available on microfiche. ***Continues*** *Federal Outlays in Nebraska, 0362-2304.*
Desc: Includes data for the executive branch of the federal government only.

LC HC107.N33 P637 ISSN 0162-0991
DD 336.1/85 US
GEOGRAPHIC DISTRIBUTION OF FEDERAL FUNDS IN NEVADA. (1976/77)-. Government Publication. English. One time a year. National Technical Information Service - NTIS, Room

Business and Economics —Economic History, Conditions

2027S, 5285 Port Royal Road, Springfield VA 22161. **Tel** (703)487-4630, (703)487-4660, (703)487-4650, FAX (703)321-8547, telex 89-9405. available on microfiche. **Continues** *Federal Outlays in Nevada, 0362-2312.*
Desc: Includes data for the executive branch of the federal government only.

LC HC107.N43 P637 **ISSN** 0161-8911
DD 336.1/85 US
GEOGRAPHIC DISTRIBUTION OF FEDERAL FUNDS IN NEW HAMPSHIRE.
(1976/77)-. Government Publication. English. One time a year. National Technical Information Service - NTIS, Room 2027S, 5285 Port Royal Road, Springfield VA 22161. **Tel** (703)487-4630, (703)487-4660, (703)487-4650, FAX (703)321-8547, telex 89-9405. available on microfiche. **Continues** *Federal Outlays in New Hampshire, 0362-2339.*
Desc: Includes data for the executive branch of the federal government only.

LC HC107.N53 P637 **ISSN** 0162-1769
DD 338.97 US
GEOGRAPHIC DISTRIBUTION OF FEDERAL FUNDS IN NEW JERSEY.
(1976/77)-. Government Publication. English. One time a year. National Technical Information Service - NTIS, Room 2027S, 5285 Port Royal Road, Springfield VA 22161. **Tel** (703)487-4630, (703)487-4660, (703)487-4650, FAX (703)321-8547, telex 89-9405. available on microfiche. **Continues** *Federal Outlays in New Jersey, 0362-2320.*
Desc: Includes data for the executive branch of the federal government only.

LC HC107.N63 P634 **ISSN** 0162-0509
DD 336.1/85 US
GEOGRAPHIC DISTRIBUTION OF FEDERAL FUNDS IN NEW MEXICO.
(1976/77)-. Government Publication. English. One time a year. National Technical Information Service - NTIS, Room 2027S, 5285 Port Royal Road, Springfield VA 22161. **Tel** (703)487-4630, (703)487-4660, (703)487-4650, FAX (703)321-8547, telex 89-9405. available on microfiche. **Continues** *Federal Outlays in New Mexico, 0362-2150.*
Desc: Includes data for the executive branch of the federal government only.

LC HC107.N73 P6362 **ISSN** 0162-9492
DD 336.1/85 US
GEOGRAPHIC DISTRIBUTION OF FEDERAL FUNDS IN NEW YORK.
(1976/77)-. Government Publication. English. One time a year. National Technical Information Service - NTIS, Room 2027S, 5285 Port Royal Road, Springfield VA 22161. **Tel** (703)487-4630, (703)487-4660, (703)487-4650, FAX (703)321-8547, telex 89-9405. available on microfiche. **Continues** *Federal Outlays in New York, 0362-2142.*
Desc: Includes data for the executive branch of the federal government only.

LC HC107.N83 P6362 **ISSN** 0161-9802
DD 336.1/85 US
GEOGRAPHIC DISTRIBUTION OF FEDERAL FUNDS IN NORTH CAROLINA.
(1976/77)-. Government Publication. English. One time a year. National Technical Information Service - NTIS, Room 2027S, 5285 Port Royal Road, Springfield VA 22161. **Tel** (703)487-4630, (703)487-4660, (703)487-4650, FAX (703)321-8547, telex 89-9405. available on microfiche. **Continues** *Federal Outlays in North Carolina, 0362-2347.*
Desc: Includes data for the executive branch of the federal government only.

LC HC107.N93 P637 **ISSN** 0162-0452
DD 336.1/85 US
GEOGRAPHIC DISTRIBUTION OF FEDERAL FUNDS IN NORTH DAKOTA.
(1976/77)-. Government Publication. English. One time a year. National Technical Information Service - NTIS, Room 2027S, 5285 Port Royal Road, Springfield VA 22161. **Tel** (703)487-4630, (703)487-4660, (703)487-4650, FAX (703)321-8547, telex 89-9405. available on microfiche. **Continues** *Federal Outlays in North Dakota, 0362-2355.*
Desc: Includes data for the executive branch of the federal government only.

LC HC107.O323 P6362 **ISSN** 0161-8962
DD 336.1/85 US
GEOGRAPHIC DISTRIBUTION OF FEDERAL FUNDS IN OHIO.
(1976/77)-. Government Publication. English. One time a year. National Technical Information Service - NTIS, Room 2027S, 5285 Port Royal Road, Springfield VA 22161. **Tel** (703)487-4630, (703)487-4660, (703)487-4650, FAX (703)321-8547, telex 89-9405. available on microfiche. **Continues** *Federal Outlays in Ohio, 0362-2177.*
Desc: Includes data for the executive branch of the federal government only.

LC HC107.O53 P634 **ISSN** 0162-1882
DD 336.1/85 US
GEOGRAPHIC DISTRIBUTION OF FEDERAL FUNDS IN OKLAHOMA.
(1976/77)-. Government Publication. English. One time a year. National Technical Information Service - NTIS, Room 2027S, 5285 Port Royal Road, Springfield VA 22161. **Tel** (703)487-4630, (703)487-4660, (703)487-4650, FAX (703)321-8547, telex 89-9405. available on microfiche. **Continues** *Federal Outlays in Oklahoma, 0362-2657.*
Desc: Includes data for the executive branch of the federal government only.

LC HC107.O73 P637 **ISSN** 0161-8512
DD 336.1/85 US
GEOGRAPHIC DISTRIBUTION OF FEDERAL FUNDS IN OREGON.
(1976/77)-. Government Publication. English. One time a year. National Technical Information Service - NTIS, Room 2027S, 5285 Port Royal Road, Springfield VA 22161. **Tel** (703)487-4630, (703)487-4660, (703)487-4650, FAX (703)321-8547, telex 89-9405. available on microfiche. **Continues** *Federal Outlays in Oregon, 0362-2169.*
Desc: Includes data for the executive branch of the federal government only.

LC HC107.P43 P6362 **ISSN** 0161-8873
DD 336.1/85 US
GEOGRAPHIC DISTRIBUTION OF FEDERAL FUNDS IN PENNSYLVANIA.
(1976/77)-. Government Publication. English. One time a year. National Technical Information Service - NTIS, Room 2027S, 5285 Port Royal Road, Springfield VA 22161. **Tel** (703)487-4630, (703)487-4660, (703)487-4650, FAX (703)321-8547, telex 89-9405. available on microfiche. **Continues** *Federal Outlays in Pennsylvania, 0362-2398.*
Desc: Includes data for the executive branch of the federal government only.

LC HC107.R43 P634 **ISSN** 0161-8849
DD 336.1/85 US
GEOGRAPHIC DISTRIBUTION OF FEDERAL FUNDS IN RHODE ISLAND.
(1976/77)-. Government Publication. English. One time a year. National Technical Information Service - NTIS, Room 2027S, 5285 Port Royal Road, Springfield VA 22161. **Tel** (703)487-4630, (703)487-4660, (703)487-4650, FAX (703)321-8547, telex 89-9405. available on microfiche. **Continues** *Federal Outlays in Rhode Island, 0362-2193.*
Desc: Includes data for the executive branch of the federal government only.

LC HC107.S73 P635A **ISSN** 0161-8970
DD 336.1/85 US
GEOGRAPHIC DISTRIBUTION OF FEDERAL FUNDS IN SOUTH CAROLINA.
(1976/77)-. Government Publication. English. One time a year. National Technical Information Service - NTIS, Room 2027S, 5285 Port Royal Road, Springfield VA 22161. **Tel** (703)487-4630, (703)487-4660, (703)487-4650, FAX (703)321-8547, telex 89-9405. available on microfiche. **Continues** *Federal Outlays in South Carolina, 0362-3998.*
Desc: Includes data for the executive branch of the federal government only.

LC HC107.S83 P634 **ISSN** 0161-9101
DD 336.1/85 US
GEOGRAPHIC DISTRIBUTION OF FEDERAL FUNDS IN SOUTH DAKOTA.
(1976/77)-. Government Publication. English. One time a year. National Technical Information Service - NTIS, Room 2027S, 5285 Port Royal Road, Springfield VA 22161. **Tel** (703)487-4630, (703)487-4660, (703)487-4650, FAX (703)321-8547, telex 89-9405. available on microfiche. **Continues** *Federal Outlays in South Dakota, 0362-2185.*
Desc: Includes data for the executive branch of the federal government only.

LC HC107.T33 P6362 **ISSN** 0162-1548
DD 336.1/85 US
GEOGRAPHIC DISTRIBUTION OF FEDERAL FUNDS IN TENNESSEE.
(1976/77)-. Government Publication. English. One time a year. National Technical Information Service - NTIS, Room 2027S, 5285 Port Royal Road, Springfield VA 22161. **Tel** (703)487-4630, (703)487-4660, (703)487-4650, FAX (703)321-8547, telex 89-9405. available on microfiche. **Continues** *Federal Outlays in Tennessee, 0362-238X.*
Desc: Includes data for the executive branch of the federal government only.

LC HC109 .U53A **ISSN** 0162-3419
DD 336.1/85 US
GEOGRAPHIC DISTRIBUTION OF FEDERAL FUNDS IN TERRITORIES & OTHER AREAS ADMINISTERED BY THE U.S.
VAT Geographic Distribution of Federal Funds in Territories and Other Areas Administered by the United States. (1976/77)-. Government Publication. English. One time a year. National Technical Information Service - NTIS, Room 2027S, 5285 Port Royal Road, Springfield VA 22161. **Tel** (703)487-4630, (703)487-4660, (703)487-4650, FAX (703)321-8547, telex 89-9405. available on microfiche. **Continues** *Federal Outlays in Territories & Other Areas Administered by the U.S., 0362-126X.*
Desc: Includes data for the executive branch of the federal government only.

LC HC107.T43 P6362 **ISSN** 0161-8881
DD 336.1/85 US
GEOGRAPHIC DISTRIBUTION OF FEDERAL FUNDS IN TEXAS.
(1976/77)-. Government Publication. English. One time a year. National Technical Information Service - NTIS, Room 2027S, 5285 Port Royal Road, Springfield VA 22161. **Tel** (703)487-4630, (703)487-4660, (703)487-4650, FAX (703)321-8547, telex 89-9405. available on microfiche. **Continues** *Federal Outlays in Texas, 0362-2371.*
Desc: Includes data for the executive branch of the federal government only.

LC HC107.U83 P634 **ISSN** 0161-9195
DD 336.1/85 US
GEOGRAPHIC DISTRIBUTION OF FEDERAL FUNDS IN UTAH.
(1976/77)-. Government Publication. English. One time a year. National Technical Information Service - NTIS, Room 2027S, 5285 Port Royal Road, Springfield VA 22161. **Tel** (703)487-4630, (703)487-4660, (703)487-4650, FAX (703)321-8547, telex 89-9405. available on microfiche. **Continues** *Federal Outlays in Utah, 0362-2258.*
Desc: Includes data for the executive branch of the federal government only.

LC HC107.V53 P6375 **ISSN** 0163-335X
DD 336.1/85 US
GEOGRAPHIC DISTRIBUTION OF FEDERAL FUNDS IN VERMONT.
(1976/77)-. Government Publication. English. One time a year. National Technical Information Service - NTIS, Room 2027S, 5285 Port Royal Road, Springfield VA 22161. **Tel** (703)487-4630, (703)487-4660, (703)487-4650, FAX (703)321-8547, telex 89-9405. available on microfiche. **Continues** *Federal Outlays in Vermont, 0362-2665.*
Desc: Includes data for the executive branch of the federal government only.

LC HC107.V83 P6362 **ISSN** 0161-892X
DD 336.1/85 US
GEOGRAPHIC DISTRIBUTION OF FEDERAL FUNDS IN VIRGINIA.
(1976/77)-. Government Publication. English. One time a year. National Technical Information Service - NTIS, Room 2027S, 5285 Port Royal Road, Springfield VA 22161. **Tel** (703)487-4630, (703)487-4660, (703)487-4650, FAX (703)321-8547, telex 89-9405. available on microfiche. **Continues** *Federal Outlays in Virginia, 0362-2541.*
Desc: Includes data for the executive branch of the federal government only.

LC HC107.W23 P6362 **ISSN** 0161-8520
DD 336.1/85 US
GEOGRAPHIC DISTRIBUTION OF FEDERAL FUNDS IN WASHINGTON.
Added/Corp United States. Community Services Administration. United States. Community Services Administration. Office of the Controller. United States. Executive Office of the President. (1977)-. English. One time a year. National Technical Information Service - NTIS, Room 2027S, 5285 Port Royal Road, Springfield VA 22161. **Tel** (703)487-4630, (703)487-4660, (703)487-4650, FAX (703)321-8547, telex 89-9405. available on microfiche. **Continues** *Federal Outlays in Washington, 0362-2533.*
Desc: Includes data for the executive branch of the federal government only.

LC HC107.W53 .P6362 **ISSN** 0161-8636
DD 336.1/85 US
GEOGRAPHIC DISTRIBUTION OF FEDERAL FUNDS IN WEST VIRGINIA.
(1976/77)-. Government Publication. English. One time a year. National Technical Information Service - NTIS, Room 2027S, 5285 Port Royal Road, Springfield VA 22161. **Tel** (703)487-4630, (703)487-4660, (703)487-4650, FAX (703)321-8547, telex 89-9405. available on microfiche. **Continues** *Federal Outlays in West Virginia, 0362-255X.*
Desc: Includes data for the executive branch of the federal government only.

LC HC107.W63 P6362 **ISSN** 0161-9187
DD 336.1/85 US
GEOGRAPHIC DISTRIBUTION OF FEDERAL FUNDS IN WISCONSIN.
(1976/77)-. Government Publication. English. One time a year. National Technical Information Service - NTIS, Room 2027S, 5285 Port Royal Road, Springfield VA 22161. **Tel** (703)487-4630, (703)487-4660, (703)487-4650, FAX (703)321-8547, telex 89-9405. available on microfiche. **Continues** *Federal Outlays in Wisconsin, 0362-2568.*
Desc: Includes data for the executive branch of the federal government only.

Business and Economics —Economic History, Conditions

LC HC107.W93 P6372 **ISSN** 0161-889X
DD 336.1/85 US
GEOGRAPHIC DISTRIBUTION OF FEDERAL FUNDS IN WYOMING. (1976/77)-. Government Publication. English. One time a year. National Technical Information Service - NTIS, Room 2027S, 5285 Port Royal Road, Springfield VA 22161. **Tel** (703)487-4630, (703)487-4660, (703)487-4650, FAX (703)321-8547, telex 89-9405. available on microfiche. **Continues** Federal Outlays in Wyoming, 0362-2363.
Desc: Includes data for the executive branch of the federal government only.

LC HC14 .G47 **ISSN** 0722-2416
DD 330.9/005 GW
GERMAN YEARBOOK ON BUSINESS HISTORY. **Added/Corp** Gesellschaft fuer Unternehmensgeschichte. Institut fuer Bankhistorische Forschung. (1981)-. English. One time a year. Springer-Verlag GmbH & Company KG, Heidelberger Platz 3, D-14197 Berlin Germany. **Tel** 011 49 30 8207223, FAX 011 49 30 8214091, telex 183 319 SPBLN D. **(Subscription address:** Springer-Verlag New York Inc. / North America, PO Box 2485, Journal Fulfillment, Secaucus NJ 07096. **Tel** (201)348-4033, (800)777-4643, FAX (201)348-4505.)

ISSN 1056-4721
DD 943 US
GERMANY (SYRACUSE, N.Y.). (GERMANY : A POLITICAL AND ECONOMIC FORECAST / POLITICAL RISK SERVICES.). [Germany]. **Added/Corp** Political Risk Services (IBC USA (Publications) Inc.). (Apr. 1, 1991)-. Periodical. English. $325.00. Political Risk Services, 6320 Fly Road, Suite 102, PO Box 248, East Syracuse NY 13057-0248. **Tel** (315)431-0511, FAX (315)431-0200.
Desc: Assesses the factors affecting the prospects for business and trade. Each report focuses specifically on business needs such as finding and developing markets, determining currency movements, or making judgements about capital investments or corporate security.

LC HC517.G6 G455
DD 330.9/667/05 GH
GHANA ECONOMIC REVIEW. (1970)-. Periodical. English. Ghana Economic Review, PO Box 5743, Accra Ghana.

LC HC517.G6
GW
GHANA : WIRTSCHAFTLICHE ENTWICKLUNG. **Main/Corp** Bundesstelle fur Aussenhandelsinformation (Germany). German. DM2.00. Bundesstelle fuer Aussenhandelsinformation, Agrippastrasse 87 93, D-50676 Cologne Germany. **Tel** 011 49 221 2057316, FAX 011 49 221 2057212.

LC HC517.G6
GW
GHANA : WIRTSCHAFTSDATEN UND WIRTSCHAFTSDOKUMENTATION. **Main/Corp** Bundesstelle fur Aussenhandelsinformation (Germany). German. DM2.00. Bundesstelle fuer Aussenhandelsinformation, Agrippastrasse 87 93, D-50676 Cologne Germany. **Tel** 011 49 221 2057316, FAX 011 49 221 2057212.

LC HC995.A1 G5
DD 338/.0025/67113 CM
GICOCAM : GUIDE INDUSTRIEL & COMMERCIAL DU CAMEROUN. VFOAT Guide Industriel & Commercial du Cameroun; Guide Industriel et Commercial du Cameroun. French. 1.000CFAF. Gicocam, B P 1455 R C No H-289 Street, 14776 Oi E Yaounde Cameroon.

LC HC10 .A66 US
DD 330.9/09/049
GLOBAL ALTERNATIVE SCENARIOS. **Added/Corp** WEFA Group. Periodical. English. Two times a year. WEFA / Philadelphia, PO Box 8500, Suite 1995, Philadelphia PA 19178. **Tel** (215)667-6000, telex 710 6700575. **Continues** Alternative Global Scenarios.

LC HC462.9 .N4864b
JA
GOKANEN KEIZAI YOSOKU. **Main/Corp** Nihon Keizai Kenkyu Senta. Issue No. 1 (1975-1979)-. Periodical. Japanese. Nihon Keizai Kenkyu Senta, c/o Nikkei Building, 9-5 Otemachi 1-chome Chiyoda-ku, Tokyo 100 Japan.

US
GOLD & BLACK ILLUSTRATED. (19??)-. English. Irregular. $31.95. Boilers Inc, 3530 State Road 26 East, Suite G, Lafayette IN 47905. **Tel** (317)477-7022.

LC HC337.P7 G585 **ISSN** 0867-0005
PL
GOSPODARKA NARODOWA (WARSAW, POLAND : 1990). (GOSPODARKA NARODOWA). Vol. 1, No. 1 (1990)-. Periodical. Polish. Twelve times a year. Price on request. **(Subscription address:** Ars Polona-Ruch, PO Box 1001, Krakowskie Przedmiescie 7, 00-068 Warsaw Poland. **Tel** 011 48 22 261201.) **Continues** Gospodarka Planowa, 0017-2421.

LC HC108.W3 W27 **ISSN** 0274-5496
DD 330.9753/005 US
GREATER WASHINGTON BOARD OF TRADE NEWS, THE. **Added/Corp** Greater Washington Board of Trade. VFOAT Board of Trade News. (19??)-. Periodical. English. Eleven times a year. $120.00. Greater Washington Board of Trade, 1129 20th Street Northwest, Suite 200, Washington DC 20036. **Tel** (202)857-5900, FAX (202)223-2648. **ED** Sandra W. Rubenstein (editor's phone: (202)857-5943). **Ad Acc**, **Adv Mgr:** Suzanne Trump-Warring, **Tel** (202)857-5944. **Circ:** 5,500 (ctrl). **Continues** Metropolitan Washington Board of Trade News, 0026-1599.

ISSN 1054-5530
DD 949 US
GREECE (SYRACUSE, N.Y.). (GREECE : A POLITICAL AND ECONOMIC FORECAST / POLITICAL RISK SERVICES.). [Greece]. **Added/Corp** Political Risk Services (IBC USA (Publications) Inc.). (19??)-. English. $325.00. Political Risk Services, 6320 Fly Road, Suite 102, PO Box 248, East Syracuse NY 13057-0248. **Tel** (315)431-0511, FAX (315)431-0200.
Desc: Assesses the factors affecting the prospects for business and trade. Each report focuses specifically on business needs such as finding and developing markets, determining currency movements, or making judgements about capital investments or corporate security.

LC HC291 .G753
DD 330.9495/005 GR
GREECE'S WEEKLY FOR BUSINESS & FINANCE YEARBOOK. VFOAT Greece's Weekly for Business and Finance Yearbook; Greece's Political and Economic Almanac; B and F Yearbook; Greece's Weekly - B and F Yearbook; Greece's Political & Economic Almanac; B & F Yearbook; Greece's Weekly - B & F Yearbook. (1982)-. English. One time a week. $120.00. Coronakis Press Ltd., 10 Fokidos Street, Athens 115 26 Greece. **Tel** 011 30 1 7706922.
Ind/Abst Infomat Int. Bus.

LC HC295 .N48
GR
GREEK FORUM (KAVALA, GREECE). (GREEK FORUM.). (198?)-. Periodical. Greek, Modern (English). Twelve times a year. Oyo Seikagaku Kenkyujo, (Inst. of Applied Biochemistry), Yagi Kinen Paku Mitakecho, Kanigun Gifuken 505-01 Japan. **Continues** New Greek Forum.

GW
GRENADA, WIRTSCHAFTSDATEN / BUNDESSTELLE FUER AUSSENHANDELSINFORMATION. German. DM3.00. Bundesstelle fuer Aussenhandelsinformation, Agrippastrasse 87 93, D-50676 Cologne Germany. **Tel** 011 49 221 2057316, FAX 011 49 221 2057212.

LC HC291
GW
GRIECHENLAND : WIRTSCHAFTSDATEN UND WIRTSCHAFTSDOKUMENTATION. **Main/Corp** Bundesstelle fur Aussenhandelsinformation (Germany). German. DM2.00. Bundesstelle fuer Aussenhandelsinformation, Agrippastrasse 87 93, D-50676 Cologne Germany. **Tel** 011 49 221 2057316, FAX 011 49 221 2057212.

LC HC60 .U4844 HC79.I5 **ISSN** 0097-8698
DD 309.2/233/7301724 S 339.3/1 US
GROSS NATIONAL PRODUCT GROWTH RATES AND TREND DATA BY REGION AND COUNTRY. **Main/Corp** United States. Agency for International Development. Statistics and Reports Division. 1973-. English. US Agency for International Development, Economic Data Branch, Washington DC 20523. **Continues** Gross National Product Growth Rates and Trend Data by Region and Country.

LC HT390 .G74 **ISSN** 0017-4815
DD 301.3/72/05 US
CODEN GRCHDH
Pr Rev.
GROWTH AND CHANGE. See Housing and Urban Development.

LC HC601 .G76 **ISSN** 0085-1280
AT
GROWTH (MELBOURNE, VIC.). (GROWTH.). [Growth]. **Added/Corp** Committee for Economic Development of Australia. Vol. 1 (Sept. 1961)-. Periodical. English. Irregular. 225.00Aus$ Australia; 300.00Aus$ other. Committee for Economic Development of Australia, 123 Lonsdale Street, GPO Box 2117T, Melbourne Victoria 3000 Australia. **Tel** 011 61 03 6623544, FAX 011 61 03 6637271. Index available. **Circ:** 2,000 (ctrl).
Ind/Abst APAIS, Aust. Public Aff. Inf. Ser. (1963)-.

LC HC905.A1 G76
DD 338.968/005 SA
GROWTH (PRETORIA, SOUTH AFRICA). (GROWTH.). **Added/Corp** Corporation for Economic Development (South Africa). Vol. 1, No. 1 (May 1981)-. Periodical. English. Four times a year. R12.00. Growth Publications Pty Limited, 522 President Street, Silverton 0184 South Africa. **Tel** FAX 012-868719. **ED** Eugene Kruger. **Bk Rev**. **Ad Acc**. **Circ:** 25,000 (ctrl).
Desc: Articles and news reports concerning economic development in Southern Africa.

LC HX861 .G8 **ISSN** 0890-0280
DD 335/.83/097291 US
GUANGARA LIBERTARIA. **Added/Corp** Paul Avrich Collection (Library of Congress). VFOAT Guangara. (Winter 1980)-. Periodical. Spanish. Four times a year. Free US; $2.75 other. International Society of Historical and Social Studies, PO Box 1516 Riverside Station, Miami FL 33135. **Tel** (305)446-2788. **Bk Rev**. **Circ:** 5,000 (ctrl).

GT
GUATEMALA NEWS WATCH. **Added/Corp** Guatemalan Development Foundation. Vol. 6, No. 8 (Sept./Oct. 1991)-. Periodical. English. Twelve times a year. Fundesa, 10 65 Zona 10, Guatemala Guatemala. **Tel** 011 502 2 3279527. **(Subscription address:** Guatemala Business, 299 Alhambra, Coral Gables FL 33134. **Tel** (800)741-6133.) **Continues** Guatemala Watch.

ISSN 1054-5549
DD 972 US
GUATEMALA (SYRACUSE, N.Y.). (GUATEMALA : A POLITICAL AND ECONOMIC FORECAST.). [Guatemala]. **Added/Corp** Political Risk Services (IBC USA (Publications) Inc.). (19??)-. English. $325.00. Political Risk Services, 6320 Fly Road, Suite 102, PO Box 248, East Syracuse NY 13057-0248. **Tel** (315)431-0511, FAX (315)431-0200.
Desc: Assesses the factors affecting the prospects for business and trade. Each report focuses specifically on business needs such as finding and developing markets, determining currency movements, or making judgements about capital investments or corporate security.

LC HC144.A1 G846
DD 330.97281/005 GW
GUATEMALA, WIRTSCHAFTLICHE ENTWICKLUNG / BUNDESSTELLE FUR AUSSENHANDELSINFORMATION. German. DM3.00. Bundesstelle fuer Aussenhandelsinformation, Agrippastrasse 87 93, D-50676 Cologne Germany. **Tel** 011 49 221 2057316, FAX 011 49 221 2057212.

LC HC144.A1 G848
DD 330.97281/0021 GW
GUATEMALA, WIRTSCHAFTSDATEN. **Added/Corp** Bundesstelle fuer Aussenhandelsinformation (Germany). (19??)-. German. DM3.00. Bundesstelle fuer Aussenhandelsinformation, Agrippastrasse 87 93, D-50676 Cologne Germany. **Tel** 011 49 221 2057316, FAX 011 49 221 2057212.

LC HC144.A1
DD 330.97281 GW
GUATEMALA WIRTSCHAFTSDATEN UND WIRTSCHAFTSDOKUMENTATION / BUNDESSTELLE FUR AUSSENHANDELSINFORMATION. Periodical. German. DM2.00. Bundesstelle fuer Aussenhandelsinformation, Agrippastrasse 87 93, D-50676 Cologne Germany. **Tel** 011 49 221 2057316, FAX 011 49 221 2057212.

LC HC226 .G84
DD 380.1/029/485 PE
GUIA VERDE INDUSTRIAL Y COMERCIAL. VFOAT Guia Verde. Spanish. Sirob Ediciones S A Crnel, Andres Reyes 366, San Isidro, Lima Peru.

LC HC547.T8 G83
DD 338/.0961/1 TI
GUIDE ECONOMIQUE DE LA TUNISIE. (1976)-. Directory. French. One time a year. $100.00. Editions IEA, 16 rue de Rome, 1015 Tunis Tunisia. **Tel** FAX 011 216 2 353172. **ED** Mohamed Zerzeri. **Ad Acc**. **Circ:** 30,000 (ctrl).
Desc: Divided into five main sections, with an introduction to the Tunisian economy, and an alphabetical list of the first 5,000 Tunisian firms. Includes a list of businesses engaged in import and export.

LC HC101 .G87 **ISSN** 0072-8535
DD 338/.0973 US
GUIDE TO INDUSTRIAL PARKS AND AREA DEVELOPMENT. **Added/Corp** Resource Publications, inc. (1969)-. English. One time a year. Resource Publications, 160 East Virginia Street, Suite 290, San Jose CA 95112. **Tel** (408)286-8505.

Business and Economics —Economic History, Conditions

ISSN 1054-5557
DD 966 US
GUINEA (SYRACUSE, N.Y.). (GUINEA : A POLITICAL AND ECONOMIC FORECAST / POLITICAL RISK SERVICES.). [Guinea]. **Added/Corp** Political Risk Services (IBC USA (Publications) Inc.). (19??)-. English. $325.00. Political Risk Services, 6320 Fly Road, Suite 102, PO Box 248, East Syracuse NY 13057-0248. **Tel** (315)431-0511, FAX (315)431-0200.
Desc: Assesses the factors affecting the prospects for business and trade. Each report focuses specifically on business needs such as finding and developing markets, determining currency movements, or making judgements about capital investments or corporate security.

LC HC1030 GW
GUINEA, WIRTSCHAFTSDATEN (KURZFASSUNG), WIRTSCHAFTSDOKUMENTATION UND PROJEKTE / BUNDESSTELLE FUER AUSSENHANDELSINFORMATION.
German. DM3.00. Bundesstelle fuer Aussenhandelsinformation, Agrippastrasse 87 93, D-50676 Cologne Germany. **Tel** 011 49 221 2057316, FAX 011 49 221 2057212.

LC HC1030.A1
DD 330.966/52 GW
GUINEA WIRTSCHAFTSDATEN UND WIRTSCHAFTSDOKUMENTATION / BUNDESSTELLE FUR AUSSENHANDELSINFORMATION.
German. DM2.00. Bundesstelle fuer Aussenhandelsinformation, Agrippastrasse 87 93, D-50676 Cologne Germany. **Tel** 011 49 221 2057316, FAX 011 49 221 2057212.

LC HC206
DD 330.9/88/103 GW
GUYANA : WIRTSCHAFTLICHE ENTWICKLUNG. Main/Corp Bundesstelle fur Aussenhandelsinformation (Germany). (19??)-. German. DM2.00. Bundesstelle fuer Aussenhandelsinformation, Agrippastrasse 87 93, D-50676 Cologne Germany. **Tel** 011 49 221 2057316, FAX 011 49 221 2057212.

LC HC10 .H263 KO
HAEOE KYONGJE CHONGBO. Added/Corp Hanguk Unhaeng. (1973)-. Periodical. Korean. Twelve times a year. Hanguk Unhaeng, 110 3-ka Namdaemunro Chung-ku, Seoul Korea. **Tel** 535-5498.

ISSN 1054-5565
DD 972 US
HAITI (SYRACUSE, N.Y.). (HAITI : A POLITICAL AND ECONOMIC FORECAST / POLITICAL RISK SERVICES.). [Haiti]. **Added/Corp** Political Risk Services (IBC USA (Publications) Inc.). (19??)-. English. $325.00. Political Risk Services, 6320 Fly Road, Suite 102, PO Box 248, East Syracuse NY 13057-0248. **Tel** (315)431-0511, FAX (315)431-0200.
Desc: Assesses the factors affecting the prospects for business and trade. Each report focuses specifically on business needs such as finding and developing markets, determining currency movements, or making judgements about capital investments or corporate security.

LC HC466 .H217 KO
HAN'GUK KAEBAL YON'GU. Vol. 1 (1979)-. Periodical. Korean. Four times a year. W12,000. Korea Development Institute / Seoul, PO Box 113 Chung-Ryang, Seoul 130-650 Seoul South Korea. **Tel** 960-4815-6, FAX 82-02-961-5092, telex 25100 KDILINK K. **ED** Bon-Ho Koo. No. available. **Circ:** 1,600.
Desc: Targeted for an academic audience, presents in-depth, theoretical and empirical analyses of major issues confronting the Korean and world economics.

LC HC466 .H237 KO
HANGUK SANGPUM CHONGNAM. 1 (1980)-. Korean. One time a year. Hanguk Sangpum Chongbosa, Chungang Sasoham, 8153-Ho, Seoul Korea.

LC HC466 .H34A KO
HANIL WOLBO. Main/Corp Hanil Unhaeng (1960-). **VFOAT** Hanil Monthly. Periodical. Korean. Hanil Unhaeng, 76 Sogong-dong Chung-ku, Seoul South Korea.

ISSN 0168-9444 NE
HARVARD BUSINESS REVIEW. (HARVARD HOLLAND REVIEW.). [Harv. Holl. rev.]. No. 1 (Fall 1984)-. Periodical. Dutch. Three times a year. Fl1200.00 Netherlands; 3700F Belgium. Harvard Holland Review, Keizersgracht 618, 1016 HV Amsterdam Netherlands.

LC HF5001 .H32 US
TITLE CHANGE
HARVARD BUSINESS REVIEW CATALOG. See Business and Economics.

LC HF5001 .H32 US
●**HARVARD BUSINESS REVIEW. FIVE-YEAR INDEX. See** Business and Economics.

ISSN 0073-067X US
HARVARD STUDIES IN BUSINESS HISTORY. 1 (1931)-. Monographic series. English. Irregular. Harvard University Press, 79 Garden Street, Cambridge MA 02138. **Tel** (617)496-1344, (800)448-2242. **ED** H.M. Larson and T.R. Navin.

LC HC446 .A212C IO
HASIL RAPAT KERJA DEPARTEMEN PERINDUSTRIAN. Main/Corp Indonesia. Departemen Perindustrian. Indonesian. Departemen Perindustrian, Jalan Kebon Sirih No 36, Jakarta Indonesia.

LC HC59.7 .A745a JA
HATTEN TOJOKOKU KEIZAI TOKEI YORAN. Main/Corp Ajia Keizai Kenkyujo, Tokyo Keizai Seicho Chosabu. (19??)-. Periodical. Japanese. ¥1,000. Ajia Keizai Kenkyujo, 42 Ichigaya Honmura-cho, Shinjuku-ku Tokyo 162 Japan.

LC HC107.H3 B34a **ISSN** 1043-6685
DD 330.99969/005 US
HAWAII ANNUAL ECONOMIC REPORT. (HAWAII ... ANNUAL ECONOMIC REPORT / BANK OF HAWAII.). [Hawaii annu. econ. rep.]. **Added/Corp** Bank of Hawaii. (1984)-. Statistical Publication. English. One time a year. Free on request. Bank of Hawaii, Economics Department, PO Box 2900, Honolulu HI 96846. **Tel** (808)537-8307, FAX (808)536-9433. **Circ:** 9,000. available on diskette (statistical tables). **Continues** Bank of Hawaii. Dept. of Business Research. Hawaii Annual Economic Review, 0898-6282.
Desc: Highlights developments in Hawaii's economy. Contains statistical tables and forecasts.

LC HC430.6.Z7 H53 **ISSN** 1012-9804
DD 330.95496 NP
HIMAL. Added/Corp Himal Associates. Vol. 1, No. 1 (July 1988)-. Periodical. English. Six times a year. $35.00. Himal Association, PO Box 42, Patan Dhoka Lalitpur Nepal. **Tel** 011 977 1 523845, FAX 011 977 1 523845. **(Subscription address:** Himal Magazine, PO Box 470758, San Francisco CA 94147. **Tel** (415)434-8802.**)**

LC HC121 .H57
DD 980/.005 PE
HISLA. Added/Corp Centro Latinoamericano de Historia Economica y Social (Lima, Peru). **VFOAT** H.I.S.L.A. (1st Semester 1983)-. Periodical. Spanish. Two times a year. $35.00 (institutions); $20.00 (individuals) Latin America, $25.00 (individuals) other. HISLA, Casilla de Correos 10052, Lima 1 Peru. **Tel** 011 51 14 443064. **ED** Heraclio Bonilla. **Bk Rev. Ad Rev. Circ:** 1,000 (ctrl).
Desc: Covers rural labor markets in Peru; labor exchange; the state of economic theory in Latin America; and assesses the current state of Latin American historical studies.

LC H3 .H57
DD 300/.5 FR
HISTOIRE, ECONOMIE ET SOCIETE. (1982)-. Periodical. French. Four times a year. 55.00F. Editions CDU et Sedes, 88 boulevard Saint Germain, 75005 Paris France. **Tel** 011 33 1 43252323.
Ind/Abst Am. Hist. Life (1982-).

LC HC10 .O42
DD 330.9/00212 FR
●**HISTORICAL STATISTICS = STATISTIQUES RETROSPECTIVES.**
Added/Corp Organisation for Economic Co-operation and Development. Organisation for Economic Co-operation and Development. Statistics Directorate. **VFOAT** Statistiques Retrospectives. (1993)-. English (French). Irregular. Price varies per volume. OECD Publications and Information Center, 2 rue Andre-Pascal, 75775 Paris Cedex 16 France. **Tel** 011 33 1 49104262, US:(202)785-6323, FAX 011 33 1 45248500, 011 33 1 45248176, telex 620 160 OCDE. **Continues** OECD Economic Outloook. Historical Statistics.

LC HB1 .H55 **ISSN** 0018-2702
DD 330/.01 US
  CCC
Pr Rev.
HISTORY OF POLITICAL ECONOMY. [Hist. polit. econ.]. Vol. 1 (Spring 1969)-. Periodical. English. Four times a year (plus clothbound annual supplement). $132.00. Duke University Press, PO Box 90660, Durham NC 27708-0660. **Tel** (919)687-3600, (919)688-5134 (orders), FAX (919)688-4574, telex 802829. **ED** Craufurd D.W. Goodwin. **Bk Rev. Ad Acc. Circ:** 1,500 (ctrl). available on microfilm and microfiche from University Microfilms International (UMI). Documents available from The Genuine Article, UMI Article Clearinghouse.
Desc: Examines the history of economic thought and the development of economic analysis.
Ind/Abst Acad. Search; Am. Hist. Life (1969-); Arts Humanit. Citation Index (19??-19??) [Full Cov.]; Curr. Contents Arts Humanit.; Curr. Contents Soc. Behav. Sci.; Econ. Lit. Index; EP Collect.; Expand. Acad. Index (1989-); Hist. Source (July 1993-); Homework Help.; Hum. Resour. Abstr.; INFO-SOUTH Abstr.; J. Econ. Lit.; Mag. Search; MasterFile FullTEXT 1000; MasterFile FullTEXT 350; MasterFile FullTEXT 650; MasterFile FullTEXT (July 1993-); Middle East Abstr. Index; Newsp. Period. Abstr. (1991-); OCLC; Res. Alert [Full Cov.]; Romant. Movem.; Soc. Sci. Source; Soc. Sci. Source; Soc. Sci. Cit. Index [Full Cov.]; Soc. Sci. Index; Soc. Sci. Index Fulltext (Fall 1988-) [Full Txt.]; Telebase; West. Hist. Q.

LC HC463.H6 H545 JA
HOKKAIDO KEIZAI CHOSA. Added/Corp Hokkaido (Japan). Kaihatsu Choseibu. Keizai Chosashitsu. No. 1 (1981)-. Japanese. Hokkaido Keihatsu Choseibu Keizai Chosashitsu, Nishi 6 chome Kita 3-jo Chuo-ku, Sapporo-shi 060-91 Japan.

LC HC463.H63 J34a JA
HOKURIKU KEIZAI TOKEI NEMPO.
Added/Corp Japan. Hokuriku Zaimukyoku. (1970)-. Periodical. Japanese. Hokuriku Zaimukyoku, 2-ban 6-go Hirosaka 2-chome, Kanazawa 920 Japan. **Continues** Kannai Keizai Tokei Nempo.

ISSN 1054-5573
DD 972 US
HONDURAS (SYRACUSE, N.Y.).
(HONDURAS : A POLITICAL AND ECONOMIC FORECAST / POLITICAL RISK SERVICES.). [Honduras]. **Added/Corp** Political Risk Services (IBC USA (Publications) Inc.). (19??)-. English. $325.00. Political Risk Services, 6320 Fly Road, Suite 102, PO Box 248, East Syracuse NY 13057-0248. **Tel** (315)431-0511, FAX (315)431-0200.
Desc: Assesses the factors affecting the prospects for business and trade. Each report focuses specifically on business needs such as finding and developing markets, determining currency movements, or making judgements about capital investments or corporate security.

LC HC145.A1 G4a
DD 330.9/7283/05 GW
HONDURAS, WIRTSCHAFTLICHE ENTWICKLUNG. Main/Corp Germany (West). Bundesstelle fur Aussenhandelsinformation. (19??)-. German. Bundesstelle fuer Aussenhandelsinformation, Agrippastrasse 87 93, D-50676 Cologne Germany. **Tel** 011 49 221 2057316, FAX 011 49 221 2057212.

  HK
HONG KONG ECONOMIC TRENDS.
Added/Corp Hong Kong. Census and Statistics Dept. (19??)-. Periodical. English. Twelve times a year. HK$36.00. Hong Kong Government Information Service, Beaconsfield House, 4 Queens Road, Hong Kong Hong Kong. **Tel** 011 852 284288014, 011 852 259881947, FAX 011 852 28459078, 011 852 25987482, telex 61190 HKGIS. **(Subscription address:** Government Information Service, Publications Office, 1 Battery Path, Hong Kong Hong Kong. **)**

ISSN 1054-5581
DD 951 US
HONG KONG (SYRACUSE, N.Y.). (HONG KONG : A POLITICAL AND ECONOMIC FORECAST.). [Hong Kong]. **Added/Corp** Political Risk Services (IBC USA (Publications) Inc.). (19??)-. English. $325.00. Political Risk Services, 6320 Fly Road, Suite 102, PO Box 248, East Syracuse NY 13057-0248. **Tel** (315)431-0511, FAX (315)431-0200.
Desc: Assesses the factors affecting the prospects for business and trade. Each report focuses specifically on business needs such as finding and developing markets, determining currency movements, or making judgements about capital investments or corporate security.

LC HC470.3.A1 H67
DD 330.951/25/005 GW
HONGKONG, WIRTSCHAFTSDATEN UND WIRTSCHAFTSDOKUMENTATION / BUNDESSTELLE FUER AUSSENHANDELSINFORMATION.
Added/Corp Bundesstelle fuer Aussenhandelsinformation (Germany). (19??)-. German. Every 2 years. DM3.00. Bundesstelle fuer Aussenhandelsinformation, Agrippastrasse 87 93, D-50676 Cologne Germany. **Tel** 011 49 221 2057316, FAX 011 49 221 2057212.

LC HC591.C6 H67 CG
HORIZONS 80 I.E. QUATRE-VINGT.
Periodical. French. Societe Zairoise d'Edition et d'Information, Compte Bancaire No 36000398/V Biaz, Kinshasa Congo Zaire.

LC HC381 .H6 **ISSN** 0212-0607
DD 330.946/005 SP
TITLE CHANGE
HORIZONTE EMPRESARIAL. [Horiz. empres.]. **Added/Corp** Fomento del Trabajo Nacional (Spain). (19??)-(19??). Periodical. Spanish (Catalan). Fomento del Trbajo Nacional, Via Layetana 32-34, 08003 Barcelona Spain. **Tel** 93-319-61-00, telex 97826-1831. **Ad Acc, Adv Mgr:** Rosa Guillen, **Tel** 484-12-00. **Circ:** 10,000. ***Continued by*** *Fomento del Trabajo.*
Ind/Abst Foreign Lang. Index (?-?).

LC HC270.2 .H67
DD 330.9437/005 XR
HOSPODARSKE DEJINY = ECONOMIC HISTORY. **Added/Corp** Ustav Ceskoslovenskych a Svetovych Dejin (Ceskoslovenska Akademie Ved). **VFOAT** Economic History. (1978)-. Academic Scholarly Publication. Czech (English and Slovak; summaries and/or abstracts in Russian). Two times a year. Available on an exchange basis only. Ceska Akademie Ved Historicky Ustav, Vysehradska 49, 128 26 Prague 2 Czech Republic. **ED** Jan Hajek. **Bk Rev.**
Ind/Abst Am. Hist. Life (1989-).

LC HC300.2 .H85 **ISSN** 0133-0365
DD 330.9/439/05 HU
HUNGARIAN ECONOMY (BUDAPEST. 1972), THE. (THE HUNGARIAN ECONOMY.). [Hung. econ.]. **VFOAT** Figyelo. Vol. 1 (Dec. 1972)-. Periodical. English. Four times a year. $45.00. Hirlapkiado V Allalat, POB 149, 1389 Budapest Hungary. **(Subscription address:** Kultura, PO Box 143, H-1300 Budapest 3 Hungary. **Tel** 011 36 1 2500194.**)**
Desc: Covers Hungarian foreign policy, economic and business life. Informs on every plan, result, change and phenomenon of Hungarian economics.
Ind/Abst Predicasts.

ISSN 1054-559X
DD 943 US
HUNGARY (SYRACUSE, N.Y.). (HUNGARY : A POLITICAL AND ECONOMIC FORECAST.). [Hungary]. **Added/Corp** Political Risk Services (IBC USA (Publications) Inc.). (19??)-. English. $325.00. Political Risk Services, 6320 Fly Road, Suite 102, PO Box 248, East Syracuse NY 13057-0248. **Tel** (315)431-0511, FAX (315)431-0200.
Desc: Assesses the factors affecting the prospects for business and trade. Each report focuses specifically on business needs such as finding and developing markets, determining currency movements, or making judgements about capital investments or corporate security.

LC HN730.5 .A53
KO
HYONDAE SAHOE. Vol. 5, No. 1 (Spring 1985)-. Periodical. Korean. Four times a year. W12.000. Hyandae Sahoe / 2000-Yon, Yonguso 7-16 Sinchon-dong Kangdong-ku, Seoul 1 Korea. ***Continues*** *Kyegan Hyondae Sahoe.*

LC HC10 .I14 **ISSN** 0738-3398
DD 330.9/005 US
IBCD. (IBCD : INTERNATIONAL BUSINESS CONDITIONS DIGEST.). [IBCD]. **Added/Corp** IBR, Inc. Economics Dept. **VFOAT** International Business Conditions Digest. Vol. 1, No. 1 (Aug. 1983)-. Periodical. English. Four times a year. $120.00. International Business Resources Inc., 24 Tennyson Avenue, Dover NH 03820. **Tel** (603)862-3363. **ED** Evangelos O. Simos.

LC HC107.I2 I193 **ISSN** 8756-1840
DD 338.5/443/09796 US
IDAHO ECONOMIC FORECAST, THE. [Ida. econ. forecast]. **Added/Corp** Idaho. Division of Budget, Policy Planning, and Coordination. Idaho. Division of Financial Management. (197?)-. English. Four times a year. $20.00. Idaho Economic Forecast, Division of Financial Management, Statehouse Room 122, Boise ID 83720-1000. **Tel** (208)334-3900, FAX (208)334-2438. **ED** Derek Santos; Telephone: (208)334-2906. **Circ:** 500 (ctrl).
Desc: Forecast of the Idaho economy plus articles regarding the regional economy and economic issues.

LC HC286.7 .I17a
DD 330.943/005 GW
IFO-DIGEST. **Main/Corp** Ifo-Institut fur Wirtschaftsforschung, Munich. Vol. 1 (March 1978)-. Periodical. German. Four times a year. DM75.00. IFO-Institut fuer Wirtschaftsforschung, Postfach 860460, D-81631 Munich Germany. **Tel** 011 49 89 92241, telex 5-22269. **Circ:** 700.
Desc: Contains analyses of the current situation of the German economy and a detailed forecast of next year's development, business cycles indicators, industry reports, and abstracts.
Ind/Abst Contents Recent Econ. J.

LC HC905.Z7 B664
DD 330.9682/94/005 SA
IKONOMI. Vol. 1, No. 1 (July 1981)-. Periodical. English. The Secretary / South Africa, Department of Economic Affairs, Private Bag X2008, Mafikeng Republic of Bophuthatswana South Africa. ***Formed by the union of*** *Impetus (Montshiwa, South Africa)* ***and*** *Kgodisano.*

LC HC59 .I347
KO
IKONOMISUTU (SEOUL, KOREA). (IKONOMISUTU.). **VFOAT** The Economist; Economist. Vol. 1, No. 1 (1984)-. Periodical. Korean (Korean). Twenty-four times a year. W48.000. Chungang Ilbo Tongyang Pangsong, 58-9 Sosomun-Dong, Chung-Ku 100, Seoul South Korea.

LC HC277.I47 I43 **ISSN** 0181-0162
DD 330.944/34/005 FR
ILE-DE-FRANCE, NOTE DE CONJONCTURE REGIONALE. French. Three times a year. 20F single issue. Delegation Regionale pour Lile-de-France, 219 Building Saint-Germain, 75007 Paris France.

LC HD3616.I8 I48
IT
IMPRESA & STATO. **Added/Corp** Camera di Commercio, Industria, Artigianato e Agricoltura di Milano. **VFOAT** Impresa e Stato. (198?)-. Periodical. Italian. Four times a year. L40880. Camera di Commercio Industria Artigianato E Agricoltura di Milano, via Meravigli 9 B, 20123 Milan Italy. **Tel** 011 39 2 85154516.

LC HC110.I5 C33a **ISSN** 0319-0374
DD 339.2/0971 CN
INCOME AFTER TAX, DISTRIBUTIONS BY SIZE IN CANADA. [Income tax distrib. size Can.]. **Added/Corp** Statistics Canada. Consumer Income and Expenditure Division. Statistics Canada. Household Surveys Division. **VFOAT** Revenu Apres Impot, Repartition Selon la Taille du Revenu au Canada. (1971)-. English (French). One time a year. 24.01Can$. Statistics Canada Publications Sales and Services, R.H. Coats Building 6th Floor, Ottawa Ontario K1A 0T6 Canada. **Tel** (613)951-5078, (800)267-6677, FAX (613)951-1584, telex 053-3585.
Desc: Income distributions for families, unattached individuals and all persons. Incomes are shown on an after-tax basis by selected characteristics such as region, age and sex. Income after tax is defined as total money income less income taxes paid. Statistics are derived from the Survey of Consumer Finances, conducted annually since 1972.

LC HC171 .I523
DD 330 AG
INDEX ESTADISTICO. ANALISIS DE COYUNTURA. **See** Business and Economics-Abstracting, Bibliographies and Statistics.

ISSN 0963-5572
UK
INDEX TO MEED. MIDDLE EAST ECONOMIC DIGEST. **See** Business and Economics-Abstracting, Bibliographies and Statistics.

ISSN 1054-5603
DD 954 US
INDIA (SYRACUSE, N.Y.). (INDIA : A POLITICAL AND ECONOMIC FORECAST.). [India]. **Added/Corp** Political Risk Services (IBC USA (Publications) Inc.). (19??)-. English. $325.00. Political Risk Services, 6320 Fly Road, Suite 102, PO Box 248, East Syracuse NY 13057-0248. **Tel** (315)431-0511, FAX (315)431-0200.
Desc: Assesses the factors affecting the prospects for business and trade. Each report focuses specifically on business needs such as finding and developing markets, determining currency movements, or making judgements about capital investments or corporate security.

LC HC431 .I338 **ISSN** 0019-4646
II
INDIAN ECONOMIC AND SOCIAL HISTORY REVIEW, THE. **Added/Corp** Delhi School of Economics. Vol. 1 (July/Sept. 1963)-. Periodical. English. Four times a year (March, June, Sept., Dec.). $105.00. SAGE Periodical Press, 2455 Teller Road, Thousand Oaks CA 91320. **Tel** (805)499-0721, FAX (805)499-0871, telex 100799. **ED** Dharma M. Kumar. Index available. **Ad Acc.** available on microfilm and microfiche from University Microfilms International (UMI). Documents available from The Genuine Article.
Desc: Focuses on the history, economy, and society of India and South Asia, and includes comparative studies of world development.
Ind/Abst Am. Hist. Life (1963-1969, 1975-); Arts Humanit. Citation Index [Full Cov.]; Curr. Contents Arts Humanit.; Econ. Lit. Index (19??-); Geogr. Abstr. Human Geogr. (?-?); Int. Bibliogr. Sociol.; Int. Dev. Abstr. (?-?); J. Econ. Lit.; Numis. Lit. (1963-1969, 1975-); Res. Alert [Full Cov.]; Soc. Sci. Cit. Index [Select. Cov.].

LC HC431 .I3383 **ISSN** 0019-4654
II
INDIAN ECONOMIC DIARY. Vol. 1, No. 1 (Jan. 1, 1970)-. Periodical. English. One time a week. $65.00. Indian Economic Diary, F-15 Bhagat Singh Market, New Delhi India. **(Subscription address:** Prints India, 11 Darya Ganj, New Delhi 110002 India. **Tel** 011 91 11 3268645, FAX 011 91 11 3275542, telex 31-61087 PRIN-IN.) cum. index.

LC HC431 .I34 **ISSN** 0019-4662
DD 330.5 II
INDIAN ECONOMIC JOURNAL, THE. (THE INDIAN ECONOMIC JOURNAL : THE QUARTERLY JOURNAL OF THE INDIAN ECONOMIC ASSOCIATION.). [Indian econ. j.]. **Added/Corp** Indian Economic Association. Vol. 1, No. 1 (July 1953)-. Periodical. English. Four times a year. $30.00. Department of Economics / Bombay, C S T Road, University Campus, Santacruz East Bombay India. **(Subscription address:** Prints India, 11 Darya Ganj, New Delhi 110002 India. **Tel** 011 91 11 3268645, FAX 011 91 11 3275542, telex 31-61087 PRIN-IN.**)** available on microfilm and microfiche from University Microfilms International (UMI).
Ind/Abst Contents Recent Econ. J.; Econ. Lit. Index; Int. Labour Doc.; J. Econ. Lit.; LABORDOC; Middle East Abstr. Index; Rural Dev. Abstr.; Stat. Theory Method Abstr. (1959-1963); World Agric. Econ. Rural Sociol. Abstr.

LC HB9 .I43 **ISSN** 0019-5766
II
INDIAN LIBERTARIAN, THE. (1952)-. Periodical. English. Twenty-four times a year. Libertarian Publishing Private Ltd, Arya Bhavan Sandhurst Road, Bombay 4 India. ***Absorbed*** *Free Economic Review;* ***Continues*** *Indian Nationalist.*

LC HC188.S45 I54
BL
INDICADORES DA CONJUNTURA SERGIPANA. Vol. 1 (1977)-. Periodical. Portuguese. Two times a year. Secretaria do Planejamento do Estado de Sergipe, Coordenacao de Planejamento e Estatistica, Praca Fausto Cardoso, s/No Ed Walter Franco, 5 O Andar, 49 000 Aracaju Sergipe.

LC HC196 .I46 **ISSN** 0120-9299
CK
INDICADORES DE COYUNTURA. **Added/Corp** Colombia. Departamento Administrativo Nacional de Estadistica. (May 1987)-. Periodical. Spanish. Twelve times a year. $120.00. Departamento Administrativo Nacional de Estadistica, Apartado Aereo 80043, Bogota Colombia. **Tel** 011 57 1 2223273, 011 57 1 2224318.

LC HC171 .I53 **ISSN** 0537-3468
DD 330.982/005 AG
INDICADORES DE COYUNTURA (BUENOS AIRES, ARGENTINA). **See** Business and Economics-Abstracting, Bibliographies and Statistics.

LC HC391 .I528
DD 330.9469/005 PO
INDICADORES ECONOMICOS PORTUGAL / PORTUGAL ECONOMIC INDICATORS / BANCO DE PORTUGAL. **Added/Corp** Banco de Portugal. **VFOAT** Portugal Economic Indicators. (19??)-. English (Portuguese). One time a year. $3.46. Banco de Portugal, rua R Francisco Ribeiro 2, 1100 Lisbon Portugal. **Tel** 011 351 1 3558655. **(Subscription address:** Livraria Barata, Avenue Roma 11 A, 1000 Lisbon Portugal. **Tel** 011 351 1 8481631.**)**

BL
INDICADORES IBGE. ESTATISTICA DA PRODUCAO AGRICOLA ANUAL. **See** Business and Economics-Abstracting, Bibliographies and Statistics.

LC HC190.I52 I553
DD 338.0981/021 BL
TITLE CHANGE
INDICADORES IBGE. INDICADORES CONJUNTURAIS DA INDUSTRIA, PRODUCAO FISICA. REGIONAL. **Added/Corp** Fundacao Instituto Brasileiro de Geografia e Estatistica. **VFOAT** Indicadores Conjunturais da Industria, Producao Fisica. Regional. (Jan. 1991)-(199?). Portuguese. IBGE/CDDI/GEMAR/SERCOM, Av Beira Mar/436 CEP 20021, Rio de Janeiro RJ Brasil. **Tel** (021)533.30.94, telex 021.30939 IBGE BR. ***Continues in part*** *Indicadores IBGE.* ***Continued by*** *Indicadores IBGE. Pesquisa Industrial Mensal, Producao Fisica. Regional.*

BL
INDICADORES IBGE. INDICES DE PRECOS AO CONSUMIDOR, INPC, IPCA. **See** Business and Economics-Abstracting, Bibliographies and Statistics.

LC HC190.I52 I55
DD 338.0981/021 BL
INDICADORES IBGE. PESQUISA INDUSTRIAL MENSAL, PRODUCAO FISICA. BRASIL. **Added/Corp** Fundacao Instituto Brasileiro de Geografia e Estatistica. **VFOAT** Pesquisa Industrial Mensal, Producao Fisica. Brasil. (199?)-. Portuguese. Twelve times a year. price varies. IBGE/CDDI/GEMAR/SERCOM, Av Beira Mar/436 CEP 20021, Rio de Janeiro RJ Brasil. **Tel** (021)533.30.94,

Business and Economics —Economic History, Conditions

telex 021.30939 IBGE BR. **Continues** *Indicadores IBGE. Indicadores Conjunturais da Industria, Producao Fisica. Brasil.*

LC HC190.I52 I553
DD 338.0981/021
BL
INDICADORES IBGE. PESQUISA INDUSTRIAL MENSAL, PRODUCAO FISICA. REGIONAL. Added/Corp Fundacao Instituto Brasileiro de Geografia e Estatistica. VFOAT Pesquisa Industrial Mensal, Producao Fisica. Regional. (19??)-. Portuguese. Twelve times a year. IBGE/CDDI/GEMAR/SERCOM, Av Beira Mar/436 CEP 20021, Rio de Janeiro RJ Brasil. **Tel** (021)533.30.94, telex 021.30939 IBGE BR. **Continues** *Indicadores IBGE. Indicadores Conjunturais da Industria, Producao Fisica. Regional.*

BL
INDICADORES IBGE. PRODUTO INTERNO BRUTO. Added/Corp Fundacao Instituto Brasileiro de Geografia e Estatistica. VFOAT Produto Interno Bruto. (1990)-. Portuguese. Four times a year. IBGE/CDDI/GEMAR/SERCOM, Av Beira Mar/436 CEP 20021, Rio de Janeiro RJ Brasil. **Tel** (021)533.30.94, telex 021.30939 IBGE BR. **Continues in part** *Indicadores IBGE.*

LC HC186 .I42
DD 330.981/005
BL
TITLE CHANGE
INDICADORES IBGE / SECRETARIA DE PLANEJAMENTO DA PRESIDENCIA DA REPUBLICA, FUNDACAO INSTITUTO BRASILEIRO DE GEOGRAFIA E ESTATISTICA, IBGE. Added/Corp Fundacao Instituto Brasileiro de Geografia e Estatistica. VFOAT Indicadores I.B.G.E. Vol. 1, No. 1 (Nov. 1982)-(1990). Portuguese. IBGE/CDDI/GEMAR/SERCOM, Av Beira Mar/436 CEP 20021, Rio de Janeiro RJ Brasil. **Tel** (021)533.30.94, telex 021.30939 IBGE BR. Index available. ctrl circ. **Split into** *Indicadores IBGE ... .*
Desc: Publishes indicators produced by IGBE: national index of consumer prices; monthly employment information; economic indicators of industry.
Ind/Abst Chem. Bus. Bull.; Chem. Bus. NewsBase (1986-); Chem. Bus. Update.

LC HC557.T6 A26A **ISSN** 0302-4423
DD 339/.0966/81
TG
INDICATEURS DE L'ECONOMIE TOGOLAISE. [Indic. econ. togol.]. Main/Corp Togo. Direction de la Statistique. (19??)-. French. Secretariat d'Etat a la Presidence Charge du Plan, Direction du la Statistique, BP No 118, Lome Togo.

LC HC437.G6 .G625a **ISSN** 0376-9925
DD 330.954/799/005
II
INDICATORS OF SOCIO-ECONOMIC DEVELOPMENT OF GOA, DAMAN & DIU SINCE LIBERATION. Added/Corp Goa, Daman and Diu (India). Directorate of Planning, Statistics & Evaluation. Goa, Daman and Diu (India). Dept. of Planning & Statistics. Goa, Daman and Diu (India). Bureau of Economics, Statistics & Evaluation. Goa, Daman and Diu (India). Dept. of Information and Tourism. (19??)-. Periodical. English. One time a year. Government of Goa, Daman & Diu, Department of Information & Tourism, Panaj India.

LC HC446 .A16a
IO
INDIKATOR EKONOMI. Main/Corp Indonesia. Biro Pusat Statistik. (Jan. 1970)-. Periodical. Indonesian (English). One time a year. Biro Pusat Statistik / Central Bureau of Statistics, 8 Jalan Dr. Sutomo No. 8, Box 3, Jakarta Pusat 10710 Indonesia. **Tel** 011 62 21 372808, 011 62 21 374908 ext.342. **Bk Rev. Ad Acc.** ctrl circ.

LC HC448.B3 I525
IO
INDIKATOR EKONOMI BALI. Added/Corp Indonesia. Kantor Statistik Propinsi Bali. (1981)-. Indonesian. One time a year. Kantor Statistik Propinsi Bali, JL Raya Puputan, Denpasar Indonesia.

IO
INDIKATOR EKONOMI KALIMANTAN SELATAN. Main/Corp Kalimantan Selatan. Kantor Sensus dan Statistik. (19??)-. Indonesian. Kantor Sensus dan Statistik Propinsi Kalimantan Selatan, Jl K S Tubun, No 117, Banjarmasin Indonesia.

LC HC448.S78 I5
DD 330.9598/4/005
IO
INDIKATOR EKONOMI ... SULAWESI SELATAN. (19??)-. English (Indonesian). One time a year. Kantor Statistik Propinsi Sulawesi Selatan, Jl Haji Bau No 6, Ujung Pandang Indonesia. **Continues** *Indikator Ekonomi Propinsi Sulawesi Selatan.*

LC HD2081 .I48
DD 630
IO
INDIKATOR PEMBANGUNAN INDUSTRI PERTANIAN. See Agriculture.

LC HC10 .I56
DD 309.1/04
UK
INDIVIDUALIST, THE. English. Six times a year. Personal Rights Association, 31 Parkside Gardens, London SW19 5ET United Kingdom.

LC HC446 .U5a
DD 330.9/598/03
IO
INDONESIA ECONOMIC TRENDS REPORT. Main/Corp United States. Embassy (Indonesia). (1975)-. English. US Embassy, Jalan Medan Merdeka Selatan 5, Jakarta Pusat Indonesia.

ISSN 1054-5611
DD 959
US
INDONESIA (SYRACUSE, N.Y.). (INDONESIA : A POLITICAL AND ECONOMIC FORECAST / POLITICAL RISK SERVICES.). [Indonesia]. Added/Corp Political Risk Services (IBC USA (Publications) Inc.). (19??)-. English. $325.00. Political Risk Services, 6320 Fly Road, Suite 102, PO Box 248, East Syracuse NY 13057-0248. **Tel** (315)431-0511, FAX (315)431-0200.
Desc: Assesses the factors affecting the prospects for business and trade. Each report focuses specifically on business needs such as finding and developing markets, determining currency movements, or making judgements about capital investments or corporate security.

LC HC446 .I74
DD 330.9598/005
SI
INDONESIAN TRADE, INDUSTRY, AND TOURISM REVIEW. VFOAT Indonesian Review. (Jan. 1981)-. English. Twelve times a year. Indorep, 283G, 7th Floor/Selegie Complex, Selegie Road, Singapore 0718 Singapore.

LC HC447
DD 330.9/598/03
GW
INDONESIEN : WIRTSCHAFTLICHE ENTWICKLUNG. Main/Corp Bundesstelle fur Aussenhandelsinformation (Germany). German. Bundesstelle fuer Aussenhandelsinformation, Agrippastrasse 87 93, D-50676 Cologne Germany. **Tel** 011 49 221 2057316, FAX 011 49 221 2057212.

LC HC446
GW
INDONESIEN : WIRTSCHAFTSDATEN UND WIRTSCHAFTSDOKUMENTATION. Main/Corp Bundesstelle fur Aussenhandelsinformation (Germany). German. DM3.00. Bundesstelle fuer Aussenhandelsinformation, Agrippastrasse 87 93, D-50676 Cologne Germany. **Tel** 011 49 221 2057316, FAX 011 49 221 2057212.

LC HC188.P35 I55
BL
INDUSTRIA. Added/Corp Federacao das Industrias do Estado do Parana. Vol. 1, No. 1 (July 1975)-. Bulletin. Portuguese. Irregular. Federacao das Industrias do Estado do Parana, Av Candido de Abreu, 200-60 Andar, Curitiba Parana Brazil. **Tel** 011 55 41 254 8040, FAX 011 55 41 253 6486, telex 41. **ED** Roberto Peredo Zurcher. **Ad Acc. Circ:** 2,500. available on diskette.

LC HC188.S3 I47
BL
INDUSTRIA DE SAO PAULO: ORGAOS DIRIGENTES. Portuguese. Viadito Dona Paulina 80, Terreo 01595, Sao Paulo Brazil.

II
INDUSTRIAL AND TRADE WORLD. (April 1974)-. Periodical. English. Twelve times a year. Rs27.00. Impex India, 2118 Ansari Road, New Delhi 110002 India. **Tel** 278034.

LC HC107.H33 Z64
DD 338.09969
US
INDUSTRIAL PARKS AND AREAS IN HAWAII. English. Hawaii Department of Business and Economic Development, PO Box 2359, Honolulu HI 96804. **Tel** (808)586-2423, FAX (808)586-2452.

LC HC865.A1 I5
DD 330.9676/2/005
KE
INDUSTRIAL REVIEW (NAIROBI, KENYA). See Industry and Production.

LC HC327.N6 I5
NE
INDUSTRIE ADRESBOEK VAN NOORD-HOLLAND. Dutch. Economisch-Technologische Dienst Voor Noord-Holland, Stolbergstraat 9, Haarlem Netherlands.

US
Pr Rev.
INDUSTRY FORECAST. English. Sixteen times a year. $295.00 (one-year); $565.00 (two-year). Jerome Levy Economics Institute, Box 26, Cahppaqua NY 10514. **Tel** (914)238-3665, FAX (914)238-4599.

LC HC101 .I52 **ISSN** 0749-5870
DD 338.5/443/0973
US
INDUSTRY PLANNING SERVICE. [Ind. plann. serv.]. Vol. 1, No. 1 (July 1982)-. Periodical. English. Twelve times a year. WEFA / Philadelphia, PO Box 8500, Suite 1995, Philadelphia PA 19178. **Tel** (215)667-6000, telex 710 6700575.

LC Z1601 .I56 **ISSN** 1059-5910
US
CEASED
INFO-SOUTH ABSTRACTS. See Business and Economics-Abstracting, Bibliographies and Statistics.

ISSN 0736-8666
US
Pr Rev. CEASED
INFOBRAZIL. [Infobrazil]. Added/Corp Johns Hopkins University. Center of Brazilian Studies. Paul H. Nitze School of Advanced International Studies. Center of Brazilian Studies. VFOAT Info Brazil. Vol. 1 (Dec. 1979)-(19??). Periodical. English. Centre for Brazilian Studies, 1740 Massachusetts Avenue NW, Washington DC 20036. **Tel** (202)663-5739, FAX (202)663-5737, telex 264170 JHU UR. **ED** Rafael de la Dehesa. Index available. **Bk Rev. Circ:** 500 (ctrl).
Desc: Contains news and commentaries on the Brazilian political, financial and industrial sectors, following the latest economic and political developments in Brazil.

AG
INFORMACIONES : A.L.A.L.C., GRUPO ANDINO, S.E.L.A. Y MERCADO COMUN CENTROAMERICANO. Vol. 9, No. 173 (Sept. 13, 1978)-. Periodical. Spanish. Twenty-four times a year. Los Convenios SRL, 25 de Mayo 489 30 Piso Oficina 319, Buenos Aires Argentina. **Continues** *Informaciones Actualizadas Sobre A.L.A.L.C.*

LC HC446 .I77
IO
INFORMASI POTENSI INDUSTRI. Indonesian. Two times a year. Departemen Perindustrian Badan Penelitian dan Pengembangan Industri, JL Proklamasi 56, PO Box 3538, Jakarta Indonesia.

LC HC820.A1 I53
DD 330.961/1/005
TI
INFORMATIONS ECONOMIQUES (SHARIKAH AL-TUNISIYAH LIL-BANK). (INFORMATIONS ECONOMIQUES / SOCIETE TUNISIENNE DE BANQUE.). Periodical. French. Irregular. Societe Tunisienne de Banque, 1 Avenue Habib Thameur, Tunis Tunisia.

ISSN 0721-5088
GW
UDC 323.12(=96)(6-13)
INFORMATIONSDIENST SUDLICHES AFRIKA. See Political Science.

LC HC381 .B3352a **ISSN** 0067-3315
DD 330/338.946
SP
INFORME ANUAL - BANCO DE ESPANA. Main/Corp Banco de Espana. (1967)-. Spanish. One time a year. Banco de Espana, Alcala 50, 28014 Madrid Spain. **Tel** 011 34 1 4469055, 011 34 1 3385072. **Continues** *Informe Sobre la Economia Espanola en ... .* **Continued in part by** *Cuentas Financieras de la Economia Espanola.*

ISSN 1054-5077
US
INFORME COMMERCIAL U.S.A. (1991)-. Periodical. Spanish (English). Twenty-four times a year. $198.00. Merkator International, 1140 19th Street NW, Suite A422, Washington DC 20036.

LC HC171 .A3356
AG
INFORME ECONOMICO. RESUMEN. Main/Corp Argentina. Ministerio de Economia. 2nd Quarterly 1973-. Periodical. Spanish. Ministerio de Economia, Servicio de Prensa Relaciones y Ceremonial, Buenos Aires Argentina. **Continues** *Informe Economico. Resumen.*

ISSN 0384-0719
DD 330.9/71/0644
CN
INITIATIVE. Vol. 1 (Feb. 1976)-. Periodical. English. Twelve times a year. $15.00. Initiative, 45 Charles Street East/Suite 702, Toronto Ontario M4Y 1S2 Canada.

US
INSIDE ECONOMIC DEVELOPMENT. (19??)-. English. Twelve times a year. $199.00. New Hope Communications, 9500 Nall, Suite 400, Overland Park KS 66207. **Tel** (913)381-9489.

Business and Economics — Economic History, Conditions

LC HC101 .I544
DD 338.5/443/0973
ISSN 0734-6557
US
INTERINDUSTRY REVIEW. **VFOAT** Data Resources Interindustry Review. Periodical. English. DRI McGraw Hill, 24 Hartwell Avenue, Lexington MA 02173. **Tel** (617)863-5100, FAX (617)860-6464, (617)860-6416.

LC HC186 .A3325
BL
INTERIOR. **Main/Corp** Brazil. Ministerio do Interior. Coordenadoria de Comunicacao Social. (Dec. 1974)-. Portuguese. Ministerio do Interior, Gabinete do Ministro Sas, Quadra 1 Bloco A, Lotes 9/10 80 Andar, Brasilia Brazil.

BE
INTERMEDIAIR BELGIE. (19??)-. Periodical. Dutch (French). One time a week (one issue in July & Aug.). 1600F Belgium; 1900F Netherlands and Luxembourg; 2500F Europe; 3000F other. Diligentia, Hulstlaan 42 Avenue du Houx, 1170 Brussels Belgium. **Tel** 011 32 2 6738170. **ED** H. Coenjaarts and C. Rugener. **Bk Rev.** **Ad Acc.** Circ: 93,000 (ctrl).

LC HC10 .I6494
DD 330.9/001/12
ISSN 0960-8869
UK
CCC
TITLE CHANGE
INTERNATIONAL ECONOMIC OUTLOOK / CENTRE FOR ECONOMIC FORECASTING, LONDON BUSINESS SCHOOL. **Added/Corp** London Business School. Centre for Economic Forecasting. Vol. 1, No. 1 (June 1991)-. Academic Scholarly Publication. English. Basil Blackwell Publishers Ltd., 108 Cowley Road, Oxford 0X4 1JF United Kingdom. **Tel** 011 44 1235 465500, FAX 011 44 1235 465556, telex 837022 OXBOOK G. available on microfilm and microfiche from University Microfilms International (UMI). **Merged with** Financial Outlook **to form** Economic Outlook, 0140-489X.

LC HT390 .I54
DD 361.6/05
ISSN 0160-0176
US
Pr Rev.
INTERNATIONAL REGIONAL SCIENCE REVIEW. See Housing and Urban Development.

LC HA42 .I57a
DD 310/.8
ISSN 0098-5643
US
INTERNATIONAL RESEARCH DOCUMENT. See Business and Economics-Abstracting, Bibliographies and Statistics.

LC HC171 .I57
DD 330.982/005
AG
INTERPRETACION ECONOMICA : ORGANO DE DIFUSION DE LA SOCIACION DE ECONOMISTAS ARGENTINOS. (June 1, 1977)-. Periodical. Spanish. Twelve times a year. Miapu 746 70 Piso, 1ER Cuerpo, 1006 Capital Federal, Republica Argentina.

ISSN 0210-1521
SP
INVESTIGACIONES ECONOMICAS. [Invest. econ.]. **Added/Corp** Instituto Nacional de Industria (Spain). Fundacion. Fundacion Empresa Publica (Madrid, Spain). No. 1 (Sept./Dec. 1976)-No. 27 (May/Aug. 1985); 2nd Series, Vol. 1, No. 1 (Jan. 1986)-. Periodical. Spanish. Three times a year (Jan., May, & Sept.). 5000ptas (institutions); 2500ptas (individuals). Fundacion del Empresa Publica, Ctr Publ Plaza del Marques de Salamanca 8, 28006 Madrid Spain. **Tel** 011 34 1 3961373. cum. index.
Ind/Abst Econ. Lit. Index (199?-); J. Econ. Lit.

LC HC267.A2 A228A
HU
IPARI TERMELES SZERKEZETENEK ALAKULASA, AZ. **Main/Corp** Hungary. Kozponti Statisztikai Hivatal. Ipargazdasagi Osztaly. (19??)-. Hungarian. Statisztikai Kiado Vallalat, PO Box 99, H-1033 Budapest 3 Hungary. **Tel** 803-311, telex 22-6699-SKV-H.

LC HC835.A1 I65
SJ
IQTISADI (KHARTOUM, SUDAN). (AL-IQTISADI.). Periodical. Arabic. £s0.25 single issue. PO Box 6258, Qaat Al-Shab Al-Khartum Sudan.

LC HC415.4.A1
DD 330.955
GW
IRAK, WIRTSCHAFTSDATEN UND WIRTSCHAFTSDOKUMENTATION / BUNDESSTELLE FUR AUSSENHANDELSINFORMATION. German. One time a year. DM2.00. Bundesstelle fuer Aussenhandelsinformation, Agrippastrasse 87 93, D-50676 Cologne Germany. **Tel** 011 49 221 2057316, FAX 011 49 221 2057212.

UK
IRAN QUARTERLY. (19??)-. English. Four times a year. £225.00. MEED Limited, MEED House, 21 John Street, London WC1N 2BP United Kingdom. **Tel** 011 44 171 4045513, FAX 011 44 171 2421450, telex 266872 MEEDAR G.

DD 955
ISSN 1054-562X
US
IRAN (SYRACUSE, N.Y.). (IRAN : A POLITICAL AND ECONOMIC FORECAST / POLITICAL RISK SERVICES.). [Iran]. **Added/Corp** Political Risk Services (IBC USA (Publications) Inc.). (19??)-. English. $325.00. Political Risk Services, 6320 Fly Road, Suite 102, PO Box 248, East Syracuse NY 13057-0248. **Tel** (315)431-0511, FAX (315)431-0200.
Desc: Assesses the factors affecting the prospects for business and trade. Each report focuses specifically on business needs such as finding and developing markets, determining currency movements, or making judgements about capital investments or corporate security.

DD 956
ISSN 1054-5638
US
IRAQ (SYRACUSE, N.Y.). (IRAQ : A POLITICAL AND ECONOMIC FORECAST.). [Iraq]. **Added/Corp** Political Risk Services (IBC USA (Publications) Inc.). (19??)-. English. $325.00. Political Risk Services, 6320 Fly Road, Suite 102, PO Box 248, East Syracuse NY 13057-0248. **Tel** (315)431-0511, FAX (315)431-0200.
Desc: Assesses the factors affecting the prospects for business and trade. Each report focuses specifically on business needs such as finding and developing markets, determining currency movements, or making judgements about capital investments or corporate security.

DD 941
ISSN 1054-5646
US
IRELAND (SYRACUSE, N.Y.). (IRELAND : A POLITICAL AND ECONOMIC FORECAST / POLITICAL RISK SERVICES.). [Ireland]. **Added/Corp** Political Risk Services (IBC USA (Publications) Inc.). (19??)-. English. $325.00. Political Risk Services, 6320 Fly Road, Suite 102, PO Box 248, East Syracuse NY 13057-0248. **Tel** (315)431-0511, FAX (315)431-0200.
Desc: Assesses the factors affecting the prospects for business and trade. Each report focuses specifically on business needs such as finding and developing markets, determining currency movements, or making judgements about capital investments or corporate security.

LC HC257.I6
GW
IRLAND : WIRTSCHAFT IN ZAHLEN UND WIRTSCHAFTSDOKUMENTATION. **Main/Corp** Bundesstelle fur Aussenhandelsinformation (Germany). German. DM4.00. Bundesstelle fuer Aussenhandelsinformation, Agrippastrasse 87 93, D-50676 Cologne Germany. **Tel** 011 49 221 2057316, FAX 011 49 221 2057212.

LC HC257.I6 G46a
DD 330.9/415/0824
GW
IRLAND : WIRTSCHAFTLICHE ENTWICKLUNGEN. **Main/Corp** Bundesstelle fuer Aussenhandelsinformation (Germany). (19??)-. German. Bundesstelle fuer Aussenhandelsinformation, Agrippastrasse 87 93, D-50676 Cologne Germany. **Tel** 011 49 221 2057316, FAX 011 49 221 2057212.

LC HC497.N5 I18
DD 338.4/09549/6
NP
ISDOC BULLETIN. Bulletin. English. 12.50. Industrial Services Centre, PO Box 1318, Kathmandu Nepal.

LC HC107.A45 A465
DD 309.1/798/05
US
ISEGR REPORT. **Main/Corp** Alaska. University. Institute of Social, Economic and Government Research. (19??)-. Monographic series. English. Price varies per volume. University of Alaska ISEGR, Institute of Social Economics and Government Resources, Fairbanks AK 99701. **Continues** SEG Report, 0065-5937.

LC HC360.5.A1
GW
ISLAND : WIRTSCHAFT IN ZAHLEN. **Main/Corp** Bundesstelle fur Aussenhandelsinformation (Germany). German. DM4.00. Bundesstelle fuer Aussenhandelsinformation, Agrippastrasse 87 93, D-50676 Cologne Germany. **Tel** 011 49 221 2057316, FAX 011 49 221 2057212.

DD 956
ISSN 1054-5662
US
ISRAEL (SYRACUSE, N.Y.). (ISRAEL : A POLITICAL AND ECONOMIC FORECAST.). [Israel]. **Added/Corp** Political Risk Services (IBC USA (Publications) Inc.). (19??)-. English. $325.00. Political Risk Services, 6320 Fly Road, Suite 102, PO Box 248, East Syracuse NY 13057-0248. **Tel** (315)431-0511, FAX (315)431-0200.
Desc: Assesses the factors affecting the prospects for business and trade. Each report focuses specifically on business needs such as finding and developing markets, determining currency movements, or making judgements about capital investments or corporate security.

DD 330.9/71/0644
ISSN 0709-0501
CN
ISSUES IN THE CANADIAN ECONOMY. **Added/Corp** Canadian Foundation for Economic Education. (Oct. 1978)-. Monographic series. English. Irregular. 10.00Can$. Canadian Foundation for Economic Education, 2 St. Clair Avenue West, Suite 501, Toronto Ontario M4V 1L5 Canada. **Tel** (416)968-2236.

LC HC301 .I88
DD 330.945
ISSN 0021-2911
IT
ITALIAN ECONOMIC SURVEY. **Added/Corp** Associazione Fra le Societa Italiane per Azioni. (1946)-. Periodical. English. Six times a year. Association of Italian Joint Stock Companies, Piazza Venezia 11, Rome Italy. **Supersedes** Business and Financial Report.

LC HC301
GW
ITALIEN : WIRTSCHAFT IN ZAHLEN UND WIRTSCHAFTSDOKUMENTATION. **Main/Corp** Bundesstelle fur Aussenhandelsinformation (Germany). German. Bundesstelle fuer Aussenhandelsinformation, Agrippastrasse 87 93, D-50676 Cologne Germany. **Tel** 011 49 221 2057316, FAX 011 49 221 2057212.

LC HC301
GW
ITALIEN : WIRTSCHAFTLICHE ENTWICKLUNG. **Main/Corp** Bundesstelle fur Aussenhandelsinformation (Germany). German. DM2.00. Bundesstelle fuer Aussenhandelsinformation, Agrippastrasse 87 93, D-50676 Cologne Germany. **Tel** 011 49 221 2057316, FAX 011 49 221 2057212.

DD 945
ISSN 1054-5654
US
ITALY (SYRACUSE, N.Y.). (ITALY : A POLITICAL AND ECONOMIC FORECAST.). [Italy]. **Added/Corp** Political Risk Services (IBC USA (Publications) Inc.). (19??)-. English. $325.00. Political Risk Services, 6320 Fly Road, Suite 102, PO Box 248, East Syracuse NY 13057-0248. **Tel** (315)431-0511, FAX (315)431-0200.
Desc: Assesses the factors affecting the prospects for business and trade. Each report focuses specifically on business needs such as finding and developing markets, determining currency movements, or making judgements about capital investments or corporate security.

LC HC10 .I864
RU
ITOGI NAUKI I TEKHNIKI: MIROVAIA EKONOMIKA, EKONOMICHESKOE POLOZHENIE STRAN. **Added/Corp** Vsesoiuznyi Institut Nauchnoi i Tekhnicheskoi Informatsii (Soviet Union). **VFOAT** Itogi Nauki i Tekhniki: Mirovaia Ekonomika, Ekonomicheskoe Polozhenie Stran; Itogi Nauki I Tekhniki: Seriia Mirovaia Ekonomika, Ekonomicheskoe Polozhenie Stran. Vol. 2, (1974)-. Russian. VINITI - Vsesoyuznyi Institut Nauchno-Tekhnicheskoi Informatsii, All-Union Scientific and Technical Information Institute, Baltiiskaia ulitsa 14, 125219 Moscow Russia. **Tel** 011 7 95 2384600, FAX 011 7 95 9430060, telex 411160. **Continues** Itogi Nauki: Mirovaia Ekonomika. Ekonomicheskoe Polozhenie Stran.

LC HC10 .I866
RU
ITOGI NAUKI I TEKHNIKI. OBSHCHEOTRASLEVYE VOPROSY EKONOMIKI I ORGANIZATSII PROMYSHLENNOSTI. **Added/Corp** Vsesoiuznyi Institut Nauchnoi i Tekhnicheskoi Informatsii (Soviet Union). **VFOAT** Itogi Nauki i Tekhniki: Seriia Obshcheotraslevye Voprosy Ekonomiki i Organizatsii Promyshlennosti; Obshcheotraslevye Voprosy Ekonomiki i Organizatsii Promyshlennosti. Vol. 3 (1974)-. Periodical. Russian. VINITI - Vsesoyuznyi Institut Nauchno-Tekhnicheskoi Informatsii, All-Union Scientific and Technical Information Institute, Baltiiskaia ulitsa 14, 125219 Moscow Russia. **Tel** 011 7 95 2384600, FAX 011 7 95 9430060, telex 411160. **Continues** Itogi Nauki: Obshcheotraslevye Voprosy Ekonomiki i Organizatsii Promyshlennosti.

LC HC321 .J27
NE
JAARBOEK (FINANCIEELE DAGBLAD BV). (JAARBOEK.). **VFOAT** Financieele Dagblad Jaarboek. (1983)-. Dutch. One time a year. H Sijthoffs Financiele Dagblad, PO Box 216, 1000 AE Amsterdam Netherlands. **Tel** 011 31 20 5574511.

LC HC321 .J3
NE
JAARVERSLAG / SOCIAAL-ECONOMISCHE RAAD. **Added/Corp** Sociaal-Economische Raad. (19??)-.

Corporate Report. Dutch. One time a year. Fl25.00 Netherlands; $13.00 US. SER - Sociaal Economische Raad, Bezuidenhoutseweg 60, Postbus 90405, 2509 LK The Hague Netherlands. **Tel** 011 31 70 3499499, FAX 011 31 70 3832535, telex 41.146. **Circ:** 1,500.

LC HC905.A1 S668a
DD 338.968 SA
JAARVERSLAG / SUID-AFRIKAANSE ONTWIKKELINGSTRUSTKORPORASIE BEPERK (STK) = ANNUAL REPORT / SOUTH AFRICAN DEVELOPMENT TRUST CORPORATION LIMITED (STK). **Main/Corp** South African Development Trust Corporation. **VFOAT** Annual Report. (1985)-. Afrikaans (English). SA Development Trust Corporation, PO Box 213, Pretoria 0001 South Africa. **Tel** 325-3300. Index available. ctrl circ.

LC HC79.C6 J33 **ISSN** 0021-3985
GW
CCC
JAHRBUCH DER ABSATZ- UND VERBRAUCHSFORSCHUNG. [Jahrb. absatz- Verbrauchsforsch.]. **Added/Corp** Gesellschaft fur Konsum-, Markt- und Absatzforschung (Germany). (1954)-. German. Four times a year. $80.75. Duncker und Humblot Verlag, Postfach 410329, D-12113 Berlin Germany. **Tel** 011 49 30 79000612, 011 49 30 79000613. **Ind/Abst** Selec. Coop. Index Manage. Period.

LC HC281 .J35 **ISSN** 0075-2800
GW
JAHRBUCH FUER WIRTSCHAFTSGESCHICHTE. [Jahrb. Wirtsch.gesch.]. **Added/Corp** Akademie der Wissenschaften, Berlin. Institut fuer Geschichte. Abteilung Wirtschaftsgeschichte. Akademie der Wissenschaften der DDR. Institut fuer Wirtschaftsgeschichte. (1960)-. Periodical. German. Two times a year. DM74.00. Akademie-Verlag GmbH, Postfach, D-13162 Berlin Germany. **Tel** 011 49 30 47889300, FAX 011 49 30 47889357. **(Subscription address:** VCH Publishers Inc., 303 Northwest 12th Avenue, Journals Department, Deerfield FL 33442. **Tel** (800)367-8249, (305)428-5566.**)** cum. index.
Desc: Generally focuses on one topic per issue. Contains reviews and discussions of research developments, and presents ongoing research projects.
Ind/Abst Am. Hist. Life (1964-); Int. Bibliogr. Sociol.; PAIS Int. Print (1991-?).

LC HC270.I52 J33
DD 338/.06/09436 AU
JAHRESBERICHT (OSTERREICHISCHES PRODUKTIVITATS- UND WIRTSCHAFTLICHKEITS-ZENTRUM). (JAHRESBERICHT / OPWZ.). German. One time a year. Osterreichisches Produktivitats-Und Wirtschaftlichkeits-Zentrum, Hohenstaufengasse 3, A-1014 Wein Austria.

ISSN 1054-5689
DD 972 US
JAMAICA (SYRACUSE, N.Y.). (JAMAICA : A POLITICAL AND ECONOMIC FORECAST / POLITICAL RISK SERVICES.). [Jamaica]. **Added/Corp** Political Risk Services (IBC USA (Publications) Inc.). (19??)-. English. $325.00. Political Risk Services, 6320 Fly Road, Suite 102, PO Box 248, East Syracuse NY 13057-0248. **Tel** (315)431-0511, FAX (315)431-0200.
Desc: Assesses the factors affecting the prospects for business and trade. Each report focuses specifically on business needs such as finding and developing markets, determining currency movements, or making judgements about capital investments or corporate security.

LC HC157.J2
DD 330.9/7292/06 GW
JAMAIKA : WIRTSCHAFTLICHE ENTWICKLUNG. **Main/Corp** Bundesstelle fur Aussenhandelsinformation (Germany). English. Bundesstelle fuer Aussenhandelsinformation, Agrippastrasse 87 93, D-50676 Cologne Germany. **Tel** 011 49 221 2057316, FAX 011 49 221 2057212.

LC HC461 .J29 **ISSN** 0389-3502
DD 330.952/005 JA
JAPAN ... AN INTERNATIONAL COMPARISON. **Added/Corp** Keizai Koho Senta (Tokyo, Japan). (19??)-. English. Two times a year (Apr. & Oct.). Keizai Koho Center, Otemachi Building, 6-1 Otemachi 1-chome Chiyoda-ku, Tokyo 100 Japan. **Tel** (03)201-1415, telex 222-5452 KKCTOK J. **ED** Noriyuki Aihara.

LC HC461 .J353
DD 330.9/52/04 JA
JAPAN ECONOMIC REVIEW. Vol. 1 (Aug. 1969)-. Periodical. English. Twelve times a year. $98.00. **(Subscription address:** Maruzen Company Ltd., PO Box 5050, Import & Export Department, Tokyo 100 31 Japan. **Tel** 011 81 3 32789224.**)**

ISSN 1054-5697
DD 952 US
JAPAN (SYRACUSE, N.Y.). (JAPAN : A POLITICAL AND ECONOMIC FORECAST.). [Japan]. **Added/Corp** Political Risk Services (IBC USA (Publications) Inc.). (19??)-. English. $325.00. Political Risk Services, 6320 Fly Road, Suite 102, PO Box 248, East Syracuse NY 13057-0248. **Tel** (315)431-0511, FAX (315)431-0200.
Desc: Assesses the factors affecting the prospects for business and trade. Each report focuses specifically on business needs such as finding and developing markets, determining currency movements, or making judgements about capital investments or corporate security.

ISSN 0912-3474
JA
JAPAN UPDATE. **Added/Corp** Keizai Koho Senta (Tokyo, Japan). No. 1 (Oct. 1991)-. Periodical. English. Twelve times a year. Keizai Koho Center, Otemachi Building, 6-1 Otemachi 1-chome Chiyoda-ku, Tokyo 100 Japan. **Tel** (03)201-1415, telex 222-5452 KKCTOK J. ***Continues** Japan Update, 0912-3474.*

LC HC461 .J428
DD 330.952/0021 GW
JAPAN, WIRTSCHAFTSDATEN. **Added/Corp** Bundesstelle fuer Aussenhandelsinformation (Germany). (19??)-. German. DM3.00. Bundesstelle fuer Aussenhandelsinformation, Agrippastrasse 87 93, D-50676 Cologne Germany. **Tel** 011 49 221 2057316, FAX 011 49 221 2057212.

LC HC461
DD 330.952/005 GW
JAPAN, WIRTSCHAFTSDATEN UND WIRTSCHAFTSDOKUMENTATION / BUNDESTELLE FUR AUSSENHANDELSINFORMATION. German. One time a year. DM3.00. Bundesstelle fuer Aussenhandelsinformation, Agrippastrasse 87 93, D-50676 Cologne Germany. **Tel** 011 49 221 2057316, FAX 011 49 221 2057212.

LC HC461 .J45 **ISSN** 0021-4841
DD 330.9/52/04 US
CCC
JAPANESE ECONOMIC STUDIES. [Japanese econ. stud.]. Vol. 1 (Fall 1972)-. Periodical. English. Six times a year. $629.00. M. E. Sharpe Inc., 80 Business Park Drive, Armonk NY 10504. **Tel** (914)273-1800, (800)541-6563, FAX (914)273-2106. **ED** Kazuo Sato. **Bk Rev. Ad Acc. Circ:** 250 (ctrl). available on microfilm from University Microfilms International (UMI). Documents available from The Genuine Article.
Desc: Translations of Japanese economic material. Intended to reflect developments in the Japanese economy and to be of interest to those professionals concerned with this field.
Ind/Abst Contents Recent Econ. J.; Curr. Contents Clin. Med.; Econ. Lit. Index; Int. Labour Doc.; LABORDOC; PAIS Int. Print (1991-); Res. Alert [Full Cov.]; Soc. Sci. Cit. Index [Full Cov.]; World Agric. Econ. Rural Sociol. Abstr.

LC HC337.F5 S786
FI
JASENLUETTELO - SUOMEN TEOLLISUUSLIITTO. **Main/Corp** Suomen Teollisuusliitto. **VFOAT** Medlemsforteckning - Finlands Industriforbund; List of Members - Federation of Finnish Industries. Multiple languages (English, Finnish and Swedish). Suomen Teollisuusliitto, Etelaranta 10 Pl 220, Helsinki 00131 13 Finland.

LC HD1940.5 .A26
DD 333 HU
JELENTES A MEZOGAZDASAG ... EVI FEJLODESEROL. **See** Agriculture.

ISSN 0883-136X
US
CCC
JOHN NAISBITT'S TREND LETTER. **VFOAT** Trend Letter. (19??)-. Periodical. English. Twenty-four times a year. $195.00. Global Network Inc., 1101 30th Street NW, Suite 301, Washington DC 20007. **Tel** (800)368-0115, (202)337-5960.
Desc: A newsletter that business and professional people turn to for early notice of the latest trends.

LC HC1602.5.Z4 A23
DD 330 US
•**JOINT U.S.-KOREA ACADEMIC STUDIES.** **Added/Corp** Korea Economic Institute (U.S.). Vol. 5 (1995)-. English. Korea Economic Institute of America, 1101 Vermont Avenue NW, Suite 401, Washington DC 20005. ***Continues** Academic Studies Series, 1054-6944.*

LC HC497.J6
GW
JORDANIEN : WIRTSCHAFTSDATEN UND WIRTSCHAFTSDOKUMENTATION. **Main/Corp** Bundesstelle fur Aussenhandelsinformation (Germany). German. DM2.00. Bundesstelle fuer Aussenhandelsinformation, Agrippastrasse 87 93, D-50676 Cologne Germany. **Tel** 011 49 221 2057316, FAX 011 49 221 2057212.

LC HC415.26.A1 J67
DD 330.95695/005 GW
JORDANIEN, WIRTSCHAFTSSTRUKTUR / BUNDESSTELLE FUR AUSSENHANDELSINFORMATION. German. One time a year. Bundesstelle fuer Aussenhandelsinformation, Agrippastrasse 87 93, D-50676 Cologne Germany. **Tel** 011 49 221 2057316, FAX 011 49 221 2057212.

LC HC431 .I54
DD 330.9/54/05 II
JOURNAL. **Main/Corp** Institute of Economic Geography, India. (1970)-. English. Four times a year. 4/1 Ashton Road, Calcutta 20 India.

LC HC241 .J6 **ISSN** 0021-9886
UK
CCC
Pr Rev.
JOURNAL OF COMMON MARKET STUDIES. [J. common mark. stud.]. Vol. 1 (1962)-. Academic Scholarly Publication. English. Four times a year. $280.00. Basil Blackwell Publishers Ltd., 108 Cowley Road, Oxford 0X4 1JF United Kingdom. **Tel** 011 44 1235 465500, FAX 011 44 1235 465556, telex 837022 OXBOOK G. **(Subscription address:** Blackwell Publishers / UK, 108 Cowley Road, Oxford OX4 1JF United Kingdom. **Tel** 011 44 1865 791100, FAX 011 44 1865 791347.**) ED** Peter Robson. cum. index. **Bk Rev. Ad Acc. Circ:** 1,300. available on microfilm and microfiche from University Microfilms International (UMI). Documents available from The Genuine Article, UMI Article Clearinghouse.
Desc: Devoted to the analysis of international integration and the experience of regional groupings. Its predominant concern is with the European community and its relations with the rest of the world.
Ind/Abst ABC POL SCI; ABI/INFORM Glob. Ed.; ABI/INFORM [Computer File] (Sept. 1978-); Acad. Search; Am. Hist. Life (1975-); Appl. Soc. Sci. Index Abstr.; Br. Humanit. Index; Bus. ASAP (1992-) [Full Txt.]; Bus. Index (1985-); Bus. Period. Index; Bus. Source Plus; Bus. Source; Contents Recent Econ. J.; Contents Pages Manage.; Curr. Cit.; Curr. Contents Soc. Behav. Sci.; Econ. Lit. Index; Energy Res. Abstr. (Dec. 1979-); EP Collect.; Expand. Acad. Index (1992-); Gen. BusinessFile (1985-); Gen. Period. Index (1985-); Homework Help.; INFO-SOUTH Abstr.; Int. Labour Doc.; Int. Polit. Sci. Abstr.; J. Econ. Lit.; LABORDOC; Leis., Rec., Tour. Abstr.; Mag. Search; Manage. Market. Abstr.; MasterFile FullTEXT 1000; MasterFile FullTEXT 350; MasterFile FullTEXT 650; MasterFile FullTEXT (July 1993-); Newsp. Period. Abstr. (1992-); OCLC; PAIS Int. Print (1991-); Res. Alert [Full Cov.]; Rural Dev. Abstr.; Selec. Coop. Index Manage. Period.; Soc. Sci. Cit. Index [Full Cov.]; Telebase; Trade Ind. ASAP [Full Txt.]; Trade Ind. Index [Full Txt.]; Wilson Bus. Abstr.; World Agric. Econ. Rural Sociol. Abstr.

LC HC59.7 .J655 **ISSN** 0304-3878
DD 338.9/005 NE
CCC
CODEN JDECDF
Pr Rev.
JOURNAL OF DEVELOPMENT ECONOMICS. [J. dev. econ.]. Vol. 1 (June 1974)-. Academic Scholarly Publication. English. Six times a year (3 vols.). $807.00. Elsevier Science Publishers BV, PO Box 211, 1000 AE Amsterdam Netherlands. **Tel** 011 31 20 4853641, 011 31 20 4853642, FAX 011 31 20 4853598. **ED** Pranab Bardhan, Albert Fishlow, and Jehre Behrman. **Bk Rev. Ad Acc.** available on microfilm and microfiche from University Microfilms International (UMI); available on an online database from Elsevier Electronic Subscriptions (EES). Documents available from The Genuine Article, UMI Article Clearinghouse.
Desc: Publishes papers relating to all aspects of economic development - from immediate policy concerns to structural problems of under-development.
Ind/Abst ABI/INFORM Glob. Ed.; ABI/INFORM [Computer File] (Feb. 1981-); Acad. Search; BioBusiness (1986-); Bus. Index (1985-); Curr. Cit.; Curr. Contents Soc. Behav. Sci.; Econ. Lit. Index (Feb. 1981-); EP Collect.; Expand. Acad. Index (1984-); Fluid Abstr., Civil Eng.; Fluid Abstr. Proc. Eng.; FLUIDEX (199?-); Gen. BusinessFile (1985-); Gen. Period. Index (1985-); Geogr. Abstr. Human Geogr. (1986-); Homework Help.; INFO-SOUTH Abstr.; Int. Bibliogr. Sociol.; Int. Dev. Abstr. (1974-); J. Econ. Lit.; J. Plan. Lit.; Leis., Rec., Tour. Abstr.; Mag. Search; MasterFile FullTEXT 1000; MasterFile FullTEXT 350; MasterFile FullTEXT 650; MasterFile FullTEXT (July 1993-); Middle East Abstr. Index; Newsp. Period. Abstr. (1991-); Nutr. Abstr. Rev., Ser. A, Hum. Exp.; OCLC; PAIS Int. Print (1991-?); Popul. Index; Res. Alert [Full Cov.]; Rice Abstr.; Rural Dev. Abstr.; Soc. Sci. Source; Soc. Sci. Cit. Index [Full Cov.]; Soc. Sci. Index; Soc. Sci. Index Fulltext (Sept. 1988-) [Full Txt.]; Sorghum Mill. Abstr.; Telebase; World Agric. Econ. Rural Sociol. Abstr.

LC HC10 .J64 ISSN 0022-0507
DD 330.5 US
CCC

Pr Rev.

JOURNAL OF ECONOMIC HISTORY, THE. [J. econ. hist.]. **Added/Corp** Economic History Association (U.S.). Vol. 1 (May 1941)-. Academic Scholarly Publication. English. Four times a year. $80.00. Cambridge University Press / New York, 40 West 20th Street, New York NY 10011-4211. **Tel** (212)924-3900, (800)221-4512, FAX (212)691-3239. **(Subscription address:** Cambridge University Press / Outside of North America, United Kingdom. **Tel** 011 44 223 312 393, FAX 011 44 223 325 959.**) ED** Thomas Weiss and Peter Lindert. cum. index. **Bk Rev. Ad Acc. Circ:** 3,500. available on microfilm and microfiche from University Microfilms International (UMI). Documents available from The Genuine Article, UMI Article Clearinghouse.
Desc: Devoted to the inter-disciplinary study of history and economics. Of interest not only to economic historians but to social, urban and demographic historians, as well as economists in general. Has broad coverage, in terms of both method and geographic scope. Topics examined include agriculture, servitude, money and banking, trade, manufacturing, technology, transportation, industrial organization, labor, demography, education, and economic regulation.
Ind/Abst Acad. Abstr.; Acad. Ind. [Computer File] (1987-); Acad. Search; AGRICOLA [Select. Cov.]; Am. Hist. Life (1954-); Am. Bibliogr. Slavic East Europ. Stud.; Arts Humanit. Citation Index [Full Cov.]; Book Rev. Index; Bus. Source Plus; Bus. Source; Curr. Contents Arts Humanit.; Curr. Contents Soc. Behav. Sci.; Econ. Lit. Index; EP Collect.; Expand. Acad. Index (1987-); Geogr. Abstr. Human Geogr.; Hist. Source (July 1990-); Homework Help.; Index Period. Artic. Relat. Law (19??-19??); INFO-SOUTH Abstr.; Int. Bibliogr. Sociol.; Int. Dev. Abstr. (?-?); J. Econ. Lit.; J. Plan. Lit.; Leis., Rec., Tour. Abstr.; Mag. Search; MasterFile FullTEXT 1000; MasterFile FullTEXT 350; MasterFile FullTEXT 650; MasterFile FullTEXT (July 1990-); Middle East Abstr. Index; Newsp. Period. Abstr. (1991-); OCLC; PAIS Int. Print (1991-?); Popul. Index; Res. Alert [Full Cov.]; Rural Dev. Abstr.; Soc. Sci. Source; Soc. Sci. Cit. Index [Full Cov.]; Soc. Sci. Index; Soc. Sci. Index Fulltext (Dec. 1988-) [Full Txt.]; Telebase; West. Hist. Q.; Women Stud. Abstr.; Work Relat. Abstr.; World Agric. Econ. Rural Sociol. Abstr.

LC HB1 .J6445 ISSN 0950-0804
DD 330/.05 UK
CCC

JOURNAL OF ECONOMIC SURVEYS. [J. econ. surv.]. Vol. 1, No. 1 (1987)-. Academic Scholarly Publication. English. Four times a year. $177.00. Basil Blackwell Publishers Ltd., 108 Cowley Road, Oxford OX4 1JF United Kingdom. **Tel** 011 44 1235 465500, FAX 011 44 1235 465556, telex 837022 OXBOOK G. **(Subscription address:** Blackwell Publishers / UK, 108 Cowley Road, Oxford OX4 1JF United Kingdom. **Tel** 011 44 1865 791100, FAX 011 44 1865 791347.**) ED** Donald George, Lesley Oxley, Colin Roberts, Stuart Sayer. **Bk Rev. Ad Acc. Circ:** 1,000. available on microfilm and microfiche from University Microfilms International (UMI).
Desc: Publishes surveys of recent contributions and developments across the broad spectrum of economics.
Ind/Abst Curr. Cit.; Econ. Lit. Index (1987-); J. Econ. Lit.

LC HB1.A1 J68 ISSN 1013-1809
DD 330/.05 HK
SUSPENDED

JOURNAL OF ECONOMICS AND INTERNATIONAL RELATIONS. VFOAT JEIR. Vol. 1, No. 1 (Spring 1987)-(19??). Periodical. English. Four times a year. $50.00. Asian Research Service, Sub Department, GPO Box 2232, Hong Kong Hong Kong. **Tel** 011 852 25707227, FAX 011 852 25128050, telex 63899 CONPA HX. **Ad Acc. Circ:** 1,000.
Desc: Main objective of the publication is to encourage and publish articles reflecting interdisciplinary research in economics and international relations.

LC HC240.A1 J68 ISSN 0391-5115
DD 330.9/4 IT

JOURNAL OF EUROPEAN ECONOMIC HISTORY, THE. [J. Eur. econ. hist.]. Vol. 1 (Spring 1972)-. Periodical. English. Three times a year. Free on request. Banco di Roma / Ufficio Relazion Esterne, Viale Umberto Tupini 180, 00144 Rome Italy. **Tel** 011 39 6 54451. **ED** Luigi de Rosa. Index available. **Bk Rev. Circ:** 3,500. Documents available from UMI Article Clearinghouse.
Ind/Abst Acad. Search; Am. Hist. Life (1979-); Econ. Lit. Index; EP Collect.; Expand. Acad. Index (1989-); Hist. Source (July 1993-); Homework Help.; Humanit. Index; Humanit. Source; INFO-SOUTH Abstr.; J. Econ. Lit.; J. Plan. Lit.; Mag. Search; MasterFile FullTEXT 1000; MasterFile FullTEXT 350; MasterFile FullTEXT 650; MasterFile FullTEXT (Jan. 1993-); Middle East Abstr. Index; Newsp. Period. Abstr. (1990-); OCLC; Popul. Index (?-?); Telebase.

LC HC431.A1 I57 ISSN 0020-2851
DD 330/.05 II

JOURNAL OF INSTITUTE OF ECONOMIC RESEARCH. Main/Corp Institute of Economic Research, Dharwar. Vol. 1 (Jan. 1966)-. Periodical. English. Two times a year. $20.00. Institute of Economic Research Karnataka State, Dharwar 580 004 India. **Tel** 8553. **(Subscription address:** Prints India, 11 Darya Ganj, New Delhi 110002 India. **Tel** 011 91 11 3268645, FAX 011 91 11 3275542, telex 31-61087 PRIN-IN.**) ED** N Vajra Kumar. **Bk Rev. Ad Acc. Circ:** 200.
Desc: Original research articles on empirical field data pertaining to population, contraception, agriculture, industry, economics, statistics, anthropology, sociology, family, marriage, and women.

LC H62 .J65 ISSN 0022-4146
DD 330/.07/2 US
CCC

Pr Rev.

JOURNAL OF REGIONAL SCIENCE. [J. reg. sci.]. **Added/Corp** Regional Science Research Institute. Wharton School. Dept. of Regional Science. University of Pennsylvania. Dept. of Regional Science. Vol. 1 (Summer 1958)-. Periodical. English. Four times a year. $86.50. Blackwell Publishers, 238 Main Street, Cambridge MA 02142. **Tel** (617)547-7110, (800)835-6770, FAX (617)547-0789. **ED** Walter Isard, Ronald E Miller, and Benjamin H Stevens. Index available. cum. index. **Circ:** 1,800. available on microfilm and microfiche from University Microfilms International (UMI); available on photocopies from University Microfilms International (UMI). Documents available from The Genuine Article, UMI Article Clearinghouse, Documents on Demand.
Desc: Covers regional economics and economic geography. Emphasizes theory or empirical applications.
Ind/Abst ABI/INFORM Glob. Ed.; ABI/INFORM [Computer File] (Feb. 1988-); Acad. Search; Avery Index Archit. Period. Suppl. Colum. Univ. (1990-); Biostatistica; Bus. Index (1985-); Contents Recent Econ. J.; Curr. Cit.; Curr. Contents Soc. Behav. Sci.; Econ. Lit. Index; Energy Inf. Abstr.; Environ. Abstr.; EP Collect.; Expand. Acad. Index (1984-); Gen. BusinessFile (1985-); Gen. Period. Index (1985-); Geogr. Abstr. Human Geogr.; Homework Help.; Index Period. Artic. Relat. Law (19??-19??); INFO-SOUTH Abstr.; Int. Dev. Abstr. (?-?); Irr. Drain. Abstr.; J. Econ. Lit.; J. Plan. Lit.; Mag. Search; MasterFile FullTEXT 1000; MasterFile FullTEXT 350; MasterFile FullTEXT 650; MasterFile FullTEXT (July 1993-); Middle East Abstr. Index; Newsp. Period. Abstr. (1991-); OCLC; Oper. Res./Manage. Sci.; Popul. Index; Qual. Control Appl. Stat.; Res. Alert [Full Cov.]; Sage Race Relat. Abstr.; Sage Urban Stud. Abstr; Soc. Sci. Source; Soc. Sci. Cit. Index [Full Cov.]; Soc. Sci. Index; Soc. Sci. Index Fulltext (Nov. 1988-) [Full Txt.]; Telebase; Urban Aff. Abstr.

LC HC431 .N64a
DD 330.9/54/05 II

JOURNAL OF THE NORTH EASTERN COUNCIL. Main/Corp North Eastern Council (India). (19??)-. Periodical. English. Four times a year. $25.00. North Eastern Council, Public Relations Officer, Shillong 793001 India. **(Subscription address:** Prints India, 11 Darya Ganj, New Delhi 110002 India. **Tel** 011 91 11 3268645, FAX 011 91 11 3275542, telex 31-61087 PRIN-IN.**)**

LC HC59.7 .K225
JA

KAENJU. Added/Corp Ajia Keizai Kenkyujo (Japan). (19??)-. Periodical. Japanese. ¥50. Ajia Keizai Kenkyujo, 42 Ichigaya Honmura-cho, Shinjuku-ku Tokyo 162 Japan.

LC HC557.C3
DD 330.9/67/1104 GW

KAMERUN : WIRTSCHAFTLICHE ENTWICKLUNG. Main/Corp Bundesstelle fur Aussenhandelsinformation (Germany). German. Bundesstelle fuer Aussenhandelsinformation, Agrippastrasse 87 93, D-50676 Cologne Germany. **Tel** 011 49 221 2057316, FAX 011 49 221 2057212.

LC HC111
DD 330.971/00212 GW

KANADA, WIRTSCHAFT IN ZAHLEN / BUNDESSTELLE FUR AUSSENHANDELSINFORMATION. German. Bundesstelle fuer Aussenhandelsinformation, Agrippastrasse 87 93, D-50676 Cologne Germany. **Tel** 011 49 221 2057316, FAX 011 49 221 2057212.

LC HC463.C48 J34a
JA

KANNAI KEIZAI JOSEI HOKOKU. Main/Corp Japan. Chugoku Zaimukyoku. (19??)-. Periodical. Japanese. Chugoku Zaimukyoku, 6-30 Kami Hatchobori, Niroshima 730 Japan.

LC HC463.K95 J35a
JA

KANNAI KEIZAI JOSEI HOKOKU. Main/Corp Japan. Minami Kyushu Zaimukyoku. (19??)-. Periodical. Japanese. Minami Kyushu Zaimukyoku, 1-2 Ninomaru 860, Kumamoto Japan.

LC HC463.K95 J345a
JA

KANNAI KEIZAI JOSEI HOKOKU. Main/Corp Japan. Kita Kyushu Zaimukyoku. (19??)-. Periodical. Japanese. Kita Kyushu Zaimukyoku, c/o Fukuoka God Chosha, 11-1 Hakataeki Higashi 2 Hakata-ku, Fukuoka 812 Japan.

LC HC463.T55 J38b
JA

KANNAI KEIZAI JOSEI HOKOKU. Main/Corp Japan. Tohoku Zaimukyoku. (19??)-. Periodical. Japanese. Tohoku Zaimukyoky, 3-3-1 Honmachi, Sendai 980 Japan.

LC HC463.S5 J37b
JA

KANNAI KEIZAI JOSEI HOKOKU. Main/Corp Japan. Shikoku Zaimukyoku. (19??)-. Periodical. Japanese. Shikoku Zaimukyoku, 26-1 Nakanocho, Kanazawa 920 Japan.

LC HC463.K3 J25a
JA

KANNAI KEIZAO JOSEI HOKOKU. Main/Corp Japan. Kanto Zaimukyoku. (19??)-. Japanese. Kanto Zaimukyoku, 3-1 Otemachi 1 Chiyoda-ku, Tokyo 100 Japan.

LC HC461 .A314
JA

KANTO KO-SHIN-ETSU-SEI CHIIKI KEIZAI GAIKAN. Main/Corp Japan. Tokyo Tsusho Sangyokyoku. (19??)-. Japanese. Tsusho Sangyo Chosakai, (Research Institute on International Trade and Industry), Kobikikan Ginza Biru, 8-9 Ginza 2 chome Chuoku, Tokyo 104 Japan.

LC HC59 .K368
PL

KAPITALIZM. Vol. 1, No. 1 (1977)-. Periodical. Polish (summaries and/or abstracts in English and Russian). Four times a year. zl.80.00. Krajowa Agencja Wydawnicza, Ul. Wilcza 46, 00-679 Warsaw Poland.

LC HC463.K345 K37
JA

KASUMIGAURA CHIIKI KENKYU HOKOKU. Added/Corp Kasumigaura Chiiki Kenkyukai (Japan). (1979)-. Japanese. Kasumigaura Chiiki Kenkyukai Tsukuba Daigaku Chikyu Kagakukei Jinbun Chirigaku, Kenkyu Gurupu 1-1 Tennodai 1 Sakura-mura Niihari-gun, Ibaraki-ken 305 Japan.

LC HC497.Q3
GW

KATAR : WIRTSCHAFTLICHE ENTWICKLUNG. Main/Corp Germany (Federal Republic, 1949-). Bundesstelle fur Aussenhandelsinformation (Germany). German. One time a year. DM2.00. Bundesstelle fuer Aussenhandelsinformation, Agrippastrasse 87 93, D-50676 Cologne Germany. **Tel** 011 49 221 2057316, FAX 011 49 221 2057212.

LC HC466 .K38
KO

KDI PUNGIBYOL KYONGJE CHONMANG / QUARTERLY ECONOMIC OUTLOOK. Added/Corp Hanguk Kaebal Yonguwon. **VFOAT** K.D.I. Pungibyol Kyongje Chonmang; Quarterly Economic Outlook; Pungibyol Kyongje Chonmang. (1982)-. Periodical. Korean (English; summaries and/or abstracts in English). Four times a year. W8000. Korea Development Institute / Seoul, PO Box 113 Chung-Ryang, Seoul 130-650 Seoul South Korea. **Tel** 960-4815-6, FAX 82-02-961-5092, telex 25100 KDILINK K. **ED** Bon-Ho Koo. Index available. cum. index. **Circ:** 2,000.
Desc: Addresses major aspects of Korea's latest macroeconomic performance and near-term prospects. In addition, the Korean version carries one to two studies on current economic policy issues, often with recommendations.

LC HB9 .K4 ISSN 0022-9709
DD 330.9/005 JA

KEIO ECONOMIC STUDIES. [Keio econ. stud.]. **Added/Corp** Keio Gijuku Keizai Gakkai. Vol. 1 (1963)-. Periodical. English. Two times a year. $64.50. **(Subscription address:** Japan Publications Trading Company Ltd., PO Box 5030, Tokyo International, Tokyo 100-31 Japan. **Tel** 011 81 3 3292 3753.**)** ***Continues Mita Gakkai Zasshi.***
Ind/Abst Contents Recent Econ. J.; Econ. Lit. Index; J. Econ. Lit.

Business and Economics —Economic History, Conditions

LC HC462.9 .K3898
JA
KEIZAI DOKO GEPPO / TSUSHO SANGYOSHO SANGYO SEISAKUKYOKU CHOSAKA KANSHU. **Added/Corp** Japan. Tsusho Sangyosho. Sangyo Seisakukyoku. Chosaka. (19??)-. Periodical. Japanese. Twelve times a year. ¥9000. Tsusan Shiryo Chosakai, 5-12 Fujimi 2 chome, Chiyodaku, Tokyo 101 Japan.

LC HC462.9.K4363
JA
KEIZAI KISHODAI / ASAHI SHINBUN KEIZAIBU HEN. 1 (July/Sept. 1983)-. Periodical. Japanese. Four times a year. ¥250 (single issue). Asahi Shinbunsha, 3-2 Tsukiji 5 chome Chuoku, Tokyo 104 Japan.

LC HC463.K95 M55
JA
KEIZAI TOKEI NEMPO. (1976/77)-. Japanese. Minami Kyushu Zaimukyoku, 1-2 Ninomaru 860, Kumamoto Japan. **Continues** Minami Kyushu Keizai Tokei Nempo.

LC HC461 .K4593
DD 338.95
KEIZAI TOKEI NENKAN. **See** Business and Economics-Abstracting, Bibliographies and Statistics.

LC HC517.K4 G45b
GW
KENIA: WIRTSCHAFTSDATEN UND WIRTSCHAFTSDOKUMENTATION. **Main/Corp** Bundesstelle fur Aussenhandelsinformation (Germany). (19??)-. German. Irregular. DM2.00. Bundesstelle fuer Aussenhandelsinformation, Agrippastrasse 87 93, D-50676 Cologne Germany. **Tel** 011 49 221 2057316, FAX 011 49 221 2057212.

LC HC463.H63 T68a
JA
KENKYU NEMPO - TOYAMA DAIGAKU NIHONKAI KEIZAI KENKYUJO. **Main/Corp** Toyama Daigaku. Nihonkai Keizai Kenkyujo. **Added/Corp** Toyama Daigaku. Nihonkai Keizai Kenkyujo. Annual Bulletin on Economics and Social Science. **VFOAT** Annual Bulletin on Economics and Social Science. Vol. 1 (1975)-. Bulletin. Japanese. Toyama Daigaku Nihonkai Keizai Kenkyujo, 3190 Gofuku 930, Tayama Japan.

LC HC517.K4 K455 **ISSN** 1010-3716
DD 330.9/676/204
KE
KENYA REVIEW. [Kenya rev.]. Periodical. English. Three times a year. Sh20.00. Cienbi Company, PO Box 10028, Nairobi Kenya.

ISSN 1054-5700
DD 967
US
KENYA (SYRACUSE, N.Y.). (KENYA : A POLITICAL AND ECONOMIC FORECAST / POLITICAL RISK SERVICES.). [Kenya]. **Added/Corp** Political Risk Services (IBC USA (Publications) Inc.). (19??)-. English. $325.00. Political Risk Services, 6320 Fly Road, Suite 102, PO Box 248, East Syracuse NY 13057-0248. **Tel** (315)431-0511, FAX (315)431-0200.
Desc: Assesses the factors affecting the prospects for business and trade. Each report focuses specifically on business needs such as finding and developing markets, determining currency movements, or making judgements about capital investments or corporate security.

LC HC411 .A754a **ISSN** 0116-3000
DD 330.95/000
PH
KEY INDICATORS OF DEVELOPING ASIAN AND PACIFIC COUNTRIES. **Added/Corp** Economics and Development Resource Center (Asian Development Bank). **VFOAT** Key Indicators. Vol. 21 (July 1990)-. English. One time a year. $21.86. Oxford University Press / UK, Walton Street, Oxford OX2 6DP United Kingdom. **Tel** 011 44 1865 56767, FAX 011 44 1865 267773, telex 851/837330 OXPRES G. (**Subscription address:** Oxford University Press / USA, Journals Marketing Department, Oxford University Press, 2001 Evans Road, Cary NC 27513. **Tel** (800)451-7556, (919)677-0977, FAX (919)677-1714.) available with illustrations. **Continues** Key Indicators of Developing Member Countries of ADB, 0116-3000.

LC HC685.A1 K49
DD 330.993/4
NN
KEY INDICATORS (PORT-VILA, VANUATU). (KEY INDICATORS.). **VFOAT** Indicateurs Principaux. Mar. 1982-. English (French). Twelve times a year. **Absorbed** Hotel Statistics; Overseas Trade (Vanuatu. Bureau of Statistics). Preliminary Values and Principal Exports.

LC HD9710.K64 K494
KO
KIA. (19??)-. Periodical. Korean. Four times a year. Kia / Korea, 1-1042 Youido-dong Yongdungpo-ku, Seoul Korea.

ISSN 0340-6989
GW
KIELER STUDIEN. (KIELER STUDIEN : FORSCHUNGSBERICHTE DES INSTITUTS FUER WELTWIRTSCHAFT AN DER UNIVERSITAET KIEL.). [Kieler stud.]. **Added/Corp** Universitat Kiel. Institut fuer Weltwirtschaft. (1949)-. Monographic series. German (English). Irregular. Price varies per volume. JCB Mohr / Paul Siebeck, Postfach 2040, D-72010 Tuebingen Germany. **Tel** 011 49 7071 9230, FAX 011 49 7071 51104, telex 7/262872 mohr d.

LC HC461 .K54 **ISSN** 0387-1789
DD 330
JA
KIKAN KEIZAI KENKYU. **Added/Corp** Osaka Shiritsu Daigaku. Keizai Kenkyukai. **VFOAT** Keizai Kenkyu; Quarterly Journal of Economic Studies. (19??)-. Periodical. Japanese. Four times a year. Osaka Shiritsu Daigaku Keizai Kenkyukai, 3-Ban 138-gosugimoto 3-chome Sumiyoshi-ku, Osaka-shi 558 Japan.
Ind/Abst Econ. Lit. Index.

LC HC443.V5 N43a
VM
KINH-TE TAP-SAN. **Main/Corp** Ngan-Hang Quoc-Gia Viet-Nam. **VFOAT** Bulletin Economique. (Feb. 15, 1955)-. Bulletin. French (Vietnamese). Twelve times a year. 17 Ben Chuong Duong, Saigon South Vietnam.

LC HC463.K55 K54
JA
KINKI CHIIKI TSUSHO SANGYO TOKEI YORAN. **Added/Corp** Japan. Osaka Tsusho Sangyokyoku. (19??)-. Japanese. Tsusho Sangyo Chosakai, (Research Institute on International Trade and Industry), Kobikikan Ginza Biru, 8-9 Ginza 2 chome Chuoku, Tokyo 104 Japan.

LC HC463.K55 K55
JA
KINKI ZAISEI KEIZAI TOKEI NEMPO. **Added/Corp** Japan. Kinki Zaimukyoku. (19??)-. Periodical. Japanese. Kinki Zaimukyoku, 25 Hoenzakacho 6 Higashi-Ku 540, Osaka Japan.

LC HC463.W3 K54
JA
KISHU KEIZAISHI BUNKASHI KENKYUJO KIYO. **Added/Corp** Wakayama Daigaku. Kishu Keizaishi Bunkashi Kenkyujo. No. 1 (1981)-. Japanese. Wakayama Daigaku Kishu Keizaishi Bunkashi Kenkyujo, 7-1 Nishi Takamatsu 1, Wakayama-Shi Japan.

LC HB9 .K449
JA
KOBE GAKUIN KEIZAIGAKU RONSHU. **Added/Corp** Kobe Gakuin Daigaku Keizaigakkai. **VFOAT** Kobegakuin Economic Papers. Vol. 1 (1969)-. Periodical. Japanese (English). Four times a year. ¥2,500. Kobe-Gakuin Daigaku Keizaigakkai, c/o Kobe-Gakuin University, Nishi-ku Kobe 673 Japan. **Tel** 078-974-1551, telex 078-974-5689. **ED** Takeshi Yoshimi. Index available. cum. index. **Bk Rev. Circ:** 1,500 (ctrl)

LC HB9 .K45 **ISSN** 0454-1111
JA
KOBE UNIVERSITY ECONOMIC REVIEW. **Added/Corp** Kobe Daigaku. Kobe Daigaku. Keizai Gakubu. Vol. 1 (1955)-. Periodical. English. Irregular. Kobe University / Faculty of Economics, 1 1 Rokkodai Cho Nada Ku, Kobe 67 Japan. **Tel** 011 81 078 8811212, FAX 011 81 078 8616434.
Ind/Abst Econ. Lit. Index; J. Econ. Lit.

LC HC461 .A3148
JA
KOKOGYO SHISU NEMPO. **Main/Corp** Japan. Tsusho Sangyosho Daijin Kambo. Chosa Tokeibu. (19??)-. Periodical. Japanese. One time a year. ¥2000. Okurasho Insatukyoku, (Printing Bureau Ministry of Finance), 2-4 Toranomon 2 chome, Minatoku Tokyo 105 Japan.

LC HD911.A1 K64
JA
KOKUDO TOKEI YORAN. **Added/Corp** Japan. Kokudocho. (19??)-. Japanese. ¥3500. Taisei Shuppansha, 1-7-11 Hanegi 1, Setagaya-ku, Tokyo-to Japan.

LC HC196
DD 330.9/861/063
GW
KOLUMBIEN : WIRTSCHAFTLICHE ENTWICKLUNG. **Main/Corp** Bundesstelle fur Aussenhandelsinformation (Germany). German. Bundesstelle fuer Aussenhandelsinformation, Agrippastrasse 87 93, D-50676 Cologne Germany. **Tel** 011 49 221 2057316, FAX 011 49 221 2057212.

LC HC362.2 .K65 **ISSN** 0075-6709
DD 338.7/4/09481
NO
KOMPASS; INDEKS OVER NORGES INDUSTRI OG NRINGSLIV. **VFOAT** Indeks Over Norges Industri og Nringsliv; Kompass-Norge. Vol. 1 (1970)-. English (French, German, Norwegian and Spanish). One time a year. Business Press International USA, 205 East 42nd Street, New York NY 10017. **Tel** (212)867-2080.

LC HC10 .K539 **ISSN** 0023-3498
GW
CCC
KONJUNKTURPOLITIK. [Konjunkturpolitik]. (Oct. 1954)-. Periodical. German. Six times a year. $128.96. Duncker und Humblot Verlag, Postfach 410329, D-12113 Berlin Germany. **Tel** 011 49 30 79000612, 011 49 30 79000613. **ED** Begerundet Von Albert Wissler.
Ind/Abst Econ. Lit. Index; J. Econ. Lit.; PAIS Int. Print (1991-).

LC HC361 .O43
DD 330.9481/005
NO
KONOMISK REVY. **Added/Corp** Forretningsbankenes Konjunkturinstitutt (Norway) Norske Bankforening. Vol. 1 (1945)-. Periodical. Norwegian. Irregular. Kr250.00. Forretningsbankenes Felleskont, Postboks 1354 Vika, Oslo 1 Norway. **Tel** +472 411830. **ED** Magne Haug. **Ad Acc.** ctrl circ.
Desc: Published by the Norwegian Banker's Association, covering Norwegian banking and the Norwegian economy.

KO
TITLE CHANGE
KOREA ECONOMIC REPORT. **VFOAT** Economic Report. Vol. 3, No. 9 (Sept. 1988)-(Jan. 1995). Periodical. English. World Media Inc, Yodio PO Box 963, Seoul 151-609 Korea. **Tel** 011 82 2 7835283, FAX 011 82 2 7801717. **ED** Chong-Tae Kim (phone: (02)783 5283). cum. index. **Ad Acc, Adv Mgr:** M.H. Jeon, **Tel** (02)783-5283. **Circ:** 32,000 (ctrl). **Continues** Korea-Europe Economic Report. **Continued by** Economic Report (Seoul, Korea).

LC HC517.S7 A183A
DD 330.9/68/06
SA
KORTTERMYN EKONOMIESE AANWYSERS / REPUBLIEK VAN SUID-AFRIKA, BURO VIR STATISTIEK. **Main/Corp** South Africa. Dept. of Statistics. **VFOAT** Short-Term Economic Indicators; Short Term Economic Indicators. June 1967-. Periodical. Afrikaans (English). Twelve times a year. Government Printer / South Africa, Bosman Street, Private Bag X85, Pretoria 0001 South Africa. **Tel** 011 27 12 3239731 ext. 262.

LC HC461 .K97a **ISSN** 0387-2955
DD 330.9/52/04
JA
KSU ECONOMIC AND BUSINESS REVIEW. [KSU econ. bus. rev.]. **Main/Corp** Kyoto Sangyo Daigaku Keizai Keiei Gakkai. No. 1 (1974)-. Periodical. English (French, German and Spanish). One time a year. Free. Kyoto Sangyo University Society of Economics and Business Administration, Motoyama Kamigamo, Kitaku Kyoto 603 Japan. **Tel** 075 701 2151. **ED** Kiichi Mizokawa. Index available. cum. index. **Bk Rev. Circ:** 720.
Ind/Abst Contents Recent Econ. J.

LC HC152.5.A1
GW
KUBA : WIRTSCHAFTLICHE ENTWICKLUNG. **Main/Corp** Bundesstelle fur Aussenhandelsinformation (Germany). (19??)-. German. DM2.00. Bundesstelle fuer Aussenhandelsinformation, Agrippastrasse 87 93, D-50676 Cologne Germany. **Tel** 011 49 221 2057316, FAX 011 49 221 2057212.

LC HC59 .K797
KO
KUKCHE KYONGJE TONGGYE YONBO. **VFOAT** Year Book of International Economic Statistics. Korean. One time a year. Kukche Kyongje Yongwon, 541 5-ka Namdaemun-ro, Chung-ku, Seoul South Korea.

ISSN 1055-9434
DD 953
US
KUWAIT (SYRACUSE, N.Y.). (KUWAIT : A POLITICAL AND ECONOMIC FORECAST.). [Kuwait]. **Added/Corp** Political Risk Services (IBC USA (Publications) Inc.). (19??)-. English. $325.00. Political Risk Services, 6320 Fly Road, Suite 102, PO Box 248, East Syracuse NY 13057-0248. **Tel** (315)431-0511, FAX (315)431-0200.
Desc: Assesses the factors affecting the prospects for business and trade. Each report focuses specifically on business needs such as finding and developing markets, determining currency movements, or making judgements about capital investments or corporate security.

LC HC415.39.A1 K886
DD 330.953/67/005
GW
KUWAIT, WIRTSCHAFTLICHE ENTWICKLUNG / BUNDESSTELLE FUR AUSSENHANDELSINFORMATION. German. DM5.00. Bundesstelle fuer Aussenhandelsinformation, Agrippastrasse 87 93, D-50676 Cologne Germany. **Tel** 011 49 221 2057316, FAX 011 49 221 2057212.

Business and Economics — Economic History, Conditions

LC HC497.K8
GW
KUWAIT : WIRTSCHAFTSDATEN UND WIRTSCHAFTSDOKUMENTATION. **Main/Corp** Bundesstelle fur Aussenhandelsinformation (Germany). German. DM2.00. Bundesstelle fuer Aussenhandelsinformation, Agrippastrasse 87 93, D-50676 Cologne Germany. **Tel** 011 49 221 2057316, FAX 011 49 221 2057212.

LC HC466 .K897
KO
TITLE CHANGE
KYONGJE PURIPUSU. Added/Corp Hanguk Sanop Unhaeng. (19??)-(1993). Periodical. Korean. Hanguk Sanop Unhaeng, 140 Ui 1 2-ka Namdaemun-no, Chung-ku, Seoul Korea. **Continued by** KDB Sanop Kyongje.

LC HC466 .S65
KO
KYONGJE RIBYU. VFOAT Economic Review. Periodical. Korean (Korean). Twelve times a year. Soul Sintak Unhaeng, 10-1 2-ka Namdaemun Chung-ku, Seoul South Korea. **Continues** Kyongje Ribyu (Soul Unhaeng).

LC HC463.K9 K94
JA
KYOTO-FU SANGYO NO TEMBO / HENSHU, KYOTO FURITSU CHUSHO KIGYO SOGO SHIDOSHO. Added/Corp Kyoto Furitsu Chusho Kigyo Sogo Shidosho. (1958)-. Japanese. Every 3 years. Kyoto Furitsu Chusho Kigyo Sogo Shidojo, (Kyoto Prefectural Comprehensive Guidance Center, for Small and Medium Enterprises), 31 Hachimancho Nishi 7 jo, Shimogyoku Kyotoshi, Kyotofu 600 Japan.

LC HC463.K95 J34b
JA
KYUSHU TSUSHO SANGYO NEMPO. **Main/Corp** Japan. Fukuoka Tsusho Sangyokyoku. **Added/Corp** Kyushu Shoko Jiho. (1948)-. Periodical. Japanese. One time a year. ¥2,000. Kyushu Shoko Kyokai, (Kyushu Association of Commerce and Industry), 13-4 Hakataeki Higashi 2-chome, Hakataku Fukuokashi, Fukuokaken 812 Japan.

LC HC415.38.A1 S73
DD 330.953/65/005
GW
LAENDERBERICHT. BAHRAIN. See Business and Economics-Abstracting, Bibliographies and Statistics.

LC HC142.A1 G47A
GW
LANDERKURZBERICHT : BELIZE. **Main/Corp** Germany (West). Statistisches Bundesamt. **VFOAT** Belize. German. DM3.50. W. Kohlhammer Verlag GmbH, Postfach 800430, D-70549 Stuttgart Germany. **Tel** 011 49 711 78630, FAX 011 49 711 7863430, telex 7-255820.

LC HC443.V5 G45A
GW
LANDERKURZBERICHT : VIETNAM. **Main/Corp** Germany (West). Statistisches Bundesamt. **VFOAT** Vietnam. German. 3.50. W. Kohlhammer Verlag GmbH, Postfach 800430, D-70549 Stuttgart Germany. **Tel** 011 49 711 78630, FAX 011 49 711 7863430, telex 7-255820.

LC HC448.Y63 Y644A
IO
LAPORAN DINAS PERINDUSTRIAN DAERAH ISTIMEWA YOGYAKARTA. **Main/Corp** Yogyakarta, Indonesia (Daerah Istimewa). Dinas Perindustrian. Indonesian. Jl Kusumanegara 3, Yogyakarta Indonesia.

LC HC448.Y63 I5A
IO
LAPORAN - KANTOR WILAYAH DEPARTEMEN PERINDUSTRIAN DAERAH ISTIMEWA YOGYAKARTA. **Main/Corp** Indonesia. Departemen Perindustrian. Kantor Wilayah Daerah Istimewa Yogyakarta. Indonesian. Kantor Wilayah Departemen Perindustrian Daerah Istimewa Yogyakarta, Jln Kusumanegara 3, Yogyakarta Indonesia.

LC HN710.Z9 C6365
DD 307./14/09598
IO
LAPORAN / LEMBAGA STUDI PEMBANGUNAN. Main/Corp Lembaga Studi Pembangunan (Indonesia). **VFOAT** Indonesian (English). Gedung Arthaloka Lantai, 17 J1 Jenderal Sudirman, 2 Kotakpos 1 Kbys/Jaksel, Jakarta Pusat Indonesia.

LC HC448.R5 R533a
DD 330
IO
LAPORAN TAHUNAN. Main/Corp Indonesia. Departemen Perindustrian. Kantor Wilayah Propinsi Riau. **Added/Corp** Riau (Indonesia : Province). Dinas Perindustrian. (1977)-. Indonesian. One time a year. Kantor Wilayah Propinsi Riau, Departemen Perindustrian, Pekanbaru Indonesia. **Continues** Riau (Indonesia : Province). Dinas Perindustrian. Laporan Tahunan.

LC HC448.B3 I535A
IO
LAPORAN TAHUNAN - KANTOR WILAYAH DEPARTEMEN PERINDUSTRIAN PROPINSI BALI. **Main/Corp** Indonesia. Departemen Perindustrian. Kantor Wilayah Propinsi Bali. Indonesian. Kantor Wilayah Departemen Perindustrian Propinsi Bali, Jl Melati No 31, Denpasar Indonesia. **Continues** Indonesia. Departemen Peridustrian. Kantor Wilayah Propinsi Bali. Laporan - Kantor Wilayah Propinsi Bali. Laporan - Kantor Wilayah Departemen Perindustrian Propinsi Bali.

LC HC448.S782 I54A
DD 330
IO
LAPORAN TAHUNAN - KANTOR WILAYAH DEPARTEMEN PERINDUSTRIAN PROPINSI SULAWESI TENGAH. See Business and Economics-Abstracting, Bibliographies and Statistics.

LC HC121 .L26
DD 330.9/8/003
SZ
LATEINAMERIKA NACHRICHTEN. Periodical. English. Lateinamerikanisches Institut, Varnbuelstrasse 14, St. Gallen Switzerland. **Ind/Abst** Hisp. Am. Period. Index, HAPI.

UK
LATIN AMERICA MONITOR. ANDEAN GROUP. VFOAT Andean Group; Latin American Monitor. Andean Group. Vol. 8, No. 2 (Mar. 1991)-. Periodical. English. Twelve times a year. Business Monitor International, 56 60 St. John Street, London EC1M 4DT United Kingdom. **Tel** 011 44 171 6083646, FAX 011 44 171 6083620. **Continues** Latin American Monitor. 3, Andean Group.

LC HC161 .L255
DD 330.98/0005
ISSN 0143-5248
UK
LATIN AMERICA REGIONAL REPORTS. ANDEAN GROUP. [Lat. Am. reg. rep. Andean Group.]. **VFOAT** A.Latin America regional reports: P.Andean Group report; A.Latin American regional reports: P.Andean Group report; A.Andean Group; A.Andean Group report. (Nov. 1979)-. Periodical. English. Ten times a year. $185.00. Lettres UK Ltd, 61 Old Street, London EC1V 9HX United Kingdom. **Tel** 011 44 171 2510012, FAX 011 44 171 2538193. **ED** Peter Rodger. available on an online database from Lexis-Nexis; and (files 771,772/Full-Text) DIALOG. **Desc:** Gives a perceptive look at Bolivia, Colombia, Ecuador, Peru and Venezuela, examining and evaluating the key issues and developments that effect the Andean countries.

LC HC186 .L37
DD 330.981/005
ISSN 0143-5272
UK
TITLE CHANGE
LATIN AMERICA REGIONAL REPORTS. BRAZIL. [Lat. Am. reg. rep. Brazil.]. **VFOAT** Latin America Regional Reports. Brazil Report; Latin American Regional Reports. Brazil Report; Brazil; Brazil Report. (Nov. 9, 1979)-(19??). Periodical. English. Lettres UK Ltd, 61 Old Street, London EC1V 9HX United Kingdom. **Tel** 011 44 171 2510012, FAX 011 44 171 2538193. **ED** Peter Rogers. available on an online database from NEXIS. **Continued by** Brazil Report, 0143-5272. **Desc:** This Latin American Regional Report focuses on the unique problems and opportunities of Brazil. Examines key economic, political and social issues in depth. Provides expert analysis on the facts behind the headlines.

LC HC161 .L256
DD 330.9/8/0005
ISSN 0143-5256
UK
LATIN AMERICA REGIONAL REPORTS. SOUTHERN CONE. [Lat. Am. reg. rep. South. cone]. **VFOAT** Latin America Regional Reports: Southern Cone Report; Latin American Regional Reports: Southern Cone Report; Southern Cone; Southern Cone Report. (Dec. 1979)-. Periodical. English. Ten times a year. $185.00. Lettres UK Ltd, 61 Old Street, London EC1V 9HX United Kingdom. **Tel** 011 44 171 2510012, FAX 011 44 171 2538193. **ED** Peter Rodger. available on an online database from Lexis-Nexis. **Desc:** This Latin American Regional Report covers Argentina, Chile, Paraguay and Uruguay giving insight into the current developments involving regional integration attempts and the stabilising of new democratic regimes as well as providing news about business and investment opportunities.

LC HC121 .L276
DD 338.5/443/098
ISSN 8756-1301
US
LATIN AMERICAN ECONOMIC OUTLOOK. [Lat. Am. econ. outlook]. Periodical. English. WEFA / Philadelphia, PO Box 8500, Suite 1995, Philadelphia PA 19178. **Tel** (215)667-6000, telex 710 6600575. **Continues** Latin American Outlook, 0749-9256.

LC F1401 .L327
DD 980/.005
ISSN 0090-9416
US
LATIN AMERICAN INDEX. See Political Science.

UK
LATIN AMERICAN MONITOR. CARIBBEAN. VFOAT Caribbean; Latin American Monitor. Caribbean. Vol. 8, No. 2 (Mar. 1991)-. English. Twelve times a year. Business Monitor International, 56 60 St. John Street, London EC1M 4DT United Kingdom. **Tel** 011 44 171 6083646, FAX 011 44 171 6083620. **Continues** Latin America Monitor. 5, Caribbean.

LC HC121 .L324
DD 330.98/0005
ISSN 0732-6270
US
LATIN AMERICAN REVIEW. [Lat. Am. rev.]. **Added/Corp** Data Resources, inc. **VFOAT** Data Resources Latin American Review. (19??)-. Periodical. English. Four times a year. DRI McGraw Hill, 24 Hartwell Avenue, Lexington MA 02173. **Tel** (617)863-5100, FAX (617)860-6464, (617)860-6416.

LC HC10 .L42
DD 309.1/04
ISSN 0163-3635
US
LEADERS. [Leaders]. **VFOAT** Leaders Magazine. (1978)-. Periodical. English. Four times a year. Free on request. Leaders Magazine Inc, 59 East 54th Street, New York NY 10022. **Tel** (212)758-0740.

LC HC311 .L47
DD 330.9493/005
ISSN 0772-0831
BE
LETTRE DE CONJONCTURE (BRUSSELS, BELGIUM). (LETTRE DE CONJONCTURE / MINISTERE DES AFFAIRES ECONOMIQUES, DIRECTION GENERALE DES ETUDES ET DE LA DOCUMENTATION.). **Added/Corp** Belgium. Ministere des Affaires Economiques. Direction Generale des Etudes et de la Documentation. No. 1 (1984)-. Periodical. French (Dutch). Twelve times a year. 400F, 500F other; 1250F Belgium, 1500F other Comes with combination Apercu Trimestriel de l'Economie. Direction Generales des Etudes et de la Documentation, 6 rue de l'Industrie, 1040 Brussels Belgium. **Tel** 02 506.51.11, 02 506.63.07, FAX 02 513.46.57. Circ: 7,500 (ctrl). **Continues in part** Belgium. Ministere des Affaires Economiques. Direction Generale des Etudes et de la Documentation. Apercu de l'Evolution Economique. **Desc:** A report on the current state of the Belgian economy.

LC HC497.L4
GW
LIBANON : WIRTSCHAFTLICHE ENTWICKLUNG. Main/Corp Bundesstelle fur Aussenhandelsinformation (Germany). German. DM2.00. Bundesstelle fuer Aussenhandelsinformation, Agrippastrasse 87 93, D-50676 Cologne Germany. **Tel** 011 49 221 2057316, FAX 011 49 221 2057212.

LC HC497.L4
GW
LIBANON : WIRTSCHAFTSDATEN UND WIRTSCHAFTSDOKUMENTATION. **Main/Corp** Bundesstelle fur Aussenhandelsinformation (Germany). German. DM2.00. Bundesstelle fuer Aussenhandelsinformation, Agrippastrasse 87 93, D-50676 Cologne Germany. **Tel** 011 49 221 2057316, FAX 011 49 221 2057212.

LC HC591.L6
GW
LIBERIA : WIRTSCHAFTLICHE ENTWICKLUNG. Main/Corp Bundesstelle fur Aussenhandelsinformation (Germany). German. Bundesstelle fuer Aussenhandelsinformation, Agrippastrasse 87 93, D-50676 Cologne Germany. **Tel** 011 49 221 2057316, FAX 011 49 221 2057212.

DD 961
ISSN 1054-5719
US
LIBYA (SYRACUSE, N.Y.). (LIBYA : A POLITICAL AND ECONOMIC FORECAST / POLITICAL RISK SERVICES.). [Libya]. **Added/Corp** Political Risk Services (IBC USA (Publications) Inc.). (19??)-. English. $325.00. Political Risk Services, 6320 Fly Road, Suite 102, PO Box 248, East Syracuse NY 13057-0248. **Tel** (315)431-0511, FAX (315)431-0200. **Desc:** Assesses the factors affecting the prospects for business and trade. Each report focuses specifically on business needs such as finding and developing markets, determining currency movements, or making judgements about capital investments or corporate security.

LC HC567.L5
DD 330.9/61/204
GW
LIBYEN : WIRTSCHAFTLICHE ENTWICKLUNG. Main/Corp Germany (Federal Republic, 1949-). Bundesstelle fur Aussenhandelsinformation (Germany). (19??)-. German. One time a year. DM2.00. Bundesstelle fuer Aussenhandelsinformation, Agrippastrasse 87 93, D-50676 Cologne Germany. **Tel** 011 49 221 2057316, FAX 011 49 221 2057212.

Business and Economics —Economic History, Conditions

LC HC307.L5 L53
IT
LIGURIA TRE / A CURA DEL CENTRO STUDI, UNIONE DELLE CAMERE DI COMMERCIO LIGURI. Periodical. Italian. Four times a year. Centro Studi Unioncamere Liguri, Via Garibaldi 3, Geneva Switzerland.

LC HC10 .L55 **ISSN** 0953-5004
DD 330.941/005
UK
CEASED
LLOYDS BANK ANNUAL REVIEW. **Added/Corp** Lloyds Bank. Vol. 1 (1988)-Vol. 5. English. Pinter Publishers, 25 Floral Street, London WC2 9DS United Kingdom. **Tel** 011 44 181 2409233, **FAX** 011 44 181 3795553. **ED** Christopher Johnson. Index available. ctrl circ. available on an online database (file 648/Full-Text) from DIALOG. Documents available from The Genuine Article. **Continues** Lloyds Bank Review, 0024-547X.
Desc: Deals with major and current economic issues.
Ind/Abst Bus. ASAP (1992-) [Full Txt.]; Bus. Index (1988-); Curr. Contents Soc. Behav. Sci.; Econ. Lit. Index (?-199?); Gen. BusinessFile (1988-); Gen. Period. Index (1988-); Int. Labour Doc.; Res. Alert [Full Cov.].

ISSN 0269-0942
UK
CCC
LOCAL ECONOMY. (LOCAL ECONOMY : LE : JOURNAL OF THE LONDON ECONOMIC POLICY UNIT.). **Added/Corp** London Economic Policy Unit. **VFOAT** LE. Issue No. 1 (Spring 1986)-. Periodical. English. Four times a year. $168.00. Longman Group Ltd., Fourth Avenue, Longman House, Harlow Essex CM19 5SR United Kingdom. **Tel** 011 44 1279 429655, **FAX** 011 44 1279 431067, telex 81259. **ED** Sam Aaronouitch, M Geddes. Index available. **Bk Rev. Ad Acc. Circ:** 650.
Ind/Abst Curr. Cit.; Int. Bibliogr. Sociol.

LC HC101 .W5423
DD 338.5/443/0973
US
LONG-TERM ALTERNATIVE SCENARIOS AND 25-YEAR EXTENSION. **VFOAT** Long Term Alternative Scenarios and 25-Year Extension; Long-Term Alternative Scenarios and Twenty Five-Year Extension. (1986)-. English. Two times a year. WEFA / Philadelphia, PO Box 8500, Suite 1995, Philadelphia PA 19178. **Tel** (215)667-6000, telex 710 6700575. **Continues** Long-Term Alternative Scenarios and 20-Year Extension.

LC HC101 .W5422 **ISSN** 8755-1500
DD 338.5/443/0973
US
LONG-TERM FORECAST. [Long-term forecast]. **VFOAT** Long Term Forecast. English. $15,000 (both print and online), $21,000 (includes short-term version). WEFA / Philadelphia, PO Box 8500, Suite 1995, Philadelphia PA 19178. **Tel** (215)667-6000, telex 710 6700575. **ED** Kurt Karl. **Circ:** 600 (ctrl). **Continues** Wharton Long-Term Forecast, 8755-1497.
Desc: Long-term economic forecasts of the US energy, demographic and industry data in great detail.

LC HC101 .L59 **ISSN** 0749-923X
DD 338.5/442/0973
US
LONG-TERM SERVICE DATA BANKS. [Long-term serv. data banks]. **VFOAT** Long Term Service Data Banks. English. WEFA / Philadelphia, PO Box 8500, Suite 1995, Philadelphia PA 19178. **Tel** (215)667-6000, telex 710 6700575.

LC HC101 .L62 **ISSN** 0747-525X
DD 330.9/005
US
LOOKING AHEAD (WASHINGTON, D.C. : 1982). (LOOKING AHEAD.). [Look. ahead]. Vol. 7, No. 1 (Dec. 1982)-. Periodical. English. Four times a year. $35.00. National Planning Association, 1424 16th Street Northwest, Suite 700, Washington DC 20036. **Tel** (202)265-7685. **ED** Martha Lee Benz. **Circ:** 1,000 (ctrl). **Formed by the union of** Looking Ahead & Projection Highlights, 0087-9583 **and** New International Realities, 0362-9570.
Desc: Focuses on developments in domestic and international policy issues, their implications and findings. Provides articles on NPA committee and staff activities and ongoing research.
Ind/Abst Energy Res. Abstr. (Dec. 1982-).

LC HG107.L8 L588 **ISSN** 0193-5712
DD 338
US
LOUISIANA BUSINESS SURVEY. [La. bus. surv.]. **Added/Corp** University of New Orleans. Division of Business and Economic Research. Louisiana State University in New Orleans. Division of Business and Economic Research. Vol. 1 (1970)-. Periodical. English. Two times a year. Free on request. University of New Orleans / Louisiana Business Survey, Division of Business and Economic Research, College of Business Administration, New Orleans LA 70148. **Tel** (504)286-6248, **FAX** (504)286-6958. **ED** Patricia J. Connor. **Circ:** 15,000 (ctrl).
Desc: Articles reporting empirical studies of business, government and economic sectors of Louisiana or greater New Orleans area.
Ind/Abst PAIS Int. Print (1991-).

SW
LUND PAPERS IN ECONOMIC HISTORY. **Added/Corp** Lunds Universitet. Ekonomisk-Historiska Institutionen. No. 1 (1990)-. Monographic series. English. Price varies per volume. **Continues** Meddelande Fran Ekonomisk-Historiska Institutionen, Lunds Universitet.

LC HC330.A1
GW
LUXEMBURG : WIRTSCHAFT IN ZAHLEN UND WIRTSCHAFTSDOKUMENTATION. **Main/Corp** Bundesstelle fur Aussenhandelsinformation (Germany). German. DM4.00. Bundesstelle fuer Aussenhandelsinformation, Agrippastrasse 87 93, D-50676 Cologne Germany. **Tel** 011 49 221 2057316, **FAX** 011 49 221 2057212.

LC HC497.M24 G46a
DD 330.9/51/26
GW
MACAN : WIRTSCHAFTLICHE ENTWICKLUNG. **Main/Corp** Bundesstelle fuer Aussenhandelsinformation (Germany). (19??)-. German. Bundesstelle fuer Aussenhandelsinformation, Agrippastrasse 87 93, D-50676 Cologne Germany. **Tel** 011 49 221 2057316, **FAX** 011 49 221 2057212.

LC HC547.T8 M33
DD 338/.0025/611
TI
MADE IN TUNISIA. (1974)-. French (French). 6 Avenue Montplaisir, Tunis Tunisia.

ISSN 0961-9836
DD 330.961
UK
MAGHREB QUARTERLY REPORT. [Maghreb q. Rep.]. **VFOAT** MEED Quarterly Report. Maghreb. (1991)-. English. Four times a year. $385.02. MEED Limited, MEED House, 21 John Street, London WC1N 2BP United Kingdom. **Tel** 011 44 171 4045513, **FAX** 011 44 171 2421450, telex 266872 MEEDAR G.

LC HC10 .O68 **ISSN** 0474-5523
FR
MAIN ECONOMIC INDICATORS. [Main econ. indic.]. **Main/Corp** Organisation for Economic Co-Operation and Development. **Added/Corp** Organisation for Economic Co-operation and Development. Principaux Indicateurs Economiques. **VFOAT** Principaux Indicateurs Economiques. (March 1962)-. English (French). Twelve times a year. $290.00. OECD Publications and Information Center, 2 rue Andre-Pascal, 75775 Paris Cedex 16 France. **Tel** 011 33 1 49104262, US:(202)785-6323, **FAX** 011 33 1 45248500, 011 33 1 45248176, telex 620 160 OCDE. (**Subscription address:** OECD Publications Center, 2001 L Street, Suite 700, Washington DC 20036. **Tel** (202)822-3873, (202)785-6323.) **Continues in part** Statistiques Generales (Organisation for Economic Co-Operation and Development). **Absorbed by** Statistiques Generales (Organisation for Economic Co-Operation and Development) **and** Organisation for Economic Co-Operation and Development. Bulletin of Foreign Trade Statistics. Series A, Overall Trade by Countries.
Desc: Essential source of timely statistics for OECD member countries. Graphs provide a picture of the most recent changes in member country economies and tables give statistics and/or indicators for gross national product, industrial production, deliveries, stocks and orders, construction, wholesale and retail sales, employment, wages, prices, finance, foreign trade, and balance of payments.

LC WMLC L 83/3469 **ISSN** 0474-5442
FR
MAIN ECONOMIC INDICATORS. HISTORICAL STATISTICS / ORGANISATION FOR ECONOMIC CO-OPERATION AND DEVELOPMENT. **Added/Corp** Organisation for Economic Co-Operation and Development. **VFOAT** Principaux Indicateurs Economiques; Historical Statistics. (19??)-. English (French). Irregular. $58.00. OECD Publications and Information Center, 2 rue Andre-Pascal, 75775 Paris Cedex 16 France. **Tel** 011 33 1 49104262, US:(202)785-6323, **FAX** 011 33 1 45248500, 011 33 1 45248176, telex 620 160 OCDE. (**Subscription address:** OECD Publications Center, 2001 L Street, Suite 700, Washington DC 20036. **Tel** (202)822-3873, (202)785-6323.)

LC HC107.M2 M36 **ISSN** 0025-0619
US
MAINE BUSINESS INDICATORS. **Added/Corp** Maine National Bank. Maine College-Community Research Program. Bowdoin College. Center for Economic Research. Bowdoin College. Public Affairs Research Center. Vol. 1 (Sept. 1956)-. Periodical. English. Four times a year. Free on request. Center of Business & Economic Research / Maine, University of Southern Maine, 118 Bedford Street, Portland MD 04103. **Tel** (207)780-4187, **FAX** (207)780-4046. **ED** Robert C. McMahan. **Circ:** 4,900.
Desc: Contains Maine oriented articles on economic development and analysis, industry studies, and economic public policy. It also maintains the Maine Business Index as a measure of changes in the level of Maine's economy.

LC HC497.T8 M34
TS
MAJALLAT AL-TIJARAH WA-AL-SINAAH, DUBAYY. **VFOAT** Dubai Trade & Industry Magazine. Vol. 1, No. 1 (December 1975)-. Periodical. Arabic (English). Ghurfat Tijarat Wa-Sinaat Dubayy, PO Box 1457, Dubayy Trucial States United Arab Emirates.

LC HC441.A1 M33
IO
MAKALAH STAF LPEM. **VFOAT** Makalah Staf L.P.E.M. No. 1-. Periodical. Indonesian. Irregular. Lpem-Feui, Jln Salemba Raya No 4, Jakarta-Pusat Indonesia.

LC HC517.M3
DD 330.9/689/704
GW
MALAWI : WIRTSCHAFTLICHE ENTWICKLUNG. **Main/Corp** Bundesstelle fur Aussenhandelsinformation (Germany). German. Bundesstelle fuer Aussenhandelsinformation, Agrippastrasse 87 93, D-50676 Cologne Germany. **Tel** 011 49 221 2057316, **FAX** 011 49 221 2057212.

LC HC445.5.A1 M32 **ISSN** 0542-3937
MY
MALAYSIA INDUSTRIAL DIGEST. **Added/Corp** Lembaga Kemajuan Perusahaan Persekutuan. Vol. 1 (1968)-. Periodical. English. Four times a year. Free on request. Malaysian Industrial Development Authority, PO Box 10618, Kuala Lumpur Malaysia. **Tel** 011 60 3 2553633.

ISSN 1054-5727
DD 959
US
MALAYSIA (SYRACUSE, N.Y.). (MALAYSIA : A POLITICAL AND ECONOMIC FORECAST.). [Malaysia]. **Added/Corp** Political Risk Services (IBC USA (Publications) Inc.). (19??)-. English. $325.00. Political Risk Services, 6320 Fly Road, Suite 102, PO Box 248, East Syracuse NY 13057-0248. **Tel** (315)431-0511, **FAX** (315)431-0200.
Desc: Assesses the factors affecting the prospects for business and trade. Each report focuses specifically on business needs such as finding and developing markets, determining currency movements, or making judgements about capital investments or corporate security.

LC HC445.5.A1
GW
MALAYSIA : WIRTSCHAFTSDATEN UND WIRTSCHAFTSDOKUMENTATION. **Main/Corp** Bundesstelle fur Aussenhandelsinformation (Germany). German. DM2.00. Bundesstelle fuer Aussenhandelsinformation, Agrippastrasse 87 93, D-50676 Cologne Germany. **Tel** 011 49 221 2057316, **FAX** 011 49 221 2057212.

LC HC445.5.A1 M327
DD 330.9595
GW
MALAYSIA, WIRTSCHAFTSSTRUKTUR / BUNDESSTELLE FUR AUSSENHANDELSINFORMATION. German. One time a year. DM10.00. Bundesstelle fuer Aussenhandelsinformation, Agrippastrasse 87 93, D-50676 Cologne Germany. **Tel** 011 49 221 2057316, **FAX** 011 49 221 2057212.

LC HC445.5.A1 M34
DD 330.9/595/05
MY
MALAYSIAN FINANCE & DEVELOPMENT. Vol. 1, (Sept. 1972)-. Periodical. English. Inter Grafik, 68 Jalan Ampang, Kuala Lumpur Malaysia.

LC HC547.M25 F73a
DD 330.9/66/2305
FR
MALI. **Main/Corp** France. Direction de l'Aide au Developpement. Secteur Information Economique Et Conjoncture. (19??)-. French. Direction de l'Aide au Developpement, 20 rue Monsieur Viie, Paris France.

LC HC1035.A1
DD 330.966/23
GW
MALI WIRTSCHAFTLICHE ENTWICKLUNG / BUNDESSTELLE FUR AUSSENHANDELSINFORMATION. German. DM3.00. Bundesstelle fuer Aussenhandelsinformation, Agrippastrasse 87 93, D-50676 Cologne Germany. **Tel** 011 49 221 2057316, **FAX** 011 49 221 2057212.

Business and Economics —Economic History, Conditions

LC HC310.2.A1 M34
DD 330.945/85/005 GW
MALTA, WIRTSCHAFT IN ZAHLEN.
(19??)-. German. DM5.00. Bundesstelle fuer Aussenhandelsinformation, Agrippastrasse 87 93, D-50676 Cologne Germany. **Tel** 011 49 221 2057316, FAX 011 49 221 2057212.

LC HC601 .M36 ISSN 0816-2484
DD 330.994/005 AT
●**MANAGEMENT REPORT ON THE AUSTRALIAN ECONOMY (NORTH SYDNEY, N.S.W. : 1986).** (MANAGEMENT REPORT ON THE AUSTRALIAN ECONOMY.). **Added/Corp** Coopers & Lybrand WD Scott. (1996)-. English. One time a year. 98.66Aus$. Coopers & Lybrand W D Scott, 580 George Street, North Sydney New South Wales 2060 Australia. **Tel** (02)929-0033, FAX (02)957-4608, telex AA176288. **ED** Bob Smith and John Donovan. ctrl circ. **Continues** Management Report of the Australian Economy, 0816-2484.
Desc: Descriptions of the Australian economy and five-year forecasts of key economic variables.

LC HC424.A1 M3 ISSN 0047-5912
CE
MARGA (COLOMBO). (MARGA.). [Marga]. **Added/Corp** Marga Institute. **VFOAT** Marga Quarterly Journal. (1971)-. Periodical. English. Four times a year. Marga Institute, PO Box 601, Colombo Sri Lanka. **Tel** 585186. **ED** Godfrey Gunatilleke. **Circ:** 1,500.
Desc: Devoted to the discussion of issues of development pertaining to developing countries in general, and in particular to Sri Lanka's society.
Ind/Abst Hum. Rights Intern. Rep.; Int. Labour Doc.; LABORDOC; Leis., Rec., Tour. Abstr.; Rural Dev. Abstr.; World Agric. Econ. Rural Sociol. Abstr.

LC HC431 .M35 ISSN 0025-2921
DD 330.954 II
MARGIN. [Margin]. **Added/Corp** National Council of Applied Economic Research. Vol. 1 (Oct. 1968)-. Periodical. English. Four times a year. $80.00. National Council of Applied Economic Research, Parisila Bhawan 11 Indraprasth, New Delhi 110002 India. **Tel** 011 91 11 3317861, FAX 011 91 11 3327164, telex 3165880. **(Subscription address:** Prints India, 11 Darya Ganj, New Delhi 110002 India. **Tel** 011 91 11 3268645, FAX 011 91 11 3275542, telex 31-61087 PRIN-IN.) **ED** S L Rao. **Bk Rev. Circ:** 1,000 (ctrl).
Desc: Research papers on applied economic problems and a detailed review of the Indian economy.
Ind/Abst Cot. Trop. Fibr. Abstr. Bibliogr.; Econ. Lit. Index (19??-); For. Abstr.; Irr. Drain. Abstr.; J. Econ. Lit.; Postharvest News Inf.; Rice Abstr.; Rural Dev. Abstr.; World Agric. Econ. Rural Sociol. Abstr.

LC HC122.2 .M37 ISSN 0278-6192
DD 338.7/4/0258 US
MARKET GUIDE, LATIN AMERICA. (MARKET GUIDE, LATIN AMERICA.). [Mark. guide, Latin Am.]. **Added/Corp** Dun & Bradstreet International. **VFOAT** Latin America Market Guide. (19??)-. English. Two times a year (Jan., June). Dun & Bradstreet Information Services, 3 Sylvan Way, Parsippany NJ 07054. **Tel** (201)605-6000, (800)526-0651.

LC HC591.A3 Y35A
DD 330.9/63/06 ET
MARKET REPORT - YAITYOPYA NEGD BANK. Main/Corp Yaityopya Negd Bank. Market Research Dept. English. Commercial Bank of Ethiopia, Haile Selassie I Square, PO Box 255, Addis Ababa Ethiopia.

LC HC226 .M36
PE
MAS DEL PERU Y DEL MUNDO. Vol. 1 (Nov. 1975)-. Periodical. Spanish. Distribuidora Inca, S A Emilio Althaus 470, Lima Peru.

II
MASIKA ANKARA SARA. MONTHLY ABSTRACT OF STATISTICS. See Business and Economics-Abstracting, Bibliographies and Statistics.

LC HC517.M5
GW
MAURITIUS : WIRTSCHAFTSDATEN UND WIRTSCHAFTSDOKUMENTATION. Main/Corp Bundesstelle fur Aussenhandelsinformation (Germany). German. DM2.00. Bundesstelle fuer Aussenhandelsinformation, Agrippastrasse 87 93, D-50676 Cologne Germany. **Tel** 011 49 221 2057316, FAX 011 49 221 2057212.

LC HC463.H6 J258b
JA
ME DE MIRU HOKKAIDO SANGYO. Main/Corp Japan. **VFOAT** Sapporo Tsusho Sangyokyoku. (1956)-. Periodical. Japanese. One time a year. ¥500. Sapporo Shoko Kyokai, c/o Sapporo Dai-1 Godo Chosha Nishi, 4-chome Kita Sanjo Chu-ku, Sapporo Japan.

LC HC448.J34 J34A
IO
MEDIA JAYA. Main/Corp Jakarta Raya, Indonesia. **VAT** Media Jakarta Raya. Periodical. Indonesian. Six times a year. Free. Biro Humas Pemerintah Dki Jakarta, Merdeka Selatan 8-9, Jakarta Pusat Indonesia. **Tel** 345981. **ED** S Sudarsin. **Bk Rev. Circ:** 5,000 (ctrl).
Desc: To motivate citizens of Jakarta to participate in the development and progress of their community.

LC HC10 .E335a ISSN 0790-9470
DD 338.5/443/05 IE
MEDIUM-TERM REVIEW. Added/Corp Economic and Social Research Institute. **VFOAT** Medium Term Review. No. 2 (1992)-. Periodical. English. Economic & Social Research Institute / Dublin, 4 Burlington Road, Dublin 4 Ireland. **Tel** 011 353 1 6760115 Ext. 427. **Continues** Medium-Term Outlook, 0790-696X.

LC HC411 .M48 ISSN 0047-7230
DD 330.956/005 UK
CODEN MEEDDO
MEED. VFOAT Middle East Economic Digest. Vol. 29, No. 41 (Oct. 12-18, 1985)-. Trade Publication. English. Fifty-one times per year. £285.00 Europe and Middle East; £310.00 other. MEED Limited, MEED House, 21 John Street, London WC1N 2BP United Kingdom. **Tel** 011 44 171 4045513, FAX 011 44 171 2421450, telex 266872 MEEDAR G. **ED** Edmund O'Sullivan. **Ad Acc. Circ:** 11,000. **Continues** Middle East Economic Digest, 0047-7230.
Ind/Abst Bus. Index (1992-); Chem. Ind. Notes; Gen. BusinessFile (1992-); Infomat Int. Bus.; PROMT; Rural Dev. Abstr.; Trade Ind. ASAP [Full Txt.]; Trade Ind. Index [Full Txt.].

LC HC196 .A242a
DD 338.9861/005 CK
MEMORIA / DEPARTAMENTO NACIONAL DE PLANEACION. Main/Corp Colombia. Departamento Nacional de Planeacion. (1982/1983)-. Spanish. One time a year. **Continues** Colombia. Departamento Nacional de Planeacion. Memorias del Departamento Nacional de Planeacion.

LC HC175 .C62
AG
MEMORIA Y BALANCE GENERAL. Main/Corp Confederacion General de la Industria. (19??)-. Spanish. Confederacion General de la Industria, Rivadavia 1115 4 P, Buenos Aires Argentina. **Continues** Memoria y Balance General.

LU
MEMORIAL JOURNAL OFFICIOL DU GRAND DUCHE DE LUXEMBOURG.
(19??)-. English. Irregular. Imprimerie Cour Victor Buck, 6 rue Francois Hogenberg, Luxembourg BP 1341 Luxembourg. **Tel** 49 41 61 63.

LC HC236 .M39
VE
MENSAJE ECONOMICO FINANCIERO. Periodical. Spanish. Six times a year. Bs5.00. EDIF Distribuidor Comercial, Pise 3 Ferrenquin a la Cruz, Apartado 602 Carmelitas, Caracas Venezuela.

LC HC171 .M47 ISSN 0325-0687
DD 330.9/82/06 AG
MERCADO. Vol. 1, No. 1 (July 17, 1969)-. Periodical. Spanish. Twelve times a year. $165.00. Editorial Coyuntura S.A., Peru 263 2 piso, 1067 Buenos Aires Argentina. **Tel** 541-342-3322. **ED** Miguel Angel Diez. **Bk Rev. Ad Acc. Circ:** 28,000.
Ind/Abst PROMT.

LC HC161 .M472
BL
MERCOSUL. Added/Corp Federacao do Comercio do Estado de Sao Paulo. (199?)-. Periodical. Portuguese (Spanish). Twelve times a year. Free on request. Federal Comercio Estado de Sao Paulo, Circ Avenue Paulista 119 5 Andar, 01311 000 Sao Paulo SP Brazil. **Tel** 011 55 11 2842111 ext. 1500.

ISSN 0026-6809
JA
MERI'S MONTHLY CIRCULAR. (MERI'S MONTHLY CIRCULAR : SURVEY OF ECONOMIC CONDITIONS IN JAPAN.). [MERI's mon. circ.]. **Main/Corp** Mitsubishi Keizai Kenkyujo. **Added/Corp** Mitsubishi Keizai Kenkyujo. **VFOAT** Survey of Economic Conditions in Japan; Monthly Circular. No. 475 (July 1969)-. Periodical. English. Twelve times a year. $52.00. Mitsubishi Economic Research Institute, 3-3-1 Marunouchi Chiyoda-ku, Tokyo 100 Japan. **Tel** 214 4416. **(Subscription address:** Japan Publications Trading Company Ltd., PO Box 5030, Tokyo International, Tokyo 100-31 Japan. **Tel** 011 81 3 3292 3753.) **ED** Toshio Yamaguchi. **Ad Acc. Continues** Monthly Circular.

ISSN 1188-1941
DD 330.9716/22/05 CN
METRO IN VIEW. [Metro view]. (Jan. 1992)-. Periodical. English. Twelve times a year. $18.95. Mega Grand Marketing, Inc., Suite 207 57 Portland Street, Dartmouth Nova Scotia B2Y 1H1, Canada.

ISSN 0267-9973
UK
MEXICO (LONDON, ENGLAND). (MEXICO.). **Added/Corp** Latin American Monitor Ltd. (1985)-. English. One time a year (June). $435.00. Latin American Monitor Ltd., 56 60 St. John Street, London EC1M 4DT United Kingdom. **Tel** 011 44 171 6083646.

LC HC131 .M587 ISSN 1044-6303
DD 972 US
CCC
MEXICO SERVICE. (MEXICO SERVICE : MS : A PUBLICATION OF INTERNATIONAL REPORTS.). [Mex. serv.]. **Added/Corp** International Reports (Firm). **VFOAT** MS. (Jan. 1980)-. Periodical. English. Twenty-five times a year. $400.00. United Communications Group, 11300 Rockville Pike, Suite 1100, Rockville MD 20852. **Tel** (301)816-8950 ext. 313, FAX (301)816-8945. available on an online database (file 636/Full-Text) from DIALOG.
Desc: Accurate, comprehensive information about Mexico's turbulent financial, political and economics climate.
Ind/Abst PTS Newsl. Database [Full Txt.].

ISSN 1054-5735
DD 972 US
MEXICO (SYRACUSE, N.Y.). (MEXICO : A POLITICAL AND ECONOMIC FORECAST.). [Mexico]. **Added/Corp** Political Risk Services (IBC USA (Publications) Inc.). (19??)-. English. $325.00. Political Risk Services, 6320 Fly Road, Suite 102, PO Box 248, East Syracuse NY 13057-0248. **Tel** (315)431-0511, FAX (315)431-0200.
Desc: Assesses the factors affecting the prospects for business and trade. Each report focuses specifically on business needs such as finding and developing markets, determining currency movements, or making judgements about capital investments or corporate security.

LC HC135 .G47A
DD 330.9/72/082 GW
MEXIKO : WIRTSCHAFTLICHE ENTWICKLUNG. Main/Corp Germany (Federal Republic, 1949-). Bundesstelle fur Aussenhandelsinformation. (19??)-. German. Bundesstelle fuer Aussenhandelsinformation, Agrippastrasse 87 93, D-50676 Cologne Germany. **Tel** 011 49 221 2057316, FAX 011 49 221 2057212.

LC HC131
DD 330.972/005 GW
MEXIKO, WIRTSCHAFTSDATEN UND WIRTSCHAFTSDOKUMENTATION / BUNDESTELLE FUR AUSSENHANDELSINFORMATION. German. DM3.00. Bundesstelle fuer Aussenhandelsinformation, Agrippastrasse 87 93, D-50676 Cologne Germany. **Tel** 011 49 221 2057316, FAX 011 49 221 2057212.

LC HC307.S69 M49 ISSN 0392-9566
DD 330.945/7/005 IT
SUSPENDED
MEZZOGIORNO D'EUROPA. [Mezzog. Eur.]. **Added/Corp** Isveimer. Vol. 1 (Jan./March 1981)-(Dec. 1993). Periodical. Italian (English). Four times a year. Isveimer, Via Comparone V A de Gasperi 71, 80133 Naples Italy. **Tel** 011 39 81 7853467.
Ind/Abst Int. Dev. Abstr. (?-?).

LC HF296.M672 M5A ISSN 0026-4334
DD 330.9/775/9404 US
MILWAUKEE. Periodical. English. Twelve times a year. $5.00. Schmidt Publications, 720 North Jefferson Street, Milwaukee WI 53202.

LC HC466 .M56
KO
MINGAN KYONGJE PAEKSO. Korean. Chonguk Kyongjein Yonhaphoe, 1-124 Youido-dong, Yongdungpo-ku, Seoul South Korea.

LC HC10 .M5357 ISSN 0026-5829
DD 330.9005 RU
MIROVAJA EKONOMIKA I MEZDUNARODNYE OTNOSENIJA.
(MIROVAIA EKONOMIKA I MEZHDUNARODNYE OTNOSHENIIA / AKADEMIIA NAUK SSSR, INSTITUT MIROVOI EKONOMIKI I MEZHDUNARODNYKH OTNOSHENII.). [Mirovaja ekon. mezdunar. otnos.]. **Added/Corp** Institut Mirovoi Ekonomiki i Mezhdunarodnykh Otnoshenii (Akademiia Nauk SSSR). **VFOAT** Memo. (July 1957)-. Periodical. Russian (English, French and German; table of contents in Chinese, English, French and German). Twelve times a year. $270.00. **(Subscription address:** East View Publications Inc., 3020 Harbor Lane North, Suite 110, Minneapolis MN 55447. **Tel** (800)477-1005, (612)550-0961, FAX (612)559-2931.) Index available in last issue of volume-attached. available on microfilm from University Microfilms International (UMI).
Ind/Abst Am. Hist. Life (1957-1961, 1973-); Int. Polit. Sci. Abstr.; Curr. Dig. Post Sov. Press.

1055

LC HC107.M8 M46 ISSN 0195-6159
DD 330.9778/005 US
MISSOURI ECONOMIC INDICATORS.
Added/Corp Missouri. Division of Budget and Planning. University of Missouri--Columbia. Public Affairs Information Service. Vol. 1 (Oct. 1975)-. Periodical. English. Four times a year. $20.00. University of Missouri - Columbia / College of Business and Public Administration, B&PA Research Center, 10 Professional Building, Columbia MO 65211. **Tel** (314)882-4805. **ED** Susan Aitkens. **Circ:** 100 (ctrl).
Desc: Economic projections for Missouri and major MSA's.

LC HC107.M8 M485
DD 330.9778/005 US
MISSOURI STATE ECONOMY IN REVIEW. 1978-. English. One time a year. Missouri Division of Community and Economic Development, Box 118, Jefferson City MO 65102.

LC HC300.2 .M58
HU
MIT KELL TUDNI AZ ... EVI NEPGAZDASAGI TERVROL?. (19??)-. Hungarian. One time a year. Kossuth Konyvkiado, Steindl U-6, 1054 Budapest Hungary. **Tel** 011 36 1 1312111, FAX 011 36 1 1113670.

LC DD801.S6331 G47a
DD 943.1 GW
MITGLIEDERVERZEICHNIS DER GESELLSCHAFT FUER SCHLESWIG-HOLSTEINISCHE GESCHICHTE. **Main/Corp** Gesellschaft fuer Schleswig-Holsteinische Geschichte. (19??)-. German. Gesellschaft fur Schleswig-Holsteinische, Geschichte Schloss Gottorf, W-2380 Schleswig Germany.

LC HC10 .M65 ISSN 0026-9522
IT
MONDO ECONOMICO. [Mondo econ.]. **Added/Corp** Istituto per Gli Studi di Economia. (1947)-. Periodical. Italian. One time a week. SEME 24 Ore, Via Parabiago 19, 20151 Milan Italy. **Tel** 011 39 2 3103295.
Ind/Abst F&S Index Plus Text, Int. [Select. Cov.]; PAIS Int. Print; PROMT.

US
MONETARY INDICATORS. (19??)-. Periodical. English.

LC HC101 .M626 ISSN 0272-9970
DD 332.4/973 US
MONEY (BOCA RATON). (MONEY.). Vol. 1, Article 1 (1977)-. English. One time a year. Social Issues Resources Series Inc, PO Box 2348, Boca Raton FL 33427. **Tel** (800)327-0513, (407)994-0079. **ED** E C Goldstein.
Desc: Interdisciplinary resource material consisting of reprinted articles from popular and professional journals, newspapers, magazines and government documents.

LC HC107.M9 M53a ISSN 0146-4302
DD 330.9/786/03 US
MONTANA ECONOMIC INDICATORS.
Main/Corp Montana. Division of Employment Security. Research and Analysis Section. Vol. 4, No.4 (Feb. 1976)-. Periodical. English. Four times a year. Division of Employment Security / Montana, PO Box 1728, Helena MT 59601. ***Continues** Montana Economic Indicators, 0146-4302.*

LC HC57 .U66 ISSN 0041-7432
DD 330.9/0021 US
MONTHLY BULLETIN OF STATISTICS - UNITED NATIONS. **See** Business and Economics-Abstracting, Bibliographies and Statistics.

LC HC431 .M6 ISSN 0027-030X
DD 330.954 II
MONTHLY COMMENTARY ON INDIAN ECONOMIC CONDITIONS. **Added/Corp** Indian Institute of Public Opinion. (Aug. 1959)-. Periodical. English. Twelve times a year. $60.00. Indian Institute of Public Opinion, PO Box 288, New Delhi 1 India. **Tel** 011 91 11 3342846, 011 91 11 312742, FAX 011 91 11 310405, telex 31-65156 NEWS IN. **ED** E.P.W. da Costa. Index available. **Bk Rev**, (Qty: 1-2). **Ad Acc, Adv Mgr:** Inderjit Rai, **Tel** 011 91 11 312742. **Circ:** 1,500.
Desc: Presents research and statistical articles on Indian economic conditions, with economic indicators on prices, production and monetary conditions.

LC HC251 .A32 ISSN 0017-3622
DD 330.942 UK
MONTHLY DIGEST OF STATISTICS. **See** Business and Economics-Abstracting, Bibliographies and Statistics.

LC HC440.8.A1 M67
DD 330.95492/0021 BG
TITLE CHANGE
MONTHLY INDICATORS OF CURRENT ECONOMIC SITUATION OF BANGLADESH = MASIKA ARTHANAITIKA NIRDESIKA, BAMLADESA. **Added/Corp** Bangladesh. Parisamkhyana Bibhaga. **VFOAT** Masika Arthanaitika Nirdesika, Bamladesa. (Jan. 1987)-(Feb. 1994). Periodical. English (Bengali). Bangladesh Bureau of Statistics, Ministry of Planningstats Division, Dacca 1000 Bangladesh. **Tel** 011 880 23000 29312081. **Bk Rev**. **Ad Acc. Circ:** 250 (ctrl). ***Formed by the union of** Bangladesh. Parisamkhyana Bibhaga. Economic Indicators of Bangladesh **and** Monthly Economic Situation of Bangladesh. **Split into** Bangladesh. Parisamkhyana Byuro. Monthly Statistical Bulletin of Bangladesh, 0377-1555 **and** Monthly Statistical Bulletin, Bangladesh.*
Desc: Gives data on major economic trends, money and banking, national account, production, foreign trade, prices, wages and consumption.

VE
MONTHLY REPORT (CARACAS, VENEZUELA). (THE MONTHLY REPORT / EL REPORTE MENSUAL.). **VFOAT** Reporte Mensual. (Nov. 1959)-. Periodical. English (Spanish). Twelve times a year. The Monthly Report, Apartado 50-679, Caracas 1050 Venezuela. **Tel** 283 21 55, FAX 283 9653, telex 24704 PRUNH VC. **ED** Carlton Prunhuber. Index available. **Circ:** 2,000 (ctrl).
Desc: Analysis and projection of the more pertinent economic, financial and business matters concerning Venezuela. Private sector matters and government affairs featured.

LC HD ISSN 1021-4224
DD 330 BE
UDC 33
●**MONTHLY REPORT ON EUROPE.** (1993)-. Periodical. English (English and French). Twelve times a year. $822.77. Europe Information Service, rue de Geneve 6, 1140 Brussels Belgium. **Tel** 011 32 2 242 6020, FAX 011 32 2 242 9549.

LC HC601 .A32
DD 330.994/005 AT
MONTHLY SUMMARY OF STATISTICS, AUSTRALIA. **See** Business and Economics-Abstracting, Bibliographies and Statistics.

ISSN 1054-5743
DD 964 US
MOROCCO (SYRACUSE, N.Y.). (MOROCCO : A POLITICAL AND ECONOMIC FORECAST / POLITICAL RISK SERVICES.). [Morocco]. **Added/Corp** Political Risk Services (IBC USA (Publications) Inc.). (19??)-. English. $325.00. Political Risk Services, 6320 Fly Road, Suite 102, PO Box 248, East Syracuse NY 13057-0248. **Tel** (315)431-0511, FAX (315)431-0200.
Desc: Assesses the factors affecting the prospects for business and trade. Each report focuses specifically on business needs such as finding and developing markets, determining currency movements, or making judgements about capital investments or corporate security.

LC HC470.C7 M84
KO
MULKA SISE. **VFOAT** Mulka Sise Wolbo. Periodical. Korean. Twelve times a year. W60,000. Hanguk Mukla Sise Wolboas, 7-3 2-ka Pil-dong Chung-ku, Seoul Korea.

KO
MULKA TONGGYE. **Added/Corp** Hanguk Unhaeng. **VFOAT** Price Statistics. (1989)-. Korean (English). Irregular. Hanguk Unhaeng, 110 3-ka Namdaemunro Chung-ku, Seoul Korea. **Tel** 535-5498. ***Continues** Mulka Chongnam (Hangguk Unhaeng).*

LC HC186 .M84
DD 309.1/81/06 BL
MUNDO ECONOMICO, POLITICO & I.E. E SOCIAL. Vol. 1 (Sept. 1975)-. Periodical. Portuguese. $25.00. Mundo Cultural, rua Marconi 53 Conj 54, Sao Paulo Brazil.

LC HC54 ISSN 0929-9742
DD 330.9 NE
UDC 94/99
●**N.W. POSTHUMUS REEKS.** [N.W. Posthumus reeks]. **VFOAT** Nicolaas Wilhelmus Posthumus Reeks. (1994)-. Monographic series. Dutch. Irregular. Uitgeverij Verloren, Larenseweg 123, 1221 CL Hilversum Netherlands. **Tel** 011 31 35 859856, FAX 011 31 35 836557.

LC HG3288.N37 N37
DD 332.2 II
NATIONAL BANK NEWS REVIEW. **VFOAT** Nesanala Bainka Nyuja Rivyu. English (Hindi). Twelve times a year. National Bank for Agriculture and Rural Development, Economic Analysis and Publications Dept, Garment House, Worli, Bombay 400018 India.
Ind/Abst Agrofor. Abstr. (1991-); Dairy Sci. Abstr.; For. Abstr.; Int. Labour Doc.; Potato Abstr.; Rice Abstr.; Rural Dev. Abstr.; World Agric. Econ. Rural Sociol. Abstr.

LC HC430.5.A1 C56a
DD 330.95124/905/021 CH
NATIONAL CONDITIONS OF THE REPUBLIC OF CHINA. **Added/Corp** China (Republic : 1949-). Chu chi chu. Tung chi chu. **VFOAT** Chung-Hua min kuo kuo Ching Tung chi chi Kan. (Winter 1986)-. Periodical. English. Four times a year. National Conditions of the Republic of China, Bureau of Statistics, Directorate-General of Budget Accounting and Statistics, Executive Yuan, 2 Kwang Chow Street, Taipei 10729 Taiwan. ***Continues** China (Republic : 1949-). Chu chi chu. Tung chi chu. National Conditions.*
Ind/Abst PAIS Int. Print.

LC HC101 .N37 ISSN 0547-8154
DD 330.973 US
NATIONAL ECONOMIC PROJECTIONS SERIES. **Added/Corp** National Planning Association. Center for Economic Projections. (19??)-. Monographic series. English. Irregular. $900.00. National Planning Association, 1424 16th Street Northwest, Suite 700, Washington DC 20036. **Tel** (202)265-7685. **ED** Nestor E Terleckyj. **Circ:** 400 (ctrl). ***Continues** National Economic Projections.*
Desc: Up-to-date long-term growth outlook for US economy with 250 basic indicators.

LC HC460.I5 P47A
DD 339.3599 PH
NATIONAL INCOME ACCOUNTS, THE.
Main/Corp Philippines. National Economic and Development Authority. English. One time a year. National Economic and Development Authority, PO Box 419, Greenhills Metro Manila Philippines. **Tel** 011 63 2 6313281.

LC HC120.I5 A34 ISSN 0318-708X
DD 339.2/0971 CN
TITLE CHANGE
NATIONAL INCOME AND EXPENDITURE ACCOUNTS. [Natl. income expend. acc.]. **Main/Corp** Statistics Canada. Gross National Product Division. **Added/Corp** Canada. Dominion Bureau of Statistics. National Income and Expenditure Division. Statistics Canada. National Income and Expenditure Division. Statistics Canada. Gross National Product Division. Statistics Canada. Income and Expenditure Accounts Division. Canada. National Income and Expenditure Division. Statistics Canada. National Accounts and Environment Division. **VFOAT** Comptes Nationaux des Revenus et des Depenses; Comptes Nationaux des Revenus et Depenses. Vol. 17, No. 2 (2nd Quarter 1969)-4th Quarter (1994). Periodical. English (French). Four times a year. Statistics Canada Publications Sales and Services, R.H. Coats Building 6th Floor, Ottawa Ontario K1A 0T6 Canada. **Tel** (613)951-5078, (800)267-6677, FAX (613)951-1584, telex 053-3585. **ED** Philip Smith. **Circ:** 900. available on diskette. ***Continues** National Accounts, Income and Expenditure (Ottawa, Ont. : Quarterly), 0575-9196. **Merged with** Financial Flow Accounts (Preliminary), 0380-0938 **to form** National Economic and Financial Accounts. Quarterly Estimates.*
Desc: Contains gross national product and its principal components, sources and disposition of personal income and gross saving, government revenue and expenditure by level of government, transactions of residents with non-residents, gross national expenditure in constant dollars, implicit price indexes, analysis of recent trends and occasional short articles of a technical or analytical nature.

LC HC120.I5 C35h ISSN 0703-0037
DD 339.371 CN
NATIONAL INCOME AND EXPENDITURE ACCOUNTS : THE ANNUAL ESTIMATES. [Natl. income expend. acc., Annu. estim.]. **Main/Corp** Canada. Statistics Canada Gross National Product Division. **Added/Corp** Statistics Canada. Gross National Product Division. Statistics Canada. Income and Expenditure Accounts Division. Statistics Canada. National Accounts and Environment Division. Statistics Canada. Gross National Product Division. Comptes Nationaux des Revenus et des Depenses: les Estimations Annuelles. **VFOAT** Comptes Nationaux des Revenus et des d'Epenses, les Estimations Annuelles. (1975)-. English (French). One time a year. 50.00Can$ Canada; $52.00 other. Statistics Canada Publications Sales and Services, R.H. Coats Building 6th Floor, Ottawa Ontario K1A 0T6 Canada. **Tel** (613)951-5078, (800)267-6677, FAX (613)951-1584, telex 053-3585. ***Continues** Canada. Dominion Bureau of Statistics. National Accounts Section. National Accounts, Income and Expenditure., 0703-0045.*
Desc: Contains series for breakdowns of sector accounts including industrial distribution of gross domestic product, geographical distribution of personal income, and government revenues and expenditures.

LC HC10 .N35 ISSN 0027-9501
DD 330.9 UK
CODEN NIERAY

NATIONAL INSTITUTE ECONOMIC REVIEW. [Natl. inst. econ. rev.]. **Added/Corp** National Institute of Economic and Social Research. No. 1 (Jan. 1959)-. Periodical. English. Four times a year (February, May, August, November). $188.23. National Institute for Economic and Social Research / London, 2 Dean Trench Street, Smith Square, London SW1P 3HE United Kingdom. **Tel** 011 44 171 2227665, FAX 011 44 171 2221435. **Circ:** 3,000 (ctrl). available on microfilm and microfiche from University Microfilms International (UMI); available on an online database (file 648/Full-Text) from DIALOG. Documents available from UMI Article Clearinghouse.
Desc: Contains general survey of economic situation and prospects with special articles on topical economic problems and studies of underlying trends.
Ind/Abst ABI/INFORM Glob. Ed.; ABI/INFORM [Computer File] (Feb. 1978-); Acad. Search; Bus. ASAP (1990-) [Full Txt.]; Bus. Index (1985-); Bus. Period. Index; Bus. Source Plus; Bus. Source; Contents Recent Econ. J.; Contents Pages Manage.; Curr. Cit.; Econ. Lit. Index; EP Collect.; F&S Index Plus Text, Int. [Select. Cov.]; Gen. BusinessFile (1985-); Gen. Period. Index (1985-); Homework Help.; INFO-SOUTH Abstr.; Int. Labour Doc.; J. Econ. Lit.; Mag. Search; Manage. Market. Abstr.; MasterFile FullTEXT 1000; MasterFile FullTEXT 350; MasterFile FullTEXT 650; MasterFile FullTEXT (July 1993-); OCLC; PAIS Int. Print (1991-); Predicasts Forecasts; Telebase; Trade Ind. Index (1981-?); UMI ABI/Inform--Bus. Period. Ondisc (Nov. 1987-) [Full Txt.]; Wilson Bus. Abstr.

LC HC10 .N38 HD78 .W6 ISSN 1058-8450
DD 330 US

NBER WORKING PAPER SERIES ON HISTORICAL FACTORS IN LONG-RUN GROWTH. [NBER work. pap. ser. hist. factors long run growth]. **Added/Corp** National Bureau of Economic Research. **VFOAT** NBER Working Papers Series on Historical Factors in Long Run Growth; NBER Working Paper Series; Historical Factors in Long-Run Growth; Working Paper Series on Historical Factors in Long Run Growth. **VAT** National Bureau of Economic Research working paper series on historical factors in long run growth. (1989)-. Monographic series. English. Irregular. $50.00. National Bureau of Economic Research, 1050 Massachusetts Avenue, Cambridge MA 02138. **Tel** (617)868-3900, FAX (617)441-3895.

LC HC10 .N42
JA

NENPO KEIZAIGAKU. Added/Corp Hiroshima Daigaku. Keizai Gakubu. **VFOAT** Hiroshima Economic Studies; Keizaigaku. Vol. 1 (1980)-. Japanese (English). ¥225 Japan; $1.00 US. Hiroshima Daigaku Keizai Gakubu, Higashi Sendacho, Naka-ku Hiroshima Japan. **Tel** (082)241-1221.

LC HC497.N5
GW

NEPAL : WIRTSCHAFTLICHE ENTWICKLUNG. Main/Corp Bundesstelle fur Aussenhandelsinformation (Germany). German. DM2.00. Bundesstelle fuer Aussenhandelsinformation, Agrippastrasse 87 93, D-50676 Cologne Germany. **Tel** 011 49 221 2057316, FAX 011 49 221 2057212.

ISSN 1054-5751
DD 949 US

NETHERLANDS (SYRACUSE, N.Y.). (NETHERLANDS : A POLITICAL AND ECONOMIC FORECAST.). [Netherlands]. **Added/Corp** Political Risk Services (IBC USA (Publications) Inc.). (19??)-. English. $325.00. Political Risk Services, 6320 Fly Road, Suite 102, PO Box 248, East Syracuse NY 13057-0248. **Tel** (315)431-0511, FAX (315)431-0200.
Desc: Assesses the factors affecting the prospects for business and trade. Each report focuses specifically on business needs such as finding and developing markets, determining currency movements, or making judgements about capital investments or corporate security.

LC HC661
DD 330.9/931/03 GW

NEUSEELAND : WIRTSCHAFTLICHE ENTWICKLUNG. Main/Corp Germany (Federal Republic, 1949-). Bundesstelle fur Aussenhandelsinformation (Germany). German. One time a year. DM2.00. Bundesstelle fuer Aussenhandelsinformation, Agrippastrasse 87 93, D-50676 Cologne Germany. **Tel** 011 49 221 2057316, FAX 011 49 221 2057212.

LC HC107.A11 N342 ISSN 0028-4726
DD 330.974/005 US
CODEN NWEEAP

NEW ENGLAND ECONOMIC REVIEW. **See** Business and Economics-Banks and Banking.

LC HC107.N5 N423 ISSN 1064-5942
DD 330.9749/005 US

NEW JERSEY ECONOMIC INDICATORS (1976). **See** Business and Economics-Abstracting, Bibliographies and Statistics.

LC HC107.N6 N435 ISSN 0145-2665
DD 330.9/789/05 US

NEW MEXICO DIGEST (CLOVIS), THE. (THE NEW MEXICO DIGEST.). English. J R Spencer, 2921 Axtell Street, Clovis NM 88101.

LC HC451 .N47
DD 330.9/599/04 PH

NEW PHILIPPINES. Added/Corp National Media Production Center. (19??)-. Periodical. English. Twenty-six times a year.

ISSN 1054-5778
DD 993 US

NEW ZEALAND (SYRACUSE, N.Y.). (NEW ZEALAND : A POLITICAL AND ECONOMIC FORECAST.). [N. Z.]. **Added/Corp** Political Risk Services (IBC USA (Publications) Inc.). (19??)-. English. $325.00. Political Risk Services, 6320 Fly Road, Suite 102, PO Box 248, East Syracuse NY 13057-0248. **Tel** (315)431-0511, FAX (315)431-0200.
Desc: Assesses the factors affecting the prospects for business and trade. Each report focuses specifically on business needs such as finding and developing markets, determining currency movements, or making judgements about capital investments or corporate security.

ISSN 1054-5786
DD 972 US

NICARAGUA (SYRACUSE, N.Y.). (NICARAGUA : A POLITICAL AND ECONOMIC FORECAST.). [Nicaragua]. **Added/Corp** Political Risk Services (IBC USA (Publications) Inc.). (19??)-. English. $325.00. Political Risk Services, 6320 Fly Road, Suite 102, PO Box 248, East Syracuse NY 13057-0248. **Tel** (315)431-0511, FAX (315)431-0200.
Desc: Assesses the factors affecting the prospects for business and trade. Each report focuses specifically on business needs such as finding and developing markets, determining currency movements, or making judgements about capital investments or corporate security.

LC HC321 .G47a
GW

NIEDERLANDE: WIRTSCHAFT IN ZAHLEN UND WIRTSCHAFTSDOKUMENTATION.
Main/Corp Bundesstelle fur Aussenhandelsinformation (Germany). (19??)-. German. DM4.00. Bundesstelle fuer Aussenhandelsinformation, Agrippastrasse 87 93, D-50676 Cologne Germany. **Tel** 011 49 221 2057316, FAX 011 49 221 2057212.

LC HC325
GW

NIEDERLANDE : WIRTSCHAFTLICHE ENTWICKLUNG UND PROGNOSE.
Main/Corp Bundesstelle fur Aussenhandelsinformation (Germany). German. One time a year. DM2.00. Bundesstelle fuer Aussenhandelsinformation, Agrippastrasse 87 93, D-50676 Cologne Germany. **Tel** 011 49 221 2057316, FAX 011 49 221 2057212. ***Continues*** *Niederlande: Wirtschaftliche Entwicklung.*

GW

NIEDERSAECHSISCHE WIRTSCHAFT.
Added/Corp Vereingung der Niedersaechisischen Industrie- und Handelskammern. (May 1946)-. Periodical. German. Twelve times a year. DM112.00. Schluetersche Verlag Druckerei, Postfach 5440, D-30054 Hannover Germany. **Tel** 011 49 511 85500, FAX 011 49 511 1236460, telex 923978. **ED** W. Linsenmann. Index available. **Bk Rev**. **Ad Acc**. **Circ:** 30,779. available with charts; available with illustrations.

LC HC547.N5 F73a
DD 330.9/66/2605 FR

NIGER. Main/Corp France. Direction de l'Aide au Developpement. Secteur Information Economique et Conjoncture. (19??)-. French. Direction de l'Aide au Developpement, 20 rue Monsieur Viie, Paris France.

LC HC1020.A1
DD 330.966/26/005 GW

NIGER, WIRTSCHAFTSDATEN UND WIRTSCHAFTSDOKUMENTATION.
(19??)-. German. One time a year. DM2.00. Bundesstelle fuer Aussenhandelsinformation, Agrippastrasse 87 93, D-50676 Cologne Germany. **Tel** 011 49 221 2057316, FAX 011 49 221 2057212.

ISSN 1054-576X
DD 966 US

NIGERIA (SYRACUSE, N.Y.). (NIGERIA : A POLITICAL AND ECONOMIC FORECAST.). [Nigeria]. **Added/Corp** Political Risk Services (IBC USA (Publications) Inc.). (19??)-. English. $325.00. Political Risk Services, 6320 Fly Road, Suite 102, PO Box 248, East Syracuse NY 13057-0248. **Tel** (315)431-0511, FAX (315)431-0200.
Desc: Assesses the factors affecting the prospects for business and trade. Each report focuses specifically on business needs such as finding and developing markets, determining currency movements, or making judgements about capital investments or corporate security.

LC HC462.9 .J25b
JA

NIHON KEIZAI NO GENKYO. Main/Corp Japan. Keizai Kikakucho. Chosakyoku. (1972)-. Japanese. ¥1000. Okurasho Insatukyoku, (Printing Bureau Ministry of Finance), 2-4 Toranomon 2 chome, Minatoku Tokyo 105 Japan.

LC HC59 .N469
JA

NIHON KEIZAI O CHUSHIN TO SURU KOKUSAI HIKAKU TOKEI. Added/Corp Nihon Ginko. Tokeikyoku. Nihon Ginko. Chosa Tokeikyoku. **VFOAT** Comparative Economic and Financial Statistics Japan and Other Major Countries; Comparative Statistics. (19??)-. Japanese. One time a year. Price varies per volume. Government Publications Service Center, 2-1 Kasumigaseki 1-Chome, Chiyoda-Ku Tokyo 100 Japan. **Tel** 011 81 3 3504 3885.

LC HC462.9 .N49433
JA

NIHON NO HAKUSHO. Added/Corp Nihon Joho Kyoiku Kenkyukai. (1980)-. Japanese. One time a year. ¥5500. Seibunsha / Tokyo-to-101, 4 Kanda Ogawacho 3, Chiyoda-ku, Tokyo-to-101 Japan. **Tel** 03-291-2653, FAX 03-291-8663. **Circ:** 175,000.
Desc: Summarization of all of Japanese "Hakusho".

LC HB9 .N535
JA

NIIGATA DAIGAKU KEIZAIGAKU NENPO. VFOAT Annual Report of Economics, Niigata University. No. 1- (Feb. 1977)-. Japanese. Irregular. Niigata Daigaku Jinbun Gakubu Keizai Gakka, 8050 Igarashi Nino-machi, Niigata-shi 950-21 Japan.

ISSN 0912-3881
DD 330.952 JA

NIKKEI CHIIKI JOHO. [Nikkei chiiki joho]. **VFOAT** Nikkei Regional Economic Report; Nikkei Chiiki Joho. Sokanzen Tokubetsu-go. (1985)-. Newsletter. Japanese. Twenty-four times a year. Nihon Keizai Shimbun Inc., 9-5 Otemachi 1 Chome, Chiyoda-ku Tokyo 100 Japan. **Tel** 011 81 3 32700251, 011 81 3 52108502 (Nikkei Business Publications Inc.), FAX 011 81 3 52552661, 011 81 3 52108119 (Nikkei Business Publications Inc.).

JA
CODEN NIWEEL

NIKKEI WEEKLY, THE. Added/Corp Nihon Keizai Shimbun. Vol. 29, No. 1,468 (June 1, 1991)-. Academic Scholarly Publication. English. Fifty-one times per year. $108.00. Nihon Keizai Shimbun Inc., 9-5 Otemachi 1 Chome, Chiyoda-ku Tokyo 100 Japan. **Tel** 011 81 3 32700251, 011 81 3 52108502 (Nikkei Business Publications Inc.), FAX 011 81 3 52552661, 011 81 3 52108119 (Nikkei Business Publications Inc.). **(Subscription address:** Nikkei Weekly, 27 08 42nd Road, Long Island City NY 11101. **Tel** (718)392-5115.**)** **ED** Norimichi Okai. Index available. **Ad Acc**. **Circ:** 35,000. available on microfilm from University Microfilms International (UMI); available on an online database from Tokyo. Documents available from CASDDS. ***Continues*** *Japan Economic Journal, 0021-4388.*
Desc: Covers Japan's economy, politics, industry, and weekly transactions of the Tokyo Stock Exchange, reports on Japan's overall business trends, individual corporations and figures in the world of Japanese political and economic news.
Ind/Abst BioBusiness (1991-); Chem. Abstr.; Chem. Ind. Notes (1991-); Infomat Int. Bus.; PROMT; World Ceram. Abstr.

LC HC59 .S5578a
JA

NIRA REPORT. Main/Corp Sogo Kenkyu Kaihatsu Kiko (Japan). No. 1 (July 1977)-. Periodical. Japanese. National Institute for Research Advancement, Center for Public Activities, Shinjuku Mitsui Bldg 37th Floor, 2-1-1 Nishi-Shinjuku, Shinjuku-ku Tokyo 163-04 Japan. **Tel** 011 81 3 33443371, FAX 011 81 3 33451449.

LC HC1888.B7242 N67
DD 330.981/3/005 BL

NORDESTE ECONOMICO. Periodical. Portuguese. Twelve times a year. Pool Editor, Caixa Postal 650, CEP 50.000 Recife Pernambuco Brazil.

LC HC107.N8 N753 ISSN 0095-4284
DD 330.9/756/04 US

NORTH CAROLINA DATA FILE.
Added/Corp North Carolina. Division of Commerce and Industry. (19??)-. English. Division of Commerce & Industry, PO Box 27687, Raleigh NC 27611.

LC HC107.N8 N754 ISSN 0732-9326
DD 330.9756/005 US

NORTH CAROLINA ECONOMIC ANNUAL REVIEW. 1981-. English. One time a year. Office of State Budget and Management Research and Planning Services Section, 116 West Jones Street, Raleigh NC 27611.

FR
NORTH/SOUTH ISSUES : BIBLIOGRAPHY OF THEORETICAL AND CURRENT EVENT ANALYSIS. See Business and Economics-Abstracting, Bibliographies and Statistics.

LC HC107.A19 N48 **ISSN** 0197-3665
DD 330.9795/005 US
NORTHWEST EXPERIENCE, THE. No. 1-. Periodical. English. Idaho Wool Growers Association, Box 2596, Boise ID 83701. **Tel** (208)344-2271.

ISSN 1054-5794
DD 948 US
NORWAY (SYRACUSE, N.Y.). (NORWAY : A POLITICAL AND ECONOMIC FORECAST.). [Norway]. **Added/Corp** Political Risk Services (IBC USA (Publications) Inc.). (19??)-. English. $325.00. Political Risk Services, 6320 Fly Road, Suite 102, PO Box 248, East Syracuse NY 13057-0248. **Tel** (315)431-0511, FAX (315)431-0200.
Desc: Assesses the factors affecting the prospects for business and trade. Each report focuses specifically on business needs such as finding and developing markets, determining currency movements, or making judgements about capital investments or corporate security.

LC HC121 .N67 **ISSN** 0257-2168
DD 338 CL
NOTAS SOBRE LA ECONOMIA Y EL DESARROLLO. **Added/Corp** United Nations. Economic Commission for Latin America and the Caribbean. United Nations. Economic Commission for Latin America and the Caribbean. Information Service. No. 399 (August 1984)-. Periodical. Spanish (English). Twelve times a year. Free on request. Comision Economica para America Latina y el Caribe, Casilla 179 D, Santiago Chile. **Tel** 011 56 2 485051, FAX 11 56 2 481946, 480252, telex 441054. **Bk Rev. Circ:** 12,000. available with charts; available on microfiche. ***Continues*** *Notas Sobre la Economia y el Desarrollo de America Latina, 0251-9453.*
Desc: Describes main activities (economy and development) that take place at the Economic Commission for Latin America and the Caribbean (ECLAC) during the year.

LC HC276.3.A1 N68 **ISSN** 0766-6268
FR
NOTE DE CONJONCTURE DE L'I.N.S.E.E. (NOTE DE CONJONCTURE DE L'INSEE.). [Note conjonct. I.N.S.E.E.]. **Added/Corp** Institut National de la Statistique et des Etudes Economiques (France). **VAT** Note de Conjoncture de l'Institut National de la Statistique et des Etudes Economiques. (Feb. 1985)-. French. Irregular. 165.00F France; 206.00F other. CNGP Insee, BP 2718, 1 rue V Auriol, F 80027 Amiens, Cedex 1 France. **Tel** 011 33 22 927322. ***Continues*** *Tendances de la Conjoncture. Note de Synthese: Situation & Perspectives de l'Economie Francaise, 0150-8849.*

LC Z7165.R9 N6 HC335 **ISSN** 0134-272X
DD 016.3(2) RU
TITLE CHANGE
NOVAIA SOVETSKAIA LITERATURA PO OBSHCHESTVENNYM NAUKAM: EKONOMIKA. **Added/Corp** Institut Nauchnoi Informatsii po Obshchestvennym Naukam (Akademiia Nauk SSSR). (1976)-(199?). Academic Scholarly Publication. Russian. Izdatelstvo Nauka / Akademiia Nauk, (Publishing House of the Russian Academy of Sciences), Leninskii Porspekt 14, 117901 Moscow Russia. **Tel** 011 95 9542153, FAX 011 95 9382144, telex 411964. ***Continues*** *Novaia Sovetskaia Ekonomicheskaia Literatura.* ***Continued by*** *Novaia Otechestvennaia Literatura po Obshchestvennym Naukam. Ekonomika.*

LC HC196 .N84
DD 330.9/861 CK
NUEVA FRONTERA. DOCUMENTOS. **VFOAT** Documentos Nueva Frontera. (1976)-. Periodical. Spanish. Twelve times a year. $300.00 single issue. Nueva Frontera, Carrera 7A No 17-02/Piso 5, Apartado 3137IA, Bogota Colombia. **Tel** 011 57 1 2444389.

LC HC547.U6
GW
OBERVOLTA : WIRTSCHAFTSDATEN UND WIRTSCHAFTSDOKUMENTATION. **Main/Corp** Bundesstelle fur Aussenhandelsinformation (Germany). German. DM2.00. Bundesstelle fuer Aussenhandelsinformation, Agrippastrasse 87 93, D-50676 Cologne Germany. **Tel** 011 49 221 2057316, FAX 011 49 221 2057212.

LC HC10 .A646 **ISSN** 0207-3676
RU
OBSHCHESTVO I EKONOMIKA. **Added/Corp** Rossiiskaia Akademiia Nauk. Rossiiskii Soiuz Promyshlennikov i Predprinimatelei. (1992)-. Academic Scholarly Publication. Russian. Twelve times a year. Izdatelstvo Nauka / Akademiia Nauk, (Publishing House of the Russian Academy of Sciences), Leninskii Porspekt 14, 117901 Moscow Russia. **Tel** 011 95 9542153, FAX 011 95 9382144, telex 411964. ***Continues*** *Izvestiia Akademii Nauk SSSR. Seriia Ekonomicheskaia, 0321-172X.*

LC HC601 .C575
DD 338.9/005 AT
OCCASIONAL PAPER (COMMITTEE FOR ECONOMIC DEVELOPMENT OF AUSTRALIA). (OCCASIONAL PAPER.). **Added/Corp** Committee for Economic Development of Australia. (196?)-. Monographic series. English. Every 2 years. Price varies per volume. Committee for Economic Development of Australia, 123 Lonsdale Street, GPO Box 2117T, Melbourne Victoria 3000 Australia. **Tel** 011 61 03 6623544, FAX 011 61 03 6637271. Index available. **Circ:** 2,000 (ctrl).

LC HC10 .O42
DD 330.9/00212 FR
TITLE CHANGE
OECD ECONOMIC OUTLOOK. HISTORICAL STATISTICS = PERSPECTIVES ECONOMIQUES DE L'OCDE. STATISTIQUES RETROSPECTIVES. **Added/Corp** Organisation for Economic Co-Operation and Development. **VFOAT** Economic Outlook. Historical Statistics; O.E.C.D. Economic Outlook. Historical Statistics; Historical Statistics; Perspectives Economiques de l'O.C.D.E. Statistiques Retrospectives; Statistiques Retrospectives; Perspectives Economiques de l'OCDE. Statistiques Retrospectives. (1980)-(1990). English (French). OECD Publications and Information Center, 2 rue Andre-Pascal, 75775 Paris Cedex 16 France. **Tel** 011 33 1 49104262, US:(202)785-6323, FAX 011 33 1 45248500, 011 33 1 45248176, telex 620 160 OCDE. **(Subscription address:** OECD Publications Center, 2001 L Street, Suite 700, Washington DC 20036. **Tel** (202)822-3873, (202)785-6323.) ***Continued by*** *Historical Statistics.*
Desc: Examines the prospects regarding domestic developments in demand, output, employment, monetary and fiscal affairs, wages, costs and prices. Also looks at international developments in foreign trade, current balances and international monetary affairs.

LC HC10 .O423 **ISSN** 0255-0822
DD 330.9/005 FR
OECD ECONOMIC STUDIES. [OECD econ. stud.]. **Added/Corp** Organisation for Economic Co-Operation and Development. **VFOAT** Economic Studies; O.E.C.D. Economic Studies. No. 1 (Autumn 1983)-. Periodical. English. Two times a year (Spring/Autumn). $65.00. OECD Publications and Information Center, 2 rue Andre-Pascal, 75775 Paris Cedex 16 France. **Tel** 011 33 1 49104262, US:(202)785-6323, FAX 011 33 1 45248500, 011 33 1 45248176, telex 620 160 OCDE. **(Subscription address:** OECD Publications Center, 2001 L Street, Suite 700, Washington DC 20036. **Tel** (202)822-3873, (202)785-6323.) available on an online database (file 648/Full-Text) from DIALOG. ***Continues*** *OECD Economic Outlook Occasional Studies.*
Desc: Articles in the area of applied macroeconomic and statistical analysis, generally with an international or cross-country dimension.
Ind/Abst Contents Recent Econ. J.; Curr. Cit.; Econ. Lit. Index (19??-); Geogr. Abstr. Human Geogr.; Int. Labour Doc.; J. Econ. Lit.; LABORDOC; PAIS Int. Print (1991-); Public Aff. Inf. Serv. Bull. (1983-); Trade Ind. ASAP [Full Txt.]; Trade Ind. Index [Full Txt.]; World Agric. Econ. Rural Sociol. Abstr.

LC HC605 .O74a
DD 330.9/94/06 FR
OECD ECONOMIC SURVEYS : AUSTRALIA. **Main/Corp** Organisation for Economic Co-Operation and Development. **VFOAT** Australia. **VAT** Organisation for Economic Co-Operation and Development Economic Surveys: Australia. (1972)-. English. One time a year. 2 rue Andre-Pascal, 75775 Cedex 16 France.
Ind/Abst Trade Ind. ASAP [Full Txt.]; Trade Ind. Index [Full Txt.].

LC HC337.F5 O73a
DD 330.9/471/03 FR
OECD ECONOMIC SURVEYS : FINLAND. **Main/Corp** Organisation for Economic Co-Operation and Development. **VAT** Organisation for Economic Co-Operation and Development Economic Surveys: Finland. (June 1969)-. English. One time a year. Organ for Economic Co-Operation and Development, 2 rue Andre Pascal, 75775 Paris Cedex 16 France. ***Continues*** *Economic Surveys: Finland.*
Ind/Abst Trade Ind. ASAP [Full Txt.]; Trade Ind. Index [Full Txt.].

LC HC271 .O7
DD 330.9/44/083 FR
OECD ECONOMIC SURVEYS : FRANCE. **Main/Corp** Organisation for Economic Co-Operation and Development. **VFOAT** France. **VAT** Organisation for Economic Co-Operation and Development Economic Surveys: France. (1968)-. English. Twenty times a year. $240.00. OECD Publications and Information Center, 2 rue Andre-Pascal, 75775 Paris Cedex 16 France. **Tel** 011 33 1 49104262, US:(202)785-6323, FAX 011 33 1 45248500, 011 33 1 45248176, telex 620 160 OCDE. **(Subscription address:** OECD Publications Center, 2001 L Street, Suite 700, Washington DC 20036. **Tel** (202)822-3873, (202)785-6323.) ***Continues*** *Economic Surveys by the OECD: France.*
Ind/Abst Trade Ind. ASAP [Full Txt.]; Trade Ind. Index [Full Txt.].

LC HC257.I6 A272
DD 330.9/415/0824 FR
OECD ECONOMIC SURVEYS : IRELAND. **Main/Corp** Organisation for Economic Co-Operation and Development. **VFOAT** Ireland. **VAT** Organisation for Economic Co-Operation and Development Economic Surveys: Ireland. (1968)-. English. Twenty times a year. $240.00. OECD Publications and Information Center, 2 rue Andre-Pascal, 75775 Paris Cedex 16 France. **Tel** 011 33 1 49104262, US:(202)785-6323, FAX 011 33 1 45248500, 011 33 1 45248176, telex 620 160 OCDE. **(Subscription address:** OECD Publications Center, 2001 L Street, Suite 700, Washington DC 20036. **Tel** (202)822-3873, (202)785-6323.) ***Continues*** *Economic Surveys by the OECD: Ireland.*
Ind/Abst Trade Ind. ASAP [Full Txt.]; Trade Ind. Index [Full Txt.].

LC HC301 .O69
DD 330.9/45/092 FR
OECD ECONOMIC SURVEYS: ITALY. **Main/Corp** Organisation for Economic Co-Operation and Development. **VFOAT** Italy. **VAT** Organisation for Economic Co-Operation and Development Economic Surveys : Italy. (1968)-. English. Twenty times a year. $240.00. OECD Publications and Information Center, 2 rue Andre-Pascal, 75775 Paris Cedex 16 France. **Tel** 011 33 1 49104262, US:(202)785-6323, FAX 011 33 1 45248500, 011 33 1 45248176, telex 620 160 OCDE. **(Subscription address:** OECD Publications Center, 2001 L Street, Suite 700, Washington DC 20036. **Tel** (202)822-3873, (202)785-6323.) ***Continues*** *Economic Surveys OECD: Italy.*

LC HC325 .O73
DD 330.9/492/07 FR
OECD ECONOMIC SURVEYS : NETHERLANDS. **Main/Corp** Organisation for Economic Co-Operation and Development. **VFOAT** Netherlands. **VAT** Organisation for Economic Co-Operation and Development Economic Surveys: Netherlands. (1969)-. English. Twenty times a year. $240.00. OECD Publications and Information Center, 2 rue Andre-Pascal, 75775 Paris Cedex 16 France. **Tel** 011 33 1 49104262, US:(202)785-6323, FAX 011 33 1 45248500, 011 33 1 45248176, telex 620 160 OCDE. **(Subscription address:** OECD Publications Center, 2001 L Street, Suite 700, Washington DC 20036. **Tel** (202)822-3873, (202)785-6323.) ***Continues*** *Economic Surveys: Netherlands.*
Ind/Abst Trade Ind. ASAP [Full Txt.]; Trade Ind. Index [Full Txt.].

LC HC392 .O73
DD 330.9/469/04 FR
OECD ECONOMIC SURVEYS : PORTUGAL. **Main/Corp** Organisation for Economic Co-Operation and Development. **VFOAT** Portugal. **VAT** Organisation for Economic Co-Operation and Development Economic Surveys: Portugal. (19??)-. English. Twenty times a year. $240.00. OECD Publications and Information Center, 2 rue Andre-Pascal, 75775 Paris Cedex 16 France. **Tel** 011 33 1 49104262, US:(202)785-6323, FAX 011 33 1 45248500, 011 33 1 45248176, telex 620 160 OCDE. **(Subscription address:** OECD Publications Center, 2001 L Street, Suite 700, Washington DC 20036. **Tel** (202)822-3873, (202)785-6323.) ***Continues*** *Economic Surveys: Portugal.*
Ind/Abst Trade Ind. ASAP [Full Txt.]; Trade Ind. Index [Full Txt.].

LC HC270.2 .O37
FR
●**OECD ECONOMIC SURVEYS. THE CZECH AND SLOVAK REPUBLICS / CENTRE FOR CO-OPERATION WITH THE ECONOMIES IN TRANSITION.** **Added/Corp** Centre for Co-Operation with the Economies in Transition. **VFOAT** Czech and Slovak Republics; Organisation for Economic Co-Operation and Development Economic Surveys. Czech and Slovak Republics. (1994)-. English. Twenty times a year. OECD Publications and Information Center, 2 rue Andre-Pascal, 75775 Paris Cedex 16 France. **Tel** 011 33 1 49104262, US:(202)785-6323, FAX 011 33 1 45248500, 011 33 1 45248176, telex 620 160 OCDE. **(Subscription address:** OECD Publications Center, 2001 L Street, Suite 700, Washington DC 20036. **Tel** (202)822-3873, (202)785-6323.) ***Continues*** *OECD Economic Surveys. Czech and Slovak Federal Republic.*

LC HC492 .O73a
DD 330.9/561/03 FR
OECD ECONOMIC SURVEYS : TURKEY. **Main/Corp** Organisation for Economic Co-Operation and Development. **VFOAT** Turkey. **VAT** Organisation for

Business and Economics —Economic History, Conditions

Economic Co-Operation and Development Economic Surveys: Turkey. (1969)-. English. Twenty times a year. $240.00. OECD Publications and Information Center, 2 rue Andre-Pascal, 75775 Paris Cedex 16 France. **Tel** 011 33 1 49104262, US:(202)785-6323, FAX 011 33 1 45248500, 011 33 1 45248176, telex 620 160 OCDE. **(Subscription address:** OECD Publications Center, 2001 L Street, Suite 700, Washington DC 20036. **Tel** (202)822-3873, (202)785-6323.) *Continues Economic Surveys by the OECD: Turkey, 0474-5302.*
 Ind/Abst Trade Ind. ASAP [Full Txt.]; Trade Ind. Index [Full Txt.].

LC HC256.5 .O7
DD 330.9/41/085
FR
OECD ECONOMIC SURVEYS : UNITED KINGDOM.
Main/Corp Organisation for Economic Co-Operation and Development. **VAT** Organisation for Economic Co-Operation and Development Economic Surveys: United Kingdom. 1968-. English. 720.00F France; £84.30 UK; $158.00 US; DM310.00 other. Organ for Economic Co-Operation and Development, 2 rue Andre Pascal, 75775 Paris Cedex 16 France. *Continues Economic Surveys: United Kingdom.*
 Ind/Abst Trade Ind. ASAP [Full Txt.]; Trade Ind. Index [Full Txt.].

LC HC106.5 .O7 **ISSN** 0474-5329
DD 330.9/73/092
FR
OECD ECONOMIC SURVEYS : UNITED STATES.
Main/Corp Organisation for Economic Co-Operation and Development. **VFOAT** United States. **VAT** Organisation for Economic Co-Operation and Development Economic Surveys: United States. (1967)-. English. Twenty times a year. $240.00. OECD Publications and Information Center, 2 rue Andre-Pascal, 75775 Paris Cedex 16 France. **Tel** 011 33 1 49104262, US:(202)785-6323, FAX 011 33 1 45248500, 011 33 1 45248176, telex 620 160 OCDE. **(Subscription address:** OECD Publications Center, 2001 L Street, Suite 700, Washington DC 20036. **Tel** (202)822-3873, (202)785-6323.) *Continues Economic Surveys OECD: United States.*
 Ind/Abst Trade Ind. ASAP [Full Txt.]; Trade Ind. Index [Full Txt.].

LC HC59 .O35
KO
OEHWAN UNJAENG WOLBO.
Periodical. Korean. Twelve times a year. Hanguk Oehwan Unhaeng, 181 2-ka Ulchi-ro, Chung-ku, Seoul South Korea.

LC HD8039.B27 I73 **ISSN** 0302-8119
IS
OFEQ (TEL-AVIV).
(OFEK.). [Ofeq]. **Added/Corp** Bank Leumi le-Yisrael. (19??)-. Periodical. Hebrew. Four times a year. Free. POB 2, Tel Aviv Israel. **Tel** 3 650 643. **ED** G Shifron. **Circ:** 10,000 (ctrl).
 Desc: Dedicated to surveying the Israeli economy on a non-political level.

LC HC463.O4 O45
JA
OKINAWA KEIZAI TOKEI NEMPO.
Added/Corp Okinawa Kaihatsucho (Japan). Okinawa Sogo Jimukyoku. Zaimubu. (19??)-. Periodical. Japanese. One time a year. Okinawa Sogo Jimukyoku Zaimubu, 21-5 Maejima 2-chome 900, Naha Japan.

LC HC463.O4 O49a
JA
OKINAWA-KEN NO KEIZAI GAIKYO.
Main/Corp Okinawa-Ken (Japan). Kikaku Choseibu. (19??)-. Periodical. Japanese. Okinawa-ken, 2-32 1-chome Izumizaki, Naha-shi 900 Japan.

LC HC10 .O4 **ISSN** 0030-1906
DD 330.9
DK
OKONOMI OG POLITIK.
[okon. polit.]. **Added/Corp** Selskabet for Historie og Samfundskonomi. Institutet for Historie og Samfundskonomi. Vol. 1 (Jan./March 1927)-. Periodical. Danish. Four times a year (Apr., June, Sept., Nov.). $69.13. Jurist Okonomforbundets Forlag, Gothersgade 133, 1123 Copenhagen Denmark. **Tel** 011 45 1 33142920. **ED** Jurn Henrig Petersen. **Bk Rev. Ad Acc. Circ:** 1,050 (ctrl).
 Desc: Publishes articles on economics and political science.
 Ind/Abst Am. Hist. Life (1954-).

ISSN 1054-5808
DD 953
US
OMAN (SYRACUSE, N.Y.).
(OMAN : A POLITICAL AND ECONOMIC FORECAST.). [Oman]. **Added/Corp** Political Risk Services (IBC USA (Publications) Inc.). (19??)-. English. $325.00. Political Risk Services, 6320 Fly Road, Suite 102, PO Box 248, East Syracuse NY 13057-0248. **Tel** (315)431-0511, FAX (315)431-0200.
 Desc: Assesses the factors affecting the prospects for business and trade. Each report focuses specifically on business needs such as finding and developing markets, determining currency movements, or making judgements about capital investments or corporate security.

LC HC117.N48 O66 **ISSN** 0383-0098
DD 330.9/719/03
CN
OPPORTUNITY (WINNIPEG).
(OPPORTUNITY.). Vol. 1, (1974)-. Periodical. English. Irregular. Fleet Publications Canada Ltd, PO Box 1679, Winnipeg Manitoba R3C 2Z6 Canada.

LC HC267.S573 I515A
XV
OSEBNI DOHODKI ZA DOLOCENE POKLICE / ZAVOD SR SLOVENIJE ZA STATISTIKO.
1978-. Slovenian. One time a year. Zavod Sr Slovenije za Statistiko, Vozarski Pot 12, Ljubljana Slovenia. *Continues Osebni Dohodki Po Poklicih.*

LC HC244 .A3
DD 330.9/171/7
GW
OSTINFORMATION.
Added/Corp Bundesstelle feur Aussenhandelsinformation (Germany). (19??)-. German. Postfach 10 80 07, Blaubach 13.

SW
OUTLOOK ON THE SWEDISH ECONOMY.
Added/Corp PKbanken, Economic Research Department. (19??)-. English. Four times a year. $45.00. Nordbanken, S 105 71 Stockholm Sweden. **Tel** 011 46 8 7818000.

LC JV1801 .E65 **ISSN** 0014-2816
DD 303.4/8244/06
FR
SUSPENDED
OUTREMER (PARIS, FRANCE : 1982).
(OUTREMER.). (19??)-(19??). Periodical. French. Twelve times a year. Europe Outremer, 178 Quai, L Bieriot, 75015 Paris France. **Tel** 46.42.78.44. **Ad Acc. Circ:** 18,000. *Continues Europe. Outremer.*
 Desc: Economics of French speaking Africa (Nughreb and Black Africa).

LC HC10 .O78 **ISSN** 0305-9049
DD 330.9/005
UK
CCC
Pr Rev.
OXFORD BULLETIN OF ECONOMICS AND STATISTICS.
See Business and Economics-Abstracting, Bibliographies and Statistics.

LC HC681 .P2827 **ISSN** 8755-0911
DD 338.5/443/099
US
PACIFIC BASIN ECONOMIC OUTLOOK.
[Pac. Basin econ. outlook.]. **Added/Corp** Wharton Econometric Forecasting Associates. (198?)-. English. Two times a year. WEFA / Philadelphia, PO Box 8500, Suite 1995, Philadelphia PA 19178. **Tel** (215)667-6000, telex 710 6700575.

LC HC411 .P3 **ISSN** 8755-6006
DD 338.5/443/095
US
PACIFIC BASIN ECONOMIC UPDATE.
[Pac. Basin econ. update]. Vol. 1, No. 1 (Winter 1983)-. English. Four times a year. WEFA / Philadelphia, PO Box 8500, Suite 1995, Philadelphia PA 19178. **Tel** (215)667-6000, telex 710 6700575.

LC AS741 .P3 **ISSN** 0030-8978
DD 052
NZ
CCC
PACIFIC VIEWPOINT.
See Sociology-Abstracting, Bibliographies and Statistics.

LC HC431 .P2
II
PACT; A PANORAMA OF INDUSTRY, AGRICULTURE, COMMERCE & TRADE.
(19??)-. Periodical. English. Four times a year. N K Bakshi, C-3/26 Rajouri Garden, New Delhi-27 India.

LC HC440.5.A1 P27 **ISSN** 1011-002X
DD 330.9/549/105
PK
PAKISTAN ECONOMIC AND SOCIAL REVIEW.
Added/Corp University of the Punjab. Economics Dept. **VAT** Pak. econ. soc. rev. Vol. 9 (1971)-. Periodical. English. Two times a year. $30.00. Pakistan Economic and Social Review / Department of Economics, Quaid E Azam CPU, Lahore 54590 Pakistan. **Tel** 011 92 42 5863997, FAX 011 92 42 5868313. *Continues Punjab University Economist, 0377-3191.*
 Ind/Abst Econ. Lit. Index; Int. Bibliogr. Sociol.; J. Econ. Lit.; Middle East Abstr. Index; Rice Abstr.; Sorghum Mill. Abstr.; Middle East J.

ISSN 1054-6030
DD 954
US
PAKISTAN (SYRACUSE, N.Y.).
(PAKISTAN : A POLITICAL AND ECONOMIC FORECAST.). [Pakistan]. **Added/Corp** Political Risk Services (IBC USA (Publications) Inc.). (19??)-. English. $325.00. Political Risk Services, 6320 Fly Road, Suite 102, PO Box 248, East Syracuse NY 13057-0248. **Tel** (315)431-0511, FAX (315)431-0200.
 Desc: Assesses the factors affecting the prospects for business and trade. Each report focuses specifically on business needs such as finding and developing markets, determining currency movements, or making judgements about capital investments or corporate security.

LC HC440.5.A1 G47a
DD 330.9/549/105
GW
PAKISTAN, WIRTSCHAFTLICHE ENTWICKLUNG.
Main/Corp Germany (West). Bundesstelle fur Aussenhandelsinformation. (19??)-. German. Bundesstelle fuer Aussenhandelsinformation, Agrippastrasse 87 93, D-50676 Cologne Germany. **Tel** 011 49 221 2057316, FAX 011 49 221 2057212.

LC HC440.5.A1
DD 330.9549/1/005
GW
PAKISTAN, WIRTSCHAFTSDATEN UND WIRTSCHAFTSDOKUMENTATION / BUNDESSTELLE FUER AUSSENHANDELSINFORMATION.
German. DM3.00. Bundesstelle fuer Aussenhandelsinformation, Agrippastrasse 87 93, D-50676 Cologne Germany. **Tel** 011 49 221 2057316, FAX 011 49 221 2057212.

ISSN 1054-6049
DD 972
US
PANAMA (SYRACUSE, N.Y.).
(PANAMA : A POLITICAL AND ECONOMIC FORECAST.). [Panama]. **Added/Corp** Political Risk Services (IBC USA (Publications) Inc.). (19??)-. English. $325.00. Political Risk Services, 6320 Fly Road, Suite 102, PO Box 248, East Syracuse NY 13057-0248. **Tel** (315)431-0511, FAX (315)431-0200.
 Desc: Assesses the factors affecting the prospects for business and trade. Each report focuses specifically on business needs such as finding and developing markets, determining currency movements, or making judgements about capital investments or corporate security.

LC HC147
DD 330.9/7287/05
GW
PANAMA : WIRTSCHAFTLICHE ENTWICKLUNG.
Main/Corp Bundesstelle fur Aussenhandelsinformation (Germany). (19??)-. German. Bundesstelle fuer Aussenhandelsinformation, Agrippastrasse 87 93, D-50676 Cologne Germany. **Tel** 011 49 221 2057316, FAX 011 49 221 2057212.

LC HC171 .P18
AG
PANORAMA DE LA ECONOMIA.
Vol. 6 (1969)-. Periodical. Spanish. Four times a year. $12.00. Bolivar 177, Buenos Aires Argentina. *Continues Panorama de la Economia Argentina.*

LC HC381 .P27
SP
PANORAMA DE LA ECONOMIA ESPANOLA.
Spanish. Ediciones del Movimiento, Gaztambide 61, Madrid Spain.

LC HC340.2.Z9 I576 **ISSN** 0784-9656
FI
PANOS-TUOTOS.
VFOAT Input-Output. **VAT** Panos Tuotos. (19??)-. Finnish. Central Statistical Office, PO Box 504, SF-00101 Helsinki Finland. **Tel** 011 358 0 17347, FAX 011 358 0 17342279.

LC HC381 .P34 **ISSN** 0210-9107
DD 330.946/005
SP
PAPELES DE ECONOMIA ESPANOLA.
[Pop. econ. esp.]. **Added/Corp** Confederacion Espanola de Cajas de Ahorros. Fondo Para la Investigacion Economica y Social. Fundacion Fondo para la Investigacion Economica y Social (Spain) Fundacion Fondo para la Investigacion para la Investigacion Economica y Social (Spain). Vol. 1 (1980). Periodical. Spanish. Four times a year. $79.94. Fundacion Fondo para la Investigacion Economica y Social, Juan Hurtado de Mendoza 14, 28036 Madrid Spain. **Tel** 011 34 1 3504400, FAX 011 34 1 3508040. **ED** Padre Damian. **Circ:** 10,000 (ctrl). available on microfiche.
 Desc: Aims to offer responsible and thorough information on Spanish economical problems through investigations conducted by the foundation or promoted by it, in order to interpret the Spanish economical mark.
 Ind/Abst Int. Bibliogr. Sociol.; Selec. Coop. Index Manage. Period.

LC HC683.5.A1 P36
DD 330.995/3
GW
PAPUA-NEUGUINEA, WIRTSCHAFTSDATEN UND WIRTSCHAFTSDOKUMENTATION.
Added/Corp Bundesstelle fur Aussenhandelsinformation (Germany). (19??)-. German. Bundesstelle fuer Aussenhandelsinformation, Agrippastrasse 87 93, D-50676 Cologne Germany. **Tel** 011 49 221 2057316, FAX 011 49 221 2057212.

LC HC221 .P32
DD 330.9892/005
GW
PARAGUAY WIRTSCHAFTLICHE ENTWICKLUNG.
Added/Corp Bundesstelle fuer Aussenhandelsinformation (Germany). (19??)-. German. One time a year. Bundesstelle fuer Aussenhandelsinformation, Agrippastrasse 87 93, D-50676 Cologne Germany. **Tel** 011 49 221 2057316, FAX 011 49 221 2057212.

Business and Economics —Economic History, Conditions

LC HC188.P35 B25a
BL
PARANA INFORMACOES. Main/Corp Banco de Desenvolvimento do Parana. (1973)-. Portuguese. Banco de Desenvolvimento do Parana, Av Vicente Machado 445, Cx Postal 6042, Curitiba Brazil.

LC HX7
DD 335.43/05
UDC 908
ISSN 0392-4815
IT
PASSATO E PRESENTE (FLORENCE, ITALY). See History.

LC HC188.P4 P447A
BL
PERNAMBUCO INDUSTRIAL, SUDENE : PROJETOS APROVADOS. Main/Corp Pernambuco, Brazil (State). Secretaria de Industria e Comercio. **VAT** Pernambuco Industrial, Superintendencia do Desenvolvimento do Nordeste: Projetos Aprovados. Portuguese. Secretaria de Industria e Comercio do Estado de Pernambuco, Av Pantas Barreto, 512 - 70 Andar 50.000, Recife Brazil.

LC HC110.I5 N46A
DD 339.373
US
PERSONAL INCOME FOR UNITED STATES, NEW JERSEY, AND COUNTIES. Main/Corp New Jersey. Office of Demographic and Economic Analysis. English. Every 2 years. Division of Labor Market and Demographic Research, New Jersey Department of Labor, CN 388, Trenton NJ 08625-0388. **Tel** (609)292-0076, FAX (609)984-6833. available on diskette.

LC HC329.5.I5 P482
NE
PERSONELE IMKOMENSVERDELING, REGIONALE GEGEVENS / CENTRAAL BUREAU VOOR DE STATISTIED, HOOFDAFDELING STATISTIEKEN VAN INKOMEN EN CONSUMPTIE, DE. VFOAT Distribution of Personal Income, Regional Data. Dutch. Irregular. Fl35.00. Centraal Bureau voor de Statistiek, AFD ALG Zaken, Postbus 959, 2270 AZ Voorburg Netherlands. **Tel** 011 31 70 3373800, FAX 011 31 70 0387429, telex 32692 CBS NL. available on audiocassette.

LC HC226 .P35
PE
PERSPECTIVA. Vol. 1, No. 1 (Sept./Dec. 1974)-. Spanish. Oficina Nacional de Integracion, Las Begonias 375 - Of 332 - San Isidro, Lima Peru.
Ind/Abst Biocont. News Inf.; Rice Abstr.

LC HC381 .P47
ISSN 1132-9564
SP
●**PERSPECTIVAS DEL SISTEMA FINANCIERO. Added/Corp** Fundacion Fondo para la Investigacion Economica y Social (Spain). (1993)-. Periodical. Spanish. Four times a year. $71.06. Fundacion Fondo para la Investigacion Economica y Social, Juan Hurtado de Mendoza 14, 28036 Madrid Spain. **Tel** 011 34 1 3504400, FAX 011 34 1 3508040. **ED** Padre Damian. **Circ:** 4,000 (ctrl). available on microfiche. **Continues** Papeles de Economia Espanola / Suplementos sobre el Sistema Financiero, 0212-5994.
Desc: Content concerns new financial institutions that have arisen, analyzing their content, functions, and regulations, in order to widen the field of the Spanish financial realm through the diffusion of information.

DD 330.9714/04/05
ISSN 1189-3516
CN
PERSPECTIVE, EN. [En perspect.]. **Added/Corp** Confederation des Caisses Populaires et d'Economie Desjardins du Quebec. Vice-Presidence Planification. Vol. 1, No 1 (Mar 1991)-. Periodical. French. Ten times a year. Free on request. Confederation des Caisses Populaires et D'Economie Desjardins du Quebec, 100 Avenue des Commandeurs, Levis Quebec G6V 7N5 Canada. **Tel** (418)835-2893, FAX (418)833-5873. **Circ:** 10,000.

LC T58.7
DD 338
US CEASED
PERSPECTIVES. See Industry and Production.

LC HC226 .P395
DD 330.985.005
Pr Rev.
PE
PERU ECONOMICO. (197?)-. Periodical. Spanish. Twelve times a year. $560.00. Apoyo SA, Apartado 671, Lima 100 Peru. **Tel** 011 51 14 445555, FAX 011 51 14 450536. **ED** Augusto Alvarez-Rodrich. **Circ:** 5,000 (ctrl).
Desc: Exclusive statistical information; analysis of current trends and future projections on the political and economic situation in Peru.

LC HC226 .P425
PE
PERU INFORMA. VFOAT National Information System. Periodical. English (English). Information Service Enterprise, Lima Peru.

DD 985
ISSN 1054-6057
US
PERU (SYRACUSE, N.Y.). (PERU : A POLITICAL AND ECONOMIC FORECAST / POLITICAL RISK SERVICES.). [Peru]. **Added/Corp** Political Risk Services (IBC USA (Publications) Inc.). (19??)-. English. $325.00. Political Risk Services, 6320 Fly Road, Suite 102, PO Box 248, East Syracuse NY 13057-0248. **Tel** (315)431-0511, FAX (315)431-0200.
Desc: Assesses the factors affecting the prospects for business and trade. Each report focuses specifically on business needs such as finding and developing markets, determining currency movements, or making judgements about capital investments or corporate security.

LC HC226
GW
PERU: WIRTSCHAFTSDATEN UND WIRTSCHAFTSDOKUMENTATION. Main/Corp Bundesstelle fur Aussenhandelsinformation (Germany). German. DM2.00. Bundesstelle fuer Aussenhandelsinformation, Agrippastrasse 87 93, D-50676 Cologne Germany. **Tel** 011 49 221 2057316, FAX 011 49 221 2057212.

LC HC226 .P428
DD 330.9/85/063
US
PERUVIAN TIMES. (19??)-. Periodical. English. One time a week. Andean Air Mail & Peruvian Times SA, PO Box 1405, Coral Gables FL 33114-1405. **Continues** Andean Air Mail & Peruvian Times.

LC HC451 .A28972b
DD 330.9/599/04
ISSN 0115-0073
PH
PHILIPPINE DEVELOPMENT. [Philipp. dev.]. **Added/Corp** Philippines. National Economic and Development Authority. Office of the Director-General. Vol. 4, No. 8 (Sept. 15, 1976)-. Periodical. English. Six times a year. $28.50. National Economic and Development Authority, PO Box 419, Greenhills Metro Manila Philippines. **Tel** 011 63 2 6313281. **ED** Patricia Rivera. **Circ:** 1,000. **Continues** Philippines. National Economic and Development Authority. NEDA Development Digest.
Desc: Digests of the economy, features of ideal industries, major economic indicators, updates on regional and domestic economic development projects.
Ind/Abst Food Sci. Technol. Abstr.; Index Philip. Period.; J. Ferrocement; PAIS Int. Print; Philip. Sci. Technol. Abstr.

LC HC451 .P525
DD 338.9599/005
PH
PHILIPPINE DEVELOPMENT REPORT. Added/Corp Philippines. National Economic and Development Authority. (1977)-. Monographic series. English. Irregular. Price varies per volume. National Economic and Development Authority, PO Box 419, Greenhills Metro Manila Philippines. **Tel** 011 63 2 6313281. **Continues** Report on the Philippine Economy.

LC HC451 .P567
DD 330.9599
GW
PHILIPPINEN, WIRTSCHAFTLICHE ENTWICKLUNG / BUNDESSTELLE FUR AUSSENHANDELSINFORMATION. German. One time a year. DM4.00. Bundesstelle fuer Aussenhandelsinformation, Agrippastrasse 87 93, D-50676 Cologne Germany. **Tel** 011 49 221 2057316, FAX 011 49 221 2057212.

LC HC451
DD 330.9599/005
GW
PHILIPPINEN, WIRTSCHAFTSDATEN UND WIRTSCHAFTSDOKUMENTATION / BUNDESSTELLE FUR AUSSENHANDELSINFORMATION. German. DM3.00. Bundesstelle fuer Aussenhandelsinformation, Agrippastrasse 87 93, D-50676 Cologne Germany. **Tel** 011 49 221 2057316, FAX 011 49 221 2057212.

DD 959
ISSN 1054-6065
US
PHILIPPINES (SYRACUSE, N.Y.). (PHILIPPINES : A POLITICAL AND ECONOMIC FORECAST / POLITICAL RISK SERVICES.). [Philippines]. **Added/Corp** Political Risk Services (IBC USA (Publications) Inc.). (19??)-. English. $325.00. Political Risk Services, 6320 Fly Road, Suite 102, PO Box 248, East Syracuse NY 13057-0248. **Tel** (315)431-0511, FAX (315)431-0200.
Desc: Assesses the factors affecting the prospects for business and trade. Each report focuses specifically on business needs such as finding and developing markets, determining currency movements, or making judgements about capital investments or corporate security.

NQ
PIEDRA BOCONA, LA. See Housing and Urban Development.

LC HC146.A1 P58
NQ
PLAN ECONOMICO. Spanish. One time a year.

US
PLANECON REVIEW & OUTLOOK. (19??)-. English. Two times a year. $7500.00. PlanEcon Inc., 1111 14th Street Northwest, Suite 801, Washington DC 20005. **Tel** (202)898-0471.
Desc: Information on present and future developments in the former Soviet republics and Eastern Europe, with emphasis on related political and social developments. Includes projections of major economic indicators and a forecast risk assessment.

LC HA1228.A9 A32
DD 314.4
FR
POINT ECONOMIQUE DE L'AUVERGNE, LE. See Business and Economics-Abstracting, Bibliographies and Statistics.

DD 943
ISSN 1054-6073
US
POLAND (SYRACUSE, N.Y.). (POLAND : A POLITICAL AND ECONOMIC FORECAST / POLITICAL RISK SERVICES.). [Poland (Syracuse N. Y.)]. **Added/Corp** Political Risk Services (IBC USA (Publications) Inc.). (19??)-. English. $325.00. Political Risk Services, 6320 Fly Road, Suite 102, PO Box 248, East Syracuse NY 13057-0248. **Tel** (315)431-0511, FAX (315)431-0200.
Desc: Assesses the factors affecting the prospects for business and trade. Each report focuses specifically on business needs such as finding and developing markets, determining currency movements, or making judgements about capital investments or corporate security.

LC HC244 HC337.P7
GW
POLEN : VOLKSWIRTSCHAFTSPLAN UND BUDGETDATEN. Main/Corp Bundesstelle fur Aussenhandelsinformation (Germany). German. DM3.00. Bundesstelle fuer Aussenhandelsinformation, Agrippastrasse 87 93, D-50676 Cologne Germany. **Tel** 011 49 221 2057316, FAX 011 49 221 2057212.

LC HC59.7 .P57
DD 327
ISSN 0032-3101
IT
POLITICA INTERNAZIONALE. See Political Science-International Relations.

LC HC171 .P64
AG
POLITICA Y ECONOMIA. (19??)-. Periodical. Spanish. Twelve times a year. 25 de Mayo 486 50 Piso, Buenos Aires Argentina.

DD 320
ISSN 1056-5280
US
POLITICAL AND ECONOMIC CONDITIONS IN SOUTHERN AFRICA. See Political Science.

LC HC391 .G4b
GW
PORTUGAL, AZOREN UND MADEIRA : WIRTSCHAFT IN ZAHLEN UND WIRTSCHAFTSDOKUMENTATION. Main/Corp Bundesstelle fuer Aussenhandelsinformation (Germany). (19??)-. German. Bundesstelle fuer Aussenhandelsinformation, Agrippastrasse 87 93, D-50676 Cologne Germany. **Tel** 011 49 221 2057316, FAX 011 49 221 2057212.

DD 946
ISSN 1054-6081
US
PORTUGAL (SYRACUSE, N.Y.). (PORTUGAL : A POLITICAL AND ECONOMIC FORECAST.). [Portugal (Syracuse N. Y.)]. **Added/Corp** Political Risk Services (IBC USA (Publications) Inc.). (19??)-. English. $325.00. Political Risk Services, 6320 Fly Road, Suite 102, PO Box 248, East Syracuse NY 13057-0248. **Tel** (315)431-0511, FAX (315)431-0200.
Desc: Assesses the factors affecting the prospects for business and trade. Each report focuses specifically on business needs such as finding and developing markets, determining currency movements, or making judgements about capital investments or corporate security.

LC HC391
DD 330.9/469/042
GW
PORTUGAL, WIRTSCHAFTLICHE ENTWICKLUNG. Main/Corp Germany (West). Bundesstelle fur Aussenhandelsinformation. German. Bundesstelle fuer Aussenhandelsinformation, Agrippastrasse 87 93, D-50676 Cologne Germany. **Tel** 011 49 221 2057316, FAX 011 49 221 2057212.

LC HC10 .T44A
YU
POSLOVNI DNEVNIK - TANJUG. Main/Corp Telegrafska Agencija Nova Jugoslavija. **VAT** Poslovni Dnevnik - Telegrafska Agencija Nova Jugoslavija. Vol. 1 (Jan. 6, 1970)-. Serbo-Croatian (Roman). Obilicev Venac 2, Postanski FAH 439, Belgrad Yugoslavia. **Supersedes** Dnevne Ekonomske Vesti.

Business and Economics —Economic History, Conditions

LC HC101 .P7
DD 338.5/443/0973
ISSN 0278-0135
US
CCC
PREDICASTS FORECASTS. See Business and Economics-Abstracting, Bibliographies and Statistics.

DD 330.97127
ISSN 0228-2488
CN
PRESENTATION TO THE PREMIER AND PROVINCIAL CABINET. (PRESENTATION TO THE PREMIER AND PROVINCIAL CABINET - MANITOBA CHAMBERS OF COMMERCE.). **Main/Corp** Manitoba Chambers of Commerce. English. One time a year. Free. Manitoba Chambers of Commerce, 705-177 Lombard Avenue, Winnipeg Man. R3B 0W8. ctrl circ.

LC HC381 .A29
SP
PRESUPUESTO Y LA ECONOMIA ESPANOLA, EL. Main/Corp Spain. Ministerio de Hacienda. Secretaria General Tecnica. Spanish. 150ptas. Ministerio de Economia Y Hacienda, Centro de Publicaciones, Pl Camillo del Mundo Nuevo 3, 28005 Madrid Spain. **Tel** 227 14 37.

SZ
PRICES AND EARNINGS AROUND THE GLOBE. (1971)-. English. Every 3 years. Union Bank of Switzerland / UBS, Economic Research Department, PO Box 8021, Zurich Switzerland. **Tel** 011 41 1 2344243.

LC HC547.I8 C47B
DD 338/.0025/6668
IV
PRINCIPALES INDUSTRIES INSTALLEES EN COTE D'IVOIRE. Main/Corp Chambre d'Industrie de Cote d'Ivoire. French. Chambre d'Industrie de Cote d'Ivoire, 11 Avenue Lamblin, BP No 1 758, Abidjan Ivory Coast. **Continues** Principales Industries Ivoiriennes.

LC HC10 .B357A
DD 330.9/04
BE
PRINCIPAUX FAITS ECONOMIQUES DANS LE DOMAINE INTERNATIONAL. Main/Corp Belgium. Ministere des Affaires Economiques. Direction Generale des Etudes et de la Documentation. **VFOAT** Voornaamste Economische Feiten Op Het Internationaal Gebied. Periodical. Multiple languages (Dutch and French).

LC HC121 .P75
ISSN 0301-7036
MX
Pr Rev.
PROBLEMAS DEL DESARROLLO. See Business and Economics-International Economic Relations.

LC HC10 .E515
AA
PROBLEME EKONOMIKE. Added/Corp Akademia e Shkencave. Instituti i Studimeve Ekonomike. Vol. 20 (Jan./Feb. 1973)-. Periodical. Albanian. Four times a year. $7.27. Book Distribution Enterprise, Rruga Kavajes, Tirane Albania. **Tel** 011 355 42 27246. **Continues** Ekonomia Popullore.
Ind/Abst Geogr. Abstr. Human Geogr. (?-?).

LC HC10 .P7
DD 330.5
ISSN 0032-9304
FR
PROBLEMES ECONOMIQUES. [Probl. econ.]. No. 1 (Jan. 6, 1948)-. Periodical. French. One time a week. 308.00F France; 386.00F (surface mail), 545.00F (airmail) other. Documentation Francaise, 29 quai Voltaire, 75344 Paris Cedex 7 France. **Tel** 011 33 1 40157000, FAX 011 33 1 40157230, telex 204 826 DOCFRAN. **Formed by the union of** Bulletin Hebdomadaire d'Information Economiques **and** Revue Hebdomadaire de la Presse Economique Francaise.
Ind/Abst Int. Labour Doc.; LABORDOC; PAIS Int. Print (1991-); Repere; World Agric. Econ. Rural Sociol. Abstr.

LC HC307.S3 P75
IT
PROGRAMMAZIONE IN SARDEGNA, LA. Added/Corp Sardinia (Italy). Centro Regionale di Programmazione. (1966)-. Periodical. Italian. Six times a year. Centro Regionale di Programmazione, Cagliari Italy.

LC HC547.U6 O74A
DD 330.9/66/2505
UV
PROGRAMME D'ACTIVITES - ORGANISME REGIONAL DE DEVELOPPEMENT DU CENTRE-NORD. Main/Corp Organisme Regional de Developpement du Centre-Nord. French. Republique de Haute-Volta, Organisme Regional de Developpement du Centre-Nord, Kaya Burkina Faso.

LC HC60 .O73b
DD 341.7/5
ISSN 0377-2993
FR
PROGRAMME OF WORK AND BUDGET. (PROGRAMME OF WORK AND BUDGET - ORGANISATION FOR ECONOMIC CO-OPERATION AND DEVELOPMENT.). **Main/Corp** Organisation for Economic Co-Operation and Development. Secretariat. (19??)-. English. Irregular. OECD Publications and Information Center, 2 rue Andre-Pascal, 75775 Paris Cedex 16 France. **Tel** 011 33 1 49104262, US:(202)785-6323, FAX 011 33 1 45248500, 011 33 1 45248176, telex 620 160 OCDE. **(Subscription address:** OECD Publications Center, 2001 L Street, Suite 700, Washington DC 20036. **Tel** (202)822-3873, (202)785-6323.**)**

LC HC547.U6 O74B
DD 354/.66/25008233
UV
PROJET DE BUDGET - ORGANISME REGIONAL DE DEVELOPPEMENT DU CENTRE-NORD. Main/Corp Organisme Regional de Developpement du Centre-Nord. French. Ministere du Developpement Rural, Organisme Regionale de Developpement du Centre-Nord, Kaya Burkina Faso.

LC HC171 .P76
AG
PROPUESTA Y CONTROL. (August 1976)-. Periodical. Spanish. Ediciones PYC, San Jose 189 Ler Piso, Buenos Aires Argentina.

IT
PROSPETTIVE DELL ECONOMIA.
Added/Corp Federazione delle Casse di Risparmio della Liguria. Cassa di Risparmio di Genova e Imperia. Ufficio Studi e Ricerche. Italian. Four times a year. Ufficio Studi e Statistica della Cassa di Risparmio di Genova e Imperia, Via Cassa di Risparmio 15, 16123 Genova Italy. **Continues in part** Rassegna Statistica dell'Economia Ligure.

DD 330.971
ISSN 0827-5785
CN
PROVINCIAL OUTLOOK. ECONOMIC FORECAST. [Prov. outlook, Econ. forecast]. Vol. 1, No. 1 (March 1986)-. Periodical. English. Conference Board of Canada, 255 Smyth Road, Ottawa Ontario K1H 8M7 Canada. **Tel** (613)526-3280, FAX (613)526-4857, telex 053-3034. **Continues** Quarterly Provincial Forecast, 0381-0100.

LC Z7165.E8 P8 HC241.2
DD 015.4
LU
PUBLICATIONS OF THE EUROPEAN COMMUNITIES. CATALOGUE. See Business and Economics-Abstracting, Bibliographies and Statistics.

LC Z7165.E86 O34 HC241.2.P9
DD 341.242
LU
PUBLICATIONS / OFFICE FOR OFFICIAL PUBLICATIONS OF THE EUROPEAN COMMUNITIES. Main/Corp Office for Official Publications of the European Communities. **VFOAT** Publications of the European Communities. (1991)-. English. Four times a year. Publications Department of the European Communities, PO Box 1003, Luxembourg 2985 Luxembourg. **Continues** Office for Official Publications of the European Communities. Publications of the European Communities.

LC HC154.5.A1 P854
PR
PUERTO RICO ECONOMIC INDICATORS / GOVERNMENT DEVELOPMENT BANK FOR PUERTO RICO. Added/Corp Government Development Bank for Puerto Rico. **VFOAT** Indicadores Economicos. (1985)-. Monographic series. Spanish (Spanish). Irregular. Price varies per issue. Junta de Planificacion, PO Box 41119, San Juan Puerto Rico 000940. **Tel** (809)742-2840. **Circ:** 50 (ctrl) **Continues** Puerto Rico Monthly Economic Indicators.

DD 972
ISSN 1054-609X
US
PUERTO RICO (SYRACUSE, N.Y.). (PUERTO RICO : A POLITICAL AND ECONOMIC FORECAST / POLITICAL RISK SERVICES.). [P. R.]. **Added/Corp** Political Risk Services (IBC USA (Publications) Inc.). (19??)-. English. $325.00. Political Risk Services, 6320 Fly Road, Suite 102, PO Box 248, East Syracuse NY 13057-0248. **Tel** (315)431-0511, FAX (315)431-0200.
Desc: Assesses the factors affecting the prospects for business and trade. Each report focuses specifically on business needs such as finding and developing markets, determining currency movements, or making judgements about capital investments or corporate security.

LC HC157.P8 P86
DD 330.9/7295/053
ISSN 0147-5908
US
PUERTO RICO (WASHINGTON. 1976). (PUERTO RICO : AN ECONOMIC ASSESSMENT). 1975/76-. English. One time a year. $20.00. Frank Henjes and Company, 100 Wall Street, New York NY 10005.

LC HC445.5.A1 P87
MY
PUSPANIAGA. Vol. 1 (1973)-. Periodical. Malay. Twelve times a year. $1.50 single issue. Berita Publishing Company SDN BHD, 22 Jalan Liku, 59206 Kuala Lumpur Malaysia. **Tel** 011 60 3 2822754, FAX 011 60 3 2821605, telex 30259. **Supersedes** Suara Gabungan.

LC HC497.Q3
GW
QATAR: WIRTSCHAFTLICHE ENTWICKLUNG. Main/Corp Bundesstelle fur Aussenhandelsinformation (Germany). (19??)-. German. DM2.00. Bundesstelle fuer Aussenhandelsinformation, Agrippastrasse 87 93, D-50676 Cologne Germany. **Tel** 011 49 221 2057316, FAX 011 49 221 2057212.

LC HC497.Q3
QA
QATAR : WIRTSCHAFTSDATEN UND WIRTSCHAFTSDOKUMENTATION. Main/Corp Bundesstelle fur Aussenhandelsinformation (Germany). German. 2.00QR. Bundesstelle fuer Aussenhandelsinformation, Agrippastrasse 87 93, D-50676 Cologne Germany. **Tel** 011 49 221 2057316, FAX 011 49 221 2057212.

UDC 33
ISSN 1121-9610
IT
QUADERNI DI ECONOMIA E FINANZA. [Quad. econ. finanza]. (1992)-. Periodical. Italian. Three times a year. Banco di Sardegna, Viale Umberto I 36, 07100 Sassari Italy. **Tel** 011 39 79 226572, FAX 011 39 79 226579, telex 791106. **Circ:** 2,000 (ctrl). **Continues** Quaderni Sardi di Economia, 0391-8394.

DD 330
ISSN 0888-787X
US
CCC
TITLE CHANGE
QUARTERLY CONSENSUS FORECAST OF KEY ECONOMIC INDICATORS. [Q. consens. forecast key econ. indic.]. **Added/Corp** Institute of Business Forecasting. (198?)-(19??). Periodical. English. Graceway Publishing Company, PO Box 159 Station C, Flushing NY 11367. **Tel** (718)463-9114, FAX (718)544-9086. **Continued by** Quarterly Domestic & Global Forecasts of Key Economics Indicators.

LC HC1060.A1 Q36
DD 330.9667/0021
GH
QUARTERLY DIGEST OF STATISTICS (ACCRA, GHANA : 1981). (QUARTERLY DIGEST OF STATISTICS.). Vol. 1, No. 1 (June 1981)-. English. Four times a year. Statistical Service, PO Box 1098, Accra Ghana. **Continues** Quarterly Digest of Statistics (Accra, Ghana : 1959).

LC HC157.T8 C4B
DD 330.0/729/8304
TR
QUARTERLY ECONOMIC BULLETIN - CENTRAL BANK OF TRINIDAD AND TOBAGO. Main/Corp Central Bank of Trinidad and Tobago. Vol. 1 (Mar. 1976)-. Bulletin. English. Four times a year (Mar., June, Sept., Dec). $35.00. Central Bank of Trinidad and Tobago, PO Box 1250, Port of Spain Trinidad. **Tel** (809)625-4835, (809)625-5028. cum. index. **Circ:** 1,000 (ctrl). available on microfilm from University Microfilms International (UMI). **Supersedes** Central Bank of Trinidad and Tobago. Economic Bulletin.
Desc: Commentary on the economic, banking and financial situations in Trinidad and Tobago. Presents papers or speeches on the same subjects by the members of the central bank staff.
Ind/Abst PAIS Int. Print (1991-).

LC HC257.S4 Q37
DD 330.9411/005
ISSN 0306-7866
UK
QUARTERLY ECONOMIC COMMENTARY (GLASGOW). (QUARTERLY ECONOMIC COMMENTARY.). [Q. econ. comment.]. **Added/Corp** Fraser of Allander Institute. Vol. 1, (July 1975)-. English. Four times a year (Mar., June, Sept., Dec.). $85.56. Fraser of Allander Institute, 100 Cathedral Street, Glasgow G4 OLN United Kingdom. **Tel** 011 041 5524400, FAX 011 041 552 5589. **ED** Stewart Dunlop. **Circ:** 500.
Desc: Analysis and commentary of current and prospective developments in the Scottish economy.
Ind/Abst Leis., Rec., Tour. Abstr.

LC HC461 .N64a
DD 330.952/005
JA
QUARTERLY ECONOMIC REVIEW. Added/Corp Nomura Sogo Kenkyujo. **VFOAT** NRI Quarterly Economic Review. Vol. 22, No. 2 (May 1992)-. Periodical. English. Four times a year (Feb., May, Aug., Nov.). $100.00. Nomura Research Institute Ltd., Information Resources Department, NRI Tower, 134 Godo-cho, Hodgaya-ku, Yokohama 240 Japan. **Tel** 011 81 45 3367097, FAX 011 81 45 3368739. **(Subscription address:** OCS / Overseas Courier Service of America Inc., 5 East 44th Street, New York NY 10017. **Tel** (212)599-4517.**) ED** Yoshikazu Takao. **Continues** NRI Quarterly Economic Review (Tokyo, Japan : 1989).

LC HC466 .H246
DD 330.9519/5/005
KO
QUARTERLY ECONOMIC REVIEW (HANGUK UNHAENG). (QUARTERLY ECONOMIC REVIEW.). (June 1969)-. Periodical. English.

Business and Economics —Economic History, Conditions

Four times a year. Bank of Korea, 110 3 Ka Namdaemun Ro, Seoul Korea. **Tel** 011 82 2 7594340. *Continues in part* Monthly Statistical Review (Hanguk Unhaeng).

LC HC240.9.I5 Q37 **ISSN** 0258-2066
DD 339.34/05 LU

QUARTERLY NATIONAL ACCOUNTS--ESA = COMPTES NATIONAUX TRIMESTRIELS--SEC.
Added/Corp Statistical Office of the European Communities. **VFOAT** Comptes Nationaux Trimestriels--SEC. **VAT** Quarterly National Accounts--European System of Integrated Economic Accounts. Vol. 1 (1986)-. English (French). Four times a year. L176000. Office for Official Publications of the European Communities, 2 rue Mercier, 2985 Luxembourg Luxembourg. **Tel** 011 352 499281, FAX 011 352 292942763. **(Subscription address:** Licosa s.p.a., PO Box 552, 50125 Florence Italy. **Tel** 011 39 55 645415.)

LC HC670.I5 N48a **ISSN** 0033-5711
DD 339.3931 NZ
CCC

QUARTERLY PREDICTIONS. Added/Corp
New Zealand Institute of Economic Research. **VFOAT** Quarterly Predictions of National Income and Expenditure. No. 10 (Dec. 1966)-. Periodical. English. Four times a year (Mar., June, Sep., Dec.). $268.63. New Zealand Institute of Economic Research Inc, PO Box 3479, Wellington New Zealand. **Tel** 011-64-4-721880, 011-64-4-721800. *Continues* New Zealand Institute of Economic Research. Quarterly Predictions of National Income and Expenditure.

LC HC10 .S352 **ISSN** 0347-3139
DD 330/.05 SW
CEASED

QUARTERLY REVIEW - SKANDINAVISKA ENSKILDA BANKEN.
(QUARTERLY REVIEW.). [Q. rev. - Skand. ensk. banken]. **Main/Corp** Skandinaviska Enskilda Banken. Vol. 1 (1972)-(19??). English. Skandinaviska Enskilda Banken, Kungstradgardsgatan 8, S-106 40 Stockholm Sweden. **Tel** 011 46 8 7635000. *Supersedes* Skandinaviska Banken, A.-B. Quarterly Review, Issued by the Statistical Department.
Ind/Abst Predicasts; Public Aff. Inf. Serv. Bull.

LC HC59 .R255
DD 330.9/005 FR

RAMSES : RAPPORT ANNUEL SUR LE SYSTEME ECONOMIQUE ET LES STRATEGIES. Added/Corp Institut Francais des Relations Internationales. VFOAT Rapport Annuel Mondial sur le Systeme Economique et les Strategies; RAMSES. (1981)-. French. One time a year. $51.62. Bordas, 17 rue Remy Dumoncel, 75661 Paris Cedex 14 France. Tel 011 33 1 43299430. (Subscription address: Librairie Dunod, 30 rue St. Sulpice, 75006 Paris France. Tel 011 33 1 43299430.)

LC HC59 .R258
PL

RAPORT O WYBRANYCH PROBLEMACH GOSPODARKI SWIATOWEJ / INSTYTUT FINANSOW.
Added/Corp Instytut Finansow (Poland). (1991)-. Polish. If, Warszawa Swietokrzyska 12 Poland. *Continues* Raport O Stanie Kluczowych Procesow Gospodarczych.

LC HC158.A1 I57a
DD 330 FR

RAPPORT ANNUEL. Main/Corp Institut d'Emission des Departements d'Outre-Mer (France). (1990)-. French. Institut d'Emission des Departments d Outre-Mer, 233 boulevard Saint-Germain, 75007 Paris France. *Continues* Institut d'Emission des Departements d'Outre-Mer (France). Rapport d'Activite - Institute d'Emission des Departements d'Outre-mer.

LC HC547.C5 C55a
DD 330.9/67/4304 CD

RAPPORT ECONOMIQUE ANNUEL.
Main/Corp Chad. Ministere du Commerce et de l'Industrie. (19??)-. French. Ministere du Commerce et de l Industrie, Fort-Lamy Chad.

LC HC271 .A223d HC271 .A218
DD 330.944 S 330.944/0021 FR

RAPPORT SUR LES COMPTES DE LA NATION. Main/Corp Institut National de la Statistique et des Etudes Economiques (France). (19??)-. French (summaries and/or abstracts in English and Spanish). One time a year. 230.00F, 184.00F (microfiche). CNGP INSEE - Institut National de la Statistique et des Etudes Economiques, BP 2718, 1 rue V Auriol, 80027 Amiens Cedex 1 France. Tel 011 33 22 927322. available on microfiche.
Desc: Corresponds to the report on the fiscal situation of France by using charts, documentation, and tracing the course of the economy over the past year.

LC HC307.B45 R37
IT

RASSEGNA ECONOMICA: SIENA.
(1953)-. Periodical. Italian. Three times a year. L30660. Camera Comm Ind Art Arg, P Za G Matteotti 30, 53100 Siena Italy. **Tel** 011 39 577 202511.

LC HC121 .R43 **ISSN** 0325-1926
AG
Pr Rev.

REALIDAD ECONOMICA. [Real. econ.].
Added/Corp Instituto Argentino para el Desarrollo Economico. (19??)-. Periodical. Spanish. Eight times a year. $150.00. Instituto Argentino Para El Desarrollo Economico, Hipolito Yrigoyen 1116, 1086 Buenos Aires Argentina. **Tel** 011 54 1 3817380, 011 54 1 3819337, FAX 011 54 1 38174016. Index available. **Ad Acc, Adv Mgr:** Juan Carlosamigo. **Circ:** 6,000 (ctrl).
Ind/Abst Foreign Lang. Index; Hisp. Am. Period. Index, HAPI; Maize Abstr.; PAIS Int. Print; Rice Abstr.; Sug. Indus. Abstr.

LC HC387.C25 R43 **ISSN** 0210-380X
DD 330.9467/005 SP
UDC 00833946

RECERQUES. [Recerques]. No. 1 (1972)-. Catalan. Two times a year. 2475ptas. Curial Ediciones Catalanes S A, Bruc 144 Baixos, 08037 Barcelona Spain. **Tel** 011 34 3 2588101, FAX 207 74 27.

LC HC101 .R348 **ISSN** 0734-2942
DD 338.5/443/0973 US

REGIONAL INFORMATION SERVICE.
[Reg. inf. serv.]. **Added/Corp** Data Resources, inc. **VFOAT** Data Resources Regional Information Service. (19??)-. English. DRI McGraw Hill, 24 Hartwell Avenue, Lexington MA 02173. **Tel** (617)863-5100, FAX (617)860-6464, (617)860-6416.

LC HC107.A14 R43 **ISSN** 0734-2985
DD 338.5/443/0977 US

REGIONAL INFORMATION SERVICE. NORTH CENTRAL REGION. (REGIONAL INFORMATION SERVICE. NORTH CENTRAL REGION / DATA RESOURCES, INC.). [Reg. inf. serv., North Cent. reg.]. English. DRI McGraw Hill, 24 Hartwell Avenue, Lexington MA 02173. **Tel** (617)863-5100, FAX (617)860-6464, (617)860-6416.

LC HC107.A115 R43 **ISSN** 0734-2977
DD 338.5/443/0974 US

REGIONAL INFORMATION SERVICE. NORTHEAST REGION. (REGIONAL INFORMATION SERVICE. NORTHEAST REGION / DATA RESOURCES, INC.). [Reg. inf. serv., Northeast reg.]. English. DRI McGraw Hill, 24 Hartwell Avenue, Lexington MA 02173. **Tel** (617)863-5100, FAX (617)860-6464, (617)860-6416.

LC HC107.A13 R43 **ISSN** 0734-2950
DD 338.5/443/0975 US

REGIONAL INFORMATION SERVICE. SOUTHERN REGION. [Reg. inf. serv., South. reg.]. English. DRI McGraw Hill, 24 Hartwell Avenue, Lexington MA 02173. **Tel** (617)863-5100, FAX (617)860-6464, (617)860-6416.

LC HC107.A17 R43 **ISSN** 0734-2969
DD 338.5/443/0973 US

REGIONAL INFORMATION SERVICE. WESTERN REGION. (REGIONAL INFORMATION SERVICE. WESTERN REGION / DATA RESOURCES, INC.). [Reg. inf. serv., West. reg.]. English. DRI McGraw Hill, 24 Hartwell Avenue, Lexington MA 02173. **Tel** (617)863-5100, FAX (617)860-6464, (617)860-6416.

LC HC101 .W545 **ISSN** 8755-2779
DD 338.5/443/0973 US

REGIONAL SERVICES OUTLOOK. [Reg. serv. outlook]. Mar. 1984-. English. WEFA / Philadelphia, PO Box 8500, Suite 1995, Philadelphia PA 19178. **Tel** (215)667-6000, telex 710 6700575. *Continues* Wharton Regional Service Outlook, 8755-2760.

 ISSN 0034-3420
US

REGION'S AGENDA, THE. See Housing and Urban Development.

LC HC407.A1 R43
YU

REGISTAR JUGOSLOVENSKE PRIVREDE. Serbo-Croatian (Roman). Zavod Za Ekonomiku Usluznih Delatnosti, Marsala Birjuzova 10, Belgrad Yugoslavia.

LC HC188.R4 R44
BL

RELACAO DAS INDUSTRIAS COM MAIS DE 20 I.E. VINTE EMPREGADOS NO ESTADO DO RIO GRANDE DO SUL.
VFOAT Anuario das Industrias do Estado do Rio Grande do Sul. Portuguese. Fiergs, Caixa Postal 845, Porto Algre Brazil.

LC HC188.M29 M33a
BL

RELATORIO DA DIRETORIA EXECUTIVA - COMPANHIA DE DENSENVOLVIMENTO DE DISTRITOS INDUSTRIAIS DO MARANHAO. Main/Corp
Maranhao, Brazil (State). Companhia de Desenvolvimento de Distritos Industriais. (19??)-. Portuguese. Companhia de Desenvolvimento de Distritos Industriais, Caixa Postal 328, Sao Luis Brazil.

LC HC394.5.E5 P67a
DD 330 BL

RELATORIO DE ACTIVIDADES. Main/Corp
Portugal. Comissao Nacional do Ambiente. (19??)-. Portuguese. Commissao Nacional do Ambiente, R Barata Salgeiro 28 20, 2 Lisbon Portugal.

LC HC446 .B313a **ISSN** 0376-4303
DD 330.9598/005 IO

REPORT FOR THE FINANCIAL YEAR - BANK INDONESIA. [Rep. financ. year - Bank Indones.]. Main/Corp Bank Indonesia. Added/Corp Bank Indonesia. Report of Bank Indonesia. VFOAT Report of Bank Indonesia. (1972)-. Periodical. English. One time a year. $16.00. Bank Indonesia, Jl Kebon Sirih 82 84, Jakarta 10010 Indonesia. Tel 011 62 21 374108. Continues Report of Bank Indonesia.

LC HD9887.S7 S66A
DD 331.7 SA

REPORT OF THE AUDITOR-GENERAL ON THE ACCOUNTS OF THE COTTON BOARD FOR THE FINANCIAL YEAR ... .
See Agriculture.

LC HD9049.W4S58
DD 354.680082/333 SA

REPORT OF THE AUDITOR-GENERAL ON THE ACCOUNTS OF THE WHEAT BOARD FOR THE FINANCIAL YEAR ... .
See Agriculture-Feed Grain and Milling.

LC HC431 .B53A
DD 354.54/120082/06 II

REPORT OF THE COUNCIL / BIHAR INDUSTRIES ASSOCIATION. Main/Corp
Bihar Industries Association. English. One time a year. Bihar Industries Association, Sinha Library Road, Patna-800 001 India. *Continues* Bihar Industries Association. Report of the Council for the Year ... .

LC HC107.C8 C52A
DD 353.97460082 US

REPORT ON DEPARTMENT OF ECONOMIC DEVELOPMENT AND CONNECTICUT DEVELOPMENT AUTHORITY FOR FISCAL YEARS ENDED JUNE 30 ... . Main/Corp Connecticut. Auditors of Public Accounts. 1978/79-. English. Auditors of Public Accounts, State Capitol, Hartford CT 06106. *Continues* Report on Department of Commerce and Connecticut Development Authority for Fiscal Years Ended June 30 ... .

LC HC446 .P8716
DD 338.9598 IO

REPORT ON THE CENTRE'S ACTIVITIES - PUSAT PENELITIAN ATMA JAYA. Main/Corp Pusat Penelitian Atma Jaya. 1973/74-. English. Pusat Penelitian Atma Jaya, Jalan Jenderal Sudirman 49-A, PO Box 2639 DAK, Jakarta Indonesia.

LC HC257.I6 N28A
DD 330.9/415/09 IE

REPORT ON THE ECONOMY AND THE PROSPECTS. Main/Corp National Economic and Social Council. No. 1- 1973/74-. English. 7.50p. Government Publications, 4 5 Harcourt Road, Dublin 2 Ireland. Tel 011 353 1 6613111 ext.4005.

LC HC466
GW

REPUBLIK KOREA : WIRTSCHAFTLICHE ENTWICKLUNG.
Main/Corp Germany (Federal Republic, 1949-). Bundesstelle fur Aussenhandelsinformation (Germany). German. One time a year. DM3.00. Bundesstelle fuer Aussenhandelsinformation, Agrippastrasse 87 93, D-50676 Cologne Germany. **Tel** 011 49 221 2057316, FAX 011 49 221 2057212.

LC HC466
GW

REPUBLIK KOREA : WIRTSCHAFTSDATEN UND WRITSCHAFTSDOKUMENTATION.
Main/Corp Bundesstelle fur Aussenhandelsinformation (Germany). (19??)-. German. Bundesstelle fuer Aussenhandelsinformation, Agrippastrasse 87 93, D-50676 Cologne Germany. **Tel** 011 49 221 2057316, FAX 011 49 221 2057212.

LC HF5601
DD 657 US

•**RESEARCH IN ACCOUNTING IN EMERGING ECONOMICS.** **See** Business and Economics-Accounting.

LC HC1 .R47 ISSN 0363-3268
DD 330/.09 US
CCC

RESEARCH IN ECONOMIC HISTORY. [Res. econ. hist.]. Vol. 1 (1976)-. Monographic series. English. Irregular. $73.25. JAI Press Inc., 55 Old Post Road, Suite 2, PO Box 1678, Greenwich CT 06836-1678. **Tel** (203)661-7602, FAX (203)661-0792. **ED** Roger Ransom.
Ind/Abst AGRICOLA; Am. Hist. Life (1976-).

LC HC54 .R38 ISSN 1048-1222
DD 305/.05 US

RESEARCH IN INEQUALITY AND SOCIAL CONFLICT. [Res. inequal. soc. confl.]. **VFOAT** Inequality and Social Conflict. Vol. 1 (1989)-. English. One time a year. $73.25. JAI Press Inc., 55 Old Post Road, Suite 2, PO Box 1678, Greenwich CT 06836-1678. **Tel** (203)661-7602, FAX (203)661-0792. **ED** Michael Dobkowski and Isidor Wallimann.

LC HC10 .R326 ISSN 0161-7230
DD 330.9/04 US
CCC

RESEARCH IN POLITICAL ECONOMY. [Res. polit. econ.]. Vol. 1 (1977)-. English. Irregular. $73.25. JAI Press Inc., 55 Old Post Road, Suite 2, PO Box 1678, Greenwich CT 06836-1678. **Tel** (203)661-7602, FAX (203)661-0792. **ED** Paul Zarembka.

UK

RESEARCH REPORT. **Added/Corp** Policy Studies Institute. (1986)-. Monographic series. English. Price varies per volume. Policy Studies Institute, 100 Park Village East, London NW1 3SR United Kingdom. **Tel** 011 44 1 387 2171. ***Continues*** *Policy Studies Institute PSI.*
Ind/Abst Curr. Cit.

LC HC107.L8 L58 ISSN 0362-7217
DD 330.9/763 US

RESEARCH STUDY - DIVISION OF BUSINESS AND ECONOMIC RESEARCH, COLLEGE OF BUSINESS ADMINISTRATION, UNIVERSITY OF NEW ORLEANS. (RESEARCH STUDY - DIVISION OF BUSINESS AND ECONOMIC RESEARCH, UNIVERSITY OF NEW ORLEANS.). **Main/Corp** University of New Orleans. Division of Business and Economic Research. (19??)-. English. University of New Orleans Division of Business and Economic Research, New Orleans LA 70148. **Tel** (504)286-6248. ***Continues*** *Louisiana. State University in New Orleans. Division of Business and Economic Research. Research Study.*

LC HC188.R4 R49 ISSN 0102-0226
DD 318.1/65 BL

RESENHA ESTATISTICA DO RIO GRANDE DO SUL / SECRETARIA DE COORDENACAO E PLANEJAMENTO, FUNDACAO DE ECONOMIA E ESTATISTICA. **See** Business and Economics-Abstracting, Bibliographies and Statistics.

LC HC241.2 .A19 ISSN 0378-4479
DD 330.9/4/055 LU

RESULTATERNE AF KONJUNKTURUNDERSGELSEN HOS VIRKSOMHEDSLEDERE I FLLESSKABET. **Main/Corp** Commission of the European Communities. Directorate-General for Economic and Financial Affairs. **Added/Corp** Commission of the European Communities. Directorate-General for Economic and Financial Affairs. Ergebnisse der Konjunkturbefragung Bei den Unternehmern in der Gemeinschaft. Commission of the European Communities. Directorate-General for Economic and Financial Affairs. Results of the Business Survey Carried out among Managements in the Community. **VFOAT** Ergebnisse der Konjunkturbefragugn Bei den Unternehmern in der Gemeinschaft; Results of the Business Survey Carried out among Managements in the Community. (1976)-. Periodical. Danish (Dutch, English, French, German and Italian). Twelve times a year. $125.00. Office for Official Publications of the European Communities, 2 rue Mercier, 2985 Luxembourg Luxembourg. **Tel** 011 352 499281, FAX 011 352 292942763. **(Subscription address:** UNIPUB, 4611 F Assembly Drive, Lanham MD 20706. **Tel** (800)274-4888, (301)459-7666.) ***Continues*** *Commission of the European Communities. Directorate-General for Economic and Financial Affairs. Results of the Business Surveys Carried out among Heads of Enterprises in the Community.*

LC HC236 .B36A
VE

RESUMEN ECONOMICO FINANCIERO. **Main/Corp** Banco Industrial de Venezuela. Vol. 1, No. 1 (June 1974)-. Spanish. Banco Industrial de Venezuela, Avenida Uniersidad, Esq de Traposos, Caracus Venezuela.

LC HC107.K4 K425
DD 330.9769/005 US

REVIEW & PERSPECTIVE / COLLEGE OF BUSINESS AND ECONOMICS, UNIVERSITY OF KENTUCKY. **Added/Corp** University of Kentucky. College of Business and Economics. University of Kentucky. Center for Business and Economic Research. **VFOAT** Review and Perspective. Vol. 11, No. 1 (Spring 1987)-. Periodical. English. Four times a year. Free on request. University of Kentucky / Center of Business and Economic Research, 301 Mathews Building, Lexington KY 40506-0047. **Tel** (606)257-7675. **ED** J. Beth Smith. Index available. **Bk Rev. Circ:** 1,700. ***Continues*** *Kentucky Economy, Review & Perspective, 0270-1421.*
Desc: A publication which summarizes the performance of the Kentucky economy of the immediate past; includes short expository articles dealing with some aspect of the Kentucky economy and/or some aspect of information systems in Kentucky.

LC D1 .F29a ISSN 0147-9032
DD 305/.05 US

REVIEW - FERNAND BRAUDEL CENTER FOR THE STUDY OF ECONOMIES, HISTORICAL SYSTEMS, AND CIVILIZATIONS. [Rev. - Fernand Braudel Cent. Study Econ. Hist. Syst. Civiliz.]. **Main/Corp** Fernand Braudel Center for the Study of Economies, Historical Systems, and Civilizations. Vol. 1 (Summer 1977)-. Periodical. English. Four times a year. $90.00. Research Foundation of SUNY, Fernand Braudel Center, SUNY, Box 6000, Binghamton NY 13901. **Tel** (607)777-4924, FAX (607)777-4315. **ED** Immanuel Wallerstein. Index available (published in No. 4 of each volume). cum. index. **Circ:** 1,000. available on microfilm and microfiche from University Microfilms International (UMI).
Desc: Features articles in all the historical social sciences without regard to discipline; worldwide list of contributors.
Ind/Abst Am. Hist. Life (1982-); Am. Bibliogr. Slavic East Europ. Stud.; Geogr. Abstr. Human Geogr.; Int. Bibliogr. Sociol.; Int. Dev. Abstr.; Middle East Abstr. Index; Recent. Publ. Artic.; Soc. Plann. Policy Dev. Abstr.; Soc. Welf. Soc. Plan./Policy Soc. Dev.; Sociol. Abstr. (?-?) [Full Cov.].

LC HD4150.3 .A45
DD 363.7/006/0417 IE

REVIEW ... INCLUDING ACCOUNTS FOR YEAR TO 31 DECEMBER ... / AN FORAS FORBARTHA. **VFOAT** Review. English. One time a year. An Foras Forbartha, St. Martins House, Waterloo Road, Dublin 4 Ireland.

LC HC501 .R46 ISSN 0305-6244
DD 330.9/6/03 UK
CCC

REVIEW OF AFRICAN POLITICAL ECONOMY. [Rev. Afr. polit. econ.]. No. 1 (Aug./Nov. 1974)-. Periodical. English. Four times a year. $194.00. Carfax Publishing Company, PO Box 25, Abingdon, Oxfordshire OX14 3UE United Kingdom. **Tel** 011 44 1235 555335, FAX 011 44 1235 553559, telex 817484. **ED** Jan Burgess & David Seddon. Index available. cum. index. **Bk Rev. Ad Acc. Circ:** 2,000. available on microfiche.
Desc: An indispensable source and influential opinion-former in Africa. Most of the great debates about contemporary Africa have taken place on its pages. ROAPE is subscribed to by all major institutions in North America, Africa, U.K., Europe, and the Far East.
Ind/Abst Acad. Search; Altern. Press Index; EP Collect.; Geogr. Abstr. Human Geogr.; Homework Help.; Int. Bibliogr. Sociol.; Int. Dev. Abstr.; Int. Labour Doc.; LABORDOC; MasterFile FullTEXT 1000; MasterFile FullTEXT 350; MasterFile FullTEXT 650; MasterFile FullTEXT (Jan. 1994-); Multicult. Educ. Abstr.; PAIS Int. Print (1991-); Soc. Sci. Source; Stud. Women Abstr.; Telebase; World Mag. Bank.

LC HC491 .T84b ISSN 0034-6500
DD 330.9561/005 TU

REVIEW OF ECONOMIC CONDITIONS. [Rev. econ. cond.]. **Main/Corp** Turkiye Is Bankasi. **Added/Corp** Turkiye Is Bankas. Iktisadi Arastrmalar Mudurlugu. (19??)-. Periodical. English. Four times a year. Free on request. Turkiye is Bankasi A S, Ataturk Bulvari 191, Kavaklidere Ankara Turkey. **Tel** 011 90 4 188096, FAX 011 90 4 4250750, telex 42082 TAB TR. **ED** Argun Bassorgun. **Circ:** 1,700 (ctrl).
Desc: Economic conditions in Turkey.

LC HC517.E2 E27A
DD 338.91/67 TZ

REVIEW OF ECONOMIC INTEGRATION ACTIVITIES WITHIN THE EAST AFRICAN COMMUNITY. **Main/Corp** East African Community. Common Market and Economic Affairs Secretariat. 1973-1974/75. English. 15/- Each Copy. Common Market and Economic Affairs Secretariat, PO Box 1003, Arusha Tanzania.

LC HD1039.W47 W44a
DD 354.9410082/326/06 AT

REVIEW OF OPERATIONS - WESTERN AUSTRALIAN URBAN LANDS COUNCIL. **Main/Corp** Western Australian Urban Lands Council. (19??)-. English. Irregular. Western Australian Urban Lands Council, Saint George's Court/19th Floor, 16 Saint Georges's Terrace, Perth Western Australia 6000 Australia.

LC HB1 .C314 ISSN 0034-6764
DD 330.5 UK
CCC
Pr Rev.

REVIEW OF SOCIAL ECONOMY. [Rev. soc. econ.]. **Added/Corp** Association for Social Economics. Catholic Economic Association. Catholic Economic Association. Papers and Proceedings. Vol. 1 (Dec. 1942)-. Periodical. English. Four times a year. $88.00. Routledge, 11 New Fetter Lane, London EC4P 4EE United Kingdom. **Tel** 011 44 171 5839855, FAX 011 44 171 5830701. **(Subscription address:** Kinokuniya Company Ltd., 38-1 Sakuragaoka 5, chome Setagaya-ku, Tokyo 156 Japan. **Tel** FAX 011 03 3439 0136.) cum. index. **Bk Rev.** available on microfilm and microfiche from University Microfilms International (UMI); available on an online database (file 648/Full-Text) from DIALOG. Documents available from The Genuine Article.
Desc: Articles, comments and book reviews in the area of social economics. Reflects the ideological spectrum, theoretical and empirical.
Ind/Abst Acad. Search; Am. Hist. Life (1973-); Appl. Soc. Sci. Index Abstr.; Bus. ASAP (1992-) [Full Txt.]; Bus. Index (1985-); Curr. Cit.; Curr. Contents Soc. Behav. Sci.; Econ. Lit. Index (19??-); EP Collect.; Gen. BusinessFile (1985-); Gen. Period. Index (1985-); Homework Help.; INFO-SOUTH Abstr.; Int. Bibliogr. Sociol.; J. Econ. Lit.; Mag. Search; Manage. Contents (1974-); MasterFile FullTEXT 1000; MasterFile FullTEXT 350; MasterFile FullTEXT 650; MasterFile FullTEXT (July 1993-); Middle East Abstr. Index; OCLC; PAIS Int. Print (?-?); Public Aff. Inf. Serv. Bull.; Res. Alert [Full Cov.]; Soc. Sci. Cit. Index [Full Cov.]; Telebase; Abr. Cathol. Period. Lit. Index; Cathol. Period. Lit. Index.

LC HC301 .R48 ISSN 0034-6799
DD 330.945/005 IT

REVIEW OF THE ECONOMIC CONDITIONS IN ITALY. (REVIEW OF ECONOMIC CONDITIONS IN ITALY.). [Rev. econ. cond. Italy]. **Added/Corp** Banco di Roma. No. 1 (1979)-. Periodical. English (Italian). Three times a year. Free. Banco di Roma / Ufficio Relazion Esterne, Viale Umberto Tupini 180, 00144 Rome Italy. **Tel** 011 39 6 54451. Documents available from The Genuine Article. ***Continues*** *Review of the Economic Conditions in Italy.*
Ind/Abst Curr. Contents Soc. Behav. Sci.; Econ. Lit. Index (19??-); Geogr. Abstr. Human Geogr.; J. Econ. Lit.; PAIS Int. Print; Res. Alert [Full Cov.]; Soc. Sci. Cit. Index [Full Cov.].

ISSN 0265-9387
UK

REVIEW OF THE ECONOMY AND EMPLOYMENT. **See** Business and Economics-Labor.

LC HC171 .R4 ISSN 0325-7487
DD 330.982/005 AG

REVIEW OF THE RIVER PLATE, THE. [Rev. River Plate]. **VFOAT** Revista del Rio de la Plata. Vol. 1 (1892)-. Periodical. English (Spanish). Two times a year. $225.00 North America; $275.00 Europe; $290.00 Asia. Review of the River Plate, Bulnes 44 P BJA A, 1176 Buenos Aires Argentina. **Tel** 982-4961. **ED** Archibald B Norman. Index available. **Bk Rev. Ad Acc. Circ:** 3,500. ***Absorbed*** *Times of Argentina.*
Desc: Financial, economic, agricultural, political and shipping affairs and developments in other South American countries.

LC HA984 .R4 ISSN 0034-7175
DD 330.981 BL
NLM W1 RE317

REVISTA BRASILEIRA DE ESTATISTICA. **See** Business and Economics-Abstracting, Bibliographies and Statistics.

LC HC681 .R47
CL

REVISTA DE ESTUDIOS DEL PACIFICO. **Added/Corp** Centro de Estudios del Pacifico. (1971)-. Periodical. Spanish. Centro de Estudios del Pacifico, Secretario Ejecutivo Casilla 1487, Valparaiso Chile.

LC HC10 .R353 ISSN 0212-6109
DD 330/.05 SP

REVISTA DE HISTORIA ECONOMICA. **Added/Corp** Centro de Estudios Constitucionales. Vol. 1, No. 1 (Spring/Summer 1983)-. Periodical. Spanish. Three times a year. $55.00. Centro de Estudios Constitucionales, Calle Fuencarial 45 6A, 28071 Madrid

Business and Economics —Economic History, Conditions

Spain. **Tel** 011 34 1 5325069, 011 34 1 5316430. **(Subscription address:** Alianza Editorial, Juan Ignacio Luca de Tema 15, 28027 Madrid Spain. **Tel** 011 34 1 7416600, FAX 011 34 1 3207480.) **Continues** Revista de Economia Politica, 0034-8058.
Ind/Abst Am. Hist. Life (1981-).

LC HC391 .R48

PO
SUSPENDED
REVISTA DE HISTORIA ECONOMICA E SOCIAL. No. 1 (Jan./June 1978)-(Dec. 27, 1989). Periodical. English (French and Portuguese). Three times a year. $29.00. Livraria Sa Da Costa Editora, Praca Luis de Camoes 22 4, 1294 Lisbon Codex Portugal. **Tel** 011 351 1 3460721.
Ind/Abst Am. Hist. Life (1988-).

LC HC241 .R47

ISSN 0210-0924
SP
REVISTA DE INSTITUCIONES EUROPEAS. [Rev. inst. eur.]. 1- Jan./April 1974-. Spanish. Three times a year. $23.00. Centro de est Constitucionales, 28013 Madrid Spain.
Ind/Abst Am. Hist. Life (1975-1984); Int. Polit. Sci. Abstr.; PAIS Int. Print.

LC HC121 U55a

CL
REVISTA DE LA CEPAL. Main/Corp United Nations. Economic Commission for Latin America. **VAT** Revista de la Comision Economica Para America Latina. Vol. 1 (1976)-. Government Publication. Spanish. Three times a year. $16.00. United Nations Publications, 2 United Nations Plaza, Room DC2 0853, Department 007C, New York NY 10017. **Tel** (212)963-8303, (800)253-9646. **(Subscription address:** United Nations Publications, Subscription Office, PO Box 361, Birmingham AL 35201-0361. **Tel** (800)633-4931, (205)995-1567 (outside US and Canada), FAX (205)995-1588.) **Supersedes** Boletin Economico de America Latina.
Ind/Abst LABORDOC.

LC HC186 .R425 ISSN 0100-4956
DD 330.9/81/3 BL
REVISTA ECONOMICA DO NORDESTE. [Rev. econ. nordeste]. Vol. 4, No. 16; April/June 1973-. Periodical. Portuguese (summaries and/or abstracts in English). Four times a year. Cr$20.00. Departamento de Estudos Economicos do Nordeste do Banco do Nordeste do Brazil, Caixa Postal 628, Fortaleza Brazil. **Continues** Revista Economica (Banco do Nordeste do Brasil).
Ind/Abst Int. Dev. Abstr. (?-?); PAIS Int. Print (?-?).

LC HC171 .I33
DD 338.7/4/0982 AG
REVISTA IDEA / INSTITUTO PARA EL DESARROLLO DE EMPRESARIOS EN LA ARGENTINA. VFOAT Revista I.D.E.A.; Noticias de I.D.E.A.; I.D.E.A.; IDEA. Periodical. Spanish. Irregular. $25.00. Moreno, 1850 20 40 50 Y 60 Piso, 1094 Capital Federal Argentina. **Continues** Noticias de IDEA.

LC HC188.S45 R47

BL
REVISTA INDUSTRIAL DE SERGIPE. (1973)-. Portuguese. One time a year. Promowal Ltda, rua Laraneiras 151 - Salas 214/215, Aracaju Brazil.

LC HC188.P4 R48 ISSN 0100-0217
DD 330.9/81/3 BL
REVISTA PERNAMBUCANA DE DESENVOLVIMENTO. [Rev. pernamb. desenvolv.]. **Added/Corp** Instituto de Desenvolvimento de Pernambuco. Conselho de Desenvolvimento de Pernambuco. (1974)-. Periodical. Portuguese. Two times a year. Conselho de Desenvolvimento de Pernambuco, Av Dantas Barreto 180 Ed San Diego, C Postal 3344, Recife Brazil.

LC HC547.I8 C47C
DD 330.9/6 IV
REVUE DE PRESSE - CHAMBRE D'INDUSTRIES DE COTE D'IVOIRE. SERVICE DOCUMENTATION. Main/Corp Chambre d'Industrie de Cote d'Ivoire. Service Documentation. No. 1- Jan./Feb. 1978-. French. Chambre d'Industrie de Cote d'Ivoire, 11 Avenue Lamblin, BP No 1 758, Abidjan Ivory Coast.

LC HD30.22 .R4 ISSN 0154-3229
FR
REVUE D'ECONOMIE INDUSTRIELLE. [Rev. econ. ind.]. (197?)-. Periodical. French. Four times a year. 520.08F France; 637.00F other. Les Editions Techniques, 3 rue Soufflot, 75005 Paris France. **Tel** 011 33 1 46341030, FAX 011 33 1 46345583, telex 260 717 F. Index available. cum. index. **Bk Rev** (Qty: 4). **Circ:** 1,500.
Ind/Abst Econ. Lit. Index; J. Econ. Lit. (1977-1984); Selec. Coop. Index Manage. Period.

LC HC501 .R47
DD 330.9/6/03 TG
REVUE GENERALE AFRICAINE DES TRAVAUX PUBLICS, DE L'INDUSTRIE ET DES MINES. Periodical. French. Irregular. 24.00. Compagnie Africaine d'Editions Techniques, BP 1960, Lome Togo.

ISSN 1245-3927
UDC 31(442.1/.5-14) CODEN 312(442.1/.5-14) FR
●**REVUE - INSEE BASSE-NORMANDIE, LA. See** Business and Economics-Abstracting, Bibliographies and Statistics.

LC HC270.2 .R48 ISSN 0139-7036
XR
REVUE OBHCODU, PRUMYSLU, HOSPODARSTVI. Added/Corp Ceskoslovensko-Sovetska Obchodni Komora. Ceskoslovenska Obchodni Komora. Ceskoslovenska Obchodni a Prumyslova Komora. Vol. 1 (Jan. 1976)-. Periodical. Czech (summaries and/or abstracts in English, German and Russian). Twelve times a year. kcs132.00. Rapid / Czech Republic, 28 Rijna 13, 112 79 Prague 1 Czech Republic. **Tel** (2)2319111, FAX (2)2327520. **Formed by the union of** Obchod, Prumysl, Hospodaarstvi **and** Revue Prumyslu a Obschodu.
Ind/Abst PROMT.

LC HB9 .R55

JA
RITSUMEIKAN KEIZAIGAKU. Added/Corp Ritsumeikan Daigaku Keizaigakkai. **VFOAT** Ritsumeikan Economic Review. (1952)-. Japanese. Six times a year. Ritsumeikan Daigaku Keizaigakkai, (Ritsumeikan University Economic Society), Higashi-iru Tera-machi, Hirokiji Kamigyo-ku Kyoto Japan.

LC H7 .R56 ISSN 0393-3415
DD 330.5 IT
CEASED
RIVISTA DI STORIA ECONOMICA. [Riv. stor. econ.]. (March 1936)-(1995). Periodical. Italian (English). Guilio Einaudi Editore SPA, Via U Biancamano 1, CP 245, 10100 Turin Italy. **Tel** 011 39 11 56561. **(Subscription address:** Cadmo SRL, via B da Maiano 3, 50014 Fiesole fi Italy. **Tel** 011 39 55 597029.) **ED** Pierluigi Ciocca and Gianni Toniolo (editor's address: Rivista di Storia Economica, Dip to di Scienze Economiche Ca Foscari, Universita di Venezia, Dorsoduro 3246, 30123 Venezia Italy). Index available. **Bk Rev. Circ:** 2,700.
Desc: Contains collection papers on economic history.
Ind/Abst Am. Hist. Life (1984-); Econ. Lit. Index; J. Econ. Lit.

LC HC307.S69 R58

IT
RIVISTA ECONOMICA DEL MEZZOGIORNO : TRIMESTRALE DELLA SVIMEZ, ASSOCIAZIONE PER LO SVILUPPO DELL'I1NDUSTRIA NEL MEZZOGIORNO. Added/Corp Associazione per lo Sviluppo dell'Industria nel Mezzogiorno. Vol. 1 (1987)-. Periodical. Italian. Four times a year. L73580. Societa Editrice il Mulino, Strada Maggiore 37, 40125 Bologna Italy. **Tel** 011 39 51 256011, FAX 011 39 51 256034.

LC HC188.R38 R18

BL
RN-ECONOMICO. VAT Rio Grande do Notre-Economico. Periodical. Portuguese. Twelve times a year. Cr$40.00. RN-Economico Ltda, Rua Princesa Isabel 670 Terreo, Natal Brazil.

LC HC287.S5 R6

PL
ROCZNIK DOLNOSLASKI. Added/Corp Dolnoslaskie Towarzystwo Oswiatowe. (1972)-. Polish. Twenty-four times a year. **(Subscription address:** Ars Polona-Ruch, PO Box 1001, Krakowskie Przedmiescie 7, 00-068 Warsaw Poland. **Tel** 011 48 22 261201.)

LC HD9715.P7

PL
ROCZNIK STATYSTYCZNY BUDOWNICTWA. Main/Corp Poland. Gowny Urzad Statystyczny. 1946/67-. Polish. Irregular (every five years). zl.8.00 Poland; zl.9.00 North America; zl.8.50 other. Zaklad Wydawnictw Statystycznych, Al. Niepodleglosci 208, 00-925 Warsaw Poland. **Tel** 011 48 22 250345, telex 814581 A GUS PL. **Circ:** 1,000 (ctrl).
Desc: Yearbook of the Polish construction.

LC HC337.P7 A255 ISSN 0080-3634
PL
ROCZNIKI DZIEJOW SPOLECZNYCH I GOSPODARCZYCH. (ROCZNIKI DZIEJOW SPOLECZNYCH I GOSPODARCZYCH = ANNALES D'HISTOIRE SOCIALE ET ECONOMIQUE.). [Rocz. dziejow spolecz. gosp.]. **Added/Corp** Towarzystwo Naukowe we Lwowie. Sekcja Historji Spolecznej i Gospodarcjej. Poznanskie Towarzystwo Przyjaciol Nauk. Komisja Historyczna. Poznanskie Towarzystwo Przyjaciol Nauk. Wydzial Historii i Nauk Spolecznych. **VFOAT** Annales d'Histoire Sociale et Economique. Vol. 1 (1932)-. Monographic series. French (Polish). Irregular. Price varies per volume. Poznanskie Towarzystwo Przyjaciol Nauk, Ul. Mielzynskiego 27-29, 61-725 Poznan Poland. **Tel** 011 48 61 527441. **(Subscription address:** Ars Polona-Ruch, PO Box 1001, Krakowskie Przedmiescie 7, 00-068 Warsaw Poland. **Tel** 011 48 22 261201.) Index available. cum. index.
Ind/Abst Am. Hist. Life (1955-1959, 1965-1971, 1979-).

LC HC465.L3 J34a
DD 338.952 JA
RODO SEISANSEI TOKEI CHOSA HOKOKU. Main/Corp Japan. Rodosho. Daijin Kambo. Tokei Johobu. Keizai Tokei. (1971)-. Japanese. Rodo Daijin Kambo Tokei Johobu, Tokyo Japan. **Continues** Rodo Seisansei Tokei Chosa Hokoku.

ISSN 1054-6103
DD 949 US
ROMANIA (SYRACUSE, N.Y.). (ROMANIA : A POLITICAL AND ECONOMIC FORECAST.). [Romania]. **Added/Corp** Political Risk Services (IBC USA Publications) Inc.). (19??)-. English. $325.00. Political Risk Services, 6320 Fly Road, Suite 102, PO Box 248, East Syracuse NY 13057-0248. **Tel** (315)431-0511, FAX (315)431-0200.
Desc: Assesses the factors affecting the prospects for business and trade. Each report focuses specifically on business needs such as finding and developing markets, determining currency movements, or making judgements about capital investments or corporate security.

LC HC407.R8 R597

RM
ROMANIAN ECONOMIC NEWS. Added/Corp Camera de Comert a Republicii Socialiste Romania. Vol. 1 (Jan. 1970)-. Periodical. English (French, German, Spanish and Russian). Twelve times a year. $50.00. Foreign Trade Publicity AG, BD N Baicescu 22, Bucharest Romania. **Tel** 132379. **Ad Acc. Circ:** 5,000 (ctrl). **Continues** Information Bulletin (Camera de Comert a Republicii Socialiste Romania).
Desc: Papers on Romania's trade relations with other countries.

LC HC340.12.A1 R67 ISSN 0968-8862
UK
ROSSIISKAIA EKONOMIKA / INSTITUT EKONOMICHESKOI POLITIKI. Added/Corp Institut Ekonomicheskikh Problem Perekhodnogo Perioda (Moscow, Russia). **VFOAT** Review of the Russian Economy; Russian Economy. Vol. 1, No. 1 (Summer 1992)-. Periodical. English. Two times a year. £55.00. European Development Centre, University of East Anglia, Norwich NR4 3TJ United Kingdom. **Tel** 011 44 1603 56161 ext. 2736.

LC HD87.25 .A45a ISSN 0271-0188
US
ROSTER - AMERICAN INSTITUTE OF CERTIFIED PLANNERS. Main/Corp American Institute of Certified Planners. (1980)-. English. Every 2 years. American Institute of Certified Planners / Washington DC, 1776 Massachusetts Avenue NW, Washington DC 20036. **Tel** (202)872-0611. **ED** Rosemary K Jones. **Circ:** 10,000 (ctrl).
Desc: Professional listing of certified planners of the American Institute of Certified Planners.
Ind/Abst Archit. Period. Index (19??-19??).

LC HC111 .R6 ISSN 0229-0243
DD 330.971/005 CN
ROYAL BANK LETTER, THE. [R. Bank lett.]. **Added/Corp** Royal Bank of Canada. Vol. 61, No. 6 (July 1980)-. Periodical. English. Six times a year. Free on request. Royal Bank of Canada, 200 Bay Street, 18th Floor South Tower, Toronto Ontario M5J 2J5 Canada. **Tel** (416)974-7242. **ED** Bob Stewart (editor's address: 1 Place Ville Marie, 7th Floor, West Montreal, Quebec H3C 3A9 Canada, phone: (514)874-7031). **Circ:** 238,000. available in braille; available on audiocassette. **Continues** Royal Bank of Canada Monthly Letter, 0035-8770.
Ind/Abst Can. Period. Index (19??-).

ISSN 0383-9834
DD 330.9/71/0644 CN
ROYAL BANK TRENDICATOR REPORT. Vol. 1, No. 1 (Dec. 1974)-. Periodical. English. Irregular. Royal Bank of Canada Economics Group, Royal Bank Plaza, South Tower, 18th Floor, Toronto Ontario M5J 2J5 Canada. **Tel** (416)974-2274.

LC HC244 HC405.A1

GW
RUMANIEN: VOLKSWIRTSCHAFTSPLAN UND BUDGETDATEN. Main/Corp Bundesstelle fur Aussenhandelsinformation (Germany). German. DM3.00. Bundesstelle fuer Aussenhandelsinformation, Agrippastrasse 87 93, D-50676 Cologne Germany. **Tel** 011 49 221 2057316, FAX 011 49 221 2057212.

Business and Economics —Economic History, Conditions

LC HC501 .R8
DD 301.3/5/0967
ISSN 0085-5839
US
TITLE CHANGE

RURAL AFRICANA. [Rural Afr.]. (1967)-No. 29. Monographic series. English. Michigan State University African Studies Center, East Lansing MI 48824. **Tel** (517)353-1700, FAX (517)353-7254, telex 650 277 3148. **ED** David Wiley. **Bk Rev. Ad Acc. Circ:** 200 (ctrl). **Merged into** African Rural and Urban Studies.
 Desc: Journal of multidisciplinary research on rural Africa, rural development, and agricultural issues.
 Ind/Abst Am. Hist. Life (1980-); Geogr. Abstr. Human Geogr. (?-?); Int. Bibliogr. Sociol.; Int. Dev. Abstr. (?-?); Int. Labour Doc.

ISSN 0816-5173
AT

RURAL DEVELOPMENT WORKING PAPER. Added/Corp Australian National University. National Centre for Development Studies. No. 1 (1986)-. Monographic series. English. Irregular. Price varies per volume. National Center for Development Studies, Australian National University, Canberra ACT 0200 Australia. **Tel** 011 61 6 2492760, FAX 011 61 6 2495525. **Continues** Working Paper (Australian National University. National Centre for Development Studies), 0815-7596.

LC DJK1 .R87
DD 947.086/05
ISSN 1062-3574
US

RUSSIA, EURASIAN STATES, AND EASTERN EUROPE. [Russ. Eurasian states East. Eur.]. (1992)-. Academic Scholarly Publication. English. One time a year. $10.50. Stryker-Post Publications, PO Drawer 1200, Harpers Ferry WV 25425. **Tel** (800)995-1400, FAX (304)535-6513. **ED** M. Wesley Shoemaker. **Continues** Soviet Union and Eastern Europe, 0090-3868.
 Desc: Covers current political/military affairs.

ISSN 1060-8753
DD 947
US

RUSSIA (SYRACUSE, N.Y.). See Political Science.

LC HC336.27 .R87
ISSN 0967-0793
UK
Pr Rev.

RUSSIAN ECONOMIC TRENDS / GOVERNMENT OF THE RUSSIAN FEDERATION. Added/Corp Centre for Economic Reform (Russia) Russia (Federation) London School of Economics and Political Science. Centre for Economic Performance. Vol. 1, No. 1 (1992)-. Government Publication. English. Four times a year (includes 12 updates). $195.00. Whurr Publishers Ltd., 19B Compton Terrace, London N1 2UN United Kingdom. **Tel** 011 44 171 3595979, FAX 011 44 171 2265290. **(Subscription address:** Turpin Distribution Services Limited, Blackhorse Road, Letchworth, Hertfordshire SH6 1HN United Kingdom. **Tel** 011 44 1462 672555, FAX 011 44 1462 480947.) **ED** George Lucas. **Ad Acc.** Full Page (B&W) £150.00. Half Page (B&W) £100.00. **Acid Free.** available with illustrations.
 Desc: Updated analysis of the economic situation in Russia, presented in a modern Western form with graphical illustrations. Provides information for all those interested in Russia - as investors, traders, social scientists or citizens of the world community.

LC HC900.A1 S23
DD 330.968/005
ISSN 0276-1629
US

SADEX. (SADEX : THE SOUTHERN AFRICA DEVELOPMENT INFORMATION/DOCUMENTATION EXCHANGE.). [SADEX]. **VFOAT** Southern Africa Development Information/Documentation Exchange. (June/July 1979)-. Periodical. English. Six times a year. Temple Heights Station, PO Box 53398, Washington DC 20009.

LC HC915.A1 S25
DD 330.96894/005
GW

SAMBIA, WIRTSCHAFTSDATEN UND WIRTSCHAFTSDOKUMENTATION. Added/Corp Bundesstelle fur Aussenhandelsinformation (Germany). (19??)-. German. DM3.00. Bundesstelle fuer Aussenhandelsinformation, Agrippastrasse 87 93, D-50676 Cologne Germany. **Tel** 011 49 221 2057316, FAX 011 49 221 2057212.

LC HC462.9 .S2517
JA

SANGYO SEMINA. Added/Corp Kansai Daigaku. Keizai Seiji Kenkyujo. (19??)-. Japanese. Kansai Daigaku Keizai Seiji Kenkyujo, Yamatecho, Suita-shi Japan.

LC HC466 .S27
KO

SANJONG YON'GU. VFOAT Industrial Policy. Periodical. Korean (Korean). Hanguk Sanop Chongchaek Yonguso, 54 Kyonji-dong, Chongo-ku, Seoul Korea.

LC HC470.I57 S26
KO

SANOP YONGWANPYO CHAKSONG POGO. VFOAT Compilatory Report on ... Input-Output Tables. Korean (Korean). W3,830. Hanguk Unhaeng, 110 3-ka Namdaemunro Chung-ku, Seoul Korea. **Tel** 535-5498.

UK

SAUDI ARABIA QUARTERLY. (19??)-. Trade Publication. English. Four times a year. £225.00. MEED Limited, MEED House, 21 John Street, London WC1N 2BP United Kingdom. **Tel** 011 44 171 4045513, FAX 011 44 171 2421450, telex 266872 MEEDAR G.

LC HC415.33.A1 S275
DD 338.953/8/005
LE

SAUDI ARABIA, RECORD OF ECONOMIC DEVELOPMENT. 1983-. English. One time a year. Research & Publishing House, PO Box 55025, Sin El Fil 090 Beirut Lebanon. **Continues in part** Saudi Arabia Yearbook.

ISSN 1054-6111
DD 953
US

SAUDI ARABIA (SYRACUSE, N.Y.). (SAUDI ARABIA : A POLITICAL AND ECONOMIC FORECAST / POLITICAL RISK SERVICES.). [Saudi Arab.]. **Added/Corp** Political Risk Services (IBC USA Publications) Inc.). (19??)-. English. $325.00. Political Risk Services, 6320 Fly Road, Suite 102, PO Box 248, East Syracuse NY 13057-0248. **Tel** (315)431-0511, FAX (315)431-0200.
 Desc: Assesses the factors affecting the prospects for business and trade. Each report focuses specifically on business needs such as finding and developing markets, determining currency movements, or making judgements about capital investments or corporate security.

LC HC415.33.A1 S28
DD 330.953/8/005
SU

SAUDI ECONOMIC SURVEY. (19??)-. Periodical. English. Fifty times a year. $475.00. Saudi Economic Survey, PO Box 1989, Jeddah 21441 Saudi Arabia. **Tel** 011 966 2 6514952, FAX 011 966 2 6514952. **ED** Abdelhakim Ghaitm. **Ad Acc, Adv Mgr:** Abdelhakim Ghaith, **Tel** 011 966 2 6514952. **Circ:** 5,000 (ctrl). available on an online database (files 771,772,799/Full-Text) from DIALOG.
 Desc: A review of Saudi Arabian economic, business and commercial activities including government laws, tenders, contract awards and import statistics.

LC HC244 .S59582b
RU

SBORNIK INFORMATSII O DEIATELNOSTI ORGANOV SEV. Main/Corp Sovet Ekonomicheskoi Vzaimopomoshchi. Sekretariat. (19??)-. Russian. Gosudarstvennaia Biblioteka, Informatsionnyi Tsentr, Imeni V. I. Lenina, Prospekt Kalinina 3, 121019 Moscow Russia.

LC HC341 .A25
DD 330.948/005
ISSN 0358-5522
SW

SCANDINAVIAN ECONOMIC HISTORY REVIEW, THE. [Scand. econ. hist. rev.]. **Added/Corp** Scandinavian Society for Economic and Social History and Historical Geography. Vol. 1 No. 1 (1953)-. Periodical. English. Three times a year (Feb., June, Nov.). $88.88. Odense University Press, 55 Campusvej, DK-5230 Odense M Denmark. **Tel** 011 45 7 66157999, FAX 011 45 7 66158126. **ED** Olle Krantz and Rolf Ohlsson. Index available. cum. index. **Bk Rev. Ad Acc. Circ:** 700 (ctrl). **Absorbed** Economy and History.
 Desc: Articles, book reviews and bibliographies primarily on Scandinavian economic and social history.
 Ind/Abst Am. Hist. Life (1954-); Econ. Lit. Index; Int. Bibliogr. Sociol.; J. Econ. Lit.; Numis. Lit.; Selec. Coop. Index Manage. Period.

ISSN 0582-0170
GW

SCHRIFTEN ZU REGIONAL- UND VERKEHRSPROBLEMEN IN INDUSTRIE- UND ENTWICKLUNGSLANDERN. (19??)-. Monographic series. German. Irregular (3 per year). Price varies per volume. Duncker und Humblot Verlag, Postfach 410329, D-12113 Berlin Germany. **Tel** 011 49 30 79000612, 011 49 30 79000613.

LC HC371
GW

SCHWEDEN : WIRTSCHAFT IN ZAHLEN UND WIRTSCHAFTSDOKUMENTATION. Main/Corp Bundesstelle fur Aussenhandelsinformation (Germany). German. DM4.00. Bundesstelle fuer Aussenhandelsinformation, Agrippastrasse 87 93, D-50676 Cologne Germany. **Tel** 011 49 221 2057316, FAX 011 49 221 2057212.

LC HC371
GW

SCHWEDEN : WIRTSCHAFTLICHE ENTWICKLUNG. Main/Corp Bundesstelle fur Aussenhandelsinformation (Germany). German. DM2.00. Bundesstelle fuer Aussenhandelsinformation, Agrippastrasse 87 93, D-50676 Cologne Germany. **Tel** 011 49 221 2057316, FAX 011 49 221 2057212.

LC HC395 .S28
DD 330.9494/005
GW

SCHWEIZ, WIRTSCHAFT IN ZAHLEN UND WIRTSCHAFTSDOKUMENTATION / BUNDESSTELLE FUER AUSSENHANDELSINFORMATION. German. DM5.00. Bundesstelle fuer Aussenhandelsinformation, Agrippastrasse 87 93, D-50676 Cologne Germany. **Tel** 011 49 221 2057316, FAX 011 49 221 2057212.

LC HC257.S4 S3276
DD 330.9411/005
ISSN 0269-5030
UK

SCOTTISH ECONOMIC & SOCIAL HISTORY. See Social Sciences.

LC HC257.S4 A417
DD 330.9/41/081
ISSN 0952-6498
UK

SCOTTISH ECONOMIC BULLETIN. (SCOTTISH ECONOMIC BULLETIN / SCOTTISH OFFICE.). [Scott. econ. bull.]. **Added/Corp** Great Britain. Scottish Office. (Summer 1971)-. Bulletin. English. Two times a year. £11.50. Her Majesty's Stationery Office, 51 Nine Elms Lane, London SW8 5DR United Kingdom. **Tel** 011 44 171 8738459, 011 44 171 8738456, FAX 011 44 171 8738499, 011 44 171 8738456, telex 297138. **(Subscription address:** Her Majesty's Stationery Office, PO Box 276, Public Centre, London SW8 5DT United Kingdom. **Tel** 011 44 171 8738499, 011 44 171 8738456.) **Continues in part** Digest of Scottish Statistics / Scottish Statistical Office.
 Desc: Contains charts and tables designed to provide a broad background to the trends in the economy, plus a general economic review and special articles of items of particular interest, such as the labour market and aspects of oil-related employment.
 Ind/Abst Contents Recent Econ. J.

LC HC10 .S316
ISSN 0036-973X
GW

SCRIPTA MERCATURAE. [Scr. mercaturae]. (1967)-. Periodical. German (French; summaries and/or abstracts in English). Irregular. DM46.00. Scripta Mercaturae Verlag, AM Rotenberg 5 9, D-55595 St. Katharinen Germany. **Tel** 011 49 6706 8800. **ED** H. Winkel, F.W. Henning. **Circ:** 500.
 Ind/Abst Am. Hist. Life (1972-1975).

LC HC59 .S3755
KO

SEGYE CHONOL. VFOAT Segye Journal. Periodical. Korean (Korean). Twenty-four times a year. W15.360. Yonhap Tongsin Opmuguk, 98-5 Unni-dong, Chongno-ku 110, Seoul South Korea.

LC D839 .S44
JA

SEKAI KARA. See History.

LC HC108.D8 D84
DD 330.9776/7/005
US

SELECTED ECONOMIC DATA FOR DULUTH AND NORTHEASTERN MINNESOTA THROUGH ... . Added/Corp University of Minnesota, Duluth. Bureau of Business and Economic Research. (1977)-. English. One time a year. $10.00. University of Minnesota Business and Economic Research, 10 University Drive, Duluth MN 55812. **Tel** (218)726-7298. **ED** Jerrold M Peterson and Glenn O Gronseth. **Circ:** 800. **Continues** Duluth Business Indicators and Selected Area Economic Data Through ... .
 Desc: Selected areas of economic data.

PE

SEMANA ECONOMICA / APOYO. Added/Corp Apoyo S.A. (198?)-. Periodical. Spanish. Fifty times a year. $590.00. Apoyo SA, Apartado 671, Lima 100 Peru. **Tel** 011 51 14 445555, FAX 011 51 14 450536. **ED** Augusto Alvarez-Rodrich. ctrl circ. **Continues** Semana Bursatil.

LC HC547.S4 S455
SG

SENEGAL EN CHIFFRE, LE. VFOAT Annuaire Statistique du Senegal. (1976)-. French. Irregular. Societe Africaine d'Edition, BP 1877 20 rue Mohamed V, Dakar Senegal. **Tel** 011 221 32216.

LC HC547.S4
DD 330.9/66/305
GW

SENEGAL : WIRTSCHAFTLICHE ENTWICKLUNG. Main/Corp Bundesstelle fur Aussenhandelsinformation (Germany). German. Bundesstelle fuer Aussenhandelsinformation, Agrippastrasse 87 93, D-50676 Cologne Germany. **Tel** 011 49 221 2057316, FAX 011 49 221 2057212.

Business and Economics —Economic History, Conditions

LC HC1045.A1
GW
SENEGAL. WIRTSCHAFTSDATEN UND WIRTSCHAFTSDOKUMENTATION . German. One time a year. DM2.00. Bundesstelle fuer Aussenhandelsinformation, Agrippastrasse 87 93, D-50676 Cologne Germany. **Tel** 011 49 221 2057316, FAX 011 49 221 2057212.

DD 337
UK
Pr Rev.
●**SERIES IN INTERNATIONAL BUSINESS AND ECONOMICS.** (1994)-. Monographic series. English. Irregular. Price varies. Elsevier Applied Science, An Imprint of Elsevier Science Ltd., The Boulevard, Langford Lane, Kidlington, Oxford OX5 1GB United Kingdom. **Tel** 011 44 1865 843000, 011 44 1865 843699, FAX 011 44 1865 843010.

ISSN 1195-5961
DD 330.971/0021
CN
●**SERVICES INDICATORS.** (SERVICES INDICATORS = INDICATEURS DES SERVICES.). [Serv. indic.]. **Added/Corp** Statistics Canada. **VFOAT** Indicateurs des Services. 1st Issue (2nd Quarter, 1994)-. Periodical. English (French). Four times a year. 89.63Can$. Statistics Canada Publications Sales and Services, R.H. Coats Building 6th Floor, Ottawa Ontario K1A 0T6 Canada. **Tel** (613)951-5078, (800)267-6677, FAX (613)951-1584, telex 053-3585.

EC
SERVICIO INFORMATIVO. Added/Corp Agence Latino-Americaine d'Information (Montreal, Quebec). No. 149 (Mar. 6, 1992)-. Periodical. Spanish. Twenty times a year. $80.00. ALAI / Oficina Regional Andina, Casilla 17 12 877, Quito Ecuador. **Tel** 011 593 2 528716, FAX 011 5932 505073. **Continues** Servicio Mensual de Informacion y Documentacion.

LC HC596.5.A1
DD 330.969/6
GW
SESCHELLEN, WIRTSCHAFTLICHE ENTWICKLUNG . German. DM3.00. Bundesstelle fuer Aussenhandelsinformation, Agrippastrasse 87 93, D-50676 Cologne Germany. **Tel** 011 49 221 2057316, FAX 011 49 221 2057212.

LC HC51 .S465
ISSN 0038-0113
JA
SHAKAI KEIZAI SHIGAKU. See Social Sciences.

LC HD916 .J33B
JA
SHICHOSONBETSU KOCHI MENSEKI TOKEI. Main/Corp Japan. Norinsho. Norin Keizaikyoku. Tokei Johobu. Japanese. Five times a year. Norin Kelzaikuoku Tokei Johobu Chiyoda-ku 100, Tokyo Japan.

LC HC462.5 .S525
JA
SHIGEN JOHO. Added/Corp Kagaku Gijutsucho Shigen Chosajo. Vol. 1, No. 1 (April 1982)-. Periodical. Japanese. Four times a year. Kagaku Gijutsucho Shigen Chosajo, (National Institute of Resources, Science and Technology Agency), 1-1 Kasumigaseki 3 chome, Chiyodaku Tokyo 100 Japan.

LC HC10 .S327
DD 330.9/047
CC
SHIH CHIEH CHING CHI (CHUNG-KUO SHIH CHIEH CHING CHI HSUEH HUI). (SHIH CHIEH CHING CHI). **Added/Corp** Chung-Kuo Shih Chieh Ching Chi Hsueh Hui. Chung-Kuo She Hui ko Hsueh Yuan. Shih Chieh Ching Chi yu Cheng Chih Yen Chiu So. **VFOAT** Shijie Jingji. (19??)-. Periodical. Chinese. Twelve times a year. $24.80. **(Subscription address:** China International Book Trading Corporation, PO Box 399, Library Service Department, Beijing 100044 People's Republic of China. **Tel** 011 86 1 8414284, FAX 011 86 1 8412023, telex 22496 CIBTC CN.) **Bk Rev. Ad Acc.**
Desc: Covers international economic relations and theories in world economy, with analyses of the economic policies of major countries and forecasts of the world economic situation. Includes lessons in economic development of various countries; introduces famous economists and books.

LC Z7165.J3 K42a HC462.9
JA
SHIRYO KANKO ANNAI. Main/Corp Keizai Chosa Kyokai. (19??)-. Japanese. Keizai Chosa Kyokai, c/o Toranomon Ogura Building, 2 Shiba Kotohiracho Minato-ku, Tokyo 105 Japan.

LC HC188.G6 G637a
BL
SIC INFORMATIVO. Main/Corp Goias, Brazil (State). Secretaria da Industria e Comercio. **Added/Corp** Goias, Brazil (State). Secretaria da Industria e Comercio. Assessoria Tecnica. Goias, Brazil (State). Secretaria da Industria e Comercio. Nucleo de Assessoria e Coordenacao. (19??)-. Portuguese. Twenty-four times a year. Praca Civica, Secretaria da Industria e Comercio, Centro Administrativo 70 Andar, Goiania Brazil.

LC HC1065.A1 S45
DD 330.966/4/0021
GW
SIERRA LEONE, WIRTSCHAFTSDATEN UND WIRTSCHAFTSDOKUMENTATION.
Added/Corp Bundesstelle fur Aussenhandelsinformation (Germany). (198?)-. German. One time a year. Bundesstelle fuer Aussenhandelsinformation, Agrippastrasse 87 93, D-50676 Cologne Germany. **Tel** 011 49 221 2057316, FAX 011 49 221 2057212. **Continues** Sierra Leone, Wirtschaftsdaten.

LC HC910.A1 S55
DD 330.96891/005
GW
SIMBABWE, WIRTSCHAFTLICHE ENTWICKLUNG. German. One time a year. 5.00. Bundesstelle fuer Aussenhandelsinformation, Agrippastrasse 87 93, D-50676 Cologne Germany. **Tel** 011 49 221 2057316, FAX 011 49 221 2057212.

LC HC910.A1
DD 330.96891/00212
GW
SIMBABWE, WIRTSCHAFTSDATEN UND WIRTSCHAFTSDOKUMENTATION.
German. Every 2 years. DM3.00. Bundesstelle fuer Aussenhandelsinformation, Agrippastrasse 87 93, D-50676 Cologne Germany. **Tel** 011 49 221 2057316, FAX 011 49 221 2057212.

LC HC445.8 .S54
DD 330.9/595/205
SI
SINGAPORE BULLETIN. Added/Corp Singapore. Ministry of Culture. Publicity Division. Singapore. Ministry of Culture. Information Division. Singapore. Ministry of Communications and Information. Information Division. (1972)-. Bulletin. English. Twelve times a year. Publicity Division, Ministry of Culture, Singapore 0617 Singapore.

LC HB1 .M27
ISSN 0217-5908
DD 330.9595/7/005
SI
Pr Rev.
SINGAPORE ECONOMIC REVIEW. (THE SINGAPORE ECONOMIC REVIEW : JOURNAL OF THE ECONOMIC SOCIETY OF SINGAPORE AND THE DEPARTMENT OF ECONOMICS AND STATISTICS, NATIONAL UNIVERSITY OF SINGAPORE.). [Singap. econ. rev.]. **Added/Corp** Economic Society of Singapore. National University of Singapore. Dept. of Economics and Statistics. **VFOAT** Economic Review. Vol. 28, No. 1 (Apr. 1983)-. Periodical. English. Two times a year. $30.52. University of Singapore / Faculty of Business Administration, 10 Kent Ridge, Singapore 0511 Singapore. **Tel** 011 65 7723101, FAX 011 65 7792621 3571, telex 33943. Documents available from The Genuine Article. **Continues** Malayan Economic Review.
 Desc: Joint presentation of information on the economic situation of Singapore.
Ind/Abst Econ. Lit. Index (19??-); Geogr. Abstr. Human Geogr.; Int. Dev. Abstr.; J. Econ. Lit.; LABORDOC; Middle East Abstr. Index; PAIS Int. Print; Res. Alert [Full Cov.]; World Agric. Econ. Rural Sociol. Abstr.

LC HC445.8.A1 S563
ISSN 0217-6181
DD 339.2/3/095957
SI
SINGAPORE INPUT-OUTPUT TABLES.
Added/Corp Singapore. Dept. of Statistics. **VFOAT** Singapore Input Output Tables. (19??)-. English. Irregular (Publishes every five years). $116.30. Chief Statistician of Singapore, 8 Shenton Way, 10 01 Treasury B, Singapore 0106 Singapore. **Tel** 011 65 3239686, telex 20826 STATS RS.

ISSN 1054-612X
DD 959
US
SINGAPORE (SYRACUSE, N.Y.).
(SINGAPORE : A POLITICAL AND ECONOMIC FORECAST / POLITICAL RISK SERVICES.). [Singapore]. **Added/Corp** Political Risk Services (IBC USA (Publications) Inc.). (19??)-. English. $325.00. Political Risk Services, 6320 Fly Road, Suite 102, PO Box 248, East Syracuse NY 13057-0248. **Tel** (315)431-0511, FAX (315)431-0200.
 Desc: Assesses the factors affecting the prospects for business and trade. Each report focuses specifically on business needs such as finding and developing markets, determining currency movements, or making judgements about capital investments or corporate security.

LC HC445.8.A1
GW
SINGAPUR : WIRTSCHAFTLICHE ENTWICKLUNG. Main/Corp Bundesstelle fur Aussenhandelsinformation (Germany). German. DM3.00. Bundesstelle fuer Aussenhandelsinformation, Agrippastrasse 87 93, D-50676 Cologne Germany. **Tel** 011 49 221 2057316, FAX 011 49 221 2057212.

LC HC445.8.A1
DD 330.9595/7/005
GW
SINGAPUR, WIRTSCHAFTSDATEN UND WIRTSCHAFTSDOKUMENTATION.
German. DM3.00. Bundesstelle fuer Aussenhandelsinformation, Agrippastrasse 87 93, D-50676 Cologne Germany. **Tel** 011 49 221 2057316, FAX 011 49 221 2057212.

LC HC196 .S56
DD 330.9861/005
CK
SINTESIS ECONOMICA (BOGOTA, COLOMBIA). (SINTESIS ECONOMICA.). (1975)-. Periodical. Spanish. One time a week. $175.00. Sintesis Economica, Calle 70 A NO 10 52, Bogota Colombia. **Tel** 011 57 1 2125121.

LC HC171 .S452
AG
SINTESIS INFORMATIVA. Oct. (1976)-. Periodical. Spanish. Twelve times a year. Sintesis Informativa, Piso 16 1085, Buenos Aires Argentina.

LC HC121 .S58
SP
SINTESIS (MADRID, SPAIN). (SINTESIS.). **Added/Corp** Asociacion de Investigacion y Especializacion Sobre Temas Iberoamericanos (Madrid, Spain). (Jan./April 1987)-. Periodical. Spanish. Three times a year. $50.00. Av Sociedad Editorial de Sintesis, Claudio Coello 86 4TO DCHA, 28006 Madrid Spain. **Tel** 011 34 1 5770640 42.
Ind/Abst PAIS Int. Print.

LC HC497.N5 S58
ISSN 0049-0628
DD 954.9/6
NP
SIRJANA. [Sirjana]. Vol. 1 (Aug./Sept. 1971)-. Periodical. English (English). Twelve times a year. 1-202 Dilli Bazar, Kathmandu Nepal.

LC HC59 .S89C
DD 330.9494/005
SZ
SITUATION ECONOMIQUE SUISSE ET LES PERSPECTIVES, LA. Main/Corp Switzerland. Kommission fur Konjunkturfragen. French. Eggenberger Thomas, Lic Rer Pol, Bureau du Delegue aux Questions Conjoncturelles, Belpstrasse 53, 3003 Bern Switzerland.

LC HC271 .A223C
DD 338/.0944
FR
SITUATION ET PERSPECTIVES DANS LE COMMERCE D'APRES LES CHEFS D'ENTREPRISE. Main/Corp France. Institut National de la Statisique et des Etudes Economies. Service de la Conjuncture. French. 29 Quai Branly, Paris 75700 France. **Continues** Situation et Perspectives dans le Commerce d'Apres les Chefs d'Entreprise.

LC HC107.O73 P6342
DD 330.9/794/04
US
SOCIAL ACCOUNTING FOR OREGON : SOCIO-ECONOMIC INDICATORS.
Main/Corp Oregon. State Community Services Program. English. State Community Services Program, Department of Human Resources, 772 Commercial Street SE, Salem OR 97310.

LC HC243.5.A1 S66
XR
SOCIALISTICKA EKONOMICKA INTEGRACE. Added/Corp CTK. Ekonomicka Redakce. Council for Mutual Economic Assistance. Agentsvto Pechati "Novosti.". Vol. 1 (1973)-. Periodical. Czech. Twelve times a year. CTK Ekonomicka Redajce, Opletalova 5, 111 44 Prague 1 Czech Republic.

LC HC437.G85 A3
ISSN 0533-5884
DD 330.954/75
II
SOCIO-ECONOMIC REVIEW: GUJARAT STATE. Main/Corp Gujarat, India (State). Bureau of Economics and Statistics. (19??)-. English. Bureau of Economics and Statistics / India, Ahmedabad India.

LC HC596.5.A1
DD 330.967/73/005
GW
SOMALIA, WIRTSCHAFTSDATEN UND WIRTSCHAFTSDOKUMENTATION.
German. DM3.00. Bundesstelle fuer Aussenhandelsinformation, Agrippastrasse 87 93, D-50676 Cologne Germany. **Tel** 011 49 221 2057316, FAX 011 49 221 2057212.

LC HC371 .S64
DD 330.9/485/05
SW
SOME DATA ABOUT SWEDEN.
Added/Corp Stockholms Enskilda Bank, AB. (19??)-. English. One time a year. Kr180.00. Skandinaviska Enskildz Bankey, 10640 Stockholm Sweden. **Tel** 011 46 8 7635000. **ED** Carina Norlander. **Ad Acc. Circ:** 20,000.

Business and Economics —Economic History, Conditions

LC HC440.5.A1 S65
DD 315.49/1 PK
SOME SOCIO-ECONOMIC TRENDS.
Added/Corp Pakistan. Statistical Division. Pakistan. Central Statistical Office. (19??)-. English. Statistics Division / Pakistan, Ministry of Finance Planning and Development, 1 Sindhi Muslim Cooperative Housing Society, Karachi 3 Pakistan.
Desc: Contains data on population, national accounts, agriculture, industry, external trade, finance and banking, public finance, prices, transport and communication, health and education in tabular form as well as graphs and charts. Of interest to students, research scholars and the general public.

LC HC188.R4 R58A BL
SONDAGEM CONJUNTURAL. Main/Corp
Rio Grande do Sul, Brazil (State). Universidad Federal. Instituto de Estudos e Pesquisas Economicas. Periodical. Portuguese. Universidade Federal do Rio Grande do Sul / Ciencias Economicas, Faculdade de Ciencias Economicas, Centro de Estudos E Pequisas, Av Joao Pessoa 31, Porto Alegre Brazil.

LC Z7164.E2 S72 HC59 RU
SOTSIALISTICHESKII OBRAZ ZHIZNI I IDEOLOGICHESKAIA BORBA .Added/Corp
Institut Nauchnoi Informatsii po Obshchestvennym Naukam (Akademiia Nauk SSSR). (19??)-. Russian. Inion An SSSR, Ulitsa Krasikova D 28/45, Moscow Russia. **Tel** 128.89.71. **ED** E.L. Serebrjanaja.

ISSN 1054-6138
DD 968 US
SOUTH AFRICA (SYRACUSE, N.Y.).
(SOUTH AFRICA : A POLITICAL AND ECONOMIC FORECAST / POLITICAL RISK SERVICES.). [S. Afr.]. **Added/Corp** Political Risk Services (IBC USA (Publications) Inc.). (19??)-. English. $325.00. Political Risk Services, 6320 Fly Road, Suite 102, PO Box 248, East Syracuse NY 13057-0248. **Tel** (315)431-0511, FAX (315)431-0200.
Desc: Assesses the factors affecting the prospects for business and trade. Each report focuses specifically on business needs such as finding and developing markets, determining currency movements, or making judgements about capital investments or corporate security.

ISSN 1011-3436
SA
SOUTH AFRICAN JOURNAL OF ECONOMIC HISTORY : [JOURNAL OF THE ECONOMIC HISTORY SOCIETY OF SOUTHERN AFRICA], THE. Added/Corp
Economic History Society of Southern Africa. Vol. 1, No. 1 (Sept. 1986)-. Periodical. English. Two times a year (Mar. & Sept.). $7.46. University of South Africa, Department of Semitics, PO Box 392, Pretoria 0001 South Africa. **Tel** 011 27 12 4298468. **Continues** Perspectives in Economic History.
Ind/Abst Am. Hist. Life (1987-).

LC HC517.S7 S64
DD 330.9/68/06 SA
SOUTH AFRICAN PROGRESS. English.
R6.00. Progress, PO Box 1741, Pretoria South Africa.

LC HC107.S7 S68a **ISSN** 0038-304X
DD 330.9/757/04 US
SOUTH CAROLINA ECONOMIC INDICATORS. Added/Corp
South Carolina Employment Security Commission University of South Carolina. Bureau of Business and Economic Research. (19??)-. Periodical. English. Twelve times a year. Free on request. South Carolina Employment Security Commission, 1550 Gadsden Street, PO Box 995, Columbia SC 29202. **Tel** (803)737-2660, FAX (803)737-2642. **ED** Richard Ellson. ctrl circ.

LC HC441.A1 S65 **ISSN** 0959-2601
DD 330.959/005 UK
SOUTH EAST ASIA MONITOR. Vol. 1, No. 1
(March 1990)-. Periodical. English. Twelve times a year. $436.35. Business Monitor International, 56 60 St. John Street, London EC1M 4DT United Kingdom. **Tel** 011 44 171 6083646, FAX 011 44 171 6083620.

ISSN 1054-6146
DD 951 US
SOUTH KOREA (SYRACUSE, N.Y.).
(SOUTH KOREA : A POLITICAL AND ECONOMIC FORECAST.). [South Korea]. **Added/Corp** Political Risk Services (IBC USA (Publications) Inc.). (19??)-. English. $325.00. Political Risk Services, 6320 Fly Road, Suite 102, PO Box 248, East Syracuse NY 13057-0248. **Tel** (315)431-0511, FAX (315)431-0200.
Desc: Assesses the factors affecting the prospects for business and trade. Each report focuses specifically on business needs such as finding and developing markets, determining currency movements, or making judgements about capital investments or corporate security.

LC HC336.26 .S673 BE
SOVIET ECONOMIC PERFORMANCE IN ... / NATO ECONOMIC COMMITTEE.
Added/Corp NATO Economic Committee. (1991)-. English. OTAN/NATO Information Service, North Atlantic Treaty Organization, Distribution Unit, 1110 Brussels Belgium. **Tel** 011 32 2 2414400. **Continues** Report on the State of the Soviet Economy.

ISSN 1054-6154
DD 946 US
SPAIN (SYRACUSE, N.Y.). (SPAIN : A
POLITICAL AND ECONOMIC FORECAST). [Spain]. **Added/Corp** Political Risk Services (IBC USA (Publications) Inc.). (19??)-. English. $325.00. Political Risk Services, 6320 Fly Road, Suite 102, PO Box 248, East Syracuse NY 13057-0248. **Tel** (315)431-0511, FAX (315)431-0200.
Desc: Assesses the factors affecting the prospects for business and trade. Each report focuses specifically on business needs such as finding and developing markets, determining currency movements, or making judgements about capital investments or corporate security.

LC Q180.S7
DD 338.94606 GW
SPANIEN, FORSCHUNGSPOLITIK UND FORSCHUNGSPRAXIS. German. DM3.00.
Bundesstelle fuer Aussenhandelsinformation, Agrippastrasse 87 93, D-50676 Cologne Germany. **Tel** 011 49 221 2057316, FAX 011 49 221 2057212.

LC HC381
DD 330.946 GW
SPANIEN UND KANARISCHE INSELN, WIRTSCHAFT IN ZAHLEN UND WIRTSCHAFTSDOKUMENTATION.
German. DM4.00. Bundesstelle fuer Aussenhandelsinformation, Agrippastrasse 87 93, D-50676 Cologne Germany. **Tel** 011 49 221 2057316, FAX 011 49 221 2057212.

LC HC157.P8 G62
DD 354.7295/0082 PR
SPECIAL REPORT ON PUERTO RICO INDUSTRIAL DEVELOPMENT COMPANY (PRIDCO), A. Main/Corp
Government Development Bank for Puerto Rico. (19??)-. English. Government Development Bank for Puerto Rico, PO Box 42001, San Juan PR 00940. **Tel** (809)722-2525, FAX (809)268-5496.

LC HC157.P82 S34
DD 330.97295 PR
SPECIAL REPORT ON SAN JUAN, CAPITAL OF PUERTO RICO. Main/Corp
Government Development Bank for Puerto Rico. English. Government Development Bank for Puerto Rico, PO Box 42001, San Juan PR 00940. **Tel** (809)722-2525, FAX (809)268-5496.

LC HC424.A1
DD 330.9/549/303 GW
SRI LANKA (CEYLON) : WIRTSCHAFTLICHE ENTWICKLUNG.
Main/Corp Germany (West). Budnesstelle fur Aussenhandelsinformation. German. Bundesstelle fuer Aussenhandelsinformation, Agrippastrasse 87 93, D-50676 Cologne Germany. **Tel** 011 49 221 2057316, FAX 011 49 221 2057212.

ISSN 1054-6162
DD 954 US
SRI LANKA (SYRACUSE, N.Y.). (SRI LANKA
: A POLITICAL AND ECONOMIC FORECAST / POLITICAL RISK SERVICES.). [Sri Lanka]. **Added/Corp** Political Risk Services (IBC USA (Publications) Inc.). (19??)-. English. $325.00. Political Risk Services, 6320 Fly Road, Suite 102, PO Box 248, East Syracuse NY 13057-0248. **Tel** (315)431-0511, FAX (315)431-0200.
Desc: Assesses the factors affecting the prospects for business and trade. Each report focuses specifically on business needs such as finding and developing markets, determining currency movements, or making judgements about capital investments or corporate security.

LC HC424.A1
DD 330.9549/3/0021 GW
SRI LANKA, WIRTSCHAFTSDATEN.
German. DM3.00. Bundesstelle fuer Aussenhandelsinformation, Agrippastrasse 87 93, D-50676 Cologne Germany. **Tel** 011 49 221 2057316, FAX 011 49 221 2057212.

LC HC424.A1
DD 330.9549/3/005 GW
SRI LANKA, WIRTSCHAFTSDATEN UND WIRTSCHAFTSDOKUMENTATION.
German. DM3.00. Bundesstelle fuer Aussenhandelsinformation, Agrippastrasse 87 93, D-50676 Cologne Germany. **Tel** 011 49 221 2057316, FAX 011 49 221 2057212.

LC HC156.5.Z7
DD 330.97298/44 GW
ST. VINCENT UND DIE GRENADINEN, WIRTSCHAFTSDATEN. VFOAT Sankt Vincent
und die Grenadinen, Wirtschaftsdaten. (19??)-. German. DM3.00. Bundesstelle fuer Aussenhandelsinformation, Agrippastrasse 87 93, D-50676 Cologne Germany. **Tel** 011 49 221 2057316, FAX 011 49 221 2057212.

LC HC10 .S713
DD 338.5/443/05 US
STAFF STUDIES FOR THE WORLD ECONOMIC OUTLOOK. Added/Corp
International Monetary Fund. Research Dept. (July 1986)-. Periodical. English. One time a year. $20.00. International Monetary Fund, 700 19th Street Northwest, Publishing Unit, Washington DC 20431. **Tel** (202)623-7430, FAX (202)623-7201.

CI
STANOVNISTVO I DOMACINSTVA SR SRBIJE PREMA POPISU ... Periodical.
Serbo-Croatian (Roman). 400.00. Republicki Zavod za Statistiku, Central Bureau of Statistics of the Republic of Croatia, Ilica 3, Zagreb Croatia. **Tel** 011 385 41 45 44 22, FAX 011 385 41 42 94 13, 011 385 41 42 37 11, telex 21130 DZSTAT RH.

LC HC59 .S734 **ISSN** 0887-364X
DD 330.9/005 US
CODEN STWOED
STATE OF THE WORLD. See Environmental
Issues.

ISSN 1044-4947
DD 330 US
STATE PROFILE (WASHINGTON, D.C.
1984). (STATE PROFILE.). [State profile]. (1984)-. Periodical. English. One time a year (May). $295.00. Woods & Poole Economics Inc., 1794 Columbia Road Northwest, Suite 4, Washington DC 20009. **Tel** (202)332-7111, FAX (202)332-6466. **ED** Martin Holdrich. available on diskette from the publisher.
Desc: Contains tables of economic and demographic data for every country and MSA in a state. There are 35 volumes in all; some states are combined in a single profile.

LC HC411 .S73
DD 330.95/0021 TH
STATISTICAL INDICATORS FOR ASIA AND THE PACIFIC. See Business and
Economics-Abstracting, Bibliographies and Statistics.

LC HC301 .A683
DD 330 IT
CEASED
STATISTICHE INDUSTRIALI. See Business
and Economics-Abstracting, Bibliographies and Statistics.

LC HC431 .A3272A
DD 338.0954 II
STATISTICS RELATING TO DGTD UNITS. See Business and Economics-Abstracting,
Bibliographies and Statistics.

LC HC280
DD 330/338.943 GW
STATISTIK DES AUSLANDES. LAENDERBERICHT. KATAR. See Business
and Economics-Abstracting, Bibliographies and Statistics.

LC HC446 .S74
DD 330.9598/021 IO
STATISTIK EKONOMI DAN KEUANGAN INDONESIA. See Business and
Economics-Abstracting, Bibliographies and Statistics.

LC HC271 .A218 HC280.Z6
DD 330/.08 S 309.2/5/0944 FR
STATISTIQUES ET INDICATEURS DES REGIONS FRANCAISES. See Business and
Economics-Abstracting, Bibliographies and Statistics.

US
STOCK & WATSON INDICATOR REPORTS. (19??)-. Periodical. English. Twelve times
a year. $100.00. National Bureau of Economic Research, 1050 Massachusetts Avenue, Cambridge MA 02138. **Tel** (617)868-3900, FAX (617)441-3895.

Pr Rev. IT
STORIA DEL PENSIERO ECONOMICO. BOLLETTINO DI INFORMAZIONE. Italian
(English and French). Two times a year (with one supplement in English). free. Univ Dip Scienze Economiche, Via Curtatone 1, 50123 Florence Italy. **ED** Piero Roggi and Roberto Romani. Bk Rev. Ad Acc.

Business and Economics —Economic History, Conditions

Circ: 1,000 (ctrl).
Desc: History of economic thought and of economic analysis. An economists archives.
AT

STRATEGIC ISSUES FORUM REPORT.
(19??)-. English. Committee for Economic Development of Australia, 123 Lonsdale Street, GPO Box 2117T, Melbourne Victoria 3000 Australia. **Tel** 011 61 03 6623544, FAX 011 61 03 6637271.

LC HB9 .S832   **ISSN** 0081-6485
PL

STUDIA HISTORIAE OECONOMICAE.
[Stud. hist. oecon.]. **Added/Corp** Uniwersytet im. Adama Mickiewicza w Poznaniu. Vol 1 (1966)-. Academic Scholarly Publication. Multiple languages (English, French and German). Irregular. Price varies per volume. Uniwersytet im Adama Mickiewicza / Adam Mickiewicz University Press, Nowowiejskiego 55, 61734 Poznan Poland. **Tel** 011 48 61 527380, FAX 011 48 61 526425. **Circ:** 600.
Desc: Works in the economic sciences contributed by economists from the university as well as by other Polish specialists.
Ind/Abst Am. Hist. Life (1979-).

ISSN 0198-8263
US
Pr Rev.   **TITLE CHANGE**

STUDIES IN ECONOMIC ANALYSIS.
[Stud. econ. anal.]. **Added/Corp** Omicron Delta Epsilon. University of South Carolina Chapter. Vol. 1 (Spring 1977)-(19??). Periodical. English. University of North Carolina / Economics, Economics Department, Charlotte NC 28223. **Tel** (704)547-2185. **ED** Libby Dismuke and Alice Perritt. Index available (bound in last issue). **Bk Rev. Circ:** 200. Documents available from UMI Article Clearinghouse. **Continued by** Studies in Economics and Finance.
Desc: Articles covering diverse areas of economic theory and analysis.
Ind/Abst ABI/INFORM Glob. Ed.; ABI/INFORM [Computer File] (Spring 1979-); Gen. BusinessFile (1992-).

ISSN 1014-997X
US

STUDIES OF ECONOMIES IN TRANSFORMATION. See Business and Economics-Economic Assistance and Development.

LC JX1977 .A2 HC410.7
DD 300/.8 S 338.956
US
CEASED

STUDIES ON DEVELOPMENT PROBLEMS IN COUNTRIES OF WESTERN ASIA. See Public Administration.

LC HC331 .P72
DD 338.947/005
RU

●STUDIES ON RUSSIAN ECONOMIC DEVELOPMENT.
Added/Corp Institut Ekonomiki i Prognozirovaniia Nauchno-Tekhnicheskogo Progressa (Akademiia Nauk SSSR). Vol. 4, No. 1 (Feb. 1993)-. Periodical. (translations available in Russian). Six times a year (bimonthly). $699.00. MAIK Nauka / Interperiodica, Ulitsa Profsoyuznaia 90, Moscow 117864 Russia. **(Subscription address:** Interperiodica Publishing, Subscription Office, PO Box 1831, Birmingham AL 35201-1831. **Tel** (800)633-4931, (205)995-1567 (outside US and Canada), FAX (205)995-1588.) **Continues** Studies on Soviet Economic Development, 1054-6588.
Desc: Information on socioeconomic problems in the Commonwealth of Independent States and the former Soviet bloc. For researchers in sovietology, comparative economics, international business, and comparative government.

LC HN518.L54 S78   **ISSN** 0562-4231
DD 309.1/492/4
NE

STUDIES OVER DE SOCIAAL-ECONOMISCHE GESCHIEDENIS VAN LIMBURG.
Added/Corp Sociaal Historisch Centrum voor Limburg. (19??)-. Dutch (English). One time a year. $20.56. Sociaal Historisch Centrum, Boschstraat 73, 6211 BV Maastricht Netherlands. **Tel** 011 31 43 250141. **Bk Rev. Circ:** 1,250.
Desc: Articles on the social and economic history of the Dutch province of Limburg and related regions.

FR
Pr Rev.

SUD; INFORMATION ECONOMIQUE : PROVENCE ALPES COTE D'AZUR.
Main/Corp Institut National de la Statistique et des Etudes Economiques (France). (1977)-. Periodical. French. Five times a year (Quarterly with one special). 345.00F France; 395.00F other. Sud, 62 rue Sainte, 13001 Marseille France. **Tel** 011 33 91 336068. Index available in last issue of volume--attached. **Bk Rev** (Qty: 3). **Ad Acc. Continues** France. Institut National de la Statistique et des Etudes Economiques. Sud.

Desc: Publishes socio-economic information on the Marseille region of France in an accessible format with concise analysis of statistics.

LC HC591.S8 S845
DD 330.9/624/04
SJ

SUDAN JOURNAL OF DEVELOPMENT RESEARCH.
Vol. 1 (Feb. 1977)-. Periodical. English. Two times a year. Economic and Social Research Guide, The Editor, Sudan Journal of Development Research, PO Box 1166, Khartoum Sudan.

LC HC591.S8 S846   **ISSN** 0377-5828
DD 330.9/624/04
SJ

SUDAN JOURNAL OF ECONOMIC AND SOCIAL STUDIES.
[Sudan j. econ. soc. stud.]. Vol. 1 (Summer 1974)-. Periodical. English. Two times a year. $5.00. Sales Manager, Khartoum University Press, PO Box 321, Khartoum Sudan.

ISSN 1054-6170
DD 962
US

SUDAN (SYRACUSE, N.Y.).
(SUDAN : A POLITICAL AND ECONOMIC FORECAST / POLITICAL RISK SERVICES.). [Sudan]. **Added/Corp** Political Risk Services (IBC USA (Publications) Inc.). (19??)-. English. $325.00. Political Risk Services, 6320 Fly Road, Suite 102, PO Box 248, East Syracuse NY 13057-0248. **Tel** (315)431-0511, FAX (315)431-0200.
Desc: Assesses the factors affecting the prospects for business and trade. Each report focuses specifically on business needs such as finding and developing markets, determining currency movements, or making judgements about capital investments or corporate security.

LC HC591.S8
GW

SUDAN : WIRTSCHAFTLICHE ENTWICKLUNG.
Main/Corp Bundesstelle fur Aussenhandelsinformation (Germany). (19??)-. German. One time a year. DM3.00. Bundesstelle fuer Aussenhandelsinformation, Agrippastrasse 87 93, D-50676 Cologne Germany. **Tel** 011 49 221 2057316, FAX 011 49 221 2057212.

LC HC835.A1
DD 330.9624/005
GW

SUDAN, WIRTSCHAFTSDATEN UND WIRTSCHAFTSDOKUMENTATION.
German. DM3.00. Bundesstelle fuer Aussenhandelsinformation, Agrippastrasse 87 93, D-50676 Cologne Germany. **Tel** 011 49 221 2057316, FAX 011 49 221 2057212.

LC HC186 .A33752D
DD 338/.0981/1
BL

SUDENE INFORMA. Main/Corp Brazil.
Superintendencia do Desenvolvimento do Nordeste. **VAT** Superintendencia do Desenvolvimento do Nordeste Informa. Portuguese. Superintendencia do Desenvolvimento do Nordeste, Av Professor Moraes Rego Cidade Universitaria, Recife Brazil.

LC HC337.F5 E58a   **ISSN** 0303-8130
FI

SUHDANNE. [Suhdanne]. Main/Corp
Elinkeinoelaman Tutkimuslaitos (Finland). **Added/Corp** Elinkeinoelaman Tutkimuslaitos (Finland). Economic Prospects in Finland. **VFOAT** Economic Prospects in Finland. Vol. 1 (Fall 1971)-. Periodical. Finnish (summaries and/or abstracts in English). Four times a year. Fmk1100.00. ETLA, Lonnrotinkatu 4B, SF-00120 Helsinki 12 Finland. **Tel** 40 609500, FAX 40-601753. **ED** Pentti Vartia. **Circ:** 250 (ctrl)

LC WMLC 93/4129   **ISSN** 0797-0064
RU

SUMA. Added/Corp Centro de Investigaciones
Economicas (Uruguay). Vol. 1, No. 1 (Oct. 1986)-. Periodical. Spanish. Four times a year. Ediciones Irilce, Guayabo 1729, Ap. 702, 11200 Montevideo Uruguay. **Tel** 011 598 2 404917, FAX 011 598 2 404947.
Ind/Abst PAIS Int. Print.

LC HC461 .S742   **ISSN** 0287-7406
DD 330.952/005
JA

SUMITOMO BANK ECONOMIC SURVEY.
[Sumitomo Bank econ. surv.]. **Added/Corp** Sumitomo Ginko. Vol. 24, No. 1 (Jan. 1983)-. Periodical. English. Twelve times a year. Sumitomo Bank Ltd, 1-3-2 Marunouchi, Chiyodaku Tokyo 100 Japan. **Tel** 011 81 3 2825111, FAX 011 81 3 2828613. **Continues** Sumitomo Bank Review.
Ind/Abst F&S Index Plus Text, Int. [Select. Cov.]; Predicasts Forecasts.

LC HC462.9 .S7478
DD 330.952/005
JA

SUMITOMO QUARTERLY.
Vol. 1, No. 1 (Jan. 1980)-. Periodical. English. Four times a year. Sumitomo Publication Committee, CPO Box 229, Tokyo 100-91 Japan.
Ind/Abst PAIS Int. Print.

ISSN 0212-5994
SP
TITLE CHANGE

SUPLEMENTOS SOBRE EL SISTEMA FINANCIERO.
(PAPELES DE ECONOMIA ESPANOLA. SUPLEMENTOS SOBRE EL SISTEMA FINANCIERO.). [Supl. sist. financ.]. **Added/Corp** Fundacion Fondo para la Investigacion Economica y Social (Spain). (1983)-(199?). Periodical. Spanish. Fundacion Fondo para la Investigacion Economica y Social, Juan Hurtado de Mendoza 14, 28036 Madrid Spain. **Tel** 011 34 1 3504400, FAX 011 34 1 3508040. **Continues** Papeles de Economia Espanola. Suplemento. **Continued by** Perspectivas del Sistema Financiero, 1132-9564.

LC HC107.T3 T435   **ISSN** 0099-0973
DD 330/.9/768/05
US
CODEN SUBUDY
CEASED

SURVEY OF BUSINESS. [Surv. bus.].
Added/Corp University of Tennessee. Center for Business and Economic Research. Vol. 10 (May/June 1975)-Vol. 30 (1995). Periodical. English. University of Tennessee Business and Economic Research, Room 100 Glocker Business Building, Knoxville TN 37996-4170. **Tel** (615)974-5441, FAX (615)974-3100. **ED** Jeanne P. McDonald. Index available. cum. index. **Circ:** 5,500 (ctrl). available on microfilm and microfiche from University Microfilms International (UMI). Documents available from UMI Article Clearinghouse, Ask*IEEE.
Continues Tennessee Survey of Business, 0040-3393.
Desc: Current economic and socioeconomic trends and techniques in Tennessee.
Ind/Abst ABI/INFORM Glob. Ed.; ABI/INFORM [Computer File] (Spring 1979-); Curr. Cit.; Energy Res. Abstr. (Oct. 1976-); INSPEC (Summer 1983-); PAIS Int. Print; Stat. Ref. Index; UMI ABI/Inform--Bus. Period. Ondisc (Fall 1987-) [Full Txt.].

LC HC261 .S87
DD 330.9436/0021
AU

SURVEY OF THE AUSTRIAN ECONOMY.
Added/Corp Osterreichisches Gesellschafts und Wirtschaftsmuseum. Wirtschaftsstudio. **VFOAT** Osterreichs Wirtschaft Im Uberblick. (19??)-. Statistical Publication. English. One time a year (Sept.). S150. Wirtschaftsstudio des Osterreichischen Gesellschafts und Wirtschaftmuseum, Vogelsanggasse 36, 1050 Vienna Austria. **Tel** 011 222 545 2557, FAX 011 222 545 3209. **Acid Free. Circ:** 6,000.
Desc: Presents a picture of Austria's economy and its international position in all important sectors.

LC HC79.E5 S8668   **ISSN** 0968-0802
UK

●SUSTAINABLE DEVELOPMENT.
Added/Corp MCB University Press. University of Queensland. International Land Management Research Centre. Vol. 1, No. 1 (1993)-. Periodical. English. Three times a year. $225.00. John Wiley & Sons Ltd., Baffins Lane, Chichester, West Sussex PO19 1UD United Kingdom. **Tel** 011 44 1243 779777, FAX 011 44 1243 776128 BTG:JWP001, telex 86290 WIBOOKG.

LC HC517.S9
GW

SWASILAND : WIRTSCHAFTLICHE ENTWICKLUNG.
Main/Corp Bundesstelle fur Aussenhandelsinformation (Germany). German. DM2.00. Bundesstelle fuer Aussenhandelsinformation, Agrippastrasse 87 93, D-50676 Cologne Germany. **Tel** 011 49 221 2057316, FAX 011 49 221 2057212.

ISSN 1054-6189
DD 948
US

SWEDEN (SYRACUSE, N.Y.). (SWEDEN : A
POLITICAL AND ECONOMIC FORECAST / POLITICAL RISK SERVICES.). [Sweden]. **Added/Corp** Political Risk Services (IBC USA (Publications) Inc.). (19??)-. English. $325.00. Political Risk Services, 6320 Fly Road, Suite 102, PO Box 248, East Syracuse NY 13057-0248. **Tel** (315)431-0511, FAX (315)431-0200.
Desc: Assesses the factors affecting the prospects for business and trade. Each report focuses specifically on business needs such as finding and developing markets, determining currency movements, or making judgements about capital investments or corporate security.

ISSN 1054-6197
DD 956
US

SYRIA (SYRACUSE, N.Y.). (SYRIA : A
POLITICAL AND ECONOMIC FORECAST / POLITICAL RISK SERVICES.). [Syria]. **Added/Corp** Political Risk Services (IBC USA (Publications) Inc.). (19??)-. English. $325.00. Political Risk Services, 6320 Fly Road, Suite 102, PO Box 248, East Syracuse NY 13057-0248. **Tel** (315)431-0511, FAX (315)431-0200.
Desc: Assesses the factors affecting the prospects for business and trade. Each report focuses specifically on business needs such as finding and developing markets, determining currency movements, or making judgements about capital investments or corporate security.

Business and Economics —Economic History, Conditions

LC HC497.S8
GW
SYRIEN : WIRTSCHAFTLICHE ENTWICKLUNG. Main/Corp Bundesstelle fur Aussenhandelsinformation (Germany). German. One time a year. DM3.00. Bundesstelle fuer Aussenhandelsinformation, Agrippastrasse 87 93, D-50676 Cologne Germany. **Tel** 011 49 221 2057316, FAX 011 49 221 2057212.

LC HC975.A1 T324
DD 330.967/21/005
GB
TABLEAU DE BORD DE L'ECONOMIE. French. Direction Generale de l'Economie, BP 1204, Libreville Gabon.

LC HC277.B7 T3
ISSN 0395-871X
FR
TABLEAUX DE L'ECONOMIE BRETONNE. French. Institut National de la Statistique et des Etudes Economiques, 18 Bd Adolphe Pinard, 75675 Paris 14 France.

LC HC430.5. T294
CH
TAI-WAN CHING CHI YEN CHIU YUEH KAN. VFOAT Taiwan Economic Research Monthly. (1978)-. Periodical. Chinese. Twelve times a year. $65.00. Tai-Wan Ching Chi Yen Chiu Tsa Chi She 62, Hsi Ning S Road/6th Floor, Taipei Shih Taiwan.

DD 951
ISSN 1054-6200
US
TAIWAN (SYRACUSE, N.Y.). (TAIWAN : A POLITICAL AND ECONOMIC FORECAST.). [Taiwan]. Added/Corp Political Risk Services (IBC USA (Publications) Inc.). (19??)-. English. $325.00. Political Risk Services, 6320 Fly Road, Suite 102, PO Box 248, East Syracuse NY 13057-0248. **Tel** (315)431-0511, FAX (315)431-0200.
Desc: Assesses the factors affecting the prospects for business and trade. Each report focuses specifically on business needs such as finding and developing markets, determining currency movements, or making judgements about capital investments or corporate security.

LC HC430.5.A1 T387
DD 330.951/249/005
GW
TAIWAN, WIRTSCHAFTSDATEN UND WIRTSCHAFTSDOKUMENTATION. German. DM3.00. Bundesstelle fuer Aussenhandelsinformation, Agrippastrasse 87 93, D-50676 Cologne Germany. **Tel** 011 49 221 2057316, FAX 011 49 221 2057212.

LC HC497.P23 I513a
IS
TAKTSIV LEUMI. Main/Corp Bank Yisrael. Mahleket ha-Mehkar. Added/Corp Israel. Misrad ha-Otsar. Lishkah le-Yiuts ule-Mehkar Kalkali. Israel. Agaf ha-Taktsivim. Israel. Rashut le-Tikhnun Kalkali. Israel. Misrad ha-Otsar. Israel. Misrad ha-Otsar. Lishkat ha-Yoets ha-Kalkali. (19??)-. Hebrew. One time a year. Bank of Israel Research Department, PO Box 780, Jerusalem 91007 Israel. **Tel** 02-552111.

LC HC557.T3 G44a
DD 330.9/678/04
GW
TANSANIA: WIRTSCHAFTLICHE ENTWICKLUNG. Main/Corp Germany (West). Bundesstelle fur Aussenhandelsinformation. (19??)-. German. Bundesstelle fuer Aussenhandelsinformation, Agrippastrasse 87 93, D-50676 Cologne Germany. **Tel** 011 49 221 2057316, FAX 011 49 221 2057212.

LC HC885.A1
DD 330.9/678
GW
TANSANIA WIRTSCHAFTSDATEN UND WIRTSCHAFTSDOKUMENTATION. (19??)-. German. DM2.00. Bundesstelle fuer Aussenhandelsinformation, Agrippastrasse 87 93, D-50676 Cologne Germany. **Tel** 011 49 221 2057316, FAX 011 49 221 2057212.

LC HC59.7 .I552A
ISSN 0271-1834
US
TAQRIR AN AL-TANMIYAH FI AL-ALAM. Main/Corp World Bank. 1978-. Arabic. One time a year. World Bank Publications, 1818 H Street Northwest, Washington DC 20043. **Tel** (202)473-1155, (202)473-1155, FAX (202)522-3224, telex WUI 64145 WORLDBANK.

LC HC681.Z7 F837
DD 330.996/2
ISSN 0293-2547
FP
TE AVEIA. Added/Corp Institut Territorial de la Statistique (French Polynesia). No. 1 (July 1980)-. Statistical Publication. French. Four times a year. Institut Territorial de la Statistique, B P 395, Papeete Tahiti French Polynesia. **Ad Acc.** Documents available from Magazine Collection, BLDSC. **Continues** Tableau de Bord Economique de la Polynesie Francaise; **Absorbed** Note de Conjoncture (Institut Territorial de la Statistique (French Polynesia), 0754-3190 **and** Tableau de Bord de l'Economie Polynesienne.

LC HC107.M5 A459
DD 338.9 330.9774
ISSN 0543-8330
US
TECHNICAL REPORT - STATE RESOURCES PLANNING PROGRAM. Main/Corp Michigan. Department of Commerce. VFOAT State Resources Planning Program. No. 1 (1966)-. Periodical. English. Michigan State Resources Planning Program, Lansing MI 48904.

LC HC301 .T38
IT
TEMPI MODERNI. (19??)-. Periodical. Italian. Four times a year. Edizioni Dedalo Spa, Casella Postale 362, Bari 70100 Italy. **Tel** 011 39 080 5311400, FAX 011 39 080 5311414. **Continues** Tempi Moderni dell'Economia, della Politica e della Cultura.

LC HC391 .T46
ISSN 0492-6749
PO
TEMPO E O MODO, O. Periodical. Portuguese. Twelve times a year. 400$00. Rua Francisco Sanches, 8 r/c D Lisbon Portugal.

LC HC186 .T46
BL
TENDENCIA. Vol. 1 (Oct. 1973)-. Periodical. Portuguese. Irregular. $80.00. Bloch Editoras SA, Rua do Russell 766 804, 22210 Rio de Janeiro Brazil. **Tel** 011 51 21 2652012, 011 51 21 2850033.

LC HC10 .T54
DD 330
RU
TENDENTSII MIROVOGO EKONOMICHESKOGO RAZVITIIA. Added/Corp Institut Mirovoi Ekonomiki I Mezhdunarodnykh Otnoshenii (Akaemiia Nauk SSSR). (1991)-. Academic Scholarly Publication. Russian. Two times a year. Izdatelstvo Nauka / Akademiia Nauk, (Publishing House of the Russian Academy of Sciences), Leninskii Porspekt 14, 117901 Moscow Russia. **Tel** 011 95 9542153, FAX 011 95 9382144, telex 411964. **Continues** Ekonomicheskoe Polozhenie Kapitalisticheskikh I Razvivaiushchikhsia Stran.

LC HC107.T4 T492
DD 330.9764/005
ISSN 0896-0453
US
CEASED
TEXAS ECONOMIC INDICATORS (AUSTIN, TEX.: 1987). (TEXAS ECONOMIC INDICATORS.). [Tex. econ. indic.]. Added/Corp University of Texas at Austin. Bureau of Business Research. (July 1987)-(Dec. 1994). English. Bureau of Business Research / Texas, University of Texas at Austin, Box 7459, Austin TX 78713. **Tel** (512)471-1616. **ED** Lois G. Shrout and Rita J. Wright.
Desc: Provides data on employment and unemployment income, production levels, business activity, prices, etc. for state of Texas.

LC HC107.T4 T495
DD 330.9/764/06
ISSN 0163-4666
US
CEASED
TEXAS FACT BOOK. Added/Corp University of Texas at Austin. Bureau of Business Research. 1st Ed. (1978)-(19??). Monographic series. English. Bureau of Business Research / Texas, University of Texas at Austin, Box 7459, Austin TX 78713. **Tel** (512)471-1616. **ED** Rita Wright and Laurie Gamel. **Ad Acc. Circ:** 3,000.
Desc: Collection of statistical data for the state.

LC HC445.A1 T47
DD 330.9593/005
TH
THAI ECONOMY, THE. Periodical. English. One time a year. U-Chuliang Foundation Building 3rd Floor/Rama IV Road, Bangkok Thailand.

DD 959
ISSN 1054-6219
US
THAILAND (SYRACUSE, N.Y.). (THAILAND : A POLITICAL AND ECONOMIC FORECAST / POLITICAL RISK SERVICES.). [Thailand]. Added/Corp Political Risk Services (IBC USA (Publications) Inc.). (19??)-. English. $325.00. Political Risk Services, 6320 Fly Road, Suite 102, PO Box 248, East Syracuse NY 13057-0248. **Tel** (315)431-0511, FAX (315)431-0200.
Desc: Assesses the factors affecting the prospects for business and trade. Each report focuses specifically on business needs such as finding and developing markets, determining currency movements, or making judgements about capital investments or corporate security.

LC HC497.S5
GW
THAILAND : WIRTSCHAFTLICHE ENTWICKLUNG. Main/Corp Bundesstelle fur Aussenhandelsinformation (Germany). German. One time a year. DM3.00. Bundesstelle fuer Aussenhandelsinformation, Agrippastrasse 87 93, D-50676 Cologne Germany. **Tel** 011 49 221 2057316, FAX 011 49 221 2057212.

THAILAND, WIRTSCHAFTSDATEN UND WIRTSCHAFTSDOKUMENTATION. (19??)-. German. DM3.00. Bundesstelle fuer Aussenhandelsinformation, Agrippastrasse 87 93, D-50676 Cologne Germany. **Tel** 011 49 221 2057316, FAX 011 49 221 2057212.

LC HC59.7 .T46
DD 330.9/172/4
PK
THIRD WORLD REVIEW, THE. Vol. 1 (Fall 1974)-. Periodical. English. 15.00 each issue. Karachi Geographers Association, 328/9 Federal B Area 38, Karachi Pakistan. available on microfilm and microfiche from University Microfilms International (UMI).

LC HC440.8.A1 T46
DD 330.9549/2/005
BG
THOUGHTS ON ECONOMICS. Added/Corp Islamic Economics Research Bureau (Bangladesh). (1980)-. Periodical. English (Bengali and Arabic). Islamic Economics Research Bureau, Central Mosque Kataban Campus 5037, Dacca 1205 Bangladesh. **Tel** (880)(2)508472, telex 642525 IBANK BJ. **ED** Salahuddin Ahmad. **Ad Acc. Circ:** 1,000.
Desc: Professional journal on Islamic economics.
Ind/Abst Index Islam. Lit.

LC HC557.T6
GW
TOGO : WIRTSCHAFTLICHE ENTWICKLUNG. Main/Corp Bundesstelle fur Aussenhandelsinformation (Germany). (19??)-. German. 4.00. Bundesstelle fuer Aussenhandelsinformation, Agrippastrasse 87 93, D-50676 Cologne Germany. **Tel** 011 49 221 2057316, FAX 011 49 221 2057212.

LC HC557.T6
GW
TOGO : WIRTSCHAFTSDATEN UND WIRTSCHAFTSDOKUMENTATION. Main/Corp Bundesstelle fur Aussenhandelsinformation (Germany). German. DM2.00. Bundesstelle fuer Aussenhandelsinformation, Agrippastrasse 87 93, D-50676 Cologne Germany. **Tel** 011 49 221 2057316, FAX 011 49 221 2057212.

LC HC463.T56 T64
DD 330/338.952
JA
TOKAI HOKURIKU TSUSAN TOKEI NEMPO. Added/Corp Japan. Nagoya Tsusho Sangyokyoku. Chosaka. (19??)-. Japanese. Nagoya Tsusho Sangyokyoku Chosaka, 5-2 Sannomaru 2-chome Naka-ku, 460 Nagoya Japan.

LC HC463.T58 T632
JA
TOKUBETSUKU KUSEI GAIYO. Added/Corp Tokyo. Somukyoku. Gyoseibu. (19??)-. Japanese. Tokyo-to Somukyoku Gyoseibu, 5-1 Marunouchi 3-chome, Chiyoda-ku 100, Tokyo Japan.

LC DJK1 .R47
BE
●TRANSITIONS. Added/Corp Centre de Recherches Interdisciplinaires sur la Transition vers l'Economie de Marche des Pays de l'Est. (1993)-. Periodical. French. Two times a year. 1500F (institutions), 1000F (individuals) Belgium; 1750F (institutions), 1250F (individuals) other. Centre National d'Etude d'Etats, Institut de Sociologie, 44 avenue Jeanne, 1050 Brussels Belgium. **Tel** 011 32 2 6503360, FAX 011 32 2 6503521. **Continues** Revue des Pays de l'Est, 0303-9617.

LC HC261 .T7
AU
TREND. Vol. 1 (Jan. 1970)-. Periodical. German. Twelve times a year. $93.23. Wirtschafts Trend Zeitschrifte Verlagsges GmbH, Marc Aurel Str 10, A-1010 Vienna Austria. **Tel** 011 43 222 661670.

LC HC59 .T38
DD 330.9/005
ISSN 0776-3395
BE
TRENDS-TENDANCES (BRUXELLES). (TENDANCES.). [Trends-tend.]. VFOAT Trends. (19??)-. Periodical. French (French). Fifty times a year. $241.79. Uitgeverij Biblo, Brasschaatsesteenweg 200, 2920 Kalmthout Belgium. **Tel** 011 32 3 6200240 6200211, 011 32 3 6200211, FAX 011 32 3 6200361, telex 72080. **Ind/Abst** PAIS Int. Print; Predicasts.

LC HC405.A1 T75
RM
TRIBUNA ECONOMICA : PUBLICATIE A ECONOMISTILOR DIN ROMANIA. Vol. 1 (Jan. 5, 1990)-. Romanian. One time a week. $124.30. **(Subscription address:** Orion Press SRL, SPL Independentei 202-A, Bucharest 6 Romania. **Tel** 011 401 3122425.) **Continues** Revista Economica, 0251-3080.

LC HC157.A1
DD 330.97298/3/005
GW
TRINIDAD UND TOBAGO, WIRTSCHAFTSDATEN. German. DM3.00. Bundesstelle fuer Aussenhandelsinformation, Agrippastrasse 87 93, D-50676 Cologne Germany. **Tel** 011 49 221 2057316, FAX 011 49 221 2057212.

Business and Economics — Economic History, Conditions

LC HC10 .T76
CC
TSAI HSING SHIH CHIEH. VFOAT World Wealth-Star. (Nov. 1974)-. Periodical. Chinese (English). $33.00. Cosmopolitan Enterprises Inc, 1739-1743 West Golf Road, Mount Prospect IL 60056.

LC HC267.B2 T8
XR
TSCHECHOSLOWAKISCHE WIRTSCHAFTSRUNDSCHAU. (19??)-. Periodical. German. Eight times a year. $20.00. Pragopress Feature Service, Slavickova 5, Prague 6 Czech Republic. **ED** Karel Beba. Index available. **Circ:** 350.

LC HC28 .T78
JA
●**TSUSAN KENKYU REBYU = MITI RESEARCH REVIEW. Added/Corp** Japan. Tsusho Sangyosho. Tsusho Sangyosho Tsusho Sangyo Kenkyujo (Japan). **VFOAT** Tsusho Sangyosho Kenkyu Rebyu; Ministry of International Trade and Industry Research Review; MITI Research Review. (1993)-. Periodical. Japanese (summaries and/or abstracts in English). Two times a year. $80.00. (**Subscription address:** Japan Publications Trading Company Ltd., PO Box 5030, Tokyo International, Tokyo 100-31 Japan. **Tel** 011 81 3 3292 3753.)

LC HC461 .A316a
JA
TSUSANSHO KOHO. Main/Corp Japan. Tsusho Sangyosho. **Added/Corp** Tsusho Sangyo Chosakai (Tokyo, Japan). (19??)-. Periodical. Japanese. Irregular. ¥24000. Tsusho Sangyo Chosakai, (Research Institute on International Trade and Industry), Kobikikan Ginza Biru, 8-9 Ginza 2 chome Chuoku, Tokyo 104 Japan.

LC HC108.T82 T85
DD 338.5/443/0976686
US
TULSA ECONOMIC OUTLOOK. (1977)-. English. Four times a year. $75.00. Office of Economic Development, City of Tulsa, 200 Civic Center, Suite 1035, Tulsa OK 74103. **Tel** (918)592-7668. **ED** Steve Ward. **Circ:** 1,000.
Desc: Details economic activity in Tulsa, OK. Emphasis on construction activity, labor force, and retail sales.

ISSN 1054-6227
DD 961
US
TUNISIA (SYRACUSE, N.Y.). (TUNISIA : A POLITICAL AND ECONOMIC FORECAST.). [Tunisia]. **Added/Corp** Political Risk Services (IBC USA (Publications) Inc.). (19??)-. English. $325.00. Political Risk Services, 6320 Fly Road, Suite 102, PO Box 248, East Syracuse NY 13057-0248. **Tel** (315)431-0511, FAX (315)431-0200.
Desc: Assesses the factors affecting the prospects for business and trade. Each report focuses specifically on business needs such as finding and developing markets, determining currency movements, or making judgements about capital investments or corporate security.

LC HC401 .A356
DD 330
TU
TURK KOYUNDE MODERNLESME EGILIMLERI ARASTRMAS. Added/Corp Turkey. Devlet Planlama Teskilat. Toplum Yaps Arastrma Grubu. (19??)-. Turkish. Free to State Planning Organizations. Devlet Planlama Teskilat, 108 Necatibey Caddesi, 06100 Ankara Turkey. **Tel** 230 87 20, FAX 90(4)230 97 38. **ED** Ahmet Tugac. **Circ:** 1,000 (ctrl)

LC HC491 .T77
DD 956.1
GW
TURKEI, WIRTSCHAFT IN ZAHLEN UND WIRTSCHAFTSDOKUMENTATION. Added/Corp Bundesstelle fuer Aussenhandelsinformation (Germany). (19??)-. German. One time a year. Bundesstelle fuer Aussenhandelsinformation, Agrippastrasse 87 93, D-50676 Cologne Germany. **Tel** 011 49 221 2057316, FAX 011 49 221 2057212.

ISSN 1054-6235
DD 956
US
TURKEY (SYRACUSE, N.Y.). (TURKEY : A POLITICAL AND ECONOMIC FORECAST.). [Turkey]. **Added/Corp** Political Risk Services (IBC USA (Publications) Inc.). (19??)-. English. $325.00. Political Risk Services, 6320 Fly Road, Suite 102, PO Box 248, East Syracuse NY 13057-0248. **Tel** (315)431-0511, FAX (315)431-0200.
Desc: Assesses the factors affecting the prospects for business and trade. Each report focuses specifically on business needs such as finding and developing markets, determining currency movements, or making judgements about capital investments or corporate security.

ISSN 0828-2404
DD 338.9/005
CN
U.B.C. PLANNING PAPERS. COMPARATIVE URBAN & REGIONAL STUDIES. [U.B.C. plan. pap., Comp. urban reg. stud.]. **Added/Corp** University of British Columbia. School of Community and Regional Planning. **VFOAT** Comparative Urban & Regional Studies. **VAT** University of British Columbia Planning Papers. Comparative Urban & Regional Studies. (198?)-. Monographic series. English (summaries and/or abstracts in French). Price varies per volume.
Ind/Abst Geogr. Abstr. Human Geogr.; Int. Dev. Abstr.

LC HC60 .U32
DK
UDVIKLING. Periodical. Danish. Six times a year. 30.00. Udenrigsministeriets Afdling for Internationale Udviklingssamarbejde, Amaliegade 1, 1256 K Copenhagen Denmark.

ISSN 1061-1304
DD 947
US
UKRAINE (SYRACUSE, N.Y.). See Political Science.

LC HB522
ISSN 1061-4095
DD 338
US
UKRAINE UPDATE. (UKRAINE UPDATE : BUSINESS AND INVESTMENT NEWS.). [Ukr. update]. **Added/Corp** Beard Group, Inc. (1992)-. Periodical. English. Four times a year. $195.00. Beard Group, PO Box 9867, Washington DC 20016. **Tel** (301)951-6400, FAX (301)951-3621.

LC HC547.M2 U55
DD 330.9/69/105
MG
UNION ECONOMIQUE, L'. French. Union des Syndicats d'Interest Economique de Madagascar, Place Roland Garros, Tananarive Madagascar.

ISSN 1054-6251
DD 953
US
UNITED ARAB EMIRATES (SYRACUSE, N.Y.). (UNITED ARAB EMIRATES : A POLITICAL AND ECONOMIC FORECAST.). [U. A. Emir.]. **Added/Corp** Political Risk Services (IBC USA (Publications) Inc.). (19??)-. English. $325.00. Political Risk Services, 6320 Fly Road, Suite 102, PO Box 248, East Syracuse NY 13057-0248. **Tel** (315)431-0511, FAX (315)431-0200.
Desc: Assesses the factors affecting the prospects for business and trade. Each report focuses specifically on business needs such as finding and developing markets, determining currency movements, or making judgements about capital investments or corporate security.

ISSN 1054-626X
DD 941
US
UNITED KINGDOM (SYRACUSE, N.Y.). (UNITED KINGDOM : A POLITICAL AND ECONOMIC FORECAST / POLITICAL RISK SERVICES.). [U. K.]. **Added/Corp** Political Risk Services (IBC USA (Publications) Inc.). (19??)-. English. $325.00. Political Risk Services, 6320 Fly Road, Suite 102, PO Box 248, East Syracuse NY 13057-0248. **Tel** (315)431-0511, FAX (315)431-0200.
Desc: Assesses the factors affecting the prospects for business and trade. Each report focuses specifically on business needs such as finding and developing markets, determining currency movements, or making judgements about capital investments or corporate security.

LC HC60 .U4589
ISSN 0498-0085
DD 338.91
US
UNITED NATIONS SPECIAL FUND, THE. Main/Corp United Nations Special Fund. (1960)-. Government Publication. English. Irregular. United Nations Publications, 2 United Nations Plaza, Room DC2 0853, Department 007C, New York NY 10017. **Tel** (212)963-8303, (800)253-9646.

ISSN 1054-6278
DD 973
US
UNITED STATES (SYRACUSE, N.Y.). (UNITED STATES : A POLITICAL AND ECONOMIC FORECAST.). [U. S.]. **Added/Corp** Political Risk Services (IBC USA (Publications) Inc.). (19??)-. English. $325.00. Political Risk Services, 6320 Fly Road, Suite 102, PO Box 248, East Syracuse NY 13057-0248. **Tel** (315)431-0511, FAX (315)431-0200.
Desc: Assesses the factors affecting the prospects for business and trade. Each report focuses specifically on business needs such as finding and developing markets, determining currency movements, or making judgements about capital investments or corporate security.

LC HC110.P63 U54A
DD 338.973
US
UPDATE TO THE ... CATALOG OF FEDERAL DOMESTIC ASSISTANCE. Catalog. English. Office of Management and Budget, Executive Office Building, Washington DC 20503. **Tel** (202)395-3080.

ISSN 1054-6286
DD 989
US
URUGUAY (SYRACUSE, N.Y.). (URUGUAY : A POLITICAL AND ECONOMIC FORECAST / POLITICAL RISK SERVICES.). [Uruguay]. **Added/Corp** Political Risk Services (IBC USA (Publications) Inc.). (19??)-. English. $325.00. Political Risk Services, 6320 Fly Road, Suite 102, PO Box 248, East Syracuse NY 13057-0248. **Tel** (315)431-0511, FAX (315)431-0200.
Desc: Assesses the factors affecting the prospects for business needs such as finding and developing markets, determining currency movements, or making judgements about capital investments or corporate security.

LC HC231
DD 330.9895/005
GW
URUGUAY, WIRTSCHAFTSDATEN UND WIRTSCHAFTSDOKUMENTATION. German. Bundesstelle fuer Aussenhandelsinformation, Agrippastrasse 87 93, D-50676 Cologne Germany. **Tel** 011 49 221 2057316, FAX 011 49 221 2057212.

LC HC106.7
GW
USA: WIRTSCHAFT IN ZAHLEN. Main/Corp Bundesstelle fur Aussenhandelsinformation (Germany). German. DM4.00. Bundesstelle fuer Aussenhandelsinformation, Agrippastrasse 87 93, D-50676 Cologne Germany. **Tel** 011 49 221 2057316, FAX 011 49 221 2057212.

LC HC107.A13
GW
USA : WIRTSCHAFTLICHE ENTWICKLUNG DER SUDOSTSTAATEN. Main/Corp Germany (Federal Republic, 1949-). Bundesstelle fur Aussenhandelsinformation. (19??)-. German. DM3.00. Bundesstelle fuer Aussenhandelsinformation, Agrippastrasse 87 93, D-50676 Cologne Germany. **Tel** 011 49 221 2057316, FAX 011 49 221 2057212.

LC HC107.C2 U75
DD 330.9794/005
GW
USA, WIRTSCHAFTLICHE ENTWICKLUNG DES BUNDESSTAATES KALIFORNIEN. German. DM2.00. Bundesstelle fuer Aussenhandelsinformation, Agrippastrasse 87 93, D-50676 Cologne Germany. **Tel** 011 49 221 2057316, FAX 011 49 221 2057212.

LC HC106.6
DD 330.9/73/092
GW
USA, WIRTSCHAFTSPOLITIK UND -ENTWICKLUNG. Main/Corp Germany (West). Bundesstelle fur Aussenhandelsinformation. (19??)-. German. Bundesstelle fuer Aussenhandelsinformation, Agrippastrasse 87 93, D-50676 Cologne Germany. **Tel** 011 49 221 2057316, FAX 011 49 221 2057212.

LC HC271 .U75
ISSN 0042-126X
FR
USINE NOUVELLE. (L'USINE NOUVELLE.). [Usine nouv.]. **Added/Corp** Societe de Periodiques Techniques et Industriels (Paris, France). (June 21, 1945)-. Periodical. English. One time a week. $352.80. Cepit Groupe Usine Nouvelle, 6 rue Marius Aufan BTMT D 1 ET, F 92300 Levallois Perr France. **Tel** 011 33 1 47582020. *Continues* Usine.
Ind/Abst Alum. Ind. Abstr.; Eng. Mater. Abstr.; F&S Index Plus Text, Int. [Select. Cov.]; GeoRef; Int. Labour Doc.; LABORDOC; Met. Abstr.; PROMT; Saf. Health Work.

LC HC186 .V37
DD 330.981/005
BL
VARIA SOCIO-ECONOMICA. Added/Corp Rio Grande do Sul (Brazil). Fundacao de Economia e Estatistica. (Vol. for 1982)-. Periodical. Portuguese. One time a year. Fundacao de Economia e Estatistica, Rua Duque de Caixias 1691, 90010 Porto Alegre, Rio Grande do Sul Brazil. **Tel** 0512-259455, FAX 0512-25006, telex 0515042.

ISSN 0267-9957
UK
VENEZUELA (LONDON. 1985). (VENEZUELA.). [Venezuela]. **Added/Corp** Latin American Monitor Ltd. (1985)-. English. One time a year (June). $435.00. Business Monitor International, 56 60 St. John Street, London EC1M 4DT United Kingdom. **Tel** 011 44 171 6083646, FAX 011 44 171 6083620.

ISSN 1054-6294
DD 987
US
VENEZUELA (SYRACUSE, N.Y.). (VENEZUELA : A POLITICAL AND ECONOMIC FORECAST.). [Venezuela]. **Added/Corp** Political Risk Services (IBC USA (Publications) Inc.). (19??)-. English. $325.00. Political Risk Services, 6320 Fly Road, Suite 102, PO Box 248, East Syracuse NY 13057-0248. **Tel** (315)431-0511, FAX (315)431-0200.
Desc: Assesses the factors affecting the prospects for business and trade. Each report focuses specifically on business needs such as finding and developing markets, determining currency movements, or making judgements about capital investments or corporate security.

VE
VENEZUELAN ECONOMIC REVIEW. Added/Corp Office of Economic Studies, Caracas. (1???)-. Periodical. English (Spanish). Fifty times a year. $350.00. Venezuelan Economic Review, Apartado 50679, Caracas 1050 Venezuela. **Tel** 011 58 2 2835575 2833964, FAX 011 58 2 285-8004, telex 24704 PRUNH VC. (**Subscription address:** Venezuelan Economic

Business and Economics —Economic History, Conditions

Review, 6 Royal Palm Way 6408, Boca Raton FL 33432. **Tel** (407)368-0561.) **ED** Roger Prunhuber Leon. **Circ:** 3,500.
 Desc: A newsletter condensing all important Venezuelan economic, financial and business events.

LC HC301 .V45

VENTO DEL SUD. (19??)-. Italian. Via Degli Ortaggi 12, Rome 00157 Italy.

IT

LC HC289.B4 V38

GW

VERARBEITENDES GEWERBE IN BERLIN (WEST). German. One time a year.

LC HC331.A1 M8   ISSN 0580-2008
GW

VEROEFFENTLICHUNGEN DES OESTEUROPA-INSTITUTES MUENCHEN. REIHE : WIRTSCHAFT UND GESELLSCHAFT. Main/Corp Munich. Osteuropa-Institut. (1966)-. Monographic series. German. Irregular. Price varies per volume. Duncker und Humblot Verlag, Postfach 410329, D-12113 Berlin Germany. **Tel** 011 49 30 79000612, 011 49 30 79000613. **Continues** Wilhelmshaven, Germany. Hochschule fuer Sozialwissenschaften. Institut zum Studium der Sowjetwirtschaft. Schriften des Instituts zum Studium der Sowjetwirtschaft.

LC HC271 .V49   ISSN 0220-5858
DD 330.944/005   FR

VIE FRANCAISE (PARIS, FRANCE: 1978). (LA VIE FRANCAISE.). (1978)-. Periodical. French. One time a week. $254.59. La Vie Francaise, 25 rue Le Blanc, 75510 Paris Cedex 15 France. **Tel** 011 33 1 40604060. **Continues** La Vie Francaise, l'Opinion, 0151-2382.

LC HC10 .S719

GW

VIERTELJAHRESHEFT ZUR AUSLANDSSTATISTIK. Added/Corp Germany. Statistisches Bundesamt. **VFOAT** Vierteljahreshefte zur Auslandsstatistik. (March 1991)-. German. Four times a year. Hermann Leins GmbH & Co., Verlags-KG, Holzwiesenstrasse 2, Postfach 11 52, D-7408 Kusterdingen Germany. **Continues** Statistik des Auslandes. Vierteljahreshefte zur Auslandsstatistik, 0177-7564.

LC H5 .V6   ISSN 0042-5699
GW
CCC

VIERTELJAHRSCHRIFT FUER SOZIAL- UND WIRTSCHAFTSGESCHICHTE. [Vierteljahrschr. Soz.- Wirtschaftsgesch.]. **VFOAT** VSWG. Vol. 9, No. 3 (1911)-. Periodical. German (French and German). Four times a year. DM148.00. Franz Steiner Verlag GmbH, Postfach 101061, D-70009 Stuttgart Germany. **Tel** 011 49 711 2582372, FAX 011 49 711 2582290, telex 723636 daz d. **ED** H. Pohl, R. Gommel, F. W. Henning, K. H. Kaufhold, F. Schonert-Rohlk, and W. Zorn. cum. index. **Continues** Vierteljahrschrift fur Social- und Wirtschaftsgeschichte.
 Ind/Abst Am. Hist. Life (1955-1958, 1962-); Foreign Lang. Index; Popul. Index (?-?); Public Aff. Inf. Serv. Bull.; Writ. Am. Hist.

ISSN 1058-3831
DD 959   US

VIETNAM (SYRACUSE, N.Y.). See Political Science.

ISSN 0218-5253
DD 330.9597   SI

VIETNAM TODAY SINGAPORE. [Vietnam today Singap.]. (1991)-. Periodical. English. Ten times a year. $65.00. Communication Indochine Pty Ltd, 15 MHD Sultan Road, Singapore 0923 Singapore. **Tel** 011 65 7328948, 011 65 7323628. **(Subscription address:** Global Directions Inc., 58 Genebern Way, San Francisco CA 94112.)

LC HC425.A1 V54

NP

VIKASA DARPANA. VFOAT Development Mirror. Vol. 1, No. 1 (Mid-April to Mid-July 1979)-. Periodical. English (Nepali). Four times a year. Rs18.00. Post Box 1601, Kalikasthan Kathmandu Nepal.

LC HC10 .V522

GR

VIOMECHANIKE EPITHEORESIS. VFOAT Viomichaniki Epitheorissis; Industrial Review. (1934)-. Greek. Monthly. Twelve times a year. Hodos Zalokosta 4, T T 134 Athens Greece.

LC HC431 .V57

II

VISLESHANA. VFOAT Vishleshan. Vol. 1 (March 1975)-. Periodical. Multiple languages (English and Gujarati). 25.00. Gujarat University Department of Economics, Ahmedabad 380009 India.

LC HC547.C65
GW

VOLKSREPUBLIK KONGO : WIRTSCHAFTLICHE ENTWICKLUNG. Main/Corp Bundesstelle fur Aussenhandelsinformation (Germany). (19??)-. German. Bundesstelle fuer Aussenhandelsinformation, Agrippastrasse 87 93, D-50676 Cologne Germany. **Tel** 011 49 221 2057316, FAX 011 49 221 2057212.

LC HC547.C65
DD 330.967/24/005   GW

VOLKSREPUBLIK KONGO, WIRTSCHAFTSDATEN UND WIRTSCHAFTSDOKUMENTATION. German. One time a year. DM3.00. Bundesstelle fuer Aussenhandelsinformation, Agrippastrasse 87 93, D-50676 Cologne Germany. **Tel** 011 49 221 2057316, FAX 011 49 221 2057212. **Continues** Volksrepublic Kongo, Wirtschaftsdaten.

LC HC290.5.I5 V645
DD 330   GW

VOLKSWIRTSCHAFTLICHE GESAMTRECHNUNGEN. REIHE 3, VIERTELJAHRESERGEBNISSE DER INLANDPRODUKTSBERECHNUNG. Added/Corp Germany. Statistisches Bundesamt. **VFOAT** Vierteljahresergebnisse der Inlandproduktsberechnung; Fachserie 18. (19??)-. German. Four times a year. Metzler Poeschel Verlag Veroeffen, Statist Bundesamt Kernerstr 43, D-70182 Stuttgart Germany. **Tel** 011 49 7071 935350. **Continues** Volkswirtschaftliche Gesamtrechnungen. Reihe 3, Vierteljahresergebnisse der Sozialproduktsberechnung.

LC HC   ISSN 0042-8736
DD 330   RU

VOPROSY EKONOMIKI. [Vopr. ekon.].
 Added/Corp Institut Ekonomiki (Akademiia Nauk SSSR). (March 1948)-. Periodical. Russian. Twelve times a year. $159.95. Izdatelstvo Pressa, Myasnitskaia 24, 101877 Moscow Russia. **Tel** 011 95 923 2122, FAX 011 95 200 2259. **(Subscription address:** East View Publications Inc., 3020 Harbor Lane North, Suite 110, Minneapolis MN 55447. **Tel** (800)477-1005, (612)550-0961, FAX (612)559-2931.) available on microfilm from University Microfilms International (UMI). **Continues** Mirovoe Khoziaistvo I Mirovaia Politika.
 Ind/Abst AGRICOLA; Am. Hist. Life (1954-1955, 1973-);(1954-1955, 1973); Dairy Sci. Abstr.; Int. Bibliogr. Sociol.; Int. Labour Doc.; LABORDOC; Potato Abstr.; Soc. Plann. Policy Dev. Abstr.; Curr. Dig. Post Sov. Press; World Agric. Econ. Rural Sociol. Abstr.

LC HA1228.A75 A332   ISSN 0395-9473
DD 314.4   FR

VUES SUR L'ECONOMIE D'AQUITAINE. See Business and Economics-Abstracting, Bibliographies and Statistics.

LC HC800.A1 W37   ISSN 0733-8104
DD 330.96/005   US

WASHINGTON REPORT ON AFRICA. See Political Science.

LC HC59.A15 K53   ISSN 0043-2652
GW
CCC

WELTWIRTSCHAFT (TUBINGEN), DIE. (DIE WELTWIRTSCHAFT / INSTITUTE FUER WELTWIRTSCHAFT AN DER UNIVERSITAET KIEL.). [Weltwirtschaft]. **Added/Corp** Universitat Kiel. Institut fuer Weltwirtschaft. (July 1950)-. Periodical. German. Four times a year. $81.07. JCB Mohr / Paul Siebeck, Postfach 2040, D-72010 Tuebingen Germany. **Tel** 011 49 7071 9230, FAX 011 49 7071 51104, telex 7/262872 mohr d. **ED** Horst Siebert. **Bk Rev. Circ:** 1,200.
 Desc: A journal of current facts of the world economy.
 Ind/Abst Coal Abstr.; GeoRef; Int. Labour Doc.; LABORDOC; World Agric. Econ. Rural Sociol. Abstr.

ISSN 0726-6685
DD 330.9941063   AT

WESTERN AUSTRALIAN ECONOMIC REVIEW. [West. Aust. econ. rev.]. **VFOAT** WAER. (1981)-. Periodical. English. Two times a year (June, Dec.). 81.40Aus$. Chamber of Commerce Industry of Western Australia, PO Box 6209, 190 Hay Street East, Perth WA 6000 Australia. **Tel** 011 61 9 4217555, FAX 011 61 9 3256550, telex AA 93609 CHACO. ctrl circ.

LC HC462.9 .B87
DD 330.952/005   JA
CEASED

WHITE PAPER ON JAPANESE ECONOMY. Added/Corp Business Intercommunications Inc. Jochi Daigaku. Shakai Keizai Kenkyujo. (19??)-(1994). Periodical. English. **(Subscription address:** Maruzen Company Ltd., PO Box 5050, Import & Export Department, Tokyo 100 31 Japan. **Tel** 011 81 3 32789224.)

ISSN 0782-8233
FI

WIDER WORKING PAPERS. Added/Corp World Institute for Development Economics Research. (Feb. 1986)-. Monographic series. English.
 Ind/Abst World Agric. Econ. Rural Sociol. Abstr.

GW

WIRTSCHAFT IM SUDWESTERN. VFOAT W I S. Vol. 1 (July 1973)-. Periodical. German. Twelve times a year. DM36.00. Pressetelle / Industrie und Handelskammrn im Regierungsbezirk Freiburg, Schnewlinstrasse 11-13, 79098 Freiburg Germany. **Tel** 0761/38-2829, FAX 0761/3858-222.

LC HC261 .W4858   ISSN 0378-5130
AU

WIRTSCHAFT UND GESELLSCHAFT. [Wirtsch. Ges.]. **Added/Corp** Kammer fuer Arbeiter und Angestellte fuer Wien. Vol. 1 (1975)-. Periodical. German. Four times a year. S396.00. Verlag Orac GmbH & Co., Schoenbrunner Str 59 61, A-1050 Vienna Austria. **Tel** 011 43 1 5130651. **ED** Gunther Chaloupek. Index available. cum. index. **Bk Rev. Ad Acc. Circ:** 3,000 (ctrl).
 Desc: Essays and reviews on economic policy.
 Ind/Abst Int. Polit. Sci. Abstr.; PAIS Int. Print.

LC HC417 .G47a
GW

WIRTSCHAFTLICHE ENTWICKLUNG : AFGHANISTAN. Main/Corp Bundesstelle fur Aussenhandelsinformation (Germany). (19??)-. German. Bundesstelle fuer Aussenhandelsinformation, Agrippastrasse 87 93, D-50676 Cologne Germany. **Tel** 011 49 221 2057316, FAX 011 49 221 2057212.

LC HC535 .G43a
GW

WIRTSCHAFTLICHE ENTWICKLUNG : AGYPTEN. Main/Corp Bundesstelle fur Aussenhandelsinformation (Germany). (19??)-. German. Agypten, Blaubach 13, 5 Cologne 1 Germany.

LC HC146 .G47a
GW

WIRTSCHAFTLICHE ENTWICKLUNG : GUATEMALA. Main/Corp Bundesstelle fur Aussenhandelsinformation (Germany). (19??)-. German. Bundesstelle fuer Aussenhandelsinformation, Agrippastrasse 87 93, D-50676 Cologne Germany. **Tel** 011 49 221 2057316, FAX 011 49 221 2057212.

LC HC497.K8 G47a
GW

WIRTSCHAFTLICHE ENTWICKLUNG : KUWAIT. Main/Corp Bundesstelle fur Aussenhandelsinformation (Germany). (19??)-. German. Bundesstelle fuer Aussenhandelsinformation, Agrippastrasse 87 93, D-50676 Cologne Germany. **Tel** 011 49 221 2057316, FAX 011 49 221 2057212.

LC HC578.M6 G45a
GW

WIRTSCHAFTLICHE ENTWICKLUNG : MOCAMBIQUE. Main/Corp Bundesstelle fur Aussenhandelsinformation (Germany). (19??)-. German. Bundesstelle fuer Aussenhandelsinformation, Agrippastrasse 87 93, D-50676 Cologne Germany. **Tel** 011 49 221 2057316, FAX 011 49 221 2057212.

LC HC146 .G47b
GW

WIRTSCHAFTLICHE ENTWICKLUNG : NICARAGUA. Main/Corp Bundesstelle fur Aussenhandelsinformation (Germany). (19??)-. German. Nicaragua, Blaubach 13, 5 Cologne 1 Germany.

LC HC237 .G45a
GW

WIRTSCHAFTLICHE ENTWICKLUNG : VENEZUELA. Main/Corp Bundesstelle fur Aussenhandelsinformation. (Germany). (19??)-. German. Venezuela, Blaubach 13, 5 Cologne 1 Germany.

LC HC497.C9 G47a
GW

WIRTSCHAFTLICHE ENTWICKLUNG : ZYPERN. Main/Corp Bundesstelle fur Aussenhandelsinformation (Germany). (19??)-. German. Bundesstelle fuer Aussenhandelsinformation, Agrippastrasse 87 93, D-50676 Cologne Germany. **Tel** 011 49 221 2057316, FAX 011 49 221 2057212.

LC HC261 .W486   ISSN 0043-6291
AU

WIRTSCHAFTSPOLITISCHE BLAETTER. Added/Corp Bundeskammer der Gewerblichen Wirtschaft (Austria). Vol. 1 March (1954)-. Periodical. German. Six times a year. S348.00. Osterreich Wirtschaftsverlag, Nikolsdorfergasse 7-11, A-1501 Vienna Austria. **Tel** 0222/55-55-85. **ED** Ernst Hofbauer. **Circ:** 4,200.

Business and Economics —Economic History, Conditions

LC HC107.W6 W665
DD 330.9775/005
US
WISCONSIN ECONOMIC INDICATORS.
See Business and Economics-Labor.

ISSN 0012-1304
GW
CCC
WOCHENBERICHT - DEUTSCHES INSTITUT FUER WIRTSCHAFTSFORSCHUNG. (WOCHENBERICHT.). [Wochenber. - Dtsch. Inst. Wirtschaftsforsch.]. **Main/Corp** Deutsches Institut fuer Wirtschaftsforschung. Vol. 1, (Jan. 1928)-Vol. 8, (Feb. 1928)- New Series Vol. 1, (Apr. 1928)-. Periodical. German. One time a week. $148.16. Duncker und Humblot Verlag, Postfach 410329, D-12113 Berlin Germany. **Tel** 011 49 30 79000612, 011 49 30 79000613. **ED** Klaus Henkner.
Ind/Abst World Agric. Econ. Rural Sociol. Abstr.

ISSN 0085-8293
US
WORLD BANK ATLAS. [World Bank atlas]. **Added/Corp** World Bank. International Bank for Reconstruction and Development. **VFOAT** Atlas. (1967)-. English (French and Spanish). One time a year. $7.95. World Bank Publications, 1818 H Street Northwest, Washington DC 20043. **Tel** (202)473-1155, (202)473-1155, FAX (202)522-3224, telex WUI 64145 WORLDBANK. **Continues** World Bank Atlas of Per Capita Product and Population.
Desc: Provides data on population, Gross National Product, and GNP per capita in current US dollars.

LC HD9000.4 .W68
ISSN 1351-8968
UK
●**WORLD COMMODITY FORECASTS. FOOD, FEEDSTUFFS, AND BEVERAGES.** **Added/Corp** Economist Intelligence Unit (Great Britain). **VFOAT** Food, Feedstuffs, and Beverages; WFC : Food, Feedstuffs, and Beverages. (June 1993)-. Trade Publication. English. Six times a year. $575.00. The Economist Intelligence Unit, 40 Duke Street, London W1A 1DW United Kingdom. **Tel** 011 44 171 8301000. (**Subscription address:** Economist Intelligence Unit / North America Subscriptions, 111 West 57th Street, New York NY 10019. **Tel** 800 938-4685, (212)554-0600, FAX (212)586-1181, (212)586-1182.) **Separated from** World Commodity Forecasts, 0267-6303.

LC HD
ISSN 0256-7687
DD 330.9
UDC 33 (100)
SZ
●**WORLD DATA.** (1994)-. Periodical. English. One time a year. $275.00. World Bank Publications, 1818 H Street Northwest, Washington DC 20043. **Tel** (202)473-1155, (202)473-1155, FAX (202)522-3224, telex WUI 64145 WORLDBANK. available on CD-ROM.
Desc: Profiles socioeconomic indicators and surveys economies.

LC HC59.69 .W68
US
WORLD DEVELOPMENT INDICATORS [COMPUTER FILE]. See Business and Economics-Economic Assistance and Development.

LC HC59 .A169
DD 330.9/005
US
●**WORLD ECONOMIC AND SOCIAL SURVEY.** **Added/Corp** United Nations. Dept. for Economic and Social Information and Policy Analysis. (1994)-. Government Publication. English. One time a year. Price varies per volume. United Nations Publications, 2 United Nations Plaza, Room DC2 0853, Department 007C, New York NY 10017. **Tel** (212)963-8303, (800)253-9646. **Continues** World Economic Survey (New York, N.Y.), 0084-1714.
Desc: Reviews the major differences in economic circumstances among countries and regions, and forecasts short-term global and regional trends.

LC HC10 .W7977
ISSN 0197-811X
DD 330.9/005
US
WORLD ECONOMIC BULLETIN. [World econ. bull.]. Vol. 1 (Spring 1979)-. Bulletin. English. DRI McGraw Hill, 24 Hartwell Avenue, Lexington MA 02173. **Tel** (617)863-5100, FAX (617)860-6464, (617)860-6416.

LC HC59.15 .W67
UK
●**WORLD ECONOMIC FACTBOOK, THE.** **Added/Corp** Euromonitor PLC. (1993)-. Trade Publication. English. $290.00. Euromonitor Publications Ltd., 60-61 Britton Street, London EC1M 5NA United Kingdom. **Tel** 011 44 171 2518024, FAX 011 44 171 6083149, telex 21120. (**Subscription address:** Gale Research Co., 835 Penobscot Building, Detroit MI 48226. **Tel** (800)347-4253.)
Desc: Presents essential economic, demographic and political information on the world's principal countries.

LC HC59 .A1692
US
TITLE CHANGE
WORLD ECONOMIC SURVEY : A READER. **Added/Corp** United Nations. Dept. of International Economic and Social Affairs. (1992)-(1993). Government Publication. English. United Nations Publications, 2 United Nations Plaza, Room DC2 0853, Department 007C, New York NY 10017. **Tel** (212)963-8303, (800)253-9646. **Continued by** World Economic Survey (New York, N.Y.). Student Edition.

LC HC59 .A169
ISSN 0084-1714
DD 330.9/005
US
TITLE CHANGE
WORLD ECONOMIC SURVEY (NEW YORK, N.Y.). (WORLD ECONOMIC SURVEY.). **Added/Corp** United Nations. Dept. of Economic and Social Affairs. United Nations. Centre for Development Planning, Projections, and Policies. United Nations. Dept. of International Economic and Social Affairs. (1955)-(1993). Government Publication. English. United Nations Publications, 2 United Nations Plaza, Room DC2 0853, Department 007C, New York NY 10017. **Tel** (212)963-8303, (800)253-9646. **Continues** World Economic Report. **Continued by** World Economic and Social Survey.
Desc: Reviews the major differences in economic circumstances among countries and regions, and forecasts short-term global and regional trends.
Ind/Abst Predicasts Forecasts (?-?).

US
●**WORLD ECONOMIC SURVEY. STUDENT EDITION.** **Added/Corp** United Nations. Dept. of International Economic and Social Affairs. (1992/1993)-. Government Publication. English. One time a year. $10.00. United Nations Publications, 2 United Nations Plaza, Room DC2 0853, Department 007C, New York NY 10017. **Tel** (212)963-8303, (800)253-9646. **Continues** World Economic Survey (New York, N.Y.). Reader.
Desc: For use in graduate and undergraduate economics classes. Reviews major differences in economic circumstances among countries and regions, and forecasts short-term global and regional trends.

LC HD82 .W68
DD 330.9/005
UK
WORLD LINK. **Added/Corp** World Link Publications. (Feb. 1988)-. Periodical. English. Six times a year. $175.00. Euromoney Publications PLC, Nestor House, Playhouse Yard, London EC4Z 5EX United Kingdom. **Tel** 011 44 171 7798888, FAX 011 44 171 7798630, telex 290700 EUROMON G. (**Subscription address:** Euromoney Publications PLC, Perrymount Road Haywards Heath, West Sussex RH16 3DH United Kingdom. **Tel** 011 44 1444 440421.)
Desc: Addresses the concerns of global businesses. Written for businessmen and political leaders. Provides senior corporate and financial executives with information on direct investment, management techniques, technological innovations and trade developments.

LC HC10 .W825
ISSN 0749-5846
DD 330.9/005
US
WORLD MODEL HISTORICAL DATA. [World model hist. data]. English. One time a year. WEFA / Philadelphia, PO Box 8500, Suite 1995, Philadelphia PA 19178. **Tel** (215)667-6000, telex 710 6700575.

LC HC59 .E387a
ISSN 0424-3331
DD 338.5/443/05
UK
WORLD OUTLOOK. **Main/Corp** Economist Intelligence Unit (Great Britain). **VFOAT** EIU World Outlook. (1969)-. English. One time a year. $350.79. The Economist Intelligence Unit, 40 Duke Street, London W1A 1DW United Kingdom. **Tel** 011 44 171 8301000. (**Subscription address:** Economist Intelligence Unit / North America Subscriptions, 111 West 57th Street, New York NY 10019. **Tel** 800 938-4685, (212)554-0600, FAX (212)586-1181, (212)586-1182.) **ED** Gerald Roberts. available on an online database from Lexis-Nexis.
Desc: Provides separate detailed forecasts of likely trends in the economies of over 160 countries.

LC HC59 .W668
US
WORLD RESOURCES DATA DISKETTE [COMPUTER FILE]. **Added/Corp** World Resources Institute. (19??)-. English. One time a year. $99.95. WRI Publications, PO Box 4852, Baltimore MD 21211. **Tel** (800)822-0504.

LC HC59 .W669
ISSN 1043-5573
DD 330.9/0021
US
WORLD TABLES (BALTIMORE, MD.). (WORLD TABLES.). [World tables]. **Added/Corp** World Bank. International Bank for Reconstruction and Development. Socio-Economic Data Division. International Finance Corporation. **VFOAT** WT. (1976)-. English. One time a year. $39.95. World Bank Publications, 1818 H Street Northwest, Washington DC 20043. **Tel** (202)473-1155, (202)473-1155, FAX (202)522-3224, telex WUI 64145 WORLDBANK. (**Subscription address:** World Bank Publications, PO Box 7247-8619, Books Department, Philadelphia PA 19170.)

Desc: Makes available the World Bank's collection of economic, demographic and social data on most countries and territories of the world.

LC D839 .W65
ISSN 0264-0872
DD 909.82
US
UDC 930.9
WORLD VIEW (NEW YORK, N.Y.). See History.

LC HC107.W9 W944
ISSN 0163-5433
DD 330.9/787/03
US
WYOMING ISSUES. [Wyo. issu.]. Periodical. English. Four times a year. $8.00. PO Box 3925, University of Wyoming, Laramie WY 82071.

LC HC463.Y28 Y33
JA
YAEYAMA YORAN. **Added/Corp** Yaeyama-Shicho, Japan. (19??)-. Periodical. Japanese. Yaeyama-Shicho, 2-32 Senzaki 1-chome, Naha Okinawa-ken Japan.

US
YALE SERIES IN ECONOMIC HISTORY. (19??)-. English. Irregular. Yale University Press, PO Box 209040, New Haven CT 06520. **Tel** (203)432-0940, (800)987-7323, FAX (203)432-0948.

ISSN 1054-6316
DD 967
US
ZAIRE (SYRACUSE, N.Y.). (ZAIRE : A POLITICAL AND ECONOMIC FORECAST.). [Zaire]. **Added/Corp** Political Risk Services (IBC USA (Publications) Inc.). (19??)-. English. $325.00. Political Risk Services, 6320 Fly Road, Suite 102, PO Box 248, East Syracuse NY 13057-0248. **Tel** (315)431-0511, FAX (315)431-0200.
Desc: Assesses the factors affecting the prospects for business and trade. Each report focuses specifically on business needs such as finding and developing markets, determining currency movements, or making judgements about capital investments or corporate security.

LC HC591.C6
GW
ZAIRE : WIRTSCHAFTLICHE ENTWICKLUNG. **Main/Corp** Bundesstelle fur Aussenhandelsinformation (Germany). German. DM2.00. Bundesstelle fuer Aussenhandelsinformation, Agrippastrasse 87 93, D-50676 Cologne Germany. **Tel** 011 49 221 2057316, FAX 011 49 221 2057212.

ISSN 1054-6324
DD 968
US
ZAMBIA (SYRACUSE, N.Y.). (ZAMBIA : A POLITICAL AND ECONOMIC FORECAST.). [Zambia]. **Added/Corp** Political Risk Services (IBC USA (Publications) Inc.). (19??)-. English. $325.00. Political Risk Services, 6320 Fly Road, Suite 102, PO Box 248, East Syracuse NY 13057-0248. **Tel** (315)431-0511, FAX (315)431-0200.
Desc: Assesses the factors affecting the prospects for business and trade. Each report focuses specifically on business needs such as finding and developing markets, determining currency movements, or making judgements about capital investments or corporate security.

AU
ZEITSCHRIFT FUER GEMEINWIRTSCHAFT. (19??)-. Periodical. German. Six times a year. S660.00. Verband der Offentlichen Wirtschaft und Gemeinwirtschaft Osterreichs, Stadiongasse 6-8, A 1016 Vienna Austria. **Tel** 0043 1 4082204, 0043 1 4088206, FAX 0043 4082602. Index available. **Bk Rev**, (Qty: 15-20). **Ad Acc**. Full Page (B&W) S1800.00. **Circ**: 1,200. **Continues** Gemeinwirtschaft.
Desc: Covers social development and changes in both public and social economy.

LC HC985.A1
DD 330.967/41/005
GW
ZENTRALAFRIKANISCHE REPUBLIK, WIRTSCHAFTLICHE ENTWICKLUNG. Periodical. German. One time a year. DM3.00. Bundesstelle fuer Aussenhandelsinformation, Agrippastrasse 87 93, D-50676 Cologne Germany. **Tel** 011 49 221 2057316, FAX 011 49 221 2057212.

LC HC547.C4 G47a
DD 330/338
GW
ZENTRALAFRIKANISHCHES KAISERREICH : WIRTSCHAFTLICHE ENTWICKLUNG. **Main/Corp** Bundesstelle fur Aussenhandelsinformation (Germany). (19??)-. German. Bundesstelle fuer Aussenhandelsinformation, Agrippastrasse 87 93, D-50676 Cologne Germany. **Tel** 011 49 221 2057316, FAX 011 49 221 2057212.

ISSN 1054-6332
DD 968
US
ZIMBABWE (SYRACUSE, N.Y.). (ZIMBABWE : A POLITICAL AND ECONOMIC FORECAST.). [Zimbabwe]. **Added/Corp** Political Risk Services (IBC USA (Publications) Inc.). (19??)-. English. $325.00. Political Risk Services, 6320 Fly Road, Suite

102, PO Box 248, East Syracuse NY 13057-0248. **Tel** (315)431-0511, FAX (315)431-0200.
Desc: Assesses the factors affecting the prospects for business and trade. Each report focuses specifically on business needs such as finding and developing markets, determining currency movements, or making judgements about capital investments or corporate security.

LC HC337.P7 A29

PL

ZYCIE GOSPODARCZE. (1946)-. Periodical. Polish. One time a week. $78.00. **(Subscription address:** Ars Polona-Ruch, PO Box 1001, Krakowskie Przedmiescie 7, 00-068 Warsaw Poland. **Tel** 011 48 22 261201.**)**

LC HC415.2.A1

GW

ZYPERN, TURKISCH VERWALTETER TEIL : WIRTSCHAFTLICHE ENTWICKLUNG. Main/Corp Bundesstelle fur Aussenhandelsinformation (Germany). German. DM2.00. Bundesstelle fuer Aussenhandelsinformation, Agrippastrasse 87 93, D-50676 Cologne Germany. **Tel** 011 49 221 2057316, FAX 011 49 221 2057212.

LC HC415.2.A1 Z94
DD 330.95645

GW

ZYPERN, WIRTSCHAFT IN ZAHLEN UND WIRTSCHAFTSDOKUMENTATION.
Added/Corp Bundesstelle fuer Aussenhandelsinformation (Germany). (Aug. 1984)-. Periodical. German. Bundesstelle fuer Aussenhandelsinformation, Agrippastrasse 87 93, D-50676 Cologne Germany. **Tel** 011 49 221 2057316, FAX 011 49 221 2057212. *Continues Zypern, Wirtschaft in Zahlen.*

LC HC415.2.A1 Z95
DD 330.95645/005

GW

ZYPERN, WIRTSCHAFTLICHE ENTWICKLUNG. (19??)-. German. One time a year. 3.00. Bundesstelle fuer Aussenhandelsinformation, Agrippastrasse 87 93, D-50676 Cologne Germany. **Tel** 011 49 221 2057316, FAX 011 49 221 2057212.

INTERNATIONAL ECONOMIC RELATIONS

FR

1999 NOW : A EUROPEAN REVIEW PUBLISHED QUATERLY BY IBM EUROPE. Added/Corp IBM Europe. **VFOAT** Nineteen Ninety-Nine Now. Spring (1991)-. Periodical. English. Four times a year. IBM Europe, Tour Pascal, Cedex 40, 92075 Paris La Defense France. *Continues 1992 Now.*

ISSN 1075-3281
DD 382 US

AAP INSIDE EXPORT. [AAP inside export]. **Added/Corp** Association of American Publishers. International Division. **VFOAT** Association of American Publishers Inside Export. (Jan./Feb. 1990)-. Periodical. English. Six times a year. $50.00. Association of American Publishers Inc., 220 East 23rd Street/2nd Floor, New York NY 10010. **Tel** (212)689-8920.

ISSN 1061-2920
DD 337 US

ACAPA SERIAL. [ACAPA ser.]. **Added/Corp** American Council on Asian and Pacific Affairs. **VAT** American Council on Asian and Pacific Affairs Serial. No. 1 (1992)-. Monographic series. English. Price varies per volume. ACAPA, 7700 Leesburg Dr., Bethesda MD 20817.

LC HF1410 .B3
DD 382/.3/05

ISSN 0183-5017
FR
SUSPENDED

ACTUALITES (PARIS). See Business and Economics-Banks and Banking.

LC HC800.A1 A34
DD 330.96/005

ISSN 0144-8234
UK

AED (LONDON, ENGLAND). (AED : AFRICA ECONOMIC DIGEST). **VFOAT** Africa Economic Digest; A.E.D. Vol. 1, No. 1 (May 16, 1980)-. Periodical. English. Twenty-six times a year (Fri.). $350.00. Concord Press of Nigeria Ltd., 26 32 Whistler Street, Highbury London N5 1NH United Kingdom. **Tel** 011 44 181 3595335, FAX 011 44 181 3599173, telex 262505. **ED** Roy Laishley. Index available. cum. index. **Bk Rev**. **Ad Acc**. **Circ:** 6,000 (ctrl).
Desc: Covers the whole sub Saharan Africa every week. With a country-by-country analysis and regular special reports on individual economies and key industries, it keeps you up to date with all the latest aid and currency information telling you exactly where to find key business opportunities.
Ind/Abst Infomat Int. Bus.

LC HC59.7 .A776
DD 330.9/172/4

ISSN 0304-3754
US
CCC

ALTERNATIVES (AMSTERDAM). (ALTERNATIVES SOCIAL TRANSFORMATION AND HUMANE GOVERNANCE.). [Alternatives]. **Added/Corp** Institute for World Order. Centre for the Study of Developing Societies. International Peace Research Institute. World Order Models Project. Vol. 1 (1975)-. Periodical. English. Four times a year (Feb., May, Aug., Nov.). $78.00. Lynne Rienner Publishers, 1800 30th Street, Suite 314, Boulder CO 80301. **Tel** (303)444-6684, FAX (303)444-0824. **ED** D. L. Sheth (editor's address: Centre for the Study of Developing Societies, 29 Rajpur Road, Delhi 110054 India). Index available. **Ad Acc**. available on microfilm and microfiche from University Microfilms International (UMI). Documents available from UMI Article Clearinghouse, Documents on Demand.
Desc: Promotes wide-ranging discussions of the future of the world. Encourages autonomy and dignity in all individuals and all peoples. Promotes equity and justice within and among societies, the elimination of oppression and war in human affairs, and the restoration of harmony, between humanity and nature.
Ind/Abst ABC POL SCI; Altern. Press Index; Am. Hist. Life (1975-1979); Curr. Cit.; Energy Inf. Abstr.; Energy Res. Abstr. (1975-); Environ. Abstr.; Fish Rev.; Gen. Period. Index (1985-); Geogr. Abstr. Human Geogr.; Int. Bibliogr. Sociol.; Int. Dev. Abstr. (?-?); Int. Polit. Sci. Abstr.; Linguist. Lang. Behav. Abstr.; Mag. Index Plus (1989-); New Testam. Abstr.; Newsp. Period. Abstr. (1989-); PAIS Int. Print (1991); Peace Res. Abstr. J (1987-1988); Soc. Plann. Policy Dev. Abstr.; Soc. Sci. Cit. Index [Select. Cov.]; Sociol. Abstr.; Mag. Index (1983-); Wildl. Rev.

LC WMLC 93/2659

ISSN 0955-5129
UK
TITLE CHANGE

ANGLO JAPANESE JOURNAL. **Added/Corp** Anglo-Japanese Economic Institute. Vol. 2, No. 4 (Jan./March 1989)-(199?). Periodical. English. Anglo-Japanese Economic Institute, Morely House, 314-322 Regent Street, London W1R 5AD United Kingdom. *Continues Anglo-Japanese Economic Journal, 1355-2759. Continued by Euro Japanese Journal.*

LC HF1573 .A56
DD 337.4940172/4/05

SZ

ANNUAIRE SUISSE-TIERS MONDE. **Added/Corp** Institut Universitaire d'Etudes du Developpement. **VFOAT** Annuaire Suisse Tiers Monde; Jahrbuch Schweiz Dritte Welt. (1981)-. Periodical. French (German). One time a year. $33.95. Institut Universite d'Etudes du Developpement, 24 rue Rothschild, Casa Postale 136, CH-1211 Geneva 21 Switzerland. **Tel** 011 41 22 7315940, FAX 011 41 22 7384416, telex 22810 IUED-CH, . Index available. **Circ:** 1,400.
Desc: Economic relations between Switzerland and the Third World.

LC HG3879 .G76A
DD 332/.042/0601

ISSN 0735-2034
US

ANNUAL REPORT / GROUP OF THIRTY.
See Business and Economics-Banks and Banking.

LC HG3881 .I634
DD 332.1/52

ISSN 0250-7498
US

ANNUAL REPORT OF THE EXECUTIVE BOARD - INTERNATIONAL MONETARY FUND. See Business and Economics-Banks and Banking.

GW

ARBEITSBERICHTE DES IBERO-AMERIKA INSTITUT FUER WIRTSCHAFTSFORSCHUNG AN DER UNIVERSITAET GOETTINGEN. Main/Corp Universitat Gottingen. Ibero-Amerika Institut fur Wirtschaftsforschung. Issue 1 (1968)-. Monographic series. German. Irregular. Price varies per volume. Verlag Otto Schwartz & Company, Annastrasse 7, D-37075 Goettingen Germany. **Tel** 011 49 551 31051, 011 49 551 31052, FAX 011 49 551 372812.

ISSN 1195-499X
DD 382 CN

ASIA-PACIFIC BULLETIN. [Asia-Pac. bull.]. **Added/Corp** Canada Asia Accord Association. China Accord (Canada) Association. Vol. 3, No. 4 (Autumn 1991)-. Bulletin. English. Four times a year (Mar., June, Sept., Dec.). 24.01Can$. Canada Asia Accord Association, 607 10136 100th Street, Edmonton Alberta T5J 0P1 Canada. **Tel** (403)424-9897. *Continues China Accord Bulletin., 1197-5326.*

ISSN 1351-3958
Pr Rev. HK

ASIAN ECONOMIC JOURNAL : JOURNAL OF THE EAST ASIAN ECONOMIC ASSOCIATION. **Added/Corp** East Asian Economic Association. **VFOAT** Journal of the East Asian Economic Association. Vol. 1 (Mar. 1987)-. Periodical. English. Three times a year (Mar.,

July, Nov.). $60.00. East Asian Economic Association, The Chinese University of Hong Kong, Shatin Hong Kong. **Tel** 011 852 0 26036424, (852)547-8313, FAX 011 852 0 26035245, (852)548-6319, telex 50301 CUHK HX. **(Subscription address:** Blackwell Publishers / UK, 108 Cowley Road, Oxford OX4 1JF United Kingdom. **Tel** 011 44 1865 791100, FAX 011 44 1865 791347.**) ED** Professor Shinichi Ichimura (editor's address: Osaka International University, 50-1, Sugi, 3-chome Hirakata, Osaka, 573-01, Japan) and Professor Steven N.S. Cheung (editor's address: School of Economics, The University of Hong Kong, Pokfulam Road, Hong Kong). **Bk Rev**. **Ad Acc**. **Adv Mgr Tel** (852)547-8313.
Desc: This journal focuses on the economies of East Asia.

LC HC411.A1 A8

ISSN 0403-4465
FR

ASIE NOUVELLE, L'. [Asie nouv.]. Vol. 1 (1951)-. Periodical. French. Irregular. Chambre de Commerce-Franco Asi, 94 rue St. Lazare, 75009 Paris France. **Tel** 011 33 1 47446701. **ED** Ameral Andre Roux.
Desc: Economy in Southeast Asia and the Near East.

LC HF1371
DD 382

ISSN 0004-8216
SZ

AUSSENWIRTSCHAFT: ZEITSCHRIFT FUER INTERNATIONALE WIRTSCHAFTSBEZIEHUNGEN.
Added/Corp St. Gall, Switzerland. Handelshochschule. Schweizerisches Institut fuer Aussenwirtschafts und Marktforschung. **VFOAT** Zeitschrift fuer Internationale Wirtschaftsbeziehungen. Vol. 1 (Mar. 1946)-. Periodical. German (English and French). Four times a year. 100.00F. Verlag Ruegger AG, Kasernenstrasse 1, CH-7007 Chur Switzerland. **Tel** 011 41 81 235111. **ED** H Hauser. Index available. **Bk Rev**. **Ad Acc**. **Circ:** 1,600 (ctrl).
Desc: Covers the economy, law and politics. Targeted toward economic scientists.
Ind/Abst Econ. Lit. Index (199?-); J. Econ. Lit.

LC HG3000.L84 B294
DD 332/.05

ISSN 0956-5574
UK

BARCLAYS ECONOMIC REVIEW. See Business and Economics-Banks and Banking.

ISSN 0072-0623
DD 337 SZ

BASIC INSTRUMENTS AND SELECTED DOCUMENTS. SUPPLEMENT : GENERAL AGREEMENTS ON TARIFFS AND TRADE. [Basic instrum. sel. doc. Suppl. - Gen. Agreem. Tariffs Trade]. **Main/Corp** General Agreement on Tariffs and Trade (Organization). **VFOAT** General Agreement on Tariffs and Trade. Vol. 1 (1953)-. Periodical. English (French and Spanish). One time a year. 60.00F. General Agreement on Tariffs and Trade / GATT, Centre William Rappard, 154 rue de Lausanne, 1211 Geneva 21 Switzerland. **Tel** 011 41 22 7395111, 011 41 22 7395019, FAX 011 41 22 7395458. **(Subscription address:** UNIPUB, 4611 F Assembly Drive, Lanham MD 20706. **Tel** (800)274-4888, (301)459-7666.**)**
Desc: All decisions and reports adopted by the GATT contracting parties.

US

BAXTER. (19??)-. English. Twenty-six times a year. $195.00. Baxter, 1030 East Putnam Avenue, Greenwich CT 06830. **Tel** (203)637-4559.

GW

BEITRAEGE ZUM INTERNATIONALEN WIRTSCHAFTSRECHT UND ATOMENERGIERECHT. Added/Corp Universitaat Goettingen. Institut fuer Voelkerrecht. Vol. 1 (1963)-. Periodical. German. Irregular. DM15.80 (latest volume). Verlag Otto Schwartz & Company, Annastrasse 7, D-37075 Goettingen Germany. **Tel** 011 49 551 31051, 011 49 551 31052, FAX 011 49 551 372812.

LC HF1410 .K52B
DD 337/.05

GW

BERICHT DES PRASIDENTEN UEBER DIE TATIGKEIT DES INSTITUTS. Main/Corp Kiel. Universitat. Institut fur Weltwirtschaft. German. Institut fur Weltwirtschaft an der Universitat Kiel, Dusternbrooker Weg 120-122, W-2300 Kiel 1 Germany.

LC HC186 .B71248
DD 330.981/005

US

BRAZIL FILE : MONTHLY PUBLICATION OF THE INSTITUTE OF BRAZILIAN BUSINESS AND PUBLIC MANAGEMENT ISSUES. Added/Corp Institute of Brazilian Business and Public Management Issues. Vol. 1, No. 1 (Sept. 1992)-. English. Twelve times a year (Jan., July, and Aug.). $45.00. Institute of Brazilian Issues, 2020 K Street Northwest, Suite 230, Washington DC 20052. **Tel** (202)994-5205.

Business and Economics —International Economic Relations

DD 337   ISSN 1044-2944   US
BRITISH-AMERICAN DEAL REVIEW, THE. [Brit.-Am. deal rev.]. **VFOAT** British American Deal Review. 1989-. Periodical. English. Four times a year. $470.00. British-American Deal Review, 730 5th Avenue/Suite 1906, New York NY 10019. **Tel** (212)265-7990, **FAX** (212)265-5864. **ED** Mark Dixon. Index available. **Ad Acc. Circ:** 800 (ctrl).
Desc: Research report about British acquisitions in America; provides information on recent transactions and analysis of trends.

US
BROOKINGS DISCUSSION PAPERS IN INTERNATIONAL ECONOMICS. **Added/Corp** Brookings Institution. (19??)-. Academic Scholarly Publication. English. Irregular. Free on request. Brookings Institution, 1775 Massachusetts Avenue Northwest, Washington DC 20036-2188. **Tel** (202)797-6255, (800)275-1447. **(Subscription address:** Brookings Institution, PO Box 037, Washington DC 20042. **Tel** (202)797-6255.)

DD 382   ISSN 0007-392X   BU   SUSPENDED
BULGARIAN FOREIGN TRADE. See Business and Economics-Commerce.

FR
BULLETIN DU POSTE D'EXPANSION ECONOMIQUE. Bulletin. French. Centre Francais du Commerce Exterieur, 10 Avenue d'Iena, 75783 Paris Cedex 16 France. **Tel** 011 33 1 40733415.

FR
BULLETIN OFFICIEL DES IMPOTS. (19??)-. Bulletin. French. Imprimerie Nationale / France, BP 514, 59505 Douai Cedex France. **Tel** 011 33 27 937090.

LC K2 .U85   ISSN 0269-2694
DD 341.7/51   UK   CCC
BUTTERWORTHS JOURNAL OF INTERNATIONAL BANKING AND FINANCIAL LAW. See Business and Economics-Banks and Banking.

ISSN 0992-3950
UDC 380.81   FR
CAHIERS D'ESPACES PARIS, LES. (LES CAHIERS D'ESPACES.). [Cah. Espaces Paris]. (198?)-. Periodical. French. Five times a year. $328.08. Edns Touristiques Europeennes, 8 rue Cels, 75014 Paris France. **Tel** 011 33 1 43275590.

DD 337/.05   ISSN 0825-5822   CN
Pr Rev.
CAHIERS DU CETAI, LES. [Cah. CETAI]. **Added/Corp** Ecole des Hautes Etudes Commerciales (Montreal, Quebec). Centre d'Etudes en Administration Internationale. **VAT** Cahiers du Centre d'Etudes en Administration Internationale. (197?)-. Monographic series. English (French). Irregular (10-14 times per year). Free on request. Center for International Business Studies, 5255 Avenue Decelles, Montreal Quebec H3T 1V6 Canada. **Tel** (514)340-6186, **FAX** (514)340-6177. **ED** Dr. T. Hafsi. cum. index.

DD 338.91   BD
CAHIERS DU CURDES. **Added/Corp** Universite du Burundi. Centreu Universitaire de Recherche pour le Developpement Economique et Social. No. 1 (June 1982)-. Periodical. French. Four times a year. Universite de Burundi, Centre Universitaire de Recherche pour le Developpement Economique et Social, Postale 1049, Bujumbura Burundi.

LC HF1371   ISSN 1190-9706
DD 382   CN
•**CANADA'S EXPORT STRATEGY, THE INTERNATIONAL TRADE BUSINESS PLAN. 2, AGRICULTURE AND FOOD PRODUCTS. See** Agriculture.

DD 972.9   ISSN 0271-6577   PR
CARIBBEAN STUDIES NEWSLETTER. See Political Science-International Relations.

PE
CARTA AL EJECUTIVO ANDINO. **Added/Corp** Instituto Coordinador del Comercio Internacional. Carta al Ejecutivo Andino. No. 1 (Aug. 28, 1975)-. Periodical. Spanish. One time a week. $120.00 US and Canada; $100.00 Peru; $115.00 Pan-American nations; $130.00 other. Promotores y Consultores Andinos, Casilla 4857, Lima 100 Peru. **Tel** 011 51 14 714984. **ED** Oscar Castaneda Arrascue. **Bk Rev. Circ:** 1,000.
Desc: Contains economic data on the Andes countries. Covers the course of the processes of integration in Latin America. Offers economic information for executives.

LC HF3500.7 .A13   ISSN 0962-2543
DD 330.947/005   UK
CENTRAL EUROPEAN. No. 1 (Apr. 1991)-. Periodical. English. Ten times a year. $410.69. Euromoney Publications PLC, Nestor House, Playhouse Yard, London EC4Z 5EX United Kingdom. **Tel** 011 44 171 7798888, **FAX** 011 44 171 7798630, telex 290700 EUROMON G. **ED** Gavin Gray. **Ad Acc, Adv Mgr:** Susan Christopherson. **Circ:** 5000.
Desc: Covers all economic activity in Central and Eastern Europe, including changes in commercial law, tax structures and accountancy regulations. Covers business news, the latest investments, joint ventures, and contracts. Provides features on specific businesses, trades and industries with profiles of western and indigenous companies.

NE
•**CENTRAL EUROPEAN ECONOMIC REVIEW. See** Business and Economics-Economic History, Conditions.

ISSN 0952-9756
UK
CHINA-BRITAIN TRADE REVIEW. See Business and Economics-Commerce.

LC HF3831 .C47
DD 382/.0951/005   HK   TITLE CHANGE
CHINA MARKET. **Added/Corp** Ching Chi Tao Pao She. **VFOAT** Chung-Kuo Shih Chang. No. 1 (1982)-No. 129 (1993). Periodical. English (Chinese and English). Economic Information & Agency, 342 Hennessy Road, 10-16th Floor, Hong Kong Hong Kong. **Tel** 011 852 25738217, **FAX** 011 852 8388304, telex 60647 EICC HX. **ED** Chan Park-qun. cum. index. **Bk Rev. Ad Acc. Circ:** 20,000 (ctrl). **Continues** Economic Reporter. **Continued by** Economic Reporter (Hong Kong : 1993).
Desc: Supplies information on the China market, investment opportunities, and new laws and regulations concerning international economic relations and trade.
Ind/Abst Int. Labour Doc.

LC HF6 .B43   ISSN 0185-0601   MX
COMERCIO EXTERIOR. See Business and Economics-Commerce.

LC HF3229.Q4 C65   ISSN 0820-0025
DD 382/.09714/0021   CN
COMMERCE INTERNATIONAL DU QUEBEC. [Commer. int. Que.]. (19??)-. French. One time a year. 7.95Can$. Ministere des Communications, PO Box 1005, Quebec Quebec G1K 7B5 Canada. **Tel** (418)643-5150. **Formed by the union of** Importations Internationales du Quebec, 0709-9908 **and** Exportations Internationales DU Quebec, 0704-5956.

IT
COMMERCIO ESTERO CINESE. (19??)-. Italian. Twelve times a year. Libreria Marco Polo, Via del Seminario 103, 00186 Rome Italy. **Tel** 011 39 6 6785764.

LC HC701 .C66
DD 330.9171/7   UK
COMMUNIST ECONOMIES AND ECONOMIC TRANSFORMATION. **Added/Corp** Centre for Research into Communist Economies. Vol. 3, No. 1 (1991)-. Periodical. English. Four times a year (Mar., Jun., Sep., Dec). $372.00. Carfax Publishing Company, PO Box 25, Abingdon, Oxfordshire OX14 3UE United Kingdom. **Tel** 011 44 1235 555335, **FAX** 011 44 1235 553559, telex 817484. **ED** Ljubo Sirc, Jacek Rostowski & Roger Clarke. Index available. **Continues** Communist Economies, 0954-0113.
Desc: Covers progress in stabilization, liberalization and privatization.

LC HC60 .U447a
DD 338.9/1/09172405   US
COMPENDIUM OF PROJECTS AS OF 31 DECEMBER ... . Main/Corp United Nations Development Programme. **Added/Corp** United Nations Development Programme. Documentation and Statistics Office. **VFOAT** UNDP Compendium of Ongoing Projects. (1988)-. Government Publication. English. Irregular. United Nations Publications, 2 United Nations Plaza, Room DC2 0853, Department 007C, New York NY 10017. **Tel** (212)963-8303, (800)253-9646. **Continues** Compendium of Approved Projects, 0379-8119.

LC HC60 .U66A   ISSN 0742-3012
DD 353.0089   US
CONGRESSIONAL PRESENTATION. **Main/Corp** United States Trade and Development Program. English. One time a year. US Agency for International Development, Economic Data Branch, Washington DC 20523.

LC HC121 .C63   ISSN 0326-4068
DD 330.98/0005   AG
Pr Rev.
CONTRIBUCIONES : PUBLICACION TRIMESTRAL DEL CENTRO INTERDISCIPLINARIO DE ESTUDIOS SOBRE EL DESARROLLO LATINOAMERICANO. **Added/Corp** Centro Interdisciplinario de Estudios Sobre el Desarrollo Latinoamericano. No. 1 (Jan./Mar. 1984)-. Periodical. Spanish (summaries and/or abstracts in English). Four times a year (Jan., Apr., Jul., Oct). $32.00. CIEDLA / Konrad Adenauer Stift, Leonardo N Alem 690 Piso 20, 1001 Buenos Aires Argentina. **Tel** 011 54 1 3133522, **FAX** 011 54 1 3112902. Index available (published separately, $8.00). **Circ:** 3,500. available in hardback.
Ind/Abst LABORDOC.

IT
Pr Rev.
CORRIERE EUROPEO. (19??)-. Italian (English). Forty-Five times a year. L1000000 Italy; L1050000 other. Pietro Castro Editore, Via M Poggioli 9, 00161 Rome Italy. **Tel** 011 39 6 4959798, **FAX** 011 39 6 491446. **ED** Pietro Castro. Index available. **Bk Rev.** ctrl circ.
Desc: Economic relations between Italy and Eastern Countries.

LC HC59.7 .C77   UY
CUADERNOS DEL TERCER MUNDO. (19??)-. Periodical. Spanish. Twelve times a year. $35.00. ACU S A, Miguel de Corro 1461, Montevideo 11200 Uruguay. **Tel** 011 598 2 496192. **ED** Ruben Aguilar Valenzuela. **Bk Rev. Ad Acc. Circ:** 10,000.
Desc: Publishes articles about the Third World countries (including Africa, Asia and Latin America), describing its politics, history and economics.

LC K1188.B6 C88   ISSN 0883-0517
DD 343/.0965 342.3965   US
CURRENT ISSUES IN INTERNATIONAL SHIP FINANCE. (1984)-. English. Practising Law Institute, 810 Seventh Avenue, New York NY 10019-5818. **Tel** (212)765-5700, **FAX** (212)581-4670 general correspondence, (212)265-4742 orders and billing inquiries. **Continues** Current Issues in Ship Financing, 0883-0592.

ISSN 1014-9600
US
DAILY SUBSISTANCE ALLOWANCE RATES. (19??)-. Government Publication. English. Twelve times a year. $245.00. United Nations Publications, 2 United Nations Plaza, Room DC2 0853, Department 007C, New York NY 10017. **Tel** (212)963-8303, (800)253-9646. **(Subscription address:** United Nations Publications, Subscription Office, PO Box 361, Birmingham AL 35201-0361. **Tel** (800)633-4931, (205)995-1567 (outside US and Canada), **FAX** (205)995-1588.)
Desc: Provides figures on international per diem rates including U.S. dollar/local currency rates and cost of daily room accomodations.

LC HC79.D4 D43   ISSN 1024-2694   SZ
•**DEFENCE AND PEACE ECONOMICS. See** Military and Defense.

LC HC79.D4 D43   ISSN 1043-0717
DD 338   SZ
CODEN DEECEP   TITLE CHANGE
DEFENCE ECONOMICS. See Military and Defense.

GW
DEUTSCH-CHINESISCHES FORUM. German. Frierich Reinake-Verlag GmbH, Hartwiscsstr 3-4, W-2000 Hamburg 76 Germany.

ISSN 1057-9206
US
DEVELOPING NATIONS. (1992)-. Periodical. English. $2.00. Developing Nations, Po Box 3713, Langley Park, Hyattsville MD 20787.

IT
DISCIPLINA SCAMBI CON L ESTERO. Italian. Euroloitalia Editrice SRL, Via XX Settembre 37 / 12, 16121 Genoa Italy.

IT
DOCUMENTAZIONE DOGANALE VALUTARIA E DEGLI SCAMBI CON L'ESTERO. (19??)-. Italian. One time a week. $303.00. Publishing Customs, Via Conca d'Oro 378, 00141 Rome Italy. **Tel** 011 39 6 8102204.

IT
DOCUMENTI COM + CES: QUESTIONI SOCIALI. (19??)-. Italian. Irregular. L123000.00. Office for Official Publications of the European Communities, 2 rue Mercier, 2985 Luxembourg

Luxembourg. **Tel** 011 352 499281, FAX 011 352 292942763. **(Subscription address:** Licosa s.p.a., PO Box 552, 50125 Florence Italy. **Tel** 011 39 55 645415.**)**

ISSN 0338-4454
FR

DOCUMENTS D'ACTUALITE INTERNATIONALE. **Added/Corp** France. Direction de la Documentation. France. Documentation Francaise. France. Ministere des Affaires Etrangeres. Sous-Direction de la Documentation. France. Ministere des Relations Exterieures. Sous-Direction de la Documentation. No. 7 (Feb. 1972)-. Periodical. French. Twenty-four times a year. 400.00F France, 500.00F other (surface mail); 650.00F (airmail). Documentation Francaise, 29 quai Voltaire, 75344 Paris Cedex 7 France. **Tel** 011 33 1 40157000, FAX 011 33 1 40157230, telex 204 826 DOCFRAN. **(Subscription address:** Documentation Francaise, 124 rue Henri Barbusse, 93308 Aubervilliers Cedex France. **Tel** 011 33 1 48395600.**)** ***Continues*** *France. Direction de la Documentation. Documents Officiels - Direction de la Documentation.*

LC HF3626.5 .E16 **ISSN** 1081-8421
DD 337 US

•**EAST/WEST COMMERSANT.** [East/West commersant]. Vol. 2, No. 11 (June 15, 1994)-. Periodical. English. Twenty-two times a year. $425.00. WorldTrade Executive Incorporated, PO Box 761, Concord MA 01742. **Tel** (508)287-0301, FAX (508)287-0302. ***Formed by the union of*** *Commersant International* ***and*** *East/West Business and Finance Alert.*

ISSN 0012-8570
BE
CCC

EAST WEST FORTNIGHTLY BULLETIN. Jan. 12, (1983)-. Bulletin. English. Twenty times a year. 21200F. East West Publications, 10 boulevard Saint Lazare, B 1210 Brussels Belgium. **Tel** 011 32 2 2184349, FAX 011 32 2 2181985, telex 21 108 EUROPE B. **ED** Jan Zoubek. Index available. **Bk Rev**. ctrl circ.
Desc: Reporting on East-West trade, economic and financial developments in East Europe, investments, plans, technology, economic and trade legislation.

LC HF **ISSN** 0835-8451
DD 382.9/142/05 CN
TITLE CHANGE

EC NEWSLETTER - DELEGATION OF THE COMMISSION OF THE EUROPEAN COMMUNITIES. (EC NEWSLETTER = NOUVELLES DE LA CE.). [EC newsl. - Deleg. Comm. Eur. Communities]. **Added/Corp** Commission of the European Communities. Delegation (Canada). **VFOAT** Nouvelles de la CE. No. 1 (Sept. 1987)-(199?). Newsletter. English (French). Delegation of the Commission of the European Communities, 350 Sparks Street/Suite 1110, Ottawa Ontario K1R 7S8 Canada. **Tel** (613)238-6464, FAX (613)238-5191. **ED** Roy Christensen. **Circ:** 1,500 (ctrl). ***Continues*** *Europe (Ottawa, Ont. : 1981), 0712-9874.* ***Split into*** *Nouvelles de l'Union Europeenne, 1196-6491* ***and*** *European Union Newsletter, 1196-6483.*

LC HF1351 .E23
SP

ECONOMIA INTERNACIONAL. **Added/Corp** Universidad Autonoma de Puebla. Programa de Estudios de Economia Internacional. No. 1 (July 1987)-. Periodical. Spanish. Twelve times a year. $71.06. Economia Internacional, Administracion Balmes 213-1-1, 08006 Barcelona Spain. **Tel** 011 34 3 2170256.

LC HB7 .E285 **ISSN** 0012-981X
DD 330.5 IT
Pr Rev.

ECONOMIA INTERNAZIONALE. [Econ. int.]. **Added/Corp** Istituto di Economia Internazionale, Genoa. Vol. 1 (Jan. 1948)-. English (Italian and French). Four times a year. L85000. Istituto di Economia Internazionale, Via Garibaldi 4, 16124 Genova Italy. **Tel** (010)2094202, FAX (010)2094300. **ED** Orlando D'Alauro. Index available. **Bk Rev**. **Circ:** 1,000.
Desc: Papers dealing with international economics and related sectors.
Ind/Abst AGRICOLA; Contents Recent Econ. J.; Econ. Lit. Index; J. Econ. Lit.; Leis., Rec., Tour. Abstr.; PAIS Int. Print; Rural Dev. Abstr.; Stat. Theory Method Abstr. (1959-1963); World Agric. Econ. Rural Sociol. Abstr.

LC HB9 .E39 **ISSN** 0252-8584
DD 338.9/005 CU
CODEN ECDEEN

ECONOMIA Y DESARROLLO. [Econ. desarro.]. No. 1 (Jan./March 1970)-. Periodical. Spanish (summaries and/or abstracts in English). Four times a year. $60.00. Ediciones Cubanas, Obispo 527 Altos ESQ Bernaza, CP 10100 Havana Cuba. **Circ:** 30,000 (ctrl).
Desc: Documentation on the evolution and development of economic problems. Its articles present information on topics in the international sphere, knowledge of which is required in view of the levels attained by the economy and contemporary economics.
Ind/Abst Hisp. Am. Period. Index, HAPI (?-?); Int. Bibliogr. Sociol. (?-?); Int. Labour Doc. (?-?); LABORDOC (?-?); Leis., Rec., Tour. Abstr.; Rural Dev. Abstr. (?-?); Soc. Plann. Policy Dev. Abstr. (?-?); World Agric. Econ. Rural Sociol. Abstr. (?-?).

ISSN 1014-4994
US

ECONOMIC STUDIES. [Econ. stud. - U.N. Econ. Comm. Eur.]. **Added/Corp** United Nations. Economic Commission for Europe. **VFOAT** Economic Studies of the Economic Commission for Europe. No. 1 (1989)-. Monographic series. English. Irregular (1-2 issues per year). $43.45. United Nations Publishers / Geneva, Palais des Nations, C115 Services Ventes, CH-1211 Geneva 10 Switzerland. **Tel** 011 41 22 7988400, FAX 011 41 22 7332673, telex 415465. ***Separated from*** *Economic Bulletin for Europe.*
Desc: Analysis of economic situation in Europe with special focus on east-west relations. Covers economic reforms, markets, joint ventures, and financial framework.

ISSN 0245-9132
FR
Pr Rev.

ECONOMIE ET HUMANISME. [Econ. humanisme]. Vol. 1. (No. 1-), April/May 1942-. Periodical. French. Four times a year. $76.56. Economie Et Humanisme, 14 rue Autoiue Dumont, 69372 Lyon Cedex 08 France. **Tel** 7 861 32 23, FAX 78 69 86 96. Index available. cum. index. **Bk Rev**. **Ad Acc**. **Circ:** 2,500.
Ind/Abst Int. Labour Doc.; LABORDOC; Leis., Rec., Tour. Abstr.; PAIS Int. Print (1991-); Repere (1983-); Rural Dev. Abstr.; Saf. Health Work; World Agric. Econ. Rural Sociol. Abstr.

FR

•**ECONOMIE INTERNATIONALE : LA REVUE DU CEPII.** **Added/Corp** Centre d'Etudes Prospectives et d'Informations Internationales (France). No. 54 (1993)-. Periodical. French. Four times a year. 372.18F. Documentation Francaise, 29 quai Voltaire, 75344 Paris Cedex 7 France. **Tel** 011 33 1 40157000, FAX 011 33 1 40157230, telex 204 826 DOCFRAN. **(Subscription address:** Documentation Francaise, 124 rue Henri Barbusse, 93308 Aubervilliers Cedex France. **Tel** 011 33 1 48395600.**)** ***Continues*** *Economie Prospective Internationale, 0242-7818.*

LC HC10 .E434 **ISSN** 0242-7818
DD 337/.05 FR
TITLE CHANGE

ECONOMIE PROSPECTIVE INTERNATIONALE. **Added/Corp** Centre d'Etudes Prospectives et d'Informations Internationales (France). No 1 (Jan. 1980)-(1993). Periodical. French. Documentation Francaise, 29 quai Voltaire, 75344 Paris Cedex 7 France. **Tel** 011 33 1 40157000, FAX 011 33 1 40157230, telex 204 826 DOCFRAN. **Ad Acc**. ***Continued by*** *Economie Internationale.*
Desc: Analysis and evaluation of the main trends of international economics.
Ind/Abst Int. Labour Doc.; LABORDOC; Selec. Coop. Index Manage. Period.

ISSN 0343-6667
GW

EGMAGAZIN. [EGmagazin]. **Added/Corp** Commission of the European Communities. **VAT** Europaisches Gemeinschaftenmagazin. (1976)-. Periodical. German (English and German). Ten times a year. DM61.20 Germany; DM74.00 other. Nomos Verlagsgesellschaft, Postfach 610, D-76484 Baden Baden Germany. **Tel** 011 49 7221 210439.
Ind/Abst Coal Abstr.; Energy Res. Abstr. (Oct. 1981-).

LC HC407.Y6 E63 **ISSN** 0013-3248
YU

EKONOMSKA POLITIKA. (EKONOMSKA POLITIKA : EP.). **VFOAT** EP. Vol. 1 (April 4, 1952)-. Periodical. Serbo-Croatian (Roman) (Serbo-Croatian (Cyrillic)). One time a week. $215.00. Oour Ekonomska Politika, Trg Marksa1 Engelsa 7, 11001 Belgrad Yugoslavia. **Tel** 621 992, telex 12-466 YU JK BGD. **ED** Milutin Mitrovic (phone: 381 11 335355). **Bk Rev**, (Qty: 100). **Ad Acc**, **Adv Mgr Tel** 381 11 334464. **Circ:** 5,000.
Desc: Information on and analysis of Yugoslav and world economy.

LC HD9651.9.D6 E4 **ISSN** 0098-1710
DD 338.8/8 US

ELEMENTS (MIDLAND). (ELEMENTS.). **Added/Corp** Dow Chemical Co. Vol. 1 (1973)-. English. Dow Chemical Company, 2020 Dow Center, Barstow Building, Midland MI 48640. **Tel** (517)636-1000.

US

ENTERPRISE AND DEVELOPMENT. **Added/Corp** United States Council for International Business. (198?)-. Periodical. English. Twelve times a year. United States Council of the International Chamber of Commerce, 1212 Avenue of the Americas, New York NY 10036. **Tel** (212)354-4480.
Desc: Reports on a range of information sources, including publications by corporations, critics, and research groups. Covers meetings, speeches, interviews, and on corporate country programs, relating to the role of the private sector in economic and social development.

LC HF1379 .E76 **ISSN** 1059-3098
DD 658 US

ERNST & YOUNG RESOURCE GUIDE TO GLOBAL MARKETS, THE. [Ernst Young resour. guide glob. mark.]. **Added/Corp** Ernst & Young. **VFOAT** Ernst and Young Resource Guide to Global Markets; Resource Guide to Global Markets. (1991)-. English.

LC J100 **ISSN** 1021-4208
DD 354.4 BE
UDC 354(4)

EURO-EAST BRUXELLES. **See** Political Science.

LC HC241.2.A1 E86
DD 337.1/42/05 GW

EUROPAISCHE INTEGRATION : MITTEILUNGEN DES ARBEITSKREISES EUROPAISCHE INTEGRATION. **Added/Corp** Arbeitskreis Europaische Integration. Commission of the European Communities. Presse- und Informationsburo. **VFOAT** Mitteilungen des Arbeitskreises Europaische Integration. (19??)-. Periodical. German. Two times a year.
Ind/Abst World Agric. Econ. Rural Sociol. Abstr.

LC HD72
DD 338.91 BE

•**EUROPEAN COMMISSION. TACIS PROGRAMME. CONTRACT INFORMATION UPDATE.** (1994)-. English. Irregular. European Commission / Tacis Information Office, Directorate General for External Economic Relations, AN 88 1-26 rue de la Loi, Wetstraat 200 B-1049 Brussels Belgium. **Tel** 011 32 2 2952585, FAX 011 32 2 2310441.
Desc: Covers the projects funded by the Tacis Programme. These projects concern the nations of the former Soviet Union and provide support for their transitions.

LC HC241.2
DD 330 BE

EUROPEAN REPORT. (19??)-. Periodical. English (French). Irregular. $1910.45. Europe Information Service, rue de Geneve 6, 1140 Brussels Belgium. **Tel** 011 32 2 242 6020, FAX 011 32 2 242 9549. **ED** Jonathan Todd. **Bk Rev**. **Circ:** 2,000. available on an online database from Lexis-Nexis; available on CD-ROM.
Desc: General information on activities of the EEC and its relations with Third World countries, trade and economics.

ISSN 0995-2721
FR
UDC 659(4)
SUSPENDED

EUROPEAN SPONSORSHIP NEWSLETTER PARIS, THE. (THE EUROPEAN SPONSORSHIP NEWSLETTER.). (1989)-(1993). Newsletter. English. Six times a year. Editions des Trois Rives, 23 Ave Corentin Cariou, 75019 Paris France. **Tel** 011 33 1 40 38 39 11.

LC HC241.2 .E865 **ISSN** 0014-3162
DD 330.94/005 UK
CODEN EURTAM

EUROPEAN TRENDS. [Eur. trends]. **Added/Corp** Economist Intelligence Unit (Great Britain). No. 1 (Sept. 1964)-. Periodical. English. Four times a year. $390.00. The Economist Intelligence Unit, 40 Duke Street, London W1A 1DW United Kingdom. **Tel** 011 44 171 8301000. **(Subscription address:** Economist Intelligence Unit / North America Subscriptions, 111 West 57th Street, New York NY 10019. **Tel** 800 938-4685, (212)554-0600, FAX (212)586-1181, (212)586-1182.**)** **ED** Charles Jenkins. available on an online database from Lexis-Nexis. Documents available from UMI Article Clearinghouse. ***Continued in part by*** *European Trends. Background Supplement.*
Desc: Covers developments in the European Community affecting businessmen and administrators. Includes coverage of internal and external political, legal and economic relations.
Ind/Abst ABI/INFORM Glob. Ed.; ABI/INFORM [Computer File] (Feb. 1982-); Contents Pages Manage. (Feb. 1982-); Curr. Cit.; PAIS Int. Print; Selec. Coop. Index Manage. Period.; World Agric. Econ. Rural Sociol. Abstr.

LC HF **ISSN** 1196-6483
DD 382.9/142/05 CN

•**EUROPEAN UNION NEWSLETTER.** [Eur. Union newsl.]. **Added/Corp** Commission of the European Communities. Delegation (Canada). (Mar. 1994)-. Periodical. English. Six times a year. Delegation of the Commission of the European Communities, 350 Sparks Street/Suite 1110, Ottawa Ontario K1R 7S8 Canada. **Tel** (613)238-6464, FAX (613)238-5191. ***Continues in part*** *EC Newsletter, 0835-8451.*

LC HG450 **ISSN** 0015-2129
DD 332.6 UK

FINANCING FOREIGN OPERATIONS. (1957)-. Periodical. English. Irregular. $1750.00. The Economist Intelligence Unit / New York, 111 West 57th

Business and Economics —International Economic Relations

Street, New York NY 10019. **Tel** (800)938-4685, (212)554-0600. available on an online database (file 627/Full-Text) from DIALOG.
Desc: Information on global financial conditions - reference source providing information on areas such as exchange controls, sources of funding, financial markets, cash management and trade credit facilities for 42 countries. Includes comparative tables of interest and exchange rates with commentary and global financial news bulletins.

LC HG4501
DD 332.6   UK
●**FINANCING FOREIGN OPERATIONS. CHINA. Added/Corp** Economist Intelligence Unit (Great Britain). **VFOAT** China; FFO. China. (1993)-. English. One time a year. $245.00. The Economist Intelligence Unit, 40 Duke Street, London W1A 1DW United Kingdom. **Tel** 011 44 171 8301000. **(Subscription address:** Economist Intelligence Unit / North America Subscriptions, 111 West 57th Street, New York NY 10019. **Tel** 800 938-4685, (212)554-0600, FAX (212)586-1181, (212)586-1182.**)**

ISSN 1188-3475
DD 337.7108   CN
FOCUS SOUTH. [Focus south]. Vol. 1, No. 1 (Jan. 1992)-. Periodical. English. Twelve times a year. $100.00. Focus South Publishing, 2108 Alta Vista Drive, Ottawa Ontario K1H 7L8.

LC HD2907 .J33a
DD 338.8/8   JA
FOREIGN-AFFILIATED ENTERPRISES IN JAPAN--FULL TEXT OF ENTERPRISE BUREAU OF M.I.T.I. REPORT--. Main/Corp Japan. Tsusho Sangyosho. Kigyokyoku. **Added/Corp** Marunouchi Risachi Senta. (1967)-. English. ¥3000. **(Subscription address:** Maruzen Company Ltd., PO Box 5050, Import & Export Department, Tokyo 100 31 Japan. **Tel** 011 81 3 32789224.**)**

LC HG3810 .W46   **ISSN** 0883-3575
DD 332.4/5/05   US
FOREIGN EXCHANGE LONG-TERM OUTLOOK. [Foreign exch. long-term outlook]. **VFOAT** Foreign Exchange Long Term Outlook. English. WEFA / Philadelphia, PO Box 8500, Suite 1995, Philadelphia PA 19178. **Tel** (215)667-6000, telex 710 6700575. **Continues** Wharton Foreign Exchange Long-Term Outlook, 0749-6516.

NE
FOREIGN INVESTMENT IN CENTRAL AND EASTERN EUROPE. (19??)-. English. Irregular. Transnational Juris Publishers, 1 Bridge Street/ Candy Dubenski, Irvington NY 10533. **Tel** (914)591-4288, FAX (914)591-2688. **(Subscription address:** Kluwer Academic Publishers / Netherlands, PO Box 322, 3300 AH Dordrecht Netherlands. **Tel** 011 31 78 392392, FAX 011 31 78 546474.**)**

LC HM24 .F84   **ISSN** 0190-3241
DD 301.01   US
FUTURE SURVEY. See Business and Economics-Abstracting, Bibliographies and Statistics.

SZ
GATT STUDIES IN INTERNATIONAL TRADE. See Business and Economics-Commerce.

LC K10 .O87   **ISSN** 0748-4305
DD 341.7/5/05   US
GEORGE WASHINGTON JOURNAL OF INTERNATIONAL LAW AND ECONOMICS, THE. See Law-International Law.

GW
HANDBUCH DER AUSLANDSZOELLE. (19??)-. German. Twenty-four times a year. Price varies. VD Linnepe Verlagsgesellschaft GmbH & Co, Bahnhofstrasse 28, Postfach 2260, W 5800 Hagen 1 FR Germany. **Tel** 011 49 2331 32078 or 79.

ISSN 0836-6667
DD 337.51/25/071   CN
HONG KONG MONITOR. (HONG KONG MONITOR : THE NEWSLETTER OF THE HONG KONG-CANADA BUSINESS ASSOCIATION.). [Hong Kong monit.]. **Added/Corp** Hong Kong-Canada Business Association. Hong Kong Trade Development Council. Vol. 1, No. 1 (June 1986)-. Newsletter. English. Irregular. 107.00Can$ (individuals); 267.50Can$ (corporate) Comes with Hong Kong Canada Business Association membership. Hong Kong-Canada Business Association, 347 Bay Street, Suite 1100, Toronto Ontario M5H 2R7 Canada. **Tel** (416)366-3594.

CN
HORIZONS NEWSLETTER. (19??)-. Newsletter. English. Two times a year. Horizons of Friendship, 50 Covert Street, PO Box 402, Cobourg Ontario K9A 4L1 Canada. **Tel** (905)372-5483, FAX (905)372-7095. **ED** Rick K. Arnold.
Desc: Addresses causes of poverty and injustice.

GW
I F O-STUDIEN ZUR ENTWICKLUNGSFORSCHUNG. Main/Corp I F O-Institut fuer Wirtschaftsforschung, Munich. (1976)-. Monographic series. German. Irregular. Price varies per volume. IFO-Institut fuer Wirtschaftsforschung, Postfach 860460, D-81631 Munich Germany. **Tel** 011 49 89 92241, telex 5-22269. **(Subscription address:** Deutscher Wirtschaftsdienst, Marienburger Str 22, D 50968 Cologne Germany. **Tel** 011 49 221 346950.**)**
Desc: The economic imperative of developing countries is the theme of this monograph series, with consideration given to such topics as investment in Third World countries and industrial co-operation across national boundaries.

LC S
DD 630   US
IED STAFF REPORT. Added/Corp United States. Dept. of Agriculture. Economics, Statistics, and Cooperatives Service. International Economics Division. **VFOAT** International Economics Division Staff Report. (19??)-. Monographic series. English. Irregular. Price varies per volume. US Department of Agriculture / Economics and Statistics Service, Washington DC 20250.

LC HC281 .I26a   **ISSN** 0170-3617
DD 330.9/43/087   GW
    CEASED
IFO SPIEGEL DER WIRTSCHAFT. See Business and Economics-Abstracting, Bibliographies and Statistics.

ISSN 1015-2148
UDC 336.7   FR
II. INFORMATIONS INTERNATIONALES. [II, Inf. int.]. **VFOAT** Informations Internationales. (19??)-. Periodical. French. Twelve times a year. 5649.55. DAFSA Documentation, 25 rue Leblanc, 75510 Paris Cedex 15 France. **Tel** 011 33 1 40605129.

AT
INDONESIA ASSESSMENT : PROCEEDINGS OF INDONESIA UPDATE CONFERENCE ... INDONESIA PROJECT, DEPARTMENT OF ECONOMICS AND DEPARTMENT OF POLITICAL AND SOCIAL CHANGE, RESEARCH SCHOOL OF PACIFIC STUDIES, A.N.U. Added/Corp Australian National University. Research School of Pacific Studies. Dept. of Political and Social Change. (1988)-. Proceedings. English. One time a year. 35.00Sing$ ($25.00). Institute of Southeast Asian Studies / Singapore, Heng Mui Keng Terrace, Pasir Panjang Road, Singapore 0511 Republic of Singapore. **Tel** 011 65 8702447, FAX 011 65 7781735, telex 37068. **(Subscription address:** Ashgate Publishing Company / US, Old Post Road, Brookfield VT 05036-9704. **Tel** (800)535-9544, (802)276-3162, FAX (802)276-3837.**)**

LC HD72
DD 338.91   BE
●**INFO PHARE.** (1994)-. Newsletter. English. Six times a year. Free. Commission of European Communities / Phare Information Office, Directorate General for External Economic Relations, DG I AN 88 1-26, rue de la Loi 200, 1049 Brussels Belgium. **Tel** 011 32 2 2991400, FAX 011 32 2 2991777. **ED** P. Kalbe. **Circ:** 20,000. available with illustrations.
Desc: Covers the projects of Phare. These projects provide financial aid for the social/economic transitions of Central and Eastern Europe.

IT
INFORMATORE. POLITICO ECONOMICO CULTURALE, L'. (19??)-. Periodical. Italian. One time a week. L500000 (without supplements), L1000000 (with supplements). Informatore, Via Cassia 929, 00189 Rome Italy. **Tel** 011 39 6 3761191, FAX 011 39 6 3761191.
Desc: Covers activities of the Italian Parliament, laws and regulations.

LC HF1746 .I57   **ISSN** 1075-5349
DD 382/.917/05   US
●**INSIDE NAFTA. See** Business and Economics-Commerce.

LC HC1005.A1 I58
DD 337.1/660097541/05   UV
INTEGRATION AFRICAINE : REVUE TRIMESTRIELLE DE LA C.E.A.O. Added/Corp Communaute Economique de l'Afrique de l'Ouest. No. 1 (1977)-. Periodical. French. Four times a year. Integration Africaine, B P 643, Ouagadougou Burkina Faso.

LC HF1410 .I54   **ISSN** 0020-5346
    GW
    CCC
INTER ECONOMICS. See Business and Economics-Commerce.

US
TITLE CHANGE
INTERNATIONAL BUSINESS OPPORTUNITIES SERVICES : IBOS. (19??)-(19??). English. World Bank Publications, 1818 H Street Northwest, Washington DC 20043. **Tel** (202)473-1155, (202)473-1155, FAX (202)522-3224, telex WUI 64145 WORLDBANK. **(Subscription address:** World Bank Publications, PO Box 7247-8619, Books Department, Philadelphia PA 19170.**)** Index available. **Merged into** Development Business.

ISSN 0738-8888
US
INTERNATIONAL CURRENCY REPORT. [Int. curr. rep.]. **Added/Corp** International Business Information Inc. (19??)-. Periodical. English. Twenty-four times a year. $797.00. International Business Information, 4242 Airport Road, Cincinnati OH 45226. **Tel** (513)871-5501, FAX (513)871-5458.

LC HF1371   **ISSN** 1050-5563
DD 382   US
INTERNATIONAL DIRECTORY OF IMPORTERS. MIDDLE EAST, THE. See Business and Economics-Commerce.

LC HF1419   **ISSN** 1050-5466
DD 382/.5/02573   US
INTERNATIONAL DIRECTORY OF IMPORTERS. NORTH AMERICA, THE. See Business and Economics-Commerce.

ISSN 0142-0771 y 0307-0379
US
INTERNATIONAL ECONOMIC DATA SERVICE. Added/Corp Advisory Information Services. (1978)-. Periodical. English. Irregular. $650.00. World Reports Ltd., 108 Horse Ferry Road, Westminster, London SW1P 2EF United Kingdom. **Tel** 011 44 171 2223836, FAX 11 44 171 2330185. **Continues** Economic Data Service.

LC HB1.A1 I57   **ISSN** 1050-8481
DD 337/.05   US
    CCC
    CEASED
INTERNATIONAL ECONOMIC INSIGHTS. [Int. econ. insights]. **Added/Corp** Institute for International Economics (U.S.). **VFOAT** Economic Insights. Vol. 1, No. 1 (July/Aug. 1990)-Vol. 5, No. 3. Periodical. English. Institute for International Economics, 11 Dupont Circle, 6th Floor, Washington DC 20036. **Tel** (202)328-0583, FAX (202)328-5432. available on CD-ROM.
Desc: Attempts to fill the need in the critical field of international economic policy. Its goal is to tell busy corporate and financial executives, government officials, and other interested citizens what they need to know about new thinking from all over the world on economic issues.
Ind/Abst Am. Bibliogr. Slavic East Europ. Stud.; PAIS Int. Print.

LC HF1455 .U47a   **ISSN** 0091-2492
DD 382/.0973   US
INTERNATIONAL ECONOMIC REPORT OF THE PRESIDENT. (INTERNATIONAL ECONOMIC REPORT OF THE PRESIDENT, TRANSMITTED TO THE CONGRESS.). [Int. econ. rep. Pres.]. **Main/Corp** United States. President. (1973)-. Government Publication. English. Irregular. Superintendent of Documents, US Government Printing Office, Washington DC 20402. **Tel** (202)275-3328, FAX (202)786-2377.
Ind/Abst Predicasts.

ISSN 0270-045X
CCC
TITLE CHANGE
INTERNATIONAL ECONOMIC SCOREBOARD. [Int. econ. scoreb.]. (June 1979)-(1993). Periodical. English. Conference Board, 845 Third Avenue, New York NY 10022. **Tel** (212)759-0900 ext. 582, (800)872-6273, FAX (212)980-7014. **ED** Edgar R. Fiedler. **Circ:** 6,500 (ctrl). **Continued by** International Economic Scoreboard/ The Conference Board, 0270-045X.
Desc: Indexes of economic performance for the major industrial countries presented in chart and tabular form with summary text.
Ind/Abst Stat. Ref. Index.

ISSN 0270-045X
DD 337 US
CCC
CODEN IECSEG

•INTERNATIONAL ECONOMIC SCOREBOARD. (INTERNATIONAL ECONOMIC SCOREBOARD / THE CONFERENCE BOARD.). [Int. econ. scoreb.]. **Added/Corp** Conference Board. Vol. 1, No. 1 (Mar. 1993)-. English. Irregular. $295.00 (non-associates), $145.00 (Conference Board associates). Conference Board, 845 Third Avenue, New York NY 10022. **Tel** (212)759-0900 ext. 582, (800)872-6273, FAX (212)980-7014. ***Continues*** *International Economic Scoreboard, 0270-045X.*

NE

INTERNATIONAL ECONOMICS SERIES. **Added/Corp** Geneva. Graduate Institute of International Studies. Geneva. Graduate Institute of International Studies. Collection d'Economie Internationale. **VFOAT** Collection d'Economie Internationale. (1973)-. Monographic series. English. Irregular. Price varies per volume. Sijthoff & Noordhoff International Publications, 20010 Century Boulevard, Germantown MD 20767.

LC HG3879 .I565 ISSN 0898-4336
DD 337/.05 US

INTERNATIONAL ECONOMY, THE. (THE INTERNATIONAL ECONOMY : THE MAGAZINE OF INTERNATIONAL ECONOMIC POLICY.). [Int. econ.]. Vol. 1, No. 1 (Oct./Nov. 1987)-. Trade Publication. English. Six times a year (Jan., Mar., May, July, Sept., Nov.). $72.00. International Economy Publishing Inc., 1133 Connecticut Avenue Northwest, No. 901, Washington DC 20036. **Tel** (202)861-0791, FAX (202)861-0790. **ED** Whayne Dillehay. Index available. **Bk Rev**. **Ad Acc**. **Circ:** 15,000 (ctrl). Documents available from UMI Article Clearinghouse.
Desc: Contains articles written by economic policy makers dealing with exchange rates, debt, and international trade.
Ind/Abst Expand. Acad. Index (1992-); Newsp. Period. Abstr. (1992-); PAIS Int. Print.

ISSN 1353-1158
DD 330 UK

INTERNATIONAL PAPERS IN POLITICAL ECONOMY. [Int. pap. polit. econ.]. **VFOAT** IPPE (London). (1993)-. English. Three times a year. $25.67. IPPE University of East London, Longbridge Road, Dagenham Essex, RM8 2AS United Kingdom. **Tel** 011 44 181 8493507. **ED** Peter Mottershead.

LC HF1410 .I579 ISSN 8755-8335
DD 337/.05 US

INTERNATIONAL POLITICAL ECONOMY YEARBOOK. [Int. pol. econ. yearb.]. **Added/Corp** International Studies Association. International Political Economy Section. (1985)-. Monographic series. English. Irregular. Price varies per volume. Lynne Rienner Publishers, 1800 30th Street, Suite 314, Boulder CO 80301. **Tel** (303)444-6684, FAX (303)444-0824.

LC D839 .I538 ISSN 0740-669X
DD 905 US

INTERNATIONAL REPORT (IRVINE, CALIF.). See Political Science.

US

INTERNATIONAL RESEARCH IN THE BUSINESS DISCIPLINES. (19??)-. Monographic series. English. Irregular. $73.25. JAI Press Inc., 55 Old Post Road, Suite 2, PO Box 1678, Greenwich CT 06836-1678. **Tel** (203)661-7602, FAX (203)661-0792. **ED** Carl Swanson.

LC K9 .N865 ISSN 0144-8188
DD 343.41/07/05 344.103705 US
CCC
CODEN IRLEE8

INTERNATIONAL REVIEW OF LAW AND ECONOMICS. [Int. rev. law econ.]. Vol. 1, No. 1 (June 1981)-. Periodical. English. Four times a year (Mar., June, Sept., Dec.). $215.00 US; $245.00 other. Butterworth Heinemann / Woburn, MA, 225 Wildwood Avenue, Unit B, Woburn MA 01801. **Tel** (800)366-2665, FAX (617)928-2620, telex 880052. **(Subscription address:** Elsevier Science Inc. / New York Books, 655 Avenue of the Americas, New York NY 10010. **Tel** (212)633-3650.**)** **ED** A. I. Ogus, Robert Cooter and Daniel L. Rubinfeld. Index available. **Ad Acc**. available on microfilm and microfiche from University Microfilms International (UMI). Documents available from UMI Article Clearinghouse.
Desc: Provides an outlet for research on the interface between economics and law. It embraces interrelationships between economics and substantive law, including international and European Community law.
Ind/Abst ABI/INFORM Glob. Ed.; Am. Hist. Life (1985-1986); Contents Recent Econ. J.; Curr. Law Index (1982-); Econ. Lit. Index; Index Leg. Period.; J. Econ. Lit.; J. Plan. Lit.; Leg. Resour. Index (1981, 1982-); LegalTrac (1982-); PAIS Int. Print (1991-).

UK

INTERNATIONAL TAX FREE TRADER. (19??)-. Trade Publication. English. $196.00. Argus Press Group, Queensway House, 2 Queensway Redhill, Surrey RH1 1QS United Kingdom. **Tel** 011 44 1737 768611, 011 44 1737 761685, FAX 011 44 1737 760510, telex 948669 TOPJNL G. **ED** Peter Tipthorp. **Ad Acc**, **Adv Mgr:** Stuart Velden, **Tel** 011 44 737 768611 ext. 3519. Documents available from FAXON Xpress, BLDSC.

ISSN 1073-9084
DD 382 US

•INTERNATIONAL TRADE & BUSINESS JOURNAL. See Business and Economics.

LC HF19 .I8
DD 382.05 IT

ITALIAN-AMERICAN BUSINESS. **Added/Corp** American Chamber of Commerce for Italy, Milan. (July 1915)-. Periodical. Italian (English). Six times a year. L40000. American Chamber of Commerce in Italy, Via Cantu 1, 20123 Milan Italy. **Tel** 011 39 2 6890661, FAX 011 39 2 8057737, telex 352128. **ED** Alexandra Olgiati. Index available. cum. index. **Bk Rev**. **Ad Acc**. **Circ:** 7,000 (ctrl).
Desc: Trade between US and Italy, legal aspects, investment and business opportunities, fiscal and tax news for US and Italy, company activities, management and labor relations, economic trends, EEC matters.
Ind/Abst PAIS Int. Print (1991-).

ISSN 0021-3098
CN

ITALY CANADA TRADE. (Oct. 1964)-. Periodical. Multiple languages (Italian and English). One time a year. $13.93. Italy Canada Trade, 159 Bay Street/Suite 313, Toronto Ontario M5J 1J7 Canada. **Tel** (416)364-6551.

LC HF1601 .J352 ISSN 0922-1425
DD 337.52/005 NE
CCC
Pr Rev.

JAPAN AND THE WORLD ECONOMY. **Added/Corp** New York University. Center for Japan-U.S. Business and Economic Studies. Vol. 1, No. 1 (Oct. 1988)-. Academic Scholarly Publication. English. Four times a year (1 volume). $291.00. Elsevier Science Publishers BV, PO Box 211, 1000 AE Amsterdam Netherlands. **Tel** 011 31 20 4853641, 011 31 20 4853642, FAX 011 31 20 4853598. available on microfilm and microfiche from University Microfilms International (UMI); available on an online database from Elsevier Electronic Subscriptions (EES).
Ind/Abst Curr. Cit.; PAIS Int. Print (1991-).

ISSN 0888-5710
DD 330 US

JAPAN ECONOMIC SURVEY. [Jpn. econ. surv.]. **Added/Corp** Japan Economic Institute of America. United States--Japan Trade Council. (197?)-. Periodical. English. Eleven times a year. $30.00 US; $35.00 other. Japan Economic Institute of America, 1000 Connecticut Avenue NW, Suite 211, Washington DC 20036. **Tel** (202)296-5633, FAX (202)296-8333. **ED** Barbara Wanner. **Circ:** 3,500.
Desc: Current economic and political analyses of US-Japan bilateral relations.

LC HF1410 .K235
JA

JETORO HAKUSHO. BOEKI-HEN. **Added/Corp** Nihon Boeki Shinkokai. **VFOAT** Sekai to Nihon No Boeki. (1984)-. Japanese. One time a year. ¥2500. Nihon Boeki Shinkokai Honbu, 2-5 Toranomon 2 Minato-ku, Tokyo-to 105 Japan. **Tel** 011 81 3 5823518, FAX 011 81 3 5872485, telex J24378. **Circ:** 9,000. ***Continues Kaigai Shijo Hankusho Boeki-Hen.***

LC HF1351 .J68 ISSN 0940-4821
GW
CCC

JOICE : JOURNAL OF INTERNATIONAL AND COMPARATIVE ECONOMICS. **VFOAT** Journal of International and Comparative Economics. (1992)-. Periodical. English. Four times a year. $258.00. Physica-Verlag GmBh & Company, Postfach 105280, D-69042 Heidelberg Germany. **Tel** 011 49 6221 487492, 011 49 6221 345186, FAX 011 49 6221 487177 und 487366, telex 461723 sphdb-d. **(Subscription address:** Springer-Verlag New York Inc. / North America, PO Box 2485, Journal Fulfillment, Secaucus NJ 07096. **Tel** (201)348-4033, (800)777-4643, FAX (201)348-4505.**)**
Desc: A comparative view of the development of integration and enlargement of international competition .

ISSN 0963-8024
UK
CCC

JOURNAL OF AFRICAN ECONOMIES. Vol. 1, No. 1 (Mar. 1992)-. Periodical. English. Three times a year. $118.00. Oxford University Press / UK, Walton Street, Oxford OX2 6DP United Kingdom. **Tel** 011 44 1865 56767, FAX 011 44 1865 267773, telex 851/837330 OXPRES G. **(Subscription address:** Oxford University Press / USA, Journals Marketing Department, Oxford University Press, 2001 Evans Road, Cary NC 27513. **Tel** (800)451-7556, (919)677-0977, FAX (919)677-1714.**)** **ED** Paul Collier, Jan Willem Gunning, Benno Ndulu and Ademola Oyejide. Index available. **Bk Rev**. **Ad Acc**. **Circ:** 1,000.

LC HF1418.5 .J676 ISSN 1015-356X
DD 337.1/05 KO

JOURNAL OF ECONOMIC INTEGRATION. **Added/Corp** Sejong Taehak. Kukche Kyongje Yonguso. Vol. 7, No. 2 (Autumn 1992)-. Periodical. English. Four times a year. $60.00. Sejong University, Institute International Economics, Seongdong-ku, Seoul 133 747 Korea. **Tel** 011 82 2 4600338, FAX 011 82 2 4600200. **ED** Myung Gum Choo. cum. index. **Ad Acc**. **Circ:** 1,500 (ctrl). ***Continues*** *Journal of International Economic Integration.*

LC HD69.I7 ISSN 0047-2506
DD 650 CN
Pr Rev.

JOURNAL OF INTERNATIONAL BUSINESS STUDIES. [J. int. bus. stud.]. **Added/Corp** Georgia State University. School of Business Administration. Association for Education in International Business. Academy of International Business. Rutgers University. Graduate School of Business Administration. University of South Carolina. College of Business Administration. **VFOAT** JIBS. Vol. 1 (Spring 1970)-. Academic Scholarly Publication. English. Four times a year. 57.00Can$. Western Business School, University of Western Ontario, London Ontario N6A 3K7 Canada. **Tel** (519)661-4031, FAX (519)661-3700. **ED** Professor Paul W. Beamish. Index available. cum. index. **Bk Rev**. **Ad Acc**. Full Page (B&W) $400.00 (one issue), $700.00 (two issues). **Circ:** 4,100 (ctrl). available on microfilm and microfiche from University Microfilms International (UMI); available on an online database (file 648/Full-Text) from DIALOG; available with charts. Documents available from The Genuine Article, UMI Article Clearinghouse, BLDSC, FAXON Xpress, SWETS, UMI Article Clearinghouse, The UnCover Company.
Desc: Publishes primarily the results of significant basic or applied research in international or comparative business.
Ind/Abst ABI/INFORM Glob. Ed.; ABI/INFORM [Computer File] (Fall 1974-); Acad. Search; Am. Bibliogr. Slavic East Europ. Stud.; Anbar Account. Finan. Abstr. [Full Txt.]; Anbar Mark. Distr. Abstr. [Full Txt.]; Anbar Top Manage. Abstr. [Full Txt.]; Bus. ASAP (1990-) [Full Txt.]; Bus. Index (1985-); Bus. Period. Index; Bus. Source Plus; Bus. Source; Contents Pages Manage.; Curr. Cit.; Curr. Contents Soc. Behav. Sci.; EP Collect.; Gen. BusinessFile (1985-); Gen. Period. Index (1985-); Homework Help.; INFO-SOUTH Abstr.; Int. Bibliogr. Sociol.; Int. Exec.; J. Econ. Lit.; Mag. Search; Manage. Market. Abstr.; Manage. Bibliogr. Rev.; MasterFile FullTEXT 1000; MasterFile FullTEXT 350; MasterFile FullTEXT 650; MasterFile FullTEXT (July 1993-); Middle East Abstr. Index; OCLC; Oper. Prod. Manage. Abstr. [Full Txt.]; PAIS Int. Print (1991-); Person. Train. Abstr. [Full Txt.]; Person. Manage. Abstr.; Res. Alert [Full Cov.]; Selec. Coop. Index Manage. Period.; Soc. Sci. Cit. Index [Full Cov.]; Telebase; Trade Ind. ASAP [Full Txt.]; Trade Ind. Index [Full Txt.]; UMI ABI/Inform--Bus. Period. Ondisc (Summer 1987-) [Full Txt.]; U.S. Polit. Sci. Doc.; Wilson Bus. Abstr.; Women Manage. Rev. [Full Txt.].

LC HF1 .J65 ISSN 0022-1996
DD 382.1/05 NE
CCC
CODEN JIECBE
Pr Rev.

JOURNAL OF INTERNATIONAL ECONOMICS. [J. int. econ.]. Vol. 1 (Feb. 1971)-. Academic Scholarly Publication. English. Eight times a year (2 vols.). $646.00. Elsevier Science Publishers BV, PO Box 211, 1000 AE Amsterdam Netherlands. **Tel** 011 31 20 4853641, 011 31 20 4853642, FAX 011 31 20 4853598. **ED** R A Brecher, J N Bhagwati, and J S Chipman. available on microfilm and microfiche from University Microfilms International (UMI); available on an online database from Elsevier Electronic Subscriptions (EES). Documents available from The Genuine Article, UMI Article Clearinghouse, Documents on Demand.
Desc: Designed to serve as the principal outlet for analytical work in pure theory of international trade and in balance-of-payments analysis, and also for institutional, empirical, and econometric work of high quality and general professional interest.
Ind/Abst ABI/INFORM Glob. Ed.; ABI/INFORM [Computer File] (Feb. 1981-); Acad. Search; Bus. Index (1985-); Bus. Source Plus; Bus. Source; Contents Recent Econ. J.; Curr. Cit.; Curr. Contents Soc. Behav. Sci.; Econ. Lit. Index; Energy Inf. Abstr.; Environ. Abstr.; EP Collect.; Expand. Acad. Index (1984-); Gen. BusinessFile (1985-); Gen. Period. Index (1985-); Homework Help.; INFO-SOUTH Abstr.; J. Econ. Lit.; Leis., Rec., Tour. Abstr.; Mag. Search; MasterFile FullTEXT 1000; MasterFile FullTEXT 350; MasterFile FullTEXT 650; MasterFile FullTEXT (July 1993-); Newsp. Period. Abstr. (1991-); OCLC; PAIS Int. Print; Res. Alert [Full Cov.]; Rural Dev. Abstr.; Selec. Coop. Index Manage. Period.; Soc. Sci. Source; Soc. Sci. Cit. Index [Full Cov.]; Soc. Sci.

Business and Economics —International Economic Relations

Index; Soc. Sci. Index Fulltext (Nov. 1988-) [Full Txt.]; Telebase; Trade Ind. Index; World Agric. Econ. Rural Sociol. Abstr.

LC HG3879 .J678   ISSN 1042-4431
DD 332/.042/05   US
Pr Rev.
JOURNAL OF INTERNATIONAL FINANCIAL MARKETS, INSTITUTIONS & MONEY. See Business and Economics-Banks and Banking.

LC HF1371 .J68   ISSN 0963-8199
    UK
Pr Rev.
JOURNAL OF INTERNATIONAL TRADE AND ECONOMIC DEVELOPMENT. VFOAT Journal of International Trade and Economic Development; International Trade and Economic Development; International Trade & Economic Development; JITED. Vol. 1 (1992)-. Periodical. English. Three times a year. $165.00. Routledge, 11 New Fetter Lane, London EC4P 4EE United Kingdom. **Tel** 011 44 171 5839855, **FAX** 011 44 171 5830701. (**Subscription address:** Kinokuniya Company Ltd., 38-1 Sakuragaoka 5, chome Setagaya-ku, Tokyo 156 Japan. **Tel** FAX 011 03 3439 0136.) **ED** P. Sgro and B. Hasari. Index available (Nov.). **Bk Rev. Ad Acc, Adv Mgr:** David Polley.
Desc: Provides an interface between international trade and development economics and publishes research in these areas.

LC HF1601 .J68   ISSN 0889-1583
DD 337.52/005   US
    CCC
JOURNAL OF THE JAPANESE AND INTERNATIONAL ECONOMIES. [J. Jpn. int. econ.]. **Added/Corp** Tokyo Keizai Kenkyu Senta. VFOAT Japanese and International Economies. Vol. 1, No. 1 (March 1987)-. Academic Scholarly Publication. English. Four times a year. $211.00. Academic Press Inc., 6277 Sea Harbor Drive, Orlando FL 32887. **Tel** (800)543-9534, (407)345-4100, **FAX** (407)352-3445. **ED** Masahiko Aoki, Michihiro Ohyama, Koichi Hamada, Masahiro Okuno-Fujiwara and Takatoshi Ito. **Bk Rev.** Documents available from The Genuine Article.
Desc: Publishes original reports of research devoted to academic analyses of the Japanese economy and its interdependence with other national economies. The journal also features articles that present related theoretical, empirical, or comparative analyses and their policy implications.
Ind/Abst Econ. Lit. Index (1988-); J. Econ. Lit. (1988-); Res. Alert [Full Cov.]; Soc. Sci. Cit. Index [Full Cov.].

    ISSN 8755-3449
DD 909   US
Pr Rev.
JOURNAL OF THIRD WORLD STUDIES. [J. third world stud.]. **Added/Corp** Association of Third World Studies (U.S.). Vol. 1 (Fall 1984)-. Academic Scholarly Publication. English. Two times a year (June & Dec.). $45.00. Association of Third World Studies, PO Box 1232, Americus GA 31709. **Tel** (912)924-8287, **FAX** (912)931-2270. **ED** Harold Isaacs. **Bk Rev. Ad Acc. Circ:** 815. available on microfilm and CD-ROM.
Desc: Scholarly periodical which examines Third World problems and issues from different perspectives or viewpoints.
Ind/Abst Am. Hist. Life (1987-); Int. Dev. Abstr. (?-?); PAIS Int. Print.

LC HF53 .K33
DD 380.10   JA
KAIGAI SHIJO HAKUSHO. DAI 1 BUNSATSU : SEKAI BOEKI NO GENJO. See Business and Economics-Commerce.

LC HF1410 .K79
    KO
KUKCHE KORAR KONSOLTONTU. (19??)-. Periodical. Korean. Hanguk Oehwan Unhaeng, 181 2-ka Ulchi-ro, Chung-ku, Seoul South Korea.

LC HC121 .K87
    GW
KURZBERICHT UEBER LATEINAMERIKA. Added/Corp Deutsch-Sudamerikanische Bank. (19??)-. German. Three times a year (Feb., June, Oct.). Deutsch-Suedamerikanische Bank AG, Postfach 30 12 46, D-20305 Hamburg Germany. **Tel** (040)34107-0, **FAX** (040)34107-314, telex 214 236-0 DS D. Index available. **Bk Rev,** (Qty: 3). ctrl circ.
Desc: Gives concise information on the current economic situation of Latin American countries and the trade between the Federal Republic of Germany and Latin America.

    ISSN 1040-3175
DD 338   US
LAGNIAPPE LETTER. Added/Corp Latin American Information Services, Inc. (19??)-. Periodical. English. Twenty-five times a year. $675.00. Latin American Information Services, Inc., 159 West 53rd Street, Suite 28B, New York NY 10019-6050. **Tel** (212)765-5520, **FAX** (212)765-2927. **ED** Rosemary Werrett. available on an online database (files 16,636/Full-Text) from DIALOG.
Desc: Reports on key economic, political and financial developments in the large markets of Latin and Central America.
Ind/Abst PTS Newsl. Database [Full Txt.].

LC HA1433 .L36
DD 314.7/05   GW
●**LANDERBERICHT. GUS-STAATEN.**
Added/Corp Germany. Statistisches Bundesamt. VFOAT GUS-Staaten. (1994)-. Statistical Publication. German (table of contents in English). W. Kohlhammer Verlag GmbH, Postfach 800430, D-70549 Stuttgart Germany. **Tel** 011 49 711 78630, **FAX** 011 49 711 7863430, telex 7-255820. **Continues** Landerbericht. Sowjetunion, 0940-9947.

    ISSN 0243-1947
DD 337   FR
LETTRE DU C.E.P.I.I, LA. Added/Corp Centre d'Etudes Prospectives et d'Informations Internationales (France). VFOAT Lettre du CEPII. **VAT** Lettre du Centre d'Etudes Prospectives et d'Informations Internationales. (19??)-. Periodical. French. Eleven times a year. 269.34F France; $55.00 other. Documentation Francaise, 29 quai Voltaire, 75344 Paris Cedex 7 France. **Tel** 011 33 1 40157000, **FAX** 011 33 1 40157230, telex 204 826 DOCFRAN. (**Subscription address:** Documentation Francaise, 124 rue Henri Barbusse, 93308 Aubervilliers Cedex France. **Tel** 011 33 1 48395600.)

    ISSN 0760-4211
    FR
UDC 658.114.7
LETTRE DU GROUPEMENT NATIONAL DE LA COOPERATION, LA. [Lett. Group. natl. coop.]. VFOAT Lettre du G.N.C.; Lettre - G.N.C. (1978)-. Periodical. French.
Ind/Abst LABORDOC.

LC HC805.A1 M33   ISSN 0153-114X
DD 330.961/005   FR
MAGHREB-DEVELOPPEMENT. VFOAT Maghreb Developpement. (19??)-. Periodical. French. Twelve times a year. 4620.00F. Bloux, 03320 Lurcy-Levis France. **Tel** 70 67 88 89, **FAX** 70 67 92 33.
Desc: Economics and development of Algeria, Tunisia and Morocco.

    ISSN 0226-1995
DD 330.9172/4   CN
MARCHE INTERNATIONAL (PIERREFONDS). (MARCHE INTERNATIONAL.). [Marche int.]. Vol. 1 (Dec. 1979)-. Periodical. English (French). Twelve times a year. $48.00. Entreprises AMAF, Marche International, 6084 Clark Street, Pierrefonds Quebec H8Z 2G4 Canada.

LC HG1501
DD 332.1   TU
MIDDLE EAST BUSINESS & BANKING. VFOAT Middle East Business and Banking; MEBB. (198?)-. Periodical. English. Twelve times a year. $40.00. International Business and Banking, Serfin As Oba Sokak 15/2, 80060 Istanbul Turkey. **Tel** 011 90 212 1448335.
Ind/Abst PAIS Int. Print.

    ISSN 0307-0387
    UK
MIDDLE EAST CURRENCY REPORTS.
Added/Corp International Currency Services. Currency Journals Ltd. International Currency Review. World Reports Ltd. (19??)-. Vol. 1, No. 1 (Oct. 1974)-. Periodical. English. Six times a year. £235.00 UK and Ireland; $550.00 other. World Reports Ltd., 108 Horse Ferry Road, Westminster, London SW1P 2EF United Kingdom. **Tel** 011 44 171 2223836, **FAX** 11 44 171 2330185.
Desc: Financial intelligence service provides institutional subscribers worldwide with comprehensive reports on the currencies, economies and sociopolitical background of Saudi Arabia, Kuwait, Qatar, Bahrain, Syria, Iraq, Iran, Jordan, Oman, the Yemens, Algeria, Libya and the Maghreb.

    ISSN 0026-315X
    US
MIDDLE EAST MONITOR. See Political Science.

LC HC410.7.A1 M517
DD 330.956/005   UK
MIDDLE EAST REVIEW (SAFFRON WALDEN, ESSEX). (MIDDLE EAST REVIEW.). (1981)-. English. One time a year (Nov.). $109.00 North America. Kogan Page Ltd., 120 Pentonville Rd, London N1 9BR United Kingdom. **Tel** 011 44 171 2780433, **FAX** 011 44 171 8376348, telex 263088 KOGAN G. (**Subscription address:** Kogan Page / North America Subscriptions, PO Box 830430, Birmingham AL 35283-0430. **Tel** (800)633-4931, **FAX** (205)995-1588.) **ED** R. Green. **Ad Acc. Circ:** 10,000. **Continues** Middle East Annual Review, 0305-3210.
Desc: Accurate, comprehensive coverage of the region from Mauritania in the West to Afghanistan in the East.

Objective articles by experts on economics, politics, business, industry and commerce.
Ind/Abst Index Islam. Lit.; Middle East Abstr. Index.

LC HF3161.M6 M56
DD 382/.6/025776   US
MINNESOTA INTERNATIONAL TRADE DIRECTORY. (19??)-. Directory. English. Minnesota Department of Trade & Economic Development, 150 East Kellogg Boulevard, American Center Building, Room 900, St Paul MN 55101. **Tel** (612)296-6424, **FAX** (612)296-1290.

    ISSN 0713-6501
DD 338.91/1722/01724   CN
MINUTES OF PROCEEDINGS AND EVIDENCE OF THE SPECIAL COMMITTEE ON NORTH-SOUTH RELATIONS. [Minutes proc. evid. Spec. Comm. North-South Relat.]. **Main/Corp** Canada. Parlement. Chambre des Communes. Groupe de Travail Parlementaire Sur les Relations Nord-Sud. VFOAT Proces-Verbaux et Temoignages du Comite Special Relations Nord-Sud. **VAT** North-South Relations (Ottawa); Relations Nord-Sud (Ottawa). Issue No. 1 (June 25, 1980)-. Proceedings. French (English). Receiver General for Canada / Ottawa, Canada Comm Group Publishing, Ottawa Ontario K1A 0S9 Canada. **Tel** (819)956-4802, (800)661-2868.

    IT
MOCT MOST : ECONOMIC JOURNAL ON EASTERN EUROPE & SOVIET UNION. English. Three times a year. L200000. Nomisma, Strada Maggiore 44, 40125 Bologna Italy. **Tel** 011 39 51 239422.

LC HD69.I7 M88   ISSN 0300-3922
DD 338.8/8/05   US
    TITLE CHANGE
MULTINATIONAL BUSINESS. [Multinatl. bus.]. **Added/Corp** Economist Intelligence Unit (Great Britain) Economist Intelligence Unit (New York, N.Y.). 1971, No. 1 (Nov. 1971)-No. 4 (Winter 1992-93). Periodical. English. Economist, Diary Department, 25 St. James Street, London SW1A 1HG United Kingdom. **Tel** 011 44 14023 81555, **FAX** 011 44 14023 81211, telex 927809. **ED** Sarah Child. Documents available from UMI Article Clearinghouse. **Continued by** Crossborder Monitor.
Desc: A guide to developments in multinational corporate enterprise, the world trading environment, relations with governments and current problems and controversies.
Ind/Abst ABI/INFORM Glob. Ed.; ABI/INFORM [Computer File] (1983-); Bus. Index (1985-); Contents Pages Manage. (1983-); Gen. BusinessFile (1985-); Gen. Period. Index (1985-); Manage. Contents; Person. Manage. Abstr.; Selec. Coop. Index Manage. Period.

    ISSN 0300-7464
    US
NEWS BULLETIN - BRAZILIAN-AMERICAN CHAMBER OF COMMERCE. Main/Corp Brazilian-American Chamber of Commerce. (1970)-. Bulletin. English. Twelve times a year. Brazilian American Chamber of Commerce, 22 West 48th Street/Suite 404, New York NY 10036. **Tel** (212)575-9030. **ED** Frank J. Devine. **Circ:** 600 (ctrl).
Desc: Topics include the economy of Brazil and economic relations between United States and Brazil.

    ISSN 0045-4214
    CN
NEWSLETTER - CANADA JAPAN TRADE COUNCIL. [Newsl. - Can. Jap. Trade Counc.]. **Main/Corp** Canada-Japan Trade Council. (Nov. 1966)-. Newsletter. English. Six times a year. Free on request. Canada Japan Trade Council, 75 Albert Street #903, Ottawa Ontario K1P 5E7 Canada. **Tel** (613)233-4047, **FAX** (613)233-2256. **ED** J.E. Struthers. **Circ:** 3,400 (ctrl). available on microfiche (from University Microfilms Int., Ann Arbor, MI).
Desc: Promotes trade and other economic relations between Canada and Japan. Information on relevant trade, economic, and political subjects.

LC HG4009 .N54
    JA
NIKKEI ANNUAL FOREIGN CORPORATION REPORTS = GAIKOKU KAISHA NENKAN. VFOAT Gaikoku Kaisha Nenkan; Annual Foreign Corporation Reports; Foreign Corporation Reports. (1980)-. Annual. One time a year. ¥25000. Nihon Keizai Shimbun Inc., 9-5 Otemachi 1 Chome, Chiyoda-ku Tokyo 100 Japan. **Tel** 011 81 3 32700251, 011 81 3 52108502 (Nikkei Business Publications Inc.), **FAX** 011 81 3 52552661, 011 81 3 52108119 (Nikkei Business Publications Inc.).

LC HC59.7 .N64 ISSN 0273-0499
DD 909/.09/724 US
NONALIGNED THIRD WORLD ANNUAL. 1970-. English. Irregular. Books International of DH-TE International Inc, PO Box 14487, St Louis MO 63178. Index available in last issue of volume--attached.

FR
NOTE DE CONJONCTURE INTERNATIONALE. (June 1988)-. Periodical. French. Three times a year. 109.00F France; 136.00F other. Institut National de la Statistique et des Etudes Economiques, 18 Bd Adolphe Pinard, 75675 Paris 14 France.

LC DT1 .N68 ISSN 1141-9946
DD 950/.05 FR
NOUVEL AFRIQUE ASIE, LE. **See** Political Science.

LC HF ISSN 1196-6491
DD 382.9/142/05 CN
●**NOUVELLES DE L'UNION EUROPEENNE.** [Nouv. Union eur.]. **Added/Corp** Commission des Communautes Europeennes. Delegation (Canada). (1994)-. Periodical. French. Six times a year. Delegation of the Commission of the European Communities, 350 Sparks Street/Suite 1110, Ottawa Ontario K1R 7S8 Canada. **Tel** (613)238-6464, FAX (613)238-5191. ***Continues in part** EC Newsletter, 0835-8451.*

LC HD2329 ISSN 1351-8569
DD 338.91 UK
OASIS LONDON. 1985. [Oasis Lond., 1985]. (1985)-. Newsletter. English. Two times a year. WaterAid, 1 Queen Anne's Guide, London SW1H 9RT United Kingdom. **Tel** 011 171 2334800, FAX 011 171 2333161.

LC HG1501 ISSN 0278-1468
DD 332.1 US
OCCASIONAL PAPERS (GROUP OF THIRTY). **See** Business and Economics-Banks and Banking.

LC HD1635 ISSN 1356-9228
DD 333.7 UK
●**ODI NATURAL RESOURCE PERSPECTIVES.** (1994)-. Bulletin. English. Five times a year. Overseas Development Institute, Regents College Inner Circle, Regent's Park, London NW1 4NS United Kingdom. **Tel** 011 171 4877413, FAX 011 171 4877590.

LC HF1371
DD 382 CN
●**OVERSEAS EXPORTERS.** **See** Business and Economics-Commerce.

ISSN 1015-6283
BE
UDC 336.74
PECUNIA. BRUXELLES, DE. [De Pecunia Brux.]. (1989)-. Periodical. Multiple languages (English, French, German, Italian and Spanish). Three times a year. $149.25. ICHEC-CEPIME, Boulevard Brand Whitlock 2, 1150 Brussels Belgium. **Tel** 011 32 2 7359144, 011 32 2 7353783. Index available.
Desc: Provides analysis of political economy and economic policy problems linked to the European monetary integration. Review of information and debate.

LC HC336.25 .P424 ISSN 0895-3317
DD 330.947/005 US
PLANECON REPORT. (PLANECON REPORT : DEVELOPMENTS IN THE ECONOMIES OF THE SOVIET UNION AND EASTERN EUROPE.). [PlanEcon rep.]. **Added/Corp** PlanEcon, Inc. **VFOAT** Plan Econ Report. Vol. 1, No. 1 (Sept. 2, 1985)-. Newsletter. English. Irregular (25-30 per year). $1800.00. PlanEcon Inc., 1111 14th Street Northwest, Suite 801, Washington DC 20005. **Tel** (202)898-0471. **ED** Jan Vanous.
Desc: Focuses on the major macroeconomic and trade developments in the former Soviet Republics and 6 East European countries, including Bulgaria, Czech Republic, Slovakia, Hungary, Poland, Romania and the former Yugoslav Republics.

ISSN 0733-1738
US
POLICY ANALYSES IN INTERNATIONAL ECONOMICS. (POLICY ANALYSES IN INTERNATIONAL ECONOMICS / INSTITUTE FOR INTERNATIONAL ECONOMICS.). [Policy anal. int. econ.]. **Added/Corp** Institute for International Economics (U.S.). (1982)-. Monographic series. English. Irregular. Price varies per volume. Institute for International Economics, 11 Dupont Circle, 6th Floor, Washington DC 20036. **Tel** (202)328-0583, FAX (202)328-5432.
Desc: A paperback series of books providing fresh analysis of key economic, monetary, trade and investment issues and practical new approaches for problem solving in these areas.
Ind/Abst World Agric. Econ. Rural Sociol. Abstr.

ISSN 1013-3429
US
POLICY & RESEARCH SERIES. **Added/Corp** International Bank for Reconstruction and Development. **VFOAT** Policy and Research Series. (1988)-. Monographic series. English. Price varies per volume. World Bank Publications, 1818 H Street Northwest, Washington DC 20043. **Tel** (202)473-1155, (202)473-1155, FAX (202)522-3224, telex WUI 64145 WORLDBANK.
Ind/Abst Geogr. Abstr. Human Geogr.; Int. Dev. Abstr.; World Agric. Econ. Rural Sociol. Abstr.

LC HG1501 ISSN 0957-1973
DD 332.15 UK
PORTFOLIO INTERNATIONAL. [Portf. int.]. (1986)-. Periodical. English. Twelve times a year. £64.00 Europe; £76.00 other. MSM International, PO Box 11, Loughborough, Leicester LE11 1ZY United Kingdom. **Tel** 011 44 509 233100.

LC HC244 .P74
AU
CEASED
PRESSESCHAU OSTWIRTSCHAFT. **Added/Corp** Osterreichisches Ost-und Sudosteuropa--Institut. (1962)-(June 1995). Periodical. German. Osterreichishes Ost und Sudosteuropa Institute, Josefsplatz 6, A-1010 Wien(Vienna) Austria. **Tel** 011 43 222/512 18 95, FAX 011 43 222/512 2189 553. **ED** Stephan Baristtz. Index available. **Circ:** 250 (ctrl).
Desc: Abstracts from East European periodicals regarding the current economic situation and development.

LC HG1501 ISSN 0081-8070
DD 332.1 US
CCC
PRINCETON STUDIES IN INTERNATIONAL FINANCE. **See** Finance.

LC HC121 .P75 ISSN 0301-7036
MX
Pr Rev.
PROBLEMAS DEL DESARROLLO. [Probl. desarro.]. **Added/Corp** Universidad Nacional Autonoma de Mexico. Instituto de Investigaciones Economicas. (1969)-. Periodical. Spanish. Four times a year. $40.00. Instituto de Investigaciones Economica, Ciudad Universidad del Coyoacan, 04510 Mexico DF Mexico. **Tel** 011 52 5 6230080. Index available. cum. index. **Circ:** 2,000 (ctrl). available on microfilm and microfiche.
Desc: Economical and socio-political studies in Latin-America and Mexico.
Ind/Abst Hisp. Am. Period. Index, HAPI; Int. Labour Doc.; PAIS Int. Print (1991-).

ISSN 0885-2316
DD 905 US
PROCEEDINGS / ... ANNUAL THIRD WORLD CONFERENCE. [Proc. - Third World Conf.]. **Main/Conf** Third World Conference. (1982)-. Proceedings. English. One time a year. $52.00. Third World Conference Foundation, PO Box 53110, Chicago IL 60653. **Tel** (312)241-6688. **ED** Roger K Oden. **Ad Acc.**

LC HC461 .N64a
DD 330.952/005 JA
QUARTERLY ECONOMIC REVIEW. **See** Business and Economics-Economic History, Conditions.

ISSN 1120-754X
IT
UDC 32
SUSPENDED
RE. REGIONE EUROPA. [Re, Reg. Eur.]. **VFOAT** Regione Europe. (1990)-(1993). Periodical. Italian. Four times a year. L50000 Italy; L100000 other. Edizioni Cire, C So Magenta 81, 20123 Milan Italy. **Tel** 011 39 2 4816296.

LC HB3 .R28 ISSN 0034-2971
BE
REFLETS ET PERSPECTIVES DE LA VIE ECONOMIQUE. [Reflets perspect. vie econ.]. (Oct. 1961)-. Periodical. French. Six times a year. $84.49. Recherche and Diffusion Econ Secretariat, 41 Chemin Ducal, 1970 Wezembeek Belgium. **Tel** 011 32 2 7676526. Index available. **Bk Rev. Ad Acc. Circ:** 1,000.
Desc: Covers international economy and economic policy.
Ind/Abst PAIS Int. Print.

ISSN 1120-6535
IT
UDC 336.74
REGIME DELLE IMPORTAZIONI, ESPORTAZIONI E NORME VALUTARIE. (1980)-. Periodical. Italian. Twelve times a year. L170310. Editrice Commercio Estero, Via Vincenzo Tizzani 36, 00151 Rome Italy. **Tel** 011 39 6 58201061.

LC DS520 .R44 ISSN 0218-3056
DD 959/.005 SI
●**REGIONAL OUTLOOK. SOUTHEAST ASIA.** **Added/Corp** Institute of Southeast Asian Studies. (1993)-. English. One time a year. $29.00. Institute of Southeast Asian Studies / Singapore, Heng Mui Keng Terrace, Pasir Panjang Road, Singapore 0511 Republic of Singapore. **Tel** 011 65 8702447, FAX 011 65 7781735, telex 37068. **(Subscription address:** Ashgate Publishing Company / US, Old Post Road, Brookfield VT 05036-9704. **Tel** (800)535-9544, (802)276-3162, FAX (802)276-3837.**) Circ:** 1,000.
Desc: Provides overviews and insights into the current geo-political and economic situations in the individual countries and the region as a whole, together with the likely trends over the next year or so.

BE
REPORT FROM EUROPE. **Added/Corp** Chemical Bank (New York, N.Y.). (July/Aug. 1973)-. Periodical. English. Eleven times a year. Free on request. Chemical Bank, 380 Madison Avenue/12th Floor, New York NY 10017. **Tel** (212)770-3139.

LC HC151.A1 C36a
DD 341.24/5 GY
REPORT OF THE SECRETARY-GENERAL OF THE CARIBBEAN COMMUNITY. **Main/Corp** Caribbean Community. **VFOAT** Secretary-General's Report. (19??)-. Corporate Report. English. One time a year. Free. Caribbean Community Secretariat, PO Box 10827, Bank of Guyana Building, Georgetown Guyana. **Tel** 011 592 2 69281-9, FAX 011 592 2 67816, 011 592 2 58039, telex 2263 CARISEC GY. **Circ:** 925.
Desc: Gives an overview of the economic situation and reports on developments within the common market, in the coordination of foreign policies and in functional cooperation.

LC HC411 .R47 ISSN 1047-126X
DD 330.95/005 US
RESEARCH IN ASIAN ECONOMIC STUDIES. [Res. Asian econ. stud.]. Vol. 1 (1988)-. Monographic series. English. Irregular. $73.25. JAI Press Inc., 55 Old Post Road, Suite 2, PO Box 1678, Greenwich CT 06836-1678. **Tel** (203)661-7602, FAX (203)661-0792. **ED** M. Jan Dutta.

LC HD2755.5 .R467 ISSN 0275-5319
DD 338.8/8/05 US
RESEARCH IN INTERNATIONAL BUSINESS AND FINANCE. [Res. int. bus. Financ.]. (1979)-. English. Irregular. $73.25. JAI Press Inc., 55 Old Post Road, Suite 2, PO Box 1678, Greenwich CT 06836-1678. **Tel** (203)661-7602, FAX (203)661-0792. **ED** H. Peter Grey.

LC HF1410 .R465 ISSN 1053-1254
DD 337/.05 US
RESEARCH IN INTERNATIONAL BUSINESS AND INTERNATIONAL RELATIONS. [Res. int. bus. int. relat.]. Vol. 1 (1986)-. Monographic series. English. Irregular. $73.25. JAI Press Inc., 55 Old Post Road, Suite 2, PO Box 1678, Greenwich CT 06836-1678. **Tel** (203)661-7602, FAX (203)661-0792.

LC HF1351 .R484 ISSN 0965-7576
UK
CCC
REVIEW OF INTERNATIONAL ECONOMICS. (1992)-. Academic Scholarly Publication. English. Three times a year. $149.00. Basil Blackwell Publishers Ltd., 108 Cowley Road, Oxford 0X4 1JF United Kingdom. **Tel** 011 44 1235 465500, FAX 011 44 1235 465556, telex 837022 OXBOOK G. **(Subscription address:** Blackwell Publishers / UK, 108 Cowley Road, Oxford OX4 1JF United Kingdom. **Tel** 011 44 1865 791100, FAX 011 44 1865 791347.**)**

LC HF1410 .R467 ISSN 0969-2290
DD 337 UK
CCC
●**REVIEW OF INTERNATIONAL POLITICAL ECONOMY : RIPE.** **VFOAT** RIPE. Vol. 1, No. 1 (Spring 1994)-. Academic Scholarly Publication. English. Four times a year (quarterly). $147.16. Routledge, 11 New Fetter Lane, London EC4P 4EE United Kingdom. **Tel** 011 44 171 5839855, FAX 011 44 171 5830701. **(Subscription address:** ITPS Ltd., Cheriton House, North Way Andover, Hampshire SP10 5BE United Kingdom. **Tel** 011 44 1264 332424, FAX 011 44 1264 342807.**) ED** Board. **Ad Acc.** Full Page (B&W) £150.00. Documents available from BLDSC.

LC HB9 .R35 ISSN 0034-7140
BL
REVISTA BRASILEIRA DE ECONOMIA. [Rev. bras. econ.]. Vol. 1, No. 1 (Sept. 1947)-. Periodical. Portuguese. Irregular (4 issues). $60.00. Fundacao Getulio Vargas, Praia de Botafogo, 190 6 Andar, 22253-900 Rio de Janeiro RJ Brazil. **Tel** 011 5521 551 0698, FAX 011 5521 551 1596, 011 5521 551 5755. **ED** Moacy R. A. Fioravante. **Bk Rev. Circ:** 2,800.
Desc: Report on the national economic performance and

Business and Economics —International Economic Relations

the development of international economic thought.
Ind/Abst AGRICOLA; Hisp. Am. Period. Index, HAPI; Int. Bibliogr. Sociol.; Int. Labour Doc.; LABORDOC; PAIS Int. Print; Soyabean Abstr.

LC HC59 .R45   **ISSN** 0225-5189
DD 338.9/005   CN
    CCC
Pr Rev.
REVUE CANADIENNE D'ETUDES DU DEVELOPPEMENT. [Rev. can. etud. dev.]. **Added/Corp** International Development Studies Group. University of Ottawa. Institute for International Co-Operation. **VFOAT** Canadian Journal of Development Studies. Vol. 1 (May 1980)-. Periodical. English (French). Four times a year (April/May, July/Aug., Oct./Nov.). 48.02Can$. University of Ottawa, 550 Cumberland Room 160B, Ottawa Ontario K1N 6N5 Canada. **Tel** (613)564-5459, FAX (613)564-9518. Index available. cum. index. **Bk Rev**, (Qty: 30). **Circ:** 500 (ctrl). Documents available from The Genuine Article.
Ind/Abst ABC POL SCI (19??-19??); Am. Hist. Life (1980-); Asia.-Pac. Econ. Lit.; Can. Period. Index (1989-); Curr. Cit.; Curr. Contents Soc. Behav. Sci.; Econ. Lit. Index; Foreign Lang. Index; Geogr. Abstr. Human Geogr.; Int. Bibliogr. Sociol.; Int. Dev. Abstr.; Int. Labour Doc.; J. Econ. Lit. (1984-); LABORDOC; PAIS Int. Print (1991-); Public Aff. Inf. Serv. Bull.; Res. Alert [Full Cov.]; Rural Dev. Abstr.; Soc. Sci. Cit. Index [Full Cov.]; SportSearch (1984-); World Agric. Econ. Rural Sociol. Abstr.

LC HC241.A1 R48   **ISSN** 1155-4274
    FR
REVUE DU MARCHE UNIQUE EUROPEEN. (1991)-. Periodical. French. Four times a year. $210.12. Clement Juglar, 62 Avenue Suffren, 75015 Paris France. **Tel** 33 1 45675806, FAX 33 1 45665070. **ED** Alfonso Mattera. cum. index. **Bk Rev**, (Qty: 4). ctrl circ.
Ind/Abst PAIS Int. Print.

    IT
    SUSPENDED
RIVISTA DI DIRITTO VALUTARIO E DI ECONOMIA INTERNAZIONALE. See Law.

LC HF25 .A65   **ISSN** 1061-2009
DD 382   US
    CCC
RUSSIAN & EAST EUROPEAN FINANCE AND TRADE. See Business and Economics-Commerce.

    PL
SERIA EKONOMIA. **Added/Corp** Polska Akademia Nauk. Oddzial w Poznaniu. **VFOAT** Ekonomia. Vol. 1 (1976)-. Monographic series. Polish. Irregular. Price varies per volume. Polska Akademia Nauk / Zaklad Narodowy im. Ossoliniskich, Ossolineum Publishing House of the Polish Academy of Sciences, Ulitsa Rynek 9, 50-106 Wroclaw Poland. **Tel** 011 48 71 38625, FAX 011 48 71 448103, telex 0712771.

    NE
SEW. See Law-International Law.

LC HC462.7 .T65
    JA
SHUKAN TOYO KEIZAI. VFOAT Toyo Keizai.; Weekly Toyo Keizai. (1961)-. Periodical. Japanese. Fifty times a year. $369.00. **(Subscription address:** Maruzen Company Ltd., PO Box 5050, Import & Export Department, Tokyo 100 31 Japan. **Tel** 011 81 3 32789224.) **Continues** Toyo Keizai Shinpo.

LC HG4501   **ISSN** 1053-5497
DD 332.6   US
●**SOUTH AFRICA INVESTOR.** See Business and Economics-Investments.

LC HG5851.A2 S65   **ISSN** 1053-5497
DD 968.06/3/05   US
    TITLE CHANGE
SOUTH AFRICA REPORTER. See Business and Economics-Investments.

    ISSN 0963-7036
DD 338.947   UK
Pr Rev.
SOVIET & EASTERN EUROPEAN REPORT. See Law-International Law.

    ISSN 0081-3559
    US
SPECIAL PAPERS IN INTERNATIONAL ECONOMICS. **Main/Corp** Princeton University. International Finance Section. (1955)-. Monographic series. English. Seven times a year. Price varies per volume. International Finance Section, Princeton University, Department of Economics, Princeton NJ 08544. **Tel** (609)258-4051, FAX (609)258-6419, telex 499-1258 TIGER.

LC E840 .U614b   **ISSN** 0271-1486
DD 327.73/005   US
SPECIAL REPORT - UNITED STATES DEPARTMENT OF STATE, BUREAU OF PUBLIC AFFAIRS. (SPECIAL REPORT.). [Spec. rep. - U.S. Dep. State, Bur. Public Aff.]. **Added/Corp** United States. Dept. of State. Bureau of Public Affairs. (19??)-. Monographic series. English. Price varies per volume. US Department of State / Bureau of Public Affairs, Washington DC 20520. **Continues** Special Report - Department of State, Bureau of Public Affairs, Office of Public Communication, 0271-1508.

    ISSN 1042-4237
DD 332   US
STRATEGIC INVESTMENT. [Strateg. investm.]. (19??)-. Periodical. English. Twelve times a year. $59.00. Agora Publishing, 824 East Baltimore Street, Baltimore MD 21202. **Tel** (800)433-1528.

LC HB   **ISSN** 1100-1283
DD 330   SW
UDC 33
STUDIES IN INTERNATIONAL ECONOMICS & GEOGRAPHY. [Stud. int. econ. geogr.]. **VFOAT** Studies in International Economics and Geography. (1988)-. Monographic series. English. Irregular. Price varies per volume.
Ind/Abst Geogr. Abstr. Human Geogr.

LC WMLC 93/4129   **ISSN** 0797-0064
    RU
SUMA. See Business and Economics-Economic History, Conditions.

LC HC59 .S8876
    KO
SUUN CHOSA WOLBO. Periodical. Korean. Twelve times a year. W600 each issue. Hanguk Suchurip Unhaeng, 541 5-ka Namdaemunno Chung-ku, Seoul Korea.

    ISSN 1035-7068
    AT
SYDNEY PAPERS, THE. **Added/Corp** Sydney Institute. Vol. 1, No. 1 (Spring/Summer 1989)-. Periodical. English. Four times a year. 16.44Aus$. Sydney Institute, 41 Phillip Street, Sydney 2000 Australia. **Tel** 011 61 2 2523366, FAX 011 61 23 2523360. **ED** Anne Henderson.

    IT
TARIFFA DAZI DOGANALI. Italian. L250000.00. Editrice Commercio Estero, Via Vincenzo Tizzani 36, 00151 Rome Italy. **Tel** 011 39 6 58201061.

    IT
TEORIA E PRATICA DEGLI SCAMBI INTERNAZIONALI. Italian. Four times a year. L200000. Associazione Italiana per Il Commercio Mondiale, Via Donizzetti 53, 20122 Milan Italy. **Tel** 2/796282.

    ISSN 0049-3740
    UK
THIRD WORLD REPORTS. See Political Science.

    ISSN 0707-7815
    CN
THOUGHTS ON INTERNATIONAL DEVELOPMENT. **Main/Corp** Canada. International Development Agency. **VFOAT** Reflexions sur le Developpement International. 1 (1971)-. Monographic series. English (French). Irregular. Price varies per volume. Information Division, Canadian International Development Agency, Ottawa Ontario Canada.

LC HC59.7 .T53   **ISSN** 0040-7356
DD 909/.09724   FR
    CCC
TIERS MONDE (PARIS). (REVUE TIERS-MONDE.). [Tiers monde]. **Added/Corp** Universite de Paris. Institut d'Etude du Developpement Economique et Social. Universite de Paris I: Pantheon-Sorbonne. Institut d'Etude du Developpement Economique et Social. Vol. 8, No. 29 (Jan./March 1967)-. Periodical. French. Four times a year. 465.00F France; 515.00F other. Presses Universitaires de France, Department des Revues, 17 Rue Souflot, 75005 Paris France. **Tel** 011 33 1 43267741, telex PUF 600 474 F. **ED** Charles Moraze. **Continues** Tiers-Monde, 0040-7356.
Desc: For scientists, teachers, administrators and men of action. This journal studies ideas and facts concerning the Third World, with an international public content.
Ind/Abst For. Abstr.; Hisp. Am. Period. Index, HAPI (19??-); Int. Bibliogr. Sociol.; Int. Dev. Abstr. (?-?); LABORDOC; PAIS Int. Print; Popul. Index (?-?); Rural Dev. Abstr.

    CH
TRADE WINDS INDUSTRY WEEKLY. See Business and Economics-Commerce.

    ISSN 0259-9880
    CH
TRADE WINDS MONTHLY. See Business and Economics-Commerce.

LC HC701 .S6
    US
Pr Rev.
TRANSITION : THE NEWSLETTER ABOUT REFORMING ECONOMIES. See Business and Economics-Economic Assistance and Development.

LC D839 .T7   **ISSN** 0275-5351
DD 327/.09045   US
TRIALOGUE. [Trialogue]. **Added/Corp** Trilateral Commission. No. 1 (Oct. 1973)-. English. Three times a year. $20.00. Trilateral Commission, 345 East 46th Street, Suite 711, New York NY 10017. **Tel** (212)661-1180, FAX (212)949-7268.
Ind/Abst Energy Inf. Abstr.; Environ. Abstr.; Public Aff. Inf. Serv. Bull.

LC HB9 .T7   **ISSN** 0041-3011
    MX
Pr Rev.
TRIMESTRE ECONOMICO, EL. [Trimest. econ.]. **Added/Corp** Fondo de Cultura Economica (Mexico). Vol. 1, No. 1, (1934)-. Periodical. Spanish. Four times a year. $120.00. Fondo de Cultura Economica / Mexico, Av Picacho Ajusco 227 / Pedregal, 14200 Mexico DF Mexico. **Tel** 011 52 5 2274670 71, FAX 011 52 5 2274683, telex 01775866. Index available. cum. index. **Bk Rev**. **Ad Acc**, **Adv Mgr:** Guillermo Escalante. **Circ:** 5,000. Documents available from The Genuine Article.
Desc: Concerns economics and international economics.
Ind/Abst Econ. Lit. Index; Hisp. Am. Period. Index, HAPI; Int. Labour Doc.; J. Econ. Lit.; Res. Alert [Full Cov.]; Soc. Sci. Cit. Index [Full Cov.].

    US
U.S. TRADE STATUS WITH SOCIALIST COUNTRIES. See Business and Economics-Commerce.

    ISSN 0041-5707
    GW
UBERSEE RUNDSCHAU. See Business and Economics-Commerce.

LC HG3879 .U27
    SZ
UBS INTERNATIONAL FINANCE.
Added/Corp Union de Banques Suisses. Departement des Etudes Economiques. **VFOAT** U.B.S. International Finance. Vol. 1, No. 1 (Fall 1989)-. Periodical. English. Four times a year. Free on request. Union Bank of Switzerland / UBS, Economic Research Department, PO Box 8021, Zurich Switzerland. **Tel** 011 41 1 2344243. **ED** William Gasser. **Continues** UBS Business Facts and Figures.
Ind/Abst PAIS Int. Print.

LC HF1410 .M66
DD 337/.05   SZ
    CEASED
UNCTAD BULLETIN. See Business and Economics-Commerce.

LC HF1371 .U53   **ISSN** 1014-370X
DD 337/.05   SZ
UNCTAD REVIEW. See Business and Economics-Commerce.

LC JX1995 .U58   **ISSN** 0499-1583
DD 353.0089   US
UNITED STATES CONTRIBUTIONS TO INTERNATIONAL ORGANIZATIONS.
Added/Corp United States. Dept. of State. Bureau of International Organization Affairs. (1951/52)-. One time a year. US Department of State / International Organization Affairs, 2201 C Street Northwest, Washington DC 20520.

    HK
USSR ECONOMY AND TRADE GUIDE. (19??)-. English (Chinese). Twenty-six times a year. $400.00. SHK International Services Ltd, 22P 151 Gloucester Road, Hong Kong Hong Kong. **Tel** 011 852 5 28325100, FAX 011 852 25725258.

    ISSN 0039-7288
    SW
UTRIKESHANDEL. MANADSSTATISTIK. **Added/Corp** Sweden. Statistiska Centralbyraan. Sweden. Statistiska Centralbyraan. Foreign Trade. Monthly Bulletin. **VFOAT** Foreign Trade. Monthly Bulletin. Vol. 1 (Jan. 1968)-. Bulletin. Swedish (English and Swedish). Twelve times a year. Scandinavian University Press, PO Box 2959 Toeyen, N 0608 Oslo 6 Norway. **Tel** 011 47 2 2575400, FAX 011 47 2 2575353, telex 71896 UROR N. **(Subscription address:** Scandinavian University Press, 200 Meacham Ave., Elmont NY 11003. **Tel** (516)352-7300, FAX (516)352-7377.) **Continues** Manadsstatistik Over Utrikeshandeln.

ISSN 0043-6275
GW
CCC
WIRTSCHAFTSDIENST (HAMBURG). (WIRTSCHAFTSDIENST.). [Wirtschaftsdienst]. **Added/Corp** Hamburgisches Welt-Wirtschafts-Archiv. Universitat Kiel. Institut fuer Weltwirtschaft. HWWA-Institut fuer Wirtschaftsforschung-Hamburg. (June 1949)-. Academic Scholarly Publication. German. Twelve times a year. $95.19. Nomos Verlagsgesellschaft, Postfach 610, D-76484 Baden Baden Germany. **Tel** 011 49 7221 210439. **Ad Acc. Circ:** 3,500. ***Continues*** *Wirtschaftsdienst (Hamburg: 1916).*
Ind/Abst EMBASE; Int. Labour Doc.; LABORDOC; PAIS Int. Print; World Agric. Econ. Rural Sociol. Abstr.

ISSN 0228-4235
DD 337/.05 CN
WORKING PAPER (UNIVERSITY OF WESTERN ONTARIO.) CENTRE FOR THE STUDY OF INTERNATIONAL ECONOMIC RELATIONS). (WORKING PAPER / CENTRE FOR THE STUDY OF INTERNATIONAL ECONOMIC RELATIONS.). [Work. pap. - Cent. Study Int. Econ. Rel.]. No. 8001 (Jan. 1980)-. Monographic series. English. Thirty times a year. Price varies per volume. University of Western Ontario Department of Economics, London Ontario N6A 5C2 Canada. **Tel** (519)661-3514. **ED** John Whalley. Index available. cum. index. **Circ:** 150 (ctrl).
Desc: Contains both theoretical and policy-oriented working papers in the areas of international trade and economic development.

LC HG3881.5.W57 I57a
DD 332.1/532/025 US
WORLD BANK GROUP DIRECTORY, THE. **Main/Corp** International Bank for Reconstruction and Development. **Added/Corp** International Bank for Reconstruction and Development. Information, Technology, and Facilities Dept. **VFOAT** Directory. (June 1990)-. Directory. English. Two times a year. $35.00. World Bank Publications, 1818 H Street Northwest, Washington DC 20043. **Tel** (202)473-1155, (202)473-1155, FAX (202)522-3224, telex WUI 64145 WORLDBANK. ***Continues*** *International Bank for Reconstruction and Development. Directory.*

LC HF1 .S83 HF1410 **ISSN** 0732-734X
DD 330 S 337/.05 US
WORLD BUSINESS (MENLO PARK, CALIF.). (WORLD BUSINESS.). [World bus.]. No. 1-. Periodical. English. $50.00 single issue, to associates, on request. C Calk Director, International Secretariat, SRI International, Menlo Park CA 94025.

LC HF1414 .W67 **ISSN** 1015-5449
DD 337/.05 SZ
WORLD COMPETITIVENESS REPORT. **Added/Corp** EMF Foundation. IMEDE (Institute) World Economic Forum. IMD International (Institute). **VFOAT** EMF's World Competitiveness Report. **VAT** European Management Forum's World Competitiveness Report. (1986)-. English. One time a year (June). $754.33. I M D, PO Box 915, CH-1001 Lausanne Switzerland. **Tel** 011 41 21 6180251, FAX 011 41 21 6180204, telex 455871. ***Continues*** *Report on International Competitiveness.*
Desc: A study on the competitiveness of nations and how countries and companies compete in international markets.

LC HJ8899 .W672 **ISSN** 0253-2859
DD 336.3/435/091724 US
WORLD DEBT TABLES. **See** Business and Economics-Abstracting, Bibliographies and Statistics.

LC HC10 .W7979 **ISSN** 0256-6877
DD 338.5/443/09048 US
WORLD ECONOMIC OUTLOOK (WASHINGTON). (WORLD ECONOMIC OUTLOOK : A SURVEY BY THE STAFF OF THE INTERNATIONAL MONETARY FUND.). [World econ. outlook]. **Added/Corp** International Monetary Fund. (May 1980)-. Periodical. English (French, Spanish and Arabic). Two times a year. $62.00. International Monetary Fund, 700 19th Street Northwest, Publishing Unit, Washington DC 20431. **Tel** (202)623-7430, FAX (202)623-7201. available on microfilm from University Microfilms International (UMI).
Desc: Individual country insights and global perspectives; discusses the problems of balance of payments adjustment by the major groups of countries, the key policy options available to them, issues of inflation and interest rates and debt and capital flows.

LC HF1410 .W667 **ISSN** 0378-5920
DD 382.1/05 UK
CCC
Pr Rev.
WORLD ECONOMY, THE. [World econ.]. Vol. 1 (Oct. 1977)-. Academic Scholarly Publication. English. Seven times a year. $420.00. Basil Blackwell Publishers Ltd., 108 Cowley Road, Oxford 0X4 1JF United Kingdom. **Tel** 011 44 1235 465500, FAX 011 44 1235 465556, telex 837022 OXBOOK G. **(Subscription address:** Blackwell Publishers / UK, 108 Cowley Road, Oxford OX4 1JF United Kingdom. **Tel** 011 44 1865 791100, FAX 011 44 1865 791347.) **ED** Peter Oppenheimer, Ingo Walter, and Hugh Corbet. **Bk Rev. Ad Acc. Circ:** 1,500 (ctrl). available on microfilm and microfiche from University Microfilms International (UMI). Documents available from The Genuine Article, UMI Article Clearinghouse.
Desc: Provides a continuous focus on the conduct of international economic affairs, for professionals in commerce and industry, government and international government.
Ind/Abst ABC POL SCI; ABI/INFORM Glob. Ed.; ABI/INFORM [Computer File] (March 1982-); Acad. Search; Br. Humanit. Index; Bus. Index (1985-); Coal Abstr.; Contents Recent Econ. J.; Contents Pages Manage.; Curr. Cit.; Curr. Contents Soc. Behav. Sci.; Econ. Lit. Index; Energy Res. Abstr. (May 1980-); EP Collect.; Gen. BusinessFile (1985-); Gen. Period. Index (1985-); Geogr. Abstr. Human Geogr.; Homework Help.; INFO-SOUTH Abstr.; Int. Dev. Abstr.; Int. Labour Doc.; Int. Polit. Sci. Abstr.; J. Econ. Lit.; LABORDOC; Mag. Search; MasterFile FullTEXT 1000; MasterFile FullTEXT 350; MasterFile FullTEXT 650; MasterFile FullTEXT (July 1993-); OCLC; PAIS Int. Print; Res. Alert [Full Cov.]; Selec. Coop. Index Manage. Period.; Soc. Sci. Cit. Index [Full Cov.]; Sug. Indus. Abstr.; Telebase; Trade Ind. Index; World Agric. Econ. Rural Sociol. Abstr.; World Mag. Bank.

ISSN 1055-1573
US
WORLD FINANCE (WASHINGTON, D.C.). (WORLD FINANCE.). (1991)-. Periodical. English. Twelve times a year. $150.00. International Investment, Ltd., PO Box 57450, Washington DC 20037.

ISSN 0229-6942
DD 327/.05 CN
WORLD POLICY. [World policy]. No. 1 (1983)-. English. One time a year. $10.00. World Policy, Department of Political Studies, Lakehead University, Thunder Bay Ontario P7B 5E1 Canada.

LC HG450
DD 332.6 US
WORLD RISK ANALYSIS REPORTS. (19??)-. English. One time a year (with periodic updates). $2,000 (complete set). S.J. Rundt & Associates Inc., 130 East 63rd Street, New York NY 10021-7334. **Tel** (212)838-0141, FAX (201)744-3073. Index available. **Bk Rev.** ctrl circ.
Desc: Covers international trade and currency issues, with risk analysis for 56 countries.

LC HC10 .W799 **ISSN** 0749-5811
DD 338.5/442/02854 US
WORLD SERVICE DATA BANKS. [World serv. data banks]. (19??)-. English. WEFA / Philadelphia, PO Box 8500, Suite 1995, Philadelphia PA 19178. **Tel** (215)667-6000, telex 710 6700575. ***Continues*** *World Economic Service Data Banks, 0749-582X.*

LC K27 .O78 **ISSN** 1022-6583
SZ
•**WORLD TRADE AND ARBITRATION MATERIALS.** **See** Business and Economics-Commerce.

INVESTMENTS

LC HG4501 .F58 **ISSN** 1065-3414
DD 332 US
TITLE CHANGE
5-STAR INVESTOR. (5-STAR INVESTOR: MORNINGSTAR'S GUIDE TO BUILDING A WINNING FUND PORTFOLIO.). [5-star invest.]. **VFOAT** 5 Star Investor; Five Star Investor. (1992)-(199?). Periodical. English. Morningstar Inc., 225 West Wacker Drive, Chicago IL 60606. **Tel** (312)696-6000, (800)876-5005. ***Continued by*** *Morningstar Investor, 1082-3018.*

LC HG1501 **ISSN** 0885-4777
DD 332.1 US
100 HIGHEST YIELDS. **See** Business and Economics-Banks and Banking.

LC HG **ISSN** 0884-7657
DD 332 US
401 (K) REPORTER, THE. [401 (k) report.]. Vol. 1, No. 1 (July 1985)-. Periodical. English. Twelve times a year. $126.00. Universal Pensions Inc., Box 979, Brainerd MN 56401. **Tel** (800)541-6089, (800)346-3860, FAX (218)829-2106. **ED** Jennifer Norquist (Editor's telephone: (218)829-4781). **Circ:** 500 (ctrl).
Desc: Provides technical analysis and news updates on 401 (k) and other qualified plans. Aimed at financial organizations and employees.

LC HG4501 .A23 **ISSN** 0192-3315
DD 332.6/78/05 US
AAII JOURNAL. [AAII j.]. **Added/Corp** American Association of Individual Investors. **VFOAT** A.A.I.I. Journal. **VAT** American Association of Individual Investors Journal. (197?)-. Periodical. English. Ten times a year. comes with membership. American Association of Individual Investors, 625 North Michigan Avenue, Chicago IL 60611. **Tel** (312)280-0170. **ED** Maria Crawford Scott. Index available. **Bk Rev. Circ:** 105,000.
Desc: Publishes educational articles intended to provide a background for the understanding of investment theory and practice. All investment categories and methodologies are examined.

LC HC462.95 .A25 HF3828 .A223 **ISSN** 0915-4841
DD 332.6 JA
ACCESS NIPPON. **VFOAT** Business Handbook, Access Nippon. (19??)-. English. One time a year. $38.45. Access Nippon Inc, 2-8-5 Uchikanda Chiyoda-ki, Tokyo 101 Japan. **(Subscription address:** Japan Publications Trading Company Ltd., PO Box 5030, Tokyo International, Tokyo 100-31 Japan. **Tel** 011 81 3 3292 3753.)

LC HG450
DD 332.6 UK
ADVANCES IN INVESTMENT ANALYSIS & PORTFOLIO MANAGEMENT. (19??)-. Periodical. English. One time a year. £44.50 UK; $76.75 other. JAI Press Ltd., The Courtyard, 28 High Street, Hampton Hill Middlesex TW12 1PD United Kingdom. **Tel** 011 44 181 9439296, FAX 011 44 181 9439317. **(Subscription address:** JAI Press Inc. / North America Subscriptions, PO Box 1678, Greenwich CT 06836. **Tel** (203)661-7602.)

DD 332.6 US
ADVISOR. **Added/Corp** Retirement Systems of Alabama. (197?)-. Periodical. English. Twelve times a year. Free on request. Retirement Systems of Alabama, PO Box 302150, Montgomery AL 36130. **Tel** (334)832-4140.

LC HG4501 **ISSN** 1034-2338
DD 332.605 AT
AFR INVESTOR. [AFR invest.]. **VFOAT** Investor; Australian Financial Review Investor. (1989)-. Periodical. English. One time a week. John Fairfax & Sons Ltd, GPO Box 506, Sydney NSW 2001 Australia. **Tel** 011 61 2 2822833, FAX 011 61 2 2822424, telex 23425. **(Subscription address:** TNT Newsfast International, PO Box 351, Mascot NSW 2020 Australia. **Tel** 011 61 2 3177717.)

LC HG **ISSN** 1053-8763
DD 332 US
AFRICA INVESTMENT MONITOR. (AFRICA INVESTMENT MONITOR : AIM.). [Afr. investm. monitor]. **Added/Corp** Africa Investment Associates. **VFOAT** AIM. (Dec. 19, 1991)-. Trade Publication. English. Twelve times a year. $395.00. Media International Inc., PO Box 25683, Washington DC 20007. **Tel** (202)338-4440, FAX (202)338-4440. **ED** Gail Reardon. **Ad Acc, Adv Mgr:** Gail Reardon. **Circ:** 5,000.
Ind/Abst F&S Index Plus Text, Int. [Select. Cov.]; Mark. Advert. Ref. Serv.; PROMT.

LC HG **ISSN** 1061-8880
DD 332 US
AFRICAN STOCK MARKETS. [Afr. stock mark.]. **Added/Corp** Africa Investment Promotion Partnership. DAC International, Inc. (1991)-. English. DAC International, 2100 M Street NW, Washington DC 20008. **Tel** (202)898-1070.

LC HG4501
DD 332.6 US
AIC INVESTMENT BULLETIN. **Added/Corp** AIC Investment Advisors, Inc. **VAT** American Institute Counselors Investment Bulletin. Vol. 51 No. 15 (Aug. 5, 1985)-. Bulletin. English. Twenty-four times a year (Publishes 1st and 3rd Monday of each month). $60.00. AIC Investment Advisors Inc, 440 South Street, Pittsfield MA 01201. **Tel** (413)499-1111. ***Continues*** *Investment Bulletin (Great Barrington, Mass.), 0401-8680.*

LC HG450
DD 332.6 US
AIMR NEWSLETTER. (19??)-. Newsletter. English. Six times a year. $25.00. Association for Investment Management Research, 5 Boar's Head Lane, Charlottesville VA 22903. **Tel** (804)980-9712, (804)977-6600. ***Continues*** *Investment Management Newsletter.*

LC KF1071.Z9 A14 **ISSN** 0271-3535
DD 346.73/0926 US
ALI-ABA COURSE OF STUDY. BROKER-DEALER REGULATION: MATERIALS. **See** Law.

LC KF1072.Z9 A143 **ISSN** 0270-9686
DD 346.73/092 US
ALI-ABA COURSE OF STUDY. INVESTMENT ADVISER REGULATION: MATERIALS. **See** Law.

Business and Economics — Investments

LC HG4501 .A66 **ISSN** 1061-8872
DD 338.8/8873/05 US
AMERICAN INVESTOR (RESEARCH TRIANGLE PARK, N.C.). (AMERICAN INVESTOR.). [Am. invest.]. **Added/Corp** Institute of Foreign Investment in America. Issue I (Jan./Feb. 1991)-. Periodical. English. Six times a year. Free (qualified subscribers), $96.00 (other). Institute of Foreign Investment in America, Inc., PO Box 14265, Research Triangle Park NC 27709-4265.

LC HG4651 **ISSN** 1057-0020
DD 346 US
AMERICAN/OVERSEAS INVESTOR, THE. [Am. overseas investor]. **VFOAT** American Overseas Investor. Vol. 1, No. 1 (1991)-. Periodical. English. Twelve times a year. $350.00. The American/Overseas Investor, 470 Park Avenue South, New York NY 10016-6820.

LC HG4907 .A62 **ISSN** 1061-7051
DD 332.6/025/73 US
AMERICA'S BEST MONEY MANAGERS. [Am. best money manag.]. **VFOAT** Nelson's America's Best Money Managers. (1991)-. English. One time a year. $151.75. Nelson Publications, One Gateway Plaza, PO Box 591, Port Chester NY 10573. **Tel** (914)937-8400, (800)333-6357, FAX (914)937-8908.

LC HG4574 **ISSN** 0550-6557
DD 332.6/42 US
AMEX DATABOOK. **Main/Corp** American Stock Exchange. 1st- Ed.; 1968-. English. $1.00. American Stock Exchange, 86 Trinity Place, New York NY 10006. **Tel** (212)306-1386, FAX (212)306-2160. Each issue contains an index to its own contents (no volume index)--loose.

LC HG4501
DD 332.6 NE
●**AMSTERDAM FINANCIAL SERIES. STOCK EXCHANGE AND EEC LAW : COMMENTARY.** (1994)-. English. Kluwer Law and Taxation Publishers / Netherlands, Staverenstraat 32015, PO Box 23, 7400 GA Deventer Netherlands. **Tel** 011 31 5700 47261.

LC HG450
DD 332.6 SP
ANALISIS TECNICO DE VALORES. (19??)-. Spanish. Twenty-six times a year. $253.13. Analisis Tecnico de Valores, Monte Exquniza 28 30IZDA, 28010 Madrid Spain. **Tel** 011 34 1 3192646.

LC HG **ISSN** 1071-2364
DD 332 US
●**ANALYST WATCH.** [Anal. watch]. **Added/Corp** Zacks Investment Research, Inc. (Oct. 30, 1993)-. Periodical. English. Twenty-six times a year. $250.00. Zacks Investment Research, 155 North Wacker Drive, 3rd Floor, Chicago IL 60606-1719. **Tel** (312)630-9880 ext. 149, FAX (312)630-9617. **Ad Acc**, **Adv Mgr**: Eden Levinson.

LC HG4905 .A66 **ISSN** 0884-6936
DD 332.63/22/0973021 US
 TITLE CHANGE
ANALYST'S HANDBOOK. [Anal. handb.]. **Added/Corp** Standard and Poor's Corporation. **VFOAT** Monthly Analyst's Handbook; Standard and Poor's Analyst's Handbook; Standard & Poor's Analyst's Handbook. (19??)-(1993). English. Standard & Poor's Corporation, (A Division of McGraw-Hill, Inc.), 25 Broadway, New York NY 10004. **Tel** (212)208-8775, (800)221-5277. **Continued by** S&P Analyst's Handbook.
 Desc: Provides the industry with the data needed to make performance comparisons of company to industry; industry to industry; and company and industry to business in general.

LC HD2756.2.J3 A5
DD 338.7/4/0952 JA
ANARISUTO GAIDO = ANALYSTS' GUIDE. **Added/Corp** Daiwa Shoken Kabushiki Kaisha. Chosabu. **VFOAT** Analysts' Guide. (1970)-. English (Japanese). One time a year. $252.00. Daiwa Securities Research Institute Company Ltd, 1-2-1 Kyobashi Chuo-ku, Tokyo 104 Japan. (**Subscription address:** Japan Publications Trading Company Ltd., PO Box 5030, Tokyo International, Tokyo 100-31 Japan. **Tel** 011 81 3 3292 3753.)
 Desc: Includes a statistical table covering the preceding 5 years.

LC HJ2053.C6 C64A
DD 353.97880072/22534/05 US
ANNUAL CAPITAL INVESTMENT BUDGET - COLORADO. OFFICE OF STATE PLANNING AND BUDGETING. **Main/Corp** Colorado. Office of State Planning and Budgeting. English. One time a year. Office of State Planning and Budgeting, 102 State Capitol Building, Denver CO 80203.

LC HG4244.66 .K8A **ISSN** 0127-2462
DD 338.7/4/025595 MY
ANNUAL COMPANIES HANDBOOK. (19??)-. English. One time a year. Komplek Bukit Naga, Off Jalan Semantan, Damansara Heights 50490 Kuala Lumpur Malaysia. **Continues** Companies Handbook of the Kuala Lumpur Stock Exchange Berhad.

LC HG4551
DD 332.6322 US
ANNUAL DIVIDEND RECORD. **Added/Corp** Standard and Poor's Corporation. **VFOAT** Dividend Record; Standard & Poor's Dividend Record; Standard & Poor's Annual Dividend Record. (19??)-. English. One time a year (published in Jan.). $32.50. Standard & Poor's Corporation, (A Division of McGraw-Hill, Inc.), 25 Broadway, New York NY 10004. **Tel** (212)208-8775, (800)221-5277. **Continues** Poor's Annual Dividend Record.
 Desc: All the information on the dividend disbursements of stocks for the entire year is included.

LC KF1440 .I53 **ISSN** 0195-5756
DD 346/.73/09202636 US
ANNUAL INSTITUTE ON SECURITIES REGULATION. [Annu. Inst. Secur. Regul.]. **Added/Corp** Practising Law Institute. (1970)-. English. Irregular. $198.00. Practising Law Institute, 810 Seventh Avenue, New York NY 10019-5818. **Tel** (212)765-5700, FAX (212)581-4670 general correspondence, (212)265-4742 orders and billing inquiries.
 Ind/Abst Index Leg. Period.; Leg. Resour. Index (1980-).

LC HG3729.I4 M37a
DD 338.7/61/3380954792 II
ANNUAL REPORT. **Main/Corp** State Industrial and Investment Corporation of Maharashtra. (19??)-. English. Nirmal, 1st Floor/Nariman Point, Bombay-1 BR India.

LC HD7105.45.A8 S86A
DD 332.6/7254 AT
ANNUAL REPORT. **Main/Corp** Superannuation Fund Investment Trust (Australia). (1987/88)-. English. One time a year. Commonwealth Funds Management, GPO Box 1921, Canberra ACT 2601 Australia. **Tel** 011 61 6 2750414, FAX 011 61 6 2750111. **Continues in part** The Annual Reports of the Superannuation Fund Investment Trust and the Commissioner for Superannuation.

LC HG6046 .U625A **ISSN** 0148-9283
DD 353.008/25 US
ANNUAL REPORT / COMMODITY FUTURES TRADING COMMISSION. **Main/Corp** United States. Commodity Futures Trading Commission. **VFOAT** CFTC Annual Report. (1976)-. English. One time a year. Commodity Futures Trading Commission, 2033 K Street NW, Washington DC 20581. available on microfiche (Vols. for (1986-) distributed to depository libraries).

LC HG3881 .E73 **ISSN** 0071-2868
DD 332.1/534/05 BE
ANNUAL REPORT - EUROPEAN INVESTMENT BANK. **Main/Corp** European Investment Bank. (1958)-. English (Danish, Dutch, French, German, Greek, Modern, Italian and Portuguese, Spanish). One time a year. Free on request. Office for Official Publications of the European Communities, 2 rue Mercier, 2985 Luxembourg Luxembourg. **Tel** 011 352 499281, FAX 011 352 292942763. **Circ:** 32,000.
 Desc: Summarizes the activities of the European Investment Bank (EIB) which was created in 1958 under the Treaty of Rome at the same time as the European Economic Community. Its task is to grant loans and give guarantees which facilitate the financing of capital investment promoting the balanced development of the community.

LC HG4501 **ISSN** 0839-9506
DD 332.6 CN
ANNUAL REPORT / INVESTMENT CANADA. [Annu. rep. - Invest Can.]. **Main/Corp** Investment Canada. **VFOAT** Rapport Annuel. (1986)-. English (French). One time a year. Free. Investment Canada, PO Box 2800 Station D, Ottawa Ontario K1P 6A5 Canada. **Tel** 995-3395, telex 053-4450. **Formed by the union of** Rapport Annuel, Loi sur l'Examen de l'Investissement Etranger, 0704-1624 **and** Annual Report, Foreign Investment Review Act, 0318-7853.

LC HG450
DD 332.6 UK
ANNUAL REPORT OF THE COUNCIL OF THE CORPORATION OF FOREIGN BONDHOLDERS. **Main/Corp** Corporation of Foreign Bondholders, London. No. 26- 1898/99-. English. One time a year. $4.21. Council of Foreign Bondholders, 9 12 Cheapside, London EC2V 6AB United Kingdom. **Tel** 011 44 181 2363641. **Continues** Annual General Report of the Council of the Corporation of Foreign Bondholders.

LC HJ3835.N58 N48B
DD 353.97890072/6 US
ANNUAL REPORT OF THE NEW MEXICO STATE PERMANENT FUND AND SEVERENCE TAX PERMANENT FUND. **Main/Corp** State of New Mexico State Investment Council. 21st- 1978/79-. English. One time a year. State Investment Council, P E R A Building, Santa Fe NM 87503. **Circ:** 250 (ctrl). **Continues** New Mexico. State Investment Council. Annual Report on the State Permanent Funds.
 Desc: Financial and performance summary of the state's two Permanent Trust Funds.

LC HG5761 .P45a
DD 332.6/4/09599 PH
ANNUAL REPORT - SECURITIES AND EXCHANGE COMMISSION. **Main/Corp** Philippines. Securities and Exchange Commission. **Added/Corp** Philippines. Securities and Exchange Commission. SEC Annual Report. **VFOAT** SEC Annual Report. (19??)-. English. Securities and Exchange Commission / Washington, 450 Fifth Street NW, Washington DC 20549. **Tel** (202)272-3100.

LC HG4651
DD 332.632 US
ANNUAL REPORT / SECURITIES INDUSTRY ASSOCIATION. (19??)-. English. One time a year. Securities Industry Association, 120 Broadway/35th Floor, New York NY 10271. **Tel** (212)608-1500, FAX (212)608-1604.
 Desc: A summary of the previous year's activities. Provides an accounting to member firm management of how the Association used its resources to further industry goals through government relations, research and management services.

LC HG6024.U6 N37A **ISSN** 8756-226X
DD 332.64/6 US
ANNUAL REVIEW - NATIONAL FUTURES ASSOCIATION (U.S.). (ANNUAL REVIEW / NATIONAL FUTURES ASSOCIATION.). [Annu. rev. - Natl. Futures Assoc. (U.S.)]. **Main/Corp** National Futures Association (U.S.). 1983-. English. One time a year. National Futures Association, 200 West Madison Street, Suite 1600, Chicago IL 60606. **Tel** (312)781-1373, FAX (312)781-1467.

LC HG4953.W4 M86a
DD 352.1/4/09754 US
ANNUAL SUMMARY OF RECEIPTS AND DISBURSEMENTS. See Finance-Public Finance.

LC HG8011 **ISSN** 1071-4510
DD 368 US
ANNUITY & LIFE INSURANCE SHOPPER. See Insurance.

LC HG5640.M33 M32A
DD 332.6/42/094641 SP
ANUARIO - BOLSA DE MADRID. **Main/Corp** Madrid. Bolsa. Spanish. One time a year. Plaza de la Lealtad 1, Madrid Spain.

LC HG450 **ISSN** 0211-125X
DD 332.6 SP
UDC 368
ANUARIO ESPANOL DE SEGUROS. [Anu. esp. seguros]. (1910)-. Spanish. One time a year. 12.500ptas. Club del Ejecutivo del Seguros, C Santa Engracia 151, 28003 Madrid Spain. **Tel** 011 34 1 5341108, FAX 5336196. **ED** Juan Manuel Blanco. Index available. **Ad Acc**. **Circ:** 5,000.

LC K4456.2 .A84 **ISSN** 0217-6661
DD 343.052/46/091823 342.35246091823 SI
 TITLE CHANGE
APTIRC BULLETIN. See Finance-Taxation.

LC N8600 .A73 **ISSN** 0161-1232
DD 332.6/78 US
ART-ANTIQUES INVESTMENT REPORT, THE. See The Arts-Art.

LC N8680 .A77 **ISSN** 0090-9211
DD 381/.45/7 US
ART INVESTMENT REPORT, THE. See The Arts-Art.

LC HG5740.8.A2 A83 **ISSN** 0125-7382
DD 332.6/732259 TH
ASEAN INVESTOR. **VFOAT** A.S.E.A.N. Investor. Vol. 1, No. 1 (Mar. 1982)-. Periodical. English. Twelve times a year. $60.00. Investor Publications Company Ltd, 28 1 Surosak Road, Prapairt 6 Flr, Bangkok 10500 Thailand. **Tel** 233 5040. **Supersedes** Investor.

LC HG4501
DD 332.6 SI
●**ASIA-PACIFIC TAX BULLETIN.** See Finance-Taxation.

Business and Economics —Investments

LC HG450   **ISSN** 0958-9309
DD 332   UK
●**ASIAMONEY.** No. 15 (April 1993)-. Monographic series. English. Ten times a year. $265.00. Euromoney Publications PLC, Nestor House, Playhouse Yard, London EC4Z 5EX United Kingdom. **Tel** 011 44 171 7798888, FAX 011 44 171 7798630, telex 290700 EUROMON G. *Continues* Asia Money & Finance, 0958-9309.

LC HG   **ISSN** 1076-3708
DD 332   US
●**ASIAN M&A AND INVESTMENT DATABASE.** [Asian M&A invest. database]. **Added/Corp** Ulmer Brothers Research Institute. **VFOAT** Asian M and A and Investment Database; Asian M & A and Investment Database. (1994)-. English. Eleven times a year. $795.00. Ulmer Brothers Inc., 80 Maiden Lane, 22nd Floor, New York NY 10038. **Tel** (212)344-4411, FAX (212)344-8074. **Circ:** 250. *Formed by the union of* China M&A and Investment Reporter, 1074-0619; Japan M&A Reporter, 1049-4383 *and* Pacific M&A Reporter, 1049-4367.
Desc: Provides information on the consolidation and merger of corporations and investments in Asia.

LC HG450   **ISSN** 1012-3334
DD 332.6   HK
ASIAN VENTURE CAPITAL JOURNAL, THE. Vol. 1, Issue 1 (January 1988)-. Periodical. English. Twelve times a year. $590.00. Asian Venture Capital Journal Holdings Ltd. / AVCJ, 18-F Sincere Insurance Building, 4 Hennessy Road, Wanchai Hong Kong. **Tel** 011 852 28650118, FAX 011 852 28662748. **ED** Dennis Corcoran. **Ad Acc.**

LC HG   **ISSN** 1060-4642
DD 332   US
  CCC
  TITLE CHANGE
ASSET INTERNATIONAL (GREENWICH, CONN.). (ASSET INTERNATIONAL.) [Asset int.]. **Added/Corp** Asset International, Inc. Vol. 1. No. 1 (June 16, 1986)-(19??). Periodical. English. Asset International, 125 Greenwich Avenue, Greenwich CT 06830. **Tel** (203)629-5014, FAX (203)629-5024. *Continued by* Plan Sponsor.

LC HG450   **ISSN** 0899-0468
DD 332.6   US
ASSETS PROTECTION SOURCEBOOK. (1990)-. English. One time a year. $48.00. Assets Protection, PO Box 5323, Madison WI 53705. **Tel** (608)833-8099, FAX (608)271-4520.

LC HG450
DD 332.6   US
ASTRO INVESTOR. (19??)-. English. Twelve times a year. $45.00. Mull Publications, PO Box 11133, Indianapolis IN 46201. **Tel** (317)357-6855. **ED** Carol Mull. **Bk Rev. Circ:** 250.

LC HG450   **ISSN** 0736-7643
DD 332.6   US
ASTUTE INVESTOR (KINGSTON, TENN.), THE. (THE ASTUTE INVESTOR.). (1982)-. Periodical. English. Twelve times a year. $30.00. Astute Investor - Charles E. Cardwell, 135 Beechwood Lane, Kingston TN 37763-9803. **Tel** (615)376-2732. **ED** Charles E. Cardwell, ph.D. **Bk Rev**, (Qty: 2-4). **Circ:** 1,000 (ctrl).
Desc: "Preliminary legwork" for value-oriented investors: computer screens for stocks selling below apparent real worth; evaluates investment strategies; reviews investment books.

LC HG450   **ISSN** 1035-364X
DD 332.6   AT
AUSTRALIAN PROPERTY MARKET INVESTMENT STRATEGY REPORT. (198?)-. Periodical. English. Four times a year. 295.99Aus$. Knight Frank Hooker, GPO Box 187, 175 Pitt Street, Sydney NSW 2001 Australia. **Tel** 011 61 02 2392624, FAX 011 61 02 2392625. ctrl circ.

LC HG450
DD 332.6   AT
  TITLE CHANGE
AUSTRALIAN SMALL BUSINESS & INVESTING. *See* Business and Economics-Small Business.

LC HG450
DD 332.6   AT
AUSTRALIAN SMALL BUSINESS AND PORTFOLIO. (19??)-. English. Eleven times a year. 41.11Aus$. Federal Publishing Co Pty Ltd., PO Box 199, 180 Bourke Road, Alexandria New South Wales 2015 Australia. **Tel** 011 61 2 3539992, FAX 011 61 2 66923059935.

LC HG4061 .B32A   **ISSN** 0093-190X
DD 332.6/78   US
BABSON'S INVESTMENT DIGEST. **Main/Corp** Babson's Reports, Inc. English. $5.00. Babson's Reports Inc, Wellesly Hills MA 02181.

LC HB   **ISSN** 0749-5714
DD 330   US
BAHAMAS DATELINE. (BAHAMAS DATELINE : BUSINESS, INVESTMENT, REAL ESTATE.). [Bahamas dateline]. (19??)-. Periodical. English. Twelve times a year. $36.00. US International Marketing Company, 17057 Bellflower Boulevard, PO Box 428, Bellflower CA 90706. **Tel** (310)925-2918, telex 6502978961. **ED** R. M. Meaton. **Circ:** 500.
Desc: Investment newsletter on events, trends, and opportunities for the investor in the Bahamas. Includes information on real estate, banking, incorporation, tax-free business and tax-haven activities.

LC HG450   **ISSN** 0193-9947
DD 332.6   US
BALKAN INVESTMENT REPORT.
Periodical. English. Irregular. $75.00. Balkan Investment Report, PO Box 30214, Bethesda MD 20014.

LC HG5580.B35 B3   **ISSN** 1058-1057
DD 332.6/73/0947405   US
BALTIC BUSINESS REPORT. [Baltic bus. rep.]. **Added/Corp** Baltic Ventures, Inc. Vol. 1, No. 1 (Apr. 1991)-. Periodical. English. Twelve times a year. $260.00. Baltic Ventures, Inc., 1075 Washington Street, West Newton MA 02165. **Tel** (617)527-2550.

LC HG4501 .B17   **ISSN** 0822-5788
DD 330.973/005   CN
BANK CREDIT ANALYST. INVESTMENT AND BUSINESS FORECAST, THE. [Bank credit anal., Invest. bus. forecast]. Vol. 32, No. 4 (Oct. 1980)-. Periodical. English. Twelve times a year. 695.00Can$. BCA Publications Ltd., 1002 Sherbrooke Street West, Suite 1600, Montreal Quebec H3A 3L6 Canada. **Tel** (514)499-9706, FAX (514)499-9709. **ED** J. A. Boeckh and Warren Smith. ctrl circ. *Continues* Bank Credit Analyst. Stock Market and Business Forecast, 0822-577X.
Desc: Forecast and analysis of trends in business conditions and major investment markets based on a continuous appraisal of money and credit flows.

LC HG1501   **ISSN** 1055-3193
DD 332.1   US
BANK INVESTMENT REPRESENTATIVE. *See* Business and Economics-Banks and Banking.

LC HG1 .B3   **ISSN** 1077-8039
DD 332   CCC
●**BARRON'S (CHICOPEE, MASS.).**
(BARRON'S.). [Barron's]. Vol. 74, No. 10 (Mar. 7, 1994)-. Periodical. English. One time a week. $135.00. Dow Jones and Company Inc., 200 Burnett Road, Chicopee MA 01021. **Tel** (413)592-7761, (800)568-7625. **Bk Rev. Ad Acc. Circ:** 280,000. available on microfilm from University Microfilms International (UMI); available on an online database from Dow Jones News/Retrieval. Documents available from UMI Article Clearinghouse, Documents on Demand. *Continues* Barron's National Business and Financial Weekly, 0005-6073.
Ind/Abst ABI/INFORM Glob. Ed.; ABI/INFORM Ondisc: Expr. Ed.; ABI/INFORM [Computer File]; Abstr. BioCommer.; Acad. Abstr. Full Text Elite; Acad. Abstr.; Acad. Search; AGRICOLA [Select. Cov.]; BioBusiness; Bus. Index; Bus. Period. Index; Bus. Source Plus; Bus. Source; Energy Inf. Abstr.; Environ. Abstr.; EP Collect.; F&S Index Plus Text, Int. [Select. Cov.]; Foods Adlibra; Gen. BusinessFile; Gen. Period. Index; Homework Help.; INFO-SOUTH Abstr.; Infobank; Mag. Index Plus; Mag. Index. Sel.; Mag. Search; MasterFile FullTEXT 1000; MasterFile FullTEXT 350; MasterFile FullTEXT 650; MasterFile FullTEXT; Newsp. Period. Abstr.; OCLC; PROMT; Pub. Lib. FullTEXT; Telebase; Mag. Index; Trade Ind. Index; UMI ABI/Inform--Bus. Period. Ondisc [Full Txt.]; Wilson Bus. Abstr.

LC HG4571 .B36   **ISSN** 0363-1273
DD 332.6/42/097471   US
BARRON'S MARKET LABORATORY.
1976-. English. One time a year. $3.95. Book Division, Dow Jones Irwin, 1818 Ridge Road, Homewood IL 60430.

LC HG1 .B3   **ISSN** 0005-6073
DD 332   CCC
  CODEN BRNSAD
  TITLE CHANGE
BARRON'S NATIONAL BUSINESS AND FINANCIAL WEEKLY. *See* Business and Economics-Banks and Banking.

LC HG450
DD 332.6   US
BASIC INVESTMENT & INDUSTRY DATA SHELF. (19??)-. Periodical. Irregular. $1,950.00. Standard & Poor's Corporation, (A Division of McGraw-Hill, Inc.), 25 Broadway, New York NY 10004. **Tel** (212)208-8775, (800)221-5277.
Desc: A combination of financial and industry information publications that completes a well-rounded reference library of essential facts, statistics and investment advice for business and industry executives.

LC KF1085.Z9 I58   **ISSN** 1060-8362
DD 346.73/073 347.30673   US
BASICS OF SWAPS. [Basics swaps]. **Added/Corp** Practising Law Institute. (1991)-. English. Practising Law Institute, 810 Seventh Avenue, New York NY 10019-5818. **Tel** (212)765-5700, FAX (212)581-4670 general correspondence, (212)265-4742 orders and billing inquiries. *Continues* Swap Market in ..., 1062-5925.

LC HG450
DD 332.6   GW
●**BERLINER WERTPAPIERBOERSE AKTUELL.** (1994)-. Bulletin. German. Four times a year. Berliner Wertpapierboerse, Fasanenstr. 3, 10623 Berlin Germany. **Tel** 011 030 3110910, FAX 011 030 31109179.

LC HG450
DD 332.6   UK
  TITLE CHANGE
BEST INVESTMENT. (19??)-(19??). English. Best Investment, 32 Duke Street, St James London SW1Y 6DF United Kingdom. **Tel** 011 44 171 3210100. *Continued by* Best Tax Shelter Service.

LC HG450
DD 332.6   UK
BEST PEP ADVICE. (19??)-. English. Best Investment, 32 Duke Street, St James London SW1Y 6DF United Kingdom. **Tel** 011 44 171 3210100.

LC HG4651
DD 332.632   CN
BEST US STOCKS FOR CANADIAN INVESTORS. (19??)-. Periodical. English. Twenty-six times a year. 87.00Can$. MPL Communications, 133 Richard Street West, Suite 700, Toronto Ontario M5H 3M8 Canada. **Tel** (416)869-1177, FAX (416)869-0456.
Desc: Provides investment advice on 100 US stocks with a uniquely Canadian perspective. It addresses specific areas that Canadians must know about when investing in US stocks, including tax laws, which funds to buy, recommended stock portfolios and more.

LC HG450   **ISSN** 0006-016X
DD 332.6   US
BETTER INVESTING. **Added/Corp** National Association of Investment Clubs. (1951)-. Periodical. English. Twelve times a year. $20.00. National Association of Investors Corporation, 1515 East Eleven Mile Road, Royal Oak MI 48067. **Tel** (313)543-0612, FAX (313)543-8442. **ED** Donald Danko. Index available in last issue of volume--attached. cum. index. **Bk Rev. Ad Acc, Adv Rep:** Martha Stephens. **Circ:** 140,000. available on microfilm and microfiche from University Microfilms International (UMI).
Desc: Material aimed at helping individuals become successful long-term investors in common stock.

LC HG4953.M6 M56a
DD 353.9/776/0072   US
BIENNIAL REPORT AND OVERVIEW OF MINNESOTA MUNICIPAL REVENUE BONDS. Main/Corp Minnesota. Finance and International Trade Division. (19??)-. English. Every 2 years. Department of Economic Development / Minnesota, 480 Cedar Street, St Paul MN 55101.

LC HG   **ISSN** 1057-2848
DD 332   US
BIG BOND BOOK, THE. (THE BIG BOND BOOK : THE DIRECTORY OF BELOW INVESTMENT GRADE CORPORATE BONDS.). [Big bond book]. **Added/Corp** Bloomberg Financial Markets. Bond Investors Association. (June 1991 Ed.)-. Directory. English. Two times a year. $995.00. Bond Investors Association, PO Box 4427, Miami Lakes FL 33014. **Tel** (305)557-1832, FAX (305)557-1454.
Desc: Directory of the entire $370 billion Below Investment Grade bond market. Provides current description, ownership, assets and detailed information for 4,000 bond issues.

LC HG   **ISSN** 1064-5365
DD 332   US
BIG PICTURE (ALEXANDRIA, VA.), THE. (THE BIG PICTURE.). [Big pict.]. Vol. 30, Issue No. 12 (Aug. 1991)-. Periodical. English. Twelve times a year. $127.00. KCI Communications Inc, 1101 King Street, Suite 400, Alexandria VA 22314. **Tel** (703)548-2400, (800)832-2330, FAX (703)683-6974. *Continues* Indicator Digest, 0019-6940.

LC HG   **ISSN** 0891-3161
DD 332   US
BIOTECH INVESTOR. *See* Biology-Bioengineering.

LC TP248   **ISSN** 0277-9773
DD 660.6   US
BIOTECHNOLOGY INVESTMENT OPPORTUNITIES. *See* Biology-Bioengineering.

LC WMLC 93/1607 ISSN 1063-2123
DD 332 US
BLOOMBERG (PRINCETON, N.J.). (BLOOMBERG.). [Bloomberg]. **VFOAT** Bloomberg Magazine. Vol. 1, No. 1 (July 1992)-. Periodical. English. Twelve times a year. Free to qualified personnel. Bloomberg Magazine, PO Box 888, Princeton NJ 08542-0888. **Tel** (609)279-3000. **ED** William Inman.
Desc: Contains news and financial information.

LC HD58 ISSN 0384-7802
DD 338/.0971 CN
BLUE BOOK OF C B S STOCK REPORTS. (THE BLUE BOOK OF C B S STOCK REPORTS.). **Main/Corp** Canadian Business Service. (1???)-. Periodical. English. Twenty-six times a year (19 reports mailed every two weeks). 93.64Can$. MPL Communications, 133 Richard Street West, Suite 700, Toronto Ontario M5H 3M8 Canada. **Tel** (416)869-1177, FAX (416)869-0456. **ED** Mohan Bhagwanani. ***Supersedes*** *Canadian Business Service. Summary Review Service., 0384-7799.*
Desc: Detailed and continuous 2-page research reports on more than 250 key Canadian companies. Includes information on the major Canadian corporations, as well as in-depth research on lesser known companies, in particular those not already covered by stock brokerage research reports.

LC HG450
DD 332.6 US
BLUE SKY GUIDE. English. One time a year (plus two updates). $600.00 (nonmembers), $100.00 (associate members). Investment Company Institute, 1401 H Street Northwest, Washington DC 20005. **Tel** (202)326-5800, (202)326-5972.

LC HG450 ISSN 1080-9201
DD 332.6 US
●**BOB CZECHIN'S WORLD INVESTOR.** (1994)-. English. Twelve times a year. $59.00. Agora Publishing, 824 East Baltimore Street, Baltimore MD 21202. **Tel** (800)433-1528.

LC HG4501 .B63 ISSN 1050-9011
DD 332 US
BOB NUROCK'S ADVISORY. [Bob Nurock's advis.]. **VFOAT** Advisory. (Mar. 15, 1990)-. Periodical. English. Twelve times a year. $247.00. Investors Analysis Inc., PO Box 460, Santa Fe NM 87504. **Tel** (505)820-2737. **ED** Robert J. Nurock. ***Continues*** *Astute Investor, 0899-4765.*

LC HG4503 .B63
DD 332.6 SP
BOLSA EN GRAFICOS, ACTUALIZACION, LA. (Jan./March 1973)-. Spanish. Irregular. Copernicus, Avda General Peron 27, Madrid Spain.

LC HG4501 .D3 ISSN 0732-0469
DD 332.63/233/0973 US
CCC
BOND BUYER (NEW YORK, N.Y. 1982), THE. (THE BOND BUYER.). [Bond buy.]. Vol. 259, No. 26280 (Monday, Jan. 4, 1982)-. Periodical. English. Seven times a week. $1,897.00. American Banker, Concourse Level, 1 State Street Plaza, New York NY 10004. **Tel** (212)803-8200, (800)221-1809, FAX (212)943-6256, (212)843-9598. **ED** John Allan. **Ad Acc. Circ:** 2,000. available on an online database from NEWSNET; Lexis-Nexis; and (files 626,648/Full-Text) DIALOG. ***Continues*** *Daily Bond Buyer, 0884-3937.*
Desc: Publication focused on municipal bonds and other fixed income securities. Features comprehensive tables and statistics, news and analysis on instruments, legislation, etc.
Ind/Abst Trade Ind. ASAP [Full Txt.]; Trade Ind. Index [Full Txt.].

LC HG ISSN 1075-3710
DD 332 US
BOND BUYER YEARBOOK, THE. (THE BOND BUYER ... YEARBOOK.). [Bond buy. yearb.]. **Added/Corp** Bond Buyer (Firm). **VFOAT** Bond Buyer ... Year Book. (1987)-. English. One time a year. $75.00. American Banker, Concourse Level, 1 State Street Plaza, New York NY 10004. **Tel** (212)803-8200, (800)221-1809, FAX (212)943-6256, (212)843-9598. ***Continues*** *Bond Buyer's Municipal Statbook.*

LC HG4907 .D5 ISSN 1053-8658
DD 332.63/233/02573 US
BOND BUYER'S MUNICIPAL MARKETPLACE, THE. [Bond Buy. munic. marketpl.]. **Added/Corp** Bond Buyer (Firm). **VFOAT** Municipal Marketplace. (Spring 1990)-. Periodical. English. Two times a year (Apr., Oct.). Thomson Financial Publishing, PO Box 65, 4709 West Golf Road, Skokie IL 60076-0065. **Tel** (800)321-3373, (708)933-8031. ***Continues*** *Bond Buyer's Directory of Municipal Bond Dealers of the United States.*

LC HG450 ISSN 1064-9476
DD 332.6 US
BOND COUNSEL. (BOND COUNSEL : A WEEKLY SERVICE ON LEGAL DEVELOPMENTS AFFECTING MUNICIPAL BONDS.). [Bond couns.]. No. 89-1--92-34 (1989)-. Periodical. English. One time a week. $645.00. Mortgage Commentary Publications, 4829 Fairmont Avenue, Bethesda MD 20814-0240. **Tel** (301)654-5580.
Ind/Abst PTS Newsl. Database [Full Txt.].

LC HG450
DD 332.6 US
TITLE CHANGE
BOND FUND ADVISOR. (19??)-(19??). Periodical. English. IBC Donoghue Organization, 290 Eliot Street, Ashland MA 01721. **Tel** (800)343-5413, (508)881-2800. ***Continued by*** *Investing for Income, 1080-7942.*

LC HG4905 .S435 ISSN 0277-3988
DD 332.6/323/0973 US
BOND GUIDE. [Bond guide]. **Main/Corp** Standard and Poor's Corporation. Vol. 35, No. 8 (Aug. 1971)-. English. Twelve times a year. $211.00. Standard & Poor's Corporation, (A Division of McGraw-Hill, Inc.), 25 Broadway, New York NY 10004. **Tel** (212)208-8775, (800)221-5277. ***Continues*** *Standard and Poor's Corporation. New Comprehensive Bond Guide.*
Desc: Presents 41 items of descriptive and statistical data on approximately 5,500 domestic and Canadian corporate bonds and their issuing companies. Also includes statistics on over 650 convertible bonds with 26 data items for each, as well as a special section listing over 280 foreign bonds. A fundamental reference tool for all investors concerned with fixed income investments.

LC HG450
DD 332.6 US
BOND MARKET ROUNDUP. Added/Corp Salomon Brothers. (19??)-. Periodical. English. One time a week. $500.00. Salomon Brothers Center / Finance, 7 World Trade Center, 36th Floor, New York NY 10048. **Tel** (212)747-7000.

LC HG ISSN 1197-6535
DD 330 CN
CEASED
BONDS & BILLS. [Bonds bills]. **Added/Corp** Midland Walwyn Capital. **VFOAT** Bonds and Bills; Economics & Capital Markets Research; Fixed Income Analysis. (1992)-(1994). Periodical. English. Midland Walwyn Capital, Suite 1600, 121 King Street West, Toronto Ontario M5H 3W6 Canada. ***Absorbed by*** *On the Margin (Toronto, Ont.), 1196-7005.*

LC HG450 ISSN 0278-8896
DD 332.6 US
BONDWEEK. [Bondweek]. **Added/Corp** Institutional Investor (Firm). **VFOAT** Bond Week. Vol. 1, No. 1 (May 4, 1981)-. Newsletter. English. One time a week (51 issues). $1395.00. Institutional Investor Inc., 488 Madison Avenue, New York NY 10022. **Tel** (212)303-3234, (212)303-3233, FAX (212)303-3353. ***Continues*** *Money Manager.*
Desc: Provides insights into all major taxable bond markets. Coverage includes macro economic forecasts, with emphasis on interest rate projections.

LC HG4556.A92 G55a ISSN 0302-0770
DD 332.6 AU
BORSE (WIEN). (DIE BORSE.). **Main/Corp** Girozentrale und Bank der Osterreichischen Sparkassen. (19??)-. German. Irregular. Gironzentrale und Bank der Osterreichischen Sparkassen, Schubertring 5, 1011 Vienna Austria.

LC HG450 ISSN 0274-4805
DD 332.6 US
CODEN BLPEEB
BOTTOM LINE, PERSONAL. Vol. 1 (March 30, 1980)-. Periodical. English. Twenty-four times a year. $49.00. Bottom Line, Personal, 330 West 42nd Street, New York NY 10036. **Tel** (212)239-9000. **(Subscription address:** Neodata / Colorado, PO Box 2606, Boulder CO 80322. **) ED** Lee Rath.
Desc: The executive update that puts your personal life on a business-like basis. Investments, money management, real estate, insurance, retirement and estate planning, travel and leisure, marriage and family, physical fitness, human relationships, prestige-building strategies and expert advice on how to live wealthier and wiser.

LC HG450
DD 332.6 CN
BOURSE CANADIENNE DES ECHETS. (19??)-. French. Six times a year. 70.00Can$. Ortech International, 2395 Speakman Drive, Mississauga Ontario, L5K 1B3 Canada. **Tel** (416)822-4111, FAX (416)823-1446.

ISSN 1053-0908
DD 332 US
BOWSER DIRECTORY OF SMALL STOCKS, THE. [Bowser dir. small stocks]. (1991)-. Directory. English. Twelve times a year. $89.00. Bowser Report, PO Box 6278, Newport News VA 23606. **Tel** (804)877-5979.
Desc: Shows 14 fields of information on over 700 low-priced stocks on the NYSE, ASE and NASDAO to be used by the Do-it-yourself Stock Market Researcher. Fields of information include president or chairman, address, phone number, revenue and net income for the past four consecutive quarters, book values, shares outstanding, long-term debt, principle business, market traded and symbol. Information is kept current and indicated whether up or down.

LC HG450 ISSN 0738-7288
DD 332.6 US
BOWSER REPORT, THE. [Bowser rep.]. (197?)-. Periodical. English. Twelve times a year. $48.00. The Bowser Report, PO Box 6278, Newport News VA 23606. **Tel** (804) 877-5979. **ED** R. Max Bowser.
Desc: Recommends and follows-through on stocks $3 a share or less. Features include Company of the Month, Insider Trading, Earnings Chart, and interviews with successful small investors. Includes plans for investing in small stocks.

LC HG ISSN 0748-1853
DD 332 US
BRICKMAN LETTER, THE. [Brickman lett.]. (Sept. 1983)-. Periodical. English. Twelve times a year. $77.00. Myrtle Brickman, 11905 Bennett Road, Herndon VA 22071. **Tel** (703)620-3239. **ED** Myrtle Brickman. Index available. **Circ:** 100 (ctrl).
Desc: Highlights investments for various tax brackets.

LC HG450
DD 332.6 UK
BRITAIN'S TOP 1,000 FOREIGN OWNED COMPANIES. See Business and Economics-Marketing and Purchasing.

LC HG450 ISSN 0146-0110
DD 332.6 US
BROADCAST INVESTOR. See Communications-Television and Cable.

LC HG450 ISSN 0736-9069
DD 332.6 US
BROADCAST INVESTOR CHARTS. See Communications-Television and Cable.

LC HG4651 ISSN 1033-0682
DD 332.63220994 AT
BROKER REPORT INDEX. (BROKER REPORT INDEX RESEARCH REVIEW.). [Brok. rep. index]. **VFOAT** BRI. (1986)-. Periodical. English. Twelve times a year. 395.00Aus$ (one-year), 750.00Aus$ (two-year). Fleet Publications, PO Box H153, Australia Square Sydney, NSW 2000 Australia. **Tel** 011 61 2 2328836, FAX 011 61 02 2215010. Index available. cum. index.
Desc: Research reports and updates on Australian companies and financial markets which have been issued by stockbrokers and other investment professionals.

LC HG ISSN 0319-1362
DD 332 US
BULL & BEAR. [Bull bear]. **VFOAT** Bull & the Bear. **VAT** Bull and Bear. Vol. 1 (April/May 1972)-. Periodical. English. Twelve times a year. $29.00. Bull & Bear, PO Box 917179, Longwood FL 32791. **Tel** (407)677-7872. **ED** David J. Robinson. **Bk Rev**, (Qty: 12-15). **Ad Acc, Adv Mgr Tel** (407)682-6170. **Circ:** 55,000.
Desc: Comprehensive digest of investment advisory newsletters. Original articles by leaping investment advisors on stocks, precious metals, mutual funds, real estates and money-making opportunities.

LC HG4651 ISSN 0835-1384
DD 332.63/2/0971405 CN
BULLETIN (COMMISSION DES VALEURS MOBILIERES DU QUEBEC). [Bull. - Comm. valeurs mobil. Que.]. **Added/Corp** Commission des Valeurs Mobilieres du Quebec. Vol. 16, No. 48 (Nov. 1985)-. Bulletin. French. One time a week. 316.13Can$. Les Publications du Quebec, CP 1190, Outremont Quebec H2V 4S7 Canada. **Tel** (514)948-1222, (418)643-5150, FAX (514)278-3030. **ED** Marc Barriere. Index available. **Circ:** 500. ***Continues*** *Bulletin Hebdomadaire - Commission des Valeurs Mobilieres du Quebec., 0707-8420.*

LC HG4501 ISSN 0706-1498
DD 332.6/0971 CN
BULLETIN DE STATISTIQUES - COMMISSION DES VALEURS MOBILIERES DU QUEBEC. [Bull. stat. - Comm. valeurs mobil. Que.]. **Main/Corp** Quebec (Province) Commission des Valeurs Mobilieres. Vol. 1 (July/Dec. 1978)-. Bulletin. French. Two times a year. Commission des Valeurs Mobilieres du Quebec, 800 Square Victoria 17e, CP 246 Tour de la Bourse, Montreal Quebec H4Z 1G3 Canada. **Tel** 514 873 5326, FAX 514 873 3090.

LC HG4651
DD 332.632 US
BUSINESS BULLETIN. Added/Corp Illinois. Securities Dept. Vol. 1 No. 1 (Aug. 1989)-. Bulletin. English. Four times a year. Free on request. Illinois Securities Department, 900 South Spring Street, Springfield IL 62704. **Tel** (217)785-4941. ***Formed by the union of*** *The Inc.* ***and*** *Securities Exchange.*

LC HG4501
DD 332.6 SA
●**BUSINESS ENVIRONMENT FOCUS.** (1994)-. English. Irregular. Andrew Levy and Associates, PO Box 1431, Rivonia 2128 South Africa.

LC HG4538 .B79 ISSN 0738-5595
DD 332.6/73/05 US
BUSINESS ENVIRONMENT RISK INFORMATION. [Bus. environ. risk inf.]. (198?)-. English. Three times a year. International Research and Marketing, The Plaza, 2 West 59th Street, New York NY 10019. ***Continues*** *Business Environment Risk Index, 0736-9786.*

LC HG450 ISSN 0007-6945
DD 332.6 US
BUSINESS MEMO FROM BELGIUM. **Added/Corp** Belgium. Consulat General (New York, N.Y.). Industrial Section. Belgium. Ambassade (U.S.). Investments Office. **VFOAT** Belgium. (19??)-. Periodical. English. Four times a year. Free. EMBASSY Belgium, 3330 Garfield Street Northwest, Washington DC 20008. **Tel** (202)625-5887, (202)625-5888.
Desc: Highlights recent events in the fiscal and the financial investment environment in Belgium.
Ind/Abst Predicasts.

LC HG450
DD 332.6 UK
BUSINESS MONITOR PRODUCTION SERIES. MISCELLANEOUS MONITORS. (19??)-. English. Irregular. £443.00 (volume set). Her Majesty's Stationery Office, 51 Nine Elms Lane, London SW8 5DR United Kingdom. **Tel** 011 44 171 8738459, 011 44 171 8738499, FAX 011 44 171 8738499, 011 44 171 8738456, telex 297138. **(Subscription address:** Her Majesty's Stationery Office, PO Box 276, Public Centre, London SW8 5DT United Kingdom. **Tel** 011 44 171 8738499, 011 44 171 8738456.**)**

LC HG4921 .D66 ISSN 1062-0028
DD 332.6/78/0973 US
TITLE CHANGE
BUSINESS ONE IRWIN INVESTOR'S HANDBOOK, THE. [Bus. One Irwin invest. handb.]. **Added/Corp** Business One Irwin. **VFOAT** Investor's Handbook. (1991)-(1993). English. Irwin Professional Publishing, 1333 Burr Ridge Parkway, Burr Ridge Parkway IL 60521. **Tel** (800)634-3966, (708)789-5480. ***Continues*** *Dow Jones Investor's Handbook, 0748-2140.* ***Continued by*** *Irwin Investor's Handbook, 1080-3912.*

LC HG450 ISSN 0193-3221
DD 332.6 US
BUSINESS OPPORTUNITIES JOURNAL. (1969)-. Periodical. English. Twelve times a year. $30.00. Business Service Corp, PO Box 60762, San Diego CA 92166. **Tel** (619)223-5661, FAX (619)223-1705. **ED** Gina M. Petrone. **Ad Acc, Adv Mgr:** Maria Nicolaidis, **Tel** (800)854-6570. **Circ:** 102,000 (ctrl). ***Continues*** *Business Ventures.*
Desc: Specializes in business opportunities, real estate and franchising.

LC HG4501
DD 332.6 UK
BUSINESSES AND ASSETS. Issue 79 (Dec. 12, 1986)-. Periodical. English. Twenty-six times a year. $220.74. Business and Assets Ltd, 23 Conduit Place, London W2 1RR United Kingdom. **Tel** 011 44 181 2621164. ***Absorbed*** *Venture UK.*

LC HG4651 ISSN 0046-9777
DD 332.63/2/0973 US
C.F.A. DIGEST, THE. See Business and Economics-Abstracting, Bibliographies and Statistics.

LC HG4501 ISSN 0834-1508
DD 332.6/0971 CN
CEASED
C.H.W. LETTER. [C.H.W. lett.]. **Added/Corp** C.H.W. International Investment Services. **VAT** C. Harry Wilkins Letter. Vol. 46, No. 31 (Aug. 25, 1986)-(Jan. 30, 1995). Periodical. English. Pente Investment Management Ltd., 330 Bay Street, Suite 1204, Toronto Ontario M5H 2S8 Canada. **Tel** (416)861-9555, FAX (416)368-7151. **ED** Robin J. V. Fielding. ctrl circ. ***Continues*** *Investment Letter., 0708-2843.*
Desc: Investment newsletter that primarily deals with Canadian equity markets.

LC HG ISSN 1062-3515
DD 332 US
CABLE NETWORK INVESTOR. See Communications-Television and Cable.

LC HG450 ISSN 0731-0250
DD 332.6 US
CABLE TV INVESTOR. See Communications-Television and Cable.

LC HG450 ISSN 0732-7757
DD 332.6 US
CABLE TV INVESTOR CHARTS. See Communications-Television and Cable.

LC HG450 ISSN 0733-8554
DD 332.6 US
CABOT MARKET LETTER, THE. **Added/Corp** Cabot Heritage Corporation. **VFOAT** Market Letter. (19??)-. Periodical. English. Twenty-four times a year. $97.00. Cabot Heritage Corporation, PO Box 3044, Salem MA 01970. **Tel** (617)745-5532, FAX (508)745-1283. **ED** Carlton G. Lutts. **Circ:** 18,000.
Desc: An investment advisory service.

LC HG ISSN 1041-9454
DD 332 US
CABOT'S MUTUAL FUND NAVIGATOR. [Cabot's mutual fund navig.]. **VFOAT** Mutual Fund Navigator. (Oct. 1988)-. Periodical. English. Twelve times a year. $86.00. Cabot Heritage Corporation, PO Box 3044, Salem MA 01970. **Tel** (617)745-5532, FAX (508)745-1283. **ED** Timothy Lutts.
Desc: Contains sound advise on investing in well-managed no-load mutual funds, using long-term market timing to increase profits and reduce risk.

LC HG4501
DD 332.6 US
CADENCE UNIVERSE PERFORMANCE REPORT. **Added/Corp** CDA Investment Technologies, Inc. (Dec. 31, 1984)-. Periodical. English. Four times a year. $850.00. CDA Investment Technologies, 1355 Piccard Drive, Rockville MD 20850. **Tel** (301)974-9600, (800)232-2285, FAX (301)590-1389. **Circ:** 350. available on diskette; available on magnetic tape; available on an online database.
Desc: A performance report for: mutual funds, bank and insurance company funds, investment advisors 13(f) equity. Also, performance comparisons.

LC WMLC 93/2814 ISSN 0257-7755
DD 332.042 LU
CAHIERS BEI = EIB PAPERS. **Added/Corp** European Investment Bank. **VFOAT** EIB Papers. (Feb. 1986)-. English (French). Irregular. Free on request. Office for Official Publications of the European Communities, 2 rue Mercier, 2985 Luxembourg Luxembourg. **Tel** 011 352 499281, FAX 011 352 292942763.

LC HG450 ISSN 0749-2375
DD 332.6 US
CALIFORNIA MUNICIPAL BOND ADVISOR. Vol. 1, Issue 1 (Nov. 1, 1984)-. Periodical. English. Twelve times a year. $125.00. California Municipal Bond Advisor, 1037 South Canyon Drive, Palm Springs CA 92264. **Tel** (619)320-7997. **ED** Zane B. Mann and Gavin Murphy. **Bk Rev.** ctrl circ.
Desc: Investment advisory newsletter for individual investors in tax-exempt bonds, municipal bond, mutual funds and for professional participants in the municipal bond market.

LC HG ISSN 8756-2154
DD 332 US
CALIFORNIA TECHNOLOGY STOCK LETTER. [Calif. technol. stock lett.]. (198?)-. Newsletter. English. Twenty-four times a year. $295.00. Murenove Inc, PO Box 308, Half Moon Bay CA 94019. **Tel** (415)726-8495. **ED** Michael Murphy. Index available. cum. index. **Ad Acc.** ctrl circ.

LC HG4538 ISSN 0318-8868
DD 332.6/73/0971 CN
CANADA'S INTERNATIONAL INVESTMENT POSITION. [Can. int. investm. position]. **Main/Corp** Statistics Canada. Balance of Payments Division. **Added/Corp** Statistics Canada. Balance of Payments Section. Statistics Canada. Balance of Payments Division. Statistics Canada. International and Financial Economics Division. **VFOAT** Bilan Canadien des Investissements Internationaux; Bilan des Investissements Internationaux du Canada. (1967)-. Statistical Publication. English (French). One time a year. 60.00Can$. Statistics Canada Publications Sales and Services, R.H. Coats Building 6th Floor, Ottawa Ontario K1A 0T6 Canada. **Tel** (613)951-5078, (800)267-6677, FAX (613)951-1584, telex 053-3585.
Desc: Preliminary release on foreign investments in Canada (liabilities) and Canadian investments abroad (assets), by broad category such as direct portfolio and other investments; by industry and by type of claims.

LC NX513 ISSN 0384-1588
DD 709/.71 US
CANADIAN ART INVESTOR'S GUIDE, THE. See The Arts-Art.

LC HG4651 ISSN 1186-1983
DD 332.63 CN
CANADIAN BASE METAL EQUITIES. [Can. base met. equities]. **Added/Corp** Midland Walwyn Capital. Research Dept. Midland Walwyn Capital. (Feb. 11, 1991)-. Periodical. English. Twelve times a year. Limited free distribution to clients of Midland Walwyn Capital. Midland Walwyn Capital, Suite 1600, 121 King Street West, Toronto Ontario M5H 3W6 Canada. ***Continues*** *Base Metal Review., 1186-1975.*

LC HG1723 ISSN 0828-0622
DD 332.6/72/0971 CN
CANADIAN CAPITAL PROJECTS. [Can. cap. proj.]. **Added/Corp** Informetrica Limited. Vol. 1, No. 1 (1st Quarter 1985)-. Periodical. English. Four times a year (Mar., June, Sept., Dec.). 477.00Can$; $622.00 (with monthly updates). Informetrica Limited, PO Box 828 Station B, Ottawa Ontario K1P 5P9 Canada. **Tel** (613)238-4831, FAX (613)238-7698. **ED** Stan Kustec. available on diskette.
Desc: Inventory listing of major construction and capital projects in Canada.

LC HG4501 ISSN 0848-0435
DD 332.6/0971 CN
CANADIAN FINANCE LETTER. [Can. financ. lett.]. **VFOAT** Canadian Finance. (1988)-. Periodical. English. Twenty-four times a year. 100.04Can$. Michael Lombardi Publishing Corporation, 2 Bloor Street West, Suite 100, Toronto Ontario M4W 3E2 Canada. **Tel** (416)975-1726, (416)661-2041, FAX (416)975-0752.

LC HG4651 ISSN 1180-3584
DD 332.63/232/0971 CN
CANADIAN GOVERNMENT BOND REGISTER. [Can. gov. bond regist.]. **Added/Corp** FRI Corporation. 1st Ed. (Jan. 1990)-. Periodical. English. Two times a year. 88.04Can$. FRI Corporation, 1801 McGill College Bureau 600, Montreal Quebec H3A 2N4 Canada. **Tel** (514)842-5091, FAX (514)842-8809.

LC HG4501 ISSN 0840-6863
DD 332.6/0971 CN
CANADIAN INVESTMENT REVIEW. [Can. invest. rev.]. **VFOAT** Revue Canadienne d'Investissement. Vol. 1, No. 1, Fall (1988)-. Periodical. English. Four times a year. 48.02Can$. MacLean Hunter Ltd. Business Publishers / Canada, Box 9100, Station A, Toronto Ontario M5W 1A5 Canada. **Tel** (416)596-5000, , FAX (416)596-5552. **(Subscription address:** Indas Customer Service, 35 Riviera Drive, Building 17, Markham Ontario L3R 8N4 Canada. **Tel** (905)946-0406.**)** **ED** Keith Ambachtsheer. cum. index. **Bk Rev. Ad Acc. Circ:** 8,100 (ctrl). Documents available from UMI Article Clearinghouse.
Ind/Abst ABI/INFORM Glob. Ed.

LC HG4651 ISSN 0840-4917
DD 332.63/22/0971 CN
CANADIAN INVESTOR (TORONTO. 1984). (THE CANADIAN INVESTOR.). [Can. invest.]. **Added/Corp** North American Investment Inc. Michael Lombardi Publishing Corporation. (Jan. 1984)-. Periodical. English. Twelve times a year. 71.23Can$. Michael Lombardi Publishing Corporation, 2 Bloor Street West, Suite 100, Toronto Ontario M4W 3E2 Canada. **Tel** (416)975-1726, (416)661-2041, FAX (416)975-0752.

LC HG ISSN 0713-3286
DD 332.024 CN
CANADIAN MONEYSAVER. (THE CANADIAN MONEY SAVER.). [Can. moneysaver]. Vol. 1, No. 5 (Jan. 1982)-. Periodical. English. Eleven times a year (monthly with July/Aug. issues combined). 26.41Can$. Canadian MoneySaver Inc., PO Box 370, Bath Ontario K0H 1G0 Canada. **Tel** (613)352-7448. **ED** Dale Ennis. **Bk Rev,** (Qty: 22). **Circ:** 26,000. ***Continues*** *Money Saver (Bath, Ont.), 0713-0244.*
Desc: Canadian experts provide practical, objective and money-making information, including smart use of personal finances, profitable tax and retirement planning, travel savings, investment ideas that work, and more.
Ind/Abst Can. Index; Can. Period. Index.

LC HG4651 ISSN 1182-1590
DD 332.63/228/097105 CN
CANADIAN RESOURCES & PENNYMINES ANALYST. [Can. resour. pennyMines anal.]. **VFOAT** Canadian Resources & Penny Mines Analyst. **VAT** Canadian Resources and PennyMines Analyst. Vol. 4, No. 8 (Mar. 6, 1990)-. Periodical. English. Twelve times a year. 62.43Can$. MPL Communications, 133 Richard Street West, Suite 700, Toronto Ontario M5H 3M8 Canada. **Tel** (416)869-1177, FAX (416)869-0456. ***Continues*** *Canadian Penny Mines Analyst., 0836-6357.*
Desc: Information source for investors in the Canadian resources and gold mining sector. Covers "penny" stocks as well as the major companies.

LC HG4501 ISSN 0317-9451
DD 332.6/0971 CN
CANADIAN SECURITIES COURSE, THE. **Main/Corp** Canadian Securities Institute. (1964)-. Periodical. English. One time a year. Canadian Securities Institute, PO Box 225, Commerce Court South, Toronto Ontario M5L 1E8 Canada.

LC HG4651 ISSN 0836-0960
DD 332.63/22/05 CN
CANADIAN SHAREOWNER. [Can. shareown.]. **Added/Corp** Canadian Shareowners Association. Vol. 1, No. 1 (Sept./Oct. 1987)-. Periodical. English. Six times a year. 67.23Can$. Canadian Shareowner Magazine Inc., 1090 University Avenue West, Suite #204, Windsor Ontario N71 5S4 Canada. **Tel** (519)252-9965, FAX (519)252-9570. **ED** John T. Bart. **Ad Acc, Adv Mgr:** Dawn Paupst, **Tel** (519)252-9965. **Circ:** 10,000. available on microfilm and microfiche from University Microfilms International (UMI); available on an online database from University Microfilms International (UMI). Documents available from UMI Article Clearinghouse.
Desc: Covers investment education.
Ind/Abst Can. Period. Index (Jan. 1990-).

LC HG4651 ISSN 1186-1029
DD 332.63 CN
CANADIAN STEEL STOCKS. (CANADIAN STEEL STOCKS / MIDLAND WALWYN RESEARCH.). [Can. steel stocks]. **Added/Corp** Midland Walwyn Capital. Research Dept. Midland Walwyn Capital. **VAT** Canadian Steel Stocks Monthly Review; Canadian Steel Stocks Bimonthly Review. (1990)-. Periodical. English. Limited

Business and Economics —Investments

free distribution to clients of Midland Walwyn Capital. Midland Walwyn Capital, Suite 1600, 121 King Street West, Toronto Ontario M5H 3W6 Canada.

LC HG4651
DD 332.63
ISSN 1186-1037
CN
CANADIAN TECHNOLOGY MONTHLY. [Can. technol. mon.]. **Added/Corp** Midland Walwyn Capital. Midland Walwyn Capital. Research Dept. (1990)-. Periodical. English. Twelve times a year. Limited free distribution to clients of Midland Walwyn Capital. Midland Walwyn Capital, Suite 1600, 121 King Street West, Toronto Ontario M5H 3W6 Canada.

LC HG4028 .C4 P29A
DD 332.6/72
PP
CAPITAL EXPENDITURE BY PRIVATE BUSINESSES (PAPUA NEW GUINEA). **Main/Corp** Papua New Guines. Bureau of Statistics. English. One time a year. k1.00 Papua New Guinea; k1.50 (surface mail), k2.00 (airmail) other. National Statistical Office / New Guinea, PO Wards Strip NCO, Papua New Guinea. **Tel** 011 675 27182 271172, FAX 011 657 255057, telex FINANCE NE 22312.

LC HD3890.V8 F34a
DD 352/.12/09755291
ISSN 0147-7749
US
CAPITAL IMPROVEMENT PROGRAM (FAIRFAX). (CAPITAL IMPROVEMENT PROGRAM.). **Main/Corp** Office of Comprehensive Planning. Fairfax Co., Va. **VFOAT** CIP. Capital Improvement Program for Fairfax County, Virginia. (19??)-. English. One time a year. Office of Comprehensive Planning, 4100 Chain Bridge Road, Fairfax VA 22030.

LC HG4948.H3 H38A
DD 353.9/969/00722
ISSN 0160-0109
US
CAPITAL IMPROVEMENTS PROGRAM STATUS REPORT, FINANCIAL SUMMARY. (CAPITAL IMPROVEMENTS PROGRAM STATUS REPORT : FINANCIAL SUMMARY (HAWAII).). **Main/Corp** Hawaii. Planning Division. English. Hawaii Department of Planning and Economic Development, Planning Division, Honolulu HI.

LC HG450
DD 332.6
US
CAPITAL INVESTMENT FORECASTS AND TRENDS IN INDUSTRY. **See** Industry and Production.

LC HG5731 .C36
DD 332.6/0954
II
CAPITAL MARKET. (198?)-. Periodical. English. Twenty-six times a year. $75.00. **(Subscription address:** Prints India, 11 Darya Ganj, New Delhi 110002 India. **Tel** 011 91 11 3268645, FAX 011 91 11 3275542, telex 31-61087 PRIN-IN.)

LC HG5733 .C36
DD 332.63/222/095405
II
CAPITAL MARKET TECHNICALS. **VFOAT** Capital Market; Technicals. Vol. 1, No. 1 (Sept. 9-22, 1991)-. Periodical. English. Twenty-six times a year. Rs220.00. Investwel Publishers, 401 Swastik Chambers, Unarshi Bappa Chowk, Sion-Trombay Road, Chembur Bombay 400071 India.

LC HG450
DD 332.6
US
CAPITAL MARKETS GUIDE. (19??)-. Periodical. English. Twelve times a year. $2900.00. Euromoney Publications PLC, Nestor House, Playhouse Yard, London EC4Z 5EX United Kingdom. **Tel** 011 44 171 7798888, FAX 011 44 171 7798630, telex 290700 EUROMON G. **(Subscription address:** Euromoney Publications PLC, Perrymount Road Haywards Heath, West Sussex RH16 3DH United Kingdom. **Tel** 011 44 1444 440421.)

LC HG1501
DD 332.1
ISSN 1024-5499
UK
CAPITAL MARKETS REPORT. **See** Business and Economics-Banks and Banking.

LC HG450
DD 332.6
Pr Rev.
US
CARIBBEAN DATELINE. Vol. 1, No. 1 (May 1980)-. Newsletter. English. Twelve times a year. $95.00. Caribbean Dateline Publications, PO Box 23276, Washington DC 20026. **ED** N. Poteat Day. **Bk Rev**, (Qty: 15). **Ad Acc. Circ:** 1,000. **Continues** Caribbean and Central American Letter.
Desc: Events, trends and opportunities for the investor in the Caribbean and Central America. Report on tax haven activities, real estate, banking, incorporation, trust formation, tax-free business, vacation living, retirement, direct investments, stock markets and expatriation.

LC HG4651
DD 332.6
ISSN 0849-181X
CN
TITLE CHANGE
CAVELTI'S MARKET REPORT. [Cavelti's mark. rep.]. **Added/Corp** Cavelti Capital Management. **VFOAT** Market Report. (April 2, 1990)-(1994). Periodical. English. Cavelti Capital Management, 74 Victoria Street, Toronto Ontario M5C 2A5 Canada. **Continues** Market Report (Toronto, Ont.)., 0827-6234. **Continued by** Global Market Watch, 1202-6948.

LC HG4538
DD 332.6/78
ISSN 0710-3468
CN
CCR FUTURES TRADING GUIDE. [CCR futures trading guide]. **VFOAT** Futures Trading Guide. **VAT** Commodity & Currency Report Futures Trading Guide. No. 1-. Periodical. English. One time a week. $95.00. Marpep Publishing Ltd, 133 Richmond Street West, Suite 700, Canada. **Tel** (416)869-1177.

LC HG1 .I44
DD 332.6
US
●**CDA/INVESTNET INSIDERS' CHRONICLE.** **VFOAT** CDA Investnet Insiders' Chronicle; Insiders' Chronicle. Vol. 18, No. 1 (Jan. 11, 1993)-. Periodical. English. Fifty times a year. $375.00. CDA Investment Technologies, 1355 Piccard Drive, Rockville MD 20850. **Tel** (301)974-9600, (800)232-2285, FAX (301)590-1389. **(Subscription address:** CDA Investnet, 3265 Meridian Parkway, Suite 130, Ft. Lauderdale FL 33331. **Tel** (305)384-1500, (800)243-2324.) **Formed by the union of** Insiders' Chronicle, 0162-5152 **and** Invest/Net Inside.
Desc: Information on insider trading in securities.
Ind/Abst MasterFile FullTEXT (July 1993-).

LC HG1616.I5 S63
DD 332
US
CDA/SPECTRUM. 13(F) INSTITUTIONAL STOCK HOLDINGS. **Added/Corp** CDA Investment Technologies, Inc. **VFOAT** CDA Spectrum. 13(F) Institutional Stock Holdings; Institutional Stock Holdings; 13(F) Institutional Stock Holdings. (Dec. 31, 1992)-. Periodical. English. Four times a year. $785.00. CDA Investment Technologies, 1355 Piccard Drive, Rockville MD 20850. **Tel** (301)974-9600, (800)232-2285, FAX (301)590-1389. **Continues** Spectrum 3. 13(F) Institutional Stock Holdings Survey.

LC HG4501 .S62
DD 332.6
US
●**CDA/SPECTRUM FIVE PERCENT STOCK HOLDINGS.** **Added/Corp** CDA Investment Technologies, Inc. **VFOAT** CDA Spectrum Five Percent Stock Holdings; Five Percent Stock Holdings. (Jan. 31, 1993)-. Periodical. English. Four times a year. $545.00. CDA Investment Technologies, 1355 Piccard Drive, Rockville MD 20850. **Tel** (301)974-9600, (800)232-2285, FAX (301)590-1389. **Continues** Spectrum 5.

LC HG4501 .S64
DD 332.6
US
TITLE CHANGE
CDA/SPECTRUM INSIDER HOLDINGS. **Added/Corp** CDA Investment Technologies, Inc. **VFOAT** Spectrum Insider Holdings; CDA Spectrum Insider Holdings; Insider Holdings. (Dec. 31, 1992)-(1995). Periodical. English. CDA Investment Technologies, 1355 Piccard Drive, Rockville MD 20850. **Tel** (301)974-9600, (800)232-2285, FAX (301)590-1389. **Continues** Spectrum 6. **Continued by** Investnet Insider Holdings Book.

LC HG450
DD 332.6
US
CDA/WIESENBERGER MUTUAL FUNDS PANORAMA. **Added/Corp** CDA Investment Technologies, Inc. **VFOAT** Mutual Funds Panorama. (1992)-. English. One time a year. $54.45. CDA Investment Technologies, 1355 Piccard Drive, Rockville MD 20850. **Tel** (301)974-9600, (800)232-2285, FAX (301)590-1389. **Continues** Mutual Funds Panorama, 0464-0977.

LC HG4930 .C43
DD 332
ISSN 1066-9264
US
CDA/WIESENBERGER MUTUAL FUNDS UPDATE. [CDA/Wiesenberger mutual funds update]. **Added/Corp** CDA/Wiesenberger (Firm). **VFOAT** CDA Wiesenberger Mutual Funds Update; Mutual Funds Update. Vol. 1, Issue No. 1 (Feb. 29, 1992)-. Periodical. English. Twelve times a year. $295.00. CDA Investment Technologies, 1355 Piccard Drive, Rockville MD 20850. **Tel** (301)974-9600, (800)232-2285, FAX (301)590-1389. **Formed by the union of** Wiesenberger Mutual Funds Investment Report; Current Dividend Record **and** Management Results.

LC HB522
DD 338
ISSN 1073-2918
US
●**CENTRAL EUROPEAN BUSINESS GUIDE.** [Cent. Europ. bus. guide]. **Added/Corp** Central European Business Information Services. Vol. 1, No. 1 (Jan. 1994)-. Periodical. English. Twelve times a year. $100.00. Central European Business Information Service Inc., 100 South King Street, Suite 410, Seattle WA 98104. **Tel** (800)992-5247, FAX (206)343-0484.

LC HG6046 .U625A SUPPL
DD 353.008/25
ISSN 0195-3591
US
CFTC DATABOOK. **Main/Corp** United States. Commodity Futures Trading Commission. **VAT** Commodity Futures Trading Commission Databook. 1977/78-. English. One time a year. Commodity Futures Trading Commission, 2033 K Street NW, Washington DC 20581.

LC HG5780.5.A2 C47
DD 332.6
KO
CHABON SIJANG YONBO. Korean. One time a year. Chungkwon Kamdogwon, 146-12 Susong-dong Chongno-ku, Seoul South Korea.

LC HG450
DD 332.6
US
CHARTIST. (19??)-. Newsletter. English. Twenty-four times a year. $150.00 (one-year); $250.00 (two-year). The Chartist, PO Box 758, Seal Beach CA 90740. **Tel** (310)596-2385. **ED** Don Sullivan. **Circ:** 5,000 (ctrl).

LC HG4501 .C48
DD 332.6/05
ISSN 1048-2717
US
CHASE INVESTMENT PERFORMANCE DIGEST. [Chase investm. perform. dig.]. **Added/Corp** Chase Global Data & Research Inc. (1990)-. Trade Publication. English. One time a year (March). $28.95. Chase Global Date and Research, 73 Junction Square Drive, Concord MA 01742. **Tel** (508)263-0404, FAX (508)263-3525. **ED** C. David Chase. **Continues** Chase Global Investment Almanac, 1041-8636.
Desc: Presents information on the world's major investment markets. Includes graphs and statistical information on the subject matter covered. A true performance indicator.

LC HG
DD 332
ISSN 0747-7236
US
CHEAP INVESTOR, THE. [Cheap invest.]. **Added/Corp** Mathews and Associates. (19??)-. Periodical. English. Twelve times a year. $98.00. The Cheap Investor, 2549 West Golf, Suite 350, Hoffman Estates IL 60194. **Tel** (708)830-5666, FAX (708)830-5797. **ED** Bill Mathews.
Desc: Contains buy recommendations and updates on previously recommended stocks. Goal is to allow subscribers to buy undervalued, quality stocks at bargain prices, then sell for a profit when the prices cycle upward.

LC HG4501
DD 332.6
CC
●**CHINA TRADE LINK.** (1994)-. Newsletter. English. Twelve times a year. $345.00. Han Consultants Inc., PO Box 71006, Wuhan Hubei 430071, People's Republic of China. **Tel** 011 86 27 7838532, FAX 011 86 27 7878343.
Desc: Import and export opportunities from and to China.

LC HC465.C3 N54a
DD 332.6
JA
CHOSA. **Main/Corp** Nihon Kaihatsu Ginko. Chosabu. **Added/Corp** Nihon Kaihatsu Ginko. Chosa. No. 4 (April 1973)-. Periodical. Japanese. Irregular. Free. Nihon Kaihatsu Ginko Chosabu, 1-9-1 Otemachi 1-chome Chiyoda-ku, Tokyo 100 Japan. **Tel** 011 81 3 32441770, FAX 011 81 3 32450954, telex J24342. **Circ:** 3,000. **Continues** Chosa Geppo.

LC HG4503 .C44a
DD 332.6
KO
CHUNGKWON CHOSA WOLBO. MONTHLY REVIEW. **Main/Corp** Chungkwon Kamdogwon. **Added/Corp** Chungkwon Kamdogwon. Monthly Review. **VFOAT** Monthly Review. (19??)-. Periodical. Korean. Twelve times a year. Chungkwon Kamdogwon, 146-12 Susong-dong Chongno-ku, Seoul South Korea.

LC HG4503 .C43
DD 332.6
KO
CHUNGKWON HAKHOE CHI. **VFOAT** Journal of Korean Securities Association. Vol. 1 (1980)-. Periodical. Korean. One time a year. Hanguk Chungkwon Hakhoe, 1-164 Youido-dong, Yongdungpo-ku, Seoul South Korea.

LC HG4503 .C446
DD 332.6
KO
CHUNGKWON KUMYUNG. **VFOAT** Securities Finance. Periodical. English (Korean). Twelve times a year. Hanguk Chungkwon Kumyung Chusik Hoesa, 1-154 Youido-dong Yongdungpo-ku, Seoul Korea.

LC HG4458.A1 C47
DD 332.6
KO
CHUNGKWON TUJA SINTAK. **VFOAT** Securities Investment Trust. Periodical. Korean. Six times a year. Hanguk Tuja Sintak Chusik Hoesa, 1-591 Youido-dong, Yongdungpo-ku, Seoul Korea.

LC HG4503 .C47
DD 332.6
KO
CHUSIK. **VFOAT** Stock. Periodical. Korean. Twelve times a year. Hanguk Chungkwon Koraeso, 1-116 Youido-dong, Yongdungpo-ku, Seoul South Korea.

LC HG4930 .U54A ISSN 0192-5997
DD 332.6/327 US

CLASSIFICATION, ASSETS AND LOCATION OF REGISTERED INVESTMENT COMPANIES UNDER THE INVESTMENT COMPANY ACT OF 1940.
Main/Corp United States. Securities and Exchange Commission. Office of Reports and Information Services. English. One time a year. Office of Reports and Information Services, Securities and Exchange Commission, Washington DC 20549. ***Continues*** *Classification, Assets and Location of Registered Investment Companies under the Investment Company Act of 1940, 0192-5997.*

LC HG ISSN 0882-3820
DD 332 US

CLEAN YIELD, THE. [Clean yield]. **Added/Corp** Fried and Fleer Investment Services. Vol. 1, No. 1, (Mar. (1985)-. Periodical. English. Six times a year. $80.00. Clean Yield Publications, Box 1880, Greensboro Bend VT 05842. **Tel** (802)533-7178, FAX (802)533-2907. **ED** Rian Fried (phone: (802)533-7082). **Bk Rev. Circ:** 1,200.
Desc: A stock market newsletter for the social investors.

LC HG4551 ISSN 0964-671X
DD 332.644 UK

CLEARING & SETTLEMENT. [Clear. settl.]. **VFOAT** Clearing and Settlement. (1991)-. Periodical. English. Six times a year. $253.00. Metal Bulletin PLC, PO Box 28E, Worcester Park, Surrey KT4 7HY United Kingdom. **Tel** 011 44 171 8279977, FAX 011 44 171 3378943.

LC HG450
DD 332.6 US

CLOSED-END FUND DIGEST. (19??)-. English. Twelve times a year. $200.00. Madent Publishing, 1224 Coast Village Circle, Suite 11, Santa Barbara CA 93108. **Tel** (800)282-2335, FAX (805)565-3433. **ED** Jon Chatfield. **Ad Acc.**
Desc: Description of current economic conditions, closed-end fund statistical charts, and digest of relevant issues.

LC HG1 .C7 ISSN 0163-2876
DD 332.6/32/05 US

COMMERCIAL AND FINANCIAL CHRONICLE (1978), THE. (THE COMMERCIAL AND FINANCIAL CHRONICLE.). [Commer. financ. chron.]. Vol. 223, No. 7621 (April 6, 1978)-. Periodical. English. One time a week. $237.00. William B Dana Company, PO Box 1839, Daytona Beach FL 32115. **Tel** (904)255-9885, (800)322-1839. **ED** John Dunne. **Ad Acc. Circ:** 910. available on microfilm from University Microfilms International (UMI). ***Continues*** *Commercial and Financial Chronicle. Statistical Section, 0163-058X.*
Desc: A compendium of stocks and bond activity compiled from stock exchanges around the country.

LC HG450
DD 332.6 UK

COMMERCIAL LEASES. (19??)-. English. Twelve times a year. £90.50 UK; £159.00 other. Monitor Press, Rectory Road, Great Waldingfield, Sudbury Suffolk CO10 0TL United Kingdom. **Tel** 011 44 1787 378607, FAX 011 44 1787 880201.

LC KF1085.A59 C66 ISSN 0887-784X
DD 343.73/08/02648 347.303802648 US
TITLE CHANGE

COMMODITIES LITIGATION REPORTER. [Commod. litig. report.]. **Added/Corp** Andrews Publications, Inc. (July 5, 1985)-(1995). Periodical. English. Andrews Publications Inc., 1646 West Chester Pike, PO Box 1000, Westtown PA 19395. **Tel** (610)399-6600, (800)345-1101, FAX (610)399-6610. ***Merged into*** *Securities and Commodities Litigation Reporter.*
Desc: Provides coverage of major reparations and enforcement actions involving the scope of the Commodity Exchange Act.

LC HG6051.D44 C66 ISSN 1020-0967
DD 332.6 US

•COMMODITY MARKETS AND THE DEVELOPING COUNTRIES : A WORLD BANK QUARTERLY. **Added/Corp** International Bank for Reconstruction and Development. Vol. 1, No. 1 (Dec. 1993)-. English. Four times a year. $150.00. World Bank Publications, 1818 H Street Northwest, Washington DC 20043. **Tel** (202)473-1155, (202)473-1155, FAX (202)522-3224, telex WUI 64145 WORLDBANK. ***Continues*** *Quarterly Review of Commodity Markets, 1020-0533.*

LC HB522 ISSN 1064-8216
DD 338 US

COMMODITY MENU ALERT. [Commod. menu alert]. (1992)-. Periodical. English. Twelve times a year. Kenat & Associates, 3242 Paris Park Drive SE, Kenwood MI 49512.

LC HG6046 .C659 ISSN 0730-7217
DD 332.63/28/05 US
TITLE CHANGE

COMMODITY PERSPECTIVE. [Commod. perspect.]. (19??)-(1995). English. Commodity Perspective, 30 South Wacker/Suite 1820, Chicago IL 60606. **Tel** (312)454-1801, (800)621-5271, FAX (312)454-0239, telex 206099. ***Continued by*** *Futures Perspective.*

LC HG4501 ISSN 1186-0294
DD 332.6 CN

COMMUNICATION STOCKS AND THE TSE 300. [Commun. stocks TSE 300]. **Added/Corp** Nesbitt Research. (Sept. 1990)-. Periodical. English. Limited free distribution. Nesbitt Burns Research, First Canadian Place, Suite 5000, PO Box 150, Toronto Ontario M5X1H3 Canada. **Tel** (416)359-4002, FAX (416)359-6429.

LC HC683.A1 C65
DD 332.6/7322967 GU

COMMUNITY/BUSINESS PROFILE, TERRITORY OF GUAM. (Jan. 1980)-. English. Guam Growth Council, PO Box BV.

LC HG450
DD 332.6 US

COMPARATIVE ANNUITY REPORT : MONTHLY NEWSLETTER. **VFOAT** Comparative Annuity Report. (19??)-. Newsletter. English. Twelve times a year. $80.00. Comparative Annuity Report Inc., PO Box 1268, Fair Oaks CA 95628. **Tel** (505)265-7189. **ED** Joe Rosanswank (phone: (916)487-7863). **Circ:** 1,000.
Desc: Surveying flexible and single premium deferred annuity programs.

LC HG450 ISSN 0734-4597
DD 332.6 US

COMPUTERIZED INVESTING. (COMPUTERIZED INVESTING : A PUBLICATION OF THE AMERICAN ASSOCIATION OF INDIVIDUAL INVESTORS.). [Comput. ind.]. **Added/Corp** American Association of Individualized Investors. Vol. 1, No. 1 (Oct. 1982)-. Periodical. English. Six times a year. $40.00. American Association of Individual Investors, 625 North Michigan Avenue, Chicago IL 60611. **Tel** (312)280-0170. **ED** Frederic Shipley II. Index available. cum. index. **Circ:** 45,000 (ctrl).
Desc: Keeps investors abreast of the latest developments in investment related computer information: software, databases and methods of implementation.

LC HS2501 .C65 ISSN 0090-0842
DD 367/.05 US

CONSENSUS (BROOKLYN). (CONSENSUS.). **Added/Corp** National Club Association. Vol. 1 (Winter 1972)-. Periodical. English. Fifty-one times per year. $365.00. Consensus / Missouri, PO Box 411128, Kansas City MO 64141. **Tel** (816)471-3862, FAX (816)221-2045. **ED** Robert Salva.
Desc: Investment newspaper for the futures industry used by most brokers and traders. Market letters, special reports, and buy/sell advice from over 80 top national and international sources. Covers all stock and financial markets, metals, agricultural markets, livestock, grains and oilseeds and more.
Ind/Abst Relig. Index One Period.

LC HG4501 ISSN 0711-4877
DD 332.6/2/06071 CN

CONSTITUTION, BY-LAWS AND REGULATIONS - INVESTMENT DEALERS' ASSOCIATION OF CANADA. (CONSTITUTION, BY-LAWS AND REGULATIONS.). [Const., by-laws regul. - Investm. Deal. Assoc. Can.]. **Main/Corp** Investment Dealers' Association of Canada. No. 1-. English. One time a year (irregular). Free to members. ***Continues in part*** *Investment Dealers' Association of Canada. Blue Book.*

LC HG450 ISSN 0010-793X
DD 332.6 US

CONTRARY INVESTOR, THE. [Contrary invest.]. **Added/Corp** Fraser Management Associates. **VFOAT** Contrary Investor Letter. (19??)-. Periodical. English. Twenty-six times a year. $95.00. Fraser Management Association, PO Box 494, Burlington VT 05402. **Tel** (802)658-0322, FAX (802)658-0260.

LC HG450 ISSN 0740-0306
DD 332.6 US

CONTRARY INVESTOR FOLLOW-UP, THE. **Added/Corp** Fraser Management Associates. (19??)-. Periodical. English. Twenty-six times a year. $65.00. Fraser Management Association, PO Box 494, Burlington VT 05402. **Tel** (802)658-0322, FAX (802)658-0260.

LC KF1477.A15 C67 ISSN 0743-0272
DD 346.73/06626 347.3066626 US

CORPORATE CONTROL ALERT. [Corp. control alert]. Vol. 1, No. 1 (Mar. 1984)-. Corporate Report. English. Eleven times a year. $1125.00. American Lawyer Media, L.P., 600 3rd Avenue, New York NY 10016. **Tel** (212)973-2800. **(Subscription address:** Corporate Control Alert, 600 3rd Avenue, 3rd Floor, New York NY 10016. **) ED** Joanne Ganek. **Circ:** 300.
Desc: A newsletter about the latest strategies used in contested mergers and acquisitions and leveraged buyouts.

LC HG ISSN 1052-8342
DD 332 US

CORPORATE GOVERNANCE SERVICE. VOTING RESULTS. [Corp. gov. serv., Voting results]. **Added/Corp** Investor Responsibility Research Center. **VFOAT** Voting Results. (Jan. 29, 1988)-. Periodical. English. Twelve times a year. Investor Responsibility Research Center, 1350 Connecticut Avenue Northwest 700, Washington DC 20036. **Tel** (202)833-0700. ***Separated from*** *Corporate Governance Bulletin, 1053-5489.*

LC HF5001 .C83
DD 338.6/042/05 UK

CORPORATE LOCATION. (199?)-. Periodical. English. Six times a year. £120.00. Euromoney Publications PLC, Nestor House, Playhouse Yard, London EC4Z 5EX United Kingdom. **Tel** 011 44 171 7798888, FAX 011 44 171 7798630, telex 290700 EUROMON G. ***Continues*** *Corporate Location International, 0962-2578.*
Desc: Publication on direct corporate investment. Provides information on the conditions, opportunities and factors affecting investment worldwide, whether the chosen route is siting of new facilities, acquisition or joint ventures.

LC HG5127 .C66 ISSN 0589-7920
DD 332.63/22/0976 US
CCC

CORPORATE REPORT FACT BOOK. (1968)-. English. One time a year. $125.78. MCP Inc., 5500 Wayzata Boulevard, Suite 800, Minneapolis MN 55416. **Tel** (612)591-2700, FAX (612)591-2639.

LC HG4057 .A157 ISSN 0091-4975
DD 332.6/7 US
SUSPENDED

CORPORATE REPORTS ON FILE. Vol. 1 (June 11, 1973)-Suspended (July 1974). Corporate Report. English. One time a week. $100.00. Wall Street Transcript, 100 Wall Street, New York NY 10005. **Tel** (212)747-9500.

LC HG4501 ISSN 0849-5793
DD 332.6/09714/05 CN

COTE 100. [Cote 100]. **VAT** Cote cent. (Sept. 1989)-. Periodical. French. Twelve times a year. 140.05Can$. Cote 100 Inc., 575 Beaumont Street East, St. Bruno Quebec J3V 2R2 Canada. **ED** Guy LeBlanc.
Desc: Financial newsletter based on a portfolio based on a stock valuation system that detects undervalued situations on the Canadian and US stock markets.

LC HG4503 .C6 ISSN 0220-6358
DD 332.6/7 FR

COTE OFFICIELLE. **Main/Corp** Compagnie des Agents de Change de Paris. **Added/Corp** Compagnie des agents de change (Paris, France) Societe des Bourses Francaises. (19??)-. French. Six times a week. 3917.73F (France); 6534.00F (Europe); 8000.00F (other). Compagnie des Agents de Change, 4 place de la Bourse, Paris 2E France. ***Continues*** *Compagnie des Agents de Change de Paris. Chambre Syndicale. Bulletin de la Cote.*

LC HD9001 .C6 ISSN 1057-4883
DD 338.1405 US

CRB FUTURES MARKET SERVICE. [CRB futures mark. serv.]. **Added/Corp** Commodity Research Bureau (U.S.). **VFOAT** Futures Market Service. **VAT** Commodity Research Bureau Futures Market Service. (19??)-. Periodical. English. One time a week. $150.00. Knight Ridder Financial Publishing, 30 South Wackler Drive, Suite 1820, Chicago IL 60606. **Tel** (312)454-1801, (800)621-5271, FAX (312)454-0239. **(Subscription address:** Knight Ridder Financial Publications, PO Box 94513, Chicago IL 60690. **)** ***Continues*** *Futures Market Service.*

LC HG ISSN 1354-0904
DD 332 UK

•CROSS-SHAREHOLDINGS IN EUROPE.
See Business and Economics-Banks and Banking.

LC HG ISSN 1052-3456
DD 332 US

CRSP DAILY EXCESS RETURNS FILE. (CRSP DAILY EXCESS RETURNS FILE [COMPUTER FILE].). **Added/Corp** University of Chicago. Center for Research in Security Prices. **VFOAT** Daily Excess Returns File; Excess Returns File; CRSP Excess Returns File. (19??)-. English. One time a year. $460.00. University of Chicago CRSP, 1101 East 58th Street, Graduate School of Business, Chicago IL 60637.
Desc: Available in ASCII format. Contains the daily returns for each stock in excess of the daily returns on a portfolio of similar risk stocks. The market is divided into ten risk classes, or portfolios.

Business and Economics — Investments

LC HG
DD 332
ISSN 1054-4437
US
CRSP INDICES FILES [COMPUTER FILE]. [CRSP indices files]. **Added/Corp** University of Chicago. Center for Research in Security Prices. **VAT** Center for Research in Security Prices indices files. (19??)-. English. University of Chicago CRSP, 1101 East 58th Street, Graduate School of Business, Chicago IL 60637.
Desc: Certified for use at 800 bpi through 6250 bpi.

LC HG450
DD 332.6
US
CYCLICAL INVESTING QUARTERLY REPORT. (19??)-. English. Four times a year. $85.00. Cyclical Investing Quarterly, PO Box 301, Concord CA 94522-0301. **Tel** (415)831-9129.
Desc: Analysis and forecasts of cyclical economic and investments trends, monetary and fiscal policy, international developments, stocks and bonds, precious metals, oil and real estate.

LC HG5751 .D33
DD 332.6
IO
DAFTAR JENIS BIDANG USAHA SEKTOR INDUSTRI. Indonesian. One time a year. Departemen Prindustrian Sekretariat Jenderal, JL Kebonsirih No 36, Jakarta Indonesia.

LC HG4651
DD 332.63/22/0971
ISSN 0838-9365
CN
DAILIES. (THE DAILIES FOR WEEK ENDING ...). [Dailies]. **VFOAT** Dailies. Issue 8804 (Jan. 28, 1988)-. Periodical. English. One time a week. 708.80Can$ Canada; 804.74Can$ US; 865.94Can$ other. Canadian Analyst Ltd., 30 Duncan Street, Toronto Ontario M5V 2C3 Canada. **Tel** (416)971-6543, FAX (416)598-0049. **ED** Lina Murray. **Continues** Canadian Daily Stock Charts, 0045-4656.
Desc: Provides coverage of 450 active Canadian stocks.

LC HG4916 .D32
DD 332.64/3/097305
ISSN 1067-9375
US
DAILY GRAPHS. NASDAQ (OTC)/AMERICAN STOCK EXCHANGE. [Dly. graphs, NASDAQ (OTC)/Am. Stock Exch.]. **Added/Corp** William O'Neil & Co. **VFOAT** NASDAQ (OTC)/American Stock Exchange. (Mar. 8, 1991)-. English. Fifty-two times a year (weekly). $497.00. Daily Graphs Inc., 12655 Beatrice Street, Los Angeles CA 90066. **Tel** (310)448-6843. **Continues** Daily Graphs. American/OTC Stock Exchange, 1055-0658.

LC HG4916 .D33
DD 332.63/22/0973022
US
DAILY GRAPHS. NEW YORK STOCK EXCHANGE. **Added/Corp** William O'Neil & Co. **VFOAT** New York Stock Exchange. (Sept. 4, 1987)-. English. One time a week. $518.00. Daily Graphs Inc., 12655 Beatrice Street, Los Angeles CA 90066. **Tel** (310)448-6843. **Continues** Daily Graphs. New York Stock Exchange/OTC.

LC HG1501
DD 332.1
US
DAILY GRAPHS OPTION GUIDE WEEKLY. (19??)-. English. One time a week. $261.00 North America; $269.94 Florida; $305.00 other. Daily Graphs Inc., 12655 Beatrice Street, Los Angeles CA 90066. **Tel** (310)448-6843. **Continues** Daily Graphs Stock Option Guide, 0195-2021.

LC HG1501
DD 332.1
ISSN 0195-2021
TITLE CHANGE
DAILY GRAPHS. STOCK OPTION GUIDE. **Added/Corp** William O'Neil & Co. **VFOAT** Stock Option Guide. (19??)-(19??). Periodical. English. William O'Neil & Company Inc., PO Box 66919, Los Angeles CA 90066. **Tel** (310)448-6843. **ED** William O'Neil. **Circ:** 25,000 (ctrl). **Continued by** Daily Graphs Option Guide Weekly.
Desc: Stock market charts on NYSE/AMEX and OTC common stocks. More than 70 pieces of technical and fundamental information.

LC HG4651
DD 332.6/322/0973
ISSN 0737-4127
US
DAILY STOCK PRICE RECORD. AMERICAN STOCK EXCHANGE. [Dly. stock price rec., Am. Stock Exch.]. **Main/Corp** Standard and Poor's Corporation. **VFOAT** American Stock Exchange; Daily Stock Price Index: American Stock Exchange; ASE. (July/Sept. 1972)-. Periodical. English. Four times a year. $395.00. Standard & Poor's Corporation, (A Division of McGraw-Hill, Inc.), 25 Broadway, New York NY 10004. **Tel** (212)208-8775, (800)221-5277. **Continues** ISL Daily Stock Price Index: American Stock Exchange.
Desc: Contains accurate stock price data for brokers, investment advisors, stock market technicians and chartists, research organizations, trust departments, tax consultants, attorneys, and accountants. Contains data on approximately 1,000 issues.

LC HG4915 .S665 HG4915 .D665
DD 332.63/222/0973
ISSN 1072-3846
US
●**DAILY STOCK PRICE RECORD. NASDAQ.** [Dly. stock price rec., NASDAQ]. **Added/Corp** Standard and Poor's Corporation. **VFOAT** NASDAQ. (Jan. Feb. Mar. 1993)-. English. Four times a year. $505.00. Standard & Poor's Corporation, (A Division of McGraw-Hill, Inc.), 25 Broadway, New York NY 10004. **Tel** (212)208-8775, (800)221-5277. **Continues** Standard and Poor's Corporation. Daily Stock Price Record. Over-the-Counter, 0737-4100.

LC HG4651
DD 332.6/322/0973
ISSN 0737-4119
US
DAILY STOCK PRICE RECORD. NEW YORK STOCK EXCHANGE. [Dly. stock price sec., N.Y. Stock Exch.]. **Main/Corp** Standard and Poor's Corporation. **Added/Corp** Standard and Poor's Corporation. Daily Stock Price Index. New York Stock Exchange. **VFOAT** Daily Stock Price Index. New York Stock Exchange; NYSE. (July/Sept. 1972)-. Periodical. English. Four times a year. $420.00. Standard & Poor's Corporation, (A Division of McGraw-Hill, Inc.), 25 Broadway, New York NY 10004. **Tel** (212)208-8775, (800)221-5277. **Continues** ISL Daily Stock Price Index: New York Stock Exchange.
Desc: Contains accurate stock price data for brokers, investment advisors, stock market technicians and chartists, research organizations, trust departments, tax consultants, attorneys, and accountants. Contains data on more than 2,400 issues.

LC HG5771 .D33
DD 332.6
JA
DAIYAMONDO KABUKA GURAFU. **Added/Corp** Daiyamondosha. **VFOAT** Kabuka Gurafu. (1962)-. Japanese. Two times a year. ¥2200. Daiyamondo Sha, (Diamond Inc.), 4-2 1-chome Kasumigaseki, Chiyoda-ku Tokyo 100 Japan.

LC HG4503 .D35
DD 332.6
JA
DAIYAMONDO KABUSHIKI TOSHIBAN. **VFOAT** Kabushiki Toshiban. (1977)-. Periodical. Japanese. Six times a year. ¥5700. Daiyamondo Sha, (Diamond Inc.), 4-2 1-chome Kasumigaseki, Chiyoda-ku Tokyo 100 Japan. **ED** Toshikazu Yatsu.

LC HG450
DD 332.6
IT
DATAFONDI. Italian. Four times a year. Databank Spa, Corso Italia 8, 20122 Milan Italy. **Tel** 011 39 2 866641.

LC HG
DD 332
ISSN 1057-7521
US
DEFAULTED BONDS NEWSLETTER. [Defaulted bonds newsl.]. **Added/Corp** Bond Investors Association. (19??)-. Newsletter. English. Twelve times a year. $350.00. Bond Investors Association, PO Box 4427, Miami Lakes FL 33014. **Tel** (305)557-1832, FAX (305)557-1454. **ED** Richard Lehmann. Index available. cum. index. **Ad Acc. ctrl circ.**
Desc: News and information on defaulted municipal and corporate bonds.

LC HG450
DD 332.6
US
DEFINED CONTRIBUTION NEWS. Newsletter. English. Twenty-six times a year. $1495.00 (one-year); $2695.00 (two-year). Institutional Investor Inc., 488 Madison Avenue, New York NY 10022. **Tel** (212)303-3234, (212)303-3233, FAX (212)303-3353.

LC HG450
DD 332.6
US
DEFINED CONTRIBUTION PLAN INVESTING. (19??)-. English. Twenty-four times a year. $895.00 US; $943.00 other. Institute of Management and Administration, 29 West 35th Street, 5th Floor, New York NY 10001-2299. **Tel** (212)244-0360, FAX (212)564-0465. **Continues** IOMAS GIC BIC Yields and Market Report, 1047-9244.

LC HG450
DD 332.6
US
●**DERIVATIVES QUARTERLY.** (1994)-. Periodical. English. Four times a year. $290.00. Institutional Investor Inc., 488 Madison Avenue, New York NY 10022. **Tel** (212)303-3234, (212)303-3233, FAX (212)303-3353. **Continues** Derivatives Review.

LC HG5993 .D48
DD 332.6
ISSN 0957-4115
UK
NLM W1; DE997NAJ
CCC
DEVELOPMENT JOURNAL (LONDON). (DEVELOPMENT JOURNAL.). [Dev. j.]. (Feb. 1990)-. Periodical. English. Four times a year. $120.00. Development Journal Ltd., 150 Regent Street, Suite 500, London W1R 5FA United Kingdom. **Tel** 011 44 171 2421280. **ED** Irvine Cohen. **Bk Rev. Ad Acc. Circ:** 5,300 (ctrl).

Desc: Leading international journal dealing with Third World development. Primary circulation is to senior government level in developing countries and to policy-making, decision-making and implementation levels in bilateral and multilateral official donor agencies.

LC HG
DD 332
ISSN 0890-0957
US
DICK DAVIS DIGEST. [Dick Davis dig.]. Vol. 1, No. 1 (June 14, 1982)-. Periodical. English. Twenty-four times a year. $165.00. Dick Davis Digest, 1080 Southeast 3rd Avenue, Ft Lauderdale FL 33316. **Tel** (305)476-8500, FAX (305)771-1756. **(Subscription address:** Dick Davis Digest, Box 350630, Ft. Lauderdale FL 33335. **Tel** (305)467-8500.) **ED** Dick Davis.
Desc: Provides serious investors with a comprehensive, yet concise overview of the stock market, including specific "buy" recommendations and analyses.

LC HG4501
DD 332.6
ISSN 0012-2742
US
DIGEST OF INVESTMENT ADVICES, THE. **VFOAT** Investment Advices. (1947)-. Periodical. English. Twelve times a year. Digest of Advices Inc, 516-5th Avenue/Suite 507, New York NY 10036. **Tel** (212)564-6090. **ED** N. H. Mager. **Bk Rev Circ:** 3,000.
Desc: Distills and organizes figures, facts and opinions on trends in the economy and security prices.

LC HG450
DD 332.6
US
DINES LETTER. (1962)-. English. Twenty-four times a year. $195.00. James Dines and Company Inc, Box 22, Belvedere CA 94920. **ED** James Dines.
Desc: Investment advisory publication on stocks, precious metals, commodities, options-including charts.

LC HG4501
DD 332.6730973
ISSN 1352-6367
UK
●**DIRECT INVESTMENT IN NORTH AMERICA.** [Direct. invest. North Am.]. (1994)-. Periodical. English. Twelve times a year. $660.00. BNA International Inc., Herron, HSE Dean 10 Farrar Street, 6th Floor, London SW1H 0DX United Kingdom. **Tel** 011 44 171 2228831, FAX 011 44 171 2220294, telex 262570 BNA LONG. **Continues** Foreign Investment in the US.

LC HG4907 .D53
DD 332.6/2
ISSN 1059-7433
US
DIRECTORY OF REGISTERED INVESTMENT ADVISORS. See Industry and Production-Trade and Industrial Directories.

LC HD2709
DD 338.74
ISSN 0111-1574
NZ
DIRECTORY OF SHAREHOLDERS, NEW ZEALAND PUBLIC COMPANIES. [Dir. sharehold., N.Z. public co.]. **VFOAT** Transvision Directory of Shareholders, New Zealand Public Companies. (1980)-. Periodical. English. One time a year. $25.00. Datex Services Ltd., PO Box 30988, Lower Hutt New Zealand. **ED** PW Saunders.

LC HG4905 .D58
DD 332.6/32/0973
ISSN 0094-2561
US
DISCLOSURE RECORD. See Business and Economics-Banks and Banking.

LC HG
DD 332
ISSN 1052-5092
US
DIVIDEND REINVESTMENT PLANS. (DIVIDEND REINVESTMENT PLANS : GUIDE ANNUAL.). [Divid. reinvestm. plans]. **VFOAT** Guide Annual. (19??)-. English. One time a year. $68.50. Evergreen Enterprises, PO Box 763, Laurel MD 20725. **Tel** (301)953-1861.

LC HB522
DD 338
ISSN 1059-1273
US
DOING BUSINESS IN ARGENTINA (NEW YORK, N.Y.). See Finance-Taxation.

LC KJK1051 .D65
DD 346.493/065 344.930665
ISSN 1057-3828
US
DOING BUSINESS IN BELGIUM (NEW YORK, N.Y. 1978). See Finance-Taxation.

LC KHD333.B86 D65
DD 346.81/07 348.1067
US
DOING BUSINESS IN BRAZIL. See Finance-Taxation.

LC HG4501
DD 332.6
US
DOING BUSINESS IN HONG KONG. See Finance-Taxation.

Business and Economics — Investments

LC KNX1040.A13 D65 ISSN 1057-3925
DD 346.52/07 345.2067 US
DOING BUSINESS IN JAPAN (1975). See Finance-Taxation.

LC KGF333.B86 D64 ISSN 1068-0683
DD 346.72/07 347.2067 US
DOING BUSINESS IN MEXICO (NEW YORK, N.Y.). See Finance-Taxation.

LC HG4501
DD 332.6 US
DOING BUSINESS IN PERU. See Finance-Taxation.

LC HG4501 ISSN 1057-3801
DD 332.6 US
DOING BUSINESS IN SOUTH AFRICA. See Finance-Taxation.

LC KKT1051 .D65 ISSN 1057-3887
DD 346.46/07 344.6067 US
DOING BUSINESS IN SPAIN (NEW YORK, N.Y. 1980). See Finance-Taxation.

LC KKV78.B86 D65 ISSN 1059-1281
DD 346.485/07/05 344.8506705 US
DOING BUSINESS IN SWEDEN. See Finance-Taxation.

LC HG4501
DD 332.6 US
DOING BUSINESS IN THE BAHAMAS. See Finance-Taxation.

LC KKM78.B86 D65 ISSN 1059-2849
DD 346.492/07/05 344.9206705 US
DOING BUSINESS IN THE NETHERLANDS (NEW YORK, N.Y. 1980). See Finance-Taxation.

LC HG4501 ISSN 1059-2857
DD 332.6 US
DOING BUSINESS IN THE PEOPLE'S REPUBLIC OF CHINA. See Finance-Taxation.

LC HB522 ISSN 1057-8684
DD 338 US
DOING BUSINESS IN THE UNITED STATES (NEW YORK, N.Y. 1980). See Finance-Taxation.

LC HG1501 ISSN 0197-7083
DD 332.1 US
TITLE CHANGE
DONOGHUE'S MONEYLETTER. [Donoghue's moneylett.]. **Added/Corp** Donoghue, William E. Moneyletter. **VFOAT** Moneyletter. **VAT** Donoghue's Money Letter. Vol. 1 (Feb. 1980)-(19??). Newsletter. English. IBC Donoghue Organization, 290 Eliot Street, Ashland MA 01721. **Tel** (800)343-5413, (508)881-2800. **(Subscription address:** IBC Donoghue Organization, PO Box 91004, Ashland MA 01721. **) ED** Mary C. Driscoll. **Bk Rev. Circ:** 20,000. available on an online database. **Continued by** Moneyletter.
Desc: Emphasizes market timing and strategic selection of no-load and low-load mutual funds. Specific buy and sell signals are listed for stock, bond, money market and international funds.

LC HG6041 D63A ISSN 0147-5649
DD 332.6/45 US
DOW JONES STOCK OPTIONS HANDBOOK, THE. Main/Corp Dow, Jones & Co. 1977-. English. One time a year. $4.95. Book Division, Dow Jones Irwin, 1818 Ridge Road, Homewood IL 60430.

LC HG450 ISSN 0300-7324
DD 332.6 US
DOW THEORY FORECASTS. (1946)-. English. One time a week. $233.00. Dow Theory Forecasts Inc., 7412 Calumet Avenue, Hammond IN 46324. **Tel** (219)931-6480. **ED** Charles Carlson. Index available. **Circ:** 24,500 (ctrl).
Desc: Financial newsletter covering primarily New York Stock Exchange issues.

LC HG4905 .Y6 ISSN 0098-2466
DD 332.6/7/0973 US
DUN & BRADSTREET'S GUIDE TO YOUR INVESTMENTS. VFOAT Dun and Bradstreet's Guide to Your Investments; Guide to Your Investments. 19th- Ed. (1974/1975)-. English. One time a year. $18.00. Harper Collins Publishers, Keystone Industrial Park, Scranton PA 18512. **Tel** (800)242-7737, (800)233-4727, FAX (800)822-4090. **Continues** Your Investments.

LC HG ISSN 1073-631X
DD 332 US
EARNINGS FORECASTER. (EARNINGS FORECASTER : ZACKS INVESTMENT RESEARCH, INC.). [Earn. forecast.]. **Added/Corp** Zacks Investment Research (Firm). **VFOAT** Zacks Earnings Forecaster. (April 17, 1987)-. Periodical. English. Twelve times a year. $495.00. Zacks Investment Research, 155 North Wacker Drive, 3rd Floor, Chicago IL 60606-1719. **Tel** (312)630-9880 ext. 149, FAX (312)630-9617. **Ad Acc, Adv Mgr:** Eden Levinson. **Circ:** 100. **Continues** Standard & Poor's Earnings Forecaster, 0277-6154.
Desc: News and information on earnings forecasts on United States public companies.

LC HG ISSN 1064-7678
DD 332 US
EARNINGS GUIDE (NEW YORK, N.Y.). (EARNINGS GUIDE.). [Earn. guide]. **Added/Corp** Standard and Poor's Corporation. **VFOAT** Standard and Poor's Corporation Earnings Guide; Standard & Poor's Corporation Earnings Guide. (Aug. 1991)-. Trade Publication. English. Twelve times a year. $147.00. Standard & Poor's Corporation, (A Division of McGraw-Hill, Inc.), 25 Broadway, New York NY 10004. **Tel** (212)208-8775, (800)221-5277. **ED** Bill Coughlin.
Desc: Reports corporate stock earnings on a quarterly and annual basis.

LC HG450 ISSN 1063-4029
DD 332.6 US
EAST EUROPEAN INVESTMENT MAGAZINE. (1992)-. Periodical. English. Four times a year. $580.00. Dixon & Company, 19 5th Avenue, 8th Floor, New York NY 10003. **Tel** (212)388-1500, FAX (212)254-3386. **ED** Mark Dixon. **Ad Acc, Adv Mgr Tel** (212)388-1500. **Circ:** 9,800 (ctrl). **Continues** East European Investment Monthly, 1063-5262.
Desc: Focusing on acquisitions, joint ventures and greenfield investments in all 28 countries of the east block. Covers investment laws and trends in each state.

LC HG450 ISSN 0262-0456
DD 332.6 UK
EAST EUROPEAN MARKETS. [East Eur. mark.]. **Added/Corp** Financial Times Business Information Ltd. London Chamber of Commerce and Industry. (1981)-. Periodical. English. Twenty-four times a year. $992.50. Financial Times / UK, Maple House, 149 Tottenham Court Road, London W1P 9LL United Kingdom. **Tel** 011 44 171 8962276, FAX 011 44 171 8962275, 011 44 171 8962399. **ED** Margie Lindsay. Index available. cum. index. **Bk Rev.** ctrl circ. available on microfiche; available on an online database from Lexis-Nexis; DATA-STAR; and (files 16,636/Full-Text) DIALOG. Documents available from UMI Article Clearinghouse.
Desc: Provides background briefings on developments in business prospects, foreign trade, finance, the domestic economies, plus industry and technology.
Ind/Abst PROMT [Full Txt.]; PTS Newsl. Database [Full Txt.].

LC HG ISSN 0889-4396
DD 332 US
  CCC
EBRI QUARTERLY PENSION INVESTMENT REPORT. [EBRI q. pension investm. rep.]. **Added/Corp** Employee Benefit Research Institute (Washington, D.C.). **VFOAT** Quarterly Pension Investment Report. **VAT** Employee Benefit Research Institute Quarterly Pension Investment Report. Vol. 1, No. 1 & 2 (Nov. 1986)-. Periodical. English. Four times a year. comes with membership. Employee Benefit Research Institute, 2121 K Street Northwest, Suite 600, Washington DC 20037. **Tel** (202)659-0670, FAX (202)775-6312.

LC HG ISSN 8756-4602
DD 332 US
ECONOMETRIC INVESTING. [Econom. invest.]. Vol. 1, No. 1 (June 1985)-. Periodical. English. Twelve times a year. $165.00. Investment Statistics, 2314 Empire Drive, Wilmington DE 19810. **Tel** (302)772-2518. **ED** D Robert Coulson. **Bk Rev. Circ:** 100.
Desc: A investment newsletter giving stock selections, investment strategies and market outlook based on viewpoint of modern investment theory. Graphical tracking of stocks included.

LC HC498.A1 E25 ISSN 0160-3167
DD 338/.0917/4927 US
ECONOMIC DEVELOPMENT PROJECTS IN THE ARAB WORLD AND IRAN. English. One time a year. $20.00. Harvard Square, Box 92, Cambridge MA 02138.

LC HG1501 ISSN 0250-3891
DD 332.1 LU
EIB-INFORMATION. Added/Corp European Investment Bank. **VFOAT** EIB Information; BEI Informations. No. 47 (Jan. 1986)-. Periodical. English. Twelve times a year. Free on request. Office for Official Publications of the European Communities, 2 rue Mercier, 2985 Luxembourg Luxembourg. **Tel** 011 352 499281, FAX 011 352 292942763. **Continues** Information (European Investment Bank).
Desc: Provides information about the activities of the European Investment Bank.

LC HG450 ISSN 0742-891X
DD 332.6 US
ELLIOTT WAVE COMMODITY LETTER, THE. [Elliott wave commod. lett.]. June (1983)-. Periodical. English. Twelve times a year. $233.00 North America; $250.00 other. New Classics Library, PO Box 1618, Gainesville GA 30503. **Tel** (404)536-0309, FAX (404)536-2514. **ED** Daniel L Ascani. **Circ:** 6,000 (ctrl). available on videocassette.
Desc: Market timing for all the physical commodities plus currencies.

LC HG450 ISSN 0742-5252
DD 332.6 US
ELLIOTT WAVE THEORIST, THE. [Elliott wave theor.]. (19??)-. Periodical. English. Twelve times a year. $233.00. New Classics Library, PO Box 1618, Gainesville oGA 30503. **Tel** (404)536-0309, FAX (404)536-2514. **ED** Robert R. Prechter Jr. **Circ:** 15,000 (ctrl). available on videocassette.
Desc: Market timing for stocks, bonds, gold and silver.

LC HG450
DD 332.6 US
EMERGING MARKETS WEEK. Newsletter. English. One time a week (51 issues). $1595.00 (one-year), $2875.00 (two-year). Institutional Investor Inc., 488 Madison Avenue, New York NY 10022. **Tel** (212)303-3234, (212)303-3233, FAX (212)303-3353.

LC HG5993 .E57 ISSN 1012-8115
DD 332.64/09172/405 US
EMERGING STOCK MARKETS FACTBOOK. [Emerg. stock mark., Factb.]. **Added/Corp** International Finance Corporation. International Finance Corporation. Capital Markets Dept. International Bank for Reconstruction and Development. **VFOAT** Emerging Markets Data Base. (1986)-. English. One time a year. $100.00. International Finance Corporation, 1818 H Street NW, Washington DC 20433. **Tel** (202)473-8979, (202)473-8981.

LC HG450
DD 332.6 US
ENERGY PROJECTIONS. (19??)-. English. One time a year. $1,000.00. CJ Lawrence Morgan Grenfell, 1290 Avenue of the Americas, New York NY 10104. **Tel** (212)468-5000, FAX (212)468-5490.
Desc: News and information on equity and industry research for investments purposes.

LC HG450
DD 332.6 US
EQUIDATA INVESTOR. (19??)-. Newsletter. English. Twelve times a year. $150.00. Equidata, PO Box 16641, Washington DC 20041.
Desc: Stock market analysis based on historical data.

LC HG4501 .O93 ISSN 1053-2544
DD 338.7/4/097305 US
EQUITIES (NEW YORK, N.Y.). (EQUITIES : NEWS OF MIDDLE AND EMERGING COMPANIES.). [Equities]. Vol. 38, No. 9 (Sept. 1990)-. Periodical. English. Twelve times a year. $36.00. Equities Magazine Inc., 145 East 49th Street, Suite 5B and 5C, New York NY 10017. **Tel** (212)832-7800. Index available. **Ad Acc. Circ:** 15,000. **Continues** OTC Review, 0161-0694.
Desc: Covers listed middle-market and emerging growth companies.
Ind/Abst Acad. Search; Bus. Source Plus; Bus. Source; EP Collect.; F&S Index Plus Text, Int. [Select. Cov.]; Homework Help.; MasterFile FullTEXT 1000; MasterFile FullTEXT 350; MasterFile FullTEXT 650; MasterFile FullTEXT (July 1994-); Telebase; World Mag. Bank.

LC HG450
DD 332.6 US
EQUITIES : SPECIAL SITUATIONS. (199?)-. Periodical. English. Twelve times a year. $150.00 (one-year), $250.00 (two-year), $350.00 (three-year). Equities Magazine Inc., 145 East 49th Street, Suite 5B and 5C, New York NY 10017. **Tel** (212)832-7800.
Ind/Abst MasterFile FullTEXT (July 1994-).

LC HG450
DD 332.6 UK
EQUITY INTERNATIONAL. (19??)-. English. Twelve times a year. $120.00. Equity International, Unit 8 Grove Ash, Bletchely, Milton Keynes MK1 1BZ United Kingdom. **Tel** 011 44 171 5871545.

LC HG4503 .E67
DD 332.6/7/09599 PH
EQUITYMAN. Vol. 1 (Apr. 1974)-. Periodical. English. $20.00. Grafik Concepts & Designs Inc, Suite 405/Madrigal Building, Makati Rizal Philippines.

Business and Economics —Investments

LC HD7105.45.U6 E75
DD 332.6/7254 US
ERISA RED BOOK OF PENSION FUNDS, THE. Added/Corp ERISA Benefit Funds, Inc. Dun's Marketing Services. **VFOAT** Red Book of Pension Funds. (19??)-. English. One time a year. Dun & Bradstreet Information Services, 3 Sylvan Way, Parsippany NJ 07054. **Tel** (201)605-6000, (800)526-0651.
Desc: Source for finding marketing and financial information on the nation's qualified pension market. Over 1,000,000 plans are listed. This pool of capital not only includes the large funds of the major U.S. corporations but also the small funds controlled by other U.S. companies.

LC HG450
DD 332.6 CN
●**ESTIMATES. PART III, INDUSTRY CANADA. EXPENDITURES. Main/Corp** Canada. **VFOAT** Industry Canada. Expenditures; Budget des Depenses. Partie III, Plan de Depenses; Industry Canada. (1995)-. English (French). Canada Communication Group Publishers, Order Processing, Ottawa Ontario K1A 0S9 Canada. **Tel** (819)956-4800, (819)956-4802. **Continues in part** Canada. Estimates. Part III, Industry, Science and Technology Canada. Expenditure Plan **and** Canada. Estimates. Part III, Consumer and Corporate Affairs Expenditure Plan. **Continued in part by** Canada. Estimates. Part III, Communications Canada. Expenditure Plan **and** Canada. Estimates. Part III, Investment Canada.

LC HG5151 .C3b
DD 354.710072/6 CN
 CEASED
ESTIMATES. PART III, INVESTMENT CANADA. Main/Corp Canada. **VFOAT** Budget des Depenses. Partie III, Investissement Canada. (1987)-(1994). English (French). Canada Communication Group Publishers, Order Processing, Ottawa Ontario K1A 0S9 Canada. **Tel** (819)956-4800, (819)956-4802. **Continues** Canada. Estimates. Part III, Foreign Investment Review Agency. **Continued in part by** Canada. Estimates. Part III, Industry Canada. Expenditures.

LC HD1241 **ISSN** 0961-9712
DD 333.3094 UK
Pr Rev.
EUROPROPERTY LONDON. [Europroperty Lond.]. (1991)-. Periodical. English. Ten times a year. $375.00. IFR Publishing Ltd., Aldgate House, 33 Aldgate High Street, London EC3N 1DL United Kingdom. **Tel** 011 44 171 369 7536, FAX 011 44 171 369 7395, telex 889365/8953051 IFRPUBG. (**Subscription address:** IFR Publishing, 90 Broad Street, Second Floor, New York NY 10004.) **ED** Adrienne Margolis. **Ad Acc, Adv Mgr:** John Taylor. **Circ:** 6,000 (ctrl).
Desc: Investment and development news and analysis of international activity in European commercial property sector.

LC HG4538 .U754a **ISSN** 0094-470X
DD 658.1/5 US
EXAMINATION OF FINANCIAL STATEMENTS OF OVERSEAS PRIVATE INVESTMENT CORPORATION. (EXAMINATION OF FINANCIAL STATEMENTS OF OVERSEAS PRIVATE INVESTMENT CORPORATION : REPORT TO THE CONGRESS BY THE COMPTROLLER GENERAL OF THE UNITED STATES.). **Main/Corp** United States. General Accounting Office. **Added/Corp** United States. Congress. (19??)-. Periodical. English. US General Accounting Office / District of Columbia, 441 G Street Northwest, Room 4528, Washington DC 20548. **Tel** (202)275-2812.

LC HG450 **ISSN** 0896-6494
DD 332.6 US
EXECUTIVE INVESTMENT LETTER, THE. (1992)-. Periodical. English. Twenty-six times a year. $56.00. Digby Financial News, Inc., 228 Willowbrook Drive, Gretina LA 70056-7816.

LC HG4651
DD 332.632 US
●**EXECUTIVE STOCK OPTIONS AND STOCK DEPRECIATION RIGHTS.** (1995)-. English. Law Journal Press, 345 Park Avenue South, New York NY 10010. **Tel** (212)545-6160, (800)888-8300, FAX (212)741-3985.

LC HG **ISSN** 0195-0746
DD 332 US
 CCC
EXECUTIVE WEALTH ADVISORY. [Exec. wealth advis.]. **Main/Corp** Research Institute of America, Inc. **Added/Corp** Research Institute of America, Inc. National Institute of Business Management (U.S.). (197?)-. Newsletter. English. Twelve times a year. $96.00. National Institute of Business Management, Inc., 1101 King Street, Alexandria VA 22133. **Tel** (800)543-2052, (703)548-3885, (800)543-2049, FAX (703)549-0182. **ED** Phil Springer.

Desc: Reports on investment strategies and opportunities to build personal wealth rapidly and safely. By following EWA's investment advice, subscribers are able to transform current good income into substantial wealth.

LC HG450
DD 332.6 US
EXECUTIVES' INVESTMENT REACTIONS TO TAX PROPOSALS AFFECTING SAVINGS AND INVESTMENT. English. Securities Industry Association, 120 Broadway/35th Floor, New York NY 10271. **Tel** (212)608-1500, FAX (212)608-1604.
Desc: Research report based on survey conducted by Opinion Research Corporation. Details executives' investment responses to five tax proposals: reduction in the capital gains rate; tax exemption of long-term dividends and interest; reduction or elimination of double taxation of corporate earnings; a tax on the purchase and sale of stock; and an increase in individual tax rates.

LC HG4530 .T44
DD 332.6327 US
●**FABIAN PREMIUM INVESTMENT RESOURCE. VFOAT** Investment Resource; FIR. (Jan. 1995)-. Periodical. English. Twelve times a year. Telephone Switch Newsletter, PO Box 2538, Huntington Beach CA 92647. **Tel** (800)950-8765, (714)536-7066, FAX (714)536-7066. **Continues** Fabians' Investment Resource, 1072-7264.

LC HG4530 .T44 **ISSN** 1072-7264
DD 332 US
Pr Rev. TITLE CHANGE
FABIAN'S INVESTMENT RESOURCE. [Fabian's invest. resour.]. **VFOAT** Investment Resource; FIR. (Oct. 1993)-(Dec. 1994). Newsletter. English. Telephone Switch Newsletter, PO Box 2538, Huntington Beach CA 92647. **Tel** (800)950-8765, (714)536-7066, FAX (714)536-7066. **ED** Douglas Fabian, Mary Jane Barnett (editor's address: 2100 Main Street, Huntington Beach, CA 92648; phone: (714)536-1931). **Circ:** 40,000. **Continues** Fabian's Telephone Switch Newsletter, 1066-3495. **Continued by** Fabian Premium Investment Resource.

LC HG4530 .T44 **ISSN** 1066-3495
DD 332 US
 TITLE CHANGE
FABIAN'S TELEPHONE SWITCH NEWSLETTER. [Fabian's teleph. switch newsl.]. **VFOAT** Telephone Switch Newsletter. (Jan. 10, 1990)-(Sept. 9, 1993). Periodical. English. Dick Fabian, PO Box 2538, Huntington Beach CA 92647. **Continues** Dick Fabian's Telephone Switch Newsletter, 0898-350X. **Continued by** Fabians' Investment Resource, 1072-7264.

LC HG **ISSN** 1056-2540
DD 332 US
 TITLE CHANGE
FACS OF THE WEEK. (FACS OF THE WEEK : MUTUAL FUND NEWS & INFORMATION.). [FACS week]. (19??)-Vol. 7, Issue 9 (May 3, 1993). Periodical. English. Dalbar Publishing Inc., 260 Franklin Street, Boston MA 02110. **Tel** (617)439-6195, FAX (617)439-6346. **ED** Louis S Harvey and Anne Harvey. **Ad Acc. Continued by** Mutual Fund Market News, 1070-3373.

LC HG4521 .S432
DD 332.6 US
FACT BOOK. Added/Corp Securities Industry Association. Securities Industry Association. Research Dept. **VFOAT** Securities Industry Association ... Fact Book; SIA Fact Book. (1991)-. English. $25.00 members; $50.00 nonmembers. Securities Industry Association, 120 Broadway/35th Floor, New York NY 10271. **Tel** (212)608-1500, FAX (212)608-1604.

LC HG4575.a .F33 **ISSN** 1075-1637
DD 332.6/4273/05 US
FACT BOOK / AMERICAN STOCK EXCHANGE. [Fact book - Am. Stock Exch.]. **Added/Corp** American Stock Exchange. **VFOAT** Amex Fact Book. (1984)-. English. One time a year (spring of the following year). $15.00. American Stock Exchange, 86 Trinity Place, New York NY 10006. **Tel** (212)306-1386, FAX (212)306-2160. **ED** Janice Coleman. **Circ:** 4,000 (ctrl). **Continues** Amex Fact Book, 1075-167X.
Desc: A general reference of the American stock exchange and listing stocks, options and bonds.

LC HG5780.5.A2 F33A
DD 332.63/2/095195 KO
FACT BOOK (HANGUK CHUNGKWON KORAESO). (FACT BOOK.). English. One time a year. Free. Korea Stock Exchange, 1-116 Yoido-dong Youngdeungpo-ku, Seoul Korea. **Tel** (02)783-3371. **ED** Yong Soo Chang. **Circ:** 1,000.

Desc: Provides comprehensive basic statistics and the general trends of the Korean Securities Market for the year.

LC HG4571 .N56 **ISSN** 8756-6788
DD 332.64/273 US
FACT BOOK - NEW YORK STOCK EXCHANGE. (FACT BOOK.). [Fact book - N.Y. Stock Exch.]. **Main/Corp** New York Stock Exchange. (19??)-. English. One time a year. $10.00. New York Stock Exchange Inc., 20 Broad Street, New York NY 10005. **Tel** (212)656-3000, FAX (212)656-5725. (**Subscription address:** New York Stock Exchange, 11 Wall Street, New York NY 10005.) **ED** Joyce Kalcich. **Circ:** 14,000 (ctrl). **Continues** New York Stock Exchange. Dept. of Public Relations and Market Development. Fact Book.
Desc: Statistical portrait of the Exchange Community in 1984. To provide the investing public, securities industry, government and financial press with a convenient reference manual.
Ind/Abst Predicasts Forecasts.

LC HG4551
DD 332.6322 SI
FACT BOOK (STOCK EXCHANGE OF SINGAPORE). (FACT BOOK.). English. One time a year. Stock Exchange of Singapore Ltd, 16 Raffles Quay, 16-03 Hong Leong Building, Singapore 0104 Singapore.

LC HJ9013.W2 E19A **ISSN** 0275-6404
DD 352.1/22534/09753 US
FEDERAL CAPITAL IMPROVEMENTS PROGRAM FOR THE NATIONAL CAPITAL REGION. Main/Corp United States. National Capital Planning Commission. **VFOAT** Capital Improvements Program. English. One time a year. National Capital Planning Commission, 1325 G Street Northwest, Washington DC 20576. **Tel** (202)724-0176. **ED** George Evans /PM88/.
Desc: Capital improvement problems in the Washington, DC area of federal agencies.

LC HG450
DD 332.6 US
FEDERAL TAXATION OF MUNICIPAL BONDS DESKBOOK. See Finance-Taxation.

LC HG450
DD 332.6 US
FERC DATA ON CD-ROM. See Energy.

LC HG4551 .I532b
DD 332.6/42 FR
FIBV STATISTICAL DATA. See Business and Economics-Abstracting, Bibliographies and Statistics.

LC HG **ISSN** 1064-170X
DD 332 US
FIDELITY INSIGHT. [Fidel. insight]. **Added/Corp** Mutual Fund Investors Association. (1988)-. Periodical. English. Twelve times a year. $149.00 US; $169.00 other. Mutual Fund Investors Association, 20 William Street, PO Box 9135, Wellesley MA 02181. **Tel** (617)235-4432, FAX (617)235-5467. **ED** Eric M. Kobren. **Circ:** 40,000. **Continues** Insight (Needham, Mass.), 0892-2934.
Desc: Provides objective analysis and advice on fidelity mutual funds and services.

LC HD2709
DD 338.7/4/09711 CN
FILING STATEMENT (VANCOUVER STOCK EXCHANGE). (FILING STATEMENT / VANCOUVER STOCK EXCHANGE, BRITISH COLUMBIA, CANADA.). **Added/Corp** Vancouver Stock Exchange. Vancouver Curb Exchange. **VFOAT** Application for Listing; Statement of Material Facts. (19??)-. Periodical. English. Irregular. 572.24Can$. Vancouver Stock Exchange, PO Box 10333, 609 Granville Street, Vancouver British Columbia V7Y 1H1 Canada. **Tel** (604)689-3334, FAX (604)688-6051.

LC HG450 **ISSN** 0786-2652
DD 332.6 FI
UDC 336.7
FINANCE & FINLAND FOR INVESTORS. See Finance.

LC HG1 .B96a **ISSN** 1070-9215
DD 332/.05 US
FINANCE & TREASURY. See Business and Economics-Banks and Banking.

Business and Economics—Investments

LC HG4501 .A7
DD 332.6305
ISSN 0015-198X
US
CCC
CODEN FIAJA4
Pr Rev.
FINANCIAL ANALYSTS JOURNAL, THE. [Financ. anal. j.]. **Added/Corp** National Federation of Financial Analysts Societies. Financial Analysts Federation. Vol. 16, No. 1 (Jan./Feb. 1960)-. Periodical. English. Six times a year. $112.50. Association for Investment Management Research, 5 Boar's Head Lane, Charlottesville VA 22903. **Tel** (804)980-9712, (804)977-6600. **ED** Charles A. d'Ambrosio. cum. index. **Bk Rev**. **Ad Acc**. **Circ:** 20,000. available on microfilm and microfiche from University Microfilms International (UMI); available on an online database (files 15,485/Full-Text) from DIALOG. Documents available from UMI Article Clearinghouse, Ask*IEEE. **Continues** Analysts Journal.
Desc: Articles of interest to investment professionals.
Ind/Abst ABI/INFORM Glob. Ed.; ABI/INFORM [Computer File] (Sept. 1971-); Acad. Search; Account. Tax Datab. (Sept. 1971-) [Full Txt.]; Account. Art.; Bus. Index (1985-); Bus. Period. Index; Bus. Source Plus; Bus. Source; Comput. Lit. Index; Contents Pages Manage.; Curr. Cit.; EP Collect.; Fed. Tax Artic.; Gen. BusinessFile (1985-); Gen. Period. Index (1985-); Homework Help.; INFO-SOUTH Abstr.; INSPEC (Sept./Oct. 1984-); Mag. Search; Manage. Contents; MasterFile FullTEXT 1000; MasterFile FullTEXT 350; MasterFile FullTEXT 650; MasterFile FullTEXT (July 1993-); Middle East Abstr. Index; OCLC; Selec. Coop. Index Manage. Period.; Telebase; Trade Ind. Index; UMI ABI/Inform--Bus. Period. Ondisc [Full Txt.]; Wilson Bus. Abstr.

LC HG179 .F459
DD 332.024/005
ISSN 1052-3073
US
FINANCIAL COUNSELING AND PLANNING. See Business and Economics-Banks and Banking.

LC HG4905 .F45
DD 332.6/7/0973
ISSN 0093-4070
US
FINANCIAL DAILY CARD SERVICE, CUMULATIVE. See Business and Economics-Banks and Banking.

LC HG450
DD 332.6
ISSN 0893-7060
US
FINANCIAL PLANNING NEWS. [Financ. plan. news]. **Added/Corp** International Association for Financial Planning. (198?)-. Periodical. English. Ten times a year. International Association of Financial Planning, 2 Concourse Parkway, Suite 800, Atlanta GA 30328. **Tel** (404)395-1605, FAX (404)668-7758. **ED** Cliff Green. **Ad Acc**. **Circ:** 25,000 (ctrl).
Desc: A primary information source for financial planners; offers topical articles on issues, people in the industry, product development, regulatory topics and the IAFP association news.

LC HG
DD 332
ISSN 1074-4282
US
FINANCIAL PLANNING ON WALL STREET. [Financ. plan. Wall Str.]. (April 1992)-. Periodical. English. Four times a year. Securities Data Company, 40 West 57th Street, 11th Floor, New York NY 10019. **Tel** (212)765-5311. **Ad Acc**. **Circ:** 50,000 (ctrl).
Desc: Targets retail brokers and their clients. The title features articles on competition from new financial services firms, tax and regulatory developments affecting clients, mutual funds, new products and investments, and long-term strategies.

LC HG450
DD 332.6
US
FINANCIAL PLANNING SERIES. MONEYLINES MAGAZINE. VFOAT Financial Planning Series. Money Line. (19??)-. English. Four times a year. Blockbuster Periodicals Inc, 2131 Hollywood Boulevard, Suite 204, Hollywood FL 33020. **Tel** (305)925-5242, FAX (305)925-5244. **ED** F. Young and R. Hughes. **Ad Acc**. **Circ:** 50,000.
Desc: Lists investment opportunities, from real estate, mutual funds, and franchises. It provides the reader with important details on making wise investment decisions.

LC HG
DD 332
ISSN 0015-2021
CN
CCC
FINANCIAL POST, THE. See Finance.

LC HJ3835.N58 N48A
DD 353.97890072/31
US
FINANCIAL REPORT - STATE INVESTMENT COUNCIL. See Finance-Public Finance.

LC HG4512 .R4
DD 332.6/7
ISSN 0093-9536
US
FINANCIAL STOCK GUIDE SERVICE. (19??)-. English. Thirteen times a year (main volume published in Jan., supplements published monthly). $1900.00. Financial Information Inc, 30 Montgomery Street, Jersey City NJ 07302. **Tel** (201)332-5400. **Bk** Rev. **Ad Acc**. **Continues** Red Book Transfer Directory.
Desc: Transfer guide listing active obsolete securities and complete listing of transfer agent addresses.

LC HG450
DD 332.6
ISSN 1071-3646
US
CEASED
FINANCIAL TECHNOLOGY REVIEW. (1993)-(19??). Trade Publication. English. Rand Publishing, 780 Third Avenue, 25th Floor, New York NY 10017. **Tel** (212)308-4325. **ED** Teri Robinson. **Circ:** 30,000.

LC HG450
DD 332.6
CN
FINANCIAL TIMES INVESTOR'S 500. (19??)-. English. Globe & Mail, 444 Front Street West, Toronto Ontario M5V 2S9 Canada. **Tel** (416)585-5000, FAX (416)585-5085.
Ind/Abst Can. Period. Index (19??-).

LC HG450
DD 332.6
CN
FINANCIAL TIMES MARKETSHARE. (19??)-. English. Four times a year. Financial Times of Canada, 444 Front Street West, Toronto Ontario M5V 3E6 Canada. **Tel** (416)585-5265, telex 06-218681.
Ind/Abst Can. Period. Index (19??-).

LC HG450
DD 332.6
CN
FINANCIAL TIMES MONEY GUIDE. (19??)-. English. Four times a year. Financial Times of Canada, 444 Front Street West, Toronto Ontario M5V 3E6 Canada. **Tel** (416)585-5265, telex 06-218681.
Ind/Abst Can. Period. Index (19??-).

LC HG4501 .F5
DD 332/.05
ISSN 0015-2064
US
CCC
CODEN FIWOAR
TITLE CHANGE
FINANCIAL WORLD. [Financ. world]. Vol. 1 (Oct. 1902)-(19??). Periodical. English. FW / Financial World, 1328 Broadway, 3rd Floor, New York NY 10001-2116. **Tel** (212)594-5030, FAX (212)629-0021. **ED** Geoffrey Smith. **Ad Acc. Circ:** 500,000 (ctrl). available on microfilm and microfiche from University Microfilms International (UMI); available on an online database from NEXIS; and (files 15,485,647,648/Full-Text) DIALOG. Documents available from UMI Article Clearinghouse, Ask*IEEE, Documents on Demand, Magazine Collection. **Continued by** FW / Financial World.
Desc: Covers a wide range of investment opportunities including stocks, bonds, real estate, mutual funds and the U.S. and international markets.
Ind/Abst ABI/INFORM Glob. Ed.; ABI/INFORM Ondisc: Expr. Ed.; ABI/INFORM [Computer File] (Oct. 1972-); Acad. Search; Account. Tax Datab. (Oct. 1972-) [Full Txt.]; BioBusiness; Bus. Index (1985-1989); Bus. Period. Index; Bus. Source Plus; Bus. Source; Energy Inf. Abstr.; Environ. Abstr.; EP Collect.; Gen. BusinessFile (1985-1989); Gen. Period. Index (1985-1989); Homework Help.; INFO-SOUTH Abstr.; INSPEC (March 1984-); Lotus Notes; Mag. Express (1986-) [Full Txt.]; Mag. Index Plus (Jan. 1989-Dec. 1989); MasterFile FullTEXT 1000; MasterFile FullTEXT 350; MasterFile FullTEXT 650; MasterFile FullTEXT; Newsp. Period. Abstr. (1986-); OCLC; Resource/One Ondisc; Telebase; Mag. Index (1977-?); Trade Ind. Index (1981-?); UMI ABI/Inform--Bus. Period. Ondisc [Full Txt.]; Wilson Bus. Abstr.

LC HG450
DD 332.6
ISSN 0015-2129
UK
FINANCING FOREIGN OPERATIONS. See Business and Economics-International Economic Relations.

LC HG4501
DD 332.6
UK
●**FINANCING FOREIGN OPERATIONS. CHINA.** See Business and Economics-International Economic Relations.

LC HJ3835.M9 M62A
DD 353.9/786/0072
ISSN 0090-9122
US
FISCAL YEAR REPORT - STATE OF MONTANA. BOARD OF INVESTMENTS. (FISCAL YEAR REPORT.). **Main/Corp** Montana. Board of Investments. 1971/72-. English. One time a year. $20.00. Montana Board of Investments, Capitol Station, Helena MT 59620. **Tel** (406)442-1970. **ED** David M Lewis. **Circ:** 500 (ctrl).
Desc: Investment performance of pension and state asset.

LC HG4651 .F54a
DD 332.6
US
FITCH RATINGS. Main/Corp Fitch Investors Service. Vol. 12, No. 3-4 (March-April 1991)-. Periodical. English. Twelve times a year. $225.00. Fitch Investors Service, One State Street Plaza, New York NY 10004. **Tel** (212)908-0590. **Continues** Rating Register, 0703-3513.

LC HG4501 .F587
DD 332.6/78/05
ISSN 0739-4799
US
FIXED INCOME JOURNAL, THE. [Fixed income j.]. Periodical. English. One time a week. $150.00. The Fixed Income Journal, Subscription Department, 1629 K Street NW, Suite 520, Washington DC 20006.

LC HG450
ISSN 0300-4228
DD 332.6
UK
FLEET STREET LETTER. (1938)-. Periodical. English. One time a week. £96.00. Fleet Street Publications Ltd., 3 Fleet Street, London EC4Y 1AU United Kingdom. **Tel** 011 44 181 3537571. **ED** Nigel Wray. index available. **Circ:** 20,000.

LC HG5822 .I58
DD 338.096/05
ET
FOCUS ON AFRICAN INDUSTRY. Vol. 1, No. 1 (June 1987)-. Periodical. English. Four times a year. United Nations Economy, One United Nations Plaza, New York NY 10017. **Tel** (212)609-8351.
Continues Investment Africa.

LC HF3800.6.Z8 S17
DD 332.6/73225953
MY
FOCUS ON SABAH. English. Every 2 years. $25.00. Malaysia Department of Industrial Development, 1st Floor/Natikar Building, Kota Kinabulu Sabah Sabah Malaysia.

LC HG450
DD 332.6
US
FOREIGN COMMISSION RANKING REPORT. (19??)-. English. Securities Industry Association, 120 Broadway/35th Floor, New York NY 10271. **Tel** (212)608-1500, FAX (212)608-1604.
Desc: Allows participating firms to gauge their market share of commission generated by international activity in US equities. Participating firms are ranked against each other on a quarterly basis according to other major countries. Reports are confidential.

LC HG450
DD 332.6
FR
FOREIGN DIRECT INVESTMENT. (19??)-. Periodical. English. Four times a year. $62.00. OECD Publications and Information Center, 2 rue Andre-Pascal, 75775 Paris Cedex 16 France. **Tel** 011 33 1 49104262, US:(202)785-6323, FAX 011 33 1 45248580, 011 33 1 45248176, telex 620 160 OCDE. **(Subscription address:** OECD Publications Center, 2001 L Street, Suite 700, Washington DC 20036. **Tel** (202)822-3873, (202)785-6323.)

LC HG4501 .F674
DD 332.6
US
FOREIGN DIRECT INVESTMENT IN THE UNITED STATES. ESTABLISHMENT DATA FOR MANUFACTURING. Added/Corp United States. Bureau of Economic Analysis. United States. Bureau of the Census. **VFOAT** FDIUS. Establishment Data for Manufacturing; Establishment Data for Manufacturing. (1988)-. English. One time a year. $24.00. Superintendent of Documents, US Government Printing Office, Washington DC 20402. **Tel** (202)275-3328, FAX (202)786-2377. **(Subscription address:** US Government Bookstore, O'Neil Building, 2023 3rd Avenue North, Birmingham AL 35203.)
Continues Foreign Direct Investment in the United States. Establishment Data for ... .

LC HG4501 .F66
DD 332.6/73/0973
ISSN 0732-0418
US
FOREIGN DIRECT INVESTMENT IN THE UNITED STATES ... TRANSACTIONS. [Foreign direct investm. U. S., trans.]. **Added/Corp** United States. International Trade Administration. United States. International Trade Administration. Office of Trade and Investment Analysis. United States. International Trade Administration. Office of Trade and Economic Analysis. (19??)-. Government Publication. English. One time a year. $16.50. US Department of Commerce, 14th Street & Constitution Avenue NW, Washington DC 20230. **Tel** (202)482-2000, FAX (202)482-3772. **(Subscription address:** Superintendent of Documents, US Government Printing Office, Washington DC 20402.)

LC HG450
DD 332.6
US
FOREIGN EXCHANGE LETTER. Newsletter. English. One time a week. $1495.00 (one-year); $2695.00 (two-year). Institutional Investor Inc, 488 Madison Avenue, New York NY 10022. **Tel** (212)303-3234, (212)303-3233, FAX (212)303-3353.

LC HG
DD 332
ISSN 1018-4902
US
FOREIGN INVESTMENT ADVISORY SERVICE OCCASIONAL PAPER. (OCCASIONAL PAPER / FOREIGN INVESTMENT ADVISORY SERVICE.). [Foreign investm. Advis. Serv. occas. pap.]. **Added/Corp** International Finance Corporation. Multilateral Investment Guarantee Agency. Foreign Investment Advisory Service. (1990)-. English. International Finance Corporation, 1818 H Street NW,

Washington DC 20433. **Tel** (202)473-8979, (202)473-8981.
Ind/Abst Int. Dev. Abstr.

LC HG450 **ISSN** 0958-3076
DD 332.6 UK
Pr Rev. **TITLE CHANGE**
FOREIGN INVESTMENT IN THE US. (19??)-(19??). English. BNA International Inc., Herron, HSE Dean 10 Farrar Street, 6th Floor, London SW1H 0DX United Kingdom. **Tel** 011 44 171 2228831, FAX 011 44 171 2220294, telex 262570 BNA LONG. **ED** Kenneth Skilling and Basco Esleki. Index available. cum. index. **Bk Rev**. ***Continued by*** *Direct Investment in North America.*
Desc: A source of information for foreign investors and advisors to help structure their transactions and monitor legal and regulatory developments.

LC HG4501 **ISSN** 0702-6005
DD 332.6 CN
FOREIGN INVESTMENT REVIEW. **Added/Corp** Canada. Foreign Investment Review Agency. Vol. 1 (Autumn 1977)-. Periodical. English. Four times a year. Foreign Investment Review Agency, PO Box 2800 Station D, Ottawa Ontario K1P 6A5 Canada.
Desc: Quarterly journal on investment conditions in Canada.

LC HG450
DD 332.6 US
FOREIGN INVESTORS' HANDBOOK : MAKING SUCCESSFUL US INVESTMENTS, THE. (19??)-. English. One time a year. $450.00. Business International Corporation, 215 Park Avenue South, New York NY 10003. **Tel** (212)460-0600, FAX (212)995-8837. **Circ:** 200. ***Continues*** *The Effects of US Corporate Foreign Investment : A Special Research Study Undertaken By Business International Corporation., 0276-7791.*
Desc: Hands-on ways to operate profitably. Its seven chapters walk you through the foreign investment maze with hard-to-find statistics on foreign investors, detailed case analyses of companies' successes and failures, and practical checklists and how-to information.

LC HG4528 .I5
DD 332.6 US
•FRANKLIN RESEARCH'S INSIGHT. **Added/Corp** Franklin Research and Development Corporation. **VFOAT** Insight; Investing for a Better World. (1993)-. Newsletter. English. Twelve times a year. $195.00. Franklin Research and Development Corp., 711 Atlantic Avenue, Boston MA 02111. **Tel** (617)423-6655. **ED** Elliott Sclar. Index available. **Bk Rev**. ***Continues*** *Franklin's Insight.*

LC HG4528 .I5
DD 332.6 US
TITLE CHANGE
FRANKLIN'S INSIGHT. **Added/Corp** Franklin Research and Development Corporation. **VFOAT** Franklin's Insight's; Insight; A.Investing for a better world. (1987)-(1993). Periodical. English. Franklin Research and Development Corp., 711 Atlantic Avenue, Boston MA 02111. **Tel** (617)423-6655. **ED** Elliott Sclar. ***Continues*** *Insight (Boston, Mass.), 0742-5244;* ***Absorbed*** *Insights (Boston, Mass.); Insight. Equity Briefs, 0742-5236.* ***Continued by*** *Franklin Research's Insight.*

LC HG4551 **ISSN** 0229-4559
DD 332.64/4/05 CN
FRIEDBERG'S COMMODITY & CURRENCY COMMENTS. [Friedberg's commod. curr. comments]. (1971)-. Periodical. English. Twelve times a year. 295.00Can$. Friedberg Commodity Management Co., 347 Bay Street/Suite 1100, Toronto Ontario M5H 2P7 Canada. **Tel** (416)364-1171, FAX (416)364-0572, telex 065-24674.
Desc: A trading advisory model combining both fundamental and technical analysis.

LC HG4633 .F74 **ISSN** 0278-8861
DD 332.6 US
FRIENDS OF FINANCIAL HISTORY. Vol. 1, No. 1 (Oct/Nov. 1978)-. Periodical. English. Four times a year (Spring, Summer, Winter, and Fall). $25.00. Museum of American Financial History, 26 Broadway, New York NY 10004. **Tel** (212)908-4110, (212)908-4519, FAX (212)908-4600. **ED** Diane Moore. Index available. cum. index. **Bk Rev**, (Qty: 5). **Ad Acc**, **Adv Mgr:** D. Moore, **Tel** (212)908-4519. **Circ:** 2,000. Documents available from the publisher.
Desc: Traces world financial history and America's stock and bond markets, individuals, institutions and issues.

LC HG **ISSN** 1054-5956
DD 332 US
FUND ACTION. [Fund action]. **Added/Corp** Chatham Associates of N.Y. Vol. 1, No. 1 (May 14, 1990)-. Periodical. English. Twenty-six times a year. $1595.00. Fund World Publications, 211 East 43rd Street, 20th Floor, New York NY 10017. **Tel** (212)661-4929, FAX (212)661-2037.

LC HG **ISSN** 1057-6703
DD 332 US
FUND WATCH. (FUND WATCH : A SERVICE OF THE INSTITUTE FOR ECONOMETRIC RESEARCH.). [Fund watch]. **Added/Corp** Institute for Econometric Research (Fort Lauderdale, Fla.). Issue No. 1 (June 27, 1991)-. Periodical. English. Twelve times a year. $80.00. Institute for Econometric Research, 2200 SW 10th Street, Deerfield Beach FL 33442. **Tel** (305)421-1000. **ED** Norman G. Fosback.

LC HG4501 **ISSN** 1350-6625
DD 332.6 UK
•FUNDHOLDING SUMMARY, THE. [Fundholding summ.]. **VFOAT** TFS. (1993)-. Periodical. English. Four times a year. $67.60. Helath Productions Ltd, 32 King Henry's Road, London NW3 3RP United Kingdom. **Tel** 011 44 171 225596, FAX 011 44 171 7227158. **ED** Jill Turner.

LC HG4530 **ISSN** 1202-9262
DD 332.6327 332.63 CN
•FUNDLETTER WILLOWDALE. (THE FUNDLETTER). [Fundletter Willowdale]. **VFOAT** FundLetter; Fund Letter. (1994)-. Newsletter. English. Twelve times a year. 89.00Can$. Hume Publishing Company, 4100 Yonge Street, Willowdale Ontario M2P 2B9 Canada. **Tel** (416)221-4596, (800)733-4863.

LC HG4930 .F32 **ISSN** 0887-8161
DD 332.63/27 US
TITLE CHANGE
FUNDS, AGENTS, CUSTODIANS, SUPPLIERS. (FACS : FUNDS, AGENTS, CUSTODIANS, SUPPLIERS.). [Funds agents custod. suppliers]. **Added/Corp** NICSA (Association : U.S.). **VFOAT** Funds, Agents, Custodians, Suppliers. Vol. 1, No. 1 (May 1986)-(1993). Periodical. English. Dalbar Publishing Inc., 260 Franklin Street, Boston MA 02110. **Tel** (617)439-6195, FAX (617)439-6346. **ED** Louis S. Harvey. **Ad Acc.** ***Continued by*** *Journal of Mutual Fund Services, 1071-846X.*

LC HG **ISSN** 1352-1039
DD 332 UK
•FUTURES & DERIVATIVES LAW REVIEW, THE. (1994)-. Academic Scholarly Publication. English. Irregular. £150.00. Cavendish Publishing Ltd., Glass House, Wharton Street, London WC1X 9PX United Kingdom. **Tel** 011 44 171 2788000, FAX 011 44 171 2788080. **ED** Edward J. Swan. **Bk Rev**. **Circ:** 1,000. Documents available from BLDSC.
Desc: Covers legal issues internationally.

LC HG6046 .C577 **ISSN** 0746-2468
DD 332.64/4 US
CODEN FUTSEA
FUTURES (CEDAR FALLS, IOWA). (FUTURES.). [Futures]. **VFOAT** Futures. Source Book. Vol. 12, No. 9 (Sept. 1983)-. Periodical. English. Fourteen times a year. $39.00. Oster Communications Inc., 219 Parkade, Cedar Falls IA 50613. **Tel** (800)635-3931. **Circ:** 80,000. available on microfilm and microfiche from University Microfilms International (UMI). Documents available from UMI Article Clearinghouse. ***Continues*** *Commodities, 0279-5590;* ***Absorbed*** *Futures. Reference Guide to Futures/Options Markets.*
Ind/Abst ABI/INFORM Glob. Ed. (Sept. 1983-); ABI/INFORM [Computer File] (Sept. 1983-); Acad. Search; Bus. Index (1985-); Bus. Period. Index; EP Collect.; Gen. BusinessFile (1985-); Gen. Period. Index (1985-); Homework Help.; INFO-SOUTH Abstr.; Mag. Search; Manage. Contents; MasterFile FullTEXT 1000; MasterFile FullTEXT 350; MasterFile FullTEXT 650; MasterFile FullTEXT (Jan. 1994-); OCLC; PAIS Int. Print (1991-?); Sci. Fict. Fantasy Book Rev. Index; Soc. Sci. Source; Telebase; Trade Ind. ASAP [Full Txt.]; Trade Ind. Index [Full Txt.]; Wilson Bus. Abstr.

LC HG450 **ISSN** 0197-5382
DD 332.6 US
FUTURES INDUSTRY'S MANAGED ACCOUNT REPORTS. **VFOAT** Managed Account Reports. (197?)-. Periodical. English. Twelve times a year. $299.00 US and Canada; $370.00 other. Metal Bulletin Inc., 220 5th Avenue, 10th Floor, New York NY 10001. **Tel** (800)638-2525, (212)213-6202. **ED** Leou Rose and Morton Baratz. Index available. **Bk Rev**.
Desc: Reports on managed Futures Investment programs. Covers public funds, private pools, and individual managed accounts in two editions: "Futures Industry Update" and "Performance Update".

LC HG450
DD 332.6 US
•FUTURES PERSPECTIVE. (1995)-. English. Fifty-two times a year. $395.00. Commodity Perspective, 30 South Wacker/Suite 1820, Chicago IL 60606. **Tel** (312)454-1801, (800)621-5271, FAX (312)454-0239, telex 206099. ***Continues*** *Commodity Perspective.*

LC HG1501
DD 332.1 US
FW / FINANCIAL WORLD. (19??)-. Periodical. English. Twenty-five times a year. $37.50. FW / Financial World, 1328 Broadway, 3rd Floor, New York NY 10001-2116. **Tel** (212)594-5030, FAX (212)629-0021. **ED** Geoffrey Smith. **Ad Acc. Circ:** 500,000 (ctrl). available on microfilm and microfiche from University Microfilms International (UMI); available on an online database from NEXIS; and (files 15,485,647,648/Full-Text) DIALOG. Documents available from UMI Article Clearinghouse, Ask*IEEE, Documents on Demand, Magazine Collection. ***Continues*** *Financial World, 0015-2064.*
Desc: Covers a wide range of investment opportunities including stocks, bonds, real estate, mutual funds and the U.S. and international markets.
Ind/Abst MasterFile FullTEXT (July 1993-); PAIS Int. Print (1991).

LC HG5771 .J35a
DD 332.6 JA
GAIKOKU GIJUTSU DONYU NENJI HOKOKU. **Main/Corp** Japan. Kagaku Gijutsucho. Shinkokyoku. (19??)-. Periodical. Japanese. One time a year. ¥4200. Okurasho Insatukyoku, (Printing Bureau Ministry of Finance), 2-4 Toranomon 2 chome, Minatoku Tokyo 105 Japan. ***Continues*** *Gaikoku Gijutsu Donyu Nenji Hokoku.*

LC HG4501 .G37 **ISSN** 1053-5527
DD 330 US
GARY NORTH'S REMNANT REVIEW. [Gary North's remn. rev.]. **Added/Corp** American Bureau of Economic Research. Hoisager & Laird. **VFOAT** Remnant Review. (19??)-. Periodical. English. Twelve times a year. $97.00. Remnant Review, PO Box 84906, Phoenix AZ 85071. **Tel** (800)528-0559, FAX (602)943-2363.

LC HG4651
DD 332.63 US
GENERAL RULES AND REGULATIONS UNDER THE INVESTMENT COMPANY ACT OF 1940. **Main/Corp** United States. Securities and Exchange Commission. 1941-. English. US Securities and Exchange Commission, 450 Fifth Street NW, Washington DC 20549. **Tel** (202)272-3100.

LC HG186.I8 G4
DD 332/.0945 IT
GENTEMONEY. See Business and Economics-Banks and Banking.

LC HG **ISSN** 1077-0119
DD 332 US
•GERBINO INVESTMENT LETTER, THE. [Gerbino invest. lett.]. Vol. 3, No. 6 (June 1994)-. Periodical. English. Twelve times a year. $175.00. Phillips Business Information Inc., 1201 Seven Locks Road, PO Box 61130, Potomac MD 20854. **Tel** (301)424-3338, (301)340-1520, (800)777-5005, FAX (301)424-4297, telex 358149. ***Continues*** *Ken Gerbino's Smart Investing, 1059-6674.*

LC HG3810. G56 **ISSN** 1047-8736
DD 332/.042/05 US
CCC
GLOBAL CUSTODIAN. (Sept. 1989)-. Trade Publication. English. Four times a year (Mar., July, Sept., Dec.). $80.00. Asset International, 125 Greenwich Avenue, Greenwich CT 06830. **Tel** (203)629-5014, FAX (203)629-5024. **ED** Fergus Reid. **Ad Acc, Adv Mgr:** Ana Pacheco.
Desc: Covers developments throughout the world in global investing, market structure, and regulation product and technology development.

LC HG450 **ISSN** 1058-3920
DD 332.6 US
GLOBAL INVESTMENT TECHNOLOGY. (1991)-. Trade Publication. English. Twenty-six times a year. $595.00. Investment Media Inc., 909 Third Avenue, Sixth Floor, New York NY 10022. **Tel** (212)888-5810, FAX (212)888-6145. **ED** Pavan Sahgal. **Ad Acc, Adv Mgr:** M. Horton. **Circ:** 1,800-2,000 (ctrl). available via fax.
Desc: Provides bi-weekly reports and analysis of how business needs are driving technology decisions in the financial markets. Geared toward money managers, securities professionals, custodian banks and the suppliers who serve them.

LC HG **ISSN** 1076-8300
DD 332 US
•GLOBAL INVESTMENT : THE JOURNAL OF MONEY MANAGEMENT, TRADING, AND GLOBAL ASSET SERVICES. [Glob. invest.]. Vol. 1, No. 1 (Oct. 1994)-. Periodical. English. Four times a year. $95.00. Investment Media Inc., 909 Third Avenue, Sixth Floor, New York NY 10022. **Tel** (212)888-5810, FAX (212)888-6145.

LC HG4502 .G56 **ISSN** 0951-3604
DD 332.6/05 UK
GLOBAL INVESTOR. [Global invest.]. **VFOAT** Gurobaru Inbesuta. No. 1 (April 1987)-. Trade Publication. English (Japanese). Ten times a year. $425.00. Euromoney Publications PLC, Nestor House, Playhouse Yard, London EC4Z 5EX United Kingdom. **Tel** 011 44 171 7798888, FAX 011 44 171 7798630, telex 290700 EUROMON G. available on an online database (files 771,772/Full-Text) from DIALOG. Documents available from UMI Article Clearinghouse.
Desc: International medium for the cross-border

Business and Economics —Investments

investor, examining strategy, asset allocation, markets and trends in international investment. **Ind/Abst** ABI/INFORM Glob. Ed.

LC HG4651 **ISSN** 1202-6948
DD 332.63 CN
●**GLOBAL MARKET WATCH.** [Glob. mark. watch]. **Added/Corp** Cavelti Capital Management. (May 1, 1994)-. Periodical. English. Twelve times a year. Cavelti Capital Management, 74 Victoria Street, Toronto Ontario M5C 2A5 Canada. **Continues** Cavelti, Peter C. (Peter Christian), 1948- Cavelti's Market Report, 0849-181X.

LC HG4651
DD 332.632 US
GLOBAL OIL STOCKS & BALANCES.
See Petroleum and Natural Gas.

LC HG4538 .G55 **ISSN** 0739-4640
DD 658 US
GLOBAL RISK ASSESSMENTS : ISSUES, CONCEPTS, AND APPLICATIONS. (GLOBAL RISK ASSESSMENTS, ISSUES, CONCEPTS & APPLICATIONS IN BUSINESS ENVIRONMENT RISK ASSESSMENT, COUNTRY, INVESTMENT & TRADE RISK ANALYSIS, POLITICAL RISK ASSESSMENT & MANAGEMENT.). **Added/Corp** Global Risk Assessments, Inc. **VFOAT** Global Risk Assessments, Issues, Concepts and Applications. Book 1 (1983)-. Monographic series. English. Irregular. Price varies per volume. Global Risk Assessments, 3638 University Avenue, Suite 215, Riverside CA 92501. **Tel** (714)788-0672. **ED** Jerry Rogers. **Bk Rev**. **Ad Acc**. **Circ**: 2,000.
Desc: Edited book series on political risk analysis.
Ind/Abst Bus. Index (?-?); Int. Polit. Sci. Abstr.; Soc. Plann. Policy Dev. Abstr.; Trade Ind. Index (?-?).

LC HG450 **ISSN** 1017-1371
DD 332.6
UDC 33 HK
GLOOM, BOOM AND DOOM REPORT, THE. (1990)-. Periodical. English. Twelve times a year. $550.00. Marc Faber Ltd., 16 18 Queen's Road, 2705 New World Tower, Central District Hong Kong. **Tel** 011 852 28015410, FAX 011 852 28459192. **ED** Marc Faber.
Desc: Highlights undervalued and overvalued investments and appraises opportunities.

LC HG1501 **ISSN** 0743-5185
DD 332.1 US
GOURGUES REPORT, THE. [Gourgues rep.]. Vol. 1, No. 1 (Jan. 1984)-. Periodical. English. Twelve times a year. $125.00. Gourgues Report, PO Box 81668, Atlanta GA 30366. **Tel** (404)261-1713. **ED** Ronald Davis. **Bk Rev**. **Circ**: 750 (ctrl)
Desc: A success guide for those who practice or support the evolving profession of comprehensive personal financial planning emphasizing strategies and trends.

LC HG4551
DD 332.6322 MX
GRAFICAS TECNICAS DE VALORES.
Added/Corp Asociacion de Consultores Tecnicos en Valores e Inversiones, S.A. (19??)-. Periodical. English (Spanish). One time a week.

LC HG450 **ISSN** 0046-631X
DD 332.6 CN
GRAPHOSCOPE, THE. **Added/Corp** Canadian Analyst Limited. No. 1 (Sept. 1953)-. Periodical. English. Six times a year. 207.65Can$. Canadian Analyst Ltd., 30 Duncan Street, Toronto Ontario M5V 2C3 Canada. **Tel** (416)971-6543, FAX (416)598-0049. **ED** Lina Murray. Index available. **Ad Acc**. **Circ**: 2,000 (ctrl).
Desc: Provides you with a reliable source of basic stock market data to help the investor pinpoint his strategic position in the market. Contains a ten year history of stock market performance, plotted monthly along with a wealth of fundamental data.

LC HG **ISSN** 0017-4831
DD 332 US
GROWTH FUND GUIDE. (GROWTH FUND GUIDE : THE INVESTORS GUIDE TO DYNAMIC GROWTH FUNDS.). [Growth fund guide]. **Main/Corp** Growth Fund Research, Inc. Vol. 1 (July 1967)-. Periodical. English. Twelve times a year. $99.00. Growth Fund Research Inc, PO Box 6600, Rapid City SD 57709. **Tel** (605)341-1971.

LC HG4501 .G76
DD 332.6 US
GROWTH STOCK OUTLOOK. **Added/Corp** Growth Stock Outlook, Inc. (1965)-. Periodical. English. Twenty-four times a year. $195.00. Growth Stock Outlook Inc, PO Box 15381, Chevy Chase MD 20815. **Tel** (301)654-5205. **ED** Charles Allmon (editor's address: 4405 East-West Highway, Suite 305, Bethesda MD 20814). ctrl circ.

LC HG5401 .G83
DD 332.6 UY
GUIA FINANCIERA. (19??)-. Periodical. Spanish. One time a week. Nicaragua 1579, Montevideo Uruguay. **Continues** Guia Financiera Magui.

LC HC547.S43 I537a
DD 330.9/66/305 SG
GUIDE DE L'INVESTISSEUR INDUSTRIEL AU SENEGAL. **Main/Corp** Societe Nationale d'Etudes et de Promotion Industrielle. (19??)-. French. 4 rue Maunoury, BP 100, Dakar Senegal.

LC HG4028.D5 .G84 **ISSN** 1080-4188
DD 332 US
GUIDE TO DIVIDEND REINVESTMENT PLANS. [Guide divid. reinvestm. plans]. (19??)-. English. Four times a year. $137.00. Evergreen Enterprises, PO Box 763, Laurel MD 20725. **Tel** (301)953-1861.

LC HG450
DD 332.6 US
CEASED
GUIDE TO GLOBAL INSTITUTIONAL INVESTORS. (19??)-(1993). Periodical. English. Institutional Investor Inc., 488 Madison Avenue, New York NY 10022. **Tel** (212)303-3234, (212)303-3233, FAX (212)303-3353.

LC HC517.K4 A16
DD 330.9/66/204 KE
GUIDE TO INDUSTRIAL INVESTMENT, A. **Main/Corp** Kenya. Ministry of Commerce and Industry. (1967)-. English.

LC HG450
DD 332.6 UK
GUIDE TO SELECTED DOMESTIC BOND MARKETS, THE. **Added/Corp** Euromoney Publications Ltd. **VFOAT** Selected Domestic Bond Markets. (1992)-. English. Euromoney Publications PLC, Nestor House, Playhouse Yard, London EC4Z 5EX United Kingdom. **Tel** 011 44 171 7798888, FAX 011 44 171 7798630, telex 290700 EUROMON G.

LC HG4551 .G8
DD 332.6 UK
GUIDE TO WORLD EQUITY MARKETS, THE. **Added/Corp** Euromoney Publications. G.T. Management. **VFOAT** World Equity Markets. (1992)-. Periodical. English. One time a year. $250.00. Euromoney Publications PLC, Nestor House, Playhouse Yard, London EC4Z 5EX United Kingdom. **Tel** 011 44 171 7798888, FAX 011 44 171 7798630, telex 290700 EUROMON G. **Continues** GT Guide to World Equity Markets.

LC HG4501 .H36 **ISSN** 0736-6264
DD 332.63/27 US
HANDBOOK FOR NO-LOAD FUND INVESTORS, THE. [Handb. no-load fund investors]. **VFOAT** Handbook for No Load Fund Investors. (1981)-. Periodical. English. One time a year (May). $49.00. No-Load Fund Investor, PO Box 318, Irvington-on-Hudson NY 10533. **Tel** (914)693-7420, FAX (914)693-8067. **ED** Sheldon Jacobs.

LC HG5128.F6 H35
DD 332.6/7/09759 US
HANDBOOK OF FLORIDA SECURITIES. (1970)-. English. One time a year. First Florida Company, 7421 SW 11th St., Plantation FL 33317-4119.

LC HG4243.5.C4 H3
DD 332.63 CE
HANDBOOK OF RUPEE COMPANIES. **Added/Corp** Colombo Brokers' Association. (19??)-. English.

LC HG4551 .H319
DD 332.64/2 UK
... HANDBOOK OF WORLD STOCK AND COMMODITY EXCHANGES, THE. **VFOAT** Blackwell Finance ... Handbook of World Stock and Commodity Exchanges. (1991)-. English. $265.00. Basil Blackwell Publishers Ltd., 108 Cowley Road, Oxford OX4 1JF United Kingdom. **Tel** 011 44 1235 465500, FAX 011 44 1235 465556, telex 837022 OXBOOK G.

LC HG5800.5.S44 S45a
DD 332.6/42/09593 TH
HANDBOOK - SECURITIES EXCHANGE OF THAILAND. **Main/Corp** Securities Exchange of Thailand. (1975)-. English. Irregular. 15.00. Securities Exchange of Thailand, Siam Center 4th Floor/Room 412, Bangkok Thailand.

LC HG450
DD 332.6 US
HARRY BROWNE'S SPECIAL REPORTS. **Added/Corp** Harry Browne Special Reports, Inc. **VFOAT** Special Reports. 1 (Dec. 20, 1974)-. Periodical. English. Irregular. Harry Browne's Special Reports, Box 5586, Austin TX 78763. **Tel** (512)453-7313, (800)531-5142. **ED** Harry Browne. **Bk Rev**. ctrl circ.
Desc: Long and short-term investment strategies for investors in gold and silver stocks, bonds, mutual funds, options and collectibles.

LC HG450 **ISSN** 0745-7073
DD 332.6 US
HAWAII INVESTOR. See Real Estate.

LC HG **ISSN** 1075-9107
DD 332 US
HEALTHCARE INVESTOR FOR THE SENIOR CARE MARKET, THE. See Medical Sciences-Health Services Administration.

LC HG4651 **ISSN** 0315-2782
DD 332.6/322 CN
HIGH AND LOW. [High low]. (1926)-. Periodical. English. One time a year. Financial Counsel, PO Box 250, Montreal Quebex H3C 2S1.

LC HG **ISSN** 8756-8403
DD 332 US
HIGH PROFIT INVESTING. Periodical. English. Twelve times a year. $96.00. Universal Information Services, Woodland Hills CA 91364. **Continues** Cash Flow Letter.

LC HG450
DD 332.6 US
HIGH TECH GROWTH FORECASTER. English. Twelve times a year. $195.00. Fitch Investors Service, One State Street Plaza, New York NY 10004. **Tel** (212)908-0590.
Desc: Advisory report features high tech and growth stock selections. Timing to buy, sell or hold based on a unique proven statistical technique.

LC HG450 **ISSN** 0736-427X
DD 332.6 US
HIGH TECH INVESTOR. [High tech invest.]. Vol. 1, No. 1 (April 19, 1983)-. Periodical. English. $180.00 (general), $200.00 (airmail) other. HMR Publishing Company, PO Box 3073, Barrington IL 60010-3073. **Tel** (312)382-7857.

LC HG4651
DD 332.632 US
UDC 33
HIGH TECHNOLOGY AND OTHER GROWTH STOCKS. English. Twelve times a year. $175.00 (one-year), $300.00 (two-year). High Technology and Other Growth Stocks, 402 Border Road, Concord MA 01742. **Tel** (617)371-0096.
Desc: An investment letter focusing on attractive investments among high technology and other growth companies. Fundamental and technical analysis of over 90 stocks.

LC HG **ISSN** 1065-089X
DD 332 US
HIGH YIELD SECURITIES JOURNAL. [High yield secur. j.]. **Added/Corp** Bond Investors Association. (1992)-. Periodical. English. Twelve times a year. $99.00. Bond Investors Association / Florida, PO Box 4427, Miami Lakes FL 33014. **Tel** (305)557-1832.

LC HG **ISSN** 1047-9791
DD 332 US
TITLE CHANGE
HOLT ADVISORY, THE. [Holt advis.].
Added/Corp T.J. Holt & Co. (1986)-(19??). Periodical. English. Weiss Research Inc., PO Box 109665, Palm Beach Gardens FL 33410. **Tel** (407)627-3300, FAX (407)625-6685. **Continues** Holt Investment Advisory. **Merged into** Safe Money Report.
Desc: For active investors seeking growth appreciation opportunities. Suitable for more experienced investors with a moderate risk profile.

LC HD941 .H68 **ISSN** 1046-1655
DD 333.33/025/5125 US
HONG KONG REGISTER. See Real Estate.

LC HG450 **ISSN** 0273-0618
DD 332.6 US
HOTTEST NEW BUSINESS IDEAS, THE.
Added/Corp International Entrepreneurs' Association. Research Dept. (1978)-. English. Entrepreneur Inc., 2392 Morse Avenue, Irvine CA 92714. **Tel** (714)261-2393.

LC HG **ISSN** 1042-4261
DD 332 US
HULBERT FINANCIAL DIGEST, THE.
[Hulbert financ. dig.]. (19??)-. Periodical. English. Twelve times a year. $135.00. Hulbert Financial Digest, 316 Commerce Street, Alexandria VA 22314. **Tel** (703)683-5905.

LC HG4651 **ISSN** 1191-8934
DD 332.63/2/05 CN
IAN MCAVITY'S DELIBERATIONS ON WORLD MARKETS. [Ian McAvity's delib. world mark.]. **VFOAT** Deliberations on World Markets. (1991)-. Periodical. English. Twenty-four times a year. 225.00Can$. Deliberations Research Inc., PO Box 182, Adelaide Street Station, Toronto Ontario M5C 2J1 Canada. **Tel** (416)867-1100. **(Subscription address:** IRIS Limited / US, PO Box 43310, Tucson AZ 85733. **Tel** (602)987-1100.) **Continues** McAvity, Ian. Deliberations., 0843-9915.

Business and Economics —Investments

LC HF331.I55 I5314
DD 332.6/73598/0595706050957   SI
IBAS ANNUAL. **VFOAT** I.B.A.S. Annual. (1980)-. English. One time a year. Indonesian Business Association of Singapore, Wisma Indonesia, 435 Orchard Road, PO Box 3804, Singapore 0923 Singapore.

LC HG4930 .I2   **ISSN** 1060-8524
DD 332   US
    TITLE CHANGE
IBC/DONOGHUE'S MUTUAL FUNDS ALMANAC. [IBC/Donoghue's mutual funds alm.]. **Added/Corp** IBC USA (Publications) Inc. **VFOAT** IBC Donoghue's Mutual Funds Almanac; Mutual Funds Almanac. **VAT** International Business Communications/Donoghue's Mutual Funds Almanac; IBC Donoghue's Mutual Funds Almanac. 22nd Ed. (1991)-(1995). Periodical. English. IBC Donoghue Organization, 290 Eliot Street, Ashland MA 01721. **Tel** (800)343-5413, (508)881-2800. **(Subscription address:** IBC Donoghue Organization, PO Box 91004, Ashland MA 01721. **)** *Continues Donoghue's Mutual Funds Almanac, 0737-0369. Continued by IBC's Mutual Funds Almanac.*

LC HG   **ISSN** 1043-285X
DD 332   US
IBC'S MONEY MARKET INSIGHT. [IBC's money mark. insight]. **Added/Corp** International Business Communications (Holdings) (U.S.). **VFOAT** Money Market Insight. **VAT** International Business Communications' Money Market Insight. Vol. 1, No. 1 (Feb. 1989)-. Periodical. English. Twelve times a year. $575.00. IBC Donoghue Organization, 290 Eliot Street, Ashland MA 01721. **Tel** (800)343-5413, (508)881-2800. **(Subscription address:** IBC Donoghue Organization, PO Box 91004, Ashland MA 01721. **)**
 Desc: Summary of over 500 taxable and tax-free money funds, identifying top performing funds with similar investment strategies, allowing comparison between trends in different industry segments.

LC HG1501
DD 332.1   US
●**IBC'S MONEYLETTER.** (1995)-. English. Twenty-four times a year. $109.00. IBC Donoghue Organization, 290 Eliot Street, Ashland MA 01721. **Tel** (800)343-5413, (508)881-2800. *Continues Moneyletter.*
 Desc: An investment advisory containing money management advice and general investment recommendations.

LC HG4930 .I2   **ISSN** 1060-8524
DD 332   US
●**IBC'S MUTUAL FUNDS ALMANAC.** (1995)-. Periodical. English. IBC Donoghue Organization, 290 Eliot Street, Ashland MA 01721. **Tel** (800)343-5413, (508)881-2800. **(Subscription address:** IBC Donoghue Organization, PO Box 91004, Ashland MA 01721. **)** *Continues IBC Donoghue's Mutual Funds Almanac, 1060-8524.*

LC HG4534 .I27   **ISSN** 0968-6118
DD 332.66/05   UK
ICB MAGAZINE. (19??)-. Trade Publication. English. Six times a year. $260.00. Euromoney Publications PLC, Nestor House, Playhouse Yard, London EC4Z 5EX United Kingdom. **Tel** 011 44 171 7798888, FAX 011 44 171 7798630, telex 290700 EUROMON G. **(Subscription address:** ICB Publications Limited, 39 41 North Road, London N7 9DP United Kingdom. **Tel** 011 44 181 6098661.**)** Documents available from Ask*IEEE. *Continues ICB, 0953-5632.*
 Ind/Abst INSPEC.

LC HG450   **ISSN** 0273-0898
DD 332.6   US
ICI TRENDS IN MUTUAL FUND ACTIVITY. **Main/Corp** Investment Company Institute (U.S.) Research Dept. **Added/Corp** Investment Company Institute (U.S.). Research Dept. Trends in Mutual Fund Activity. **VFOAT** Trends in Mutual Fund Activity. **VAT** Investment Company Institute Trends in Mutual Fund Activity. (19??)-. English. Twelve times a year. $225.00. Investment Company Institute, 1401 H Street Northwest, Washington DC 20005. **Tel** (202)326-5800, (202)326-5972.

LC HG4501   **ISSN** 0840-9137
DD 332.6/0971   CN
IE, INVESTMENT EXECUTIVE. [IE, Invest. exec.]. **VFOAT** Investment Executive. Vol. 1, No. 1 (Jan. 1989)-. Periodical. English. Eleven times a year. 45.00Can$. Investment Executive Inc., 208 Carlton Street, Toronto Ontario M5A 2L1 Canada. **Tel** (416)962-4103. **ED** Tessa Wilmott. **Bk Rev**. **Ad Acc**, **Adv Mgr:** B. Hyland. **Circ:** 16,000 (ctrl).
 Desc: A magazine for Canada's financial community.

LC HG4651
DD 332.632   US
ILLINOIS BOND WATCHER, THE. (Jan. 1981)-. Periodical. English. Illinois Economic and Fiscal Commission, 703 Stratton Building, Springfield IL 62706.

LC HG5471 .I46   **ISSN** 0244-7118
DD 332.6/73/0944   FR
IMPLANTATION ETRANGERE DANS L'INDUSTRIE AU IER JANVIER, L'. French. One time a year. Documentation Francaise, 29 quai Voltaire, 75344 Paris Cedex 7 France. **Tel** 011 33 1 40157000, FAX 011 33 1 40157230, telex 204 826 DOCFRAN. available on microfiche.

LC HG450   **ISSN** 0390-9212
DD 332.6   IT
UDC 658
    CEASED
IMPRESA E SOCIETA. [Impresa Soc.]. (1971)-(19??). Periodical. Italian. Cedis SRL, Via F Denza 52, 00197 Rome Italy. **Tel** 011 39 6 36307954.

LC R   **ISSN** 0733-1398
DD 610   US
    CCC
IN VIVO (NEW YORK, N.Y.). (IN VIVO.). [In vivo]. Vol. 1, No. 1 (Spring 1982)-. Trade Publication. English. Eleven times a year. $595.00. Windhover Information, PO Box 360, South Norwalk CT 06856. **Tel** (203)838-4401. **ED** Roger Longman, David Cassak. Index available. **Ad Acc**.
 Desc: Provides strategic, financial and technological analyses of the medical business for strategic planners and investors. Includes lists of all medical acquisitions, joint arrangements and financings.
 Ind/Abst Abstr. BioCommer.; F&S Index Plus Text, Int. [Full Txt.] [Select. Cov.]; PROMT; Ref. Upd. Deluxe Ed.

LC HG4930 .M66
DD 332   US
●**INCOME FUND OUTLOOK.** **Added/Corp** Institute for Econometric Research (Fort Lauderdale, Fla.). (Jan. 14, 1994)-. Periodical. English. Twelve times a year. $100.00. Institute for Econometric Research, 2200 SW 10th Street, Deerfield Beach FL 33442. **Tel** (305)421-1000. *Continues Income & Safety, 0891-1215.*

LC HB251   **ISSN** 0019-3429
DD 339   US
INCOME OPPORTUNITIES (NEW YORK, N.Y.). (INCOME OPPORTUNITIES.). [Income oppor.]. (19??)-. Periodical. English. Twelve times a year. $17.89. Essence, 1500 Broadway, New York NY 10036. **Tel** (212)642-0613. **(Subscription address:** Neodata / Colorado, PO Box 2606, Boulder CO 80322. **)** available on microfilm and microfiche from University Microfilms International (UMI).

LC HG4050 .H53   **ISSN** 0741-1812
DD 338.7/4/0973   US
INCOME STOCKS HANDBOOK. [Income stocks handb.]. **Added/Corp** Standard and Poor's Corporation. Vol. 2, No. 2 (Dec. 1983)-. English. Two times a year. Standard & Poor's Corporation, (A Division of McGraw-Hill, Inc.), 25 Broadway, New York NY 10004. **Tel** (212)208-8775, (800)221-5277. *Continues High-Yield Stocks Handbook, 0737-4070.*
 Desc: Reports on the companies that pay the highest dividends; lists of companies offering dividend reinvestment plans, utility dividends eligible for tax exclusion, and latest earnings for companies in the book.

LC HG4501   **ISSN** 0821-0756
DD 332.6/7373/071   CN
INDEPENDENCE NEWS. [Indep. news]. (Oct. 1973)-. Periodical. English. Four times a year. Committee for Canadian Self-Reliance, PO Box 624, Saskatoon Saskatchewan S7K 3L6 Canada.

LC HG450   **ISSN** 1046-3291
DD 332.6   US
INDEPENDENT INVESTOR (MIAMI BEACH, FLA.). (INDEPENDENT INVESTOR.). (1991)-. Periodical. English. Twelve times a year. $192.00. Independent Investor, 605 Euclid Avenue, #204, Miami Beach FL 33139.

LC HG4651   **ISSN** 0081-4466
DD 332.632   PK
INDEX NUMBERS OF STOCK EXCHANGE SECURITIES. **Main/Corp** State Bank of Pakistan. Dept. of Statistics. (June 1963)-. Periodical. English. One time a year. Rs12.00 Pakistan; $2.40 US. State Bank of Pakistan - Public Relation Department, PO Box 4456, Central Directorate, Karachi Pakistan. **Tel** 011 92 21 2414141310, telex 2754 SBP. **Circ:** 435 (ctrl).

LC HG4930 .I48   **ISSN** 0147-9504
DD 332   US
INDEX OF ACTIVE REGISTERED INVESTMENT COMPANIES UNDER THE INVESTMENT COMPANY ACT OF 1940 AND RELATED INVESTMENT ADVISERS, PRINCIPAL UNDERWRITERS, SPONSORS (I.E. DEPOSITORS) AND UNDERLYING COMPANIES. **Added/Corp** United States. Securities and Exchange Commission. Office of Reports and Information Services. United States. Securities and Exchange Commission. Office of Registrations and Reports. United States. Securities and Exchange Commission. Office of Registrations and Reports Services. **VAT** Index of Active Registered Investment Companies Under the Investment Company Act of Nineteen Hundred and Forty and Related Investment Advisers, Principal Underwriters, Sponsors (ID Est Depositors) and Underlying Companies. (19??)-. English. Securities and Exchange Commission, Office of Reports and Information Services, 450 Fifth Street NW, Washington DC 20549.

LC HG450
DD 332.6   US
INDIAN TRUST FUNDS INVESTMENT OPERATIONS. (INDIAN TRUST FUNDS INVESTMENT OPERATIONS : FISCAL YEAR ...). **Main/Corp** United States. Bureau of Indian Affairs. Office of Trust Responsibilities. Branch of Investments. **VFOAT** Investments; Results of Investments Operations; Indian Trust Fund Investments. (19??)-. English. One time a year. Bureau of Indian Affairs, Office of Trust and Responsibilities, Branch of Investments, 500 Gold Avenue SW, PO Box 886, Albuquerque NM 87103.

LC HG
DD 016.3326
INDIVIDUAL INVESTOR'S GUIDE TO INVESTMENT PUBLICATIONS, THE. English. One time a year. $19.95. American Association of Individual Investors, 625 North Michigan Avenue, Chicago IL 60611. **Tel** (312)280-0170. **ED** B Craig. Index available. ctrl circ.
 Desc: Reference to various investments and financial products.

LC HG4930 .I49
DD 332.620973   US
●**INDIVIDUAL INVESTOR'S GUIDE TO LOW LOAD MUTUAL FUNDS, THE.** **Added/Corp** American Association of Individual Investors. **VFOAT** Low Load Mutual Funds; Individual Investor's Guide to Low Load Mutual Funds. 13th Ed. (1994)-. English. One time a year. $24.95. American Association of Individual Investors, 625 North Michigan Avenue, Chicago IL 60611. **Tel** (312)280-0170. *Continues Individual Investor's Guide to No-Load Mutual Funds.*

LC HG4930 .I49
DD 332.63/27   US
    CEASED
INDIVIDUAL INVESTOR'S GUIDE TO NO-LOAD MUTUAL FUNDS, THE. **VFOAT** Individual Investor's Guide to No Load Mutual Funds. (Dec. 1982)-(1993). English. American Association of Individual Investors, 625 North Michigan Avenue, Chicago IL 60611. **Tel** (312)280-0170. Each issue contains an index to its own contents (no volume index)--loose.

LC HG1501   **ISSN** 0744-6268
DD 332.1   US
INDIVIDUAL RETIREMENT PLANS GUIDE : IRA, SEP, KEOGH. See Business and Economics-Banks and Banking.

LC HC446 .I665
DD 332.6/7322598   IO
INDONESIA (CHASE MANHATTAN BANK, N.A.). (INDONESIA : EXECUTIVE'S FACT BOOK.). English. One time a year. Chase Manhattan Bank N A, Government Printing Office, Box 311, Jakarta Indonesia.

LC HC431 .I5215
DD 338.0954   II
INDUSTRIAL RESEARCHER. (19??)-. Periodical. English. Four times a year. $200.00. Pranava Industrial Services Pvt Ltd, 49 Warden Court August Kranti Marg, Bombay 400036 India. **Tel** 8221564. **(Subscription address:** Prints India, 11 Darya Ganj, New Delhi 110002 India. **Tel** 011 91 11 3268645, FAX 011 91 11 3275542, telex 31-61087 PRIN-IN.**)** **ED** Manda Pariku. **Bk Rev**. **Ad Acc**. **Circ:** 500.
 Desc: Investment and marketing, economics industry and production.

LC HG4915 .M5A   **ISSN** 0094-1352
DD 332.6/322/0973   US
INDUSTRISCOPE (RICHMOND). (INDUSTRISCOPE.). **Main/Corp** Media General Financial Services. Vol. 1 (May 1973)-. Periodical. English. Twelve times a year. Industriscope, PO Box C-32333, Richmond VA 23293.

LC HG450
DD 332.6   GW
INDUSTRITEHEMEN; PR-MAGAZIN FUER DIE INVESTITIONSGUESTERINDUSTRIE. (19??)-. German. Industriehemen Verlag, Packenreiterstr 18B, W-8000 Munich 60 Germany.

Business and Economics —Investments

LC HG5160.5.A2 O74B
DD 332/.041/097
US
INFORMATIVE BULLETIN - CAPITAL MARKETS DEVELOPMENT PROGRAM. **Main/Corp** Organization of American States. Capital Markets Development Program. Bulletin. English. Organization of American State, 1889 F Street NW, Washington DC 20006.

LC HG1501
DD 332.1
US
CEASED
INSIDE FINANCIAL SERVICES MARKETING. See Business and Economics-Banks and Banking.

LC KF1073.I5 I575
DD 346
ISSN 0897-490X
US
INSIDER TRADING REGULATION. [Insid. trading regul.]. (1988)-. English. One time a year. $110.00. Clark Boardman Callaghan, 155 Pfingsten Road, Deerfield IL 60015. **Tel** (800)323-8067. **Continues** Insider Trading Handbook, 0891-9658.

LC HG4551
DD 332.6322
ISSN 0730-2908
US
CCC
INSIDERS, THE. (THE INSIDERS / A SERVICE OF THE INSTITUTE FOR ECONOMETRIC RESEARCH.). **Added/Corp** Institute for Econometric Research (Fort Lauderdale, Fla.). (19??)-. Periodical. English. Twenty-four times a year. $100.00. Institute for Econometric Research, 2200 SW 10th Street, Deerfield Beach FL 33442. **Tel** (305)421-1000. **ED** Norman G. Fosback. **Circ:** 7,000.
Desc: Contains information based on insider trading activities in listed stocks.

LC HG450
DD 332.6
US
INSIDERS OPTIONS. English. Six times a year. $95.00. Vickers Stock Research Corporation, 17 Battery Place, 18th Floor, New York NY 10004. **Tel** (212)425-7500.

LC HG450
DD 332.6
ISSN 8756-6435
US
INSIDERS REPORT (SCOTTSDALE, ARIZ.). (INSIDERS REPORT.). **Added/Corp** Scottsdale Chamber of Commerce. (1984)-. Periodical. English. Twelve times a year. $45.00. Alan Shaw Feinstein, 37 Alhambra Circle, Cranston RI 02905. **Tel** (401)467-5155.

LC HG4501 .I56
DD 332.6/0973
ISSN 0741-0239
US
INSTITUTIONAL EQUITY SERVICES. [Inst. equity serv.]. **Added/Corp** Greenwich Research Associates. (19??)-. English. One time a year. Greenwich Research Associates Inc, Office Park 8, Greenwich CT 06830.

LC HG4501 .I583
DD 332.6/7
ISSN 0192-5660
US
INSTITUTIONAL INVESTOR (INTERNATIONAL ED.). (INSTITUTIONAL INVESTOR.). [Inst. invest.]. (Mar. 1976)-. Periodical. English. Twelve times a year. $430.00. Institutional Investor Inc., 488 Madison Avenue, New York NY 10022. **Tel** (212)303-3234, (212)303-3233, FAX (212)303-3353. available on microfilm and microfiche from University Microfilms International (UMI); available on CD-ROM. Documents available from Documents on Demand.
Desc: Charts the international financial community.
Ind/Abst Bus. Index (1985-); Environ. Abstr.; Gen. BusinessFile (1985-); Manage. Contents (1979-); Trade Ind. ASAP [Full Txt.]; Trade Ind. Index [Full Txt.]; UMI ABI/Inform--Bus. Period. Ondisc (Dec. 1987-) [Full Txt.].

LC HG4501 .I58
DD 658.1/52
ISSN 0020-3580
US
CODEN ITIVAK
INSTITUTIONAL INVESTOR (U.S. ED.). (THE INSTITUTIONAL INVESTOR.). [Inst. investor]. Vol. 1 (March 1967)-. Periodical. English. Twelve times a year. $405.00. Institutional Investor Inc., 488 Madison Avenue, New York NY 10022. **Tel** (212)303-3234, (212)303-3233, FAX (212)303-3353. available on microfilm and microfiche from University Microfilms International (UMI); available on CD-ROM. Documents available from UMI Article Clearinghouse. **Absorbed** Pensions and Corporate Financing, 0010-8960.
Desc: Covers pension fund investing, the new ways companies finance themselves, changes in banking and tax laws, new techniques in securities research and stockholder relations, plus the personalities that characterize the investment community.
Ind/Abst ABI/INFORM Glob. Ed.; ABI/INFORM Ondisc: Expr. Ed.; ABI/INFORM [Computer File] (Nov. 1972-); Acad. Search; Account. Index Suppl.; Account. Tax Datab. (Nov. 1972-) [Full Txt.]; Bus. ASAP (1990-) [Full Txt.]; Bus. Period. Index; Bus. Source Plus; Bus. Source; EP Collec.; Gen. Period. Index (1985-); Homework Help.; INFO-SOUTH Abstr.; Mag. Search; Manage. Contents (1974-); Manage. Contents; MasterFile FullTEXT 1000; MasterFile FullTEXT 350; MasterFile FullTEXT 650; MasterFile FullTEXT (July 1993-); OCLC; PAIS Int. Print (1991-?); Public Aff. Inf. Serv. Bull.; Telebase; Wilson Bus. Abstr.

LC HE
DD 384
ISSN 1068-9834
US
●**INTERACTIVE MULTIMEDIA INVESTOR.** See Communications.

LC HG3 .I57
DD 332.1/5/05
ISSN 0020-6113
CN
INTERNATIONAL BANK CREDIT ANALYST, THE. [Int. bank credit anal.]. (1962)-. Periodical. English. Twelve times a year. 795.00Can$. BCA Publications Ltd., 1002 Sherbrooke Street West, Suite 1600, Montreal Quebec H3A 1L6 Canada. **Tel** (514)499-9706, FAX (514)499-9709.

LC HG450
DD 332.6
UK
INTERNATIONAL BOND EQUITIES LETTER : WEEKLY REVIEW OF THE INTERNATIONAL BOND & EQUITIES MARKET. (19??)-. English. One time a week. £575.00 UK; £645.00 other. New Times Publishing Ltd, 57-60 Charlotte Road, London EC2A 3QT United Kingdom. **Tel** 011 44 171 7399090.

LC HG450
DD 332.6
ISSN 1352-0431
UK
●**INTERNATIONAL BOND INVESTOR.** **Added/Corp** Euromoney Publications Ltd. **VFOAT** Bond Investor. (March 1993)-. Periodical. English. Four times a year. $170.00. Euromoney Publications PLC, Nestor House, Playhouse Yard, London EC4Z 5EX United Kingdom. **Tel** 011 44 171 7798888, FAX 011 44 171 7798630, telex 290700 EUROMON G. (**Subscription address:** Euromoney Publications PLC, Perrymount Road Haywards Heath, West Sussex RH16 3DH United Kingdom. **Tel** 011 44 1444 440421.)

LC HG3891.5 .I55
DD 332.6/73/068
ISSN 0278-6680
US
CCC
INTERNATIONAL COUNTRY RISK GUIDE. [Int. ctry. risk guide]. **Added/Corp** Political Risk Services (IBC USA (Publications) Inc.). **VFOAT** ICRG. (19??)-. Periodical. English. Twelve times a year. $1585.00. Political Risk Services, 6320 Fly Road, Suite 102, PO Box 248, East Syracuse NY 13057-0248. **Tel** (315)431-0511, FAX (315)431-0200.
Desc: Provides an early warning of the hazards of international commerce with key information on changes in the political, economic and financial risks worldwide.
Ind/Abst PTS Newsl. Database [Full Txt.].

LC JX1977 .A2 HG4538 .U34
DD 332.67
US
INTERNATIONAL FLOW OF PRIVATE CAPITAL, THE. **Main/Corp** United Nations. Department of Economic and Social Affairs. (1946-52)-. Government Publication. English. Irregular. United Nations Publications, 2 United Nations Plaza, Room DC2 0853, Department 007C, New York NY 10017. **Tel** (212)963-8303, (800)253-9646.

LC HG4501
DD 332.6
SZ
INTERNATIONAL HARRY SCHULTZ LETTER, THE. **VFOAT** Harry Schultz Letter; HSL. (1967)-. Periodical. English. Irregular. $275.00. FERC, PO Box 622, CH-1001 Lausanne Switzerland. **Tel** 011 32 16 533684, FAX 011 32 16 535777.

LC HG4509 .I62
DD 332.6/73/025
ISSN 1040-6921
US
CCC
INTERNATIONAL INVESTOR'S DIRECTORY. See Industry and Production-Trade and Industrial Directories.

LC HG
DD 332.042
ISSN 0958-3785
UK
Pr Rev.
INTERNATIONAL MONEY MARKETING. [Int. money mark.]. **VFOAT** International MoneyMarketing. (1989)-. Trade Publication. English (German). Twelve times a year. $205.35. Centaur Communications Ltd., St. Giles House, 50 Poland Street, London W1V 4AX United Kingdom. **Tel** 011 44 171 4394222, FAX 011 44 171 7346748, telex 261352. **ED** Sunil Gopalan (phone: 071 287 5000). **Ad Acc, Adv Mgr:** Tony Hay, **Tel** 011 44 71 287 1536. **Circ:** 8,000 (ctrl). Documents available from FAXON Xpress. **Continues** Offshore Money, 0955-6133.
Desc: News, views, opinions and trends of cross-border and international financial products and services.

LC HG4501
DD 332.6
ISSN 0960-0140
UK
INTERNATIONAL RISK & PAYMENT REVIEW. See Business and Economics-Commerce.

LC K1331 .I56
DD 341.7/52
ISSN 0149-1067
US
INTERNATIONAL SECURITIES REGULATION. **Added/Corp** Practising Law Institute. (19??)-. Periodical. English. One time a year. $650.00 (5 volume set). Oceana Publications, Inc., 75 Main Street, Dobbs Ferry NY 10522. **Tel** (914)693-1320, FAX (914)693-0402.

LC HG4651
DD 332.632
UK
INTERNATIONAL STOCK EXCHANGE FACT SHEET. (19??)-. English. Fact Service, The Stock Exchange, London EC2N 1HP United Kingdom.

LC HG4501
DD 332.6
ISSN 0535-4900
IO
INTISARI. [Intisari]. (Aug. 1963)-. Indonesian. Twelve times a year. Intisari, Jalan Palmerah Selatan 22-26, Jakarta 10270 Indonesia. **Tel** 62 21 5490666, FAX 62 21 5494035.

LC HG4538
DD 332.6/73/0971
ISSN 0828-5721
CN
INVEST CANADA (TORONTO, ONT. : 1984). (INVEST CANADA.). [Invest Can.]. (Fall 1984)-. Periodical. English. Four times a year (Feb., May., Aug., Nov.). Mensamedia Inc., 111 Elizabeth Street, Suite 700, Toronto Ontario M5G 1P7 Canada.
Ind/Abst Can. Index (?-?); Can. Period. Index (19??-).

LC HG450
DD 332.6
UDC 330.3
ISSN 0239-1929
HU
INVEST IN HUNGARY. [Invest Hung.]. (1989)-. Periodical. English. Six times a year. $45.00. Invest in Hungary, Ruthen U 28, H-1085 Budapest Hungary. **Tel** 011 36 1 1342160 ext. 105, FAX 011 36 1 1342524. **ED** Attila Karvalics. **Ad Acc. Circ:** 10,000 (ctrl). available on diskette.
Desc: Covers the investment climate in Hungary, business opportunities for investors and traders, new laws in Hungary, the Hungarian stock exchange and financial sector, real estate market in Hungary, and reports on different sectors.

LC HG4501 .I588
DD 332.6/732/097305
ISSN 1040-2934
US
INVESTAMERICA (SAN FRANCISCO, CALIF.). (INVESTAMERICA.). [InvestAmerica]. **VFOAT** Invest America. (1989)-. English. One time a year. $130.00. World Trade and Data Inc., 425 California Street/Suite 2500, San Francisco CA 94104. **Tel** (415)781-6507, FAX (415)788-0943, telex 650 296 9473. cum. index. **Bk Rev. Ad Acc.**

LC HG
DD 332
ISSN 0896-4165
US
INVESTECH MUTUAL FUND ADVISOR. [InvesTech mutual fund advis.]. **VFOAT** Mutual Fund Advisor. Periodical. English. Irregular. $235.00 North America; $259.00 other. InvesTech Research, 2472 Birch Glen, Whitefish MT 59937. **Tel** (406)862-7777. **ED** James B Stack.
Desc: Provides a unique blending of key technical and monetary indicators which has earned widespread recognition for reliable market timing and no-load mutual fund switching.

LC HG450
DD 332.6
ISSN 0276-7414
US
INVESTIGATE NEWSLETTER. Vol. 1, No. 1 (Apr. 1981)-. Newsletter. English. Four times a year. $125.00. American Investment Research Inc, Investigate Newsletter, 44 Montgomery Street/Suite 500, San Francisco CA 94104.

LC HG4501 .I59
DD 332.6/73/0917561
ISSN 0735-9225
US
INVESTING & TRADING WITH SPANISH SPEAKING COUNTRIES. **Added/Corp** Aurora International Consulting (Firm). **VFOAT** Investing and Trading with Spanish Speaking Countries. (19??)-. English. Three times a year. $35.00 US, Canada and Mexico, $45.00 other countries. Aurora International Consulting, PO Box 668, Norwalk CT 06856.

LC HG450
DD 332.6
ISSN 0733-351X
US
INVESTING COMMON CENTS. Periodical. English. Twelve times a year. $37.00. Donald H Haskins, 204 Gordon Road, Monticello IN 47960.

LC HG450
DD 332.6
ISSN 1080-7942
US
●**INVESTING FOR INCOME (ASHLAND, MASS.).** (INVESTING FOR INCOME.). [Invest. income]. (1995)-. Periodical. English. Twelve times a year. $48.00. IBC Donoghue Organization, 290 Eliot Street, Ashland MA 01721. **Tel** (800)343-5413, (508)881-2800. **Continues** Bond Fund Advisor.

LC HG450
DD 332.6
ISSN 0740-3666
US
INVESTING IN CRISIS. (INVESTING IN CRISIS : DOUGLAS CASEY'S ADVISORY NEWSLETTER.). [Invest. crisis]. **Added/Corp** International Fund

Business and Economics —Investments

Management, Inc. (198?)-. Newsletter. English. Twelve times a year. Agora Publishing, 824 East Baltimore Street, Baltimore MD 21202. **Tel** (800)433-1528. **ED** Douglas R Casey and Leon Rubis. **Circ:** 35,000.
Continues Casey Advisory.
Desc: Covers investments in precious metals, gold mining, commodities, stock in speculative start-up companies and technologically-innovative firms.

LC HG4501 **ISSN** 0021-003X
DD 332.6 US
INVESTING, LICENSING AND TRADING CONDITIONS ABROAD. Main/Corp Business
International Corporation. (1955)-. English. Irregular (base volume with bi-monthly updates). $2200.00. The Economist Intelligence Unit / New York, 111 West 57th Street, New York NY 10019. **Tel** (800)938-4685, (212)554-0600. **ED** Bob Harris. available on an online database from Lexis-Nexis; and (file 627/Full-Text) DIALOG.
Desc: Answers questions on corporate tax rules, exchange and price controls, trade and licensing restrictions, labor and operating conditions in 60 countries. Provides practical advice on solving problems or seizing opportunities in overseas markets.

LC HG450
DD 332.6 IT
INVESTIRE. (19??)-. Italian. Eleven times a year.
L70000 Italy; L140000 other. Iniziative Editoriali, Via S Orsola 8, 20123 Milan Italy. **Tel** 011 39 2 89010360.

LC HG5152 .C23a
DD 332.6/7/0971 CN
INVESTISSEMENTS PRIVES ET PUBLICS AU CANADA : PERSPECTIVES. Main/Corp Statistics Canada.
Added/Corp Canada. Dept. of Industry, Trade, and Commerce. (19??)-. French. One time a year. Information Canada, 171 Slater Street, Ottawa Ontario K1A 0S9 Canada. **Tel** (819)997-1095.

LC HG450
DD 332.6 US
INVESTMENT ADVISERS GUIDE. English.
$500.00 (nonmembers), $75.00 (associate members). Investment Company Institute, 1401 H Street Northwest, Washington DC 20005. **Tel** (202)326-5800, (202)326-5972.

LC HG4501 .S73 **ISSN** 1069-1731
DD 332 US
INVESTMENT ADVISOR (SHREWSBURY, N.J.). (INVESTMENT
ADVISOR.). [Invest. advis.]. (Sept. 1992)-. Periodical. English. Twelve times a year. $79.00. Charter Financial Publishing, 179 Avenue at the Common, Shrewsbury NJ 07702. **Tel** (908)389-8700, FAX (908)389-8701. **ED** Barry Vinocur (editor's phone: (908)389-8700 Ext. 114). **Bk Rev**, (Qty: 6). **Ad Acc**, **Adv Mgr:** David Smith, **Tel** (908)389-8700 Ext. 111. **Circ:** 60,000 (ctrl). **Continues** Stanger's Investment Advisor, 1052-5912.
Desc: Financial, mutual fund, insurance and variable annuities coverage.

LC HG4501
DD 332.6 NE
INVESTMENT AND TAXATION IN THE PEOPLE'S REPUBLIC OF CHINA. See
Finance-Public Finance.

LC HG4961 .V467 **ISSN** 1051-7073
DD 332/.0415/097305 US
INVESTMENT BENCHMARKS.
(INVESTMENT BENCHMARKS : VENTURE CAPITAL.). [Investm. benchmarks]. **Added/Corp** Venture Economics, Inc. **VFOAT** Venture Capital; IBR. **VAT** Investment Benchmarks Report. (1990)-. English. $1995.00 (single issue). Venture Economics Inc, 40 West 57th Street, Suite 802, New York NY 10019. **Tel** (201)622-4500.
Continues Venture Capital Performance, 1051-4899.

LC HG **ISSN** 1069-305X
DD 332 US
●INVESTMENT BLUE BOOK. [Invest. blue
book]. **Added/Corp** Securities Investigations, Inc. (Winter/Spring 1994)-. English. Four times a year. $275.00. Securities Investigations Inc, PO Box 888, Mill Hill Road, Woodstock NY 12498. **Tel** (914)679-2300.
Continues Investment & Tax Shelter Blue Book, 1046-8803.

LC HG450
DD 332.6 UK
INVESTMENT BUSINESS COMPLIANCE MANUAL. (19??)-. English. Two times a year.
£180.00. Institute of Chartered Accountants, 399 Silbury Boulevard, Central Milton, Keynes Buckinghamshire MK9 2HL United Kingdom. **Tel** 011 44 1908 248016, FAX 011 44 1908 248001, telex 727530.
Desc: A practical manual to help set up and manage systems required to ensure compliance under categories one and two of the Financial Services Act of 1986 and the Institute's regulations.

LC HG4530 .I525 **ISSN** 0091-4533
DD 332.6/327 US
INVESTMENT COMPANIES INTERNATIONAL YEARBOOK. (19??)-.
English. Scheinman Ciaramella International, 505 Park Avenue, NY NY 00122.

LC HG4530 .I5 **ISSN** 1068-9958
DD 332 US
●INVESTMENT COMPANIES YEARBOOK.
[Invest. co. yearb.]. **Added/Corp** CDA/Wiesenberger (Firm). 53rd Ed. (1993)-. English. One time a year. $295.00. CDA Investment Technologies, 1355 Piccard Drive, Rockville MD 20850. **Tel** (301)974-9600, (800)232-2285, FAX (301)590-1389. **Continues** Investment Companies (CDA/Wiesenberger (Firm)), 1070-2334.

LC HG181 .I58 **ISSN** 1068-1159
DD 332.6/025/73 US
INVESTMENT COMPANY SERVICE DIRECTORY, THE. See Industry and
Production-Trade and Industrial Directories.

LC HG4501 .I732 **ISSN** 0021-0080
DD 332 US
  CCC
INVESTMENT DEALERS' DIGEST, THE.
See Business and Economics-Banks and Banking.

LC HG450 **ISSN** 0739-9138
DD 332.6 US
INVESTMENT GUIDE (GREAT BARRINGTON, MASS.). (INVESTMENT
GUIDE.). [Investm. guide]. **Added/Corp** American Investment Services. Vol. 1, No. 1 (Feb. 1979)-. Periodical. English. Twelve times a year. $49.00. American Institute for Economic Research, Division Street, Great Barrington MA 01230. **Tel** (413)528-1216, FAX (413)528-0103. **ED** John Blodgett. cum. index. **Circ:** 15,000.
Desc: News and information on the investments.

LC HC441.A1 I58
DD 338.7/4/02559 SI
INVESTMENT IN ASEAN. VFOAT Investment
in A.S.E.A.N.; Investment in Asean. Vol. 1, (1981)-. English.

LC K
DD 346.595/707/05 SI
INVESTMENT IN SINGAPORE. See
Law-Taxation Law.

LC HG **ISSN** 1060-1481
DD 332 US
INVESTMENT INFORMATION DIRECTORY (SEATTLE, WASH.). See
Industry and Production-Trade and Industrial Directories.

LC HG4503 .I4965
DD 332.6/05 AT
INVESTMENT INSIGHT. (19??)-. English.
Twelve times a year. 195.00Aus$. Richardson Mann Corporation Australia Pty Ltd., American Express Tower 11th Floor, 388 George Street/GPO 3704, Sydney NSW 2000 Australia.

LC KF6415.A15 T39 **ISSN** 0893-1364
DD 343.7305/23 347.303523 US
INVESTMENT LIMITED PARTNERSHIPS LAW REPORT. [Investm. ltd. partnersh. law rep.].
Vol. 1, No. 1 (May 1987)-. Periodical. English. Ten times a year. $185.00. Clark Boardman Callaghan, 155 Pfingsten Road, Deerfield IL 60015. **Tel** (800)323-8067. **Continues** Tax Sheltered Investments Law Report, 0731-5759.

LC HG450 **ISSN** 0267-3770
DD 332.6 UK
INVESTMENT MANAGEMENT. [Investm.
manage.]. (1985)-. Trade Publication. English. Ten times a year. $75.29. Mitre House Publishing, Clifton Center, 110 Clifton Street, London EC2A 4HD United Kingdom. **Tel** 011 44 171 72966443.

LC HG **ISSN** 1057-5626
DD 332 US
INVESTMENT MANAGEMENT TECHNOLOGY. [Investm. manage. technol.].
(1991)-. Periodical. English. Twenty-four times a year. $595.00. Waters Information Services, PO Box 2248, Binghamton NY 13902-2248. **Tel** (607)770-8535, FAX (607)798-1692. available on an online database (files 16,636/Full-Text) from DIALOG.
Ind/Abst PROMT [Full Txt.]; PTS Newsl. Database [Full Txt.].

LC HG **ISSN** 0896-8500
DD 332 US
INVESTMENT MANAGEMENT WEEKLY.
[Investm. manage. wkly.]. **VFOAT** IMW. Vol. 1, No 1 (Jan. 18, 1988)-. Periodical. English. Fifty times a year. $1195.00. Investment Management Weekly, 1 Liberty Square, 12th Floor, Boston MA 02109. **Tel** (617)426-5450, FAX (617)422-0162. **ED** Richard Chinberg. Index available. cum. index. **Bk Rev**, (Qty: 24). **Ad Acc**, **Adv Mgr:** Ana Pacheco, **Tel** (505)474-2828. **Circ:** 12,000.

LC HG450
DD 332.6 US
INVESTMENT MANAGER PROFILES.
(19??)-. English. $2975.00 (full subscription). Evaluation Associates Inc., 200 Connecticut Avenue, Norwalk CT 06854. **Tel** (203)855-2200, FAX (203)855-2301.

LC HG450
DD 332.6 AT
INVESTMENT MONITOR. English. Four times a
year (Feb., May, Aug., Nov.). 125.00Aus$ (universities and libraries); 95.00Aus$ (individuals); 325.00Aus$ (other). Access Economics Pty. Ltd., PO Box E347, Queen Victoria Terrace, Barton ACT 2600 Australia. **Tel** 011 61 6 2731222, FAX 011 61 6 2731223. ctrl circ.
Desc: A list of major investment prospects in Australia under construction, committed, or under consideration by state and industry.

LC HG4521 .I4227 **ISSN** 1073-4570
DD 332.63/2/05 US
  SUSPENDED
INVESTMENT OPERATIONS. [Invest. oper.].
(Spring 1994)-Suspended (May 1995). Periodical. English. Four times a year. $60.00. Securities Operations Forum, 170 Broadway, 8th Floor, New York NY 10038. **Tel** (212)587-9531.

LC HB522 **ISSN** 0883-1661
DD 338 US
INVESTMENT PORTFOLIO GUIDE.
[Invest. portf. guide]. Periodical. English. Twelve times a year. $54.00 correspondent forms, $180.00 other. Argus Research Corporation, 42 Broadway, New York NY 10004.

LC HG4501 **ISSN** 0021-0110
DD 332.6 US
INVESTMENT QUALITY TRENDS. [Investm.
qual. trends]. (19??)-. Periodical. English. Twenty-four times a year. $275.00. Investment Quality Trends, 7440 Girard Avenue, Suite 4, La Jolla CA 92037. **Tel** (619)459-3818. **ED** Gerladine Weiss. **Circ:** 5,000 (ctrl).
Continues Value Trends.
Desc: Investment advisory following 350 blue-chip stocks, listing them in groups of undervalue, overvalue, as well as rising and declining trends. Contains charts and identifies value in the stock market.

LC HG4501 **ISSN** 0700-5539
DD 332.6'7 CN
INVESTMENT REPORTER. [Invest. rep.].
(1972)-. Periodical. English. One time a week. 77.64Can$. MPL Communications, 133 Richard Street West, Suite 700, Toronto Ontario M5H 3M8 Canada. **Tel** (416)869-1177, FAX (416)869-0456.
Desc: Canada's oldest stock market newsletter, and a proven source of profitable low-risk investment advice.

LC HG4501 .I738 **ISSN** 0094-8683
DD 332.6/0973 AT
INVESTMENT REVIEW. (THE INVESTMENT
REVIEW.). (19??)-. Periodical. English. Four times a year. Free. Potter Partners, 325 Collins Street, Melbourne Victoria 3000 Australia. **Tel** (03)6162611, telex 30203. **ED** John D. Bartley. **Circ:** 1,400 (ctrl).
Desc: Comments on the share market and stock recommendations directed basically to private clients.

LC HD7105.45.U6 I59 **ISSN** 1059-7441
DD 332.6/7254 US
INVESTMENT SPECIALTIES GUIDE.
[Investm. spec. guide]. **Added/Corp** Money Market Directories, Inc. (19??)-. Periodical. English. One time a year. $195.00. Money Market Directories Inc., 320 East Main Street, PO Box 1608, Charlottesville VA 22902. **Tel** (800)446-2810, (804)977-1450.

LC HG4501 **ISSN** 0115-9291
DD 332.6 PH
INVESTMENTS GUIDE. Added/Corp Manila
Stock Exchange. **VFOAT** Manila Stock Exchange Investments Guide; MSE Investments Guide. (19??)-. English. One time a year. $65.00. Research and Publication Department, Manilla Stock Exchange Building, 3rd Floor, Binondo Manilla Philippines. **Tel** 011 63 2 408774.

LC KF6415.A152 T39 **ISSN** 0893-3944
DD 343.7305/23 347.303523 US
INVESTMENTS LIMITED PARTNERSHIPS HANDBOOK. [Investm. ltd.
partnersh. handb.]. **Added/Corp** Clark Boardman Company. (1987)-. English. One time a year. $97.50. Clark Boardman Callaghan, 155 Pfingsten Road, Deerfield IL 60015. **Tel** (800)323-8067. **ED** Robert J Haft and Peter M Fass. **Continues** Tax Sheltered Investments Handbook, 0731-5821.

LC HG450
DD 332.6 US
●INVESTNET INSIDER HOLDINGS BOOK.
(1995)-. English. Two times a year. $295.00. CDA Investment Technologies, 1355 Piccard Drive, Rockville

MD 20850. **Tel** (301)974-9600, (800)232-2285, FAX (301)590-1389. ***Continues*** *CDA Spectrum Insider Holdings.*

LC HG4503.I4 I58
DD 332.6 II
INVESTOR, THE. (1991)-. English.

LC HG450
DD 332.6 US
INVESTOR ACTIVITY REPORT. (19??)-. English. Twelve times a year. $100.00 (members); $150.00 (nonmembers). Securities Industry Association, 120 Broadway/35th Floor, New York NY 10271. **Tel** (212)608-1500, FAX (212)608-1604.
Desc: A data series and analysis covering the retail, institutional and member trading components of share volume on the NYSE and Amex. Net purchases by sector are also available. In addition, the data series traces institutional NASDAQ volume, as well as the daily value of institutional trading activity in corporate bonds.

LC HG450
DD 332.6 UK
TITLE CHANGE
INVESTOR LATIN AMERICA. (19??)-(19??). English. The Economist Intelligence Unit / New York, 111 West 57th Street, New York NY 10019. **Tel** (800)938-4685, (212)554-0600. **ED** Anna Szterenfeld and Steven Murphy. ***Merged into*** *Latin American Finance & Capital Markets.*
Desc: Assists portfolio investors with coverage of the rapid flow of funds into and out of Latin America. Provides analysis on the political, economic and regulatory issues that affect investment decisions.

LC HG450
DD 332.6 US
INVESTOR RELATIONS NEWSLETTER. (19??)-. Newsletter. English. Twelve times a year. $195.00 US, Canada and Mexico; $225.00 other. Remy Publishing Company, 350 Hubbard Street, Suite 440, Chicago IL 60610. **Tel** (312)464-0300, FAX (312)464-0166. **ED** Regina Ann Ludes. Index available. cum. index. **Bk Rev**. ctrl circ.

LC HG450 **ISSN** 0739-8026
DD 332.6 US
INVESTOR, U.S.A. [Investor, U.S.A.]. **VFOAT** Investor, USA. **VAT** Investor, United States of America. Periodical. English. Twelve times a year. $195.00, $95.00 (libraries). Seahorse Financial Advisors Inc, 18 Seatuck Lane, Remsenburg NY 11960. **Tel** (212)686-8522. **ED** Ed Jorgensen. **Bk Rev**. **Circ:** 800 (ctrl).
Desc: Review of investments markets: stocks, mutual funds and tax exempt bonds. Includes digests of commentary by economists and investment advisors, plus a complete investment data bank.

LC HF5001 .I58 **ISSN** 1061-2890
DD 332 US
INVESTOR'S BUSINESS DAILY. [Investor's bus. dly.]. Vol. 8, No. 111 (Sept. 16, 1991)-. Periodical. English. Five times a week (260 per year). $179.00. Finadco / Financial Advertising Company, 12655 Beatrice Street, Los Angeles CA 90066. **Tel** (310)448-6801. **(Subscription address:** Investor's Business Daily, PO Box 66370, Los Angeles CA 90066. **Tel** (800)831-2525.) available via Internet (http://ibd.ensemble.com). ***Continues*** *Investor's Daily, 0743-9423.*

LC HG4502 .I57
DD 332.6/05 UK
INVESTORS CHRONICLE (LONDON, ENGLAND : 1983). (INVESTORS CHRONICLE.). (19??)-. Periodical. English. One time a week. $217.33. Financial Times Business Information Ltd, Greystoke Place, Fetter Lane, London EC4A 1ND United Kingdom. **Tel** 011 44 171 4056969, FAX 011 44 171 2420347. available on microfilm from University Microfilms International (UMI). ***Continues*** *Investors Chronicle & Financial World.*
Ind/Abst Index Bus. Reports (19??-); Infomat Int. Bus. (19??-); Int. Packag. Abstr. (19??-); Manage. Market. Abstr. (19??-); Nonwovens Abstr. (19??-); PAIS Int. Print (1991-); Pap. Board Abstr. (19??-); Print. Abstr. (19??-).

LC HG1501
DD 332.1 US
INVESTOR'S DAILY. Vol. 1, No. 1 (Apr. 9, 1984)-. Periodical. English. Irregular. $617.40 (one-year), $1,195.80 (two-year) Canada; $516.00 (one-year), $993.00 (two-year) Mexico; $1,069.80 (one-year), $2,100.60 (two-year) Europe; $799.40 (one-year), $1,559.80 (two-year) Central America adn Caribbean Islands; $1,345.40 (one-year), $2,651.80 (two-year) other. Investors Daily, PO Box 25000, Los Angeles CA 90025. **Tel** (310)207-1832. **ED** Stephen P Fox. **Bk Rev**. **Ad Acc. Circ:** 30,000. available on microfiche; available on an online database.
Desc: National daily financial newspaper covering the markets, the economy, and general business news.

LC HG450
DD 332.6 CN
●**INVESTOR'S DIGEST.** (1994)-. English. Twenty-four times a year. 127.00Can$. MPL Communications, 133 Richard Street West, Suite 700, Toronto Ontario M5H 3M8 Canada. **Tel** (416)869-1177, FAX (416)869-0456. ***Continues*** *Finanical Post Investors Guide.*

LC HG **ISSN** 1057-6711
DD 332 US
INVESTOR'S DIGEST (FORT LAUDERDALE, FLA.). (INVESTOR'S DIGEST.). [Investor's dig.]. **Added/Corp** Institute for Econometric Research (Fort Lauderdale, Fla.). (1990)-. Periodical. English. Twelve times a year. $60.00. Institute for Econometric Research, 2200 SW 10th Street, Deerfield Beach FL 33442. **Tel** (305)421-1000. **ED** Norman G. Fosback.
Desc: Contains information on investments and securities.

LC HG **ISSN** 1055-2154
DD 332 US
INVESTOR'S ENVIRONMENTAL REPORT. [Investor's environ. rep.]. **Added/Corp** Investor Responsibility Research Center. Environmental Information Service. Winter (1991)-. Periodical. English. Four times a year. $150.00. Investor Responsibility Research Center, 1350 Connecticut Avenue Northwest 700, Washington DC 20036. **Tel** (202)833-0700.

LC HG5851.A2 F3
DD 332.6 SA
INVESTORS' GUIDE : FOR THE SERIOUS INVESTOR AND BUSINESSMAN, THE. (19??)-. English. Four times a year. $26.72. Investors Group Ltd, PO Box 62000, Marshalltown 2107 South Africa. **Tel** 011 27 11 8369321. ***Continues*** *FACtS Investors' Guide, 0250-1732.*

LC HG4501
DD 332.6 SI
INVESTOR'S GUIDE TO SINGAPORE, THE. **Added/Corp** Singapore International Chamber of Commerce. (19??)-. English. One time a year. $24.00. Singapore International Chamber of Commerce, 50 Raffles PL#03-02, Shell Tower, Singapore 0104 Singapore. **Tel** 011 65 2241255. ***Continues*** *Singapore International Chamber of Commerce. Investor's Guide, 0129-5276.*
Desc: Information on international investments.

LC HG4501 .I758 **ISSN** 0741-9813
DD 332.6/0973 US
INVESTOR'S YEARBOOK. [Invest. yearb.]. (1984)-. English. One time a year. $75.00. Newsletter Digest, 2335 Pansy Street, Huntsville AL 35801-3899. **Tel** (205)536-0901. **ED** Al Owen. **Bk Rev**. **Circ:** 5,000.
Desc: A timely digest of more than 300 investment advisory and economic newsletters, with editorial commentary and current recommendations. All investments. Emphasis on timing.

LC HG4001 **ISSN** 1059-2741
DD 658 US
CCC
IOMA'S REPORT ON MANAGING 401 (K) PLANS. [IOMA's rep. manag. 401(k) plans]. **Added/Corp** Institute of Management & Administration. **VFOAT** Managing 401(k) Plans. Issue 92-2 (Feb. 1992)-. Periodical. English. Twelve times a year. $245.00. Institute of Management and Administration, 29 West 35th Street, 5th Floor, New York NY 10001-2299. **Tel** (212)244-0360, FAX (212)564-0465.

LC HG4538 .I657 **ISSN** 0958-6679
DD 659.2/89/05 UK
IR. INVESTOR RELATIONS. (INVESTOR RELATIONS.). [IR, Invest. relat.]. (19??)-. Periodical. English. Ten times a year. $213.90. Corporate Finance Publishers, 67-71 Goswell Road, London EC1V 7EN United Kingdom. **Tel** 011 44 171 4904777. **(Subscription address:** Stonehart Subscription Services, Hainault Road Little Heath, Bromford RM6 5NP United Kingdom. **Tel** 011 44 181 5977335.) **Ad Acc. Circ:** 10,000 (ctrl).
Desc: The magazine for the financial communications professionals that is concerned for investments and other related business.

LC HG **ISSN** 1062-7499
DD 332 US
TITLE CHANGE
IRA BULLETIN (BRAINERD, MINN.). (IRA BULLETIN.). [IRA bull.]. **Added/Corp** Universal Pensions, Inc. **VAT** Individual Retirement Account Bulletin. (19??)-(19??). Bulletin. English. Universal Pensions Inc., Box 979, Brainerd MN 56401. **Tel** (800)541-6089, (800)346-3860, FAX (218)829-2106. ***Merged into*** *Retirement Plans Bulletin.*

LC HG4501-6051 **ISSN** 0739-2168
DD 332.6 US
IRA REPORTER, THE. [IRA rep.]. **VFOAT** I.R.A. Reporter. **VAT** Individual Retirement Account Reporter. (1983)-. Periodical. English. Twelve times a year. $115.00. Universal Pensions Inc., Box 979, Brainerd MN 56401. **Tel** (800)541-6089, (800)346-3860, FAX (218)829-2106. **ED** Jennifer Norquist (Editor's telephone: (218)829-4781). Index Available Published separately--free--upon request. cum. index. **Circ:** 500 (ctrl).
Desc: Provides industry news, trends and marketing strategies concerning IRAs for financial organizations.

LC HG4921 .I7 **ISSN** 1080-3912
DD 332 US
●**IRWIN INVESTOR'S HANDBOOK, THE.** [Irwin invest. handb.]. **Added/Corp** Irwin Professional Publishing. Dow Jones & Co. **VFOAT** Investor's Handbook. (1994)-. English. One time a year. $27.50. Irwin Professional Publishing, 1333 Burr Ridge Parkway, Burr Ridge Parkway IL 60521. **Tel** (800)634-3966, (708)789-5480. ***Continues*** *Business One Irwin Investor's Handbook, 1062-0028.*

LC HG450
DD 332.6 US
Pr Rev.
ISRAEL MARKETFAX. (1992)-. Newsletter. English. Twenty-six times a year. $99.00. marketFax, 4 Randall Avenue, Baltimore MD 21208. **Tel** (410)486-5127, FAX (410)486-2859. **ED** David B. Weiner. **Ad Acc. Circ:** 100 (ctrl). available via fax; available via electronic mail.
Desc: A "faxazine" for the American investor in Israeli securities. Concentrates exclusively on Israeli companies in the United States. Includes press releases, interviews with company representatives, and analyses from brokers. Each issue includes an analytical article profiling one of sixty companies covered.

LC HG4503 .I78 **ISSN** 0147-4316
DD 332.6/7 US
ISRAEL SECURITIES REVIEW (1975). (ISRAEL SECURITIES REVIEW.). Vol. 2, No. 2 (Apr./May 1975)-. Periodical. English. American Israel Ventures Corporation, 557 Beach 129 Street, Bell Harbor NY 11694. ***Continues*** *Israel Securities Review Monthly Magazine, 0147-4308.*

LC HG181 .J23 **ISSN** 1041-2115
DD 332.024/005 US
J.K. LASSER'S PERSONAL INVESTMENT ANNUAL. [J.K. Lasser's pers. investm. annu.]. **VFOAT** Personal Investment Annual. (1989/90)-. English. One time a year. $16.95. Simon & Schuster Reference Division, One Gulf & Western Plaza, New York NY 10023.

LC HG5280.J35 J35
DD 332.64/27292 JM
JAMAICA STOCK EXCHANGE YEARBOOK. **Added/Corp** Jamaica Stock Exchange. **VFOAT** Review. (19??)-. English. Irregular. Jamaican Stock Exchange, PO Box 621, Kingston Jamaica.

LC HG5421 .J352 **ISSN** 0075-3041
DD 332.67 US
JANE'S MAJOR COMPANIES OF EUROPE. [Jane's major co. Eur.]. Vol. 1 (1970)-. English. One time a year. Jane's Information Group, Sentinel House, 163 Brighton Road, Coulsdon Surrey CR5 2NH United Kingdom. **Tel** 011 44 181 7631030, FAX 011 44 181 7630276, telex 916907-JANES-G.

LC HG4651 **ISSN** 0021-4736
DD 332.632 JA
JAPAN STOCK JOURNAL, THE. (May 6, 1957)-. Periodical. English. One time a week. $62.47. **(Subscription address:** Japan Publications Trading Company Ltd., PO Box 5030, Tokyo International, Tokyo 100-31 Japan. **Tel** 011 81 3 3292 3753.)

LC HG450 **ISSN** 1054-3562
DD 332.6 US
JAPANESE GOLF COURSE INVESTMENT REPORT. (1992)-. English. $295.00. Mead Ventures Inc., PO Box 44952, Phoenix AZ 85064. **Tel** (602)234-0044, FAX (602)234-0076.

LC HF5035 .J36 **ISSN** 1067-697X
DD 338.8/8952073/05 US
JAPAN'S EXPANDING U.S. MANUFACTURING PRESENCE. (JAPAN'S EXPANDING U.S. MANUFACTURING PRESENCE ... UPDATE / JAPAN ECONOMIC INSTITUTE.). [Jpn. expand. U.S. manuf. presence]. **Added/Corp** Japan Economic Institute of America. **VFOAT** Japan's Expanding US Manufacturing Presence; Japan's Expanding United States Manufacturing Presence ... Update. (1981)-. English. One time a year. $50.00 US; $55.00 other (1990 edition -- latest edition available). Japan Economic Institute of America, 1000 Connecticut Avenue NW, Suite 211, Washington DC 20036. **Tel** (202)296-5633, FAX (202)296-8333.

LC HG4501 **ISSN** 0313-5934
DD 332.61 AT
JASSA. [JASSA]. (1976)-. Periodical. English. Four times a year. 29.60Aus$. Securities Institute of Australia, PO Box H99, Australia Square, Sydney NSW 2001 Australia. **Tel** 011 61 2 2516799. **Bk Rev**, (Qty: 8). **Circ:** 8,000 (ctrl).
Desc: Professional journal of the Securities Institute of Australia.
Ind/Abst APAIS, Aust. Public Aff. Inf. Ser. (19??-).

LC HG ISSN 8756-5161
DD 332 US
CCC
JAY SCHABACKER'S MUTUAL FUND INVESTING. [Jay Schabacker's mutual fund invest.]. **VFOAT** Mutual Fund Investing. Vol. 1, No. 1 (March 1985)-. Periodical. English. Twelve times a year. $149.00. Phillips Business Information Inc., 1201 Seven Locks Road, PO Box 61130, Potomac MD 20854. **Tel** (301)424-3338, (301)340-1520, (800)777-5005, FAX (301)424-4297, telex 358149. **ED** Jay Schabacker. Index available. ***Absorbed*** *Switch Fund Advisory.*
Desc: A guide to successful mutual fund investing.

LC HG4530 .J38
DD 332.63/27 US
JAY SCHABACKER'S YEARBOOK. (1992)-. English. Phillips Publishing Inc., 7811 Montrose Road, Potomac MD 20854. **Tel** (800)777-5005, (301)340-2100. ***Continues*** *Jay Schabacker's Mutual Fund Yearbook, 1044-5420.*

LC HC187 .J54
DD 332.6 BL
JITSUGYO NO BURAJIRU. SELECOES ECONOMICAS. Periodical. Japanese (Japanese). $1.20. Selecoes Economicas, AV Paulista 807, 15 and CJ/512 S Paulo Brazil.

LC HG5851.A2 J63
DD 332.64/268 SA
JOHANNESBURG STOCK EXCHANGE MONTHLY BULLETIN, THE. Added/Corp Johannesburg Stock Exchange. Committee. (19??)-. Bulletin. English. Twelve times a year. $101.99. Johannesburg Stock Exchange, PO Box 1174, 2000 Johannesburg South Africa. **Tel** 011 27 11 833 6580, FAX 011 27 11 838 1463. **ED** Anne Clarke. **Circ:** 3,000 (ctrl).
Desc: Summary of stocks and statistics.

LC HG4501 .J64 ISSN 1064-3133
DD 332 US
JOHN PUGSLEY'S JOURNAL. [John Pugsley's j.]. (1988)-. Periodical. English. Twelve times a year. $95.00. John Pugsley's Journal, 2731 Cita Avenue, Escondido CA 92029. **Tel** (619)747-1910. ***Continues*** *Pugsley, John A. John A. Pugsley's Common Sense Viewpoint.*

LC HG ISSN 0887-1922
DD 332 US
JOHN T. REED'S REAL ESTATE INVESTOR'S MONTHLY. See Real Estate.

LC HG450
DD 332.6 US
JOHNSON'S CHARTS. Added/Corp Johnson's Charts, Inc. 36th Ed. (1984)-. Periodical. English. One time a year (May). $449.00. Johnson's Charts Inc, 175 Bridle Path, Williamsville NY 14221. **Tel** (716)626-0845, (800)682-1203, FAX (716)626-4899. ***Continues*** *Johnson's Investment Company Charts.*
Desc: Charts mutual fund performances. Includes tables on markets, economy, inflation, bonds, etc.

LC HG6024.A3 J68 ISSN 1074-1240
DD 332.63/2044 US
Pr Rev.
●**JOURNAL OF DERIVATIVES, THE.** (THE JOURNAL OF DERIVATIVES : A PUBLICATION OF INSTITUTIONAL INVESTOR, INC.). [J. deriv.]. **Added/Corp** Institutional Investor (Firm). (1993)-. Periodical. English. Four times a year. $245.00. Institutional Investor Inc., 488 Madison Avenue, New York NY 10022. **Tel** (212)303-3234, (212)303-3233, FAX (212)303-3353. **ED** Stephen Figlewski. Index available (extra for $25.00).
Desc: Serves the practitioner and the academic with analysis and academic theory. Contains insights on developments in the derivatives markets.

LC HG4501 .J678 ISSN 0304-405X
DD 332/.05 NE
CCC
CODEN JFECDT
Pr Rev.
JOURNAL OF FINANCIAL ECONOMICS. See Business and Economics-Banks and Banking.

LC HG4515.2 .J68 ISSN 1042-9573
DD 332.1/05 US
CCC
Pr Rev.
JOURNAL OF FINANCIAL INTERMEDIATION. [J. financ. intermed.]. Vol. 1, No. 1 (Mar. 1990)-. Academic Scholarly Publication. English. Four times a year. $167.00. Academic Press Inc., 6277 Sea Harbor Drive, Orlando FL 32887. **Tel** (800)543-9534, (407)345-4100, FAX (407)352-3445. **ED** Stuart I. Greenbaum, B. Douglas Bernheim, Christopher M. James and Anjan V. Thakor. **Ad Acc.**
Desc: The journal collects and stimulates research in this area, stressing the use of contemporary analytical and empirical tools.
Ind/Abst Econ. Lit. Index.

LC HG4961 .J68 ISSN 1059-8596
DD 332.63/2/097305 US
JOURNAL OF FIXED INCOME, THE. [J. fixed income]. Vol. 1, No. 1 (June 1991)-. Periodical. English. Four times a year. $245.00. Institutional Investor Inc., 488 Madison Avenue, New York NY 10022. **Tel** (212)303-3234, (212)303-3233, FAX (212)303-3353. **ED** Dr. Douglas T. Breeden. available on microfilm and microfiche from University Microfilms International (UMI).
Desc: Offers a balance of economic theory, including direct applications for portfolio managers and virtually anyone involved in banking, securities trading, modeling and research in fixed income.
Ind/Abst Account. Tax Datab. (Mar. 1992-).

LC HG6001 .J68 ISSN 0270-7314
DD 332.63/28 US
CCC
CODEN JFMADT
Pr Rev.
JOURNAL OF FUTURES MARKETS, THE. [J. futures mark.]. **Added/Corp** Columbia University. Center for the Study of Futures Markets. Vol. 1, No. 1 (Spring 1981)-. Trade Publication. English. Eight times a year. $648.00. John Wiley & Sons, Inc., 605 Third Avenue, New York NY 10158-0012. **Tel** (212)850-6000, (212)850-6645, FAX (212)850-6088, telex 12-7063. **(Subscription address:** John Wiley & Sons / UK, Baffins Lane, Chichester, West Sussex PO19 1UD United Kingdom. **Tel** 011 44 1243 779777, FAX 011 44 243 776128, telex 86290 WIBOOKG.) **ED** Mark J. Powers. **Ad Acc, Adv Mgr:** Roberta Frederick. **Circ:** 1,200. available on microfilm and microfiche from University Microfilms International (UMI). Documents available from The Genuine Article, UMI Article Clearinghouse.
Desc: Publishes articles for those concerned with futures markets. Topics range from the practical to the theoretical and include financial futures, commodity forecasting techniques, corporate hedging strategies, tax and accounting implications of hedging, analysis of commodity trading systems, legal and regulatory issues and commodity portfolio optimization.
Ind/Abst ABI/INFORM Glob. Ed.; ABI/INFORM [Computer File] (Spring 1982-); Acad. Search; AGRICOLA; Bus. Index (1985-); Bus. Period. Index; Bus. Source Plus; Bus. Source; Contents Pages Manage.; Cot. Trop. Fibr. Abstr. Bibliogr.; Curr. Cit.; Curr. Contents Soc. Behav. Sci.; Econ. Lit. Index; EP Collect.; Gen. BusinessFile (1985-); Gen. Period. Index (1985-); Homework Help.; INFO-SOUTH Abstr.; J. Econ. Lit.; Mag. Search; MasterFile FullTEXT 1000; MasterFile FullTEXT 350; MasterFile FullTEXT 650; MasterFile FullTEXT (July 1993-); OCLC; Res. Alert [Full Cov.]; Soc. Sci. Cit. Index [Full Cov.]; Telebase; Wilson Bus. Abstr.

LC HG4501 ISSN 1068-0896
DD 333 US
Pr Rev.
JOURNAL OF INVESTING, THE. (THE JOURNAL OF INVESTING : A PUBLICATION OF INSTITUTIONAL INVESTOR, INC.). [J. invest.]. **Added/Corp** Institutional Investor (Firm). (1992)-. Periodical. English. Four times a year. $215.00. Institutional Investor Inc., 488 Madison Avenue, New York NY 10022. **Tel** (212)303-3234, (212)303-3233, FAX (212)303-3353. **ED** Brian R. Bruce. Index available (extra for $25.00).
Desc: Written by and for investment practitioners. Includes articles on developments affecting financial and investment decisions.

LC HG4930 .F32 ISSN 1071-846X
DD 332.63/27 US
●**JOURNAL OF MUTUAL FUND SERVICES, THE.** (1993)-. Trade Publication. English. Six times a year. $795.00. Dalbar Publishing Inc., 260 Franklin Street, Boston MA 02110. **Tel** (617)439-6195, FAX (617)439-6346. **ED** Louis S. Harvey. **Ad Acc. *Continues*** *FACS, 0887-8161.*

LC HG4501 .J68 ISSN 0095-4918
DD 332.6 US
Pr Rev.
JOURNAL OF PORTFOLIO MANAGEMENT. [J. portf. manage.]. Vol. 1 (Fall 1974)-. Periodical. English. Four times a year. $280.00. Institutional Investor Inc., 488 Madison Avenue, New York NY 10022. **Tel** (212)303-3234, (212)303-3233, FAX (212)303-3353. available on microfilm and microfiche from University Microfilms International (UMI); available on CD-ROM. Documents available from The Genuine Article, UMI Article Clearinghouse.
Desc: Provides a forum for the exploration and development of theoretical and practical applications of investment decision making.
Ind/Abst ABI/INFORM Glob. Ed.; ABI/INFORM [Computer File] (Fall 1974-); Acad. Search; Account. Tax Datab. (Fall 1974-); Bus. ASAP (1992-) [Full Txt.]; Bus. Index (1985-); Bus. Period. Index; Curr. Cit.; Curr. Contents Soc. Behav. Sci.; Econ. Lit. Index (Fall 1974-); EP Collect.; Gen. BusinessFile (1985-); Gen. Period. Index (1985-); Homework Help.; INFO-SOUTH Abstr.; Int. Exec.; J. Econ. Lit.; Mag. Search; Manage. Contents (1974-); MasterFile FullTEXT 1000; MasterFile FullTEXT 350; MasterFile FullTEXT 650; MasterFile FullTEXT (July 1993-); OCLC; Public Aff. Inf. Serv. Bull.; Res. Alert [Full Cov.]; Soc. Sci. Cit. Index [Full Cov.]; Telebase; UMI ABI/Inform--Bus. Period. Ondisc (Fall 1987-) [Full Txt.]; Wilson Bus. Abstr.

LC K10 .O8957 ISSN 0747-9115
DD 343.7305/246/05 347.303524605 US
CCC
JOURNAL OF TAXATION OF INVESTMENTS. [J. tax. investm.]. Vol. 1, No. 1 (Autumn 1983)-. Trade Publication. English. Four times a year. $152.25. Warren Gorham & Lamont Inc., Park Square Building, 31 St. James Avenue, Boston MA 02116-4112. **Tel** (617)423-2020, (800)950-1207, FAX (617)423-2026. **ED** Joel D. Kuntz. available on microfilm and microfiche from University Microfilms International (UMI). Documents available from UMI Article Clearinghouse.
Desc: A professional resource devoted to tax issues affecting investments. Offers ideas for new investment opportunities as well as new perspectives on traditional investment techniques.
Ind/Abst ABI/INFORM Glob. Ed.; ABI/INFORM [Computer File] (Autumn 1982-); Account. Tax Datab. (Fall 1983-); Curr. Law Index (1984-); Gen. BusinessFile (1992-); Index Leg. Period.; Leg. Resour. Index (1984-); LegalTrac (1984-).

LC HG5841 .J65
DD 332.6 SA
JSE HANDBOOK, THE. Added/Corp Johannesburg Stock Exchange. **VFOAT** Johannesburg Stock Exchange Handbook. (Feb. 1991)-. Periodical. English. Two times a year. $23.86. Flesch Financial Publications, PO Box 3473, Capetown 8000 South Africa. **Tel** 011 27 21 461-7472, FAX 011 27 21 461-3758. **ED** Mike Maher. **Ad Acc, Adv Mgr:** D. Wood. **Circ:** 24,000. ***Continues*** *Stock Exchange Handbook, 0075-3793.*
Desc: Contains information on all companies listed on the Johannesburg Stock Exchange, including five year balance sheet abstracts.

LC HG5771 .K32
DD 332.6 JA
KABUKA SORAN. VFOAT Stock Price Review. (19??)-. Periodical. Japanese. One time a year. Toyo Keizai Shimpo Sha, 1-2-1 Nihombashi Hongoku-cho, Chuo-ku Tokyo 103 Japan. **Tel** (03)3246-5470.

LC HC59.7 .N554a
DD 332.6 JA
KAIGAI TOSHI KENKYUJO HO. Main/Corp Nihon Yushutsunyu Ginko, Tokyo. Kaigai Toshi Kenkyijo. (19??)-. Japanese. Twelve times a year. Nihon Yushutsunyu Ginko Kaigai Toshi Kenkyujo, 4-1 Otemachi 1-chome, Chiyoda-ku 100, Tokyo Japan. **Tel** 011 81 3 2871221, FAX 011 81 3 2879578. Index available. cum. index. **Circ:** 2,000.

LC HC329.5.C3 C37 ISSN 0923-9669
DD 332.6 NE
KAPITAALGOEDERENVOORRAAD. Added/Corp Netherlands. Centraal Bureau voor de Statistiek. Hoofdafdeling Statistieken van Kapitaalgoederenvoorraad en Balansen. **VFOAT** Statistics on Stocks of Capital Goods. (1989)-. Dutch (summaries and/or abstracts in English). ***Continues*** *CBS bijdragen tot de statistieken betreffende de kapitaalgoederenvoorraad.*

LC HG4501 ISSN 0823-7042
DD 332.6/78/05 CN
KEN-CUR REPORT, THE. [Ken-Cur rep.]. Feb. 1983-. Periodical. English. Twelve times a year. $225.00. Unique Consulting Service, 69 Gilmour Street West, Ottawa Ontario K2P 1N0 Canada. **ED** Earl G Curley and Shelagh Kendal.

LC HG ISSN 1059-6674
DD 332 US
CCC
TITLE CHANGE
KEN GERBINO'S SMART INVESTING. [Ken Gerbino's smart invest.]. **VFOAT** Smart Investing. Vol. 1, No. 1 (Jan. 1992)-(June 1994). Periodical. English. Phillips Business Information Inc., 1201 Seven Locks Road, PO Box 61130, Potomac MD 20854. **Tel** (301)424-3338, (301)340-1520, (800)777-5005, FAX (301)424-4297, telex 358149. ***Continued by*** *Gerbino Investment Letter, 1077-0119.*

LC HG450 ISSN 0453-9249
DD 332.6 US
KIPLINGER CALIFORNIA LETTER, THE. Added/Corp Kiplinger Washington Editors, Inc. (1965)-. Newsletter. English. Twenty-four times a year. $73.00. Kiplinger Washington Editors, 1729 H Street Northwest, Washington DC 20006. **Tel** (202)887-6400, (800)544-0155, FAX (202)331-1206. **(Subscription address:** Kiplinger Washington Editors, 3401 East West Highway, c/o Rick Topolski, Editors Park MD 20782. **Tel** (800)544-0155, (301)853-6600.) **ED** J. Fogarty. **Circ:** 20,000.
Desc: Focuses on items of interest to those with investments/business in the state.

Business and Economics —Investments

LC HG450
DD 332.6
ISSN 0023-1754
US
TITLE CHANGE
KIPLINGER FLORIDA LETTER, THE.
Added/Corp Kiplinger Washington Editors. Vol. 1 (1956)-(19??). Newsletter. English. Kiplinger Washington Editors, 1729 H Street Northwest, Washington DC 20006. **Tel** (202)887-6400, (800)544-0155, FAX (202)331-1206. (**Subscription address:** Kiplinger Washington Editors, 3401 East West Highway, c/o Rick Topolski, Editors Park MD 20782. **Tel** (800)544-0155, (301)853-6600.) **ED** K. Dalecki. **Circ**: 23,000. **Continued by** Kiplinger's Florida Business Letter, 1073-5593.
Desc: Focuses on items of interest to those with investments/business in the state.

LC HB
DD 330
ISSN 1073-5593
US
●**KIPLINGERS FLORIDA BUSINESS LETTER.** [Kiplinger's Fla. bus. lett.]. **Added/Corp** Kiplinger Washington Editors, Inc. **VFOAT** Florida Business Letter. Vol. 38, No. 9 (Sept. 29, 1993)-. Newsletter. English. Twelve times a year. $48.00. Kiplinger Washington Editors, 1729 H Street Northwest, Washington DC 20006. **Tel** (202)887-6400, (800)544-0155, FAX (202)331-1206. (**Subscription address:** Kiplinger Washington Editors, 3401 East West Highway, c/o Rick Topolski, Editors Park MD 20782. **Tel** (800)544-0155, (301)853-6600.) **Continues** Kiplinger Florida Letter, 0023-1754.

LC CURRENT ISSUES ONLY
DD 332.6
US
●**KNIGHT-RIDDER CRB COMMODITY YEARBOOK STATISTICAL SUPPLEMENT, THE. Added/Corp** Commodity Research Bureau (U.S.). **VFOAT** CRB Commodity Yearbook Statistical Supplement. **VAT** Knight Ridder Commodity Research Bureau Commodity Yearbook Statistical Supplement. Vol. 31, No. 1 (Sept. 1993)-. Statistical Publication. English. Three times a year. $75.00 North America; $87.00 other. Knight Ridder Financial Publishing, 30 South Wackler Drive, Suite 1820, Chicago IL 60606. **Tel** (312)454-1801, (800)621-5271, FAX (312)454-0239. **Continues** Commodity Year Book Statistical Supplement.

LC HG4538 .K97
DD 332.6
ISSN 0773-3666
BE
KWARTAALOVERZICHT VAN DE ECONOMIE. Periodical. Dutch (French). Four times a year. Ministerie van Economische Zaken, Nijverheidsstraat 6 4E Verdieping, 1040 Brussels Belgium.

LC HG4501
DD 332.6
ISSN 0279-0467
US
CEASED
LABOR & INVESTMENTS. See Business and Economics-Labor.

LC HG450
DD 332.6
ISSN 0891-7337
US
LAND INVESTMENT NEWS. (19??)-. Periodical. English. Four times a year. $10.00. Land Investment News, 2035 Westwood Boulevard, Suite 207, Los Angeles CA 90025. **Tel** (310)475-7869. **ED** Sam Solomon. **Circ:** 42,000.
Desc: Covers real estate and business development in 4,000 square mile area of California high desert.

LC HG450
DD 332.6
GW
LANGFRISTIGE KREDIT, DER. (19??)-. German. Six times a year. DM321.60. Fritz Knapp Verlag, Postfach 111151, D-60046 Frankfurt Germany. **Tel** 011 49 69 9708304, FAX 011 49 69 9708400. **ED** Klaus-Friedrich Otto, Juergen Meissner, Juergen Fischer, Berthold Morschhaeuser, Roland Fischer.
Desc: Journal providing information on financing and investments.

LC HG450
DD 332.6
UK
LATIN AMERICAN FINANCE & CAPITAL MARKETS. (19??)-. English. Twenty-two times a year. $595.00. WorldTrade Executive Incorporated, PO Box 761, Concord MA 01742. **Tel** (508)287-0301, FAX (508)287-0302. **ED** Anna Szterenfeld and Steven Murphy. **Absorbed** Investor Latin America.
Desc: Assists portfolio investors with coverage of the rapid flow of funds into and out of Latin America. Provides analysis on the political, economic and regulatory issues that affect investment decisions.

LC K1110
DD 346.71/092
ISSN 1189-3257
CN
LEGAL FOR LIFE. See Business and Economics-Banks and Banking.

LC HC407.Z7 S553
XV
LETNI PREGLED INVESTICIJ. Slovenian. One time a year. Zavod Sr Slovenije za Statistiko, Vozarski Pot 12, Ljubljana Slovenia.

LC HG450
DD 332.6
US
LETTER FROM SIA. English. Securities Industry Association, 120 Broadway/35th Floor, New York NY 10271. **Tel** (212)608-1500, FAX (212)608-1604.
Desc: Letter from SIA's President summarizing his views on issues of importance to the Association and its membership.

LC HG4051 .S4A
DD 353.008/25
ISSN 0098-9657
US
LIST OF COMPANIES REGISTERED UNDER THE INVESTMENT COMPANY ACT OF 1940. (LIST OF COMPANIES REGISTERED UNDER THE INVESTMENT COMPANY ACT OF 1940 AS OF ... / SECURITIES AND EXCHANGE COMMISSION.). English. Office of Reports and Information Services, Securities and Exchange Commission, Washington DC 20549.

LC HG1616.I5 C66A
DD 332.6/725
ISSN 0098-0005
US
LIST OF LEGAL INVESTMENTS FOR SAVINGS BANKS IN CONNECTICUT.
Main/Corp Connecticut. Office of the Bank Commissioner. (1974)-. English. One time a year. Office of the Bank Commissioner, State Office Building, Hartford CT 06101. **Continues** List of Legal Investments for Savings Banks and the Savings Departments of State Banks and Trust Companies in Connecticut.

LC HG1616.I5 L57
DD 332.63/09742
US
LIST OF LEGAL INVESTMENTS FOR SAVINGS BANKS, SAVINGS DEPOSITS OF TRUST COMPANIES AND COOPERATIVE BANKS. English. One time a year. New Hampshire Banking Dept., 97 Main Street, Concord NH 03301.

LC HG4651
DD 332.632
US
LIST OF MARGINABLE OTC STOCKS AS OF ... . Added/Corp Board of Governors of the Federal Reserve System (U.S.). **VAT** List of Marginable Over-the-Counter Stocks as of ... . (Nov. 13, 1984)-. Periodical. English. Four times a year. Free on request. Board of Governors of the Federal Reserve System, Mail Stop 127, Washington DC 20551. **Tel** (202)452-3244, (202)452-3245. **Continues** Board of Governors of the Federal Reserve System (U.S.). List of OTC Margin Stocks, 0196-0628.

LC HG4501
DD 332.6
ISSN 0188-1833
MX
Pr Rev.
LLOYD'S MEXICAN ECONOMIC REPORT. [Lloyd's Mex. econ. rep.]. **Added/Corp** Allen W. Lloyd y Asociados, S.A. (1963)-. Periodical. English. Twelve times a year. $36.00. Allen Lloyd y Asociados SA, Mariano Otero 1915, Guadalajara Jalisco Mexico. **Tel** 011 52 36 219050.
Ind/Abst Predicasts Forecasts.

LC HG450
DD 332.6
ISSN 0744-3846
US
LONG TERM VALUES. [Long term values]. **Added/Corp** William O'Neil & Co. (19??)-. English. Forty-eight times a year. $258.00. Daily Graphs Inc., 12655 Beatrice Street, Los Angeles CA 90066. **Tel** (310)448-6843. **Circ:** 25,000 (ctrl).
Desc: Covers 4,000 stocks over a six week period. Fifteen-year history of price, relative performance and quarterly annual earnings.

LC HG450 .L64
DD 332.6/0973/05
ISSN 1060-9903
US
LOUIS RUKEYSER'S WALL STREET. [Louis Rukeyser's Wall Str.]. **VFOAT** Wall Street. Vol. 1, No. 1 (Mar. 1992)-. Periodical. English. Twelve times a year. $49.50. Financial Service Associates, L.P., 1101 North King Street, Suite 400, Alexandria VA 22314. **Tel** (703)548-2400, (800)892-9702, FAX (705)549-9705. **ED** Louis Rukeyser and Soula Stefanopoulos (editors' telephone: (703)548-2918). **Circ:** 400,000 (ctrl).
Desc: Written by the award-winning host of the PBS program "Wall Street Week with Louis Rukeyser." Offers information on different kinds of investments with a focus on making more money.

LC HG4651
DD 332.632
ISSN 0273-7752
US
LOW PRICED STOCK SURVEY, THE.
Added/Corp Dow Theory Forecasts, inc. (19??)-. Periodical. English. Twenty-six times a year. $82.00. Dow Theory Forecasts Inc., 7412 Calumet Avenue, Hammond IN 46324. **Tel** (219)931-6480. **ED** Charles B. Carlson. Index available.
Desc: Focuses on stocks selling primarily under $20.00. Emphasizing issues with high capital gains potential.

LC HG450
DD 332.6
ISSN 0193-9262
US
LOWE INVESTMENT & FINANCIAL LETTER. [Lowe investm. financ. lett.]. **Main/Corp** Lowe Management Corporation. **VAT** Lowe Investment and Financial Letter. (197?)-. Periodical. English. Lowe Management Corporation, 26 Broadway, New York NY 10004.

LC HG1501
DD 332.1
US
LOWRY'S POWER AND VELOCITY RATINGS REPORT. (19??)-. English. One time a week. $260.00 (one-year), $420.00 (two-year). Lowry's Reports Inc., 631 US Highway One, Suite 305, North Palm Beach FL 33408. **Tel** (407)842-3514, FAX (407)842-1523.
Desc: Covers New York Stock Exchange issues. Service includes operating manual updates plus special studies as issued.

LC HG1501
DD 332.1
US
LOWRY'S WEEKLY MARKET TREND ANALYSIS. (19??)-. English. One time a week. $260.00 (one-year), $420.00 (two-year). Lowry's Reports Inc., 631 US Highway One, Suite 305, North Palm Beach FL 33408. **Tel** (407)842-3514, FAX (407)842-1523. **ED** Paul Desmond.
Desc: Mailed Friday after closing and includes operating manual updates and quarterly posting graphs.

LC HG450
DD 332.6
US
LYNCH INTERNATIONAL INVESTMENT SURVEY, THE. (1971)-. Periodical. English. One time a week. $175.00. Lynch Bowes Inc., 301 Main Street, Suite 206, Port Washington NY 11050. **Tel** (516)883-7094. **ED** Walter A. Lynch.
Desc: Financial advice and recommendations in precious metals and industrials. Effects of economic situations on banking and industry.

LC HG4501 .M14
DD 332.6/7
ISSN 0148-284X
US
M-G FINANCIAL WEEKLY. INDUSTRISCOPE EDITION, THE.
Added/Corp Media General Financial Services. **VFOAT** M/G Financial Weekly. (19??)-. Periodical. English. One time a week. $145.00. Media General Financial Services, PO Box C-32333, Richmond VA 23293-0001. **Tel** (804)649-6569.

LC HG5431 .S82
DD 338.7/4/0941
UK
●**MACMILLAN STOCK EXCHANGE YEARBOOK, THE. Added/Corp** Macmillan International Stock Exchange. **VFOAT** Stock Exchange Yearbook. (1994/1995)-. English. Macmillan Distribution Ltd., Houndsmill Basingstoke, Hampshire RG21 2XS United Kingdom. **Tel** 011 44 1256 29242, FAX 011 44 1256 842596. **Continues** Stock Exchange Official Yearbook (London, England : 1992), 0953-6329.

LC HG1723
DD 332.6/72/0971
ISSN 0715-6448
CN
MAJOR CAPITAL PROJECTS INVENTORY. [Major cap. proj. inventory]. **Added/Corp** Canada. Office of Industrial and Trade Benefits. Issue 1 (Oct. 1981)-. English. One time a year. Ministry of Industry Trade & Commerce, Tower B place DeVille, Ottawa Ontario K1A 0H5 Canada.

LC HG4509 .M33
DD 332.6/2
ISSN 0092-4407
US
MANAGERS (NEW YORK). (MANAGERS.). Vol. 1 (1973)-. English. One time a year. Techimetrics Inc., 919 Third Avenue, New York NY 10022.
Ind/Abst Gen. Period. Index (1985-); Manage. Contents.

LC HG4503 .M33
DD 332.64/25991
PH
MANILA STOCK EXCHANGE JOURNAL. Periodical. English. Twelve times a year. Manila Stock Exchange, Prensa Cor, Muelle de la Industria, Binondo Manila Philippines.

LC HG5391 .M36
DD 332.6
PE
MANUAL PRACTICO DEL AHORRISTA Y DEL INVERSIONISTA. No. 1-. Spanish. Av Orriantia, 305 San Isidro, Lima Peru.

LC HG4501 .O16
DD 332.6/32/0973
ISSN 0360-1773
US
CEASED
MARKET CHRONICLE, THE. (1975)-(199?). Periodical. English. William B Dana Company, PO Box 1839, Daytona Beach FL 32115. **Tel** (904)255-9885, (800)322-1839. **Continues** O-T-C Market Chronicle, 0029-7305.

LC HG4551
DD 332.6322
ISSN 1046-2171
US
MARKET GUIDE, THE. (Summer 1990)-. Periodical. English. Four times a year (Jan., Mar./Apr., July/Aug., Nov.). $345.00. Market Guide Inc, PO Box 106, 49 Glen Head Road, Glen Head NY 11545. **Tel** (516)751-1253, FAX (516)676-9240. **ED** Peter Sluka and Domenic Graziosi. Index available. **Continues** Market Guide (Over the Counter Stock Edition).

LC HF ISSN 0966-212X
DD 658.83505 UK
MARKET INFORMATION. [Mark. inf.]. (1992)-. Periodical. English. Two times a year. $224.00. Headland Business Information, 1 Henry Smiths Terrace, Headland Cleveland, TS24 0PD United Kingdom. **Tel** 011 44 429 231902, FAX 011 44 429 861403.

LC HG4651 ISSN 1182-4166
DD 332.63/22/097105 CN
MARKET INSIDER BULLETIN. [Mark. insid. bull.]. **Added/Corp** Michael Lombardi Publishing Corporation. Evasona Corporation. (1981)-. Periodical. English. Twenty times a year. 199.28Can$. Market Insider Bulletin, PO Box 541, Thornhill Ontario L3T 2C0 Canada. **Tel** (416)737-8743, FAX (905)737-8743. **ED** Antonin Jasansky. Index available. cum. index.

LC HG4501 ISSN 0162-6817
DD 332.6 US
CCC
MARKET LOGIC FROM THE INSTITUTE FOR ECONOMETRIC RESEARCH. **Added/Corp** Institute for Econometric Research (Fort Lauderdale, Fla.). **VFOAT** Market Logic. No. 1 (1978)-. Periodical. English. Twenty-four times a year. $200.00. Institute for Econometric Research, 2200 SW 10th Street, Deerfield Beach FL 33442. **Tel** (305)421-1000. **ED** Norman G. Fosback. **Circ:** 12,800.
Desc: Features econometric model forecasts of the market. Includes recommended stocks, market indicators, recommended mutual funds and options and research reports.

LC HG450 ISSN 0890-023X
DD 332.6 US
MARKET MONTH. [Mar. mon.]. **Added/Corp** Standard and Poor's Corporation. (198?)-. Periodical. English. Twelve times a year. $59.00. Standard & Poor's Corporation, (A Division of McGraw-Hill, Inc.), 25 Broadway, New York NY 10004. **Tel** (212)208-8775, (800)221-5277.

LC HG450 ISSN 0967-6384
DD 332.6 UK
MARKET PROFILES. (1992)-. English. One time a year. £179.00 UK; $359.00 other. Headland Business Information, 1 Henry Smiths Terrace, Headland Cleveland, TS24 0PD United Kingdom. **Tel** 011 44 429 231902, FAX 011 44 429 861403.

LC HG4551 ISSN 1194-2339
DD 332.64 CN
MARKET PROGRESS EXECUTIVE REPORT. [Mark. prog. exec. rep.]. **Main/Corp** Toronto Stock Exchange. Information Services. (1986)-. Periodical. English. Twelve times a year. 100.32Can$. Toronto Stock Exchange, The Exchange Tower, 2 First Canadian Place, Toronto Ontario M5X 1J2 Canada. **Tel** (416)947-4681.

LC HG5131.C4 C45A ISSN 0146-731X
DD 332.6/7 US
MARKET STATISTICS. **Main/Corp** Chicago Board Options Exchange. English. Chicago Board Options Exchange, 400 South LaSalle Street, Chicago IL 60605. **Tel** (312)786-7466.

LC HG4501 .M43 ISSN 0734-502X
DD 332.6/05 US
MARKET TECHNICIANS ASSOCIATION JOURNAL. [Mark. Tech. Assoc. j.]. **Added/Corp** Market Technicians Association. Market Technicians Association. Journal. Vol. 1, Issue 1 (Jan. 1978)-. Periodical. English. Irregular. $50.00. Market Technicians Association, 71 Broadway, 2nd Floor, New York NY 10006. **Tel** (212)344-1266, FAX (212)673-9334.

LC HG450
DD 332.6 US
●**MARTIN WEISS' SAFE MONEY REPORT.** (1995)-. English. Twelve times a year. $148.00. Weiss Research Inc., PO Box 109665, Palm Beach Gardens FL 33410. **Tel** (407)627-3300, FAX (407)625-6685. ***Continues*** *Safe Money Report.*

LC HG ISSN 1040-323X
DD 332 US
MATURE INVESTOR, THE. [Mature invest.]. Issue No. 1 (March 29, 1989)-. Periodical. English. Twelve times a year. $99.00. Susan Donovan, 2 South 671 Devonshire, Glen Ellyn IL 60137.

LC HG450 ISSN 0279-1277
DD 332.6 US
MEDIA GENERAL MARKET DATAGRAPHICS. **Added/Corp** Media General Financial Services. **VFOAT** Market Datagraphics. Vol. 1, Issue 1 (May 18, 1981)-. Periodical. English. One time a week. $145.00. Media General Financial Public, Box C-32333, Richmond VA 23293. **Tel** (804)649-6569. ***Continues in part*** *M/G Financial Weekly, 0145-4765.*
Desc: Detailed statistical data on 3,000 stocks, including price and volume charts for each. Also covers mutual funds, bonds, commodities and options.

LC R ISSN 1065-996X
DD 610 US
MEDICAL TECHNOLOGY STOCK LETTER. **See** Biology-Bioengineering.

LC HG4576 .S76A
DD 332.6/2/0254212 UK
MEMBERS AND FIRMS / THE STOCK EXCHANGE. **Main/Corp** Stock Exchange (London, England). English. Stock Exchange, London EC2N 1HP United Kingdom.

LC HG4928.5 .I55a ISSN 1056-6074
DD 332.6/2/06073 US
MEMBERSHIP DIRECTORY / ASSOCIATION FOR INVESTMENT MANAGEMENT AND RESEARCH. **See** Industry and Production-Trade and Industrial Directories.

LC HD28 .A48 ISSN 0543-6222
DD 338 RU
METODY I PRAKTIKA OPREDELENIIA EFFEKTIVNOSTI KAPITALNYKH VLOZHENII I NOVOI TEKHNIKI. [Metody prakt. opred. eff. kapitaln. volz. nov. teh.]. **Added/Corp** Nauchnyi Sovet po Effektivnosti Osnovnykh Fondov Kapitalnykh Vlozhenii i Novoi Tekhniki (Akademiia Nauk SSSR) Institut Ekonomiki (Akademiia Nauk SSSR). (1963)-. Russian. One time a year. Izdatelstvo Nauka / Akademiia Nauk, (Publishing House of the Russian Academy of Sciences), Leninskii Porspekt 14, 117901 Moscow Russia. **Tel** 011 95 9542153, FAX 011 95 9382144, telex 411964. ***Continues*** *Metody i Praktika Opredeleniia-Ekonomicheskoi Effektivnosti Kapitalnykh Vlozhenii i Novoi Tekhniki.*

LC HC131 .M385
DD 332.6 MX
MEXICAN BUSINESS & INVESTMENT. **VFOAT** Mexican Business and Investment. (19??)-. Periodical. Spanish (English). Twenty-two times a year. $400.00 US and Canada; $450.00 other. El Inversionista Mexicano, Felix Cuevas 301-204, Col Valle, 03100 Mexico D F Mexico. **Tel** 011 52 5 5349297, 011 52 5 5245396. **ED** Evangelina Astorsa. Index available. **Circ:** 1,000.

LC HB ISSN 1054-2663
DD 330 US
CCC
MEXICO BUSINESS MONTHLY. [Mex. bus. mon.]. (1991)-. Periodical. English. Twelve times a year. $188.00. Mexico Business Monthly, 52 Maples Avenue, Department M, Maplewood NJ 07040. **Tel** (201)762-1565, (800)766-3949, FAX (201)762-9585. available on an online database (files 16,636/Full-Text) from DIALOG.

LC HG4001 ISSN 1041-7524
DD 658 US
CCC
MINORITY MARKETS ALERT. [Minor. mark. alert]. (Jan. 1989)-. Periodical. English. Twelve times a year. $295.00. EPM Communications Inc., 488 East 18th Street, Brooklyn NY 11226. **Tel** (718)469-9330, FAX (718)469-7124. available on an online database (files 16,570,636/Full-Text) from DIALOG.
Ind/Abst Mark. Advert. Ref. Serv. [Full Txt.]; PROMT [Full Txt.]; PTS Newsl. Database [Full Txt.].

LC HG179 .M59 ISSN 0149-4953
DD 332/.024 US
CODEN MNEYAB
MONEY (CHICAGO, ILL.). (MONEY.). [Money]. Vol. 1, No. 1 (Oct. 1972)-. Periodical. English. Thirteen times a year. $35.95. Time Inc. / New York, Time & Life Building, Rockefeller Center, New York NY 10020. **(Subscription address:** Time Customer Service, PO Box 60050, Tampa FL 33609. **Tel** (800)541-9955.) Index available (free). **Ad Acc. Circ:** 2,160,000. available on microfilm and microfiche from University Microfilms International (UMI); available on an online database (files 15,485,647,648,746/Full-Text) from DIALOG. Documents available from UMI Article Clearinghouse, Documents on Demand.
Desc: Tells how to protect your money and make it grow, how to invest more profitably, save smarter, and keep more of your earnings at tax time.
Ind/Abst ABI/INFORM Glob. Ed.; ABI/INFORM Ondisc: Expr. Ed.; ABI/INFORM [Computer File] (June 1973-); Abr. Read. Guide Period. Lit.; Acad. Abstr. Full Text Elite; Acad. Abstr.; Acad. Search; Account. Tax Datab. (Jun. 1973-) [Full Txt.]; BioBusiness; Book Rev. Index; Bus. ASAP (1992-) [Full Txt.]; Bus. Index (1985-); Bus. Period. Index; Bus. Source Plus; Bus. Source; Consum. Index Prod. Eval. Inf. Source; Environ. Abstr.; EP Collect.; Gen. BusinessFile (1985-); Gen. Period. Index (1985-); Homework Help.; INFO-SOUTH Abstr.; Mag. Artic. Summar. Elite; Mag. Artic. Summar. Select; Mag. Artic. Summar. CD-ROM; Mag. ASAP Plus [Full Txt.]; Mag. ASAP Sel. [Full Txt.]; Mag. Express (1986-) [Full Txt.]; Mag. Index Plus (1989-); Mag. Index. Sel. (1986-); Mag. Search; MasterFile FullTEXT 1000; MasterFile FullTEXT 350; MasterFile FullTEXT 650; MasterFile FullTEXT (Jan. 1984-); Newsp. Period. Abstr. (1986-); OCLC; Pub. Lib. FullTEXT; Read. Guide Abstr. Select Ed.; Read. Guide Period. Lit.; Resource/One Ondisc; Telebase; Mag. Index (1977-); TOM Gen. Index (1985-) [Full Txt.]; Trade Ind. ASAP [Full Txt.]; Trade Ind. Index (1981-) [Full Txt.]; UMI ABI/Inform--Bus. Period. Ondisc (Dec. 1987-) [Full Txt.]; Vocat. Search; Wilson Bus. Abstr.; World Mag. Bank.

LC HG4501 ISSN 0833-3432
DD 332.6/78/0971 CN
MONEY DIGEST (BATH). (MONEY DIGEST.). [Money dig.]. **Added/Corp** Investors Association of Canada. Vol. 1, Issue 1 (July 1986)-. Periodical. English. Twelve times a year. 49.00Can$ Canada; 59.00Can$ US; 69.00Can$ other. Investors Association of Canada, 26 Soho Street, Suite 380, Toronto Ontario M5T 1Z7 Canada. **Tel** (416)340-1723. **ED** Chuck Chakrapani. Index available. **Bk Rev**, (Qty: 12). **Circ:** 3,300 (ctrl). available on an online database, CD-ROM, magnetic tape, and microfilm (micromedia).
Desc: Personal finance magazine that contains articles on new products, different types of investments, personal financial planning, insurance, retirement strategies and more.
Ind/Abst Can. Period. Index.

LC HG201 .D66
DD 332.4 US
●**MONEY FUND REPORT.** **Added/Corp** International Business Communications, Inc. **VFOAT** IBC's Money Fund Report. (Jan. 15, 1993)-. Periodical. English. One time a week. $1254.75 Massachussettes residents; $1293.59 New York residents;$1,195.00 other. IBC Donoghue Organization, 290 Eliot Street, Ashland MA 01721. **Tel** (800)343-5413, (508)881-2800. **(Subscription address:** IBC Donoghue Organization, PO Box 91004, Ashland MA 01721. **)** ***Continues*** *IBC/Donoghue's Money Fund Report.*

LC HG450
DD 332.6 US
MONEY MANAGEMENT LETTER. Newsletter. English. Twenty-six times a year. $1495.00 (one-year), $2695.00 (two-year). Institutional Investor Inc., 488 Madison Avenue, New York NY 10022. **Tel** (212)303-3234, (212)303-3233, FAX (212)303-3353.
Desc: Reports on trends, new products, searches, investment strategies, hires and fires throughout the fund management industry.

LC HG4501 .M494 ISSN 1063-2301
DD 332.6/025/73 US
MONEY MANAGER REVIEW. [Money manag. rev.]. (1988)-. Periodical. English. Four times a year. $145.00. Money Manager Review, 1550 California Street / Suite 263, San Francisco CA 94109. **Tel** (415)386-7111, FAX (415)387-9045.

LC HG450
DD 332.6 CN
MONEY REPORTER. English. Twenty-six times a year. 97.00Can$. MPL Communications, 133 Richard Street West, Suite 700, Toronto Ontario M5H 3M8 Canada. **Tel** (416)869-1177, FAX (416)869-0456.
Desc: Insider's letter for people whose interest is earning more investment income and paying less tax. Includes cumulative quarterly indexes, special tax-saving reports, portfolio planning advice, special investment Fact Sheets and a free Hotline service.

LC HG179 ISSN 0703-7163
DD 332/.024/0971 CN
MONEYLETTER. (THE MONEYLETTER.). **VFOAT** Money Letter. Vol. 1 (Aug. 16, 1976)-. Periodical. English. Twenty-four times a year. 48.50Can$; 97.00Can$. Hume Publishing Company, 4100 Yonge Street, Willowdale Ontario M2P 2B9 Canada. **Tel** (416)221-4596, (800)733-4863. **ED** A. Michael Keerma. Index available. **Circ:** 70,000.
Desc: An investment advisory containing money management advice and general investment recommendations.

LC HG450
DD 332.6 US
TITLE CHANGE
MONEYLETTER. (19??)-(1995). Periodical. English. IBC Donoghue Organization, 290 Eliot Street, Ashland MA 01721. **Tel** (800)343-5413, (508)881-2800. **(Subscription address:** IBC Donoghue Organization, PO Box 91004, Ashland MA 01721. **)** ***Continues*** *Donoghues Moneyletter.* ***Continued by*** *IBC's Moneyletter.*
Desc: Emphasizes market timing and strategic selection of no-load and low-load mutual funds. Specific buy and sell signals are listed for stock, bond, money market and international funds.

LC HG ISSN 0958-3769
DD 332.1 UK
MONEYMARKETING LONDON. (MONEY MARKETING.). [MoneyMarketing Lond.]. **VFOAT** Money Marketing (London). (1985)-. Newspaper. English. One time a week. Centaur Communications Ltd., St. Giles House, 50 Poland Street, London W1V 4AX United Kingdom. **Tel** 011 44 171 4394222, FAX 011 44 171 7346748, telex 261352. available on an online database from DIALOG.
Ind/Abst Infomat Int. Bus.

Business and Economics—Investments

LC HG
DD 332/.05
ISSN 0226-2894
CN

MONITEUR DES AFFAIRES ET DE LA FINANCE, LE. [Monit. aff. financ.]. Vol. 2, No. 2 (Jan. 14, 1980)-. Periodical. French. One time a week. $200.00. Cobaro Inc., 1255 Carre Phillips Bureau 407, Montreal Quebec H3B 3G1 Canada. **Continues** Moniteur des Affaires, 0226-2886.

LC HG450
DD 332.6
HK

MONTHLY MARKET STATISTICS. See Business and Economics-Abstracting, Bibliographies and Statistics.

LC HC435.2 .I573a
DD 330.9/54/05
ISSN 0019-4999
II

MONTHLY NEWSLETTER - INDIAN INVESTMENT CENTRE. Main/Corp Indian Investment Centre. (19??)-. Newsletter. English. Twelve times a year. $40.00. Indian Investment Centre, Jeevan Vijar Bldg., Sansad Marg., New Delhi 110001 India. **Tel** 11-351673, FAX 11-351205, telex 031-63176 ICHO IN. **(Subscription address:** Prints India, 11 Darya Ganj, New Delhi 110002 India. **Tel** 011 91 11 3268645, FAX 011 91 11 3275542, telex 31-61087 PRIN-IN.**) ED** K.K. Trivedi. **Bk Rev. Ad Acc. Circ:** 3,000.
Desc: An academic journal which publishes articles and reviews on literature, history and the humanities.

LC HG4651
DD 332.63/22/0971
ISSN 0828-8178
CN

MONTHLY STOCK CHARTS. [Mon. stock charts]. Issue No. 1 (Sept. 28, 1984)-. Periodical. English. Four times a year. $79.00. Independent Survey Company, PO Box 6000, Vancouver British Columbia V6B 4B9, Canada. **Tel** (604)689-5795, (604)731-5777.
Desc: A publication which charts a 12 year record of monthly share price and volume for Canadian companies.

LC HG4651
DD 332.632
ISSN 0734-4880
US

MONTHLY STOCK REVIEW. [Mon. stock rev.]. English. Twelve times a year. Salomon Brothers Center / Finance, 7 World Trade Center, 36th Floor, New York NY 10048. **Tel** (212)747-7000.

LC HG4651 .M617
DD 338.7/4/0973
ISSN 1050-0820
US

MOODY'S ... ANNUAL BOND RECORD. [Moody's annu. bond rec.]. **Added/Corp** Moody's Investors Service. **VFOAT** Annual Bond Record. (1989)-. Periodical. English. One time a year. $65.00. Moody's Investors Service, 99 Church Street, New York NY 10007. **Tel** (212)553-0547, (212)553-0435, FAX (212)553-4700.

LC HG5123.B3 M6
DD 332
ISSN 0027-0814
US
CCC

MOODY'S BANK & FINANCE NEWS REPORTS. See Business and Economics-Banks and Banking.

LC HG4905 .M78
DD 332.63
ISSN 0148-1878
US
CCC

MOODY'S BOND RECORD. [Moody's bond rec.]. Vol. 3, No. 5 (Feb. 20, 1936)-. Periodical. English. Twelve times a year. $370.00. Moody's Investors Service, 99 Church Street, New York NY 10007. **Tel** (212)553-0547, (212)553-0435, FAX (212)553-4700. **Continues** Moody's Bond Ratings with Quotations.

LC HG4905 .M785
DD 332.63
ISSN 0027-0822
US

MOODY'S BOND SURVEY. [Moody's bond surv.]. Vol. 28 (Jan. 6, 1936)-. Periodical. English. One time a week. $1650.00. Moody's Investors Service, 99 Church Street, New York NY 10007. **Tel** (212)553-0547, (212)553-0435, FAX (212)553-4700. Index Available, published separately, free-automatically sent. **Continues** Moody's Investment Survey.

LC HG450
DD 332.6
US

●**MOODY'S CREDIT PERSPECTIVES.** (1995)-. English. One time a week. Moody's Investors Service, 99 Church Street, New York NY 10007. **Tel** (212)553-0547, (212)553-0435, FAX (212)553-4700. **Continues** Moody's Bond Survey.

LC HG4551
DD 332.6322
ISSN 0192-7019
US
CCC

MOODY'S DIVIDEND RECORD. [Moody's divid. rec.]. **Added/Corp** Moody's Investors Service. Vol. 1 (Nov. 1930)-. Periodical. English. Two times a week. $725.00. Moody's Investors Service, 99 Church Street, New York NY 10007. **Tel** (212)553-0547, (212)553-0435, FAX (212)553-4700.

LC HG450
DD 332.6
US

MOODY'S DIVIDEND RECORD. ANNUAL CUMULATIVE ISSUE. Added/Corp Moody's Investors Service. **VFOAT** Moody's Annual Dividend Record. Vol. 1 (1930)-. English. Two times a week. $105.00 (combined with UIT Payment Record). Moody's Investors Service, 99 Church Street, New York NY 10007. **Tel** (212)553-0547, (212)553-0435, FAX (212)553-4700. **ED** Robert Hanson.
Desc: Reports on current dividend data on over 18,300 stocks.

LC HG4501 .M59
DD 332.67
ISSN 0027-0830
US
CCC

MOODY'S HANDBOOK OF COMMON STOCKS. VFOAT Handbook of Common Stocks. 3rd Quarterly Ed. (1965)-. Periodical. English. Four times a year. $310.00. Moody's Investors Service, 99 Church Street, New York NY 10007. **Tel** (212)553-0547, (212)553-0435, FAX (212)553-4700. **ED** John J. Esposito. **Circ:** 12,000. **Continues** Moody's Handbook of Widely Held Common Stocks, 0190-728X.
Desc: Basic financial and business information on companies of high investor interest. Fifteen-year stock price charts, 10-year statistics and text on quarterly earnings and prospects are also included.

LC HG4050 .M66
DD 338.7/4/0973
ISSN 0737-1586
US

MOODY'S HANDBOOK OF DIVIDEND ACHIEVERS. Added/Corp Moody's Investors Service. **VFOAT** Handbook of Dividend Achievers. (19??)-. English. One time a year. $19.95. Moody's Investors Service, 99 Church Street, New York NY 10007. **Tel** (212)553-0547, (212)553-0435, FAX (212)553-4700. **ED** John J. Esposito. **Circ:** 1,500.
Desc: Financial and business information on companies which increased their dividends in each of the last ten years.

LC HG4501 .M58
DD 338.7/4/0973
ISSN 1059-8057
US

MOODY'S HANDBOOK OF NASDAQ STOCKS. [Moody's handb. NASDAQ stocks]. **Added/Corp** Moody's Investors Service. **VFOAT** Handbook of NASDAQ Stocks; NASDAQ Stocks. **VAT** Moody's Handbook of National Association of Securities Dealers Automated Quotations Stocks. (Winter 1991/1992)-. Periodical. English. Four times a year. $215.00. Moody's Investors Service, 99 Church Street, New York NY 10007. **Tel** (212)553-0547, (212)553-0435, FAX (212)553-4700. **Continues** Moody's Handbook of OTC Stocks, 0276-3516.

LC HG4961 .M67
DD 332.6
ISSN 0545-0217
US
CCC

MOODY'S INDUSTRIAL MANUAL. Added/Corp Moody's Investors Service. (1954)-. Periodical. English. One time a year. $1995.00. Moody's Investors Service, 99 Church Street, New York NY 10007. **Tel** (212)553-0547, (212)553-0435, FAX (212)553-4700. **Continues in part** Moody's Manual of Investments.

LC HG4961 .M723
DD 332
ISSN 0027-0849
US

MOODY'S INDUSTRIAL NEWS REPORTS. [Moody's ind., News rep.]. **Added/Corp** Moody's Investors Service. Vol. No. 11 (July 3 1970)-. English. Two times a week. $1475.00 (with Industrial Manual). Moody's Investors Service, 99 Church Street, New York NY 10007. **Tel** (212)553-0547, (212)553-0435, FAX (212)553-4700. **Continues** Moody's Industrials.

LC HG4961 .M68
DD 332.63/22/0973021
ISSN 1047-3114
CCC

MOODY'S INDUSTRY REVIEW. [Moody's ind. rev.]. **Added/Corp** Moody's Investors Service. **VFOAT** Industry Review. (Sept. 15, 1989)-. Periodical. English. Twenty-six times a year. $710.00. Moody's Investors Service, 99 Church Street, New York NY 10007. **Tel** (212)553-0547, (212)553-0435, FAX (212)553-4700. **Continues** Moody's Investors Industry Review, 1062-7685.

LC HG4009 .M65
DD 332.6
US

MOODY'S INTERNATIONAL COMPANY DATA [COMPUTER FILE]. Added/Corp Moody's Investors Service. **VFOAT** International Company Data. (19??)-. English. Twelve times a year. $7000.00. Moody's Investors Service, 99 Church Street, New York NY 10007. **Tel** (212)553-0547, (212)553-0435, FAX (212)553-4700.

LC HG4009 .M66
DD 338.8/8/05
ISSN 0278-3509
US
CCC

MOODY'S INTERNATIONAL MANUAL. (MOODY'S INTERNATIONAL MANUAL / MOODY'S INVESTORS SERVICE). **Added/Corp** Moody's Investors Service. **VFOAT** International Manual. (1981)-. Periodical. English. One time a year. $2825.00 (with Weekly News Report). Moody's Investors Service, 99 Church Street, New York NY 10007. **Tel** (212)553-0547, (212)553-0435, FAX (212)553-4700.

LC HG
DD 332
ISSN 0278-3517
US
CCC

MOODY'S INTERNATIONAL NEWS REPORTS. [Moody's int. news rep.]. **Added/Corp** Moody's Investors Service. **VFOAT** Moody's International. Vol. 1, No. 1 (Fri., Oct. 23, 1981)-. Periodical. English. One time a week. $2495.00 (with International Manual). Moody's Investors Service, 99 Church Street, New York NY 10007. **Tel** (212)553-0547, (212)553-0435, FAX (212)553-4700.

LC HG4931 .M58
DD 332.6/323
ISSN 0545-0233
US
CCC

MOODY'S MUNICIPAL & GOVERNMENT MANUAL. [Moody's munic. gov. man.]. **VFOAT** Municipal & Government Manual. **VAT** Moody's Municipal and Government Manual. (1955)-. Periodical. English. One time a year. $2450.00 (with Weekly News Reports). Moody's Investors Service, 99 Church Street, New York NY 10007. **Tel** (212)553-0547, (212)553-0435, FAX (212)553-4700. **Continues in part** Moody's Manual of Investments: American and Foreign.

LC HG450
DD 332.6
US

MOODY'S MUNICIPAL ISSUES. Added/Corp Moody's Investors Service. **VFOAT** Municipal Issues. (198?)-. Periodical. English. Six times a year. Free. Moody's Investors Service, 99 Church Street, New York NY 10007. **Tel** (212)553-0547, (212)553-0435, FAX (212)553-4700.

LC HG4961 .M7237
DD 332.67
ISSN 0192-7167
CCC

MOODY'S OTC INDUSTRIAL MANUAL. Added/Corp Moody's Investors Service. **VFOAT** OTC Industrial Manual. **VAT** Moody's Over the Counter Industrial Manual. (1970)-. English. One time a year. $1350.00 (with Weekly News Report). Moody's Investors Service, 99 Church Street, New York NY 10007. **Tel** (212)553-0547, (212)553-0435, FAX (212)553-4700. Index available in last issue of volume--attached.
Desc: Covers companies traded over the counter or on regional conferences.

LC HG4907 .M68
DD 338.7/4/0973
ISSN 0890-5282
US
CCC

MOODY'S OTC UNLISTED MANUAL. [Moody's OTC unlisted man.]. **Added/Corp** Moody's Investors Service. **VFOAT** OTC Unlisted Manual. **VAT** Moody's Over the Counter Unlisted Manual. (1986)-. Periodical. English. Irregular (53 issues per year). $1825.00 (manual with News Report). Moody's Investors Service, 99 Church Street, New York NY 10007. **Tel** (212)553-0547, (212)553-0435, FAX (212)553-4700.

LC HG4961 .M7245
DD 332.6/7
ISSN 0545-0241
US
CCC

MOODY'S PUBLIC UTILITY MANUAL. Added/Corp Moody's Investors Service. **VFOAT** Public Utility Manual. (1954)-. Periodical. English. One time a year. $1725.00 (with Weekly News Reports). Moody's Investors Service, 99 Church Street, New York NY 10007. **Tel** (212)553-0547, (212)553-0435, FAX (212)553-4700. **Continues in part** Moody's Manual of Investments, American and Foreign. Public Utility Securities.

LC HG4501 .S7948
DD 332.6/7
ISSN 0097-6997
US

MOODY'S STOCK SURVEY. (19??)-. Periodical. English. One time a week. Moody's Investors Service, 99 Church Street, New York NY 10007. **Tel** (212)553-0547, (212)553-0435, FAX (212)553-4700. **Continues** Stock Survey.

LC HG4530 .M64
DD 332.63/27
ISSN 1053-6175
US

MOODY'S UNIT INVESTMENT TRUSTS. [Moody's unit investm. trusts]. **Added/Corp** Moody's Investors Service. **VFOAT** Unit Investment Trusts; Unit Investment Trusts Annual Payment Record; Moody's Unit Investment Trusts Annual Payment Record. Vol. 1, No. 1 (Jan. 4, 1991)-. English. One time a week. $475.00. Moody's Investors Service, 99 Church Street, New York NY 10007. **Tel** (212)553-0547, (212)553-0435, FAX (212)553-4700.

LC HG
DD 332
ISSN 1052-9713
US

MORGAN STANLEY CAPITAL INTERNATIONAL PERSPECTIVE (MONTHLY). (MORGAN STANLEY CAPITAL INTERNATIONAL PERSPECTIVE). [Morgan Stanley Cap. Int. perspect.]. **Added/Corp** Morgan Stanley & Co. Capital International Perspective S.A. Issue 1 (1986)-. Periodical. English (French and German). Sixteen times a year. $6000.00. Capital International Perspective SA, 3 place des Bergues, CH-1201 Geneva Switzerland. **Tel** 011 41 22 7151515, FAX 011 41 22 7313179, telex 27335. **Continues** Capital International Perspective (Monthly).

Business and Economics —Investments

Desc: Designed to keep the investor continuously and conveniently informed on stock market developments worldwide.

LC HG
DD 332
ISSN 1052-9721
SZ
MORGAN STANLEY CAPITAL INTERNATIONAL PERSPECTIVE (QUARTERLY). (MORGAN STANLEY CAPITAL INTERNATIONAL PERSPECTIVE.). [Morgan Stanley Cap. Int. perspect.]. (Jan. 1986)-. Periodical. English (French and German). Four times a year. Capital International Perspective SA, 3 place des Bergues, CH-1201 Geneva Switzerland. **Tel** 011 41 22 7151515, FAX 011 41 22 7313179, telex 27335. **Continues** Capital International Perspective (Quarterly).

LC HG450
DD 332.6
US
MORNINGSTAR 500 SOURCEBOOK. (19??)-. English. One time a year. $35.00 US, $45.00 Canada and Mexico; $60.00 other. Morningstar Inc., 225 West Wacker Drive, Chicago IL 60606. **Tel** (312)696-6000, (800)876-5005. **Continues** Morningstar Mutual Fund 500, 1067-6228.

LC HG4538 .M598
DD 338.7/4/05
ISSN 1076-2744
US
●**MORNINGSTAR AMERICAN DEPOSITARY RECEIPTS.** [Morningstar Am. depositary receipts]. **Added/Corp** Morningstar, Inc. **VFOAT** American Depositary Receipts; Morningstar ADRs. (1994)-. Periodical. English. Twenty-six times a year. $295.00 US / $360.00 Canada and Mexico; $480.00 other. Morningstar Inc., 225 West Wacker Drive, Chicago IL 60606. **Tel** (312)696-6000, (800)876-5005.

LC HG450
DD 332.6
US
●**MORNINGSTAR CLOSED-END FUND 250.** (1995)-. English. One time a year. $35.00. Morningstar Inc., 225 West Wacker Drive, Chicago IL 60606. **Tel** (312)696-6000, (800)876-5005.

LC HG4530 .M69
DD 332
ISSN 1059-1419
US
MORNINGSTAR CLOSED-END FUNDS. [Morningstar closed-end funds]. **Added/Corp** Morningstar, Inc. **VFOAT** Morningstar Closed End Funds. (1991)-. English. Twenty-three times a year. $195.00 US; $225.00 Canada and Mexico; $275.00 other. Morningstar Inc., 225 West Wacker Drive, Chicago IL 60606. **Tel** (312)696-6000, (800)876-5005.

LC HG
DD 332
ISSN 1082-8001
US
●**MORNINGSTAR INVESTOR.** [Morningstar invest.]. Vol. 3, No. 9 (May 1995)-. Periodical. English. Twelve times a year. $89.00. Morningstar Inc., 225 West Wacker Drive, Chicago IL 60606. **Tel** (312)696-6000, (800)876-5005. **Continues** 5-Star Investor, 1065-3414.

LC HG4530 .M664
DD 332
ISSN 1067-6228
TITLE CHANGE
MORNINGSTAR MUTUAL FUND 500. [Morningstar mutual fund 500]. **Added/Corp** Morningstar, Inc. **VFOAT** Morningstar Mutual Fund Five Hundred. (1993)-(19??). English. Morningstar Inc., 225 West Wacker Drive, Chicago IL 60606. **Tel** (312)696-6000, (800)876-5005. **Continued by** Morningstar 500 Sourcebook.

LC HG450
DD 332.6
US
CEASED
MORNINGSTAR MUTUAL FUND SOURCEBOOK. **Added/Corp** Morningstar, Inc. (1993)-(1997). English. Morningstar Inc., 225 West Wacker Drive, Chicago IL 60606. **Tel** (312)696-6000, (800)876-5005. **Continues** Mutual Fund Sourcebook, 8755-4151.

LC HG4530 .M8
DD 332
ISSN 1059-1443
US
MORNINGSTAR MUTUAL FUNDS. [Morningstar mutual funds]. **Added/Corp** Morningstar, Inc. **VFOAT** Mutual Funds. Vol. 14, No. 6 (Sept. 6, 1991)-. Periodical. English. Twenty-six times a year. $395.00 US; $465.00 Canada and Mexico; $525.00 other. Morningstar Inc., 225 West Wacker Drive, Chicago IL 60606. **Tel** (312)696-6000, (800)876-5005. **Continues** Mutual Fund Values, 0890-7153.

LC HG4530
DD 332
ISSN 1059-142?
US
MORNINGSTAR MUTUAL FUNDS ONDISC. (MORNINGSTAR MUTUAL FUNDS ONDISC [COMPUTER FILE].). [Morningstar mutual funds ondisc]. **Added/Corp** Morningstar, Inc. **VFOAT** Morningstar Mutual Funds Ondisc; Mutual Funds on Disc. 3rd Quarter (1991)-. English. Twelve times a year. $795.00 US; $1295.00 Canada and Mexico; $1355.00 other. Morningstar Inc., 225 West Wacker Drive, Chicago IL 60606. **Tel** (312)696-6000, (800)876-5005.

LC HG4651
DD 332.63/244/09713
ISSN 0712-2284
CN
MORTGAGE BROKER. [Mortg. broker]. Periodical. English. Six times a year. Free. Ontario Mortgage Brokers Association, 8 King Street East/Suite 1710, Toronto Ontario M5C 1B5 Canada.

LC HG450
DD 332.6
ISSN 0742-8839
US
MOTION PICTURE INVESTOR. See Motion Picture.

LC HG450
DD 332.6
US
MPT FUND REVIEW. (19??)-. English. Twelve times a year. $125.00. MPT Fund Review, PO Box 590, Sausalito CA 94966. **Tel** (415)331-2070.
Desc: Specializing in modern portfolio theory; risk-adjusted performance for mutual fund and stock investors.

LC HG4951 .M815
DD 332.63/233/02573
ISSN 1076-8491
US
●**MUNICIPAL ISSUERS REGISTRY.** [Munic. issu. regist.]. (July 1994)-. English. One time a year. $160.00. Thomson Financial Publishing, PO Box 65, 4709 West Golf Road, Skokie IL 60076-0065. **Tel** (800)321-3373, (708)933-8031.

LC HG450
DD 332.6
US
CEASED
MUNICIPAL MARKET DEVELOPMENTS. **Added/Corp** Public Securities Association. Securities Industry Association. (19??)-(Nov. 1993). Periodical. English. Public Securities Association, 40 Broad Street, 12th Floor, New York NY 10004. **Tel** (212)809-7000, (212)440-9430, FAX (212) 797-3895, (212) 742-1549. **Supersedes** SIA Municipal Statistical Bulletin.

LC HB522
DD 338
ISSN 1050-656X
US
MUTUAL FUND ADVISOR. [Mutual fund advis.]. (Nov. 1989)-. Periodical. English. Twelve times a year. $150.00. Wall Street Digest Inc., 1 Sarasota Tower, Suite 602, Sarasota FL 34236. **Tel** (813)954-5500, FAX (813)364-8447. **ED** Donald H. Rowe.

LC HG
DD 332
ISSN 1067-1358
US
MUTUAL FUND BUYER'S GUIDE. [Mutual fund buy. guide]. **Added/Corp** Institute for Econometric Research (Fort Lauderdale, Fla.). (Nov. 1992)-. English. Twelve times a year. $80.00. Institute for Econometric Research, 2200 SW 10th Street, Deerfield Beach FL 33442. **Tel** (305)421-1000. **ED** Norman G. Fosback.

LC HG4930 .M85
DD 332.63/27
ISSN 0077-2550
US
MUTUAL FUND FACT BOOK. (1966)-. English. One time a year. $25.00. Investment Company Institute, 1401 H Street Northwest, Washington DC 20005. **Tel** (202)326-5800, (202)326-5972. **ED** Sue Duncan. **Bk Rev**.
Desc: Updated facts and figures on the U.S. mutual fund industry, including sales and performance trends; history, growth, policies, operations, regulation, services, and shareholders of industry.
Ind/Abst Stat. Ref. Index.

LC HG
DD 332
ISSN 8755-9889
CCC
MUTUAL FUND FORECASTER. [Mutual fund forecast.]. **Added/Corp** Institute for Econometric Research (Fort Lauderdale, Fla.). (1985)-. Periodical. English. Twelve times a year. $100.00. Institute for Econometric Research, 2200 SW 10th Street, Deerfield Beach FL 33442. **Tel** (305)421-1000. **ED** Norman G. Fosback. **Circ:** 195,000.
Desc: Contains ratings for common stock mutual funds.

LC HG
DD 332
ISSN 0742-9657
US
MUTUAL FUND LETTER, THE. [Mutual fund lett.]. **Added/Corp** Investment Information Services. Vol. 1, No. 1 (Jan. 1984)-. Periodical. English. Twelve times a year. $99.00. Investment Information Service, 680 North Lake Shore Drive, Suite 2038, Chicago IL 60611. **Tel** (312)649-6940. **ED** Gerald Perritt. **Circ:** 12,000.
Desc: Advisory that recommends mutual funds for various investment objectives. Also includes model portfolios, news, special statistical reports, spotlighted funds, feature articles and distribution alerts.

LC HG4530 .M853
DD 332.63/27
ISSN 1070-3373
US
●**MUTUAL FUND MARKET NEWS.** [Mutual fund mark. news]. **VFOAT** MN. Vol. 1, Issue 1 (May 24, 1993)-. Trade Publication. English. One time a week. $1250.00. Dalbar Publishing Inc., 260 Franklin Street, Boston MA 02110. **Tel** (617)439-6195, FAX (617)439-6346. **Continues** FACS of the Week, 1056-2540.

LC HG4651
DD 332.63
ISSN 1202-3329
CN
●**MUTUAL FUND MONITOR (TORONTO).** (THE MUTUAL FUND MONITOR.). [Mutual fund monit.]. **Added/Corp** Canadian Analyst Limited. Issue No. 1 (Feb. 1994)-. Trade Publication. English. Four times a year. 80.00Can$. Canadian Analyst Limited, 30 Duincan Street, Toronto Ontario M5V 2C3 Canada. **Tel** (416)971-6543.

LC HG450
DD 332.6
US
MUTUAL FUND NEWS. English. Five times a year. Available only to brokers, financial planners, and registered reps. Investment Company Institute, 1401 H Street Northwest, Washington DC 20005. **Tel** (202)326-5800, (202)326-5972.

LC HG4530 .M854
DD 332.63/27
ISSN 1046-8773
US
CEASED
MUTUAL FUND PERFORMANCE REPORT. [Mutual fund perform. rep.]. (May 1990)-(Jan. 1996). Periodical. English. Morningstar Inc., 225 West Wacker Drive, Chicago IL 60606. **Tel** (312)696-6000, (800)876-5005.

LC HG450
DD 332.6
US
MUTUAL FUND REPORT. (19??)-. English. Twelve times a year. $275.00. CDA Investment Technologies, 1355 Piccard Drive, Rockville MD 20850. **Tel** (301)974-9600, (800)232-2285, FAX (301)590-1389.

LC HG4651
DD 332.63/27
ISSN 0835-4669
CN
MUTUAL FUND SOURCEBOOK (TORONTO). (MUTUAL FUND SOURCEBOOK.). [Mutual fund sourceb.]. **Added/Corp** Financial Times of Canada (Firm) Southam Business Information and Communications Group. (1987)-. Periodical. English. One time a year. 287.32Can$. Southam Information & Technical Group Inc, 1450 Don Mills Road, Don Mills Ontario M3B 2X7 Canada. **Tel** (416)445-6641, (800)668-2374, FAX (416)442-2261.

LC HG450
DD 332.6
ISSN 0741-1278
US
CEASED
MUTUAL FUND SPECIALIST, THE. [Mutual fund spec.]. **Added/Corp** Royal R. Lemier & Co. (March 1979)-(1993). Periodical. English. Royal R Lemier and Company, PO Box 1025, Eau Claire WI 54701. **Tel** (715)834-7425. **ED** Royal R. LeMier.

LC HG450
DD 332.6
US
MUTUAL FUND STRATEGIST. English. Twelve times a year. $149.00. Mutual Fund Strategist, PO Box 446, Burlington VT 05402. **Tel** (802)658-3513. **ED** Charlie Hooper and Hollie Hooper-Fourmer. **Circ:** 5,000.
Desc: Provides a market timing approach to investing in US equity and bond mutual funds, international equity and bond funds, and precious metals funds.

LC HG450
DD 332.6
US
MUTUAL FUND TRENDS. (19??)-. Statistical Publication. English. Twelve times a year. $119.00 US, Canada and Mexico; $169.00 other. Growth Fund Research Inc, PO Box 6600, Rapid City SD 57709. **Tel** (605)341-1971. **ED** Walter J. Rouleau. **Absorbed** Mutual Fund Chartist; The Strongest Funds.
Desc: Contains statistics and semi-log fund charts with multiple moving averages and indicators.

LC HG450
DD 332.6
US
MUTUAL FUND WEEKLY. (19??)-. English. Irregular (48 issues). $360.00. Institute for Econometric Research, 2200 SW 10th Street, Deerfield Beach FL 33442. **Tel** (305)421-1000. **ED** Norman G. Fosback.

LC HG
DD 332
ISSN 1079-0039
US
●**MUTUAL FUNDS MAGAZINE.** [Mutual funds mag.]. **Added/Corp** Institute for Econometric Research (Fort Lauderdale, Fla.). (Oct./Nov. 1994)-. Periodical. English. Twelve times a year. $9.97. Institute for Econometric Research, 2200 SW 10th Street, Deerfield Beach FL 33442. **Tel** (305)421-1000. **ED** Norman G. Fosback. **Bk Rev**. **Ad Acc**.

LC HG450
DD 332.6
US
MUTUAL FUNDS ONFLOPPY. (19??)-. English. Twelve times a year. $185.00 US; $190.00 Canada and Mexico; $245.00 other. Morningstar Inc., 225 West Wacker Drive, Chicago IL 60606. **Tel** (312)696-6000, (800)876-5005.

LC HG4907 .N29
DD 332.63/23/0973
US
TITLE CHANGE
NATIONAL BOND SUMMARY, THE. **Added/Corp** National Quotation Bureau (U.S.). Vol. 138 (July 1983)-Vol. 159 (Jan. 1994). English. National

Business and Economics — Investments

Quotation Bureau, 150 Commerce Road, Cedar Grove NJ 07009. Tel (201)239-6100. *Separated from National Monthly Bond Summary. Continued by National Quotation Bureau Semi-Annual Bond Summary.*

LC Z7164.F5 N34 HG4501   ISSN 0735-035X
DD 016.3326/05   US
NATIONAL DIRECTORY OF INVESTMENT NEWSLETTERS, THE. See Industry and Production-Trade and Industrial Directories.

LC HC431 .N27
DD 332.6   II
NATIONAL INVESTMENT AND FINANCE. (1953)-. Periodical. English. One time a week. $69.00. National Investment and Finance, C-25 Press Enclave Saket, PO Box 4007, New Delhi 110 017 India. (Subscription address: Prints India, 11 Darya Ganj, New Delhi 110002 India. Tel 011 91 11 3268645, FAX 011 91 11 3275542, telex 31-61087 PRIN-IN.) *Absorbed Investment and Finance.*

LC HG4905 .N3
DD 332.6   US
                                 TITLE CHANGE
NATIONAL MONTHLY BOND SUMMARY, THE. Added/Corp National Quotation Bureau (U.S.). VFOAT National Bond Summary. Vol. 80 (July 1954)-(May 1994). Periodical. English. National Quotation Bureau, 150 Commerce Road, Cedar Grove NJ 07009. Tel (201)239-6100. *Continues National Monthly Corporation Bond Summary; Continued in part by National Bond Summary; Continued by NQB National Monthly Bond Summary.*

LC HG4905 .N34   ISSN 0275-8326
DD 332.63   US
                                 TITLE CHANGE
NATIONAL MONTHLY STOCK SUMMARY, THE. Added/Corp National Quotation Bureau (U.S.). VFOAT National Stock Summary. (19??)-(1994). Periodical. English. National Quotation Bureau, 150 Commerce Road, Cedar Grove NJ 07009. Tel (201)239-6100. *Continued in part by National Stock Summary; Continued by NQB National Monthly Stock Summary, 1080-319X.*
   Desc: Contains a summarization of market quotations which have appeared in the National Daily Services, or have been supplied by dealers on special lists.

LC HG   ISSN 0745-7049
DD 332   US
NATIONAL OTC STOCK JOURNAL, THE. [Natl. OTC stock j.]. VFOAT National O.T.C. Stock Journal. VAT National Over-the-Counter Stock Journal. (198?)-. Periodical. English. One time a week. Price varies per volume. The National OTC Stock Journal, 1780 South Bellaire, Suite 400, Denver CO 80222. Tel (303)758-9131. ED Terry Freeman. Ad Acc. Circ: 20,000 (ctrl). *Continues National OTC Stock Exchange, 0744-7892.*
   Desc: Financial journal covering the OTC market, business and finance. Includes listings of quotes, editorial coverage and news of the over-the-counter market.

LC HG4915 .N3   ISSN 1080-3173
DD 332   US
●NATIONAL QUOTATION BUREAU MONTHLY BOND SUMMARY. [Natl. Quota. Bur. mon. bond summ.]. Added/Corp National Quotation Bureau (U.S.). VFOAT Monthly Bond Summary. (Aug. 1, 1994)-. Periodical. English. Twelve times a year. $420.00 (includes 10 supplements and 2 hardbound volumes). National Quotation Bureau, 150 Commerce Road, Cedar Grove NJ 07009. Tel (201)239-6100. *Continues NQB National Monthly Bond Summary.*

LC HG4915 .N34   ISSN 1080-3157
DD 332.63   US
●NATIONAL QUOTATION BUREAU MONTHLY STOCK SUMMARY. [Natl. Quota. Bur. mon. stock summ.]. Added/Corp National Quotation Bureau (U.S.). VFOAT Monthly Stock Summary; NQB Monthly Stock Summary. (Aug.1, 1994)-. Periodical. English. Twelve times a year. National Quotation Bureau, 150 Commerce Road, Cedar Grove NJ 07009. Tel (201)239-6100. *Continues NQB National Monthly Stock Summary, 1080-319X.*

LC HG4915 .N29   ISSN 1080-3181
DD 332.63/23/0973   US
●NATIONAL QUOTATION BUREAU SEMI-ANNUAL BOND SUMMARY. [Natl. Quota. Bur. semi-annu. bond summ.]. Added/Corp National Quotation Bureau (U.S.). VFOAT Semi-Annual Bond Summary. (1994)-. Periodical. English. Two times a year. National Quotation Bureau, 150 Commerce Road, Cedar Grove NJ 07009. Tel (201)239-6100. *Continues National Bond Summary.*

LC HD251 .N36   ISSN 0027-9994
DD 332   US
                                 CCC
NATIONAL REAL ESTATE INVESTOR. See Real Estate.

LC HG4907 .N34
DD 332.63/22/0973   US
NATIONAL STOCK SUMMARY, THE. Added/Corp National Quotation Bureau (U.S.). (1983)-. English. Two times a year. National Quotation Bureau, 150 Commerce Road, Cedar Grove NJ 07009. Tel (201)239-6100. *Separated from National Monthly Stock Summary, 0275-8326.*

LC Z   ISSN 1079-0772
DD 016   US
●NELSON'S CATALOG OF INSTITUTIONAL RESEARCH REPORTS. [Nelson's cat. inst. res. rep.]. VFOAT Institutional Research Reports. Vol. 19, No. 10 (Dec. 1994)-. Periodical. English. Twelve times a year. $125.00. Nelson Publications, One Gateway Plaza, PO Box 591, Port Chester NY 10573. Tel (914)937-8400, (800)333-6357, FAX (914)937-8908. *Continues Nelson's Guide to Institutional Research, 1059-9290.*

LC HG4907 .N44   ISSN 0896-0143
DD 332.6/025/73   US
NELSON'S DIRECTORY OF INVESTMENT MANAGERS. See Industry and Production-Trade and Industrial Directories.

LC HG4907 .N43   ISSN 0896-0135
DD 332.6/2/02573   US
NELSON'S DIRECTORY OF INVESTMENT RESEARCH. See Industry and Production-Trade and Industrial Directories.

LC HG4907 .N46
DD 332.6/7254   US
●NELSON'S DIRECTORY OF PENSION FUND CONSULTANTS. [Nelson's directory pension fund consult.]. Added/Corp Nelson Publications (Firm). VFOAT Directory of Pension Fund Consultants; Pension Fund Consultants. (1995)-. Directory. English. One time a year. $359.75. Nelson Publications, One Gateway Plaza, PO Box 591, Port Chester NY 10573. Tel (914)937-8400, (800)333-6357, FAX (914)937-8908. *Continues Nelson's Guide to Pension Fund Consultants, 1053-2536.*

LC Z7164.F5 N37 HG4529   ISSN 1059-9290
DD 016.3326   US
                                 TITLE CHANGE
NELSON'S GUIDE TO INSTITUTIONAL RESEARCH. (NELSON'S GUIDE TO INSTITUTIONAL RESEARCH : U.S., INTERNATIONAL.). [Nelson's guide inst. res.]. VFOAT Guide to Institutional Research; Institutional Research. Vol. 17, No. 1 (Jan./Feb. 1992)-(1994). Periodical. English. Nelson Publications, One Gateway Plaza, PO Box 591, Port Chester NY 10573. Tel (914)937-8400, (800)333-6357, FAX (914)937-8908. *Continues Nelson's Global Research, 1044-0267. Continued by Nelson's Catalog of Institutional Research Reports, 1079-0772.*
   Desc: Reports all job changes among buy and sell side investment professionals, and lists all research reports written by analysts at over 200 research firms worldwide.

LC HG   ISSN 1049-5630
DD 332   US
                                 CEASED
NELSON'S GUIDE TO INVESTMENT CONSULTANTS. [Nelson's guide invest. consult.]. VFOAT Guide to Investment Consultants. (1990)-(199?). English. Nelson Publications, One Gateway Plaza, PO Box 591, Port Chester NY 10573. Tel (914)937-8400, (800)333-6357, FAX (914)937-8908. *Continues in part Nelson's Directory of Investment Managers, 0896-0143.*
   Desc: Edited for pension plan sponsors, consultants, and others needing information on 2,000 money management firms.

LC HG4907 .N46   ISSN 1053-2536
DD 332.6/7254   US
                                 TITLE CHANGE
NELSON'S GUIDE TO PENSION FUND CONSULTANTS. [Nelson's guide pension fund consult.]. Added/Corp Nelson Publications (Firm). VFOAT Guide to Ppension Fund Consultants; Pension Fund Consultants. (1991)-(199?). English. Nelson Publications, One Gateway Plaza, PO Box 591, Port Chester NY 10573. Tel (914)937-8400, (800)333-6357, FAX (914)937-8908. *Continued by Nelson's Directory of Pension Fund Consultants.*
   Desc: A detailed description of the 300+ professional firms providing investment consulting services to the sponsors of employee benefit funds, foundations and endowments.

LC HG65 .N45   ISSN 1065-2396
DD 332.1/029/473   US
                                 CEASED
NELSON'S TECHRESOURCE. [Nelson's techresources]. Added/Corp Nelson Publications (Firm). VFOAT Techresources; Tech Resources; Nelson's Tech Resources. (Winter 1993)-(1995). Periodical. English. Nelson Publications, One Gateway Plaza, PO Box 591, Port Chester NY 10573. Tel (914)937-8400, (800)333-6357, FAX (914)937-8908.

LC HC111   ISSN 1197-6292
DD 330.971   CN
                                 CEASED
NEW ECONOMIC TRENDS. [New econ. trends]. Added/Corp Midland Walwyn Capital. Research Dept. Midland Walwyn Capital. (198?)-(1993). Periodical. English. Midland Walwyn Capital, Suite 1600, 121 King Street West, Toronto Ontario M5H 3W6 Canada. *Absorbed by On the Margin (Toronto, Ont.), 1196-7005.*

LC HG450   ISSN 0743-3433
DD 332.6   US
NEW ISSUES ALERT. Vol. 1, No. 1 (Mar. 1984)-. Periodical. English. Twelve times a year. $49.00. Infodata Inc, 10076 Boca Entrada Boulevard, Boca Raton FL 33433-5897. Tel (407)483-2600.

LC HG4501 .N4   ISSN 0162-9050
DD 332.6   US
                                 CCC
NEW ISSUES (FORT LAUDERDALE, FLA.). (NEW ISSUES.). [New issues]. Added/Corp Institute for Econometric Research (Fort Lauderdale, Fla.). No. 1 (Sept. 1978)-. Periodical. English. Twelve times a year. $95.00. New Issues, 3471 North Federal Highway, Ft. Lauderdale FL 33306. Tel (800)327-6720, FAX (305)563-9003. ED Norman G. Fosback. Circ: 13,000.
   Desc: Contains a calendar of forthcoming new issue offerings, also analyses and recommendations, plus penny stock digest.

LC HG4651
DD 332.632   NZ
NEW ZEALAND STOCK EXCHANGE WEEKLY DIARY. (19??)-. English. One time a week. 270.00NZ$ Australia; 210.00NZ$ New Zealand; 290.00NZ$ the Americas and Asia; 310.00NZ$ other. New Zealand Stock Exchange, Caltex Tower, 286-292 Lambton Q, Wellington New Zealand. Tel 011 64 4 727599, FAX 011 64 4 731470, telex 3424. ED Roulla Matsis. Ad Acc. Circ: 250.

LC HG450
DD 332.6   US
NEWS, FACTS, ACTIONS. (1983)-. English. Six times a year. Free. National Futures Association, 200 West Madison Street, Suite 1600, Chicago IL 60606. Tel (312)781-1373, FAX (312)781-1467. ED Kate Rice. Circ: 4,500.

LC HD60.5.U5 N48   ISSN 1053-5470
DD 332   US
                                 TITLE CHANGE
NEWS FOR INVESTORS. [News investors]. Added/Corp Investor Responsibility Research Center. VFOAT IRRC News for Investors. Vol. 1 (1974)-(1995). Periodical. English. Investor Responsibility Research Center, 1350 Connecticut Avenue Northwest 700, Washington DC 20036. Tel (202)833-0700. ED Carolyn S. Mathiasen. Circ: 1,000 (ctrl). *Continued by Social Issues Reporter.*

LC HG   ISSN 1042-4326
DD 332   US
NEWSPAPER INVESTOR. [Newspap. investor]. No. 1 (Jan. 1989)-. Newsletter. English. Twelve times a year. $625.00. Paul Kagan Associates Inc., 126 Clock Tower Place, Carmel CA 93923-8734. Tel (408)624-1536, FAX (408)625-3225, telex ITT 4938124 PKA UI. available via fax.
   Desc: Views of the oldest media business - valuations of private and public newspapers and companies, analysis of newspaper industry economics and trends.

LC HC431 .N27
DD 332.6/7153/0954   II
NIF WEEKLY. VFOAT N.I.F. Weekly. Vol. 27, No. 1 (Apr. 13, 1969)-. English. One time a week. Rs3.00. Managing Editor of the National Investment and Finance, Post Box No 4007, C-25 Press Enclave Saket, New Delhi 110017 India. *Continues National Investment and Finance.*

LC HG4501
DD 332.6   NR
NIGERIA COMPANY HANDBOOK AND GUIDE TO OPERATING BUSINESS IN NIGERIA. Added/Corp Jikonzult Management Services. VFOAT NCH; Nigeria Company Handbook. (1988)-. English. Jikonzult Management Services Ltd, 13 Ogunda Street Office, Allen Avenue, Box 1949 Ikeja, Lagos State Nigeria. Tel 961481. *Continues ICON Nigeria Company Handbook and Guide to Operating Business in Nigeria, 0189-1693.*

LC HG4501   ISSN 0736-6256
DD 332.6   US
NO-LOAD FUND INVESTOR, THE. [No-load fund investor]. VFOAT No Load Fund Investor. VAT No Load Fund Investor. (19??)-. Periodical. English. Twelve times a year. $119.00. No-Load Fund Investor, PO Box 318, Irvington-on-Hudson NY 10533. Tel (914)693-7420, FAX (914)693-8067. ED Sheldon Jacobs.

LC HG450 ISSN 0194-0104
DD 332.6 US
NOLOAD FUND X. **Added/Corp** Dal Investment Co. **VAT** No Load Fund X. (1976)-. Periodical. English. Twelve times a year. $119.00. Noload Fund X, 235 Montgomery Street, Suite 662, San Francisco CA 94104. **Tel** (415)986-7979, FAX (415)986-1595. **ED** Janet Brown. **Bk Rev. Circ:** 10000.
Desc: Newsletter covering the entire Noload Mutual Fund industry. Provides performance records of all funds and identifies good buys. Includes industry news and market analyses.

LC HG450 ISSN 1237-1394
DD 332.6 FI
UDC 336.7
●**NORDBALT INVESTMENT REPORT.** (1994)-. Periodical. English. Twenty-three times a year. Lochlann Publishing, BioCity, Tykistokatu 6A 5 fl., FIN-20520 Turku Finland. **Tel** 011 358 21 2410447, FAX 011 358 21 2410449. **ED** Gerard O'Dwyer.

LC HG4551 ISSN 0710-5088
DD 332.64/4/0971 CN
NOTICE TO MEMBERS. FUTURES MEMORANDUM (TORONTO STOCK EXCHANGE). (NOTICE TO MEMBERS. FUTURES MEMORANDUM.). [Not. memb., Futures memo.]. **VAT** Futures Memorandum - Toronto Stock Exchange. Periodical. English. Irregular. Toronto Stock Exchange, The Exchange Tower, 2 First Canadian Place, Toronto Ontario M5X 1J2 Canada. **Tel** (416)947-4681.

LC HG4551 ISSN 0710-5096
DD 332.64/52/0971 CN
NOTICE TO MEMBERS. OPTIONS MEMORANDUM (TORONTO STOCK EXCHANGE). (NOTICE TO MEMBERS. OPTIONS MEMORANDUM.). [Not. memb., Options memo.]. **VAT** Options Memorandum - Toronto Stock Exchange. (19??)-. Periodical. English. Irregular. Toronto Stock Exchange, The Exchange Tower, 2 First Canadian Place, Toronto Ontario M5X 1J2 Canada. **Tel** (416)947-4681.

LC HG4551 ISSN 0710-507X
DD 332.64/2/71 CN
NOTICE TO MEMBERS - TORONTO STOCK EXCHANGE. (NOTICE TO MEMBERS / THE TORONTO STOCK EXCHANGE.). [Not. memb. - Tor. Stock Exch.]. **Added/Corp** Toronto Stock Exchange. (19??)-. Periodical. English. Irregular. 175.00Can$. Toronto Stock Exchange, The Exchange Tower, 2 First Canadian Place, Toronto Ontario M5X 1J2 Canada. **Tel** (416)947-4681.

LC HG4551 ISSN 0710-5746
DD 332.64/4/0971 CN
NOTICE TO MEMBERS - TRANS CANADA OPTIONS INC. (NOTICE TO MEMBERS.). [Not. memb. - Trans Can. Options Inc.]. Periodical. English. Trans Canada Options, 234 Bay Street, Toronto Ontario M5J 1R1 Canada.

LC HG4915 .N3
DD 332.6 US
TITLE CHANGE
NQB NATIONAL MONTHLY BOND SUMMARY, THE. **Added/Corp** National Quotation Bureau (U.S.). **VFOAT** National Quotation Bureau National Monthly Bond Summary. (June 1994)-(1994). Periodical. English. National Quotation Bureau, 150 Commerce Road, Cedar Grove NJ 07009. **Tel** (201)239-6100. ***Continues*** *National Monthly Bond Summary.* ***Continued by*** *National Quotation Bureau Monthly Bond Summary, 1080-3173.*

LC HG4915 .N34 ISSN 1080-319X
DD 332.63 US
TITLE CHANGE
NQB NATIONAL MONTHLY STOCK SUMMARY, THE. [NQB natl. mon. stock summ.]. **Added/Corp** National Quotation Bureau (U.S.). **VFOAT** National Quotation Bureau National Monthly Stock Summary. (1994)-(1994). English. National Quotation Bureau, 150 Commerce Road, Cedar Grove NJ 07009. **Tel** (201)239-6100. ***Continues*** *National Monthly Stock Summary, 0275-8326.* ***Continued by*** *National Quotation Bureau Monthly Stock Summary, 1080-3157.*

LC HG ISSN 1060-6629
DD 332 US
NYSE WEEKLY STOCK BUYS. [NYSE wkly. stock buys]. (Dec. 9, 1991)-. English. One time a week. Elton Stephens, PO Box 476, South Bend IN 46624-0476.

LC HG ISSN 0882-6323
DD 332 US
OBER INCOME LETTER. [Ober income lett.]. Vol. 3, No. 3-4 (March/April 1985)-. Periodical. English. Twelve times a year. $197.00. Securities Investigations Inc, PO Box 888, Mill Hill Road, Woodstock NY 12498. **Tel** (914)679-2300. **ED** Stuart A Ober and Richard A White. **Bk Rev. Circ:** 60,000. ***Continues*** *Oil Income Letter, 0740-8749.*
Desc: Newsletter specializes in real estate and oil and gas income programs. Issues contain newsworthy items, surveys, interviews, analyses and an extensive data bank.

LC hg4551 ISSN 0384-9465
DD 332.6/42/0971133 CN
OFFICIAL DAILY BULLETIN - VANCOUVER STOCK EXCHANGE. **Main/Corp** Vancouver Stock Exchange. (1???)-. Bulletin. English. Six times a week (312 per year). 750.75Can$ Canada; 824.25Can$ US; 1239.00Can$ other. Vancouver Stock Exchange, PO Box 10333, 609 Granville Street, Vancouver British Columbia V7Y 1H1 Canada. **Tel** (604)689-3334, FAX (604)688-6051. **Circ:** 2,000 (ctrl).
Desc: Containing a breakdown of trading in all issues including volume, value, high, low, close, price changes, closing market; advances and declines; VSE listing notices, dividends, index and options.

LC HG5850.K454 N335A
DD 332.6/42/0967625 KE
OFFICIAL YEAR BOOK. **Main/Corp** Nairobi Stock Exchange. (19??)-. English. 10/-. Nairobi Stock Exchange, PO Box 43633, Nairobi Kenya.

LC HG4501 ISSN 0954-0628
DD 332.6 UK
OFFSHORE INVESTMENT. [Offshore invest.]. **Added/Corp** Offshore Institute. No. 1 (1986)-. Periodical. English. Twelve times a year. $359.36. European Media Sales, 62 Brompton Road, London SW3 1BW United Kingdom. **Tel** 011 44 171 2250550, FAX 011 44 171 5841093.

LC HD9561 .O49 ISSN 0744-5881
DD 332.6/722 US
CCC
OIL & GAS INVESTOR. **See** Petroleum and Natural Gas.

LC HG3881 .J337a
DD 332.042 JA
OKURASHO KOKUSAI KINYUKYOKU NEMPO. **Main/Corp** Japan. Okurasho. Kokusai Kinyukyoku. No. 1 (1977)-. Japanese. ¥8000. Nihon Shobo Kaikan, 18 Shiba Nishikubo Akefunecho Minato-ku, Tokyo Japan.

LC HG ISSN 1196-7005
DD 332.63 CN
ON THE MARGIN TORONTO. (ON THE MARGIN.). [On margin Tor.]. (199?)-. Periodical. English. Irregular. Midland Walwyn Capital, Suite 1600, 121 King Street West, Toronto Ontario M5H 3W6 Canada. ***Absorbed*** *Bonds & Bills, 1197-6535; New Economic Trends, 1197-6292; Market Monitor (Toronto), 1186-0928; Economic Advisor (Toronto), 1186-1053.*

LC HG4551
DD 332.6322 CN
OPEN INTEREST/ THE TORONTO STOCK EXCHANGE. **Added/Corp** Toronto Stock Exchange. Vol. 1, Issue 1 (Winter 1992)-. English. Four times a year. Toronto Stock Exchange, The Exchange Tower, 2 First Canadian Place, Toronto Ontario M5X 1J2 Canada. **Tel** (416)947-4681. ***Continues*** *Open Interest, 0707-0926.*

LC HG4501
DD 332.6 US
OPTION ADVISOR. (1981)-. Newsletter. English. Irregular. $99.00. Investment Research Institute, 1259 Kemper Meadow Drive, Ste 100, Cincinnati OH 45240. **Tel** (800)872-6600, FAX (513)589-3810. **ED** Bernard Schaeffer.
Desc: An investment newsletter specializing in recommendations in the options market.

LC HG4551 ISSN 0226-9325
DD 332.64/2/09713 CN
OSC BULLETIN. [OSC bull.]. **VAT** Ontario Securities Commission Bulletin. Vol. 1 (Jan. 9, 1981)-. Bulletin. English. One time a week. prices varies. Micromedia Limited, 20 Victoria Street, Toronto Ontario M5C 2N8 Canada. **Tel** (416)362-5211, (800)387-2689, FAX (416)362-6161, telex 06524668. **Circ:** 1,000. available in microform. ***Formed by the union of*** *Ontario Securities Commission. Weekly Summary, 0030-3100* ***and*** *Bulletin of the Ontario Securities Commission. Ontario Securities Commission, 0030-3097.*
Desc: Information related to the administration of the Securities Act of Ontario and the Commodities Futures Act of Ontario by the Ontario Securities Commission.

LC HG4916 .O2
DD 332.6 US
TITLE CHANGE
OTC CHART MANUAL. [Over the counter chart manual]. **VFOAT** O-T-C Chart Manual. **VAT** Over the Counter Chart Manual. (196?)-(May 1994). Periodical. English. Standard & Poor's Corporation, (A Division of McGraw-Hill, Inc.), 25 Broadway, New York NY 10004. **Tel** (212)208-8775, (800)221-5277. ***Continues*** *OTC Traders Graphic.* ***Merged with*** *Trendline Current Market Perspectives.*
Desc: Concentrates on more than 800 stocks traded over the counter that have attracted heavy investor interest over the years. Designed investors follow price and volume action on individual OTC stocks over a period of up to four years.

LC HG ISSN 0030-7246
DD 332 US
OUTLOOK (NEW YORK, N.Y. 1937), THE. (THE OUTLOOK.). [Outlook]. **Added/Corp** Standard and Poor's Corporation. (1937)-. Periodical. English. One time a week (48 issues). $298.00. Standard & Poor's Corporation, (A Division of McGraw-Hill, Inc.), 25 Broadway, New York NY 10004. **Tel** (212)208-8775, (800)221-5277. Index Available, published separately, free-automatically sent. ***Absorbed*** *Standard and Poor Corporation. Investment Advisory Survey.*
Desc: Keeps private investors, securities dealers, investment counselors and money managers abreast of market developments and helps spot suitable securities investments.

LC HG ISSN 0891-463X
DD 332 US
OUTSTANDING INVESTOR DIGEST. [Outst. investor dig.]. (1986)-. Periodical. English. Six times a year. $595.00 (libraries), $495.00 (other). Outstanding Investor, 14 East Fourth Street, Suite 501, New York NY 10012. **Tel** (212) 777-3330, FAX (212) 777-4108. **ED** Henry J. Emerson. ctrl circ.

LC HG4651
DD 332.632 US
OVER-THE-COUNTER AND REGIONAL EXCHANGE STOCK REPORTS. **Main/Corp** Standard and Poor's Corporation. **VFOAT** Stock Reports; Over-the-Counter and Regional Exchanges. (19??)-. English. One time a week. $999.00. Standard & Poor's Corporation, (A Division of McGraw-Hill, Inc.), 25 Broadway, New York NY 10004. **Tel** (212)208-8775, (800)221-5277.

LC HG4651
DD 332.632 US
OVERPRICED STOCK SERVICE. (19??)-. Newsletter. English. Twelve times a year. $495.00. Murenove Inc, PO Box 308, Half Moon Bay CA 94019. **Tel** (415)726-8495. **ED** Michael Murphy. Index available. cum. index. ctrl circ.
Desc: Independent advice for short selling.

LC HG4502 .O83
DD 332.6 UK
OVERSEAS DIRECT INVESTMENT. **Added/Corp** Great Britain. Central Statistical Office. (1992)-. English. Her Majesty's Stationary Office Books - HMSO, PO Box 276, London SW8 5DT United Kingdom. **Tel** 011 44 171 8730011, FAX 011 44 171 8738463. ***Continues*** *Overseas Transactions.*

LC [HG4905 .P38a] ISSN 0164-176X
DD 332.6/327 US
P.I.P.E.R., PENSIONS & INVESTMENT'S PERFORMANCE EVALUATION REPORT. **Main/Corp** Pensions & Investments. **Added/Corp** Pensions & Investments. Pensions & Investments' Performance Evaluation Report. **VFOAT** Pensions & Investment's Performance Evaluation Report. **VAT** PIPER, Pensions and Investments' Performance Evaluation Report. (19??)-. English. Four times a year. $879.00. PIPER, 85 Old Kings Highway North, Darien CT 06820. **Tel** (203)656-5954.

LC HG4651 ISSN 0743-8508
DD 332.632 US
PENNY MINING STOCK REPORT. [Penny min. stock rep.]. Periodical. English. Twelve times a year. $139.00. Target Inc / California, 6612 Owens Drive, Pleasanton CA 94566-0625. **Tel** (510)463-2200.

LC HG4961 .P46 ISSN 0090-9327
DD 332.6/322 US
PENNY STOCK HANDBOOK. (1971)-. English. $8.00 single issue. Penny Press, PO Box 703, Palo Alto CA 94302.

LC HG ISSN 1041-6544
DD 332 US
PENNY STOCK INSIGHT. [Penny stock insight]. Vol. 1, Issue 1 (1988)-. Periodical. English. Twelve times a year. $96.00 (includes Telephone Hotline Service). Hellinger Lead Center Inc, 301 Oxford Valley Road/Suite 103B, Yardley PA 19067.

LC HG4001 ISSN 1063-2476
DD 658 US
CCC
PENSION BENEFITS. [Pension benefits]. Vol. 1, No. 1 (May 1992)-. Periodical. English. Twelve times a year. $170.00. Panel Publishers, A Division of Aspen Publishers Inc., 7201 McKinney Circle, PO Box 990, Frederick MD 21705-9727. **Tel** (800)638-8437. **(Subscription address:** Aspen Publishers Inc., PO Box 990, Frederick MD 21701. **Tel** (800)901-9074, (301)698-7100.) **ED** Bruce G. Carveth.
Desc: Focuses on the trends and issues that will affect the future of pensions.

Business and Economics —Investments

LC HG450 **ISSN** 0140-6647
DD 332.6 UK
PENSION FUNDS AND THEIR ADVISERS. (1978)-. Periodical. English. One time a year. $295.00. Money Market Directories Inc., 320 East Main Street, PO Box 1608, Charlottesville VA 22902. **Tel** (800)446-2810, (804)977-1450. **ED** Alan Philipp. Index available. **Bk Rev**. **Ad Acc**. **Circ**: 3,500. available on labels (and floppy disks).
Desc: Covering pension funds and their advisors.

LC HG4001 **ISSN** 1041-4371
DD 658 US
PENSION MANAGEMENT COMPANY'S IRA & KEOGH COMPLIANCE UPDATE. [Pension Manage. Co. IRA Keogh compliance update]. **Added/Corp** Pension Management Company. **VFOAT** IRA & Keogh Compliance Update; Compliance Update; PMC Compliance Update. (19??)-. Periodical. English. Twelve times a year. $295.00. Pension Management Company, PO Box 431, King of Prussia PA 19406. **Tel** (215)251-0361.

LC HG450 **DD** 332.6 US
●**PENSION PLAN ADMINISTRATOR.** (1994)-. English. Twelve times a year. $170.00. Panel Publishers, A Division of Aspen Publishers Inc., 7201 McKinney Circle, PO Box 990, Frederick MD 21705-9727. **Tel** (800)638-8437. **(Subscription address:** Aspen Publishers Inc., PO Box 990, Frederick MD 21701. **Tel** (800)901-9074, (301)698-7100.**)** **ED** Lisa A. Germano, CPA, JD.
Desc: Information for pension plan administrators.

LC HG450 **ISSN** 0275-0333
DD 332.6 US
PENSIONS & INVESTMENT AGE. EDITORIAL INDEX. See Business and Economics-Abstracting, Bibliographies and Statistics.

LC HG **ISSN** 1050-4974
DD 332 US
 CCC
PENSIONS & INVESTMENTS (1990). (PENSIONS & INVESTMENTS.). [Pensions investm.]. **Added/Corp** Crain Communications, Inc. **VFOAT** Pensions and Investments. Vol. 18, No. 1 (Jan. 8, 1990)-. Periodical. English. Twenty-six times a year. $205.00. Crain Communications Inc., 1400 Woodbridge, Detroit MI 48207-3187. **Tel** (313)446-6000, (800)992-9970. available on microfilm and microfiche from University Microfilms International (UMI); available on microfiche from University Microfilms International (UMI); available on an online database (file 16/Full-Text) from DIALOG. **Continues** Pensions & Investment Age, 0273-5466.
Ind/Abst Acad. Search; Bus. Index (1990-); Bus. Period. Index; Bus. Source Plus; Bus. Source; EP Collect.; F&S Index Plus Text, Int. [Full Txt.] [Select. Cov.]; Gen. BusinessFile (1990-); Gen. Period. Index (1990-); Homework Help.; INFO-SOUTH Abstr.; Ins. Period. Index (19??-199?); Mag. Search; MasterFile FullTEXT 1000; MasterFile FullTEXT 350; MasterFile FullTEXT 650; MasterFile FullTEXT (July 1993-); OCLC; PROMT [Full Txt.]; Stat. Ref. Index; Telebase; Trade Ind. Index; UMI ABI/Inform--Bus. Period. Ondisc (Nov. 1987-) [Full Txt.]; Wilson Bus. Abstr.

LC K **ISSN** 0959-8014
DD 342.04152 UK
PENSIONS LAW REPORTS. See Law-Labor Laws and Legislation.

LC HG **ISSN** 0738-4017
DD 332 US
PERSONAL INVESTING (WOODLAND HILLS, CALIF.). (PERSONAL INVESTING.). [Pers. invest.]. Vol. 1, No. 1 (July 1983)-. Periodical. English. Twelve times a year. Business and Financial Data Search Institute, PO Box 8039, Calabasas CA 91302-8039.

LC HG450 **DD** 332.6 AT
PERSONAL INVESTMENT. (Aug. 1983)-. Periodical. English. Twelve times a year. 83.87Aus$. Business Review Weekly, 469 La Trobe Street, Melbourne Victoria 3000 Australia. **Tel** 011 61 3 6033888, FAX 011 61 3 6704328. Documents available from UMI Article Clearinghouse. **Continues** Australian Stock Exchange Journal, 0045-0901; **Absorbed** Property Investor.
Ind/Abst ABI/INFORM Glob. Ed.; Energy Res. Abstr. (Aug. 1983-).

LC R **ISSN** 1069-269X
DD 610 US
●**PERSONAL REPORT. PRACTICE DEVELOPMENT AND WEALTH ACCUMULATION FOR THE PERIODONTIST, THE. See** Dentistry.

LC HG4501 **DD** 332.6 US
PERSPECTIVE ON BOND INSURANCE. Added/Corp Moody's Investors Service. **VFOAT** Moody's Public Finance Perspective on Bond Insurance. (1991)-. Periodical. English. One time a week. Moody's Investors Service, 99 Church Street, New York NY 10007. **Tel** (212)553-0547, (212)553-0435, FAX (212)553-4700.

LC HG4501 **DD** 332.6 US
PERSPECTIVE ON HEALTH CARE FINANCE. Added/Corp Moody's Investors Service. Public Finance Dept. **VFOAT** Moody's Public Finance Perspective on Health Care Finance. (Mar. 16, 1992)-. Periodical. English. One time a week. Moody's Investors Service, 99 Church Street, New York NY 10007. **Tel** (212)553-0547, (212)553-0435, FAX (212)553-4700.

LC HG450 **DD** 332.6 US
PERSPECTIVES ON MUTUAL FUND ACTIVITY. English. $30.00. Investment Company Institute, 1401 H Street Northwest, Washington DC 20005. **Tel** (202)326-5800, (202)326-5972.

LC HG450 **ISSN** 0196-9323
DD 332.6 US
 CCC
PETER DAG INVESTMENT LETTER, THE. (19??)-. Periodical. English. Irregular (29 issues per year). $250.00. Peter Dag Investment Letter, 65 Lake Front Drive, Akron OH 44319. **Tel** (216)644-2782. **ED** George Dagnino. **Bk Rev**. **Circ**: 5,000 (ctrl).
Desc: Forecasts inflation, interest rates, business conditions, trends of stock market, bond prices, dollar and gold. Formulates investment strategy with specific recommendations.

LC HG450 **DD** 332.6 US
PLAN SPONSOR. (19??)-. Trade Publication. English. Ten times a year. $150.00 US; $200.00 other. Asset International, 125 Greenwich Avenue, Greenwich CT 06830. **Tel** (203)629-5014, FAX (203)629-5024. **ED** Eric Laursen. **Ad Acc**, **Adv Mgr:** Dan Dent. **Continues** Asset International, 1060-4642.
Desc: Magazine for users of investment services. Covers issues, events, and other developments of the pension plan sponsor community.

LC HG450 **DD** 332.6 US
●**POCKET CHANGE INVESTOR.** (1995)-. English. Four times a year. $12.95. Good Advice Press, PO Box 78, Elizaville NY 12523. **Tel** (914)758-1400. **Bk Rev**, (Qty: 12). **Continues** Bankers Secret Bulletin.

LC JQ1758.A1 P64 **ISSN** 0897-8530
DD 320.9/048 US
... POLITICAL RISK YEARBOOK. MIDDLE EAST & NORTH AFRICA, THE. [Polit. risk yearb. Middle East North Afr.]. **Added/Corp** Frost & Sullivan. **VFOAT** Middle East & North Africa; Middle East and North Africa. (1987)-. English. One time a year. $250.00 (per volume), $1000.00 (full set). Political Risk Services, 6320 Fly Road, Suite 102, PO Box 248, East Syracuse NY 13057-0248. **Tel** (315)431-0511, FAX (315)431-0200. **ED** William D. Coplin and Michael K. O'Leary. available on CD-ROM.
Desc: Designed especially for research and archival purposes. Brings together pertinent economics, social, and political information of particular interest to those researching the answers to complex questions.

LC JL1416 .P65 **ISSN** 0897-8557
DD 970.053/7 320 US
... POLITICAL RISK YEARBOOK. NORTH & CENTRAL AMERICA, THE. [Polit. risk yearb. North Cent. Am.]. **Added/Corp** Frost & Sullivan. **VFOAT** Political Risk Yearbook. North and Central America; North & Central America; North and Central America. (1987)-. English. One time a year. $250.00 (per volume), $1000.00 (full set). Political Risk Services, 6320 Fly Road, Suite 102, PO Box 248, East Syracuse NY 13057-0248. **Tel** (315)431-0511, FAX (315)431-0200. **ED** William D. Coplin and Michael K. O'Leary. available on CD-ROM.
Desc: Designed especially for research and archival purposes. Brings together pertinent economic, social, and political information of particular interest to those researching the answers to complex questions.

LC JL1866 .P65 **ISSN** 0897-8549
DD 980/.037 US
... POLITICAL RISK YEARBOOK. SOUTH AMERICA, THE. [Polit. risk yearb. South Am.]. **Added/Corp** Frost & Sullivan. **VFOAT** South America. (1987)-. English. One time a year. $250.00 (per volume), $1000.00 (full set). Political Risk Services, 6320 Fly Road, Suite 102, PO Box 248, East Syracuse NY 13057-0248. **Tel** (315)431-0511, FAX (315)431-0200. **ED** William D. Coplin and Michael K. O'Leary. available on CD-ROM.
Desc: Designed especially for research and archival purposes. Brings together pertinent economic, social, and political information of particular interest to those researching the answers to complex questions.

LC JQ21.A1 P64 **ISSN** 0897-8565
DD 332.6 US
POLITICAL RISK YEARBOOK. VOL. 5, ASIA & THE PACIFIC. Added/Corp Political Risk Services (IBC USA (Publications) Inc.). **VFOAT** Asia & the Pacific; Asia and the Pacific. (1991)-. English. One time a year. $250.00 (per volume), $1000.00 (full set). Political Risk Services, 6320 Fly Road, Suite 102, PO Box 248, East Syracuse NY 13057-0248. **Tel** (315)431-0511, FAX (315)431-0200. **Continues** Political Risk Yearbook. Asia & The Pacific, 0897-8565.
Desc: Designed especially for research and archival purposes. Brings together pertinent economic, social, and political information of particular interest to those researching the answers to complex questions.

LC JN12 .P645 **ISSN** 1053-878X
DD 940 US
TITLE CHANGE
POLITICAL RISK YEARBOOK. VOL. 7, EUROPE. OUTSIDE THE EUROPEAN COMMUNITY. [Polit. risk yearb, Vol. 7 Eur., Outs. Eur. Community]. **Added/Corp** Political Risk Services (IBC USA (Publications) Inc.). **VFOAT** Europe, Outside the European Community; Outside the European Community. (1991)-(1994). English. Political Risk Services, 6320 Fly Road, Suite 102, PO Box 248, East Syracuse NY 13057-0248. **Tel** (315)431-0511, FAX (315)431-0200. **Continues** Political Risk Yearbook. Eastern Europe, 0897-8514. **Continued by** Political Risk Yearbook. Vol. 7, Europe. Outside the European Union, 1080-0182.

LC D900 **ISSN** 1080-0182
DD 940 US
●**POLITICAL RISK YEARBOOK. VOL. 7, EUROPE. OUTSIDE THE EUROPEAN UNION.** [Polit. risk yearb., Vol. 7 Eur., Outs. Eur. Union]. **Added/Corp** Political Risk Services (IBC USA (Publications) Inc.). **VFOAT** Europe, Outside the European Union; Outside the European Union. (1995)-. English. Political Risk Services, 6320 Fly Road, Suite 102, PO Box 248, East Syracuse NY 13057-0248. **Tel** (315)431-0511, FAX (315)431-0200. **Continues** Political Risk Yearbook. Vol. 7, Europe. Outside the European Community, 1053-878X.

LC HG4651 **ISSN** 0822-6970
DD 332.63/22/0971 CN
POLYMETRIC REPORT (T.S.E. ED.). (THE POLYMETRIC REPORT.). [Polymetric rep.]. **Added/Corp** Canadian Polymetric Analysis (Firm). (1981)-. Periodical. English. Twelve times a year. 239.36Can$. Polymetric Report, Box 658 Don Mills, Toronto Ontario M3C 2T6 Canada. **ED** Picton Davies. **Circ**: 2,000. available on an online database. **Continues** Polymetric Report. Canadian Stocks, 0229-222X.
Desc: Analysis of long-term and intermediate-term outlook for stock market as a whole and for 41 industry-groups. Also detailed monthly analysis, evaluation and ranking of 263 TSE-listed common stocks in each issue.

LC HG450 **DD** 332.6 US
PORTFOLIO LETTER. (19??)-. Newsletter. English. One time a week. $1395.00 (one-year), $2495.00 (two-year). Institutional Investor Inc., 488 Madison Avenue, New York NY 10022. **Tel** (212)303-3234, (212)303-3233, FAX (212)303-3353.
Desc: Covers large institutional investors and explains what they plan to buy, at what prices and why. Includes summary of investment recommendations from key analysts.

LC HG450 **DD** 332.6 US
PPG SHAREHOLDER NEWS. Added/Corp PPG Industries. (19??)-. Periodical. English. Four times a year. PPG Industries Inc., One Gateway Center, Pittsburgh PA 15222. **Tel** (412)434-3131.

LC HG65 .G83 **ISSN** 0884-1616
DD 332.66 US
PRATT'S GUIDE TO VENTURE CAPITAL SOURCES. [Pratt's guide to venture cap. sources]. **Added/Corp** Venture Economics, Inc. **VFOAT** Guide to Venture Capital Sources. 8th Ed. (1984)-. English. One time a year. $249.00. SDC Publishers, 40 West 57th Street, New York NY 10019. **Tel** (212)765-5311, FAX (212)765-6123. **(Subscription address:** Oryx Press, 4041 North Central Indian School Road, Phoenix AZ 85012. **Tel** (800)279-6799, (602)265-2651 (outside US and Canada).**) Continues** Guide to Venture Capital Sources, 0749-6893.
Desc: Detailed profiles of 800 active US and Canadian venture capital firms supply the name, address, telephone and FAX number of home and branch offices.

LC HG4651 **ISSN** 1184-7409
DD 332.63 CN
PREFERRED SHARE QUARTERLY. (PREFERRED SHARE QUARTERLY / BURNS FRY LIMITED.). [Prefer. share q.]. **Added/Corp** Burns Fry Limited. (June 1990)-. Periodical. English. Twelve times a year. Limited free distribution. Burns Fry Ltd., PO Box

150, 1st Canadian Place, Toronto Ontario M5X 1H3 Canada. **Tel** (416)365-4000. ***Continues*** *Preferred Share Monthly., 0843-0136.*

LC HG4651 **ISSN** 0829-383X
DD 332.63/22/0971 CN

PREFERRED SHARES & WARRANTS. [Prefer. shares warrants.]. **Added/Corp** Financial Post Corporation Service Group. (1985)-. English. One time a year. 35.97Can$. Financial Post Company Ltd., 333 King Street East, Toronto Ontario M5A 4N2, Canada. **Tel** (416)350-6500, FAX (416)350-6601. **Ad Acc.**
Desc: A volume detailing all preferred share and warrant issues in Canada.

LC HG4501 .P74 **ISSN** 0735-4819
DD 332.63/225/0973 US

PREFERRED STOCK HANDBOOK. (19??)-. English. Shearson/American Express Inc, Two World Trade Center, New York NY 10048.

LC HG4501 .P75 **ISSN** 0748-9102
DD 332.63/222/0973 US

PRICE MOMENTUM CHARTS AND REPORT / QUANTITATIVE ANALYSIS SERVICE. English. Quantitative Analysis Service Inc, 70 Pine Street, New York NY 10270.

LC HG5151 .C35a **ISSN** 0823-065X
DD 332.6/72/0971 CN

PRIVATE AND PUBLIC INVESTMENT IN CANADA. INTENTIONS. (PRIVATE AND PUBLIC INVESTMENT IN CANADA. INTENTIONS = INVESTISSEMENTS PRIVES ET PUBLICS AU CANADA. PERSPECTIVE.). [Priv. public investm. Can., Intent.]. **Added/Corp** Statistics Canada. Science, Technology and Capital Stock Division. Statistics Canada. Construction Division. Statistics Canada. Investment and Capital Stock Division. **VFOAT** Investissements Prives et Publics au Canada. Perspective. (1984)-. English (French). One time a year. 28.01Can$. Statistics Canada Publications Sales and Services, R.H. Coats Building 6th Floor, Ottawa Ontario K1A 0T6 Canada. **Tel** (613)951-5078, (800)267-6677, FAX (613)951-1584, telex 053-3585. ***Continues*** *Statistics Canada. Construction Division. Private and Public Investment in Canada. Outlook, 0318-2274.*

LC HF5601 **ISSN** 0823-0668
DD 338.4/367/0971 CN

PRIVATE AND PUBLIC INVESTMENT IN CANADA, REVISED INTENTIONS. [Priv. public invest. Can., Revis. intent.]. **Added/Corp** Statistique Canada. Division de la Construction. Statistique Canada. Division des Sciences, de la Technologie et du Stock de Capital. **VFOAT** Investissements Prives et Publics au Canada, Perspective Revisee. (1984)-. French (English). One time a year. 51.00Can$. Statistics Canada Publications Sales and Services, R.H. Coats Building 6th Floor, Ottawa Ontario K1A 0T6 Canada. **Tel** (613)951-5078, (800)267-6677, FAX (613)951-1584, telex 053-3585. ***Continues*** *Statistique Canada. Division de la Construction. Private and Public Investment in Canada: Mid-Year Review.*

LC HG450
DD 332.6 US

PRIVATE ASSET MANAGEMENT. Newsletter. English. Twenty-six times a year. $1495.00 (one-year), $2695.00 (two-year). Institutional Investor Inc., 488 Madison Avenue, New York NY 10022. **Tel** (212)303-3234, (212)303-3233, FAX (212)303-3353.

LC HE **ISSN** 1068-4514
DD 384 US

●**PRIVATE CABLE INVESTOR. See** Communications-Television and Cable.

LC HG **ISSN** 1057-526X
DD 332 US

PRIVATE EQUITY ANALYST, THE. [Priv. equity anal.]. Vol. 1, Issue 1 (July 1991)-. Periodical. English. Twelve times a year. $295.00. Asset Alternatives Inc., 180 Linden Street, Suite 3, Wellesley MA 02181. **Tel** (617)431-7353. **ED** Steven P. Galante. Index available. **Ad Acc, Adv Mgr:** Leanne Cowley. **Circ:** 1,250.
Desc: News, analysis, and data on private equity fund-raising, institutional investment in private equity, current topics such as terms and conditions of limited partnerships and secondary market. Private equity includes venture capital, lbo, mezzanine and turnaround investing.

LC HG450
DD 332.6 US

PRIVATE INVESTMENTS ABROAD. PROBLEMS AND SOLUTIONS IN INTERNATIONAL BUSINESS. (1990)-. Periodical. English. One time a year. Matthew Bender & Company Inc., 1275 Broadway, Albany NY 12204. **Tel** (800)833-9844, (518)487-3000. ***Continues*** *Symposium on Private Investments Abroad. Private Investors Abroad.*

LC HG450
DD 332.6 US

PRIVATE INVESTMENTS AND INTERNATIONAL TRANSACTIONS IN ASIAN AND SOUTH PACIFIC COUNTRIES. Main/Conf Symposium on Private Investments and International Transactions in Asian and South Pacific Countries. **VFOAT** Private Investors in Asia. English. One time a year. Matthew Bender & Company Inc., 1275 Broadway, Albany NY 12204. **Tel** (800)833-9844, (518)487-3000.

LC HG450
DD 332.6 US

PRIVATE PLACEMENT LETTER. (19??)-. Periodical. English. One time a week (51 issues). $995.00. Investment Dealers Digest Inc., Two World Trade Center, 18th Floor, New York NY 10048. **Tel** (212)227-1200, FAX (212)432-1039.

LC HG450
DD 332.6 US

PROCEEDINGS - SEMINAR ON THE ANALYSIS OF SECURITY PRICES. Main/Conf Seminar on the Analysis of Security Prices. **Added/Corp** Chicago. University. Center for Research in Security Prices. Merrill Lynch, Pierce, Fenner & Smith, Inc. (19??)-. Proceedings. English. Two times a year (May & Nov.). $100.00. University of Chicago Graduate School of Business, 1101 East 58th Street, Chicago IL 60637. **Tel** (312)702-7277, FAX (312)702-0458. **ED** Toni Mason. ctrl circ.
Desc: Dissemination of new work of importance in the field of investments.

LC HG450
DD 332.6 US

PRODUCER PRICE INDEXES / U.S. DEPARTMENT OF LABOR, BUREAU OF LABOR STATISTICS. Added/Corp United States. Bureau of Labor Statistics. **VFOAT** News. Producer Price Indexes. (Jan. 1978)-. Government Publication. English. Twelve times a year. $34.00 US; $42.50 other. US Department of Labor, 200 Constitution Avenue NW, Washington DC 20210. **Tel** (202)219-7316, FAX (202)219-7312. **(Subscription address:** Superintendent of Documents, US Government Printing Office, Washington DC 20402.) Documents available from Documents on Demand. ***Continues*** *Wholesale Price Index.*
Desc: Comprehensive report on price movements at the primary market level, arranged by stage of processing and by commodity.
Ind/Abst Am. Stat. Index.

LC HG4502 .I611 **ISSN** 0958-2541
DD 332.6 UK

PROFESSIONAL INVESTOR. (THE PROFESSIONAL INVESTOR : THE JOURNAL OF THE SOCIETY OF INVESTMENT ANALYSTS.). **Added/Corp** Society of Investment Analysts (Great Britain). Vol. 1, No. 1 (Oct. 1989)-. Periodical. English. Ten times a year. $333.69. Corporate Finance Publishers, 67 71 Goswell Road, London EC1V 7EN United Kingdom. **Tel** 011 44 171 4904777. **(Subscription address:** Stonehart Subscription Services, Hainault Road Little Heath, Bromford RM6 5NP United Kingdom. **Tel** 011 44 181 5977335.) ***Continues*** *Investment Analyst.*

LC HG **ISSN** 0889-0897
DD 332 US

PROFESSIONAL INVESTOR, THE. [Prof. investor]. (19??)-. Periodical. English. Twenty-four times a year. $399.00. Institute for Econometric Research, 2200 SW 10th Street, Deerfield Beach FL 33442. **Tel** (305)421-1000.

LC HG450
DD 332.6 US

PROFITABILITY REPORT. (19??)-. English. Irregular. $200.00. Securities Industry Association, 120 Broadway/35th Floor, New York NY 10271. **Tel** (212)608-1500, FAX (212)608-1604.
Desc: Through this service, participating firms receive quarterly information on how their profitability compares with other firms. Includes information on Pre-Tax Return on Equity, Profit Margin on Revenues, Pre-Tax Profit, Gross Revenues and Equity Capital. Complete confidentiality is preserved.

LC HG4501 .P77
DD 332.6/78/05 US

PROFITABLE INVESTING. (199?)-. Periodical. English. Twelve times a year. $99.95. Phillips Publishing Inc., 7811 Montrose Road, Potomac MD 20854. **Tel** (800)777-5005, (301)340-2100. ***Continues*** *Richard E. Band's Profitable Investing, 1048-3667.*

LC HG450 **ISSN** 0268-8867
DD 332.6 UK
CCC
CODEN PRAPET

PROJECT APPRAISAL. Vol. 1 (1986)-. Periodical. English. Four times a year. $164.00. Beech Tree Publishing, 10 Waterford Close, Guildford Surrey GU1 2EP United Kingdom. **Tel** 011 44 1483 67497, FAX 011 44 1483 67497. **(Subscription address:** World-Wide Subscription Services, Gibbs Reed Farm, Pashley Road, Ticehurst TN5 7HE United Kingdom. **Tel** 011 44 1580 200657.) Documents available from Documents on Demand.
Ind/Abst AgBiotech News Inf.; Asia.-Pac. Econ. Lit.; Curr. Cit.; Environ. Abstr.; For. Abstr.; Geogr. Abstr. Human Geogr.; Int. Dev. Abstr.; Irr. Drain. Abstr.; Leis., Rec., Tour. Abstr.; Rural Dev. Abstr.; Soc. Plann. Policy Dev. Abstr.; World Agric. Econ. Rural Sociol. Abstr.

LC HG450
DD 332.6 AT
TITLE CHANGE

PROPERTY INVESTOR. (19??)-(19??). English. Business Review Weekly, 469 La Trobe Street, Melbourne Victoria 3000 Australia. **Tel** 011 61 3 6033888, FAX 011 61 3 6704328. ***Merged into*** *Personal Investment.*

LC HG450 **ISSN** 0743-0809
DD 332.6 US

PRUDENT SPECULATOR, THE. (19??)-. Periodical. English. Twelve times a year. $175.00. Al Frank Asset Management Inc., PO Box 1767, Santa Monica CA 90406. **Tel** (310)507-2410, FAX (310)587-2407. **ED** Al Frank. **Circ:** 1,500.
Desc: Gives current recommendations; fundamental stock analysis technical analysis for market timing, being defensive in overvalued markets and aggressive in undervalued markets.

LC HG4576 .L662
DD 332.6 UK

QUALITY OF MARKETS MONTHLY FACT SHEET. Added/Corp International Stock Exchange. **VFOAT** Monthly Fact Sheet. (1990)-. Periodical. English. Twelve times a year. £48.00 Europe; £53.00 other. London Stock Exchange, Publications Marketing, London EC2N 1HP United Kingdom. **Tel** 011 44 171 7971000. ***Continues*** *International Stock Exchange Fact Sheet.*

LC HG450
DD 332.6 US
CEASED

R.H.M. CONVERTIBLE SURVEY, THE. Vol. 1 (1958)-(1993). Periodical. English. RHM Survey, 172 Forest Avenue, Glen Cove NY 11542. **Tel** (516)759-2904. **ED** Sidney Fried. Index available. cum. index.
Desc: Recommends convertible bonds and preferred stocks for purchase, describes applicable strategies, and gives complete statistical information with all pertinent changes indicated, updated weekly.

LC HG4651 **ISSN** 0196-6901
DD 332.632 US
CEASED

R.H.M. SURVEY OF WARRANTS, OPTIONS & LOW-PRICE STOCKS, THE. Main/Corp R.H.M. Associates, Inc. **VFOAT** Survey of Warrants, Options & Low-Price Stocks. **VAT** The R.H.M. Survey of Warrants, Options and Low Price Stocks. Vol. 24, No. 16- (April 25, 1975)-(Sept. 1993). Periodical. English. RHM Survey, 172 Forest Avenue, Glen Cove NY 11542. **Tel** (516)759-2904. **ED** Sidney Fried. Index available. cum. index. ***Continues*** *R.H.M. Associates, Inc. R.H.M. Warrant and Stock Survey plus Stocks under 10.*

LC HG4501 **ISSN** 0710-2674
DD 332.6/2/0971 CN

RAMA ANNUAL. (RAMA ANNUAL : THE REVENUE AND MARKET ANALYSIS.). [RAMA annu.]. **VFOAT** Revenue and Market Analysis. **VAT** Revenue and Market Analysis Annual. English. One time a year. Toronto Stock Exchange, The Exchange Tower, 2 First Canadian Place, Toronto Ontario M5X 1J2 Canada. **Tel** (416)947-4681.

LC HG **ISSN** 0887-7408
DD 332 US

RATE%GRAM. Added/Corp Bradshaw Group, Ltd. (La Costa, Calif.). **VFOAT** Rate % Gram; Rate Percent Gram; Rategram; Bradshaw Rate%gram. Vol. 7, No. 1 (Aug. 18, 1986)-. Periodical. English. Twelve times a year. $295.00. Bradshaw Financial Network, PO Box 3517, San Rafael CA 94912. **Tel** (415)479-3815. ***Continues*** *Rate%Gram Hotline.*
Desc: Regarded as the standard reference among investors and financial professionals requiring up-to-the-minute rate reporting in one source.

LC HD1361 .R4235 **ISSN** 0898-0209
DD 332.7/2/05 US
CCC

REAL ESTATE FINANCE JOURNAL, THE. See Real Estate.

LC HG450
DD 332.6 US

REAL ESTATE INVESTING LETTER. See Real Estate.

LC HG4651 **ISSN** 0832-0748
DD 332.63/22/0971 CN

RECORD OF NEW ISSUES. [Rec. new issues]. **Added/Corp** Financial Post Information Service. Financial Post Corporation Service Group. (1951)-.

Business and Economics — Investments

English. One time a year. 236.10Can$. Financial Post Company Ltd., 333 King Street East, Toronto Ontario M5A 4N2, Canada. **Tel** (416)350-6500, FAX (416)350-6601.
Desc: Cumulative listing that includes new issue details, issue features, underwriters, gross proceeds, offer price, and more.

LC HG **ISSN** 1075-9743
DD 332 US

●REDEMPTION DIGEST AND SECURITIES INDUSTRY DAILY.
[Redempt. dig. secur. ind. dly.]. **VFOAT** Securities Industry Daily. Vol. 6, No. 70 (Apr. 11, 1994)-. Periodical. English. Seven times a week. $195.00. Redemption Digest, PO Box 2055, Canal Street Station, New York NY 10013. **Tel** (800)879-2663, (212)219-1550, FAX (212)925-0262. **Absorbed** Redemption Digest and Corporate Actions, 1056-506X.

LC HG5430.5.A2 S73a
DD 332.6/094/021 LU

REGIONER. FLLESSKABETS KONOMISKE BISTAND TIL INVESTERINGER = REGIONEN. FINANZBEITRAEGE DER GEMEINSCHAFT FUER INVESTITIONEN =REGIONS. THE COMMUNITY'S FINANCIAL PARTICIPATION IN INVESTMENTS.
Added/Corp Statistical Office of the European Communities. **VFOAT** Fllesskabets Konomiske Bistand til Investeringer; Regionen. Finanzbeitrage der Gemeinschaft fuer Investitionen; Regions. Community's Financial Participation in Investments. (1984)-. English (French; summaries and/or abstracts in Danish, Dutch, German, Greek and Modern, Italian). Irregular. Office for Official Publications of the European Communities, 2 rue Mercier, 2985 Luxembourg Luxembourg. **Tel** 011 352 499281, FAX 011 352 292942763. **Continues** Statistical Office of the European Communities. Regional Statistics.

LC HG4621 .R43 **ISSN** 0193-1865
DD 332.6/2/05 US

REGISTERED REPRESENTATIVE, THE.
[Regist. represent.]. (19??)-. Trade Publication. English. Twelve times a year. $24.00. Plaza Communications Inc, 18818 Teller Avenue, Suite 280, Irvine CA 92715. **Tel** (714)851-2220, FAX (714)851-1636. **ED** Laurie Brannen. **Circ:** 80,407.

LC HG5095 .N24
DD 332.6/324 US

REIT HANDBOOK OF MEMBER TRUSTS.
See Real Estate.

LC HG4057 .A23A **ISSN** 0162-0584
DD 332.6/7 US

RELATIVE VALUE ANALYSIS. Main/Corp
Donaldson, Lufkin & Jenrette Securities Corporation. Periodical. English. Four times a year. Donaldson Lufkin & Jenrette Securities Corporation, 140 Broadway, New York NY 10005.

LC HG5881.A2 N54A
DD 354.6690082/58/06 NR

REPORT AND ACCOUNTS FOR THE YEAR ENDED 31ST DECEMBER ... / THE SECURITIES AND EXCHANGE COMMISSION (NIGERIA). Main/Corp
Nigeria. Securities and Exchange Commission. English. Mandilas House/9th Floor, Nigeria.

LC HG4621 **ISSN** 1186-0405
DD 332.6/2 CN

REPORT - BRITISH COLUMBIA. LEGISLATIVE ASSEMBLY. SELECT STANDING COMMITTEE ON FINANCE, CROWN CORPORATIONS AND GOVERNMENT SERVICES.
(REPORT / SELECT STANDING COMMITTEE ON FINANCE, CROWN CORPORATIONS AND GOVERNMENT SERVICES.). [Rep. - B.C. Legis. Assem. Sel. Standing Comm. Financ. Crown Corp. Gov. Serv.]. **Main/Corp** British Columbia. Legislative Assembly. Select Standing Committee on Finance, Crown Corporations and Government Services. **VFOAT** Financial Planning and Advisory Industry. (Feb. 19, 1991)-. Periodical. English.

LC HG5891 .A92a **ISSN** 0155-0802
DD 332.6/73/0994 AT

REPORT / FOREIGN INVESTMENT REVIEW BOARD. Main/Corp
Australia. Foreign Investment Review Board. (19??)-. English. Irregular. Australian Government Publishing Service, GPO Box 84, Canberra ACT 2601 Australia. **Tel** 011 61 6 2954411, FAX 011 61 6 2954455.

LC HG4028.B2 F47a **ISSN** 1057-8927
DD 338.7/4/05 US

REPORT OF ASSOCIATION FOR INVESTMENT MANAGEMENT AND RESEARCH CORPORATE INFORMATION COMMITTEE.
[Rep. Assoc. Investm. Manage. Res. Corp. Inf. Comm.]. **Main/Corp** Association for Investment Management and Research. Corporate Information Committee. **VFOAT** Corporate Information Committee Report. (1989)-. English. Financial Analysts Federation, 1633 Broadway/Suite 1402, New York NY 10019. **Tel** (212)1957-2860. **Continues** Report of the Financial Analysts Federation's Corporate Information Committee, 0276-3028.

LC HG4501
DD 332.6 UK

REPORT OF THE SECURITIES AND INVESTMENTS BOARD FOR ... . Main/Corp
Securities and Investments Board (Great Britain). (1987/88)-. English. One time a year. **Continues** Chairman's Statement and Accounts.

LC HG4651
DD 332.632 US

REPORT OF THE SECURITIES DIVISION. Main/Corp
Illinois. Office of Secretary of State. (19??)-. English. Twelve times a year. Illinois Securities Division, Springfield IL 62704. **Tel** (217)785-4941.

LC HG4501
DD 332.6 US

REPORT [MICROFORM]. Main/Corp
Overseas Private Investment Corporation. (1989)-. English. Overseas Private Investment Corporation, 1129 20th Street NW, Washington DC 20527. **Tel** (202)457-7093. **Formed by the union of** Overseas Private Investment Corporation. Annual Report **and** Overseas Private Investment Corporation. Development Report.

LC HG450 **ISSN** 0199-3534
DD 332.6 US

RESSI REVIEW. See Real Estate.

LC HG450
DD 332.6 US

RETIREMENT PLANS BULLETIN.
(19??)-. Bulletin. English. Twelve times a year. $89.00. Universal Pensions Inc., Box 979, Brainerd MN 56401. **Tel** (800)541-6089, (800)346-3860, FAX (218)829-2106. **ED** Jennifer Norquist (Editor's telephone: (218)829-4781). Index Bound in First Issue (Jan.). cum. index. **Circ:** 3,000 (ctrl). **Absorbed** Qualified Plan Update and IRA Bulletin.
Desc: Provides operational guidance for financial organizations to make certain their IRA and qualified plan programs are run in compliance with IRS requirements.

LC HG226 .R47 **ISSN** 1077-9493
DD 332.6/05 US

●RETURN ON INVESTMENT.
[Return investm.]. **VFOAT** ROI. (Sept./Oct. 1994)-. Trade Publication. English. Six times a year. $150.00. Investment Management Weekly, 1 Liberty Square, 12th Floor, Boston MA 02109. **Tel** (617)426-5450, FAX (617)422-0162. **ED** Richard Chimberg. **Circ:** 30,000.
Desc: Reports on investment management worldwide.

LC HG5128.P4 R48
DD 332.63/232 US

REVENUE MORTGAGE AND BOND PROJECTS UNDER THE INDUSTRIAL AND COMMERCIAL AUTHORITY LAW, SUMMARY OF LOANS ... . Added/Corp
Pennsylvania. Dept. of Commerce. (19??)-. English.

LC HG **ISSN** 1380-6645
DD 332.63 NE
Pr Rev. CCC

●REVIEW OF DERIVATIVES RESEARCH.
(1996)-. Academic Scholarly Publication. English. Four times a year. $267.00. Kluwer Academic Publishers, Postbus 322, 3300 AH Dordrecht The Netherlands. **Tel** 011 31 78 524400, FAX 011 31 78 183273, telex 20083. **(Subscription address:** Kluwer Academic Publishers / Netherlands, PO Box 322, 3300 AH Dordrecht Netherlands. **Tel** 011 31 78 392392, FAX 011 31 78 546474.) **ED** Menachem Brenner and Marti Subrahmanyam.
Desc: Academic research dealing with pricing of derivative assets on any underlying asset.

LC HG6046 .R48 **ISSN** 0898-011X
DD 332.64/4 US
  CEASED

REVIEW OF FUTURES MARKETS, THE.
[Rev. futures mark.]. **Added/Corp** Chicago Board of Trade. Vol. 6, No. 1 (1987)-(19??)-. Periodical. English. Chicago Board of Trade, 141 West Jackson, #2210 Education / Marketing, Chicago IL 60604. **Tel** (312)435-7208, FAX (312)341-3027. **Continues** Review of Research in Futures Markets, 0734-2063.
Ind/Abst Curr. Cit.

LC HE **ISSN** 0824-362X
DD 388/.0971 CN

REVIEW OF MAJOR INVESTMENT PROJECTS IN CANADA.
[Rev. major investm. proj. Can.]. English. One time a year. $750.00 per volume. Informetrica Ltd, PO Box 828 Station B, Ottawa Ontario K1P 5P9 Canada. **Tel** (613)238-4831, FAX (613)238-7698.

LC HG450
DD 332.6 UK

REVIEW OF THE INTERNATIONAL BOND MARKETS, A.
1986-. Periodical. English. Credit Suisse First Boston Limited, 2A Great Titchfield Street, London W1P 1AA United Kingdom.

LC HG5340.S34 S25A
DD 332.6 BL

REVISTA - BOLSA DE VALORES DE SAO PAULO. Main/Corp
Bolsa de Valores de Sao Paulo. Periodical. Portuguese. 90.00. Divasao de Commicacoes, rua Alvares Penteado 151, Sao Paulo Brazil. **Continues** Bolsa Oficial de Valores. Revista.

LC HG4503 .R45 **ISSN** 0102-9797
DD 332.6 BL

REVISTA BRASILEIRA DE MERCADO DE CAPITAIS.
[Rev. bras. merc. cap.]. **Added/Corp** Instituto Brasileiro de Mercado de Capitais. Vol. 1 (Jan./April 1975)-. Periodical. Portuguese. Four times a year. $250.00. Instituto Brasileiro de Mercado de Capitals, Avenue Rio Branco, 108 2 Andar, 20040 Rio de Janeiro Brazil. **Tel** 011 55 21 2426646 6653.
Ind/Abst Foreign Lang. Index.

LC HG450
DD 332.6 US

RISK MANAGEMENT MANUAL. See
Business and Economics-Management.

LC HG4501 **ISSN** 0261-3344
DD 332.6 UK

RISK MEASUREMENT SERVICE.
[Risk meas. serv.]. (1979)-. Bulletin. English. Four times a year. $547.59. London Business School Library, Sussex Place Regents Park, London NW1 4SA United Kingdom. **Tel** 011 44 171 2625050 ext. 444, FAX 011 44 171 7247875, telex 27461. Index available (bound in all issues). available on diskette; available with illustrations.

LC HG4551 **ISSN** 0225-2007
DD 332.6/328 CN

ROTHBERG FORECASTS.
[Rothberg forecasts]. (July 1978)-. Periodical. English. Twelve times a year. $60.00. D Rothberg Futures Ltd., Suite 1 122 Scollard Street, Toronto Ontario M5R 1G2 Canada.

LC HG **ISSN** 0891-5547
DD 332 US

RUFF TIMES (1986), THE.
(THE RUFF TIMES.). [Ruff times]. (Oct. 27, 1986)-. Periodical. English. One time a week. $129.00. Ruff Times, 757 South Main, Springville UT 84663. **Tel** (801)489-0222. **Continues** Howard Ruff's Financial Success Report, 0747-0541.
Desc: Covers a wide range of financial, economic and political information for middle-class investors.

LC HG4651 .S19 **ISSN** 1049-3263
DD 338.7/4/09705 US
  TITLE CHANGE

S & P'S HIGH YIELD QUARTERLY.
[S P's high yield q.]. **Added/Corp** Standard & Poor's Corporation. **VFOAT** High Yield Quarterly; S and P's High Yield Quarterly. **VAT** Standard & Poor's High Yield Quarterly. 3rd Quarter (1989)-(199?). English. Standard & Poor's Corporation, (A Division of McGraw-Hill, Inc.), 25 Broadway, New York NY 10004. **Tel** (212)208-8775, (800)221-5277. **Continued by** Standard and Poor's High Yield Directions, 1072-1290.

LC HG4501 .S32 **ISSN** 1068-4034
DD 332 US
  TITLE CHANGE

SAFE MONEY REPORT.
[Safe money rep.]. **Added/Corp** Weiss Research, Inc. (West Palm Beach, Fla.). (1991)-(1993). Periodical. English. Weiss Research Inc., PO Box 109665, Palm Beach Gardens FL 33410. **Tel** (407)627-3300, FAX (407)625-6685. **ED** Martin Weiss (editor's address: 2200 N. Florida Mango Road, West Palm Beach. FL 33409). **Continues** Money & Markets, 1047-9821; **Absorbed** Holt Advisory, 1047-9791. **Continued by** Martin Weiss' Safe Money Report.

LC HG450
DD 332.6 US

SALES & MARKETING NOTES.
(19??)-. English. One time a year. $25.00 (members); $40.00 (nonmembers). Securities Industry Association, 120 Broadway/35th Floor, New York NY 10271. **Tel** (212)608-1500, FAX (212)608-1604.
Desc: Designed to advance the state of retail sales and marketing management in the securities industry.

Business and Economics —Investments

LC HG4905 .A66
DD 332.63/22/0973021 US
● **S&P ANALYSTS' HANDBOOK. Added/Corp** Standard and Poor's Corporation. **VFOAT** S & P Analysts' Handbook; Analysts' Handbook; S and P Analysts' Handbook; Standard & Poor's Analysts' Handbook; Standard and Poor's Analysts' Handbook; Monthly Analysts' Handbook. (1994)-. English. One time a year. $525.00. Standard & Poor's Corporation, (A Division of McGraw-Hill, Inc.), 25 Broadway, New York NY 10004. **Tel** (212)208-8775, (800)221-5277. *Continues Analyst's Handbook, 0884-6936.*

LC HC59.72.S3 S28
DD 332/.0415/091724 IT
SAVINGS AND DEVELOPMENT.
Added/Corp Finafrica (Institution). (1977)-. Periodical. English (summaries and/or abstracts in French). Four times a year. L100000. Finafrica Foundation, Via San Vigilio 10 1, 20142 Milan Italy. **Tel** 011 39 2 8135341. Index available. **Bk Rev**. **Ad Acc**. 2,500 (ctrl).
Ind/Abst AGRICOLA [Select. Cov.]; Geogr. Abstr. Human Geogr.; Int. Dev. Abstr.; Int. Labour Doc.; LABORDOC; Poult. Abstr.; Rural Dev. Abstr.; World Agric. Econ. Rural Sociol. Abstr.

LC HG3729.U5 A3392C   **ISSN** 0149-2500
DD 332.6/725 US
SBIC DIGEST. See Business and Economics-Small Business.

LC HG   **ISSN** 1067-6090
DD US
SCIENTIFIC INVESTMENT. [Sci. invest.]. Vol. 11, No. 1 (Jan. 1993)-. Periodical. English. Twelve times a year. SIL Inc., PO Box 41522, Baltimore MD 21203. *Continues Financial Predictions, 1062-9033.*

LC HG4057 .A55A   **ISSN** 0193-0192
DD 338.7/4/02573 US
SEC CORPORATION INDEX. Main/Corp United States. Securities and Exchange Commission. Office of Reports and Information Services. **VFOAT** Corporation Index. **VAT** Securities and Exchange Commission Corporation Index. English. Securities and Exchange Commission / Washington, 450 Fifth Street NW, Washington DC 20549. **Tel** (202)272-3100.

LC KF1436.A2 U54   **ISSN** 0091-4061
DD 346.73/0666/02648 347.30666602648 US
SEC DOCKET. Main/Corp United States. Securities and Exchange Commission. **Added/Corp** Commerce Clearing House. **VFOAT** S.E.C. Docket; C.C.H. S.E.C. Docket; CCH SEC Docket. Vol. 1, No. 1 (Feb. 13, 1973)-. Periodical. English. One time a week. Commerce Clearing House Inc., 4025 West Peterson Avenue, Chicago IL 60646-6085. **Tel** (312)583-8500, FAX (708)940-4600. **ED** A.E. Schechter. available on microfilm and microfiche from University Microfilms International (UMI).
Desc: Issues reproduce text of SEC rulings, opinions and other official actions as prepared by the agency.

LC HG450   **ISSN** 0745-2667
DD 332.6 US
CCC
SEC TODAY, THE. Added/Corp Washington Service Bureau. **VFOAT** S.E.C. Today. **VAT** Securities Exchange Commission Today. (19??)-. Periodical. English. Five times a week (Mon.-Fri.). $575.00 (first class), $500.00 (second class) renewal; $600.00 (new). Washington Service Bureau Inc., 655 15th Street Northwest, Suite 270, Washington DC 20005. **Tel** (800)955-5219, (202)508-0600. **ED** Jacquelyn Lumb. **Circ**: 2,000.
Desc: Provides coverage of new SEC administrative proceedings, announcements and releases; new registrations and acquisitions by specific companies, as prepared by the SEC.

LC HG4651
DD 332.632 US
● **SECURITIES AND COMMODITIES LITIGATION REPORTER.** (1995)-. English. Twenty-four times a year. $1250.00. Andrews Publications Inc., 1646 West Chester Pike, PO Box 1000, Westtown PA 19395. **Tel** (610)399-6600, (800)345-1101, FAX (610)399-6610. *Absorbed Securities and Inside Trading Litigation Reporter* **and** *Commodities Litigation Reporter.*
Desc: Provides coverage of major reparations and enforcement actions involving the scope of the Commodity Exchange Act.

LC HG4651
DD 332.632 UK
SECURITIES AND INVESTMENT BOARD. English. Irregular. £75.00 UK; £155.00 other. Securities Investments Board, 2-14 Bunhill Row, Gavrelle House, London EC1Y 8RA United Kingdom. **Tel** 011 44 171 6381240, FAX 011 44 171 3825900, telex 262433.
Desc: Information of regulations made under Chapter 8 of Part II of the Financial Services Act and associated guidance releases and consultation documents.

LC HG4651
DD 332.632 US
SECURITIES INDUSTRY DATABANK. (19??)-. English. Securities Industry Association, 120 Broadway/35th Floor, New York NY 10271. **Tel** (212)608-1500, FAX (212)608-1604. available on diskette.
Desc: This service consists of a unique and comprehensive database containing aggregated financial data, quarterly and annual income statements and balance sheets of all NYSE broker-dealers dealing with the public. This industry data is aggregated into 16 firm categories including: national full lines, large investment banks, New York City, regionals, discounters, etc.

LC HG4503 .S43
DD 332.6/7/095952 SI
SECURITIES INDUSTRY REVIEW.
Added/Corp Singapore Securities Research Institute. Vol. 1 (1975)-. Periodical. English. Two times a year. $18.00. University of Singapore / Faculty of Business Administration, 10 Kent Ridge, Singapore 0511 Singapore. **Tel** 011 65 7723101, FAX 011 65 7792621 3571, telex 33943.

LC HG4651   **ISSN** 0276-2749
DD 332.632 US
SECURITIES INDUSTRY TRENDS. [Secur. ind. trends]. **Added/Corp** Securities Industry Association. Research Dept. **VFOAT** Trends. (19??)-. Trade Publication. English. Irregular (six-eight issues per year). $75.00. Securities Industry Association, 120 Broadway/35th Floor, New York NY 10271. **Tel** (212)608-1500, FAX (212)608-1604. Index available.
Desc: Report on trends within the securities industry. Profitability and financial statements of the securities industry are discussed, as well as economic developments affecting securities firms.

LC HG4907 .S398   **ISSN** 0730-5796
DD 332.6/2/02573 US
SECURITIES INDUSTRY YEARBOOK.
[Secur. ind. yearb.]. **Added/Corp** Securities Industry Association. Vol. 1 (1980)-. English. One time a year (July). $135.31. Securities Industry Association, 120 Broadway/35th Floor, New York NY 10271. **Tel** (212)608-1500, FAX (212)608-1604. **ED** Rosalie Pepe.
Desc: A reference for people involved in the securities industry. Includes detailed information on individual firms, such as key personnel and department heads, number of accounts, registered representatives and offices, capital, underwriting volume, syndications and other data. Also provides rankings by capital, offices, employees and RRs.

LC HG4651
DD 332.632 HK
SECURITIES JOURNAL. Chinese. $150.00. Capital Communications Corporation, 7 F Paramount Building, 12 Ka Yip Street, Chai Wan Hong Kong. **Tel** 011 852 25952378, FAX 011 852 28892854.

LC HG5771 .S43
DD 332.6/32/0952 JA
SECURITIES MARKET IN JAPAN.
Added/Corp Nihon Shoken Keizai Kenkyujo. (19??)-. Periodical. English (Japanese). Every 2 years. Price varies. Japan Securities Research Institute, 1-5-8 Nihonbashi Kayaba-cho Chuo-ku, Tokyo 103 Japan. **Tel** 03 3669 0737, FAX 03 3662 8294.

LC HG   **ISSN** 1055-0720
DD 332 US
SECURITIES OPERATIONS MAGAZINE. [Secur. oper. mag.]. **VFOAT** Securities Operations. (Jan. 1991)-. Periodical. English. Four times a year. $395.00. Securities Operations Letter Inc., 53 Wall Street, 5th Floor, New York NY 10005.

LC KF1439.A1 S38   **ISSN** 0037-0665
DD 346/.73/09205 US
CCC
SECURITIES REGULATION & LAW REPORT. See Law-Corporation Law.

LC HG4651   **ISSN** 0149-3582
DD 332.632 US
SECURITIES WEEK. [Secur. week]. (19??)-. Periodical. English. One time a week. $1395.00. McGraw Hill Publishing Company, Inc., 1221 Avenue of the Americas, New York NY 10020. **Tel** (212)512-6410, (800)525-5003, FAX (212)512-6111. available on an online database from NEXIS; and (file 624/Full-Text) DIALOG.

LC HG4501 .S48   **ISSN** 0278-1514
DD 332.63/22/0973 US
SHAREOWNERSHIP. (SHAREOWNERSHIP / N.Y. STOCK EXCHANGE.). **Added/Corp** New York Stock Exchange. (1970)-. English. Every 2 years (every two years). $25.00. New York Stock Exchange Inc., 20 Broad Street, New York NY 10005. **Tel** (212)656-3000, FAX (212)656-5725. *Continues Census of Shareowners (1965).*

LC HD2756.2.J3 S52
DD 338 JA
SHINON KEITOBETSU ZEN JOJO KAISHA SHURAN. VFOAT Zen Jojo Kaisha Shuran. (19??)-. Japanese. Kobayashi Rabo To-1-409, 1-87 Somechi 3-chome, Chofu-shi 182 Japan.

LC HG4503 .S49
DD 332.6 JA
TITLE CHANGE
SHOKEN KEIZAI JIHO. Added/Corp Nihon Shoken Keizai Kenkyujo. (19??)-Vol. 34 No.4 (19??). Periodical. Japanese. Nihon Shoken Keizai Kenkujo, 1-5-8 Nihonbashi Kayaba-cho Chuo-ku, Tokyo 103 Japan. **Tel** 011 81 3 36690737, FAX 011 81 3 3 36628294. *Continued by Shoken Review.*

LC HG4245 .A43a   **ISSN** 0388-1458
DD 332.6 JA
SHOKEN KEIZAIGAKKAI NEMPO.
Main/Corp Shoken Keizaigakkai (Japan). **VFOAT** Annals of the Society for the Economic Studies of Securities. (19??)-. Japanese. One time a year. Shoken Keizaigakkai Jimukyoku, c/o Tokyo Shoken Kaikan, 3-gai Nihon Shoken Keizai Kenkyujo, 14 Nihonbashi Kayaba-cho Chuo-ku, Tokyo Japan.

LC HG450
DD 332.6 JA
SHOKEN REVIEW. Added/Corp Nihon Shoken Keizai Kenkyujo. (19??)-. Academic Scholarly Publication. Japanese. Twelve times a year. ¥300.00. Nihon Shoken Keizai Kenkujo, 1-5-8 Nihonbashi Kayaba-cho Chuo-ku, Tokyo 103 Japan. **Tel** 011 81 3 36690737, FAX 011 81 3 3 36628294. **ED** Shozo Koyama. **Acid Free**. **Circ**: 1,900. *Continues Shoken Keizai Jiho, 1340-6809.*

LC HG450
DD 332.6 US
SIA FACT BOOK. See Business and Economics-Abstracting, Bibliographies and Statistics.

LC HG450
DD 332.6 US
CEASED
SIA INTERNATIONAL CAPITAL MARKETS REVIEW. (19??)-(July 1993). Newsletter. English. Securities Industry Association, 120 Broadway/35th Floor, New York NY 10271. **Tel** (212)608-1500, FAX (212)608-1604.
Desc: A newsletter covering issues which impact US broker-dealers doing business in foreign markets, as well as foreign broker-dealers doing business in the US. Also includes a special quarterly feature, Global Equity Analysis Report, which tracks equity news on a worldwide basis.

LC HG450
DD 332.6 US
SIA POLICIES AND POSITIONS. (19??)-. English. Irregular. Free. Securities Industry Association, 120 Broadway/35th Floor, New York NY 10271. **Tel** (212)608-1500, FAX (212)608-1604.
Desc: Summarizing the key policy stands taken by the SIA Board of Directors. Managing executives on a periodic basis as policies are added or revised.

LC HG450
DD 332.6 US
Pr Rev.
SID CATO'S NEWSLETTER ON ANNUAL REPORTS. Newsletter. English. Twelve times a year. $197.20 (one-year), $315.20 (two-year), $413.70 (three-year). Cato Communications, Box 9850, Kalamazoo MI 49019-0850. **Tel** (616)344-2286, FAX (616)344-4145. **ED** Sid Cato.

LC Z7164.C81 G83 HF5351   **ISSN** 0361-3917
DD 016.33 US
SIE GUIDE TO BUSINESS & INVESTMENT BOOKS. Main/Corp Select Information Exchange. **VAT** Select Information Exchange Guide to Business & Investment Books. English. $12.95. Forecaster, 19623 Ventura Boulevard, Tarzana CA 91356. **Tel** (818)345-4421, FAX (818)345-0468. *Continues Guide to Business & Investment Books.*

LC HG450   **ISSN** 0199-6177
DD 332.6 CCC
SIGNIFICANT SEC FILINGS REPORTER. See Law.

LC HG   **ISSN** 0195-8054
DD 332 US
SILVER & GOLD REPORT. [Silver gold rep.]. **Added/Corp** Precious Metals Report, Inc. Weiss Research, Inc. (West Palm Beach, Fla.). **VFOAT** Silver and Gold Report. (1975)-. Periodical. English. Twelve times a year. $195.00. Silver & Gold Report, Attention: Jennifer Epler, PO Box 2923, West Palm Beach FL 33402. **Tel** (407)684-8100 Sales, (800)289-9222, FAX (407)684-9039. **ED** James DiGeorgia (editor's address: 2200 North Flamango Road, West Palm Beach, FL 33409). **Circ**: 22,000 (ctrl).

Desc: SGR is an independent financial and economic newsletter specializing in impartial news coverage and analysis of events affecting precious metals markets.

LC HG4538 .S494 **ISSN** 1055-3584
DD 338.8/8/05 US
SITE WORLD. [SITE world]. **Added/Corp** Conway Data, Inc. (1991)-. English. One time a year. $95.00. Conway Data Inc., 40 Technology Park Suite, Suite 200, Norcross GA 30092. **Tel** (404)446-6996, (800)554-5686, FAX (404)263-8825.

LC HD2340 **ISSN** 0959-0773
DD 338.642 UK
SMALL COMPANY INVESTOR. [Small Co. Invest.]. (1989)-. Periodical. English. Twelve times a year. £350.00 UK; £375.00 other. Financial Times Magazines, Greystoke Place, Fetter Lane, London EC4A 1ND United Kingdom. **Tel** 011 44 171 8316577. **ED** Bryan Hubbard. Index available. **Ad Acc.**
Desc: Analyses smaller companies in UK and continental.

LC HG450
DD 332.6 UK
SMALL COMPANY INVESTOR. English. Twelve times a year. £350.00 UK; £375.00 other. Financial Times Magazines, Greystoke Place, Fetter Lane, London EC4A 1ND United Kingdom. **Tel** 011 44 171 8316577. **ED** Bryan Hubbard. Index available. **Ad Acc.**
Desc: Analyses smaller companies in UK and continental.

LC HG450
DD 332.6 US
SMART MONEY. (19??)-. English. $120.00 US; $140.00 other. Hirsch Organization, 6 Deer Trail, Old Tappan NJ 07675. **Tel** (201)664-3400.
Ind/Abst Access (1992-).

LC HG **ISSN** 1080-2134
DD 332 US
●**SNL FINANCE COMPANY WEEKLY, THE.** [SNL finance co. wkly.]. **Added/Corp** SNL Securities. **VFOAT** Finance Company Weekly. (Oct. 1994)-. Periodical. English. Fifty-two times a year. $296.00. SNL Securities Inc., 410 East Main Street, Charlottesville VA 22902. **Tel** (804)977-1600, (804)977-5877.

LC HG450
DD 332.6 US
●**SOCIAL ISSUES REPORTER.** (1995)-. English. Eleven times a year. $275.00. Investor Responsibility Research Center, 1350 Connecticut Avenue Northwest 700, Washington DC 20036. **Tel** (202)833-0700.

LC HG450 **ISSN** 0733-4605
DD 332.6 US
SOUND ADVICE. See Real Estate.

LC HG4501 **ISSN** 1053-5497
DD 332.6 US
●**SOUTH AFRICA INVESTOR.** **Added/Corp** Investor Responsibility Research Center. **VFOAT** IRRC South Africa Investor. Vol. 1, No. 1 (Jan. 1995)-. Periodical. English. Eleven times a year. $400.00. Investor Responsibility Research Center, 1350 Connecticut Avenue Northwest 700, Washington DC 20036. **Tel** (202)833-0700.

LC HG5851.A2 S65 **ISSN** 1053-5497
DD 968.06/3/05 US
TITLE CHANGE
SOUTH AFRICA REPORTER. [S. Afr. report.]. **Added/Corp** Investor Responsibility Research Center. **VFOAT** South Africa Review Service Reporter; Reporter; SA Reporter. (Dec. 1985)-(1995). Periodical. English. Investor Responsibility Research Center, 1350 Connecticut Avenue Northwest 700, Washington DC 20036. **Tel** (202)833-0700. **ED** Meg Voorhes. **Bk Rev. Circ:** 1,500. ***Continues in part*** *South Africa Review Service. Reporter.* ***Continued by*** *South Africa Investor.*

LC HG4907 .S47 **ISSN** 0091-6854
DD 332.6/7 US
SPECTRUM 1: STOCK HOLDINGS SURVEY. **Added/Corp** Computer Directions Advisors, Inc. **VFOAT** Stock Holdings Survey. 1st Quarter (1973)-. English. Four times a year. $295.00. CDA Investment Technologies, 1355 Piccard Drive, Rockville MD 20850. **Tel** (301)974-9600, (800)232-2285, FAX (301)590-1389. **Circ:** 222 (ctrl). available on an online database; available on magnetic tape; available in hardback.
Desc: Alphabetically lists by common stock the quarterly holdings and transactions of US and European investment companies. Coverage includes all NYSE, ASE and NASDAQ issues.

LC HG4907 .S473 **ISSN** 0091-6862
DD 332.6/327/0973 US
SPECTRUM 2: INVESTMENT COMPANY PORTFOLIOS. [Spectr. 2, Investm. co. portf.]. **Added/Corp** Computer Directions Advisors, Inc. **VFOAT** Investment Company Portfolios. 1st Quarter (1973)-. English. Four times a year. $295.00. CDA Investment Technologies, 1355 Piccard Drive, Rockville MD 20850. **Tel** (301)974-9600, (800)232-2285, FAX (301)590-1389. **Circ:** 178 (ctrl). available on an online database; available on magnetic tape; available in hardback.
Desc: Alphabetically lists by investment company the quarterly holdings and transactions of US and European funds with assets exceeding $25 million.

LC HG450
DD 332.6 US
SPECTRUM 4: 13(F) INSTITUTIONAL PORTFOLIOS. **VFOAT** Institutional Portfolios. (Dec. 3, 1978)-. English. $755.00. CDA Investment Technologies, 1355 Piccard Drive, Rockville MD 20850. **Tel** (301)974-9600, (800)232-2285, FAX (301)590-1389. **Circ:** 228.
Desc: Alphabetically lists by institution the quarterly holdings and changes of all institutions with equity assets exceeding $100 million.

LC HG4651
DD 332.632 US
SPECTRUM CONVERTIBLES -- 13 (F) INSTITUTIONAL HOLDINGS SURVEY OF CONVERTIBLE BONDS AND CONVERTIBLE PREFERRED STOCK. (19??)-. English. Four times a year. $450.00. CDA Investment Technologies, 1355 Piccard Drive, Rockville MD 20850. **Tel** (301)974-9600, (800)232-2285, FAX (301)590-1389.

LC HG450
DD 332.6 US
SPENCER'S RESEARCH REPORTS ON EMPLOYEE BENEFITS. **Added/Corp** Charles D. Spencer & Associates. Vol. 34, No. 38 (Sept. 19, 1986)-. Periodical. English. One time a week (54 issues). $650.00. Charles D. Spencer & Associates, 250 South Wacker Drive, Suite 600, Chicago IL 60606-5834. **Tel** (312)993-7900, FAX (312)993-7910. ***Continues*** *EBPR Research Reports.*

LC HG450 **ISSN** 0740-1329
DD 332.6 US
SPENCER'S RETIREMENT PLAN SERVICE. See Insurance.

LC HG4501 .S367 **ISSN** 8750-2356
DD 332.63/22/0973 US
SRC BLUE BOOK OF 5-TREND CYCLI-GRAPHS, THE. [SRC blue book 5-trend cycli-graphs]. **Added/Corp** Securities Research Company (Boston, Mass.). **VFOAT** S.R.C. Blue Book of 5-Trend Cycli-Graphs; SRC Blue Book of Five-Trend Cycli-Graphs. **VAT** Securities Research Company Blue Book of Five-Trend Cycli-Graphs. 167th Quarterly Ed. (July 1984)-. English. Four times a year. $119.00. Securities Research Company, 101 Prescott Street, Wellesley Hills MA 02181. **Tel** (617)235-0900. **ED** Donald S. Jones. **Circ:** 13,000 (ctrl). ***Continues*** *SRC Blue Book of 3-Trend Cycli-Graphs, 0744-4133.*
Desc: Covers 1,108 companies with monthly prices over 12 years. Also shows earnings, dividends, volume, and relative performance.

LC HG4916 .S67 **ISSN** 0884-8475
DD 332.63/22/0973 US
SRC GREEN BOOK OF 5-TREND 35-YEAR CHARTS, THE. [SRC green book 5-trend 35-year charts]. **Added/Corp** Securities Research Company (Boston, Mass.). **VFOAT** S.R.C. Green Book of 5-Trend 35-Year Charts; SRC Green Book of Five-Trend 35-Year Charts; SRC Green Book--Thirty-Five-Year Charts; SRC Green Book--35 Year Charts. 4th Edition (1949-1984)-. English. One time a year. $114.45. Securities Research Company, 101 Prescott Street, Wellesley Hills MA 02181. **Tel** (617)235-0900. **ED** Donald S. Jones. ctrl circ. ***Continues*** *SRC Green Book of 3-Trend 35-Year Charts, 0739-6317.*
Desc: A 448 page chart book of 400 stocks and 39 industry groups. Each chart contains earnings, dividends, monthly prices and volume for 35-year period.

LC HG4501 .S37 **ISSN** 8750-2461
DD 332.63/2/0973 US
SRC RED BOOK OF 5-TREND SECURITY CHARTS, THE. [SRC red book 5-trend secur. charts]. **Added/Corp** Securities Research Company (Boston, Mass.). **VFOAT** S.R.C. Red Book of 5-Trend Security Charts; SRC Red Book of Five Trend Security Charts. **VAT** Securities Research Company Red Book of Five-Trend Security Charts. 609th Monthly Edition (July 1984)-. English. Twelve times a year. $139.00. Securities Research Company, 101 Prescott Street, Wellesley Hills MA 02181. **Tel** (617)235-0900. **ED** Donald S. Jones. **Circ:** 7,800 (ctrl). ***Continues*** *SRC Red Book of 3-Trend Security Charts, 0744-4125.*
Desc: Covers 1,105 companies with weekly prices over 21 month period. Also shown are earnings, dividends, volume, 39-week moving average and relative performance.

LC HG4651 **ISSN** 0196-4674
DD 332.632 US
STANDARD & POOR'S CORPORATION RECORDS. CURRENT NEWS EDITION. (STANDARD & POOR'S CORPORATION RECORDS.). **VFOAT** Standard & Poor's Corporation Records: Daily News; Standard & Poor's Daily News. **VAT** Standard and Poor's Corporation Records. (1???)-. Periodical. English. Irregular. $1,350.00 (daily news only). Standard & Poor's Corporation, (A Division of McGraw-Hill, Inc.), 25 Broadway, New York NY 10004. **Tel** (212)208-8775, (800)221-5277. Index Available, published separately, free-automatically sent. available on CD-ROM; available on an online database.
Desc: A source of information on over 12,000 publicly held U.S. corporations.

LC HG4501 .S7662 **ISSN** 0731-1974
DD 332.6/05 US
STANDARD & POOR'S CREDITWEEK. [Standard Poor's creditweek]. **Added/Corp** Standard and Poor's Corporation. **VFOAT** Standard and Poor's Creditweek; Standard & Poor's Credit Week; Standard and Poor's Credit Week; Creditweek; Credit Week. (Nov. 2, 1981)-. Periodical. English. One time a week. $2190.00. Standard & Poor's Corporation, (A Division of McGraw-Hill, Inc.), 25 Broadway, New York NY 10004. **Tel** (212)208-8775, (800)221-5277. **ED** Paul Stanwick. ***Continues*** *Standard and Poor's Corporation. Standard & Poor's Fixed Income Investor, 0193-9335.*
Desc: Analyzes ratings, trends and the outlook for fixed income securities. Includes corporate and municipal bonds and commercial paper.

LC HG4501 .S686
DD 332.6 US
STANDARD & POOR'S CREDITWEEK INTERNATIONAL. **Added/Corp** Standard and Poor's Corporation. **VFOAT** Standard and Poor's Creditweek International; Creditweek International. Vol. 9, No. 2 (Feb. 4, 1991)-. Periodical. English. Twelve times a year. Standard & Poor's Corporation, (A Division of McGraw-Hill, Inc.), 25 Broadway, New York NY 10004. **Tel** (212)208-8775, (800)221-5277. ***Continues*** *Standard & Poor's International Creditweek, 0739-9057.*

LC HG **ISSN** 1058-6679
DD 332 US
STANDARD & POOR'S CREDITWEEK. MUNICIPAL. **Added/Corp** Standard and Poor's Corporation. **VFOAT** Standard and Poor's Creditweek. Municipal; Standard and Poor's Credit Week. Municipal; Municipal; Credit Week Municipal; Creditweek Municipal. (Oct. 1991)-. Periodical. English. Four times a year. $2350.00. Standard & Poor's Corporation, (A Division of McGraw-Hill, Inc.), 25 Broadway, New York NY 10004. **Tel** (212)208-8775, (800)221-5277.

LC HG4028.D5 S73 **ISSN** 1062-5607
DD 332 US
STANDARD & POOR'S DIRECTORY OF DIVIDEND REINVESTMENT PLANS. See Industry and Production-Trade and Industrial Directories.

LC HG4908 .S8 **ISSN** 0196-4658
DD 338.7/4/0973 US
STANDARD & POOR'S DIVIDEND RECORD. **Main/Corp** Standard and Poor's Corporation. **Added/Corp** Standard and Poor's Corporation. Dividend Record. **VFOAT** Dividend Record; Standard & Poor's Daily Dividend Record; Daily Dividend Record. (1977/78)-. Periodical. English. Five times a week (260 issues). $1075.00. Standard & Poor's Corporation, (A Division of McGraw-Hill, Inc.), 25 Broadway, New York NY 10004. **Tel** (212)208-8775, (800)221-5277.
Desc: Provides complete and carefully detailed information on the dividend disbursements of over 10,000 stocks, with frequency of service tailored to specific individual or institutional needs.

LC HG **ISSN** 0882-5440
DD 332 US
STANDARD & POOR'S EMERGING & SPECIAL SITUATIONS. [Stand. Poor's emerg. spec. situat.]. **Added/Corp** Standard and Poor's Corporation. **VFOAT** Standard and Poor's Emerging and Special Situations; Emerging & Special Situations; Emerging and Special Situations. Vol. 3, No. 8 (Aug. 17, 1984)-. Periodical. English. Twelve times a year (monthly with mid-month supplements). $259.00. Standard & Poor's Corporation, (A Division of McGraw-Hill, Inc.), 25 Broadway, New York NY 10004. **Tel** (212)208-8775, (800)221-5277. available on an online database from Dow Jones News/Retrieval; NEWSNET; Lexis-Nexis; and (file 624/Full-Text) DIALOG. ***Continues*** *New Issue Investor, 0737-4089.*

LC HG4930 .S72 **ISSN** 0897-5108
DD 332.63/27 US
STANDARD & POOR'S/LIPPER MUTUAL FUND PROFILES. [Stand. Poor's/Lipper mutual fund profiles]. **Added/Corp** Standard and Poor's Corporation. Lipper Analytical Services, Inc. **VFOAT** Mutual Fund Profiles; Standard and Poor's Lipper Mutual Fund Profiles; Standard & Poor's Lipper Mutual Fund

Profiles; Standard and Poor's/Lipper Mutual Fund Profiles. (Dec. 1987)-. Periodical. English. Four times a year. $152.00. Standard & Poor's Corporation, (A Division of McGraw-Hill, Inc.), 25 Broadway, New York NY 10004. **Tel** (212)208-8775, (800)221-5277.

LC HG4501 .S69 **ISSN** 1078-0262
DD 332 US
•STANDARD & POOR'S NASDAQ AND REGIONAL EXCHANGE PROFILES. [Standard Poor's NASDAQ reg. exch. profiles]. **Added/Corp** Standard and Poor's Corporation. **VFOAT** Standard and Poor's NASDAQ and Regional Exchange Profiles; NASDAQ and Regional Exchange Profiles. (July 1994)-. English. Three times a year. $79.00. Standard & Poor's Corporation, (A Division of McGraw-Hill, Inc.), 25 Broadway, New York NY 10004. **Tel** (212)208-8775, (800)221-5277. ***Continues*** *Standard & Poor's OTC Profiles, 0733-205X.*

LC HG4501 .S68
DD 332 US
•STANDARD & POOR'S NASDAQ AND REGIONAL EXCHANGE STOCK REPORTS. **Added/Corp** Standard and Poor's Corporation. **VFOAT** NASDAQ and Regional Exchange Stock Reports; Standard NASDAQ Stock Reports. (May 6, 1994)-. English. Four times a year. $955.00. Standard & Poor's Corporation, (A Division of McGraw-Hill, Inc.), 25 Broadway, New York NY 10004. **Tel** (212)208-8775, (800)221-5277. ***Continues*** *Standard OTC Stock Reports.*

LC HG4501 .S69 **ISSN** 0733-205X
DD 338.7/4/02573 US
TITLE CHANGE
STANDARD & POOR'S OTC PROFILES. [Standard Poor's OTC profiles]. **Added/Corp** Standard and Poor's Corporation. **VFOAT** Standard and Poor's O.T.C. Profiles; O.T.C Profiles; OTC Profiles. (Sept. 1981)-(Mar. 1994). English. Standard & Poor's Corporation, (A Division of McGraw-Hill, Inc.), 25 Broadway, New York NY 10004. **Tel** (212)208-8775, (800)221-5277. ***Continued by*** *Standard & Poor's NASDAQ and Regional Exchange Profiles, 1078-0262.*

LC HG4907 .S69 **ISSN** 1061-7043
DD 332.6/025/73 US
STANDARD & POOR'S QIB. **See** Industry and Production-Trade and Industrial Directories.

LC HG4908 .S765
DD 332.6 US
STANDARD & POOR'S QUARTERLY DIVIDEND RECORD. **Added/Corp** Standard and Poor's Corporation. **VFOAT** Standard and Poor's Quarterly Dividend Record; Dividend Record; Standard & Poor's Dividend Record; Quarterly Dividend Record. (19??)-. Periodical. English. Four times a year (Jan. issue is the Annual Dividend Record). $1075.00. Standard & Poor's Corporation, (A Division of McGraw-Hill, Inc.), 25 Broadway, New York NY 10004. **Tel** (212)208-8775, (800)221-5277. **ED** Anthony J. Onofrio. **Circ:** 3,100. ***Absorbed*** *Standard & Poor's ... Annual Dividend Record.*
Desc: Provides complete and carefully detailed information on the dividend disbursement of over 10,000 stocks.

LC HG4501 .S693 **ISSN** 1061-0855
DD 332.6/05 US
STANDARD & POOR'S RATINGS HANDBOOK. [Standard Poor's rat. handb.]. **Added/Corp** Standard and Poor's Corporation. **VFOAT** Standard and Poor's Ratings Handbook; S & P Ratings Handbook; Ratings Handbook. Vol. 1, No. 1 (Apr. 1992)-. English. Twelve times a year. $395.00. Standard & Poor's Corporation, (A Division of McGraw-Hill, Inc.), 25 Broadway, New York NY 10004. **Tel** (212)208-8775, (800)221-5277. ***Continues*** *Creditweek International Ratings Guide, 0895-2639.*

LC HG4651 .S7a **ISSN** 0162-6531
DD 332.6/7 US
STANDARD AND POOR'S REGISTERED BOND INTEREST RECORD. **Main/Corp** Standard and Poor's Corporation. **Added/Corp** Standard and Poor's Corporation. Registered Bond Interest Record. (19??)-. English. One time a week (published every Friday). $2620.00. Standard & Poor's Corporation, (A Division of McGraw-Hill, Inc.), 25 Broadway, New York NY 10004. **Tel** (212)208-8775, (800)221-5277.

LC HG4907 .S4
DD 332.6 US
STANDARD & POOR'S SECURITY DEALERS OF NORTH AMERICA. **Added/Corp** Standard and Poor's Corporation. **VFOAT** Standard and Poor's Security Dealers of North America; Security Dealers of North America. (Fall 1975)-. Directory. English. Two times a year (Mar. and Sept.). $540.00. Standard & Poor's Corporation, (A Division of McGraw-Hill, Inc.), 25 Broadway, New York NY 10004. **Tel** (212)208-8775, (800)221-5277. Index available (New Address Index, Discontinued Listings Index, Location of Investment Firms Index). ***Continues*** *Security Dealers of North America, 0363-6933.*
Desc: National directory that lists over 14,000 brokerage and investment banking houses in the U.S. and Canada, including branch offices, along with their executive rosters of over 45,000 individuals.

LC HG450 **ISSN** 0737-299X
DD 332.6 US
STANDARD & POOR'S SEMI-WEEKLY CALLED BOND RECORD. **Main/Corp** Standard and Poor's Corporation. **VFOAT** Semi-Weekly Called Bond Record; Standard & Poor's Called Bond Record; Called Bond Record. **VAT** Standard and Poor's Semi-Weekly Called Bond Record. (19??)-. English. Two times a week (104 per year). $1650.00. Standard & Poor's Corporation, (A Division of McGraw-Hill, Inc.), 25 Broadway, New York NY 10004. **Tel** (212)208-8775, (800)221-5277.
Desc: Provides the greatest bond and stock call coverage available. It includes thousands of call notices, from the smallest municipal call to the largest corporate calls.

LC HG4915 .S68a **ISSN** 0272-0914
DD 332.63/222/0973 US
STANDARD & POOR'S STATISTICAL SERVICE: SECURITY PRICE INDEX RECORD. [Stand. Poor's stat. serv., secur. price index rec.]. **Main/Corp** Standard and Poor's Corporation. **Added/Corp** Standard and Poor's Corporation. Security Price Index Record. **VFOAT** Security Price Index Record. **VAT** Standard and Poor's Statistical Service. Security Price Index Record. (1978)-. Statistical Publication. English. Every 2 years. $95.00. Standard & Poor's Corporation, (A Division of McGraw-Hill, Inc.), 25 Broadway, New York NY 10004. **Tel** (212)208-8775, (800)221-5277. ***Continues*** *Standard & Poor's Trade and Securities Statistics: Security Price Index Record.*
Desc: Covers long-term statistics on all Standard & Poor's Indexes, the Dow Jones averages, price indexes for over 100 different industry groups, and more.

LC HG4905 .S44 **ISSN** 0191-1112
DD 332.6/7 US
STANDARD & POOR'S STOCK REPORTS. AMERICAN STOCK EXCHANGE. (STANDARD & POOR'S STOCK REPORTS: AMERICAN STOCK EXCHANGE.). **Main/Corp** Standard and Poor's Corporation. **VFOAT** Stock Reports: American Stock Exchange. **VAT** Standard and Poor's Stock Reports. American Stock Exchange. (Feb. 1973)-. Periodical. English. Four times a year. $1035.00. Standard & Poor's Corporation, (A Division of McGraw-Hill, Inc.), 25 Broadway, New York NY 10004. **Tel** (212)208-8775, (800)221-5277.
Desc: A succinct profile of the company's activities and financial position, supported by extensive statistics that facilitate quick year-to-year comparisons; includes the most pertinent background information on the company in an arrangement that reflects its relative importance. Contains over 700 reports.

LC HG4905 .S443 **ISSN** 0160-4899
DD 332.6/7 US
STANDARD & POOR'S STOCK REPORTS: NEW YORK STOCK EXCHANGE. **Main/Corp** Standard and Poor's Corporation. **VFOAT** Stock Reports: New York Stock Exchange. **VAT** Standard and Poor's Stock Reports: New York Stock Exchange. (Jan. 1973)-. Periodical. English (French, German and Italian). Four times a year. $1295.00. Standard & Poor's Corporation, (A Division of McGraw-Hill, Inc.), 25 Broadway, New York NY 10004. **Tel** (212)208-8775, (800)221-5277.
Desc: A succinct profile of the company's activities and financial position, supported by extensive statistics that facilitate quick year-to-year comparisons; includes the most pertinent background information on the company in an arrangement that reflects its relative importance. Contains over 1,600 reports.

LC HG4905 .S444 **ISSN** 0163-1993
DD 332.6/7 US
STANDARD & POOR'S STOCK REPORTS: OVER THE COUNTER. **Main/Corp** Standard and Poor's Corporation. **VFOAT** Stock Reports: Over the Counter. **VAT** Standard and Poor's Stock Reports: Over the Counter. (Mar. 1973)-. Periodical. English. Four times a year. $999.00. Standard & Poor's Corporation, (A Division of McGraw-Hill, Inc.), 25 Broadway, New York NY 10004. **Tel** (212)208-8775, (800)221-5277.

LC HG4655 .S73 **ISSN** 1056-9162
DD 332.63/244 US
STANDARD & POOR'S STRUCTURED FINANCE. [Stand. Poor's struct. finance]. **Added/Corp** Standard and Poor's Corporation. **VFOAT** Standard and Poor's Structured Finance; Structured Finance; Standard & Poor's. (May 1991)-. Periodical. English. Four times a year. $1450.00. Standard & Poor's Corporation, (A Division of McGraw-Hill, Inc.), 25 Broadway, New York NY 10004. **Tel** (212)208-8775, (800)221-5277.

LC HG4551
DD 332.6322 US
•STANDARD & POOR'S/TRENDLINE CURRENT MARKET PERSPECTIVES. **Added/Corp** Standard & Poor's Corporation. Trendline Corporation. **VFOAT** Standard and Poor's Trendline Current Market Perspectives; Trendline Current Market Perspectives; Current Market Perspectives. (May 1994)-. Periodical. English. Twelve times a year. $288.32. Standard & Poor's Corporation, (A Division of McGraw-Hill, Inc.), 25 Broadway, New York NY 10004. **Tel** (212)208-8775, (800)221-5277. ***Formed by the union of*** *OTC Chart Manual* ***and*** *Trendline Corporation. Trendline's Current Market Perspectives.*

LC HG4551
DD 332.6322 US
STANDARD & POOR'S WEEKLY DIVIDEND RECORD. **Main/Corp** Standard and Poor's Corporation. **VFOAT** Standard and Poor's Weekly Dividend Record; Weekly Dividend Record. (19??)-. English. Fifty-two times a year. $530.00. Standard & Poor's Corporation, (A Division of McGraw-Hill, Inc.), 25 Broadway, New York NY 10004. **Tel** (212)208-8775, (800)221-5277.
Desc: Provides complete detailed information on the dividend disbursements of over 10,000 stocks.

LC HG4501 .S76635 **ISSN** 0277-500X
DD 332 US
STANDARD CORPORATION DESCRIPTIONS. (STANDARD CORPORATION DESCRIPTIONS.). [Stand. corp. descr.]. **Main/Corp** Standard and Poor's Corporation. **Added/Corp** Standard and Poor's Corporation. Standard Corporation Records. Standard and Poor's Corporation. Standard & Poor's Corporation Descriptions. Standard and Poor's Corporation. Standard & Poor's Corporation Records. **VFOAT** Standard Corporation Records; Standard & Poor's Corporation Descriptions; Standard & Poor's Corporation Records. (Mar. 1941)-. Periodical. English. Irregular. $3,160.00. Standard & Poor's Corporation, (A Division of McGraw-Hill, Inc.), 25 Broadway, New York NY 10004. **Tel** (212)208-8775, (800)221-5277. ***Continues*** *Standard Statistics Co. Standard Corporation Record (Stock) Service.*

LC HG4651
DD 332.632 US
TITLE CHANGE
STANDARD OTC STOCK REPORTS. **Added/Corp** Standard and Poor's Corporation. **VFOAT** Stock Reports. Over the Counter and Regional Exchanges. **VAT** Standard Over-the-Counter Stock Reports. (197?)-(197?). Periodical. English. Standard & Poor's Corporation, (A Division of McGraw-Hill, Inc.), 25 Broadway, New York NY 10004. **Tel** (212)208-8775, (800)221-5277. Index Available, published separately, free-automatically sent. ***Continued by*** *Standard & Poors NASDAQ and Regional Exchange Stock Reports.*
Desc: Contains nearly 1,400 2-page reports and about 700 OTC ProFiles on more than 3,700 companies. Each report includes the most pertinent information on the company in an arrangement that reflects its relative importance.

LC CURRENT ISSUES ONLY **ISSN** 0195-6620
DD 332 US
STANGER REPORT, THE. [Stanger rep.]. **Added/Corp** Robert A. Stanger & Co. Vol. 1 (March 1979)-. Periodical. English. Twelve times a year. $447.00. Robert A Stanger and Company, PO Box 7490, Shrewsbury NJ 07702. **Tel** (201)389-3600, (800)631-2291, FAX (201)389-1751. **ED** Keith Allaire. (published separately). cum. index. **Bk Rev. Ad Acc, Adv Mgr:** Kathy Phillips. **Circ:** 5,000. ***Absorbed*** *Stanger's Partnership Watch.*
Desc: Provides exclusive coverage on every aspect of the partnership industry. Also includes comprehensive listings of the selling prices of partnerships in the secondary market, prior partnership performance data, partnership analysis, investment strategies and product trends, taxes, and regulatory issues, structuring techniques, and complete profiles and rankings of all public partnerships in the market.

LC HG4930 .S72
DD 332.6 US
STANGER'S SELLING MUTUAL FUNDS. **Added/Corp** Robert A. Stanger & Co. **VFOAT** Selling Mutual Funds. (Jan. 1991)-. Periodical. English. Twelve times a year. $197.00. Strange's Selling Mutual Funds, PO Box 7490, SHrewsbury NJ 77702-7490. ***Continues*** *Stanger's Mutual Fund Monitor.*

LC HA1631 .A33 HC407.Y63
DD 314.971 YU
STATISTICAL REPORT. **See** Business and Economics-Abstracting, Bibliographies and Statistics.

LC HG **ISSN** 1046-820X
DD 332 US
STATISTICAL YEARBOOK / CHICAGO MERCANTILE EXCHANGE. **See** Business and Economics-Abstracting, Bibliographies and Statistics.

Business and Economics — Investments

LC HG4651
DD 332.632
UK
STOCK EXCHANGE INVESTMENT LIST.
(19??)-. English. Twelve times a year. £36.35. Stock Exchange Investment List, 72 Borough High Street, London SE1 1XF United Kingdom. **Tel** 011 44 171 4036544, FAX 011 44 171 4035742.

LC HG5431 .S82
DD 338.7/4/0941
UK
TITLE CHANGE
STOCK EXCHANGE OFFICIAL YEARBOOK. **Added/Corp** International Stock Exchange. **VFOAT** Stock Exchange Official Year Book; Official Yearbook; Official Year Book. (1992)-(1994). English. Macmillan Distribution Ltd., Houndsmill Basingstoke, Hampshire RG21 2XS United Kingdom. **Tel** 011 44 1256 29242, FAX 011 44 1256 842084. **Continues** International Stock Exchange Official Yearbook. **Continued by** Macmillan Stock Exchange Yearbook.

LC HG4551
DD 332.6322
ISSN 0737-4135
US
STOCK GUIDE. [Stock guide]. **Main/Corp** Standard and Poor's Corporation. **Added/Corp** Standard and Poor's Corporation. (19??)-. Periodical. English. Twelve times a year. $135.00. Standard & Poor's Corporation, (A Division of McGraw-Hill, Inc.), 25 Broadway, New York NY 10004. **Tel** (212)208-8775, (800)221-5277. available on microfiche.
Desc: Pocket-size, 260-page, statistical summary of investments data on over 5,300 common and preferred stocks, listed and over-the-counter. It provides rapid review of all issues on the New York and American Stock Exchanges, and many NASDAQ issues, with 48 items of essential information on each.

LC HG4057 .A46
DD 338.7/4/0973
ISSN 0882-5467
US
STOCK MARKET ENCYCLOPEDIA (1985). (STOCK MARKET ENCYCLOPEDIA.). [Stock mark. encycl.]. **Added/Corp** Standard and Poor's Corporation. **VFOAT** Stock Market Encyclopedia Including the S&P 500; Standard & Poor's Stock Market Encyclopedia. Vol. 7, No. 2 (May 1985)-. English. Two times a year (Feb. and Aug.). $87.00. Standard & Poor's Corporation, (A Division of McGraw-Hill, Inc.), 25 Broadway, New York NY 10004. **Tel** (212)208-8775, (800)221-5277. **Continues** S & P 500 Stock Market Encyclopedia, 0737-5026.
Desc: Reports on more than 700 stocks.

LC HG
DD 332
ISSN 0039-1638
US
SUSPENDED
STOCK MARKET MAGAZINE, THE. [Stock mark. mag.]. Periodical. English. Irregular. $13.98 (surface mail) Canada; $13.98 (airmail) other except US. Wall Street Publications Institute Inc, 16 School Street, Yonkers NY 10701. **Tel** (914)423-4566. **ED** Bernard D Brown. **Bk Rev**. **Ad Acc**.
Desc: The little guy's business and financial publication.

LC HG4916 .S75
DD 332.63/22/0973
ISSN 0196-1705
US
STOCK PICTURE, THE. **Added/Corp** Horsey (M. C.) and Company. 1st Ed. (1938)-. Periodical. English. Six times a year (Jan., Mar., May, July, Sept., Nov.). $140.00. M. C. Horsey & Company, 120 South Boulevard, PO Box H, Salisbury MD 21801. **Tel** (301)742-3700 or 742-0132.

LC HG4651
DD 332.632
ISSN 0562-083X
US
STOCK QUOTATIONS ON THE NEW YORK STOCK EXCHANGE. Periodical. English. Seven times a week. $4.50. Francis Emory Fitch Inc, 130 Cedar Street, New York NY 10006. **Tel** (212)619-3800, FAX (212)233-1817. **Circ:** Daily stock sheets. available on magnetic tape.

LC HG4651
DD 332.632
US
STOCK TRADER'S ALMANAC, THE. (19??)-. English. $31.00. Hirsch Organization, 6 Deer Trail, Old Tappan NJ 07675. **Tel** (201)664-3400.

LC HG4915 .S75
DD 332.6/322/0973
ISSN 0081-5624
US
STOCK VALUES AND DIVIDENDS FOR TAX PURPOSES. **Added/Corp** Commerce Clearing House. (1969)-. English. Commerce Clearing House Inc., 4025 West Peterson Avenue, Chicago IL 60646-6085. **Tel** (312)583-8500, FAX (708)940-4600. **ED** A.E. Schechter. **Continues** Stock Values and Yields for Tax Purposes.
Desc: Contains a comprehensive table showing values and yields or dividends paid of all regularly quoted and listed stocks.

LC HG4651
DD 332.632
US
STOCKS & BONDS. **Main/Corp** American Stock Exchange. English. Irregular. $4.50. Francis Emory Fitch Inc, 130 Cedar Street, New York NY 10006. **Tel** (212)619-3800, FAX (212)233-1817.

LC HG4651
DD 332.632
ISSN 0276-7740
US
STOCKS & BONDS ON THE NEW YORK STOCK EXCHANGE. **Added/Corp** New York Stock Exchange. **VFOAT** Stocks and Bonds, New York Stock Exchange Incorporated. **VAT** Stocks and Bonds on the New York Stock Exchange. (1979)-. Periodical. English. Four times a year. $38.00. Francis Emory Fitch Inc, 130 Cedar Street, New York NY 10006. **Tel** (212)619-3800, FAX (212)233-1817. **Continues** New York Stock Exchange. Stocks.

LC HG4651 .S7949
DD 332.63/222/0973
ISSN 1047-2436
US
STOCKS, BONDS, BILLS, AND INFLATION YEARBOOK. (STOCKS, BONDS, BILLS, AND INFLATION ... YEARBOOK.). [Stocks bonds bills inflat. yearb.]. **Added/Corp** R.G. Ibbotson Associates (Firm) Ibbotson Associates (Firm) Capital Market Research Center (Chicago, Ill.). **VFOAT** SBBI Yearbook. (1983)-. English. One time a year. $100.00. Ibbotson Associates, 2225 North Michigan Avenue, Suite 700, Chicago IL 60601. **Tel** (312)616-1620. **ED** Laurence B. Siegel and Katie B. Weigel. **Ad Acc**. **Circ:** 2,500 (ctrl). available on diskette.
Desc: Market results on basic financial assets. Covers monthly and annual returns, indices and summary statistics on 15 US assets.

LC HG4501 .S7665b
DD 332.6/7
ISSN 0163-6235
US
STOCKS IN THE STANDARD & POOR'S 500. **Main/Corp** Standard and Poor's Corporation. **VAT** Stocks in the Standard and Poor's Five Hundred. (19??)-. Trade Publication. English. Twelve times a year. Standard & Poor's Corporation, (A Division of McGraw-Hill, Inc.), 25 Broadway, New York NY 10004. **Tel** (212)208-8775, (800)221-5277.

LC HG4501
DD 332.6/0971
ISSN 0822-9694
CN
STRATEGIE (TORONTO). (STRATEGIE.). [Strategie]. Vol. 1, No. 1 (Fall 1981)-. Periodical. French. Four times a year. Free. Bibliothecaire Dominion Securities Ames, PO Box 21 Commerce Court South, Toronto Ontario M5L 1A7 Canada.

LC HG5151
DD 332.6/0971
ISSN 0229-0510
CN
STRATEGY (TORONTO). (STRATEGY : A REVIEW OF CANADIAN INVESTMENTS.). [Strategy]. **VFOAT** Ames Strategy. Fall 1976-Summer 1980; Vol. 1, No. 1 (Autumn 1981)-. Periodical. English. Four times a year. RBC Dominion Securities, PO Box 21, Commerce Ct. South, Toronto Ontario M5L 1A7 Canada. **Absorbed** Market Strategy (Toronto, Ont.), 0822-9686.

LC HG4501
DD 332.6
ISSN 1185-3077
CN
STRIVE (OTTAWA). (STRIVE.). [Strive]. **Added/Corp** Midland Walwyn Capital. (Winter 1991)-. Periodical. English. Four times a year. $6.00. Midland Walwyn Capital, Suite 1600, 121 King Street West, Toronto Ontario M5H 3W6 Canada.

LC HG
DD 332
ISSN 1060-4251
US
STURZA'S MEDICAL INVESTMENT LETTER. [Sturza's med. investm. lett.]. Vol. 1, No. 1 (Nov. 1991)-. Periodical. English. Twelve times a year. $295.00. Taurus Littrow Publishing, 424 West End Avenue, 7th Floor, New York NY 10024. **Tel** (212)873-7200, FAX (212)873-7799. Index available. cum. index.
Desc: Provides monthly analysis and investment recommendations on companies in the healthcare industry. Emphasis is placed on the equities of biotechnology, pharmaceutical, medical equipment and medical supply companies.

LC HG450
DD 332.6
US
SUMMARY OF PRESCRIBED UNIT COST AND HOURLY RATE FOR RETURN ON INVESTMENT AND TAX ALLOWANCE. English. One time a year. Civil Aeronautics Board, 1825 Connecticut Avenue, Washington DC 20428. **Tel** (202)673-5174.

LC HG4527 .K55 Suppl
DD 332.6/78
US
SUPPLEMENT TO THE BEAT INFLATION STRATEGY. (19??)-. English. One time a year. Prentice Hall Simon & Schuster, PO Box 11071, Des Moines IA 50336. **Tel** (800)947-7700, (515)284-6751.

LC HG4651
DD 332.63/27
ISSN 0834-0420
CN
TITLE CHANGE
SURVEY OF FUNDS (TORONTO. 1985). (SURVEY OF FUNDS : MUTUAL FUNDS, RRIFS, RRSPS, INVESTMENT FUNDS.). [Surv. funds]. **Added/Corp** Financial Post Information Service. (Dec. 31, 1985)-(19??). Periodical. English. Financial Post Company Ltd., 333 King Street East, Toronto Ontario M5A 4N2, Canada. **Tel** (416)350-6500, FAX (416)350-6601. **Continues** Survey of RRSP & Investment Fund Performance, 0829-5166. **Continued by** Survey of Mutual Funds.
Desc: Data on more than 700 funds, including a glossary of terms that precisely defines fund types.

LC HG450
DD 332.6
CN
SURVEY OF MUTUAL FUNDS. (19??)-. Periodical. English. Four times a year. 120.01Can$. Financial Post Company Ltd., 333 King Street East, Toronto Ontario M5A 4N2, Canada. **Tel** (416)350-6500, FAX (416)350-6601. **Continues** Survey of Funds.

LC HG4501
DD 332.6
US
SURVEY OF NON-US STOCK MARKET SUITABILITY. **Added/Corp** Ennis, Knupp & Associates. **VFOAT** Survey of Non-U.S. Stock Market Suitability. **VAT** Survey of Non-United States Stock Market Suitability. (1991)-. English. Ennis, Knupp & Associates, 10 South Riverside Plaza, Suite 700, Chicago IL 60606.

LC HG
DD 332
ISSN 0896-4106
US
SYLVIA PORTER'S PERSONAL FINANCE. [Sylvia Porter's pers. finance]. **VFOAT** Personal Finance. (198?)-. Periodical. English. Twelve times a year. Sylvia Porter's Personal Finance, PO Box 1928, Marion OH 43306. **Continues** Sylvia Porter's Personal Finance Magazine, 0738-4173.
Ind/Abst Bus. Index (Jan. 1989-June 1989); Gen. BusinessFile (Jan. 1989-June 1989); Gen. Period. Index (1987-1989); Mag. Index Plus (Jan. 1989-June 1989); Mag. Index. Sel. (1987-1989); Mag. Index (?-?).

LC HG4501
DD 332.6
US
TABLES OF REDEMPTION VALUES FOR UNITED STATES SAVINGS BONDS FOR ALL MONTHS FROM ... SERIES EE. **Added/Corp** United States. Bureau of the Public Debt. **VFOAT** Series EE. (July through Dec. 1980)-. Government Publication. English. Two times a year. $15.00. Superintendent of Documents, US Government Printing Office, Washington DC 20402. **Tel** (202)275-3328, FAX (202)786-2377. **Continues** United States. Bureau of the Public Debt. Tables of Redemption Values for United States Savings Bonds. Series A-E, 0498-8752.

LC HG4501
DD 332.6
US
TAIPAN. (19??)-. English. Twelve times a year. $79.95. Agora Publishing, 824 East Baltimore Street, Baltimore MD 21202. **Tel** (800)433-1528.

LC HG4503 .T33
DD 338/.0951/249
CH
TAIWAN INDUSTRIAL PANORAMA. **Added/Corp** China (Republic : 1949-). Ching Chi Pu. Tou Tzu Yeh Wu Chu. Vol. 1 (Sept. 1973)-. Periodical. English. Twelve times a year. Free on request. Industrial Development & Investment Center, Roosevelt Road, Section 1, Floor 10, Tapei 10757 Taiwan. **Tel** (212)752-2340 (US office).

LC HD936 .T36
DD 332.63/24/02551249
ISSN 1044-470X
US
TAIWAN REGISTER. See Real Estate.

LC HG450
DD 332.6
US
TARGET 2000 AND BEYOND INVESTOR. Newsletter. English. Twelve times a year. Brattin Capital Management Inc., PO Box 8429, Bartlett IL 60103-8429. **Tel** (708)736-1094, FAX (708)213-2274.
Desc: Investment research topics and market commentary. Takes a futuristic view and recommends investment opportunities that stand to benefit from technological and demographic megatrends. Concentrates on emerging growth stocks and closed-end funds as a way to participate in emerging markets internationally.

LC HJ3851
DD 336.2
US
TAX & INVESTMENT PROFILE. GERMANY. See Finance-Taxation.

LC KF6415.A15 T36
DD 343.7305/246 347.3035246
ISSN 0739-6619
US
TAX FACTS ON INVESTMENTS. See Finance-Taxation.

LC KF6289.8.E9 E96
DD 343.7305/23 347.303523
ISSN 0747-8607
US
CCC
TAX MANAGEMENT COMPENSATION PLANNING JOURNAL. [Tax manage. compens. plann. j.]. **Added/Corp** Tax Management Inc. Vol. 12 No. 1 (Jan. 1984)-. Trade Publication. English. Twelve times a year. $371.00. Bureau of National Affairs Inc., 9435 Key

West Avenue, Rockville MD 20850. **Tel** (800)372-1033, (301)258-1033, FAX (301)948-5823. **ED** Glenn Davis. Index available. cum. index. available on microfilm and microfiche from University Microfilms International (UMI); available on an online database (file 485/Full-Text) from DIALOG. ***Continues*** *Compensation Planning Journal, 0148-690X.*
Desc: A professional review of major employee benefit plans in use, and new developments in retirement, profit sharing and welfare plans, stock options, and other employee compensation arrangements.
Ind/Abst Acad. Search; Account. Tax Datab. (1989-) [Full Txt.]; Bus. Index (1985-); Bus. Source Plus; Bus. Source; EP Collect.; Gen. BusinessFile (1985-); Gen. Period. Index (1985-); Homework Help.; INFO-SOUTH Abstr.; Leg. Resour. Index (1984-); LegalTrac (1980-); Mag. Search; MasterFile FullTEXT 1000; MasterFile FullTEXT 350; MasterFile FullTEXT 650; MasterFile FullTEXT (July 1993-); OCLC; Telebase.

LC KE3098 **ISSN** 1186-1487
DD 344.71/012522 CN
TAX REFORM AND RETIREMENT SAVINGS (TORONTO). (TAX REFORM AND RETIREMENT SAVINGS.). [Tax reform retire. sav.]. **Added/Corp** William M. Mercer Limited. No. 1 (July 23, 1990)-. Periodical. English. Twelve times a year. Free on request. William M Mercer Limited, BCE Place, 161 Bay Street, PO Box 501, Toronto Ontario M5J 2S5 Canada. **Tel** (416)868-2000.

LC HG4501
DD 332.6 NE
TAXATION AND INVESTMENT IN CANADA. See Finance-Taxation.

LC HG450
DD 332.6 NE
TAXATION & INVESTMENT IN MEXICO.
See Finance-Taxation.

LC HG450
DD 332.6 NE
TAXATION AND INVESTMENT IN SOUTH AFRICA. See Finance-Taxation.

LC HG4501
DD 332.6 NE
TAXES AND INVESTMENT IN THE MIDDLE EAST. SUPPLEMENT. See Law-Corporation Law.

LC HG **ISSN** 0738-3355
DD 332 US
CCC
TECHNICAL ANALYSIS OF STOCKS AND COMMODITIES (JOURNAL). (TECHNICAL ANALYSIS OF STOCKS & COMMODITIES.). [Tech. anal. stocks commod.]. **VFOAT** Technical Analysis of Stocks & Commodities; Stocks & Commodities; Technical Analysis. (1982)-. Trade Publication. English. Twelve times a year. $70.28. Technical Analysis Inc, 4757 California Avenue Southwest, Seattle WA 98116. **Tel** (206)938-0570, telex 4993678. **ED** John Sweeney, Melanie F. Bowman, and Thomas R. Hartle. Index available. cum. index. **Bk Rev. Ad Acc. Circ:** 20,000. available on microfilm from University Microfilms International (UMI).
Desc: Magazine for traders of stocks, options, mutual funds, and commodities. Articles describe application of chart, numerical, and computer methods to buying and selling actively traded financial issues. Includes reviews, computer subroutines and examples.

LC HG **ISSN** 0889-9525
DD 332 US
TECHNICAL TRENDS. [Tech. trends]. **Added/Corp** Merrill Analysis (Chappaqua, N.Y.). (19??)-. Periodical. English. Forty times a year. $147.00 US, Canada and Mexcio; $180.00 other. Technical Trends, Box 792, Wilton CT 06897. **Tel** (203)762-0229, (800)762-0229, FAX (203)762-0229. **ED** John McGinley.
Ind/Abst Urban Aff. Abstr.

LC HG **ISSN** 0749-999X
DD 332 US
TECHNOLOGY STOCK MONITOR. [Technol. stock monit.]. Vol. 1, No. 1 (Dec. 1984)-. Periodical. English. Twelve times a year. $95.00. HMR Publishing Company, PO Box 3073, Barrington IL 60010-3073. **Tel** (312)382-7857.

LC HG5161 .T46
DD 332.64/272/05 MX
TENDENCIAS PARA EL INVERSIONISTA. Spanish. One time a week. Grupo Editorial Expansion, Sinaloa 149 P9, Col Roma, 06700 Mexico DF Mexico. **Tel** 011 52 5 2072066, 2072619, FAX 011 52 5 5116351.

LC HG4953.T4 A17
DD 332.63/233/09764 US
TEXAS BOND REPORTER. Added/Corp Municipal Advisory Council of Texas. Vol. 1 (1933)-. Periodical. English. One time a week. Free. Municipal Advisory Council of Texas, PO Box 2177, Austin TX 78768. **Tel** (512)476-6947.

LC HG5750.55.A2 T46
DD 332.6/7322593/05 TH
THAILAND INVESTMENT. Added/Corp Thailand. Samnakngan Khana Kammakan Songs Kanlongthun. English. Business Thailand Co Ltd, 972 Soi Saeng Cham Rama 9 Road, Bangkok 10310 Thailand. **Tel** 011 66 2 2483257. ***Continues*** *Thailand Investment Handbook and Directory of Promoted Companies.*

LC HG4651 **ISSN** 0820-8026
DD 332.63/23/0971 CN
THAT WAS THE WEEK THAT WAS. Periodical. English. One time a week. Free. John Grundy Investment Department Commercial Union Assurance, PO Box 441, Toronto-Dominion Centre, Toronto Ontario M5K 1L9 Canada. **Tel** (416)361-2536. **ED** John Grundy. **Circ:** 500 (ctrl).
Desc: A review of major happenings in the Canadian bond market.

LC HG450
DD 332.6 US
TIMER DIGEST. English. Irregular (18 issues per year). $225.00. Timer Digest Inc, PO Box 1688, Greenwich CT 06836. **Tel** (203)629-3503.

LC HD9134 .A24
DD 338.1/7371/0973 US
TOBACCO STOCKS. Government Publication. English. Four times a year. $4.00. US Department of Agriculture / Agricultural Marketing Service / Washington, DC, Market News Branch, Fruit and Vegetable Division, Washington DC 20250. **Tel** (202)720-2745, (202)720-3343, FAX (202)720-7502. Documents available from Documents on Demand. ***Continues*** *United States. Agricultural Marketing Service. Tobacco Division. Tobacco Stocks., 0360-439X;* ***Absorbed*** *Quarterly Report of Manufacture and Sales of Snuff, Smoking, and Chewing Tobacco.*
Ind/Abst Am. Stat. Index.

LC HG **ISSN** 1042-8127
DD 332 US
TODAY'S INVESTOR. [Today's investor]. Vol. 10, No. 5, March 17 (1989)-. Periodical. English. Twenty-six times a year. $69.00. Today's Investor, PO Box 86, Columbia Maryland 21045. ***Continues*** *Penny Stock News, 0745-4600.*
Desc: Covers 2500+ small cap companies trading on the various exchanges. Also covers unreported bulletin board companies.

LC hg4551 **ISSN** 0703-7716
DD 332.6/42/065713541 CN
TORONTO STOCK EXCHANGE '300' STOCK PRICE INDEX SYSTEM, THE. Main/Corp Toronto Stock Exchange. (1976)-. English. One time a year. 1200.49Can$. Toronto Stock Exchange, The Exchange Tower, 2 First Canadian Place, Toronto Ontario M5X 1J2 Canada. **Tel** (416)947-4681.

LC HG5160.T6 T68a **ISSN** 0049-4216
DD 332.6/42/09713541 CN
TORONTO STOCK EXCHANGE REVIEW, THE. See Business and Economics-Abstracting, Bibliographies and Statistics.

LC HF5001 **ISSN** 1051-7197
DD 650 US
TRACKING EASTERN EUROPE. (TRACKING EASTERN EUROPE : EXECUTIVE BUSINESS GUIDE.). [Track. East. Eur.]. **Added/Corp** A.M.F. International Consultants. (1990)-. Periodical. English. Twenty-four times a year (Fridays). $445.00. AMF International Consultants, 812 North Wood Avenue, Linden NJ 07036. **Tel** (908)486-3534, FAX (908)486-4084. **ED** Fred T. Rossi.
Desc: News and information on investments and other related businesses on Eastern Europe and former Soviet Republics.

LC HG **ISSN** 0892-3280
DD 332 US
CEASED
TRADING CYCLES. [Trading cycles]. (19??)-(19??). Periodical. English. Trading Cycles, 995 Oak Park Drive, Morgan Hill CA 95037. **Tel** (408)778-2925. **ED** R. E. Andrews. **Bk Rev**, (Qty: 1-2). ctrl circ.
Desc: For traders and low risk investors. Establishes turning points for stock indexes, currencies, interest rates, bonds, gold/silver, mining stocks, and stock selections. Calculated by BOBA, the computer program that analyzes technical data then interprets for action signals.

LC HG4651 **ISSN** 0846-0469
DD 333.63/22/09712305 CN
TRADING TRENDS. [Trading trends]. (Mar. 15, 1990)-. Periodical. English. Six times a year. $24.95 for 12 issues. Trading Trends, Suite D-501, 500 Eau Claire Avenue South West, Calgary Alberta T2P 3RS Canada.

LC HG450
DD 332.6 US
TRANSACTIONS AND INTENTIONS REPORT. (19??)-. English. $525.00. Vickers Stock Research Corporation, 17 Battery Place, 18th Floor, New York NY 10004. **Tel** (212)425-7500.

LC HG4551 **ISSN** 0277-4968
DD 332.6322 US
TRENDLINE DAILY ACTION STOCK CHARTS. Added/Corp Trendline Corp. **VFOAT** Daily Action Stock Charts. Vol. 22, No. 16 (Apr. 18, 1980)-. Periodical. English. One time a week. $691.84. Standard & Poor's Corporation, (A Division of McGraw-Hill, Inc.), 25 Broadway, New York NY 10004. **Tel** (212)208-8775, (800)221-5277. ***Continues*** *Trendline Daily Basis Stock Charts, 0564-1896.*
Desc: Used by professional investors and market analysts to identify short- and intermediate-range trends in the market and individual stocks, and to technically analyze and compare price performance of stocks they hold or are considering.

LC HG4916 .T73 **ISSN** 0041-2333
DD 332.63/22/0973 US
TITLE CHANGE
TRENDLINE'S CURRENT MARKET PERSPECTIVES. [Trendline's curr. mark. perspect.]. **Main/Corp** Trendline Corporation. **Added/Corp** Trendline Corporation. Current Market Perspectives. **VFOAT** Current Market Perspectives. Vol. 1 (Oct. 1962)-(1994). English. Standard & Poor's Corporation, (A Division of McGraw-Hill, Inc.), 25 Broadway, New York NY 10004. **Tel** (212)208-8775, (800)221-5277. ***Merged with*** *OTC Chart Manual* ***to form*** *Standard & Poor's/Trendline Current Market Perspectives.*
Desc: Specially designed to show market action and key fundamental facts for 1,476 stocks- including almost every issues on the New York Stock Exchange. Used to technically analyze intermediate- and long-term performance of individual stocks and the market.

LC HC106.6 .S742
DD 332.6 US
TRENDS & PROJECTIONS. Main/Corp Standard and Poor's Corporation. **VFOAT** Trends and Projections. (197?)-. Periodical. English. Twelve times a year. $115.00. Standard & Poor's Corporation, (A Division of McGraw-Hill, Inc.), 25 Broadway, New York NY 10004. **Tel** (212)208-8775, (800)221-5277.

LC HG **ISSN** 1018-208X
DD 332 US
TRENDS IN PRIVATE INVESTMENT IN DEVELOPING COUNTRIES. [Trends priv. investm. dev. ctries.]. **Added/Corp** International Finance Corporation. (1991)-. English. One time a year. Price varies. World Bank Publications, 1818 H Street Northwest, Washington DC 20043. **Tel** (202)473-1155, (202)473-1155, FAX (202)522-3224, telex WUI 64145 WORLDBANK. **(Subscription address:** World Bank Publications, PO Box 7247-8619, Books Department, Philadelphia PA 19170.)

LC HD7106.C2 A37 **ISSN** 0835-4634
DD 332.6/75254 CN
TRUSTEED PENSION FUNDS, FINANCIAL STATISTICS. [Trusted pension funds financ. stat.]. **Added/Corp** Statistics Canada. Pensions Section. **VFOAT** Caisses de Retraite en Fiducie, Statistiques Financieres. (1985)-. English (French). One time a year. 51.00Can$. Statistics Canada Publications Sales and Services, R.H. Coats Building 6th Floor, Ottawa Ontario K1A 0T6 Canada. **Tel** (613)951-5078, (800)267-6677, FAX (613)951-1584, telex 053-3585. ***Continues*** *Trusteed Pension Plans Financial Statistics, 0575-9978.*

LC HG4458.A1 T85
DD 332.6 KO
TUJA SINTAK = INVESTMENT TRUST. Added/Corp Taehan Tuja Sintak Chusik Hoesa. **VFOAT** Investment Trust. (19??)-. Korean (Korean). Twelve times a year. Daehan Investment Trust Company Ltd, 44-1 Yoido-Dong, Yongdungpo-ku, Seoul Korea 150-010. **Tel** (02)785-3111, FAX (02)781-0331. **ED** Joong-Hee Lee. **Circ:** 1,900 (ctrl).
Desc: Trends and statistics of investment trust.

LC HG **ISSN** 1056-0173
DD 332 US
TURNAROUND LETTER, THE. [Turnaround lett.]. **VFOAT** Turn Around Letter. (198?)-. Periodical. English. Twelve times a year. $195.00. New Generation Research Inc / Boston, 225 Friend Street, Suite 801, Box 6721, Boston MA 02114. **Tel** (800)468-3810.

LC HG450 **ISSN** 0148-5911
DD 332.6 US
TUROV ON OPTIONS AND HEDGING. Periodical. English. One time a week. Cowen & Company, One Battery Park Plaza, New York NY 10004.

LC HG **ISSN** 0885-2340
DD 332 US
TV PROGRAM INVESTOR. See Communications-Television and Cable.

LC HG5851.A2 U23 **ISSN** 1048-681X
DD 338.8/8973068/025 US
U.S. BUSINESS IN SOUTH AFRICA. [U. S. bus. S. Afr.]. **Added/Corp** Investor Responsibility Research Center. **VFOAT** US Business in South Africa.

VAT United States business in South Africa. 6th Ed. (1990)-. English. One time a year. $595.00. Investor Responsibility Research Center, 1350 Connecticut Avenue Northwest 700, Washington DC 20036. **Tel** (202)833-0700. ***Continues*** *U.S. and Canadian Business in South Africa.*

LC HG4538 .U2 **ISSN** 0730-9848
DD 332.6/7373/00212 US

U.S. DIRECT INVESTMENT ABROAD. [U.S. dir. investm. abroad]. **VFOAT** United States Direct Investment Abroad. (19??)-. English. One time a year. Bureau of Economic Analysis, US Department of Commerce, 1401 K Street Northwest, Washington DC 20230. **Tel** (202)523-0777.

LC KF6389.A1 U24 **ISSN** 0275-1755
DD 343.7305/23 347.303523 US

... U.S. INVESTMENT TAX CREDIT INDEX, THE. **VFOAT** US Investment Tax Credit Index. **VAT** United States Investment Tax Credit Index. 1st. Ed. (1981)-. English. Three times a year. $140.00. Valtec Associates Inc., 85 West Algonquin Road, Suite 650, Arlington Heights IL 60005.

LC HG4503 .U36
DD 332.6 IO

UANG & EFEK (PERSERIKATAN PERDAGANGAN UANG DAN EFEK-EFEK (INDONESIA) : 1982). (UANG & EFEK.). **VFOAT** Uang dan Efek. Edition No. 1-. Periodical. Indonesian. Twelve times a year. J1 Kebon Sirth, No 48 Flat, Danareksa Indonesia. ***Continues*** *Uang & Efek (Perserikatan Perdagangan Uang dan Efek-Efik (Indonesia) : 1978).*

LC HB522 **ISSN** 1061-4095
DD 338 US

UKRAINE UPDATE. **See** Business and Economics-Economic History, Conditions.

LC HC101 .U5 **ISSN** 0895-5689
DD 330.973/005 US

UNITED & BABSON INVESTMENT REPORT. [United Babson investm. rep.]. **Added/Corp** Babson-United Investment Advisors. **VFOAT** United and Babson Investment Report. Vol. 79, No. 1 (Jan. 5, 1987)-. Periodical. English. Fifty-two times a year. $268.00. Babson - United Investment Advisors Inc., 101 Prescott Street, Wellesley Hills MA 02181. **Tel** (617)235-0900. **ED** Sydney S. McMath. ***Continues*** *United Business & Investment Report, 0360-8662.*
Desc: Includes a concise summary of business and investment developments, Washington news, commodity price trends, industry surveys, the outlook for the stock market and specific buy-hold-sell advice on stocks and bonds recommended for growth, income or profit.
Ind/Abst Predicasts.

LC HG4530 .U45 **ISSN** 0740-557X
DD 332.63/27 US
CEASED

UNITED MUTUAL FUND SELECTOR. **Added/Corp** United Business Service Company. **VFOAT** Mutual Fund Selector. (1968)-(July 1994). Periodical. English. Babson - United Investment Advisors Inc., 101 Prescott Street, Wellesley Hills MA 02181. **Tel** (617)235-0900. **ED** Patricia A Ganley. **Circ:** 13,000.
Desc: Provides a regular flow of statistical information on over 1,000 mutual funds. Tracks developments in the field and makes specific recommendations.

LC HG **ISSN** 0734-9211
DD 332 US

UNITED STATES INVESTOR. [U.S. investor]. Vol. 48, No. 29 (July 20, 1977)-. Periodical. English. One time a week. $78.00. Cleworth Publishing Company / CT, 1 River Road, Cos Cob CT 06807. ***Continues*** *United States Investor. Investment Edition.*

LC HG4155 .U57
DD 658.1509 GW

UNTERNEHMEN UND ARBEITSSTATTEN. REIHE 2.2, ZAHL UND NOMINALKAPITAL DER KAPITALGESELLSCHAFTEN. **Added/Corp** Germany (West). Statistisches Bundesamt. **VFOAT** Zahl und Nominalkapital der Kapitalgesellschaften Fachserie 2. (1986)-. German. One time a year. DM9.50. W. Kohlhammer Verlag GmbH, Postfach 800430, D-70549 Stuttgart Germany. **Tel** 011 49 711 78630, FAX 011 49 711 7863430, telex 7-255820.

LC HG450
DD 332.6 CN
CEASED

UPDATE : WEEKLY DEVELOPMENTS AND INVESTMENT INSIGHTS. (19??)-(Aug. 1995). English. BCA Publications Ltd., 1002 Sherbrooke Street West, Suite 1600, Montreal Quebec H3A 3L6 Canada. **Tel** (514)499-9706, FAX (514)499-9709.

LC HG4501 HD9502 **ISSN** 1352-7983
DD 332.6 333.79 UK

•**UTILITY PRIVATISATIONS IN DEVELOPING COUNTRIES.** (1994)-. Bulletin. English. One time a year. £265.00. OXERA Press, Blue Boar Court, Alfred Street, Oxford OX1 4HE United Kingdom. **Tel** 011 44 865 251142, FAX 011 44 865 251172.
Desc: Gives information on opportunities for investment in Latin America and East Asia.

LC HG450
DD 332.6 US

V-A-R-D-S REPORT, THE. (THE V-A-R-D-S REPORT : A MONTHLY VARIABLE ANNUITY INDUSTRY ANALYSIS.). [V-A-R-D-S rep.]. **Added/Corp** Financial Planning Resources, Inc. **VFOAT** VARDS Report. (1988)-. English. Twelve times a year. $698.00. Financial Planning Resources Inc, PO Box 1927, Roswell GA 30077. **Tel** (404)998-5186, FAX (404)998-5187. **ED** Robert H. Carey. **Circ:** 4,000.

LC HG5496.5 .H64a
DD 332.6 GW

VADEMECUM DER INVESTMENTFONDS. **Main/Corp** Verlag Hoppenstedt. (19??)-. English. One time a year. $221.86. Verlag Hoppenstedt & Company, Postfach 100139, D-64201 Darmstadt Germany. **Tel** 011 49 6151 380436, 011 49 6151 380361.

LC HG4926.A3 N3
DD 332.6/32 US

VALUATIONS OF SECURITIES. **Main/Corp** National Association of Insurance Commissioners. Securities Valuation Office. (19??)-. English. One time a year. Securities Valuation Office, 195 Broadway 19th Floor, New York NY 10007. **Tel** (212)285-0010. ***Continues*** *Valuations of Securities.*

LC HG4501 **ISSN** 0846-1155
DD 332.6 CN

VALUE ADVISOR. (THE VALUE ADVISOR.). [Value advis.]. **Added/Corp** Midland Walwyn Capital. (June 1990)-. Periodical. English. Four times a year. Limited free distribution. Midland Walwyn Capital, Suite 1600, 121 King Street West, Toronto Ontario M5H 3W6 Canada.

LC HG4501 .V25 **ISSN** 0737-0717
DD 332.63/22 US
TITLE CHANGE

VALUE LINE CONVERTIBLES. [Value line convert.]. Vol. 12, No. 27 (July 20, 1981)-(1995). Periodical. English. (published weekly on Monday). Value Line Publishing, Inc., 711 3rd Avenue, New York NY 10017. **Tel** (212)687-3965, (800)634-3853, FAX (212)661-2807. **ED** Allan Lyons. **Circ:** 3,000. ***Continues in part*** *Value Line Options & Convertibles, 0146-7581.* ***Continued by*** *Value Line Convertibles Survey, 1081-986X.*

LC HG4501 .V25 **ISSN** 1081-986X
DD 332.63/22 US

•**VALUE LINE CONVERTIBLES SURVEY (1995), THE.** (THE VALUE LINE CONVERTIBLES SURVEY.). [Value line convert. surv.]. (1995)-. English. One time a week. $625.00. Value Line Publishing, Inc., 711 3rd Avenue, New York NY 10017. **Tel** (212)687-3965, (800)634-3853, FAX (212)661-2807. ***Continues*** *Value Line Convertibles, 0737-0717.*

LC HG **ISSN** 1055-6354
DD 332 US

VALUE LINE INVESTMENT SURVEY (CANADIAN ED.), THE. (THE VALUE LINE INVESTMENT SURVEY.). [Value line investm. surv.]. Ed. 1 (May 10, 1991)-. Periodical. English. One time a week. $260.00 (Can.). Value Line Publishing, 711 3rd Avenue, New York NY 10017-4064.
Ind/Abst Trade Ind. Index.

LC HG450
DD 332.6 US

VALUE LINE INVESTMENT SURVEY. PART 2, SELECTION & OPINION, THE. **VFOAT** Value Line Selection & Opinion. (19??)-. Periodical. English. Fifty-two times a year (Fri.). $525.00 US Possessions APO and FPO; $625.00 Canada, Mexico, South African and Caribbean; $940.00 other. Value Line Publishing, Inc., 711 3rd Avenue, New York NY 10017. **Tel** (212)687-3965, (800)634-3853, FAX (212)661-2807.
Ind/Abst Bus. Index (1992-); Gen. BusinessFile (1992-); Trade Ind. Index.

LC HG450
DD 332.6 US

VALUE LINE INVESTMENT SURVEY. PART 3, RATINGS & REPORTS, THE. (19??)-. Periodical. English. One time a week. Arnold Bernhard Company Inc, 711 Third Avenue, New York NY 10017. **Tel** (212)687-3965.
Ind/Abst Bus. Index (1992-); Gen. BusinessFile (1992-); Trade Ind. Index.

LC HG4501 .V26 **ISSN** 0042-2401
DD 332.6305 US

VALUE LINE INVESTMENT SURVEY (U.S. ED.), THE. (THE VALUE LINE INVESTMENT SURVEY.). [Value line investm. surv.]. (1936)-. English. One time a week. $525.00. Value Line Publishing, Inc., 711 3rd Avenue, New York NY 10017. **Tel** (212)687-3965, (800)634-3853, FAX (212)661-2807. Index available. available on microfilm and microfiche.
Desc: Provides weekly the current relative rating for performance and safety together with estimated yields, the latest earnings, dividends and p/e data, guidance on current investment policy, analysis and forecasts of the national economy and the stock market.

LC HG4501 .V28 **ISSN** 0737-0709
DD 332.64/52 US
TITLE CHANGE

VALUE LINE OPTIONS. [Value line options]. (July 20, 1981)-(1995). Periodical. English. Value Line Publishing, Inc., 711 3rd Avenue, New York NY 10017. **Tel** (212)687-3965, (800)634-3853, FAX (212)661-2807. **ED** Allan Lyons. **Circ:** 3,000. ***Continues in part*** *Value Line Options & Convertibles, 0146-7581.* ***Continued by*** *Value Line Options Survey.*

LC HG4050 .V33 **ISSN** 0361-2589
DD 332.6/7 US

VALUE LINE OTC SPECIAL SITUATIONS SERVICE, THE. **VAT** Value Line Over-the-Counter Special Situations Service. (19??)-. English. Twenty-four times a year (published on the 2nd and 4th Monday of each month). $390.00. Value Line Publishing, Inc., 711 3rd Avenue, New York NY 10017. **Tel** (212)687-3965, (800)634-3853, FAX (212)661-2807. Index available (free). ***Continues*** *Over-the-Counter Special Situations Service.*

LC hg4551 **ISSN** 0049-5832
DD 332.6/42/0971 CN

VANCOUVER STOCK EXCHANGE REVIEW. [Vanc. Stock Exch. rev.]. **Main/Corp** Vancouver Stock Exchange. (Dec. 1964)-. Periodical. English. Twelve times a year. 91.60Can$. Vancouver Stock Exchange, PO Box 10333, 609 Granville Street, Vancouver British Columbia V7Y 1H1 Canada. **Tel** (604)689-3334, FAX (604)688-6051. **ED** David Morton. **Circ:** 2,000. ***Supersedes*** *Vancouver Stock Exchange Monthly Bulletin, 0384-1138.*
Desc: Summary on the month's transactions on equities and options, recaps listing details, market commentaries and other topical articles.
Ind/Abst Can. Bus. Index.

LC HG450
DD 332.6 US

VARIABLE ANNUITY / LIFE ONFLOPPY. (19??)-. English. Twelve times a year. $185.00 US; $190.00 Canada and Mexico; $245.00 other. Morningstar Inc., 225 West Wacker Drive, Chicago IL 60606. **Tel** (312)696-6000, (800)876-5005.

LC HG8790 .V37 **ISSN** 1075-5179
DD 332 US

VARIABLE ANNUITY/LIFE PERFORMANCE REPORT. [Var. annuity/life perform. rep.]. **Added/Corp** Morningstar, Inc. **VFOAT** Variable Annuity Life Performance Report; Morningstar Variable Annuity Life Performance Report; Morningstar's Variable Annuity/Life Performance Report; Morningstar Variable Annuity/Life Performance Report. (199?)-. Periodical. English. Twelve times a year. $125.00 US; $130.00 Canada and Mexico; $175.00 other. Morningstar Inc., 225 West Wacker Drive, Chicago IL 60606. **Tel** (312)696-6000, (800)876-5005. ***Continues*** *Variable Annuity Performance Report, 1059-1435.*

LC HG4501 **ISSN** 1077-9922
DD 332 US

•**VARIABLE ANNUITY MARKET NEWS.** [Var. annuity mark. news]. **VFOAT** VAMN. Vol. 1, Issue No. 1 (Oct. 1994)-. Periodical. English. Twelve times a year. $550.00. Dalbar Publishing Inc., 260 Franklin Street, Boston MA 02110. **Tel** (617)439-6195, FAX (617)439-6346. **ED** Robert J. Powell.

LC HG **ISSN** 1059-1435
DD 332 US
TITLE CHANGE

VARIABLE ANNUITY PERFORMANCE REPORT. [Var. annuity perform. rep.]. **Added/Corp** Morningstar, Inc. **VFOAT** Morningstar's Variable Annuity Performance Report; Morningstar Variable Annuity Performance Report. (1991)-(199?). Periodical. English. Morningstar Inc., 225 West Wacker Drive, Chicago IL 60606. **Tel** (312)696-6000, (800)876-5005. ***Continued by*** *Variable Annuity/Life Performance Report.*

LC HG4961 .V465 **ISSN** 0883-2773
DD 332/.0415/05 US

VENTURE CAPITAL JOURNAL. [Venture cap. j.]. (July 1980)-. Trade Publication. English. Twelve times a year. $449.00. Securities Data Company, 40 West 57th Street, 11th Floor, New York NY 10019. **Tel** (212)765-5311. **ED** Jane Koloski Morris. available on an online database (files 16,636/Full-Text) from DIALOG.

Business and Economics —Investments

Continues Venture Capital.
Ind/Abst PTS Newsl. Database [Full Txt.]; Trade Ind. Index.

LC HG4028.C4 V46
DD 332/.0415/05 US
VENTURE CAPITAL YEARBOOK. 1985-. English. One time a year. Venture Economics Inc, 40 West 57th Street, Suite 802, New York NY 10019. **Tel** (201)622-4500. *Continues* Venture Capital Journal ... Yearbook, 8756-8896.

LC HF3828.U5 V46
DD 337.52073/05 US
CEASED
VENTURE JAPAN. Vol. 1, No. 1 (1988)-(March 1994). Periodical. English. Investment Dealers Digest Inc., Two World Trade Center, 18th Floor, New York NY 10048. **Tel** (212)227-1200, FAX (212)432-1039.

LC HG4651 .V54 **ISSN** 1044-6834
DD 332.63/23/0973021 US
VICKERS BOND TRADERS GUIDE. [Vickers bond traders guide]. **Added/Corp** Vickers Stock Research (Firm). **VFOAT** Bond Traders Guide. (198?)-. English. Four times a year. $767.58. Vickers Stock Research Corporation, 17 Battery Place, 18th Floor, New York NY 10004. **Tel** (212)425-7500. *Continues* Bond Traders Guide.

LC HG4509 .D57 **ISSN** 1046-5340
DD 332.6/2/02573 US
VICKERS DIRECTORY OF INSTITUTIONAL INVESTORS. See Industry and Production-Trade and Industrial Directories.

LC HG4930 .F33
DD 332.63223 US
VICKERS FACTS ON THE FUNDS. **Added/Corp** Vickers Stock Research (Firm). **VFOAT** Facts on the Funds. 4th Quarter (1988)-. English. Four times a year. Vickers Stock Research Corporation, 17 Battery Place, 18th Floor, New York NY 10004. **Tel** (212)425-7500. *Continues* Facts on the Funds.

LC HG4915 .S737 **ISSN** 1044-6850
DD 332.63/222/0973021 US
VICKERS STOCK TRADERS GUIDE. [Vickers stock traders guide]. **Added/Corp** Vickers Stock Research (Firm). **VFOAT** Stock Traders Guide. (198?)-. English. Four times a year. $730.00. Vickers Stock Research Corporation, 17 Battery Place, 18th Floor, New York NY 10004. **Tel** (212)425-7500. *Continues* Stock Traders Guide, 0882-6226.

LC HG450
DD 332.6 US
VICKERS WEEKLY INSIDER REPORT. (19??)-. English. One time a week. $190.52 (includes tax) New York; $176.00 US (outside New York). Vickers Stock Research Corporation, 17 Battery Place, 18th Floor, New York NY 10004. **Tel** (212)425-7500.

LC HF1594.5.Z4 U68 **ISSN** 1076-0032
DD 332.6 US
VIETNAM BUSINESS JOURNAL, THE. [Vietnam bus. j.]. (19??)-. Periodical. English. Two times a month. $30.00. VIAM Communications Group, 381 Park Avenue South, Suite 919, New York NY 10016. **Tel** (212)725-1717, FAX (212)725-8160.

LC HG450 **ISSN** 1021-318X
DD 332.6 VM
UDC 38
CODEN 33
VIETNAM INVESTMENT REVIEW. (1991)-. Periodical. English. One time a week. $350.00. Vietnam Investment Review, 122 Nguyen Thi Minh, Khai Street, D3 Ho Chi Minh City Vietnam. **Tel** 011 8 48243111.

LC HG4551 **ISSN** 0846-1031
DD 332.64/271133/05 CN
VSE BUSINESS REPORT. (VSE BUSINESS REPORT : A QUARTERLY REPORT FROM THE VANCOUVER STOCK EXCHANGE.). [VSE bus. rep.]. **Added/Corp** Vancouver Stock Exchange. Vancouver Stock Exchange. Public Affairs Dept. **VFOAT** Vancouver Stock Exchange Business Report. Vol. 1, No. 1 (Nov. 1990)-. Periodical. English. Irregular. Free on request. Vancouver Stock Exchange, PO Box 10333, 609 Granville Street, Vancouver British Columbia V7Y 1H1 Canada. **Tel** (604)689-3334, FAX (604)688-6051.

LC HG4538 .J26a
DD 332.6 JA
WAGA KUNI KIGYO NO KAIGAI JIGYO KATSUDO, SONO GENJO TO MONDAITEN. **Main/Corp** Japan. Tsusho Sangyosho. Sangyo Seisakukyoku. (19??)-. Periodical. Japanese. ¥450. Okurasho Insatukyoku, (Printing Bureau Ministry of Finance), 2-4 Toranomon 2 chome, Minatoku Tokyo 105 Japan.

LC HG4501 .W33 **ISSN** 0090-9235
DD 332.6/0973 US
WALL ST. U.S.A. Vol. 1 (July/Dec. 1972)-. English. $120.00. Wall Street U.S.A., 590 Madison Avenue, New York NY 10022.

LC HG4515.5 .W35 **ISSN** 1060-989X
DD 332.6/028/54 US
CODEN WSTEE5
WALL STREET & TECHNOLOGY. [Wall Str. technol.]. **VFOAT** Wall Street and Technology. Vol. 9, No. 6 (Feb. 1992)-. Periodical. English. Twelve times a year. $65.00. Miller Freeman Inc., 600 Harrison Street, San Francisco CA 94107. **Tel** (415)905-2337, (415)905-2200, FAX (415)905-2240, telex 278273. (Subscription address: JCI, PO Box 1766, Riverton NJ 08077.) available on an online database (file 675/Full-Text) from DIALOG. Documents available from Ask*IEEE, UMI Article Clearinghouse. *Continues* Wall Street Computer Review, 0738-4343.
Ind/Abst ABI/INFORM Glob. Ed. (19??-); ABI/INFORM [Computer File] (19??-); Curr. Cit.; INSPEC (Feb. 1992-); Microcomput. Abstr. (Feb. 1992-).

LC HG **ISSN** 0899-0530
DD 332 US
WALL STREET DIGEST, THE. [Wall Str. dig.]. (19??)-. Periodical. English. Twelve times a year. $150.00. Wall Street Digest Inc., 1 Sarasota Tower, Suite 602, Sarasota FL 34236. **Tel** (813)954-5500, FAX (813)364-8447. **ED** Donald H. Rowe.

LC HG450 **ISSN** 0277-4992
DD 332.6 US
WALL STREET LETTER. [Wall str. lett.]. (19??)-. Newsletter. English. One time a week. $1595.00. Institutional Investor Inc., 488 Madison Avenue, New York NY 10022. **Tel** (212)303-3234, (212)303-3233, FAX (212)303-3353.
Desc: Offers insights into every aspect of the retail and institutional brokerage business, including staff cuts, hirings and other news from behind closed doors. It also reports on new technological breakthroughs, regulatory matters and tells what's going on at the major and regional exchanges.

LC HG4501 .W27 **ISSN** 0043-0099
DD 332.6 US
WALL STREET REPORTS. [Wall Str. rep.]. Vol. 1, Issue No.1, (May 1967)-. Periodical. English. Twelve times a year. $75.00. Wall Street Reports Publishing Corporation, 99 Wall Street/22nd Floor, New York NY 10005. **Tel** (212)747-9500, FAX (212)668-9842.

LC HG450 **ISSN** 0043-0102
DD 332.6 US
WALL STREET TRANSCRIPT, THE. [Wall Str. transcr.]. (1963)-. Trade Publication. English. One time a week. $1890.00. Wall Street Transcript, 100 Wall Street, New York NY 10005. **Tel** (212)747-9500. available on microfilm from University Microfilms International (UMI); available on an online database (files 16,636/Full-Text) from DIALOG.
Ind/Abst F&S Index Plus Text, Int. [Select. Cov.]; Trade Ind. Index.

LC HF1371 **ISSN** 0049-691X
DD 382 US
WASHINGTON INTERNATIONAL BUSINESS REPORT. See Business and Economics-Commerce.

LC HG4501 **ISSN** 0278-937X
DD 332.6 US
WASHINGTON PAPERS, THE. [Wash. pap.]. 1- 1972-. Monographic series. English. Irregular. Price varies per volume. Greenwood Press Inc., PO Box 5007, Westport CT 06881-5007. **Tel** (203)226-3571, FAX (203)222-1502.
Ind/Abst ABC POL SCI (-1984).

LC HG4515.5 .W37 **ISSN** 1068-5863
DD 332.64/0285 US
•**WATERS (NEW YORK, N.Y.).** (WATERS : FOR WALL STREET'S TECHNOLOGY PROFESSIONALS.). [Waters]. **Added/Corp** Waters Information Services, Inc. (Summer 1993)-. Periodical. English. Four times a year (Mar., June, Sept., Dec.). $75.00. Waters Information Services, PO Box 2248, Binghamton NY 13902-2248. **Tel** (607)770-8535, FAX (607)798-1692.

LC HG4502 .S73
DD 332.6305 UK
WEEKLY OFFICIAL INTELLIGENCE. **Added/Corp** International Stock Exchange. **VFOAT** Stock Exchange Weekly Official Intelligence. (19??)-. English. One time a week. Council of the Stock Exchange, Old Beauregard Street, London EC2N 1HP United Kingdom. **Tel** 011 44 181 5882355. *Continues* Stock Exchange Weekly Official Intelligence.
Desc: Information on securities and the international stock exchange.

LC HG450
DD 332.6 HK
WEEKLY REPORT. (19??)-. Chinese. One time a week. HK$200.00 Hong Kong; HK$475.00 Asia; HK$600.00 other. Stock Exchange Hong Kong Ltd., Exchange Square, Box 8888, Hong Kong Hong Kong. **Tel** 011 852 25221122, FAX 011 852 28453554.

LC HG4651 **ISSN** 0830-1972
DD 332.63/22/0971 CN
WEEKLY STOCK CHARTS. CANADIAN AND U.S. INDUSTRIAL COMPANIES. [Wkly. stock charts, Can. U.S. ind. co.]. **Added/Corp** Independent Survey Company. Issue No. 248 (Oct. 4, 1985)-. Periodical. English. Twelve times a year. 195.28Can$. Independent Survey Company, PO Box 6000, Vancouver British Columbia V6B 4B9, Canada. **Tel** (604)689-5795, (604)731-5777. **ED** Michael den Hertog. *Continues* Weekly Stock Charts. ... Canadian Industrial Companies, 0829-3120.
Desc: A publication which charts a 2-1/4 year record of weekly share price and volume for 1,000 Canadian and 300 United States Industrial Companies.

LC HG4651 **ISSN** 0829-3139
DD 332.63/22/0971 CN
WEEKLY STOCK CHARTS. ... CANADIAN RESOURCE COMPANIES. [Wkly. stock charts, Can. resour. co.]. **Added/Corp** Independent Survey Company. Issue No. 236 (Sept. 28, 1984)-. Periodical. English. Twelve times a year. 195.28Can$. Independent Survey Company, PO Box 6000, Vancouver British Columbia V6B 4B9, Canada. **Tel** (604)689-5795, (604)731-5777. **ED** Michael den Hertog. *Continues* Canadian Mining and Oil Stock Charts, 0383-2953.
Desc: A publication which charts a 2 1/4 year record share price and volume for 1,200 Canadian resource companies.

LC KD1755 **ISSN** 1187-1733
DD 346.711/092 CN
WEEKLY SUMMARY - BRITISH COLUMBIA SECURITIES COMMISSION (1989). (BRITISH COLUMBIA SECURITIES COMMISSION WEEKLY SUMMARY.). [Wkly. summ. - B.C. Secur. Comm.]. **Added/Corp** British Columbia Securities Commission. (198?)-. Periodical. English. Fifty-two times a year (Wed.). 280.12Can$. British Columbia Securities Commission Info & Rec., 865 Hornby Street, Room 1100, Vancouver BC V6Z 2H4 Canada. **Tel** (604)660-4800. *Continues* British Columbia. Corporate, Financial and Regulatory Services. Weekly Summary - Ministry of Consumer and Corporate Affairs, Corporate, Financial and Regulatory Services., 0700-2734.

LC HG4928.5 .W45 **ISSN** 1074-2123
DD 332 US
WEISS RESEARCH'S BROKERAGE FIRM SAFETY DIRECTORY. See Industry and Production-Trade and Industrial Directories.

LC HB522 **ISSN** 0300-662X
DD 338 US
CEASED
WESTERN MINING NEWS. [West. min. news]. (1968)-(May 1995). Newspaper. English. Western Mining News, North 3019 Argonne Road, Spokane WA 99212. **Tel** (509)922-4184. **ED** Roger Rutcosky. **Ad Acc. Circ:** 1,000.
Desc: Quotes and information on North American Penny Mining Stocks.

LC HG4501 .W46 **ISSN** 1061-1258
DD 338.7/4/02573 US
WHO OWNS CORPORATE AMERICA. (WHO OWNS CORPORATE AMERICA : A COMPREHENSIVE LISTING OF MORE THAN 75,000 OFFICERS, DIRECTORS, AND 1% PRINCIPAL STOCKHOLDERS AND THEIR HOLDINGS OF SECURITIES ISSUED BY U.S. PUBLIC COMPANIES.). [Who owns corp. Am.]. **Added/Corp** Taft Group (Rockville, Md.). 1st Ed. (1993)-. English. One time a year. $295.00. Taft Group, 835 Penobscott Building, Customer Service, Detroit MI 48226. **Tel** (800)877-8238, FAX (313)961-6083.
Desc: Offers comprehensive listings of "insider" stock holders. Lists 75,000 stockholders arranged by last name.

LC HG4501-6051
DD 332.6 US
WISCONSIN SECURITIES BULLETIN. **Main/Corp** Wisconsin. Office of the Commissioner of Securities. Vol. 1, No. 1 (1973)-. Bulletin. English. Six times a year. $15.00. Wisconsin State Office of the Commissioner of Securities, 101 E Wilson Street, Fourth Floor, Box 1768, Madison WI 53701. **Tel** (608)266-3583. **Circ:** 3,600 (ctrl) *Continues* Wisconsin Securities Bulletin.
Desc: Contains information on new developments regarding securities-related matters, suggestions on securities, business operations and listings of various securities transactions in Wisconsin.

LC HG4501 **ISSN** 0821-5596
DD 332.6/78/0971 CN
WOMEN'S INVESTMENT NETWORK NEWSLETTER. [Women's Investm. Netw. newsl.]. Vol. 1, No. 1 (Dec. 1981)-. Newsletter. English. $2.00 per number. Nesbitt Thomson Bongard Inc, PO Box 35, Royal Trust Tower, Toronto Dominion Centre, Toronto Ontario M5K 1C4 Canada.

LC HG4501
DD 332.6　　　　　　　　　　　　　　US
　　　　　　　　　　　　　TITLE CHANGE
WORLD COUNTRY REPORT SERVICE.
(19??)-(19??). English. Political Risk Services, 6320 Fly Road, Suite 102, PO Box 248, East Syracuse NY 13057-0248. **Tel** (315)431-0511, FAX (315)431-0200. **ED** William D Coplin and Michael K O'Leary. **Continued by** World Service.

LC HG4538 .W67
DD 338.8/8/021　　　　　　　　　　　US
WORLD INVESTMENT DIRECTORY. VOL. 1, ASIA AND THE PACIFIC. See Industry and Production-Trade and Industrial Directories.

LC HG4538 .W67
DD 332.6　　　　　　　　　　　　　　US
WORLD INVESTMENT REPORT.
Added/Corp Centre on Transnational Corporations (United Nations). (1991)-. Government Publication. English. One time a year (July). $45.00 (latest edition). United Nations Publications, 2 United Nations Plaza, Room DC2 0853, Department 007C, New York NY 10017. **Tel** (212)963-8303, (800)253-9646.

LC HG450
DD 332.6　　　　　　　　　　　　　　US
WORLD RISK ANALYSIS REPORTS. See Business and Economics-International Economic Relations.

LC HG4501 .W67　　　　　　　ISSN 1060-5967
DD 332.6/0973/05　　　　　　　　　　　US
WORTH (BOSTON, MASS.). (WORTH.). [Worth]. Vol. 1, No. 1 (Feb./Mar. 1992)-. Periodical. English. Ten times a year. $24.00. Worth Magazine, 82 Devonshire Street, Department R25A, Boston MA 02109. **Tel** (617)728-6719. **(Subscription address:** Neodata / Boulder, CO, Agency Processing, PO Box 8034, Boulder CO 80306. **Tel** (800)264-9717.**) Continues** Investment Vision, 1055-2375.
Ind/Abst Access (1992-).

LC HG5470.5.A2 Y42　　　　　ISSN 0230-418X
DD 332.6/09439　　　　　　　　　　　　HU
YEARBOOK OF INVESTMENT STATISTICS. See Business and Economics-Abstracting, Bibliographies and Statistics.

LC HG179 .M593　　　　　　　　ISSN 1057-123X
DD 332.6/78/05　　　　　　　　　　　　US
YOUR MONEY (CHICAGO, ILL.). (YOUR MONEY.). [Your money]. Vol. 12, No. 5 (Aug./Sept. 1991)-. Periodical. English. Six times a year. $15.97. Consumers Digest, 5705 North Lincoln Avenue, Chicago IL 60659. **Tel** (312)275-3590, FAX (312)275-7273. **(Subscription address:** CDS Agency Hard Copy, PO Box 4966, Des Moines IA 50340. **Tel** (515)247-7569.**)** available on microfilm from University Microfilms International (UMI). **Continues** Money Maker (Chicago, Ill.), 0730-692X.
Desc: Designed to assist the average person in making informed decisions about saving, spending, investing, earnings and even enjoying money.
Ind/Abst Acad. Abstr.; Acad. Search; EP Collect.; Homework Help.; Mag. Artic. Summar. Elite; Mag. Artic. Summar. Select; Mag. Artic. Summar. CD-ROM; MasterFile FullTEXT 1000; MasterFile FullTEXT 350; MasterFile FullTEXT 650; MasterFile FullTEXT (July 1994)- [Full Txt.]; OCLC; Pub. Lib. FullTEXT; Telebase; Vocat. Search.

LC HG4551　　　　　　　　　　　ISSN 0158-2836
DD 332.64294　　　　　　　　　　　　　AT
YOUR MONEY WEEKLY. [Your money wkly.]. (1979)-. Periodical. English. One time a week. 367.00Aus$. Ian Huntley Publishers Pty Limited, PO Box 99, Cremorne NSW 2090 Australia. **Tel** 011 61 2 9535788, FAX 011 61 2 9532280.

LC HG4501　　　　　　　　　　　ISSN 1357-437X
DD 332.6　　　　　　　　　　　　　　UK
●**YOUR PENSION.** (1994)-. Consumer Publication. English. Four times a year. Brass Tacks Publishing Company Ltd., 62-68 Roseberry Avenue, London EC1R 4RR United Kingdom. **Tel** 011 171 8335566, FAX 011 171 8338050. **ED** James Hipwell. **Continues** Which Pension, 7352-4011.

LC HG4501　　　　　　　　　　　ISSN 1357-4388
DD 332.6　　　　　　　　　　　　　　UK
●**YOUR PRIVATE HEALTH OPTION.** (1994)-. Consumer Publication. English. Four times a year. Brass Tacks Publishing Company Ltd., 62-68 Roseberry Avenue, London EC1R 4RR United Kingdom. **Tel** 011 171 8335566, FAX 011 171 8338050. **ED** Andrew Stuart. **Continues** Which Private Health Option, 1354-9936.
Desc: Information on selecting private health care plans.

LC HG450
DD 332.6　　　　　　　　　　　　　　US
ZACKS PROFIT GUIDE. (19??)-. English. Four times a year. $375.00. Zacks Investment Research, 155 North Wacker Drive, 3rd Floor, Chicago IL 60606-1719. **Tel** (312)630-9880 ext. 149, FAX (312)630-9617.

LC HG450
DD 332.6　　　　　　　　　　　　　　GW
ZEITSCHRIFT FUER VERMOEGENS- UND INVESTITIONSRECHT : VIZ. VFOAT Vermoegens- und Investitionsrecht; VIZ. (1991)-. Periodical. German. Twelve times a year. DM367.00 Germany; DM380.00 other. CH Beck Verlagsbuchhandlung, D-80791 Munich Germany. **Tel** 011 49 89 381891.

LC HG4633 .Z45
DD 332.63/22/05　　　　　　　　　　　GW
ZEITUNG FUR HISTORISCHE WERTPAPIERE. English (German). Irregular. DM5.00 each issue. Freunde Historischer Wertpapiere, Goethestrasse 23, 6000 Frankfurt Am Main 1 Germany.

LABOR

　　　　　　　　　　　　　　ISSN 0824-3573
DD 331.88/11　　　　　　　　　　　　CN
204 REPORTER. [204 report.]. **Added/Corp** Service Employees International Union. **VAT** Two Hundred and Four Reporter. (1976)-. Periodical. English. Four times a year. Free. Service Employees International Union / Canada, 1 Credit Union Drive, Toronto Ontario M4A 2S6 Canada. **Tel** (416)752-4073.

　　　　　　　　　　　　　　ISSN 0012-6535
　　　　　　　　　　　　　　　　　　US
1199 NEWS. **Main/Corp** National Union of Hospital and Health Care Employees. District 1199. **VAT** Eleven Ninety-Nine News. (1965)-. Periodical. English. Irregular. $15.00. National Union of Hospitals and Health Care Employees, 330 West 42nd Street/15th Floor, New York NY 10036. **Tel** (212)582-1890. **ED** Daniel North. **Bk Rev. Circ:** 100,000 (ctrl). **Continues** 1199 Drug & Hospital News, 0742-6003.
Ind/Abst Hosp. Health Admin. Index.

　　　　　　　　　　　　　　　　　　US
1199 NEWS / LOCAL 1199 DRUG, HOSPITAL AND HEALTHCARE EMPLOYEES UNION. Added/Corp Local 1199 Drug, Hospital and Healthcare Employees Union (New York, N.Y.). **VAT** Eleven Ninety-Nine News. Vol. 3, No. 3 (Mar 1991)-. Periodical. English (Spanish). Twelve times a year. **Continues** 1199 News (Retail, Wholesale and Department Store Union. Local 1199 Drug, Hospital and Health Care Employees Union (New York, N.Y.)).

　　　　　　　　　　　　　　ISSN 0162-248X
　　　　　　　　　　　　　　　　　　US
2108 NEWS. Added/Corp Communications Workers of America. Local 2108. **VAT** Two Thousand One Hundred and Eight News. (19??)-. Periodical. English. Twelve times a year. Free. 2108 News, Local 2108 News, 10 Old Post Office Road, Silver Spring MD 20910.

LC HD6856 .A35a　　　　　　　ISSN 0001-009X
DD 331.88/096　　　　　　　　　　　　US
AALC REPORTER. [AALC rep.]. **Main/Corp** African-American Labor Center. **Added/Corp** African-American Labor Center. Center Reports. African-American Labor Center. Centre Communique. **VFOAT** Centre Communique; Center Reports. **VAT** African-American Labor Center Reporter. Vol. 1 (March 1965)-. Language (English (French). Six times a year. Free on request. African American Labor Centre, 1125 15th Street West, Washington DC 20005. **Tel** (202)293-3603. cum. index.
Ind/Abst Hum. Rights Intern. Rep.

　　　　　　　　　　　　　　　　　　NE
ABU MAGAZINE. See Occupations and Careers.

LC HF5549.5.C67 A23　　　　　ISSN 1068-0918
DD 331　　　　　　　　　　　　　　　　US
Pr Rev.
ACA JOURNAL / AMERICAN COMPENSATION ASSOCIATION. See Business and Economics-Personnel Management.

LC JV7532 .A26
DD 325.87　　　　　　　　　　　　　　VE
ACONTECER MIGRATORIO. Added/Corp Centro de Estudios de Pastoral y Asistencia Migratoria (Caracas, Venezuela). Vol. 1, No. 7 (1978)-. Periodical. Spanish. Six times a year. $15.00. Centro de Estudios de Pastoral y Asistencia Migratoria, Apartado 68827, Caracas 1062 A Venezuela. **Tel** 011 58 2 2842297. **Continues** Revision de la Prensa.
Ind/Abst Hum. Rights Intern. Rep.

LC HD1401　　　　　　　　　　　ISSN 1032-0083
DD 331.1330994　　　　　　　　　　　　AT
ACTION NEWS NORTH SYDNEY. (ACTION NEWS). [Action news North Syd.]. **Added/Corp** Affirmative Action Agency (Australia). (1987)-. Periodical.

Business and Economics —Labor

English. Four times a year. Affirmative Action Agency, PO Box 974, North Sydney NSW 2059 Australia. **Tel** 011 02 9574333, FAX 011 02 9570170.

　　　　　　　　　　　　　　　　　　SP
ACTUALIDAD PANADERA DE CATALUNA. See Food and Food Industry.

　　　　　　　　　　　　　　ISSN 1184-9800
DD 331.88　　　　　　　　　　　　　　CN
ACTUALITE - ALLIANCE DE LA FONCTION PUBLIQUE DU CANADA. ELEMENT NATIONAL. (ACTUALITE / ELEMENT NATIONAL.). [Actual. - Alliance Fonct. publique Can., Elem. natl.]. **Added/Corp** Alliance de la Fonction Publique du Canada. Element National. (April 1991)-. Periodical. French. Four times a year. Free for Members. Alliance de la Fonction Publique du Canada, 233 rue Gilmore, Ottawa Ontario K2P 0P1 Canada. **Continues** Nouvelles (Alliance de la Fonction Publique du Canada. Element National)., 1182-2163.

LC HD7105.35.A8 A25
DD 354.94230083/5　　　　　　　　　　AT
ACTUARIAL REPORTS ON THE SOUTH AUSTRALIAN SUPERANNUATION FUND AS AT ... . English. One time a year.

　　　　　　　　　　　　　　ISSN 1185-1724
DD 331.89　　　　　　　　　　　　　　CN
ADJUDICATION/ARBITRATION HIGHLIGHTS. [Adjudic./arbitr. highlights]. **Added/Corp** Public Service Alliance of Canada. Grievance and Adjudication Section. Vol. 1, No. 1 (June 1990)-. Periodical. English. Six times a year. Free to members. Direction de la Negociation Collective, Alliance de la Fonction Publique du Canada, 233 Gilmour Street, Ottawa Ontario K2P 0P1 Canada.

LC HD6958.5 .A38　　　　　　　ISSN 0742-6186
DD 331/.05　　　　　　　　　　　　　CCC
ADVANCES IN INDUSTRIAL AND LABOR RELATIONS. [Adv. ind. labor relat.]. Vol. 1 (1983)-. English. One time a year (Spring). $73.25. JAI Press Inc., 55 Old Post Road, Suite 2, PO Box 1678, Greenwich CT 06836-1678. **Tel** (203)661-7602, FAX (203)661-0792.
Ind/Abst Int. Labour Doc.; LABORDOC.

LC HD5650 .A327　　　　　　　ISSN 0885-3339
DD 658.3/152/05　　　　　　　　　　　US
ADVANCES IN THE ECONOMIC ANALYSIS OF PARTICIPATORY AND LABOR-MANAGED FIRMS. [Adv. econ. anal. particip. labor-manag. firms]. Vol. 1 (1985)-. Monographic series. English. One time a year. $73.25. JAI Press Inc., 55 Old Post Road, Suite 2, PO Box 1678, Greenwich CT 06836-1678. **Tel** (203)661-7602, FAX (203)661-0792. **ED** Derek Jones and Jan Svejnor.

　　　　　　　　　　　　　　ISSN 0148-8147
　　　　　　　　　　　　　　　　　　US
　　　　　　　　　　　　　　　　　CCC
AFFIRMATIVE ACTION COMPLIANCE MANUAL FOR FEDERAL CONTRACTORS. Added/Corp Bureau of National Affairs (Washington, D.C.). No. 1 (Dec. 31 1975)-. English. Irregular. $340.00. Bureau of National Affairs Inc., 9435 Key West Avenue, Rockville MD 20850. **Tel** (800)372-1033, (301)258-1033, FAX (301)948-5823. **ED** Susan J Sala.
Desc: Contains the official text of the Office of Federal Contract Compliance Programs Manual and reports on related developments.

　　　　　　　　　　　　　　ISSN 1187-8924
DD 331.13/3/0971424　　　　　　　　　CN
AFFIRMATIVE ACTION FORUM (SASKATOON). (AFFIRMATIVE ACTION FORUM.). [Affirm. action forum.]. **Added/Corp** Saskatchewan Human Rights Commission. **VFOAT** Forum. No. 6 (Feb. 1992)-. Periodical. English. Saskatchewan Human Rights Commission, 8th Floor Canterbury Towers, 224 4th Avenue South, Saskatoon Saskatchewan S7K 5M5 Canada. **Tel** 933-5952. **Continues** Affirmative Action News., 0715-1977.

LC HD5725.V8 V53a　　　　　　ISSN 0099-1910
DD 331.1/1/09755　　　　　　　　　　　US
AFFIRMATIVE ACTION INFORMATION. Main/Corp Virginia Employment Commission. Manpower Research Division. (19??)-. English. Virginia Employment Commission, 703 East Main Street, PO Box 1358, Richmond VA 23211.

LC HD5725.W2 A645
DD 331.1209(4-9)　　　　　　　　　　　US
AFFIRMATIVE ACTION INFORMATION. COLUMBIA BASIN LABOR AREAS. Added/Corp Washington (State). Employment Security Dept. Labor Market and Economic Analysis Branch. United States. Employment and Training Administration. **VFOAT** Columbia Basin Labor Areas; Columbia Basin Washington Labor Area; Affirmative Action Information.

Columbia Basin Washington Labor Area. (1987)-. Periodical. English. Price varies. Research and Analysis Branch, Washington State Employment Security Department, Box 9046, Olympia WA 98507. **Tel** (206)438-4800, FAX (206)438-4846. ***Continues*** *Affirmative Action Information ... Labor Areas in the Columbia Basin.*

LC HD5725.W2 A626
US

AFFIRMATIVE ACTION INFORMATION. LABOR AREAS IN NORTHEAST WASHINGTON. Added/Corp Washington (State). Employment Security Dept. Labor Market and Economic Analysis Branch. **VFOAT** Labor Areas in Northeast Washington; Northeast Washington Labor Area; Affirmative Action Information. Northeast Washington Labor Area. (1986)-. Periodical. English. Price varies. Research and Analysis Branch, Washington State Employment Security Department, Box 9046, Olympia WA 98507. **Tel** (206)438-4800, FAX (206)438-4846. ***Continues*** *Affirmative Action Information. Labor Market Areas in Northeast Washington.*

LC HD5726.O49 A33
DD 331.11/43 US
AFFIRMATIVE ACTION INFORMATION. OLYMPIA MSA, METROPOLITAN STATISTICAL AREA (THURSTON COUNTY). See Business and Economics-Abstracting, Bibliographies and Statistics.

LC JK4860.5.M5 T48a **ISSN** 0361-9036
DD 331.2 US
AFFIRMATIVE ACTION REPORT. See Public Administration-Civil Service.

US
AFL-CIO CONVENTION PROCEEDINGS. (19??)-. Proceedings. English. Every 2 years. $25.00. American Federation of Labor and Congress of Industrial Organizations, 815 16th Street Northwest, Washington DC 20006. **Tel** (202)637-5000.

ISSN 0735-214X
US
AFL-CIO INTERNAL DISPUTES PLAN, THE. (THE AFL-CIO INTERNAL DISPUTES PLAN : DETERMINATIONS AND REPORTS.). **Main/Corp** AFL-CIO. **VFOAT** A.F.L.-C.I.O. Internal Disputes Plan. **VAT** American Federation of Labor and Congress of Industrial Organizations Internal Disputes Plan. (1963)-. English. Every 2 years. American Federation of Labor and Congress of Industrial Organizations, 815 16th Street Northwest, Washington DC 20006. **Tel** (202)637-5000. cum. index. ***Continues*** *Decisions and Recommendations of the AFL-CIO Impartial Umpire.*

LC HD **ISSN** 0883-8275
DD 331 US
AFL-CIO LEGISLATIVE ALERT!. [AFL-CIO legis. alert]. **Added/Corp** AFL-CIO. Legislative Dept. **VFOAT** AFL CIO Legislative Alert. (1984)-. Periodical. English. Twenty-six times a year. $8.00. American Federation of Labor and Congress of Industrial Organizations, 815 16th Street Northwest, Washington DC 20006. **Tel** (202)637-5000. ***Formed by the union of*** *Memo from COPE and AFL-CIO Legislative Alert (AFL-CIO. Legislative Dept.), 0193-3523* ***and*** *Memo from COPE and AFL-CIO Legislative Alert (AFL-CIO. Committee on Political Education), 0193-3523.*

ISSN 0001-1185
DD 331 US
AFL-CIO NEWS. [AFL-CIO news]. **Main/Corp** AFL-CIO. **Added/Corp** AFL-CIO. News. **VAT** American Federation of Labor and Congress of Industrial Organizations News. Vol. 1, (Dec. 10, 1955)-. Periodical. English. Twenty-six times a year. $10.00. American Federation of Labor and Congress of Industrial Organizations, 815 16th Street Northwest, Washington DC 20006. **Tel** (202)637-5000. **ED** Murray Seeger. **Circ:** 65,000. available on microfilm from University Microfilms International (UMI); available on an online database from DIALOG. ***Formed by the union of*** *AFL News-Reporter* ***and*** *CIO News;* ***Absorbed*** *AFL-CIO American Federationist, 0149-2489.*
Ind/Abst Mag. Index (1959-?)(1959-); Work Relat. Abstr.

LC HD6856 .A354
DD 331.88/096 TG
AFRICAN TRADE UNION NEWS. Added/Corp African-American Labor Center. Organisation of African Trade Union Unity. Centre Regional d'Etudes et de Documentation Economiques. (197?)-. Periodical. English. Six times a year. Regional Economic Research and Documentation Center, PO Box 7138, Lome Republic of Togo. ***Continues*** *African Labor News.*
Ind/Abst Hum. Rights Intern. Rep.

ISSN 0044-7676
US
AFTRA. Added/Corp American Federation of Television and Radio Artists. **VFOAT** AFTRA Magazine. **VAT** American Federation of Television and Radio Artists. (196?)-. Periodical. English. Four times a year. American Federation of Television and Radio Artists, 260 Madison Avenue/7th Floor, New York NY 10016-2401.

LC HD6280 .A25 **ISSN** 0193-063X
DD 331.3/94 US
AGE DISCRIMINATION IN EMPLOYMENT ACT OF 1967. Main/Corp United States. Employment Standards Administration. **VAT** Age Discrimination in Employment Act of Nineteen Sixty-Seven. (1971)-. English. One time a year. US Department of Labor Employment Standards Administration, 200 Constitution Avenue NW, Room S2321, Washington DC 20210. **Tel** (202)219-6191, FAX (202)219-8457.

LC HD8008.A1 F475a **ISSN** 0091-3812
DD 331.4/81/353 US
AGENCY ACCOUNTABILITY SURVEY. Main/Corp Federally Employed Women (Association). Accountability Committee. (1972)-. English. Federally Employed Women Association, 1319 4th Street Southwest, Washington DC 20024.

LC HD1501
DD 305.555 US
AGRICULTURAL WORK FORCE OF .... . See Agriculture.

LC HD8729.A3 A36a
JA
AICHI-KEN RODO KEIZAI NO BUNSEKI. Main/Corp Aichi, Japan. Rodobu. **Added/Corp** Aichi-ken (Japan). Rodobu. Rodo Hakusho. **VFOAT** Rodo Hakusho. (19??)-. Periodical. Japanese. Aichi-Ken Rodobu, 1-2 Sannomaru 3-chome Naka-ku, Nagoya Japan.

US
AIFLD OUTLOOK : A PUBLICATION OF THE AMERICAN INSTITUTE FOR FREE LABOR DEVELOPMENT. Added/Corp American Institute for Free Labor Development. (Fall 1992)-. Periodical. English. Four times a year. American Institute for Free Labor Development, 1015 20th Street NW, Washington DC 20036. **Tel** (202)659-6300. ***Formed by the union of*** *American Institute for Free Labor Development. AIFLD Report* ***and*** *AIFLD Briefs.*

LC HE9761 **ISSN** 0002-2411
DD 387.7 US
AIR LINE EMPLOYEE, THE. [Air line empl.]. **Added/Corp** Air Line Employees Association, International. Canadian Air Line Dispatchers Association, CLC. Air Carrier Communication Operators Association. Vol. 1 (June 1955)-. Periodical. English. Six times a year. $6.00. Air Line Employees Association International, 6520 South Cicero Avenue, Bedford Park IL 60638. **Tel** (708)563-9999, FAX (708)563-9958. **ED** David Nelson. **Circ:** 500.
Ind/Abst Work Relat. Abstr.

LC HD8766.A5 A45
DD 331.095 KU
AL-AMIL. Added/Corp Ittihad al-Amm li-Ummal al-Kuwayt. (19??)-. Periodical. Arabic. Twenty-four times a year. Al-Ittihad Al-Amm Li-Ummal Al-Kuwayt, PO Box 430005., Al-Kuwayt Kuwait.

LC Z682.3 .A4 **ISSN** 0747-7201
DD 331.2/8102 US
ALA SURVEY OF LIBRARIAN SALARIES. [ALA surv. libr. salaries]. **Added/Corp** American Library Association. Office for Research. American Library Association. Office for Library Personnel Resources. **VFOAT** A.L.A. Survey of Librarian Salaries. **VAT** American Library Association Survey of Librarian Salaries. (1982)-. English. Every 2 years. $44.00 (nonmembers), $39.60 (ALA members). American Library Association, 50 East Huron Street, Chicago IL 60611. **Tel** (312)944-6780, (800)545-2433, FAX (312)337-6787. **(Subscription address:** American Library Association, Subscription Department, 434 West Downer, Aurora IL 60506-9936. **Tel** (708)892-7465, FAX (708)892-7466.**)**
Desc: Survey report on salaries earned and salary ranges for public and academic library positions.

LC HD8053.A4 A44 **ISSN** 0160-3345
DD 331.1/09798 US
ALASKA ECONOMIC TRENDS. [Alsk. econ. trends]. **Added/Corp** Alaska. Employment Security Division. Alaska. Dept. of Labor. Alaska. Dept. of Labor. Research and Analysis Section. (Aug. 1968)-. Periodical. English. Twelve times a year. Free on request. Alaska Department of Labor, Administrative Services, Research & Analysis Section, PO Box 25501, Juneau AK 99802-5501. **Tel** (907)465-4500, FAX (907)465-2101. **ED** John Bouchen. **Circ:** 3,000 (ctrl). ***Continues*** *Trends in Alaska's Employment and Economy.*
Desc: Current economic conditions of Alaska including articles of economic interest, labor force data, nonagricultural wage and salary employment, and average hours and earnings in selected industries.
Ind/Abst PAIS Int. Print; Stat. Ref. Index.

LC HD5725.A4 A56a **ISSN** 0362-4196
DD 331.1/1/09798 US
ALASKA LABOR FORCE ESTIMATES BY INDUSTRY & AREA. Main/Corp Alaska. Employment Security Division. **VAT** Alaska Labor Force Estimates by Industry and Area. (19??)-. English. One time a year. Employment Security Division, Research and Analysis Section, Box 3-7000, Juneau AK 99801. ***Continues*** *Alaska Workforce Estimates By Industry and Area.*

US
ALASKA PUBLIC EMPLOYEE / APEA, FEDERATION OF STATE EMPLOYEES, AFT, AFL-CIO, THE. Added/Corp Alaska Public Employees Association. Vol. 6, No. 5 (May/June 1990)-. Periodical. English. Six times a year. ***Continues*** *News 'n Views (Alaska Public Employees Association).*

US
ALERT. (19??)-. Periodical. English. Six times a year. $150.00. Labor Relations Association Inc., 7910 Ivanhoe 321, La Jolla CA 92038. **Tel** (619)450-3356.

ISSN 0838-7990
DD 331.88/1135471 CN
ALLIANCE (OTTAWA. ENGLISH ED.). (ALLIANCE / PUBLIC SERVICE ALLIANCE OF CANADA.). [Alliance]. **Added/Corp** Public Service Alliance of Canada. Vol. 1, No. 1 (Jan./Feb. 1988)-. Periodical. English (French). Six times a year. Free on request. Public Service Alliance of Canada, 233 Gilmour Street, Ottawa Ontario K2P 0P1 Canada. **Tel** (613)560-4211. **Circ:** 180,000 (Canada) (ctrl). ***Continues*** *Argus-Journal, 0004-1211.*

ISSN 0002-6107
US
TITLE CHANGE
ALLIED INDUSTRIAL WORKER. Added/Corp International Union, Allied Industrial Workers of America. Vol. 1 (Sept. 1957)-(19??). Periodical. English (Spanish). Allied Industrial Workers, 3520 West Oklahoma Avenue, Milwaukee WI 53215. **Tel** (414)645-9500. **ED** Dominick d'Ambrosio and Anne Bingham. **Circ:** 72,000 (ctrl). ***Supersedes*** *Allied Industrial Worker.* ***Merged into*** *Paperworker, 0363-6437.*
Desc: A newspaper to provide information to union members involving collective bargaining, contract administration, political and legislative issues and economics.
Ind/Abst Work Relat. Abstr.

LC Z7164.S66 I5 1970 Suppl HN8 **ISSN** 0099-0779
DD 019/.1 US
ALPHABETICAL CATALOG OF THE BOOKS AND PAMPHLETS OF THE INTERNATIONAL INSTITUTE OF SOCIAL HISTORY, AMSTERDAM. SUPPLEMENT. See Business and Economics-Abstracting, Bibliographies and Statistics.

LC HD4801 **ISSN** 0843-0586
DD 331/.09714 CN
CEASED
ALTERNATIVE (MONTREAL, QUEBEC). (L'ALTERNATIVE.). [Alternative]. Vol. 42, No. 17 (Oct. 27, 1988)-(199?). Periodical. French. L'Alternative / Montreal, 4164 rue Parthenais, Montreal Quebec H2K 3T9 Canada. **Tel** (514)524-2896, FAX (514)524-8285. **ED** Montserrat Escola. **Bk Rev. Ad Acc. Circ:** 1,000. ***Continues*** *Combat, 0588-5620.*

LC TL **ISSN** 0279-7968
DD 629 US
AMERICAN AERONAUT. Added/Corp International Association of Machinists and Aerospace Workers. District 727. (19??)-. Periodical. English. Twelve times a year. Free. International Association of Machinists & Aerospace Workers AFL-CIO, 2600 North Victory Boulevard, Burbank CA 91505. **Tel** (310)845-7401. **ED** Don Nakamoto. **Ad Acc. Circ:** 15,000 (ctrl).
Desc: Labor publication-union member readership.

LC HD6350.G5 A6 **ISSN** 0002-8525
DD 331.881661 US
AMERICAN FLINT. Added/Corp American Flint Glass Workers' Union. (1909)-. Periodical. English. Twelve times a year. American Flint, 1440 South Byrne Road, Toledo OH 43614.
Ind/Abst Work Relat. Abstr.

ISSN 0744-6454
US
AMERICAN LABOR BEACON. (19??)-. Periodical. English. Twelve times a year. $35.00. Beacon News Service, 1249 Washington Boulevard, Suite 626, Detroit MI 48226.

US
AMERICAN LABOR YEARBOOK, THE. Added/Corp Labor Research Association (U.S.). (19??)-. English. One time a year. $15.00. Labor Research Association Inc., 145 West 28th Street, New York NY 10001. **Tel** (212)714-1677, FAX (212)714-1674.

Business and Economics —Labor

LC HE6499 .A64　　ISSN 0044-7811
DD 331.881/1/3830973　　US
AMERICAN POSTAL WORKER, THE.
Added/Corp American Postal Workers Union. Vol. 1 (Aug. 1971)-. Periodical. English. Twelve times a year. $3.00. American Postal Workers Union, 817 14th Street Northwest, Washington DC 20005. **Tel** (202)842-8500. **ED** Moe Biller. **Bk Rev. Circ:** 290,000 (ctrl). *Continues Union Postal Clerk & the Postal Transport Journal.* **Ind/Abst** Work Relat. Abstr.

LC HD4973 .A67　　ISSN 1055-7628
DD 331.2/973/021　　US
AMERICAN SALARIES AND WAGES SURVEY. [Am. salaries wages surv.]. **Added/Corp** Gale Research Inc. 1st Ed. (1990)-. English. $95.00. Gale Research Inc., 835 Penobscot Building, 645 Griswold Street, Detroit MI 48226. **Tel** (800)877-GALE, (313)961-2242, FAX (313)961-6083, (800)414-5043, telex TWX 810-221-7086. **ED** Marlita A. Reddy. available on magnetic tape; available on diskette.
 Desc: More than 32,000 salary statistics for more than 4,500 occupational classifications at different experience levels, as well as in specific areas of the country. Salary data comes from more than 300 publications issued by federal, state, and local government offices, professional organizations and other business groups, periodicals and newspapers.

　　ISSN 1047-7136
DD 331　　US
AMERICAN WORKER (BALTIMORE, MD.), THE. (THE AMERICAN WORKER.). [Am. work.]. (198?)-. Periodical. English. Twelve times a year. Turner Communications, Box 518, Millersville MD 21108. **Tel** (410)987-5757. **ED** James C. Turner. **Bk Rev. Ad Acc. Circ:** 60,000 (ctrl).
 Desc: A communication forum for labor and management.

LC HD6350.A8 A5　　ISSN 0161-9810
DD 331.88/1292/0973　　US
AMMO. Added/Corp International Union, United Automobile, Aerospace, and Agricultural Implement Workers of America. **VFOAT** UAW Ammo. Vol. 18, (Aug. 1977)-. Periodical. English. Twelve times a year. $3.00. United Auto & Aerospace Worker, 8000 Jefferson Avenue East, Detroit MI 48214. **Tel** (313)926-5291. **ED** Peter Laarman. **Circ:** 160,000. *Continues Ammunition.*
 Desc: Popular handbook for UAW local union leaders with information on unions, politics, economics, current affairs and consumer issues.

　　US
　　CEASED
AMS FLEXIBLE WORK SURVEY.
Added/Corp Administrative Management Society. **VFOAT** Flexible Work Survey. **VAT** Administrative Management Society Flexible Work Survey. (19??)-(19??). English.

　　ISSN 1053-8402
DD 331　　US
　　CEASED
AMS OFFICE, PROFESSIONAL & DATA PROCESSING SALARIES REPORT. [AMS off. prof. data process. salaries rep.]. **Added/Corp** Administrative Management Society. **VFOAT** AMS Office, professional and data processing salaries report; Office, Professional and Data Processing Salaries Report. **VAT** Administrative Management Society Office, Professional & Data Processing Salaries Report. (198?)-(19??). English. *Formed by the union of AMS ... Office Salaries Report and AMS ... Data Processing Salaries Report.*

　　ISSN 0007-585X
　　GW
UDC 331.5
　　CODEN 351.84:331.56
AMTLICHE NACHRICHTEN DER BUNDESANSTALT FUER ARBEIT. (1969)-. Periodical. German. Twelve times a year. $149.69. Landesarbeitsamt Nordbayern, Ref IV F36 Regensburger Street 104, D-90478 Nuernberg Germany. **Tel** 011 49 911 1794163, FAX 011 49 911 1792123.

　　ISSN 0007-585X
　　GW
AMTLICHE NACHRICHTEN DER BUNDESANSTALT FUER ARBEIT.
Added/Corp Bundesanstalt fuer Arbeit (Germany). (19??)-. Periodical. German. Twelve times a year. $149.69. Landesarbeitsamt Nordbayern, Ref IV F36 Regensburger Street 104, D-90478 Nuernberg Germany. **Tel** 011 49 911 1794163, FAX 011 49 911 1792123.

LC HD5777 .A67　　ISSN 0170-2696
DD 331.1/0943/021　　GW
AMTLICHE NACHRICHTEN DER BUNDESANSTALT FUER ARBEIT. ARBEITSSTATISTIK ... JAHRESZAHLEN. *See* Business and Economics-Abstracting, Bibliographies and Statistics.

LC HD5752 .F85a
　　BL
ANALISE CONJUNTURAL DO EMPREGO. Main/Corp Fundacao Instituto de Pesquisas Economicas (Sao Paulo, Brazil). (19??)-. Portuguese. Esplanado Dos Ministerios, Bloco F 5O, Andar Brazil.

　　AG
ANALISIS LABORAL Y SOCIAL.
Added/Corp Instituto de Estudios Laborales y Sociales (Argentina). **VFOAT** Revista Analisis Laboral y Social. Vol. 1, No. 1 (July 1988)-. Periodical. Spanish. **Ind/Abst** Int. Labour Doc.

　　ISSN 0341-017X
　　GW
　　CCC
ANGESTELLTEN MAGAZIN. Added/Corp Deutscher Gewerkschaftsbund. No. 5 (1976)-. Periodical. German. Twelve times a year. DM21.60. Bund Verlag GmbH, Postfach 900840, D-51118 Cologne Germany. **Tel** 011 49 2203 934758. **ED** Tomas Vosta. **Bk Rev. Ad Acc.** *Continues Wirtschaft und Wissen.*
 Desc: Journal for employees.

LC HF
DD 658　　IT
ANIE PUBBLICAZIONI. (19??)-. Italian. Irregular. L190.000 Italy; L260.000 other. Anie Promozione SRL, via Algardi 2, 20148 Milan Italy. **Tel** 011 39 2 3264237.

LC HA1631 .A33 HD8631
DD 317.971　　YU
ANKETA O OSTVARIVANJU PRAVA RADNIKA IZ RADNOG ODNOSA. *See* Business and Economics-Abstracting, Bibliographies and Statistics.

　　US
ANN ARBOR'S LABOR MARKET NEWS.
Added/Corp Michigan Employment Security Commission. Bureau of Research and Statistics. Information and Reports Section. Vol. 12, No. 1 (Mar. 1992)-. Periodical. English. Twelve times a year. Detroit Employment Security Commission, 7310 Woodward Castro, Room 520, Detroit MI 48202. **Tel** (313)876-5427. *Continues Ann Arbor Labor Market Review.*

　　IT
ANNALI DELLA FONDAZIONE GIULIO PASTORE. Added/Corp Fondazione Giulio Pastore. (19??)-. Italian. Irregular. Franco Angeli Riviste SRL, Viale Monza 106, 20127 Milan Italy. **Tel** 011 39 2 2827651, 011 39 2 289562, FAX 011 39 2 258004, telex 051-511650.

　　ISSN 0831-0513
DD 331/.025/714　　CN
ANNUAIRE DU TRAVAIL. [Annu. trav.]. (1985)-. French. Irregular (once every two years). 32.82Can$. Les Productions Infort, CP 145 Succursale Cartierville, Montreal Quebec H4K 2J5 Canada. **Tel** (514)336-8415.

LC HD5725.R38 N48a　　ISSN 0149-3779
DD 331.1/1/09793　　US
ANNUAL AREA LABOR REVIEW.
Main/Corp Nevada. Employment Security Dept. (1976)-. English. One time a year. Free. Nevada Employment Security Department, 500 East Third Street, Carson City NV 89713. **Tel** (702)687-4635. **Bk Rev. Ad Acc. Circ:** 1,000 (ctrl). *Continues Nevada. Employment Security Dept. Semi-Annual Area Manpower Review: Reno Standard Metropolitan Statistical Area.*
 Desc: Evaluates current economic situations in Las Vegas, Reno, and state as a whole. Labor market expectations for upcoming year are reviewed.

　　US
ANNUAL AVERAGES, LABOR FORCE AND NONAGRICULTURAL EMPLOYMENT ESTIMATES. Added/Corp Tennessee. Dept. of Employment Security. **VFOAT** Annual Averages, Tennessee Labor Force and Nonagricultural Employment Estimates; Labor Force and Nonagricultural Employment Estimates, Annual Averages. (1986/1990)-. English. Labor Market Information Unit / Nashville, TN, Research and Statistics Division, Tennessee Department of Employment Security, 11th Floor, 500 James Robertson Parkway, Nashville TN 37245-1040. *Continues Annual Averages, Tennessee Labor Force Estimates.*

LC HD5725.M7 A58
DD 331.12/5/09762　　US
ANNUAL AVERAGES, ... MISSISSIPPI BY COUNTIES. English. One time a year. **ED** Raiford G Crews.
 Desc: Average labor force and place of work employment for all counties of Mississippi.

LC HD5725.I3 I4617A
DD 331.11/09773　　US
ANNUAL CETA REPORT FOR ... - ILLINOIS. DEPT. OF COMMERCE AND COMMUNITY AFFAIRS. Main/Corp Illinois. Dept. of Commerce and Community Affairs. **VFOAT** Annual C.E.T.A. Report for ... . (1980)-. English. One time a year. Illinois Department of Commerce & Community Affairs, 620 East Adams Street, Springfield IL 62701. **Tel** (217)782-7500, FAX (217)785-6454.

LC HD7102.U4 A765　　ISSN 0736-9026
DD 368.3/82/0068　　US
ANNUAL CONTRACTOR EVALUATION REPORT FOR BLUE CROSS/BLUE SHIELD OF MICHIGAN. PART B CARRIER. VFOAT Annual Contractor Evaluation Report. English. One time a year. American Medical Association, 535 North Dearborn Street, Chicago IL 60610.

　　ISSN 0319-0153
　　CN
ANNUAL CONVENTION - NEWFOUNDLAND AND LABRADOR FEDERATION OF LABOUR. Main/Corp Newfoundland and Labrador Federation of Labour. **Added/Corp** Memorial University of Newfoundland. Extension Service. (1937)-. Periodical. English. One time a year. Memorial University of Newfoundland / Faculty of Education, Elizabeth Avenue, St. John's Newfoundland A1C 5S7 Canada. **Tel** (709)737-8621.

LC HD5725.W2 A648
DD 331.1/09797/98021　　US
ANNUAL DEMOGRAPHIC INFORMATION. SERVICE DELIVERY AREA I, CLALLAM, JEFFERSON, AND KITSAP COUNTIES : A LABOR MARKET INFORMATION REPORT OF THE RESEARCH AND ANALYSIS BRANCH, WASHINGTON STATE EMPLOYMENT SECURITY DEPARTMENT / PREPARED IN COOPERATION WITH THE EMPLOYMENT AND TRAINING ADMINISTRATION, U.S. DEPARTMENT OF LABOR. Added/Corp Washington (State). Employment Security Dept. Research & Analysis Branch. United States. Employment and Training Administration. **VFOAT** Service Delivery Area I, Clallam, Jefferson, and Kitsap Counties; Service Delivery Area 1, Clallam, Jefferson, and Kitsap Counties; Service Delivery Area One, Clallam, Jefferson, and Kitsap Counties; Clallam, Jefferson, and Kitsap Counties. (Jan. 1984)-. English. One time a year. $3.00. Research and Analysis Branch, Washington State Employment Security Department, Box 9046, Olympia WA 98507. **Tel** (206)438-4800, FAX (206)438-4846.

LC HD5725.W2 A6482
DD 331.1/09797/9021　　US
ANNUAL DEMOGRAPHIC INFORMATION. SERVICE DELIVERY AREA II, GRAYS HARBOR, LEWIS, MASON, PACIFIC, AND THURSTON COUNTIES : A LABOR MARKET INFORMATION REPORT OF THE RESEARCH AND ANALYSIS BRANCH, WASHINGTON STATE EMPLOYMENT SECURITY DEPARTMENT / PREPARED IN COOPERATION WITH THE EMPLOYMENT AND TRAINING ADMINISTRATION, U.S. DEPARTMENT OF LABOR. Added/Corp Washington (State). Employment Security Dept. Research & Analysis Branch. United States. Employment and Training Administration. **VFOAT** Service Delivery Area II, Grays Harbor, Lewis, Mason, Pacific, and Thurston Counties; Service Delivery Area 2, Grays Harbor, Lewis, Mason, Pacific; Service Delivery Area Two, Grays Harbor, Lewis, Mason, Pacific; Grays Harbor, Lewis, Mason, Pacific, and Thurston Counties. (Jan. 1984)-. English. One time a year. $3.00. Research and Analysis Branch, Washington State Employment Security Department, Box 9046, Olympia WA 98507. **Tel** (206)438-4800, FAX (206)438-4846.

LC HD5725.W2 A6483
DD 331.1/09797/7021　　US
ANNUAL DEMOGRAPHIC INFORMATION. SERVICE DELIVERY AREA III, ISLAND, SAN JUAN, SKAGIT, AND WHATCOM COUNTIES : A LABOR MARKET INFORMATION REPORT OF THE RESEARCH AND ANALYSIS BRANCH, WASHINGTON STATE EMPLOYMENT SECURITY. Added/Corp Washington (State). Employment Security Dept.

Business and Economics — Labor

Research & Analysis Branch. Washington (State). Employment Security Dept. Labor Market and Economic Analysis Branch. United States. Employment and Training Administration. **VFOAT** Service Delivery Area III, Island, San Juan, Skagit, and Whatcom Counties; Service Delivery Area 3, Island, San Juan, Skagit and Whatcom Counties; Service Delivery Area Three, Island, San Juan, Skagit and Whatcom Countries; Island, San Juan, Skagit, and Whatcom Counties. (Jan. 1984)-. English. One time a year. $3.00. Research and Analysis Branch, Washington State Employment Security Department, Box 9046, Olympia WA 98507. **Tel** (206)438-4800, FAX (206)438-4846.

LC HD5725.W2 A649
DD 331.1/09797/5021 US
ANNUAL DEMOGRAPHIC INFORMATION. SERVICE DELIVERY AREA IX, KITTITAS, KLICKITAT, AND YAKIMA COUNTIES : A LABOR MARKET INFORMATION REPORT OF THE RESEARCH AND ANALYSIS BRANCH, WASHINGTON STATE EMPLOYMENT SECURITY DEPARTMENT / PREPARED IN COOPERATION WITH THE EMPLOYMENT AND TRAINING ADMINISTRATION, U.S. DEPARTMENT OF LABOR. **Added/Corp** Washington (State). Employment Security Dept. Research & Analysis Branch. United States. Employment and Training Administration. **VFOAT** Service Delivery Area IX, Kittitas, Klickitat, and Yakima Counties; Service Delivery Area 9, Kittitas, Klickitat, and Yakima Counties; Service Delivery Area Nine, Kittitas, Klickitat, and Yakima Counties; Kittitas, Klickitat, and Yakima Counties. (Jan. 1984)-. English. One time a year. $3.00. Research and Analysis Branch, Washington State Employment Security Department, Box 9046, Olympia WA 98507. **Tel** (206)438-4800, FAX (206)438-4846.

LC HD5725.W2 A6486
DD 331.1/09797/3 US
ANNUAL DEMOGRAPHIC INFORMATION. SERVICE DELIVERY AREA VIII, ADAMS, CHELAN, DOUGLAS, GRANT, AND OKANOGAN COUNTIES : A LABOR MARKET INFORMATION REPORT OF THE RESEARCH AND ANALYSIS BRANCH, WASHINGTON STATE EMPLOYMENT SECURITY DEPARTMENT. **Added/Corp** Washington (State). Employment Security Dept. Research & Analysis Branch. Washington (State). Employment Security Dept. Labor Market and Economic Analysis Branch. United States. Employment and Training Administration. **VFOAT** Service Delivery Area VIII, Adams, Chelan, Douglas, Grant, and Okanogan Counties; Service Deliver Area 8, Adams, Chelan, Douglas, Grant; Service Delivery Area Eight, Adams, Chelan, Douglas, Grant; Adams, Chelan, Douglas, Grant, and Okanogan Counties. (Jan. 1984)-. English. One time a year. $3.00. Research and Analysis Branch, Washington State Employment Security Department, Box 9046, Olympia WA 98507. **Tel** (206)438-4800, FAX (206)438-4846.

LC HD5725.W2 A65
DD 331.1/09797/2021 US
ANNUAL DEMOGRAPHIC INFORMATION. SERVICE DELIVERY AREA X, ASOTIN, COLUMBIA, FERRY, GARFIELD, LINCOLN, PEND OREILLE, STEVENS, AND WHITMAN COUNTIES : A LABOR MARKET INFORMATION REPORT OF THE RESEARCH AND ANALYSIS BRANCH, WASHINGTON STATE EMPLOYMENT SECURITY DEPARTMENT / PREPARED IN COOPERATION WITH THE EMPLOYMENT AND TRAINING ADMINISTRATION, U.S. DEPARTMENT OF LABOR. **Added/Corp** Washington (State). Employment Security Dept. Research & Analysis Branch. United States. Employment and Training Administration. **VFOAT** Service Delivery Area X, Asotin, Columbia, Perry, Garfield, Lincoln, Pend Oreille, Stevens, and Whitman Counties; Service Delivery Area 10, Asotin, Columbia, Ferry, Garfield; Service Delivery Area Ten, Asotin, Columbia, Ferry, Garfield; Asotin, Columbia, Ferry, Garfield, Lincoln, Pend Oreille, Stevens, and Whitman Counties. (Jan. 1984)-. English. One time a year. $3.00. Research and Analysis Branch, Washington State Employment Security Department, Box 9046, Olympia WA 98507. **Tel** (206)438-4800, FAX (206)438-4846.

LC HD5725.W2 A653
DD 331.1/09797/33021 US
ANNUAL DEMOGRAPHIC INFORMATION. SERVICE DELIVERY AREA XI, BENTON, FRANKLIN, AND WALLA WALLA COUNTIES : A LABOR MARKET INFORMATION REPORT OF THE RESEARCH AND ANALYSIS BRANCH, WASHINGTON STATE EMPLOYMENT SECURITY DEPARTMENT. **Added/Corp** Washington (State). Employment Security Dept. Research & Analysis Branch. United States. Employment and Training Administration. **VFOAT** Service Delivery Area XI, Benton, Franklin, and Walla Walla Counties; Service Delivery Area 11, Benton, Franklin, and Walla Walla; Service Delivery Area Eleven, Benton, Franklin, and Walla Walla Counties; Benton, Franklin, and Walla Walla Counties. (Jan. 1984)-. English. One time a year. $3.00. Research and Analysis Branch, Washington State Employment Security Department, Box 9046, Olympia WA 98507. **Tel** (206)438-4800, FAX (206)438-4846.

LC HD5726.S66 A56
DD 331.1/09797/37021 US
ANNUAL DEMOGRAPHIC INFORMATION. SERVICE DELIVERY AREA XII, SPOKANE COUNTY : A LABOR MARKET INFORMATION REPORT OF THE RESEARCH AND ANALYSIS BRANCH, WASHINGTON STATE EMPLOYMENT SECURITY DEPARTMENT. **Added/Corp** Washington (State). Employment Security Dept. Research & Analysis Branch. United States. Employment and Training Administration. **VFOAT** Service Delivery Area XII, Spokane County; Service Delivery Area 12, Spokane County; Service Delivery Area Twelve, Spokane County; Spokane County. (Jan. 1984)-. English. One time a year. $3.00. Research and Analysis Branch, Washington State Employment Security Department, Box 9046, Olympia WA 98507. **Tel** (206)438-4800, FAX (206)438-4846.

LC HD5726.W3 D5a
DD 331.11/09753 US
ANNUAL EMPLOYMENT AND TRAINING REPORT TO THE MAYOR, DISTRICT OF COLUMBIA / EMPLOYMENT AND TRAINING SERVICES ADVISORY COUNCIL. **Main/Corp** District of Columbia. Employment and Training Services Advisory Council. (19??)-. English. One time a year. Employment and Training Services Advisory Council, East Potomac Building, 606 G Street NW, Washington DC 20001.

LC HD5820.5 .A56
DD 331.12/5/095491 PK
ANNUAL ESTABLISHMENT ENQUIRY. **Added/Corp** Pakistan. Federal Bureau of Statistics. (198?)-. English. **Continues** Report on Annual Establishment Enquiry.

LC HD7096.U6 N713 ISSN 0093-8017
DD 368.4/4/009747 US
ANNUAL EVALUATION OF THE NEW YORK STATE UNEMPLOYMENT INSURANCE FUND. **Main/Corp** New York (State). Dept. of Labor. Division of Research and Statistics. 2nd- 1965-. English. One time a year. New York State Department of Labor / Albany, 401 Harriman, Division of Research and Statistics, State Office Building Campus, Albany NY 12240. **Tel** (518)457-6649. **Continues** Evaluation of the New York State Unemployment Insurance Fund with Analysis of the Operation of the System.

LC HD5725.N7 A62
DD 331.12/09747/021 US
ANNUAL LABOR AREA REPORT. NEW YORK STATE / NEW YORK STATE, DEPT.OF LABOR, DIVISION OF RESEARCH AND STATISTICS. **Added/Corp** New York (State). Bureau of Labor Market Information. State Analysis Unit. New York (State). Dept. of Labor. Division of Research and Statistics. **VFOAT** New York State. (1985)-. Periodical. English. One time a year. New York State Department of Labor / Albany, 401 Harriman, Division of Research and Statistics, State Office Building Campus, Albany NY 12240. **Tel** (518)457-6649. **Continues** Annual Planning Information, New York State.

LC HD5726.A78 A65
DD 331.12/09749/84 US
ANNUAL LABOR MARKET REVIEW. ATLANTIC CITY LABOR MARKET AREA, NEW JERSEY. **Added/Corp** New Jersey. Dept. of Labor. Division of Planning and Research. **VFOAT** Annual Labor Market Review. Atlantic City Labor Area; Atlantic City Labor Area. (Mar. 1982)-. English. One time a year. New Jersey Department of Labor, Division of Planning and Research CN 056, Trenton NJ 08625. **Tel** (609)292-7567. **Continues** Annual Planning Information and Occupational Supply and Demand Report. Atlantic City Labor Area.

LC HD5725.N5 G73
DD 331.12/09749/41 US
ANNUAL LABOR MARKET REVIEW. NEW BRUNSWICK, PERTH AMBOY, SAYREVILLE LABOR AREA #5460, NEW JERSEY / STATE OF NEW JERSEY, DEPARTMENT OF LABOR, DIVISION OF PLANNING AND RESEARCH AFFILIATED WITH THE EMPLOYMENT AND TRAINING ADMINISTRATION, U.S. DEPARTMENT OF LABOR ; PREPARED BY ROBERT FISK, LABOR MARKET ANALYST. **Added/Corp** New Jersey. Dept. of Labor. Division of Planning and Research. United States. Employment and Training Administration. **VFOAT** New Brunswick, Perth Amboy, Sayreville Labor Area #5460, New Jersey. (Feb. 1982)-. English. One time a year. State of New Jersey / Department of Labor, 744 Broad Street, Room 1704, Newark NJ 07102. **Continues** Annual Planning Information and Occupational Supply and Demand Report. New Brunswick, Perth Amboy, Sayreville Labor Area, 0275-925X.

LC HD5726.N53 A57
DD 331.12/09749/3 US
ANNUAL LABOR MARKET REVIEW. NEWARK LABOR AREA #5640, NEW JERSEY / PREPARED BY ANDREW M. SMAKULA. **Added/Corp** New Jersey. Dept. of Labor. Division of Planning and Research. **VFOAT** Newark Labor Area #5640, New Jersey; Newark Labor Area Number Fifty Four Forty, New Jersey. (Mar. 1982)-. English. One time a year. New Jersey Department of Labor & Industry, Labor Market & Demographic, CN 388, Trenton NJ 08625. **Tel** (609)984-2595. **Continues** Annual Planning Information and Occupational Supply and Demand Report. Newark Labor Area.

LC HD5725.N5 A67
DD 331.12/09749/94 US
ANNUAL LABOR MARKET REVIEW. VINELAND-MILLVILLE-BRIDGETON LABOR AREA, NEW JERSEY. **Added/Corp** New Jersey. Dept. of Labor. Division of Planning and Research. **VFOAT** Vineland-Millville-Bridgeton Labor Area, New Jersey. Apr. 1982-. Periodical. English. One time a year. New Jersey Dept of Labor, Division of Planning & Research, 1421 Atlantic Avenue, Atlantic City NJ 08401. **Continues** Annual Planning Information and Occupational Supply and Demand Report. Vineland-Millville-Bridgeton Labor Area.

LC HD5726.C4 I43A ISSN 0091-4908
DD 331.1/09773/11 US
ANNUAL MANPOWER PLANNING REPORT. CHICAGO STANDARD METROPOLITAN STATISTICAL AREA. (CHICAGO STANDARD METROPOLITAN STATISTICAL AREA : ANNUAL MANPOWER PLANNING REPORT.). **Main/Corp** Illinois. State Employment Service. Labor Market Unit. 1974-. Statistical Publication. English. One time a year. Illinois State Employment Service, Labor market Unit, 208 South Lasalle Street, Chicago IL 60604. **Continues** Annual Manpower Planning Report : Chicago Standard Metropolitan Statistical Area.

LC HD5725.N3 N44b
DD 331.11/09793 US
ANNUAL PLAN FOR THE GOVERNOR'S SPECIAL GRANT. **Main/Corp** Nevada. State Comprehensive Employment and Training Office. **VFOAT** Annual Plan. (19??)-. Government Publication. English. One time a year. State Comprehensive Employment and Training Office, State Mail Room, Capitol Complex, Carson City NV 89710.

LC HD5725.C2 C29a
DD 331.1/09794/38021 US
ANNUAL PLANNING INFORMATION. (ANNUAL PLANNING INFORMATION. PLACER COUNTY.). **Added/Corp** California. Northern Area Labor Market Group. **VFOAT** Placer County. (1986)-. English. Northern Area Labor Market Information Group, 800 Capitol Mall/MIC 57, Sacramento CA 95814. **Continues** Labor Market Information. Placer County.

LC HD5725.M3 M33B
DD 331.12/09741 US
ANNUAL PLANNING INFORMATION. **Main/Corp** Maine. Labor Market Evaluation and Planning Section. **VFOAT** Annual Planning Information, Maine Statewide. (19??)-. English. One time a year. Dana A Evans, Chief Labor Market Evaluation and Planning Section, Maine Department of Manpower Affairs, Bureau of Employment Security, 20 Union Street, Augusta ME 04330. **Continues** Maine. Dept. of Manpower Affairs. Annual Planning Information.

Business and Economics — Labor

LC HD5725.I23 I28a
DD 317.96/05 US
ANNUAL PLANNING INFORMATION.
Added/Corp Idaho. Dept. of Employment. Bureau of Research & Analysis. **English.** Idaho Department of Employment, 317 Main Street, Boise ID 83735. **Tel** (208)334-6112, FAX (208)334-6430. **Continues** Annual Planning Information Report, Idaho.

LC HD5725.N4 N45k
DD 331.12/09742/45 US
ANNUAL PLANNING INFORMATION, BELKNAP COUNTY. **Main/Corp** New Hampshire. Dept. of Employment Security. Economic Analysis and Reporting Section. **Added/Corp** United States. Employment and Training Administration. (19??)-. English. One time a year. New Hampshire Department of Employment Security, 32 South Main Street, Concord NH 03301. **Tel** (603)224-3311, FAX (603)228-4145.

LC HD5725.I8 A66
DD 331.1/09777/96 US
ANNUAL PLANNING INFORMATION, BURLINGTON, IOWA LABOR AREA, DES MOINES COUNTY / PREPARED BY LARRY HOLTKAMP [FOR] IOWA DEPARTMENT OF JOB SERVICE.
Added/Corp Job Service of Iowa. (19??)-. Statistical Publication. English. One time a year. Free. Job Service of Iowa / Burlington, 1000 North Roosevelt, Burlington IA 52601.
Desc: Statistical and analytical presentation of labor market data.

LC HD5725.C2 C29E
DD 331.1/09794/32 US
ANNUAL PLANNING INFORMATION. BUTTE COUNTY. **Main/Corp** California. Northern Area Labor Market Information Group. 1979/80-. English. One time a year. Free. Employment Development Department, PO Box 826880, Sacramento CA 94280. **Tel** (916)445-1952. **Circ:** 1,500. **Continues** Annual Planning Information. Butte County.
Desc: Summary of California economic conditions.

LC HD5725.C2 C228a
DD 331.1/2/09794 US
ANNUAL PLANNING INFORMATION. CALIFORNIA / PREPARED BY EMPLOYMENT DEVELOPMENT DEPARTMENT, EMPLOYMENT DATA AND RESEARCH DIVISION. **Main/Corp** California. Employment Data and Research Division. **Added/Corp** California. Employment Data and Research Division. California. Labor Market Information Division. **VFOAT** California. (1979)-. English. One time a year. Employment Development Department, PO Box 826880, Sacramento CA 94280. **Tel** (916)445-1952. **Continues** California. Employment Data and Research Division. State Manpower Review, California.

LC HD5726.C37 W48A
DD 331.12/09754/38 US
ANNUAL PLANNING INFORMATION. CHARLESTON, WEST VIRGINIA STANDARD METROPOLITAN STATISTICAL AREA. See Business and Economics-Abstracting, Bibliographies and Statistics.

LC HD5726.S88 A57
DD 331.1/09794/73 US
ANNUAL PLANNING INFORMATION, CITY OF SUNNYVALE. **Added/Corp** California. Coastal Area Labor Market Information Group. **VFOAT** Annual Planning Information, San Jose Standard Metropolitan Statistical Area, City of Sunnyvale. (19??)-. English. One time a year. California Employment Data and Research Department, PO Box 7774, San Francisco CA 94120.

LC HD5726.C54 A56
DD 331.12/09742/75 US
ANNUAL PLANNING INFORMATION. CLAREMONT, NEW HAMPSHIRE, LABOR MARKET AREA. **VFOAT** Claremont, New Hampshire, Labor Market Area; Annual Planning Information, Claremont Labor Market Area. English. One time a year. New Hampshire Department of Employment Security, 32 South Main Street, Concord NH 03301. **Tel** (603)224-3311, FAX (603)228-4145. **ED** Wesley S Noyes Jr. **Circ:** 250.
Desc: Current fiscal year data on population, labor force, employment, unemployment, applicants, job openings, placements and occupational projections.

LC HD5726.C697 A56 **ISSN** 0737-4275
DD 331.1/09758/4 US
ANNUAL PLANNING INFORMATION. COLUMBUS, GEORGIA, STANDARD METROPOLITAN STATISTICAL AREAS, COLUMBUS CONSORTIUM. (ANNUAL PLANNING INFORMATION FOR FISCAL YEAR ... COLUMBUS, GEORGIA, STANDARD METROPOLITAN STATISTICAL AREA, COLUMBUS CONSORTIUM.). Statistical Publication. English. One time a year. Employment Security Agency, Georgia Department of Labor, Box 390, Columbus GA 31902.

LC HD5725.C2 A647
DD 331.1/09794/33021 US
ANNUAL PLANNING INFORMATION. COLUSA COUNTY. **Added/Corp** California. Northern Area Labor Market Information Group. **VFOAT** Colusa County. (19??)-. English. One time a year. Northern Area Labor Market Information Group, 800 Capitol Mall/MIC 57, Sacramento CA 95814.

LC HD5726.C76 A56
DD 331.12/09742/72 US
ANNUAL PLANNING INFORMATION. CONCORD, NEW HAMPSHIRE, LABOR MARKET AREA / ECONOMIC ANALYSIS AND REPORTS SECTION. **Added/Corp** New Hampshire. Dept. of Employment Security. Economic Analysis and Reporting Section. **VFOAT** Concord, New Hampshire, Labor Market Area; Annual Planning Information, Concord Labor Market Area. (19??)-. English. One time a year. New Hampshire Department of Employment Security, 32 South Main Street, Concord NH 03301. **Tel** (603)224-3311, FAX (603)228-4145. **ED** Wesley S. Noyes, Jr. **Circ:** 250.
Desc: Current fiscal year data on population, labor force, employment, unemployment, applicants, job openings, placements and occupational projections.

LC HD5725.I8 A665
DD 331.1/09777/69 US
ANNUAL PLANNING INFORMATION, DAVENPORT, IOWA LABOR AREA FOR FISCAL YEAR ... . English. One time a year. free. Job Service of Iowa / Davenport, 902 West Kimberly Road, Davenport IA 52806.
Desc: Statistical and analytical presentation of labor market data.

US
ANNUAL PLANNING INFORMATION. DEL NORTE COUNTY (1985). (ANNUAL PLANNING INFORMATION. DEL NORTE COUNTY.). **VFOAT** Del Norte County. (1986)-. English. One time a year. Northern Area Labor Market Information Group, 800 Capitol Mall/MIC 57, Sacramento CA 95814. **Continues** Labor Market Information. del Norte County.

LC HD5725.I8 A667
DD 331.1/0977/39 US
ANNUAL PLANNING INFORMATION, DUBUQUE COUNTY FOR FISCAL YEAR ... . English. One time a year. Free. Dubuque Job Service, PO Box 757, Dubuque IA 52001.
Desc: Statistical and analytical presentation of labor market data.

LC HD5725.M5 M49A
DD 331.1/09774 US
ANNUAL PLANNING INFORMATION, FISCAL YEAR ... - MICHIGAN EMPLOYMENT SECURITY COMMISSION, BUREAU OF RESEARCH AND STATISTICS. See Business and Economics-Abstracting, Bibliographies and Statistics.

LC HD5725.M3 M34H
DD 331.12/09741/1 US
ANNUAL PLANNING INFORMATION FOR AROOSTOOK COUNTY. **Main/Corp** Maine. Manpower Research Division. **VFOAT** Annual Planning Information, Aroostook County. (19??)-. English. One time a year. Maine Department of Manpower Affairs / Augusta, Manpower Research Division, 20 Union Street, Augusta ME 04330.

LC HD5726.B74 C66A
US
ANNUAL PLANNING INFORMATION FOR BRISTOL-NEW BRITAIN SERVICE DELIVERY AREA, PLANNING YEAR ... .
Main/Corp Connecticut. Employment Security Division. Office of Research and Information. English. One time a year. Free. Office of Research and Information, Employment Security Division, 200 Folly Brook Boulevard, Wethersfield CT 06109. **Tel** (203)566-2120. **ED** Margaret Gagnon and Roger Therrier. **Circ:** 250.
Desc: Report prepared primarily for use by persons administering the Job Training Partnership Act in the New Britain-Bristol service delivery area.

LC HD5726.C68 M57A
DD 331.12/09778/29 US
ANNUAL PLANNING INFORMATION FOR COLUMBIA SMSA. See Business and Economics-Abstracting, Bibliographies and Statistics.

LC HD5726.P77 M34a
DD 331.12/09741/91 US
ANNUAL PLANNING INFORMATION FOR CUMBERLAND COUNTY. **Main/Corp** Maine. Manpower Research Division. (19??)-. English. One time a year. Maine Department of Manpower Affairs, Employment Security Commission, Manpower Research Division, 20 Union Street, Augusta ME 04330. **Continues** Annual Planning Report for Cumberland County Featuring the Portland SMSA, 0160-4058.

LC HD5726.C28 A56
DD 331.1/09777/62 US
ANNUAL PLANNING INFORMATION FOR FISCAL YEAR ..., CEDAR RAPIDS, IOWA LABOR AREA (LINN COUNTY).
VFOAT Annual Planning Information, Cedar Rapids. (1978/79)-. English. One time a year. Free. Job Service of Iowa / Cedar Rapids, 800 7th Street SE, PO Box 729, Cedar Rapids IA 52406. **Continues** Annual Planning Report, Cedar Rapids, Iowa Labor Area.
Desc: Statistical and analytical presentation of labor market data.

LC HD5725.U8 U82D
DD 331.12/09792 US
ANNUAL PLANNING INFORMATION FOR FISCAL YEAR ... / LABOR MARKET INFORMATION SERVICES SECTION, UTAH DEPARTMENT OF EMPLOYMENT SECURITY. **Main/Corp** Utah. Dept. of Employment Security. Labor Market Information Services Section. English. One time a year. Utah Department of Employment Security, 174 Social Hall Avenue, PO Box 11249, Salt Lake City UT 84147. **Tel** (801)533-2400.

LC HD5725.M8 A77
DD 331.12/09778 US
ANNUAL PLANNING INFORMATION FOR MISSOURI. (196?)-. English. One time a year. Missouri Division of Employment Security / Jefferson City, PO Box 59, Jefferson City MO 65104.

LC HD5725.M9 M65A
DD 331.1/1/09786 US
ANNUAL PLANNING INFORMATION FOR MONTANA, RURAL CEP AREA, BALANCE-OF-THE-STATE, BILLINGS SMSA, GREAT FALLS SMSA. **Main/Corp** Montana. Division of Employment Security Research and Analysis Section. (19??)-. English. One time a year. Free. Montana Department of Labor and Industry, PO Box 1728, Helena MT 59601. **Circ:** 750.
Desc: Provides data on labor force characteristics and narratives describing past year and forecast economic conditions in Montana.

US
ANNUAL PLANNING INFORMATION FOR NEW HAVEN LABOR MARKET AREA. (19??)-. English.

LC HD5725.M3 M34G
DD 331.12/09741/3 US
ANNUAL PLANNING INFORMATION FOR PENOBSCOT CONSORTIUM.
Main/Corp Maine. Manpower Research Division. (19??)-. English. One time a year. Maine Department of Manpower Affairs, Employment Security Commission, Manpower Research Division, 20 Union Street, Augusta ME 04330. **Continues** Annual Planning Report for the Penobscot Consortium Featuring the Bangor-Brewer Labor Market Area.

LC HD5725.A8 A7C
DD 331.12/09767 US
ANNUAL PLANNING INFORMATION FOR SMSA'S IN ARKANSAS. **Main/Corp** Arkansas. Employment Security Division. Research and Analysis Section. **VFOAT** Arkansas SMSA's. (198?)-. English. One time a year. Arkansas Employment Security Division, Research & Analysis Section, PO Box 2981, Little Rock AR 72203.

LC HD5726.S73 M57A
DD 331.12/09778/78 US
ANNUAL PLANNING INFORMATION FOR SPRINGFIELD SMSA. **Main/Corp** Missouri. Division of Employment Security. (19??)-. English. One time a year. Missouri Division of Employment Security / Springfield, 505 East Walnut Street, Springfield MO 65806.

LC HD5726.S78 C64A
DD 331.1/09746/9 US
ANNUAL PLANNING INFORMATION FOR STAMFORD LABOR MARKET AREA. **VFOAT** Annual Planning Information, Stamford. (19??)-. English. One time a year. Free to the US. Office of Research and Information, Employment Security Division, 200 Folly Brook Boulevard, Wethersfield CT 06109. **Tel** (203)566-2120. **ED** Margaret Gagnon and

Business and Economics —Labor

Roger Skelly. **Circ:** 250. **Continues** Stamford Annual Planning Information.
Desc: Primarily for the use of those persons who administer the Job Training Partnership Act in the Stamford Service delivery area.

LC HD5725.M3 M38a
DD 331.12/09741   US
ANNUAL PLANNING INFORMATION FOR STATE OF MAINE. Main/Corp Maine. State Employment and Training Council. (19??)-. English. One time a year. State Employment and Training Council, 512 West 6th Street, Topeka KS 66603.

LC HD5725.M3 M34D
DD 331.1/09741/95   US
ANNUAL PLANNING INFORMATION FOR YORK COUNTY. Main/Corp Maine. Manpower Research Division. (19??)-. English. One time a year. Maine Department of Manpower Affairs, Employment Security Commission, Manpower Research Division, 20 Union Street, Augusta ME 04330.

LC HD5725.N4 N45F
DD 331.12/09742/8   US
ANNUAL PLANNING INFORMATION : HILLSBOROUGH COUNTY. Main/Corp New Hampshire. Dept. of Employment Security. Economic Analysis and Reporting Section. English. One time a year. New Hampshire Department of Employment Security, 32 South Main Street, Concord NH 03301. **Tel** (603)224-3311, FAX (603)228-4145. **ED** Wesley S Noyes Jr. **Circ:** 600.
Desc: Current fiscal year data on population, labor force, employment, unemployment, applicants, job openings, placements and occupational projections.

LC HD5725.C2 C29F   **ISSN** 0736-6787
DD 331.109794/12   US
ANNUAL PLANNING INFORMATION. HUMBOLDT COUNTY. Main/Corp California. Coastal Area Labor Market Information Group. **VFOAT** Humboldt County. (198?)-. English. One time a year. Donna Grassman, PO Box 7774, San Francisco CA 94120. **Continues** California. Northern Area Labor Market Information Group. Annual Planning Information. Humboldt County, 0736-6787.

LC HD5726.H9 A55
DD 331.12/09754/42   US
ANNUAL PLANNING INFORMATION. HUNTINGTON-ASHLAND-IRONTON STANDARD METROPOLITAN STATISTICAL AREA. See Business and Economics-Abstracting, Bibliographies and Statistics.

LC HD5725.C2 A673
DD 331.1/09794/48021   US
ANNUAL PLANNING INFORMATION. INYO/MONO COUNTIES / STATE OF CALIFORNIA, HEALTH AND WELFARE AGENCY, EMPLOYMENT DEVELOPMENT DEPARTMENT, SOUTHERN CALIFORNIA EMPLOYMENT DATA AND RESEARCH.
VFOAT Inyo/Mono Countries; Inyo Mono Counties; Inyo and Mono Counties; Annual Planning Information. Inyo and Mono Counties. (198?)-. English (French). One time a year. Southern California Employment Data and Research, 312 1525 South Broadway/Room 232, Los Angeles CA 90015.

LC HD5726.K43 A56
DD 331.12/09742/9   US
ANNUAL PLANNING INFORMATION. KEENE, NEW HAMPSHIRE, LABOR MARKET AREA / ECONOMIC ANALYSIS AND REPORTS SECTION. VFOAT Keene, New Hampshire, Labor Market Area; Annual Planning Information, Keene Labor Market Area. (19??)-. English. One time a year. New Hampshire Department of Employment Security, 32 South Main Street, Concord NH 03301. **Tel** (603)224-3311, FAX (603)228-4145. **ED** Wesley S Noyes Jr. **Circ:** 250.
Desc: Current fiscal year data on population, labor force, employment, unemployment, applicants, job openings, placements and occupational projections.

LC HD5726.L26 A56
DD 331.12/09742/45   US
ANNUAL PLANNING INFORMATION. LACONIA, NEW HAMPSHIRE, LABOR MARKET AREA. Added/Corp New Hampshire. Dept. of Employment Security. Economic Analysis and Reporting Section. **VFOAT** Laconia, New Hampshire, Labor Market Area; Annual Planning Information, Laconia Labor Market Area. (19??)-. English. One time a year. New Hampshire Department of Employment Security, 32 South Main Street, Concord NH 03301. **Tel** (603)224-3311, FAX (603)228-4145. **ED** Wesley S Noyes Jr. **Circ:** 250.

Desc: Current fiscal year data on population, labor force, employment, unemployment, applicants, job openings, placements and occupational projections.

LC HD5726.M342 A56
DD 331.12/09742/8   US
ANNUAL PLANNING INFORMATION. MANCHESTER, NEW HAMPSHIRE, LABOR MARKET AREA / ECONOMIC ANALYSIS AND REPORTS SECTION.
VFOAT Manchester, New Hampshire, Labor Market Area; Annual Planning Information, Manchester Labor Market Area. (19??)-. English. One time a year. New Hampshire Department of Employment Security, 32 South Main Street, Concord NH 03301. **Tel** (603)224-3311, FAX (603)228-4145. **ED** Wesley S Noyes Jr. **Circ:** 250.
Desc: Current fiscal year data on population, labor force, employment, unemployment, applicants, job openings, placements and occupational projections.

LC HD5725.C2 A674
DD 331.1/09794/62021   US
ANNUAL PLANNING INFORMATION. MARIN COUNTY. VFOAT Marin County. (198?)-. English. One time a year. California Employment Data and Research Department, PO Box 7774, San Francisco CA 94120.

LC HD5725.C2 C2B   **ISSN** 0883-301X
DD 331.1/09794/58021   US
ANNUAL PLANNING INFORMATION. MERCED COUNTY. (1979)-. English. One time a year. New York State Department of Labor / Albany, 401 Harriman, Division of Research and Statistics, State Office Building Campus, Albany NY 12240. **Tel** (518)457-6649. **Continues** Annual Planning Report. Merced County, 0160-7448.

LC HD5726.M43 C66A
DD 331.1/09746/7   US
ANNUAL PLANNING INFORMATION. MERIDEN-MIDDLESEX SERVICE DELIVERY AREA. VFOAT Meriden-Middlesex Service Delivery Area; Meriden Middlesex Service Delivery Area. 1987-. English. One time a year. Free. Office of Research and Information, Employment Security Division, 200 Folly Brook Boulevard, Wethersfield CT 06109. **Tel** (203)566-2120. **ED** Margaret Gagnon and Roger Skelly. **Circ:** 225. **Continues** Annual Planning Information for Meriden-Middletown Service Delivery Area, Planning Year ... .
Desc: This report was prepared primarily for the use of persons administering the Job Training Partnership Act (JTPA) in the Meriden Middlesex Service Delivery area.

LC HD5726.N29 A56
DD 331.12/09742/8   US
ANNUAL PLANNING INFORMATION. NASHUA, NEW HAMPSHIRE, LABOR MARKET AREA. VFOAT Nashua, New Hampshire, Labor Market Area; Annual Planning Information, Nashua Labor Market Area. (19??)-. English. One time a year. New Hampshire Department of Employment Security, 32 South Main Street, Concord NH 03301. **Tel** (603)224-3311, FAX (603)228-4145. **ED** Welsey S Noyes Jr. **Circ:** 250.
Desc: Current fiscal year data on population, labor force, employment, unemployment, applicants, job openings, placements and occupational projections.

LC HD5725.N4 N45C
DD 331.1/09742   US
ANNUAL PLANNING INFORMATION, NEW HAMPSHIRE. Main/Corp New Hampshire. Dept. of Employment Security. Economic Analysis and Reports Section. English. One time a year. New Hampshire Department of Unemployment Security, 32 South Main Street, Concord NH 03301. **Tel** (603)224-3311. **Continues** Annual Planning Report - New Hampshire Department of Employment Security, 0149-6360.

LC HD5725.C8 C64f
DD 331.1/09746/45   US
ANNUAL PLANNING INFORMATION. NORTHEAST SERVICE DELIVERY AREA. Added/Corp Connecticut. Employment Security Division. Office of Research and Information. **VFOAT** Northeast Service Delivery Area. (1987)-. English. Office of Research and Information, Employment Security Division, 200 Folly Brook Boulevard, Wethersfield CT 06109. **Tel** (203)566-2120. **Continues** Annual Planning Information for Danielson-Windham Service Delivery Area ... .

LC HD5725.I8 A675
DD 331.1/09777/93   US
ANNUAL PLANNING INFORMATION. OTTUMWA, IOWA LABOR AREA, WAPELLO COUNTY. English. One time a year. Free. Job Service of Iowa / Ottumwa, 609 West 2nd Street, Ottumwa IA 52501.
Desc: Statistical and analytical presentation of labor market data.

LC HD5726.P83 A56
DD 331.12/09742/6   US
ANNUAL PLANNING INFORMATION. PORTSMOUTH, NEW HAMPSHIRE, LABOR MARKET AREA. Added/Corp New Hampshire. Dept. of Employment Security. Economic Analysis and Reporting Section. **VFOAT** Portsmouth, New Hampshire, Labor Market Area; Annual Planning Information, Portsmouth Labor Market Area. (19??)-. English. New Hampshire Department of Employment Security, 32 South Main Street, Concord NH 03301. **Tel** (603)224-3311, FAX (603)228-4145. **ED** Wesley S. Noyes Jr. **Circ:** 250.
Desc: Current fiscal year data on population, labor force, employment, unemployment, applicants, job openings, placements and occupational projections.

LC HD5726.B42 T48A
DD 331.12/09764/145   US
ANNUAL PLANNING INFORMATION REPORT : BEAUMONT-PORT ARTHUR-ORANGE SMSA. See Business and Economics-Abstracting, Bibliographies and Statistics.

LC HD5725.C6 A66   **ISSN** 0749-7857
DD 331.11/09788/021   US
ANNUAL PLANNING INFORMATION REPORT. COLORADO. [Annu. plann. inf. rep., Colo.]. **VFOAT** Colorado Annual Planning Information Report. (1980)-. English. One time a year. Colorado Division of Employment and Training, Research and Development Section, 251 East 12th Avenue, Denver CO 80203. **Continues** Annual Planning Information, Fiscal Year ... Colorado.

LC HD5726.B65 M38c
DD 331.12/09744/61   US
ANNUAL PLANNING INFORMATION REPORT, FISCAL YEAR ... BOSTON, MASSACHUSETTS STANDARD METROPOLITAN STATISTICAL AREA / PREPARED BY EDWARD F. KAZONCHA, LABOR MARKET ECONOMIST (DIVISION OF EMPLOYMENT SECURITY, JOB MARKET RESEARCH, LABOR AREA RESEARCH). Main/Corp Massachusetts. Labor Area Research Dept. (19??)-. Statistical Publication. English. One time a year. Free on request. Division of Employment Security / Boston, Charles F. Hurley Building, Government Center, Boston MA 02114. **Tel** (617)727-6531.

LC HD5726.A77 A566
DD 331.1/09758/231   US
ANNUAL PLANNING INFORMATION REPORT FOR FISCAL YEAR ... ATLANTA STANDARD METROPOLITAN STATISTICAL AREA.
VFOAT Annual Planning Information for Fiscal Year ... Atlanta. Statistical Publication. English. One time a year. Georgia Department of Labor, CES Unit, 148 International Boulevard, Atlanta GA 30303. **Tel** (404)656-2994.

LC HD5726.A84 A56
DD 331.1/09758   US
ANNUAL PLANNING INFORMATION REPORT FOR FISCAL YEAR ... AUGUSTA, GEORGIA AREA, RICHMOND AND COLUMBIA COUNTIES, GEORGIA AND AIKEN COUNTY, SOUTH CAROLINA AND THE CENTRAL SAVANNAH RIVER AREA.
VFOAT Annual Planning Information for Fiscal Year ... Augusta. English. One time a year. Georgia Department of Labor, CES Unit, 148 International Boulevard, Atlanta GA 30303. **Tel** (404)656-2994.

LC HD5726.S48 A56
DD 331.1/09758/724   US
ANNUAL PLANNING INFORMATION REPORT FOR FISCAL YEAR ... SAVANNAH SMSA SAVANNAH/CHATHAM CONSORTIUM. See Business and Economics-Abstracting, Bibliographies and Statistics.

LC HD5726.J64 P46A
DD 331.12/09746/7   US
ANNUAL PLANNING INFORMATION REPORT FOR SOUTHERN ALLEGHENIES SERVICE DELIVERY AREA : INCLUDES ALTOONA SMSA AND JOHNSTOWN SMSA. Main/Corp Pennsylvania. Office of Employment Security. (19??)-. English. One time a year. Labor Market Information Unit / Altoona, PA, Office of Employment Security, 1101 Green Avenue, Altoona PA 16603.

Business and Economics — Labor

LC HD5726.M47 F58B
DD 331.12/09759/381 US
ANNUAL PLANNING INFORMATION REPORT ... MIAMI SMSA AND SOUTH FLORIDA CETA CONSORTIUM. **Main/Corp** Florida. Division of Employment Security. **VFOAT** Miami S.M.S.A. Annual Planning Information; Miami SMSA Annual Planning Information. English. One time a year. Florida State Employment Service / Miami, 500 Northwest 12th Avenue, PO Box 011750, Miami FL 33101.
Desc: Includes supplementary material for the CETA prime sponsor area.

LC HD5726.O7 F57A
DD 331.12/09759/24 US
ANNUAL PLANNING INFORMATION REPORT. ORLANDO SMSA AND ORANGE COUNTY, ORLANDO CITY, SEMINOLE COUNTY CETA PRIME SPONSOR AREAS. See Business and Economics-Abstracting, Bibliographies and Statistics.

LC HD5726.P44 F57a
DD 331.12/09759/982 US
ANNUAL PLANNING INFORMATION REPORT ... PENSACOLA SMSA AND OKALOOSA COUNTY. See Business and Economics-Abstracting, Bibliographies and Statistics.

LC HD5726.T35 F58B
DD 331.12/09759/88 US
ANNUAL PLANNING INFORMATION REPORT ... TALLAHASSEE SMSA AND LEON-GADSDEN CETA CONSORTIUM. **Main/Corp** Florida. Division of Employment Security. **VFOAT** Tallahassee S.M.S.A. Annual Planning Information; Tallahassee SMSA Annual Planning Information. English. One time a year. Florida Labor, Employment & Training Division, 1320 Executive Center Drive, Suite 300, Tallahassee FL 32399. **Tel** (904)488-7225, FAX (904)487-1753.
Desc: Includes supplementary material for the CETA prime sponsor area.

LC HD5725.N4 A66
DD 331.12/09742/6 US
ANNUAL PLANNING INFORMATION. SALEM, NEW HAMPSHIRE, LABOR MARKET AREA / ECONOMIC ANALYSIS AND REPORTS SECTION. **VFOAT** Salem, New Hampshire, Labor Market Area; Annual Planning Information, Salem Labor Market Area. (19??)-. English. One time a year. New Hampshire Department of Employment Security, 32 South Main Street, Concord NH 03301. **Tel** (603)224-3311, FAX (603)228-4145. **ED** Wesley S Noyes Jr. **Circ:** 250.
Desc: Current fiscal year data on population, labor force, employment, unemployment, applicants, job openings, placements and occupational projections.

LC HD5726.S4 A56
DD 331.1/09794/61 US
ANNUAL PLANNING INFORMATION. SAN FRANCISCO CITY AND COUNTY. **VFOAT** San Francisco City and County. (1985)-. English. One time a year. California Employment Data and Research Department, PO Box 7774, San Francisco CA 94120.

LC HD5726.B45 C32a ISSN 0272-6815
DD 331.1/09794/67 US
ANNUAL PLANNING INFORMATION: SAN FRANCISCO-OAKLAND STANDARD METROPOLITAN STATISTICAL AREA, CITY OF BERKELEY. **Main/Corp** California. Coastal Area Labor Market Information Group. (19??)-. Statistical Publication. English. One time a year. California Employment Data and Research Department, PO Box 7774, San Francisco CA 94120. **Continues** Annual Planning Report. San Francisco-Oakland Standard Metropolitan Statistical Area, City of Berkeley, 0160-0745.

LC HD5726.O22 C32A
DD 331.1/09794/65 US
ANNUAL PLANNING INFORMATION : SAN FRANCISCO-OAKLAND STANDARD METROPOLITAN STATISTICAL AREA, CITY OF OAKLAND. (19??)-. Statistical Publication. English. One time a year. Employment Development Department, PO Box 826880, Sacramento CA 94280. **Tel** (916)445-1952. **Continues** Annual Planning Report. San Francisco-Oakland Standard Metropolitan Statistical Area, City of Oakland.

LC HD5726.C2 C22a ISSN 0272-703X
DD 331.1/09794/63 US
ANNUAL PLANNING INFORMATION : SAN FRANCISCO-OAKLAND STANDARD METROPOLITAN STATISTICAL AREA, CITY OF RICHMOND. **Main/Corp** California. Coastal Area Labor Market Information Group. (19??)-. Statistical Publication. English. One time a year. California Employment Data and Research Department, PO Box 7774, San Francisco CA 94120. **Continues** Annual Planning Report. San Francisco-Oakland Standard Metropolitan Statistical Area, Richmond of Richmond, 0160-0761.

LC HD5725.C2 C22K ISSN 0198-8662
DD 331.1/09794/63 US
ANNUAL PLANNING INFORMATION : SAN FRANCISCO-OAKLAND STANDARD METROPOLITAN STATISTICAL AREA, CONTRA COSTA COUNTY, EXCLUDING THE CITY OF RICHMOND. **Main/Corp** California. Coastal Area Labor Market Information Group. (19??)-. Statistical Publication. English. California Employment Data and Research Department, PO Box 7774, San Francisco CA 94120. **Continues** Annual Planning Report. San Francisco-Oakland Standard Metropolitan Statistical Area, Balance of Contra Costa County, Contra Costa County Except City of Richmond, 0160-046X.

US
ANNUAL PLANNING INFORMATION. SANTA CRUZ COUNTY. **Added/Corp** California. Coastal Area Labor Market Information Group. **VFOAT** Santa Cruz County; Annual Planning Information. Santa Cruz Metropolitan Statistical Area. (1989)-. Statistical Publication. English. California Employment Data and Research Department, PO Box 7774, San Francisco CA 94120. **Continues** Annual Planning Information. Santa Cruz Metropolitan Statistical Area (Santa Cruz County).

US
ANNUAL PLANNING INFORMATION. SARASOTA SMSA. **VFOAT** Sarasota SMSA; Sarasota Standard Metropolitan Statistical Area. (198?)-. English. One time a year. Florida State Employment Service / Sarasota, PO Drawer Y, Sarasota FL 33577. **Continues** Annual Planning Information Report. Sarasota County.

LC HD5726.S56 A66
DD 331.1/09777/41 US
ANNUAL PLANNING INFORMATION, SIOUX CITY SMSA. See Business and Economics-Abstracting, Bibliographies and Statistics.

LC HD5725.C8 C64G
DD 331.1/09746/5 US
ANNUAL PLANNING INFORMATION. SOUTH EAST SERVICE DELIVERY AREA. **VFOAT** Southeast Service Delivery Area. 1987-. English. One time a year. Free. Office of Research and Information, Employment Security Division, 200 Folly Brook Boulevard, Wethersfield CT 06109. **Tel** (203)566-2120. **ED** Margaret Gagnon and Roger Therrien. **Circ:** 250. **Continues** Annual Planning Information for New London-Norwich Service Delivery Area, Planning Year ... .
Desc: This report was prepared primarily for use of those persons administering the Job Training Partnership Act (JTPA) in the Southeast Service Delivery Area.

LC HD5725.F6 F35E
DD 331.12/09759 US
ANNUAL PLANNING INFORMATION, STATE OF FLORIDA. **Main/Corp** Florida. Division of Employment Security. **VFOAT** Annual Planning Information, Florida. 1982-. English. One time a year. Division of Employment Security / Florida, Bureau of Research & Analysis, Caldwell Building, Tallahassee FL 32301. **Continues** Annual Planning Information Report, State of Florida.

LC HD5725.C2 C22B
DD 331.1/0979419 US
ANNUAL PLANNING INFORMATION : VALLEJO-FAIRFIELD-NAPA STANDARD METROPOLITAN STATISTICAL AREA, NAPA COUNTY. **Main/Corp** California. Coastal Area Labor Market Information Group. Statistical Publication. English. One time a year. California Health and Welfare Agency Employment Development Department, Employment Data and Research, Coastal Area Labor Market, PO Box 7774, San Francisco CA 94120. **Continues** Annual Planning Report. Vallejo-Fairfield-Napa Standard Metropolitan Statistical Area, Napa County, 0160-0494.

LC HD5725.I23 A83
DD 331.12/09796/28 US
ANNUAL PLANNING REPORT ... ADA COUNTY. **Added/Corp** Idaho. Dept. of Employment. Planning, Research, and Evaluation Bureau. (1981)-. English. One time a year. Free. Idaho Department of Employment, 317 Main Street, Boise ID 83735. **Tel** (208)334-6112, FAX (208)334-6430. **ED** Fred J. Friel. **Circ:** 1,000. **Continues** Annual Planning Report ... Boise SMSA (Ada County).
Desc: Demographic profile and socioeconomic information for social scientists and planners.

LC HD5726.F34 M38A ISSN 0148-5075
DD 331.1/26/097448 US
ANNUAL PLANNING REPORT : FALL RIVER, MASSACHUSETTS-RHODE ISLAND LABOR MARKET AREA. [Annu. plan. rep. Fall River Mass. R. I. labor mark. area]. **Main/Corp** Massachusetts. Labor Area Research Dept. **VFOAT** Fall River, Massachusetts-Rhode Island Labor Market Area. English. One time a year. Labor Area Research Department, Massachusetts Division of Employment Security, Charles F Hurley Building, Cambridge Street, Boston MA 02114.

LC HD5726.C36 I44A
DD 331.1/09773/6 US
ANNUAL PLANNING REPORT, FISCAL YEAR ... CHAMPAIGN SMSA. See Business and Economics-Abstracting, Bibliographies and Statistics.

LC HD5725.W9 W96b
DD 331.12/09787 US
ANNUAL PLANNING REPORT FOR THE STATE OF WYOMING. **Added/Corp** Wyoming. Dept. of Employment. Research and Planning Section. (1990)-. Government Publication. English. One time a year. Employment Security Commission of Wyoming, PO Box 2760, Research and Analysis, Casper WY 82602. **Tel** (307)237-3701. **Continues** Wyoming Annual Planning Report, 0749-7512.

LC HD5725.M3 M34C
DD 331.1/1/09741 US
ANNUAL PLANNING REPORT: MAINE, BALANCE OF STATE. **Main/Corp** Maine. Manpower Research Division. (19??)-. English. One time a year. Maine Department of Manpower Affairs, Employment Security Commission, Manpower Research Division, 20 Union Street, Augusta ME 04330.

LC HD5725.N2 N43A
DD 331.1/09782 US
ANNUAL PLANNING REPORT - NEBRASKA DEPARTMENT OF LABOR, DIVISION OF EMPLOYMENT. **Main/Corp** Nebraska. Division of Employment. (19??)-. English. One time a year. Nebraska Department of Labor, Box 94600, Statehouse Station, Lincoln NE 68509. **Tel** (402)475-8451.

LC HD5725.W2 W35H
DD 331.1/09797/79 US
ANNUAL PLANNING REPORT. OLYMPIA SMSA. See Business and Economics-Abstracting, Bibliographies and Statistics.

LC HD5726.R6 N48A
DD 331.1/2/097478 US
ANNUAL PLANNING REPORT: ROCHESTER LABOR AREA. **Main/Corp** New York (State). Dept. of Labor. Division of Research and Statistics. (1977)-. English. One time a year. New York State Department of Labor / Rochester, Division of Research and Statistics, 155 West Main Street, Rochester NY 14614. **Continues** Annual Manpower Planning Report, Fiscal Year ... Rochester Standard Metropolitan Statistical Area (Monroe, Livingston, Ontario, Orleans and Wayne Counties).

LC HD5726.S485 W37A ISSN 0145-7187
DD 331.1/09797/77 US
ANNUAL PLANNING REPORT : SEATTLE-EVERETT, WASHINGTON AREA. **Main/Corp** Washington (State). Employment Security Dept. English. One time a year. Washington Employment Security Department, Labor Market and Economic Analysis, Box 9046, Olympia WA 98507-9046. **Tel** (206)753-5114, FAX (206)753-4851.

LC HD5725.F6 F35c ISSN 0147-4901
DD 353.9/759/0083 US
ANNUAL PLANNING REPORT - STATE OF FLORIDA, DEPARTMENT OF COMMERCE, DIVISION OF EMPLOYMENT SECURITY. (ANNUAL PLANNING REPORT.). **Main/Corp** Florida. Division of Employment Security. Office of Research and Statistics. (19??)-. English. One time a year. Florida Department of Commerce Development, 107 West Gaines Street, Collins Building, Suite 536, Tallahassee FL 32399. **Tel** (904)488-3104, FAX (904)487-1612.

Business and Economics —Labor

LC HD5725.W9 W96B
DD 331.12/09787 US
ANNUAL PLANNING REPORT, STATE OF WYOMING. Main/Corp Employment Security Commission of Wyoming. Research and Analysis Section. English. One time a year. Free. Employment Security Commission of Wyoming, PO Box 2760, Research and Analysis, Casper WY 82602. **Tel** (307)237-3701. **ED** Michael J Paris. **Circ:** 350.
Desc: A comprehensive report which uses most of the programs in research and analysis to analyze labor market developments and related problems in the State of Wyoming.

LC HD5725.O3 O38a
DD 353.97710083/3 US
ANNUAL REPORT. Main/Corp Ohio. Office of Manpower Development. (1977)-. English. One time a year. Office of Manpower Development, 30 East Broad Street, Columbus OH 43215.

LC HD5876.M6 M56a
DD 353.97760083/06 US
●**ANNUAL REPORT. Main/Corp** Minnesota. Dept. of Economic Security. (1993)-. English. Minnesota Department of Jobs & Training, 390 North Robert Street, St. Paul MN 55101. **Continues** Minnesota. Dept. of Jobs and Training. Annual Report.

LC HD5850.V5 V55a
DD 354.9450083/3/06 AT
ANNUAL REPORT. Main/Corp Victoria. Ministry of Employment and Training. (19??)-. English. One time a year. Ministry of Employment and Training, 80 Collins Street, Melbourne 3000 Australia.

LC E78.A3 A73a
DD 353.97980081/497 US
ANNUAL REPORT - ALASKA NATIVE HUMAN RESOURCES DEVELOPMENT PROGRAM. Main/Corp Alaska Native Human Resources Development Program. (19??)-. English. One time a year. Alaska Native Human Resources Development Program, 733 West 4th Avenue 200, Anchorage AK 99501-2132. **Continues** Alaska Native Human Resources Development Program. Fiscal Year Report.

LC HD8101.5 .A57A   **ISSN** 0702-9667
DD 354/.7123/0083 CN
ANNUAL REPORT - ALBERTA LABOUR. [Annu. rep. - Alta. Labour]. **Main/Corp** Alberta. Alberta Labour. 1975/76-. English. One time a year. **Continues in part** Alberta. Alberta Manpower and Labour. Annual Report - Alberta Manpower and Labour, 0381-4300.

LC HD8053.A8 A3
DD 353.9/767/0083 US
ANNUAL REPORT - ARKANSAS DEPARTMENT OF LABOR. Main/Corp Arkansas. Dept. of Labor. (1955/56)-. English. One time a year. Arkansas Department of Labor, PO Box 2981, Little Rock AR 72203. **Continues** Annual Report of Department of Labor of the State of Arkansas.

LC J905 .L3 HD5630   **ISSN** 0310-5148
DD 328.94/01 S 354/.94/00833 AT
ANNUAL REPORT - AUSTRALIAN ARBITRATION INSPECTORATE. (ANNUAL REPORT - ARBITRATION INSPECTORATE.). **Main/Corp** Australia. Arbitration Inspectorate. (1972)-. English. 0.45Aus$. Government Printer / Australia, PO Box 84, Canberra, Australian Capital Territory, 2600 Australia.

LC HD4903.5.U58 C34a
DD 353.97940083/3 US
ANNUAL REPORT / CALIFORNIA DEPARTMENT OF FAIR EMPLOYMENT AND HOUSING. Main/Corp California. Dept. of Fair Employment and Housing. **Added/Corp** California. State and Consumer Services Agency. (1985/86)-. English. **Continues** Annual Report - Ontario. Ministry of Municipal Affairs and Housing.

LC HD4903.5.A8 W47a
 AT
ANNUAL REPORT / COMMISSIONER FOR EQUAL OPPORTUNITY. Main/Corp Western Australia. Equal Opportunity Commission. 1st (1985/1986)-. Government Publication. English. One time a year. Free. Equal Opportunity Commission, 4/356 Collins Street, Melbourne Victoria 3000 Australia. **Tel** (03)6023222, FAX (03)6702922. **Circ:** 2,000.
Desc: Information on discrimination in employment.

LC HD8005.6.U53 C83
DD 353.9/746/0083 US
**ANNUAL REPORT - CONNECTICUT OFFICE OF LABOR RELATIONS.
Main/Corp** Connecticut. Office of Labor Relations. **Added/Corp** Connecticut. Office of Labor Relations. Connecticut Collective Bargaining. (1976/77)-. English. One time a year. Connecticut Office of Labor Relations, State Office Building, Room 510, Hartford CT 06115.

LC HD8849.Q45 Q435a
DD 354.9430083/06 AT
ANNUAL REPORT / DEPT. OF EMPLOYMENT, VOCATIONAL EDUCATION, TRAINING, AND INDUSTRIAL RELATIONS. Main/Corp Queensland. Dept. of Employment, Vocational Education, Training, and Industrial Relations. (1990)-. English. Department of Employment, Vocational Education, Training and Industrial Relations, Citibank Centre, 199 Charlotte Street, Brisbane Queensland 4000 Australia. **Tel** 011 61 7 225 2000, FAX 011 61 7 229 0126. **Formed by the union of** Queensland. Dept. of Industrial Affairs.; Annual Report; Queensland. Dept. of Employment, Vocational Education, and Training. **and** Annual Report, 1033-0828.

LC HC107.M3 A4137   **ISSN** 0363-4485
DD 353.9/752/0083 US
**ANNUAL REPORT - DIVISION OF LABOR AND INDUSTRY (MARYLAND).
Main/Corp** Maryland. Division of Labor and Industry. English. One time a year. Maryland Department of Licensing and Regulation, Division of Labor and Industry, 203 East Baltimore Street, Baltimore MD 21202. **Continues** Maryland. Dept. of Labor and Industry. Annual Report.

LC JK4360.P4 G43a   **ISSN** 0435-4842
DD 353.9/758/005 US
ANNUAL REPORT - EMPLOYEES' RETIREMENT SYSTEM. See Public Administration-Civil Service.

 UK
ANNUAL REPORT / EMPLOYMENT DEPARTMENT GROUP, TRAINING COMMISSION. Main/Corp Great Britain. Training Commission. (1987/88)-. English. One time a year. **Continues** Annual Report / Great Britain. Manpower Services Commission.

LC HD7694.5 .A25a
DD 306/.094 LU
ANNUAL REPORT / EUROPEAN FOUNDATION FOR THE IMPROVEMENT OF LIVING AND WORKING CONDITIONS. Main/Corp European Foundation for the Improvement of Living and Working Conditions. (19??)-. English. One time a year. £7.10 UK; 7.70p Ireland. Office for Official Publications of the European Communities, 2 rue Mercier, 2985 Luxembourg Luxembourg. **Tel** 011 352 499281, FAX 011 352 292942763.

LC HD7102.A8 W47A
DD 354.9410082/56 AT
**ANNUAL REPORT FOR THE YEAR ENDING JUNE 30 ... OF THE WORKERS' COMPENSATION AND REHABILITATION COMMISSION.
Main/Corp** Western Australia. Workers' Compensation and Rehabilitation Commission. **VFOAT** Annual Report. 1987-. English. One time a year. **Continues** Annual Report on the Operation of the Workers' Compensation and Assistance Act 1981-... for the Year Ending 30 June ... .

LC HD7096.U6 A8
DD 331.25444 US
ANNUAL REPORT FOR THE YEAR ... / STATE OF ARKANSAS, EMPLOYMENT SECURITY DIVISION, DEPARTMENT OF LABOR. Main/Corp Arkansas. Employment Security Division. 5th (1941)-. English. One time a year. Arkansas Department of Labor, PO Box 2981, Little Rock AR 72203. **Continues** Arkansas. Unemployment Compensation Division. Annual Report.

LC HD8799.K4 A25   **ISSN** 0075-5893
DD 354/.676/2008 KE
ANNUAL REPORT - KENYA. MINISTRY OF LABOUR. Main/Corp Kenya. Ministry of Labour. (1965)-. English. Republic of Kenya, Print and Stat Department, PO Box 30128, Nairobi Kenya. **Continues in part** Kenya. Ministry of Labour and Social Services. Annual Report.

LC HD8109.B7 A3   **ISSN** 0836-1126
DD 354.7110683/05 CN
ANNUAL REPORT - MINISTRY OF LABOUR AND CONSUMER SERVICES (VICTORIA). (ANNUAL REPORT.). [Annu. rep. - Minist. Labour Consum. Serv.]. **Main/Corp** British Columbia. Ministry of Labour and Consumer Services. (1985/1986)-. English. Ministry of Labour / Victoria, 1019 Wharf Street, 6th Floor, Victoria British Columbia V8V 1X5 Canada. **Tel** (604)387-3169. **Continues** Ministry of Labour. Annual Report / British Columbia. Ministry of Labour, 0705-9698; **Absorbed** British Columbia. Liquor Control and Licensing Branch. Annual Report.

 US
ANNUAL REPORT - MISSOURI. DEPT. OF LABOR AND INDUSTRIAL RELATIONS. Main/Corp Missouri. Dept. of Labor and Industrial Relations. Vol. 1 (1975)-. English. One time a year. Missouri Department of Labor and Industrial Relations, 3315 West Truman Boulevard, Jefferson City MO 65109. **Tel** (314)751-4091. **Continues in part** Annual Report - Missouri Division of Workmen's Compensation.

LC HD5713.6.S6 S68b
DD 331.11/0968/05 SA
ANNUAL REPORT / NATIONAL MANPOWER COMMISSION. Main/Corp South Africa. National Manpower Commission. (19??)-. English. Department of Manpower / Pretoria, Manpower Building, 215 Schoeman Street, Private Bag X117, 0001 Pretoria South Africa. **Tel** (012)310-6911, FAX (012)320-2059. **Continues in part** South Africa. National Manpower Commission. Jaarverslag.

LC HD8053.N7 A23
DD 353.9740083/06 US
ANNUAL REPORT - NEW YORK (STATE). DEPT. OF LABOR. Main/Corp New York (State). Dept. of Labor. 1966-. English. One time a year. New York State Department of Labor / Albany, 401 Harriman, Division of Research and Statistics, State Office Building Campus, Albany NY 12240. **Tel** (518)457-6649. **Continues** Annual Report of the New York State Department of Labor.

LC HD5725.C8 C65a
DD 331.1/1/09746 US
ANNUAL REPORT OF COMMISSIONER OF LABOR ... ON THE ECONOMY, WORKFORCE AND TRAINING NEEDS IN CONNECTICUT. Added/Corp Connecticut. Labor Dept. **VFOAT** Annual Report on the Economy, Workforce and Training Needs in Connecticut. (Jan. 1990)-. English. Connecticut Labor Department, 200 Folly Brook Boulevard, Wethersfield CT 06109. **Tel** (203)566-4380. **Continues** Connecticut. Labor Dept. Manpower Development and Planning Report.

LC HD5725.A6 A73A
DD 353.9/791/0084 US
**ANNUAL REPORT OF ECONOMIC SECURITY NEEDS AND RESOURCES.
Main/Corp** Arizona. Dept. of Economic Security. English. One time a year. Office of Planning, PO Box 6121, Phoenix AZ 85005. **Continues** Arizona. Dept. of Economic Security. Annual Report.

LC HD8934   **ISSN** 0438-7473
DD 331 US
ANNUAL REPORT OF THE DEPARTMENT OF LABOR AND INDUSTRIAL RELATIONS, STATE OF HAWAII. Main/Corp Hawaii. Department of Labor and Industrial Relations. **VFOAT** Annual Report - Department of Labor and Industrial Relations, State of Hawaii. (19??)-. Periodical. English. One time a year. Hawaii Department of Labor and Industrial Relations, 830 Punchbowl Street, Room 321, Honolulu HI 96813. **Tel** (808)586-8844, FAX (808)586-5099. **Continues** Hawaii (Ter.) Department of Labor and Industrial Relations. Annual Report - Department of Labor and Industrial Relations, Territory of Hawaii.

LC KF5365 .A8444   **ISSN** 0275-200X
DD 353.001/74/06 US
ANNUAL REPORT OF THE FEDERAL LABOR RELATIONS AUTHORITY AND THE FEDERAL SERVICE IMPASSES PANEL FOR THE FISCAL PERIOD ... .
[Annu. rep. Fed. Labor Relat. Auth. Fed. Serv. Impasses Panel fisc. period]. **Main/Corp** United States. Federal Labor Relations Authority. 1st (Jan. 1-Sept. 30, 1979)-. English. One time a year. Federal Labor Relations Authority, 500 C Street SW, Washington DC 20424. **Tel** (202)382-0711. **Continues** United States. Federal Service Impasses Panel. Annual Report.

LC HD7655.I2 I33a   **ISSN** 0362-3912
DD 353.9/796/0083 US
ANNUAL REPORT OF THE IDAHO DEPARTMENT OF LABOR AND INDUSTRIAL SERVICES. Main/Corp Idaho. Dept. of Labor and Industrial Services. 1st (1975)-. English. Idaho Department of Labor and Industrial Services, 317 Main Street, Statehouse/Room 400, Boise ID 83720.

Business and Economics —Labor

LC HD5503 .A715
DD 331.15506173
ISSN 0083-2200
US
ANNUAL REPORT OF THE NATIONAL LABOR RELATIONS BOARD. (ANNUAL REPORT OF THE NATIONAL LABOR RELATIONS BOARD FOR THE FISCAL YEAR ENDED ...). [Annu. rep. Natl. Labor Relat. Board]. **Main/Corp** United States. National Labor Relations Board. 1st (June 30, 1936)-. Government Publication. English. Twelve times a year. $18.00. Superintendent of Documents, US Government Printing Office, Washington DC 20402. **Tel** (202)275-3328, FAX (202)786-2377. available on microfiche (Vols. for (1985-) distributed to depository Libraries).

LC HD8053.T6 D46a
DD 353.9/764/0083
US
ANNUAL REPORT OF THE TEXAS DEPARTMENT OF LABOR AND STANDARDS. **Main/Corp** Texas. Dept. of Labor and Standards. (19??)-. English. One time a year. Texas Department of Labor and Standards, Box 12157, Austin TX 78711.

LC HD7256.U6 O74a
DD 353.97950083/4
US
ANNUAL REPORT / OREGON VOCATIONAL REHABILITATION DIVISION. **Main/Corp** Oregon. Vocational Rehabilitation Division. (19??)-. English. Oregon Department of Human Resources Development, 155 Cottage Street Northeast, Salem OR 97310. **Continues** Oregon. Vocational Rehabilitation Division. Bi-Annual Report.

LC JK8060.P4 P8a
DD 353.9789001/82/06
ISSN 0196-6685
US
ANNUAL REPORT - PUBLIC EMPLOYEES' RETIREMENT ASSOCIATION OF NEW MEXICO. See Public Administration-Civil Service.

LC HD7106.C3 Q363
DD 354/.714/0083
CN
ANNUAL REPORT - QUEBEC PENSION BOARD. **Main/Corp** Quebec Pension Board. **VFOAT** Rapport Annuel. Multiple languages (English and French). One time a year.

LC HD7116.R12
DD 331.2520973
ISSN 0891-8066
US
ANNUAL REPORT - RAILROAD RETIREMENT BOARD. (ANNUAL REPORT FOR FISCAL YEAR ENDING SEPTEMBER 30 / RAILROAD RETIREMENT BOARD.). [Annu. rep. - U. S., Railr. Retire. Board]. **Main/Corp** United States. Railroad Retirement Board. 1977-. English. One time a year. Price varies. Railroad Retirement Board, 844 Rush Street, Chicago IL 60611. **Tel** (312)751-4777. **ED** William Poulos. **Circ:** 1,850 (ctrl). available on microfiche (Vols. for (1981-1982, 1983-) distributed to depository libraries).
Desc: Report of U.S. Railroad Retirement Board, a federal agency administering retirement-survivor and unemployment-sickness benefit programs for nations's railroad workers and their families.

DD 354.71240083/2
ISSN 1191-033X
CN
ANNUAL REPORT - SASKATCHEWAN. LABOUR RELATIONS BOARD. (ANNUAL REPORT.). [Annu. rep. - Sask., Labour Relat. Board]. **Main/Corp** Saskatchewan. Labour Relations Board. (1990/91)-. English.

LC HD7102.U5 A74
DD 353.9/791/00823
ISSN 0160-3337
US
ANNUAL REPORT - STATE COMPENSATION FUND (ARIZONA). **Main/Corp** Arizona. State Compensation Fund. English. One time a year. State Compensation Fund, 1616 West Adams Street, PO Box 6967, Phoenix AZ 85005. **Tel** (602)229-2110.

LC HD5725.N6 N464A
DD 331.11/09789
US
ANNUAL REPORT TO GOVERNOR ... ON EMPLOYMENT AND TRAINING ACTIVITIES THROUGHOUT NEW MEXICO DURING FISCAL YEAR ... . **Main/Corp** New Mexico. Governor's Office of Employment and Training Administration. **VFOAT** Employment and Training in New Mexico. 1981-. English. One time a year. New Mexico Governor's Office of Employment and Training Administration, 3157 Cerrillos Road, PO Box 4218, Santa Fe NM 87502. **Continues** New Mexico. Governor's Office of Employment and Training Administration. CETA ... New Mexico.

LC HD5725.I8 I593A
DD 353.97770083/05
US
... ANNUAL REPORT TO THE GOVERNOR ON EMPLOYMENT AND TRAINING, THE. **Main/Corp** Iowa. State Employment and Training Council. Fiscal year 1981-. English. One time a year. **Continues** Iowa. State Employment and Training Council. Annual Report to the Governor on Employment & Training.

US
ANNUAL REPORT TO THE GOVERNOR / WEST VIRGINIA BUREAU OF EMPLOYMENT PROGRAMS. **Main/Corp** West Virginia. Bureau of Employment Programs. 1st (1990/91)-. English. **Continues** Annual Report to the Governor.

LC HD5726.W3 D55a
DD 352.94/3/09753
US
ANNUAL REPORT TO THE MAYOR OF THE DISTRICT OF COLUMBIA. **Main/Corp** District of Columbia. Manpower Services Planning Advisory Council. (19??)-. English. One time a year. Manpower Services Planning Advisory Council, 605 G Street NW, Washington DC 20001.

LC HD7103.65.C22 N486a
DD 354.7180083/5
ISSN 0225-3291
CN
ANNUAL REPORT / WORKERS' COMPENSATION BOARD, NEWFOUNDLAND AND LABRADOR. **Main/Corp** Workers' Compensation Board of Newfoundland and Labrador. **VFOAT** Report of the Workers' Compensation Board of Newfoundland and Labrador. (1978)-. English. Free. Workers Compensation Commission, 146-148 Forest Road, St. John's Newfoundland A1A 3B8 Canada. **Tel** (709)778-1000, FAX (709)738-1714. **ED** Tony Thomas. **Circ:** 7,500 (ctrl). **Continues** Annual Report of the Workmen's Compensation Board, Newfoundland and Labrador, 0225-3282.

LC HB74.9.G7 U58a
DD 330/.07/1142574
UK
ANNUAL REPORTS FOR ... / UNIVERSITY OF OXFORD, INSTITUTE OF ECONOMICS AND STATISTICS. **Main/Corp** University of Oxford. Institute of Economics and Statistics. (19??)-. Periodical. English. One time a year. Free. University of Oxford / Institute of Economics and Statistics, St. Cross Building, Manor Road, Oxford OX1 3UL United Kingdom. **Tel** 011 44 1865 271073, FAX 011 44 1865 271094. **Circ:** 300 (ctrl).
Desc: Summary of work and activities undertaken by staff members during the academic year.

LC HD8101 .C33a
DD 354.710083/06 354.710683
ISSN 0225-9923
CN
ANNUAL REVIEW - LABOUR CANADA. (ANNUAL REVIEW.). [Annu. rev. - Labour Can.]. **Main/Corp** Canada. Labour Canada. **VFOAT** Revue Annuelle. (1971)-. English (French). One time a year. Free on request. Labour Canada / Hull Quebec Canada, 140 Promenade du Portage, Hull Quebec K1A 0J2 Canada. **Tel** (819)997-2560. **Continues** Canada. Dept. of Labour. Annual Report, 0382-3415.

LC HD5727
DD 331.137971
CN
ANNUAL REVIEW OF THE EMPLOYMENT SITUATION (CANADA). **Main/Corp** Canada. Bureau of Statistics. (19??)-. Periodical. English. One time a year. Publishing Dist, Ottawa Ontario K1A 0T6 Canada.

DD 331.2
ISSN 1184-9525
CN
ANNUAL SALARY SURVEYS. ADMINISTRATIVE & FINANCE REPORT. [Annu. salary surv., Adm. finance rep.]. **Added/Corp** Peat Marwick Stevenson & Kellogg. **VFOAT** Administrative & Finance Report. (1991)-. English. $350 per vol. $1,350.00 for the complete set (Executive, Administrative and finance, Information systems, Engineering and technical, Sales and marketing, Production and distribution). Peat Marwick Stevenson and Kellogg, PO Box 10427, Pacific Centre, Vancouver British Columbia V7Y 1K5. **Continues in part** Salary Survey. Administrative, Finance & Information Systems Report., 1184-9509.

DD 331.2
ISSN 1185-3565
CN
ANNUAL SALARY SURVEYS. EXECUTIVE COMPENSATION REPORT. (ANNUAL SALARY SURVEYS. EXECUTIVE COMPENSATION REPORT / KPMG, PEAT MARWICK STEVENSON & KELLOGG, MANAGEMENT CONSULTANTS.). [Annu. salary surv., Exec. compens. rep.]. **Added/Corp** Peat Marwick Stevenson & Kellogg. **VFOAT** Executive Compensation Report. (1990/91)-. English. $600.00 per vol. $1,350.00 for complete set (Executive, Administrative and Finance, Information systems, Engineering and Technical, Sales and marketing, Production and distribution). Peat Marwick Stevenson and Kellogg, PO Box 10427, Pacific Centre, Vancouver British Columbia V7Y 1K5. **Continues** Salary Survey. Executive Compensation Report, 0842-5280.

DD 331.2
ISSN 1184-9517
CN
ANNUAL SALARY SURVEYS. INFORMATION SYSTEMS REPORT. (ANNUAL SALARY SURVEYS. INFORMATION SYSTEMS REPORT.). [Annu. salary surv., Inf. syst. rep.]. **Added/Corp** Peat Marwick Stevenson & Kellogg. **VFOAT** Information Systems Report. (1990/91)-. English. $350 per vol. $1,350.00 for the complete set (Executive, Administrative and Finance, Information Systems, Engineering and Technical, Sales and Marketing, Production and Distribution). Peat Marwick Stevenson and Kellogg, PO Box 10427, Pacific Centre, Vancouver British Columbia V7Y 1K5. **Continues in part** Salary Survey. Administrative, Finance & Information Systems Report., 1184-9509.

DD 331.2
ISSN 1185-3573
CN
ANNUAL SALARY SURVEYS. PRODUCTION & DISTRIBUTION REPORT. (ANNUAL SALARY SURVEYS. PRODUCTION & DISTRIBUTION REPORT / KPMG, PEAT MARWICK STEVENSON & KELLOGG, MANAGEMENT CONSULTANTS.). [Annu. salary surv., Prod. distrib. rep.]. **Added/Corp** Thorne Stevenson & Kellogg Limited. Stevenson Kellogg Ernst & Whinney. **VFOAT** Production & Distribution Report. VAT Annual Salary Surveys. Production and Distribution Report. (1991)-. English. $300.00 per vol. $1,350.00 for the complete set (Executive, Administrative and Finance, Information Systems, Engineering and Technical, Sales and Marketing, Production and Distribution). Peat Marwick Stevenson and Kellogg, PO Box 10427, Pacific Centre, Vancouver British Columbia V7Y 1K5. **Continues** Salary Survey. Production and Distribution Report, 0830-9868.

LC HD7103.65.U6 A56
DD 368.4/1/00973
US
ANNUAL STATISTICAL BULLETIN. See Business and Economics-Abstracting, Bibliographies and Statistics.

LC HD4965.5.U6 A66
DD 331.2/816584/00973
US
ANNUAL STUDY EXECUTIVE COMPENSATION / PREPARED BY SIBSON & COMPANY, INC. **Added/Corp** Sibson & Company. (19??)-. English. Sibson and Company, 212 Carnegie Center, CN 5323, Princeton NJ 08543-5323. **Tel** (609)520-2700.

LC HD5725.M4 M38C
DD 331.1/37
US
ANNUAL SUMMARY, CHARACTERISTIC OF THE INSURED UNEMPLOYED (MASSACHUSETTS). **Main/Corp** Massachusetts. Occupation/Industry Research Dept. (19??)-. English. One time a year. Charles F. Hurley Building, Government Center, Boston MA 02114.

LC HD5725.A6 A73B
DD 353.9/791/0082
ISSN 0146-891X
US
ANNUAL SUMMARY OF ACTIVITIES - ARIZONA DEPARTMENT OF ECONOMIC SECURITY. (ANNUAL SUMMARY OF ACTIVITIES.). **Main/Corp** Arizona. Dept. of Economic Security. (19??)-. English. One time a year. Department of Economic Security, 1717 West Jefferson, PO Box 6123, Phoenix AZ 85005. **Tel** (602)255-3871.

LC HD9721 .A56
US
ANNUAL SURVEY OF MANUFACTURES. STATISTICS FOR INDUSTRY GROUPS AND INDUSTRIES (INCLUDING CAPITAL EXPENDITURES, INVENTORIES AND SUPPLEMENTAL LABOR, FUEL, AND ELECTRIC ENERGY COSTS). **Added/Corp** United States. Bureau of the Census. **VFOAT** ASM; Statistics for Industry Groups and Industries (Including Capital Expenditures, Inventories and Supplemental Labor, Fuel, and Electric Energy Costs); Annual Survey of Manufactures. Industry Statistics. (1986)-. Government Publication. English. Irregular. $4.50. US Department of Commerce / Bureau of the Census, Data User Services Division, Customer Services, Washington DC 20233-0800. **Tel** (301)763-4100. **(Subscription address:** Superintendent of Documents, US Government Printing Office, Washington DC 20402.) **Continues** Annual Survey of Manufactures. Statistics for Industry Groups and Industries (Including Supplemental Labor, Fuel, and Electric Energy Costs).
Desc: Covers, by industry and industry group, employment, hours, payroll, value added by manufacture, capital expenditures, costs of materials and labor, value of industry shipments, and end-of-year inventories.
Ind/Abst Predicasts Forecasts.

Business and Economics — Labor

LC KFM5742.Z9 W673   **ISSN** 1058-6504
DD 344.776/021 347.760421   US
ANNUAL WORKERS' COMPENSATION CONFERENCE, THE. (THE ... ANNUAL WORKERS' COMPENSATION CONFERENCE : [PROCEEDINGS].). [Annu. Workers' Compens. Conf.]. **Added/Corp** Hamline University. Advanced Legal Education. 13th (Dec. 14, 1990)-. English. $90.10. Advanced Legal Education, Hamline University, School of Law, 1536 Hewitt Avenue, St. Paul MN 55104. *Continues Conference on Workers' Compensation. Annual Conference on Workers' Compensation : [Proceedings].*

LC HD8582 .A57   SP
ANUARIO DE LAS RELACIONES LABORALES EN ESPANA. 1975-. Spanish. One time a year. Ediciones de la Torre, Calle de Augusto Figueroa, Madrid 17 Spain.

LC HD4966.C62 P47   **ISSN** 1053-2382
DD 331.21   US
APPAREL PERSONNEL POLICIES & BENEFITS SURVEY. **Added/Corp** American Apparel Manufacturers Association. Personnel Relations Committee. American Apparel Manufacturers Association. Human Resources Committee. **VFOAT** Apparel Personnel Policies and Benefits Survey. (1981)-. Trade Publication. English. Every 2 years. American Apparel Manufacturers Association, 2500 Wilson Boulevard, Suite 301, Arlington VA 22201. **Tel** (703)524-1864. *Continues Personnel Policies & Benefits Survey, 0161-4401.*

LC HD4966.C62 U623   **ISSN** 0275-8873
DD 331.2/87/0973   US
APPAREL PLANT WAGES SURVEY. [Apparel plant wages surv.]. Trade Publication. English. One time a year. $60.00. American Apparel Manufacturers Association, 2500 Wilson Boulevard, Suite 301, Arlington VA 22201. **Tel** (703)524-1864. **Circ:** 1,300. **Desc:** Details number and daily hourly earnings of direct and indirect workers; number and average weekly earnings of supervisors; and wage and salary comparisons from 1981.
Ind/Abst Stat. Ref. Index.

LC HD5725.S6 S67
DD 331.12/4/09757   US
APPLICANTS AND OPENINGS. (Oct. 1980/Dec. 1980)-. English. Two times a year. Free. South Carolina Employment Security Commission, 1550 Gadsden Street, PO Box 995, Columbia SC 29202. **Tel** (803)737-2660, **FAX** (803)737-2642. **ED** David L Laird. *Continues South Carolina Employment Service Applicants and Openings.*
Desc: Contains an overview of supply and demand by comparing available applicants with job openings received by major occupational category.

ISSN 0801-7778   NO
ARBEIDERHISTORIE. **Added/Corp** Arbeiderbevegelsens Arkiv og Bibliotek (Oslo, Norway). (1987)-. Norwegian. One time a year.
Ind/Abst Am. Hist. Life.

LC HD5798 .A25a   DK
ARBEIDSMARKED OG ARBEIDSMARKEDSPOLITIKK I NORDEN. TYOMARKKINAT JA TYOMARKKINAPOLITIIKKA. **Main/Corp** Nordisk Arbeidsmarkedsutvalg. **Added/Corp** Nordisk Arbeidsmarkedsutvalg. Tyomarkkinat ja Tyomarkkinapolitiikka. **VFOAT** Tyomarkkinat Ja Tyomarkkinapolitiikka. (1978)-. Government Publication. Danish (Norwegian and Swedish; summaries and/or abstracts in Swedish and Finnish). One time a year. Free. Nordisk Ministerrad / Nordic Publications / Nordic Council of Ministers, Store Strandstraede 18, DK-1255 Kobenhavn K Denmark. **Tel** 011 45 33 96 02 00, **FAX** 011 45 33 93 58 18, telex 155 44 NORDMR DK. **Circ:** 400 (ctrl).
Desc: A compilation of labour market policies in the Nordic countries.

LC HD6958   **ISSN** 0929-9289
DD 331   NE
UDC 349.2
●**ARBEIDSRECHT DEVENTER.** (ARBEIDSRECHT). [ArbeidsRecht Deventer]. (1994)-. Periodical. Dutch. Twelve times a year. Kluwer BV, Postbus 23, 7400 GA Deventer Netherlands. **Tel** 011 31 5700 33155, 011 31 5700 47421, **FAX** 011 31 5700 11504, telex 42829.

ISSN 0323-4568   GW
ARBEIT UND ARBEITSRECHT. [Arbeit Arbeitsr.]. **Added/Corp** Germany (Territory under Allied Occupation, 1945-1955. Russian Zone). Deutsche Verwaltung fuer Arbeit und Sozialfuersorge. Vol. 1 (March 1946)-. Periodical. German. Twelve times a year. DM119.60. CH Beck Verlagsbuchhandlung, D-80791 Munich Germany. **Tel** 011 49 89 381891.

Desc: Articles on scientific work organization, the efficient use of social working faculties, and the efficiency of work.
Ind/Abst Acoust. Abstr.; Int. Labour Doc.; Saf. Health Work.

LC HD8443 .A58   GW
ARBEIT UND BERUF. **Added/Corp** Bundesanstalt fuer Arbeit (Germany). (19??)-. German. Twelve times a year. $85.98. Verlag Arbeit und Beruf, Bingstrasse 30, D-90480 Nuernberg Germany. **Tel** 011 49 911 4030355. **ED** Walter Lutz. **Bk Rev**. **Ad Acc**. **Circ:** 10,000. *Continues Arbeit, Beruf und Arbeitslosenhilfe.*
Desc: Labor administration in general with special regard to the responsibility of the Federal Institute for Labour Administration.
Ind/Abst LABORDOC.

LC HD8459.B3 A7   GW
ARBEIT UND SOZIALES. (19??)-. Periodical. German. Twelve times a year. Bayerisches Staatsministerium fur Arbeit und Sozialordn, Winzererstrasse 9, 8 Munich 40 Germany.

LC HD8442.D8 A73   **ISSN** 0340-8434
   CCC
ARBEIT UND SOZIALPOLITIK. **Added/Corp** North Rhine-Westphalia. Arbeitsministerium. (Feb. 1, 1947)-. Periodical. German. Six times a year. $123.03. Nomos Verlagsgesellschaft, Postfach 610, D-76484 Baden Baden Germany. **Tel** 011 49 7221 210439. Index available.

LC HD5769 .B86b   AU
ARBEITER IM ANGESTELLTENVERHALTNIS IN DER INDUSTRIE OSTERREICHS. **Main/Corp** Buneskammer der Gewerblichen Wirtschaft (Austria). Sektion Industri. (197?)-. German. Irregular. Bundeskammer der Gewerblichen Wirtschaft, Wiedner Hauptstrasse 63, A-1040 Vienna Austria. **Tel** 0222 65 05 DW 4110, telex 111 871 BUKA.

LC HD6697 .A7   GW
ARBEITERBEWEGUNG UND PARLAMENTARISMUS. **Added/Corp** Martin-Luther-Universitat Halle-Wittenberg. Sektion Marxismus-Leninismus. (19??)-. Periodical. German. Universitats u Landesbibliothek Sachsen-Anhalt, August-Bebel-Strasse 13, 06098 Halle (Saale) Tauschstelle Germany.

LC HD4809 .A675   **ISSN** 0402-7787
DD 331.0943   GW
ARBEITGEBER, DER. [Arbeitgeber]. **Added/Corp** Vereinigung Nordrhein-Westfalischer Arbeitgeberverbande. Vereinigung der Arbeitgeververbande (Germany) Bundesvereinigung der Deutschen Arbeitgeberverbande. (July 1, 1949)-. Trade Publication. German. Twenty-four times a year. $147.39. J P Bachem GmbH and Company, KG Ussulaplatz 1, 5000 Cologne 1 Germany. **Supersedes** *Arbeitgeber*.
Desc: Covers labor issues and the laboring classes.
Ind/Abst Energy Res. Abstr. (Oct. 1978-); Saf. Health Work.

LC HD6948.G32 N674A
DD 658/.006/04355   GW
ARBEITGEBER NRW. **Main/Corp** Landesvereinigund der Industriellen Arbeitgeberverbande Nordrhein-Westfaliens. (19??)-. German. Landesvereinigung der Industriellen, Arbeitgeberverbande Nordrhein-Westfalens E V, Uerdinger Strasse 58-62, 4000 Dusseldorf 30 Germany.

   GW
ARBEITS UND SOZIALRECHT. *See* Industry and Production.

LC HD8441 .A83   **ISSN** 0341-7840
DD 331/.0943   GW
ARBEITS- UND SOZIALSTATISTIK. HAUPTERGEBNISSE. **Added/Corp** Germany (West). Bundesministerium fur Arbeit und Sozialordnung. (1975)-. German. Bundesministerium fur Arbeit und Sozialordnung, Postfach 14 02 80, 5300 Bonn 1 Germany. Index available. cum. index. **Bk Rev**. **Ad Acc**. *Continues Germany (West). Bundesministerium fur Arbeit und Sozialordnung. Hauptergebnisse der Arbeits- und Sozialstatistik, 0072-1557.*

LC HD4809 .I54A
DD 331/.0943   GW
ARBEITSHEFT - INDUSTRIEGEWERKSCHAFT METALL FUR DIE BUNDESREPUBLIK DEUTSCHLAND. ABTEILUNG BILDUNGSWESEN/BILDUNGSPOLITIK. (19??)-. Monographic series. German. Price varies per volume. *Continues Industriegewerkschaft Metall. Abteilung Bildungswesen. Arbeitsheft.*

LC HA1320.N6 A32 HD5070.N67   GW
ARBEITSKOSTEN IM HANDEL SOWIE IM BANK- UND VERSICHERUNGSGEWERBE, DIE. **Main/Corp** North Rhine-Westphalia (Germany). Landesamt fur Datenverarbeitung Und Statistik. (19??)-. German. Landesamt fuer Datenverarbeitung und Statistik Nordrhein-Westfalen, Postfach 101105, 40002 Duesseldorf Germany. **Tel** (0211)944901, **FAX** (0211)442006, telex 8586654 LDST D.

LC HA1320.N6 A32 HD5030.N6   **ISSN** 0722-2432
DD 314.3   GW
ARBEITSKOSTEN IM PRODUZIERENDEN GEWERBE UND IM DIENSTLEISTUNGSBEREICH. *See* Business and Economics-Abstracting, Bibliographies and Statistics.

LC HD1536.G3 S23A
DD 331.7/63/094359   GW
ARBEITSKRAFTEERHEBUNG IN DER LANDWIRTSCHAFT. **Main/Corp** Niedersachsisches Landesverwaltungsamt. (19??)-. German. DM8.40. Niedersaechsisches Landesamt fuer Statistik, Postfach 4460, D-30044 Hannover Germany. **Tel** 011 49 511 9898321, **FAX** 011 49 511 9898400.

LC HD5780.B23 B23a
DD 331.12/0943/46   GW
ARBEITSMARKT IN BADEN-WURTTEMBERG; JAHRESBERICHT, DER. *See* Business and Economics-Abstracting, Bibliographies and Statistics.

LC HD5780.H4 A73   **ISSN** 0722-3285
DD 331.12/0943/41   GW
ARBEITSMARKT IN HESSEN. JAHRESBERICHT, DER. (19??)-. German. One time a year. Landesarbeitsamt Hessen, Saonstrasse 2-4-6, Frankfurt Am Main 71 Germany.

LC HD5780.H4 L35C
DD 331.12/0943/41   GW
ARBEITSMARKT IN HESSEN : JAHRESZAHLEN, DER. **Main/Corp** Landesarbeitsamt Hessen. 1978-. German. One time a year. Landesarbeitsamt Hessen, Saonstrasse 2-4-6, Frankfurt Am Main 71 Germany. *Continues Arbeitsmarktlage in Hessen: Jahreszahlen.*

LC HD5779 .I59A   GW
ARBEITSMARKTSTATISTISCHE ZAHLEN IN ZEITREIHENFORM. **Main/Corp** Institut fur Arbeitsmarkt- und Berufsforschung. (19??)-. German (summaries and/or abstracts in English and French). DM30.00. Institut fur Arbeitsmarkt und Berufsforschung der Bundesanstalt fur Arbeit, Regensburger Strasse 104, 85 Nuernberg Germany. **Tel** 0911 173086, telex 7-255 820.

ISSN 0003-7761   GW
UDC 349.2(094.9)   CCC
ARBEITSRECHT IN STICHWORTEN. **VFOAT** ARST. Arbeitsrecht in Stichworten. (1947)-. Periodical. German. Twelve times a year. $138.18. Dr. Alfred Huethig Verlag GmbH, Postfach 102869, D-69018 Heidelberg Germany. **Tel** 011 49 6221 489281, **FAX** 011 49 6221 489279. **(Subscription address:** Huethig Publishing Inc., 29 Macintosh Drive, Oxford CT 06478. **Tel** (203)881-2647.)

ISSN 0107-8461   DK
ARBEJDERHISTORIE. [Arbejderhistorie]. **Added/Corp** Selskabet til Forskning i Arbejderbevaegelsens Historie. **VFOAT** Arbejder Historie. (Apr. 1982)-. Periodical. Danish. Two times a year. Selskabet til Forskning i Arbejderbevaegelsens Historie, Noerrebrogade 66 D, DK 2200 Copenhagen N Denmark. **Tel** 011 45 31 241522, **FAX** 011 45 42 191594. *Continues Meddelelser om Forskning i Arbejderbevaegelsens Historie, 0106-5904.*
Ind/Abst Am. Hist. Life (1978-).

ISSN 0903-8388
DD 331.094 89   DK
ARBEJDSMARKEDETS HANDBOG (KOEBENHAVN. 1974). (ARBEJDSMARKEDETS HANDBOG.). [Arb.mark. handb. Kbh., 1974]. (1974)-. Danish. One time a year. $28.14. AOFS Forlag, Teglvaerksgade 27 1099, 2100 Copenhagen 0 Denmark. **Tel** 011 45 33 296066. *Continues Den Nye Handbog for Arbejdere og Funktionrer, 0903-837X.*

LC HD5715.5.D4 A74   **ISSN** 0106-9896
DD 331.2592   DK
ARBEJDSMARKEDSUDDANNELSERNE STATISTIK. TABELMATERIALE VEDRRENDE OMSKOLING OG ERHVERVSINTRODUKTION. *See* Business and Economics-Abstracting, Bibliographies and Statistics.

Business and Economics —Labor

ISSN 0281-7446
SW

ARBETARHISTORIA : MEDDELANDE FRAN ARBETARRORELSENS ARKIV OCH BIBLIOTEK. **Added/Corp** Arbetarrorelsens
Arkiv och Bibliotek (Stockholm, Sweden). Vol. 8 No. 29-30 (1984)-. Periodical. Swedish. Four times a year. $24.04. Arbetarrorelsens Arkiv och Bibliotek, Box 1124, 11181 Stockholm Sweeden. **Tel** 011 46 8 4546500, FAX 011 48 8 215560. Index available. **Bk Rev**, (Qty: 8-10). **Ad Acc**, **Adv Mgr:** Lars Wessman, **Tel** 46 8 4546500. **Circ:** 2,000. **Continues** Meddelande Fran Arbetarrorelsens Arkiv och Bibliotek, 0347-7134.
Desc: Introduces research and studies on labor movement, working life, the working-classes, social democracy, and trade unions in articles, reviews, and bibliographies. Also presents the archives, collections, and holdings of the national labor movement archives and library in Stockholm.
Ind/Abst Am. Hist. Life (1985-1986,1988-).

ISSN 0347-2965
SW

ARBETARRAORELSENS AARSBOK.
[Arbetarraorel. arsb.]. **Added/Corp** Arbetarnas Kulturhistoriska Saallskap. Arbetarraorelsens Arkiv. (1970)-. Swedish. One time a year. Arbetarraorelsens Arkiv och Bibliotek, Box 1124, 11181 Stockholm Sweeden. **Tel** 011 46 8 4546500, FAX 011 48 8 215560.
Ind/Abst Am. Hist. Life (1972-1980).

SW

ARBETSGIVAREN. Vol. 1 (Nov. 21, 1952)-.
Periodical. Swedish. Svenska Arbetsgivareforeningen, Sweden.

LC HD5801 .A33
DD 331
SW

ARBETSKRAFTSUNDERSOKNINGEN : AKU. **See** Business and Economics-Abstracting, Bibliographies and Statistics.

ISSN 1185-1716
DD 331.89
CN

ARBITRAGE, POINTS SAILLANTS.
(L'ARBITRAGE : POINTS SAILLANTS / DIVISION DES GRIEFS ET A L'ARBITRAGE.). [Arbitr. points saillants]. **Added/Corp** Alliance de la Fonction Publique du Canada. Division des Griefs et a l'Arbitrage. Vol. 1, No 1 (June 1990)-. Periodical. French. Six times a year. Free for members. Direction de la Negociation Collective, Alliance de la Fonction Publique du Canada, 233 Gilmour Street, Ottawa Ontario K2P 0P1 Canada.

LC HD5726.B45 C33A   **ISSN** 0146-2415
DD 331.1/1/0979467
US

AREA MANPOWER REVIEW : CITY OF BERKELEY. **Main/Corp** California. Employment Development Dept. Northern California Employment Data and Research Section. (19??)-. English. California Health and Welfare Agency Employment Development Department, Employment Data and Research, Coastal Area Labor Market, PO Box 7774, San Francisco CA 94120.

LC HD5726.O22 C33a   **ISSN** 0145-7179
DD 331.1/1/0979466
US

AREA MANPOWER REVIEW: CITY OF OAKLAND. **Main/Corp** California. Employment Development Dept. Northern California Employment Data and Research Section. (19??)-. English. Health and Welfare Agency Employment Development Department, PO Box 7774, San Francisco CA 94120.

LC HD5726.R5 C24A   **ISSN** 0145-6415
DD 331.1/1/0979463
US

AREA MANPOWER REVIEW : CITY OF RICHMOND. **Main/Corp** California. Employment Development Dept. Northern California Employment Data and Research Section. (19??)-. English. Health and Welfare Agency Employment Development Department, PO Box 7774, San Francisco CA 94120.

LC HD5725.C2 C23I   **ISSN** 0145-7160
DD 331.1/1/0979462
US

AREA MANPOWER REVIEW : MARIN COUNTY. **Main/Corp** California. Employment Development Dept. Northern California Employment Data and Research Section. (19??)-. English. California Health and Welfare Agency Employment Development Department, Employment Data and Research, Coastal Area Labor Market, PO Box 7774, San Francisco CA 94120.

LC HD5726.R53 V57A
DD 331.1/1/097554
US

AREA MANPOWER REVIEW : RICHMOND, VIRGINIA STANDARD METROPOLITAN STATISTICAL AREA.
Main/Corp Virginia. Employment Commission. Manpower Research Division. **VFOAT** Area Manpower Review: Richmond Metropolitan Area. (19??)-. Statistical Publication. English. One time a year. Virginia Employment Commission, 703 East Main Street, PO Box 1358, Richmond VA 23211.

LC HD5726.R57 V57A
DD 331.1/1/0975579
US

AREA MANPOWER REVIEW : ROANOKE, VIRGINIA AREA. **Main/Corp**
Virginia. Employment Commission. Manpower Research Division. **VFOAT** Area Manpower Review Roanoke Metropolitan Area. English. One time a year. Virginia Employment Commission, 703 East Main Street, PO Box 1358, Richmond VA 23211.

LC HD5725.C2 C23J   **ISSN** 0145-7144
DD 331.1/1/09794438
US

AREA MANPOWER REVIEW : SACRAMENTO STANDARD METROPOLITAN STATISTICAL AREA. PLACER COUNTY SUPPLEMENT.
Main/Corp California. Employment Development Dept. Northern California Employment Data and Research Section. (19??)-. Statistical Publication. English. California Health and Welfare Agency Employment Development Department, Employment Data and Research, Coastal Area Labor Market, PO Box 7774, San Francisco CA 94120.

LC HD5726.S25 C24A   **ISSN** 0145-6393
DD 331.1/1/0979453
US

AREA MANPOWER REVIEW : SACRAMENTO-YOLO PLANNING AREA. **Main/Corp** California. Employment Development Dept. Northern California Employment Data and Research Section. (19??)-. English. Health and Welfare Agency Employment Development Department, PO Box 7774, San Francisco CA 94120.

LC HD5725.C2 C23K   **ISSN** 0145-7128
DD 331.1/1/0979461
US

AREA MANPOWER REVIEW : SAN FRANCISCO CITY AND COUNTY.
Main/Corp California. Employment Development Dept. Northern California Employment Data and Research Section. (19??)-. English. California Health and Welfare Agency Employment Development Department, Employment Data and Research, Coastal Area Labor Market, PO Box 7774, San Francisco CA 94120.

LC HD5725.C2 C23H   **ISSN** 0145-7101
DD 331.1/1/0979469
US

AREA MANPOWER REVIEW : SAN MATEO COUNTY. **Main/Corp** California. Employment Development Dept. Northern California Employment Data and Research Section. (19??)-. Periodical. English. Health and Welfare Agency Employment Development Department, PO Box 7774, San Francisco CA 94120.

LC HD5725.C2 C23F   **ISSN** 0145-6407
DD 331.1/1/0979452
US

AREA MANPOWER REVIEW : SOLANO COUNTY. **Main/Corp** California. Employment Development Dept. Northern California Employment Data and Research Section. (19??)-. English. Health and Welfare Agency Employment Development Department, PO Box 7774, San Francisco CA 94120.

LC HD5723 .A42   **ISSN** 0004-0916
DD 331.1/1/0973

AREA TRENDS IN EMPLOYMENT AND UNEMPLOYMENT. [Area trends employ. unemploy.]. **Added/Corp** United States. Bureau of Employment Security. United States. Dept. of Labor. Manpower Administration. United States. Employment and Training Administration. **VFOAT** Area Trends. (Oct. 1964)-. Government Publication. English. Twelve times a year. $51.00. US Department of Labor, 200 Constitution Avenue NW, Washington DC 20210. **Tel** (202)219-7316, FAX (202)219-7312. **(Subscription address:** Superintendent of Documents, US Government Printing Office, Washington DC 20402.) available on microfilm and microfiche from University Microfilms International (UMI). Documents available from Documents on Demand. **Continues** Area Labor Market Trends.
Desc: A listing of eligible labor surplus areas in which employers are given preference in bidding on federal procurement contracts. Lists civil jurisdiction in each area.
Ind/Abst Am. Stat. Index.

LC HD5726.D3 A74
DD 331.2/977172/05
US
TITLE CHANGE

AREA WAGE SURVEY. **Added/Corp** United States. Bureau of Labor Statistics. **VFOAT** Dayton-Springfield, OH; Area Wage Survey. Dayton, Springfield, OH; Dayton, Springfield, OH. **VAT** Dayton, Springfield, OH; Area Wage Survey. Dayton, Springfield, OH. (198?)-(199?). Government Publication. English. US Department of Labor, 200 Constitution Avenue NW, Washington DC 20210. **Tel** (202)219-7316, FAX (202)219-7312. **Continues in part** Area Wage Survey. Dayton, Ohio, Metropolitan Area. **Continued by** Occupational Compensation Survey--Pay Only. Dayton-Springfield, Ohio, Metropolitan Area.

LC HD8051 .A62 HD4976.A95   **ISSN** 0091-5009
DD 331/.0973 S 331.2/9764/31
US

AREA WAGE SURVEY : AUSTIN, TEXAS, METROPOLITAN AREA.
Main/Corp United States. Bureau of Labor Statistics. English. FCC / Federal Communications Commission, 1919 M Street Northwest, Room 538, Washington DC 20554. **Tel** (202)632-6302.

LC HD8051 .A62   **ISSN** 0197-4424
DD 331.2976178
US

AREA WAGE SURVEY : BIRMINGHAM, ALABAMA, METROPOLITAN AREA.
Main/Corp United States. Bureau of Labor Statistics. **VFOAT** Birmingham, Alabama, Metropolitan Area. (April 1966)-. English. One time a year. US Department of Labor, 200 Constitution Avenue NW, Washington DC 20210. **Tel** (202)219-7316, FAX (202)219-7312. **Supersedes in part** Occupational Wage Survey. Birmingham, Alabama.

LC HD4976.D39 U53A   **ISSN** 0098-020X
DD 331.2/9759/21
US

AREA WAGE SURVEY. DAYTONA BEACH, FLORIDA, METROPOLITAN AREA. (AREA WAGE SURVEY. DAYTONA BEACH, FLORIDA, METROPOLITAN AREA / U.S. DEPARTMENT OF LABOR, BUREAU OF LABOR STATISTICS.). **Added/Corp** United States. Bureau of Labor Statistics. **VFOAT** Daytona Beach, Florida, Metropolitan Area. English. One time a year. US Government Printing Office / Department of Labor, 200 Constitution Avenue NW, Washington DC 20210. **Tel** (202)523-8165. available on microfiche (Vols. for (Aug. 1983-) distributed to depository libraries). **Continues in part** Occupational Wage Survey. Daytona Beach, Florida.

LC HD8051 .A62 HD4976.F64 F64   **ISSN** 0093-867X
DD 331/.0973 S 331.2/9759/32
US

AREA WAGE SURVEY : FORT LAUDERDALE-HOLLYWOOD AND WEST PALM BEACH, FLORIDA, METROPOLITAN AREAS. **Main/Corp** United States. Bureau of Labor Statistics. English. One time a year. US Department of Labor, 200 Constitution Avenue NW, Washington DC 20210. **Tel** (202)219-7316, FAX (202)219-7312.

US

AREA WAGE SURVEY. GREEN BAY, WISCONSIN, METROPOLITAN AREA.
Added/Corp United States. Bureau of Labor Statistics. **VFOAT** Green Bay, Wisconsin, Metropolitan Area. (1965)-. English. One time a year. US Department of Labor, 200 Constitution Avenue NW, Washington DC 20210. **Tel** (202)219-7316, FAX (202)219-7312. available on microfiche (Vols. for (Aug. 1983-) distributed to depository libraries). **Continues in part** Occupational Wage Survey. Green Bay, Wisconsin.

LC HD4976.G7 U53A   **ISSN** 0361-655X
DD 331.2/9757/2
US

AREA WAGE SURVEY. GREENVILLE-SPARTANBURG, SOUTH CAROLINA, METROPOLITAN AREA. **See** Business and Economics-Abstracting, Bibliographies and Statistics.

DD 331.2975912
US

AREA WAGE SURVEY. JACKSONVILLE, FLORIDA, METROPOLITAN AREA. **See** Business and Economics-Abstracting, Bibliographies and Statistics.

US

AREA WAGE SURVEY. MANSFIELD, OHIO. **VFOAT** Area Wage Survey. Mansfield, OH; Mansfield, Ohio. (19??)-. Government Publication. English. One time a year. US Department of Labor / Bureau of Labor Statistics, 441 G Street Northwest, Washington DC 20212. **Tel** (202)606-7800, FAX (202)606-7797.

LC HD4976.N85 U54A   **ISSN** 0149-600X
DD 331.2/97555
US

AREA WAGE SURVEY. NORFOLK-VIRGINIA BEACH-PORTSMOUTH AND NEWPORT NEWS-HAMPTON, VIRGINIA-NORTH CAROLINA, METROPOLITAN AREAS.
(19??)-. English. One time a year. US Department of Labor, 200 Constitution Avenue NW, Washington DC 20210. **Tel** (202)219-7316, FAX (202)219-7312. **Continues in part** Area Wage Survey. Norfolk-Virginia Beach-Portsmouth and Newport News-Hampton, Virginia, Metropolitan Area.

US
TITLE CHANGE

AREA WAGE SURVEY. NORTHERN NEW YORK / U.S. DEPARTMENT OF LABOR, BUREAU OF LABOR STATISTICS. **Added/Corp** United States. Bureau of Labor Statistics. **VFOAT** Northern New York. **VAT** Area

Business and Economics —Labor

Wage Survey. Northern New York. (19??)-(199?). English. US Department of Labor / Bureau of Labor Statistics, 441 G Street Northwest, Washington DC 20212. **Tel** (202)606-7800, FAX (202)606-7797. **Continued by** Occupational Compensation Survey--Pay Only. Northern New York.

US

AREA WAGE SURVEY. ORLANDO, FLORIDA, METROPOLITAN AREA.
VFOAT Orlando, Florida, Metropolitan Area; Area Wage Survey, Orlando, Florida, Metropolitan Area. (Sept. 1988)-. Government Publication. English. Every 2 years. US Department of Labor / Bureau of Labor Statistics, 441 G Street Northwest, Washington DC 20212. **Tel** (202)606-7800, FAX (202)606-7797.

US

AREA WAGE SURVEY. PATERSON-CLIFTON-PASSAIC, NEW JERSEY METROPOLITAN AREA.
Added/Corp United States. Bureau of Labor Statistics. **VFOAT** Paterson-Clifton-Passaic, New Jersey Metropolitan Area. (1966)-. English. One time a year. US Department of Labor, 200 Constitution Avenue NW, Washington DC 20210. **Tel** (202)219-7316, FAX (202)219-7312. available on microfiche (Vols. for (1985-) distributed to depository libraries). **Continues in part** Occupational Wage Survey. Paterson-Clifton-Passaic, New Jersey.

LC HD8051 .A62 ISSN 0197-4335
DD 331.2/9745/1 US

AREA WAGE SURVEY. PROVIDENCE-WARWICK-PAWTUCKET, RHODE ISLAND-MASSACHUSETTS, METROPOLITAN AREA.
Added/Corp United States. Bureau of Labor Statistics. **VFOAT** Providence-Warwick-Pawtucket, Rhode Island-Massachusetts, Metropolitan Area. (1966)-. English. One time a year. US Department of Labor, 200 Constitution Avenue NW, Washington DC 20210. **Tel** (202)219-7316, FAX (202)219-7312. available on microfiche (Vols. for (June 1984-) distributed to depository libraries). **Continues in part** Occupational Wage Survey. Providence-Warwick-Pawtucket, Rhode Island-Massachusetts.

LC HD4976.S23 U53a ISSN 0099-1899
DD 331.2/9794/54 US
TITLE CHANGE

AREA WAGE SURVEY. SACRAMENTO, CALIFORNIA, METROPOLITAN AREA.
(AREA WAGE SURVEY. SACRAMENTO, CALIFORNIA, METROPOLITAN AREA / U.S. DEPARTMENT OF LABOR, BUREAU OF LABOR STATISTICS.). **Added/Corp** United States. Bureau of Labor Statistics. **VFOAT** Sacramento, California, Metropolitan Area. (19??)-(19??). English. US Department of Labor, 200 Constitution Avenue NW, Washington DC 20210. **Tel** (202)219-7316, FAX (202)219-7312. available on microfiche (Vols. for (1983-) distributed to depository libraries). **Continues in part** Occupational Wage Survey. Sacramento, California. **Continued by** Occupational Compensation Survey--Pay Only. Sacramento, California, Metropolitan Area.

LC HD4976.S8 U55A ISSN 0146-3233
DD 331.2/9746/9 US

AREA WAGE SURVEY : STAMFORD, CONNECTICUT, METROPOLITAN AREA.
Main/Corp United States. Bureau of Labor Statistics. **VFOAT** Stamford, Connecticut, Metropolitan Area. (19??)-. English. One time a year. US Department of Labor, 200 Constitution Avenue NW, Washington DC 20210. **Tel** (202)219-7316, FAX (202)219-7312.

LC HD4976.S85 A74
DD 331.2/979456 US

AREA WAGE SURVEY. STOCKTON, CALIF.
VFOAT Area Wage Survey, Stockton, Calif. (19??)-. Government Publication. English. One time a year. US Department of Labor / Bureau of Labor Statistics, 441 G Street Northwest, Washington DC 20212. **Tel** (202)606-7800, FAX (202)606-7797.

LC HD4976.R3 U55a ISSN 0364-4731
DD 331.2/9756/56 US

AREA WAGE SURVEY: THE RALEIGH-DURHAM, NORTH CAROLINA, METROPOLITAN AREA.
Main/Corp United States. Bureau of Labor Statistics. English. $0.55. Iowa Department of Corrections, 523 East 12th Street, Capitol Annex, Des Moines IA 50319. **Tel** (515)281-4811, FAX (515)281-7345. **Formed by the union of** United States. Bureau of Labor Statistics. Area Wage Survey: The Raleigh, North Carolina, Metropolitan Area **and** United States. Bureau of Labor Statistics. Area Wage Survey: The Durham, North Carolina, Metropolitan Area.

LC HD4976.T85 A74
DD 331.2/976686/021 US

AREA WAGE SURVEY. TULSA, OKLA.
VFOAT Area Wage Survey, Tulsa, Okla. (19??)-. Government Publication. English. One time a year. US Department of Labor / Bureau of Labor Statistics, 441 G Street Northwest, Washington DC 20212. **Tel** (202)606-7800, FAX (202)606-7797.

LC HD4976.U66 A73
DD 331.2/97749 US
TITLE CHANGE

AREA WAGE SURVEY. UPPER PENINSULA, MICH.
Added/Corp United States. Bureau of Labor Statistics. **VFOAT** Area Wage Survey, Upper Peninsula, Mich. (19??)-(199?). Government Publication. English. US Department of Labor / Bureau of Labor Statistics, 441 G Street Northwest, Washington DC 20212. **Tel** (202)606-7800, FAX (202)606-7797. **Continued by** Occupational Compensation Survey--Pay Only. Upper Peninsula, MI.

LC HD4976.W43 U53A ISSN 0361-7637
DD 331.2/7747/277 US

AREA WAGE SURVEY : WESTCHESTER COUNTY, NEW YORK.
Main/Corp United States. Bureau of Labor Statistics. (19??)-. English. US Government Printing Office / Department of Labor Statistics, Washington DC 20402.

LC HD8051 .A62 ISSN 0270-5923
DD 331.2974841 US

AREA WAGE SURVEY. YORK, PENNSYLVANIA, METROPOLITAN AREA.
(AREA WAGE SURVEY. YORK, PENNSYLVANIA, METROPOLITAN AREA / U.S. DEPARTMENT OF LABOR, BUREAU OF LABOR STATISTICS.). **Added/Corp** United States. Bureau of Labor Statistics. **VFOAT** York, Pennsylvania, Metropolitan Area. (1966)-. English. One time a year. US Department of Labor, 200 Constitution Avenue NW, Washington DC 20210. **Tel** (202)219-7316, FAX (202)219-7312. available on microfiche (Vols. for (1984-) distributed to depository libraries). **Continues** Occupational Wage Survey. York, Pennsylvania.

US

AREA WAGE SURVEYS.
(19??)-. Periodical. English. Every 2 years. $1.00. Research and Analysis Branch, Washington State Employment Security Department, Box 9046, Olympia WA 98507. **Tel** (206)438-4800, FAX (206)438-4846.

LC HD4973 .A462
DD 331.2/973 US

AREA WAGE SURVEYS: SELECTED METROPOLITAN AREAS.
(AREA WAGE SURVEYS. SELECTED METROPOLITAN AREAS / C.U.S. DEPARTMENT OF LABOR, BUREAU OF LABOR STATISTICS.). **Added/Corp** United States. Bureau of Labor Statistics. **VFOAT** Selected Metropolitan Areas; AWS, Selected Metropolitan Areas. (1969)-. Government Publication. English. Irregular. $156.00. Superintendent of Documents, US Government Printing Office, Washington DC 20402. **Tel** (202)275-3328, FAX (202)786-2377. **Continues** Occupational Wage Survey (Washington, D.C.).

LC JS451.A67 A74a ISSN 0096-3399
DD 352/.005/1209791 US

ARIZONA ASSOCIATION OF COUNTIES SALARY AND BENEFIT SURVEY.
Main/Corp Arizona Association of Counties. **Added/Corp** Arizona Association of Counties. Salary and Benefit Survey. (July 1973)-. English. One time a year. Arizona Association of Counties, 3001 West Indian School Road, Suite 303, Phoenix AZ 85017.

LC HD5725.A6 A73C ISSN 0149-7987
DD 331.1/1/09791 US

ARIZONA BICENTENNIAL REVIEW.
Main/Corp Arizona. Dept. of Economic Security. Bureau of Statistical Information, Research and Analysis. **VFOAT** Arizona Bicentennial Manpower Review. July 1976-. English. Two times a year. Department of Economic Security, 1717 West Jefferson, PO Box 6123, Phoenix AZ 85005. **Tel** (602)255-3871. **Continues** Arizona Manpower Review, 0149-7995.

LC HC107.A6 A773
DD 330.9791/005 US

ARIZONA ECONOMIC TRENDS.
Added/Corp Arizona. Dept. of Economic Security. Research Administration. Vol. 16, No. 4 (Apr. 1992)-. Periodical. English. Four times a year. Free. Arizona Department of Economic Security, PO Box 6123, Code 733 A, Phoenix AZ 85005. **Tel** (602)255-3871. **Continues** Arizona Labor Market Information Newsletter.

LC HD5725.A6 A734A
DD 331.1/1/09791 US

ARIZONA LABOR FORCE DATA.
Main/Corp Arizona. Dept. of Economic Security. (19??)-. English. One time a year. Arizona Department of Economic Security, PO Box 6123, Code 733 A, Phoenix AZ 85005. **Tel** (602)255-3871. **Continues** Arizona Labor Force Data.

ISSN 0743-5657
US

ARIZONA LABOR MARKET NEWSLETTER.
(1977)-. Newsletter. English. Twelve times a year. Department of Economic Security, 1717 West Jefferson, PO Box 6123, Phoenix AZ 85005. **Tel** (602)255-3871. **ED** Nancy Augustin. **Circ:** 5,500 (ctrl). **Formed by the union of** Tucson Area Manpower Newsletter; Phoenix Manpower Review Newsletter **and** Phoenix Area Manpower Review.
Desc: Monthly statistics on Arizona's labor force, economic analysis of statistics. Often comparing Arizona to other states or to the US as a whole, special features, and a 'New Developments' section.

LC HD5725.A6 A73d
DD 331.1/1/09791 US

ARIZONA LABOR MARKET REVIEW.
Main/Corp Arizona. Dept. of Economic Security. Labor Market Information Research and Analysis Section. **Added/Corp** United States. Employment and Training Administration. (19??)-. Periodical. English. One time a year. Arizona Dept of Economic Security, PO Box 6123, Phoenix AZ 85005.

LC HD5725.A8 A725A ISSN 0094-1166
DD 331.1/1/09767 US

ARKANSAS COMPREHENSIVE MANPOWER PLAN.
Main/Corp Arkansas. Manpower Council. English. Comprehensive Manpower Plan, 3 C Executive Building, Little Rock AR 72220.

SW

ARKIV.
VFOAT Arkiv for Studier i Arbetarrorelsens Historia. Periodical. Swedish. Three times a year. Kr70.00 (individuals), Kr120.00 (institutions). Sallskapet for Studier I Arbetarrorelsens Historia, Box 16 393, Stockholm 16 Sweden. **Tel** (46)13 39 20. (**Subscription address:** Arkiv, PO Box 1559, S-221 00 Lund Sweden.) **ED** Sven E Olsson. cum. index. **Circ:** 1,000.
Desc: The policy of the journal can be summarized under four main themes: (1) analysis of historical and contemporary problems in Swedish society, (2) comparative studies of class, state and economy in industrial societies, (3) classical issues and polemics in the working class movement, (4) original theoretical contributions to historiography and social science.
Ind/Abst Am. Hist. Life (1989-).

LC Z682.3 .A79a ISSN 0361-5669
DD 331.2/81/020973 US

ARL ANNUAL SALARY SURVEY.
Main/Corp Association of Research Libraries. **Added/Corp** Association of Research Libraries. Annual Salary Survey. **VAT** Association of Research Libraries Annual Salary Survey. (19??)-. English. One time a year. $70.00. Association Research Libraries, 21 Dupont Circle, Washington DC 20036. **Tel** (202)296-2296. **ED** Gordon Fretwell. **Bk Rev. Ad Acc. Circ:** 800.
Desc: Includes data on beginning and median professional salaries as well as numbers and average salaries for positions in ARL libraries and distribution by several categories.
Ind/Abst Stat. Ref. Index.

LC HD8651 .A77
DD 331.12/042/09505 TH

ARPLA LABOUR ADMINISTRATION BULLETIN.
Added/Corp UNDP/ILO Asian Regional Project for Strengthening Labour/Manpower Administration. **VFOAT** Labour Administration Bulletin. **VAT** Asian Regional Project for Strengthening Labour/Manpower Administration Labour Administration Bulletin. Vol. 1, No. 1 (Jan. 1979)-. Bulletin. English. Three times a year.
Ind/Abst LABORDOC.

LC HD5799 .A29

DK

ARSLEDIGHEDEN.
VFOAT Annual Unemployment. Danish (Danish).

LC NX163 .N38 ISSN 1070-8901
DD 700 US
TITLE CHANGE

ARTJOB/BANK (SANTA FE, N.M.). See
The Arts.

LC HD6276.J3 A78
JA

ARUBAITO HAKUSHO.
(1980)-. Japanese. One time a year. ¥1800. Gakusei Engokai 15, Ichigaya Honmura-cho Shinjuku-ku, Tokyo-to Japan.

LC HD6515.A55 A73 ISSN 1054-4100
DD 331.88/16672 US

ASBESTOS WORKERS JOURNAL.
[Asbestos work. j.]. **Added/Corp** International Association of Heat and Frost Insulators and Asbestos Workers. Periodical. English. Four times a year. The Asbestos Worker, 505 Machinists's Building, 1300 Connecticut Avenue, Washington DC 20036. **Continues** Asbestos Worker, 0004-4245.

HK

ASIA LABOUR MONITOR.
Added/Corp Asia Monitor Resource Center. Vol. 1, No. 1 (May 1984)-. Monographic series. English. Irregular. Price varies per

volume. Asia Monitor Resource Center, 444 Nathan Road, 8 F Flat B, Kowloon Hong Kong. **Tel** 011 852 23321346, FAX 011 852 23855319. **Continues** Asia Monitor.
Ind/Abst Hum. Rights Intern. Rep.

LC HD5062 .A75   ISSN 0092-7627
DD 331.2/95   US
ASIA-PACIFIC REGIONAL COMPENSATION SURVEY. AUSTRALIA.
(ASIA/PACIFIC REGIONAL COMPENSATION SURVEY.). (19??)-. English. One time a year. Business International Corporation, 215 Park Avenue South, New York NY 10003. **Tel** (212)460-0600, FAX (212)995-8837.

SI
ASIAN & PACIFIC LABOUR NEWS.
Added/Corp ICFTU Asian and Pacific Regional Organisation. **VFOAT** Asian and Pacific Labour News. Vol. 1, No. 1 (Oct. 1990)-. Periodical. English. Twelve times a year. International Confederation of Free Trade Unions, 3rd Floor Trade Union House, Shenton Way, Singapore 0106, Republic of Singapore. **Tel** 011 65 2226294. **Continues** Asian and Pacific Labour.

LC HD5876.T4 A9
DD 353.97640083   US
AUDIT REPORT, TEXAS EMPLOYMENT COMMISSION. Main/Corp Texas Employment
Commission. **VFOAT** Texas Employment Commission. (19??)-. English. One time a year. State Auditor, John H Reagan, State Office Building, PO Box 12067, Austin TX 78711.

ISSN 0311-6336
AT
AUSTRALIAN BULLETIN OF LABOUR.
[Aust. bull. labour]. **Added/Corp** National Institute of Labour Studies (Australia) Flinders University of South Australia. Institute of Labour Studies. Vol. 1 (Sept. 1974)-. Bulletin. English. Four times a year. 49.34Aus$. National Institute of Labour Studies, Flinders University of South Australia, GPO Box 2100, Adelaide SA 5001 Australia. **Tel** 011 61 8 2012642, FAX 011 61 8 2769060. **ED** Richard Blandy, Frances Robertson, Judy Sloan, and Mark Wooden. Index available (free). cum. index. **Circ**: 1,000.
Desc: Reviews current developments in the Australian labor market; includes articles on employment, unemployment, wages, education, equal employment opportunity and labor relations.
Ind/Abst APAIS, Aust. Public Aff. Inf. Ser. (1980-); Aust. Educ. Index (1985-); Econ. Lit. Index; Int. Labour Doc.; J. Econ. Lit. (1980-); LABORDOC.

AT
AUSTRALIAN BULLETIN OF LABOUR. SUPPLEMENT. Added/Corp National Institute of
Labour Studies (Australia). No. 1 (June 1978)-. Bulletin. English. Irregular. National Institute of Labour Studies, Flinders University of South Australia, GPO Box 2100, Adelaide SA 5001 Australia. **Tel** 011 61 8 2012642, FAX 011 61 8 2769060. Index available. cum. index. **Circ**: 1,000.
Desc: Publishes articles on topical labor relation issues in Australia and reviews labor market developments. Topics include: wages, industrial relations, employment, unemployment, economic developments and forecasts.

AT
AUSTRALIAN SUPER UNIONS. (19??)-.
English. Two times a year. 375.00Aus$. Ian Huntley Publishers Pty Limited, PO Box 99, Cremorne NSW 2090 Australia. **Tel** 011 61 2 9535788, FAX 011 61 2 9532280. **Continues** Australian Trade Union Monitor.

LC HD4811 .A8
DD 331   AT
●AUSTRALIAN WORKER & LABOR NEWS. Added/Corp Australian Workers
Union-Federation of Industrial, Manufacturing & Engineering Employees. **VFOAT** Australian Worker and Labor News. Vol. 1, No. 1 (Nov. 1993)-. Periodical. English. A W U - F I M E Amalgamated Union, 245 Chalmers Street, Suite 15, Redfern New South Wales 2016 Australia. **Tel** 011 61 2 6901022, FAX 011 61 2 6901020. **Continues** Australian Worker.
Desc: Covers union news.

LC HD4811 .A8
DD 331   AT
TITLE CHANGE
AUSTRALIAN WORKER : OFFICIAL JOURNAL OF THE AUSTRALIAN WORKERS' UNION, THE. Added/Corp
Australian Workers' Union. (Nov. 6, 1913)-(19??). Periodical. English. A W U - F I M E Amalgamated Union, 245 Chalmers Street, Suite 15, Redfern New South Wales 2016 Australia. **Tel** 011 61 2 6901022, FAX 011 61 2 6901020. **Ad Acc. Pub. Size:** Tabloid. **Circ**: 105,000 (ctrl). **Continues** Worker. **Continued by** Australian Worker & Labor News.
Desc: Covers union news.

LC HD8401 .F67
DD 331.1/09436   US
AUSTRIA. Added/Corp United States. Bureau of
International Labor Affairs. United States. Embassy (Austria). **VFOAT** Labor Trends in Austria. (19??)-. Government Publication. English. Irregular. $43.00. Superintendent of Documents, US Government Printing Office, Washington DC 20402. **Tel** (202)275-3328, FAX (202)786-2377.
Desc: These reports prepared by the American Embassy describe and analyze the labor trends in some of the most important foreign countries. They cover significant labor developments, including labor-management relations, trade unions, employment and unemployment, wages and working conditions, labor and government, labor administration and legislation, training, labor and politics, labor migrations, and international labor activities.

LC HX9.S7 A93
DD 335/.005   SP
AUTOGESTION Y SOCIALISMO. See
Political Science-Socialism, Communism, Anarchism, Utopianism.

LC HD5731 .A18   ISSN 0187-4969
DD 331.1209   MX
AVANCE DE INFORMACION ECONOMICA. EMPLEO. Added/Corp Instituto
Nacional de Estadistica, Geografia e Informatica (Mexico). **VFOAT** Empleo. (19??)-. Spanish. Twelve times a year. $30.55. INEGI / Instituto Nacional de Estadistica, Geografia e Informatica, Avenida Patriotismo 711 Segundo Piso, 03730 Mexico DF Mexico. **Tel** 011 52 5 5639935, 011 52 5 5988935, FAX 011 52 55987941. **(Subscription address:** INEGI / Instituto Nacional de Estadistica, Geografia e Informatica, Avenida Heroe de Nacozari 2301 Sur, Fracc. Jardines del Parque, CP 20270, Aguascalientes Mexico. **Tel** 011 52 49 182998.)
Desc: Provides information on unemployment and the labor supply.

US
AVERAGE ANNUAL WAGES (ANNUAL PAYROLL DIVIDED BY EMPLOYMENT) AND WAGE ADJUSTMENT INDEX FOR CETA PRIME SPONSORS. Main/Corp United
States. Bureau of Labor Statistics. (19??)-. Government Publication. English. US Department of Labor / Bureau of Labor Statistics, 441 G Street Northwest, Washington DC 20212. **Tel** (202)606-7800, FAX (202)606-7797.

LC HD7096.U6 K469   ISSN 0149-4120
DD 368.4/4/009769   US
AVERAGE MONTHLY WORKERS COVERED BY KENTUCKY UNEMPLOYMENT INSURANCE LAW BY INDUSTRIAL DIVISION AND COUNTY.
See Insurance.

ISSN 0005-2299
IS
AVODAH U-VITUAH LEUMI. Added/Corp
Israel. Misrad Ha-Avodah. **VFOAT** Monthly Review of Labour; Monthly Review of Labour and National Insurance; Labour and National Insurance. Vol. 1 (Sept. 1949)-. Periodical. Hebrew (summaries and/or abstracts in Arabic, English and French; table of contents in Arabic, French and English). Twelve times a year. Ministry of Labour and Social Affairs / Israel, 10 Yad Harutzim Street, Box 1260, Talpiod, Jerusalem Israel. **ED** Z. Heyn. Index available. cum. index (every 2 years). **Circ**: 2,500. available with charts.

II
AWARDS DIGEST. (19??)-. Periodical. English.
Twelve times a year. Rs5.00. National Labour Institute, Ab-6 Safdarjang Enclave, New Delhi 110 01 India.

ISSN 0163-447X
DD 331   US
B C & T NEWS. [BC T news]. Added/Corp Bakery,
Confectionery, and Tobacco Workers International Union. **VFOAT** B C and T news. **VAT** Bakery Confectionery & Tobacco News; Bakery Confectionery and Tobacco News. Vol. 1 (Sept 1978)-. Periodical. English (Spanish). Nine times a year. Bakery, Confectionery and Tobacco Workers International Union, 10401 Connecticut Avenue, Kensington MD 20895. **Tel** (301)933-8600, FAX (301)946-8452. **Continues** B & C News, 0001-043X.
Ind/Abst Work Relat. Abstr.

LC HD5729.B75 B75A   ISSN 0317-8269
DD 331.1/2/09711   CN
B.C. LABOUR MARKET INFORMATION.
Main/Corp British Columbia. Dept. of Labour. Research and Planning Branch. (1973)-. Periodical. English. One time a year. Ministry of Labour / Victoria, 1019 Wharf Street, 6th Floor, Victoria British Columbia V8V 1X5 Canada. **Tel** (604)387-3169.

ISSN 0744-8767
US
BANK WAGE-HOUR AND PERSONNEL REPORT. [Bank wage-hour pers. rep.]. VAT Bank
Wage Hour and Personnel Report. (19??)-. Periodical. English. Twenty-four times a year. $97.00. Bank Wage-Hour and Personnel Service, 1117 North 19th Street/Suite 400-A, Arlington VA 22209-0655.
Desc: Coverage of employment law developments applicable to banks and savings institutions.

LC TN4 .K6   ISSN 0005-5670
HU
CODEN BKLKBX
BANYASZATI ES KOHASZATI LAPOK. KOHASZAT. (BANYASZATI ES OHASZATI LAPOK.
KOHASZAT : AZ ORSZAGOS MAGYAR BANYASZATI ES KOHASZATI EGYESUELET LAPJA.). [Banyasz. Kohasz. lapok, Kohasz.]. **Added/Corp** Orszagos Magyar Banyaszati es Kohaszati Egyesuelet. **VFOAT** Mining and Metallurgical Journal. Metallurgy; Kohaszat; Gornyi i Metallurgicheskii Zhurnal. Metallurgiia; Mining & Metallurgical Journal. Metallurgy. (1968)-. Periodical. Hungarian (summaries and/or abstracts in English, German and Russian). Twelve times a year. $52.00. Lapkiado Vallalat, Lenin Korut 9-11, 1073 Budapest 7 Hungary. **Tel** 011 36 1 222408. **(Subscription address:** Kultura, PO Box 143, H-1300 Budapest 3 Hungary. **Tel** 011 36 1 2500194.) Documents available from CASDDS. **Continues** Kohaszati Lapok, 0368-6469.
Ind/Abst Alum. Ind. Abstr.; Chem. Abstr.; Coal Abstr.; Energy Res. Abstr. (May 1973-); Eng. Mater. Abstr.; Met. Abstr.

ISSN 0255-3449
TH
UDC 341.16 :331
CODEN NU051
BAOGAO - GUOJI LAOGONG JU. GUOJI LAOGONG DAHUI. [Baogaao - Guoji laogong ju.
Guoji laogong dahui]. (1984)-. Periodical. Chinese. ILO Regional Office for Asia and the Pacific, United Nations Building, Rajdamnern Avenue, PO Box 1759, Bangkok Thailand.
Ind/Abst Int. Labour Doc.

LC HD8051 .A834b HD8064
DD 331/.0973 S 331.89/0973   US
BARGAINING CALENDAR. Added/Corp
United States. Bureau of Labor Statistics. (1978)-. English. US Department of Labor, 200 Constitution Avenue NW, Washington DC 20210. **Tel** (202)219-7316, FAX (202)219-7312. **Continues** Wage Calendar.

US
BATTLE CREEK'S LABOR MARKET NEWS. Added/Corp Michigan Employment Security
Commission. Bureau of Research and Statistics. Information and Reports Section. Vol. 12, No. 1 (Mar. 1992)-. Periodical. English. Twelve times a year. Detroit Employment Security Commission, 7310 Woodward Castro, Room 520, Detroit MI 48202. **Tel** (313)876-5427. **Continues** Battle Creek Labor Market Review.

ISSN 0710-5703
DD 331.88/11354711   CN
BCGEU NEWS & VIEWS. [BCGEU news views].
Main/Corp British Columbia Government Employees' Union. Vol. 1, No. 1 (Mar. 5, 1976)-. Periodical. English. Free. BCGEU Communications Department, 4911 Canada Way, Burnaby British Columbia V5G 3W3 Canada.

ISSN 1074-6293
DD 344   US
●BENEFITS & COMPENSATION UPDATE.
[Benefits compens. update]. **Added/Corp** Warren Gorham Lamont. **VFOAT** Benefits and Compensation Update. Vol. 1, No. 1 (Jan. 1994)-. Periodical. English. Twelve times a year. $136.75. Warren Gorham & Lamont Inc., Park Square Building, 31 St. James Avenue, Boston MA 02116-4112. **Tel** (617)423-2020, (800)950-1207, FAX (617)423-2026. **Continues** Employee Benefits Report, 0884-478X.

ISSN 1191-0763
DD 658.3/253   CN
BENEFITS AND PENSIONS MONITOR.
[Benefits pensions monit.]. Vol. 1, No. 1 (Nov./Dec. 1991)-. Trade Publication. English. Six times a year (bimonthly). 39.22Can$. Powershift Communications Inc., 235 Yorkland Boulevard, 3rd Floor, North York Ontario M23 4Y8 Canada. **Tel** (416)494-1066.

ISSN 0703-7732
DD 658.32/5/0971   CN
CCC
BENEFITS CANADA. See Business and
Economics-Personnel Management.

ISSN 1062-1148
DD 658   US
CODEN BENEEK
TITLE CHANGE
BENEFITS (CLEARWATER, FLA.).
(BENEFITS.). [Benefits]. **Added/Corp** Applied Benefits Research, Inc. (1987)-(19??). Periodical. English. Applied Benefits Research, 34125 US Highway 19 North, Palm Harbor FL 34684. **Tel** (813)785-2819, FAX (813)785-4306. **ED** Patrick Manders. **Merged into** Benefits & Compensation Solutions.
Desc: Information on employee fringe benefits.

Business and Economics —Labor

LC HD4928.N62 U627
DD 658
ISSN 0199-3100
US
SUSPENDED
BENEFITS NEWS ANALYSIS. [Benefits news anal.]. Vol. 1 (Nov. 1979)-Suspended with Vol. 14, No. 1 (19??). Periodical. English. Six times a year. Benefits News Analysis, PO Box 4033, New Haven CT 06525. **Tel** (203)393-2272, FAX (203)393-2272. **ED** Faisal A. Saleh. Index available. cum. index. **Ad Acc. Circ:** 10,000 (ctrl). **Desc:** In-depth analysis of corporate employee benefit practices.

LC HD4928.N62 U6233
DD 331
ISSN 8756-1263
US
CCC
NLM W1; BE522
Pr Rev.
BENEFITS QUARTERLY. See Insurance.

US
BENTON HARBOR'S LABOR MARKET NEWS. Added/Corp Michigan Employment Security Commission. Bureau of Research and Statistics. Information and Reports Section. Vol. 12, No. 1 (Mar. 1992)-. Periodical. English. Twelve times a year. Detroit Employment Security Commission, 7310 Woodward Castro, Room 520, Detroit MI 48202. **Tel** (313)876-5427. **Continues** Benton Harbor Labor Market Review.

LC HA1320.N6 A32 HD5780.N
DD 314.3
GW
BESCHAFTIGTENENTWICKLUNG IN NORDRHEIN-WESTFALEN. ERGEBNISSE EINER REGIONAL DISAGGREGIERTEN ANALYSE, DIE. See Business and Economics-Abstracting, Bibliographies and Statistics.

LC HD5777 .S8d
DD 331.12/0943
GW
BEVOELKERUNG UND ERWERBSTAETIGKEIT. REIHE 4.1.1, STAND UND ENTWICKLUNG DER ERWERBSTAETIGKEIT. Main/Corp Germany (West). Statistisches Bundesamt. **Added/Corp** Germany (West). Statistisches Bundesamt. Germany. Statistisches Bundesamt. **VFOAT** Fachserie 1; Stand und Entwicklung der Erwerbstaetigkeit. (1978)-. German. DM14.70. Messrs W Kohlhammer GmbH, Publications of the Federal Statistical Office, Philipp-Reis-Strabe 3, Postfach 42 11 20, W-6500 Mainz 42 Germany. **Tel** 06131/59094-95, telex 4187768 DGV. **Continues in part** Bevoelkerung und Erwerbstaetigkeit. Reihe 4.1, Stand und Entwicklung der Erwerbstaetigkeit. **Desc:** State and development of employment; results of the labor force sample survey of the EC.

LC HD5777 .B49
GW
BEVOLKERUNG UND ERWERBSTATIGKEIT. REIHE 4.2.1., STRUKTUR DER ARBEITNEHMER. VFOAT Struktur der Arbeitnehmer. Vol. 31 (March 1987)-. Periodical. German. Four times a year. DM4.80. W. Kohlhammer Verlag GmbH, Postfach 800430, D-70549 Stuttgart Germany. **Tel** 011 49 711 78630, FAX 011 49 711 7863430, telex 7-255820. **Continues** Bevovlkerung und Erwerbstatigkeit. Reihe 4.2, Sozialversickerungspflichtig Beschaftigte Arbeitnehmer.

LC HA1231 .B48
GW
BEVOLKERUNG UND ERWERBSTATIGKEIT. REIHE 1, GEBIET UND BEVOLKERUNG / HERAUSGEBER STATISTISCHES BUNDESAMT. See Population Studies.

ISSN 1065-2426
DD 331
US
BEYOND BORDERS. [Beyond bord.]. Vol. 1, Issue 1 (Winter 1992)-. Trade Publication. English. Four times a year. $12.00. Beyond Borders, 4677 30th Street, Suite 214, San Diego CA 92116. **Tel** (619)280-2976. **ED** Mary E. Tong. **Bk Rev. Circ:** 2,000. **Desc:** Covers the global economy, and international living and working conditions. Provides information on available resources for community activists and organizers.

US
BIENNIAL REPORT. Main/Corp Texas. State Pension Review Board. (1987?)-. English. Every 2 years. **Continues** Annual Report / Texas. State Pension Review Board.

LC HD5725.N8 N646A
DD 331.1/1/09756
ISSN 0146-9150
BIENNIAL REPORT - NORTH CAROLINA MANPOWER COUNCIL. Main/Corp North Carolina. Manpower Council. English. Every 2 years. North Carolina Department of Administration, Manpower Council, 331 Sir Walter Building, Raleigh NC 27601.

LC HD8053.W6 A4
DD 353.97750083/06
US
BIENNIAL REPORT - STATE OF WISCONSIN, DEPARTMENT OF INDUSTRY, LABOR AND HUMAN RELATIONS. Main/Corp Wisconsin. Dept. of Industry, Labor and Human Relations. (1973)-. English. Every 2 years. Wisconsin Department of Industry, Labor & Human Relations, 201 East Washington Avenue, PO Box 7944, Madison WI 53707-7944. **Tel** (608)266-0851. **Continues** Wisconsin. Industrial Commission. Biennial Review.

LC HD7096.U6 T233
DD 353.97680083/3/06
US
BIENNIAL REPORT / TENNESSEE DEPARTMENT OF EMPLOYMENT SECURITY. Main/Corp Tennessee. Dept. of Employment Security. 1st (Oct. 1, 1980-Sept. 30, 1982)-. English. Every 2 years. Tennessee Department of Employment Security, Volunteer Plaza Building, 12th Floor, Nashville TN 37245. **Tel** (615)741-2131, FAX (615)741-3203. Index available. ctrl circ. **Continues** Tennessee. Dept. of Employment Security. Annual Report.

LC HC107.V8 A2
DD 353.97550083/06
US
BIENNIAL REPORT / VIRGINIA DEPARTMENT OF LABOR AND INDUSTRY. Main/Corp Virginia. Dept. of Labor and Industry. (1982/1983)-. English. Every 2 years. **Continues** Virginia. Dept. of Labor and Industry. Annual Report of the Department of Labor and Industry.

ISSN 0292-9287
FR
BIULETYN INFORMACYJNY SOLIDARNOSC. (SOLIDARNOSC : BULLETIN D'INFORMATION / COMITE DE COORDINATION DU SYNDICAT SOLIDARNOSC EN FRANCE.). [Biul. inf. Solidarnosc]. 1982-. Bulletin. Polish (Polish). Universite de Montreal / SOCP, PO Box 6128, Stn Centre-Ville, Montreal Quebec H3C 3J7 Canada. **Tel** (514)343-6853, FAX (514)343-2479.

US
BLACK EMPLOYMENT & EDUCATION JOURNAL. VFOAT Black Employment and Education Journal. (19??)-. English. Twelve times a year. Free on request. Black Employment and Education Journal, 6433 Topanga Canyon Boulevard, Suite 401, Canooa Park CA 91303. **Tel** (818)716-0071. **Circ:** 400,000.

ISSN 0045-2238
CEASED
BLACK NEWS DIGEST. See Ethnic Interests.

LC HD8051 .A7876 HD8008
DD 331.1/08 S, 331.89/0973
ISSN 0362-4234
US
BLS FILE OF STATE, COUNTY, AND MUNICIPAL COLLECTIVE BARGAINING AGREEMENTS. Main/Corp United States. Bureau of Labor Statistics. **VAT** Bureau of Labor Statistics File of State, County, and Municipal Collective Bargaining Agreements. Government Publication. English. US Department of Labor / Bureau of Labor Statistics, 441 G Street Northwest, Washington DC 20212. **Tel** (202)606-7800, FAX (202)606-7797. **Continues** State, County, and Municipal Collective Bargaining Agreements on File With the Bureau of Labor Statistics.

LC HD7106.U5 B58
DD 332.6/7254
ISSN 0272-2445
US
BLUE BOOK OF PENSION FUNDS, THE. Added/Corp Insurance Research, inc. (19??)-. English. One time a year. Dun & Bradstreet Information Services, 3 Sylvan Way, Parsippany NJ 07054. **Tel** (201)605-6000, (800)526-0651.

LC HD5773 .A369
FR
BMST, BULLETIN MENSUEL DES STATISTIQUES DU TRAVAIL. Added/Corp France. Minist'ere du Travail, de l'Emploi et de la Formation Professionnelle. Service des Etudes et de la Statistique. **VFOAT** Bulletin Mensuel des Statistiques du Travail. (July 1991)-. Bulletin. French. Twelve times a year. 472.00F France; $111.00 US; £94.00 other. Ministere du Travail et Service d'Etudes, Statistique place Fontenoy, 75007 Paris France. **(Subscription address:** Documentation Francaise, 124 rue Henri Barbusse, 93308 Aubervilliers Cedex France. **Tel** 011 33 1 48395600.) **Continues** Statistiques du Travail, Bulletin Mensuel.

LC HD6350.R43 B7
DD 331
ISSN 1049-3921
US
BMWE JOURNAL. [BMWE j.]. **Added/Corp** Brotherhood of Maintenance of Way Employees. **VAT** Brotherhood of Maintenance of Way Employees Journal. (19??)-. Trade Publication. English. Twelve times a year. $20.00. Brotherhood of Maintenance of Way Employees, 26555 Evergreen Road, Suite 200, Southbuild MI 48076. **Tel** (313)868-0490. **Continues** Railway Journal, 0146-0625. **Ind/Abst** Work Relat. Abstr.

LC HD8083.C2 B63
DD 331
ISSN 1058-7373
US
TITLE CHANGE
BNA CALIFORNIA EMPLOYEE RELATIONS REPORT. [BNA Calif. empl. relat. rep.]. **Added/Corp** Bureau of National Affairs (Washington, D.C.). **VFOAT** Employee Relations Report. Vol. 1, No. 1 (Oct. 7, 1991)-(1994). Periodical. English. Bureau of National Affairs Inc., 9435 Key West Avenue, Rockville MD 20850. **Tel** (800)372-1033, (301)258-1033, FAX (301)948-5823. **Merged into** California Employment Law Monitor, 1081-504X.

ISSN 1069-5117
DD 331
US
CCC
●**BNA PENSION & BENEFITS REPORTER.** [BNA pension benefits report.]. **Added/Corp** Bureau of National Affairs (Washington, D.C.). **VFOAT** BNA Pension and Benefits Reporter; Bureau of National Affairs Pension & Benefits Reporter. Vol. 20, No. 20 (May 17, 1993)-. Periodical. English. One time a week. $835.00. Bureau of National Affairs Inc., 9435 Key West Avenue, Rockville MD 20850. **Tel** (800)372-1033, (301)258-1033, FAX (301)948-5823. available on an online database from Lexis-Nexis; West Services, Inc.; Human Resources Information Network; and (tle 655/Full-Text) DIALOG. **Continues** BNA Pension Reporter, 0095-7100.

LC HD7106.U5 B78a
DD 331.2/52/0973
ISSN 0095-7100
US
CCC
TITLE CHANGE
BNA PENSION REPORTER. [BNA pension rep.]. **Main/Corp** Bureau of National Affairs (Washington, D.C.). **VAT** Bureau of National Affairs Pension Reporter. (19??)-(1993). Periodical. English. Bureau of National Affairs Inc., 9435 Key West Avenue, Rockville MD 20850. **Tel** (800)372-1033, (301)258-1033, FAX (301)948-5823. **ED** David A Sayre. **Continued by** BNA Pension & Benefits Reporter, 1069-5117. **Desc:** Covers the latest pension developments stemming from the passage of ERISA and its amendments, plus pension and welfare benefit regulations, standards, enforcement actions, court decisions, legislative and administrative actions, agency options, and employee benefit trust fund requirements.

LC HD8051 .B96
DD 331/.0973
ISSN 0739-3016
US
CCC
BNA'S EMPLOYEE RELATIONS WEEKLY. Added/Corp Bureau of National Affairs (Washington, D.C.). **VFOAT** B.N.A.'s Employee Relations Weekly; Employee Relations Weekly. Vol. 1, No. 1 (Sept. 5, 1983)-. Periodical. English. One time a week. $796.00. Bureau of National Affairs Inc., 9435 Key West Avenue, Rockville MD 20850. **Tel** (800)372-1033, (301)258-1033, FAX (301)948-5823. **ED** Susan J Sala. available on an online database from Human Resources Information Network. **Desc:** Gives an overview of the latest developments influencing employee relations in both private and public sectors, with information on EEO policy, federal and state legislative and regulatory actions, NLRB actions, federal and state court decisions, and the impact of foreign competition.

ISSN 1051-4775
DD 331
US
CCC
BNA'S WORKERS' COMPENSATION REPORT. [BNA'S work. compens. rep.]. **Added/Corp** Bureau of National Affairs. **VFOAT** Workers' Compensation Report. **VAT** Bureau of National Affairs Workers' Compensation Report. Vol. 1, No. 1 (July 24, 1990)-. Periodical. English. Twenty-six times a year. $476.00. Bureau of National Affairs Inc., 9435 Key West Avenue, Rockville MD 20850. **Tel** (800)372-1033, (301)258-1033, FAX (301)948-5823. available on an online database from Human Resources Information Network.

ISSN 1078-4101
DD 331
US
BOILERMAKER REPORTER. [Boil.mak. report.]. **Added/Corp** International Brotherhood of Boilermakers, Iron Shipbuilders, Blacksmiths, Forgers, and Helpers. Vol. 29, No. 1 (Jan./Feb. 1990)-. Periodical. English. Six times a year. Boilmakers' Publications, 592 New Brotherhood Building, Kansas City KS 66101. **Continues** Boilermakers Blacksmiths Reporter, 0197-5757. **Ind/Abst** Work Relat. Abstr.

LC HD8281 .A23A
DD 331/.0981
BL
BOLETIM DO TRABALHO. Main/Corp Brazil. Ministerio do Trabalho. Portuguese. Editora Revista dos Tribunais, rua Conde do Pinhal 78, 01501 Sao Paulo SP Brazil. **Tel** 011 55 11 372433.

Business and Economics — Labor

LC HD5752 .M54A
BL
BOLETIM TECNICO. Main/Corp Brazil. Ministerio do Trabalho e Previdencia Social. Centro de Documentacao e Informatica. Bulletin. Portuguese. Irregular. $40.00. Banco do Brasil SA, Carteira de Cambio Agencia de Itabuna, 45600 Itabuna Bahia Brasil. *Continues* Boletim Tecnico / Brazil. Servico de Estatistica da Previdencia e Trabalho.

ISSN 0210-2439
SP
UDC 614.8
BOLETIN BIBLIOGRAFICO DE LA PREVENCION. [Bol. bibliogr. prev.]. (1970)-. Periodical. Spanish. Six times a year. 1000ptas Spain; $12.00 other. Instituto Nacional de Medicina Seguridad, Pabellon 8, Divulgacion, Universitaria S N, 28040 Madrid Spain. **Tel** 011 34 1 544-1400, FAX 91 243 72 71. Index available. cum. index. available on microfiche. **Desc:** Covers safety and health at work.

MX
BOLETIN BOLSA DE TRABAJO. Main/Corp Mexico. Consejo Nacional de Ciencia Y Tecnologia. Departamento Bolsa de Trabajo. **VFOAT** Bolsa de Trabajo; Boletin de la Bolsa de Trabajo. (19??)-. Periodical. Spanish. Six times a year. Free. Consejo Nacional Ciencia y Tecno, Av Constituyentes 1046 Lomas A, CP 11950 Mexico DF Mexico. **Tel** 011 52 5 3277400. Index available. **Circ:** 6,000. **Desc:** Labor promotion of people with postgraduate degrees.

LC HD8581 .B65   ISSN 0212-7180
DD 331.0946   SP
BOLETIN DE ESTADISTICAS LABORALES. See Business and Economics-Abstracting, Bibliographies and Statistics.

LC HD6475.A2 I2288
BE
BOLETIN ECONOMICO Y SOCIAL. Main/Corp International Confederation of Free Trade Unions. Periodical. Spanish. Six times a year. International Confederation of Free Trade Unions, 37-41 Montagne Herbes Potageres, 1000 Brussels Belgium. **Tel** 011 32 2 2178085, FAX 011 32 2 2188415, telex 26785.

BO
BOLIVIA EN MARCHA / SECRETARIA NACIONAL DE TRABAJADORES. Added/Corp Movimiento de la Izquierda Revolucionaria (Bolivia). Nueva Mayoria. Secretaria Nacional de Trabajadores. Vol. 1 No. 1 (Feb 1991)-. Periodical. Spanish. Four times a year.

IT
BOLLETINO TARIFFE TRASFERTE ITALIA. Italian. ASA SRL, Via Soderini 35-A, 20146 Milan Italy.

IT
BOLLETTINO DELLA PREVENZIONE. Italian. Cedis, Milanofiori Palazzo E2, 20090 Assago MI Italy.

ISSN 0390-9131
IT
UDC 34
BOLLETTINO LEGGI E DECRETI. [Boll. leggi decreti]. (1965)-. Periodical. Italian. One time a week. L158390. SIT SRL, Casella Postale 4061, 00182 Rome Italy. **Tel** 011 39 6 70302751.

ISSN 0392-3797
IT
UDC 36
BOLLETTINO NAZIONALE PREVENZIONE INFORTUNI. [Boll. Naz. Prev. Infort.]. (1971)-. Periodical. Italian. Twelve times a year. L104570. SIT SRL, Casella Postale 4061, 00182 Rome Italy. **Tel** 011 39 6 70302751.

LC HD38.25.U6 B66
US
BOOK OF PROFILES. (1991)-. English.

ISSN 0758-1858
FR
UDC 65.015
BREF BULLETIN DE RECHERCHES SUR L'EMPLOI ET LA FORMATION. VFOAT CEREQ BREF; CEREQ Communication; Bulletin de Recherches sur l'Emploi et la Formation. (1983)-. Bulletin. French. Eleven times a year. Free on request. CEREQ / Centre d'Etudes et de Recherches sur les Qualifications, 10 Place de la Joliette, 13474 Marseille Cedex France. **Tel** 011 33 91 132828, FAX 011 33 91 132880.

LC HD8005.2.U5 B74   ISSN 0276-9743
DD 322/.2/0973   US
BRIEFING BOOK ON MAJOR POLICY ISSUES. See Public Administration.

DD 331.05   ISSN 0819-3754
AT
BRIGHT REPORT. (THE BRIGHT REPORT.). [Bright rep.]. (1988)-. Periodical. English. Irregular (11 issues with index in Dec.). 233.50Aus$. Bright & Associates, PO Box 501, Alstonville 2477 Australia. **Tel** 011 61 66 291090, FAX 011 61 66281988. **ED** J. W. Armstrong. Index available (Dec.). cum. index. **Ad Acc.** ctrl circ.

DD 331.89/09711   ISSN 0829-8319
CN
... BRITISH COLUMBIA COLLECTIVE BARGAINING REVIEW AND OUTLOOK, THE. [B.C. collect. bargain rev. outlook]. **Added/Corp** Business Council of British Columbia. (1985)-. English. One time a year. $85.00. Business Council of British Columbia, 1050 West Pender, Suite 810, Vancouver British Columbia V6E 3S7, Canada. **Tel** (604)684-3384. ctrl circ. *Formed by the union of* British Columbia Collective Bargaining Review, 0822-4757 *and* British Columbia Collective Bargaining Outlook, 0822-4765.

LC HD6951 .B7   ISSN 0007-1080
DD 331.1   UK
      CCC
      CODEN BJIRAV
Pr Rev.
BRITISH JOURNAL OF INDUSTRIAL RELATIONS. [Br. j. ind. relat.]. Vol. 1 (Feb. 1963)-. Academic Scholarly Publication. English. Four times a year. $166.00. Basil Blackwell Publishers Ltd., 108 Cowley Road, Oxford OX4 1JF United Kingdom. **Tel** 011 44 1235 465500, FAX 011 44 1235 465556, telex 837022 OXBOOK G. **(Subscription address:** Blackwell Publishers / UK, 108 Cowley Road, Oxford OX4 1JF United Kingdom. **Tel** 011 44 1865 791100, FAX 011 44 1865 791347.**)** **ED** Ben Roberts and Ray Richardson. **Bk Rev. Ad Acc.** available on microfilm and microfiche from University Microfilms International (UMI). Documents available from The Genuine Article, UMI Article Clearinghouse. **Desc:** Publishes wide range of articles covering theory and practice of law.
Ind/Abst ABI/INFORM Glob. Ed.; ABI/INFORM [Computer File] (March 1976-); Anbar Account. Finan. Abstr. [Full Txt.]; Anbar Mark. Distr. Abstr. [Full Txt.]; Anbar Top Manage. Abstr. [Full Txt.]; Appl. Soc. Sci. Index Abstr.; Br. Humanit. Index; Coal Abstr.; Contents Recent Econ. J.; Contents Pages Manage.; Curr. Cit.; Curr. Contents Soc. Behav. Sci.; Econ. Lit. Index; Gen. BusinessFile; Hum. Resour. Abstr. (?-?); Int. Bibliogr. Sociol.; Int. Labour Doc.; Int. Polit. Sci. Abstr.; J. Econ. Lit.; LABORDOC; Manage. Market. Abstr.; Manage. Bibliogr. Rev.; Middle East Abstr. Index; Oper. Prod. Manage. Abstr. [Full Txt.]; PAIS Int. Print; Person. Train. Abstr. [Full Txt.]; Person. Manage. Abstr.; Res. Alert [Full Cov.]; Selec. Coop. Index Manage. Period.; Soc. Sci. Cit. Index [Full Cov.]; Tech. Educ. Train. Abstr.; Women Manage. Rev. [Full Txt.]; Work Relat. Abstr.

LC HD4966.M79 U53   ISSN 0193-2314
DD 331.2/81/791450973   US
BROOKS' STANDARD RATE BOOK, THE. (1956)-. English. One time a year. $44.20. Stanley J Brooks Company, 1416 Westwood Boulevard, Los Angeles CA 90024. **Tel** (310)470-2849. **ED** S J Brooks. **Bk Rev. Ad Acc. Circ:** 5,000. **Desc:** Film technicians, actors and directors salaries for payroll and budgeting departments.

LC HD8051 .A78767   ISSN 0161-4770
DD 353.83   US
BUDGET PROPOSED FOR THE DEPARTMENT OF LABOR AND RELATED AGENCIES, THE. Main/Corp United States. Dept. of Labor. English. One time a year. US Department of Labor, 200 Constitution Avenue NW, Washington DC 20210. **Tel** (202)219-7316, FAX (202)219-7312.

LC HD6350.B9 B653
DD 331.88/091   SZ
BUILDING AND WOOD. 1974-. Periodical. English. Four times a year. International Federation of Building and Wood Workers, rue de la Coulouvreniere 27-29, CH-1204 Geneva Switzerland. *Continues* IFBWW Bulletin.

LC HD4966.B92 U398
DD 331.2/89/009787   US
BUILDING TRADES INDEX, STATE OF WYOMING. English. One time a year. Free. Wyoming Department of Labor & Statistics, Herschler Building, Cheyenne WY 82002. **Tel** (307)777-7340. **ED** J Wolff. **Circ:** 250 (ctrl). **Desc:** Wages and fringe benefits for union construction workers in Wyoming.

LC HD8053.C8 L33a
DD 331./09746   US
BULLETIN / CONNECTICUT LABOR DEPARTMENT. Added/Corp Connecticut. Labor Dept. (1977)-. Bulletin. English. Six times a year. Connecticut Labor Department, 200 Folly Brook Boulevard, Wethersfield CT 06109. **Tel** (203)566-4380.

ED Richard Ficks. **Circ:** 4,000. *Continues* Connecticut. Labor Dept. Monthly Bulletin - Connecticut Labor Department.

DD 331/.09714   ISSN 0705-6257
CN
BULLETIN DE LIAISON - SECTEUR PUBLIC. Main/Corp Front Commun Secteur Public. Published since March 1976. Bulletin. French. Confederation des Syndicats Nationaux, 1001 St. Denis, Montreal Quebec H2X 3J1 Canada.

DD 331.88/11/79109714   ISSN 0383-9397
CN
BULLETIN DE L'UNION DES ARTISTES, LE. Main/Corp Union des Artistes. Dec. 1972-. Bulletin. French. Union des Artistes, 1290 rue St. Denis, Montreal Quebec H2X 3J7 Canada. **Tel** (514)288-6682. *Supersedes* Union des Artistes. Bulletin d'Information, 0383-9400.

DD 331.88/11/354714   ISSN 0380-1705
CN
BULLETIN DES MEMBRES - SYNDICAT DES FONCTIONNAIRES PROVINCIAUX DU QUEBEC. Main/Corp Syndicat des Fonctionnaires Provinciaux du Quebec. Vol. 1 (July 1973)-. Bulletin. French. Free. Syndicat des Fonctionnaires Provinciaux du Quebec, 155 Est boulevard Charest, Quebec Quebec G1K 3G6 Canada.

FR
BULLETIN D'INFORMATION DE L'ARRCO. (19??)-. Bulletin. French. Four times a year. $41.56. ARRCO / Association des Regimes de Retraites Complementaires, 44 boulevard Bastille, F 75012 Paris France. **Tel** 011 33 1 43461320.

DD 331.88/116106953/097123   ISSN 0712-4775
CN
BULLETIN / HEALTH SCIENCES ASSOCIATION OF ALBERTA. [Bull. - Health Sci. Assoc. Alta.]. **Added/Corp** Health Sciences Association of Alberta. **VFOAT** H.S.A.A. Bulletin; H.S.A.A. Newsletter. Vol. 1, No. 1 (July 1982)-. Bulletin. English. Four times a year. Free on request. Health Sciences Association, 10340 124th Street, Edmonton Alta T5N 1RS Canada. **Tel** (403)488-0168. ctrl circ.

LC HD5786 .A25   ISSN 0771-1182
DD 331.12/09493/021   BE
BULLETIN MENSUEL DE L'OFFICE NATIONAL DE L'EMPLOI. Added/Corp Belgium. Office National de l'Emploi. **VFOAT** Bulletin Mensuel. (Jan. 1980)-. Bulletin. French. Twelve times a year. Office National de l'Emploi Belgium, boulevard de l'Empereur 7, 1000 Brussels Belgium. *Continues* Bulletin Mensuel (Belgium. Office National de l'Emploi).

LC HD5773 .A369 Suppl.
DD 331/.0944   FR
BULLETIN MENSUEL DES STATISTIQUES DU TRAVAIL. SUPPLEMENT (PARIS, FRANCE : 1982). See Business and Economics-Abstracting, Bibliographies and Statistics.

DD 331.88/1135471   ISSN 0713-6595
CN
BULLETIN - NATIONAL COMPONENT. PUBLIC SERVICE ALLIANCE OF CANADA. (BULLETIN / NATIONAL COMPONENT, PUBLIC SERVICE ALLIANCE OF CANADA.). [Bull. Natl. Compon., Public Serv. Alliance Can.]. **Added/Corp** Public Service Alliance of Canada. National Component. (January 29, 1973)-. Bulletin. English. Public Service Alliance of Canada, 233 Gilmour Street, Ottawa Ontario K2P 0P1 Canada. **Tel** (613)560-4211. *Continues* Newsbulletin (Public Service Alliance of Canada. National Component). English, 0713-6587.

DD 331   ISSN 0882-3669
US
BULLETIN - NATIONAL FOUNDATION FOR UNEMPLOYMENT COMPENSATION & WORKERS' COMPENSATION (U.S.). (BULLETIN : A PUBLICATION OF THE NATIONAL FOUNDATION FOR UNEMPLOYMENT COMPENSATION & WORKERS' COMPENSATION.). [Bull. - Natl. Found. Unemploy. Compens. Work. Compens. (U.S.)]. **Added/Corp** National Foundation for Unemployment Compensation & Workers' Compensation (U.S.). Bulletin No. 29 W.C. (Mar. 22, 1985)-. Bulletin. English. comes with membership. UBA Inc., 820 First Street Northeast, Suite 400, Washington DC 20002. **Tel** (202)682-1517. *Continues* Bulletin (UBS (Firm)).
Desc: Provides information on cost, taxes, benefits, state legislative changes, current issues and topics of general interest for the unemployment compensation and worker's compensation programs.

Business and Economics —Labor

LC HD4815 .C83   **ISSN** 0070-0134
Pr Rev.   US
BULLETIN (NEW YORK STATE SCHOOL OF INDUSTRIAL AND LABOR RELATIONS). (BULLETIN / NEW YORK STATE SCHOOL OF INDUSTRIAL AND LABOR RELATIONS, CORNELL UNIVERSITY.). **Added/Corp** New York State School of Industrial and Labor Relations. **VFOAT** ILR Bulletin. No. 15 (April 1951)-. Bulletin. English. Irregular. Cornell University / ILR, 201 ILR Research Building, Ithaca NY 14853. **Tel** (607)255-2733, FAX (607)255-2755. **Circ:** 10,000 (ctrl). *Formed by the union of Extension Bulletin (New York State School of Industrial and Labor Relations) and Research Bulletin (New York State School of Industrial and Labor Relations).*
Desc: Pamphlets (25-60 pages) on topics related to the many fields encompassed by industrial and labor relations.

LC HD4826 .I53   **ISSN** 0007-4950
DD 331/.0212   SZ
     CCC
BULLETIN OF LABOUR STATISTICS. See Business and Economics-Abstracting, Bibliographies and Statistics.

LC HD6475.A1 B84   **ISSN** 0890-6165
DD 331   US
     TITLE CHANGE
BULLETIN OF THE DEPARTMENT OF INTERNATIONAL AFFAIRS, AFL-CIO, THE. See Political Science-International Relations.

     FR
BULLETIN OFFICIEL DES MINISTERES CHARGES DE L'EMPLOI ET DU TRAVAIL. **Main/Corp** France. Ministeres Charges de l'Emploi et du Travail. Issue No. 82/28 (Aug. 13, 1982)-. Bulletin. French. Irregular. Direction des Journaux Officiels, 26 rue Desaix, 75727 Paris Cedex 15 France. **Tel** 011 33 1 40587500. *Continues France. Ministere du Travail. Bulletin Officiel du Ministere du Travail.*

     SZ
BULLETIN OFFICIEL DU BIT. SERIES A. (19??)-. Bulletin. English (French and Spanish). Irregular. $24.00 (per issue); $112.00 (Series A and B). International Labour Office - ILO, Publications Sales Service, CH-1211 Geneva 22 Switzerland. **Tel** 011 41 22 7996111, FAX 011 41 22 7986253, telex 415 647 ilo ch. **Circ:** 3,000. available on microfiche.
Desc: Information on the activities of the ILO, texts adopted by the International Labour Conference and other official documents.

     SZ
BULLETIN OFFICIEL DU BIT. SERIES B. (19??)-. Bulletin. French. Irregular. $24.00 (per issue); $112.00 (Series A and B). International Labour Office - ILO, Publications Sales Service, CH-1211 Geneva 22 Switzerland. **Tel** 011 41 22 7996111, FAX 011 41 22 7986253, telex 415 647 ilo ch.

ISSN 0713-6668
DD 331.88/1135471   CN
BULLETIN - PUBLIC SERVICE ALLIANCE OF CANADA (1978). (BULLETIN / PSAC). [Bull. - Public Serv. Alliance Can.]. **VFOAT** Bulletin. March 17, 1978-. Bulletin. English (French). Public Service Alliance of Canada, 233 Gilmour Street, Ottawa Ontario K2P 0P1 Canada. **Tel** (613)560-4211.

ISSN 0710-9857
DD 331.12/09714/6   CN
BULLETIN REGIONAL SUR LE MARCHE DU TRAVAIL (REGION DES CANTONS DE L'EST). (BULLETIN REGIONAL SUR LE MARCHE DU TRAVAIL : REGION DES CANTONS DE L'EST (05).). [Bull. reg. marche trav., Reg. Cantons Est]. Vol. 1, No. 1, 21 Quarterly 1981 -. Bulletin. French. Four times a year. Centre de Recherche et de Statistiques sur le Marche du Travail, 425 St. Amable 4 Etage, Quebec G1R 4Z1 Canada.

ISSN 0710-9865
DD 331.12/09714/22   CN
BULLETIN REGIONAL SUR LE MARCHE DU TRAVAIL (REGION LAURENTIDES-LANAUDIERE). (BULLETIN REGIONAL SUR LE MARCHE DU TRAVAIL : REGION LAURENTIDES-LANAUDIERE (06 NORD).). [Bull. reg. marche trav., Reg. Laurent.-Lanaudiere]. Vol. 1, No. 1 (2E Quarterly 1981)-. Bulletin. French. Four times a year. Centre de Recherche et de Statistiques sur le Marche du Travail, 425 St. Amable 4 Etage, Quebec G1R 4Z1 Canada.

LC DK4442 .B84   **ISSN** 0738-2154
DD 322/.2/09438   US
BULLETIN SOLIDARNOSC. [Bull. Solidarnosc]. **Added/Corp** Polish Workers Task Force. League for Industrial Democracy. Poland Watch Center (Washington, D.C.). **VFOAT** Solidarnosc; Solidarity Bulletin. Issue No. 1 (Oct. 1981)-. Bulletin. English. Irregular. Polish Workers Task Force, 275 7th Avenue/25th Floor, New York NY 10001.
Ind/Abst Hum. Rights Intern. Rep.

ISSN 0704-0873
DD 331/.09714   CN
BULLETIN SUR LES RELATIONS DU TRAVAIL (EDITION ANGLAISE). (BULLETIN SUR LES RELATIONS DU TRAVAIL.). **Main/Corp** Conseil du Patronat du Quebec. Vol. 1 (Oct. 1970)-. Bulletin. English. Irregular. 24.01Can$. Conseil du Patronat du Quebec, Suite 606/2075 rue Universite, Montreal Quebec H3A 2L1 Canada. **Tel** (514)288-5161.

LC HD6093 .A35   **ISSN** 0083-3606
DD 331.4   US
BULLETIN - U.S. DEPT. OF LABOR, EMPLOYMENT STANDARDS ADMINISTRATION, WOMEN'S BUREAU. (BULLETIN / U.S. DEPARTMENT OF LABOR, WOMEN'S BUREAU.). No. 5 (1919)-. Bulletin. English. Price varies per volume. US Department of Labor, 200 Constitution Avenue NW, Washington DC 20210. **Tel** (202)219-7316, FAX (202)219-7312. *Continues Bulletin of the Woman in Industry Service.*

ISSN 0730-8469
     US
BULLETIN - UNITED STEELWORKERS OF AMERICA. LOCAL 7896 (FITCHBURG, MASS.), THE. (THE BULLETIN : OFFICIAL NEWSLETTER OF LOCAL 7896 USWA.). (1982)-. Bulletin. English. Twelve times a year. Free. United Steelworkers of America Local 7896, 17 Redman Place, Fitchburg MA 01420.

ISSN 0954-7932
     UK
BULLETIN - UNIVERSITY OF WARWICK. INSTITUTE FOR EMPLOYMENT RESEARCH. (BULLETIN). [Bull. - Univ. Warwick, Inst. Employ. Res.]. **VFOAT** IER Bulletin. (1988)-. Bulletin. English. Four times a year. $29.09. University of Warwick, Institute for Employment Research, Coventry CV4 7AL United Kingdom. **Tel** 011 44 1203 523523, 011 44 1203 524523, FAX 011 44 1203 524241, telex 31406.

LC HD6350.B9 B75
DD 331.88/124   NE
BULLETIN (WORLD FEDERATION OF BUILDING AND WOODWORKERS UNIONS). (BULLETIN.). **Added/Corp** World Federation of Building and Woodworkers Unions. (19??)-. Bulletin. French (French). Sekretariat, Postbus 414, 3500 AK Utrecht Netherlands.

     SZ
BUREAU INTERNATIONAL DU TRAVAIL ABONNEMENT GROUPE. (19??)-. French. Irregular. $141.00 (C/A). International Labour Office - ILO, Publications Sales Service, CH-1211 Geneva 22 Switzerland. **Tel** 011 41 22 7996111, FAX 011 41 22 7986253, telex 415 647 ilo ch.
Desc: Contains articles based on recent ILO and other research into economic and social topics of international interest affecting labor.

     CN
●BUSINESS AND EMPLOYMENT TRENDS. (1995)-. English. Oasis, 204-21 10405 Jasper Avenue, Edmonton Alberta T5J 2Y6 Canada. **Tel** (403)467-0843. **ED** Norah Cantin. Index available. cum. index. **Ad Acc.**

LC HD4976.N5 N48A
DD 331.2/9749   US
BUSINESS AND GOVERNMENT SALARY AND WAGE SURVEYS (NEW JERSEY). **Main/Corp** New Jersey. Dept. of Civil Service. 1973-. English. One time a year. Department of Civil Service / Trenton, Trenton NJ 08625.

DD 353.9/771/0082/56   US
BWC NEWS. **Added/Corp** Ohio. Bureau of Workers' Compensation. **VFOAT** Bureau of Workers' Compensation News. Vol. 1, Issue 1 (Mar./Apr. 1992)-. Periodical. English. Six times a year. Ohio Bureau of Workers' Compensation, Communications Department, 3rd Floor, 39 West Spring Street, Columbus OH 43266-0581. *Continues Ohio Monitor Magazine.*

LC HD8423 .U5414   **ISSN** 0398-3145
DD 331.7/61/6072   FR
CADRES CFDT. **Main/Corp** Confederation Francaise Democratique du Travail. **Added/Corp** Union Confederale des Ingenieurs et Cadres. (19??)-. French. One time a year. $65.61. Cadres CFDT, 47 Avenue Simon Bolivar, 75950 Paris Cedex 19 France. **Tel** 33 1 42024443, FAX 33 1 42024858. **Ad Acc, Adv Mgr:** Pierre Vial. *Continues Cadres et Profession.*

     FR
●CAHIERS DE L'ATELIER. (1995)-. French. Six times a year. 240.00F. Editions Ouvrieres, 12 Avenue Soeur Rosalie, Box Postale 50, 75621 Paris Cedex 13 France. **Tel** 011 33 1 44089515, telex 240 435 LIVREST. *Continues Masses Ouvrieres.*

ISSN 0824-9547
     CN
CAHIERS DU GRIDEQ. See Business and Economics-Cooperatives.

ISSN 1071-0531
DD 344   US
CALENDAR OF COLLECTIVE BARGAINING, NEW YORK STATE. [Cal. collect. bargain. N.Y. State]. **Added/Corp** New York (State). Dept. of Labor. Division of Research and Statistics. (19??)-. Government Publication. English. One time a year (Dec.). Free on request. New York State Labor Department, 1 Main Street, Room 907, New York NY 11201. **Tel** (718)797-7000. **ED** Lawrence Viger. **Circ:** 1,500 (ctrl).
Desc: Listing of major agreements (those covering 500 or more workers) known to the New York State Department of Labor that expire or are subject to a wage reopening during given calendar year.

ISSN 0381-4130
     CN
CALENDAR OF EXPIRING COLLECTIVE AGREEMENTS. [Cal. expir. collect. agreem.]. **Added/Corp** British Columbia. Dept. of Labour. Research and Planning Branch. British Columbia. Ministry of Labour. Program Services. British Columbia. Ministry of Labour. Policy and Research. British Columbia. Ministry of Labour. Policy and Planning Branch. British Columbia. Ministry of Labour and Consumer Services. Policy and Planning British Columbia. Ministry of Labour and Consumer Services. Policy and Legislation. (1977)-. Periodical. English. One time a year. 10.75Can$. Crown Publications Inc., 521 Fort Street, Victoria British Columbia, V8W 1E7 Canada. **Tel** (604)386-4636, FAX (604)386-0221. *Supersedes British Columbia. Dept. of Labour. Research and Planning Branch. Calendar of Expiring Collective Agreements, 0381-4130.*

LC HD5715.5.P5 N37a
DD 354.5990083/82   PH
CALENDAR YEAR REPORT / NATIONAL MANPOWER AND YOUTH COUNCIL. **Main/Corp** National Manpower and Youth Council (Philippines). (19??)-. English. One time a year. Free. National Manpower and Youth Council, Bookman Building, Quezon Avenue, Quezon City Philippines. **Circ:** 2,000 (ctrl).

ISSN 0008-0802
     US
CALIFORNIA AFL-CIO NEWS. **Added/Corp** California Labor Federation, AFL-CIO. **VAT** California American Federation of Labor, Congress of Industrial Organizations News. (196?)-. Periodical. English. One time a week (except weeks of New Year, Thanksgiving and Christmas). $20.00. California Labor Federation, 417 Montgomery Street, Suite 300, San Francisco CA 94104. **Tel** (415)986-3585. **ED** Floyd Tucker. **Circ:** 3,000. *Continues California Labor Federation, AFL-CIO. Weekly News Letter.*
Desc: Official publication of the California Labor Federation, AFL-CIO.

LC HD5725.C2 A245   **ISSN** 0098-1435
DD 331/.09794   US
CALIFORNIA EMPLOYER. **Added/Corp** California. Employment Development Dept. Vol. 28 No. 2 (Dec. 1974)-. Periodical. English. Four times a year (Mar., June, Sept, Dec.). free on request. Employment Development Department, PO Box 826880, Sacramento CA 94280. **Tel** (916)445-1952. **ED** Kevin M. Callori. *Continues California. Employment Development Dept. Newsletter to Employers.*
Desc: For employers who are subject to the provisions of the California Unemployment Insurance Code.

ISSN 1058-4293
DD 344   US
CALIFORNIA EMPLOYER ADVISOR. [Calif. empl. advis.]. (1991)-. Periodical. English. Twelve times a year. $167.00. California Employer Alert Inc., 2115 4th Street, Berkeley CA 94710.

LC HD7096.U6 C155A   **ISSN** 0091-3545
DD 338.4/336844/009794   US
CALIFORNIA EMPLOYER CONTRIBUTIONS TO THE UNEMPLOYMENT FUND. (19??)-. English. One time a year. California Estimates Group, Estimates Group/MIC 45, 800 Capitol Mall/Room 6099, Sacramento CA 95814.

Business and Economics —Labor

US
Pr Rev.
CALIFORNIA LABOR LETTER. (19??)-. Newsletter. English. Twelve times a year. $298.00. California Labor Letter, PO Box 3651, Manhattan Beach CA 90266. **Tel** (310)798-3868, FAX (310)798-3872. **ED** Joseph C. Beachboard. Index available ($24.00). cum. index. **Circ:** 2,000. available on an online database from BBS.
Desc: News and information on the employment and human resource.

LC HD5725.C2 C23A ISSN 0096-980X
DD 331.1/1/097946 US
CALIFORNIA MANPOWER. Main/Corp California. Employment Development Dept. (19??)-. English. California Employment Development Department, 800 Capitol Mall, Sacramento CA 95814.

LC JK8755 .C35 ISSN 0194-3073
DD 353.9794/0017 US
CALIFORNIA PUBLIC EMPLOYEE RELATIONS : CPER SERIES. [Calif. public empl. relat.]. **Added/Corp** University of California, Berkeley. Institute of Industrial Relations. **VFOAT** CPER Series. (Feb. 1969)-. Trade Publication. English. Six times a year (Feb., Apr., June, Aug., Oct., Dec.). $250.00. University of California Institute of Industrial Relations, Institute of Industrial Relations, Berkeley CA 94720. **Tel** (800)247-6553, FAX (419)281-6883. **ED** B. Schneider. Index available (free). cum. index. **Bk Rev. Circ:** 700 (ctrl).
Desc: Public sector labor relations including negotiations, litigation, arbitration, legislation.

ISSN 0883-9867
US
CALIFORNIA WORKERS' COMPENSATION ENQUIRER. See Insurance.

LC HF5681.L2 I77
TU
CALSMA ISTATISTIKLERI VE ISGUCU MALIYETI. Added/Corp Turkiye Isveren Sendikalar Konfederasyonu. **VFOAT** Labour Statistics and Labour Cost. Turkish (English). **Continues** Isgucu Maliyeti ve Calsma Istatistikleri.

ISSN 0713-1755
DD 354.710083/5 CN
CANADA PENSION PLAN CONTRIBUTION AND UNEMPLOYMENT INSURANCE PREMIUM TABLES. [Can. Pension Plan contrib. Unemploy. Insur. prem. tables]. **VFOAT** Tables de Cotisations au Regime de Pensions du Canada et de Primes d'Assurance-Chomage. Periodical. English (French). Revenue Canada Taxation, 875 Heron Road, Ottawa Ontario K1A 0L8 Canada. **Tel** (613)957-3508, FAX (613)941-0914. **Continues** Canada Pension Plan and Unemployment Insurance Premium Tables, including Instructions to Employers, 0713-1747.

ISSN 1189-7775
DD 331.7/02/097105 CN
CANADA PROSPECTS. [Can. prospects]. **Added/Corp** Canadian Career Information Partnership. Vol. 1, Issue 1 (Fall 1992)-. Periodical. English. One time a year. Free on request. Canadian Career Information Partnership, 140 Promenade, Phase 4 5th Floor, Ottawa Hull K1A 0J9 Canada. **Tel** (818)953-7445.

LC HD5727 .C395 ISSN 0835-8478
DD 331.11/0971/021 CN
CANADA'S MEN. See Business and Economics-Abstracting, Bibliographies and Statistics.

LC HD6283.C2 .C37 ISSN 0835-8494
DD 331.3/98/0971021 CN
CANADA'S OLDER WORKERS. See Business and Economics-Abstracting, Bibliographies and Statistics.

LC WMLC L 83/9245 ISSN 0835-8559
DD 331.88/0971 CN
CANADA'S UNIONIZED WORKERS. See Business and Economics-Abstracting, Bibliographies and Statistics.

LC HD6097 .C37 ISSN 0835-846X
DD 331.4/0971/021 CN
CANADA'S WOMEN. See Business and Economics-Abstracting, Bibliographies and Statistics.

LC HD6276.C29 C36 ISSN 0835-8486
DD 331.3/4/0971021 CN
CANADA'S YOUTH. See Business and Economics-Abstracting, Bibliographies and Statistics.

ISSN 0841-6060
CN
CANADAWORKS! : THE SERVICE EMPLOYEES INTERNATIONAL UNION MAGAZINE. [Canadaworks!]. **VFOAT** Canada Works!; Canada au Travail!. (April/May 1988)-. Periodical. English (French). Irregular. Service Employees International Union / Canada, 1 Credit Union Drive, Toronto Ontario M4A 2S6 Canada. **Tel** (416)752-4073. **Continues** Canadian Service Employee, 0229-3609.

LC HD4932.N6 C25a
DD 331.25/5/0971 US
CANADIAN EMPLOYEE BENEFIT PLANS. Added/Corp International Foundation of Employee Benefit Plans. (1983)-. English. One time a year. International Foundation of Employee Benefit Plans, PO Box 69, 18700 West Bluemound Road, Brookfield WI 53008-0069. **Tel** (414)786-6700 ext.358, FAX (414)786-8670. **Continues** Proceedings of the Annual Canadian Conference of the International Foundation of Employee Benefit Plans, 0148-9178.
Desc: Edited texts of presentations at annual Canadian conference.

ISSN 0826-4899
DD 650.1/4 CN
CANADIAN MOONLIGHTER'S DIGEST. Vol. 1, No. 1 (April 1984)-. Periodical. English. Twelve times a year. $35.00. Quasar Consulting, Suite 6 4620 Manilla Road South, Calgary Alta. T2G 4B7 Canada.

ISSN 0382-8700
DD 331.89/041/35471 CN
CANADIAN PUBLIC SERVICE WORKER'S BULLETIN. Vol. 1 (May 1975)-. Bulletin. English. Six times a year. $1.00. Canadian Public Service Workers Bulletin, 542 MacLaren Street, Ottawa Ontario K1R 5K5 Canada.

ISSN 0890-5878
DD 331 US
CAREER RESOURCE GUIDE. (CAREER RESOURCE GUIDE / NCPA, NATIONAL COLLEGE PLACEMENT ASSOCIATION.). [Career resour. guide]. **Added/Corp** National College Placement Association (U.S.). **VFOAT** NCPA Career Resource Guide. (19??)-. Periodical. English. Twenty-four times a year. $190.00. NCPA Career Resource Guide, PO Box 5112, Mill Valley CA 94942. **Tel** (415)383-9652. **Continues** Inside Line.

LC HD4801 ISSN 1071-0418
DD 331 US
CAREERISM NEWSLETTER. See Physically Impaired.

LC HD6350.C2 C3 ISSN 0008-6843
DD 694/.05 US
CARPENTER. See Building and Construction-Carpentry and Woodwork.

IT
CASI E QUESTIONI DEL LAVORA. (19??)-. Periodical. Italian. Irregular. IPSOA Editore SRL, Casella Postale 12055, Mastrangelo, 20120 Milan Italy. **Tel** 011 39 2 82476248.

ISSN 0008-7815
DD 331 US
CATERING INDUSTRY EMPLOYEE, THE. [Cater. ind. empl.]. **Added/Corp** Hotel Employees & Restaurant Employees International Union. Hotel & Restaurant Employees and Bartenders International Union. Hotel and Restaurant Employees' International Alliance and Bartenders' International League of America. **VFOAT** CIE. (19??)-. Trade Publication. English (French and Spanish). Six times a year. $5.00. Hotel and Restaurant Employees and International Union, 1219 28th Street Northwest, Washington DC 20007-3316. **Tel** (202)393-4373. Index Available, published separately, free-automatically sent. **Continues** Mixer and Server.

PP
CENSUS OF EMPLOYMENT / NATIONAL STATISTICAL OFFICE. (1983)-. Statistical Publication. English. One time a year. k3.00 Papua New Guinea; k3.50 (surface mail), k5.00 (airmail) other. National Statistical Office / New Guinea, PO Wards Strip NCO, Papua New Guinea. **Tel** 011 675 27182 271172, FAX 011 657 255057, telex FINANCE NE 23312.

LC HD7105.35.C2 C47
DD 331.25/2/09714 CN
CESSATIONS DE COTISATION EN ..., LES. (1973)-. French. Regie des Rentes du Quebec, Case Postale 5200, Quebec Quebec G1K 7S9 Canada. **Tel** (418)643-8309.

LC HD5727.M3 M38d
DD 331.11/09741 US
CETA ACTIVITY IN THE STATE OF MAINE, FISCAL YEAR ... / STATE EMPLOYMENT AND TRAINING COUNCIL. Main/Corp Maine. State Employment and Training Council. **VFOAT** C.E.T.A. Activity in the State of Maine, Fiscal Year ... . (19??)-. English. One time a year. Maine State Employment and Training Council, 283 State Street, Augusta ME 04333.

US
CETA TECHNICAL BULLETIN. Added/Corp New York (State). Manpower Services Council. New York (State). Governer's Manpower Planning Secretariat.

VFOAT Technical Bulletin. **VAT** Comprehensive Employment and Training Act Technical Bulletin. (19??)-. Bulletin. English.

FR
CFDT AUJOURD'HUI. VFOAT Aujourd'Hui. No. 1- May/June 1973-. Periodical. French. Six times a year. $85.09. CFDT Presse, 4 boulevard de la Villette, 75955 Paris Cedex 19 France. **Tel** 011 33 1 42038140. **Ind/Abst** LABORDOC.

LC HD8423 .C4318
FR
CFDT MAGAZINE. Main/Corp Confederation Francaise Democratique du Travail. **VAT** Confederation Francaise Democratique du Travail Magazine. No. 1- Dec. 1976-. Periodical. French. 100.00. Cadres CFDT, 47 Avenue Simon Bolivar, 75955 Paris Cedex 19 France. **Tel** 33 1 42024443, FAX 33 1 42024858. **Supersedes** CFDT Syndicalisme Magazine.

LC HD6681.A1 C6
DD 331.80944 FR
CFDT SYNDICALISME HEBDO. Main/Corp Confederation Francaise Democratique du Travail. **VAT** Confederation Francaise Democratique du Travail Syndicalisme Hebdo. No. 1396 (June 1972)-. French. One time a week. 480.97F. CFDT Presse, 4 boulevard de la Villette, 75955 Paris Cedex 19 France. **Tel** 011 33 1 42038140. **Continues** Syndicalisme.
Ind/Abst LABORDOC.

LC HD8051 .A34A ISSN 0160-2934
DD 331/.89/0973 US
CHARACTERISTICS OF MAJOR COLLECTIVE BARGAINING AGREEMENTS. (1974)-. English. US Department of Labor, 200 Constitution Avenue NW, Washington DC 20210. **Tel** (202)219-7316, FAX (202)219-7312.

LC HD4885.U52 C242a ISSN 0146-8863
DD 331.5/5/09794 US
CHARACTERISTICS OF REGISTERED APPRENTICES IN CALIFORNIA. Main/Corp California. Dept. of Industrial Relations. Division of Apprenticeship Standards. (19??)-. English. One time a year. California Department of Industrial Relations, 395 Oyster Pt. Boulevard, San Francisco CA 94101. **Tel** (415)982-4773, FAX (415)557-8964.

LC HD4811 .S65
RU
CHELOVEK I TRUD. (1992)-. Periodical. Russian. Twelve times a year. $159.95. Izdatelstvo Ekonomika, Berezhkovskaia Nab. 6, 121864 Moscow Russia. **(Subscription address:** East View Publications Inc., 3020 Harbor Lane North, Suite 110, Minneapolis MN 55447. **Tel** (800)477-1005, (612)550-0961, FAX (612)559-2931.) **Continues** Sotsialisticheskii Trud, 0037-8216.

ISSN 0162-637X
US
CHEMICAL WORKER, THE. Added/Corp International Chemical Workers Union. Vol. 36, No. 4 (Apr./May 1976)-. Newspaper. English. Twelve times a year. $12.00. International Chemical Workers Union, 1655 West Market Street, Akron OH 44313. **Continues** International Chemical Worker, 0020-6334.
Ind/Abst Work Relat. Abstr.

US
●**CHICAGO WORKERS VOICE THEORETICAL JOURNAL. See** Political Science-Socialism, Communism, Anarchism, Utopianism.

LC HD8039.M4 K63
KO
CHIKCHANGIN. First issue in April 1984-. Periodical. Korean. W3000 single copy. Chikchangin, 511 Socho dong Kangnam ku, Seoul 135 Korea.

LC HD6228 .C5 ISSN 1060-6661
DD 331 US
CHILD LABOR MONITOR. (CHILD LABOR MONITOR : A NATIONAL CONSUMERS LEAGUE PUBLICATION FOR THE CHILD LABOR COALITION.). [Child labor monit.]. **Added/Corp** National Consumers League. Child Labor Coalition. Vol. 1, No. 1 (Fall 1991)-. Newsletter. English. Three times a year. $25.00. National Consumers League, 1701 K Street Northwest, Suite 1200, Washington DC 20006. **Tel** (202)835-3323, FAX (202)835-0747. **ED** Darlene Adkins. **Bk Rev. Circ:** 3,000.
Desc: Focus on the problems and trends in the state, federal and international child labor issues.

DD 331/.0973 312/.92 US
CHILDREN OF WORKING MOTHERS. (19??)-. Government Publication. English. US Department of Labor / Bureau of Labor Statistics, 441 G Street Northwest, Washington DC 20212. **Tel** (202)606-7800, FAX (202)606-7797.

Business and Economics —Labor

CHILTON'S LABOR GUIDE MANUAL.
ISSN 1060-443X
US
(1992)-. Periodical. English. Every 2 years. $115.00 (single issue). Chilton Book Company, 1 Chilton Way, Radnor PA 19089. **Tel** (610)964-4000, (800)695-1214, FAX (215)964-4273, telex 6851035 CHILTON UW.

CHINA LABOR NOTES. Added/Corp
US
Asian-American Free Labor Institute (U.S.). Issue No. 1 (Feb. 1990)-Issue No. 11 (Dec. 1990)-Vol. 2, No. 1 (Jan. 1991)-. Periodical. English. Twelve times a year. Asian-American Free Labor Institute, 1125 15th Street NW, Suite 401, Washington DC 20005-2707.

LC HD5077 .A35h

CHINGIN HIKIAGE TO NO JITTAI NI KANSURU CHOSA KEKKA HOKOKUSHO. Main/Corp Japan. Rodosho.
JA
Roseikyoku. (19??)-. Periodical. Japanese. Rodosho Roseikyoku, 3-1 Otemachi 1 Chiyoda-ku, Tokyo 100 Japan.

LC HD5077 .C449

CHINGIN KENTO SHIRYO. (1967)-. Periodical.
JA
Japanese. ¥2300. Nihon Horei Yoshiki Hambaisho, 20-15-101 Shinbashi 2-chome Minato-ku, Tokyo 105 Japan.

LC HD7057 .C46

CHINGIN KETTEI NO TAME NO BUKKA TO SEIKEIHI SHIRYO. See Finance.
JA

LC HD5077 .C4538

CHINGIN ROMU SORAN. Added/Corp Shukan
JA
Toyo Keizai. (1979)-. Periodical. Japanese. ¥5000. Toyo Keizai Shimpo Sha, 1-2-1 Nihombashi Hongoku-cho, Chuo-ku Tokyo 103 Japan. **Tel** (03)3246-5470. **Continues** Chingin Soran.

LC HD4811 .C5

CHINGIN SHIKI HO. Added/Corp Seikei
JA
Kenkyujo. (1973)-. Periodical. Japanese. ¥9800. Seikei Kenkyujo, 1-4 Nihonbashi Honcho, Chuo-ku Tokyo 103 Japan.

LC HD5077.Z9 A332a

CHUSHO KIGYO NO CHINGIN JIJO.
JA
Main/Corp Aichi-Ken (Japan). Rodo Keizai Chosashitsu. (19??)-. Periodical. Japanese. Rodo Keizai Chosashitsu, 1-2 Sannomaru 3-chome, Naka-ku 460, Nagoya Japan.

DD 331/.06/071
ISSN 0710-555X
CN
CIRA NEWSLETTER. [CIRA newsl.]. **Main/Corp**
Canadian Industrial Relations Association. **VFOAT** Bulletin de l'ARCI. **VAT** Canadian Industrial Relations Association Newsletter; Bulletin de l'Association Canadienne des Relations Industrielles. (197?)-. Newsletter. English (French). Canadian Industrial Relations Association, PO Box 5050, Saint John New Brunswick E2L 4L5 Canada.

LC HA1631.A33 HD5061.6

CIST LICNI DOHODAK PO RADNIKU ZA ODREENA ZANIMANJA. VFOAT Net Personal
YU
Income per Worker by Occupations. Serbo-Croatian (Roman). 100.00. Savezni Zavod za Statistiku, Kneza Milosa 20, Belgrad Yugoslavia.

US
CITY EMPLOYMENT. See Public Administration-Civil Service.

LC JQ3092.Z1 C58
ISSN 0331-085X
DD 331.88/11/3546690005
NR
CIVIL SERVANT, THE. See Public Administration-Civil Service.

LC HD5725.N6 N46b
ISSN 0145-4137
DD 331.12/5/09789021
US
CIVILIAN LABOR FORCE, EMPLOYMENT, UNEMPLOYMENT AND UNEMPLOYMENT RATE. Added/Corp New
Mexico. Employment Security Dept. Research and Statistics Section. New Mexico. Employment Security Commission. Research and Statistics Section. (19??)-. English. Department of Labor / Albuquerque / PO Box 1928, Bureau of Economic Research, Albuquerque NM 87103. **Tel** (505)841-8645.

LC KF3362.7 .L3
ISSN 0147-7250
DD 344/.73/018902648
US
CLASSIFIED INDEX OF DISPOSITIONS OF ULP CHARGES BY THE GENERAL COUNSEL OF THE NATIONAL LABOR RELATIONS BOARD. Added/Corp United
States. National Labor Relations Board. Office of the General Counsel. **VFOAT** Classified Index of Dispositions of ULP Charges. **VAT** Classified Index of Dispositions of Unfair Labor Practices Charges by the General Counsel of the National Labor Relations Board. (Dec. 1975)-. English. Irregular. Superintendent of Documents, US Government Printing Office, Washington DC 20402. **Tel** (202)275-3328, FAX (202)786-2377.

LC HD6530.5 .A18
DD 331.88/098
VE
CLAT NEWS. Added/Corp Central Latinoamericana de Trabajadores. No. 1 (Apr. 1984)-. Periodical. English. Four times a year. CLAT News, CLAT Bureau, 661 Caracus, 1010-A Venezuela.
Ind/Abst Hum. Rights Intern. Rep.

DD 331
ISSN 0257-7151
US
CLAT REPORT. (CLAT REPORT / CENTRAL LATINOAMERICANA DE TRABAJADORES.). [CLAT rep.]. **Added/Corp** Central Latinoamericana de Trabajadores. U.S. Office. **VAT** Central Latinoamericana de Trabajadores Report. No. 1 (Aug. 1984)-. Periodical. English. Four times a year. $5.00. Jose Prince, PO Box 39, Jackson Heights Station, Flushing NY 11372-0039. **Continues** CLAT Newsletter, 0254-9530.
Ind/Abst Hum. Rights Intern. Rep.

DD 331.88/0971/05
ISSN 0848-7448
CN
CEASED
CLC TODAY. [CLC today]. **Added/Corp** Canadian Labour Congress. **VFOAT** Canadian Labour Congress Today; CTC Aujourd'Hui. (Aug. 1990)-(April/May 1993). Periodical. English (French). Canadian Labour Congress, 2841 Riverside Drive, Ottawa Ontario K1V 8X7 Canada. **Tel** (613)521-3400, FAX (613)053-4750, telex 060313.
Ind/Abst Can. Period. Index (199?-); Work Relat. Abstr.

ISSN 0199-8919
US
CLUW NEWS. Added/Corp Coalition of Labor Union Women (U.S.). **VFOAT** C.L.U.W. News. **VAT** Coalition of Labor Union Women News. Vol. 1, No. 1 (Winter 1975)-. Periodical. English. Six times a year. $20.00. Coalition of Labor Union Women, 15 Union Square, New York NY 10003. **Tel** (212)242-0700.

ISSN 0891-0723
US
CO-WORKER. (CO-WORKER / TENNESSEE STATE EMPLOYEES ASSOCIATION.). **VFOAT**
Coworker. Vol. 2, No. 7 (Oct. 1986)-. Periodical. English. Twelve times a year. $5.00 members; $6.50 other. Tennessee State Employee Association, 627 Woodland Street, Nashville TN 37206. **Tel** (615)256-4533. **ED** Nina J Wood. **Circ:** 20,000. available in microform. **Continues** Employee, 0747-427X.

DD 331.88/06/0718
ISSN 1186-8325
CN
COALITION OF UNIONS NEWSLETTER.
[Coalit. Union newsl.]. **Added/Corp** Coalition of Unions. Vol. 1, No. 1 (June 1991)-. Newsletter. English. Four times a year. Free to union locals affiliated with member-unions in the Coalition. Coalition of Unions, PO Box 6144, St. John's Newfoundland A1C 5X8 Canada.

LC K
DD 344.714/018/0263
ISSN 0836-3935
CN
CODE DU TRAVAIL DU QUEBEC ET REGLEMENTS. (CODE DU TRAVAIL DU QUEBEC ET REGLEMENTS : L.R.Q. 1977, C-27.). [Code trav. Que. reglem.]. **Main/Corp** Quebec (Province). **VFOAT**
Code du Travail du Quebec; Code du Travail du Quebec et Reglements Avec References Analogiques; Code du Travail du Quebec et Reglements Avec Renvois Analogiques; Quebec Labour Code. (19??)-. French (English). Twelve times a year. 395.00Can$. Canadian Research & Publication Center, 33 Racine Street, Farnham Quebec J2N 3A3 Canada. **Tel** (514)293-5377, (514)866-7148.

UK
COHSE JOURNAL. Vol. 1, Issue 1 (May/June 1989)-. Periodical. English. Twelve times a year. Confederation of Health Services Employees, Glen High Street, Banstead Surrey United Kingdom. **Continues** Health Services.

DD 331.88/113520714281
ISSN 0227-6046
CN
CEASED
COL BLANC. [Col blanc]. Vol. 1, No. 1, (April 1967)-(199?). Periodical. French. Syndicat des Fonctionnaires Municipaux de Montreal, 429 Est rue de la Gauchetiere, Montreal Quebec H2L 2M1 Canada. **Absorbed** Quat. Centre Social des Fonctionnaires Municipaux de Montreal, 0712-6158.

LC HD8361 .R48
DD 331/.0987/05
VE
COLECCION RELACIONES DE TRABAJO. Added/Corp Asociacion de Relaciones de Trabajo (Venezuela). **VFOAT** Relaciones de Trabajo. No. 12/13 (Nov. 1988-May 1989)-. Periodical. Spanish. Irregular. $35.00. Hector Lucena Assoc. Relaciones, Apartado 5110 Naguanagua, Carabobo 2005 Venezuela. **Tel** 011 58 41 674348, 223463. **Continues** Revista Relaciones de Trabajo.

DD 331.89/0413711
ISSN 0710-5193
CN
COLLECTIVE BARGAINING HANDBOOK. [Collect. bargain. handb.]. **Main/Corp**
British Columbia Teachers' Federation. (1958)-. English. One time a year. Collective Bargaining Handbook Teachers' Federation, 105-2235 Burrard Street, Vancouver British Columbia V6J 3H9 Canada. Index available. ctrl circ.

DD 331.89/09715/1
ISSN 1193-3437
CN
COLLECTIVE BARGAINING IN NEW BRUNSWICK. (COLLECTIVE BARGAINING IN NEW BRUNSWICK / DEPARTMENT OF ADVANCED EDUCATION AND LABOUR, LABOUR MARKET ANALYSIS BRANCH.). [Collect. bargain. N.B.].
Added/Corp New Brunswick. Labour Market Analysis Branch. Vol. 1, No. 1 (1992)-. Periodical. English. Four times a year (Mar., Apr., July, November). 12.01Can$. Labour Market Analysis Branch, PO Box 6000, Department of Adv Educ Labour, Fredericton NB E3B 5H1 Canada. **ED** Gerald Kitchen. Index available. **Circ:** 200. **Formed by the union of** Arbitration Awards-- in New Brunswick., 0833-7012 **and** Negotiated Settlements-- in New Brunswick., 0713-4029.
Desc: Report which contains summaries of collective bargaining settlements and grievance arbitration awards.

LC HD6521 .C65a
ISSN 0010-0803
DD 331.89/0971/05
CN
COLLECTIVE BARGAINING REVIEW.
Added/Corp Canada. Labour Data Branch. Collective Bargaining Division. Canada. Dept. of Labour. Collective Bargaining Section. Canada. Dept. of Labour. Collective Bargaining Division. Canada. Labour Canada.Canada. Bureau of Labour Information. (Dec. 1965)-. Periodical. English. Twelve times a year. Canada Communication Group Publishers, Order Processing, Ottawa Ontario K1A 0S9 Canada. **Tel** (819)956-4800, (819)956-4802.

LC HD8053.N7 A27
US
COLLECTIVE BARGAINING SETTLEMENTS IN NEW YORK STATE.
Main/Corp New York (State). Dept. of Labor. Division of Research and Statistics. (19??)-. English. Four times a year (Feb., May, Aug., Nov.). $75.00. New York State Department of Labor, 1 Main Street Room 966, Coll Bargain, Brooklyn NY 11201. **Tel** (718)797-7722, FAX (718)797-7704. **ED** Lawrence Viger. **Circ:** 600.
Desc: Presents summaries of wage and wage-related changes in recent collective bargaining agreements affecting 100 or more workers and fringe benefit changes involving 1,000 or more workers in New York State.

DD 331.809713
ISSN 0829-7800
CN
COLLECTIVE BARGAINING SETTLEMENTS IN ONTARIO (1985).
[Collect. bargain. settl. Ont. 1985]. (1985)-. Periodical. English. Twelve times a year. Free on request. Ontario Ministry of Labour, 400 University Avenue / 11th Floor, Toronto Ontario M7A 1T7 Canada. **Tel** (416)326-1260, 326-7837. **Continues** Collective Bargaining Settlements and Negotiations in Ontario, 0702-0317.

LC HD6278.U5 A23A
ISSN 0361-5057
DD 331.7/61
US
COLLEGE RECRUITING REPORT.
Main/Corp Abbott, Langer & Associates. English. One time a year. $35.00. Abbott Langer & Associates, 548 First Street, Department Z, Crete IL 60417. **Tel** (708)672-4200.

LC HD4976.C57 C57
ISSN 0275-942X
DD 331.2/97881
US
COLORADO WEST SALARY SURVEY.
(COLORADO WEST SALARY SURVEY / PREPARED BY MOUNTAIN STATES EMPLOYERS COUNCIL, INC.). **VFOAT** Survey, Colorado West. (19??)-. English. One time a year. Mountain States Employers Council, 1790 Logan Street, PO Box 539, Denver CO 80201.

AT
COMMON CAUSE. See Mines and Mining.

DD 331.7/95/097124
ISSN 0838-8032
CN
COMMON GROUND (REGINA). (COMMON GROUND.). [Common ground]. **Added/Corp**
Saskatchewan Government Employees' Union. **VFOAT** U-Name-It; Union Matters. Vol. 1, No. 1 (Dec. 1986)-. Periodical. English. Saskatchewan Government Employees' Union, 1440 Broadway Avenue, Regina Saskatchewan S4P 1E2 Canada. **Continues** Dome, 0319-8588.

DD 354/.718/00173
ISSN 0707-9133
CN
COMMUNICATOR (ST. JOHN'S). See Public Administration.

LC HF5382.5.U5 C65 ISSN 0195-1157
DD 331 US
COMMUNITY JOBS. [Community jobs]. **Added/Corp** Community Careers Resource Center. Youth Project. (197?)-. Periodical. English. Twelve times a year. $69.00. Access Networking Public International, 30 Irving Place, New York NY 10005. **Tel** (212)475-1199, FAX (212)475-1001. **ED** Jim Clark. **Bk Rev**, (Qty: 12). **Ad Acc, Adv Mgr:** Jim Clark, **Tel** (212)475-1001. **Circ:** 15,000 (ctrl).
Desc: Job listings with non-profit organizations around the country.
Ind/Abst Altern. Press Index (-199?).

CN
COMPARATIVE INDUSTRIAL RELATIONS NEWSLETTER. No. 4 (Jan. 1992)-. Newsletter. English. Two times a year. $20.00 (individuals), $35.00 (institutions). Comparative Industrial Relations Newsletter, McGroote School of Business, McMaster University, Hamilton Ontario L8S 4C7 Canada. **Tel** (905)525-9140, FAX (905)527-0100. **ED** Roy J. Adams. ***Continues** Adams, Roy J. Comparative IR Newsletter.*
Desc: Strives to foster cross disciplinary communication among those interested in comparative, international labour issues.

LC Q149.U5 C65 ISSN 0743-7692
DD 331.2/815/0973 US
COMPARISON OF COMPENSATION PAID SCIENTISTS AND ENGINEERS IN RESEARCH AND DEVELOPMENT. (19??)-. English. One time a year. National Technical Information Service - NTIS, Room 2027S, 5285 Port Royal Road, Springfield VA 22161. **Tel** (703)487-4630, (703)487-4660, (703)487-4650, FAX (703)321-8547, telex 89-9405. available on microfiche (Vols. for (1982-) distributed to depository libraries).

LC HD4973 .C65 ISSN 0886-3687
DD 331.2/973 US
CCC
COMPENSATION AND BENEFITS REVIEW. [Compens. benefits rev.]. **Added/Corp** American Management Association. Periodicals Division. **VAT** Compensation & Benefits Review. Vol. 17, No. 3 (July/Aug. 1985)-. Periodical. English. Six times a year. $133.00. American Management Association, 135 West 50th Street, New York NY 10020-1201. **Tel** (212)586-8100, (212)903-8375 (periodicals), FAX (212)903-8168, (212)903-8083 (periodicals). **(Subscription address:** American Management Association, PO Box 408, Saranac Lake NY 12983. **Tel** (800)262-9699, FAX (518)891-1500.**) ED** Don Bohl. Index available (bound in last issue). available on microfilm and microfiche from University Microfilms International (UMI); available on an online database (file 648/Full-Text) from DIALOG. Documents available from BLDSC, The UnCover Company, SWETS, CASDDS. ***Continues** Compensation Review, 0010-4248.*
Desc: Original features, digests, summaries or articles related to the compensation and benefits field, news briefs, and occasional book reviews. Edited for compensation and benefits administrators and executives with responsibility for compensation and benefits practices.
Ind/Abst Account. Art.; Anbar Account. Finan. Abstr. [Full Txt.]; Anbar Mark. Distr. Abstr. [Full Txt.]; Anbar Top Manage. Abstr. [Full Txt.]; Bus. ASAP (1990-) [Full Txt.]; Bus. Index (1985-); Bus. Period. Index; Gen. BusinessFile (1985-); Gen. Period. Index (1985-); INFO-SOUTH Abstr.; Mag. Search; Manage. Bibliogr. Rev.; Manage. Contents; MasterFile FullTEXT (July 1993-) [Full Txt.]; Oper. Prod. Manage. Abstr. [Full Txt.]; Person. Train. Abstr. [Full Txt.]; Person. Manage. Abstr.; Trade Ind. ASAP [Full Txt.]; Trade Ind. Index [Full Txt.]; UMI ABI/Inform--Bus. Period. Ondisc [Full Txt.]; Wilson Bus. Abstr.; Women Manage. Rev. [Full Txt.]; Work Relat. Abstr.

LC HD4973 .A275 ISSN 1059-0722
DD 331 US
COMPENSATION AND WORKING CONDITIONS. (COMPENSATION AND WORKING CONDITIONS : CWC / U.S. DEPARTMENT OF LABOR, BUREAU OF LABOR STATISTICS.). [Compens. work. cond.]. **Added/Corp** United States. Bureau of Labor Statistics. Office of Compensation and Working Conditions. **VFOAT** CWC. Vol. 43, No. 5 (May 1991)-. Government Publication. English. Twelve times a year. $33.00. US Department of Labor, 200 Constitution Avenue NW, Washington DC 20210. **Tel** (202)219-7316, FAX (202)219-7312. **(Subscription address:** Superintendent of Documents, US Government Printing Office, Washington DC 20402. **)** available on microfilm and microfiche from University Microfilms International (UMI). Documents available from UMI Article Clearinghouse, Documents on Demand. ***Continues** Current Wage Developments, 0192-8163.*
Desc: Presents information on wage and benefit changes resulting from collective bargaining settlements and unilateral management decisions; statistical summaries; special reports on wage trends, most aspects of employee benefits, and various aspects of collective bargaining.
Ind/Abst Am. Stat. Index; Newsp. Period. Abstr. (1992-).

LC HD7102.Z3 Z35A
DD 368.4/1/0096894 ZA
COMPENSATION MIRROR. Main/Corp Zambia. Workmen's Compensation Fund Control Board. No. 1 (July 1973)-. English. Six times a year. Workmen's Compensation Board, PO Box 1534, Ndola Zambia.

LC JS361 .C65 ISSN 0732-5282
DD 352/.005123/0973 US
COMPENSATION (WASHINGTON, D.C. : 1982). (COMPENSATION.). **Added/Corp** International City Management Association. Vol. 1 (1982)-. Periodical. English. One time a year. $180.00. International City Management Association, 777 North Capitol Street NE, Suite 500, Washington DC 20002. **Tel** (202)289-4262, (800)745-8780, FAX (202)962-3500. **(Subscription address:** International City Management Association, PO Box 2011, Annapolis Junction MD 20701. **) ED** Ross Hoff. **Circ:** 800.
Desc: Data on the salaries of top managers and department heads in municipalities and counties throughout the country.

LC HD4975 .C582 ISSN 0147-1570
DD 331.2/973 US
CCC
CEASED
COMPFLASH. [Comp flash]. **Added/Corp** Amacom. (19??)-(Dec. 1995). Periodical. English. American Management Association, 135 West 50th Street, New York NY 10020-1201. **Tel** (212)586-8100, (212)903-8375 (periodicals), FAX (212)903-8168, (212)903-8083 (periodicals). **(Subscription address:** American Management Association, PO Box 408, Saranac Lake NY 12983. **Tel** (800)262-9699, FAX (518)891-1500.**) ED** Don Bohl. available on microfilm from University Microfilms International (UMI).
Desc: News items on developments in compensations and benefits. Reports on surveys (some gratis), legislation and developments affecting compensation and employee benefits for executives, salaried employees, and hourly workers.

LC HD7106.U5 C59a ISSN 0274-8304
DD 658.32/53/0973 US
COMPLIANCE GUIDE FOR PLAN ADMINISTRATORS. [Compliance guide plan adm.]. **Main/Corp** Commerce Clearing House. **Added/Corp** Commerce Clearing House. CCH Compliance Guide for Plan Administrators. **VFOAT** CCH Compliance Guide for Plan Administrators. No. 1 (April 1, 1976)-. Periodical. English. Twenty-six times a year. Commerce Clearing House Inc., 4025 West Peterson Avenue, Chicago IL 60646-6085. **Tel** (312)583-8500, FAX (708)940-4600. **ED** Daniel Newquist. Index available. cum. index.
Desc: Emphasizes ERISA reporting, disclosure and fiduciary liability rules for employee benefit, self-employed and IRA plans by type.

LC HD5725.A4 A18a
DD 331.11/09798 US
COMPREHENSIVE EMPLOYMENT AND TRAINING PLAN, ANNUAL PLAN. BALANCE OF STATE / STATE OF ALASKA, CETA DIVISION. Main/Corp Alaska. CETA Division. **Added/Corp** Alaska. CETA Division. Balance of State. (19??)-. English. One time a year. Alaska CETA Division, CETA Division, Juneau AK 99811.
Desc: Information on manpower policies.

LC HD5725.A4 A59a
DD 331.11/09798 US
COMPREHENSIVE EMPLOYMENT & TRAINING PROGRAMS IN ALASKA. Main/Corp Alaska. State Manpower Services Council. **Added/Corp** Alaska. CETA Division. (19??)-. English. One time a year. Alaska CETA Division, Department of Community and Regional Affairs, Pouch BC, Juneau AK 99811.

LC HD5725.N3 N45a ISSN 0091-066X
DD 331.1/09793 US
COMPREHENSIVE MANPOWER PLAN. Main/Corp Nevada Manpower Planning Council. (19??)-. English. One time a year. Nevada Manpower Planning Council, Carson City NV 89710.

LC HD5725.S8 S63A ISSN 0148-7140
DD 331.1/1/09783 US
COMPREHENSIVE MANPOWER PLAN AND GRANT APPLICATION. (COMPREHENSIVE MANPOWER PLAN AND GRANT APPLICATION - (SOUTH DAKOTA).). **Main/Corp** South Dakota. Dept. of Labor. (19??)-. English. One time a year. South Dakota Department of Labor, Capital Lake Plaza, 700 Governors Drive, Pierre SD 57501.

LC HD8109.Q4 C653 ISSN 0228-0922
DD 331.2/09714 CN
CONDITIONS DE TRAVAIL CONTENUES DANS LES CONVENTIONS COLLECTIVES AU QUEBEC. SECTION 1, ENSEMBLE DES SECTEURS. [Cond. trav. contenues conv. collect. Que.]. **VFOAT** Ensemble des Secteurs. 1979-. Statistical Publication. French. One time a year. Ministere du Travail et de la Main-d'Oeuvre, 425 rue St. Amable, Quebec Quebec G1R 4Z1 Canada.

LC HD7703 .B54
FR
CONDITIONS DE TRAVAIL / MINISTERE DU TRAVAIL, DE L'EMPLOI ET DE LA FORMATION PROFESSIONNELLE, CONSEIL SUPERIEUR DE LA PREVENTION DES RISQUES PROFESSIONNELS. French. One time a year. Documentation Francaise, 29 quai Voltaire, 75344 Paris Cedex 7 France. **Tel** 011 33 1 40157000, FAX 011 33 1 40157230, telex 204 826 DOCFRAN. ***Continues** Bilan en ... des Conditions de Travail, 0762-252X.*

LC HD4811 .C728 ISSN 0257-3512
DD 331.2/05 SZ
CCC
CEASED
CONDITIONS OF WORK DIGEST. Added/Corp International Labour Office. Vol. 5, No. 1 (1986)-(1995). Periodical. English. International Labour Office - ILO, Publications Sales Service, CH-1211 Geneva 22 Switzerland. **Tel** 011 41 22 7996111, FAX 011 41 22 7986253, telex 415 647 ilo ch. **(Subscription address:** International Labour Office / Washington, DC, 1828 L Street Northwest, Suite 801, Washington DC 20036. **Tel** (202)653-7652.**) *Continues** Conditions of Work, A Cumulative Digest, 0252-8088.*
Desc: Contains factual data on specific topics in the field of conditions of work and quality of working life. Notes on research in progress, annotated bibliographies, guides to information sources.
Ind/Abst Curr. Cit.; Int. Labour Doc.; LABORDOC; PAIS Int. Print.

ISSN 0319-2482
CN
CONGRES DES RELATIONS INDUSTRIELLES DE L'UNIVERSITE LAVAL. [Congr. relat. ind. Univ. Laval]. **Main/Corp** Congres des Relations Industrielles de l'Universite Laval. **VFOAT** Rapport. 1st (1946)-. Monographic series. French. One time a year. Price varies per volume. Presses de l'Universite Laval, CP 2447 Avenue de la Medicine, Saint Foy Quebec G1K 7P4 Canada. **Tel** (418)656-5106, (418)656-2590.
Ind/Abst Can. Period. Index (19??-19??).

ISSN 0414-5798
DD 331 US
CONNECTICUT LABOR SITUATION. Added/Corp Connecticut. Employment Security Division. (19??)-. Periodical. English. Six times a year. Connecticut Labor Department, 200 Folly Brook Boulevard, Wethersfield CT 06109. **Tel** (203)566-4380. ***Supersedes** Connecticut Area Labor Trends in Employment and Unemployment; **Absorbed** Connecticut Economic Indicators and Employment, Wages, Hours in Connecticut.*

ISSN 0010-6348
IT
CONQUISTE DEL LAVORO. Added/Corp Confederazione Italiana Sindacati Lavoratori. (Dec. 24, 1948)-. Periodical. Italian. One time a week. L204380. Conquiste del Lavoro, Via Livenza 7, 00198 Rome Italy. **Tel** 011 39 6 8546742 or, 8546743, FAX 011 39 6 8415365.

ISSN 0228-1511
DD 331.7/14/060714 CN
CONSEIL DU PATRONAT DU QUEBEC. (1973)-. English (French). One time a year. Free. Conseil du Patronat du Quebec, Suite 606/2075 rue Universite, Montreal Quebec H3A 2L1 Canada. **Tel** (514)288-5161.

ISSN 0318-4196
DD 331.88/09713 CN
CONSTITUTION - ONTARIO FEDERATION OF LABOUR. [Const. - Ont. Fed. Labour]. **Main/Corp** Ontario Federation of Labour. (1957)-. Periodical. English. Irregular. Free. Ontario Federation of Labour, 15 Gervais Drive, Suite 202, Don Mills Ontario M3C 1Y8 Canada. **Tel** (905)441-2731.

ISSN 0161-990X
DD 331 US
CONSTRUCTION LABOR NEWS. [Constr. labor news]. **VFOAT** CLN. Vol. 1 (June 30, 1978)-. Periodical. English. Twenty-four times a year. $48.00. Construction Labor News, 2102 Almaden Road/#303, San Jose CA 95125. **Tel** (408)265-6280. **ED** Mindy Dravis-Gonzales. **Ad Acc. Circ:** 17,000 (ctrl). available on diskette from MACPHUS.
Desc: Publishes building trades, union news, columns by labor leaders, politicians, and pictures.

Business and Economics —Labor

LC HD4966.B92 U423A ISSN 0272-8478
DD 331.2/824/0973 US
CONSTRUCTION LABOR RATE TRENDS AND OUTLOOK. Main/Corp Construction Labor Research Council (U.S.). (19??)-. English. Construction Labor Research Council, Suite 206/1101 15th Street NW, Washington DC 20005.

LC HD8039.B892 U63 ISSN 0010-6836
DD 331.7/624/0973 US
CCC
CONSTRUCTION LABOR REPORT. [Constr. labor rep.]. **Added/Corp** Bureau of National Affairs (Washington, D.C.). (19??)-. Trade Publication. English. One time a week. $855.00. Bureau of National Affairs Inc., 9435 Key West Avenue, Rockville MD 20850. **Tel** (800)372-1033, (301)258-1033, FAX (301)948-5823. **ED** Anthony A Harris. available on an online database from Human Resources Information Network. **Continues** BNA's Construction Labor Report.
Desc: An information service that covers union-management relations in the construction industry, reporting on significant legislative, judicial, economic, management and union developments.

LC Z
DD 016.64 US
CONSUMER PRICE INDEX (NEWS). See Business and Economics-Abstracting, Bibliographies and Statistics.

ISSN 0703-5780
DD 331.88/09714 CN
CONTACT (MONTREAL. 1977). (CONTACT.). **Added/Corp** Federation des Professionnelles Salaries et des Cadres du Quebec. Vol. 1 (Jan. 1977)-. Periodical. French. Irregular. Free. Federation Des Professionnelles Salaries Et Des Cadres Du Quebec, 1001 rue St-Denis, Montreal Quebec H2X 3J1 Canada. ctrl circ. **Supersedes** Federation des Professionnelles Salaries et des Cadres du Quebec. Bulletin d'Information, 0703-5772.

ISSN 1065-3406
DD 658 US
CCC
CONTINUOUS JOURNEY. See Business and Economics-Management.

LC HD7096.U6 S75 ISSN 0361-9400
DD 368.4/4/008 US
CONTINUOUS WAGE AND BENEFIT HISTORY. **Added/Corp** South Dakota. Employment Security Division. South Dakota. Employment Security Dept. (19??)-. English. South Dakota Department of Manpower Affairs, Box 730, Aberdeen SD 57401. **Continues** Continuous Wage and Benefit History Report in Unemployment Insurance.

IT
CONTRATTAZIONE COLLETTIVA. (19??)-. Periodical. Italian. Four times a year. IPSOA Editore SRL, Casella Postale 12055, Mastrangelo, 20120 Milan Italy. **Tel** 011 39 2 82476248. Index available (Included).

IT
CONTRATTI : PRINCIPI FORMULE PROCEDURE, I. (19??)-. Periodical. Italian. Irregular. L165000 Italy; L330000 other. IPSOA Editore SRL, Casella Postale 12055, Mastrangelo, 20120 Milan Italy. **Tel** 011 39 2 82476248. Index available (Included).

LC HD7338.A3 P27A
DD 338.4/7/69080944 FR
CONTRIBUTION DES EMPLOYEURS A L'EFFORT DE CONSTRUCTION. Main/Corp Chambre de Commerce et d'Industrie de Paris. (19??)-. French. Chambre de Commerce et d'Industrie de Paris, 67 boulevard de Courcelles, Paris France.

LC HD4965.3.M39 C66 ISSN 0742-5848
DD 331.2/813811 US
CONVENIENCE STORE INDUSTRY'S COMPENSATION SURVEY REPORT FOR ..., THE. English. National Association of Convenience Stores, 1605 King Street, Alexandria VA 22314. **Tel** (703)684-3600.

ISSN 0380-7789
DD 331.88/11/35471 CN
CONVENTION REPORT - C U P E. Main/Corp Canadian Union of Public Employees. Convention. **VFOAT** Rapport du Congres. 1973-. English (French). Every 2 years. Free. Canadian Union of Public Employees, 233 Gilmour Street/Suite 800, Ottawa Ontario K0P 0P5 Canada. **Tel** (613)237-1590. ctrl circ. **Supersedes** Canadian Union of Public Employees. Proceedings, 0380-7770.

DD 331.89/04135471 CN
CONVENTION REPORT / CANADA EMPLOYMENT AND IMMIGRATION UNION. Main/Corp Canada Employment and Immigration Union. National Convention. 2nd (Aug. 10/11/12/13, 1981)-. English. Every 3 years. Canada Employment and Immigration Union, 1004-233 Gilmour, Ottawa Ontario K2P 0P2 Canada. **Continues** Canadian Employment and Immigration Union. National Convention. Report of the National Convention.

FR
CONVENTIONS COLLECTIVES UIC. (19??)-. French. Irregular. $64.52. Societe de Gestion UIC, 65 Avenue Marceau, 75116 Paris France. **Tel** 011 33 1 47203826.

FR
CONVENTIONS COLLECTIVES VRP. (19??)-. French. Irregular. 20.00F. Direction des Journaux Officiels, 26 rue Desaix, 75727 Paris Cedex 15 France. **Tel** 011 33 1 40587500.

US
CONVOY. **Added/Corp** Teamsters for a Democratic Union. **VFOAT** Convoy: Voice of Teamsters for a Democratic Union. (19??)-. Periodical. English. Ten times a year. $50.00. Teamsters for a Democratic Union, PO Box 10128, Detroit MI 48210. **Tel** (313)842-2600. **ED** Marilyn Penttinen. **Circ:** 60,000.
Desc: Contains views of the teamster union, with information on policy and laws, a how-to column and Stewards Section.

LC HD
DD 331 US
●**CORPORATE UNIVERSITY REVIEW.** (1995)-. Trade Publication. English. Enterprise Communications Inc., 1165 Northchase Parkway, Suite 350, Marietta GA 30067. **Tel** (404)988-9558, FAX (404)859-9166. **Continues** Workforce Training News, 1078-8638.

ISSN 1182-610X
DD 368.4/1/00971 CN
CORPUS WORKERS' COMPENSATION HANDBOOK. See Insurance.

LC HC131 .C64 ISSN 0186-1840
MX
COTIDIANO, EL. **Added/Corp** Universidad Autonoma Metropolitana. Unidad Azcapotzalco. Division de Ciencias Sociales y Humanidades. (19??)-. Periodical. Spanish. Six times a year. $40.00. Universidad Autonoma Metropolitana, Av San Pablo 180 EDF H 3ER PSO, Azcapotzalco 02200 Mexico. **Tel** 011 52 5 3825000 ext. 280 & 285.
Ind/Abst Hisp. Am. Period. Index, HAPI.

US
COUNTRY LABOR MARKET AND ECONOMIC PROFILES. 19??)-. Periodical. English. Research and Analysis Branch, Washington State Employment Security Department, Box 9046, Olympia WA 98507. **Tel** (206)438-4800, FAX (206)438-4846.
Desc: Labor market and economic conditions in each of Washington's counties.

LC HD5725.I6 A25
DD 331.1/1/09772 US
COUNTY EMPLOYMENT PATTERNS. Main/Corp Indiana. Employment Security Division. **Added/Corp** Indiana. Employment Security Division. Research and Statistics Section. Indiana. Labor Market Information and Statistical Services. Indiana. Labor Market Statistics. Indiana. Dept. of Employment & Training Services. Statistical Services. (19??)-. English.

US
COVERED EMPLOYMENT AND WAGES IN SOUTH CAROLINA. **Added/Corp** South Carolina Employment Security Commission. Labor Market Information. (2nd Quarter 1990)-. Periodical. English. One time a year. $10.00. South Carolina Employment Security Commission, 1550 Gadsden Street, PO Box 995, Columbia SC 29202. **Tel** (803)737-2660, FAX (803)737-2642. **Continues** Employment and Wages in South Carolina (Quarterly).

LC HD5725.N6 N46a
DD 331.12/5/09789 US
COVERED EMPLOYMENT AND WAGES : QUARTERLY REPORT / EMPLOYMENT SECURITY COMMISSION OF NEW MEXICO. **Added/Corp** New Mexico. Employment Security Commission. New Mexico. Employment Services Division. New Mexico. Employment Security Dept. New Mexico. Dept. of Labor. (19??)-. Periodical. English. Four times a year. Department of Labor / Albuquerque, PO Box 1928, Bureau of Economic Research, Albuquerque NM 87103. **Tel** (505)841-8645.

US
CPER BULLETIN. Main/Corp California Public Employee Relations Program. Vol. 1 (Jan. 30, 1976)-. Bulletin. English. Twelve times a year. CPER Bulletin, Institute of Industrial Relations, University of California, Berkeley CA 94720.

ISSN 0711-1053
DD 331.88/1762/0971 CN
TITLE CHANGE
CPU JOURNAL (1981). (CPU JOURNAL / SYNDICAT CANADIEN DES TRAVAILLEURS DU PAPIER = CANADIAN PAPERWORKERS UNION.). [CPU j.]. **Added/Corp** Canadian Paperworkers Union. **VFOAT** Journal du SCTP. **VAT** Canadian Paperworkers Union Journal (1981); Journal du SCTP (1981); Journal du Syndicat Canadien des Travailleurs du Papier (1981). Vol. 1, No. 1 (March 1981)-(199?). Periodical. English (French). **Formed by the union of** Intercom (Canadian Paperworkers Union). English, 0229-9402 **and** Intercom (Canadian Paperworkers Union). French, 0229-9410. **Merged with** Connections (Ottawa, Ont.), 0834-9355 **and** Contact (Communications and Electrical Workers of Canada) **to form** CEP Journal (Communications, Energy and Paperworkers Union of Canada), 1196-4057.

SP
CRONICA DE INFORMACION LABORAL. Spanish. $9.00 Spain; $15.06 US and Canada; $11.91 Pan America; $16.11 other. Centro de Estudios Sociales, San Bartolome 7, Barcelona 1 Spain.

MX
CUADERNOS DE CIDAMO. **Added/Corp** Centro de Informacion, Documentacion y Analisis Sobre el Movimiento Obrero Latinoamericano. (1980)-. Periodical. Spanish.
Ind/Abst Hum. Rights Intern. Rep.

LC HD8110.5 .A16
UY
CUADERNOS DE ORIENTACION "ESTUDIAR PARA LUCHAR". SERIE ESTUDIOS E INVESTIGACIONES. **Added/Corp** International Union of Food and Allied Workers' Associations. **VFOAT** Serie Estudios e Investigaciones. No. 1 (1990)-. Monographic series. Spanish. Price varies per volume.

ISSN 1131-8635
SP
CUADERNOS DE RELACIONES LABORALES / ESCUELA DE RELACIONES LABORALES, UNIVERSIDAD COMPLUTENSE DE MADRID. **Added/Corp** Universidad Complutense de Madrid. Escuela de Relaciones Laborales. (1992)-. Periodical. Spanish. Two times a year. 2500ptas. Editorial Complutense, Donoso Cortes 65, Primera Planta, 28015 Madrid Spain. **Tel** 011 34 1 3946372, 011 34 1 3946373, 011 34 1 3946374.

LC HD28 .C84 ISSN 1070-3160
DD 658 US
CULTURAL DIVERSITY AT WORK. [Cult. divers. work]. **Added/Corp** GilDeane Group. Vol. 4, No. 1 (Sept. 1991)-. Periodical. English. Six times a year (bimonthly). $84.00. Gildeane Group, 13751 Lake City Way NE, Suite 106, Seattle WA 98125. **Tel** (206)362-0336, FAX (206)363-5028. **Continues** Training & Culture Newsletter, 1043-1322.
Desc: Examines management and cross-cultural orientation.

ISSN 1047-1065
DD 331 US
CURRENT DEFERRALS. (Nov. 1989)-. Periodical. English. Four times a year (subscription includes Asset Base, reference book to this publication). $210.00. Independent Information Service, PO Box 770057, Ocala FL 34477. **Tel** (904)237-4570, FAX (904)237-4577. **ED** Connie Jones. Index available in last issue of volume--attached. cum. index. **Circ:** 1,000.

UK
CURRENT LITERATURE ON OCCUPATIONAL PENSIONS. (19??)-. English. £7.50. **(Subscription address:** Department of Health and Social Security, Baps Distribution Center, Manchester Road, Heywood Lancashire OL10 2PZ United Kingdom. **Tel** 011 44 171 9722000, 011 44 171 9728161, FAX 011 44 171 9723765.)

US
CURRENT POPULATION SURVEY ... ANNUAL DEMOGRAPHIC FILES [COMPUTER FILE]. **Added/Corp** United States. Bureau of the Census. Data User Services Division. (198?)-. Government Publication. English. $150.00. US Department of Commerce / Bureau of the Census, Data User Services Division, Customer Services, Washington DC 20233-0800. **Tel** (301)763-4100. **(Subscription address:** Superintendent of Documents, US Government Printing Office, Washington DC 20402.)
Desc: Provides the usual Current Population Survey (CPS) monthly labor force microdata and, in addition, provides supplemental data on work experience, income, noncash benefits, and migration.

Business and Economics —Labor

CURRENT WAGE DEVELOPMENTS. US TITLE CHANGE
Main/Corp United States. Bureau of Labor Statistics. **Added/Corp** United States. Bureau of Labor Statistics. Monthly Report on Current Wage Developments. No. 1 (Jan. 1948)-(19??). Government Publication. English. Superintendent of Documents, US Government Printing Office, Washington DC 20402. **Tel** (202)275-3328, FAX (202)786-2377. *Continued by Compensation and Working Conditions, 1059-0722.*
Ind/Abst Expand. Acad. Index (1992-).

ISSN 0745-3302
US
CUTW VOICE. VFOAT C.U.T.W. Voice; Voice. **VAT** Connecticut Union of Telephone Workers Voice. (198?)-. Periodical. English. Eleven times a year. CUTW, PO Box 5462, Hamden CT 06518. *Continues Union Voice, 0194-8806.*

ISSN 0007-9227
US
CWA NEWS. Main/Corp Communications Workers of America. **Added/Corp** Communications Workers of America. News. **VAT** Communications Workers of America News. (19??)-. Periodical. English. Twelve times a year. Free on request. Communications Workers of America, 501 3rd Street Northwest, Washington DC 20001. **Tel** (202)728-2382, (202)434-1100. **ED** Jeffery M. Miller. **Bk Rev. Circ:** 650,000 (ctrl). available on microfilm and microfiche from University Microfilms International (UMI). *Continues Telephone Worker.*
Desc: Publication is for members of CWA to alert them of national union news, advise of upcoming events issues and report on current news.
Ind/Abst Work Relat. Abstr.

LC HD5797.7.A6 P63B
PL
CZYNNI ZAWODOWO W GOSPODARCE NARODOWEJ. Main/Corp Poland. Gowny Urzad Statystyczny. 1977-. Polish. Zaklad Wydawnictw Statystycznych, Al. Niepodleglosci 208, 00-925 Warsaw Poland. **Tel** 011 48 22 250345, telex 814581 A GUS PL.

US
D/C : NATIONAL NEWSLETTER FOR STATE ADMINISTERED DEFERRED COMPENSATION PROGRAMS. Added/Corp Illinois. Dept. of Personnel. Vol. 1, No. 1 (Summer 1980)-. Newsletter. English. Four times a year. The National Association of State Deferred Compensation Administrators, PO Box 7326, Montgomery AL 36107.

LC HD4802 .D3
DD 331/.0973
ISSN 0418-2693
US
CCC
DAILY LABOR REPORT (WASHINGTON, D.C. : 1948). (DAILY LABOR REPORT.). [Dly. labor rep.]. **Added/Corp** Bureau of National Affairs (Washington, D.C.). (1948)-. Periodical. English. Five times a week (daily except Sat. and Sun.). $5347.00. Bureau of National Affairs Inc., 9435 Key West Avenue, Rockville MD 20850. **Tel** (800)372-1033, (301)258-1033, FAX (301)948-5823. **ED** William Bank. *Continues Daily Report on Labor-Management Problems.*
Desc: A notification service that comprehensively covers the latest labor developments in Congress, the courts, federal agencies, unions, management, the NLRB and more.

DD 331.88
ISSN 0700-513X
CN
TITLE CHANGE
DANS LA MELEE. [Dans Melee]. **Added/Corp** Syndicat des Professionnels du Gouvernement du Quebec. Vol. 4, No. 3 (August 1976)-(19??). Periodical. French. Syndicat des Professionnels du Gouvernement du Quebec, 625 East Grande Allee, CP 199, Quebec Quebec G1R 2K4 Canada. *Continues Syndicat des Professionnels du Gouvernement du Quebec. Bulletin. Continued by Enjeux (Quebec, Quebec), 1188-5866.*

DD 381
ISSN 1070-9207
US
DARTNELL'S ... SALES FORCE COMPENSATION SURVEY. [Dartnell's sales force compens. surv.]. **Added/Corp** Dartnell Corporation. **VFOAT** Sales Force Compensation Survey. 27th (1992)-. English. Every 2 years. $250.00. Dartnell Corporation, 4660 North Ravenswood Avenue, Chicago IL 60640. **Tel** (312)561-4000, (800)621-5463, FAX (312)561-3801. *Continues Sales Force Compensation, 0739-7798.*

DD 331.2/816584/0097105
ISSN 1183-4676
CN
CEASED
DAVIS ON EXECUTIVE COMPENSATION. [Davis exec. compens.]. Winter (1991)-(199?). Periodical. English. Federated Press, PO Box 885, Stock Exchange Tower, Montreal Quebec H4Z 1K2 Canada. **Tel** (514)849-6600, (800)363-0722.

LC JL689.A15 D39
GY
DAYCLEAN. (19??)-. English.
Ind/Abst Hum. Rights Intern. Rep.

LC HD5725.W4 W38B HD7096.U U6W4
DD 331.1/09754 S 338.4/3
US
DEBIT BALANCES, WEST VIRGINIA'S UNEMPLOYMENT COMPENSATION LAW. Main/Corp West Virginia. Dept. of Employment Security. Labor and Economic Research. English. West Virginia Employment Programs Bureau, 112 California Avenue, Charleston WV 25305. **Tel** (304)558-2630, FAX (304)348-0301. **Circ:** 200.
Desc: Study of firms, using contributions paid and benefits paid, which have debit balances in their UC accounts. Several fiscal years are shown for comparison purposes.

DD 331.88/11/3711
ISSN 0317-221X
CN
DECISIONS DU CONGRES DE LA C. E. Q. Main/Corp Centrale de l'Enseignement du Quebec. Vol. 24 (1974)-. Periodical. French. Every 2 years. Centrale de l'Enseignement du Quebec, 2336 Chemin Sainte-Foy, CP 5800, Quebec Quebec G1V 4E5 Canada. **Tel** (418)658-5711. *Continues Decisions du Congres de la C.E.Q.*

US
DECISIONS OF THE HAWAII PUBLIC EMPLOYMENT RELATIONS BOARD. Main/Corp Hawaii. Public Employment Relations Board. **Added/Corp** Hawaii. University, Honolulu. Industrial Relations Center. **VFOAT** Hawaii PERB Decisions. Vol. 1, (1977)-. English. Industrial Relations Center, University of Hawaii, Honolulu HI 96822. **Tel** (808)948-8132.

LC HD8634.S563 S57A
XV
DELAVCI V ZDRUZENEM DELU IN SAMOSTOJNEM OSEBNEM DELU, PRIPRAVNIKI TER FLUKTUACIJA DELAVCEV. Main/Corp Zavod SR Slovenije Za Statistiko. (19??)-. Slovenian. Zavod Sr Slovenije za Statistiko, Vozarski Pot 12, Ljubljana Slovenia.

LC HA1631 .A33 JN9670
DD 314.971
YU
DELEGACIJE OSNOVNIH SAMOUPRAVNIH ORGANIZACIJA I ZAJEDNICA I SKUPSTINE DRUSTVENO-POLITICKIH ZAJEDNICA. *See Political Science-Abstracting, Bibliographies and Statistics.*

LC HD4928.N62 U627
DD 331.25/5
US
DENVER HEALTH & WELFARE PLANS SURVEY. VFOAT Denver Health and Welfare Plans Survey; Denver Health & Welfare Plans; Survey. (19??)-. English. Research Department Mountain States Employers Council Inc, PO Box 539, Denver CO 80201.

DD 331.88/1100151/09714
ISSN 0831-0467
CN
DEPECHE. (LA DEPECHE : REVUE DE LA FEDERATION NATIONALE DES COMMUNICATIONS.). [Depeche]. (Feb. 1982)-. Periodical. French. Six times a year. 1601 de Lorimier, Montreal H2K 4M5 Canada.

LC HD8634.S563 S57B
XV
DESEZONIRANE CASOVNE VRSTE SR SLOVENIJE. Main/Corp Zavod Sr Slovenije Za Statistiko. 1-. Slovenian. Zavod Sr Slovenije za Statistiko, Vozarski Pot 12, Ljubljana Slovenia.

DD 331
ISSN 1072-1525
US
DETROIT LABOR NEWS. [Detroit labor news]. **Added/Corp** Metropolitan Detroit AFL-CIO Council. (19??)-. Periodical. English. Twenty-six times a year. $11.00. Metropolitan Detroit AFL CIO, 2550 West Grand Boulevard, Detroit MI 48208. **Tel** (313)491-3700, FAX (313)491-3704. **ED** Aldo Vagnozzi and David Hecker (editors' choice: (313)961-6000). **Bk Rev,** (Qty: 3/year). **Ad Acc. Circ:** 4,500 (ctrl). available on microfilm from University Microfilms International (UMI).
Desc: Concerned with labor issues, primarily in the Detroit area.

US
DETROIT'S LABOR MARKET NEWS. Added/Corp Michigan Employment Security Commission. Bureau of Research and Statistics. Information and Reports Section. Vol. 48, No. 1 (Mar. 1992)-. Periodical. English. Twelve times a year. Detroit Employment Security Commission, 7310 Woodward Castro, Room 520, Detroit MI 48202. **Tel** (313)876-5427. *Continues Detroit Labor Market Review.*

LC GV1800
DD 791
ISSN 1083-5253
US
●**DGA MAGAZINE.** *See Motion Picture.*

LC GV1800
DD 791
ISSN 1075-6116
US
TITLE CHANGE
DGA NEWS. *See Motion Picture.*

LC HD8101 .A45a
DD 331/.0971
ISSN 0318-6377
CN
DI. DECISIONS INFORMATION. (D I; DECISIONS, INFORMATION.). **Added/Corp** Canada Labour Relations Board. **VFOAT** D I; Decisions, Information. Vol. 1 (March 1974)-. English (French). Four times a year. Canada Communication Group Publishers, Order Processing, Ottawa Ontario K1A 0S9 Canada. **Tel** (819)956-4800, (819)956-4802. Index available. **Circ:** 700 (ctrl).
Desc: Contains the full text of all written Board decisions, and headnotes.

LC HD6338.2.C5 D5
CL
DIALOGANDO : BOLETIN INFORMATIVO DE LA VICARIA DE PASTORAL OBRERA DE SANTIAGO-CHILE. *See Religions and Theology.*

FR
DICTIONNAIRE PERMANENT / SECURITE ET CONDITIONS DE TRAVAIL. (19??)-. French. Editions Legislatives et Admin, 80 82 Avenue de la Marne, 92546 Montrouge Cedex France. **Tel** 011 33 1 40926868, FAX 011 33 1 46560015, telex 632 855 F.

CN
DIGEST OF BENEFIT ENTITLEMENT PRINCIPLES. Main/Corp Canada. Unemployment Insurance Commission. (19??)-. English (French). Irregular. Canada Communication Group Publishers, Order Processing, Ottawa Ontario K1A 0S9 Canada. **Tel** (819)956-4800, (819)956-4802.

LC HD1501
DD 305.555
US
DIGNIDAD. *See Agriculture.*

LC HD4141 .D57
DD 338.909
UK
DIRECT LABOUR ORGANISATIONS STATISTICS ... ACTUALS. *See Business and Economics-Abstracting, Bibliographies and Statistics.*

LC HD8038.U5 D57
ISSN 0147-5657
US
DIRECTORIO PROFESIONAL HISPANO. Spanish. One time a year. Directorio Profesional Hispano, PO Box 408, Flushing NY 11352. **Tel** (718)762-1432. **ED** George E Balbi. **Circ:** 107 (ctrl).

LC Z7164.W1 D56 HD4973
DD 016.3312/973
ISSN 0566-7801
US
DIRECTORY OF AREA WAGE SURVEYS. (19??)-. Directory. English. US Department of Labor / Bureau of Labor Statistics, 441 G Street Northwest, Washington DC 20212. **Tel** (202)606-7800, FAX (202)606-7797.

LC HF5549.5.E425 D57
DD 331.12/8
ISSN 1056-6112
US
DIRECTORY OF EMPLOYEE LEASING FIRMS, A. [Dir. empl. leas. firms]. **Added/Corp** Aegis Group. 1st Ed. (1991). Directory. English. $37.50. Aegis Group, 155 West Hospitality Lane, Suite 230, San Bernardino CA 92408.

LC HD5725.N84 D57
DD 016.3311/09784
US
DIRECTORY OF LABOR MARKET AND OCCUPATIONAL INFORMATION. 1980-. Directory. English. Every 2 years. Job Service North Dakota, Box 1537, 1000 East Divide Avenue, Bismarck ND 58502. **Tel** (701)224-2868. **Circ:** 500.
Desc: Annotated listing of over 100 publications relating to labor market and occupational information in North Dakota.

LC Z7164.L1 D53 HD5725.M3
DD 016.3311/2/09741
ISSN 0190-3217
US
DIRECTORY OF LABOR MARKET INFORMATION. (19??)-. Directory. English. One time a year. Free. Maine Employment Security Commission, 20 Union Street, Augusta ME 04330. **ED** Ray Fongemie. **Circ:** 2,000 (ctrl).
Desc: Labor market information for Maine. Includes a list of persons to contact for specific categories of information and a list of publications that are available.

LC HD8083.S5 D57
DD 016.33112/09757
US
DIRECTORY OF LABOR MARKET INFORMATION (COLUMBIA, S.C.). (DIRECTORY OF LABOR MARKET INFORMATION / SOUTH CAROLINA EMPLOYMENT SECURITY COMMISSION.). (19??)-. Directory. English. Two times a year. Free. South Carolina Employment Security Commission, 1550 Gadsden Street, PO Box 995,

Business and Economics —Labor

Columbia SC 29202. **Tel** (803)737-2660, FAX (803)737-2642. **ED** David Laird. ctrl circ.
Desc: Catalog of publications available from Labor Market Information Division of South Carolina Employment Security Commission.

LC Z7164.L1 D54 HD5725.N4   **ISSN** 0149-4961
DD 016.3311/2/09742   US
DIRECTORY OF LABOR MARKET INFORMATION REPORTS AND PUBLICATIONS. [Dir. labor mark. inf. rep. publ.].
1977-. Directory. English. New Hampshire Department of Employment Security, 32 South Main Street, Concord NH 03301. **Tel** (603)224-3311, FAX (603)228-4145.

LC HD6521 .A4   **ISSN** 0711-1703
DD 331.88/025/71   CN
DIRECTORY OF LABOUR ORGANIZATIONS IN CANADA. [Dir. labour organ. Can.]. Added/Corp Canada. Labour Data Branch.
Canada. Labour Data Branch. Repertoire des Organisations de Travailleurs au Canada. **VFOAT** Repertoire des Organisations de Travailleurs au Canada. (1980)-. Directory. English (French). One time a year. Price varies. Canada Communication Group Publishers, Order Processing, Ottawa Ontario K1A 0S9 Canada. **Tel** (819)956-4800, (819)956-4802. **Circ:** 6,000. *Continues Labour Organizations in Canada, 0075-7578.*

US
DIRECTORY OF MAINE LABOR ORGANIZATIONS. Main/Corp Maine. Bureau of Labor. Research and Statistics Division. (19??)-.
Directory. English. One time a year. Free. Research & Statistics Division, Bureau of Labor Standards, State House Station 45, Augusta ME 04333-0045. **Tel** (207)289-6400, FAX (207)289-6449. **ED** Terry Hathaway. **Circ:** 1,000.
Desc: Listing of active labor organizations and their officers in the state of Maine.

LC HD8008 .A262   **ISSN** 0097-8639
DD 331.88/11/35300025   US
DIRECTORY OF NATIONAL AND INTERNATIONAL UNIONS AND ASSOCIATIONS WITH EXCLUSIVE RECOGNITION IN THE FEDERAL SERVICE. Directory. English. US Civil Service Commission Bureau of Intergovernmental Personnel Programs, 1900 E Street NW, Washington DC 20415.

LC LB2335.875.U6 D57   **ISSN** 1054-7568
DD 331.89/0413712/02   US
SUSPENDED
DIRECTORY OF NON-FACULTY BARGAINING AGENTS IN INSTITUTIONS OF HIGHER EDUCATION. [Dir. non-fac. bargain. agents inst. high. educ.]. Added/Corp National Center for the Study of Collective Bargaining in Higher Education and the Professions (U.S.). VFOAT Directory of Non Faculty Bargaining Agents in Institutions of Higher Education; Directory of Non-Faculty Bargaining Agents. Vol. 1 (Jan. 1991)-Suspended (19??). Directory. English. Irregular.
National Center for the Study of Collective Bargaining in Higher Education and the Professions, Baruch College, Box G-1050, 17 Lexington Avenue, New York NY 10010. **Tel** (212)387-1510, FAX (212)387-1516.

LC HD6058 .D57
DD 331.1/28   US
DIRECTORY OF ORGANIZATIONS PROMOTING EQUAL EMPLOYMENT OPPORTUNITIES FOR WOMEN, CALIFORNIA. (19??)-. Directory. English.
Agriculture and Service Agency, 455 Golden Gate Avenue, Room 1193, San Francisco CA 94102.

LC HD8083.C7 D56   **ISSN** 0362-9562
DD 362.8/4/025746   US
DIRECTORY OF RESOURCE ORGANIZATIONS AND MEDIA SERVING MINORITY COMMUNITIES IN CONNECTICUT. Added/Corp Connecticut.
Commission on Human Rights and Opportunities. (19??)-. Directory. English. Irregular. Connecticut Commission on Human Rights and Opportunities, 90 Washington Street, Hartford CT 06115.

LC HD2346.I52 H354   **ISSN** 0376-8570
DD 338.6/42/02554558   II
DIRECTORY OF SMALL SCALE INDUSTRIAL UNITS EMPLOYING FIVE OR MORE PERSONS IN THE UNORGANISED SECTOR IN HARYANA.
(19??)-. Directory. English. Economic and Statistical Organization, Government of Haryan, Chandigarh 160011 India.

LC HD8061 .U55A   **ISSN** 0091-9497
DD 331.88/025/73   US
DIRECTORY OF THE LABOR RESEARCH ADVISORY COUNCIL TO THE BUREAU OF LABOR STATISTICS.
(DIRECTORY / UNITED STATES. LABOR RESEARCH ADVISORY COUNCIL.). **Main/Corp** United States. Labor Research Advisory Council. (19??)-. Directory. English. US Department of Labor, 200 Constitution Avenue NW, Washington DC 20210. **Tel** (202)219-7316, FAX (202)219-7312.

LC HD6504 .D64   **ISSN** 0734-6786
DD 331.88/025/73   US
CCC
DIRECTORY OF U.S. LABOR ORGANIZATIONS. [Dir. U.S. labor organ.].
VFOAT Directory of US Labor Organizations. (1982/83)-. Directory. English. Every 2 years. $35.00. Bureau of National Affairs Inc., 9435 Key West Avenue, Rockville MD 20850. **Tel** (800)372-1033, (301)258-1033, FAX (301)948-5823. **ED** Courtney D. Gifford. *Continues Directory of National Unions and Employee Associations.*
Desc: Contains an extensive labor organization listing of headquarters' addresses and telephone numbers, key officers, membership statistics and other information.

LC HD8005.2.U5 D57   **ISSN** 0193-385X
DD 331.88/11/35300025   US
DIRECTORY OF UNIONS AND ASSOCIATIONS WITH EXCLUSIVE RECOGNITION IN THE FEDERAL SERVICE. (19??)-. Directory. English. US Civil
Service Commission, 1900 E Street Northwest, Room 5354, Washington DC 20415. **Tel** (202)632-5532.

   ISSN 1078-277X
DD 331   US
●DISCOVERING CAREERS & JOBS [COMPUTER FILE]. [Discov. careers jobs]. Added/Corp Gale Research, Inc. VFOAT Discovering Careers and Jobs. (1995)-. English. Two times a year.
Gale Research Inc., 835 Penobscot Building, 645 Griswold Street, Detroit MI 48226. **Tel** (800)877-GALE, (313)961-2242, FAX (313)961-6083, (800)414-5043, telex TWX 810-221-7086.

   ISSN 0012-3765
US
DISPATCHER, THE. Added/Corp International Longshoremen's and Warehousemen's Union. Vol. 2, No. 6 (Mar. 10, 1944)-. Periodical. English. Eleven times a year (except Aug.). $2.50. International Longshoremen's & Warehousemen's Union, 1188 Franklin Street, San Francisco CA 94109. Tel (415)775-0533, FAX (415)775-1302. ED Kathy Wilkes. Index available. cum. index. Bk Rev, (Qty: 4). Circ: 40,000 (ctrl). available in microform. Continues ILWU Dispatcher.
Desc: National and international news related to labor, unions, legislation, and work trends by the International Longshoremen's and Warehousemen's Union.
Ind/Abst Work Relat. Abstr.

LC HD7105.35.C2 D57
DD 331.25/2/09714   CN
DISPOSITIONS DES REGIMES ET LES COTISANTS EN ..., LES. French. Irregular.
Regie des Rentes du Quebec, Case Postale 5200, Quebec Quebec G1K 7S9 Canada. **Tel** (418)643-8309. Index available.

LC HD5723 .U54A   **ISSN** 0270-8469
DD 331.11/1/0973   US
DISTRIBUTION OF OCCUPATIONAL EMPLOYMENT IN STATES AND AREAS BY RACE AND SEX. Main/Corp United States.
Bureau of Labor Statistics. 1978-. Government Publication. English. US Department of Labor / Bureau of Labor Statistics, 441 G Street Northwest, Washington DC 20212. **Tel** (202)606-7800, FAX (202)606-7797.

   ISSN 0012-3986
US
DISTRIBUTIVE WORKER, THE. Added/Corp
International Union, United Autombile, Aerospace, and Agricultural Implement Workers of America. District 65. Distributive Workers of America. National Council of Distributive Workers of America. **VFOAT** Distributive 65 Worker. Vol. 1 (July 1969)-. Trade Publication. English. Ten times a year. National Council for the Distributive Worker, 13 Astor Place, New York NY 10003. **Tel** (212)673-5120. **ED** Kitty Krupat. **Circ:** 50,000 (ctrl).
Desc: News concerning district 65 United Auto Workers. Labor movement news and trends, collective bargaining, organization and political action.
Ind/Abst Work Relat. Abstr.

   ISSN 0211-8556
SP
UDC 351.83
DOCUMENTACION LABORAL. [Doc. labor.]. Added/Corp Asociacion de Cajas de Ahorros para Relaciones Laborales. Madrid. (1981)-. Periodical.
Spanish. Three times a year. 8000ptas. Asociacion de Cajas de Ahorros para Relaciones Laborales, Principe 5, 28012 Madrid Spain. **Tel** 011 34 1 4296596.

LC HN261 .D63   **ISSN** 0325-8483
DD 306/.098   AG
DOCUMENTO DE TRABAJO / INSTITUTO TORCUATO DI TELLA, CENTRO DE INVESTIGACIONES SOCIALES. Main/Corp Instituto Torcuato di Tella.
Centro de Investigaciones Sociales. **Added/Corp** Centro de Investigaciones Sociales (Instituto Torcuato di Tella). **VFOAT** Documentos de Trabajo; Serie Documentos de Trabajo. (1966)-. Monographic series. Spanish (English and French). Irregular. Price varies per volume. Institut Torcuato di Tella, 11 de Septiembre 2139, 1423 Buenos Aires Argentina. **Tel** 781-5013, FAX 784 8225, telex 15 2817051. **Circ:** 300 (ctrl).

   ISSN 1014-703X
SZ
DOCUMENTOS DE DERECHO SOCIAL.
(19??)-. Spanish (English and French). Three times a year. $68.00. International Labour Office - ILO, Publications Sales Service, CH-1211 Geneva 22 Switzerland. **Tel** 011 41 22 7996111, FAX 011 41 22 7986253, telex 415 647 ilo ch. Index available. cum. index. **Circ:** 1,000.
Desc: Includes the most important texts of international conventions, laws and regulations enacted throughout the world on labour and social security.

LC HC143.A1 D63
CR
DOCUMENTOS DE TRABAJO (UNIVERSIDAD DE COSTA RICA, INSTITUTO DE INVESTIGACIONES EN CIENCIAS ECONOMICAS). (DOCUMENTOS DE TRABAJO / UNIVERSIDAD DE COSTA RICA, FACULTAD DE CIENCIAS ECONOMICAS, INSTITUTO DE INVESTIGACIONES EN CIENCIAS ECONOMICAS.).
(19??)-. Monographic series. Spanish. Irregular. Price varies per volume. Inst Torcuato de Tella, 11 de Septiembre 2139, 1423 Buenos Aires Argentina. **Tel** 781-5013. **Circ:** 300 (ctrl).

US
DOCUMENTS OF THE INTERNATIONAL LABOUR CONFERENCE. (19??)-. English.
Irregular. $316.00. International Labour Office - ILO, Publications Sales Service, CH-1211 Geneva 22 Switzerland. **Tel** 011 41 22 7996111, FAX 011 41 22 7986253, telex 415 647 ilo ch. **(Subscription address:** International Labour Office / Washington, DC, 1828 L Street Northwest, Suite 801, Washington DC 20036. **Tel** (202)653-7652.**)**
Desc: Contains reports prepared to each item on the agenda of the annual session of the Conference and the Record of Proceedings.

   ISSN 0923-3822
NE
UDC 331.5
DOEN AMSTERDAM. (DOEN.). [Doen Amst.].
(1987)-. Periodical. Dutch. Twelve times a year (except July and Aug.). $19.39. Stichting Doen, Hartenstraat 18, 1016 CB Amsterdam Netherlands. **Tel** 011 31 20 6207112.

LC HN421 .F73a HC271 .A218   **ISSN** 0758-6531
FR
DONNEES SOCIALES. Main/Corp Institut
National de la Statistique et des -Etudes -Economiques (France). (1973)-. French. Irregular. Price varie per volume. CNGP Insee, BP 2718, 1 rue V Auriol, F 80027 Amiens, Cedex 1 France. **Tel** 011 33 22 927322.

   ISSN 0715-1055
DD 331.11/0971   CN
DONNEES SUR LA POPULATION ACTIVE : QUEBEC, ONTARIO ET CANADA. See Business and Economics-Abstracting, Bibliographies and Statistics.

FR
DONZERE MONDRAGON. (DONZERE MONDRAGON; BULLETIN D'INFORMATION TECHNIQUE ET PROFESSIONNEL. GROUPEMENT D'ENTERPRISES DES TRAVAUX D'AMENAGEMENT DU RHONE A DONZERE.). Main/Corp Compagnie Nationale du Rhone. (19??)-. Bulletin. French.

   ISSN 0821-4433
DD 330.9714   CN
DOSSIERS CSN (1980 OCT.). (DOSSIERS CSN.). [Doss. CSN]. VAT Dossiers Confederation des Syndicats Nationaux. No. 3 (20 Oct. 1980)-. Periodical.
French. Free. Librairie Service Documentation, 1601 Ave de Lorimier, Montreal Quebec H2K 4M5 Canada. **Tel** (514)598-2151. ctrl circ. *Continues Dossier CSN, 0821-4433.*

FR
DOSSIERS STATISTIQUES DU TRAVAIL ET DE L'EMPLOI. Added/Corp France. Ministere
des Affaires Sociales et de la Solidarite Nationale. Service des Etudes et de la Statistique. France. Ministere du Travail, de l'Emploi et de la Formation Professionnelle. Service des Etudes et de la Statistique. **VFOAT** D.S.T.E. No. 1 (1984)-. Periodical. French. Six times a year.

Business and Economics — Labor

Ministere du Travail et Service d'Etudes, Statistique place Fontenoy, 75007 Paris France. **(Subscription address:** Documentation Francaise, 124 rue Henri Barbusse, 93308 Aubervilliers Cedex France. **Tel** 011 33 1 48395600.**)**
Ind/Abst Trop. Dis. Bull.

LC HD7275 .D67   **ISSN** 0366-9610
DD 338.4/7/68176   GW
    CODEN DRARAZ
DRAGER REVIEW. [Drager rev.]. Academic Scholarly Publication. Multiple languages (English, French and Spanish). Dragerwerk, PO Box 1339, W-24 Lubeck Germany. Documents available from CASDDS.
Ind/Abst Chem. Abstr.; Coal Abstr.; Saf. Health Work.

LC UB358.C2 E24
DD 362.1608697   US
EAGLE : INFORMATION FOR CALIFORNIA VETERANS FROM THE CALIFORNIA EMPLOYMENT DEVELOPMENT DEPARTMENT, THE. See Military and Defense.

     US
     SUSPENDED
EAP DIGEST ANNUAL. VAT Employee Assistance Programs Digest Annual. (1982)-(1987/88). English. One time a year. Performance Resource Press, Inc., 1863 Technology Drive, Suite 200, Troy MI 48083. **Tel** (810)588-7733, (800)453-7733, FAX (810)588-6633.

LC HD4977 .E37   **ISSN** 0829-6235
DD 331.2/971021   CN
EARNINGS OF MEN AND WOMEN. See Business and Economics-Abstracting, Bibliographies and Statistics.

LC HD4811 .E22   **ISSN** 0012-8953
     PK
EASTERN WORKER. Vol. 1 (Sept. 1959)-. Periodical. English. Six times a year. Rs180.00 Pakistan; $27.00 US. Bureau of Labour Publications, 8 Business Centre, Mumtaz Hasan Road, PO Box 5833, Karachi-74000 Pakistan. **Tel** 011 91 11 224975. **ED** Mohammad Shafi. Index available. **Bk Rev. Circ:** 1,000 (ctrl).
  Desc: Independent journal on labor law and problems in Pakistan; includes labor news, statistics on the cost of living, book reviews and editorials.
Ind/Abst Hum. Rights Intern. Rep.; Work Relat. Abstr.

     ISSN 0887-137X
DD 331   US
     CCC
NLM W1; EB6
EBRI ISSUE BRIEF. [EBRI issue brief].
Added/Corp Employee Benefit Research Institute (Washington, D.C.). **VFOAT** Employee Benefit Research Institute Issue Brief; Issue Brief. (19??)-. Periodical. English. Twelve times a year. $224.00 (US); $227.00 (Canada and Mexico); $234.00 (other) includes postage (includes Employee Benefit Notes). Employee Benefit Research Institute, 2121 K Street Northwest, Suite 600, Washington DC 20037. **Tel** (202)659-0670, FAX (202)775-6312. **ED** Stephanie Poe. Index available. **Circ:** 3,200. available on an online database.
  Desc: Aids decision makers in the formulation of policy concerning health, welfare, and retirement benefits for workers. Expert evaluations of a single employee benefit issue.
Ind/Abst PAIS Int. Print.

     ISSN 0240-396X
     FR
UDC 33
     CEASED
ECHANGE TRAVAIL PARIS. [Echange trav. Paris]. (1979)-(19??). Periodical. French. Masson Editeur, BP 22, 41354 Vineuil Cedex France. **Tel** 011 33 54 504612, FAX 011 33 54 504611.
Ind/Abst LABORDOC (?-?).

     ISSN 0713-5688
DD 331.88/12/0009714   CN
ECHO : JOURNAL DU SYNDICAT PROFESSIONNEL DES INGENIEURS DE L'HYDRO-QUEBEC, L'. [Echo]. (19??)-. Periodical. French. Irregular. l'Echo, 8E Etage, 855 East rue Sainte Catherine, Montreal Quebec H2L 4N4 Canada.

LC HD8581 .E28
     SP
ECONOMIA Y SOCIOLOGIA DEL TRABAJO. Added/Corp Spain. Ministerio de Trabajo y Seguridad Social. Centro de Publicaciones. **VFOAT** Revista de Economia y Sociologia del Trabajo. (Dec. 1988)-. Periodical. Spanish. Four times a year. Centro de Publicaciones, Min. Trabajo, Agustin de Bethancourt 11, 28071 Madrid Spain. **Tel** 011 34 1 5543400. **(Subscription address:** Mundi Prensa Libros SA, Castello 37, Apartado 1223, 28001 Madrid Spain. **Tel** 011 34 1 4313222.**)**
Ind/Abst LABORDOC.

LC HC191 .E38
DD 330.983/005   CL
ECONOMIA Y TRABAJO EN CHILE.
Added/Corp Programa de Economia del Trabajo (Academia de Humanismo Cristiano). (1990/1991)-. Spanish.

LC HD28 .E45   **ISSN** 0351-286X
DD 658/.009497   YU
ECONOMIC ANALYSIS AND WORKERS' MANAGEMENT. See Business and Economics-Management.

LC HD5650 .E24   **ISSN** 0143-831X
DD 331/.01/12   UK
Pr Rev.
ECONOMIC AND INDUSTRIAL DEMOCRACY. [Econ. ind. democr.]. **Added/Corp** Arbetslivcentrum (Stockholm, Sweden). Vol. 1 No. 1 (Feb. 1980)-. Periodical. English. Four times a year. $229.00. Sage Publications Ltd., 6 Bonhill Street, London EC2A 4PU United Kingdom. **Tel** 011 44 181 3740645, FAX 011 44 181 3748741, telex 296207 SAGE G. **ED** Rudolf Meidner. Index available. cum. index. **Bk Rev. Ad Acc.** Acid Free. Documents available from The Genuine Article, UMI Article Clearinghouse.
  Desc: Covers all aspects of industrial democracy, from the practical problems of democratic management to wide-ranging social, political and economic analysis.
Ind/Abst ABI/INFORM Glob. Ed.; ABI/INFORM [Computer File] (Feb. 1988-); Contents Pages Manage.; Curr. Cit.; Curr. Contents Soc. Behav. Sci.; Econ. Lit. Index (199?-); Hum. Resour. Abstr.; Int. Bibliogr. Sociol.; Int. Labour Doc.; J. Econ. Lit.; LABORDOC; Middle East Abstr. Index; Person. Manage. Abstr.; Res. Alert [Full Cov.]; Soc. Plann. Policy Dev. Abstr.; Soc. Sci. Cit. Index [Full Cov.]; Sociol. Abstr.; Sociol. Educ. Abstr.; Work Relat. Abstr.

LC HD5725.N4 N45A   **ISSN** 0091-5033
DD 331.1/09742   US
ECONOMIC CONDITIONS IN NEW HAMPSHIRE LOCAL OFFICE AREAS.
Main/Corp New Hampshire. Dept. of Employment Security. (19??)-. English. New Hampshire Department of Employment Security, 32 South Main Street, Concord NH 03301. **Tel** (603)224-3311, FAX (603)228-4145.

LC HB   **ISSN** 1351-2145
DD 330   UK
UDC 33
ECONOMIC REPORT - EMPLOYMENT POLICY INSTITUTE. (ECONOMIC REPORT.). [Econ. rep. - Employ. Policy Inst.]. (1985)-. Periodical. English. Twelve times a year. $51.33. Employment Policy Institute, South Bank House, Black Prince Road, London SE1 7SJ United Kingdom. **Tel** 011 44 171 7350777, FAX 011 44 171 7938192. **ED** John Philpott.
  Desc: Economic reports on topics such as: skilling the jobless, human resource management, unemployment, unemployment.

     ISSN 0378-5564
     SZ
UDC 331
EDUCACION OBRERA. [Educ. obrera]. (1964)-. Periodical. Spanish. Three times a year.
Ind/Abst LABORDOC.

     ISSN 0378-5572
     SZ
UDC 331
EDUCATION OUVRIERE. [Educ. ouvriere]. (1964)-. Periodical. French. Four times a year. $40.00. International Labour Office - ILO, Publications Sales Service, CH-1211 Geneva 22 Switzerland. **Tel** 011 41 22 7996111, FAX 011 41 22 7986253, telex 415 647 ilo ch.
Ind/Abst LABORDOC.

LC HD4903.5.U58 E15   **ISSN** 0148-6934
DD 331.2   US
     CCC
EEO REVIEW, THE. [EEO rev.]. **VAT** Equal Employment Opportunity Review. (19??)-. Periodical. English. Twelve times a year. $160.00. John Wiley & Sons, Inc., 605 Third Avenue, New York NY 10158-0012. **Tel** (212)850-6000, (212)850-6645, FAX (212)850-6088, telex 12-7063. **(Subscription address:** John Wiley & Sons Inc / New Jersey, PO Box 2575, Secaucus NJ 07096-2575. **) ED** Jane G. Bensahely. Index available. **Ad Acc.** available on microfiche; available on microfilm; available in microform.
  Desc: Designed to give managers and supervisors the latest information avoiding EEO problems in hiring, promotion, discipline, termination, performance appraisal, career counseling and supervising the physically and mentally handicapped.

     ISSN 0740-204X
     US
Pr Rev.
EEO TRENDS AND ISSUES. (EEO TRENDS AND ISSUES : A PUBLICATION OF STENBERG ASSOCIATES.). **Added/Corp** Stenberg Associates. **VFOAT** E.E.O. Trends and Issues. (19??)-. Periodical. English. Twelve times a year. $85.00 (one-year), $168.00 (two-year), $252.00 (three-year). Stenberg Associates, 3100 Pruitt Road, Building F-306, Port St. Lucie FL 34952. **Tel** (305)335-8390. **Bk Rev,** (Qty: 10). **Circ:** 1,400.

     US
EI NETWORK NEWSLETTER. (19??)-. Newsletter. English. Six times a year. $24.00 US; $25.00 other. Teambuilding, Inc., 12 Pine Lane, Chadds Ford PA 19317. **Tel** (610)358-1961, FAX (215)558-0325. **ED** Peter Grazier. **Circ:** 600.
  Desc: Deals with employee involvement and total quality management.

LC HD4966.D372 U633   **ISSN** 0193-7979
DD 331.2/81/001640973   US
ELECTRONIC DATA PROCESSING SALARY SURVEY. English. One time a year. M & M Association, 2300 Occidental Center, 1150 South Olive Street, Los Angeles CA 90015.

     PR
EMPLEO, HORAS Y SALARIOS EN LAS INDUSTRIAS MANUFACTURERAS DE PUERTO RICO. EMPLOYMENT, HOURS AND EARNINGS IN THE MANUFACTURING INDUSTRIES IN PUERTO RICO. Main/Corp Puerto Rico. Bureau of Labor Statistics. **VFOAT** Employment, Hours and Earnings in the Manufacturing Industries in Puerto Rico. (1???)-. Spanish (English). Twelve times a year. Bureau of Labor Statistics / Puerto Rico, 414 Barbosa Avenue, Hato Rey PR 00917.

LC HD8231 .A372 HD5744   **ISSN** 0091-9233
     PR
EMPLEO, HORAS Y SALARIOS EN LOS ESTABLECIMIENTOS MANUFACTUREROS PROMOVIDOD POR LA ADMINISTRACION DE FOMENTO ECONOMICO O LA COMPANIA DE FOMENTO INDUSTRIAL DE PUERTO RICO. Main/Corp Puerto Rico. Bureau of Labor Statistics. **VFOAT** Employment, Hours, and Earnings in the Manufacturing Establishment Promoted by the Economic Development Administration or the Puerto Rico Industrial Development Company. English.

     PR
EMPLEO Y DESEMPLEO EN PUERTO RICO / DEPARTMENTO DEL TRABAJO.
VFOAT Employment and Unemployment in Puerto Rico. No. 1 (Nov. 1962)-. Periodical. English (Spanish). Twelve times a year.

     ISSN 0837-2470
DD 331.12/09714/021   CN
EMPLOI AU QUEBEC. (L'EMPLOI AU QUEBEC.). [Empl. Que]. **Added/Corp** Quebec (Province). Ministere de la Main-d'Oeuvre et de la Securite du Revenu. Direction de la Recherche. (Sept. 1986)-. Periodical. French. Twelve times a year. Free on request. Ministere de la Main d'Oeurre de la Securite du Revenu et de la Formaton Professionelle, 425 St- Amable 1st Floor, Quebec City Quebec G1R 4Z1 Canada. **Tel** (418)643-7513, FAX (418)646-5426. **ED** Denise Boulanger, (418)646-3885. **Circ:** 600 (ctrl). **Absorbed** La Situation de l'Emploi au Quebec en ..., 0825-2785.

     AT
EMPLOYED WAGE AND SALARY EARNERS, AUSTRALIA. Added/Corp Australian Bureau of Statistics. (198?)-. Periodical. English. Four times a year. 72.00Aus$. Australian Bureau of Statistics, PO Box 2796Y, Melbourne 3001 Australia. **Tel** 011 61 3 6157843. **Continues** Civilian Employees Australia.

     US
EMPLOYEE ASSISTANCE. (19??)-. Periodical. English. Ten times a year. $82.50. Stevens Publishing Corporation, 225 North New Road, Waco TX 76702-2604. **Tel** (800)727-7573, (817)776-9000, FAX (817)776-9018. **(Subscription address:** Stevens Publishing Corp., PO Box 2573, Waco TX 76702. **)**
Ind/Abst Work Relat. Abstr.

     ISSN 1061-7728
DD 331   US
EMPLOYEE ASSISTANCE PROFESSIONAL REPORT. [Empl. assist. prof. rep.]. (1991)-. Periodical. English. Twelve times a year. $123.75. Stevens Publishing Corporation, 225 North New Road, Waco TX 76702-2604. **Tel** (800)727-7573, (817)776-9000, FAX (817)776-9018.

LC HF5549.5.A4 L32   **ISSN** 0749-0003
DD 362.2/9286   US
NLM W1; EM696N
Pr Rev.
EMPLOYEE ASSISTANCE QUARTERLY. See Industrial Health and Safety.

LC HD7106.U5 N163 ISSN 1048-2814
DD 658.3/25/097305 US
EMPLOYEE BENEFIT ISSUES. [Empl. benefit issues]. **Added/Corp** International Foundation of Employee Benefit Plans. International Foundation of Employee Benefit Plans. Employee Benefits Conference. Vol. 30 (1988)-. English. Four times a year (Mar., June, Sept. Dec.). $60.00. International Foundation of Employee Benefit Plans, PO Box 69, 18700 West Bluemound Road, Brookfield WI 53008-0069. **Tel** (414)786-6700 ext.358, FAX (414)786-8670. ***Continues*** *Employee Benefits Annual, 1046-3208.*

LC HD4928.N62 U626 ISSN 1044-6265
DD 331 US
CCC
EMPLOYEE BENEFIT NEWS. (EMPLOYEE BENEFIT NEWS : THE NEWS SOURCE FOR GROUP BENEFITS DECISIONMAKERS.). [Empl. benefit news]. (198?)-. Periodical. English. Eight times a year. $75.00. Enterprise Communication, 1165 Northchase Pkwy NE #350, Marietta GA 30067. **Tel** (404)988-9558, FAX (404)859-9166. Index available. cum. index. **Ad Acc.** ctrl circ.

LC HD4928.N62 U6282 ISSN 0887-1388
DD 331 US
CCC
EMPLOYEE BENEFIT NOTES. (EMPLOYEE BENEFIT NOTES.). [Empl. benefit notes]. **Added/Corp** Employee Benefit Research Institute (Washington, D.C.). **VFOAT** EBRI Notes. (198?)-. Periodical. English. Twelve times a year. $224.00 (includes EBRI Issue Brief). Employee Benefit Research Institute, 2121 K Street Northwest, Suite 600, Washington DC 20037. **Tel** (202)659-0670, FAX (202)775-6312. **(Subscription address:** John Hopkins University Press, Journals Publishing Division, PO Box 19966, Baltimore MD 21211. **Tel** (410)516-6987, (800)548-1784, FAX (410)516-6968.**) ED** Shannon Braymen. Index available. **Bk Rev. Circ:** 2,000. ***Continues*** *EBRI Notes.*
Desc: Provides updates on legislation, litigation, new regulations, corporate trends, and surveys pertinent to the field.
Ind/Abst PAIS Int. Print.

LC HD4932.N6 C49 ISSN 0194-3499
DD 331.25/5/0973 US
EMPLOYEE BENEFITS. (EMPLOYEE BENEFITS : RESEARCH STUDY.). **Added/Corp** U.S. Chamber Survey Research Center. Chamber of Commerce of the United States of America. Chamber of Commerce of the United States of America. Economic Analysis and Study Group. U.S. Chamber Survey Center. Chamber of Commerce of the United States of America. Economic Policy Dept. Chamber of Commerce of the United States of America. Economic Policy Division. Survey Research Section. Chamber of Commerce of the United States of America. Economic Policy Division. Research Center. (1967)-. Government Publication. English. One time a year. $29.00. Chamber of Commerce of the United States of America, 1615 H Street Northwest, Washington DC 20062. **Tel** (800)638-6582. **ED** Martin Lefkowitz. **Bk Rev. Ad Acc. Circ:** 75,000 (ctrl). ***Continues*** *Fringe Benefits.*
Desc: Employee benefits as percent of payroll for manufacturing and non-manufacturing companies.

ISSN 0894-5306
DD 331 US
EMPLOYEE BENEFITS ALERT. [Empl. benefits alert]. **Added/Corp** Warren, Gorham & Lamont, Inc. Research Institute of America, Inc. (April 1987)-. Periodical. English. Twenty-six times a year. Research Institute of America, 117 East Stevens Avenue, Valhalla NY 10595. **Tel** (800)431-9025, FAX (800)820-3135 (914)749-5300. ***Continues*** *Executive Compensation Alert, 0273-821X.*

ISSN 0273-768X
US
CCC
EMPLOYEE BENEFITS COMPLIANCE COORDINATOR. See Business and Economics-Personnel Management.

ISSN 8756-4971
DD 331 US
EMPLOYEE BENEFITS FOR NONPROFITS. (Jan. 1985)-. Periodical. English. Twelve times a year. $135.00. NP Publishing Inc., 801 North Pitt Street, Suite 124, Alexandria VA 22314. **Tel** (703)549-9644. **(Subscription address:** Employee Benefits for Nonprofits, Subscription Office, PO Box 1584, Birmingham AL 35201-1584. **Tel** (800)633-4931, (205)995-1567 (outside US and Canada), FAX (205)995-1588.**)**

LC HD4928.N62 U6334
DD 331.25/5/0973 US
EMPLOYEE BENEFITS IN MEDIUM AND LARGE PRIVATE ESTABLISHMENTS / U.S. DEPARTMENT OF LABOR, BUREAU OF LABOR STATISTICS. **Added/Corp** United States. Bureau of Labor Statistics. (1991)-. English. Irregular. $23.00 (price per copy). Superintendent of Documents, US Government Printing Office, Washington DC 20402. **Tel** (202)275-3328, FAX (202)786-2377. ***Continues*** *Employee Benefits in Medium and Large Firms, 0748-2663.*

LC JK2474 .E48
DD 350.1/23/0973 US
EMPLOYEE BENEFITS IN STATE AND LOCAL GOVERNMENTS. **Added/Corp** United States. Bureau of Labor Statistics. (1987)-. Government Publication. English. One time a year. $5.00. US Department of Labor / Bureau of Labor Statistics, 441 G Street Northwest, Washington DC 20212. **Tel** (202)606-7800, FAX (202)606-7797. **Circ:** 3,000. available on magnetic tape.

LC HD4932.N6 E43 ISSN 0361-4050
DD 331.2/55/0973 US
CCC
NLM W1 EM696T
EMPLOYEE BENEFITS JOURNAL. [Empl. benefits j.]. **VFOAT** International Foundation Employee Benefits Journal. Vol. 1 (Fall 1975)-. Periodical. English. Four times a year. $60.00. International Foundation of Employee Benefit Plans, PO Box 69, 18700 West Bluemound Road, Brookfield WI 53008-0069. **Tel** (414)786-6700 ext.358, FAX (414)786-8670. **ED** Mary E Brennan. **Circ:** 35,000. available on microfilm and microfiche from University Microfilms International (UMI). Documents available from UMI Article Clearinghouse.
Desc: Timely important subjects from the practical aspects of benefit plan management to the socioeconomic climate in which plans operate.
Ind/Abst ABI/INFORM Glob. Ed. (Winter 1980-); ABI/INFORM Ondisc: Expr. Ed. (March 1987-); ABI/INFORM [Computer File] (Winter 1980-); Acad. Search; Account. Art.; Bus. Index (1985-); Bus. Period. Index; Bus. Source Plus; Bus. Source; EP Collect.; Gen. BusinessFile (1985-); Gen. Period. Index (1985-); Health Plan. Adminis.; Homework Help.; Hosp. Health Admin. Index; INFO-SOUTH Abstr.; Ins. Period. Index; Mag. Search; Manage. Contents; MasterFile FullTEXT 1000; MasterFile FullTEXT 350; MasterFile FullTEXT 650; MasterFile FullTEXT (Jan. 1993-); OCLC; Pub. Lib. FullTEXT; Telebase; Vocat. Search; Wilson Bus. Abstr.

LC KF1424.A15 E9 ISSN 0884-478X
DD 344.73/01252 US
CCC
CEASED
EMPLOYEE BENEFITS REPORT. [Empl. benefits rep.]. (198?)-(19??). Periodical. English. Warren Gorham & Lamont Inc., Park Square Building, 31 St. James Avenue, Boston MA 02116-4112. **Tel** (617)423-2020, (800)950-1207, FAX (617)423-2026. **ED** John D Reynolds. ***Continues*** *Executive Compensation & Employee Benefits Report, 0273-9046.*
Desc: Provides information on ideas and developments in the field of employee benefits. Offers advice and coverage on IRS actions, employment law, benefits planning, social security developments and related topics.

UK
EMPLOYEE BENEFITS UNIT 1. (19??)-. English. Twelve times a year. £84.50. Stapleford Publications Ltd., 6 West St Wilton North Salisbury, Wiltshire SP2 0DF United Kingdom. **Tel** 011 44 1722 711128.

LC HD8051 .A62 ISSN 0091-8261
DD 331.2/973 US
EMPLOYEE COMPENSATION IN THE PRIVATE NONFARM ECONOMY. **Main/Corp** United States. Bureau of Labor Statistics. (19??)-. English. US Department of Labor, 200 Constitution Avenue NW, Washington DC 20210. **Tel** (202)219-7316, FAX (202)219-7312.

ISSN 0199-6304
US
CCC
EMPLOYEE HEALTH & FITNESS. VAT Employee Health and Fitness. (19??)-. Periodical. English. Twelve times a year. $219.00. American Health Consultants, 3525 Piedmont Road, Suite 400, Atlanta GA 30305. **Tel** (800)688-2421, (404)262-7436, FAX (800)850-1232, (404)262-7837. **(Subscription address:** American Health Consultants, Dept. 5042, Box 71266, Chicago IL 60691. **)** available on microfilm and microfiche from University Microfilms International (UMI).
Desc: A newsletter containing articles, news items, and commentary on physical fitness, health promotion, corporate wellness, employee assistance programs, obesity, and alcohol intervention programs.
Ind/Abst Consum. Health Nutr. Index (?-?); SPORT Discus; SportSearch.

ISSN 8756-3231
DD 331 US
EMPLOYEE RELATIONS BULLETIN (NEW YORK, N.Y.). (EMPLOYEE RELATIONS BULLETIN.). [Empl. relat. bull.]. **Added/Corp** National Retail Merchants Association. Employee Relations Service. (19??)-. Bulletin. English. Twelve times a year. $172.80. Bureau of Business Practice, 24 Rope Ferry Road, Waterford CT 06386. **Tel** (800)243-0876, (203)442-4365, (800)876-9105, FAX (203)443-1123. ***Continues*** *Employee Relations and Human Resources Bulletin, 0744-7779.*

ISSN 0013-6824
DD 658 US
EMPLOYEE RELATIONS IN ACTION. [Empl. relat. action]. (1961)-. Periodical. English. Twenty-four times a year. $225.00. Business Research Publications, 1333 H Street Northwest, 2nd Floor West, Washington DC 20005. **Tel** (202)842-3022, (800)822-6338, FAX (202)842-3023.
Desc: Publishes case studies of employee problems and management reactions. Provides details and analysis of events, arbitration and ruling. Covers absenteeism, alcoholism, discharge and discipline, discrimination, etc.

ISSN 0735-4738
US
CODEN EMRREW
CEASED
EMPLOYEE RELATIONS REPORT (RICHMOND, VA.). (EMPLOYEE RELATIONS REPORT.). [Empl. relat. rep.]. Vol. 1, No. 1 (Aug. 1982)-(Oct. 1993). Periodical. English. Employee Relations Report, PO Box 671, Richmond VA 23206. **Tel** (804)355-0214. **ED** Ann Black. Index available. cum. index. **Bk Rev.**
Desc: Reports on trends and issues in personnel and employee communications.

ISSN 1183-8485
DD 342.71/085 CN
EMPLOYERS' HUMAN RIGHTS & EQUITY REPORT. [Empl. hum. rights equity rep.]. **VFOAT** Employers' Human Rights and Equity Report; Human Rights & Equity Report. Vol. 3, No. 1 (June 1991)-. Periodical. English. Irregular. $175.00. Richard de Boo Ltd, 70 Richmond Street East, Toronto Ontario N5C 1M8 Canada. **Tel** (416)445-4940. ***Continues*** *The Employers' Human Rights Review., 0843-672X.*

AT
EMPLOYERS' REVIEW, THE. Vol. 1 (Sept. 1928)-. Periodical. English. Employers' Federation of New South Wales, PO Box A233, Sydney New South Wales 2000 Australia. ***Continues*** *Industrial Bulletin / Employers' Federation of New South Wales.*
Ind/Abst Int. Labour Doc.

ISSN 0257-3415
SZ
EMPLOYMENT, ADJUSTMENT, AND INDUSTRIALISATION. **Added/Corp** International Labour Office. (1986)-. Monographic series. English. Irregular. Price varies per volume. International Labour Office - ILO, Publications Sales Service, CH-1211 Geneva 22 Switzerland. **Tel** 011 41 22 7996111, FAX 011 41 22 7986253, telex 415 647 ilo ch.

ISSN 0267-5374
DD 331.0941 UK
EMPLOYMENT AFFAIRS REPORT. [Employ. aff. rep.]. (1985)-. Periodical. English. Six times a year. $171.12. Confederation British Industry, 103 New Oxford Street, London WC1A 1DU United Kingdom. **Tel** 011 44 171 3797400, FAX 011 44 171 2401578, telex 21332, .

LC HD5723 .A4532 ISSN 0013-6840
DD 331.12/5/0973 US
EMPLOYMENT AND EARNINGS (1969). (EMPLOYMENT AND EARNINGS.). [Employ. earn.]. **Added/Corp** United States. Bureau of Labor Statistics. **VFOAT** E and E; E & E. Vol. 16, No. 1 (July 1969)-. English. Twelve times a year (annual supplement). $41.00. US Government Printing Office / Department of Labor, 200 Constitution Avenue NW, Washington DC 20210. **Tel** (202)523-8165. available on microfilm and microfiche from University Microfilms International (UMI). Documents available from UMI Article Clearinghouse, Documents on Demand. ***Continues*** *Employment and Earnings and Monthly Report on the Labor Force.*
Desc: Current data on employment, hours, and earnings for the United States as a whole, for the states, and for more than 200 local areas. Presents revised data for recent years from the survey of business establishments.
Ind/Abst Am. Stat. Index; Expand. Acad. Index (1992-); Newsp. Period. Abstr. (1992-); Predicasts Forecasts.

US
EMPLOYMENT AND EARNINGS IN THE MOUNTAIN-PLAINS REGION / U.S. DEPARTMENT OF LABOR, BUREAU OF LABOR STATISTICS. (Feb. 1979)-. Periodical. English. Twelve times a year. US Department of Labor Bureau of Labor Statistics / Kansas City, 911 Walnut Street, Federal Office Building, Room 1604, Kansas City MO 64106. **Tel** (816)426-2378, FAX (816)426-6537. ***Formed by the union of*** *Employment in the Plains States* ***and*** *Employment in the Mountain States.*

LC HD5725.A4 A26 ISSN 1063-3782
DD 331.12/5/09798 US

EMPLOYMENT AND EARNINGS REPORT FOR ALASKA AND ... CENSUS AREAS. [Employ. earn. rep. Alsk. census areas]. **Added/Corp** Alaska. Dept. of Labor. Research and Analysis Section. **VFOAT** Employment & Earnings Report. Vol. 11, Issue 3 (3rd Quarter 1990)-. Periodical. English. One time a year. Free on request. Alaska Department of Labor, Administrative Services, Research & Analysis Section, PO Box 25501, Juneau AK 99802-5501. **Tel** (907)465-4500, FAX (907)465-2101. ***Continues*** *Quarterly Employment and Earnings Report for Alaska and ... Census Areas.*

US

EMPLOYMENT AND EARNINGS / U.S. DEPARTMENT OF LABOR, BUREAU OF LABOR STATISTICS. **Added/Corp** United States. Bureau of Labor Statistics. **VFOAT** Revised Establishment Data on Employment, Hours, and Earnings for the United States, ... (1992)-. English. US Department of Labor / Bureau of Labor Statistics, 441 G Street Northwest, Washington DC 20212. **Tel** (202)606-7800, FAX (202)606-7797. ***Continues*** *Supplement to Employment and Earnings, Revised Establishment Data, 0740-4352.*

LC HD5729.O6 O65 ISSN 0700-0847
DD 331.1/1/09713 CN

EMPLOYMENT AND IMMIGRATION REVIEW : ONTARIO. **VFOAT** Revue de l'Emploi et de l'Immigration : Ontario. Vol. 10 (1977)-. Periodical. English (French). Two times a year. Box 25 Canada Square, 2180 Yonge Street, Toronto Ontario M4S 2E7 Canada. ***Continues*** *Manpower and Immigration Review: Ontario Region, 0381-2154.*

LC HD5725.F6 A3
DD 331.112 US

EMPLOYMENT AND PAYROLLS IN FLORIDA COVERED BY THE UNEMPLOYMENT COMPENSATION LAW. **Main/Corp** Florida Industrial Commission. Vol. 1 (1948)-. English. Florida Industrial Commission, Tallahassee FL 32301.

LC HD5725.W2 A32
DD 331.12/5/09797021 US

EMPLOYMENT AND PAYROLLS IN WASHINGTON STATE BY COUNTY AND BY INDUSTRY. **Added/Corp** Washington (State). Employment Security Dept. Research and Statistics Branch. Washington (State). Employment Security Dept. Research & Analysis Branch. No. 1 (4th Quarter 1946)-. Periodical. English. Four times a year. $20.00. Research and Analysis Branch, Washington State Employment Security Department, Box 9046, Olympia WA 98507. **Tel** (206)438-4800, FAX (206)438-4846.

LC HD5725.I3 I463a
DD 331.1/1/09773 US

EMPLOYMENT AND TRAINING REPORT TO THE GOVERNOR. **Main/Corp** Illinois Governor's Advisory Council on Manpower. **Added/Corp** Illinois. Governor's Office of Manpower and Human Development. (1976)-. English. One time a year. Governor's Advisory Council on Manpower, 623 East Monroe Street, Springfield IL 62701. ***Continues*** *Manpower Report to the Governor.*

LC HD5842.9 .A28a
DD 331.1/1/09683 SQ

EMPLOYMENT AND WAGES. **Main/Corp** Swaziland. Central Statistical Office. (1970)-. English. One time a year. Free. PO Box 456, Mbabane Swaziland. **Tel** 43765, telex 2109 WD. **Ad Acc. Circ:** 500. ***Continues*** *Report on the Swaziland Employment and Wages Survey.*

ISSN 0267-8314
UK

EMPLOYMENT BULLETIN AND IR DIGEST. [Employ. bull. IR dig.]. **VFOAT** Employment Bulletin and Industrial Relations Digest. (1985)-. Bulletin. English. Six times a year. $824.00. MCB University Press, 60 62 Toller Lane, Bradford, West Yorkshire BD8 9BY United Kingdom. **Tel** 011 44 1274 785280, FAX 011 44 1274 785200, telex 51317-MCBUNI-G. **(Subscription address:** MCB University Press / US and Canada Subscriptions, PO Box 10812, Birmingham AL 35201-0812. **Tel** (205)995-1567, (800)633-4931, FAX (205)995-1588.**)** ***Formed by the union of*** *Employment Bulletin (London), 0266-0571* ***and*** *IR Digest, 0262-477X.*
Desc: Contains information on issues within the field of employee relations.
Ind/Abst Manage. Market. Abstr.

ISSN 0315-3525
CN

EMPLOYMENT BULLETIN (TORONTO. 1971). (EMPLOYMENT BULLETIN (CANADIAN REHABILITATION COUNCIL FOR THE DISABLED).). **Main/Corp** Canadian Rehabilitation Council for the Disabled. No. 1- Aug. 1971-. Bulletin. English. Six times a year. Canadian Rehabilitation Council for the Disabled, 45 Sheppard Avenue East/Suite 801, Toronto Ontario M2N 5W9 Canada. **Tel** (416)250-7490, FAX (416)229-1371.

US

EMPLOYMENT DISCRIMINATION. (1975)-. English. Irregular. Price varies. Matthew Bender & Company Inc., 1275 Broadway, Albany NY 12204. **Tel** (800)833-9844, (518)487-3000.

ISSN 0380-6936
CN

EMPLOYMENT, EARNINGS AND HOURS. **See** Business and Economics-Abstracting, Bibliographies and Statistics.

ISSN 1183-1804
DD 331.13/3/09713 CN

EMPLOYMENT EQUITY REVIEW. (THE EMPLOYMENT EQUITY REVIEW.). [Empl. equity rev.]. Vol. 1, No. 1 (Jan. 1991)-. Periodical. English. Twelve times a year (monthly). 316.13Can$. Concord Publishing Ltd., 14 Prince Arthur Avenue, Suite 209, Toronto Ontario M5R 2A9 Canada. **Tel** (416)964-2758, FAX (416)964-0659.

LC HD8381 .A17 ISSN 0264-7052
DD 331/.0941 UK
CODEN EMGAES
TITLE CHANGE

EMPLOYMENT GAZETTE. [Employ. gaz.]. **Main/Corp** Great Britain Dept. of Employment. (Jan. 1979)-(1995). English. Harrington Kilbride Plc, Highbury Station Road, London N1 1SE United Kingdom. **Tel** 011 44 171 2262222, FAX 011 44 171 2201255. Documents available from UMI Article Clearinghouse. ***Continues*** *Department of Employment Gazette, 0013-6859.* ***Continued by*** *Labour Market Trends.*
Desc: Monitors public employment and manpower policy, not only through its statistical coverage, but also in its specialist accounts (often exclusive) of research and developments in the labour field.
Ind/Abst ABI/INFORM Glob. Ed.; Curr. Cit.; Int. Labour Doc.; LABORDOC; Manage. Market. Abstr.; PAIS Int. Print; Stud. Women Abstr.; Work Relat. Abstr.; World Text. Abstr.

US

EMPLOYMENT GUIDE : [REFERENCE SECTION]. **Added/Corp** Bureau of National Affairs (Washington, D.C.). (198?)-. English. One time a week. $453.00. Bureau of National Affairs Inc., 9435 Key West Avenue, Rockville MD 20850. **Tel** (800)372-1033, (301)258-1033, FAX (301)948-5823.

LC HD8051 .A62 HD5723
DD 331/.0973 S 331.12/5/0973021 US

EMPLOYMENT, HOURS, AND EARNINGS, STATES AND AREAS. **Added/Corp** United States. Bureau of Labor Statistics. **VFOAT** Employment, Hours, and Earnings, States and Areas, Data for ... . (1982)-. Government Publication. English. Irregular. $31.00 US; $38.75 other. Superintendent of Documents, US Government Printing Office, Washington DC 20402. **Tel** (202)275-3328, FAX (202)786-2377. ***Continues*** *Employment and Earnings, States and Areas.*
Desc: Current data on employment, hours, and earnings for the United States as a whole, for individual States, and for more than 200 local areas.

LC HD8051 .A62 HD5723 ISSN 1047-059X
DD 331 US

EMPLOYMENT, HOURS, AND EARNINGS, UNITED STATES. [Employ. hours earn. U. S.]. **Added/Corp** United States. Bureau of Labor Statistics. (1984)-. Government Publication. English. Irregular. Superintendent of Documents, US Government Printing Office, Washington DC 20402. **Tel** (202)275-3328, FAX (202)786-2377. ***Continues*** *Employment and Earnings, United States, 0271-4787.*
Ind/Abst Predicasts Forecasts.

US

EMPLOYMENT IN NEW YORK STATE. **Added/Corp** New York (State). Dept. of Labor. Division of Research and Statistics. (Mar. 1991)-. Periodical. English. Twelve times a year. New York State Department of Labor / Albany, 401 Harriman, Division of Research and Statistics, State Office Building Campus, Albany NY 12240. **Tel** (518)457-6649.

US

EMPLOYMENT IN THE MAINSTREAM. **See** Physically Impaired.

ISSN 0163-3287
US

EMPLOYMENT INFORMATION IN THE MATHEMATICAL SCIENCES. **Added/Corp** Mathematical Sciences Employment Register. American Mathematical Society. Mathematical Association of America. Issue 37 (Nov. 1978)-. Periodical. English. Five times a year. $175.00. American Mathematical Society, PO Box 6248, Providence RI 02940-6248. **Tel** (800)321-4267, (401)455-4000, FAX (401)331-3842, telex 797192. **(Subscription address:** American Mathematical Society, PO Box 5904, Boston MA 02206-5904. **Tel** (800)321-4267.**)** **ED** J. Scapini. **Ad Acc. Circ:** 700. ***Continues*** *Employment Information for Mathematicians, 0147-3018.*
Desc: Provides information on available positions in the mathematical sciences.

LC HD5764.5.A3 I56
NE

EMPLOYMENT OBSERVATORY. POLICIES. **Added/Corp** Commission of the European Communities. Mutual Information System on Employment Policies. Institute for Policy Research (Leiden, Netherlands). **VFOAT** Policies. (Winter 1991)-. Periodical. English. Four times a year. Free on request. Office for Official Publications of the European Communities, 2 rue Mercier, 2985 Luxembourg Luxembourg. **Tel** 011 352 499281, FAX 011 352 292942763. ***Continues*** *InforMISEP.*
Ind/Abst PAIS Int. Print.

BE

EMPLOYMENT OBSERVATORY. TRENDS. **Added/Corp** European System of Documentation on Employment. **VFOAT** Trends. No. 7 (1991)-. Periodical. English. Four times a year. Free on request. SYSDEM, 136 avenue de Tervuren, 1040 Brussels Belgium. **Tel** 011 32 2 7327818. ***Continues*** *SYSDEM Bulletin.*

LC HD5701 .O215
FR

EMPLOYMENT OUTLOOK. **Added/Corp** Organisation for Economic Co-Operation and Development. **VFOAT** Employment Outlook. (July 1991)-. English. One time a year. $52.00. OECD Publications and Information Center, 2 rue Andre-Pascal, 75775 Paris Cedex 16 France. **Tel** 011 33 1 49104262, US:(202)785-6323, FAX 011 33 1 45248500, 011 33 1 45248176, telex 620 160 OCDE. **(Subscription address:** OECD Publications Center, 2001 L Street, Suite 700, Washington DC 20036. **Tel** (202)822-3873, (202)785-6323.**)** ***Continues*** *OECD Employment Outlook.*
Desc: Discusses short-term labour market prospects and the nature of employment growth over the last decade.

LC HD4903.5.U58 E16 ISSN 0745-7790
DD 658.3 US
CCC
CODEN EEOTDY

EMPLOYMENT RELATIONS TODAY. [Empl. relat. today]. Vol. 10, No. 1 (Spring 1983)-. Periodical. English. Four times a year. $165.00. John Wiley & Sons, Inc., 605 Third Avenue, New York NY 10158-0012. **Tel** (212)850-6000, (212)850-6645, FAX (212)850-6088, telex 12-7063. **(Subscription address:** John Wiley & Sons Inc / New Jersey, PO Box 2575, Secaucus NJ 07096-2575. **)** **ED** Jane G. Bensahel. Index available. **Ad Acc.** available on microfilm and microfiche from University Microfilms International (UMI); available on an online database (files 15,648/Full-Text) from DIALOG. Documents available from UMI Article Clearinghouse. ***Continues*** *EEO Today, 0362-5818.*
Desc: Helps top-level human resources administrators anticipate and meet critical business and regulatory challenges posed by the fast-changing global economy and diverse workforce. Discusses solutions to specific workplace problems, as well as how to deal with modern corporate culture, develop new, more appropriate organizational structures, and respond to economic forces which have altered traditional employer-employee relationships.
Ind/Abst ABI/INFORM Glob. Ed. (Fall 1977-); ABI/INFORM Ondisc: Expr. Ed. (Spring 1987-); ABI/INFORM [Computer File] (Fall 1977-); Bus. ASAP (1992-) [Full Txt.]; Bus. Index (1985-); Bus. Period. Index; Curr. Cit.; Gen. BusinessFile (1985-); Gen. Period. Index (1985-); Health Plan. Adminis.; Hum. Resour. Abstr.; INFO-SOUTH Abstr.; Mag. Search; Manage. Contents; PAIS Int. Print (1991-?); Person. Manage. Abstr.; Sage Public Adm. Abstr.; UMI ABI/Inform--Bus. Period. Ondisc [Full Txt.]; Wilson Bus. Abstr.; Work Relat. Abstr.

LC HD5725.N7 N43A ISSN 0013-6883
DD 331.1/09747 US

EMPLOYMENT REVIEW. [Employ. rev.]. **Main/Corp** New York (State). Dept. of Labor. Division of Research and Statistics. Vol. 25, No. 3 (March 1972)-. English. Twelve times a year. Free on request. New York State Department of Labor / Albany, 401 Harriman, Division of Research and Statistics, State Office Building Campus, Albany NY 12240. **Tel** (518)457-6649. **ED** Sanford Fialkoff. **Circ:** 1,000.
Desc: Contains current labor market information, presented in tabular format. Focuses on employment and the rate of unemployment. Includes non-agricultural employment by state and area.
Ind/Abst Acad. Search; Bus. Index (Jan. 1985-Dec. 1985); Bus. Source Plus; Bus. Source; EP Collect.; Gen. BusinessFile (Jan. 1985-Dec. 1985); Gen. Period. Index (Jan. 1985-Dec. 1985); Homework Help.; INFO-SOUTH Abstr.; Mag. Search; MasterFile FullTEXT 1000; MasterFile FullTEXT 350; MasterFile FullTEXT 650; MasterFile FullTEXT (Jan. 1993-); OCLC; Pub. Lib. FullTEXT; Telebase; Vocat. Search.

Business and Economics — Labor

LC HD5725.N8 N64B
DD 353.97560083/06 US
EMPLOYMENT SECURITY LOCAL OFFICE OPERATIONS ANNUAL. **Main/Corp** North Carolina. Labor Market Information Division. (1981)-. English. One time a year.

LC HD7096.U6 A3 ISSN 0735-3286
DD 368.4/4/009761 US
EMPLOYMENT SECURITY STATISTICAL BULLETIN. See Business and Economics-Abstracting, Bibliographies and Statistics.

US
EMPLOYMENT TRENDS (ALBANY, N.Y.). (EMPLOYMENT TRENDS.). **Added/Corp** New York (State). Division of Employment. New York (State). Dept. of Labor. Division of Research and Statistics. (19??)-. Periodical. English. Twelve times a year. Free on request. New York State Department of Labor / Albany, 401 Harriman, Division of Research and Statistics, State Office Building Campus, Albany NY 12240. **Tel** (518)457-6649.

ISSN 1201-3897
CN
TITLE CHANGE
EMPLOYMENT TRENDS BULLETIN. (1994)-(1995). English. Oasis, 204-21 10405 Jasper Avenue, Edmonton Alberta T5J 2Y6 Canada. **Tel** (403)467-0843. **ED** Norah Cantin. Index available. cum. index. **Ad Acc**. Continued by Business and Employment Trends.

LC HD5756.S25 C55B
DD 331.12/5/098331 SP
ENCUESTA NACIONAL DEL EMPLEO, GRAN SANTIAGO. (19??)-. Periodical. Spanish. Four times a year. $18.00. Instituto Nacional de Estadisticas, Avenida Bulnes 418, Casilla 498, Correo 3 Santiago Chile. **Tel** 6991441. **Circ**: 350 (ctrl). Continues Encuesta Nacional del Empleo. Region Metropolitana.

LC TA157 .S849
DD 331.2/82/000973 US
ENGINEERING SALARIES SURVEY / PREPARED BY D. DIETRICH ASSOCIATES, INC. See Engineering.

ISSN 0711-5318
DD 331.2/816/09714 CN
ENQUETE-SALAIRES (1981). (ENQUETE-SALAIRES.). [Enquete-salaires]. 1981-. French. One time a year. Free. Corporation Professionnelle des Technologues des Sciences Appliquees du Quebec, 1265 Berri Bureau 720, Montreal Quebec H2L 4X4 Canada. **Tel** (514)845-3247, FAX (514)845-3643. ctrl circ. Continues Enquetes-Salaires, 0711-7361.

LC HC271 .A218 HD5776
DD 330/.08 S 331.1/26/0944 FR
ENQUETE SUR L'EMPLOI. (1968)-. French. 12.00F. CNGP INSEE - Institut National de la Statistique et des Estudes Economiques, BP 2718, 1 rue V Auriol, F 80027 Amiens Cedex 1 France. **Tel** 011 33 22 927322.

ISSN 0842-2192
CN
ENQUETE SUR L'EMPLOI ET LA REMUNERATION. [Enq. empl. remun.]. **Main/Corp** Quebec (Province) Bureau de la Statistique. Service du Travail et de la Main-d'Oeuvre. (1972)-. French. One time a year. Bureau de la Statistique, Service du Travail et de la Main-d'Oeuvre, Montreal Quebec Canada.

ISSN 1067-3970
DD 331 US
ENTERTAINMENT EMPLOYMENT JOURNAL. (ENTERTAINMENT EMPLOYMENT JOURNAL : EEJ.). [Entertain. employ. j.]. **VFOAT** EEJ. (1992)-. Periodical. English. Twenty-two times a year. $125.00. Monumental Communications, 5632 Van Nuys Boulevard, Suite 320, Van Nuys CA 91401. **Tel** (818)901-9425, FAX (818)901-9421. **ED** Lawrence Haberman. **Bk Rev**. **Ad Acc**. ctrl circ.
Desc: Career magazine for the film and TV entertainment industry. Includes networking information and professional, technical, and production job opportunities.

LC HD4801 ISSN 1055-1131
DD 331 US
ENTERTAINMENT EMPLOYMENT NETWORK. [Entertain. Employ. Netw.]. **Added/Corp** Entertainment Employment Network. Vol. 1 (1991)-. Monographic series. English. $21.95 (single issue). Entertainment Employment Network, 8306 Wilshire Boulevard, Department 7024, Beverly Hills CA 90211.

LC HD4801 ISSN 1055-114X
DD 331 US
ENTERTAINMENT EMPLOYMENT WEEKLY. **VFOAT** Entertainment Employment Monthly; Entertainment Employment Network; Entertainment Employment Network. (1991)-. Periodical. English. One time a week. $24.99 (6 months). EEN Publishing Co., 8306 Wilshire Boulevard, Department 7024, Beverly Hills CA 90211.

LC HD4903.5.U58 U536A ISSN 0149-8320
DD 331.1/33 US
EQUAL EMPLOYMENT OPPORTUNITY COMMISSION AFFIRMATIVE ACTION PLAN. **Main/Corp** United States. Equal Employment Opportunity Commission. (19??)-. English. Equal Employment Opportunity Commission, 2401 E Street NW, Washington DC 20506. **Tel** (202)634-7062.

LC HD6490.R22 U64 ISSN 0741-2479
DD 331.87/32/0973 US
EQUAL EMPLOYMENT OPPORTUNITY REPORT. MINORITIES AND WOMEN IN APPRENTICESHIP PROGRAMS AND REFERRAL UNIONS. (EQUAL EMPLOYMENT OPPORTUNITY REPORT. MINORITIES AND WOMEN IN APPRENTICESHIP PROGRAMS AND REFERRAL UNIONS.). **Added/Corp** United States. Equal Employment Opportunity Commission. **VFOAT** E.E.O.C. Report. Minorities and Women in Apprenticeship Programs and Referral Unions; E.E.O.C. Report. Job Patterns for Minorities and Women in Apprenticeship Programs and Referral Unions; Minorities and Women in Apprenticeship Programs and Referral Unions; EEOC Report. Minorities and Women in Apprenticeship Programs and Referral Unions. (19??)-. English. One time a year. US Equal Employment Opportunity Commission, 2401 E Street NW, Washington DC 20506. **Tel** (202)634-6930. Continues Minority and Female Membership in Referral Unions, 0741-2274.

AT
EQUAL EMPLOYMENT OPPORTUNITY YEARLY REPORT. **Added/Corp** Western Australia. Directorate of Equal Opportunity in Public Employment. English.

ISSN 0261-0159
UK
EQUAL OPPORTUNITIES INTERNATIONAL. Vol. 1, No. 1 (1981)-. Periodical. English. Six times a year. $349.00. MCB University Press, 60 62 Toller Lane, Bradford, West Yorkshire BD8 9BY United Kingdom. **Tel** 011 44 1274 785280, FAX 011 44 1274 785200, telex 51317-MCBUNI-G. (**Subscription address**: MCB University Press / US and Canada Subscriptions, PO Box 10812, Birmingham AL 35201-0812. **Tel** (205)995-1567, (800)633-4931, FAX (205)995-1588.) **ED** Barrie O. Pettman. **Bk Rev**. available on an online database (file15/Full-Text) from DIALOG.
Desc: Provides articles and features on all aspects of women's involvement in the labour force. Is written and compiled on the basis of professional expertise, relevant research and practical experience. Aims to give these subjects a primacy which they seldom receive elsewhere. Provides a comprehensive service for its readers, and an opportunity for the publication of serious and innovative work.
Ind/Abst Curr. Cit.; Manage. Market. Abstr.; Person. Manage. Abstr.; Stud. Women Abstr.

US
EQUAL OPPORTUNITY IN EMPLOYMENT. **Main/Corp** United States. Office of Personnel Management. Library. (1979)-. English. Office of Personnel Management, 1900 East Street Northwest, OELR Room 7429, Washington DC 20415. **Tel** (202)632-6256. Continues United States. Civil Service Commission. Library. Equal Opportunity in Employment.

LC HD1751 .D48a ISSN 0146-2938
DD 331.2 US
EQUAL OPPORTUNITY REPORT USDA PROGRAMS. **Main/Corp** United States. Dept. of Agriculture. Office of Equal Opportunity. **VAT** Equal Opportunity Report United States Department of Agriculture Programs. (1972)-. English. One time a year. US Department of Agriculture, 14th Street and Independence Avenue SW, Washington DC 20250. **Tel** (202)720-5457. Documents available from Documents on Demand. Continues OEO Annual Report.
Ind/Abst Am. Stat. Index.

LC PN2055 .E7 ISSN 0092-4520
DD 331.88/11/79020973 US
EQUITY NEWS. [Equity news]. **Added/Corp** Actors' Equity Association. Vol. 58, No. 3 (Aug. 1973)-. Periodical. English. Ten times a year (monthly with Jan/Feb & July/Aug. combined). $20.00. Actors Equity Association, 165 West 46th Street, New York NY 10036. **Tel** (212)869-8530, FAX (212)719-9815. **ED** Dick Moore and Helawe Feldman. **Circ**: 33,000 (ctrl). Continues Equity.
Desc: Provides union information for theatre members.

LC HA1173 .A27 HD1536.A93 A93
DD 314.36 331.7/63/09436 AU
ERHEBUNG DER LAND- UND FORSTWIRTSCHAFTLICHEN ARBEITSKRAFTE. See Business and Economics-Abstracting, Bibliographies and Statistics.

LC K5 .R33 ISSN 1068-3542
DD 344.73/01255/05 347.304125505 US
CCC
ERISA AND BENEFITS LAW JOURNAL. [ERISA benefits law j.]. **VFOAT** Employee Retirement Income Security Act and Benefits Law Journal. Vol. 1, Issue 1 (May 1992)-. Periodical. English. Four times a year. $125.00. Butterworth Legal Publishers / Salem, NH, 8 Industrial Way, Building C, Salem NH 03079. **Tel** (800)548-4001, (603)898-9664.

ISSN 0883-3052
US
ERISA CITATOR. [ERISA cit.]. **Added/Corp** Washington Service Bureau. (1985)-. Periodical. English. Twelve times a year. $736.70. Washington Service Bureau Inc., 655 15th Street Northwest, Suite 270, Washington DC 20005. **Tel** (800)955-5219, (202)508-0600.

ISSN 8755-5379
DD 332 US
ERISA NEWSLETTER, THE. [ERISA newsl.]. **VFOAT** E.R.I.S.A. Newsletter. **VAT** Employee Retirement Income Security Act Newsletter. (19??)-. Newsletter. English. Twelve times a year. $89.00. Two Crows, 11 Pleasant Street, Berlin MA 01503. **Tel** (508)838-2104.

ISSN 0194-4959
US
CCC
ERISA UPDATE, THE. **Added/Corp** Washington Service Bureau. **VAT** Employee Retirement Income Security Act Update. (19??)-. English. Twelve times a year. $1150.10. Washington Service Bureau Inc., 655 15th Street Northwest, Suite 270, Washington DC 20005. **Tel** (800)955-5219, (202)508-0600. Index available (free). Continues ERISA Advisory Opinion Letters. Full-Text and Abstracts.

ISSN 1065-5085
US
ERS UPDATE (HONOLULU, HAWAII). (ERS UPDATE.). **VAT** Employees' Retirement System Update. (1992)-. Periodical. English. $180.00. Honolulu Information Service, PO Box 10447, Honolulu HI 96816.

LC HD8051 .U56a
DD 353.0083/025 US
ESA DIRECTORY OF OFFICES. **Main/Corp** United States. Employment Standards Administration. **VFOAT** Directory of Offices. **VAT** Employment Standards Administration Directory of Offices. (19??)-. Directory. English. US Department of Labor Employment Standards Administration, 200 Constitution Avenue NW, Room S2321, Washington DC 20210. **Tel** (202)219-6191, FAX (202)219-8457. available on microfiche (Vols. for March 1986- distributed to depository libraries).

LC HD5725.S6 E77
DD 362.8/5/09757 US
ESARS QUARTERLY SUMMARY OF LOCAL OFFICE ACTIVITIES. **VFOAT** Employment Security Automated Reporting System Quarterly Summary of Local Office Activities. (19??)-. English. Two times a year. Free. South Carolina Employment Security Commission, 1550 Gadsden Street, PO Box 995, Columbia SC 29202. **Tel** (803)737-2660, FAX (803)737-2642. **ED** David L Laird. Continues ESARS Summary of Local Office Activities.
Desc: Contains a summary of services provided to applicants by the South Carolina job service.

FR
ESPOIR. No. 1 (Sept. 1972)-. Periodical. French. Irregular. Institut Charles de Gaulle, 5 rue Solferino, 75007 Paris France.

ISSN 1010-8149
LU
CODEN CE
ESRA NEWSLETTER. [ESRA newsl.]. Periodical. English. Twelve times a year. Free on request. Office for Official Publications of the European Communities, 2 rue Mercier, 2985 Luxembourg Luxembourg. **Tel** 011 352 499281, FAX 011 352 292942763.

ISSN 0710-1996
DD 331.88/1135471 CN
ESSA BULLETIN. [ESSA bull.]. **Main/Corp** Economists', Sociologists' and Statisticans' Association. **VFOAT** Bulletin AESS. Vol. 2, No. 11 (Nov. 1977)-?. Bulletin. English (French). Twelve times a year. Free. Economists', Sociologists' and Statisticians' Association, 9-200 Cooper Street, Ottawa Ontario K2P 0G1 Canada. **Absorbed** Economists' Sociologists' and Statisticians' Association. Bulletin AESS. Continued in part by Bulletin AESS.

Business and Economics — Labor

LC HD5726.M75 E88
DD 331.12/5/0976147
US
ESTIMATED CIVILIAN LABOR FORCE. MONTGOMERY, ALABAMA STANDARD METROPOLITAN STATISTICAL AREA, MONTGOMERY, AUTAUGA & ELMORE COUNTIES. **Added/Corp** Alabama. **VFOAT** Montgomery, Alabama Standard Metropolitan Statistical Area, Montgomery, Autauga & Elmore Counties. (19??)-. Statistical Publication. English. One time a year.

LC HD5728 .B85a
DD 331.1/1/0971
ISSN 0702-0961
CN
ESTIMATES OF EMPLOYEES BY PROVINCE AND INDUSTRY (CUMULATED EDITION). See Business and Economics-Abstracting, Bibliographies and Statistics.

LC HD5726.D38 I44a
DD 331.2/09773/582
ISSN 0091-4517
US
ESTIMATES OF EMPLOYMENT, HOURS, AND EARNINGS IN NONAGRICULTURAL ESTABLISHMENTS: DECATUR STANDARD METROPOLITAN STATISTICAL AREA. **Main/Corp** Illinois. Bureau of Employment Security. Research and Statistics Section. **Added/Corp** United States. Bureau of Labor Statistics. United States. Dept. of Labor. Manpower Administration. **VFOAT** Decatur Standard Metropolitan Statistical Area Employment, Hours, and Earnings. No. 1 (1971)-. Statistical Publication. English. Illinois Bureau of Employment Security, 910 South Michigan Avenue, Chicago IL 60605.

LC HD5726.S7 I44A
DD 331.2/09773/56
ISSN 0091-4355
US
ESTIMATES OF EMPLOYMENT, HOURS, AND EARNINGS IN NONAGRICULTURAL ESTABLISHMENTS. SPRINGFIELD STANDARD METROPOLITAN STATISTICAL AREA. (ESTIMATES OF EMPLOYMENT, HOURS, AND EARNINGS IN NONAGRICULTURAL ESTABLISHMENTS.). **Main/Corp** Illinois. Bureau of Employment Security. Research and Statistics Section. **VFOAT** Springfield Standard Metropolitan Statistical Area Employment, Hours, and Earnings. No. 1- 1966/71-. English. Illinois Bureau of Employment Security, 910 South Michigan Avenue, Chicago IL 60605.

LC HD4977 .A24
DD 331.2/971
ISSN 0318-9007
CN
Pr Rev.
ESTIMATES OF LABOUR INCOME (OTTAWA). See Business and Economics-Abstracting, Bibliographies and Statistics.

LC HD5727 .C32a
DD 354.710083
CN
ESTIMATES. PART III, EMPLOYMENT AND IMMIGRATION CANADA. **Main/Corp** Canada. **VFOAT** Budget des Depenses. Partie III, Emploi et Immigration Canada. (19??)-. English (French). $6.00 Canada; $7.20 other. Canada Communication Group Publishers, Order Processing, Ottawa Ontario K1A 0S9 Canada. **Tel** (819)956-4800, (819)956-4802.

LC HD8005.6.C22 P823a
DD 354.71001/7
CN
ESTIMATES. PART III, PUBLIC SERVICE STAFF RELATIONS BOARD. **Main/Corp** Canada. **VFOAT** Budget des Depenses. Partie III, Commission des Relations de Travail dans la Fonction Publique. (19??)-. English (French). $3.00 Canada; $3.60 other. Canada Communication Group Publishers, Order Processing, Ottawa Ontario K1A 0S9 Canada. **Tel** (819)956-4800, (819)956-4802.

LC HD7088 .E84
DD 368.4/005
ISSN 0379-0266
AG
ESTUDIOS DE LA SEGURIDAD SOCIAL. **Added/Corp** International Social Security Association. General Secretariat. (19??)-. Periodical. Spanish. Two times a year.
Ind/Abst LABORDOC.

LC HD6305.M5 E84
DD 331.1/37804
UK
ETHNIC MINORITIES & EMPLOYMENT. **Added/Corp** Great Britain. Community Relations Commission. Employment Section. **VAT** Ethnic Minorities and Employment. (Dec. 1975)-. Periodical. English. Four times a year. Community Relations Commission, London WCZE 9HX United Kingdom.

IT
EUROINFORMAZIONI. (19??)-. Italian. Forty-eight times a year. L400000. Centro Internazionale e Documentazione Comunita Europea, Cisdce CSO Magenta 61, 20123 Milan Italy. **Tel** 011 39 2 48009072.

LC HF5549.5.E45 E9
US
EUROPEAN EMPLOYMENT DIRECTORY, THE. **Added/Corp** Docker Research Group. (1991)-. Directory. English.

LC HD8380.5.A5 E96
DD 331/.094
ISSN 0309-7234
UK
EUROPEAN INDUSTRIAL RELATIONS REVIEW. [Eur. ind. relat. rev.]. (1974)-. Academic Scholarly Publication. English. Twelve times a year. $504.81. Eclipse Publications Ltd., 18 20 Highbury Place, London N5 1QP United Kingdom. **Tel** 011 44 171 3545858. **(Subscription address:** Industrial Relations Services, 18-20 Highbury Place, London N5 1QP United Kingdom.) **ED** Richard Hyman. Index available. cum. index. **Bk Rev. Ad Acc, Adv Mgr:** Bernie Folan. Full Page (B&W) £180.00. **Circ:** 2,000. Documents available from UMI Article Clearinghouse.
Desc: Publishes news and feature texts relating to industrial relations and labor law throughout Western Europe.
Ind/Abst ABI/INFORM Glob. Ed.; Curr. Cit.; Int. Labour Doc.; LABORDOC; Manage. Market. Abstr.; Work Relat. Abstr.

UK
EUROPEAN INFORMATION BULLETIN. **Added/Corp** Commission of the European Communities. Trade Union Division. Issue 1 (March 1985)-. Bulletin. English. Four times a year. Free on request. Trade Union Directorate, Commission European Comm 200, B 1049 Brussels Belguim.

UK
●**EUROPEAN TRADE UNION INFORMATION BULLETIN.** **Added/Corp** Commission of the European Communities. **VFOAT** Trade Union Information Bulletin. (1993)-. Bulletin. English. Four times a year. Commission of the European Communities, Directorate of General Information, Avenue D Auderghem, 45 Breydel boulevard, B 1049 Brussels Belgium. **Tel** 011 32 2 2357639, telex 21877 COMEU B. **Continues** Trade Union Information Bulletin.

DD 331.1/0973 S 363.1/19624/0973
ISSN 0743-6149
EVALUATING YOUR FIRM'S INJURY & ILLNESS RECORD. CONSTRUCTION INDUSTRIES. **Added/Corp** United States. Bureau of Labor Statistics. **VFOAT** Evaluating Your Firm's Injury and Illness. Construction Industries.; Construction Industries. (1978)-. English. One time a year. **Continues** Evaluating Your Firm's Injury and Illness Record. Construction Industries, 0743-6149.

LC HD6475.F7 I588C
DD 331.88/1413
SZ
EXECUTIVE COMMITTEE MEETING - INTERNATIONAL UNION OF FOOD AND ALLIED WORKERS' ASSOCIATIONS. EXECUTIVE COMMITTEE. **Main/Corp** International Union of Food and Allied Workers' Associations. Executive Committee. (19??)-. English. International Union of Food and Allied Workers' Associations Secretariat, Rampe du Pont-Rouge 8, CH-1213 Petit-Lancy Geneva Switzerland.

LC HD4965.U5 D53A
DD 331.2/81/658400973
ISSN 0148-7353
US
EXECUTIVE COMPENSATION ANALYSIS OF PROFESSIONAL SERVICES' FIRMS. **Main/Corp** D. Dietrich Associates. (19??)-. English. One time a year. $150.00. Dietrich Associates Inc, Box 511, Phoenixville PA 19460. **Tel** (610)935-1563.
Desc: Contains compensation data on key executive level positions for engineering/architectural firms, management consulting firms, and scientific/economic research firms; includes base salaries, bonus/incentive pay, other pay factors, and benefit value factors.

CN
●**EXECUTIVE COMPENSATION IN CANADA.** (1993)-. Trade Publication. English. One time a year. Sobeco Inc., Immeuble Sobeco, 505 Rene-Levesque boulevard West, Montreal Quebec H2Z 1Y7 Canada. **Continues** Executives and Boards of Directors Total Compensation in Canada.

LC HD4965.5.U6 A59a
DD 331.2/81/65892130973
ISSN 0164-2812
US
EXECUTIVE COMPENSATION IN THE HIGH-TECHNOLOGY INDUSTRIES. **Main/Corp** American Electronics Association. (19??)-. Periodical. English. One time a year. American Electronics Association, 5201 Great America Parkway, Santa Clara CA 95054. **Tel** (415)327-9300.

ISSN 8756-2111
US
EXECUTIVE COMPENSATION REPORT (PARAMUS, N.J.). (EXECUTIVE COMPENSATION REPORT.). **VFOAT** Executive Compensation. (1985)-. Periodical. English. Twelve times a year. $613.00. Prentice-Hall Law and Business, 270 Sylvan Avenue, Englewood Cliffs NJ 07632. **Tel** (800)223-0231, (201)894-8538, FAX (201)894-8666.
Desc: Provide advice needed to design and draft compensation plans that yield maximum tax-saving benefits and attract and keep high-level employees.

LC HD4965.3.P88 E34A
DD 331.2/8136362
ISSN 0741-3424
US
EXECUTIVE COMPENSATION SURVEY (PRINCETON, N.J.). (EXECUTIVE COMPENSATION SURVEY - EDISON ELECTRIC INSTITUTE.). [Exec. compens. surv.]. **Main/Corp** Edison Electric Institute. (19??)-. English. Sibson and Company, 212 Carnegie Center, CN 5323, Princeton NJ 08543-5323. **Tel** (609)520-2700.

LC HD4965.5.U6 E92
DD 331.2/816584/00973
ISSN 0743-6130
US
EXECUTIVE COMPENSATION ... SURVEY RESULTS. **VFOAT** Executive Compensation; Planning Report. English. $10.00 members, $50.00 nonmembers. Research Institute of America, 117 East Stevens Avenue, Valhalla NY 10595. **Tel** (800)431-9025, FAX (800)820-3135 (914)749-5300.

LC HD7105.45.U6 E93
US
EXECUTIVE REPORT ON LARGE CORPORATE PENSION PLANS. **Added/Corp** Johnson & Higgins. (1983)-. English. Johnson & Higgins, 125 Broad Street, New York NY 10004-2424. **Continues** Funding Costs and Liabilities of Large Corporate Pension Plans, 0192-222X.

LC HD4966.M4 U53
DD 331.2/81/000976579
ISSN 0736-4482
US
EXEMPT SALARY SURVEY. English. One time a year. Personnel Surveys, Inc., 1608 Northstar Center, Minneapolis MN 55402.

US
EXPLORING CAREERS. (19??)-. English. One time a year. $19.95 (two-year). JIST Works Inc, 720 North Park Avenue, Indianapolis IN 46202-3431. **Tel** (317)637-6643, FAX (317)264-3709. **ED** JoAnn Amore, Greg Croy and Lisa Farr. Index available.
Desc: Reference book that describes myriad of occupations in terms of what a typical day is like for a worker performing that job.

LC LB2335.885.U6 F33
DD 331.89/04137812/0973
ISSN 0891-2785
US
FACT SHEET - ACADEMIC COLLECTIVE BARGAINING INFORMATION SERVICE. (FACT SHEET.). [Fact sheet - Acad. Collect. Bargain. Inf. Serv.]. **Added/Corp** Academic Collective Bargaining Information Service (Washington, D.C.). (19??)-. Periodical. English. Twelve times a year. $125.00. Academic Collective Bargaining Information Service, 4200 Connecticut Avenue Northwest, B52 Room 504 G, Washington DC 20005. **Tel** (202)727-2326, FAX (202)727-5998. **ED** Isadore Goldberg Ph.D. Index available. **Circ:** 500.
Desc: Deals with general news, fair employment practices, wages and hours, and arbitration in higher education institutions.

LC HD5725.N6 N475a
DD 331.12/5/09789
US
FACTS AND FIGURES: NEW MEXICO EMPLOYERS, INDUSTRY, SIZE, AND LOCATION. **Main/Corp** New Mexico. Unemployment Insurance Division. Actuarial Research Section. **Added/Corp** New Mexico. Unemployment Insurance Division. Actuarial Research Section. New Mexico Employers, Industry, Size and Location. (19??)-. Periodical. English. Four times a year. Free on request. New Mexico Department of Labor, Economic Research, Actuarial Research Section, PO Box 1928, Albuquerque NM 87103. **Tel** (505)841-8699. **ED** Vincent Brunacini Jr. **Circ:** 245 (ctrl).
Desc: Tables by county of the number of New Mexico private employers and employees arranged by workforce size categories and standard industrial code.

DD 331/.0971
ISSN 0429-9949
CN
FACTS AND TRENDS (VANCOUVER). (FACTS AND TRENDS.). [Facts trends]. **Added/Corp** Vancouver Board of Trade. (1960)-. Periodical. English. Irregular. 30.00Can$ members, 60.00Can$ nonmembers. Vancouver Board of Trade, 999 Canada Place, Suite 400, Vancouver British Columbia V6C 3C1 Canada. **Tel** (604)641-1264.
Desc: Digest of current trends in the area of personnel management and industrial relations.

DD 331.88/11/35471
ISSN 0705-856X
CN
FACTS (OTTAWA). (THE FACTS.). [Facts]. **Added/Corp** Canadian Union of Public Employees. **VFOAT** Leader. Vol. 1 (Mar. 1978)-. Periodical. English. Six times a year. Free on request. Canadian Union Public Employee, 21 Florence Street, Ottawa Ontario K2P 0W6 Canada. **Tel** (613)237-1590.

Business and Economics —Labor

LC RT79 .R45
DD 331.2/8161073/071173 US
NLM W1; FA199G
FACULTY SALARIES IN BACCALAUREATE AND GRADUATE PROGRAMS IN NURSING. Added/Corp American Association of Colleges of Nursing. Institutional Data Systems. (19??)-. English. American Association of Colleges of Nursing, One Dupont Circle NW / Suite 530, Washington DC 20036. **Tel** (202)463-6930. *Continues Report on Faculty Salaries in Baccalaureate and Graduate Programs in Nursing, 1055-6958.*

US
FACULTY SALARY SURVEY. Main/Corp American Association of Dental Schools. (19??)-. English. American Association of Dental Schools, 1625 Massachusetts Avenue Northwest, Washington DC 20036. **Tel** (202)667-9433, FAX (202)667-0642.

US
FAIR EMPLOYMENT PRACTICE NEWSLETTER. (19??)-. Newsletter. English. Twenty-six times a year. $112.00. Bureau of National Affairs Inc., 9435 Key West Avenue, Rockville MD 20850. **Tel** (800)372-1033, (301)258-1033, FAX (301)948-5823.

ISSN 0014-6919
US
CCC
FAIR EMPLOYMENT REPORT. (19??)-. Periodical. English. Twenty-four times a year. $299.00. Business Publishers Inc., 951 Pershing Drive, Silver Spring MD 20910-4464. **Tel** (301)587-6300, (800)274-0122, FAX (301)585-9075. **ED** Nancy Aldrich. *Supersedes Civil Rights Employment Reporter.*
Desc: Report on legislation and court cases involving workplace discrimination as governed by civil rights laws.

LC S
DD 630 US
FARM LABOR AND WAGE RATES / IOWA CROP AND LIVESTOCK REPORTING SERVICE. Periodical. English. Four times a year. $885.00. The Service, Full Depository, 707 Savings and Loan Building, Des Moines IA 50309.
Desc: Farm employment and indexes, and farm wage rate for Iowa and the United States.

LC HD1527.W9 W94A ISSN 0095-389X
DD 331.7/63/09787 US
FARM LABOR REPORT (CASPER). (FARM LABOR REPORT.). Main/Corp Employment Security Commission of Wyoming. Research and Analysis Section. (19??)-. English. One time a year. Employment Security Commission of Wyoming, PO Box 2760, Research and Analysis, Casper WY 82602. **Tel** (307)237-3701.

ISSN 0163-8270
DD 353.001 US
FEDERAL CIVILIAN WORK FORCE STATISTICS. See Business and Economics-Abstracting, Bibliographies and Statistics.

US
FEDERAL CONTRACT COMPLIANCE MANUAL. Main/Corp United States. Office of Federal Contract Compliance Programs. (19??)-. English. US Department of Labor Employment Standards Administration, 200 Constitution Avenue NW, Room S2321, Washington DC 20210. **Tel** (202)219-6191, FAX (202)219-8457.

LC KF3464 .A515 ISSN 1043-7274
DD 344.73/0113/30264 347.30411330264 US
CCC
FEDERAL EQUAL OPPORTUNITY REPORTER. [Fed. equal oppor. report.]. (1979/1982)-. Periodical. English. Twenty-two times a year. $885.00. LRP Publications, 747 Dresher Road, Suite 500, Horsham PA 19044. **Tel** (800)341-7874, (215)784-0941, FAX (215)784-9639, (215)784-0870. **(Subscription address:** LRP Publications, PO Box 980, Horsham PA 19044. **Tel** (800)341-7874, (215)784-0860.)
Desc: Reports on the decisions of both the ORA and the courts on federal employee EEO appeals. Includes advance sheets highlighting cases of particular importance in each issue. All reported cases fully indexed, summarized and headnoted.

ISSN 1075-6574
DD 331 US
●**FEDERAL HUMAN RESOURCES WEEK.** [Fed. human resour. week]. (1994)-. Periodical. English. Forty-eight times a year. $295.00. LRP Publications, 747 Dresher Road, Suite 500, Horsham PA 19044. **Tel** (800)341-7874, (215)784-0941, FAX (215)784-9639, (215)784-0870. **(Subscription address:** LRP Publications, PO Box 980, Horsham PA 19044. **Tel** (800)341-7874, (215)784-0860.)

US
FEDERAL LABOR AND EMPLOYEE RELATIONS UPDATE. English. Twelve times a year. $195.00. FPMI Communications Inc., 707 Fiber Street, Huntsville AL 35801. **Tel** (205)539-1850, FAX (205)539-0911, .

LC KF5365.A59 F43 ISSN 0885-3061
DD 344.73/0189041353 347.304189041353 US
FEDERAL LABOR-MANAGEMENT AND EMPLOYEE RELATIONS CONSULTANT, THE. [Fed. labor-manage. empl. relat. consult.]. Added/Corp United States. Office of Personnel Management. VFOAT The Federal Labor Management and Employee Relations Consultant; Consultant. 1 FLMERC 84-7 (April 13, 1984)-. Government Publication. English. Twenty-six times a year. $49.00. Office of Personnel Management, 1900 East Street Northwest, OELR Room 7429, Washington DC 20415. **Tel** (202)632-6256. **(Subscription address:** Superintendent of Documents, US Government Printing Office, Washington DC 20402.) *Continues Federal Labor-Management Consultant, 0046-3418.*
Desc: Presents current information in the field of labor management and employee relations.

ISSN 1065-8238
DD 344 US
FEDERAL LABOR RELATIONS ... DESK BOOK. [Fed. labor relat. desk book]. Added/Corp LRP Publications (Firm). (1992)-. Periodical. English. One time a year. $57.50. LRP Publications, 747 Dresher Road, Suite 500, Horsham PA 19044. **Tel** (800)341-7874, (215)784-0941, FAX (215)784-9639, (215)784-0870. **ED** Al Celmer.
Desc: Focuses on the major decisions of the Federal Labor Relations Authority, Federal Service Impasses Panel, and the Circuit Courts.

LC KF5365.A57 F44 ISSN 0199-4883
DD 344.73/0189041353 347.304189041353 US
FEDERAL LABOR RELATIONS REPORTER. (1970/1978)-. Periodical. English. One time a week (50 issues). $790.00. LRP Publications, 747 Dresher Road, Suite 500, Horsham PA 19044. **Tel** (800)341-7874, (215)784-0941, FAX (215)784-9639, (215)784-0870. **ED** Al Celmer. **Bk Rev. Ad Acc.**
Desc: Contains abstracts of FLRA, FSIP, AIJ and GCFLRA decisions, with full-text court cases, complete indexing, citations/statute trackers, and citators.

ISSN 0898-2821
DD 353 US
FEDERAL LABOR RELATIONS UPDATE. [Fed. labor relat. update]. Added/Corp Federal Personnel Management Institute. VFOAT Update. Vol. 1, Issue 1 (March 1988)-. Periodical. English. Twelve times a year. $125.00. Federal Personnel Management Institute Inc., 3322 South Memorial Parkway, Suite 40, Huntsville AL 35802. **Tel** (205)882-3042.
Desc: A summary and explanation of significant third party decisions affecting the Federal Labor Relations program.

US
FEDERAL PERSONNEL MANUAL SYSTEM. FPM SUPPLEMENT 711-2. LABOR-MANAGEMENT CASE FINDER. See Public Administration-Civil Service.

US
FEDERAL PERSONNEL MANUAL SYSTEM. FPM SUPPLEMENT 990-3. NATIONAL EMERGENCY STANDBY REGULATIONS (PERSONNEL AND MANPOWER). See Public Administration-Civil Service.

US
CEASED
FEDERAL REGULATIONS AND THE EMPLOYMENT PRACTICES OF COLLEGES AND UNIVERSITIES. Main/Corp National Association of College and University Business Officers. No. 1 (June 1974)-(1987). English. Three times a year. National Association of College & University Business Officers, 1 Dupont Circle, Suite 500, Washington DC 20036. **Tel** (202)861-2564.

ISSN 0738-0550
US
FEDERATION NEWS (LOS ANGELES, CALIF.), THE. (THE FEDERATION NEWS.). Added/Corp Los Angeles County Federation of Labor. Vol. 1, Issue 1 (May 1983)-. Periodical. English. Twelve times a year. Free to members. Los Angeles County Federation of Labor, 2130 West 9th Street, Los Angeles CA 90006. *Continues Los Angeles Citizen, 0024-6549.*

ISSN 0430-2761
US
FEDNEWS, THE. [Fednews]. Added/Corp National Association of Government Employees (U.S.). Vol. 1 (1962)-. Periodical. English. Twelve times a year. $7.20. National Association of Government Employees, 159 Burgin Parkway, Quincy MA 02169. **Tel** (617)268-5002. **ED** Ed Gillooly. **Bk Rev. Ad Acc. Circ:** 25,000 (ctrl).
Desc: Labor and member news.
Ind/Abst Work Relat. Abstr.

SZ
FIET INFO / INTERNATIONAL FEDERATION OF COMMERCIAL, CLERICAL, PROFESSIONAL AND TECHNICAL EMPLOYEES. Added/Corp International Federation of Commercial, Clerical, Professional and Technical Employees. (March 1988)-. Periodical. English. Eleven times a year. Free. FIET, 15 Avenue de Balexert, 1210 Chatelaine-Geneva Switzerland. **Tel** 011 41 22 962733. *Continues FIET Newsletter.*

US
FINAL ACT / ORGANIZATION OF AMERICAN STATES, CIES. Main/Conf Inter-American Conference of Ministries of Labor. Added/Corp Inter-American Economic and Social Council. (19??)-. English. Organization of American States, 19th Street & Constitution Avenue NW, Suite 300, Washington DC 20006. **Tel** (202)458-6256. *Continues Inter-American Conference of Ministers of Labor on the Alliance for Progress. Final Act.*

LC HD7106.U6 A24 ISSN 0742-0072
DD 332.6/7254 US
FINANCIAL DIRECTORY OF PENSION FUNDS. ALABAMA. Added/Corp ERISA Benefit Funds, Inc. (19??)-. Directory. English. One time a year. $445.00 print; $890.00 disk. Dun & Bradstreet Information Services, 3 Sylvan Way, Parsippany NJ 07054. **Tel** (201)605-6000, (800)526-0651. available on diskette. *Continues ERISA Benefit Funds. Financial Directory of Pension Funds, State of Alabama, 0190-6259.*

LC HD7106.U6 A43 ISSN 0742-0099
DD 332.6/7254 US
FINANCIAL DIRECTORY OF PENSION FUNDS. ALASKA. Added/Corp ERISA Benefit Funds, Inc. (19??)-. Directory. English. One time a year. $295.00 print; $590.00 disk. Dun & Bradstreet Information Services, 3 Sylvan Way, Parsippany NJ 07054. **Tel** (201)605-6000, (800)526-0651. available on diskette. *Continues ERISA Benefit Funds. Financial Directory of Pension Funds, State of Alaska, 0190-6038.*

LC HD7106.U6 A64 ISSN 0742-0110
DD 332.6/7254 US
FINANCIAL DIRECTORY OF PENSION FUNDS. ARIZONA. Added/Corp ERISA Benefit Funds, Inc. (19??)-. Directory. English. One time a year. $495.00 print; $990.00 disk. Dun & Bradstreet Information Services, 3 Sylvan Way, Parsippany NJ 07054. **Tel** (201)605-6000, (800)526-0651. available on diskette. *Continues ERISA Benefit Funds. Financial Directory of Pension Funds, State of Arizona, 0190-6550.*

LC HD7106.U6 A84 ISSN 0742-0102
DD 332.6/7254 US
FINANCIAL DIRECTORY OF PENSION FUNDS. ARKANSAS. Added/Corp ERISA Benefit Funds, Inc. (19??)-. Directory. English. One time a year. $345.00 print; $690.00 disk. Dun & Bradstreet Information Services, 3 Sylvan Way, Parsippany NJ 07054. **Tel** (201)605-6000, (800)526-0651. available on diskette. *Continues ERISA Benefit Funds. Financial Directory of Pension Funds, State of Arkansas, 0190-6534.*

LC HD7106.U6 C232 ISSN 0739-2737
DD 332.6/7254 US
FINANCIAL DIRECTORY OF PENSION FUNDS. CALIFORNIA, NORTHERN, EXCLUDING SAN FRANCISCO (OAKLAND, SAN JOSE, FRESNO & OTHERS). Added/Corp ERISA Benefit Funds, Inc. (19??)-. Directory. English. One time a year. $495.00 (print), $990.00 (disk) zip codes 936-939 and 950-951; $545.00 (print), $1090.00 (disk) zip codes 945-949. Dun & Bradstreet Information Services, 3 Sylvan Way, Parsippany NJ 07054. **Tel** (201)605-6000, (800)526-0651. available on diskette. *Continues ERISA Benefit Funds. Financial Directory of Pension Funds, Northern California, excluding San Francisco, 0190-8677.*

LC HD7106.U6 C233 ISSN 0739-2699
DD 332.6/7254 US
FINANCIAL DIRECTORY OF PENSION FUNDS. CALIFORNIA, NORTHERN. SAN FRANCISCO AREA. (FINANCIAL DIRECTORY OF PENSION FUNDS. CALIFORNIA, NORTHERN (SAN FRANCISCO AREA) / ERISA BENEFIT FUNDS, INC.). Added/Corp ERISA Benefit Funds, Inc. (19??)-.

Business and Economics —Labor

Directory. English. One time a year. $545.00 print; $1090.00 disk. Dun & Bradstreet Information Services, 3 Sylvan Way, Parsippany NJ 07054. **Tel** (201)605-6000, (800)526-0651. available on diskette. ***Continues*** *ERISA Benefit Funds. Financial Directory of Pension Funds, Northern California, San Francisco Area, 0190-9878.*

LC HD7105.35.U6 F56 **ISSN** 0739-3385
DD 332.6/7254 US
FINANCIAL DIRECTORY OF PENSION FUNDS. CALIFORNIA, SOUTHERN, EXCLUDING LOS ANGELES AREA (SAN DIEGO, SANTA ANA, SAN BERNARDINO & OTHERS). (FINANCIAL DIRECTORY OF PENSION FUNDS. CALIFORNIA, SOUTHERN, EXCLUDING LOS ANGELES AREA (SAN DIEGO, SANTA ANA, SANTA BERNARDINO & OTHERS) / ERISA BENEFIT FUNDS, INC.). **Added/Corp** ERISA Benefit Funds, Inc. (19??)-. Directory. English. One time a year. $545.00 (print), $1090.00 (disk) zip codes 919-925; $495.00 (print), $990.00 (disk) zip codes 926-928. Dun & Bradstreet Information Services, 3 Sylvan Way, Parsippany NJ 07054. **Tel** (201)605-6000, (800)526-0651. available on diskette.

LC HD7106.U6 C235 **ISSN** 0739-2591
DD 332.6/7254 US
FINANCIAL DIRECTORY OF PENSION FUNDS. CALIFORNIA, SOUTHERN (LOS ANGELES CITY PROPER). **Added/Corp** ERISA Benefit Funds, Inc. (19??)-. Directory. English. One time a year. $445.00 print, $890.00 disk. Dun & Bradstreet Information Services, 3 Sylvan Way, Parsippany NJ 07054. **Tel** (201)605-6000, (800)526-0651. available on diskette. ***Continues*** *ERISA Benefit Funds. Financial Directory of Pension Funds, Southern California, Los Angeles Proper, 0190-8669.*

LC HD7105.45.U6 F56 **ISSN** 0739-2729
DD 332.6/7254 US
FINANCIAL DIRECTORY OF PENSION FUNDS. CALIFORNIA, SOUTHERN, NO. SUBURBAN LOS ANGELES (VENTURA, PASADENA, ALHAMBRA & OTHERS). **Added/Corp** ERISA Benefit Funds, Inc. (19??)-. Directory. English. One time a year. $495.00 print, $990.00 disk. Dun & Bradstreet Information Services, 3 Sylvan Way, Parsippany NJ 07054. **Tel** (201)605-6000, (800)526-0651. available on diskette.

LC HD7105.45.U6 F562 **ISSN** 0739-2672
DD 332.6/7254 US
FINANCIAL DIRECTORY OF PENSION FUNDS. CALIFORNIA, SOUTHERN, SO. SUBURBAN LOS ANGELES (INGLEWOOD, WHITTIER, LONG BEACH & OTHERS). **Added/Corp** ERISA Benefit Funds, Inc. (19??)-. Directory. English. One time a year. $445.00 print, $890.00 disk. Dun & Bradstreet Information Services, 3 Sylvan Way, Parsippany NJ 07054. **Tel** (201)605-6000, (800)526-0651. available on diskette.

LC HD7106.U6 C24 **ISSN** 0278-2405
DD 332.6/7254 US
FINANCIAL DIRECTORY OF PENSION FUNDS. CALIFORNIA, UPPER NORTHERN (STOCKTON, SACRAMENTO & OTHERS). **Added/Corp** ERISA Benefit Funds, Inc. **VFOAT** Financial Directory of Pension Funds. California, Upper Northern (Stockton, Sacramento and Others); Financial Directory of Pension Funds. (19??)-. English. One time a year. $595.00 print, $1190.00 disk. Dun & Bradstreet Information Services, 3 Sylvan Way, Parsippany NJ 07054. **Tel** (201)605-6000, (800)526-0651. available on diskette.

LC HD7106.U6 C66 **ISSN** 0741-4714
DD 332.6/7254 US
FINANCIAL DIRECTORY OF PENSION FUNDS. COLORADO. **Added/Corp** ERISA Benefit Funds, Inc. (19??)-. Directory. English. One time a year. $545.00 print, $1090.00 disk. Dun & Bradstreet Information Services, 3 Sylvan Way, Parsippany NJ 07054. **Tel** (201)605-6000, (800)526-0651. available on diskette. ***Continues*** *ERISA Benefit Funds. Financial Directory of Pension Funds, State of Colorado, 0190-6542.*

LC HD7106.U6 C845 **ISSN** 0739-280X
DD 332.6/7254 US
FINANCIAL DIRECTORY OF PENSION FUNDS. CONNECTICUT, NORTHERN (HARTFORD, WILLIMANTIC, WATERBURY & OTHERS). **Added/Corp** ERISA Benefit Funds, Inc. (19??)-. Directory. English. One time a year. $395.00 print, $790.00 disk. Dun & Bradstreet Information Services, 3 Sylvan Way, Parsippany NJ 07054. **Tel** (201)605-6000, (800)526-0651. available on diskette. ***Continues*** *ERISA Benefit Funds. Financial Directory of Pension Funds, Northern Connecticut, 0190-9312.*

LC HD7106.U6 C846 **ISSN** 0739-2621
DD 332.6/7254 US
FINANCIAL DIRECTORY OF PENSION FUNDS. CONNECTICUT, SOUTHERN. STAMFORD, NEW HAVEN, NEW LONDON & OTHERS. (FINANCIAL DIRECTORY OF PENSION FUNDS. CONNECTICUT, SOUTHERN (STAMFORD, NEW HAVEN, NEW LONDON & OTHERS) / ERISA BENEFIT FUNDS, INC.). **Added/Corp** ERISA Benefit Funds, Inc. (19??)-. Directory. English. One time a year. $495.00 print, $990.00 disk. Dun & Bradstreet Information Services, 3 Sylvan Way, Parsippany NJ 07054. **Tel** (201)605-6000, (800)526-0651. available on diskette. ***Continues*** *ERISA Benefit Funds. Financial Directory of Pension Funds, Southern Connecticut, 0190-9304.*

LC HD7106.U6 D44 **ISSN** 0882-2980
DD 332.6/7254 US
FINANCIAL DIRECTORY OF PENSION FUNDS. DELAWARE, THE. [Financ. dir. pension funds, Del.]. **Added/Corp** ERISA Benefit Funds, Inc. (1984-85)-. Directory. English. One time a year. $295.00 print, $590.00 disk. Dun & Bradstreet Information Services, 3 Sylvan Way, Parsippany NJ 07054. **Tel** (201)605-6000, (800)526-0651. available on diskette. ***Continues*** *Financial Directory of Pension Funds. State of Delaware, 0731-7387.*

LC HD7106.U6 D64 **ISSN** 0742-0080
DD 332.6/7254 US
FINANCIAL DIRECTORY OF PENSION FUNDS. DISTRICT OF COLUMBIA. **Added/Corp** ERISA Benefit Funds, Inc. (19??)-. Directory. English. One time a year. $345.00 print, $690.00 disk. Dun & Bradstreet Information Services, 3 Sylvan Way, Parsippany NJ 07054. **Tel** (201)605-6000, (800)526-0651. available on diskette. ***Continues*** *ERISA Benefit Funds. Financial Directory of Pension Funds, District of Columbia, 0190-6291.*

LC HD7106.U5 F54 **ISSN** 0278-0348
DD 332.6/7254 US
FINANCIAL DIRECTORY OF PENSION FUNDS. FLORIDA, CENTRAL (TAMPA, LAKELAND, ORLANDO & OTHERS). (FINANCIAL DIRECTORY OF PENSION FUNDS. FLORIDA, CENTRAL (TAMPA, LAKELAND, ORLANDO & OTHERS) / ERISA BENEFIT FUNDS, INC.). **Added/Corp** ERISA Benefit Funds, Inc. **VFOAT** Financial Directory of Pension Funds. Florida, Central (Tampa, Lakeland, Orlando & Others); Financial Directory of Pension Funds. (19??)-. Directory. English. One time a year. $545.00 print, $1090.00 disk. Dun & Bradstreet Information Services, 3 Sylvan Way, Parsippany NJ 07054. **Tel** (201)605-6000, (800)526-0651. available on diskette.

LC HD7106.U6 F62 **ISSN** 0739-2656
DD 332.6/7254 US
FINANCIAL DIRECTORY OF PENSION FUNDS. FLORIDA, NORTHERN (JACKSONVILLE, TALLAHASSEE, GAINESVILLE & OTHERS). **Added/Corp** ERISA Benefit Funds, Inc. (19??)-. Directory. English. One time a year. $395.00 print, $790.00 disk. Dun & Bradstreet Information Services, 3 Sylvan Way, Parsippany NJ 07054. **Tel** (201)605-6000, (800)526-0651. available on diskette. ***Continues*** *ERISA Benefit Funds. Financial Directory of Pension Funds, Northern Florida, 0190-6305.*

LC HD7106.U6 F623 **ISSN** 0739-2664
DD 332.6/7254 US
FINANCIAL DIRECTORY OF PENSION FUNDS. FLORIDA, SOUTHERN. WEST PALM BEACH, MIAMI, FT. MYER & OTHERS. (FINANCIAL DIRECTORY OF PENSION FUNDS. FLORIDA, SOUTHERN (WEST PALM BEACH, MIAMI, FT. MYER & OTHERS) / ERISA BENEFIT FUNDS, INC.). **Added/Corp** ERISA Benefit Funds, Inc. (19??)-. Directory. English. One time a year. $595.00 print, $1190.00 disk. Dun & Bradstreet Information Services, 3 Sylvan Way, Parsippany NJ 07054. **Tel** (201)605-6000, (800)526-0651. available on diskette. ***Continues*** *ERISA Benefit Funds. Financial Directory of Pension Funds, Southern Florida, 0190-6267.*

LC HD7106.U6 G433 **ISSN** 0739-3245
DD 332.6/7254 US
FINANCIAL DIRECTORY OF PENSION FUNDS. GEORGIA, ATLANTA AREA. (FINANCIAL DIRECTORY OF PENSION FUNDS. GEORGIA, ATLANTA AREA / ERISA BENEFIT FUNDS, INC.). **Added/Corp** ERISA Benefit Funds, Inc. (19??)-. Directory. English. One time a year. $495.00 print, $990.00 disk. Dun & Bradstreet Information Services, 3 Sylvan Way, Parsippany NJ 07054. **Tel** (201)605-6000, (800)526-0651. available on diskette. ***Continues*** *ERISA Benefit Funds. Financial Directory of Pension Funds, State of Georgia, Atlanta Area, 0192-2947.*

LC HD7106.U5 F543 **ISSN** 0731-7328
DD 332.6/7254 US
FINANCIAL DIRECTORY OF PENSION FUNDS. GEORGIA, EXCLUDING ATLANTA AREA. (FINANCIAL DIRECTORY OF PENSION FUNDS. GEORGIA, EXCLUDING ATLANTA AREA / ERISA BENEFIT FUNDS, INC.). **Added/Corp** ERISA Benefit Funds, Inc. (19??)-. Directory. English. One time a year. $395.00 print, $790.00 disk. Dun & Bradstreet Information Services, 3 Sylvan Way, Parsippany NJ 07054. **Tel** (201)605-6000, (800)526-0651. available on diskette. ***Continues*** *ERISA Benefit Funds. Directory of Pension Funds, State of Georgia, 0148-1614.*

LC HD7106.U6 H33 **ISSN** 0882-2956
DD 332.6/7254 US
FINANCIAL DIRECTORY OF PENSION FUNDS. HAWAII, THE. [Financ. dir. pension funds, Hawaii]. **Added/Corp** ERISA Benefit Funds, Inc. (1984-85)-. Directory. English. One time a year. $395.00 print, $790.00 disk. Dun & Bradstreet Information Services, 3 Sylvan Way, Parsippany NJ 07054. **Tel** (201)605-6000, (800)526-0651. available on diskette. ***Continues*** *Financial Directory of Pension Funds. State of Hawaii, 0731-7352.*

LC HD7106.U6 I23 **ISSN** 0742-5139
DD 332.6/7254 US
FINANCIAL DIRECTORY OF PENSION FUNDS. IDAHO. **Added/Corp** ERISA Benefit Funds, Inc. (19??)-. Directory. English. One time a year. $345.00 print, $690.00 disk. Dun & Bradstreet Information Services, 3 Sylvan Way, Parsippany NJ 07054. **Tel** (201)605-6000, (800)526-0651. available on diskette. ***Continues*** *ERISA Benefit Funds. Financial Directory of Pension Funds, State of Idaho, 0190-7131.*

LC HD7106.U6 I354 **ISSN** 0739-2834
DD 332.6/7254 US
FINANCIAL DIRECTORY OF PENSION FUNDS. ILLINOIS, CHICAGO CITY PROPER. **Added/Corp** ERISA Benefit Funds, Inc. (19??)-. Directory. English. One time a year. $545.00 print; $1090.00 disk. Dun & Bradstreet Information Services, 3 Sylvan Way, Parsippany NJ 07054. **Tel** (201)605-6000, (800)526-0651. available on diskette. ***Continues*** *ERISA Benefit Funds. Financial Directory of Pension Funds, State of Illinois, Chicago Proper, 0192-3463.*

LC HD7106.U6 I3549 **ISSN** 0731-3748
DD 332.6/7254 US
FINANCIAL DIRECTORY OF PENSION FUNDS. ILLINOIS, NO. SUBURBAN CHICAGO (OAK PARK, SKOKIE, EVANSTON & OTHERS). **Added/Corp** ERISA Benefit Funds, Inc. **VFOAT** Financial Directory of Pension Funds. Illinois, No. Surburban Chicago (Oak Park, Skokie, Evanston and Others); Financial Directory of Pension Funds. (19??)-. Directory. English. One time a year. $650.00 print; $1300.00 disk. Dun & Bradstreet Information Services, 3 Sylvan Way, Parsippany NJ 07054. **Tel** (201)605-6000, (800)526-0651. available on diskette.

LC HD7105.45.U6 F565 **ISSN** 0739-2818
DD 332.6/7254 US
FINANCIAL DIRECTORY OF PENSION FUNDS. ILLINOIS, NORTHERN, EXCLUDING CHICAGO AREA. KANKAKEE, ROCKFORD, PEORIA & OTHERS. (FINANCIAL DIRECTORY OF PENSION FUNDS. ILLINOIS, NORTHERN, EXCLUDING CHICAGO AREA (KANKAKEE, ROCKFORD, PEORIA & OTHERS) / ERISA BENEFIT FUNDS, INC.). **Added/Corp** ERISA Benefit Funds, Inc. (19??)-. Directory. English. One time a year. $395.00 print; $790.00 disk. Dun & Bradstreet Information Services, 3 Sylvan Way, Parsippany NJ 07054. **Tel** (201)605-6000, (800)526-0651. available on diskette.

LC HD7106.U6 I355 **ISSN** 0731-3756
DD 332.6/7254 US
FINANCIAL DIRECTORY OF PENSION FUNDS. ILLINOIS, SO. SUBURBAN CHICAGO (EVERGREEN PARK, CHICAGO HEIGHTS, JOLIET & OTHERS). **Added/Corp** ERISA Benefit Funds, Inc. **VFOAT** Financial Directory of Pension Funds. Illinois, So. Surburban Chicago (Evergreen Park, Chicago Heights, Joliet and Others); Financial Directory of Pension Funds. (19??)-. Directory. English. One time a year. $445.00 print; $890.00 disk. Dun & Bradstreet Information Services, 3 Sylvan Way, Parsippany NJ 07054. **Tel** (201)605-6000, (800)526-0651. available on diskette.

Business and Economics — Labor

LC HD7106.U5 F5443 ISSN 0732-7145
DD 332.6/7254 US

FINANCIAL DIRECTORY OF PENSION FUNDS. ILLINOIS, SOUTHERN DOWNSTATE (CHAMPAIGN, SPRINGFIELD, EAST ST. LOUIS & OTHERS). Added/Corp ERISA Benefit Funds, Inc. **VFOAT** Financial Directory of Pension Funds. (19??)-. Directory. English. One time a year. $395.00 print; $790.00 disk. Dun & Bradstreet Information Services, 3 Sylvan Way, Parsippany NJ 07054. **Tel** (201)605-6000, (800)526-0651. available on diskette.

LC HD7106.U6 I623 ISSN 0739-2583
DD 332.6/7254 US

FINANCIAL DIRECTORY OF PENSION FUNDS. INDIANA, NORTHERN (SOUTH BEND, FT. WAYNE, MUNCIE & OTHERS). Added/Corp ERISA Benefit Funds, Inc. (19??)-. Directory. English. One time a year. $445.00 print; $890.00 disk. Dun & Bradstreet Information Services, 3 Sylvan Way, Parsippany NJ 07054. **Tel** (201)605-6000, (800)526-0651. available on diskette. **Continues** ERISA Benefit Funds. Financial Directory of Pension Funds, Northern Indiana, 0190-8251.

LC HD7106.U6 I624 ISSN 0739-2869
DD 332.6/7254 US

FINANCIAL DIRECTORY OF PENSION FUNDS. INDIANA, SOUTHERN (INDIANAPOLIS, TERRE HAUTE, EVANSVILLE & OTHERS). (FINANCIAL DIRECTORY OF PENSION FUNDS. INDIANA, SOUTHERN (INDIANAPOLIS, TERRE HAUTE, EVANSVILLE & OTHERS) / ERISA BENEFIT FUNDS, INC). **Added/Corp** ERISA Benefit Funds, Inc. (19??)-. Directory. English. One time a year. $445.00 print; $890.00 disk. Dun & Bradstreet Information Services, 3 Sylvan Way, Parsippany NJ 07054. **Tel** (201)605-6000, (800)526-0651. available on diskette. **Continues** ERISA Benefit Funds. Financial Directory of Pension Funds, Southern Indiana, 0190-9894.

LC HD7106.U6 I77 ISSN 0742-0129
DD 332.6/7254 US

FINANCIAL DIRECTORY OF PENSION FUNDS. IOWA. Added/Corp ERISA Benefit Funds, Inc. (19??)-. Directory. English. One time a year. $495.00 print; $990.00 disk. Dun & Bradstreet Information Services, 3 Sylvan Way, Parsippany NJ 07054. **Tel** (201)605-6000, (800)526-0651. available on diskette. **Continues** ERISA Benefit Funds. Financial Directory of Pension Funds, State of Iowa, 0190-7123.

LC HD7106.U6 K23 ISSN 0882-083X
DD 332.6/7254 US

FINANCIAL DIRECTORY OF PENSION FUNDS. KANSAS, THE. [Financ. dir. pension funds, Kans.]. **Added/Corp** ERISA Benefit Funds, Inc. (1984-85)-. Directory. English. One time a year. $445.00 print; $890.00 disk. Dun & Bradstreet Information Services, 3 Sylvan Way, Parsippany NJ 07054. **Tel** (201)605-6000, (800)526-0651. available on diskette. **Continues** Erisa Benefit Funds. Financial Directory of Pension Funds, State of Kansas, 0190-7719.

LC HD7106.U6 K44 ISSN 0731-7395
DD 332.6/7254 US

FINANCIAL DIRECTORY OF PENSION FUNDS. KENTUCKY. Added/Corp ERISA Benefit Funds, Inc. (19??)-. Directory. English. One time a year. $445.00 print; $890.00 disk. Dun & Bradstreet Information Services, 3 Sylvan Way, Parsippany NJ 07054. **Tel** (201)605-6000, (800)526-0651. available on diskette. **Continues** ERISA Benefit Funds. Directory of Pension Funds, State of Kentucky, 0148-1401.

LC HD7106.U6 L63 ISSN 0742-0137
DD 332.6/7254 US

FINANCIAL DIRECTORY OF PENSION FUNDS. LOUISIANA. Added/Corp ERISA Benefit Funds, Inc. (19??)-. Directory. English. One time a year. $445.00 print; $890.00 disk. Dun & Bradstreet Information Services, 3 Sylvan Way, Parsippany NJ 07054. **Tel** (201)605-6000, (800)526-0651. available on diskette. **Continues** ERISA Benefit Funds. Financial Directory of Pension Funds, State of Louisiana, 0190-7700.

LC HD7106.U6 M18 ISSN 0741-8663
DD 332.6/7254 US

FINANCIAL DIRECTORY OF PENSION FUNDS. MAINE. Added/Corp ERISA Benefit Funds, Inc. (19??)-. Directory. English. One time a year. $345.00 print; $690.00 disk. Dun & Bradstreet Information Services, 3 Sylvan Way, Parsippany NJ 07054. **Tel** (201)605-6000, (800)526-0651. available on diskette. **Continues** ERISA Benefit Funds. Financial Directory of Pension Funds. State of Maine, 0190-7239.

LC HD7106.U5 F546 ISSN 0278-0283
DD 332.6/7254 US

FINANCIAL DIRECTORY OF PENSION FUNDS. MARYLAND, EASTERN (BALTIMORE, ANNAPOLIS, EASTERN SHORE & OTHERS). Added/Corp ERISA Benefit Funds, Inc. **VFOAT** Financial Directory of Pension Funds; Financial Directory of Pension Funds. Maryland, Eastern (Baltimore, Annapolis, Eastern Shore and Others). (19??)-. Directory. English. One time a year. $495.00 print; $990.00 disk. Dun & Bradstreet Information Services, 3 Sylvan Way, Parsippany NJ 07054. **Tel** (201)605-6000, (800)526-0651. available on diskette.

LC HD7106.U6 M243 ISSN 0278-2162
DD 332.6/7254 US

FINANCIAL DIRECTORY OF PENSION FUNDS. MARYLAND, WESTERN (FREDERICK, ROCKVILLE, WALDORF & OTHERS). (FINANCIAL DIRECTORY OF PENSION FUNDS. MARYLAND, WESTERN (FREDERICK, ROCKVILLE, WALDORF & OTHERS) / ERISA BENEFIT FUNDS, INC.). **Added/Corp** ERISA Benefit Funds, Inc. **VFOAT** Financial Directory of Pension Funds. Maryland, Western (Frederick, Rockville, Waldorf and Others); Financial Directory of Pension Funds. (19??)-. Directory. English. One time a year. $445.00 print; $890.00 disk. Dun & Bradstreet Information Services, 3 Sylvan Way, Parsippany NJ 07054. **Tel** (201)605-6000, (800)526-0651. available on diskette.

LC HD7106.U6 M287 ISSN 0278-2081
DD 332.6/7254 US

FINANCIAL DIRECTORY OF PENSION FUNDS. MASSACHUSETTS, BOSTON CITY PROPER. (FINANCIAL DIRECTORY OF PENSION FUNDS. MASSACHUSETTS, BOSTON CITY PROPER / ERISA BENEFIT FUNDS, INC.). **Added/Corp** ERISA Benefit Funds, Inc. **VFOAT** Financial Directory of Pension Funds. (19??)-. Directory. English. One time a year. $445.00 print; $890.00 disk. Dun & Bradstreet Information Services, 3 Sylvan Way, Parsippany NJ 07054. **Tel** (201)605-6000, (800)526-0651. available on diskette.

LC HD7106.U6 M285 ISSN 0739-2648
DD 332.6/7254 US

FINANCIAL DIRECTORY OF PENSION FUNDS. MASSACHUSETTS, EXCLUDING BOSTON & SUBURBS (WORCESTER, SPRINGFIELD, PITTSFIELD & OTHERS). Added/Corp ERISA Benefit Funds, Inc. (19??)-. Directory. English. One time a year. $445.00 print; $890.00 disk. Dun & Bradstreet Information Services, 3 Sylvan Way, Parsippany NJ 07054. **Tel** (201)605-6000, (800)526-0651. available on diskette. **Continues** ERISA Benefit Funds. Financial Directory of Pension Funds, State of Massachusetts, Excluding Boston Area, 0192-3226.

LC HD7106.U6 M289 ISSN 0278-209X
DD 332.6/7254 US

FINANCIAL DIRECTORY OF PENSION FUNDS. MASSACHUSETTS, SUBURBAN BOSTON (LYNN, FRAMINGHAM & OTHERS). (FINANCIAL DIRECTORY OF PENSION FUNDS. MASSACHUSETTS, SUBURBAN BOSTON (LYNN, FRAMINGHAM & OTHERS) / ERISA BENEFIT FUNDS, INC.). **Added/Corp** ERISA Benefit Funds, Inc. **VFOAT** Financial Directory of Pension Funds. Massachusetts, Suburban Boston (Lynn, Framingham and Others); Financial Directory of Funds. (19??)-. Directory. English. One time a year. $445.00 print; $890.00 disk. Dun & Bradstreet Information Services, 3 Sylvan Way, Parsippany NJ 07054. **Tel** (201)605-6000, (800)526-0651. available on diskette.

LC HD7106.U6 M48 ISSN 0278-2138
DD 332.6/7254 US

FINANCIAL DIRECTORY OF PENSION FUNDS. MICHIGAN, CENTRAL AND NORTHERN (SAGINAW, TRAVERSE CITY, IRON MOUNTAIN & OTHERS). (FINANCIAL DIRECTORY OF PENSION FUNDS. MICHIGAN, CENTRAL AND NORTHERN (SAGINAW, TRAVERSE CITY, IRON MOUNTAIN & OTHERS) / ERISA BENEFIT FUNDS, INC.). **Added/Corp** ERISA Benefit Funds, Inc. **VFOAT** Financial Directory of Pension Funds. Michigan, Central and Northern (Saginaw, Traverse City, Iron Mountain and Others); Financial Directory of Pension Funds. (19??)-. Directory. English. One time a year. $345.00 print; $690.00 disk. Dun & Bradstreet Information Services, 3 Sylvan Way, Parsippany NJ 07054. **Tel** (201)605-6000, (800)526-0651. available on diskette.

LC HD7106.U6 M47 ISSN 0731-7379
DD 332.6/7254 US

FINANCIAL DIRECTORY OF PENSION FUNDS. MICHIGAN, DETROIT CITY PROPER. (FINANCIAL DIRECTORY OF PENSION FUNDS. MICHIGAN, DETROIT CITY PROPER / ERISA BENEFIT FUNDS, INC.). **Added/Corp** ERISA Benefit Funds, Inc. (19??)-. Directory. English. One time a year. $345.00 print; $690.00 disk. Dun & Bradstreet Information Services, 3 Sylvan Way, Parsippany NJ 07054. **Tel** (201)605-6000, (800)526-0651. available on diskette. **Continues** ERISA Benefit Funds. Directory of Pension Funds, Detroit Area, 0148-1479.

LC HD7106.U6 M473 ISSN 0731-7484
DD 332.6/7254 US

FINANCIAL DIRECTORY OF PENSION FUNDS. MICHIGAN, SOUTHERN, EXCLUDING DETROIT & SUBURBS (FLINT, GRAND RAPIDS, KALAMAZOO & OTHERS). (FINANCIAL DIRECTORY OF PENSION FUNDS. MICHIGAN, SOUTHERN, EXCLUDING DETROIT & SUBURBS (FLINT, GRAND RAPIDS, KALAMAZOO & OTHERS) / ERISA BENEFIT FUNDS, INC.). **Added/Corp** ERISA Benefit Funds, Inc. (19??)-. Directory. English. One time a year. $545.00 print; $1090.00 disk. Dun & Bradstreet Information Services, 3 Sylvan Way, Parsippany NJ 07054. **Tel** (201)605-6000, (800)526-0651. available on diskette. **Continues** ERISA Benefits Funds. Financial Directory of Pension Funds, State of Michigan, excluding Detroit Area, 0148-1185.

LC HD7106.U5 F5466 ISSN 0278-2170
DD 332.6/7254 US

FINANCIAL DIRECTORY OF PENSION FUNDS. MICHIGAN, SUBURBAN DETROIT (PONTIAC, ANN ARBOR, MONROE & OTHERS). Added/Corp ERISA Benefit Funds, Inc. **VFOAT** Financial Directory of Pension Funds. Michigan, Suburban Detroit (Pontiac, Ann Arbor, Monroe and Others); Financial Directory of Pension Funds. (19??)-. Directory. English. One time a year. $650.00 print; $1300.00 disk. Dun & Bradstreet Information Services, 3 Sylvan Way, Parsippany NJ 07054. **Tel** (201)605-6000, (800)526-0651. available on diskette.

LC HD7106.U5 F547 ISSN 0731-7301
DD 332.6/7254 US

FINANCIAL DIRECTORY OF PENSION FUNDS. MINNESOTA (EXCLUDING MINNEAPOLIS-ST. PAUL AREA). Added/Corp ERISA Benefit Funds, Inc. (19??)-. Directory. English. One time a year. $395.00 print; $790.00 disk. Dun & Bradstreet Information Services, 3 Sylvan Way, Parsippany NJ 07054. **Tel** (201)605-6000, (800)526-0651. available on diskette. **Continues** ERISA Benefit Funds. Directory of Pension Funds. State of Minnesota, 0148-1223.

LC HD7106.U6 M645 ISSN 0739-5787
DD 332.6/7254 US

FINANCIAL DIRECTORY OF PENSION FUNDS. MINNESOTA, MINNEAPOLIS-ST. PAUL AREA. (FINANCIAL DIRECTORY OF PENSION FUNDS. MINNESOTA (MINNEAPOLIS-ST. PAUL AREA) / ERISA BENEFIT FUNDS, INC.). **Added/Corp** ERISA Benefit Funds, Inc. (19??)-. Directory. English. One time a year. $695.00 print; $1190.00 disk. Dun & Bradstreet Information Services, 3 Sylvan Way, Parsippany NJ 07054. **Tel** (201)605-6000, (800)526-0651. available on diskette. **Continues** ERISA Benefit Funds. Financial Directory of Pension Funds, State of Minnesota, Minneapolis-St. Paul Area, 0192-2556.

LC HD7106.U6 M73 ISSN 0741-868X
DD 332.6/7254 US

FINANCIAL DIRECTORY OF PENSION FUNDS. MISSISSIPPI. Added/Corp ERISA Benefit Funds, Inc. (19??)-. Directory. English. One time a year. $345.00 print; $690.00 disk. Dun & Bradstreet Information Services, 3 Sylvan Way, Parsippany NJ 07054. **Tel** (201)605-6000, (800)526-0651. available on diskette. **Continues** ERISA Benefit Funds. Financial Directory of Pension Funds. State of Mississippi, 0190-8308.

LC HF7106.U6 M823 ISSN 0739-2877
DD 332.6/7254 US

FINANCIAL DIRECTORY OF PENSION FUNDS. MISSOURI, EASTERN. ST. LOUIS, JEFFERSON CITY & OTHERS. (FINANCIAL DIRECTORY OF PENSION FUNDS. MISSOURI, EASTERN (ST. LOUIS, JEFFERSON CITY & OTHERS) / ERISA BENEFIT FUNDS, INC.). **Added/Corp** ERISA Benefit Funds, Inc. (19??)-. Directory. English. One time a year. $495.00 print; $990.00 disk. Dun & Bradstreet Information Services, 3 Sylvan Way, Parsippany NJ 07054. **Tel** (201)605-6000, (800)526-0651. available on diskette. **Continues** ERISA Benefit Funds. Financial Directory of Pension Funds, Eastern Missouri, 0192-7582.

Business and Economics —Labor

LC HD7106.U6 M825 **ISSN** 0739-2826
DD 332.6/7254 US
FINANCIAL DIRECTORY OF PENSION FUNDS. MISSOURI, WESTERN (KANSAS CITY, ST. JOSEPH, SPRINGFIELD & OTHERS). Added/Corp ERISA Benefit Funds, Inc. (19??)-. Directory. English. One time a year. $395.00 print; $790.00 disk. Dun & Bradstreet Information Services, 3 Sylvan Way, Parsippany NJ 07054. **Tel** (201)605-6000, (800)526-0651. available on diskette. ***Continues** ERISA Benefit Funds. Financial Directory of Pension Funds, Western Missouri, 0197-3614.*

LC HD7106.U6 M94 **ISSN** 0742-0153
DD 332.6/7254 US
FINANCIAL DIRECTORY OF PENSION FUNDS. MONTANA. Added/Corp ERISA Benefit Funds, Inc. (19??)-. Directory. English. One time a year. $345.00 print; $690.00 disk. Dun & Bradstreet Information Services, 3 Sylvan Way, Parsippany NJ 07054. **Tel** (201)605-6000, (800)526-0651. available on diskette. ***Continues** ERISA Benefit Funds. Financial Directory of Pension Funds, State of Montana, 0190-7263.*

LC HD7106.U6 N24 **ISSN** 0741-5117
DD 332.6/7254 US
FINANCIAL DIRECTORY OF PENSION FUNDS. NEBRASKA. Added/Corp ERISA Benefit Funds, Inc. (19??)-. Directory. English. One time a year. $395.00 print; $790.00 disk. Dun & Bradstreet Information Services, 3 Sylvan Way, Parsippany NJ 07054. **Tel** (201)605-6000, (800)526-0651. available on diskette. ***Continues** ERISA Benefit Funds. Financial Directory of Pension Funds, State of Nebraska, 0190-7271.*

LC HD7106.U6 N33 **ISSN** 0741-8671
DD 332.6/7254 US
FINANCIAL DIRECTORY OF PENSION FUNDS. NEVADA. Added/Corp ERISA Benefit Funds, Inc. (19??)-. Directory. English. One time a year. $345.00 print; $690.00 disk. Dun & Bradstreet Information Services, 3 Sylvan Way, Parsippany NJ 07054. **Tel** (201)605-6000, (800)526-0651. available on diskette. ***Continues** ERISA Benefit Funds. Financial Directory of Pension Funds. State of Nevada, 0190-7247.*

LC HD7106.U6 N42 **ISSN** 0741-4706
DD 332.6/7254 US
FINANCIAL DIRECTORY OF PENSION FUNDS. NEW HAMPSHIRE. Added/Corp ERISA Benefit Funds, Inc. (19??)-. Directory. English. One time a year. $345.00 print; $690.00 disk. Dun & Bradstreet Information Services, 3 Sylvan Way, Parsippany NJ 07054. **Tel** (201)605-6000, (800)526-0651. available on diskette. ***Continues** ERISA Benefit Funds. Financial Directory of Pension Funds, State of New Hampshire, 0190-8014.*

LC HD7106.U5 F548 **ISSN** 0278-6001
DD 332.6/7254 US
FINANCIAL DIRECTORY OF PENSION FUNDS. NEW JERSEY, NORTHERN, EXCLUDING NEWARK AND ENVIRONS (HACKENSACK, PATTERSON, SUMMIT & OTHERS). Added/Corp ERISA Benefit Funds, Inc. **VFOAT** Financial Directory of Pension Funds. New Jersey, Northern, Excluding Newark and Environs (Hackensack, Patterson, Summit and Others); Financial Directory of Pension Funds. (19??)-. Directory. English. One time a year. $595.00 print; $1190.00 disk. Dun & Bradstreet Information Services, 3 Sylvan Way, Parsippany NJ 07054. **Tel** (201)605-6000, (800)526-0651. available on diskette.

LC HD7106.U5 F5483 **ISSN** 0278-579X
DD 332.6/7254 US
FINANCIAL DIRECTORY OF PENSION FUNDS. NEW JERSEY, NORTHERN, NEWARK AND ENVIRONS (NEWARK, PASSAIC, JERSEY CITY & OTHERS). Added/Corp ERISA Benefit Funds, Inc. **VFOAT** Financial Directory of Pension Funds. New Jersey, Northern, Newark and Environs (Newark Passaic, Jersey City & Others); Financial Directory of Pension Funds. (19??)-. Directory. English. One time a year. $545.00 print; $1090.00 disk. Dun & Bradstreet Information Services, 3 Sylvan Way, Parsippany NJ 07054. **Tel** (201)605-6000, (800)526-0651. available on diskette.

LC HD7106.U6 N523 **ISSN** 0739-2567
DD 332.6/7254 US
FINANCIAL DIRECTORY OF PENSION FUNDS. NEW JERSEY, SOUTHERN. TRENTON, CAMDEN, ATLANTIC CITY & OTHERS. (FINANCIAL DIRECTORY OF PENSION FUNDS. NEW JERSEY, SOUTHERN (TRENTON, CAMDEN, ATLANTIC CITY & OTHERS) / ERISA BENEFIT FUNDS, INC.). **Added/Corp** ERISA Benefit Funds, Inc. (19??)-. Directory. English. One time a year. $545.00 print; $1090.00 disk. Dun & Bradstreet Information Services, 3 Sylvan Way, Parsippany NJ 07054. **Tel** (201)605-6000, (800)526-0651. available on diskette. ***Continues** ERISA Benefit Funds. Financial Directory of Pension Funds, Southern New Jersey, 0190-6240.*

LC HD7106.U6 N5913 **ISSN** 0882-2964
DD 332.6/7254 US
FINANCIAL DIRECTORY OF PENSION FUNDS. NEW MEXICO, THE. [Financ. dir. pension funds, N.M.]. **Added/Corp** ERISA Benefit Funds, Inc. (1984-85)-. Directory. English. One time a year. $345.00 print; $690.00 disk. Dun & Bradstreet Information Services, 3 Sylvan Way, Parsippany NJ 07054. **Tel** (201)605-6000, (800)526-0651. available on diskette. ***Continues** Financial Directory of Pension Funds. State of New Mexico, 0731-7360.*

LC HD7106.U6 N625 **ISSN** 0739-2680
DD 332.6/7254 US
FINANCIAL DIRECTORY OF PENSION FUNDS. NEW YORK (BROOKLYN, S.I., BRONX, QUEENS). Added/Corp ERISA Benefit Funds, Inc. (19??)-. Directory. English. One time a year. $545.00 print; $1090.00 disk. Dun & Bradstreet Information Services, 3 Sylvan Way, Parsippany NJ 07054. **Tel** (201)605-6000, (800)526-0651. available on diskette. ***Continues** ERISA Benefit Funds. Financial Directory of Pension Funds, State of New York, Brooklyn, S.I., Bronx, Queens, L.I., 0191-0442.*

LC HD7106.U6 N626 **ISSN** 0739-2761
DD 332.6/7254 US
FINANCIAL DIRECTORY OF PENSION FUNDS. NEW YORK, EASTERN UPSTATE. POUGHKEEPSIE, ALBANY, GLENS FALLS & OTHERS. (FINANCIAL DIRECTORY OF PENSION FUNDS. NEW YORK, EASTERN UPSTATE (POUGHKEEPSIE, ALBANY, GLENS FALLS & OTHERS) / ERISA BENEFIT FUNDS, INC.). **Added/Corp** ERISA Benefit Funds, Inc. (19??)-. Directory. English. One time a year. $445.00 print; $890.00 disk. Dun & Bradstreet Information Services, 3 Sylvan Way, Parsippany NJ 07054. **Tel** (201)605-6000, (800)526-0651. available on diskette. ***Continues** ERISA Benefit Funds. Financial Directory of Pension Funds, State of New York, Eastern Upstate, 0190-9290.*

LC HD7106.U6 N627 **ISSN** 0739-2605
DD 332.6/7254 US
FINANCIAL DIRECTORY OF PENSION FUNDS. NEW YORK, MANHATTAN-DOWNTOWN. WALL ST. TO 40 ST. (FINANCIAL DIRECTORY OF PENSION FUNDS. NEW YORK, MANHATTAN-DOWNTOWN (WALL ST. TO 40 ST.) / ERISA BENEFIT FUNDS, INC.). **Added/Corp** ERISA Benefit Funds, Inc. (19??)-. Directory. English. One time a year. $495.00 print; $990.00 disk. Dun & Bradstreet Information Services, 3 Sylvan Way, Parsippany NJ 07054. **Tel** (201)605-6000, (800)526-0651. available on diskette. ***Continues** ERISA Benefit Funds. Financial Directory of Pension Funds, State of New York Manhattan-Downtown Wall St. to 40 St.), 0191-0345.*

LC HD7106.U6 N6272 **ISSN** 0739-2745
DD 332.6/7254 US
FINANCIAL DIRECTORY OF PENSION FUNDS. NEW YORK, MANHATTAN-MIDTOWN, 41 ST. TO 50 ST. (FINANCIAL DIRECTORY OF PENSION FUNDS. NEW YORK, MANHATTAN-MIDTOWN (41 ST. TO 50 ST.) / ERISA BENEFIT FUNDS, INC.). (19??)-. Directory. English. One time a year. $345.00 print; $690.00 disk. Dun & Bradstreet Information Services, 3 Sylvan Way, Parsippany NJ 07054. **Tel** (201)605-6000, (800)526-0651. available on diskette. ***Continues** ERISA Benefit Funds. Financial Directory of Pension Funds, State of New York, Manhattan-Midtown (41 St. to 50 St.), 0190-9932.*

LC HD7106.U6 N6273 **ISSN** 0739-2842
DD 332.6/7254 US
FINANCIAL DIRECTORY OF PENSION FUNDS. NEW YORK, MANHATTAN-UPTOWN (51 ST. TO HARLEM RIVER). Added/Corp ERISA Benefit Funds, Inc. (19??)-. Directory. English. One time a year. $445.00 print; $890.00 disk. Dun & Bradstreet Information Services, 3 Sylvan Way, Parsippany NJ 07054. **Tel** (201)605-6000, (800)526-0651. available on diskette. ***Continues** ERISA Benefit Funds. Financial Directory of Pension Funds, State of New York, Manhattan-Uptown (51 St. to Harlem River), 0191-0493.*

LC HD7106.U5 F55 **ISSN** 0278-0305
DD 332.6/7254 US
FINANCIAL DIRECTORY OF PENSION FUNDS. NEW YORK (NASSAU & SUFFOLK COUNTIES ONLY). Added/Corp ERISA Benefit Funds, Inc. **VFOAT** Financial Directory of Pension Funds; Financial Directory of Pension Funds. New York (Nassau and Suffolk Counties Only). (19??)-. Directory. English. One time a year. $545.00 print; $1090.00 disk. Dun & Bradstreet Information Services, 3 Sylvan Way, Parsippany NJ 07054. **Tel** (201)605-6000, (800)526-0651. available on diskette.

LC HD7106.U5 F555 **ISSN** 0278-0291
DD 332.6/7254 US
FINANCIAL DIRECTORY OF PENSION FUNDS. NEW YORK, WEST CENTRAL UPSTATE (UTICA, SYRACUSE, BINGHAMTON & OTHERS). Added/Corp ERISA Benefit Funds, Inc. **VFOAT** Financial Directory of Pension Funds; Financial Directory of Pension Funds. New York, West Central Upstate (Utica, Syracuse, Binghamton and Others). (19??)-. Directory. English. One time a year. $445.00 print; $890.00 disk. Dun & Bradstreet Information Services, 3 Sylvan Way, Parsippany NJ 07054. **Tel** (201)605-6000, (800)526-0651. available on diskette.

LC HD7106.U5 F556 **ISSN** 0278-0356
DD 332.6/7254 US
FINANCIAL DIRECTORY OF PENSION FUNDS. NEW YORK, WESTCHESTER COUNTY AREA (YONKERS, WHITE PLAINS, MIDDLETOWN & OTHERS). Added/Corp ERISA Benefit Funds, Inc. **VFOAT** Financial Directory of Pension Funds; Financial Directory of Funds. New York, Westchester County Area (Yonkers, White Plains, Middletown and Others). (19??)-. Directory. English. One time a year. $445.00 print; $890.00 disk. Dun & Bradstreet Information Services, 3 Sylvan Way, Parsippany NJ 07054. **Tel** (201)605-6000, (800)526-0651. available on diskette.

LC HD7106.U6 N628 **ISSN** 0739-2850
DD 332.6/7254 US
FINANCIAL DIRECTORY OF PENSION FUNDS. NEW YORK, WESTERN UPSTATE (ROCHESTER, BUFFALO, ELMIRA & OTHERS). Added/Corp ERISA Benefit Funds, Inc. (19??)-. Directory. English. One time a year. $545.00 print; $1090.00 disk. Dun & Bradstreet Information Services, 3 Sylvan Way, Parsippany NJ 07054. **Tel** (201)605-6000, (800)526-0651. available on diskette. ***Continues** ERISA Benefit Funds. Financial Directory of Pension Funds, State of New York, Western Upstate, 0190-9908.*

LC HD7106 .U6 N844 **ISSN** 0739-2796
DD 332.6/7254 US
FINANCIAL DIRECTORY OF PENSION FUNDS. NORTH CAROLINA, EASTERN (RALEIGH, FAYETTEVILLE, WILMINGTON & OTHERS). Added/Corp ERISA Benefit Funds, Inc. (19??)-. Directory. English. One time a year. $395.00 print; $790.00 disk. Dun & Bradstreet Information Services, 3 Sylvan Way, Parsippany NJ 07054. **Tel** (201)605-6000, (800)526-0651. available on diskette. ***Continues** ERISA Benefit Funds. Financial Directory of Pension Funds, North Carolina, Eastern, 0190-8324.*

LC HD7106.U6 N847 **ISSN** 0739-263X
DD 332.6/7254 US
FINANCIAL DIRECTORY OF PENSION FUNDS. NORTH CAROLINA, WESTERN (WINSTON-SALEM, LEXINGTON, GREENSBORO, CHARLOTTE & OTHERS). Added/Corp ERISA Benefit Funds, Inc. (19??)-. Directory. English. One time a year. $545.00 print; $1090.00 disk. Dun & Bradstreet Information Services, 3 Sylvan Way, Parsippany NJ 07054. **Tel** (201)605-6000, (800)526-0651. available on diskette. ***Continues** ERISA Benefit Funds. Financial Directory of Pension Funds, North Carolina, Western, 0190-9886.*

LC HD7106.U6 N93 **ISSN** 0741-479X
DD 332.6/7254 US
FINANCIAL DIRECTORY OF PENSION FUNDS. NORTH DAKOTA. Added/Corp ERISA Benefit Funds, Inc. (19??)-. Directory. English. One time a year. $295.00 print; $590.00 disk. Dun & Bradstreet Information Services, 3 Sylvan Way, Parsippany NJ 07054. **Tel** (201)605-6000, (800)526-0651. available on diskette. ***Continues** ERISA Benefit Funds. Financial Directory of Pension Funds, State of North Dakota, 0190-8022.*

LC HD7106.U5 F5563 **ISSN** 0278-0321
DD 332.6/7254 US
FINANCIAL DIRECTORY OF PENSION FUNDS. OHIO, MIDEASTERN (AKRON, YOUNGSTOWN, ZANESVILLE, CANTON & OTHERS). (FINANCIAL DIRECTORY OF PENSION FUNDS. OHIO, MIDEASTERN (AKRON, YOUNGSTOWN, ZANESVILLE, CANTON & OTHERS) / ERISA BENEFIT FUNDS, INC.). **Added/Corp** ERISA Benefit Funds, Inc. **VFOAT** Financial Directory of Pension Funds; Financial Directory of Pension Funds. Ohio, Mideastern (Akron, Youngstown, Zanesville, Canton and Others). (19??)-. Directory. English. One time a year. $445.00 print; $890.00 disk.

Business and Economics — Labor

Dun & Bradstreet Information Services, 3 Sylvan Way, Parsippany NJ 07054. **Tel** (201)605-6000, (800)526-0651. available on diskette.

LC HD7106.U5 F5565   **ISSN** 0731-7026
DD 332.6/7254   US
FINANCIAL DIRECTORY OF PENSION FUNDS. OHIO, NORTHERN, CLEVELAND AREA. **Added/Corp** ERISA Benefit Funds, Inc. (19??)-. Directory. English. One time a year. $495.00 print; $990.00 disk. Dun & Bradstreet Information Services, 3 Sylvan Way, Parsippany NJ 07054. **Tel** (201)605-6000, (800)526-0651. available on diskette. **Continues in part** ERISA Benefit Funds. Directory of Pension Funds, Northern Ohio, 0148-1371.

LC HD7106.U5 F557   **ISSN** 0278-0275
DD 332.6/7254   US
FINANCIAL DIRECTORY OF PENSION FUNDS. OHIO, NORTHWESTERN (TOLEDO, MANSFIELD, LIMA & OTHERS). (FINANCIAL DIRECTORY OF PENSION FUNDS. OHIO, NORTHWESTERN (TOLEDO, MANSFIELD, LIMA & OTHERS) / ERISA BENEFIT FUNDS, INC.). **Added/Corp** ERISA Benefit Funds, Inc. **VFOAT** Financial Directory of Pension Funds; Financial Directory of Pension Funds. Ohio, Northwestern (Toledo, Mansfield, Lima and Others). (19??)-. Directory. English. One time a year. $395.00 print; $790.00 disk. Dun & Bradstreet Information Services, 3 Sylvan Way, Parsippany NJ 07054. **Tel** (201)605-6000, (800)526-0651. available on diskette.

LC HD7106.U5 F5574   **ISSN** 0731-700X
DD 332.6/7254   US
FINANCIAL DIRECTORY OF PENSION FUNDS. OHIO, SOUTHERN, CINCINNATI AREA. (FINANCIAL DIRECTORY OF PENSION FUNDS. OHIO, SOUTHERN, CINCINNATI AREA / ERISA BENEFIT FUNDS, INC.). **Added/Corp** ERISA Benefit Funds, Inc. (19??)-. Directory. English. One time a year. $445.00 print; $890.00 disk. Dun & Bradstreet Information Services, 3 Sylvan Way, Parsippany NJ 07054. **Tel** (201)605-6000, (800)526-0651. available on diskette. **Continues in part** ERISA Benefit Funds. Directory of Pensions, Southern Ohio, 0148-1665.

LC HD7106.U5 F5575   **ISSN** 0731-7018
DD 332.6/7254   US
FINANCIAL DIRECTORY OF PENSION FUNDS. OHIO, SOUTHERN, EXCLUDING CINCINNATI AREA (COLUMBUS, DAYTON, ATHENS & OTHERS). **Added/Corp** ERISA Benefit Funds, Inc. (19??)-. Directory. English. One time a year. $495.00 print; $990.00 disk. Dun & Bradstreet Information Services, 3 Sylvan Way, Parsippany NJ 07054. **Tel** (201)605-6000, (800)526-0651. available on diskette. **Continues in part** ERISA Benefit Funds. Directory of Pensions, Southern Ohio, 0148-1665.

LC HD7106.U6 O53   **ISSN** 0741-8698
DD 332.6/7254   US
FINANCIAL DIRECTORY OF PENSION FUNDS. OKLAHOMA. **Added/Corp** ERISA Benefit Funds, Inc. (19??)-. Directory. English. One time a year. $445.00 print; $890.00 disk. Dun & Bradstreet Information Services, 3 Sylvan Way, Parsippany NJ 07054. **Tel** (201)605-6000, (800)526-0651. available on diskette. **Continues** ERISA Benefit Funds. Financial Directory of Pension Funds. State of Oklahoma, 0190-8332.

LC HD7106.U6 O744   **ISSN** 0742-0161
DD 332.6/7254   US
FINANCIAL DIRECTORY OF PENSION FUNDS. OREGON. **Added/Corp** ERISA Benefit Funds, Inc. (19??)-. Directory. English. One time a year. $545.00 print; $1090.00 disk. Dun & Bradstreet Information Services, 3 Sylvan Way, Parsippany NJ 07054. **Tel** (201)605-6000, (800)526-0651. available on diskette. **Continues** ERISA Benefit Funds. Financial Directory of Pension Funds, State of Oregon, 0190-7816.

LC HD7106.U6 P365   **ISSN** 0739-2575
DD 332.6/7254   US
FINANCIAL DIRECTORY OF PENSION FUNDS. PENNSYLVANIA, EASTERN, EXCLUDING PHILADELPHIA AREA. HARRISBURG, WILKESBARRE & OTHERS). (FINANCIAL DIRECTORY OF PENSION FUNDS. PENNSYLVANIA, EASTERN, EXCLUDING PHILADELPHIA AREA (HARRISBURG, WILKESBARRE & OTHERS) / ERISA BENEFIT FUNDS, INC.). **Added/Corp** ERISA Benefit Funds, Inc. (19??)-. Directory. English. One time a year. $650.00 print; $1300.00 disk. Dun & Bradstreet Information Services, 3 Sylvan Way, Parsippany NJ 07054. **Tel** (201)605-6000, (800)526-0651. available on diskette. **Continues** ERISA Benefit Funds. Financial Directory of Pension Funds, Eastern Pennsylvania, excluding Philadelphia Area, 0190-955X.

LC HD7106.U6 P366   **ISSN** 0739-5779
DD 332.6/7254   US
FINANCIAL DIRECTORY OF PENSION FUNDS. PENNSYLVANIA, EASTERN, PHILADELPHIA CITY PROPER. **Added/Corp** ERISA Benefit Funds, Inc. (19??)-. English. One time a year. $395.00 print; $790.00 disk. Dun & Bradstreet Information Services, 3 Sylvan Way, Parsippany NJ 07054. **Tel** (201)605-6000, (800)526-0651. available on diskette. **Continues** ERISA Benefit Funds. Financial Directory of Pension Funds, Eastern Pennsylvania, Philadelphia Area, 0190-8278.

LC HD7106.U5 F558   **ISSN** 0278-0364
DD 332.6/7254   US
FINANCIAL DIRECTORY OF PENSION FUNDS. PENNSYLVANIA, EASTERN, SUBURBAN PHILADELPHIA (UPPER DARBY, WEST CHESTER, KING OF PRUSSIA & OTHERS). (FINANCIAL DIRECTORY OF PENSION FUNDS. PENNSYLVANIA, EASTERN, SUBURBAN PHILADELPHIA (UPPER DARBY, WEST CHESTER, KING OF PRUSSIA & OTHERS) / ERISA BENEFIT FUNDS, INC.). **Added/Corp** ERISA Benefit Funds, Inc. **VFOAT** Financial Directory of Pension Funds. Pennsylvania, Eastern Suburban Philadelphia (Upper Darby, West Chester, King of Prussia and Others); Financial Directory of Pension Funds. (19??)-. Directory. English. One time a year. $595.00 print; $1190.00 disk. Dun & Bradstreet Information Services, 3 Sylvan Way, Parsippany NJ 07054. **Tel** (201)605-6000, (800)526-0651. available on diskette.

LC HD7106.U6 P367   **ISSN** 0739-2710
DD 332.6/7254   US
FINANCIAL DIRECTORY OF PENSION FUNDS. PENNSYLVANIA, WESTERN, EXCLUDING PITTSBURGH AREA. ERIE, NEW CASTLE, GREENSBURG & OTHERS. (FINANCIAL DIRECTORY OF PENSION FUNDS. PENNSYLVANIA, WESTERN, EXCLUDING PITTSBURGH AREA (ERIE, NEW CASTLE, GREENSBURG & OTHERS) / ERISA BENEFIT FUNDS, INC.). **Added/Corp** ERISA Benefit Funds, Inc. (19??)-. Directory. English. One time a year. $445.00 print; $890.00 disk. Dun & Bradstreet Information Services, 3 Sylvan Way, Parsippany NJ 07054. **Tel** (201)605-6000, (800)526-0651. available on diskette. **Continues** ERISA Benefit Funds. Financial Directory of Pension Funds, Western Pennsylvania, excluding Pittsburgh Area, 0190-9916.

LC HD7106.U6 P368   **ISSN** 0741-5427
DD 332.6/7254   US
FINANCIAL DIRECTORY OF PENSION FUNDS. PENNSYLVANIA, WESTERN (PITTSBURGH AREA). **Added/Corp** ERISA Benefit Funds, Inc. (19??)-. Directory. English. One time a year. $445.00 print; $890.00 disk. Dun & Bradstreet Information Services, 3 Sylvan Way, Parsippany NJ 07054. **Tel** (201)605-6000, (800)526-0651. available on diskette. **Continues** ERISA Benefit Funds. Financial Directory of Pension Funds. Western Pennsylvania, Pittsburgh Areaa41, 0190-9924.

LC HD7106.U6 P83   **ISSN** 0882-2972
DD 332.6/7254   US
FINANCIAL DIRECTORY OF PENSION FUNDS. PUERTO RICO, THE. [Financ. dir. pension funds, P.R.]. **Added/Corp** ERISA Benefit Funds, Inc. (1984-85)-. Directory. English. One time a year. $295.00 print; $590.00 disk. Dun & Bradstreet Information Services, 3 Sylvan Way, Parsippany NJ 07054. **Tel** (201)605-6000, (800)526-0651. available on diskette. **Continues** Financial Directory of Pension Funds. Puerto Rico & Other Foreign, 0739-2702.

LC HD7106.U6 R43   **ISSN** 0741-871X
DD 332.6/7254   US
FINANCIAL DIRECTORY OF PENSION FUNDS. RHODE ISLAND. **Added/Corp** ERISA Benefit Funds, Inc. (19??)-. Directory. English. One time a year. $345.00 print; $690.00 disk. Dun & Bradstreet Information Services, 3 Sylvan Way, Parsippany NJ 07054. **Tel** (201)605-6000, (800)526-0651. available on diskette. **Continues** ERISA Benefit Funds. Financial Directory of Pension Funds. State of Rhode Island, 0190-8006.

LC HD7106.U6 S64   **ISSN** 0882-293X
DD 332.6/7254   US
FINANCIAL DIRECTORY OF PENSION FUNDS. SOUTH CAROLINA, THE. (THE FINANCIAL DIRECTORY OF PENSION FUNDS. SOUTH CAROLINA.). [Financ. dir. pension funds, S.C.]. **Added/Corp** ERISA Benefit Funds, Inc. (1984-85)-. Directory. English. One time a year. $445.00 print; $890.00 disk. Dun & Bradstreet Information Services, 3 Sylvan Way, Parsippany NJ 07054. **Tel** (201)605-6000, (800)526-0651. available on diskette. **Continues** Financial Directory of Pension Funds. State of South Carolina, 0731-731X.

LC HD7106.U6 S84   **ISSN** 0741-8701
DD 332.6/7254   US
FINANCIAL DIRECTORY OF PENSION FUNDS. SOUTH DAKOTA. **Added/Corp** ERISA Benefit Funds, Inc. (19??)-. Directory. English. One time a year. $295.00 print; $590.00 disk. Dun & Bradstreet Information Services, 3 Sylvan Way, Parsippany NJ 07054. **Tel** (201)605-6000, (800)526-0651. available on diskette. **Continues** ERISA Benefit Funds. Financial Directory of Pension Funds. State of South Dakota, 0190-8219.

LC HD7106.U6 T34   **ISSN** 0742-017X
DD 332.6/7254   US
FINANCIAL DIRECTORY OF PENSION FUNDS. TENNESSEE. **Added/Corp** ERISA Benefit Funds, Inc. (19??)-. Directory. English. One time a year. $545.00 print; $1090.00 disk. Dun & Bradstreet Information Services, 3 Sylvan Way, Parsippany NJ 07054. **Tel** (201)605-6000, (800)526-0651. available on diskette. **Continues** ERISA Benefit Funds. Financial Directory of Pension Funds, State of Tennessee, 0190-7980.

LC HD7106.U6 T45   **ISSN** 0278-2189
DD 332.6/7254   US
FINANCIAL DIRECTORY OF PENSION FUNDS. TEXAS, NORTH CENTRAL & EASTERN (WACO, BRYAN, CONROE, LUFKIN, TYLER, LONGVIEW, TEXARKANA). (FINANCIAL DIRECTORY OF PENSION FUNDS. TEXAS, NORTH CENTRAL & EASTERN (WACO, BRYAN, CONROE, LUFKIN, TYLER, LONGVIEW, TEXARKANA) / ERISA BENEFIT FUNDS, INC.). **Added/Corp** ERISA Benefit Funds, Inc. **VFOAT** Financial Directory of Pension Funds. (19??)-. Directory. English. One time a year. $345.00 print; $690.00 disk. Dun & Bradstreet Information Services, 3 Sylvan Way, Parsippany NJ 07054. **Tel** (201)605-6000, (800)526-0651. available on diskette.

LC HD7106.U6 T444   **ISSN** 0739-3237
DD 332.6/7254   US
FINANCIAL DIRECTORY OF PENSION FUNDS. TEXAS, NORTHERN (DALLAS, DENTON, SHERMAN). (FINANCIAL DIRECTORY OF PENSION FUNDS. TEXAS, NORTHERN (DALLAS, DENTON, SHERMAN) / ERISA BENEFIT FUNDS, INC.). **Added/Corp** ERISA Benefit Funds, Inc. (19??)-. Directory. English. One time a year. $445.00 print; $890.00 disk. Dun & Bradstreet Information Services, 3 Sylvan Way, Parsippany NJ 07054. **Tel** (201)605-6000, (800)526-0651. available on diskette. **Continues** Erisa Benefit Funds. Financial Directory of Pension Funds, Northern Texas, Dallas Area, 0190-8642.

LC HD7106.U6 T453   **ISSN** 0278-2103
DD 332.6/7254   US
FINANCIAL DIRECTORY OF PENSION FUNDS. TEXAS, NORTHWESTERN (FORT WORTH, AMARILLO, LUBBOCK, MIDLAND, EL PASO). **Added/Corp** ERISA Benefit Funds, Inc. **VFOAT** Financial Directory of Pension Funds. (19??)-. Directory. English. One time a year. $445.00 print. Dun & Bradstreet Information Services, 3 Sylvan Way, Parsippany NJ 07054. **Tel** (201)605-6000, (800)526-0651. available on diskette.

   ISSN 0731-7484
   US
FINANCIAL DIRECTORY OF PENSION FUNDS. TEXAS, SOUTHERN (AUSTIN, SAN ANTONIO, VICTORIA, CORPUS CHRISTI). **Added/Corp** ERISA Benefit Funds, Inc. (19??)-. English. One time a year. $445.00 print; $890.00 disk. Dun & Bradstreet Information Services, 3 Sylvan Way, Parsippany NJ 07054. **Tel** (201)605-6000, (800)526-0651. available on diskette.

LC HD7106.U5 F5585   **ISSN** 0731-7484
DD 332.6/7254   US
FINANCIAL DIRECTORY OF PENSION FUNDS. TEXAS, SOUTHERN, EXCLUDING HOUSTON AREA (BEAUMONT, SAN ANTONIO, CORPUS CHRISTI & OTHERS). (FINANCIAL DIRECTORY OF PENSION FUNDS. TEXAS, SOUTHERN, EXCLUDING HOUSTON AREA (BEAUMONT, SAN ANTONIO, CORPUS CHRISTI & OTHERS) / ERISA BENEFIT FUNDS, INC.). **Added/Corp** ERISA Benefit Funds, Inc. (19??)-. Directory. English. One time a year. $445.00 print. Dun & Bradstreet Information Services, 3 Sylvan Way, Parsippany NJ 07054. **Tel** (201)605-6000, (800)526-0651. **Continues in part** Erisa Benefit Funds. Directory of Pension Funds, Southern Texas, 0148-1495.

LC HD7106.U6 T446   **ISSN** 0739-2788
DD 332.6/7254   US
FINANCIAL DIRECTORY OF PENSION FUNDS. TEXAS, SOUTHERN, HOUSTON & EAST COAST (PASADENA & BEAUMONT). (FINANCIAL DIRECTORY OF PENSION FUNDS. TEXAS, HOUSTON & EAST COAST

(PASADENA & BEAUMONT) / ERISA BENEFIT FUNDS, INC.). **Added/Corp** ERISA Benefit Funds, Inc. (19??)-. Directory. English. One time a year. $495.00 print; $990.00 disk. Dun & Bradstreet Information Services, 3 Sylvan Way, Parsippany NJ 07054. **Tel** (201)605-6000, (800)526-0651. available on diskette. ***Continues*** *Erisa Benefit Funds. Financial Directory of Pension Funds, Southern Texas, Houston Area, 0192-5520.*

LC HD7106.U6 U84 **ISSN** 0742-0188
DD 332.6/7254 US
FINANCIAL DIRECTORY OF PENSION FUNDS. UTAH. **Added/Corp** ERISA Benefit Funds, Inc. (19??)-. Directory. English. One time a year. $395.00 print; $790.00 disk. Dun & Bradstreet Information Services, 3 Sylvan Way, Parsippany NJ 07054. **Tel** (201)605-6000, (800)526-0651. available on diskette. ***Continues*** *ERISA Benefit Funds. Financial Directory of Pension Funds, State of Utah, 0190-7999.*

LC HD7106.U6 V46 **ISSN** 0742-0196
DD 332.6/7254 US
FINANCIAL DIRECTORY OF PENSION FUNDS. VERMONT. **Added/Corp** ERISA Benefit Funds, Inc. (19??)-. Directory. English. One time a year. $295.00 print; $590.00 disk. Dun & Bradstreet Information Services, 3 Sylvan Way, Parsippany NJ 07054. **Tel** (201)605-6000, (800)526-0651. available on diskette. ***Continues*** *ERISA Benefit Funds. Financial Directory of Pension Funds, State of Vermont, 0190-7972.*

LC HD7106.U6 V823 **ISSN** 0739-2613
DD 332.6/7254 US
FINANCIAL DIRECTORY OF PENSION FUNDS. VIRGINIA, NORTHERN (ARLINGTON, WINCHESTER, HARRISONBURG & OTHERS). **Added/Corp** ERISA Benefit Funds, Inc. (19??)-. Directory. English. One time a year. $445.00 print; $890.00 disk. Dun & Bradstreet Information Services, 3 Sylvan Way, Parsippany NJ 07054. **Tel** (201)605-6000, (800)526-0651. available on diskette. ***Continues*** *ERISA Benefit Funds. Financial Directory of Pension Funds. Northern Virginia, 0192-2440.*

LC HD7106.U6 V826 **ISSN** 0278-212X
DD 332.6/7254 US
FINANCIAL DIRECTORY OF PENSION FUNDS. VIRGINIA, SOUTHERN (RICHMOND, NORFOLK, ROANOKE & OTHERS). (FINANCIAL DIRECTORY OF PENSION FUNDS. VIRGINIA, SOUTHERN (RICHMOND, NORFOLK, ROANOKE & OTHERS) / ERISA BENEFIT FUNDS, INC.). **Added/Corp** ERISA Benefit Funds, Inc. **VFOAT** Financial Directory of Pension Funds. Virginia, Southern (Richmond, Norfolk, Roanoke and Others). (19??)-. Directory. English. One time a year. $545.00 print; $1090.00 disk. Dun & Bradstreet Information Services, 3 Sylvan Way, Parsippany NJ 07054. **Tel** (201)605-6000, (800)526-0651. available on diskette.

LC HD7106.U5 F559 **ISSN** 0278-0313
DD 332.6/7254 US
FINANCIAL DIRECTORY OF PENSION FUNDS. WASHINGTON, EASTERN (SPOKANE, YAKIMA, PASCO & OTHERS). (FINANCIAL DIRECTORY OF PENSION FUNDS. WASHINGTON, EASTERN (SPOKANE, YAKIMA, PASCO & OTHERS) / ERISA BENEFIT FUNDS, INC.). **Added/Corp** ERISA Benefit Funds, Inc. **VFOAT** Financial Directory of Pension Funds. Washington, Eastern (Spokane, Yakima, Pasco and Others); Financial Directory of Pension Funds. (19??)-. Directory. English. One time a year. $345.00 print; $690.00 disk. Dun & Bradstreet Information Services, 3 Sylvan Way, Parsippany NJ 07054. **Tel** (201)605-6000, (800)526-0651. available on diskette.

LC HD7106.U6 W34 **ISSN** 0278-2073
DD 332.6/7254 US
FINANCIAL DIRECTORY OF PENSION FUNDS. WASHINGTON, WESTERN, EXCLUDING SEATTLE AREA (TAKOMA, OLYMPIA & OTHERS). **Added/Corp** ERISA Benefit Funds, Inc. **VFOAT** Financial Directory of Pension Funds; Financial Directory of Pension Funds. Washington, Western, Excluding Seattle Area (Tacoma, Olympia and Others). (19??)-. Directory. English. One time a year. $395.00 print; $790.00 disk. Dun & Bradstreet Information Services, 3 Sylvan Way, Parsippany NJ 07054. **Tel** (201)605-6000, (800)526-0651. available on diskette.

LC HD7106.U6 W343 **ISSN** 0278-2111
DD 332.6/7254 US
FINANCIAL DIRECTORY OF PENSION FUNDS. WASHINGTON, WESTERN (SEATTLE AREA ONLY). (FINANCIAL DIRECTORY OF PENSION FUNDS. WASHINGTON, WESTERN (SEATTLE AREA ONLY) / ERISA BENEFIT FUNDS, INC.). **Added/Corp** ERISA Benefit Funds, Inc. **VFOAT** Financial Directory of Pension Funds. (19??)-. Directory. English. One time a year. $445.00 print; $890.00 disk. Dun & Bradstreet Information Services, 3 Sylvan Way, Parsippany NJ 07054. **Tel** (201)605-6000, (800)526-0651. available on diskette.

LC HD7106.U6 W43 **ISSN** 0882-0821
DD 332.6/7254 US
FINANCIAL DIRECTORY OF PENSION FUNDS. WEST VIRGINIA, THE. [Financ. dir. pension funds, W. Va.]. **Added/Corp** ERISA Benefit Funds, Inc. (1984-85)-. Directory. English. One time a year. $345.00 print; $690.00 disk. Dun & Bradstreet Information Services, 3 Sylvan Way, Parsippany NJ 07054. **Tel** (201)605-6000, (800)526-0651. available on diskette. ***Continues*** *Financial Directory of Pension Funds. State of West Virginia, 0731-7344.*

LC HD7105.45.U6 F566 **ISSN** 0739-277X
DD 332.6/7254 US
FINANCIAL DIRECTORY OF PENSION FUNDS. WISCONSIN, MILWAUKEE CITY PROPER. (FINANCIAL DIRECTORY OF PENSION FUNDS. WISCONSIN, MILWAUKEE CITY PROPER / ERISA BENEFIT FUNDS, INC.). **Added/Corp** ERISA Benefit Funds, Inc. (19??)-. Directory. English. One time a year. $345.00 print; $690.00 disk. Dun & Bradstreet Information Services, 3 Sylvan Way, Parsippany NJ 07054. **Tel** (201)605-6000, (800)526-0651. available on diskette.

LC HD7106.U5 F5593 **ISSN** 0278-2154
DD 332.6/7254 US
FINANCIAL DIRECTORY OF PENSION FUNDS. WISCONSIN, MILWAUKEE (SHEBOYGAN, WAUWATOSA, RACINE & OTHERS). (FINANCIAL DIRECTORY OF PENSION FUNDS. WISCONSIN, MILWAUKEE SUBURBAN (SHEBOYGAN, WAUWATOSA, RACINE & OTHERS) / ERISA BENEFIT FUNDS, INC.). **Added/Corp** ERISA Benefit Funds, Inc. **VFOAT** Financial Directory of Pension Funds. Wisconsin, Milwaukee Suburban (Sheboygan, Waumatosa, Racine and Others); Financial Directory of Pension Funds. (19??)-. Directory. English. One time a year. $395.00 print; $790.00 disk. Dun & Bradstreet Information Services, 3 Sylvan Way, Parsippany NJ 07054. **Tel** (201)605-6000, (800)526-0651. available on diskette.

LC HD7106.U5 F5594 **ISSN** 0278-033X
DD 332.6/7254 US
FINANCIAL DIRECTORY OF PENSION FUNDS. WISCONSIN, NORTHERN (GREENBAY, WAUSAU, EAU CLAIRE & OTHERS). **Added/Corp** ERISA Benefit Funds, Inc. **VFOAT** Financial Directory of Pension Funds; Financial Directory of Pension Funds. Wisconsin, Northern (Greenbay, Wausau, Eau Claire and Others). (19??)-. Directory. English. One time a year. $345.00 print; $690.00 disk. Dun & Bradstreet Information Services, 3 Sylvan Way, Parsippany NJ 07054. **Tel** (201)605-6000, (800)526-0651. available on diskette.

LC HD7106.U6 W334 **ISSN** 0739-2753
DD 332.6/7254 US
FINANCIAL DIRECTORY OF PENSION FUNDS. WISCONSIN, SOUTHERN, EXCLUDING MILWAUKEE AREA (MADISON, LACROSSE, OSHKOSH & OTHERS). **Added/Corp** ERISA Benefit Funds, Inc. (19??)-. Directory. English. One time a year. $395.00 print. Dun & Bradstreet Information Services, 3 Sylvan Way, Parsippany NJ 07054. **Tel** (201)605-6000, (800)526-0651. available on diskette. ***Continues*** *ERISA Benefit Funds. Financial Directory of Pension Funds, State of Wisconsin, Excluding Milwaukee Area.*

LC HD7106.U6 W88 **ISSN** 0882-2948
DD 332.6/7254 US
FINANCIAL DIRECTORY OF PENSION FUNDS. WYOMING, THE. [Financ. dir. pension funds, Wyo.]. **Added/Corp** ERISA Benefit Funds, Inc. (1984-85)-. Directory. English. One time a year. $295.00 print; $590.00 disk. Dun & Bradstreet Information Services, 3 Sylvan Way, Parsippany NJ 07054. **Tel** (201)605-6000, (800)526-0651. available on diskette. ***Continues*** *Financial Directory of Pension Funds. State of Wyoming, 0731-7336.*

LC HD4966.B262 U473 **ISSN** 0734-967X
DD 331.2/813321/09788 US
FINANCIAL INDUSTRY SALARY SURVEY (DENVER, COLO. : 1982). (FINANCIAL INDUSTRY SALARY SURVEY.). 1982-. English. One time a year. Mountain States Employers Council / Research Department, PO Box 539, Denver CO 80201. ***Continues*** *Financial Industry Survey / Mountain States Employers Council, 0732-4936.*

LC HD7177 .F56
GW
FINANZEN UND STEUERN. REIHE 3.5, RECHNUNGSERGEBNISSE DER OFFENTLICHEN HAUSHALTE FUER SOZIALE SICHERUNG UND FUER GESUNDHEIT, SPORT, ERHOLUNG. **VFOAT** Rechnungsbegebnisse der Offentlichen Haushalte fur Soziale Sicherung und fur Gesundheit, Sport, Erholung Fashserie 14. German. One time a year. W. Kohlhammer Verlag GmbH, Postfach 800430, D-70549 Stuttgart Germany. **Tel** 011 49 711 78630, FAX 011 49 711 7863430, telex 7-255820. ***Formed by the union of*** *Finanze und Steuern. Reihe 3.5, Rechnungsergebnisse der Offentlichen Haushalte fur Soziale Sicherung* ***and*** *Finanzen und Steuern. Reihe 3.6, Rechnungsergebnisse der Offentlichen Haushalte fur Gesundheit, Sport und Erholung.*

ISSN 0890-8494
DD 363 US
FIRE SERVICE LABOR MONTHLY. [Fire serv. labor mon.]. (Jan. 1987)-. English. Twelve times a year. $97.00. Justex System Inc., PO Box 6224, Huntsville TX 77340. **Tel** (409)291-7981, FAX (409)294-0984. **ED** Jerry L. Dowling (editor's address: 1300 11th Street, Huntsville, TX 77342). **Circ:** 500.
Desc: Deals with fire service labor issues.

KO
FKTU NEWS. (19??)-. Periodical. English. Hanguk Nodong Chohop, Chongnyonmaeng Fktu Building, 1-117 Yoido-dong, Yongdeungpo-ku, Seoul South Korea. **Tel** (7)782-3884. **Circ:** 300.
Desc: Report on the Korean Trade Union activities.

BE
FLASH. (19??)-. Periodical. English (French, Spanish, German and Dutch). Twenty-four times a year. $6.00. World Confederation of Labour, 33 rue de Treves, B-1040 Brussels Belgium. **Tel** 011 32 2 230 62 95, FAX 011 32 2 230 87 22.

XR
FLASHES FROM THE TRADE UNIONS. **Added/Corp** World Federation of Trade Unions. (197?)-. Periodical. English (English, Spanish, Russian and Arabic). Six times a year. $24.00. World Federation of Trade Unions, Branicka 112, 140 00 Prague 4 Czech Republic. **Tel** 46 21 40, FAX 46 13 78. **Circ:** 13,000. available with illustrations.
Desc: A bulletin of news and information relating to international trade union affairs.

US
FLINT'S LABOR MARKET NEWS. **Added/Corp** Michigan Employment Security Commission. Bureau of Research and Statistics. Information and Reports Section. Vol. 12, No. 1 (Mar. 1992)-. Periodical. English. Twelve times a year. Detroit Employment Security Commission, 7310 Woodward Castro, Room 520, Detroit MI 48202. **Tel** (313)876-5427. ***Continues*** *Flint Labor Market Review.*

ISSN 1078-2362
DD 331 US
FLORIDA COMP. (FLORIDA COMP : THE WORKERS' COMPENSATION INDUSTRY'S MAGAZINE.). [Fla. comp]. **VFOAT** Florida Compensation. (199?)-. Periodical. English. Four times a year (Jan., April, July, Oct.). $40.00. Florida Comp, 721 Tarawitt Drive, Longboatkey FL 34228. **Tel** (813)383-0450.

US
FLORIDA EMPLOYMENT LAW DESK BOOK. (19??)-. English. One time a year. $74.90 Florida; $70.00 other. Florida Chamber of Commerce, PO Box 11309, Tallahassee FL 32302. **Tel** 800/940-3034, FAX (904)425-1260. **ED** Gary Cliett, (editor's address: P. O. Box 11309, Tallahassee, FL 32302-3309, phone: (904)425-1242).

US
FLORIDA LABOR MARKET TRENDS. **Added/Corp** Florida. Bureau of Labor Market Information. Letter No. 474 (Feb. 1989)-. Periodical. English. Twelve times a year. Florida Labor, Employment & Training Division, 1320 Executive Center Drive, Suite 300, Tallahassee FL 32399. **Tel** (904)488-7225, FAX (904)487-1753. ***Continues*** *Florida Employment Trends.*

US
FLORIDA PUBLIC EMPLOYEE REPORTER DIGEST. **Added/Corp** Labor Relations Press. **VFOAT** Public Employee Reporter (Florida Edition). Vol. 1-6 (1975/1980)-. Periodical. English. Twenty-four times a year. $677.00. LRP Publications, 747 Dresher Road, Suite 500, Horsham PA 19044. **Tel** (800)341-7874, (215)784-0941, FAX (215)784-9639, (215)784-0870. **(Subscription address:** LRP Publications, PO Box 980, Horsham PA 19044. **Tel** (800)341-7874, (215)784-0860.) **ED** Jim Gasper.
Desc: Abstracts and full-text of Florida state labor board decisions. Complete indexing, many access parts, table of cases, citation tracker, rules and regulations of boards, articles and database.

LC HD7106.U6 F63
DD 353.9759005/06 US
FLORIDA RETIREMENT SYSTEM ANNUAL REPORT. **Main/Corp** Florida. Division of Retirement. **VFOAT** Annual Report of the Division of Retirement. (1982)-. English. One time a year. Carlton Building, Room 530, Tallahassee FL. ***Continues*** *Annual Report of the Division of Retirement.*

Business and Economics —Labor

LC HD5725.F6 F43a   **ISSN** 0093-7126
DD 331.1/1/09759   US
FLORIDA STATE MANPOWER PLAN.
Main/Corp Florida State Manpower Council. (19??)-. English. One time a year. Florida State Manpower Council, 1720 South Gadsden Street, Tallahassee FL 32301.

LC HD6726 .F43
DD 331.88/09492   NE
FNV JAARVERSLAG. Main/Corp Federatie Nederlandse Vakbeweging. **VFOAT** F.N.V. Jaarverslag; Jaarverslag F.N.V.; Jaarverslag FNV. **VAT** Federatie Nederlandse Vakbeweging News. (1982)-. Dutch. One time a year. Federatie Nederlandse, Vakbeweging Plun '40-'45, Amsterdam-West Netherlands.

ISSN 0831-4535
DD 344.71/01133/05   CN
FOCUS ON CANADIAN EMPLOYMENT AND EQUALITY RIGHTS. [Focus Can. employ. equal. rights]. **VFOAT** Canadian Employment and Equality Rights. Vol. 1, No. 1 (Jan. 1986)-. Periodical. English. Twelve times a year. 100.00Can$. CCH Canadian Ltd., 6 Garamond Court, Don Mills Ontario M3C 1Z5 Canada. **Tel** (416)441-2992, **FAX** (416)441-3418.

LC HD6611 .F67   BL
FORCA SINDICAL. Vol. 1, No. 1 (June 1991)-. Periodical. Portuguese. Twelve times a year. Central de Trabaalhadores Forca Sindical, Rua Cel. Oscar Porto 841, Bairro do Paraiso, 04003 Sao Paulo SP Brazil. **Tel** 011 885-3217, **FAX** 011 885-0890.

US
FORCE (ALBANY, N.Y.). (THE FORCE.). Vol. 1, No. 1 (Spring 1982)-. Periodical. English. Four times a year. University of the State of New York / State Education Department, Albany NY 12234.

LC HD8423 .F6   **ISSN** 0399-4708
DD 331/.0944   FR
FORCE OUVRIERE HEBDO. Added/Corp CGT-FO (Union). No. 1708 (April 7, 1982)-. Periodical. French. Forty-three times a year. $87.49. Force Ouvriere, 198 Avenue du Maine, 75680 Paris Cedex 14 France. **Tel** 011 33 1 45392203. **Continues** Fo Hebdo.

ISSN 0733-0324
US
FORDYCE LETTER, THE. (19??)-. Periodical. English. Twelve times a year. $126.00. The Fordyce Letter, PO Box 31011, Des Peres MO 63131-0011. **Tel** (314)965-3883, **FAX** (314)965-8177. **ED** Paul Hawkinson. Index available (bound in Feb. issue). cum. index. **Bk Rev**, (Qty: 3). **Ad Acc**. **Circ:** 9,000 (ctrl).
Desc: Information and commentary for executive recruiters and personnel consultants.

LC HD8191 .F67
DD 331.1/09729   US
FOREIGN LABOR TRENDS. EASTERN CARIBBEAN. VFOAT Labor Trends in the Eastern Caribbean. English. Irregular (approximately 73 issues). $36.00 US; $45.00 other. US Department of Labor Bureau of International Labor Affairs, 200 Constitution Avenue NW, Room S-2235, Washington DC 20210. **Tel** (202)219-6043, **FAX** (202)219-9880.
Desc: Describe and analyze the labor trends in some of the most important foreign countries. Covers significant labor developments, including labor-management relations, trade unions, employment and unemployment, wages and working conditions, labor and government, labor administration and legislation, training, labor and politics, labor migration, and international labor activities, as appropriate.

FR
FORMATION EMPLOI. Added/Corp France. Documentation Francaise. No. 1 (Jan./Mar. 1983)-. Periodical. French (summaries and/or abstracts in English and German). Four times a year. 22.00F France; 48.97F Europe; 86.79F other. CEREQ / Centre d'Etudes et de Recherches sur les Qualifications, 10 Place de la Joliette, 13474 Marseille Cedex France. **Tel** 011 33 91 132828, **FAX** 011 33 91 132880. **(Subscription address:** La Documentaion Francaise, 124 rue Henry Barbusse, 93308 Aubervilliers Cedex France. **Tel** 011 33 1 48395600.) **Bk Rev**. **Circ:** 1,200.
Desc: Covers the entrance of young people into the labor market, changing job contents and occupations, work organization, management, labor management, technological change, skills and employment.
Ind/Abst Int. Bibliogr. Sociol.; Int. Labour Doc.

LC HD5715.5.F8 F738A
DD 331.25/92/0944   FR
FORMATION PROFESSIONNELLE CONTINUE, RAPPORT D'ACTIVITE. VFOAT Formation, Rapport d'Activite. (19??)-. French. **Continues** France. Direction Generale des Postes. Service du Personnel. Formation Professionnelle Continue du Personnel.

LC HD6475.A1 B84   **ISSN** 1079-8900
DD 331   US
●**FORUM (AFL-CIO). See** Political Science-International Relations.

ISSN 0823-8006
DD 331.7/61651374/09714   CN
FRAPPE. (LA FRAPPE : BULLETIN DE LIAISON DU REGROUPEMENT DES SECRETAIRES DU QUEBEC.). [Frappe]. Vol. 1, No. 1 (Jan./Feb. 1983)-. Bulletin. French. Six times a year. Free to members. Regroupement Des Secretaires Du Quebec, 1015 Est rue Ste-Catherine, Montreal Quebec H2L 2G4 Canada.

LC HD4802 .F7   **ISSN** 0770-1470
DD 331.88091   BE
FREE LABOUR WORLD. [Free labour world].
Added/Corp International Confederation of Free Trade Unions. (July 1950)-. Periodical. English (French, German and Spanish). Twenty-six times a year. $55.98. International Confederation of Free Trade Unions, 37-41 Montagne Herbes Potageres, 1000 Brussels Belgium. **Tel** 011 32 2 2178085, **FAX** 011 32 2 2188415, telex 26785.
Ind/Abst Hum. Rights Intern. Rep.; Middle East Abstr. Index; Work Relat. Abstr.

ISSN 0270-6865
US
FROM THE HORSE'S MOUTH (PITTSBURGH). (FROM THE HORSE'S MOUTH.). (19??)-. Periodical. English. Western Pennsylvania Teamsters for a Democratic Union, 250 Hazelwood Avenue, Pittsburgh PA 15207.

ISSN 0734-0931
US
CCC
TITLE CHANGE
FROM THE STATE CAPITALS. WORKERS' COMPENSATION. [From state cap., Work. compens.]. **VFOAT** Worker's Compensation. (1982)-(19??). Periodical. English. Wakeman Walworth Inc., 300 North Washington Street #204, Alexandria VA 22314. **Tel** (703)549-8606. **Continues** From the State Capitals. Summary of Workers' Compensation Trends. **Continued by** From the State Capitals: Labour Relations, 0734-1105.

ISSN 0016-3090
US
FURNITURE WORKERS PRESS. See Building and Construction-Carpentry and Woodwork.

LC Z120.G69 A3   **ISSN** 0094-4211
DD 331.88/11/6862   US
G.A.I.U. HANDBOOK OF WAGES, HOURS AND FRINGE BENEFITS. (GAIU HANDBOOK OF WAGES, HOURS, AND FRINGE BENEFITS.). **Main/Corp** Graphic Arts International Union. Contract & Research Dept. **VFOAT** Handbook of Wages, Hours, and Fringe Benefits. (19??)-. English. Graphic Arts International Union, 1900 L Street, Washington DC 20036.

LC HD6761 .G3
DD 331/.0946   SP
GACETA SINDICAL : ORGANO DE LA CONFEDERACION DE CC.OO. Vol. 1, No. 1 (April 1980)-. Spanish. Irregular. 1,600ptas. Fernandez de la Hoz 12, Madrid 4 Spain.

ISSN 0823-9177
DD 320.5/31/05   CN
GAUCHE SOCIALISTE. See Political Science-Socialism, Communism, Anarchism, Utopianism.

LC HA1320.B2 A32 HD5030.B3
DD 314.3/46 S 331.2/94346   GW
GEHALTS- UND LOHNSTRUKTURERHEBUNG / HERAUSGEGEBEN VOM STATISTISCHEN LANDESAMT BADEN-WURTTEMBERG. Added/Corp Statistisches Landesamt Baden-Wurttemberg. (19??)-. German. Statistisches Landesamt Baden-Wuerttemberg, Postfach 10 60 33, 70049 Stuttgart Germany. **Tel** 011 49 771 6410, **FAX** 011 49 711 6412440.

LC HD5833 .A27
DD 331.11/095125/021   HK
GENERAL HOUSEHOLD SURVEY LABOUR FORCE CHARACTERISTICS: QUARTERLY REPORT. Added/Corp Hong Kong. Census and Statistics Dept. **VFOAT** Labour Force Characteristics. (19??)-. Periodical. English. Four times a year. HK$96.00. Hong Kong Government Information Service, Beaconsfield House, 4 Queens Road, Hong Kong Hong Kong. **Tel** 011 852 284288014, 011 852 259881947, **FAX** 011 852 28459078, 011 852 25987486, telex 61190 HKGIS.

US
GENERAL WAGE DETERMINATIONS ISSUED UNDER THE DAVIS-BACON AND RELATED ACTS. VOLUME 1, ESA REGIONS 1-4. Added/Corp United States. Employment Standards Administration. Wage and Hour Division. **VFOAT** ESA Regions 1-4. (1985)-. Government Publication. English. $601.00 domestic; $751.25 other. US Department of Labor, 200 Constitution Avenue NW, Washington DC 20210. **Tel** (202)219-7316, **FAX** (202)219-7312. **(Subscription address:** Neodata / Colorado, PO Box 2606, Boulder CO 80322.)
Desc: Presents current wage decisions for laborers and mechanics engaged in Federal construction projects.

LC HD8051 .A7876 HD5723   **ISSN** 0145-7330
DD 331.1/08 S 331.1/1/0973   US
GEOGRAPHIC PROFILE OF EMPLOYMENT AND UNEMPLOYMENT. English. One time a year. US Department of Labor, 200 Constitution Avenue NW, Washington DC 20210. **Tel** (202)219-7316, **FAX** (202)219-7312.

LC HD4975 .C5817A   **ISSN** 0161-3146
DD 658.32   US
GEOGRAPHIC SALARY DIFFERENTIALS. Main/Corp Compensation Institute. (19??)-. English. Compensation Institute, 3250 Wilshire Boulevard, Suite 900, Los Angeles CA 90010.

US
GEOGRAPHIC SALARY DIFFERENTIALS REPORT. Added/Corp William M. Mercer-Meidinger-Hansen, Inc. (1987)-. Periodical. English. One time a year. $275.00 (print); $375.00 (diskette). William Mercer Inc., 1500 Meidinger Tower, Louisville KY 40202. **Tel** (502)561-4655, **FAX** (502)561-7858. Index available. **Circ:** 500. available on diskette. **Continues** Geographic Salary Differentials (Louisville, Ky.).

LC HD5725.G4 G44a   **ISSN** 0147-9865
DD 331.1/2/09758   US
GEORGIA LABOR MARKET TRENDS.
Main/Corp Georgia. Labor Information Systems. (Mar. 1976)-. Periodical. English. Twelve times a year. Free on request. Georgia Department of Labor, CES Unit, 148 International Boulevard, Atlanta GA 30303. **Tel** (404)656-2994. **Circ:** 2,000. **Continues** Georgia Labor Market Trends, 0147-9865.
Desc: Contains estimates of monagricultural employment for state, hours and earnings of state's manufacturing production workers, civilian labor force estimates for US, GA, MSA's and narrative discussion of trends.

LC HD8450 .G386
RU
GERMANSKOE RABOCHEE I DEMOKRATICHESKOE DVIZHENIE V NOVEISHEE VREMIA. Added/Corp Vologodskii Gosudarstvennyi Pedagogicheskii Institut. (19??)-. Periodical. Russian. 0.60rub. Vologda, Vologodskii Gosudarstvennyi Pedagogicheskii Institut, Maiakovskogo 6, Vologda Russia.

LC HD7116.R12 G37
GW
Pr Rev.
GESCHAFTSBERICHT DER BUNDESBAHN-VERSICHERUNGSANST ALT. Main/Corp Bundesbahn-Versicherungsanstalt. (19??)-. German. Free on request. Bahnversicherungsanstalt, Hauptverwaltung, Karlstrasse 4-6, D-60329 Frankfurt Germany. **Tel** 069 765 6003, **FAX** 069 265 5170. ctrl circ.

AU
GESETZE UND KOMMENTARE.
Added/Corp Osterreichischer Gewerkschaftsbund. (1989)-. Monographic series. German. Irregular. Price varies per volume. **Continues** Schriftenreihe des Osterreichischen Gewerkschaftsbundes.

LC HD4809 .G38   **ISSN** 0016-9447
GW
CCC
GEWERKSCHAFTLICHE MONATSHEFTE. [Gewerksch. Monatsh.].
Added/Corp Deutscher Gewerkschaftsbund. Vol. 1 (Jan. 1950)-. Periodical. German. Twelve times a year. $130.35. Bund Verlag GmbH, Postfach 900840, D-51118 Cologne Germany. **Tel** 011 49 2203 934758.
Ind/Abst Energy Res. Abstr. (Oct. 1978-); Int. Bibliogr. Sociol.

LC HD4809 .G4
DD 331/.09494   SZ
CEASED
GEWERKSCHAFTLICHE RUNDSCHAU.
Added/Corp Schweizerischer Gewerkschaftsbund. (19??)-(1994). Periodical. German. Schweizerischer

Gewerkschafts, Bund Monbijoustr 61, PO Box 64, CH-3000 Bern 23 Switzerland. **Tel** 011 41 31 455666, telex 912-831 CH. **ED** Arnold Isler. **Bk Rev**. **Ad Acc**. **Circ:** 5,500. **Continues** *Gewerkschaftliche Rundschau fuer die Schweiz*.
Desc: Articles on Swiss Trade Union politics in social, economics and labor affairs. Official meanings and discussions on it. Sometimes views on foreign trade union politics.

LC HD6691 .G46
DD 331.87/0943

GW
TITLE CHANGE
GEWERKSCHAFTS JAHRBUCH. VFOAT
Gewerkschaftsjahrbuch. (1984)-(1993). German. Bund Verlag GmbH, Postfach 900840, D-51118 Cologne Germany. **Tel** 011 49 2203 934758. **Continued by** *Gewerkschaften Heute*.

LC HB
DD 331.702

US
●**GLOBAL CAREER RESOURCES.** See Occupations and Careers.

UK
GMB DIRECT. See Business and Economics-Commerce.

LC HD9623.U45 G533 **ISSN** 1065-1640
DD 331.88/166/0973 US
GMP HORIZONS. [GMP horiz.]. Added/Corp
Glass, Molders, Pottery, Plastics & Allied Workers International Union. **VFOAT** Horizons. Vol. 36, No. 5 (May 1988)-. Periodical. English. Twelve times a year. $15.00. Glass, Pottery, Plastics and Allied Workers, 3342 Bladensburg Road, Brentwood MD 20722. **Tel** (215)565-5051. **Continues** *GPPAW Horizons, 0745-0761*.
Ind/Abst Work Relat. Abstr.

LC HD7255.A2 W57x

US
GOAL, THE. Main/Corp Wisconsin Rehabilitation
Association. (Feb. 1981)-. Periodical. English. Six times a year. **Continues** *The Wire*.
Ind/Abst SportSearch (May 1987-).

LC HD8005.2.U5 G68 **ISSN** 0738-3312
DD 331.88/1135/0000973 US
SUSPENDED
GOVERNMENT UNION CRITIQUE, THE.
Added/Corp Public Service Research Council. **VFOAT** Critique. Vol. 1 (Nov. 1978)-Suspended with Vol. 17 (1995). Periodical. English. Twenty-six times a year (Published every other Friday). $80.00. Public Service Research Foundation, 1761 Business Center Drive, Suite 230, Reston VA 22090-5333. **Tel** (703)438-3966, FAX (703)438-3935. **ED** Peter W. Katsiruba. Index available. **Circ:** 2,000 (ctrl).
Desc: A news report on public sector unionism.

US
CEASED
GOVERNMENTS QUARTERLY REPORT. GR, FINANCES OF SELECTED PUBLIC EMPLOYEE RETIREMENT SYSTEMS. Added/Corp United States. Bureau of the
Census. **VFOAT** Finances of Selected Public Employee Retirement Systems. (19??)-(June 30, 1994). Government Publication. English. US Department of Commerce, 14th Street & Constitution Avenue NW, Washington DC 20230. **Tel** (202)482-2000, FAX (202)482-3772. Documents available from Documents on Demand. **Continues** *Governments Quarterly Reports. GR, Holdings of Selected Public Employee Retirement Systems*.
Ind/Abst Am. Stat. Index.

ISSN 0992-7662
UDC 331.6 FR
GRAND ANGLE SUR L'EMPLOI ISSY-LES-MOULINEAUX. (GRAND ANGLE
SUR L'EMPLOI.). [Grand angle emploi Issy-les-Moulineaux]. **Added/Corp** Agence Nationale pour l'Emploi (France). Direction des Etudes, des Statistiques et du Controle de Gestion. (1986)-. Periodical. French.
Ind/Abst LABORDOC.

US
GRAND RAPIDS' LABOR MARKET NEWS. Added/Corp Michigan Employment Security
Commission. Bureau of Research and Statistics. Information and Reports Section. Vol. 12, No. 1 (Mar. 1992)-. Periodical. English. Twelve times a year. Detroit Employment Security Commission, 7310 Woodward Castro, Room 520, Detroit MI 48202. **Tel** (313)876-5427. **Continues** *Grand Rapids Labor Market Review*.

LC HD6350.S7 G7 **ISSN** 0017-3207
DD 331.88/122352/0973 US
GRANITE CUTTERS' JOURNAL, THE.
Vol. 1 (1877)-. Periodical. English. Four times a year. $2.00. Granite Cutters' International Association of America, 18 Federal Avenue, Quincy MA 02169.

LC HB2667 .N65
DD 331.7/12/025 UY
GUIA DE PROFESIONALES URUGUAYOS. (1979)-. Spanish. One time a year.
Impresora Polo Ltda, Avenida Garibaldi 2579, Montevideo Uruguay. **Tel** 80 27 79. **Continues** *Nomina Clasificada de Profesionales Uruguayos*.

FR
GUIDE DU TRAVAIL. French. 615.00F. Les
Editions ESF, 17 rue Viete, 75854 Paris Cedex 17 France. **Tel** 1 44 15 62 00, FAX 1 46 22 67 45.

FR
GUIDE PRATIQUE DU SALARIE. (19??)-.
French. 528.91F France; 558.00F other. Editions Prat Europa, 28481 Thiron Cedex France. **Tel** 011 33 37 295718.

LC JK2445.P82 N37 **ISSN** 0897-3156
DD 353.0081/9/025 US
GUIDE TO BACKGROUND INVESTIGATIONS, THE. [Guide backgr. invest.].
Added/Corp National Employment Screening Services (U.S.). No. 1 (1988)-. Periodical. English. Two times a year. $138.45. National Employment Screening Service, 4110 S 100 E Avenue/Suite 200, Tulsa OK 74146. **Tel** (918)491-9936, 800 247-8713. **Continues** *National Employment Screening Directory, 0891-4419*.

LC HD8103 .G84
DD 331.1/077 CN
GUIDE TO FEDERAL GOVERNMENT LABOUR STATISTICS. See Business and
Economics-Abstracting, Bibliographies and Statistics.

ISSN 0533-5051
CN
GUIDE (TORONTO). (THE GUIDE.). Added/Corp
Christian Labour Association of Canada. (Jan. 1, 1953)-. Periodical. English. Eight times a year. 12.01Can$. Christian Labour Association of Canada, 5920 Atlantic Drive, Mississauga Ontario L4W 1NG Canada. **Tel** (416)670-7383. **ED** Ray Pennings. Index available. cum. index. **Bk Rev**, (Qty: 1-3). **Ad Acc**. **Circ:** 13,500 (ctrl).
Desc: Ideas in the areas of labour relations, economics and trade unions.

LC HD6350.N4 G8 **ISSN** 0017-5404
DD 070.5 US
GUILD REPORTER, THE. Vol.1 (Nov. 23,
1933)-. Periodical. English. Twelve times a year (every third Friday). $20.00. Newspaper Guild, 8611 Second Avenue, Silver Spring MD 20910. **Tel** (301)585-2990, FAX (301)585-0668. **ED** James M Cesnik. **Circ:** 35,350 (ctrl). available on microfilm and microfiche from University Microfilms International (UMI).
Desc: Publishes industry information on employee relations and the 1st Amendment.
Ind/Abst GATFWORLD (1984); Hum. Rights Intern. Rep.; Work Relat. Abstr.

LC HD8721 .G87

JA
GURAFU DE MIRU RODO JIJO / RODOSHO HEN. Added/Corp Japan. Rodosho.
(19??)-. Japanese. ¥3200. Rodo Kijun Chosakai, 4-5 Kitaotsuka 2-chome Toshimaku, Tokyo 170 Japan.

LC HD5083 .A35
DD 331.2/95125/021 HK
●**HALF-YEARLY REPORT OF WAGE STATISTICS. Added/Corp** Hong Kong. Wages and Labour Cost Statistics Section. **VFOAT** Half Yearly Report of Wage Statistics. (1994)-. English. Four times a year. Hong Kong Government Information Service, Beaconsfield House, 4 Queens Road, Hong Kong Hong Kong. **Tel** 011 852 284288014, 011 852 259881947, FAX 011 852 28459078, 011 852 25987482, telex 61190 HKGIS. **Continues** *Report on Half-Yearly Survey of Wages, Salaries, and Employee Benefits*.

LC HD7096.U6 O514 **ISSN** 0361-2902
DD 368.4/4/009766 US
HANDBOOK OF EMPLOYMENT SECURITY PROGRAM STATISTICS. See
Business and Economics-Abstracting, Bibliographies and Statistics.

LC HD6278.C32 P744
DD 331.11/423 CN
HANDBOOK OF THE LABOUR MARKET OUTCOMES OF THE ... GRADUATES FROM UNIVERSITY OF PRINCE EDWARD ISLAND, HOLLAND COLLEGE POST SECONDARY COURSES, CANADA EMPLOYMENT AND IMMIGRATION COMMISSION SPONSORED COURSES. 1981-. English. One
time a year. Department of Labour Research & Planning, PO Box 2000, Charlottetown Prince Edward Island C1A 7N8 Canada.

Business and Economics —Labor

ISSN 8755-979X
US
HANDBOOK OF WAGES AND BENEFITS FOR CONSTRUCTION UNIONS. (1980)-. English. One time a year. US
Department of Labor, 200 Constitution Avenue NW, Washington DC 20210. **Tel** (202)219-7316, FAX (202)219-7312.

ISSN 1059-0277
DD 344 US
HANDLING CORPORATE EMPLOYMENT PROBLEMS. [Handl. corp.
employ. probl.]. **Added/Corp** Practising Law Institute. (1991)-. English. Practising Law Institute, 810 Seventh Avenue, New York NY 10019-5818. **Tel** (212)765-5700, FAX (212)581-4670 general correspondence, (212)265-4742 orders and billing inquiries. **Continues** *Handling Corporate Employment Law Problems, 1059-0269*.

ISSN 0319-4132
DD 331.88/0971 CN
HARMONIE SYNDICALE, L'. First issue in
1960?. French. Federation Canadienne des Associations Independants, 4815 Est boulevard Gouin, Montreal Quebec H1H 1G2 Canada.

ISSN 0095-3792
US
HEALTH CARE LABOR MANUAL.
Added/Corp Aspens Systems Corporation. Health Law Center. (19??)-. Periodical. English. Six times a year. $714.00. Aspen Publishers Inc., 7201 McKinney Circle, Frederick MD 21701. **Tel** (800)234-1660, (301)698-7100, FAX (301)251-5784, telex 5106014543. **(Subscription address:** Aspen Publishers Inc., PO Box 990, Frederick MD 21701. **Tel** (800)901-9074, (301)698-7100.) **Bk Rev**. **Ad Acc**. ctrl circ.
Desc: Loose-leaf service providing latest methods in handling personnel problems, laws, and new rulings and indexed sections.

ISSN 0148-4761
US
NLM W1 HE4015
HEALTH LABOR RELATION REPORTS.
VFOAT HLR Reports. Vol. 1 (Oct. 26, 1976)-. Periodical. English. Twenty-four times a year. $159.00. Interwood Publications, 3 Interwood Place, PO Box 20241, Cincinnati OH 45220. **Tel** (513)221-3715. **ED** Frank J. Bardack.
Desc: Covers employee and labor relations in health care, with legal decisions on at-will employment, wrongful discharge, discrimination, NLRB decisions, arbitration awards, contract settlements, worker's compensation and legal organizing.

ISSN 0823-518X
DD 331.12/42/0009714 CN
HEBDO CARRIERES (MONTREAL).
(HEBDO CARRIERES.). [Hebdo carr.]. Vol. 1, No. 1 (Feb. 1980)-. Periodical. French. Twelve times a year. Free. Hebdo Carrieres, 8020 St. Hubert, Montreal Quebec H2R 2P3 Canada. ctrl circ.

LC D731 .V53
DD 940.53/05 FR
●**HEBDO DE L'ACTUALITE SOCIALE, L'.**
See History-History of Europe.

UK
HIGH BROWSE. (19??)-. English. Twelve times a
year. Free. Royal National Institute for the Blind, PO Box 173, Peterborough PE2 6WS United Kingdom. **Tel** 011 44 1733 3730777, FAX 011 44 1733 371555.
Desc: Details of the latest study and employment-related books and leaflets.

LC HD8112 .H57

MX
HISTORIA OBRERA. Added/Corp Centro de
Estudios Historicos del Movimiento Obrero Mexicano. Vol. 1 (June 1974)-. Spanish. Four times a year. $50.00. Centro de Estudios Historicos del Movimiento Obrero, Dr Jose Maria Vertiz, No 96 1 Piso, Mexico City Mexico.

LC HD5727 .H58 **ISSN** 1181-957X
DD 331.11/0971 CN
HISTORICAL LABOUR FORCE STATISTICS. See Business and
Economics-Abstracting, Bibliographies and Statistics.

LC RA413.5.U5 **ISSN** 0278-1247
DD 331.2/813621/0973 US
NLM W1; HM676R
HMO EXECUTIVE SALARY SURVEY.
March 1981-. Periodical. English. Two times a year. Henry W Warren and Associates, 500 Davis Center/Suite 600, Evanston IL 60201. **Tel** (312)864-0310.

ISSN 0710-2232
DD 331.88/1213/09711 CN
HOTLINE (VANCOUVER). (HOTLINE.).
[Hotline]. **Added/Corp** B.C. Hydro. International Brotherhood of Electrical Workers. Local 258. (19??)-.

Business and Economics —Labor

Periodical. English. Six times a year. Hotline / Canada, 204-2001 East, 36th Avenue, Vancouver BC V5P 1C9 Canada.

LC HD4973 .B85B   **ISSN** 0362-692X
DD 331.2/973   US
HOURLY EARNINGS INDEX, THE.
Main/Corp United States. Bureau of Labor Statistics. (19??)-. Government Publication. English. US Department of Labor / Bureau of Labor Statistics, 441 G Street Northwest, Washington DC 20212. **Tel** (202)606-7800, FAX (202)606-7797.

US
HOW TO GET A JOB IN DALLAS/FORT WORTH : THE INSIDER'S GUIDE. English. $15.95. Surrey Books, 230 East Ohio Street, Suite 120, Chicago IL 60611. **Tel** (800)326-4430, (312)751-7330.

US
HOW TO GET A JOB IN HOUSTON : THE INSIDER'S GUIDE. (19??)-. English. Irregular. $15.95. Surrey Books, 230 East Ohio Street, Suite 120, Chicago IL 60611. **Tel** (800)326-4430, (312)751-7330.

    ISSN 0741-6997
US
CCC
HR REPORTER. See Business and Economics-Personnel Management.

LC HD9502.A1 H77   **ISSN** 0250-8869
DD 333.7/05   CH
HSIN SHIH / LIEN-HO-KUO CHIAO KO WEN TSU CHIH. (July 1980)-. Periodical. Chinese. Irregular. $.095. Science Press, 16 Donghuangchenggen North Street, Beijing 100707, People's Republic of China. **Tel** 011 86 1 4019821, 011 86 1 4010642, FAX 011 86 1 4012180, 011 86 1 4019810, telex 210147.

LC HD5701 .H85
DD 331.1/1/09599   PH
SUSPENDED
HUMAN RESOURCE DEVELOPMENT JOURNAL. Added/Corp National Manpower and Youth Council (Philippines) Philippines. Dept. of Labor. Vol. 1 (Dec. 1976)-Suspended. Periodical. English. Four times a year. $4.00. National Manpower and Youth Council, Bookman Building, Quezon Avenue, Quezon City Philippines.

    ISSN 1058-5001
DD 331   US
HUMAN RESOURCE LINE, THE. [Hum. resour. line]. Vol. 1, No. 1 (Sept. 1990)- Vol. 9 (Sept. 1993)-. Periodical. English. Twelve times a year. $35.00. Business Council of New York State, 152 Washington Avenue, Albany NY 12210-2289. **Tel** (518)465-7511, (800)692-5483. **ED** Cathy Tempesta.

LC HF5549.A2 H86
DD 658.3/005   US
HUMAN RESOURCES. VFOAT Annual Editions, Human Resources. (1989/90)-. English. One time a year. Dushkin Publishing Group Inc., Sluice Dock, Guilford CT 06437. **Tel** (203)453-4351, (800)243-6532, FAX (203)453-6000. **Circ:** 11,000.
Desc: Facsimile reproduction anthology of articles from the public press selected for relevance to the college-level introductory course. Original graphics reproduced.

LC Z7165.U5 P2   **ISSN** 0099-2453
DD 331/.05   US
CCC
NLM Z 7164.C4 P115
HUMAN RESOURCES ABSTRACTS. See Business and Economics-Abstracting, Bibliographies and Statistics.

LC HD4904.7 .M36   **ISSN** 1051-3760
DD 658   US
CCC
CODEN HRBREK
TITLE CHANGE
HUMAN RESOURCES BRIEFING. See Business and Economics-Personnel Management.

    ISSN 0791-847X
DD 331.041   IE
●**HUMAN RESOURCES INTERNATIONAL.**
[Hum. res. int.]. (1993)-. Periodical. English. Irregular. 699p. Lafferty Publications Ltd., Tower Ida Centre Pearse Street, Dublin 2 Ireland. **Tel** 011 353 1 6718022, FAX 011 353 1 718520.

    ISSN 0816-0368
DD 331.80994   AT
HUMMER SYDNEY. [Hummer Syd.]. **Added/Corp** Australian Society for the Study of Labour History. Sydney Branch. (1983)-. Bulletin. English. Four times a year (Feb., Apr., July, Oct.). 16.44Aus$. Australian Society for the Study of Labour History, 11 Henley Street / Sydney Branch, Lane Cove New South Wales 2066 Australia. **Tel** 02 427 6366. **ED** Lucy Taltsa (phone: 02 385 2010). **Bk Rev**, (Qty: 8). **Circ:** 140.

LC HD5819 .D4   **ISSN** 0418-5633
DD 331   II
I.A.M.R. REPORT. Main/Corp Delhi, Institute of Applied Manpower Research. **VFOAT** Report. **VAT** Institute of Applied Manpower Research Report. No. 1 (1963)-. Monographic series. English. Irregular. Price varies per volume. Institute of Applied Manpower Research, Indraprastha Estate, Mahatma Gandhi Marg, New Delhi 110 002 India.

LC HD4801   **ISSN** 1083-0413
DD 331   US
●**IAM JOURNAL.** [IAM j.]. **Added/Corp** International Association of Machinists and Aerospace Workers. **VFOAT** International Association of Machinists Journal. Vol. 1, No. 1 (Winter 1995)-. Periodical. English. Four times a year. International Association of Machinists, 9000 Machinists Place, Upper Malboro MD 20772. **Tel** (301)967-4520, FAX (301)967-4586. **Continues** Machinist, 0047-5378.

LC HD6350.E3 J7   **ISSN** 0897-2826
DD 331.88/213/05   US
IBEW JOURNAL. [IBEW j.]. **Added/Corp** International Brotherhood of Electrical Workers. **VAT** International Brotherhood of Electrical Workers Journal. Vol. 86, No. 4; (April 1987)-. Periodical. English. Twelve times a year. $4.00. International Brotherhood of Electrical Workers / Washington, 1125 15th Street Northwest, Washington DC 20005. **Tel** (202)833-7000. **Continues** Journal (International Brotherhood of Electrical Workers).
Ind/Abst Work Relat. Abstr.

LC HD5725.I23 A3
DD 331.11/09796   US
IDAHO EMPLOYMENT. Vol. 22, No. 1 (Aug. 1976)-. Periodical. English. Twelve times a year. Free. Idaho Department of Employment, 317 Main Street, Boise ID 83735. **Tel** (208)334-6112, FAX (208)334-6430. **ED** Janell Hyer. **Circ:** 5,000. **Continues** Idaho Manpower Review.
Desc: A profile of current labor conditions in the state with a review of conditions in Idaho's primary labor market areas.

    ISSN 0308-9312
UK
IDS BRIEF. Added/Corp Incomes Data Services. (Nov. 1972)-. Trade Publication. English. Twenty-four times a year. £208.00. Incomes Data Services, 193 St. John Street, London EC1V 4LS United Kingdom. **Tel** 011 44 171 2503434, FAX 011 44 171 6080949. **ED** Stephen Gibbons. cum. index.
Desc: Keeps up with the legal side of employee relations. The most recent significant tribunal and court decisions on cases in areas such as unfair dismissal, redundancy and employment protection are reported and their implications are explained. Changes to EC and UK law and practice, laws on equal pay, union ballots and injunctions and immunities are also covered.
Ind/Abst Curr. Cit.

UK
IDS EMPLOYMENT EUROPE. (19??)-. Periodical. English. Twelve times a year. Incomes Data Services, 193 St. John Street, London EC1V 4LS United Kingdom. **Tel** 011 44 171 2503434, FAX 011 44 171 6080949. **Continues** IDS European Report.
Desc: Provides an information service for international employee relations specialists, and for anyone in the personnel field who needs to be aware of developments in Europe.

    ISSN 0959-2199
UK
TITLE CHANGE
IDS EUROPEAN REPORT. Added/Corp Incomes Data Services. **VFOAT** European Report. No. 322 (Oct. 1988)-(19??). Periodical. English. Incomes Data Services, 193 St. John Street, London EC1V 4LS United Kingdom. **Tel** 011 44 171 2503434, FAX 011 44 171 6080949. **ED** Sally Murullo. **Continues** IDS/PA European Report. **Continued by** IDS Employment Europe.

    ISSN 0265-6019
DD 331.29410212   UK
IDS PAY DIRECTORY. [IDS pay dir.]. **VFOAT** Incomes Data Services Pay Directory. (1982)-. Periodical. English. Three times a year. £48.00. Incomes Data Services, 193 St. John Street, London EC1V 4LS United Kingdom. **Tel** 011 44 171 2503434, FAX 011 44 171 6080949. **ED** Alastair Hatchett.
Desc: Gives examples of standard pay for various positions, citing a variety of named companies. Also gives details of employment conditions such as holidays, hours of work, shift pay, bonuses and London allowances and information on the locations at which these apply. Covers around 250 blue collar and office jobs.

    ISSN 0308-9339
UK
IDS STUDY. Main/Corp Incomes Data Services. **VAT** Incomes Data Services Study. (June 1975)-. Trade Publication. English. Twenty-four times a year. £170.00. Incomes Data Services, 193 St. John Street, London EC1V 4LS United Kingdom. **Tel** 011 44 171 2503434, FAX 011 44 171 6080949. **ED** Jim Cowie. **Continues** Incomes Data Study.
Desc: Provides a detailed information source for personnel professionals on key issues in the field of pay, conditions of employment and employee relations. Analyzes issues and options, and illustrates them with examples drawn from named companies.
Ind/Abst Curr. Cit.; Int. Labour Doc.; LABORDOC.

SZ
IFBWW EDUCATION NEWS. Added/Corp International Federation of Building and Wood Workers. **VFOAT** Education News. **VAT** International Federation of Building and Wood Workers Education News. (1992)-. Periodical. English. Two times a year.

LC HD5725.I3 I525   **ISSN** 0883-3338
DD 331.12/5/09773021   US
ILLINOIS LABOR MARKET REVIEW.
(ILLINOIS LABOR MARKET REVIEW / DEPARTMENT OF LABOR, BUREAU OF EMPLOYMENT SECURITY, RESEARCH AND ANALYSIS). **Added/Corp** Illinois. Bureau of Employment Security. Research & Analysis. Illinois. Division of Unemployment Insurance. Illinois. Bureau of Employment Security. Labor Market Information. Illinois. Dept. of Employment Security. Labor Market Information. (Feb. 1979)-. Periodical. English. Twelve times a year. Free on request. Illinois Bureau of Employment Security, 401 South State Street, Second Floor South, Chicago IL 60605. **Tel** (312)793-5700. **Continues** Illinois Labor Market Conditions.

US
ILLINOIS STATE AFL-CIO LABORLETTER. Added/Corp Illinois State AFL-CIO. **VFOAT** Laborletter; Illinois State AFL-CIO Labor Letter. (198?)-. Periodical. English. Six times a year. Illinois State AFL-CIO, 100 East Washington/2nd Floor, Springfield IL 62701. **Tel** (217)544-4014. **Continues** Illinois State AFL-CIO News Letter.

US
ILLINOIS STATE EMPLOYEE, THE.
(19??)-. Periodical. English.

LC HD4976.I3 I44A
DD 331.2/9773   US
ILLINOIS WAGE SURVEY. (19??)-. English. Research and Analysis, Illinois Bureau of Employment Security, 910 South Michigan Avenue, Chicago IL 60605. **Continues** Illinois Statewide Wage and Salary Survey of Selected Occupation.

    ISSN 0379-1734
US
TITLE CHANGE
ILO INFORMATION. U.S. EDITION. (ILO INFORMATION.). [ILO inf., U.S. ed.]. **Main/Corp** International Labour Office. **VAT** International Labour Office Information. Vol. 1 (Aug. 1973)-(19??). Periodical. English. International Labour Office, 1828 L Street NW, Suite 801, Washington DC 20036-5102. **Continued by** World of Work.
Ind/Abst Chem. Hazards Ind.; HILITES; Hum. Rights Intern. Rep.; Lab. Hazards Bull.; Trop. Dis. Bull.; Work Relat. Abstr.

LC HD4805 .N35   **ISSN** 0951-2187
DD 331/.0941   UK
SUSPENDED
ILP MAGAZINE. Vol. 79, No. 1 (Spring 1987)-Vol. 80, No. 4 (19??). Periodical. English. Four times a year. £3.50 (individuals), £7.00 (multi-users) UK; £8.50 (individuals), £12.00 (multi-users) US. Independent Labour Publications, 49 Top Moor Side 11, Leeds LS11 9LW United Kingdom. **Tel** 011 44 113 430613. **ED** B Winter. **Bk Rev**. **Ad Acc**. **Circ:** 4,000. **Continues** Labour Leader.
Desc: Devoted to the socialist and democratic renewal of the labour party.

    ISSN 0070-0177
US
ILR PAPERBACK. Main/Corp Cornell University. New York State School of Industrial and Labor Relations. (1967)-. Monographic series. English. Price varies per volume. School of Industry and Labor Relations, New York Street, Cornell University, Ithaca NY 14853.

    ISSN 0306-0144
UK
IMS MANPOWER SURVEY SUMMARY REPORT. [IMS manpow. surv. summ. rep.]. **VFOAT** Institute of Manpower Studies Manpower Survey Summary Report. (1974)-. Monographic series. English. One time a year. Institute of Manpower Studies, University of Sussex, Mantell Building, Falmer Brighton BN1 9RF United Kingdom. **Tel** 011 44 1273 686751.
Ind/Abst Curr. Cit.

    ISSN 0888-9724
DD 331   US
TITLE CHANGE
IN THE MAINSTREAM (WASHINGTON, D.C.). See Physically Impaired.

Business and Economics —Labor

IN TRANSIT (WASHINGTON). See Transportation.

ISSN 0019-3291
US

LC HD5261 .I52   ISSN 0090-8533
DD 331.2   US

INCENTIVE TRAVEL AND BUSINESS MEETINGS. Vol. 1 (March/Apr. 1973)-. Trade Publication. English. Six times a year. $9.00. Hartman Communications, 633 Third Avenue, New York NY 10017.

LC WMLC 91/3497   ISSN 0579-3149
UK

INCOMES DATA PANORAMA. Added/Corp Incomes Data Services. **VFOAT** Panorama. (1966)-. Trade Publication. English. One time a year.
Desc: Contains information on wages and collective labor agreements.

LC HA1363 .A27 HD5264.I8
DD 314.5   IT

INDAGINE SPECIALE SULLE VACANZE DEGLI ITALIANI. See Business and Economics-Abstracting, Bibliographies and Statistics.

LC LB2335.86-.88   ISSN 1037-0242
DD 331.88113711009945   AT

INDEPENDENT REPORTER JOLIMONT. (INDEPENDENT REPORTER.). [Indep. report. Jolimont.]. **VFOAT** VIESA Newsletter. (1991)-. Periodical. English. Six times a year. **Continues** VATIS Newsletter, 0815-4473.
Ind/Abst Aust. Educ. Index.

ISSN 0820-7933
DD 331.7/14/060714   CN

INDEX CHRONOLOGIQUE / INDEX CHRONOLOGIQUE - CONSEIL DU PATRONAT DU QUEBEC. [Index chronol. - Cons. patronat Que.]. **Main/Corp** Conseil du Patronat du Quebec. French. One time a year. Le Conseil du Patronat du Quebec, Bureau 606 2075 rue University, Montreal Quebec H3C 2L1 Canada. **Tel** (514)288-5161. ctrl circ.
Desc: Contains information on: main official statements, briefs, and written communications, various texts and speeches.

LC HD8682 .I57   ISSN 0019-5286
II

INDIAN JOURNAL OF INDUSTRIAL RELATIONS. See Industry and Production.

LC HD4811 .I53   ISSN 0019-5308
II

INDIAN JOURNAL OF LABOUR ECONOMICS. (THE INDIAN JOURNAL OF LABOUR ECONOMICS : THE QUARTERLY JOURNAL OF THE INDIAN SOCIETY OF LABOUR ECONOMICS.). [Indian j. labour econ.]. **Added/Corp** Indian Society of Labour Economics. (1958)-. Periodical. English. Four times a year. $45.00. Lucknow University / Indian Society of Labour Economics, Badshah Bagh, Lucknow Uttar Pradesh India. (**Subscription address:** Prints India, 11 Darya Ganj, New Delhi 110002 India. **Tel** 011 91 11 3268645, FAX 011 91 11 3275542, telex 31-61087 PRIN-IN.)
Ind/Abst Int. Bibliogr. Sociol.; Int. Labour Doc.; World Agric. Econ. Rural Sociol. Abstr.

LC HD8681 .A675   ISSN 0019-5723
II

INDIAN LABOUR JOURNAL. [Indian labour j.]. **Added/Corp** India. Labour Bureau. **VFOAT** Indian Labour Gazette. Vol. 1, No. 1 (Jan. 1960)-. Periodical. English. Twelve times a year. $440.64. Director of the Government of India, Ministry of Labour, Labour Bureau Clerment, Shimla 171004 India. (**Subscription address:** Prints India, 11 Darya Ganj, New Delhi 110002 India. **Tel** 011 91 11 3268645, FAX 011 91 11 3275542, telex 31-61087 PRIN-IN.) **Continues** Indian Labour Gazette.
Ind/Abst Int. Bibliogr. Sociol.; Int. Labour Doc.; LABORDOC.

LC HD4805 .I55   ISSN 0537-2682
II

INDIAN WORKER, THE. [Indian work.]. **Added/Corp** Indian National Trade Union Congress. Vol. 1 (Oct. 2, 1952)-. Periodical. English. Fifty times a year (Publishes on Monday). Rs100.00. Indian National Trade Union Congress, 1-B Maulana Azad Road, New Delhi 110011 India. **Continues** Worker (Bombay, India).
Ind/Abst Int. Labour Doc.; LABORDOC.

DD 331.25444   US

INDIANA EMPLOYMENT SECURITY ACT. Main/Corp Indiana. **Added/Corp** Indiana. Employment Security Board. English. Indiana Employment Security Division, Research and Statistics Section, 10 North Senate Avenue, Indianapolis IN 46204. **Tel** (317)232-7187. **Continues** Employment Security Act (Indiana).
Desc: Issues for 1945, 1947 include Rules and regulations of the Indiana Employment Security Board.

US

INDIANA LABOR MARKET TRENDS. VFOAT Trends. (19??)-. Periodical. English. Four times a year. Indiana Employment Security Division, Research and Statistics Section, 10 North Senate Avenue, Indianapolis IN 46204. **Tel** (317)232-7187.

US

INDIANA PUBLIC EMPLOYEE REPORTER. English. Twelve times a year. $375.00 (includes postage). LRP Publications, 747 Dresher Road, Suite 500, Horsham PA 19044. **Tel** (800)341-7874, (215)784-0941, FAX (215)784-9639, (215)784-0870.
Desc: Timely and comprehensive source for public sector labor law decisions issued by Indiana state agencies and courts.

LC HD1527.I6 I57a   ISSN 0092-3222
DD 331.7/63/09772   US

INDIANA RURAL MANPOWER REPORT. Main/Corp Indiana. Employment Security Division. (19??)-. English. Employment Security Division / Indiana, 10 North Senate Avenue, Indianapolis IN 46204. **Continues** Indiana Farm Labor Report, 0445-8699.

IT

INDICI COSTO LAVORO INDUSTRIA. (19??)-. Italian. Four times a year. L300000.00. Indicitalia SRL, Via G A Resti 36, 00143 Rome Italy. **Tel** 011 39 6 5193544.

IT

INDUSTRIA & FORMAZIONE. (19??)-. Italian. Twelve times a year. 4500000L. Industria & Formazione, Via Alessandria 12, 15033 Casale Monferrato Italy. **Tel** 011 39 142 72876.

LC HD4802 .I53   ISSN 0019-7939
DD 331.05   US
CCC
CODEN ILREA
Pr Rev.

INDUSTRIAL & LABOR RELATIONS REVIEW. [Ind. labor relat. rev.]. **Added/Corp** New York State School of Industrial and Labor Relations. **VFOAT** Industrial and Labor Relations Review. **VAT** Industrial and Labor Relations Review. Vol. 1 (Oct. 1947)-. Periodical. English. Four times a year (Jan., Apr., July, Oct.). $43.00. Cornell University / ILR, 201 ILR Research Building, Ithaca NY 14853. **Tel** (607)255-2733, FAX (607)255-2755. **ED** Donald Cullen. **Bk Rev. Ad Acc. Circ:** 4,100 (ctrl). available on microfilm and microfiche from University Microfilms International (UMI); available on an online database (file 648/Full-Text) from DIALOG. Documents available from Article Express International, The Genuine Article, UMI Article Clearinghouse.
Desc: Articles, book reviews, and reports of research in progress on economic, legal, social, psychological, and historical aspects of industrial relations.
Ind/Abst ABC POL SCI; ABI/INFORM Glob. Ed.; ABI/INFORM Ondisc: Expr. Ed.; ABI/INFORM [Computer File] (Oct. 1971-); Acad. Abstr.; Acad. Ind. [Computer File] (1992-); Acad. Search; Account. Art.; Am. Hist. Life (1969-); Appl. Soc. Sci. Index Abstr.; Bioeng. Abstr.; Book Rev. Index; Bus. ASAP (1990-) [Full Txt.]; Bus. Index (1985-); Bus. Period. Index; Bus. Source Plus; Bus. Source; Contents Pages Manage.; Curr. Cit.; Curr. Contents Soc. Behav. Sci.; Curr. Index J. Educ.; Curr. Law Index (1980-); Econ. Lit. Index; Educ. Adm. Abstr. (?-?); Ei Page One; Eng. Index Annu.; EP Collect.; Expand. Acad. Index (1984-); Gen. BusinessFile (1985-); Gen. Period. Index (1985-); Health Plan. Adminis.; High. Educ. Abstr. (1965-); Homework Help.; Hum. Resour. Abstr.; Index Period. Artic. Relat. Law; INFO-SOUTH Abstr.; Int. Bibliogr. Sociol.; Int. Labour Doc.; Int. Polit. Sci. Abstr.; J. Econ. Lit.; LABORDOC; Leg. Resour. Index (1980-); LegalTrac (1980-); Mag. Search; MasterFile FullTEXT 1000; MasterFile FullTEXT 350; MasterFile FullTEXT 650; MasterFile FullTEXT (July 1990-); Middle East Abstr. Index; Newsp. Period. Abstr. (1989-); OCLC; PAIS Int. Print (1991-); Person. Manage. Abstr.; Res. Alert [Full Cov.]; Sage Fam. Stud. Abstr.; Selec. Coop. Index Manage. Period.; Soc. Plann. Policy Dev. Abstr.; Soc. Sci. Source; Soc. Sci. Cit. Index [Full Cov.]; Soc. Sci. Index; Soc. Sci. Index Fulltext (Oct. 1988-) [Full Txt.]; Sociol. Abstr.; SPORT Discus; Telebase; Trade Ind. Index (1981-?); UMI ABI/Inform--Bus. Period. Ondisc (Jan. 1988-) [Full Txt.]; Vocat. Search; Wilson Bus. Abstr.; Women Stud. Abstr.; Work Relat. Abstr.

SA

●**INDUSTRIAL DEMOCRACY REVIEW. Added/Corp** University of the Witwatersrand. Faculty of Management. Industrial Democracy Programme. Vol. 3, No. 3 (Sept.-Oct. 1994)-. English. Four times a year. $23.86. Wits Business School, PO Box 98, Bilateralism Project, Wits 2050 South Africa. **Tel** 011 27 11 6436641. **Continues** Bilateralism Review.

DD 331.809417 331.80212   ISSN 0791-329X
IE

INDUSTRIAL DISPUTES (DUBLIN). See Business and Economics-Abstracting, Bibliographies and Statistics.

DD 331.209417   ISSN 0791-2927
IE

INDUSTRIAL EMPLOYMENT, EARNINGS AND HOURS WORKED, DETAILS FOR SUPPLEMENTARY NACE SUB-SECTORS. See Business and Economics-Abstracting, Bibliographies and Statistics.

AT
Pr Rev.

INDUSTRIAL RELATIONS & MANAGEMENT LETTER. (19??)-. Newsletter. English. Eleven times a year. 247.00Aus$. Ian Huntley Publishers Pty Limited, PO Box 99, Cremorne NSW 2090 Australia. **Tel** 011 61 2 9535788, FAX 011 61 2 9532280. **ED** Patricia Huntley. **Bk Rev. Circ:** 1,000.
Desc: Profile interviews with new officials in major unions, studies of companies with innovative management practices, wages, and legislation acts.

ISSN 0710-5940
DD 331.89/09711   CN

INDUSTRIAL RELATIONS BULLETIN (VANCOUVER). (INDUSTRIAL RELATIONS BULLETIN / EMPLOYERS' COUNCIL OF BRITISH COLUMBIA.). [Ind. relat. bull.]. **Added/Corp** Business Council of British Columbia. Employers' Council of British Columbia. (1969)-. Bulletin. English. One time a week. Free to members of the Business Council of British Columbia. Business Council of British Columbia, 1050 West Pender, Suite 810, Vancouver British Columbia V6E 3S7, Canada. **Tel** (604)684-3384. ctrl circ.

BE

INDUSTRIAL RELATIONS EUROPE. (1973)-. Periodical. English. Twelve times a year. $350.00. ESC Wyatt Company SA, Avenue Herrmann Debroux 52, 1160 Brussels Belgium. **Tel** 011 32 2 7719910, FAX 011 32 2 7623743. (**Subscription address:** Industrial Relations / Europe, 49 Bushey Grove Road, Bushey Hertfordshire WD2 2JG, United Kingdom. **Tel** 011 44 1923 252440.) **Continues** Industrial Relations Europe Newsletter.

LC HD8690.5 .A18a
DD 331/.09549/1   PK

INDUSTRIAL RELATIONS JOURNAL (KARACHI, PAKISTAN). (INDUSTRIAL RELATIONS JOURNAL.). **Added/Corp** Employers' Federation of Pakistan. (198?)-. Periodical. English. Six times a year (Jan., Mar., May, July, Sep., Nov.). $50.00. Employers Federation of Pakistan, State Life Building No 2, 2nd Floor, Karachi 74000 Pakistan. **Tel** 011 92 21 241 1049, 011 92 21 241 2708. **ED** Mohammed Mustafa Sharif. **Bk Rev,** (Qty: 4200). **Ad Acc. Circ:** 700 (ctrl).
Desc: Employers view points on current issues of labour, human resource management and labour welfare issues and schemes.
Ind/Abst Selec. Coop. Index Manage. Period.

LC HD4805 .I63   ISSN 0019-8692
DD 331/.05   UK
CCC

INDUSTRIAL RELATIONS JOURNAL (LONDON, ENGLAND). (INDUSTRIAL RELATIONS JOURNAL.). [Ind. relat. j.]. (1970)-. Academic Scholarly Publication. English (French; summaries and/or abstracts in French). Four times a year. £111.00 UK and Europe; $219.00 North America; £141.00 other. Basil Blackwell Publishers Ltd., 108 Cowley Road, Oxford OX4 1JF United Kingdom. **Tel** 011 44 1235 465500, FAX 011 44 1235 465556, telex 837022 OXBOOK G. (**Subscription address:** Blackwell Publishers / UK, 108 Cowley Road, Oxford OX4 1JF United Kingdom. **Tel** 011 44 1865 791100, FAX 011 44 1865 791347.) **ED** Brian Towers. cum. index. **Bk Rev. Ad Acc. Circ:** 1,500. available on microfilm from University Microfilms International (UMI). Documents available from UMI Article Clearinghouse.
Desc: Research and practical articles on industrial relations for practitioners.
Ind/Abst ABI/INFORM Glob. Ed.; Acad. Search; Appl. Soc. Sci. Index Abstr.; Bus. ASAP (1992-) [Full Txt.]; Bus. Index (1985-); Bus. Source Plus; Bus. Source; Contents Pages Manage.; Curr. Cit.; EP Collect.; Gen. BusinessFile (1985-); Gen. Period. Index (1985-); Homework Help.; INFO-SOUTH Abstr.; Int. Bibliogr. Sociol.; Int. Labour Doc.; LABORDOC; Leis., Rec., Tour. Abstr.; Mag. Search; Manage. Market. Abstr.; MasterFile FullTEXT 1000; MasterFile FullTEXT 350; MasterFile FullTEXT 650; MasterFile FullTEXT (Jan. 1993-); OCLC; PAIS Int. Print (1991-); Person. Manage. Abstr.; Pollut. Abstr. Indexes; Selec. Coop. Index Manage. Period.;

Business and Economics —Labor

Stud. Women Abstr.; Tech. Educ. Train. Abstr.; Telebase; Vocat. Search; Women Manage. Rev. [Full Txt.]; Work Relat. Abstr.

INDUSTRIAL RELATIONS REPORT. US
Added/Corp United States. Bureau of Labor Statistics. Southwest Regional Office. (19??)-. Monographic series. English. Irregular. Price varies per volume. US Bureau of Labor, Statistics Region 6, 555 Griffin Square Building, Dallas TX 75202.

ISSN 0749-2162
DD 331 US

INDUSTRIAL RELATIONS RESEARCH ASSOCIATION SERIES NEWSLETTER. [Ind. Relat. Res. Assoc. ser. newsl.]. **Main/Corp** Industrial Relations Research Association. **VFOAT** IRRA Newsletter; I.R.R.A. Newsletter; Series Newsletter Newsletter. Vol. 25, No. 3 (Sept. 1983)-. Newsletter. English. Four times a year. Comes with Industrial Relations Research Association membership. Industrial Relations Research Association, 4233 Social Science Building, University of Wisconsin, 1180 Observatory Drive, Madison WI 53706. **Tel** (608)262-2762, FAX (608)262-4591. **ED** Barbara D. Dennis. **Bk Rev. Ad Acc. Circ:** 5,000 (ctrl). **Continues** Industrial Relations Research Association. IRRA Newsletter, 0019-0500.
Desc: Enables people in the field to become better acquainted, to keep abreast of practices and new developments, and to exchange ideas.
Ind/Abst LABORDOC.

LC HD8381 .I42 ISSN 0309-7269
UK
TITLE CHANGE
INDUSTRIAL RELATIONS REVIEW AND REPORT. [Ind. relat. rev. rep.]. **Added/Corp** Industrial Relations Services. No. 1 (Feb. 1971)-(1995). Periodical. English. Eclipse Publications Ltd., 18 20 Highbury Place, London N5 1QP United Kingdom. **Tel** 011 44 171 3545858. **(Subscription address:** Industrial Relations Services, 18-20 Highbury Place, London N5 1QP United Kingdom.) **ED** Patrick Burns. Index available. cum. index. **Circ:** 5,000. Documents available from UMI Article Clearinghouse. **Continued by** IRS Employment Review.
Ind/Abst ABI/INFORM Glob. Ed.; Coal Abstr.; Contents Pages Manage.; Int. Packag. Abstr.; LABORDOC; LegalTrac (Jan. 1988-Dec. 1988); Manage. Market. Abstr.

LC HD8051 .A62 HD4966.C45 ISSN 0091-8156
DD 331/.0973 S 331.2/86/00973 US

INDUSTRIAL WAGE SURVEY. INDUSTRIAL CHEMICALS. **VFOAT** Industrial Chemicals. (19??)-. English. US Department of Labor, 200 Constitution Avenue NW, Washington DC 20210. **Tel** (202)219-7316, FAX (202)219-7312.

ISSN 0019-8870
US
Pr Rev.

INDUSTRIAL WORKER. [Ind. work.]. **Added/Corp** Industrial Workers of the World. (1906)-. Newspaper. English. Twelve times a year. $15.00. Industrial Workers of the World, 1095 Market Street, Suite 204, San Francisco CA 94103. **Tel** (415)863-9627, FAX (415)626-2685. **ED** Carlos Murray (editor's address: Box 4217, Station E, Ottawa, Ontario K1S 5B2 Canada; phone: (613)231-2922). cum. index. **Bk Rev. Circ:** 2,000. available on microfilm from University Microfilms International (UMI).
Desc: World labor news and commentary from an industrial unionist (IWW) perspective.
Ind/Abst Altern. Press Index.

LC HD8441 ISSN 0943-2779
DD 331.1 GW
UDC 33
Pr Rev.

●**INDUSTRIELLE BEZIEHUNGEN.** [Ind. Beziehr.]. (1994)-. Trade Publication. German (summaries and/or abstracts in English). Four times a year. DM78.00. Rainer Hampp Verlag, Meringerzellerstrasse 16, 86415 Mering Germany. **Tel** 011 49 82334783, FAX 011 49 823330755.

LC HD4965.5.U6 I54 ISSN 1041-908X
DD 331.2/81658302/0973021 US

INDUSTRY REPORT ON SUPERVISORY MANAGEMENT COMPENSATION. See Business and Economics-Personnel Management.

LC TA158 .I47 ISSN 1063-0058
DD 331.2/973/021 US

INDUSTRY REPORT ON TECHNICIAN AND SKILLED TRADES PERSONNEL COMPENSATION. (INDUSTRY REPORT ON TECHNICIAN AND SKILLED TRADES PERSONNEL COMPENSATION / WYATT DATA SERVICES, ECS.). [Ind. rep. tech. skilled pers. compens.].
Added/Corp Executive Compensation Service (U.S.). **VFOAT** Industry Report on Technician & Skilled Trades Personnel Compensation. 1st ed. (1991/92)-. Trade Publication. English. One time a year. $490.00. ECS, Executive Compensation Service, Wyatt Data Services,

218 Route 17 North, Roselle Park NJ 07662-9832. **Tel** (201)843-1177, FAX (201)843-0101. available with charts.

LC HD4976.S6 I53
DD 331.2/9757 US

INDUSTRY WAGE AND PRACTICES SURVEY, SOUTH CAROLINA. **VFOAT** Industry Wage & Practices Survey, South Carolina. (19??)-. English. One time a year. State Board for Technical and Comprehensive Education, 1429 Senate Street, Columbia SC 29201.

LC HD4966.R386 U58A
DD 331.2/8838/0973 US

INDUSTRY WAGE SURVEY. APPLIANCE REPAIR. **VFOAT** Appliance Repair. English. US Department of Labor, 200 Constitution Avenue NW, Washington DC 20210. **Tel** (202)219-7316, FAX (202)219-7312. available on microfiche (Vols. for (Nov. 1981-) distributed to depository libraries).
Continues Industry Wage Survey. Appliance Repair Shops, 0361-1604.

US
INDUSTRY WAGE SURVEY. BASIC IRON AND STEEL. **VFOAT** Basic Iron and Steel. Government Publication. English. US Department of Labor / Bureau of Labor Statistics, 441 G Street Northwest, Washington DC 20212. **Tel** (202)606-7800, FAX (202)606-7797. available on microfiche (Vols. for (Aug 1983-) distributed to depository libraries).

LC HD4966.M63 U47 ISSN 8755-559X
DD 331.2/822334/0973021 US

INDUSTRY WAGE SURVEY. BITUMINOUS COAL. **VFOAT** Bituminous Coal; Industry Wage Survey, Bituminous Coal. English. US Department of Labor, 200 Constitution Avenue NW, Washington DC 20210. **Tel** (202)219-7316, FAX (202)219-7312. available on microfiche (Vols. for (July 1982-) distributed to depository libraries). **Continues** Industry Wage Survey. Bituminous Coal Mining.

US
INDUSTRY WAGE SURVEY. CANDY AND OTHER CONFECTIONERY PRODUCTS. **VFOAT** Candy and Other Confectionery Products. (19??)-. English. US Department of Labor, 200 Constitution Avenue NW, Washington DC 20210. **Tel** (202)219-7316, FAX (202)219-7312.

US
INDUSTRY WAGE SURVEY. CIGARETTE MANUFACTURING / U.S. DEPARTMENT OF LABOR, BUREAU OF LABOR STATISTICS. **VFOAT** Cigarette Manufacturing. (19??)-. Periodical. English. US Department of Labor, 200 Constitution Avenue NW, Washington DC 20210. **Tel** (202)219-7316, FAX (202)219-7312.

LC HD4966.P3 U58 ISSN 0148-9208
DD 331.2/87/6320973 US

INDUSTRY WAGE SURVEY. CORRUGATED AND SOLID FIBER BOXES. (INDUSTRY WAGE SURVEY. CORRUGATED AND SOLID FIBER BOXES / U.S. DEPT. OF LABOR, BUREAU OF LABOR STATISTICS.). **VFOAT** Corrugated and Solid Fiber Boxes. (19??)-. English. US Department of Labor, 200 Constitution Avenue NW, Washington DC 20210. **Tel** (202)219-7316, FAX (202)219-7312.

LC HD4966.M4 U5482A ISSN 0360-2060
DD 331.2/81/381 US

INDUSTRY WAGE SURVEY. DEPARTMENT STORES. (INDUSTRY WAGE SURVEY. DEPARTMENT STORES / U.S. DEPARTMENT OF LABOR, BUREAU OF LABOR STATISTICS.). **VFOAT** Department Stores. (19??)-. English. US Department of Labor, 200 Constitution Avenue NW, Washington DC 20210. **Tel** (202)219-7316, FAX (202)219-7312.

LC HD4966.P14 U52
DD 331.2/8649/00973021 US

INDUSTRY WAGE SURVEY, MEAT PRODUCTS. (INDUSTRY WAGE SURVEY. MEAT PRODUCTS / U.S. DEPARTMENT OF LABOR, BUREAU OF LABOR STATISTICS.). **VFOAT** Meat Products. English. One time a year. US Department of Labor, 200 Constitution Avenue NW, Washington DC 20210. **Tel** (202)219-7316, FAX (202)219-7312. available on microfiche (Vols. for (1984-) distributed to depository libraries). **Continues** Industry Wage Survey. Meat Products, Meatpacking, Prepared Meat Products.

LC HD4966.M6 U558A ISSN 0360-0718
DD 331.2/82/2340973 US

INDUSTRY WAGE SURVEY : METAL MINING. **Main/Corp** United States. Bureau of Labor Statistics. (19??)-. Government Publication. English. US

Department of Labor / Bureau of Labor Statistics, 441 G Street Northwest, Washington DC 20212. **Tel** (202)606-7800, FAX (202)606-7797.

LC HD4966.M44 U3 ISSN 0148-9194
DD 331.2/87/30973 US

INDUSTRY WAGE SURVEY : NONFERROUS FOUNDRIES. **Main/Corp** United States. Bureau of Labor Statistics. (19??)-. Government Publication. English. US Department of Labor / Bureau of Labor Statistics, 441 G Street Northwest, Washington DC 20212. **Tel** (202)606-7800, FAX (202)606-7797.

ISSN 0749-5102
DD 331 US

INDUSTRY WAGE SURVEY. NURSING AND PERSONAL CARE FACILITIES. [Ind. wage surv., Nurs. pers. care facil.]. **Added/Corp** United States. Bureau of Labor Statistics. **VFOAT** Nursing and Personal Care Facilities. (May 1981)-. English. US Department of Labor, 200 Constitution Avenue NW, Washington DC 20210. **Tel** (202)219-7316, FAX (202)219-7312. **Continues in part** Industry Wage Survey. Hospitals and Nursing Homes, 0276-7341.

US
INDUSTRY WAGE SURVEY. PETROLEUM REFINING. **VFOAT** Petroleum Refining. Government Publication. English. US Department of Labor / Bureau of Labor Statistics, 441 G Street Northwest, Washington DC 20212. **Tel** (202)606-7800, FAX (202)606-7797. available on microfiche (Vols. for (June 1985-) distributed to depository libraries).

LC HD4966.B62 U58 ISSN 0148-9747
DD 331.2/82/38200973 US

INDUSTRY WAGE SURVEY. SHIPBUILDING AND REPAIRING. **Added/Corp** United States. Bureau of Labor Statistics. **VFOAT** Shipbuilding and Repairing. (19??)-. Government Publication. English. Irregular. US Department of Labor, 200 Constitution Avenue NW, Washington DC 20210. **Tel** (202)219-7316, FAX (202)219-7312.

LC LB2335.86
DD 331.88113711 SZ

INFO / FITPAS = IFPAAW / FITPASC. **Added/Corp** International Federation of Plantation, Agricultural, and Allied Workers. **VFOAT** FITPAS Info; FITPASC Info; IFPAAW Info. No. 1 (Spring 1992)-. Periodical. English. Four times a year. **Continues** IFPAAW News.

ISSN 8755-9269
DD 331 US
CCC
INFO-LINE (WASHINGTON, D.C.). (INFO-LINE). [Info-line]. **Added/Corp** American Society for Training and Development. **VFOAT** Info Line; Infoline. (1984)-. Monographic series. English. Twelve times a year. $119.00. American Society for Training and Development, 1640 King Strreet, PO Box 1443, Department 840, Alexandria VA 22313. **Tel** (703)683-8100, (703)683-8129, FAX (703)683-8103. **Circ:** 3,000.

ISSN 0822-5591
DD 331.88/11302234 CN

INFO-SARDEC. (INFO-SARDEC / SOCIETE DES AUTEURS, RECHERCHISTES, DOCUMENTALISTES ET COMPOSITEURS.). [Info-SARDEC]. **VAT** Info-Societe des Auteurs, Recherchistes, Documentalistes et Compositeurs. No. 1-. Periodical. French. Four times a year. Free to members. Societe des Auteurs Recherchistes Documentalistes Et Compositeurs, 1229 rue Panet, Montreal Quebec H2L 2Y6 Canada.

LC HD8589.C32 I54 ISSN 1130-4553
SP
INFORMACIO ESTADISTICA DEL DEPARTAMENT DE TREBALL. **Added/Corp** Catalonia (Spain). Departament de Treball. (Mar 1990)-. Statistical Publication. Catalan. Twelve times a year.

LC HD8201 .I54 ISSN 0864-0122
CU
INFORMACION LABORAL (HAVANA, CUBA). (INFORMACION LABORAL.). Spanish (summaries and/or abstracts in English and Russian). Four times a year. Ediciones Cubanas, Obispo 527 Altos ESQ Bernaza, CP 10100 Havana Cuba.

ISSN 1031-5543
DD 368.430994 AT

INFORMATION CIRCULAR - OCCUPATIONAL SUPERANNUATION GROUP. [Inf. circ. - Occup. Superann. Group]. **Added/Corp** Australia. Occupational Superannuation Group. (1987)-. Government Publication. English. Twelve times a year. 48.00Aus$. Australian Government Publishing Service, GPO Box 84, Canberra ACT 2601 Australia. **Tel** 011 61 6 2954411, FAX 011 61 6 2954455.

Continues *Information Circular - Occupational Superannuation Commissioner Interim Group, 0818-4399.*

ISSN 1188-1305
DD 331.2/041004/09712338 CN

INFORMATION PROCESSING COMPENSATION SURVEY. [Inf. process. compens. surv.]. **Added/Corp** Calgary Chamber of Commerce. Western Management Consultants. (1991/1992)-. English. $325.00 per volume. Calgary Chamber of Commerce, 273 One Palliser Square, 125 9th Avenue SE, Calgary Alberta T2G 0P6 Canada. **Tel** (403)263-7435.

LC HD5927 .A256a
GW

INFORMATIONEN FUER DIE BERATUNGS- UND VERMITTLUNGSDIENSTE. **Main/Corp** Bundesanstalt fuer Arbeit (Germany). (19??)-. Periodical. German. One time a week. Frauentorgraben, 33/35 8500 Nuernberg 1 Germany.

LC HD8110.5.A5 C463
VE

INFORMATIVO CLAT. **Main/Corp** Central Latinoamericana de Trabajadores. Vol. 1, No. 1 (April 1976)-. Spanish. Eleven times a year. $18.00. CLAT, Apartado Postal 6681, Caracas 101A Venezuela. **Tel** 011 58 32 721549, 011 58 32 720794. **Bk Rev. Circ:** 30,000. ***Supersedes*** *Central Latinoamericana de Trabajadores. CLAT.*

LC HD8537 .K27
PL

INFORMATOR ROBOTNICZY. (1973)-. Polish. One time a year. zl.35.00. Ksiazka i Wiedza, Ul. Nowy Swiat 27, Warzsawa Poland. ***Continues*** *Kalendarz Robotniczy.*

BE

INFOS DE L'ISE. (19??)-. English (French, German, Spanish, Italian, Norwegian and Dutch). Irregular. 100F ETUC Trade Union Organizations; 300F other. European Trade Union Institut, boulevard Emile Jacqmain 155, B-1210 Brussels Belgium.

FR

INNOVATION AND EMPLOYMENT. Government Publication. English. Four times a year. Free on request. OECD Publications and Information Center, 2 rue Andre-Pascal, 75775 Paris Cedex 16 France. **Tel** 011 33 1 49104262, US:(202)785-6323, FAX 011 33 1 45248500, 011 33 1 45248176, telex 620 160 OCDE. **(Subscription address:** OECD Publications Center, 2001 L Street, Suite 700, Washington DC 20036. **Tel** (202)822-3873, (202)785-6323.**)**
Desc: Aims to explore new strategies for employment development by illustrations from real life experience. Reports on notable achievements in an endeavour to induce local economic development and encourage all forms of partnership.

ISSN 0998-4747
FR
UDC 31(44)

INSEE RESULTATS. EMPLOI-REVENUS. **VFOAT** Institut National de la Statistique et des Etudes Economiques Resultats. Emplois-Revenus. (1989)-. Monographic series. French. Irregular. Price varies per volume. CNGP INSEE - Institut National de la Statistique et des Estudes Economiques, BP 2718, 1 rue V Auriol, F 80027 Amiens Cedex 1 France. **Tel** 011 33 22 927322.

ISSN 1185-3816
DD 331.13/3 CN

INSIDE OLA SUPPLEMENT, OPINION SURVEY, AN. [Inside OLA suppl. opin. surv.]. **Added/Corp** Ontario Library Association. **VFOAT** Inside Ontario Library Association Supplement, Opinion Survey; Inside OLA Opinion Survey. (Jan./Feb. 1991)-. Periodical. English. Free to members of the Ontario Library Association. Ontario Library Association, 100 Lombard Street, Suite 303 Toronto, Ontario M5C 1M3 Canada. **Tel** (416)363-3388.

ISSN 1065-2736
US

INSIDE WORKERS' COMPENSATION. (1992)-. Periodical. English. Twelve times a year. $108.00. Brooke Publishers, PO Box 3743, Littleton CO 80161-3743.

LC HD5701 .U623 **ISSN** 0738-4858
DD 331/.072077418 US

INSTITUTE REPORT (KALAMAZOO, MICH.), THE. (THE INSTITUTE REPORT.). [Inst. rep.]. **Main/Corp** W.E. Upjohn Institute for Employment Research. (1981)-. English. W.E. Upjohn Institute for Employment Research, 300 South Westnedge Avenue, Kalamazoo MI 49007. **Tel** (616)343-5541, FAX (616)343-7310. ***Continues*** *W.E. Upjohn Institute for Employment Research. Annual Report.*

BL

INSTITUTO DO DESENCOLVIMENTO ECONOMICO-SOCIAL DO PARA: PEDQUISA EMPREGO E DESEMPREGO NA REGIAO METROPOLITANA DE BELEM. **Main/Corp** Instituto de Desenvolvimento Econ„omico Social do Par,a. **Added/Corp** Instituto do Desenvolvimento Economico Social do Para. Serie Relatorios de Pesquisa. **VFOAT** Serie Relatorios de Pesquisa. (197?)-. Monographic series. Portuguese. Irregular. Price varies per volume. Instituto do Desenvolvimento Economico-Social do Para, Av Nazare 871, Belem Para Brazil. **Tel** (091)224-4411. **Circ:** 800 (ctrl).
Desc: Studies about conditions of employment and unemployment in the city of Belem, state Para.

LC HD7096.U6 W444
DD 331.12/5/09754 US

INSURED WORKERS IN WEST VIRGINIA / PREPARED BY WEST VIRGINIA DEPARTMENT OF EMPLOYMENT SECURITY, LABOR AND ECONOMIC RESEARCH SECTION. **See** Business and Economics-Abstracting, Bibliographies and Statistics.

LC HD4975 .A22a **ISSN** 0196-3457
DD 331.2/2/0973 US

INTER-CITY WAGE & SALARY DIFFERENTIALS. **Main/Corp** Abbott, Langer & Associates. **VAT** Inter-City Wage and Salary Differentials. (19??)-. English. Abbott Langer & Associates, 548 First Street, Department Z, Crete IL 60417. **Tel** (708)672-4200.

ISSN 1061-7337
DD 331 US

INTERNAMERICA (NEEDHAM, MASS.). (INTERNAMERICA.). [InternAmerica]. **VFOAT** Intern America. (1991)-. Newsletter. English. Six times a year (Jan., Mar., May, July, Sept., Nov.). $49.50. Bernard H. Ford / InternAmerica, 105 Chestnut Street, Suite 34, Needham MA 02192-2520. **Tel** (617)449-8200, (800)456-SEEK, FAX (617)444-7335. **Bk Rev**, (Qty: 3-4). **Ad Acc, Adv Mgr:** Ellen Miller. Full Page (B&W) $175.00. Half Page (B&W) $90.00. available on diskette.

ISSN 8756-2359
DD 331 US

INTERNATIONAL BENEFITS. [Int. benefits]. (19??)-. English. International Foundation of Employee Benefit Plans, PO Box 69, 18700 West Bluemound Road, Brookfield WI 53008-0069. **Tel** (414)786-6700 ext.358, FAX (414)786-8670.

LC HD6977 .I47
DD 339.4/1 SZ

INTERNATIONAL COMPARISON OF AVERAGE NET HOURLY EARNINGS BASED ON WORK TIME REQUIRED FOR THE PURCHASE OF VARIOUS CONSUMER ITEMS. **VFOAT** Purchasing Power of Working Time, An International Comparison. (19??)-. English. One time a year. International Metalworkers Federation, Route des Acacias 54 Bis, CH-1227 Geneva Switzerland.

LC HD5701 .I74 **ISSN** 1052-9187
DD 331/.05 UK
CCC

INTERNATIONAL CONTRIBUTIONS TO LABOUR STUDIES. [Int. contrib. labour stud.]. **Added/Corp** Cambridge Political Economy Society. University of Notre Dame. Labor Studies Center. (1991)-. Academic Scholarly Publication. English. One time a year. $33.00. Academic Press Ltd., A Division of Harcourt Brace & Company Ltd., 24-28 Oval Road, London NW1 7DX United Kingdom. **Tel** 011 44 171 2674466, FAX 011 44 171 4822293, 011 44 171 4854752, telex 25775 ACPRES G. **(Subscription address:** Harcourt Brace & Company, Ltd., Foots Cray High Street, Sidcup Kent DA14 5HP United Kingdom. **Tel** 011 44 181 3003322, FAX 011 44 181 3090807, telex 896 377 ACADEM.**) ED** J. Berk, C. Craypo, T. Ghilarducci, E. Lorenz, J. Rubery and F. Wilkinson. **Bk Rev.**
Desc: Publishes economic, historical, industrial relations, legal, sociological, and political papers in any field of the study of labor.

ISSN 1081-4876
US

•INTERNATIONAL HR JOURNAL. **Added/Corp** Warren, Gorham & Lamont, Inc. (1995)-. Periodical. English. Four times a year (Jan., Mar., May, July, Sept., Nov.). $226.25. Warren Gorham & Lamont Inc., Park Square Building, 31 St. James Avenue, Boston MA 02116-4112. **Tel** (617)423-2020, (800)950-1207, FAX (617)423-2026. ***Continues*** *Journal of International Compensation & Benefits, 1068-9306.*

LC HD4805 .I76 **ISSN** 0143-7720
DD 331/.05 UK
CCC

INTERNATIONAL JOURNAL OF MANPOWER. [Int. j. manpow.]. (1980)-. Periodical. English. Ten times a year. $3779.00. MCB University Press, 60 62 Toller Lane, Bradford, West Yorkshire BD8 9BY United Kingdom. **Tel** 011 44 1274 785280, FAX 011 44 1274 785200, telex 51317-MCBUNI-G. **(Subscription address:** MCB University Press / US and Canada Subscriptions, PO Box 10812, Birmingham AL 35201-0812. **Tel** (205)995-1567, (800)633-4931, FAX (205)995-1588.**) ED** Geraint Johnes. available on an online database (file 15/Full-Text) from DIALOG. Documents available from UMI Article Clearinghouse. ***Absorbed*** *Quality of Working Life.*
Desc: Deals with key issues in manpower planning and economics, and offers guidance to all involved in corporate, local, national and international aspects of manpower planning and forecasting.
Ind/Abst ABI/INFORM Glob. Ed.; ABI/INFORM [Computer File] (Jan. 1980-); Anbar Account. Finan. Abstr. [Full Txt.]; Anbar Mark. Distr. Abstr. [Full Txt.]; Anbar Top Manage. Abstr. [Full Txt.]; Appl. Soc. Sci. Index Abstr.; Curr. Cit.; Curr. Index J. Educ.; Econ. Lit. Index; Ergon. Abstr.; Gen. BusinessFile (1992-); Hum. Resour. Abstr.; Int. Labour Doc.; LABORDOC; Manage. Market. Abstr.; Manage. Bibliogr. Rev.; Oper. Prod. Manage. Abstr. [Full Txt.]; Person. Train. Abstr. [Full Txt.]; Person. Manage. Abstr.; Stud. Women Abstr.; Tech. Educ. Train. Abstr.; Women Manage. Rev. [Full Txt.]; Work Relat. Abstr.

US

INTERNATIONAL LABOR AFFAIRS REPORT / UNITED STATES COUNCIL OF THE INTERNATIONAL CHAMBER OF COMMERCE INC. **Added/Corp** International Chamber of Commerce. United States Council. (19??)-. Periodical. English. Six times a year. United States Council of the International Chamber of Commerce, 1212 Avenue of the Americas, New York NY 10036. **Tel** (212)354-4480.
Desc: Reports on the growing influence of intergovernmental organizations and international trade union movements upon the international labor and management environment.

LC HD4802 .I7 **ISSN** 0147-5479
DD 305.5/62/05 US
CCC

INTERNATIONAL LABOR AND WORKING CLASS HISTORY. [Int. labor work. class hist.]. **Added/Corp** Study Group on International Labor and Working Class History. Social Science History Association. Workers and Industrialization Network. **VFOAT** ILWCH. No. 9 (May 1976)-. Academic Scholarly Publication. English. Two times a year. $40.00. Cambridge University Press / New York, 40 West 20th Street, New York NY 10011-4211. **Tel** (212)924-3900, (800)221-4512, FAX (212)691-3239. **(Subscription address:** Cambridge University Press / Outside of North America, United Kingdom. **Tel** 011 44 223 312 393, FAX 011 44 223 325 959.**) ED** Helmut Gruber and David Montgomery. **Bk Rev. Ad Acc. Circ:** 500. Documents available from The Genuine Article. ***Continues*** *Newsletter. European Labor and Working Class History, 0097-8523.*
Desc: Specializes in comparative labor history. Publishes essays, book reviews, substantive articles, scholar controversies, and conference reports.
Ind/Abst Am. Hist. Life (1983-); Am. Bibliogr. Slavic East Europ. Stud.; Arts Humanit. Citation Index [Full Cov.]; Curr. Contents Arts Humanit.; Left Index; Middle East Abstr. Index; Res. Alert [Full Cov.]; Work Relat. Abstr.

LC Z7164.L1 I646 HD4811 **ISSN** 0020-7756
DD 016.331 SZ
CCC

INTERNATIONAL LABOUR DOCUMENTATION. **See** Business and Economics-Abstracting, Bibliographies and Statistics.

LC HD4811 .I65 **ISSN** 0020-7780
SZ
CCC
CODEN ILREDT

INTERNATIONAL LABOUR REVIEW. [Int. labour rev.]. **Added/Corp** International Labour Office. Vol. 1, No. 1 (Jan. 1921)-. Periodical. English (French and Spanish). Six times a year. $70.00. International Labour Office - ILO, Publications Sales Service, CH-1211 Geneva 22 Switzerland. **Tel** 011 41 22 7996111, FAX 011 41 22 7986253, telex 415 647 ilo ch. **(Subscription address:** International Labour Office / Washington, DC, 1828 L Street Northwest, Suite 801, Washington DC 20036. **Tel** (202)653-7652.**) ED** Martha Fetherolf Loutfi. cum. index. available on microfilm and microfiche from University Microfilms International (UMI); available on an online database (as LABORDOC) from ORBIT; (as LABORDOC) HRIN file (ABI); and (as LABORDOC) ESA-IRS. Documents available from The Genuine Article, UMI Article Clearinghouse. ***Continues in part*** *Industry and Labour;* ***Absorbed*** *Industrial and Labour Information; International Labour Office. Notes Bibliographiques.* ***Continued in part by*** *Bulletin of Labour Statistics, 0007-4950; Industry and Labour* ***and*** *Legislative Series.*

Business and Economics —Labor

Supplement. Recent Labour Legislation.
Desc: Contains articles based on recent ILO and other research into economic and social topics of international interest affecting labour: notices of new books received by the ILO.
Ind/Abst ABI/INFORM Glob. Ed.; ABI/INFORM [Computer File] (July 1971-); Acad. Search; AGRICOLA; Appl. Soc. Sci. Index Abstr.; Asia.-Pac. Econ. Lit.; Book Rev. Index; Bus. Index (1985-); Bus. Period. Index; Bus. Source Plus; Bus. Source; Contents Pages Manage.; Curr. Cit.; Curr. Contents Soc. Behav. Sci.; Curr. Index J. Educ. (March 1990) ; Econ. Lit. Index; EP Collect.; Ergon. Abstr.; Expand. Acad. Index (1984-); Gen. BusinessFile (1985-); Gen. Period. Index (1985-); Geogr. Abstr. Human Geogr.; Homework Help.; Hum. Resour. Abstr.; Hum. Rights Intern. Rep.; INFO-SOUTH Abstr.; Int. Bibliogr. Sociol.; Int. Dev. Abstr.; Int. Labour Doc.; J. Econ. Lit.; LABORDOC; Manage. Market. Abstr.; Manage. Contents; MasterFile FullTEXT 1000; MasterFile FullTEXT 350; MasterFile FullTEXT 650; MasterFile FullTEXT (Jan. 1994-); Middle East Abstr. Index; Multicult. Educ. Abstr.; Newsp. Period. Abstr. (1990-); OCLC; PAIS Int. Print (1991-); Person. Manage. Abstr.; Popul. Index (?-?); Res. Alert [Full Cov.]; Rice Abstr.; Rural Dev. Abstr.; Saf. Health Work; Selec. Coop. Index Manage. Period.; Soc. Plann. Policy Dev. Abstr.; Soc. Sci. Source; Soc. Sci. Cit. Index [Full Cov.]; Soc. Sci. Index; Soc. Sci. Index Fulltext (1988-) [Full Txt.]; Soc. Work Abstr. (?-?); Spec. Educ. Needs Abstr.; Stud. Women Abstr.; Tech. Educ. Train. Abstr.; Telebase; Middle East J.; Trop. Dis. Bull.; UMI ABI/Inform--Bus. Period. Ondisc (Nov. 1987-) [Full Txt.]; Wilson Bus. Abstr.; Women Stud. Abstr.; Work Relat. Abstr.; World Agric. Econ. Rural Sociol. Abstr.

ISSN 0020-8159
US

INTERNATIONAL OPERATING ENGINEER, THE. Added/Corp International Union of Operating Engineers. International Union of Steam Engineers. International Union of Steam and Operating Engineers. Vol. 1 (Dec. 1901)-. Periodical. English. Twelve times a year. $5.00. International Union of Operating Engineers, 1125 17th Street, Washington DC 20006. **Tel** (202)429-9100. **ED** Frank Hanley. **Circ:** 360,000 (ctrl). **Absorbed** Steam Shovel and Dredge.
Desc: Addresses interest and needs of membership of IUOE as workers in construction industry and as citizens.

US

INTERNATIONAL REPORT OF SALARY INCREASES. Added/Corp Hewitt Associates. 3rd Annual (1991)-. English. **Continues** International Summary of Salary Increases in ... Countries.

ISSN 0379-0282
SW

INTERNATIONAL REVUE FUER SOZIALE SICHERHEIT. [Int. Rev. Soz. Sicherh.]. (1967)-. Periodical. German. Four times a year. $47.14. International Social Security Association, Case Postale 1, CH-1211 Geneva 22 Switzerland. **Tel** 011 41 22 7996617, FAX 011 41 22 7986385.
Ind/Abst LABORDOC.

UK

INTERNATIONAL WORKER. English. Twelve times a year. £6.00 UK; £8.50 Europe; £9.50 Australia; £10.00 other. International Communist Party, PO Box 71, Rotherham S YK S60 2QA United Kingdom.

LC L901 .I66 **ISSN** 0272-5460
DD 331.25/922 US
TITLE CHANGE

INTERNSHIPS. See Occupations and Careers.

LC KF3512.Z9 I57 **ISSN** 8756-9396
DD 344.73/01252 347.3041252 US

INTRODUCTION TO QUALIFIED PENSION AND PROFIT-SHARING PLANS. VFOAT Qualified Pension and Profit-Sharing Plans. (19??)-. English. One time a year. Practising Law Institute, 810 Seventh Avenue, New York NY 10019-5818. **Tel** (212)765-5700, FAX (212)581-4670 general correspondence, (212)265-4742 orders and billing inquiries.

LC HD8578.5.A2 S94A

SW

INVANDRARNAS LEVNADSFORHALLANDEN. Main/Corp Sweden. Statistiska Centralbyran. VFOAT Living Conditions of Swedish Immigrants. (19??)-. Swedish (summaries and/or abstracts in English). One time a year. SCB Statistiska Centralbyran, 11581 Stockholm Sweden.

ISSN 1068-4239
DD 658 US
CCC

●IOMA'S REPORT ON COMPENSATION & BENEFITS FOR LAW OFFICES. [IOMA's rep. compens. benefits law off.]. Added/Corp Institute of Management & Administration. VFOAT IOMA's Report on Compensation and Benefits for Law Offices; Compensation & Benefits for Law Offices. Issue 93-5 (May 1993)-. Periodical. English. Twelve times a year. $245.00. Institute of Management and Administration, 29 West 35th Street, 5th Floor, New York NY 10001-2299. **Tel** (212)244-0360, FAX (212)564-0465. **Continues** IOMA's Report on Controlling Benefits Costs for Law, Design, CPA, and Other Professional Service Firms, 1062-7936.

ISSN 1067-5361
DD 658 US
CCC

●IOMA'S REPORT ON MANAGING FLEXIBLE BENEFITS PLANS. [IOMA's rep. manag. flex. benefits plans]. Added/Corp Institute of Management & Administration. VFOAT Report on Managing Flexible Benefits Plans.; Managing Flexible Benefits Plans. Issue 93-3 (Mar. 1993)-. Newsletter. English. Twelve times a year. $245.00. Institute of Management and Administration, 29 West 35th Street, 5th Floor, New York NY 10001-2299. **Tel** (212)244-0360, FAX (212)564-0465. **ED** Rebecca Morrow. Index available.
Desc: Covers design and administration of benefits plans, including structure, rules, regulations, and costs for employees.

US

IOWA LOCAL GOVERNMENT SALARY AND BENEFIT SURVEY. (1982)-. English. One time a year. **Continues** Iowa Municipal Salary Survey.

ISSN 0958-5222
UK

IPMS BULLETIN. [IPMS bull.]. VFOAT Bulletin - Institution of Professionals, Managers and Specialists. (1989)-. Trade Publication. English. Twelve times a year. $10.27. TG Scott Subscriber Services, 6 Bourne Enterprise Center, Sevenoaks Kent TN15 8DG United Kingdom. **Tel** 011 44 1732 884023, FAX 011 44 1732 884034. **Continues** IPCS Bulletin, 0265-0975.
Desc: News and views on employment issues affecting scientists and technologists in the public and private sector.

UK

IRELAND AGENDA, THE. No. 1 (March 1991)-. Periodical. English. Six times a year. £10.50. Labour & Ireland, BM Box 5355, London WC1 N3XX United Kingdom. **Tel** 011 44 171 2498816.

IT

IRES MATERIALI. (19??)-. Italian. Twelve times a year. L100000 Itlay; L200000 other. Ediesse / Rome, Via Dei Frentani 4A, 00185 Rome Italy. **Tel** 011 39 6 44870286, 44870288, FAX 011 39 6 4469007.

LC HD8381 .I77 **ISSN** 1358-2216
UK

●IRS EMPLOYMENT REVIEW. Added/Corp Industrial Relations Services. VFOAT Industrial Relations Services Employment Review; Employment Review. (Jan. 1995)-. Periodical. English. Twenty-four times a year. $795.71. Eclipse Publications Ltd., 18 20 Highbury Place, London N5 1QP United Kingdom. **Tel** 011 44 171 3545858. (**Subscription address:** Industrial Relations Services, 18-20 Highbury Place, London N5 1QP United Kingdom.) **Continues** Industrial Relations Review and Report, 0309-7269.

LC HD6350.E3 I2 **ISSN** 0019-0861
DD 331.88/121/05 US

IUE NEWS. Added/Corp International Union of Electrical, Radio and Machine Workers. VAT International Union of Electrical, Radio, and Machine Workers News. Vol. 10, No. 20 (Sept. 18, 1959)-. Periodical. English. Six times a year. $2.00. IUE, 1126 16th Street, Washington DC 20036. **Tel** (202)296-1200. **ED** Nick Dell Donne. **Circ:** 150,000. available on microfilm and microfiche from University Microfilms International (UMI). **Continues** IUE AFL-CIO News.
Desc: News and opinions about and of interest to members of the International Union of Electronic Workers.
Ind/Abst Work Relat. Abstr.

LC HD8448 .I57 **ISSN** 0046-8428
GW

IWK INTERNATIONALE WISSENSCHAFTLICHE KORRESPONDENZ ZUR GESCHICHTE DER DEUTSCHEN ARBEITERBEWEGUNG. (INTERNATIONALE WISSENSCHAFTLICHE KORRESPONDENZ ZUR GESCHICHTE DER DEUTSCHEN ARBEITERBEWEGUNG.). [IWK. Int. wiss. Korresp. Gesch. dtsch. Arb.beweg.]. **Added/Corp** Friedrich-Ebert-Stiftung. Forschungsinstitut. Historische Kommission zu Berlin. VFOAT IWK. Vol. 1-19/20, (Dec. 1965-73); 1974- 10.- Year. Periodical. German (English). Four times a year. $60.64. H Skrzypcak Historische Kommission, Kirchweg 33, D-14 129 Berlin Germany. **Tel** 49 30 81600141, FAX 49 30 81600134. **ED** Gunter Krueschet. Index available (bound in fourth issue). **Bk Rev,** (Qty: 200). **Ad Acc, Adv Mgr:** Gunter Krueschet. **Circ:** 1,400.
Desc: Signed articles concerning the history of the German labor movement.
Ind/Abst Am. Hist. Life (1973-1976, 1979-); Writ. Am. Hist.

LC WMLC 91/1838
SA

JAARVERSLAG. Main/Corp South Africa. National Training Board. VFOAT Annual Report. (1990)-. Periodical. Dutch. Nasionale Opleidingsraad.
Desc: To provide for the advancement of the training of the human resources of the Republic of South Africa.

LC HD5842 .A45a
DD 354.680083/06 SA

JAARVERSLAG / DEPARTEMENT VAN MANNEKRAG = ANNUAL REPORT / DEPARTMENT OF MANPOWER. See Public Administration.

US

JACKSON'S LABOR MARKET NEWS. Added/Corp Michigan Employment Security Commission. Bureau of Research and Statistics. Information and Reports Section. Vol. No. 1 (Mar. 1992)-. Periodical. English. Twelve times a year. Detroit Employment Security Commission, 7700 Woodward Castro, Room 520, Detroit MI 48202. **Tel** (313)876-5427. **Continues** Jackson Labor Market Review.

LC HD8419.N53 K35a
AU

JAHRBUCH DER KAMMER FUER ARBEITER UND ANGESTELLTE FUER NIEDEROSTERREICH. Main/Corp Kammer fur Arbeiter und Angestellte fur Niederosterrich. (19??)-. German. Irregular. Kammer fur Arbeiter und Angestellte fur Niederosterreich, Windmuhlgasse 28, 1060 Vienna Austria. **Continues** Kammer fur Arbeiter und Angestellte fur Niederosterreich. Jahresbericht.

LC HD7102.A9 L3 **ISSN** 0457-1231
AU

JAHRESBERICHT. Main/Corp Landwirtschaftskrankenkasse fur Steiermark. (19??)-. German. Irregular. Stadt Graz, Stadtarchiv, Hans-Sachs-Gasse 1, A-8010 Graz Austria.

LC HD5772.T9 L36a
AU

Pr Rev.
JAHRESBERICHT DES LANDESARBEITSAMTES TIROL. Main/Corp Landesarbeitsamt Tirol. (19??)-. Government Publication. German. One time a year. Free. Arbeitsmarktservice Tirol Landesgeschaftsstelle, Schopfstrse 5, 6010 Innsbruck Austria. **Tel** 0512 5903-0, FAX 0512 579578. Index available. **Circ:** 400 (ctrl).
Desc: Covers the labor market in Tirol. Working power, unemployment, and administrative activities.

LC HD8721 .J36 **ISSN** 0021-4469
JA

JAPAN LABOR BULLETIN. Added/Corp Nihon Rodo Kyokai. Japan. Rodosho. (June 1959)-. Bulletin. English. Twelve times a year. $38.40. Japan Institute of Labor, Shinjuku Monolith 2 3 1, Tokyo 163 09 Japan. **Tel** 011 81 3 53213084. (**Subscription address:** OCS / Overseas Courier Service of America Inc., 5 East 44th Street, New York NY 10017. **Tel** (212)599-4517.)
Ind/Abst Int. Labour Doc.; LABORDOC; Saf. Health Work; Work Relat. Abstr.

LC HD5827 .A52
DD 331/.0952/021 JA

JAPANESE WORKING LIFE PROFILE. Added/Corp Nihon Rodo Kyokai. (19??)-. English (table of contents in Japanese). One time a year. ¥1000. Japan Institute of Labor, Shinjuku Monolith 2 3 1, Tokyo 163 09 Japan. **Tel** 011 81 3 53213084. available with illustrations; available with charts.
Desc: Presents profiles of average Japanese workers through selected statistical figures. Contains labor statistics relevant to a worker's successive life stages from school graduation and entering a firm up until his or her retirement age.

LC HD7106.J3 K597a
JA

JIGYO YORAN - KANI HOKEN YUBIN NENKIN FUKUSHI JIGYODAN. Main/Corp Kani Hoken Yubin Nenkin Fukushi Jigyodan. (19??)-. Periodical. Japanese. Kani Hoken Yubin Nenkin Fukushi Jigyodan, 3-4 Akasaka 2-chome Minato-ku, Tokyo Japan.

US

JLS & K PREVENTIVE LABOR RELATIONS FOR EXECUTIVES. Main/Corp Jackson, Lewis, Schnitzler and Krupman. VFOAT Preventive Labor Relations. Vol. 1, No. 1 (Nov. 1978)-. Periodical. English. Twelve times a year. $60.00. Preventive Labor Relations, PO Box 82, Dresher PA 19025. **Tel** (215)628-4840.

ISSN 1065-4658
DD 331 US

JOB FINDER FOR HIGH TECH SILICON VALLEY. See Occupations and Careers.

ISSN 0731-3365
US
CEASED
JOB OPPORTUNITIES BULLETIN. (JOB OPPORTUNITIES BULLETIN / PRODUCED BY THE TRANSCENTURY RECRUITMENT CENTER ...). **Added/Corp** New TransCentury Foundation. Transcentury Recruitment Center. (19??)-(1993). Bulletin. English. Transcentury Foundation, 1724 Kalorama Road NW, Washington DC 20009. **Tel** (202)328-4437.

ISSN 1046-1353
DD 331 US
JOB READY. [Job ready]. Vol. 1, No. 1 (Nov. 1989)-. Periodical. English. Twelve times a year. $48.00. Quantum Publications, 1211 North Westshore Boulevard, Suite 102, Tampa FL 33607.
Desc: National magazine for human resource professionals. Covers aspects of affirmative action for people with disabilities.

US
JOBFLO. (19??)-. Periodical. English. Twelve times a year. New York State Department of Labor / Albany, 401 Harriman, Division of Research and Statistics, State Office Building Campus, Albany NY 12240. **Tel** (518)457-6649.

ISSN 0738-0208
US
JOBLESS NEWSLETTER. (1982)-. Newsletter. English. Twelve times a year. $24.00. Al Baker, PO Box 689, Los Fresnos TX 78566.

ISSN 1053-654X
DD 331 US
JOBS IN RECESSIONARY TIMES POSSIBILITY NEWSLETTER. [Jobs recess. times possibility newsl.]. Vol. 1 (1990)-. Newsletter. English. One time a year. $7.00. Prosperity & Profits Unlimited, PO Box 416, Denver CO 80201-0416. **Tel** (303)575-5676. **ED** A.C. Doyle.
Desc: Information about types of jobs available in recessionary times.

US
JOBS MAGAZINE. English. Twenty-six times a year. $166.00. Classified Publications Inc, PO Box 5061, Oak Brook IL 60521. **Tel** (708)582-3322. **Ad Acc. Circ:** 10,000 (ctrl).
Desc: The magazine that covering the community with full-time, part-time and career positions.

AT
JOHN CURTIN MEMORIAL LECTURE, THE. (1???)-. Monographic series. English. Irregular. Free on request. Australian Labour Party, 2nd Floor Labor Center 82, Baufort St. Perth 6000 Australia. **Tel** 011 61 09 3287222, FAX 011 61 09 2279585. **ED** Mark Nolan, (editor's address: PO Box 8117, Stirling, St. Perth, 6000 Australia, phone: 011 61 09 328 7222).
Desc: News and information on the annual lecture by a prominent member of the labor movement.

LC HD4801
DD 331 SW
JORDBRUKETS ARBETSKRAFT. VFOAT Agricultural Labour Force in ... . (19??)-. Swedish. Liber Distribution, Prenumerationsorder, Forlagsorder 162 89, Stockholm Sweden.

LC HC190.P6 J67
DD 331.5 BL
JORNAL DOS TRABALHADORES RURAIS SEM TERRA. See Agriculture.

ISSN 0709-2504
DD 331.11/0971 CN
JOURNAL DE L'APUC (EDITION FRANCAISE). See Education-Higher Education.

ISSN 0225-3089
DD 331.88/0971 CN
JOURNAL DE L'ASSOCIATION OUVRIERE CANADIENNE. [J. Assoc. ouvriere can.]. **Main/Corp** Association Ouvriere Canadienne. **VFOAT** Faisons Payer les Riches. (Jan. 1979)-. Periodical. French. Twelve times a year. 0.25Can$ per no. Association Ouvriere Canadienne, Centre National de Publications, CP 727 Succursale Adelaide, Toronto Ontario M5C 2J8 Canada. ***Continues** Bulletin de l'Association Ouvriere Canadienne, 0225-3070.*

LC HD66 .Q335 **ISSN** 1040-9602
DD 658.4/036 US
CCC
Pr Rev.
JOURNAL FOR QUALITY AND PARTICIPATION, THE. [J. qual. participat.]. **Added/Corp** Association for Quality and Participation. **VFOAT** Quality and Participation. Vol. 10, No. 4 (Dec. 1987)-. Periodical. English. Seven times a year. $52.00. Association for Quality and Participation, 801-B West 8th Street, Suite 501, Cincinnati OH 45203. **Tel** (513)381-1959, FAX (513)381-0070. **ED** Ned Hamson. Index available. cum. index. **Bk Rev. Ad Acc. Acid Free. Circ:** 8,000 (ctrl). available on microfilm and microfiche from University Microfilms International (UMI). Documents available from UMI Article Clearinghouse. ***Continues** Quality Circles Journal, 0740-2287.*
Desc: Contains information on participative management, total quality management and employee involvement theory and practice.
Ind/Abst ABI/INFORM Glob. Ed.; ABI/INFORM [Computer File] (Dec. 1984-); Curr. Cit.; EP Collect.; Gen. BusinessFile (1992-); Homework Help.; LABORDOC; MasterFile FullTEXT 1000; MasterFile FullTEXT 350; MasterFile FullTEXT 650; MasterFile FullTEXT; OCLC; Telebase.

LC HD6350.B9 B6 **ISSN** 0362-3696
DD 331.88/193/0973 US
JOURNAL - INTERNATIONAL UNION OF BRICKLAYERS AND ALLIED CRAFTSMEN. [Journal - Int. Union Bricklay. Allied Craftsm.]. **Main/Corp** International Union of Bricklayers and Allied Craftsmen. Vol. 79, No. 10 (Oct./Nov. 1975)-. Periodical. English. Twelve times a year. $1.50. Bricklayer Mason & Plasterers, 815 Fifteenth Street Northwest, Washington DC 20005. **Tel** (202)783-3788. **ED** Mary T. Dresser. **Circ:** 100,000 (ctrl). ***Continues** Journal - Bricklayers, Masons and Plasterers International Union of America, 0360-6058.*
Desc: For union bricklayers and other members of trowel trades.
Ind/Abst Work Relat. Abstr. (-19??).

LC LB2842.2 .J68 **ISSN** 0047-2301
DD 331.89/041/371100973 US
Pr Rev.
JOURNAL OF COLLECTIVE NEGOTIATIONS IN THE PUBLIC SECTOR. [J. collect. negot. publ. sector]. (Feb. 1972)-. Periodical. English. Four times a year. $132.50. Baywood Publishing Company Inc., 26 Austin Avenue, PO Box 337, Amityville NY 11701. **Tel** (516)691-1270, (800)638-7819, FAX (516)691-1770. **ED** Harry Kershen. Documents available from The Genuine Article, UMI Article Clearinghouse.
Desc: Serves as a forum for the interchange of ideas and information among the international community of individuals concerned with the negotiations process. Editorial emphasis is on practical ideas that may guide readers toward usable techniques for the negotiations process, or that recommend constructive approaches for dealing with the complexities of public sector labor relations.
Ind/Abst ABI/INFORM Glob. Ed.; ABI/INFORM [Computer File] (Jan. 1980-); Acad. Search; Bus. Period. Index; Curr. Cit.; Curr. Contents Soc. Behav. Sci.; Curr. Index J. Educ.; Curr. Law Index (1980-); Educ. Adm. Abstr.; EP Collect.; Gen. BusinessFile (1992-); Homework Help.; Hosp. Health Admin. Index; Hum. Resour. Abstr. (?-?); Index Period. Artic. Relat. Law; INFO-SOUTH Abstr.; Leg. Resour. Index (1980-); LegalTrac (1980-); Mag. Search; MasterFile FullTEXT 1000; MasterFile FullTEXT 350; MasterFile FullTEXT 650; MasterFile FullTEXT (July 1993-); OCLC; PAIS Int. Print (1991-); Person. Manage. Abstr.; Res. Alert [Full Cov.]; Sage Public Adm. Abstr.; Soc. Sci. Cit. Index [Full Cov.]; Telebase; Urban Aff. Abstr.; Wilson Bus. Abstr.; Work Relat. Abstr.

LC KF3509.A15 J68 **ISSN** 0893-780X
DD 344.83/01255/05 347.304125505 US
CCC
JOURNAL OF COMPENSATION AND BENEFITS. [J. compens. benefits]. **VFOAT** Compensation and Benefits. Vol. 1, No. 1 (July/August 1985)-. Trade Publication. English. Six times a year. $149.25. Warren Gorham & Lamont Inc., Park Square Building, 31 St. James Avenue, Boston MA 02116-4112. **Tel** (617)423-2020, (800)950-1207, FAX (617)423-2026. **ED** Jeffrey Mamorsky. available on microfilm and microfiche from University Microfilms International (UMI). Documents available from UMI Article Clearinghouse.
Desc: Practical working advisor for benefits administrators, compensation specialists and consultants. Gives analysis of plan design, administration and record keeping, accounting, tax planning responsibilities and more.
Ind/Abst ABI/INFORM Glob. Ed.; ABI/INFORM [Computer File] (Sept. 1985-); Acad. Search; Account. Tax Datab. (Sept. 1985-); Account. Art.; Bus. Period. Index; Bus. Source Plus; Bus. Source; Curr. Cit.; EP Collect.; Fed. Tax Artic.; Gen. BusinessFile (1992-); Homework Help.; INFO-SOUTH Abstr.; Ins. Period. Index; Mag. Search; MasterFile FullTEXT 1000; MasterFile FullTEXT 350; MasterFile FullTEXT 650; MasterFile FullTEXT (July 1993-); OCLC; Telebase; Wilson Bus. Abstr.

ISSN 1046-7491
DD 331 US
Pr Rev.
JOURNAL OF EMPLOYEE OWNERSHIP LAW AND FINANCE, THE. [J. empl. ownersh. law finance]. **Added/Corp** National Center for Employee Ownership (U.S.). Vol. 1, No. 1 (Fall 1989)-. Periodical. English. Four times a year (seasonally). $100.00. National Center for Employee Ownership, 1201 Martin Luther King Jr. Way, 2nd Floor, Oakland CA 94612. **Tel** (510)272-9461, FAX (510)272-9510. **ED** Scott Rodrick (phone: (510)208-1801). **Circ:** 300.
Desc: Provides technical information on employee ownership for academics, practitioners and companies.

LC HD5701 .J6 **ISSN** 0022-166X
DD 331.1/1/0973 US
CCC
NLM W1 JO673W **CODEN** JHREA9
Pr Rev.
JOURNAL OF HUMAN RESOURCES, THE. See Business and Economics-Personnel Management.

LC K10 .O865 **ISSN** 1055-7512
DD 344.73/01/05 347.304105 US
JOURNAL OF INDIVIDUAL EMPLOYMENT RIGHTS. (JOURNAL OF INDIVIDUAL EMPLOYMENT RIGHTS : IER.). [J. individ. employ. rights]. **VFOAT** IER; Individual Employment Rights. Vol. 1, No. 1 (1992)-. Periodical. English. Four times a year. $115.50. Baywood Publishing Company Inc., 26 Austin Avenue, PO Box 337, Amityville NY 11701. **Tel** (516)691-1270, (800)638-7819, FAX (516)691-1770.

LC HD4811 .J63 **ISSN** 0022-1856
AT
CCC
JOURNAL OF INDUSTRIAL RELATIONS, THE. [J. ind. relat.]. **Added/Corp** Industrial Relations Society. Industrial Relations Society of Australia. **VFOAT** JIR. Vol. 1 (April 1959)-. Periodical. English. Four times a year (Mar., June, Sept., Dec.). 45.22Aus$. Industrial Relations Society of New South Wales, GPO Box 4479, Sydney New South Wales 2001 Australia. **Tel** 011 61 2 8731308. **ED** J. Niland. Index available. **Bk Rev. Circ:** 4,000 (ctrl).
Desc: Articles and reviews on industrial relations and related subjects from contributors in management, trade unions, government services, professions and specialists in academic disciplines.
Ind/Abst APAIS, Aust. Public Aff. Inf. Ser. (1963-); Appl. Soc. Sci. Index Abstr.; Contents Recent Econ. J.; Curr. Cit.; Int. Bibliogr. Sociol.; Int. Labour Doc.; LABORDOC; Person. Manage. Abstr.; Soc. Plann. Policy Dev. Abstr.; Sociol. Abstr.; Work Relat. Abstr.

LC HD4802 .J678 **ISSN** 0734-306X
DD 331/.05 US
CCC
Pr Rev.
JOURNAL OF LABOR ECONOMICS. [J. labor econ.]. Vol. 1, No. 1 (Jan. 1983)-. Periodical. English. Four times a year. $110.00. University of Chicago Press / Journals Division, PO Box 37005, 5720 South Woodlawn, Chicago IL 60637. **Tel** (312)753-3347, FAX (312)753-0811. **ED** Edward P. Lazear. **Acid Free.** available on microfilm and microfiche from University Microfilms International (UMI). Documents available from The Genuine Article, UMI Article Clearinghouse.
Desc: Presents theoretical and empirical articles pertaining to labor economics, very broadly defined. Among the topics explored are supply and demand for labor services, compensation, labor markets, distribution of income, labor demographics, unions and collective bargaining, research relating to both U.S. and international data and applied and policy issues in labor economics.
Ind/Abst ABI/INFORM Glob. Ed.; ABI/INFORM [Computer File] (Jan 1988-); Acad. Abstr.; Acad. Search; Arts Humanit. Citation Index [Select. Cov.]; Bus. Index (1985-); Bus. Source Plus; Bus. Source; Contents Recent Econ. J.; Curr. Cit.; Econ. Lit. Index; EP Collect.; Expand. Acad. Index (1984-); Gen. BusinessFile (1985-); Gen. Period. Index (1985-); Homework Help.; INFO-SOUTH Abstr.; Int. Bibliogr. Sociol.; Int. Labour Doc.; J. Econ. Lit.; J. Plan. Lit.; LABORDOC; Mag. Search; MasterFile FullTEXT 1000; MasterFile FullTEXT 350; MasterFile FullTEXT 650; MasterFile FullTEXT (Jan. 1992-); Newsp. Period. Abstr. (1991-); OCLC; Person. Manage. Abstr.; Res. Alert [Full Cov.]; Soc. Sci. Source; Soc. Sci. Cit. Index [Full Cov.]; Soc. Sci. Index; Soc. Sci. Index Fulltext (Oct. 1988-) [Full Txt.]; Telebase.

LC HD4802 .J68 **ISSN** 0195-3613
DD 331/.05 US
CCC
Pr Rev.
JOURNAL OF LABOR RESEARCH. [J. labor res.]. **Added/Corp** George Mason University. Dept. of Economics. (Spring 1980)-. Periodical. English. Four times a year (Feb., Apr., July, Sept.). $110.00. George Mason University Journal of Labor Research, Department of Economics, Fairfax VA 22030. **Tel** (703)993-1155, FAX (703)993-1133. **ED** James T. Bennett. Index available (Fall issue). **Bk Rev**, (Qty: 12 per year). **Ad Acc. Circ:** 1,200. Documents available from The Genuine Article, UMI Article Clearinghouse.
Desc: Labor unions--their economic, political, and social impacts and activities.
Ind/Abst ABI/INFORM Glob. Ed.; ABI/INFORM [Computer File] (Fall 1980-); Acad. Abstr.; Acad. Search; Bus. Index (1985-); Bus. Source Plus; Bus. Source; Curr. Cit.; Curr. Contents Soc. Behav. Sci.; Econ. Lit. Index; Educ. Adm. Abstr. (?-?); EP Collect.; Expand. Acad. Index (1984-); Gen. BusinessFile (1985-); Gen. Period. Index (1985-); Homework Help.; Hum. Resour. Abstr.; INFO-SOUTH Abstr.; Int. Bibliogr. Sociol.; Int. Labour Doc.; J. Econ. Lit. (1980-); J. Plan. Lit.; Mag. Search;

Business and Economics — Labor

Manage. Contents (1980-); Manage. Contents; MasterFile FullTEXT 1000; MasterFile FullTEXT 350; MasterFile FullTEXT 650; MasterFile FullTEXT (Jan. 1992-); Newsp. Period. Abstr. (1991-); OCLC; PAIS Int. Print (1991-); Person. Manage. Abstr.; Public Aff. Inf. Serv. Bull.; Res. Alert [Full Cov.]; Sage Public Adm. Abstr. (?-?); Sage Urban Stud. Abstr; Soc. Plann. Policy Dev. Abstr.; Soc. Sci. Source; Soc. Sci. Cit. Index [Full Cov.]; Soc. Sci. Index; Soc. Sci. Index Fulltext (Spring 1989-) [Full Txt.]; Sociol. Abstr.; Telebase; UMI ABI/Inform--Bus. Period. Ondisc (Spring 1988-Winter 1990) [Full Txt.]; Work Relat. Abstr.

DD 810   **ISSN** 1055-1948   US

JOURNAL OF THE WRITERS GUILD OF AMERICA. WEST. See Literature.

LC HD8005.2.G7 J68a   **ISSN** 0957-8978
DD 331.88/0941/05   UK
TITLE CHANGE

JOURNAL : PAPER OF THE NATIONAL UNION OF CIVIL AND PUBLIC SERVANTS. See Public Administration-Civil Service.

LC HD8399.S3 S36a   **ISSN** 0586-7762
UK

JOURNAL - SCOTTISH LABOUR HISTORY SOCIETY. [J. - Scott. Labour Hist. Soc.]. Main/Corp Scottish Labour History Society. VFOAT Journal of the Scottish Labour History Society. No. 1 (May 1969)-. English. One time a year. £5.00 (ordinary membership); £2.00 (unwaged membership) Comes with membership. University Glasgow / Department of Scottish History, 9 University Gardens, Glasgow G12 8Q4 United Kingdom. Tel 011 44 41 3398855 ext. 4148.
Ind/Abst Am. Hist. Life (1978-).

LC HD5350.P6 U5
DD 331.881961   US

JOURNAL - UNITED ASSOCIATION OF JOURNEYMEN AND APPRENTICES OF THE PLUMBING AND PIPE FITTING INDUSTRY. Main/Corp United Association of Journeymen and Apprentices of the Plumbing and Pipe Fitting Industry. Vol. 1 (1898)-. Periodical. English. Twelve times a year. United Association of Journeymen and Apprentices of the Plumbing and Pipe Fitting Industry, Washington DC 20402.

LC HD6350.C6 J8   **ISSN** 0022-7013
DD 331   US
TITLE CHANGE

JUSTICE (NEW YORK, N.Y. 1919).
(JUSTICE.). [Justice]. Added/Corp International Ladies' Garment Workers' Union. Vol. 1 (Jan. 18, 1919)-(1995). Periodical. English (Spanish). International Ladies Garment Workers Union, 1710 Broadway, New York NY 10019. Tel (212)265-7000. ED Dwight Burton. Bk Rev, (Qty: 1-2). Circ: 250,000. available on microfilm.
Supersedes Ladies' Garment Worker. Merged into Unite Magazine.
Ind/Abst Hum. Rights Intern. Rep.; Work Relat. Abstr.

ISSN 0195-3737
US

JUSTICIA (NEW YORK). (JUSTICIA.). (19??)-. Periodical. English. Twelve times a year. $2.00. International Ladies Garment Workers Union, 1710 Broadway, New York NY 10019. Tel (212)265-7000.

US

KALAMAZOO'S LABOR MARKET NEWS. Added/Corp Michigan Employment Security Commission. Bureau of Research and Statistics. Information and Reports Section. Vol. 12, No. 1 (Mar. 1992)-. Periodical. English. Twelve times a year. Detroit Employment Security Commission, 7310 Woodward Castro, Room 520, Detroit MI 48202. Tel (313)876-5427.
Continues Kalamazoo Labor Market Review.

JA

KANKO RODO. (1949)-. Periodical. Japanese. Twelve times a year. $75.50. (Subscription address: Japan Publications Trading Company Ltd., PO Box 5030, Tokyo International, Tokyo 100-31 Japan. Tel 011 81 3 3292 3753.)

LC HD4976.K2 K36
DD 331.2/781   US

KANSAS WAGE SURVEY / RESEARCH AND ANALYSIS SECTION, DEPARTMENT OF HUMAN RESOURCES, DIVISION OF POLICY AND MANAGEMENT ANALYSIS. (1968)-. English. One time a year. Free from issuing agency.

Kansas Department of Human Resources, 401 SW Topeka Boulevard, Topeka KS 66603. Tel (913)296-7474, FAX (913)296-0179. Circ: 200.

JA

KATSUYO RODO TOKEI. Added/Corp Nihon Seisansei Honbu. Rodo Tokei Iinkai. (1965)-. Japanese. One time a year. Government Publications Service Center, 2-1 Kasumigaseki 1-Chome, Chiyoda-Ku Tokyo 100 Japan. Tel 011 81 3 3504 3885.

LC HD5824 .A37   **ISSN** 0126-3919
DD 331.11/09598   IO

KEADAAN ANGKATAN KERJA DI INDONESIA. Added/Corp Indonesia. Bagian Statistik Penduduk dan Tenaga Kerja. VFOAT S.A.K.E.R.N.A.S.; The Labour Force Situation in Indonesia. Average for the Months of February, May, August, and November; Labour Force Situation in Indonesia. Average for the Months of February, May, August, and November. (19??)-. English (Indonesian). One time a year. Biro Pusat Statistik / Central Bureau of Statistics, 8 Jalan Dr. Sutomo No. 8, Box 3, Jakarta Pusat 10710 Indonesia. Tel 011 62 21 372808, 011 62 21 374908 ext.342. ctrl circ.

LC HD5824 .A25A
IO

KEADAAN ANGKATEN KERJA DI INDONESIA : ANGKA SEMENTARA. Main/Corp Indonesia. Biro Pusat Statistik. VFOAT Labour Force Situation in Indonesia : Preliminary Figures. 1977-. English (Indonesian). Rp1.500. Biro Pusat Statistik / Central Bureau of Statistics, 8 Jalan Dr. Sutomo No. 8, Box 3, Jakarta Pusat 10710 Indonesia. Tel 011 62 21 372808, 011 62 21 374908 ext.342. Bk Rev. Ad Acc. ctrl circ.

LC HD7256.I6 I45A
IO

KEBIJAKSANAAN OPERASIONIL DAN RENCANA KERJA ROUTINE & PEMBANGUNAN. Main/Corp Indonesia. Direktorat Jenderal Bina Karya. (19??)-. Indonesian. Direktorat Jenderal Bira, Karya Indonesia.

ISSN 0023-0251
US

KENTUCKY LABOR NEWS. Added/Corp Kentucky State AFL-CIO. VFOAT KLN. Vol. 1 (April 24, 1942)-. Periodical. English. Twenty-six times a year. $14.50. Kentucky Labor News, PO Box 4533, Louisville KY 40204. Tel (502)456-4568.

LC HC446 .A14
IO

KEPADATAN PERUSAHAAN INDUSTRI DAN TENAGA KERJA DI SEKTOR INDUSTRI TERHADAP JUMLAH PENDUDUK DI TIAP-TIAP PROPINSI, KABUPATEN, KOTA MADYA. Main/Corp Indonesia. Biro Pusat Statistik. 1973-. Indonesian. Biro Pusat Statistik / Central Bureau of Statistics, 8 Jalan Dr. Sutomo No. 8, Box 3, Jakarta Pusat 10710 Indonesia. Tel 011 62 21 372808, 011 62 21 374908 ext.342. Bk Rev. Ad Acc.

LC HD4811 .K56
II

KIRATI YUGA. No. 1- October 1973-. Periodical. Panjabi (Panjabi). 10.00. Zila Kurukushetra Sam Bajiua, Railway Road, Shahabada India.

LC HD9736.J3 K59
JA

KOGYO TOKEI HYO. KOGYO CHIKU HEN / TSUSHO SANGYO DAIJIN KANBO CHOSA TOKEIBU. Added/Corp Japan. Tsusho Sangyosho. Chosa Tokeibu. VFOAT Census of Manufacturers. Report by Industrial District. (19??)-. Japanese. Tsusho Sangyo Chosakai, (Research Institute on International Trade and Industry), Kobikikan Ginza Biru, 8-9 Ginza 2 chome Chuoku, Tokyo 104 Japan.

JA

KOKKA OMUIN SAIGAI HOSHO KANKEI HOREI SHU. Main/Corp Japan. Added/Corp Japan. Jinjiin. Japan. Jinjiin. Jinjiin Geppo. Bessatsu. (19??)-. Periodical. Japanese. Okurasho Insatsukyoku, (Printing Bureau Ministry of Finance), 2-4 Toranomon 2 chome, Minatoku Tokyo 105 Japan.

LC HD84 .D485 HC281
GW

KONZERTIERTE AKTION; BERICHT UEBER DIE ERFAHRUNGEN SEIT IHREM BESTEHEN. Main/Corp Deutsches Industrieinstitut, Cologne. (19??)-. German. Deutscher Instituts Verlag GmbH, Gustav-Heinemann-Ufer 84-88, Postfach 51 06 70, 50942 Cologne Germany. Continues Deutsches Industrieinstitut, Cologne. Konzertierte Aktion; Bericht Ueber die Erfahrungen Seit Ihrem Bestehen.

LC HD5827.A258c
JA

KOYO DOKO CHOSA KEKKA NO GAIYO. Main/Corp Japan. Rodosho. Tokei Johobu. (19??)-. Periodical. Japanese. Two times a year. Daijin Kanbo, 7-3, Ichigaya Honmuracho, Shinjuku-ku Tokyo 162 Japan.

LC HD7260 .K85
KO

KULLO POKCHI. Periodical. Korean. Six times a year. Kullo Pokchi Kongsa, 94-267 Yongdungpo-Dong Yongdungpo-Ku, Seoul Korea.

LC HD8730.6 .K84
KN

KULLOJA. (19??)-. Periodical. Korean. Kulloja, Munsin 1-dong, Tongdaewon-Kuyok, Pyongyang North Korea.

LC LC5056.G4 K8   **ISSN** 0451-0410
GW

KULTURELLES LEBEN. Vol. 1 (Jan. 1954)-. Periodical. German. Twelve times a year. Deutscher Judo Verband, Redaktion Ippon Segewaldweg 40, D-12557 Berlin Germany. Tel 011 49 711 210770, telex 051 678.
Supersedes Kulturelle Massenarbeit.
Desc: Includes songs.

LC HD5824 .A32D
IO

KUMPULAN KERTAS KARYA - DEPARTEMEN TENAGA KERJA, TRANSMIGRASI DAN KOPERASI, TEAM POLICY RESEARCH. Main/Corp Indonesia. Departemen Tenaga Kerja, Transmigrasi Dan Koperasi. Team Policy Research. (19??)-. Indonesian. D/A Biro Perencanaan Dan Penelitian, Jl H Agus Salin 58, Kotak Pos 45, Jakarta Indonesia.

LC HD7057 .K6
JA

KURASHI NO TOKEI / KOKUMIN SEIKATSU SENTA HEN. Added/Corp Kokumin Seikatsu Senta. Japan. Kokumin Seikatsukyoku. (1982)-. Japanese. One time a year. ¥4200. Okurasho Insatukyoku, (Printing Bureau Ministry of Finance), 2-4 Toranomon 2 chome, Minatoku Tokyo 105 Japan. Continues Kokumin Seikatsu Tokei Nenpo.

LC HD5777 .K87   **ISSN** 0173-6574
DD 331.12/0943   GW

KURZBERICHTE. (19??)-. Periodical. German. One time a year. Institut fur Arbeitsmarkt und Berufsforschung der Bundesanstalt fur Arbeit, Regensburger Strasse 104, 85 Nuernberg Germany. Tel 0911 173086, telex 7-255 820. Index available.

LC HD6735.7 .A135   **ISSN** 0860-9357
PL

KWARTALNIK HISTORII I TEORII RUCHU ZAWODOWEGO. Added/Corp Instytut Wydawniczy Zwiazkow Zawodowych (Poland) Centrum Studiow Zwiazkow Zawodowych (Warsaw, Poland). (1989)-. Periodical. Polish (table of contents in English, French, German and Russian). Four times a year. Instytut Wydawniczy Zwiazkow Zawodowych, Ul. Spasowskiego 1-3, 00-950 Warsaw Poland. Tel 011 48 22 279011. (Subscription address: Ars Polona-Ruch, PO Box 1001, Krakowskie Przedmiescie 7, 00-068 Warsaw Poland. Tel 011 48 22 261201.) Bk Rev. Ad Acc. Circ: 3,000.
Continues Kwartalnik Historii Ruchu Zawodowego, 0454-7330.

LC HD7367.A3 K9a
DD 363.5   JA

KYOTO DAIGAKU UEDA ATSUSHI KENKYUSHITSU KENKYU ROMBUN SHU. Main/Corp Kyoto Daigaku. Ueda Atsushi Kenkyushitsu. (19??)-. Japanese. Uead Atsushi Kenkyushitsu, Yoshida Honcho, Kyoto Japan.

LC HD5827 .A25
JA

KYUJIN TO JITTAI CHOSA HOKOKU. Main/Corp Japan. Rodosho. Tokei Johobu. (1972)-. Periodical. Japanese. Daijin Kanbo, 7-3, Ichigaya Honmuracho, Shinjuku-ku Tokyo 162 Japan. Continues Kyujin to Jittai Chosa Hokoku.

LC HD6475.A2 I269
DD 331.88/05   BE

LABOR. Added/Corp World Confederation of Labour. International Federation of Christian Trade Unions. (Apr. 1956)-. Periodical. French (German, Dutch, Spanish and English). Irregular (4 issues plus 2 supplements). $16.00. World Confederation of Labour, 33 rue de Treves, B-1040 Brussels Belgium. Tel 011 32 2 230 62 95, FAX 011 32 2 230 87 22. Absorbed Christlabor.
Desc: Articles on labor movement.

LC HD8772 .L25
DD 331/.096   TG

LABOR AND DEVELOPMENT. Added/Corp Centre Regional d'Etudes et de Documentation Economiques. African-American Labor Center.

Organisation of African Trade Union Unity. No. 1 (Jan. 1975)-. Periodical. English. Twelve times a year. *Supersedes* Labor in Perspective, 0377-0737. **Ind/Abst** Hum. Rights Intern. Rep.

LC HG4501   ISSN 0279-0467
DD 332.6   US
    CEASED
LABOR & INVESTMENTS. Added/Corp
AFL-CIO. Industrial Union Dept. **VAT** Labor and Investments. Vol. 1, No. 1 (Jan. 1981)-(Oct. 1993). Periodical. English. Industrial Union Department, 815 16th Street Northwest, Room 301, Washington DC 20006. **Tel** (202)842-7860, FAX (202)842-7838. **ED** Richard Prosten. Index available. **Bk Rev. Circ:** 3,000 (ctrl).
    Desc: Reviews major issues in the pension and benefit fund area. Emphasis on labor's struggle to better workers' lives through progressive fund investment, administration, and design.

    ISSN 0023-6500
DD 331.155   US
LABOR ARBITRATION AWARDS. [Labor
arbitrat. awards]. **Main/Corp** Commerce Clearing House. (Jan. 6, 1961)-. English. Irregular. Commerce Clearing House Inc., 4025 West Peterson Avenue, Chicago IL 60646-6085. **Tel** (312)583-8500, FAX (708)940-4600. **ED** A. E. Schechter.
    Desc: Texts of current awards setting labor relations disputes selected to show resolution of personnel problems arising in everyday grievance situations.

    US
LABOR AREA SUMMARIES. (19??)-.
Periodical. English. Twelve times a year. Research and Analysis Branch, Washington State Employment Security Department, Box 9046, Olympia WA 98507. **Tel** (206)438-4800, FAX (206)438-4846.

    US
LABOR AREA SUMMARY. STATISTICAL REPORT. Added/Corp New York (State) Dept. of
Labor Division of Research and Statistics. **VFOAT** Statistical Report. (1992)-. Statistical Publication. English. Twelve times a year. New York State Department of Labor / Albany, 401 Harriman, Division of Research and Statistics, State Office Building Campus, Albany NY 12240. **Tel** (518)457-6649. *Continues* Labor Area Summary. Monthly Statistical Report.

LC HD5726.B76 M35A
DD 331.1/2/0974482   US
LABOR AREA TRENDS IN SUPPLY AND DEMAND : BROCKTON, MASSACHUSETTS, STANDARD METROPOLITAN STATISTICAL AREA.
Main/Corp Massachusetts. Division of Employment Security. (19??)-. Statistical Publication. English. Massachusetts Division of Employment Security, Boston MA 02114.

LC HD5718.M22 U545A
DD 331.12/09744/5   US
LABOR AREA TRENDS IN SUPPLY AND DEMAND : LAWRENCE-HAVERHILL, STANDARD METROPOLITAN STATISTICAL AREA. Main/Corp
Massachusetts. Division of Employment Security. (19??)-. Statistical Publication. English. Massachusetts Division of Employment Security, Boston MA 02114.

LC HD5725.M4 M37d
DD 331.1/2/0974461   US
LABOR AREA TRENDS IN SUPPLY AND DEMAND: MASSACHUSETTS/BOSTON AREA. Main/Corp Massachusetts. Division of
Employment Security. (19??)-. English. Massachusetts Division of Employment Security, Boston MA 02114.

LC HD6475.A1 L33
DD 331.88/091   BE
LABOR EDITION TRADE ACTION : MONTHLY REVIEW ON TRADE-UNION INFORMATION AND TRAINING, EDITED BY THE W.C.L. WORLD SECRETARIAT FOR TRADE ACTION. Added/Corp World
Secretariat for Trade Action. **VFOAT** Labor Inter-Trade Edition; Labor Intertrade Edition. (19??)-. Periodical. English (French, German, Spanish and Dutch). Six times a year. 600F Belgium; $15.00 US. World Confederation of Labour, 33 rue de Treves, B-1040 Brussels Belgium. **Tel** 011 32 2 230 62 95, FAX 011 32 2 230 87 22. Documents available from FAXON Xpress.
    Desc: Information on trade union and social situation all over the world.

LC HD6517.C2 L33
    US
LABOR EDUCATION NEWS. Added/Corp
University of California, Los Angeles. Institute of Industrial Relations. University of California, Los Angeles. Center for Labor Research and Education. **VFOAT** News, Labor Education. Vol. 1, No. 1 (Fall 1991)-. Periodical. English. Four times a year.

LC HD5725.W2 L3
    US
LABOR FORCE AND EMPLOYMENT IN WASHINGTON STATE. Added/Corp
Washington (State). Employment Security Dept. Labor Market and Economic Analysis Branch. (19??)-. Periodical. English. $5.00. Research and Analysis Branch, Washington State Employment Security Department, Box 9046, Olympia WA 98507. **Tel** (206)438-4800, FAX (206)438-4846.

LC HD5725.I6 I53A   ISSN 0362-3793
DD 331.1/1/09772   US
LABOR FORCE STATUS OF INDIANA RESIDENTS. Main/Corp Indiana. Employment
Security Division. (19??)-. English. One time a year. Indiana Employment Security Division, Research and Statistics Section, 10 North Senate Avenue, Indianapolis IN 46204. **Tel** (317)232-7187.

LC HD4802 .L435   ISSN 0023-656X
DD 331/.0973   US
    CCC
Pr Rev.
LABOR HISTORY. [Labor hist.]. Added/Corp
Tamiment Institute. Vol. 1 (Winter 1960)-. Periodical. English. Four times a year (Jan., May, July, Nov.). $52.00. Labor History, Box 1236, Washington CT 06793. **Tel** (203)868-7408, FAX (203)868-4846. **ED** Daniel J. Leab, (phone: (212)737-2715). Index available. cum. index. **Bk Rev**, (Qty: 60-70). **Ad Acc. Circ:** 2,000. available on microfilm and microfiche from University Microfilms International (UMI). Documents available from The Genuine Article, UMI Article Clearinghouse. *Supersedes* Labor Historian's Bulletin; *Absorbed* Newsletter (labor Historians).
    Desc: Articles, reviews, documents, and other notes on American working class history.
    Ind/Abst Acad. Abstr.; Acad. Ind. [Computer File] (1987-); Acad. Search; Altern. Press Index; Am. Hist. Life (1960-); Arts Humanit. Citation Index [Full Cov.]; Bus. Period. Index (1960-); Bus. Source Plus; Bus. Source; Curr. Contents Arts Humanit.; Curr. Contents Soc. Behav. Sci.; Econ. Lit. Index; EP Collect.; Expand. Acad. Index (1987-); Hist. Source (July 1990-); Homework Help.; Hum. Resour. Abstr. (1960-?); Humanit. Index; Humanit. Source; INFO-SOUTH Abstr.; J. Econ. Lit.; Mag. Search; MasterFile FullTEXT 1000; MasterFile FullTEXT 350; MasterFile FullTEXT 650; MasterFile FullTEXT (Jan. 1991-); Newsp. Period. Abstr. (1991-); OCLC; Person. Manage. Abstr.; Recent. Publ. Artic.; Res. Alert [Full Cov.]; Sage Urban Stud. Abstr (?-?); Soc. Sci. Source; Soc. Sci. Cit. Index [Full Cov.]; Telebase; West. Hist. Q.; Wilson Bus. Abstr.; Women Stud. Abstr. (1960-); Work Relat. Abstr.; Writ. Am. Hist.

LC JK2403 .A35 HD8008.A1   ISSN 0272-3689
DD 300/.973 S 331/.04135/0000973   US
LABOR-MANAGEMENT RELATIONS IN STATE AND LOCAL GOVERNMENTS.
See Business and Economics-Abstracting, Bibliographies and Statistics.

LC Z7164.C81 U4568 HD8005. D8005.6.U5   ISSN 0730-5486
DD 016.353001 S 016.33189/041353   US
LABOR-MANAGEMENT RELATIONS IN THE PUBLIC SERVICE.
(LABOR-MANAGEMENT RELATIONS IN THE PUBLIC SERVICE / OFFICE OF PERSONNEL MANAGEMENT, LIBRARY). **VAT** Labor Management Relations in the Public Service. (1972)-. English. One time a year. Office of Personnel Management, 1900 East Street Northwest, OELR Room 7429, Washington DC 20415. **Tel** (202)632-6256. *Continues* Employee-Management Relations in the Public Service.

    US
LABOR MANAGEMENT RELATIONS ISSUES IN STATE AND LOCAL GOVERNMENTS. Added/Corp United States. Civil
Service Commission. Bureau of Intergovernmental Personnel Programs. No. 1 (1976)-. Periodical. English. One time a year. US Civil Service Commission Bureau of Intergovernmental Personnel Programs, 1900 E Street NW, Washington DC 20415.

LC HD5725.O35 L33
DD 331.12/5/09766021   US
LABOR MARKET INFORMATION.
Added/Corp Oklahoma Employment Security Commission. Economic Research & Analysis Division. **VFOAT** LMI; Oklahoma Labor Market; Labor Market Newsletter. Vol. 2, Issue 4 (Apr. 1992)-. Periodical. English. Twelve times a year. Free on request. Oklahoma Employment Security Commission, Will Rogers Building, Room 310, Oklahoma City OK 73105. **Tel** (405)521-3735. *Continues* Labor Market Information Newsletter.

LC Z7164.L1 A43   ISSN 1063-3804
DD 331   US
LABOR MARKET INFORMATION DIRECTORY. [Labor mark. infor. dir.]. Main/Corp
Alaska. Dept. of Labor. Research and Analysis Section. **Added/Corp** Alaska Occupational Information Coordinating Committee. Alaska State Employment Service. Alaska. Dept. of Labor. Research and Analysis Section. **VFOAT** Training Info & Labor Market Information Directory. (1991)-. English. Free. Alaska Department of Labor, Administrative Services, Research & Analysis Section, PO Box 25501, Juneau AK 99802-5501. **Tel** (907)465-4500, FAX (907)465-2101. *Continues* Alaska. Dept. of Labor. Research and Analysis Section. Product and Information Directory.

LC HD5725.V8 V53D
DD 331.11/09755   US
LABOR MARKET INFORMATION FOR AFFIRMATIVE ACTION PROGRAMS.
Main/Corp Virginia Employment Commission. Manpower Research Division. (19??)-. English. Virginia Employment Commission, 703 East Main Street, PO Box 1358, Richmond VA 23211.

LC HD5725.V8 L32
DD 331.12/09755   US
LABOR MARKET INFORMATION FOR AFFIRMATIVE ACTION PROGRAMS (VIRGINIA EMPLOYMENT COMMISSION. MANPOWER RESEARCH DIVISION). (LABOR MARKET
INFORMATION FOR AFFIRMATIVE ACTION PROGRAMS. SUPPLEMENT.). English. One time a year. Virginia Employment Commission, 703 East Main Street, PO Box 1358, Richmond VA 23211.

LC HD5726.B76 M37a
DD 331.1/2/0974482   US
LABOR MARKET INFORMATION REVIEW: BROCKTON, MASSACHUSETTS, STANDARD METROPOLITAN STATISTICAL AREA.
Main/Corp Massachusetts. Labor Area Research Dept. **Added/Corp** Massachusetts. Labor Area Research Dept. Labor Market Information Review: Brockton. **VFOAT** Labor Market Information Review: Brockton. (19??)-. Statistical Publication. English. Four times a year. Labor Area Research Department, Massachusetts Division of Employment Security, Charles F Hurley Building, Cambridge Street, Boston MA 02114.

LC HD5725.M4 M377B
DD 331.1/2/09744   US
LABOR MARKET INFORMATION REVIEW : COMMONWEALTH OF MASSACHUSETTS. Main/Corp Massachusetts.
Labor Area Research Dept. **VFOAT** Labor Market Information Review: Massachusetts. (19??)-. Periodical. English. Four times a year. Labor Area Research Department, Massachusetts Division of Employment Security, Charles F Hurley Building, Cambridge Street, Boston MA 02114.

LC HD5726.F34 M38B
DD 331.1/2/0974484   US
LABOR MARKET INFORMATION REVIEW : LABOR MARKET AREA, FALL RIVER, MASSACHUSETTS-RHODE ISLAND. Main/Corp Massachusetts. Labor Area
Research Dept. **VFOAT** Labor Market Information Review: Fall River. (19??)-. Periodical. English. Four times a year. Labor Area Research Department, Massachusetts Division of Employment Security, Charles F Hurley Building, Cambridge Street, Boston MA 02114.

LC HD5726.N35 M37A
DD 331.1/2/0974485   US
LABOR MARKET INFORMATION REVIEW : LABOR MARKET AREA, NEW BEDFORD, MASSACHUSETTS. Main/Corp
Massachusetts. Labor Area Research Dept. **VFOAT** Labor Market Information Review: New Bedford. (19??)-. English. Four times a year. Labor Area Research Department, Massachusetts Division of Employment Security, Charles F Hurley Building, Cambridge Street, Boston MA 02114.

LC HD5726.P63 M37A
DD 331.1/2/097441   US
LABOR MARKET INFORMATION REVIEW : LABOR MARKET AREA, PITTSFIELD, MASSACHUSETTS.
Main/Corp Massachusetts. Labor Area Research Dept. **VFOAT** Labor Market Information Review: Pittsfield. (19??)-. Periodical. English. Four times a year. Labor Area Research Department, Massachusetts Division of Employment Security, Charles F Hurley Building, Cambridge Street, Boston MA 02114.

LC HD5726.S72 M37b
DD 331.12/09744/26   US
LABOR MARKET INFORMATION REVIEW: LABOR MARKET AREA, SPRINGFIELD-CHICOPEE-HOLYOKE, MASSACHUSETTS. Main/Corp Massachusetts.
Labor Area Research Dept. **Added/Corp** Massachusetts. Labor Area Research Dept. Labor Market Information Review: Springfield, Chicopee, Holyoke. **VFOAT** Labor Market Information Review: Springfield, Chicopee,

Business and Economics —Labor

Holyoke. (19??)-. Periodical. English. Four times a year. Labor Area Research Department, Massachusetts Division of Employment Security, Charles F Hurley Building, Cambridge Street, Boston MA 02114.

LC HD5726.W67 M37A
DD 331.1/2/097443 US
LABOR MARKET INFORMATION REVIEW : LABOR MARKET AREA, WORCESTER, MASSACHUSETTS.
Main/Corp Massachusetts. Labor Area Research Dept. **VFOAT** Labor Market Information Review: Worcester. (19??)-. Periodical. English. Four times a year. Labor Area Research Department, Massachusetts Division of Employment Security, Charles F Hurley Building, Cambridge Street, Boston MA 02114.

LC HD5726.B65 M38A
DD 331.1/2/0974461 US
LABOR MARKET INFORMATION REVIEW : STANDARD METROPOLITAN STATISTICAL AREA, BOSTON, MASSACHUSETTS. Main/Corp Massachusetts. Labor Area Research Dept. **VFOAT** Labor Market Information Review: Boston. (19??)-. Statistical Publication. English. Four times a year. Labor Area Research Department, Massachusetts Division of Employment Security, Charles F Hurley Building, Cambridge Street, Boston MA 02114.

LC HD5726.F47 M37A
DD 331.1/2/097443 US
LABOR MARKET INFORMATION REVIEW : STANDARD METROPOLITAN STATISTICAL AREA, FITCHBURG-LEOMINSTER, MASSACHUSETTS. Main/Corp Massachusetts. Labor Area Research Dept. **VFOAT** Labor Market Information Review: Fitchburg, Leominster. (19??)-. Statistical Publication. English. Four times a year. Labor Area Research Department, Massachusetts Division of Employment Security, Charles F Hurley Building, Cambridge Street, Boston MA 02114.

LC HD5726.L38 M37A
DD 331.1/2/097445 US
LABOR MARKET INFORMATION REVIEW : STANDARD METROPOLITAN STATISTICAL AREA, LAWRENCE-HAVERHILL, MASSACHUSETTS. Main/Corp Massachusetts. Labor Area Research Dept. **VFOAT** Labor Market Information Review: Lawrence, Haverhill. (19??)-. Statistical Publication. English. Four times a year. Labor Area Research Department, Massachusetts Division of Employment Security, Charles F Hurley Building, Cambridge Street, Boston MA 02114.

LC HD5726.L83 M37A
DD 331.1/2/097444 US
LABOR MARKET INFORMATION REVIEW : STANDARD METROPOLITAN STATISTICAL AREA, LOWELL, MASSACHUSETTS. Main/Corp Massachusetts. Labor Area Research Dept. **VFOAT** Labor Market Information Review: Lowell. (19??)-. Statistical Publication. English. Four times a year. Labor Area Research Department, Massachusetts Division of Employment Security, Charles F Hurley Building, Cambridge Street, Boston MA 02114.
US

LABOR MARKET PLANNING INFORMATION : WISCONSIN STATE-LEVEL STATISTICAL REPORT / WISCONSIN DEPARTMENT OF INDUSTRY, LABOR AND HUMAN RELATIONS, DIVISION OF EMPLOYMENT AND TRAINING POLICY, LABOR MARKET INFORMATION BUREAU. Added/Corp Wisconsin. Dept. of Industry, Labor and Human Relations. Labor Market Information Section. (1991)-. Statistical Publication. English. Every 2 years. Wisconsin Department of Industry, Labor & Human Relations, 201 East Washington Avenue, PO Box 7944, Madison WI 53707-7944. **Tel** (608)266-0851. **Continues** Planning Information for Employment, Training and Industrial Development.

LC HD5725.I6 L28
DD 331.12/0772 US
LABOR MARKET REVIEW AND PLANNING INFORMATION. VFOAT Labor Market Review & Planning Information for Indiana and Balance of State. (19??)-. English. Research and Statistics Section / Indianapolis, Indiana Employment Security Division, 10 North Senate Avenue, Indianapolis IN 46204.

LC HD5726.S33 C34a ISSN 0192-9844
DD 331.1/2/0979476 US
LABOR MARKET REVIEW: SALINAS-SEASIDE-MONTEREY STANDARD METROPOLITAN STATISTICAL AREA. Main/Corp California. Coastal Area Labor Market Information Group. **Added/Corp** California. Coastal Area Labor Market Information Group. Salinas-Seaside-Monterey Standard Metropolitan Statistical Area. (1978)-. Statistical Publication. English. California Employment Data and Research Department, PO Box 7774, San Francisco CA 94120. **Continues** Area Manpower Review. Salinas-Seaside-Monterey Standard Metropolitan Statistical Area, 0145-7136.

LC HD5726.S4 C35A ISSN 0192-8295
DD 331.1/1/097946 US
LABOR MARKET REVIEW : SAN FRANCISCO-OAKLAND STANDARD METROPOLITAN STATISTICAL AREA. Main/Corp California. Coastal Area Labor Market Information Group. (1978)-. Statistical Publication. English. Coastal Area Labor Market Info Group, PO Box 7774, San Francisco CA 94120. **Continues** Area Manpower Review. San Francisco-Oakland Standard Metropolitan Statistical Area, 0145-711X.

LC HD5726.S42 C24A ISSN 0192-9739
DD 331.1/09794/74 US
LABOR MARKET REVIEW : SAN JOSE STANDARD METROPOLITAN STATISTICAL AREA. Main/Corp California. Coastal Area Labor Market Information Group. 1978-. Statistical Publication. English. California Employment Data and Research Department, PO Box 7774, San Francisco CA 94120. **Continues** Area Manpower Review. San Jose Standard Metropolitan Statistical Area, 0145-6512.

LC HD5726.S45 C25a
DD 331.1/09794/71 US
LABOR MARKET REVIEW: SANTA CRUZ STANDARD METROPOLITAN STATISTICAL AREA. Main/Corp California. Coastal Area Labor Market Information Group. **Added/Corp** California. Coastal Area Labor Market Information Group. Santa Cruz Standard Metropolitan Statistical Area. (1978)-. Statistical Publication. English. California Employment Data and Research Department, PO Box 7774, San Francisco CA 94120. **Continues** Area Manpower Review. Santa Cruz Standard Metropolitan Statistical Area, 0145-6695.

LC HD5726.S47 C25A
DD 331.1/09794/18 US
LABOR MARKET REVIEW : SANTA ROSA STANDARD METROPOLITAN STATISTICAL AREA. Main/Corp California. Coastal Area Labor Market Information Group. 1977/78-. Statistical Publication. English. California Employment Data and Research Department, PO Box 7774, San Francisco CA 94120. **Continues** Area Manpower Review. Santa Rosa Standard Metropolitan Statistical Area, 0145-6377.

LC HD5726.V34 C33a
DD 331.1/09794/52 US
LABOR MARKET REVIEW: VALLEJO-FAIRFIELD-NAPA STANDARD METROPOLITAN STATISTICAL AREA. Main/Corp California. Coastal Area Labor Market Information Group. **Added/Corp** California. Coastal Area Labor Market Information Group. Vallejo-Fairfield-Napa Standard Metropolitan Statistical Area. (1978)-. Statistical Publication. English. California Employment Data and Research Department, PO Box 7774, San Francisco CA 94120. **Continues** Area Manpower Review. Vallejo-Fairfield-Napa Standard Metropolitan Statistical Area, 0145-7098.

ISSN 0892-4902
DD 331 US
LABOR MILITANT. Issue No. 1 (Apr./May/June 1986)-. Periodical. English. Six times a year. $7.50. Labor Militant Publications, PO Box 60, Brooklyn NY 11222.

LC Discard ISSN 0275-4452
US
LABOR NOTES (DETROIT, MICH.). (LABOR NOTES / LABOR EDUCATION & RESEARCH PROJECT.). [Labor notes]. **Added/Corp** Labor Education & Research Project (U.S.). (Feb. 20, 1979)-. Periodical. English. Twelve times a year. $30.00. Labor Education & Research Project, 7435 Michigan Avenue, Detroit MI 48210. **Tel** (313)842-6262, FAX (313)842-0227. **ED** James West. **Bk Rev. Circ:** 10,000.
Desc: News of the labor movement from a rank and file viewpoint.
Ind/Abst Altern. Press Index; Chicano Index.

ISSN 8755-1284
US
LABOR PAGE, THE. (THE LABOR PAGE : A PUBLICATION OF CITY LIFE.). **Added/Corp** City Life (Organization). Workplace Committee. No. 1 (Feb. 1982)-. Periodical. English (Spanish). Six times a year. $15.00. City Life, 335 Lamartine Street, Jamaica Plain MA 02130-2231. **Tel** (617)524-3541. **ED** Arvid Muller. **Bk Rev. Ad Acc. Circ:** 4,000.
Desc: Reports and analyzes the Boston area labor movement - what is happening to unions and to union workers.

ISSN 0075-7470
US
LABOR RELATIONS AND PUBLIC POLICY SERIES. Added/Corp Wharton School. Industrial Research Unit. Report No. 1 (1968)-. Monographic series. English. Irregular. Price varies per volume. University of Pennsylvania / Center for Human Resources, 3733 Spruce Street, 309 Vance Hall, Philadelphia PA 19104.
Desc: Books and monographs on the impact of legislation regulating labor-management relations.

US
LABOR RELATIONS TODAY (WASHINGTON, D.C.). (LABOR RELATIONS TODAY.). **Added/Corp** United States. Dept. of Labor. Bureau of Labor-Management Relations and Cooperative Programs. (19??)-. Periodical. English. Six times a year. Free on request. US Department of Labor, 200 Constitution Avenue NW, Washington DC 20210. **Tel** (202)219-7316, FAX (202)219-7312.

LC KF3352 .L3 ISSN 0891-4141
DD 344.73/018904/05 347.30418904/05 US
CCC
LABOR RELATIONS WEEK. [Labor relat. week]. **Added/Corp** Bureau of National Affairs (Washington, D.C.). Vol. 1, No. 1 (Jan. 7, 1987)-. Periodical. English. One time a week. $853.00. Bureau of National Affairs Inc., 9435 Key West Avenue, Rockville MD 20850. **Tel** (800)372-1033, (301)258-1033, FAX (301)948-5823. **ED** Susan J Sala. **Formed by the union of** Retail/Services Labor Report, 0148-7930 **and** White Collar Report, 0043-4892.
Desc: Reporting service that provides a comprehensive overview of developments influencing labor relations in the private sector.
Ind/Abst Int. Labour Doc.

LC HD5725.N7 A29 ISSN 0093-5034
DD 331.1/1/09747 US
LABOR RESEARCH REPORT (ALBANY). (LABOR RESEARCH REPORT.). (197?)-. English. New York State Department of Labor / Albany, 401 Harriman, Division of Research and Statistics, State Office Building Campus, Albany NY 12240. **Tel** (518)457-6649. **Continues** New York (State). Division of Employment. Research and Statistics Office. Research Bulletin.

LC HD4824.5.U5 L3 ISSN 0885-4238
DD 322 US
LABOR RESEARCH REVIEW. [Labor res. rev.]. **Added/Corp** Midwest Center for Labor Research (U.S.). Vol. 1, No. 1 (Fall 1982)-. Trade Publication. English. Two times a year. $24.00. Midwest Center Labor Research, 3411 West Diversey Avenue, Suite 14, Chicago IL 60647. **Tel** (312)278-5418, FAX (312)278-5918. **ED** Lisa Oppenheim. **Bk Rev. Ad Acc. Circ:** 4,000.
Desc: Written by and for labor leaders and activists, journalists and scholars. Covers labor strategies and economic development.
Ind/Abst Altern. Press Index; Am. Hist. Life (1985-); LABORDOC; Work Relat. Abstr.

LC HD4802 .L49 ISSN 0160-449X
DD 331/.05 US
CCC
LABOR STUDIES JOURNAL. [Labor stud. j.]. **Added/Corp** University and College Labor Education Association. Vol. 1 (May 1976)-. Periodical. English. Four times a year. $80.00. Transaction Publishers / Rutgers State University, Department 3091 or 3092, New Brunswick NJ 08903. **Tel** (908)932-2280 ext. 105, FAX (908)932-3138. **ED** Higdon C. Roberts, Jr. **Bk Rev. Ad Acc. Circ:** 800. available on labels; available on microfilm and microfiche from University Microfilms International (UMI).
Desc: Explores the role of the trade union movement in forging American economic and social policy. Provides basic information on the philosophy, history and substance of labor education. The official journal of the University and College Labor Education Association.
Ind/Abst Acad. Search; Am. Hist. Life (1983-); Bus. ASAP (1992-) [Full Txt.]; Bus. Index (1985-); Bus. Period. Index; Bus. Source Plus; Bus. Source; EP Collect.; Gen. BusinessFile (1985-); Gen. Period. Index (1985-); Homework Help.; Index Period. Artic. Relat. Law (1987-); INFO-SOUTH Abstr.; Int. Polit. Sci. Abstr. (1982-); Mag. Search; MasterFile FullTEXT 1000; MasterFile FullTEXT 350; MasterFile FullTEXT 650; MasterFile FullTEXT (July 1993-); OCLC; PAIS Int. Print (1991-); Person. Manage. Abstr.; Telebase; U.S. Polit. Sci. Doc.; Urban Aff. Abstr. (1982-); Wilson Bus. Abstr.; Work Relat. Abstr. (1976-).

Business and Economics —Labor

LC HD5723 .L33   ISSN 0882-0279
DD 331.12/0973   US
LABOR SURPLUS AREAS. VFOAT
Purchasing Agents Guide to Labor Surplus Areas. (1985)-. English. Three times a year (Jan., May, Sept.). $160.00. Business Research Services Inc, 4201 Connecticutt Avenue, Suite 610, Washington DC 20008. **Tel** (800)845-8420, (202)364-6473.

LC HD8072 .L2553   ISSN 0023-6659
   US
LABOR TRENDS (SOUTHFIELD, MICH.).
(LABOR TRENDS.). [Labor trends]. (19??)-. English. One time a week. $254.00. Business Research Publications, 1333 H Street Northwest, 2nd Floor West, Washington DC 20005. **Tel** (202)842-3022, (800)822-6338, FAX (202)842-3023. **Continues** Detroit Labor Trends.
Desc: A newsletter reporting and analyzing labor affairs for labor relations executives.

   ISSN 0890-6041
DD 331   US
   TITLE CHANGE
LABOR UNITY (U.S. ED.). (LABOR UNITY.).
[Labor unity]. **Added/Corp** Amalgamated Clothing and Textile Workers Union. (May 1982)-(June 1995). Periodical. English. Amalgamated Clothing and Textile Workers Union, 15 Union Square, New York NY 10003. **Tel** (212)242-0700. available on microfilm from The State Historical Society of Wisconsin. **Continues** Amalgamated Clothing and Textile Workers Union. ACTWU Labor Unity, 0271-5848. **Merged into** UNITE Magazine.
Ind/Abst Work Relat. Abstr.

   ISSN 0023-6667
   US
LABOR WORLD, THE. Added/Corp Duluth
Central Labor Body (Duluth, Minn.). Vol. 1, No. 1 (Apr. 11, 1896)-. Periodical. English. Twenty-five times a year. $10.00. Labor World, 2002 London Road, Room 102, Duluth MN 55812. **Tel** (218)728-4469. **ED** Larry Sillanpa. **Bk Rev. Ad Acc. Circ:** 14,000. available on microfilm.
Desc: Published by and for local unions affiliated with the Duluth AFL-CIO central labor body.

   SZ
LABORDOC [ONLINE DATABASE]. See
Business and Economics-Abstracting, Bibliographies and Statistics.

   ISSN 0210-1718
   SP
UDC 631
LABOREO. [Laboreo]. (1969)-. Periodical. Spanish.
Twelve times a year. $187.00. Laboreo SL, Orellana 10, 28004 Madrid Spain. **Tel** 011 34 1 3081898.

LC HD6350.B89 I53   ISSN 0023-6888
DD 331.8819   US
LABORER (WASHINGTON), THE. (THE
LABORER.). Vol. 1 (June 1947)-. Periodical. English. Twelve times a year. Laborers International Union of North America, 905 16th Street NW, Washington DC 20006. **Tel** (202)737-8320.
Ind/Abst Work Relat. Abstr.

   US
LABORERS' BENEFITS REVIEW. VFOAT
Benefits Review. Vol. 1, No. 1 (June 1988)-. Periodical. English. Laborers International Union of North America, 905 16th Street NW, Washington DC 20006. **Tel** (202)737-8320.
Ind/Abst Work Relat. Abstr. (-19??).

   US
LABORITE. (19??)-. Periodical. English. One time a
year. Laborite, George Meany Center, 10000 New Hampshire Avenue, Silver Spring MD 20903.

LC HD8051 .L33   ISSN 1041-5904
DD 331.88/0973/05   US
LABOR'S HERITAGE. [Labor's herit.].
Added/Corp George Meany Memorial Archives. Vol. 1, No. 1 (Jan. 1989)-. Periodical. English. Four times a year. $19.95. George Meany Center for Labor Studies, 10000 New Hampshire Avenue, Silver Springs MD 20903. **Tel** (301)431-5457, FAX (301)431-0385. **ED** Stuart Kaufman. **Circ:** 12,000.
Desc: Brings public attention to the heritage of the American workers.
Ind/Abst Am. Hist. Life (1989-); Work Relat. Abstr.

   ISSN 0711-3889
DD 331.1/09713   CN
LABOUR ADVOCATE (ST.
CATHARINES). (LABOUR ADVOCATE / THE ST. CATHARINES AND DISTRICT LABOUR COUNCIL.). [Labour advocate]. **VFOAT** Advocate. **VAT** Advocate (St. Catharines). Vol. 1, No. 1 (Mar. 1981)-. Periodical.

English. Four times a year. Free. St. Catharines and District Lobour Council, 76 Queenston Street, St. Catharines Ontario L2R 2Z2 Canada. ctrl circ.

   IT
LABOUR AND EMPLOYMENT POLICIES IN ITALY. VFOAT Report on Labour
and Employment Policies in Italy. (1987)-. English. One time a year. Free on request. Min Lavoro Gabin Uff Affari, Interni Via Flavia 6, 00187 Rome Italy.

LC HD4904 .L32   ISSN 1030-1763
   AT
LABOUR & INDUSTRY. Added/Corp Griffith
University. Sociological Association of Australia and New Zealand. Association of Industrial Relations Academics of Australia and New Zealand. **VFOAT** Labour and Industry. Vol. 1, No. 1 (Oct. 1987)-. Periodical. English. Three times a year. 53.44Aus$. Labour and Industry, School of Soc Inquiry, Deakin University, Geelong VIC 3217 Australia. **Tel** 011 61 52 272541, FAX 011 61 52 272018. **ED** Ray Jureidini. **Bk Rev. Ad Acc.**
Ind/Abst APAIS, Aust. Public Aff. Inf. Ser. (1993-).

LC HD5822.6 .A26   ISSN 0127-0362
DD 331/.09595   MY
LABOUR AND MANPOWER REPORT / MINISTRY OF LABOUR AND
MANPOWER. English. One time a year. $10.16. Research and Planning Division / Kuala Lumpur, Ministry of Labour and Manpower, 8th Floor/Wisma MPI, Kuala Lumpur Malaysia.

   ISSN 0706-1706
DD 331.1/09172/4   CN
LABOUR CAPITAL AND SOCIETY.
(LABOUR CAPITAL AND SOCIETY. TRAVAIL CAPITAL ET SOCIETE.). [Labour cap. soc.]. **Added/Corp** McGill University. Centre for Developing-Area Studies. **VFOAT** Travail Capital et Societe. **VAT** Travail Capital et Societe. Vol. 12, No. 2 (April 1979)-. Periodical. English (French). Two times a year. 27.00Can$. McGill University / Centre for Developing Area Studies, 3715 Peel Street Room 219, Montreal H3A 1X1 Canada. **Tel** (514)398-3508. **ED** Rosalind E. Boyd. Index available. cum. index. **Bk Rev. Circ:** 900 (ctrl). **Continues** Manpower and Unemployment Research, 0702-7605.
Desc: Articles, as well as book reviews and bibliographical entries, on labor issues in developing areas, especially the Third World.
Ind/Abst Altern. Press Index; Appl. Soc. Sci. Index Abstr.; Geogr. Abstr. Human Geogr.; Hum. Resour. Abstr. (?-?); Int. Bibliogr. Sociol.; Int. Dev. Abstr.; Int. Labour Doc.; LABORDOC; Rural Dev. Abstr.; Soc. Plann. Policy Dev. Abstr.; Sociol. Abstr.; World Agric. Econ. Rural Sociol. Abstr.

LC HD8682 .L28

   II
LABOUR CHRONICLE. Vol. 1 (1968)-.
Periodical. English. Twelve times a year. Institute of Workers Education, Rajawadi Bombay, 400077 India. **Tel** 525253.

   ISSN 0226-2290
DD 331/.0971   CN
LABOUR COMMENTARY. [Labour comment.].
No. 1 (Mar. 1980)-. Periodical. English. Four times a year. Free. Waldie, Brennan and Associates, Ontario M4P 2A6 Canada.

LC HD5701 .L32   ISSN 0927-5371
   NE
   CCC
   CODEN LECOE3
Pr Rev.
●LABOUR ECONOMICS. Vol. 1, No. 1 (June
1993)-. Academic Scholarly Publication. English. Four times a year (1 volume). $210.00. Elsevier Science Publishers BV, PO Box 211, 1000 AE Amsterdam Netherlands. **Tel** 011 31 20 4853641, 011 31 20 4853642, FAX 011 31 20 4853598. available on an online database from Elsevier Electronic Subscriptions (EES).

LC LC5001 .L32   ISSN 0378-5467
DD 331.25/9   SZ
   CCC
LABOUR EDUCATION. [Labour educ.].
Added/Corp International Labour Office. Workers' Education Branch. (1964)-. Periodical. English (French and Spanish). Four times a year. $40.00. International Labour Office - ILO, Publications Sales Service, CH-1211 Geneva 22 Switzerland. **Tel** 011 41 22 7996111, FAX 011 41 22 7986253, telex 415 647 ilo ch. **(Subscription address:** International Labour Office / Washington, DC, 1828 L Street Northwest, Suite 801, Washington DC 20036. **Tel** (202)653-7652.) available on microfilm and microfiche from University Microfilms International (UMI). **Continues** Bulletin (International Labour Office. Workers' Education Branch).
Desc: Designed to promote the educational activities of trade union organizations and other workers' education bodies. Current developments in the labour world, activities of the ILO, methods and techniques of workers'

education, labour history and book reviews.
Ind/Abst Curr. Index J. Educ.; Int. Labour Doc.; LABORDOC.

   SA
LABOUR FOCUS / ARBEIDS-FOKUS.
(19??)-. Newsletter. English (Afrikaans). Twelve times a year. Department of Labour / Pretoria, Private Bag X117, Pretoria 0001 South Africa. **Tel** 011 27 012 3106-250, FAX 011 27 012 3202-059. **ED** Francois de Villiers.
Desc: Discusses issues regarding the labor force and gives statistics on employment.

LC DJK1 .L3
DD 947/.0005   UK
LABOUR FOCUS ON EASTERN
EUROPE. Vol. 1 (March/Apr. 1977)-. Periodical. English. Three times a year. $59.89. Labour Focus on Eastern Europe, 30 Bridge Street, Oxford OX2 0BA United Kingdom. **Tel** 011 44 1865 723207. **ED** Gus Fagan.

LC HD5743 .A33a
DD 331.11/097292   JM
LABOUR FORCE, THE. Added/Corp Jamaica.
Dept. of Statistics. Statistical Institute of Jamaica. (19??)-. English. One time a year. 38.50Jam$ Jamaica; $7.00 US. Department of Statistics / Jamaica, Print Section, 84 Hannover Street, Kingston Jamaica. **Tel** (809)92-28371. **ED** Vernon James. **Bk Rev. Ad Acc. Circ:** 500.
Desc: The publication deals with the labor force employed by age, sex, parish, occupation group and industry group. It also gives the unemployed figures by age, occupation group and industry group.

   AT
LABOUR FORCE. See Business and
Economics-Abstracting, Bibliographies and Statistics.

   ISSN 1181-6627
DD 331.12/5/0971021   CN
LABOUR FORCE ANNUAL AVERAGES.
See Business and Economics-Abstracting, Bibliographies and Statistics.

LC HA867 .A385 HD5745.T72
DD 317.29/83 S 331./1/0972983   TR
LABOUR FORCE BY SEX. See Business and
Economics-Abstracting, Bibliographies and Statistics.

   ISSN 0708-3157
DD 331.11/0971   CN
LABOUR FORCE INFORMATION. See
Business and Economics-Abstracting, Bibliographies and Statistics.

LC HD5727 .A33   ISSN 0380-6804
DD 331.1/0971   CN
LABOUR FORCE (MONTHLY ED.). See
Business and Economics-Abstracting, Bibliographies and Statistics.

LC HD5764.A6 O58   ISSN 0474-5515
   FR
LABOUR FORCE STATISTICS. Added/Corp
Organisation for Economic Co-Operation and Development. Organisation for Economic Co-Operation and Development. Economic Statistics and National Accounts Division. Organisation for Economic Co-Operation and Development. Structural Statistics Section. **VFOAT** Statistiques de la Population Active. (1956/66)-. English (French). One time a year (published in July). $96.00 all except Canada. OECD Publications and Information Center, 2 rue Andre-Pascal, 75775 Paris Cedex 16 France. **Tel** 011 33 1 49104262, US:(202)785-6323, FAX 011 33 1 45248500, 011 33 1 45248176, telex 620 160 OCDE. **(Subscription address:** OECD Publications Center, 2001 L Street, Suite 700, Washington DC 20036. **Tel** (202)822-3873, (202)785-6323.) **Continues** Manpower Statistics.
Desc: OECD's annual statistical report on the labor forces of its member countries.

LC HD5850 .A56
DD 312/.9   AT
LABOUR FORCE STATUS AND OTHER CHARACTERISTICS OF FAMILIES / AUSTRALIAN BUREAU OF STATISTICS.
See Business and Economics-Abstracting, Bibliographies and Statistics.

LC HD5768 .A38
DD 331.11/09417   IE
LABOUR FORCE SURVEY (IRELAND. CENTRAL STATISTICS OFFICE). (LABOUR
FORCE SURVEY.). **Added/Corp** Ireland. Central Statistics Office. (19??)-. English. One time a year. Government Publications, 4 5 Harcourt Road, Dublin 2 Ireland. **Tel** 011 353 1 6613111 ext.4005. **ED** D. Garvey. **Circ:** 600. available on diskette.

   ISSN 0700-3862
DD 331/.0971   CN
   CCC
Pr Rev.
LABOUR (HALIFAX). (LABOUR. LE TRAVAIL.).
[Labour]. **Added/Corp** Comite sur l'Histoire Ouvriere Canadienne. **VFOAT** Travail; Travailleur. **VAT** Labour (St. John's). Vol. 1, (1976)-. Periodical. French (English). Two

times a year (Spring and Fall). 35.00Can$ (institutions), 25.00Can$ (individuals). Memorial University / Department of History, St. John's Newfoundland A1C 5S7 Canada. **Tel** (709)737-2144, FAX (709)737-4342, telex 016-4101. **ED** Gregory S. Kealey. **Bk Rev. Ad Acc, Adv Mgr:** Irene Whitfield, **Tel** (709)737-2144. **Circ:** 1,000 (ctrl). available on microfilm and microfiche from University Microfilms International (UMI). ***Absorbed*** *Comite sur l'Histoire Ouvriere Canadienne. Bulletin of the Committee on Canadian Labour History., 0701-161X.*
Ind/Abst Altern. Press Index; Am. Hist. Life (1976-); Curr. Contents Arts Humanit.; Soc. Sci. Cit. Index [Select. Cov.]; Work Relat. Abstr.

LC HD8101 .L22 **ISSN** 0700-3862
DD 331/.0971 CN
CCC
Pr Rev.
LABOUR (HALIFAX). (LABOUR / LE TRAVAILLEUR.). [Labour]. **Added/Corp** Committee on Canadian Labour History. **VFOAT** Travailleur; La Travailleur; Travail. **VAT** Labour (St. John's). Vol. 1, (1976)-. English (French). Two times a year (Spring and Fall). 50.00Can$. Memorial University / Department of History, St. John's Newfoundland A1C 5S7 Canada. **Tel** (709)737-2144, FAX (709)737-4342, telex 016-4101. **ED** Gregory S. Kealey. Index available. **Bk Rev**, (Qty: 70). **Ad Acc. Circ:** 1,200. available on microfiche. Documents available from The Genuine Article. ***Absorbed*** *Committee on Canadian Labour History. Bulletin of the Committee on Canadian Labour History, 0701-161X.*
Desc: Dedicated to the broad, interdisciplinary study of Canadian labor history. Holding to no rigid position on the definition of labor, the editorial board hopes to foster imaginative approaches to both teaching and research in labor studies through an open exchange of viewpoints.
Ind/Abst Altern. Press Index (199?-); Am. Hist. Life; Arts Humanit. Citation Index [Full Cov.]; Can. Period. Index; Curr. Contents Arts Humanit.; Econ. Lit. Index (199?-); Hum. Resour. Abstr. (?-?); Int. Bibliogr. Sociol.; J. Econ. Lit.; Res. Alert [Full Cov.]; Sage Public Adm. Abstr. (?-?).

LC HD6891.A13 L3 **ISSN** 0023-6942
DD 331.88/0994 AT
LABOUR HISTORY (CANBERRA). (LABOUR HISTORY.). [Labour hist.]. **Added/Corp** Australian Society for the Study of Labour History. No. 4 (May 1963)-. Periodical. English. Two times a year. 45.00Aus$. Labour History, Faculty of Economics HO3, University of Sydney, NSW 2006 Australia. **Tel** 011 61 2 3513786, telex 26169. **ED** Terry Irving. **Bk Rev. Ad Acc. Circ:** 600. ***Continues*** *Australian Society for the Study of Labour History. Bulletin.*
Desc: A journal of labor and social history.
Ind/Abst Am. Hist. Life (1975-); APAIS, Aust. Public Aff. Inf. Ser. (1963-); SportSearch (1975-); Work Relat. Abstr. (1975-).

LC HD4805 .S6
DD 331/.09 UK
Pr Rev.
LABOUR HISTORY REVIEW. Added/Corp Society for the Study of Labour History. Vol. 55, Pt. 1 (Spring 1990)-. Periodical. English. Three times a year. $42.78. SUBIS, Mansion House 19 Kingfield Road, Sheffield S11 9AS United Kingdom. **Tel** 011 44 114 2554433, FAX 011 44 114 255 4626. **ED** John L. Halstead, Alan Campbell, Laurence Marlow, David Martin. available on microfiche. ***Continues*** *Society for the Study of Labour History. Bulletin - Society for the Study of Labour History, 0049-1179.*
Desc: An interdisciplinary tool of the trade for study of British and other labour or social movements and working class history.
Ind/Abst Am. Hist. Life (1965-).

LC HD6961.A1 I73 **ISSN** 0538-8325
DD 331 SZ
LABOUR-MANAGEMENT RELATIONS SERIES. Added/Corp International Labour Office. International Labour Organisation. **VFOAT** Labour Management Relations Series. No. 1 (1957)-. Monographic series. English. Irregular. Price varies per volume. International Labour Office - ILO, Publications Sales Service, CH-1211 Geneva 22 Switzerland. **Tel** 011 41 22 7996111, FAX 011 41 22 7986253, telex 415 647 ilo ch.
Desc: Occasional monographs and reports on labor-management relations.

FR
LABOUR MARKET AND SOCIAL POLICY OCCASIONAL PAPERS / ORGANISATION FOR ECONOMIC CO-OPERATION AND DEVELOPMENT. Added/Corp Organisation for Economic Co-Operation and Development. Directorate for Social Affairs, Manpower, and Education. **VFOAT** Occasional Papers. No. 1 (June 1990)-. Monographic series. English (French). Irregular. Price varies per volume. OECD Publications and Information Center, 2 rue Andre-Pascal, 75775 Paris Cedex 16 France. **Tel** 011 33 1 49104262, US:(202)785-6323, FAX 011 33 1 45248500, 011 33 1 45248176, telex 620 160 OCDE. **(Subscription address:** OECD Publications Center, 2001 L Street, Suite 700, Washington DC 20036. **Tel** (202)822-3873, (202)785-6323.**)**

ISSN 1187-4457
DD 331.12/0971/05 CN
LABOUR MARKET DEVELOPMENTS. [Labour mark. dev.]. **Added/Corp** Canada. Library of Parliament. Research Branch. (Apr. 24 1991)-. Periodical. English. ***Continues*** *Labour Market, Recent Developments., 1185-3972.*

ISSN 0952-2506
UK
LABOUR MARKET QUARTERLY REPORT. GREAT BRITAIN. [Labour mark. q. rep., G.B.]. (198?)-. Periodical. English. Four times a year (Feb., May, Aug., Nov.). Free on request. Meads, PO Box 12, West PDO Leengate, Nottinghamshire NG7 2GB United Kingdom. **Tel** 011 44 1115 9244090.
Ind/Abst HILITES.

LC HD5768 .A385
DD 331.12/09415/05 IE
LABOUR MARKET REVIEW. Added/Corp Ireland. Training & Employment Authority. **VFOAT** FAS Labour Market Review. **VAT** Foras Aiseanna Saothair Labour Market Review. Issue No. 1 (June 1990)-. Periodical. English. Twenty-four times a year. Labour Market Review, c/o Planning & Research Department, 27-33 Upper Baggot Street, Dublin 4 Ireland.
Ind/Abst Int. Labour Doc.; LABORDOC.

LC HD8381 .A17
DD 331/.0941 UK
•**LABOUR MARKET TRENDS.** (1995)-. English. Twelve times a year. £58.00. Harrington and Kilbride, Highbury Station Road, London N1 1SE United Kingdom. **Tel** 011 44 171 2262222. ***Continues*** *Employment Gazette.*

AT
LABOUR NETWORK. English. Three times a year (Apr., Aug., Oct.). 20.00Aus$. Evatt Foundation, 377-383 Sussex Street, Level 6, Sydney New South Wales, 2000 Australia. **Tel** 011 61 2 261-4766, FAX 011 61 2 261-4835. **ED** Brett Evans. **Bk Rev**, (Qty: 3-4). **Ad Acc. Circ:** 400 (ctrl).

ISSN 0832-6223
DD 331/.0971 CN
LABOUR NEWS & GRAPHICS. [Labour news graph.]. **VFOAT** LNG. Vol. 1, No. 1 (June 1986)-. Periodical. English (French). Twelve times a year. $125.00 North America; $150.00 other. Canadian Association of Labour Media, 2841 Riverside Drive, Ottawa Ontario K1V 8X7 Canada. **Tel** (416)762-6947. **ED** Art Kilgour. **Bk Rev. Circ:** 200. ***Continues*** *Labour News (Canadian Association of Labour Media), 0713-3405.*
Desc: A co-operative news, features and graphics service published by the Canadian Association of Labor Media for its members.

CN
LABOUR RELATIONS BULLETIN. (19??)-. Bulletin. English. Twenty-six times a year. 275.00Can$. Ontario Hospital Association, 150 Ferrand Drive, Don Mills Ontario M3C 1H6 Canada. **Tel** (905)429-2661 ext. 7736. **ED** Danielle Giroux. Index available. ctrl circ.
Desc: Summary of rights arbitration cases in Ontario hospitals. Covers interest arbitration awards, negotiated settlements, OLRB cases and judicial review.

LC HD4805 .L34 **ISSN** 0023-7000
DD 331.05 UK
LABOUR RESEARCH (LONDON). (LABOUR RESEARCH.). [Labour res.]. (1930)-. Trade Publication. English. Twelve times a year. $45.35. Labour Research Department, 78 Blackfriars Road, London SE1 8HF United Kingdom. **Tel** 011 44 171 9283649, FAX 011 44 171 9280621. **ED** Clare Ruhemann. Index available. **Bk Rev. Ad Acc. Circ:** 9,000 (ctrl).
Desc: Political, social, industrial and economic news and analysis for trade unionists and labour movement activists.
Ind/Abst Appl. Soc. Sci. Index Abstr.; Curr. Cit.; PAIS Int. Print; Sage Race Relat. Abstr.; School Organ. Manage. Abstr.

ISSN 0229-2726
DD 331/.05 CN
LABOUR REVIEW / ST. CATHARINES AND DISTRICT LABOUR COUNCIL. [Labour rev. - St. Catharines Dist. Counc.]. **VAT** St. Catharines and District Labour Council Labour Review. English. One time a year. Free. St. Catharines and District Labour Council, 76 Queenston, St. Catharines Ontario L2R 2Z2 Canada. ctrl circ.

ISSN 1121-7081
IT
UDC 331 CCC
LABOUR ROMA. (LABOUR.). (1987)-. Academic Scholarly Publication. English. Three times a year. $77.00 North America; £51.00 other. Basil Blackwell Publishers Ltd., 108 Cowley Road, Oxford 0X4 1JF United Kingdom. **Tel** 011 44 1235 465500, FAX 011 44 1235 465556, telex 837022 OXBOOK G. **(Subscription address:** Blackwell Publishers / UK, 108 Cowley Road, Oxford OX4 1JF United Kingdom. **Tel** 011 44 1865 791100, FAX 011 44 1865 791347.**)**

LC HD4811 .L3 **ISSN** 1121-7081
DD 331/.094/05 IT
CCC
LABOUR (ROME, ITALY). (LABOUR.). **Added/Corp** Fondazione Giacomo Brodolini. **VFOAT** Review of Labour Economics and Industrial Relations. Vol. 1, No. 1 (Spring 1987)-. Periodical. English. Three times a year. $88.00. Basil Blackwell Publishers Ltd., 108 Cowley Road, Oxford 0X4 1JF United Kingdom. **Tel** 011 44 1235 465500, FAX 011 44 1235 465556, telex 837022 OXBOOK G. **(Subscription address:** Marston Book Services Ltd., PO Box 87, Oxford OX2 0DT United Kingdom. **Tel** 011 44 1865 791155.**)**
Desc: Review of economics and industrial relations.
Ind/Abst PAIS Int. Print.

ISSN 0709-0862
DD 331/.0971 CN
LABOUR SCENE, THE. Vol. 1 (Apr. 1979)-. Periodical. English. Twelve times a year. $90.00. Labour Research Associates, PO Box 4737 Station E, Ottawa K1S 5H9 Canada.

ISSN 0576-1123
CN
LABOUR STANDARDS IN CANADA. Main/Corp Canada. Dept. of Labour. Legislative Research Branch. (1970)-. English. Irregular. 9.95Can$ Canada; 11.94Can$ other. Canada Communication Group Publishers, Order Processing, Ottawa Ontario K1A 0S9 Canada. **Tel** (819)956-4800, (819)956-4802. ***Supersedes*** *Canada. Dept. of Labour. Legislation Branch. Labour Standards in Canada., 0576-1123.*

LC HD5811.95 .A35 **ISSN** 0255-8386
DD 331.12/5/095645021 CY
LABOUR STATISTICS. Added/Corp Cyprus. Tmema Statistikes kai Ereunon. (1986)-. English. ***Continues*** *Labour Statistics Report for ... .*

LC HD8841 .A32a **ISSN** 0314-2779
DD 331/.0994/021 AT
LABOUR STATISTICS ... AUSTRALIA. **See** Business and Economics-Abstracting, Bibliographies and Statistics.

LC HD5091.Z9 S673A
DD 331.2/968 SA
LABOUR STATISTICS : WAGE RATES, EARNINGS AND AVERAGE HOURS WORKED IN THE PRINTING AND NEWSPAPER INDUSTRY, ENGINEERING INDUSTRY, BUILDING INDUSTRY AND COMMERCE. **See** Business and Economics-Abstracting, Bibliographies and Statistics.

ISSN 0817-8798
DD 322.20994 AT
LABOUR STUDIES BRIEFING. **See** Political Science-International Relations.

ISSN 0229-4567
DD 331.2/8684/0971 CN
LABOUR SURVEY (SOCIETY OF THE PLASTICS INDUSTRY OF CANADA). (LABOUR SURVEY / SOCIETY OF THE PLASTICS INDUSTRY OF CANADA.). [Labour surv.]. **Added/Corp** Society of the Plastics Industry of Canada. **VFOAT** Annual Labour Survey for Plastics Processing Companies; Annual Labour Survey ... for Plastics Processing Companies. **VAT** Society of the Plastics Industry of Canada Labour Survey; Societe des Industries du Plastiques du Canada Labour Survey. (1972)-. English. One time a year. $125.00. Society of the Plastics Industry of Canada, 1262 Don Mills Road, Suite 104, Don Mills Ontario, M3B 2W7 Canada. **Tel** (416)449-3444, FAX (416)449-5685, telex 06- 966739. **ED** F.R. Shammas.

ISSN 1194-6237
DD 344.71/01133/0264 CN
LANCASTER'S EMPLOYMENT EQUITY REPORTER. [Lancaster's employ. equity report.]. **Added/Corp** Lancaster House (Firm). **VFOAT** Employment Equity Reporter. Vol. 1, No. 9 (Sept. 1992)-. Periodical. English. Eleven times a year. 145.00Can$. Lancaster House Publishing, 20 Dundas Street West, Box 133, Toronto Ontario M5G 2G8 Canada. **Tel** (416)977-6618, FAX (416)977-5873. ***Continues*** *Employment Equity Reporter., 1194-6229.*

LC HD6668.A3 L3
DD 331.8813 UK
LANDWORKER, THE. Added/Corp National Union of Agricultural Workers (Gt. Brit.). **VFOAT** Land Worker. (May 1919)-. Trade Publication. English. Six times a year. $10.27. Landworker, Transport House, Smith Square, London SW1P 3JB United Kingdom. **Tel** 011 44 171 8287788, FAX 011 44 171 6305861, telex 919009. **ED** Bridget Henderson. Index available. cum. index. **Bk Rev. Circ:** 25,000 (ctrl). ***Absorbed*** *Labourer.*
Desc: Covers trade union, agricultural and labor movement news.

US

Business and Economics —Labor

LANSING'S LABOR MARKET NEWS.
Added/Corp Michigan Employment Security Commission. Bureau of Research and Statistics. Information and Reports Section. Vol. 12, No. 1 (Mar. 1992)-. Periodical. English. Twelve times a year. Detroit Employment Security Commission, 7310 Woodward Castro, Room 520, Detroit MI 48202. **Tel** (313)876-5427. *Continues* Lansing Labor Market Review.
LC HD5824 .A32A
IO

LAPORAN DEPARTEMEN TENAGA KERJA, TRANSMIGRASI DAN KOPERASI. **Main/Corp** Indonesia. Departemen Tenaga Kerja, Transmigrasi dan Koperasi. Periodical. Indonesian. Departemen Tenaga Kerja, Jalan H Agus Salim No 58, Jakarta Indonesia.
LC HD6824.F65 H55A
IO

LAPORAN KEGIATAN - DEWAN PIMPINAN PUSAT, HIMPUNAN NELAYAN SELURUH INDONESIA.
Main/Corp Himpunan Nelayan Seluruh Indonesia. Dewan Pimpinan Pusat. Indonesian. Sekretariat DPP, Jln Haji Juanda No 2, Jakarta Indonesia.
LC HD5715.5.I6 Y38A
IO

LAPORAN KEGIATAN YAYASAN TENAGA KERJA INDONESIA. **Main/Corp** Yayasan Tenaga Kerja Indonesia. (19??)-. Indonesian. Yayasan Tenaga Kerja Indonesia, Indonesia.
LC HD5824 .A32f
DD 331.12
IO

LAPORAN STATISTIK BULANAN - BAGIAN PENGUMPULAN DAN PENGOLAHAN DATA, BIRO PERENCANAAN, DEPARTEMEN TENAGA KERJA, TRANSMIGRASI DAN KOPERASI. See Business and Economics-Abstracting, Bibliographies and Statistics.
LC HD5824.Y6 Y64A
IO

LAPORAN TAHUNAN DINAS TENAGA KERJA DAERAH ISTIMEWA YOGYAKARTA. **Main/Corp** Yogyakarta, Indonesia (Daerah Istimewa). Dinas Tenaga Kerja. (19??)-. Indonesian.
LC HD5824 .A32C
IO

LAPORAN TENTANG PELAKSANAAN PROYEK-PROYEK PEMBANGUNAN YANG DIPERTANGGUNG JAWABKAN PADA DEPARTEMEN TENAGA KERJA, TRANSMIGRASI DAN KOPERASI R.I.
Main/Corp Indonesia. Departemen Tenaga Kerja, Transmigrasi dan Koperasi. Periodical. Indonesian. Departemen Tenaga Kerja, Jalan H Agus Salim No 58, Jakarta Indonesia.
LC HC107.M4 M44A **ISSN** 0145-8760
DD 331.1/1/09744
US

LARGE EMPLOYERS IN MASSACHUSETTS, THE. **Main/Corp** Massachusetts. Occupational/Industry Research Dept. (19??)-. English. Division of Employment Security / Boston, Charles F. Hurley Building, Government Center, Boston MA 02114. **Tel** (617)727-6531.
US

LAUNDRY AND DRY CLEANING WAGE SURVEY, BALTIMORE, MD. (19??)-. Government Publication. English. One time a year. US Department of Labor / Bureau of Labor Statistics, 441 G Street Northwest, Washington DC 20212. **Tel** (202)606-7800, FAX (202)606-7797.
US

LAUNDRY AND DRY CLEANING WAGE SURVEY, DETROIT, MICH. / U.S. DEPARTMENT OF LABOR, BUREAU OF LABOR STATISTICS. (19??)-. Government Publication. English. One time a year. US Department of Labor / Bureau of Labor Statistics, 441 G Street Northwest, Washington DC 20212. **Tel** (202)606-7800, FAX (202)606-7797.
US

LAUNDRY AND DRY CLEANING WAGE SURVEY, MIDDLESEX, MONMOUTH, AND OCEAN COUNTIES, N.J. / U.S. DEPARTMENT OF LABOR, BUREAU OF LABOR STATISTICS. (19??)-. Government Publication. English. One time a year. US Department of Labor / Bureau of Labor Statistics, 441 G Street Northwest, Washington DC 20212. **Tel** (202)606-7800, FAX (202)606-7797.
US

LAUNDRY AND DRY CLEANING WAGE SURVEY, MONTANA. **Added/Corp** United States. Bureau of Labor Statistics. (19??)-. Government Publication. English. One time a year. US Department of Labor / Bureau of Labor Statistics, 441 G Street Northwest, Washington DC 20212. **Tel** (202)606-7800, FAX (202)606-7797.
US

LAUNDRY AND DRY CLEANING WAGE SURVEY, PORTLAND, OREG.-WASH. / U.S. DEPARTMENT OF LABOR, BUREAU OF LABOR STATISTICS. (19??)-. Government Publication. English. One time a year. US Department of Labor / Bureau of Labor Statistics, 441 G Street Northwest, Washington DC 20212. **Tel** (202)606-7800, FAX (202)606-7797.
US

LAUNDRY AND DRY CLEANING WAGE SURVEY, PORTSMOUTH-CHILLICOTHE-GALLIPOLIS, OHIO / U.S. DEPARTMENT OF LABOR, BUREAU OF LABOR STATISTICS. (19??)-. Government Publication. English. One time a year. US Department of Labor / Bureau of Labor Statistics, 441 G Street Northwest, Washington DC 20212. **Tel** (202)606-7800, FAX (202)606-7797.
US

LAUNDRY AND DRY CLEANING WAGE SURVEY, PUERTO RICO / U.S. DEPARTMENT OF LABOR, BUREAU OF LABOR STATISTICS. (19??)-. Government Publication. English. One time a year. US Department of Labor / Bureau of Labor Statistics, 441 G Street Northwest, Washington DC 20212. **Tel** (202)606-7800, FAX (202)606-7797.
US

LAUNDRY AND DRY CLEANING WAGE SURVEY, SOUTHEASTERN MASSACHUSETTS / U.S. DEPARTMENT OF LABOR, BUREAU OF LABOR STATISTICS. (19??)-. Government Publication. English. One time a year. US Department of Labor / Bureau of Labor Statistics, 441 G Street Northwest, Washington DC 20212. **Tel** (202)606-7800, FAX (202)606-7797.
US

LAUNDRY AND DRY CLEANING WAGE SURVEY, TUCSON-DOUGLAS, ARIZ. / U.S. DEPARTMENT OF LABOR, BUREAU OF LABOR STATISTICS. (19??)-. Government Publication. English. One time a year. US Department of Labor / Bureau of Labor Statistics, 441 G Street Northwest, Washington DC 20212. **Tel** (202)606-7800, FAX (202)606-7797.
US

LAUNDRY AND DRY CLEANING WAGE SURVEY, WASHINGTON, D.C.-MD. -VA. / U.S. DEPARTMENT OF LABOR, BUREAU OF LABOR STATISTICS. (19??)-. Government Publication. English. One time a year. US Department of Labor / Bureau of Labor Statistics, 441 G Street Northwest, Washington DC 20212. **Tel** (202)606-7800, FAX (202)606-7797.
US

LAUNDRY AND DRY CLEANING WAGE SURVEY, WESTERN AND NORTHERN MASSACHUSETTS / U.S. DEPARTMENT OF LABOR, BUREAU OF LABOR STATISTICS. (19??)-. Government Publication. English. One time a year. US Department of Labor / Bureau of Labor Statistics, 441 G Street Northwest, Washington DC 20212. **Tel** (202)606-7800, FAX (202)606-7797.
US

LAUNDRY AND DRY CLEANING WAGE SURVEY, WICHITA, KAN. / U.S. DEPARTMENT OF LABOR, BUREAU OF LABOR STATISTICS. (19??)-. Government Publication. English. One time a year. US Department of Labor / Bureau of Labor Statistics, 441 G Street Northwest, Washington DC 20212. **Tel** (202)606-7800, FAX (202)606-7797.
US

LAVORO INFORMAZIONE. (19??)-. Italian. Twenty-four times a year. L580000 Italy; L650000 other. Franco Angeli Riviste SRL, Viale Monza 106, 20127 Milan Italy. **Tel** 011 39 2 2827651, 011 39 2 289562, FAX 011 39 2 258004, telex 051-511650.
IT

LAVORO SICURO. Italian. Propaganda Edit Grafica, PEG, Via Fratelli, Bressan 2, 20126 Milan Italy.
IT
SUSPENDED

LAVOROSOCIETA. (19??)-(1993). Italian. Eleven times a year. Lavorosocieta, Via Lucullo 6, 00187 Rome Italy. **Tel** 011 39 6 4753386.
US

LAW FIRM PARTNERSHIP AND BENEFITS REPORT. See Law.
LC HD4885.A9 S83a
AU

LEHRLINGSSTATISTIK / KAMMER DER GEWERBLICHEN WIRTSCHAFT FUER STEIERMARK. **Main/Corp** Syria. Kammer der Gewerblichen Wirtschaft. **Added/Corp** Kammer der Gewerblichen Wirtschaft fuer Steiermark. Handelskammer Steiermark. (19??)-. German. One time a year. Kammer der Gewerblichen Wirtschaft, Burggasse 13, A-8010 Graz Austria.
ISSN 0399-449X
FR

LETTRE D'INFORMATION - ANACT.
Main/Corp France. Agence Nationale pour l'Amelioration des Conditions de Travail. (19??)-. Periodical. French. Eleven times a year. $65.61. France, 7 boulevard Romain Rolland, 92128 Montrouge Cedex France. **Tel** 011 33 1 42314040, FAX 011 33 1 46571002.
ISSN 0982-460X
FR

UDC 331
LETTRE D'INFORMATION DU C.E.E, LA. (LETTRE DU CEE.). (1986)-. Periodical. French. Four times a year. Free on request. Centre des Etudes de l Emploi, 29 Promenade Michel Simon, 93160 Noisy Grand Cdx France. **Tel** 011 33 1 45926897. **Circ:** 3,000. *Continues* Bulletin d'Information - Centre d'Etudes de l'Emploi, 0294-8400.
Desc: Labor market and employment policy in France.
LC HD8739.L5 L5
DD 331.88/0951/82
CC

LIAO-NING KUNG JEN. VFOAT
Liaoninggongren; Liaoning Gongren. (19??)-. Periodical. Chinese. Twelve times a year. RMBY0.25. Chung-Kuo Chu Pan Tui Wai Mao I Kung SSU, Shing-Hai Fen Kung SSU, 380 Pei Su-Chou Road, Shanghai, People's Republic of China.
ISSN 0712-9599
DD 362.5/8/09714
CN

LIBEREZ LES VACANCES. (LIBEREZ LES VACANCES : PUBLICATION DU MOUVEMENT QUEBECOIS DES CAMPS FAMILIAUX.). No. 1-. Periodical. French. Three times a year. Free. Mouvement Quebecois Des Campus, Familiaux, 49 Est rue Sainte-Catherine, Montreal Quebec H2X 1K7 Canada. ctrl circ.
LC WMLC 93/4965 **ISSN** 1069-1995
DD 331
US

LIBERTARIAN LABOR REVIEW. [Libert. labor rev.]. **Added/Corp** Libertarian Labor Review Collective. (May 1, 1986)-. Periodical. English. Two times a year (June, Dec.). $6.00. Libertarian Labor Review Collective, PO Box 2824, Champaign IL 61825. **Tel** (217)337-5999. Index available. cum. index. **Bk Rev**, (Qty: 20). **Ad Acc, Adv Mgr:** Jon Bekken, **Tel** (312)549-5045. **Circ:** 1,000.
Desc: Features articles on the international labor movement, economic trends and theory, and labor history.
LC Z7164.L1 C84 Suppl 2 HD4815 **ISSN** 0360-1080
DD 016.331

LIBRARY CATALOG OF THE MARTIN P. CATHERWOOD LIBRARY OF THE NEW YORK STATE SCHOOL OF INDUSTRIAL AND LABOR RELATIONS, CORNELL UNIVERSITY. SUPPLEMENT.
Main/Corp Martin P. Catherwood Library. 4th (1970)-. Catalog. Multiple languages. GK Hall & Co., 100 Front Street, Riverside NJ 08075. **Tel** (800)257-5755 ext. 2223. *Continues* Cornell University. New York State School of Industrial and Labor Relations. Library. Library Catalog. Supplement.
Desc: Library of 78,000 cataloged volumes and bound

Business and Economics —Labor

periodicals and 80,000 pamphlets from late 18th Century to present. Provides comprehensive coverage of human relations, personnel, employee welfare, etc.

ISSN 0363-8863
US

LIBRARY EMPLOYEE RELATIONS NEWSLETTER, THE. VFOAT LERN. Newsletter. English. Twelve times a year. $48.00. Top Management Consultants, 54 Margaret Avenue, PO Box 444, Lawrence NY 11559.

ISSN 0714-2862
CN
DD 331.88/11023/09713541

LIBRARY WORKER. (LIBRARY WORKER : THE NEWS & VIEWS QUARTERLY OF LOCAL 1996-CANADIAN UNION OF PUBLIC EMPLOYEES.). [Libr. work.]. (1980)-. Periodical. English. Six times a year. Canadian Union of Public Employees Local 1996, Suite 303/11 Yorkville Avenue, Toronto Ontario M4W 1L2 Canada.

LC HD6060.5.D4 L54
DK

LIGESTILLINGSARBEJDET I AF. 1982-. Danish. Arbejdsdirektoratet, Adelgade 13, 1304 Copenhagen K Denmark.

ISSN 0704-1969
CN
DD 335.43/05

LIGNE DE MASSE, LA. See Political Science-Socialism, Communism, Anarchism, Utopianism.

ISSN 0344-6727
GW
UDC 801

LINGUISTISCHE ARBEITEN TUBINGEN. VFOAT LA. Linguistische Arbeiten. (1973)-. Monographic series. Multiple languages. Irregular. Price varies per volume. Max Niemeyer Verlag, Postfach 2140, D-72011 Tuebingen Germany. Tel 011 49 7071 989494, FAX 011 49 7071 989450.

LC HD5507 .Q42a
ISSN 0229-9062
DD 331.89/14/025714
CN

LISTE ANNOTEE D'ARBITRES DE GRIEFS. Main/Corp Quebec (Province). Conseil Consultatif du Travail et de la Main-d'Oeuvre. (1975)-. French. One time a year. Free on request. Conseil Consultatif du Travail et de la main-d'oeuvre, 800 Tour de la place Victoria, Bureau 2026, Montreal Quebec H4Z 1B7 Canada. Tel (514)873-2880, FAX (514)873-1129. ED Romuald Dufour. Circ: 10,000. Continues Liste Annotee d'Arbitres de Griefs Presentee par le Conseil Consultatif du Travail et de la Main d'Oeuvre, 0229-9062. Desc: Formed by representatives of Quebec Employers and Quebec Unions, provides professional resumes of selected arbitrators recommended by the Conseil to act upon ministerial request in cases specified in the Quebec Labour Code. Also used to select arbitrators with the settlement in their disputes and grievances.

US

LISTING OF ELIGIBLE LABOR SURPLUS AREAS UNDER DEFENSE MANPOWER POLICY NO. 4A AND EXECUTIVE ORDER 10582. Main/Corp United States. Employment and Training Administration. (19??)-. English. Four times a year. Free. Department of Labor Employment & Training Ad., 601 D Street Northwest, Room 9304, Washington DC 20213.

LC Z7164.L1 L68
DD 016.3311
GW

LITERATURDOKUMENTATION ZUR ARBEITSMARKT- UND BERUFSFORSCHUNG. German. Geschaftsstelle fur Veroffentlichungen, Regensburger Strasse 104, Nuernberg Germany.

ISSN 0791-3206
DD 331.119417 331.110212
IE

LIVE REGISTER, MONTHLY AREA ANALYSIS (DUBLIN). See Business and Economics-Abstracting, Bibliographies and Statistics.

ISSN 0791-3222
DD 331.119417 331.110212
IE

LIVE REGISTER STATEMENT (DUBLIN). See Business and Economics-Abstracting, Bibliographies and Statistics.

ISSN 0306-0837
UK

LLAFUR. [Llafur]. Added/Corp Society for the Study of Welsh Labour History. Vol. 1 (May 1972)-. English. One time a year (Aug.). £5.00 UK; £7.00 other Comes with Llafur Society for the Study of Welsh Labour History membership. Llafur Society for the Study of Welsh Labour History Society, Economics Department, University College of Wales, Aberystwyth Dyfed Wales United Kingdom. ED Aled Jones. Circ: 750 (ctrl). Desc: The journal of the society for the study of Welsh Labour History. Contributors include academic historians and trade unionists.
Ind/Abst Am. Hist. Life (1972-).

US

LMI REVIEW / WASHINGTON STATE EMPLOYMENT SECURITY DEPARTMENT. Added/Corp Washington (State). Employment Security Dept. Labor Market and Economic Analysis Branch. Washington (State). Employment Security Dept. VFOAT L.M.I. Review. (198?)-. Periodical. English. Four times a year. Free on request. Research and Analysis Branch, Washington State Employment Security Department, Box 9046, Olympia WA 98507. Tel (206)438-4800, FAX (206)438-4846.

LC HA1501 HD5050
DD 314.81
NO

LNNINGER OG INNTEKTER. See Business and Economics-Abstracting, Bibliographies and Statistics.

LC HA1501 HD8039.M4N77
DD 314.81 S 331.2/9481
NO

LNNSSTATISTIKK FOR ANSATTE I FORRETNINGSMESSIG TJENESTEYTING OG I INTERESSEORGANISASJONER. See Business and Economics-Abstracting, Bibliographies and Statistics.

LC HA1501
DD 381/.09481
NO

LNNSSTATISTIKK FOR ANSATTE I VAREHANDEL. See Business and Economics-Abstracting, Bibliographies and Statistics.

LC HD8542 .A68
ISSN 0105-032X
DK

LO-BLADET. Main/Corp Landsorganisationen I Danmark. VAT Landsorganisationen-Bladet. (Jan. 1973)-. Periodical. Danish. Twenty-four times a year. kr100.00. Landsorganisationen i Danmark / Danish Federation of Trade Unions, Galionsvej 7, 1910 Frederiksberg C Denmark. Tel FAX 011 45 31 317989. ED Finn Thorgrimson. Bk Rev. Pub. Size: Tabloid. Circ: 36,000. available with illustrations; available with charts. Continues Ln Og Virke, 0024-5976.

LC HC10 .F3
SW

LO I.E. LANDSORGANISATIONEN I SVERIGE TIDNINGEN. Main/Corp Landsorganisationen i Sverige. Swedish. Landsorganisationen I Sverige, Barnhusgatan 18, 105 53 Stockholm Sweden. Continues Fackforeningsrorelsen.

ISSN 0011-8915
US

LOCAL 1-S NEWS. VAT Local One-S News. Vol. 1 (Aug. 1949)-. Periodical. English. Twelve times a year. Local 1-S, Department Store Workers Union, 140 West 31st Street, New York NY 10001. available on microfilm from University Microfilms International (UMI).

US

LOCAL 824 BULLETIN. (19??)-. Bulletin. English. Four times a year. International Longshoreman's Association, 642 Twelfth Avenue, New York NY 10019.

LC HD4973 .B85C HD4966.A45 A452U5
ISSN 0273-432X
DD 331.2/973 331.2/8291/09794
US

LOCKHEED AIRCRAFT CORPORATION. Main/Corp United States. Bureau of Labor Statistics. 1937/51-. Government Publication. English. US Department of Labor / Bureau of Labor Statistics, 441 G Street Northwest, Washington DC 20212. Tel (202)606-7800, FAX (202)606-7797.

ISSN 0894-3605
DD 331
US

LOCOMOTIVE ENGINEERS JOURNAL (1987). (LOCOMOTIVE ENGINEERS JOURNAL.). [Locomot. eng. j.]. Added/Corp Brotherhood of Locomotive Engineers (U.S.). Vol. 1, No. 4 (Winter 1987)-. Trade Publication. English. Four times a year (Mar., June, Sept., Dec.). $9.00. Brotherhood of Locomotive Engineers, 1370 Ontario Street, Standard Building MZ, Cleveland OH 44113. Tel (216)241-2630. Continues in part Locomotive Engineer.
Ind/Abst Work Relat. Abstr.

LC HD6350.S4
ISSN 0160-2047
DD 331.88/11/38750973
US

LOG (BROOKLYN). (LOG.). Vol. 38, No. 10 (Oct. 1976)-. Periodical. English. Twelve times a year. Seafarers International Union, 675-4th Avenue, Brooklyn NY 11232. Continues Seafarers Log, 0037-0096; Absorbed Stewards News.
Ind/Abst Work Relat. Abstr. (-19??).

LC HD5027 .S74E
GW

LOHNE UND GEHALTER. REIHE 2. 1 : ARBEITERVERDIENSTE IN DER INDUSTRIE. Main/Corp Germany (West). Statistisches Bundesamt. VFOAT Arbeiterverdienste in der Industrie. Jan. 1977-. Periodical. German. Irregular. W. Kohlhammer Verlag GmbH, Postfach 800430, D-70549 Stuttgart Germany. Tel 011 49 711 78630, FAX 011 49 711 7863430, telex 7-255820. Supersedes in part Preise, Lohne, Wirtschaftsrechnungen. Reihe 15: Arbeitnehmerverdienste in Industrie und Handel.

GW

LOHNE UND GEHALTER. REIHE 5, LOHNE, GEHALTER UND ARBEITSKOSTEN IM AUSLAND. Added/Corp Germany. Statistisches Bundesamt. VFOAT Lohne und Gehalter und Arbeitskosten im Ausland; Fachserie 16. (Jan. 1991)-. German. Two times a year. Hermann Leins GmbH & Co., Verlags-KG, Holzwiesenstrasse 2, Postfach 11 52, D-7408 Kusterdingen Germany. Formed by the union of Lohne und Gehalter. Reihe 5.1, Arbeitnehmerverdienste und Arbeitskosten im Ausland and Lohne und Gehalter. Reihe 5.2, Tariflohne und Gehalter im Ausland.

US

LONG HOURS AND PREMIUM PAY. (197?)-. Government Publication. English. One time a year. US Department of Labor / Bureau of Labor Statistics, 441 G Street Northwest, Washington DC 20212. Tel (202)606-7800, FAX (202)606-7797.

US

LONGSHORE NEWSLETTER PROCEDURE MANUAL. (19??)-. Newsletter. English. Twelve times a year. $325.00. Longshore Newsletter, 15 Fowler Court, San Rafael CA 94903. Tel (415)499-9105, FAX (415)472-6823. ED Robert Brahm. Circ: 400-500.

LC HD4976.L6 C65
DD 331.2/979493/04
US

LOS ANGELES COUNTY, WAGE RATE SURVEY. Added/Corp Merchants and Manufacturers Association. (198?)-. English. M & M Association, 2300 Occidental Center, 1150 South Olive Street, Los Angeles CA 90015. Continues Community Wage Rate Survey, Los Angeles County.

LC HD5725.L8 L685
ISSN 0091-4711
DD 331.1/09763
US

LOUISIANA LABOR MARKET. (19??)-. English. Twelve times a year. Louisiana Department of Labor, Office of Employment Security, PO Box 94094, Baton Rouge LA 70804-9094. Tel (504)342-3104.

ISSN 1058-0557
US

LRA TRADE UNION ADVISOR. (1988)-. English. Twenty-six times a year. $225.00. Labor Research Association Inc., 145 West 28th Street, New York NY 10001. Tel (212)714-1677, FAX (212)714-1674. ED Greg Tarpinian, (212)714-1677. Circ: 500 (ctrl). Desc: An economic forecasting publication designed for trade union leaders. Written in straight forward language that is easy to understand. Provides forecasts that readers can absorb quickly and easily and use immediately in representing their members.

LC HC101 .E4
ISSN 0895-5220
DD 331/.0973/05
US

LRA'S ECONOMIC NOTES. [LRA's econ. notes]. Added/Corp Labor Research Association (U.S.). VFOAT EN; Economic Notes. Vol. 54, Nos. 7-8 (July/Aug. 1986)-. Periodical. English. Eleven times a year (monthly except August). $50.00. Labor Research Association Inc., 145 West 28th Street, New York NY 10001. Tel (212)714-1677, FAX (212)714-1674. ED Greg Tarpinian. Bk Rev. Ad Acc. Circ: 3,000 (ctrl). Continues Economic Notes, 0013-0184.
Ind/Abst Altern. Press Index (1986-); Econ. Lit. Index (199?-); J. Econ. Lit.

UK

LRD BOOKLETS. English. Ten times a year. £57.25 employers; £21.75 other. Labour Research Department, 78 Blackfriars Road, London SE1 8HF United Kingdom. Tel 011 44 171 9283649, FAX 011 44 171 9280621. ED Celia Dignan. Circ: 9,000. Desc: Contains subjects of interest to trade unions.

US

LRRC LABOR UPDATE / LABOR RELATIONS AND RESEARCH CENTER, UNIVERSITY OF MASSACHUSETTS, AMHERST. Added/Corp University of Massachusetts at Amherst. Labor Relations and Research Center. VFOAT Labor Update. VAT Labor Relations and Research Center Labor Update. Vol. 1, No. 1 (Spring 1991)-. Periodical. English. Four times a year. Continues Labor Center Review.

Business and Economics —Labor

DD 331.8812   **ISSN** 0047-5378   US   CEASED

MACHINIST, THE. [Machinist]. **Added/Corp** International Association of Machinists and Aerospace Workers. International Association of Machinists. Vol. 1 (April 4, 1946)-(1994). Periodical. English. International Association of Machinists, 9000 Machinists Place, Upper Malboro MD 20772. **Tel** (301)967-4520, FAX (301)967-4586. **ED** Robert Kalaski. **Bk Rev**, (Qty: 3). ctrl circ.
 Desc: Features news about the American labor movement. Heavy emphasis on collective bargaining trends and political and legislative issues facing trade unions and their members.
 Ind/Abst Surf. Treat. Technol. Abstr.; Work Relat. Abstr.

DD 331.88/1162180288/0971   **ISSN** 0824-2453   CN   TITLE CHANGE

MACHINIST CANADA. (THE MACHINIST CANADA.). [Mach. Can.]. **Added/Corp** International Association of Machinists and Aerospace Workers. **VFOAT** Machiniste Canada; Canadian Machinist; Machiniste Canadien. (1973)-(1994). Periodical. English (French). International Association of Machinists and Aerospace Workers, Suite 400, 287 Maclaren Street, Ottawa Ontario K2P 0L9 Canada. **Continued by** IAM Journal, 1196-8613.

LC HD5827 .A258a

JA

MAIGETSU KINRO TOKEI TOKUBETSU CHOSA HOKOKU. **Main/Corp** Japan. Rodosho. Tokei Johobu. (1972)-. Periodical. Japanese. Daijin Kanbo, 7-3, Ichigaya Honmuracho, Shinjuku-ku Tokyo 162 Japan. **Continues** Maigetsu Kinro Tokei Tokubetsu Chosa Hokoku.

JA

MAIGETSU KINRO TOKEI YORAN / RODO DAIJIN KANBO SEISAKU CHOSABU HEN. **Added/Corp** Japan. Rodosho. Seisaku Chosabu. Rodo Horei Kyokai (Japan). (19??)-. Japanese. One time a year (Oct.). Government Publications Service Center, 2-1 Kasumigaseki 1-Chome, Chiyoda-Ku Tokyo 100 Japan. **Tel** 011 81 3 3504 3885.

LC RA981.M2 M34
DD 331.2/813621/109741   US

MAINE HOSPITAL WAGE SURVEY / MAINE DEPARTMENT OF LABOR, BUREAU OF EMPLOYMENT SECURITY, DIVISION OF ECONOMIC ANALYSIS AND RESEARCH. **VFOAT** Hospital Wage Survey. (19??)-. English. One time a year. $2.50. Maine Labor Department, 20 Union Street, Augusta ME 04333. **Tel** (207)289-3788, FAX (202)289-5292. **ED** Ray A Fongemie. **Circ:** 300.
 Desc: Fifty-four nonadministrative occupations in private hospitals with low, average, median, middle-range and high wages are indicated for the state and five areas.

LC HD4976.M2 M33
DD 331.2/87/09741   US

MAINE OCCUPATIONAL WAGES. **Added/Corp** Maine. Dept. of Labor. Economic Analysis and Research. (19??)-. English. Economic Analysis Research Division, 20 Union Street, Augusta ME 04330. **Tel** (207)289-2271. **Formed by the union of** Maine Occupational Wages in Selected Nonmanufacturing Industries **and** Maine Occupational Wages in Manufacturing Industries.

LC HD4976.M2 M35B
DD 331.2/87/09741   US

MAINE OCCUPATIONAL WAGES AND FRINGE BENEFITS BY INDUSTRY IN MANUFACTURING. **Main/Corp** Maine. Manpower Research Division. **VFOAT** Maine Occupational Wages and Fringe Benefits for Manufacturing Industries. (19??)-. English. One time a year. Manpower Research Division, 20 Union Street, Augusta ME 04330.

LC HD4976.M2 M35b
DD 331.2/87/09741   US   TITLE CHANGE

MAINE OCCUPATIONAL WAGES IN MANUFACTURING INDUSTRIES. **Added/Corp** Maine. Occupational Outlook and Job Information Section. Maine. Manpower Research Division. (19??)-(199?). English. Economic Analysis Research Division, 20 Union Street, Augusta ME 04330. **Tel** (207)289-2271. **ED** Ray A. Fongemie. **Circ:** 600.
Continues Maine Occupational Wages and Fringe Benefits by Industry in Manufacturing. **Merged with** Maine Occupational Wages **to form** Maine Occupational Wages in Selected Nonmanufacturing Industries.
 Desc: Over 200 occupations with low, average, median, middle range, and high wages are indicated, broken out by industry groups and 4 areas.

LC HD4976.M2 M38
DD 331.2/81/0009741   US

MAINE OCCUPATIONAL WAGES IN NONMANUFACTURING INDUSTRIES / OCCUPATIONAL OUTLOOK AND JOB INFORMATION SECTION. 1979-. English. Every 2 years. $3.00. Maine Employment Security Commission, 20 Union Street, Augusta ME 04330. **ED** Ray A Fongemie. **Circ:** 1,100.
 Desc: Over 200 occupations in trade, finance, insurance, and services with low, average, median, middle range, and high wages are indicated and are broken out by industry groups and four area

LC HD4976.M2 M33
DD 331.2/87/09741   US   TITLE CHANGE

MAINE OCCUPATIONAL WAGES IN SELECTED NONMANUFACTURING INDUSTRIES. (19??)-(19??). English. Economic Analysis Research Division, 20 Union Street, Augusta ME 04330. **Tel** (207)289-2271. **Merged with** Maine Occupational Wages in Manufacturing Industries **to form** Maine Occupational Wages.

LC HD8013.I5 K67A   **ISSN** 0216-4051   IO

MAJALAH BULANAN KORPRI. **VFOAT** Majalah Bulanan K.O.R.P.R.I.; K.O.R.P.R.I. (19??)-. Periodical. Indonesian. Twelve times a year. Jorpri Pusat, Jl Kramat Vi No 4-6, Jakarta Indonesia. **Continues** KORPI.

UA

NLM W1; MA492KW

MAJALLAT AL-KHADAMAT AL-SIHHIYAH LI-IQLIM SHARQ AL-BAHR AL-MUTAWASSIT. **See** Public Health and Safety.

US

MAJOR ACTIVITY ANNOUNCEMENTS. English. Four times a year. $50.00. Atlanta Regional Commission, 3715 Northside Parkway, 200 Northcreek, Suite 300, Atlanta GA 30327. **Tel** (404)656-7700. **Absorbed** Major Employment Announcements in the Atlanta Region **and** Major Development Announcements in the Atlanta Region.

US   TITLE CHANGE

MAJOR EMPLOYMENT ANNOUNCEMENTS IN THE ATLANTA REGION / ATLANTA REGIONAL COMMISSION. **Added/Corp** Atlanta Regional Commission. **VFOAT** Atlanta Regional Commission Research Report. (1983)-(1993). Periodical. English. Atlanta Regional Commission, 3715 Northside Parkway, 200 Northcreek, Suite 300, Atlanta GA 30327. **Tel** (404)656-7700. **Absorbed by** Major Activity Announcements.

DD 331.2/1/0971021   **ISSN** 0848-6433   CN

MAJOR WAGE SETTLEMENTS. [Major wage settl.]. **Added/Corp** Canada. Labour Canada. Canada. Bureau of Labour Information. **VFOAT** Grands Reglements Salariaux. 1st Quarter (1984)-. Periodical. English (French). Four times a year. Labour Canada / Publications Distribution Centre, Publications Distribution Centre, Ottawa Ontario K1A 0J2 Canada. **Continues** Labour Data., 0228-1678.

LC HD28 .M3413   **ISSN** 0258-042X
DD 658/.005   II

MANAGEMENT AND LABOUR STUDIES. **See** Business and Economics-Personnel Management.

LC HD4965.3.I48 I57   **ISSN** 8756-6001
DD 331.2/81368973   US

MANAGEMENT COMPENSATION SURVEY OF THE INSURANCE INDUSTRY. [Manage. compens. surv. insur. ind.]. **VFOAT** Management Compensation Survey. Insurance Industry. (198?)-. English. One time a year. Sibson and Company, 212 Carnegie Center, CN 5323, Princeton NJ 08543-5323. **Tel** (609)520-2700. **Continues** Insurance Industry ... Annual Management Compensation Survey, 0278-9582.

ISSN 1351-4954   UK

MANAGEMENT PAY REVIEW. (19??)-. English. Twelve times a year. £184.00. Incomes Data Services, 193 St. John Street, London EC1V 4LS United Kingdom. **Tel** 011 44 171 2503434, FAX 011 44 171 6080949. **ED** Steve Tatton. **Continues** Top Pay Unit Review : Monthly Review of Salaries and Benefits.
 Desc: Monitors salary and benefit developments within individual companies, with case studies of innovations. Analyzes changing practice in benefit areas ranging from share options to flexible benefits.

US

MANAGING DIVERSITY. **Added/Corp** Jamestown Area Labor Management Committee (Jamestown, N.Y.). (1991)-. Periodical. Twelve times a year. $89.50. Jamestown Area Labor Management Committee Inc, PO Box 819, Jamestown NY 14702. **Tel** (800)542-7869, (716)665-3654, FAX (716)665-8060. **ED** Leo Patterson. Index available. cum. index. **Bk Rev**, (Qty: 12). **Circ:** 4,000.
 Desc: A monthly source of information, ideas, and tips for people managing a diverse workforce.

US

MANAGING THE CIVILIAN WORK FORCE. A GUIDE FOR MILITARY MANAGER. (19??)-. English. Irregular. $8.95 (US); $12.45 (Canada). FPMI Communications Inc., 707 Fiber Street, Huntsville AL 35801. **Tel** (205)539-1850, FAX (205)539-0911, .

DD 331.12/5/097127   **ISSN** 0711-6411   CN

MANITOBA LABOUR MARKET INFORMATION BULLETIN. [Manit. lab. mark. inf. bull.]. Bulletin. English. Twelve times a year. Manitoba Department of Labour, 401 York Avenue Room 409, Winnipeg Manitoba R3C 0P8 Canada.

DD 331.7/69/00257127   **ISSN** 0714-3222   CN

MANITOBA WINNIPEG BUILDING AND CONSTRUCTION TRADES COUNCIL YEARBOOK. [Manit. Winn. Build. Constr. Trades Counc. yearb.]. **Added/Corp** Manitoba-Winnipeg Building and Construction Trades Council. (1972)-. English. One time a year. Free. Naylor Communications Ltd, 100 Sutherland Avenue, Winnipeg Manitoba R2W 3C7 Canada. **Tel** (204)947-0222, FAX (604)985-7399. **ED** Will Oliver and Pam Kellett. **Ad Acc.** (Qty: 1,500 (ctrl).
 Desc: A look at the building trades in Manitoba including new projects, news and views of the Building and Construction Trades Council.

ISSN 0149-080X   US

MANPOWER AND HUMAN RESOURCES STUDIES. (197?)-. Monographic series. English. Irregular. Price varies per volume. University of Pennsylvania / Industrial Research Unit, 3733 Spruce Street, Philadelphia PA 19104. **Tel** (215)898-5605.
 Desc: Books and monographs on personnel policies, labor market availability of specific skills, and the manpower concerns of various industries.

NE

MANPOWER ARGUS. (19??)-. Newsletter. English. Twelve times a year. Free on request. Hans Vink / General Manager, Manpower BV, Diemerhof 16-18, 1112 XN Diemen Netherlands.

LC Z7165.I6 M35 HD5819   **ISSN** 0047-5793
DD 331.1/1/0954   II

MANPOWER DOCUMENTATION. **Added/Corp** Institute of Applied Manpower Research (India). Documentation Centre. (19??)-. English. Four times a year. Free. Institute of Applied Manpower Research / Documentation, Documentation Centre, New Delhi 110002 India. **Tel** 3317869. **Bk Rev**. **Circ:** 500 (ctrl).

LC HD4995.Z9 T836A
DD 331.2/9729/83   TR

MANPOWER INCOME REPORT. **Main/Corp** Trinidad and Tobago. Central Statistical Office. English. Government Printery / Trinidad, Central Statistical Office, 35 41 Queen Street, Port of Spain Trinidad. **Tel** (809)625-4970, FAX (809)625-3802.

LC HD5725.V8 V53b   **ISSN** 0099-1104
DD 331.1/1/09755   US

MANPOWER INFORMATION FOR AFFIRMATIVE ACTION PROGRAMS. **Main/Corp** Virginia Employment Commission. Manpower Research Division. (19??)-. English. Virginia Employment Commission, 703 East Main Street, PO Box 1358, Richmond VA 23211.

LC HD5724 .M239 SUPPL
DD 331.1/1/0973   US

MANPOWER INFORMATION SERVICE. SUPPLEMENT. (19??)-. Periodical. English. Twenty-six times a year. $396.00. Manpower Information Inc, 1231 25th Street NW, Washington DC 20037.

LC HD5701 .M37   **ISSN** 0542-5808
DD 331   II

MANPOWER JOURNAL. [Manpow. j.]. **Added/Corp** Institute of Applied Manpower Research (India). Vol. 1 (Apr. 1965)-. Periodical. English. Four times a year. $10.00. Institute of Applied Manpower Research, Indraprastha Estate, Mahatma Gandhi Marg, New Delhi 110 002 India. **(Subscription address:** Prints India, 11

Business and Economics —Labor

Darya Ganj, New Delhi 110002 India. **Tel** 011 91 11 3268645, FAX 011 91 11 3275542, telex 31-61087 PRIN-IN.) **ED** Shri S P Awasthi. Index available. **Bk Rev**. **Circ**: 500. Documents available from UMI Article Clearinghouse.
Desc: Articles on subjects related to manpower, based on research studies and/or on practical experience in India and abroad. Articles seek to make original contributions of the thinking on the subject, or give analytical reports on pioneering efforts in the practical field.
Ind/Abst ABI/INFORM Glob. Ed.; ABI/INFORM [Computer File] (May 1982-).
LC Z7164.C81 U4568 HF5549. F5549.5.M3 Z7164.L1
ISSN 0147-4766
DD 016.353001 S 016.3311/1/0973   US
MANPOWER PLANNING AND UTILIZATION. **Main/Corp** United States Civil Service Commission. Library. English. $1.05. US Civil Service Commission Library, Washington DC 20402.

ISSN 0565-3061
DD 331   US
MANPOWER RESEARCH. VFOAT Manpower Research Bulletin. Bulletin No. 1 (1963)-. Government Publication. English. Price varies per volume. US Department of Labor, 200 Constitution Avenue NW, Washington DC 20210. **Tel** (202)219-7316, FAX (202)219-7312.

LC HD5744 .A262A   **ISSN** 0147-8281
DD 331.1/1/097295   PR
MANPOWER TRAINING NEEDS, PUERTO RICO. [Manpow. train. needs, P. R.]. **Main/Corp** Puerto Rico. Bureau of Employment Security. Research Section. English. Bureau of Employment Security / Puerto Rico, Research and Statistics Division, San Juan PR.

ISSN 1189-041X
DD 331.89/04161073/0971405   CN
MANUEL D'INTERPRETATION ET D'APPLICATION DE LA CONVENTION COLLECTIVE F.I.I.Q. ... EN VIGUEUR DANS LES CENTRES D'ACCUEIL MEMBRES DE L'ASSOCIATION DES CENTRES D'ACCUEIL DU QUEBEC. [Man. interpret. appl. conv. collect. F.I.I.Q. vigueur cent. accueil memb. Assoc. cent. accueil Que.]. **Added/Corp** Association des Centres d'Accueil du Quebec. Service-Conseil en Gestion des Ressources Humaines. Association des Centres d'Accueil du Quebec. Federation des Infirmieres et Infirmiers du Quebec. **VFOAT** Manuel d'Interpretation et d'Application de la Convention Collective en Vigueur dans les Centres d'Accueil. (1990/1991)-. French. Every 3 years. Limited free distribution. Service-Conseil en Gestion des Ressources Humaines, Association des Centres D'Accueil du Quebec, 1001 Est boulevard de Maisonneuve, Montreal Quebec H2L 4P9 Canada.

ISSN 1184-6577
DD 331.89/04161073/09714   CN
MANUEL D'INTERPRETATION ET D'APPLICATION DES CONVENTIONS COLLECTIVES F.T.Q. (U.E.S. LOCAL 298 ET S.C.F.P.) ... EN VIGUEUR DANS LES CENTRES D'ACCUEIL MEMBRES DE L'ASSOCIATION DES CENTRES D'ACCUEIL DU QUEBEC. **Added/Corp** Association des Centres d'Accueil du Quebec. Service-Conseil en Gestion des Ressources Humaines. Association des Centres d'Accueil du Quebec. Syndicat Canadien de la Fonction Publique. Union des Employes (ees) de Service. Local 298. **VFOAT** Manuel d'Interpretation et d'Application des Conventions Collectives en Vigueur dans les Centres d'Accueil. (1990/1991)-. French. Every 3 years. Limited free distribution. Service-Conseil en Gestion des Ressources Humaines, Association des Centres D'Accueil du Quebec, 1001 Est boulevard de Maisonneuve, Montreal Quebec H2L 4P9 Canada.

LC HD5729.Q4 M37   **ISSN** 0226-2576
CN
MARCHE DU TRAVAIL (QUEBEC). (LE MARCHE DU TRAVAIL / CENTRE DE RECHERCHE ET DE STATISTIQUES SUR LE MARCHE DU TRAVAIL.). **Added/Corp** Quebec (Province). Centre de Recherche et de Statistiques sur le Marche du Travail. (1980)-. Periodical. French. Twelve times a year. 78.43Can$. Les Publications du Quebec, CP 1190, Outremont Quebec H2V 4S7 Canada. **Tel** (514)948-1222, (418)643-5150, FAX (514)278-3030.
Ind/Abst Repere.

LC HD5725.A6 A73e
DD 331.1/1/0979173   US
MARICOPA COUNTY LABOR MARKET REVIEW. **Main/Corp** Arizona. Dept. of Economic Security. Labor Market Information Research Analysis Section. (19??)-. Periodical. English. One time a year. Arizona Dept of Economic Security, PO Box 6123, Phoenix AZ 85005.

LC HE730 .M33   **ISSN** 0161-9373
DD 387.5/0973   US
MARITIME NEWSLETTER. (Sept. 1976)-. Newsletter. English. Twelve times a year. $2.50. American Federation of Labor and Congress of Industrial Organizations, 815 16th Street Northwest, Washington DC 20006. **Tel** (202)637-5000. **ED** Jean F Ingrao.
Continues Maritime, 0025-3391.
Desc: Deals with maritime and trade union issues.

AT
MARITIME WORKER. 1938. Periodical. English. Twelve times a year. 13.16Aus$. Waterside Workers Federation of Australia, 365-375 Sussex Street, Sydney New South Wales 2000 Australia. **Tel** 02 2679134, FAX 02 2613481, telex 25645. **ED** T I Bull. **Bk Rev**. **Ad Acc**. **Circ**: 8,300 (ctrl).
Desc: Industrial news.

ISSN 0792-0970
IS
UDC 331
MASABEY 'ENWS. [Masabey 'enws]. (1988)-. Periodical. Hebrew. Twelve times a year. Eush Ltd, 19 Nordau Blvd, Tel Aviv Israel. **Tel** 972-3-5466893, FAX 972-3-448915. **ED** Chanoch Sadan. **Bk Rev**. **Ad Acc**. **Circ**: 300 (ctrl).

ISSN 0705-0615
DD 331/.09714   CN
MASSE (MONTREAL). (LA MASSE.). First issue in 1968. Periodical. French. Twenty-four times a year. La Masse, 864 Bloomfield, Montreal Quebec H2C 3S6 Canada.

ISSN 0181-057X
FR
TITLE CHANGE
MASSES OUVRIERES. (19??)-(1995). Periodical. French. Editions Ouvrieres, 12 Avenue Soeur Rosalie, Box Postale 50, 75621 Paris Cedex 13 France. **Tel** 033 1 44089515, telex 240 435 LIVREST.
Continued by Cahiers de l'Atelier.

LC HD4966.B92 U43
DD 331.2/2   US
MEANS LABOR RATES FOR THE CONSTRUCTION INDUSTRY. See Building and Construction.

ISSN 1074-9179
US
●**MEDIATION MONTHLY.** (1994)-. Periodical. English. Twelve times a year. $48.00. Meditation Group, PO Box 6161, Rockford IL 61125. **Tel** (815)399-8407.

ISSN 1047-1863
DD 368   US
CCC
NLM W1; ME5509B
MEDICARE COMPLIANCE ALERT. See Insurance.

LC HD5715.5.A53 C45b
DD 341.7/63   UY
MEETING OF THE TECHNICAL COMMITTEE - CINTERFOR. **Main/Corp** Centro Interamericano de Investigacion y Documentacion Sobre Formacion Profesional. Comision Tecnica. (19??)-. English. Cinterfor, Casilla de Correo, Montevideo Uruguay.

LC HD4801   **ISSN** 0190-3144
DD 331   US
MEMO (CINCINNATI). (MEMO.). **Added/Corp** Retail Store Employees Union. Local 1099. (19??)-. Periodical. English. Twelve times a year. Retail Store Employees Union Local 1099, 2562 North Bend Road, Cincinnati OH 45239.
Ind/Abst Archit. Period. Index (19??-19??).

ISSN 0316-5892
DD 338.9/71   CN
MEMORANDUM TO THE GOVERNMENT OF CANADA BY THE CANADIAN LABOUR CONGRESS. **Main/Corp** Canadian Labour Congress. (1957)-. Periodical. English. One time a year. Free. Canadian Labour Congress, 2841 Riverside Drive, Ottawa Ontario K1V 8X7 Canada. **Tel** (613)521-3400, FAX (613)053-4750, telex 060313. **Continues** Trades and Labor Congress of Canada. Memorandum to the Government of Canada., 0316-5884.

LC HD6604.S452 S557a

AG
MEMORIA Y BALANCE. **Main/Corp** Sindicato Unico Trabajadores Espectaculo Publico. (19??)-. Spanish. Pasco 148, Buenos Aires Argentina.

LC HD4966.B892 F84A
DD 2/89/00944   FR
MENSUALISATION DES OUVRIERS DU BATIMENT, LA. **Main/Corp** Federation Nationale du Batiment. (19??)-. French. 33 Avenue Kleber, Paris 75784 France.

ISSN 0714-6914
DD 331.25/5/0971   CN
Pr Rev.
MERCER BULLETIN, THE. [Mercer bull.]. **Added/Corp** William M. Mercer Limited. Vol. 32, No. 1 (Jan. 1982)-. Bulletin. English (French). Twelve times a year. Free on request. William M Mercer Limited, BCE Place, 161 Bay Street, PO Box 501, Toronto Ontario M5J 2S5 Canada. **Tel** (416)868-2000. **ED** Robert C. Dowsett. Index available. cum. index. **Circ**: 10,000 (ctrl).
Continues Mercer Actuarial Bulletin, 0025-9845.
Desc: Provides clients and friends of William W. Mercer Limited with news and opinions on employee benefits, compensation and related matters.

LC HD7123.U5 M47
US
MERCER GUIDE TO SOCIAL SECURITY AND MEDICARE. See Insurance.

ISSN 1183-8620
DD 331.11/8/0971021   CN
MESURES GLOBALES DE PRODUCTIVITE (1989). (MESURES GLOBALES DE PRODUCTIVITE.). **Added/Corp** Statistique Canada. Division des Entrees-Sorties. (1989)-. French. One time a year. 44.00Can$ Canada; $53.00 US; $62.00 other. Statistics Canada Publications Sales and Services, R.H. Coats Building 6th Floor, Ottawa Ontario K1A 0T6 Canada. **Tel** (613)951-5078, (800)267-6677, FAX (613)951-1584, telex 053-3585.
Separated from Aggregate Productivity Measures., 0317-7882.

ISSN 0026-1998
US
MICHIGAN AFL-CIO NEWS. **Main/Corp** Michigan AFL-CIO. **VAT** Michigan American Federation of Labor-Congress of Industrial Organizations News. (Feb. 27, 1958)-. Periodical. English. Twelve times a year. $2.50. Michigan AFL-CIO, 419 Washington Square South 200, Lansing MI 48933. **Tel** (517)487-5966. **ED** Jon Ogar. **Ad Acc**. **Circ**: 30,000 (ctrl). available on microfilm from University Microfilms International (UMI). **Supersedes** Michigan CIO News.
Desc: Political and legislative news of interest to Michigan union leaders.

LC HD5725.M5 M43A   **ISSN** 0731-2938
DD 331.11/09774   US
MICHIGAN CETA ACTIVITY REPORT FOR ... . **Main/Corp** Michigan. Bureau of Employment and Training. **VFOAT** Michigan C.E.T.A. Activity Report for ... . (19??)-. English. Four times a year. Bureau of Employment and Training, State Secondary Complex, 7150 Harris Drive, Box 30015, Lansing MI 48909.

US
MICHIGAN PUBLIC EMPLOYEE REPORTER. English. Twenty-four times a year. $545.00 (includes postage). LRP Publications, 747 Dresher Road, Suite 500, Horsham PA 19044. **Tel** (800)341-7874, (215)784-0941, FAX (215)784-9639, (215)784-0870.
Desc: Timely and comprehensive source for public sector labor law decisions issued by Michigan state agencies and courts.

LC HD5725.M5 A3
DD 331.1/2   US
MICHIGAN'S LABOR MARKET NEWS. **Added/Corp** Michigan Employment Security Commission. **VFOAT** Labor Market News. Vol. 48, No. 1 (Mar. 1992)-. English. Twelve times a year. Free on request. Detroit Employment Security Commission, 7310 Woodward Castro, Room 520, Detroit MI 48202. **Tel** (313)876-5427. **Continues** Michigan Labor Market Review, 0098-0307.

LC RA448.5.M5 U54A   **ISSN** 0145-1340
DD 362.8/5   US
NLM W2 A H64M
MIGRANT HEALTH PROJECTS. See Public Health and Safety.

LC LC5152.N6 M54
DD 371.9/675/09789   US
MIGRANT REPORT. English. New Mexico Department of Education, 300 Don Gaspar Avenue, Santa Fe NM 87501. **Tel** (505)827-6516, FAX (505)827-6696.

LC HV86 .M536
DD 361/.9774 S 362.8/5   US
MIGRANT SERVICES STATISTICAL REPORT. See Business and Economics-Abstracting, Bibliographies and Statistics.

LC Discard   **ISSN** 0279-3741
US
MILWAUKEE LABOR PRESS. **Added/Corp** Milwaukee County Labor Council, AFL-CIO. **VFOAT** AFL-CIO Milwaukee Labor Press. Vol. 1 (1942)-. Periodical. English. Twelve times a year. $9.50. Milwaukee Labor Press Inc, 633 South Hawley Road, Milwaukee WI 53214. **Tel** (414)771-7070, FAX (414)771-6191. **ED** Carole Casamento. **Ad Acc**. **Circ**: 70,000 (ctrl).
Desc: All news and information relevant to all AFL-CIO members in Milwaukee county.

LC HD4918 .U64A ISSN 0093-5611
DD 331.2/2 US

MINIMUM WAGE AND MAXIMUM HOURS STANDARDS UNDER THE FAIR LABOR STANDARDS ACT. (19??)-. English. One time a year. US Department of Labor Employment Standards Administration, 200 Constitution Avenue NW, Room S2321, Washington DC 20210. **Tel** (202)219-6191, FAX (202)219-8457. available on microfiche (Vols. for (1983-) distributed to depository libraries). ***Absorbed*** *Groups with Historically High Incidences of Unemployment.*

LC HD4966.M612 U55 ISSN 0192-5032
DD 331.2/82/230978 US

MINING PERSONNEL PRACTICES SURVEY. **Main/Corp** Mountain States Employers Council. (19??)-. Periodical. English. Mountain States Employers Council, 1790 Logan Street, PO Box 539, Denver CO 80201.

ISSN 0274-9017
US

MINNEAPOLIS LABOR REVIEW, THE. **Added/Corp** Minneapolis Central Labor Union Council. Trades and Labor Assembly of Minneapolis and Hennepin County. **VFOAT** Labor Review. 11th Year, No. 526 (May 25, 1917)-. Periodical. English. Twenty-four times a year. $10.00. Minneapolis Labor Review, 312 Central Avenue, Suite 526, Minneapolis MN 55414. **Tel** (612)379-4725, 4726. **ED** Wallace A. Nelson. **Ad Acc. Circ:** 50,000 (ctrl). available on microfilm. ***Continues*** *Labor Review (Minneapolis, Minn.).*

LC HD5725.M6 R48
DD 331.1/09776/05 US

MINNESOTA LABOR MARKET REVIEW. **Added/Corp** Minnesota. Dept. of Jobs and Training. Research and Statistics Office. **VFOAT** Labor Market Review. 3rd quarter (Nov. 1986)-. Periodical. English. Twelve times a year. Minnesota Department of Employment Services, 390 North Robert Street, St Paul MN 55101. ***Continues*** *Review of Labor and Economic Conditions for ... .*

ISSN 1050-3463
DD 331 US

MINORITIES IN BUSINESS INSIDER. [Minor. bus. insider]. (1989)-. Periodical. English. Twenty-four times a year. $297.00. CD Publications, 8204 Fenton Street, Silver Spring MD 20910. **Tel** (800)666-6380, (301)588-6380, FAX (301)588-6385. **ED** Ken Silverstone. Index available. cum. index. **Bk Rev.**

LC HD5727 .C36c ISSN 0825-0677
DD 331.12/4/0971 CN

MINUTES OF PROCEEDINGS AND EVIDENCE OF SUB-COMMITTEE B OF THE SPECIAL COMMITTEE ON EMPLOYMENT OPPORTUNITIES FOR THE '80S. [Minutes proc. evid. Sub-Comm. B Spec. Comm. Employ. Oppor. '80s]. **Main/Corp** Canada. Parliament. House of Commons. Special Committee on Employment Opportunities for the '80s. Sub-Committee B. **VFOAT** Proces-Verbaux et Temoignages du Sous-Comite B du Comite Special sur les Perspectives d'Emploi pour les Annees 80; Employment Opportunities for the '80's. Issue No. 1 (Sept. 22, 1980)-. English (French). Canada Communication Group Publishers, Order Processing, Ottawa Ontario K1A 0S9 Canada. **Tel** (819)956-4800, (819)956-4802.

LC HD7105.35.C2 C366a ISSN 0825-0138
DD 331.25/22/0971 CN

MINUTES OF PROCEEDINGS AND EVIDENCE OF THE SPECIAL COMMITTEE ON PENSION REFORM. [Minutes proc. evid. Spec. Comm. Pension Reform]. **Main/Corp** Canada. Parliament. House of Commons. Special Committee on Pension Reform. **VFOAT** Proces-Verbaux et Temoignages du Comite Special sur la Reforme des Pensions; Pension Reform; Reforme des Pensions. Issue No. 1 (Mar. 17/Apr. 21, 1983)-. English (French). Canada Communication Group Publishers, Order Processing, Ottawa Ontario K1A 0S9 Canada. **Tel** (819)956-4800, (819)956-4802.

LC HD5725.M7 A32 ISSN 0090-5321
DD 331.2/9762 US

MISSISSIPPI COVERED EMPLOYMENT & WAGES. **Main/Corp** Mississippi. Employment Security Commission. (19??)-. Periodical. English. Irregular (3 quarterly and 1 annual report). Free on request. Mississippi Employment Security Commission, PO Box 1699, Jackson MS 39205. **Tel** (601)354-8711. **ED** Raiford G. Crews. **Circ:** 250 (ctrl). ***Continues*** *Monthly Employment and Quarterly Wages of Workers Covered by the Mississippi Employment Security Law, by County, by Industry.*
Desc: Includes employment and wages covered by the Mississippi Employment Security Law.

LC HD4928.N62 U65 ISSN 0731-1494
DD 331.25/5/09762 US

MISSISSIPPI FRINGE BENEFIT SURVEY. **Added/Corp** Mississippi Employment Security Commission. Research and Statistics Dept. Mississippi Manufactures Association. **VFOAT** Mississippi Manufactures Association Fringe Benefit Survey. (19??)-. English. Every 2 years. Free on request. Mississippi Employment Security Commission, PO Box 1699, Jackson MS 39205. **Tel** (601)354-8711. **ED** Raiford G. Crews. **Circ:** 400 (ctrl).
Desc: Includes a description of fringe benefits offered by companies in Mississippi.

LC HD5725.M7 M62
DD 331.12/09762 US

MISSISSIPPI GUIDE TO LABOR MARKET INFORMATION. **Added/Corp** Mississippi Employment Security Commission. Mississippi Employment Security Commission. Research and Statistics Dept. (19??)-. English. One time a year. Free on request. Mississippi Employment Security Commission, PO Box 1699, Jackson MS 39205. **Tel** (601)354-8711. **ED** Raiford C. Crews. **Circ:** 400 (ctrl).
Desc: Lists and describes all labor market publications of the Labor Market Information Department of the Mississippi Employment Security Commission.

LC KFM6942 .A516 ISSN 1052-7869
DD 344.762/021 347.620421 US

MISSISSIPPI WORKERS' COMPENSATION REPORTER. See Insurance.

LC HD5725.M8 M59 ISSN 0148-4214
DD 331.1/1/09778 US

MISSOURI AREA LABOR TRENDS. **Added/Corp** Missouri. Division of Employment Security. (Jan. 1977)-. Periodical. English. Twelve times a year. Free on request. Division of Employment Security / Missouri, PO Box 59, Jefferson City MO 65101. **Tel** (314)751-3602. **ED** Lloyd Banwart. **Circ:** 1,100. ***Continues*** *Missouri State and Area Labor Trends.*
Desc: Provides narrative, tabular and graphical description of labor market conditions of the state of Missouri and metropolitan statistical areas.

ISSN 0026-6728
US

MISSOURI TEAMSTER. **Added/Corp** International Brotherhood of Teamsters, Chauffeurs, Warehousemen and Helpers of America. Joint Council 13 (St. Louis, Mo.). Vol. 1, No. 1 (June 7, 1963)-. Newspaper. English. Twelve times a year. $5.00. Teamsters Joint Council, 13 300 South Grand Street, St. Louis MO 63103. **Tel** FAX (314)647-2002. **ED** Gus Lumpe. **Bk Rev. Circ:** 42,000 (ctrl).
Desc: News of interest and importance to teamsters and their families.

LC HD4824 .I5 ISSN 0340-3254
GW
CCC

MITTEILUNGEN AUS DER ARBEITSMARKT- UND BERUFSFORSCHUNG. [Mitt. Arbeitsmarkt-Berufsforsch.]. (1970)-. Periodical. German (summaries and/or abstracts in English and French). Four times a year. $75.23. W. Kohlhammer Verlag GmbH, Postfach 800430, D-70549 Stuttgart Germany. **Tel** 011 49 711 78630, FAX 011 49 711 7863430, telex 7-255820. **ED** Erika Haerting and Ursula Wagner. Index available (free). **Bk Rev. Ad Acc. Circ:** 880 (ctrl). ***Continues*** *Mitteilungen (Institut fuer Arbeitsmarkt- und Berufsforschung).*
Desc: Studies and reports on all aspects of the German job and labor market, job training and education.
Ind/Abst Int. Labour Doc.; LABORDOC.

US

MLRC NEWS. **Main/Corp** Massachusetts. Labor Relations Commission. Vol. 3, No. 2 (Dec. 1979)-. Periodical. English. Irregular. Free on request. Massachusetts Labor Relations Commission, 100 Cambridge Street/Room 1604, Boston MA 02202. ***Continues*** *Massachusetts. Labor Relations Commission. News - Massachusetts Labor Relations Commission.*

LC HF5549.5.R47 M6a ISSN 0195-8194
DD 658.3/83 US

MOBILITY (WASHINGTON). (MOBILITY: MAGAZINE OF THE EMPLOYEE RELOCATION COUNCIL.). **Added/Corp** Employee Relocation Council. Vol. 1, No. 1 (Mar./Apr. 1980)-. Periodical. English. Twelve times a year. $48.00. Employee Relocation Council, 1720 North Street Northwest, Washington DC 20036. **Tel** (202)857-0905, FAX (202)467-4012. **ED** Jerry Holloman; Telephone: (202)857-0857. Index available (quarterly). cum. index. **Bk Rev. Ad Acc, Adv Mgr:** Richard McGuire. **Circ:** 12,400.
Desc: Examines key issues affecting the relocation industry for the benefit of companies, government agencies, and those providing services to relocating employees and their families.

AT
CEASED

MODERN UNIONIST, THE. (19??)-. English. Percival Publishing Ltd, 862 870 Elizabeth Street, Waterloo New South Wales, 2017 Australia. **Tel** 011 61 2 31726007.

LC HD4966.M4 A93a
AU

MONATSBEZUEGE DER ANGESTELLTEN IN DER INDUSTRIE OSTERREICHS. **Main/Corp** Bundeskammer der Gewerblichen Wirtschaft (Austria). Sektion Industrie. (19??)-. German. Irregular. Bundeskammer der Gewerblichen Wirtschaft, Wiedner Hauptstrasse 63, A-1040 Vienna Austria. **Tel** 0222 65 05 DW 4110, telex 111 871 BUKA. ***Continues*** *Statistik Uber die Monatsbezuege der Angestellten.*

ISSN 1065-7797
DD 331 US

MONMOUTH'S EARLY REPORT. [Monmouth's early rep.]. **Added/Corp** Probation Association of New Jersey. Local 113. (July 17, 1992)-. Periodical. English. Four times a year. $2.00 (members). Court House, Box 1252, Freehold NJ 07728.

ISSN 0708-9945
DD 331/.05 CN

MONOGRAPHIE - ECOLE DE RELATIONS INDUSTRIELLES, UNIVERSITE DE MONTREAL. See Business and Economics-Personnel Management.

US

MONOGRAPHS IN ORGANIZATIONAL BEHAVIOR AND INDUSTRIAL RELATIONS. Vol. 1 (1983)-. Monographic series. English. Irregular. $73.25. JAI Press Inc., 55 Old Post Road, Suite 2, PO Box 1678, Greenwich CT 06836-1678. **Tel** (203)661-7602, FAX (203)661-0792. **ED** Samuel Bacharach.

LC HD8051 .A78 ISSN 0098-1818
DD 331/.0973 US
Pr Rev.

MONTHLY LABOR REVIEW. (MONTHLY LABOR REVIEW / U.S. DEPARTMENT OF LABOR, BUREAU OF LABOR STATISTICS.). [Mon. labor rev.]. **Added/Corp** United States. Bureau of Labor Statistics. **VFOAT** MLR. Vol. 7, No. 1 (July 1918)-. Government Publication. English. Twelve times a year. $35.00. US Department of Labor, 200 Constitution Avenue NW, Washington DC 20210. **Tel** (202)219-7316, FAX (202)219-7312. **(Subscription address:** Superintendent of Documents, US Government Printing Office, Washington DC 20402. **)** cum. index. available on microfilm and microfiche from University Microfilms International (UMI); available on an online database (files 15,647,648/Full-Text) from DIALOG. Documents available from The Genuine Article, UMI Article Clearinghouse, Documents on Demand. ***Continues*** *Monthly Review of the U.S. Bureau of Labor Statistics.*
Desc: Articles on labor force, wages, prices, productivity, economic growth, and occupational injuries and illnesses. Regular features include a review of developments in industrial relations, book reviews, and current labor statistics.
Ind/Abst ABI/INFORM Glob. Ed.; ABI/INFORM Ondisc: Expr. Ed.; ABI/INFORM [Computer File] (Aug. 1971-); Abstr. Soc. Gerontol. (1977-?); Acad. Abstr. Full Text Elite; Acad. Abstr.; Acad. Ind. [Computer File] (1984-); Acad. Search; Am. Hist. Life (1968-); Am. Stat. Index; Anbar Account. Finan. Abstr. [Full Txt.]; Anbar Mark. Distr. Abstr. [Full Txt.]; Anbar Top Manage. Abstr. [Full Txt.]; Book Rev. Digest (Aug. 1971-); Book Rev. Index; Bus. ASAP (1990-) [Full Txt.]; Bus. Index (1985-); Bus. Period. Index; Bus. Source Plus; Bus. Source; Cumul. Index Nurs. Allied Health Lit.; Curr. Cit.; Curr. Contents Soc. Behav. Sci.; Curr. Index J. Educ.; Curr. Law Index (1980-Dec. 1985); Econ. Lit. Index (19??-); EP Collect.; Expand. Acad. Index (1984-); F&S Index Plus Text, Int. [Select. Cov.]; Gen. BusinessFile (1985-); Gen. Period. Index (1985-); Health Plan. Adminis.; High. Educ. Abstr. (1968-); Homework Help.; Hosp. Health Admin. Index; Hum. Resour. Abstr. (?-?); Index Period. Lit. Aging; INFO-SOUTH Abstr.; Int. Labour Doc.; J. Econ. Lit.; LABORDOC; Leg. Resour. Index (1980-Dec. 1985); LegalTrac (1980-1985); Mag. Artic. Summar. Elite; Mag. Artic. Summar. Select; Mag. Artic. Summar. CD-ROM; Mag. ASAP Plus [Full Txt.]; Mag. Express (1986-) [Full Txt.]; Mag. Index Plus (1989-); Mag. Search; Manage. Bibliogr. Rev.; MasterFile FullTEXT 1000; MasterFile FullTEXT 350; MasterFile FullTEXT 650; MasterFile FullTEXT (Jan. 1989-) [Full Txt.]; Newsp. Period. Abstr. (1986-); OCLC; Oper. Prod. Manage. Abstr. [Full Txt.]; PAIS Int. Print (1991-); Person. Train. Abstr. [Full Txt.]; Person. Manage. Abstr.; Predicasts Forecasts; Pub. Lib. FullTEXT; Read. Guide Abstr. Select Ed.; Read. Guide Period. Lit.; Res. Alert [Full Cov.]; Resource/One Ondisc (1977-); Saf. Health Work; Soc. Sci. Source; Soc. Sci. Cit. Index [Full Cov.]; Soc. Sci. Index; Soc. Sci. Index Fulltext (Sept. 1988-) [Full Txt.]; Soc. Work Abstr. (Spring, Summer 1987-) [Select. Cov.]; Stud. Women Abstr.; Tech. Educ. Train. Abstr.; Telebase; Mag. Index (1977-);

Business and Economics —Labor

UMI ABI/Inform--Bus. Period. Ondisc (Jan. 1987-) [Full Txt.]; Vocat. Search; Wilson Bus. Abstr.; Women Manage. Rev. [Full Txt.]; Work Relat. Abstr.

LC HD8700.6 .A38a   ISSN 0301-8288
DD 331.1/1/09595   MY
MONTHLY REPORT - MINISTRY OF LABOUR & MANPOWER (KUALA LUMPUR). (MONTHLY REPORT.). **Main/Corp** Malaysia. Kementerian Buruh dan Tenaga Rakyat. (July 1971)-. Periodical. English. Twelve times a year. $9.00. Kementerian Buroh Dan Tenaga Raayat, Jalan Raja, Kuala Lumpur Malaysia. *Continues* Malaysia. Kementerian Buroh. Monthly Report.

SZ
MOP : GEBAEUDEUNTERHALT & REINIGUNG. See Building and Construction.

LC HD6615.R55 R56a
DD 331.8098   BL
MOVIMENTO SINDICAL. Main/Corp Rio Grande do sul, Brazil (State). Secretaria de Coordenacao e Planejamento. Superintendencia de Planejamento Global. (19??)-. Portuguese. Fundacao de Economia e Estatistica, Rua Duque de Caixias 1691, 90010 Porto Alegre, Rio Grande do Sul Brazil. **Tel** 0512-259455, FAX 0512-25006, telex 0515042.

US
MOVING AND STORAGE WAGE SURVEY, ATLANTA, GA. / U.S. DEPARTMENT OF LABOR, BUREAU OF LABOR STATISTICS. (19??)-. Government Publication. English. One time a year. US Department of Labor / Bureau of Labor Statistics, 441 G Street Northwest, Washington DC 20212. **Tel** (202)606-7800, FAX (202)606-7797.

US
MOVING AND STORAGE WAGE SURVEY, COLORADO SPRINGS, COLO. / U.S. DEPARTMENT OF LABOR, BUREAU OF LABOR STATISTICS. (19??)-. Government Publication. English. One time a year. US Department of Labor / Bureau of Labor Statistics, 441 G Street Northwest, Washington DC 20212. **Tel** (202)606-7800, FAX (202)606-7797.

US
MOVING AND STORAGE WAGE SURVEY, MOBILE-PENSACOLA-PANAMA CITY, ALA.-FLA. / U.S. DEPARTMENT OF LABOR, BUREAU OF LABOR STATISTICS. (19??)-. Government Publication. English. One time a year. US Department of Labor / Bureau of Labor Statistics, 441 G Street Northwest, Washington DC 20212. **Tel** (202)606-7800, FAX (202)606-7797.

US
MOVING AND STORAGE WAGE SURVEY, NASSAU-SUFFOLK, N.Y. / U.S. DEPARTMENT OF LABOR, BUREAU OF LABOR STATISTICS. (19??)-. Government Publication. English. One time a year. US Department of Labor / Bureau of Labor Statistics, 441 G Street Northwest, Washington DC 20212. **Tel** (202)606-7800, FAX (202)606-7797.

US
MOVING AND STORAGE WAGE SURVEY, NORTHWEST TEXAS / U.S. DEPARTMENT OF LABOR, BUREAU OF LABOR STATISTICS. (19??)-. Government Publication. English. One time a year. US Department of Labor / Bureau of Labor Statistics, 441 G Street Northwest, Washington DC 20212. **Tel** (202)606-7800, FAX (202)606-7797.

US
MOVING AND STORAGE WAGE SURVEY, OXNARD-SIMI VALLEY-VENTURA, CALIF. / U.S. DEPARTMENT OF LABOR, BUREAU OF LABOR STATISTICS. (19??)-. Government Publication. English. One time a year. US Department of Labor / Bureau of Labor Statistics, 441 G Street Northwest, Washington DC 20212. **Tel** (202)606-7800, FAX (202)606-7797.

US
MOVING AND STORAGE WAGE SURVEY, PATERSON-CLIFTON PASSAIC, N.J. / U.S. DEPARTMENT OF LABOR, BUREAU OF LABOR STATISTICS. (19??)-. Government Publication. English. One time a year. US Department of Labor / Bureau of Labor Statistics, 441 G Street Northwest, Washington DC 20212. **Tel** (202)606-7800, FAX (202)606-7797.

US
MOVING AND STORAGE WAGE SURVEY, RICHMOND, VA. Added/Corp United States. Bureau of Labor Statistics. (19??)-. English. One time a year. US Department of Labor / Bureau of Labor Statistics, 441 G Street Northwest, Washington DC 20212. **Tel** (202)606-7800, FAX (202)606-7797.

US
MOVING AND STORAGE WAGE SURVEY, SAN ANTONIO, TEX. / U.S. DEPARTMENT OF LABOR, BUREAU OF LABOR STATISTICS. (19??)-. Government Publication. English. One time a year. US Department of Labor / Bureau of Labor Statistics, 441 G Street Northwest, Washington DC 20212. **Tel** (202)606-7800, FAX (202)606-7797.

US
MOVING AND STORAGE WAGE SURVEY, UTICA-ROME, N.Y. / U.S. DEPARTMENT OF LABOR, BUREAU OF LABOR STATISTICS. (19??)-. Government Publication. English. One time a year. US Department of Labor / Bureau of Labor Statistics, 441 G Street Northwest, Washington DC 20212. **Tel** (202)606-7800, FAX (202)606-7797.

US
MOVING AND STORAGE WAGE SURVEY, WESTERN AND NORTHERN MASSACHUSETTS. (19??)-. Government Publication. English. One time a year. US Department of Labor / Bureau of Labor Statistics, 441 G Street Northwest, Washington DC 20212. **Tel** (202)606-7800, FAX (202)606-7797.

US
MOVING AND STORAGE WAGE SURVEY, WICHITA, KAN. / U.S. DEPARTMENT OF LABOR, BUREAU OF LABOR STATISTICS. (19??)-. Government Publication. English. One time a year. US Department of Labor / Bureau of Labor Statistics, 441 G Street Northwest, Washington DC 20212. **Tel** (202)606-7800, FAX (202)606-7797.

US
MOVING AND STORAGE WAGE SURVEY, WILMINGTON, DEL- N.J.-MD. (19??)-. Government Publication. English. One time a year. US Department of Labor / Bureau of Labor Statistics, 441 G Street Northwest, Washington DC 20212. **Tel** (202)606-7800, FAX (202)606-7797.

UK
MSF HEALTH NEWS. VFOAT Health News. (Summer 1988)-. Periodical. English. Four times a year. ASTMS / England, 79 Camden Road, London NW1 9ES United Kingdom. **Tel** 011 44 171 2674422.

US
MULTIPLE JOBHOLDERS. (19??)-. Government Publication. English. One time a year. US Department of Labor / Bureau of Labor Statistics, 441 G Street Northwest, Washington DC 20212. **Tel** (202)606-7800, FAX (202)606-7797.

LC HD8581 .M66
DD 322/.2/0946   SP
MUNDO OBRERO (MADRID, SPAIN). (MUNDO OBRERO : MO.). **Added/Corp** Partido Comunista de Espana. **VFOAT** MO; M.O. Vol. 1, No. 1, (Dec. 1978)-. Periodical. Spanish. Twelve times a year. $34.64. Mundo Obrero, C Marques de Monteagudo 8, 28028 Madrid Spain. **Tel** 011 34 1 3569807.

LC HD8083.A4 N63 HD4939.U U6
DD 331/.0977 S 331.2/81/352077311   US
MUNICIPAL GOVERNMENT WAGE SURVEY, CHICAGO, ILLINOIS / U.S. DEPARTMENT OF LABOR, BUREAU OF LABOR STATISTICS, NORTH CENTRAL REGION. English. US Department of Labor Bureau of Labor Statistics / Chicago, 230 South Dearborn Street, 9th Floor, Chicago IL 60604. **Tel** (312)353-7226, FAX (312)353-1886.

LC HD8083.A4 N63 HD4939.U6 U6
DD 331.1/0977S   US
MUNICIPAL GOVERNMENT WAGE SURVEY, COLUMBUS, OHIO / U.S. DEPARTMENT OF LABOR, BUREAU OF LABOR STATISTICS, NORTH CENTRAL REGION V. English. US Department of Labor Bureau of Labor Statistics / Chicago, 230 South Dearborn Street, 9th Floor, Chicago IL 60604. **Tel** (312)353-7226, FAX (312)353-1886. available on microfiche (Vols. for (1978)-) distributed to depository libraries.

LC HD8083.A4 N63 JS844.A4 A4
DD 331/.0977 S 352/. 005123/0977434   US
MUNICIPAL GOVERNMENT WAGE SURVEY, DETROIT, MICHIGAN. (19??)-. English. One time a year. US Department of Labor Bureau of Labor Statistics / Chicago, 230 South Dearborn Street, 9th Floor, Chicago IL 60604. **Tel** (312)353-7226, FAX (312)353-1886.

LC JS451.M43 M39A   ISSN 0542-9676
DD 331.2/81/3520744   US
MUNICIPAL SALARY SURVEY : BENCH-MARK JOBS. Main/Corp Massachusetts Municipal Personnel Association. (19??)-. English. One time a year. Massachusetts Municipal Personnel Association, 131 Tremont Street/4th Floor, Boston MA 02111.

LC JS451.S67 M85A   ISSN 0199-9850
DD 331.2/813520757   US
MUNICIPAL WAGE AND SALARY SURVEY. Main/Corp Municipal Association of South Carolina. (1979)-. English. One time a year. $10.00. Municipal Association of South Carolina, PO Box 12109, Columbia SC 29211. *Continues* Municipal Wage, Salary, and Benefit Survey, 0160-5828.

US
MUSKEGON'S LABOR MARKET NEWS. Added/Corp Michigan Employment Security Commission. Bureau of Research and Statistics. Information and Reports Section. Vol. 12, No. 1 (Mar. 1992)-. Periodical. English. Twelve times a year. Detroit Employment Security Commission, 7310 Woodward Castro, Room 520, Detroit MI 48202. **Tel** (313)876-5427. *Continues* Muskegon Labor Market Review.

LC HE2791 .P369   ISSN 0740-672X
DD 331.7/61385/0974   US
MUTUAL MAGAZINE (PHILADELPHIA, PA. : 1980), THE. See Transportation-Railroads.

ISSN 0270-9732
US
N.L.R.B ELECTION REPORT. CASES CLOSED. (N.L.R.B. ELECTION REPORT. CASES CLOSED / COMPILED BY DIVISION OF ADMINISTRATION.). **Added/Corp** United States. National Labor Relations Board. Division of Administration. **VFOAT** NLRB Election Report. Cases Closed. **VAT** National Labor Relations Board Election Report. Cases Closed. (1961)-. Periodical. English. Twelve times a year. $33.00. National Labor Relations Board, 251 North Main, 447 Federal Building, Winston Salem NC 27101. **Tel** (919)631-5201. **(Subscription address:** Superintendent of Documents, US Government Printing Office, Washington DC 20402.) Documents available from Documents on Demand.
Ind/Abst Am. Stat. Index.

ISSN 0747-5837
DD 331   US
NAB CLEARINGHOUSE QUARTERLY. [NAB clgh. q.]. **VFOAT** N.A.B. Clearinghouse Quarterly. **VAT** National Alliance of Business Clearinghouse Quarterly. Vol. 1, No. 1 (Spring 1984)-. Periodical. English. Four times a year. $40.00. National Alliance of Business, 1201 New York Avenue Northwest, Suite 700, Washington DC 20005. **Tel** (202)289-2888.

LC L13 .A699513   ISSN 0270-6881
DD 331.89/04137/06073   US
NAEN BULLETIN. See Education.

ISSN 8750-863X
DD 331   US
NALC RETIREE. (NALC RETIREE : A PUBLICATION FOR RETIRED MEMBERS OF THE NATIONAL ASSOCIATION OF LETTER CARRIERS.). **VAT** National Association of Letter Carriers Retiree. Vol. 1, No. 1 (Fall 1984)-. Periodical. English. Four times a year. $1.20. National Association of Letter Carriers, 100 Indiana Avenue NW, Washington DC 20001. **Tel** (202)393-4695.

LC HE6499 .P64   ISSN 0027-8513
US
NATIONAL ALLIANCE. (NATIONAL ALLIANCE : OFFICIAL ORGAN OF NATIONAL ALLIANCE OF POSTAL AND FEDERAL EMPLOYEES.). **Added/Corp** National Alliance of Postal and Federal Employees (U.S.). Vol. 15, No. 1 (Jan. 1966)-. Periodical. English. Twelve times a year. $10.00. National Alliance Postal & Federal Employees, 1628 11th Street Northwest, Washington DC 20001. **Tel** (202)939-6325, FAX (202)939-6389. **ED** Jacquelyn C. Moore. **Ad Acc. Circ:** 14,000 (ctrl).
Continues Postal Alliance.
Desc: Information concerning locals, rules and regulations update for postal and federal employees and political action.

Business and Economics —Labor

ISSN 0194-0775
US
NATIONAL EMPLOYMENT LISTING SERVICE FOR HUMAN SERVICES. Added/Corp Sam Houston State University. National Employment Listing Service. Sam Houston State University. National Employment Listing Service for Human Services. **VFOAT** NELS Bulletin. (197?)-. Bulletin. English. Twelve times a year. $65.00 US; $85.00 other. Sam Houston State University Criminal Justice Center, Huntsville TX 77341. **Tel** (409)294-1692. **ED** Stephanie Tinsley. **Bk Rev. Ad Acc. Circ:** 2,500 (ctrl).
Desc: Publication of current employment openings in the various criminal justice fields. Monthly employment listings in law enforcement, corrections, security, community services and academics.

ISSN 0197-7032
US
NATIONAL RIGHT TO WORK NEWSLETTER. Added/Corp National Right to Work Committee. (1955)-. Newsletter. English. Twelve times a year. $15.00. National Right of Work Committee, 8001 Braddock Road/Suite 500, Springfield VA 22160. **Tel** (703)321-9820, FAX (703)321-7342. **ED** Reed Larson. **Circ:** 150,000 (ctrl). available on microfilm. **Continues** Right to Work National Newsletter.
Desc: Serves to supplement and reinforce committee bulletins, brochures, advisories and other internal communications to our 1.7 million members.

LC Q148 .S56a
DD 331.11/915/095957 SI
NATIONAL SURVEY OF SCIENTIFIC MANPOWER. Main/Corp Singapore. Ministry of Science and Technology. (1971)-. English. Every 3 years. $5.00. Ministry of Science and Technology, 63 Blk 1 Science Park Drive, Singapore 0511 Singapore.

LC AS262 .K417 HD8526.5
UN
NAUKOVYI KOMUNIZM. Main/Corp Kharkivskyi Derzhavnyi Universytet Imeni O.M. Horkoho. Ukrainian.

LC HD5725.I6 I53C
DD 331.12/3/097729 US
NEED FOR WORKERS IN SELECTED OCCUPATIONS RELATED TO VOCATIONAL & TECHNICAL EDUCATION PROGRAMS. REGION 1. Main/Corp Indiana. Employment Security Division. Research and Statistics Section. **VFOAT** Indiana Labor Market. (19??)-. English. One time a year. Indiana Employment Security Division, Research and Statistics Section, 10 North Senate Avenue, Indianapolis IN 46204. **Tel** (317)232-7187.

LC HD5725.I6 I53D
DD 331.12/3/097728 US
NEED FOR WORKERS IN SELECTED OCCUPATIONS RELATED TO VOCATIONAL & TECHNICAL EDUCATION PROGRAMS. REGION 2. Main/Corp Indiana. Employment Security Division. Research and Statistics Section. **VFOAT** Indiana Labor Market. (19??)-. English. One time a year. Indiana Employment Security Division, Research and Statistics Section, 10 North Senate Avenue, Indianapolis IN 46204. **Tel** (317)232-7187.

LC HD5725.I6 I53E
DD 331.12/3/097727 US
NEED FOR WORKERS IN SELECTED OCCUPATIONS RELATED TO VOCATIONAL & TECHNICAL EDUCATION PROGRAMS. REGION 3. Main/Corp Indiana. Employment Security Division. Research and Statistics Section. **VFOAT** Indiana Labor Market. (19??)-. English. One time a year. Indiana Employment Security Division, Research and Statistics Section, 10 North Senate Avenue, Indianapolis IN 46204. **Tel** (317)232-7187.

LC HD5725.I6 I53F
DD 331.12/3/097729 US
NEED FOR WORKERS IN SELECTED OCCUPATIONS RELATED TO VOCATIONAL & TECHNICAL EDUCATION PROGRAMS. REGION 4. Main/Corp Indiana. Employment Security Division. Research and Statistics Section. **VFOAT** Indiana Labor Market. (19??)-. English. One time a year. Indiana Employment Security Division, Research and Statistics Section, 10 North Senate Avenue, Indianapolis IN 46204. **Tel** (317)232-7187.

LC HD5725.I6 I53G
DD 331.12/3/097728 US
NEED FOR WORKERS IN SELECTED OCCUPATIONS RELATED TO VOCATIONAL & TECHNICAL EDUCATION PROGRAMS. REGION 5. Main/Corp Indiana. Employment Security Division. Research and Statistics Section. **VFOAT** Indiana Labor Market. (19??)-. English. One time a year. Indiana Employment Security Division, Research and Statistics Section, 10 North Senate Avenue, Indianapolis IN 46204. **Tel** (317)232-7187.

LC HD5725.I6 I53h
DD 331.12/3/097726 US
NEED FOR WORKERS IN SELECTED OCCUPATIONS RELATED TO VOCATIONAL & TECHNICAL EDUCATION PROGRAMS. REGION 6. Main/Corp Indiana. Employment Security Division. Research and Statistics Section. **VFOAT** Indiana Labor Market. (19??)-. English. Indiana Employment Security Division, Research and Statistics Section, 10 North Senate Avenue, Indianapolis IN 46204. **Tel** (317)232-7187.

LC HD5725.I6 I53I
DD 331.12/3/097724 US
NEED FOR WORKERS IN SELECTED OCCUPATIONS RELATED TO VOCATIONAL & TECHNICAL EDUCATION PROGRAMS. REGION 7. Main/Corp Indiana. Employment Security Division. Research and Statistics Section. **VFOAT** Indiana Labor Market. (19??)-. English. One time a year. Indiana Employment Security Division, Research and Statistics Section, 10 North Senate Avenue, Indianapolis IN 46204. **Tel** (317)232-7187.

LC HD5725.I6 I53j
DD 331.12/3/097725 US
NEED FOR WORKERS IN SELECTED OCCUPATIONS RELATED TO VOCATIONAL & TECHNICAL EDUCATION PROGRAMS. REGION 8. Main/Corp Indiana. Employment Security Division. Research and Statistics Section. **VFOAT** Indiana Labor Market. (19??)-. English. Indiana Employment Security Division, Research and Statistics Section, 10 North Senate Avenue, Indianapolis IN 46204. **Tel** (317)232-7187.

LC HD5725.I6 I53k
DD 331.12/3/097726 US
NEED FOR WORKERS IN SELECTED OCCUPATIONS RELATED TO VOCATIONAL & TECHNICAL EDUCATION PROGRAMS. REGION 9. Main/Corp Indiana. Employment Security Division. Research and Statistics Section. **VFOAT** Indiana Labor Market. (19??)-. English. One time a year. Indiana Employment Security Division, Research and Statistics Section, 10 North Senate Avenue, Indianapolis IN 46204. **Tel** (317)232-7187.

LC HD5725.I6 I53L
DD 331.12/3/09772255 US
NEED FOR WORKERS IN SELECTED OCCUPATIONS RELATED TO VOCATIONAL & TECHNICAL EDUCATION PROGRAMS. REGION 10. Main/Corp Indiana. Employment Security Division. Research and Statistics Section. **VFOAT** Indiana Labor Market. (19??)-. English. One time a year. Indiana Employment Security Division, Research and Statistics Section, 10 North Senate Avenue, Indianapolis IN 46204. **Tel** (317)232-7187.

LC HD5725.I6 I53O
DD 331.12/3/097722 US
NEED FOR WORKERS IN SELECTED OCCUPATIONS RELATED TO VOCATIONAL & TECHNICAL EDUCATION PROGRAMS. REGION 11. Main/Corp Indiana. Employment Security Division. Research and Statistics Section. **VFOAT** Indiana Labor Market. (19??)-. English. One time a year. Indiana Employment Security Division, Research and Statistics Section, 10 North Senate Avenue, Indianapolis IN 46204. **Tel** (317)232-7187.

LC HD5725.I6 I53P
DD 331.12/3/097721 US
NEED FOR WORKERS IN SELECTED OCCUPATIONS RELATED TO VOCATIONAL & TECHNICAL EDUCATION PROGRAMS. REGION 12. Main/Corp Indiana. Employment Security Division. Research and Statistics Section. **VFOAT** Indiana Labor Market. (19??)-. English. One time a year. Indiana Employment Security Division, Research and Statistics Section, 10 North Senate Avenue, Indianapolis IN 46204. **Tel** (317)232-7187.

LC HD5725.I6 I53N
DD 331.12/3/097723 US
NEED FOR WORKERS IN SELECTED OCCUPATIONS RELATED TO VOCATIONAL & TECHNICAL EDUCATION PROGRAMS. REGION 13. Main/Corp Indiana. Employment Security Division. Research and Statistics Section. **VFOAT** Indiana Labor Market. (19??)-. English. One time a year. Indiana Employment Security Division, Research and Statistics Section, 10 North Senate Avenue, Indianapolis IN 46204. **Tel** (317)232-7187.

LC HD5725.I6 I53M
DD 331.12/3/097722 US
NEED FOR WORKERS IN SELECTED OCCUPATIONS RELATED TO VOCATIONAL & TECHNICAL EDUCATION PROGRAMS. REGION 14. Main/Corp Indiana. Employment Security Division. Research and Statistics Section. **VFOAT** Indiana Labor Market. (19??)-. English. One time a year. Indiana Employment Security Division, Research and Statistics Section, 10 North Senate Avenue, Indianapolis IN 46204. **Tel** (317)232-7187.

ISSN 0228-2593
DD 331.89/049009714 CN
NEGOCIATIONS 79. **VAT** Negociations Soixante-Dix-Neuf. Vol. 1 (May 4, 1979)-. Periodical. French. Free. Association des Entrepreneurs en Construction du Quebec Siege Social, Bureau 100, 7777 boulevard Louis-H Lafontaine, Anjou Quebec H1K 4E4 Canada.

LC HD8101.5.B74 D45a   ISSN 0703-0665
DD 331.89/09711 CN
NEGOTIATED WORKING CONDITIONS (VICTORIA). (NEGOTIATED WORKING CONDITIONS.). Added/Corp British Columbia. Ministry of Labour. Program Services. British Columbia. Dept. of Labour. Research and Planning Branch. British Columbia. Ministry of Labour. Research and Planning. **VFOAT** Collective Agreements in British Columbia. (1974)-. English. One time a year. 28.01Can$. Crown Publications Inc., 521 Fort Street, Victoria British Columbia, V8W 1E7 Canada. **Tel** (604)386-4636, FAX (604)386-0221.
Continues Analysis of Collective Agreements in British Columbia, 0703-0673.

ISSN 0228-2607
DD 331.89/049009714 CN
NEGOTIATIONS 79. Added/Corp Association of Building Contractors of Quebec. **VAT** Negotiations Seventy-Nine. Vol. 1 (May 4, 1979)-. Periodical. English. Free. Association of Building Contractors of Quebec, Head Office, Suite 100, 7777 Louis-H Lafontaine Boulevard, Anjou Quebec H4E 4E4 Canada.

LC HD4824 .R62a
JA
NEMPO. Main/Corp Rodo Kagaku Kenkyujo. (1922)-. Periodical. Japanese. One time a year. Rodo Kagaku Kenkyujo, 2-8-14 Sugao Miyamae-ku, Kawasaki 216 Japan. **Tel** 81 44 977 2121, FAX 81 44 976 8659. **ED** Kazutaka Kogi.

GW
NEUE ARBEITERPRESSE. (19??)-. German. One time a week. DM65.00 Germany; $110.00 US; DM85.00 other. Bund Sozialistischer Arbeiter, Postfach 100, 105 W-4300 Essen 1 Germany. **Tel** 0201 733556. **ED** B Rippert. **Bk Rev.**
Desc: Politics and history of the workers movement.

LC HD5725.N3 N447
DD 331.12/09793 US
NEVADA AREA LABOR REVIEW. ECONOMIC DEVELOPMENTS AND ... OUTLOOK. **VFOAT** Economic Developments and ... Outlook. 1983-. English. One time a year. **Formed by the union of** Nevada Area Labor Review, Las Vegas SMSA **and** Nevada Area Labor Review, Reno SMSA.

LC HD4976.N35 N43a
DD 331.2/9793 US
CEASED
NEVADA WAGE SURVEY. Main/Corp Nevada. Employment Security Research Section. (197?)-(1992). Periodical. English. Nevada Employment Security Dept, 500 East Third Street, Carson City NV 89713. **Tel** (702)885-4550. Index available. **Bk Rev. Ad Acc. Circ:** 2,300 (ctrl). **Continues** Nevada Statewide Wage Survey, 0097-8760.
Desc: Metropolitan and rural occupational wage information, public and private sector for Nevada.

ISSN 0316-5795
DD 330.9715/04 CN
NEW BRUNSWICK FEDERATION OF LABOUR. ANNUAL SUBMISSION TO THE PREMIER AND MEMBERS OF THE CABINET OF THE GOVERNMENT OF NEW BRUNSWICK. (MEMOIRE ANNUEL PRESENTE AU PREMIER MINISTRE ET AUX

MEMBRES DU CABINET DE LA PROVINCE DU NOUVEAU-BRUNSWICK / LA FEDERATION DES TRAVAILLEURS DU NOUVEAU-BRUNSWICK.). **Main/Corp** Federation des Travailleurs du Nouveau-Brunswick. **VFOAT** Annual Submission to the Premier and Members of the Cabinet of the Province of New Brunswick. Mar. 24, 1983-. French (French and English). One time a year. Federation des Travailleurs du Nouveau-Brunswick, Salle 209 96 Av Norwood, Moncton New Brunswick E1C 6L9 Canada. ***Continues*** *Annual Submission to the Premier and Members of the Cabinet of the Government of New Brunswick, 0316-5795.*

LC HD5015 .A33
DD 331.2/942 UK
NEW EARNINGS SURVEY (LONDON, 1970-). (NEW EARNINGS SURVEY.). **Main/Corp** Great Britain. Department of Employment. (1970)-. English. One time a year. £69.00. Her Majesty's Stationery Office, 51 Nine Elms Lane, London SW8 5DR United Kingdom. **Tel** 011 44 171 8738459, 011 44 171 8738499, FAX 011 44 171 8738499, 011 44 171 8738456, telex 297138. **(Subscription address:** Her Majesty's Stationery Office, PO Box 276, Public Centre, London SW8 5DT United Kingdom. **Tel** 011 44 171 8738499, 011 44 171 8738456.) ***Continues*** *Great Britain. Dept. of Employment and Productivity. New Earning Survey.*
Desc: Differs from other official surveys of earnings in that information is obtained on individual employers (covering hours of work and the composition of earnings) which, in conjunction with details on the characteristics of each individual enable a wide range of analyses to be prepared on the distribution and structure of earnings.

ISSN 0703-9263
DD 331.1/1/0971 CN
NEW FOUNDATIONS. Vol. 1 (Mar. 1977)-. Periodical. English. 25c. per no. $3. for 12 issues. New Foundations, Box 8138, Kitchener Ontario N2K 2B6 Canada.

US
NEW JERSEY EMPLOYMENT AND THE ECONOMY. ATLANTIC COASTAL REGION (ATLANTIC, CAPE MAY, MONMOUTH, AND OCEAN COUNTIES). **VFOAT** Atlantic Coastal Region. No. 1 (Oct. 1983)-. Periodical. English. Twelve times a year. New Jersey Department of Labor & Industry, Labor Market & Demographic, CN 388, Trenton NJ 08625. **Tel** (609)984-2595. ***Formed by the union of*** *New Jersey Employment and the Economy. Atlantic City Labor Area* ***and*** *New Jersey Employment and the Economy. Long Branch Asbury Park Labor Market.*

US
NEW JERSEY EMPLOYMENT AND THE ECONOMY. NORTHERN NEW JERSEY REGION (BERGEN, ESSEX, HUDSON, HUNTERDON, MIDDLESEX, MORRIS, PASSAIC, SOMERSET, SUSSEX, UNION AND WARREN COUNTIES). **Added/Corp** New Jersey. Dept. of Labor. Division of Planning and Research. **VFOAT** Northern New Jersey Region. No. 1 (Oct. 1983)-. Periodical. English. Twelve times a year. New Jersey Department of Labor & Industry, Labor Market & Demographic, CN 388, Trenton NJ 08625. **Tel** (609)984-2595. ***Formed by the union of*** *New Jersey Employment and the Economy. Hackensack Labor Area; New Jersey Employment and the Economy. Jersey City Labor Area; New Jersey Employment and the Economy. Newark Labor Area; New Jersey Employment and the Economy. Paterson-Clifton-Passaic Labor Area* ***and*** *New Jersey Employment and the Economy. New Brunswick-Perth Amboy-Sayreville Labor Area.*

US
NEW JERSEY EMPLOYMENT AND THE ECONOMY. SOUTHERN NEW JERSEY REGION (BURLINGTON, CAMDEN, CUMBERLAND, GLOUCESTER, MERCER, AND SALEM COUNTIES). **VFOAT** Southern New Jersey Region (Burlington, Camden, Cumberland, Gloucester, Mercer and Salem Counties). No. 1 (Oct. 1983)-. Periodical. English. Twelve times a year. New Jersey Department of Labor & Industry, Labor Market & Demographic, CN 388, Trenton NJ 08625. **Tel** (609)984-2595. ***Formed by the union of*** *New Jersey Employment and the Economy. Camden Labor Area; New Jersey Employment and the Economy. Trenton Labor Area* ***and*** *New Jersey Employment and the Economy. Vineland Labor Area.*

LC KFN2132.8.P77 A496
DD 344.749/0189041351 347.904189041351 US
NEW JERSEY PUBLIC EMPLOYEE REPORTER. **Added/Corp** Labor Relations Press. New Jersey. Public Employment Relations Commission. **VFOAT** Public Employee Reporter (New Jersey Edition). (1975)-. English. Twenty-four times a year. $655.00. LRP Publications, 747 Dresher Road, Suite 500, Horsham PA 19044. **Tel** (800)341-7874, (215)784-0941, FAX (215)784-9639, (215)784-0870.
Desc: A full-text subscription service reporting all significant New Jersey Public Employment Relations Commission and related court decisions, comprehensively indexed and headnoted.

US
NEW JERSEY STATE AFL-CIO NEWS. **Main/Corp** New Jersey State AFL-CIO. **Added/Corp** New Jersey State AFL-CIO. News. (19??)-. Periodical. English. New Jersey State AFL-CIO, 106 West State Street, Trenton NJ 08608. **Tel** (609)989-8730. **ED** Charles H Marciante. **Circ:** 3,000 (ctrl).
Desc: Details issues and events of importance to organized labor and its membership in New Jersey.

LC HD5725.N6 N46d
DD 331.1/09789/05 US
NEW MEXICO LABOR MARKET ANNUAL PLANNING REPORT FOR PROGRAM YEAR ... / NEW MEXICO DEPARTMENT OF LABOR, BUREAU OF ECONOMIC RESEARCH AND ANALYSIS. **Added/Corp** New Mexico. Bureau of Economic Research and Analysis. (198?)-. English. Department of Labor / Albuquerque, PO Box 1928, Bureau of Economic Research, Albuquerque NM 87103. **Tel** (505)841-8645. ***Continues*** *New Mexico Annual Manpower Planning Report (Albuquerque, N.M. : 1985).*

LC HD5725.N6 A3
DD 331.12/09789 US
NEW MEXICO LABOR MARKET REVIEW. **Added/Corp** New Mexico. Employment Security Dept. Research and Statistics Section. New Mexico. Employment Services Division. New Mexico. Employment Security Commission. (Sept. 1975)-. Periodical. English. Twelve times a year. Free on request. Department of Labor / Albuquerque, PO Box 1928, Bureau of Economic Research, Albuquerque NM 87103. **Tel** (505)841-8645. **ED** Lawrence E. Blackwell. ctrl circ. ***Continues*** *New Mexico Manpower Review.*

UK
NEW REVIEW OF THE LOW PAY UNIT, THE. **Added/Corp** Low Pay Unit. No. 1 (Dec. 1989/Jan. 1990)-. Periodical. English. Three times a year. $51.33. Low Pay Unit Ltd, 9 Upper Berkeley Street, London W1H 8BY United Kingdom. **Tel** 011 44 171 7137616, FAX 011 44 171 7137581. ***Continues*** *Low Pay Review.*
Ind/Abst Int. Labour Doc.

LC HD5715.3.I8 I67A **ISSN** 0098-0021
DD 331.2/5924/09777 US
NEW SKILLS FOR PROGRESS : MDTA. **Main/Corp** Iowa. Employment Security Commission. Employability Development Section. **VFOAT** MDTA: New Skills for Progress. (19??)-. English. Employment Security Commission Section, 1000 East Grand Avenue, Des Moines IA 50319.

LC HD6331 .N494 **ISSN** 0268-1072
DD 338/.06 UK
CCC
NEW TECHNOLOGY, WORK, AND EMPLOYMENT. Vol. 1, No. 1 (Spring 1986)-. Academic Scholarly Publication. English. Two times a year. $100.00. Basil Blackwell Publishers Ltd., 108 Cowley Road, Oxford 0X4 1JF United Kingdom. **Tel** 011 44 1235 465500, FAX 011 44 1235 465556, telex 837022 OXBOOK G. **(Subscription address:** Blackwell Publishers / UK, 108 Cowley Road, Oxford OX4 1JF United Kingdom. **Tel** 011 44 1865 791100, FAX 011 44 1865 791347.) Index available. cum. index. **Bk Rev. Ad Acc.** ctrl circ. available on microfilm and microfiche from University Microfilms International (UMI).
Ind/Abst Appl. Soc. Sci. Index Abstr.; Contents Pages Manage.; Curr. Cit.; Ergon. Abstr.; Geogr. Abstr. Human Geogr.; Int. Bibliogr. Sociol.; Int. Dev. Abstr. (1987-?); Int. Labour Doc.; LABORDOC; Manage. Market. Abstr.; PAIS Int. Print (1991-); Person. Manage. Abstr.; Spec. Educ. Needs Abstr.; Work Relat. Abstr.

ISSN 1070-7727
DD 331 US
NEW UNIONIST (MINNEAPOLIS, MINN.). (NEW UNIONIST.). [New Unionist]. **Added/Corp** New Union Party (Minn.) New Unionists (Organization : Minneapolis, Minn.). No. 12 (Dec. 1975)-. Periodical. English. Twelve times a year. $5.00. New Unionist, 621 West Lake Street, Suite 210, Minneapolis MN 55408. **Tel** (612)823-2593. **ED** Jeff Miller. **Bk Rev**, (Qty: 3). **Circ:** 9,000. ***Continues*** *New Unionists' Newsletter, 0276-2609.*
Desc: Official paper of the New Union party.

NZ
NEW ZEALAND EMPLOYMENT MANAGEMENT INFORMATION SYSTEM (EMIS) EMPLOYMENT OPERATION STATISTICS, THE. **VFOAT** Employment Operation Statistics. (Dec. 1988)-. Periodical. English. Twelve times a year. New Zealand Department of Labour, Private Bag, Wellington 1 New Zealand. ***Continues in part*** *Monthly Employment Operations.*

LC HD8930.5 .A3 **ISSN** 0110-0637
NZ
NEW ZEALAND JOURNAL OF INDUSTRIAL RELATIONS. [N. Z. j. ind. relat.]. **Added/Corp** Industrial Relations Society of New Zealand. New Zealand Institute of Industrial Relations Research. Vol. 1 (May 1976)-. Periodical. English. Three times a year (Apr., Aug., Dec.). $80.00. Foundation for Industrial Relations Research and Education, PO Box 6088, Dunedin New Zealand. **Tel** 011 64 3 478128, FAX 011 64 3 4798173. **ED** Alan Geare. Index available. cum. index. **Bk Rev**, (Qty: 24). **Ad Acc. Circ:** 375.
Desc: Industrial relations in New Zealand and other countries.
Ind/Abst Appl. Soc. Sci. Index Abstr.; Int. Labour Doc.; LABORDOC; PAIS Int. Print (1991-).

LC HD4801 **ISSN** 1041-5971
DD 331 US
NEWS. (NEWS. THE NEW ENGLAND LABOR MARKET AT YEAR END.). [News, N. Engl. labor mark. year end]. **VFOAT** New England Labor Market at Year End. (1987)-. Government Publication. English. One time a year. US Department of Labor / Bureau of Labor Statistics, 441 G Street Northwest, Washington DC 20212. **Tel** (202)606-7800, FAX (202)606-7797. ***Continues*** *News. New England Economy at Year End.*

DD 016.33 US
NEWS. AVERAGE ANNUAL PAY BY STATE AND INDUSTRY. **See** Business and Economics-Abstracting, Bibliographies and Statistics.

SZ
NEWS BULLETIN - INTERNATIONAL UNION OF FOOD & ALLIED WORKERS' ASSOCIATIONS. **Main/Corp** International Union of Food and Allied Workers' Associations. (19??)-. Bulletin. English. Twelve times a year. $169.72. International Union of Food & Allied Workers Associations, Rampe du Pont-Rouge 8, CH-1213 PL Geneva Switzerland. **Tel** 011 22 1 7932233.

US
NEWS - BUREAU OF LABOR STATISTICS. **See** Business and Economics-Abstracting, Bibliographies and Statistics.

LC HD4928 .N49
DD 331.216 US
NEWS. EMPLOYMENT COST INDEX. **See** Business and Economics-Abstracting, Bibliographies and Statistics.

ISSN 0258-1965
IE
NEWS FROM THE FOUNDATION / FOUNDATION FOR THE IMPROVEMENT OF LIVING AND WORKING CONDITIONS. **Added/Corp** European Foundation for the Improvement of Living and Working Conditions. No. 26 (1991)-. Periodical. English. Four times a year. Free on request. European Foundation for the Improvement of Living and Working Conditions, Loughlinstown House, Shankill Co, Dublin Ireland. **Tel** 011 353 1 2826888, FAX 011 353 1 2826456. ***Continues*** *EF News.*

ISSN 1185-0264
DD 368.4/1/0097105 CN
NEWS FROM WORKERS' COMPENSATION. [News Work. Compens.]. **Added/Corp** Prince Edward Island. Worker's Compensation Board. Vol. 1, No. 1 (Summer 1990)-. Periodical. English. Four times a year.

ISSN 0020-6008
DD 331 US
NEWS - INTERNATIONAL ASSOCIATION OF PERSONNEL IN EMPLOYMENT SECURITY. (NEWS.). [News - Int. Assoc. Pers. Employ. Secur.]. **Added/Corp** International Association of Personnel in Employment Security. **VFOAT** IAPES News. (19??)-. Periodical. English. Six times a year. $25.00. International Association of Personnel in Employment Security / IAPES, 1801 Louisville Road, Frankfort KY 40601. **Tel** (502)223-4459. **ED** Michael R. Stone. **Ad Acc. Circ:** 25,000 (ctrl).

ISSN 0732-1988
US
NEWS - NEW YORK STATE PUBLIC EMPLOYMENT RELATIONS BOARD. **Main/Corp** New York (State). Public Employment Relations Board. **VFOAT** PERB News. **VAT** Public Employment Relations Board News. Vol. 1 (Jan. 1968)-. Periodical. English. Twelve times a year. $25.00. Public Employment Relations Board/State of New York, 80 Wolf Road, Albany NY 12205-2604. **Tel** (518)457-2676.

Business and Economics —Labor

LC HD4906
DD 331.21 US
NEWS. REAL EARNINGS IN ... .
Added/Corp United States. Bureau of Labor Statistics.
VFOAT Real Earnings. (19??)-. Periodical. English.
Twelve times a year. Free on request. US Department of Labor Labor Statistics, Postal Square Building, 2 Massachusetts Avenue Northeast, Washington DC 20212. **Tel** (202)606-6392. Documents available from Documents on Demand.
Ind/Abst Am. Stat. Index.

US
●**NEWS. STATE AND METROPOLITAN AREA EMPLOYMENT AND UNEMPLOYMENT.** **Added/Corp** United States. Bureau of Labor Statistics. **VFOAT** State and Metropolitan Area Employment and Unemployment. (Feb. 1994)-. Periodical. English. Twelve times a year. Free on request. US Department of Labor Labor Statistics, Postal Square Building, 2 Massachusetts Avenue Northeast, Washington DC 20212. **Tel** (202)606-6392. *Formed by the union of* News. Unemployment in States *and* News. State Employment and Metropolitan area unemployment.

US
NEWS / UNITED STATES DEPARTMENT OF LABOR, OFFICE OF INFORMATION. **Main/Corp** United States. Dept. of Labor. **Added/Corp** United States. Dept. of Labor. Office of Information. (19??)-. Periodical. English. Free on request. US Department of Labor Office of Information, 200 Constitution Avenue Northwest, Washington DC 20010. **Tel** (202)219-7343.

ISSN 0703-5861
DD 658.31/52/0971 CN
NEWSLETTER - CANADIANS FOR A DEMOCRATIC WORKPLACE. **Main/Corp** Canadians for a Democratic Workplace. Vol. 1 (1977)-. Newsletter. English. Six times a year. $2.00. Canadians for a Democratic Workplace Newsletter, PO Box 3793 Station C, Ottawa Ontario K1Y 4J8 Canada.

ISSN 0892-631X
DD 331 US
SUSPENDED
NEWSLETTER - COLUMBIA UNIVERSITY. CENTER FOR SOCIAL POLICY AND PRACTICE IN THE WORKPLACE. (NEWSLETTER / CENTER FOR SOCIAL POLICY AND PRACTICE IN THE WORKPLACE, COLUMBIA UNIVERSITY, SCHOOL OF SOCIAL WORK.). [Newsl. - Columbia Univ., Cent. Soc. Policy Pract. Workplace]. Newsletter. English. Two times a year. $6.00. Center for Social Policy and Practice in the Workplace, Columbia University, School of Social Work, 622 West 113th Street, New York NY 10025. **ED** Sheila H Akahas. **Circ:** 2,500 (ctrl)

LC HD8794.A5 F43a
DD 331/.09676/1 UG
NEWSLETTER - FEDERATION OF UGANDA EMPLOYERS, COMMERCE & INDUSTRY. See Industry and Production.

ISSN 0317-0993
DD 331/.049/009714 CN
NEWSLETTER. LABOUR RELATIONS. CONSTRUCTION ASSOCIATION OF MONTREAL AND THE PROVINCE OF QUEBEC. (NEWS LETTER : LABOUR RELATIONS.). **Main/Corp** Construction Association of Montreal and the Province of Quebec. Vol. 6, No. 15 (Oct. 24, 1974)-. English. Construction Association of Montreal and the Province of Quebec, 4970 place de la Savane, Montreal Quebec H4P 1Z6 Canada. **Tel** (514)739-2381. *Continues* News Letter: Labour Relations, 0317-0985.

US
NEWSLETTER - MASSACHUSETTS STATE LABOR COUNCIL. **Main/Corp** Massachusetts State Labor Council. Vol. 1 (May 1959)-. Newsletter. English. Irregular. Massachusetts State Labor Council, 6 Beacon Street, Room 720, Boston MA 02108.

ISSN 0731-3373
US
NEWSLETTER - WISCONSIN LABOR HISTORY SOCIETY. (NEWSLETTER.).
Main/Corp Wisconsin Labor History Society. Vol. 1, No. 1 (Fall 1981)-. Newsletter. English. Four times a year. Wisconsin Labor History Society, c/o State Historical Society of Wisconsin, 816 State Street, Madison WI 53706.

LC PN4841 .N4516
DD 331.88/11070172 ISSN 0270-2223
US
NEWSPAPER GUILD, AFL-CIO, CLC CONSTITUTION, THE. **Main/Corp** Newspaper Guild. **VFOAT** Constitution of the Newspaper Guild. Convention 1971-. Periodical. English. One time a year. $2.00. Newspaper Guild, 8611 Second Avenue, Silver Spring MD 20910. **Tel** (301)585-2990, FAX (301)585-0668. **ED** James Cesnik. **Circ:** 7,000. available on microfilm. *Continues* Constitution of the American Newspaper Guild, AFL-CIO, CLC.
Desc: Constitution, collective bargaining program and collective bargaining recommendations of The Newspaper Guild.

LC LB2335.86
DD 331.88/0971 ISSN 0225-3100
CN
NEWSPAPER OF THE CANADIAN WORKERS' ASSOCIATION. **Main/Corp** Canadian Workers' Association. **VFOAT** Make the Rich Pay. Vol. 2, No. 3 (March 1979)-. Periodical. English. Twelve times a year. $5.00. Canadian Workers' Association, National Publications Centre, PO Box 727 Adelaide Station, Toronto Ontario M5C 2J8 Canada.

ISSN 1380-149X
NE
UDC 331.5
NIEUWSBRIEF ARBEIDSMARKT.
[Nieuwsbr. arb.markt]. (1986)-. Periodical. Dutch. Six times a year. Stichting FNV Pers, Postbus 8456, 1005 Al Amsterdam Netherlands. **Tel** 011 31 20 5816300.

LC HD8723 .N45
JA
NIHON NO ROSHI KANKEI. **Added/Corp**
Nihon Rodo Kyokai. **VFOAT** Nenpo, Nihon No Roshi Kankei. (1973)-. English. One time a year. Nihon Rodo Kenkyu Kiko, Shinjuku Monolith, 2-3-1 Nishishinjuku, Tokyo Japan 163-09. **Tel** 011 81 3 53213084, FAX 011 81 3 53213015. **ED** Tagata Yuki. Index available. cum. index. **Circ:** 1,000 (ctrl). *Continues* Nempo Nihon No Roshi Kankei.
Desc: Provides information on trends in industrial relations and labour economics, as well as the governmental response to these new challenges.

LC HD4811 .N5 ISSN 0916-3808
JA
NIHON RODO KEBNKYU ZASSHI.
Added/Corp Nihon Rodo Kenkyu Kiko. **VFOAT** Monthly Journal of the Japan Institute of Labour. (1990)-. Periodical. Japanese (table of contents in English). Twelve times a year. Japan Institute of Labor, Shinjuku Monolith 2 3 1, Tokyo 163 09 Japan. **Tel** 011 81 3 53213084. *Continues* Nihon Rodo Kyokai Zasshi, 0029-0378.

LC HD4824 .N56A
JA
NIHON RODO KYOKAI JIGYO NENJI HOKOKU. **Main/Corp** Nihon Todo Kyokai. (1965/66)-. Japanese. Japan Institute of Labor, Shinjuku Monolith 2 3 1, Tokyo 163 09 Japan. **Tel** 011 81 3 53213084. *Continues* Nihon Rodo Kyokai Jigyo Nempo.

LC HD8730.5 .A317
KO
NODONG KYONGJE RIBYU. **VFOAT** Monthly Labor & Management; Monthly Labor and Management. Periodical. Korean (Korean). Twelve times a year.

LC HD6529.S2 M34 ISSN 0830-0763
DD 331.89/097124/021 CN
NON-WAGE PROVISIONS IN SASKATCHEWAN COLLECTIVE AGREEMENTS. [Non-wage provis. Sask. collect. agreem.]. **VFOAT** Non Wage Provisions in Saskatchewan Collective Agreements. 1985-. English. One time a year. Saskatchewan Labour / Department Human Resources Labour, 1870 Albert Street, Regina Saskatchewan S4P 3V7 Canada. **Tel** (306)787-3369, FAX (306)787-7229. *Continues* Study of Saskatchewan Collective Bargaining Agreements, 0822-3866.

LC HD4976.N6 M69A ISSN 0196-416X
DD 331.2/2/09789 US
NORTH CENTRAL NEW MEXICO SALARY SURVEY. **Main/Corp** Mountain States Employers Council. **VFOAT** Survey, North Central New Mexico. (19??)-. English. Mountain States Employers Council, 1790 Logan Street, PO Box 539, Denver CO 80201.

LC HD4976.C57 N67
DD 331.2/9788 US
NORTHERN COLORADO COMPENSATION SURVEY. 1982-. English. One time a year. Mountain States Employers Council, 1790 Logan Street, PO Box 539, Denver CO 80201. *Continues* Northern Colorado Survey.

ISSN 0711-1304
DD 331.88/113711/00971445 CN
NOS LUTTES (1981). (NOS LUTTES.). [Nous luttes]. Vol. 7, No. 1 (11 June 1981)-. Periodical. French. Syndicat des Enseignants des Vieilles-Forges, 4160 rue de Labadie, Trois-Rivieres Quebec G8Y 1T7 Canada. *Continues in part* S.E.V.F. en Action, 0227-5929.

ISSN 0227-4906
DD 331.89/0413711/00971445 CN
NOS LUTTES EXPRESS. [Nos luttes express].
Feb. 6, 1979-. Periodical. French. One time a week. Syndicat des Enseignants des Vieilles-Forges, 4160 rue de Labadie, Trois-Rivieres Quebec G8Y 1T7 Canada.

LC HD8039.M39 I53a
DD 331.7/92/05 SZ
NOTE ON THE PROCEEDINGS / ADVISORY COMMITTEE ON SALARIED EMPLOYEES AND PROFESSIONAL WORKERS. **Main/Corp** International Labour Organisation. Advisory Committee on Salaried Employees and Professional Workers. Session. **Added/Corp** International Labour Organisation. Programme of Industrial Activities. (19??)-. Proceedings. English. Irregular. $14.00 (£8.40). International Labour Office - ILO, Publications Sales Service, CH-1211 Geneva 22 Switzerland. **Tel** 011 41 22 7996111, FAX 011 41 22 7986253, telex 415 647 ilo ch.

LC HD1521 .I75a
DD 331.7/63/05 SZ
NOTE ON THE PROCEEDINGS OF THE ... / INTERNATIONAL LABOUR ORGANISATION, PROGRAMME OF INDUSTRIAL ACTIVITIES, COMMITTEE ON WORK ON PLANTATIONS. **Main/Corp** International Labour Organisation. Committee on Work on Plantations. **Added/Corp** International Labour Office. **VFOAT** Note on the Proceedings. (19??)-. Proceedings. English. Irregular. Price varies. International Labour Office - ILO, Publications Sales Service, CH-1211 Geneva 22 Switzerland. **Tel** 011 41 22 7996111, FAX 011 41 22 7986253, telex 415 647 ilo ch. (**Subscription address:** International Labor Office / Albany, NY, 49 Sheridan Avenue, Albany NY 12210. **Tel** (518)436-9686.)

ISSN 0316-0386
DD 331.88/0971 CN
NOTES ON UNIONS. (1974)-. Periodical. English (French). Canadian Labour Congress, 2841 Riverside Drive, Ottawa Ontario K1V 8X7 Canada. **Tel** (613)521-3400, FAX (613)053-4750, telex 060313. *Formed by the union of* Notes on Unions, 0316-0386 *and* Cahiers Syndicaux, 0316-0394.

AG
NOTISUR. **Added/Corp** Instituto Internacional de Estudios y Capacitacion Social del Sur. (197?)-. Periodical. Spanish (Portuguese). INCASUR, Alberti 36, 1082-Buenos Aires Argentina. available on an online database (file 636/Full-Text) from DIALOG.
Ind/Abst Int. Labour Doc.; LABORDOC.

ISSN 0394-3623
UDC 331 IT
NOTIZIARIO DEL LAVORO E PREVIDENZA. (1983)-. Periodical. Italian. Irregular (every 10 days). L224810. De Lillo Editore Srl, Via Mecenate 76/3, 20138 Milan Italy. **Tel** 011 39 2 58013112.

IT
NOTIZIARIO ENEA. SICUREZZA E PROTEZIONE. Italian. Free. ENEA, V le Regina Margherita 125, 00198 Rome Italy. **Tel** 011 39 6 85281.

IT
NOTIZIE INTERNATIONALI: BOLLETTINO BIMESTRALE DELLA FIOM-CGIL. (19??)-. Italian. Six times a year. L30000.00 Italy; L60000.00 other. Meta Edizioni Srl, C So Trieste 36, 00198 Rome Italy. **Tel** 011 39 6 85262375.

ISSN 0712-8789
DD 331.88/09714 CN
NOUVELLES CSN. [Nouv. CSN]. **Added/Corp** Confederation des Syndicats Nationaux. **VFOAT** CSN News. **VAT** Nouvelles. Confederation des Syndicats Nationaux. (1978)-. Periodical. French. Twenty-six times a year (Publishes on the 1st & 15th of each month). Free on request. Librairie Service Documentation, 1601 Ave de Lorimier, Montreal Quebec H2K 4M5 Canada. **Tel** (514)598-2151.

ISSN 0317-0977
DD 331/.049/009714 CN
NOUVELLES. RELATIONS OUVRIERES. ASSOCIATION DE LA CONSTRUCTION DE MONTREAL ET DU QUEBEC.
(NOUVELLES: RELATIONS OUVRIERES.). **Main/Corp** Association de la Construction de Montreal et du Quebec. Vol. 6, No 15-24 (Oct. 1974)-. French. Association de la Construction de Montreal et du Quebec, 4970 place de la Savane, Montreal Quebec H4P 1Z6 Canada. *Continues* Association de la Construction de Montreal. Nouvelles: Relations Ouvrieres, 0317-0969.

Business and Economics — Labor

DD 378/.12/060714
ISSN 0709-8006
CN
NOUVELLES UNIVERSITAIRES (MONTREAL). (NOUVELLES UNIVERSITAIRES.). Vol. 1 (Sept. 1979)-. Periodical. French. Twenty-six times a year. Federation des Associations de Professeures des Universites du Quebec, 2715 Chemin de la Cote Sainte-Catherine, Montreal Quebec H3T 1B6 Canada. **Tel** (514)735-3654. **ED** Michel Croteau. **Bk Rev. Circ:** 5,000. **Formed by the union of** F A P U Q Information. Federation des Associations de Professeures des Universites du Quebec, 0709-8014 **and** Mot a Mot, 0701-1474.
Desc: Intended for faculty unions and associations members in French and Englophone Quebec universities - mostly news on labor relations in Quebec universities and on the management of universities.

DD 331.88/09716
ISSN 0228-717X
CN
NOVA SCOTIA WORKER, THE. [N.S. work.]. Vol. 1, No. 1 (Feb. 1980)-. Periodical. English. Free to members. Nova Scotia Worker, 3700 Kempt Road, Halifax Nova Scotia B3K 2R7 Canada.

LC HD
DD 331
UDC 331.105
ISSN 1230-9494
PL
●**NOWY TYGODNIK POPULARNY.** [Nowy Tyg. Pop.]. (1993)-. Periodical. Polish. One time a week. **(Subscription address:** Ars Polona-Ruch, PO Box 1001, Krakowskie Przedmiescie 7, 00-068 Warsaw Poland. **Tel** 011 48 22 261201.) **Continues** Tygodnik Popularny, 1230-9486.

LC HD8009.O3 N3
DD 331.88/113532
ISSN 0279-540X
US
NTEU BULLETIN, THE. VFOAT N.T.E.U. Bulletin. **VAT** National Treasury Employees Union Bulletin. (19??)-. Bulletin. English. Twelve times a year. National Treasury Employees Union, 1730 K Street NW/Suite 1100, Washington DC 20006. **Tel** (202)785-4411. **ED** Jim Stentzel. **Circ:** 86,000 (ctrl). **Continues** Bulletin (National Treasury Employees Union), 0095-4748.
Desc: Focus on federal sector employees, job rights, pay equity, other issues affecting their welfare and working conditions.

LC HD8005.2.G7 J68a
DD 331.88/0941/05
UK
NUCPS JOURNAL. See Public Administration-Civil Service.

DD 016.363 110 948
ISSN 0901-6473
DK
CODEN 01.6614461.44
CEASED
NYT OM ARBEJDSMILJ SKANDINAVIEN I SKANDINAVIEN. [Nyt arb.milj Skand.]. (1986)-(Jan. 1995). Periodical. Danish (Norwegian and Swedish). SYMB Videnformidling Kipenhav, Kobenhavns Forskerby Symbion, Fruebjergvei 11, DK-2100 Copenhagen Denmark. **Tel** 011 45 31817888, FAX 011 45 31817833.

ISSN 0194-1593
US
OBRERO REBELDE, EL. (197?)-. Periodical. Spanish. $6.00. El Obrero Rebelde, 3364-26th Street, San Francisco CA 94110.

US
OBREROS EN MARCHA. Added/Corp El Comite - Movimiento de Izquierda Nacional Puertorriqueno. (19??)-. Periodical. English (Spanish). Twelve times a year. El Comite, 577 Columbus Avenue, New York NY 10024.

LC HD6350.P415 I5
DD 331.88/12
ISSN 8756-1727
US
OCAW REPORTER. (OCAW REPORTER : OFFICIAL PUBLICATION OF THE OIL AND ATOMIC WORKERS INTERNATIONAL UNION.). [OCAW report.]. **VAT** Oil, Chemical and Atomic Workers Reporter. Vol. 40, No. 9-10 (Nov./Dec. 1984)-. Periodical. English. Six times a year. Oil Chem Atomic Workers Intl, PO Box 281200, Lakewood CO 80228-8200. **Tel** (303)987-2229, FAX (303)987-1967. available on microfilm and microfiche from University Microfilms International (UMI). **Continues** Oil, Chemical & Atomic Union News, 0030-1426.
Ind/Abst Work Relat. Abstr.

ISSN 0529-0937
US
OCCASIONAL PAPERS - CHICAGO. UNIVERSITY. INDUSTRIAL RELATIONS CENTER. Main/Corp Chicago. University. Industrial Relations Center. 1- Oct. 1953-. Periodical. English. Industrial Relations, PO Box 37005, Chicago IL 60637.

US
OCCUPATIONAL COMPENSATION SURVEY--PAY AND BENEFITS. BRUNSWICK, GA / U.S. DEPARTMENT OF LABOR, BUREAU OF LABOR STATISTICS. Added/Corp United States. Bureau of Labor Statistics. **VFOAT** Occupational Compensation Survey--Pay Only. Brunswick, GA; Brunswick, GA. (May 1992)-. Government Publication. English. Every 2 years. US Department of Labor / Bureau of Labor Statistics, 441 G Street Northwest, Washington DC 20212. **Tel** (202)606-7800, FAX (202)606-7797. **Continues** Area Wage Survey. Brunswick, GA.

US
OCCUPATIONAL COMPENSATION SURVEY--PAY AND BENEFITS. CHARLESTON, SC / U.S. DEPARTMENT OF LABOR, BUREAU OF LABOR STATISTICS. Added/Corp United States. Bureau of Labor Statistics. **VFOAT** Charleston, SC. (1992)-. English. US Department of Labor / Bureau of Labor Statistics, 441 G Street Northwest, Washington DC 20212. **Tel** (202)606-7800, FAX (202)606-7797. **Continues** Area Wage Survey. Charleston-North Charleston-Walterboro, SC.

US
OCCUPATIONAL COMPENSATION SURVEY--PAY AND BENEFITS. CLARKSVILLE-HOPKINSVILLE, TN-KY / U.S. DEPARTMENT OF LABOR, BUREAU OF LABOR STATISTICS. Added/Corp United States. Bureau of Labor Statistics. **VFOAT** Clarksville-Hopkinsville, TN-KY; Clarksville, Hopkinsville, TN KY. (1992)-. English. US Department of Labor / Bureau of Labor Statistics, 441 G Street Northwest, Washington DC 20212. **Tel** (202)606-7800, FAX (202)606-7797. **Continues** Area Wage Survey. Clarksville-Hopkinsville, Tenn.-Ky.

US
OCCUPATIONAL COMPENSATION SURVEY--PAY AND BENEFITS. FLORENCE, SC. Added/Corp United States. Bureau of Labor Statistics. **VFOAT** Florence, SC. (Jan. 1992)-. English. US Department of Labor / Bureau of Labor Statistics, 441 G Street Northwest, Washington DC 20212. **Tel** (202)606-7800, FAX (202)606-7797.

LC HD4976.C23 F78a
DD 331.2/9794/82
US
OCCUPATIONAL COMPENSATION SURVEY--PAY AND BENEFITS. FRESNO, CA / U.S. DEPARTMENT OF LABOR, BUREAU OF LABOR STATISTICS. Added/Corp United States. Bureau of Labor Statistics. **VFOAT** Fresno, CA. (Feb. 1992)-. English. Every 2 years. US Department of Labor / Bureau of Labor Statistics, 441 G Street Northwest, Washington DC 20212. **Tel** (202)606-7800, FAX (202)606-7797. **Continues** Area Wage Survey. Fresno, California, Metropolitan Area, 0361-7386.

LC HD4976.G34 A73
DD 331.2/977299
ISSN 1068-4581
US
OCCUPATIONAL COMPENSATION SURVEY--PAY AND BENEFITS. GARY-HAMMOND, INDIANA, METROPOLITAN AREA. (OCCUPATIONAL COMPENSATION SURVEY--PAY AND BENEFITS. GARY-HAMMOND, INDIANA, METROPOLITAN AREA / U.S. DEPARTMENT OF LABOR, BUREAU OF LABOR STATISTICS.). [Occup. compens. surv.--pay benefits, Gary-Hammond Ind. metrop. area]. **Added/Corp** United States. Bureau of Labor Statistics. **VFOAT** Occupational Compensation Survey--Pay Only. Gary-Hammond, Indiana, Metropolitan area; Gary-Hammond, Indiana, Metropolitan Area; Gary Hammond, Indiana, Metropolitan Area. Feb. (1992)-. Government Publication. English. Irregular. $226.00. Superintendent of Documents, US Government Printing Office, Washington DC 20402. **Tel** (202)275-3328, FAX (202)786-2377. **Continues** Area Wage Survey. Gary-Hammond, Indiana Metropolitan Area.

US
OCCUPATIONAL COMPENSATION SURVEY--PAY AND BENEFITS. GREENSBORO-WINSTON SALEM-HIGH POINT, NC / U.S. DEPARTMENT OF LABOR, BUREAU OF LABOR STATISTICS. Added/Corp United States. Bureau of Labor Statistics. **VFOAT** Greensboro-Winston Salem-High Point, NC; Greensboro, Winston Salem, High Point, NC. (Feb. 1992)-. English. US Department of Labor / Bureau of Labor Statistics, 441 G Street Northwest, Washington DC 20212. **Tel** (202)606-7800, FAX (202)606-7797. **Continues** Area Wage Survey. Greensboro-Winston Salem-High Point, NC.

LC HD4976.H8 A3
DD 331.2/9761/97
US
OCCUPATIONAL COMPENSATION SURVEY--PAY AND BENEFITS. HUNTSVILLE, ALABAMA, METROPOLITAN AREA. Added/Corp United States. Bureau of Labor Statistics. **VFOAT** Occupational Compensation Survey, Pay and Benefits. Huntsville, Alabama, Metropolitan Area; Huntsville, Alabama, Metropolitan Area. (Jan. 1992)-. Government Publication. English. One time a year. $226.00. Superintendent of Documents, US Government Printing Office, Washington DC 20402. **Tel** (202)275-3328, FAX (202)786-2377. **Continues** Area Wage Survey. Huntsville, Alabama, Metropolitan Area, 0270-5931.

LC HD4976.J26 A37
DD 331.2976251
US
OCCUPATIONAL COMPENSATION SURVEY--PAY AND BENEFITS. JACKSON, MISSISSIPPI, METROPOLITAN AREA / U.S. DEPARTMENT OF LABOR, BUREAU OF LABOR STATISTICS. Added/Corp United States. Bureau of Labor Statistics. **VFOAT** Occupational Compensation Survey, Pay and Benefits. Jackson, Mississippi, Metropolitan area; Jackson, Mississippi, Metropolitan Area. Jan. (1992)-. Government Publication. English. Irregular. $226.00. Superintendent of Documents, US Government Printing Office, Washington DC 20402. **Tel** (202)275-3328, FAX (202)786-2377. **Continues** Area Wage Survey. Jackson, Mississippi, Metropolitan Area, 0161-4797.

LC HD4976.L6 U55a
DD 331.2/9794/93
US
OCCUPATIONAL COMPENSATION SURVEY--PAY AND BENEFITS. LOS ANGELES-LONG BEACH, CALIFORNIA, METROPOLITAN AREA. Added/Corp United States. Bureau of Labor Statistics. **VFOAT** Los Angeles-Long Beach, California, Metropolitan Area; Los Angeles, Long Beach, California, Metropolitan Area. (Dec 1991)-. Government Publication. English. One time a year. $226.00. Superintendent of Documents, US Government Printing Office, Washington DC 20402. **Tel** (202)275-3328, FAX (202)786-2377. **Continues** Area Wage Survey. Los Angeles-Long Beach, California, Metropolitan Area, 0147-7072.

US
OCCUPATIONAL COMPENSATION SURVEY--PAY AND BENEFITS. MONTGOMERY, AL. Added/Corp United States. Bureau of Labor Statistics. **VFOAT** Montgomery, AL. (1992)-. English. US Department of Labor / Bureau of Labor Statistics, 441 G Street Northwest, Washington DC 20212. **Tel** (202)606-7800, FAX (202)606-7797. **Continues** Area Wage Survey. Montgomery, Ala.

US
●**OCCUPATIONAL COMPENSATION SURVEY--PAY AND BENEFITS. RALEIGH-DURHAM, NC. Added/Corp** United States. Bureau of Labor Statistics. **VFOAT** Raleigh-Durham, NC; Raleigh Durham, NC. (June 1993)-. English. US Department of Labor / Bureau of Labor Statistics, 441 G Street Northwest, Washington DC 20212. **Tel** (202)606-7800, FAX (202)606-7797. **Continues** Area Wage Survey. Raleigh-Durham, NC.

US
OCCUPATIONAL COMPENSATION SURVEY--PAY AND BENEFITS. SALINAS-SEASIDE-MONTEREY, CA / U.S. DEPARTMENT OF LABOR, BUREAU OF LABOR STATISTICS. Added/Corp United States. Bureau of Labor Statistics. **VFOAT** Salinas-Seaside-Monterey, CA; Salinas Seaside Monterey, CA. (Feb. 1992)-. English. US Department of Labor / Bureau of Labor Statistics, 441 G Street Northwest, Washington DC 20212. **Tel** (202)606-7800, FAX (202)606-7797. **Continues** Area Wage Survey. Salinas-Seaside-Monterey, CA.

LC HD4906
DD 331.21
US
OCCUPATIONAL COMPENSATION SURVEY--PAY AND BENEFITS. SOUTH BEND-MISHAWAKA, INDIANA, METROPOLITAN AREA. Added/Corp United States. Bureau of Labor Statistics. **VFOAT** Occupational Compensation Survey--Pay Only. South Bend-Mishawaka, Indiana, Metropolitan Area; South Bend Mishawaka, Indiana, Metropolitan Area. (Sept. 1992)-. Monographic series. English. Irregular. $226.00. US Department of Labor, 200 Constitution Avenue NW, Washington DC 20210. **Tel** (202)219-7316, FAX (202)219-7312. **Continues** Area Wage Survey. South Bend, Indiana, Metropolitan Area, 0197-4440.

US
OCCUPATIONAL COMPENSATION SURVEY--PAY AND BENEFITS. TOLEDO, OH. Added/Corp United States. Bureau of Labor Statistics. **VFOAT** Toledo, OH. (Mar. 1992)-.

Business and Economics —Labor

English. US Department of Labor / Bureau of Labor Statistics, 441 G Street Northwest, Washington DC 20212. **Tel** (202)606-7800, FAX (202)606-7797.

US

OCCUPATIONAL COMPENSATION SURVEY--PAY AND BENEFITS. TUCSON-DOUGLAS, AZ. Added/Corp United States. Bureau of Labor Statistics. **VFOAT** Tucson-Douglas, AZ; Tucson Douglas, AZ. (Feb. 1992)-. English. US Department of Labor / Bureau of Labor Statistics, 441 G Street Northwest, Washington DC 20212. **Tel** (202)606-7800, FAX (202)606-7797. *Continues* Area Wage Survey. Tucson-Douglas, AZ.

US

OCCUPATIONAL COMPENSATION SURVEY--PAY AND BENEFITS. VALLEJO-FAIRFIELD-NAPA, CA / U.S. DEPARTMENT OF LABOR, BUREAU OF LABOR STATISTICS. Added/Corp United States. Bureau of Labor Statistics. **VFOAT** Vallejo-Fairfield-Napa, CA; Vallejo Fairfield Napa, CA. (Feb. 1992)-. English. US Department of Labor / Bureau of Labor Statistics, 441 G Street Northwest, Washington DC 20212. **Tel** (202)606-7800, FAX (202)606-7797. *Continues* Area Wage Survey. Vallejo-Fairfield-Napa, Calif.

US

OCCUPATIONAL COMPENSATION SURVEY--PAY AND BENEFITS. VERMONT / U.S. DEPARTMENT OF LABOR, BUREAU OF LABOR STATISTICS. Added/Corp United States. Bureau of Labor Statistics. **VFOAT** Vermont. (Aug. 1992)-. English. US Department of Labor / Bureau of Labor Statistics, 441 G Street Northwest, Washington DC 20212. **Tel** (202)606-7800, FAX (202)606-7797. *Continues* Area Wage Survey. Vermont.

US

OCCUPATIONAL COMPENSATION SURVEY--PAY AND BENEFITS. WICHITA, KS / U.S. DEPARTMENT OF LABOR, BUREAU OF LABOR STATISTICS. Added/Corp United States. Bureau of Labor Statistics. **VFOAT** Wichita, KS. (1992)-. English. US Department of Labor / Bureau of Labor Statistics, 441 G Street Northwest, Washington DC 20212. **Tel** (202)606-7800, FAX (202)606-7797. *Continues* Area Wage Survey. Wichita, KS.

US

OCCUPATIONAL COMPENSATION SURVEY--PAY ONLY. ARKANSAS--FORESTRY / U.S. DEPARTMENT OF LABOR, BUREAU OF LABOR STATISTICS. Added/Corp United States. Bureau of Labor Statistics. **VFOAT** Arkansas--Forestry; Arkansas, Forestry. (1992)-. English. Every 2 years. US Department of Labor / Bureau of Labor Statistics, 441 G Street Northwest, Washington DC 20212. **Tel** (202)606-7800, FAX (202)606-7797. *Continues* Forestry Wage Survey. Arkansas.

US

●**OCCUPATIONAL COMPENSATION SURVEY--PAY ONLY. AUSTIN, TX / U.S. DEPARTMENT OF LABOR, BUREAU OF LABOR STATISTICS. Added/Corp** United States. Bureau of Labor Statistics. **VFOAT** Austin, TX. (Nov. 1993)-. Government Publication. English. Irregular. $236.00. Superintendent of Documents, US Government Printing Office, Washington DC 20402. **Tel** (202)275-3328, FAX (202)786-2377. *Continues* tOccupational Compensation Survey--Pay and Benefits. Austin, TX.

US

●**OCCUPATIONAL COMPENSATION SURVEY--PAY ONLY. BELL COUNTY, TX--FAST FOOD RESTAURANTS. Added/Corp** United States. Bureau of Labor Statistics. **VFOAT** Bell County, TX--Fast Food Restaurants; Bell County, TX, Fast Food Restaurants. (Jan. 1993)-. Government Publication. English. Irregular. $226.00. US Department of Labor / Bureau of Labor Statistics, 441 G Street Northwest, Washington DC 20212. **Tel** (202)606-7800, FAX (202)606-7797. **(Subscription address:** Superintendent of Documents, US Government Printing Office, Washington DC 20402. **)** *Continues* Fast Food Restaurants Wage Survey. Bell County, TX.

LC HD4976.B5 U53a
DD 331.2/9786/39

US

OCCUPATIONAL COMPENSATION SURVEY--PAY ONLY. BILLINGS, MONTANA, METROPOLITAN AREA / U.S. DEPARTMENT OF LABOR, BUREAU OF LABOR STATISTICS. Added/Corp United States. Bureau of Labor Statistics. **VFOAT** Occupational Compensation Survey, Pay Only. Billings, Montana, Metropolitan Area; Billings, Montana, Metropolitan Area. (Oct. 1991)-. Government Publication. English. Irregular. $226.00. Superintendent of Documents, US Government Printing Office, Washington DC 20402. **Tel** (202)275-3328, FAX (202)786-2377. *Continues* Area Wage Survey. Billings, Montana, Metropolitan Area, 0361-6819.

LC HD4976.B67 .A37

US

OCCUPATIONAL COMPENSATION SURVEY--PAY ONLY. BOSTON, MASSACHUSETTS, METROPOLITAN AREA / U.S. DEPARTMENT OF LABOR, BUREAU OF LABOR STATISTICS. Added/Corp United States. Bureau of Labor Statistics. **VFOAT** Boston, Massachusetts, Metropolitan Area; Occupational Compensation Survey, Pay Only. Boston, Massachusetts Metropolitan Area. (May 1992)-. Government Publication. English. One time a year. $226.00. Superintendent of Documents, US Government Printing Office, Washington DC 20402. **Tel** (202)275-3328, FAX (202)786-2377. *Continues* Occupational Compensation Survey--Pay and Benefits. Boston.

LC HC
DD 331

US

OCCUPATIONAL COMPENSATION SURVEY--PAY ONLY. CHEYENNE, WY. Added/Corp United States. Bureau of Labor Statistics. **VFOAT** Occupational Compensation Survey--Pay and Benefits. Cheyenne, WY; Cheyenne, WY. (May 1992)-. Government Publication. English. Irregular. $226.00. US Department of Labor / Bureau of Labor Statistics, 441 G Street Northwest, Washington DC 20212. **Tel** (202)606-7800, FAX (202)606-7797. **(Subscription address:** Superintendent of Documents, US Government Printing Office, Washington DC 20402. **)** *Continues* Area Wage Survey. Cheyenne, Wyo.

LC HD5726.D3 A74
DD 331.2/977172/05

US

●**OCCUPATIONAL COMPENSATION SURVEY--PAY ONLY. DAYTON-SPRINGFIELD, OHIO, METROPOLITAN AREA / U.S. DEPARTMENT OF LABOR, BUREAU OF LABOR STATISTICS. Added/Corp** United States. Bureau of Labor Statistics. (Feb. 1993)-. Government Publication. English. Irregular. $226.00. US Department of Labor / Bureau of Labor Statistics, 441 G Street Northwest, Washington DC 20212. **Tel** (202)606-7800, FAX (202)606-7797. **(Subscription address:** Superintendent of Documents, US Government Printing Office, Washington DC 20402. **)** *Continues* Area Wage Survey. Dayton-Springfield, OH.

US

OCCUPATIONAL COMPENSATION SURVEY--PAY ONLY. DUVAL COUNTY, FL--FAST FOOD RESTAURANTS. Added/Corp United States. Bureau of Labor Statistics. **VFOAT** Duval County, FL--Fast Food Restaurants; Duval County, FL, Fast Food Restaurants. (Dec. 1992)-. English. US Department of Labor / Bureau of Labor Statistics, 441 G Street Northwest, Washington DC 20212. **Tel** (202)606-7800, FAX (202)606-7797. *Continues* Fast Food Restaurants Wage Survey. Duval County, FL.

US

OCCUPATIONAL COMPENSATION SURVEY--PAY ONLY. ESCAMBIA COUNTY, FL--FAST FOOD RESTAURANTS / U.S. DEPARTMENT OF LABOR, BUREAU OF LABOR STATISTICS. Added/Corp United States. Bureau of Labor Statistics. **VFOAT** Escambia County, FL--Fast Food Restaurants; Escambia County, FL, Fast Food Restaurants. (Nov. 1992)-. Government Publication. English. Irregular. $226.00. US Department of Labor / Bureau of Labor Statistics, 441 G Street Northwest, Washington DC 20212. **Tel** (202)606-7800, FAX (202)606-7797. **(Subscription address:** Superintendent of Documents, US Government Printing Office, Washington DC 20402. **)** *Continues* Fast Food Restaurants Wage Survey. Escambia County, FL.

US

●**OCCUPATIONAL COMPENSATION SURVEY--PAY ONLY. HARDIN COUNTY, KY--FAST FOOD RESTAURANTS. Added/Corp** United States. Bureau of Labor Statistics. **VFOAT** Hardin County, KY--Fast Food Restaurants; Hardin County, KY, Fast Food Restaurants. (Jan. 1993)-. English. US Department of Labor / Bureau of Labor Statistics, 441 G Street Northwest, Washington DC 20212. **Tel** (202)606-7800, FAX (202)606-7797. *Continues* Fast Food Restaurants Wage Survey. Hardin County, KY.

US

●**OCCUPATIONAL COMPENSATION SURVEY--PAY ONLY. HARRISON COUNTY, MS--FAST FOOD RESTAURANTS / U.S. DEPARTMENT OF LABOR, BUREAU OF LABOR STATISTICS. Added/Corp** United States. Bureau of Labor Statistics. **VFOAT** Harrison County, MS--Fast Food Restaurants; Harrison County, MS, Fast Food Restaurants. (Jan. 1993)-. Statistical Publication. English. US Department of Labor / Bureau of Labor Statistics, 441 G Street Northwest, Washington DC 20212. **Tel** (202)606-7800, FAX (202)606-7797. *Continues* Fast Food Restaurants Wage Survey. Harrison County, MS.

US

OCCUPATIONAL COMPENSATION SURVEY--PAY ONLY. ISLAND COUNTY, WA--FAST FOOD RESTAURANTS. Added/Corp United States. Bureau of Labor Statistics. **VFOAT** Island County, WA, Fast Food Restaurants; Island County, WA--Fast Food Restaurants. (Dec. 1992)-. English. US Department of Labor / Bureau of Labor Statistics, 441 G Street Northwest, Washington DC 20212. **Tel** (202)606-7800, FAX (202)606-7797. *Continues* Fast Food Restaurants Wage Survey. Island County, WA.

LC HD4976.K23 A37

US

OCCUPATIONAL COMPENSATION SURVEY--PAY ONLY. KANSAS CITY, MISSOURI-KANSAS, METROPOLITAN AREA / U.S. DEPARTMENT OF LABOR, BUREAU OF LABOR STATISTICS. Added/Corp United States. Bureau of Labor Statistics. **VFOAT** Kansas City, Missouri-Kansas Metropolitan Area. (Aug. 1992)-. Government Publication. English. One time a year. $226.00. Superintendent of Documents, US Government Printing Office, Washington DC 20402. **Tel** (202)275-3328, FAX (202)786-2377. *Continues* Area Wage Survey. Kansas City, Missouri-Kansas, Metropolitan Area.

US

OCCUPATIONAL COMPENSATION SURVEY--PAY ONLY. LAKE COUNTY, IL--FAST FOOD RESTAURANTS / U.S. DEPARTMENT OF LABOR, BUREAU OF LABOR STATISTICS. Added/Corp United States. Bureau of Labor Statistics. **VFOAT** Lake County, IL--Fast Food Restaurants; Lake County, IL, Fast Food Restaurants. (Nov. 1992)-. Government Publication. English. Irregular. $226.00. US Department of Labor / Bureau of Labor Statistics, 441 G Street Northwest, Washington DC 20212. **Tel** (202)606-7800, FAX (202)606-7797. **(Subscription address:** Superintendent of Documents, US Government Printing Office, Washington DC 20402. **)** *Continues* Fast Food Restaurants Wage Survey. Lake County, IL.

US

●**OCCUPATIONAL COMPENSATION SURVEY--PAY ONLY. LAUDERDALE COUNTY, MS--FAST FOOD RESTAURANTS. Added/Corp** United States. Bureau of Labor Statistics. **VFOAT** Lauderdale County, MS--Fast Food Restaurants; Lauderdale County, MS, Fast Food Restaurants. (Feb. 1993)-. English. US Department of Labor / Bureau of Labor Statistics, 441 G Street Northwest, Washington DC 20212. **Tel** (202)606-7800, FAX (202)606-7797. *Continues* Fast Food Restaurants Wage Survey. Lauderdale County, MS.

US

OCCUPATIONAL COMPENSATION SURVEY--PAY ONLY. LEAVENWORTH, KS--FAST FOOD RESTAURANTS / U.S. DEPARTMENT OF LABOR, BUREAU OF LABOR STATISTICS. Added/Corp United States. Bureau of Labor Statistics. **VFOAT** Leavenworth, KS--Fast Food Restaurants; Leavenworth, KS, Fast Food Restaurants. (Nov. 1992)-. English. US Department of Labor / Bureau of Labor Statistics, 441 G Street Northwest, Washington DC 20212. **Tel** (202)606-7800, FAX (202)606-7797. *Continues* Fast food Restaurants Wage Survey. Leavenworth County, KS.

US

OCCUPATIONAL COMPENSATION SURVEY--PAY ONLY. MISSISSIPPI--FORESTRY / U.S. DEPARTMENT OF LABOR, BUREAU OF LABOR STATISTICS. Added/Corp United States. Bureau of Labor Statistics. **VFOAT** Mississippi--Forestry; Mississippi, Forestry. (1992)-. English. Every 2 years. US Department of Labor / Bureau

Business and Economics —Labor

of Labor Statistics, 441 G Street Northwest, Washington DC 20212. **Tel** (202)606-7800, FAX (202)606-7797. *Continues* Forestry Wage Survey. Mississippi.

US

●**OCCUPATIONAL COMPENSATION SURVEY--PAY ONLY. MONTGOMERY COUNTY, MD--FAST FOOD RESTAURANTS / U.S. DEPARTMENT OF LABOR, BUREAU OF LABOR STATISTICS. Added/Corp** United States. Bureau of Labor Statistics. **VFOAT** Montgomery County, MD--Fast Food Restaurants; Montgomery County, MD, Fast Food Restaurants. (Jan. 1993)-. Government Publication. English. US Department of Labor / Bureau of Labor Statistics, 441 G Street Northwest, Washington DC 20212. **Tel** (202)606-7800, FAX (202)606-7797. *Continues* Fast Food Restaurants Wage Survey. Montgomery County, MD.

US

●**OCCUPATIONAL COMPENSATION SURVEY--PAY ONLY. NORFOLK, VA--FAST FOOD RESTAURANTS / U.S. DEPARTMENT OF LABOR, BUREAU OF LABOR STATISTICS. Added/Corp** United States. Bureau of Labor Statistics. **VFOAT** Norfolk, VA--Fast Food Restaurants; Norfolk, VA, Fast Food Restaurants. (Jan. 1993)-. Government Publication. English. US Department of Labor / Bureau of Labor Statistics, 441 G Street Northwest, Washington DC 20212. **Tel** (202)606-7800, FAX (202)606-7797. *Continues* Fast Food Restaurants Wage Survey. Norfolk, VA.

US

OCCUPATIONAL COMPENSATION SURVEY--PAY ONLY. NORTHERN NEW YORK / U.S. DEPARTMENT OF LABOR, BUREAU OF LABOR STATISTICS. VFOAT Northern New York. (199?)-. Government Publication. English. One time a year. $226.00. US Department of Labor / Bureau of Labor Statistics, 441 G Street Northwest, Washington DC 20212. **Tel** (202)606-7800, FAX (202)606-7797. **(Subscription address:** Superintendent of Documents, US Government Printing Office, Washington DC 20402. **)**

LC HD4976.O17 O22
DD 331.2/979466/05

US

OCCUPATIONAL COMPENSATION SURVEY--PAY ONLY. OAKLAND, CALIFORNIA, METROPOLITAN AREA / U.S. DEPARTMENT OF LABOR, BUREAU OF LABOR STATISTICS. Added/Corp United States. Bureau of Labor Statistics. **VFOAT** Oakland, California, Metropolitan Area; Occupational Compensation Survey, Pay Only. Oakland, California, Metropolitan Area. (Feb. 1992)-. Government Publication. English. One time a year. $226.00. Superintendent of Documents, US Government Printing Office, Washington DC 20402. **Tel** (202)275-3328, FAX (202)786-2377. *Continues* Area Wage Survey. Oakland, California, metropolitan area.

LC HD4906
DD 331.21

US

●**OCCUPATIONAL COMPENSATION SURVEY-- PAY ONLY. PORTSMOUTH-CHILLICOTHE-GALLIPOLIS, OH. Added/Corp** United States. Bureau of Labor Statistics. **VFOAT** Portsmouth-Chillicothe-Gallipolis, OH. (Jan. 1993)-. English. US Department of Labor / Bureau of Labor Statistics, 441 G Street Northwest, Washington DC 20212. **Tel** (202)606-7800, FAX (202)606-7797. *Continues* Area Wage Survey. Portsmouth-Chillicothe-Gallipolis, Ohio.

US

OCCUPATIONAL COMPENSATION SURVEY--PAY ONLY. PROVIDENCE, RI / U.S. DEPARTMENT OF LABOR, BUREAU OF LABOR STATISTICS. Added/Corp United States. Bureau of Labor Statistics. **VFOAT** Providence, RI. (1992)-. English. US Department of Labor / Bureau of Labor Statistics, 441 G Street Northwest, Washington DC 20212. **Tel** (202)606-7800, FAX (202)606-7797. *Continues* Area Wage Survey. Providence, RI.

US

●**OCCUPATIONAL COMPENSATION SURVEY--PAY ONLY. PUERTO RICO. Added/Corp** United States. Bureau of Labor Statistics. **VFOAT** Puerto Rico. (July 1993)-. English. Every 2 years. US Department of Labor / Bureau of Labor Statistics, 441 G Street Northwest, Washington DC 20212. **Tel** (202)606-7800, FAX (202)606-7797. *Continues* Area Wage Survey. Puerto Rico.

LC HD4976.S23 U53a
DD 331.2/9794/54

US

OCCUPATIONAL COMPENSATION SURVEY--PAY ONLY. SACRAMENTO, CALIFORNIA, METROPOLITAN AREA. Added/Corp United States. Bureau of Labor Statistics. **VFOAT** Sacramento, California, Metropolitan Area. (Aug. 1992)-. Government Publication. English. One time a year. $226.00. Superintendent of Documents, US Government Printing Office, Washington DC 20402. **Tel** (202)275-3328, FAX (202)786-2377. *Continues* Area Wage Survey. Sacramento, California, Metropolitan Area, 0099-1899.

LC HD4976.S28 A37
DD 331.2/9792/25

US

OCCUPATIONAL COMPENSATION SURVEY--PAY ONLY. SALT LAKE CITY-OGDEN, UTAH, METROPOLITAN AREA / U.S. DEPARTMENT OF LABOR, BUREAU OF LABOR STATISTICS. Added/Corp United States. Bureau of Labor Statistics. **VFOAT** Occupational Compensation Survey, Pay Only. Salt Lake City-Ogden, Utah, Metropolitan Area; Salt Lake City-Ogden, Utah, Metropolitan Area; Salt Lake City, Ogden, Utah, Metropolitan Area. Apr. (1992)-. Government Publication. English. Irregular. $226.00. Superintendent of Documents, US Government Printing Office, Washington DC 20402. **Tel** (202)275-3328, FAX (202)786-2377. *Continues* Area Wage Survey. Salt Lake City-Ogden, Utah, Metropolitan Area, 0362-4137.

LC HD4976.S295 O27
DD 331.2/979461/05

US

OCCUPATIONAL COMPENSATION SURVEY--PAY ONLY. SAN FRANCISCO, CALIFORNIA, METROPOLITAN AREA / U.S. DEPARTMENT OF LABOR, BUREAU OF LABOR STATISTICS. Added/Corp United States. Bureau of Labor Statistics. **VFOAT** San Francisco, California, Metropolitan Area; Occupational Compensation Survey, Pay Only. San Francisco, California, Metropolitan Area. (Apr. 1992)-. Government Publication. English. One time a year. $226.00. Superintendent of Documents, US Government Printing Office, Washington DC 20402. **Tel** (202)275-3328, FAX (202)786-2377. *Continues* Area Wage Survey. San Francisco, California, Metropolitan Area.

LC HD4976.S3 A37
DD 331.2/9794/74

US

OCCUPATIONAL COMPENSATION SURVEY--PAY ONLY. SAN JOSE, CALIFORNIA, METROPOLITAN AREA. Added/Corp United States. Bureau of Labor Statistics. **VFOAT** San Jose, California, Metropolitan Area. (Aug. 1992)-. Government Publication. English. One time a year. $236.00. Superintendent of Documents, US Government Printing Office, Washington DC 20402. **Tel** (202)275-3328, FAX (202)786-2377. *Continues* Area Wage Survey. San Jose, California, Metropolitan Area, 0197-436X.

LC HD4976.S73 A74
DD 331.2/977356

US

OCCUPATIONAL COMPENSATION SURVEY--PAY ONLY. SPRINGFIELD, IL / U.S. DEPARTMENT OF LABOR, BUREAU OF LABOR STATISTICS. Added/Corp United States. Bureau of Labor Statistics. (Oct. 1991)-. English. US Department of Labor / Bureau of Labor Statistics, 441 G Street Northwest, Washington DC 20212. **Tel** (202)606-7800, FAX (202)606-7797. *Continues* Area Wage Survey. Springfield, Ill.

US

OCCUPATIONAL COMPENSATION SURVEY--PAY ONLY. TOPEKA, KS / U.S. DEPARTMENT OF LABOR, BUREAU OF LABOR STATISTICS. Added/Corp United States. Bureau of Labor Statistics. **VFOAT** Topeka, KS. (1992)-. English. US Department of Labor / Bureau of Labor Statistics, 441 G Street Northwest, Washington DC 20212. **Tel** (202)606-7800, FAX (202)606-7797. *Continues* Area Wage Survey. Topeka, KS.

US

OCCUPATIONAL COMPENSATION SURVEY--PAY ONLY. UPPER PENINSULA, MI / U.S. DEPARTMENT OF LABOR, BUREAU OF LABOR STATISTICS. Added/Corp United States. Bureau of Labor Statistics. **VFOAT** Upper Peninsula, MI. (May 1992)-. Government Publication. English. One time a year. $226.00. US Department of Labor / Bureau of Labor Statistics, 441 G Street Northwest, Washington DC 20212. **Tel** (202)606-7800, FAX (202)606-7797.

(Subscription address: Superintendent of Documents, US Government Printing Office, Washington DC 20402. **)** *Continues* Area Wage Survey. Upper Peninsula, Mich.

US

●**OCCUPATIONAL COMPENSATION SURVEY--PAY ONLY. WASHINGTON, DC--FAST FOOD RESTAURANTS. Added/Corp** United States. Bureau of Labor Statistics. **VFOAT** Washington, DC--Fast Food Restaurants; Washington, DC, Fast Food Restaurants. (Jan. 1993)-. Government Publication. English. Irregular. $226.00. US Department of Labor / Bureau of Labor Statistics, 441 G Street Northwest, Washington DC 20212. **Tel** (202)606-7800, FAX (202)606-7797. **(Subscription address:** Superintendent of Documents, US Government Printing Office, Washington DC 20402. **)** *Continues* Fast Food Restaurants Wage Survey. Washington, DC.

LC HD4976.W6 A37
DD 331.2/9/7443

US

OCCUPATIONAL COMPENSATION SURVEY--PAY ONLY. WORCESTER, MASSACHUSETTS, METROPOLITAN AREA / U.S. DEPARTMENT OF LABOR, BUREAU OF LABOR STATISTICS. Added/Corp United States. Bureau of Labor Statistics. **VFOAT** Worcester, Massachusetts, Metropolitan Area. (Sept. 1991)-. Government Publication. English. One time a year. $226.00. Superintendent of Documents, US Government Printing Office, Washington DC 20402. **Tel** (202)275-3328, FAX (202)786-2377. *Continues* Area Wage Survey. Worcester, Massachusetts, Metropolitan Area, 0197-4386.

US

OCCUPATIONAL EARNINGS AND WAGE TRENDS IN METROPOLITAN AREAS. (1964/65)-. Government Publication. English. Three times a year. US Department of Labor / Bureau of Labor Statistics, 441 G Street Northwest, Washington DC 20212. **Tel** (202)606-7800, FAX (202)606-7797. Documents available from Documents on Demand. *Continues* Occupational Earnings in Major Labor Markets.
Ind/Abst Am. Stat. Index.

LC HD5725.O7 O28
DD 331.12/09795

US

OCCUPATIONAL EMPLOYMENT TRENDS IN THE STATE OF OREGON / PREPARED BY RESEARCH AND STATISTICS SECTION. Added/Corp Oregon. Employment Division. Research and Statistics Section. **VFOAT** Revision of Occupational Employment Trends in the State of Oregon. (1980)-. English. Oregon Employment Division, 875 Union Street Northeast, Salem OR 97311. **Tel** (503)378-3211.

LC HD6958
DD 331

UK

●**OCCUPATIONAL ERGONOMICS AND SAFETY. See** Industrial Health and Safety.

US

OCCUPATIONAL OUTLOOK FOR VOCATIONAL AND TECHNICAL JOBS IN TENNESSEE, THE. Added/Corp Tennessee. Occupational Employment Statistics Unit. (1989)-. English. OCLC Pacific Network, 250 West First Street/Suite 330, Claremont CA 91711. **Tel** (909)621-9998.

US

OCCUPATIONAL PROFILES. (19??)-. Periodical. English. One time a year. $23.00 (all areas), price varies (individual counties). Research and Analysis Branch, Washington State Employment Security Department, Box 9046, Olympia WA 98507. **Tel** (206)438-4800, FAX (206)438-4846.

LC HD5725.O7 O67A   **ISSN** 0147-1333
DD 331/1/1/09795

US

OCCUPATIONAL PROFILES OF OREGON'S MANUFACTURING INDUSTRIES. Main/Corp Oregon. Employment Division. Research and Statistics Section. (1971)-. English. Oregon Department of Human Resources Development, 155 Cottage Street Northeast, Salem OR 97310.

US

OCCUPATIONAL PROJECTIONS. (19??)-. Consumer Publication. English. Every 2 years. $59.00 (full set); $2.50 (counties in Washington). Research and Analysis Branch, Washington State Employment Security Department, Box 9046, Olympia WA 98507. **Tel** (206)438-4800, FAX (206)438-4846.
Desc: Five-year occupational employment projections for nonagricultural wage and salary employment.

Business and Economics —Labor

LC HD4976.O5 O28
DD 331.2/976682 US
OCCUPATIONAL WAGE SURVEY. MUSKOGEE AREA. **Added/Corp** Oklahoma Employment Security Commission. Research and Planning. **VFOAT** Muskogee Area; Occupational Wage Survey. Muskogee, Oklahoma. (19??)-. English. Oklahoma Employment Security Commission, Will Rogers Building, Room 310, Oklahoma City OK 73105. **Tel** (405)521-3735.

LC HD4976.O37 O373a
DD 331.2/976638 US
OCCUPATIONAL WAGE SURVEY: OKLAHOMA CITY METROPOLITAN AREA. **Main/Corp** Oklahoma. Employment Security Commission. Research and Planning Division. (19??)-. English. Oklahoma Employment Security Commission, Will Rogers Building, Room 310, Oklahoma City OK 73105. **Tel** (405)521-3735.

LC HD4976.S45 O32
DD 331.2/976636 US
OCCUPATIONAL WAGE SURVEY. SHAWNEE, OKLAHOMA. **Added/Corp** Oklahoma Employment Security Commission. Research and Planning. **VFOAT** Occupational Wage Survey. Shawnee Area. (19??)-. English. Oklahoma Employment Security Commission, Will Rogers Building, Room 310, Oklahoma City OK 73105. **Tel** (405)521-3735.

LC HD4976.T85 O25
DD 331.2/2/0976686 US
OCCUPATIONAL WAGE SURVEY. TULSA METROPOLITAN AREA. **Added/Corp** Oklahoma Employment Security Commission. Research and Planning. **VFOAT** Tulsa Metropolitan Area; Occupational Wage Survey. Tulsa, Oklahoma. (19??)-. English. Oklahoma Employment Security Commission, Will Rogers Building, Room 310, Oklahoma City OK 73105. **Tel** (405)521-3735.

LC HD5725.W2 O33 US
OCCUPATIONS IN THE LABOR MARKET. **Added/Corp** Washington (State). Employment Security Dept. Labor Market and Economic Analysis Branch. (198?)-. Periodical. English. Price varies. Research and Analysis Branch, Washington State Employment Security Department, Box 9046, Olympia WA 98507. **Tel** (206)438-4800, FAX (206)438-4846.

LC HD5756.A6 C49A CL
OCUPACION Y DESOCUPACION, SECTORES URBANOS DE LAS REGIONES IV A X, EXCEPTO EL GRAN SANTIAGO. **Main/Corp** Universidad de Chile. Departamento de Economia. 1977/78-. Periodical. Spanish. Two times a year. 2,500Chil$ Chile; $35.00 US. Depto de Economia, Universidad de Chile, Casilla 3861 Santiago Chile. **Tel** 2228521. **ED** Ricardo Zabala. **Circ:** 400 (ctrl).
Desc: Survey to determine the unemployment rate in Chile.

LC HD8013.A9 O47 ISSN 0029-8565
DD 331.7/6135/00009436 GW
UDC 342.9 :35.08
OEFFENTLICHE DIENST KOELN, DER. (DER OFFENTLICHE DIENST.). [Off. Dienst Koln]. **VFOAT** Der Offentliche Dienst. Ausgabe A; DOD. (1948)-. Periodical. German. Twelve times a year. $119.75. Carl Heymanns Verlag KG, Luxemburger Strasse 449, D-50939 Cologne Germany. **Tel** 011 49 221 460100, telex 8 881 888. Index available. **Bk Rev**. **Ad Acc**. **Circ:** 1,500 (ctrl). **Continues** Offentlich Bedienstete.

ISSN 0228-7935
DD 971.4/04 CN
OFFENSIVES COMMUNAUTAIRES ET CULTURELLES. [Offensives communaut. cult.]. **VAT** Offensives. Vol. 1, No 1 (Oct./Nov./Dec. 1980)-. Periodical. French. Three times a year. $5.00.

LC HD4801
DD 331 US
OFFICE OF EMPLOYEE RELATIONS NEWS. **VFOAT** News. Vol. 1, No. 1 (Oct. 1984)-. Periodical. English. Twelve times a year. Goer, 12th Floor/Agency Building, 2 Empire State Plaza, Albany NY 12237.

LC HD8039.M4 U569 ISSN 0734-7421
US
OFFICE POLICY SURVEY, TWIN CITY AREA. English. One time a year. Personnel Surveys, Inc., 1608 Northstar Center, Minneapolis MN 55402.

ISSN 0378-5890
SZ
OFFICIAL BULLETIN. SERIES B / INTERNATIONAL LABOUR OFFICE. [Off. bull. - Int. Labour Off. Ser. B]. **Main/Corp** International Labour Office. **Added/Corp** International Labour Office. Freedom of Association Committee. **VFOAT** Reports of the Committee on Freedom of Association. Vol. 58, Nos. 1/2, (1975)-. Bulletin. English. Three times a year. 140.00F. International Labour Office - ILO, Publications Sales Service, CH-1211 Geneva 22 Switzerland. **Tel** 011 41 22 7996111, FAX 011 41 22 7986253, telex 415 647 ilo ch. **(Subscription address:** International Labour Office / Washington, DC, 1828 L Street Northwest, Suite 801, Washington DC 20036. **Tel** (202)653-7652.)
Continues in part Official Bulletin (International Labour Office : 1921), 0020-7772.
Desc: Reports of the Committee on Freedom of Association of the Governing Body of the ILO and related material.
Ind/Abst Middle East Abstr. Index.

LC HD8801.A5 S66 ISSN 0379-8410
DD 331/.0968 SA
OFFICIAL JOURNAL OF THE INSTITUTE OF LABOUR RELATIONS, UNIVERSITY OF SOUTH AFRICA. (SOUTH AFRICAN JOURNAL OF LABOUR RELATIONS.). **Added/Corp** University of South Africa. Institute of Labour Relations. Vol. 1 (1977)-. Periodical. English (Afrikaans). Four times a year. $49.21. School of Business Leadership, University of South Africa, PO Box 392, Pretoria 0001 South Africa. **Tel** 011 27 12 322-6777, FAX 011 27 12 429-2925, telex 35 0068. **ED** M Rajah. **Bk Rev**. **Circ:** 1,000.
Ind/Abst Int. Bibliogr. Sociol.

LC HD6870.5 .A35
DD 331.88/0968/05 SA
OFFICIAL SOUTH AFRICAN TRADE UNIONS DIRECTORY AND INDUSTRIAL RELATIONS HANDBOOK. **VFOAT** Trade Union Directory. Directory. English. One time a year. **Continues** Official Trade Union Directory and Industrial Relations Handbook.

IT
OGGIDOMANI ANZIANI : TRIMESTRALE DELLA FEDERAZIONE NAZIONALE PENSIONATI-CISL. **Added/Corp** Federazione Nazionale Pensionati Cisl (Italy). **VFOAT** Oggi Domani Anziani. (1988)-. Periodical. Italian. Three times a year. Franco Angeli Riviste SRL, Viale Monza 106, 20127 Milan Italy. **Tel** 011 39 2 2827651, 011 39 2 289562, FAX 011 39 2 258004, telex 051-511650.

LC KFO332.8.P77 A496
DD 344.771/0189/041353 347.7104189041353 US
OHIO PUBLIC EMPLOYEE REPORTER. **Added/Corp** Ohio. State Employment Relations Board. **VFOAT** Public Employee Reporter (Ohio Ed.). Vol. 1 (1984)-. Periodical. English. Twenty-four times a year. $495.00. LRP Publications, 747 Dresher Road, Suite 500, Horsham PA 19044. **Tel** (800)341-7874, (215)784-0941, FAX (215)784-9639, (215)784-0870. **(Subscription address:** LRP Publications, PO Box 980, Horsham PA 19044. **Tel** (800)341-7874, (215)784-0860.) Index available. cum. index. **Circ:** 300. available on microfiche.
Desc: Abstracts and full-text of Ohio State Labor Board and related court decisions. Complete indexing, access points, table of cases, citation tracker, rules and regulations of boards, articles, database and off-line searches.

ISSN 0199-7734
US
OHIO TEAMSTER, THE. **Added/Corp** International Brotherhood of Teamsters, Chauffeurs, Warehousemen and Helpers of America. Joint Council No. 41, Ohio. (19??)-. Periodical. English. Eight times a year. Free on request. Ohio Teamster, 2070 E 22nd, Cleveland OH 44115. **Tel** (216)771-6339.

SZ
OIT INFORMACIONES. **Main/Corp** International Labour Office. (19??)-. Periodical. Spanish. Irregular. Free on request. International Labour Office - ILO, Publications Sales Service, CH-1211 Geneva 22 Switzerland. **Tel** 011 41 22 7996111, FAX 011 41 22 7986253, telex 415 647 ilo ch.

LC HD5725.O35 O43a
DD 331.12/09766 US
OKLAHOMA ANNUAL PLANNING REPORT. **Main/Corp** Oklahoma Employment Security Commission. Research and Planning Division. **Added/Corp** Oklahoma Employment Security Commission. Research and Planning Division. Annual Planning Report: State of Oklahoma. **VFOAT** Annual Planning Report: State of Oklahoma. (19??)-. English. One time a year.

LC HD5725.O35 O54 ISSN 0147-8052
DD 331.12/51/09766 US
OKLAHOMA OCCUPATIONAL EMPLOYMENT STATISTICS. See Business and Economics-Abstracting, Bibliographies and Statistics.

LC HD1527.O3 O43a ISSN 0090-8037
DD 331.7/63/09766 US
OKLAHOMA RURAL MANPOWER REPORT. **Main/Corp** Oklahoma. Employment Security Commission. Research and Planning Division. (1971)-. Periodical. English. Oklahoma Employment Security Commission, Will Rogers Building, Room 310, Oklahoma City OK 73105. **Tel** (405)521-3735. **Continues** Oklahoma Farm Labor Report.

LC HD5077 .A35d
JA
OKUGAI RODOSHA SHOKUSHUBETSU CHINGIN CHOSA HOKOKU. **Main/Corp** Japan. Rodosho. Tokei Johobu. (1972)-. Periodical. Japanese. Rodosho Daijin Kambo, Tokei Johobu, 3-1 Otemachi 1-chome, Chiyoda-ku 100 Tokyo Japan. **Continues** Okugai Rodosha Shokushubetsu Chingin Chosa Hokoku.

IT
OLTRE IL PONTE. **Added/Corp** Ires-Cgil Veneto. (1983)-. Periodical. Italian. Three times a year. L49000. Franco Angeli Riviste SRL, Viale Monza 106, 20127 Milan Italy. **Tel** 011 39 2 2827651, 011 39 2 289562, FAX 011 39 2 258004, telex 051-511650.

LC HG8011
DD 368 US
ON WORKERS COMPENSATION. (19??)-. English. Four times a year. $175.00. Edward M. Welch, 2875 North Wind Drive, Suite 210 A, East Lansing MI 48823. **Tel** (517)332-5266.

LC HD5264.N4 N46A
NE
ONDERZOEK NAAR VAKANTIES EN UITGAAN, DAG- EN VERBLIJFSRECREATIE. **VFOAT** National Survey on Holidays and Outdoor Recreation. (19??)-. Dutch. Fl24.80. Centraal Bureau voor de Statistiek, AFD ALG Zaken, Postbus 959, 2270 AZ Voorburg Netherlands. **Tel** 011 31 70 3373800, FAX 011 31 70 0387429, telex 32692 CBS NL. **Continues** Netherlands. Centraal Bureau Voor de Statistiek. Onderzoek Naar Vakanties en Uitgaan.

ISSN 0848-7049
DD 331.2/9713 CN
ONTARIO WAGE DEVELOPMENTS, COLLECTIVE BARGAINING SETTLEMENTS. [Ont. wage dev. collect. bargain. settl.]. **Added/Corp** Ontario. Office of Collective Bargaining Information. **VFOAT** Wage Developments in Collective Bargaining Settlements in Ontario. (1990)-. Periodical. English. Four times a year. Free. Ontario Ministry of Labour, 400 University Avenue / 11th Floor, Toronto Ontario M7A 1T7 Canada. **Tel** (416)326-1260, 326-7837. **Continues** Wage Developments in Collective Bargaining Settlements in Ontario., 0709-1400.

US
OPERATING INSTRUCTIONS HANDBOOK FOR LABOR CERTIFICATION PROGRAM FOR IMMIGRANT WORKERS. CHAPTER 1. **Main/Corp** United States. Employment and Training Administration. **Added/Corp** United States Employment Service. (1977)-. English. Irregular. US Department of Labor, 200 Constitution Avenue NW, Washington DC 20210. **Tel** (202)219-7316, FAX (202)219-7312.

LC HD8013.G7 C5
DD 354/.41/006062 UK
TITLE CHANGE
OPINION. See Public Administration-Civil Service.

ISSN 0711-7159
DD 331.12/4/09713541 CN
OPPORTUNITIES (SCARBOROUGH). (OPPORTUNITIES.). [Opportunities]. Vol. 1, No. 1 (Dec. 1981)-. Periodical. English. Twelve times a year. $0.50 each number. Opportunities, c/o Meta Publications, 2161 Lawrence Avenue East, Scarborough Ontario M1P 2P5 Canada.

ISSN 0229-8104
DD 354.713001/73 CN
OPSEU NEWS. [OPSEU news]. **VAT** Ontario Public Service Employees Union News. 10/10 (Nov. 1975)-. Periodical. English. Four times a year. Free. Ontario Public Service Employees Union, 1901 Yonge Street, Toronto Ontario M4S 2Z5 Canada. **Tel** (416)482-7423, FAX (416)482-1493. **ED** John C Ward. **Circ:** 75,000 (ctrl). **Continues** C.S.A.O. News, 0229-8112.
Desc: News, editorials, features, and letters about the activities of our members and the union that represents them, including social, economic, and political issues concerning them.

Business and Economics —Labor

LC HD5725.O7 O76
DD 016.3311/09795
ISSN 0732-6084
US
OREGON LABOR MARKET INFORMATION DIRECTORY. (19??)-. Directory. English. Irregular. Oregon Employment Division, 875 Union Street Northeast, Salem OR 97311. **Tel** (503)378-3211.

ISSN 0471-9506
YU
UDC 65
ORGANIZACIJA RADA. [Organ. rada]. **VFOAT** Organization of Work; Organisation du Travail; Arbeitsorganisation; Organizacija Truda. (1951)-. Periodical. Serbo-Croatian (Roman). Twelve times a year. **Ind/Abst** Ergon. Abstr.

ISSN 0833-0530
DD 331.7/02/09714
CN
ORIENTATION (MONTREAL. 1986). (L'ORIENTATION / LA CORPORATION PROFESSIONNELLE DES CONSEILLERS ET CONSEILLERES D'ORIENTATION DU QUEBEC.). [Orientation]. **Added/Corp** Corporation Professionnelle des Conseillers d'Orientation du Quebec. Vol. 1, No. 1 (Fall 1986)-. Periodical. French. Three times a year. 32.01Can$. La Corporation Professionnelle des Conseillers et Conseilleres d'Orientation du Quebec, 1100 Avenue Beaumont, Bureau 520, Ville Mount Royal Quebec H3P 3E5 Canada. **Tel** (514)737-4717, (800)363-2643, **FAX** (514)737-6431. **Circ:** 2,000. **Continues** Orientation Professionnelle, 0384-1383. **Ind/Abst** Repere (1986-).

LC HA1631 .A33 HF5549.5.T7 T7
DD 317.971
YU
OSTRUCAVANJE RADNIKA U RADNIM ORGANIZACIJAMA. See Business and Economics-Abstracting, Bibliographies and Statistics.

ISSN 0822-6377
DD 331/.05
CN
OUR TIMES. [Our times]. **Added/Corp** Our Times Cooperative. Vol. 1, No. 1 (March 1982)-. Periodical. English. Six times a year. 25.61Can$. Our Times, 390 Dufferin Street, Toronto Ontario M6K 2A3 Canada. **Tel** (416)531-5762, **FAX** (416)533-2397. **ED** Lorraine Endicott. **Bk Rev**. (Qty: 10). **Ad Acc**. **Circ:** 3,000. available on microfiche (Micromedia) from Micromedia Limited. **Desc:** For the readers who are interested in trade union activities and the labour movement in Canada. **Ind/Abst** Altern. Press Index (199?-); Can. Index; Can. Period. Index.

LC HD6350.I48 O93
US
OUR VOICE. (19??)-. Periodical. English. Twelve times a year. International Union of Life Insurance Agents, 161 West Wisconsin Avenue, Milwaukee WI 53203.

LC HX1 .O93
DD 335/.005
ISSN 0738-3436
US
OUT SOCIALISM. See Political Science-Socialism, Communism, Anarchism, Utopianism.

LC HD6500 .O9
DD 331.89/0974
US
OUTLOOK FOR COLLECTIVE BARGAINING IN NEW ENGLAND IN ... / U.S. DEPARTMENT OF LABOR, BUREAU OF LABOR STATISTICS, NEW ENGLAND REGIONAL OFFICE, THE. English. One time a year. Free. Bureau of Labor Statistics / New England Regional Office, 1603 JFK Federal Building, Government Center, Boston MA 02203. **Tel** (617)565-2327. **Circ:** 600. **Desc:** Includes calendar of collective bargaining expirations in New England.

ISSN 0743-0892
US
OVERSEAS JOB-PERSONALQUARTER. [Overs. job-personalquart.]. **VFOAT** Overseas Job Personal Quarter. (1986)-. Periodical. English. Four times a year. $30.00.

LC HD6270 .D5
UK
●**OVERSEAS SUMMER JOBS. VFOAT** Directory of Overseas Summer Jobs; Vacation Work's Overseas Summer Jobs. 26th Ed. (1995)-. Directory. English. One time a year. $14.95. Peterson's Guides, 202 Carnegie Center, Department 2342, PO Box 2123, Princeton NJ 08543-2123. **Tel** (609)243-9111, (800)338-3282, **FAX** (609)243-9150, (609)452-0966. **Continues** Directory of Overseas Summer Jobs (Oxford, England : 1985).

ISSN 1046-5049
DD 331
US
OWNERS AT WORK. [Owners work]. Vol. 1, No. 1 (Spring 1989)-. Periodical. English. Two times a year. Free on request. Northeast Ohio Employee Ownership Center, Department of Political Science, Kent State University, Kent OH 44242. **ED** Jim Bado. **Bk Rev**. **Circ:** 4500. **Desc:** Case studies and general information about employee ownership in Ohio; essays by leaders in employee-owned firms.

LC HD5729.P7 P696
DD 331.12/09717
ISSN 0826-9475
CN
P.E.I. LABOUR MARK. BULL. (PRINCE EDWARD ISLAND LABOUR MARKET BULLETIN.). [P.E.I. labour mark. bull.]. 1982-. Bulletin. English. Four times a year. Prince Edward Island Department of Labour, Manpower Resources Division, Research And Planning Branch, PO Box 2000, Charlottetown Prince Edward Island C1A 7N8 Canada.

LC HD8489.P6 P33
IT
PADANIA. Added/Corp Istituto di Storia Contemporanea del Movimento Operaio e Contadino (Ferrara, Italy). (1987)-. Periodical. Italian. Two times a year. L54440. Rosenberg & Sellier, Via Andrea Doria 14, 10123 Turin Italy. **Tel** 011 39 11 8127808, telex 224202 ROSSELI. **Desc:** Gives historical and cultural view of the Po River Valley in Italy through articles on labor, daily life, civil adjustments and humanistic ideals. Covers technology, art and economics of the region.

ISSN 0734-4317
US
PAINTERS & ALLIED TRADES DISTRICT COUNCIL 9 SPOTLITE NEWS. **Main/Corp** International Brotherhood of Painters and Allied Trades. Painters District Council 9 of New York City. **VFOAT** Spotlite News. **VAT** Painters and Allied Trades District Council Nine Spotlite News. (19??)-. Periodical. English. Four times a year. Painters District Council 9 of New York City, 69 West 14th Street, New York NY 10011.

LC HD5047.3 .A2A
FI
PALKKATILASTO. Main/Corp Finland. Tilastokeskus. (19??)-. Finnish. Tilastokeskus, PL 504, Annankatu 44, 00101 Helsinki Finland. **Tel** 011 358 0 17341, **FAX** 011 358 0 17342474, telex 1002111 TILASTO SF.

LC HD6350.P27 P44
DD 331.88/091
ISSN 0363-6437
US
PAPERWORKER, THE. Added/Corp United Paperworkers International Union. Vol. 1 (Oct. 4, 1972)-. Periodical. English. Twelve times a year. Free. United Paperworkers International Union, PO Box 1475, Nashville TN 37202. **Tel** (615)834-8590, **FAX** (615)831-6725. **Continues** Allied Industrial Worker, 0002-6107. **Ind/Abst** Work Relat. Abstr.

PY
PARAGUAY GREMIAL / BANCO PARAGUAYO DE DATOS. Added/Corp Banco Paraguayo de Datos. No. 1 (1982)-. Periodical. Spanish. Twelve times a year. Banco Paraguayo de Datos, Casilla Postal 1140, Asuncion Paraguay. **Continues in part** Resumen Mensual de Noticias. **Ind/Abst** Hum. Rights Intern. Rep.

LC HD6073.D372 U66
DD 331.4/8100164/0973
ISSN 0278-0224
US
PARITY. (PARITY : THE MAGAZINE OF WIP, WOMEN IN INFORMATION PROCESSING, INC.). [Parity]. Vol. 1, No. 1 (April 1980)-. Periodical. English. Four times a year. $15.00. Women in Information Processing, Inc., 1000 Connecticut Avenue, Suite 9, Washington DC 20036.

ISSN 1180-4890
DD 331.2/153/0971605
CN
PAY EQUITY NEWSLETTER, THE. [Pay equity news.- N.S., Pay Equity Comm.]. **Main/Corp** Nova Scotia. Pay Equity Commission. Vol 1 No. 1 (Mar. 1990)-. Newsletter. English.

LC JK639 .A42 JK774
DD 353.001/23/05
ISSN 0161-2964
US
PAY STRUCTURE OF THE FEDERAL CIVIL SERVICE. See Public Administration-Civil Service.

US
PAYROLL GUIDE. Added/Corp Prentice-Hall, inc. (1956)-. English. Irregular. Warren Gorham & Lamont Inc., Park Square Building, 31 St. James Avenue, Boston MA 02116-4112. **Tel** (617)423-2020, (800)950-1207, **FAX** (617)423-2026.

ISSN 1047-6571
DD 331
US
PAYROLL PRACTITIONER'S MONTHLY. [Payr. pract. mon.]. Vol. 1, No. 1 (Jan. 1989)-. Trade Publication. English. Twelve times a year. $140.64. Propub Inc., PO Box 102, 49 Van Syckel Lane, Wyckoff NJ 07481. **Tel** (201)891-6430.

ISSN 1185-0175
DD 361.7/66/09713535
CN
PEEL LABOUR. [Peel labour]. **Added/Corp** Labour Community Services of Peel. Vol. 1, No. 1 (1990/1991)-. English. Limited free distribution. Labour Community Services of Peel, 12 John Street, Brampton Ontario L6W 1Y9 Canada.

LC HD8740.P42 P45
DD 322/.2/09511565
CH
PEI-CHING KUNG YUN SHIH LIAO / PEI-CHING SHIH TSUNG KUNG HUI KUNG JEN TUNG SHIH YEN CHIU TSU PIEN. Vol. 1 (Aug. 1981)-. Periodical. Chinese. NT$0.90. Kung Jen Chu Pan She, Pei-Ching Shis Fa Hsing Pu, Beijing, People's Republic of China.

LC KFP332.8.P77 A496
DD 344.748/01890413539/02648 347.4804189041353902648
US
PENNSYLVANIA PUBLIC EMPLOYEE REPORTER. VFOAT Public Employee Reporter (Pennsylvania Edition). (1970)-. Periodical. English. Twenty-four times a year. $655.00. LRP Publications, 747 Dresher Road, Suite 500, Horsham PA 19044. **Tel** (800)341-7874, (215)784-0941, **FAX** (215)784-9639, (215)784-0870. **Desc:** A full-text subscription service reporting all significant Pennsylvania Labor Relations Board and related court decisions, comprehensively indexed and headnoted.

LC HD7096.U6 P425
DD 331.13/79748
ISSN 0553-5115
US
PENNSYLVANIA'S INSURED UNEMPLOYED. Jan. 1966-. English. Twelve times a year. Free. Chief of Research and Statistics, Labor and Industry Building, Harrisburg PA 17121. **Continues** Insured Unemployed.

LC HD5725 .P4 P53
DD 331.120973
US
PENNSYLVANIA'S LABOR FORCE. Feb. (1988)-. English. Twelve times a year. Pennsylvania Department of Labor and Industry, Bureau of Research and Statistics, 300 Liberty Avenue / Room 1303, Pittsburgh PA 15222. **Tel** (412)565-5350. **Continues** Pennsylvania Employment & Earnings, 0476-1979.

ISSN 0923-6007
NE
UDC 331.25(492)
PENSIOENMEMO DEVENTER. (PENSIOENMEMO.). [Pensioenmemo Deventer]. (1988)-. Periodical. Dutch. One time a year. $15.19. Kluwer BV, Postbus 23, 7400 GA Deventer Netherlands. **Tel** 011 31 5700 33155, 011 31 5700 47421, **FAX** 011 31 5700 11504, telex 42829.

LC HG4001
DD 658
ISSN 1063-2476
US
CCC
PENSION BENEFITS. See Business and Economics-Investments.

LC HD7106.U5 P39
DD 658.32/53/0973
ISSN 1078-9766
US
CCC
●**PENSION MANAGEMENT.** [Pension manag.]. Vol. 30, No. 10 (Oct. 1994)-. Periodical. English. Twelve times a year. $68.00. Argus Business, 6151 Powers Ferry Road Northwest, Atlanta GA 30339. **Tel** (404)995-2500, **FAX** (404)995-0400. **(Subscription address:** Hallmark Data Systems, PO Box 1147, Skokie IL 60076. **Tel** (708)647-6933.) **Continues** Pension World, 0098-1753. **Ind/Abst** Acad. Search; Bus. Source Plus; Bus. Source; Curr. Cit.; EP Collect.; Homework Help.; MasterFile FullTEXT 1000; MasterFile FullTEXT 350; MasterFile FullTEXT 650; MasterFile FullTEXT (Oct. 1994-); Telebase.

LC HD7127 .P46
DD 331.25/2/097105
ISSN 0835-8583
CN
PENSION PLAN COVERAGE IN CANADA. See Business and Economics-Abstracting, Bibliographies and Statistics.

CN
PENSION PLANS IN CANADA : STATISTICAL HIGHLIGHTS AND KEY TABLES. See Business and Economics-Abstracting, Bibliographies and Statistics.

LC HD7105.45.C2 P46
DD 331.25/2/09714
ISSN 0225-4530
CN
PENSION PLANS IN QUEBEC. [Pension plans Que.]. No. 5 (1979)-. Monographic series. English. Price varies per volume. Regie des Rentes du Quebec, Case Postale 5200, Quebec Quebec G1K 7S9 Canada. **Tel** (418)643-8309.

ISSN 1353-1654
DD 658.3253
UK
●**PENSION SCHEME TRUSTEE.** (THE PENSION SCHEME TRUSTEE.). [Pension scheme trustee]. (1994)-. Periodical. English. Twelve times a year.

$299.46. Monitor Press, Rectory Road, Great Waldingfield, Sudbury Suffolk CO10 0TL United Kingdom. **Tel** 011 44 1787 378607, FAX 011 44 1787 880201.

LC HD7106.U5 P39 **ISSN** 0098-1753
DD 658.32/53/0973 US
CCC
CODEN PEWODA
TITLE CHANGE

PENSION WORLD. [Pension world]. (1975)-(1994). Trade Publication. English. Argus Business, 6151 Powers Ferry Road Northwest, Atlanta GA 30339. **Tel** (404)995-2500, FAX (404)995-0400. **ED** Kathleen N. Crighton. **Bk Rev. Ad Acc. Circ:** 28,000 (ctrl). available on microfilm and microfiche from University Microfilms International (UMI); available on an online database (files 15,485,648/Full-Text) from DIALOG. Documents available from UMI Article Clearinghouse. ***Continues** Pension & Welfare News, 0031-4862.* ***Continued by** Pension Management, 1078-9766.*
Desc: Contains articles of interest to pension plan sponsors and their investment managers on employee benefit and investment topics.
Ind/Abst ABI/INFORM Glob. Ed.; ABI/INFORM [Computer File] (Feb. 1975-1994); Acad. Search; Account. Tax Datab. (Apr. 1972-199?) [Full Txt.]; Account. Art.; Anbar Account. Finan. Abstr. [Full Txt.]; Anbar Mark. Distr. Abstr. [Full Txt.]; Anbar Top Manage. Abstr. [Full Txt.]; Bus. ASAP (1990-199?) [Full Txt.]; Bus. Index (1989-199?); Bus. Period. Index; Bus. Source Plus; Bus. Source; Curr. Cit.; EP Collect.; Fed. Tax Artic.; Gen. BusinessFile (1988-199?); Gen. Period. Index (1988-199?); Homework Help.; INFO-SOUTH Abstr.; Ins. Period. Index (19??-199?); Mag. Search; Manage. Market. Abstr.; Manage. Bibliogr. Rev.; MasterFile FullTEXT 1000; MasterFile FullTEXT 350; MasterFile FullTEXT 650; MasterFile FullTEXT (July 1993-Sept. 1994); OCLC; Oper. Prod. Manage. Abstr. [Full Txt.]; PAIS Int. Print (1991-199?); Person. Train. Abstr. [Full Txt.]; Stat. Ref. Index; Telebase; Trade Ind. ASAP [Full Txt.]; Trade Ind. Index [Full Txt.]; UMI ABI/Inform--Bus. Period. Ondisc (Jan. 1987-199?) [Full Txt.]; Wilson Bus. Abstr.; Women Manage. Rev. [Full Txt.]; Work Relat. Abstr.

MX

PERFIL LABORAL : REVISTA DE LA DIRECCION DEL TRABAJO Y PREVISION SOCIAL DEL ESTADO DE BAJA CALIFORNIA. **Added/Corp** Direccion del Trabajo y Prevision Social del Estado de Baja California. (1990)-. Periodical. Spanish. Four times a year. Direccion del Trabajo y Prevision Social, Centro de Gobierno, Edificio del Poder Judicial, Tercer Piso, Centro Civico Mexico BV.

ISSN 0228-3212
DD 332.63/27 CN

PERFORMANCE COMPARISON, CANADIAN POOLED PENSION FUNDS. [Perform. comp. Can. pooled pension funds]. **VFOAT** Canadian Pooled Pension Funds. June 1979-. Periodical. English. Two times a year. $100. per no. B J Vincent Company Ltd, 820 Mount Pleasant Road, Toronto Ontario M4P 2L2 Canada. ***Continues** Performance Comparison, Canadian Equity Pooled Pension Funds, 0228-3220.*

ISSN 1247-7575
FR
UDC 331.82

•**PERFORMANCES HUMAINES & TECHNIQUES TOULOUSE.** (PERFORMANCES HUMAINES & TECHNIQUES.). **VFOAT** Performances Humaines et Techniques (Toulouse). (1993)-. Periodical. French. Six times a year. Performances Humaines Techniques, 24 rue de Nazareth, 31000 Toulouse France. **Tel** 011 61 321175.

ISSN 0996-5882
FR
UDC 331.82
Pr Rev. **TITLE CHANGE**

PERFORMANCES MARSEILLE. (PERFORMANCES.). **VFOAT** Performances Humaines et Techniques (Marseille). (1989)-(1993). Periodical. French. Performances, 24 rue Nazareth, 31000 Toulouse France. **Tel** 011 33 61 321175, FAX 011 33 61 551760. **ED** Nouie Christol. **Bk Rev**, (Qty: 6/yr). **Ad Acc. Circ:** 2,000 (ctrl). ***Continues** Revue des Conditions de Travail, 0754-8435.* ***Continued by** Performances Humaines & Techniques (Toulouse), 1247-7575.*

LC HD6796 .A35A
DD 331.88/095 SI

PERJUANGAN. Vol. 1 (Jan. 1977)-. Periodical. English. Twelve times a year. $0.20 single issue. National Trades Union Congress Way, Singapore 1 Singapore. ***Formed by the union of** Afro-Asian Labour Bulletin **and** Perjuangan. Singapore. National Trades Union Congress.*

ISSN 0264-2778
UK
CEASED

PERMANENT REVOLUTION (LONDON, ENGLAND : 1983). (PERMANENT REVOLUTION : THEORETICAL JOURNAL OF THE WORKERS POWER GROUP.). **Added/Corp** Workers Power Group (London, England). No. 1 (Summer 1983)-(19??). Periodical. English. Workers Power Group, BCM Box 7750, London WC1N 3XX United Kingdom.

ISSN 0965-7991
DD 344.206323 UK

PERSONAL INJURIES AND QUANTUM REPORTS. [Pers. injur. quantum rep.]. (1992)-. Periodical. English. Six times a year (Feb., Apr., June, Aug., Oct., Dec.). $270.37. Sweet & Maxwell Ltd., South Quay Plaza, 183 Marsh Wall 7th Floor, London E14 9FT United Kingdom. **Tel** 011 44 171 5388686, FAX 011 44 171 5389508, telex 929089 ITPINF G. **(Subscription address:** International Thomson Publishing Services Ltd., North Way Andover, Hampshire SP10 5BE United Kingdom. **Tel** 011 44 1264 332424.)

GW

PERSONAL; MENSCH UND ARBEIT IM BETRIEB. (April 1949)-. Periodical. German. Twelve times a year. DM298.00. Wirtschaftsverlag Bachem GmbH, Ursulaplatz 1, D-50668 Cologne Germany. **Tel** 011 49 221 1619224, FAX 011 49 221 1619205.

LC HD5850 .A34d
DD 331.1/37994 AT

PERSONS NOT IN THE LABOUR FORCE. **See** Business and Economics-Abstracting, Bibliographies and Statistics.

LC AP62 .P47 **ISSN** 0164-3169
US

PERSPECTIVA MUNDIAL. Vol. 1 (Jan. 24, 1977)-. Periodical. Spanish. Eleven times a year (July/Aug. issues combined). $30.00. 408 Printing and Publishing Inc, 410 West Street, New York NY 10014. **Tel** (212)243-6392, FAX (212)727-0150. **ED** Martin Koppel. Index available. **Bk Rev. Circ:** 5,000.
Desc: Socialist magazine covering labor and national struggles in the Americas and internationally.

LC HD5727 .P47 **ISSN** 0840-8750
DD 331.12/5/097105 CN
CODEN PLAIEY

PERSPECTIVES ON LABOUR AND INCOME. **See** Business and Economics-Abstracting, Bibliographies and Statistics.

ISSN 1185-7099
DD 354.7130082/56 CN

PERSPECTIVES - ONTARIO WORKERS' COMPENSATION INSTITUTE. (PERSPECTIVES : ONTARIO WORKERS' COMPENSATION INSTITUTE NEWSLETTER.). [Perspect. - Ont. Work. Compens. Inst.]. **Added/Corp** Ontario Workers' Compensation Institute. Fall Issue (1991)-. Newsletter. English. Six times a year. Limited free distribution. Ontario Workers' Compensation Institute, Suite 702, 250 Bloor Street East, Toronto Ontario M4W 1E6 Canada.

LC L901 .I66 **ISSN** 1082-2577
DD 331.25/922 US

•**PETERSON'S INTERNSHIPS.** **See** Occupations and Careers.

ISSN 0127-1253
MY

PETUNJUK-PETUNJUK BURUH. **Added/Corp** Malaysia. Kementerian Buruh. **VFOAT** Labour Indicators. (1984)-. English (Malay). ***Continues** Petunjuk-Petunjuk Buruh Semenanjung Malaysia.*

LC HD8423 .C58
FR

PEUPLE, LE. **Added/Corp** Confederation Generale du Travail. No. 1 (1920)-. Periodical. French. Six times a year. $138.89. SAEPJS / Societe Anonyme d'Edition de Publications et Journaux Syndicaux, CP 432, 93514 Montreuil Cedex France. **Tel** 011 33 1 48518306. **ED** Lucien Postal. Index available. **Circ:** 30,000 (ctrl).
Desc: Official journal of the CGT; trade union journal.

LC HD6958.5 .P48
DD 331/.09599/05 PH

PHILIPPINE JOURNAL OF LABOR AND INDUSTRIAL RELATIONS. Vol. 10, No. 2 (1988)-. Periodical. English. Two times a year. P200.00 Philippines; $24.00 other. Research and Publications Program, School of Labor and Industrial Relations, University of the Philippines System, Diliman Quezon City 1101 Philippines. **Tel** 98-83-40. **ED** Geraldine C Maayo. Index available. cum. index. **Bk Rev. Circ:** 1,000. ***Continues** Philippine Journal of Industrial Relations, 0115-6373.*
Desc: Serves as the primary vehicle for analyzing and disseminating significant research and confronting problems related to Philippine labor industrial relations using a multidisciplinary approach.
Ind/Abst Int. Labour Doc.; LABORDOC.

LC HD8712 .P53 **ISSN** 0115-2629
DD 331/.09599 PH

PHILIPPINE LABOR REVIEW. [Philipp. labor rev.]. Vol. 1, No. 2 (Aug. 1976)-. Periodical. English. Four times a year. Philippine Labor Review, Mole Building/5th Floor, Intramuros Manila Philippines.
Ind/Abst Index Philip. Period.; Int. Labour Doc.; LABORDOC.

LC HF5549.5.E45 P47
DD 650.1/4 PH

PHILIPPINE OVERSEAS EMPLOYMENT ANNUAL-DIRECTORY. **VFOAT** Philippine Overseas Employment Annual Directory. (19??)-. Directory. English. One time a year. Projects Division, Metrocolor Services 6th Floor, Medalla Building, EDSA Cubao Q C Philippines.

LC HD5725.W2 A6485
DD 331.1/09797/78021 US

PIERCE COUNTY : A LABOR MARKET INFORMATION REPORT OF THE RESEARCH AND ANALYSIS BRANCH, WASHINGTON STATE EMPLOYMENT SECURITY DEPARTMENT / PREPARED IN COOPERATION WITH THE EMPLOYMENT AND TRAINING ADMINISTRATION, U.S. DEPARTMENT OF LABOR. **Added/Corp** Washington (State). Employment Security Dept. Research & Analysis Branch. United States. Employment and Training Administration. **VFOAT** Service Delivery Area VI, Pierce County; Service Delivery Area 6, Pierce County; Service Delivery Area Six, Pierce County; Pierce County. (Jan. 1984)-. English. One time a year. Research and Analysis Branch, Washington State Employment Security Department, Box 9046, Olympia WA 98507. **Tel** (206)438-4800, FAX (206)438-4846.

LC HD4976.P55 A75A **ISSN** 0145-9155
DD 331.2/9791/77 US

PIMA COUNTY EMPLOYER WAGE SURVEY. **Main/Corp** Arizona. Dept. of Economic Security. Bureau of Statistical Information, Research and Analysis. (19??)-. English. One time a year. Arizona Department of Economic Security, PO Box 6123, Code 733 A, Phoenix AZ 85005. **Tel** (602)255-3871.

NO

•**PLAN.** (1995)-. Norwegian. Six times a year. Scandinavian University Press, PO Box 2959 Toeyen, N 0608 Oslo 6 Norway. **Tel** 011 47 2 2575400, FAX 011 47 2 2575353, telex 71896 UROR N. ***Continues** Plan og Arbeid.*

LC HD4811 .P57 **ISSN** 0032-0609
NO
TITLE CHANGE

PLAN OG ARBEID. **Added/Corp** Norway. Arbeidsdirektoratet. Distriktenes Utbyggingsfond (Norway). Norway. Kommunal- og Arbeidsdepartementet. Distriktsplanavdelingen. **VFOAT** Plan & Arbeid. Vol. 1 (1966)-(1995). Periodical. Norwegian. Scandinavian University Press, PO Box 2959 Toeyen, N 0608 Oslo 6 Norway. **Tel** 011 47 2 2575400, FAX 011 47 2 2575353, telex 71896 UROR N. **(Subscription address:** Scandinavian University Press, 200 Meacham Ave., Elmont NY 11003. **Tel** (516)352-7300, FAX (516)352-7377.) **ED** Andreas Hompland. **Bk Rev. Ad Acc. Circ:** 2,800. ***Continues** Arbeidsmarkedet (Oslo, Norway : 1943), 0332-7043.* ***Continued by** Plan.*
Desc: A periodical of community development, regional planning and employment.

LC HD4861 **ISSN** 1193-4018
DD 331.11 CN

•**PLAN REGIONAL DE DEVELOPPEMENT DE LA MAIN-D'OEUVRE, REGION DE LANAUDIERE.** [Plan reg. dev. main-d'oeuvre reg. Lanaudiere]. **Added/Corp** Commission de Formation Professionnelle Laurentides-Lanaudiere (Quebec). (1992/1993)-. French. ***Continues in part** Plan Regional de Developpement de la Main-d'Oeuvre, Regions Laurentides et Lanaudiere., 1193-400X.*

US

PLANNING INFORMATION FOR VOCATIONAL EDUCATION : STATE OF IOWA. **See** Education-Vocational Education.

ISSN 0987-3260
FR

PLEIN DROIT : LA REVUE DE GISTI. **Added/Corp** Groupe d'Information et de Soutien des Travailleurs Immigres (Paris, France). (1987)-. Periodical. French. Four times a year. GISTI, 46 rue de Montreuil, 75011 Paris France.
Ind/Abst Hum. Rights Intern. Rep.

ISSN 0710-6491
DD 331.88/1137812/0971416 CN

POINT D'INTERROGATION (CHICOUTIMI). (LE POINT D'INTERROGATION.). [Point interrog.]. (1976)-. Periodical. French. Twelve times a year. Free. Syndicat des Professeurs du College de Chicoutimi, 534 East rue Jacques-Cartier, Chicoutimi Quebec G7H 1Z6 Canada.

Business and Economics —Labor

POINT D'INTERROGATION ?. ENGLISH SECTION. [Point interrog., Engl. sect.]. Vol. 7, No. 4.1-A (July 1980)-. Periodical. English. Irregular. Free. Association Professionnelle des Technologistes Medicaux du Quebec, Suite 100/1595 Saint Hubert, Montreal Quebec H2L 3Z2 Canada. ctrl circ.
ISSN 0710-6521
DD 331.88/116106953/09714
CN

POINT D'INTERROGATION (MONTREAL). (POINT D'INTERROGATION : JOURNAL D'INFORMATIONS ET DE CONSULTATIONS DES MEMBRES A.P.T.M.Q.). [Point interrog.]. **VAT** Journal d'Informations et de Consultations. A.P.T.M.Q.; Journal d'Informations et de Consultations. Association Professionnelle des Technologistes Medicaux du Quebec; Journal d'Information et de Consultation des Membres - Association. Vol. 1, No. 3 (1974)-. Periodical. French. Irregular. Free. Association Professionnelle des Technologistes Medicaux du Quebec, Suite 100/1595 Saint Hubert, Montreal Quebec H2L 3Z2 Canada. ctrl circ. **Continues** Informations (Association Proiessionnelle des Technologistes Medicaux du Quebec), 0710-6513.
ISSN 0226-7950
DD 331.88/116106953/09714
CN

LC HD8055.A5 A363 HC101
DD 331/.0973 S 338.973
ISSN 0587-4971
US
POLICY RESOLUTIONS ADOPTED BY THE CONSTITUTIONAL CONVENTION. **Main/Corp** AFL-CIO. (19??)-. English. Every 2 years. American Federation of Labor and Congress of Industrial Organizations, 815 16th Street Northwest, Washington DC 20006. **Tel** (202)637-5000.

DD 331
ISSN 1061-1843
US
POLICY STUDIES PAPERS. [Policy stud. pap.]. **Added/Corp** Maxwell Graduate School of Citizenship and Public Affairs. Metropolitan Studies Program. **VFOAT** Income Security Policy Studies. No. 1 (Feb. 1992)-. Monographic series. English. Price varies per volume. MSP, 400 Maxwell Hall, Syracuse University, Syracuse NY 13244-1090.

LC HA1170.3 .P67
DD 304.6/2/0941705
ISSN 0790-9969
IE
POPULATION AND LABOUR FORCE PROJECTIONS. See Population Studies.

LC F1236 .P67
MX
POR ESTO. Periodical. Spanish. One time a week. Editorial Nuestra America, SA Santander No 25 Colonia San Rafae/Delegacion Azcapotzalco, Mexico 16 DF Mexico.

LC Z7164.C81 U4568 HF5549. F5549.A2
DD 016.353001 S 016.6583/00973
US
POSITION CLASSIFICATION, PAY, AND EMPLOYEE BENEFITS. **Main/Corp** United States. Civil Service Commission. Library. English. One time a year.

LC HD5725.A8 P63
DD 331.12/3/09767
US
POTENTIAL LABOR SUPPLY, ARKANSAS. **VFOAT** Estimated Potential Labor Supply for Industrial Expansion in Arkansas, by County. (19??)-. English. One time a year. Research and Analysis Section / Employment Security, Arkansas Employment Security Division, PO Box 2981, Little Rock AR 72203. **Continues** Estimated Potential Labor Supply for Industrial Expansion in Arkansas.

LC HD8537 .P7
ISSN 0032-6186
PL
PRACA I ZABEZPIECZENIE SPOLECZNE. Vol. 1 (1959)-. Periodical. Polish (English; summaries and/or abstracts in Russian and English; table of contents in Russian and English). Twelve times a year. $87.00. Panstwowe Wydawnictwo Ekonomiczne, Niecala 4-A, 00 098 Warsaw Poland. **Tel** 011 48 22 278001. **(Subscription address:** Ars Polona-Ruch, PO Box 1001, Krakowskie Przedmiescie 7, 00-068 Warsaw Poland. **Tel** 011 48 22 261201.) **ED** Wieslaw Krencik. **Supersedes** Przeglad Zagadnien Socjalnych **and** Przeglad Ubezpieczen Spolecznych. **Ind/Abst** Int. Bibliogr. Sociol.

ISSN 0543-1905
PL
PRACE. **Main/Corp** Mazowiecki Osrodek Badan Naukowych. (1967)-. Monographic series. Polish. Irregular. $158.40. **(Subscription address:** Artia Pegas Press Ltd., Palac Metro Narodni Trida 25, 11210 Prague 1 Czech Republic. **Tel** 011 42 2 24196265, 011 42 2 24196266.)

DD 331.89
ISSN 1186-1371
CN
PRECIS DE CONCORDANCE DE LA CONVENTION COLLECTIVE C.S.D.-F.A.S. ... EN VIGUEUR DANS LES CENTRES D'ACCEUIL MEMBRES DE L'ASSOCIATION DES CENTRES D'ACCEUIL DU QUEBEC. [Precis concord. conven. collect. C.S.D.-F.A.S.(C.S.N.) vigueur centr. accueil memb. Assoc. centr. accueil Que.]. **Added/Corp** Association des Centres d'Accueil du Quebec. Service-Conseil en Gestion des Ressources Humaines. Centrale des syndicats Democratiques. Federation des Affaires Sociales. (1991)-. French. Every 3 years. 20.00Can$ per volume. Service-Conseil en Gestion des Ressources Humaines, Association des Centres D'Accueil du Quebec, 1001 Est boulevard de Maisonneuve, Montreal Quebec H2L 4P9 Canada.

DD 331.89
ISSN 1186-1355
CN
PRECIS DE CONCORDANCE DE LA CONVENTION COLLECTIVE F.P.S.S.S.(C.E.Q.) ... EN VIGUEUR DANS LES CENTRES D'ACCUEIL MEMBRES DE L'ASSOCIATION DES CENTRES D'ACCUEIL DU QUEBEC. (PRECIS DE CONCORDANCE DE LA CONVENTION COLLECTIVE F.P.S.S.S. ... ENVIGUEUR DANS LES CENTRES D'ACCUEIL MEMBRES DE L'ASSOCIATION DES CENTRES D'ACCEUIL DU QUEBEC.). [Precis concord. conven. collect. F.P.S.S.S.(C.E.Q.) vigueur centr. acceuil memb. Assoc. centr. accueil Que.]. **Added/Corp** Association des Centres d'Accueil du Quebec. Service-Conseil en Gestion des Ressources Humaines. Federation du Personnel de la Sante et des Services Sociaux. (1990/1991)-. French. Every 3 years. Limited free distribution. 20.00Can$ per volume. Service-Conseil en Gestion des Ressources Humaines, Association des Centres D'Accueil du Quebec, 1001 Est boulevard de Maisonneuve, Montreal Quebec H2L 4P9 Canada.

LC TS191 .P7
DD 658.2/7/0288
ISSN 1068-6037
US
●**PRECISION CLEANING.** See Chemistry and Chemicals-Chemical Technology.

ISSN 0298-430X
FR
PREMIERES INFORMATIONS. **Added/Corp** France. Ministere du Travail, de l'Emploi et de la Formation Professionnelle. (19??)-. Periodical. French. Irregular (80 per year). Comes with Premieres Syntheses. Ministere du Travail et Service d'Etudes, Statistique place Fontenoy, 75007 Paris France.

LC HD8051 .A6218 TX957
DD 331/.0973 S 338.4/3
ISSN 0362-9724
US
PRICE INDEX OF OPERATING COSTS FOR RENT STABILIZED APARTMENT HOUSES IN NEW YORK CITY. (19??)-. English. One time a year. US Department of Labor Bureau of Labor Statistics / New York, 201 Varick Street, Room 808, New York NY 10014. **Tel** (212)337-2500, FAX (212)337-2532.

LC KF3408.Z9 P7
DD 331.1502673
ISSN 0272-0574
US
PRIMER OF LABOR RELATIONS. [Prim. labor relat.]. **Added/Corp** Bureau of National Affairs (Washington, D.C.). (19??)-. Monographic series. English. Irregular. $45.00. Bureau of National Affairs Inc., 9435 Key West Avenue, Rockville MD 20850. **Tel** (800)372-1033, (301)258-1033, FAX (301)948-5823.

LC HD4811 .P72
DD 331/.05
IT
PRIMO MAGGIO. (19??)-. Periodical. Italian. Calusca, Porta Ticinese 106, Milan 20123 Italy.

LC HD4811 .P73
XV
PRISPEVKI ZA NOVEJSO ZGODOVINO. **VFOAT** Contributions to the Contemporary History. Vol. 26, No. 1-2- 1986-. Periodical. Slovenian (summaries and/or abstracts in English, French and German). Two times a year. Institut za Zgodovino Delavskega Gibanja, YU-61000 Ljubljana Trg Osvoboditve 1, Slovenia. **Continues** Prispevki za Zgodovino Delavskega Gibanja. **Ind/Abst** Am. Hist. Life (1978-).

LC HD8055.A6
DD 331.88062773
US
PROCEEDINGS ... ANNUAL CONVENTION ... / ILLINOIS STATE FEDERATION OF LABOR. **Main/Corp** Illinois State Federation of Labor. Proceedings. English. One time a year.

DD 331/.09715
ISSN 0225-9060
CN
PROCEEDINGS, ANNUAL CONVENTION - NEW BRUNSWICK FEDERATION OF LABOUR. [Proc., Annu. conv. - N.B. Fed. Lab.]. **Main/Corp** New Brunswick Federation of Labour. Convention. 22D- 1979-. Proceedings. English. One time a year. New Brunswick Federation of Labour, PO Box 524, Moncton New Brunswick E1C 8R9 Canada. **Continues** New Brunswick. Federation of Labour. Convention. Official Proceedings of Convention, 0701-175X.

LC HD6515.N4 A53
DD 331.88/110713
ISSN 0741-7950
US
PROCEEDINGS, ANNUAL CONVENTION - NEWSPAPER GUILD. CONVENTION. (PROCEEDINGS, ... ANNUAL CONVENTION / NEWSPAPER GUILD (AFL-CIO, CLC)). **Main/Corp** Newspaper Guild. Convention. 38th-. Proceedings. English. One time a year. $30.00. Newspaper Guild, 8611 Second Avenue, Silver Spring MD 20910. **Tel** (301)585-2990, FAX (301)585-0668. **ED** James M Cesnik. **Circ:** 600. available on microfilm and microfiche from University Microfilms International (UMI). **Continues** American Newspaper Guild. Convention. Proceedings.
 Desc: Proceedings of the Newspaper Guild's Annual Convention.

DD 331.88/0971
ISSN 0225-0403
CN
PROCEEDINGS - CANADIAN LABOUR CONGRESS, CONSTITUTIONAL CONVENTION. [Proc. - Can. Labour Congr., Const. Conv.]. **Main/Corp** Canadian Labour Congress. Constitutional Convention. 12th (1978)-. Proceedings. English. One time a year. Free on request. Canadian Labour Congress, 2841 Riverside Drive, Ottawa Ontario K1V 8X7 Canada. **Tel** (613)521-3400, FAX (613)053-4750, telex 060313. Index available. ctrl circ. **Continues** Canadian Labour Congress. Constitutional Convention. Report of Proceedings, 0410-9120.

LC HD8055.A5 A364
DD 331.88097
ISSN 0569-4612
US
PROCEEDINGS, CONSTITUTIONAL CONVENTION OF THE INDUSTRIAL UNION DEPARTMENT, AFL-CIO. (PROCEEDINGS ... CONSTITUTIONAL CONVENTION OF THE INDUSTRIAL UNION DEPT., AFL-CIO.). [Proc., const. conv. Ind. Union Dep., AFL-CIO]. **Main/Corp** AFL-CIO. Industrial Union Dept. (1955)-. Proceedings. English. Every 2 years. AFL CIO, 17 Battery Place, Room 1930, New York NY 10004.

DD 331.88/11/35471
ISSN 0380-7770
CN
PROCEEDINGS - CONVENTION, CANADIAN UNION OF PUBLIC EMPLOYEES. **Main/Corp** Canadian Union of Public Employees. Convention. 4th- 1969-. Proceedings. English. Every 2 years. Canadian Union of Public Employees, 233 Gilmour Street/Suite 800, Ottawa Ontario K2P 0P5 Canada. **Tel** (613)237-1590. **Continues** Canadian Union of Public Employees. National Convention. Proceedings.

ISSN 0277-7347
US
PROCEEDINGS OF THE ANNUAL MEETING - INDUSTRIAL RELATIONS RESEARCH ASSOCIATION (1978). (PROCEEDINGS OF THE ANNUAL MEETING – INDUSTRIAL RELATIONS RESEARCH ASSOCIATION.). [Proc. annu. meet. - Ind. Relat. Res. Assoc.]. **Main/Corp** Industrial Relations Research Association. (1978)-. Proceedings. English. One time a year. $52.00 Comes with Industrial Relations Research Association membership. Industrial Relations Research Association, 4233 Social Science Building, University of Wisconsin, 1180 Observatory Drive, Madison WI 53706. **Tel** (608)262-2762, FAX (608)262-4591. Index available. **Circ:** 5,000 (ctrl). **Continues** Industrial Relations Research Association. Proceedings of the Annual Winter Meeting, 0275-3081.
 Desc: Latest research and ideas in industrial relations for professionals in management, unions, government and academic life, and for libraries and institutions.

US
PROCEEDINGS OF THE ... BIENNIAL CONVENTION OF THE INTERNATIONAL LONGSHOREMEN'S AND WAREHOUSEMEN'S UNION. **Main/Corp** International Longshoremen's and Warehousemen's Union. Vol. 1 (1938)-. Proceedings. English. Every 2 years.

LC HD8055.A5 A36
DD 331.88/097
ISSN 0569-4515
US
PROCEEDINGS OF THE ... CONSTITUTIONAL CONVENTION OF THE AFL-CIO. [Proc. const. conv. AFL-CIO]. **Main/Corp** AFL-CIO. Constitutional Convention. **VFOAT** Proceedings of the ... Convention; Proceedings of the AFL-CIO Constitutional Convention; AFL-CIO Convention Proceedings. 2nd (1957)-. Proceedings. English. Every 2 years. American Federation of Labor and Congress of Industrial Organizations, 815 16th Street Northwest, Washington DC 20006. **Tel** (202)637-5000. available on microfilm from University Microfilms International (UMI); available on microfiche from University Microfilms International (UMI). **Continues** AFL-CIO. Constitutional Convention. Report of the Constitutional Convention Proceedings, 0741-787X.

Business and Economics —Labor

LC HD8055.A5 A36   **ISSN** 0569-4515
DD 331.88091   US
PROCEEDINGS OF THE CONSTITUTIONAL CONVENTION OF THE AFL-CIO. **Main/Corp** AFL-CIO. **VFOAT** Proceedings and Executive Council Reports of the AFL-CIO. 1st (1955)-. English. One time a year. $15.00 (per copy). American Federation of Labor and Congress of Industrial Organizations, 815 16th Street Northwest, Washington DC 20006. **Tel** (202)637-5000.

LC HD6514.S57
DD 331.88172   US
PROCEEDINGS OF THE CONSTITUTIONAL CONVENTION OF THE UNITED STEEL WORKERS OF AMERICA. **Main/Corp** United Steel Workers of America. Vol. 1 (1942)-. Proceedings. English. United Steelworkers of America/ Indiana, 2457 East Washington Street, Indianapolis IN 46201.

LC HD7106.C2 C2485A   **ISSN** 0708-1421
DD 331.3/98/0971   CN
PROCEEDINGS OF THE SPECIAL SENATE COMMITTEE ON RETIREMENT AGE POLICIES. **Main/Corp** Canada. Parliament. Senate. Special Senate Committee on Retirement Age Policies. **VFOAT** Deliberations du Comite Special du Senat sur les Politiques Relatives a l'Age de la Retraite. **VAT** Retirement Age Policies; Politiques Relatives A l'Age de la Retraite. Nov. 14, 1978-. Proceedings. English (French). Receiver General for Canada / Ottawa, Canada Comm Group Publishing, Ottawa Ontario K1A 0S9 Canada. **Tel** (819)956-4802, (800)661-2868.

   ISSN 0733-0898
   US
PROCEEDINGS OF THE ... SPRING MEETING (INDUSTRIAL RELATIONS RESEARCH ASSOCIATION : 1979). (PROCEEDINGS OF THE ... SPRING MEETING / INDUSTRIAL RELATIONS RESEARCH ASSOCIATION.). [Proc. spring meet. - Ind. Relat. Res. Assoc.]. **Main/Corp** Industrial Relations Research Association. Spring Meeting. **VFOAT** IRRA Spring Meeting. (1979)-. English. One time a year (Aug.). $52.00 Comes with Industrial Relations Research Association membership. Industrial Relations Research Association, 4233 Social Science Building, University of Wisconsin, 1180 Observatory Drive, Madison WI 53706. **Tel** (608)262-2762, FAX (608)262-4591. **Circ** : 5,000 (ctrl). **Continues** Industrial Relations Research Association. Spring Meeting. Proceedings of the ... Annual Spring Meeting, 0537-5428.
   Desc: Research papers and discussions presented at IRRA's annual Spring meeting.

   ISSN 0225-0411
DD 331.88/0971   CN
PROCES-VERBAL - CONGRES DU TRAVAIL DU CANADA, ASSEMBLEE STATUTAIRE. [P.-v.- Congr. trav. Can., Assem. statut.]. **Main/Corp** Congres du Travail du Canada. Assemblee Statutaire. **VFOAT** Compte Rendu des Travaux de l'Assemblee Statutaire. **VAT** Compte Rendu des Travaux de l'Assemblee Statutaire - Congres du Travail du Canada. (1978)-. Periodical. French. Every 2 years. Congres du Travail du Canada, 2841 Riverside Drive, Ottawa Ontario K1V 8X7 Canada. **Continues** Compte Rendu des Deliberations, 0225-0411.

LC HD   **ISSN** 0317-2228
DD 331.88/11/3711   CN
PROCES-VERBAL DU CONGRES - CENTRALE DE L'ENSEIGNEMENT DU QUEBEC, CONGRES. **Main/Corp** Centrale de l'Enseignement du Quebec. 23E (1973)-. Periodical. French. Every 2 years. Centrale de l'Enseignement du Quebec, 2336 Chemin Sainte-Foy, CP 5800, Quebec Quebec G1V 4E5 Canada. **Tel** (418)658-5711. **Circ:** 1,500. **Continues** Corporation des Enseignants du Quebec. Proces-Verbal des Assemblees du Congres de la C.E.Q., 0315-8608.

   ISSN 0225-655X
DD 331.88/09714   CN
PROCES-VERBAL DU CONGRES DE LA CSN (1978). (PROCES-VERBAL DU CONGRES DE LA CSN.). [P.-v. congr. CSN (1978)]. **Main/Corp** Confederation des Syndicats Nationaux. Congres. 1978-. French. One time a year. Confederation des Syndicats Nationaux, 1001 St. Denis, Montreal Quebec H2X 3J1 Canada. **Continues** Proces-Verbal du Congres Special et du Congres Regulier de la CSN, 0708-2517.

LC HB235.U6 A472   **ISSN** 0882-5270
DD 338.5/28/0973   US
PRODUCER PRICE INDEXES (EXPANDED VERSION). See Industry and Production.

LC Z243.U5 P76   **ISSN** 0277-4119
DD 331.2/816862   US
PRODUCTION EMPLOYEES COST SURVEY. (19??)-. English. Every 2 years. $120.00. International Business Forms Industries, 1730 North Lynn Street, Arlington VA 22209. **Tel** (703)841-9191, telex 440172. **ED** Douglas Taylor.
   Desc: Wage and benefit cost data for production employees of business firms' plants; categorized by plant location and job category.

LC TL502
DD 629.13   US
PRODUCTIVITY AND COST OF EMPLOYMENT. LOCAL SERVICE CARRIERS. **Main/Corp** United States. Civil Aeronautics Board. (19??)-. Periodical. English. Civil Aeronautics Board, 1825 Connecticut Avenue, Washington DC 20428. **Tel** (202)673-5174.

LC HC110.L3 U54a
DD 331.11/8/0973021   US
PRODUCTIVITY MEASURES FOR SELECTED INDUSTRIES AND GOVERNMENT SERVICES / U.S. DEPARTMENT OF LABOR, BUREAU OF LABOR STATISTICS. **Added/Corp** United States. Bureau of Labor Statistics. (1986)-. Government Publication. English. Six times a year. $21.00. Superintendent of Documents, US Government Printing Office, Washington DC 20402. **Tel** (202)275-3328, FAX (202)786-2377. **Continues** Productivity Measures for Selected Industries.
   Ind/Abst Predicasts Forecasts.

   ISSN 1130-765X
UDC 377   SP
PROFESIONES Y EMPRESAS. [Prof. empres.]. (1974)-. Periodical. Spanish. Four times a year. 8000ptas Spain; 4000ptas Europe; 1000ptas other. Edic Tecnicas y Profesionales, Gran via 38 90 1I, 28013 Madrid Spain. **Tel** 011 34 1 5223844.
   Ind/Abst LABORDOC.

LC HD8051 .A6218 HD4965.U5   **ISSN** 0362-9953
DD 331/.0973 S 331.2/81   US
PROFESSIONAL, ADMINISTRATIVE, TECHNICAL AND CLERICAL PAY IN NEW YORK. **Main/Corp** United States. Bureau of Labor Statistics. (197?)-. English. One time a year. Department of Labor, Two World Trade Center, New York NY 10047. **Continues** Professional, Administrative and Technical Pay in New York.

LC HD5725.I6 P76
DD 331.12/09772/9   US
PROFILE OF ECONOMIC REGION 1. **VFOAT** Profile of Economic Region One; Indiana Labor Market. (19??)-. English. Indiana Employment Security Division, Research and Statistics Section, 10 North Senate Avenue, Indianapolis IN 46204. **Tel** (317)232-7187. **Continues** Indiana Labor Market. Profile of Economic Region 1.

LC HD5725.I6 P76A
DD 331.12/09772/8   US
PROFILE OF ECONOMIC REGION 2. **VFOAT** Profile of Economic Region Two; Indiana Labor Market. (19??)-. English. Indiana Employment Security Division, Research and Statistics Section, 10 North Senate Avenue, Indianapolis IN 46204. **Tel** (317)232-7187. **Continues** Indiana Labor Market. Profile of Economic Region 2.

LC HD5725.I6 P76B
DD 331.12/09772/7   US
PROFILE OF ECONOMIC REGION 3. **VFOAT** Profile of Economic Region Three; Indiana Labor Market. (19??)-. English. Indiana Employment Security Division, Research and Statistics Section, 10 North Senate Avenue, Indianapolis IN 46204. **Tel** (317)232-7187. **Continues** Indiana Labor Market. Profile of Economic Region 3.

LC HD5725.I6 P76C
DD 331.12/09772/4   US
PROFILE OF ECONOMIC REGION 4. **VFOAT** Profile of Economic Region Four; Indiana Labor Market. (19??)-. English. Indiana Employment Security Division, Research and Statistics Section, 10 North Senate Avenue, Indianapolis IN 46204. **Tel** (317)232-7187. **Continues** Indiana Labor Market. Profile of Economic Region 4.

LC HD5725.I6 P76D
DD 331.12/09772/8   US
PROFILE OF ECONOMIC REGION 5. **VFOAT** Profile of Economic Region Five; Indiana Labor Market. (19??)-. English. Indiana Employment Security Division, Research and Statistics Section, 10 North Senate Avenue, Indianapolis IN 46204. **Tel** (317)232-7187. **Continues** Indiana Labor Market. Profile of Economic Region 5.

LC HD5725.I6 P76e
DD 331.12/09772/6   US
PROFILE OF ECONOMIC REGION 6. **Added/Corp** Indiana. Occupational Information Unit. **VFOAT** Profile of Economic Region Six; Indiana Labor Market. (19??)-. English. Indiana Employment Security Division, Research and Statistics Section, 10 North Senate Avenue, Indianapolis IN 46204. **Tel** (317)232-7187. **Continues** Indiana Labor Market. Profile of Economic Region 6.

LC HD5725.I6 P76F
DD 331.12/09772/4   US
PROFILE OF ECONOMIC REGION 7. **VFOAT** Profile of Economic Region Seven; Indiana Labor Market. (19??)-. English. Indiana Employment Security Division, Research and Statistics Section, 10 North Senate Avenue, Indianapolis IN 46204. **Tel** (317)232-7187. **Continues** Indiana Labor Market. Profile of Economic Region 7.

LC HD5725.I6 P76G
DD 331.12/09772/5   US
PROFILE OF ECONOMIC REGION 8. **VFOAT** Profile of Economic Region Eight; Indiana Labor Market. (19??)-. English. Indiana Employment Security Division, Research and Statistics Section, 10 North Senate Avenue, Indianapolis IN 46204. **Tel** (317)232-7187. **Continues** Indiana Labor Market. Profile of Economic Region 8.

LC HD5725.I6 P76H
DD 331.12/09772/6   US
PROFILE OF ECONOMIC REGION 9. **VFOAT** Profile of Economic Region Nine; Indiana Labor Market. (19??)-. English. Indiana Employment Security Division, Research and Statistics Section, 10 North Senate Avenue, Indianapolis IN 46204. **Tel** (317)232-7187. **Continues** Indiana Labor Market. Profile of Economic Region 9.

LC HD5725.I6 P76I
DD 331.12/09772/2   US
PROFILE OF ECONOMIC REGION 10. **VFOAT** Indiana Labor Market; Profile of Economic Region Ten. (19??)-. English. Indiana Employment Security Division, Research and Statistics Section, 10 North Senate Avenue, Indianapolis IN 46204. **Tel** (317)232-7187. **Continues** Indiana Labor Market. Profile of Economic Region 10.

LC HD5725.I6 P76J
DD 331.12/09772/2   US
PROFILE OF ECONOMIC REGION 11. **VFOAT** Profile of Economic Region Eleven; Indiana Labor Market. (19??)-. English. Indiana Employment Security Division, Research and Statistics Section, 10 North Senate Avenue, Indianapolis IN 46204. **Tel** (317)232-7187. **Continues** Indiana Labor Market. Profile of Economic Region 11.

LC HD5725.I6 P76K
DD 331.12/09772/1   US
PROFILE OF ECONOMIC REGION 12. **VFOAT** Profile of Economic Region Twelve; Indiana Labor Market. (19??)-. English. Indiana Employment Security Division, Research and Statistics Section, 10 North Senate Avenue, Indianapolis IN 46204. **Tel** (317)232-7187. **Continues** Indiana Labor Market. Profile of Economic Region 12.

LC HD5725.I6 P76L
DD 331.12/09772/3   US
PROFILE OF ECONOMIC REGION 13. **VFOAT** Profile of Economic Region Thirteen; Indiana Labor Market. (19??)-. English. Indiana Employment Security Division, Research and Statistics Section, 10 North Senate Avenue, Indianapolis IN 46204. **Tel** (317)232-7187. **Continues** Indiana Labor Market. Profile of Economic Region 13.

LC HD5725.I6 P76M
DD 331.12/09772/2   US
PROFILE OF ECONOMIC REGION 14. **VFOAT** Profile of Economic Region Fourteen; Indiana Labor Market. (19??)-. English. Indiana Employment Security Division, Research and Statistics Section, 10 North Senate Avenue, Indianapolis IN 46204. **Tel** (317)232-7187. **Continues** Indiana Labor Market. Profile of Economic Region 14.

   ISSN 0132-1196
   RU
●PROFSOIUZY. **Added/Corp** Vseobshchaia Konferatsiia Profsoiuzov. No. 1 (1993)-. Periodical. Russian. Twelve times a year. $99.95. (**Subscription address:** East View Publications Inc., 3020 Harbor Lane North, Suite 110, Minneapolis MN 55447. **Tel** (800)477-1005, (612)550-0961, FAX (612)559-2931.) **Continues** Sovetskie Profsoiuzy, 0038-5174.

   IT
PROGETTO : BIMESTRALE DELLA CISL DI POLITICA DEL LAVORO. **Added/Corp** Confederazione Italiana Sindicati Lavoratori. Vol. 1, No. 1 (Jan./Feb. 1981)-. Periodical. Italian. Six times a year. L40880. Conquiste del Lavoro, Via Livenza 7, 00198

Business and Economics —Labor

Rome Italy. **Tel** 011 39 6 8546742 or, 8546743, FAX 011 39 6 8415365. **Circ:** 4,000.
Ind/Abst Int. Labour Doc.

LC HD7694.5 .A25B
DD 306/.094/05   IE
PROGRAMME OF WORK. **Main/Corp** European Foundation for the Improvement of Living and Working Conditions. English. One time a year. European Foundation for the Improvement of Living and Working Conditions, Loughlinstown House, Shankill Co, Dublin Ireland. **Tel** 011 353 1 2826888, FAX 011 353 1 2826456.

IT
PROSPETTI COSTO ORARIO DELLA MAMODOPERA : ASSISTAL. (19??)-. Italian. Irregular. L250000.00. Sial Srl, Via Saverio Mercadante 18, 00198 Rome Italy. **Tel** 011 39 6 8554284.

ISSN 0393-9510
IT
UDC 33
PROSPETTIVE SOCIALI E SANITARIE. (1971)-. Periodical. Italian. Twenty-six times a year. L54500. Centro Informazione Sanitaria, Via San Siro 1, 20149 Milan Italy. **Tel** 011 39 2 4694542.

LC HD6517.C2 P76
DD 331.89/09794   US
PROVISIONS OF CALIFORNIA COLLECTIVE BARGAINING AGREEMENTS. 1977-. English. One time a year. Chief, Division of Labor Statistics and Research, PO Box 603, San Francisco CA 94101. **Tel** (415)557-0315.
Desc: Report summarizes trends in private sector provisions and gives data on holidays, sick leave, scheduled hours of work and other provisions.

XR
PRUMYSLOVE OBLASTI. **Added/Corp** Ceskoslovenska Akademie ved. Slezsky Ustav v Opave. (19??)-. Czech. One time a year. **(Subscription address:** Artia Pegas Press Ltd., Palac Metro Narodni Trida 25, 11210 Prague 1 Czech Republic. **Tel** 011 42 2 24196265, 011 42 2 24196266.)
Ind/Abst Am. Hist. Life (1969-1980).

LC HD8536 .P79   ISSN 0137-8783
PL
PRZEGLAD (NACZELA ORGANIZACJA TECHNICZNA (POLAND)). (PRZEGLAD.). (19??)-. Periodical. Polish. One time a week. $130.00. Centrala Kolportazu Prasy I Wydawnictw RSW Prasa-Ksiazka-Ruch, Ul Towarowa 28, 00-958 Warszawa Poland.

LC HD6735.7 .A15
PL
PRZEGLAD ZWIAZKOWY. (1949)-. Periodical. Polish (English). Twelve times a year. **(Subscription address:** Ars Polona-Ruch, PO Box 10C1, Krakowskie Przedmiescie 7, 00-068 Warsaw Poland. **Tel** 011 48 22 261201.) **Supersedes** Robotniczy Przeglad Gospodarczy.

FR
PSI-INFO. See Public Administration -Civil Service.

LC HD8001 .P85A   ISSN 0306-4026
DD 331.88/11/3500005   UK
PSI NEWS & VIEWS. [PSI news views]. **Main/Corp** Public Services International. **VAT** Public Services International News & Views; PSI News and Views. (1974)-. English. **Formed by the union of** Bulletin - Public Services International **and** PSI Newsletter.

LC HF5548.8 .P72
IT
PSICOLOGIA E LAVORO. Vol. 1, 1968-. Periodical. Italian. L5700. Corso Europa 5, Milan 20122 Italy.

ISSN 0033-345X
US
PUBLIC EMPLOYEE PRESS (NEW YORK). (PUBLIC EMPLOYEE PRESS.). (19??)-. Periodical. English. Twenty-six times a year. Free. District Council 37 AFSCME AFL-CIO, 140 Park Place, New York NY 10007. **Continues** Spotlight.

US
PUBLIC EMPLOYEE REPORTER FOR THE STATE OF CALIFORNIA. (19??)-. Periodical. English. Twenty-four times a year. $655.00. LRP Publications, 747 Dresher Road, Suite 500, Horsham PA 19044. **Tel** (800)341-7874, (215)784-0941, FAX (215)784-9639, (215)784-0870.
Desc: Source for public sector labor law decisions issued by California state agencies and courts.

ISSN 0195-0770
US
PUBLIC EMPLOYMENT PERSPECTIVE. PENNSYLVANIA. **VFOAT** Pennsylvania Public Employee Reporter. Periodical. English. Twenty-four times a year. $375.00 (plus $10.00 postage). LRP Publications, 747 Dresher Road, Suite 500, Horsham PA 19044. **Tel** (800)341-7874, (215)784-0941, FAX (215)784-9639, (215)784-0870. Index available. cum. index. **Circ:** 200.
Desc: Abstracts and full texts of all Pennsylvania Labor Relations Board and related state court decisions. Completely indexed, contains the board's rule, regulations and forms.

ISSN 0892-5933
DD 331   US
PUBLIC EMPLOYMENT RECRUITER BULLETIN : PERB. [Public employ. recruit. bull.]. **VFOAT** PERB. Bulletin. English. Twelve times a year. $29.95. Public Sector Recruitment, Inc., 1st and Main Bldg. 137 North Main, Suite 600, Dayton OH 45402.

US
PUBLIC EMPLOYMENT RELATIONS REPORTER. **Added/Corp** California Research (Firm). Public Communications Group. (1976)-. Periodical. English. Twelve times a year. $120.00. Pacific Communications Group, PO Box 162901, Sacramento CA 95816. **Tel** (916)343-1100. **ED** Thomas K. DeLapp. Each issue contains an index to its own contents (no volume index)--loose.
Desc: Summary and analysis of public sector labor relation laws and regulatory actions in California.

ISSN 1067-7100
DD 333   US
●**PUBLIC SAFETY LABOR NEWS.** See Industrial Health and Safety.

LC HD8055.A5 A363   ISSN 0569-4523
DD 331.88/0973   US
PUBLICATION - AMERICAN FEDERATION OF LABOR AND CONGRESS OF INDUSTRIAL ORGANIZATIONS. **Main/Corp** AFL-CIO. No. 1 (1956)-. Monographic series. English. Price varies per volume. American Federation of Labor and Congress of Industrial Organizations, 815 16th Street Northwest, Washington DC 20006. **Tel** (202)637-5000. available on microfilm and microfiche from University Microfilms International (UMI).

US
PUBLICATIONS IN INDUSTRIAL RELATIONS. **Main/Corp** Harvard University. Jacob Wertheim Research Fellowship. 1- 1927-. English. Irregular. Harvard University Press, 79 Garden Street, Cambridge MA 02138. **Tel** (617)496-1344, (800)448-2242.

SP
PUBLICATIONS - INDUSTRIAL RELATIONS RESEARCH ASSOCIATION. **Main/Corp** Industrial Relations Research Association. (19??)-. Monographic series. English. Price varies per volume. **Circ:** 5,000.
Desc: Two volumes printing the research papers of the meetings. A volume on a timely topic of industrial relations, plus quarterly newsletter.

LC HD8473 .Q3   ISSN 0033-4901
IT
QUADERNI DI AZIONE SOCIALE. [Quad. azione soc.]. **Added/Corp** Associazioni Cristiane Lavoratori Italiani. (Jan. 1950)-. Periodical. Italian. Four times a year. L40880. Editrice Aesse, Via Marcora 18 20, 00153 Rome Italy. **Tel** 011 39 6 5840480.
Ind/Abst Bibliogr. Mission.

ISSN 0390-105X
IT
UDC 33
QUADERNI DI ECONOMIA DEL LAVORO. [Quad. econ. lav.]. **VFOAT** Collana di Quaderni di Economia del Lavoro. (1974)-. Monographic series. Italian. Three times a year. L81660. Franco Angeli Riviste SRL, Viale Monza 106, 20127 Milan Italy. **Tel** 011 39 2 2827651, 011 39 2 289562, FAX 011 39 2 258004, telex 051-511650.

IT
QUADERNI ISRIL. (19??)-. Periodical. Italian. Four times a year. L60.000 Italy; L75.000 other. Isril Cooperativa, via Piemonte 101, 00187 Rome Italy. **Tel** 011 39 6 4818443, 4818590.

LC HD4801   ISSN 1062-7480
DD 331   US
TITLE CHANGE
QUALIFIED PLAN UPDATE. [Qualif. plan update]. **VFOAT** Update. (19??)-(19??). Periodical. English. Universal Pensions Inc., Box 979, Brainerd MN 56401. **Tel** (800)541-6089, (800)346-3860, FAX (218)829-2106. **Merged into** Retirement Plans Bulletin.

LC HD66 .Q333   ISSN 1049-8699
DD 658.4/036   US
CCC
QUALITY DIGEST. [Qual. dig.]. (198?)-. Periodical. English. Twelve times a year. $49.00. Quality Digest, PO Box 882, Red Bluff CA 96080. **Tel** (916)527-6970, FAX (916)527-6983, telex 3791991. **ED** Scott M Paton. **Bk Rev. Ad Acc. Circ:** 6,000. **Continues** Quality Circle Digest, 0278-2642.
Desc: Quality improvement through employee involvement.
Ind/Abst Qual. Control Appl. Stat.

ISSN 0700-205X
DD 331.25/2/0971   CN
QUARTERLY ESTIMATES OF TRUSTEED PENSION FUNDS. [Q. estim. trusteed pension funds]. **Added/Corp** Statistics Canada. **VFOAT** Estimations Trimestrielles sur les Regimes de Pensions en Fiducie. Vol. 4, No. 2 (2nd Quarter 1976)-. Periodical. English (French). Four times a year. 60.00Can$ Canada; $72.00 US; $84.00 other. Statistics Canada Publications Sales and Services, R.H. Coats Building 6th Floor, Ottawa Ontario K1A 0T6 Canada. **Tel** (613)951-5078, (800)267-6677, FAX (613)951-1584, telex 053-3585. **Continues** Quarterly Survey of Trusteed Pension Plans, 0700-2068.

LC HD5725.C6 Q37
DD 331.12/09788   US
QUARTERLY OCCUPATIONAL SUPPLY/DEMAND OUTLOOK. **VFOAT** Colorado State Planning Region Three (Denver Labor Market Area); Colorado State Planning Region 3 (Denver Labor Market Area). (19??)-. Periodical. English. Four times a year. Colorado Division of Employment and Training, Research and Development Section, 251 East 12th Avenue, Denver CO 80203.

LC HD5833 .A36
DD 331.12/5/095125021   HK
QUARTERLY REPORT OF EMPLOYMENT, VACANCIES, AND PAYROLL STATISTICS / EMPLOYMENT AND EARNINGS STATISTICS SECTION, CENSUS AND STATISTICS DEPARTMENT. **Added/Corp** Hong Kong. Employment and Earnings Statistics Section. (March 1991)-. Statistical Publication. English. Four times a year. Hong Kong Government Information Service, Beaconsfield House, 4 Queens Road, Hong Kong Hong Kong. **Tel** 011 852 284288014, 011 852 259881947, FAX 011 852 28459078, 011 852 25987482, telex 61190 HKGIS. **Continues** Report of Employment, Vacancies, and Payroll Statistics; **Absorbed in part** Monthly Survey of Employment, Payroll, and Orders-on-Hand.

ISSN 0838-6609
DD 331/.0971   CN
QUEEN'S PAPERS IN INDUSTRIAL RELATIONS. [Queen's pap. ind. relat.]. Monographic series. English. Twelve times a year. Price varies per volume. Queen's University / Industrial Relations Centre, Kingston Ontario K7L 3N6 Canada. **Tel** (613)545-6709. **Bk Rev. Circ:** 800 (ctrl).

LC HD4809 .Q4   ISSN 0033-6246
DD 331.0943   GW
CCC
QUELLE (KOLN). (DIE QUELLE.). [Quelle]. **Added/Corp** Deutscher Gewerkschaftsbund. (19??)-. Periodical. German. Twelve times a year. $31.94. Bund Verlag GmbH, Postfach 900840, D-51118 Cologne Germany. **Tel** 011 49 2203 934758. **Supersedes** Quelle.

LC HD5701 .U53   ISSN 0148-8023
DD 331.12   US
R & D MONOGRAPH. **Added/Corp** United States. Employment and Training Administration. **VAT** Research and Development Monograph. (1976)-. Periodical. English. US Department of Labor Employment & Training Administration, 200 Constitutions Avenue NW, Room S307, Washington DC 20210. **Tel** (202)219-6050, FAX (202)219-6827. **Continues** Manpower R & D Monograph, 0361-3879.

RU
RABOCHII KLASS I SOTSIALNYI PROGRESS. **Added/Corp** Institut Mezhdunarodnogo Rabochego Dvizheniia (Akademiia Nauk SSSR) Institut Sravnitelnoi Politologii i Problem Rabochego Dvizheniia (Rossiiskaia Akademiia Nauk). (1990)-. Academic Scholarly Publication. Russian. Izdatelstvo Nauka / Akademiia Nauk, (Publishing House of the Russian Academy of Sciences), Leninskii Porspekt

Business and Economics —Labor

14, 117901 Moscow Russia. **Tel** 011 95 9542153, FAX 011 95 9382144, telex 411964. **Continues** *Rabochii Klass v Mirovom Revoliutsionnom Protsesse.*

LC AP50 .R33

RU

RABOTNITSA. Added/Corp Vsesoiuznaia Kommunisticheskaia Partiia (Bolshevikov). Tsentralnyi Komitet. (19??)-. Periodical. Russian. Twelve times a year. $99.95. **(Subscription address:** East View Publications Inc., 3020 Harbor Lane North, Suite 110, Minneapolis MN 55447. **Tel** (800)477-1005, (612)550-0961, FAX (612)559-2931.**)**

US

RACINE LABOR. (1992)-. English. One time a week. $23.00 (one-year), $45.00 (two-year), .75 (single copies). The Racine Labor, 1840 Sycamore Avenue, Racine WI 53406. **Tel** (414)634-7186. **ED** Roger Bybee. **Ad Acc, Adv Mgr:** Sherry Horton, **Tel** (414)634-7186. **Circ:** 11,000.
Desc: A weekly labor newspaper serving basically Racine County. We also write articles dealing with labor related issues and politics.

LC HD4802 .R33 **ISSN** 0033-7617
DD 322/.2/0973

US

RADICAL AMERICA. See Political Science.

LC HA1651 .A334 LB2391.Y8

CI

RADNICI PREMA STEPENU STRUONOG OBRAZOVANJA / SOCIJALISTICKA REPUBLIKA SRBIJA, REPUBLICKI ZAVOD ZA STATISTIKU. Serbo-Croatian (Roman). 150.00. Republicki Zavod za Statistiku, Central Bureau of Statistics of the Republic of Croatia, Ilica 3, Zagreb Croatia. **Tel** 011 385 41 45 44 22, FAX 011 385 41 42 94 13, 011 385 41 42 37 11, telex 21130 DZSTAT RH.

LC HD8602 .S374

SZ

RAPPORT D'ACTIVITE / UNION SYNDICALE SUISSE. Main/Corp Schweizerischer Gewerkschaftsbund. (1981)-. French. **Continues** *Rapport du Comite Syndical.*

LC HD2429.C3 Q4A **ISSN** 0703-0770
DD 354/.714/0083

CN

RAPPORT D'ACTIVITES - OFFICE DES PROFESSIONS DU QUEBEC. Main/Corp Quebec (Province). Office des Professions. 1973/74-. Periodical. French. Office des Professions du Quebec, 320 rue St. Joseph Est, Quebec G1K 8G5 Canada.

LC HD7102.F8 Q32D
DD 354/44/00825

FR

RAPPORT D'ACTIVITIE - CAISSE NATIONALE DE L'ASSURANCE MALADIE DES TRAVAILLEURS SALARIES. Main/Corp Caisse Nationale de l'Assurance Maladie des Travailleurs Salaries. (19??)-. French. Caisse National de l'Assurance Maladie des Travailleurs Salaries, 66 Avenue du Maine, 75682 Paris Cedex 14 France.

LC HD8102 .C23A
DD 331/.0971

CN

RAPPORT DU ... CONGRES DE L'INSTITUT CANADIEN DE RECHERCHE EN RELATIONS INDUSTRIELLES. Main/Corp Canadian Industrial Relations Research Institute. Meeting. **VFOAT** Proceedings of the ... Annual Meeting of the Canadian Industrial Relations Research Institute. Vol. 15 (May 29-30, 1978)-. English. One time a year. ACRI Departement des Relations Industrielles, Universite Laval, Sainte-Foy Quebec G1K 7P4 Canada.
Ind/Abst Can. Legal Lit.

LC HD7343.A3 S65A

BE

RAPPORT DU CONSEIL D'ADMINISTRATION SUR LES OPERATIONS DE L'EXERCICE ... / SOCIETE NATIONALE DU LOGEMENT. Main/Corp Societe Nationale du Logement (Belgium). **VFOAT** Rapport Annuel. French. One time a year. Societe Nationale du Logement, rue Breydel 12, 1040 Brussels Belgium.

ISSN 0848-8061
DD 331.88/11354714/05

CN

RAPPORT DU PRESIDENT GENERAL - SYNDICAT DES FONCTIONNAIRES PROVINCIAUX DU QUEBEC. (RAPPORT DU PRESIDENT GENERAL.). [Rapp. pres. gen. - Synd. fonct. prov. Que.]. **Main/Corp** Syndicat des Fonctionnaires Provinciaux du Quebec. Congres. **Added/Corp** Syndicat des Fonctionnaires Provinciaux du Quebec. 14E 25/29 May 1987-. French. Every 2 years. Distribution gratuite restreinte. Syndicat des Fonctionnaires Provinciaux du Quebec, 155 Est boulevard Charest, Quebec Quebec G1K 3G6 Canada. **Continues in part** *Syndicat des Fonctionnaires Provinciaux du Quebec. Congres.* Proces-Verbal, Congres, 0227-4701.

LC HD4826 .R37 **ISSN** 0033-961X
DD 331
CEASED

IT

RASSEGNA DI STATISTICHE DEL LAVORO. See Business and Economics-Abstracting, Bibliographies and Statistics.

ISSN 0033-9849

IT

RASSEGNA SINDACALE. [Rass. sind.]. **Added/Corp** Confederazione Generale Italiana del Lavoro. Vol. 1 (Dec. 15, 1955)-. Periodical. Italian. One time a week. L81750. Edit Coop Coop Giornalisti, Via dei Frentani 4A, 00185 Rome Italy. **Tel** 011 39 6 44870286, 288. cum. index. **Bk Rev**. **Ad Acc**. **Circ:** 50,000 (ctrl).
Supersedes *Notiziario Cgil.*
Ind/Abst Int. Labour Doc.

LC HD4966.H82 F554
DD 331.291724

FI

RAVITSEMIS- JA MAJOITUSLIIKKEIDEN TYONTEKIJOIDEN JA TOIMIHENKILOIDEN PALKAT. LONERNA FOR ARBETSTAGARE OCH FUNKTIONARER INOM FORPLAGNADS- OCH HARBARGERINGSRORELSER. Main/Corp Finland. Tilastokeskus. **Added/Corp** Finland. Tilastokeskus. Lonerna for Arbetstagare och Funktionarer Inom Forplagnads- och Harbargeringsrorelser. (19??)-. Finnish (Swedish). Tilastokeskus, PL 504, Annankatu 44, 00101 Helsinki Finland. **Tel** 011 358 0 17341, FAX 011 358 0 17342474, telex 1002111 TILASTO SF.

ISSN 1062-385X
DD 331

US

REAL PEOPLE, REAL JOBS. [Real peop. real jobs]. **VFOAT** Real People/Real Jobs. Vol. 1, No. 1, Issue 1 (Jan./Feb./Mar. 1992)-. Periodical. English. Four times a year. $40.00. Louise Longmoore, PO Box 465, Shannon GA 30172.

ISSN 0486-1140

US

REBEL. Vol. 1 (1964)-. Periodical. English. Twenty-four times a year. Association of Pulp and Paper Workers, PO Box 1735, Portland OR 97207.

ISSN 0155-8722

AT

RECORDER. Added/Corp Australian Society for the Study of Labour History. Melbourne Branch. No. 1 (1964)-. Periodical. English. Six times a year (Feb., Apr., June, Aug., Oct., Dec.). 8.23Aus$. Australian Society for the Study of Labour History, 93 Robert Street, Essendon Vic 3040 Australia. **Tel** 03 337-7554. **ED** L. Edmonds. Index available. cum. index. **Ad Acc**. **Circ:** 270.

LC HD6278.U5 M52a **ISSN** 0163-5611
DD 331.1/0973

US

RECRUITING TRENDS (EAST LANSING). (RECRUITING TRENDS.). **Main/Corp** Michigan State University. Placement Services. **Added/Corp** Michigan State University. Career Development and Placement Services. Michigan State University. Placement Services. (19??)-. English. One time a year. $25.00. Michigan State University / 345 Student Services Building, East Lansing MI 48824-1113. **Tel** (517)355-3447. **ED** J.D. Shingleton and L.P. Scheetz.

LC HD5850.4 .A453A **ISSN** 0110-1943
DD 331.1/379931

NZ

REDUNDANCY IN NEW ZEALAND. Main/Corp New Zealand. Dept. of Labour Research and Planning Division. (1972/73)-. English. One time a year. New Zealand Department of Labour, Private Bag, Wellington 1 New Zealand.

US

REFUSE HAULING WAGE SURVEY, RIVERSIDE-SAN BERNARDINO-ONTARIO, CALIF. (19??)-. Government Publication. English. One time a year. US Department of Labor / Bureau of Labor Statistics, 441 G Street Northwest, Washington DC 20212. **Tel** (202)606-7800, FAX (202)606-7797.

LC HD5725.N5 R44
DD 331.12/09749/46021

US

REGIONAL LABOR MARKET REVIEW. ATLANTIC COASTAL REGION. VFOAT Atlantic Coastal Region. (19??)-. English. One time a year. Free. Division of Labor Market and Demographic Research, New Jersey Department of Labor, CN 388, Trenton NJ 08625-0388. **Tel** (609)292-0076, FAX (609)984-6833. **ED** David R Crane. **Circ:** 2,000 (ctrl).
Desc: Analyzes trends in demographics, employment and labor force for Atlantic City, Cape May, Ocean and Monmouth counties, with supporting graphs and tables.

LC HD5725.N5 R43
DD 331.12/09749/9021

US

REGIONAL LABOR MARKET REVIEW. SOUTHERN NEW JERSEY REGION. VFOAT Southern New Jersey Region. (1984)-. English. One time a year. Free. New Jersey Department of Labor, Division of Planning and Research CN 056, Trenton NJ 08625. **Tel** (609)292-7567. **ED** David R Crane. **Circ:** 1,000 (ctrl).
Desc: Analysis and trends in population, employment, and labor force. Current and future economic developments discussed.

LC HD4965.5.U5 R44 **ISSN** 1056-9561
DD 331.2/816584/00973021

US

REGIONAL REPORT ON TOP MANAGEMENT COMPENSATION. See Business and Economics-Management.

LC HD6504 .U56A **ISSN** 0565-9310
DD 331.88/02573

US

REGISTER OF REPORTING LABOR ORGANIZATIONS. (REGISTER OF REPORTING LABOR ORGANIZATIONS.) / U.S. DEPARTMENT OF LABOR, LABOR-MANAGEMENT SERVICES ADMINISTRATION, OFFICE OF LABOR-MANAGEMENT STANDARDS ENFORCEMENT.). English. Every 3 years. US Department of Labor, 200 Constitution Avenue NW, Washington DC 20210. **Tel** (202)219-7316, FAX (202)219-7312. available on microfiche (Vols. for (1983)- distributed to depository libraries).
Desc: A register of labor organizations which filed reports with the U.S. Department of Labor under the provisions of the Labor-Management Reporting and Disclosure Act...

LC HD7106.U5 R4 **ISSN** 0091-357X
DD 331.2/52/0973

US

REGISTER OF RETIREMENT BENEFIT PLANS REPORTED UNDER THE WELFARE AND PENSION PLANS DISCLOSURE ACT. Added/Corp United States. Office of Labor-Management and Welfare-Pension Reports. (19??)-. English. $5.00. Office of Labor-Management and Welfare Pension Reports, Washington DC 20402.

LC HD6870.S6 R44 **ISSN** 0377-3485
DD 331.88/0968

SA

REGISTERED TRADE UNIONS IN SOUTH AFRICA. Added/Corp South African Institute of Race Relations. (19??)-. English. $0.75. South African Institute of Race Relations, PO Box 31044, Braamfontein 2017 South Africa. **Tel** 011 27 11 4033600, FAX 011 27 11 4033671.

ISSN 0213-0556

SP

UDC 331.1
RELACIONES LABORALES. [Relac. labor.]. (1984)-. Periodical. Spanish. Twenty-four times a year. 54000ptas Spain; 64800ptas Europe; 70200ptas other. Distribuciones la Ley, Monterry 1 LA Coruna KM 17200, 282030 Las Rozas Madrid Spain. **Tel** 011 34 1 6342200.
Ind/Abst LABORDOC.

LC HD6958.5 **ISSN** 0034-379X
DD 331

CN

Pr Rev.
RELATIONS INDUSTRIELLES = INDUSTRIAL RELATIONS. [Relat. ind.]. **Added/Corp** Universite Laval. Departement des Relations Industrielles. **VFOAT** Industrial Relations. Vol. 6, (Dec. 1952)-. Periodical. English (French). Four times a year (Jan., Apr., July, Oct.). 48.00Can$. Universite Laval Faculte des Sciences Sociales, Bureau des Communications, 3448 de Koninck, Quebec G1K 7P4 Canada. **Tel** (418)656-2131. **ED** Gerard Dion. Index available. cum. index. **Bk Rev**. **Circ:** 3,000. available on microfilm and microfiche from University Microfilms International (UMI). Documents available from The Genuine Article. **Continues** *Industrial Relations (Quebec, Quebec),* 0034-379X.
Desc: Publishes articles on all aspects of industrial and labor relations with a particular, but not exclusive, emphasis on Canada.
Ind/Abst Am. Hist. Life (1963-1978); Can. Period. Index; Curr. Cit.; Curr. Contents Soc. Behav. Sci.; Hum. Resour. Abstr.; Index Can. Leg. Period. Lit.; Int. Labour Doc. (1963-1978); LABORDOC; PAIS Int. Print (1991-); Person. Manage. Abstr.; Repere (1983-); Res. Alert [Full Cov.]; Soc. Plann. Policy Dev. Abstr.; Soc. Sci. Cit. Index [Full Cov.]; Work Relat. Abstr.

LC HD5715.5.B69 R54A
DD 331.25/92/098165

BL

RELATORIO. Main/Corp Brazil. Servico Nacional de Aprendizagem Industrial. Departamento Regional do Rio Grande do sul. (19??)-. Portuguese. Servico Nacional de Aprendizagem Industrial Departamento Regional do Rio Grande do Sul, Caixa Postal 2130, CEP 90.000 Porto Alegre RS Brazil. **Continues** *Brazil. Servico Nacional de Aprendizagem Industrial. Departamento Regional do Rio Grande do Sul. Relatorio das Atividades.*

Business and Economics —Labor

LC HD6957.B82 M377a
DD 354.81/720083   BL
RELATORIO ANUAL. Main/Corp Servico Social do Comercio. Administracao Regional de Mato Grosso. (19??)-. Portuguese.

LC HD6957.B82 R57A
DD 354.81/53008485/06   BL
RELATORIO ANUAL DE ATIVIDADES REFERENTE AO EXERCICIO DE ... / SESI, DEPARTAMENTO REGIONAL DO ESTADO DO RIO DE JANEIRO. Main/Corp Servico Social da Industria. Departamento Regional do Estado do Rio de Janeiro. Portuguese. One time a year. **Continues** Servico Social da Industria. Departamento Regional do Estado do Rio de Janeiro. Relatorio do Execicio.

LC HD5715.5.B68 B7a
DD 331.2592   BL
RELATORIO DE ATIVIDADES. Main/Corp Brazil. Servico Nacional de Aprendizagem Industrial. Departamento Regional do Amazonas. (199?)-. Portuguese. Servico Nacional de Aprencizagem Industrial, Departamento Regional do Amazonas, Avenida Carvalho Leal 555 Cachoeirinha, Manaus Brazil. **Tel** 092 237 4218, FAX 092 237 4336, telex 092 2708. **Continues** Brazil. Servico Nacional de Aprendizagem Industrial. Departamento Regional do Amazonas. Relatorio - Servico Nacional de Aprendizagem Industrial, Departamento Regional do Amazonas.

LC HD5715.5.B68 B7a
DD 331.2592   BL
TITLE CHANGE
RELATORIO - SERVICO NACIONAL DE APRENDIZAGEM INDUSTRIAL, DEPARTAMENTO REGIONAL DO AMAZONAS. Main/Corp Brazil. Servico Nacional de Aprendizagem Industrial. Departamento Do Regional Amazonas. **Added/Corp** Federacao das Industrias do Estado do Amazonas. (19??)-(199?). Portuguese. Servico Nacional de Aprendizagem Industrial, Departamento Regional do Amazonas, Avenida Carvalho Leal 555 Cachoeirinha, Manaus Brazil. **Tel** 092 237 4218, FAX 092 237 4336, telex 092 2708. **Continued by** Brazil. Servico Nacional de Aprendizagem Industrial. Departamento Regional do Amazonas. Relatorio de Atividades.

LC HD5715.5.B69 P373a   BL
RELATORIO - SERVICO NACIONAL DE APRENDIZAGEM INDUSTRIAL, DEPARTAMENTO REGIONAL DO PARANA. Main/Corp Brazil. Servico Nacional de Aprendizagem Industrial. Departamento Regional do Parana. (19??)-. Portuguese. Rua Chile 1678, Caixa Postal 999, Curitiba Brazil.

UK
REMUNERATION IN EUROPE REPORT.
See Business and Economics-Management.

ISSN 0714-8461
DD 331.7/14/060714   CN
REPERTOIRE DES ASSOCIATIONS PATRONALES QUEBECOISES. [Repert. assoc. patronales que.]. **Main/Corp** Conseil du Patronat du Quebec. (197?)-. French. Every 2 years. $5.00. Conseil du Patronat du Quebec, Suite 606/2075 rue Universite, Montreal Quebec H3A 2L1 Canada. **Tel** (514)288-5161. ctrl circ. **Continues** Conseil du Patronat du Quebec et Ses Membres Affilies, 0714-8453.

LC HD5715.5.G72 N62   IE
REPORT AND STATEMENT OF ACCOUNTS - ENTERPRISE ULSTER.
Main/Corp Enterprise Ulster (Corporation). (Sept. 14, 1973/March 31, 1974)-. English. One time a year. £55.00. Armagh House, Ormeau Avenue, BT 2 8HB Belfast United Kingdom.

SZ
REPORT / CONFERENCE OF AMERICAN STATES MEMBERS OF THE INTERNATIONAL LABOUR ORGANISATION. Added/Corp International Labour Office. (1936)-. Monographic series. English. Irregular. Price varies per volume. International Labour Office - ILO, Publications Sales Service, CH-1211 Geneva 22 Switzerland. **Tel** 011 41 22 7996111, FAX 011 41 22 7986253, telex 415 647 ilo ch. (**Subscription address:** International Labor Office / Albany, NY, 49 Sheridan Avenue, Albany NY 12210. **Tel** (518)436-9686.)

ISSN 0251-3811
SZ
UDC 331:(7):(8)
REPORT - CONFERENCE OF AMERICAN STATES MEMBERS OF THE INTERNATIONAL LABOUR ORGANISATION. (1936)-. Periodical. English. Three times a week. Price varies. International Labour Office - ILO, Publications Sales Service, CH-1211 Geneva 22 Switzerland. **Tel** 011 41 22 7996111, FAX 011 41 22 7986253, telex 415 647 ilo ch. **Desc:** Information on international labor, working conditions, vocational training, employment for women and many other labor issues around the world.

LC J961 .H835 TT166.F4
DD 331.2/592/09611   FJ
REPORT - FIJI NATIONAL TRAINING COUNCIL. Main/Corp Fiji. National Training Council. 1973-. English.

ISSN 0162-0703
DD 331   US
REPORT FROM HEADQUARTERS. [Rep. hqrs.]. **Main/Corp** International Association of Machinists and Aerospace Workers. (19??)-. Periodical. English. Report from Headquarters, 1300 Connecticut Avenue NW, Washington DC 20036.

LC HD4824 .G44a
DD 331/.06/21   SZ
REPORT - INTERNATIONAL INSTITUTE FOR LABOUR STUDIES. Main/Corp International Institute for Labour Studies. (19??)-. Monographic series. English. Irregular. Price varies per volume. International Labour Office - ILO, Publications Sales Service, CH-1211 Geneva 22 Switzerland. **Tel** 011 41 22 7996111, FAX 011 41 22 7986253, telex 415 647 ilo ch.

LC HD4813 .R37   **ISSN** 0074-6681
DD 331/.05   SZ
REPORT / INTERNATIONAL LABOUR CONFERENCE. Added/Corp International Labour Conference. International Labour Office. Session 26 (1944)-. Monographic series. English. Irregular. Price varies per volume. International Labour Office - ILO, Publications Sales Service, CH-1211 Geneva 22 Switzerland. **Tel** 011 41 22 7996111, FAX 011 41 22 7986253, telex 415 647 ilo ch.

LC K   **ISSN** 0255-349X
DD 340   SZ
UDC 341.12 : 331 (6)
REPORT - INTERNATIONAL LABOUR ORGANISATION, AFRICAN REGIONAL CONFERENCE. (1960)-. Monographic series. English. Irregular. Price varies. International Labour Office - ILO, Publications Sales Service, CH-1211 Geneva 22 Switzerland. **Tel** 011 41 22 7996111, FAX 011 41 22 7986253, telex 415 647 ilo ch.

LC HD4801
DD 331   SZ
REPORT (INTERNATIONAL LABOUR ORGANISATION. ASIAN REGIONAL CONFERENCE). (REPORT / ASIAN REGIONAL CONFERENCE.). **Added/Corp** International Labour Organisation. Asian Regional Conference. International Labour Office. Issue 1 (1947)-. Monographic series. English. Irregular. Price varies per volume. International Labour Office - ILO, Publications Sales Service, CH-1211 Geneva 22 Switzerland. **Tel** 011 41 22 7996111, FAX 011 41 22 7986253, telex 415 647 ilo ch. (**Subscription address:** International Labor Office / Albany, NY, 49 Sheridan Avenue, Albany NY 12210. **Tel** (518)436-9686.)

ISSN 0255-352X
SZ
UDC 341.12 : 331 (4)
REPORT - INTERNATIONAL LABOUR ORGANISATION, EUROPEAN REGIONAL CONFERENCE. (1955)-. Periodical. English. Irregular. Price varies. International Labour Office - ILO, Publications Sales Service, CH-1211 Geneva 22 Switzerland. **Tel** 011 41 22 7996111, FAX 011 41 22 7986253, telex 415 647 ilo ch.
Desc: Information on growth, structural changes, manpower and many other labor issues in Europe and around the world.

LC HD8038.U5 A35
DD 353.976384   US
REPORT - LOUISIANA DEPT. OF OCCUPATIONAL STANDARDS. Main/Corp Louisiana. Dept. of Occupational Standards. (19??)-. English. One time a year. Louisiana Department of Occupational Standards, PO Box 44095 Capitol Station, Baton Rouge LA 70804.

LC HD6661 .T7
DD 331.88/0941   UK
REPORT OF ANNUAL TRADES UNION CONGRESS. Main/Conf Trades Union Congress. **Main/Corp** Trades Union Congress. **Added/Corp** Trades Union Congress. TUC Report. **VFOAT** TUC Report. 94th (1962)-. English. One time a year. $77.01. Trade Union Congress, Congress House, Great Russell Street, London WC1B 3LS United Kingdom. **Tel** 011 44 171 6364030, FAX 011 44 171 6360632, telex 268328 TUEG. Index available. **Circ:** 2,000. available on microfilm. **Continues** Trades Union Congress. Report of Proceedings at the Annual Trades Union Congress.

LC RT5.O5 R46
DD 331.12/9161073/09766   US
REPORT OF NURSE POPULATION IN OKLAHOMA / OKLAHOMA BOARD OF NURSE REGISTRATION AND NURSING EDUCATION. See Medical Sciences-Nursing.

LC LB2335.86-.88
DD 331.88   US
REPORT OF OFFICERS TO THE ... REGULAR AND ... QUADRENNIAL CONVENTION. Main/Corp Transportation Communications International Union. **Added/Corp** Transportation Communications International Union. Convention. 29th (1991)-. English. Irregular. **Continues** Reports of International Officers to the ... Regular and ... Qquadrennial Convention.

LC HD4965.H85 R47
DD 331.2/95125   HK
REPORT OF SALARIES AND EMPLOYEE BENEFITS STATISTICS; MANAGERIAL AND PROFESSIONAL EMPLOYEES, EXCLUDING TOP MANAGEMENT. Added/Corp Hong Kong. Wages and Labour Cost Statistics Section. (19??)-. English. Four times a year. HK$32.00. Hong Kong Government Information Service, Beaconsfield House, 4 Queens Road, Hong Kong Hong Kong. **Tel** 011 852 284288014, 011 852 259881947, FAX 011 852 28459078, 011 852 25987482, telex 61190 HKGIS. (**Subscription address:** Government Information Service, Publications Office, 1 Battery Path, Hong Kong Hong Kong.)

LC HD5849.53 .A4
DD 331.11/097299   BM
REPORT OF THE MANPOWER SURVEY. 1978-. English. One time a year. $10.00. Ministry of Home Affairs, Hamilton Bermuda. **Tel** (809)292-8867. **Circ:** 450.
Desc: Labor force in Bermuda by occupation, industry, sex, status, etc. Includes average and normal hours worked by occupation and major industry group.

DD 331.2   US
REPORT ON EXECUTIVE REMUNERATION / WYATT DATA SERVICES, ECS. Added/Corp Executive Compensation Service (U.S.). (1990/91)-. Trade Publication. English. One time a year. ECS, Executive Compensation Service, Wyatt Data Services, 218 Route 17 North, Roselle Park NJ 07662-9832. **Tel** (201)843-1177, FAX (201)843-0101. **Continues** Report on Canadian Executive Remuneration., 1050-0766.

LC HD5111.U5 E9   **ISSN** 1058-5109
DD 658.3/222   US
REPORT ON EXEMPT OVERTIME PLANS AND PRACTICES. (REPORT ON EXEMPT OVERTIME PLANS AND PRACTICES / WYATT DATA SERVICES, ECS.). [Rep. exempt overtime plans pract.]. **Added/Corp** Executive Compensation Service (U.S.). (1990/91)-. English. ECS, Executive Compensation Service, Wyatt Data Services, 218 Route 17 North, Roselle Park NJ 07662-9832. **Tel** (201)843-1177, FAX (201)843-0101. **Continues** Exempt Overtime Plans and Practices.

LC HD5083 .A35
DD 331.2/95125/021   HK
TITLE CHANGE
REPORT ON HALF-YEARLY SURVEY OF WAGES, SALARIES, AND EMPLOYEE BENEFITS. Added/Corp Hong Kong. Wages and Labour Cost Statistics Section. **VFOAT** Report on Half Yearly Survey of Wages, Salaries, and Employee Benefits; Wages, Salaries, and Employee Benefits; Wages, Salaries & Employee Benefits. (198?)-(19??). English. Four times a year. Hong Kong Government Information Service, Beaconsfield House, 4 Queens Road, Hong Kong Hong Kong. **Tel** 011 852 284288014, 011 852 259881947, FAX 011 852 28459078, 011 852 25987482, telex 61190 HKGIS. (**Subscription address:** Government Information Service, Publications Office, 1 Battery Path, Hong Kong Hong Kong.) **Continues** Quarterly Report of Wages, Salaries, and Employee Benefits Statistics. **Continued by** Half-Yearly Report of Wage Statistics.

US
REPORT ON SALARIES AND TOTAL PAY IN THE SMALLER MANUFACTURING COMPANY. See Industry and Production-Manufacturing.

LC JK3457 .N54A   **ISSN** 0095-7968
DD 353.9/747/00123   US
REPORT ON SALARIES, FRINGE BENEFITS, AND RELATED PRACTICES AFFECTING CLASSIFIED SERVICE EMPLOYEES OF NEW YORK STATE.
Main/Corp New York (State). Public Employment Relations Board. 1970/72. English. Public Employment

Relations Board/State of New York, 80 Wolf Road, Albany NY 12205-2604. **Tel** (518)457-2676. **Continues** Report of Salaries, Classified Service Employees of New York State.

LC HD4976.C2 R46
DD 331.2/2/09794 US
REPORT ON SALARIES IN OCCUPATIONS COMPARABLE TO STATE CIVIL SERVICE / PREPARED BY CALIFORNIA STATE PERSONNEL BOARD, PAY AND BENEFITS CENTER.
Added/Corp California State Personnel Board. Pay and Benefits Center. California. State Dept. of Personnel Administration. Negotiations Support. (19??)-. English. One time a year. California Department of Personnel Administration, 1515 S Street, North Building/Suite 400, Sacramento CA 94244-2340.
Desc: Salaries of employees in private and other governmental agencies in occupations comparable to those of California State Civil Service.

LC HD5822.6.S5 S56a ISSN 0129-6965
DD 331.1/1/095952 SI
REPORT ON THE LABOUR FORCE SURVEY OF SINGAPORE. [Rep. labour force surv. Singap.]. **Main/Corp** Singapore. Ministry of Labour. **Added/Corp** Singapore. National Statistical Commission. Singapore. Ministry of Labour. Research and Statistics Dept. (1974)-. English. One time a year. $11.75. Singapore National Printers, 303 Upper Serangoon Road, Singapore 1334 Singapore. **Tel** 011 65 2820611. **Continues** Singapore. Dept. of Statistics. Report on the Labour Force Survey.

ISSN 1041-6633
DD 331 US
REPORT ON THE ... SALARY BUDGET SURVEY. [Rep. salary budget surv.]. **Added/Corp** American Compensation Association. **VFOAT** Salary Budget Survey. (1987/1988)-. Trade Publication. English. $65.00. American Compensation Association, 14040 North Northsight Boulevard, Scottsdale AZ 85260. **Tel** (602)951-9191, FAX (602)483-8352. **Continues** Salary Budget Survey.

LC HD5725.H3 H37a
DD 331.13/77/09969 US
REPORT ON THE STATE PROGRAM FOR THE UNEMPLOYED. Main/Corp Hawaii. Office of Manpower Planning. **Added/Corp** Hawaii. Dept. of Labor and Industrial Relations. (19??)-. English. One time a year. Hawaii Department of Labor and Industrial Relations, 830 Punchbowl Street, Room 321, Honolulu HI 96813. **Tel** (808)586-8844, FAX (808)586-5099.

LC HD5504.C2 C34A
DD 353.97940083/2 US
REPORT / STATE OF CALIFORNIA, MEDIATION/CONCILIATION SERVICE.
Main/Corp California. State Mediation/Conciliation Service. (19??)-. English. **Continues** California. Conciliation Service. Report.

LC HD8038.G7 C66A
DD 331.7/12/0942 UK
REPORT - THE COMMONWEALTH FOUNDATION. Main/Corp Commonwealth Foundation (British Commonwealth). (19??)-. English. Every 2 years. Marlborough House Pall Mall, London SW1 United Kingdom.

LC HD5725.N2 N45a
DD 331.1/1/09782 US
REPORT TO THE GOVERNOR FROM THE MANPOWER SERVICES COUNCIL, THE. Main/Corp Nebraska. Manpower Services Council. 1st (1974/75)-. English. One time a year. Manpower Services Council / Lincoln, Box 94601 State Capitol, Lincoln NE 68509.

LC HD5725.W2 W355A
DD 331.1/1/09797 US
REPORT TO THE GOVERNOR - WASHINGTON (STATE). STATE EMPLOYMENT DEVELOPMENT SERVICES COUNCIL. Main/Corp Washington (State). State Employment Development Services Council. **VFOAT** Annual Report to the Governor on the Comprehensive Employment and Training Act (CETA). 1975-. English. One time a year. Office of the Governor / Washington, Office of Community Development, Olympia WA 98504.

LC HD5725.M6 M49A
DD 331.1/1/09776 US
REPORT TO THE LEGISLATURE - MINNESOTA. DEPT. OF ECONOMIC SECURITY. Main/Corp Minnesota. Dept. of Economic Security. (1978)-. English. One time a year. Minnesota Department of Economic Security, 390 North Robert Street, St Paul MN 55101.

LC HD8051 .R46 ISSN 0738-8527
DD 331/.0973 US
REPORTER (LONG BEACH, CALIF.).
(REPORTER / NATIONAL LABOR RELATIONS BUREAU.). [Rep. - Natl. Labor Relat. Bur.]. **VFOAT** NLRB Report; N.L.R.B. Report. Vol. 1, Issue 1-. Periodical. English. Answer Bureau Inc., 2nd floor, 215 Long Beach Blvd., Long Beach CA 90802.

ISSN 0414-0516
DD 338.9 UK
REPORTS: L. Main/Conf Inter-African Conference. Labour. **Added/Corp** Commission for Technical Co-operation in Africa South of the Sahara. **VFOAT** Reports: Labour. (1948)-. Periodical. English. Europa Publications Ltd., 18 Bedford Square, London WC1B 3JN United Kingdom. **Tel** 011 44 171 5808236, telex 21540 EUROPA G.

LC HD4965.5.A7 E9A ISSN 0095-4144
DD 331.2/81/658420982 US
REPORTS ON INTERNATIONAL COMPENSATION : ARGENTINA. Main/Corp
American Management Association. Executive Compensation Service. (19??)-. English. One time a year. Amacom, 135 West 50th Street, New York NY 10020. **Tel** (212)903-8075.

LC HD4965.5.B7 E9A
DD 331/2/81/658420981 US
REPORTS ON INTERNATIONAL COMPENSATION : BRAZIL. Main/Corp
American Management Association. Executive Compensation Service. (19??)-. English. Amacom, 135 West 50th Street, New York NY 10020. **Tel** (212)903-8075.

LC HD8102 .K52 ISSN 0075-6156
DD 331/.0971 CN
REPRINT SERIES - INDUSTRIAL RELATIONS CENTRE. QUEEN'S UNIVERSITY. (REPRINT SERIES - QUEEN'S UNIVERSITY, INDUSTRIAL RELATIONS CENTRE.). **Added/Corp** Queen's University (Kingston, Ont.). Industrial Relations Centre. (19??)-. Monographic series. English. Irregular. Price varies per volume. Queens University at Kingston, Industrial Relations Centre, Kingston Ontario K7L 3N6 Canada. **Tel** (613)545-6709. **Circ:** 400 (ctrl).

LC HD8381 .A25A
DD 331.1/07/2042 UK
RESEARCH. Main/Corp Great Britain. Dept. of Employment. 1972/73-. English. One time a year. £36.50. Her Majesty's Stationery Office, 51 Nine Elms Lane, London SW8 5DR United Kingdom. **Tel** 011 44 171 8738459, 011 44 171 8738499, FAX 011 44 171 8738499, 011 44 171 8738456, telex 297138.
(Subscription address: Her Majesty's Stationery Office, PO Box 276, Public Centre, London SW8 5DT United Kingdom. **Tel** 011 44 171 87384998456.)
Ind/Abst Anthropol. Lit.

ISSN 0317-2546
DD 331/.0971 CN
RESEARCH AND CURRENT ISSUES SERIES - INDUSTRIAL RELATIONS CENTRE. QUEEN'S UNIVERSITY.
(RESEARCH AND CURRENT ISSUES SERIES.). [Res. curr. issues ser. - Ind. Relat. Cent., Queen's Univ.].
Added/Corp Queen's University (Kingston, Ont.). Industrial Relations Centre. No. 21 (1973)-. Monographic series. English. Irregular. Price varies per volume. Queens University at Kingston, Industrial Relations Centre, Kingston Ontario K7L 3N6 Canada. **Tel** (613)545-6709. **Circ:** 700 (ctrl). **Continues** Research Series (Queen's University (Kingston, Ont.). Industrial Relations Centre), 0075-6164.

LC HD5723 .A414
DD 331.1/0973 US
RESEARCH, EVALUATION, AND DEMONSTRATION PROJECT. Added/Corp
United States. Employment and Training Administration. Office of Strategic Planning and Policy Development.
VFOAT Research, Demonstration, and Evaluation Projects; ETA Research, Demonstration, and Evaluation Projects. English. US Department of Labor Employment & Training Administration, 200 Constitutions Avenue NW, Room S307, Washington DC 20210. **Tel** (202)219-6050, FAX (202)219-6827. **Continues** Research and Development Projects (Washington, D.C. : 1976).

LC HD4802 .R42 ISSN 0147-9121
DD 331/.05 US
RESEARCH IN LABOR ECONOMICS. Vol. 1 (1977)-. Monographic series. English. One time a year. $73.25. JAI Press Inc., 55 Old Post Road, Suite 2, PO Box 1678, Greenwich CT 06836-1678. **Tel** (203)661-7602, FAX (203)661-0792. **ED** Ronald G. Ehrenberg.

LC HD7096.U6 N849
DD 331.13/79756 US
RESEARCH IN UNEMPLOYMENT INSURANCE. CHARACTERISTICS OF THE INSURED UNEMPLOYED. VFOAT
Characteristics of the Insured Unemployed. (Feb. 1981)-. English. Labor Market Information Division, Employment Security Commission of North Carolina, 200 West Jones Street, PO Box 25903, Raleigh NC 27611.

LC HD4903.5.U58 A33
DD 331.1/33/0973 US
RESEARCH REPORT (UNITED STATES. EQUAL EMPLOYMENT OPPORTUNITY COMMISSION). (RESEARCH REPORT / EQUAL EMPLOYMENT OPPORTUNITY COMMISSION.).
Main/Corp United States. Equal Employment Opportunity Commission. Office of Planning, Research, and Systems. (19??)-. English. Equal Employment Opportunity Commission, 2401 E Street NW, Washington DC 20506. **Tel** (202)634-7062. **Continues** United States. Equal Employment Opportunity Commission. Office of Research. Research Report.

LC HD4965.3.B9 S74 ISSN 0735-5068
DD 331.2/89/083/0973 US
RESIDENTIAL BUILDERS COMPENSATION SURVEY. English. One time a year. L. Stephens, 7825 Ivanhoe, Suite 203, La Jolla CA 92037.

US
RETIREMENT PLANS FOR THE SELF-EMPLOYED : FOR USE IN PREPARING ... RETURNS. Added/Corp
United States. Internal Revenue Service. **VFOAT** Retirement Plans for the Self Employed. (1990)-. English. Eastern Area Distribution Center, PO Box 85074, Richmond VA 23261-5074. **Continues** Self-Employed Retirement Plans.

LC HD5014.5 .S7a ISSN 0259-0492
DD 331.2/94 LU
RETRIBUCIONES, INDUSTRIA Y SERVICIOS = VERDIENSTE, PRODUZIERENDES GEWERBE UND DIENSTLEISTUNGEN = EARNINGS, INDUSTRY AND SERVICES / [EUROSTAT]. Added/Corp Statistical Office of the European Communities. **VFOAT** Verdienste, Produzierendes Gewerbe und Dienstleistungen; Earnings, Industry and Services. (1985)-. English (French). Two times a year. Office for Official Publications of the European Communities, 2 rue Mercier, 2985 Luxembourg. **Tel** 011 352 499281, FAX 011 352 292942763. **Continues** Lnninger Inden for Industri Og Tjenesteydelser, 0254-9050.

LC HD5820.T3 A25
DD 331.1/0954/82 II
REVIEW OF EMPLOYMENT IN TAMIL NADU. Main/Corp Tamil Nadu. (India). Director of Employment and Training. (19??)-. English. Tamil Nadu Directorate of Employment & Training, Madras India. **Continues** Review of Employment in Madras State.

ISSN 0840-7231
DD 331.12/0971 CN
REVIEW OF PROFESSIONAL EMPLOYMENT. [Rev. prof. employ.]. (1988/89)-. English. One time a year. $16.00. Technical Service Council, 1 St. Clair Avenue East, Suite 1001, Toronto Ontario M4T 2V7 Canada. **Tel** (416)966-5030, FAX (416)966-6253. **Continues** Review of Professional Manpower, 0229-0324.

ISSN 0265-9387
UK
REVIEW OF THE ECONOMY AND EMPLOYMENT. Added/Corp University of Warwick. Institute for Employment Research. (1981)-. English. Irregular. £70.00. University of Warwick, Institute for Employment Research, Coventry CV4 7AL United Kingdom. **Tel** 011 44 1203 523523, 011 44 1203 524127, FAX 011 44 1203 524241, telex 31406.
Desc: Information on the international economic environment, including an outlook for employment in the UK. Sections present the macroeconomic scenario underlying the forecast, detailed prospects for industries, including emphasis on the structure of employment, and prospects for occupational employment, including the possible implications of the recession for white collar jobs.

LC HD8631 .R48 ISSN 0350-4557
YU
REVIJA RADA. [Rev. rada]. Periodical. Serbo-Croatian (Roman). Institut Za Dokumentaciju Zastite Na Radu Nis, 11000 Belgrad, Jelene Cetkovic 3, Niro Zastita Rada Yugoslavia.
Ind/Abst Saf. Health Work.

Business and Economics — Labor

LC HD4811 .E76
SP

REVISTA DE ESTUDIOS SINDICALES.
Vol. 9, No. 33 (Jan./March 1975)-. Periodical. Spanish. Four times a year. $5.50. Ediciones Publicaciones Populares, Lope de Vega 38 8A Planta, Madrid Spain. *Continues* Estudios Sindicales.

LC HD8302 .R48
CK

REVISTA DE TRABAJO Y SEGURIDAD SOCIAL. Added/Corp Colombia. Servicio Nacional de Aprendizaje. (19??)-. Spanish. Four times a year. 6796ptas Spain; 6500ptas other. Centro de Publicaciones del Ministero de Trabajo y Seguridad Social, Agustin Bethencourt 11, 28003 Madrid Spain. **Tel** 011 34 1 5543400. **(Subscription address:** Mundi Prensa Libros SA, Castello 37, Apartado 1223, 28001 Madrid Spain. **Tel** 011 34 1 4313222.)

ISSN 0250-605X
AG

UDC 36

REVISTA INTERNACIONAL DE SEGURIDAD SOCIAL. [Rev. int. segur. soc.]. (1980)-. Periodical. Spanish. Four times a year. *Continues* Estudios de la Seguridad Social, 0379-0266. **Ind/Abst** Int. Labour Doc.; LABORDOC.

ISSN 0378-5548
SZ

UDC 331

REVISTA INTERNACIONAL DEL TRABAJO. [Rev. int. trab.]. (1930)-. Periodical. Spanish (French). Six times a year. $64.00. International Labour Office - ILO, Publications Sales Service, CH-1211 Geneva 22 Switzerland. **Tel** 011 41 22 7996111, FAX 011 41 22 7986253, telex 415 647 ilo ch. **(Subscription address:** International Labour Office / Washington, DC, 1828 L Street Northwest, Suite 801, Washington DC 20036. **Tel** (202)653-7652.) Index available.
Desc: Contains articles on international economic and social issues of the world and their effects on the OIT.
Ind/Abst LABORDOC.

LC HD6958.5 .R48
DD 331/.0987
VE

REVISTA SOBRE RELACIONES INDUSTRIALES Y LABORALES / UNIVERSIDAD CATOLICA ANDRES BELLO. VFOAT Revista de Investigaciones Sobre Relaciones Industriales y Laborales. Year 1, No. 1 (July/August 1979)-. Periodical. Spanish. Four times a year. UCAB/Revista Sobre Relaciones Industriales y Laborales, Apartado 29.068, Urbanizacion Montalban la Vega, Caracas Venezuela. **Tel** 4429511. **ED** J Urquijo. **Bk Rev. Circ:** 2,000 (ctrl).
Desc: History of labor institutions, labor problems and solutions, labor, government, and management relations.
Ind/Abst LABORDOC.

ISSN 0484-8365
AE

REVOLUTION ET TRAVAIL. (19??)-. Periodical. French. Four times a year. $39.83. Revolution et Travail, Administration Gestion, 48 rue Khelife, Boukhalfa Algeria.

ISSN 0228-9253
CN

DD 331.12/0971

REVUE DU MARCHE POUR CADRES, LA. VFOAT Review of Professional Manpower. 1981-. French (English). One time a year. $16.00. Le Conseil de Placement Professionnel/Technical Service Council, One St. Clair Avenue East, 10th Floor, Toronto Ontario M4T 2V7 Canada. **Tel** (416)966-5030, FAX (416)966-6253. **ED** Neil A MacDougall. **Circ:** 800.
Desc: An outline of the supply of and demand for accountants, engineers, scientists, executives and other professionals, factors affecting demand and employers' recruiting practices.

LC HD4807 .R45   **ISSN** 0035-2985
DD 331.05   FR
NLM W1 RE848R

REVUE FRANCAISE DES AFFAIRES SOCIALES. See Sociology.

ISSN 0378-5599
SZ

UDC 331

REVUE INTERNATIONALE DU TRAVAIL. [Rev. int. trav.]. (1921)-. Periodical. French (English and Spanish). Six times a year. $64.00. International Labour Office - ILO, Publications Sales Service, CH-1211 Geneva 22 Switzerland. **Tel** 011 41 22 7996111, FAX 011 41 22 7986253, telex 415 647 ilo ch. Index available. **Bk Rev.**
Desc: Articles based on recent ILO and other research into international interest affecting labour.
Ind/Abst LABORDOC; Repere (1979-).

ISSN 0035-421X
SZ
CEASED

REVUE SYNDICALE SUISSE. [Rev. synd. suisse]. **Added/Corp** Schweizerischer Gewerkschaftsbund. (1909)-Vol. 86 (1994). Periodical. French. Swiss Federation of Trade Unions, Case Postale 64, CH-3000 Bern Switzerland. **Tel** 011 41 31 455667, telex 912 831 CH. **ED** Fernand Quartenoud. **Bk Rev. Ad Acc. Circ:** 2,500.
Desc: Official position of the Swiss Trade Union Confederation and information of labor problems.
Ind/Abst Int. Bibliogr. Sociol.; Saf. Health Work.

ISSN 0392-7229
IT

RIVISTA GIURIDICA DEL LAVORO. (19??)-. Italian. Four times a year. L204380. Ediesse / Rome, Via Dei Frentani 4A, 00185 Rome Italy. **Tel** 011 39 6 44870286, 44870288, FAX 011 39 6 4469007. Index available. **Circ:** 2,000. *Continues* Rivista Giuridica de Lavoro e della Previdenza Sociale. Dottrina, Giurisprudenza.

US

ROCKFORD LABOR NEWS (MICROFICHE). (ROCKFORD LABOR NEWS.). (19??)-. Periodical. English. One time a week. $20.00. Rockford Labor News, 1418 Broadway, Rockford IL 61101-1412. **Tel** (815)963-3489. **ED** D Brady. **Bk Rev. Ad Acc.**

ISSN 0035-7774
JA

NLM W1 RO231   **CODEN** ROKAAV

RODO KAGAKU. [RODO kagaku]. **Added/Corp** Nippon Rodo Kagaku Konkyujo, Tokyo. Nippon Sangyo Eisei Kyokai. Rodo Igaku Shinrigaku Kenkyusho, Tokyo. Rodo Igaku Shinrigaku Kenkyusho, Tokyo. Rodo Kagaku Kenkyujo. **VFOAT** Journal of Science of Labour. Vol. 17 (Jan. 1940)-. Academic Scholarly Publication. Japanese (summaries and/or abstracts in English; table of contents in English). Twelve times a year. ¥10000. Institute for Science of Labour, 2 8 14 Sugao Miyama Ku, Kawasaki 213 Japan. **Tel** 011 81 3 2613803. **ED** Akira Nishioka. **Ad Acc.** ctrl circ. Documents available from CASDDS. *Continues* Rodo Kagaku Kenkyu; *Absorbed* Reports of the Institute for Science of Labour.
Desc: Covers work physiology, the psychology of the work environment, occupational diseases and social science.
Ind/Abst Chem. Abstr.; Coal Abstr.; Ergon. Abstr.; Ind. Hyg. Dig. (19??-); Saf. Health Work; Trop. Dis. Bull.

LC HD5827.T65 R63
JA

RODO KEIZAI TOKEI NENPO. Added/Corp Tokyo (Japan). Rodo Keizaikyoku. Tokyo (Japan). Rodokyoku. Tokei Chosaka. Tokyo (Japan). Roseibu. Tokei Chosaka. (19??)-. Japanese. One time a year. Tokyo-to Rodo Keizaikyoku, 8-ban 1-go, Marunouchi 3-chome Chiyoda-ku, Tokyo Japan.

LC HD6951 .R6
JA

RODO MONDAI KENKYU. VFOAT Journal of Labor Problems. No. 1- Apr. 1975-. Japanese. Kinki Daigaku Rodo Mondai Kenkyujo, 4-1 Kowakae 3-chome 577, Higashiosaka Japan.

LC HD6831 .R64
JA

RODO NENKAN. Periodical. Japanese. One time a year. ¥1600. Nihon Hyoronsha, 3-10-10 Minami-Ootsuka, Toshima-ku, Tokyo-to 170 Japan. **Tel** 011 81 3 9878611, FAX 011 81 3 9878590.

LC HD8729.A3 R63
JA

RODO SHIRYO JOHO. VFOAT Labour Document. No. 1- July 1970-. Periodical. Japanese. ¥30 single issue. Aichi-Ken Kinro Kaikan, 2-32 Tsurumai Showa-ku, Nagoya 466 Japan.

LC HD8721 .A328
JA

RODO TOKEI NEMPO. Added/Corp Japan. Rodosho. Tokei Johobu. Japan. Rodo Tokei Chosabu. **VFOAT** Year Book of Labour Statistics. (1952)-. Statistical Publication. Multiple languages (English and Japanese). Every 2 years. Government Publications Service Center, 2-1 Kasumigaseki 1-Chome, Chiyoda-Ku Tokyo 100 Japan. **Tel** 011 81 3 3504 3885. *Continues* Rodo Tokei Chosa Nempo.

LC HD8721 .R63
JA

RODO UNDO HAKUSHO. Added/Corp Nihon Rodo Kyokai. Japan. Rodosho. Roseikyoku. (19??)-. Japanese. ¥2800. Japan Institute of Labor, Shinjuku Monolith 2 3 1, Tokyo 163 09 Japan. **Tel** 011 81 3 53213084.

LC HD5827 .A3
JA

RODORYOKU CHOSA NEMPO / HENSHU SORIFU TOKEIKYOKU / ANNUAL REPORT ON THE LABOUR FORCE SURVEY. Added/Corp Japan. Sorifu. Tokeikyoku. **VFOAT** Annual Report on the Labour Force Survey. (1978)-. Japanese (English). Somucho Tokeikyoku, (Statistics Bureau Management and Coordination Agency), 19-1 Wakamatsucho Shinjukuku, Tokyo 162 Japan. *Continues* Rodoryoku Chosa Hokoku.

LC HD8721 .A3235
JA

RODOSHA FUKUSHI SOGO CHOSA HOKOKU. Main/Corp Japan. Rodosho. Daijin Kambo. Tokei Johobu. Joho Kaisekika. **Added/Corp** Japan. Rodosho. Tokei Johobu. (1976)-. Periodical. Japanese. Rodosho Daijin Dambo Tokei Johobu, 3-1 Otemachi 1-chome Chiyoda-ku, Tokyo 100 Japan.

LC HD5725.W4 W38B   **ISSN** 0145-2320
DD 331.1/09754   US

RS-SERIES. Main/Corp West Virginia. Dept. of Employment Security. Research and Statistics Section. English. West Virginia Employment Programs Bureau, 112 California Avenue, Charleston WV 25305. **Tel** (304)558-2630, FAX (304)348-0301. *Supersedes* West Virginia. Dept. of Employment Security. Research and Statistics Division. RS.

ISSN 0819-0283
AT

DD 616.7505

RSI STUDENT NEWSLETTER. [RSI stud. newsl.]. **Added/Corp** Australian National University. Counselling Centre. **VFOAT** Repetition Strain Injury Student Newsletter. (1985)-. Newsletter. English. Six times a year. 20.00Aus$. ACT/RSI Support Group, PO Box 541, Canberra 2601 Australia. **Tel** 062 487 080.
Desc: News and information on work related accidents or injuries.

LC HD5797.7.A6 P63A
PL

RUCH ZATRUDNIONYCH W GOSPODARCE USPOECZNIONEJ. Main/Corp Poland. Gowny Urzad Statystyczny. 1973-. Polish. Zaklad Wydawnictw Statystycznych, Al. Niepodlegosci 208, 00-925 Warsaw Poland. **Tel** 011 48 22 250345, telex 814581 A GUS PL.

ISSN 0033-7196
US

RWDSU RECORD. VAT Retail, Wholesale and Department Store Union Record. Vol. 1 (June 1945)-. Periodical. English. Six times a year. $3.00. Retail Wholesale & Department Store, 30 East 29th Street, New York NY 10016. **Tel** (212)684-5300. **ED** Stuart Appelbaun. **Circ:** 200,000 (ctrl) available on microfilm and microfiche from University Microfilms International (UMI). *Formed by the union of* Retail, Wholesale and Department Store Employee *and* Union Voice of the Distributive, Processing and Office Workers of America.
Desc: General labor news including AFL-CIO, RWDSU local news, health news, consumer, social security, labor humor.
Ind/Abst Work Relat. Abstr.

ISSN 0225-4042
CN

DD 331.88/1107113

S. O. N. G. SHEET. [S.O.N.G. sheet]. **Main/Corp** Southern Ontario Newspaper Guild. **VAT** Southern Ontario Newspaper Guild Sheet. Vol. 1 (Oct. 1978)-. Periodical. English. Irregular. Limited free distribution to members and interested parties. Southern Ontario Newspaper Guild, 37 King Street East/Suite 29, Toronto Ontario M5C 1E9 Canada.

ISSN 0816-3103
AT

DD 331.8819099423

SA BUILDING WORKER. [SA build. work.]. **VFOAT** South Australian Building Worker. (1984)-. Periodical. English. Four times a year. $32.96. Avonwold Publishing Company Pty Limited, PO Box 52068, Saxonwold 2132, South Africa. **Tel** 11 27 11 7881610.

US

SAGINAW-BAY-MIDLAND'S LABOR MARKET NEWS. Added/Corp Michigan Employment Security Commission. Bureau of Research and Statistics. Information and Reports Section. **VFOAT** Saginaw Bay Midland's Labor Market News. Vol. 12, No. 1 (Mar. 1992)-. Periodical. English. Twelve times a year. Detroit Employment Security Commission, 7310 Woodward Castro, Room 520, Detroit MI 48202. **Tel** (313)876-5427. *Continues* Saginaw, Bay City, Midland Labor Market Review.

LC HD4922.J3 S25
JA

SAITEI CHINGIN KETTEI YORAN / RIDOSHO ROKIKYOKU CHINGIN FUKUSHIBU CHINGINKA HEN. Added/Corp Japan. Chingin Fukushibu. Chinginka. (19??)-. Japanese. ¥1200. Rodo Horei Kyokai, c/o Fuji Building, 18-6 Hatchobori 3 Chuo-ku, Tokyo-to 104 Japan.

LC HD4966.B6 A26a   **ISSN** 0147-2305
DD 331.2/82/3805   US

SALARIES & BENEFITS IN BOAT MANUFACTURING. Main/Corp Abbott, Langer & Associates. **VAT** Salaries and Benefits in Boat

Business and Economics — Labor

Manufacturing. (19??)-. English. Every 2 years. Abbott Langer & Associates, 548 First Street, Department Z, Crete IL 60417. **Tel** (708)672-4200.

LC HD4965.5.U6 A54a ISSN 0160-516X
DD 331.2/041/658430973 US
SALARIES AND RELATED MATTERS IN THE SERVICE DEPARTMENT. Main/Corp
Abbott, Langer & Associates. (19??)-. Periodical. English. One time a year. $85.00. Abbott Langer & Associates, 548 First Street, Department Z, Crete IL 60417. **Tel** (708)672-4200. **ED** Steven Langer.
Desc: Includes information concerning an analysis of vacations, holidays, sick leave and insurance programs.

LC HD4973 .S24 ISSN 0732-099X
DD 331.2/973 US
SALARIES (CAMBRIDGE, MASS.).
(SALARIES.). 1982-. English. One time a year. Ballinger Publishing Company, 10 East 53rd Street, New York NY 10022-5244.

LC Q149.U5 S315a ISSN 0146-5015
DD 331.2/81/50973 US
  CCC
NLM W1 SA31K
SALARIES OF SCIENTISTS, ENGINEERS AND TECHNICIANS.
Main/Corp Scientific Manpower Commission. **Added/Corp** Scientific Manpower Commission. Commission on Professionals in Science and Technology. **VFOAT** Salaries of Scientists, Engineers & Technicians. 3rd Edition (June 1967)-. English. Every 2 years. $107.50. Commission on Professionals in Science and Technology, 1333 H Street NW, Suite 111, Washington DC 20005. **Tel** (202)326-7080. **ED** Eleanor L Babco. **Circ:** 1,000. *Continues Salaries of Scientists and Engineers.*
Desc: Salaries of scientists and engineers.

LC JS451.O57 S24 ISSN 0147-7080
DD 331.28/1/35200809766 US
SALARIES, WAGES AND FRINGE BENEFITS OF OKLAHOMA CITIES AND TOWNS. See Business and Economics-Abstracting, Bibliographies and Statistics.

LC HF5549.5.C67 S24 ISSN 1184-0900
DD 658.3/2/097105 CN
SALARY ADMINISTRATION POLICIES AND PRACTICES IN CANADA. [Salary adm. policies pract. Can.]. Added/Corp Canada. Public Service Staff Relations Board. Pay Research Bureau.
(1986)-. English. Director General, Pay Research Bureau, 140 O'Connor Street, PO Box 1525 Station B, Ottawa Ontario K1P 5V2 Canada. *Continues Salary Administration in Canadian Industry.,* 0712-3531.

LC HD4965.5.U6 N24A ISSN 0196-867X
DD 331.2/8817 US
SALARY & BENEFITS SURVEY. Main/Corp
National Fluid Power Association. **VAT** Salary and Benefits Survey. (19??)-. English. One time a year. $400.00, $35.00 (members). National Fluid Power Association, 3333 North Mayfair Road, Milwaukee WI 53222. **Tel** (414)778-3357, FAX (414)778-3361. **ED** Steven Latin-Kasper. ctrl circ.
Desc: Details salaries, bonuses and benefits provided to more than 25 salaried job classifications. Breakouts by company size. Results held confidential to participants for one year after publication.

  US
SALARY STRATIFICATION REPORT / UNIVERSITY OF WASHINGTON PAYROLL/PERSONNEL SYSTEM.
Main/Corp University of Washington Payroll/Personnel System. (1990)-. English. *Continues State of Washington Personnel Detail Listing. Agency, University of Washington.*

  ISSN 0711-3196
DD 331.2/8165/00971 CN
SALARY SURVEY. ADMINISTRATIVE, FINANCE, AND DATA PROCESSING REPORT. [Salary surv., Adm., finance data process. rep.]. 1980-. English. One time a year. $400.00 for Salary Survey set, 5 reports. Thorne Stevenson & Kellogg, 1600 Board of Trade Tower, 1177 West Hastings Street, Vancouver British Columbia V6E 2K3 Canada.
Continues in part Stevenson & Kellogg Salary Survey. An Annual Study of Compensation Across Canada, 0711-3153.

LC HD4976.C2 W47A ISSN 0149-4309
DD 331.2/9794/73 US
SALARY SURVEY (LOS GATOS). (SALARY SURVEY.). Main/Corp Western Management Group.
(19??)-. English. One time a year. Western Management Group, 101 Church Street/Suite 13, Los Gatos CA 95030.

LC HD4966.I482 U543 ISSN 0145-3947
DD 331.2/81/368006573 US
SALARY SURVEY (NEW YORK). (SALARY SURVEY.). [Salary surv.]. Main/Corp American Insurance Association. Added/Corp American Mutual
Insurance Alliance. National Association of Independent Insurers (U.S.). (19??)-. English. One time a year. American Insurance Association, 85 John Street, New York NY 10038. **Tel** (212)669-0400.

LC HD4965.3.E372 U57 ISSN 0276-4822
DD 331.2/8165843/0973 US
SALARY SURVEY OF MIDDLE MANAGEMENT AND SUPERVISORY PERSONNEL. SOUTHERN CALIFORNIA.
(SALARY SURVEY OF MIDDLE MANAGEMENT AND SUPERVISORY PERSONNEL.). 1980-. English. One time a year. American Electronics Association, 5201 Great America Parkway, Santa Clara CA 95054. **Tel** (415)327-9300.

LC JK2474 .A75A ISSN 0091-5599
DD 331.2/81/3539791 US
SALARY SURVEY OF STATE GOVERNMENT EMPLOYERS (PHOENIX). (SALARY SURVEY OF STATE GOVERNMENT EMPLOYERS.). Main/Corp Arizona. State Personnel Commission. (19??)-. English. One time a year. Arizona Personnel Commission, State Personnel Commission, Phoenix AZ 85007.

LC TA157 .W44 ISSN 0190-5732
DD 331.2/82/000973 US
SALARY SURVEY OF SUPERVISORY AND NON-SUPERVISORY PROFESSIONAL ENGINEERS. Main/Corp
American Electronics Association. **VFOAT** Engineers Salary Survey; Salary Survey of Professional Engineers. 1978-. English. One time a year. American Electronics Association, 5201 Great America Parkway, Santa Clara CA 95054. **Tel** (415)327-9300. *Continues WEMA Salary Survey of Supervisory Professional Engineers and Non-Supervisory Professional Engineers.*

  ISSN 0229-4575
DD 331.2/8684/0971 CN
SALARY SURVEY (SOCIETY OF THE PLASTICS INDUSTRY OF CANADA).
(SALARY SURVEY : PLASTICS PROCESSING COMPANIES.). [Salary surv.]. **VAT** Society of the Plastics Industry of Canada Salary Survey. (1972)-. English. Every 2 years. $100.00 members only. Salary Survey, Society of the Plastics Industry of Canada, 1262 Don Mills Road, Don Mills Ontario M3B 2W7 Canada. **Tel** (416)449-3444, FAX (416)449-5685, telex 06-966739.

LC HA1631 .A33 HD5660.Y8
DD 314.971 YU
SAMOUPRAVLJANJE U PRIVREDI. See Business and Economics-Abstracting, Bibliographies and Statistics.

LC HA1631 .A33 HD5660.Y8
DD 314.971 YU
SAMOUPRAVLJANJE U USTANOVAMA DRUSTVENIH SLUZBI. See Business and Economics-Abstracting, Bibliographies and Statistics.

LC HF5441 .A4 ISSN 0036-3898
  US
SAMPLE CASE, THE. Added/Corp United Commercial Travelers of America. (1???)-. Periodical. English. Four times a year. $3.00. United Commercial Travelers, 632 North Park Street, Columbus OH 43215.

  ISSN 0332-1169
  IE
SAOTHAR. Added/Corp Irish Labour History Society. 1 (1975)-. Periodical. English. One time a year. $17.48. Irish Congress of Trade Unions, 19 Raglan Road, Dublin 4 Ireland. **Tel** 011 353 1 680641.
Ind/Abst Am. Hist. Life (1987-).

LC HD8109.S2 S27 ISSN 0317-7335
DD 331/.097124 CN
SASKATCHEWAN LABOUR REPORT, THE. [Sask. labour rep.]. Added/Corp Saskatchewan. Labour Relations Board. Policy Planning and Research Division. Saskatchewan. Dept. of Labour. Research and Planning Division. Saskatchewan. Labour Relations Board. Saskatchewan. Saskatchewan Human Resources, Labour and Employment. VAT Labour Report (Regina).
Vol. 25, No. 1 (Jan. 1974)-. Periodical. English. Four times a year. Free on request. Saskatchewan Labour / Department Human Resources Labour, 1870 Albert Street, Regina Saskatchewan S4P 3V7 Canada. **Tel** (306)787-3369, FAX (306)787-7229. *Continues Consumer Price Index and Monthly Statistical Bulletin,* 0318-7691; *Absorbed Saskatchewan Industrial-Relations Report; Decisions of the Saskatchewan Labour-Relations Board.*

LC HD4870.Y8 S28
  YU
SAVEZNE OMLADINSKE RADNE AKCIJE U ... GODINI / SOCIJALISTICKA REPUBLIKA SRBIJA, REPUBLICKI ZAVOD ZA STATISTIKU. Serbo-Croatian (Roman).

  ISSN 0818-3317
DD 331.110994 AT
SCAN : SUMMARISING CONTEXTS, ACTION AND NETWORKS. [SCAN : Summ. contexts action netw.]. (1986)-. Periodical. English. Four times a year. National Clearinghouse on Local Employment Initiatives, c/o Work Resources Centre, GPO Box 4, Canberra ACT 2601 Australia.
Ind/Abst Aust. Educ. Index (1986).

  ISSN 8750-1708
  US
SCANNER AND KING COUNTY LABOR NEWS, THE. VFOAT Scanner. (1968)-. Periodical. English. Six times a year. King County Labor Council, 2800 1st Avenue, Seattle WA 98121-1166. *Continues King County Labor News.*

  ISSN 1184-9312
DD 331.2 CN
SCCUQ-INFO. [SCCUQ-info]. Added/Corp
SCCUQ. **VAT** Syndicat des Chargees et Charges de Cours de l'UQAM-Info (1991). Vol. 2, No 1 (Apr 1991)-. Periodical. French. Limited free distribution. SCCUQ, Syndicat des Chargees et Charges de Cours de L'Uqam, Local P-5610, CP 8888, Succursale A, Montreal Quebec H3C 3P8 Canada. *Continues SCCUQ-Nego.,* 0849-1615.

  IT
SCHEMI DI LAVORO. VFOAT Journal of Human Communications. (19??)-. Italian. Two times a year. L25000. Ist Ricerca Comunicazione CNR, 65016 Montesilvano Pe Italy. **Tel** 011 39 85 836044.

  ISSN 0037-0142
  UK
  CEASED
SEAMAN, THE. Added/Corp National Union of Seamen. Vol. 1-27, (1912-1939); Series 2, Vol. 1 (August 1941)-(19??). Periodical. English. National Union of Seaman, Maritime House Old Town, Clapham London SW4 OJP United Kingdom. **Tel** 011 44 181 6225581, telex 8814611. **ED** Jim Jump. **Bk Rev. Ad Acc. Circ:** 13,000.
Desc: Journal of the National Union of Seamen.

  MX
SECTOR SOCIAL. Added/Corp Asociacion Nacional de Empresas Sindicales de Interes Social (Mexico). No. 1 (May/Jun. 1987)-. Periodical. Spanish. Six times a year.
Ind/Abst LABORDOC.

LC HD7090 .S4 ISSN 0379-0304
  MX
NLM W1 SE245J
SEGURIDAD SOCIAL. [Segur. soc.].
Added/Corp International Social Security Association. Inter-American Conference on Social Security. Permanent Inter-American Committee on Social Security. Inter-American Center for Social Security Studies. Vol. 1, No. 1 (Oct. 1951)-. Periodical. Spanish. Three times a year. $50.00. Comite Permanente Interamericano de Seguridad Social, Apartado Postal 20532, Mexico 20 DF Mexico. **Tel** 011 52 5 5950177. **Bk Rev. Circ:** 500 (ctrl). *Supersedes International Social Security Association Bulletin. Association.*
Ind/Abst Int. Labour Doc.

LC UA17.5.U5 U5414a ISSN 0501-9427
DD 355.2/2/0973 US
SELECTED MANPOWER STATISTICS.
See Military and Defense-Abstracting, Bibliographies and Statistics.

LC HD4976.C57 S44 ISSN 0740-5030
DD 331.2/9788 US
SELECTED MFRS. INDEX SURVEY. [Sel. mfrs. index surv.]. VFOAT Selected Manufacturers' Index Survey; Survey; Selected Manufacturers' Index. English. One time a year. Mountain States Employers Council, 1790 Logan Street, PO Box 539, Denver CO 80201.

LC HD8051 .U55A ISSN 0275-5076
DD 353.83/05 US
SEMIANNUAL REPORT - UNITED STATES. DEPT. OF LABOR. OFFICE OF THE INSPECTOR GENERAL. (SEMIANNUAL REPORT OF THE INSPECTOR GENERAL / U.S. DEPARTMENT OF LABOR, OFFICE OF INSPECTOR GENERAL.). Main/Corp United States. Dept. of Labor. Office of the Inspector General. April 1, 1983-Sept. 30, 1983-. English. Two times a year. US Department of Labor, 200 Constitution Avenue NW, Washington DC 20210. **Tel** (202)219-7316, FAX (202)219-7312. available on microfiche (Vols. for (April-Sept. 1983) distributed to depository libraries. *Continues United States. Dept. of Labor. Office of the Inspector General. Semiannual Report,* 0275-5076.

Business and Economics —Labor

LC HD6831 .S46   JA
SENGO RODO UNDOSHI KENKYU.
Added/Corp Sengo Rodo Undoshi Kenkyukai (Japan). (1984)-. Periodical. Japanese. ¥700 (single issue). Sengo Rodo Undoshi Kenkyukai, c/o Sasaki Masahiko 30-15 Nadadai 1 Itabashi-ku, Tokyo-to Japan.

LC HD4966.S4 J35a   JA
SENIN RODO TOKEI. **Main/Corp** Japan.
Unyusho. Daijin Kambo. Joho Kanribu. No. 54 (1975)-. Periodical. Japanese. Senin Rodo Takei, 2-1-3 Kasumigaseki, Chiyoda-ku Tokyo Japan. **Continues** Senin Rodo Tokei.

LC HD8039.S4 J35a   JA
SENIN TOKEI. **Main/Corp** Japan. Unyusho. Daijin
Kambo. Joho Kanribu. (19??)-. Periodical. Japanese. Daijin Kanbo, 7-3, Ichigaya Honmuracho, Shinjuku-ku Tokyo 162 Japan.

LC HD6281.T4 S45A   **ISSN** 0149-161X
DD 331.3/98/09764   US
SENIOR TEXANS EMPLOYMENT PROGRAM ANNUAL REPORT TO GOVERNOR'S COMMITTEE ON AGING.
(ANNUAL REPORT TO GOVERNOR'S COMMITTEE ON AGING.). **Main/Corp** Senior Texans Employment Program. (19??)-. English. One time a year. Farmers Union Community Development Association, 800 Lake Air Drive, Waco TX 76710.

LC KEQ663.P8 A445   **ISSN** 0823-3322
DD 347.140268   CN
SENTENCES ARBITRALES DE LA FONCTION PUBLIQUE. **Main/Corp** Quebec
(Province). Ministere de la Fonction Publique. Greffe du Tribunal d'Arbitrage. Vol. 1, No 1 (Sept. 1983)-. Periodical. French. Twelve times a year. 100.04Can$. Les Publications du Quebec, CP 1190, Outremont Quebec H2V 4S7 Canada. **Tel** (514)948-1222, (418)643-5150, FAX (514)278-3030.

   ISSN 0920-4849
UDC 331.105.6 (492)   NE
SER-BULLETIN. [SER-bull.]. **VFOAT**
Sociaal-Economische Raad-Bulletin. (1981)-. Bulletin. Dutch. Twelve times a year. $25.86. Social Economische Raad, Bezuidenhoutseweg 60, Postbus 90405, 2509 LK The Hague Netherlands. **Tel** 011 31 70 3499499, FAX 011 31 70 3832535, telex 41.146. Index available. cum. index. **Bk Rev**. **Circ**: 2 500 (ctrl).
Continues SER Informatie- en Documentatiebulletin, 0166-9125.
Desc: Covers actual developments in the advisory tasks of the SER, the Foundation of Labour and articles about new publications.

   ISSN 0577-1145
   FR
SERIE : ETUDES SYNDICALES. **Main/Corp**
Centre d'Etude de la Vie Politique Francaise, Paris. **VFOAT** Etudes Syndicales. No. 1- 1964-. Periodical. French. Centre d'Etude de la Vie Politique Francaise, 86 Bd Haussmann, Paris 7E France.

   ISSN 1062-4597
DD 331   US
SERVICE EMPLOYEES UNION. [Serv. empl.
union]. **Added/Corp** Service Employees International Union. **VFOAT** Union. Vol. 1, No. 1, Sept. (1987)-. Periodical. English. Four times a year. $12.00 (nonmembers). Service Employees International Union / US, 1313 L Street NW, Washington DC 20005-4409. **Tel** (202)898-3200. **Continues** Service Employee, 0037-2609.
Ind/Abst Work Relat. Abstr.

   ISSN 0710-5630
DD 331.7/69/009714   CN
SERVICES AUX MEMBRES - ASSOCIATION DE LA CONSTRUCTION DE MONTREAL ET DU QUEBEC. (LES
SERVICES AUX MEMBRES.). [Serv. memb. - Assoc. constr. Montr. Que.]. **Main/Corp** Association de la Construction de Montreal et du Quebec. French. Association de la Construction de Montreal et du Quebec, 4970 place de la Savane, Montreal Quebec H4P 1Z6 Canada.

LC HD4811 .S46   JA
SHAKAI HYORON. **Added/Corp** Katsudoka
Shudan Shiso Undo. (Nov. 11, 1975)-. Periodical. Japanese. Six times a year. ¥3000. Katsudoka Shudan Shiso Undo, c/o Tazawa Building, 1 Kanda Ogawacho, 1 Chiyoda-ku Tokyo Japan.

   US
SHIFTWORK MANAGERS NEWSLETTER. (1989)-. Newsletter. English. Four
times a year. $35.00. SynchroTech, 315 South 9th Street, Suite 211, Lincoln NE 68508. **Tel** (402)474-4387, FAX (402)474-4425. **ED** Marty Klein and Phyllis Webb. **Circ**: 20,000 (ctrl).
Desc: This newsletter addresses current issues faced by managers, as well as employees, in dealing with shiftwork and schedule related issues.

LC HD5077 .S495   JA
SHUNKI CHINAGE KANKEI SHUYO SANKO SHIRYO. **Added/Corp** Tokyo. Shoko
Kaigisho. Kigyo Keieibu. Rodoka. Tokyo Shoko Kaigisho. Chusho Kigyo Shinkobu. Tokyo. Shoko Kaigisho. Rodobu. (19??)-. Japanese. ¥1000. Tokyo Shoko Kaigisho, 2-2 Marunouchi 3, Chiyoda-ku, Tokyo Japan.

LC HD5077 .S5   JA
SHUNKI CHINGIN KOSHO SHIRYO.
Added/Corp Nihon Chingin Kenkyu Senta. (1971)-. Japanese. One time a year. ¥3000. Sangyo Rodo Chosajo, 4-7 Hirakawacho 2-chome Chiyoda-ku 102 Tokyo Japan. **Tel** 03-237-1611, FAX 03-237-1631. **ED** Sangyo Rodo Chosajo. cum. index. **Circ**: 13,000.
Desc: The last new statistical figures specialized for determination of the wages and other labor conditions inside the enterprise.

LC HD8039.M4 I78   IS
SHUROT. (June 1938)-. Periodical. Hebrew. Twelve
times a year. Histadrut Ha-Pekidim Ovde Ha-Minhal Vera-Sherutim Be-Yisrael, Bet Ha-Vaad Ha-Poel Shel Ha-Histadrut, Tel-Aviv Israel.

   UK
SICK PAY BULLETIN. **Added/Corp** Incomes
Data Services. **VFOAT** IDS Studies. No. 1 (Mar 1982)-. Bulletin. English. Twelve times a year. Incomes Data Services, 193 St. John Street, London EC1V 4LS United Kingdom. **Tel** 011 44 171 2503494, FAX 011 44 171 6080949.

LC HD2429.S55 S56
DD 331.7/1/0605957   SI
SINGAPORE PROFESSIONALS : JOURNAL OF THE SINGAPORE PROFESSIONAL CENTRE, THE. Vol. 1, No.
1 (Jan. 1976)-. Periodical. English. Four times a year. Singapore Professional Centre, Block 23 129-B, Outram Park Singapore 0316.

   ISSN 0761-3857
UDC 331.96   FR
SITUATIONS. [Situations]. (1970)-. Periodical.
French. Six times a year. 100.00F France; 110.00F other. L'Agence Natl pour l'Emploi, 4 rue Galilee, 93198 Noisy Le Grand France. **Tel** 011 33 1 49317698.

   ISSN 0279-2028
   US
SKILL (DETROIT, MICH.). (SKILL : THE UAW'S
INTERNATIONAL MAGAZINE FOR SKILLED TRADE MEMBERS.). [Skill]. **Added/Corp** International Union, United Automobile, Aerospace, and Agricultural Implement Workers of America. Skilled Trades Dept. Vol. 1, No. 1 (Summer 1981)-. Periodical. English. Four times a year (Jan., Apr., July, Oct.). Free on request. Skill, 8000 East Jefferson, Detroit MI 48214. **Tel** (313)926-5291, FAX (313)331-1520. **ED** Dave Elula. **Bk Rev**. **Circ**: 212,000 (ctrl).

   ISSN 0835-2453
DD 331.25/92/09713   CN
SKILLS LETTER. [Skills lett.]. **Added/Corp**
Ontario. Ministry of Skills Development. Vol. 1, No. 1 (Spring 1987)-. Periodical. English (French). Five times a year. Free on request. Ministry of Skills Development, 101 Blook Street North, 11th Floor, Toronto Ontario M5S 1P7 Canada. **Tel** (416)924-8701.

   NE
SOCIAAL MAANDBLAD-ARBEID. (1954)-.
Periodical. Dutch. Eleven times a year. $126.04. Samsom Bedrijfsinformatie BV, Postbus 4, 2400 MA Alphen Rij Netherlands. **Tel** 011 31 1720 66633. (**Subscription address**: Intermedia BV, Postbus 4, 2400 MA Alphen AD Rijn Netherlands. **Tel** 011 31 1720 66481.) **Formed by the union of** Sociaal Maandbland **and** Arbeid.

LC HD5764.5.A6 S65   **ISSN** 0255-0776
DD 306/.094   LU
SOCIAL EUROPE. (SOCIAL EUROPE /
COMMISSION OF THE EUROPEAN COMMUNITIES, DIRECTORATE-GENERAL FOR EMPLOYMENT, SOCIAL AFFAIRS AND EDUCATION.). [Soc. Eur.]. **Added/Corp** Commission of the European Communities. Directorate-General for Employment, Social Affairs, and Education. Vol. 1 (May 1984)-. Periodical. English. Three times a year. £37.00 UK; 40.10p Ireland. Office for Official Publications of the European Communities, 2 rue Mercier, 2985 Luxembourg Luxembourg. **Tel** 011 352 499281, FAX 011 352 292942763.
Desc: Covers the social situation in Europe today and is illustrated with official texts.
Ind/Abst Curr. Cit.; LABORDOC; PAIS Int. Print.

   LU
SOCIAL EUROPE. SUPPLEMENT.
Added/Corp Commission of the European Communities. Directorate-General for Employment, Social Affairs, and Education. (1986)-. Periodical. English. Office for Official Publications of the European Communities, 2 rue Mercier, 2985 Luxembourg Luxembourg. **Tel** 011 352 499281, FAX 011 352 292942763.
Ind/Abst LABORDOC.

   ISSN 1013-4492
   II
UDC 362
SOCIAL SECURITY DOCUMENTATION. PACIFIC SERIES. [Soc. secur. doc., Pac. ser.].
(1990)-. Periodical. English. Irregular.
Ind/Abst Int. Labour Doc.

DD 331.1/0971   CN
SOCIAL SECURITY RESEARCH REPORTS. (RAPPORTS DE RECHERCHE SUR LA
SECURITE SOCIALE.). No. 01-. Monographic series. French (English). Price varies per volume. Services de l'Information, Ministere de la Sante e National et du Bien-Etre Social Edifice Brooke Claxton, Ottawa Ontario K1A 0S9 Canada.

   ISSN 0821-4980
DD 335.43/0971   CN
SOCIALIST CHALLENGE (MONTREAL).
See Political Science-Socialism, Communism, Anarchism, Utopianism.

   UK
SOCIALIST WORKER. (19??)-. English. One
time a week. £50.00. Socialist Workers Party, PO Box 82, London E3 3LH United Kingdom. **Tel** 011 44 171 5381626, FAX 011 44 171 5380018. **ED** Chris Harman. **Bk Rev**, (Qty: 50).

   ISSN 0836-7094
DD 331/.05   CN
SOCIALIST WORKER (TORONTO). See
Political Science-Socialism, Communism, Anarchism, Utopianism.

LC HD6951 .S54   **ISSN** 0392-5048
DD 306/.36/05   IT
SOCIOLOGIA DEL LAVORO. [Sociol. lav.].
Added/Corp Centro Internazionale di Documentazione e Studi Sociologici sui Problemi del Lavoro. Year 1, No. 1 (Mar. 1978)-. Periodical. Italian (summaries and/or abstracts in English and French). Three times a year. L102080. Franco Angeli Riviste SRL, Viale Monza 106, 20127 Milan Italy. **Tel** 011 39 2 2827651, 011 39 2 289562, FAX 011 39 2 258004, telex 051-511650. **ED** Franco Angeli. **Ad Acc**. **Circ**: 1,000.
Ind/Abst Int. Bibliogr. Sociol.; Int. Labour Doc.; LABORDOC; Soc. Plann. Policy Dev. Abstr.; Sociol. Abstr. [Full Cov.].

LC HD4807 .S6   **ISSN** 0038-0296
   FR
   CCC
Pr Rev.
SOCIOLOGIE DU TRAVAIL (PARIS).
(SOCIOLOGIE DU TRAVAIL.). [Sociol. trav.]. **Added/Corp** Association pour le Developpement de la Sociologie du Travail. (Oct./Dec. 1959)-. Periodical. French. Four times a year. $135.60. Dunod Gauthier Villars, 15 rue Gossin, 92543 Montrouge Cedex France. **Tel** 011 33 1 46565266, 011 33 1 40926527, FAX 011 33 1 40926597. (**Subscription address**: Centrale des Revues, 11 rue Gossin, 92543 Montrouge Cedex France. **Tel** 011 33 1 46565266.) **ED** Odile Benoit Guilbot. cum. index. **Bk Rev**. **Ad Acc**. **Circ**: 2,400. Documents available from The Genuine Article.
Desc: Covers factory work, social work, office work, professional and social groups, companies, public offices, labor movement, trade unions, and work relations.
Ind/Abst Arts Humanit. Citation Index [Select. Cov.]; Curr. Contents Soc. Behav. Sci.; EMBASE; Int. Bibliogr. Sociol.; Int. Labour Doc.; Int. Polit. Sci. Abstr.; LABORDOC; PAIS Int. Print; Res. Alert; Selec. Coop. Index Manage. Period.; Soc. Plann. Policy Dev. Abstr.; Soc. Sci. Cit. Index; Sociol. Abstr.; Sociol. Educ. Abstr.; Work Relat. Abstr.

   ISSN 0164-856X
   US
SOLIDARITY (DETROIT, MICH.).
(SOLIDARITY / INTERNATIONAL UNION, UNITED AUTOMOBILE, AIRCRAFT & AGRICULTURAL IMPLEMENT WORKERS OF AMERICA - UAW.). [Solidarity]. **Added/Corp** International Union, United Automobile, Aircraft and Agricultural Implement Workers of America. International Union, United Automobile, Aerospace, and Agricultural Implement Workers of America. **VFOAT** UAW Solidarity. Vol. 1, No. 1 (Dec. 16, 1957)-. Periodical. English. Ten times a year (Jan.-Feb and July-Aug. are combined issues). $5.00. International Union Law, 8000 Jefferson Avenue East, Detroit MI 48214. **Tel** (313)926-5291. **ED** David Elsila. **Bk Rev**. **Circ**: 1,300,000.
Desc: News and commentary from the UAW and the labor community.
Ind/Abst Work Relat. Abstr.

LC HD56 .S69

RU

SOTSIALNO-EKONOMICHESKIE PROBLEMY NAUCHNO-TEKHNICHESKOGO PROGRESSA. See Industry and Production.

ISSN 1014-9856
SZ

SOURCES AND METHODS / SOURCES ET METHODES / FUENTES Y METODOS. Added/Corp International Labour Office. **VFOAT** Sources and Methods, Labour Statistics; Sources et Methodes; Fuentes y Metodos. 3rd Ed. (1992)-. English (French and Spanish). 35.00F. International Labour Office - ILO, Publications Sales Service, CH-1211 Geneva 22 Switzerland. **Tel** 011 41 22 7996111, FAX 011 41 22 7986253, telex 415 647 ilo ch. **(Subscription address:** International Labor Office / Albany, NY, 49 Sheridan Avenue, Albany NY 12210. **Tel** (518)436-9686.**)** *Continues* Statistical Sources and Methods, 0255-3465.

SA

SOUTH AFRICAN CLEANING REVIEW. English. Six times a year. R50.16 South Africa; R68.00 APU countries; R80.00 other. George Warman Publications Pty, PO Box 704, Cape Town 8000 South Africa. **Tel** 011 27 21 245320, FAX 011 27 21 261332, telex 5-21849. **Ad Acc. Circ:** 1,800 (ctrl). *Continues* South African Laundry & Cleaning Review, 0250-1325.

LC HD8799.S72 S68   ISSN 0377-5429
DD 331/.0968   SA
Pr Rev.

SOUTH AFRICAN LABOUR BULLETIN. [S. Afr. labour bull.]. **Added/Corp** Institute for Industrial Education. Vol. 1 (Apr. 1974)-. Bulletin. English. Six times a year. $95.00. Umanyano Publications CC, PO Box 3851, Johannesburg 2000 South Africa. **Tel** 011 27 11 8365020, 011 27 11 4871603, FAX 011 27 11 8366062. **ED** Karl Von Holdt. Index available. **Bk Rev**. **Ad Acc. Circ:** 6,000. available on microfiche.
 Desc: Analyses labor and trade union issues in South Africa from the standpoint of the democratic unions. Provides a critique of both state action and actions of employers.
 Ind/Abst Hum. Rights Intern. Rep.; Int. Bibliogr. Sociol.

LC HD5630.S6 A3
AT

SOUTH AUSTRALIAN INDUSTRIAL REPORTS. Main/Corp South Australia. Industrial Court. Vol. 1 (1918)-. English. Industrial Court of South Australia, PO Box 566, GPO Registrar, Adelaide South Australia 5001 Australia.
 Ind/Abst Aust. Leg. Mon. Dig.

LC HD5725.S6 A63
DD 331.12/09757   US

SOUTH CAROLINA LABOR MARKET REVIEW. Added/Corp South Carolina Employment Security Commission. Labor Market Information. United States. Employment and Training Administration. United States. Bureau of Labor Statistics. **VFOAT** Labor Market Review. (1984)-. Government Publication. English. One time a year. $15.00. South Carolina Employment Security Commission, 1550 Gadsden Street, PO Box 995, Columbia SC 29202. **Tel** (803)737-2660, FAX (803)737-2642. **ED** Joe Ward. **Circ:** 1,500 (ctrl). *Continues* Annual Planning Information for ... South Carolina.
 Desc: Annual review of labor market, employment and unemployment in South Carolina with articles on related topics.

LC HD7116.C382 U67
DD 353.97830083/5   US

SOUTH DAKOTA STATE CEMENT PLANT RETIREMENT FUND ANNUAL FINANCIAL REPORT FOR THE PERIOD JANUARY 1, THROUGH DECEMBER 31. Added/Corp South Dakota. Legislature. Dept. of Legislative Audit. **VFOAT** South Dakota State Cement Plant Retirement Fund for the Period January 1, through December 31. (19??)-. English. One time a year. South Dakota Department of Legislative Auditing, State Capitol, 500 East Capitol, Pierre SD 57501.

ISSN 0038-3953
US

SOUTHERN CALIFORNIA TEAMSTER. Added/Corp Joint Council of Teamsters No. 42. (19??)-. Periodical. English. Joint Council No 42 of Southern California, 1616 West 9th Street/Room 500, Los Angeles CA 90015. **Tel** (310)383-4242. **ED** Paul Mihalow.

LC HD   ISSN 1320-0259
DD 331.099405   AT

●**SOUTHLAND (SYDNEY).** (SOUTHLAND.). [Southland (Syd.)]. (1993)-. Periodical. English. Four times a year. 23.70Aus$. Southland Magazine, Box Q162 Queen Victoria Building, Sydney NSW 2000 Australia. **Tel** 011 61 2 716 6710, FAX 011 61 2 716 6287. *Continues* Union Issues, 1033-2391.

GW

SOZIALE BEWEGUNGEN : ANALYSE UND DOKUMENTATION DES IMSF. Added/Corp Institut fur Marxistischen Studien und Forschungen (Frankfurt am Main, Germany). (1976)-. Monographic series. German. Irregular. Price varies per volume. Verein Foerderung Pressewesens, Postfach 401940, W-8000 Munich 40 Germany. **Tel** 011 49 89283727. **Ad Acc. Circ:** 2,000.
 Desc: Analysis and documentation on the struggle of the West German working class, especially on the economic and sociopolitical level, in industrial and union fields.

GW

SOZIALWISSENSCHAFTLICHE ARBEITSMARKTFORSCHUNG. VFOAT Socio-Economic Labour Market Research; Reihe Sozialwissenschaftliche Arbeitsmarktforschung. Vol. 1 (1981)-. Monographic series. German (English). Price varies per volume. Campus Verlag, Heelstrasse 149, D-60488 Frankfurt Germany. **Tel** 011 49 69 96751606, FAX 011 49 69 7682046.

ISSN 0394-3127
IT
CEASED

SPAZIO IMPRESA. (Mar. 1987)-(Dec. 1993). Periodical. Italian. Procom, Piazza Campo Marzio 5, 00186 Rome Italy. **Tel** 11 39 6 6865607, FAX 11 39 6 6896743. Index available.

TR

SPECIAL LABOUR FORCE REPORT / REPUBLIC OF TRINIDAD & TOBAGO, CENTRAL STATISTICAL OFFICE. Statistical Publication. English. *Continues* Special Labour Force.

DD 331.1/1/08   US

SPECIAL MANPOWER RESEARCH REPORT. No. 1-. Monographic series. English. Price varies per volume. Utah Department of Employment Security, 174 Social Hall Avenue, PO Box 11249, Salt Lake City UT 84147. **Tel** (801)533-2400.

ISSN 0714-7430
DD 331.89/041610730692/09714   CN

SPECIAL NEGO. [Spec. nego]. **Main/Corp** Regroupement des Infirmieres et Infirmiers du Quebec. Vol. 1, No 1 (20 Sept. 1982)-. Periodical. French. Regroupement Des Infirmieres Et Infirmiers Du Quebec, Bureau 240 580 Est, Grande-Allee Quebec, Quebec G1R 2K2.

LC DS101 .S7   ISSN 0334-1046
IS

SPECTRUM (TEL AVIV, ISRAEL). (SPECTRUM : ISRAEL LABOUR MOVEMENT MONTHLY.). Vol. 1, No 1 (Dec. 1982). Periodical. English (Spanish, German and French). Twelve times a year. IL35.00 Israel; $30.00 other. Horizons Association for Labour, POB 3038, Tel Aviv 61030 Israel. **Tel** 03-663467. **ED** Susan Hattis Rolef and Nancy Ben-Asher. **Bk Rev. Ad Acc.**

ISSN 0714-7570
DD 331.89/041354714/0005   CN

SPGQ EN NEGOTIATION. [SPGQ negoc.]. **VFOAT** En Negotiation. **VAT** Syndicat de Professionels du Gouvernement du Quebec en Negociation. Vol. 1, No 1 (20 Sept. 1982)-. Periodical. French. Free. Syndicat de Professionels du Gouvernement du Quebec, 5E Etage 155 Est boulevard Charest, Quebec G1K 3G6 Canada. *Continues* Negotiation, 0226-7853.

ISSN 0888-9325
DD 331   US

SPIDR NEWS. [SPIDR news]. **Added/Corp** Society of Professionals in Dispute Resolution (U.S.). Vol. 1, No. 1 (May 1977)-. Periodical. English. Four times a year (Jan., Apr., Aug., Nov.). $100.00 Comes with SPIDR membership. Society of Professionals in Dispute Resolution / SPIDR, 815 15th Street Northwest, Suite 530, Washington DC 20006. **Tel** (202)783-7277, FAX (202)293-3054. **Bk Rev,** (Qty: varies). **Ad Acc. Circ:** 3,000. *Continues* Society of Professionals in Dispute Resolution (U.S.). SPIDR Newsletter, 0273-4745.

LC HD8670.8.A5 C48   ISSN 0379-3737
DD 331.1/1/095493   CE

SRI LANKA LABOUR GAZETTE. [Sri Lanka lab. gaz.]. **Added/Corp** Ceylon. Kamkaru Departamentuva. (1950)-. English. Four times a year. Ministry of Labour and Vocational Training, Labour Secretariat, Colombo-5 Sri Lanka. *Continues* Ceylon Labour Gazette.
 Ind/Abst Int. Labour Doc.

LC HD5726.S27 S8
DD 331.12/09776/47   US

ST. CLOUD SMSA LABOR MARKET INFORMATION SUMMARY FOR ... . **VFOAT** St. Cloud S.M.S.A. Labor Market Information Summary for ...; Saint Cloud SMSA Labor Market Information Summary for ...; Labor Market Information Summary for ... . English. One time a year. Minnesota Department of Economic Security, 390 North Robert Street, St Paul MN 55101. *Continues* St. Cloud SMSA Annual Planning Information Report.

ISSN 0885-6869
US

ST. LOUIS/SOUTHERN ILLINOIS LABOR TRIBUNE. VFOAT St. Louis Southern Illinois Labor Tribune; Saint Louis Southern Illinois Labor Tribune; Labor Tribune. (Sept. 5, 1985)-. Periodical. English. One time a week. Labor Tribune Publishing Co, 505 South Ewing Street, St Louis MO 63103. *Formed by the union of* St. Louis Labor Tribune, 0190-0870 *and* Southern Illinois Labor Tribune, 0490-0200.

LC HD5725.I8 I594A
DD 331.11/09777   US

STATE MANPOWER REPORT TO THE GOVERNOR - IOWA. Main/Corp Iowa. State Manpower Services Council. English. One time a year. Iowa Office for Planning and Programming, 523 East 12th Street, Des Moines IA 50319.

LC HD5725.V5 S84   ISSN 0148-4567
DD 331.1/1/09755   US

STATE MANPOWER REVIEW. (STATE MANPOWER REVIEW, STATE OF VIRGINIA.). 1976-. English. One time a year. Virginia Employment Commission, 703 East Main Street, PO Box 1358, Richmond VA 23211.

LC HD5725.F6 F37A   ISSN 0095-6430
DD 331.1/1/09759   US

STATE OF FLORIDA COMPREHENSIVE MANPOWER PLAN. Main/Corp Florida. State Manpower Planning Council. **VFOAT** Florida State Comprehensive Manpower Preplan. English. State Manpower Planning Council, Calwell Building, Tallahassee FL 32304.

LC JK6357 .I57A   ISSN 0146-065X
DD 331.2/81/3539777   US

STATE OF IOWA CLASSIFIED SERVICE PAY PLAN. Main/Corp Iowa. Merit Employment Dept. English. Grimes State Office Building - Employment, Merit Employment Department, Des Moines IA 50319.

LC HD7102.U5 M665a
DD 368.4/1/009786   US

STATE OF MONTANA, DEPARTMENT OF LABOR AND INDUSTRY, WORKMEN'S COMPENSATION DIVISION, REPORT ON REVIEW OF CERTAIN INSURANCE AND DISABILITY COMPENSATION OPERATIONS. Main/Corp Montana. Legislative Assembly. Office of the Legislative Auditor. (19??)-. English. Montana Department of Labor and Industry, PO Box 1728, Helena MT 59601.

LC JK6657 .S76
DD 331.2/813539782   US

STATE SALARY SURVEY. English. One time a year. State Department of Personnel, 301 Centennial Mall South, Box 94905, Lincoln NE 68509.

LC HD8053.R4 A26
DD 331.0973   US

STATISTICAL AND FISCAL DIGEST - RHODE ISLAND. DEPT. OF EMPLOYMENT SECURITY. See Business and Economics-Abstracting, Bibliographies and Statistics.

LC JS7025.W4 A3   ISSN 0511-5507
DD 37/61/331795095414   II

STATISTICS OF EMPLOYMENT IN LOCAL BODIES IN WEST BENGAL. See Business and Economics-Abstracting, Bibliographies and Statistics.

SZ

STATISTICS ON OCCUPATIONAL WAGES AND HOURS OF WORK AND ON FOOD PRICES : OCTOBER INQUIRY RESULTS / INTERNATIONAL LABOUR OFFICE, GENEVA. Added/Corp International Labour Office. International Labour Organisation. **VFOAT** Statistiques des Salaires et de la Duree du Ttravail par Profession et des Prix de Produits Alimentaires; October Inquiry Results; Resultats de l'Enquete d'Octobre. (1991)-. English (French and Spanish). Nine times a year. 105.00F. International Labour Office - ILO, Publications Sales Service, CH-1211 Geneva 22 Switzerland. **Tel** 011 41 22 7996111, FAX 011 41 22 7986253, telex 415 647 ilo ch. **(Subscription address:** International Labour Office / Washington, DC, 1828 L Street Northwest, Suite

Business and Economics —Labor

801, Washington DC 20036. **Tel** (202)653-7652.)
Continues Bulletin of Labour Statistics. October Inquiry Results, 0007-4950.

FR
STATISTIQUES DE LA POPULATION ACTIVE.
French. Four times a year. $43.00. OECD Publications and Information Center, 2 rue Andre-Pascal, 75775 Paris Cedex 16 France. **Tel** 011 33 1 49104262, US:(202)785-6323, FAX 011 33 1 45248500, 011 33 1 45248176, telex 620 160 OCDE. **(Subscription address:** OECD Publications Center, 2001 L Street, Suite 700, Washington DC 20036. **Tel** (202)822-3873, (202)785-6323.)
Desc: French edition of the OECD's annual statistical report on the labor forces of its member countries.

LC HD7106.B3 S73
DD 331.252
BE
STATISTIQUES DES BENEFICIAIRES DE PRESTATIONS DE RETRAITE ET DE SURVIE.
See Business and Economics-Abstracting, Bibliographies and Statistics.

LC HD7352.A3 P67B
DD 363
PO
STATISTIQUES DU BATIMENT ET DE L'HABITATION : CONTINENT, AZORES ET MADERE.
See Business and Economics-Abstracting, Bibliographies and Statistics.

LC HD7105.35.C2 S8 **ISSN** 0846-8001
DD 331.25/2/09714
CN
STATISTIQUES FINANCIERES EN ..., LES.
See Business and Economics-Abstracting, Bibliographies and Statistics.

LC HA1107 **ISSN** 0067-5563
DD 314
NLM W2 GB4 I5SK
BE
STATISTIQUES SOCIALES.
See Business and Economics-Abstracting, Bibliographies and Statistics.

LC HD5799 .A4 **ISSN** 0108-5514
DD 331.11
DK
STATISTISKE EFTERRETNINGER. ARBEJDSMARKED.
See Business and Economics-Abstracting, Bibliographies and Statistics.

LC HD5715.5.I8 S75 **ISSN** 0390-3532
DD 331.25/92/0945
IT
STATO E PROSPETTIVE DELLA FORMAZIONE PROFESSIONALE IN ITALIA : RELAZIONE ANNUALE PRESENTATA DALL'ISFOL AL MINISTERO DEL LAVORO E DELLA PREVIDENZA SOCIALE IN ATTUAZIONE DELL'ART. 20 DELLA LEGGE-QUADRO SULLA FORMAZIONE PROFESSIONALE.
Italian. Isfol, via Bartolomeo Eustachio 8, 00161 Rome Italy.

US
CEASED
STEEL ARBITRATION DIGEST.
(19??)-(1994). English. Pike & Fischer nc., 4600 East-West Highway, Suite 200, Bethesda MD 20814-1438. **Tel** (301)654-6262, FAX (301)654-6297. **ED** John W. Willis. **Circ:** 250.
Desc: Digest of arbitration decisions affecting the steelworkers union and steel industry managers.

ISSN 0892-1652
DD 331
US
STEEL EMPLOYMENT NEWS.
[Steel employ. news]. **Added/Corp** American Iron and Steel Institute. Communications Dept. (19??)-. Periodical. English. Twelve times a year. $25.00. American Iron & Steel Institute, 1101 17th Street Northwest, Suite 1300, Washington DC 20036. **Tel** (202)452-7100, (202)452-7151. **Circ:** 1,000 (ctrl).
Desc: Reports employment levels and hourly employment costs in primary steel industry.

ISSN 0883-3141
DD 331
US
STEELABOR.
[Steelabor]. Vol. 44 (Jan. 1979)-. Periodical. English (French and Spanish). Six times a year (Jan., Feb., March, May, July, Aug., Sept., and Nov.). $12.00. Steelabor, Five Gateway Center, Pittsburgh PA 15222. **Tel** (412)562-2400. **ED** Russell W Gibbons. **Circ:** 1,040,000. available on microfilm.
Continues Steel Labor, 0039-0941.
Desc: Magazine of the United Steel Workers of America, representing workers in the steel, aluminum, nonferrous metals, container, foundry, hardware and upholstery industries.
Ind/Abst Work Relat. Abstr.

LC HD6331 .S74
DD 331.1
FR
STI REVIEW.
See Industry and Production.

US
STOCKTON AREA LABOR MARKET BULLETIN.
Added/Corp California. Employment Data and Research Division. **VFOAT** Labor Market Bulletin. 3rd Quarter (1987)-. Bulletin. English. Four times a year. Employment Development Department, PO Box 826880, Sacramento CA 94280. **Tel** (916)445-1952.
Continues Stockton Labor Market Bulletin.

LC HD6756 .S77
SW
STUDIER I ARBETARRORELSENS HISTORIA.
Swedish. Sallskapet for Studier I Arbetarrorelsens Historia, Box 16 393, Stockholm 16 Sweden. **Tel** (46)13 39 20.

ISSN 0254-3931
SW
STUDIES AND RESEARCH - INTERNATIONAL SOCIAL SECURITY ASSOCIATION.
[Stud. res. - Int. Soc. Secur. Assoc.]. (1???)-. Periodical. English. Irregular (one or two volumes per year). 25.00F. International Social Security Association, Case Postale 1, CH-1211 Geneva 22 Switzerland. **Tel** 011 41 22 7996617, FAX 011 41 22 7986385.

LC HD4861
DD 331.11
US
●STUDIES IN INDUSTRY AND EMPLOYMENT.
See Industry and Production.

DD 301.45
US
STUDIES OF THE LABOR MARKET. REPORT.
Main/Corp Chicago Urban League. No. 1 (1968)-. Periodical. English. Chicago Urban League, 4500 South Michigan Avenue, Chicago IL 60653.

AT
SUCCESSFUL AND UNSUCCESSFUL JOB SEARCH EXPERIENCE, AUSTRALIA.
See Business and Economics-Abstracting, Bibliographies and Statistics.

ISSN 0039-5005
DD 331
US
SUMMARY OF LABOR ARBITRATION AWARDS.
(SUMMARY OF LABOR ARBITRATION AWARDS / AMERICAN ARBITRATION ASSOCIATION.). [Summ. labor arbitr. awards]. **Main/Corp** American Arbitration Association. No. 1 (Apr. 15, 1959)-. Periodical. English. Twelve times a year. $125.00. American Arbitration Association, 140 West 51st Street, New York NY 10020. **Tel** (212)484-4011, (212)484-4014, FAX (212)765-4874, telex 12463. **ED** Margaret Leibowitz. Index available. **Circ:** 5,000 (ctrl).
Desc: Arbitration dispute awards private industry.

ISSN 0229-365X
DD 331.88/09711
CN
SUMMARY OF PROCEEDINGS. ANNUAL CONVENTION - B.C. FEDERATION OF LABOUR (CLC).
(SUMMARY OF PROCEEDINGS / B.C. FEDERATION OF LABOUR.). [Summ. proc., Annu. conv. - B.C. Fed. Labour]. **Main/Corp** British Columbia Federation of Labour (C.L.C.). Convention. **VAT** Summary of Proceedings. Annual Convention - British Columbia Federation of Labour. Canadian Labour Congress (1966)-. Proceedings. English. One time a year. British Columbia Federation of Labour, 3110 Boundary Road, Burnaby British Columbia V5M 4A2 Canada. **Tel** (604)430-1421.
Continues British Columbia Federation of Labour (C.L.C.). Convention. Proceedings (1965), 0229-3641.

LC K1702 .I5317
DD 341.7/63
SZ
SUMMARY OF REPORTS (ARTICLES 19, 22 AND 35 OF THE CONSTITUTION).
Added/Corp International Labour Office. **VFOAT** Summary of Reports (Articles Nineteen, Twenty-Two, and Thirty-Five of the Constitution). 68th Session (1982)-. English. One time a year. Price varies. International Labour Office - ILO, Publications Sales Service, CH-1211 Geneva 22 Switzerland. **Tel** 011 41 22 7996111, FAX 011 41 22 7986253, telex 415 647 ilo ch. **(Subscription address:** International Labor Office / Albany, NY, 49 Sheridan Avenue, Albany NY 12210. **Tel** (518)436-9686.)
Formed by the union of Summary of Reports on Ratified Conventions (Articles 22 and 35 of the Constitution) **and** International Labour Office, Summary of Reports on Unratified Conventions and on Recommendations (Article 19 of the Constitution).

ISSN 0319-5082
DD 917.1/04/644
CN
SUMMER IN CANADA.
Added/Corp Canadian Bureau for International Education. **VFOAT** Ete au Canada. (1972)-. English (French). One time a year (Apr.). 1.50Can$. Canadian Bureau for International Education, 220 Laurier Avenue West, Suite 1100, Ottawa Ontario K1P 6A4 Canada. **Tel** (613)237-4820, FAX (613)237-1073.

NZ
SUPER BENEFITS.
VFOAT Super Benefits : a Review of Superannuation in New Zealand. English. Two times a year (April & Oct.). 28.00NZ$. Super Benefits, PO Box 3761, Wellington 1 New Zealand. **Tel** 011 64 4 795599, FAX 011 64 4 795599.

LC HD4903.5.U58 S94 **ISSN** 0362-5826
DD 658.3/005
US
SUPERVISOR'S EEO REVIEW, THE.
VFOAT EEO Review. **VAT** Supervisor's Equal Employment Opportunity Review. (19??)-. Periodical. English. Twelve times a year. $24.00. Executive Enterprises Publications Company Inc, 22 West 21st Street, 10th Floor, PO Box 10088, New York NY 10010-6990. **Tel** (212)645-7880, (800)332-8804, FAX (212)675-4883.

LC HD4965.5.U6 M4B **ISSN** 0092-5802
DD 331.2/81/65843097949
US
SUPERVISORY AND MIDDLE MANAGEMENT SALARY SURVEY (LOS ANGELES).
(SUPERVISORY AND MIDDLE MANAGEMENT SALARY SURVEY.). [Superv. middle manage. salary surv.]. **Main/Corp** Merchants and Manufacturers Association. 1971-. English. One time a year. 2300 Occidental Center, 1150 South Olive Street, Los Angeles CA 90015. **Supersedes** Supervisory Salary Survey.

US
SUPPLEMENT TO EMPLOYMENT AND UNEMPLOYMENT IN STATES AND LOCAL AREAS (SUPPL. TO THE MONTHLY).
(SUPPLEMENT TO EMPLOYMENT AND UNEMPLOYMENT IN STATES AND LOCAL AREAS MICROFORM.). Periodical. English. Irregular (monthly issues). $23.00 US; $28.75 other. US Department of Labor, 200 Constitution Avenue NW, Washington DC 20210. **Tel** (202)219-7316, FAX (202)219-7312.
Desc: Provides provisional, monthly estimates of the labor force, employment, and unemployment for States, metropolitan areas, counties, and cities of 50,000 or more. These estimates are used for economic analysis and administration of various Federal economic assistance programs.

LC HD8051 .A62 [HD5723] **ISSN** 8755-4712
DD 331.12/5/0973021
US
SUPPLEMENT TO EMPLOYMENT, HOURS, AND EARNINGS, STATES AND AREAS.
(SUPPLEMENT TO EMPLOYMENT, HOURS, AND EARNINGS, STATES AND AREAS, DATA FOR ... / U.S. DEPT. OF LABOR, BUREAU OF LABOR STATISTICS.). 1980-83-. English. One time a year. US Department of Labor, 200 Constitution Avenue NW, Washington DC 20210. **Tel** (202)219-7316, FAX (202)219-7312. **Continues** Supplement to Employment and Earnings, States and Areas, Data for ..., 0733-3625.

ISSN 0713-1763
DD 354.710083/5
CN
SUPPLEMENTARY CANADA PENSION PLAN CONTRIBUTION AND UNEMPLOYMENT INSURANCE PREMIUM TABLES.
(SUPPLEMENTARY CANADA PENSION PLAN CONTRIBUTION AND UNEMPLOYMENT INSURANCE PREMIUM TABLES FOR 10 - 13 - 22 PAY PERIODS.). [Suppl. Can. Pension Plan contrib. Unemploy. Insur. prem. tables]. **VFOAT** Tables Supplementaires et de Primes au Regime de Pensions du Canada et de Primes d'Assurance-Chomage pour 10 - 13 - 22 Periods de Paie. Periodical. French (English). Revenue Canada Taxation, 875 Heron Road, Ottawa Ontario K1A 0L8 Canada. **Tel** (613)957-3508, FAX (613)941-0914.

LC HD6278.C3 C32a **ISSN** 0317-4697
DD 331.1/0971
CN
SUPPLY, DEMAND AND SALARIES; NEW GRADUATES OF UNIVERSITIES AND COMMUNITY COLLEGES.
[Supply demand salaries, New grad. univ. community coll.]. **Added/Corp** Canada. Manpower and Immigration. Strategic Planning and Research. **VFOAT** Offre, Demande et Salaires; Nouveaux Diplomes d'Universites et de Colleges. **VAT** Offre, Demande et Salaires. Nouveaux Diplomes d'Universites et de Colleges. (1973)-. English (French). One time a year. Free. E A Bourque Memorial Building, 305 Rideau Street, Ottawa Ontario K1A 0J9 Canada. **Formed by the union of** Supply and Demand; New University Graduates., 0317-4719; Requirements and Salaries. University Graduates., 0317-4727 **and** Requirements and Salaries; Community College Graduates., 0317-4735.

Business and Economics — Labor

LC HD4966.S452 U526
ISSN 0730-6849
DD 331.2/81/000973
US
SUPPORT SERVICES SALARIES SURVEY. VFOAT Support Services Survey. 1st (1980)-. English. One time a year. $143.00. Dietrich Associates Inc, Box 511, Phoenixville PA 19460. **Tel** (610)935-1563.
Desc: Salary data on 86 positions by industry groups, firm size, and geographic areas across nine job families (administrative, secretarial, finance/accounting, personnel services, engineering services, marketing support, computer services, legal services and editing specifications.

LC HD4966.D372 U636
ISSN 0737-4887
DD 331.2/8100164/097471
US
SURVEY OF DATA PROCESSING SALARIES. [Surv. data process. salaries]. English. One time a year. $175.00 (members), $250.00 (nonmembers). New York Chamber of Commerce, Educational Foundation Inc, 200 Madison Avenue, New York NY 10016. **Tel** (212)561-2043. **ED** Maria Bruck and Chandra Mack. **Circ:** 200 (ctrl).
Desc: Salary survey of data processing positions from New York City employees.

LC HD.5848.7 .A25A
GM
SURVEY OF EMPLOYMENT, EARNINGS AND HOURS OF WORK. (Aug. 1986)-. English. Central Statistics Dept, Ministry of Economic Planning and Industrial Development, Banjul Gambia. **Continues** Quarterly Survey of Employment and Earnings.

LC TA158 .S93
ISSN 0738-1832
DD 331.2/81/616075
US
SURVEY OF LABORATORY TECHNICIAN SALARIES. (SURVEY OF LABORATORY TECHNICIAN SALARIES.). Added/Corp D. Dietrich Associates. VFOAT Laboratory Technician Salaries Survey. (19??)-. English. Dietrich Associates Inc, Box 511, Phoenixville PA 19460. **Tel** (610)935-1563.
Desc: Salary data as of May 1st for 7 position levels. Analyses made by industry groups, firm size and geographic regions. Data also on salary ranges, salary trends, and overtime pay.

LC HD6977 .S9
DD 339.4/2/0212
SZ
SURVEY OF LIVING COSTS IN MAJOR CITIES WORLDWIDE. Added/Corp Business International S.A. (19??)-. English. Business International, 12 14 Chemin Riev, 1208 Geneva Switzerland.

LC HD4966.M4 U67
ISSN 0737-4860
DD 331.2/81651/09747
US
SURVEY OF OFFICE SALARIES, PERSONNEL PRACTICES, AND BENEFITS. [Surv. off. salaries, pers. pract., benefits]. (1979)-. English. One time a year. $175.00 (members), $250.00 (nonmembers). New York Chamber of Commerce, Educational Foundation Inc, 200 Madison Avenue, New York NY 10016. **Tel** (212)561-2043. **ED** Maria Bruck and Chandra Mack. **Circ:** 300 (ctrl). **Continues** Annual Survey of Office Salaries and Hiring Rates.
Desc: Annual survey of salaries, personnel practices and benefits representing New York City employers non-exempt (clerical) positions.

ISSN 0843-3097
DD 331.25/2/0971
CN
SURVEY OF PENSION PLANS IN CANADA. (SURVEY OF PENSION PLANS IN CANADA / AUTHORED BY T.R. ARCHIBALD ... ET AL.]. [Surv. pension plans Can.]. Added/Corp Financial Executives Institute Canada. 7th Ed. (July 1, 1986/June 30, 1987)-. English. One time a year. 60.00Can$. Carswell / Canada, 2075 Kennedy Road, Scarborough Ontario M1T 3V4 Canada. **Tel** (416)298-5092, (800)387-5164, FAX (416)298-5094. **Continues** Financial Executives Institute Canada. Pension Sub-committee. Report on Survey of Pension Plans in Canada., 0226-1022.

LC HD4965.U6 S87
ISSN 0737-4879
DD 331.2/81658302/09747
US
SURVEY OF SUPERVISORY PERSONNEL SALARIES. [Surv. superv. pers. salaries]. English. One time a year. $175.00 (members), $250.00 (nonmembers). New York Chamber of Commerce, Educational Foundation Inc, 200 Madison Avenue, New York NY 10016. **Tel** (212)561-2043. **ED** Maria Bruck and Chandra Mack. **Circ:** 200 (ctrl).
Desc: Survey of supervisory salaries of New York City companies.

LC JQ4045 .D54
DD 331.7/61/35494
AT
SURVEY OF TEMPORARY AND EXEMPT EMPLOYMENT. Main/Corp Australia. Public Service Board. Project Services Branch. Statistical Section. (19??)-. Statistical Publication. English. Australia Public Service Board Project Service Branch, Statistical Section, PO Box 84 Territory 2600 Australia.

LC HD4966.D32 N457
NZ
SURVEY OF TOWN MILK PRODUCERS' INCOMES. English. Department of Statistics / New Zealand, PO Box 2922, Wellington New Zealand. **Tel** 011 64 4 4954600.

LC HD4965.2 .R46
DD 331.2/16
US
SURVEY REPORT ON VARIABLE PAY PROGRAMS / WYATT DATA SERVICES, ECS. Added/Corp Executive Compensation Service (U.S.). 2nd Ed. (1991/92)-. Trade Publication. English. One time a year. $640.00. ECS, Executive Compensation Service, Wyatt Data Services, 218 Route 17 North, Roselle Park NJ 07662-9832. **Tel** (201)843-1177, FAX (201)843-0101. available with charts. **Continues** Report on Variable Pay Programs.

IT
SUSPENDED
SVOLTA DEL SIDACATO, LA. (19??)-(19??). Italian. Twelve times a year. L20000. La Svolta Srl, Via Germanico 216, 00192 Rome Italy. **Tel** 011 39 6 85565305.

LC HD5801 .S8A
SW
SYSSELSATTNING OCH ARBETSTIDER. Main/Corp Sweden. Statistiska Centralbyran. VFOAT Employment Conditions and Hours of Work. (19??)-. Swedish (summaries and/or abstracts in English). SCB Statistiska Centralbyran, 11581 Stockholm Sweden.

LC HD6668.T73 T77
DD 331.88/113805/0941
UK
T & G RECORD. Added/Corp Transport and General Workers' Union (Great Britain). VFOAT T and G Record; T. & G. Record. (Sept. 1983)-. Newsletter. English. Twelve times a year. Transport & General Workers Union, Transport House Smith Square, London SW1 3JB United Kingdom. **ED** Chris Kaufman. **Bk Rev**, (Qty: 25). **Ad Acc, Adv Mgr:** Steve McGowan, **Tel** 071 831 8864. **Circ:** 200,000 (ctrl). **Continues** TGWU Record.

ISSN 1131-9615
SP
UDC 331.105.44(460) :37
T.E. TRABAJADORES DE LA ENSENANZA. VFOAT Trabajadores de la Ensenanza. (1979)-. Periodical. Spanish. Twelve times a year. Free on request. Sec Commun e Imagen Ct Ugt, Avenida de America 25, 28002 Madrid Spain. **Tel** 011 34 1 5897100.

II
TAMIL NADU LABOUR JOURNAL. Vol. 13, No. 2 (Feb. 1971)-. Periodical. English (Tamil). Twelve times a year. Commissioner of Labour, Thiru S Narashimhan I A S, Teynampet Madras 600 006 India. **Continues** Tamil Nadu Labour Gazette.

LC HD7106.G3 G46A
GW
TATIGKEITSBERICHT DES BUNDESVERSICHERUNGSAMTES. Main/Corp Germany (Federal Republic, 1949-). Bundesversicherungsamt. German. Bundesversicherungamst, Reichpietschufer 72-76, 1 30 Berlin Germany.

LC WMLC L 83/1188
AU
TATIGKEITSBERICHT / KAMMER FUER ARBEITER UND ANGESTELLTE FUER VORARLBERG. Main/Corp Kammer fuer Arbeiter und Angestellte fuer Vorarlberg. (19??)-. German. One time a year. Free on request. Kammer Arbeiter Angest Vorarlb, Widnau 4, 6800 Feldkirch Austria. **Tel** 055221 26656.

ISSN 0829-917X
DD 331.2/81371/009713
CN
SUSPENDED
TEACHERS' MONEY MATTERS. [Teach. money matters.]. VFOAT Money Matters; TMM. Vol. 1, No. 1, (Oct. 1, 1984)-(19??). Periodical. English. Eight times a year. Teachers Money Matters Ltd, 70 Scriven Road, Rural Route 1, Bailieboro Ontario K0L 1B0 Canada. **Tel** (705)939-6739.

LC LB2842.2 .T45A
DD 331.2/29
US
TEACHERS' RETIREMENT SYSTEM OF OKLAHOMA. VFOAT Rules and Procedures. 1981-82-. English. Four times a year. Teachers Retirement System of Oklahoma, PO Box 53524, Oklahoma City OK 73152. **Tel** (405)521-2387. **ED** Chris Menefee. **Continues** Oklahoma Teachers' Retirement System.

LC HD8101 .A44A
DD 331/.0971
CN
TEAMWORK IN INDUSTRY. English. Labour Management Consultation Branch, Department of Labour, Ottawa Ontario K1A 0J2 Canada. **Continues** Teamwork in Industry.

TU
TEBANEWS. Turkish. $450.00. Teba Publishing Advertising Market, LTD Selanik Cad 26 13, Kizilay Ankara Turkey.

LC TA158 .T38
DD 331.2/973/021
US
TECHNICIAN AND SKILLED TRADES PERSONNEL REPORT. Added/Corp Executive Compensation Service (U.S.). VFOAT Technician and Skilled Trades. (198?)-. Trade Publication. English. One time a year. $470.00. ECS, Executive Compensation Service, Wyatt Data Services, 218 Route 17 North, Roselle Park NJ 07662-9832. **Tel** (201)843-1177, FAX (201)843-0101. **ED** Michael Marvin. **Continues** American Management Association. Technician Report - Executive Compensation Service, 0093-8750.

US
TITLE CHANGE
TEXAS PLANNING INFORMATION. Added/Corp Texas Employment Commission. JTPA Special Projects Unit. (198?)-(199?). English. Texas Employment Commission, 101 East 15th Street, Room 208T, Austin TX 78778. **Tel** (512)463-2619. available on microfiche. **Continues** Annual Planning Information Report (Texas Employment Commission). **Continued by** Texas Service Delivery Area Planning Information.

ISSN 0040-4640
US
TEXAS PUBLIC EMPLOYEE. Added/Corp Texas Public Employees Association. (1946)-. Periodical. English. Four times a year. $5.00. Texas Public Employee Association, Drawer 12217 Capitol Station, Austin TX 78711. **Tel** (512)476-2691. **ED** Bill Warren. **Ad Acc. Circ:** 15,000.
Desc: Items of interest to Texas state government employees and families. Includes politics, management, general concerns.

US
TEXAS WORKERS COMPENSATION & SAFETY REPORTER. See Industrial Health and Safety.

LC HD7727.3.Z8 H447
FI
TOIMIPISTEET HELSINGISSA. VFOAT Arbetslokalerna i Helsingfors. (19??)-. Finnish (Finnish). Helsingin Kaupungin Tilastokeskus, Toolontorink 2B, 00260 Helsinki 26 Finland.

LC HD2346.J3 T634
JA
TOKUTEI SANGYO SHOKIBO KIGYO RODO JOKEN JITTAI CHOSA HOKOKU. Added/Corp Japan. Rodosho. Tokei Johobu. (19??)-. Japanese. Rodo Daijin Kambo Tokei Johobu, Tokyo Japan.

LC HD1537.S72 T65
DD 305.555
CE
TOLILALAR PATAI. Periodical. Tamil (Tamil). Twelve times a year.

ISSN 1065-5107
US
●**TOM ALLAIRE HRD REPORT.** VFOAT HRD Report. (1993)-. Periodical. English. Six times a year. $65.00. HRD Report, 301 North Harrison Street, Suite 424, Princeton NJ 08540-3512.

US
TOMORROW'S JOBS, TOMORROW'S WORKERS. CENTRAL NEW YORK REGION / NEW YORK STATE DEPARTMENT OF LABOR, DIVISION OF RESEARCH AND STATISTICS. Added/Corp New York (State) Dept. of Labor. Division of Research and Statistics. New York (State). Bureau of Labor Market Information. VFOAT Central New York Region. (1991)-. English. **Continues** Labor Market Assessment, Occupational Supply and Demand. Syracuse Area.

US
TOMORROW'S JOBS, TOMORROW'S WORKERS. FINGER LAKES REGION. Added/Corp New York (State). Dept. of Labor. Division of Research and Statistics. New York (State). Bureau of Labor Market Information. VFOAT Finger Lakes Region. (1991)-. English. New York State Department of Labor / Albany, 401 Harriman, Division of Research and Statistics, State Office Building Campus, Albany NY

Business and Economics —Labor

12240. **Tel** (518)457-6649. **Continues** Labor Market Assessment, Occupational Supply and Demand. Rochester Area.

US

TOMORROW'S JOBS, TOMORROW'S WORKERS. HUDSON VALLEY REGION / NEW YORK STATE DEPARTMENT OF LABOR, DIVISION OF RESEARCH AND STATISTICS. **Added/Corp** New York (State). Dept. of Labor. Division of Research and Statistics. New York (State). Bureau of Labor Market Information. **VFOAT** Hudson Valley Region. (1991)-. English. New York State Department of Labor / Albany, 401 Harriman, Division of Research and Statistics, State Office Building Campus, Albany NY 12240. **Tel** (518)457-6649. **Formed by the union of** Labor Market Assessment, Occupational Supply and Demand. Poughkeepsie Area **and** Labor Market Assessment, Occupational Supply and Demand. Westchester County.

US

TOMORROW'S JOBS, TOMORROW'S WORKERS. LONG ISLAND REGION / NEW YORK STATE DEPARTMENT OF LABOR, DIVISION OF RESEARCH AND STATISTICS. **Added/Corp** New York (State). Dept. of Labor. Division of Research and Statistics. New York (State). Bureau of Labor Market Information. **VFOAT** Long Island Region. (1991)-. English. New York State Department of Labor / Albany, 401 Harriman, Division of Research and Statistics, State Office Building Campus, Albany NY 12240. **Tel** (518)457-6649. **Continues** Labor Market Assessment, Occupational Supply and Demand. Nassau-Suffolk.

US

TOMORROW'S JOBS, TOMORROW'S WORKERS. MOHAWK VALLEY REGION. **Added/Corp** New York (State) Dept. of Labor. Division of Research and Statistics. New York (State). Bureau of Labor Market Information. **VFOAT** Mohawk Valley Region. (1991)-. English. One time a year. New York State Department of Labor / Albany, 401 Harriman, Division of Research and Statistics, State Office Building Campus, Albany NY 12240. **Tel** (518)457-6649. **Continues** Labor Market Assessment, Occupational Supply and Demand. Utica-Rome Area.

US

TOMORROW'S JOBS, TOMORROW'S WORKERS. NEW YORK CITY / NEW YORK STATE DEPARTMENT OF LABOR, DIVISION OF RESEARCH AND STATISTICS. **Added/Corp** New York (State). Dept. of Labor. Division of Research and Statistics. New York (State). Bureau of Labor Market Information. **VFOAT** Tomorrow's Jobs, Tomorrow's Workers'. New York City. (1991)-. English. New York State Department of Labor / Albany, 401 Harriman, Division of Research and Statistics, State Office Building Campus, Albany NY 12240. **Tel** (518)457-6649. **Continues** Labor Market Assessment, Occupational Supply and Demand. New York City.

US

TOMORROW'S JOBS, TOMORROW'S WORKERS. NORTH COUNTRY REGION. **Added/Corp** New York (State). Dept. of Labor. Division of Research and Statistics. New York (State). Bureau of Labor Market Information. **VFOAT** North Country Region. (1991)-. English. New York State Department of Labor / Albany, 401 Harriman, Division of Research and Statistics, State Office Building Campus, Albany NY 12240. **Tel** (518)457-6649.

US

TOMORROW'S JOBS, TOMORROW'S WORKERS. SOUTHERN TIER REGION / NEW YORK STATE DEPARTMENT OF LABOR, DIVISION OF RESEARCH AND STATISTICS. **Added/Corp** New York (State). Dept. of Labor. Division of Research and Statistics. New York (State). Bureau of Labor Market Information. **VFOAT** South Tier Region. (1991)-. English. **Formed by the union of** Labor Market Assessment, Occupational Supply and Demand. Binghamton Area **and** Labor Market Assessment, Occupational Supply and Demand. Elmira Area.

US

TOMORROW'S JOBS, TOMORROW'S WORKERS. WESTERN NEW YORK REGION / NEW YORK STATE DEPARTMENT OF LABOR, DIVISION OF RESEARCH AND STATISTICS. **Added/Corp** New York (State). Dept. of Labor. Division of Research and Statistics. New York (State). Bureau of Labor Market Information. (1991)-. English. New York State Department of Labor / Albany, 401 Harriman, Division of Research and Statistics, State Office Building Campus, Albany NY 12240. **Tel** (518)457-6649. **Continues** Labor Market Assessment, Occupational Supply and Demand. Buffalo-Niagara Falls CMSA.

ISSN 0262-2548
UK

TOPICS. (19??)-. Periodical. English. Four times a year. Employment Relations, 80 Newmarket Road, Resource Center, Cambridge CB5 8DZ United Kingdom. **Tel** 011 44 1223 315944.
Ind/Abst Curr. Cit.

ISSN 0896-7776
DD 658 US

TOTAL EMPLOYEE INVOLVEMENT. See Business and Economics-Management.

HO

TRABAJO. (1978)-. Periodical. Spanish. Colonia de las Colinas, 5A Avenida No 179-G, Tegucigalpa D C Honduras.

CL

TRABAJOS & NEGOCIOS. **VFOAT** Trabajos y Negocios. (Oct. 17, 1990)-. Periodical. Spanish. Twenty-six times a year.

LC HD4805 .T7
DD 331.88/09417 IE

TRADE UNION INFORMATION. Vol. 1, No. 1 (May 1949)-. Periodical. English. Irregular. Irish Congress of Trade Unions, 19 Raglan Road, Dublin 4 Ireland. **Tel** 011 353 1 680641.
Desc: Includes summaries of Labour Court recommendations.

LC HD8682 .T7
DD 331.88/0954 II

TRADE UNION RECORD. Added/Corp All-India Trade Union Congress. (1943)-. Periodical. English. Twenty-six times a year. $15.00. New Age Printing Press, Rani Jhansi Road, New Delphi India. **(Subscription address:** Prints India, 11 Darya Ganj, New Delhi 110002 India. **Tel** 011 91 11 3268645, FAX 011 91 11 3275542, telex 31-61087 PRIN-IN.**)**

LC HD6891 .A23
DD 331.88/0994 AT

TRADE UNION STATISTICS: AUSTRALIA. See Business and Economics-Abstracting, Bibliographies and Statistics.

UK

TRADE UNIONS & EMPLOYERS ORGANIZATIONS. (19??)-. Periodical. English. Four times a year. £105.00 Europe; £110.00 other (institutions). Longman Group Ltd., Fourth Avenue, Longman House, Harlow Essex CM19 5SR United Kingdom. **Tel** 011 44 1279 429655, FAX 011 44 1279 431067, telex 81259.

LC HD6350.R318 T7 ISSN 0041-0837
DD 331.88/11/3850973 US

TRAIN DISPATCHER (BERWYN), THE. (THE TRAIN DISPATCHER.). **Added/Corp** American Train Dispatchers Association. (1919)-. Periodical. English. Four times a year. $12.00. American Train Dispatcher, 1401 South Harlem Avenue, Berwyn IL 60402. **Tel** (708)795-5656. **Supersedes** Transit.

LC HD5723 .A43
DD 331.11/0973/05 US
CEASED

TRAINING AND EMPLOYMENT REPORT OF THE SECRETARY OF LABOR. **Main/Corp** United States. Dept. of Labor. **Added/Corp** United States. Employment and Training Administration. (1985)-(19??). English. Superintendent of Documents, US Government Printing Office, Washington DC 20402. **Tel** (202)275-3328, FAX (202)786-2377. **Continues** United States. President. Employment and Training Report of the President.

LC HF5549.5.T7 C274A ISSN 0318-7225
DD 331.2/592/0971 CN

TRAINING IN INDUSTRY. [Train. ind.].
Main/Corp Statistics Canada. Student Information Section. **VFOAT** Formation dans l'Industrie. Multiple languages (English and French). $1.00. Information Canada, 171 Slater Street, Ottawa Ontario K1A 0S9 Canada. **Tel** (819)997-1095.

LC HD7106.U5 A688a ISSN 0094-422X
DD 331.2/52 US

TRANSCRIBINGS, ANNUAL CONFERENCE - AMERICAN SOCIETY OF PENSION ACTUARIES. Main/Corp American Society of Pension Actuaries. (19??)-. English. One time a year. $12.50. American Society of Pension Actuaries, 1700 K Street North West, Suite 404, Washington DC 20006.

ISSN 1024-2589
BE

●**TRANSFER BRUSSELS.** (1995)-. English. Four times a year. $44.77. European Trade Union Institut, boulevard Emile Jacqmain 155, B-1210 Brussels Belgium.

LC HD6668.R3 R3
DD 380.5/0941 UK

TRANSPORT REVIEW. See Transportation-Railroads.

ISSN 0757-3065
FR

TRAVAIL (PARIS, FRANCE). (TRAVAIL.).
[Travail]. No. 1 (Jan. 1983)-. Periodical. French. Irregular. AEROT, Revue Travail, 64 rue de la Folie Mericourt, 75011 Paris France.
Ind/Abst PAIS Int. Print.

ISSN 0707-7017
DD 331.7/67/609714 CN

TRAVAILLEUR (QUEBEC). (LE TRAVAILLEUR.). Vol. 1 (April 1978)-. Periodical. French. Four times a year. Free to members. Federation des Travailleurs du Papier et de la Foret, 155 Est boulevard Charest, Quebec Quebec G1K 3G6 Canada.
Ind/Abst Am. Hist. Life (19??-19??).

LC HD5768.I7 IE

TREND OF EMPLOYMENT AND UNEMPLOYMENT, THE. **Main/Corp** Ireland. Central Statistics Office. 1926/35-. English. Irregular. Government Publications, 4 5 Harcourt Road, Dublin 2 Ireland. **Tel** 011 353 1 6613111 ext.4005. **Circ:** 1,000.

ISSN 1019-4126
SZ

TRENDS IN SOCIAL SECURITY.
Added/Corp International Social Security Association. No. 1 (June 1992)-. Periodical. English (French, German and Spanish). Four times a year. Free on request. International Social Security Association, Case Postale 1, CH-1211 Geneva 22 Switzerland. **Tel** 011 41 22 7996617, FAX 011 41 22 7986385.

LC HD7096.U6 N86
DD 331.13/79756 US

TRENDS (NORTH CAROLINA. LABOR MARKET INFORMATION DIVISION). (TRENDS.). Oct. 1981-. Periodical. English. Twelve times a year. Employment Security Commission of North Carolina, Labor Market Information Division, 200 West Jones Street, PO Box 25903, Raleigh NC 27611. **Continues** Employment Security Trends (North Carolina. Employment Security Commission).

LC HD6820.6.Z7 T75
DD 331.88/11/380509598 IO

TRIENNIAL REPORT - TRANSPORT WORKERS UNION. **Main/Corp** Kesatuan Pekerja P2 S Pengangkutan. (19??)-. English. Transport Workers Union, Transport Workers House, 21 Jalan Barat, Petaling Jaya Indonesia.

LC HD8537 .T78
PL

TRYBUNA SAMORZADU ROBOTNICZEGO. Periodical. Polish. RSW Prasa-Kriazka-Ruch, Centrala Kolportazu Prasy i Wydawnictw, Towarowa 28, 00-958 Warsaw Poland.

UK

TURKEY NEWSLETTER : MONTHLY PUBLICATION OF THE COMMITTEE FOR DEFENCE OF DEMOCRATIC RIGHTS IN TURKEY. See Political Science-Socialism, Communism, Anarchism, Utopianism.

ISSN 0039-8659
US

TWU EXPRESS. Main/Corp Transport Workers Union of America. **Added/Corp** Transport Workers Union of America. Express. **VAT** Transport Workers Union Express. (19??)-. Periodical. English. Twelve times a year. $2.00. Transport Workers Union America, 80 West End Avenue, New York NY 10023. **Tel** (212)873-6000.

LC HD ISSN 1230-9486
DD 331 PL
UDC 331.10
TITLE CHANGE

TYGODNIK POPULARNY. [Tyg. Pop.].
(1993)-(1993). Periodical. Polish. **(Subscription address:** Ars Polona-Ruch, PO Box 1001, Krakowskie Przedmiescie 7, 00-068 Warsaw Poland. **Tel** 011 48 22

Business and Economics —Labor

261201.) *Continues* Tygodnik Popularny Zwiazkowiec, 0867-5961. *Continued by* Nowy Tygodnik Popularny, 1230-9494.

LC HD ISSN 0867-5961
DD 331 PL
UDC 331.105
TITLE CHANGE

TYGODNIK POPULARNY ZWIAZKOWIEC. [Tyg. Pop. Zw.]. **VFOAT** Zwiazkowiec. (1990)-(1993). Periodical. Polish. **(Subscription address:** Ars Polona-Ruch, PO Box 1001, Krakowskie Przedmiescie 7, 00-068 Warsaw Poland. **Tel** 011 48 22 261201.) *Continues* Tygodnik Zwiazkowiec, 0867-597X. *Continued by* Tygodnik Popularny, 1230-9486.

LC HD5715.5.F5 F57A
FI

TYOLLISYYSKURSSIN SUORITTANEET. Main/Corp Finland. Tilastokeskus. (19??)-. Finnish. Tilastokeskus, PL 504, Annankatu 44, 00101 Helsinki Finland. **Tel** 011 358 0 17341, FAX 011 358 0 17342474, telex 1002111 TILASTO SF.

LC HD5797.3 .A28B
FI

TYOVOIMA-ARVIO. Main/Corp Finland. Tilastokeskus. **VFOAT** Arbetskraftprognose. Multiple languages (Finnish and Swedish). Tilastokeskus, PL 504, Annankatu 44, 00101 Helsinki Finland. **Tel** 011 358 0 17341, FAX 011 358 0 17342474, telex 1002111 TILASTO SF.

LC HD8582 .U617
FR

U.G.T. : BOLETIN DE LA UNION GENERAL DE TRABAJADORES DE ESPANA. Main/Corp Union General de Trabajadores de Espana. **VAT** Union General de Trabajadores: Boletin de la Union General de Trabajadores de Espana. Periodical. Spanish. Union General de Trabajodores, B P No 1520-31, Toulouse France 31000.

US

U.S. DEPARTMENT OF LABOR ADVISORY COMMITTEE DIRECTORY. Main/Corp United States. Dept. of Labor. Directory. English. One time a year. US Department of Labor, 200 Constitution Avenue NW, Washington DC 20210. **Tel** (202)219-7316, FAX (202)219-7312.

US

U.S. DEPARTMENT OF LABOR PROGRAM HIGHLIGHTS. Main/Corp United States. Dept. of Labor. English. US Department of Labor, 200 Constitution Avenue NW, Washington DC 20210. **Tel** (202)219-7316, FAX (202)219-7312.

LC HF5382.5.U5 U2 ISSN 0890-5959
DD 331.7/02/0973 US
TITLE CHANGE

U.S. EMPLOYMENT OPPORTUNITIES. See Occupations and Careers.

LC HD6504 .U18 ISSN 0897-1439
DD 331.88/0973/021 US

U.S. UNION SOURCEBOOK. (U.S. UNION SOURCEBOOK : MEMBERSHIP, FINANCES, STRUCTURE, DIRECTORY / BY LEO TROY, NEIL SHEFLIN.). [U. S. union sourceb.]. **VFOAT** U.S. Union Source Book; Union Sourcebook. **VAT** United States Union Sourcebook. 1st Ed. (1985)-. English. Irregular. IRDIS, PO Box 226 WOB, West Orange NJ 07052. **Tel** (201)731-1554.

LC HD6350.P6 U5 ISSN 0095-7763
DD 331.88/19/60971 US

UA JOURNAL. Added/Corp United Association of Journeymen and Apprentices of the Plumbing and Pipe Fitting Industry. **VAT** United Association Journal. Vol. 79, No. 5 (May 1967)-. Periodical. English. Twelve times a year. United Association of Journeymen and Apprentices of the Plumbing and Pipe Fitting Industry, Washington DC 20402. **ED** Charles J. Habig. **Circ:** 300,000 (ctrl). *Continues* United Association of Journeymen and Apprentices of the Plumbing and Pipe Fitting Industry. Journal.
 Desc: Promotes the point of view held by union members.

ISSN 0890-040X
US

UAW FACTS. VAT United Auto Workers Facts. (198?)-. Periodical. English. Twelve times a year. $1.50. UAW Local 600, 10550 Dix Avenue, Deereborne MI 48120. **Circ:** 35,000. *Continues* Ford Facts, 0733-8422.

ISSN 0041-5065
US

UE NEWS (U.S. EDITION). (UE NEWS.). **Added/Corp** United Electrical, Radio and Machine Workers of America. **VAT** United Electrical News. Vol. 1 (Jan. 1, 1939)-. Trade Publication. English. Seventeen times a year. $10.00. United Electrical Radio, 535 Smithfield Street, 2400 Oliver Building, Pittsburgh PA 15222. **Tel** (412)471-8919. **ED** Peter Gilmore. **Circ:** 40,000 (ctrl). available on microfilm and microfiche from the publisher.
 Desc: Trade union newspaper.
 Ind/Abst Work Relat. Abstr.

LC HD6350.F7 U36 ISSN 0195-0363
DD 331.88/164/00973 US

UFCW ACTION. Added/Corp United Food and Commercial Workers International Union. **VFOAT** Action. **VAT** United Food and Commercial Workers Action. Vol. 1, No. 1 (July 1979)-. Periodical. English. Six times a year. United Food & Commercial Workers International, 1775 K Street Northwest, Washington DC 20006. **Tel** (202)223-3111. **ED** William H Wynn. **Circ:** 1,300,000 (ctrl). available on microfilm from University Microfilms International (UMI). Formed by the union of Retail Clerks Advocate, 0034-6039 and Butcher Workman, 0007-7267.
 Desc: Labor union membership publication with articles regarding union members and political and social issues affecting the union member.
 Ind/Abst Work Relat. Abstr.

ISSN 8750-328X
DD 331 US

UFCW LEADERSHIP UPDATE. [UFCW leadersh. update]. **VFOAT** U.F.C.W. Leadership Update. **VAT** United Food and Commercial Workers Leadership Update. Periodical. English. Twelve times a year. UFCW, 1775 K Street NW, Washington DC 20006. **Tel** (202)223-3111. **ED** William H Wynn. **Circ:** 2,300 (ctrl).

ISSN 1060-3840
US

UFCW LOCAL 1428 MESSENGER. Main/Corp United Food and Commercial Workers Union. Local 1428. **VFOAT** Messenger. **VAT** United Food and Commercial Workers Local 1428 Messenger. Vol. 1, No. 1 (Nov. 1991)-. Periodical. English. Twelve times a year. Local 1428, 375 North Towne Avenue, Pomona CA 91766. *Continues* Union News.

ISSN 8755-1845
DD 331 US

UFF REACH. [UFF reach]. **VFOAT** U.F.F. Reach; Reach. **VAT** United Faculty of Florida Reach. Vol. 1, No. 1 (Sept.-Oct. 1979)-. Periodical. English. Three times a year. $5.00. United Faculty of Florida, 201 S Monroe/Suite 201, Tallahassee FL 32301. **Tel** (904)224-8220.

ISSN 0745-0052
US

UIW NEWSLETTER. Added/Corp Seafarers' International Union of North America. **VFOAT** U.I.W. Newsletter. **VAT** United Industrial Workers Newsletter. (19??)-. Newsletter. English. Twelve times a year. United Industrial Workers, Seafarers International Union, 675 4th Avenue, Brooklyn NY 11232.

ISSN 1064-5039
DD 331 US

UNCONVENTIONAL WISDOM (NEW YORK, N.Y.). (UNCONVENTIONAL WISDOM.). [Unconv. wisdom]. **Added/Corp** Manpower Plus (Firm). Issue 1 (Sept. 1992)-. Newsletter. English. Ten times a year. $120.00. Audrey Freedman & Associates, 111 Broadway, 5th Floor, New York NY 10006. **Tel** (212)406-2148, FAX (212)587-1929.

LC HD7096.C2 A34 ISSN 0829-1098
DD 368.4/1/00971021 CN

UNEMPLOYMENT INSURANCE STATISTICS (OTTAWA). See Insurance.

LC KD3110.A59 R83
DD 344.41/012596 344.10412596 UK

UNFAIR DISMISSAL. VFOAT IRLR Guide to Unfair Dismissal. 1st Ed. (1983)-. English. One time a year. Marketing Department, Industrial Relations Services, 18-20 Highbury Place, London N5 1QP United Kingdom. **ED** Michael Rubenstein and Yvonne Frost.

LC HD5725.M4 M38b
DD 331.1/26/09744 US

UNFILLED JOB OPENINGS. Main/Corp Massachusetts. Occupation/Industry Research Dept. (19??)-. English. One time a year. Charles F. Hurley Building, Government Center, Boston MA 02114.

BE

UNICE INFORMATION. Main/Corp UNICE. **VFOAT** Information. **VAT** Union of Industrial and Employers' Confederation of Europe Information. (1992)-. Periodical. English. Six times a year.

LC HD8083.A4 N63 ISSN 0362-4188
DD 331.1/0977 S 331.89/0977 US

UNION CONTRACT EXPIRATIONS IN THE NORTH CENTRAL REGION 5. (UNION CONTRACT EXPIRATIONS IN THE NORTH CENTRAL REGION V. / U.S. DEPARTMENT OF LABOR, BUREAU OF LABOR STATISTICS, NORTH CENTRAL REGION V.). **VAT** Union Contract Expirations in the North Central Region Five. English. One time a year. US Department of Labor Bureau of Labor Statistics / Chicago, 230 South Dearborn Street, 9th Floor, Chicago IL 60604. **Tel** (312)353-7226, FAX (312)353-1886.

US

UNION DEMOCRACY REVIEW. Added/Corp Association for Union Democracy. (1972)-. English. Six times a year (Jan., March, May, July, Sept., Nov.). $15.00. Association for Union Democracy, 500 State Street, 2nd Floor, Brooklyn NY 11217. **Tel** (718)855-6650. **ED** Herman Benson. Index available. **Bk Rev. Circ:** 2,500. *Supersedes* Union Democracy in Action.
 Desc: Articles on the trade union movement emphasizing promotion of principles and practices of internal union democracy and reports and analysis in the field of union democracy law.

ISSN 0709-9118
DD 331.88/1184099714 CN

UNION DES ECRIVAINS QUEBECOIS. (UNION DES ECRIVAINS QUEBECOIS : BULLETIN PERIODIQUE.). **VFOAT** Bulletin Periodique. Vol. 1, No. 1 (15 Dec. 1979)-. Bulletin. French. Irregular. Free. Union des Ecrivains Quebecois, 1030 rue Cherrier/Bureau 510, Montreal Quebec H2L 1H9 Canada. **Tel** (514)526-6653.

LC S ISSN 0317-2279
DD 630/.6/2714 CN

UNION DES PRODUCTEURS AGRICOLES. Main/Corp Union des Producteurs Agricoles. 1-. Monographic series. French. Price varies per volume. Union de Producteurs Agricoles, 555 boulevard Roland Therrien, Longueuil Quebec J4H 3Y9 Canada. **Tel** (514)679-0535.

ISSN 0715-6359
DD 331.88/117902/060714 CN

UNION EXPRESS. (L'UNION EXPRESS.). [Union express]. **Main/Corp** Union des Artistes. No. 1 (1982)-. Periodical. French. Six times a year. Free on request. Union des Artistes, 1290 rue St. Denis, Montreal Quebec H2X 3J7 Canada. **Tel** (514)288-6682. **Ad Acc. Circ:** 5,000.
 Desc: Quebec culture, cultural policies, proceedings of the administrative council of the artists' union and opinions of the members (tv, film, theater, dance, advertising, etc.).

LC HD6500 .U6
US

UNION LABOR ADVOCATE. DEVOTED TO THE INTEREST OF ALL UNION LABOR AND LABELS. Added/Corp Chicago Federation of Labor. Vol. 1 (1901)-. Periodical. English. Twelve times a year.

ISSN 0894-7775
US

UNION LABOR JOURNAL. Vol. 80, No. 2 (April 1983)-. Periodical. English. Twelve times a year. Kern County Labor Council, 200 West Jeffrey, Bakersfield CA 93305. **Tel** (805)324-6451. **ED** Jack Brigham. **Circ:** 6,300. *Continues* Kern, Inyo, and Mono Counties Union Labor Journal (1979).

ISSN 0041-6924
DD 331 US

UNION LABOR NEWS (MADISON, WIS.). (UNION LABOR NEWS.). [Union labor news]. (19??)-. English. Twelve times a year. $5.00. Union Labor News Publishers Ltd, 1602 South Park Street/Room 107, Madison WI 53715. **Tel** (608)256-5111. **ED** James Cavanaugh. **Bk Rev. Ad Acc. Circ:** 18,000 (ctrl).
 Desc: Local, state, and national labor issues, politics on same levels, health and safety issues.

ISSN 0744-9658
US

UNION REPORTER (DIAMOND BAR, CALIF.). (UNION REPORTER.). Periodical. English. Twelve times a year. $4.00. Local 47, IBEW, 600 North Diamond Bar Boulevard, Diamond Bar CA 91765.

LC HD8051 .A62 ISSN 0093-0784
DD 331/.0973 US

UNION WAGES AND HOURS : GROCERY STORES. Main/Corp United States. Bureau of Labor Statistics. 1971-. English. US Department of Labor, 200 Constitution Avenue NW, Washington DC 20210. **Tel** (202)219-7316, FAX (202)219-7312.

Business and Economics —Labor

ISSN 0707-0063
DD 331.4/0971 CN
SUSPENDED
UNION WOMAN. Vol. 1 (Nov. 1977). Periodical. English. Irregular. $7.74. Organized Working Women, 15 Gervais Drive/Suite 301, Don Mills Ontario M3C 1Y8 Canada.

ISSN 0748-6839
US
UNION WRITES NEWSLETTER.
Added/Corp New York State Public Employees Federation, AFL-CIO. Division 234. Capital District Dept. of Social Services. Vol. 1, No. 1 (June 1984)-. Newsletter. English. New York State Public Employees Federation AFL-CIO, PO Box 7248, Albany NY 12224. **Tel** (518)474-7825. **ED** Victor Batorsky and Doris Williams. **Bk Rev. Ad Acc. Circ:** 1,400 (ctrl).
Desc: It represents 1,435 professional employees in the Department of Social Services of New York State.

BB
UNIONIST, THE. Periodical. English. Four times a year. Barbados Workers' Union, Corner Nelson and Fairchild Streets, Bridgetown Barbados. **ED** Orlando Scott. **Circ:** 500 (ctrl).

LC HD6350.M6 U5 **ISSN** 0041-7327
DD 331 US
UNITED MINE WORKERS JOURNAL.
[United Mine Work. j.]. **Main/Corp** United Mine Workers of America. **Added/Corp** United Mine Workers of America. Journal. (1891)-. Periodical. English. Twelve times a year. $25.00. United Mine Workers Journal, 900 15th Street NW, Washington DC 20005. **Tel** (202)842-7244. **ED** Greg Hawthorne. **Bk Rev. Circ:** 250,000.
Desc: Issues relevant to coal miners. Topics include health, safety, organizing, coal legislation, black lung, unemployment, etc.
Ind/Abst Coal Abstr. (19??-); Work Re at. Abstr. (19??-).

LC HD2425 .U53 **ISSN** 0093-6685
DD 338/.0025/73 US
UNITED STATES TRADE ASSOCIATIONS. (19??)-. English. $10.00. Johnson Publishing Company / Colorado, PO Box 455, 8th and Vanburen, Loveland CO 80537. **Tel** (303)667-0652.

LC HD4861
DD 331.11 CN
●**UP TO DATE [HUMAN RESOURCE].** (1993)-. English. Twelve times a year. 64.00Can$. Up to Date Publications, 3160 Steeles Avenue E, Suite 215, Markham Ontario L3R 4G9 Canada. **Tel** (905)479-7895, FAX (905)479-2990. **ED** Alan Roadburg. Index available. cum. index.

US
UPPER PENINSULA'S LABOR MARKET NEWS. Added/Corp Michigan Employment Security Commission. Bureau of Research and Statistics. Information and Reports Section. Vol. 12, No. 1 (Mar. 1992)-. Periodical. English. Twelve times a year. Detroit Employment Security Commission, 7310 Woodward Castro, Room 520, Detroit MI 48202. **Tel** (313)876-5427. **Continues** Upper Peninsula Labor Market Review (1981).

LC HD8730.5 .A375
KO
URI SASANG. Added/Corp Sahoe Sasang Yonguso (Korea). Vol. 1 (1991)-. Periodical. Korean. Saebyokpyol, Kodae Kyouhoegwan 608-Ho, 34 Kongyong-Dong Chongno-Ku, Seoul Korea.

UK
USDAW TODAY : THE VOICE OF THE UNION OF SHOP, DISTRIBUTIVE AND ALLIED WORKERS. Added/Corp Union of Shop, Distributive and Allied Workers. (Jan. 19##)-. Periodical. English. Twelve times a year. Union Shop Distribution and Allied WRRK, 188 Wilmslow Road M14 6LJ United Kingdom. **Tel** 011 44 161 2242804. **Continues** Dawn (Manchester, England).

US
UTAH LABOR MARKET REPORT.
Added/Corp Utah. Dept. of Employment Security. (August 1983)-. Periodical. English. Twelve times a year. Free. Utah Department of Employment Security, 174 Social Hall Avenue, PO Box 11249, Salt Lake City UT 84147. **Tel** (801)533-2400. **Continues** Utah Labor Market Information.

US
UTILITY WORKERS' LIGHT. Added/Corp Utility Workers Union of America. **VFOAT** Light. Vol. 37, No. 3 (Mar. 1992)-. Periodical. English. Twelve times a year. Utility Workers Union of America AFL-CIO, 815 Sixteenth Street NW, Washington DC 20006. **Tel** (202)347-8105. **Continues** Light.

LC HD6515.R1 U5 **ISSN** 0098-5937
DD 331.88/11/3850973 US
UTU NEWS. Main/Corp United Transportation Union. **VAT** United Transportation Union News. Vol. 4, No. 21 (May 27, 1972)-. Periodical. English. One time a week. United Transportation Union / Ohio, 14600 Detroit Avenue, Cleveland OH 44107. available on microfilm and microfiche from University Microfilms International (UMI). **Continues** UTU Transportation News.

ISSN 0383-2015
DD 331.88/11/3850971 CN
UTU NEWS CANADA. Main/Corp United Transportation Union. **VFOAT** U T U, "Progress Through Unity". Vol. 4, No. 5 (May 1973)-. Periodical. English (summaries and/or abstracts in French). Six times a year. Free on request. United Transportation Union / Canada, 99 Bank Street, Metro House/Suite 709, Ottawa Ontario K1P 6B9 Canada. **Tel** (613)238-3717. **ED** G.K. Strickland. **Circ:** 20,000 (ctrl). **Continues** United Transportation Union. UTU Transportation News Canada., 0383-2007.

LC HD4811 .D5
II
VARKARSA, DI. Periodical. Hindi (Hindi). 3.00.

LC HX7 .V46 **ISSN** 1121-0680
DD 335/.005 IT
VENTESIMO SECOLO. See Political Science-Socialism, Communism, Anarchism, Utopianism.

LC RC967 .V467
NE
VERKORT OVERZICHT ZIEKTEVERZUIM. Dutch. One time a year. Free. Nederlands Instituut voor Praeventieve Gezondheidszorg/TNO, Wassenaarseweg 56, Postbus 124, 2300 AC Leiden Netherlands. **Tel** 011 31 71 17888, FAX 011 31 71 176382. **Circ:** 1,000 (ctrl).

LC HD7106.S6 S65A
SA
VERSLAE VAN DIE GEKOSE KOMITEE VOOR PENSIOENE. Main/Corp South Africa. Parliament. House of Assembly. Select Committee on Pensions. **VFOAT** Reports of the Select Committee on Pensions. Afrikaans (English). R0.85. Government Printer / South Africa, Bosman Street, Private Bag X85, Pretoria 0001 South Africa. **Tel** 011 27 12 3239731 ext. 262.

LC HD6895.V52 V52a
DD 331.88/025/945 AT
VICTORIAN TRADES HALL COUNCIL OFFICIAL TRADE UNION DIRECTORY & DIGEST. Main/Corp Victorian Trades Hall Council. **Added/Corp** Victorian Trades Hall Council. Official Trade Union Directory & Digest. **VAT** Victorian Trades Hall Council Official Trade Union Directory and Digest. (19??)-. English. One time a year. Victorian Trades Hall Council, Box 93 Trades Hall, Victoria and Lygon Streets, 3053 Carlton South Australia. **Ad Acc, Adv Mgr:** Phil Wicks. Full Page (B&W) 2495.00Aus$. Half Page (B&W) 1575.00Aus$. **Circ:** 5,000.

ISSN 0253-3987
SZ
VIE ECONOMIQUE (BERNE), LA. (LA VIE ECONOMIQUE.). [Vie econ.]. (1930)-. Periodical. French. Twelve times a year. $165.01. Fischer Druck AG, Satz Druck und Verlag, CH-3110 Muensingen Switzerland. **Tel** 011 41 31 7212211, FAX 011 41 31 7214617, telex 845/911600. **Continues** Rapports Economiques et Statistiques Sociales.
Desc: Information on Swiss economy and social statistics. Consists of text part, charts and economic statistics.
Ind/Abst Int. Labour Doc.

LC HD5701 **ISSN** 1024-0020
DD 331.12 IC
●**VINNUMARKAUR = LABOUR MARKET STATISTICS. See** Business and Economics-Abstracting, Bibliographies and Statistics.

LC HD5744.3 .A36 **ISSN** 8756-1638
DD 331.12/5/09729722 VI
VIRGIN ISLANDS LABOR MARKET REVIEW. Government Publication. English. One time a year. US Department of Labor / Bureau of Labor Statistics, 441 G Street Northwest, Washington DC 20212. **Tel** (202)606-7800, FAX (202)606-7797. **Continues** U.S. Virgin Islands Annual Planning LMI Report.

US
●**VIRGINIA LABOR MARKET REVIEW / VIRGINIA EMPLOYMENT COMMISSION, ECONOMIC INFORMATION SERVICES DIVISION. Added/Corp** Virginia Employment Commission. Economic Information Services Division. **VFOAT** Labor Market Review. Vol. 6, No. 1 (Jan. 1993)-. Periodical. English. Twelve times a year. Virginia Employment Commission, 703 East Main Street, PO Box 1358, Richmond VA 23211. **Continues** Labor Market Review.

LC HD5725.V8 V53c
DD 016.33112/09755 US
VIRGINIA LMI DIRECTORY. Added/Corp Virginia Employment Commission. Division of Research & Analysis. Virginia Employment Commission. Labor Market Information Marketing Section. **VFOAT** Labor Market Information Directory; LMI Directory. (198?)-. Directory. English. Virginia Employment Commission, 703 East Main Street, PO Box 1358, Richmond VA 23211. **Continues** Virginia Employment Commission.; Labor Market Information Directory for Virginia Employment Commission, 0149-9254.

ISSN 0849-035X
DD 261.83456 CN
VO. VIE OUVRIERE. [VO, Vie ouvriere]. **VFOAT** Vie Ouvriere (Montreal. 1990). (1990)-. Periodical. French. Six times a year. 28.00Can$ Canada; 33.00Can$ other (institutions). Vie Ouvriere, 1212 Panet, Montreal Quebec H2L 2Y7 Canada. **Tel** (514)523-5998, FAX (514)527-3403. **Continues** Vie Ouvriere (Montreal), 0229-3803.
Ind/Abst Repere (1990-).

LC HD7256.U6 M7
DD 353.97620083/4 US
VOCATION REHABILITATION ANNUAL REPORT FOR ... . Main/Corp Mississippi. Division of Vocational Rehabilitation. English. One time a year. Division of Vocational Rehabilitation, State Department of Education, PO Box 1698, Jackson MS 39205-1698. **Continues** Mississippi. Division of Vocational Rehabilitation. Report.

LC HD7256.U6 G493
DD 362/.0425 US
VOCATIONAL REHABILITATION IN GEORGIA. English. One time a year. Vocational Rehabilitation / Georgia, 47 Trinity Avenue South West, Atlanta GA 30334.

LC HD6350.M25 V6 **ISSN** 0042-8191
US
VOICE OF THE CEMENT, LIME, GYPSUM AND ALLIED WORKERS. (Dec. 1937)-. Periodical. English. Twelve times a year. United Cement, Lime and Gypsum Workers, Intl Union, 7830 W Lawrence Avenue, Chicago IL 60656. **Tel** (312)595-5171.

LC HD6079.2.I4 V64
DD 331.4/0954 II
VOICE OF THE WORKING WOMAN, THE. Periodical. English (Hindi). Six times a year. Rs6.00. All-India Co-Ordination Committee of Working Women, 6 Talkatora Road, New Delhi 110001 India. **Tel** 384071, 3329867. **ED** Vimala Ranadive. Index available. **Bk Rev. Ad Acc. Circ:** 1,500 (ctrl).
Desc: Problems of working women; participation and promotion in trade unions, struggle against sex discrimination. International co-operation among women. Fight for peace against war.

UY
VOZ DE LA MAYORIA, LA. VFOAT Voz. Vol. 1, No. 1 (June 21, 1984)-. Periodical. Spanish. One time a week. 18 de Julio No 1488 of 11, Montevideo Uruguay. **ED** Alexis Jano Ros.

LC S **ISSN** 0889-3233
DD 630 US
WACO FARM AND LABOR JOURNAL (1986). See Agriculture.

LC HD4976.V5 V57a **ISSN** 0099-2054
DD 331.2/87/09755 US
WAGE & FRINGE BENEFITS FOR SELECTED OCCUPATIONS PAID BY VIRGINIA MANUFACTURERS. Main/Corp Virginia Employment Commission. Manpower Research Division. **VAT** Wage and Fringe Benefits for Selected Occupations Paid by Virginia Manufacturers. (19??)-. English. Virginia Employment Commission, 703 East Main Street, PO Box 1358, Richmond VA 23211.

LC HD4966.A482 U548 **ISSN** 0191-3433
DD 331.2/81/38770973 US
WAGE & SALARY HANDBOOK.
Added/Corp National Air Transportation Association (U.S.). **VAT** Wage and Salary Handbook. (1978)-. English. One time a year. $10.00 (nonmembers); $5.00 (members). Wage and Salary Handbook, 900 Desmoine Street, Suite 200, Des Moines IA 50309.

LC HD4976.N72 N48a
DD 331.2/9747 US
WAGE BULLETIN. Main/Corp New York (State). Dept. of Labor. Division of Research and Statistics. (19??)-. Bulletin. English. New York State Department of Labor, 1 Main Street Room 966, Coll Bargain, Brooklyn NY 11201. **Tel** (718)797-7722, FAX (718)797-7704. **Continues** New York (State). Division of Employment. Research and Statistics Office. Wage Bulletin.

Business and Economics —Labor

LC HD4966.T4 U698D **ISSN** 0272-9024
DD 331.2/877/00974485 US
WAGE CHRONOLOGY : BERKSHIRE HATHAWAY AND THE CLOTHING AND TEXTILE WORKERS. **Main/Corp** United States. Bureau of Labor Statistics. Government Publication. English. US Department of Labor / Bureau of Labor Statistics, 441 G Street Northwest, Washington DC 20212. **Tel** (202)606-7800, FAX (202)606-7797. *Continues* Wage Chronology. Berkshire Hathaway Inc. and the Textile Workers Union of America, TWUA, 0360-4934.

LC HD4973 .B85C
DD 331.2/973 US
WAGE CHRONOLOGY SERIES. SER 4, THE. **Main/Corp** United States. Bureau of Labor Statistics. Government Publication. English. One time a year. US Department of Labor / Bureau of Labor Statistics, 441 G Street Northwest, Washington DC 20212. **Tel** (202)606-7800, FAX (202)606-7797.

LC HD4966.A452 U58A **ISSN** 0362-7233
DD 331.2/82/9109797 US
WAGE CHRONOLOGY : THE BOEING CO., WASHINGTON PLANTS, AND INTERNATIONAL ASSOCIATION OF MACHINISTS. **Main/Corp** United States. Bureau of Labor Statistics. Government Publication. English. US Department of Labor / Bureau of Labor Statistics, 441 G Street Northwest, Washington DC 20212. **Tel** (202)606-7800, FAX (202)606-7797. *Continues* Wage Chronology: The Boeing Co. (Washington Plants).

LC HD4793 .U52A **ISSN** 0272-8109
DD 331.2/2/0973 US
WAGE DIFFERENCES AMONG METROPOLITAN AREAS : SUMMARY. **Main/Corp** United States. Bureau of Labor Statistics. Government Publication. English. US Department of Labor / Bureau of Labor Statistics, 441 G Street Northwest, Washington DC 20212. **Tel** (202)606-7800, FAX (202)606-7797.

ISSN 0149-2691
US
CCC
WAGES AND HOURS. **Added/Corp** Bureau of National Affairs (Washington, D.C.). (19??)-. Periodical. English. Twenty-six times a year (except one issue during year-end holiday). $607.00. Bureau of National Affairs Inc., 9435 Key West Avenue, Rockville MD 20850. **Tel** (800)372-1033, (301)258-1033, FAX (301)948-5823.

LC HD4980.S3 S26a **ISSN** 0706-4926
DD 331.2/097124/021 CN
WAGES AND WORKING CONDITIONS BY OCCUPATION. **Added/Corp** Saskatchewan. Saskatchewan Labour. Policy Planning and Research Division. Saskatchewan. Saskatchewan Human Resources, Labour and Employment. Policy, Planning and Research Branch. Saskatchewan. Labour Relations Branch. 5th (June 1978)-. Statistical Publication. English. Every 2 years. Free. Saskatchewan Labour / Planning and Policy Division, 1870 Albert Street, Regina Saskatchewan S4P 3V7 Canada. **Tel** (306)787-2389, FAX (306)787-7229. **Circ:** 2,200 (ctrl). *Continues* Salaries, Wages, Working Conditions and Fringe Benefits in Saskatchewan, 0706-4934.
 Desc: Results of survey of wages and working conditions in the province of Saskatchewan.

ISSN 0229-1967
DD 331.4/3 CN
WAGES FOR HOUSEWORK : CAMPAIGN BULLETIN, THE. (1976)-. Bulletin. English. Irregular (2 to 3 per year). 3.00Can$. Toronto Wages for Housework Committee, Box 38, Station E, Toronto Ontario M6K 4E1 Canada. **Tel** (416)465-6822. **Bk Rev. Circ:** 10,000.

LC HD5729.O6 O54A **ISSN** 0318-4013
DD 331.2/09713 CN
WAGES, HOURS OF WORK AND OVERTIME PAY PROVISIONS IN SELECTED INDUSTRIES. ONTARIO. (WAGES, HOURS OF WORK AND OVERTIME PAY PROVISIONS IN SELECTED INDUSTRIES.). [Wages hours work overtime pay provis. sel. ind., Ont.]. **Main/Corp** Ontario. Ministry of Labour. Research Branch. English. Ontario Ministry of Labour, 400 University Avenue / 11th Floor, Toronto Ontario M7A 1T7 Canada. **Tel** (416)326-1260, 326-7837.

LC HD8051 .A6218 HD4976.N7 N72 **ISSN** 0364-3883
US
WAGES IN NEW YORK CITY. English. One time a year. US Department of Labor Bureau of Labor Statistics / New York, 201 Varick Street, Room 808, New York NY 10014. **Tel** (212)337-2500, FAX (212)337-2532.

ISSN 0383-3569
DD 331.2/9715 CN
WAGES, SALARIES AND HOURS OF LABOUR, NEW BRUNSWICK. VFOAT Salaires, Traitements et Heures de Travail, Nouveau-Brunswick. (1975)-. French (English). One time a year. New Brunswick Department of Labor and Manpower, PO Box 6000, Fredericton New Brunswick E3B 5H1 Canada.

ISSN 1075-0843
DD 332 US
●WARRANT WATCH. [Warrant watch]. (1993)-. Periodical. English. Twenty-four times a year. $225.00. Noddings Investment Group, 480 West Hintz Road, Wheeling IL 60090. **Tel** (800)566-9987, FAX (708)520-5228.

ISSN 1068-1477
DD 332 US
WASATCH LETTER, THE. (THE WASATCH LETTER : A FORUM FOR RETIREMENT AND PLANNING ISSUES.). [Wasatch lett.]. (Oct. 1992)-. Periodical. English. Twelve times a year. $60.00. Wasatch Planning and Publishing Corporation, 3495 South Medford Drive, Bountiful UT 84010. **Tel** (801)292-4378, FAX (801)292-6927. **ED** Mary L.C. Flood. Index available (published separately). cum. index. **Circ:** 500.

LC JS303.W2 A8 JS451.W27
DD 331.2/81/3520797 US
WASHINGTON CITY AND COUNTY EMPLOYEE SALARIES AND BENEFIT SURVEY. **Main/Corp** Washington Local Government Personnel Institute. (1972)-. English. One time a year (June). $75.00. Association for Washington Cities, 1076 South Franklin, Olympia WA 98501. **Tel** (206)753-4137.

US
WASHINGTON LABOR MARKET. (19??)-. Periodical. English. Twelve times a year. Research and Analysis Branch, Washington State Employment Security Department, Box 9046, Olympia WA 98507. **Tel** (206)438-4800, FAX (206)438-4846.
 Desc: Covers economic conditions affecting the labor market in Washington state.

LC HD5725.W2 W3595
US
WASHINGTON STATE LABOR MARKET AND ECONOMIC REPORT / C.LABOR MARKET AND ECONOMIC ANALYSIS BRANCH, WASHINGTON STATE EMPLOYMENT SECURITY. **Added/Corp** Washington (State). Employment Security Dept. Labor Market and Economic Analysis Branch. (19??)-. Periodical. English. One time a year. $7.50. Research and Analysis Branch, Washington State Employment Security Department, Box 9046, Olympia WA 98507. **Tel** (206)438-4800, FAX (206)438-4846.

LC HD7090 .S6 **ISSN** 1061-1444
DD 331 US
WBF IN ACTION. [WBF action]. **Added/Corp** Workmen's Benefit Fund of the United States of America. **VAT** Workmen's Benefit Fund in Action. Vol. 86, No. 1 (Jan./Feb. 1992)-. Periodical. English. Six times a year. Workmen's Benefit Fund, 99 North Broadway, Hicksville NY 11801-2905. *Continues* Solidarity, 0038-1152.

AT
WEEKLY INDUSTRIAL REGISTER. (19??)-. English. Forty-eight times a year. 315.00Aus$. The Law Book Company Limited, 44-50 Waterloo Road, North Ryde New South Wales, 2113 Australia. **Tel** 011 61 2 9366444, FAX 011 61 2 888724, telex ASBOOK 27995. **(Subscription address:** Law Book Company / Australia, Australia Level 7 132 Arthur St., N Sydney NSW 2060 Australia.) *Continues* Workforce Industrial Register.

US
WEEKLY INSURED UNEMPLOYMENT REPORT. *See* Insurance.

LC HD8512 .W4
BE
WERKER, DE. **Added/Corp** Federation Generale du Travail de Belgique. (June 23, 1945)-. Periodical. Dutch. One time a week. $42.90. ABVV, Redaktie en ADM Hoogstraat 42, 1000 Brussels Belgium.

LC HD5725.W4 A464A **ISSN** 0097-7837
DD 331.1/09754 US
WEST VIRGINIA LABOR FORCE ANNUAL AVERAGES HOURS & EARNINGS : WEST VIRGINIA STANDARD METROPOLITAN STATISTICAL AREAS. *See* Business and Economics-Abstracting, Bibliographies and Statistics.

LC HD5725.W4 **ISSN** 0095-6112
DD 331.1/09754 S 331.1/1/09754 US
WEST VIRGINIA WORK FORCE ANNUAL AVERAGES. (WEST VIRGINIA WORK FORCE, ANNUAL AVERAGES; STATE OF WEST VIRGINIA STANDARD METROPOLITAN STATISTICAL AREAS, SMALLER LABOR AREAS.). **Main/Corp** West Virginia. Dept. of Employment Security. Research and Statistics Division. (19??)-. Statistical Publication. English. West Virginia Employment Programs Bureau, 112 California Avenue, Charleston WV 25305. **Tel** (304)558-2630, FAX (304)348-0301.
 Desc: Information on the labor supply in West Virginia.

LC HD5850.W4 W48
DD 331.12/09941 AT
WESTERN AUSTRALIAN LABOUR MARKET, THE. (19??)-. English. Twelve times a year. Department of Employment and Training / Perth, St George's Centre, 81 St George's Terrace, Perth Western Australia 6000 Australia.

LC HD6350.M39 W5 **ISSN** 0043-4876
US
WHITE COLLAR. **Added/Corp** Office and Professional Employees International Union. Office Employes International Union. No. 109 (Jan. 1954)-. Periodical. English. Four times a year. Office and Professional Employees International Union, 815 16th Street Northwest, Suite 606, Washington DC 20006. **Tel** (212)675-3210. *Continues* Office Worker (1945).
 Ind/Abst Work Relat. Abstr.

LC HD4966.M4 U5495
DD 331.2/81/00097305 US
WHITE-COLLAR PAY. PRIVATE GOODS-PRODUCING INDUSTRIES. **Added/Corp** United States. Bureau of Labor Statistics. **VFOAT** Private Goods-Producing Industries. **VAT** White Collar Pay. Private Goods Producing Industries. (March 1990)-. English. Every 2 years. US Department of Labor Bureau of Labor Statistics / Atlanta, 1371 Peachtree Street NE, Suite 500, Atlanta GA 30367. **Tel** (404)347-2161, FAX (404)347-2447. *Continues in part* National Survey of Professional, Administrative, Technical, and Clerical Pay. Private Service Industries.

LC HC107.W6 W665
DD 330.9775/005 US
WISCONSIN ECONOMIC INDICATORS. **Added/Corp** Wisconsin. Dept. of Industry, Labor and Human Relations. (Dec. 1984)-. Periodical. English. Twelve times a year. Free on request. Wisconsin Department of Industry, Labor & Human Relations, 201 East Washington Avenue, PO Box 7944, Madison WI 53707-7944. **Tel** (608)266-0851. available with charts. *Continues* Wisconsin. Dept. of Industry, Labor and Human Relations. Wisconsin Employment and Economic Indicators, 0147-6106.
 Desc: Labor force data, local area employment estimates, economic outlook material, etc.

LC KFW2732.8.P77 A498 **ISSN** 0145-8655
DD 344/.775/01890413530002648 US
WISCONSIN PUBLIC EMPLOYMENT DECISIONS DIGEST. **Added/Corp** Wisconsin Association of School Boards. Wisconsin. Laws, Statutes, etc. Municipal Employment Relations Act. (July 1976)-. English. Twelve times a year. $135.00 tax exempt organizations; $142.43 non-tax exempt organizations. Wisconsin Association of School Boards, 122 West Washington, Madison WI 53703. **Tel** (608)257-2622, FAX (608)257-8386. **ED** Ken Cole. ctrl circ.

LC HD5725.M3 M34b **ISSN** 0149-8959
DD 331.4/09741 US
WOMEN AND MINORITY MANPOWER STATISTICS. *See* Business and Economics-Abstracting, Bibliographies and Statistics.

ISSN 0196-8394
US
CEASED
WOMEN & WORK. (WOMEN & WORK : NEWS FROM THE UNITED STATES DEPARTMENT OF LABOR, OFFICE OF INFORMATION, PUBLICATIONS AND REPORTS.). [Women work]. **VAT** Women and Work. (1973)-(Aug. 1993). Periodical. English. US Department of Labor, 200 Constitution Avenue NW, Washington DC 20210. **Tel** (202)219-7316, FAX (202)219-7312. available on microfilm and microfiche from University Microfilms International (UMI). Documents available from UMI Article Clearinghouse.
 Ind/Abst Expand. Acad. Index (1992-); Newsp. Period. Abstr. (1992-).

LC HD6050 .W558 **ISSN** 0882-0910
DD 331.4/05 US
WOMEN AND WORK (BEVERLY HILLS, CALIF.). (WOMEN AND WORK). [Women work]. Vol. 1 (1985)-. Monographic series. English. Irregular. Price varies per volume. SAGE Periodical Press, 2455 Teller Road, Thousand Oaks CA 91320. **Tel** (805)499-0721, FAX (805)499-0871, telex 100799. **Acid Free.**
 Ind/Abst LABORDOC; Soc. Plann. Policy Dev. Abstr.

Business and Economics —Labor

LC HB6096.N3 W65
DD 331.4/09782
US
WOMEN IN NEBRASKA; A LABOR FORCE ANALYSIS. Periodical. English. One time a year. Division of Employment, Nebraska Department of Labor, PO Box 94600 State House Station, Lincoln NE 68509.

LC HD6096.M7 M57a ISSN 0149-2152
DD 331.4/09762 US
WOMEN IN THE LABOR FORCE. **Main/Corp** Mississippi Employment Security Commission. (1977)-. English. One time a year. Mississippi Employment Security Commission, PO Box 1699, Jackson MS 39205. **Tel** (601)354-8711.

CN
WOMEN IN THE LABOUR FORCE. See Women's Interests.

LC HD6097 .W65a ISSN 0382-2192
DD 331.4/0971 CN
WOMEN IN THE LABOUR FORCE. FACTS AND FIGURES. (WOMEN IN THE LABOUR FORCE; FACTS AND FIGURES. LES FEMMES DANS LA POPULATION ACTIVE; FAITS ET DONNEES.). **Added/Corp** Canada. Women's Bureau. **VFOAT** Femmes Dans la Population Active; Faits et Donnees. (1967)-. Periodical. English (French). One time a year. 16.01Can$. Labour Canada / Women's Bureau, Ottawa Ontario K1A 0J2 Canada. **Tel** (819)997-1550. **Circ:** 8,000 (ctrl). **Continues** Facts and Figures About Women in the Labour Force.
Desc: Statistics on women in the labour force in Canada.

LC HD6096.A6 A73A ISSN 0145-7802
DD 331.4/09791 US
WOMEN IN THE WORKING WORLD. [Women work. world]. **Main/Corp** Arizona. Dept. of Economic Security. Bureau of Statistical Information, Research and Analysis. 1975-. English. One time a year. Arizona Department of Economic Security, PO Box 6123, Code 733 A, Phoenix AZ 85005. **Tel** (602)255-3871.

ISSN 0711-463X
DD 331.4/09713 CN
WOMEN'S RIGHTS BULLETIN. See Women's Interests.

LC GN495.4 ISSN 1058-4870
DD 305 US
WOMEN'S WORK (MONTESANO, WASH.). (WOMEN'S WORK.). Vol. 1, No. 1 (July 1991)-. Periodical. English. Six times a year. $18.00. Women's Work, 606 Avenue A, Snohomish WA 98290. **Tel** (206)568-5914, FAX (206)568-5620. **ED** Andrea Damm. **Bk Rev**, (Qty: 24-30). **Ad Acc, Adv Mgr:** Andrea Damm, **Tel** (206)568-5914. **Circ:** 3,000.

LC HD6050 .W59 ISSN 0360-1986
DD 331.4/05 US
WOMEN'S WORK (WASHINGTON). (WOMEN'S WORK.). (1975)-. Periodical. English. Six times a year. $6.00. Women's Work / Washington, 1818 Kalorama Road NW/31 Zanca, Washington DC 20009.

LC HF5548.85 .W667 ISSN 0267-8373
DD 158.7/05 UK
CCC
NLM W1; WO8469
Pr Rev.
WORK AND STRESS. See Psychology.

LC HD4802 .W62 ISSN 0273-0022
DD 306/.36/0973 US
WORK (BOCA RATON). (WORK.). [Work]. **Added/Corp** Social Issues Resources Series, Inc. Vol. 1 (1972)-. English. One time a year. Social Issues Resources Series Inc, PO Box 2348, Boca Raton FL 33427. **Tel** (800)327-0513, (407)994-0079. **ED** E.C. Goldstein.
Desc: Interdisciplinary resource material consisting of reprinted articles from popular and professional journals, newspapers, magazines and government documents.

ISSN 0822-2711
US
WORK DIGEST. Vol. 1, No. 1 (Nov.-Dec. 1983)-. Periodical. English. Six times a year. $44.00. Work Digest, Post Office Box 400, Alexandria Bay NY 13607.

LC HD6951 .W67 ISSN 0950-0170
DD 306/.36/05 UK
Pr Rev.
WORK, EMPLOYMENT AND SOCIETY. (WORK, EMPLOYMENT & SOCIETY : JOURNAL OF THE BRITISH SOCIOLOGICAL ASSOCIATION.). [Work employ. soc.]. **Added/Corp** British Sociological Association. **VFOAT** Work, Employment, and Society. Vol. 1, No. 1 (March 1987)-. Periodical. English. Four times a year. $146.30. British Sociological Association, 351 Station Road, Dorridge-Solihull, West Midlands B93 8EY United Kingdom. **Tel** 011 44 1564 772402, FAX 011 44 1564 772402. **ED** Paul Edwards (editor's address: Sociology Department University of Warwick Coventry CV4 7A1 United Kingdom). Index available (Bound in 4th issue in December.). **Bk Rev**, (Qty: 56). **Ad Acc, Adv Mgr:** J. Ward. **Circ:** 900. available on microfiche from Institute for Scientific Information; available on microfilm; available in microform. Documents available from The Genuine Article.
Desc: A forum for the discussion of all forms and aspects of work and its interconnections with wider social processes and structures both national and international.
Ind/Abst Anbar Account. Finan. Abstr. [Full Txt.]; Anbar Mark. Distr. Abstr. [Full Txt.]; Anbar Top Manage. Abstr. [Full Txt.]; Appl. Soc. Sci. Index Abstr.; Contents Pages Manage.; Curr. Cit.; Curr. Contents Soc. Behav. Sci.; Ergon. Abstr.; Int. Bibliogr. Sociol.; Int. Labour Doc.; LABORDOC; Manage. Market. Abstr.; Manage. Bibliogr. Rev.; Oper. Prod. Manage. Abstr. [Full Txt.]; PAIS Int. Print; Person. Train. Abstr. [Full Txt.]; Person. Manage. Abstr.; Res. Alert [Full Cov.]; Soc. Plann. Policy Dev. Abstr.; Soc. Sci. Cit. Index [Full Cov.]; Sociol. Abstr. (1987-) [Full Cov.]; Stud. Women Abstr.; Women Manage. Rev. [Full Txt.].

LC HD5723 .B87C ISSN 0162-0592
DD 331.1/1/0973 US
WORK EXPERIENCE OF THE POPULATION. (WORK EXPERIENCE OF THE POPULATION IN ... / U.S. DEPARTMENT OF LABOR, BUREAU OF LABOR STATISTICS.). Government Publication. English. One time a year. US Department of Labor / Bureau of Labor Statistics, 441 G Street Northwest, Washington DC 20212. **Tel** (202)606-7800, FAX (202)606-7797.

LC JK671 .U54A ISSN 0276-9247
DD 353.001 US
WORK FORCE PROFILE AS OF SEPTEMBER 30 ... . [Work force profile Sept. 30]. **Main/Corp** United States. General Services Administration. Office of Human Resources and Organization. **VAT** Work Force Profile as of September Thirtieth. English. One time a year. General Services Administration Office of Information Resources Management, Office of Information Resources Management, Eighteenth and F Streets Northwest, Washington DC 20405.

LC HD5725.F6 F37B ISSN 0149-3329
DD 331.11/09759 US
WORK IN FLORIDA. (WORK IN FLORIDA : THE ... STATE MANPOWER SERVICES COUNCIL REPORT TO THE GOVERNOR OF FLORIDA.). [Work Fla.]. **VFOAT** Review of the Youth Employment and Demonstration Projects Act of 1977; Annual Manpower Report to the Governor. (1976)-. English. One time a year. Florida Labor, Employment & Training Division, 1320 Executive Center Drive, Suite 300, Tallahassee FL 32399. **Tel** (904)488-7225, FAX (904)487-1753.

LC DT1155 .W67
DD 968.06/3
SA
CEASED
WORK IN PROGRESS (JOHANNESBURG, SOUTH AFRICA). (WORK IN PROGRESS.). **Added/Corp** Southern African Research Service. **VFOAT** W.I.P.; WIP. No. 1 (Sept. 1977)-No. 95 (1994). Periodical. English. South African Research Services, PO Box 32716, Braamfontein, South Africa 2017. **Tel** 011 27 11 4031912. **Circ:** 8,000. **Absorbed** New Era (Cape Town, South Africa).
Desc: Contemporary South African labour and politics; anti-apartheid oppositional, but independent in approach. Includes debates and information on resistance politics.
Ind/Abst Hum. Rights Intern. Rep.

US
WORK INJURY MANAGEMENT. See Insurance.

LC Z7164.L1 W68 HD4901 ISSN 0273-3234
DD 016.331 US
WORK RELATED ABSTRACTS. See Business and Economics-Abstracting, Bibliographies and Statistics.

LC HD8051 .A7876 HD8004.2.U5 ISSN 0147-9547
DD 331.1/08 S 331.89/281/350000973 US
WORK STOPPAGES IN GOVERNMENT. **Added/Corp** United States. Bureau of Labor Statistics. (1968)-. English. One time a year. US Department of Labor / Bureau of Labor Statistics, 441 G Street Northwest, Washington DC 20212. **Tel** (202)606-7800, FAX (202)606-7797.

LC HD5725.N7 A29 HD5326.N
US
WORK STOPPAGES IN NEW YORK STATE (ANNUAL : 1982). (WORK STOPPAGES IN NEW YORK STATE.). 1982-. English. One time a year. **Continues** Statistics on Work Stoppages in New York State.

LC JK776 .W67 ISSN 0277-3325
DD 353.001/23 US
WORK YEARS AND PERSONNEL COSTS, EXECUTIVE BRANCH, UNITED STATES GOVERNMENT. (19??)-. English. One time a year. US Office of Personnel Management / Personnel Systems and Oversight Group, 1900 E Street NW/Room 7494, Washington DC 20415. **Tel** (202)632-6245. **ED** Mary A McCarthy. available on microfiche (Vols. for 1983- distributed to depository libraries).
Desc: Federal civilian employment distributions by work years, basic pay, premium pay, benefits, leave, agency, work schedule, tenure, and pay system category.

ISSN 0740-4077
US
WORKAMERICA. **VFOAT** Work America. Vol. 1, No. 1 (Oct. 1983)-. Periodical. English. Twelve times a year. $22.00. National Alliance of Business, 1201 New York Avenue Northwest, Suite 700, Washington DC 20005. **Tel** (202)289-2888. **ED** Alan Vanneman. **Bk Rev. Ad Acc. Circ:** 3,500.
Desc: Education and job training programs involving the private sector that aid the poor.
Ind/Abst Urban Aff. Abstr.

ISSN 0895-3678
DD 331 US
WORKAMPER NEW$. [Workamper new$]. **VFOAT** Workamper News; Work Camper News; WKNS; WKN$. (Sept./Oct. 1987)-. Periodical. English. Six times a year. $23.00. Workamper New$, 201 Hiram Road, HC 34 Box 125, Heber Springs AR 72543-8747. **Tel** (501)362-2637, FAX (501)362-2637. **ED** Greg Robus. **Bk Rev**, (Qty: 6 /year). **Ad Acc. Circ:** 10,000.
Desc: Serves employers and job seekers in the recreation, leisure and travel industries.

LC HD4869 .W67
DD 361.7/025 FR
WORKCAMPS PROGRAMME. PROGRAMME DE CHANTIERS. PROGRAMA DE CAMPAMENTOS. **Added/Corp** United Nations Educational, Scientific and Cultural Organization. Coordinating Committee for International Voluntary Service. **VFOAT** Programme de Chantiers; Programa de Campamentos. (19??)-. Multiple languages (English, French and Spanish). Irregular. UNESCO / France, 31 rue Francois Bonvin, 75732 Paris Cedex 15 France. **Tel** 011 33 1 45684564, 011 33 1 45684565, FAX 011 33 1 45669270, telex 204461 Paris.

ISSN 0829-576X
DD 334/.6/0971 CN
WORKER CO-OPS (TORONTO. 1980). See Business and Economics-Cooperatives.

ISSN 0273-4680
US
WORKER FOR THE MARYLAND-D.C.-VIRGINIA AREA, THE. **Added/Corp** Revolutionary Communist Party, USA. **VFOAT** Worker. (19??)-. Periodical. English. Twelve times a year. $10.00 (institutions), $4.00 (individuals). Worker for Maryland-DC, PO Box 1992, Baltimore MD 21203. **Tel** (301)563-1315.

ISSN 0273-4672
US
WORKER FOR THE NORTHWEST, THE. **VFOAT** Worker. Periodical. English (Spanish). $15.00. The Worker, 6010 Empire Way Street, Seattle WA 98118.

ISSN 1070-681X
DD 331 US
WORKER RIGHTS NEWS. [Worker rights news]. **Added/Corp** International Labor Rights Education and Research Fund. (19??)-. Periodical. English. Four times a year. $25.00. ILRERF, Box 74, 100 Maryland Avenue Northeast, Washington DC 20002.

ISSN 1101-3516
UDC 331 SW
WORKER TODAY. (1990)-. Periodical. Multiple languages. Twelve times a year. Kr280.00 (institutions), Kr140.00 (individuals) Europe; Kr420.00 (institutions), Kr210.00 (individuals) other. Worker Today, WT Box 6278, 10234 Stockholm Sweden.

ISSN 1054-7819
DD 344 US
CCC
WORKERS' COMP ADVISOR (CALIFORNIA ED.). (WORKERS' COMP ADVISOR.). [Work. comp advis.]. **VAT** Workers' Compensation Advisor. (19??)-. Periodical. English. Twelve times a year. $197.00. Genesis Communications, 11772 Sorrento Valley Road, Suite 134, San Diego CA 92121. **Continues** California Workers' Comp Advisor, 1046-2775.

ISSN 1058-7179
DD 344 US
WORKERS' COMP ADVISOR (OHIO ED.). (WORKERS' COMP ADVISOR (MEDICINE, LAW, ADMINISTRATION.). [Work. comp advis.]. **VAT** Workers' Compensation Advisor. (1991)-. Periodical.

English. Twelve times a year. $197.00. Workers' Comp Advisor, 3768 Rocky River Drive, Suite 106, Cleveland OH 44111.

US

WORKERS' COMP NEWSLETTER. (19??)-.
Newsletter. English. Twenty-six times a year. $93.09. Merritt Company, 1661 Ninth Street, PO Box 955, Santa Monica CA 90406. **Tel** (310)450-7234, (800)638-7597, FAX (310)396-4563.

LC KFO342.A15 W67 **ISSN** 0886-9162
DD 344.771/021 347.710421   US

WORKERS' COMPENSATION JOURNAL OF OHIO. (WORKERS' COMPENSATION JOURNAL OF OHIO. WCJO.). [Work. compens. j. Ohio]. Added/Corp Banks-Baldwin Law Publishing Company. VFOAT WCJO. Vol. 1, Issue 1 (Jan./Feb. 1986)-.
Periodical. English. Six times a year. $139.65 (one-year), $257.90 (two-year) Ohio; $130.90 (one-year), $241.80 (two-year) other. Banks-Baldwin Law Publishing Company, PO Box 1974, University Center, Cleveland OH 44106. **Tel** (216)721-7373. **ED** Jerald D Harris.
Desc: A newsletter tuned to fast-paced developments in Ohio workers' compensation and intentional tort law. Provides a balanced perspective and comprehensive coverage for all concerned: attorneys, claimants, employers, physicians, insurers, and workers' compensation administrators.

ISSN 0847-5857
DD 658.3/254/09713   CN

WORKERS' COMPENSATION MANAGING CLAIMS. See Insurance.

ISSN 1052-6358
DD 331   US

WORKERS COMPENSATION OUTLOOK (BOSTON, MASS.). (WORKERS COMPENSATION OUTLOOK.). [Work. compens. outl.]. Vol. 1, No. 1 (Oct. 1990)-.
Periodical. English. Twelve times a year. $168.00. Standard Publishing Company, 155 Federal Street, Boston MA 02110. **Tel** (617)457-0604, (617)457-0600, FAX (617)457-0608.

ISSN 0826-4198
DD 368.4/1/009711   CN

WORKERS' COMPENSATION REPORTER. [Work. compens. report.]. Main/Corp Workers' Compensation Board of British Columbia.
Periodical. English. Workers Compensation Board of British Columbia, 6951 Westminster Highway, Richmond British Columbia V7C 1C6 Canada. **Tel** (604)276-3154. Index available. **Circ:** 1,400 (ctrl). **Continues** W.C.B. Reporter, 0826-418X.
Desc: Reporting of significant policy decisions and/or amendments taken by the commissioner of the Workers' Compensation Board of British Columbia.

LC HD7096.U6 K47   **ISSN** 0149-371X
DD 368.4/4/009769   US

WORKERS COVERED BY KENTUCKY UNEMPLOYMENT INSURANCE LAW BY COUNTY. See Insurance.

LC H62.5.I5 W67
DD 300.7/1054   II

WORKERS EDUCATION. Added/Corp India. Central Board for Workers Education. (19??)-.
Periodical. English (Hindi). Four times a year. Free. Central Board for Workers Education, 1440 West High Court Road, Gokuipeth Nagpur 440 010 India. **Tel** 32162. **ED** K. G. Dani. **Bk Rev**. **Ad Acc**. **Circ:** 1,500 (ctrl).
Desc: Contain articles of studies and surveys pertaining to industrial relations, trade unions, productivity, labour economics and topics related to workers education.

IE

WORKERS LIFE : THE MAGAZINE FOR WORKERS. (19??)-.
Periodical. English. Twelve times a year. $18.00. Repsol Ltd., 30 Gardiner Place, Dublin 1 Ireland. **Tel** 786052.

UK

WORKERS NEWS. (19??)-.
Periodical. English. Eight times a year. £7.00 UK; £12.20 others. Workers News / UK, 1 17 Meredith Street, London EC1R 0AE United Kingdom.

UK

WORKERS' UNITY. Added/Corp South African Congress of Trade Unions. No. 1 (Jan. 1977)-.
Periodical. English.
Ind/Abst Hum. Rights Intern. Rep.

ISSN 0276-0746
US

WORKERS VANGUARD (NEW YORK, N.Y.). (WORKERS VANGUARD.). [Work. vanguard]. Added/Corp Spartacist League of the U.S. No. 1 (1971)-.
Periodical. English. Twenty-two times a year (biweekly except two weeks in June & July). $10.00. Spartacist Publishing Company, PO Box 1377 GPO, New York NY 10116. **Tel** (212)732-7861. **ED** Jan Norton. Index available. **Bk Rev**. **Circ:** 16,000 (ctrl). available on microfilm.
Desc: Marxist analysis of social and political issues of interest to working people and the oppressed.

BM

WORKERS VOICE, THE. Added/Corp Bermuda Industrial Union. (19??)-.
Periodical. English. The Workers Voice, c/o the Bermuda Industrial Union, Hamilton 5-26 Bermuda. **Tel** 011 809 29 20044. **ED** Barbara B. Ball. **Bk Rev**. **Ad Acc**. **Circ:** 2,000.
Desc: Current local and overseas topics affecting labour: collective bargaining issues, politics, labor problems, drug abuse aids, and other matters of interest to workers.

ISSN 1351-3273
UK

●WORKFLOW WORLD. [Workflow World]. (1993)-.
English. Ten times a year (publishes monthly with July/Aug. and Dec./Jan. issues combined). £250.00. Sodan, 20 Mead Road, Uxbridge Middlesex UB8 1AU United Kingdom. **Tel** 011 44 1895 233194.

LC HD1401   **ISSN** 0811-9023
DD 331   AT

WORKFORCE. (1974)-.
Periodical. English. One time a week. 435.00Aus$. Newsletter Information Service, PO Box 693, Manly New South Wales 2095 Australia. **Tel** 011 61 2 9777500, FAX 011 61 2 9773310.
Desc: Objective coverage of all industrial relations issues, dispute outcomes, tribunal judgements, etc.

AT
TITLE CHANGE

WORKFORCE INDUSTRIAL REGISTER. (19??)-(19??).
English. The Law Book Company Limited, 44-50 Waterloo Road, North Ryde New South Wales, 2113 Australia. **Tel** 011 61 2 9366444, FAX 011 61 2 888724, telex ASBOOK 27995. (**Subscription address:** Law Book Company / Australia, Australia Level 7 132 Arthur St., N Sydney NSW 2060 Australia.) **Continued by** Weekly Industrial Register.

ISSN 1078-0394
DD 331   US

●WORKFORCE INVESTMENT QUARTERLY. [Workforce invest. q.]. Added/Corp National Governors' Association,. Vol. 1, No. 1 (Spring 1994)-.
Periodical. English. Four times a year. $75.00. National Governors Association, 444 North Capitol Street, Suite 267, Washington DC 20001. **Tel** (202)624-5300. **Continues** Labor Notes (Washington, D.C.).

ISSN 1078-8638
US
TITLE CHANGE

WORKFORCE TRAINING NEWS. (1993)-(1995).
Trade Publication. English. Enterprise Communications Inc., 1165 Northchase Parkway, Suite 350, Marietta GA 30067. **Tel** (404)988-9558, FAX (404)859-9166. **Continued by** Corporate University Review.
Desc: A newsmagazine for employee learning and development.

ISSN 1063-4363
DD 368   US

WORKFORCE (WASHINGTON, D.C.). (WORKFORCE.). [Workforce]. Added/Corp Interstate Conference of Employment Security Agencies. International Association of Personnel in Employment Security. (Spring 1992)-.
Periodical. English. Four times a year. $20.00. International Association of Personnel in Employment Security / IAPES, 1801 Louisville Road, Frankfort KY 40601. **Tel** (502)223-4459. **ED** Michael R. Stone. **Bk Rev**, (Qty: 6-8). **Ad Acc**. **Circ:** 1,000 (ctrl). **Continues** Perspective (Frankfort, Ky.), 0887-798X.

ISSN 0270-0417
US

WORKING. [Working]. Periodical. English. Four times a year. National Alliance of Buiness, 1730 K Street NW, Washington DC 20006.

ISSN 0956-6120
DD 331.137941   UK

WORKING BRIEF - UNEMPLOYMENT UNIT. [Work. brief - Unempl. Unit]. VFOAT Working Brief - Youthaid. (1989)-.
Periodical. English. Eleven times a year. $102.67. Unemployment Unit, 409 Brixton Road, London SW9 7DQ United Kingdom. **Tel** 011 44 171 7378001, FAX 011 44 171 3260818. **ED** Paul Convery. **Circ:** 1,600. **Formed by the union of** Statistical Supplement - Unemployment Unit **and** Youthaid Bulletin.

LC HD8682.C45 W67
DD 301.44/42/0954   II

WORKING CLASS, THE. Added/Corp Centre of Indian Trade Unions. (Sept. 1971)-.
Periodical. English. Twelve times a year. Rs20.00. Centre of Indian Trade Unions, 6 Talkatora Road, New Delhi 110001 India. **Tel** 384070. **ED** P.K. Ganguly. **Bk Rev**. **Ad Acc**. **Circ:** 5,000. available with illustrations; available with charts.

US

WORKING CLASS OPPOSITION : MONTHLY NEWSPAPER OF THE INTERNATIONALIST WORKERS PARTY.
VFOAT Opposition; Oposicion Obrera. Vol. 5, No. 32

Business and Economics —Labor

(Nov./Dec. 1987)-. Periodical. English. $8.00. October Publications, 3309 1/2 Mission Street/Suite 135, San Francisco CA 94110. **Absorbed** Bolchevique.

LC HD4980.B7 B74A
DD 331.2/09711   CN

WORKING CONDITIONS IN BRITISH COLUMBIA INDUSTRY. Main/Corp British Columbia. Dept. of Labour. Research Branch. English. British Columbia Department of Labor, Research Branch, Parliament Building, Victoria British Columbia V8V 1X5 Canada.

DD 914/.0455   UK

WORKING HOLIDAYS (LONDON, ENGLAND). (WORKING HOLIDAYS.). (197?)-.
English. One time a year. $22.16. Central Bureau of Education Visits, Seymour Mews House, Seymour Mews, London W1H 9PE United Kingdom. **Tel** 011 44 171 4865101.
Desc: Information on students and summer employment.

ISSN 1064-489X
DD 331   US

WORKING IT OUT. (WORKING IT OUT : THE NEWSLETTER FOR GAY AND LESBIAN EMPLOYMENT ISSUES.). [Work. out]. (Spring 1992)-.
Newsletter. English. Four times a year. $60.00. Mail Handlers Division of the Laborers' International Union of North America, 906 16th Street NW, Washington DC 20006.

ISSN 0251-0251
SZ

WORKING PAPER - WORLD EMPLOYMENT PROGRAMME RESEARCH. [Work. pap. - World Employ. Programme Res.]. Periodical. English. Three times a week.
Ind/Abst World Agric. Econ. Rural Sociol. Abstr.

ISSN 0384-0654
DD 016.3314/0971   CN

WORKING WOMEN IN CANADA. See Women's Interests.

ISSN 0834-292X
DD 331/.0971   CN
CCC

WORKLIFE REPORT, THE. [Worklife rep.]. Vol. 5, No. 1, (1986)-.
Periodical. English. 35.00Can$ (6 issues) Canada; 37.50Can$ (6 issues) other. IR Research Publications, PO Box 1092, Kingston Ontario K7L 4Y5 Canada. **Tel** (613)542-5596. available on microfilm and microfiche from University Microfilms International (UMI). Documents available from UMI Article Clearinghouse. **Continues** Worklife, 0227-7743.
Ind/Abst ABI/INFORM Glob. Ed.; ABI/INFORM [Computer File] (1982-); Acad. Abstr.; Acad. Search; Bus. Source Plus; Bus. Source; Can. Index (?-?); EP Collect.; Health Source Plus; Health Source; Homework Help.; INFO-SOUTH Abstr.; Mag. Search; MasterFile FullTEXT 1000; MasterFile FullTEXT 350; MasterFile FullTEXT 650; MasterFile FullTEXT (Jan. 1993-); OCLC; PAIS Int. Print (?-?); Pub. Lib. FullTEXT; Soc. Sci. Source; Telebase; UMI ABI/Inform--Bus. Period. Ondisc (1987-) [Full Txt.]; Vocat. Search.

LC HD7102.U5 W65A   **ISSN** 0097-9163
DD 368.4/1/009775   US
NLM W2 AW6 D4W

WORKMEN'S COMPENSATION DATA. Main/Corp Wisconsin. Dept. of Industry, Labor and Human Relations. Bureau of Research and Statistics. Risk Management Section. English. Wisconsin Department of Industry, Labor & Human Relations, 201 East Washington Avenue, PO Box 7944, Madison WI 53707-7944. **Tel** (608)266-0851.

US

WORKMEN'S COMPENSATION FOR OCCUPATIONAL INJURIES AND DEATH. VFOAT Industrial Injuries and Death.; Larson's Workmen's Compensation. (1972)-.
English. Irregular. Matthew Bender & Company Inc., 1275 Broadway, Albany NY 12204. **Tel** (800)833-9844, (518)487-3000.

ISSN 1074-0449
DD 331   US

●WORKPLACE AMERICA. [Workplace Am.]. Vol. 1, No. 1 (Feb. 1994)-.
Periodical. English. Four times a year. Free on request. Hunt-Scanlon Publishing Company, Two Pickwick Plaza, Greenwich CT 06830. **Tel** (203)629-3629, FAX (203)629-3701.

AT

WORKPLACE CHANGE. Added/Corp Australia. Dept. of Industrial Relations. (June 1988)-.
Periodical. English. Irregular. Australian Government Printing Office / Australia, PO Box 4050, Government NSW 2001 Australia.
Ind/Abst Int. Labour Doc.

Business and Economics —Labor

DD 331.8806094   **ISSN** 1036-5117   AT
WORKPLACE MELBOURNE.
(WORKPLACE.). [Workplace Melb.]. **Added/Corp** Australian Council of Trade Unions. (1991)-. Periodical. English. Four times a year. 16.44Aus$. Client Publishing, 220 Clarendon Street, East Melbourne, 3002 Australia. **Tel** 11 61 3 2724700. ctrl circ.

DD 331   **ISSN** 1188-4126   CN
WORKSIGHT (EDMONTON). (WORKSIGHT.).
[Worksight]. **Added/Corp** Alberta. Alberta Labour. Vol. 1, Issue #1 (Winter 1992)-. Periodical. English. Four times a year. 8.00Can$. Worksight Editorial Board, PO Box 1481, Station Main, Edmonton Alberta T5J 2N7 Canada.

DD 331   **ISSN** 1062-9742   US
WORKWATCH (BELLINGHAM, WASH.).
(WORKWATCH: A RESOURCE FOR EMPLOYMENT ISSUES, TRAINING AND EDUCATION.). [WorkWatch]. **VFOAT** Work Watch. Vol. 1, Issue 1 (May/June 1992)-. Periodical. English. Six times a year. $19.00. New Legends Publishing Group, PO Box 2567, Bellingham WA 98227.

LC HD4802 .W65   **ISSN** 0255-5514
DD 331/.05   SZ   CCC
WORLD LABOUR REPORT. Added/Corp
International Labour Office. Vol. 1 (1984)-. English. One time a year. $20.00. International Labour Office - ILO, Publications Sales Service, CH-1211 Geneva 22 Switzerland. **Tel** 011 41 22 7996111, FAX 011 41 22 7986253, telex 415 647 ilo ch. **(Subscription address:** International Labour Office / Washington, DC, 1828 L Street Northwest, Suite 801, Washington DC 20036. **Tel** (202)653-7652.)
Desc: Employment, unemployment, earnings and labor cost statistics. Examines how older workers can come to terms with changes in employment, working conditions and social protection; how the modern state participates in the industrial relations process; how the re-entry of the unemployed into the labor market can be facilitated by retraining; and how privatization affects employment and social protection.

ISSN 1020-0029   SZ
WORLD OF WORK : THE MAGAZINE OF THE ILO. Added/Corp
International Labor Office. No. 1 (Dec. 1992)-. Periodical. English. Five times a year. Free on request. International Labour Office - ILO, Publications Sales Service, CH-1211 Geneva 22 Switzerland. **Tel** 011 41 22 7996111, FAX 011 41 22 7986253, telex 415 647 ilo ch. **Continues** International Labour Office. ILO Information, 0379-1734.
Desc: A newsletter covering ILO activities throughout the world.

CS   CEASED
WORLD TRADE UNION MOVEMENT.
Added/Corp World Federation of Trade Unions. (Mar./Apr. 1946)-(19??). Periodical. English. Progress Books, 71 Bathurst Street, Toronto Ontario M5V 2P6 Canada. **Tel** (416)368-5336. Index available in last issue of volume--attached. **Supersedes** World Federation of Trade Unions. Information Bulletin.

LC HC281 .W15   **ISSN** 0342-300X
DD 330.943/005   GW   CCC
WSI MITTEILUNGEN. (WSI MITTEILUNGEN :
ZEITSCHRIFT DES WIRTSCHAFTS- UND SOZIALWISSENSCHAFTLICHEN INSTITUTS DES DEUTSCHEN GEWERKSCHAFTSBUNDES GMBH.). [WSI-Mitt.]. **Added/Corp** Deutscher Gewerkschaftsbund. Wirtschafts- und Sozialwissenschaftliches Institut. **VFOAT** W.S.I. Mitteilungen. **VAT** Wirtschafts- und Sozialwissenschaftliches Institut Mitteilungen. Vol. 25, 4 (Apr. 1972)-. Periodical. German. Twelve times a year. $130.35. Bund Verlag GmbH, Postfach 900840, D-51118 Cologne Germany. **Tel** 011 49 2203 934758. **Continues** WWI Mitteilungen, 0042-9872.
Ind/Abst Energy Res. Abstr. (1979-); Int. Labour Doc.

LC HD5725.W9 W97
DD 331.1/09787/021   US
TITLE CHANGE
WYOMING INCOME AND EMPLOYMENT REPORT. Added/Corp
Wyoming. Dept. of Administration and Fiscal Control. Statistics and Research Division. Wyoming. Dept. of Administration and Information. Economic Analysis Division. **VFOAT** Wyoming Income Report. (May 1981)-(Dec. 1993). English. Wyoming Department of Administration and Fiscal Control, Division of Research and Statistics, Emerson Building 327E, Cheyenne WY 82002-0060.

Formed by the union of Wyoming Income Report *and* Wyoming Employment Report. *Continued by* Wyoming Income, Employment, and Gross State Product Report.

US
●WYOMING INCOME, EMPLOYMENT, AND GROSS STATE PRODUCT REPORT. Added/Corp
Wyoming. Dept. of Administration and Information. Economic Analysis Division. 15th Ed. (Sept. 1994)-. Periodical. English. Wyoming Department of Administration and Fiscal Control, Division of Research and Statistics, Emerson Building 327E, Cheyenne WY 82002-0060. **Continues** Wyoming Income and Employment Report.

DD 331   **ISSN** 0512-4409   US
WYOMING LABOR FORCE TRENDS.
[Wyo. labor force trends]. **Added/Corp** Employment Security Commission of Wyoming. Research and Analysis Section. **VFOAT** Labor Force Trends. (196?)-. English. Twelve times a year. Free on request. Employment Security Commission of Wyoming, PO Box 2760, Research and Analysis, Casper WY 82602. **Tel** (307)237-3701. **ED** Michael J. Paris. **Circ:** 1,400.
Desc: Wyoming's labor force at a glance. Includes number unemployed, number employed, and unemployment rates. Also, includes related articles and articles on the general health of Wyoming's economy.
Ind/Abst Stat. Ref. Index.

LC HD7106.U5 A688b   **ISSN** 0194-3979
DD 331.2/52   US
YEARBOOK - AMERICAN SOCIETY OF PENSION ACTUARIES. Main/Corp
American Society of Pension Actuaries. (19??)-. English. One time a year. American Society of Pension Actuaries, 1700 K Street North West, Suite 404, Washington DC 20006.

US
YOUNG WORKER.
Vol. 1 (1970)-. Periodical. English. Irregular. Young Workers Liberation League, 235 West 23rd/5th Floor, New York NY 10011. **Tel** (212)929-2010. **Supersedes** Insurgent.

DD 331.88/113547124   **ISSN** 0844-3750   CN
YOUR UNION MATTERS.
[Your union matters]. No. 1 (June 12, 1987)-. Periodical. English. Irregular. Saskatchewan Government Employees Union, 1440 Broadway Avenue, Regina Saskatchewan S4P 1E2 Canada. **Continues** News, News, News, 0838-8040.

LC HD6274.N2 Y68
DD 331.3/4/09782   US
YOUTH IN NEBRASKA; A LABOR FORCE ANALYSIS. Added/Corp
Nebraska. Division of Employment. (19??)-. English. One time a year. Youth in Nebraska / A Labor Force Analysis, PO Box 94600, State House Station, Lincoln NE 68509.

DD 362   **ISSN** 0889-5058   US
YOUTHWORKER UPDATE.
[Youthworker update]. **VFOAT** Youth Worker Update. Vol. 1, No. 1 (Sept. 1986)-. Periodical. English. Ten times a year (monthly except July and Aug.). $23.95. Youth Specialties Inc., 1224 Greenfield Drive, El Cajon CA 92021. **Tel** (619)440-2333. **Formed by the union of** Sources & Resources **and** Youthletter.
Ind/Abst Curr. Thoughts Trends.

LC HD8537 .Z23   **ISSN** 0084-4403
DD 331   PL
Z BADAN KLASY ROBOTNICZEJ I INTELIGENCJI. Added/Corp
Polska Akademia Nauk. Zaklad Badan Socjologicznych. Vol. 1 (1958)-. Polish. **(Subscription address:** Ars Polona-Ruch, PO Box 1001, Krakowskie Przedmiescie 7, 00-068 Warsaw Poland. **Tel** 011 48 22 261201.)

LC HD5772.S5 A33
DD 331.1/26   XV
ZAPOSLENI PO OBCINAH. Main/Corp
Zavod Sr Slovenije za Statistiko. (19??)-. Slovenian. 20.00 Din. Zavod Sr Slovenije za Statistiko, Vozarski Pot 12, Ljubljana Slovenia.

LC HA1631 .A33 HD5811.6.A6 A6   YU
ZAPOSLENO OSOBLJE. Main/Corp
Savezni Zavod Za Statistiku (Yugoslavia). Serbo-Croatian (Roman). 4.00 Din each issue. Kneza Milosa 20, Belgrad Yugoslavia.

LC HA1631 .A33 HD5811.6.A6 A6   YU
ZAPOSLENO OSOBLJE I NETO LICNI DOHOCI PO GRUPAMA DELATHOSTI.
Main/Corp Savezni Zavod Za Statistiku (Yugoslavia). (19??)-. Serbo-Croatian (Roman). 3.00 Din each issue. Savezni Zavod Za Statistiku, Kneza Milosa 20, Belgrad Yugoslavia.

LC HD9715.G3 Z33   **ISSN** 0342-7943   GW
ZDB FORDERUNGEN, ZIELVORSTELLUNGEN FUER DIE ... LEGISLATURPERIODE DES DEUTSCHEN BUNDESTAGES.
Added/Corp Zentralverband des Deutschen Baugewerbes. (1976)-. German. Irregular (every four years). Free. Zentralverband des Deutschen Baugewerbes (ZDB), Haus des Deutschen Baugewerbes, Godesberger Allee 99, W-53175 Bonn 2 Germany. **Tel** 228 81 02 166, FAX 228 81 02 121. **Circ:** 4,000 (ctrl).

LC HD5077 .A26   JA
ZEIMU TOKEI KARA MITA MINKAN KYUYO NO JITTAI. Main/Corp
Japan. Kokuseicho. Somuka. **VFOAT** Minkan Kyuyo No Jittai. (1963)-. Government Publication. Japanese. One time a year. ¥1204. Ministry of Finance / Okura-Sho, 2-1 1-chome Kasumigaseki Chiyoda-ku, Tokyo 100 Japan. **Continues** Minkan Kyuyo Jittai Chosa Kekkahyo.

LC HD4809 .A52   **ISSN** 0340-2444
GW   CCC
ZEITSCHRIFT FUER ARBEITSWISSENSCHAFT. [Z. Arbeitswiss.].
Added/Corp Gesellschaft fuer Arbeitswissenschaft (Germany) Verband fuer Arbeitsstudien. (Mar. 1975)-. Trade Publication. German. Four times a year. $117.45. Verlag Dr. Otto Schmidt KG, Postfach 511026, D-50946 Cologne Germany. **Tel** 011 49 221 93738450. Index available. **Bk Rev. Ad Acc. Circ:** 1,700. **Continues** Arbeit und Leistung, 0003-763X.
Ind/Abst EMBASE; Ergon. Abstr.; Saf. Health Work.

LC HD4802 .Z47   **ISSN** 0148-8902
DD 301.44/42/05   US
ZEROWORK. [Zerowork]. (19??)-.
English. $2.50 each issue. Zerowork, Apartment 7, 417 East 65th Street, New York NY 10021.

LC HD5115.6.N4 Z53   NE
ZIEKTEVERZUIM IN ..., HET. Dutch.
One time a year. Free. Nederlands Instituut voor Praeventieve Gezondheidszorg/TNO, Wassenaarseweg 56, Postbus 124, 2300 AC Leiden Netherlands. **Tel** 011 31 71 17888, FAX 011 31 71 176382. **Circ:** 1,000 (ctrl).

MANAGEMENT

LC HD70.I4 A3
DD 658/.00954   II
ABHIGYAN : THE JOURNAL OF FOUNDATION OF ORGANISATIONAL RESEARCH. Added/Corp
Foundation for Organisational Research (India). (19??)-. Periodical. English. Four times a year. $15.00. Foundation for Organizational Research and Education, Adhitam Kendra, B-18 Qutab Institutional Area, New Delhi 110016 India. **Tel** 011 91 11 6866305, FAX 011 91 11 6856294. **(Subscription address:** Prints India, 11 Darya Ganj, New Delhi 110002 India. **Tel** 011 91 11 3268645, FAX 011 91 11 3275542, telex 31-61087 PRIN-IN.)

LC HD28 .A32   **ISSN** 1079-5545
DD 650   US
●ACADEMY OF MANAGEMENT EXECUTIVE (1993), THE. (THE ACADEMY OF MANAGEMENT EXECUTIVE.). [Acad. Manage. exec.].
Added/Corp Academy of Management. **VFOAT** Academy of Management Executive. Vol. 7, No. 2 (May 1993)-. Periodical. English. Four times a year. $75.00 (one year), $143.00 (two year), $203.00 (three year) US, Canada, Mexico; $85.00 (one year), $162.00 (two year), $230.00 (three year) other. Academy of Management, Academy of Management Publications, PO Box 3020, Briarcliff Manor NY 10510. **Tel** (914)923-2607, FAX (914)923-2615. **ED** John Young. Index available. cum. index. **Bk Rev. Ad Acc. Circ:** 9,000 (ctrl). **Continues** Executive (Ada, Ohio).
Ind/Abst ABI/INFORM [Computer File]; Bus. Period. Index; Mag. Search; Work Relat. Abstr.

LC HD28 .A24   **ISSN** 0001-4273
DD 658.05   US
ACADEMY OF MANAGEMENT JOURNAL. [Acad. Manage. j.]. Main/Corp
Academy of Management. Vol. 6, No. 1 (March 1963)-. Trade Publication. English. Four times a year. $95.00 (one-year), $181.00 (two-year), $257.00 (three-year) US, Canada and Mexico; $105.00 (one-year), $200.00 (two-year), $284.00 (three-year) other. Academy of Management, Academy of Management Publications, PO Box 3020, Briarcliff Manor NY 10510. **Tel** (914)923-2607, FAX (914)923-2615. **ED** Michael Hitt. cum. index. **Ad Acc. Circ:** 10,350 (ctrl). available on microfilm and microfiche from University Microfilms International (UMI);

available on an online database. Documents available from The Genuine Article, UMI Article Clearinghouse. ***Continues*** *Journal of the Academy of Management.* ***Superseded in part by*** *Academy of Management Review, 0363-7425.*
Desc: Original research of an empirical nature with articles or research notes in the field of management.
Ind/Abst ABI/INFORM Glob. Ed.; ABI/INFORM Ondisc: Expr. Ed. (March 1987-); ABI/INFORM [Computer File] (Sept. 1971-); Acad. Search; Bus. ASAP (1992-) [Full Txt.]; Bus. Index (1985-); Bus. Period. Index; Bus. Source Plus; Bus. Source; Contents Pages Manage.; Cumul. Index Nurs. Allied Health Lit.; Curr. Cit.; Curr. Contents Soc. Behav. Sci.; EP Collect.; Ergon. Abstr.; Gen. BusinessFile (1985); Gen. Period. Index (1985-); Health Plan. Adminis.; High. Educ. Abstr. (1980-); Homework Help.; Hosp. Health Admin. Index; Mag. Search; Manage. Market. Abstr.; Manage. Contents; MasterFile FullTEXT 1000; MasterFile FullTEXT 350; MasterFile FullTEXT 650; MasterFile FullTEXT (July 1993-); Middle East Abstr. Index; OCLC; Psychol. Abstr. (1968-); PsycINFO; PsycLit; PsycScan: Appl. Psych.; Res. Alert [Full Cov.]; Res. High. Educ. Abstr.; Risk Abstr. (19??-19??); Selec. Coop. Index Manage. Period.; Soc. Sci. Cit. Index [Full Cov.]; Telebase; UMI ABI/Inform--Bus. Period. Ondisc (March 1987-) [Full Txt.]; Wilson Bus. Abstr.; Work Relat. Abstr.

US

ACADEMY OF MANAGEMENT NEWS, THE. **Main/Corp** Academy of Management. Vol. 18, No. 4 (Oct. 1988)-. Periodical. English. Four times a year. Comes with Academy of Management individual membership - $65.00. Academy of Management, Academy of Management Publications, PO Box 3020, Briarcliff Manor NY 10510. **Tel** (914)923-2607, FAX (914)923-2615. ***Continues*** *Academy of Management. Academy of Management Newsletter, 0161-5998.*

LC HD28 .A23a **ISSN** 0363-7425
DD 658/.005 US
Pr Rev.
ACADEMY OF MANAGEMENT REVIEW, THE. [Acad. Manage. rev.]. **Main/Corp** Academy of Management. **Added/Corp** Academy of Management. Review. Vol. 1 (Jan. 1976)-. Trade Publication. English. Four times a year. $80.00. Academy of Management, Academy of Management Publications, PO Box 3020, Briarcliff Manor NY 10510. **Tel** (914)923-2607, FAX (914)923-2615. **ED** Orlando Behling. Index available (Bound in Oct. issue). **Bk Rev. Ad Acc. Circ:** 9,200. available on an online database; available on microfilm and microfiche from University Microfilms International (UMI). Documents available from The Genuine Article, UMI Article Clearinghouse. ***Supersedes in part*** *Academy of Management Journal, 0001-4273.*
Desc: Conceptual journal, published for scholars and researchers in management and related fields.
Ind/Abst ABI/INFORM Glob. Ed. (Jan. 1976-); ABI/INFORM Ondisc: Expr. Ed. (Jan. 1987-); ABI/INFORM [Computer File] (Jan. 1976-); Acad. Search; Anbar Account. Finan. Abstr. [Full Txt.]; Anbar Mark. Distr. Abstr. [Full Txt.]; Anbar Top Manage. Abstr. [Full Txt.]; Arts Humanit. Citation Index [Select. Cov.]; Bus. ASAP (1992-) [Full Txt.]; Bus. Index (1985-); Bus. Period. Index; Bus. Source Plus; Bus. Source; Contents Pages Manage.; Curr. Cit.; Curr. Contents Soc. Behav. Sci.; EP Collect.; Gen. BusinessFile (1985-); Gen. Period. Index (1985-); Health Plan. Adminis.; High. Educ. Abstr. (1982-); Homework Help.; Hosp. Health Admin. Index; INFO-SOUTH Abstr.; Int. Exec.; Mag. Search; Manage. Bibliogr. Rev.; Manage. Contents; MasterFile FullTEXT 1000; MasterFile FullTEXT 350; MasterFile FullTEXT 650; MasterFile FullTEXT (July 1993-); Middle East Abstr. Index; OCLC; Oper. Prod. Manage. Abstr. [Full Txt.]; Person. Train. Abstr. [Full Txt.]; Psychol. Abstr. (1981-); PsycINFO; PsycLit; PsycScan: Appl. Psych.; Res. Alert [Full Cov.]; Selec. Coop. Index Manage. Period.; Soc. Sci. Cit. Index [Full Cov.]; Telebase; UMI ABI/Inform--Bus. Period. Ondisc (Jan 1987-) [Full Txt.]; Wilson Bus. Abstr.; Women Manage. Rev. [Full Txt.]; Work Relat. Abstr.

ISSN 1076-8432
US
TITLE CHANGE
ACCOUNTABILITY NEWS FOR HEALTH CARE MANAGERS. **Added/Corp** Atlantic Information Services. (1994)-(1995). Periodical. English. Atlantic Information Services Inc., 1050 17th Street Northwest, Suite 480, Washington DC 20036. **Tel** (202)775-9008, (800)521-4323, FAX (202)331-9542. ***Continued by*** *Report on Quality Management.*

LC HF5601 **ISSN** 0749-2928
DD 657 US
CCC
ACCOUNTING OFFICE MANAGEMENT & ADMINISTRATION REPORT. **See** Business and Economics-Accounting.

ISSN 8756-629X
DD 615 US
ADMINISTRATION & MANAGEMENT SPECIAL INTEREST SECTION NEWSLETTER. [Adm. Manage. Spec. Interest Sect. newsl.]. **Added/Corp** American Occupational Therapy Association. Administration and Management Special Interest Section. **VFOAT** Administration and Management Special Interest Section Newsletter. Vol. 1, No. 1 (1985)-. Newsletter. English. Four times a year. $20.00. American Occupational Therapy Association, 1383 Piccard Drive, PO Box 1725, Rockville MD 20849. **Tel** (301)948-9626, FAX (301)948-5512. **ED** Sharon Gausch and Jacquelyn Bell. **Bk Rev. Circ:** 3,500 (ctrl).
Desc: Health care administration, management techniques, labor relations policy.

US
ADMINISTRATIVE ASSISTANT ADVISER. (19??)-. English. Twenty-three times a year. $230.00. Progressive Business Publications, 370 Technology Drive, PO Box 3019, Malvern PA 19355. **Tel** (617)527-8600, (800)220-5000, FAX (617)647-8089.
Desc: Information designed to help administrative assistants be more effective in today's business world.

ISSN 1191-7881
DD 651.3/741 CN
ADMINISTRATIVE ASSISTANT'S UPDATE. [Adm. assist. update]. (Nov. 1992)-. Periodical. English. Twelve times a year. 139.00Can$. MPL Communications, 133 Richard Street West, Suite 700, Toronto Ontario M5H 3M8 Canada. **Tel** (416)869-1177, FAX (416)869-0456. ***Continues*** *Secretary's Update., 0833-2878.*
Desc: Professional newsletter for secretaries, administrative assistants and office support staff. Offers professional insights, advice and information to help administrative assistants become more efficient, professional and responsible.

LC HD28 .A25 **ISSN** 0001-8392
DD 658.05 US
CCC
NLM W1 AD347 **CODEN** ASCQAG
Pr Rev.
ADMINISTRATIVE SCIENCE QUARTERLY. [Adm. sci. q.]. **Added/Corp** Cornell University. Graduate School of Business and Public Administration. Vol. 1 (June 1956)-. Periodical. English. Four times a year. $90.00. Administrative Science Quarterly, 20 Thornwood #100, Cornell University, Ithaca NY 14850. **Tel** (607)254-8307, FAX (607)254-7100, telex WUI 6713054. **ED** John H. Freeman. Index available (bound in Dec. issue). cum. index. **Bk Rev. Ad Acc. Circ:** 6,031. available on microfilm and microfiche from University Microfilms International (UMI); available on an online database from BRS; Dow Jones News/Retrieval; Information Access Company; and (Full-Text) DIALOG. Documents available from The Genuine Article, UMI Article Clearinghouse.
Desc: Empirical and theoretical articles that contribute to knowledge of business, governmental, military, health, and other organizations.
Ind/Abst ABC POL SCI; ABI/INFORM Glob. Ed.; ABI/INFORM [Computer File] (June 1971-); Acad. Abstr.; Acad. Search; Am. Hist. Life (1967-); Anbar Account. Finan. Abstr. [Full Txt.]; Appl. Soc. Sci. Index Abstr.; Bus. Index (1985-); Bus. Period. Index; Commun. Abstr.; Contents Pages Manage.; Cumul. Index Nurs. Allied Health Lit.; Curr. Cit.; Curr. Contents Soc. Behav. Sci.; Curr. Index J. Educ.; Educ. Adm. Abstr. (?-?); EP Collect.; Expand. Acad. Index (1984-); Gen. BusinessFile (1985-); Gen. Period. Index (1985-); Health Plan. Adminis.; High. Educ. Abstr. (1965-); Homework Help.; Hosp. Health Admin. Index; Hum. Resour. Abstr.; INFO-SOUTH Abstr.; Int. Aerosp. Abstr.; Int. Bibliogr. Sociol.; Int. Polit. Sci. Abstr.; Linguist. Lang. Behav. Abstr.; Mag. Search; Manage. Market. Abstr.; Manage. Bibliogr. Rev.; Manage. Contents; MasterFile FullTEXT 1000; MasterFile FullTEXT 350; MasterFile FullTEXT 650; MasterFile FullTEXT (July 1990-); Middle East Abstr. Index; Multicult. Educ. Abstr.; Newsp. Period. Abstr. (1988-); OCLC; Oper. Prod. Manage. Abstr. [Full Txt.]; Oper. Res./Manage. Sci.; PAIS Int. Print; Person. Manage. Abstr.; Psychol. Abstr. (1956-); PsycINFO; PsycLit; PsycScan: Appl. Psych.; Pub. Lib. FullTEXT; Qual. Control Appl. Stat.; Res. Alert [Full Cov.]; Res. High. Educ. Abstr.; Sage Public Adm. Abstr.; School Organ. Manage. Abstr.; Selec. Coop. Index Manage. Period.; Soc. Plann. Policy Dev. Abstr.; Soc. Sci. Source; Soc. Sci. Cit. Index [Full Cov.]; Soc. Sci. Index; Soc. Sci. Index Fulltext (Sept. 1988-) [Full Txt.]; Soc. Work Abstr. [Select. Cov.]; Sociol. Abstr.; Sociol. Educ. Abstr.; Telebase; UMI ABI/Inform--Bus. Period. Ondisc (Mar. 1987-) [Full Txt.]; U.S. Polit. Sci. Doc.; Wilson Bus. Abstr.; Work Relat. Abstr.

NE
ADVANCED SERIES IN MANAGEMENT. Vol. 1 (1983)-. Monographic series. English. Irregular. Price varies per volume. Elsevier Science Publishers BV, PO Box 211, 1000 AE Amsterdam Netherlands. **Tel** 011 31 20 4853641, 011 31 20 4853642, FAX 011 31 20 4853598. **ED** D. Neven, B. Kogut.
Desc: Includes volumes on topics such as entrepreneurship research, strategic management, and international manufacturing.
Ind/Abst Zentralbl. Math. Ihre Grenzgeb.

LC HD30.28 .A32 **ISSN** 0749-6826
DD 658.4/012/05 US
ADVANCES IN APPLIED BUSINESS STRATEGY. [Adv. appl. bus. strategy]. Vol. 1 (1984)-. English. Irregular. $73.25. JAI Press Inc., 55 Old Post Road, Suite 2, PO Box 1678, Greenwich CT 06836-1678. **Tel** (203)661-7602, FAX (203)661-0792. **ED** Lawrence Foster.

US
ADVANCES IN BUSINESS MANAGEMENT AND FORECASTING. (19??)-. Periodical. English. $73.25. JAI Press Inc., 55 Old Post Road, Suite 2, PO Box 1678, Greenwich CT 06836-1678. **Tel** (203)661-7602, FAX (203)661-0792. **ED** Kenneth D. Lawrence, Michael Geurts, and John Guerard.

LC QA76.76.E95 A4 **ISSN** 1074-7532
DD 004 US
●**ADVANCES IN EXPERT SYSTEMS FOR MANAGEMENT.** **See** Computers-Artificial Intelligence.

LC HD62.37 .A35
DD 620/.0068 US
ADVANCES IN GLOBAL HIGH-TECHNOLOGY MANAGEMENT. **VFOAT** Advances in Global High Technology Management. Vol. 1 (1992)-. English. Irregular. $73.25. JAI Press Inc., 55 Old Post Road, Suite 2, PO Box 1678, Greenwich CT 06836-1678. **Tel** (203)661-7602, FAX (203)661-0792. **ED** Luis R. Gomez-Mejia.

LC HD30.55 .A38 **ISSN** 0747-7929
DD 658/.049/05 US
CCC
ADVANCES IN INTERNATIONAL COMPARATIVE MANAGEMENT. [Adv. int. comp. manage.]. Vol. 1 (1984)-. English. One time a year. $73.25. JAI Press Inc., 55 Old Post Road, Suite 2, PO Box 1678, Greenwich CT 06836-1678. **Tel** (203)661-7602, FAX (203)661-0792. **ED** Benjamin Prasad and Richard Peterson. Documents available from UMI Article Clearinghouse.
Ind/Abst ABI/INFORM Glob. Ed.

LC HG4001 .A39 **ISSN** 1048-4760
DD 658.1/5/0726 US
ADVANCES IN MATHEMATICAL PROGRAMMING AND FINANCIAL PLANNING. [Adv. math. program. financ. plan.]. Vol. 1 (1987)-. English. One time a year. $73.25. JAI Press Inc., 55 Old Post Road, Suite 2, PO Box 1678, Greenwich CT 06836-1678. **Tel** (203)661-7602, FAX (203)661-0792.

LC HD30.28 .A33 **ISSN** 0742-3322
DD 658.4/012/05 US
CCC
ADVANCES IN STRATEGIC MANAGEMENT. [Adv. strateg. manage.]. Vol. 1 (1983)-. English. One time a year. $73.25. JAI Press Inc., 55 Old Post Road, Suite 2, PO Box 1678, Greenwich CT 06836-1678. **Tel** (203)661-7602, FAX (203)661-0792. **ED** Paul Shrivastava.

ISSN 0711-494X
DD 303.3/4/06071351 CN
AGENDA / THE NIAGARA INSTITUTE. [Agenda - Niagara Inst.]. **Main/Corp** Niagara Institute. Spring/Summer 1981-. Periodical. English. Three times a year. Free. Niagara Institute, PO Box 1041, Niagara-on-the-Lake Ontario L0S 1J0 Canada.

ISSN 1065-5921
DD 658 US
TITLE CHANGE
AGENT & MANAGER. (AGENT & MANAGER : THE BIBLE FOR ENTERTAINMENT, LITERARY & SPORTS AGENTS & MANAGERS.). [Agent manag.]. **VFOAT** Agent and Manager. (1991)-(July 1994). Trade Publication. English. Bedrock Communications, 650 First Avenue, New York NY 10016. **Tel** (212)532-4150, FAX (212)213-6382. **ED** Michael Caffin. **Ad Acc. Circ:** 22,000 (ctrl). ***Continued by*** *Facilities.*

LC TL **ISSN** 1061-3145
DD 629 US
CEASED
AIRPORT MANAGEMENT. **See** Aeronautics, Astronautics.

LC HD28 .I33
LE
AL-IDARI. (19??)-. Periodical. Arabic. Twelve times a year. $200.00. Al-Idari, PO Box 1038, Beirut Lebanon. **Tel** 011 961 1 387020, 011 961 1 387060, FAX 011 961 1 452957, telex 44224 SAYAD LE. **ED** H. El Khoury. Index available. **Ad Acc. Circ:** 24,908.

Business and Economics — Management

DD 658.4/73/05   **ISSN** 1186-0057   CN
ALLPOINTS (WILLOWDALE). (ALLPOINTS.).
[Allpoints]. **Added/Corp** Intercon Security Limited.
VFOAT All Points; Intercon Allpoints. (Summer 1990)-.
Periodical. English. Four times a year. Intercon Security Limited, 40 Sheppard Avenue West, Willowdale Ontario M2N 6K9 Canada.

LC HD28 .A52   **ISSN** 0002-6549   SP   CCC
ALTA DIRECCION. [Alta dir.]. Year 1 (May/June 1965)-. Periodical. Spanish. Six times a year (Feb., Apr., June, Aug., Oct., Dec.) $139.60. Alta Direccion SA, Infanta Carlota 123, No. 6 5A, 08029 Barcelona Spain. **Tel** 011 34 3 4109619, 011 34 3 4109739, **FAX** 011 34 3 4109739. **ED** D. Jorge Alarcon. Index available. cum. index. **Bk Rev**. **Ad Acc**. **Circ**: 15,000 (ctrl).
Desc: Commercial management, aimed at the elite of the current enterprise and industry.
Ind/Abst Selec. Coop. Index Manage. Period.

LC KF318.A1 A38   **ISSN** 0191-863X
DD 651/.9/34   US   CCC
ALTMAN WEIL PENSA REPORT TO LEGAL MANAGEMENT, THE. See Law.

DD 366.0068   **ISSN** 1037-6445   AT
AM NEWS BOX HILL. (AM NEWS.). [AM news Box Hill]. **VFOAT** Association Management News. (1991)-. Periodical. English. Four times a year. 39.46Aus$. Association Management Publishing, PO Box 614, Box Hill Victoria 3128 Australia. **Tel** 011 61 3 8993448, **FAX** 011 61 3 8993449. *Continues* Association Management (Box Hill), 1036-1871.

   US
AMA GUIDE TO MANAGEMENT DEVELOPMENT & TRAINING COURSES / AMERICAN MANAGEMENT ASSOCIATION, THE. **Added/Corp** American Management Association. (19??)-. Periodical. English. Two times a year. Free on request. American Management Association, 135 West 50th Street, New York NY 10020-1201. **Tel** (212)586-8100, (212)903-8375 (periodicals), **FAX** (212)903-8168, (212)903-8083 (periodicals). **(Subscription address:** American Management Association, PO Box 408, Saranac Lake NY 12983. **Tel** (800)262-9699, **FAX** (518)891-1500.**)** *Continues* Management Development Guide.

   US
AMA MANAGEMENT BRIEFING. (1971)-. Monographic series. English. Irregular. Price varies per volume. American Management Association, 135 West 50th Street, New York NY 10020-1201. **Tel** (212)586-8100, (212)903-8375 (periodicals), **FAX** (212)903-8168, (212)903-8083 (periodicals).

   US
AMA SURVEY REPORT, AN. Main/Corp American Management Association. **Added/Corp** American Management Association. Survey report. **VFOAT** Survey Report. (19??)-. Monographic series. English. Irregular. Comes with membership. American Management Association, 135 West 50th Street, New York NY 10020-1201. **Tel** (212)586-8100, (212)903-8375 (periodicals), **FAX** (212)903-8168, (212)903-8083 (periodicals).

LC HG1501   **ISSN** 0743-2348
DD 332.1   US
AMERICAN BUSINESS REVIEW. [Am. bus. rev.]. **Added/Corp** University of New Haven. School of Business. (June 1983)-. Periodical. English. Two times a year (Jan., June). $14.00. University of New Haven, School of Business, West Haven CT 06516. **Tel** (203)932-7118. **ED** Thomas Katsaros. **Bk Rev**. **Ad Acc**. **Circ:** 1,000.
Desc: Contains articles which reflect current ideas, techniques and international business practices and financial operations.

DD 658   **ISSN** 0002-8908   US
AMERICAN INDUSTRY. [Am. ind.]. (19??)-. Periodical. English. Ten times a year. $25.00. Publications for Industry, 21 Russel Woods Road, Great Neck NY 11021. **Tel** (516)487-0990, **FAX** (516)487-0809. **ED** Jack S. Panes. **Bk Rev**. **Ad Acc**. **Circ:** 25,000 (ctrl). available on microfilm from University Microfilms International (UMI).
Desc: New industrial product releases, new brochures and literature of interest to plant managers of largest manufacturing plants in the US.

   ISSN 1354-5787   UK
●**AMERICAN JOURNAL OF MANAGEMENT DEVELOPMENT.** (1995)-. Trade Publication. English. Four times a year. $129.00. MCB University Press, 60 62 Toller Lane, Bradford, West Yorkshire BD8 9BY United Kingdom. **Tel** 011 44 1274 785280, **FAX** 011 44 1274 785200, telex 51317-MCBUNI-G. **ED** Dr. Seb Sora.
Desc: Results-oriented journal with emphasis on how management development relates to everyday issues with which organizations have to deal.

LC HF5410   **ISSN** 0003-0902
DD 658.805   US   CCC   **CODEN** AMSLB6
AMERICAN SALESMAN, THE. [Am. salesm.].
Added/Corp National Research Bureau. (Sept. 1955)-. Trade Publication. English. Twelve times a year. $45.00. National Research Bureau Inc. / Iowa, 200 North Fourth, PO Box 1, Burlington IA 52601. **Tel** (319)752-5415, **FAX** (319)752-3421. **(Subscription address:** National Research Bureau Inc., PO Box 1, Burlington IA 52601. **)** **ED** Barbara Boeding. **Bk Rev**. **Circ:** 1,500 (ctrl). available on microfilm and microfiche from University Microfilms International (UMI); available on an online database from Lexis-Nexis; University Microfilms International (UMI); Mead Data Central; and (files 15,648/Full-Text) DIALOG. Documents available from BLDSC, FAXON Xpress, The UnCover Company, UMI Article Clearinghouse, FAXON Xpress.
Desc: Focuses on providing articles which help develop the attitudes, skills, and personal and professional qualities of sales representatives, enabling them to use more of their potential to increase productivity and achieve goals.
Ind/Abst ABI/INFORM Glob. Ed.; ABI/INFORM [Computer File] (Feb. 1975-); Bus. ASAP (1990-) [Full Txt.]; Bus. Index (1985-); Bus. Source Plus; Curr. Cit.; EP Collect.; Gen. BusinessFile (1985-); Gen. Period. Index (1985-); Homework Help.; Mag. Search; Manage. Contents; MasterFile FullTEXT 1000; MasterFile FullTEXT 350; MasterFile FullTEXT 650; MasterFile FullTEXT (Jan. 1993-); OCLC; Telebase; Trade Ind. ASAP [Full Txt.]; Trade Ind. Index [Full Txt.]; UMI ABI/Inform--Bus. Period. Ondisc (Jan. 1988-) [Full Txt.]; Vocat. Search.

LC QA   **ISSN** 0883-6221
DD 515   US
UDC 519.8; 51-74:658
Pr Rev.
AMERICAN SERIES IN MATHEMATICAL AND MANAGEMENT SCIENCES. See Mathematics.

LC HF5472.U6 A6   **ISSN** 0194-1534
DD 658.8/4   US
AMERICAN SHOWMAN, THE. Periodical. English. Twelve times a year. $9.00. Warren Gormley, RR 1 Box 5751, Brookline Station MO 65619-9801.

   US
AMR REPORT. (19??)-. English. Irregular. Advanced Manufacturing Research, 2 Oliver Street, 5th Floor, Boston MA 02109. **Tel** (617)542-6600. *Continues* Report on Industrial Communications, 0892-6158; *Absorbed* AMR Report on Mes.

LC HD4965.5.U6 A656   **ISSN** 1048-6135
DD 331.2/8165843/0973021   US   CEASED
AMS ... MANAGEMENT SALARIES REPORT. [AMS manage. salaries rep.]. **VFOAT** Management Salaries Report. **VAT** Administrative Management Society Management Salaries Report. (1988)-(19??). English. Administrative Management Society, 4622 Street Road, Trevose PA 19047. *Continues* Annual Management Salaries Report.

LC HB   **ISSN** 1351-3044
DD 330   UK
●**ANBAR MANAGEMENT OF QUALITY ABSTRACTS.** See Business and Economics-Abstracting, Bibliographies and Statistics.

LC TS155.A1 A55   **ISSN** 1353-5498
DD 658.5/05   UK
ANBAR OPERATIONS & PRODUCTION MANAGEMENT ABSTRACTS. See Business and Economics-Abstracting, Bibliographies and Statistics.

LC HD28 .T66
DD 658.4/005   UK
ANBAR TOP MANAGEMENT ABSTRACTS. See Business and Economics-Abstracting, Bibliographies and Statistics.

LC HF5601   **ISSN** 0307-0409
DD 657   UK
ANBAR YEARBOOK. [Anbar yearb.]. (1972)-. English. One time a year. Comes with Anbar Management Services. MCB University Press, 60 62 Toller Lane, Bradford, West Yorkshire BD8 9BY United Kingdom. **Tel** 011 44 1274 785280, **FAX** 011 44 1274 785200, telex 51317-MCBUNI-G. **(Subscription address:** MCB University Press / US and Canada Subscriptions, PO Box 10812, Birmingham AL 35201-0812. **Tel** (205)995-1567, (800)633-4931, **FAX** (205)995-1588.**)** **ED** Andrew Ede.
Desc: Contains reprints of all the ANBAR abstracts published in the previous volume plus index and author index.

DD 658   **ISSN** 0898-6614
ANNUAL CONFERENCE - COUNCIL OF LOGISTICS MANAGEMENT (U.S.). (ANNUAL CONFERENCE : PROCEEDINGS / COUNCIL OF LOGISTICS MANAGEMENT.). [Annu. conf. - Counc. Logist. Manage. (U. S.)]. **Main/Corp** Council of Logistics Management (U.S.). Conference. **VFOAT** Annual Conference Proceedings Proceedings; Fall Meeting; Annual Meeting. 23rd (Oct. 27-30, 1985)-. Proceedings. English. One time a year. $35.00. Council of Logistics Management, 2803 Butterfield Road, Suite 380, Oak Brook IL 60521. **Tel** (708)574-0985, **FAX** (708)574-0989. *Continues Fall Meeting.*
Desc: Covers subjects relating to logistics management as presented at the annual conference.

DD 658   **ISSN** 1059-3446   US
ANNUAL INTERNATIONAL MAINTENANCE CONFERENCE PROCEEDINGS. See Engineering-Industrial Engineering.

DD 354.71001   **ISSN** 1187-2160   CN
ANNUAL REPORT-CANADIAN CENTRE FOR MANAGEMENT DEVELOPMENT. (RAPPORT ANNUEL / CENTRE CANADIEN DE GESTION.). [Annu. rep. - Can. Cent. Manage. Dev.]. **Main/Corp** Centre Canadien de Gestion. **VFOAT** Annual Report. **VAT** Rapport Annuel - Centre Canadien de Gestion. (1991)-. French (English and French). *Continues* Le Rapport du Principal., 0848-4317.

LC HF5429.27 .A56   **ISSN** 0743-5460
DD 658.8/7   US
ANNUAL SECURITY AND SHRINKAGE STUDY. English. One time a year. National Mass Retailing Institute, 570 Seventh Avenue, New York NY 10018.

   ISSN 0360-6929   US   CCC
ANNUAL TECHNICAL CONFERENCE TRANSACTIONS - AMERICAN SOCIETY FOR QUALITY CONTROL. Main/Conf American Society for Quality Control. (1947)-. English. One time a year. $51.25 member, $56.25 nonmember. American Society for Quality Control, 611 East Wisconsin Avenue, PO Box 3005, Milwaukee WI 53201. **Tel** (414)272-8575, (800)248-1946, **FAX** (414)272-1734, telex 316567. available on microfilm and microfiche from University Microfilms International (UMI).
Ind/Abst Curr. Index Stat.; Stat. Theory Method Abstr. (1969).

   ISSN 0396-8995   FR
UDC 791
ANTENNES. **VFOAT** Micro Camera Antennes. (1975)-. Periodical. French. Eleven times a year. $76.56. Association PDI Techniques Audiovisual, Journal Antennes TDF, BP 518, 92542 Montrouge Cedex France. **Tel** 011 33 1 49651231, **FAX** 011 33 1 49651948.

   ISSN 0744-9143   US
APARTMENT MANAGEMENT NEWSLETTER. See Real Estate.

   US
APICS BIBLIOGRAPHY. **Added/Corp** American Production and Inventory Control Society. **VFOAT** Bibliography. (198?)-. English. Irregular. $7.50 (per copy). American Production and Inventory Control Society, 500 West Annandale Road, Falls Church VA 22046. **Tel** (703)237-8344, (800)444-2742. *Continues* Bibliography of Articles, Books, and Other Sources of Information, Concerning Production and Inventory Management (PIM) and Related Subjects, 0733-2890.

DD 658   **ISSN** 1056-0017   US
APICS, THE PERFORMANCE ADVANTAGE. [APICS perform. advant.]. **Added/Corp** American Production and Inventory Control Society. **VFOAT** APICS. Vol. 1, No. 1 (July 1991)-. Periodical. English. Twelve times a year. $45.00. American Production and Inventory Control Society, 500 West Annandale Road, Falls Church VA 22046. **Tel** (703)237-8344, (800)444-2742.

LC HD30.23 .A66   **ISSN** 0276-8976
DD 658.4/03/05   US
APPLICATIONS OF MANAGEMENT SCIENCE. [Appl. manage. sci.]. Vol. 1 (1981)-. Monographic series. English. Irregular. $73.25. JAI Press Inc., 55 Old Post Road, Suite 2, PO Box 1678, Greenwich CT 06836-1678. **Tel** (203)661-7602, **FAX** (203)661-0792. **ED** Randall L. Schultz.

Business and Economics —Management

LC QE48.G83 D46a
DK
ARSBERETNING - GRONLANDS GEOLOGISKE UNDERSOGELSE.
Main/Corp Grnlands Geologiske Undersogelse. (19??)-. Corporate Report. Danish. One time a year. Free (postage may be charged). Gronlands Geologiske Undersogelse, Oster Voldgade 10, DK-1350 Kobenhavn K Denmark. **Tel** (45)33 11 88 66, FAX (45)33 93 53 52, telex 19066 GGUTEL DK. **Circ:** 100 (ctrl).
Desc: Review of the institution's activities.

LC HD20.15.I4 H93 ISSN 0257-8069
DD 658/.007/1054 II
ASCI JOURNAL OF MANAGEMENT. [ASCI j. manage.]. **Added/Corp** Administrative Staff College of India. **VFOAT** A.S.C.I. Journal of Management; Journal of Management. **VAT** Administrative Staff College of India Journal of Management. Vol. 1, No. 1 (Sept. 1971)-. Periodical. English. Two times a year. $36.00. Administrative Staff College, India Belle Vista, Hyderabad 500049 India. **(Subscription address:** UBS Publishers Distributors, 5 Ansari Road, PO Box 7015, New Delhi 110002 India. **Tel** 011 91 11 3273601, 011 91 11 3266645.**)** **Bk Rev.** **Ad Acc.** Documents available from UMI Article Clearinghouse.
Ind/Abst ABI/INFORM Glob. Ed.; ABI/INFORM [Computer File] (Sept. 1980-); Bus. Index (1979-?).

ISSN 0954-2957
HK
CEASED
ASIA PACIFIC INTERNATIONAL MANAGEMENT REVIEW. **Added/Corp** International Management Centres. **VFOAT** International Management Review. Vol. 1 (Aug. 1988)-(19??). Periodical. English. MCB University Press, 60 62 Toller Lane, Bradford, West Yorkshire BD8 9BY United Kingdom. **Tel** 011 44 1274 785280, FAX 011 44 1274 785200, telex 51317-MCBUNI-G. **ED** Barry Smith. **Ad Acc.** **Continues** Management Forum.
Desc: Aims to publish articles that show the benefits that can be achieved by an organization through increased professional skills.

LC HD28 .A739 ISSN 0217-4561
DD 658/.005 SI
Pr Rev.
ASIA PACIFIC JOURNAL OF MANAGEMENT. (ASIA PACIFIC JOURNAL OF MANAGEMENT : APJM). [Asia Pac. j. manage.]. **Added/Corp** National University of Singapore. School of Management. **VFOAT** APJM; A.P.J.M.; Asia-Pacific Journal of Management. Vol. 1, No. 1 (Sept. 1983)-. Periodical. English. Two times a year (Apr., Oct.). 35.00Sing$ (individuals), 24.00Sing$ (student), 48.00Sing$ (institutions), Singapore; $22.00 (individuals), $15.00 (student), $30.00 (institutions) other. University of Singapore / Faculty of Business Administration, 10 Kent Ridge, Singapore 0511 Singapore. **Tel** 011 65 7723101, FAX 011 65 7792621 3571, telex 33943. Index available. cum. index. **Bk Rev.** **Circ:** 1,000. available on microfilm and microfiche from University Microfilms International (UMI); available on an online database (file 15/Full-Text) from DIALOG.
Desc: Study of functions, processes and structures of management as practiced in the countries of the Asia-Pacific region.
Ind/Abst Asia.-Pac. Econ. Lit.; Curr. Cit.; Curr. Contents Soc. Behav. Sci.

ISSN 0965-3570
HK
CCC
ASIA PACIFIC JOURNAL OF QUALITY MANAGEMENT. Vol. 1, No. 1 (1992)-. Trade Publication. English. Three times a year. $549.00. MCB University Press, 60 62 Toller Lane, Bradford, West Yorkshire BD8 9BY United Kingdom. **Tel** 011 44 1274 785280, FAX 011 44 1274 785200, telex 51317-MCBUNI-G. **(Subscription address:** MCB University Press / US and Canada Subscriptions, PO Box 10812, Birmingham AL 35201-0812. **Tel** (205)995-1567, (800)633-4931, FAX (205)995-1588.**)** **ED** Amrik Sohal.
Desc: Promotes the practice and benefits of total quality management throughout the Asia Pacific Region. Provides a source of information on innovation and developments in quality management.

ISSN 1015-5023
HK
ASIAMAC JOURNAL. **See** Engineering-Mechanical Engineering and Machinery.

LC HF5001 .A723
US
ASSOCIATION MANAGEMENT.
Added/Corp American Society of Association Executives. Vol 1. (Oct. 1949)-. Periodical. English. Twelve times a year. $30.00 US; $35.00 Canada; $40.00 other. American Society of Association Executives, 1575 Eye Street NW, Washington DC 20005. **Tel** (202)626-2735, (202)626-2722, FAX (202)371-8825. **ED** Ann I Mahoney. Index available. **Bk Rev.** **Ad Acc.** **Circ:** 23,000. available on microfiche. Documents available from UMI Article Clearinghouse. **Absorbed** ASAE News; Here's How.

Desc: Provides information on finance, education, management, business, government, community, operations, etc., that benefit and educate association executives.
Ind/Abst ABI/INFORM Glob. Ed.; ABI/INFORM [Computer File] (January 1975); Bus. ASAP (1990-) [Full Txt.]; Bus. Index (1985-); Bus. Period. Index; GATFWORLD (1984); Gen. BusinessFile (1985-); Hosp. Health Admin. Index; Urban Aff. Abstr.; Work Relat. Abstr.

LC HF5001 .A723 ISSN 0004-5578
DD 658 US
Pr Rev.
ASSOCIATION MANAGEMENT. [Assoc. manage.]. **Added/Corp** American Society of Association Executives. Vol. 15 (Jan. 1963)-. Periodical. English. Twelve times a year. $30.00. American Society of Association of Executives, 1575 Eye Street Northwest, Washington DC 20005. **Tel** (202)626-2722, FAX (202)842-1109. **ED** Elissa M. Myers. **Bk Rev.** **Ad Acc.** **Circ:** 22,000. available on microfilm and microfiche from University Microfilms International (UMI). Documents available from UMI Article Clearinghouse. **Formed by the union of** American Society of Association Executives. Journal of the American Society of Association Executives **and** American Society of Association Executives. ASAE News Here's How. **Continued in part by** Leadership, 0195-9204.
Desc: Exclusively for association decision makers. In it you will find features on a broad range of association management topics. News on issues affecting the associations, job changes among their colleagues, and peer to peer advice on problems with real-life solutions.
Ind/Abst ABI/INFORM Glob. Ed.; ABI/INFORM [Computer File] (Jan. 1975-); Acad. Search; Account. Tax Datab. (Jan. 1975-) [Full Txt.]; Bus. Period. Index; Bus. Source Plus; Bus. Source; Curr. Cit.; EP Collect.; Gen. Period. Index (1985-); Health Plan. Adminis.; Homework Help.; Hosp. Health Admin. Index (Vol. 29, No. 12, 1977-Vol. 41, No. 12, 1989); INFO-SOUTH Abstr.; Mag. Search; MasterFile FullTEXT 1000; MasterFile FullTEXT 350; MasterFile FullTEXT 650; MasterFile FullTEXT (Jan. 1994-); OCLC; Telebase; Trade Ind. ASAP [Full Txt.]; Trade Ind. Index [Full Txt.]; UMI ABI/Inform--Bus. Period. Ondisc (Jan. 1987-) [Full Txt.]; Wilson Bus. Abstr.

ISSN 0144-9613
UK
ASSOCIATION MANAGEMENT WATFORD. [Assoc. manage.Watford]. (1980)-. Periodical. English. Four times a year (Mar., June, Sept., Dec.). £12.50 UK; £15.00 other. Scriven Park Ltd., Scriven Park / Ripley Road / Knaresbor, North Yorkshire HG5 9DF United Kingdom. **Tel** 011 44 181 423866985, FAX 011 44 181 423866586.

ISSN 0744-1088
US
ASSOCIATIONS REPORT. (19??)-. Periodical. English. Twelve times a year. $64.00 US; $64.80 Canada; $72.00 other. Associations Report, PO Box 3889, Vancouver WA 98662. **Tel** (206)256-0300. **ED** Howard Galloway. **Bk Rev.** **Ad Acc.**
Desc: Practical management aids for executives of membership organizations. Contains ideas for improvement in all phases of association management.

ATN : AUSTRALIAN TRANSPORT NEWS. **See** Transportation.

ISSN 0742-0978
US
AUERBACH DATAGRAM. DATA SECURITY MANAGEMENT. [Auerbach datagram, Data secur. manage.]. **VFOAT** Data Security Management; Datagram. Vol. 1, No. 1 (Feb. 1984)-. Periodical. English. Six times a year. Auerbach Publishers Inc., Park Square Building, 31 St. James Avenue, Boston MA 02116. **Tel** (800)950-1207.

LC HD28 .A77
DD 658/.005 US
AUGSBA REVIEW / THE ATLANTA UNIVERSITY, GRADUATE SCHOOL OF BUSINESS, THE. Periodical. English. Two times a year. Augsba Review, Graduate School of Business, The Atlanta University, Atlanta GA 30314.

AT
Pr Rev.
AUSTRALASIAN BUS AND COACH. **See** Transportation.

AT
●**AUSTRALASIAN TELECOMMUNICATIONS MARKETING AND MANAGEMENT NEWSLETTER.** **See** Communications-Telecommunication.

ISSN 0312-8962
AT
Pr Rev.
AUSTRALIAN JOURNAL OF MANAGEMENT. [Aust. j. manage.]. **Added/Corp** Australian Graduate School of Management. Vol. 1, No. 1 (Apr. 1976)-. Periodical. English. Two times a year (June & Dec.). 50.00Aus$. The Australian Journal of Management, Australian Graduate School of Management, University of New South Wales, PO Box 1, Kensington New South Wales, 2033 Australia. **Tel** 011 61 2 9319259, FAX 011 61 2 6627621. **ED** Justin Wood, John Rossiter, Ian Marsh, Robert Marks, Vic Taylor and Philip Yetton. Index available. cum. index. **Bk Rev.** **Circ:** 350. available on microfiche. Documents available from UMI Article Clearinghouse.
Desc: Objectives are to encourage and publish research in the field of management.
Ind/Abst ABI/INFORM Glob. Ed.; ABI/INFORM [Computer File] (Oct. 1979-); APAIS, Aust. Public Aff. Inf. Ser. (1976-); Contents Recent Econ. J.; EP Collect.; Homework Help.; J. Econ. Lit.; MasterFile FullTEXT 1000; MasterFile FullTEXT 350; MasterFile FullTEXT 650; MasterFile FullTEXT; OCLC; PAIS Int. Print (1991-); Telebase; World Mag. Bank.

AT
AUSTRALIAN PROJECT MANAGER. (19??)-. English. Four times a year (Mar., June, Sept., Dec.). 25.00Aus$. Australian Institute of Project Management, 28 Bond Street, Mosman NSW 2088 Australia. **Tel** 011 61 2 9601834, FAX 011 61 2 9681846. **ED** Geoff Sheldon. **Ad Acc.** **Circ:** 3,000 (ctrl).
Desc: Information on project management, building, computer programming, electronics and new products.

ISSN 0005-0385
AT
AUSTRALIAN TRANSPORT. **See** Transportation.

ISSN 0740-6819
US
AUTOMATED LAW OFFICE CONSULTANT, THE. **See** Law-Computer Applications.

LC HD9710.U5 A836 ISSN 0195-1564
DD 629.2/068 US
AUTOMOTIVE EXECUTIVE (1979). **See** Transportation-Automobiles.

IT
AZIENDA ITALIA. (19??)-. Periodical. Italian. Twelve times a year. L160000 Italy; L320000 other. IPSOA Editore SRL, Casella Postale 12055, Mastrangelo, 20120 Milan Italy. **Tel** 011 39 2 82476248.

LC HD ISSN 0923-5108
DD 658 NE
UDC 69
CEASED
B & B. BOUW EN BEHEER. (B & B.) [B B, Bouw beheer]. **VFOAT** Bouw en Beheer. (1988)-(1993). Periodical. Dutch. Bureau van Viet BV, Postbus 20, 2040 A A Zandvoort Netherlands. **Continues** Patrimonium (Amstelvenn), 0031-3149.

LC HD28 .B36
DD 658.4/005 NP
BANIJYA SANSAR. **VFOAT** Vanijaya Samsara. Periodical. English (Nepali). Rs10.00. Business Administration and Commerce Welfare Association, Tribhuvan University, Gandhi Bhawan Kathmandu, Katipur Nepal.

LC HD4966.B262 U432
DD 331.2/813321/978 US
BANK MANAGEMENT SURVEY. **VFOAT** Survey. (19??)-. English. One time a year. Mountain States Employers Council, 1790 Logan Street, PO Box 539, Denver CO 80201.

ISSN 0882-6218
DD 658 US
BARNARD'S RETAIL MARKETING REPORT. [Barnard's Retail mark. rep.]. **Added/Corp** Barnard Enterprises. **VFOAT** Retail Marketing Report. Vol. 1, No. 1 (Apr. 1985)-. Periodical. English. Twelve times a year. $125.00. Barnard Enterprises, 25 Sutton Place South, New York NY 10022. **Tel** (212)752-9810. **ED** Kurt Barnard. **Bk Rev,** (Qty: 2). **Ad Acc, Adv Mgr:** W. Barnard, **Tel** (212)752-9810.
Desc: Retail industry forecasts and anaylsis.

US
BBP MANAGER'S LETTER. (19??)-. Newsletter. English. Twenty-six times a year. $146.28. Bureau of Business Practice, 24 Rope Ferry Road, Waterford CT 06386. **Tel** (800)243-0876, (203)442-4365, (800)876-9105, FAX (203)443-1123. **Continues** PC Manager's Letter.

Business and Economics —Management

BEDRIJFSDOCUMENTAIRE. (19??)-(Nov. 1993). Dutch. Koggeschip Vakbladen BV, Postbus 1198, 1000 BD Amsterdam Netherlands. **Tel** 011 31 20 6916666.
LC HF23 .M3

NE CEASED

BEDRIJFSKUNDE. Vol. 41, No. 1 (Jan. 1969)-. Periodical. Dutch. Twelve times a year. Distributiecentrum Uitgevers, Santvoortbeeklaan 21 23, 2100 Deurne Antwerpen Belgium. **Tel** 011 32 3 3256880. *Continues Handelswetenschappen & Administratieve Praktijk.* **Ind/Abst** Selec. Coop. Index Manage. Period.

NE

ISSN 0921-2000
NE
UDC 656

BEDRIJFSVERVOER (1987). (BEDRIJFSVERVOER.). [Bedrijfsvervoer 1987]. (1987)-. Periodical. Dutch. Twenty-four times a year. $304.06. Wegener Tijl Tijdschriften Group, Postbus 1860, 1110 CD Diemen Netherlands. **Tel** 011 31 20 6603300. *Continues Goederenstroom Management, 0927-7072.*

UK

BENCHMARK - THE EUROPEAN MANAGEMENT REVIEW. (199?)-. Periodical. English. Six times a year. £95.00 UK; $125.00 other. Euromoney Publications PLC, Nestor House, Playhouse Yard, London EC4Z 5EX United Kingdom. **Tel** 011 44 171 7798888, FAX 011 44 171 7798630, telex 290700 EUROMON G. **(Subscription address:** Euromoney Publications PLC, Perrymount Road Haywards Heath, West Sussex RH16 3DH United Kingdom. **Tel** 011 44 1444 440421.)
Desc: Offers insights and practical help with today's business challenges.

ISSN 1351-3036
DD 658.562
UK

●**BENCHMARKING FOR QUALITY MANAGEMENT & TECHNOLOGY.** [Benchmark. qual. manag. technol.]. **VFOAT** Benchmarking for Quality Management and Technology. (1994)-. Periodical. English. Four times a year. $199.00. MCB University Press, 60 62 Toller Lane, Bradford, West Yorkshire BD8 9BY United Kingdom. **Tel** 011 44 1274 785280, FAX 011 44 1274 785200, telex 51317-MCBUNI-G.
LC HD28
DD 658

ISSN 1351-3036
UK

●**BENCHMARKING FOR QUALITY MANAGEMENT & TECHNOLOGY: AN INTERNATIONAL JOURNAL.** (1994)-. Academic Scholarly Publication. English. Four times a year. £159.00. MCB University Press, 60 62 Toller Lane, Bradford, West Yorkshire BD8 9BY United Kingdom. **Tel** 011 44 1274 785280, FAX 011 44 1274 785200, telex 51317-MCBUNI-G. **(Subscription address:** MCB University Press / US and Canada Subscriptions, PO Box 10812, Birmingham AL 35201-0812. **Tel** (205)995-1567, (800)633-4931, FAX (205)995-1588.) **ED** Mohamed Youssef. Documents available from BLDSC.

ISSN 0896-7911
DD 658
US

BEST PAPERS PROCEEDINGS / ACADEMY OF MANAGEMENT. [Best pap. proc. - Acad. Manage.]. **Main/Corp** Academy of Management. **VFOAT** Academy of Management Best Papers Proceedings. (1986)-. Proceedings. English. One time a year (August). $24.00. Academy of Management, Academy of Management Publications, PO Box 3020, Briarcliff Manor NY 10510. **Tel** (914)923-2607, FAX (914)923-2615. (Free). cum. index. *Continues Academy of Management. Proceedings - Academy of Management, 0065-0668.*

ISSN 0801-3322
DD 658
NO

BETA. [Beta]. Vol. 1 (1987)-. Periodical. Norwegian. Two times a year. Kr480.00, $80.00. Scandinavian University Press, PO Box 2959 Toeyen, N 0608 Oslo 6 Norway. **Tel** 011 47 2 2575400, FAX 011 47 2 2575353, telex 71896 UROR N. **(Subscription address:** Scandinavian University Press, 200 Meacham Ave., Elmont NY 11003. **Tel** (516)352-7300, FAX (516)352-7377.) **ED** Ole Gjoelberg. **Ad Acc. Circ:** 600.
Desc: A scholarly journal of business management.

ISSN 0172-6196
GW
UDC 658(01)

BETRIEBSWIRT GERNSBACH, DER. [Betriebswirt Gernsb.]. **VFOAT** BW. Der Betriebswirt. (1979)-. Periodical. German. Four times a year. DM69.75 Germany; DM90.00 other. Deutscher Betriebswirte Verlag, Bleichstr 20 22, Postfach 1332, D-76593 Gernsbach Germany. **Tel** 011 49 7224 93970. *Continues Der Betriebswirt. Ausgabe A, 0340-854X; Absorbed LBW-Fachinformation, 0723-760X.*
Ind/Abst Selec. Coop. Index Manage. Period.

ISSN 0723-9629
GW
UDC 336.722

BETRIEBSWIRTSCHAFTLICHE BLATTER. (1981)-. Periodical. German. Twelve times a year.
Ind/Abst Selec. Coop. Index Manage. Period.

ISSN 0409-2805
GW

BETRIEBSWIRTSCHAFTLICHE FORSCHUNGEN. Vol. 1 (1954)-. Monographic series. German. Irregular. Price varies per volume. Duncker und Humblot Verlag, Postfach 410329, D-12113 Berlin Germany. **Tel** 011 49 30 79000612, 011 49 30 79000613.

ISSN 0523-1035
GW

BETRIEBSWIRTSCHAFTLICHE SCHRIFTEN. (1955)-. Periodical. German. Irregular. Duncker und Humblot Verlag, Postfach 410329, D-12113 Berlin Germany. **Tel** 011 49 30 79000612, 011 49 30 79000613.

UK

BETTER MANAGEMENT. (19??)-. English. Four times a year (Jan., April, July, Oct.). Free on request. Residuary Milk Marketing Board, Statistics Unit, Thames Ditton, Surrey KT7 OEL United Kingdom. **Tel** 011 01398-4101.
Ind/Abst Agric. Eng. Abstr.; Dairy Sci. Abstr.; Nutr. Abstr. Rev., Ser. B, Live Feeds and Feed.
LC HG1501
DD 332.1
US

BEYOND THE BOTTOM LINE. See Business and Economics-Banks and Banking.

ISSN 0340-5370
GW
UDC 657/658.01

BFUP. BETRIEBSWIRTSCHAFTLICHE FORSCHUNG UND PRAXIS. [BFuP, Betriebswirtsch. Forsch. Prax.]. **VFOAT** Betriebswirtschaftliche Forschung und Praxis (1973). (1949)-. Periodical. German. Irregular. Verlag Neue Wirtschaftsbriefe, Eschstrasse 22, D-44629 Herne Germany. **Tel** 011 49 2323 1410. *Continues Betriebswirtschaftliche Forschung und Praxis, 0006-002X.*
Ind/Abst Soc. Sci. Cit. Index [Full Cov.].

ISSN 0167-1146
NE
UDC 35

BINNENLANDS BESTUUR. [Binnenl. best.]. (1980)-. Periodical. German. One time a week. $132.51. Samsom Bedrijfsinformatie BV, Postbus 4, 2400 MA Alphen Rij Netherlands. **Tel** 011 31 1720 66633. **(Subscription address:** Intermedia BV, Postbus 4, 2400 MA Alphen AD Rijn Netherlands. **Tel** 011 31 1720 66481.)

ISSN 1050-1975
US

BITS & PIECES (FAIRFIELD, N.J.). (BITS & PIECES, A MONTHLY MIXTURE OF HORSE SENSE AND COMMON SENSE ABOUT WORKING WITH PEOPLE.). **VFOAT** Bits and Pieces. Vol. 11 (1978)-. Periodical. English. Thirteen times a year. $23.50. Economics Press Inc, 12 Daniel Road, Fairfield NJ 07004. **Tel** (201)227-1224, (800)526-2554, FAX (201)227-9742.
Desc: Strives to get to the heart of managing: understanding how people think, feel, and react. Contains humorous anecdotes, memorable quotations, success stories that inspire more success.

ISSN 1061-4249
DD 650
US

BOARD LEADERSHIP. [Board leadersh.]. **Added/Corp** Carver, John. (1992)-. Periodical. English. Six times a year. $135.00. Jossey Bass Inc., 350 Sansome Street, San Francisco CA 94104. **Tel** (415)433-1767, FAX (415)433-0499.
Desc: Offers insights of board consultants in the form of a workshop.

ISSN 1058-5419
DD 658
US

BOARD MEMBER: NATIONAL CENTER FOR NONPROFIT BOARDS. [Board memb.]. **Added/Corp** National Center for Nonprofit Boards (U.S.). Vol. 1, No. 1 (Jan./Feb. 1992)-. Periodical. English. Six times a year. $79.00 (nonmembers), $48.00 (membership). National Center for Nonprofit Boards, 2000 L Street NW, Suite 411, Washington DC 20036.
LC HD2745 .K63a
DD 658.4/2
ISSN 0161-6196
US

BOARD OF DIRECTORS ANNUAL STUDY. **Main/Corp** Korn/Ferry International (Firm). (19??)-. English. One time a year. Korn/Ferry International, 277 Park Avenue, New York NY 10017.

ISSN 0045-2300
US
TITLE CHANGE

BOARDROOM REPORTS. [Boardr. rep.]. Vol. 1 (1972)-(19??). Periodical. English. Boardroom Reports Inc., 330 West 42nd Street, 14th Floor, New York NY 10036. **Tel** (212)239-9000. **(Subscription address:** Neodata / Colorado, PO Box 2606, Boulder CO 80322.) available on microfilm and microfiche from University Microfilms International (UMI). *Continued by Bottom Line Business.*
Desc: Management's source of inside information. A continuing education in the tough nitty-gritty of running a business successfully in uncertain times. Inside ways to save taxes, cut costs, improve cash flow, increase productivity, and out-perform competition. How to separate the facts from the hocus-pocus in banking, insurance, advertising, marketing, computers, credit, management, sales, etc.
Ind/Abst Pop. Mag. Rev. (1984).

ISSN 1192-6201
DD 658.4
CN

●**BOARDROOM (WILLOWDALE).** (BOARDROOM.). [Boardroom]. No. 1 (Jan. 1993)-. Periodical. English. Six times a year. 100.04Can$. Emond Montgomery Publishing Ltd., 58 Shaftesbury Avenue, Toronto Ontario, M4T 1A3 Canada. **Tel** (416)975-3925, FAX (416)975-3924.

ISSN 0211-1535
SP

BOLETIN / CIRCULO DE EMPRESARIOS. [Bol. - Circ. Empres.]. **Added/Corp** Circulo de Empresarios (Madrid, Spain). (1979)-. Periodical. Spanish. Four times a year. Circulo de Empresarios / Spain, Serrano Jover 5-20, E-28015 Madrid Spain.
LC HC153.5.A1 B64
DD 330.97293/005
ISSN 1012-9480
DR

BOLETIN DEL SECRETARIADO TECNICO. [Bol. Secr. tec. - Secr. tec. Pres.]. Vol. 1 (April 1983)-. Periodical. Spanish. Twelve times a year. Edifico de Oficinas Publicas, Ave Mexico Esq Leopoldo Navarro, Santo Domingo Dominican Republic.

ISSN 1036-1456
DD 658.00994
AT

BOND MANAGEMENT REVIEW. [Bond manag. rev.]. **Added/Corp** Australia-Pacific Society for Management Studies. (1990)-. Periodical. English. Two times a year. 246.65Aus$. Bond Management Review, School of Business, Bond University Gold Coast, Mail Centre 4229 Australia. **Tel** 11 61 75 952277, FAX 11 61 75 951160. **ED** Kristin M. Hickey (phone: 075 952233). **Bk Rev. Ad Acc. Circ:** 200 (ctrl).
Desc: Articles of multidisciplinary nature which foster a mutually productive relationship between the academic and business communities.
LC Z683 .B69
DD 021.8/3
ISSN 0888-045X
US
CCC
CODEN BOLIEO

BOTTOM LINE (NEW YORK, N.Y.), THE. See Library and Information Sciences.
LC JC323 .B685
ISSN 0957-4441
UK

●**BOUNDARY AND SECURITY BULLETIN.** **Added/Corp** University of Durham. International Boundaries Research Unit. **VFOAT** IBRU Boundary and Security Bulletin. Vol. 1, No. 1 (Apr. 1993)-. Periodical. English. Four times a year. £65.00. International Boundaries Research Unit, Suite 3P, Mountjoy Research Centre, University of Durham, Durham DH1 3UR United Kingdom. **Tel** 011 44 191 3747701, FAX 011 44 191 3747702. *Continues Boundary Bulletin, 0957-4441.*

ISSN 1061-6675
DD 658
US

BRAINSTORMER (BELLINGHAM, MASS.). (BRAINSTORMER.). [Brainstormer]. (1991)-. Periodical. English. Twelve times a year. $1.25 (single issue). Giphlyn Products, PO Box 177, Bellingham MA 02019.

ISSN 1066-260X
DD 658
US
CEASED

BREAKTHROUGH STRATEGIES. [Breakthr. strateg.]. **Added/Corp** Alexander Hamilton Institute (U.S.). (1992)-(1994). Periodical. English. Alexander Hamilton Institute, 70 Hilltop Road, Ramsey NJ 07446-1119. **Tel** (201)825-8161, (800)879-2441, FAX (201)825-8696.
LC HD30.4 .B745
DD 658
ISSN 1054-7835
US
TITLE CHANGE

BRICKER'S INTERNATIONAL DIRECTORY. VOL. 1, LONG-TERM UNIVERSITY-BASED EXECUTIVE PROGRAMS. [Bricker's int. dir., Vol. 1 Long-term univ.-based exec. programs]. **Added/Corp** Peterson's Guides, Inc. **VFOAT** Long-Term University-Based

Executive Programs; Long Term University Based Executive Programs; Bricker's International Directory. Vol. 1, Long-Term. (199?)-25th Edition (1994). English. Peterson's Guides, 202 Carnegie Center, Department 2342, PO Box 2123, Princeton NJ 08543-2123. **Tel** (609)243-9111, (800)338-3282, FAX (609)243-9150, (609)452-0966. ***Continues*** *Bricker's International Directory, 0277-7312.* ***Merged with*** *Bricker's International Directory. Vol. 2, Short-Term University-Based Executive Programs, 1054-7843* ***to form*** *Bricker's International Directory (Princeton, N.J. : 1994), 1078-2257.*
Desc: Hundreds of the top level management programs are detailed and described at length in a full page profile on program locations, duration, subject matter, participants, faculty and special features.

LC HD30.4 .B746 **ISSN** 1054-7843
DD 658 US
TITLE CHANGE

BRICKER'S INTERNATIONAL DIRECTORY. VOL. 2, SHORT-TERM UNIVERSITY-BASED EXECUTIVE PROGRAMS. [Bricker's int. dir., Vol. 2 Short-term univ.-based exec. programs]. **Added/Corp** Peterson's Guides, Inc. **VFOAT** Short-Term University-Based Executive Programs; Short Term University Based Executive Programs; Bricker's International Directory. Vol. 2, Short-Term. 3rd Edition (1991)-6th Edition (1994). English. Peterson's Guides, 202 Carnegie Center, Department 2342, PO Box 2123, Princeton NJ 08543-2123. **Tel** (609)243-9111, (800)338-3282, FAX (609)243-9150, (609)452-0966. ***Continues*** *Bricker's Short-Term Executive Programs, 1040-7618.* ***Merged with*** *Bricker's International Directory. Vol. 1, Long-Term University-Based Executive Programs, 1054-7843* ***to form*** *Bricker's International Directory (Princeton, N.J. : 1994), 1078-2257.*
Desc: Covers 200 programs between two and four days long for mid- to upper- level executives. Also, includes a special essay on the trends in short-term executive education programs, advice on how to select a program, and directories to help locate the right program.

ISSN 1062-5690
DD 658 US

BRIEF (FORT LAUDERDALE, FLA.). (THE BEST OF THE BUSINESS PRESS.). [Brief]. Vol. 1, No. 1 May (1992)-. Periodical. English. Six times a year. $30.00. American Narrowcasting, 305 South Andrews Avenue, Suite 302, Ft. Lauderdale FL 33301.

ISSN 0899-3009
DD 658 US

BRIEF (HOUSTON, TEX.). (BRIEF.). [Brief]. (1988)-. Periodical. English. Six times a year. Free to members, $12.50 other. American Productivity and Quality Center, 123 North Post Oak Lane, Houston TX 77024. **Tel** (713)681-4020, FAX (713)681-8578. **Circ:** 1,500. ***Continues*** *Productivity Brief, 0741-644X.*

LC HD6951 .B7 **ISSN** 0007-1080
DD 331.1 UK
CCC
CODEN BJIRAV
Pr Rev.

BRITISH JOURNAL OF INDUSTRIAL RELATIONS. **See** Business and Economics-Labor.

LC HD28 .B69 **ISSN** 1045-3172
DD 658/.00941/05 UK
CCC
CODEN BJMAE4

BRITISH JOURNAL OF MANAGEMENT. [Br. j. manage.]. **Added/Corp** British Academy of Management. (1990)-. Periodical. English. Five times a year. $195.00. John Wiley & Sons Ltd., Baffins Lane, Chichester, West Sussex PO19 1UD United Kingdom. **Tel** 011 44 1243 779777, FAX 011 44 1243 776128 BTG:JWP001, telex 86290 WIBOOKG. **(Subscription address:** John Wiley & Sons, Inc. / Philadelphia, PO Box 7247, Philadelphia PA 19170. **Tel** (212)850-6645, (800)225-5945.**)** **ED** David Otley. available on microfilm and microfiche from University Microfilms International (UMI). Documents available from UMI Article Clearinghouse.
Desc: Aims to provide an outlet for research and scholarship on managerial oriented themes and topics. Aims to publish work of a multidisciplinary and interdisciplinary nature as well as empirical research across the traditional business divisions of production, marketing, personnel and finance.
Ind/Abst ABI/INFORM Glob. Ed.; Curr. Cit.; Ergon. Abstr.; Int. Bibliogr. Sociol.

ISSN 1055-3525
DD 658 US

BRUCE REPORT, THE. (THE BRUCE REPORT : THE NEWSLETTER FOR THE CATALOG INDUSTRY.). [Bruce rep.]. **Added/Corp** Bruce Consulting Group. Vol. 1, No. 1 (Dec. 1990)-. Newsletter. English. Twelve times a year. $295.00. Bruce, Dean, Company, 116 New Montgomery, Suite 914, San Francisco CA 94105. **Tel** (415)512-7305, FAX (415)512-7308. **ED** Hannah Bruce. cum. index.
Desc: Covers the financial trends of the catalog industry. It features lead articles on today's most pressing issues.

ISSN 1191-9841
DD 658.2/00971 CN

BUILDING MANAGEMENT & DESIGN. [Build. manag. des.]. **VFOAT** Building Management and Design. (1992)-. Periodical. English. Six times a year. 20.81Can$. Southham Information & Technical Group Inc, 1450 Don Mills Road, Don Mills Ontario M3B 2X7 Canada. **Tel** (416)445-6641, (800)668-2374, FAX (416)442-2261. ***Continues*** *Building Owner & Property Manager., 1189-6264.*

LC TH3301 .B4 **ISSN** 0007-3490
DD 647/.05 US

BUILDING OPERATING MANAGEMENT. **See** Building and Construction.

LC TH **ISSN** 0007-3725
DD 690 US
CCC

BUILDINGS (CEDAR RAPIDS. 1947). **See** Building and Construction.

ISSN 0226-8434
DD 658/.005 CN

BULLETIN - ASSOCIATION DES CONSEILLERS EN ORGANISATION ET METHODES DE QUEBEC, LE. [Bull. - Assoc. conseillers organ. methodes Que.]. **Main/Corp** Association des Conseillers en Organisation et Methodes de Quebec. Vol. 1 (Jan. 1980)-. Bulletin. French. Irregular. Free to members, $25.00 other.

ISSN 0711-5830
DD 651/.06/071422 CN

BULLETIN DU TRIMESTRE / ASSOCIATION INTERNATIONALE DES SECRETAIRES PROFESSIONNELLES, SECTION DE L'OUTAOUAIS. **Added/Corp** Association Internationale des Secretaires Professionnelles. Section de l'Outaouais. (Sept./Dec. 1981)-. Bulletin. French. Four times a year. Free. Association Internationale des Secretaires Professionnelles Section de l'Outaouais, 9 rue de Bourgogne, Aylmer Quebec J9H 3R6 Canada.

US
CEASED

BUREAU OF BUSINESS PRACTICE MANAGEMENT LETTER, THE. **VFOAT** Management Letter. (1988)-(July 25, 1995). English. Bureau of Business Practice, 24 Rope Ferry Road, Waterford CT 06386. **Tel** (800)243-0876, (203)442-4365, (800)876-9105, FAX (203)443-1123. **ED** Wayne Muller. ***Continues*** *Interaction/Insight.*
Desc: Focuses on day-to-day management skills for middle-level managers.

ISSN 0007-6465
US
CODEN BSERA6

BUSINESS AND ECONOMIC REVIEW (COLUMBIA). (BUSINESS AND ECONOMIC REVIEW / UNIVERSITY OF SOUTH CAROLINA.). [Bus. econ. rev.]. **Added/Corp** University of South Carolina. College of Business Administration. Division of Research. University of South Carolina. Bureau of Business and Economic Research. **VFOAT** Business & Economic Review. Vol. 1, No. 1 (Jan. 1, 1954)-. Periodical. English. Four times a year. Free on request. Bureau of Business & Economic Research / South Carolina, University of South Carolina, Columbia SC 29208. **Tel** (803)777-2510. available on microfilm and microfiche from University Microfilms International (UMI).
Ind/Abst PAIS Int. Print; Person. Manage. Abstr.

BE

BUSINESS AND MANAGEMENT EDITIONS: BMB. French (Dutch). Eleven times a year (monthly except July/Aug.). 1368.00F Belgium; 1868.00F other. Business & Management Editions, rue Stephanie 17, B 1020 Brussels Belgium. **Tel** 011 32 2 4266115, FAX 011 32 2 4258226. Index available. **Bk Rev.** **Ad Acc.**

LC HF5717 .B87 **ISSN** 0162-3885
DD 658.4/5/05 US
CCC
CODEN BCORBD

BUSINESS COMMUNICATIONS REVIEW. [Bus. commun. rev.]. (1971)-. Trade Publication. English. Twelve times a year. $45.00. BCR Enterprises Inc., 950 York Road, Suite 203, Hinsdale IL 60521. **Tel** (800)227-1234, (708)986-1432. **ED** Fred Knight. cum. index. **Bk Rev.** **Circ:** 6,000 (ctrl). available on microfilm and microfiche from University Microfilms International (UMI); available on an online database (file 648/Full-Text) from DIALOG. Documents available from UMI Article Clearinghouse, Ask*IEEE.
Desc: Provides in-depth, analytical information in the telecommunications field. The focus is on voice and/or data communications management issues affecting both the end user and vendor communities.
Ind/Abst ABI/INFORM Glob. Ed.; ABI/INFORM [Computer File] (May 1983-); Acad. Search; Bus. Period. Index; Bus. Source Plus; Bus. Source; Curr. Cit.; EP Collect.; Gen. BusinessFile (1992-); Homework Help.; INFO-SOUTH Abstr.; INSPEC (Jan./Feb. 1984-); Mag. Search; MasterFile FullTEXT 1000; MasterFile FullTEXT 350; MasterFile FullTEXT 650; MasterFile FullTEXT (July 1993-); OCLC; Telebase; Trade Ind. ASAP [Full Txt.]; Trade Ind. Index [Full Txt.]; Wilson Bus. Abstr.

ISSN 0951-1792
UK

BUSINESS EXECUTIVE. **Added/Corp** Association of Business Executives (Great Britain). (19??)-. English. Six times a year. $34.23. Association of Business Executives, 14 Worple Road, London SW19 4DD United Kingdom. **Tel** 011 44 81 8791973.
Ind/Abst Curr. Cit.

ISSN 1042-8704
DD 650 US
TITLE CHANGE

BUSINESS FOR CENTRAL NEW JERSEY. [Bus. cent. N. J.]. **Added/Corp** Snowden Publications, Inc. **VFOAT** Business. (1988)-(1995). Periodical. English. Business News New Jersey, 391 George Street, New Brunswick NJ 08901. **Tel** (908)246-7677. **ED** George Taber. **Ad Acc.** **Circ:** 13,000 (ctrl). available on an online database (file 635/Full-Text) from DIALOG. Documents available from UMI Article Clearinghouse. ***Merged into*** *Business News New Jersey.*
Desc: Business and economic journal.
Ind/Abst Bus. Dateline; Bus. Source Plus; EP Collect.; Homework Help.; MasterFile FullTEXT 1000; MasterFile FullTEXT 350; MasterFile FullTEXT 650; MasterFile FullTEXT (Jan. 1995-); OCLC; Telebase.

LC HD28 .B84a **ISSN** 0276-3923
DD 650/.05 US

BUSINESS/MANAGEMENT (GUILFORD, CONN.). (BUSINESS/MANAGEMENT.). [Bus./manage.]. **VFOAT** Annual Editions. Business/Management. (1982)-. Periodical. English. One time a year. $11.95. Times Mirror Higher Education Group, 2460 Kerper Boulevard, Dubuque IA 52001. **Tel** (800)338-5578. **ED** Joseph Mattingly Jr.
Desc: Collection of public press articles covering current issues in business/management. Includes topic guide and complete index.

LC HD28 **ISSN** 1355-2503
DD 658 UK
Pr Rev.

•BUSINESS PROCESS RE-ENGINEERING & MANAGEMENT JOURNAL. **VFOAT** Business Process Re-Engineering and Management Journal. Vol. 1, No. 1 (1995). Trade Publication. English. Three times a year. £99.00. MCB University Press, 60 62 Toller Lane, Bradford, West Yorkshire BD8 9BY United Kingdom. **Tel** 011 44 1274 785280, FAX 011 44 1274 785200, telex 51317-MCBUNI-G. **ED** Dr. Mohamed Zairi.
Desc: Looks at how processes evolve: how they can be assessed, re-engineered if necessary and subsequently maintained and adapted to changing circumstances.

LC HD28 **ISSN** 0007-6996
DD 658 CN
CODEN BUQUAL

BUSINESS QUARTERLY, THE. [Bus. q.]. **Added/Corp** University of Western Ontario. School of Business Administration. (1950)-. Trade Publication. English. Four times a year. 45.00Can$. Business Quarterly, Western Business School, University of Western Ontario, London Ontario N6A 3K7 Canada. **Tel** (519)661-3309, FAX (519)661-3838. **ED** Andrew Grindlay and Angela Smith (Managing Editor). Index available. cum. index. **Photos.** **Ad Acc.** available on microfiche from Johnson Associates; and Micromedia Limited; available on microfilm and microfiche from University Microfilms International (UMI). Documents available from Ask*IEEE, UMI Article Clearinghouse. ***Continues*** *Quarterly Review of Commerce, 0317-6797.*
Desc: A management magazine written by practicing managers and academics in the field of management for persons in upper and middle management. Emphasis placed on Canadian issues.
Ind/Abst ABI/INFORM Glob. Ed. (Fall 1974-); ABI/INFORM Ondisc: Expr. Ed. (Spring 1987-); ABI/INFORM [Computer File] (Fall 1974-); Acad. Search; Anbar Account. Finan. Abstr. [Full Txt.]; Anbar Mark. Distr. Abstr. [Full Txt.]; Anbar Top Manage. Abstr. [Full Txt.]; Bus. ASAP (1990-) [Full Txt.]; Bus. Index (1985-); Bus. Period. Index; Bus. Source Plus; Bus. Source; Can. Bus. Index; Can. Period. Index; Contents Pages Manage.; Curr. Cit.; EP Collect.; Gen. BusinessFile (1985-); Gen. Period. Index (1985-); Homework Help.; Index Can. Leg. Period. Lit.; INFO-SOUTH Abstr.; INSPEC (May 1982-); Mag. Search; Manage. Market. Abstr.; Manage. Bibliogr. Rev.; Manage. Contents; MasterFile FullTEXT 1000; MasterFile FullTEXT 350; MasterFile FullTEXT 650; MasterFile FullTEXT (Jan. 1994-) [Full Txt.]; Middle East Abstr. Index; OCLC; Oper. Prod. Manage. Abstr. [Full Txt.]; PAIS Int. Print; Person. Train. Abstr. [Full Txt.]; Person. Manage. Abstr.; Selec. Coop. Index Manage. Period.; Telebase; Trade Ind. ASAP [Full Txt.]; Trade Ind. Index [Full Txt.]; UMI ABI/Inform--Bus. Period. Ondisc; Wilson Bus. Abstr.; Women Manage. Rev. [Full Txt.].

Business and Economics —Management

ISSN 0227-3748
DD 651.5/04261/0971 CN
C H R A RECORDER. [CHRA rec.]. **Main/Corp** Canadian Health Record Association. **VAT** Canadian Health Record Association Recorder; Recorder (Oshawa). Dec. 1976-. Periodical. English (French). Free to members. Canadian Health Record Association, 187 King Street East, Oshawa Ontario L1H 1C3 Canada. **Tel** (416)728-9743. **Continues** CAMRL Recorder, 0316-0637.

ISSN 0226-3467
DD 658/.006/0714281 CN
CADUCEE, LE. [Caducee]. Vol. 1 (May 1952)-. Periodical. French. Twelve times a year. Assn Diplom Ecol Haut Etud Com, 3333 Queen Mary Road, Montreal Quebec H3V 1A2 Canada. **Tel** (514)340-6028. **Supersedes** H.E.C. Nouvelles.

LC HD28 .C18
DD 658.05 **ISSN** 0008-1256
US
CCC
Pr Rev.
CALIFORNIA MANAGEMENT REVIEW. [Calif. manage. rev.]. **Added/Corp** University of California, Berkeley. Graduate School of Business Administration. University of California, Los Angeles. Graduate School of Management. University of California, Los Angeles. Graduate School of Business Administration. University of California, Irvine. Graduate School of Administration. University of California, Irvine. Graduate School of Business Administration. **VFOAT** CMR. Vol. 1 (Fall 1958)-. Academic Scholarly Publication. English. Four times a year (Jan., April, July, and Oct.). $58.00. California Management Review, 350 Barrows Hall, University of California, Berkeley CA 94720. **Tel** (510)642-7159, FAX (510)642-2826. **ED** David Vogel. Index available. **Bk Rev. Ad Acc. Circ:** 5,000. available on microfilm and microfiche from University Microfilms International (UMI); available on an online database (files 15,648/Full-Text) from DIALOG. Documents available from The Genuine Article, UMI Article Clearinghouse, Ask*IEEE, Documents on Demand.
Desc: A bridge of communication between those who study management and those who practice it. Concentrates on providing information on the latest research and creative thought in three critical areas: business and public policy; strategy and organization; and the international economy.
Ind/Abst ABC POL SCI; ABI/INFORM Glob. Ed.; ABI/INFORM Ondisc: Expr. Ed. (Winter 1987-); ABI/INFORM [Computer File] (Spring 1971-);(spring 1971-); Acad. Search; Account. Index Suppl.; Account. Art.; Anbar Mark. Distr. Abstr. [Full Txt.]; Anbar Top Manage. Abstr. [Full Txt.]; Bus. ASAP (1992-) [Full Txt.]; Bus. Index (1985-); Bus. Period. Index; Bus. Source Plus; Bus. Source; Commun. Abstr. (?-?); Comput. Lit. Index; Contents Pages Manage.; Curr. Cit.; Curr. Contents Soc. Behav. Sci.; EMBASE; Employ. Relat. Abstr. (1962-); Energy Inf. Abstr.; Environ. Abstr.; EP Collect.; Fed. Tax Artic.; Gen. BusinessFile (1985-); Gen. Period. Index (1985-); Health Plan. Adminis.; Hist. Abstr.; Homework Help.; INFO-SOUTH Abstr.; INSPEC (Winter 1972-Summer 1978); Int. Aerosp. Abstr.; J. Econ. Lit. (1968-1982); J. Plan. Lit.; Mag. Search; Manage. Market. Abstr.; Manage. Bibliogr. Rev.; Manage. Contents (1974-); Manage. Contents; Manage. Index (1962-); MasterFile FullTEXT 1000; MasterFile FullTEXT 350; MasterFile FullTEXT 650; MasterFile FullTEXT (July 1993-); Middle East Abstr. Index; OCLC; Oper. Prod. Manage. Abstr. [Full Txt.]; PAIS Int. Print (1991-); Person. Train. Abstr. [Full Txt.]; Person. Manage. Abstr. (1962-); Public Aff. Inf. Serv. Bull.; Res. Alert [Full Cov.]; Selec. Coop. Index Manage. Period.; Soc. Sci. Cit. Index [Full Cov.]; Telebase; UMI ABI/Inform--Bus. Period. Ondisc [Full Txt.]; Wilson Bus. Abstr.; Women Manage. Rev. [Full Txt.]; Work Relat. Abstr.

ISSN 0823-6429
DD 658.8/4 CN
CANADIAN AUCTIONEER, THE. [Can. auctioneer]. 1st Issue (Feb. 1983)-. Trade Publication. English. Free to Members. Auctioneers Association of Canada, 1871 Ellice Avenue, Winnipeg Manitoba R3H 0C1 Canada. **Tel** FAX (204)775-2261. **ED** Ken Knight, Paul Gardner. **Ad Acc. Circ:** 800 (ctrl).

ISSN 0707-2902
DD 338.7/4/02571 CN
CANADIAN BOOK OF CORPORATE MANAGEMENT. 1977-. English. One time a year. Dun's Marketing Services, 899 Eaton Avenue, Bethlehem PA 18025. **Tel** (800)999-3867, (610)882-6200.

ISSN 1193-7505
DD 658.2 CN
CANADIAN FACILITY MANAGEMENT & DESIGN. [Can. facil. manag. des.]. Vol. 6, No. 4 (Sept. 1992)-. Trade Publication. English. Six times a year (Feb., Apr., June, Sept., Oct., Dec.). 24.01Can$. CFM Communications Ltd., 62 Olsen Drive, Don Mills Ontario M3A 3J3 Canada. **Tel** (416)447-3417, FAX (416)447-4410. **ED** Vicky Von Buchstab, (phone: (416)222-2265). **Bk Rev. Ad Acc.** ctrl circ. **Continues** Canadian Facility Management., 0838-0139.

LC HD28 .R475 **ISSN** 0825-0383
DD 658/.005 CN
CANADIAN JOURNAL OF ADMINISTRATIVE SCIENCES. (REVUE CANADIENNE DES SCIENCES DE L'ADMINISTRATION.). [Can. j. Adm. Sci. Assoc. Can.]. **Added/Corp** Administrative Sciences Association of Canada. **VFOAT** Canadian Journal of Administrative Sciences. Vol. 5, No. 1 (Mar. 1988)-. Academic Scholarly Publication. English (summaries and/or abstracts in French). Four times a year. 47.48 Can$ Canada; $60.00 other. Administrative Sciences Association of Canada, Faculty of Administration, McGill University, 1001 Sherbrooke West Street, Montreal Quebec H3G 1M8 Canada. **Tel** (514)848-2719, FAX (514)848-2839. **ED** V.V. Baba. **Bk Rev. Ad Acc. Circ:** 900. available in microform from University Microfilms International (UMI); available on an online database from University Microfilms International (UMI). Documents available from The Genuine Article, BLDSC.
Ind/Abst Res. Alert; Soc. Sci. Cit. Index [Full Cov.].

ISSN 0709-5384
DD 658/.007/15 CN
CANADIAN MANAGEMENT CENTRE PRESENTS MANAGEMENT DEVELOPMENT PROGRAMMES.
Main/Corp Canadian Management Centre (Toronto, Ont.). **VFOAT** Management Development Programmes. Jan./June 1979-. Periodical. English. Two times a year. Free. Canadian Management Centre of AMA/International, 100 University Avenue/Suite 303, Toronto Ontario M5J 1V6 Canada. **Continues** Catalog of Management Training Programmes, 0709-5376.

LC HD28 .C36 **ISSN** 0045-5156
DD 658 CN
CCC
CANADIAN MANAGER. [Can. manager]. **Added/Corp** Canadian Institute of Management. **VFOAT** Manager Canadien. (Sept./Oct. 1970)-. Periodical. English. Four times a year. 12.81Can$. Canadian Institute of Management, 2175 Sheppard Avenue E/Suite 110, Willowdale Ontario M2J 1W8 Canada. **Tel** (416)493-0155, 800 387-5774, FAX (416)491-1670. **ED** Ruth Max. **Bk Rev. Ad Acc. Circ:** 5,200 (ctrl). available on an online database from HRIN file (ABI); DIALOG; and BRS. Documents available from UMI Article Clearinghouse, The UnCover Company, BLDSC. **Supersedes** Industrial Manager, 0319-4027.
Desc: Geared toward middle and upper management. Articles on time management, labor-management relations, marketing, technology, delegation, meetings, etc.
Ind/Abst ABI/INFORM Glob. Ed.; ABI/INFORM [Computer File] (May 1980-); Bus. ASAP (1992-) [Full Txt.]; Bus. Index (1985-); Can. Period. Index (19??-); Curr. Cit.; Gen. BusinessFile (1985-); Gen. Period. Index (1985-); INFO-SOUTH Abstr.; Mag. Search; MasterFile FullTEXT (July 1993-); UMI ABI/Inform--Bus. Period. Ondisc [Full Txt.].

LC HG4001 **ISSN** 0829-4003
DD 658.1/5244 CN
CEASED
CANADIAN TREASURY MANAGEMENT REVIEW. See Business and Economics-Banks and Banking.

LC HG1501 **ISSN** 0256-9647
DD 332.1 JM
CARIBBEAN FINANCE AND MANAGEMENT : CFM. See Finance.

ISSN 0889-2288
DD 381 US
CCC
CARLSONREPORT. See Business and Economics-Retail.

LC HD28 .C37 **ISSN** 0894-6043
DD 658/.005 US
CASE RESEARCH JOURNAL. [Case res. j.]. **Added/Corp** Case Research Association. North American Case Research Association. Vol. 1 (1980)-. English. Four times a year. $75.00. Abbott Turner School of Business, Columbus College, C/O Dr. Robert N. Carter, Columbus GA 31907. **Tel** (706)568-2284, FAX (706)568-2184. **ED** William Nalmes. **Ad Acc. Circ:** 400.
Desc: Publishes articles on case method and teaching and research cases in management and business disciplines.

US
CASES IN PUBLIC POLICY AND MANAGEMENT. See Public Administration.

LC HG1501
DD 332.1 NE
CASH FLOW. CASH- EN CREDITMANAGEMENT. See Business and Economics-Banks and Banking.

ISSN 1053-0347
DD 658 US
CCC
CASH FLOW ENHANCEMENT REPORT. [Cash flow enhanc. rep.]. **Added/Corp** Institute of Management & Administration. (Dec. 1990)-. Periodical. English. Twelve times a year. $245.00. Institute of Management and Administration, 29 West 35th Street, 5th Floor, New York NY 10001-2299. **Tel** (212)244-0360, FAX (212)564-0465.

LC HF5861 .C35 **ISSN** 0740-3119
DD 658.8/72/05 US
CATALOG AGE. See Business and Economics-Advertising and Public Relations.

US
CATALOG OF PROFESSIONAL DEVELOPMENT SEMINARS / INSTITUTE FOR ADVANCED TECHNOLOGY, CONTROL DATA CORPORATION. **Main/Corp** Control Data Corporation. Institute for Advanced Technology. (19??)-. Catalog. English. Irregular. Free on request. Institute of Advanced Technology, 6003 Executive Boulevard, Rockville MD 20852. **Tel** (800)638-6590. **Circ:** 500,000 (ctrl).
Desc: A collection of technical and management seminars designed for the professional community. All seminars are real world skill oriented. Seminars are regularly scheduled in major cities.

ISSN 0229-7779
DD 380.1/06/0714281 CN
CCMS BUSINESS PAGES. [CCMS bus. pages]. **VFOAT** Business Pages. **VAT** concordia Centre for Management Studies Business Pages. Vol. 1, No. 1 (Jan. 1981)-. Periodical. English (French). Irregular. Free. Concordia Centre for Management Studies, 1560 de Maisonneuve boulevard West, Montreal Quebec H3G 1N1 Canada.

LC HD28 HC26 **ISSN** 1381-4346
DD 658 330.1 US
Pr Rev.
●**CEMS BUSINESS REVIEW.** (1995-)-. Academic Scholarly Publication. English. Four times a year. $306.00. Kluwer Academic Publishers / Massachusetts, PO Box 358, Accord Station, Hingham MA 02018. **Tel** (617)871-6600. **(Subscription address:** Kluwer Academic Publishers / Netherlands, PO Box 322, 3300 AH Dordrecht Netherlands. **Tel** 011 31 78 392392, FAX 011 31 78 546474.)
Desc: Covers European management research.

US
CENTER FOR LIFE CYCLE SCIENCES NEWSLETTER. (19??)-. Newsletter. English. Four times a year. $79.00. Center for Life Cycle Sciences, 3311 Bethel Road SE #04A-257, Port Orchard WA 98366. **Tel** (206)876-2399, FAX (206)876-2499. **Circ:** 1,000 (ctrl).

LC HD62.15 .C38 **ISSN** 1072-5296
DD 658.5/62/005 US
CENTER FOR QUALITY MANAGEMENT JOURNAL, THE. [Cent. Qual. Manag. j.]. **Added/Corp** Center for Quality Management (Cambridge, Mass.). **VFOAT** Journal. Vol. 1, No. 1 (Fall 1992)-. English. Four times a year. $77.00. Center for Quality Management, 150 Cambridge Park Drive, Cambridge MA 02140. **Tel** (617)873-2152.

LC HF5661 .C39 **ISSN** 1041-7222
DD 658.15/11/076 US
CERTIFIED MANAGEMENT ACCOUNTANT EXAMINATION. QUESTIONS AND UNOFFICIAL ANSWERS (MONTVALE, N.J.). See Business and Economics-Accounting.

DD 658 US
CHANGE LETTER. [Change]. **Added/Corp** Center for Leadership Development (Los Angeles, Calif.). (199?)-. Periodical. English. Six times a year. $35.00. Centre for Leadership Development, 850 State Street, Suite 202, San Diego CA 92101. **Tel** (619)338-0380, FAX (619)338-8134. **Continues** Change Letter, 1073-4317.

ISSN 1073-4317
DD 658 US
TITLE CHANGE
CHANGE (SAN DIEGO, CALIF.). (CHANGE.). [Change]. **Added/Corp** Center for Leadership Development (Los Angeles, Calif.). (1992)-(199?). Periodical. English. Centre for Leadership Development, 850 State Street, Suite 202, San Diego CA 92101. **Tel** (619)338-0380, FAX (619)338-8134. **Continued by** Change Letter.

LC HD2741 .C46 **ISSN** 0376-7868
DD 658.1/145/05 II
CHARTERED SECRETARY (NEW DELHI). (CHARTERED SECRETARY.). **Added/Corp** Institute of Company Secretaries of India. (19??)-.

Business and Economics —Management

Periodical. English. Twelve times a year. Rs150.00 India; £15.00 UK; $30.00 US. The Institute of Company Secretaries of India, ICSI House, 22 Institutional Area/Lodi Road, New Delhi 110003 India. **Tel** 617321-2-3-4, telex 31-62164 ICSI IN. **ED** V. Balu, V. Gopalan. Index available. **Bk Rev. Ad Acc. Circ:** 15,000. available with illustrations.
Desc: Covers a wide range of subjects like corporate, economic, labour and tax legislations; management; accountancy, etc. Useful to corporate executives, accountants, solicitors, management consultants, academicians and government officials.
LC HD70.C5 C415
DD 658/.00951   CC

CHI SHU CHING CHI YU KUAN LI YEN CHIU. (19??)-. Periodical. Chinese. Four times a year. NT$0.25. Chi Shu Ching Chi Yu Kuan Li Yen Chiu, Post Office, Tai-Yuan Shih, People's Republic of China.

LC HD70.C5 C422
DD 658/.00951   CH

CHI YEH KUAN LI (CHUNG-KUO CHI YEH KUAN LI HSIEH HUI). (CHI YEH KUAN LI.). (19??)-. Periodical. Chinese. Six times a year. NT$0.25. Post Office Beijing, Beijing, People's Republic of China.

LC HC10 .C454   ISSN 0160-4724
DD 330.9/04   US
     CODEN CHIEER

CHIEF EXECUTIVE (NEW YORK, N.Y. 1977). (CHIEF EXECUTIVE.). [Chief exec.]. **VFOAT** Chief Executive Magazine. No. 1 (July, Aug., Sept. 1977)-. Periodical. English. Ten times a year. $76.00. Chief Executive Group Inc., 733 3rd Avenue, 21st Floor, New York NY 10017. **Tel** (212)687-8288, FAX (212)687-8456. **ED** J. P. Donlon (Editor's telephone: (212)687-8438). **Bk Rev**, (Qty: 10). **Ad Acc, Adv Mgr:** (212)687-8288. **Circ:** 40,000 (ctrl). available on microfilm and microfiche from University Microfilms International (UMI). Documents available from UMI Article Clearinghouse.
Desc: Business publication written by and for international (primarily North American) chief executives.
Ind/Abst ABI/INFORM Glob. Ed.; ABI/INFORM [Computer File] (Summer 1981-); Acad. Search; Bus. ASAP (1992-) [Full Txt.]; Bus. Index (1979-); Bus. Source Plus; Bus. Source; Curr. Cit.; EP Collect.; Homework Help.; INFO-SOUTH Abstr.; Mag. Search; MasterFile FullTEXT 1000; MasterFile FullTEXT 350; MasterFile FullTEXT 650; MasterFile FullTEXT (July 1993-) [Full Txt.]; OCLC; Telebase; UMI ABI/Inform--Bus. Period. Ondisc [Full Txt.]; World Mag. Bank.
LC HD70.C5 .C453
DD 658/.00951   CC

CHING CHI KUAN LI. VFOAT Jingji Guanli; Economic Management. (1979)-. Periodical. Chinese. Twelve times a year. RMBY0.38. Ching Chi Kuan Li Tsa Chih She PO Box 2820, Beijing China, People's Republic of China.

     JA
CHUO-KORON KEIEI MONDAI. (1962)-. Periodical. English. Four times a year. **(Subscription address:** Kinokuniya Company Ltd., 38-1 Sakuragaoka 5, chome Setagaya-ku, Tokyo 156 Japan. **Tel** FAX 011 03 3439 0136.**)**

     ISSN 0412-4715
DD 338.6 658   JA
CHUSHO KIGYO KEIEI BUNSEKI. (19??)-. Periodical. Japanese. Tokyo International, PO Box 5030, Tokyo 100 31 Japan. **Tel** 03 811 7238.

LC T58.6 .C5   ISSN 0894-9301
DD 658.4/038/05   US
     CCC
     CODEN CIOOEQ
CIO (FRAMINGHAM, MASS.). (CIO.). [CIO]. **VFOAT** CIO Magazine. **VAT** Chief Information Officer; Chief Information Officer Magazine. Vol. 1, No. 1 (Sept./Oct. 1987)-. Academic Scholarly Publication. English. Twenty-one times a year. $75.00. International Data Corporation, 5 Speen Street, PO Box 9015, Framingham MA 01701. **Tel** (508)872-8200, (508)935-4443. **(Subscription address:** CIO Publishing, PO Box 489, Northbrook IL 60065. **)** available on microfilm and microfiche from University Microfilms International (UMI). Documents available from Ask*IEEE, CASDDS.
Desc: Covers news, views and trends with reports, case histories and surveys.
Ind/Abst Chem. Abstr. (1989-); Curr. Cit.; Gen. BusinessFile; INSPEC (Sept.-Oct. 1987-).

     ISSN 1051-5720
DD 658   US
     CCC
     TITLE CHANGE
CLEANING MANAGEMENT MAGAZINE. (CLEANING MANAGEMENT MAGAZINE : CM.). [Clean. manage. mag.]. **VFOAT** CM; Cleaning Management. (19??)-(19??). Trade Publication. English. National Trade Publications, 13 Century Hill Drive, Latham NY 12110. **Tel** (518)783-1281, FAX (518)783-1386. **Ad Acc. Circ:** 34,000 (ctrl). **Continues** Cleaning Management.

Continued by CM : Cleaning & Maintenance Management.
Desc: Edited for end-user managers and supervisors directly responsible for building maintenance and housekeeping operations in all types of buildings and institutions.

     ISSN 1183-9236
DD 658.8   CN
CLIENT (MONTREAL). (CLIENT : BULLETIN DE DIMENSION CLIENTELE, ASSOCIATION QUEBECOISE DES PROFESSIONNELS ET DES PROFESSIONELLES DU SERVICE A LA CLIENTELE.). [Client]. **Added/Corp** Dimension Clientele. Vol. 1, No 1 (Jun 1991)-. Bulletin. French. Four times a year. 48.02Can$. Dimension Clientele, 7339 Baldwin, Montreal Quebec H1K 3C9 Canada. **Tel** (514)353-4612.

     ISSN 1073-6379
DD 005   US
NLM W1; CL69IE
●**CLINICAL DATA MANAGEMENT.** [Clin. data manag.]. **VFOAT** Clinical Data. Vol. 1, No. 1 (Apr. 1994)-. Periodical. English. Twelve times a year. $205.00. Aspen Publishers Inc., 7201 McKinney Circle, Frederick MD 21701. **Tel** (800)234-1660, (301)698-7100, FAX (301)251-5784, telex 5106014543. **(Subscription address:** Aspen Publishers Inc., PO Box 990, Frederick MD 21701. **Tel** (800)901-9074, (301)698-7100.**)**

     ISSN 0888-7950
DD 658   US
NLM W1; CL726DF
CLINICAL LABORATORY MANAGEMENT REVIEW. [Clin. lab. manage. rev.]. **Added/Corp** Clinical Laboratory Management Association. Vol. 1, No. 1 (Jan./Feb. 1987)-. Periodical. English. Six times a year. $100.00. Williams & Wilkins Company, 428 East Preston Street, Baltimore MD 21202-3993. **Tel** (410)528-4000, (800)638-6423, FAX (410)528-8596, telex 87669. **(Subscription address:** Williams & Wilkins, PO Box 64380, Baltimore MD 21264. **Tel** 800 638-6423.**) Ad Acc**. Documents available from Quick Copies.
Desc: Provides balanced coverage of financial management, new equipment, medical information systems, operational issues, marketing, personnel management, regulatory issues, and a broad range of topics in health care.
Ind/Abst Curr. Cit.; EMBASE; Health Plan. Adminis.; Hosp. Health Admin. Index (Vol 3 No 1, 1989-).

     ISSN 0965-5751
     UK
CLINICIAN IN MANAGEMENT. See Medical Sciences-Physicians and Medical Personnel.

     US
CM : CLEANING MAINTENANCE MANAGEMENT. VFOAT CM; Cleaning Management. (19??)-. Trade Publication. English. Twelve times a year. $42.00. National Trade Publications, 13 Century Hill Drive, Latham NY 12110. **Tel** (518)783-1281, FAX (518)783-1386. **Ad Acc. Circ:** 34,000 (ctrl). **Continues** Cleaning Management Magazine, 1051-5720.
Desc: Edited for end-user managers and supervisors directly responsible for building maintenance and housekeeping operations in all types of buildings and institutions.

LC HF5416 .C6   ISSN 0362-4455
DD 658.8   US
CODE & SYMBOL. VAT Code and Symbol. Vol. 1, (Aug. 1975)-. Periodical. English. Twelve times a year. $225.00. Distribution Codes Inc, 401 Wythe Street, Alexandria VA 22314.

     ISSN 0710-5193
DD 331.89/0413711   CN
COLLECTIVE BARGAINING HANDBOOK. See Business and Economics-Labor.

     ISSN 0966-6907
     UK
     CEASED
COLLEGE MANAGEMENT TODAY. (1992)-(19??). English. Longman Group UK Ltd., Westgate House, The High 6th Floor, Harlow Essex CM20 1YR United Kingdom. **Tel** 011 44 1279 442601, FAX 011 44 1279 444501. **ED** George Low.

     ISSN 0884-934X
DD 658   US
     CEASED
COMMITMENT PLUS. [Commit. plus]. Vol. 1, No. 1 (Oct. 1985)-(June 1995). Periodical. English. Quality Productivity Management Association, 300 North Martingale Road, Suite 230, Schaumberg IL 60173. **Tel** (708)619-2909. **ED** Bill Ginnodo. **Circ:** 1,300.
Desc: Practical, case-study oriented newsletter for managers who want to improve productivity, quality, and service through people. Mostly original material.

     ISSN 1053-0169
DD 658   US
COMMUNICATION EDGE, THE. [Commun. edge]. Vol. 1, No. 1 (Jan./Feb. 1991)-. Periodical. English. Six times a year. $48.00. Writing, Etc., 7856 North Clarendon Road, Indianapolis IN 46260-3513.

     ISSN 8755-8955
DD 658   US
COMMUNICATION OPTIONS. [Commun. options]. (1983)-. Periodical. English. Six times a year. $270.00. Communication Options Inc, 1385 York Avenue, New York NY 10021.

LC HF5718 .C65x   ISSN 0744-7612
DD 659   CCC
COMMUNICATION WORLD (SAN FRANCISCO, CALIF.). See Communications.

     UK
COMMUNICATIONS MANAGEMENT. English. Twelve times a year. £48.00 UK; £60.00 other. EMAP Business Publishing Ltd., 260 Field Road, Audit House, Ruislip Middlesex HA4 9LT United Kingdom. **Tel** 011 44 181 9563000, FAX 011 44 181 4293117.

     UK
COMPANY ADMINISTRATION. (19??)-. Periodical. English. £170.05. Croner Publ Ltd., Croner House London Road, Kingston Upon Thames, Surrey KT2 6SR United Kingdom. **Tel** 011 44 181 5473333, FAX 011 44 181 5472637.

LC HF5549.5.C67 C62   ISSN 0748-061X
DD 658.3/2/0973   US
     CCC
COMPENSATION & BENEFITS MANAGEMENT. [Compens. benefits manage.]. **VFOAT** Compensation and Benefits Management. Vol. 1, No. 1 (Autumn 1984)-. Periodical. English. Four times a year. $150.50. Panel Publishers, A Division of Aspen Publishers Inc., 7201 McKinney Circle, PO Box 990, Frederick MD 21705-9727. **Tel** (800)638-8437. **(Subscription address:** Aspen Publishers Inc., PO Box 990, Frederick MD 21701. **Tel** (800)901-9074, (301)698-7100.**) ED** Gerald W. Bush, Ph.D. **Circ:** 4,000. Documents available from UMI Article Clearinghouse.
Desc: Professional journal for executives who must plan and implement the 'total compensation' package.
Ind/Abst ABI/INFORM Glob. Ed.; ABI/INFORM Ondisc: Expr. Ed. (Fall 1987-); ABI/INFORM [Computer File] (Fall 1987-); Curr. Cit.; Gen. BusinessFile (1992-); PAIS Int. Print (1977-); Work Relat. Abstr.

     US
COMPENSATION & BENEFITS MANAGERS LETTER. (19??)-. English. Twenty-four times a year. $210.36 (US), $255.60 (Canada). Bureau of Business Practice, 24 Rope Ferry Road, Waterford CT 06386. **Tel** (800)243-0876, (203)442-4365, (800)876-9105, FAX (203)443-1123.

     US
●**COMPLETE EUROPEAN TRADE DIGEST - ADMINISTRATIVE.** (1995)-. English. Twenty-four times a year. SIMCOM, PO Box 420511, Atlanta GA 30342. **Tel** (404)875-3105, FAX (404)872-1620. *Separated from* Complete European Trade Digest.

LC HF5601
DD 657   US
COMPREHENSIVE MANAGEMENT REPORT. Main/Corp Kansas. Dept. of Administration. Division of Accounts and Reports. (1989)-. English. One time a year. Free on request. Kansas Department of Administration, Division of Accounts and Reports, 900 Jackson, 251 Landon Street, Topeka KS 66612-1220. **Tel** (913)296-2111. **Continues in part** Kansas. Dept. of Administration. Division of Accounts and Reports. Financial Report for Period July 1, ... to June 30 ... .

     ISSN 1071-2488
DD 658   US
     CCC
     CEASED
COMPUTER MARKETING & DISTRIBUTION REPORT. [Comput. mark. distrib. rep.]. **VFOAT** Computer Marketing and Distribution Report; CMDR. Vol. 2, No. 13 (July 19, 1993)-(Oct. 10, 1994). Periodical. English. SIMBA Information Inc., 213 Danbury Road, PO Box 7430, Wilton CT 06897-7430. **Tel** (203)834-0033 ext. 173, FAX (203)884-1771. **(Subscription address:** Simba Information Inc., PO Box 7430, Wilton CT 06897. **Tel** (203)834-0033 ext. 160, FAX (203)834-1771.**)** *Continues* Computer Direct Marketing Rreport.

LC HD28
DD 620   US
●**CONCEPTS AND TRANSFORMATION.** (1996)-. Academic Scholarly Publication. English. Three times a year. Fl.150.00. John Benjamins BV, Amsteldijk

Business and Economics —Management

44, PO Box 75577, 1070 AN Amsterdam Netherlands. **Tel** 011 31 20 6738156, FAX 011 31 20 739773. **ED** Hans van Beinum and Oeyvind Paalshaugen.

LC HF5007 .C66 **ISSN** 0899-6741
DD 658 US
 CCC
 CODEN CBOBE6
 TITLE CHANGE
CONFERENCE BOARD BRIEFING, THE. [Conf. Board brief.]. **Added/Corp** Conference Board. Vol. 1, No. 1 (June 1988)-(1993). Periodical. English. Conference Board, 845 Third Avenue, New York NY 10022. **Tel** (212)759-0900 ext. 582, (800)872-6273, FAX (212)980-7014. **ED** Judith Alster. ctrl circ. *Formed by the union of News Briefs (Conference Board) and Letter (Conference Board), 0896-2448. Merged with Quality Briefing, 1059-3918; Business and Society Briefing, 1065-5875 to form Conference Board's Membership Update, 1072-0235.*
 Desc: Newsletter reporting on a variety of management concerns and offering insights into what top business leaders are thinking and doing on the major trends and issues of the day.

 ISSN 1072-0235
DD 338 US
 CODEN CBMUEJ
●**CONFERENCE BOARD'S MEMBERSHIP UPDATE, THE.** [Conf. Board's membsh. update]. **Added/Corp** Conference Board. **VFOAT** Membership Update. Vol. 1, No. 1 (Sept./Oct. 1993)-. Periodical. English. Six times a year. Free to associates of the Conference Board. Conference Board, 845 Third Avenue, New York NY 10022. **Tel** (212)759-0900 ext. 582, (800)872-6273, FAX (212)980-7014. *Formed by the union of Conference Board Briefing, 0899-6741; Quality Briefing, 1059-3918 and Business and Society Briefing, 1065-5875.*

 ISSN 0748-1837
DD 658 US
CONSULTANT PRACTICE. (CONSULTANT PRACTICE : A PUBLICATION OF CONSULTANT CAPACITIES GROUP, INC.). [Consult. pract.]. Periodical. English. Six times a year. $24.00. Free to CCG associate consultants and clients/affiliates. Consultant Capacities Group Inc, 3 Harbor Road, Cold Spring Harbor NY 11724. **Tel** (617)237-6237. **ED** Nancy Jasinski. **Bk Rev. Circ:** 3,000.
 Desc: A newsletter for independent consultants in all industrial discipline areas. It includes articles about consulting and maintaining a successful consulting practice.

 ISSN 1184-8839
DD 658/.0089/97071 CN
CONTACT / CANADIAN COUNCIL FOR NATIVE BUSINESS. [Contact - Can. Counc. Native Bus.]. **Added/Corp** Canadian Council for Native Business. **VFOAT** CCNB Contact; Contact. (Sept. 1990)-. Periodical. English (French). Four times a year. Canadian Council for Native Business, Box 132, Suite 405, 777 Bay Street, Toronto Ontario M5G 2C8 Canada. *Continues CouncilLine., 0838-7400.*

 UK
CONTAINERISATION. (19??)-. Periodical. English. Twelve times a year. £85.00 UK £120.00 Europe; £150.00 other. EMAP Readerlink, Audit House, 260 Field End Road, Ruislip Middlesex HA4 9LT United Kingdom. **Tel** 011 44 1773 63100, FAX 011 44 1733 87367. **(Subscription address:** EMAP Business Publishing, 4 Admiral House Cardinal Way, Middlesex HA3 5SQ United Kingdom. **Tel** 011 44 181 8684499.**)**

 ISSN 0010-7379
DD 658.7 UK
 CCC
CONTAINERISATION INTERNATIONAL. [Contain. int.]. (1967)-. Trade Publication. English. Twelve times a year. $265.00. EMAP Readerlink, Audit House, 260 Field End Road, Ruislip Middlesex HA4 9LT United Kingdom. **Tel** 011 44 1773 63100, FAX 011 44 1733 87367. **(Subscription address:** EMAP Business Publishing, 4 Admiral House Cardinal Way, Middlesex HA3 5SQ United Kingdom. **Tel** 011 44 181 8684499.**) ED** Francis Phillips. Index available. **Ad Acc. Circ:** 10,130. available on microfilm and microfiche from University Microfilms International (UMI).
 Desc: Reports, analysis and commentary upon business, technical, and development aspects of world container trades.
 Ind/Abst Fluid Abstr., Civil Eng.; Fluid Abstr. Proc. Eng.; FLUIDEX (1973-); Int. Packag. Abstr.

 ISSN 1071-2917
DD 658 US
CONTEMPORARY TIMES. (CONTEMPORARY TIMES / NATIONAL ASSOCIATION OF TEMPORARY SERVICES.). [Contemp. times]. **Added/Corp** National Association of Temporary Services (U.S.). **VFOAT** Times Contemporary. (19??)-. Trade Publication. English. Four times a year. $120.00. National Association of Temporary Services, 119 South Saint Asaph Street, Alexandria VA 22314. **Tel** (703)549-6287, FAX (703)549-4808. **ED** Louise Seghers. cum. index. **Bk Rev**, (Qty: 2-3). **Ad Acc, Adv Mgr:** Janice Alvey. **Circ:** 5,500 (ctrl).

 ISSN 0306-3224
 UK
CONTENTS PAGES IN MANAGEMENT. See Business and Economics-Abstracting, Bibliographies and Statistics.

LC HD28 .C644 BL
CONTEXTO BOLETIM. See Business and Economics-Personnel Management.

 ISSN 1065-3406
DD 658 US
 CCC
CONTINUOUS JOURNEY. (CONTINUOUS JOURNEY : THE MAGAZINE FOR CONTINUOUS IMPROVEMENT.). [Contin. journey]. **Added/Corp** American Productivity & Quality Center. (1992)-. Trade Publication. English. Four times a year. $50.00. American Product Quality Center, 123 North Post Oak Lane, Suite 300, Houston TX 77024-7797. **Tel** (713)681-4020, FAX (713)681-8578, telex 775013. **Bk Rev. Ad Acc.** ctrl circ. *Absorbed Letter / American Productivity & Quality Center, 0899-3017.*
 Desc: To promote productivity, quality, and quality of work life; a source for improvement information including case studies and how-to articles.

 ISSN 1058-9260
DD 658 US
CONTRACTOR'S BUSINESS MANAGEMENT REPORT. [Contract. bus. manage. rep.]. **Added/Corp** Institute of Management & Administration. Vol. 1, No. 1 (Dec. 1991)-. Periodical. English. Twelve times a year. $245.00. Institute of Management and Administration, 29 West 35th Street, 5th Floor, New York NY 10001-2299. **Tel** (212)244-0360, FAX (212)564-0465.

 ISSN 0895-2787
DD 658 US
 CCC
CONTROLLER'S REPORT (NEW YORK, N.Y.). (THE CONTROLLER'S REPORT.). [Control. rep.]. **Added/Corp** Institute for Office Management and Administration (U.S.). (Oct. 1987)-. Periodical. English. Twelve times a year. $245.00. Institute of Management and Administration, 29 West 35th Street, 5th Floor, New York NY 10001-2299. **Tel** (212)244-0360, FAX (212)564-0465.

LC HD28 **ISSN** 1356-3289
DD 658 UK
●**CORPORATE COMMUNICATIONS.** (1996)-. Academic Scholarly Publication. English. Three times a year. £89.00. MCB University Press, 60 62 Toller Lane, Bradford, West Yorkshire BD8 9BY United Kingdom. **Tel** 011 44 1274 785280, FAX 011 44 1274 785200, telex 51317-MCBUNI-G.

 ISSN 0964-8410
 UK
 CCC
●**CORPORATE GOVERNANCE.** See Law-Corporation Law.

 US
CORPORATE MEETING PLANNERS DIRECTORY. Directory. English. One time a year. $297.00. Salesman's Guide, A Reed Reference Publishing Company, Part of Reed International PLC, 121 Chanlon Road, New Providence NJ 07974. **Tel** (800)223-1797, (908)464-6800, FAX (908)665-3560, telex 138755.

LC T58.6 .C675 **ISSN** 0362-501X
DD 658.4/5/05 US
CORPORATE SYSTEMS. (19??)-. Periodical. English. Twelve times a year. $1.00 single issue. United Technical Publications, 645 Stewart Avenue, Garden City NY 11530.

LC HD30.42.U5 C67 **ISSN** 1080-7616
DD 658/.0071/52 US
●**CORPORATE UNIVERSITY GUIDE TO MANAGEMENT SEMINARS, THE.** [Corp. Univ. guide manag. semin.]. **Added/Corp** Corporate University (Firm). **VFOAT** Guide to Management Seminars; Management Seminars. (1993)-. English. One time a year (Oct.). $195.00. Corporate University Press, 124 Washington Avenue/Suite B-2, Point Richmond CA 94801. **Tel** (510)236-9400, FAX (510)236-1979. **ED** William Hamilton. **Circ:** n. available on diskette. *Continues Corporate University Guide to Short Management Seminars.*
 Desc: Listings of over 900 seminars and short courses for all levels of management and all produced by U.S. or Canadian universities and independent organizations.

LC HV8935 **ISSN** 1083-3382
DD 365 US
●**CORRECTIONS MANAGERS' REPORT.** See Law-Law Enforcement and Criminology.

 ISSN 1063-2735
DD 658 US
COST CONTROLLER, THE. [Cost control.]. **Added/Corp** Siefer Consultants, Inc. (1992)-. Periodical. English. Twelve times a year. $149.00. Siefer Consultants Inc., PO Box 1384, 525 Cayuga Street, Storm Lake IA 50588. **Tel** (712)732-7340, (712)747-7342, FAX (712)732-7906. **ED** Lynn Hardt. Index available (Dec. issue). cum. index (each individual year).

 ISSN 0010-9606
 UK
COST ENGINEER. [Cost eng.]. Vol. 6, No. 4 (July 1967)-. Periodical. English. $71.87. Association of Cost Engineers, Lea House, 5 Middlewich Road, Cheshire CW11 9XL United Kingdom. **Tel** 011 44 1270 764798, telex 367169. cum. index. **Bk Rev. Ad Acc. Circ:** 2,300 (ctrl).
 Ind/Abst Curr. Cit.

 ISSN 1079-2341
 US
●**COST MANAGEMENT INSIDER'S REPORT. Added/Corp** Warren, Gorham & Lamont, Inc. (1994)-. Periodical. English. Twelve times a year. $180.98. Warren Gorham & Lamont Inc., Park Square Building, 31 St. James Avenue, Boston MA 02116-4112. **Tel** (617)423-2020, (800)950-1207, FAX (617)423-2026.

 ISSN 8750-9555
 US
CREATIVE SALES MANAGER. [Creat. sales manager]. Trade Publication. English. Twenty-six times a year. $119.40. Executive Reports Corporation, 113 Sylvan Avenue, Englewood Cliffs NJ 07632.

 ISSN 0963-1690
 UK
 CCC
CREATIVITY AND INNOVATION MANAGEMENT. (1992)-. Academic Scholarly Publication. English. Four times a year (Mar., June, Sept., Dec.). $175.00. Basil Blackwell Publishers Ltd., 108 Cowley Road, Oxford OX4 1JF United Kingdom. **Tel** 011 44 1235 465500, FAX 011 44 1235 465556, telex 837022 OXBOOK G. **(Subscription address:** Blackwell Publishers / UK, 108 Cowley Road, Oxford OX4 1JF United Kingdom. **Tel** 011 44 1865 791100, FAX 011 44 1865 791347.**) ED** Tudor Richards 061 831-7824. Index available. **Bk Rev**, (Qty: 25 /year). **Ad Acc, Adv Mgr:** Paula Stewart, **Tel** 0865 791100. **Circ:** 120 (ctrl).
 Desc: Aims to give managers insights into innovation within their organization and accelerates the development of creative performance in their staff.

LC HG1501 **ISSN** 0273-9267
DD 332.1 US
CREDIT UNION MANAGEMENT. See Business and Economics-Banks and Banking.

 ISSN 1168-6448
 FR
UDC 658 (44)
CREEZ! LOISIRS CLICHY. (CREEZ! LOISIRS.). (1992)-. Periodical. French. Groupe Commun Gerard Touati, 13 15 rue Marcel Sembat, 13001 Marseille France. **Tel** 011 33 91 084284. *Continues Creez!, 0248-1855.*

 ISSN 0967-621X
 UK
CRONER'S PREMISES MANAGEMENT. (19??)-. Periodical. English. Four times a year. $332.41. Croner Publ Ltd., Croner House London Road, Kingston Upon Thames, Surrey KT2 6SR United Kingdom. **Tel** 011 44 181 5473333, FAX 011 44 181 5472637.

LC HD28 **ISSN** 1352-7606
DD 658 UK
●**CROSS CULTURAL MANAGEMENT.** (1994)-. Academic Scholarly Publication. English. Four times a year. MCB University Press, 60 62 Toller Lane, Bradford, West Yorkshire BD8 9BY United Kingdom. **Tel** 011 44 1274 785280, FAX 011 44 1274 785200, telex 51317-MCBUNI-G. **ED** Samuel Natale. Documents available from BLDSC.

 ISSN 1077-5536
DD 658 US
●**CSP (NEW YORK, N.Y.).** (CSP : THE MAGAZINE FOR CONVENIENCE STORE PEOPLE.). [CSP]. **VFOAT** Magazine for Convenience Store People. (1994)-. Trade Publication. English. Twelve times a year. $100.00. Group Weiss & Watson, 1140 6th Avenue, 6th Floor, New York NY 10036. **Tel** (212)391-2626. *Continues Convenience Store People, 1057-0411.*

 PE
CUADERNOS DE DIFUSION / ESCUELA DE ADMINISTRACION DE NEGOCIOS PARA GRADUADOS, ESAN. Added/Corp Escuela de Administracion de Negocios Para Graduados. Direccion de Investigacion. (1992)-. Periodical. Spanish. ESAN, Direccion de Investigacion, Apartado Postal 1846, Lima 100 Peru.

ISSN 1061-9119
DD 658 US
CUSTOMER SERVICE MANAGER'S GUIDE, THE. [Cust. serv. manag. guide]. (19??)-. English. One time a year. $112.00. Bureau of Business Practice, 24 Rope Ferry Road, Waterford CT 06386. **Tel** (800)243-0876, (203)442-4365, (800)876-9105, FAX (203)443-1123.

US
CUSTOMER SERVICE MANAGER'S LETTER. English. Twelve times a year. $159.36 (US); $192.48 (Canada). Bureau of Business Practice, 24 Rope Ferry Road, Waterford CT 06386. **Tel** (800)243-0876, (203)442-4365, (800)876-9105, FAX (203)443-1123.

ISSN 0145-8442
DD 658 US
CUSTOMER SERVICE NEWSLETTER. [Cust. serv. newsl.]. **VFOAT** CSN. (19??)-. Newsletter. English. Twelve times a year. $124.00. Alexander Research & Communications, Inc, 215 Park Avenue South, Suite 1301, New York NY 10003. **Tel** (212)228-0246, FAX (212)228-0376.
Desc: The newsletter for customer service managers concerned with improving their operations.

LC HF5547 .D282 ISSN 0418-4025
DD 651 US
CEASED
DARTNELL OFFICE ADMINISTRATION HANDBOOK, THE. **Added/Corp** Dartnell Corporation. **VFOAT** Office Administration Handbook. 1st Ed. (1967)-(1994). Periodical. English. Dartnell Corporation, 4660 North Ravenswood Avenue, Chicago IL 60640. **Tel** (312)561-4000, (800)621-5463, FAX (312)561-3801. **ED** Clark Fetridge and Robert Minor. ***Supersedes*** *Dartnell Office Manager's Handbook.*
Desc: All the information you need to handle more than 2,000 office, personnel and administrative problems.

US
DARTNELL SALES MANAGER'S HANDBOOK, THE. **Added/Corp** Dartnell Corporation. **VFOAT** Sales Mmanager's Handbook. (19??)-. English. Irregular. $49.95. Dartnell Corporation, 4660 North Ravenswood Avenue, Chicago IL 60640. **Tel** (312)561-4000, (800)621-5463, FAX (312)561-3801. ***Continues*** *The Sales Manager's Handbook.*

IT
DATA MANAGER. (19??)-. Trade Publication. Italian. Ten times a year. L55000 Italy. Fratelli Pini Editori SRL, Via Vitt Emanuele 99, 22100 Como Italy. **Tel** 011 39 31 264584.

ISSN 1065-7177
DD 658 US
TITLE CHANGE
DATA PROCESSING MANAGER'S BULLETIN. [Data process. manager's bull.]. (19??)-(19??). Bulletin. English. Bureau of Business Practice, 24 Rope Ferry Road, Waterford CT 06386. **Tel** (800)243-0876, (203)442-4365, (800)876-9105, FAX (203)443-1123. ***Continued by*** *PC Manager's Letter, 1069-9228.*

LC T58.64 .D37 ISSN 1053-5594
DD 658.4/038 US
CCC
CODEN DRMAEE
CEASED
DATA RESOURCE MANAGEMENT. (DATA RESOURCE MANAGEMENT : DRM.). [Data resour. manage.]. **VFOAT** DRM. Vol. 1, No. 1 (Winter 1990)-(Fall 1993). Periodical. English. Auerbach Publishers Inc., Park Square Building, 31 St. James Avenue, Boston MA 02116. **Tel** (800)950-1207. **ED** Susan M McDermott. Index available. **Bk Rev**, (Qty: 4). **Ad Acc, Adv Mgr:** Phil Brady, **Tel** (212)971-5120. **Circ:** 1500. Documents available from Ask*IEEE.
Desc: Designed to be the data resource manager's single reference covering all aspects of emerging information and data technologies. It is also a solutions-oriented publication that provides practical, how-to advice from practitioners and consultants alike.
Ind/Abst INSPEC (Winter 1991-).

LC HD28 .D4 ISSN 0304-0941
DD 658.4/008 II
DECISION (CALCUTTA). (DECISION.). Vol. 1 (Apr. 1974)-. English. Rs15.00. Indian Institute of Management / Calcutta, Calcutta India.

ISSN 0167-9236
NE
CCC
CODEN DSSYDK
Pr Rev.
DECISION SUPPORT SYSTEMS. [Decis. support syst.]. Vol. 1, No. 1 (Jan. 1985)-. Academic Scholarly Publication. English. Twelve times a year (3 volumes). $756.00. Elsevier Science Publishers BV, PO Box 211, 1000 AE Amsterdam Netherlands. **Tel** 011 31 20 4853641, 011 31 20 4853642, FAX 011 31 20 4853598. **ED** H J Schneider and A B Whinston. available on microfilm and microfiche from University Microfilms International (UMI); available on an online database from Elsevier Electronic Subscriptions (EES). Documents available from Article Express International, The Genuine Article, UMI Article Clearinghouse, Ask*IEEE.
Desc: Intended to both encourage further investigations by providing a forum for advances in the DSS field and to facilitate research by providing an efficient mechanism for researchers to keep up with the efforts of others.
Ind/Abst ABI/INFORM Glob. Ed.; ABI/INFORM [Computer File] (Jan. 1985-); ACM Guide Comput. Lit.; CompuMath Cit. Index [Full Cov.]; Comput. Abstr.; Comput. Lit. Index; Comput. Rev.; Contents Pages Manage.; Curr. Cit.; Curr. Contents Eng. Comput. Technol.; Eng. Index Annu.; Ergon. Abstr.; INSPEC (1986-); Int. Abstr. Oper. Res. [Select. Cov.]; Linguist. Lang. Behav. Abstr.; Res. Alert [Select. Cov.]; SCISEARCH; Soc. Plann. Policy Dev. Abstr.; Soc. Sci. Cit. Index [Select. Cov.]; Sociol. Abstr.

ISSN 1070-7409
DD 658 US
DELANEY REPORT, THE. [Delaney rep.]. (1990)-. Periodical. English. One time a week. $245.00. Delaney Report, 510 East 23rd Street, New York NY 10010. **Tel** (212)533-4430, FAX (212)979-7874.

ISSN 1057-2864
DD 658 US
CCC
DESIGN FIRM MANAGEMENT & ADMINISTRATION REPORT. [Design firm manage. adm. rep.]. **Added/Corp** Institute of Management & Administration (U.S.). **VFOAT** Design Firm Management and Administration Report. (Sept. 1991)-. Periodical. English. Twelve times a year. $245.00. Institute of Management and Administration, 29 West 35th Street, 5th Floor, New York NY 10001-2299. **Tel** (212)244-0360, FAX (212)564-0465. ***Absorbed*** *Architects' Office Management & Administration Report, 0890-9814.* ***Continued in part by*** *Engineering Office Management & Administration Report, 0749-1557.*

LC TS239 .D515 ISSN 0745-449X
DD 671.2/53 US
DIE CASTING MANAGEMENT. **See** Industry and Production-Manufacturing.

ISSN 1202-631X
DD 658.8 CN
●**DIGITAL MARKETING.** **See** Business and Economics-Marketing and Purchasing.

ISSN 0839-1300
DD 658.4/006/0714 CN
DIMENSIONS. [Dimens. - Corp. prof. adm. agrees Que.]. **Added/Corp** Corporation Professionnelle des Administrateurs Agrees du Quebec. Vol. 1, No. 1 (Dec. 1987)-. Periodical. French. Irregular. Corporation Professionnelle Des Administrateurs Agrees Du Quebec / Montreal, Bureau 890, 1801 McGill College, Montreal Quebec H3A 2N4. ***Continues*** *Pentagone, 0713-5629.*

LC HD2709 .D56 ISSN 0364-9156
DD 658.4/2/0973 US
DIRECTORS & BOARDS. [Dir. boards]. **Added/Corp** Information for Industry, Inc. **VAT** Directors and Boards. Vol. 1 (Spring 1976)-. Periodical. English. Four times a year. $195.00. Investment Dealers Digest Inc., Two World Trade Center, 18th Floor, New York NY 10048. **Tel** (212)227-1200, FAX (212)432-1039. **ED** Jim Kristie. **Ad Acc. Circ:** 5,000. available on microfilm and microfiche from University Microfilms International (UMI); available on an online database (file 648/Full-Text) from DIALOG. Documents available from UMI Article Clearinghouse.
Desc: Provides coverage and research reports on corporate oversight issues; features articles by board members, chairmen and CEO's.
Ind/Abst ABI/INFORM Glob. Ed.; ABI/INFORM Ondisc: Expr. Ed. (Winter 1987-); ABI/INFORM [Computer File] (Spring 1980-); Acad. Search; Account. Index Suppl.; Anbar Account. Finan. Abstr. [Full Txt.]; Anbar Mark. Distr. Abstr. [Full Txt.]; Anbar Top Manage. Abstr. [Full Txt.]; Bowne Dig. Corp. Sec. Lawyers; Bus. Index (1985-); Bus. Source Plus; Bus. Source; Curr. Cit.; Curr. Law Index (1980-); EP Collect.; Gen. BusinessFile (1985-); Gen. Period. Index (1985-); Homework Help.; INFO-SOUTH Abstr.; Leg. Resour. Index (1980-?);; LegalTrac (1980-1986); Mag. Search; Manage. Market. Abstr.; Manage. Bibliogr. Rev.; Manage. Contents (1976-); MasterFile FullTEXT 1000; MasterFile FullTEXT 350; MasterFile FullTEXT 650; MasterFile FullTEXT (Jan. 1993-); OCLC; Oper. Prod. Manage. Abstr. [Full Txt.]; Person. Train. Abstr. [Full Txt.]; Person. Manage. Abstr.; Predicasts; Public Aff. Inf. Serv. Bull.; Telebase; Trade Ind. ASAP [Full Txt.]; Trade Ind. Index (1981-) [Full Txt.].

ISSN 0193-4279
US
DIRECTORSHIP (WESTPORT). (DIRECTORSHIP.). **Added/Corp** Directors Publications, Inc. (Jan. 1976)-. Newsletter. English. Twelve times a year. $470.00. Directors Publications Inc., 8 Sound Shore Drive, Suite 250, Greenwich CT 06830. **Tel** (203)861-7000, FAX (203)226-7893. **ED** B.J. Dunn. Index available. cum. index. **Bk Rev**, (Qty: 40).
Desc: Analysis, surveys, commentary and interviews on issues critical to corporate guidance.
Ind/Abst Bus. Source Plus; EP Collect.; Homework Help.; MasterFile FullTEXT 1000; MasterFile FullTEXT 350; MasterFile FullTEXT 650; MasterFile FullTEXT (Jan. 1995-); OCLC; Telebase.

ISSN 0703-1742
DD 658.5/6/02571 CN
DIRECTORY - CANADIAN TESTING ASSOCIATION. **Main/Corp** Canadian Testing Association. **VFOAT** Repertoire - Association Canadienne des Laboratoires d'Essais. 2d Ed.- 1965-. Directory. English (French). Every 2 years. Free. Canadian Testing Association, Suite 640, 220 Laurier Avenue West, Ottawa K1P 5Z9. ***Continues*** *Association of Canadian Commercial Testing Laboratories & Consultants. Directory, 0703-1734.*

LC HD69.C6 D49 ISSN 0842-6562
DD 001/.029/471 CN
DIRECTORY OF CANADIAN MANAGEMENT CONSULTANTS. [Dir. Can. manag. consult.]. **Added/Corp** Canada. Commercial Service Industries Directorate. Consulting Services Division. Business Opportunities Sourcing System (Canada) Canada. Consulting and Engineering Service Industries Directorate. **VFOAT** Directory of Management Consultants. (1987)-. Directory. English. One time a year. 32.82Can$. Tyrell Press, Ltd., 2714 Fenton Road, Box 937, Gloucester Ontario K1G 3N3 Canada. **Tel** (800)574-0137, (613)822-0740, FAX (613)822-1089.

LC HD69.C6 D53 ISSN 0090-4945
DD 658.4/03 US
DIRECTORY OF CONSULTING SPECIALISTS. **VFOAT** Consulting Specialists. (19??)-. Directory. English. Stemm's Information Systems and Indexes, PO Box 42576, Los Angeles CA 90050.

ISSN 0070-5438
DD 658 UK
DIRECTORY OF DIRECTORS, THE. **Added/Corp** Thomas Skinner & Co. (Publishers). (1878)-. Directory. English. One time a year. $395.00. Reed Information Services Ltd., Windsor Court, East Grinstead House, East Grinstead RH19 1BR United Kingdom. **Tel** 011 44 1342 326972, FAX 011 44 1342 335977, telex 95127 INFSER G. **(Subscription address:** Cahners Publishing / Connecticut, PO Box 2118, Westport CT 06880. **Tel** (203)454-4147.) **Ad Acc. Circ:** 4,000. available on an online database.
Desc: Instant access to the boardrooms of industrial and commercial concerns throughout Britain. A unique reference work, this publication now lists 57,000 directors and extensive detail on over 15,000 major British companies.

US
DIRECTORY OF DIRECTORS IN THE CITY OF NEW YORK AND TRI-STATE AREA. 1982 Ed. (1982)-. Directory. English. One time a year (May). $215.00. Directory of Directors Company Inc, PO Box 462, Southport CT 06490. **Tel** (203)255-8525. **ED** A. M. Dahl. Index available. **Circ:** 1,000. ***Continues*** *Directory of Directors in the City of New York and Suburbs.*
Desc: Lists approximately 15,000 executives address, company name, outside directorates, and approximately 2,500 firms and corporations listing all executives and directors, address, telephone, and type of business.

LC HG4001 ISSN 0071-5042
DD 658.15 CN
DIRECTORY OF DIRECTORS. [EXECUTIVES OF CANADA]. **Main/Corp** The Financial Post. (19??)-. Directory. English. One time a year. 111.96Can$. Financial Post Company Ltd., 333 King Street East, Toronto Ontario M5A 4N2, Canada. **Tel** (416)350-6500, FAX (416)350-6601. **ED** Jean Graham. **Ad Acc. Circ:** 6,000. available on an online database.

LC TX911.3.M27 D57 ISSN 0742-3306
DD 647/.94/071073 US
CEASED
DIRECTORY OF HOSPITALITY EDUCATORS. **See** Hotels/Motels.

LC HD69.C6 D55 ISSN 0743-6890
DD 658.4/6/02573 US
DIRECTORY OF MANAGEMENT CONSULTANTS. (DIRECTORY OF MANAGEMENT CONSULTANTS / COMPILED AND PUBLISHED BY CONSULTANTS NEWS.). [Dir. manage. consult.]. (1977)-. Directory. English. Every 2 years. $99.95. Kennedy Publications, Templeton Road, Fitzwilliam NH 03447. **Tel** (603)585-6544, (800)531-0007, FAX (603)585-9555. Index available. **Bk Rev**.
Desc: Lists management consulting firms by geographic location cross indexed by functions, industries and key principals locator with paragraph description, billings and staff-size.

ISSN 0268-375X
UK
DIRECTORY OF MANAGEMENT CONSULTANTS IN THE UK. [Dir. manage. consult. U.K.]. **Added/Corp** Management Consultancy Information Service. (1983)-. Directory. English. One time

Business and Economics — Management

a year. $145.02. Task Force Pro Libra Ltd., 17-18 Britton Street, London EC1M 5NQ United Kingdom. **Tel** 011 44 171 2515522, FAX 011 44 171 2518318.

LC HD69.C6 I57a **ISSN** 0097-6547
DD 658.4/6/06273 US
DIRECTORY OF MEMBERS - INSTITUTE OF MANAGEMENT CONSULTANTS.
Main/Corp Institute of Management Consultants (New York, N.Y.). (19??)-. English. Every 2 years. $50.00. Institute of Management Consultants, 521 5th Avenue, 35th Floor, New York NY 10175. **Tel** (212)697-8262. Circ: 2,500 (ctrl).
Desc: Alphabetical listing of approximately 2,200 certified management consultants with geographical cross-reference. Cross-referenced by field of experts.

LC HF5548.2 .D537 **ISSN** 0278-9663
DD 652 US
DIRECTORY OF WORD PROCESSING MANAGEMENT. See Computers-Word Processing.

LC HD28 .D54 **ISSN** 0419-3903
YU
DIREKTOR. No. 1 (Jan. 1969)-. Periodical. Serbo-Croatian (Roman). Twelve times a year. $266.90. **(Subscription address:** Jugoslovenska Knjiga, PO Box 36, YU 11001 Belgrade Yugoslovia. **Tel** 011 38 11 621055, FAX 011 38 11 325970.)

ISSN 0012-3366
BL
DIRIGENTE INDUSTRIAL. (1959)-. Portuguese. Twelve times a year. $70.00. Visao SA Editorial, Rua Alvaro Carvalho 350, 01050 Sao Paulo SP Brazil. **Tel** 256 5011, FAX 2581919, telex 11221436.

ISSN 0894-7651
DD 658 US
DISTRIBUTION CENTER MANAGEMENT. [Distrib. cent. manage.]. Vol. 21, No. 1 (Jan. 1986)-. Periodical. English. Twenty-four times a year. $127.00. Alexander Research & Communications, Inc, 215 Park Avenue South, Suite 1301, New York NY 10003. **Tel** (212)228-0246, FAX (212)228-0376. **Continues** Warehousing and Physical Distribution Productivity Report.
Desc: Provides practical strategies and industry news to help distribution center and warehouse professionals improve distribution center efficiency.

ISSN 1080-7160
DD 676 US
●**DISTRIBUTION MANAGEMENT (GREAT NECK, N.Y.).** See Paper and Pulp Industry.

LC HD28 **ISSN** 1043-7118
DD 658 US
DISTRIBUTOR'S & WHOLESALER'S ADVISOR, THE. [Distrib. wholes. advis.]. **VFOAT** Distributor's and Wholesaler's Advisor. (1989)-. Periodical. English. Twenty-four times a year. $197.00. Alexander Research & Communications, Inc, 215 Park Avenue South, Suite 1301, New York NY 10003. **Tel** (212)228-0246, FAX (212)228-0376.
Desc: Business management strategies and tactics for senior management at wholesale distribution firms.

ISSN 0824-4316
DD 658/.005 CN
DOCUMENT DE TRAVAIL - UNIVERSITE D'OTTAWA. FACULTE D'ADMINISTRATION. (DOCUMENT DE TRAVAIL.). [Doc. trav. - Univ. Ottawa, Fac. adm.]. (1978)-. Monographic series. French (English). Irregular (50-80 per year). Price varies per volume. Faculte d'Administration Universite d'Ottawa, 136 Jean-Jacques Lussier, Ottawa Ontario K1N 6N5 Canada. **Tel** (613)564-3494, FAX 1(613)564-6518. Index available. cum. index. ctrl circ.
Desc: A series of original research reports, designed for preliminary distribution prior to publication in final form as journal articles or book chapters.

ISSN 0927-9547
NE
DOCUMENT MANAGEMENT. (DOCUMENT MANAGEMENT : NIEUWSBRIEF VOOR DOCUMENTAIRE INFORMATIEKUNDE.). [Doc. manage.]. **Added/Corp** Instituut voor Toegepaste Informatica. **VFOAT** Nieuwsbrief Document Management. No. 1 (June 1992)-. Periodical. Dutch. Four times a year. Samsom Bedrijfsinformatie BV, Postbus 4, 2400 MA Alphen Rij Netherlands. **Tel** 011 31 1720 66633. **(Subscription address:** Intermedia BV, Postbus 4, 2400 MA Alphen AD Rijn Netherlands. **Tel** 011 31 1720 66481.)

BE
DOCUMENTATION ON BOOKS / INTERNATIONAL UNIVERSITY CONTACT FOR MANAGEMENT EDUCATION. LITERATURE SERVICE.
Added/Corp International University Contact for Management Education. Literature Service. European Foundation for Management Development. **VFOAT** Documentation Bulletin. (Jan. 1971)-. Bulletin. English. Four times a year. $167.92. European Foundation for Management Development, rue Washington 40, 1050 Brussels Belgium. **Tel** 011 32 2 648 0385. **Continues** Documentation Bulletin (International University Contact for Management Education).

ISSN 0223-5625
FR
UDC 331.25
DOCUMENTS D'INFORMATION ET DE GESTION. [Doc. inf. gest.]. (1966)-. Periodical. French. Twelve times a year. Free on request. CNRO, BP 300, 06808 Cagnes S Mer Cedex France. **Tel** 011 33 93 162804.

ISSN 1079-641X
DD 658 US
●**DSN RETAIL FAX.** [DSN ratail fax]. **VFOAT** Discount Store News Retail Fax. (1994)-. Periodical. English. One time a week. $179.00. Lebhar Friedman Inc., PO Box 31203, Tampa FL 33633. **Tel** (800)944-4676, (813)664-6707.

LC HD69.C6 D86 **ISSN** 0884-3724
DD 658.4/6/02573 US
NLM HD 69.C6; D897
DUN'S CONSULTANTS DIRECTORY.
[Dun's consult. dir.]. **Added/Corp** Dun's Marketing Services. (1986)-. English. One time a year. $425.00. Dun & Bradstreet Information Services, 3 Sylvan Way, Parsippany NJ 07054. **Tel** (201)605-6000, (800)526-0651.

ISSN 0722-6950
GW
UDC 658.628
CODEN 381
DYNAMIK IM HANDEL (1982). See Food and Food Industry.

ISSN 1018-7405
SZ
UDC 654.19
CODEN 621.396.74
E.B.U. REVIEW. PROGRAMMES, ADMINISTRATION, LAW. **VFOAT** European Broadcasting Union Review. Programmes, Administration, Law. (1972)-. Periodical. English. Six times a year. European Broadcasting Union, Case Postale 67, CH-1218 Geneva Switzerland. **Tel** 011 41 22 7172111, FAX 011 41 22 7985897, telex 41 57 00 EBU CH.

UK
EASING THE PAIN OF THE MEETINGS EPIDEMIC. (1987)-. Academic Scholarly Publication. English. £9.50. International Hospital Federation, 4 Abbots Place, London NW6 4NP United Kingdom. **Tel** 011 44 171 3727181, FAX 011 44 171 3287433. Documents available from FAXON Xpress, BLDSC.
Desc: Reviews and abstracts the literature on the effectiveness of meetings and sets out a practical strategy for improving this aspect of managerial performance.

ISSN 1045-2559
DD 658 US
EAST TENNESSEE TODAY. (Jan. 1989)-. Periodical. English. Free. Data Services of Greeneville, 415 Elk Street, Greeneville TN 37743.

ISSN 1061-9402
US
Pr Rev.
●**EASY MONEY.** (1993)-. Periodical. English. Twelve times a year. $10.00 (libraries), $30.00 (individuals), Free (institutions) US; $50.00 (individuals), Free (libraries and institutions) other. Zenolith Publications, PO Box 444, Sharon TN 38255-0444. Index available. cum. index. **Bk Rev**, (Qty: 12). **Ad Acc**, **Adv Mgr:** Scott Pierpoint. Acid Free. Circ: 750,000 (ctrl).
Desc: Motivational sales training and skill development. The goal is expanded Christianity in the sales field.

ISSN 1186-8449
DD 650/.0285 CN
ECHANGE DE DOCUMENTS INFORMATISES AU CANADA. [Echange doc. inform. Can.]. **Added/Corp** Conseil Canadien de l'Echange Electronique de Donnees. (1991)-. French. $14.95 (members) $19.95 (other). Conseil Canadien de L'Echange Electronique de Donnees Conseil Canadien de L'Echange Electronique de Donnees, Bureau 203, 5401 Ouest Avenue Eglinton, Etobicoke Ontario M9C 5K6 Canada, Bureau 203, 5401 Ouest Avenue Eglinton, Etobicoke Ontario M9C 5K6 Canada,. **Tel** , , FAX , , telex , ,

LC HD28 .E45 **ISSN** 0351-286X
DD 658/.009497 YU
ECONOMIC ANALYSIS AND WORKERS' MANAGEMENT. [Econ. anal. work. manage.].
Added/Corp Jugoslovensko Udruzenje Za Ekonometriju i Organizacione Nauke. Vol. 8, No. 3-4 (198?)-. Periodical. English (Macedonian, Russian and Slovenian). Four times a year. $85.00. Prosveta Export Import Agency, PO Box 180, Terazije 16, 1101 Belgrade Yugoslavia. **Tel** 011 862 687441, telex 862-11609. **Continues** Ekonomska Analiza, 0013-3213.
Ind/Abst Contents Recent Econ. J. (1980-); Econ. Lit. Index (1980); J. Econ. Lit.; LABORDOC; Middle East Abstr. Index.

ISSN 0958-5052
DD 384.3 UK
CEASED
EDI ANALYSIS. [EDI anal.]. (1989)-(1993). Periodical. English. Integration Europe, 144 Avenue Moliere, 1060 Brussels Belgium. **Tel** 011 32 2 3466420. **Continues** Trade Flash International, 0775-2911.

LC HF1142.L8 E38
DD 650/.07/11421 UK
EDUCATION FOR BUSINESS AND MANAGEMENT IN THE REGION. English. Every 2 years. £1.60. Regional Advisory Council for Further Education, Tavistock House South Tavistock Square, London WC1H 9LR United Kingdom.

LC HD28
DD 658 UK
●**EFFECTIVE MANAGEMENT SERIES.**
(1994)-. Monographic series. English. Irregular. Basil Blackwell Publishers Ltd., 108 Cowley Road, Oxford OX4 1JF United Kingdom. **Tel** 011 44 1235 465500, FAX 011 44 1235 465556, telex 837022 OXBOOK G. **ED** Alan Anderson.

ISSN 0890-4790
US
EFFECTIVE SPECIAL SERVICES MANAGEMENT. [Eff. spec. serv. manage.].
Added/Corp National Professional Resources, Inc. (Port Chester, N.Y.). (198?)-. Periodical. English. Ten times a year. $69.00 (one-year), $99.00 (two-year) US; $73.00 (one-year), $107.00 (two-year) Canada; $77.00 (one-year), $115.00 (two-year) other. National Professional Resources, PO Box 1479, 25 South Regent Street, Port Chester NY 10573. **Tel** (914)937-8879, FAX (914)937-9327. **ED** Robert Hanson. **Bk Rev**. ctrl circ.

LC HD28 .E39
RU
EKO. **Added/Corp** Akademiia Nauk SSSR. Sibirskoe Otdelenie. Rossiiskaia Nauk. Sibirskoe Otdelenie. (1989)-. Periodical. Russian. Twelve times a year. $154.80. **(Subscription address:** East View Publications Inc., 3020 Harbor Lane North, Suite 110, Minneapolis MN 55447. **Tel** (800)477-1005, (612)550-0961, FAX (612)559-2931.) available on microfilm from University Microfilms International (UMI). **Continues** Ekonomika i Organizatsiia Promyshlennogo Proizvodstva (Novosibirsk, R.S.F.S.R.), 0131-7652.

LC HC267.B2 H65
XR
EKONOM. (1991)-. Periodical. Czech (Slovak). One time a week. $178.20. **(Subscription address:** Kubon & Sagner, ABT Zeitschriftenimport, D 80328 Munich Germany. **Tel** 011 49 89 54218130.) **Continues** Tydenik Hospodarskych Novin.
Ind/Abst PROMT.

ISSN 0167-3939
NE
ELAN (DEVENTER, NETHERLANDS).
(ELAN.). **Added/Corp** Nederlands Centrum van Directeuren en Commissarissen. Vol. 1, No. 1 (Jan. 1986)-. Periodical. Dutch. Ten times a year. Fl169.00. Intermedia BV, Postbus 4, 2400 MA Alphen AD Rijn Netherlands. **Tel** 011 31 1720 66855, FAX 011 31 1720 94714.

ISSN 0884-7142
DD 658 US
ELECTED LEADER. [Elect. lead.]. **Added/Corp** Institute of Association Management Companies. (198?)-. Periodical. English. Four times a year. Institute of Association Management Companies, 335 Commerce Street, Suite 201, Alexandria VA 22314. **Tel** (703)548-5016.

LC HD9696.A3 U5376 **ISSN** 0163-6197
DD 338.4/7/62130973 US
CCC
CODEN ELBUDL
TITLE CHANGE
ELECTRONIC BUSINESS. See Electronics.

ISSN 0896-0941
DD 658 US
CCC
EMPLOYEE ASSISTANCE PROGRAM MANAGEMENT LETTER. [Empl. Assist. Program manage. lett.]. **Added/Corp** Employee Assistance Program (N.J.). **VFOAT** EAP Management Letter. (Feb. 1987)-. Periodical. English. Twelve times a year. $137.00. Health Resources Publishing, 3100 Highway 138, Wall Township NJ 07719-1442. **Tel** (908)681-1133, FAX (908)681-0490. **ED** Robert K Jenkins. Index available. **Bk Rev**. **Ad Acc**.
Desc: A comprehensive monthly management briefing on the range of influences surrounding your employee assistance program.

LC HD30.42.S6 E47 ISSN 0968-4921
DD 658 UK
●**EMPOWERING BLACK MANAGERS : THE SOUTHERN AFRICAN EXPERIENCE.** **VFOAT** EBM. (1994)-. Academic Scholarly Publication. English. Four times a year. $479.00. MCB University Press, 60 62 Toller Lane, Bradford, West Yorkshire BD8 9BY United Kingdom. **Tel** 011 44 1274 785280, FAX 011 44 1274 785200, telex 51317-MCBUNI-G. **(Subscription address:** MCB University Press / US and Canada Subscriptions, PO Box 10812, Birmingham AL 35201-0812. **Tel** (205)995-1567, (800)633-4931, FAX (205)995-1588.**) ED** Michael Phalatsi.
Desc: Deals with economic policy, development, black management and corporate structure in South Africa.

ISSN 0968-4891
UK
EMPOWERMENT IN ORGANIZATIONS. (1993)-. Periodical. English. Three times a year. $549.00. MCB University Press, 60 62 Toller Lane, Bradford, West Yorkshire BD8 9BY United Kingdom. **Tel** 011 44 1274 785280, FAX 011 44 1274 785200, telex 51317-MCBUNI-G. **(Subscription address:** MCB University Press / US and Canada Subscriptions, PO Box 10812, Birmingham AL 35201-0812. **Tel** (205)995-1567, (800)633-4931, FAX (205)995-1588.**)**

LC Z7164.C81 E93 HF5351 ISSN 0071-0210
DD 016.33 US
NLM HF 5353 E56
ENCYCLOPEDIA OF BUSINESS INFORMATION SOURCES. **See** Business and Economics-Abstracting, Bibliographies and Statistics.

ISSN 1055-0526
US
ENGINEERING DEPARTMENT MANAGEMENT & ADMINISTRATION REPORT. **VFOAT** Engineering Department Management and Administration Report. (1991)-. Trade Publication. English. Twelve times a year. $245.00. Institute of Management and Administration, 29 West 35th Street, 5th Floor, New York NY 10001-2299. **Tel** (212)244-0360, FAX (212)564-0465.

ISSN 0765-7579
FR
ENSEIGNEMENT ET GESTION (PARIS). (ENSEIGNEMENT ET GESTION.). [Enseign. gest]. **Added/Corp** Fondation Nationale pour l'Enseignement de la Gestion. **VFOAT** Cahiers Enseignement et Gestion. (197?)-. Periodical. French. Four times a year. ***Continues*** *Formation et Gestion, 0765-7587.*
Ind/Abst Int. Labour Doc.; Selec. Coop. Index Manage. Period.

ISSN 0709-8138
DD 650/.05 CN
ENTERPRISE WEST. [Enterp. west]. May 1979-. Periodical. English. Twelve times a year. $1.50 per number. Pennex Ltd, 107 Paramount Road, Winnipeg Manitoba R2X 2W6 Canada. ***Continues*** *Enterprise in Manitoba, 0706-3911.*

ISSN 0925-1928
NE
UDC 654.14057.33
ENTREE 'S-GRAVENHAGE. (ENTREE.). [Entree 's-Gravenhage]. (1990)-. Periodical. Dutch. Four times a year. PTT Telecom BV, DHR de Munck, IECT PB 30000, 2500 GA Den Haag Netherlands.

ISSN 1188-7427
DD 658.4 CN
ENTREPRENDRE (LAVAL). (LAVAL.). [Entreprendre]. **Added/Corp** Centre de l'Entrepreneurship. (1992)-. Periodical. French. Six times a year. 18.37Can$. Centre de l'Entrepreneur, 1600 boulevard St. Martinest Bur 630, Laval Quebec H7G 4S7 Canada. **Tel** (514)669-8373, FAX (800)479-1777. **ED** Edmond Bourque. **Bk Rev**, (Qty: 5). **Ad Acc.** ctrl circ. ***Continues*** *Le Club Regional de l'Entrepreneurship., 0840-9145.*

ISSN 0705-0542
DD 658/.008 CN
ENTREPRISE (QUEBEC). (L'ENTREPRISE.). (1977)-. Newspaper. French. Seven times a week. Journal le Soleil, CP 1547 Succursale Terminus, 925 CH St. Louis, Quebec Quebec G1K 7J6 Canada. **Tel** (418)686-3233, FAX (418)686-3260. **ED** Gilbert Lacasse. **Bk Rev. Ad Acc, Adv Mgr:** Dennis Dube. Full Page (B&W) 9,572.00. Half Page (B&W) $4,113.00. **Circ:** 140,000 (Sat.), 100,000 (weekdays) (ctrl).

ISSN 0212-1867
SP
ESIC MARKET. **VFOAT** Estudios de Gestion Comercial y Empresa. (1970)-. Periodical. Spanish. Four times a year. $63.51. Escuela Superior Gestion Comercial, Marketing Avda de Valdenigrales S N, 28223 Madrid Spain. **Tel** 011 34 1 3527716, 011 34 1 3527746.
Ind/Abst Selec. Coop. Index Manage. Period.

LC HD28 .E73 ISSN 0425-3698
SP
ESTUDIOS EMPRESARIALES. [Estud. empres.]. **Added/Corp** Escuela Superior de Tecnica Empresarial. (Jan./April 1965)-. Periodical. Spanish. Three times a year. $65.00. Facultad de Ciencias Economicas y Empresariales, Apartado 1359, 20080 San Sebastian Spain. **Tel** 011 34 943 273100. cum. index.
Ind/Abst J. Econ. Lit.

LC HD5650 ISSN 1261-7121
DD 658 FR
UDC 172
●**ETHIQUE DES AFFAIRES.** **VFOAT** Revue Ethique des Affaires. (1995)-. Academic Scholarly Publication. French. Four times a year. $108.70. Editions ESKA, 27 rue Dunois, 75013 Paris France. **Tel** 011 33 1 44068042, FAX 011 33 1 44240694.
Desc: Articles regarding management ethics.

BE
EUROPEAN FORUM FOR MANAGEMENT DEVELOPMENT / EFMD. **Added/Corp** European Foundation for Management Development. **VFOAT** EFMD Quarterly Review. (1991)-. English. Three times a year. efmd / European Forum for Management Development, rue Washington 40, B 1050 Brussels Belgium. **Tel** 011 32 2 6480385, FAX 011 32 2 6460768, telex 65080 INAC B. **ED** Tony Hubert. ***Continues*** *EMD Journal.*

ISSN 0263-2373
UK
CCC
EUROPEAN MANAGEMENT JOURNAL. [Eur. manage. j.]. **Added/Corp** European School of Management Studies. Scottish Business School. European School of Management. Glasgow Business School. **VFOAT** EMJ. Vol. 1, No. 1 (Summer 1982)-. Periodical. English. Six times a year. $331.00. Pergamon Press, An Imprint of Elsevier Science Ltd., The Boulevard, Langford Lane, Kidlington, Oxford OX5 1GB United Kingdom. **Tel** 011 44 1865 843000, 011 44 1865 843699, FAX 011 44 1865 843010. **(Subscription address:** Elsevier Science Ltd. / Oxford Fulfillment Centre, PO Box 800, Kidlington OX5 1DX United Kingdom. **Tel** 011 44 865 843355.**) ED** Tom Milne. **Bk Rev. Ad Acc.** available on microfilm and microfiche from University Microfilms International (UMI); available on an online database from Elsevier Electronic Subscriptions (EES); and (file 15/Full-Text) DIALOG.
Desc: Clear coverage of the issues that matter in the European management scene.
Ind/Abst Anbar Account. Finan. Abstr. [Full Txt.]; Anbar Mark. Distr. Abstr. [Full Txt.]; Anbar Top Manage. Abstr. [Full Txt.]; Contents Pages Manage.; Curr. Cit.; Manage. Market. Abstr.; Manage. Bibliogr. Rev.; Oper. Prod. Manage. Abstr. [Full Txt.]; PAIS Int. Print (1991-); Person. Train. Abstr. [Full Txt.]; Person. Manage. Abstr.; Selec. Coop. Index Manage. Period.; Women Manage. Rev. [Full Txt.].

ISSN 0938-1236
GW
UDC 655
CODEN 338.45
EUROPRINTER OSTFILDERN. **See** Printing Industry.

LC HD38.2 .E92
DD 658 US
EVALUATION GUIDE TO EXECUTIVE PROGRAMS, THE. **Added/Corp** Corporate Education Resources, Inc. Corporate University (Firm). (1988)-. English. One time a year. $195.00. Corporate University Press, 124 Washington Avenue/Suite B-2, Point Richmond CA 94801. **Tel** (510)236-9400, FAX (510)236-1979. **ED** William Hamilton. **Circ:** 1,000. available on diskette. ***Continues*** *CER Evaluation Guide to Executive Programs.*
Desc: Provides detailed listings of 170 high-level courses around the world for human resources professionals.

ISSN 1035-719X
DD 658.3125 AT
Pr Rev.
EVALUATION JOURNAL OF AUSTRALASIA. [Eval. j. Australas.]. **Added/Corp** Australasian Evaluation Society. (1989)-. Periodical. English. Two times a year (June & Nov.). 24.67Aus$. Australasian Evaluation Society, PO Box 448, Curtin ACT 2605 Australia. **Tel** 011 61 6 2823320, FAX 011 61 6 2823320. **ED** John Dunn (editor's address: PO Box 376, Glenside SA 5065 Australia, phone: 011 61 08 379 7146). **Ad Acc. Circ:** 550 (ctrl). ***Continues*** *Bulletin of the Australasian Evaluation Society Inc., 1030-6463.*

ISSN 1077-1956
DD 658 US
●**EXCELLENCE IN SERVICE.** [Exce. serv.]. **Added/Corp** Bureau of Business Practice. (May 1994)-. Periodical. English. Twelve times a year. $70.00. Bureau of Business Practice, 24 Rope Ferry Road, Waterford CT 06386. **Tel** (800)243-0876, (203)442-4365, (800)876-9105, FAX (203)443-1123.

ISSN 0740-1388
US
EXCESS EXPRESS. **See** Insurance.

LC HD28 .E89 ISSN 1072-4818
DD 658.4/005 US
●**EXEC (EMMAUS, PA.).** (EXEC.). [Exec]. (1993)-. Periodical. English. Six times a year. $19.97. Rodale Press Inc., 400 South 10th Street, Emmaus PA 18098. **Tel** (610)967-5171, (800)666-2503, FAX (610)967-8964, telex 847338. ***Continues*** *Young Executive (Emmaus, Pa.), 1060-2119.*

LC HD28 .A32
US
TITLE CHANGE
EXECUTIVE : AN ACADEMY OF MANAGEMENT PUBLICATION, THE. **Added/Corp** Academy of Management. **VFOAT** Academy of Management Executive. (1990)-(1993). Periodical. English. Academy of Management, Academy of Management Publications, PO Box 3020, Briarcliff Manor NY 10510. **Tel** (914)923-2607, FAX (914)923-2615. **ED** John Young. Index available. cum. index. **Bk Rev. Ad Acc. Circ:** 9,000 (ctrl). ***Continues*** *Academy of Management Executive, 0896-3789.* ***Continued by*** *Academy of Management Executive (1993), 1079-5545.*
Ind/Abst Mag. Search; Work Relat. Abstr.

US
EXECUTIVE BRIEFING. (19??)-. Newsletter. English. Twenty-six times a year. $69.00. Economics Press Inc, 12 Daniel Road, Fairfield NJ 07004. **Tel** (201)227-1224, (800)526-2554, FAX (201)227-9742.
Desc: For mid- to upper-level executives whose responsibilities encompass everything from improving workforce productivity to increasing the bottom line.

ISSN 0898-7912
DD 658 US
EXECUTIVE BRIEFING (NEW YORK, N.Y.). (EXECUTIVE BRIEFING.). [Exec. brief.]. **Added/Corp** Coopers & Lybrand. **VFOAT** Coopers & Lybrand Executive Briefing. (Feb. 1986)-. Newsletter. English. Ten times a year. Free on request. Cooper and Lybrand / New York, 1251 Avenue of the Americas, New York NY 10020. **Tel** (212)536-2000. available on microfilm and microfiche from University Microfilms International (UMI). Documents available from UMI Article Clearinghouse. ***Continues*** *Executive Alert Newsletter, 0739-7844.*
Ind/Abst ABI/INFORM Glob. Ed.; ABI/INFORM [Computer File] (Sept. 1988-); Account. Tax Datab. (Sept. 1988-).

US
EXECUTIVE COUNSELOR. Periodical. English. Twelve times a year (mailed quarterly). American Institute of Management, 45 Willard Street, Boston MA 02169. **Tel** (617)536-2503. **ED** Barbara C Dall. Index available. ctrl circ.

LC WMLC 93/3089 ISSN 0953-3230
UK
TITLE CHANGE
EXECUTIVE DEVELOPMENT. (19??)-(1995). Periodical. English. MCB University Press, 60 62 Toller Lane, Bradford, West Yorkshire BD8 9BY United Kingdom. **Tel** 011 44 1274 785280, FAX 011 44 1274 785200, telex 51317-MCBUNI-G. **(Subscription address:** MCB University Press / US and Canada Subscriptions, PO Box 10812, Birmingham AL 35201-0812. **Tel** (205)995-1567, (800)633-4931, FAX (205)995-1588.**) ED** Jeffrey Gold. **Bk Rev. Ad Acc. Circ:** 500. ***Absorbed*** *Top Management Digest.* ***Absorbed by*** *International Journal of Career Management.*
Desc: Covers all subjects relevant to management development, to help both companies and their executives to get the most out of the work situation. It aims to present a broad overview of new developments helping to put the latest methods and strategies into perspective. The journal draws its concise contributions from a cross-section of both academic and business sources - allowing the reader's organization to be compared with others and to benefit from their experience.
Ind/Abst Curr. Cit.; Manage. Market. Abstr.

ISSN 8756-2308
DD 658 US
EXECUTIVE EXCELLENCE. (1984)-. Periodical. English. Twelve times a year. $129.00. Stephen Covy and Associates, 3507 North University Avenue, Suite 100, Provo UT 84604. **Tel** (800)331-7716. **ED** Ken Shelton. Index available. **Bk Rev. Circ:** 5,000. available on microfilm and microfiche from University Microfilms International (UMI); available on an online database (file 15/Full-Text) from DIALOG. Documents available from UMI Article Clearinghouse.
Desc: Centrally concerned with issues and ideas relating to personal development, managerial effectiveness and personal productivity.
Ind/Abst ABI/INFORM Glob. Ed.; ABI/INFORM [Computer File] (Nov. 1987-); Curr. Cit.; UMI ABI/Inform--Bus. Period. Ondisc [Full Txt.].

LC HF5500.3.U54 E93 ISSN 0199-2880
DD 658/.0088042 US
EXECUTIVE FEMALE, THE. [Exec. female]. **Added/Corp** National Association for Female Executives (U.S.). **VFOAT** EF. Vol. 2 No. 4 (July/Aug. 1979)-. Periodical. English. Six times a year. comes with membership. National Association for Female Executives, 127 West 24th Street, 4th Floor, New York NY 10011. **Tel** (212)477-2200. available on an online database (files 647,648/Full-Text) from DIALOG. ***Continues** Executive Female Digest, 0160-8134.*
Desc: Articles on career and management strategies, personal finances, entrepreneurship. Ideas for use on the job and accounts of how successful women are meeting their career and life challenges.
Ind/Abst Acad. Search; Account. Art.; Bus. ASAP (1990-) [Full Txt.]; Bus. Index (1985-); Bus. Period. Index; Bus. Source Plus; Bus. Source; EP Collect.; Gen. BusinessFile (1985-); Gen. Period. Index (1985-); Homework Help.; INFO-SOUTH Abstr.; Mag. Search; MasterFile FullTEXT 1000; MasterFile FullTEXT 350; MasterFile FullTEXT 650; MasterFile FullTEXT (Jan. 1994-); OCLC; Telebase; Mag. Index (1977-); Wilson Bus. Abstr.

ISSN 0193-8150
US
EXECUTIVE LETTER (DALLAS). (EXECUTIVE LETTER.). **Added/Corp** Chamber of Commerce of the United States. Southwest Region. (Sept. 1979)-. Periodical. English. Six times a year. Chamber of Commerce of the United States Southwest Region, 4835 LBJ Freeway, Suite 750, Dallas TX 75234. ***Continues** Management Memo.*

ISSN 0735-4746
US
EXECUTIVE MANAGEMENT AND MOTIVATION. [Exec. manage. motiv.]. Vol. 3, No. 4 (Apr. 1983)-. Periodical. English. Twelve times a year. $156.00. Management Consultant Communications Inc, PO Box 80785, Atlanta GA 30366.

ISSN 0882-6463
DD 658 US
EXECUTIVE PC LETTER, THE. [Exec. PC letter]. **VAT** Executive Personal Computer Letter. Periodical. English. Twenty-six times a year. $36.00. Research Institute of America, 117 East Stevens Avenue, Valhalla NY 10595. **Tel** (800)431-9025, FAX (800)820-3135 (914)749-5300.

ISSN 1064-8623
DD 658 US
EXECUTIVE REPORT ON CUSTOMER SATISFACTION. [Exec. rep. cust. satisf.]. **VFOAT** Customer Satisfaction. (1988)-. Periodical. English. Twenty-four times a year. $199.00. Alexander Research & Communications, Inc, 215 Park Avenue South, Suite 1301, New York NY 10003. **Tel** (212)228-0246, FAX (212)228-0376. ***Continues** Customer Assurance Report.*
Desc: For senior managers concerned with corporate level customer satisfaction policy.

ISSN 0271-3659
DD 808 US
EXECUTIVE SPEAKER, THE. [Exec. speak.]. (1980)-. Periodical. English. Twelve times a year. $120.00. The Executive Speaker Company, PO Box 292437, Dayton OH 45429. **Tel** (513)294-8493, FAX (513)294-6044. **ED** Robert O. Skovgard. Index available (sent bound in issue twice a year). available in microform from University Microfilms International (UMI); available on an online database from NEXIS.
Desc: Serves as clearinghouse and digest for speeches by corporate executives.
Ind/Abst Curr. Lit. Fam. Plan. (19??-199?).

LC HD28 .E95
BL
EXPANSAO. Vol. 1 (Jan. 26, 1972)-. Periodical. Portuguese. $60.00. Publicacoes Executivas Brasileiras Ltd, Marconi 34 CJ 92-CP 30837, Sao Paulo Brazil.

MX
EXPANSION. (19??)-. Periodical. Spanish. Twenty-five times a year. $345.00. Grupo Editorial Expansion, Sinaloa 149 P9, Col Roma, 06700 Mexico DF Mexico. **Tel** 011 52 5 2072066, 2072619, FAX 011 52 5 5116351. **ED** Diego Arrazola Menterola. Index available ($5.42 per issue). cum. index. **Ad Acc**, **Adv Mgr:** Elena Bayardo. **Circ:** 27,500 (ctrl).
Desc: Geared toward leadership executives in responsible management positions in both business and government in Mexico.

FR
EXPANSION MANAGEMENT REVIEW, L'. (1976)-. French. Four times a year. 575.00F. Groupe Expansion, Le Ponant, 25 rue LeBlanc, 75842 Paris Cedex 15 France. **Tel** 011 33 1 40604115. **(Subscription address:** Harvard l'Expansion, SVC Abonnements B 070, 60732 St Geneva Cedex 9 France. **Tel** 011 33 44895230.) **Ad Acc**, **Adv Mgr:** Philippe Guillanton, **Tel** 011 33 1 40604060. **Circ:** 8,000. ***Continues** Harvard l'Expansion / La Revue des Responsables.*
Desc: A selection of articles and papers about management in the US and Europe.

LC T396 .E94 ISSN 1046-3925
DD 659.1/52 US
EXPO (WAUCONDA, ILL.). (EXPO.). **VFOAT** EXPO Magazine. (1989)-. Trade Publication. English. Six times a year. $32.00 US; $39.00 Canada; $48.00 other. Sanford Organization, 8016 Pennsylvania, Kansas City MO 64114. **Tel** (816)523-5693. **ED** Donna P. Sanford. **Bk Rev**. **Ad Acc**. **Circ:** 8,500 (ctrl).
Desc: Targets association executives responsible for planning, organizing, promoting and operating trade shows. Each issue contains news, features and columns that deal with show management.

US
•**FACILITIES.** (1995)-. English. Twelve times a year. $36.00. Bedrock Communications, 650 First Avenue, New York NY 10016. **Tel** (212)532-4150, FAX (212)213-6382. ***Continues** Agent and Manager.*

LC TS177 .F32 ISSN 0263-2772
DD 658.2 UK
FACILITIES (BRADFORD, WEST YORKSHIRE, ENGLAND). **See** Industry and Production-Manufacturing.

ISSN 1040-5828
DD 658 US
FACILITY ISSUES. [Facil. issues]. Vol. 1, No. 1 (Oct. 1, 1988)-. Periodical. English. Twenty-four times a year. $189.00. Facility Issues, PO Box 477, Tempe AZ 85280. **Tel** (602)941-5898, FAX (602) 423-9808.

LC TS177 .I35 ISSN 1059-3667
DD 658.2 US
FACILITY MANAGEMENT JOURNAL : A PUBLICATION OF THE INTERNATIONAL FACILITY MANAGEMENT ASSOCIATION. **Added/Corp** International Facility Management Association. **VFOAT** Facility Management. (19??)-. Periodical. English. Six times a year. $75.00 US; $100.00 other. Ieternational Facility Management Association, 1 Greenway Plaza/11th Fl, Houston TX 77046-0194. **Tel** (713)623-4362, FAX (713)623-6124. **ED** Suzanne M. Pearson. Index available (in Nov.). **Bk Rev**, (Qty: 12/yr). **Ad Acc**. **Circ:** 12,000 (ctrl). ***Continues** IFMA Journal.*
Desc: Written by facility managers, for facility managers.

NE
FACILITY MANAGEMENT MAGAZINE. Dutch. Six times a year. Fl95.00. Arko Uitgeverij, Postbus 616, 3430 AP Nieuwegein Netherlands. **Tel** 011 31 3402 51090.

LC WMLC 93/1274 ISSN 0888-0085
DD 658 US
FACILITY MANAGER. [Facil. manager]. **Added/Corp** International Association of Auditorium Managers (Chicago Heights, Ill.). (19??)-. Periodical. English. Four times a year (Jan., Apr., July, Oct.). $35.00 one-year; $65.00 two-year. International Association Auditorium Managers, 4425 West Airport Freeway, Suite 590, Irving TX 75026. **Tel** (214)255-8020. **ED** Julie Herrick. **Ad Acc**, **Adv Mgr:** Carole Snyder, **Tel** (616)345-3230.

ISSN 1081-9517
DD 658 US
•**FACILITY MANAGER'S ALERT.** [Facil. manag. alert]. (April 5, 1995)-. Periodical. English. Twenty-three times a year. $253.00. Progressive Business Publications, 370 Technology Drive, PO Box 3019, Malvern PA 19355. **Tel** (617)527-8600, (800)220-5000, FAX (617)647-8089.

LC TS177 .F33 ISSN 0146-3314
DD 658.2/005 US
FACTORY MANAGEMENT (NEW YORK). (FACTORY MANAGEMENT.). Vol. 10 (Jan. 1977)-. Periodical. English. Twelve times a year. $25.00. Morgan Grampian, 40 Beresford Street Woolwich, London SE18 6BQ United Kingdom. **Tel** 011 44 181 8557777, FAX 011 44 181 8555548, telex 896238. available on microfilm and microfiche from University Microfilms International (UMI). ***Continues** Factory.*
Ind/Abst Saf. Health Work.

ISSN 1047-255X
DD 650 US
CCC
FAMILY BUSINESS. **See** Business and Economics-Small Business.

ISSN 1065-0032
DD 650 US
FEDERAL MANAGER'S EDGE, THE. [Fed. manag. edge]. (Feb. 1990)-. Periodical. English. Twelve times a year. $65.00. FPMI Communications Inc., 707 Fiber Street, Huntsville AL 35801. **Tel** (205)539-1850, FAX (205)539-0911, .

US
FEDERAL MANAGERS GUIDE TO DISCIPLINE. (19??)-. English. Irregular. $8.95 (US); $12.45 (Canada). FPMI Communications Inc., 707 Fiber Street, Huntsville AL 35801. **Tel** (205)539-1850, FAX (205)539-0911, .

US
FEDERAL MANAGERS GUIDE TO PREVENTING SEXUAL HARASSMENT. English. Irregular. $8.95 (US); $12.45 (Canada). FPMI Communications Inc., 707 Fiber Street, Huntsville AL 35801. **Tel** (205)539-1850, FAX (205)539-0911, .

US
FEDERAL MANAGERS GUIDE TO TQM. (19??)-. English. Irregular. $8.95 (US); $12.45 (Canada). FPMI Communications Inc., 707 Fiber Street, Huntsville AL 35801. **Tel** (205)539-1850, FAX (205)539-0911, .

LC JK404 .F435 ISSN 0893-8415
DD 353.07/4/05 US
FEDERAL MANAGERS QUARTERLY. [Fed. managers q.]. **Added/Corp** Federal Managers Association. **VFOAT** Federal Managers. Vol. 1, (198?)-. Trade Publication. English. Four times a year (Feb., May, Aug., Nov.). $24.00. Federal Managers Association, 1641 Prince Street, Alexandria VA 22314. **Tel** (703)683-8700, FAX (703)683-8707. **ED** Erin Lynch. **Bk Rev**. **Ad Acc**. **Circ:** 20,000 (ctrl).
Desc: In-depth articles addressing management, professional development and legislation affecting federal employees. Addresses the state of Federal Management.

US
FEDERAL MANAGERS SURVIVAL GUIDE. (19??)-. English. Irregular. $8.95 (US); $12.45 (Canada). FPMI Communications Inc., 707 Fiber Street, Huntsville AL 35801. **Tel** (205)539-1850, FAX (205)539-0911, .

LC HF5001 .F514 ISSN 0895-4186
DD 658.1/5/05 US
CCC
CODEN FIEXAW
FINANCIAL EXECUTIVE (1987). (FINANCIAL EXECUTIVE : FE.). [Financ. exec.]. **Added/Corp** Financial Executives Institute. **VFOAT** FE; FE, Financial Executive. Vol. 3, No. 1 (Jan. 1987)-. Periodical. English. Six times a year. $45.00. Financial Executives Institute Publishers, 10 Madison Avenue, PO Box 1938, Morristown NJ 07960. **Tel** (201)898-4600, FAX (201)898-4649. **ED** Robin Couch. **Ad Acc**. **Circ:** 16,000. available on microfiche. Documents available from UMI Article Clearinghouse, Ask*IEEE. ***Continues** FE (Morristown, N.J.), 0883-7481.*
Desc: Three basic subject areas are corporate reporting, corporate finance, and management strategy. Articles examine professional and technical developments that affect financial executives' day-to-day responsibilities, as well as long range issues that reflect financial executives' increasing involvement in the general management of their companies.
Ind/Abst ABI/INFORM Glob. Ed.; ABI/INFORM Ondisc: Expr. Ed. (Jan. 1987-); ABI/INFORM [Computer File] (1987-); Acad. Search; Account. Tax Datab. (Sept. 1971-) [Full Txt.]; Anbar Account. Finan. Abstr. [Full Txt.]; Anbar Mark. Distr. Abstr. [Full Txt.]; Anbar Top Manage. Abstr. [Full Txt.]; Bus. ASAP (1990-) [Full Txt.]; Bus. Index (1985-); Bus. Period. Index (1987-); Bus. Source Plus; Bus. Source; Comput. Lit. Index; Contents Pages Manage.; Curr. Cit.; EP Collect.; Fed. Tax Artic.; Gen. BusinessFile (1985-); Gen. Period. Index (1985-1986); Homework Help.; INFO-SOUTH Abstr.; INSPEC (1987-); Int. Exec.; Mag. Search; Manage. Market. Abstr. (1987-); Manage. Bibliogr. Rev.; Manage. Contents; MasterFile FullTEXT 1000; MasterFile FullTEXT 350; MasterFile FullTEXT 650; MasterFile FullTEXT (July 1993-); OCLC; Oper. Prod. Manage. Abstr. [Full Txt.]; PAIS Int. Print (1991-?); Person. Train. Abstr. [Full Txt.]; Selec. Coop. Index Manage. Period.; Telebase; UMI ABI/Inform--Bus. Period. Ondisc [Full Txt.]; Wilson Bus. Abstr.; Women Manage. Rev. [Full Txt.].

LC HG1501
DD 332.1 NE
FINANCIEEL MANAGEMENT. **See** Business and Economics-Banks and Banking.

IT
FINANZA, MARKETING E PRODUZIONE : RIVISTA DELL'UNIVERSITA L. BOCCONI. **See** Business and Economics-Marketing and Purchasing.

ISSN 0015-2358
US
FINISHERS' MANAGEMENT. 1957. Trade Publication. English. Ten times a year (monthly with June/July and Nov./Dec. combined). $30.00. Publication Management Inc, 4350 DiPaulo Center/Dearlove Road, Glenview IL 60025-9998. **Tel** (312)699-1700, FAX (312)699-1703. **ED** Hugh Morgan. **Bk Rev**. **Ad Acc**.

Circ: 8,500 (ctrl). available on microfilm from University Microfilms International (UMI).
Desc: Management oriented "why to" editorial focused on improved management practices and more profitable operation of captive and job shops in metal finishing industry.
Ind/Abst Eng. Mater. Abstr.; Surf. Treat. Technol. Abstr.

ISSN 1082-3476
DD 363 US
•FIREHOUSE MANAGEMENT ADVISOR.
See Fire Prevention.

ISSN 0939-8414
GW
UDC 64
FIRST CLASS ALFELD. See Hotels/Motels.

LC HB **ISSN** 1350-4959
DD 330 UK
•FOCUS ON BRITISH BUSINESS AND MANAGEMENT SCIENCES RESEARCH.
(1994)-. Bibliography. English. Twelve times a year. £26.00. British Library / Document Supply Centre, Boston Spa, Wetherby West Yorkshire LS23 7BQ United Kingdom. **Tel** 011 44 1937 546060, FAX 011 44 1937 546333, telex 557381. **(Subscription address:** Turpin Distribution Services Limited, Blackhorse Road, Letchworth, Hertfordshire SH6 1HN United Kingdom. **Tel** 011 44 1462 672555, FAX 011 44 1462 480947.**)** Index available. **Ad Acc.** Documents available from BLDSC.

LC HF5549 **ISSN** 1352-9501
DD 658.40605 UK
•FOCUS ON CHANGE MANAGEMENT.
[Focus chang. manag.]. (1994)-. Trade Publication. English. Ten times a year. $504.81. Armstrong Information Ltd., 3rd Floor Brigade House, Parsons Green, London SW6 4TH United Kingdom. **Tel** 011 44 171 7367111, FAX 011 44 171 3717806. Documents available from BLDSC.

UK
FORESIGHT (LONDON, ENGLAND).
(FORESIGHT.). **Added/Corp** Risk Research Group. Risk & Insurance Research Group. Vol. 1, (July 1975)-. Periodical. English. Twelve times a year. $400.00. Risk & Insurance Research Group, 4 Henrietta Street, Covent Gard, London WC2E 8PS United Kingdom. **Tel** 011 44 171 8360614, FAX 011 44 171 3796355, telex 23446.

ISSN 1040-0753
DD 658 US
FORESIGHT (WESTLAKE VILLAGE, CALIF.). (FORESIGHT.). Periodical. English. Four times a year. Free (to qualified recipients). Forecast Communications Inc, 32129 Lindero Canyon Road/Suite 211, Westlake Village CA 91361.

LC Z7164.A2 B85 **ISSN** 1157-3783
DD 658 FR
CEASED
FRANCIS BULLETIN SIGNALETIQUE. 528, BIBLIOGRAPHIE INTERNATIONALE DE SCIENCE ADMINISTRATIVE. Added/Corp Institut de l'Information Scientifique et Technique (France). Sciences Humaines et Sociales. **VFOAT** Bibliographie Internationale de Science Administrative; International Bibliography of Administrative Science. Vol. 45, No 1 (1991)-Vol. 48, No 4 (1994). Bulletin. French. CNRS / Institut d'Information Scientifique et Technique, (Centre National de la Recherche Scientifique), 15 Quai Anatole France, 75700 Paris France. **Tel** 011 33 1 47531515, FAX 011 33 1 45517307, telex 260034. **(Subscription address:** Institut d'Information Scientifique et Technique Diffusion, 2 Allee du Parc de Brabois, 54514 Vandoeuvre Nancy France. **Tel** 011 33 83 504664, FAX 011 33 83 504666, telex 961942.**)** Index available (free). ***Continues*** *Bulletin Signaletique. 528, Bibliographie Internationale de Science Administrative.*

LC Z7164.A2 B85
DD 658 FR
•FRANCIS BULLETIN SIGNALETIQUE. 528, BIBLIOGRAPHIE INTERNATIONALE DE SCIENCE ADMINISTRATIVE [COMPUTER FILE].
1995. Bibliography. French (English). Four times a year. CNRS / Institut d'Information Scientifique et Technique, (Centre National de la Recherche Scientifique), 15 Quai Anatole France, 75700 Paris France. **Tel** 011 33 1 47531515, FAX 011 33 1 45517307, telex 260034. available on an online database.

ISSN 1077-5498
DD 658 US
TITLE CHANGE
FRONT LINE LEADERSHIP. [Front line leadersh.]. **Added/Corp** Bureau of Business Practice. (1994)-(1994). Periodical. English. Bureau of Business Practice, 24 Rope Ferry Road, Waterford CT 06386. **Tel** (800)243-0876, (203)442-4365, (800)876-9105, FAX (203)443-1123. ***Continues*** *Front Line Supervisor's Bulletin, 1067-8956.* ***Continued by*** *Leadership for the Front Lines, 1080-1863.*

LC HV41 .F94 **ISSN** 0016-268X
DD 658/.91/3617305 US
CCC
FUND RAISING MANAGEMENT. [Fund rais. manage.]. (March/April 1969)-. Trade Publication. English. Twelve times a year. $58.00. Hoke Communications Inc, 224 7th Street, Garden City NY 11530. **Tel** (516)746-6700, (800)229-6700. **ED** William Olcott. **Bk Rev. Ad Acc. Circ:** 11,000 (ctrl). available on microfilm and microfiche from University Microfilms International (UMI); available on an online database (files 15,648/Full-Text) from DIALOG. Documents available from UMI Article Clearinghouse.
Desc: A magazine for development directors and other management of all types of non-profit organizations, detailing methods of raising funds, managing volunteers and other issues.
Ind/Abst ABI/INFORM Glob. Ed.; ABI/INFORM [Computer File]; Acad. Search; Bus. ASAP (19??-199?); Bus. Index; Bus. Source Plus (1985-); Bus. Source (1985-); Curr. Cit.; Curr. Lit. Fam. Plan.; EP Collect.; Gen. BusinessFile; Gen. Period. Index; Health Plan. Adminis. (1974-); Homework Help.; Hosp. Health Admin. Index; INFO-SOUTH Abstr.; Mag. Search (Jan. 1993-); Manage. Contents; MasterFile FullTEXT 1000; MasterFile FullTEXT 350; MasterFile FullTEXT 650; MasterFile FullTEXT (Dec. 1987-) [Full Txt.]; OCLC; PAIS Int. Print; Public Aff. Inf. Serv. Bull.; Telebase; UMI ABI/Inform--Bus. Period. Ondisc; Vocat. Search.

UK
•FUNDHOLDING MANAGEMENT HANDBOOK. (1994)-. English. Two times a year. £37.00 Europe; £40.00 other (institutions). Longman Group Ltd., Fourth Avenue, Longman House, Harlow Essex CM19 5SR United Kingdom. **Tel** 011 44 1279 429655, FAX 011 44 1279 431067, telex 81259.

ISSN 1069-4951
DD 658 US
CEASED
•FUTURE AT WORK, THE. [Future work]. **Added/Corp** Coates & Jarratt, Inc. Issue 1 (May 1993)-(Nov 1995). Periodical. English. Jossey Bass Inc., 350 Sansome Street, San Francisco CA 94104. **Tel** (415)433-1767, FAX (415)433-0499.

ISSN 0932-3961
GW
UDC 65.012.4
GABLERS MAGAZIN. [Gablers Mag.]. (1987)-. Periodical. German. Ten times a year. $144.32. Gabler Verlag, Postfach 1546, D-65005 Wiesbaden Germany. **Tel** 011 49 611 534129, FAX 011 49 611 534430. ***Continues*** *Betriebswirtschafts-Magazin, 0005-9986.*

LC HF3401 .G39
BL
GAZETA MERCANTIL : ADMINISTRACAO E SERVICOS. VFOAT Administracao e Servicos. Vol. 1, No. 1 (April 1979)-. Periodical. Portuguese. Rua Major Quedinho 90, Sao Paulo Sp Brazil.

LC HD28 .L63 **ISSN** 0773-0543
DD 658/.005 BE
GESTION 2000. VFOAT Gestion Deux Mille. Vol. 1, No. 1 (1985)-. Periodical. French (English). Six times a year. $253.72. Gestion 2000, 16 Avenue de l'Espinette, B 1348 Louvain-la-Neuve Belgium. **Tel** 011 32 10 473081, FAX 011 32 10 454060, telex 59037. Index available. **Bk Rev. Ad Acc. Circ:** 2,500. ***Continues*** *Annales de Sciences Economiques Appliquees.*
Desc: Articles written by businesses, academics, consultants, and managers on key areas of management.
Ind/Abst Curr. Cit.; Int. Bibliogr. Sociol.; Manage. Market. Abstr.; PAIS Int. Print (1991-); Selec. Coop. Index Manage. Period.

FR
SUSPENDED
GESTION ACTUALITE. (19??)-(19??). French. Six times a year. 800.00F. Biblio Paris Dauphine, Svc Per Pl du Marechal Lattr Tassigny, 75016 Paris France. **Tel** 011 33 1 45051410.

LC HD28 .G49
DD 658/.005 MR
GESTION & SOCIETE. VFOAT Tasyir Wa-Al-Mujtama. Periodical. English (French; summaries and/or abstracts in Arabic). Four times a year. 100.00MD. ISCAE KM 9, 500 Route Nouasseur, Casablanca Morocco.

ISSN 1013-8501
FR
GESTION DE L'ENSEIGNEMENT SUPERIEUR. See Education-Higher Education.

ISSN 0701-0028
DD 658/.005 CN
GESTION (LAVAL). (GESTION.). [Gestion]. **VFOAT** Revue Internationale de Gestion. Vol. 1 (Nov. 1976)-. Periodical. French. Four times a year (Mar., June, Sept., Dec.). 27.67Can$. Gestion / H.E.C., 5255 Decelles, Montreal Quebec H3T 1V6 Canada. **Tel** (514)340-6677. **ED** Laurent Lapierre. **Bk Rev,** (Qty: 6-8). **Ad Acc. Circ:** 4,300 (ctrl).
Desc: Published in French for highest level of management. Offers readers, articles written by scholars and practitioners on such topics as accounting, finance, marketing, business environment, behavioral sciences, human relations, import-export. Addresses itself and to the highest level of management.
Ind/Abst Repere (1983-).

LC LB2917 .G45 **ISSN** 0393-5523
DD 371.2/00945/05 IT
GESTIONESCUOLA. Added/Corp Coordinamento Nazionale Associazioni/Collegi Presidi (Italy) Associazione Nazionale Presidi (Italy). **VFOAT** Gestione Scuola. Vol. 1, No. 1 (Jan. 1984)-. Periodical. Italian. Six times a year. L34060. Tecnodid, Piazza Carlo III 42, 80137 Naples Italy. **Tel** 011 39 81 441922, FAX 011 39 81 294083. **Bk Rev,** (Qty: 12). **Ad Acc, Adv Mgr:** Gabriella Crusco. ctrl circ.
Desc: Information on school management and organization.

LC HF5549.5.T7 G5 **ISSN** 1055-3371
DD 331.25/92/025 US
GLOBAL CONNECTOR, THE. (THE GLOBAL CONNECTOR : THE COMPLETE RESOURCE DIRECTORY FOR INTERNATIONAL TRAINING & DEVELOPMENT.). [Glob. connect.]. **Added/Corp** PASport Publishing International. (1992)-. Directory. English. $295.00. Pasport Publishing Internationsl, PO Box 2706, Sausalito CA 94965.

ISSN 1188-1917
DD 658.3 CN
GLOBAL FOCUS. [Glob. focus]. **Added/Corp** ACCIS (Organization). Vol. 1, No. 1 (Oct. 1991)-. Periodical. English. Two times a year. $10.00 per issue. ACCIS - The Graduate Workforce Professionals, 1209 King Street West 2nd Floor, Toronto Ontario M6K 1G2 Canada.

ISSN 1056-6406
DD 658 US
GLOBAL MEETING LINE, INC. [COMPUTER FILE] : MEETINGS DATA BASE MANAGEMENT. [Global Meet. Line Inc.]. **Added/Corp** Global Meeting Line, Inc. **VFOAT** Global Meeting Line. (1991)-. Periodical. English. Four times a year. $95.00. Global Meeting Line, Inc., 1345 Oak Ridge Turnpike, Suite 357, Oak Ridge TN 37830.
Desc: Quarterly cumulations of information contained online.

LC GV975 .G6 **ISSN** 0192-3048
DD 796.352/06/8 US
CODEN GCMAEA
GOLF COURSE MANAGEMENT. See Sports and Games.

LC HM134 .G73 **ISSN** 1059-6011
DD 658 US
CCC
GROUP & ORGANIZATION MANAGEMENT. [Group organ. manage.]. **VFOAT** Group and Organization Management. Vol. 17, No. 1 (Mar. 1992)-. Periodical. English. Four times a year (Mar., June, Sept., Dec.). $181.00. SAGE Periodical Press, 2455 Teller Road, Thousand Oaks CA 91320. **Tel** (805)499-0721, FAX (805)499-0871, telex 100799. **ED** Michael J. Kavanagh (SUNY- Albany, New York). **Acid Free.** available on microfilm and microfiche from University Microfilms International (UMI). Documents available from The Genuine Article, UMI Article Clearinghouse. ***Continues*** *Group & Organization Studies, 0364-1082.*
Desc: Bridges the gap between research and practice for psychologists, group facilitators, educators and consultants who are involved in the broad field of human relations training.
Ind/Abst ABI/INFORM Glob. Ed.; ABI/INFORM [Computer File] (March 1981-); Acad. Search; Bus. Index (1992-); Bus. Source Plus; Bus. Source; Commun. Abstr.; Cumul. Index Nurs. Allied Health Lit.; Curr. Contents Soc. Behav. Sci.; Curr. Index J. Educ.; EP Collect.; Gen. BusinessFile (1992-); Homework Help.; Hum. Resour. Abstr.; INFO-SOUTH Abstr.; Mag. Search; MasterFile FullTEXT 1000; MasterFile FullTEXT 350; MasterFile FullTEXT 650; MasterFile FullTEXT (July 1993-); OCLC; Person. Manage. Abstr.; Res. Alert [Full Cov.]; Soc. Plann. Policy Dev. Abstr.; Soc. Sci. Cit. Index [Full Cov.]; Sociol. Abstr.; Telebase; UMI ABI/Inform--Bus. Period. Ondisc (Dec. 1987-) [Full Txt.]; Work Relat. Abstr.

ISSN 1057-6193
DD 658 US
CEASED
GUIDE LINES (ROUND ROCK, TEX.).
(GUIDE LINES.). [Guide lines]. **Added/Corp** Texas Professional Training Associates. No. 1 (Nov. 1991)-(Dec. 1994). Periodical. English. Professional Training Associates, 210 Commerce Boulevard, Round Rock TX 78664. **Tel** (512)255-6006, (800)424-2112.

UK
GUIDE TO COLLEGE MANAGEMENT.
(19??)-. Periodical. English. Two times a year. £83.00 Europe; £88.00 other (institutions). Churchill Livingstone, 1-3 Baxter's Place, Leith Walk, Edinburgh EH1 3AF United Kingdom. **Tel** 011 44 131 5562424, FAX 011 44 131 5581278, telex 727511. **(Subscription address:**

Business and Economics — Management

Maruzen Company Ltd., PO Box 5050, Import & Export Department, Tokyo 100 31 Japan. **Tel** 011 81 3 32789224.)

LC Z7164.O7 H24 HD28

KO

HAKSUL CHAPCHI MOKCHA SOKPO. KYONGYONG, KYONGJE PYON / CURRENT CONTENTS OF FOREIGN JOURNALS. MANAGEMENT & ECONOMICS.
Added/Corp Hanguk Kwahak Kisul Chongbo Sento. **VFOAT** Kyongyong, Kyongje Pyon; Management & Economics; Management and Economics; Current Contents of Foreign Journals. Management & Economics. (19??)-. English (Japanese and Korean). Twelve times a year. Hanguk Kwahak Kisul Chongbo Sento, 206-9 Chongyangni-dong, Tongdaemun-ku, Seoul South Korea.

LC T58.6 .H342
DD 658.4/038

US

HANDBOOK OF IS MANAGEMENT. VAT
Handbook of Information Systems Management. (1991)-. English. Irregular. $169.95. Auerbach Publishers Inc., Park Square Building, 31 St. James Avenue, Boston MA 02116. **Tel** (800)950-1207. **Continues** Handbook of MIS Management, 1055-5870.

LC HF5415.7 .H34
DD 658.7/8

US

HANDLING & SHIPPING. PRESIDENTIAL ISSUE.
English. One time a year. $3.00 single issue. Industrial Publishing Company, 614 Superior Avenue West, Cleveland OH 44113.

ISSN 0749-4882
DD 658/.005

US

HARBUS NEWS, THE.
Added/Corp Harvard University. Graduate School of Business Administration. (19??)-. Periodical. English. Irregular (37 issues per year). $67.00. Harvard School of Business Administration, Harvard University, Boston MA 02163. **Tel** (617)495-6528.

ISSN 1043-6146
DD 912

US

HARLOW REPORT, GEOGRAPHIC INFORMATION SYSTEMS, THE.
[Harlow rep. geogr. inf. syst.]. **VFOAT** Geographic Information Systems; Harlow Report. Vol. 12, No. 1 (Jan. 1989)-. Periodical. English. Twelve times a year. $190.00. Advanced Information Management Group, PO Box 380487, Birmingham AL 35238-0487. **Tel** (205)980-8297, FAX (205)991-3877. **ED** Chris Harlow. Index available. **Continues** F-M Automation Newsletter, 0742-468X.
Desc: Monthly newsletter that reports on the current activities in the GIS industry. Contains articles about new software, service providers, users, and key management issues. Each month it contains "News to Use" reporting the latest items of interest, and an industry event calendar.

ISSN 0397-5495
UDC 33

FR
TITLE CHANGE

HARVARD, L'EXPANSION.
(1976)-(19??). Periodical. French. Groupe Expansion, Le Ponant, 25 rue LeBlanc, 75842 Paris Cedex 15 France. **Tel** 011 33 1 40604115. (**Subscription address:** Harvard l'Expansion, SVC Abonnements B 070, 60732 St Geneva Cedex 9 France. **Tel** 011 33 44895230.) **Ad Acc, Adv Mgr:** Philippe Guillanton, **Tel** 33 1 40604060. **Circ:** 8,000. **Continued by** l'Expansion Management Review.
Desc: A selection of articles and papers about management in the US and Europe.
Ind/Abst Repere (1992-?); Selec. Coop. Index Manage. Period. (?-?).

GW
TITLE CHANGE

HARVARD MANAGER.
(19??)-(19??). English. Manager Magazin Verlag GmbH, Postfach 111060, Brandstwiete 19, W2000 Hamburg 11 Germany. **Tel** 011 49 40 3007551, FAX 011 49 40 3007247, telex 841 2162477. **Continued by** Harvard Business Manager.

ISSN 1062-6026
DD 363

US
TITLE CHANGE

HAZMAT TRANSPORTATION MANAGEMENT.
See Transportation.

LC RA971 .H414
DD 658
NLM W1; HE335PJ

ISSN 0899-6210
US

HEALTH FACILITIES MANAGEMENT.
See Medical Sciences-Health Services Administration.

LC HF
DD 658.5
UDC 65

ISSN 0018-1951
JA

HINSHITSU KANRI.
[Hinshitsu kanri]. **VFOAT** Statistical Quality Control. (1950)-. Periodical. Japanese. Twelve times a year. $178.00. Nihon Kagaku Gijutsu Renmei, (Union of Japanese Scientists & Engineers), 10-11 Sendagaya 5 Chome, Shibuyaku Tokyo 151 Japan. (**Subscription address:** Maruzen Company Ltd., PO Box 5050, Import & Export Department, Tokyo 100 31 Japan. **Tel** 011 81 3 32789224.)

LC HF41 .H58
DD 380.105/6

ISSN 0018-2796
JA

HITOTSUBASHI JOURNAL OF COMMERCE AND MANAGEMENT.
See Business and Economics-Commerce.

ISSN 1183-3564
DD 658

CN

HOME OFFICE : THE OFFICIAL PUBLICATIN OF THE NATIONAL HOME BUSINESS INSTITUTE, INC.
[Home off.]. **Added/Corp** National Home Business Institute. Vol. 1, Issue 1 (Winter 1991)-. Periodical. English. Four times a year. Free. National Home Business Institute, Mr. J Hrynyshn, 1453 Eddie Shain Drive, Oakville Ontario L6J 7C3 Canada.

LC HD28 .H63
DD 658/.005

HK

HONG KONG JOURNAL OF BUSINESS MANAGEMENT.
Added/Corp Chinese University of Hong Kong. Faculty of Business Administration. **VFOAT** Hsiang-Kang Kung Shang Kuan Li Hsueh Pao. Vol. 1 (1983)-. Periodical. English (Chinese; summaries and/or abstracts in Chinese). One time a year. $15.00. Chinese University of Hong Kong, Faculty of Business Administration, Shatin NT Hong Kong. **Tel** 011 852 0 26097742, 011 852 0 26097801, FAX 011 852 0 26035114, 011 852 0 26035917, telex 50301 CUHK HX. **ED** Simon S.M. Ho. **Bk Rev**, (Qty: 1).
Desc: To promote business research relevant to Hong Kong, China, and Asia.
Ind/Abst Asia.-Pac. Econ. Lit.

HK

HONG KONG MANAGER. K'O HSUEH KUAN LI.
Added/Corp Hong Kong Management Association. **VFOAT** K'o Hsueh Kuan Li. (Jan./Feb. 1965)-. Periodical. Chinese (English). Six times a year. HK$300 Hong Kong; HK$350.00 Macau, China and Taiwan; $52.00 other. Hong Kong Management Association, Management House 3rd Floor, 26 Canal Road West, Happy Valley Hong Kong. **Tel** 011 852 25749346, FAX 011 852 25721660. **ED** John Hung. **Ad Acc. Circ:** 7,000 (ctrl).
Desc: A bilingual English and Chinese publication that contains articles by local and overseas senior managers, management educationalists, and abstracts of articles from other publications.
Ind/Abst Manage. Market. Abstr.

ISSN 8755-3392
DD 658

US

HOSPITAL MARKETING MONITOR.
[Hosp. mark. monitor]. Oct. 1984-. Periodical. English. Twelve times a year. $50.00. Hospital/Community Relations Professional, PO Box 590, Naperville IL 60566.

US

HOSPITALITY INDEX, THE.
1988-. Trade Publication. English. Four times a year. American Hotel and Motel Association, 1201 New York Avenue Northwest, Washington DC 20005. **Tel** (202)289-3100, (202)289-3165, FAX (202)289-3199. **ED** Omar E Akchurin. **Continues** Lodging and Restaurant Index, 0894-5128.

US
CODEN HOMAE3

HOSPITALITY MANAGEMENT. See
Hotels/Motels.

ISSN 0018-6082
DD 647

US
CCC

HOTEL & MOTEL MANAGEMENT. See
Hotels/Motels.

ISSN 0959-5414

UK

HOTEL MANAGEMENT TODAY. See
Hotels/Motels.

ISSN 0891-8244
DD 658

US

HOWARD WAY LETTER, THE.
[Howard Way lett.]. (19??)-. Periodical. English. Twelve times a year. $95.00. Howard Way Letter, PO Box 5387, Baltimore MD 21209. **Tel** (301)542-4446, FAX (301)542-9218. **ED** Arthur S. Liebeskind. Index available. **Bk Rev. Circ:** 400.

LC HE5549.A2 H85
DD 658.3/005

ISSN 1043-8998
US
SUSPENDED

HUMAN CAPITAL.
[Hum. cap.]. (1989)-Suspended (1991). Periodical. English. Six times a year. $29.95. Learning Ventures International, Box 1328, Camden ME 04843. **Tel** (207)236-6267, FAX (207)236-6018. **ED** Bruce Taylor. **Ad Acc. Circ:** 65,000. **Desc:** Focuses on senior management methods for investing in and creating a productive, innovative workforce.

US

HUMAN RESOURCE BRIEFINGS.
English. Six times a year. $60.00. Beta Systems, 9648 Olive/Suite 240, St Louis MO 63132. **Tel** (314)569-6940. **Continues** Human Resource Advisor.

US

HUMAN SIDE OF SUPERVISION.
English. Twenty-four times a year. $45.72 (US); $56.04 (Canada). Bureau of Business Practice, 24 Rope Ferry Road, Waterford CT 06386. **Tel** (800)243-0876, (203)442-4365, (800)876-9105, FAX (203)443-1123.

UK

ILAM GUIDE TO GOOD PRACTICE IN LEISURE MANAGEMENT.
(19??)-. Periodical. English. Two times a year. £67.00 Europe; £70.00 other (institutions). Churchill Livingstone, 1-3 Baxter's Place, Leith Walk, Edinburgh EH1 3AF United Kingdom. **Tel** 011 44 131 5562424, FAX 011 44 131 5581278, telex 727511. (**Subscription address:** Maruzen Company Ltd., PO Box 5050, Import & Export Department, Tokyo 100 31 Japan. **Tel** 011 81 3 32789224.)

ISSN 1055-9973
DD 650

US

IMAGE BUILDER.
[Image build.]. **VFOAT** Imagebuilder. Vol. 1, No. 1 (May/June 1991)-. Periodical. English. Six times a year. $25.00. Images by Cary, PO Box 5980, Oxnard CA 93031.

ISSN 0198-8042

US

IMPAC REPORTS.
[IMPAC rep.]. **Main/Corp** Intensive Management Practices Assessment Center. **VAT** Intensive Management Practices Assessment Center Reports. Vol. 1, No. 1- June 1976-. Monographic series. English. Four times a year. Price varies per volume. IMPAC, School of Forest Resources and Conservation, University of Florida, Gainesville FL 32611.
Ind/Abst AGRICOLA.

IT

IMPRENDITORIALITA.
Italian. Sviluppo Editoriale Pubblicita 55, 00186 Rome Italy.

IT

IMPRESA : PER IL CONSULENTE DELLE IMPRESE INDUSTRIALI E COMMERCIALI.
Italian. Editoriale Tributaria Italiana, Viale Mazzini 25, 00195 Rome Italy. **Tel** 011 39 6 87130300.
Ind/Abst Selec. Coop. Index Manage. Period.

FR

INDECOSA.
(19??)-. Periodical. French. Six times a year. 117.53F France; 120.00F other. Gestion Information, 263 rue de Paris, F-93516 Montreuil France. **Tel** 011 33 1 40353399.

ISSN 0838-0457
DD 650/.05

CN

INDEX DES AFFAIRES, L'.
[Index aff.]. (Jan./Feb. 1988)-. Periodical. French. Twelve times a year. 475.00Can$ regular subscribers; 345.00Can$ subscribers to Index de L'Actualite. Inform II Microfor, 801 rue Sherbrooke Est, Suite 615, Montreal Quebec H2L 1K7 Canada. **Tel** (514)524-7722, FAX (514)524-5441.

LC HG4001 .I53
DD 658.15/0954/05

ISSN 0971-0566
II

INDIAN JOURNAL OF FINANCE AND RESEARCH.
Added/Corp Indian Financial Management Association. Vol. 1, No. 1 (Jan. 1991)-. Periodical. English. Two times a year. Indian Journal of Finance and Research, 116-D, Pocket IV, Mayur Vihar, Delhi- 110 091 India.

LC LA1150 .I64a
DD 370.954

II

INDIAN JOURNAL OF TRAINING & DEVELOPMENT.
Added/Corp Indian Society for Training & Development. Vol. 7, No. 5 (Sept./Oct. 1977)-. Periodical. English. Six times a year. $10.00. Jawaharlal Nehru University Campus, New Mehrauli Road, New Delhi 110067 India. (**Subscription address:** Prints India, 11 Darya Ganj, New Delhi 110002 India. **Tel** 011 91 11 3268645, FAX 011 91 11 3275542, telex 31-61087 PRIN-IN.) **Continues** Training and Development.

LC HD70.I4 I6

ISSN 0019-5812
II

INDIAN MANAGEMENT.
(INDIAN MANAGEMENT : JOURNAL OF THE ALL INDIA MANAGEMENT ASSOCIATION.). **Added/Corp** All India Management Association. **VFOAT** AIMA Indian Management. **VAT** All India Management Association Indian Management. Vol. 1, No. 1 (Sept./Oct. 1961)-. Periodical. English. Six times a year. $24.00. All India Management Association, Management House, 14 Institutional Area Lodi Road, New Delhi-110003 India.

(**Subscription address:** Prints India, 11 Darya Ganj, New Delhi 110002 India. **Tel** 011 91 11 3268645, FAX 011 91 11 3275542, telex 31-61087 PRIN-IN.) available on microfilm from University Microfilms International (UMI).

II

INDIAN MANAGEMENT ABSTRACTS. (19??)-. Periodical. English. Four times a year. Rs350.00 India; $150.00 other. Information Research Academy, 37 Syed Amir Ali Avenue, Calcutta 700018 India. **ED** Partha Subir Guha. Index available. **Ad Acc.**

LC TA4 .C63
DD 658.5/005 AT

INDUSTRIAL MANAGEMENT. (Oct. 1968)-. English. $6.00. ***Continues*** *Factory and Plant.*

LC HD28 .I4424 **ISSN** 0263-5577
DD 650/.05 UK
CCC
CODEN IMDSD8

INDUSTRIAL MANAGEMENT & DATA SYSTEMS. [Ind. manage. data syst.]. **Added/Corp** Institute of Factory Management (Great Britain). **VFOAT** Industrial Management and Data Systems; Industrial Management & Data Systems. (Sept. 1980)-. Periodical. English. Eleven times a year. $2679.00. MCB University Press, 60 62 Toller Lane, Bradford, West Yorkshire BD8 9BY United Kingdom. **Tel** 011 44 1274 785280, FAX 011 44 1274 785200, telex 51317-MCBUNI-G. (**Subscription address:** MCB University Press / US and Canada Subscriptions, PO Box 10812, Birmingham AL 35201-0812. **Tel** (205)995-1567, (800)633-4931, FAX (205)995-1588.) **ED** Sue de Verteuil and Len Williams. **Bk Rev.** available on an online database (file 15/Full-Text) from DIALOG. Documents available from UMI Article Clearinghouse, Ask*IEEE. ***Formed by the union of*** *Industrial Management (London, England)* ***and*** *Data Systems (London, England : 1977).*
Desc: Aims to improve skills by promoting awareness of new practices and techniques in the management systems area. It helps broaden the capabilities of an organisation's management team, providing practical assistance by highlighting other specialist areas within their own, and others', organisations.
Ind/Abst ABI/INFORM Glob. Ed.; ABI/INFORM [Computer File] (May 1986-); Acad. Search; Anbar Account. Finan. Abstr. [Full Txt.]; Anbar Mark. Distr. Abstr. [Full Txt.]; Anbar Top Manage. Abstr. [Full Txt.]; BMT Abstr. (-199?); Bus. Index (1988-); Bus. Period. Index; Bus. Source Plus; Bus. Source; Comput. Lit. Index; Contents Pages Manage.; Curr. Cit.; Curr. Technol. Index; Energy Res. Abstr. (1980-); EP Collect.; Ergon. Abstr.; Gen. BusinessFile (1988-); Gen. Period. Index (1988-); Homework Help.; INSPEC (Sept. 1980-); Mag. Search; Manage. Market. Abstr.; Manage. Bibliogr. Rev.; MasterFile FullTEXT 1000; MasterFile FullTEXT 350; MasterFile FullTEXT 650; MasterFile FullTEXT (July 1993-); OCLC; Oper. Prod. Manage. Abstr. [Full Txt.]; Person. Train. Abstr. [Full Txt.]; Telebase; Trade Ind. Index; Women Manage. Rev. [Full Txt.].

LC HD28 .I442 **ISSN** 0019-8471
DD 658/.005 US
CCC
CODEN IMNGDM

INDUSTRIAL MANAGEMENT (DES PLAINES). (INDUSTRIAL MANAGEMENT.). [Ind. manage.]. **Added/Corp** Industrial Management Society. Institute of Industrial Engineers (1981-). (1959)-. Periodical. English. Six times a year. $39.00. Institute of Industrial Engineers, 25 Technology Park-Atlanta, Norcross GA 30092. **Tel** (404)449-0460, FAX (404)263-8532. **ED** Chuck Lopez. **Bk Rev. Circ:** 4,000. available on microfilm and microfiche from University Microfilms International (UMI). Documents available from UMI Article Clearinghouse, Ask*IEEE.
Desc: Covers white and blue collar productivity, strategic planning, people management, labor relations, participative management techniques, and other topics. Deals with international management, microcomputers, legal considerations, support systems, and behavioral management.
Ind/Abst ABI/INFORM Glob. Ed.; ABI/INFORM Ondisc: Expr. Ed.; ABI/INFORM [Computer File] (Sept. 1971-); Acad. Search; Account. Art.; Anbar Account. Finan. Abstr. [Full Txt.]; Anbar Mark. Distr. Abstr. [Full Txt.]; Anbar Top Manage. Abstr. [Full Txt.]; Bus. ASAP (1990-) [Full Txt.]; Bus. Index (1985-); Bus. Source Plus; Bus. Source; Curr. Cit.; Ei Page One; EP Collect.; Gen. BusinessFile (1985-); Gen. Period. Index (1985-); Homework Help.; INFO-SOUTH Abstr.; INSPEC (1987-); Mag. Search; Manage. Bibliogr. Rev.; Manage. Contents (1974-); MasterFile FullTEXT 1000; MasterFile FullTEXT 350; MasterFile FullTEXT 650; MasterFile FullTEXT (Jan. 1994-); OCLC; Oper. Prod. Manage. Abstr. [Full Txt.]; Person. Train. Abstr. [Full Txt.]; Person. Manage. Abstr.; Telebase; Trade Ind. ASAP [Full Txt.]; Trade Ind. Index [Full Txt.]; UMI ABI/Inform--Bus. Period. Ondisc (Nov. 1987-) [Full Txt.]; Women Manage. Rev. [Full Txt.]; Work Relat. Abstr.

LC HF5415.12.E8 I53 **ISSN** 0019-8501
DD 658.8/005 US
CCC
CODEN IMMADX

Pr Rev.

INDUSTRIAL MARKETING MANAGEMENT. See Business and Economics-Marketing and Purchasing.

LC HD6951 .I5 **ISSN** 0019-8676
DD 331 US
CCC
CODEN IDRLAP

Pr Rev.

INDUSTRIAL RELATIONS (BERKELEY). (INDUSTRIAL RELATIONS.). [Ind. relat.]. **Added/Corp** University of California, Berkeley. Institute of Industrial Relations. Vol. 1 (Oct. 1961)-. Periodical. English. Four times a year. $70.00. Blackwell Publishers, 238 Main Street, Cambridge MA 02142. **Tel** (617)547-7110, (800)835-6770, FAX (617)547-0789. **ED** Michael Reich and Jonathan Leonard. Index available. cum. index. **Ad Acc. Circ:** 2,500 (ctrl). available on microfilm and microfiche from University Microfilms International (UMI). Documents available from The Genuine Article, UMI Article Clearinghouse.
Desc: Covers all aspects of the employment relationship, with special attention to developments in the fields of labor economics, sociology, psychology, political science and law.
Ind/Abst ABI/INFORM Glob. Ed.; ABI/INFORM [Computer File] (Oct. 1971-); Acad. Abstr.; Acad. Ind. [Computer File] (1984-); Acad. Search; Account. Art.; Bus. Period. Index; Bus. Source Plus; Bus. Source; Curr. Cit.; Econ. Lit. Index; EP Collect.; Expand. Acad. Index (1984-); Gen. BusinessFile (1992-); Homework Help.; Index Period. Artic. Relat. Law (19??-); INFO-SOUTH Abstr.; Int. Bibliogr. Sociol.; Int. Labour Doc.; J. Econ. Lit.; J. Plan. Lit.; LABORDOC; Leg. Resour. Index (1980-); LegalTrac (1980-); Mag. Search; MasterFile FullTEXT 1000; MasterFile FullTEXT 350; MasterFile FullTEXT 650; MasterFile FullTEXT (Jan. 1990-); Newsp. Period. Abstr. (1989-); OCLC; PAIS Int. Print (1991-); Person. Manage. Abstr.; Pub. Lib. FullTEXT; Res. Alert [Full Cov.]; Soc. Plann. Policy Dev. Abstr.; Soc. Sci. Source; Soc. Sci. Cit. Index [Full Cov.]; Soc. Work Abstr. [Select. Cov.]; Sociol. Abstr. (1981-); Telebase; Trade Ind. ASAP [Full Txt.]; Trade Ind. Index (1981-) [Full Txt.]; UMI ABI/Inform--Bus. Period. Ondisc (Spring 1988-) [Full Txt.]; Vocat. Search; Wilson Bus. Abstr.; Women Stud. Abstr.; Work Relat. Abstr.

LC TS155.4 .I52
DD 658.5/05 GW

INDUSTRIE MEISTER. **VFOAT** Industriemeister. Vol. 1 (Jan. 1991)-. Periodical. German. Twelve times a year. $72.93. Vogel Verlag, Postfach 6740, D-97064 Wuerzburg Germany. **Tel** 011 49 931 4182145, 011 49 931 4182483, FAX 011 49 931 4182670, telex 841 680131. ***Continues*** *Meister-Zeitung.*

US

INDUSTRY FORUM / AMERICAN MANAGEMENT ASSOCIATION. **Added/Corp** American Management Association. (July 1989)-. Periodical. English. Twelve times a year. Comes with membership. American Management Association, 135 West 50th Street, New York NY 10020-1201. **Tel** (212)586-8100, (212)903-8375 (periodicals), FAX (212)903-8168, (212)903-8083 (periodicals).

ISSN 1040-2179
DD 658 US

INFOCUS (PORTLAND, OR.). (INFOCUS.). [Infocus]. **Added/Corp** Business Forms Management Association. **VFOAT** In Focus. Vol. 1, No. 1 (Sept. 10, 1988)-. Bulletin. English. Ten times a year. $50.00. Business Forms Management Association Inc., 519 SW Third Avenue, Suite 712, Portland OR 97204. **Tel** (503)227-3393, FAX (503)274-7667. **ED** Paul Telles. **Bk Rev. Ad Acc. Circ:** 1,800.
Desc: A bulletin format with focus on technology that impacts the information resources management industry.

LC HD45-.2 **ISSN** 1200-278X
DD 658.403801105 CN

●**INFOCYCLE TORONTO. ONLINE.** (INFOCYCLE.). [InfoCycle Tor., Online]. **VFOAT** Info Cycle. (1994)-. Periodical. English. Twelve times a year. Free. Jason Smith, 203-30 Edith Drive, Toronto Ontario M4R 1Y8 Canada. **Tel** (416)487-7202, FAX (416)487-1673. **ED** Jason Smith. available via Internet (message pax@pax.com).
Desc: Publication providing information on technology management.

ISSN 1070-0013
DD 658 US
CCC

INFOMANAGE (WASHINGTON, D.C.). (INFOMANAGE.). [InfoManage]. **VFOAT** Info Manage. (199?)-. Periodical. English. Twelve times a year. $137.50. SMR International, Murray Hill Station, PO Box 948, New York NY 10156. **Tel** (212)683-6285, FAX (212)683-2987.

US

INFOPACK. (19??)-. English. Irregular. $175.00. Securities Industry Association, 120 Broadway/35th Floor, New York NY 10271. **Tel** (212)608-1500, FAX (212)608-1604.
Desc: This service is designed to help individuals who are associated with the securities industry to keep abreast of events and developments occuring within the industry.

ISSN 1080-286X
US

●**INFORMATION MANAGEMENT.** (1995)-. English. Two times a year. $60.00. Idea Group Publishing, 4811 Jonestown Road, Suite 230, Harrisburg PA 17109. **Tel** (800)345-4332, (717)541-9150, FAX (717)541-9159. ***Continues*** *Information Management Bulletin, 1046-9303.*

ISSN 1353-8853
UK

●**INFORMATION MANAGEMENT IN HEALTH CARE / FULL SERVICE.** (1994)-. English. Three times a year. £195.00 (institutions). Churchill Livingstone, 1-3 Baxter's Place, Leith Walk, Edinburgh EH1 3AF United Kingdom. **Tel** 011 44 131 5562424, FAX 011 44 131 5581278, telex 727511. (**Subscription address:** Maruzen Company Ltd., PO Box 5050, Import & Export Department, Tokyo 100 31 Japan. **Tel** 011 81 3 32789224.)

ISSN 0824-3514
DD 025.5/2 CN

INFORMATION SOLUTIONS/ INFORMATION PLUS. See Business and Economics-Marketing and Purchasing.

ISSN 0743-8613
DD 658 US
CCC

INFORMATION STRATEGY. [Inf. strategy]. **Added/Corp** Auerbach Publishers. Vol. 1, No. 1 (Fall 1984)-. Trade Publication. English. Four times a year. $183.25. Auerbach Publishers Inc., Park Square Building, 31 St. James Avenue, Boston MA 02116. **Tel** (800)950-1207. **ED** Nancy Tyson. Index available. **Bk Rev,** (Qty: (up to 4)). **Ad Acc, Adv Mgr Tel** (212)971-5000. **Circ:** 1100. available on microfilm and microfiche from University Microfilms International (UMI). Documents available from Ask*IEEE.
Desc: Designed to help executives make educated policy and strategy decisions about information management concerns facing their organizations.
Ind/Abst Acad. Search; Bus. Period. Index; Bus. Source Plus; Bus. Source; Comput. Lit. Index; Curr. Cit.; EP Collect.; Gen. BusinessFile (1992-); Homework Help.; INFO-SOUTH Abstr.; Inf. Sci. Abstr. [Full Cov.]; INSPEC (Spring 1986-); Mag. Search; MasterFile FullTEXT 1000; MasterFile FullTEXT 350; MasterFile FullTEXT 650; MasterFile FullTEXT (July 1993-); OCLC; Telebase; Wilson Bus. Abstr.

ISSN 0959-3845
DD 650 US

INFORMATION TECHNOLOGY & PEOPLE (WEST LINN, OR.). (INFORMATION TECHNOLOGY & PEOPLE.). [Inf. technol. people]. **VFOAT** Information Technology and People. Vol. 6, No. 1 (1992)-. Periodical. English. Four times a year. $199.00. MCB University Press, 60 62 Toller Lane, Bradford, West Yorkshire BD8 9BY United Kingdom. **Tel** 011 44 1274 785280, FAX 011 44 1274 785200, telex 51317-MCBUNI-G. **ED** Dr. Eleanor Wynn. ***Continues*** *Office, Technology and People, 0167-5710.*
Desc: Focuses on the "people" aspect of information technology and how it can be organized to maximize its effects.
Ind/Abst Curr. Cit.

ISSN 1322-3526
AT

Pr Rev.

INFORMATION TECHNOLOGY MANAGEMENT. See Science and Technology.

ISSN 0390-2447
IT

UDC 33

INFORMAZIONI AZIENDALI E PROFESSIONALI. [Inf. aziend. prof.]. (1974)-. Periodical. Italian. Twenty-four times a year (26 issues per year - published every 15 days). L218000. De Lillo Editore Srl, Via Mecenate 76/3, 20138 Milan Italy. **Tel** 011 39 2 58013112.

ISSN 0739-4748
US

INFORME INTERCONTINENTAL SOBRE GERENCIA AVANZADA. **VFOAT** Gerencia Avanzada. (Nov. 1981)-. Periodical. Spanish. Twelve times a year. $150.00. Advanced Management

Business and Economics — Management

Publishers Inc, One Gateway Center Suite 408, Newton MA 02165. **Tel** (617)964-5080, telex 80-4294 SPEDEX ATL.

US

●**INFORMS MEETING BULLETIN.** (1995)-.
Bulletin. English. Two times a year. NASA Center for Aerospace Information, 800 Elkridge Landing Road, Linthicum Heights MD 21090. **Tel** (301)621-0153, FAX (301)621-0134. **(Subscription address:** INFORMS Circulation Department, PO Box 64794, Baltimore MD 21264. **) Continues** TIMS / ORSA Bulletin.

LC TS192 .I53   ISSN 0396-3586
DD 658.2/02/05   FR
INGENIEURS D'ENTRETIEN. [Ing. entret.].
French. 160.00F. Societe les Nouvelles du Monde, 13 rue de Liege, 75009 Paris France. **Continues** Entretien et Travaux Neufs.
Ind/Abst Saf. Health Work.

LC HD2771 .C67   ISSN 1046-9958
DD 338.7/4/097784LL/05   US
INGRAM'S (KANSAS CITY, MO.).
(INGRAM'S FOR SUCCESSFUL KANSAS CITIANS.). [Ingram's]. **VFOAT** Ingram's. Vol. 15, No. 10 (Oct. 1989)-. Periodical. English. Twelve times a year. $30.00. Corporate Report Kansas City, 306 East 12th Street, Suite 1014, Kansas City MO 64106. **Tel** (816)842-9994. Documents available from UMI Article Clearinghouse. **Continues** Corporate Report, Kansas City, 0273-9968.
Ind/Abst Acad. Search; Bus. Dateline (Nov. 198?-) [Full Txt.]; Bus. Index (1989-); EP Collect.; Gen. BusinessFile (1989-); Gen. Period. Index (1989-); Homework Help.; INFO-SOUTH Abstr.; Mag. Search; MasterFile FullTEXT 1000; MasterFile FullTEXT 350; MasterFile FullTEXT 650; MasterFile FullTEXT (July 1993-); OCLC; Telebase; Trade Ind. ASAP [Full Txt.]; Trade Ind. Index [Full Txt.].

DD 338.4/76479471   ISSN 0847-9356
    CN
INNKEEPER. See Hotels/Motels.

LC HC79.T4 I5457   ISSN 1053-2587
DD 658.4/063/05   US
INNOVATING (RENSSELAERVILLE, N.Y.). (INNOVATING.). [Innovating]. **Added/Corp** Rensselaerville Institute. Innovation Group. Vol. 1, No. 1 (Fall 1990)-. Periodical. English. Four times a year. $23.00. Innovating, Rensselaerville Institute, Rensselaerville NY 12147. **Tel** (518)797-3783, FAX (518)797-3692. **ED** Harold S. Williams. **Bk Rev. Circ:** 1,000.
Desc: Dedicated to enabling people and organizations to lead change by example. Its content includes innovation research, assumptions, examples, theory and paradigms. Targeted toward individuals who work within organizations and are concerned with their high performance.
Ind/Abst Person. Manage. Abstr.; Work Relat. Abstr.

ISSN 0260-3748
UK
CODEN INNMEE
INNOVATION AND MANAGEMENT.
(INNOVATION AND MANAGEMENT : THE JOURNAL OF THE INSTITUTE OF MANAGEMENT CONSULTANTS.). [Innov. manage.]. (1981)-. Periodical. English. Four times a year. IMC, 23-24 Cromwell Place, London SW7 2LG United Kingdom. Documents available from Ask*IEEE.
Ind/Abst INSPEC (1985-).

ISSN 1073-6514
DD 362   US
NLM W1; IN4576G
●**INSIDE CASE MANAGEMENT.** [Inside case manag.]. (1994)-. Periodical. English. Twelve times a year. $105.00. Aspen Publishers Inc., 7201 McKinney Circle, Frederick MD 21701. **Tel** (800)234-1660, (301)698-7100, FAX (301)251-5784, telex 5106014543. **(Subscription address:** Aspen Publishers Inc., PO Box 990, Frederick MD 21701. **Tel** (800)901-9074, (301)698-7100.**)**

ISSN 0885-6885
DD 658   US
INSIDE TRACK (MIAMI, FLA.). (INSIDE TRACK.). [Inside track]. (Nov. 15, 1985)-. Periodical. English. Forty-eight times a year. $239.00. Inside Track Publishing Company, PO Box 561747, Miami FL 33256. **Tel** (305)271-7338. **ED** Gisela Schoell (editor's address: 18 Lost Mine Place, Ridgefield CT 06877-3425; phone: (203)431-4540; fax: (203)431-4711).

ISSN 0967-652X
UK
INSTITUTE OF MANAGEMENT INTERNATIONAL DATABASES PLUS.
[Inst. Manag. int. Databases Plus]. (1992)-. English. Four times a year. £799.00. Bowker Saur Ltd., A Reed Reference Publishing Company, Part of Reed International PLC, 59-60 Grosvenor Street, London W1X 9DA United Kingdom. **Tel** 011 44 171 4935841, FAX 011 44 171 4991590. available on CD-ROM.
Desc: Gives access to an entire multi-media management information centre. Provides over 35,000 abstracts.

ISSN 0739-313X
US
INTERCONTINENTAL ADVANCED MANAGEMENT REPORT, THE.
(ADVANCED MANAGEMENT REPORT.). English. Twelve times a year. $150.00 (one-year), $250.00 (two-year). Advanced Management Publishers Inc, One Gateway Center Suite 408, Newton MA 02165. **Tel** (617)964-5080, telex 80-4294 SPEDEX ATL. **ED** Edward C Bursk, Carole Samworth, Ernest J Enright, G Scott Hutchison, Lisa E Sacks, Elizabeth H Knox. Index available. cum. index. **Bk Rev. Circ:** 2,000.
Desc: Contains management ideas and techniques, edited for the busy executive to quickly read and put to use.

LC HD28 .I45   ISSN 0092-2102
DD 658.4   US
    CCC
CODEN INFAC
Pr Rev.
INTERFACES (PROVIDENCE).
(INTERFACES.). [Interfaces]. **Added/Corp** Institute of Management Sciences. Operations Research Society of America. Vol. 1 No. 4 (June 1971)-. Trade Publication. English. Six times a year. $104.00. Institute of Management Sciences, 290 Westminster Street, Providence RI 02903. **Tel** (401)274-2525, FAX (401)274-3189. **ED** Frederic H. Murphy. available on microfilm and microfiche from University Microfilms International (UMI). Documents available from UMI Article Clearinghouse, Ask*IEEE. **Continues** Institute of Management Science. Bulletin, 0020-2916.
Ind/Abst ABI/INFORM Glob. Ed.; ABI/INFORM [Computer File] (Nov. 1973-); Abstr. Hum. Comput. Interact.; Arts Humanit. Citation Index [Select. Cov.]; Bus. Index (1985-); Bus. Period. Index; CompuMath Cit. Index [Full Cov.]; Contents Pages Manage.; Curr. Cit.; EMBASE; Gen. BusinessFile (1985-); Gen. Period. Index (1985-); HILITES; INFO-SOUTH Abstr.; Inf. Sci. Abstr. (?-?); INSPEC (Nov. 1972-); Int. Abstr. Oper. Res. [Select. Cov.]; Int. Aerosp. Abstr.; J. Plan. Lit.; Mag. Search; Oper. Res./Manage. Sci.; Psychol. Abstr. (1984-); PsycINFO (1990-); PsycLit; School Organ. Manage. Abstr.; Selec. Coop. Index Manage. Period.; Soc. Plann. Policy Dev. Abstr.; Soc. Sci. Cit. Index [Full Cov.]; SportSearch; Trade Ind. Index; Wilson Bus. Abstr.; Work Relat. Abstr.

LC HG64 .I58   ISSN 1058-2894
DD 338.8/8/025   US
    CCC
    CEASED
INTERNATIONAL CORPORATE YELLOW BOOK. (INTERNATIONAL CORPORATE YELLOW BOOK : WHO'S WHO AT THE LEADING NON-U.S. COMPANIES.). [Int. corp. yellow book]. Vol. 5, No. 1 (1992)-(Aug. 1994). Directory. English. Leadership Directories, Inc., 104 Fifth Avenue, Second Floor, New York NY 10011. **Tel** (212)627-4140, FAX (212)645-0931. **Continues** International Corporate 1000 Yellow Book, 1049-7951.
Desc: Identifies foreign companies and lists over 30,000 names and titles of senior executives including mailing addresses, telephone, facsimile and telex numbers plus indexes by individual and company name and by industry.

UK
INTERNATIONAL HANDBOOK OF PARTICIPATION IN ORGANIZATIONS.
Vol. 1 (1989)-. Monographic series. English. Irregular. Price varies per volume. John Wiley & Sons Ltd., Baffins Lane, Chichester, West Sussex PO19 1UD United Kingdom. **Tel** 011 44 1243 779777, FAX 011 44 1243 776128 BTG:JWP001, telex 86290 WIBOOKG. **(Subscription address:** Gordon & Breach Science Publishers / US, 820 Town Center Drive, Langhorne PA 19047. **Tel** (215)750-2642.**) Continues** International Yearbook of Organizational Democracy.

ISSN 1056-9219
DD 658   US
INTERNATIONAL JOURNAL OF COMMERCE AND MANAGEMENT. See Business and Economics-Commerce.

LC HD42 .I57   ISSN 1044-4068
DD 658.4   US
    CCC
Pr Rev.
INTERNATIONAL JOURNAL OF CONFLICT MANAGEMENT, THE. [Int. j. confl. manage.]. **VFOAT** Journal of Conflict Management. Vol. 1, No. 1 (Jan. 1990)-. Periodical. English. Four times a year. $129.00. 3-R Executive System, 3109 Cooperfield Ct., Professor Rahim, Bowling Green KY 42104. **Tel** (502)782-2601, FAX (502)782-2601. **ED** Dr. Rahim.

ISSN 0959-6119
HK
CCC
INTERNATIONAL JOURNAL OF CONTEMPORARY HOSPITALITY MANAGEMENT. See Hotels/Motels.

LC TX911.3.M27 I56   ISSN 0278-4319
DD 647/.94/05   UK
    CCC
CODEN IJHMDN
INTERNATIONAL JOURNAL OF HOSPITALITY MANAGEMENT. See Hotels/Motels.

LC HD28 .I525   ISSN 0167-7187
DD 658.4/02/05   NE
    CCC
CODEN IJIODY
Pr Rev.
INTERNATIONAL JOURNAL OF INDUSTRIAL ORGANIZATION. [Int. j. ind. organ.]. **VFOAT** Industrial Organization. Vol. 1, No. 1 (1983)-. Academic Scholarly Publication. English. Six times a year. $482.00. Elsevier Science Publishers BV, PO Box 211, 1000 AE Amsterdam Netherlands. **Tel** 011 31 20 4853641, 011 31 20 4853642, FAX 011 31 20 4853598. **ED** Paul Geroski and Norman Ireland. available on microfilm and microfiche from University Microfilms International (UMI); available on an online database from Elsevier Electronic Subscriptions (EES). Documents available from The Genuine Article, UMI Article Clearinghouse.
Desc: Full coverage of both theoretical and empirical questions within the field of industrial organization.
Ind/Abst ABI/INFORM Glob. Ed.; ABI/INFORM [Computer File] (1983-); Contents Recent Econ. J.; Contents Pages Manage.; Curr. Cit.; Curr. Contents Soc. Behav. Sci.; Econ. Lit. Index; Gen. BusinessFile (1992-); Hum. Resour. Abstr.; J. Econ. Lit. (1983-); Res. Alert [Full Cov.]; Selec. Coop. Index Manage. Period.; Soc. Sci. Cit. Index [Full Cov.].

ISSN 0813-0183
UK
INTERNATIONAL JOURNAL OF MANAGEMENT. Vol. 1, No. 1 (March 1984)-. Periodical. English. Four times a year. $120.00. International Journal of Management, PO Box 982, Poole, Dorset BH12 5YF United Kingdom. **Tel** (052)435638. **ED** Peter Burgess. **Circ:** 600.
Desc: International Journal of Management publishes original articles dealing with the theory and practice of management. Areas covered include finance, accounting, marketing, operations and personnel. Preference is given to articles that adopt an international perspective. All articles are externally refereed. IJM is aimed at both academics and practitioners.
Ind/Abst Curr. Cit.; Person. Manage. Abstr.; Work Relat. Abstr.

ISSN 0970-7328
II
UDC 658
INTERNATIONAL JOURNAL OF MANAGEMENT AND SYSTEMS. [Int. J. Manag. Syst.]. **VFOAT** IJOMAS (1988). (1988)-. Periodical. English. Three times a year. $50.00 (institutions), $30.00 (individuals). International Journal of Management and Systems, 16 Vaishali Pitampura, Delhi 11034 India. **Continues** Indian Journal of Management and Systems, 0970-0439.

LC TS155.A1 I63   ISSN 0144-3577
DD 658.5/005   UK
    CCC
CODEN IOPMDU
INTERNATIONAL JOURNAL OF OPERATIONS & PRODUCTION MANAGEMENT. [Int. j. oper. prod. manage.]. **VFOAT** International Journal of Operations and Production Management. Vol. 1, No. 1- (1980)-. Periodical. English. Twelve times a year. $2399.00. MCB University Press, 60 62 Toller Lane, Bradford, West Yorkshire BD8 9BY United Kingdom. **Tel** 011 44 1274 785280, FAX 011 44 1274 785200, telex 51317-MCBUNI-G. **(Subscription address:** MCB University Press / US and Canada Subscriptions, PO Box 10812, Birmingham AL 35201-0812. **Tel** (205)995-1567, (800)633-4931, FAX (205)995-1588.**) ED** Keith Howard. **Bk Rev.** available on an online database (file 15/Full-Text) from DIALOG. Documents available from UMI Article Clearinghouse, Ask*IEEE.
Desc: Seeks to raise standards in all aspects of operations management. Shows how the theory and practice of the management of production and operations are linked.
Ind/Abst ABI/INFORM Glob. Ed.; ABI/INFORM [Computer File] (Jan. 1980-); Anbar Account. Finan. Abstr. [Full Txt.]; Anbar Mark. Distr. Abstr. [Full Txt.]; Anbar Top Manage. Abstr. [Full Txt.]; Curr. Cit.; Ei Page One; Ergon. Abstr.; Gen. BusinessFile (1992-); INSPEC (1981-); Int. Abstr. Oper. Res. [Select. Cov.]; Manage. Market. Abstr.; Manage. Bibliogr. Rev.; Oper. Prod. Manage. Abstr. [Full Txt.]; Person. Train. Abstr. [Full Txt.]; Women Manage. Rev. [Full Txt.].

LC HF5415.7 .I55 ISSN 0960-0035
DD 658.7/88/05 UK
CCC
CODEN IPDMEC

INTERNATIONAL JOURNAL OF PHYSICAL DISTRIBUTION & LOGISTICS MANAGEMENT. [Int. j. phys. distrib. logist. manag.]. **VFOAT** Physical Distribution and Logistics Management; Physical Distribution & Logistics Management. Vol. 20, No. 1 (1990)-. Periodical. English. Ten times a year. $3999.00. MCB University Press, 60 62 Toller Lane, Bradford, West Yorkshire BD8 9BY United Kingdom. **Tel** 011 44 1274 785280, FAX 011 44 1274 785200, telex 51317-MCBUNI-G. **(Subscription address:** MCB University Press / US and Canada Subscriptions, PO Box 10812, Birmingham AL 35201-0812. **Tel** (205)995-1567, (800)633-4931, FAX (205)995-1588.**) ED** James Stock. **Ad Acc.** available on an online database (file 15/Full-Text) from DIALOG. Documents available from UMI Article Clearinghouse, Ask*IEEE. ***Continues*** *International Journal of Physical Distribution and Materials Management, 0269-8218.*
Desc: Covers the study of distribution and materials management. Providing a link between theory and practice, this journal is both a working tool and a source of reference.
Ind/Abst ABI/INFORM Glob. Ed.; ABI/INFORM [Computer File] (1979-); Curr. Cit.; Gen. BusinessFile (1992-); INSPEC (1985-); Manage. Market. Abstr.; Selec. Coop. Index Manage. Period.

LC TS155.A1 I64 ISSN 0020-7543
UK
CCC
NLM W1 SC832 CODEN IJPRB8
Pr Rev.

INTERNATIONAL JOURNAL OF PRODUCTION RESEARCH. [Int. j. prod. res.]. **Added/Corp** Institution of Production Engineers (Great Britain) American Institute of Industrial Engineers. Society of Manufacturing Engineers. Institute of Industrial Engineers (1981-). **VFOAT** Production Research. Vol. 1, No. 1 (Nov. 1961)-. Periodical. English (French and German). Twelve times a year. $1270.00. Taylor & Francis Ltd. / UK, Rankine Road, Basingstoke, Hampshire RG24 8PR United Kingdom. **Tel** 011 44 1256 840366, FAX 011 44 1256 479438, telex 858540. **(Subscription address:** Taylor & Francis Inc., 1900 Frost Road, Suite 101, Bristol PA 19007-1598. **Tel** (215)785-5800, (800)821-8312, FAX (215)785-5515.**) ED** R. J. Sury and J. E. Middle (editorial address: Department of Manufacturing Engineering, University of Technology, Loughborough, LE11 3TU, UK). available on microfilm and microfiche from University Microfilms International (UMI). Documents available from Article Express International, The Genuine Article, Ask*IEEE, CASDDS.
Desc: Publishes papers dealing with technology and the fundamental behavior of production resources, the complex and cross-disciplinary problems of analysis and control that arise in combining these resources within the design of production systems. The journal also publishes survey papers reviewing and assessing advances in production research and development.
Ind/Abst Alum. Ind. Abstr.; Bioeng. Abstr.; Chem. Abstr.; Civ. Struct. Eng. Abstr.; Comput. Inf. Syst. Abstr. J. [Full Cov.]; Curr. Cit.; Curr. Contents Eng. Comput. Technol.; Curr. Technol. Index; Ei Page One; Elect. Comm. Abstr.; Eng. Index Annu.; Ergon. Abstr.; INSPEC (Jan. 1976-); Int. Abstr. Oper. Res. [Select. Cov.]; Int. Aerosp. Abstr.; Leadscan; Manuf. Process Eng. Abstr.; Mech. Eng. Abstr.; Met. Abstr.; Predicasts; Psychol. Abstr.; Res. Alert [Select. Cov.]; SCISEARCH; Soc. Sci. Cit. Index [Select. Cov.]; World Alum. Abstr.; Zentralbl. Math. Ihre Grenzgeb.

LC T56.8 .I537 ISSN 0263-7863
DD 658.4/04 UK
CCC

INTERNATIONAL JOURNAL OF PROJECT MANAGEMENT. (INTERNATIONAL JOURNAL OF PROJECT MANAGEMENT : THE JOURNAL OF THE INTERNATIONAL PROJECT MANAGEMENT ASSOCIATION.). [Int. j. proj. manage.]. **Added/Corp** Association of Project Managers (Great Britain) International Project Management Association. **VFOAT** Project Management. Vol. 1, No. 1 (Feb. 1983)-. Periodical. English. Six times a year. $441.00. Butterworth Heinemann Publishers, Linacre House Jordan Hill, Oxford OX2 8DP United Kingdom. **Tel** 011 44 1865 310366, FAX 011 44 1865 310898. **(Subscription address:** Elsevier Science Ltd. / Oxford Fulfillment Centre, PO Box 800, Kidlington OX5 1DX United Kingdom. **Tel** 011 44 865 843355.**) ED** Angela Jamieson. Index available. cum. index. **Bk Rev. Ad Acc.** available on microfilm and microfiche from University Microfilms International (UMI); available on an online database from Elsevier Electronic Subscriptions (EES). Documents available from UMI Article Clearinghouse, Ask*IEEE, Documents on Demand. ***Continues*** *Project Manager.*
Desc: Offers wide ranging and comprehensive coverage of all facets of project management. Its scope includes project management concepts and methods, project controls, tools and training and motivation, techniques, management, contract law, project economics, national and international co-operation and communication.
Ind/Abst ABI/INFORM Glob. Ed.; Curr. Cit.; Environ. Abstr.; INSPEC (May 1985-); Int. Abstr. Oper. Res. [Select. Cov.]; Oper. Res./Manage. Sci.; Qual. Control Appl. Stat.; Risk Abstr.; Selec. Coop. Index Manage. Period.

LC TS156 .I62 ISSN 0265-671X
DD 658.5/62/05 UK
CCC
CODEN IJQMEZ

INTERNATIONAL JOURNAL OF QUALITY & RELIABILITY MANAGEMENT, THE. **VFOAT** International Journal of Quality and Reliability Management; IJQRM. Vol. 1, No. 1 (1984)-. Periodical. English. Nine times a year. $2199.00. MCB University Press, 60 62 Toller Lane, Bradford, West Yorkshire BD8 9BY United Kingdom. **Tel** 011 44 1274 785280, FAX 011 44 1274 785200, telex 51317-MCBUNI-G. **(Subscription address:** MCB University Press / US and Canada Subscriptions, PO Box 10812, Birmingham AL 35201-0812. **Tel** (205)995-1567, (800)633-4931, FAX (205)995-1588.**) ED** Barrie Dale and Alf Keller. **Ad Acc.** Documents available from UMI Article Clearinghouse.
Desc: Responsible for increasing the reliability and quality of an organisation's product, process or service. Aims to provide the essential information needed to achieve competitive standards in an easily assimilated form. Describes new techniques and systems - focusing particular attention on their application.
Ind/Abst ABI/INFORM Glob. Ed.; ABI/INFORM [Computer File] (1986-); Contents Pages Manage.; Curr. Cit.; Gen. BusinessFile (1992-); Manage. Market. Abstr.; Women Manage. Rev. [Full Txt.].

LC HD28 ISSN 1359-8538
DD 658 UK

•**INTERNATIONAL JOURNAL OF QUALITY SCIENCE.** (1996)-. Academic Scholarly Publication. English. Three times a year. MCB University Press, 60 62 Toller Lane, Bradford, West Yorkshire BD8 9BY United Kingdom. **Tel** 011 44 1274 785280, FAX 011 44 1274 785200, telex 51317-MCBUNI-G. available on an online database.

LC HD9980.1 .I57 ISSN 0956-4223
DD 658/.005 UK

INTERNATIONAL JOURNAL OF SERVICE INDUSTRY MANAGEMENT. **VFOAT** Service Industry Management. Vol. 1, No. 1 (1990)-. Periodical. English. Six times a year. $949.00. MCB University Press, 60 62 Toller Lane, Bradford, West Yorkshire BD8 9BY United Kingdom. **Tel** 011 44 1274 785280, FAX 011 44 1274 785200, telex 51317-MCBUNI-G. **(Subscription address:** MCB University Press / US and Canada Subscriptions, PO Box 10812, Birmingham AL 35201-0812. **Tel** (205)995-1567, (800)633-4931, FAX (205)995-1588.**) ED** Robert Johnston. Documents available from UMI Article Clearinghouse.
Desc: Provides information on research and developments worldwide in management within the service sector. Focuses on aspects of service industry management, reporting on latest research on an international scale.
Ind/Abst ABI/INFORM Glob. Ed.; Curr. Cit.

LC HD28 .I527
UK

INTERNATIONAL MANAGEMENT. (ALAM AL-IDARAH.). Periodical. Arabic (English). Twelve times a year. $57.00 (surface mail), $81.00 (airmail). McGraw Hill Publishing Company, Inc., 1221 Avenue of the Americas, New York NY 10020. **Tel** (212)512-6410, (800)525-5003, FAX (212)512-6111. **ED** Michael R Johnson. **Ad Acc. Circ:** 25,000 (ctrl).
Desc: Reports on management trends, new ideas and innovative techniques from around the world.

UK
CEASED

INTERNATIONAL MANAGEMENT. **VFOAT** Management Digest. (1946)-(Sept. 1994). Periodical. English. Reed Business Publishing / West Sussex, England, Perrymount Road, Haywards Heath, West Sussex RH16 3DH United Kingdom. **Tel** 011 44 1444 441212, FAX 011 44 1444 445447. available on microfilm and microfiche from University Microfilms International (UMI).
Ind/Abst Contents Pages Manage.; INFO-SOUTH Abstr.; Infomat Int. Bus.; PROMT.

LC HD28 .I5295 ISSN 0020-7888
DD 658/.005 SZ
CCC
CODEN INTMEA
CEASED

INTERNATIONAL MANAGEMENT (LAUSANNE, SWITZERLAND). (INTERNATIONAL MANAGEMENT.). [Int. manag.]. Vol. 41, No. 1 (Jan. 1986)-(Sept. 1994). Trade Publication. English. Reed Business Publishing / West Sussex, England, Perrymount Road, Haywards Heath, West Sussex RH16 3DH United Kingdom. **Tel** 011 44 1444 441212, FAX 011 44 1444 445447. Documents available from Ask*IEEE. ***Formed by the union of*** *International Management. Europe; International Management. Asia/Pacific* ***and*** *International Management. Africa.*
Ind/Abst Acad. Search; Bus. ASAP (1990-) [Full Txt.]; Bus. Index (1985-); Bus. Source Plus; Bus. Source; EP Collect.; F&S Index Plus Text, Int. [Select. Cov.]; Gen. BusinessFile (1985-); Gen. Period. Index (1985-); Homework Help.; INFO-SOUTH Abstr.; INSPEC (1986-); Manage. Contents; MasterFile FullTEXT 1000; MasterFile FullTEXT 350; MasterFile FullTEXT 650; MasterFile FullTEXT (July 1993-Sept. 1994); Middle East Abstr. Index; OCLC; PAIS Int. Print; Telebase; Trade Ind. ASAP [Full Txt.]; Trade Ind. Index [Full Txt.]; Work Relat. Abstr.; World Mag. Bank.

US

INTERNATIONAL MANAGER PROFILES. (19??)-. English. $1750.00 (full subscription). Evaluation Associates Inc., 200 Connecticut Avenue, Norwalk CT 06854. **Tel** (203)855-2200, FAX (203)855-2301.

LC HD30.28 .I554 ISSN 1047-7918
DD 658.4/012/05 UK
CCC

INTERNATIONAL REVIEW OF STRATEGIC MANAGEMENT. [Int. rev. strateg. manage.]. (1990)-. English. One time a year. $120.00. John Wiley & Sons Ltd., Baffins Lane, Chichester, West Sussex PO19 1UD United Kingdom. **Tel** 011 44 1243 779777, FAX 011 44 1243 776128 BTG:JWP001, telex 86290 WIBOOKG. **(Subscription address:** John Wiley & Sons, Inc. / Philadelphia, PO Box 7247, Philadelphia PA 19170. **Tel** (212)850-6645, (800)225-5945.**) ED** David E. Hussey. available on microfilm and microfiche from University Microfilms International (UMI). Documents available from UMI Article Clearinghouse.
Desc: Provides a critical review of the developments and practices in strategic management. The aim, over time, is to cover all aspects of strategic management, and to record major changes and advances. Readership includes practicing managers and academics in: strategic management, corporate strategy, organizational development, and business administration.
Ind/Abst ABI/INFORM Glob. Ed.

LC HV8290 .I58 ISSN 0141-8017
DD 658.4/73/05 UK

INTERNATIONAL SECURITY REVIEW. **VFOAT** Revue Internationale de la Surete et de la Securite. No. 1 (Apr. 1978)-. Trade Publication. English (French and German). Four times a year. $144.00. Argus Press Group, Queensway House, 2 Queensway Redhill, Surrey RH1 1QS United Kingdom. **Tel** 011 44 1737 768611, 011 44 1737 761685, FAX 011 44 1737 760510, telex 948669 TOPJNL G. **(Subscription address:** FMJ International Publications Ltd., Queensway House 2 Queensway, Redhill Surrey RH1 1QS United Kingdom. **Tel** 011 44 1737 768611, FAX 011 44 1737 773993, telex 948669 TOPJNL G.**)** ***Continues*** *Security Times.*
Desc: For the senior security executive seeking a worldwide view of security problems and their solutions.
Ind/Abst Women Manage. Rev. [Full Txt.].

LC HD28 .I54 ISSN 0020-8825
DD 658/.005 US
CCC

INTERNATIONAL STUDIES OF MANAGEMENT & ORGANIZATION. [Int. stud. manage. organ.]. **VFOAT** International Studies of Management and Organization. **VAT** International Studies of Management and Organization. Vol. 1 (Spring 1971)-. Academic Scholarly Publication. English. Four times a year. $495.00. M. E. Sharpe Inc., 80 Business Park Drive, Armonk NY 10504. **Tel** (914)273-1800, (800)541-6563, FAX (914)273-2106. **ED** J. J. Boddewyn. **Ad Acc. Circ:** 350. available on microfilm and microfiche from University Microfilms International (UMI). Documents available from UMI Article Clearinghouse.
Desc: This journal contains translations of material that has appeared originally in scholarly journals and books throughout the world.
Ind/Abst ABI/INFORM Glob. Ed.; ABI/INFORM [Computer File] (Winter 1976-); Acad. Search; Bus. ASAP (1992-) [Full Txt.]; Bus. Index (1985-); Bus. Source Plus; Bus. Source; Curr. Cit.; EP Collect.; Gen. BusinessFile (1985-); Gen. Period. Index (1985-); Homework Help.; INFO-SOUTH Abstr.; Manage. Contents; MasterFile FullTEXT 1000; MasterFile FullTEXT 350; MasterFile FullTEXT 650; MasterFile FullTEXT (July 1993-) [Full Txt.]; OCLC; PAIS Int. Print (1991-); Telebase; UMI ABI/Inform--Bus. Period. Ondisc (Winter 1987-) [Full Txt.].

ISSN 1049-9849
DD 658 US
CCC

INVENTORY REDUCTION REPORT. [Invent. reduct. rep.]. **Added/Corp** Institute of Management & Administration. (1990)-. Periodical. English. Twelve times a year. $245.00. Institute of Management and Administration, 29 West 35th Street, 5th Floor, New York NY 10001-2299. **Tel** (212)244-0360, FAX (212)564-0465.

UK
TITLE CHANGE

INVOLVEMENT & PARTICIPATION / IPA. **Added/Corp** Involvement & Participation Association (Great Britain). **VFOAT** Involvement and Participation. No. 604 (Winter 1989/1990)-(1993). Periodical. English. Involvement & Participation Association, 42 Colebrooke

Business and Economics —Management

Row, London N1 8AF United Kingdom. **Tel** 011 44 71 354 8040, FAX 011 44 71 354 8041. **Bk Rev. Ad Acc. Circ:** 4,000 (ctrl). *Continues Industrial Participation, 0950-1932. Continued by Involvement (London, England).*

UK

●**INVOLVEMENT : THE JOURNAL OF THE INVOLVEMENT & PARTICIPATION ASSOCIATION. Added/Corp** Involvement & Participation Association (Great Britain). (Winter 1994)-. Periodical. English. Four times a year. £35.00 UK; £50.00 other. Involvement & Participation Association, 42 Colebrooke Row, London N1 8AF United Kingdom. **Tel** 011 44 71 354 8040, FAX 011 44 71 354 8041. **ED** Tony Barry. **Bk Rev. Ad Acc. Circ:** 4,000 (ctrl). *Continues Involvement & Participation.*
Desc: Current topics relating to participation and involvement in the working environment.

LC HD45.A1 O7   ISSN 0019-9281
DD 658/.005   SZ
  CODEN IIOODN

IO, MANAGEMENT-ZEITSCHRIFT INDUSTRIELLE ORGANISATION. Added/Corp Eidgenoessische Technische Hochschule. Betriebswissenschaftliches Institut. **VFOAT** Management-Zeitschrift Industrielle Organisation; Management-Zeitschrift IO. Vol. 43 (1974)-. Trade Publication. German (French and English; summaries and/or abstracts in English, French and German). Ten times a year (two are double issues). $161.17. Verlag Industrielle Organization, Zurichbergstrasse 18, Postfach CH-8028, Zurich Switzerland. **Tel** 011 41 1 6320801, FAX 011 41 1 6320822, telex 59559 BWI CH. **ED** R. H. Scheuchzer. Index available. **Bk Rev. Ad Acc. Circ:** 12,000. Documents available from UMI Article Clearinghouse. *Continues Industrielle Organisation.*
Desc: Information on management, organization, personnel, innovation, technique, marketing, and logistics.
Ind/Abst ABI/INFORM Glob. Ed.; ABI/INFORM [Computer File] (1981-); Ergon. Abstr.; Saf. Health Work; Selec. Coop. Index Manage. Period.

LC HD28   ISSN 1062-7936
DD 658   US

IOMA'S REPORT ON CONTROLLING BENEFITS COSTS FOR LAW, DESIGN, CPA, AND OTHER PROFESSIONAL SERVICE FIRMS. [IOMA's rep. control. benefits costs law des. CPA other prof. serv. firms]. **Added/Corp** Institute of Management & Administration. **VFOAT** Controlling Benefits Costs. **VAT** Institute of Management & Administration's Report on Controlling Benefits Costs for Law, Design, CPA, and Other Professional Service Firms. Issue 92-6 (June 1992)-. Periodical. English. Twelve times a year. $245.00. Institute of Management and Administration, 29 West 35th Street, 5th Floor, New York NY 10001-2299. **Tel** (212)244-0360, FAX (212)564-0465. *Continues Professional Service Firm's Report on Controlling Benefits & Deferred Compensation, 1053-5349.*

  ISSN 1060-5924
DD 658   US
  CCC

IOMA'S REPORT ON CONTROLLING LAW FIRM COSTS. See Law.

  ISSN 1080-5753
DD 657   US

●**IOMA'S REPORT ON MANAGING ACCOUNTS PAYABLE.** [IOMA's rep. manag. acc. pay.]. **Added/Corp** Institute of Management & Administration. **VFOAT** Managing Accounts Payable. (1995)-. Periodical. English. Twelve times a year. $195.00. Institute of Management and Administration, 29 West 35th Street, 5th Floor, New York NY 10001-2299. **Tel** (212)244-0360, FAX (212)564-0465.

  ISSN 1056-7984
DD 658   US
  CCC

IOMA'S REPORT ON REDUCING BENEFITS COSTS. Added/Corp Institute of Management & Administration. **VFOAT** Report on Reducing Benefits Costs; Reducing Benefits Costs. Issue 91-8 (Aug. 1991)-. Periodical. English. Twelve times a year. $245.00. Institute of Management and Administration, 29 West 35th Street, 5th Floor, New York NY 10001-2299. **Tel** (212)244-0360, FAX (212)564-0465.

  ISSN 1077-6206
DD 658   US

●**IQM QUALITY COMPLEMENTS.** [IQM qual. complements]. (1993)-. Periodical. English. Four times a year. $36.00. Greater Expectations, 6105 Nowata Road, Bartlesville OK 74006. **Tel** (800)726-3828, (918)333-3828.

  ISSN 1065-464X
DD 303   US

ISSUES & OBSERVATIONS. (ISSUES & OBSERVATIONS / CENTER FOR CREATIVE LEADERSHIP). [Issues obs.]. **Added/Corp** Center for Creative Leadership. **VFOAT** Issues and Observations. Vol. 1, No. 1 (Feb. 1981)-. Academic Scholarly Publication. English. Four times a year. Free. Center for Creative Leadership, PO Box 26300, Greensboro NC 27438-6300. **Tel** (919)288-7210, FAX (919)288-3999. **ED** Martin Wilcox, Marcia Horowitz. Index available. cum. index. **Bk Rev.** (Qty: 2). **Circ:** 35,000 (ctrl). *Continues Center for Creative Leadership.*
Desc: Features scholarly articles on leadership development. Also contains information about publications, programs, and news of the Center for Creative Leadership.

  ISSN 1187-8606
DD 658.8   CN

IVANOUVELLES (MONTREAL). (THE IVANEWS.). [Ivanouvelles]. **Main/Corp** Ivanhoe (Firm). **VFOAT** Ivanouvelles. Vol. 1, No. 1 (Dec. 1991/Jan. 1992)-. Periodical. English (French). Twelve times a year. Free. Ivanhoe Inc., Service des Communications et des Affaires Publiques, 2 Plaza Alexis-Nihon, 3500 de Maisonneuve West, Westmount Quebec H3Z 2M4 Canada. *Continues Info Ivanhoe., 0835-4650.*

  ISSN 1187-8606
DD 658.8   CN

IVANOUVELLES (MONTREAL). (LES IVANOUVELLES.). [Ivanouvelles]. **Main/Corp** Ivanhoe (Firme). **VFOAT** Ivanews. Vol. 1, No 1 (Dec. 1991/Jan. 1992)-. Periodical. French (English). Twelve times a year. Free. Ivanhoe Inc., Service des Communications et des Affaires Publiques, 2 Plaza Alexis-Nihon, 3500 de Maisonneuve West, Westmount Quebec H3Z 2M4 Canada. *Continues Info Ivanhoe., 0835-4650.*

  ISSN 0932-3635
  GW

UDC 651

JAHRBUCH DER BUEROKOMMUNIKATION. [Jahrb. Buerokommun.]. (1985)-. German. One time a year. FBO Verlag, Hermannstr 2, Postfach 316, W-7570 Baden-Baden Germany.

  ISSN 0968-7130
  UK

JAPAN MANAGEMENT REVIEW. (19??)-. English. Two times a year. $239.00. MCB University Press, 60 62 Toller Lane, Bradford, West Yorkshire BD8 9BY United Kingdom. **Tel** 011 44 1274 785280, FAX 011 44 1274 785200, telex 51317-MCBUNI-G. **(Subscription address:** MCB University Press / US and Canada Subscriptions, PO Box 10812, Birmingham AL 35201-0812. **Tel** (205)995-1567, (800)633-4931, FAX (205)995-1588.**)**

JA
Pr Rev.
JMA MANAGEMENT NEWS. English. Four times a year. free. Japan Management Association, Noritsu Kyokai Building, 3-1-22 Shiba Park, Minato-ku Tokyo 105 Japan. **Tel** (03)434-6211, telex JMA J 25870. **ED** Tadashi Yamamoto. Index available. ctrl circ. *Continues JMA Newsletter / Japan Management Association.*
Desc: An English-language quarterly addressing management issues in Japan, the US, Europe and other areas of the world.

US
JOSSEY BASS MANAGEMENT SERIES. (19??)-. English. Jossey Bass Inc., 350 Sansome Street, San Francisco CA 94104. **Tel** (415)433-1767, FAX (415)433-0499.
Desc: Workplace basics and essential skills employers are looking for.

LC HD58.8 .J68   ISSN 0198-9383
DD 658.4/06/05   US

JOURNAL FOR CONSTRUCTIVE CHANGE. [J. constr. change]. (Autumn 1979)-. Periodical. English. Two times a year. Center for Constructive Change, 16 Strafford Avenue, Durham NH 03824. **Tel** (603)868-5433.

  ISSN 1197-1169
DD 658.8/005   CN

●**JOURNAL MEGA SUCCES, LE.** See Business and Economics-Marketing and Purchasing.

LC HD28 .J587   ISSN 0149-7901
DD 658.4/005   US
  CODEN JOAMDY

JOURNAL OF APPLIED MANAGEMENT. [J. appl. manage.]. (19??)-. Periodical. English. Six times a year. $28.00. Journal of Applied Management, PO Box 35220, Tucson AZ 85740. available on microfilm and microfiche from University Microfilms International (UMI). Documents available from UMI Article Clearinghouse. *Continues Journal of Management, 0161-1100.*
Ind/Abst ABI/INFORM Glob. Ed.; ABI/INFORM [Computer File] (July 1978-Oct. 1980); Bus. Period. Index.

LC HC   ISSN 0021-941X
  CN
  CCC

JOURNAL OF BUSINESS ADMINISTRATION (VANCOUVER). See Business and Economics.

LC HF5718 .J6   ISSN 0021-9436
DD 658   US
  CODEN JBCOAO

JOURNAL OF BUSINESS COMMUNICATION (1973). See Communications.

LC HD28 .J687   ISSN 0887-2058
DD 658   US
Pr Rev.
JOURNAL OF BUSINESS STRATEGIES. [J. bus. strategies]. **Added/Corp** Sam Houston State University. Center for Business and Economic Research. Vol. 1 (1984)-. Periodical. English. Two times a year (April, Nov.). $7.50. Sam Houston State University/ Business & Economics, Center of Business & Economic Research, Huntsville TX 77341. **Tel** (409)294-1111. **ED** Jo Ann Duffy (phone: (409)294-1518). **Ad Acc.**
Desc: Emphasis on new interpretations of, fresh insights about, or clearly stated solutions to problems faced by decision-makers.

LC HD28 .J593   ISSN 0275-6668
DD 658/.005   US
  CODEN JBSTDK

JOURNAL OF BUSINESS STRATEGY, THE. [J. bus. strategy]. Vol. 1, No. 1 (Summer 1980)-. Periodical. English. Six times a year. $102.95. Faulkner & Gray Inc., 11 Penn Plaza, 17th Floor, New York NY 10001. **Tel** (212)967-7000, (800)535-8403. **ED** Robert Lamb. available on microfilm and microfiche from University Microfilms International (UMI). Documents available from UMI Article Clearinghouse.
Desc: Each issue contains a solid mix of incisive articles on topics of interest, plus columns that look at core-interest subjects with hard-headed practicality.
Ind/Abst ABI/INFORM Glob. Ed.; ABI/INFORM Ondisc: Expr. Ed.; ABI/INFORM [Computer File] (Summer 1980-); Acad. Search; AGRICOLA [Select. Cov.]; Anbar Account. Finan. Abstr. [Full Txt.]; Anbar Mark. Distr. Abstr. [Full Txt.]; Anbar Top Manage. Abstr. [Full Txt.]; Bus. Index (1985-); Bus. Period. Index; Bus. Source Plus; Bus. Source; Contents Pages Manage.; Curr. Cit.; EP Collect.; Gen. BusinessFile (1985-); Gen. Period. Index (1985-); Health Plan. Adminis.; Homework Help.; Hosp. Health Admin. Index; INFO-SOUTH Abstr.; Mag. Search; Manage. Market. Abstr.; Manage. Bibliogr. Rev.; Manage. Contents (1980-); Manage. Contents; MasterFile FullTEXT 1000; MasterFile FullTEXT 350; MasterFile FullTEXT 650; MasterFile FullTEXT (Jan. 1994-); OCLC; Oper. Prod. Manage. Abstr. [Full Txt.]; PAIS Int. Print (1991-?); Person. Train. Abstr. [Full Txt.]; Predicasts; Public Aff. Inf. Serv. Bull.; Selec. Coop. Index Manage. Period.; Telebase; Wilson Bus. Abstr.; Women Manage. Rev. [Full Txt.]; Work Relat. Abstr.

LC HG4028.C45 J68   ISSN 0731-1281
DD 658.1/5244   US
  CCC
  TITLE CHANGE
JOURNAL OF CASH MANAGEMENT. [J. cash manage.]. **Added/Corp** National Corporate Cash Management Association. Georgia Institute of Technology. College of Management. (19??)-(1994). Periodical. English. Treasury Management Association, PO Box 64714S, Baltimore MD 21264. **Tel** (301)907-2862. available on microfilm and microfiche from University Microfilms International (UMI); available on an online database (files 15,485/Full-Text) from DIALOG. Documents available from UMI Article Clearinghouse. *Continued by TMA Journal.*
Desc: Contains articles by treasury management experts. Each issue offers theoretical and practical approaches to treasury management strategies and technology.
Ind/Abst ABI/INFORM Glob. Ed.; ABI/INFORM [Computer File] (Sept. 1985-); Account. Tax Datab. (Sept. 1985-) [Full Txt.].

  ISSN 1066-1468
DD 362   US

JOURNAL OF CHILD-CARE ADMINISTRATION. See Sociology-Social Services and Welfare.

LC HD49 .J68   ISSN 0966-0879
DD 658.4/005   UK
  CCC

●**JOURNAL OF CONTINGENCIES AND CRISIS MANAGEMENT. Added/Corp** Basil Blackwell Publisher. **VFOAT** Contingencies and Crisis Management. Vol. 1, No. 1 (Mar. 1993)-. Academic Scholarly Publication. English. Four times a year. $165.00. Basil Blackwell Publishers Ltd., 108 Cowley Road, Oxford OX4 1JF United Kingdom. **Tel** 011 44 1235 465500, FAX 011 44 1235 465556, telex 837022 OXBOOK G. **(Subscription address:** Blackwell Publishers / UK, 108 Cowley Road, Oxford OX4 1JF United Kingdom. **Tel** 011 44 1865 791100, FAX 011 44 1865 791347.**)**

ISSN 1038-2410
DD 658.400994 AT
Pr Rev. TITLE CHANGE
JOURNAL OF CORPORATE MANAGEMENT, THE. See Law-Corporation Law.

ISSN 1069-2533
US
•JOURNAL OF CUSTOMER SERVICE IN MARKETING & MANAGEMENT. Vol. 1 (Sept. 1994)-. Periodical. English. Four times a year. $75.00. The Haworth Press Inc., 10 Alice Street, Binghamton NY 13904-1580. **Tel** (607)722-5857, (800)3-HAWORTH, FAX (607)722-1424. **ED** William J. Winston. **Acid Free.** Documents available from Haworth Document Delivery Service.
Desc: Shares practical marketing theories, concepts, methodologies, strategies, and case studies. Strives to enhance customer service; improve a service's or product's level of quality; and provide true value to the customer or client in return for their time, money and stress.

LC HD28 .J69 ISSN 1058-6407
DD 330 US
CCC
JOURNAL OF ECONOMICS & MANAGEMENT STRATEGY. [J. econ. manage. strategy]. **VFOAT** Journal of Economics and Management Strategy; JEMS. Vol. 1, No. 1 (Spring 1992)-. Periodical. English. Four times a year. $98.00. Massachusetts Institute of Technology (MIT) Press, 55 Hayward Street, Cambridge MA 02142. **Tel** (617)253-2889, (617)625-8481, FAX (617)258-6779. **ED** Daniel F. Spulber.
Desc: Provides a forum for interaction and research on the competitive strategies of managers and the organizational structure of firms; features theoretical and empirical industrial organization, organization game theory, and management strategy.
Ind/Abst Econ. Lit. Index; Math. Rev.; Soc. Work Abstr. [Select. Cov.].

LC HD39.4 .J68 ISSN 0740-008X
DD 658.1/5242 US
CCC
JOURNAL OF EQUIPMENT LEASE FINANCING, THE. [J. equip. lease financ.]. **Added/Corp** American Association of Equipment Lessors. Vol. 1, No. 1 (Spring 1983)-. Periodical. English. Four times a year. American Association of Equipment Lessors, 1300 North 17th Street, Suite 1010, Arlington VA 22209-3801. **Tel** (703)527-8655, FAX (703)527-8649.
Desc: Information on industrial equipment leases.
Ind/Abst Account. Tax Datab. (1988-).

LC HF5549.5.T7 J59 ISSN 0309-0590
DD 658.31/24 UK
CCC
CODEN JEITDP
JOURNAL OF EUROPEAN INDUSTRIAL TRAINING. [J. Eur. ind. train.]. Vol. 1 (1977)-. Periodical. English. Eleven times a year. $3939.00. MCB University Press, 60 62 Toller Lane, Bradford, West Yorkshire BD8 9BY United Kingdom. **Tel** 011 44 1274 785280, FAX 011 44 1274 785200, telex 51317-MCBUNI-G. **(Subscription address:** MCB University Press / US and Canada Subscriptions, PO Box 10812, Birmingham AL 35201-0812. **Tel** (205)995-1567, (800)633-4931, FAX (205)995-1588.**)** **ED** Roger Bennett. **Bk Rev**. available on an online database (file 15/Full-Text) from DIALOG. Documents available from UMI Article Clearinghouse. ***Formed by the union of*** *Industrial Training International, 0019-8811* ***and*** *Journal of European Training.*
Desc: Strives to achieve a training balance between people in business and people working from management centres, so each can learn from the other. Also, sets out to provide information on training in other European countries.
Ind/Abst ABI/INFORM Glob. Ed.; ABI/INFORM [Computer File] (1982-); Anbar Account. Finan. Abstr. [Full Txt.]; Anbar Mark. Distr. Abstr. [Full Txt.]; Anbar Top Manage. Abstr. [Full Txt.]; Curr. Cit.; Curr. Index J. Educ.; Gen. BusinessFile (1992-); Hum. Resour. Abstr. (?-?); Int. Labour Doc.; LABORDOC; Manage. Market. Abstr.; Manage. Bibliogr. Rev.; Multicult. Educ. Abstr.; Oper. Prod. Manage. Abstr. [Full Txt.]; Person. Train. Abstr. [Full Txt.]; Res. High. Educ. Abstr.; School Organ. Manage. Abstr.; Selec. Coop. Index Manage. Period.; Stud. Women Abstr.; Tech. Educ. Train. Abstr.; Women Manage. Rev. [Full Txt.]; Work Relat. Abstr.

LC HD28 .J595 ISSN 0306-3070
DD 658.4/00942 UK
CODEN JGMAAX
JOURNAL OF GENERAL MANAGEMENT. [J. gen. manage.]. **Added/Corp** Henley, The Administrative Staff College. Vol. 1 (Autumn 1973)-. Periodical. English. Four times a year (Mar., June, Sept., Dec.). $250.00. Braybrooke Press, Coach House Remenham House, Remenham Hill, Thames Oxon RG9 3EP United Kingdom. **Tel** 011 44 1491 412061. available on microfilm and microfiche from University Microfilms International (UMI). Documents available from UMI Article Clearinghouse. ***Supersedes*** *Journal of Business Finance, 0021-9452;* ***Absorbed*** *European Journal of Marketing.*
Ind/Abst ABI/INFORM Glob. Ed.; ABI/INFORM Ondisc: Expr. Ed.; ABI/INFORM [Computer File] (Spring 1975-); Acad. Search; Anbar Account. Finan. Abstr. [Full Txt.]; Anbar Mark. Distr. Abstr. [Full Txt.]; Anbar Top Manage. Abstr. [Full Txt.]; Bus. Source Plus; Bus. Source; Contents Pages Manage.; Curr. Cit.; EMBASE; EP Collect.; Gen. BusinessFile (1992-); Gen. Period. Index (1985-); Homework Help.; INFO-SOUTH Abstr.; Int. Labour Doc.; Mag. Search; Manage. Market. Abstr.; Manage. Bibliogr. Rev.; Manage. Contents; MasterFile FullTEXT 1000; MasterFile FullTEXT 350; MasterFile FullTEXT 650; MasterFile FullTEXT (July 1993-); OCLC; Oper. Prod. Manage. Abstr. [Full Txt.]; PAIS Int. Print; Person. Train. Abstr. [Full Txt.]; Person. Manage. Abstr.; Selec. Coop. Index Manage. Period.; Telebase; Women Manage. Rev. [Full Txt.]; Work Relat. Abstr.

LC IN PROCESS ISSN 1074-4797
DD 362 US
NLM W1; JO67BGS
JOURNAL OF HEALTHCARE RISK MANAGEMENT : THE JOURNAL OF THE AMERICAN SOCIETY FOR HEALTHCARE RISK MANAGEMENT. [J. healthc. risk manag.]. **Added/Corp** American Society for Healthcare Risk Management. Vol. 12, No. 4 (Fall 1992)-. Periodical. English. Four times a year. American Hospital Association, 840 North Lake Shore Drive, Chicago IL 60611. **Tel** (312)422-3000, (800)242-2626. ***Continues*** *Perspectives in Healthcare Risk Management, 0899-1073.*
Ind/Abst Hosp. Health Admin. Index (Fall 1992-).

ISSN 1320-6095
AT
•JOURNAL OF INDUSTRY STUDIES. **Added/Corp** University of New South Wales. Industrial Relations Research Centre. Vol. 1, No. 1 (Oct. 1993)-. Periodical. English. Two times a year. 61.66Aus$. University of New South Wales, PO Box 1, Kensington NSW 2033 Australia. **Tel** 011 61 2 3852237. **(Subscription address:** Industrial Relations Research Center, University of New South Wales, Sydney NSW 2052 Australia. **)**

LC T58.64 .J68 ISSN 1042-1319
DD 658.4/038 US
Pr Rev.
JOURNAL OF INFORMATION TECHNOLOGY MANAGEMENT. (JOURNAL OF INFORMATION TECHNOLOGY MANAGEMENT : JITM : A PUBLICATION OF THE ASSOCIATION OF MANAGEMENT.). [J. inf. technol. manage.]. **Added/Corp** Association of Management. **VFOAT** JITM. Vol. 1, No. 1 (1990)-. Periodical. English. Four times a year (Mar., June, Sept., Dec.). $165.00. Association of Management, Route 17 George Washington Highway, PO Box 1301, Grafton VA 23692. **Tel** (804)479-5363, FAX (804)479-0656. **ED** W. H. Hamel Ph.D (editor's address: PO Box 64841, Virginia Beach, VA 23464-0841). **Bk Rev**, (Qty: 8). **Ad Acc. Circ:** 5,400 (ctrl).

ISSN 1075-4253
DD 658 US
Pr Rev.
•JOURNAL OF INTERNATIONAL MANAGEMENT. [J. internat. manag.]. **Added/Corp** American Graduate School of International Management. **VFOAT** International Management. Vol. 1, No. 1 (Spring 1995)-. Periodical. English. Four times a year. $148.00. John Wiley & Sons, Inc., 605 Third Avenue, New York NY 10158-0012. **Tel** (212)850-6000, (212)850-6645, FAX (212)850-6088, telex 12-7063.
Desc: Covers cutting edge research on topics such as international strategic management, comparative management principles, organizational behavior and design, education for international management, and theory and methodology for conducting international management research.

LC HD57.7 .J68 ISSN 1071-7919
DD 303.3/4/05 US
•JOURNAL OF LEADERSHIP STUDIES, THE. [J. leadersh. stud.]. Vol. 1, No. 1 (Nov. 1993)-. Periodical. English. Four times a year. $59.95. Baker College Publishing Company, 1050 West Bristol Road, Flint MI 48507. **Tel** (810)767-7600.

LC HD28 .J597 ISSN 0149-2063
DD 658/.005 US
CCC
CODEN JOMADO
Pr Rev.
JOURNAL OF MANAGEMENT. [J. manage.]. **Added/Corp** Southern Management Association. Vol. 1 (Fall 1975)-. Periodical. English. Six times a year. $200.00. JAI Press Inc., 55 Old Post Road, Suite 2, PO Box 1678, Greenwich CT 06836-1678. **Tel** (203)661-7602, FAX (203)661-0792. **ED** Dan R. Dalton. **Bk Rev. Ad Acc. Circ:** 1,400 (ctrl). available on microfilm and microfiche from University Microfilms International (UMI). Documents available from The Genuine Article, UMI Article Clearinghouse.
Desc: Articles related to the study of management and organization.
Ind/Abst ABI/INFORM Glob. Ed.; ABI/INFORM [Computer File] (Fall 1980-); Acad. Search; Bus. ASAP (1992-) [Full Txt.]; Bus. Index (1985-); Bus. Period. Index; Bus. Source Plus; Bus. Source; Contents Pages Manage.; Curr. Cit.; Curr. Index J. Educ.; EP Collect.; Gen. BusinessFile (1985-); Gen. Period. Index (1985-); Homework Help.; Hum. Resour. Abstr. (?-?); INFO-SOUTH Abstr.; Mag. Search; Manage. Market. Abstr.; Manage. Contents; MasterFile FullTEXT 1000; MasterFile FullTEXT 350; MasterFile FullTEXT 650; MasterFile FullTEXT (July 1994-); OCLC; Oper. Res./Manage. Sci.; Person. Manage. Abstr.; Psychol. Abstr. (1978-); PsycINFO; PsycLit; PsycScan: Appl. Psych.; Qual. Control Appl. Stat.; Res. Alert [Full Cov.]; Soc. Plann. Policy Dev. Abstr.; Soc. Sci. Cit. Index [Full Cov.]; Sociol. Abstr.; Telebase; UMI ABI/Inform--Bus. Period. Ondisc (Winter 1987-) [Full Txt.]; Wilson Bus. Abstr.; Work Relat. Abstr.

LC HF5657.4 .J68 ISSN 1049-2127
DD 658.15/11/05 US
JOURNAL OF MANAGEMENT ACCOUNTING RESEARCH. See Business and Economics-Accounting.

LC HD69.C6 J68 ISSN 0168-7778
DD 658.4/6/05 US
CCC
Pr Rev.
JOURNAL OF MANAGEMENT CONSULTING (AMSTERDAM). (JOURNAL OF MANAGEMENT CONSULTING.). [J. manage. consult.]. **Added/Corp** Institute of Management Consultants (New York, N.Y.). **VFOAT** MC; Journal of MC Management Consulting; JMC. Vol. 1, No. 1 (Fall 1982)-. Periodical. English. Two times a year (published in May and November). $60.00. Journal of Management Consulting, 858 Longview Road, Burlingame CA 94010-6974. **Tel** (415)342-5259, (415)342-1954, FAX (415)344-5005. **ED** Gerald A. Simon (editor's address: 311 High Street, Calistoga, CA 94515; phone: (707)942-9364). Index available. **Bk Rev**, (Qty: 8-10). **Ad Acc, Adv Mgr:** Michael Shays. **Circ:** 6,000. available on microfilm and microfiche from University Microfilms International (UMI); available on an online database (files 15,485/Full-Text) from DIALOG. Documents available from UMI Article Clearinghouse.
Desc: Tools and skill development for the professional management consultant.
Ind/Abst ABI/INFORM Glob. Ed.; ABI/INFORM [Computer File] (Winter 1984-1985); Acad. Search; Account. Tax Datab. (1984-); Anbar Account. Finan. Abstr.; Anbar Mark. Distr. Abstr. [Full Txt.]; Anbar Top Manage. Abstr. [Full Txt.]; Bus. Period. Index; Bus. Source Plus; Bus. Source; Contents Pages Manage.; EP Collect.; Homework Help.; INFO-SOUTH Abstr.; Mag. Search; Manage. Market. Abstr.; Manage. Bibliogr. Rev.; MasterFile FullTEXT 1000; MasterFile FullTEXT 350; MasterFile FullTEXT 650; MasterFile FullTEXT (July 1993-); OCLC; Oper. Prod. Manage. Abstr. [Full Txt.]; Person. Train. Abstr. [Full Txt.]; Telebase; Wilson Bus. Abstr.; Women Manage. Rev. [Full Txt.].

ISSN 1052-5629
DD 658 US
CCC
JOURNAL OF MANAGEMENT EDUCATION (NEWBURY PARK, CALIF.). (JOURNAL OF MANAGEMENT EDUCATION : A PUBLICATION OF THE ORGANIZATIONAL BEHAVIOR TEACHING SOCIETY.). [J. manag. educ.]. **Added/Corp** Organizational Behavior Teaching Society (U.S.). Vol. 15, No. 1 (Feb. 1991)-. Periodical. English. Four times a year (Feb., May, Aug., Nov.). $138.00. SAGE Periodical Press, 2455 Teller Road, Thousand Oaks CA 91320. **Tel** (805)499-0721, FAX (805)499-0871, telex 100799. **ED** Joan V. Gallos. **Acid Free.** ***Continues*** *Organizational Behavior Teaching Review.*
Desc: An international forum for the analysis and improvement of teaching and training business students and managers. The official publication of the Organizational Behavior Teaching Society.
Ind/Abst Bus. Source Plus; Commun. Abstr.; Educ. Adm. Abstr.; EP Collect.; Homework Help.; Hum. Resour. Abstr.; MasterFile FullTEXT 1000; MasterFile FullTEXT 350; MasterFile FullTEXT 650; MasterFile FullTEXT (Jan. 1995-); OCLC; Person. Manage. Abstr.; Telebase.

ISSN 1355-252X
UK
•JOURNAL OF MANAGEMENT HISTORY. **VFOAT** JMH. (1995)-. Periodical. English. Five times a year. $119.00. MCB University Press, 60 62 Toller Lane, Bradford, West Yorkshire BD8 9BY United Kingdom. **Tel** 011 44 1274 785280, FAX 011 44 1274 785200, telex 51317-MCBUNI-G.

LC HD28 .J5987 ISSN 1056-4926
DD 658/.005 US
CCC
Pr Rev.
JOURNAL OF MANAGEMENT INQUIRY. [J. manag. inq.]. **Added/Corp** Western Academy of Management. **VFOAT** JMI. Vol. 1, No. 1 (Mar. 1992)-. Periodical. English. Four times a year (Mar., June, Sept., Dec.). $135.00. SAGE Periodical Press, 2455 Teller Road, Thousand Oaks CA 91320. **Tel** (805)499-0721,

FAX (805)499-0871, telex 100799. **ED** Thomas G. Cummings (University of Southern California). **Acid Free.**
Desc: Provides a forum that provides forum for creative publication within the fields of management and organization. Articles present scholarship on a range of non-traditional research and practice.
Ind/Abst Bus. Source Plus; EP Collect.; Homework Help.; MasterFile FullTEXT 1000; MasterFile FullTEXT 350; MasterFile FullTEXT 650; MasterFile FullTEXT (Jan. 1995-); OCLC; Telebase.

LC HD28 .J6 **ISSN** 0022-2380 UK **CCC** **CODEN** JMASB2

JOURNAL OF MANAGEMENT STUDIES, THE. [J. manage. stud.]. Vol. 1 (Mar. 1964)-. Academic Scholarly Publication. English. Six times a year. $335.00. Basil Blackwell Publishers Ltd., 108 Cowley Road, Oxford 0X4 1JF United Kingdom. **Tel** 011 44 1235 465500, FAX 011 44 1235 465556, telex 837022 OXBOOK G. **(Subscription address:** Blackwell Publishers / UK, 108 Cowley Road, Oxford OX4 1JF United Kingdom. **Tel** 011 44 1865 791100, FAX 011 44 1865 791347.**)** **ED** Geoff Lockett and Karen Legge. **Bk Rev. Ad Acc.** available on microfilm and microfiche from University Microfilms International (UMI). Documents available from The Genuine Article, UMI Article Clearinghouse, Ask*IEEE.
Desc: Multidisciplinary journal publishing articles on all aspects of management research.
Ind/Abst ABI/INFORM Glob. Ed.; ABI/INFORM [Computer File] (Oct. 1972-); Acad. Search; Anbar Account. Finan. Abstr. [Full Txt.]; Anbar Mark. Distr. Abstr. (Jan. 1982-) [Full Txt.]; Anbar Top Manage. Abstr. [Full Txt.]; Bus. ASAP (1992-) [Full Txt.]; Bus. Index (1985-); Bus. Period. Index; Bus. Source Plus; Bus. Source; Contents Pages Manage.; Curr. Cit.; Curr. Contents Soc. Behav. Sci.; Educ. Adm. Abstr. (1974-?); EP Collect.; Gen. BusinessFile (1985-); Gen. Period. Index (1985-); Geogr. Abstr. Human Geogr. (?-?); Homework Help.; Hum. Resour. Abstr. (?-?); INFO-SOUTH Abstr.; INSPEC (Jan. 1982-); Int. Abstr. Oper. Res. [Select. Cov.]; Int. Bibliogr. Sociol.; Int. Labour Doc.; J. Plan. Lit.; LABORDOC; Mag. Search; Manage. Market. Abstr.; Manage. Contents; MasterFile FullTEXT 1000; MasterFile FullTEXT 350; MasterFile FullTEXT 650; MasterFile FullTEXT (July 1993-); OCLC; Oper. Prod. Manage. Abstr. [Full Txt.]; Person. Train. Abstr. [Full Txt.]; Person. Manage. Abstr.; Res. Alert [Full Cov.]; School Organ. Manage. Abstr. (Oct. 1972-); Selec. Coop. Index Manage. Period.; Soc. Plann. Policy Dev. Abstr.; Soc. Sci. Cit. Index [Full Cov.]; Telebase; Wilson Bus. Abstr.; Women Manage. Rev. (Jan. 1982-) [Full Txt.]; Work Relat. Abstr.; World Mag. Bank.

LC HD28 .J62 **ISSN** 1045-3695
DD 658 US **CCC** **CODEN** JMAIE9
Pr Rev.

JOURNAL OF MANAGERIAL ISSUES. (JOURNAL OF MANAGERIAL ISSUES : BJMI.). [J. manag. issue]. **Added/Corp** Gladys A. Kelce School of Business & Economics. **VFOAT** JMI. Vol. 1, No. 1 (Fall 1989)-. Periodical. English. Four times a year. $35.00. Pittsburg State University, Deptartment of Economics Finance & Banking, Pittsburg KS 66762. **Tel** (316)235-4547, (316)231-7000, (316)235-4369, FAX (316)232-7515. **ED** Charles C. Fischer. Index available. **Ad Acc. Circ:** 1,000. available on microfilm from University Microfilms International (UMI).
Desc: Bridge of communication between business leaders and academic researchers.
Ind/Abst Account. Art.; Bus. Index (1992-); Gen. BusinessFile (1992-); Hum. Resour. Abstr.; Neuropsych. Abstr.; PAIS Int. Print; Psychoanal. Abstr.; Psychol. Abstr. (1989-); PsycINFO; PsycScan: Appl. Exp. Eng. Psych.; PsycScan: LD/MR; Soc. Plann. Policy Dev. Abstr.

ISSN 0268-3946 UK **CCC**

JOURNAL OF MANAGERIAL PSYCHOLOGY. See Psychology.

LC HD28 **ISSN** 1382-3019
DD 658 NE

•**JOURNAL OF MARKET-FOCUSED MANAGEMENT.** (1996)-. Academic Scholarly Publication. English. Four times a year. $268.00. Kluwer Academic Publishers, Postbus 322, 3300 AH Dordrecht The Netherlands. **Tel** 011 31 78 524400, FAX 011 31 78 183273, telex 20083. **ED** Rajiv Grover.

ISSN 1057-1523 US

•**JOURNAL OF MINISTRY MARKETING & MANAGEMENT.** See Business and Economics-Marketing and Purchasing.

LC HD58.7 .J68 **ISSN** 0160-8061
DD 658.3/005 US
NLM W1 JO804LM
Pr Rev.

JOURNAL OF ORGANIZATIONAL BEHAVIOR MANAGEMENT. See Psychology.

LC HD58.8 .J68 **ISSN** 0953-4814 UK **CCC**

JOURNAL OF ORGANIZATIONAL CHANGE MANAGEMENT. **VFOAT** JOCM. Vol. 1, No. 1 (1988)-. Periodical. English. Six times a year. $1299.00. MCB University Press, 60 62 Toller Lane, Bradford, West Yorkshire BD8 9BY United Kingdom. **Tel** 011 44 1274 785280, FAX 011 44 1274 785200, telex 51317-MCBUNI-G. **(Subscription address:** MCB University Press / US and Canada Subscriptions, PO Box 10812, Birmingham AL 35201-0812. **Tel** (205)995-1567, (800)633-4931, FAX (205)995-1588.**)** **ED** David Boje. Index available. **Ad Acc. Circ:** 400. Documents available from UMI Article Clearinghouse.
Desc: Aims to bridge the gap between academic research and management practice. At the same time it makes new research accessible and understandable to practitioners. Ultimately the goal is to help build a more promising future for the societies of tomorrow.
Ind/Abst ABI/INFORM Glob. Ed.; Curr. Cit.; Ergon. Abstr.; Manage. Market. Abstr.; Person. Manage. Abstr.

LC HD30.2 .J69 **ISSN** 1054-1721
DD 658/.00285 US **CODEN** JORCEM
TITLE CHANGE

JOURNAL OF ORGANIZATIONAL COMPUTING. [J. organ. comput.]. **VFOAT** Organizational Computing. (Jan./Mar. 1991)-(1995). Periodical. English. Ablex Publishing Corporation, 355 Chestnut Street, Norwood NJ 07648. **Tel** (201)767-8450, (201)767-8455 (Customer Service), FAX (201)767-6717. Documents available from Ask*IEEE. ***Continued by*** *Organizational Computing and Electronic Commerce.*
Desc: This journal publishes original research articles concerned with the impact of computer and communication technology on organizational design, operations, and performance. It is intended as a forum for stimulating and disseminating research into the implications of these technologies for organizational structure and dynamics, detailing both the technological advances needed to keep pace with organizational changes, and the emerging technological possibilities for improving organizational productivity.
Ind/Abst Curr. Cit.; INSPEC (Jan./Mar. 1991-).

ISSN 1351-6051 UK

JOURNAL OF PAY & REWARD MANAGEMENT. (19??)-. Academic Scholarly Publication. English. Four times a year. $145.00 North America; £105.00 other. Basil Blackwell Publishers Ltd., 108 Cowley Road, Oxford 0X4 1JF United Kingdom. **Tel** 011 44 1235 465500, FAX 011 44 1235 465556, telex 837022 OXBOOK G. **(Subscription address:** Blackwell Publishers / UK, 108 Cowley Road, Oxford OX4 1JF United Kingdom. **Tel** 011 44 1865 791100, FAX 011 44 1865 791347.**)**

LC HF5415.34 .J68 **ISSN** 1049-6491
DD 658.8/2/05 US **CODEN** JPRMEP
Pr Rev.

JOURNAL OF PROMOTION MANAGEMENT. (JOURNAL OF PROMOTION MANAGEMENT : JPM.). [J. promot. manag.]. **VFOAT** JPM. Vol. 1, No. 1 (1991)-. Periodical. English. Two times a year. $60.00. The Haworth Press Inc., 10 Alice Street, Binghamton NY 13904-1580. **Tel** (607)722-5857, (800)3-HAWORTH, FAX (607)722-1424. **ED** Fred Crane (editor's address: School of Business, Dalhousie University, 6152 Coburg Road, Halifax Nova Scotia B3H 1Z5 Canada). **Bk Rev. Ad Acc. Acid Free.** available on microfiche. Documents available from Haworth Document Delivery Service.
Desc: Presents research findings on current topics in promotion management. Coverage provides teachers and practitioners a vehicle that demonstrates theory and practice with an emphasis on promotion management in action.
Ind/Abst Commun. Abstr. (?-?); Hum. Resour. Abstr. (?-?); Manage. Market. Abstr.; Oper. Res./Manage. Sci.

ISSN 1355-2511 UK
Pr Rev.

•**JOURNAL OF QUALITY IN MAINTENANCE ENGINEERING.** (1995)-. Periodical. English. Four times a year. £79.00. MCB University Press, 60 62 Toller Lane, Bradford, West Yorkshire BD8 9BY United Kingdom. **Tel** 011 44 1274 785280, FAX 011 44 1274 785200, telex 51317-MCBUNI-G. **ED** Dr. Abdul Raouf.
Desc: Covers maintenance and total quality management, including maintenance strategies and product quality, organization, planning and control, industrial relations, work measurement and motivation, surveillance, logistics and inventory control, etc.

LC HD28 **ISSN** 1084-8568
DD 658 US

•**JOURNAL OF QUALITY MANAGEMENT.** (1996)-. Periodical. English. Two times a year. $125.00. JAI Press Inc., 55 Old Post Road, Suite 2, PO Box 1678, Greenwich CT 06836-1678. **Tel** (203)661-7602, FAX (203)661-0792. **ED** Robert Cardy.

LC TS156.Q3 J65 **ISSN** 0022-4065
DD 620/.0045/08 US **CCC** **CODEN** JQUTAU
Pr Rev.

JOURNAL OF QUALITY TECHNOLOGY. See Science and Technology.

LC WMLC 93/326 HB615 .J6 **ISSN** 0895-5646 US **CCC** **CODEN** JRUNEN
Pr Rev.

JOURNAL OF RISK AND UNCERTAINTY. See Psychology.

LC HD69.S6 J67 **ISSN** 0047-2778
DD 658/.022/05 US **CODEN** JSBMAU
Pr Rev.

JOURNAL OF SMALL BUSINESS MANAGEMENT. [J. small bus. manage.]. **Added/Corp** National Council for Small Business Management Development (U.S.) West Virginia University. Bureau of Business Research. International Council for Small Business. Small Business Institute Directors' Association (U.S.). **VFOAT** Small Business Management; JSBM. (1963)-. Periodical. English (summaries and/or abstracts in French, German and Spanish). Four times a year. $60.00. International Council for Small Business, Bureau of Business Research, West Virginia University, PO Box 6025, Morgantown WV 26506-6025. **Tel** (304)293-7534, FAX (304)293-7061. **ED** Frederick C. Scherr. Index available. cum. index. **Bk Rev. Ad Acc. Circ:** 3,600. available on microfilm and microfiche from University Microfilms International (UMI); available on an online database (files 15,647,648/Full-Text) from DIALOG. Documents available from UMI Article Clearinghouse.
Desc: Official publication of the International Council for Small Business and the Small Business Institute Directors Association. Dedicated to the development of small business.
Ind/Abst ABI/INFORM Glob. Ed.; ABI/INFORM Ondisc: Expr. Ed.; ABI/INFORM [Computer File] (July 1973-); Acad. Search; Anbar Account. Finan. Abstr. [Full Txt.]; Anbar Mark. Distr. Abstr. [Full Txt.]; Anbar Top Manage. Abstr. [Full Txt.]; Bus. ASAP (1990-) [Full Txt.]; Bus. Index (1985-); Bus. Period. Index; Bus. Source Plus; Bus. Source; Contents Pages Manage.; Curr. Cit.; EP Collect.; Gen. BusinessFile (1985-); Gen. Period. Index (1985-); Homework Help.; INFO-SOUTH Abstr.; Mag. ASAP Plus [Full Txt.]; Mag. Index Plus (1989-); Mag. Search; Manage. Market. Abstr.; Manage. Bibliogr. Rev.; Manage. Contents (1974-); MasterFile FullTEXT 1000; MasterFile FullTEXT 350; MasterFile FullTEXT 650; MasterFile FullTEXT (July 1993-); Newsp. Period. Abstr. (1988-); OCLC; Oper. Prod. Manage. Abstr. [Full Txt.]; PAIS Int. Print (1991-); Person. Train. Abstr. [Full Txt.]; Person. Manage. Abstr.; Public Aff. Inf. Serv. Bull.; Telebase; Mag. Index (1977-);; Trade Ind. Index (1981-?);; UMI ABI/Inform--Bus. Period. Ondisc (Jan. 1987-) [Full Txt.]; Wilson Bus. Abstr.; Women Manage. Rev. [Full Txt.].

ISSN 0888-4773
DD 790 US **CCC**

JOURNAL OF SPORT MANAGEMENT. See Sports and Games.

ISSN 0965-254X UK **CCC**

•**JOURNAL OF STRATEGIC MARKETING.** See Business and Economics-Marketing and Purchasing.

LC HD28 .S953 **ISSN** 0022-4839
DD 658.4/005 US **CCC** **CODEN** JSYMA9
Pr Rev.

JOURNAL OF SYSTEMS MANAGEMENT. [J. syst. manage.]. **Added/Corp** Association for Systems Management. Vol. 20 (Jan. 1969)-. English. Six times a year. $60.00. Association for Systems Management, 1433 West Bagley Road, PO Box 38370, Cleveland OH 44138. **Tel** (216)243-6900, (216)243-6902, FAX (216)234-2930. **ED** Bernard A. Thiel. Index available (bound in Dec. issue). cum. index. **Bk Rev. Ad Acc. Circ:** 13,000. available on an online database from NEXIS; available on microfilm and microfiche from University Microfilms International (UMI). Documents available from The Genuine Article, UMI Article Clearinghouse, Ask*IEEE. ***Continues*** *Systems and Procedures Journal.*
Desc: Covers the issues related to the management and use of business information systems. Includes case studies, feature articles, columns and editorials.
Ind/Abst ABI/INFORM Glob. Ed.; ABI/INFORM [Computer File] (Sept. 1971-); Acad. Search; Account. Art.; Anbar Account. Finan. Abstr. [Full Txt.]; Anbar Mark. Distr. Abstr. [Full Txt.]; Anbar Top Manage. Abstr. [Full Txt.]; Bus. ASAP (1990-) [Full Txt.]; Bus. Index (1985-); Bus. Period. Index; CompuMath Cit. Index [Full Cov.]; Comput. ASAP [Full Txt.]; Comput. Database [Full Txt.]; Comput. Lit. Index; Comput. Rev.; Contents Pages Manage.; Curr. Cit.; Curr. Contents Soc. Behav. Sci.; EP

Business and Economics — Management

Collect.; Gen. BusinessFile (1985-); Gen. Period. Index (1985-); Homework Help.; INFO-SOUTH Abstr.; INSPEC (June 1970-); J. Plan. Lit.; Law Office Inf. Serv.; Libr. Inf. Sci. Abstr.; Mag. Search; Manage. Market. Abstr.; Manage. Bibliogr. Rev.; MasterFile FullTEXT 1000; MasterFile FullTEXT 350; MasterFile FullTEXT 650; MasterFile FullTEXT (July 1993-); OCLC; Oper. Prod. Manage. Abstr. [Full Txt.]; Person. Train. Abstr. [Full Txt.]; Res. Alert [Full Cov.]; Selec. Coop. Index Manage. Period.; Soc. Sci. Cit. Index [Full Cov.]; Telebase; Trade Ind. Index (1981-?); UMI ABI/Inform--Bus. Period. Ondisc (Jan. 1987-) [Full Txt.]; Wilson Bus. Abstr.; Women Manage. Rev. [Full Txt.]; Work Relat. Abstr.; World Publ. Monit.

ISSN 0970-0447
II

UDC 65
JOURNAL OF THE MANAGEMENT PROFESSIONALS ASSOCIATION. [J. Manage. Prof. Assoc.]. (1981)-. Periodical. English. Twelve times a year. $15.00. (**Subscription address:** Prints India, 11 Darya Ganj, New Delhi 110002 India. **Tel** 011 91 11 3268645, FAX 011 91 11 3275542, telex 31-61087 PRIN-IN.)

ISSN 1068-6061
US

●**JOURNAL OF TRANSNATIONAL MANAGEMENT DEVELOPMENT.** (1994)-. Periodical. English. Four times a year. $135.00. The Haworth Press Inc., 10 Alice Street, Binghamton NY 13904-1580. **Tel** (607)722-5857, (800)3-HAWORTH, FAX (607)722-1424. **ED** Victor V. Cordell, George Mason University. **Acid Free.** Documents available from Haworth Document Delivery Service.
Desc: Covers some of the most timely international and multicultural issues in international business.
Ind/Abst Foods Adlibra; Manage. Market. Abstr.; Oper. Res./Manage. Sci.; Refer. Z.; Work Relat. Abstr.

ISSN 0925-6032
NE

UDC 651 :658
KANTOORMANAGEMENT (AMSTERDAM). (KANTOORMANAGEMENT.). [Kantoormanagement Amst.]. (1990)-. Periodical. Dutch. Four times a year. Free on request. Wegener Tijl Tijdschriften Groep, Postbus 1860, 1110 CD Diemen Netherlands. **Tel** 011 31 20 6603300. **Continues** Kantoor & Management, 0925-6024.

LC Z7166 .K45 ISSN 1052-9020
DD 350 US
KENNEDY SCHOOL CASE CATALOG, THE. [Kennedy Sch. case cat.]. **Added/Corp** John F. Kennedy School of Government. Case Program. John F. Kennedy School of Government. 2nd Ed (1988)-. Catalog. English. Two times a year. $9.95. Harvard University / JFK School of Government, 79 JFK Street, Cambridge MA 02138. **Tel** (617)495-1100, FAX (617)495-1972. **Circ:** 2,000. **Continues** Kennedy School Case List.
Desc: The guide to Kennedy School public policy case studies available for classroom and research use. Kennedy School cases are designed to help students understand government decision making from an insider's perspective.

ISSN 0897-4217
DD 658 US
KEPNER TREGOE BUSINESS REVIEW. [Kepner Tregoe bus. rev.]. **Added/Corp** Kepner-Tregoe, Inc. **VFOAT** Kepner-Tregoe Business Review; Business Review. (Summer 1987)-. Periodical. English. Four times a year. Free. Kepner-Tregoe Inc, PO Box 704, Princeton NJ 08542. **Tel** (609)921-2806 ext. 278, telex 843485. **Continues** Kepner Tregoe Journal, 0736-1327.

LC HD28 .K43
DD 658.4/00954/83 II
KERALA PRODUCTIVITY JOURNAL. Periodical. English. Rs10.00. National Productivity Council, Productivity House, Lodi Road, New Delhi 110003 India.

US
KEYMAN. (19??)-. English. Irregular. $100.00. Securities Industry Association, 120 Broadway/35th Floor, New York NY 10271. **Tel** (212)608-1500, FAX (212)608-1604.
Desc: A variety of SIA mailings made expressly to the managing executive in each member organization. These mailings include legislative reports, special bulletins, position papers and other releases of importance to top management.

LC HC462.9 .K454
JA
KIGYO HAKUSHO. See Industry and Production.

LC T58.6 .K575
DD 003/.05 RU
KLASSIFIKATORY I DOKUMENTY V ASU / [GOSUDARSTVENNYI KOMITET STANDARTOV SOVETA MINISTROV SSSR, VSESOIUZNYI NAUCHNO-ISSLEDOVATEL'SKII INSTITUT TEKHNICHESKOI INFORMATSII, KLASSIFIKATSII I KODIROVANIIA]. See Computers.

ISSN 0023-2777
DD 658.5 JA
KOJO KANRI. VFOAT Factory Management (Tokyo. 1955). (1955)-. Periodical. Japanese. Fifteen times a year. $414.00. Nikkan Kogyo Shinbunsha, (Nikkan Kogyo Shinbun Ltd.), 8-10 Kudan Kita 1 Chome, Chiyodaku Tokyo 102 Japan.

LC HD28 .K942 KO
KYONGYONG NONJIP (CHUNGNAM TAEHAKKYO. PUSOL KYONGYONG KYONGJE YONGUSO). (KYONGYONG NONJIP.). **VFOAT** Journal of Management; Chungnam Kyongsang Taehak Pusol Kyongyong; Ongje Yonguso Kyongyong Nonjip. Vol. 1, Dec. 1985-. Periodical. Korean. Seoul National University Institute of Economic Research, Seoul Daehakkyo Kyeongje Yeongusa, San 56-1, Sinlim-dong Kwanak-ku, Seoul 151-742 South Korea. **Continues in part** Kyongsang Nonjip (Chungnam Taehakkyo. Pusol Kyongyong Kyongje Yonguso).

LC HD28 .K95 KO
KYONGYONG SARYE YON'GU. VFOAT Practice of Management. Periodical. Korean. 56-1 Sillim-dong Kwanak-ku, Seoul South Korea.

LC HD70.K6 K96 KO
KYONGYONG YONGU (CHOSON TAEHAKKYO. KYONGYONG YONGUSO). (KYONGYONG YONGU.). **VFOAT** Management Research. Periodical. Korean (Korean). Choson Taehakkyo Kyongyong, Yonguso 17 Pullo-dong, Tong-ku Kwangju-si Korea.

LC HD28 .K97 KO
KYONGYONGHAK YON'GU. VFOAT Korea Management Review. Periodical. English (Korean). Hanguk Kyongong Kakhoe, 1 Anam-dong 5-ka, Songbuk-ku, Seoul South Korea.

LC HD6961.A1 I73 ISSN 0538-8325
DD 331 SZ
LABOUR-MANAGEMENT RELATIONS SERIES. See Business and Economics-Labor.

US
LAKEWOOD REPORT, THE. (19??)-. English. Twelve times a year. $128.00. Lakewood Publications, 50 South Ninth Street, Minneapolis MN 55402. **Tel** (612)333-0471, (800)328-4329, FAX (612)333-6526. **Absorbed** The Service Edge, 1053-1734 **and** Total Quality Newsletter, 1053-1718.
Desc: Provides practical ideas and information about implementing a service strategy that can result in better customer service and improved profits. Includes special section devoted to front-line service techniques.

LC HD20.15.M3 M34A
MY
LAPORAN TAHUNAN - YAYASAN PENGURUSAN MALAYSIA. Main/Corp Malaysian Institute of Management. **VFOAT** Annual Report - Malaysian Institute of Management. 1966-. English (Malay). Yayasan Pengurusan Malaysia, 11 Leboh Ampang, Kuala Lampur Malaysia.

ISSN 1052-2972
US
LAW DEPARTMENT MANAGEMENT ADVISER. (1990)-. Periodical. English. Twelve times a year. $195.00. Business Laws Inc., 11630 Chillicothe Road, Chesterland OH 44026. **Tel** (216)729-7996, (800)759-0929, FAX (216)729-0645. **Continues** Corporate Counsel's Managerial Adviser, 0898-9915.

ISSN 1071-7242
DD 658 US
LAW OFFICE ADMINISTRATOR. [Law off. adm.]. Vol. 1, No. 1 (Nov. 1992)-. Periodical. English. Twelve times a year. $127.00. Law Office Administrator, PO Box 724093, Atlanta GA 31139. **Tel** (404)319-8105, FAX (404)436-4618. **ED** Fran Worrall. Index available. **Bk Rev** (Qty: 2-3); **Circ:** 1,500.

LC K12 .A9365 ISSN 0458-8630
US
LAW OFFICE ECONOMICS AND MANAGEMENT. [Law off. econ. manage.]. Vol. 1 (May 1960)-. Periodical. English. Four times a year. $95.00. Clark Boardman Callaghan, 155 Pfingsten Road, Deerfield IL 60015. **Tel** (800)323-8067.
Ind/Abst Curr. Law Index (1980-); Law Office Inf. Serv.; Leg. Inf. Manage. Index; Leg. Resour. Index (1980-); LegalTrac (1980-).

LC KF318.Z9 L38 ISSN 0883-0525
US
LAW OFFICE MANAGEMENT (1981). See Law.

LC KF318.A1 L393 ISSN 0735-4843
DD 651/.934/005 US
  CCC
LAW OFFICE MANAGEMENT & ADMINISTRATION REPORT. See Law.

LC HD58.8 .L4 ISSN 0143-7739
DD 658.4/06/05 UK
  CCC
LEADERSHIP & ORGANIZATION DEVELOPMENT JOURNAL. [Leadersh. organ. dev. j.]. **VFOAT** Leadership and Organization Development Journal; LODJ. **VAT** Leadership and Organization Development Journal. Vol. 1, No. 1 (1980)-. Periodical. English. Eight times a year. $3239.00. MCB University Press, 60 62 Toller Lane, Bradford, West Yorkshire BD8 9BY United Kingdom. **Tel** 011 44 1274 785280, FAX 011 44 1274 785200, telex 51317-MCBUNI-G. (**Subscription address:** MCB University Press / US and Canada Subscriptions, PO Box 10812, Birmingham AL 35201-0812. **Tel** (205)995-1567, (800)633-4931, FAX (205)995-1588.) **ED** Tudor Rickards.
Bk Rev. available on an online database (file 15/Full-Text) from DIALOG. Documents available from UMI Article Clearinghouse.
Desc: Presents the case for new methods and approaches in the field. Aimed at busy professionals looking to apply theories to their own organization's development.
Ind/Abst ABI/INFORM Glob. Ed.; ABI/INFORM [Computer File] (1983-); Acad. Search; Anbar Account. Finan. Abstr. [Full Txt.]; Anbar Mark. Distr. Abstr. [Full Txt.]; Anbar Top Manage. Abstr. [Full Txt.]; Bus. Index (1987-); Bus. Source Plus; Bus. Source; Curr. Cit.; Educ. Technol. Abstr.; EP Collect.; Gen. BusinessFile (1987-); Gen. Period. Index (1985-); Homework Help.; INFO-SOUTH Abstr.; Mag. Search; Manage. Market. Abstr.; Manage. Bibliogr. Rev.; MasterFile FullTEXT 1000; MasterFile FullTEXT 350; MasterFile FullTEXT 650; MasterFile FullTEXT (July 1993-); OCLC; Oper. Prod. Manage. Abstr. [Full Txt.]; Person. Train. Abstr. [Full Txt.]; Person. Manage. Abstr.; Psychol. Abstr. (1983-); PsycINFO; PsycLit; School Organ. Manage. Abstr. (1980-); Stud. Women Abstr.; Tech. Educ. Train. Abstr. (1983-); Telebase; Women Manage. Rev. [Full Txt.].

ISSN 1078-0165
DD 658 US
  CODEN LEDGEI
●**LEADERSHIP EDGE, THE.** [Leadersh. edge]. **Added/Corp** Bureau of Business Practice. Issue No. 101 (June 1994)-. Periodical. English. Twelve times a year. $104.28. Bureau of Business Practice, 24 Rope Ferry Road, Waterford CT 06386. **Tel** (800)243-0876, (203)442-4365, (800)876-9105, FAX (203)443-1123.

ISSN 1062-1474
DD 303 US
LEADERSHIP EDUCATION. (LEADERSHIP EDUCATION : A SOURCE BOOK FOR THOSE PLANNING PROGRAMS AND TEACHING COURSES IN LEADERSHIP.). [Leadersh. educ.]. **Added/Corp** Center for Creative Leadership. (1986)-. Periodical. English. Every 2 years. $59.95. Center for Creative Leadership, PO Box 26300, Greensboro NC 27438-6300. **Tel** (919)288-7210, FAX (919)288-3999. **ED** Frank H Freeman, Sara N King. ctrl circ.
Desc: Listing of courses and programs in leadership, leadership technologies, leadership bibliography, films, videos, resource persons, and resource organizations for leadership education.

ISSN 1080-1863
DD 658 US
●**LEADERSHIP FOR THE FRONT LINES.** [Leadersh. front lines]. **Added/Corp** Bureau of Business Practice. Issue No. 248 (Dec. 1994)-. Periodical. English. Twenty-four times a year. Bureau of Business Practice, 24 Rope Ferry Road, Waterford CT 06386. **Tel** (800)243-0876, (203)442-4365, (800)876-9105, FAX (203)443-1123. **Continues** Front Line Leadership, 1077-5498.

LC HD57.7 .L435 ISSN 1048-9843
DD 303.3/4/05 US
  CCC
  CODEN LEQUEN
LEADERSHIP QUARTERLY, THE. [Leadersh. q.]. **VFOAT** LQ. Vol. 1, No. 1 (Spring 1990)-. Periodical. English. Four times a year. $165.00. JAI Press

Inc., 55 Old Post Road, Suite 2, PO Box 1678, Greenwich CT 06836-1678. **Tel** (203)661-7602, FAX (203)661-0792. **ED** Robert House and Henry Tosi, Jr.
Desc: Stressing theory and empirical research on effective leadership in all walks of life, publishes scholarly research and developmental applications from fields of inquiry about leadership.
Ind/Abst Neuropsych. Abstr.; Person. Manage. Abstr.; Psychoanal. Abstr.; PsycScan: Appl. Exp. Eng. Psych.; PsycScan: LD/MR; Soc. Plann. Policy Dev. Abstr.

LC HF5001 .L32 **ISSN** 0195-9204
DD 658.4/092/05 US
LEADERSHIP (WASHINGTON). (LEADERSHIP.). [Leadership]. **Added/Corp** American Society of Association Executives. Vol. 1 (Mar. 1980)-. Periodical. English. One time a year (Jan.). $5.00. American Society of Association of Executives, 1575 Eye Street Northwest, Washington DC 20005. **Tel** (202)626-2722, FAX (202)842-1109. **ED** Ann I. Mahoney. **Bk Rev. Ad Acc. Circ:** 40,000. Documents available from UMI Article Clearinghouse. ***Supersedes*** *Association Management, 0004-5578.*
Desc: Written for an association's volunteer board. Contains articles and other information with the board members successful tenure in mind.
Ind/Abst ABI/INFORM Glob. Ed.; ABI/INFORM [Computer File] (March 1980-); Christ. Period. Index (19??-); Relig. Theol. Abstr. (Mar. 1980-).

ISSN 1057-4816
DD 818 US
CODEN LEAEEV
LEADERSHIP WITH A HUMAN TOUCH. [Leadersh. human touch]. **VFOAT** Leadership. (July 9, 1991)-. Periodical. English. Thirteen times a year. $23.50. Economics Press Inc, 12 Daniel Road, Fairfield NJ 07004. **Tel** (201)227-1224, (800)526-2554, FAX (201)227-9742. ***Continues*** *Soundings (Fairfield, N.J.), 0886-8123.*
Desc: Devoted to people, not business. Filled with stories, humor, quotes, and insights about leadership from men and women whose wisdom has stood the test of time.

LC TS155
DD 658.5 US
LECTURE SERIES - HAN'GUK SONBAK YON'GUSO. Main/Corp Hab'Guk Sonbak Yon'Guso. **VFOAT** Job Evaluation, Time and Motion Study, Wage Incentives. (1945)-. English. Society for the Advancement of Management, 300 North Zeeb Road, Ann Arbor MI 48106.

ISSN 0229-5393
DD 651/.934 CN
LEGAL SUPPORT STAFF NEWSLETTER. See Law.

NE
LEIDINGGEVEN & ORGANISEREN. Dutch. Nive, Postbus 266, Neuhuyskade 40, 2270 AG Voorburg Netherlands. **Tel** 011 31 70 3001500.

FR
LETTRE D'HUBERT LANDIER, LA. (19??)-. French. One time a week. $726.32. MCS / Management et Conjoncture Sociale, 54 rue Saint Lazare, 75009 Paris France. **Tel** 011 33 1 40829162, FAX 011 33 1 47640982.

ISSN 0763-8515
FR
LETTRE DU MANAGER. (1984)-. French. Twenty-four times a year. $594.92. La Lettre du Manager, BP 95, 06902 Sophia Antipolis France. **Tel** 011 33 93 654748.

ISSN 0738-9167
US
LEVINSON LETTER, THE. [Levinson lett.]. **Added/Corp** Levinson Institute. (1974)-. Periodical. English. Twenty-four times a year. $98.00. Levinson Institute, 404 Wyman Street, Suite 400, Waltham MA 02154. **Tel** (617)895-1000, FAX (617)895-1644. **ED** Harry Levinson Ph.D.
Desc: Focuses on the psychological aspects of leadership in organizations. Deals with managerial problems and processes from the point of view of management psychologist Dr. Harry Levinson.

ISSN 0743-9520
DD 658 US
LEVISON LETTER, THE. Added/Corp Ivan Levison & Associates. (1984)-. Periodical. English. Twelve times a year. $50.00. Ivan Levison & Associates Inc, 14 Los Cerros Drive, Greenbae CA 94904. **Tel** (415)461-0672. **ED** Ivan Levison. **Circ:** 2,500.
Desc: Ideas and tips for marketing communications.

LC HC591.L6 L443
DD 330.9/666/203 LB
LIBERIAN ECONOMIC AND MANAGEMENT REVIEW, THE. Added/Corp University of Liberia. Economic and Management Research Institute. (1972)-. Periodical. English. University of Liberia, Liberian Economic and Management Institute, Monrovia Liberia.

LC Z678 .L475 **ISSN** 0143-5124
DD 025.1/05 UK
CCC
LIBRARY MANAGEMENT (MCB PUBLICATIONS (FIRM)). See Library and Information Sciences.

ISSN 1058-6636
DD 650 US
LIFE POSITIVE!. [Life posit.]. Vol. 1, Issue 1 (1991)-. Periodical. English. Twelve times a year. $48.00. Nightingale-Conant Corporation, 7300 North Lehigh Avenue, Chicago IL 60648. **Tel** (800)323-5552.

ISSN 1064-3753
DD 004 US
CODEN LIEREG
LIFERAFT (COLORADO SPRINGS, COLO.). (LIFERAFT.). [Liferaft]. **Added/Corp** Help Desk Institute. (1989)-. Periodical. English. Six times a year. $96.00 (nonmembers), $36.00 (members). Help Desk Institute, 1755 Telstar Drive, Suite 101, Colorado Springs CO 80920. **Tel** (719)531-5138, FAX (719)531-6522.

LC HD58.5 .L53 **ISSN** 0024-3469
DD 658 FI
LIIKETALOUDELLINEN AIKAKAUSKIRJA. (LIIKETALOUDELLINEN AIKAKAUSKIRJA : THE FINNISH JOURNAL OF BUSINESS ECONOMICS.). [Liiketalo. aikak.]. **VFOAT** Finnish Journal of Business Economics; Journal of Business Economics 1955-67. (1952)-. Academic Scholarly Publication. English (Finnish; summaries and/or abstracts in English). Four times a year. Liiketaloudellinen Yhdistys, Helsinki School of Economics, Helsingen Kauppakorkeakoulu, Runeberginkatu 14-16, 00100 Helsinki Finland. **Tel** 011 358 4313622, FAX 011 358 4313730, telex 122220 ECON SF. **ED** J. Honko. Index available. **Bk Rev. Circ:** 1,850. available in reprints from University Microfilms International (UMI).
Desc: Publishes research reports on economics and business administration.
Ind/Abst Econ. Lit. Index (19??-); J. Econ. Lit.; Selec. Coop. Index Manage. Period.

UK
LIST OF ACCESSIONS / LONDON BUSINESS SCHOOL LIBRARY. Main/Corp London Business School. Library. **VFOAT** Library List of Accessions. (19??)-. English. Twelve times a year. $42.78. London Business School Journal, Sussex Place Regents Park, London NW1 4SA United Kingdom. **Tel** 011 44 171 2625050 ext. 418.

ISSN 0822-7543
DD 650/.07/11714281 CN
LIT-POT-HEC. (LIT-POT-HEC : JOURNAL DES ETUDIANTS DES HEC.). **VAT** Lit-Pot-Hautes Etudes Commerciales. (1976)-. Periodical. French. Six times a year. Free. Ecole des Hautes Etudes Commerciales, 5255 Decelles Avenue, Montreal Quebec H3T 1V6 Canada. **Tel** (514)340-6437, FAX (514)340-6469. ***Continues*** *Mercure (Montreal, Quebec: 1956).*

ISSN 0169-3212
NE
UDC 658
LITERATUURSIGNALERING. ALGEMEEN MANAGEMENT. [Lit.signal., Alg. manage.]. (1985)-. Periodical. Dutch. Twelve times a year. $181.57. Nive, Postbus 266, Neuhuyskade 40, 2270 AG Voorburg Netherlands. **Tel** 011 31 70 3001500. ***Continues*** *Literatuursignalering. Integraal Bestuur : Directiebeleid, 0166-3526.*

ISSN 0929-5402
NE
UDC 658.3:681.31
●**LITERATUURSIGNALERING. KANTOOR RN AUTOMATISERING.** [Lit.signal., Kant. autom.]. (1993)-. Periodical. English (French). Six times a year. $85.64. Nive, Postbus 266, Neuhuyskade 40, 2270 AG Voorburg Netherlands. **Tel** 011 31 70 3001500. ***Continues*** *Literatuursignalering. Administratie en Informatie, 0169-3069.*

ISSN 0300-3930
UK
Pr Rev.
LOCAL GOVERNMENT STUDIES. Added/Corp University of Birmingham. Institute of Local Government Studies. (Oct. 1971)-. Periodical. English. Four times a year. $195.00. Frank Cass & Company Ltd., Newbury House, 890-900 Eastern Avenue, Ilford Essex IG2 7HH United Kingdom. **Tel** 011 44 181 5998866, FAX 011 44 181 5990984, telex 897719. **ED** Kieron Walsh. **Bk Rev. Ad Acc, Adv Mgr:** Anne Kidson. **Circ:** 800. Documents available from The Genuine Article.
Desc: A management journal for those involved in the process of decision making and in the delivery of local services by local authorities, with an emphasis on policy and management control.
Ind/Abst Anbar Account. Finan. Abstr. [Full Txt.]; Anbar Mark. Distr. Abstr. [Full Txt.]; Anbar Top Manage. Abstr. [Full Txt.]; Appl. Soc. Sci. Index Abstr.; Br. Humanit. Index; Curr. Cit.; Curr. Contents Soc. Behav. Sci.; Int. Bibliogr. Sociol.; Manage. Bibliogr. Rev.; Oper. Prod. Manage. Abstr. [Full Txt.]; Person. Train. Abstr. [Full Txt.]; Res. Alert [Full Cov.]; School Organ. Manage. Abstr.; Soc. Sci. Cit. Index [Full Cov.]; Women Manage. Rev. [Full Txt.].

ISSN 1120-3587
IT
UDC 681.3
LOGISTICA MANAGEMENT. [Logist. manag.]. (1990)-. Trade Publication. Italian. Ten times a year. L83110. Edizioni Ritman, via Varesina 76, 20156 Milan Italy. **Tel** 011 39 2 38008859, FAX 011 39 2 66982686. **ED** Massimo Merlino. Index available. cum. index. **Bk Rev. Ad Acc. Circ:** 6,000 (ctrl).
Desc: Information on purchasing, materials handling, transportation and packaging.

ISSN 0394-4867
IT
UDC 658.7
LOGISTICA MILANO. [Logistica Milano]. (1970)-. Periodical. Italian. Twelve times a year. L143060. Tecniche Nuove SPA, Via Ciro Menotti 14, 20129 Milan Italy. **Tel** 011 39 2 75701, FAX 011 39 2 7570205, telex 334647 TECHS I. ***Continues*** *Magazzini & Trasporti, 0024-9874.*

LC HF5415.6 .L634 **ISSN** 0957-6053
DD 658.7/2/05 UK
CCC
CODEN LINMEC
LOGISTICS INFORMATION MANAGEMENT. See Library and Information Sciences.

LC TS155 **ISSN** 1353-5595
DD 658.5 UK
●**LOGISTICS MANAGER.** [Logist. manag.]. (1994)-. Periodical. English. Six times a year. £36.50. Seven Kings Publications Ltd., 26 High Street, Sutton Surrey SM1 1HW United Kingdom. **Tel** 011 44 181 6611160, FAX 011 44 181 6611173.

NE
LOGISTIEK KRANT. (19??)-. Dutch. Eleven times a year. $125.87. Misset Uitgeverij BV / Doetinchem, Postbus 4, 7000 BA Doetinchem Netherlands. **Tel** 011 31 8340 49911, 011 31 8340 49562, FAX 011 31 8340 43839, 011 31 8340 40515.

ISSN 0930-7834
GW
UDC [658.286 + 658.21] :65.012.122
LOGISTIK IM UNTERNEHMEN. [Logist. Unternehm.]. (1986)-. Trade Publication. German. Eight times a year. $195.75. VDI Verlag GmbH, Postfach 101054, D-40001 Dusseldorf Germany. **Tel** 011 49 211 6188313, FAX 011 49 211 6188133.

FR
LOGISTIQUES MAGAZINE. (19??)-. French. 360.00F France; 476.00F other. CEP Information Professions, 122 rue Edouard Vaillant, 92593 Levallois Per France. **Tel** 011 33 1 41341515.

LC HD1 .L6 **ISSN** 0024-6301
DD 658.4 UK
CCC
CODEN LRPJA4LRPDE4
Pr Rev.
LONG RANGE PLANNING. [Long range plan.]. **Added/Corp** Society for Long Range Planning. Society for Strategic and Long Range Planning. Strategic Planning Society. European Planning Federation. European Strategic Planning Federation. **VFOAT** International Journal of Strategic Management. (Sept. 1968)-. Academic Scholarly Publication. English. Six times a year. $724.00. Pergamon Press, An Imprint of Elsevier Science Ltd., The Boulevard, Langford Lane, Kidlington, Oxford OX5 1GB United Kingdom. **Tel** 011 44 1865 843000, 011 44 1865 843699, FAX 011 44 1865 843010. **(Subscription address:** Elsevier Science Ltd. / Oxford Fulfillment Centre, PO Box 800, Kidlington OX5 1DX United Kingdom. **Tel** 011 44 865 843355.**) ED** Bernard Taylor and John Grant. cum. index. available on microfilm and microfiche from University Microfilms International (UMI); available on microfiche from the publisher; available on an online database from Elsevier Electronic Subscriptions (EES). Documents available from Article Express International, The Genuine Article, UMI Article Clearinghouse, Documents on Demand.
Desc: Aims to focus the attention of senior managers, administrators, and academics on the concepts and techniques involved in the development and implementation of strategy and plans.
Ind/Abst ABI/INFORM Glob. Ed.; ABI/INFORM Ondisc: Expr. Ed.; ABI/INFORM [Computer File] (March 1972-); Acad. Search; Anbar Account. Finan. Abstr. [Full Txt.]; Anbar Mark. Distr. Abstr. [Full Txt.]; Anbar Top Manage. Abstr. [Full Txt.]; AQUAREF; Bioeng. Abstr.; Bus. Index (1985-); Bus. Period. Index; Bus. Source Plus; Bus. Source; Coal Abstr.; Commun. Abstr.; Contents Pages Manage.; Curr. Cit.; Curr. Contents Soc. Behav. Sci.; Curr. Lit. Sci. Sci.; Ei Page One; EMBASE; Energy Inf. Abstr.; Eng. Index Annu.; Environ. Abstr.; EP Collect.; Gen. BusinessFile (1985-); Gen. Period. Index (1985-); Health Plan. Adminis.; Homework Help.; Hosp. Health Admin. Index; Hum. Resour. Abstr.; INFO-SOUTH Abstr.;

Business and Economics —Management

Int. Dev. Abstr. (?-?); J. Plan. Lit.; Mag. Search; Manage. Market. Abstr.; Manage. Bibliogr. Rev.; MasterFile FullTEXT 1000; MasterFile FullTEXT 350; MasterFile FullTEXT 650; MasterFile FullTEXT (July 1994-); Middle East Abstr. Index; OCLC; Oper. Prod. Manage. Abstr. [Full Txt.]; PAIS Int. Print (1991-); Life Sci. Collect.; Person. Train. Abstr. [Full Txt.]; Res. Alert [Full Cov.]; Sage Fam. Stud. Abstr. (?-?); Sage Urban Stud. Abstr (?-?); Selec. Coop. Index Manage. Period.; Soc. Sci. Cit. Index [Full Cov.]; Telebase; Wilson Bus. Abstr.; Women Manage. Rev. [Full Txt.].

ISSN 1183-5451
DD 658.15 CN
MAGAZINE DES UTILISATEURS FORTUNE 1000. [Mag. util. Fortune 1000]. VAT Magazine des Utilisateurs Fortune One Thousand. Vol. 1, No 1 (April/May 1991)-. Periodical. French (summaries and/or abstracts in English). Twenty-four times a year. Limited Free Distribution. Magazine des Utilisateurs Fortune 1000, CP 8862, Sainte-Foy Quebec G1V 4N7 Canada.

ISSN 0827-5637
DD 658.2/02/05 CN
MAINTAINER (VANCOUVER). (THE MAINTAINER.). [Maintainer]. Vol. 1, No. 1 (Nov. 1984)-. Periodical. English. Twelve times a year. Free. Maintainer Publishing Company, 2-4725 Kingsway, Burnaby BC V5H 2C3 Canada.

ISSN 1080-188X
DD 331 US
●**MAINTENANCE MANAGEMENT.** [Maint. manag.]. **Added/Corp** Bureau of Business Practice. No. 2023 (Dec. 1994)-. Periodical. English. Twenty-four times a year. $129.48. Bureau of Business Practice, 24 Rope Ferry Road, Waterford CT 06386. **Tel** (800)243-0876, (203)442-4365, (800)876-9105, FAX (203)443-1123. **Continues** Maintenance Supervisor's Bulletin, 0194-5912.

ISSN 0167-5389
NE
CCC
CODEN MMINET
MAINTENANCE MANAGEMENT INTERNATIONAL. [Maint. manage. int.]. Vol. 3, No. 1 (May 1982)-. Academic Scholarly Publication. English. Four times a year. Fl250.00. Elsevier Science Publishers BV, PO Box 211, 1000 AE Amsterdam Netherlands. **Tel** 011 31 20 4853641, 011 31 20 4853642, FAX 011 31 20 4853598. **ED** W M J Geraerds, R F de la Mare, and F G Miller. available on microfilm and microfiche from University Microfilms International (UMI). **Continues** Terotechnica, 0378-5947.
Desc: Concerned with the maintenance of physical assets and the minimization of life-cycle costs.
Ind/Abst Energy Res. Abstr. (May 1982-); Eng. Mater. Abstr.; Int. Abstr. Oper. Res. [Select. Cov.]; Int. Build. Serv. Abstr.; Manage. Market. Abstr.; Text. Technol. Dig.

US
MAINTENANCE SUPERVISOR'S DEVELOPMENT PROGRAM. English. Sixty times a year. $148.32 (US); $182.40 (Canada) Includes : Maintenance Supervisor's Bulletin, Dynamic Supervision, and Supervisor's Memory Jogger. Bureau of Business Practice, 24 Rope Ferry Road, Waterford CT 06386. **Tel** (800)243-0876, (203)442-4365, (800)876-9105, FAX (203)443-1123.

LC HB9 .M29

IQ
MAJALLAT AL-BUHUTH AL-IQTISADIYAH WA-AL-IDARIYAH. See Business and Economics.

LC HD28 .M276 **ISSN 0025-1348**
MY
MALAYSIAN MANAGEMENT REVIEW. Vol. 1- (July 1966)-. Periodical. English. Four times a year. $23.67. Malaysian Institute of Management, Wisma HLA/7th Floor, Jalan Raja Chulan, 50200 Kuala Lumpur Malaysia. **Tel** 011 60 3 2425255, FAX 011 60 3 2425761, telex MA32643. **ED** Tarcisius Chin. **Ad Acc. Circ:** 5,000.

LC HD28 .M3 **ISSN 0025-1623**
DD 658.01 US
MANAGE. [Manage]. **Added/Corp** National Management Association (U.S.) National Association of Foremen. Vol. 1 (Sept. 1948)-. Periodical. English. Three times a year. $5.00. National Management Association, 2210 Arbor Boulevard, Dayton OH 45439. **Tel** (513)294-0421, FAX (513)294-2374. **ED** Douglas E. Shaw. **Bk Rev. Ad Acc. Circ:** 75,000 (err.). available on microfilm and microfiche from University Microfilms International (UMI); available on CD-ROM. Documents available from UMI Article Clearinghouse.
Desc: How-to articles aimed at middle managers: communication, stress management and interviewing skills.
Ind/Abst ABI/INFORM Glob. Ed.; ABI/INFORM [Computer File] (July 1975-); Acad. Search; Bus. ASAP (1990-) [Full Txt.]; Bus. Index (1985-); Bus. Source Plus; Curr. Cit.; EP Collect.; Gen. BusinessFile (1985-); Gen. Period. Index (1985-); Homework Help.; Mag. Search; MasterFile FullTEXT 1000; MasterFile FullTEXT 350;

MasterFile FullTEXT 650; MasterFile FullTEXT (July 1993-); OCLC; Telebase; UMI ABI/Inform--Bus. Period. Ondisc (Oct. 1987-) [Full Txt.]; Work Relat. Abstr.

IT
SUSPENDED
MANAGEMENT. (19??)-Suspended. Italian. Iniziative Editoriali, Via S Orsola 8, 20123 Milan Italy. **Tel** 011 39 2 89010360.

LC HD1 .M28 **ISSN 0377-1172**
DD 658.4/005 II
MANAGEMENT ABSTRACTS. Vol. 1 (Oct. 1972)-. Periodical. English. Four times a year. $12.00. All India Management Association, Management House, 14 Institutional Area Lodi Road, New Delhi-110003 India.

LC HF5686.C8 C684 **ISSN 0025-1682**
DD 657 UK
CODEN MATGBA
MANAGEMENT ACCOUNTING (LONDON). See Business and Economics-Accounting.

LC HF5686.C8 A27 **ISSN 0025-1690**
DD 658.1/552 US
CCC
CODEN MGACBD
MANAGEMENT ACCOUNTING (NEW YORK, N.Y.). See Business and Economics-Accounting.

LC HF5657 .M23 **ISSN 0065-8766**
DD 657.6 US
MANAGEMENT ADVISORY SERVICES: GUIDELINE SERIES. Added/Corp American Institute of Certified Public Accountants. Management Advisory Services Executive Committee. American Institute of Certified Public Accountants. Committee on Management Services. No. 1 (1968)-. Monographic series. English. Irregular. Price varies per volume. American Institute of Certified Public Accountants, Harborside Financial Center, #201 Plaza 3, Jersey City NJ 07311. **Tel** (201)938-3333, (800)862-4272, FAX (201)938-3329.

LC J674 .R194 **ISSN 0914-9007**
JA
MANAGEMENT & COORDINATION.
Added/Corp Japan. SomuchÂo. Japan. Somucho. Chokan Kanbo. Somuka. **VFOAT** Management and Coordination. No. 45 (1988)-. Periodical. Japanese. Twelve times a year. Somu Chokan Kanbo Somuka, c/o Chuo Godo Chosha Dai 4-Gokan 1-1, Kasumigaseki 3 Chiyoda-ku, Tokyo-to Japan. **Continues** Somucho, 0910-2310.

LC HD28 .M3217 **ISSN 0308-2172**
DD 658/.005 UK
CCC
Pr Rev.
MANAGEMENT & MARKETING ABSTRACTS. See Business and Economics-Abstracting, Bibliographies and Statistics.

ISSN 0025-1658
DD 650 NZ
CCC
MANAGEMENT AUCKLAND.
[ManagementAuckl.]. **VFOAT** Management for Business & Industry. (1955)-. Periodical. English. Eleven times a year. $107.43. Profile Publishing Ltd, PO Box 5544, Wellesley Street, Auckland New Zealand. **Tel** 011 64 9 3585455, FAX 011 64 9 3585462.
Ind/Abst EP Collect.; Homework Help.; MasterFile FullTEXT 1000; MasterFile FullTEXT 350; MasterFile FullTEXT 650; MasterFile FullTEXT; Telebase; World Mag. Bank.

LC HD28 .M3415 **ISSN 0360-7542**
DD 658.4 US
MANAGEMENT AWARENESS PROGRAM. No. 1- Sept./Oct. 1975-. English. McGraw Hill Publishing Company, Inc., 1221 Avenue of the Americas, New York NY 10020. **Tel** (212)512-6410, (800)525-5003, FAX (212)512-6111.

LC HD28 .M3417 **ISSN 0309-0582**
DD 658/.005 UK
MANAGEMENT BIBLIOGRAPHIES & REVIEWS. See Business and Economics-Abstracting, Bibliographies and Statistics.

US
MANAGEMENT BULLETINS. (19??)-. Bulletin. English. Irregular. Free. Securities Industry Association, 120 Broadway/35th Floor, New York NY 10271. **Tel** (212)608-1500, FAX (212)608-1604.
Desc: Special bulletins for the information and guidance of managers. Designed to alert firms to changes that could affect their business.

LC WMLC 93/1318 **ISSN 0893-3189**
DD 658 US
CCC
MANAGEMENT COMMUNICATION QUARTERLY. See Communications.

LC HG **ISSN 0383-7874**
DD 658/.91/33210971 CN
MANAGEMENT COMPENSATION IN CANADIAN BANKING & FINANCE. 1974/75-. Periodical. English. HV Chapman and Associates, 2 Bloor Street West/Suite 700, Toronto Ontario M4W 1B1 Canada. **Tel** (416)961-3000.

LC HD4965.5.U6 R53 **ISSN 0273-0332**
DD 331.2/81385 US
MANAGEMENT COMPENSATION, RAILROADS. See Transportation-Railroads.

UK
MANAGEMENT CONSULTANCY. (19??)-. Periodical. English. Twelve times a year. £45.00 UK; £65.00 (airmail) Europe; £55.00 (surface mail) other. VNU Business Publications BV, 32-34 Broadwick Street, London W1A 2HG United Kingdom. **Tel** 011 44 171 4394242 ext. 2222, FAX 011 44 171 4379638, telex 23918 VNU G, 8952440.

ISSN 0956-3253
IE
MANAGEMENT CONSULTANT INTERNATIONAL. [Manag. consult. int.]. (1988)-. Periodical. English. Ten times a year. $749.00. Lafferty Publications Ltd., Tower Ida Centre Pearse Street, Dublin 2 Ireland. **Tel** 011 353 1 6718022, FAX 011 353 1 718520.
Desc: Contains worldwide news and trends in the consultancy industry.

LC HD69.C6 M357 **ISSN 0741-3092**
DD 658.4/6 US
MANAGEMENT CONSULTING (BOSTON, MASS.). See Occupations and Careers.

US
MANAGEMENT CONTENTS [ONLINE DATABASE]. See Business and Economics-Abstracting, Bibliographies and Statistics.

ISSN 0302-9859
IO
MANAGEMENT DAN USAHAWAN INDONESIA. (MANAGEMENT & USAHAWAN INDONESIA). [Manage. usahawan Indones.]. **VFOAT** Majalah Management & Usahawan Indonesia. March/April 1981-. Periodical. Indonesian (English). Twelve times a year. Rp24.00 Indonesia; $14.24 US. Kepada Redaksi Dan Tata Usaha Majalah Management & Usahawan Indonesia, Jl Salemba Raya 4, PO Box 404, Jakarta Pusat Indonesia. **Tel** 330211. **ED** Dudhi Paramita, Bakir Hasan, Wagiono Ismangil, Heru Sutoyo, Goenawan A Wardhana, Wahjudi Prakarsa, Dorodjatun Kuntjoro, Jakti, Sofjan Assauri, Jazid Adam, Irzan Tanjun, and Kuta Ginting. **Bk Rev. Ad Acc. Circ:** 6,500.
Continues Management dan Usahawan Indonesia, 0302-9859.
Desc: Semi professional journal; popular management.

LC HD28 .M344 **ISSN 0025-1747**
UK
CCC
CODEN MANDA4
MANAGEMENT DECISION. [Manage. decis.]. **VFOAT** Bradford Review of Management Technology; Management Decision Monographs. (Spring 1967)-. Periodical. English. Nine times a year. $3639.00. MCB University Press, 60 62 Toller Lane, Bradford, West Yorkshire BD8 9BY United Kingdom. **Tel** 011 44 1274 785280, FAX 011 44 1274 785200, telex 51317-MCBUNI-G. (**Subscription address:** MCB University Press / US and Canada Subscriptions, PO Box 10812, Birmingham AL 35201-0812. **Tel** (205)995-1567, (800)633-4931, FAX (205)995-1588.) **ED** John Peters. available on an online database (file 15/Full-Text) from DIALOG. Documents available from UMI Article Clearinghouse, Ask*IEEE. **Continues** Scientific Business, 0582-2459.
Desc: Goal is to publish contributions that will help managers to perceive the benefits that increased professional skills can provide. The disciplines covered will give conceptual insights when applied to readers' own experience.
Ind/Abst ABI/INFORM Glob. Ed.; ABI/INFORM [Computer File] (Jan 1978-); Acad. Search; Anbar Account. Finan. Abstr. [Full Txt.]; Anbar Mark. Distr. Abstr. [Full Txt.]; Anbar Top Manage. Abstr. [Full Txt.]; Bus. Index (1985-); Bus. Period. Index (Jan. 1978-); Bus. Source Plus; Bus. Source; Contents Pages Manage.; Curr. Cit.; EP Collect.; Gen. BusinessFile (1985-); Gen. Period. Index (1985-); Homework Help.; INFO-SOUTH Abstr.; INSPEC (Spring 1970-); Int. Labour Doc.; Mag. Search; Manage. Market. Abstr. (1974-); Manage. Bibliogr. Rev.; Manage. Contents; MasterFile FullTEXT 1000; MasterFile FullTEXT 350; MasterFile FullTEXT 650; MasterFile FullTEXT (July 1993-); OCLC; Oper. Prod. Manage. Abstr. [Full Txt.]; Person. Train. Abstr.; Person. Train. Abstr. [Full Txt.]; Person. Manage. Abstr.; Selec. Coop. Index Manage. Period.; Telebase; Wilson Bus. Abstr.; Women Manage. Rev. [Full Txt.]; Work Relat. Abstr.

LC HD30.4 .T37
DD 658.4/071245/05 UK
MANAGEMENT DEVELOPMENT REVIEW. (199?)-. Periodical. English. Six times a year. $619.00 US; £189.00 UK. MCB University Press, 60 62 Toller Lane, Bradford, West Yorkshire BD8 9BY United Kingdom. **Tel** 011 44 1274 785280, FAX 011 44 1274 785200, telex 51317-MCBUNI-G. **(Subscription address:** MCB University Press / US and Canada Subscriptions, PO Box 10812, Birmingham AL 35201-0812. **Tel** (205)995-1567, (800)633-4931, FAX (205)995-1588.) ***Continues*** *Target Management Development Review, 0962-2519.*

SZ
MANAGEMENT DEVELOPMENT SERIES. **Added/Corp** International Labour Office. **VFOAT** MDS. No. 1, (1964)-. Monographic series. English. Irregular. Price varies per volume. International Labour Office - ILO, Publications Sales Service, CH-1211 Geneva 22 Switzerland. **Tel** 011 41 22 7996111, FAX 011 41 22 7986253, telex 415 647 ilo ch. **(Subscription address:** International Labor Office / Albany, NY, 49 Sheridan Avenue, Albany NY 12210. **Tel** (518)436-9686.)
Desc: Occasional monographs dealing with specialized management subjects.

ISSN 0025-164X
IE
MANAGEMENT (DUBLIN). (MANAGEMENT.). [Management]. **Added/Corp** Irish Management Institute. (1960)-. Periodical. English. Twelve times a year. $45.45. Jemma Publications Ltd, PO Box 1973, Rathmines Dublin 6 Ireland. **Tel** 011 353 1 4975500, FAX 011 353 1 4977190. **ED** Frank Dillon. **Ad Acc, Adv Mgr:** Roger Cole. **Circ:** 7,500. ***Continues*** *Irish Management.*
Ind/Abst Account. Index Suppl.; Gen. BusinessFile (1992-); Manage. Market. Abstr.

ISSN 1036-1138
AT
MANAGEMENT EDGE. (19??)-. English. Twelve times a year. 98.66Aus$. Information Edge, C State Library L10 Macquarie Street, Sydney New South Wales 2000 Australia. **Tel** 011 61 2 2301439.

LC HD20.15.G7 M32 **ISSN** 0047-5688
DD 658.4/007/1042 UK
TITLE CHANGE
MANAGEMENT EDUCATION AND DEVELOPMENT. [Manage. educ. dev.]. **Added/Corp** Association of Teachers of Management. **VFOAT** MEAD. (1970)-(1993). Periodical. English. Management Education & Development, University of Lancaster, Center for the Study of Mgt Learning, Lancaster LA1 4YX United Kingdom. **Tel** 011 44 1524 65201 ext 4011. **ED** Mike Pedler. Index available. cum. index. **Bk Rev. Circ:** 2,100 (ctrl). available on an online database (file 15/Full-Text) from DIALOG. ***Continued by*** *Management Learning, 1350-5076.*
Desc: Theory and practice of management development covering education establishments, industry and public sector. Major forum on cultural and international issues.
Ind/Abst Abstr. Res. Pastor. Care Couns. (19??-??); Anbar Account. Finan. Abstr. (?-?) [Full Txt.]; Anbar Mark. Distr. Abstr. (?-?) [Full Txt.]; Anbar Top Manage. Abstr. (?-?) [Full Txt.]; Br. Educ. Index (?-?); Contents Pages Manage. (?-?); Curr. Cit.; Curr. Index J. Educ. (?-?); Educ. Technol. Abstr. (?-?); Manage. Market. Abstr. (?-?); Manage. Bibliogr. Rev. (?-?); Oper. Prod. Manage. Abstr. (?-?) [Full Txt.]; Person. Train. Abstr. (?-?) [Full Txt.]; Psychol. Abstr. (1981-?); PsycINFO (?-?); PsycLit (?-?); School Organ. Manage. Abstr. (?-?); Selec. Coop. Index Manage. Period. (?-?); Stud. Women Abstr. (?-?); Tech. Educ. Train. Abstr. (?-?); Women Manage. Rev. (?-?) [Full Txt.]; Work Relat. Abstr. (?-?).

ISSN 1157-5662
FR
UDC 658(44)
MANAGEMENT ET CONJONCTURE SOCIALE PARIS. (MANAGEMENT ET CONJONCTURE SOCIALE.). (1991)-. Periodical. French. Twenty-four times a year. $803.34. MCS / Management et Conjoncture Sociale, 54 rue Saint Lazare, 75009 Paris France. **Tel** 011 33 1 40829162, FAX 011 33 1 47640982. ***Continues*** *Notes de Conjoncture Sociale, 0767-1121.*

US
MANAGEMENT HORIZONS. Vol. 1, No. 1 (Sept./Oct. 1969)-. Periodical. English. Four times a year. Kansas State University / Business, College of Business, Manhattan KS 66502. ***Continues*** *Kansas. State University of Agriculture and Applied Science. College of Commerce. College of Commerce Management Letters.*

LC JK1672 .M345
DD 353.007/1 US
MANAGEMENT IMPROVEMENT AND COST REDUCTION GOALS. **See** Public Administration.

NE
MANAGEMENT INFO. English. Irregular. Media Group, Postbus 568, 7600 AN Almelo The Netherlands. **Tel** 011 04390 25357.

US
MANAGEMENT INFORMATION REPORT / OFFICE OF FINANCIAL MANAGEMENT. May 1984-. English. Four times a year. Office of Financial Management, Insurance Building AQ-44, Olympia WA 98504. **Tel** (206)456-4775. ***Continues*** *Washington (State). Office of Financial Management. Monthly Fiscal Report.*

LC HD28 .M357 **ISSN** 0300-2667
DD 658.4/00954 II
MANAGEMENT INFORMATION SERVICE. [Manage. inf. serv.]. **Added/Corp** University of Cochin. Foundation for Management Education. (19??)-. Periodical. English. Irregular. Rs50.00. University of Cochin, Foundation for Management Education, Cochin India.

LC HD28 .M36 **ISSN** 0025-181X
DD 658/.005 GW
CCC
CODEN MINRAY
Pr Rev. **TITLE CHANGE**
MANAGEMENT INTERNATIONAL REVIEW. [Manage. int. rev.]. **Added/Corp** European Foundation for Management Development. (1966)-(19??). Academic Scholarly Publication. English. Gabler Verlag, Postfach 1546, D-65005 Wiesbaden Germany. **Tel** 011 49 611 534129, FAX 011 49 611 534430. **(Subscription address:** VVA Bertelsmann Distributors GmbH, Postfach 7600, D-33310 Guetersloh Germany. **Tel** 011 49 5241 803294.) Index available (free). cum. index. **Bk Rev. Ad Acc. Circ:** 1,200. available on microfilm and microfiche from University Microfilms International (UMI). Documents available from UMI Article Clearinghouse. ***Continues*** *Management International.* ***Continued by*** *MIR. Management International Review, 0938-8249.*
Desc: Aims at the advancement and dissemination of international applied research in the fields of management and business.
Ind/Abst ABI/INFORM Glob. Ed.; ABI/INFORM [Computer File] (April 1972-); Anbar Account. Finan. Abstr. [Full Txt.]; Anbar Mark. Distr. Abstr. [Full Txt.]; Anbar Top Manage. Abstr. [Full Txt.]; Bus. ASAP (1992-) [Full Txt.]; Bus. Index (1985-); Bus. Period. Index; Contents Pages Manage.; Curr. Cit.; EMBASE; Gen. BusinessFile (1985-); Gen. Period. Index (1985-); INFO-SOUTH Abstr.; Int. Exec.; Mag. Search; Manage. Market. Abstr.; Manage. Bibliogr. Rev.; Manage. Contents; Middle East Abstr. Index; Oper. Prod. Manage. Abstr. [Full Txt.]; PAIS Int. Print (1991-?); Person. Train. Abstr. [Full Txt.]; Selec. Coop. Index Manage. Period.; UMI ABI/Inform--Bus. Period. Ondisc (Spring 1987-) [Full Txt.]; Wilson Bus. Abstr.; Women Manage. Rev. [Full Txt.]; Work Relat. Abstr.

ISSN 0025-1828
JA
MANAGEMENT JAPAN. **Added/Corp** Sekai Keiei Kyogikai (Japan). (1967)-. Periodical. English. Two times a year. $42.00. **(Subscription address:** Japan Publications Trading Company Ltd., PO Box 5030, Tokyo International, Tokyo 100-31 Japan. **Tel** 011 81 3 3292 3753.) **ED** M. Horie. **Ad Acc. Circ:** 10,000. Documents available from UMI Article Clearinghouse.
Desc: Covers the management philosophy of top management in Japanese companies, scientific research on management style in Japan, and management practice commonly observed among Japanese enterprises.
Ind/Abst ABI/INFORM Glob. Ed.; ABI/INFORM [Computer File] (Spring 1983-); Acad. Search; Anbar Account. Finan. Abstr. [Full Txt.]; Anbar Mark. Distr. Abstr. [Full Txt.]; Anbar Top Manage. Abstr. [Full Txt.]; Bus. Index (1985-); Bus. Source Plus; Bus. Source; Curr. Cit.; EP Collect.; Gen. BusinessFile (1985-); Gen. Period. Index (1985-); Homework Help.; INFO-SOUTH Abstr.; Mag. Search; Manage. Market. Abstr.; Manage. Bibliogr. Rev.; MasterFile FullTEXT 1000; MasterFile FullTEXT 350; MasterFile FullTEXT 650; MasterFile FullTEXT (July 1993-); OCLC; Oper. Prod. Manage. Abstr. [Full Txt.]; Person. Train. Abstr. [Full Txt.]; Telebase; Trade Ind. Index; Women Manage. Rev. [Full Txt.].

LC HD70.U35 M35 **ISSN** 0300-2144
DD 658.4/009676/1 UY
MANAGEMENT JOURNAL. [Manage. j.]. Periodical. English. Management Training and Advisory Center, PO Box 4655, Kampala Uruguay.

LC HD28 .M3213
DD 658/.009676/2 KE
MANAGEMENT (KENYA INSTITUTE OF MANAGEMENT). (MANAGEMENT : JOURNAL OF THE KENYA INSTITUTE OF MANAGEMENT.). (19??)-. Periodical. English. Twelve times a year. Oryx Publications Ltd, Finlay House, Mfangano Street, PO Box 40106, Nairobi Kenya.

US
MANAGEMENT LAURETES: A COLLECTION OF AUTOBIOGRAPHICAL ESSAYS. English. $86.25. JAI Press Inc., 55 Old Post Road, Suite 2, PO Box 1678, Greenwich CT 06836-1678. **Tel** (203)661-7602, FAX (203)661-0792. **ED** Arthur Bedian.
Desc: Covers people and ideas who have influenced the course of management teaching and practice.

LC HD20.15.G7 M32 **ISSN** 1350-5076
DD 658.4/007/1042 UK
•**MANAGEMENT LEARNING.** **See** Industry and Production.

US
MANAGEMENT MEMO. (19??)-. Bulletin. English. Twenty-six times a year. $44.20. Economics Press Inc, 12 Daniel Road, Fairfield NJ 07004. **Tel** (201)227-1224, (800)526-2554, FAX (201)227-9742.
Desc: Covers one management principle every issue. Focuses on the ideas that have proven to be effective in business leadership.

BE
MANAGEMENT MEMO. Dutch. Irregular. 19800.00F. Centrum Bedrijsinformatie, Brouwersvliet 5 Bus 4, 2000 Antwerpen Belgium. Index available.

NE
MANAGEMENT MONITOR / NCD. Periodical. Dutch. Irregular. Libresso BV, Postbus 878, 7400 GA Deventer Netherlands. **Tel** 011 31 5700 47421.

ISSN 0943-6707
GW
UDC 33
MANAGEMENT MORGEN. [Manag. morgen]. (1992)-. Periodical. German. Four times a year. Verlag WWT / Verlag fuer Wissenschaft, Wirtschaft und Technik GmbH und Co., Postfach 242, Ambergstrasse 22, 38667 Bad Harzburg Germany. **Tel** 011 49 5322 73333, telex 957623 DVGD. ***Continues*** *Management Heute (1976), 0343-3994.*

ISSN 1039-4729
DD 658.0099405 AT
•**MANAGEMENT (NORTH SYDNEY).** (MANAGEMENT.). [Management (North Syd.)]. **Added/Corp** Stralian Institute of Management N.S.W Stralian Institute of Management - Victoria. (1993)-. Periodical. English. Ten times a year. 41.11Aus$. North Sydney Australian Institute of Management, PO Box 328, North Sydney 2059 Australia. **Tel** 011 61 02 9563048, FAX 011 61 02 9565613. **ED** Cathy Gordon. ***Formed by the union of*** *AIM (North Sydney), 0817-5713* ***and*** *Management Review (St. Kilda), 0313-0835.*

UK
MANAGEMENT OF VOLUNTARY ORGANISATIONS. **See** Philanthropy.

LC HD28 .M383
DD 658/.005 PK
MANAGEMENT PAKISTAN, THE. Vol. 1 (March/Apr. 1978)-. Periodical. English. Rs60.00 Pakistan; $18.00 US. M/S Baig Bros, PIIA Building/2nd Floor, Aiwan E Saddar Road, Karachi Pakistan.

ISSN 0923-375X
NE
UDC 658
MANAGEMENT PARTNER. [Manag. partn.]. (1989)-. Periodical. English. Seventeen times a year. Fl135.00. Samsom Bedrijfsinformatie BV, Postbus 4, 2400 MA Alphen Rij Netherlands. **Tel** 011 31 1720 66633. **(Subscription address:** Intermedia BV, Postbus 4, 2400 MA Alphen AD Rijn Netherlands. **Tel** 011 31 1720 66481.)

ISSN 1050-2114
DD 658 US
MANAGEMENT PORTFOLIO. [Manage. portf.]. **Added/Corp** Printing Industries of America. (1989)-. Trade Publication. English. Twelve times a year. $40.00. Printing Industries of America, 100 Daingerfield Road, Alexandria VA 22314. **Tel** (703)519-8100. **ED** Cliff Weiss. **Circ:** 10,000.
Desc: Covers new and information for managers of graphic arts businesses.
Ind/Abst Abstr. Bull. Inst. Pap. Sci. Tech.

LC HD28 .M14 **ISSN** 0025-1860
DD 658.005 US
CODEN MQMQAE
MANAGEMENT QUARTERLY. (MANAGEMENT QUARTERLY : MQ.). [Manage. q.]. **Added/Corp** National Rural Electric Cooperative Association. Management Services Dept. **VFOAT** MQ. Vol. 1, (Summer 1960)-. Periodical. English. Four times a year (Jan., Apr., July, Oct.). $50.00. National Rural Electric Cooperative Association, 4301 Wilson Boulevard, 10th Floor, Arlington VA 22203. **Tel** (703)907-5578. **ED** June B. Lane. **Bk Rev. Circ:** 7,200. available on microfilm and microfiche from University Microfilms International (UMI). Documents available from UMI Article Clearinghouse.
Desc: A journal of general management and specific utility management issues including information on rates, consumer relations, marketing, employee relations and purchasing.
Ind/Abst ABI/INFORM Glob. Ed.; ABI/INFORM [Computer File] (Spring 1982-); Acad. Search; Bus. ASAP (1992-) [Full Txt.]; Bus. Index (1985-); Bus. Source Plus;

Bus. Source; Curr. Cit.; EP Collect.; Gen. BusinessFile (1985-); Gen. Period. Index (1985-); Homework Help.; INFO-SOUTH Abstr.; Mag. Search; Manage. Contents; MasterFile FullTEXT 1000; MasterFile FullTEXT 350; MasterFile FullTEXT 650; MasterFile FullTEXT (July 1993-); OCLC; Telebase; UMI ABI/Inform--Bus. Period. Ondisc (Fall 1987-) [Full Txt.]; Work Relat. Abstr.

LC JK1672 .M35 **ISSN** 0091-6242
DD 353.007/1 US

MANAGEMENT REPORT - GENERAL SERVICES ADMINISTRATION. **See** Public Administration.

ISSN 0140-9174
UK

MANAGEMENT RESEARCH NEWS : MRN. **VFOAT** MRN. (19??)-. Periodical. English. Twelve times a year. $1289.00. MCB University Press, 60 62 Toller Lane, Bradford, West Yorkshire BD8 9BY United Kingdom. **Tel** 011 44 1274 785280, FAX 011 44 1274 785200, telex 51317-MCBUNI-G. **(Subscription address:** MCB University Press / US and Canada Subscriptions, PO Box 10812, Birmingham AL 35201-0812. **Tel** (205)995-1567, (800)633-4931, FAX (205)995-1588.**)** **ED** Barrie O Pettman. Documents available from UMI Article Clearinghouse.
Desc: Provides the link between the academic world and the practising manager whether in industry or public service. Provides precise, coherent and readable information - making it a source of reference material for today's busy, practising manager.
Ind/Abst ABI/INFORM Glob. Ed.; Curr. Cit.; Manage. Market. Abstr.

US

MANAGEMENT REVIEW. **Main/Corp** United States. Dept. of Agriculture. Science and Education Administration. Federal Research. No. 2; April 1978-. Periodical. English. Twelve times a year. US Department of Agriculture / Agricultural Research Service / Maryland, Hyattsville MD 20782. **ED** Kristine Vandertop. **Bk Rev. Ad Acc. Circ:** 8,100 (ctrl).
Desc: Development and practice of management. Articles of relevance to practising managers covering all areas of management.
Ind/Abst Book Rev. Index; Oper. Res./Manage. Sci.; Qual. Control Appl. Stat.

AT

MANAGEMENT S.A. Bulletin. English. Ten times a year. 15.00Aus$. Australian Institute of Management, 224 Hindley Street, Adelaide South Australia 5000 Australia. **Tel** 011 61 8 2123166, FAX 08 231 2414. **Ad Acc, Adv Mgr:** Pauline Fowles.

LC HD28 .I453 **ISSN** 0025-1909
DD 658.1082 US
CCC
CODEN MSCIAM

Pr Rev.

MANAGEMENT SCIENCE. [Manage. sci.]. **Added/Corp** Institute of Management Sciences. Institute of Management Sciences. Bulletin of the Institute of Management Sciences. Vol. 1 (Oct. 1954)-. Trade Publication. English. Twelve times a year. $192.00. Institute of Management Sciences, 290 Westminster Street, Providence RI 02903. **Tel** (401)274-2525, FAX (401)274-3189. **ED** Gabriel R. Bitran. cum. index. **Ad Acc. Circ:** 9,500. available on microfilm and microfiche from University Microfilms International (UMI). Documents available from Article Express International, The Genuine Article, Ask*IEEE, UMI Article Clearinghouse. ***Absorbed*** *Management Technology.*
Desc: Provides an interchange of information between management and management scientists in industry, academia, the military and government.
Ind/Abst ABI/INFORM Glob. Ed.; ABI/INFORM [Computer File] (Dec. 1971-); Acad. Search; ACM Guide Comput. Lit.; Bioeng. Abstr.; Bus. Index (1985-); Bus. Period. Index; Bus. Source Plus; Bus. Source; Coal Abstr.; CompuMath Cit. Index [Full Cov.]; Comput. Rev.; Contents Pages Manage.; Crim. Justice Abstr.; Curr. Contents Soc. Behav. Sci.; Educ. Adm. Abstr. (?-?); Ei Page One; Eng. Index Annu. [Select. Cov.]; EP Collect.; Gen. BusinessFile (1985-); Gen. Period. Index (1985-); High. Educ. Abstr. (1987-); Highw. Res. Abstr.; Homework Help.; Hum. Resour. Abstr. (?-?); INFO-SOUTH Abstr.; INSPEC (Nov. 1969-); Int. Abstr. Oper. Res. [Full Cov.]; Int. Aerosp. Abstr.; J. Plan. Lit.; Mag. Search; Manage. Contents; MasterFile FullTEXT 1000; MasterFile FullTEXT 350; MasterFile FullTEXT 650; MasterFile FullTEXT (July 1994-); Math. Rev. (?-199?); Middle East Abstr. Index; OCLC; Oper. Res./Manage. Sci.; Peace Res. Abstr. J. (1962-1963); Qual. Control Appl. Stat.; Res. Alert [Full Cov.]; Selec. Coop. Index Manage. Period.; Soc. Plann. Policy Dev. Abstr.; Soc. Sci. Cit. Index [Full Cov.]; SportSearch; Stat. Theory Method Abstr. (1959-1963, 1971, 1977, 1982-1983); Tech. Educ. Train. Abstr.; Telebase; UMI ABI/Inform--Bus. Period. Ondisc (Jan. 1987-) [Full Txt.]; Wilson Bus. Abstr.; Zentralbl. Math. Ihre Grenzgeb.

ISSN 0307-6768
UK
CODEN MASEDZ

MANAGEMENT SERVICES (ENFIELD). (MANAGEMENT SERVICES.). [Manage. serv.]. **Added/Corp** Institute of Management Services (Great Britain) Institute of Practitioners in Work Study, Organisation, and Methods (Great Britain). Vol. 20 (Jan. 1976)-. Trade Publication. English. Twelve times a year. $92.40. Institute of Management Services, 1 Cecil Court, London Road, Enfield, Middlesex EN2 6DD United Kingdom. **Tel** 011 44 181 3637452, FAX 011 44 181 3678149. **ED** David Charlton. **Ad Acc. Circ:** 9,000. available on microfilm and microfiche from University Microfilms International (UMI). Documents available from Ask*IEEE, UMI Article Clearinghouse. ***Continues*** *Work Study and Management Services, 0043-8030.*
Ind/Abst ABI/INFORM Glob. Ed.; ABI/INFORM [Computer File] (Jan. 1983-); Curr. Cit.; INSPEC (Jan. 1976-); Manage. Market. Abstr.; Oper. Prod. Manage. Abstr. [Full Txt.]; Selec. Coop. Index Manage. Period.; UMI ABI/Inform--Bus. Period. Ondisc (Nov. 1987-) [Full Txt.]; Work Relat. Abstr.

ISSN 0889-9444
DD 363 US

MANAGEMENT STRATEGY. **See** Leisure and Recreation-Outdoor Recreation.

LC HD7103.65.U6 M35 **ISSN** 0748-6316
DD 368.4/1012 US

MANAGEMENT SUMMARY. **See** Insurance.

LC T58.6 .M3565 **ISSN** 0736-5225
DD 658.4/038/05 US

MANAGEMENT TECHNOLOGY (NEW YORK, N.Y. : 1983). (MANAGEMENT TECHNOLOGY.). [Manage. technol.]. Vol. 1, No. 1 (May 1983)-. Periodical. English. Twelve times a year. $36.00 US; $48.00 Canada. International Thomson Organization, 345 Park Avenue/6th Floor, New York NY 10010-1706. **Tel** (212)686-7744.

LC HD70.G7 M32 **ISSN** 0025-1925
DD 658 UK
CCC
CODEN MANTAI

MANAGEMENT TODAY. [Manage. today]. (Apr. 1966)-. Trade Publication. English. Twelve times a year. $147.16. Haymarket Publishing Ltd., 12 14 Ansdell Street, London W8 5TR United Kingdom. **Tel** 011 44 171 9380705, 011 44 171 2786686, FAX 011 44 171 9380772. **(Subscription address:** Haymarket Magazines Ltd., PO Box 219, Subscription Department, Woking Surrey GU21 1ZW United Kingdom. **Tel** 011 44 1483 776345.**)** **Bk Rev. Ad Acc. Circ:** 77,024 (ctrl). available on microfilm and microfiche from University Microfilms International (UMI); available on an online database (files 15,647,648,771,772,799/Full-Text) from DIALOG. Documents available from UMI Article Clearinghouse. ***Supersedes*** *Manager (London, England).*
Desc: A business management magazine for the United Kingdom.
Ind/Abst ABI/INFORM Glob. Ed.; ABI/INFORM [Computer File] (Sept. 1972-); Acad. Search; Anbar Account. Finan. Abstr. [Full Txt.]; Anbar Mark. Distr. Abstr. [Full Txt.]; Anbar Top Manage. Abstr. [Full Txt.]; BMT Abstr. (-199?); Br. Humanit. Index (Sept. 1972-); Bus. ASAP (1990-) [Full Txt.]; Bus. Index (1985-); Bus. Period. Index; Bus. Source Plus; Bus. Source; Contents Pages Manage.; Curr. Cit.; EMBASE; EP Collect.; F&S Index Plus Text, Int. [Select. Cov.]; Gen. BusinessFile (1985-); Gen. Period. Index (1985-); Homework Help.; Index Bus. Reports; INFO-SOUTH Abstr.; Int. Labour Doc.; Mag. ASAP Plus [Full Txt.]; Mag. Index Plus (1989-); Mag. Search; Manage. Market. Abstr.; Manage. Bibliogr. Rev.; MasterFile FullTEXT 1000; MasterFile FullTEXT 350; MasterFile FullTEXT 650; MasterFile FullTEXT (July 1993-); Newsp. Period. Abstr. (1988-); OCLC; Person. Train. Abstr. [Full Txt.]; PROMT; Res. High. Educ. Abstr. (1981-); School Organ. Manage. Abstr. (1966-); Selec. Coop. Index Manage. Period.; Telebase; Mag. Index (1977-); Trade Ind. ASAP [Full Txt.]; Trade Ind. Index (1981-) [Full Txt.]; UMI ABI/Inform--Bus. Period. Ondisc (Nov. 1987-) [Full Txt.]; Wilson Bus. Abstr.; Women Manage. Rev. [Full Txt.]; Work Relat. Abstr. (1974-); World Ceram. Abstr.; World Text. Abstr.

ISSN 0771-9833
BE

MANAGER GENT. [Manager Gent]. (1979)-. Periodical. French. Ten times a year. Uitgeverij Reynaert, Communicatie Zuidstraat 30-32, 9000 Ghent Belgium. **Tel** 011 32 91 241980.

LC HD28 .M416 **ISSN** 0341-4418
GW

MANAGER MAGAZIN. [Manager-Mag.]. **VFOAT** Manager. (1971)-. Periodical. German. Twelve times a year. DM108.00 Germany; DM138.00 other. Manager Magazin Verlag GmbH, Postfach 111060, Brandstwiete 19, W2000 Hamburg 11 Germany. **Tel** 011 49 40 3007551, FAX 011 49 40 3007247, telex 841 2162477. Documents available from UMI Article Clearinghouse.
Ind/Abst ABI/INFORM Glob. Ed.; ABI/INFORM [Computer File] (Jan. 1981-); Coal Abstr.; Curr. Cit.

ISSN 1187-4147
DD 383 CN

MANAGER NEWSLETTER. (CADRES, BULLETIN D'INFORMATION.). [Manag. newsl.]. **Added/Corp** Societe Canadienne des Postes. **VFOAT** Manager Newsletter. Vol. 1, No 1 (Jun 1991)-. Bulletin. French (English). Irregular. ***Continues*** *Cadres (Ottawa, Ont.)., 0846-5843.*

LC HD28 .M423 **ISSN** 0957-4212
DD 338 UK

MANAGER UPDATE. **Added/Corp** Henley--The Management College. Vol. 1, No. 1 (Autumn 1989)-. Periodical. English. Four times a year. ***Continues*** *Management Update (Henley-on-Thames, England).*
Ind/Abst Curr. Cit.; Work Relat. Abstr.

LC HG4001 .M36 **ISSN** 0307-4358
DD 658.15/05 UK
CCC

MANAGERIAL FINANCE. **See** Business and Economics-Banks and Banking.

II

MANAGERIAL PSYCHOLOGY. **See** Psychology.

US

MANAGERS AS LEADERS. (19??)-. English. $19.95 per copy. Harvard Business School Publishing Division, Operations Department, 60 Harvard Way, Boston MA 02163. **Tel** (617)495-6192, (617)495-8948, FAX (617)495-6891, telex 6817229. **(Subscription address:** McGraw Hill / Pennsylvania, 13311 Monterey Avenue, Blue Ridge Summit PA 17294. **Tel** (800)233-1128.**)**

US

MANAGER'S DEVELOPMENT PROGRAM. English. Irregular. $135.36 (US); $165.96 (Canada) Includes: BBP Management Letter and Supervisor's Memory Jogger. Bureau of Business Practice, 24 Rope Ferry Road, Waterford CT 06386. **Tel** (800)243-0876, (203)442-4365, (800)876-9105, FAX (203)443-1123.

US

MANAGER'S INTELLIGENCE REPORT. (19??)-. Newsletter. English. Twelve times a year. $97.00. Ragan Communications Inc., 212 West Superior Street, Suite 200, Chicago IL 60610. **Tel** (312)335-0037, (800)878-5331, FAX (312)335-9583.
Desc: Full of tips for managers including tactics for managing meetings, techniques for boosting morale, strategies on hiring, promoting, firing, planning your work week and more.

LC HD30.2 .M3 **ISSN** 0895-3805
DD 650 US

MANAGING AUTOMATION. **See** Business and Economics-Computer Applications.

ISSN 1065-3937
DD 362 US
CCC

NLM W1; MA58TM

MANAGING EMPLOYEE HEALTH BENEFITS. [Manag. empl. health benefits]. (1992)-. Periodical. English. Four times a year. $150.50. Panel Publishers, A Division of Aspen Publishers Inc., 7201 McKinney Circle, PO Box 990, Frederick MD 21705-9727. **Tel** (800)638-8437. **(Subscription address:** Aspen Publishers Inc., PO Box 990, Frederick MD 21701. **Tel** (800)901-9074, (301)698-7100.**)** **ED** Mark Lutes, Esq., Ann Leopold, Esq. and Epstein, Becker & Green, P.C.

LC Z674.2 .M36 **ISSN** 1352-0229
UK
CODEN MAIOEG

•**MANAGING INFORMATION.** **Added/Corp** ASLIB. (1994)-. Trade Publication. English. Ten times a year. $74.00. ASLIB, Information House, 20-24 Old Street, London EC1V 9AP United Kingdom. **Tel** 011 44 171 2534488, FAX 011 44 171 4300514, telex 23667 AJLIB G. ***Continues*** *ASLIB Information, 0305-0033.*
Ind/Abst Curr. Cit.

LC HF5547.A2 M6 **ISSN** 1070-4051
DD 651/.05 US
CCC
CODEN MOTEE3

•**MANAGING OFFICE TECHNOLOGY.** [Manag. off. technol.]. **VFOAT** Modern Office Technology. Vol. 38, No. 6 (June 1993)-. Trade Publication. English. Twelve times a year. $45.00. Penton Publishing, 1100 Superior Avenue, Cleveland OH 44114-2543. **Tel** (216)696-7000, FAX (216)696-0836. **(Subscription address:** Penton Publishing, PO Box 96732, Chicago IL 60693. **)** Documents available from Ask*IEEE, UMI Article Clearinghouse. ***Continues*** *Modern Office Technology, 0746-3839;* ***Absorbed*** *Office.*
Ind/Abst ABI/INFORM [Computer File]; Acad. Abstr.; Acad. Search; Bus. Period. Index; Bus. Source Plus; Bus. Source; Consum. Index Prod. Eval. Inf. Source; Curr. Cit.; Electron. Pub. Abstr.; EP Collect.; Homework Help.; INSPEC; Manage. Contents; MasterFile FullTEXT 1000; MasterFile FullTEXT 350; MasterFile FullTEXT 650;

Business and Economics —Management

MasterFile FullTEXT (Nov. 1993-); OCLC; Pub. Lib. FullTEXT; Telebase; Mag. Index; Trade Ind. Index; Vocat. Search.

UK

MANAGING SERVICE QUALITY. (19??)-. English. Six times a year. $439.00. MCB University Press, 60 62 Toller Lane, Bradford, West Yorkshire BD8 9BY United Kingdom. **Tel** 011 44 1274 785280, FAX 011 44 1274 785200, telex 51317-MCBUNI-G. **(Subscription address:** MCB University Press / US and Canada Subscriptions, PO Box 10812, Birmingham AL 35201-0812. **Tel** (205)995-1567, (800)633-4931, FAX (205)995-1588.**)**

ISSN 1062-3310
DD 658 US

MANAGING TECHNOLOGY TODAY. [Manag. technol. today]. **Added/Corp** Technology Management Institute. Institute of Industrial Engineers (1981-). Vol. 1, No. 1 (May 1992)-. Periodical. English. Four times a year (published within the seasons). $49.00, $99.00 (library). Quality Observer Corporation, PO Box 1111, Fairfax VA 22030. **Tel** (703)691-9496, (703)691-9295, FAX (703)691-9399. **ED** Kay Moore. **Ad Acc.** ctrl circ.

LC HD183.L3 U54A
DD 353.0071/32/05 US

MANAGING THE NATION'S PUBLIC LANDS : A PROGRAM REPORT PREPARED PURSUANT TO REQUIREMENTS OF THE FEDERAL LAND POLICY AND MANAGEMENT ACT OF 1976. **Main/Corp** United States. Bureau of Land Management. Government Publication. English. One time a year. US Department of the Interior Bureau of Land Management, 1849 C Street NW, Room 5660, Washington DC 20240. **Tel** (202)208-3801, FAX (202)208-5902.

LC HD28 .M4167
IO

MANAJEMEN. **Added/Corp** Lembaga Pendidikan dan Pembinaan Manajemen. No. Identification (Aug. 17, 1980)-. Periodical. Indonesian. Six times a year. Rp14,000. Centre for Oceanological Research and Development Alamat, Jl Pasir Putih I, Ancol Timur, PO Box 580, DAK Jakarta 11001 Indonesia. **Tel** 011 62 21 683850, telex 62875 PDII IA.

LC HD30.28 .K35 ISSN 0149-8258
DD 658.4/01/0973 US

MANUAL OF MANAGEMENT ASSUMPTIONS FOR PLANNING BUSINESS STRATEGIES. **VFOAT** Business Strategies. (19??)-. Periodical. English. One time a year. Corporate Planning Inc, 2456 Northeast 26th Street, Lighthouse Port FL 33064. **Tel** (305)942-3226.

LC HF5415.2 .M3535a
HU

●**MARKETING & MENEDZSMENT : THE HUNGARIAN JOURNAL OF MARKETING AND MANAGEMENT.** **See** Business and Economics-Marketing and Purchasing.

US

MARKETING FORUM / AMERICAN MANAGEMENT ASSOCIATION. **See** Business and Economics-Marketing and Purchasing.

LC WMLC L 82/282
AU

MARKT, DER. **See** Business and Economics-Marketing and Purchasing.

LC HF5415.2 .M36 ISSN 0933-7105
GW

MARKTFORSCHUNG & MANAGEMENT. **See** Business and Economics-Marketing and Purchasing.

LC HF5468.A1 S9
DD 658.8/00973 US

MASS RETAILING MERCHANDISER. Vol. 78, No. 6 (June 1972)-. Periodical. English. Twelve times a year. Mass Retailing Merchandiser, 222 W Adams Street, Chicago IL 60606. **Continues** Merchandiser.

LC TS161 .M39 ISSN 0196-8211
DD 658.7/05 US

MATERIALS MANAGEMENT & PHYSICAL DISTRIBUTION ABSTRACTS. [Mater. manage. phys. distrib. abstr.]. **Added/Corp** Materials Management Services. **VFOAT** MM & PDA. **VAT** Materials Management and Physical Distribution Abstracts. Vol. 1 (Apr. 1980)-. English. Six times a year. $179.00 US; $189.00 Canada and Mexico; $199.00 other. Materials Management Services, PO Box 75, Allen TX 75002.

LC HF5437.A2
II

MATERIALS-MANAGEMENT JOURNAL OF INDIA. Periodical. English. Irregular. Hindustan Book Agency, 17 UB Jawahar Nagar, Delhi 7 India. **Absorbed** Eastern Purchasing Journal.

US

MAYORS MANAGEMENT REPORT. English. Two times a year. $17.25. CityBooks/ City Publishing Center, Department of General Services, 2208 Municipal Building, 22nd Floor, New York NY 10007. **Tel** (212)669-8245, FAX (212)669-3211.

ISSN 1060-4669
DD 650 US

MBA CAREER GUIDE, THE. [MBA career guide]. (19??)-. Periodical. English. Two times a year. $18.50. MBA Career Guide / Snyder Center, Vance Hall, 3733 Spruce Street, Philadelphia PA 19104. **Tel** (215)898-0018.

ISSN 1062-1989
DD 378 US

MCGRAW-HILL DIRECTORY OF MANAGEMENT FACULTY, THE. [McGraw-Hill dir. manag. fac.]. **VFOAT** Directory of Management Faculty. 1st Ed. (1991-1992)-. Directory. English. McGraw Hill Publishing Company, Inc., 1221 Avenue of the Americas, New York NY 10020. **Tel** (212)512-6410, (800)525-5003, FAX (212)512-6111.

US

MCGRAW-HILL MANAGEMENT AWARENESS PROGRAM. **Main/Corp** McGraw-Hill Book Company. **VFOAT** Management Awareness Program. English. Six times a year. McGraw Hill Publishing Company, Inc., 1221 Avenue of the Americas, New York NY 10020. **Tel** (212)512-6410, (800)525-5003, FAX (212)512-6111.

LC HD28 .M23 ISSN 0047-5394
DD 658.4/005 US

MCKINSEY QUARTERLY, THE. [McKinsey q.]. **Main/Corp** McKinsey and Company. **Added/Corp** McKinsey and Company. Quarterly. Vol. 1 (Summer 1964)-. Periodical. English. Four times a year. McKinsey and Company, 555 East 52nd Street, New York NY 10022. **Tel** (212)446-7000.
Ind/Abst Acad. Search; Anbar Account. Finan. Abstr. [Full Txt.]; Anbar Mark. Distr. Abstr. [Full Txt.]; Anbar Top Manage. Abstr. [Full Txt.]; Bus. ASAP (1992-) [Full Txt.]; Bus. Index (1988-); Bus. Period. Index; Bus. Source Plus; Contents Pages Manage.; Curr. Cit.; EP Collect.; Gen. BusinessFile (1988-); Gen. Period. Index (1978-); Homework Help.; INFO-SOUTH Abstr.; Mag. Search; Manage. Market. Abstr.; Manage. Bibliogr. Rev.; MasterFile FullTEXT 1000; MasterFile FullTEXT 350; MasterFile FullTEXT 650; MasterFile FullTEXT (July 1993-); OCLC; Oper. Prod. Manage. Abstr. [Full Txt.]; Person. Train. Abstr. [Full Txt.]; Telebase; Trade Ind. ASAP [Full Txt.]; Trade Ind. Index [Full Txt.]; Women Manage. Rev. [Full Txt.].

LC HD30.22 .M35 ISSN 0143-6570
DD 338.5/024658 UK
CCC
CODEN MDECDE

MDE. MANAGERIAL AND DECISION ECONOMICS. (MANAGERIAL AND DECISION ECONOMICS : MDE). [MDE. Manage. decis. econ.]. **VFOAT** MDE; M.D.E. Vol. 1, No. 1 (Mar. 1980)-. Periodical. English. Six times a year. $495.00. John Wiley & Sons Ltd., Baffins Lane, Chichester, West Sussex PO19 1UD United Kingdom. **Tel** 011 44 1243 779777, FAX 011 44 1243 776128 BTG:JWP001, telex 86290 WIBOOKG. **(Subscription address:** John Wiley & Sons, Inc. / Philadelphia, PO Box 7247, Philadelphia PA 19170. **Tel** (212)850-6645, (800)225-5945.) **ED** Ira Horowitz, David Gautschi, Steven Thompson, and Mark Hirschey. **Bk Rev**. **Ad Acc**. **Circ:** 750. available on microfilm and microfiche from University Microfilms International (UMI). Documents available from UMI Article Clearinghouse.
Desc: Covers the economic problems in the field of managerial and decision economics. It includes theoretical and empirical analyses of economic models used in forecasting pricing, advertising, diversification, competitive strategy, innovation, financial and location decisions.
Ind/Abst ABI/INFORM Glob. Ed.; ABI/INFORM [Computer File] (March 1987-); Contents Pages Manage.; Curr. Cit.; Curr. Contents Soc. Behav. Sci.; Econ. Lit. Index (19??-); Energy Res. Abstr. (July 1981-); Gen. BusinessFile (1992-); J. Econ. Lit.; PAIS Int. Print (1991-?).

LC HD28 .M22 ISSN 0970-6623
Pr Rev. II

MDI MANAGEMENT JOURNAL. **Added/Corp** Management Development Institute (New Delhi, India). **VFOAT** Management Journal. **VAT** Management Development Institute Management Journal. (1988)-. Periodical. English. Two times a year. $25.00. Management Development Institute, PO Box 60, Mehrauli Road, Guragon 122001 Haryana India. **Tel** 011 91 124340173, FAX 011 91 124341189, telex 0342-212.

ED C.V. Baxi. Index available. cum. index. **Bk Rev**. **Ad Acc**. **Circ:** 500.
Desc: Publishes research and general articles dealing with various facets of management.

ISSN 0941-8342
GW

UDC 33
MEISTERBRIEF FUER DEN BETRIEBSLEITER, DER. [Meist.br. Betr.leit.]. (1992)-. Newsletter. German. Twelve times a year. DM11.00. Verlag Norbert Mueller AG & Co. KG, Postfach 450632, Munich 80906 Germany. **Tel** 011 44 89 35093-02, FAX 011 44 89 35093-218. **ED** Stefan Uhlig. Index available. Circ: 1,700 (ctrl). **Continues** Meisterbrief (Munchen), 0171-3914.
Desc: A newsletter for plant managers.

LC HD2709 .A673 ISSN 0742-986X
DD 658.4 US

MEMBER'S YEAR BOOK - AMERICAN SOCIETY OF CORPORATE SECRETARIES. (MEMBER'S YEAR BOOK.). **Main/Corp** American Society of Corporate Secretaries. **VFOAT** Member's Yearbook; Year Book. English. One time a year. American Society of Corporate Secretaries Inc, 1270 Avenue of the Americas, New York NY 10020. **Tel** (212)765-2620. ctrl circ. **Continues** American Society of Corporate Secretaries. Year Book.

ISSN 1077-9310
DD 650 US
CEASED

MEMORY JOGGER, THE. [Mem. jog.]. **Added/Corp** Bureau of Business Practice. (19??)-(Oct. 1995). Periodical. English. Bureau of Business Practice, 24 Rope Ferry Road, Waterford CT 06386. **Tel** (800)243-0876, (203)442-4365, (800)876-9105, FAX (203)443-1123.
Desc: Organizer to help professionals keep up with meetings, appointments, expenses, etc.

UK
MENTOR MANAGEMENT DIGEST. English. Ten times a year. £50.00 (individuals), £250.00 (institutions) UK. Ashton Consultancy, 33 Kingsley Place, Newcastle NE6 5AN United Kingdom. **Tel** 011 44 191 2650838. **(Subscription address:** Mentor Subscriptions, Ashton Consultancy Freepost, Newcastle NE5 1BR United Kingdom. **Tel** 011 44 1091 2650383.**)**

LC HG4028.M4 M45 ISSN 0026-0010
DD 338.805 US
CCC
CODEN AMACDR

MERGERS & ACQUISITIONS. **See** Business and Economics-Banks and Banking.

ISSN 0889-0439
DD 658 US

MICHIGAN RETAILER, THE. [Mich. retail.]. **Added/Corp** Michigan Retailers Association. **VFOAT** MRA Michigan Retailer. (19??)-. Periodical. English. Six times a year (Jan., Mar., May, July, Sept., Nov.). $20.00. Michigan Retailers Association, 221 North Pine Street, Lansing MI 48933. **Tel** (517)372-5656, FAX (517)372-1303. **ED** Delaine A. Wright. **Ad Acc**, **Adv Mgr:** Wright, **Tel** (800)366-3699. Circ: 4,500 (ctrl).
Desc: This a newsletter about events and current happenings for the Michigan Retailers.

ISSN 0731-6305
US
CCC

MIDDLE EAST BUSINESS INTELLIGENCE. **See** Business and Economics-Marketing and Purchasing.

ISSN 1058-6318
DD 650 US

MINORITIES & SUCCESS. [Minor. success]. **VFOAT** Minorities and Success. (Oct. 1990)-. Periodical. English. Two times a year. Free (libraries/educational institutions). Minorities & Success, 2763 West Avenue L, Number 263, Lancaster CA 93536.

ISSN 0938-8249
GW

UDC 33
MIR. MANAGEMENT INTERNATIONAL REVIEW (1990). [Mir, Manag. int. rev. 1990]. **VFOAT** Management International Review (1990). (1990)-. Periodical. English. Four times a year (Mar., June, Sept., Dec.). $217.25. Gabler Verlag, Postfach 1546, D-65005 Wiesbaden Germany. **Tel** 011 49 611 534129, FAX 011 49 611 534430. **(Subscription address:** VVA Bertelsmann Distributors GmbH, Postfach 7600, D-33310 Guetersloh Germany. **Tel** 011 49 5241 803294.) **ED** Professor Dr. Klaus Macharzina. Index available (free). **Bk Rev**. **Ad Acc**, **Adv Mgr:** Beate Schoffel. **Continues** Management International Review, 0025-181X.
Desc: This journal presents insight and analyses which reflect basic and topical advances in the key areas of international management. Its target audience include scholars and executives in business and administration.
Ind/Abst Acad. Search; Bus. Source Plus; Bus. Source;

Business and Economics —Management

EP Collect.; Homework Help.; MasterFile FullTEXT 1000; MasterFile FullTEXT 350; MasterFile FullTEXT 650; MasterFile FullTEXT (July 1993-); OCLC; Telebase.

LC HF5001 .M595

JA

MITA SHOGAKU KENKYU. VFOAT Mita Business Review. (1958)-. Japanese. Six times a year. ¥4800. Do Gakkai, Keto Tsushin 19-ban 30-go Mita, 2-chome Minato-ku, Tokyo 108 Japan.

ISSN 0924-3194
NE

UDC (051.6)
MLI. MANAGEMENT LITERATUUR INFORMATIE. (MLI.). [MLI, Manag. lit. inf.]. VFOAT Management Literatuur Informatie. (1989)-. Periodical. Dutch. Twelve times a year. $102.78. KML/AFD Informative & Document, Postbus 7700, 1117 ZL Shiphol Netherlands.

ISSN 1240-4551
FR

UDC 681.3
MODELLING, MEASUREMENT &[AND] CONTROL D, MANUFACTURING, MANAGEMENT, HUMAN AND SOCIO-ECONOMIC PROBLEMS. See Industry and Production-Manufacturing.

ISSN 0544-6538
DD 658
US
MODERN DISTRIBUTION MANAGEMENT. [Mod. distrib. manage.]. (19??)-. Periodical. English. Twenty-four times a year. $195.00. Modern Distribution Management, PO Box 13507, Minneapolis MN 55414. Tel (612)699-4006, FAX (612)699-4006. ED Thomas P. Gale. Circ: 675 (ctrl).

LC HF5547.A2 M6
ISSN 0746-3839
DD 651/.05
US
CCC
CODEN MDOPAW
TITLE CHANGE

MODERN OFFICE TECHNOLOGY. See Business and Economics-Office Equipment and Services.

MONOGRAPH - CENTRE FOR MANAGEMENT IN AGRICULTURE, INDIAN INSTITUTE OF MANAGEMENT. See Agriculture-Agricultural Economics.

ISSN 1183-4692
DD 658.4
CN
CEASED

MORIARTY ON EXECUTIVE PENSIONS. [Moriarty exec. pensions]. Winter (1991)-(199?). Periodical. English. Federated Press, PO Box 885, Stock Exchange Tower, Montreal Quebec H4Z 1K2 Canada. Tel (514)849-6600, (800)363-0722.

LC HD28
ISSN 1084-4279
DD 658
US

●**MOTIVATION STRATEGIES FOR MANAGERS.** Added/Corp Alexander Hamilton Institute (U.S.). (1995)-. Periodical. English. Twelve times a year. $87.00. Alexander Hamilton Institute, 70 Hilltop Road, Ramsey NJ 07446-1119. Tel (201)825-8161, (800)879-2441, FAX (201)825-8696.

ISSN 0027-3589
CN

MUNICIPAL WORLD. [Munic. world]. (Jan. 1891)-. Trade Publication. English. Twelve times a year. 32.82Can$. Municipal World Inc., PO Box 399, St. Thomas Ontario N5P 3V3 Canada. Tel (519)633-0031, FAX (519)633-1001. ED Michael J. Smither. Index available. Bk Rev. Ad Acc. Circ: 10,500 (ctrl). Continues Municipal Miscellany.
Desc: Reports on management techniques in municipalities, urban development, law enforcement, transportation, waste disposal, planning, zoning, energy conservation, environment, highways, housing and legal articles.
Ind/Abst Urban Aff. Abstr.

ISSN 1078-5922
DD 658
US

●**MURRAY LUBLINER'S GLOBAL PACKAGING & BRAND IDENTITY REPORT.** [Murray Lubliner's glob. packag. brand identity rep.]. VFOAT Murray Lubliner's Global Packaging and Brand Identity Report; Global Packaging & Brand Identity Report. (1994)-. Periodical. English. Twelve times a year. $145.00. Global Package and Brand Identity Report, 1562 First Avenue, Suite 344, New York NY 10028. Tel (212)734-7841.

ISSN 0734-9998
US

MUTUAL AID. See Public Health and Safety.

ISSN 0162-864X
US

N-FILE NEWSLETTER, THE. Added/Corp Academy of Management. Management History Division. (19??)-. Newsletter. English. Four times a year. Free to members. Dr. Charles D. Wrege, 23 Worthington Avenue, Spring Lake NJ 07762. ED Dr. Charles D. Wrege.

ISSN 0745-0893
US

N.Y. HABITAT. See Real Estate.

ISSN 0895-7789
DD 658
US
NACS WEEKLY BULLETIN. (NACS WEEKLY BULLETIN : THE OFFICIAL NEWSLETTER OF THE NATIONAL ASSOCIATION OF COLLEGE STORES.). [NACS wkly. bull.]. Added/Corp National Association of College Stores (U.S.). VFOAT Weekly Bulletin. VAT National Association of College Stores Weekly Bulletin. (19??)-. Bulletin. English. One time a week (51 per year). $490.00 membership. National Association of College Stores, 500 East Lorain Street, Oberlin OH 44074. Tel (216)775-7777.

LC HD28
ISSN 1051-225X
DD 658
US
NASA TOTAL QUALITY MANAGEMENT ... ACCOMPLISHMENT REPORT. [NASA total qual. manage. accomp. rep.]. Main/Corp United States National Aeronautics and Space Administration. Quality and Productivity Improvement Programs Office. VFOAT Total Quality Management Accomplishments Report. (1990)-. English. One time a year. NASA Quality and Productivity Improvement Programs Office, Washington DC 20546. Continues NASA Quality and Productivity Improvement Programs Annual Accomplishments Report.

LC WMLC L 83/2761
US

NATIONAL BIOGRAPHIC, THE. Added/Corp American Institute of Management. Vol. 1 (March 1953)-. Periodical. English. Irregular. American Institute of Management, 45 Willard Street, Boston MA 02169. Tel (617)536-2503. Circ: 5,000 (ctrl).
Desc: Correspondence courses in management with diplomas and continuing education units.

LC K14 .A853
ISSN 1045-1668
DD 346.73/023/05 347.3062305
US
CODEN NCMJB9
Pr Rev.
NATIONAL CONTRACT MANAGEMENT JOURNAL (1979). (NATIONAL CONTRACT MANAGEMENT JOURNAL.). [Natl. contract manage. j.]. Added/Corp National Contract Management Association (U.S.). VFOAT NCMA Journal; National Contract Management Quarterly Journal. Vol. 13, No. 1 and 2 (Summer 1979)-. Periodical. English. Two times a year. $35.00. National Contract Management Association, 1912 Woodford Road, Vienna VA 22180. Tel (703)448-9231, (800)344-8096, FAX (703)448-0939. ED Terry Hoskins. Index available ($3.00). cum. index. available on microfilm and microfiche from University Microfilms International (UMI). Documents available from UMI Article Clearinghouse, Ask*IEEE. Continues National Contract Management Quarterly Journal, 0163-2124.
Ind/Abst ABI/INFORM Glob. Ed.; ABI/INFORM [Computer File] (Summer 1981-); Air Univ. Libr. Index Mil. Period.; INSPEC (Summer 1982-); UMI ABI/Inform--Bus. Period. Ondisc (Summer 1987-) [Full Txt.].

ISSN 1043-9838
DD 658
US
NATIONAL HOME-WORK NEWS. [Natl. home-work news]. VFOAT National Home Work News. Vol. 1, No. 1 (Oct. 1989)-. Periodical. English. Four times a year. $25.00. Love Publications, 933 North Hairston Road, Suite 7 136, Stone Mountain GA 30083. Tel (404)498-2945.

ISSN 0228-894X
DD 658.4/7
CN
NATIONAL LOSS PREVENTION. [Natl. loss prev.]. Vol. 1, No. 1 (June 1980)-. Periodical. English. Irregular. $10.00 Canada; $15.00 US. National Loss Prevention, PO Box 982 Station B, Willowdale Ontario M2K 2T6 Canada. Continues Canadian Loss Prevention, 0228-8958.

LC HD56 .N377
ISSN 0277-8556
DD 658.3/14/05
US
CCC
NATIONAL PRODUCTIVITY REVIEW. [Natl. prod. rev.]. Added/Corp Executive Enterprises Publications Co. Vol. 1, No. 1 (Winter 1981/82)-. Periodical. English. Four times a year. $220.00. John Wiley & Sons, Inc., 605 Third Avenue, New York NY 10158-0012. Tel (212)850-6000, (212)850-6645, FAX (212)850-6088, telex 12-7063. (Subscription address: John Wiley & Sons Inc / New Jersey, PO Box 2575, Secaucus NJ 07096-2575.) ED Jane G. Bensahel. Index available. Bk Rev. Ad Acc. Circ: 3,000. available on microfilm and microfiche from University Microfilms International (UMI); available on an online database (files 15,648/Full-Text) from DIALOG. Documents available from UMI Article Clearinghouse.

Desc: Focuses on concrete management problems that influence profitability of business. Covers productivity research, efficiency implementation measurement systems, and new techniques for increasing profits.
Ind/Abst ABI/INFORM Glob. Ed.; ABI/INFORM Ondisc: Expr. Ed.; ABI/INFORM [Computer File] (Winter 1981-1982); Acad. Search; Anbar Account. Finan. Abstr. [Full Txt.]; Anbar Mark. Distr. Abstr. [Full Txt.]; Anbar Top Manage. Abstr. [Full Txt.]; Bus. ASAP (1990-) [Full Txt.]; Bus. Index (1985-); Bus. Period. Index; Bus. Source Plus; Bus. Source; Curr. Cit.; EP Collect.; Gen. BusinessFile (1985-); Gen. Period. Index (1985-); Homework Help.; Hum. Resour. Abstr.; INFO-SOUTH Abstr.; Int. Labour Doc.; LABORDOC; Mag. Search; Manage. Bibliogr. Rev.; MasterFile FullTEXT 1000; MasterFile FullTEXT 350; MasterFile FullTEXT 650; MasterFile FullTEXT (July 1993-); OCLC; Oper. Prod. Manage. Abstr. [Full Txt.]; Oper. Res./Manage. Sci. (Winter 1981-82-); PAIS Int. Print; Person. Train. Abstr. [Full Txt.]; Person. Manage. Abstr.; Telebase; UMI ABI/Inform--Bus. Period. Ondisc (Winter 1987-) [Full Txt.]; Wilson Bus. Abstr.; Women Manage. Rev. [Full Txt.]; Work Relat. Abstr.

LC HD62.15 .N38
US

●**NATIONAL RESEARCH PANEL.** Added/Corp Conference Board. Total Quality Management Center. No. 1 (Sept. 1993)-. Monographic series. English. Two times a year. $60.00. Conference Board, 845 Third Avenue, New York NY 10022. Tel (212)759-0900 ext. 582, (800)872-6273, FAX (212)980-7014.

LC HD42 .N44
ISSN 0748-4526
DD 302.3/05
US
CCC
CODEN NEJOEQ
Pr Rev.
NEGOTIATION JOURNAL. [Negot. j.]. Vol. 1, No. 1 (Jan. 1985)-. Periodical. English. Four times a year. $225.00. Plenum Press, 233 Spring Street, New York NY 10013-1578. Tel (212)620-8000, (800)221-9369, FAX (212)463-0742, (212)807-1047, telex 23/421139. ED Jeffrey Z. Rubin. Index available. available on microfilm and microfiche from University Microfilms International (UMI). Documents available from The Genuine Article.
Desc: International journal devoted to the publication of works that advance the theory analysis and practice of negotiation and dispute statement.
Ind/Abst Am. Hist. Life (1986-); Curr. Cit.; Curr. Contents Agric. Biol. Environ. Sci.; Curr. Contents Soc. Behav. Sci.; Index Period. Artic. Relat. Law; Int. Bibliogr. Sociol.; Int. Polit. Sci. Abstr.; Neuropsych. Abstr.; PAIS Int. Print (1991-); Psychoanal. Abstr.; PsycScan: Appl. Exp. Eng. Psych.; PsycScan: LD/MR; Res. Alert [Full Cov.]; Sage Public Adm. Abstr.; Sage Urban Stud. Abstr; Soc. Plann. Policy Dev. Abstr.; Soc. Sci. Cit. Index [Full Cov.].

LC KF190 .N4
ISSN 0548-1546
DD 340/.065
US
NELSON'S LAW OFFICE DIRECTORY. See Law.

LC HD70.N35 N46
DD 658.4/009549/6
NP
NEPAL JOURNAL OF MANAGEMENT. No. 1 (Aug. 1972)-. Periodical. English. Four times a year. Rs5.00 single issue. 410 Nhaikantala Tole, Kathmandu 12 Nepal.

ISSN 0886-2230
DD 658
US
NETMANAGER. (NETMANAGER.). [NetManager]. Added/Corp Vanguard Telecommunications. VFOAT Net Manager. Vol. 1, No. 1 (1875?)-. Periodical. English. Twelve times a year. $350.00. Vanguard Telecommunications Inc., PO Box 1034, Carmel Valley CA 93924. Tel (408)659-2558. ED Jerry McDowell and Dustin Sykes.
Desc: A professional management tool. A guide to current and future network management tools. Reports highlight impacts on organization and career.

ISSN 1065-1306
DD 658
US
NEW LEADERS, THE. (THE NEW LEADERS.). [New lead.]. (1990)-. Periodical. English. Six times a year. $89.00. Sterling and Stone, Inc., 1668 Lombard Street, San Francisco CA 94123. Tel (800)928-5323, FAX (415)928-3346. ED John Renesch.

LC HF5549
ISSN 0929-7774
DD 658.3
NE
UDC 658.3:331.472](492)

●**NIEUWSBRIEF ABSENT!.** [Nieuwsbr. absent!]. VFOAT Absent!. (1994). Newsletter. Dutch. Six times a year. Samson HD Tjeenk Willink, Antwoordnummer 10153, 2400 VB Alphen Aan de Rijn, Netherlands. Tel 011 31 20 668223, FAX 011 31 20 6383871.

ISSN 0893-4177
US
DD 647
NIGHT CLUB & BAR MAGAZINE. See Hotels/Motels.

ISSN 0914-9325
JA
DD 001.64 651.8
NIKKEI DETAPURO OA. See Business and Economics-Office Equipment and Services.

LC T58.A2 N4
DD 658.4/008 S NE

NIVE-PUBLICATIE. **Main/Corp** Nederlandse Vereniging Voor Management. Dutch. Nive, Postbus 266, Neuhuyskade 40, 2270 AG Voorburg Netherlands. **Tel** 011 31 70 3001500. ***Continues** Nederlands Instituut voor Efficiency. Publicatie.*

ISSN 0926-4221
NE
UDC 658.012.4

NM2. NIVE MANAGEMENT MAGAZINE. (NM2.). [NM2, NIVE manag. mag.]. (1991)-. Periodical. Dutch. Six times a year. Nive, Postbus 266, Neuhuyskade 40, 2270 AG Voorburg Netherlands. **Tel** 011 31 70 3001500.

LC HD62.6 .N663 **ISSN** 1048-6682
DD 658/.048/05 US
CODEN NMLEES

NONPROFIT MANAGEMENT & LEADERSHIP. [Nonprofit manag. leadersh.]. **Added/Corp** Mandel Center for Nonprofit Organizations. London School of Economics and Political Science. Centre for Voluntary Organisation. **VFOAT** Nonprofit Management and Leadership. Vol. 1, No. 1 (Fall 1990)-. Periodical. English. Four times a year. $87.00. Jossey Bass Inc., 350 Sansome Street, San Francisco CA 94104. **Tel** (415)433-1767, FAX (415)433-0499. **ED** Dennis R. Young and David Billis (International Editor). available on microfilm and microfiche from University Microfilms International (UMI).
Desc: Brings together thinking and knowledge about the special needs, challenges, and opportunities of nonprofit organizations. Insights of executives and scholars on the concerns of nonprofit leaders in all settings - social services, the arts, education, foundations, community development, advocacy work, religion, professional associations, and others.
Ind/Abst Int. Bibliogr. Sociol.; Soc. Plann. Policy Dev. Abstr.

ISSN 1074-2654
US

•NONPROFIT MANAGEMENT DIGEST. (1994)-. English. Twelve times a year. $175.00. Aspen Publishers Inc., 7201 McKinney Circle, Frederick MD 21701. **Tel** (800)234-1660, (301)698-7100, FAX (301)251-5784, telex 5106014543. **(Subscription address:** Aspen Publishers Inc., PO Box 990, Frederick MD 21701. **Tel** (800)901-9074, (301)698-7100.**)**

ISSN 0896-5048
DD 361 US

NONPROFIT TIMES, THE. [NonProfit times]. **VFOAT** Non Profit Times. Vol. 1, No. 1 (Apr. 1987)-. Periodical. English. Twelve times a year. $59.00. The Nonprofit Times, 190 Tamarack Circle, Skillman NJ 08558. **Tel** (609)921-1251, FAX (609)921-6226. **ED** Patrick Sarver. Index available. cum. index. **Bk Rev. Ad Acc, Adv Mgr:** Kevin Landers. **Circ:** 40,000 (ctrl). available on an online database (file 648/Full-Text) from DIALOG.
Desc: Covers national and international news items effecting non-profit management.

ISSN 0739-2214
US
TITLE CHANGE

NPTA MANAGEMENT NEWS. **See** Paper and Pulp Industry.

ISSN 1059-4108
DD 658 US
CCC

OBJECT-ORIENTED STRATEGIES. [Object oriented strateg.]. **Added/Corp** Cutter Information Corp. **VFOAT** Object Oriented Strategies. (Oct. 1991)-. Periodical. English. Twelve times a year. $497.00. Cutter Information Corporation, 37 Broadway, Arlington MA 02174-5539. **Tel** (617)648-8700, (800)964-5118, FAX (617)648-8707, (617)648-1950, telex 650 100 9891.

FR

OCCASIONAL PAPERS ON PUBLIC MANAGEMENT. (19??)-. Periodical. English. Irregular (around 9 issues per year). $85.00. OECD Publications and Information Center, 2 rue Andre-Pascal, 75775 Paris Cedex 16 France. **Tel** 011 33 1 49104262, US:(202)785-6323, FAX 011 33 1 45248500, 011 33 1 45248176, telex 620 160 OCDE. **(Subscription address:** OECD Publications Center, 2001 L Street, Suite 700, Washington DC 20036. **Tel** (202)822-3873, (202)785-6323.**)**

LC KF300.A1 O33 **ISSN** 0730-3815
DD 340/.023/73 US

OF COUNSEL (NEW YORK, N.Y.). **See** Law.

ISSN 1065-7185
DD 658 US

OFFICE & BRANCH MANAGER'S BULLETIN. [Off. branch manager's bull.]. **VFOAT** Office and Branch Manager's Bulletin. (19??)-. Bulletin. English. One time a year. $159.36 US; $192.48 Canada. Bureau of Business Practice, 24 Rope Ferry Road, Waterford CT 06386. **Tel** (800)243-0876, (203)442-4365, (800)876-9105, FAX (203)443-1123.

UK
CODEN OIMIES

OFFICE & INFORMATION MANAGEMENT INTERNATIONAL : JOURNAL OF THE INSTITUTE OF ADMINISTRATIVE MANAGEMENT. **Added/Corp** Institute of Administrative Management (Beckenham, London, England). **VFOAT** Office & Information Management; Office and Information Management. **VAT** Office and Information Management International. Vol. 1, No. 4 (Sept. 1987)-. Periodical. English. Twelve times a year. $53.05. Institute of Administrative Management / England, 40 Chatsworth PRD, Peets Wood, Orpington Kent BR5 1RW United Kingdom. **Tel** 011 44 1689 875555, FAX 011 44 1689 870891. Documents available from UMI Article Clearinghouse, Ask*IEEE. ***Continues** Office Management International, 0951-5062.*
Ind/Abst ABI/INFORM Glob. Ed.; Abstr. Hum. Comput. Interact.; INSPEC (1987-); Manage. Market. Abstr.

LC HF5548 .O4 **ISSN** 0472-6049
DD 651.26 US

OFFICE AUTOMATION. **See** Business and Economics-Office Equipment and Services.

LC HF5547.A2 B77 **ISSN** 0722-2572
DD 651.8/4/05 GW
CODEN OFMADG

OFFICE-MANAGEMENT (BADEN-BADEN). (OFFICE MANAGEMENT.). [Off.-Manage.]. (19??)-. Periodical. German (German). Ten times a year. $201.89. FBO Fachverlag GmbH, Postfach 316, D-76482 Baden-Baden Germany. **Tel** 011 49 7221 271066, 011 49 7221 271067, 011 49 7221 271068, FAX 011 49 7221 33228. **ED** Heinz Scharfenberg. Index available. **Bk Rev. Ad Acc. Circ:** 12,000 (ctrl). Documents available from UMI Article Clearinghouse, Ask*IEEE. ***Continues** Burotechnik.*
Desc: publication for information, organization, and communication appealing to organization leaders and managers or the organization.
Ind/Abst ABI/INFORM Glob. Ed.; ABI/INFORM [Computer File] (Feb. 1981-); Curr. Cit.; F&S Index Plus Text, Int. [Select. Cov.]; INSPEC (Jan. 1982-).

US

OFFICE SUPERVISOR'S DEVELOPMENT PROGRAM. (19??)-. English. Twenty-four times a year. $120.36 (US); $148.44 (Canada) Includes: Dynamic Supervision, Supervisor's Bulletin for Administration and Office Support Groups, and Memory Jogger - Deluxe Edition. Bureau of Business Practice, 24 Rope Ferry Road, Waterford CT 06386. **Tel** (800)243-0876, (203)442-4365, (800)876-9105, FAX (203)443-1123.

US

OFFICE SUPERVISOR'S UPDATE PROGRAM. English. Twelve times a year. $98.88 (US); $122.40 (Canada) Includes: Dynamic Supervision, Quality Postiings, and Memory Jogger - Deluxe Edition. Bureau of Business Practice, 24 Rope Ferry Road, Waterford CT 06386. **Tel** (800)243-0876, (203)442-4365, (800)876-9105, FAX (203)443-1123.

ISSN 0745-9602
DD 651 US

OFFICERS MANAGER'S LETTER. (OFFICE MANAGER'S LETTER / ERC.). [Off. manager's lett.]. **VFOAT** ERC Office Manager's Letter. (1983)-. Periodical. English. Twenty-four times a year. $119.40. Bureau of Business Practice, 24 Rope Ferry Road, Waterford CT 06386. **Tel** (800)243-0876, (203)442-4365, (800)876-9105, FAX (203)443-1123.

NE

•OFFICIAL EUROPEAN MBA DIRECTORY. **See** Education-Higher Education.

LC HD20.15.E9 E9
NE
TITLE CHANGE

OFFICIAL GUIDE TO EUROPEAN MBA PROGRAMMES. **See** Education-Higher Education.

ISSN 1071-3956
DD 658 US

OM REVIEW. (OM REVIEW.). [OM rev.]. **Added/Corp** Operations Management Association. **VFOAT** Operations Management Review. (19??)-. Periodical. English. Four times a year. $65.00. Operations Management Association, 6701 Sanger Ave, Suite 106, Waco TX 76710. **Tel** (817)776-8099. ***Continues** Operations Management Review, 0734-1458.*
Ind/Abst INSPEC.

LC HD28 .O5 **ISSN** 0305-0483
DD 658.4/005 UK
CCC
CODEN OMEGA6
Pr Rev.

OMEGA (OXFORD). (OMEGA.). [Omega]. Vol. 1 (Feb. 1973)-. Periodical. English. Six times a year. $557.00. Pergamon Press, An Imprint of Elsevier Science Ltd., The Boulevard, Langford Lane, Kidlington, Oxford OX5 1GB United Kingdom. **Tel** 011 44 1865 843000, 011 44 1865 843699, FAX 011 44 1865 843010. **(Subscription address:** Elsevier Science Ltd. / Oxford Fulfillment Centre, PO Box 800, Kidlington OX5 1DX United Kingdom. **Tel** 011 44 865 843355.**) ED** S. Eilon, R. J. Betts, and N. Meade. available on microfilm and microfiche from University Microfilms International (UMI); available on an online database from Elsevier Electronic Subscriptions (EES). Documents available from The Genuine Article, Ask*IEEE, UMI Article Clearinghouse.
Desc: A forum for discussion of developments in management science, operational research and managerial economics, including theoretical developments, research results and applications.
Ind/Abst Appl. Soc. Sci. Index Abstr.; Bus. Index (1985-); CompuMath Cit. Index [Full Cov.]; Comput. Rev.; Contents Pages Manage.; Curr. Cit.; Curr. Contents Soc. Behav. Sci.; Curr. Lit. Sci. Sci.; EMBASE; Gen. BusinessFile (1985-); Gen. Period. Index (1985-); INSPEC (Feb. 1973-); Int. Abstr. Oper. Res. [Select. Cov.]; Int. Labour Doc.; Newsp. Period. Abstr. (1991-); Oper. Res./Manage. Sci.; Res. Alert [Full Cov.]; Selec. Coop. Index Manage. Period.; Soc. Sci. Cit. Index [Full Cov.]; Trade Ind. Index.

NE

ONDERNEMING. **Added/Corp** Verbond van Nederlandse Ondernemingen. (Mar 31 1972)-. Periodical. Dutch. One time a week. Fl130.00. Verbond van Nederlandse Ondern, Postbus 93093, 2509 AB The Hague Netherlands. **Tel** 011 31 70 3497373. **ED** NJPA van Grieken. Index available. **Bk Rev. Ad Acc. Circ:** 12,500. ***Supersedes** Nederlandse Onderneming.*
Ind/Abst Saf. Health Work.

LC HD28 .O64 **ISSN** 0734-1458
DD 658/.005 US
TITLE CHANGE

OPERATIONS MANAGEMENT REVIEW. [Oper. manage. rev.]. **Added/Corp** Operations Management Association. **VFOAT** Review. Vol. 1, No. 1 (Fall 1982)-(19??). Periodical. English. Operations Management Association, 6701 Sanger Ave, Suite 106, Waco TX 76710. **Tel** (817)776-8099. **ED** Robert R. Britney. **Bk Rev. Ad Acc. Circ:** 500. Documents available from Ask*IEEE. ***Continued by** OM Review, 1071-3956.*
Ind/Abst INSPEC (1984-1991).

LC HD20 .O6 **ISSN** 0473-0496
DD 658.4/034/05 US
Pr Rev.

OPERATIONS RESEARCH/MANAGEMENT SCIENCE YEARBOOK. [Operations research management science yearbook]. **Added/Corp** Executive Sciences Institute. **VFOAT** Operations Research Yearbook. (1961)-. English. One time a year. $185.00. Executive Sciences Institute, 1005 Mississippi Avenue, PO Box 4318, Davenport IA 52808-4318. **Tel** (319)324-4463, FAX (319)322-3725. **ED** Bruce Brocka. Index available. **Bk Rev. Circ:** 1,000.
Desc: An international literature digest service covering the methods of operations research and their applications in management of industry and government.

ISSN 1055-3924
DD 658 US

OPPORTUNITY EVALUATION NEWSLETTER. [Oppor. eval. newsl.]. (1990)-. Newsletter. English. Six times a year. $18.00. G C Associates, PO Box 150, Logan UT 84321. ***Continues** Opportunity Evaluation Bimonthly Newsletter.*

ISSN 0897-6031
DD 331 US

OPPORTUNITY NOCS. (OPPORTUNITY NOCS : A PUBLICATION OF THE MANAGEMENT CENTER.). [Oppor. NOCs]. **Added/Corp** Management Center (San Francisco Bay Area, Calif.). **VAT** Opportunity Nonprofit Organization Classifieds. (198?)-. Periodical. English. Fifty times a year. $67.00. The Management Center, 944 Market Street, Suite 700, San Francisco CA 94102. **Tel** (415)362-9735, FAX (415)362-4603.

LC HD20.5 .O6 **ISSN** 0030-3887
II
CCC
CODEN OPSEAN

OPSEARCH. [Opsearch]. **Added/Corp** Operational Research Society of India. Vol. 1, (Jan. 1964)-. Periodical. English. Four times a year (Mar., June, Sept., Dec.). $40.00. Institute for Systems Studies and Analyses, Metcalfe House, New Delhi 110054 India. **Tel** 011 91 11 2512896. **(Subscription address:** Prints India, 11 Darya Ganj, New Delhi 110002 India. **Tel** 011 91 11 3268645, FAX 011 91 11 3275542, telex 31-61087 PRIN-IN.**) ED** N K Jaiswal. Index available (In Dec. Issue). **Bk Rev**, (Qty: 15). **Ad Acc. Circ:** 1,300. Documents available from Ask*IEEE.
Desc: Theoretical and application papers on operational research and management science.
Ind/Abst Biostatistica; Curr. Cit.; INSPEC (March/June 1975-);; Int. Abstr. Oper. Res. [Full Cov.]; Math. Rev.; Oper. Res./Manage. Sci.; Qual. Control Appl. Stat.; Zentralbl. Math. Ihre Grenzgeb.

Business and Economics —Management

LC HD28
DD 658
ISSN 1350-6269
UK
●**ORGANISATIONS & PEOPLE : THE QUARTERLY JOURNAL OF AMED.**
Added/Corp Association for Management Education and Development (Great Britain). **VFOAT** Organisations and People. Vol. 1, No. 1 (Jan. 1994)-. Trade Publication. English. Four times a year. $150.00. Kogan Page Ltd., 120 Pentonville Road, London N1 9BR United Kingdom. **Tel** 011 44 171 2780433, FAX 011 44 171 8376348, telex 263088 KOGAN G.

ISSN 0350-1531
XV
CODEN ORKAEN
TITLE CHANGE
ORGANIZACIJA IN KADRI. (ORGANIZACIJA IN KADRI. ORGANIZATION AND PERSONNEL.). [Organ. kadri]. **VFOAT** Organization and Personnel. (1972)-(199?). Periodical. Slovenian (summaries and/or abstracts in English). Moderna Organizacija, 64001 Kranj, Tomsiceva 7 Slovenia. **Tel** 011 064 211560, FAX 011 064 214458. **ED** Peter Mikeln. **Bk Rev**. **Ad Acc**. **Circ:** 2,800 (ctrl). **Continues** Kadrovi i Rad; Moderna Organizacija, 0047-777X and Industrijska Istrazivanja. **Continued by** Organizacija.
Desc: Publishes original scientific treatises, dissertations and professional articles concerning organizational sciences production and personnel management, educational activities and similar sciences.
Ind/Abst Ergon. Abstr.

LC HD28 .O745
PL
ORGANIZACJA I ZARZADZANIE = ORGANIZATION AND MANAGEMENT.
Added/Corp Lodz, Poland. Politechnika. Instytut Ekonomiki i Organizacji Produkcji. No. 1 (1975)-. Monographic series. Polish (summaries and/or abstracts in English and Russian). Irregular. Price varies per volume. Politechnika Lodzka, Ul. Worcella 6/8, Lodz Poland.

UK
ORGANIZATION. (19??)-. Periodical. English. Four times a year. $158.00. Sage Publications Ltd., 6 Bonhill Street, London EC2A 4PU United Kingdom. **Tel** 011 44 181 3740645, FAX 011 44 181 3748741, telex 296207 SAGE G.

LC WMLC 93/345
DD 658
ISSN 0889-6402
US
Pr Rev.
ORGANIZATION DEVELOPMENT JOURNAL. [Organ. dev. j.]. **Added/Corp** Organization Development Institute. (198?)-. Periodical. English. Four times a year (Mar., June, Sept., Dec.). $65.00. Organization Development Institute, 11234 Walnut Ridge Road, Chesterland OH 44026. **Tel** (216)461-4333, FAX (216)729-9319. **ED** Dr. Donald W. Cole. **Bk Rev**, (Qty: 4-10). **Ad Acc**, **Adv Mgr Tel** (216)461-4333. **Circ:** 600. available on microfilm from University Microfilms International (UMI).
Ind/Abst Curr. Cit.; Psychol. Abstr. (1984-); PsycINFO; PsycLit.

LC HD28 .O758 HD28 .O74
DD 302.3/5/05
ISSN 1047-7039
US
CODEN ORSCEZ
ORGANIZATION SCIENCE. (ORGANIZATION SCIENCE : A JOURNAL OF THE INSTITUTE OF MANAGEMENT SCIENCES.). [Organ. sci.].
Added/Corp Institute of Management Sciences. Vol. 1, No. 1 (1990)-. Periodical. English. Four times a year. $107.00. Institute of Management Sciences, 290 Westminster Street, Providence RI 02903. **Tel** (401)274-2525, FAX (401)274-3189. **ED** Arie Y. Lewin. Documents available from The Genuine Article.
Desc: New forum for linking theory and practice in fields such as organization theory, strategic management, sociology, economics, political science, history, systems theory and psychology.
Ind/Abst Curr. Cit.; Curr. Contents Soc. Behav. Sci.; Neuropsych. Abstr.; Psychoanal. Abstr.; Psychol. Abstr. (1990-); PsycINFO; PsycLit; PsycScan: Appl. Exp. Eng. Psych.; PsycScan: LD/MR; Res. Alert [Full Cov.]; Sage Public Adm. Abstr.; Soc. Plann. Policy Dev. Abstr.; Soc. Sci. Cit. Index [Full Cov.].

LC HM131 .O667
DD 302.3/5/05
ISSN 1350-5084
UK
●**ORGANIZATION : THE INTERDISCIPLINARY JOURNAL OF ORGANIZATION, THEORY, AND SOCIETY.** (July 1994)-. Academic Scholarly Publication. English. Four times a year. Sage Publications Ltd., 6 Bonhill Street, London EC2A 4PU United Kingdom. **Tel** 011 44 181 3740645, FAX 011 44 181 3748741, telex 296207 SAGE G.

LC HD28 .O76
DD 658.4/005
ISSN 0090-2616
US
CCC
CODEN ORDYA
Pr Rev.
ORGANIZATIONAL DYNAMICS. [Organ. dyn.]. **Added/Corp** American Management Association. Vol. 1 (Summer 1972)-. Periodical. English. Four times a year. $63.00. American Management Association, 135 West 50th Street, New York NY 10020-1201. **Tel** (212)586-8100, (212)903-8375 (periodicals), FAX (212)903-8168, (212)903-8083 (periodicals). **(Subscription address:** American Management Association, PO Box 408, Saranac Lake NY 12983. **Tel** (800)262-9699, FAX (518)891-1500.**)** **ED** Fred Luthans. available on microfilm and microfiche from University Microfilms International (UMI); available on an online database (files 648/Full-Text) from DIALOG. Documents available from The Genuine Article, UMI Article Clearinghouse.
Desc: Review of organizational behavior for the professional manager. Features articles by authorities in the behavioral and management sciences and case studies of management theories or techniques.
Ind/Abst ABI/INFORM Glob. Ed.; ABI/INFORM [Computer File] (Summer 1975-); Acad. Search; Anbar Account. Finan. Abstr. [Full Txt.]; Anbar Mark. Distr. Abstr. (1974-) [Full Txt.]; Anbar Top Manage. Abstr. [Full Txt.]; Bus. ASAP (1990-) [Full Txt.]; Bus. Index (1985-); Bus. Period. Index; Bus. Source Plus; Bus. Source; Contents Pages Manage.; Curr. Cit.; Curr. Contents Soc. Behav. Sci.; EP Collect.; Gen. BusinessFile (1985-); Gen. Period. Index (1985-); High. Educ. Abstr.; Homework Help.; Hosp. Health Admin. Index; INFO-SOUTH Abstr.; Int. Labour Doc.; Lotus Notes; Mag. Search; Manage. Market. Abstr.; Manage. Bibliogr. Rev.; Manage. Contents; MasterFile FullTEXT 1000; MasterFile FullTEXT 350; MasterFile FullTEXT 650; MasterFile FullTEXT (July 1993-) [Full Txt.]; OCLC; Oper. Prod. Manage. Abstr.; Person. Abstr. (1973-) [Full Txt.]; Person. Train. Abstr. (1978-1989) [Full Txt.]; Person. Manage. Abstr.; Psychol. Abstr. (1973-); PsycINFO; PsycLit; PsycScan: Appl. Psych.; Res. Alert [Full Cov.]; Selec. Coop. Index Manage. Period.; Soc. Sci. Cit. Index [Full Cov.]; Telebase; UMI ABI/Inform--Bus. Period. Ondisc (Spring 1987-) [Full Txt.]; Vocat. Search; Wilson Bus. Abstr.; Women Manage. Rev. [Full Txt.]; Work Relat. Abstr. (Summer 1975-).

US
ORGANIZATIONAL LEADERSHIP OF HUMAN RESOURCES. THE KNOWLEDGE AND THE SKILLS. (19??)-. English. $223.50 (3 part set). JAI Press Inc., 55 Old Post Road, Suite 2, PO Box 1678, Greenwich CT 06836-1678. **Tel** (203)661-7602, FAX (203)661-0792.
Desc: Presents information on developing and motivation effective leadership. Covers organization behavior, the management technologies, philosophy (ethics), human resources resources, organization development, and leadership development.

LC HD28 .O77
RU
ORGANIZATSIIA UPRAVLENIIA. (1971)-. Russian. Twelve times a year. $275.00. Izdatelstvo Ekonomika, Berezhkovskaia Nab. 6, 121864 Moscow Russia. **(Subscription address:** Victor Kamkin, 4956 Boiling Brook Parkway, Rockville MD 20852. **Tel** (301)881-5973.**)**

LC TS540
DD 681
UDC 681.31+621.39
ISSN 1381-2882
NE
●**ORGANIZE AMSTERDAM.** (ORGANIZE). [Organize Amst.]. (1994)-. Consumer Publication. Dutch. Six times a year. Televak Uitgeverij NV, Postbus 75985, 1070 AZ Amsterdam Netherlands. **Tel** 011 31 20 6659220, FAX 011 31 20 6657316.

LC HF5548.2 .O86
AU
OUTPUT OESTERREICH. (July/Aug. 1975)-. German. Ten times a year. S320.00 Austria; S352.00 other. Bohmann Druck und Verlag Ges MBH, Leberstrasse 122, A-1110 Vienna Austria. **Tel** 011 43 1 74095174, FAX 011 43 1 741595-183, telex 132312. **Ad Acc. Circ:** 14,000 (ctrl).

DD 658
ISSN 0882-6242
US
OWNER AND MANAGER. [Own. manager]. **Added/Corp** Research Institute of America, Inc. (198?)-. Periodical. English. Twenty-six times a year. $96.00. Research Institute of America, 117 East Stevens Avenue, Valhalla NY 10595. **Tel** (800)431-9025, FAX (800)820-3135 (914)749-5300.

ISSN 1017-6713
IE
P+ : EUROPEAN PARTICIPATION MONITOR. **Added/Corp** European Foundation for the Improvement of Living and Working Conditions. **VFOAT** P Plus; European Participation Monitor. **VAT** Participation Plus. no. 1 (1991)-. Periodical. English. Two times a year. Free on request. European Foundation for the Improvement of Living and Working Conditions, Loughlinstown House, Shankill Co, Dublin Ireland. **Tel** 011 353 1 2826888, FAX 011 353 1 2826456. **ED** Michael Gold.
Desc: Aims to contribute to the planning and development of the improvement of living and working conditions in the future, through action designed to increase and disseminate knowledge likely to assist these ideas.
Ind/Abst Ergon. Abstr.

ISSN 0348-260X
SW
UDC 658
PACKMARKNADEN SCANDINAVIA. [Packmark. Scand.]. (1978)-. Periodical. Swedish. Ten times a year. $123.42. Indufa AB, Box 601, S-25106 Helsingborg Sweden. **Tel** 011 46 42 199909.
Ind/Abst Infomat Int. Bus.

LC HD28 .P33
DD 338
PK
PAKISTAN MANAGEMENT REVIEW. **Added/Corp** Institute of Personnel Training (Karachi, Pakistan) Pakistan Institute of Management. (19??)-. Periodical. English. Four times a year (Jan., Apr., July, Oct.). $55.00. Pakistan Institute of Management, Shahrah Iran Clifton, Karachi 6 Pakistan. **Tel** 011 92 21 531039, FAX 011 92 21 539689. **ED** Amjad Humayun. Index available. cum. index. **Ad Acc**. **Circ:** 1,500 (ctrl). available on audiocassette.
Desc: Articles devoted to the improvement of management development in Pakistan.
Ind/Abst Person. Manage. Abstr.

LC HF5006 .A26a
DD 658.4/008
IT
PAPERS ON BUSINESS ADMINISTRATION. **Main/Corp** Accademia Nazionale de Ragioneria. Vol. 1 (1974)-. English. Giuffre Editore SPA, Via Busto Arsizio 42, 20151 Milan Italy. **Tel** 011 398 2 38089200.

LC HF5371 .P25
US
PAPERWORK SIMPLIFICATION. **Added/Corp** Standard Register Company, Dayton, Ohio. No. 67 (Summer 1964)-. Periodical. English. Irregular. Free on request. Standard Register Company, PO Box 110850, Nashville TN 37222. **Tel** (615)323-8764. **Continues** PS. Paperwork Simplification for Better Management Control.

DD 361.3
ISSN 1195-4981
CN
PARTNERS IN PRINT. [Partn. print]. **VFOAT** Newsletter, Partners in Print; Partners. (1989)-. Newsletter. English. Six times a year. 28.00Can$. Partners Plus, 9030 Leslie Street, Suite 220, Richmond Hill Ontario, L4B 1G2 Canada. **Tel** (416)886-8585, FAX (416)447-8151. **Bk Rev**, (Qty: 2-3). **Circ:** 350 (ctrl).

LC KF300.A1 P37
DD 338.7/6134
ISSN 0892-4805
US
CCC
PARTNER'S REPORT. See Law.

ISSN 1043-7428
DD 658
US
CCC
PARTNER'S REPORT (NEW YORK, N.Y. 1989). (PARTNER'S REPORT : THE MONTHLY UPDATE FOR CPA FIRM OWNERS.). [Partn. rep.]. **Added/Corp** Institute for Management & Administration. (1989)-. Periodical. English. Twelve times a year. $245.00. Institute of Management and Administration, 29 West 35th Street, 5th Floor, New York NY 10001-2299. **Tel** (212)244-0360, FAX (212)564-0465.

DD 658
ISSN 1043-4364
US
PEAK PERFORMANCE SELLING. [Peak perform. sell.]. **Added/Corp** National Sales Development Institute (U.S.). No. 838 (March 30, 1989)-. Periodical. English. Twenty-four times a year. $74.76. Bureau of Business Practice, 24 Rope Ferry Road, Waterford CT 06386. **Tel** (800)243-0876, (203)442-4365, (800)876-9105, FAX (203)443-1123. **Continues** Creative Selling (Waterford, Conn.), 0889-5805.

DD 658.4/005
ISSN 0381-7075
CN
PEOPLE & PERSPECTIVES. No. 261- 1976-. Periodical. English. Twelve times a year. Free. Hay Associates Canada Ltd, 55 University Avenue/Suite 1800, Toronto Ontario Canada. **Continues** Men and Management, 0380-0164.

DD 658
ISSN 0734-029X
US
PERFORMANCE MANAGEMENT MAGAZINE. [Perform. manage. mag.]. Vol. 1, No. 1 (Fall 1982)-. Periodical. English. Four times a year (March, June, Sept., Dec.). $24.00. Performance Management, 3531 Habersham at North Lake, Tucker GA 30084. **Tel** (404)493-5080. **ED** Gail Snyder. **Ad Acc**, **Adv Mgr:** Tracy Keever. **Circ:** 3,000.

Business and Economics —Management

Desc: True stories on how to get people to do what you want them to do and like doing it through a data-oriented approach to management.

US

PERFORMANCE STANDARDS MADE SIMPLE. (19??)-. English. Irregular. FPMI Communications Inc., 707 Fiber Street, Huntsville AL 35801. **Tel** (205)539-1850, FAX (205)539-0911, .

US

PERS/ALRA INFORMATION BULLETIN. Bulletin. English. Public Employment Relations Services, 1215 Western Avenue, Albany NY 12203.

II

Pr Rev.
PERSONNEL TODAY. Added/Corp National Institute of Personnel Management (India). **VFOAT** PT. (1980)-. Periodical. English. Four times a year. $13.96. National Institute Personnel Management, 45 Jhowtala Road, Calcutta 700019, India. **Tel** 11 91 33 475650. **(Subscription address:** Prints India, 11 Darya Ganj, New Delhi 110002 India. **Tel** 011 91 11 3268645, FAX 011 91 11 3275542, telex 31-61087 PRIN-IN.**)**

LC ZL24 **ISSN** 1073-0737
DD 686 US

PERSPECTIVES (LIBERTY, MO. 1986). (PERSPECTIVES : AN IPMA PUBLICATION.). [Perspectives]. **Added/Corp** In-Plant Management Association. (1986)-. Trade Publication. English. Twelve times a year. Comes with membership; $50.00 (retired/educational membership), $150.00 (individual membership), $300.00 (associate membership). International Publishing Management Association, 1205 West College Street, Liberty MO 64068. **Tel** (816)781-1111, FAX (816)781-2790. **ED** Barbara A. Schaaf Petty. **Ad Acc**, **Adv Mgr Tel** (816)781-1111. **Circ:** 2,500 (ctrl).
Desc: Publication for active members of IPMA. Contains stories on successes, failures, equipment, personnel, etc. Areas of interest to an in-house printing manager or in-house mail manager.

ISSN 0893-2123
DD 658 US

PERSPECTIVES ON TECHNOLOGY. [Perspet. technol.]. (1986)-. Periodical. English. Three times a year. Free. Metropolitan Life Insurance Company, One Madison Avenue, New York NY 10010.
Ind/Abst Comput. Rev.

ISSN 1060-4537
DD 615 US
SUSPENDED

PHARMACY BUSINESS. See Pharmacy and Pharmacology.

ISSN 1045-8158
DD 650 US

PHOTO DISTRICT NEWS (EASTERN ED.). See Photography.

LC TR **ISSN** 1048-0161
DD 770 US

PHOTO DISTRICT NEWS (MIDWESTERN ED.). See Photography.

ISSN 1048-0153
DD 650 US

PHOTO DISTRICT NEWS (SOUTHERN ED.). See Photography.

LC TR1 .P468 **ISSN** 1048-0145
DD 650 US

PHOTO DISTRICT NEWS (WESTERN ED.). See Photography.

ISSN 0899-4587
DD 658 US

PHOTO OPPORTUNITY. See Photography.

IT

PICCOLO AZIONISTA. (19??)-. Italian. Twelve times a year. In-Ed Informazioni Editoriali, Via XX Settembre 21, 16121 Genoa Italy.

ISSN 0891-4443
DD 361 US

PLANNED GIFTS COUNSELOR, THE. [Plan. gifts couns.]. **Added/Corp** Taft Group (Rockville, Md.). (1987)-. Periodical. English. Twelve times a year. $150.00. Taft Group, 835 Penobscott Building, Customer Service, Detroit MI 48226. **Tel** (800)877-8238, FAX (313)961-6083.

ISSN 0141-2175
UK

PLANNED INNOVATION. [Plann. innov.]. (1978)-. Periodical. English. Six times a year. £35.00. NPM Infolink Ltd, Parker Street, Management House, London WC2B 5PU United Kingdom. **Tel** 011 44 171 4045414. **ED** CC Gee. **Bk Rev.**
Ind/Abst Manage. Contents (1978-); Predicasts.

LC HD28 .P57 **ISSN** 0094-064X
DD 658.4 US
CCC

PLANNING REVIEW. [Plann. rev.]. **Added/Corp** Planning Forum. North American Society for Corporate Planning. No. 1 (Oct. 1972)-. Periodical. English. Six times a year (Jan., Mar., May, July, Sept., Nov.). $95.00. Planning Forum, PO Box 70, Oxford OH 45056. **Tel** (513)523-4185, FAX (513)523-7539. **ED** Robert Allio. **Bk Rev. Ad Acc. Circ:** 11,000 (ctrl). available on microfilm and microfiche from University Microfilms International (UMI). Documents available from UMI Article Clearinghouse.
Desc: Journal for managerial decision makers involved in strategic, operational, and financial planning.
Ind/Abst ABI/INFORM Glob. Ed.; ABI/INFORM [Computer File] (March 1979-); Acad. Search; Account. Art.; Anbar Account. Finan. Abstr. [Full Txt.]; Anbar Top Manage. Abstr. [Full Txt.]; Bus. ASAP (1992-) [Full Txt.]; Bus. Index (1985-1987); Bus. Period. Index; Bus. Source Plus; Bus. Source; Comput. Lit. Index; Contents Pages Manage.; Curr. Cit.; EP Collect.; F&S Index Plus Text, Int. [Select. Cov.]; Gen. BusinessFile (198?-); Gen. Period. Index (1985-1988); Homework Help.; INFO-SOUTH Abstr.; Mag. Search; Manage. Market. Abstr.; Manage. Bibliogr. Rev.; Manage. Contents; MasterFile FullTEXT 1000; MasterFile FullTEXT 350; MasterFile FullTEXT 650; MasterFile FullTEXT (July 1993-); OCLC; Oper. Prod. Manage. Abstr. [Full Txt.]; Person. Train. Abstr. (1974-) [Full Txt.]; PROMT; Selec. Coop. Index Manage. Period.; Telebase; UMI ABI/Inform--Bus. Period. Ondisc (Nov. 1987-) [Full Txt.]; Wilson Bus. Abstr.; Women Manage. Rev. [Full Txt.].

ISSN 0845-4213
DD 670.42/068 CN

PLANT (WILLOWDALE). (PLANT.). [Plant]. Vol. 47, No. 8 (Oct. 26, 1988)-. Periodical. English. Eighteen times a year. 39.22Can$. MacLean Hunter Ltd. Business Publishers / Canada, Box 9100, Station A, Toronto Ontario M5W 1A5 Canada. **Tel** (416)596-5000, , FAX (416)596-5552. **(Subscription address:** Indas Customer Service, 35 Riviera Drive, Building 17, Markham Ontario L3R 8N4 Canada. **Tel** (905)946-0406.**)** available on microfilm and microfiche from University Microfilms International (UMI). **Continues** Plant Management & Engineering.

LC HD69.P75 P244 **ISSN** 1040-8754
DD 658 US

PM NET WORK, THE. [PM net work]. **Added/Corp** Project Management Institute. **VFOAT** PM Network. **VAT** Project Management Net Work. (198?)-. Trade Publication. English. Irregular. $80.00. Project Management Institute, 130 South State Road, Upper Darby PA 19082. **Tel** (610)622-1796, FAX (215)622-5640, telex 5101002864. **ED** Francis M. Webster. **Bk Rev. Ad Acc. Circ:** 7,000 (ctrl).
Desc: Covers all areas of project management.

ISSN 0758-1726
FR

UDC 336
Pr Rev.
POLITIQUES ET MANAGEMENT PUBLIC. See Political Science.

LC KF318.A1 P7 **ISSN** 0092-248X
DD 340/.068 US

PRACTICAL LAWYER'S LAW OFFICE MANAGEMENT MANUAL, THE. See Law.

ISSN 0159-1193
AT

PRACTISING MANAGER. (THE PRACTISING MANAGER.). [Pract. manager]. **Added/Corp** Australian Administrative Staff College (Mount Eliza, Vic.). Vol. 1, No. 1 (Oct. 1980)-. Periodical. English. Two times a year (Apr. & Oct.). 20.55Aus$. Australian Administrative Staff College, Kunyung Road, Mt Eliza Victoria 3930 Australia. **Tel** 11 61 3 215 1100. **ED** Ian Adie. **Bk Rev. Ad Acc. Circ:** 6,500.
Ind/Abst Anbar Account. Finan. Abstr. [Full Txt.]; Anbar Mark. Distr. Abstr. [Full Txt.]; Anbar Top Manage. Abstr. [Full Txt.]; APAIS, Aust. Public Aff. Inf. Ser. (1982-); Bibliogr. Mission. (1982-); Curr. Cit.; Manage. Bibliogr. Rev.; Oper. Prod. Manage. Abstr. [Full Txt.]; Person. Train. Abstr. [Full Txt.]; Women Manage. Rev. [Full Txt.].

ISSN 0169-1910
NE

UDC 614.2
PRAKTIJKMANAGEMENT. See Pharmacy and Pharmacology.

ISSN 0772-6856
BE

UDC (083.132)
PRAKTISCH MANAGEMENT. [Prakt. manage.]. (1983)-. Periodical. Dutch (French). Eleven times a year. $93.29. Praktisch Management, Aemen NV, Brusselsesteenweg 118, B-1850 Grimbergen, Belgium. **Tel** 32 21269 24 22, FAX 32 21269 26 49. Index available (December). **Bk Rev,** (Qty: 2 /year). **Circ:** 2000 (ctrl).
Desc: Contains practical advice and information for managers and board members, which can be useful in their human resources policy and their relations with employees and assistants.

ISSN 1062-5178
DD 658 US
CEASED

PREDICTIONS & PRESCRIPTIONS. [Predict. prescr.]. **Added/Corp** International Professional Trainers Guild. **VFOAT** Predictions and Prescriptions; P&P. Premier issue (1992)-(19??). Periodical. English. International Professional Trainers Guild, 2060 Broadway, Suite 460, Boulder CO 80302.

ISSN 0552-007X
US

PRESIDENT (NEW YORK), THE. (THE PRESIDENT.). Periodical. English. The President, 135 West 50th Street, New York NY 10020.

LC HF5416 .P75 **ISSN** 0968-4905
DD 658.8/16/05 UK
CCC

●**PRICING STRATEGY & PRACTICE. VFOAT** Pricing Strategy and Practice. Vol. I, No. I (1993)-. Periodical. English. Four times a year. $239.00. MCB University Press, 60 62 Toller Lane, Bradford, West Yorkshire BD8 9BY United Kingdom. **Tel** 011 44 1274 785280, FAX 011 44 1274 785200, telex 51317-MCBUNI-G.

ISSN 1044-4998
DD 658 US
CCC

PRINCIPAL'S REPORT (NEW YORK, N.Y.). (PRINCIPAL'S REPORT.). [Princ. rep.]. **Added/Corp** Institute of Management & Administration. (1989)-. Periodical. English. Twelve times a year. $245.00. Institute of Management and Administration, 29 West 35th Street, 5th Floor, New York NY 10001-2299. **Tel** (212)244-0360, FAX (212)564-0465.

ISSN 0190-9851
DD 658 US

PRIVATE LABEL (GENERAL ED.). (PRIVATE LABEL.). [Priv. label]. (1979)-. Trade Publication. English. Six times a year. $24.00. E W Williams Publications Co., 2125 Center Avenue, Suite 305, Fort Lee NJ 07024. **Tel** (201)592-7007, FAX (201)592-7171. **Absorbed** Private Label (Executive Edition), 0897-4845.
Ind/Abst Mark. Advert. Ref. Serv.

ISSN 1050-2297
DD 658 US

PRO ADMINISTRATOR. [Pro adm.]. **Added/Corp** Center for Management Systems. (1990)-. Periodical. English. Twelve times a year. $135.00. Aspen Publishers Inc., 7201 McKinney Circle, Frederick MD 21701. **Tel** (800)234-1660, (301)698-7100, FAX (301)251-5784, telex 5106014543. **(Subscription address:** Aspen Publishers Inc., PO Box 990, Frederick MD 21701. **Tel** (800)901-9074, (301)698-7100.**)**

IT

PROBLEMI DI GESTIONE DELL IMPRESA. Italian. L30.000. Vita e Pensiero Pubblic University, Largo Gemelli 1, 20123 Milan Italy. **Tel** 011 39 2 72342310, 011 39 2 72342370.

LC HD70.C725 P76 **ISSN** 0257-9928
RU

PROBLEMY TEORII I PRAKTIKI UPRAVLENIIA. [Probl. teorii prakt. upr.]. **Added/Corp** Mezhdunarodnyi Institut Problem Upravleniia. Mezhdunarodnyi Naucho-Issledovatelskii Institut Problem Upravleniia. (1983)-. Periodical. Russian. Six times a year. $99.95. Mezhdunarodnyi Tsentr Nauchnoi I Tekhicheskoi Informatsii, Ulitsa Kuusinena 21B, 125252 Moscow Russia. **(Subscription address:** East View Publications Inc., 3020 Harbor Lane North, Suite 110, Minneapolis MN 55447. **Tel** (800)477-1005, (612)550-0961, FAX (612)559-2931.**)**

ISSN 0318-5036
DD 658 CN

PROCEEDINGS. ANNUAL CONFERENCE - CANADIAN ASSOCIATION OF ADMINISTRATIVE SCIENCES. (PROCEEDINGS - CANADIAN ASSOCIATION OF ADMINISTRATIVE SCIENCES, CONFERENCE.). **Main/Corp** Canadian Association of Administrative Sciences. **VFOAT** Rapport - Association Canadienne des Sciences Administratives, Congres. 1st-1973-. Proceedings. Multiple languages (French). One time a year. $12. per no. School of Business, Queen's University, Kingston Ontario Canada. **Supersedes** Association of Canadian Schools of Business. Proceedings, 0066-9490.

LC HD29 .D43
DD 658 US

PROCEEDINGS, DECISION SCIENCES INSTITUTE ... ANNUAL MEETING [MICROFORM]. Main/Corp Decision Sciences Institute. Meeting. **VFOAT** Decision Sciences Institute ...

Business and Economics —Management

Annual Meeting; Proceedings ... Annual Meeting, Decision Sciences Institute. (1990)-. English. Decision Sciences Institute, Georgia State University, College of Business Administration, University Plaza, Atlanta GA 30303. **Tel** (404)651-4000, FAX (404)651-2804. *Continues Decision Sciences Institute. Meeting. Proceedings of the ... Annual Meeting of the Decision Sciences Institute, 0898-9567.*

ISSN 1059-356X
US

PROCEEDINGS OF THE FIRST BIANNUAL INTERNATIONAL CONFERENCE ON ADVANCES IN MANAGEMENT.
(1992)-. Proceedings. English. Every 2 years. $10.00. Center for Advanced Studies in Management, 1574 Mallory Court, Bowling Green KY 42103. **Tel** (502)782-2601, FAX (502)782-2601. **ED** Dr. M.A. Rahim, Management Department, Western Kentucky University, Bowling Green KY 42101 (editor's phone: (502)745-2499). Index available. **Ad Acc. Circ:** 150.
Desc: Papers presented at the first Biennial International Conference on Advances in management.

LC P90.I55 A1
DD 659 808 808.066
US

PROCEEDINGS OF THE INSTITUTE IN TECHNICAL AND INDUSTRIAL COMMUNICATIONS. See Communications.

UK

PROCEEDINGS OF THE ... INTERNATIONAL MEETING OF THE INSTITUTE OF MANAGEMENT SCIENCES.
Main/Corp Institute of Management Sciences. **VFOAT** Proceedings [of the] ... International Meeting, the Institute of Management Sciences. (19??)-. Proceedings. English. Pergamon Press, An Imprint of Elsevier Science Ltd., The Boulevard, Langford Lane, Kidlington, Oxford OX5 1GB United Kingdom. **Tel** 011 44 1865 843000, 011 44 1865 843699, FAX 011 44 1865 843010.

LC TS175 .N37a
DD 658.5/6
ISSN 0091-8954
US

PRODUCT SAFETY UP TO DATE.
Main/Corp National Safety Council. (19??)-. Consumer Publication. English. Six times a year. $19.00. National Safety Council, 1121 Spring Lake Drive, Itasca IL 60143. **Tel** (800)621-7615, (708)775-2294, FAX (708)285-0797. **(Subscription address:** National Safety Council, PO Box 429, Itasca IL 60143. **Tel** (800)621-3433, (708)285-1121.)

LC TS155.A1 P68
DD 658.5
ISSN 0897-8336

CODEN PIMJE8
PRODUCTION AND INVENTORY MANAGEMENT JOURNAL.
(PRODUCTION AND INVENTORY MANAGEMENT JOURNAL : THE JOURNAL OF THE AMERICAN PRODUCTION AND INVENTORY CONTROL SOCIETY, INC.). [Prod. invent. manage. j.]. **Added/Corp** American Production and Inventory Control Society. Vol. 28, No. 4 (4th Quarter 1987)-. Periodical. English. Four times a year. $110.00. American Production and Inventory Control Society, 500 West Annandale Road, Falls Church VA 22046. **Tel** (703)237-8344, (800)444-2742. available on microfilm and microfiche from University Microfilms International (UMI). Documents available from Article Express International. *Continues in part Production and Inventory Management (Washington, D.C.), 0032-9843.*
Ind/Abst Appl. Sci. Technol. Index; Eng. Index Annu.; Int. Abstr. Oper. Res. [Select. Cov.]; UMI ABI/Inform--Bus. Period. Ondisc (Fall 1987-) [Full Txt.].

ISSN 1059-1478
US
Pr Rev.
PRODUCTION AND OPERATIONS MANAGEMENT.
Added/Corp Production and Operations Management Society. **VFOAT** POM. (1992)-. Periodical. English. Four times a year. $90.00. Production and Operations Management Society, University of Baltimore, 1420 North Charles Street, Baltimore MD 21201. **Tel** (301)625-3261, (301)625-3000. **ED** Kalyan Singhal. Index available (in last issue of each volume). **Circ:** 1500.
Ind/Abst Int. Abstr. Oper. Res. [Select. Cov.].

US
PRODUCTION SUPERVISOR'S BULLETIN. See Industry and Production.

ISSN 0891-7167
DD 338
US
Pr Rev.
PRODUCTIVITY VIEWS. [Prod. views]. (198?)-.
Periodical. English. Six times a year (Jan., Mar., May., July, Sept., Nov.). $295.00. Productivity Development Group Inc, PO Box 488, Westford MA 01886. **Tel** (508)692-1818, FAX (508)692-5080. **ED** Martin F. Stankard. **Circ:** 500.

Desc: The newsletter devoted to practical developments in white-collar productivity and quality. Solutions, tips and actions ideas from service and quality leaders.

US
PROFESSIONAL ELECTRONICS. See Electronics.

UK
PROFESSIONAL MANAGER. Added/Corp
Institute of Management (Great Britain). Vol. 1, No. 1 (Nov. 1992)-. Periodical. English. Six times a year. $37.64. British Institute of Management, Management House, Cottingham Road, Northamptonshire NN17 1TT United Kingdom. **Tel** 011 44 1536 204222, FAX 011 44 1536 201651. *Formed by the union of Management News (British Institute of Management) and Industrial Management.*

ISSN 0710-4804
DD 658.4/005
CN
PROFESSIONAL MANAGER'S DIGEST, THE. Periodical. English. Twenty-six times a year.
Canadian News Services, 98 Granby Street, Toronto Ontario M5B 1J1 Canada.

US
PROFESSIONAL MANAGING. (19??)-.
English. Twelve times a year. $95.00. Resource Strategies Institute, PO Box 363, Moorestown NJ 08057. **Tel** (609)893-4790. **ED** Celine Allen. **Circ:** 8,000.

LC CURRENT ISSUES ONLY
DD 658
ISSN 0732-2119
US
PROFESSIONAL SERVICES MANAGEMENT JOURNAL.
(PROFESSIONAL SERVICES MANAGEMENT JOURNAL : PSMJ.). [Prof. serv. manage. j.]. **VFOAT** PSMJ; P.S.M.J. (19??)-. Periodical. English. Twelve times a year. $195.00. Practice Management Associates Ltd., 10 Midland Avenue, Newton MA 02158. **Tel** (617)965-0055, FAX (617)965-5152. **ED** Frank A. Stasiowski. Index available. **Circ:** 3,500.
Desc: A management newsletter for planning and design firms. Includes how-to articles, tips on employee relations and how to avoid or correct common problems.
Ind/Abst Constr. Index.

ISSN 1054-1225
DD 658
US
PROFIT MANAGEMENT. [Profit manage.].
VFOAT Profit Management Newsletter. Vol. 1, No. 1 (Nov. 1990)-. Periodical. English. Twelve times a year. $197.00. Productivity Inc., 101 Merritt 7, Corporate Park, Norwalk CT 06851. **Tel** (203)846-3777, (800)899-5009, FAX (203)846-6883.

LC UC263 .P77
DD 355.6/212/0973
ISSN 0199-7114
US
PROGRAM MANAGER. (PROGRAM MANAGER : THE DEFENSE SYSTEMS MANAGEMENT COLLEGE NEWSLETTER.). [Program manager].
Added/Corp Defense Systems Management College. (19??)-. Newsletter. English. Six times a year. $22.00. US Department of Defense, The Pentagon, Washington DC 20301. **Tel** (703)545-6700. **(Subscription address:** Superintendent of Documents, US Government Printing Office, Washington DC 20402. **)** *Continues Program Managers Newsletter, 0191-9407.*
Desc: Provides information on policies, trends, events, and current thinking affecting program management and defense systems acquisition.
Ind/Abst Acad. Search; Air Univ. Libr. Index Mil. Period.; Bus. Source Plus; Bus. Source; EP Collect.; Homework Help.; MasterFile FullTEXT 1000; MasterFile FullTEXT 350; MasterFile FullTEXT 650; MasterFile FullTEXT (July 1994-) [Full Txt.]; OCLC; Pub. Lib. FullTEXT; Telebase; Vocat. Search.

LC HD69.P75 P76
DD 658.4/04/05
ISSN 8756-9728
US
PROJECT MANAGEMENT JOURNAL.
[Proj. manage. j.]. Vol. 15, No. 1 (March 1984)-. Trade Publication. English. Irregular (Feb. Apr. Jun. Sep. Dec.). $90.00 surface mail, $135.00 airmail. Project Management Institute, 130 South State Road, Upper Darby PA 19082. **Tel** (610)622-1796, FAX (215)622-5640, telex 5101002864. **ED** Francis Webster. Index available. **Ad Acc. Circ:** 7,000 (ctrl). Documents available from UMI Article Clearinghouse. *Continues Project Management Quarterly, 0147-5363.*
Desc: Attempts to promote professionalism in project management.
Ind/Abst ABI/INFORM Glob. Ed.*; ABI/INFORM [Computer File] (March 1985-); Comput. Lit. Index; Curr. Cit.; Gen. BusinessFile (1992-); Oper. Res./Manage. Sci.

ISSN 1081-1001
DD 658
US
●PROJECT MANAGER (MOUNT HERMAN, CALIF.). (PROJECT MANAGER.). [Proj. manag.].
VFOAT Project Manager Newsletter. (1995)-. Periodical. English. Twelve times a year. $15.00. Systems Management Services, PO Box 416, Mount Herman CA 95401.

ISSN 0957-1853
UK
PROJECT MANAGER TODAY. (19??)-.
English. Twelve times a year. $82.13. Larchdrift Projects Ltd, PO Box 55, Wokingham, Berkshire RG11 4XN United Kingdom. **Tel** 011 44 1734 760577. **ED** Ken Lane.
Desc: Methods and techniques for managing projects successfully and software reviews.

LC HF5415 .I43
DD 658.8/2/05
ISSN 0266-7991
UK
CCC
PROMOTIONS & INCENTIVES. VFOAT
Promotions and Incentives. Vol. 20, No. 2 (Sept. 1984)-. Periodical. English. Ten times a year. $154.01. Haymarket Publishing Ltd., 12 14 Ansdell Street, London W8 5TR United Kingdom. **Tel** 011 44 171 9380705, 011 44 171 2786686, FAX 011 44 171 9380772. **(Subscription address:** Haymarket Magazines Ltd., PO Box 219, Subscription Department, Woking Surrey GU21 1ZW United Kingdom. **Tel** 011 44 1483 776345.**) ED** Max Cuff. **Ad Acc. Circ:** 11,500 (ctrl). available on microfilm from University Microfilms International (UMI). *Continues Incentive Marketing and Sales Promotion.*
Ind/Abst Curr. Cit.; Women Manage. Rev. [Full Txt.].

ISSN 0742-9770
DD 658
US
PRYOR REPORT, THE. See Occupations and Careers.

ISSN 1067-4489
DD 658
US
●PUBLIC SECTOR QUALITY REPORT. See Business and Economics-Abstracting, Bibliographies and Statistics.

ISSN 0882-7230
DD 658
US
PUBLIC WORKS PRO-VIEWS. (PUBLIC WORKS PRO-VIEWS : THE OFFICIAL PUBLICATION OF APWA'S INSTITUTES FOR PROFESSIONAL DEVELOPMENT.). VFOAT Public Works Proviews.
(1985)-. Periodical. English. American Public Works Association, 1313 East 60th Street, Chicago IL 60637. **Tel** (312)667-2200.

LC HD52.5 .P753
DD 658.7/2/05
ISSN 0309-7242
UK
PURCHASING & SUPPLY MANAGEMENT. See Business and Economics-Marketing and Purchasing.

IT
CEASED
QUADERNI GIURIDICI DELL IMPRESA.
(19??)-(19??). Italian. Edindustria Editoriale, Via Liguria 40, Sigra Gabrielli, 00187 Rome Italy. **Tel** 011 39 6 472911. *Continues Rivista Giurdica dell Impresa.*

ISSN 0226-3432
DD 658.5/62/05
CN
TITLE CHANGE
QUALITE (DOLLARD-DES-ORMEAUX).
(QUALITE.). [Qualite]. Vol. 1 (June 1980)-(19??). Periodical. French (English; summaries and/or abstracts in English). Qualite, 1424 Hymus Boulevard, Suite 2, Dorval Quebec H9G 2H8 Canada. **Tel** (514)684-4145. **ED** Joseph Kelada. **Bk Rev. Ad Acc. Circ:** 3,500.
Desc: Concepts and techniques in quality management, control and assurance and practical applications for management and for quality specialists.

CN
QUALITE TOTALE. (199?)-. French. Four times a year (Mar., June, Sept., Dec.). 20.00Can$ (regular),
60.00Can$ (library) Canada; 28.00Can$ (regular), 100.00Can$ (library) other; 90.00Can$ (individuals), 125.00Can$ (1-10 employees), 150.00Can$ (11-50 employees), 215.00Can$ (51-100 employees), 350.00Can$ (101-500 employees), 500.00Can$ (501-or more employees) corporations, Comes with Association Quebecoise de la Qualite membership. QUAFEC INC CDRH, CP 234, Pierrefonds Quebec, H9H 4K9 Canada. **Tel** (514)696-7450, FAX (514)696-7450. **ED** Joseph Kelada. cum. index. **Bk Rev,** (Qty: 4). **Ad Acc, Adv Mgr:** S. King. **Circ:** 6,000 (ctrl). *Continues Qualite, 0226-3432.*

ISSN 1071-1945
DD 658
US
TITLE CHANGE
QUALITY ABSTRACTS. [Qual. abstr.].
(1992)-(1994). Periodical. English. Advanced Personnel Systems, PO Box 1438, Roseville CA 95678. **Tel** (916)781-2900, FAX (916)781-2901. **ED** Richard B. Frantzreb. **Bk Rev. Circ:** 300. *Merged into Anbar Management of Quality Abstracts.*
Desc: Designed to keep you abreast of the literature of the quality field and help you benefit from the experience and insights of both the experts and those who are implementing TQM in their own organizations.

LC HD28 ISSN 0895-2272
DD 658 US
CEASED

QUALITY AND PRODUCTIVITY MANAGEMENT. [Qual. prod. manage.]. **Added/Corp** Virginia Productivity Center. **VFOAT** Quality and Productivity Management; QPM. Vol. 6, No. 2 (1987)-(June 1996). Periodical. English. Performance Center, Virginia University, 1900 Kraft Drive Suite 200, Blacksburg VA 24060. **Tel** (540)231-6473, FAX (540)231-3538. **ED** D Scott Sink. ctrl circ.
Desc: Focuses both on research and practical techniques and approaches. State-of-the art knowledge and information on quality and productivity management. Information on books, conferences, short courses, films, events, etc.

ISSN 1062-9440
US
TITLE CHANGE

QUALITY & PRODUCTIVITY ONE HUNDRED NEWSLETTER. **VFOAT** Quality and Productivity One Hundred Newsletter. (1992)-(1993). Newsletter. English. Kingspoint Company, 10610 Morado Circle, Suite 1302, Austin TX 78759. **Tel** (512)794-0944. **ED** Stephen Bilinsky. Index available (bound in each issue). **Circ:** less than 100. ***Continued by*** *The Senior Executive's Idea Letter, 1072-5873.*
Desc: Provides 100 tips each month on what others are doing and recommending to improve their quality, productivity and customer satisfaction.

LC TS156.A1 U5 ISSN 0147-4995
DD 658.5/6 US

QUALITY AND RELIABILITY ASSURANCE. English. $2.00 single issue. Office of the Assistant Secretary of Defence, Installations and Logistics, Washington DC 20301. ***Continues*** *Quality Control and Reliability.*

ISSN 1040-0664
DD 658 US
TITLE CHANGE

QUALITY ASSURANCE BULLETIN. [Qual. assur. bull.]. **Added/Corp** National Foremen's Institute. No. 1115 (Aug. 10, 1988)-(199?). Bulletin. English. Bureau of Business Practice, 24 Rope Ferry Road, Waterford CT 06386. **Tel** (800)243-0876, (203)442-4365, (800)876-9105, FAX (203)443-1123. ***Continues*** *Quality Control Supervisor's Bulletin, 0199-6223.* ***Continued by*** *Quality Management, 1080-0883.*
Ind/Abst Int. Aerosp. Abstr.

ISSN 0813-0272
DD 658.5620994 AT
CEASED

QUALITY AUSTRALIA. [Qual. Aust.]. **Added/Corp** Australian Organisation for Quality Control. (1984)-(1995). Periodical. English. Australian Organisation for Quality, PO Box 6076, Melbourne Victoria 3004 Australia. **Tel** 011 61 3 5263533, FAX 011 61 3 5263510. **Ad Acc, Adv Mgr:** Geoff Govllet. **Circ:** 6,000 (ctrl).
Desc: Includes articles on issues and related topics as well as information on national and international events.

ISSN 1059-3918
DD 658 US
CODEN QUBRE4
TITLE CHANGE

QUALITY BRIEFING. **See** Industry and Production.

ISSN 1044-0941
DD 658 US

QUALITY EXECUTIVE, THE. [Qual. exec.]. Vol. 1, No. 1 (May 1989)-. Newsletter. English. Twelve times a year. $105.00. Jerry Bowles Publishing, PO Box 801, Radio City Station, New York NY 10102. **Tel** (212)773-3000. **ED** Jerry G. Bowles.
Desc: Newsletter for performance improvement.

ISSN 1076-2760
DD 658 US

•**QUALITY HIGHLIGHTS.** [Qual. highlights]. Vol. 1, No. 1 (May 1994)-. Periodical. English. Twelve times a year. $24.00. Quality Highlights, 11500 Jollyville Road, Suite 2622, Austin TX 78759. **Tel** (512)794-0944. ***Continues*** *The Senior Executive's Idea Letter, 1072-5873.*

ISSN 1080-0883
DD 658 US

QUALITY MANAGEMENT. [Qual. manag.]. **Added/Corp** Bureau of Business Practice. (199?)-. Periodical. English. Twenty-four times a year. $148.96. Bureau of Business Practice, 24 Rope Ferry Road, Waterford CT 06386. **Tel** (800)243-0876, (203)442-4365, (800)876-9105, FAX (203)443-1123. ***Continues*** *Quality Assurance Bulletin, 1040-0664.*

LC TS156.A1 Q34 ISSN 1057-9583
DD 658.5/62 US

QUALITY OBSERVER, THE. [Qual. obs.]. Vol. 1, No. 1 (Nov. 1991)-. Periodical. English. Twelve times a year. $99.00. Quality Observer Corporation, PO Box 1111, Fairfax VA 22030. **Tel** (703)691-9496, (703)691-9295, FAX (703)691-9399. **ED** Kay Moore. **Ad Acc, Adv Mgr:** M. Jones, **Tel** same as publisher. **Circ:** 15,000 (ctrl).

ISSN 1058-0417
DD 658 US

QUALITY QUIPS. [Qual. quips]. **VFOAT** Quality Quips Newsletter. Vol. 1, No. 1 (Summer 1991)-. Periodical. English. Four times a year. Free. QP Publishing, 1210 South Adams St., Tallahassee FL 32301. **Tel** (904)224-8717, 800 852-6894.

ISSN 1063-2654
DD 658 US

QUALITY SERVICE UPDATE. (QUALITY SERVICE UPDATE : A PUBLICATION OF THE AMERICAN MANAGEMENT ASSOCIATION.). [Qual. serv. update]. **Added/Corp** American Management Association. Vol. 3, No. 6 (June 1992)-. Periodical. English. Twelve times a year. American Management Association, 135 West 50th Street, New York NY 10020-1201. **Tel** (212)586-8100, (212)903-8375 (periodicals), FAX (212)903-8168, (212)903-8083 (periodicals). **(Subscription address:** American Management Association, PO Box 408, Saranac Lake NY 12983. **Tel** (800)262-9699, FAX (518)891-1500.**)** ***Continues*** *Service Savvy, 1049-5967.*

ISSN 1078-0157
DD 658 US

•**QUALITY SOLUTIONS.** [Qual. solut.]. **Added/Corp** Bureau of Business Practice. No. 101 (June 1994)-. Periodical. English. Twelve times a year. $147.96. Bureau of Business Practice, 24 Rope Ferry Road, Waterford CT 06386. **Tel** (800)243-0876, (203)442-4365, (800)876-9105, FAX (203)443-1123.

LC TS156.A1 Q33 ISSN 0360-9936
DD 658.5/62 US
CCC
CODEN QULTDP

QUALITY (WHEATON). (QUALITY.). [Qual.]. Vol. 14, No. 7 (July 1975)-. Periodical. English. Twelve times a year. $70.00. Chilton Company, One Chilton Way, Radnor PA 19089. **Tel** (610)964-4000, (800)695-1214, FAX (610)964-4978, telex 6851035 CHILTON UW. **ED** Chet Placek. **Ad Acc. Circ:** 90,000 (ctrl). available on microfilm and microfiche from University Microfilms International (UMI). Documents available from UMI Article Clearinghouse. ***Continues*** *Quality Management & Engineering.*
Desc: Written for those involved with quality assurance including test, inspection, measurement and evaluation equipment and supplies.
Ind/Abst ABI/INFORM Glob. Ed.; ABI/INFORM [Computer File] (Jan. 1982-); Curr. Cit.; Gas Abstr. (?-?); Gen. BusinessFile (1992-); Qual. Control Appl. Stat.; UMI ABI/Inform--Bus. Period. Ondisc (Dec. 1987-) [Full Txt.].

LC HD2745 .Q36 ISSN 0733-6438
DD 658.4/22/02573 US

QUANTUS, COMPENDIUM OF DIRECTORS. [Quantus, compend. dir.]. **VFOAT** Q. 1979-. English. One time a year. PC Research Services, PO Box 7444, Trenton NJ 08628.

ISSN 1183-8949
DD 658.5/62/097105 CN

QUATRE VENTS (OTTAWA). (LES QUATRE VENTS : UNE PUBLICATION DU CONSEIL CANADIEN DES NORMES.). [Quatre vents]. **Added/Corp** Conseil Canadien des Normes. (Mar-June 1992)-. Periodical. French. Irregular. Standards Council of Canada, 45 O'Conner Street, Suite 1200, Ottawa Ontario K1P 6N7 Canada. **Tel** (613)238-3222, (800)267-8220, FAX (613)995-4564, telex 053-4403. ***Continues*** *Europe '92, Les Quatre Vents., 1181-652X.*

LC HD28 .R39 ISSN 0195-4784
DD 658/.005 US

READINGS IN MANAGEMENT : ANNUAL EDITIONS. **VFOAT** Management. (19??)-. English. One time a year. $10.95. Dushkin Publishing Group Inc., Sluice Dock, Guilford CT 06437. **Tel** (203)453-4351, (800)243-6532, FAX (203)453-6000. **ED** Fred H Maidment.
Desc: A cross section of current articles with a selected few classics addressing the various components of management today.

ISSN 1073-6042
DD 658 US

•**REAL WORLD STRATEGIST, THE.** [Real world strateg.]. Vol. 1, No. 1 (Mar. 1994)-. Periodical. English. Six times a year. $139.00. Real World Strategist, 3636 South Geyer Road, Suite 240, St. Louis MO 63127. **Tel** (314)821-5190.

IT

REALTA. (19??)-. Italian. Ten times a year. L30.000 (individuals) Italy; L65.000 other. Cida Servizi s.r.l., via Nazionale 75, 00184 Rome Italy. **Tel** 011 39 6 4818551.

ISSN 8756-0089
DD 651 US

RECORDS & RETRIEVAL REPORT, THE. [Rec. retr. rep.]. **VFOAT** Records and Retrieval Report. Vol. 1 No. 1 (Jan. 1985)-. Periodical. English. Ten times a year. $145.00. Greenwood Press Inc., PO Box 5007, Westport CT 06881-5007. **Tel** (203)226-3571, FAX (203)222-1502. **ED** C Peter Waegeman and Johanna Jacobskruse.
Desc: Explores solutions to information storage and retrieval problems, keeping records and documents managers current with new practices and technology.

UK

RECORDS MANAGEMENT BULLETIN. Bulletin. English. Six times a year. £98.00 (institutions), £24.00 (individuals). Records Management Society, 6 Sheraton Drive, Wycombe Buckshp 13 6DE United Kingdom. **Tel** 011 44 1494 525040.

LC HF5736 .R3632 ISSN 1050-2343
DD 651.5/05 US
CODEN RMAQEJ

RECORDS MANAGEMENT QUARTERLY (1986). (RECORDS MANAGEMENT QUARTERLY.). [Rec. manage. q.]. **Added/Corp** Association of Records Managers and Administrators. **VFOAT** ARMA International Records Management Quarterly; ARMA Records Management Quarterly; ARMA Quarterly. Vol. 20, No. 1 (Jan. 1986)-. Periodical. English. Four times a year (Jan., Apr., July, Oct.). $53.00. Association of Records Managers and Administrators Inc., PO Box 8540, Prairie Village KS 66208. **Tel** (800)422-2762, (913)341-3808, FAX (913)341-3742. ***Continues*** *ARMA Records Management Quarterly, 0191-1503.*
Ind/Abst Acad. Search; Bus. ASAP (1990-) [Full Txt.]; Bus. Index (1985-); Curr. Cit.; EP Collect.; Homework Help.; INFO-SOUTH Abstr.; MasterFile FullTEXT 1000; MasterFile FullTEXT 350; MasterFile FullTEXT 650; MasterFile FullTEXT (July 1993-); OCLC; Telebase.

ISSN 1046-4549
DD 650 US

REDIRECTIONS (KIRKLAND, WASH.). (REDIRECTIONS.). [ReDirections]. (1991)-. Periodical. English. Twelve times a year. $49.00. ReDirections Inc, PO Box 464, Kirkland WA 98083.

LC HD2745 .D85 ISSN 0735-6498
DD 658.4/0025/73 US

REFERENCE BOOK OF CORPORATE MANAGEMENTS. [Ref. book corp. manage.]. **Added/Corp** Dun and Bradstreet, Inc. 14th Ed. (1980/1981)-. English. One time a year. $795.00. Dun & Bradstreet Information Services, 3 Sylvan Way, Parsippany NJ 07054. **Tel** (201)605-6000, (800)526-0651. **Bk Rev.** ***Continues*** *Dun & Bradstreet Reference Book of Corporate Managements, 0070-7627.*
Desc: A four-volume set with biographical data on principal officers and directors of more than 13,000 US companies.

LC HD4965.5.U5 R44 ISSN 1056-9561
DD 331.2/816584/00973021 US

REGIONAL REPORT ON TOP MANAGEMENT COMPENSATION. [Reg. rep. top manage. compens.]. **Added/Corp** Executive Compensation Service (U.S.). 1st Ed. (1991)-. English. One time a year. $690.00. ECS, Executive Compensation Service, Wyatt Data Services, 218 Route 17 North, Roselle Park NJ 07662-9832. **Tel** (201)843-1177, FAX (201)843-0101. available with charts.

ISSN 1069-5923
DD 658 US

•**RELOCATION COMPASS.** [Relocat. compass]. Vol. 1, No. 1 (1st Quarter 1993)-. Periodical. English. Four times a year. $40.00. Dotsero Inc., 423 West Fourth Street, Hinsdale IL 60521. **Tel** (708)323-7680, FAX (708)323-7682. **ED** Ellie Monty. Index available. cum. index. **Ad Acc.** ctrl circ.

UK

REMUNERATION IN EUROPE REPORT. (19??)-. English. One time a year (June). £525.00 (first copy), £425.00 (each additional copy). International Salary Research, Pk House, Wick Road, Attn S Bryant, Egham Surrey TW20 0HW United Kingdom. **Tel** 011 44 1784 434411, FAX 011 44 1784 471404, telex 933783 PECG G. **ED** Joanna Woodford. **Acid Free. Circ:** 500.
Desc: A study of salaries and benefits data throughout Europe: It reflects local market rates and matched levels of responsibility to provide a realistic guide to compensation practices across Europe. Salary data covers 29 executive positions from top to middle management.

ISSN 0926-3314
NE
UDC 658.14/.17

RENDEMENT. AMSTERDAM. (RENDEMENT.). [Rendement Amst.]. (1991)-. Trade Publication. Dutch. Ten times a year. $137.03. VNU Business Publications BV, Postbus 9194, 1006 AC Amsterdam Netherlands. **Tel** 011 31 20 4875879.

LC HD30.42.I5 L45a
DD 658/.007/15 IO

REPORT - INSTITUTE FOR MANAGEMENT EDUCATION AND DEVELOPMENT. **Main/Corp** Lembaga Pendidikan dan Pembinaan Manajemen. (19??)-. English. One time a year. $20.00. Institute for Management Education and Development, Jalan Mentang Raya 9, Jakarta Indonesia.

Business and Economics —Management

DD 658
ISSN 0892-6158
US
TITLE CHANGE

REPORT ON INDUSTRIAL COMMUNICATIONS, THE. (THE REPORT ON INDUSTRIAL COMMUNICATIONS / ADVANCED MANUFACTURING RESEARCH.). [Rep. ind. commun.]. **Added/Corp** Advanced Manufacturing Research (Firm). Vol. 1, No. 1 (Oct. 1986)-(19??). Periodical. English. Advanced Manufacturing Research, 2 Oliver Street, 5th Floor, Boston MA 02109. **Tel** (617)542-6600. **Continued by** AMR Report.

ISSN 0486-4336
US

REPORT ON MANAGEMENT SUCCESSION. **Main/Corp** Schmitz (R. M.) & Company. 1966-. English. Irregular. University of Michigan / Dr. Swingard, Dr. Al Swingard, Ann Arbor MI 48109. **Tel** (313)764-1362.

LC HD62.4 .R46
ISSN 1064-4857
DD 658/.049/05
US

RESEARCH IN GLOBAL STRATEGIC MANAGEMENT. [Res. glob. strateg. manag.]. **VFOAT** Global Strategic Management. Vol. 1 (1990)-. Monographic series. English. One time a year. $73.25. JAI Press Inc., 55 Old Post Road, Suite 2, PO Box 1678, Greenwich CT 06836-1678. **Tel** (203)661-7602, FAX (203)661-0792. **ED** Alan Rugman.
Desc: Contains essays by authorities commissioned to identify research themes in the area of international business for the twenty first century.

LC HD58.8 .R47
ISSN 0897-3016
DD 658.4/06/05
US
CCC

RESEARCH IN ORGANIZATIONAL CHANGE AND DEVELOPMENT. [Res. organ. change dev.]. Vol. 1 (1987)-. English. One time a year. $73.25. JAI Press Inc., 55 Old Post Road, Suite 2, PO Box 1678, Greenwich CT 06836-1678. **Tel** (203)661-7602, FAX (203)661-0792. **ED** Richard Woodman and William Pasmore.

LC HD28 .R475
ISSN 1068-4867
DD 658/.005
US

RESEARCH MANAGEMENT REVIEW. (RESEARCH MANAGEMENT REVIEW : THE JOURNAL OF THE NATIONAL COUNCIL OF UNIVERSITY RESEARCH ADMINISTRATORS.). [Res. manage. rev.]. **Added/Corp** National Council of University Research Administrators. (1987)-. English. $20.00. National Council University Research Administration, One Dupont Circle Northwest, Suite 220, Washington DC 20036. **Tel** (202)466-3894.
Ind/Abst Curr. Index J. Educ.

LC HD42 .R47
ISSN 1040-9556
DD 658.4
US
CCC

RESEARCH ON NEGOTIATION IN ORGANIZATIONS. [Res. negot. organ.]. **VFOAT** Negotiations in Organizations. Vol. 1 (1986)-. English. Irregular. $73.25. JAI Press Inc., 55 Old Post Road, Suite 2, PO Box 1678, Greenwich CT 06836-1678. **Tel** (203)661-7602, FAX (203)661-0792. **ED** Roy J. Lewicki, Blair Sheppard and Robert Bies.

LC HD45 .R38
ISSN 0737-1071
DD 658.4/063/05
US
CCC

RESEARCH ON TECHNOLOGICAL INNOVATION MANAGEMENT AND POLICY. [Res. technol. innov., manage. policy]. Vol. 1 (1983)-. English. One time a year. $73.25. JAI Press Inc., 55 Old Post Road, Suite 2, PO Box 1678, Greenwich CT 06836-1678. **Tel** (203)661-7602, FAX (203)661-0792. **ED** Robert Burgelman and Richard Rosenbloom.

LC TX945 .Q53
ISSN 0095-5159
DD 647/.95/05
US

RESTAURANT EXECUTIVE. See Restaurants.

ISSN 1058-1359
DD 650
US

RETIREMENT OPPORTUNITIES. [Retire. oppor.]. Vol. 2, No. 5 (Sept./Oct. 1991)-. Periodical. English. Six times a year. $12.95. Opportunity Newsletter, PO Box 693, Holmes PA 19043. **Continues** Retirement Income Plus, 1052-2026.

LC HD28 .R48
ISSN 0034-7590
DD 658/.005
BL

REVISTA DE ADMINISTRACAO DE EMPRESAS. [Rev. adm. empresas]. **Added/Corp** Fundacao Getulio Vargas. Escola de Administracao de Empresas de Sao Paulo. Centro de Pesquisas e Publicacoes. **VFOAT** RAE; R.A.E. Vol. 1, No. 1 (May/August 1961)-. Periodical. Portuguese. Six times a year. $115.00. Fundacao Getulio Vargas, Praia de Botafogo, 190 6 Andar, 22253-900 Rio de Janeiro RJ Brazil. **Tel** 011 5521 551 0698, FAX 011 5521 551 1596, 011 5521 551 5755. **ED** Sergio Micelli. **Bk Rev**. **Ad Acc**. **Circ:** 5,000 (ctrl).
Desc: Administration in all of its details: from sophisticated subjects to buying/selling procedures of materials and marketing techniques. An assessment of the most current and significant issues, such as reengineering, quality control, marketing, eco management, health services management and computing.
Ind/Abst Foreign Lang. Index.

LC HD28 .R483
BL

REVISTA DE ESTUDOS DE ADMINISTRACAO. Year 1- ; July/Sept. 1975-. Portuguese. 10. Fundacao de Economia e Estatistica, Rua Duque de Caixias 1691, 90010 Porto Alegre, Rio Grande do Sul Brazil. **Tel** 0512-259255, FAX 0512-25006, telex 0515042.

MX

REVISTA USEM. **Added/Corp** Union Social de Empresarios Mexicanos. (19??)-. Periodical. Spanish. Twelve times a year. $15.00 US; $36.00 other. Union Social de Empresarios Mexicanos, Eugenia No 13 Desp 401, 03810 Mexico D. F. Mexico. **Tel** 536 25 80.

ISSN 0715-6669
DD 658.8/8/060714281
CN

REVUE CREDIT. **VFOAT** Credit Review. Vol. 1, No. 1 (Sept./Oct. 1982)-. Periodical. French (English). Six times a year. Section De Montreal De L'Institut Canadien Du Credit, CP 631 Succursale A, Montreal Quebec H3C 2T8 Canada.

ISSN 0338-4551
FR

REVUE FRANCAISE DE GESTION. [Rev. fr. gest.]. **Added/Corp** Fondation Nationale pour l'Enseignement de la Gestion des Entreprises. No. 1 (May 1975)-. Periodical. French. Five times a year. $146.32. Editions Chotard & Associes, 5 Avenue de la Republique, f 75011 Paris France. **Tel** 11 33 1 492344923.
Supersedes Hommes et Techniques, 0018-4381.
Ind/Abst Contents Pages Manage.; Int. Labour Doc.; Manage. Market. Abstr.; Repere (1979-1983); Selec. Coop. Index Manage. Period.

ISSN 0242-9780
FR
CCC

REVUE FRANCAISE DE GESTION INDUSTRIELLE. (19??)-. Periodical. French. Six times a year. $159.67. Dunod Gauthier Villars, 15 rue Gossin, 92543 Montrouge Cedex France. **Tel** 011 33 1 46565266, 011 33 1 40926527, FAX 011 33 1 40926597. **(Subscription address:** Centrale des Revues, 11 rue Gossin, 92543 Montrouge Cedex France. **Tel** 011 33 1 46565266.**)**
Ind/Abst Selec. Coop. Index Manage. Period.

LC HF
ISSN 1192-9480
DD 658.4/04/05
CN

●**REVUE INTERNATIONALE EN GESTION ET MANAGEMENT DE PROJETS.** [Rev. int. gest. manag. proj.]. (1993)-. Periodical. French. Four times a year (May and Nov.). 150.00Can$ (institutions), 60.00Can$ (individuals). Universite du Quebec - a Rimouski, 300 Avenue des Ursulines, Department Sci, Rimouski Quebec G5L 3A1 Canada. **Tel** (418)724-1609, FAX (418)724-1840. **Bk Rev**. **Ad Acc**. ctrl circ.

LC HG9395 .R57
ISSN 1053-556X
DD 658.3/254
US

RISK & BENEFITS JOURNAL, THE. See Insurance.

LC HG4001 HG8011
ISSN 1357-5309
DD 658 368
UK
Pr Rev.

●**RISK DECISION AND POLICY.** (1996)-. Academic Scholarly Publication. English. Two times a year. $95.00. Chapman & Hall, 2-6 Boundary Row, London SE1 8HN United Kingdom. **Tel** 011 44 171 8650066, FAX 011 44 171 5229623, telex 290164 CHAPMA G. **(Subscription address:** International Thomson Publishing Services Ltd., North Way Andover, Hampshire SP10 5BE United Kingdom. **Tel** 011 44 1264 332424.**)** **ED** Paul Anand and Chong Choi. **Ad Acc**.
Desc: Discusses various policy problems in both private and public sectors.

NE

RISK MANAGEMENT. (19??)-. English. Six times a year. Fl120.97. Brinkman Business Persgroep, Postbus 155, 6500 AD Nijmegen Netherlands. **Tel** 011 31 080 787444.

LC HD28
DD 658
US

●**RISK MANAGEMENT ADVISOR.** (1994)-. Newsletter. English. Twelve times a year. $236.88. Bureau of Business Practice, 24 Rope Ferry Road, Waterford CT 06386. **Tel** (800)243-0876, (203)442-4365, (800)876-9105, FAX (203)443-1123. **ED** Alex Vaughn.
Desc: Advice on managing business funds and protecting profits.

LC HG450
DD 332.6
US

RISK MANAGEMENT MANUAL. (1974)-. English. Twenty-four times a year. $424.79. Merritt Company, 1661 Ninth Street, PO Box 955, Santa Monica CA 90406. **Tel** (310)450-7234, (800)638-7597, FAX (310)396-4563.

ISSN 0812-8901
AT

RISK MEASUREMENT SERVICE KENSINGTON. **Added/Corp** Australian Graduate School of Management. Centre for Research in Finance. (1984)-. Periodical. English. Four times a year. 369.98Aus$. AGSM Ltd., Center for the Research of Finance, PO Box 1, Kensington NSW 2033 Australia. **Tel** 011 61 2 9319279, FAX 011 61 2 6627621.

IT

RIVISTA DI CONSULENZA AZIENDALE. (19??)-. Italian. Twenty-six times a year. 235000L. Age Editrice Srl, Via Beffa 1, 46042 Castel Goffredo Italy. **Tel** 011 39 376 770892.

ISSN 0749-7075
DD 658
US
CCC
Pr Rev.

S.A.M. ADVANCED MANAGEMENT JOURNAL (1984). (S.A.M. ADVANCED MANAGEMENT JOURNAL.). [S.A.M. adv. manage. j.]. **Added/Corp** Society for Advancement of Management. **VFOAT** Advanced Management Journal; SAM Advanced Management Journal. Vol. 49, No. 2 (Spring 1984)-. Periodical. English. Four times a year (Jan., Apr., July, Oct.). $34.00. Society for Advancement of Management, 126 Easr Lee Avenue, Suite 11, Vinton VA 24179. **Tel** (703)342-5563. **ED** M. H. Abolsamad. cum. index. **Bk Rev**. **Ad Acc**. **Circ:** 12,000 (ctrl). available on microfilm and microfiche from University Microfilms International (UMI). Documents available from UMI Article Clearinghouse. **Continues** Advanced Management Journal, 0362-1863.
Ind/Abst ABI/INFORM Glob. Ed.; ABI/INFORM Ondisc: Expr. Ed.; ABI/INFORM [Computer File] (Summer 1975-); Account. Art.; Anbar Account. Finan. Abstr. [Full Txt.]; Anbar Mark. Distr. Abstr. [Full Txt.]; Anbar Top Manage. Abstr. [Full Txt.]; Contents Pages Manage.; INFO-SOUTH Abstr.; Law Office Inf. Serv.; Mag. Search; Manage. Market. Abstr.; Manage. Bibliogr. Rev.; MasterFile FullTEXT (Jan. 1994-); Middle East Abstr. Index; Oper. Prod. Manage. Abstr. [Full Txt.]; Person. Train. Abstr. [Full Txt.]; Selec. Coop. Index Manage. Period.; Women Manage. Rev. [Full Txt.]; Work Relat. Abstr.

ISSN 1040-4236
DD 658
US

SAFETY AND SECURITY FOR SUPERVISORS. [Saf. secur. superv.]. (19??)-. Periodical. English. Twelve times a year. $21.10 (1-4 copies). Business & Legal Reports, 39 Academy Street, Madison CT 06443. **Tel** (203)245-7448, (800)727-5257, FAX (203)245-2559. Index available (bound in all issues).
Desc: Keeps your plant facility safe by making every supervisor a safety and security expert.

US

SAFETY MANAGEMENT PROGRAM. English. Thirty-six times a year. $157.92 (US); $191.04 (Canada) Includes: Safety Management, Safety Compliance Letter. Bureau of Business Practice, 24 Rope Ferry Road, Waterford CT 06386. **Tel** (800)243-0876, (203)442-4365, (800)876-9105, FAX (203)443-1123.

ISSN 0036-3421
US

SALES MANAGER'S BULLETIN. [Sales manager's bull.]. **Added/Corp** National Sales Development Institute. (19??)-. Bulletin. English. Twenty-four times a year. $181.52. Bureau of Business Practice, 24 Rope Ferry Road, Waterford CT 06386. **Tel** (800)243-0876, (203)442-4365, (800)876-9105, FAX (203)443-1123. **ED** Paulette S Withers. Index available. **Bk Rev**. **Circ:** 4,500.
Desc: A newsletter for sales managers. Includes interviews, general and sales management skills, psychology of sales management, and legal issues.

ISSN 1077-9329
DD 650
US

SALES MEMORY JOGGER. [Sales mem. jog.]. **Added/Corp** National Sales Development Institute (U.S.). (19??)-. Periodical. English. Twelve times a year. $22.80 (plus postage). Bureau of Business Practice, 24 Rope Ferry Road, Waterford CT 06386. **Tel** (800)243-0876, (203)442-4365, (800)876-9105, FAX (203)443-1123.
Desc: Organizer to help sales professionals keep up with meetings, appointments, expenses, etc.

ISSN 1081-3993
DD 658
US

●**SALES PROCESS ENGINEERING & AUTOMATION REVIEW.** [Sales process eng. autom. rev.]. **Added/Corp** Sales Automation Association. **VFOAT** Sales Process Engineering and Automation

Review; SPEAR. Vol. 1, No. 1 (Dec. 1994)-. Periodical. English. Four times a year. $69.00. Sales Automation Association, 1105 Washington, Dearborn MI 48124.

ISSN 1063-6587
DD 658 US
SALES PRODUCTIVITY REVIEW!, THE. [Sales prod. rev.]. (June 1992)-. Periodical. English. Twelve times a year. $36.00. Penoyer Communications, PO Box 2509, Santa Clara CA 95055-2509.

ISSN 0278-5048
US
SALES REP'S ADVISOR, THE. Added/Corp Business & Professional Communications Corp. (198?)-. English. Twenty-four times a year. $127.00 US, Canada and Mexico; $157.00 other. Alexander Research & Communications, Inc, 215 Park Avenue South, Suite 1301, New York NY 10003. **Tel** (212)228-0246, FAX (212)228-0376.
Desc: Business management strategies and tactics for independent manufacturer sales agents.

ISSN 1061-8465
DD 658 US
SALESFYI (CHICAGO, ILL.). (SALESFYI.). [Salesfyi]. **VFOAT** Sales FYI. Vol. 4, No.2 (1992)-. Periodical. English. Six times a year. $89.00. CIT Research Ltd, 1 Harewood, Placehanover Square, London W1R 9HA United Kingdom. **Tel** 011 44 171 4939247.

US
Pr Rev.
SAM ADVANCED MANAGEMENT JOURNAL. (1936)-. English. Four times a year (Jan., Apr., July, Oct.). $34.00 (one-year), $64.60 (two-year), $91.80 (three-year) surface mail; $59.00 (one-year), $114.60 (two-year), $166.80 (three-year) airmail. Society for Advancement of Management, 126 Easr Lee Avenue, Suite 11, Vinton VA 24179. **Tel** (703)342-5563. **(Subscription address:** SAM, Po Box 889, Vinton VA 24179. **Tel** (703)342-5563.) available in microform from University Microfilms International (UMI); available on an online database (file 15/Full-Text) from DIALOG.
Ind/Abst Bus. ASAP (1992-) [Full Txt.]; Bus. Index (1985-); Curr. Cit.; Gen. BusinessFile (1985-); Gen. Period. Index (1985-); Manage. Contents; UMI ABI/Inform--Bus. Period. Ondisc (Spring 1987-) [Full Txt.].

US
SAM FOCUS ON MANAGEMENT. English. Irregular. $25.00. Society for Advancement of Management, 126 Easr Lee Avenue, Suite 11, Vinton VA 24179. **Tel** (703)342-5563.

LC HD28 .S24 **ISSN** 0350-2546
DD 338 YU
SAMOUPRAVLJANJE (BELGRADE, SERBIA). (SAMOUPRAVLJANJE.). (19??)-. Periodical. Serbo-Croatian (Roman). Twelve times a year. $51.16. Nigro Privredni Pregled Marsala Birjuzova 3-5, Belgrad Ziro-Racun Kod Sdk 60801-833-635, Belgrad Yugoslavia.

LC HD70.K62 S26
DD 658/.009519/5 KO
SANOP MUNJE NONJIP. VFOAT Journal of Industrial Business Problems. Vol. 1 (1978)-. Periodical. English (Korean). Kyonggi Taehak Pusol Hanguk Sanop Munje Yonguso, 71 Chungjongno 2-ka, Sodaemun-ku, Seoul South Korea.

LC TS156.A1 S38a
DD 658.5/62/05 SZ
SAQ BULLETIN. Added/Corp Schweizerische Arbeitsgemeinschaft fur Qualitatsforderung. **VFOAT** S.A.Q. Bulletin; Bulletin ASPQ; Bulletin A.S.P.Q. (1984)-. Bulletin. French (German). Irregular. SAW-Geschaftsstelle, Postfach 2613, CH-3001 Bern Switzerland. ***Continues** Bulletin - Schweizerische Arbeitsgemeinschaft fur Qualitatsforderung.*

ISSN 0883-8720
DD 338 US
SAVVY MANAGEMENT MONTHLY. [Savvy manage. mon.]. May 1985-. Periodical. English. Twelve times a year. Key Communications, PO Box 42578, Washington DC 20015. **Tel** (301)656-0450, (301)656-2923, FAX (301)656-4554.

US
SBA PUBLICATIONS. SBA 115A : FREE MANAGEMENT ASSISTANCE PUBLICATIONS. Main/Corp United States. Small Business Administration. Office of Management Assistance. **VFOAT** Free Management Assistance Publications. **VAT** Small Business Administration Publications. (April 1980)-. English. Small Business Administration, 1030 15th Street, Washington DC 20417. **Tel** (202)653-6963. ***Continues** Publication - Small Business Administration.*

LC HD28 .S29 **ISSN** 0956-5221
DD 658/.005 UK
SCANDINAVIAN JOURNAL OF MANAGEMENT. [Scand. j. manag.]. Vol. 4, No. 1/2 (1988)-. Periodical. English. Four times a year. $353.00. Pergamon Press, An Imprint of Elsevier Science Ltd., The Boulevard, Langford Lane, Kidlington, Oxford OX5 1GB United Kingdom. **Tel** 011 44 1865 843000, 011 44 1865 843699, FAX 011 44 1865 843010. **(Subscription address:** Elsevier Science Ltd. / Oxford Fulfillment Centre, PO Box 800, Kidlington OX5 1DX United Kingdom. **Tel** 011 44 865 843355.) **ED** Sten Jonsson. available on microfilm and microfiche from University Microfilms International (UMI); available on an online database from Elsevier Electronic Subscriptions (EES). ***Continues** Scandinavian Journal of Management Studies, 0281-7527.*
Desc: Dedicated to advancing the understanding of management in private and public organizations through empirical investigation and theoretical analysis.
Ind/Abst Neuropsych. Abstr.; Psychoanal. Abstr.; Psychol. Abstr. (1989-); PsycScan: Appl. Exp. Eng. Psych.; PsycScan: LD/MR.

ISSN 0782-2979
FI
CEASED
SCIMP SELECTIVE CO-OPERATIVE INDEX OF MANAGEMENT PERIODICALS. See Business and Economics-Abstracting, Bibliographies and Statistics.

ISSN 0743-5207
DD 658 US
SECURITY FACTS. Vol. 1, No. 1 (Aug. 1, 1984)-. Periodical. English. Twelve times a year. $275.00. Security Facts, PO Box 398, Temple GA 30179.

LC HD38 .I53 **ISSN** 0145-9406
DD 658.4/7/05 US
CCC
CODEN SECME6
SECURITY MANAGEMENT (ARLINGTON, VA.). (SECURITY MANAGEMENT.). [Secur. manage.]. **Added/Corp** American Society for Industrial Security. Vol. 16, No. 4 (Aug./Sept. 1972)-. Trade Publication. English. Twelve times a year. $48.00. American Society for Industrial Security, 1655 North Fort Myer Drive, Suite 1200, Arlington VA 22209. **Tel** (703)522-5800, FAX (703)522-5226, telex 901892 ASIS AGTN. **ED** Sherry Harowitz, (phone: (703)312-6355). Index available. cum. index. **Bk Rev. Ad Acc, Adv Mgr:** S. Wade, **Tel** (703)312-6353. **Circ:** 30,000 (ctrl). available on microfilm and microfiche from University Microfilms International (UMI); available on an online database from BBS. Documents available from Ask*IEEE, UMI Article Clearinghouse. ***Continues** Industrial Security.*
Desc: Security in all areas: private, industrial, personal, government, banking, computer and others.
Ind/Abst ABI/INFORM Glob. Ed.; ABI/INFORM [Computer File] (April 1980-); Acad. Search; Bus. ASAP (1990-) [Full Txt.]; Bus. Index (1988-); Bus. Period. Index; Bus. Source Plus; Bus. Source; Comput. Lit. Index; Crim. Justice Abstr.; Crim. Justice Period. Index; Crim. Penol. Police Sci. Abstr.; Curr. Cit.; EP Collect.; Gen. BusinessFile (1988-); Gen. Period. Index (1988-); Homework Help.; INFO-SOUTH Abstr.; INSPEC (April 1988-); Mag. Search; MasterFile FullTEXT 1000; MasterFile FullTEXT 350; MasterFile FullTEXT 650; MasterFile FullTEXT (July 1993-); OCLC; Telebase; Trade Ind. ASAP [Full Txt.]; Trade Ind. Index [Full Txt.]; UMI ABI/Inform--Bus. Period. Ondisc (Jan. 1987-) [Full Txt.]; Wilson Bus. Abstr.

ISSN 1062-1628
DD 658 US
SECURITY MANAGEMENT BULLETIN. (SECURITY MANAGEMENT BULLETIN : PROTECTING PROPERTY, PEOPLE & ASSETS.). [Secur. manage. bull.]. **Added/Corp** National Foremen's Institute. (19??)-. Bulletin. English. Twenty-four times a year. $129.48. Bureau of Business Practice, 24 Rope Ferry Road, Waterford CT 06386. **Tel** (800)243-0876, (203)442-4365, (800)876-9105, FAX (203)443-1123. ***Continues** Security Management, Protecting Property, People & Assets, 0745-6093.*

LC HD30.4 .S45 **ISSN** 0882-0228
DD 658/.0071/173 US
SELECTIONS (GRADUATE MANAGEMENT ADMISSION COUNCIL). (SELECTIONS : THE MAGAZINE OF THE GRADUATE MANAGEMENT ADMISSION COUNCIL.). [Selections - Grad. Manage. Admiss. Counc.]. **Added/Corp** Graduate Management Admission Council. Vol. 1, No. 1 (Spring 1984)-. Periodical. English. Three times a year (Feb., Apr., and Oct.). Free on request. Graduate Management Admission Council, 2400 Broadway, Suite 230, Santa Monica CA 90404. **Tel** (310)998-9299. **ED** Deborah Perrin. **Circ:** 7000. available on microfilm and microfiche from University Microfilms International (UMI).
Desc: Provides information to schools and prospective students to help both make reasoned choices in the admission process, it also provides a forum for the exchange of information through research, educational programs, and other services among the broad constituency of individuals and institutions concerned with management education.

ISSN 1195-6399
DD 658.4 CN
•**SENIOR EXECUTIVE.** [Sr. exec.]. Vol. 1, No. 1 (1993)-. Periodical. English. Four times a year. 260.10Can$. Federated Press, PO Box 885, Stock Exchange Tower, Montreal Quebec H4Z 1K2 Canada. **Tel** (514)849-6600, (800)363-0722.

ISSN 1072-5873
DD 658 US
TITLE CHANGE
SENIOR EXECUTIVE'S IDEA LETTER, THE. [Sr. exec. idea lett.]. Vol. 1, No. 1 (Nov. 1993)-(1994). Periodical. English. Kingspoint Company, 10610 Morado Circle, Suite 1302, Austin TX 78759. **Tel** (512)794-0944. ***Continues** Quality & Productivity One Hundred Newsletter, 1062-9440. **Continued by** Quality Highlights, 1076-2760.*

BL
SERIE ESTUDOS PARA O PLANEJAMENTO. VFOAT Ipea Serie Estudos Para o Planejamento; Estudos Para o Planejamento. No. 1- 1972-. Monographic series. Portuguese. Irregular. Price varies per volume. IPEA Servicio Editorial / Instituto de Pesquisa Economica y Aplicada, Avenue P Antonio Carlos 51-14 Andar, CP 2672, 20020 010 Rio de Janeiro Brazil. **Tel** 011 55 21 2925141 ext. 1118, FAX 011 55 21 2401920.

ISSN 1053-1734
DD 658 US
CODEN SEEDEN
TITLE CHANGE
SERVICE EDGE, THE. [Serv. edge]. **Added/Corp** Lakewood Publications, Inc. **VFOAT** Service Edge Newsletter. (1988)-(19??). Newsletter. English. Lakewood Publications, 50 South Ninth Street, Minneapolis MN 55402. **Tel** (612)333-0471, (800)328-4329, FAX (612)333-6526. ***Merged into** Lakewood Report.*
Desc: Provides practical ideas and information about implementing a service strategy that can result in better customer service and improved profits. Includes special section devoted to front-line service techniques.

FR
SERVICE GROUPE. (19??)-. French. Documentation Francaise, 29 quai Voltaire, 75344 Paris Cedex 7 France. **Tel** 011 33 1 40157000, FAX 011 33 1 40157230, telex 204 826 DOCFRAN.

UK
SERVICE MANAGEMENT EUROPE. (19??)-. English. Four times a year. £30.00 UK; £33.00 other. Findlay Publications Ltd., Franks Hall, Horton Kirby, Dartford Kent DA4 9LL United Kingdom. **Tel** 011 44 1322 614060, FAX 011 44 1322 613943.

LC TX955 .S47 **ISSN** 0279-0548
DD 648/.05 US
SERVICES (VIENNA, VA.). (SERVICES : THE MAGAZINE OF THE BUILDING SERVICE CONTRACTORS ASSOCIATION INTERNATIONAL.). [Services]. **Added/Corp** Building Service Contractors Association International. Vol. 1, No. 1 (Jan. 1981)-. Periodical. English. Twelve times a year. $30.00. Services Magazine, 10201 Lee Highway, Suite 225, Fairfax VA 22030. **Tel** (703)359-7090, (800)368-3414, FAX (703)352-0493. **ED** P. Johnston. Index available (free / published in Mar.). **Ad Acc. Circ:** 13,000 (ctrl).
Desc: Management and technical articles for providers and purchasers of contract cleaning services such as office cleaning, carpet and floor care, window cleaning, and exterior maintenance.

ISSN 0712-7227
DD 658/.007/152 CN
SESSIONS DE FORMATION... / COSE. [Sess. form. - COSE]. **Main/Corp** Centre d'Organisation Scientifique de l'Enterprise. **VAT** Sessions de Formation - Centre d'Organisation Scientifique de l'Enterprise. Periodical. French. Three times a year. Free. Sessions de Formation, c/o Cose 3Me Etage, 440 Ouest boulevard Dorchester, Montreal Quebec H2Z 1V7 Canada. ctrl circ. ***Continues** Centre d'Organisation Scientifique de l'Entreprise. C O S E, 0383-9524.*

US
SHIFTWORK MANAGERS NEWSLETTER. Newsletter. English. Four times a year. $35.00 (one-year). SynchroTech, 315 South 9th Street, Suite 211, Lincoln NE 68508. **Tel** (402)474-4387, FAX (402)474-4425.

LC HD2745 .S48 **ISSN** 0193-4201
DD 658.4/22/0973 US
SIGNIFICANT ISSUES FACING DIRECTORS. VFOAT Directorship. (197?)-. English. One time a year. $36.50. Directors Publications Inc., 8 Sound Shore Drive, Suite 250, Greenwich CT 06830. **Tel** (203)861-7000, FAX (203)226-7893. **ED** Elsa Nad.
Desc: Issues of concern to public corporations in the coming year.

LC HD28 .S525 ISSN 0393-5108
DD 658/.005 IT
SINERGIE. **Added/Corp** Consorzio Universitario Economia Industriale e Manageriale (Verona, Italy). (19??)-. Periodical. Italian. Three times a year. L40880. Cueim, Via S Cristoforo #4, 37129 Verona Italy. **Tel** 011 39 45 597655, 597550.

LC HD28 .S53
DD 658/.009595/7 SI
SINGAPORE MANAGEMENT REVIEW. **Added/Corp** Singapore Institute of Management. (Jan. 1979)-. Periodical. English. Two times a year. Singapore Institute of Management, 3rd Floor/Thong Teck Building, Scotts Road, Singapore 0922 Singapore. **Tel** 7378866, telex SIM RS 50259. **ED** You Poh Seng. **Ad Acc. Circ:** 5,000. ***Supersedes** Singapore Manager.*
Desc: Contains topics on management.
Ind/Abst Women Manage. Rev. [Full Txt.].

IT
SISTEMI E IMPRESA. (1955)-. Italian. Twelve times a year. 360000L. ESTE, Via Giorgio Vasari 15, 20135 Milan Italy. **Tel** 011 39 2 55018039. **ED** Franco Rebuffo.

LC GV854.A1 S48 ISSN 0037-6175
DD 796.93/068 US
SKI AREA MANAGEMENT. **See** Leisure and Recreation-Outdoor Recreation.

LC HD28 .I14 ISSN 0019-848X
DD 658/.005 US
CCC
NLM W1 SL575 CODEN SMRVAO
Pr Rev.
SLOAN MANAGEMENT REVIEW. [Sloan manage. rev.]. **Added/Corp** Sloan Management Review Association. Industrial Management Review Association. Sloan School of Management. Vol. 12, No. 1 (Fall 1970)-. Academic Scholarly Publication. English. Four times a year (Jan., Apr., July and Oct.). $59.00. Sloan Management Review, MIT E 38 120, 292 Main Street, Cambridge MA 02139. **Tel** (617)253-7170, FAX (617)253-6466. **(Subscription address:** Neodata / Colorado, PO Box 2606, Boulder CO 80322. **) ED** Steven Star. Index available. cum. index. **Bk Rev. Ad Acc. Circ:** 20,000. available on microfilm and microfiche from University Microfilms International (UMI); available on an online database (file 15/Full-Text) from DIALOG. Documents available from Article Express International, The Genuine Article, UMI Article Clearinghouse, Ask*IEEE, Documents on Demand. ***Continues** Industrial Management Review, 0884-8211.*
Desc: Edited for and marketed to senior managers in business and industry. It provides intellectual leadership in current management issues. Articles by management scholars, executives, and management consultants describe effective responses to global, technological, and organizational challenges.
Ind/Abst ABI/INFORM Glob. Ed.; ABI/INFORM Ondisc: Expr. Ed.; ABI/INFORM [Computer File] (Spring 1972-); Acad. Search; Anbar Account. Finan. Abstr. [Full Txt.]; Anbar Mark. Distr. Abstr. [Full Txt.]; Anbar Top Manage. Abstr. [Full Txt.]; Bioeng. Abstr.; Bus. ASAP (1992-) [Full Txt.]; Bus. Index (1985-); Bus. Period. Index; Bus. Source Plus; Bus. Source; Comput. Lit. Index; Comput. Rev.; Contents Pages Manage.; Curr. Cit.; Curr. Contents Soc. Behav. Sci.; Ei Page One; Energy Res. Abstr. (Mar. 1981-); Eng. Index Annu.; Environ. Abstr.; EP Collect.; F&S Index Plus Text, Int. [Select. Cov.]; Gen. BusinessFile (1985-); Gen. Period. Index (1985-); Health Plan. Adminis.; Homework Help.; Hosp. Health Admin. Index; Hum. Resour. Abstr. (?-?); INFO-SOUTH Abstr.; INSPEC (Summer 1983-); Int. Aerosp. Abstr.; Int. Bibliogr. Sociol.; Int. Exec.; J. Econ. Lit.; J. Plan. Lit.; Mag. Search; Manage. Market. Abstr.; Manage. Bibliogr. Rev.; Manage. Contents; MasterFile FullTEXT 1000; MasterFile FullTEXT 350; MasterFile FullTEXT 650; MasterFile FullTEXT (July 1993-); OCLC; Oper. Prod. Manage. Abstr. [Full Txt.]; Oper. Res./Manage. Sci.; PAIS Int. Print; Person. Train. Abstr. [Full Txt.]; PROMT; Qual. Control Appl. Stat.; Res. Alert [Full Cov.]; School Organ. Manage. Abstr.; Selec. Coop. Index Manage. Period.; Soc. Plann. Policy Dev. Abstr.; Soc. Sci. Cit. Index [Full Cov.]; Sociol. Abstr.; Telebase; UMI ABI/Inform--Bus. Period. Ondisc (Spring 1988-) [Full Txt.]; Wilson Bus. Abstr.; Women Manage. Rev. [Full Txt.]; Work Relat. Abstr.

LC HD28 ISSN 0968-1000
DD 658.022 UK
SMALL BUSINESSES AND SMALL BUSINESS DEVELOPMENT. **See** Business and Economics-Small Business.

US
SNYDER MANAGEMENT ADVISORY. (19??)-. English. Ten times a year. $95.00. Snyder Management Advisory, 1571 Southwest 13th Drive, Boca Raton FL 33486. **Tel** (305)974-7995. ***Continues** Veterinary Management Update.*

LC HD28 .S63
DD 658/.005 SA
SOUTH AFRICAN JOURNAL OF BUSINESS MANAGEMENT. **Added/Corp** South African Association of Business Management. **VFOAT** Suid-Afrikaanse Tydskrif vir Bedryfsleiding. (19??)-. Trade Publication. English (summaries and/or abstracts in Afrikaans). Four times a year. $31.61. Foundation for Education Science & Technology, PO Box 1758, Pretoria 0001 South Africa. **Tel** 011 27 12 3226404, FAX 011 27 12 3207803. **ED** W. D. Pienaar. Index available. **Bk Rev. Circ:** 1,700 (ctrl). ***Absorbed** Bedryfsleiding.*
Desc: Original articles in any branch of business management.

LC HD28 ISSN 0971-5428
DD 658 II
UDC 65
•**SOUTH ASIAN JOURNAL OF MANAGEMENT.** [South Asian J. Manage.]. (1994)-. Periodical. English. Four times a year. $60.00. New Age International Pvt. Ltd., Journals Division, 4835-24 Ansari Road, Daryaganj New Delhi 110 022 India. **Tel** 011 091 11 3267437, FAX 011 091 11 3267437.

LC HD28 .S633 ISSN 0884-1373
DD 658/.005 US
Pr Rev.
SOUTHERN BUSINESS REVIEW. [South. bus. rev.]. **Added/Corp** Georgia Southern College. School of Business. Vol. 1, No. 1 (Spring 1975)-. Academic Scholarly Publication. English. Two times a year (June, & Dec.). $12.00. Southern Business Review, Georgia Southern University, College of Business, LB 8109, Statesboro GA 30460. **Tel** (912)681-5926, FAX (912)681-0292. **ED** Lloyd N. Dosier. **Circ:** 1,200 (ctrl).
Desc: This review is a scholarly journal aimed primarily at the academic market, college and university libraries.

LC QA75
DD 004 GW
•**SPRINGER SERIES IN OPERATIONS RESEARCH.** **See** Computers.

ISSN 0277-0458
US
ST. CLAIR SERIES IN MANAGEMENT AND ORGANIZATIONAL BEHAVIOR, THE. [St. Clair ser. manage. organ. behav.]. **VFOAT** Management and Organizational Behavior. Monographic series. English. Irregular. Price varies per volume. John Wiley & Sons, Inc., 605 Third Avenue, New York NY 10158-0012. **Tel** (212)850-6000, (212)850-6645, FAX (212)850-6088, telex 12-7063. **(Subscription address:** John Wiley & Sons / UK, Baffins Lane, Chichester, West Sussex PO19 1UD United Kingdom. **Tel** 011 44 1243 779777, FAX 011 44 243 776128, telex 86290 WIBOOKG.**)**

ISSN 0897-8484
DD 658 US
STAFF LEADER. [Staff lead.]. **Added/Corp** Center for Management Systems (Akron, Iowa). **VFOAT** Staff. (198?)-. Periodical. English. Twelve times a year. $125.00. Aspen Publishers Inc., 7201 McKinney Circle, Frederick MD 21701. **Tel** (800)234-1660, (301)698-7100, FAX (301)251-5784, telex 5106014543. **(Subscription address:** Aspen Publishers Inc., PO Box 990, Frederick MD 21701. **Tel** (800)901-9074, (301)698-7100.**)**
***Continues** Staff (Sioux City, Iowa), 0895-7568.*

LC HD62.15 .S79 ISSN 0968-0829
DD 658.5/62/05 UK
•**STRATEGIC INSIGHTS INTO QUALITY.** (1993)-. Periodical. English. Four times a year. $859.00. MCB University Press, 60 62 Toller Lane, Bradford, West Yorkshire BD8 9BY United Kingdom. **Tel** 011 44 1274 785280, FAX 011 44 1274 785200, telex 51317-MCBUNI-G.

LC HD30.28 .S733 ISSN 0143-2095
DD 658.4/012 UK
CCC
CODEN SMAJD8
Pr Rev.
STRATEGIC MANAGEMENT JOURNAL. [Strateg. manage. j.]. **VFOAT** S.M.J.; SMJ. Vol. 1, No. 1 (Jan.-March 1980)-. Periodical. English. Ten times a year. $545.00. John Wiley & Sons Ltd., Baffins Lane, Chichester, West Sussex PO19 1UD United Kingdom. **Tel** 011 44 1243 779777, FAX 011 44 1243 776128 BTG:JWP001, telex 86290 WIBOOKG. **(Subscription address:** John Wiley & Sons, Inc. / Philadelphia, PO Box 7247, Philadelphia PA 19170. **Tel** (212)850-6645, (800)225-5945.**) ED** Dan Schendel and Derek Channon. **Circ:** 2,500. available on microfilm and microfiche from University Microfilms International (UMI). Documents available from The Genuine Article, UMI Article Clearinghouse.
Desc: Publishes original refereed material concerned with all aspects of strategic management. Devoted to the development and improvement of both theory and practice. Appeals to practitioners and academics.
Ind/Abst ABI/INFORM Glob. Ed.; ABI/INFORM Ondisc: Expr. Ed.; ABI/INFORM [Computer File] (Jan. 1980-); Acad. Search; Anbar Account. Finan. Abstr. [Full Txt.]; Anbar Mark. Distr. Abstr. [Full Txt.]; Anbar Top Manage. Abstr. [Full Txt.]; Bus. Index (1985-); Bus. Period. Index; Bus. Source Plus; Bus. Source; Contents Pages Manage.; Curr. Cit.; Curr. Contents Soc. Behav. Sci.; EP Collect.; Gen. BusinessFile (1985-); Gen. Period. Index (1985-); Homework Help.; INFO-SOUTH Abstr.; Mag. Search; Manage. Market. Abstr.; Manage. Bibliogr. Rev.; Manage. Contents; MasterFile FullTEXT 1000; MasterFile FullTEXT 350; MasterFile FullTEXT 650; MasterFile FullTEXT (Jan. 1994-); OCLC; Oper. Prod. Manage. Abstr. [Full Txt.]; Oper. Res./Manage. Sci.; Person. Train. Abstr. [Full Txt.]; Res. Alert [Full Cov.]; Selec. Coop. Index Manage. Period.; Soc. Sci. Cit. Index [Full Cov.]; Telebase; UMI ABI/Inform--Bus. Period. Ondisc (Jan. 1988-) [Full Txt.]; Wilson Bus. Abstr.; Women Manage. Rev. [Full Txt.].

US
STRATEGIC MANAGEMENT, POLICY AND PLANNING. (19??)-. English. $63.50. JAI Press Inc., 55 Old Post Road, Suite 2, PO Box 1678, Greenwich CT 06836-1678. **Tel** (203)661-7602, FAX (203)661-0792. **ED** Howard Thomas and Dan Schendel.

ISSN 0748-4895
DD 658 US
STRATEGIC PLANNING MANAGEMENT. [Strateg. plan. manage.]. **VFOAT** S.P.M.; SPM. (1983)-. Periodical. English. Twelve times a year. Commerce Communications Inc, 5247 Washburn Avenue S, Minneapolis MN 55410. **Tel** (612)924-0957. **ED** Charles Hofer. Index available. **Bk Rev. Circ:** 1,000.
Desc: Strategic business, planning, tactics and strategy, with commentary and case histories.

FR
STRATEGIES. French. Forty-Four times a year. 1616.06F France; 2100.00F other. Groupe Strategie, 15 bis rue Ernest Renan, 92133 Issy Mlineaux Cdx France. **Tel** 011 33 (1) 40930102, FAX (1)40 93 05 06, telex 202 003.

ISSN 1148-750X
FR
UDC 658(44)
STRATEGIES DU MANAGEMENT PARIS. (STRATEGIES DU MANAGEMENT.). (1986)-. Periodical. French. Ten times a year. $669.30. Les Informations Rapides, 41 rue Berger, 75001 Paris France. **Tel** 011 33 1 42330211, FAX 42 33 72 32. **Bk Rev.** ctrl circ. ***Continues** La Conjoncture Sociale, 0150-3529.*

IT
STRUMENTI DI CONTROLLO DIREZIONALE. (19??)-. Periodical. Italian. Three times a year. IPSOA Editore SRL, Casella Postale 12055, Mastrangelo, 20120 Milan Italy. **Tel** 011 39 2 82476248. Index available (Included).

IT
STUDI ORGANIZZATIVI. (19??)-. Italian. Three times a year. L90000 Italy; L110000 other. Franco Angeli Riviste SRL, Viale Monza 106, 20127 Milan Italy. **Tel** 011 39 2 2827651, 011 39 2 289562, FAX 011 39 2 258004, telex 051-511650.

LC HB9 .C56a
RM
STUDIA UNIVERSITATIS BABES-BOLYAI. OECONOMICA. **Main/Corp** Universitatea Babes-Bolyai. (1975)-. Periodical. Romanian (summaries and/or abstracts in English, French, Russian and German). Two times a year. Biblioteca Centrala Universitara, Str. Clinicilor Nr. 2, 3400 Cluj Napoca Romania. **Tel** 95 117092, FAX 95 117633. **Circ:** 135. ***Continues in part** Universitatea Babes-Bolyai. Studia Universitatis Babes-Bolyai. Historia, Philologia, Oeconomica.*

ISSN 0924-4646
US
STUDIES IN INDUSTRIAL ORGANIZATION. [Stud. ind. organ.]. Vol. 1 (1981)-. Monographic series. English. Irregular. Price varies per volume. Kluwer Academic Publishers / Massachusetts, PO Box 358, Accord Station, Hingham MA 02018. **Tel** (617)871-6600. **(Subscription address:** Kluwer Academic Publishers / Netherlands, PO Box 322, 3300 AH Dordrecht Netherlands. **Tel** 011 31 78 392392, FAX 011 31 78 546474.**)**
Ind/Abst Curr. Cit.

ISSN 0921-3163
NE
Pr Rev.
STUDIES IN MANAGEMENT SCIENCE AND SYSTEMS. [Stud. manage. sci. syst.]. Vol. 1 (1975)-. Monographic series. English. Irregular. Price varies per volume. Elsevier Science Publishers BV, PO Box 211, 1000 AE Amsterdam Netherlands. **Tel** 011 31 20 4853641, 011 31 20 4853642, FAX 011 31 20 4853598. Documents available from Ask*IEEE.
Ind/Abst Ei Page One; INSPEC; Math. Rev.

ISSN 0081-8194
NE
Pr Rev.
STUDIES IN MATHEMATICAL AND MANAGERIAL ECONOMICS. **See** Mathematics.

Business and Economics — Management

SUCCESS FOCUS. (1992)-. Periodical. English. Twelve times a year. $124.00. Success Publishing Company, 9250 Greenback Lane, Suite 128, Orangevale CA 95662.
ISSN 1058-5923 US
LC HF5469 .S885
DD 658.8/78/08

SUPERMARKET MANAGEMENT. Periodical. English. Four times a year. $8.00. US Industrial Pub Inc, 209 Dunn Avenue, Stamford CT 06905. **Tel** (203)322-7676.
ISSN 0149-8894 US

SUPERVISOR'S BULLETIN FOR ADMINISTRATION AND OFFICE SUPPORT GROUPS. **Added/Corp** Bureau of Business Practice. Issue No. 626 (Feb. 15, 1982)-(19??). Bulletin. English. Bureau of Business Practice, 24 Rope Ferry Road, Waterford CT 06386. **Tel** (800)243-0876, (203)442-4365, (800)876-9105, FAX (203)443-1123. **ED** Pat Thunberg. **Continues** Office Supervisor's Bulletin, 0030-025X. **Continued by** Leadership Edge.
Desc: Published for administration and office support groups.
ISSN 0744-3625 US
TITLE CHANGE

SUPERVISOR'S DEVELOPMENT PROGRAM. English. Twelve times a year. $120.36 US; $148.44 Canada (includes Dynamic Supervision, Supervisor's Bulletin - Plant, and Supervisor's Memory Jogger). Bureau of Business Practice, 24 Rope Ferry Road, Waterford CT 06386. **Tel** (800)243-0876, (203)442-4365, (800)876-9105, FAX (203)443-1123.
US

•SUPERVISOR'S GUIDE TO EMPLOYMENT PRACTICES. [Superv. guide employ. pract.]. (March 29, 1993)-. Periodical. English. Twenty-six times a year. $98.80. Clement Communications Inc, Concord Industrial Park, Concordville PA 19331. **Tel** (800)345-8101, (610)459-4200. **ED** Wendy Kaplan Ampolsk.
ISSN 1069-4978 US
DD 658

SUPERVISOR'S MEMORY JOGGER. [Superv. mem. jog.]. **Added/Corp** National Foremen's Institute. (19??)-. Periodical. English. Twelve times a year. $16.20 (plus postage). Bureau of Business Practice, 24 Rope Ferry Road, Waterford CT 06386. **Tel** (800)243-0876, (203)442-4365, (800)876-9105, FAX (203)443-1123.
Desc: Organizer to help supervisors keep up with meetings, appointments, expenses, etc.
ISSN 1077-9337 US
DD 650

SUPERVISOR'S MOTIVATION SERIES. (19??)-. English. Twelve times a year. $45.72 US; $56.04 Canada. Bureau of Business Practice, 24 Rope Ferry Road, Waterford CT 06386. **Tel** (800)243-0876, (203)442-4365, (800)876-9105, FAX (203)443-1123.
US
LC HD4965.5.U6 M4B
DD 331.2/81/65843097949
ISSN 0092-5802 US

SUPERVISORY AND MIDDLE MANAGEMENT SALARY SURVEY (LOS ANGELES). See Business and Economics-Labor.
LC HD
DD 338
US

SUPPLEMENT TO BIBLIOGRAPHY ON LOGISTICS AND PHYSICAL DISTRIBUTION MANAGEMENT. **Added/Corp** Council of Logistics Management (U.S.) (1986)-. English. One time a year. $25.00. Council of Logistics Management, 2803 Butterfield Road, Suite 380, Oak Brook IL 60521. **Tel** (708)574-0985, FAX (708)574-0989. **Continues** Supplement to Bibliography on Physical Distribution Management.
ISSN 1046-3771 US
DD 658
CCC

SUPPLIER SELECTION & MANAGEMENT REPORT. [Supplier sel. manage. rep.]. **Added/Corp** Institute of Management & Administration. **VFOAT** Supplier Selection and Management Report. Issue 89-12 (Dec. 1989)-. Periodical. English. Twelve times a year. $245.00. Institute of Management and Administration, 29 West 35th Street, 5th Floor, New York NY 10001-2299. **Tel** (212)244-0360, FAX (212)564-0465.
LC HD28
DD 658
ISSN 1355-7912 UK

•SUPPLY CHAIN MANAGEMENT. (1996)-. Academic Scholarly Publication. English. Three times a year. $139.00. MCB University Press, 60 62 Toller Lane, Bradford, West Yorkshire BD8 9BY United Kingdom. **Tel** 011 44 1274 785280, FAX 011 44 1274 785200, telex 51317-MCBUNI-G.

SVILUPPO E ORGANIZZAZIONE. [Sviluppo organ.]. (1970)-. Periodical. Italian. Six times a year. L88560. ESTE, Via Giorgio Vasari 15, 20135 Milan Italy. **Tel** 011 39 2 55018039. available on microfilm and microfiche from University Microfilms International (UMI).
ISSN 0391-7045 IT
UDC 658
DD 658

SYSTEMS THINKER, THE. [Syst. thinker]. Vol. 1, No. 1 (April/May 1990)-. Periodical. English. Ten times a year (Dec./Jan. and June/July issues combined). $147.00. Pegasus Communications, PO Box 120, Kendall Square, Cambridge MA 02142. **Tel** (617)576-1231, FAX (617)576-3114. **ED** Colleen Lannon-Kim. Index available. cum. index. **Bk Rev**, (Qty: 2-4). **Circ:** 4,600 (ctrl).
Desc: Presents a systems perspective on issues and provides systems tools for framing problems. Includes reviews of software and books, columns by systems thinkers, and a calendar of workshops.
ISSN 1050-2726 US
LC HC497.H6 T3

TA JEN. **VFOAT** The Executive. (Aug. 1975)-. Periodical. Chinese (Chinese). One time a week. $90.00. Overseas Cultural Development Ltd, Room 534/Man Yee, Hsiang-Kang, People's Republic of China. **Supersedes** Ching Chi Shih Pao.
CH
LC HD62.15 .T36
DD 658.5/62/05
ISSN 1048-5198 US
CEASED

TAPPING THE NETWORK JOURNAL. [Tapping netw. j.]. **Added/Corp** Quality & Productivity Management Association. (1990)-(June 1995). Periodical. English. Quality Productivity Management Association, 300 North Martingale Road, Suite 230, Schaumberg IL 60173. **Tel** (708)619-2909. **Circ:** 1,300. available on microfilm and microfiche from University Microfilms International (UMI); available on an online database (file 15/Full-Text) from DIALOG.
Desc: To share what has been learned within the author's organizations within the course of a particular change effort.
LC HD30.4 .T37
DD 658.4/071245/05
ISSN 0962-2519 UK
CCC
TITLE CHANGE

TARGET MANAGEMENT DEVELOPMENT REVIEW. **VFOAT** Target; Management Development Review. (19??)-(19??). Periodical. English. MCB University Press, 60 62 Toller Lane, Bradford, West Yorkshire BD8 9BY United Kingdom. **Tel** 011 44 1274 785280, FAX 011 44 1274 785200, telex 51317-MCBUNI-G. Documents available from UMI Article Clearinghouse. **Continued by** Management Development Review.
Ind/Abst ABI/INFORM Glob. Ed.; Person. Manage. Abstr.
ISSN 1069-6539 US
DD 658

•TEAM MANAGEMENT BRIEFINGS. [Team manag. brief.]. Vol. 1, No. 1 (Oct. 1993)-. Periodical. English. Twelve times a year. $99.00. Moran Publishing Company / Oregon, PO Box 10828, Portland OR 97210. **Tel** (503)274-3953.
BE

TECHNIQUE ET MANAGEMENT. (19??)-. Dutch (French). Twelve times a year. 1180.00F. De Sikkel Media, Krijgslaan 281 512, 9000 Gent Belgium. **Tel** 011 32 3 3124761.
ISSN 0223-5587 FR
UDC 331.881

TECHNIQUES TRESOR. (1954)-. Periodical. French. Four times a year. $45.94. Techniques Tresor, 45 rue des Petites Ecuries, 75010 Paris France. **Tel** 33 1 47709169. **Circ:** 1,500 (ctrl).
ISSN 0932-2558 GW
UDC 658.624

TECHNOLOGIE & MANAGEMENT. [Technol. Manag.]. **VFOAT** Technologie und Management. (1987)-. Trade Publication. German. Four times a year. $74.46. Gabler Verlag, Postfach 1546, D-65005 Wiesbaden Germany. **Tel** 011 49 611 534129, FAX 011 49 611 534430. **Continues** Der Technologie-Manager, 0178-4463.
ISSN 0886-103X US
DD 658

TECHNOLOGY MANAGEMENT ACTION. See Science and Technology.
LC T
DD 600
ISSN 1073-4457 US
CCC
CODEN TCMAEH
Pr Rev.

•TECHNOLOGY MANAGEMENT (NEW YORK, N.Y.). (TECHNOLOGY MANAGEMENT.). [Technol. manag.]. **Added/Corp** University of Maryland. Graduate School of Management & Technology. Vol. 1, No. 1 (1994)-. Academic Scholarly Publication. English. Six times a year (1 volume). $250.00. Elsevier Science Publishing Company Inc, Madison Square Station, PO Box 882, New York NY 10159-0882. **Tel** (212)633-3950, FAX (212)633-3990. **ED** J. Leslie Glick. **Bk Rev**. **Ad Acc**. available on an online database from Elsevier Electronic Subscriptions (EES).
Desc: Addresses technology management problems--aims to give managers coverage of key concerns.
ISSN 1054-979X US
DD 658

TECHSCAN (NEW YORK, N.Y.). (TECHSCAN : THE MANAGER'S GUIDE TO TECHNOLOGY.). [TechScan]. **Added/Corp** Richmond Research. **VFOAT** Tech Scan. Mar. (1991)-. Periodical. English. Twelve times a year. $87.50. Richmond Research, PO Box 537, Village Station, New York NY 10014-0537.
ISSN 1034-7496 AT
DD 384.30994
TITLE CHANGE

TELECOMMUNICATIONS MANAGEMENT AND MARKETING NEWSLETTER. See Communications-Telecommunication.
ISSN 1188-0589 CN
DD 658.3

TENDANCES (MONTREAL. 1991). (TENDANCES.). [Tendances]. **Added/Corp** Federation des Cegeps. Vol. 1, No 1 (Oct. 1991)-. Periodical. French. Four times a year. Limited free distribution. Federation des Cegeps, 500 Est boulevard Cremazie, Montreal Quebec H2B 1G7 Canada.
ISSN 1053-718X US

THINK & GROW RICH NEWSLETTER. [Think grow rich newsl.]. **Added/Corp** Napoleon Hill Foundation. **VFOAT** Think and Grow Rich Newsletter. Vol. 3, No. 1 (Oct. 1990)-. Newsletter. English. Twelve times a year. $47.00. Believe & Achieve, 32724 Friar Tuck, Birmingham MI 48025. **Tel** (800)343-3648. **ED** Samuel Cypert. **Bk Rev**. ctrl circ. **Continues** Think & Grow Rich, 1041-1836.
LC HD69.I7 T56
DD 658.1/149/05
ISSN 0160-9823 US

THUNDERBIRD INTERNATIONAL, THE. Vol. 1 (Fall 1976)-. Periodical. English. Two times a year. $2.00 each issue. Associated Students Legislative Council, International Studies Department, Glendale AZ 85306.
LC HB9 .T44
DD 330
ISSN 0772-7674 BE

TIJDSCHRIFT VOOR ECONOMIE EN MANAGEMENT. See Business and Economics.
AT

TIME MANAGEMENT LETTER. English. Twelve times a year. 145.00Aus$. Information Australia, 45 Flinders Lane, Melbourne 3000 Australia. **Tel** 03 654 2800, FAX 03 650 5261.
ISSN 0228-4189 CN
DD 658.4/093

TIME MANAGEMENT REPORT, THE. [Time management report]. Vol. 1, No. 1, Nov. (1980)-. Periodical. English. Twelve times a year. 49.95Can$. Harold Taylor Time Consultants, 2175 Sheppard Avenue East, Suite 310, Willowdale Ontario M2J 1W8 Canada. **Tel** (416)491-0777, FAX (416)491-8233. **ED** Joan Patterson. **Circ:** 200 (ctrl).
LC HD29 .I516a
DD 658
ISSN 0161-0295 US
CODEN TIMBD
TITLE CHANGE

TIMS/ORSA BULLETIN. [TIMS/ORSA bull.]. **Main/Corp** Institute of Management Sciences. **Added/Corp** Operations Research Society of America. Institute of Management Sciences. Canadian Operational Research Society. **VFOAT** ORSA/TIMS Bulletin. **VAT** Institute of Management Sciences/Operations Research Society of America Bulletin. (1976)-(1995). Bulletin. English. Institute of Management Sciences, 290 Westminster Street, Providence RI 02903. **Tel** (401)274-2525, FAX (401)274-3189. Documents available from Ask*IEEE. **Continues** Bulletin of the Operations Research Society of America, 0030-3666. **Continued by** INFORMS Meeting Bulletin.
Ind/Abst INSPEC (1976-).
LC HG4028.C45 J68
DD 658
ISSN 1080-1162 US

•TMA JOURNAL. [TMA j.]. **Added/Corp** Treasury Management Association (U.S.). **VFOAT** Treasury Management Association Journal. Vol. 14, No. 1 (Jan./Feb. 1994)-. Periodical. English. Six times a year. $90.00. Treasury Management Association, PO Box 64714S, Baltimore MD 21264. **Tel** (301)907-2862. Index available (Bound in April issue). **Continues** Journal of Cash Management, 0731-1281.
Ind/Abst Curr. Cit.

Business and Economics — Management

ISSN 0887-5200
DD 658 US
TODAY'S EXECUTIVE. [Today's exec.]. (1978)-. Periodical. English. Four times a year. Free. Price Waterhouse & Company, 1177 Avenue of the Americas, New York NY 10020. **Tel** (212)596-7000. **ED** George de Mare. Index available. **Circ**: 60,000. Documents available from UMI Article Clearinghouse.
Desc: Trends and techniques in managing.
Ind/Abst ABI/INFORM Glob. Ed.; ABI/INFORM [Computer File] (Winter 1983-); Comput. Lit. Index.

ISSN 1055-0844
US
●**TODAY'S MANAGER.** (1993)-. Periodical. English. Twelve times a year. $47.00. Management Transformation Inc, PO Box 5225, Englewood CO 80155-5225. **Tel** (303)220-8351. available on microfilm from University Microfilms International (UMI).

ISSN 0887-5332
DD 658 US
CCC
TOM PETERS ON ACHIEVING EXCELLENCE. **VFOAT** On Achieving Excellence. Vol. 1, No. 1 (Dec. 1986)-. Periodical. English. Twelve times a year. $150.00. Tom Peters Group, 555 Hamilton Avenue, Palo Alto CA 94301. **Tel** (800)367-4310. **ED** Jayne A. Pearl and Donna Hawley. Index available. **Circ**: 7,000.
Desc: Newsletter that dares managers to take instant action.

ISSN 0821-4905
DD 651.3/05 CN
TOMORROW'S OFFICE. [Tomorrow's off.]. Vol. 1, No. 1 (June 1982)-. Periodical. English. Irregular. $20.00. Tomorrow's Office, PO Box 76, Clarkson Ontario L5J 3X9 Canada.

LC HC281. .I63
GW
TOP-BUSINESS. See Industry and Production.

LC HD28 .B79 **ISSN 0738-6699**
DD 650/.05 US
TOP LINE. [Top line]. Winter 1983-. Periodical. English. Four times a year. Free. 13-30 Corporation, 505 Market Street, Knoxville TN 37902. **Tel** (615)521-0600. **ED** George Spencer. **Ad Acc**. **Circ**: 180,000 (ctrl).
Continues Business Access Quarterly, 0738-6680.
Desc: An executive briefing service with how-to articles to help owners and executives at small to mid-sized corporations.

ISSN 0271-1206
US
CCC
NLM W1 TO539MSF
TITLE CHANGE
TOPICS IN HOSPITAL PHARMACY MANAGEMENT. See Pharmacy and Pharmacology.

ISSN 0896-7776
DD 658 US
TOTAL EMPLOYEE INVOLVEMENT. (TOTAL EMPLOYEE INVOLVEMENT : TEI.). **VFOAT** TEI; TEI Newsletter. **VAT** Total Employee Involvement Newsletter. (1988)-. Periodical. English. Ten times a year. $167.00. Productivity Inc, 101 Merritt 7, Corporate Park, Norwalk CT 06851. **Tel** (203)846-3777, (800)899-5009, FAX (203)846-6883. **ED** Lloyd Resnick. **Bk Rev**. ctrl circ. **Absorbed** Service Insider, 1047-7187.
Desc: Devoted to issues regarding employee involvement; topics covered include compensation strategies, self-directed work teams, suggestion systems, etc.

US
TOTAL QUALITY & SITE-BASED MANAGEMENT JOURNAL. English. Twelve times a year. $119.00. National Center to Save Our Schools, 731 Franklin Street, Westbury NY 11590. **Tel** (516) 997-1777, (516) 997-9555.

ISSN 0954-4127
UK
CCC
CODEN TQMAED
TOTAL QUALITY MANAGEMENT. [Total qual. manag.]. Vol. 1, No. 1 (1990)-. Periodical. English. Six times a year. $468.00. Carfax Publishing Company, PO Box 25, Abingdon, Oxfordshire OX14 3UE United Kingdom. **Tel** 011 44 1235 555335, FAX 011 44 1235 553559, telex 817484. available on microfiche. Documents available from Ask*IEEE.
Ind/Abst Bus. Source Plus; Bus. Source Cit.; Curr. Cit.; EP Collect.; Homework Help.; INSPEC (1991-); MasterFile FullTEXT 1000; MasterFile FullTEXT 350; MasterFile FullTEXT 650; MasterFile FullTEXT (July 1994-); Telebase; World Mag. Bank.

ISSN 1053-1718
DD 338 US
TITLE CHANGE
TOTAL QUALITY NEWSLETTER. (TOTAL QUALITY NEWSLETTER : THE INSIDE REPORT ON AMERICA'S NEW COMPETITIVENESS.). [Total qual. newsl.]. **VFOAT** TQN; Total Quality. (1990)-(19??). Newsletter. English. Lakewood Publications, 50 South Ninth Street, Minneapolis MN 55402. **Tel** (612)333-0471, (800)328-4329, FAX (612)333-6526. **Merged into** The Lakewood Report.
Desc: Provides total quality perspective that goes beyond slogans, labels, categories and specialization. Shows by example how to increase market share, profits, and satisfaction.

LC HD62.15 .T685 **ISSN 1075-2056**
DD 658.5/62/05 US
TOTAL QUALITY REVIEW, THE. (THE TOTAL QUALITY REVIEW : THE INTERNATIONAL JOURNAL OF EFFECTIVE ORGANIZATIONS.). [Total qual. rev.]. (1994)-. Periodical. English. Six times a year. $165.00. Cambridge Strategy Publications, 39 Cambridge Road, Cambridge CB2 1NS United Kingdom. **(Subscription address**: Direct Answer Inc., PO Box 26007, Alexandria VA 22313.) **Absorbed** TQM Magazine, 0961-8082.

LC G155.A1 I516 **ISSN 0261-5177**
DD 380.1/459104 UK
CCC
TOURISM MANAGEMENT (1982). (TOURISM MANAGEMENT.). [Tour. manage.]. Vol. 3, No. 1 (March 1982)-. Periodical. English. Eight times a year. $530.00. Butterworth Heinemann Publishers, Linacre House Jordan Hill, Oxford OX2 8DP United Kingdom. **Tel** 011 44 1865 310366, FAX 011 44 1865 310898. **(Subscription address**: Elsevier Science Ltd. / Oxford Fulfillment Centre, PO Box 800, Kidlington OX5 1DX United Kingdom. **Tel** 011 44 865 843355.) **ED** Colin Blackman. Index available. **Bk Rev**. **Ad Acc**. ctrl circ. available on microfilm and microfiche from University Microfilms International (UMI); available on an online database from Elsevier Electronic Subscriptions (EES). **Continues** International Journal of Tourism Management, 0143-2516.
Desc: International journal for all those concerned with the planning and management of tourism. It's contents reflect its integrative approach, including primary research, articles, review articles, reports, book reviews and listing of recent publications forthcoming meetings and international news.
Ind/Abst Contents Pages Manage.; Curr. Cit.; Geogr. Abstr. Human Geogr.; Int. Dev. Abstr.; Int. Labour Doc.; Leis., Rec., Tour. Abstr.

LC HD62.15 .T778 **ISSN 0954-478X**
DD 658.5/62/05 UK
CCC
CODEN TQMMEF
TITLE CHANGE
TQM MAGAZINE (INTERNATIONAL ED.). (THE TQM MAGAZINE.). [TQM mag.]. **VFOAT** Total Quality Management Magazine. (Nov. 1988)-(1995). Periodical. English. MCB University Press, 60 62 Toller Lane, Bradford, West Yorkshire BD8 9BY United Kingdom. **Tel** 011 44 1274 785280, FAX 011 44 1274 785200, telex 51317-MCBUNI-G. **Merged into** Total Quality Review.
Ind/Abst Curr. Cit.

ISSN 0775-2911
BE
UDC 62
TITLE CHANGE
TRADE FLASH BRUXELLES. [Trade flash Brux.]. **VFOAT** Electronic Trade Data Interchange News Brief. (1986)-(1994). Periodical. English. Blenheim On Line, 4 Devonshurst Place Heathfield, Terrace London W4 4JD United Kingdom. **Tel** 011 44 181 8684466. **ED** Richard Sarson. **Circ**: 500. **Continued by** EDI Analysis, 0958-5052.

ISSN 1023-2443
SA
TRAINING & DEVELOPMENT ORGANISATIONS DIRECTORY. (19??)-. English. One time a year. $23.86. Programme for Research Development, PO Box 32410, 2017 Braamfontein South Africa. **ED** Andries le Roux.
Desc: Gives advice on how to turn information into structured knowledge.

LC HD30.42.U5 T7 **ISSN 0278-5749**
DD 658 US
TRAINING AND DEVELOPMENT ORGANIZATIONS DIRECTORY. [Train. dev. organ. dir.]. **Added/Corp** Gale Research Company. Gale Research Inc. 1st Ed. (1978)-. Directory. English. Irregular. $375.00. Gale Research Inc., 835 Penobscot Building, 645 Griswold Street, Detroit MI 48226. **Tel** (800)877-GALE, (313)961-2242, FAX (313)961-6083, (800)414-5043, telex TWX 810-221-7086. **ED** Janice McLean. available on an online database (Option Code: TDOD) from HRIN; available on magnetic tape; available on diskette.
Desc: Guide to over 2,500 companies that produce more than 10,000 workshops, seminars, videos, and other training programs that can enhance skills and personal development.

UK
TRAINING & MANAGEMENT DEVELOPMENT METHODS. (19??)-. English. Five times a year. $1659.00. MCB University Press, 60 62 Toller Lane, Bradford, West Yorkshire BD8 9BY United Kingdom. **Tel** 011 44 1274 785280, FAX 011 44 1274 785200, telex 51317-MCBUNI-G. **(Subscription address**: MCB University Press / US and Canada Subscriptions, PO Box 10812, Birmingham AL 35201-0812. **Tel** (205)995-1567, (800)633-4931, FAX (205)995-1588.) **ED** Margaret Reid. **Circ**: 500.
Desc: Provides a resource bank of training materials and techniques drawn from real learning situations.
Ind/Abst Manage. Market. Abstr.

LC HD30.42.G7 T73 **ISSN 0968-4875**
UK
●**TRAINING FOR QUALITY.** Vol. 1, No. 1 (1993)-. Periodical. English. Four times a year. $649.00. MCB University Press, 60 62 Toller Lane, Bradford, West Yorkshire BD8 9BY United Kingdom. **Tel** 011 44 1274 785280, FAX 011 44 1274 785200, telex 51317-MCBUNI-G.

LC HD5650 **ISSN 1356-6539**
DD 658.1147 UK
Pr Rev.
●**TRAINING FOR RESULTS.** (March/Apr. 1995)-. Academic Scholarly Publication. English. Six times a year. £99.50. Basil Blackwell Publishers Ltd., 108 Cowley Road, Oxford OX4 1JF United Kingdom. **Tel** 011 44 1235 465500, FAX 011 44 1235 465556, telex 837022 OXBOOK G.

ISSN 0775-0552
BE
UDC 656.13
TRANSPORT ECHO NEDERLANDSE ED. (1987)-. Periodical. Dutch. Irregular. $287.32. Transmedia PVBA, Cuylitsstraat 39, B-2018 Antwerpen Belgium. **Tel** 011 32 3 2385836, FAX 011 32 3 2164488, telex 71726. **Absorbed** Logistiek Management, 0779-2484.

ISSN 0929-9645
NE
●**TRANSPORT LOGISTICS.** See Transportation.

ISSN 1065-330X
NE
TRANSPORT + OPSLAG. (1977)-. Periodical. Dutch. Twelve times a year. $174.89. Misset Uitgeverij BV / Doetinchem, Postbus 4, 7000 BA Doetinchem Netherlands. **Tel** 011 31 8340 49911, 011 31 8340 49562, FAX 011 31 8340 43839, 011 31 8340 40515. **Formed by the union of** Distributie en Transport Management **and** Bedrijfstransport; **Absorbed** Logistiek Signaal.

ISSN 0750-8964
FR
TRAVAIL ET MAITRISE. [Trav. maitrise]. Vol. 1 (1938)-. Periodical. French. Twelve times a year. $148.80. Les Editions ESF, 17 rue Viete, 75854 Paris Cedex 17 France. **Tel** 1 44 15 62 00, FAX 1 46 22 67 45. **Bk Rev**. **Ad Acc**.
Desc: Covers communication, personnel management, marketing, and technology.
Ind/Abst Coal Abstr.

LC HD28 .T73 **ISSN 0041-185X**
DD 658/.005 FR
TRAVAIL ET METHODES. [Trav. methodes]. Periodical. French. Twelve times a year. $150.92. Enterprises et Techniques, 5 bis rue Fontaine au Roi, 75011 Paris France. **Tel** 011 48 05 25 70, FAX 011 68 301 051 967. **ED** Jean Fuchs. Index available. **Bk Rev**. **Ad Acc**. **Circ**: 8,000.
Desc: Articles about office equipment, managerial technics for office work personnel management, manufacturing, etc.
Ind/Abst EMBASE; Int. Labour Doc.; Saf. Health Work.

ISSN 0896-2987
DD 658 US
CCC
TITLE CHANGE
TREASURY MANAGER, THE. [Treas. manager]. Vol. 10, No. 12 (Dec. 1987)-(June 1993). Periodical. English. Phillips Business Information Inc., 1201 Seven Locks Road, PO Box 61130, Potomac MD 20854. **Tel** (301)424-3338, (301)340-1520, (800)777-5005, FAX (301)424-4297, telex 358149. **ED** Theresa Engstrom. **Continues** Cash Manager, 0197-7075. **Absorbed by** Corporate EFT Report.
Desc: Covers new technologies and strategies for improving the flow of cash and financial information; new twists on traditional cash management strategies; bank service pricing and enhancements; payment system infrastructure and risk; short-term investment strategies and vehicles; the role of the treasury manager today; and interviews with faces behind the news.

ISSN 8755-4380
DD 658 US
TSR HOTLINE. [TSR hotline]. **VAT** Telephone Sales Representative Hotline. Vol. 1, No. 1 (1984)-. Periodical. English. One time a week. $176.00. SPI International, 236 US Route 9 South/Suite 203, Howell NJ 07731. **Tel** (201)780-7020, (800)682-5432. Index available. cum. index. **Bk Rev**.
Desc: A telemarketing sales skills reinforcement for telephone sales representatives.

Business and Economics — Management

LC HD28 .T84
CH

TUNG WU CHI KUAN. VFOAT Planning, Organize, Staffing, Leading, Control. Periodical. Chinese (Chinese). Tung Wu Ta Hsueh Chi Yeh Kuan Li Hsueh Hui, Taipei Taiwan.

ISSN 1059-4558
US

DD 658

UCC INTERCHANGE. [UCC interchange]. **Added/Corp** Uniform Code Council, Inc. **VAT** Uniform Code Council Interchange. Vol. 91.1 (1991)-. Periodical. English. Four times a year. Free. UCC Interchange, PO Box 1625, Duxbury MA 02332.

ISSN 0042-059X
SZ
CCC

UNTERNEHMUNG. (March 1947)-. Periodical. German (French and English). Six times a year. $67.42. Verlag Paul Haupt, Falkenplatz 11, CH-3001 Bern Switzerland. **Tel** 011 41 31 3012435, FAX 011 41 31 243023, telex 912 906 HAUP CH. **ED** Paul Haupt Bern. **Bk Rev. Ad Acc. Circ:** 2,000.
 Desc: Business management-research and practice.
 Ind/Abst Int. Abstr. Oper. Res. (19??-) [Select. Cov.]; Selec. Coop. Index Manage. Period. (19??-).

ISSN 1062-5062
US

DD 658

UPLINE (CHARLOTTESVILLE, VA.). See Business and Economics-Marketing and Purchasing.

LC HD28 JX
DD 658 341.026
UK

●**USING ENVIRONMENTAL MANAGEMENT SYSTEMS TO IMPROVE PROFITS. See** Environmental Issues.

LC Z7164.O7 V3 HD37.H82
ISSN 0231-0759
HU

VALLALATSZERVEZESI ES IPARGAZDASAGI SZAKIRODALMI TAJEKOZTATO. (1983)-. Periodical. Hungarian. Twelve times a year. 9.200ft. OMIKK, 1428 Budapest, PF 12, Hungary. **Tel** (361)-118-1994, FAX (361)-138-2414, telex 22-4944 omikk h. **ED** Huszar Ernone. **Circ:** 140.
 Desc: Information on industry and production, efficiency, international economic organizations, management, financial problems, innovation, and personnel management.

LC KK5571.2 .S7
DD 342.43/06/05
ISSN 0342-5592
GW
CCC

VERWALTUNGSRUNDSCHAU. (19??)-. Periodical. German. Twelve times a year. $150.46. W. Kohlhammer Verlag GmbH, Postfach 800430, D-70549 Stuttgart Germany. **Tel** 011 49 711 78630, FAX 011 49 711 7863430, telex 7-255820. **Continues** Staats- und Kommunalverwaltung.
 Desc: Journal for the theory and practice of administrative science.

LC HD28 .V48
HU

VEZETESTUDOMANY. Added/Corp Orszagos Vezetokepzo Kozpont (Hungary). (19??)-. Periodical. Hungarian. Twelve times a year. 400.00Ft. Budapesti Kozgazdasagtudomanyi Egyetem, Budapest University of Economic Sciences, Management Development Instituk, Vezetesi es Szervezesi Ianszek, 1828 Budapest 5. PF 489. Hungary. **Tel** 361 210 0200, FAX 261 210 0228. **ED** Professor Ivan Antal. **Bk Rev** (Qty: 6). **Circ:** 1,200 (ctrl).
 Desc: A journal in the field of business administration, accepts high quality papers of various nature ranging from research findings to case studies and literature reviews. It covers topics from general management to marketing, from corporate finance to human resource management. Its policy is to maintain a balance between relevance and rigour in order to promote communication between academics and practitioners.

LC HD28 .V53
DD 658.4/03/05
ISSN 0256-0909
II

VIKALPA. [Vikalpa]. **Added/Corp** Indian Institute of Management, Ahmedabad, India. Vol. 1 (Jan. 1976)-. Periodical. English. Four times a year. $45.00. Indian Institute of Management, Ahmedabad India. **Tel** 407241, telex 121 6351 IIMA IN. **(Subscription address:** Prints India, 11 Darya Ganj, New Delhi 110002 India. **Tel** 011 91 11 3268645, FAX 011 91 11 3275542, telex 31-61087 PRIN-IN.) **ED** K R S Murthy. Index available. cum. index. **Bk Rev. Ad Acc. Circ:** 2,000.
 Desc: Journal for decision makers; meant for managers in industry, government and non-profit organizations.
 Ind/Abst Psychol. Abstr. (1976-); PsycINFO; PsycLit.

ISSN 0882-6307
US

VIRGINIA SAGE'S MANAGEMENT TECHNOLOGY. [Virginia Sage's manage. technol.]. **VFOAT** Management Technology. Periodical. English. Six times a year. $50.00. Virginia Sage, PO Box 27874, Santa Ana CA 92799.

ISSN 0921-7711
NE

UDC 654.19

VISIE HILVERSUM. (VISIE.). [Visie Hilversum]. (1970)-. Periodical. Dutch. One time a week. $39.43. Evangelische OMROEP, Postbus 21200, 1202 BE Hilversum Netherlands. **Tel** 011 31 35 882411. **Absorbed** Alpha (Hilversum), 0166-4182.

ISSN 1079-0101
US

●**WAREHOUSE MANAGEMENT & CONTROL SYSTEMS. VFOAT** Warehouse Management and Control Systems. (1994)-. Periodical. English. Twelve times a year. $270.00. Alexander Research & Communications, Inc, 215 Park Avenue South, Suite 1301, New York NY 10003. **Tel** (212)228-0246, FAX (212)228-0376.

US

WAREHOUSE SUPERVISOR'S BULLETIN. Bulletin. English. Twenty-four times a year. $118.68 US; $143.64 Canada. Bureau of Business Practice, 24 Rope Ferry Road, Waterford CT 06386. **Tel** (800)243-0876, (203)442-4365, (800)876-9105, FAX (203)443-1123.

US

WAREHOUSE SUPERVISOR'S DEVELOPMENT PROGRAM. English. Twelve times a year. $148.32 US; $182.40 Canada (includes Dynamic Supervision, Warehouse Supervisor's Bulletin, and Supervisor's Memory Jogger). Bureau of Business Practice, 24 Rope Ferry Road, Waterford CT 06386. **Tel** (800)243-0876, (203)442-4365, (800)876-9105, FAX (203)443-1123.

LC HD61 .W37
DD 658.155
ISSN 0738-9140
US

WARREN REPORT, THE. (198?)-. Periodical. English. Ten times a year (monthly except July & Dec.). $35.00. Warren Report, C/O Dr. David Warren, 58 Diablo View Drive, Orinda CA 94563. **Tel** (510)254-9472, FAX (510)253-9645. Index available.
 Desc: News, information, and commentary articles on taking risks and how it works in management.

ISSN 0894-1041
US

DD 658

WATKINS REPORT ON CONSULTANTS' MARKETING STRATEGIES, THE. [Watkins rep. consult. mark. strateg.]. **Added/Corp** Watkins Associates. **VFOAT** Watkins Report. Vol. 1, No. 1 (July 1987)-. Periodical. English. Twelve times a year. $95.00. Watkins Associates, 16 Haverhill Street, PO Box 216, Andover MA 01810. **Tel** (617)475-1849. **ED** John M. Watkins. **Bk Rev. Circ:** 550.
 Desc: Guidance that helps other consultants and professionals to market their services and develop new products. Emphasizes lead generation and prospect-to-client conversion programs. Covers the development and management of profitable newsletters and seminars.

ISSN 1076-0474
US

DD 332

WHAT'S WORKING IN CREDIT & COLLECTION. [What's work. credit collect.]. **VFOAT** What's Working in Credit and Collection. (199?)-. Periodical. English. Twenty-four times a year. $253.00. Progressive Business Publications, 370 Technology Drive, PO Box 3019, Malvern PA 19355. **Tel** (617)527-8600, (800)220-5000, FAX (617)647-8089.

LC JS344.C5 I5649a
US

WHO'S WHO IN LOCAL GOVERNMENT MANAGEMENT. Main/Corp International City Management Association. (1985)-. Newsletter. English. One time a year. Free on request. International City Management Association, 777 North Capitol Street NE, Suite 500, Washington DC 20002. **Tel** (202)289-4262, (800)745-8780, FAX (202)962-3500. **Formed by the union of** Directory of Members - International City Management Association, 0362-4420 **and** Directory of Recognized Local Governments, 0145-3602.

ISSN 0271-6046
US

WILEY SERIES IN MANAGEMENT. [Wiley ser. manage.]. Monographic series. English. Price varies per volume. John Wiley & Sons, Inc., 605 Third Avenue, New York NY 10158-0012. **Tel** (212)850-6000, (212)850-6645, FAX (212)850-6088, telex 12-7063. **(Subscription address:** John Wiley & Sons / UK, Baffins Lane, Chichester, West Sussex PO19 1UD United Kingdom. **Tel** 011 44 1243 779777, FAX 011 44 1243 776128, telex 86290 WIBOOKG.)

ISSN 0273-2963
US

WILEY SERVICE MANAGEMENT SERIES. [Wiley serv. manage. ser.]. Monographic series. English. Price varies per volume. John Wiley & Sons, Inc., 605 Third Avenue, New York NY 10158-0012. **Tel** (212)850-6000, (212)850-6645, FAX (212)850-6088, telex 12-7063. **(Subscription address:** John Wiley & Sons / UK, Baffins Lane, Chichester, West Sussex PO19 1UD United Kingdom. **Tel** 011 44 1243 779777, FAX 011 44 1243 776128, telex 86290 WIBOOKG.)

ISSN 0897-5116
US

DD 322

WISCONSIN SMALL BUSINESS COUNSELOR. See Business and Economics-Small Business.

US

WOMEN AS MANAGERS. See Women's Interests.

ISSN 1185-4863
CN

DD 658.4

WOMEN IN MANAGEMENT. [Women manage.]. **Added/Corp** University of Western Ontario. National Centre for Management Research and Development. University of Western Ontario. Women in Management Program. Vol. 1, No. 1 (1990)-. Newsletter. English. Four times a year. Free on request. National Centre for Management Research and Development, Women in Management Program, Western Business School, London Canada N6A 3K7. **Tel** (519)673-3089, FAX (519)432-0784. **ED** Doreen Sanders C.M. **Photos. Ad Acc.**
 Desc: Directed at individuals in business and academic life who have an interest in the impact women have on organizations and society.

LC HD
DD 658
ISSN 0964-9425
UK
CCC

WOMEN IN MANAGEMENT REVIEW. See Business and Economics-Abstracting, Bibliographies and Statistics.

ISSN 0162-3796
US

WOODALL'S CAMPGROUND MANAGEMENT. VFOAT Campground Management. (19??)-. Trade Publication. English. Twelve times a year. Woodall Publication Company, 28167 North Keith Drive, Lake Forest IL 60015. **Tel** (708)362-6700. **ED** Mike Byrne. ctrl circ.

LC T60.T5 T5
ISSN 0043-8022
UK
CCC

WORK STUDY. [Work study]. Vol. 14, (1965)-. Periodical. English. One time a year. $779.00. MCB University Press, 60 62 Toller Lane, Bradford, West Yorkshire BD8 9BY United Kingdom. **Tel** 011 44 1274 785280, FAX 011 44 1274 785200, telex 51317-MCBUNI-G. **(Subscription address:** MCB University Press / US and Canada Subscriptions, PO Box 10812, Birmingham AL 35201-0812. **Tel** (205)995-1567, (800)633-4931, FAX (205)995-1588.) **ED** John Heap. **Bk Rev. Circ:** 3,125. **Continues** Time and Motion Study.
 Desc: Serves to promote productivity through time and motion study. Job evaluation, process control and related subjects covered.
 Ind/Abst Anbar Account. Finan. Abstr. [Full Txt.]; Anbar Mark. Distr. Abstr. [Full Txt.]; Anbar Top Manage. Abstr. [Full Txt.]; Curr. Cit.; Curr. Technol. Index; Manage. Market. Abstr.; Manage. Bibliogr. Rev.; Oper. Prod. Manage. Abstr. [Full Txt.]; Person. Train. Abstr. [Full Txt.]; Saf. Health Work; Women Manage. Rev. [Full Txt.]; Work Relat. Abstr.

ISSN 0381-8985
CN

DD 658.8/7

WORKING PAPER - RETAILING AND INSTITUTIONAL RESEARCH PROGRAM, FACULTY OF MANAGEMENT STUDIES, UNIVERSITY OF TORONTO. Main/Corp University of Toronto. Faculty of Management Studies. Retailing and Institutional Research Program. 1973-. Monographic series. English. Price varies per volume. Retailing and Institutional Research Program, Faculty of Management Studies, University of Toronto, Toronto Ontario Canada.

Business and Economics —Marketing and Purchasing

DD 658   **ISSN** 1049-4855   US   **CODEN** WRKSET
WORKING SMART (NEW YORK, N.Y.).
(WORKING SMART : PERSONAL REPORT FOR THE EXECUTIVE.). [Work. smart]. **Added/Corp** National Institute of Business Management. Vol. 16, No. 5 (March 15, 1990)-. Newsletter. English. Twelve times a year. $62.72. National Institute of Business Management, Inc., 1101 King Street, Alexandria VA 22133. **Tel** (800)543-2052, (703)548-3885, (800)543-2049, FAX (703)549-0182. **(Subscription address:** National Institute of Business Management, PO Box 25337, Alexandria VA 22313. Tel (800)543-2053.) **ED** Catharine D. Bower. **Circ**: 40,000. **Continues** Personal Report for the Executive, 0048-3443.
Desc: Each issue covers a broad range of management topics such as team building, delegating, getting more done with fewer people, dealing with difficult bosses and employees, ways to streamline paperwork, cut costs, improve customer service and more.

LC TS155.A1 W52   **ISSN** 0374-4795
DD 658/.97/05   UK
WORKS MANAGEMENT. [Works manage.].
Added/Corp Institution of Works Managers. (Jan. 1949)-. Periodical. English. Twelve times a year. $171.12. Findlay Publications Ltd., Franks Hall, Horton Kirby, Dartford Kent DA4 9LL United Kingdom. **Tel** 011 44 1322 614060, FAX 011 44 1322 613943. Documents available from UMI Article Clearinghouse.
Ind/Abst ABI/INFORM Glob. Ed.; Anbar Account. Finan. Abstr. [Full Txt.]; Anbar Mark. Distr. Abstr. [Full Txt.]; Anbar Top Manage. Abstr. [Full Txt.]; Coal Abstr.; Curr. Cit.; Curr. Technol. Index; Manage. Market. Abstr.; Oper. Prod. Manage. Abstr. [Full Txt.]; Person. Train. Abstr. [Full Txt.]; Saf. Health Work; Women Manage. Rev. [Full Txt.].

LC HG1501 .W67   **ISSN** 0730-8736
DD 332.1/068   US   **CODEN** WOBADA
WORLD OF BANKING, THE. See Business and Economics-Banks and Banking.

LC TS161 .W79
DD 658.7/05   CH
WU TZU KUAN LI. VFOAT Wuziguanli. Periodical.
Chinese. Twelve times a year. NT$0.23. Pei-Ching Pao Kan Fa Hsing Chu, Beijing, People's Republic of China. **Tel** 011 86 1 483531.

LC HF5500.3.J3 Y34   JA
YAKUIN SHIKI HO. Added/Corp Seikei Kenkyujo.
(19??)-. Japanese. Four times a year. Seikei Kenkyujo / Wako 15 Building 8, Wako 15 Building 8, Nihonbashi Honcho, 1-chome Chuo-ku, Tokyo 103 Japan.

ISSN 0260-373X   US   CEASED
YEARBOOK / INSTITUTE OF MANAGEMENT CONSULTANTS.
Main/Corp Institute of Management Consultants (London, England). **VFOAT** IMC Yearbook; I.M.C. Yearbook. (1981)-(19??). English. Sterling Publications Ltd., 57 North Wharf Road, London W2 1XR United Kingdom. **Tel** 011 44 171 9159660, FAX 011 44 171 3338155, telex 295819. **(Subscription address:** Sterling Publications Ltd., PO Box 799, Brunel House, London W2 1XR United Kingdom. Tel 011 44 181 9159660.) **Continues** Institute of Management Consultants (London, England). List of Members.

ISSN 1043-4933
DD 658   US
YELLOW SHEET (SAINT LOUIS, MO.), THE. (THE YELLOW SHEET.). [Yellow sheet]. (198?)-.
Periodical. English. Twelve times a year. $119.00. Communication Management, 13523 Barrett Parkway, Suite 221, Ballwin MO 63021. **Tel** (314)822-0555. **Continues** Practical Newsletter on Agency Management.

LC HF5500.2 .Y63   **ISSN** 0735-9063
DD 658.4/09/0973   US
YOUNG EXECUTIVE. Jan. 1983-. Periodical.
English. Twelve times a year. $12.00. Medill School of Journalism, Northwestern University, Evanston IL 60201.

LC HD70.J3 Z3   JA
ZA IGURU. VFOAT The Eagle; Eagle. (19??)-.
Periodical. Japanese. Twelve times a year. ¥6800. Tanabe Keiei, Tanabe Keiei Building 10 Enoki-cho 17 Suita-shi, Osaka 564 Japan.

LC HC462.9 .Z27   JA
ZAIKAI. (August 1953)-. Periodical. Japanese.
Twenty-four times a year. $305.00. **(Subscription address:** Japan Publications Trading Company Ltd., PO Box 5030, Tokyo International, Tokyo 100-31 Japan. **Tel** 011 81 3 3292 3753.)

LC HG41 .Z33
DD 332.05/6   JA
ZAIKAI NAGOYA. VFOAT Zaikai Nagoya.
Japanese. ¥5000. 6-5 Ikegamicho 2-chome Chigusa-ku, Nagoya Japan.

LC HF5001 .Z4   **ISSN** 0722-7485
DD 650/.05   GW   **CODEN** ZFORET
ZEITSCHRIFT FUEHRUNG + ORGANISATION. (ZEITSCHRIFT FUEHRUNG + ORGANISATION : ZFO.). [Z. Fuehr. + Organ.].
Added/Corp Gesellschaft fuer Organisation (Germany). **VFOAT** Zeitschrift Fuehrung und Organisation; ZFO; Z.F.O. Vol. 1 (1982)-. Academic Scholarly Publication. German. Six times a year. DM177.00 Germany; DM181.00 other. Gabler Verlag, Postfach 1546, D-65005 Wiesbaden Germany. **Tel** 011 49 611 534123, FAX 011 49 611 534430. Index available. **Bk Rev**. **Ad Acc**. **Circ**: 5,809. available on microfilm from University Microfilms International (UMI). Documents available from UMI Article Clearinghouse. **Continues** Zeitschrift fuer Organisation, 0722-7477.
Desc: Modern publication for organization appealing to organization leaders and managers.
Ind/Abst ABI/INFORM Glob. Ed.; ABI/INFORM [Computer File] (1982-); EMBASE; Energy Res. Abstr. (March 1982-); Selec. Coop. Index Manage. Period.

ISSN 0173-8062
UDC 658.286-658.21:65.012.122   GW
ZEITSCHRIFT FUER LOGISTIK. [Z. Logist.].
(1980)-. Periodical. German. Six times a year. $132.01. B Quadrat Verlags GmbH, Kolpingstrasse 46, D 86916 Kaufering Germany. **Tel** 011 49 8191 96410.

LC HD28 .Z465   **ISSN** 0936-8787
  GW   CCC
Pr Rev.
ZEITSCHRIFT FUER PLANUNG : ZP.
VFOAT ZP; Journal of Planning. (1990)-. Periodical. German (English). Four times a year. DM298.00. Physica-Verlag GmbH & Company, Postfach 105280, D-69042 Heidelberg Germany. **Tel** 011 49 6221 487492, 011 49 6221 345186, FAX 011 49 6221 487177 und 487366, telex 461723 sphdb-d. **(Subscription address:** Springer-Verlag New York Inc. / North America, PO Box 2485, Journal Fulfillment, Secaucus NJ 07096. **Tel** (201)348-4033, (800)777-4643, FAX (201)348-4505.) ED J. Bloech, B. Huch, W. Lucke, J. Ruhland and K. D. Wilde. cum. index. **Ad Acc**. **Circ**: 700. **Continues** Strategische Planung, 0176-487X.
Desc: Promotes the exchange of information and keeps its readers informed about new developments and empirical research in planning and controlling.

ISSN 1068-1310
DD 658   US
ZWEIG LETTER, THE. [Zweig lett.]. Added/Corp
Mark Zweig & Associates. (May 1992)-. Periodical. English. One time a week (50 issues). $225.00. Mark Zweig & Associates Inc, One Apple Hill, Box 8325, Natick MA 01760. **Tel** (508)651-1559, FAX (508)653-6522. **ED** Frederick White. cum. index. **Bk Rev**, (Qty: 8 /yr). **Circ**: 800.
Desc: A management newsletter published exclusively for the architecture, engineering, and environmental consulting industries, providing insight and hands-on advice on firm management.

MARKETING AND PURCHASING

ISSN 1062-2462   US
1ST PLACE MARKETING. VFOAT First Place
Marketing. (1992)-. Periodical. English. Twelve times a year. $187.00. Enterprise Communications Inc., 1165 Northchase Parkway, Suite 350, Marietta GA 30067. **Tel** (404)998-9558, FAX (404)859-9166.

LC HF   **ISSN** 0732-7943
DD 380.1   US
A/E MARKETING JOURNAL. [A/E mark. j.].
VFOAT AE Marketing Journal. (19??)-. Periodical. English. Twelve times a year. $189.00. Practice Management Associates Ltd., 10 Midland Avenue, Newton MA 02158. **Tel** (617)965-0055, FAX (617)965-5152. **ED** Mary Brever. Index available. **Circ**: 2,500.
Desc: Marketing newsletter for architects and engineers.
Ind/Abst Constr. Index.

LC WMLC 93/772   **ISSN** 1051-483X
DD 380   US
ABERDEEN'S CONSTRUCTION MARKETING TODAY. See Building and Construction.

LC HD28
DD 658   US
●ABOUT MARKETING TO WOMEN. See Women's Interests.

LC HF5415.13 A28   **ISSN** 0567-5235
  GW
ABSATZWIRTSCHAFT, DIE. [Absatzwirtsch.].
Academic Scholarly Publication. German. Twenty-four times a year. DM126.00. Handelsblatt GmbH, Postfach 102716, D-40018 Duesseldorf Germany. **Tel** 011 49 211 8871730, FAX 011 49 211 133523, telex 172114489. **Continues** Absatzwirtschaft + ie. und Wirtschaft und Werbung + Industrielle Werbung + Verkaufspraxis.
Ind/Abst EMBASE; Manage. Market. Abstr.

ISSN 0001-3374   GW
UDC 658.8   CCC
ABSATZWIRTSCHAFT (DUSSELDORF. 1969). [Absatzwirtschaft Dussel., 1969]. (1969)-.
Trade Publication. German. Twelve times a year. $142.79. Handelsblatt GmbH, Postfach 102716, D-40018 Duesseldorf Germany. **Tel** 011 49 211 8871730, FAX 011 49 211 133523, telex 172114489. **Continues** Die Absatzwirtschaft + Wirtschaft und Werbung + Industrielle Werbung + Verkaufspraxis, 0591-2415.
Ind/Abst Curr. Cit.

ISSN 0001-8066   US
AC. THE ADCRAFTER. See Business and Economics-Advertising and Public Relations.

LC HF3233   **ISSN** 1064-928X
DD 338   US
●ACCESS MEXICO. See Industry and Production-Trade and Industrial Directories.

ISSN 1161-7748   FR
UDC 658.8(44)
ACHATS ET ENTREPRISE PARIS.
(ACHATS ET ENTREPRISE.). (1991)-. Periodical. French. Eleven times a year. $111.55. Edipresse, 16 rue Guillaume Tell, 75017 Paris France. **Tel** 011 33 1 47660005 ext. 246. **Continues** Acheteurs (Paris), 0001-4893.

ISSN 1142-7086   FR
UDC 65
Pr Rev.
ACTION COMMERCIALE, MANUELS.
(1988)-. Monographic series. French. Thirteen times a year. 386.88F France; 495.00F other. Option Marketing, 12 rue Barbes, 92300 Levallois Perret France. **Tel** 011 33 1 41059048. Index available. **Bk Rev**. **Ad Acc**. **Circ**: 15,000.
Desc: The selling strategies in all sectors including promotion and marketing.

  US
ACUPOLL REPORTS - FOODS & BEVERAGES. (19??)-. English. Twelve times a
year. $1995.00. Marketing Intelligence Service Ltd., 6473D Route 64, Naples NY 14512. **Tel** (716)374-6326, (800)836-5710, FAX (714)374-5217, telex 469979.
Desc: Published in conjunction with AcuPOLL RESEARCH, Inc. - contains quantitative data on the consumer appeal for the most significant, innovative and impactful grocery store products entering test market or national distribution.

LC TT955
DD 646.7   US
ACUPOLL REPORTS - HEALTH & BEAUTY AIDS & HOUSEHOLD PRODUCTS. See Consumer Education and Protection.

ISSN 1071-3654   US
●AD AGENCEO, THE. See Business and Economics-Advertising and Public Relations.

  FR
ADETEM MARKETING DEMAIN. (19??)-.
Monographic series. French. Irregular. Price varies per volume. Adetem, 221 rue la Fayette, 75010 Paris France. **Tel** 011 33 1 40389710, FAX (1) 40 38 05 08.

  NE
ADFO DIRECT MAGAZINE. (19??)-. English.
Eleven times a year. Fl135.00. Samsom Bedrijfsinformatie BV, Postbus 4, 2400 MA Alphen Rij Netherlands. **Tel** 011 31 1720 66633. **(Subscription address:** Intermedia BV, Postbus 4, 2400 MA Alphen AD Rijn Netherlands. Tel 011 31 1720 66481.) **Continues** DM-Magazine.

ISSN 0926-7689   NE
UDC 658.8
ADFODIRECT MAGAZINE. [Adfodirect mag.].
(1991)-. Periodical. Dutch. Eight times a year. $96.96. Samsom Bedrijfsinformatie BV, Postbus 4, 2400 MA Alphen Rij Netherlands. **Tel** 011 31 1720 6633. **(Subscription address:** Intermedia BV, Postbus 4, 2400 MA Alphen AD Rijn Netherlands. Tel 011 31 1720 66481.) **Continues** DM-Magazine (Alphen aan den Rijn), 0923-8670.

Business and Economics — Marketing and Purchasing

LC HF5410 .A36 **ISSN** 1069-0964
DD 658.8/005 US
ADVANCES IN BUSINESS MARKETING AND PURCHASING. [Adv. bus. mark. purch.]. Vol. 5 (1992)-. Periodical. English. One time a year. $78.75. JAI Press Inc., 55 Old Post Road, Suite 2, PO Box 1678, Greenwich CT 06836-1678. **Tel** (203)661-7602, FAX (203)661-0792. **ED** Arch Woodside. *Continues Advances in Business Marketing, 0894-5969.*

LC HF5415.129 .A39 **ISSN** 1071-9679
DD 330 US
ADVANCES IN DISTRIBUTION CHANNEL RESEARCH. [Adv. distrib. channel res.]. **VFOAT** ADCR. Vol. 1 (1992)-. Periodical. English. One time a year. $73.25. JAI Press Inc., 55 Old Post Road, Suite 2, PO Box 1678, Greenwich CT 06836-1678. **Tel** (203)661-7602, FAX (203)661-0792. **ED** Gary Frazier.
 Desc: Dedicated to promoting knowledge about the operation and functioning of distribution channels for products and services.

LC HF1009.5 .A39
DD 658.8/48/05 US
ADVANCES IN INTERNATIONAL MARKETING. Vol. 1 (1986)-. English. One time a year. $73.25. JAI Press Inc., 55 Old Post Road, Suite 2, PO Box 1678, Greenwich CT 06836-1678. **Tel** (203)661-7602, FAX (203)661-0792. **ED** S. Tamer Cavusgil. Documents available from UMI Article Clearinghouse.
 Desc: A collection of original essays in international marketing. Both theoretical/conceptual and empirical contributions are included. Essays address various aspects of export and multi-national marketing.
 Ind/Abst ABI/INFORM Glob. Ed.

LC HF5410 .A377 **ISSN** 1048-1540
DD 380.1/3/05 US
ADVANCES IN MARKETING AND PUBLIC POLICY. [Adv. mark. public policy]. **VFOAT** Marketing and Public Policy. Vol. 1 (1987)-. Periodical. English. One time a year. $73.25. JAI Press Inc., 55 Old Post Road, Suite 2, PO Box 1678, Greenwich CT 06836-1678. **Tel** (203)661-7602, FAX (203)661-0792. **ED** Paul Bloom.

LC HF5410 .A38 **ISSN** 0892-9556
DD 658.8/005 US
ADVANCES IN NONPROFIT MARKETING. [Adv. nonprofit mark.]. **VFOAT** Nonprofit Marketing. Vol. 1 (1985)-. Periodical. English. One time a year. $73.25. JAI Press Inc., 55 Old Post Road, Suite 2, PO Box 1678, Greenwich CT 06836-1678. **Tel** (203)661-7602, FAX (203)661-0792. **ED** Richard J. Seminik.

LC HD9980.1 .A38 **ISSN** 1067-5671
DD 658.8/005 US
ADVANCES IN SERVICES MARKETING AND MANAGEMENT. [Adv. serv. mark. manag.]. **Added/Corp** Arizona State University. First Interstate Center for Services Marketing. Vol. 1 (1992)-. English. One time a year. $73.25. JAI Press Inc., 55 Old Post Road, Suite 2, PO Box 1678, Greenwich CT 06836-1678. **Tel** (203)661-7602, FAX (203)661-0792. **ED** Teresa Swartz, David Bowen, and Stephen Brown.
 Desc: Covers the latest research and practice in services marketing. Focusing on new ideas in services marketing and management, this publication is committed to encouraging scholars who are new to the area of services to pursue innovative and interdisciplinary services-related research. This publication also provides information on services issues such as service quality, internal marketing, service design, human resources in services, services operations, etc.

LC HF5801 .I45
 US
●**ADVERTISING AGE'S BUSINESS MARKETING.** **VFOAT** Business Marketing. Vol. 79, No. 1 (Jan. 1994)-. Periodical. English. Twelve times a year. $49.00. Crain Communications Inc., 1400 Woodbridge, Detroit MI 48207-3187. **Tel** (313)446-6000, (800)992-9970. **(Subscription address:** Crain Communications, 965 East Jefferson Avenue, Detroit MI 48207. **Tel** (800)678-9595, (313)446-1616.) *Continues Business Marketing, 0745-5933.*
 Desc: Presents business marketing news, strategy and tactics; emphasizes techniques and methods of advertising and selling products and services to business and industry. All aspects of tools and business marketing are explored, such as audio-visual, video, trade shows, direct marketing, incentives, computer-aided techniques and sales management.

  ISSN 1078-1579
DD 338 US
●**ADWEEK'S DIRECTORY OF INTERACTIVE MARKETING.** *See Industry and Production-Trade and Industrial Directories.*

LC HF5806.A11 A393 **ISSN** 1055-2022
DD 659.1/0974/05 US
ADWEEK'S GUIDE TO NEW ENGLAND MARKETS & MEDIA. [Adweek's guide N. Engl. mark. media]. **VFOAT** New England Markets and Media; New England Markets & Media. (198?)-. English. Billboard Publications Inc., 1515 Broadway Billboard, New York NY 10036. **Tel** (212)764-7300, FAX (305)755-7048, telex WU TWX 710-581-6279. *Continues Adweek's Complete Guide to New England Markets & Media, 0898-1450.*

LC HF5419 .A33 **ISSN** 0749-2332
DD 658 US
AGENCY SALES. [Agency sales]. **Added/Corp** Manufacturers' Agents National Association (U.S.). **VFOAT** Agency Sales Magazine. Vol. 9, No. 9 (Sept. 1979)-. Periodical. English. Twelve times a year. $49.00. Manufacturers Agents National Association, 23016 Mill Creek Road, PO Box 3467, Laguna Hills CA 92654. **Tel** (714)859-4040, FAX (714)855-2973. **ED** Bert Holtje. Index available. cum. index. **Bk Rev**. **Ad Acc**. **Circ:** 15,000. Documents available from UMI Article Clearinghouse. *Continues Agency Sales Magazine (1976), 0162-3656.*
 Desc: The marketing magazine for manufacturers agents and their principals. Educational and informative articles that includes tax developments and tips; management aids for manufacturers and agents; legal bulletins; trend-identifying market data; classified ads.
 Ind/Abst ABI/INFORM Glob. Ed.; ABI/INFORM [Computer File] (March 1975-); Bus. ASAP (1990-) [Full Txt.]; Bus. Index (1988-); Curr. Cit.; EP Collect.; Gen. BusinessFile (1988-); Gen. Period. Index (1988-); Homework Help.; Mag. Search; MasterFile FullTEXT 1000; MasterFile FullTEXT 350; MasterFile FullTEXT 650; MasterFile FullTEXT (July 1993-); OCLC; Telebase; Trade Ind. ASAP [Full Txt.]; Trade Ind. Index [Full Txt.]; UMI ABI/Inform--Bus. Period. Ondisc (Dec. 1987-) [Full Txt.]; Vocat. Search.

 US
AISLE VIEW : THE NEWSLETTER OF TIPS, TACTICS AND HOW-TO'S FOR SMALL EXHIBITORS. (19??)-. Newsletter. English. Twelve times a year. $47.00 US; $58.00 other. Exhibitor Publications Inc, PO Box 368, Rochester MN 55904. **Tel** (507)289-6556, FAX (507)289-5253. **ED** Lee Knight and Paula Marlo. **Bk Rev**. **Ad Acc**. **Circ:** 2,000.
 Desc: Newsletter of tips, tactics and how-to's for small and beginning trade show exhibitors.

  ISSN 0002-4325
Pr Rev. US
ALABAMA PURCHASOR. Vol. 1 (Feb. 1945)-. Periodical. English. Twelve times a year. $6.00. Purchasing Management Association of Alabama, PO Drawer 11506, Birmingham AL 35202. **Tel** (205)879-3515, FAX (205)899-3515. **ED** Sid Donaldson. **Bk Rev**. **Ad Acc**. **Circ:** 5,300 (ctrl).
 Desc: A promoter of industrial growth in the South, this publication aims articles at those in the profession of procurement.

  ISSN 0888-8396
DD 338 US
ALBUQUERQUE BI-WEEKLY REPORT, THE. (THE ALBUQUERQUE BI-WEEKLY REPORT : A PUBLICATION OF THE MARKET RESEARCH GROUP.). [Albuq. bi-wkly rep.]. **Added/Corp** Market Research Group. **VFOAT** Bi-Weekly Report. (198?)-. Periodical. English. Twenty-six times a year. $257.40. Market Research Group, 111 Gold Avenue SE, Albuquerque NM 87102. **Tel** (505)242-4818.

LC HF6146.T4 A45
DD 659.13/2 US
ALTERNATIVE REVENUE SOURCES FOR YELLOW PAGES PUBLISHERS. **Added/Corp** Communications Trends, Inc. (1991)-. English. Every 3 years. SIMBA Information Inc., 213 Danbury Road, PO Box 7430, Wilton CT 06897-7430. **Tel** (203)834-0033 ext. 173, FAX (203)884-1771. **ED** D Burns and E Sigel.

LC HF5411 .A53 **ISSN** 1054-0806
DD 658 US
AMA WINTER EDUCATORS' CONFERENCE. (AMA WINTER EDUCATORS' CONFERENCE : [PROCEEDINGS].). [AMA winter educ. conf.]. **Main/Conf** A Winter Educators' Conference. **Added/Corp** American Marketing Association. **VFOAT** Educators' Conference; Winter Educators' Conference. **VAT** American Marketing Association. Winter Educators' Conference. (1982)-. Proceedings. English. One time a year. $40.00 (AMA members), $50.00 (nonmembers). American Marketing Association, 250 South Wacker Drive, Suite 200, Chicago IL 60606-5819. **Tel** (312)648-0536, FAX (312)993-7542.

LC T12.3P4 A48
DD 670/.25/748 US
AMERITECH INDUSTRIAL PURCHASING GUIDE. EASTERN PENNSYLVANIA/SOUTHERN NEW JERSEY/DELAWARE. **VFOAT** Industrial Purchasing Guide. Eastern Pennsylvania/ Southern New Jersey/Delaware Region. (1991)-. English. American Industrial Infosource, Inc., 35 West Huron Street, Suite 700, Pontiac MI 48058.

LC HF5065.F6 A44 **ISSN** 1060-2399
DD 338.4/767/0294759 US
AMERITECH INDUSTRIAL PURCHASING GUIDE. FLORIDA. [Ameritech ind. purch. guide, Fla.]. **VFOAT** Industrial Purchasing Guide. Florida; Florida, and Contiguous Counties of Georgia and Alabama. (1991)-. English. Ameritech Industrial, 100 East Big Beaver Road #200E, Troy MI 48083-1241. *Continues Ameritech Industrial Yellow Pages Purchasing Guide. Florida.*

LC HF5065.G4 A44 **ISSN** 1059-6909
DD 338.4/767/0294758 US
AMERITECH INDUSTRIAL PURCHASING GUIDE. GEORGIA/ALABAMA/EASTERN & CENTRAL TENNESSEE. [Ameritech ind. purch. guide, Ga./Ala./East. Cent. Tenn.]. **VFOAT** Industrial Purchasing Guide. Georgia/Alabama/Eastern & Central Tennessee. (1991)-. English. $30.00. Ameritech Industrial, 100 East Big Beaver Road #200E, Troy MI 48083-1241.

LC HC107.I6 H37
DD 338.4/767/0294772 US
AMERITECH INDUSTRIAL PURCHASING GUIDE. INDIANA. **VFOAT** Industrial Purchasing Guide. Indiana; Indiana, Including Portions of Northern Kentucky. (19??)-. English. Ameritech Industrial, 100 East Big Beaver Road #200E, Troy MI 48083-1241. *Continues Ameritech Industrial Yellow Pages. Indiana Region.*

LC HF5065.W18 A48
DD 338.4/767/029475 US
AMERITECH INDUSTRIAL PURCHASING GUIDE. MARYLAND/VIRGINIA/DISTRICT OF COLUMBIA. **VFOAT** Industrial Purchasing Guide. Maryland/Virginia/District of Columbia. (1991)-. English. Ameritech Industrial, 100 East Big Beaver Road #200E, Troy MI 48083-1241. *Continues Ameritech Industrial Yellow Pages Purchasing Guide. Maryland/Virginia/District of Columbia.*

LC HD9727.M5 H37
DD 338.4/767/0294774 US
AMERITECH INDUSTRIAL PURCHASING GUIDE. MICHIGAN. **VFOAT** Industrial Purchasing Guide. Michigan. (1991)-. English. Ameritech Industrial, 100 East Big Beaver Road #200E, Troy MI 48083-1241. *Continues Ameritech Industrial Yellow Pages Purchasing Guide. Michigan.*

LC HC107.O3 H35
DD 338.09771 US
AMERITECH INDUSTRIAL PURCHASING GUIDE. OHIO. **VFOAT** Industrial Purchasing Guide. Ohio; Ohio, Including Northeast Kentucky, Erie, Pennsylvania, Parkersburg, Huntington and Wheeling, West Virginia. (1991)-. English. Ameritech Industrial, 100 East Big Beaver Road #200E, Troy MI 48083-1241. *Continues Ameritech Industrial Yellow Pages Purchasing Guide. Ohio.*

LC HF5065.N7 A45 **ISSN** 1071-0302
DD 338.4/767/0294747 US
AMERITECH INDUSTRIAL PURCHASING GUIDE. UPSTATE NEW YORK, WESTERN PENNSYLVANIA. [Ameritech ind. purch. guide, Upstate N.Y. west. Pa.]. **VFOAT** Industrial Purchasing Guide. Upstate New York, Western Pennsylvania. (1993)-. English. Ameritech Industrial, 100 East Big Beaver Road #200E, Troy MI 48083-1241. *Continues Ameritech Industrial Purchasing Guide. New York, Western Pennsylvania, 1063-9993.*

LC HF5415 .A613 **ISSN** 0305-0661
DD 016.6588 UK
ANBAR MARKETING & DISTRIBUTION ABSTRACTS. *See Business and Economics-Abstracting, Bibliographies and Statistics.*

 FR
ANNUAIRE DU MARKETING. 1964/65-. Periodical. French. One time a year. 535.00F. Adetem, 221 rue la Fayette, 75010 Paris France. **Tel** 011 33 1 40389710, FAX (1) 40 38 05 08. **Bk Rev**. **Ad Acc**. **Circ:** 2,000 (ctrl).
 Desc: The French handbook of marketing professionals, with lists of ADETEM (French Marketing Association) members.

Business and Economics —Marketing and Purchasing

DD 658.8/4   **ISSN** 1194-3386   CN
ANNUAL FACT BOOK / CANADIAN DIRECT MARKETING ASSOCIATION. See Business and Economics-Advertising and Public Relations.

LC HF5415.12.C2 M37a
DD 338.7/65/883509717   CN
ANNUAL REPORT - MARKET DEVELOPMENT CENTRE. Main/Corp Market Development Centre. (19??)-. English. One time a year. Market Development Centre, PO Box 1261, Charlottetown Prince Edward Island, C1A 7M8 Canada.

ISSN 0214-4905   SP
UDC 659
ANUNCIOS MADRID. [AnunciosMadr.]. (1980)-. Periodical. Spanish. One time a week (45 issues per year). $656.96. Publicaciones Profesionales, C principe de Vergara 15, 30 Izda 28001 Madrid Spain. **Tel** 011 34 1 435 7847, FAX 435 83 10, telex 41683 PUPRO E. **ED** Javier Castro. **Bk Rev**. **Ad Acc**. **Circ:** 5,000. available on microfiche; available on microfilm.
Desc: Specialized information on marketing and advertising directed at the professional.

ISSN 0173-1882   GW
UDC 33
APOTHEKE HEUTE. (1991)-. Trade Publication. German. Four times a year. $21.65. Deutscher Apotheker Verlag, Postfach 101061, D-70009 Stuttgart Germany. **Tel** 011 49 711 25820, INLAND:011 49 711 2582, FAX 011 49 711 2582 290, telex 723636 daz d. **ED** Peter Ditzel. **Continues** Das Schaufenster, 0568-7632.

LC HF5439.7 .A53a
DD 331.2/8138145687/0973   **ISSN** 0731-3802   US
APPAREL SALES MARKETING COMPENSATION SURVEY. [Apparel sales/mark. compens. surv.]. **Added/Corp** American Apparel Manufacturers Association. Personnel Relations Committee. (19??)-. Trade Publication. English. One time a year. American Apparel Manufacturers Association, 2500 Wilson Boulevard, Suite 301, Arlington VA 22201. **Tel** (703)524-1864. **Continues** AAMA Apparel Sales Compensation Survey, 0270-2681.

LC TP812.A1 F5   **ISSN** 0003-6781   US   CCC
APPLIANCE. See Home Economics-Household Appliances.

LC HF5410 .A66
DD 658.8/005   US
APPLICATIONS IN BASIC MARKETING. (1990)-. English.

ARMS REGISTER. (19??)-. English. Nine times a year. Association of Retail Marketing Service, 3 Caro Court, Red Bank NJ 07701. **Tel** (908)219-1938. **ED** George Meredith. **Bk Rev**. **Circ:** 350 (ctrl).
Desc: Contains news of members meetings, happenings, case historys, legal updates, and a listing of current promotions.

LC N8600 .A746
DD 706/.8/8   **ISSN** 1075-0894   US
●**ARTIST'S & GRAPHIC DESIGNER'S MARKET.** See The Arts-Graphic Arts.

LC N8600 .A76
DD 380.1/45/702573   **ISSN** 0161-0546   US
TITLE CHANGE
ARTIST'S MARKET (1979). See The Arts-Graphic Arts.

US
TITLE CHANGE
ARTS MARKETING POWER. See The Arts.

ISSN 1065-8130
DD 700   US
Pr Rev.
ARTS REACH. See The Arts.

US
ASAP. **VFOAT** American Society of Advertising and Promotion. (19??)-. English. Six times a year. $120.00. American Society of Advertising & Promotion, PO Box 15700, Santa Fe NM 87506. **Tel** (505)983-3263.
Desc: Practical, 'how-to' information on all aspects of marketing: advertising, promotion, public relations, and research.

LC HF5415.12.A8 A783
DD 368.5/0095/05   UK
●**ASIA PACIFIC JOURNAL OF MARKETING AND LOGISTICS. Added/Corp** University College of Southern Queensland. **VFOAT** Journal of Marketing and Logistics. Vol. 5, No. 1 (1993)-. Periodical. English. Three times a year. $750.00. MCB University Press, 60 62 Toller Lane, Bradford, West Yorkshire BD8 9BY United Kingdom. **Tel** 011 44 1274 785280, FAX 011 44 1274 785200, telex 51317-MCBUNI-G. **(Subscription address:** MCB University Press / US and Canada Subscriptions, PO Box 10812, Birmingham AL 35201-0812. **Tel** (205)995-1567, (800)633-4931, FAX (205)995-1588.**)** **Formed by the union of** Asia Pacific International Journal of Business Logistics **and** Asia Pacific International Journal of Marketing, 0954-7517.

LC HF   **ISSN** 0257-893X
DD 658.8   HK
ASIAN ADVERTISING & MARKETING. See Business and Economics-Advertising and Public Relations.

SI
ASIAN JOURNAL OF MARKETING. **Added/Corp** Marketing Institute of Singapore. National University of Singapore. Faculty of Business Administration. Vol. 1 (1992)-. Periodical. English. One time a year. $10.00. Singapore Marketing Review, 51 Anson Road, 03 53 Anson Center, Singapore 0207 Singapore. **Continues** Singapore Marketing Review, 0217-5320.

ISSN 0890-9709
DD 658   US
ASSOCIATION MARKETING. [Assoc. mark.]. Vol. 1, No. 5 (Nov. 1986)-. Periodical. English. Twelve times a year. $55.00 (libraries), $45.00 US; $70.00 other. Association Marketing, PO Box 549, Herndon VA 22070. **Tel** (703)860-8503. **Continues** Association Marketing News, 0888-9198.

LC KF316.5.A15 A88   **ISSN** 0745-1369
DD 340/.068/8   US   CCC
TITLE CHANGE
ATTORNEYS MARKETING REPORT. See Law.

LC HF5415.2 .A972
AT
●**AUSTRALASIAN JOURNAL OF MARKET RESEARCH. Added/Corp** Market Research Society of Australia. **VFOAT** AJMR. Vol. 1, No. 1 (July 1993)-. Periodical. English. Two times a year. 24.67Aus$. Market Research Society of Australia, PO Box 697, North Sydney 2059 Australia. **Tel** 011 61 2 9554830. **Continues** Australian Marketing Researcher, 0727-8349.

AT
●**AUSTRALASIAN TELECOMMUNICATIONS MARKETING AND MANAGEMENT NEWSLETTER.** See Communications-Telecommunication.

LC HF5415.2 .A97   **ISSN** 0727-8349
AT
TITLE CHANGE
AUSTRALIAN MARKETING RESEARCHER. [Aust. mark. res.]. **Added/Corp** Market Research Society of Australia. Vol. 1 (Autumn 1975)-(199?). Periodical. English. Market Research Society of Australia, PO Box 697, North Sydney 2059 Australia. **Tel** 011 61 2 9554830. **Supersedes** Australian Journal of Marketing Research. **Continued by** Australasian Journal of Market Research.
Ind/Abst APAIS, Aust. Public Aff. Inf. Ser. (1975-).

AT
AUSTRALIAN MONEY MARKET WEEKLY. [Aust. money mark. wkly.]. (1978)-. English. Forty-eight times a year. 431.64Aus$. Ian Huntley Publishers Pty Limited, PO Box 99, Cremorne NSW 2090 Australia. **Tel** 011 61 2 9535788, FAX 011 61 2 9532280.

AT
AUSTRALIAN PROFESSIONAL MARKETING. (19??)-. English. Eleven times a year. 55.00Aus$ Australia; 82.00Aus$ New Zealand, Papua New Guinea; 87.00Aus$ Malaysia, Indonesia, Fiji; 97.00Aus$ Japan, India, Hong Kong; 105.00Aus$ US, Canada, Lebanon; 106.00Can$ Europe, Africa, former USSR. Thomson Publications / Australia, 47 Chippen Street, Chippendale New South Wales 2008 Australia. **Tel** 011 61 2 6992411, FAX 011 61 2 6991184, telex 122226. **(Subscription address:** Thomson Publications Australia, PO Box 815, Strawberry Hills, New South Wales, 2012 Australia. **Tel** 011 61 2 6992411.**)**

ISSN 1035-0357
DD 658.72   AT
AUSTRALIAN PURCHASING AND SUPPLY (WATERLOO). [Aust. purch. supply Waterloo]. **Added/Corp** Australian Institute of Purchasing and Supply Management. (1984)-. Periodical. English. Six times a year (Feb., Apr., June, Aug., Oct., Dec.). 22.20Aus$. Australian Purchasing & Supply, PO Box 278, Burwood Victoria 3125 Australia. **Tel** 011 61 3 8080600, FAX 011 61 3 8080717. **Bk Rev** (Qty: 6-12). **Ad Acc**. **Circ:** 3,500 (ctrl). **Continues** Supply Contact, 0726-2302.
Desc: News and information related to purchasing, materials, and management.

LC HG1501   **ISSN** 0791-2765
DD 332.1   IE
BANK MARKETING INTERNATIONAL (DUBLIN). (BANK MARKETING INTERNATIONAL.). [Bank mark.int. Dublin]. (1990)-. Periodical. English. Ten times a year. $449.00. Lafferty Publications Ltd., Tower Ida Centre Pearse Street, Dublin 2 Ireland. **Tel** 011 353 1 6718022, FAX 011 353 1 718520.
Desc: Intelligence bulletin scanning the globe to bring readers marketing ideas, techniques and strategies.

CN
●**BC AD NETWORK.** (199?)-. Trade Publication. English. Twelve times a year. 19.95Can$. Xzibit Publications, PO Box 405, Cultors Lake British Lake, V0X 1H0 Canada. **Tel** (614)824-1103. **Absorbed** Xzibit News, 1195-0056.
Desc: Information on marketing and advertising in British Columbia.

LC SB175   **ISSN** 1066-0607
DD 635   US
BEAN MARKET NEWS. See Agriculture.

LC TT950 HD28   **ISSN** 1078-1781
DD 646.7 658   US
BEAUTY INC. : FOR BEAUTY DISTRIBUTION PROFESSIONALS. See Beauty and Cosmetics.

AT
BEST OF MARKETING YEARBOOK, THE. (19??)-. English. One time a year. 9.95Aus$ Australia. Niche Publishing Pty Ltd., 165 Fitzroy Street, St. Kilda West 3182 Australia. **Tel** 011 61 3 5255566, FAX 011 61 3 5255627.

LC Z7164.C8 B55
DD 016.382/6/0954   II
BIBLIOGRAPHY ON OVERSEAS MARKET SURVEYS OF INDIAN PRODUCTS. See Business and Economics-Abstracting, Bibliographies and Statistics.

ISSN 0933-3770
UDC 336.71 :681.3   GW
BM. BANK UND MARKT + TECHNIK. [BM, Bank Markt + Tech.]. **VFOAT** BM. Bank und Markt und Technik; Bank und Markt + Technik. (1987)-. Trade Publication. German. Twelve times a year. $233.98. Fritz Knapp Verlag, Postfach 111151, D-60046 Frankfurt Germany. **Tel** 011 49 69 9708330, FAX 011 49 69 7078400. **ED** Klaus-Friedrich Otto, Juergen Meissner, Juergen Fischer, Berthold Morschhaeuser, Roland Fischer. **Continues** BM. Bank und Markt, 0341-3667.
Desc: Journal providing information on all aspects of marketing.

ISSN 0963-3464
DD 658.8005   UK
CEASED
BMD (LONDON). [BMD Lond.]. **VFOAT** Business Marketing Digest. (1990)-(Jan. 1994). Trade Publication. English. Reed Business Publishing / West Sussex, England, Perrymount Road, Haywards Heath, West Sussex RH16 3DH United Kingdom. **Tel** 011 44 1444 441212, FAX 011 44 1444 445447. **Continues** Industrial Marketing Digest, 0950-9038.
Ind/Abst Curr. Cit.; UMI ABI/Inform--Bus. Period. Ondisc (Fall 1987-?) [Full Txt.].

IT
BOLLETTINO DEI CONTRATTI. Italian (English). Twelve times a year. L180.000 Italy; L200.000 other. Ministerio Difesa, Segredifesa III Rep, V XX Settembre 123, 00187 Rome Italy. Index available. **Circ:** 317 (ctrl).
Desc: Lists national orders valued at one million ECUS or more, in order to meet the requirements of the Ministry of Defense within the scope of research and development.

ISSN 0891-8813
DD 070   US   CCC
BOOK MARKETING UPDATE. See Publishing-Books and Bookmaking.

LC Z291 .B6
DD 070.5/094   UK
BOOK MARKETS IN WESTERN EUROPE. See Publishing-Books and Bookmaking.

UK
BOOK REPORT. English. Every 2 years. £450.00 UK; $990.00 US. Euromonitor Publications Ltd., 60-61 Britton Street, London EC1M 5NA United Kingdom. **Tel** 011 44 171 2518024, FAX 011 44 171 6083149, telex 21120. available for on online database.
Desc: Analysis of the book industry in the UK and other English speaking countries.

Business and Economics —Marketing and Purchasing

LC HF5415.A2 B7
DD 658.8/3/025
ISSN 0068-063X
US
SUSPENDED
BRADFORD'S DIRECTORY OF MARKETING RESEARCH AGENCIES AND MANAGEMENT CONSULTANTS IN THE UNITED STATES AND THE WORLD. See Industry and Production-Trade and Industrial Directories.

DD 658.8/38/65120971
ISSN 0380-9463
CN
BRAND RECOGNITION STUDY : OFFICE EQUIPMENT & METHODS. Main/Corp MacLean-Hunter Research Bureau. **VFOAT** Recognition Study. No. 8- 1975-. Periodical. English. Every 2 years. Maclean Hunter Canada / Montreal, 1001 bvd. de Maisonneuve W., Montreal Quebec H3A 3E1 Canada. **Tel** (514)845-5141, FAX (514)845-4302, telex 055-60604. **Continues** Recognition Study: Office Equipment, 0316-9340.

DD 658.827
ISSN 0965-9390
UK
BRAND STRATEGY. [Brand strategy]. (1991)-. Periodical. English. Twelve times a year. $487.70. Centaur Communications Ltd., St. Giles House, 50 Poland Street, London W1V 4AX United Kingdom. **Tel** 011 44 171 4394222, FAX 011 44 171 7346748, telex 261352.

DD 658.8
ISSN 1195-5953
CN
BRIAN JEFFREY'S SALESTALK. [Brian Jeffrey's salestalk]. **Added/Corp** Jeffrey & Jeffrey Associates. **VFOAT** Sales Talk; Brian Jeffrey's Sales Talk. (1991)-. Periodical. English. Four times a year. 11.22Can$. Salesforce Training & Consulting, 1451 Donald B. Munro Drive, Carp Ontario K0A 1L0 Canada. **Tel** (613)839-7355.

LC HG450
DD 332.6
UK
BRITAIN'S TOP 1,000 FOREIGN OWNED COMPANIES. Added/Corp Financial Analysis Group, ltd. (1975/1976)-. Periodical. English. One time a year. £185.00. Jordan Publishing Ltd., 21 St. Thomas Street, Bristol BS1 6JS United Kingdom. **Tel** 011 44 117 9230600, FAX 011 44 117 230063, telex 499119.
Desc: Provides an analysis of the important segment of companies registered in Great Britain with more than 50 percent of their voting share capital in the hands of corporations registered overseas.

LC HD9437.U6 U53A
DD 381/.41/653
ISSN 0360-3911
US
BROILER MARKETING FACTS. Main/Corp United States. Agricultural Marketing Service. Government Publication. English. US Department of Agriculture / Cooperative Services, Economic Street, Washington DC 20250. **Continues** Broiler Marketing Guide.

ISSN 0740-3216
US
BUMPER STICKERS FOR SALE. Periodical. English. Two times a year. Affinity Publishers Services, Box 570213, Houston TX 77257-0213.

HK
BUSINESS CHINA. Added/Corp Business International Asia/Pacific Ltd. (197?). Periodical. English. Twenty-four times a year. $695.00. The Economist Intelligence Unit, 40 Duke Street, London W1A 1DW United Kingdom. **Tel** 011 44 171 8301000. (**Subscription address:** Economist Intelligence Unit / North America Subscriptions, 111 West 57th Street, New York NY 10019. **Tel** 800 938-4685, (212)554-0600, FAX (212)586-1181, (212)586-1182.) **ED** Lois Tretiak.
Desc: Provides corporate case studies, profiles of individual sectors, market indicators, laws and regulations, and analysis on financial issues in and affecting China, discussions of individual provinces including vital statistics, leadership lineups, natural resources, manufacturing bases and opportunities, etc.
Ind/Abst Asia.-Pac. Econ. Lit.

LC HF5801 .I45
DD 658.8/005
ISSN 0745-5933
US
CCC
CODEN BUMAED
TITLE CHANGE
BUSINESS MARKETING. [Bus. mark.]. Vol. 68, No. 4 (Apr. 1983)-(19??). Periodical. English. Crain Communications Inc., 1400 Woodbridge, Detroit MI 48207-3187. **Tel** (313)446-6000, (800)992-9970. **ED** Bob Donath. Index available. cum. index. **Bk Rev. Ad Acc. Circ:** 46,000 (ctrl). available on microfilm and microfiche from University Microfilms International (UMI); available on an online database (files 16,570/Full-Text) from DIALOG. Documents available from UMI Article Clearinghouse, Ask*IEEE. **Continues** Industrial Marketing, 0019-8498. **Continued by** Advertising Ages Business Marketing.
Desc: Presents business marketing news, strategy and tactics; emphasizes techniques and methods of advertising and selling products and services to business and industry. All aspects of tools and business marketing are explored, such as audio-visual, video, trade shows, direct marketing, incentives, computer-aided techniques and sales management.
Ind/Abst ABI/INFORM Glob. Ed. (Sept. 1971-); ABI/INFORM Ondisc: Expr. Ed. (Jan. 1987-); ABI/INFORM [Computer File] (April 1983-); Acad. Search; Anbar Account. Finan. Abstr. [Full Txt.]; Anbar Mark. Distr. Abstr. [Full Txt.]; Anbar Top Manage. Abstr. [Full Txt.]; Bus. Index (1988-); Bus. Period. Index; Bus. Source Plus; Bus. Source; Curr. Cit.; EP Collect.; F&S Index Plus Text, Int. [Full Txt.] [Select. Cov.]; Gen. BusinessFile (1988-); Gen. Period. Index (1985-); Homework Help.; INFO-SOUTH Abstr.; Infobank (1983-); INSPEC (Sep. 1983-); Mag. Search; Manage. Market. Abstr.; Manage. Bibliogr. Rev.; Mark. Advert. Ref. Serv. [Full Txt.]; MasterFile FullTEXT 1000; MasterFile FullTEXT 350; MasterFile FullTEXT 650; MasterFile FullTEXT (July 1993-); OCLC; Oper. Prod. Manage. Abstr. [Full Txt.]; Person. Train. Abstr. [Full Txt.]; PROMT [Full Txt.]; Telebase; Trade Ind. Index; UMI ABI/Inform--Bus. Period. Ondisc (Dec. 1987-) [Full Txt.]; Wilson Bus. Abstr.; Women Manage. Rev. [Full Txt.].

LC HF5415.1263 .B87
DD 658.8/6
ISSN 0897-7127
US
BUSINESS-TO-BUSINESS DIRECT MARKETER, THE. (THE BUSINESS-TO-BUSINESS DIRECT MARKETER : B/BDM.). [Bus. bus. direct mark.]. **Added/Corp** Maxwell Sroge Publishing (Firm). **VFOAT** B/BDM; BBDM. **VAT** Business to Business Direct Marketer. Periodical. English. Twenty-six times a year. $159.00. Maxwell Sroge Publishers Inc., 522 Forest Avenue, Evanston IL 60202. **Tel** (708)866-1890, FAX (708)866-1899. **Continues** Business-to-Business Catalog Marketer, 0749-1204.

LC KD1554.A13 B88
DD 346.41/02 344.1062
UK
BUYER (MONITOR PRESS). (THE BUYER.). (19??)-. English. Twelve times a year. $265.23. Monitor Press, Rectory Road, Great Waldingfield, Sudbury Suffolk CO10 0TL United Kingdom. **Tel** 011 44 1787 378607, FAX 011 44 1787 880201. Index available. **Bk Rev.** ctrl circ.
Desc: The implications of new law, new regulations, statutory instruments and ministerial orders are set out briefly and simply.

ISSN 0071-0288
UK
BUYERS GUIDE (ENGINEER (LONDON, ENGLAND)). See Engineering.

ISSN 0733-0103
US
CCC
BUYING STRATEGY FORECAST FOR PURCHASING MANAGERS. (BUYING STRATEGY FORECAST FOR PURCHASING MANAGERS. CAHNERS ECONOMICS.). (19??)-. Trade Publication. English. Twenty-six times a year. $299.00. Cahners Publishing Company, 249 West 17th Street, New York NY 10011. **Tel** (212)645-0067, FAX (212)242-6987. (**Subscription address:** Cahners Publishing Company / Colorado, Paid Subscription Service Center, PO Box 7610, Highlands Ranch CO 80126-7610. **Tel** (303)470-4466, FAX (303)470-4691.) **ED** Thomas Stondla.
Desc: Scrutinizes prices and leadtimes of the materials and products that purchasing agents buy daily. Draws on current information provided by purchasing managers in the field and analyses provided by Cahners' staff of industrial economists.

DD 629
ISSN 1042-9603
US
CALIFORNIA REPORT ON AUTOMOTIVE MARKETING, THE. See Transportation-Automobiles.

DD 658.8/3/05
ISSN 0829-4836
CN
Pr Rev.
CANADIAN JOURNAL OF MARKETING RESEARCH. (CANADIAN JOURNAL OF MARKETING RESEARCH : JOURNAL OF THE PROFESSIONAL MARKETING RESEARCH SOCIETY.). [Can. j. mark. res.]. **Added/Corp** Professional Marketing Research Society. Vol. 4 (Dec. 1985)-. Trade Publication. English (French; summaries and/or abstracts in French). One time a year (Dec.). 20.01Can$. Professional Marketing Research Society, 2175 Sheperd Avenue East, Suite 110, Toronto Ontario M2N 5Y7 Canada. **Tel** (416)493-4080, FAX (416)487-3549. **ED** Chuck Chakrapani. **Bk Rev. Continues** PMRS Journal, 0833-9589.

LC HC111 .B8
DD 330.971/0021
ISSN 0832-2503
CN
CANADIAN MARKETS (1986). See Business and Economics-Abstracting, Bibliographies and Statistics.

ISSN 0272-2119
US
CASE REGISTER. [CASE regist.]. **Main/Corp** Coordinating Agency for Supplier Evaluation. **Added/Corp** Aerojet Liquid Rocket Company. **VAT** Coordinating Agency for Supplier Evaluation Register. (19??)-. Periodical. English. Three times a year (Apr., Aug., Dec.). $150.00 (nonmembers); $200.00 (associate); $500.00 (sustaining). GF Dakin, PO Box 13222, Building 2000, Sacramento CA 95813. **Tel** (916)355-3866. **ED** George F. Dakin. Index available. **Bk Rev. Circ:** 1,000 (ctrl).
Desc: An international association of major aerospace, nuclear industry, marine contractors, air carriers, and European corporations who share supplier quality evaluation information.

LC F899.S43 M37
US
CATALIST BUSINESS AND HOUSEHOLD DIGEST OF SEATTLE AND VICINITY. Added/Corp US West Marketing Resources (Firm). **VFOAT** Business and Household Digest of Seattle and Vicinity. (1991)-. English. **Continues** Marketing Reference Guide. Seattle and Surrounding Area.

DD 658
ISSN 1063-9934
US
CATALOG REPORT, THE. (THE CATALOG REPORT : A NATIONAL MARKETING INTELLIGENCE SERVICE PUBLICATION.). [Cat. rep.]. **Added/Corp** National Marketing Intelligence Service, Inc. (19??)-. Periodical. English. Twelve times a year. $245.00. National Marketing Intelligence Service Inc., 370 Marie Court, East Meadow NY 11554. **Tel** (516)735-1680. **ED** Barry Hauser (Editor's telephone: (516)935-8603). **Circ:** 200.

US
CATEGORY REPORT - BEVERAGES / CRB. See Food and Food Industry-Beverage Industry.

US
CATEGORY REPORT - FOODS + SNACKS / CRF. See Food and Food Industry.

LC TT950
DD 646.72
US
CATEGORY REPORT - HEALTH & BEAUTY AIDS. CRH. See Consumer Education and Protection.

US
CATEGORY REPORT - HOUSEHOLD, PETS, AND MISCELLANEOUS PRODUCTS / CRO. See Animal Welfare-Pets.

UK
CATERING BUYERS GUIDE. (19??)-. Consumer Publication. English. One time a year. £60.00. Miller Freeman Technical Ltd., Riverbank House, Angel Lane, Tonbridge Kent TN9 1SE United Kingdom. **Tel** 011 44 1732 362666, FAX 011 44 1732 770483, telex 95454 BBIS.

DD 380.14162
ISSN 0791-3532
IE
CBF MARKET BULLETIN. [CBF mark.bull.]. **VFOAT** Cumann Beostoc Agus Feola Market Bulletin. (1990)-. Bulletin. English. One time a week. $85.00. CBF Irish Livestock & Meat Board, Clanwilliam Court, Lower Mount Street, Dublin 2 Ireland. **Tel** 011 353 1 685155. **Continues** CBF Weekly Market Intelligence Bulletin, 0790-5254.

GW
CD BOOK. English. One time a year. $160.00. Wer Liefert Was GmbH, Normannenweg 18 20, 20537 Hamburg Germany. **Tel** 011 49 40 2515080.

GW
CD MARKETING. English. Two times a year. $900.00. Wer Liefert Was GmbH, Normannenweg 18 20, 20537 Hamburg Germany. **Tel** 011 49 40 2515080.

US
●**CELLULAR INTEGRATION.** (1995)-. English. Twelve times a year. $39.00. Argus Business, 6151 Powers Ferry Road Northwest, Atlanta GA 30339. **Tel** (404)995-2500, FAX (404)995-0400. (**Subscription address:** Sunbelt Fulfillment Services / Nashville, PO Box 41369, Nashville TN 37204. **Tel** (615)377-3322, (800)888-5139.) **Continues** Cellular Marketing.

LC TK6570.M6 C4
DD 658
ISSN 0890-2402
US
CCC
TITLE CHANGE
CELLULAR MARKETING. (CELLULAR MARKETING : CM.). [Cell. mark.]. **VFOAT** CM. Vol. 1, Issue 1 (1986)-(1995). Trade Publication. English. Argus Business, 6151 Powers Ferry Road Northwest, Atlanta GA 30339. **Tel** (404)995-2500, FAX (404)995-0400. (**Subscription address:** Sunbelt Fulfillment Services, PO Box 5039, Brentwood TN 37024. **Tel** (800)685-3435.) available on microfilm from University Microfilms International (UMI); available on an online database (file 648/Full-Text) from DIALOG. **Continued by** Cellular

Business and Economics — Marketing and Purchasing

Integration.
Ind/Abst Trade Ind. ASAP [Full Txt.]; Trade Ind. Index [Full Txt.].

DD 338   **ISSN** 0892-2683   US

CELLULAR SALES & MARKETING. See
Communications-Telecommunication.

LC TP1 .O4   **ISSN** 0090-0907
DD 380.1/4566/005   US
  CCC
  CODEN CMKRA5

CHEMICAL MARKETING REPORTER.
[Chem. mark. report.]. Vol. 201 (Jan. 3, 1972)-. Trade Publication. English. One time a week. $99.00. Schnell Publishing Company Inc., 80 Broad Street, New York NY 10004. **Tel** (212)248-4177, telex 226113 CMR UR. **ED** Harry Van. **Bk Rev**. **Ad Acc**. **Circ:** 16,000. available on microfilm and microfiche from University Microfilms International (UMI); available on an online database (files 15,16,648/Full-Text) from DIALOG. Documents available from CASDDS, BLDSC, SWETS, UMI Article Clearinghouse. *Continues* Oil, Paint and Drug Reporter.
Desc: Chemical industry newspaper covering world chemicals, drugs, coatings, plastics and allied materials marketing. Coverage includes weekly prices for 2,600 chemicals.
Ind/Abst Abstr. Bull. Inst. Pap. Sci. Tech.; Abstr. BioCommer.; Acad. Search; BioBusiness (1986-); Bus. ASAP (1990-) [Full Txt.]; Bus. Index (1985-); Bus. Period. Index; Bus. Source Plus; Bus. Source; Chem. Abstr.; Chem. Bus. Bull.; Chem. Bus. NewsBase (1985-); Chem. Bus. Update; Chem. Ind. Notes; Coal Abstr.; EP Collect.; F&S Index Plus Text, Int. [Full Txt.] [Select. Cov.]; Foods Adlibra; Gen. BusinessFile (1985-); Gen. Period. Index (1985-); Homework Help.; INFO-SOUTH Abstr.; Informat Int. Bus.; MasterFile FullTEXT 1000; MasterFile FullTEXT 350; MasterFile FullTEXT 650; MasterFile FullTEXT (Jan. 1994-); NAPRALERT; OCLC; PROMT [Full Txt.]; Telebase; Trade Ind. ASAP [Full Txt.]; Trade Ind. Index (1981-) [Full Txt.]; Vocat. Search; Wilson Bus. Abstr.

  ISSN 0009-367X
  US

CHICAGO PURCHASOR, THE. Added/Corp
Purchasing Management Association of Chicago. (19??)-. Trade Publication. English. Four times a year (Jan., April, July, Oct.). $48.00. Purchasing Management Association of Chicago, 201 North Well Street, Chicago IL 60606. **Tel** (312)782-1940. **ED** John Pressley. Index available. **Ad Acc**, **Adv Mgr:** Jackie Stinson. **Circ:** 4,450 (ctrl). *Continues* Chicago Purchasing Agent.
Desc: Educational information for purchasing agents.

DD 381   **ISSN** 0193-3264   US
  CCC

CHILTON'S AUTOMOTIVE MARKETING. See Transportation-Automobiles.

DD 380   **ISSN** 1073-7189   US
  CEASED

CHINA MARKETING NEWS. [China mark. news]. (Nov. 15, 1993)-(Dec. 1995). Periodical. English. AT&T Bell Laboratories, 600 Mountain Avenue, Room 3C 417, Murray Hill NJ 07974. **Tel** (908)582-4732, (908)582-4823, FAX (908)582-4430.

  ISSN 0009-6903
  US

CINCINNATI PURCHASOR. Added/Corp
Purchasing Management Association of Cincinnati. Periodical. English. Twelve times a year. Free. Ohio Purchasing Management Association of Cincinnati, PO Box 14249, Cincinnati OH 45214.

LC HF5905 .A57   **ISSN** 0569-6704
DD 658.8   US

CIRCULATION (WILMETTE, ILL.).
(CIRCULATION / AMERICAN NEWSPAPER MARKETS.). [Circulation]. **Added/Corp** American Newspaper Markets, Inc. Standard Rate & Data Service. (1962)-. Trade Publication. English. One time a year (published in Oct. of prior year). $179.00. SRDS / Standard Rate & Data Service, 3004 Glenview Road, Wilmette IL 60091. **Tel** (708)375-5049, (800)851-7737, FAX (708)375-5003. **(Subscription address:** Neodata / Colorado, PO Box 2606, Boulder CO 80322.**) ED** Peter S. Sinding. Index available. **Ad Acc**. **Circ:** 5,000. available on diskette. *Absorbed* Standard Rate & Data Service. SRDS Newspaper Circulation Analysis, 0585-0428.
Desc: A geographic analysis of major print media.

  US

●**CLARK REPORTS.** (1995)-. English. Twenty-four times a year. Clark Associates Inc., PO Box 185, 127 Scranton Building, Lake Bluff IL 60044. **Tel** (800)222-0255, (708)234-4665. *Absorbed* Sales Prospector.

  ISSN 0007-8654
  UK
  CODEN CMMADZ
  TITLE CHANGE

CMM. CONFECTIONERY MANUFACTURE AND MARKETING. See Industry and Production-Manufacturing.

  FR

CNPF LA REVUE DES ENTREPRISES.
Added/Corp Conseil National du Patronat Francais. **VFOAT** Revue des Entreprises; Patronat. **VAT** Conseil National du Patronat Francais, la Revue des Entreprises. (1981)-. Periodical. French. Eleven times a year. $78.74. ETP, 31 Av Pierre, 1ER de Serbie, F-75116 Paris France. **Tel** 011 33 1 40694329. *Continues* Patronat.
Ind/Abst PAIS Int. Print.

LC HD2951 .C667   **ISSN** 0009-9821
  UK

CO-OPERATIVE NEWS. **VFOAT** Cooperative News. (Dec. 24, 1955)-. Periodical. English. One time a week. $95.83. Cooperative Press Ltd., 418 Chester Road, Manchester M16 9HP United Kingdom. **Tel** 011 44 161 8722991, FAX 011 44 161 8726366. *Continues* Co-Operative News and Journal of Associated Industry.

  ISSN 1065-0369
  US

●**COLLEGE MARKETING ANNUAL. See** Education-Higher Education.

  ISSN 0010-1141
  US

COLLEGE STORE EXECUTIVE. (1970)-.
Periodical. English. Ten times a year (published monthly with July/Aug. and Nov./Dec. issues combined). $40.00. Executive Business Media, PO Box 1500, Westbury NY 11590. **Tel** (516)334-3030, FAX (516)334-3059. **ED** Robert Moran. **Ad Acc**. **Circ:** 9,000 (ctrl).

LC JK1673 .A24   **ISSN** 0095-3423
DD 353.007/12   US

COMMERCE BUSINESS DAILY. [Commer. bus. dly.]. **Added/Corp** United States. Dept. of Commerce. Office of Field Services. United States. Dept. of Commerce. Office of Field Operations. United States. Dept. of Commerce. (19??)-. Government Publication. English. Five times a week (Mon.-Fri.). $285.00. US Department of Commerce, 14th Street & Constitution Avenue NW, Washington DC 20230. **Tel** (202)482-2000, FAX (202)482-3772. **(Subscription address:** Superintendent of Documents, US Government Printing Office, Washington DC 20402.**)** available on an online database from NEWSNET; and (files 194,195/Full-Text) DIALOG. *Continues* Commerce Business Daily, 0095-3423.
Desc: The synopsis is of particular value to firms interested in bidding on United States government purchases, surplus property offered for sale, or in seeking subcontract opportunities from prime contractors. Lists current information received daily from military and civilian procurement offices.

LC HF5429.6.P9 C65   **ISSN** 0198-9650
DD 381/.029/47295   PR

COMMERCIAL BUYERS GUIDE : PUERTO RICO, VIRGIN ISLANDS, THE.
[Commer. buy. guide, P. R. Virg. Isl.]. (19??)-. Consumer Publication. English (Spanish). One time a year. Witcom Group Inc., El Caribe Building/15th Floor, San Juan Puerto Rico 00901. **Tel** (809)725-8075.

LC TL297 .T692   **ISSN** 1058-3076
DD 629.224   US

COMMERCIAL TRAILER BLUE BOOK.
[Commer. trailer blue book]. **VFOAT** Official Used Trailer Valuations. Vol. 4, No. 1 (Dec. 1, 1991-Mar. 31, 1992)-. Periodical. English. Two times a year. $110.00. Intertec Publishing Corp, 29 North Wacker Drive, Chicago IL 60606-3298. **Tel** (312)726-2802, FAX (312)726-3091. *Continues* The Trailer Book.

  ISSN 0815-9017
DD 354.940071   AT

COMMONWEALTH OF AUSTRALIA GAZETTE. PURCHASING AND DISPOSALS. [Commonw. Aust. gaz., Purch. dispos.]. **Added/Corp** Australia. **VFOAT** Purchasing and Disposals. (1985)-. Government Publication. English. One time a week. 200.00Aus$. Australian Government Publishing Service, GPO Box 84, Canberra ACT 2601 Australia. **Tel** 011 61 6 2954411, FAX 011 61 6 2954455.
Ind/Abst AESIS Q.

LC HG1501   **ISSN** 1055-4947
DD 332.1   US

COMMUNITY BANK MARKETING. See Business and Economics-Banks and Banking.

  ISSN 0886-1994
DD 659   US

COMPETITIVE ADVANTAGE, THE. See Business and Economics-Advertising and Public Relations.

LC JK1673 .U54a   **ISSN** 0095-2117
DD 353.007/12   US

COMPTROLLER GENERAL'S PROCUREMENT DECISIONS. Main/Corp
United States. General Accounting Office. (19??)-. Periodical. English. Twelve times a year. $1216.00. Federal Publications Inc, 1120 20th Street Northwest, Washington DC 20036. **Tel** (202)337-7000, (800)922-4330, FAX (202)659-2233.

  ISSN 0886-7194
DD 005   US
  CEASED

COMPUTER MARKETING NEWSLETTER, THE. See Computers-Computer Sales, Service and Supply.

LC HC108.M6 A25   **ISSN** 0735-178X
DD 381/.09775/9   US

CONSUMER ANALYSIS (MILWAUKEE, WIS.). (CONSUMER ANALYSIS.). **VFOAT** Milwaukee Journal Consumer Analysis. English. One time a year. Milwaukee Journal, Box 661, 333 West State Street, Milwaukee WI 53201. *Continues* Consumer Analysis of the Greater Milwaukee Market.

LC HF5410
DD 658.8   UK

●**CONSUMER CHINA.** (1994)-. Trade Publication. English. Every 2 years. £295.00. Euromonitor Publications Ltd., 60-61 Britton Street, London EC1M 5NA United Kingdom. **Tel** 011 44 171 2518024, FAX 011 44 171 6083149, telex 21120. **(Subscription address:** Euromonitor International Inc., 122 South Michigan Avenue, Suite 1200, Chicago IL 60603. **Tel** (312)922-1115, FAX (312)922-1157.**)** available with charts.

LC HD7022 .C68   **ISSN** 0308-4353
DD 381/.094   UK

CONSUMER EUROPE. **VFOAT** Consumer Europe ... Printout. (1976)-. Statistical Publication. English. Every 2 years. $847.05. Euromonitor Publications Ltd., 60-61 Britton Street, London EC1M 5NA United Kingdom. **Tel** 011 44 171 2518024, FAX 011 44 171 6083149, telex 21120. **Circ:** 500.
Desc: A statistical guide to the behavior of the European consumer. Statistical tables furnish five-year data on the production, sales, distribution, consumption, and other aspects of more than 350 consumer product categories.

  ISSN 1055-0666
DD 384   US

CONSUMER MEDIA TECH. [Consum. media tech]. **Added/Corp** Paul Kagan Associates. No. 1 (Jan. 22, 1991)-. Newsletter. English. Twelve times a year. $595.00. Paul Kagan Associates Inc., 126 Clock Tower Place, Carmel CA 93923-8734. **Tel** (408)624-1536, FAX (408)625-3225, telex ITT 4938124 PKA UI. available via fax.
Desc: Analysis of the latest trends in home entertainment and communication. Gauging potential of new products to give media executives a competitive edge.

LC TP   **ISSN** 1358-3387
DD 668.55   UK

●**COSMETICS INTERNATIONAL. COSMETIC PRODUCTS REPORT. See** Beauty and Cosmetics.

LC TP
DD 668.55   UK
  TITLE CHANGE

COSMETICS INTERNATIONAL. NEW PRODUCTS REVIEW. See Beauty and Cosmetics.

LC HF5601   **ISSN** 0279-1021
DD 657   US

CPA MARKETING REPORT. [CPA mark. rep.]. **VAT** Certified Public Accountant Marketing Report. (1981)-. Periodical. English. Twelve times a year. $247.00. Strafford Publications Inc., 590 Dutch Valley Road Northeast, Atlanta GA 30324. **Tel** (404)881-1141, (800)926-7926, FAX (404)881-0074. **ED** Suzanne Verity and William J. Haines. **Bk Rev**.
Desc: Information on the latest trends in marketing, public relations and advertising for CPA firms.

LC TP200 .C67   **ISSN** 0746-9012
DD 660/.05   US
  CCC
  CODEN CPIPEE
  CEASED

CPI PURCHASING. See Chemistry and Chemicals-Chemical Technology.

  ISSN 0737-5883
  US

CREATIVE. See Business and Economics-Advertising and Public Relations.

Business and Economics —Marketing and Purchasing

DD 659.105
ISSN 0262-1037
UK
CREATIVE REVIEW (LONDON, ENGLAND). (CREATIVE REVIEW.). (19??)-. Periodical. English. Twelve times a year. $119.79. Centaur Communications Ltd., St. Giles House, 50 Poland Street, London W1V 4AX United Kingdom. **Tel** 011 44 171 4394222, FAX 011 44 171 7346748, telex 261352. available on an online database (files 771,772,799/Full-Text) from DIALOG.
Ind/Abst Manage. Market. Abstr.

DD 354.7110071
ISSN 1187-0265
CN
CUSTOMER INFORMATION - BRITISH COLUMBIA. PURCHASING COMMISSION. (CUSTOMER INFORMATION.). [Cust. inf. - B.C., Purch. Comm.]. **Main/Corp** British Columbia. Purchasing Commission. **Added/Corp** British Columbia. Ministry of Government Management Services and Minister Responsible for Women's Programs. No. 2 (Jan. 1991)-. Periodical. English. **Continues** Customer Information., 0849-7508.

US
●**CYBERMARKETING LETTER. See** Computers-Online Computing and Information.

LC HC910.A1 A88A
DD 301.1/45/0002946891
RH
CZI REGISTER AND BUYER'S GUIDE, THE. (1980)-. English. Confederation of Zimbabwe Industries, Industry House, 109 Rotten Row, Harare Zimbabwe. **Continues** Arni Register and Buyer's Guide.

DD 658
ISSN 1064-6531
US
DELAY LETTER, THE. [DeLay lett.]. **Added/Corp** Robert F. DeLay & Associates. (1986)-. Periodical. English. Twenty-two times a year. $145.00. Robert F. DeLay & Associates, PO Box 58, Jamaica NY 11426. **Tel** (212)688-7559, FAX (212)753-6439. **Bk Rev**. **Circ:** 1,000.

LC HF5415.1 .D46
US
●**DEMOGRAPHICS USA. COUNTY EDITION. Added/Corp** Market Statistics (Firm). (1993)-. English. One time a year. Market Statistics, (A division of Bill Communications), 355 Park Avenue South, New York NY 10010-1789. **Tel** (800)266-4714, (212)592-6244, FAX (212)592-6499. **Continues** Survey of Buying Power Demographics USA.
Desc: Demographic data for over 3,000 counties.

DD 658
ISSN 1062-0842
US
DESKTOP MARKETING ALERT. [Deskt. mark. alert]. (Sept 1991)-. Periodical. English. Twenty-four times a year. $395.00. Cruxpoint Publishing Company, 40 Hawthorne Avenue, Los Altos CA 94022.

LC HF5415.1 .A53a
DD 658.8/00973
ISSN 0149-7421
US
DEVELOPMENTS IN MARKETING SCIENCE. Main/Corp Academy of Marketing Science. Vol. 1 (1978)-. English. One time a year (May). $53.50. Academy of Marketing Science, PO Box 248012, Coral Gables FL 33124. **Tel** (305)284-6673.

US
Pr Rev.
DEWITT POLYMER SERVICE. See Plastics.

DD 658.8
ISSN 1202-631X
CN
●**DIGITAL MARKETING.** [Digit. mark.]. (Sept. 1994)-. Periodical. English. Four times a year. MacLean Hunter Ltd. Business Publishers / Canada, Box 9100, Station A, Toronto Ontario M5W 1A5 Canada. **Tel** (416)596-5000, , FAX (416)596-5552.

US
DIRECT MAGAZINE. English. Twelve times a year. Hanson Publishing Group Inc, 911 Hope Street, Six River Bend Center, Box 4949, Stamford CT 06907-0949. **ED** Meri Erickson. **Ad Acc Circ:** 27,000 (ctrl).
Desc: Deals with direct marketing.
Ind/Abst Mark. Advert. Ref. Serv.

LC HF5861 .R4
DD 659.13/3/05
ISSN 0012-3188
CCC
CODEN DIMADI
DIRECT MARKETING. [Direct mark.]. Vol. 31 (May 1968)-. Periodical. English. Twelve times a year. $60.00. Hoke Communications Inc, 224 7th Street, Garden City NY 11530. **Tel** (516)746-6700, (800)229-6700. available on microfilm and microfiche from University Microfilms International; available on an online database (files 15,648/Full-Text) from DIALOG. Documents available from UMI Article Clearinghouse, Ask*IEEE. **Continues** Reporter of Direct Mail Advertising; **Absorbed** Promoting Store Traffic.

Desc: Teaches marketers about direct response advertising and database management. Through in-depth features, revealing interviews and case histories, marketers learn how to increase sales and generate qualified leads.
Ind/Abst ABI/INFORM Glob. Ed. (Aug. 1972-); ABI/INFORM [Computer File] (Aug. 1972-); Acad. Search; Anbar Account. Finan. Abstr. [Full Txt.]; Anbar Top Manage. Abstr. [Full Txt.]; Bus. ASAP (1990-) [Full Txt.]; Bus. Index (1985-); Bus. Period. Index; Bus. Source Plus; Bus. Source; Curr. Cit.; EP Collect.; Expand. Acad. Index (1992-); F&S Index Plus Text, Int. [Select. Cov.]; Gen. BusinessFile (1985-); Gen. Period. Index (1985-); Homework Help.; INFO-SOUTH Abstr.; Infobank (Jan. 1979-); INSPEC (Aug. 1983-); Mag. Search; Manage. Bibliogr. Rev.; Manage. Contents (1974-); Manage. Contents; Mark. Advert. Ref. Serv.; MasterFile FullTEXT 1000; MasterFile FullTEXT 350; MasterFile FullTEXT 650; MasterFile FullTEXT (July 1993-); Newsp. Period. Abstr. (1992-); OCLC; Oper. Prod. Manage. Abstr. [Full Txt.]; Person. Train. Abstr. [Full Txt.]; Predicasts; PROMT; Telebase; Topicator; Trade Ind. ASAP [Full Txt.]; Trade Ind. Index [Full Txt.]; UMI ABI/Inform--Bus. Period. Ondisc [Full Txt.]; Wilson Bus. Abstr.; Women Manage. Rev. [Full Txt.].

UK
DIRECT MARKETING INTERNATIONAL. (19??)-. English. Twelve times a year. £45.00 UK; £65.00 Europe; £85.00 other. Detailextra Limited, 3 Bridgefoot, Market Deeping, Peterborough PE6 8AA United Kingdom. **Tel** 011 44 1778 380065, FAX 011 44 1778 380075. available on an online database (file 648/Full-Text) from DIALOG.

LC HF5861 .D54
DD 659.13/3
ISSN 1071-4561
US
CODEN DMLSES
●**DIRECT MARKETING LIST SOURCE.** [Dir. mark. list source]. **Added/Corp** Standard Rate & Data Service. (1993)-. Trade Publication. English. Six times a year. $399.44. SRDS / Standard Rate & Data Service, 3004 Glenview Road, Wilmette IL 60091. **Tel** (708)375-5049, (800)851-7737, FAX (708)375-5003. (**Subscription address:** Neodata / Colorado, PO Box 2606, Boulder CO 80322.) **Continues** Direct Mail List Rates and Data, 0419-182X.

LC HF5415.1 .D57
DD 381
ISSN 0192-3137
US
DIRECT MARKETING MARKET PLACE, THE. See Business and Economics-Abstracting, Bibliographies and Statistics.

ISSN 0197-1875
US
DIRECT MARKETING NEWS DIGEST. English. Twenty-four times a year. $44.00. Informat Publishing Co., 1345 6th Avenue, New York NY 10019.

DD 658.8
ISSN 1187-7111
CN
Pr Rev.
DIRECT MARKETING NEWS (MARKHAM). (DIRECT MARKETING NEWS.). [Direct mark. news]. Vol. 4, No. 1, (Oct. 1991)-. Periodical. English. Twelve times a year. 60.00Can$. CDMN Publishing, 1200 Markhan Road, Suite 301, Scarborough Ontario M1H 3C3 Canada. **Tel** (416)439-4083, FAX (416)439-4086. **ED** David Bosworth. **Bk Rev**, (Qty: 5-10). **Ad Acc**, **Adv Mgr**: George Gadjovich. **Circ:** 5,600 (ctrl). **Continues** Canadian Direct Marketing News., 0844-3238.

ISSN 0952-9764
UK
DIRECT RESPONSE. [Direct response]. (1980)-. Periodical. English. Twelve times a year. $128.34. Direct Response, 4 Market Place Hertford, Hertfordshire SG14 1EB United Kingdom. **Tel** 011 44 1992 501177.

LC HF5429.6.C3 A36
DD 381.14/0971
ISSN 0590-5702
CN
DIRECT SELLING IN CANADA. [Direct sell. Can.]. **Main/Corp** Statistics Canada Merchandising and Services Division. **Added/Corp** Canada. Dominion Bureau of Statistics. Merchandising and Services Division. Statistics Canada. Merchandising and Services Division. Statistics Canada. Industry Division. Statistics Canada. Retail Trade Section. **VFOAT** Vente Directe au Canada. (1966/1967)-. English (French). One time a year. 19.20Can$. Statistics Canada Publications Sales and Services, R.H. Coats Building 6th Floor, Ottawa Ontario K1A 0T6 Canada. **Tel** (613)951-5078, (800)267-6677, FAX (613)951-1584, telex 053-3585.
Desc: Discusses non-store retail sales, giving data on commodities sold and breakdown by method of distribution, from premises, by mail or door-to-door.

LC HF5415.126 .D567
DD 658.8/4
ISSN 1046-4174
US
DIRECT (STAMFORD, CONN.). (DIRECT.). [Direct]. (Feb. 20th, 1989)-. Trade Publication. English. Twelve times a year. $74.00. Cowles Business Media Inc. / Connecticut, 6 River Bend Center, 911 Hope Street, Stamford CT 06907-0949. **Tel** (203)358-9900, (800)775-3777, FAX (203)357-9014.
Desc: Magazine of direct marketing management.

LC HF5465.5 .D59
DD 381/.142/029473
ISSN 1045-6201
US
DIRECTORY OF MAJOR MAILERS & WHAT THEY MAIL. See Industry and Production-Trade and Industrial Directories.

US
DIRECTORY OF MARKETING INFORMATION COMPANIES : FEATURING THE BEST 100. See Industry and Production-Trade and Industrial Directories.

SP
DISTRIBUCION ACTUALIDAD. (19??)-. Periodical. Spanish. Eleven times a year. 15450ptas Spain; 20000ptas other. Ediciones Estudios Grupo IP, Enrique Larreta 7-7A, 28036 Madrid Spain. **Tel** 011 34 1 7339114, 011 34 1 7339263, FAX 011 34 1 3157415, telex 47714. Index available.
Ind/Abst Infomat Int. Bus.

US
DISTRIBUTION CHANNELS. (19??)-. English. Twelve times a year (Jan./Feb. and July/Aug. combined). L40880. American Wholesale Marketers Association, 1128 16th Street Northwest, Washington DC 20036. **Tel** (800)482-2962, (202)463-2124. **Continues** Candy Wholesalers.

UDC 658.78
ISSN 0342-1635
GW
CCC
DISTRIBUTION MAINZ. (1970)-. Periodical. German. Nine times a year. DM132.00 Germany; DM195.00 other. Vereinigte Fachverlag, Postfach 4068, D-55030 Mainz Germany. **Tel** 011 49 6131 992150.
Ind/Abst UMI ABI/Inform--Bus. Period. Ondisc [Full Txt.].

LC HD9514 .S672A
DD 658.8/38/672
ISSN 0360-2001
US
DISTRIBUTION OF STEEL CASTINGS SALES BY END USE OF PRODUCT. [Distrib. steel cast. sales end use prod.]. **Main/Corp** Steel Founders' Society of America. (19??)-. English. Steel Founders' Society of America, 455 State Street, Cast Metal Fed Bl, Des Plaines IL 60016. **Tel** (708)299-9160.

US
DISTRIBUTORS LINK. (19??)-. English. Four times a year (Feb., May, Aug., Nov). $25.00. The Distributors Link, 4297 Corporate Square North, Naples FL 33942. **Tel** (813)643-2713. **ED** Leo J. Coar. **Ad Acc**, **Adv Mgr:** Leo Coar, **Tel** (813)643-2713. ctrl circ.

LC HF5415.126 .D6
DD 658.8/4
ISSN 0194-3588
US
DM NEWS. VAT Direct Marketing News. Vol. 1 (Sept. 1979)-. Periodical. English. Forty-eight times a year. $75.00. Mill Hollow Corporation, 19 West 21st Street, New York NY 10010. **Tel** (212)741-2095, FAX (212)633-9367. **ED** Joe Fitz-Morris. **Bk Rev**. **Ad Acc**. **Circ:** 34,000 (ctrl). available on an online database from NEXIS.
Desc: Up-to-date news publication for direct marketers.
Ind/Abst Mark. Advert. Ref. Serv.

DD 658
ISSN 0883-6256
US
DMA MATTERS. [DMA matters]. **Added/Corp** Direct Marketing Association (U.S.). **VAT** Direct Marketing Association Matters. Vol. 1, No. 1 (Spring 1985)-. Periodical. English. Four times a year. Free to members. Direct Marketing Association Inc, 11 West 42nd Street, New York NY 10036. **Tel** (212)768-7277, FAX (212)599-1268.

UDC 658
ISSN 0769-5918
FR
DOSSIERS DU MARKETING DIRECT, LES. [Doss. mark. direct]. (1984)-. Periodical. French. Eleven times a year. $415.57. Ctr Francais Promotion Mark Dir, 4 rue de Commaille, F5 75007 Paris France. **Tel** 011 33 1 42229033, FAX (1)42 22 23 89. Index available. cum. index. **Ad Acc**. **Circ:** 2,000.
Desc: Display of direct marketing techniques and experience.

ISSN 1062-9394
US
Pr Rev.
●**DRIVER (MIAMI, FLA.). See** Sports and Games.

US
●**DRUG OUTCOMES AND MANAGED CARE. See** Pharmacy and Pharmacology.

Business and Economics —Marketing and Purchasing

LC HC107.A165 D86   **ISSN** 0740-6924
DD 338.7/4/02576   US
DUN'S PROSPECT FINDER. ARKANSAS, LOUISIANA, OKLAHOMA, TEXAS.
English. Dun's Marketing Services, 899 Eaton Avenue, Bethlehem PA 18025. **Tel** (800)999-3867, (610)882-6200.

ISSN 0888-580X
DD 330   US
   CCC
EAST ASIAN BUSINESS INTELLIGENCE.
[East Asian bus. intell.]. Vol. 1, No. 1 (Nov. 10, 1986)-. Periodical. English. Twenty-four times a year (22 issues). $365.70. International Executive Reports, 717 D Street NW/Suite 300, Washington DC 20004-2807. **Tel** (202)628-6900, FAX (202)628 6618, telex 440462 MEER UI. **ED** John Boatman. **Circ:** 150 (ctrl). available on an online database from Lexis-Nexis; IBEX; and NEWSNET.
Desc: Newsletter containing contracting and sales leads in East Asia. Provides specific contract information, alerts to upcoming business opportunities and current tenders.

DD 658.8   US
EDITOR & PUBLISHER.
(EDITOR & PUBLISHER MARKET GUIDE.). **VFOAT** Editor and Publisher Market Guide; Market Guide. (1927)-. English. One time a year. $100.00. Editor & Publisher Company, 11 West 19th Street, New York NY 10011. **Tel** (212)675-4380. **ED** Robert U. Brown. **Bk Rev. Ad Acc. Circ:** 4,500 (ctrl). available on microfilm and microfiche from University Microfilms International (UMI). **Continues** Space Buyers' Guide Number.
Desc: Fact filled guide for all of your market research and strategy. Complete data on US and Canadian newspaper markets, includes metropolitan statistical area definitions.
Ind/Abst Infobank.

ISSN 0013-1806
   US
   CCC
EDUCATIONAL MARKETER. See Education.

SZ
EINKAEUFER.
VFOAT Revue de l'Acheteur. (19??)-. Periodical. German (French). 60.00F Switzerland; 85.00F other. SVME, Postfach H, CH-5001 Aarau Switzerland. **Tel** 011 41 64247131, FAX 011 41 6426045.

ISSN 1073-1059
DD 338   US
   CCC
   CODEN EBBUEK
   TITLE CHANGE
ELECTRONIC BUSINESS BUYER. See Electronics.

US
•ELECTRONIC BUSINESS TODAY. See Electronics.

US
ELECTRONIC INDUSTRY OUTLOOK. See Electronics.

CC
ELECTRONICS INTERNATIONAL CHINA REPORT. See Electronics.

ISSN 0889-0196
DD 658   US
   CCC
   CODEN ELEPEM
   TITLE CHANGE
ELECTRONICS PURCHASING. See Electronics.

ISSN 1048-5112
DD 790   US
   CCC
ENTERTAINMENT MARKETING LETTER.
[Entertain. mark. lett.]. Vol. 3, No. 3 (Mar. 1990)-. Periodical. English. Twelve times a year. $319.00. EPM Communications Inc., 488 East 18th Street, Brooklyn NY 11226. **Tel** (718)469-9330, FAX (718)469-7124. available on an online database (files 16,570,636/Full-Text) from DIALOG. **Continues** EPM Report, 0899-7209.
Ind/Abst Mark. Advert. Ref. Serv. [Full Txt.]; PROMT [Full Txt.]; PTS Newsl. Database [Full Txt.].

NE
ESOMAR MARKETING RESEARCH MONOGRAPH SERIES.
(19??)-. Monographic series. English. Irregular. Price varies per volume. ESOMAR Central Secretariat, J J Viottastraat 29, 1071 JP Amsterdam Netherlands. **Tel** 011 31 20 6642141, FAX 011 31 20 6642922.

NE
ESOMAR SEMINARS-CONFERENCE SYMPOSIA PUBLICATIONS.
(19??)-. English. Irregular. ESOMAR Central Secretariat, J J Viottastraat 29, 1071 JP Amsterdam Netherlands. **Tel** 011 31 20 6642141, FAX 011 31 20 6642922.

LC HF5808.E85 E92
DD 659.1/094/021   UK
EUROPEAN ADVERTISING, MARKETING, AND MEDIA DATA.
VFOAT European Advertising, Marketing & Media Data. 1st Ed. (1990)-. English. Euromonitor Publications Ltd., 60-61 Britton Street, London EC1M 5NA United Kingdom. **Tel** 011 44 171 2518024, FAX 011 44 171 6083149, telex 21120.
Desc: Presents a comprehensive and detailed look at European marketing statistics such as economic indicators, demographics, geographical location and market size of 16 major Western European markets.

LC HF5415.124 .E94   **ISSN** 0950-656X
DD 016.6588/0094   UK
EUROPEAN DIRECTORY OF MARKETING INFORMATION SOURCES.
See Industry and Production-Trade and Industrial Directories.

LC HF5410 .E87   **ISSN** 0309-0566
DD 658.8/005   UK
   CCC
EUROPEAN JOURNAL OF MARKETING.
[Eur. j. mark.]. **VFOAT** E.J.M.; EJM. (Summer 1971)-. Periodical. English (French and German; summaries and/or abstracts in French and German). Twelve times a year. $3499.00. MCB University Press, 60 62 Toller Lane, Bradford, West Yorkshire BD8 9BY United Kingdom. **Tel** 011 44 1274 785280, FAX 011 44 1274 785200, telex 51317-MCBUNI-G. **(Subscription address:** MCB University Press / US and Canada Subscriptions, PO Box 10812, Birmingham AL 35201-0812. **Tel** (205)995-1567, (800)633-4931, FAX (205)995-1588.) **ED** David Carson. cum. index. available on an online database (file 15/Full-Text) from DIALOG. Documents available from UMI Article Clearinghouse. **Continues** British Journal of Marketing.
Desc: As well as presenting the latest innovations in the marketing field, EJM discusses contemporary attitudes and ideas. Its readers can share the experiences of other professionals and relate them to their own organisation.
Ind/Abst ABI/INFORM Glob. Ed.; ABI/INFORM [Computer File] (Feb. 1975-); Acad. Search; Anbar Account. Finan. Abstr. [Full Txt.]; Anbar Mark. Distr. Abstr. [Full Txt.]; Anbar Top Manage. Abstr. [Full Txt.]; Bus. Index (1985-); Bus. Source Plus; Bus. Source; Commun. Abstr. (?-?); Contents Pages Manage.; Curr. Cit.; EP Collect.; Gen. BusinessFile (1985-); Gen. Period. Index (1985-); Homework Help.; INFO-SOUTH Abstr.; Int. Exec.; Manage. Market. Abstr.; Manage. Bibliogr. Rev.; MasterFile FullTEXT 1000; MasterFile FullTEXT 350; MasterFile FullTEXT 650; MasterFile FullTEXT (July 1993-); OCLC; Oper. Prod. Manage. Abstr. [Full Txt.]; Person. Train. Abstr. [Full Txt.]; Selec. Coop. Index Manage. Period.; Telebase; Trade Ind. Index; Women Manage. Rev. [Full Txt.]; World Mag. Bank.

LC HF5410   **ISSN** 0969-7012
DD 658.8   UK
   CCC
Pr Rev.
•EUROPEAN JOURNAL OF PURCHASING & SUPPLY MANAGEMENT.
VFOAT European Journal of Purchasing and Supply Management. Vol. 1, No. 1 (March 1994)-. Academic Scholarly Publication. English. Four times a year. $210.00. Butterworth Heinemann Publishers, Linacre House Jordan Hill, Oxford OX2 8DP United Kingdom. **Tel** 011 44 1865 310366, FAX 011 44 1865 310898. **(Subscription address:** Elsevier Science Ltd. / Oxford Fulfillment Centre, PO Box 800, Kidlington OX5 1DX United Kingdom. **Tel** 011 44 865 843355.) **ED** Richard Lamming. available on an online database from Elsevier Electronic Subscriptions (EES). Documents available from BLDSC, UMI Article Clearinghouse.

LC HA1107 .E87   **ISSN** 0071-2930
DD 338.09/4   UK
EUROPEAN MARKETING DATA AND STATISTICS. See Business and Economics-Abstracting, Bibliographies and Statistics.

LC HF5415.12.E85 E97   **ISSN** 0966-7717
DD 330.94   UK
EUROPEAN MARKETING POCKET BOOK.
[Eur. mark. pocket book]. (19??)-. English. One time a year. $47.06. NTC Publications Ltd., PO Box 69, Henley-on-Thames, Oxfordshire RG9 1GB United Kingdom. **Tel** 011 44 1491 574671, FAX 011 44 1491 571188.

LC HF1416.5 .E9   **ISSN** 1054-8327
DD 658.8/48/05   US
Pr Rev.
EXPORT SALES AND MARKETING MANUAL. See Business and Economics-Commerce.

DD 380   **ISSN** 1040-7537
   US
F&B MARKETPLACE : FOOD & BEVERAGE MARKETPLACE, THE MAGAZINE OF FOOD MARKETING COMMUNICATORS.
[F&B marketpl.]. **Added/Corp** Food Marketing Communicators. **VFOAT** F and B Marketplace. **VAT** Food & Beverage Marketplace. Vol. 1, Issue 1 (Winter 1988-89)-. Periodical. English. Four times a year. Free to members. F & B Marketplace, PO Box 19117, Lenexa KS 66215. **Tel** (913)888-8814. **ED** Nancy Parsons. ctrl circ.
Desc: Primarily focused on marketing challenges and creative solutions of interest to food and beverage industry marketing communicators.

ISSN 1044-4467
   US
FEDERAL MARKETING HANDBOOK AND YEARBOOK, THE.
(1990)-. English. One time a year. $59.95. Federal Buyers Guide Inc, 600 Ward Drive/#B3, Santa Barbara CA 93111. **Continues** Federal Buyers Guide Yearbook, 1044-4777.

ISSN 1044-3231
   US
FINANCIAL MARKETING LETTER, THE.
(1991)-. Periodical. English. Twelve times a year. $47.00. Digby Financial News, Inc., 228 Willowbrook Drive, Gretina LA 70056-7816.

LC HG1501   **ISSN** 0892-7812
DD 332.1   US
FINANCIAL SOURCEBOOKS' SOURCES. See Business and Economics-Banks and Banking.

IT
FINANZA, MARKETING E PRODUZIONE : RIVISTA DELL'UNIVERSITA L. BOCCONI.
Added/Corp Universita Commerciale Luigi Bocconi. Vol. 1, No. 1 (Mar. 1983)-. Trade Publication. Italian (English and Spanish). Four times a year. L47640. Giuffre Editore SPA, Via Busto Arsizio 40, 20151 Milan Italy. **Tel** 011 398 2 38089200. **ED** Luigi Guatri. ctrl circ.
Desc: Deals with the problems of running firms as basic economic units producing goods and services for the market. Aims to describe and interpret the conditions under which they operate, estimate their results, establish conditions of equilibrium and development within them. Also studies their policies for evolution and forecast trends.

LC HF5415.2 .F55   **ISSN** 0273-4125
DD 658.8/3/025   US
NLM Z 7164.C81 F494
FINDEX.
[Findex]. (1979)-. English. One time a year (includes semiannual update and update-by-phone service for subscribers). $385.00. Cambridge Information Group Directories Inc, 1200 Quince Orchard Boulevard, Gaithersburg MD 20878. **Tel** (301)590-2300, (800)638-8094, FAX (301)990-8378. **ED** JoAnne DuChez and Sharon J Marcus. Index available. available on an online database from DIALOG; available on magnetic tape. **Absorbed** Directory of United States and Canadian Marketing Surveys and Services.
Desc: Descriptive abstracts of published market research studies, reports, surveys, polls, directories, databases, etc. indexed by subject, publisher, company report title, report by publisher, and geography.

ISSN 0818-4992
DD 388.320994   AT
FLEET.
[Fleet]. (1986)-. Periodical. English. Twelve times a year. 78.10Aus$. MPA Group Inc., PO Box 861, Double Bay New South Wales, 2028 Australia. **Tel** 011 61 2 3287699.

ISSN 0275-8059
   US
FMI ISSUES BULLETIN.
Added/Corp Food Marketing Institute. **VAT** Food Marketing Institute Issues Bulletin. (19??)-. Bulletin. English. Eleven times a year. $38.50. Food Marketing Institute, 1750 K Street Northwest, Washington DC 20006. **Tel** (202)452-8444. **(Subscription address:** Food Marketing Institute, 800 Connecticut Avenue Northwest, Washington DC 20006. **Tel** (202)452-8444.) **ED** Edie Meleski. Index available (Published in December). cum. index. **Circ:** 3,300.
Desc: Covers late trends and issues in food distribution and new programs and materials for FMI numbers and other interested groups. Also provides interviews with business, government and consumer leaders.

ISSN 0884-7185
DD 381   US
FOOD BROKER QUARTERLY. See Food and Food Industry.

ISSN 0896-4203
DD 658   US
   CODEN FMABEC
FOOD MARKETING BRIEFS. See Food and Food Industry.

Business and Economics — Marketing and Purchasing

FORM (ALEXANDRIA). See Printing Industry.

ISSN 1359-852X
LC HB
DD 330
UK
●**FRANCHISING RESEARCH.** (1996)-. Academic Scholarly Publication. English. Three times a year. $119.00. MCB University Press, 60 62 Toller Lane, Bradford, West Yorkshire BD8 9BY United Kingdom. **Tel** 011 44 1274 785280, FAX 011 44 1274 785200, telex 51317-MCBUNI-G. **(Subscription address:** MCB University Press / US and Canada Subscriptions, PO Box 10812, Birmingham AL 35201-0812. **Tel** (205)995-1567, (800)633-4931, FAX (205)995-1588.**)**

ISSN 1057-5316
DD 381
US
FROHLINGER'S MARKETING REPORT. [Frohlinger's mark. rep.]. **VFOAT** Marketing Report. (1991)-. Periodical. English. Twenty-four times a year (semimonthly). $200.00 (one-year); $350.00 (two-year); $475.00 (three-year). Frohlinger's Marketing Report, 7 Coppell Drive, Tenafly NJ 07670. **Tel** (201)567-4447, FAX (201)568-8538. **ED** Joseph Frohlinger. **Bk Rev**. **Circ:** 5,000. available on an online database (files 16,570,636/Full-Text) from DIALOG; available via fax ($250.00) from the publisher. **Continues** Marketing Strategist, 0899-7993.
Desc: Covers multinational advertisers, marketers and media firms. Also specializes in major marketing events and trends.
Ind/Abst Mark. Advert. Ref. Serv. [Full Txt.]; PROMT [Full Txt.]; PTS Newsl. Database [Full Txt.].

ISSN 0429-7830
LC S
DD 630
GW
UDC 634.1/.8:339
FRUCHTHANDEL DUSSELDORF. See Agriculture-Crop Production and Soils.

ISSN 0953-6620
UK
FUTURES AND OPTIONS WORLD. [Futur. options world]. No. 153 (Thursday, Feb. 28, 1985)-. Trade Publication. English. Twelve times a year. $275.00. Metal Bulletin PLC, PO Box 28E, Worcester Park, Surrey KT4 7HY United Kingdom. **Tel** 011 44 171 8279977, FAX 011 44 171 3378943. **ED** Emma Davey. **Ad Acc**. **Circ:** 8,000 (ctrl). **Continues** Futures World, 0262-8376.
Desc: Coverage of international financial and commodity futures and options markets.

US
●**GASES AND WELDING DISTRIBUTOR, THE.** See Metals and Metallurgy-Welding.

ISSN 0741-9120
LC HC110.C6 G46
DD 658.8/348
US
GENERAL TEEN SYNDICATED STUDY. [Gen. teen synd. study]. **Added/Corp** Teen-Age Research Unlimited. No. 1 (Winter 1983)-. English. Teen-Age Research Unlimited, 721 North McKinley Road, Lake Forest IL 60045. **Tel** (312)295-5580.
Desc: Comprehensive media/marketing study. Tracks trends, lifestyles, articles and identifies key teen markets.

LC HF5415.2 .S432B
SZ
GESCHAFTSBERICHT UEBER DIE TATIGKEIT DER GESELLSCHAFT. **Main/Corp** Schweizerische Gesellschaft fur Marketing. (1975/76)-. German. Schweizerische Gesellschaft fur Marketing, Bleicherweg 21, 8022 Zurich Atag-Haus Switzerland. **Continues** Geschaftsbericht.

ISSN 0391-6413
LC HD28
DD 658
IT
UDC 658
SUSPENDED
GIORNALE DI MARKETING. [G. mark.]. (1975)-Suspended (1995). Periodical. Italian. Six times a year. L34060. Assn It Studi Marketing, Via Olmetto 3, 20124 Milan Italy. **Tel** 011 39 2 863293. **Continues** Studi di Mercato.

ISSN 0017-1824
DD 796
US
GOLFSHOP OPERATIONS. [Golfshop oper.]. **VFOAT** Golf Shop Operations. (19??)-. Trade Publication. English. Ten times a year (monthly except June and Dec.). $72.00. Golf Digest- Tennis Inc., 5520 Park Avenue, Trumbull CT 06611. **Tel** (203)373-7256, FAX (203)371-2102. **ED** Bob Carney. **Bk Rev**. **Ad Acc**. **Circ:** 15,200 (ctrl).
Desc: Reaches those retailers who sell golf products at the nation's golf courses and off-course stores. It covers the latest in new products and the techniques to sell them better.

ISSN 0840-870X
LC JL186 .G68
DD 354.710071/2
CN
GOVERNMENT BUSINESS OPPORTUNITIES. [Gov. bus. oppor.]. **Added/Corp** Canada. Supply and Services Canada. **VFOAT** Marches Publics. Vol. 1, No. 1 (April 5, 1989)-. English (French). Seven times a week. Approvisionnements et Services Canada, Publishing Centre, Ottawa Ontario K1A 0S9 Canada. **Formed by the union of** Bulletin des Marches Publics, 0713-133X **and** Bulletin of Business Opportunities, 0713-1321.

US
●**GOVERNMENT PROCUREMENT.** (1994)-. Periodical. English. Four times a year. $20.00 US; $28.00 Canada; $36.00 Mexico; $38.00 other. Penton Publishing, 1100 Superior Avenue, Cleveland OH 44114-2543. **Tel** (216)696-7000, FAX (216)696-0836. **(Subscription address:** Penton Publishing, PO Box 96732, Chicago IL 60693.**)**
Desc: Targets the public sector purchasing professional.

ISSN 0017-2642
LC JK404
DD 353
CCC
GOVERNMENT PRODUCT NEWS. See Public Administration.

ISSN 0046-6220
CN
GOVERNMENT PURCHASING GUIDE (TORONTO). (GOVERNMENT PURCHASING GUIDE.). Vol. 3 (Feb. 1971)-. Trade Publication. English. Twelve times a year. 28.01Can$. Moorshead Magazines Ltd., 10 Gateway Boulevard, Suite 490, North York Ontario M3C 3T4 Canada. **Tel** (416)696-5488, FAX (416)696-7395. **ED** Margaret Williamson. **Ad Acc**. **Circ:** 17,500 (ctrl). **Continues** Canadian Government Purchasing Guide, 0319-5511.
Desc: Providing picture and 75 word description of products and items - paperclips to sanitation trucks - that companies are attempting to sell to municipal, provincial and federal governments in Canada.

ISSN 1050-9372
LC Z716.3 .G745
DD 021.7
US
GREAT LIBRARY PROMOTION IDEAS. (GREAT LIBRARY PROMOTION IDEAS : JCD PUBLIC RELATIONS AWARD WINNERS AND NOTABLES.). [Great libr. promot. ideas]. **Added/Corp** Library Administration and Management Association. Public Relations Section. H.W. Wilson Company. **VFOAT** JCD Public Relations Award Winners and Notables. **VAT** John Cotton Dana Public Relations Award Winners and Notables. (1984)-. Periodical. English. $19.95. American Library Association, 50 East Huron Street, Chicago IL 60611. **Tel** (312)944-6780, (800)545-2433, FAX (312)337-6787. **(Subscription address:** American Library Association, Subscription Department, 434 West Downer, Aurora IL 60506-9936. **Tel** (708)892-7465, FAX (708)892-7466.**)**

CN
GREEN MARKETING HANDBOOK. (19??)-. English. One time a year. 175.00Can$. Southham Information & Technical Group Inc, 1450 Don Mills Road, Don Mills Ontario M3B 2X7 Canada. **Tel** (416)445-6641, (800)668-2374, FAX (416)442-2261.

ISSN 8756-534X
LC HF5415.2 .G69
DD 658.8/3/025
US
GREENBOOK (NEW YORK, N.Y.). (GREEN BOOK.). [GreenBook]. 11th- Ed.; 1973-. English. One time a year. $40.00 prepublication, $50.00 post publication. American Marketing Association / New York, 310 Madison Avenue, Suite 1211, New York NY 10017. **Tel** (212)687-3280. **ED** Pat Ryan. **Ad Acc**. **Circ:** 6,000. **Continues** International Directory of Marketing Research Houses and Services.
Desc: Listing of over 1,200 market research organizations in 50 countries, listed alphabetically with a description of services, names of principals, addresses and telephone numbers.

ISSN 1133-360X
LC NX571.5 .G85
DD 700/.9182/205
SP
GUIA : ARTE DEL ARCO MEDITERRANEO, EL. See The Arts.

LC HF5415.12.F7 G84
DD 650
FR
GUIDE MARKETING MIX, LE. See Business and Economics-Banks and Banking.

ISSN 0276-9891
LC JK1673 .G83
DD 353.0071/2/024658
GUIDE TO FEDERAL PROCUREMENT. See Public Administration.

ISSN 0889-8235
DD 778
US
GUILFOYLE REPORT, THE. [Guilfoyle rep.]. (198?)-. Trade Publication. English. Ten times a year. $125.00. AG Editions Inc., 41 Union Square West, New York NY 10003. **Tel** (212)929-0959, FAX (212)924-4796.

LC HF5437 .I43a
DD 658.7/2/025
UK
CEASED
HANDBOOK - INSTITUTE OF PURCHASING AND SUPPLY. **Main/Corp** Institute of Purchasing and Supply. (19??)-(1994). English. Chartered Institute of Purchasing and Supply, Easton House, Easton on the Hill, Stamford Lincolnshire PE9 3NZ United Kingdom. **Tel** 011 44 1780 56777, FAX 011 44 1780 51610, telex 32251.

ISSN 0749-2243
US
TITLE CHANGE
HANDBOOK OF ADVERTISING & MARKETING SERVICES. See Business and Economics-Advertising and Public Relations.

ISSN 0193-2004
US
HAP. HEART OF AMERICA PURCHASER. **VFOAT** Heart of America Purchaser; Kansas City. HAP. Heart of America Purchaser. (19??)-. Periodical. English. Twelve times a year. Halgo Publishing Inc, 6314 Brookside Plaza, Kansas City MO 64113.

ISSN 0744-1517
US
HAY MARKET NEWS (BELL, CALIF.). (HAY MARKET NEWS.). **Added/Corp** California. Bureau of Market News. United States. Agricultural Marketing Service. Livestock, Meat, Grain & Seed Division. **VFOAT** Weekly Hay Market News. (19??)-. Periodical. English. One time a week. $99.00. California Department of Food & Agriculture, 1220 North Street, PO Box 942871, Sacramento CA 94271. **Tel** (916)654-0298. **Circ:** 300 (ctrl).
Desc: News and information on the hay prices across the country.

ISSN 0735-9683
US
NLM W1; HE414D
Pr Rev.
HEALTH MARKETING QUARTERLY. See Medical Sciences-Medical Instruments and Apparatus.

ISSN 0891-5016
DD 658
US
CCC
HEALTHCARE MARKETING ABSTRACTS. See Business and Economics-Abstracting, Bibliographies and Statistics.

US
TITLE CHANGE
HEALTHCARE MARKETING IN AN AGE OF REFORM. (19??)-(19??). Healthcare Publishing Inc., 2503 C Duck Pond Circle, Morrisville NC 27560. **Tel** (919)852-1100. **Continues** Marketing Rehabilitation Services. **Continued by** Managed Care and Healthcare Marketing.

HEMISPHERE. (19??)-. Newsletter. English. Hemisphere Marketing Inc., 100 Spear Street, Suite 220, San Francisco CA 94105. **Tel** (415)777-1171, FAX (415)777-2371.
Desc: Aim is to assist companies with their direct marketing efforts in the Asia-Pacific and in Mexico. Offers mailing list management and brokerage, and more.

ISSN 0270-8833
US
HERB IRELAND'S SALES PROSPECTOR. CALIFORNIA, ARIZONA, NEVADA AND HAWAII. **Added/Corp** Prospector Research Services. **VFOAT** Sales Prospector. California, Arizona, Nevada and Hawaii. (19??)-. English. Twelve times a year. $82.00. Westgate Publishing Co., 635 Madison Avenue, 4th Floor, New York NY 10022. **Tel** (212)715-8652. available on an online database (files 16,636/Full-Text) from DIALOG.
Ind/Abst PTS Newsl. Database [Full Txt.].

ISSN 0270-8825
US
TITLE CHANGE
HERB IRELAND'S SALES PROSPECTOR. COLORADO, IDAHO, MONTANA, OREGON, UTAH, WASHINGTON, WYOMING AND ALASKA. **Added/Corp** Prospector Research Services. **VFOAT** Sales Prospector. Colorado, Idaho, Montana, Oregon, Utah, Washington, Wyoming and Alaska. (19??)-(19??). English. Clark Associates Inc., PO Box 185, 127 Scranton Building, Lake Bluff IL 60044. **Tel** (800)222-0255, (708)234-6665. available on an online database (files 16,636/Full-Text) from DIALOG. **Merged into** Clark Reports.
Ind/Abst PROMT [Full Txt.]; PTS Newsl. Database [Full Txt.].

ISSN 0270-8752
US
TITLE CHANGE
HERB IRELAND'S SALES PROSPECTOR. GEORGIA, FLORIDA, ALABAMA AND NORTH AND SOUTH CAROLINA. **VFOAT** Sales Prospector. Georgia, Florida, Alabama, North and South Carolina. (19??)-(19??). English. Clark Associates Inc., PO Box 185, 127 Scranton Building, Lake Bluff IL 60044. **Tel** (800)222-0255, (708)234-6665. available on an online database (files 16,636/Full-Text) from DIALOG. **Merged into** Clark Reports.
Ind/Abst PROMT [Full Txt.]; PTS Newsl. Database [Full Txt.].

Business and Economics — Marketing and Purchasing

ISSN 0270-8736
US
TITLE CHANGE

HERB IRELAND'S SALES PROSPECTOR. ILLINOIS AND INDIANA. **Added/Corp** Prospector Research Services. **VFOAT** Sales Prospector. Illinois and Indiana. (19??)-(19??). English. Clark Associates Inc., PO Box 185, 127 Scranton Building, Lake Bluff IL 60044. **Tel** (800)222-0255, (708)234-6665. available on an online database (files 16,636/Full-Text) from DIALOG. *Merged into Clark Reports.*
Ind/Abst PROMT [Full Txt.]; PTS Newsl. Database [Full Txt.].

ISSN 0270-8779
US
TITLE CHANGE

HERB IRELAND'S SALES PROSPECTOR. LOUISIANA, MISSISSIPPI, ARKANSAS, OKLAHOMA, KENTUCKY AND TENNESSEE. **Added/Corp** Prospector Research Services. **VFOAT** Sales Prospector. Louisiana, Mississippi, Arkansas, Oklahoma, Kentucky and Tennessee. (19??)-(19??). Trade Publication. English. Clark Associates Inc., PO Box 185, 127 Scranton Building, Lake Bluff IL 60044. **Tel** (800)222-0255, (708)234-6665. available on an online database (files 16,636/Full-Text) from DIALOG. *Merged into Clark Reports.*
Ind/Abst PROMT [Full Txt.]; PTS Newsl. Database [Full Txt.].

ISSN 0270-8760
US
TITLE CHANGE

HERB IRELAND'S SALES PROSPECTOR. MARYLAND, VIRGINIA, WEST VIRGINIA, NORTH AND SOUTH CAROLINA, AND DISTRICT OF COLUMBIA. **Added/Corp** Prospector Research Services. **VFOAT** Sales Prospector. Maryland, Virginia, West Virginia, North and South Carolina, and District of Columbia. (19??)-(19??). English. Clark Associates Inc., PO Box 185, 127 Scranton Building, Lake Bluff IL 60044. **Tel** (800)222-0255, (708)234-6665. available on an online database (files 16,636/Full-Text) from DIALOG. *Merged into Clark Reports.*
Ind/Abst PROMT [Full Txt.]; PTS Newsl. Database [Full Txt.].

ISSN 0270-8795
US
TITLE CHANGE

HERB IRELAND'S SALES PROSPECTOR. MISSOURI, KANSAS, IOWA AND NEBRASKA. **Added/Corp** Prospector Research Services. **VFOAT** Sales Prospector. Missouri, Kansas, Iowa and Nebraska. (19??)-(19??). English. Clark Associates Inc., PO Box 185, 127 Scranton Building, Lake Bluff IL 60044. **Tel** (800)222-0255, (708)234-6665. available on an online database (files 16,636/Full-Text) from DIALOG. *Merged into Clark Reports.*
Ind/Abst PROMT [Full Txt.]; PTS Newsl. Database [Full Txt.].

ISSN 0270-8698
US
TITLE CHANGE

HERB IRELAND'S SALES PROSPECTOR. NEW ENGLAND. **Added/Corp** Prospector Research Services. **VFOAT** Sales Prospector. New England. (19??)-(19??). English. Clark Associates Inc., PO Box 185, 127 Scranton Building, Lake Bluff IL 60044. **Tel** (800)222-0255, (708)234-6665. available on an online database (files 16,636/Full-Text) from DIALOG. *Merged into Clark Reports.*
Ind/Abst PROMT [Full Txt.]; PTS Newsl. Database [Full Txt.].

ISSN 0270-8701
US
TITLE CHANGE

HERB IRELAND'S SALES PROSPECTOR. NEW YORK, NEW JERSEY AND SOUTHERN CONNECTICUT. **Added/Corp** Prospector Research Services. **VFOAT** Sales Prospector. New York, New Jersey and Southern Connecticut. (19??)-(19??). English. Clark Associates Inc., PO Box 185, 127 Scranton Building, Lake Bluff IL 60044. **Tel** (800)222-0255, (708)234-6665. available on an online database (files 16,636/Full-Text) from DIALOG. *Merged into Clark Reports.*
Ind/Abst PROMT [Full Txt.]; PTS Newsl. Database [Full Txt.].

ISSN 0270-8728
US
TITLE CHANGE

HERB IRELAND'S SALES PROSPECTOR. OHIO AND MICHIGAN. **Added/Corp** Prospector Research Services. **VFOAT** Sales Prospector. Ohio and Michigan. (19??)-(19??). English. Clark Associates Inc., PO Box 185, 127 Scranton Building, Lake Bluff IL 60044. **Tel** (800)222-0255, (708)234-6665. available on an online database (files 16,636/Full-Text) from DIALOG. *Merged into Clark Reports.*
Ind/Abst PROMT [Full Txt.]; PTS Newsl. Database [Full Txt.].

ISSN 0270-8744
US
TITLE CHANGE

HERB IRELAND'S SALES PROSPECTOR. OHIO RIVER VALLEY. **Added/Corp** Prospector Research Services. **VFOAT** Sales Prospector. Ohio River Valley. (19??)-(19??). English. Clark Associates Inc., PO Box 185, 127 Scranton Building, Lake Bluff IL 60044. **Tel** (800)222-0255, (708)234-6665. *Merged into Clark Reports.*
Ind/Abst PROMT [Full Txt.].

ISSN 0270-871X
US
TITLE CHANGE

HERB IRELAND'S SALES PROSPECTOR. PENNSYLVANIA, DELAWARE AND SOUTHERN NEW JERSEY. **Added/Corp** Prospector Research Services. **VFOAT** Sales Prospector. Pennsylvania, Delaware and Southern New Jersey. (19??)-(19??). Periodical. English. Clark Associates Inc., PO Box 185, 127 Scranton Building, Lake Bluff IL 60044. **Tel** (800)222-0255, (708)234-6665. available on an online database (files 16,636/Full-Text) from DIALOG. *Merged into Clark Reports.*
Ind/Abst PROMT [Full Txt.]; PTS Newsl. Database [Full Txt.].

ISSN 0270-8787
US
TITLE CHANGE

HERB IRELAND'S SALES PROSPECTOR. TEXAS, OKLAHOMA AND NEW MEXICO. **Added/Corp** Prospector Research Services. **VFOAT** Sales Prospector. Texas, Oklahoma and New Mexico. (19??)-(19??). English. Clark Associates Inc., PO Box 185, 127 Scranton Building, Lake Bluff IL 60044. **Tel** (800)222-0255, (708)234-6665. available on an online database (files 16,636/Full-Text) from DIALOG. *Merged into Clark Reports.*
Ind/Abst PROMT [Full Txt.]; PTS Newsl. Database [Full Txt.].

ISSN 0270-8809
US
TITLE CHANGE

HERB IRELAND'S SALES PROSPECTOR. WISCONSIN, MINNESOTA, IOWA, NORTH AND SOUTH DAKOTA. **Added/Corp** Prospector Research Services. **VFOAT** Sales Prospector. Wisconsin, Minnesota, Iowa, North and South Dakota. (19??)-(19??). English. Clark Associates Inc., PO Box 185, 127 Scranton Building, Lake Bluff IL 60044. **Tel** (800)222-0255, (708)234-6665. available on an online database (files 16,636/Full-Text) from DIALOG. *Merged into Clark Reports.*
Ind/Abst PROMT [Full Txt.]; PTS Newsl. Database [Full Txt.].

LC P94.5.H58 H57
DD 001.51/02573
ISSN 1071-4553
US

●**HISPANIC MEDIA & MARKET SOURCE.** [Hisp. media mark. source]. **Added/Corp** Standard Rate & Data Service. **VFOAT** Hispanic Media and Market Source. (1993)-. Trade Publication. Four times a year (Mar., Jun., Sept., Dec.). $189.00. SRDS / Standard Rate & Data Service, 3004 Glenview Road, Wilmette IL 60091. **Tel** (708)375-5049, (800)851-7737, FAX (708)375-5003. **(Subscription address:** Neodata / Colorado, PO Box 2606, Boulder CO 80322. **)** *Continues Hispanic Media and Markets, 1044-0933.*

US

●**HOME CARE MARKETER.** See Medical Sciences-Family Practice.

LC HD9810.U6 S44
DD 381
ISSN 1080-4730
US

●**HOME SCHOOL MARKET GUIDE, THE.** [Home sch. mark. guide]. (1995)-. English. Bluestocking Press, Department U, Box 1014, Placeville CA 95667. *Continues Selling to the Other Educational Markets, 1054-4593.*

ISSN 0191-6653
US

HOSE & NOZZLE (SHREVEPORT). See Petroleum and Natural Gas.

LC HG4651
DD 332.63/2/05
ISSN 1191-8934
CN

IAN MCAVITY'S DELIBERATIONS ON WORLD MARKETS. See Business and Economics-Investments.

DD 380
ISSN 0896-1441
US

IDEAS (RESTON, VA.). (IDEAS : THE MONTHLY MAGAZINE OF THE INTERNATIONAL NEWSPAPER MARKETING ASSOCIATION / INMA.). [Ideas]. **Added/Corp** International Newspaper Marketing Association. (June 1987)-. Trade Publication. English. Ten times a year. $120.00 (academic), $210.00 (press association); $895.00 (newspaper supplier Comes with International Newspaper Marketing Association Affiliate membership. International Newspaper Marketing Association, 12770 Merit Drive, Suite 330, Dallas TX 75251. **Tel** (214)991-5900. *Continues Ideas Newsletter (Reston, Va.).*
Ind/Abst Mark. Advert. Ref. Serv.

US
CEASED

IDENTIFIED SOURCES OF SUPPLY, THE. **Added/Corp** National Standards Association (U.S.). (1960)-(April 1993). English. Information Handling Services, 15 Inverness Way East, Englewood CO 80150. **Tel** (800)525-7052, (303)790-0600, FAX (303)397-2599, telex 4322083. *Continues Source (Washington, D.C.).*

LC GT3930 .O38
DD 394.2/6/02373
ISSN 1058-613X
US
TITLE CHANGE

IEG DIRECTORY OF SPONSORSHIP MARKETING. See Industry and Production-Trade and Industrial Directories.

II

INDIAN BUYER. (1961)-. Periodical. English. Twelve times a year. Free (members); Rs100.00 (nonmembers). I A M M, Mehta Chambers, Mathew Road, Opera House/2nd Floor, Bombay 400 004 India.

LC HF5415.12.I5 I5
DD 658.8/005
II

INDIAN JOURNAL OF MARKETING. Vol. 1, No. 1 (May 1968)-. Periodical. English. Twelve times a year. $35.00. Associated Management Corporation, New Delhi India. **(Subscription address:** Prints India, 11 Darya Ganj, New Delhi 110002 India. **Tel** 011 91 11 3268645, FAX 011 91 11 3275542, telex 31-61087 PRIN-IN.**)**

LC HF5475.I4 I53
DD 381/.1/05
ISSN 0970-1095
II

INDIAN JOURNAL OF MARKETING GEOGRAPHY, THE. See Geography.

ISSN 0019-8153
US
CCC
CODEN INDDAZ

INDUSTRIAL DISTRIBUTION. [Ind. distrib.]. Vol. 38, No. 5 (May 1948)-. Trade Publication. English. Twelve times a year. $79.90. Cahners Publishing Company, 249 West 17th Street, New York NY 10011. **Tel** (212)645-0067, FAX (212)242-6987. **(Subscription address:** Cahners Publishing Company / Colorado, Paid Subscription Service Center, PO Box 7610, Highlands Ranch CO 80126-7610. **Tel** (303)470-4466, FAX (303)470-4691.**)** available on microfilm and microfiche from University Microfilms International (UMI); available on an online database (file 648/Full-Text) from DIALOG. Documents available from UMI Article Clearinghouse. *Continues Mill Supplies.*
Desc: Serves owners, executives and sales personnel in general line, specialist and combination industrial distributor firms. The focus is on how-to and industry news features, with an emphasis on increasing sales and profits.
Ind/Abst ABI/INFORM Glob. Ed.; ABI/INFORM [Computer File] (Jan. 1975-); Acad. Search; Bus. Index (1985-); Bus. Period. Index; Bus. Source Plus; Bus. Source; Curr. Cit.; EP Collect.; Gen. BusinessFile (1985-); Gen. Period. Index (1985-); Homework Help.; INFO-SOUTH Abstr.; Mag. Search; MasterFile FullTEXT 1000; MasterFile FullTEXT 350; MasterFile FullTEXT 650; MasterFile FullTEXT (July 1993-); OCLC; Stat. Ref. Index; Telebase; Trade Ind. ASAP [Full Txt.]; Trade Ind. Index [Full Txt.]; UMI ABI/Inform--Bus. Period. Ondisc (Jan. 1990-) [Full Txt.]; Vocat. Search; Wilson Bus. Abstr.

LC HF5415.12.E8 I53
DD 658.8/005
ISSN 0019-8501
US
CCC
CODEN IMMADX

Pr Rev.

INDUSTRIAL MARKETING MANAGEMENT. [Ind. mark. manage.]. **Added/Corp** European Association for Industrial Marketing Research. Vol. 1 (Sept. 1971)-. Academic Scholarly Publication. English. Six times a year. $350.00. Elsevier Science Publishing Company Inc, Madison Square Station, PO Box 882, New York NY 10159-0882. **Tel** (212)633-3950, FAX (212)633-3990. **ED** James Hlavacek. **Ad Acc.** available on microfilm and microfiche from University Microfilms International (UMI); available on an online database from Elsevier Electronic Subscriptions (EES). Documents available from The Genuine Article, UMI Article Clearinghouse.
Desc: Provides in-depth case studies geared to the needs of marketing managers, executives and professors. Brings readers abreast of the most timely data

Business and Economics — Marketing and Purchasing

and current thinking necessary for better industrial marketing decisions and strategy.
Ind/Abst ABI/INFORM Glob. Ed.; ABI/INFORM Ondisc: Expr. Ed.; ABI/INFORM [Computer File] (July 1972-); Acad. Search; Anbar Account. Finan. Abstr. [Full Txt.]; Anbar Mark. Distr. Abstr. [Full Txt.]; Anbar Top Manage. Abstr. [Full Txt.]; Bus. Index (1984-); Bus. Period. Index; Bus. Source Plus; Bus. Source; Commun. Abstr. (?-?); Contents Pages Manage.; Curr. Cit.; Curr. Contents Soc. Behav. Sci.; EP Collect.; Gen. BusinessFile (1984-); Gen. Period. Index (1985-); Homework Help.; INFO-SOUTH Abstr.; Int. Exec.; Mag. Search; Manage. Market. Abstr.; Manage. Bibliogr. Rev.; Manage. Contents; Mark. Res. Today; MasterFile FullTEXT 1000; MasterFile FullTEXT 350; MasterFile FullTEXT 650; MasterFile FullTEXT (Jan. 1993-); OCLC; Oper. Prod. Manage. Abstr. [Full Txt.]; PAIS Int. Print (1991-); Person. Train. Abstr. [Full Txt.]; Res. Alert [Full Cov.]; Selec. Coop. Index Manage. Period.; Soc. Sci. Cit. Index [Full Cov.]; Telebase; Vocat. Search; Wilson Bus. Abstr.; Women Manage. Rev. [Full Txt.].

ISSN 0019-8641
DD 658 US
INDUSTRIAL PURCHASING AGENT. [Ind. purch. agent]. **Added/Corp** Publications for Industry (Firm). (1956-). Periodical. English. Ten times a year. $25.00. Publications for Industry, 21 Russel Woods Road, Great Neck NY 11021. **Tel** (516)487-0990, FAX (516)487-0809. **ED** Pearl Shaine. **Bk Rev**. **Ad Acc**. **Circ:** 26,000 (ctrl).
Desc: New products, new brochures, personnel changes, special features of interest to purchasing agents goes to largest manufacturers plants in U.S.

LC HC431 .I5215
DD 338.0954 II
INDUSTRIAL RESEARCHER. See Business and Economics-Investments.

ISSN 0147-5924
US
INFO FRANCHISE NEWSLETTER, THE. See Business and Economics-Commerce.

ISSN 0179-9452
GW
UDC 681.6
INFO-MARKT. RATGEBER KOPIERER. [Info-Markt, Ratg. Kopier.]. (198?)-. German. Two times a year. $127.43. Infomarkt GmbH, Grafenberger Allee 368, D-40235 Duesseldorf Germany. **Tel** 011 49 211 669070.

ISSN 0179-9460
GW
UDC 681.61
INFO-MARKT. RATGEBER SCHREIBSYSTEME, BILDSCHIRM-SCHREIBMASCHINEN, TELETEX, DIKTIERGERATE. [Info-Markt, Ratg. Schreibsyst. Bildschirm-Schreibmasch. Teletex Diktiergerate]. (?985)-. German. Two times a year. $127.43. Infomarkt GmbH, Grafenberger Allee 368, D-40235 Duesseldorf Germany. **Tel** 011 49 211 669070.

US
INFORMATION MARKETING HANDBOOK, THE. English. $35.00 (members), $50.00 (nonmembers). National Federation of Abstracting & Information Services, 1518 Walnut Street, Suite 307, Philadelphia PA 19102-3403. **Tel** (215)893-1561, FAX (215)893-1564. **ED** Betty Unruh.

ISSN 0824-3514
DD 025.5/2 CN
INFORMATION SOLUTIONS/INFORMATION PLUS. [Inf. solut.]. **Added/Corp** Information Plus (Firm). (1983)-. Periodical. English (French). Six times a year. 115.00Can$. Information Plus Inc, 150 Bloor Street, Suite 835, Toronto Ontario M5S 2X9 Canada. **Tel** (416)968-1062, FAX (416)968-2591. **ED** Deborah C Sawyer. **Circ:** 300.
Desc: A newsletter of ideas and techniques for executives and managers, giving practical, proven techniques on how to profit from the information commodity.

US
INSIDE CONTACTS U.S.A. MARKETING INFORMATION DIRECTORY. METRO PHOENIX MARKETING DIRECTORY. See Industry and Production-Trade and Industrial Directories.

ISSN 0882-7001
DD 658 US
INSIDE DIRECT MARKETING. [Inside direct mark.]. (19??)-. Periodical. English. Twelve times a year. $125.00. Inside Direct Marketing, Marketing Confidential Inc, Suite 116/440 Main Street, Ridgefield CT 06877.

ISSN 1047-2908
DD 338 US
INSIDE MARKET DATA. [Inside mark. data]. Vol. 5, No. 5 (Nov. 27, 1989)-. Periodical. English. Twenty-four times a year. $995.00. Waters Information Services, PO Box 2248, Binghamton NY 13902-2248. **Tel** (607)770-8535, FAX (607)798-1692. available on an online database (files 16,636/Full-Text) from DIALOG.

Continues Micro Ticker Report, 0885-2510.
Ind/Abst PROMT [Full Txt.]; PTS Newsl. Database [Full Txt.].

LC HC108.P55 I5 ISSN 0446-3013
DD 309.179173 US
INSIDE PHOENIX. (19??)-. English. One time a year. $12.00. Phoenix Newspapers Inc., PO Box 660, Phoenix AZ 85001. **Tel** (602)271-8503, (602)271-8000, FAX (602)271-8910.

ISSN 1059-387X
US
INSIDE TRAC, THE. (1992)-. Periodical. English. Six times a year. $87.00 US | $97.00 other. The Trachtman Group Inc, 2300 Peachford Road, Suite 1150, Atlanta GA 30338. **Tel** (404)455-9200, FAX (404)455-8449. **ED** Leslie Trachtman. **Circ:** 3000.
Desc: This is an interactive newsletter for emerging software companies. It explores the issues of financing market entries, navigating successfully through the distribution channels, partnering, promotion and other timely topics for software developers and publishers.

ISSN 0020-2061
SZ
INSPIRATION. **Added/Corp** United Display Organization. Vol. 1 (1969)-. Periodical. Multiple languages (English, French, German, Italian and Spanish). Six times a year. $75.00. Inspiration Press Corporation, Alte Landstrasse 146, CH-8700 Kuesnacht Switzerland. **Tel** 011 41 1 9103230. (**Subscription address:** M & H Publishing Agency, PO Box 956280, 2564 Pow Wow Court, Duluth GA 30136. **Tel** (404)263-0051.) **Ad Acc**. **Circ:** 10,900 (ctrl).

LC HG8943 .G63 ISSN 0097-6245
DD 368/.9/73 US
INSURANCE MAGAZINE'S GOLD BOOK OF INSURANCE MARKETING. See Insurance.

LC HF5410
DD 658.8 UK
INTERACTIVE MARKETING NEWSLETTER. See Business and Economics-Advertising and Public Relations.

LC HG1501 ISSN 0265-2323
DD 332.1 UK
CCC
CODEN IJBMES
INTERNATIONAL JOURNAL OF BANK MARKETING. See Business and Economics-Banks and Banking.

LC HF5437.A2 J6 ISSN 1055-6001
DD 658.7/2/05 US
Pr Rev.
INTERNATIONAL JOURNAL OF PURCHASING AND MATERIALS MANAGEMENT. [Int. j. purch. mater. manage.]. **Added/Corp** National Association of Purchasing Management. Vol. 27, No. 1 (Winter 1991)-. Trade Publication. English. Four times a year. $49.00. National Association Purchasing Management Inc., PO Box 22160, Tempe AZ 85285. **Tel** (602)752-6276, (800)888-6276, FAX (602)752-7890. **ED** Donald W. Dobler. **Bk Rev** (Qty: 4). **Circ:** 2,800. available on microfilm and microfiche from University Microfilms International (UMI); available on an online database (file 15/Full-Text) from DIALOG. *Continues* Journal of Purchasing and Materials Management, 0094-8594.
Desc: Deals with concepts from business, economics, operations management, information systems, the behavioral sciences, and areas as related to the field of purchasing and materials management.
Ind/Abst Acad. Search; Bus. Index (1991-); Bus. Period. Index; Bus. Source Plus; Bus. Source; Comput. Lit. Index; Curr. Cit.; EP Collect.; Gen. BusinessFile (1992-); Gen. Period. Index (1991-); Homework Help.; INFO-SOUTH Abstr.; MasterFile FullTEXT 1000; MasterFile FullTEXT 350; MasterFile FullTEXT 650; MasterFile FullTEXT (July 1993-); OCLC; Telebase; UMI ABI/Inform--Bus. Period. Ondisc (Fall 1987-) [Full Txt.]; Wilson Bus. Abstr.

ISSN 0167-8116
NE
CCC
CODEN IJRME6
Pr Rev.
INTERNATIONAL JOURNAL OF RESEARCH IN MARKETING. **Added/Corp** European Marketing Academy. **VFOAT** IJRM; Research in Marketing. Vol. 1, No. 1 (1984)-. Academic Scholarly Publication. English. Five times a year (1 volume). $384.00. Elsevier Science Publishers BV, PO Box 211, 1000 AE Amsterdam Netherlands. **Tel** 011 31 20 4853641, 011 31 20 4853642, FAX 011 31 20 4853598. **ED** G Laurent. available on microfilm and microfiche from University Microfilms International (UMI); available on an online database from Elsevier Electronic Subscriptions (EES). Documents available from UMI Article Clearinghouse.
Desc: Contributes to the body of knowledge in marketing relevant to the development of the discipline. Assists in practical decision making in marketing.
Ind/Abst ABI/INFORM Glob. Ed.; ABI/INFORM

[Computer File] (1985-); Contents Pages Manage.; Curr. Cit.; Gen. BusinessFile (1992-); Selec. Coop. Index Manage. Period.; Soc. Res. Methodol. Abstr. (1992-).

LC HD9370.1 .I57 ISSN 0954-7541
DD 380.1/456632/005 HK
INTERNATIONAL JOURNAL OF WINE MARKETING. See Food and Food Industry-Beverage Industry.

ISSN 0308-2938
UK
INTERNATIONAL MARKETING DATA AND STATISTICS. [Int. mark. data stat.]. (1975)-. English. One time a year. $310.00 US | £155.00 other. Euromonitor Publications Ltd., 60-61 Britton Street, London EC1M 5NA United Kingdom. **Tel** 011 44 171 2518024, FAX 011 44 171 6083149, telex 21120.
Desc: Provides data on business and marketing parameters including literacy and education, consumer expenditures and demographic trends and forecasts.

ISSN 0193-9661
US
INTERNATIONAL MARKETING REPORT. Vol. 1 (July 1976)-. Periodical. English. Twelve times a year. $60.00 US and Canada. International House, 615 West 22nd Street, Oak Brook IL 60521.

LC HF1416 .I635 ISSN 0265-1335
DD 658.8/48/05 UK
CCC
INTERNATIONAL MARKETING REVIEW. [Int. mark. rev.]. Vol. 1, No. 1 (Autumn 1983)-. Periodical. English. Six times a year. $2559.00. MCB University Press, 60 62 Toller Lane, Bradford, West Yorkshire BD8 9BY United Kingdom. **Tel** 011 44 1274 785280, FAX 011 44 1274 785200, telex 51317-MCBUNI-G. (**Subscription address:** MCB University Press / US and Canada Subscriptions, PO Box 10812, Birmingham AL 35201-0812. **Tel** (205)995-1567, (800)633-4931, FAX (205)995-1588.) **ED** S Tamer Cavusgil and Malcolm McDonald. **Bk Rev**. **Ad Acc**. **Circ:** 416. available on an online database (file 15/Full-Text) from DIALOG. Documents available from UMI Article Clearinghouse.
Desc: Aims to assist academics, practitioners and policy makers in the research and practice of international marketing.
Ind/Abst ABI/INFORM Glob. Ed.; ABI/INFORM Ondisc: Expr. Ed.; ABI/INFORM [Computer File] (Spring 1986-); Contents Pages Manage.; Curr. Cit.; Gen. BusinessFile (1992-); Manage. Market. Abstr.; Selec. Coop. Index Manage. Period.

UK
INTERNATIONAL NEW PRODUCT REPORT. (19??)-. English. Twenty-four times a year. $1069.50. IIS Limited, 18-19 Long Lane, London EC1A 9HE United Kingdom. **Tel** 011 44 171 6064533, FAX 011 44 171 6065932. **ED** David Jago.
Desc: Information on new product launch and range extension in nearly every supermarket category from Europe, Australasia, South America, Africa, India, and the Middle East.
Ind/Abst Foods Adlibra.

ISSN 1055-3649
DD 381 US
INTERNATIONAL PARALLELS. (INTERNATIONAL PARALLELS : NEWS AND VIEWS ABOUT CONSUMERS AROUND THE WORLD.). [Int. parallels]. Vol. 1, No. 1 (Apr. 1991)-. Periodical. English. Five times a year. $195.00 US | $225.00 other. Williamson International, 3 Red Bay Court, Hilton Head Island SC 29926. **Tel** (803)689-5077. **ED** Irene Williamson. **Bk Rev**. ctrl circ.
Desc: Ideas and information about consumers and their needs in markets around the world.

US
INTERNATIONAL PRODUCT ALERT. (19??)-. English. Twenty-four times a year. $655.00. Marketing Intelligence Service Ltd., 6473D Route 64, Naples NY 14512. **Tel** (716)374-6326, (800)836-5710, FAX (714)374-5217, telex 469979. **ED** Sherie Meeker-Barton. available on an online database (files 16,570,636/Full-Text) from DIALOG.
Desc: Product introductions from Europe, the UK, Japan, South Africa, Australia, and New Zealand with commercial potential for North American marketers - source of ideas and notice of potential product competition.
Ind/Abst Mark. Advert. Ref. Serv. [Full Txt.]; PROMT [Full Txt.]; PTS Newsl. Database [Full Txt.].

LC HF1410 .I62 ISSN 0020-8957
DD 382/.05 SZ
CODEN ITFREV
INTERNATIONAL TRADE FORUM. [Int. trade forum]. **Added/Corp** International Trade Centre UNCTAD/GATT. **VFOAT** Forum. Vol. 1 (Dec. 1964)-. Periodical. English (French and Spanish). Four times a year. $20.00. International Trade Centre, UNCTAD/GATT, Palais des Nations, 1211 Geneva 10

Switzerland. **Tel** 011 41 22 7300111. **ED** Janice Goertz. Index available. cum. index. **Bk Rev. Circ:** 20,000 (ctrl). available on microfilm and microfiche from University Microfilms International (UMI). Documents available from UMI Article Clearinghouse.
Desc: Trade promotion and international marketing techniques of interest to developing countries.
Ind/Abst ABI/INFORM Glob. Ed.; ABI/INFORM [Computer File] (Jan. 1979-); Acad. Search; Anbar Account. Finan. Abstr. [Full Txt.]; Anbar Mark. Distr. Abstr. [Full Txt.]; Anbar Top Manage. Abstr. [Full Txt.]; BioBusiness; Bus. ASAP (1990-) [Full Txt.]; Bus. Index (1985-); Bus. Period. Index; Bus. Source Plus; Bus. Source; Cot. Trop. Fibr. Abstr. Bibliogr.; Curr. Cit.; EP Collect.; Food Sci. Technol. Abstr.; Gen. BusinessFile (1985-); Gen. Period. Index (1985-); Homework Help.; INFO-SOUTH Abstr.; Leis., Rec., Tour. Abstr.; Manage. Market. Abstr.; Manage. Bibliogr. Rev.; MasterFile FullTEXT 1000; MasterFile FullTEXT 350; MasterFile FullTEXT 650; MasterFile FullTEXT (July 1993-) [Full Txt.]; OCLC; Oper. Prod. Manage. Abstr. [Full Txt.]; PAIS Int. Print (1991-); Person. Train. Abstr. [Full Txt.]; Rural Dev. Abstr.; Telebase; Trade Ind. ASAP [Full Txt.]; Trade Ind. Index (1981-) [Full Txt.]; UMI ABI/Inform--Bus. Period. Ondisc (Jul. 1987-) [Full Txt.]; Wilson Bus. Abstr.; Women Manage. Rev. [Full Txt.]; World Agric. Econ. Rural Sociol. Abstr.

ISSN 0896-8535
DD 362 US
IRELAND REPORT, WOMEN'S HEALTH MARKETING, THE. See Health.

ISSN 0790-7362
DD 380.1 IE
IRISH MARKETING REVIEW. [Ir. mark. rev.]. (1986)-. English. One time a year. $102.67. Mercury Publications Ltd. / Dublin, 37 Main Street Donnybrook, Dublin 4 Ireland. **Tel** FAX 011 44 353 1 2696705. ***Continues*** *Professional Marketing (Dublin), 0790-9462.*

ISSN 1060-6017
US
ISSUES IN AGRICULTURAL DATABASE MARKETING. VFOAT Issue Papers. (1992)-. Periodical. English. Six times a year. Marketing Technologies, 1 Summit Square, Langhorne PA 19047.

UK
•**IT MARKETING SOURCE BOOK.** (1994)-. Directory. English. Irregular. £45.00. VNU Business Publications BV, 32-34 Broadwick Street, London W1A 2HG United Kingdom. **Tel** 011 44 171 4394242 ext. 2222, FAX 011 44 171 4379638, telex 23918 VNU G, 8952440. **ED** Anne Maher. **Ad Acc.**
Desc: Covers marketing and sales in the computer industry.

LC JN5933 .A23
NE
JAARVERSLAG (NETHERLANDS. RIJKSINKOOPBUREAU). See Public Administration.

GW
JAHRBUCH MARKETING. German. Vulkan Verlag, Classen, POB 103962, D-45039 Essen 1 Germany. **Tel** 011 49 201 820020. ***Continues*** *Jahrbuch des Marketing.*

LC HF5415.12.J3 D45 **ISSN** 0918-4406
DD 658.8/00952 JA
JAPAN ... MARKETING AND ADVERTISING YEARBOOK. See Business and Economics-Advertising and Public Relations.

DD 382/.0952/005 JA
JETRO MARKETING SERIES. Added/Corp Nihon Boeki Shinkokai. **VFOAT** J.E.T.R.O. Marketing Series. **VAT** Japan External Trade Organization Marketing Series. (1976)-. Monographic series. English. Irregular. Price varies per volume. Overseas Courier Services America Inc., 27 08 42nd Road, Long Island NY 11107. **Tel** (718)392-5115.

ISSN 1075-8143
DD 659 US
•**JEWELRY MARKETING REVIEW.** [Jewel. mark. rev.]. Vol. 38, No. 3 (Mar. 1994)-. Periodical. English. Twelve times a year. $234.00. Retail Reporting Corporation, 302 Fifth Avenue, New York NY 10001. **Tel** (212)279-7000, (800)251-4545, FAX (221)279-7014. ***Continues*** *Jewelry Ad Review, 0883-7929.*

LC HF5415.2 .J66 **ISSN** 0022-2437
DD 658.83/05 US
CCC
CODEN JMKRAE
Pr Rev.
JMR, JOURNAL OF MARKETING RESEARCH. [J. mark. res.]. **Added/Corp** American Marketing Association. **VFOAT** Journal of Marketing Research. Vol. 1 (Feb. 1964)-. Academic Scholarly Publication. English. Four times a year (Feb., May, Aug., Nov.). $150.00. American Marketing Association, 250 South Wacker Drive, Suite 200, Chicago IL 60606-5819. **Tel** (312)648-0536, FAX (312)993-7542. **ED** Michael Houston. Index available. cum. index. **Bk Rev. Ad Acc. Circ:** 8,500 (ctrl). available on microfilm and microfiche from University Microfilms International (UMI). Documents available from The Genuine Article, UMI Article Clearinghouse.
Desc: Scholarly journal furnishing data on concepts, methods, and application of marketing research.
Ind/Abst ABI/INFORM Glob. Ed.; ABI/INFORM Ondisc: Expr. Ed.; ABI/INFORM [Computer File] (Oct. 1971-); Acad. Search; Arts Humanit. Citation Index [Select. Cov.]; Bus. ASAP (1990-) [Full Txt.]; Bus. Index (1985-); Bus. Period. Index; Bus. Source Plus; Bus. Source; Commun. Abstr.; Contents Pages Manage. (Oct. 1971-); Curr. Cit.; Curr. Contents Soc. Behav. Sci.; EP Collect.; Food Sci. Technol. Abstr.; Gen. BusinessFile (1985-); Homework Help.; INFO-SOUTH Abstr.; Infobank (1979-); J. Econ. Lit. (1968-1979); Mag. Search; Manage. Market. Abstr.; MasterFile FullTEXT 1000; MasterFile FullTEXT 350; MasterFile FullTEXT 650; MasterFile FullTEXT (July 1993-); OCLC; Psychol. Abstr. (1966-); PsycINFO (1990-); PsycLit; PsycScan: Appl. Psych.; Res. Alert [Full Cov.]; Soc. Sci. Cit. Index [Full Cov.]; Soc. Res. Methodol. Abstr. (1975-); Telebase; Trade Ind. Index [Full Txt.]; UMI ABI/Inform--Bus. Period. Ondisc (Feb. 1987-) [Full Txt.]; Wilson Bus. Abstr.

CN
JOBBER NEWS ANNUAL MARKETING GUIDE. English. One time a year. 59.95Can$. Southham Information & Technical Group Inc, 1450 Don Mills Road, Don Mills Ontario M3B 2X7 Canada. **Tel** (416)445-6641, (800)668-2374, FAX (416)442-2261.

LC HD28 **ISSN** 0889-485X
DD 658 US
CCC
JONESREPORT. [Jonesreport]. **Added/Corp** Stillerman Jones & Company (Indianapolis, Ind.). **VFOAT** Jones Report. (19??)-. Periodical. English. Twelve times a year. $125.00. JonesReport for Shopping, PO Box 80209, Indianapolis IN 46280. **Tel** (800)878-9024, (317)844-9024, FAX (317)848-6953. **ED** Maureen Gilmer. Index available (September). **Bk Rev. Ad Acc, Adv Mgr:** Marsha Davis. **Circ:** 2,000.
Desc: Newsletter for shopping center marketing directors.

ISSN 1197-1169
DD 658.8/005 CN
•**JOURNAL MEGA SUCCES, LE.** [J. mega succ·es]. (1993)-. Periodical. French. Six times a year. 34.06Can$. Succes Promotion & Profits, 41 71 EME Avenue Est, Blainville Quebec J7C 1S3 Canada. **Tel** (514)979-4500. ***Continues*** *Succes, Promotion & Profits., 0830-8802.*

LC HF5801 .J6 **ISSN** 0021-8499
DD 659.1/07/2 US
CODEN JADRAV
Pr Rev.
JOURNAL OF ADVERTISING RESEARCH. See Business and Economics-Advertising and Public Relations.

ISSN 0885-8624
DD 659 US
CCC
Pr Rev.
JOURNAL OF BUSINESS & INDUSTRIAL MARKETING, THE. [J. bus. ind. mark.]. **VFOAT** Journal of Business and Industrial Marketing. Vol. 1, No. 1 (Fall 1986)-. Periodical. English. Four times a year. $279.00. MCB University Press, 60 62 Toller Lane, Bradford, West Yorkshire BD8 9BY United Kingdom. **Tel** 011 44 1274 785280, FAX 011 44 1274 785200, telex 51317-MCBUNI-G. **(Subscription address:** MCB University Press / US and Canada Subscriptions, PO Box 10812, Birmingham AL 35201-0812. **Tel** (205)995-1567, (800)633-4931, FAX (205)995-1588.**) ED** Peter LaPlaca. Index available. **Bk Rev. Ad Acc. Circ:** 1,000. available on microfilm and microfiche from University Microfilms International (UMI); available on an online database (file 15/Full-Text) from DIALOG. Documents available from UMI Article Clearinghouse. ***Absorbed*** *Journal of International Marketing.*
Desc: An academic journal written for practitioners.
Ind/Abst ABI/INFORM Glob. Ed.; ABI/INFORM [Computer File] (Fall 1986-); Acad. Search; Bus. Period. Index; Bus. Source Plus; Bus. Source; Curr. Cit.; EP Collect.; Gen. BusinessFile (1992-); Homework Help.; INFO-SOUTH Abstr.; Mag. Search; MasterFile FullTEXT 1000; MasterFile FullTEXT 350; MasterFile FullTEXT 650; MasterFile FullTEXT (Jan. 1994-); OCLC; Telebase; UMI ABI/Inform--Bus. Period. Ondisc (Fall 1987-) [Full Txt.]; Wilson Bus. Abstr.; Women Manage. Rev. [Full Txt.].

LC HF5415.1263 .J68 **ISSN** 1051-712X
DD 658.8/02 US
•**JOURNAL OF BUSINESS-TO-BUSINESS MARKETING.** [J. bus.-bus. mark.]. **VFOAT** Journal of Business to Business Marketing. Vol. 1, No. 1 (1993)-. Periodical. English. Four times a year. $95.00. The Haworth Press Inc., 10 Alice Street, Binghamton NY 13904-1580. **Tel** (607)722-5857, (800)3-HAWORTH, FAX (607)722-1424. **ED** David Wilson. **Acid Free.** available on microfiche. Documents available from Haworth Document Delivery Service.
Desc: Will publish quality research to reflect the state of scholarship and practice throughout the world. Will feature diverse approaches to business marketing theory development and problem solving.

LC HF5410 .J67 **ISSN** 0736-3761
DD 658.8/005 UK
CCC
JOURNAL OF CONSUMER MARKETING, THE. [J. consum. mark.]. Vol. 1, No. 1 (Summer 1983)-. Periodical. English. Four times a year. $279.00. MCB University Press, 60 62 Toller Lane, Bradford, West Yorkshire BD8 9BY United Kingdom. **Tel** 011 44 1274 785280, FAX 011 44 1274 785200, telex 51317-MCBUNI-G. **(Subscription address:** MCB University Press / US and Canada Subscriptions, PO Box 10812, Birmingham AL 35201-0812. **Tel** (205)995-1567, (800)633-4931, FAX (205)995-1588.**)** available on microfilm and microfiche from University Microfilms International (UMI). Documents available from UMI Article Clearinghouse.
Ind/Abst ABI/INFORM Glob. Ed.; ABI/INFORM Ondisc: Expr. Ed.; ABI/INFORM [Computer File] (Summer 1985-); Acad. Search; Bus. Period. Index; Bus. Source Plus; Bus. Source; Curr. Cit.; EP Collect.; Gen. BusinessFile (1992-); Homework Help.; INFO-SOUTH Abstr.; Mag. Search; Mark. Advert. Ref. Serv.; MasterFile FullTEXT 1000; MasterFile FullTEXT 350; MasterFile FullTEXT 650; MasterFile FullTEXT (July 1993-); OCLC; Telebase; UMI ABI/Inform--Bus. Period. Ondisc (Fall 1987-) [Full Txt.]; Wilson Bus. Abstr.

LC HF5415.3 .J68 **ISSN** 0093-5301
DD 381 US
CCC
CODEN JCSRBL
Pr Rev.
JOURNAL OF CONSUMER RESEARCH, THE. [J. consum. res.]. **Added/Corp** American Association for Public Opinion Research. **VFOAT** Consumer Research. Vol. 1 (June 1974)-. Periodical. English. Four times a year. $90.00. University of Chicago Press / Journals Division, PO Box 37005, 5720 South Woodlawn, Chicago IL 60637. **Tel** (312)753-3347, FAX (312)753-0811. **ED** Brian Sternthal. **Ad Acc. Acid Free.** available on microfilm and microfiche from University Microfilms International (UMI); available on CD-ROM. Documents available from The Genuine Article, UMI Article Clearinghouse.
Desc: An interdisciplinary journal that publishes current research on how and why consumers make choices. Empirical, theoretical, and methodological articles from psychology, marketing, economics, sociology, and other fields are featured.
Ind/Abst ABI/INFORM Glob. Ed.; ABI/INFORM Ondisc: Expr. Ed.; ABI/INFORM [Computer File] (June 1974-); Acad. Abstr.; Acad. Search; AGRICOLA [Select. Cov.]; Bus. ASAP (1990-) [Full Txt.]; Bus. Index (1985-); Bus. Period. Index; Bus. Source Plus; Bus. Source; Chicano Index; Commun. Abstr. (?-?); Curr. Cit.; Curr. Contents Soc. Behav. Sci.; Econ. Lit. Index; EP Collect.; Ergon. Abstr.; Food Sci. Technol. Abstr.; Gen. BusinessFile (1985-); Gen. Period. Index (1985-); Highw. Res. Abstr.; Homework Help.; INFO-SOUTH Abstr.; Infobank (1979-); Int. Abstr. Oper. Res. [Select. Cov.]; J. Econ. Lit.; Mag. Search; Manage. Contents; Mark. Res. Abstr.; Mark. Advert. Ref. Serv.; MasterFile FullTEXT 1000; MasterFile FullTEXT 350; MasterFile FullTEXT 650; MasterFile FullTEXT (Jan. 1992-); OCLC; Psychol. Abstr. (1974-); PsycINFO; PsycLit; Pub. Lib. FullTEXT; Res. Alert [Full Cov.]; Selec. Coop. Index Manage. Period.; Soc. Plann. Policy Dev. Abstr.; Soc. Sci. Cit. Index [Full Cov.]; Sociol. Abstr.; SportSearch; Soc. Res. Methodol. Abstr. (1987-); Telebase; Trade Ind. ASAP [Full Txt.]; Trade Ind. Index [Full Txt.]; UMI ABI/Inform--Bus. Period. Ondisc (Dec. 1987-) [Full Txt.]; Wilson Bus. Abstr.

ISSN 1069-2533
US
•**JOURNAL OF CUSTOMER SERVICE IN MARKETING & MANAGEMENT.** See Business and Economics-Management.

LC HF5415.126 .J68 **ISSN** 0892-0591
DD 658 US
CCC
JOURNAL OF DIRECT MARKETING. (JOURNAL OF DIRECT MARKETING : JDM.). [J. direct mark.]. **Added/Corp** Medill School of Journalism. Direct Marketing Educational Foundation. **VFOAT** JDM. Vol. 1, No. 1 (Winter 1987)-. Academic Scholarly Publication. English. Four times a year. $320.00. John Wiley & Sons, Inc., 605 Third Avenue, New York NY 10158-0012. **Tel** (212)850-6000, (212)850-6645, FAX (212)850-6088, telex 12-7063. **(Subscription address:** John Wiley & Sons / UK, Baffins Lane, Chichester, West Sussex PO19 1UD United Kingdom. **Tel** 011 44 1243 779777, FAX 011 44 243 776128, telex 86290 WIBOOKG.**) ED** Don E. Schultz. available on microfilm and microfiche from University Microfilms International (UMI). ***Absorbed*** *Journal of Direct Marketing Research, 0888-9295.*
Desc: This scholarly publication offers a high-level exchange of ideas in the dynamic field of direct marketing. Designed to provide a bridge between direct marketing practitioners and the academic research community. It contains in-depth, current articles on both the theory and practice of direct marketing. Also featured are a letters column, books and software reviews and editorials from the Foundation and the editor.

Ind/Abst Acad. Search; Bus. Period. Index; Bus. Source Plus; Bus. Source; Commun. Abstr.; Curr. Cit.; EP Collect.; Homework Help.; INFO-SOUTH Abstr.; Mag. Search; MasterFile FullTEXT 1000; MasterFile FullTEXT 350; MasterFile FullTEXT 650; MasterFile FullTEXT (July 1993-); OCLC; Telebase; Wilson Bus. Abstr.

LC HF1416.6.E86 J68 **ISSN** 1049-6483
DD 382/.6/09405 US
CODEN JEMAEN
Pr Rev.

JOURNAL OF EURO MARKETING. [J. Euro-mark.]. **VFOAT** Journal of Euromarketing. Vol. 1, No. 1/2 (1991)-. Periodical. English. Four times a year (Published during the academic year). $120.00. The Haworth Press Inc., 10 Alice Street, Binghamton NY 13904-1580. **Tel** (607)722-5857, (800)3-HAWORTH, FAX (607)722-1424. **ED** Erdener Kaynak (editor's address: International Business Press, PO Box 231, Middletown, PA 17057). **Bk Rev. Ad Acc. Acid Free.** available on microfilm and microfiche from University Microfilms International (UMI). Documents available from Haworth Document Delivery Service.
Desc: Creates a forum that fosters a conceptual understanding of the European markets and marketing systems. Provides analytical insights and highlights the past, present, and future of European marketing.
Ind/Abst Contents Pages Manage.; Foods Adlibra; Hum. Resour. Abstr. (?-?); Manage. Market. Abstr.; Sage Public Adm. Abstr. (?-?); Sage Urban Stud. Abstr (?-?); Soc. Plann. Policy Dev. Abstr.

LC HD9000.1 .J677 **ISSN** 1045-4446
DD 664/.0068/8 US
CODEN JFPMED
Pr Rev.

JOURNAL OF FOOD PRODUCTS MARKETING. **See** Food and Food Industry.

LC HF1009.5 .J68 **ISSN** 0891-1762
US
CODEN JGMAE3
Pr Rev.

JOURNAL OF GLOBAL MARKETING. **VFOAT** Global Marketing. Vol. 1, No. 1/2 (Fall/Winter 1987)-. Periodical. English. Four times a year (Published during the academic year). $145.00. The Haworth Press Inc., 10 Alice Street, Binghamton NY 13904-1580. **Tel** (607)722-5857, (800)3-HAWORTH, FAX (607)722-1424. **ED** Erdenher Kaynak (editor's address: International Business Press, PO Box 231, Middletown, PA 17057). **Bk Rev. Ad Acc. Acid Free. Circ:** 328. available on microfilm and microfiche from University Microfilms International (UMI). Documents available from UMI Article Clearinghouse, Haworth Document Delivery Service.
Desc: Addresses marketing challenges, opportunities, and problems encountered by firms, industries, and governments on a global scale. Contains significant contributions to the fields of global marketing form scholars, practitioners, and public policymakers at all levels.
Ind/Abst ABI/INFORM Glob. Ed.; Anbar Account. Finan. Abstr. [Full Txt.]; Anbar Mark. Distr. Abstr. [Full Txt.]; Anbar Top Manage. Abstr. [Full Txt.]; Contents Pages Manage.; Curr. Cit.; Hum. Resour. Abstr. (?-?); Index Period. Artic. Relat. Law; Int. Exec.; Int. Polit. Sci. Abstr.; Manage. Bibliogr. Rev.; Oper. Prod. Manage. Abstr. [Full Txt.]; PAIS Int. Print (1991-); Person. Train. Abstr. [Full Txt.]; Refer. Z.; Women Manage. Rev. [Full Txt.].

LC RA410.A1 J68 **ISSN** 0737-3252
DD 362.1/068/8 US
CCC

JOURNAL OF HEALTH CARE MARKETING. [J. health care mark.]. **Added/Corp** John A. Walker College of Business. Center for Management Development. John A. Walker College of Business. Bureau of Economics and Business Research. John A. Walker College of Business. Bureau of Economic and Business Research. American Marketing Association. Academy for Health Services Marketing (American Marketing Association). **VFOAT** JHCM. Vol. 1, No. 1 (Winter 1981)-. Periodical. English. Four times a year (Mar., June, Sept., Dec.). $90.00. American Marketing Association, 250 South Wacker Drive, Suite 200, Chicago IL 60606-5819. **Tel** (312)648-0536, FAX (312)993-7542. **ED** Eric Berkowitz. Index available. cum. index. **Bk Rev. Ad Acc. Circ:** 5,300 (ctrl). available on microfilm and microfiche from University Microfilms International (UMI); available on an online database (file 149/Full-Text) from DIALOG. Documents available from UMI Article Clearinghouse.
Desc: National publication for the professional health community containing the latest theories, ideas, research and practice of health care marketing
Ind/Abst ABI/INFORM Glob. Ed.; ABI/INFORM Ondisc: Expr. Ed.; ABI/INFORM [Computer File] (Fall 1983-); Acad. Search; Bus. Source Plus; Bus. Source; Cumul. Index Nurs. Allied Health Lit.; Curr. Cit.; EMBASE; EP Collect.; Gen. BusinessFile (1992-); Health Index (1992-); Health Source Plus; Health Source; Healthcare Leader. Rev.; Homework Help.; Hosp. Health Admin. Index; MasterFile FullTEXT 1000; MasterFile FullTEXT 350; MasterFile FullTEXT 650; MasterFile FullTEXT (July 1994-); PAIS Int. Print (1991-?); Telebase; Trade Ind. ASAP [Full Txt.]; Trade Ind. Index [Full Txt.]; UMI ABI/Inform--Bus. Period. Ondisc (Mar. 1987-) [Full Txt.].

LC TX911.3.M3 J68 **ISSN** 1050-7051
DD 381/.45647/05 US
CODEN JHLME7
Pr Rev.

JOURNAL OF HOSPITALITY & LEISURE MARKETING. **See** Leisure and Recreation.

LC HF5415.2 .J655 **ISSN** 0896-1530
DD 658.8/48/05 US
CODEN JIMREY
Pr Rev.

JOURNAL OF INTERNATIONAL CONSUMER MARKETING. [J. int. consum. mark.]. Vol. 1, No. 1 (1988)-. Periodical. English. Four times a year (Published during the academic year). $150.00. The Haworth Press Inc., 10 Alice Street, Binghamton NY 13904-1580. **Tel** (607)722-5857, (800)3-HAWORTH, FAX (607)722-1424. **ED** Erdener Kaynak (editor's address: International Business Press, PO Box 231, Middletown, PA 17057). **Bk Rev. Ad Acc. Acid Free. Circ:** 245. available on microfilm and microfiche from University Microfilms International (UMI). Documents available from UMI Article Clearinghouse, Haworth Document Delivery Service.
Desc: Created to improve our understanding of cross-cultural/national aspects of consumer behavior research and application by publishing articles of the highest quality. Written by practitioners and public policymakers as well as academicians from a variety of countries. It offers managerial insights to practicing international business persons as well as to policymakers in governments and international agencies and organizations to enable them to formulate need-oriented action programs and policies.
Ind/Abst ABI/INFORM Glob. Ed.; Food Sci. Technol. Abstr.; Soc. Plann. Policy Dev. Abstr.

UK
Pr Rev.

JOURNAL OF INTERNATIONAL MARKETING AND MARKETING RESEARCH. **Added/Corp** European Marketing Association. Commission Internationale de Marketing. **VFOAT** JIMMR. (19??)-. Periodical. English. Three times a year (Feb., June, Oct.). $111.23. European Marketing Association, 18 St. Peters Steps, Brixham Devon United Kingdom. **ED** Dr. D. W. Newill. Index available (Bound in 3rd iss., in Oct.). cum. index. **Bk Rev**, (Qty: 15-25). **Ad Acc, Adv Mgr:** T. A. Voss. **Circ:** 800. Documents available from UMI Article Clearinghouse.
Ind/Abst ABI/INFORM Glob. Ed.; Anbar Mark. Distr. Abstr.; Manage. Market. Abstr.

LC HF1416 .J68 **ISSN** 1069-031X
DD 338 US
Pr Rev.

•**JOURNAL OF INTERNATIONAL MARKETING (EAST LANSING, MICH.).** (JOURNAL OF INTERNATIONAL MARKETING.). [J. int. mark.]. **Added/Corp** Eli Broad Graduate School of Management. Center for International Business Education and Research. Vol. 1, No. 1 (1993)-. Periodical. English. Four times a year. $115.00. Michigan State University Press, 1405 South Harrison Road, Manly Miles 25, East Lansing MI 48823-5202. **Tel** (517)355-9543, FAX (800)678-2120, (517)336-2611. **Bk Rev. Circ:** 300.

LC HF5410 **ISSN** 1356-0565
DD 658.8 UK

•**JOURNAL OF INTERNATIONAL SELLING AND SALES MANAGEMENT.** **Added/Corp** European Marketing Association. **VFOAT** JISSM. Vol. 1, No. 1 (Spring 1995)-. Academic Scholarly Publication. English. Two times a year. European Marketing Association, 18 St. Peters Steps, Brixham Devon United Kingdom. Index available. cum. index. **Bk Rev. Ad Acc.**

LC HF5410 .J68 **ISSN** 0276-1467
DD 658.8/02 US

JOURNAL OF MACROMARKETING. [J. macromark.]. **Added/Corp** University of Colorado, Boulder. Business Research Division. **VFOAT** Macromarketing. Vol. 1, No. 1 (Spring 1981)-. Periodical. English. Two times a year (June & Nov.). $51.00. Business Research Division, University of Colorado, Campus Box 420, Boulder CO 80309-0420. **Tel** (303)492-8227, FAX (303)492-3620. **ED** Robert Nason. **Bk Rev. Ad Acc. Circ:** 600 (ctrl). available on microfilm and microfiche from University Microfilms International (UMI). Documents available from UMI Article Clearinghouse.
Desc: Provides a forum in which people can debate and clarify the role of marketing in society.
Ind/Abst ABI/INFORM Glob. Ed.; ABI/INFORM [Computer File] (Spring 1986-); Contents Pages Manage.; Curr. Cit.

LC HD28 **ISSN** 1382-3019
DD 658 NE

•**JOURNAL OF MARKET-FOCUSED MANAGEMENT.** **See** Business and Economics-Management.

LC HF5415.A2 J6 **ISSN** 0022-2429
DD 658.8/005 US
CCC
CODEN JMKTAK
Pr Rev.

JOURNAL OF MARKETING. [J. mark.]. **Added/Corp** American Marketing Association. American Marketing Society. National Association of Marketing Teachers. Vol. 1 (July 1936)-. Periodical. English. Four times a year (Jan., Apr., July, Oct.). $150.00. American Marketing Association, 250 South Wacker Drive, Suite 200, Chicago IL 60606-5819. **Tel** (312)648-0536, FAX (312)993-7542. **ED** Thomas Kinnear. Index available. cum. index. **Bk Rev. Ad Acc. Circ:** 14,200 (ctrl). available on microfilm and microfiche from University Microfilms International (UMI). Documents available from The Genuine Article, UMI Article Clearinghouse. ***Formed by the union of** American Marketing Journal, 0193-1806 **and** National Marketing Review, 0190-9509.*
Desc: Contains articles furnishing information on marketing discoveries, techniques, trends and new ideas.
Ind/Abst ABI/INFORM Glob. Ed.; ABI/INFORM Ondisc: Expr. Ed.; ABI/INFORM [Computer File] (Oct. 1971-); Acad. Abstr.; Acad. Ind. [Computer File] (1984-); Acad. Search; Anbar Account. Finan. Abstr. [Full Txt.]; Anbar Mark. Distr. Abstr. [Full Txt.]; Anbar Top Manage. Abstr. [Full Txt.]; Biogr. Index; Book Rev. Index; Bus. Index (1985-); Bus. Period. Index; Bus. Source Plus; Bus. Source; Commun. Abstr.; Contents Pages Manage.; Curr. Cit.; EP Collect.; Expand. Acad. Index (1984-); Gen. BusinessFile (1985-); Gen. Period. Index (1985-); Homework Help.; INFO-SOUTH Abstr.; Infobank (1979-); Mag. Search; Manage. Market. Abstr.; Manage. Bibliogr. Rev.; Manage. Contents; Mark. Advert. Ref. Serv.; MasterFile FullTEXT 1000; MasterFile FullTEXT 350; MasterFile FullTEXT 650; MasterFile FullTEXT (July 1990-); Middle East Abstr. Index; Newsp. Period. Abstr. (1986-); OCLC; Oper. Prod. Manage. Abstr. [Full Txt.]; Person. Train. Abstr. [Full Txt.]; Psychol. Abstr. (1938-); PsycINFO; PsycLit; PsycScan: Appl. Psych.; Pub. Lib. FullTEXT; Res. Alert [Full Cov.]; Soc. Sci. Cit. Index [Full Cov.]; Soc. Res. Methodol. Abstr. (1975-); Telebase; Trade Ind. ASAP [Full Txt.]; Trade Ind. Index [Full Txt.]; UMI ABI/Inform--Bus. Period. Ondisc (Jan. 1987-) [Full Txt.]; Wilson Bus. Abstr.; Women Manage. Rev. [Full Txt.]; Women Stud. Abstr.

LC HF5415.129 .J68 **ISSN** 1046-669X
DD 658.8/4/05 US
CODEN JMKCE7
Pr Rev.

JOURNAL OF MARKETING CHANNELS. [J. mark. channels]. **VFOAT** Marketing Channels. Vol. 1, No. 1 (Fall 1991)-. Periodical. English. Four times a year (Published during the academic year). $120.00. The Haworth Press Inc., 10 Alice Street, Binghamton NY 13904-1580. **Tel** (607)722-5857, (800)3-HAWORTH, FAX (607)722-1424. **ED** Bert Rosenbloom (editor's address: College of Business and Adm., Drexel University, 32nd and Market Streets, Philadelphia, PA 19104). **Bk Rev. Ad Acc. Acid Free.** available on microfilm and microfiche from University Microfilms International (UMI). Documents available from Ask*IEEE, Haworth Document Delivery Service.
Desc: Professional marketing journal that focuses exclusively on distribution systems, strategy and management. Leading authorities from around the world present thought, analysis and research on distribution systems, strategy, and management in this international quarterly.
Ind/Abst Contents Pages Manage.; Food Sci. Technol. Abstr.; Hum. Resour. Abstr. (?-?); INSPEC (1991-); Linguist. Lang. Behav. Abstr.; Manage. Market. Abstr.; Oper. Res./Manage. Sci.; Soc. Plann. Policy Dev. Abstr.; Sociol. Abstr.

LC HD28 **ISSN** 1352-7266
DD 658 UK

•**JOURNAL OF MARKETING COMMUNICATIONS.** (1995)-. Academic Scholarly Publication. English. Four times a year. £120.00. Chapman & Hall, 2-6 Boundary Row, London SE1 8HN United Kingdom. **Tel** 011 44 171 8650066, FAX 011 44 171 5229623, telex 290164 CHAPMA G.

LC HF5415 .J67 **ISSN** 0273-4753
DD 658.8/007/1173 US

JOURNAL OF MARKETING EDUCATION. (JOURNAL OF MARKETING EDUCATION : JME / COSPONSORED BY THE WESTERN MARKETING EDUCATORS ASSOCIATION AND MARKETING DIVISION AND BUSINESS RESEARCH DIVISION, UNIVERSITY OF COLORADO, BOULDER.). [J. mark. educ.]. **Added/Corp** Western Marketing Educators Association (U.S.) University of Colorado, Boulder. Marketing Division. University of Colorado, Boulder. Business Research Division. **VFOAT** JME. (Apr. 1979)-. Periodical. English. Three times a year (Apr., July, Nov.). $55.00. Business Research Division,

University of Colorado, Campus Box 420, Boulder CO 80309-0420. **Tel** (303)492-8227, FAX (303)492-3620. **ED** Philip Cateora. **Bk Rev**. **Ad Acc**. **Circ:** 600. available on microfilm and microfiche from University Microfilms International (UMI).
Desc: A forum for the exchange of ideas information and experiences related to the process of educating students in marketing.
Ind/Abst Curr. Cit.

LC LB2342.82 .J68 **ISSN** 0884-1241
DD 378.73068/8 US
CODEN JMHEEW
Pr Rev.
JOURNAL OF MARKETING FOR HIGHER EDUCATION. See Education-Higher Education.

ISSN 0267-257X
UK
CCC
JOURNAL OF MARKETING MANAGEMENT.
[MM, J. mark. manage.]. **VFOAT** MM. Vol. 1, No. 1 (Summer 1985)-. Academic Scholarly Publication. English. Four times a year. $299.46. Academic Press Ltd., A Division of Harcourt Brace & Company Ltd., 24-28 Oval Road, London NW1 7DX United Kingdom. **Tel** 011 44 171 2674466, FAX 011 44 171 4822293, 011 44 171 4854752, telex 25775 ACPRES G. **(Subscription address:** Harcourt Brace & Company, Ltd., Foots Cray High Street, Sidcup Kent DA14 5HP United Kingdom. **Tel** 011 44 181 3003322, FAX 011 44 181 3090807, telex 896 377 ACADEM.) **ED** M. J. Baker and S. Hart. Index available. **Bk Rev**. **Ad Acc**. **Circ:** 500. Documents available from UMI Article Clearinghouse.
Desc: Concerned with all aspects of the management of the marketing mix and is intended to provide a forum for the exchange of the latest ideas and best practice in the field of marketing as a whole. Seeks to meet the needs of a wide but sophisticated audience comprising senior marketing executives and their advisors, senior line managers, teachers and researchers in marketing, and undergraduate and postgraduate students of the subject. Its policy is to encourage the widest possible exchange of knowledge and ideas related to the theory and practice of marketing, in a thought-provoking way. Papers on particular topics, case studies, conference reports, and book reviews are also published.
Ind/Abst ABI/INFORM Glob. Ed.; Anbar Mark. Distr. Abstr. [Full Txt.]; Contents Pages Manage.; Curr. Cit.; Int. Exec.; Manage. Market. Abstr.; Women Manage. Rev. [Full Txt.].

LC HF5415 .J68 **ISSN** 1355-2538
DD 658.8 UK
•JOURNAL OF MARKETING PRACTICE : APPLIED MARKETING SCIENCE.
Added/Corp MCB University Press. (1995)-. Academic Scholarly Publication. English. Four times a year. £59.00. MCB University Press, 60 62 Toller Lane, Bradford, West Yorkshire BD8 9BY United Kingdom. **Tel** 011 44 1274 785280, FAX 011 44 1274 785200, telex 51317-MCBUNI-G. **ED** Dr. Malcolm McDonald.
Desc: Aim is to bridge the gap between marketing theory and practice, address the development of knowledge concerning the tools, techniques, and processes of marketing, and to provide a vehicle for the advancement of knowledge in the field of marketing practice.

US
JOURNAL OF MARKETING RESEARCH.
Added/Corp American Marketing Association. Vol. 1 (Feb. 1964)-. Periodical. English. Four times a year. American Marketing Association, 250 South Wacker Drive, Suite 200, Chicago IL 60606-5819. **Tel** (312)648-0536, FAX (312)993-7542.
Ind/Abst Gen. Period. Index (1985-); Manage. Contents; Selec. Coop. Index Manage. Period.

ISSN 1057-1523
US
•JOURNAL OF MINISTRY MARKETING & MANAGEMENT.
VFOAT Journal of Ministry Marketing and Management. Vol. 1 (March 1993)-. Periodical. English. Four times a year. $48.00. The Haworth Press Inc., 10 Alice Street, Binghamton NY 13904-1580. **Tel** (607)722-5857, (800)3-HAWORTH, FAX (607)722-1424. **Acid Free.** Documents available from Haworth Document Delivery Service.
Desc: Provides timely and practical information on marketing and management concepts, tools, cases, and methodologies useful for professionals in the ministry.

ISSN 1049-5142
US
Pr Rev.
JOURNAL OF NONPROFIT & PUBLIC SECTOR MARKETING.
VFOAT Journal of Nonprofit and Public Sector Marketing. Vol. 1 (Spring 1992)-. Periodical. English. Four times a year. $120.00. The Haworth Press Inc., 10 Alice Street, Binghamton NY 13904-1580. **Tel** (607)722-5857, (800)3-HAWORTH, FAX (607)722-1424. **ED** Donald Self (editor's address: Auburn University, Department of Marketing, Montgomery, AL 36193). **Bk Rev**. **Ad Acc**. **Acid Free.** available on microfilm and microfiche from University Microfilms International (UMI). Documents available from Haworth Document Delivery Service. ***Continues*** *Journal of Nonprofit & Public Sector Marketing.*
Desc: A forum for the development of marketing thought and for the dissemination of marketing knowledge in the non-profit and public sector of the economy. Devoted to the study of the adaptation of marketing for use by these organizations.
Ind/Abst Hum. Resour. Abstr. (?-?); Soc. Work Abstr. [Select. Cov.].

LC HF5438 .J74 **ISSN** 0885-3134
DD 658.8/1/005 US
JOURNAL OF PERSONAL SELLING & SALES MANAGEMENT, THE.
[J. pers. sell. sales manage.]. **Added/Corp** Pi Sigma Epsilon (Fraternity). **VFOAT** JPSSM; Journal of Personal Selling and Sales Management. Vol. 1, Issue 1 (Fall/Winter 1980/1981)-. Periodical. English. Four times a year. $75.00. Journal of Personal Selling, 155 E Capitol Drive, Hartland WI 53029. **Tel** (414)367-5600. **ED** Thomas Ingram. **Bk Rev**. **Ad Acc**. **Circ:** 1,000. available on microfilm and microfiche from University Microfilms International (UMI); available on an online database (file 15/Full-Text) from DIALOG. Documents available from UMI Article Clearinghouse.
Desc: A journal devoted to the encouragement of professional and academic thinking, exchange, and research in the world of selling and sales management.
Ind/Abst ABI/INFORM Glob. Ed.; ABI/INFORM [Computer File] (May 1983-); Acad. Search; Curr. Cit.; EP Collect.; Gen. Period. Index (1985-); Homework Help.; INFO-SOUTH Abstr.; Mag. Search; Manage. Contents; MasterFile FullTEXT 1000; MasterFile FullTEXT 350; MasterFile FullTEXT 650; MasterFile FullTEXT (July 1993-); OCLC; Telebase; UMI ABI/Inform--Bus. Period. Ondisc (Nov. 1987-) [Full Txt.].

ISSN 0748-4623
DD 658 US
Pr Rev.
JOURNAL OF PROFESSIONAL SERVICES MARKETING.
[J. prof. serv. mark.]. Vol. 1, No. 1/2 (Winter 1985/1986)-. Periodical. English. Four times a year. $350.00. The Haworth Press Inc., 10 Alice Street, Binghamton NY 13904-1580. **Tel** (607)722-5857, (800)3-HAWORTH, FAX (607)722-1424. **ED** William Winston (editor's address: Professional Services Marketing Group, 1044 Masonic Avenue, Albany, CA 94706). **Bk Rev**. **Ad Acc**. **Acid Free. Circ:** 185. available on microfilm and microfiche from University Microfilms International (UMI). Documents available from UMI Article Clearinghouse, Haworth Document Delivery Service.
Desc: For anyone interested in learning more about services marketing. Helps readers keep abreast of the techniques and current trends in this competitive industry.
Ind/Abst ABI/INFORM Glob. Ed.; ABI/INFORM [Computer File] (Spring 1986-); Curr. Cit.; Healthcare Leader. Rev.; Index Period. Artic. Relat. Law; PsycINFO.

LC HF5410 .J69 **ISSN** 0743-9156
DD 658.8/02 US
CCC
Pr Rev.
JOURNAL OF PUBLIC POLICY & MARKETING.
(JOURNAL OF PUBLIC POLICY & MARKETING : J.P.P.& M : AN ANNUAL PUBLICATION OF THE DIVISION OF RESEARCH, GRADUATE SCHOOL OF BUSINESS ADMINISTRATION, THE UNIVERSITY OF MICHIGAN.). [J. public policy mark.]. **Added/Corp** University of Michigan. Graduate School of Business Administration. Division of Research. American Marketing Association. **VFOAT** Journal of Public Policy and Marketing; JPP&M; J.P.P.&M. Vol. 2 (1983)-. Periodical. English. Two times a year. $90.00. American Marketing Association, 250 South Wacker Drive, Suite 200, Chicago IL 60606-5819. **Tel** (312)648-0536, FAX (312)993-7542. **ED** Patrick E Murphy. **Circ:** 130. available on microfilm and microfiche from University Microfilms International (UMI); available on an online database (file 15/Full-Text) from DIALOG. Documents available from The Genuine Article, UMI Article Clearinghouse. ***Continues*** *Journal of Marketing & Public Policy, 0748-6766.*
Desc: Forum for dialogue on issues in marketing and public policy including evaluation of public policy programs, and applications of marketing research concepts.
Ind/Abst ABI/INFORM Glob. Ed.; ABI/INFORM [Computer File] (1983-); Acad. Search; Bus. Source Plus; Bus. Source; Commun. Abstr.; Curr. Cit.; Curr. Contents Soc. Behav. Sci.; EP Collect.; Gen. BusinessFile (1992-); Homework Help.; Index Period. Artic. Relat. Law (19??-19??); MasterFile FullTEXT 1000; MasterFile FullTEXT 350; MasterFile FullTEXT 650; MasterFile FullTEXT (July 1994-); PAIS Int. Print; Res. Alert [Full Cov.]; Soc. Sci. Source; Soc. Sci. Cit. Index [Full Cov.]; Telebase.

LC HG1501 .J63 **ISSN** 0195-2064
DD 332.1/0973 US
CCC
TITLE CHANGE
JOURNAL OF RETAIL BANKING. See Business and Economics-Banks and Banking.

ISSN 0887-6045
DD 659 US
CCC
Pr Rev.
JOURNAL OF SERVICES MARKETING, THE.
[J. serv. mark.]. Vol. 1, No. 1 (Summer 1987)-. Periodical. English. Four times a year. $279.00. MCB University Press, 60 62 Toller Lane, Bradford, West Yorkshire BD8 9BY United Kingdom. **Tel** 011 44 1274 785280, FAX 011 44 1274 785200, telex 51317-MCBUNI-G. **(Subscription address:** MCB University Press / US and Canada Subscriptions, PO Box 10812, Birmingham AL 35201-0812. **Tel** (205)995-1567, (800)633-4931, FAX (205)995-1588.) Index available. cum. index. **Bk Rev**. **Ad Acc**. **Circ:** 1,000. available on microfilm and microfiche from University Microfilms International (UMI). Documents available from UMI Article Clearinghouse.
Desc: Academic journal written for practitioners.
Ind/Abst ABI/INFORM Glob. Ed.; ABI/INFORM Ondisc: Expr. Ed.; ABI/INFORM [Computer File] (Summer 1987-); Curr. Cit.; Gen. BusinessFile (1992-); UMI ABI/Inform--Bus. Period. Ondisc (Summer 1987-) [Full Txt.]; Women Manage. Rev. [Full Txt.].

ISSN 0965-254X
UK
CCC
•JOURNAL OF STRATEGIC MARKETING.
[J. strateg. mark.]. (1993)-. Periodical. English. Four times a year. $250.00. Chapman & Hall, 2-6 Boundary Row, London SE1 8HN United Kingdom. **Tel** 011 44 171 8650066, FAX 011 44 171 5229623, telex 290164 CHAPMA G. **ED** Gordon Greenley.
Desc: Concerned with key aspects of the interface between marketing and strategic management. Acts as a vehicle for the discussion of the long range activities where marketing has a role to play in managing the long term objectives and strategies of companies.

LC HF5415 .A319a **ISSN** 0092-0703
DD 658.8/005 US
CCC
Pr Rev.
JOURNAL OF THE ACADEMY OF MARKETING SCIENCE.
(JOURNAL.). [J. Acad. Mark. Sci.]. **Main/Corp** Academy of Marketing Science. Vol. 1 (Spring 1973)-. English. Four times a year (Jan., Apr., July, Oct.). $151.00. SAGE Periodical Press, 2455 Teller Road, Thousand Oaks CA 91320. **Tel** (805)499-0721, FAX (805)499-0871, telex 100799. **ED** Robert A. Peterson and David W. Cravens (editor-elect). cum. index. **Bk Rev**. **Ad Acc**. **Acid Free. Circ:** 1,500. available on microfilm and microfiche from University Microfilms International (UMI); available on an online database from DIALOG. Documents available from UMI Article Clearinghouse.
Desc: Aim is to further the science of marketing throughout the world by promoting the conduct of research and the dissemination of research results through the study and improvement of marketing as an economic, ethical, and social force.
Ind/Abst ABI/INFORM Glob. Ed.; ABI/INFORM Ondisc: Expr. Ed.; ABI/INFORM [Computer File] (Jan. 1979-); Acad. Search; Bus. ASAP (1990-) [Full Txt.]; Bus. Index (1985-); Bus. Source Plus; Bus. Source; Curr. Cit.; Curr. Contents Soc. Behav. Sci.; EP Collect.; Gen. BusinessFile (1985-); Gen. Period. Index (1985-); Homework Help.; INFO-SOUTH Abstr.; Mag. Search; Manage. Market. Abstr.; Manage. Contents; MasterFile FullTEXT 1000; MasterFile FullTEXT 350; MasterFile FullTEXT 650; MasterFile FullTEXT (July 1993-); OCLC; PAIS Int. Print (?-?); Psychol. Abstr.; PsycINFO; PsycLit; Soc. Plann. Policy Dev. Abstr.; Telebase.

LC HF5415.2 .M358a **ISSN** 0025-3618
DD 658.8/3/05 UK
CODEN JMRSBJ
Pr Rev.
JOURNAL OF THE MARKET RESEARCH SOCIETY.
[J. mark. res. soc.]. **Main/Corp** Market Research Society. (Jan. 1968)-. Trade Publication. English. Four times a year. $197.65. NTC Publications Ltd., PO Box 69, Henley-on-Thames, Oxfordshire RG9 1GB United Kingdom. **Tel** 011 44 1491 574671, FAX 011 44 1491 571188. **ED** Stephen Buck and James Rothman. **Bk Rev**. **Ad Acc**. **Circ:** 650. available on microfilm and microfiche from University Microfilms International (UMI). Documents available from The Genuine Article, UMI Article Clearinghouse. ***Continues*** *Commentary.*
Desc: Provides a medium for the publication of original contributions to the theory and practice of research.
Ind/Abst ABI/INFORM Glob. Ed.; ABI/INFORM Ondisc: Expr. Ed.; ABI/INFORM [Computer File] (Jan. 1975-); Acad. Search; Anbar Account. Finan. Abstr. [Full Txt.]; Anbar Mark. Distr. Abstr. [Full Txt.]; Anbar Top Manage. Abstr. [Full Txt.]; Bus. ASAP (1992-) [Full Txt.]; Bus. Index (1985-); Commun. Abstr. (?-?); Curr. Cit.; Curr. Contents Soc. Behav. Sci.; EP Collect.; Gen. BusinessFile (1985-); Gen. Period. Index (1985-); Highw. Res. Abstr.; Homework Help.; INFO-SOUTH Abstr.; Int. Bibliogr. Sociol.; Mag. Search; Manage. Market. Abstr.; Manage. Bibliogr. Rev.; MasterFile FullTEXT 1000; MasterFile FullTEXT 350; MasterFile FullTEXT 650; MasterFile FullTEXT (July 1993-); OCLC; Oper. Prod. Manage. Abstr. [Full Txt.]; Person. Train. Abstr. [Full Txt.]; Psychol.

Business and Economics —Marketing and Purchasing

Abstr. (1968-); PsycINFO; PsycLit; PsycScan: Appl. Psych.; Res. Alert [Full Cov.]; Selec. Coop. Index Manage. Period.; Soc. Sci. Cit. Index [Full Cov.]; Soc. Res. Methodol. Abstr. (1981-); Stat. Theory Method Abstr. (1973-1975); Telebase; Women Manage. Rev. [Full Txt.].

ISSN 1355-6355
UK

●JOURNAL OF VACATION MARKETING. See Travel and Tourism.

LC HG1501
DD 332.1
US
JUMBO FLASH REPORTS. (19??)-. English. One time a week (published on Mondays). $245.00. Financial Rates Inc., 11811 US Highway 1, Suite 200, North Palm Beach FL 33408-8888. **Tel** (407)627-7330, **FAX** (407)627-7335. **(Subscription address:** Financial Rates Inc., PO Box 088888, North Palm Beach FL 33408. **Tel** (407)627-7330.) **ED** Hugo Ottolenghi.
Desc: Publishes the latest in bank marketing.

LC HD9999.I473 U54
DD 381/.45/68
ISSN 0022-7161
US
JUVENILE MERCHANDISING. [Juv. merch.]. (19??)-. Periodical. English. Twelve times a year. $25.00. Columbia Communications Inc., 370 Lexington Avenue, New York NY 10017. **Tel** (212)532-9290.

NO
KAMPANJE!. Vol. 1-8 (1964-1971)-. Periodical. Norwegian. Irregular. Kr495.99 Scndanavia; Kr597.00 other. Hjemmet as Fagpresseforlaget, PO Box 1161 Sentrum, N 0107 Oslo 1 Norway. **Tel** 011 47 2 429470.

UK
KENNEDY'S SNACKMAKER. (19??)-. Trade Publication. English. Four times a year (Mar., June, Sept., Dec.). $78.72. Kennedy's Publications Ltd., 12 Blackstock Mews, London N4 2BT United Kingdom. **Tel** 011 44 171 2263423. **Continues** Snack International, 0957-4581.
Desc: The magazine bringing independent news and advice to savoury snack manufacturers.

ISSN 0160-8932
US
KEY (GOREVILLE). (KEY.). No. 101 (Sept. 1977)-(1990); resumed publication (1993)-. Periodical. English. Twelve times a year. $45.00. Owen Communications Corporation, Battleground WA 98604-0010. **Tel** (206)887-8646. **ED** Brooks Owen. **Bk Rev. Formed by the union of** Mail Order Product, 0162-8496 **and** Key : The Newsletter that Helps You Make More Money from Your Mail Order Advertising.
Desc: Shows how and where to advertise in the print, media and direct mail to make more money in direct marketing.

LC HD28
DD 658
UK
●**KEY NOTE MARKET REVIEW. GREY MARKET IN THE UK.** (1994)-. Trade Publication. English. Irregular. Key Note Publications Ltd., Field House, 72 Oldfield Road, Hampton Middlesex TW12 2HQ United Kingdom. **Tel** 011 0181 7830755, **FAX** 011 0181 7831940.

UK
●**KEY NOTE REPORT : PERISHABLE FAST-MOVING CONSUMER GOODS.** See Food and Food Industry.

UK
●**KEY NOTE REPORT : TV AND VIDEO RENTAL.** See Communications-Television and Cable.

LC HF5410
DD 658.8
UK
●**KEY NOTE REVIEW : UK PET MARKET.** (1994)-. Trade Publication. English. One time a year. Key Note Publications Ltd., Field House, 72 Oldfield Road, Hampton Middlesex TW12 2HQ United Kingdom. **Tel** 011 0181 7830755, **FAX** 011 0181 7831940.

LC HD5723 .L33
DD 331.12/0973
ISSN 0882-0279
US
LABOR SURPLUS AREAS. See Business and Economics-Labor.

US
CEASED
LAW FIRM MARKETING AND PROFIT REPORT. See Law.

IT
LETTERA MARKETING. (19??)-. Italian. Six times a year. Free on request. ABI / Serv Marketing, Piazza del Gesu 49, 00186 Rome Italy. **Tel** 011 39 6 6767439.

ISSN 8755-6235
DD 659
US
CCC
LICENSING LETTER, THE. (THE LICENSING LETTER : TLL.). [Licens. lett.]. **VFOAT** Licensing Business Yearbook Combined with the Licensing Letter; Licensing Business Yearbook; TLL; TLL 100 Top Licensed Properties Plus Licensors, Agents and Licensees. (19??)-. Periodical. English. One time a year. $325.00. New Market Enterprises, PO Box 1665, Scottsdale AZ 85252-1665. **Tel** (602)948-1527. **ED** Arnold Bolka. **Bk Rev.** available on an online database (files 16,636/Full-Text) from DIALOG.
Desc: Vital statistical data about relicensed merchandising worldwide, plus trends, reviews and analyses, combined with 100 Top Licensed Properties.
Ind/Abst PROMT [Full Txt.]; PTS Newsl. Database [Full Txt.].

LC HF5415.33.U6 L54
DD 658.8/34/097305
ISSN 1067-182X
US
LIFESTYLE MARKET ANALYST, THE. [Lifestyle mark. anal.]. **Added/Corp** Standard Rate & Data Service. National Demographics & Lifestyles. (1989)-. Trade Publication. English. One time a year. $295.00. SRDS / Standard Rate & Data Service, 3004 Glenview Road, Wilmette IL 60091. **Tel** (708)375-5049, (800)851-7737, **FAX** (708)375-5003. **(Subscription address:** Neodata / Colorado, PO Box 2606, Boulder CO 80322.) **Continues** Lifestyle Marketplanner.

ISSN 0889-0986
DD 368
US
LIMRA'S MARKETFACTS. See Insurance.

ISSN 0229-155X
DD 658.8/4
CN
LIST OF MEMBERS / AUCTIONEERS' ASSOCIATION OF ALBERTA. [List memb. - Auction. Assoc. Alta.]. **Main/Corp** Auctioneers' Association of Alberta. (1979/1980)-. English. One time a year. Free to members. Auctioneers' Association of Alberta, 1104 Ranchlands Blvd., Calgary Alta. T3G 1G5. **Continues** Auctioneers' Association of Alberta. List of Auctioneers, 0319-0048.

ISSN 1065-7444
DD 658
US
LMA BUSINESSLETTER, THE. See Agriculture-Livestock.

ISSN 0955-8241
DD 658.7
UK
LOGISTICS (STAMFORD). (LOGISTICS.). [Logistics Stamford]. (1988)-. Trade Publication. English. Four times a year. $51.33. Chartered Institute of Purchasing and Supply, Easton House, Easton on the Hill, Stamford Lincolnshire PE9 3NZ United Kingdom. **Tel** 011 44 1780 56777, **FAX** 011 44 1780 51610, telex 32251.

ISSN 0740-3860
US
CCC
LOOKOUT. FOODS. See Food and Food Industry.

ISSN 0740-3852
US
CCC
LOOKOUT. NON-FOODS. Added/Corp Marketing Intelligence Service Ltd. **VFOAT** Non-Foods. (19??)-. English. Twenty-four times a year. $660.00. Marketing Intelligence Service Ltd., 6473D Route 64, Naples NY 14512. **Tel** (716)374-6326, (800)836-5176, **FAX** (714)374-5217, telex 469979. **ED** Tom Vierhile. Index available.
Desc: Reviews 10-15 products per issue, reporting on new health and beauty aids, household products, miscellaneous products, and pet products that are potentially influential because of their innovations in positioning, packaging, formulations, technology, marketing, or the importance of the manufacturer.
Ind/Abst F&S Index Plus Text, Int. [Select. Cov.]; Mark. Advert. Ref. Serv.; PROMT.

LC HD9282.U5 L8
DD 338.1/771/09763
ISSN 0085-2880
US
LOUISIANA ANNUAL MILK MARKETING REPORT, THE. Main/Corp Louisiana. Milk Division. 1968-. English. One time a year. Louisiana Department of Agriculture & Forestry Department, Box 25060, Baton Rouge LA 70894. **Tel** (504)342-7011. **Continues** Louisiana Annual Milk Marketing Report.

US
MAILING LIST TIDBITS. (19??)-. English. Twenty-six times a year. $60.00 (one-year), $120.00 (two-year), $180.00 (three-year library; $120.00 (one-year), $200.00 (two-year), $250.00 (three-year) individual and institution. Letter Perfect Word Processing Center Inc, 4205 Menlo Drive, Baltimore MD 21215. **Tel** (301)358-8973. **ED** Wayne Stoler. **Bk Rev,** (Qty: 20/yr). **Ad Acc, Adv Mgr:** Wayne Stoler, **Tel** (410)358-8973. **Circ:** 2,500 (ctrl).
Desc: Information for mailers, marketers, and sales professionals. New information about mailing lists, free offers from suppliers, and advice from mailing list professionals.

LC HF3907.Z6 M34
DD 343.6897/087/05 346.897038705
MW
MALAWI BUYERS GUIDE. Added/Corp Malawi Export Promotion Council. (19??)-. Consumer Publication. English. Malawi Export Promotion Council, PO Box 1299, Blantyre Malawi.

US
MANAGED CARE AND HEALTHCARE MARKETING. (19??)-. English. Twelve times a year. $145.00. Healthcare Publishing Inc., 2503 C Duck Pond Circle, Morrisville NC 27560. **Tel** (919)852-1100. **Continues** Healthcare Marketing in an Age of Reform.

LC HD28 .M3217
DD 658/.005
ISSN 0308-2172
UK
CCC
Pr Rev.
MANAGEMENT & MARKETING ABSTRACTS. See Business and Economics-Abstracting, Bibliographies and Statistics.

LC HD28 .M14
DD 658.005
ISSN 0025-1860
US
CODEN MQMQAE
MANAGEMENT QUARTERLY. See Business and Economics-Management.

UK
MANUAL OF MATERIALS HANDLING : BUYERS' GUIDE TO STORAGE-HANDLING-DISTRIBUTION EQUIPMENT-COMPONENTS & SERVICES. 6th Ed. -. Consumer Publication. English. One time a year. Turret Wheatland Ltd, PO Box 64, Rickmansworth Hertfordshire WD3 1SN United Kingdom. **Tel** 011 44 1923 777000, **FAX** 011 44 1923 771297, telex 888095. **Continues** Manual of Mechanical Handling & Ancillary Equipment.

ISSN 0706-0084
CN
MANUFACTURING + MARKETING OPPORTUNITIES; BULLETIN. See Industry and Production-Manufacturing.

LC HF5415.12.F5 M37
FI
MARK. Periodical. Finnish (summaries and/or abstracts in English). Nine times a year (monthly except July and Aug.). Fmk270.00 Finland; $50.00 US. Suomen Markkinointiliitto - Finlands Marknadsforbund R Y, Fabianinkatu 4 B 10, 00130 Helsinki 13 Finland. **Tel** 011 358 0 651500, **FAX** 011 358 0 179498. **ED** Marja-Liisa Kinturi. Index available. **Bk Rev. Ad Acc. Circ:** 8,635 (ctrl).
Desc: Professional marketing magazine which provides information on all the various aspects of marketing in Finland and abroad.

ISSN 1059-275X
DD 382
US
CCC
MARKET. ASIA PACIFIC. [Mark., Asia Pac.]. **VFOAT** Asia Pacific. Vol. 1, No. 1 (Jan. 15, 1992)-. Periodical. English. Twelve times a year. $295.00. W-Two Publications Ltd., 202 The Commons, Suite 401, Ithaca NY 14850. **Tel** (607)277-0934, **FAX** (607)277-0935. **ED** Doris L. Walsh. Index available (published in Dec.). cum. index. **Bk Rev,** (Qty: 12). **Circ:** 200. available on an online database (files 16,636/Full-Text) from DIALOG; and (Full-Text) Predicasts, Inc.
Desc: Reports on demographic trends and lifestyle changes as they apply to business in the Asia Pacific region. Includes coverage of consumers in Malaysia, Indonesia, China, South Korea, Singapore, Hong Kong, Taiwan, Thailand, Japan, Australia, New Zealand and India. Analysis, insights and projections of consumer markets.
Ind/Abst PROMT [Full Txt.]; PTS Newsl. Database [Full Txt.].

ISSN 1050-9410
DD 382
US
CCC
MARKET. EUROPE. [Mark.--Eur.]. **VFOAT** Market, Europe. Vol. 1, No. 1 (Aug. 1990)-. Periodical. English. Twelve times a year. $377.00. W-Two Publications Ltd., 202 The Commons, Suite 401, Ithaca NY 14850. **Tel** (607)277-0934, **FAX** (607)277-0935. **ED** Doris L. Walsh. Index available (published in Dec.). **Circ:** 300. available on an online database (files 16,636/Full-Text) from DIALOG.
Desc: Reports on demographic trends and lifestyle changes as they apply to various consumer markets in Europe. Provides coverage of consumer markets in the entire region. Offers insights about European consumers.
Ind/Abst PROMT [Full Txt.]; PTS Newsl. Database [Full Txt.].

ISSN 1066-7024
DD 382
US
●**MARKET. LATIN AMERICA.** [Mark., Lat. Am.]. **VFOAT** Latin America. Vol. 1, No. 1 (Jan. 1993)-. Periodical. English. Twelve times a year. $289.00. W-Two Publications Ltd., 202 The Commons, Suite 401, Ithaca NY 14850. **Tel** (607)277-0934, **FAX** (607)277-0935. **ED** Doris L. Walsh. Index available (published in Dec.). **Circ:**

250.
Desc: Reports on demographic trends and lifestyle changes as they apply to various consumer markets in Latin America. Provides coverage of consumer markets in the entire region, including Mexico. Offers insights about Latin American consumers.

US
MARKET PRICE AND INDEX. English. Fifty-two times a year (Tues.). $600.00. Shrimp World Inc., 417 Eliza Street, New Orleans LA 70114. **Tel** (504)368-1571, FAX (504)368-1573, telex 414943. **ED** William D. Chauvin.
Desc: Information on the shrimp market prices.

LC HF5415.2 .M328 **ISSN** 0025-3596
DD 658.8/3/05 UK
MARKET RESEARCH ABSTRACTS. See Business and Economics-Abstracting, Bibliographies and Statistics.

LC HF5410 **ISSN** 0308-3446
DD 658.83 UK
MARKET RESEARCH EUROPE. See Business and Economics-Abstracting, Bibliographies and Statistics.

LC HC260.C6 M352
DD 380.1/0941 UK
MARKET RESEARCH GREAT BRITAIN. (1974)-. English. Twelve times a year. £450.00 UK; $900.00 US. Euromonitor Publications Ltd., 60-61 Britton Street, London EC1M 5NA United Kingdom. **Tel** 011 44 171 2518024, FAX 011 44 171 6083149, telex 21120. Index available. cum. index. **Circ:** 500. ***Continues*** *Market Research in Great Britain.*
Desc: Reports statistical information on numerous markets, i.e. food, white goods, health care within the UK.
Ind/Abst Int. Packag. Abstr.; Selec. Coop. Index Manage. Period.

LC HC111 **ISSN** 0590-9325
DD 658.8/3971 CN
MARKET RESEARCH HANDBOOK. (MARKET RESEARCH HANDBOOK = MANUEL STATISTIQUE DES ETUDES DE MARCHE.). [Mark. res. handb.]. **Added/Corp** Canada. Bureau Federal de la Statistique. Division du Commerce et des Services. Statistique Canada. Division du Commerce et des Services. Statistique Canada. Division de l'Industrie. Statistique Canada. **VFOAT** Manuel Statistique pour Etudes de Marche; Recueil Statistique des Etudes de Marche. (1969)-. Statistical Publication. French (English). One time a year. 150.00Can$. Statistics Canada Publications Sales and Services, R.H. Coats Building 6th Floor, Ottawa Ontario K1A 0T6 Canada. **Tel** (613)951-5078, (800)267-6677, FAX (613)951-1584, telex 053-3585. ***Continues*** *Market Research Handbook, Summary of Census Data, 0837-8940.*
Desc: Comprehensive compendium of Canadian marketing information derived from various Statistics Canada sources, other federal government agencies and international organizations.

LC HC260.C6 M352
DD 380.1/0941 UK
MARKET RESEARCH IN GREAT BRITAIN. **Added/Corp** ERC (Firm). **VFOAT** Market Research; Market Research Great Britain. (1971)-. Periodical. English. Twelve times a year. $950.00. Euromonitor Publications Ltd., 60-61 Britton Street, London EC1M 5NA United Kingdom. **Tel** 011 44 171 2518024, FAX 011 44 171 6083149, telex 21120. ***Continues in part*** *Market Research.*

LC HF **ISSN** 1352-1101
DD 380.1 UK
●**MARKET RESEARCH INTERNATIONAL.** [Mark. res. int.]. (1994)-. Trade Publication. English. Twelve times a year. Euromonitor Publications Ltd., 60-61 Britton Street, London EC1M 5NA United Kingdom. **Tel** 011 44 171 2518024, FAX 011 44 171 6083149, telex 21120.

LC HF5410 **ISSN** 0963-7257
DD 658.83 UK
MARKET RESEARCH REPORTER. [Mark. res. report.]. (1991)-. English. Twenty times a year. £189.00 UK; $379.00. Headland Business Information, 1 Henry Smiths Terrace, Headland Cleveland, TS24 0PD United Kingdom. **Tel** 011 44 429 231902, FAX 011 44 429 861403.

LC HF5410 .M35 HF5410 .M35 **ISSN** 1052-9578
DD 380.1/05 US
MARKET SHARE REPORTER. [Mark. share rep.]. **Added/Corp** Gale Research Inc. (1991)-. English. $185.00. Gale Research Inc., 835 Penobscot Building, 645 Griswold Street, Detroit MI 48226. **Tel** (800)877-GALE, (313)961-2242, FAX (313)961-6083, (800)414-5043, telex TWX 810-221-7086. **ED** Arsen J. Darnay and Marlita A. Reddy. available on magnetic tape; available on diskette; available on an online database (file MKTSHR in the MARKET Libraries) from NEXIS.
Desc: Affords an immediate overview of the marketplace and cites original sources for those readers who need more in-depth information.

LC HF5415.13 .M3443 **ISSN** 1050-186X
DD 658.8/005 US
MARKETER, THE. (THE MARKETER : THE MAGAZINE FOR MARKETING MANAGEMENT.). [Marketer]. (April 1990)-(1990). Trade Publication. English. Twelve times a year. Act III Publishing, 6400 Hollis Street, Emeryville CA 94608. **Tel** (510)653-3307, FAX (510)653-5142. **ED** Toni Apgar.
Desc: Targeted to 45,000 senior marketing management and corporate executives. Editorial covers new product development, trends, management, distribution, information processing, research and databases.

AT
MARKETFACT DIGEST. English. Twelve times a year. 175.00Aus$ Australia; 195.00Aus$ Asia; 205.00Aus$ other. Michael Kiely Publications, 17 New Line Road, West Pennant Hills NSW 2125 Australia. **Tel** 011 61 02 4845491, 011 61 8 242690, FAX 011 61 02 4810650.
Desc: A compilation of recently published statistics of value to marketers for creating plans, presentations, and reports.

AT
MARKETING. (19??)-. English. Twelve times a year. 35.00Aus$. John M Bester & Associates, 29-35 Bellevue Street, Surry Hills New South Wales 2010 Australia. **Tel** 02 211 4577, FAX 02 211 5908.

LC HF5415 .M2934
BL
MARKETING. **VFOAT** Revista Marketing. No. 1-August/Sept. 1967-. Periodical. Portuguese. Twelve times a year. 300.00. Associacao dos Dirigentes de Vendas do Brasil, rua da Consolacao 393, 01521 Sao Paulo Brazil.
Ind/Abst Bus. Index (1985-); Gen. BusinessFile (1985-).

US
MARKETING ACTION PLANNER. **VFOAT** NAPL Marketing Action Planner; NAPL Action Planner. Vol. 1, No. 1 (April 1983)-. Periodical. English. Twelve times a year. National Association of Printers and Lithographers, 780 Palisade Avenue, Teaneck NJ 07666. **Tel** (201)342-0707, (800)642-6275, FAX (201)692-0286.
Ind/Abst Abstr. Bull. Inst. Pap. Sci. Tech.; Graph. Arts Bull. Inst. Pap. Sci. Technol. (Jan. 1989, April 1989, June 1989).

LC HF5415 .M2967 **ISSN** 0306-3615
DD 658.8/005 UK
SUSPENDED
MARKETING AND ADVERTISING NEWS. [Mark. advert. news]. Suspended (1983). Periodical. English. £7.50. Allan Wells International, Farndon Road, Market Harborough, Leicestershire LE16 9NR United Kingdom. **Tel** 0858 34567. ***Continues*** *Advertising and Marketing for the Manufacturer.*

LC HF5415.2 .M3535a
HU
●**MARKETING & MENEDZSMENT : THE HUNGARIAN JOURNAL OF MARKETING AND MANAGEMENT.** **Added/Corp** MC-Orszagos Piackutato Intezet. Pecsi Janus Pannonius Tudomanyegyetem. **VFOAT** Marketing es Menedzsment; Hungarian Journal of Marketing and Management. (1995)-. Periodical. Hungarian (table of contents in English). Six times a year. **(Subscription address:** Kultura, PO Box 143, H-1300 Budapest 3 Hungary. **Tel** 011 36 1 2500194.**)** ***Continues*** *Marketing (Budapest, Hungary), 0237-1995.*

LC HF5415.2 .E96 **ISSN** 0923-5957
DD 658.8/394/05 NE
CCC
MARKETING AND RESEARCH TODAY : THE JOURNAL OF THE EUROPEAN SOCIETY FOR OPINION AND MARKETING RESEARCH. See Business and Economics-Abstracting, Bibliographies and Statistics.

LC HF5415.35 .M37 **ISSN** 0889-8510
DD 658.8/0023/73 US
MARKETING & SALES CAREER DIRECTORY. See Industry and Production-Trade and Industrial Directories.

LC HF5415.2 .M3535a **ISSN** 0237-1995
HU
TITLE CHANGE
MARKETING : AZ ORSZAGOS PIACKUTATO INTEZET FOLYOIRATA. [MarketingBp.]. **Added/Corp** Orszagos Piackutato Intezet. Marketing Centrum/OPK. (1985)-(1994). Periodical. Hungarian (summaries and/or abstracts in English; table of contents in English and German). ***Continues*** *Marketing, Piackutatas, 0133-2414.* ***Continued by*** *Marketing & Menedzsment.*
Ind/Abst Leis., Rec., Tour. Abstr.

ISSN 0955-4785
DD 658.8 UK
MARKETING BREAKTHROUGHS. [Mark. breakthr.]. (1986)-. Periodical. English. Twelve times a year. £225.00 UK; $395.00 US and Canada. World Business Publications Ltd., 960 High Road, Britannia 4th Floor, London N12 9RY United Kingdom. **Tel** 011 44 181 4465141, FAX 011 44 181 4463659, telex 9419208.

LC HF5410 **ISSN** 0113-6895
DD 658.83099305 NZ
MARKETING BULLETIN - DEPARTMENT OF MARKETING, MASSEY UNIVERSITY. (MARKETING BULLETIN.). [Mark. bull. - Dep. Mark. Massey Univ.]. (1990)-. Monographic series. English. One time a year (June). $21.49. Massey University Department of Marketing, PO Box 11222, Palmerston North New Zealand. **Tel** 011 64 6 3569099, FAX 011 64 6 3505608. **ED** Dr. Mike Brennan. **Ad Acc.**
Desc: Experimental, theoretical, and review papers that are concerned with matters related to marketing, market research practice, and marketing education.
Ind/Abst Bus. Source Plus; EP Collect.; Homework Help.; MasterFile FullTEXT 1000; MasterFile FullTEXT 350; MasterFile FullTEXT 650; MasterFile FullTEXT; OCLC; Telebase; World Mag. Bank.

ISSN 0093-2736
US
MARKETING BULLETIN (SYRACUSE). (MARKETING BULLETIN.). [Mark. bull. (Syracuse)]. Bulletin. English. Six times a year. Free. Faculty of Forestry, State University of New York, College of Environmental Science and Forestry, Syracuse NY 13210. **Tel** (315)470-6562. **ED** D Monteith. **Ad Acc.**
Desc: Information exchange service for the wood products industry of New York.

US
MARKETING CALIFORNIA AND ARIZONA MELONS, INCLUDES CANTALOUPS-HONEYDEWS-WATERMELONS. **Added/Corp** Federal-State Market News Service. United States. Agricultural Marketing Service. Fruit and Vegetable Division. Market News Branch. California. Bureau of Market News. **VFOAT** California and Arizona Melons. (1979)-. Government Publication. English. One time a year. $20.00. Federal-State Market News Service, 1220 N Street, Suite 216, Box 942871, Sacramento CA 94271-0001. **Tel** (916)654-0298, FAX (916)654-1046. ***Continues*** *Marketing California Melons.*

US
MARKETING CALIFORNIA APRICOTS. **Main/Corp** Federal-State Market News Service. **Added/Corp** United States. Agricultural Marketing Service. Fruit and Vegetable Division. Market News Branch. California. Division of Marketing Service. (1976)-. Periodical. English. One time a year. $20.00. Federal-State Market News Service, 1220 N Street, Suite 216, Box 942871, Sacramento CA 94271-0001. **Tel** (916)654-0298, FAX (916)654-1046.

LC HD9235.A72 C23a **ISSN** 0098-7360
DD 381/.41/53209794 US
MARKETING CALIFORNIA ARTICHOKES. **Main/Corp** Federal-State Market News Service. (19??)-. English. Federal-State Market News Service, 1220 N Street, Suite 216, Box 942871, Sacramento CA 94271-0001. **Tel** (916)654-0298, FAX (916)654-1046.

LC HD9235.A82 C23a
DD 381/.41531/09794 US
MARKETING CALIFORNIA ASPARAGUS. **Main/Corp** Federal-State Market News Service. (19??)-. English. One time a year. $20.00. Federal-State Market News Service, 1220 N Street, Suite 216, Box 942871, Sacramento CA 94271-0001. **Tel** (916)654-0298, FAX (916)654-1046. ***Continues*** *Marketing Asparagus from California.*

LC HD9235.B762 C24 **ISSN** 0148-4966
DD 380.1/41/535 US
MARKETING CALIFORNIA BROCCOLI. **Main/Corp** Federal-State Market News Service. (19??)-. English. One time a year. $20.00. Federal-State Market News Service, 1220 N Street, Suite 216, Box 942871, Sacramento CA 94271-0001. **Tel** (916)654-0298, FAX (916)654-1046.

LC HD9235.C342 U553 **ISSN** 0146-0676
DD 381/.41/51309794 US
MARKETING CALIFORNIA CARROTS. **Main/Corp** Federal-State Market News Service. (19??)-. English. One time a year. $20.00. Federal-State Market News Service, 1220 N Street, Suite 216, Box 942871, Sacramento CA 94271-0001. **Tel** (916)654-0298, FAX (916)654-1046.

US
MARKETING CALIFORNIA CAULIFLOWER. **Added/Corp** Federal-State Market News Service. (1988)-. Government Publication. English. One time a year. $20.00. Federal-State Market News Service, 1220 N Street, Suite 216, Box 942871, Sacramento CA 94271-0001. **Tel** (916)654-0298, FAX (916)654-1046. ***Continues*** *Marketing California & Arizona Cauliflower.*

LC HD9235.C442 U54 ISSN 0148-4974
DD 381/.41/55309794 US
MARKETING CALIFORNIA CELERY.
Main/Corp Federal-State Market News Service. (19??)-. Government Publication. English. One time a year. $20.00. Federal-State Market News Service, 1220 N Street, Suite 216, Box 942871, Sacramento CA 94271-0001. **Tel** (916)654-0298, FAX (916)654-1046.

US
MARKETING CALIFORNIA CHERRIES.
Main/Corp Federal-State Market News Service. (19??)-. Government Publication. English. One time a year. $20.00. Federal-State Market News Service, 1220 N Street, Suite 216, Box 942871, Sacramento CA 94271-0001. **Tel** (916)654-0298, FAX (916)654-1046. ***Continues*** *Marketing California Cherries for Fresh Market.*

US
MARKETING CALIFORNIA GRAPES FOR FRESH USE. **Added/Corp** Federal-State Market News Service. (198?)-. Government Publication. English. One time a year. $20.00. Federal-State Market News Service, 1220 N Street, Suite 216, Box 942871, Sacramento CA 94271-0001. **Tel** (916)654-0298, FAX (916)654-1046. ***Continues in part*** *California Grapes, Raisins & Wines.*

US
MARKETING CALIFORNIA NECTARINES, PEACHES, AND PLUMS.
(19??)-. Government Publication. English. One time a year. $30.00. Federal-State Market News Service, 1220 N Street, Suite 216, Box 942871, Sacramento CA 94271-0001. **Tel** (916)654-0298, FAX (916)654-1046.

LC HD9259.P333 U53a ISSN 0277-1489
DD 381./41413/09794 US
MARKETING CALIFORNIA PEARS. [Mark. Calif. pears]. **Added/Corp** Federal-State Market News Service. United States. Agricultural Marketing Service. Fruit and Vegetable Division. Market News Branch. California. Bureau of Market News. (19??)-. English. One time a year. Federal-State Market News Service, 1220 N Street, Suite 216, Box 942871, Sacramento CA 94271-0001. **Tel** (916)654-0298, FAX (916)654-1046. ***Continues*** *Marketing California Pears for Fresh Market, 0098-8928.*

US
MARKETING CALIFORNIA PLUMS.
Main/Corp Federal-State Market News Service. **Added/Corp** Federal-State Market New Service. Plums. Federal-State Market News Service. California Plums. Federal-State Market News Service. Marketing California Fresh Plums. Federal-State Market News Service. Marketing Fresh Plums from California. Federal-State Market News Service. Marketing California Plums for Fresh Market. (19??)-. English. One time a year. Federal-State Market News Service, 1220 N Street, Suite 216, Box 942871, Sacramento CA 94271-0001. **Tel** (916)654-0298, FAX (916)654-1046.
Desc: Includes a review of season shipping point, wholesale market prices, shipments, unload distribution and product information.

US
MARKETING CALIFORNIA POTATOES.
Main/Corp Federal-State Market News Service. **Added/Corp** United States. Agricultural Marketing Service. Fruit and Vegetable Division. Market News Branch. California. Dept. of Food and Agriculture. Division of Marketing Services. Bureau of Market News. (1976)-. Periodical. English. One time a year.

US
MARKETING CALIFORNIA POTATOES, FEATURING THE KERN DISTRICT.
Added/Corp Federal-State Market News Service. United States. Agricultural Marketing Service. Fruit and Vegetable Division. Market News Branch. California. Bureau of Market News. **VFOAT** California Potatoes. (197?)-. English. One time a year. Federal-State Market News Service, 1220 N Street, Suite 216, Box 942871, Sacramento CA 94271-0001. **Tel** (916)654-0298, FAX (916)654-1046.

LC HD9235.P82 U435 ISSN 0363-7964
DD 381/.41/349109794 US
MARKETING CALIFORNIA POTATOES FROM THE KERN DISTRICT AND STOCKTON DELTA DISTRICT. **Main/Corp** Federal-State Market News Service. (19??)-. English. Irregular. Federal-State Market News Service, 1220 N Street, Suite 216, Box 942871, Sacramento CA 94271-0001. **Tel** (916)654-0298, FAX (916)654-1046.

US
MARKETING CALIFORNIA TOMATOES.
Main/Corp Federal-State Market News Service. **Added/Corp** United States. Agricultural Marketing Service. Fruit and Vegetable Division. Market News Branch. California. Dept. of Food and Agriculture. Division of Marketing Services. (1974)-. Periodical. English. One time a year. $4.00. Federal-State Market News Service, 1220 N Street, Suite 216, Box 942871, Sacramento CA 94271-0001. **Tel** (916)654-0298, FAX (916)654-1046.

US
MARKETING EASTERN NORTH CAROLINA VEGETABLES ... CROP / FEDERAL STATE MARKET NEWS SERVICE. English. One time a year.

LC HF5415.1 .M366 ISSN 1052-8008
DD 658.8/007/1073 US
CCC
MARKETING EDUCATION REVIEW. [Mark. educ. rev.]. Vol. 1, No. 1 (Nov. 1990)-. Periodical. English. Three times a year. $56.00. American Marketing Association, 250 South Wacker Drive, Suite 200, Chicago IL 60606-5819. **Tel** (312)648-0536, FAX (312)993-7542.
Desc: This journal improves marketing education by providing a communication network for marketing educators.

LC HF5415.4 .M35
DD 658.8/007 US
MARKETING EDUCATORS' JOURNAL.
Added/Corp Marketing Education Association (U.S.). Vol. 10, No. 2 (Spring 1985)-. Periodical. English. One time a year. $25.00. Marketing Education Association, 1375 King Avenue, Suite 1-A, Columbus OH 43212. **Tel** (614)486-6708, (800)448-0398, FAX (614)486-1819. **ED** Carmel Martin. **Ad Acc.** ***Continues*** *Marketing & Distributive Educators' Digest.*
Desc: Covers distributive education and marketing.

GW
MARKETING ERDGAS. **Added/Corp** Bundesverband der Deutschen Gas- und Wasserwirtschaft. Hauptausschuss "Marketing.". Vol. 1 (1986)-. Periodical. German. Three times a year. $40.31. R Oldenbourg Verlag, Postfach 801360, D-81613 Munich Germany. **Tel** 011 49 89 450190, FAX 011 49 89 45019305.

ISSN 1054-2388
DD 381 US
CCC
CEASED
MARKETING EXECUTIVE REPORT. [Mark. exec. rep.]. **Added/Corp** American Marketing Association. **VFOAT** Marketing Executive; MER. Mar. (1991)-Vol. 3 No. 6 (June 1993). Periodical. English. American Marketing Association, 250 South Wacker Drive, Suite 200, Chicago IL 60606-5819. **Tel** (312)648-0536, FAX (312)993-7542. Index available.
Desc: Designed for the busy, time sensitive marketing professional. The staff reviews more than 80 marketing related periodicals each month. The most important marketing articles are summarized and provided in easy-to-use, concise abstracts and reference index.

ISSN 1067-1234
DD 658 US
MARKETING FACT BOOK, THE. **See** Business and Economics-Advertising and Public Relations.

LC HD9259.A953 U54 ISSN 0160-0370
DD 380.1/41/4 US
MARKETING FLORIDA AVOCADOS, LIMES, MANGOS. **Main/Corp** Federal-State Market News Service. (19??)-. English. Federal-State Market News Service, PO Box 3275, Homestead FL 33030.

LC HD9247.F6 M37 ISSN 0732-9768
DD 380.1/414/09759 US
MARKETING FLORIDA TROPICAL FRUITS & VEGETABLES. [Mark. Fla. trop. fruits veg.]. **Added/Corp** Federal-State Market News Service. **VFOAT** Marketing Florida Tropical Fruits and Vegetables. (19??)-. English. Federal-State Market New Service, PO Box 1148, Winter Park FL 32790.

LC HD9220.U53 F66 ISSN 0193-242X
DD 381/.41/509759 US
MARKETING FLORIDA VEGETABLES : SUMMARY. (19??)-. English. One time a year. Federal-State Market News Service, 1220 N Street, Suite 216, Box 942871, Sacramento CA 94271-0001. **Tel** (916)654-0298, FAX (916)654-1046.

US
MARKETING FORUM / AMERICAN MANAGEMENT ASSOCIATION.
Added/Corp American Management Association. (July 1989)-. Periodical. English. Twelve times a year. Comes with membership. American Management Association, 135 West 50th Street, New York NY 10020-1201. **Tel** (212)586-8100, (212)903-8375 (periodicals), FAX (212)903-8168, (212)903-8083 (periodicals).

AT
MARKETING GLOBE. English. Eleven times a year. 255.00Aus$ Australia; 275.00Aus$ Papua New Guinea, Asia and New Zealand. Michael Kiely Publications, 17 New Line Road, West Pennant Hills NSW 2125 Australia. **Tel** 011 61 02 4845491, 011 61 8 242690, FAX 011 61 02 4810650. **ED** Michael Kiely (phone: 02 4845491).
Desc: Ideas and developments in sales and marketing from all around the world.

LC HF5415 .A642 ISSN 0730-2606
DD 658.8/005 US
MARKETING (GUILFORD, CONN.).
(MARKETING.). [Marketing]. **VFOAT** Annual Editions. Marketing. (1981/82)-. English. One time a year. $12.95. Dushkin Publishing Group Inc., Sluice Dock, Guilford CT 06437. **Tel** (203)453-4351, (800)243-6532, FAX (203)453-6000. **ED** John E Richardson. ***Continues*** *Annual Editions: Readings in Marketing.*
Desc: Current articles from a broad range of sources provide complete coverage of marketing today. Includes a guide to the industries and companies discussed in the articles and a glossary of terms.

ISSN 0896-7156
DD 658 US
MARKETING HIGHER EDUCATION. [Mark. high. educ.]. (19??)-. Newsletter. English. Ten times a year (Not published in July & August). $94.95. Marketing Higher Education, 280 Easy Street #114, Mountain View CA 94043. **Tel** (415)962-1105, FAX (415)962-1155. **ED** Peg Mc Kenna. **Bk Rev.** ctrl circ.
Desc: Devoted to the science, art and craft of marketing schools, colleges and universities.

LC HB251 ISSN 1231-7853
DD 339.13 PL
UDC 339.13
●**MARKETING I RYNEK.** [Mark. Rynek]. (1994)-. Periodical. Polish. Twelve times a year. Panstwowe Wydawnictwo Ekonomiczne, Niecala 4-A, 00 098 Warsaw Poland. **Tel** 011 48 22 278001.

ISSN 0025-3723
BE
MARKETING IN EUROPE. **Added/Corp** Economist Intelligence Unit (Europe) SA. No. 1 (Nov. 1962)-. Periodical. English. Thirty-six times a year. $1080.00. The Economist Intelligence Unit, 40 Duke Street, London W1A 1DW United Kingdom. **Tel** 011 44 171 8301000. **(Subscription address:** Economist Intelligence Unit / North America Subscriptions, 111 West 57th Street, New York NY 10019. **Tel** 800 938-4685, (212)554-0600, FAX (212)586-1181, (212)586-1182.**)** **ED** Graham Lewis. cum. index. available on microfilm from World Microfilm Publications Ltd. Documents available from UMI Article Clearinghouse.
Desc: A systematically updated reference library on European consumer markets. Covers the following markets: food, drink, tobacco, clothing, furniture, leisure goods, chemists' goods, household goods and domestics.
Ind/Abst ABI/INFORM Glob. Ed.; Contents Pages Manage.; Curr. Cit.; F&S Index Plus Text, Int. [Select. Cov.]; Index Bus. Reports; PROMT; World Agric. Econ. Rural Sociol. Abstr.

LC HF5415.12.N6 M36
DD 380.1/09669 NR
MARKETING IN NIGERIA. (19??)-. Periodical. English. Six times a year. The Circulation Manager, Alpha Publications, PO Box 1163, Surulere Lagos Nigeria.

LC HF5415.124 .M36 ISSN 0732-7331
DD 658.8/0025/73 US
MARKETING INFORMATION. [Mark. inf.]. **Added/Corp** Georgia State University. College of Business Administration. Business Publishing Division. (1982)-. English. Irregular. Georgia State University Business Press, University Plaza, Atlanta GA 30303. **Tel** (404)651-4253, FAX (404)651-4256.

LC HF5410 .M36 ISSN 0263-4503
DD 658.8/3/05 UK
CCC
MARKETING INTELLIGENCE & PLANNING. [Mark. intell. plann.]. **VFOAT** Marketing Intelligence and Planning. Vol. 1, No. 1 (1983)-. Periodical. English. Eleven times a year. $3939.00. MCB University Press, 60 62 Toller Lane, Bradford, West Yorkshire BD8 9BY United Kingdom. **Tel** 011 44 1274 785280, FAX 011 44 1274 785200, telex 51317-MCBUNI-G. **(Subscription address:** MCB University Press / US and Canada Subscriptions, PO Box 10812, Birmingham AL 35201-0812. **Tel** (205)995-1567, (800)633-4931, FAX (205)995-1588.**)** **ED** Michael Thomas. **Ad Acc.** available on an online database (file 15/Full-Text) from DIALOG. Documents available from UMI Article Clearinghouse.
Desc: Aims to help the marketing practitioner increase marketing effectiveness.
Ind/Abst ABI/INFORM Glob. Ed.; ABI/INFORM [Computer File] (1983-); Anbar Account. Finan. Abstr.

Business and Economics — Marketing and Purchasing

[Full Txt.]; Anbar Mark. Distr. Abstr. [Full Txt.]; Anbar Top Manage. Abstr. [Full Txt.]; Contents Pages Manage.; Gen. BusinessFile (1992-); Manage. Market. Abstr.; Manage. Bibliogr. Rev.; Oper. Prod. Manage. Abstr. [Full Txt.]; Person. Train. Abstr. [Full Txt.]; Women Manage. Rev. [Full Txt.].

ISSN 0748-9358
DD 535 US
MARKETING INTELLIGENCE. FIBEROPTIC. See
Communications-Telecommunication.

ISSN 0025-3774
UDC 658.8 GW
MARKETING-JOURNAL. [Mark.-J.]. (1968)-. Trade Publication. German. Six times a year. $92.12. Marketing Journal, Postfach 130704, D-20107 Hamburg Germany. **Tel** 011 49 40 4103148, FAX 011 49 40 4101276. **Continues** Forschen, Planen, Entscheiden, 0532-2006.
Ind/Abst Selec. Coop. Index Manage. Period.

ISSN 0815-4384
DD 658.800994 AT
CEASED
MARKETING LETTER MILSONS POINT. [Mark. lett. Milsons Point]. (1984)-(June 1995). Periodical. English. Newsletter Information Service, PO Box 693, Manly New South Wales 2095 Australia. **Tel** 011 61 2 9777500, FAX 011 61 2 9773310. **Continues** Upmarket, 0812-1214.

LC HF5415.2 .M3554 **ISSN 0923-0645**
DD 658.8/3/05 US
CCC
CODEN MLETEK
MARKETING LETTERS. Vol. 1, No. 1 (Dec. 1989)-. Periodical. English. Four times a year. $287.00. Kluwer Academic Publishers / Massachusetts, PO Box 358, Accord Station, Hingham MA 02018. **Tel** (617)871-6600. **ED** Donald Lehmann. **Acid Free**. available on microfilm and microfiche from University Microfilms International (UMI).
Desc: The journal offers a medium for the truly rapid publication of research results. The focus is on empirical findings, methodological papers, and theoretical and conceptual insights across areas of research in marketing.
Ind/Abst Int. Bibliogr. Sociol.

LC S
DD 630 US
MARKETING LETTUCE FROM IMPERIAL VALLEY AND BLYTHE DISTRICTS. See Agriculture-Crop Production and Soils.

LC HD9235.L42 U53 **ISSN 0732-7625**
DD 381/.41552/09794 US
MARKETING LETTUCE FROM SALINAS-WATSONVILLE, OTHER CENTRAL CALIFORNIA DISTRICTS AND COLORADO. Added/Corp Federal-State Market News Service. (19??)-. English. Irregular. Federal-State Market News Service, 1220 N Street, Suite 216, Box 942871, Sacramento CA 94271-0001. **Tel** (916)654-0298, FAX (916)654-1046. **Continues** Marketing Lettuce from Salinas-Watsonville-King City and Other Central California Districts, 0145-6369.

ISSN 0896-3908
DD 658 US
CCC
MARKETING LIBRARY SERVICES. See
Library and Information Sciences.

LC HF5349.G7 M34 **ISSN 0025-3650**
UK
CODEN MARKBC
MARKETING (LONDON). (MARKETING.). [Marketing]. **Added/Corp** Institute of Marketing and Sales Management. Institute of Marketing. Vol. 1 (1931)-. Trade Publication. English. One time a week (50 issues). $239.57. Haymarket Publishing Ltd., 12 14 Ansdell Street, London W8 5TR United Kingdom. **Tel** 011 44 171 9380705, 011 44 171 2786686, FAX 011 44 171 9380772. **(Subscription address:** Haymarket Magazines Ltd., PO Box 219, Subscription Department, Woking Surrey GU21 1ZW United Kingdom. **Tel** 011 44 1483 776343.) available on microfilm and microfiche from University Microfilms International (UMI); available on an online database from VU-TEXT. Documents available from UMI Article Clearinghouse, Ask*IEEE, BLDSC, SWETS. **Supersedes** Isma.
Ind/Abst ABI/INFORM Glob. Ed.; ABI/INFORM [Computer File] (Sept. 1972-); BioBusiness; Bus. ASAP (1992-) [Full Txt.]; Dairy Sci. Abstr.; Gen. Period. Index (1985-); Index Bus. Reports; Infomat Int. Bus.; INSPEC (June 1983-); Manage. Market. Abstr.; Mark. Advert. Ref. Serv.; Trade Ind. ASAP [Full Txt.]; Trade Ind. Index [Full Txt.]; UMI ABI/Inform--Bus. Period. Ondisc (Nov. 1987-) [Full Txt.].

LC HF5415.12.C2 M37 **ISSN 1196-4650**
DD 658.8/00971/05 CN
●**MARKETING MAGAZINE (TORONTO).** (MARKETING MAGAZINE.). [Mark. mag.]. **VFOAT** Marketing. Vol. 98, No. 38 (Sept. 20, 1993)-. Trade Publication. English. One time a week. 47.62Can$. MacLean Hunter Ltd. Business Publishers / Canada, Box 9100, Station A, Toronto Ontario M5W 1A5 Canada. **Tel** (416)596-5000, , FAX (416)596-5552. **(Subscription address:** Indas Customer Service, 35 Riviera Drive, Building 17, Markham Ontario L3R 8N4 Canada. **Tel** (905)946-0406.) **Continues** Marketing, 0025-3642.
Ind/Abst MasterFile FullTEXT (Jan. 1994-).

ISSN 1061-3846
DD 658 US
CCC
MARKETING MANAGEMENT (CHICAGO, ILL.). (MARKETING MANAGEMENT.). [Mark. manag.]. **Added/Corp** American Marketing Association. Vol. 1, No. 1 (Winter 1992)-. Trade Publication. English. Four times a year. $90.00. American Marketing Association, 250 South Wacker Drive, Suite 200, Chicago IL 60606-5819. **Tel** (312)648-0536, FAX (312)993-7542.
Desc: Provides treatment of the marketing issues facing senior marketing managers today.
Ind/Abst Acad. Search; Bus. Source Plus; Bus. Source; EP Collect.; Homework Help.; MasterFile FullTEXT 1000; MasterFile FullTEXT 350; MasterFile FullTEXT 650; MasterFile FullTEXT (July 1994-); Telebase.

LC HF3893 .A33
DD 330.9676/2/005 KE
MARKETING MAN'S GUIDE TO KENYA, A. Added/Corp Corcoran & Tyrrell Limited. (July 1973)-. Periodical. English. Corcoran and Tyrrell Ltd, PO Box 44365, Nairobi Kenya.

US
MARKETING MICHIGAN APPLES, PEACHES, AND PRUNES. (197?)-. English. One time a year. **Formed by the union of** Marketing Michigan Apples **and** Marketing Michigan Peaches and Prunes.

US
MARKETING MICHIGAN ONIONS AND POTATOES. 1977-. Periodical. English. One time a year. **Formed by the union of** Marketing Michigan Onions **and** Marketing Michigan Potatoes.

US
TITLE CHANGE
MARKETING MICHIGAN VEGETABLES.
Main/Corp Federal-State Market News Service.
Added/Corp United States. Agricultural Marketing Service. Fruit and Vegetable Division. Market News Branch. Michigan. Dept. of Agriculture. Marketing Division. (1976)-(1995). Periodical. English. Michigan Department of Agriculture, PO Box 30017, Lansing MI 48909. **Tel** (517)373-1050, FAX (517)335-0628.
Continued by Marketing Great Lakes Vegetables.
Desc: Emphasis on vegetables.

ISSN 0025-3782
UDC 658.8.012.1 NE
TITLE CHANGE
MARKETING MIX DIGEST. [Mark. mix dig.]. (1965)-(19??). Periodical. English. Samsom Uitgeverij B.V., Postbus 4, 2400 AM Alphen aan den Rijn, Netherlands. **Tel** 011 31 1720 66822, FAX 011 31 1720 66639. **Continued by** Ariadne, 0922-3797.

LC Discard
SA
MARKETING MIX (JOHANNESBURG, SOUTH AFRICA). (THE MARKETING MIX.).
VFOAT Journal of the Institute of Marketing Management; Joernal van die Instituut vir Bemarkingsbestuur. (19??)-. Periodical. English. Twelve times a year. $30.48. Systems Publishers Pty Ltd, PO Box 41345, Craighall 2024 South Africa. **Tel** 011 27 11 7891808, 011 27 11 7891809, FAX 011 27 11 7894725. **ED** Frank McDonogh. **Ad Acc**. **Circ:** 8,000 (ctrl).
Desc: Marketing management reporting in South Africa. In-depth editorial features on marketing related subjects.

ISSN 0344-1369
UDC 658.8 GW
MARKETING MUENCHEN.
[MarketingMunch.]. **VFOAT** Marketing, Zeitschrift fur Forschung und Praxis; Marketing, ZFP. (1979)-. Trade Publication. Multiple languages. Four times a year. DM230.00. CH Beck Verlagshandlung, D-80791 Munich Germany. **Tel** 011 49 89 381891.
Desc: Forum for discussion between marketing as a field of study and its practical application, describes and gives insight into marketing as a field of interest to both economy and society. Case studies and treaties help propose solutions to various problems; gives critical descriptions by authorities of developments in the main fields of marketing research and their application.
Ind/Abst Selec. Coop. Index Manage. Period.

ISSN 0025-3790
DD 658 US
CCC
CODEN MKNWAT
MARKETING NEWS. [Mark. news]. **Added/Corp**
American Marketing Association. Vol. 1 (Oct. 1967)-. Trade Publication. English. Twenty-six times a year. $130.00. American Marketing Association, 250 South Wacker Drive, Suite 200, Chicago IL 60606-5819. **Tel** (312)648-0536, FAX (312)993-7542. **ED** Thomas E Caruso. **Bk Rev. Ad Acc. Circ:** 31,200 (ctrl). available on microfilm and microfiche from University Microfilms International (UMI). Documents available from UMI Article Clearinghouse, Ask*IEEE.
Desc: Reports on new ideas, techniques, trends, and what's new at the American Marketing Association.
Ind/Abst ABI/INFORM Glob. Ed.; ABI/INFORM Ondisc: Expr. Ed.; ABI/INFORM [Computer File] (April 1974-); Acad. Search; BioBusiness (1989-); Bus. ASAP (1990-) [Full Txt.]; Bus. Index (1985-); Bus. Periodical. Index; Bus. Source Plus; Bus. Source; Chicano Index; EP Collect.; GATFWORLD; Gen. BusinessFile (1985-); Gen. Period. Index (1985-); Healthcare Leader. Rev.; Homework Help.; INFO-SOUTH Abstr.; Infobank (1979-); INSPEC (Jan. 1984-); Mag. Search; Manage. Contents; Mark. Advert. Ref. Serv.; MasterFile FullTEXT 1000; MasterFile FullTEXT 350; MasterFile FullTEXT 650; MasterFile FullTEXT (July 1993-); OCLC; Telebase; Trade Ind. ASAP [Full Txt.]; Trade Ind. Index [Full Txt.]; UMI ABI/Inform--Bus. Period. Ondisc (Oct. 1987-) [Full Txt.]; Wilson Bus. Abst.

LC HF5410 .A46a
DD 380.1 US
TITLE CHANGE
... MARKETING NEWS INTERNATIONAL DIRECTORY OF THE AMERICAN MARKETING ASSOCIATION AND THE MARKETING YELLOW PAGES, THE. See
Industry and Production-Trade and Industrial Directories.

LC HF5410 .A46a **ISSN 1074-5688**
DD 658 US
●**... MARKETING NEWS MARKETING YELLOW PAGES AND INTERNATIONAL DIRECTORY OF THE AMERICAN MARKETING ASSOCIATION, THE. See**
Industry and Production-Trade and Industrial Directories.

ISSN 0822-3998
DD 368.3/2/005 CN
MARKETING OPTIONS. [Mark. options].
VFOAT MO. No. 1 (Dec. 1983)-. Periodical. English. Ten times a year. 36.81Can$. Marketing Options Inc, 16 Aldergrove Avenue, Toronto Ontario M4C 1B2 Canada. **Tel** (416)690-2662. **ED** Stephen W. Carlson. **Ad Acc. Circ:** 1,000.
Desc: Features new life insurance products and services in Canada. Regular contributing columnists cover reinsurance, group, computers, taxation, and actuarial subjects.

LC HF5415.3 .M276 **ISSN 0739-8212**
DD 381/.0973 US
MARKETING ORC INDEX. [Mark. ORC index].
Added/Corp Opinion Research Corporation (U.S.).
VFOAT Marketing O.R.C. Index. **VAT** Marketing Opinion Research Corporation Index. Vol. 1, No. 1 (July 1981)-. English. Irregular (approximately annually). $2500.00. Opinion Research Corporation, North Harrison Drive, Princeton NJ 08540. **Tel** (609)924-5900.

US
●**MARKETING POWER. Added/Corp** American Demographics, Inc. **VFOAT** Marketing Power from American Demographics. (Jan. 1994)-. English. Twelve times a year. Free on request. American Demographics / New York, PO Box 68, Ithaca NY 14851. **Tel** (607)273-6343, (800)828-1133, FAX (607)273-3196.
Continues Marketing Tools Alert.

LC HD59.2 **ISSN 1065-9994**
DD 659 US
Pr Rev.
MARKETING PULSE, THE. [Mark. pulse]. (19??)-. Periodical. English. Twelve times a year. $300.00. Unlimited Positive Communications Inc., 11 North Chestnut Street, New Paltz NY 12561. **Tel** (914)255-2222, FAX (914)255-2231. **ED** Bill Harvey (editor) and Kristine Ciavarella (managing editor). **Circ:** 1,000+. **Continues** Media Science Newsletter, 0194-1607.
Desc: Provides projections, recommendations and analysis for entertainment and advertising industries decision makers.

US
TITLE CHANGE
MARKETING REHABILITATION SERVICES. (19??)-(Dec. 1994). English. Marketing Rehabilitation Services, 13700 Berkley Davis Drive, Chesterfield VA 23832. **Tel** (804)748-5779. **ED** Don Brady. **Circ:** 350. **Continued by** Healthcare Marketing in an Age of Reform.

ISSN 1064-3893
DD 658 US
MARKETING REPORT, THE. [Mark. rep.]. (Apr. 13, 1992)-. Periodical. English. Twenty-two times a year. $264.00. Progressive Business Publications, 370 Technology Drive, PO Box 3019, Malvern PA 19355. **Tel** (617)527-8600, (800)220-5000, FAX (617)647-8089.

LC HF5415.2 .M35555 **ISSN** 1040-8460
DD 658.8/3/005 US
CCC
Pr Rev.
MARKETING RESEARCH (CHICAGO, ILL.). (MARKETING RESEARCH : A MAGAZINE OF MANAGEMENT & APPLICATIONS.). [Mark. res.]. **Added/Corp** American Marketing Association. Vol. 1, No. 1 (Mar. 1989)-. Trade Publication. English. Four times a year (Mar., June, Sept., Dec.). $120.00. American Marketing Association, 250 South Wacker Drive, Suite 200, Chicago IL 60606-5819. **Tel** (312)648-0536, FAX (312)993-7542. **ED** Harry O'Neill. **Bk Rev**. **Ad Acc**. **Circ:** 3,200 (ctrl). available on microfilm and microfiche from University Microfilms International (UMI).
Desc: Gives practical ideas, new methods and techniques, and advice from marketing research pros. Articles are meant to help improve job performance, raise profits and streamline operations.
Ind/Abst Acad. Search; Bus. Source Plus; Bus. Source; Curr. Cit.; EP Collect.; Homework Help.; MasterFile FullTEXT 1000; MasterFile FullTEXT 350; MasterFile FullTEXT 650; MasterFile FullTEXT (July 1994-); Telebase.

LC HF5415.2 .M356
DD 658.8/3/0254 NE
MARKETING RESEARCH IN EUROPE. English (French and German). One time a year. Sigma Technical Press, 5 Alton Road, Wilmslow Cheshire SK9 5DY United Kingdom.

LC HD1751 .A9183 **ISSN** 0082-9781
DD 338.14 US
CODEN XAGMAF
MARKETING RESEARCH REPORT. [Marketing res. rep.]. No. 1 (1950)-. Monographic series. English. Irregular. Price varies per volume. US Department of Agriculture, 14th Street and Independence Avenue SW, Washington DC 20250. **Tel** (202)720-5457. Documents available from CASDDS.
Ind/Abst AGRICOLA; Chem. Abstr.

NE
MARKETING RESULTS. (19??)-. Periodical. English. Eleven times a year (monthly except combined July and Aug.). Fl84.80. Pemi Marketing, Janspleyn 52, 6811 GD Arnhem Netherlands. **Tel** 011 31 85 425942.

US
MARKETING REVIEW. **Added/Corp** American Marketing Association. New York Chapter. (19??)-. Periodical. English. Ten times a year. $25.00. American Marketing Association / New York, 310 Madison Avenue, Suite 1211, New York NY 10017. **Tel** (212)687-3280. **ED** Pat Ryan. Index available (bound in Sept. issue). **Ad Acc. Circ:** 3,000.
Desc: Articles on marketing and research; viewpoints, bibliographies, abstracts, people and faces, notices of upcoming events and job positions listings.
Ind/Abst Mark. Advert. Ref. Serv.

LC HF5410 .M37
DD 658.8/005 PK
MARKETING REVIEW (MARKETING ASSOCIATION OF PAKISTAN). (MARKETING REVIEW : A QUARTERLY PUBLICATION OF THE MARKETING ASSOCIATION OF PAKISTAN.). **Added/Corp** Marketing Association of Pakistan. Vol. 1, No. 1 (Oct. 1981)-. Periodical. English. Four times a year. $5.00. Marketing Association of Pakistan, 403 Burhani Chambers Karachi-5 Pakistan.

LC HF5410 .M39 **ISSN** 0732-2399
DD 658.8/005 US
CCC
Pr Rev.
MARKETING SCIENCE (PROVIDENCE, R.I.). (MARKETING SCIENCE : THE MARKETING JOURNAL OF TIMS/ORSA.). [Mark. sci.]. **Added/Corp** Institute of Management Sciences. Operations Research Society of America. Vol. 1, No. 1 (Winter 1982)-. Trade Publication. English. Four times a year. $120.00. Institute of Management Sciences, 290 Westminster Street, Providence RI 02903. **Tel** (401)274-2525, FAX (401)274-3189. **ED** John R. Hauser. cum. index. **Ad Acc. Circ:** 1,950. available on microfilm and microfiche from University Microfilms International (UMI). Documents available from The Genuine Article, UMI Article Clearinghouse.
Desc: A quantitatively oriented journal dealing with models and their empirical applications, marketing theory, measurement and estimation, statistics, psychometrics and economics.
Ind/Abst ABI/INFORM Glob. Ed.; ABI/INFORM Ondisc: Expr. Ed.; ABI/INFORM [Computer File] (Winter 1984-); Contents Pages Manage.; Curr. Cit.; Curr. Contents Soc. Behav. Sci.; Econ. Lit. Index (Winter 1984-); Gen. BusinessFile (1992-); Int. Abstr. Oper. Res. [Full Cov.]; J. Econ. Lit. (1984-); Oper. Res./Manage. Sci. (1984-); Qual. Control Appl. Stat.; Res. Alert [Full Cov.]; Soc. Sci. Cit. Index [Full Cov.].

LC HD9225.U53 C238
DD 380.1/415/09794 US
MARKETING SELECTED CALIFORNIA VEGETABLES. **Added/Corp** Federal-State Market News Service. United States. Agricultural Marketing Service. Fruit and Vegetable Division. Market News Branch. California. Bureau of Market News. (19??)-. English. One time a year. $10.00. Federal-State Market News Service, 1220 N Street, Suite 216, Box 942871, Sacramento CA 94271-0001. **Tel** (916)654-0298, FAX (916)654-1046.

ISSN 1075-0916
US
●**MARKETING SHORTS.** (1994)-. Periodical. English. Irregular (includes Just Rewards). $179.00. Marketing Works! Inc., 1031 Sterling Rd. Ste. 204, Herndon VA 22070. **Tel** (703)742-3640, FAX (703)742-6280.

ISSN 0961-7752
DD 658.8 UK
Pr Rev.
MARKETING SUCCESS. [Mark. success]. (1990)-. Periodical. English. Six times a year. £12.00 UK; £15.00 other. Chartered Institute of Marketing, Moor Hall, Cookham, Berkshire SL6 9QH United Kingdom. **Tel** FAX 011 44 16285 31382, telex 849462 TELFAC G.
Desc: Information on CIM educational issues and policy, central and local student initiatives and general business/marketing issues.

LC AP **ISSN** 0964-0142
DD 050 UK
MARKETING SURVEYS INDEX. [Mark. surv. index]. (1983)-. Directory. English. Ten times a year (monthly with July/Aug. and Nov./Dec. combined). $646.84. Marketing Strategies Industry, Viscount House River Lane, Saltney Chester CH4 8QY United Kingdom. **Tel** 011 44 1244 681424, FAX 011 44 1244 681457. **ED** Claudia Richards (Editor's telephone: 011 44 494 681758). Index available (bound in all issues). cum. index.
Desc: A directory of published industry and market research reports from around the world.

ISSN 8756-2855
DD 004 US
MARKETING TECHNOLOGY. [Mark. technol.]. (Jan. 1985)-. Periodical. English. Twelve times a year. $269.00. Marketing Technology, PO Box 968, Menlo Park CA 94026. **Tel** (415)328-8600, FAX (415)322-9149. **ED** Kristin Zhivago (phone: (415)328-6000). Index available. cum. index. **Bk Rev**, (Qty: 5).
Desc: Every issue gives ideas that can be applied to the day-to-day political environment. Provides a fresh perspective, and real solutions that help in writing better copy, creating more compelling visuals, and selling more products.

ISSN 1043-5417
DD 658 US
TITLE CHANGE
MARKETING TO DOCTORS. (MARKETING TO DOCTORS : MD.). [Mark. dr.]. **VFOAT** MD. Vol. 1, No. 1 (Nov. 1988)-(199?). Periodical. English. The Beckham Company, 1901 East Cumberland Boulevard, Whitefish Bay WI 53211. **Tel** (414)963-8935. **ED** Dan Beckham. **Circ:** 250. ***Continued by** Management & Doctors, 1043-5417.*
Ind/Abst Healthcare Leader. Rev.

US
MARKETING TO KIDS REPORT. (1939)-. English. Twelve times a year. $225.00 US; $230.00 Canada; $247.00 other. North Shore Communications, Inc., 3364 Country Rose Circle, Second Floor, Encinitas CA 92024. **Tel** (619)756-5446, FAX (619)756-5857. **ED** Rena Karl. **Circ:** 2,000.
Desc: News, trends and developments in the children and teens markets.

ISSN 1047-1677
DD 658 US
TITLE CHANGE
MARKETING TO WOMEN (1989). **See** Women's Interests.

LC HF5410 .M415 **ISSN** 1076-4879
DD 658.8/005 US
●**MARKETING TOOLS.** [Mark. tools]. (Apr./May 1994)-. Periodical. English. Eight times a year. $54.00. American Demographics / New York, PO Box 68, Ithaca NY 14851. **Tel** (607)273-6343, (800)828-1133, FAX (607)273-3196.
Ind/Abst Bus. Source Plus; Bus. Source; EP Collect.; Homework Help.; MasterFile FullTEXT 1000; MasterFile FullTEXT 350; MasterFile FullTEXT 650; MasterFile FullTEXT; OCLC; Telebase.

LC HF5410 .M37 **ISSN** 0025-3642
CN
CCC
TITLE CHANGE
MARKETING (TORONTO). (MARKETING.). [Marketing]. Vol. 38 (1933)-(1993). Periodical. English. Maclean Hunter Canada / Montreal, 1001 bvd. de Maisonneuve W., Montreal Quebec H3A 3E1 Canada. **Tel** (514)845-5141, FAX (514)845-4302, telex 055-60604. **ED** Colin Muncie. **Bk Rev**. **Ad Acc. Circ:** 10,400. available on microfilm and microfiche from University Microfilms International (UMI). ***Continues** Marketing and Business Management; **Absorbed** Canadian Premiums & Incentives (Nov. 22, 1982), 0319-6267. **Continued by** Marketing Magazine (Toronto, Ont.).*
Desc: Covers the Canadian news in advertising sales and marketing. Carries supplements in creativity, premiums and incentives as well as regular features on major media.
Ind/Abst Acad. Search; Bus. Period. Index (?-?); Bus. Source Plus; Bus. Source; Can. Period. Index (?-?); EP Collect.; Homework Help.; INFO-SOUTH Abstr. (?-?); Mag. Search (?-?); Mark. Advert. Ref. Serv. (?-?); MasterFile FullTEXT 1000; MasterFile FullTEXT 350; MasterFile FullTEXT 650; MasterFile FullTEXT; OCLC; Telebase; Wilson Bus. Abstr. (?-?).

ISSN 0895-1799
DD 021 US
Pr Rev.
MARKETING TREASURES. [Mark. treasures]. **Added/Corp** Chris Olson & Associates. Vol. 1, No. 1 (Sept. 1987)-. Newsletter. English. Six times a year. $54.00. Chris Olson & Associates, 857 Twin Harbor Drive, Arnold MD 21012. **Tel** (410)647-6708, FAX (410)647-0415. **ED** Chris Olson. Index available. cum. index. **Bk Rev. Circ:** 1,000.
Desc: For librarians seeking tips on promotion, public relations and marketing strategies. Provides advice on writing brochures, pricing services, etc.

ISSN 1078-5930
US
●**MARKETING TREASURES, CLIP ART ON DISK.** (MARKETING TREASURES, CLIP ART ON DISK [COMPUTER FILE].). **Added/Corp** Chris Olson & Associates. (1994)-. Periodical. English. Three times a year. $24.00 (Marketing Treasures subscribers), $36.00 (non-subscribers). Chris Olson & Associates, 857 Twin Harbor Drive, Arnold MD 21012. **Tel** (410)647-6708, FAX (410)647-0415.

ISSN 0882-4770
DD 380 US
MARKETING TRENDS (DEUTSCHE AUSG.). (MARKETING TRENDS : EINE INTERNATIONALE VEROFFENTLICHUNG DER A.C. NIELSEN COMPANY.). [Mark. trends]. (1979)-. Periodical. English (German, French, Italian, Portuguese and Spanish). Two times a year. Free. AC Nielsen Company, Media Research Division, Neilsen Plaza, Northbrook IL 60062. **Tel** (312)498-6300. **ED** C J Wallis. **Circ:** 35,000 (ctrl).
Desc: Articles of interest to marketers of fast moving consumer goods and consumer durables.

ISSN 0882-4789
DD 380 US
MARKETING TRENDS (ED. ESPANOLA). (MARKETING TRENDS : REVISTA INTERNACIONAL DE A.C. NIELSEN COMPANY.). [Mark. trends]. (1979)-. Periodical. Spanish. Two times a year. AC Nielsen Company, Media Research Division, Neilsen Plaza, Northbrook IL 60062. **Tel** (312)498-6300.

ISSN 0882-4762
DD 380 US
MARKETING TRENDS (ED. FRANCAISE). (MARKETING TRENDS : REVUE INTERNATIONALE PUBLIEE PAR A.C. NIELSEN COMPANY.). [Mark. trends]. (1979)-. Periodical. French. Two times a year. AC Nielsen Company, Media Research Division, Neilsen Plaza, Northbrook IL 60062. **Tel** (312)498-6300.

ISSN 0882-4797
DD 380 US
MARKETING TRENDS (ED. ITALIANA). (MARKETING TRENDS : REVISTA INTERNAZIONALE DELLA A.C. NIELSEN COMPANY.). [Mark. trends]. (1979)-. Periodical. Italian. Two times a year. AC Nielsen Company, Media Research Division, Neilsen Plaza, Northbrook IL 60062. **Tel** (312)498-6300.

ISSN 0141-9285
UK
MARKETING WEEK. [Mark. week]. (1978)-. Periodical. English. One time a week. $188.23. Centaur Communications Ltd., St. Giles House, 50 Poland Street, London W1V 4AX United Kingdom. **Tel** 011 44 171 4394222, FAX 011 44 171 7346748, telex 261352.
Desc: The news magazine of marketing, media and advertising.
Ind/Abst Infomat Int. Bus., Mark. Advert. Ref. Serv.

Business and Economics —Marketing and Purchasing

LC HF5415.12.I5 M37
DD 658.8/005   II
MARKETOLOGY. Added/Corp Institute of Marketing Management. Vol. 14, No. 9 (Oct. 1982)-. Periodical. English. Four times a year (Jan., Apr., July, Oct.). $30.00. Institute of Marketing Management, 62-F Sujan Singh Park, New Delhi 110 003 India. **Continues** Marketing Digest.

ISSN 1059-8200
DD 380   US
MARKETOOLS (HERNDON, VA.). (MARKETOOLS : THE INFORMATION TECHNOLOGY MARKETING REPORT.). **VFOAT** Market Tools. Vol. 1, No. 1 (Oct. 1991)-. Periodical. English. Twelve times a year. $245.00. Vantage Point, 1603 Jubilation Court, Herndon VA 22070-2953.

US
MARKETSCAN INTERNATIONAL. (19??)-. English. Twelve times a year. $395.00 North America; $450.00 other. Miller Freeman Inc., 600 Harrison Street, San Francisco CA 94107. **Tel** (415)905-2337, (415)905-2200, FAX (415)905-2240, telex 278273.

LC HF5410
DD 658.83   UK
CODEN MRKEED
MARKETSEARCH. See Business and Economics-Abstracting, Bibliographies and Statistics.

ISSN 1064-5705
DD 004   US
MARKETVISION (BOSTON, MASS.). (MARKETVISION : MARKETING AND COMPETITIVE STRATEGIES FOR THE PERSONAL WORKSTATION INDUSTRY.). [Mark.Vis.]. **Added/Corp** Summit Strategies, Inc. **VFOAT** Market Vision. (19??)-. Periodical. English. Twelve times a year. $495.00. Summit Strategies Inc., 360 Newbury Street, Boston MA 02115. **Tel** (617)266-9050, FAX (617)266-7952.

ISSN 0164-4939
DD 338   US
MARKING INDUSTRY MAGAZINE. [Marking ind. mag.]. (1972)-. Trade Publication. English. Twelve times a year. $40.00. Marking Devices Publishing Company, 113 Adell Place, Elmhurst IL 60126. **Tel** (708)832-5200. **ED** Brian Sinderson. **Ad Acc. Circ:** 1,800. **Continues** Marking Industry.
Desc: Covers new products, MDA and other associations' news, sales and management methods and industry news by field.

LC WMLC L 82/282
AU
MARKT, DER. Added/Corp Osterreichische Gesellschaft fuer Absatzwirtschaft. (1962)-. Periodical. German (English). Four times a year. $47.46. Oesterreichisch G Marketing, Augasse 2-6, 1090 Vienna Austria. **Tel** 011 43 1 313364400, FAX 011 43 1 31336732. Index available. cum. index. **Bk Rev. Ad Acc. Circ:** 1,000.

GW
MARKT INTERN ELEKTROHANDEL. (19??)-. German. One time a week. DM489.11 Germany; DM459.84 Europe; DM470.24 other. Markt Intern Verlag GmbH, Grafenberger Allee 30, 4000 Duesseldorf Germany. **Tel** 011 49 2 11 66980.

LC HF5549.5.C6 M27
GW
MARKT KOMMUNIKATION. See Communications.

LC HF5415.2 .M36   ISSN 0933-7105
GW
MARKTFORSCHUNG & MANAGEMENT.
VFOAT Marktforschung und Management. (198?)-. Trade Publication. German. Four times a year. $86.29. CE Poeschel Verlag, Kernerstrasse 43, D-70182 Stuttgart Germany. **Tel** 011 49 711 229020. **(Subscription address:** Spektrum Fachverlage GmbH, Postfach 1152, D-72125 Kuesterdingen Germany. **Tel** 011 49 7071 935370.) **Continues** Marktforschung (Berlin, Germany), 0170-723X.
Ind/Abst Selec. Coop. Index Manage. Period.

ISSN 0199-3887
US
MASTER SALESMANSHIP. (197?)-. Periodical. English. Twenty-six times a year. $22.75 (six months). Clement Communications Inc., Concord Industrial Park, Concordville PA 19331. **Tel** (800)345-8101, (610)459-4200. **ED** Homer Smith. **Circ:** 50,000.
Desc: The newsletter for professional salespeople.

ISSN 0894-2609
DD 658   US
Pr Rev.
MATURE MARKET REPORT. [Mature mark. rep.]. **VFOAT** Mature Market. Vol. 1, No. 1 (May 1987)-. Periodical. English. Twelve times a year. $175.00 (one-year); $300.00 (two-year) US; $190.00 (one-year); $315.00 (two-year) Canada. Lifestyle Change Communications Inc., 5885 Glenridge Drive, Suite 150, Atlanta GA 30328. **Tel** (404)252-0554, FAX (404)252-4295. Index Available Received separately--bound from publisher (free to new subscribers). cum. index. **Bk Rev. Circ:** 400.
Desc: Business newsletter concerning marketing to the over-50 consumer. Useful for marketing professionals in healthcare, insurance, financial services, travel and retirement housing.

ISSN 0025-6137
US
MAY TRENDS. Added/Corp George S. May International Company. (1967)-. Periodical. English. Free on request. George S. May International Co., 111 South Washington Street, Park Ridge IL 60068. **Tel** (708)825-8806.

ISSN 1079-1604
DD 338   US
CODEN MMRTEO
●**MEAT MARKETING & TECHNOLOGY. See** Food and Food Industry.

UK
MEDIA & MARKETING EUROPE. (19??)-. English. Twelve times a year. £60.00. Media Week Ltd., Wilmington House, Churchill Dar, Foxtrot Kent DA2 7ES United Kingdom.

GW
MEDIA DATEN. OESTERREICHS. WERBE AGENDA. (19??)-. German. Two times a year. DM336.00. Media Daten Verlagsgesellschaf GmbH, Postfach 4260, D-65032 Wiesbaden Germany. **Tel** 011 49 6123 7000, FAX 011 49 6123 700122.

BE
Pr Rev.
MEDIA MARKETING NEWS. English. Irregular (46 issues per year). 6750F France; 7250F other. Groupe R Dupuis, rue de Stalle 70, B 1180 Brussels Belgium. **Tel** 011 32 2 4675611. **ED** Groupe R. DuPuis. Index available. cum. index. **Ad Acc.**

ISSN 0168-8235
UDC 658.8.012.1   NE
MEDIAMARKT. (1984)-. Periodical. Dutch. Twelve times a year. Samsom Uitgeverij B.V., Postbus 4, 2400 AM Alphen aan den Rijn, Netherlands. **Tel** 011 31 1720 66822, FAX 011 31 1720 66639. **Continues** Ariadne, 0922-3800.

LC HF5801 .M43   ISSN 1055-176X
DD 659   US
CCC
MEDIAWEEK (NEW YORK, N.Y.). (MEDIAWEEK.). [Mediaweek]. **VFOAT** Media Week. Vol. 1, No. 1 (Jan. 14, 1991)-. Periodical. English. One time a week. $260.00. EMAP Readerlink, Audit House, 260 Field End Road, Ruislip Middlesex HA4 9LT United Kingdom. **Tel** 011 44 1773 63100, FAX 011 44 1733 87367. available on an online database (files 16,648,7771,772,799/Full-Text) from DIALOG. Documents available from UMI Article Clearinghouse. **Continues** M & MD : Marketing and Media Decisions, 0195-4296.
Desc: Edited especially for the media professional. Has hard-hitting, in-depth features on media's hottest topics.
Ind/Abst ABI/INFORM Glob. Ed.; ABI/INFORM [Computer File]; Acad. Ind. [Computer File] (1991-); BioBusiness; Bus. Index (1991-); Bus. Period. Index; Expand. Acad. Index (1991-); F&S Index Plus Text, Int. [Full Txt.] [Select. Cov.]; Gen. BusinessFile (1991-); Gen. Period. Index (1991-); INFO-SOUTH Abstr.; Mag. Search; Mark. Advert. Ref. Serv. [Full Txt.]; MasterFile FullTEXT (July 1993-); PROMT [Full Txt.]; Stat. Ref. Index; Trade Ind. ASAP [Full Txt.]; Trade Ind. Index [Full Txt.]; Wilson Bus. Abstr.

ISSN 1049-880X
DD 338   US
MEDICAL GROUP MANAGEMENT MARKETERS GUIDEPOST. Added/Corp Medical Group Management Association. **VFOAT** Marketer's Guidepost. Vol. 1, No. 1 (Summer 1990)-. Periodical. English. Four times a year. $69.00. Medical Group Management Association, 104 Inverness Terrace East, Englewood CO 80112. **Tel** (303)397-7879, FAX (303)799-1683. **ED** Brenda Hull. **Circ:** 300 (ctrl).
Desc: Marketing tips for medical group managers.

LC HD9665.1 .P45   ISSN 0025-7354
DD 380.1/45/615105   US
CCC
NLM W1; ME383   CODEN MMKMBX
MEDICAL MARKETING & MEDIA. [Med. mark. media]. **VFOAT** MM&M. **VAT** Medical Marketing and Media. Vol. 4, No. 3 (March 1969)-. Trade Publication. English. Fourteen times a year. $100.00. CPS Communications Inc., 7200 West Camino Real, Suite 215, Boca Raton FL 33433. **Tel** (407)368-9301, FAX (407)368-7870. **ED** Gail Rendrd. Index available. **Ad Acc. Circ:** 9,500 (ctrl). available on microfilm and microfiche from University Microfilms International (UMI); available on an online database (files 15,570,648/Full-Text) from DIALOG. Documents available from UMI Article Clearinghouse. **Continues** Pharmaceutical Marketing & Media.
Desc: Professional journal to and for the pharmaceutical and medical marketing industry, providing intra-industry communication and an information link with other industries and government.
Ind/Abst ABI/INFORM Glob. Ed.; ABI/INFORM [Computer File] (Aug. 1985-); BioBusiness; Curr. Cit.; F&S Index Plus Text, Int. [Select. Cov.]; Hosp. Health Admin. Index; Infobank (Jan. 1979-); Int. Pharm. Abstr.; Mark. Advert. Ref. Serv.; PROMT; Trade Ind. ASAP [Full Txt.]; Trade Ind. Index [Full Txt.]; UMI ABI/Inform--Bus. Period. Ondisc (Jan. 1988-) [Full Txt.].

ISSN 1048-3225
DD 658   US
MEDIMARK RESEARCH MAGAZINE QUALITATIVE AUDIENCES REPORT. [Mediamark Res. mag. qual. audiences rep.]. **VFOAT** Magazine Qualitative Audiences Report. Periodical. English. Two times a year. Medimark Research Inc, 341 Madison Avenue, New York NY 10017. **Continues in part** Magazine Qualitative Audiences.

ISSN 1048-3217
DD 658   US
MEDIMARK RESEARCH MAGAZINE TOTAL AUDIENCES REPORT. [Mediamark Res. mag. total audiences rep.]. **VFOAT** Magazine Total Audiences Report. Periodical. English. Two times a year. Medimark Research Inc, 341 Madison Avenue, New York NY 10017. **Continues in part** Magazine Total Audiences.

LC HC106.6 .M36a   ISSN 0092-4857
DD 658.8   US
MEI MARKETING ECONOMICS GUIDE.
Main/Corp Marketing Economics Institute. **VFOAT** M.E.I. Marketing Guide; Marketing Economics Guide. **VAT** Marketing Economics Institute Marketing Economics Guide. (19??)-. English. One time a year (June). $35.00 ($5.00 postage). Marketing Economics Institute, 186 26 Avon Road, Jamaica NY 11432. **Tel** (718)454-1697.

LC HD59
DD 659   BL
●**MEM INFORME REGIONAL. See** Business and Economics-Advertising and Public Relations.

US
MERCHANDISING ... STATISTICAL AND MARKETING REPORT. See Business and Economics-Abstracting, Bibliographies and Statistics.

LC HF5068.P53 C66   ISSN 1059-6720
DD 338.7/4/02579173   US
METRO PHOENIX MARKETING DIRECTORY. See Industry and Production-Trade and Industrial Directories.

ISSN 0192-7973
US
SUSPENDED
METROPOLITAN PURCHASOR. Vol. 1- Sept. 1972-?. Periodical. English. Twelve times a year. White Eagle Inc, PO Box 8307, Trenton NJ 08650. **Formed by the union of** New York Purchasing Review **and** New Jersey Purchaser.

ISSN 1121-4228
IT
UDC 339.13
MICRO & MACRO MARKETING. [Micro macro mark.]. **VFOAT** Micro e Macro Marketing. (1992)-. Periodical. Italian. Three times a year. L46330. Societa Editrice il Mulino, Strada Maggiore 37, 40125 Bologna Italy. **Tel** 011 39 51 256011, FAX 011 39 51 256034.

ISSN 0738-6354
US
MICRO SOFTWARE MARKETING. See Computers-Software.

ISSN 0193-2047
US
MID-AMERICA COMMERCE & INDUSTRY. [Mid-Am. commer. ind.]. **VAT** Mid-America Commerce and Industry. (19??)-. Trade Publication. English. Twelve times a year. $18.00. Mid-America Commerce & Industry, 1824 Cheyenne Road, Topeka KS 66604. **Tel** (913)272-5280. **ED** N Ray Lippe. **Bk Rev. Ad Acc. Circ:** 10,000 (ctrl). Documents available from UMI Article Clearinghouse.
Desc: Purchasing management articles to help buyers at manufacturing firms in six states. Coverage of trade shows, conventions, association meetings. Regional news. Company profiles, how to cut costs.
Ind/Abst Bus. Dateline (Sept. 1991-) [Full Txt.].

Business and Economics — Marketing and Purchasing

MID ATLANTIC PURCHASING. [Mid Atl. purch.]. **VFOAT** Midatlantic Purchasing. Vol. 57, No. 1 (Jan. 1982)-. Periodical. English. Six times a year. A & H Communications, Inc., Suite 610, 1518 Walnut Street, Philadelphia PA 19102. **Continues** Philadelphia Purchasor, 0031-7322.
ISSN 0745-1733
DD 658
US

MIDDLE EAST BUSINESS INTELLIGENCE. [Middle East bus. intell.]. (1982)-. Newsletter. English. Twenty-two times a year. $365.70. International Executive Reports, 717 D Street NW/Suite 300, Washington DC 20004-2807. **Tel** (202)628-6900, **FAX** (202)628 6618, telex 440462 MEER UI. **ED** Colin MacKinnon. **Circ:** 600 (ctrl). available on an online database from DIALOG.
Desc: Newsletter containing contracting and sales leads in the Middle East. Provides specific contract information, alerts to upcoming business opportunities and current tenders.
ISSN 0731-6305
US
CCC
LC HF5813.B8 M53
DD 659.109
BL

MIDIA & MERCADO. See Business and Economics-Advertising and Public Relations.

MINTEL MARKET INTELLIGENCE. (19??)-. Trade Publication. English. Twelve times a year. £1045.00. Mintel International Group Ltd., 18-19 Long Lane, London EC1A 9HE United Kingdom. **Tel** 011 44 171 6064533, **FAX** 011 44 171 6065932, telex 21405.
UK

MIRROR NEWS. See Industry and Production-Manufacturing.
ISSN 0191-4677
US
SUSPENDED

MMD 1,000, THE. [MMD 1,000]. **Added/Corp** Money Market Directories, Inc. **VFOAT** MDD One Thousand. **VAT** Money Market Directory One Thousand. 1st Ed. (1982)-. English. Irregular. comes with Directory of Pension Funds and Their Investment Managers. Money Market Directories Inc., 320 East Main Street, PO Box 1608, Charlottesville VA 22902. **Tel** (800)446-2810, (804)977-1450.
LC HG4509 .M63
DD 332.6/7254
ISSN 0883-0495
US

MOBILE PHONE NEWS. See Communications-Telecommunication.
ISSN 0737-5077
US
CCC

MODERN PURCHASING. [Mod. purch.]. Vol. 1 (Apr. 1959)-. Periodical. English. Ten times a year. 37.61Can$. MacLean Hunter Ltd. Business Publishers / Canada, Box 9100, Station A, Toronto Ontario M5W 1A5 Canada. **Tel** (416)596-5000, , **FAX** (416)596-5552. **(Subscription address:** Indas Customer Service, 35 Riviera Drive, Building 17, Markham Ontario L3R 8N4 Canada. **Tel** (905)946-0406.) available on microfilm and microfiche from University Microfilms International (UMI). **Ind/Abst** World Text. Abstr.
LC HF5437 .M6
ISSN 0026-833X
CN

MOLASSES MARKET NEWS. See Agriculture.
LC SB175
DD 635
ISSN 0145-0662
US

MONITOR (CLEARWATER, FLA.). (MONITOR.). Vol. 17 No. 6 (Sept. 1988)-(Oct. 1993). Trade Publication. English. Monitor CT, 4 Stamford Forum, Stamford CT 06901. **Tel** (203) 325-7799, (203) 977-2900. **ED** Bob O'Neill. **Ad Acc.** ctrl circ. **Continues** National Mall Monitor, 0194-5017.
LC HF5430.3 .N37
DD 658.8/7
ISSN 0895-8777
US
CEASED

MOVIE/TV MARKETING. **VFOAT** Movie TV Marketing. **VAT** Movie Television Marketing. Vol. 20, No. 8 (Feb. 1966)-. Trade Publication. English. Twelve times a year. $250.00. Movie TV Marketing, Box 30, Central Post Office, Tokyo 100-91 Japan. **Tel** 011 81 3 5872855, FAX 011 81 3 5839549, telex J26864 MTVM. **(Subscription address:** Maruzen Company Ltd., PO Box 5050, Import & Export Department, Tokyo 100 31 Japan. **Tel** 011 81 3 32789224.) **ED** Wm Ireton. **Bk Rev. Ad Acc. Circ:** 100,000 (ctrl). **Continues** Movie Marketing.
Desc: Trade journal on the motion picture, television and allied industries.
LC HF5415.2 .M3557a
JA

MRA BLUE BOOK, RESEARCH SERVICES DIRECTORY. See Industry and Production-Trade and Industrial Directories.
US

MULTI-LEVEL MARKETING TAX AND FINANCIAL NEWSLETTER / MLM. **VFOAT** Multi-Level Marketing. No. 1 (Jan. 15, 1982)-. Newsletter. English. Six times a year. $32.00. MLM Financial Associates, 31 Porter Street/Drawer 804, Stoughton MA 02072.
ISSN 0730-9171
US

Pr Rev.
MULTIMEDIA MARKETS : INTERNATIONAL FORECAST SUPPLEMENT. English. One time a year. $990.00. Information Workstation Group, 501 Queens Street, Alexandria VA 22314. **Tel** (703)548-4320, FAX (703)838-9271. **ED** John Gale. Index available.
Desc: This 317 page market research report supplements the Multimedia Markets report for North America by addressing international markets. It provides a similar forecast for each of Western Europe, Asia, the rest of the world and world wide totals.
US

Pr Rev.
MULTIMEDIA OPPORTUNITIES. (19??)-. English. One time a year. $1890.00. Information Workstation Group, 501 Queens Street, Alexandria VA 22314. **Tel** (703)548-4320, FAX (703)838-9271. **ED** John Gale. Index available.
Desc: Describes multimedia application groups. It discusses relevant markets using US Government SIC Code market definitions and descriptions, lists current or probable applications, lists key companies in the industry, and establishes the acceptance of computer technology, the relevance of multimedia capabilities, competitive pressures for the use of multimedia, and legal and regulatory forces.
US

MUNICIPAL INDEX. **Added/Corp** Communications Channels, Inc. (1985)-. English. One time a year. $59.95. Argus Business, 6151 Powers Ferry Road Northwest, Atlanta GA 30339. **Tel** (404)995-2500, FAX (404)995-0400.
ISSN 0161-7990
US

Pr Rev.
NAEB BULLETIN. **Main/Corp** National Association of Educational Buyers. **VAT** National Association of Educational Buyers Bulletin. (197?)-. Bulletin. English. Eleven times a year. $40.00. National Association of Educational Buyers, 450 Wireless Boulevard, Hauppauge NY 11788. **Tel** (516)273-2600. **ED** Neil D. Markee. Index available. **Circ:** 2,350 (ctrl).
Desc: Various articles and information on effective purchasing practices for managers in higher education and health care.
ISSN 0469-7928
US

NASPO NEWSLETTER. **Main/Corp** National Association of State Purchasing Officials. **VAT** National Association of State Purchasing Officials Newsletter. Newsletter. English. Four times a year. National Association of State Purchasing Officials, Iron Works Pike, Lexington KY 40505.
US

NATIONAL FIRM RETAIL RR PRODUCTIVITY TRACKING REPORT. (19??)-. English. Four times a year. Free. Securities Industry Association, 120 Broadway/35th Floor, New York NY 10271. **Tel** (212)608-1500, FAX (212)608-1604. ctrl circ.
Desc: A service which tracks quarterly RR production performance of large national firms and provides inter-firm comparisons on a confidential basis. Reports available only to senior management of participating firms.
ISSN 1076-2582
DD 338
US
NLM W1; NE374IJ
TITLE CHANGE

NEW DRUG BUYER, THE. See Pharmacy and Pharmacology.
LC HF1 .N46
DD 338
ISSN 0028-4858
US

NEW ENGLAND PURCHASER. **Added/Corp** Purchasing Management Association of Boston. New England Purchasing Agents Association. (Feb. 1921)-. Trade Publication. English. Twelve times a year. Purchasing Management Association Boston Inc, 200 Baker Avenue, Concord MA 01742. **Tel** (508)371-2522. **Bk Rev. Ad Acc. Circ:** 5,500 (ctrl).
LC TJ1 .N4
DD 621.905
ISSN 0028-4963
US
CCC

NEW EQUIPMENT DIGEST. See Engineering-Mechanical Engineering and Machinery.

LC HF5065.N4 N48
DD 381/.45/000294742
ISSN 0276-2110
US
TITLE CHANGE

NEW HAMPSHIRE MARKETING DIRECTORY. See Industry and Production-Trade and Industrial Directories.
ISSN 1054-5190
DD 071
US

NEW JERSEY MEDIA GUIDE. See Communications.
UK

NEW MEDIA MARKETS. Vol. 1, No. 1 (Jan. 1983)-. English. Twenty-four times a year. Financial Times Magazines, Greystoke Place, Fetter Lane, London EC4A 1ND United Kingdom. **Tel** 011 44 171 8316577. available on an online database (files 16,636/Full-Text) from DIALOG.
Ind/Abst PROMT [Full Txt.]; PTS Newsl. Database [Full Txt.].
ISSN 0733-8252
US
CCC
SUSPENDED

NEW PRODUCT DEVELOPMENT. (198?)-Suspended with Vol. 9 (19??). Periodical. English. Twelve times a year. $75.00 US; $85.00 (airmail) other. New Product Development, PO Box 1309, Point Pleasant NJ 08742. **Tel** (201)295-8258. **ED** Jim Betts. **Bk Rev.**
Desc: Material related to the creative, development and marketing aspects of new product development.
UK

Pr Rev.
NEW PRODUCT REPORT, THE. (19??)-. English. Twenty-six times a year. £575.00 UK; £625.00 other. IIS Limited, 18-19 Long Lane, London EC1A 9HE United Kingdom. **Tel** 011 44 171 6064533, FAX 011 44 171 6065932. **ED** David Jago. Index available. cum. index. **Circ:** 500. available on diskette.
Desc: Lists new products launched worldwide in food, drink, household goods and toiletries markets.
ISSN 0898-5367
DD 658
US

NEWMAN REPORT, THE. [Newman rep.]. (May 1988)-. Periodical. English. Twelve times a year. $60.00 add $15.00 (airmail) for postage other. Newsletter Group Inc., PO Box 4044, 1552 Gilmore Street, Mountain View CA 94040. **Tel** (415)941-7525. **ED** Patrick Totty. **Circ:** 1,400. **Continues** Marketing & Sales Promotion Update, 0884-2973.
Desc: Provides new marketing and sales ideas which have already been tested and proven successful. Readership in the United States and thirty-eight foreign countries.
ISSN 0028-9108
GW
CODEN NROSAE

NEWS FROM ROHDE & SCHWARZ. [News Rohde & Schwarz]. (1968)-. Periodical. English. Irregular. Free on request. Rohde and Schwarz GmbH, Muhldorfstr 15, D-81671 Munich Germany. **Tel** 011 49 89 41290. **(Subscription address:** Rohde & Schwarz Inc, 4425 Nicole Drive, Lanham MD 20706.) Documents available from Article Express International, Ask*IEEE.
Ind/Abst Bioeng. Abstr.; Curr. Cit.; Ei Page One; Eng. Index Annu.; INSPEC (1968-).
ISSN 0733-5768
US

NEWSLETTER / MARKETING SCIENCE INSTITUTE. **Added/Corp** Marketing Science Institute. **VFOAT** MSI Newsletter. **M.S.I.** Newsletter. (19??)-. Newsletter. English. Irregular (25-35 issues per year). $300.00. Marketing Science Institute, 1000 Massachusetts Avenue, Cambridge MA 02138. **Tel** (617)491-2060. **ED** Judith Maas (Editor's telephone: (617)491-6002 ext.32). (catalog).
Desc: Encompasses marketing topics such as brands, service quality, product development, and market orientation.
ISSN 1040-6948
DD 380
US

NIELSEN MARKETING TRENDS (ENGLISH ED.). (NIELSEN MARKETING TRENDS.). [Nielsen mark. trends.]. **Added/Corp** Nielsen Marketing Research. **VFOAT** Marketing Trends. (198?)-. Periodical. English. Two times a year. Free. AC Nielsen Company, Media Research Division, Neilsen Plaza, Northbrook IL 60062. **Tel** (312)498-6300. **Continues** Marketing Trends (English Edition), 0882-4754.

Business and Economics —Marketing and Purchasing

DD 658
ISSN 1064-4911
US
TITLE CHANGE
NONPROFIT MARKETING REPORT.
[Nonprofit mark. rep.]. **VFOAT** Non-Profit Marketing Report. (Jan. 1992)-(19??). Periodical. English. Progressive Business Publications, 370 Technology Drive, PO Box 3019, Malvern PA 19355. **Tel** (617)527-8600, (800)220-5000, FAX (617)647-8089. *Continued by* What's Working for Nonprofit Fundraising.

LC HF5065.V8 L4 **ISSN** 1058-5494
DD 338.7/4/02575529 US
NORTHERN VIRGINIA MARKETING DIRECTORY. See Industry and Production-Trade and Industrial Directories.

ISSN 0279-2893
US
NSM REPORT. VFOAT Non-Store Marketing Report. (197?)-. Periodical. English. Twenty-four times a year. $275.00. Maxwell Sroge Publishers Inc., 522 Forest Avenue, Evanston IL 60202. **Tel** (708)866-1890, FAX (708)866-1899. **ED** Ann Meyer.
Desc: Analyses of key trends and happenings in the mail order and interactive shopping industries.

ISSN 0192-009X
US
O & A MARKETING NEWS. See Transportation-Automobiles.

LC HB848 .O34
US
OFFICIAL GUIDE TO THE AMERICAN MARKETPLACE, THE. VFOAT American Marketplace. 1st Ed. (1992)-. English. $69.95. New Strategist, PO Box 242, Ithaca NY 14851. **Tel** (607)273-0913. **ED** Margaret Ambry, Cheryl Russell.
Desc: Organized into chapters that examine the major factors that drive consumer markets.

US
●**OFICINA, LA.** (1994)-. Directory. English. Two times a year. $15.00 US; $20.00 Canada; $25.00 Mexico; $30.00 other. Penton Publishing, 1100 Superior Avenue, Cleveland OH 44114-2543. **Tel** (216)696-7000, FAX (216)696-0836. **(Subscription address:** Penton Publishing, PO Box 96732, Chicago IL 60693.)
Desc: Covers office equipment dealers in Mexico, Central and South America.

ISSN 0192-2467
US
OHIO VALLEY RETAILER. (19??)-. Periodical. English. Twelve times a year. $5.00. Ohio Valley Retailer, 11214 Enyart Road, Loveland OH 45103. **Tel** (513)677-1237, (513)683-1615.

LC HD9696.A923 U536 **ISSN** 0192-7302
DD 381/.45/62138410973 US
ORION MARKETING TRADE-IN GUIDE.
VFOAT Audio Trade-In Guide. **VAT** Orion Marketing Trade, in Guide. English. Orion Marketing, Limited, 761 Shell Beach Road, Pismo Beach CA 93449.

LC HE8700.72.U6 P39 **ISSN** 1058-9422
DD 384.55/54 US
... PAY-PER-VIEW REPORT, THE. See Communications-Television and Cable.

LC HC107.A12 P37A **ISSN** 0147-5886
DD 338/.09749 US
PENJERDEL LOCATION & MARKET GUIDE OF THE DELAWARE VALLEY, THE. Main/Corp Penjerdel Corporation. **VAT** Pennsylvania, New Jersey, and Delaware Location and Market Guide of the Delaware Valley. (1973)-. English. One time a year. Greater Philadelphia Chamber of Commerce, 1346 Chestnut Street/Suite 800, Philadelphia PA 19107. **Tel** (215)545-1234.

ISSN 0738-8594
DD 658.81 US
PERSONAL SELLING POWER. Vol.1 (Jan./Feb. 1981)-. Trade Publication. English. Irregular (8 times a year). $38.00. Personal Selling Power Inc, PO Box 5467, 1127 International Parkway, Fredericksburg VA 22403. **Tel** (703)752-7000. **ED** Gerhard Gschwandtner. Index available. **Bk Rev. Ad Acc. Circ:** 130705 (ctrl).
Desc: Sales education and motivation publication designed to improve attitudes and professional selling skills.
Ind/Abst Trade Ind. Index.

LC HF5415.13 .P378 **ISSN** 1051-1806
DD 658.8/005 UK
PERSPECTIVES ON MARKETING MANAGEMENT. (PERSPECTIVES ON MARKETING MANAGEMENT : AN INTERNATIONAL REVIEW.). [Perspect. mark. manage.]. **VFOAT** Marketing Management. (1991)-. Periodical. English. One time a year. $157.43. John Wiley & Sons Ltd., Baffins Lane, Chichester, West Sussex PO19 1UD United Kingdom. **Tel** 011 44 1243 779777, FAX 011 44 1243 776128

BTG:JWP001, telex 86290 WIBOOKG. available on microfilm and microfiche from University Microfilms International (UMI).

ISSN 0741-9643
DD 338 US
CODEN PMMOEH
PETROLEUM MARKETING MONTHLY.
[Pet. mark. mon.]. **Added/Corp** United States. Energy Information Administration. Office of Oil and Gas. **VFOAT** PMM. (April 1983)-. English. Twelve times a year. $94.00. National Energy Information Center, Energy Information Administration, Forrestal Building Room 1F-048, Washington DC 20585. **Tel** (202)586-8800. available on microfiche (Vols. for (1986)- distributed to depository libraries). *Formed by the union of* Prices and Margins of No. 2 Distillate Fuel Oil *and* Monthly Petroleum Product Price Report.
Desc: Provides current information and statistical data on a variety of petroleum products, including motor gasoline, distillants residuals, jet fuel, kerosene, and propane.

ISSN 0721-5665
GW
UDC 615:658.8
PHARMA-MARKETING-JOURNAL. See Pharmacy and Pharmacology.

UK
Pr Rev.
PHARMACEUTICAL MARKETING. See Pharmacy and Pharmacology.

ISSN 1078-6821
DD 384 US
●**PHILLIPS MEDIA GROUP'S INTERACTIVE MARKETING NEWS.**
[Phillips Media Group's interact. mark. news]. **Added/Corp** Phillips Media Group. **VFOAT** Interactive Marketing News. (1994)-. Periodical. English. Twenty-four times a year. $495.00. Phillips Business Information Inc., 1201 Seven Locks Road, PO Box 61130, Potomac MD 20854. **Tel** (301)424-3338, (301)340-1520, (800)777-5005, FAX (301)424-4297, telex 358149. *Absorbed* Libey Direct Marketing Letter; Interactive Marketplace Regulatory Handbook *and* Publishing Trends and Trendsetters.

ISSN 0724-9632
GW
UDC 658.8.012.1
PLANUNG UND ANALYSE. [Plan. Anal.]. (1983)-. Periodical. German. Six times a year. DM146.10. Deutscher Fachverlag GmbH, Verlagsgruppe, D-60264 Frankfurt Germany. **Tel** 011 49 69 75951001, telex 411 862. *Continues* Interview und Analyse, 0343-9690.

ISSN 0277-0415
US
PLATT'S OIL MARKETING BULLETIN.
[Platt's oil mark. bull.]. **VFOAT** Oil Marketing Bulletin. Vol. 21, No. 10 (March 9, 1981)-. Bulletin. English. One time a week. $269.00. McGraw Hill Publishing Company, Inc., 1221 Avenue of the Americas, New York NY 10020. **Tel** (212)512-6410, (800)525-5003, FAX (212)512-6111. *Continues* NPN Bulletin, 0027-6901.
Ind/Abst Pet. Energy Bus. News Index (1983-1991).

ISSN 0150-1844
FR
UDC 658.82
POINTS DE VENTE PARIS. [Points vente Paris]. (1962)-. Periodical. French. Forty-four times a year. $229.66. Liaisons & Convergence, 1 Avenue East Belin, F-92856 Rueil Mal France. **Tel** 011 33 1 41299872, FAX 011 33 1 47575420, telex 613128.
Ind/Abst Infomat Int. Bus.

ISSN 0711-2998
DD 381/.45728/90971 CN
POOL & SPA MARKETING. [Pool spa mark.].
VFOAT Canadian Pool & Spa Marketing. **VAT** Canadian Pool & Spa Marketing (1981); Pool and Spa Marketing; Canadian Pool and Spa Marketing (1981). Vol. 5, No. 1 (Apr. 1981)-. Trade Publication. English. Seven times a year. 16.01Can$. Hubbard Marketing, 270 Esna Park Drive, Unit 12, Markham L3R 1H3 Canada. **Tel** (416)513-0090, FAX (416)513-1377. **ED** David Barnsley. **Bk Rev,** (Qty: 2). **Ad Acc, Adv Mgr** Andree Lapierre. **Circ:** 8,000 (ctrl). *Continues* Canadian Pool & Spa Marketing, 0227-3330.

ISSN 0711-3005
DD 381/.45728/90971 CN
POOL & SPA MARKETING. SUPPLEMENT. [Pool spa mark., Suppl.]. **VAT** Canadian Pool & Spa Marketing (1981. Supplement). Vol. 5, No. 1 (Apr. 1981)-. Periodical. English. Hubbard Marketing, 270 Esna Park Drive, Unit 12, Markham L3R 1H3 Canada.

ISSN 0269-2333
NE
CCC
NLM W1; PO958P
POST-MARKETING SURVEILLANCE.
(198?)-. Periodical. English (summaries and/or abstracts in Italian). Four times a year (1 volume). Fl458.00. John Wiley & Sons Ltd., Baffins Lane, Chichester, West Sussex PO19 1UD United Kingdom. **Tel** 011 44 1243 779777, FAX 011 44 1243 776128 BTG:JWP001, telex 86290 WIBOOKG. available on microfilm from University Microfilms International (UMI).
Desc: Publishes reports on post-marketing investigations into new medicines particularly those resistant to widespread long-term use.
Ind/Abst EMBASE.

ISSN 0032-5619
US
CCC
POTENTIALS IN MARKETING. (19??)-.
Trade Publication. English. Eleven times a year. $24.00. Lakewood Publications, 50 South Ninth Street, Minneapolis MN 55402. **Tel** (612)333-0471, (800)328-4329, FAX (612)333-6526. **ED** Catherine Eberlein. **Ad Acc. Circ:** 67,204 (ctrl). available on microfilm and microfiche from University Microfilms International (UMI). *Absorbed* Marketing Communications (United Business Publications), 0164-4343.
Desc: Directed toward the professional interests of marketing, sales, advertising, promotion and general management executives. It is designed to inform, instruct, and communicate information on products and services of value in achieving marketing goals.
Ind/Abst Acad. Search; Bus. Source Plus; Bus. Source; EP Collect.; Gen. Period. Index (1989-); Homework Help; INFO-SOUTH Abstr.; Mag. Search; Mark. Advert. Ref. Serv.; MasterFile FullTEXT 1000; MasterFile FullTEXT 350; MasterFile FullTEXT 650; MasterFile FullTEXT (July 1993-); OCLC; Telebase; Trade Ind. ASAP [Full Txt.]; Trade Ind. Index [Full Txt.].

ISSN 1042-9581
US
POWER REPORT ON AUTOMOTIVE MARKETING, THE. See Transportation-Automobiles.

ISSN 0262-5849
DD 636 UK
PPM. PET PRODUCT MARKETING. See Animal Welfare-Pets.

LC HF **ISSN** 0961-8333
DD 658 UK
TITLE CHANGE
PRACTICE MARKETING. [Pr. mark.].
(1991)-(1993). Periodical. English. Ten times a year. Lafferty Publications Ltd., Tower Ida Centre Pearse Street, Dublin 2 Ireland. **Tel** 011 353 1 6718022, FAX 011 353 1 718520. **(Subscription address:** Lafferty Publications, 1422 West Peachtree Street, Suite 800, Atlanta GA 30309. **Tel** (404)636-6610.) **ED** Lisa Jaffe. *Continued by* Practice Marketing International (Dublin), 0791-914X.

LC HF **ISSN** 0791-914X
DD 658 IE
PRACTICE MARKETING INTERNATIONAL (DUBLIN). [Pract. mark. int. Dublin]. (1993)-. Periodical. English. Ten times a year. $599.00. Lafferty Publications Ltd., Tower Ida Centre Pearse Street, Dublin 2 Ireland. **Tel** 011 353 1 6718022, FAX 011 353 1 718520. **ED** Lisa Jaffe. *Continues* Practice Marketing, 0961-8333.

ISSN 0748-4755
US
CODEN PRADER
PRICING ADVISOR, THE. Added/Corp Profit & Price Consulting (Firm). (198?)-. Periodical. English. Twelve times a year. $195.00. The Pricing Advisor, 3277 Roswell Road/Suite 620, Atlanta GA 30305. **Tel** (404)252-5708, FAX (404)252-0637. **(Subscription address:** Pricing Advisor, Subscription Office, PO Box 1831, Birmingham AL 35201-1831. **Tel** (800)633-4931, (205)995-1567 (outside US and Canada), FAX (205)995-1588.) **ED** Eric Mitchell.
Desc: Contains pricing solutions, principles and practical answers. Informs subscribers of emerging competitive pricing practices and new product positioning strategies.

UK
PRICING STRATEGY AND PRACTICE.
(19??)-. English. Three times a year. $199.00. MCB University Press, 60 62 Toller Lane, Bradford, West Yorkshire BD8 9BY United Kingdom. **Tel** 011 44 1274 785280, FAX 011 44 1274 785200, telex 51317-MCBUNI-G. **(Subscription address:** MCB University Press / US and Canada Subscriptions, PO Box 10812, Birmingham AL 35201-0812. **Tel** (205)995-1567, (800)633-4931, FAX (205)995-1588.)

ISSN 0092-2633
US
PROCEEDINGS - NATIONAL PEACH COUNCIL. (PROCEEDINGS, ANNUAL CONVENTION - NATIONAL PEACH COUNCIL.). [Proc. -

Nat. Peach Counc.]. **Main/Corp** National Peach Council. (19??)-. Proceedings. English. One time a year. $15.00. National Peach Council, Box 11280, Columbia SC 29211. **Tel** (803)253-4036. **ED** Lillie Hoover-Largent. **Circ:** 300 (ctrl). ***Supersedes in part*** *National Peach Council Annual, 0092-3036.*
Desc: Speaker presentations regarding production and marketing of fresh peaches.
Ind/Abst AGRICOLA.

US
PROCEEDINGS - SOUTHERN MARKETING ASSOCIATION. **Main/Corp** Southern Marketing Association. (1974)-. Proceedings. English. One time a year (November). $20.00. Houston Baptist University, 7502 Fondren Road, Houston TX 77074. **Tel** (713)995-3306, FAX (713)995-3408. Index available. cum. index. **Circ:** 650 (ctrl).
Desc: Publication of scholarly papers presented at the annual Southern Marketing Association conference.

LC HD52.5 .P753
DD 658.7/2 UK
PROCUREMENT. **Added/Corp** Institute of Purchasing and Supply. (19??)-. Newsletter. English. One time a week. £44.00, $39.00 (agent), £10.00 (airmail) Europe; £20.00 (airmail) other. Chartered Institute of Purchasing and Supply, Easton House, Easton on the Hill, Stamford Lincolnshire PE9 3NZ United Kingdom. **Tel** 011 44 1780 56777, FAX 011 44 1780 51610, telex 32251. **ED** Alexis Nolan. **Ad Acc. Circ:** 1,826. ***Supersedes*** *Purchasing Journal.*
Desc: News of purchasing legislation, company developments, commodity price trends, contract lenders, training courses, overseas trade forecasts, UK trade trends.

ISSN 0740-3801
US
CCC
PRODUCT ALERT. **Added/Corp** Marketing Intelligence Service Ltd. (19??)-. English. Fifty-one times per year. $695.00. Marketing Intelligence Service Ltd., 6473D Route 64, Naples NY 14512. **Tel** (716)374-6326, (800)836-5710, FAX (714)374-5217, telex 469979. **ED** Diane Beach and Pat Peck. Index available. available on an online database (files 16,570,636/Full-Text) from DIALOG.
Desc: Briefing on North American packaged goods introductions. Aims to help companies make informed decisions about the development, distribution and test marketing of new products and how to defend existing entries from new products. Product descriptions include detailed packaging information, key ingredients, other label copy and retail price.
Ind/Abst Mark. Advert. Ref. Serv. [Full Txt.]; PROMT [Full Txt.]; PTS Newsl. Database [Full Txt.].

LC HD9999.C273 U626 **ISSN** 0191-6823
DD 338.4/7629287 US
CCC
PROFESSIONAL CARWASHING. Vol. 1, No. 1 (Oct. 1976)-. Periodical. English. Twelve times a year. $42.00. National Trade Publications, 13 Century Hill Drive, Latham NY 12110. **Tel** (518)783-1281, FAX (518)783-1386. **ED** Steve Kare. **Ad Acc. Circ:** 17,000 (ctrl).
Desc: Technical sales and marketing information to professional vehicle washing owners, operators and managers. Reports industry developments and special interest stories.

US
PROFESSIONAL TELEPHONE SELLING. English. Twenty-four times a year. $96.00 (add $15.96 postage and handling). Bureau of Business Practice, 24 Rope Ferry Road, Waterford CT 06386. **Tel** (800)243-0876, (203)442-4365, (800)876-9105, FAX (203)443-1123. Index available. cum. index.
Desc: Edited for professional telephone salespeople, telemarketers and other salespeople who use the phone as part of their overall sales strategy.

ISSN 1040-7480
DD 658 US
NLM W1; PR623K
PROFILES IN HEALTHCARE MARKETING. [Profiles healthc. mark.]. No. 29 (1st Quarter 1988)-. Periodical. English. Six times a year. $239.00. Wentworth Publishing Company, 1866 Colonial Village Lane, Lancaster PA 17605. **Tel** (800)331-5196, (717)393-1000, FAX (717)393-5752. **(Subscription address:** Wentworth Publishing Co., PO Box 10488, Lancaster PA 17605. **)** Index available (bound in all issues). ***Continues*** *Profiles in Hospital Marketing, 0275-9632.*
Ind/Abst Healthcare Leader. Rev.; Hosp. Health Admin. Index (1988-); Int. Nurs. Index.

LC HD9321.3 .P75 **ISSN** 0079-6921
DD 658.8/09/664002573 US
PROGRESSIVE GROCER'S MARKETING GUIDEBOOK. **VFOAT** Marketing Guidebook. (1967)-. English. One time a year. $352.00. Progressive Grocer, 263 Tresser Boulevard, Stamford CT 06901. **Tel** (203)977-7640, FAX (203)977-7645.
Desc: Directory of grocery chains and wholesalers headquartered in USA. Includes names, addresses, sales, number of stores, brokers, and other detailed market data.

ISSN 1047-1707
DD 659 US
PROMO (DANBURY, CONN.). (PROMO.). [PROMO]. (1987)-. Periodical. English. Twelve times a year. $59.00. Smith Communications, 50 Washington Street, 8th Floor, Norwalk CT 06854. **Tel** (203)831-5400.

ISSN 1046-8447
DD 380 US
PROMO NEWS. [Promo news]. **VFOAT** Promonews. (Nov. 1987)-. Periodical. English. Twelve times a year. $295.00. Promonews, 12300 Parc Crest Drive, Suite 184, Stafford TX 77477. **Tel** (713) 983-5500, FAX (713) 983-9329. **ED** Patrick Henry. ***Continues*** *Patrick Henry Creative Promotions Promonews.*

ISSN 0742-6046
DD 658 US
CCC
PSYCHOLOGY & MARKETING. [Psychol. mark.]. **VFOAT** Psychology and Marketing. Vol. 1, No. 1 (Spring 1984)-. Periodical. English. Eight times a year. $432.00. John Wiley & Sons, Inc., 605 Third Avenue, New York NY 10158-0012. **Tel** (212)850-6000, (212)850-6645, FAX (212)850-6088, telex 12-7063. **(Subscription address:** John Wiley & Sons / UK, Baffins Lane, Chichester, West Sussex PO19 1UD United Kingdom. **Tel** 011 44 1243 779777, FAX 011 44 243 776128, telex 86290 WIBOOKG.**)** **ED** Ronald Jay Cohen. available on microfilm and microfiche from University Microfilms International (UMI).
Desc: Contains social, economic and cultural trends that affect marketing decisions. Provides psychological profiles of potential customers, studies of change in consumer personalities and behavior, brief psychological reports, and gives attention to industrial and organizational psychology, market or polling research and clinical mental health.
Ind/Abst Acad. Search; Bus. Period. Index; Commun. Abstr.; Curr. Cit.; EP Collect.; Homework Help.; INFO-SOUTH Abstr.; Mag. Search; MasterFile FullTEXT 1000; MasterFile FullTEXT 350; MasterFile FullTEXT 650; MasterFile FullTEXT (July 1993-); OCLC; Psychol. Abstr. (1988-); PsycINFO (1990-); PsycLit; Soc. Sci. Source; Telebase; Wilson Bus. Abstr.

LC HF5813.I8 P815
IT
PUBBLICITA ITALIA. See Business and Economics-Advertising and Public Relations.

LC KF911.A3 P87 **ISSN** 0898-994X
DD 346.73/072/05 347.3067205 US
CCC
PURCHASER'S LEGAL ADVISER. See Law.

LC HF5001 .P8 **ISSN** 0033-4448
DD 658.7/2/05 US
CCC
PURCHASING (1936). (PURCHASING.). [Purchasing]. (Apr. 1936)-. Trade Publication. English. Nineteen times a year. $89.95. Cahners Publishing Company, 249 West 17th Street, New York NY 10011. **Tel** (212)645-0067, FAX (212)242-6987. **(Subscription address:** Cahners Publishing Company / Colorado, Paid Subscription Service Center, PO Box 7610, Highlands Ranch CO 80126-7610. **Tel** (303)470-4466, FAX (303)470-4691.**)** **ED** James P. Morgan. available on microfilm and microfiche from University Microfilms International (UMI). Documents available from UMI Article Clearinghouse, Ask*IEEE. ***Continues*** *Executive Purchaser.* ***Continued in part by*** *Purchasing (CPI Edition), 0746-9020.*
Desc: Provides price and market forecasts on industrial products, components and materials, office products, business systems and transportation. Also reports latest procurement tactics, technologies and techniques-how the brightest buy.
Ind/Abst ABI/INFORM Glob. Ed.; ABI/INFORM [Computer File] (Sept. 1971-Oct. 1973); Acad. Search; Bus. Index (1985-); Bus. Period. Index; Curr. Cit.; EP Collect.; Gen. BusinessFile (1985-); Gen. Period. Index (1985-); Homework Help.; INFO-SOUTH Abstr.; INSPEC (July 1984-); Mag. Search; MasterFile FullTEXT 1000; MasterFile FullTEXT 350; MasterFile FullTEXT 650; MasterFile FullTEXT (July 1993-); OCLC; Telebase; Trade Ind. ASAP [Full Txt.]; Trade Ind. Index (1981-) [Full Txt.]; Vocat. Search; Wilson Bus. Abstr.

LC HD52.5 .P753 **ISSN** 0309-7242
DD 658.7/2/05 UK
PURCHASING & SUPPLY MANAGEMENT. **Added/Corp** Institute of Purchasing and Supply. **VFOAT** Purchasing and Supply Management. (May 1977)-. Periodical. English. Twelve times a year. $111.23. Chartered Institute of Purchasing and Supply, Easton House, Easton on the Hill, Stamford Lincolnshire PE9 3NZ United Kingdom. **Tel** 011 44 1780 56777, FAX 011 44 1780 51610, telex 32251. **ED** Sam Tulip. Index available. **Bk Rev. Ad Acc. Circ:** 18,500. ***Continues*** *Purchasing and Supply.*
Desc: International news and research on purchasing, inventory and materials management in business and the public sector.
Ind/Abst Curr. Cit.; Manage. Market. Abstr.; Women Manage. Rev. [Full Txt.].

US
PURCHASING EXECUTIVE'S BULLETIN. (19??)-. Bulletin. English. Twenty-four times a year. $136.68 (US); $165.72 (Canada). Bureau of Business Practice, 24 Rope Ferry Road, Waterford CT 06386. **Tel** (800)243-0876, (203)442-4365, (800)876-9105, FAX (203)443-1123.

ISSN 0841-615X
DD 658.7/2/0971 CN
PURCHASING MANAGEMENT. [Purch. manage.]. **VFOAT** PM. Vol. 12, Issue 1 (Dec./Jan. 1987/1988)-. Periodical. English. Six times a year (Jan., Mar., May, June, Sept., Nov.). 12.00Can$ Canada; 30.00Can$ US; 72.00Can$ others. Bruce County Education Board, PO Box 190, 1st Avenue North, Chesley Ontario N0G 1LO Canada. **Tel** (519)363-2014. **ED** Kevin Paterson. **Ad Acc. Circ:** 20,000 (ctrl). ***Continues*** *Purchasing Management Digest, 0700-8007.*
Desc: A combination of regular columns and feature articles covering purchasing methods, practices and law, computer-based purchasing and transportation.

LC HF5437 **ISSN** 1062-5860
DD 658.7 US
PURCHASING PERFORMANCE BENCHMARKS FOR THE NONFERROUS METALS INDUSTRY. **Added/Corp** Center for Advanced Purchasing Studies (Tempe, Ariz.). (1992)-. English. $20.00. Center for Advanced Purchasing Studies, PO Box 22160, Tempe AZ 85285. **Tel** (602)752-2277.

ISSN 1058-434X
DD 658 US
PURCHASING PERFORMANCE BENCHMARKS FOR THE U.S. AEROSPACE/DEFENSE CONTRACTING INDUSTRY / CAPS, CENTER FOR ADVANCED PURCHASING STUDIES. [Purch. perform. benchmarks U.S. aerosp./def. contract. ind.]. **Added/Corp** Center for Advanced Purchasing Studies (Tempe, Ariz.). **VFOAT** Purchasing Performance Benchmarks. (1991)-. English. Free. Center for Advanced Purchasing Studies, PO Box 22160, Tempe AZ 85285. **Tel** (602)752-2277.

ISSN 1062-2063
US
PURCHASING PERFORMANCE BENCHMARKS FOR THE U.S. APPLIANCE INDUSTRY. **Added/Corp** Center for Advanced Purchasing Studies (Tempe, Ariz.). **VFOAT** Purchasing Performance Benchmarks. (1992)-. Periodical. English. $20.00 (single issue). Center for Advanced Purchasing Studies, PO Box 22160, Tempe AZ 85285. **Tel** (602)752-2277.

ISSN 1057-7351
DD 658 US
PURCHASING PERFORMANCE BENCHMARKS FOR THE U.S. FOOD MANUFACTURING INDUSTRY. (PURCHASING PERFORMANCE BENCHMARKS FOR THE U.S. FOOD MANUFACTURING INDUSTRY.). [Purch. perform. benchmarks U.S. food manuf. ind.]. **Added/Corp** Center for Advanced Purchasing Studies (Tempe, Ariz.). **VFOAT** Purchasing Performance Benchmarks. (1991)-. English. $300.00. Center for Advanced Purchasing Studies, PO Box 22160, Tempe AZ 85285. **Tel** (602)752-2277.

ISSN 1058-1251
DD 658 US
PURCHASING PERFORMANCE BENCHMARKS FOR THE U.S. TRANSPORTATION INDUSTRY. [Purch. perform. benchmarks U.S. transp. ind.]. **Added/Corp** Center for Advanced Purchasing Studies (Tempe, Ariz.). **VFOAT** Purchasing Performance Benchmarks. (1991)-. English. Free. National Association of Purchasing Management, 2055 East Centennial Circle, PO Box 22160, Tempe AZ 85285-2160.

ISSN 0317-6363
DD 658.8/38/621860971 CN
PURCHASING PREFERENCE SURVEY : MATERIALS HANDLING EQUIPMENT. 1975-. English. Maclean Hunter Canada / Montreal, 1001 bvd. de Maisonneuve W., Montreal Quebec H3A 3E1 Canada. **Tel** (514)845-5141, FAX (514)845-4302, telex 055-60604.

Business and Economics —Marketing and Purchasing

ISSN 0317-6339
DD 658.8/38/65120971   CN
PURCHASING PREFERENCE SURVEY : OFFICE EQUIPMENT AND SUPPLIES.
See Business and Economics-Office Equipment and Services.

ISSN 0317-6347
DD 658.8/38/38050971   CN
PURCHASING PREFERENCE SURVEY : TRAFFIC/TRANSPORTATION. 1975-. English. One time a year. Maclean Hunter Canada / Montreal, 1001 bvd. de Maisonneuve W., Montreal Quebec H3A 3E1 Canada. **Tel** (514)845-5141, FAX (514)845-4302, telex 055-60604.

ISSN 0191-9237
US
PURCHASOR, NEW YORK STATE. VFOAT Purchasor. Periodical. English. Twelve times a year. Sandy Robinson, 6650 Old Collamer Road, East Syracuse NY 13057.

ISSN 1077-4769
DD 384   US
●**PYRAMID RESEARCH AFRICA/MIDDLE EAST.** (PYRAMID RESEARCH AFRICA/MIDDLE EAST : AN ANALYSIS OF TELECOM MARKETS IN AFRICA AND THE MIDDLE EAST.). [Pyramid Res. Afr./Middle East]. **Added/Corp** Pyramid Research (Firm). **VFOAT** Pyramid Research Africa, Middle East; Africa/Middle East; Africa, Middle East. (1994)-. Periodical. English. Twelve times a year. $595.00. Pyramid Research Inc., 14 Arrow Street, Cambridge MA 02138. **Tel** (617)868-4725.

LC HF5410   **ISSN** 1352-2752
DD 658.8   UK
●**QUALITATIVE MARKET RESEARCH JOURNAL.** (1994)-. Academic Scholarly Publication. English. Three times a year. $119.95. MCB University Press, 60 62 Toller Lane, Bradford, West Yorkshire BD8 9BY United Kingdom. **Tel** 011 44 1274 785280, FAX 011 44 1274 785200, telex 51317-MCBUNI-G. (**Subscription address:** MCB University Press / US and Canada Subscriptions, PO Box 10812, Birmingham AL 35201-0812. **Tel** (205)995-1567, (800)633-4931, FAX (205)995-1588.) **ED** David Carson.

LC WMLC 93/1922   **ISSN** 0893-7451
DD 659   US
CODEN QMREEN
QUIRK'S MARKETING RESEARCH REVIEW. [Quirk's mark. res. rev.]. **VFOAT** Marketing Research Review. (1986)-. Trade Publication. English. Ten times a year. $50.00. Quirk Enterprises, PO Box 23536, Minneapolis MN 55423. **Tel** (612)854-5101, FAX (612)854-8191. **ED** Joseph Rydholm. Index available (bound in Jan. issue). **Bk Rev**, (Qty: 3). **Ad Acc**, **Adv Mgr:** Evan Tweed. **Circ:** 16,000 (ctrl).
Desc: Articles and case histories related to marketing research.
Ind/Abst PROMT; PTS Newsl. Database [Full Txt.].

ISSN 0767-3701
FR
UDC 658.8.012.1   CCC
RECHERCHE ET APPLICATIONS EN MARKETING. [Rech. appl. mark.]. **VFOAT** R.A.M. Recherche et Applications en Marketing. (1986)-. Periodical. French. Four times a year. $104.98. Presses Universite de Grenoble, BP 47, 38040 Grenoble, Cedex 9 France. **Tel** 011 33 76 825651, 011 33 76 825652.
Ind/Abst Selec. Coop. Index Manage. Period.

LC HD2745 .D85   **ISSN** 0735-6498
DD 658.4/0025/73   US
REFERENCE BOOK OF CORPORATE MANAGEMENTS. See Business and Economics-Management.

LC HD
DD 338   US
REGIONAL FIRMS' RETAIL SALES MANAGEMENT REPORT. (19??)-. English. Four times a year. $600.00. Securities Industry Association, 120 Broadway/35th Floor, New York NY 10271. **Tel** (212)608-1500, FAX (212)608-1604.
Desc: Through this service, participating regional firms receive data that enables them to compare their sales effectiveness with other firms. The reports include rankings and averages on such benchmark elements as revenues by product line, revenues per RR, new accounts, and much more. Confidentiality is preserved.

LC HF5068.W3 C36   **ISSN** 1042-5489
DD 381/.45/000294753   US
REGIONAL INDUSTRIAL BUYING GUIDE. CAPITAL CITIES. See Industry and Production.

LC HF3161.P4 G73   **ISSN** 1042-5497
DD 381/.45/0002947486   US
REGIONAL INDUSTRIAL BUYING GUIDE. GREATER ALLEGHENY. See Industry and Production.

LC HF3151 .G73   **ISSN** 1042-5500
DD 381/.45/000294749   US
REGIONAL INDUSTRIAL BUYING GUIDE. GREATER DELAWARE VALLEY. See Industry and Production.

LC HF3163.N7 G73   **ISSN** 1042-5519
DD 381/.45/0002947471   US
REGIONAL INDUSTRIAL BUYING GUIDE. GREATER NEW YORK. See Industry and Production.

LC HD9727.I3 N67   **ISSN** 1042-5527
DD 381/.45/00029477   US
REGIONAL INDUSTRIAL BUYING GUIDE. NORTH CENTRAL TRI-STATE. See Industry and Production.

LC HF5065.O3 N67   **ISSN** 1042-5551
DD 381/.45/000294771   US
REGIONAL INDUSTRIAL BUYING GUIDE. NORTHERN OHIO. See Industry and Production.

LC HD9727.A11 W47   **ISSN** 1042-5586
DD 381/.45/00029/474   US
REGIONAL INDUSTRIAL BUYING GUIDE. WESTERN NEW ENGLAND. See Industry and Production.

US
REHAB PURCHASING GUIDE. VFOAT RPG Rehab Purchasing Guide. (1983)-. English. IMS Communications Inc, 426 Pennsylvania Avenue, Fort Washington PA 19034. **Tel** (215)628-4920. *Continues Green Pages Rehab Sourcebook.*

US
CEASED
REHABILITATION & HEALTHCARE MARKETING. (19??)-(Nov. 1994). English. Lafon Management & Consultant, PO Box 1767, Lake Arrowhead CA 92353. **Tel** (909)337-0745, FAX (909)337-1624.

ISSN 0034-4524
DD 338   US
RENTAL EQUIPMENT REGISTER. (RENTAL EQUIPMENT REGISTER : RER.). [Rent. equip. regist.]. **VFOAT** RER. (1956)-. Periodical. English. Twelve times a year. $75.00. Miramar Publishing Company / California, 23815 Stuart Ranch Road, Malibu CA 90265. **Tel** (310)337-9717, (800)543-4116. **ED** Tim Nobolselski. **Ad Acc. Circ:** 13,654 (ctrl).
Desc: Business news magazine for firms engaged in the rental of construction contractor equipment, trucks, trailers and tools.

IT
REPERTORIO LE SOCIETA. (19??)-. Periodical. Italian. Three times a year. IPSOA Editore SRL, Casella Postale 12055, Mastrangelo, 20120 Milan Italy. **Tel** 011 39 2 82476248. Index available (Included).

LC HF5410   **ISSN** 0733-5733
DD 380.1   US
REPORT / MARKETING SCIENCE INSTITUTE. [Rep. - Mark. Sci. Inst.]. **Added/Corp** Marketing Science Institute. **VFOAT** MSI Report; Working Paper; Technical Working Paper; Research Program; Special Report; Technical Report; Preliminary Research Paper; Report. (19??)-. Monographic series. English. Price varies per volume. Marketing Science Institute, 1000 Massachusetts Avenue, Cambridge MA 02138. **Tel** (617)491-2060.
Ind/Abst Curr. Cit.

ISSN 0196-9382
US
REPORT ON REPORTS. [Rep. rep.]. Periodical. English. Four times a year. Free to subscribers of Marketing Executive's Digest, $48.00 other. Sales and Marketing Management, 633 3rd Avenue, New York NY 10017.

ISSN 8755-3511
DD 384   US
REPORT ON TELCO MARKETING, THE. See Communications-Telecommunication.

ISSN 0731-6097
US
REPORTER - CHICAGO REGIONAL MARKETING AREA. (REPORTER - CHICAGO REGIONAL MARKETING AREA.). [Report. - Chicago Reg. Mark. Area.]. **Main/Corp** Chicago Regional Marketing Area. Vol 1. (Aug. 1968)-. Periodical. English. Twelve times a year. Chicago Regional Marketing Area, 800 Roosevelt Road, Building A Suite 200, Glen Ellyn IL 60137. **Tel** (312)858-8400.

LC HF5415.3 .R4   **ISSN** 0885-2111
DD 658.8/342/05   US
RESEARCH IN CONSUMER BEHAVIOR. [Res. consum. behav.]. Vol. 1 (1985)-. English. One time a year. $73.25. JAI Press Inc., 55 Old Post Road, Suite 2, PO Box 1678, Greenwich CT 06836-1678. **Tel** (203)661-7602, FAX (203)661-0792. **ED** Janeen Costa and Russell Belk.

LC HF5415.2 .R434   **ISSN** 0191-3026
DD 658.8/005   US
RESEARCH IN MARKETING. [Res. mark.]. Vol. 1 (1978)-. Monographic series. English. One time a year. $73.25. JAI Press Inc., 55 Old Post Road, Suite 2, PO Box 1678, Greenwich CT 06836-1678. **Tel** (203)661-7602, FAX (203)661-0792. **ED** Jagdish N. Sheth.
Ind/Abst Acad. Search; Bus. Index (1986-); EP Collect.; Gen. BusinessFile (1986-); Gen. Period. Index (1986-); Homework Help.; INFO-SOUTH Abstr.; Mag. Search; MasterFile FullTEXT 1000; MasterFile FullTEXT 350; MasterFile FullTEXT 650; MasterFile FullTEXT (July 1993-); OCLC; Psychol. Abstr. (1982-); PsycINFO (?-?); PsycLit; Telebase; Trade Ind. Index.

US
RESEARCH IN MARKETING. SUPPLEMENT. (1982)-. Monographic series. English. Irregular. $63.50. JAI Press Inc., 55 Old Post Road, Suite 2, PO Box 1678, Greenwich CT 06836-1678. **Tel** (203)661-7602, FAX (203)661-0792. **ED** Jagdish N. Sheth.

ISSN 0712-7243
DD 070.5/72/0688   CN
CEASED
RESOURCE-MAG. See Publishing-Serial Publications.

LC HF5429.6.G7 R43
UK
TITLE CHANGE
RETAIL BUSINESS. MARKET REPORTS. See Business and Economics-Retail.

LC HF5429.6.G7 R47
DD 381.1   UK
RETAIL BUSINESS. RETAIL TRADE REVIEWS. See Business and Economics-Retail.

LC HD2951 .C6387
DD 658.8/7/00941   UK
CEASED
RETAIL MARKETING & MANAGEMENT. **VFOAT** Retail Marketing and Management. Vol. 14, No. 1 (July 1988)-Vol. 21, No. 1 (1995). Trade Publication. English. Twelve times a year. $104.38. Cooperative Press Ltd., 418 Chester Road, Manchester M16 9HP United Kingdom. **Tel** 011 44 161 8722991, FAX 011 44 161 8726366. *Continues Coop Marketing & Management, 0307-8604.*

US
RETAIL SALES AND MARKETING IDEA EXCHANGE. (19??)-. English. Three times a year. $50.00. Securities Industry Association, 120 Broadway/35th Floor, New York NY 10271. **Tel** (212)608-1500, FAX (212)608-1604.
Desc: A compilation of successful sales and marketing ideas submitted by industry practitioners. Available to those who contribute a viable idea.

ISSN 0192-9151
US
RETAILER AND MARKETING NEWS. (19??)-. Periodical. English. Twelve times a year. $36.00. Retailer and Marketing News, PO Box 191105, Dallas TX 75207. **Tel** (214)871-2930. **ED** Michael J. Anderson. **Ad Acc. Circ:** 8,000 (ctrl).
Desc: Retailing and marketing news and all aspects of business.

FR
REVUE DES MARCHES PUBLICS. French. Documentation Francaise, 29 quai Voltaire, 75344 Paris Cedex 7 France. **Tel** 011 33 1 40157000, FAX 011 33 1 40157230, telex 204 826 DOCFRAN.

ISSN 0035-3051
FR
REVUE FRANCAISE DU MARKETING. [Rev. fr. mark.]. **VFOAT** Cahiers de l'Adetem. (1964)-. Periodical. French. Five times a year. $193.34. Adetem, 221 rue la Fayette, 75010 Paris France. **Tel** 011 33 1 40389710, FAX (1) 40 38 05 08. **ED** J. Boss. Index available. **Bk Rev. Ad Acc. Circ:** 3,000 (ctrl). Documents available from UMI Article Clearinghouse.
Desc: Covers marketing strategy and communication. High-level articles about research, strategy and action in marketing.
Ind/Abst ABI/INFORM Glob. Ed.; ABI/INFORM [Computer File] (Jan. 1982-); Contents Pages Manage.; Manage. Market. Abstr.; Selec. Coop. Index Manage. Period.

Business and Economics —Marketing and Purchasing

ISSN 8755-5654
DD 380 US
SALES & MARKETING ANALYSIS. VFOAT
Sales and Marketing Analysis; S&MM, Sales & Marketing Analysis; S & MM, Sales and Marketing Analysis; S. & M.M., Sales and Marketing Analysis. Vol. 1 (Apr. 1981)-. Periodical. English. Six times a year. $48.00. Sales and Marketing Management, 633 3rd Avenue, New York NY 10017.

LC HF5438 .A34 **ISSN** 0163-7517
DD 658.8/005 US
CCC
SALES & MARKETING MANAGEMENT.
[Sales mark. manage.]. **VFOAT** Sales and Marketing Management; S & MM; S and MM; Sales and Marketing Management Special Report; Sales & Marketing Management Special Report. Vol. 115, No. 9 (Nov. 17, 1975)-. Periodical. English. Twelve times a year. $48.00. Bill Communications Inc., 355 Park Avenue South, New York NY 10010-1789. **Tel** (800)360-5200, (212)592-6200, FAX (212)592-6209. **ED** A.J. Vogl. **Bk Rev. Ad Acc. Circ:** 52,000. available on microfilm and microfiche from University Microfilms International (UMI); available on an online database (files 15,647,648/Full-Text) from DIALOG. Documents available from UMI Article Clearinghouse, Ask*IEEE. **Continues** Sales Management, 0885-9019.
Desc: News, features, and data of interest to sales and marketing executives in all sectors of business and industry.
Ind/Abst ABI/INFORM Glob. Ed.; ABI/INFORM Ondisc: Expr. Ed.; ABI/INFORM [Computer File] (Nov. 1975-); Acad. Search; Anbar Account. Finan. Abstr. [Full Txt.]; Anbar Mark. Distr. Abstr. [Full Txt.]; Anbar Top Manage. Abstr. [Full Txt.]; Bus. ASAP (1990-) [Full Txt.]; Bus. Index (1985-); Bus. Period. Index; Bus. Source Plus; Bus. Source; Contents Pages Manage.; Curr. Cit.; EP Collect.; F&S Index Plus Text, Int. [Select. Cov.]; Gen. BusinessFile (1985-); Gen. Period. Index (1985-); Homework Help.; INFO-SOUTH Abstr.; Infobank (1979-); INSPEC (Aug. 1984-); Mag. ASAP Plus [Full Txt.]; Mag. Index Plus (1989-); Mag. Search; Manage. Market. Abstr.; Manage. Bibliogr. Rev.; Mark. Advert. Ref. Serv.; MasterFile FullTEXT 1000; MasterFile FullTEXT 350; MasterFile FullTEXT 650; MasterFile FullTEXT (Jan. 1994-); Newsp. Period. Abstr. (1989-); OCLC; Oper. Prod. Manage. Abstr. [Full Txt.]; Person. Inform. Abstr. [Full Txt.]; PROMT; Telebase; Mag. Index (1977-); Topicator; Trade Ind. ASAP [Full Txt.]; Trade Ind. Index (1981-) [Full Txt.]; UMI ABI/Inform--Bus. Period. Ondisc (Nov. 1987-) [Full Txt.]; Urban Aff. Abstr.; Vocat. Search; Wilson Bus. Abstr.; Women Manage. Rev. [Full Txt.].

ISSN 1064-4466
US
SALES & MARKETING ONE HUNDRED NEWSLETTER. VFOAT Sales and Marketing One Hundred Newsletter; Sales & Marketing 100 Newsletter. (1992)-. Newsletter. English. Twelve times a year. $69.00. Kingspoint Company, 10610 Morado Circle, Suite 1302, Austin TX 78759. **Tel** (512)794-0944.

LC HG1616.M3 S25 **ISSN** 1060-2860
DD 332.1/0973/021 US
SALES & MARKETING SURVEY / SHESHUNOFF. [Sales mark. surv.]. **Added/Corp** Sheshunoff Information Services. **VFOAT** Sales and Marketing Survey; Sheshunoff Sales and Marketing Survey; Sheshunoff Sales & Marketing Survey. (1991)-. English. Sheshunoff Information Services Inc., PO Box 13203, Capitol Station, Austin TX 78711. **Tel** (800)456-2340, (512)472-2244.

LC HF5410
DD 380.1 CN
●**SALES FORCE.** (1994)-. English. Eight times a year. 38.00Can$. CDMN Publishing, 1200 Markhan Road, Suite 301, Scarborough Ontario M1H 3C3 Canada. **Tel** (416)439-4083, FAX (416)439-4086. **ED** Brian Jeffrey. **Ad Acc.** Full Page (B&W) 3,350.00Can$. Full Page (Color) 4,300.00Can$. **Circ:** 15,000.

US
CEASED
SALES MANAGER'S BUDGET PLANNER. (1991)-(1993). English. Bill Communications Inc., 355 Park Avenue South, New York NY 10010-1789. **Tel** (800)360-5200, (212)592-6200, FAX (212)592-6209. **Continues** Survey of Selling Costs.

LC HF5439.7 .S25
DD 004/.068/3 US
SALES PAY AND PRODUCTIVITY TRENDS. English. One time a year. $595.00. Culpepper & Associates, Inc., 7000 Peachtree Dunwoody Road 10, Atlanta GA 30328. **Tel** (404)668-0616, FAX (404)668-1095.

US
SALES PRO. (19??)-. English. Twelve times a year. $645.00. Marketing Intelligence Service Ltd., 6473D Route 64, Naples NY 14512. **Tel** (716)374-6326, (800)836-5710, FAX (714)374-5217, telex 469979. **ED** Tom Vierhile. available on an online database from DATA-STAR, and DIALOG.
Desc: Monitors and analyzes current consumer sales promotional material for packaged goods. Contains a cross-section of about 40 current promotions in each issue.
Ind/Abst Mark. Advert. Ref. Serv.

LC HF5438 .S174 **ISSN** 0095-3962
DD 658.31/24/04 US
SALES TRAINING & DEVELOPMENT.
VAT Sales Training and Development. Vol. 1 (Sept./Oct. 1974)-. Periodical. English. Two times a year. $7.50. Reinhardt Keymer Pub Co, 60 East 42nd Street/Suite 1306, New York NY 10017. **Tel** (203)966-5691.

ISSN 0738-6362
US
SALESMAN'S INSIDER. (SALESMAN'S INSIDER / MARV Q. MODELL ASSOCIATES.). **Added/Corp** Marv Q. Modell Associates. **VFOAT** Salesman's Insider Letter. (198?)-. Periodical. English. Twelve times a year. $48.00. Marv Q Modell Associates, PO Box 4111, Stanford CA 94305. **Tel** (408)270-4526.

ISSN 1070-809X
DD 658 US
SARAH STAMBLER'S MARKETING WITH TECHNOLOGY NEWS. [Sarah Stambler's market. technol. news]. **Added/Corp** Stambler, Sarah. **VFOAT** MWT; Marketing with Technology News. (199?)-. Periodical. English. Twelve times a year. $99.00. Techprose Inc., 370 Central Park Street, Suite 210, New York NY 10025. **Tel** (212)222-1765, FAX (212)678-6357. **ED** Sarah Stambler. cum. **Circ:** 4,000.
Desc: Alternative electronic media to market and deliver their products. We compare competing techniques for different applications, explore new trends, and review new products.

US
SCHOOL MARKETING NEWSLETTER.
(19??)-. Newsletter. English. Twelve times a year. $119.00 (one-year), $199.00 (two-year). School Market Research Institute Inc., PO Box 10, 1721 Saybrook Road, Haddam CT 06438. **Tel** (203)345-8183, (203)345-4018, FAX (203)345-3985. **ED** Lynn Vosburgh. Index available (published in June issue). **Circ:** 500. **Continues** Direct Response Marketing to Schools, 0882-701X.
Desc: Devoted to all aspects of marketing to educators.

LC PN1993.5.U718 S28 **ISSN** 0748-6456
DD 791.4/02573 US
SCRIPTWRITERS MARKET. See Motion Picture.

ISSN 0891-2947
DD 332 US
SECONDARY MARKETING EXECUTIVE. [Second. mark. exec.]. Vol. 1, No. 1 (Dec. 1986)-. Trade Publication. English. Twelve times a year. $48.00. Secondary Marketing Executive, PO Box 2330, Waterbury CT 06722. **Tel** (203)755-0158, (800)325-6745, FAX (203)755-3480.

ISSN 1046-9036
DD 658 US
SELLING ADVANTAGE, THE. [Sell. advant.]. (198?)-. Periodical. English. Twenty-four times a year. $94.56. Progressive Business Publications, 370 Technology Drive, PO Box 3019, Malvern PA 19355. **Tel** (617)527-8600, (800)220-5000, FAX (617)647-8089.

US
SELLING MAGAZINE. (19??)-. Periodical. English. Ten times a year. $50.00. Institutional Investor Inc., 488 Madison Avenue, New York NY 10022. **Tel** (212)303-3234, (212)303-3233, FAX (212)303-3353.

LC HF5813.U6 S43 **ISSN** 1050-3803
DD 659.13 US
SENIOR MEDIA GUIDE. (SENIOR MEDIA GUIDE : SELLING TO SENIORS.). [Sr. media guide]. **VFOAT** Selling to Seniors, Senior Media Guide. (1990)-. English. Twelve times a year. $49.95. CD Publications, 8204 Fenton Street, Silver Spring MD 20910. **Tel** (800)666-6380, (301)588-6380, FAX (301)588-6385. **ED** Jim Kelder. Index available. cum. index. **Bk Rev**. **Continues** D B Wolfe's Maturity Market Perspectives.
Desc: Contains practical advice on effective ways to reach the "over 50" market.

UK
SERVICE STATION SHOPPER SURVEY. See Consumer Education and Protection.

US
SERVICES MARKETING TODAY.
Added/Corp American Marketing Association. American Marketing Association. Services Marketing Division. **VFOAT** Services Marketing Newsletter. Vol. 7, Issue 2 (Summer 1991)-. Periodical. English. Four times a year. $40.00. American Marketing Association, 250 South Wacker Drive, Suite 200, Chicago IL 60606-5819. **Tel** (312)648-0536, FAX (312)993-7542. **Continues** Services Marketing Newsletter.
Desc: For business practitioners and educators with an interest in services marketing.

ISSN 0194-1968
US
Pr Rev.
SHELBY REPORT OF THE SOUTHEAST, THE. (1968)-. Periodical. English. Twelve times a year. $25.00. Shelby Publishing Company, 517 Green Street, Gainesville GA 30501. **Tel** (404)534-8380, FAX (404)535-0110. **ED** Chuck Gilmer. **Ad Acc, Adv Mgr:** D. Heller. **Circ:** 21,000 (ctrl).
Desc: News of retail, wholesale food industry covering all new products in supermarkets and all other news pertaining to supermarket industry in the Sunbelt.

ISSN 0037-4814
US
SIGHT & SOUND MARKETING. VFOAT
Sight & Sound. **VAT** Sight and Sound Marketing. Periodical. English. Twelve times a year. $18.00. Drorbargh Publications Inc, 51 East 42nd Street, New York NY 10017. **Tel** (212)867-2270.

ISSN 0738-6516
US
SIZZLE SHEET, THE. (THE SIZZLE SHEET : THE MARKETING COMMUNICATIONS GUIDE FOR MARKETERS OF COMPUTER, ELECTRONICS, COMMUNICATIONS, AND OFFICE PRODUCTS, SYSTEMS AND SERVICES.). [Sizz. sheet]. (1980)-. Periodical. English. Twelve times a year. $36.00. Lively Communications, 150 Speen Street, Suite 205, PO Box 801, Framingham MA 01701. **Tel** (617)875-0013. **ED** Robert A Lively. **Ad Acc. Circ:** 17,000.

ISSN 0081-0169
US
SMALL MARKETERS AIDS. No. 1-. English. Small Business Administration, 1030 15th Street, Washington DC 20417. **Tel** (202)653-6963.

US
SMART BUYING. (19??)-. English. Twenty-six times a year. $42.90. Economics Press Inc, 12 Daniel Road, Fairfield NJ 07004. **Tel** (201)227-1224, (800)526-2554, FAX (201)227-9742. **Continues** Purchasing Pointers.
Desc: Each issue focuses on one crucial buying technique and illustrates it with examples from real companies.

ISSN 0957-4581
UK
CODEN SFINEC
TITLE CHANGE
SNACK FOOD INTERNATIONAL. [Snack food int.]. (1989)-(19??). Trade Publication. English. (Mar., June, Sept., Dec.). Kennedy's Publications Ltd., 12 Blackstock Mews, London N4 2BT United Kingdom. **Tel** 011 44 171 2263423. **Continues** Snack Food Manufacture and Marketing, 0262-2580. **Continued by** Kennedy's Snackmaker.
Desc: The magazine bringing independent news and advice to savoury snack manufacturers.

ISSN 0882-3510
DD 363 US
SOCIAL MARKETING UPDATE. [Soc. mark. update]. **Added/Corp** International Contraceptive Social Marketing Project. **VFOAT** Update. Vol. 1, No. 1 (Apr. 1981)-. Periodical. English. Four times a year. Free. The Futures Group, 1029 Vermont Avenue NW, Washington DC 20005.
Ind/Abst Curr. Lit. Fam. Plan. (19??-199?).

ISSN 0882-2255
DD 363 US
SOCIAL MARKETING UPDATE.
(MARKETING SOCIAL MISE A JOUR.). **VFOAT** Mise A Jour; Mise a Jour Pour le Marketing Social. Periodical. French (French). Four times a year. Futures Group, 1111 14th Street NW, Washington DC 20005.

ISSN 1060-3964
DD 658 US
SOFTWARE MARKETING JOURNAL. See Computers-Software.

LC T12.3.M5 S69 **ISSN** 0737-0970
DD 670/.29/4774 US
SOUTHERN MICHIGAN REGIONAL INDUSTRIAL PURCHASING GUIDE.
VFOAT Regional Industrial Purchasing Guide. English. One time a year. Thomas Regional Directory Company Inc, 330 West 34th Street, New York NY 10001.

ISSN 0049-1624
US
SOUTHERN PURCHASOR. Added/Corp
Purchasing Management Association of Carolinas-Virginia. (19??)-. Trade Publication. English. Six times a year. Free on request. Purchasing Management Association Carolinas, 5601 Roanne Way 312 43, Greensboro NC 27402. **Tel** (910)292-9228.

LC HF5437.A2 S68 **ISSN** 0274-8800
DD 658.7/2/05 US
SUSPENDED
SOUTHWEST PURCHASING. (July 1980)- Suspended (Nov.-Dec. 1985). Periodical. English. Twelve times a year. Purchasing Management Association, PO Box 60620, New Orleans LA 70160. **Tel** (504)586-8400. ***Continues*** *Southwest Business, 0192-8791.*

CN
SPONSORSHIP REPORT. English. Twelve times a year. 220.00Can$ Canada; 200.00Can$. Sponsorship Report, 555 Richmond Street West, Suite 504, Toronto Ontario M5V 3B1 Canada. **Tel** (416)360-3894, FAX (416)360-0204.

LC GV716 .S6355 **ISSN** 1061-6934
DD 796/.06/91 US
Pr Rev.
SPORT MARKETING QUARTERLY. See Sports and Games.

ISSN 1060-2550
DD 338 US
SPORTING GOODS INTELLIGENCE. [Sporting goods intelligence]. Vol. 6, No. 34 (Dec. 11, 1989)-. Periodical. English. Thirty-six times a year. $365.00. Sporting Goods Intelligence, 442 Featherbed Lane, Glen Falls PA 19342. **Tel** (610)558-1601, FAX (610)558-1650. **ED** John Horan. **Circ:** 1,200. ***Continues*** *Sporting Goods Management News.*

LC HF5415.126 .F33 **ISSN** 1049-6092
DD 381/.1 US
STATISTICAL FACT BOOK - DIRECT MARKETING ASSOCIATION (U.S.). See Consumer Education and Protection.

LC JK1661 .S86
DD 353.0071/2044/05 US
STATUS OF MAJOR ACQUISITIONS AS OF ... . English. One time a year. US General Accounting Office / District of Columbia, 441 G Street Northwest, Room 4528, Washington DC 20548. **Tel** (202)275-2812.

ISSN 1058-0344
DD 332 US
STEVEN DWORMAN'S INFORMERCIAL MARKETING REPORT. [Steven Dworman's informercial market. rep.]. **VFOAT** Informercial Marketing Report. Vol. 1, No. 1 (Aug. 15, 1991)-. Periodical. English. Twelve times a year. $395.00. Steven Dworman's Informercial Market Report, 11533 Thurston Circle, Los Angeles CA 90049. **Tel** (310)472-5253, FAX (310)472-6004. **ED** Steven Dworman. **Bk Rev**, (Qty: 4-5).
Desc: Monthly newsletter dealing with the exploding Direct Response Television Industry. Called "The Bible of the Industry." Newsletter has broken many national news stories picked up in New York Times, Wall Street Journal, Ad Week, Associated Press, People and many others. We also publish Sourcebook and Industry directory.

ISSN 1078-5248
DD 658 US
•**STRATEGIC ADVANTAGE.** [Strateg. advant.]. (1994)-. Periodical. English. Twelve times a year. $395.00. Summit Strategies Inc., 360 Newbury Street, Boston MA 02115. **Tel** (617)266-9050, FAX (617)266-7952. **ED** Joyce Gavenda and Jenne Gooding.
Desc: Information on the market strategy and consulting firm focusing on the strategic role of information technology.

ISSN 1187-4309
DD 658.8 CN
STRATEGY (TORONTO. 1991). (STRATEGY.). [Strategy]. Vol. 2, No. 23 (July 29, 1991)-. Periodical. English. Twenty-five times a year. 93.50Can$. Brunico Communications Inc., 366 Adelaide Street West, Suite 500, Toronto Ontario M5V 1R9 Canada. **Tel** (416)408-2300, FAX (416)408-0807. **ED** Mark Smyka. Index available (published separately). cum. index. **Ad Acc. Circ:** 19,000 (ctrl). ***Continues*** *Playback Strategy., 0848-4457.*
Desc: Covers marketing, advertising, direct marketing, public relations, new products, promotions, etc., in Canada.

ISSN 1077-1557
DD 380 US
•**SUBSCRIPTION MARKETING.** [Subscr. mark.]. Vol. 1, No. 1 (July 1994)-. Periodical. English. Twelve times a year. $390.00. Blue Dolphin Communications, PO Box 216, Wayland MA 01778. **Tel** (508)443-8214. **(Subscription address:** Blue Dolphin Communications, PO Box 59859, Boulder CO 80322. **Tel** (800)462-0213.**)**

ISSN 0830-8802
DD 658.8/005 CN
SUCCESS, PROMOTION & PROFITS. [Succes promot. profits]. Vol. 8, No 8 (June 1985)-. Periodical. French. Six times a year. 41.97Can$. Succes Promotion & Profits, 41 71 EME Avenue Est, Blainville Quebec J7C 1S3 Canada. **Tel** (514)979-4500. ***Continues*** *Le Succes Avec Promotion & Profits, 0830-8802.*

ISSN 1036-1693
DD 381.05 AT
SUCCESSFUL SELLING & MANAGING. [Success. sell. manag.]. **VFOAT** Successful Selling. (1990)-. Periodical. English. Twelve times a year. 46.00Aus$ (Australia); 68.00Aus$ (New Zealand); 88.00Aus$ (other). Matheson Publishing, 428 St. Kilda Road, Suite 20, Melbourne Victoria 3004 Australia. **Tel** 011 61 3 8672077, FAX 011 61 3 8200258. **ED** Sally Matheson. **Bk Rev. Ad Acc. Circ:** 10,000. available on videocassette. ***Continues*** *Successful Selling, 1030-3928.*

US
SUMMARY - ANNUAL MEETING - NATIONAL ASSOCIATION OF STATE PURCHASING OFFICIALS. Main/Corp National Association of State Purchasing Officials. 16th- ; 1960-. English. One time a year. National Association of State Purchasing Officials, Iron Works Pike, Lexington KY 40505. ***Continues*** *National Association of State Purchasing Officials. Resume - Annual Meeting.*

ISSN 0039-5781
UDC 381.5 SW
SUPERMARKET. [Supermarket]. (1969)-. Periodical. Swedish. Nine times a year. $160.29. ICA Forlaget AB, Stora Gatan 41, Vaesteraas 72185 Sweden. **Tel** 011 46 21 194000. ***Continues*** *Sjaelvbetjaening, 0583-4600.*

ISSN 0361-1329
US
SURVEY OF BUYING POWER. VFOAT SM Survey of Buying Power; Sales Management Survey of Buying Power. (19??)-. English. $119.95. Bill Communications Inc., 355 Park Avenue South, New York NY 10010-1789. **Tel** (800)360-5200, (212)592-6200, FAX (212)592-6209. ***Continued in part by*** *Survey of Media Markets.*
Desc: Includes advertising matter.

LC HC106.7 .S85 **ISSN** 0735-9942
DD 339.4/1/0973 US
... SURVEY OF BUYING POWER FORECASTING SERVICE, THE. [Surv. buy. power forecast. serv.]. **VFOAT** Survey of Buying Power; Forecasting Service. (19??)-. English. Sales and Marketing Management, 633 3rd Avenue, New York NY 10017. ***Continues*** *Survey of Buying Power Forecaster's Handbook, 0164-2529.*

US
SURVEY OF DOMESTIC SPORT MARKET PRICES. (19??)-. English. Twelve times a year. $100.00. Natural Gas Clearinghouse, 13430 Northwest Freeway, Suite 1200, Houston TX 77040. **Tel** (713)744-1777.

ISSN 1062-2632
DD 353 US
Pr Rev.
T.I.P.S. (VIENNA, VA.). (T.I.P.S. : TOPICAL ISSUES IN PROCUREMENT.). [T.I.P.S.]. **Added/Corp** National Contract Management Association (U.S.). **VFOAT** Topical Issues in Procurement; TIPS. Vol. 1, No. 1 (Oct. 1989)-. Periodical. English. Twelve times a year. $72.00. National Contract Management Association, 1912 Woodford Road, Vienna VA 22180. **Tel** (703)448-9231, (800)344-8096, FAX (703)448-0939. **ED** Gina Bova. Index available. cum. index.
Desc: Presents topical issues of importance to both government and industrial personnel involved in the acquisition of supplies and service. Especially relevant to contract managers, but also of interest to lawyers, accountants, and business managers.

ISSN 1073-6662
US
TAG'S CHANNEL COMPASS. (19??)-. English. Twelve times a year. $450.00. AMBIT International Inc., 665 Third Street, Suite 508, San Francisco CA 94107. **Tel** (415)957-9433, FAX (415)957-0504. **ED** Linda Kazares.
Desc: Reports on channel marketing, sales and developments.

LC HF5410 .Z56 **ISSN** 0889-5333
DD 658.8/4 US
CCC
TARGET MARKETING. [Target mark.]. Vol. 9, No. 8 (Aug. 1986)-. Trade Publication. English. Twelve times a year. $65.00. North American Publishing Company, 401 North Broad Street, Philadelphia PA 19108. **Tel** (215)238-5300, (800)777-8074, FAX (215)238-5283. **ED** Denison Hatch. **Ad Acc. Circ:** 39,000 (ctrl). available on microfilm and microfiche from University Microfilms International (UMI). Documents available from UMI Article Clearinghouse. ***Continues*** *Zip Target Marketing, 0739-6953.*
Desc: Target marketing is edited for end users of all kinds of direct marketing, including lists, fulfillment, mail marketing, telemarketing.
Ind/Abst ABI/INFORM Glob. Ed.; ABI/INFORM [Computer File] (Sept. 1979-); Acad. Search; Bus. Index (1992-); Curr. Cit.; EP Collect.; F&S Index Plus Text, Int. [Select. Cov.]; Gen. BusinessFile (1992-); Gen. Period. Index (1986-); Graph. Arts Bull. Inst. Pap. Sci. Technol.; Homework Help.; INFO-SOUTH Abstr.; Mag. Search; Manage. Contents; MasterFile FullTEXT 1000; MasterFile FullTEXT 350; MasterFile FullTEXT 650; MasterFile FullTEXT (July 1993-); OCLC; PROMT; Telebase.

LC SB188
DD 633.1 US
TECHNICAL BULLETINS / ASSOCIATION OF OPERATIVE MILLERS. Main/Corp Association of Operative Millers. **VFOAT** A.O.M. Technical Bulletins. Vol. 1 (1948)-. Bulletin. English (Spanish). Twelve times a year. $100.00 Comes with Association of Operative Millers membership. Association of Operative, 5001 College Boulevard, Suite 104, Leawood KS 66211. **Tel** (913)338-3377, FAX (913)338-3553. Index available. cum. index. **Circ:** 1,600 (ctrl).

ISSN 1034-7496
DD 384.30994 AT
TITLE CHANGE
TELECOMMUNICATIONS MANAGEMENT AND MARKETING NEWSLETTER. See Communications-Telecommunication.

LC HF5415.1265 .T43 **ISSN** 0730-6156
DD 658.8/5 US
TELEMARKETING. [Telemarketing]. June/July (1982)-. Periodical. English. Twelve times a year. $49.00. Technology Marketing Corporation, One Technology Plaza, Norwalk CT 06854. **Tel** (203)852-6800, FAX (203)853-2845. **ED** Linda Driscoll. Index available. **Bk Rev. Ad Acc. Circ:** 60,000 (ctrl). available on microfilm and microfiche from University Microfilms International (UMI).
Desc: The magazine of business telecommunications. Describes the use of telemarketing and business telecommunications to increase sales, profits and productivity.
Ind/Abst Acad. Search; Bus. Period. Index; Bus. Source Plus; Bus. Source; Curr. Cit.; EP Collect.; Homework Help.; INFO-SOUTH Abstr.; Mag. Search; MasterFile FullTEXT 1000; MasterFile FullTEXT 350; MasterFile FullTEXT 650; MasterFile FullTEXT (Jan. 1993-); OCLC; Telebase; Trade Ind. ASAP [Full Txt.]; Trade Ind. Index [Full Txt.]; Vocat. Search; Wilson Bus. Abstr.

LC HF **ISSN** 0736-167X
DD 658 US
CCC
TELEMARKETING UPDATE. See Business and Economics-Advertising and Public Relations.

ISSN 0888-353X
DD 658 US
TELEPHONE MARKETING COUNCIL NEWSLETTER. (TELEPHONE MARKETING COUNCIL NEWSLETTER / DMA.). [Teleph. Mark. Counc. newsl.]. **Added/Corp** Direct Marketing Association. Telephone Marketing Council. (19??)-. Newsletter. English. Four times a year (Seasonally). $100.00 (associate), $200.00 (voting) Comes with Telephone Marketing Council Membership. Direct Marketing Association Inc, 11 West 42nd Street, New York NY 10036. **Tel** (212)768-7277, FAX (212)599-1268.
Desc: This is based on your company's use of direct response advertising as part of your marketing mix. Includes the use of any media such as solo direct mail packages, catalogs, telephones, space ads, electronic broadcasting, bill inserts, package inserts, cooperative mailings, and coupons for the purpose of generating measurable responses.

ISSN 0882-1461
US
CODEN TSERE4
TELEPHONE SELLING REPORT. (198?)-. Periodical. English. Twelve times a year. $109.00. Business By Phone Inc., 5301 South 144th Street, Omaha ME 68137-5109. **Tel** (402)895-9399, FAX (402)896-3353. **ED** Art Sobczak. Index available. **Circ:** 2,000.
Desc: A how-to training report providing tips on opening statements, closing, handling objections, and getting by screeners. For businesses selling to businesses.

LC HF5415.1265 .T47 **ISSN** 0886-9642
DD 658.8/5 US
TELEPROFESSIONAL. [Teleprofessional]. (Spring 1986)-. Trade Publication. English. Ten times a year. $39.00. Teleprofessional, 209 West 5th Street, Suit N, Waterloo IA 50701. **Tel** (800)338-8307, (319)235-4473, FAX (319)235-9850. **ED** Robert Van Voorhis, Jr. **Bk Rev**, (Qty: varies). **Ad Acc. Circ:** 30,000 (ctrl).
Desc: Telecommunications technology and call center applications.

US
TEXAS LABOR MARKET REVIEW / TEXAS EMPLOYMENT COMMISSION. Added/Corp Texas Employment Commission. **VFOAT** Texas Labor Market Reviews. (May 1977)-. Periodical. English. Twelve times a year. Free on request. Texas

Business and Economics —Marketing and Purchasing

Employment Commission, 101 East 15th Street, Room 208T, Austin TX 78778. **Tel** (512)463-2619. **Circ:** 6,000. available on an online database ((512)475-4893).
Continues *Texas Manpower Trends.*
Desc: News and information on labor marketing.

ISSN 0272-4014
US

THEORIES IN MARKETING SERIES.
[Theor. mark. ser.]. (1980)-. Monographic series. English. Price varies per volume. John Wiley & Sons, Inc., 605 Third Avenue, New York NY 10158-0012. **Tel** (212)850-6000, (212)850-6645, FAX (212)850-6088, telex 12-7063. **(Subscription address:** John Wiley & Sons / UK, Baffins Lane, Chichester, West Sussex PO19 1UD United Kingdom. **Tel** 011 44 1243 779777, FAX 011 44 243 776128, telex 86290 WIBOOKG.)

NE

TIJDSCHRIFT INKOOP EN LOGISTIEK.
Dutch. Ten times a year. Fl150.94. Intermedia BV, Postbus 4, 2400 MA Alphen AD Rijn Netherlands. **Tel** 011 31 1720 66855, FAX 011 31 1720 94714.

NE

Pr Rev.
TIJDSCHRIFT VOOR MARKETING. Dutch.
Eleven times a year. Fl150.00. Kluwer BV, Postbus 23, 7400 GA Deventer Netherlands. **Tel** 011 31 5700 33155, 011 31 5700 47421, FAX 011 31 5700 11504, telex 42829. **ED** B Bele van Kersbrelk. Index available. cum. index. **Bk Rev. Ad Acc.**
Desc: Articles on marketing theory and practice.

ISSN 0893-1259
DD 380 US
SUSPENDED
TMS-LETTER, THE. [TMS lett.]. VFOAT TMS
Letter; Travel Marketing and Sales Newsletter. Vol. 1, No. 1 (March 16, 1987)-(19??). Periodical. English. Twenty-three times a year (semimonthly except Dec.). $130.00. Nissen-Lie Communications Inc, 441 Lexington Avenue, Suite 1209A, New York NY 10017. **Tel** (212)986-1025, FAX (212)986-1033. **ED** Angela Reale Mathisen. **Circ:** 2,000.
Desc: Covers marketing and sales, promotion related to travel and tourism. Reports on travel marketing, advertising, public relations, and sales developments, trends, ideas, campaigns and news.

IT

TRADE MARKETING. (19??)-. Italian. Three
times a year. L87000 Italy; L110000 other. Franco Angeli Riviste SRL, Viale Monza 106, 20127 Milan Italy. **Tel** 011 39 2 2827651, 011 39 2 289562, FAX 011 39 2 258004, telex 051-511650.

LC T391 .T72 **ISSN** 0145-5559
DD 659.1/52 US
TRADESHOW (LOS ANGELES, CALIF.).
See Business and Economics-Advertising and Public Relations.

ISSN 0275-3545
US
TRAVEL MARKETING AND AGENCY MANAGEMENT GUIDELINES. See Travel
and Tourism.

IT
SUSPENDED
TRENDS & WORDS. (19??)-Suspended (1995).
Italian. Ten times a year. L170310. Trends & Words Srl, Via Siepe Lunga #57, 40137 Bologna Italy. **Tel** 011 39 51 6237010, FAX 011 39 51 6237162. **Bk Rev. Ad Acc.**
Circ: 1,000.

ISSN 0269-980X
DD 338.47674 UK
TROPICAL TIMBERS. See Forests and
Forestry-Abstracting, Bibliographies and Statistics.

LC HD966.1 .U17 **ISSN** 0275-5181
DD 381/.456151/0973 US
U.S. PHARMACEUTICAL MARKET. DRUG STORES. See Pharmacy and
Pharmacology.

ISSN 0237-1545
HU
UNGARISCHE WIRTSCHAFTSHEFTE.
(1985)-. Periodical. English. Four times a year. $81.00. **(Subscription address:** Kultura, PO Box 143, H-1300 Budapest 3 Hungary. **Tel** 011 36 1 2500194.)

ISSN 0742-3675
DD 380 US
UNITED STATES TRADE FAIR. [U. S. trade
fair]. Oct. 1984-. Periodical. English. Twelve times a year. $65.00 US; $120.00 South America; $130.00 Europe; $160.00 Africa, Asia, Mid-East; $175.00 Australia, Pacific, Oceania. United States Publishing Corporation, PO Box 11680, Chicago IL 60611-0680. **Tel** (312)721-2191. **ED** Boafo Akuffo. **Bk Rev. Ad Acc. Circ:** 356,700 (ctrl).
Desc: International merchandise mart in print featuring advertising and promotion of products and services to wholesalers, importers, retailers, and supply houses for a broad range of products and services.

ISSN 1062-5062
DD 658 US
UPLINE (CHARLOTTESVILLE, VA.).
(UPLINE: THE JOURNAL FOR NETWORK MARKETING LEADERS.). [Upline]. (198?)-. Periodical. English. Twelve times a year. $69.00. MLM Success, 400 East Jefferson St., Charlottesville VA 22902. **Tel** (804)979-4427.
Continues *MLM Success, 1054-3988.*

ISSN 0954-6235
UK
VENDING INTERNATIONAL. [Vend. int.].
(1972)-. Trade Publication. English. Twelve times a year. £50.00 (one-year), £90.00 (two-year), £110.00 (three-year) UK; £70.00 (one-year), £130.00 (two-year), £170.00 (three-year) other Europe; £95.00 (one-year), £180.00 (two-year), £243.00 (three-year) other. Datateam Publishing Ltd., Datateam House Tovil Hill, Maidstone Kent ME15 6QS United Kingdom. **Tel** 011 44 1622 687031, FAX 011 44 1622 757646. **ED** Geoff Manners.
Ad Acc; Adv Mgr: Conrad Chant. ctrl circ. **Continues** *Vending Times (Tonbridge).*

ISSN 0255-7673
UDC 658.8 SZ
VERKAUF UND MARKETING. [Verkauf
Mark.]. VFOAT V & M. Verkauf und Marketing. (1972)-. Periodical. German. Twelve times a year. 155.00F Switzerland; 175.00F other. Verlag Verkauf and Marketing, Postfach, CH-9435 Heerbrugg Switzerland.

NE
VERKOPEN! VAKMAGAZINE VOOR COMMERCIELE AKTIE. (19??)-. Dutch. Twelve
times a year. Kluwer BV, Postbus 23, 7400 GA Deventer Netherlands. **Tel** 011 31 5700 33155, 011 31 5700 47421, FAX 011 31 5700 11504, telex 42829. Index available. **Bk Rev. Ad Acc.** available on audiocassette.
Desc: A magazine for sales managers, executives, and sales advisors and contains interviews, cases, success and failure stories, and news concerning and sales profession.

IT
VSB: VIDEOTEX STRATEGIES AND BUSINESS. Italian. Twelve times a year. L480000.00
Italy; L530000.00 other. VSB Srl, Via Flaminia 173, 00196 Rome Italy. **Tel** 011 39 6 3220746.

LC HF5415.2 .V78
DD 658.8/3/05 SZ
VSMF-ASSEM INFORMATION. Added/Corp
Verband Schweizerischer Marktforscher. VFOAT VSMF-Assem. (19??)-. Periodical. German. Three times a year. IHA Institut fur Marktanalysen AG, 6052 Hergiswil Switzerland.

LC HF5068.W3 L4 **ISSN** 1058-3173
DD 338.7/4/025753 US
WASHINGTON, D.C. MARKETING DIRECTORY. See Industry and Production-Trade
and Industrial Directories.

ISSN 0043-0706
US
SUSPENDED
WASHINGTON PURCHASER. Suspended
(1984). Periodical. English. Twelve times a year. Purchasing Agents Association of Washington, Box 9038, Seattle WA 98109.

LC TS227 .A255116 **ISSN** 0192-7671
DD 338.4/76715/20973 US
CCC
TITLE CHANGE
WELDING DISTRIBUTOR (1966). See
Metals and Metallurgy-Welding.

GW
WER LIEFERT WAS? CD-ROM. VFOAT Who
Supplies What?. (19??)-. English. Two times a year. Wer Liefert Was GmbH, Normannenweg 18 20, 20537 Hamburg Germany. **Tel** 011 49 40 2515080.

LC HF5415.12.G4 W47 **ISSN** 0042-9538
DD 380.1 GW
CCC
WERBEN UND VERKAUFEN : W & V.
VFOAT W&V; W & V; W und V. (April, 1963)-. Periodical. German. Fifty-two times a year (Friday). DM143.00. Europa Fachpresse Verlag GmbH, Thomas Dehler Strasse 27, D-81737 Munich Germany. **Tel** 011 49 89 67804273, FAX 011 49 89 6377791.

ISSN 0269-2058
DD 658.6005 UK
WHAT'S NEW IN MARKETING. [What's new
mark.]. (1986)-. Periodical. English. Twelve times a year. $90.00. Morgan Grampian, 40 Beresford Street Woolwich, London SE18 6BQ United Kingdom. **Tel** 011 44 181 8557777, FAX 011 44 181 8555548, telex 896238. available on microfilm and microfiche from University Microfilms International (UMI).
Ind/Abst Leis., Rec., Tour. Abstr.

US
WHAT'S WORKING FOR NONPROFIT FUNDRAISING. (19??)-. Periodical. English.
Twelve times a year. $192.00. Progressive Business Publications, 370 Technology Drive, PO Box 3019, Malvern PA 19355. **Tel** (617)527-8600, (800)220-5000, FAX (617)647-8089. **Continues** *Nonprofit Marketing Report.*

WHEELING & TRANSMISSION MONTHLY. English. Twelve times a year. $245.00.
Cogeneration Information Services, 747 Leigh Mill Road, Great Falls VA 22066. **Tel** (703)759-5135, FAX (703)759-0232.
Desc: Reports transmissions and bulk power transactions as they are filed at the FERC. Editorials focus on key regulatory decisions in bulk power generation.

LC HD59 **ISSN** 8755-2671
DD 659 US
WHO'S MAILING WHAT!. See Business and
Economics-Advertising and Public Relations.

US
CEASED
WHO'S WHO IN DIRECT MARKETING CREATIVE SERVICES. VFOAT Direct Marketing
Creative Services. (1988)-(199?). Trade Publication. English. North American Publishing Company, 401 North Broad Street, Philadelphia PA 19108. **Tel** (215)238-5300, (800)777-8074, FAX (215)238-5283.

ISSN 0273-2955
US
WILEY SERIES IN MARKETING. [Wiley ser.
mark.]. (19??)-. Monographic series. English. Irregular. Price varies per volume. John Wiley & Sons, Inc., 605 Third Avenue, New York NY 10158-0012. **Tel** (212)850-6000, (212)850-6645, FAX (212)850-6088, telex 12-7063. **(Subscription address:** John Wiley & Sons / UK, Baffins Lane, Chichester, West Sussex PO19 1UD United Kingdom. **Tel** 011 44 1243 779777, FAX 011 44 243 776128, telex 86290 WIBOOKG.)

US
WISCONSIN WOOD MARKETING BULLETIN. See Forests and Forestry-Lumber and
Wood.

LC HD9803.U6 W67 **ISSN** 1062-7650
DD 684 US
WORKSTATION REPORT'S ... BUYER' GUIDE TO OFFICE FURNITURE, THE.
See Business and Economics-Office Equipment and Services.

ISSN 1195-0056
DD 380.1 CN
TITLE CHANGE
XZIBIT NEWS. [Xzibit news]. VFOAT Exhibit News.
Vol. 1, No. 1 (Sept./Oct. 1993)-(199?). Trade Publication. English. Xzibit Publications, PO Box 405, Cultors Lake British Lake, V0X 1H0 Canada. **Tel** (614)824-1103.
Merged into *BC Ad Network.*
Desc: Publication about trade shows.

LC HF6146.T4 Y45
DD 384.6/4 US
YELLOW PAGES MARKET FORECAST.
See Publishing.

US
YOUTH MARKETING REPORT. English.
Twelve times a year. $159.00. Youth Marketing Institute, 13521 Cedar Road, Cleveland OH 44118. **Tel** (216)397-0062. **ED** Mike Wayne. Index available. **Bk Rev. Ad Acc. Circ:** 2,500.
Desc: Covers marketing, advertising, and promotional news and research.

ISSN 1041-7516
DD 658 US
CCC
YOUTH MARKETS ALERT. [Youth mark. alert].
(Jan. 1989)-. Periodical. English. Twelve times a year. $295.00. EPM Communications Inc., 488 East 18th Street, Brooklyn NY 11226. **Tel** (718)469-9330, FAX (718)469-7124. available on an online database (files 16,570,636/Full-Text) from DIALOG.
Ind/Abst Mark. Advert. Ref. Serv. [Full Txt.]; PROMT [Full Txt.]; PTS Newsl. Database [Full Txt.].

Business and Economics — Office Equipment and Services

OFFICE EQUIPMENT AND SERVICES

ISSN 1061-3269
DD 651 US
ADVANCE FOR HEALTH INFORMATION PROFESSIONALS. [Adv. health inf. prof.]. Vol. 1, No. 12 (Nov. 18, 1991)-. Periodical. English. Twenty-six times a year. Merion Publications, Inc., 650 Park Avenue West, PO Box 61556, King of Prussia PA 19406. **Tel** (800)355-1088, (610)265-7812, FAX (610)265-8293. **Continues** Advance for Medical Record Professionals, 1061-3188.

ISSN 1046-6096
DD 658 US
AMERICAN OFFICE DEALER. [Am. off. deal.]. Trade Publication. English. Twelve times a year. Free to qualified office supply retailers and wholesalers, office machine and office furniture industries, $24.00 US; $45.00 Canada. American Office Dealer, 6 Piedmont Center/Suite 300, Atlanta GA 30305. **Tel** (404)841-3333. **Continues** American Office Dealer Magazine (Western Ed.), 0891-1045.

ISSN 0885-9965
DD 651 US
AOR OBSERVER, THE. **VFOAT** Observer. **VAT** Automated Office Resources Observer. (19??)-. Periodical. English. Six times a year. $95.00. Observer Word Processing News, PO Box 1119, Aptos CA 95003. **Tel** (408)688-4129. **Continues** Word Processing News.

LC HD2375
DD 658.72 AT
AUSTRALIAN SHOPFITTING TRADE JOURNAL. (19??)-. English. One time a year. 25.00Aus$ Australia; 30.00Aus$ other. Furnishing Publications Pty Ltd., 5 Faigh Street, Mulgrave Victoria 3170 Australia. **Tel** 011 61 3 9562 5844, FAX 011 61 3 9562 5412. **ED** Keith Dunn. **Bk Rev**. **Ad Acc**. Full Page (B&W) 1500.00Aus$. Full Page (Color) 2500.00Aus$. **Circ:** 2,500.

ISSN 0739-8743
US
AUTOMATED OFFICE SYSTEMS. (AUTOMATED OFFICE SYSTEMS : AOS.). [Autom. off. syst.]. **VFOAT** AOS; A.O.S. Vol. 1 (Jan. 1981)-. Periodical. English. Twelve times a year. $125.00. Office Systems Consulting Group, 10 Milk Street, Cambridge MA 02139. **Tel** (617)492-3300. available on an online database from NEWSNET.

ISSN 1078-5809
DD 338 US
●**B.P.I.A. BUSINESS PRODUCTS INDUSTRY REPORT.** [B.P.I.A. bus. prod. ind. rep.]. **Added/Corp** Business Products Industry Association. **VFOAT** Business Products Industry Association Business Products Industry Report; BPIA Business Products Industry Report; Business Products Industry Report; B.P.I.A. Industry Report. Vol. 1, No. 1 (July 12, 1994)-. Trade Publication. English. Twenty-six times a year. $40.00. Business Products Industry Association, 301 North Fairfax Street, Alexandria VA 22314. **Continues** NOPA Industry Report, 0746-5467.
Desc: Covers pertinent news and information of the office supplies and products industry.

ISSN 0733-5059
US
BLACK'S GUIDE. HOUSTON OFFICE SPACE MARKET. **Added/Corp** Black's Guide, Inc. **VFOAT** Houston Office Space Market; Black's Guide to the Office Space Market. Issue 82 (Jan. 1982)-. English. Two times a year. $25.00 (single issue). Blacks Guide Inc., 818 West Diamond Avenue, Suite 300, Gaithersburg MD 20878. **Tel** (301)948-0995.
Desc: A directory of office space available.

LC HD
DD 333.33 ISSN 0738-6095 US
BLACK'S GUIDE. ORANGE COUNTY OFFICE SPACE MARKET. **Added/Corp** Black's Guide, Inc. **VFOAT** Black's Guide. Orange County; Black's Guide; Black's Guide to the Office Space Market. (1983)-. Directory. English. Irregular. $37.50. Blacks Guide Inc., 818 West Diamond Avenue, Suite 300, Gaithersburg MD 20878. **Tel** (301)948-0995.
Desc: A directory of office space available.

ISSN 0733-5067
US
BLACK'S GUIDE. SUBURBAN MANHATTAN OFFICE SPACE MARKET. **Added/Corp** Black's Guide, Inc. **VFOAT** Black's Guide. Suburban Manhattan Office Space Market. (19??)-. English. Two times a year. $25.00. Blacks Guide Inc., 818 West Diamond Avenue, Suite 300, Gaithersburg MD 20878. **Tel** (301)948-0995.
Desc: A directory of office space available.

ISSN 0733-2572
US
BLACK'S GUIDE TO THE METRO DENVER OFFICE SPACE MARKET. **VFOAT** Black's Guide. (Fall 1982)-. English. Two times a year. $25.00 (single issue). Blacks Guide Inc., 818 West Diamond Avenue, Suite 300, Gaithersburg MD 20878. **Tel** (301)948-0995.
Desc: A directory of office space available.

ISSN 0380-9463
DD 658.8/38/65120971 CN
BRAND RECOGNITION STUDY : OFFICE EQUIPMENT & METHODS. See Business and Economics-Marketing and Purchasing.

LC HF5548 .B7955
GW
BTL. **VFOAT** B.T.L. 81/5 (Sept. 1981)-. Periodical. German. Six times a year. D Meininger GmbH, Maximillianstr 11-17, Postfach 312, Neustadt an der Weinstrasse Germany. **Continues** Burorationalisierung, Transport und Lagertechnik.

LC HF5548.2 .B768 ISSN 0341-1370
GW
TITLE CHANGE
BTS BUEROTECHNISCHE SAMMLUNG, DAS RATIONELLE BUERO. **VFOAT** Buerotechnische Sammlung; BTS-Das Rationelle Buero. (1987)-(19??). Periodical. German. Basten Verlag Buerowirtschaft, Eberstrasse 30, D-52134 Herzogenrath Germany. **Tel** 011 49 2407 95890, FAX 011 49 2407 4958. **Formed by the union of** BTS-Buerotechnische Sammlung **and** Rationelle Buero (1985), 0178-0549. **Continued by** BTS, 0935-0276.

LC HF5548.2 .B787
DD 651.8/05 GW
BUEROSZENE. (1992)-. Periodical. German. Twelve times a year. $134.34. Basten Verlag Buerowirtschaft, Eberstrasse 30, D-52134 Herzogenrath Germany. **Tel** 011 49 2407 95890, FAX 011 49 2407 4958. **Formed by the union of** Buero (Aachen, Germany), 0177-7696; Computer Magazin **and** BTS, 0935-0276.

SZ
TITLE CHANGE
BUREAU SUISSE. (19??)-(19??). French. Fachpresse Goldach Hudson & Co, Abteilung Vertrieb 272, CH-9403 Goldach Switzerland. **Tel** 011 41 71 416611. **Continues** Bureaux et Systemes, 0257-8328. **Merged with** IB Magazine **to form** IB Suisse.

LC HF5548 .B844 ISSN 1078-2400
DD 651 US
BUSINESS CONSUMER GUIDE. [Bus. consum. guide]. **Added/Corp** Beacon Research Group. (199?)-. English. Twelve times a year. $119.00. Beacon Research Group, 125 Walnut Street, Watertown MA 02172. **Tel** (800)938-0088, FAX (617)924-0055.

ISSN 0007-6708
UK
BUSINESS EQUIPMENT DIGEST. [Bus. equip. dig.]. **VFOAT** BED. Business Equipment Digest. (1961)-. Periodical. English. Eleven times a year. $188.23. IML Group, Blair House, 184-186 High Street, Tonbridge Kent, TN9 1BQ United Kingdom. **Tel** 011 44 1732 359990, FAX 011 44 1732 770049. Documents available from Ask*IEEE.
Ind/Abst Curr. Cit.; HILITES; Infomat Int. Bus.; Inf. Manage. Technol.; INSPEC (April 1983-); World Ceram. Abstr.

LC HF5371 .B86 ISSN 1044-758X
DD 338.4/765129/097305 CCC
CODEN BFLSEP
BUSINESS FORMS, LABELS & SYSTEMS. [Bus. forms lab. sys.]. **VFOAT** Business Forms, Labels and Systems. (198?)-. Trade Publication. English. Twenty-four times a year. $49.00. North American Publishing Company, 401 North Broad Street, Philadelphia PA 19108. **Tel** (215)238-5300, (800)777-8074, FAX (215)238-5283. available on microfilm and microfiche from University Microfilms International (UMI). Documents available from Ask*IEEE. **Continues** Business Forms & Systems, 0745-3914.
Desc: Published for distributors, designers, and printers of business forms. Regular issues cover significant trends, product developments, design techniques and information on marketing and manufacturing.
Ind/Abst Abstr. Bull. Inst. Pap. Sci. Tech.; Graph. Arts Bull. Inst. Pap. Sci. Technol. (Aug. 1989-); INSPEC (May 1989-)(20 May 1989-); Print. Abstr.

ISSN 1081-0374
US
●**BUSINESS PRODUCTS UPDATE.** (1994)-. English. Six times a year (Jan., Mar., Mar., July, Sept., Nov.). $10.00 (members), $40.00 (nonmembers). National Office Products Association, 301 North Fairfax Street, Alexandria VA 22314. **Tel** (703)549-9040, (800)542-6672, FAX (703)683-7552. **Continues** NOPA Office Markets Update, 1060-3522.

US
CANNATA REPORT. (19??)-. English. Twelve times a year. $215.00 (one-year), $390.00 (two-year) US; $260.00 (one-year), $475.00 (two-year) Canada; $235.00 (one-year), $430.00 (two-year) other. Marketing Research Consultants Inc, PO Box 776, 124 Hebron Avenue, Glastonbury CT 06033. **Tel** (203)633-7988. **ED** Frank G. Cannata. Index available. cum. index. ctrl circ. **Continues** CMN, 0889-5880.

ISSN 1187-1776
DD 651 CN
CATALOGUE DES FOURNITURES ET DU MOBILIER. [Cat. fournit. mobil.]. **Added/Corp** Quebec (Province). Ministere des Approvisionnements et Services. (1991)-. French. **Continues** Catalogue des Fournitures de Bureau., 0843-7173.

ISSN 1055-3339
DD 686 US
COLOR BUSINESS REPORT. (COLOR BUSINESS REPORT : COLOR, COMPUTERS, AND REPROGRAPHICS.). [Color bus. rep.]. **Added/Corp** Blackstone Research Associates. Vol. 1, No. 1 (Feb. 1991)-. Periodical. English. Twelve times a year. $375.00 US; $425.00 other. Blackstone Research Associates, PO Box 314, Uxbridge MA 01569. **Tel** (508)278-3449, FAX (508)278-7975. **ED** Michael Zeis. Index available.
Desc: Covers products, markets, and applications for color computers, peripherals and copiers.

US
COMPUTER & OFFICE ELECTRONICS RETAILER. See Business and Economics-Retail.

ISSN 1182-9052
DD 651.8/05 CN
COMPUTER & TELECOM INDUSTRY UPDATE. [Comput. telecom ind. update]. **Added/Corp** Stanley L. Jacobs Research Inc. **VFOAT** Computer and Telecom Industry Update. Vol. 30.0815 (Aug. 1990)-. Trade Publication. English. Irregular. $495.00 Canada. SLJ Research, 356 Erin Street, Oakville Ontario L6H 4P9 Canada. **Continues** Canadian Office Automation Analyst., 0824-250X.

US
COMPUTERS AND BUSINESS EQUIPMENT. (19??)-. English. Twelve times a year. $225.00. Predicasts Inc., A Ziff Communications Company, 11001 Cedar Avenue, Cleveland OH 44106. **Tel** (800)321-6388, (216)795-3000, FAX (216)229-9944, telex 985 604. **(Subscription address:** Information Access Company, PO Box 61000, Department 1851, San Francisco CA 94161. **Tel** (800)321-6388.**)**

LC HD9801.U54 C87 ISSN 0744-0170
DD 380.1/4562138195/0973 US
COMPUTERS AND OFFICE AND ACCOUNTING MACHINES. (CURRENT INDUSTRIAL REPORTS. MA-35R, COMPUTERS AND OFFICE AND ACCOUNTING MACHINES.). **Added/Corp** United States. Bureau of the Census. **VFOAT** Computers and Office and Accounting Machines. (1978)-. Government Publication. English. One time a year. $1.25. US Department of Commerce / Bureau of the Census, Data User Services Division, Customer Services, Washington DC 20233-0800. **Tel** (301)763-4100. **(Subscription address:** Superintendent of Documents, US Government Printing Office, Washington DC 20402. **)** **Continues** Office, Computing, and Accounting Machines.
Desc: Provides data on the quantity and value of shipments of computers and of office and accounting machines and related equipment.

IT
COPIA. (19??)-. Periodical. Italian. Nine times a year. L60000 Italy; L110000 other. Edizioni Directa SRL, Via Paolo Sarpi 62 A, 20154 Milan Italy. **Tel** 011 39 2 331690, FAX 011 39 2 3313692. Index available. cum. index. **Ad Acc**. **Circ:** 16,000.

US
COPIER. English. One time a year. $39.00. Orion Research Corporation, 14555 North Scottsdale Road, Suite 330, Scottsdale AZ 85260. **Tel** (800)844-0759, (602)951-1114, FAX (602)951-1117.
Desc: Gives information used pricing information on 1,569 products.

ISSN 0899-6164
DD 338 US
COPIER REVIEW. (19??)-. Periodical. English. Twelve times a year. $415.00. Buyers Laboratory Inc., 20 Railroad Avenue, Hackensack NJ 07601. **Tel** (201)488-0404.

Business and Economics —Office Equipment and Services

LC HD9802.3.A1 C66   **ISSN** 1050-978X
DD 686.4/4   US
COPIER SPECIFICATION GUIDE. (COPIER SPECIFICATION GUIDE / BLI.). [Copier specif. guide]. **Added/Corp** Buyers Laboratory. (19??)-. English. Two times a year. $73.90. Buyers Laboratory Inc., 20 Railroad Avenue, Hackensack NJ 07601. **Tel** (201)488-0404.

   GW
COPIERS OF THE WORLD. German (English). Two times a year. DM94.48 Germany; $109.00 other. Interdata Verlag GmbH, Lahnstrabe 27, W-5429 Katzenelnbogen Germany. **Tel** 49 6486 8085, **FAX** 49 6486 8000. **ED** Peter Wurr. Index available. **Ad Acc**. **Circ:** 4,000.
   Desc: A standard directory for the complete offerings of the copier world market. It includes directly comparable in-depth information about technical features, manufacturers, vendors and prices.

   ISSN 0897-9405
DD 686   US
   TITLE CHANGE
COPY MAGAZINE. [Copy mag.]. **VFOAT** Copy. (19??)-(Oct. 1993). Periodical. English. Coast Publishing Inc, 1680 Southwest Bayshore Boulevard, Port St Lucie FL 34984. **Tel** (407)879-6666, **FAX** (407)879-7388. **Merged into** Quick Printing.
   Desc: A journal about imaging and reproduction for librarians who are responsible for copiers and other document processing, equipment and supplies (desktop publishing, electronic printers, etc.).

   ISSN 0276-5845
   US
CREATIVE SECRETARY. See Occupations and Careers.

   ISSN 1079-1795
DD 651   US
●**CREATIVE SECRETARY'S LETTER.** [Creat. secr. lett.]. (May 1994)-. Periodical. English. Twenty-four times a year. $119.40. Bureau of Business Practice, 24 Rope Ferry Road, Waterford CT 06386. **Tel** (800)243-0876, (203)442-4365, (800)876-9105, **FAX** (203)443-1123. **Continues** Prentice Hall Creative Secretary's Letter, 1059-633X.

   UK
CRONER'S OFFICE COMPANION. (19??)-. Periodical. English. Four times a year. £131.50. Croner Publ Ltd., Croner House London Road, Kingston Upon Thames, Surrey KT2 6SR United Kingdom. **Tel** 011 44 181 5473333, **FAX** 011 44 181 5472637.

LC HD9800.U5 C87
DD 381/.456816   US
CURRENT INDUSTRIAL REPORTS. MA-26B, SELECTED OFFICE SUPPLIES AND ACCESSORIES / U.S. DEPARTMENT OF COMMERCE, BUREAU OF THE CENSUS. Added/Corp United States. Bureau of the Census. **VFOAT** Selected Office Supplies and Accessories. (1981)-. Government Publication. English. One time a year. US Department of Commerce / Bureau of the Census, Data User Services Division, Customer Services, Washington DC 20233-0800. **Tel** (301)763-4100. **(Subscription address:** Superintendent of Documents, US Government Printing Office, Washington DC 20402. **)**
   Desc: Presents data on production, inventories, and orders.

LC HD9800.7.U6 C87
DD 381/.4565129   US
CURRENT INDUSTRIAL REPORTS. MA-27A, BUSINESS FORMS, BINDERS, CARBON PAPER, AND INKED RIBBONS. Added/Corp United States. Bureau of the Census. **VFOAT** Business Forms, Binders, Carbon Paper, and Inked Ribbons. (1980)-. Government Publication. English. One time a year. US Department of Commerce / Bureau of the Census, Data User Services Division, Customer Services, Washington DC 20233-0800. **Tel** (301)763-4100. **(Subscription address:** Superintendent of Documents, US Government Printing Office, Washington DC 20402. **)**
   Desc: Presents data on production, inventories and orders.

   HK
CUSTODIAL SERVICES IN ASIA. (19??)-. English. Irregular. $90.00. ISI Ltd., 9F Carfield Comml, Building 75-77 Wyndham Street, Central Hong Kong Hong Kong. **Tel** 011 852 28773417.

   ISSN 8750-6416
DD 651   US
   CODEN DMOAEN
   CEASED
DATAPRO MANAGEMENT OF OFFICE AUTOMATION. [Datapro manage. off. autom.]. **Added/Corp** Datapro Research Corporation. **VFOAT** Management of Office Automation. Vol. 8, No. 1 (Jan. 1985)-(June 1994). Trade Publication. English. Datapro Information Services Group, 600 Delran Parkway, Delran NJ 08075. **Tel** (609)764-0100, (800)328-2776, **FAX** (609)764-8953. **Continues** Datapro Automated Office Solutions, 0730-8833.

   ISSN 0898-4468
DD 652   US
   CCC
   CEASED
DATAPRO OFFICE PRODUCTS EVALUATION SERVICE. [Datapro off. prod. eval. serv.]. **Added/Corp** Datapro Research Corporation. **VFOAT** Office Products Evaluation Service. (198?)-(March 1993). Periodical. English. Datapro Information Services Group, 600 Delran Parkway, Delran NJ 08075. **Tel** (609)764-0100, (800)328-2776, **FAX** (609)764-8953. **Continues** Datapro Reports on Copiers & Duplicators, 0730-8825.
   Desc: Consists of: twelve parts and a one-page monthly issue, which describes the twelve parts, and all are kept in two loose-leaf binders.

LC HD9803.A1 W67
DD 338.4/7684   US
DESIGNNETWORK'S WORKSTATION REPORT. Added/Corp DesignNetwork International. **VFOAT** Workstation Report. (July/Aug. 1992)-. Periodical. English. Irregular (9 issues). $196.00. Design Network International Ltd., PO Box 638, Highland Park IL 60035. **Tel** (708)831-0300. **Continues** Workstation Report, 1040-7472.

   ISSN 1148-5566
   FR
ESPACE BUREAU PARIS. (ESPACE BUREAU.). (1990)-. Periodical. French. Twelve times a year. 350.00F. Publications du Moniteur, 17 rue d'Uzes, 75108 Paris Cedex 02 France. **Tel** 011 33 1 40133030, **FAX** 011 33 1 40419495 customer service, 40133037 advertising, telex UPRESSE 680876 F. **Continues** Bureaux de France (Paris), 0374-1060.

   ISSN 1062-9645
DD 681   US
ETCETERA (LOS ANGELES, CALIF.). See Antiques.

   ISSN 1052-2336
   US
EXECUTIVE'S MANUAL OF PERSONAL SECRETARIES, THE. (1991)-. Periodical. English. Every 2 years. $25.00. Margy Markwood-Vella Publications, 11083 Glenwood Drive, PO Box 8843, Coral Springs FL 33065-8843.

   US
FAULKNER ELECTRONIC OFFICE AUTOMATION. (19??)-. Periodical. English. Twelve times a year. $990.00 US; $1125.00 Canada; $1385.00 other. Faulkner Technical Reports, 7905 Browning Road, Suite 114, Pennsauken NJ 08109. **Tel** (800)843-0460.

LC HF5520   **ISSN** 0266-7797
DD 651.2   UK
   TITLE CHANGE
FINTECH. 2, ELECTRONIC OFFICE. [FinTech, 2 Electron. off.]. (1984)-(1993). Periodical. English. Financial Times Magazines, Greystoke Place, Fetter Lane, London EC4A 1ND United Kingdom. **Tel** 011 44 171 8316577. **Absorbed by** Business Computing Brief, 1350-5092.
   Ind/Abst Infomat Int. Bus.; PTS Newsl. Database [Full Txt.].

   US
FLORIDA ATTORNEYS-SECRETARYS HANDBOOK. See Law.

   NE
GROTE SECRETARESSE HANDBOEK. (19??)-. Dutch. Two times a year. Samsom Bedrijfsinformatie BV, Postbus 4, 2400 MA Alphen Rij Netherlands. **Tel** 011 31 1720 66633.

LC HF   **ISSN** 1120-236X
DD 651   IT
UDC 651.2
HABITAT UFFICIO. [Habitat uff.]. (1981)-. Periodical. Multiple languages. Seven times a year. L90000. Alberto Greco Editore, Via Del Fusaro 8, 20146 Milan Italy. **Tel** 011 39 2 4819086 or 4691895, **FAX** 011 39 2 4819091, telex 315267.

   ISSN 0739-3431
   US
HANSON'S GUIDELINES. VFOAT Hanson's Guidelines. (19??)-. Periodical. English. Three times a year. $120.00. Perceptual Evaluations, 28 Jones Street, Setauket KY 11733. **Tel** (516)941-9472, (516)941-9476, **FAX** (516)941-4444.
   Desc: Covers copier buys for desktop and console model users.

LC TK7887.7 .H35   **ISSN** 1058-2444
DD 681/.62/029473   US
HARD COPY OBSERVER, THE. [Hard copy obs.]. **VFOAT** Observer. Vol. 1, No. 1 (Oct. 1991)-. Periodical. English. Twelve times a year. $495.00. Lyra, PO Box 304, Newton Highlands MA 02161. **Tel** (617)332-0708. **ED** Charles LeCompte. Index available. cum. index.
   Desc: Covers computer printers, related products and supplies.

   SZ
IB SUISSE. (19??)-. French. Irregular (22 issues per year). 119.00F Switzerland; 135.00F other Europe; 162.00 other. Fachpresse Goldach Hudson & Co, Abteilung Vertrieb 272, CH-9403 Goldach Switzerland. **Tel** 011 41 71 416611. **Formed by the union of** Bureau Suisse **and** IB Magazine.

LC HF5548 .I18   **ISSN** 0738-3819
DD 681   US
ISS MATCHBOOK. VFOAT ISS Matchbook. Vol. 1 (1983)-. English.

   ISSN 0022-8893
Pr Rev.
KANTOOR EN EFFICIENCY. [Kant. effic.]. **VFOAT** KE. (1962)-. Periodical. Dutch. Eleven times a year. $102.79. Kluwer BV, Postbus 23, 7400 GA Deventer Netherlands. **Tel** 011 31 5700 33155, 011 31 5700 47421, **FAX** 011 31 5700 11504, telex 42829. Index available. **Bk Rev**. **Ad Acc**. **Circ:** 10,000.
   Desc: Information on office equipment and computers.

LC HD9999.O43 N416
   NE
KANTOORMACHINE-INDUSTRIE / CENTRAAL BUREAU VOOR DE STATISTIEK, HOOFDAFDELING STATISTIEKEN VAN INDUSTRIE EN BOUWNIJVERHEID. VFOAT Manufacture of Office Machinery. Dutch (summaries and/or abstracts in English). One time a year. 9.25. Centraal Bureau voor de Statistiek, AFD ALG Zaken, Postbus 959, 2270 AZ Voorburg Netherlands. **Tel** 011 31 70 3373800, **FAX** 011 31 70 0387429, telex 32692 CBS NL. **Continues** Netherlands. Centraal Bureau Voor de Statistiek. Kantoormachine-Industrie, Produktiestatistieken.

   ISSN 0169-7285
UDC 655.42   NE
   TITLE CHANGE
KBM. KANTOORMARKT. (KBM.). (1984)-(1993). Periodical. Dutch. Wegener Tijl Tijdschriften Group, Postbus 1860, 1110 CD Diemen Netherlands. **Tel** 011 31 20 6603300. **Continues** KBM, 0169-3204. **Merged with** Best of Seven, 0929-788X **to form** Kantoor Businessmagazine, 0929-7871.

LC HF5733.L4 L47
DD 651.7/5   US
LETTERHEADS. (1977)-. Trade Publication. English. One time a year. $55.00. Art Direction Book Company, 10 East 39th Street, 6th Floor, New York NY 10016. **Tel** (212)889-6500. **ED** Don Barron. **Ad Acc**.

   US
LIVE WIRE / FAX SERVICE. English. Twelve times a year. $120.00. Marketing Research Consultants Inc, PO Box 776, 124 Hebron Avenue, Glastonbury CT 06033. **Tel** (203)633-7988. **ED** Frank G. Cannata.
   Desc: Office machine dealer / manufacturer information that cannot fit in the "Cannata Report," or is late breaking news.

   ISSN 0005-7622
   NE
MAANDBLAD VOOR BEDRIJFSADMINISTRATIE EN-ORGANISATIE. Vol. 1 No. 1 (1897)-. Periodical. Dutch. Twelve times a year. F66.00 Netherlands; F97.50 other. Infolio BV, Postbus 16500, 2500 BM Den Haag Netherlands. **Tel** 011 31 70 3819900, **FAX** 011 31 70 3632338.

LC HD   **ISSN** 1382-3590
DD 338   NE
UDC 651.4/.9
●**MANAGEMENT SUPPORT MAGAZINE.** [Manag. support mag.]. (1995)-. Periodical. Dutch. Ten times a year. Fl77.10. Samsom Bedrijfsinformatie BV, Postbus 4, 2400 MA Alphen Rij Netherlands. **Tel** 011 31 1720 66633. **(Subscription address:** Intermedia BV, Postbus 4, 2400 MA Alphen AD Rijn Netherlands. **Tel** 011 31 1720 66481.**) Continues** Secretaresse Magazine, 0169-0582.

   ISSN 0933-8241
   GW
MENSCH & BUERO. VFOAT Mensch und Buro. (19??)-. Trade Publication. German (English, French and Italian). Six times a year. $159.67. Mensch und Buero Verlag GmbH, Vertrieb Lange Strasse 66, Postfach 2247, D-76530 Baden Baden Germany. **Tel** 011 49 7221 392252, **FAX** 011 49 7221 26684. **ED** Hans Ottoman. **Bk**

Business and Economics — Office Equipment and Services

Rev. Ad Acc. Circ: 30,000 (ctrl).
 Desc: Covers office equipment, office environment, office structures, office architecture and accessories. Contains information, news, and design. All mirror the concerns of the user.

LC HF5548 .M49 ISSN 0883-4377
DD 681/.65/0294 US

MINNELLA'S POCKET-GUIDE TO COPIERS.
Added/Corp Minnella Enterprises. VFOAT Minnella's Pocket Guide to Copiers; Pocket Guide to Copiers. (19??)-. English. Four times a year. $69.50. Minnella Enterprises, PO Box 137, Little Falls NJ 07424. Tel (201)785-9029, (201)278-3353, FAX (800)726-0902. ED Thomas A. Minnella, 19 E. Main Street, Little Falls, NJ 07424, (201)785-3527. Circ: 7,000.
 Desc: Copier reference book, specifications, pricing, productivity test results on all currently marketed copiers in the U.S. marketplace.

IT

MOBILI PER UFFICIO.
(19??)-. Periodical. Italian. One time a year (September). Masson SPA, via Statuto 2/4, 20121 Milan Italy. Tel 011 39 2 63671, FAX 011 39 2 6367211.
 Desc: Presents production, design and ergonomic research on office furnishings and fittings. Deals with: office systems, operative and semi-managerial offices, tables and chairs for conference rooms, and other office accessories.

LC HF5547.A2 M6 ISSN 0746-3839
DD 651/.05 US
  CCC
  CODEN MDOPAW
  TITLE CHANGE

MODERN OFFICE TECHNOLOGY.
[Mod. off. technol.]. Vol. 28, No. 10 (Oct. 1983)-Vol. 38, No. 5 (May 1993). Periodical. English. Penton Publishing, 1100 Superior Avenue, Cleveland OH 44114-2543. Tel (216)696-7000, FAX (216)696-0836. ED J. B. Dykeman, L. K. Romei, P. Fernberg, and S. Brindza. Ad Acc. Circ: 160,300 (ctrl). available on microfilm and microfiche from University Microfilms International (UMI); available on an online database (files 15,647,648,675/Full-Text) from DIALOG. Documents available from Ask*IEEE, UMI Article Clearinghouse. Continues Modern Office Procedures, 0026-8208. Continued by Managing Office Technology, 1070-4051.
 Desc: Covers technology, applications, and issues about office automation and information processing for corporate and middle management involved in evaluating, specifying and buying products and services.
 Ind/Abst ABI/INFORM Glob. Ed.; ABI/INFORM [Computer File] (Oct. 1983-); Abstr. Bull. Inst. Pap. Sci. Tech.; Bus. ASAP (1990-) [Full Txt.]; Bus. Educ. Index; Bus. Index (1985-); Bus. Period. Index; Comput. ASAP [Full Txt.]; Comput. Database [Full Txt.]; Comput. Lit. Index; Consum. Index Prod. Eval. Inf. Source (Oct. 1983-); Curr. Cit.; Gen. BusinessFile (1985-); Gen. Period. Index (1985-); INSPEC (Oct. 1983-); Mag. ASAP Plus [Full Txt.]; Mag. Index Plus (1989-); Mag. Search; Newsp. Period. Abstr. (1988-); Mag. Index (1983-); Trade Ind. ASAP [Full Txt.]; Trade Ind. Index (1983-) [Full Txt.]; UMI ABI/Inform--Bus. Period. Ondisc (Dec. 1987-) [Full Txt.]; Wilson Bus. Abstr.; Work Relat. Abstr.; World Publ. Monit.

ISSN 0884-4100
US

MONOSSON'S DEC MARKET WEEKLY.
VAT Monosson's Digital Equipment Corporation Market Weekly. (19??)-. Periodical. English. One time a week. $245.00. Monosson Technology Enterprises, Box 71 Kenmore Station, Boston MA 02215.

ISSN 1059-9983
DD 004 US
  CEASED

NCR CONNECTION.
[NCR connect.]. VAT National Cash Register Connection. (19??)-(1995). Trade Publication. English. Publications & Communications, 12416 Hymeadow Drive, Austin TX 78750. Tel (512)250-9023, (800)678-9724, FAX (512)331-3900, telex 384303. Circ: 10,000. Continues NCR Monthly, 0892-3817.

NE

NEDLLOYD PARADE.
(19??)-. Dutch. Koninklijke Nedlloyd Groep NV, Red Nedlloyd Parade, POB 487, 3000 AL Rotterdam Netherlands.

ISSN 0749-8608
US

NEWSLETTER - AUTOMATED OFFICE CO.
(NEWSLETTER / THE AUTOMATED OFFICE CO.). Added/Corp Automated Office Co. (July 1984)-. Newsletter. English. Twelve times a year. $12.00. Automated Office Company, 253 Bedford Street, Bridgewater MA 02324. Tel (617)697-9438, FAX (617)294-0193. ED Brad Vachon.

NE

NIEUWSBRIEF PZ.
Dutch. Irregular. Kluwer Law and Taxation Publishers / Netherlands, Staverenstraat 32015, PO Box 23, 7400 GA Deventer Netherlands. Tel 011 31 5700 47261.

ISSN 0914-9325
DD 001.64 651.8 JA

NIKKEI DETAPURO OA.
VFOAT Nikkei Datapro OA. (1983)-. Japanese. Irregular. Nihon Keizai Shimbun Inc., 9-5 Otemachi 1 Chome, Chiyoda-ku Tokyo 100 Japan. Tel 011 81 3 32700251, 011 81 3 52108502 (Nikkei Business Publications Inc.), FAX 011 81 3 52552661, 011 81 3 52108119 (Nikkei Business Publications Inc.). ED Hisashi Okamura.
 Desc: Office automation journal.

ISSN 0914-0212
DD 001.64 JA

NIKKEI DETAPURO WAKU SUTESHON.
VFOAT Nikkei Datapro Waku Suteshon. (1988)-. Japanese. Irregular. Nihon Keizai Shimbun Inc., 9-5 Otemachi 1 Chome, Chiyoda-ku Tokyo 100 Japan. Tel 011 81 3 32700251, 011 81 3 52108502 (Nikkei Business Publications Inc.), FAX 011 81 3 52552661, 011 81 3 52108119 (Nikkei Business Publications Inc.). ED Hisashi Okamura.

LC HD9800.U5 N66 ISSN 1049-3743
DD 381/.4568 US

NOPA DEALER OPERATING RESULTS.
[NOPA deal. oper. results]. Added/Corp National Office Products Association. National Office Products Association. Research Dept. NOPA Data Processing Center. VFOAT Dealer Operating Results. VAT National Office Products Association Dealer Operating Results. (19??)-. English. Every 2 years (published every other year). $40.00 (members); $100.00 (nonmembers). National Office Products Association / NOPA, 301 North Fairfax Street, Alexandria VA 22314. Tel (703)549-9040, (800)542-6672, FAX (703)683-7552.

ISSN 0746-5467
DD 338 US
  TITLE CHANGE

NOPA INDUSTRY REPORT.
[NOPA ind. rep.]. Added/Corp National Office Products Association (U.S.). VFOAT National Office Products Association Industry Report. (19??)-(1994). Periodical. English. National Office Products Association, 301 North Fairfax Street, Alexandria VA 22314. Tel (703)549-9040, (800)542-6672, FAX (703)683-7552. ED Sandra Selva. Circ: 10,000. Continued by B.P.I.A. Business Products Industry Report, 1078-5809.
 Desc: Covers pertinent news and information on the office supplies, furnishings and industry as well as news and events of NOPA.

LC HF5439.O4 N66 ISSN 0741-3238
DD 338.4/368 US

NOPA MANUFACTURER SELLING COSTS SURVEY.
Added/Corp National Office Products Association. VFOAT N.O.P.A. Manufacturer Selling Costs Survey; Manufacturer Selling Costs Survey. VAT National Office Products Association Manufacturer Selling Costs Survey. (1975)-. English. Two times a year. $20.00 (members); $50.00 (nonmembers). National Office Products Association, 301 North Fairfax Street, Alexandria VA 22314. Tel (703)549-9040, (800)542-6672, FAX (703)683-7552.
 Desc: A survey on six classifications of selling costs, subdivided into seven sales volume categories, supplies and furniture product lines.

ISSN 1060-3522
DD 338 US
  TITLE CHANGE

NOPA OFFICE MARKET UPDATE.
[NOPA off. mark. update]. Added/Corp National Office Products Association. VFOAT Update. VAT National Office Products Association Office Market Update. Vol. 1, No. 1 (Jan./Feb. 1990)-(1994). Periodical. English. National Office Products Association, 301 North Fairfax Street, Alexandria VA 22314. Tel (703)549-9040, (800)542-6672, FAX (703)683-7552. Continues Special Report to the Office Products Industry. Continued by Business Products Update, 1081-0374.

US

NOPA UPDATE.
English. Six times a year. $40.00. National Office Products Association, 301 North Fairfax Street, Alexandria VA 22314. Tel (703)549-9040, (800)542-6672, FAX (703)683-7552.

LC HF5548.125 .O24
JA

OA JOHO.
VFOAT O.A. Joho; Office Automation Info. (19??)-. Periodical. Japanese. Two times a year. ¥2000. Dempa Publications Inc., 1 11 15 Higashi Gotanda, Shinagawa ku Tokyo 141 Japan. Tel 011 81 3 34456111. (Subscription address: OCS America Inc, 27 08 42nd Road, Long Island City NY 11101. Tel (718)392-0790, (800)367-3405.)

UK

OCCUPATIONAL ERGONOMICS.
(19??)-. English. Four times a year. $195.00. Chapman & Hall, 2-6 Boundary Row, London SE1 8HN United Kingdom. Tel 011 44 171 8650066, FAX 011 44 171 5229623, telex 290164 CHAPMA G. (Subscription address: International Thomson Publishing Services Ltd., North Way Andover, Hampshire SP10 5BE United Kingdom. Tel 011 44 1264 332424.)

ISSN 0709-5228
DD 651/.05 CN
  CCC

OE&M. OFFICE EQUIPMENT & METHODS (1979).
(O E & M, OFFICE EQUIPMENT & METHODS.). VAT OE&M. Office Equipment and Methods (1979); Office Equipment & Methods (1979). Vol. 25 (Jan./Feb. 1979)-. Periodical. English. Irregular. $30.18. Maclean Hunter Canada / Montreal, 1001 bvd. de Maisonneuve W., Montreal Quebec H3A 3E1 Canada. Tel (514)845-5141, FAX (514)845-4302, telex 055-60604. available on microfilm and microfiche from University Microfilms International (UMI). Documents available from Ask*IEEE. Continues Office Equipment & Methods, 0030-0179.
 Ind/Abst INSPEC.

ISSN 0387-5245
DD 338 JA
  CODEN OEPRA4

OEP : OFFICE EQUIPMENT & PRODUCTS.
[OEP, Off. equip. prod.]. VFOAT Office Equipment & Products; Office Equipment and Products. (19??)-. Trade Publication. English. Twelve times a year. $100.00. Dempa Publications Inc., 1 11 15 Higashi Gotanda, Shinagawa ku Tokyo 141 Japan. Tel 011 81 3 34456111. (Subscription address: Dempa Publications, 275 Madison Avenue, New York NY 10016. Tel (212)682-4755.) ED Tetsuo Hirayama. Ad Acc. Circ: 82,500. Documents available from UMI Article Clearinghouse, Ask*IEEE.
 Desc: Reports on new products, market trends and industry issues relating to the office and work place automation.
 Ind/Abst ABI/INFORM Glob. Ed.; ABI/INFORM [Computer File] (1982-); Curr. Cit.; F&S Index Plus Text, Int. [Select. Cov.]; Infomat Int. Bus.; INSPEC (1981-); PROMT.

LC HF5548 .O4 ISSN 0472-6049
DD 651.26 US

OFFICE AUTOMATION.
(1955)-. Periodical. English. Larry Lawier, Administrative Management, 1123 Broadway/Suite 1107, New York NY 10010. Tel (212)924-8989. ED Don Johnson. Bk Rev. Ad Acc. Circ: 300,000 (ctrl).
 Desc: The administration, management and automation of offices and businesses.

LC HF ISSN 1120-0138
DD 65 IT
UDC 681.3

OFFICE AUTOMATION MILANO.
[Off. Autom. Milano.]. (1981)-. Periodical. Italian. Eleven times a year. L130000 Italy; L240000 other. Soiel International, Via Martiri Oscuri 3, 20125 Milan Italy. Tel 011 39 2 26148855.

ISSN 0882-0198
DD 651 US

OFFICE AUTOMATION NEWS : THE PUBLICATION OF THE OFFICE AUTOMATION SOCIETY INTERNATIONAL.
[Off. autom. news]. Added/Corp Office Automation Society International. (19??)-. Periodical. English. Six times a year. $30.00. Office Automation Society International, PO Box 374, McLean VA 22101. Tel (703)821-6650.

ISSN 0886-6767
DD 651 US
  DEAD

OFFICE AUTOMATION REPORT, THE.
[Off. autom. rep.]. Vol. 28, No. 1 (Jan. 1, 1985)- (19??). Periodical. English. The Automated Office Ltd, 1123 Broadway, New York NY 10010. Tel (212)924-8989. ED Don S Johnson and Megan Paznik. Circ: 2,000. available on microfilm from University Microfilms International (UMI). Continues Information & Word Processing Report, 0276-587X.
 Desc: Covers the world of office automation systems and equipment. Includes equipment analyses and technical reports.

ISSN 0824-4073
DD 650.1/3/05 CN

OFFICE CONNECTIONS.
[Off. connect.]. (April/May 1983)-. Periodical. English. Six times a year. Paul Talbot Enterprises, PO Box 2275, Vancouver British Columbia V6B 3W5 Canada. Continues PTA Report, 0822-4234.

ISSN 0705-5153
DD 381/.45/6512 CN

OFFICE EQUIPMENT AND SUPPLIES MARKET IN CANADA, THE.
VFOAT The Office Equipment & Supplies Market in Canada. VAT Market and Media Report. The Office and Equipment and Supplies Market in Canada. (1978)-. English. One time a year. 75.00Can$. Maclean Hunter Canada / Montreal, 1001 bvd. de Maisonneuve W., Montreal Quebec H3A 3E1 Canada. Tel (514)845-5141, FAX (514)845-4302, telex 055-60604. Continues Office Equipment Market in Canada, 0315-9787.

Desc: Reports Canadian production, imports, exports, apparent domestic consumption of office machinery, furniture and supplies, and office building construction.

US
OFFICE EQUIPMENT EXPORTER. (19??)-. English. One time a year (fall). $10.00 US; $15.00 Canada; $20.00 Mexico; $25.00 other. Penton Publishing, 1100 Superior Avenue, Cleveland OH 44114-2543. **Tel** (216)696-7000, FAX (216)696-0836. **(Subscription address:** Penton Publishing, PO Box 96732, Chicago IL 60693. **)**

ISSN 0305-635X
UK
CCC
CEASED
OFFICE EQUIPMENT INDEX. [Off. equip. index]. (1974)-(1994). Periodical. English. O'Connell Reed Publishing, 6 Welden Place, Bradbourne Vale Road, Sevenoaks Kent TN3 3QQ United Kingdom. available on microfilm from University Microfilms International (UMI). ***Continues*** *Index to Office Equipment and Supplies, 0019-4085.*
Ind/Abst Infomat Int. Bus.

ISSN 0030-0187
UK
OFFICE EQUIPMENT NEWS. English. Twelve times a year. AGB Business Publs Ltd, Audit House, Field End Road, Ruislip Middlesex HA4 9LT United Kingdom. **Tel** 011 44 181 8684499. available on microfilm from University Microfilms International (UMI); available on an online database (file 771/Full-Text) from DIALOG. Documents available from Ask*IEEE.
Ind/Abst HILITES; INSPEC (Feb. 1984-); World Ceram. Abstr.

ISSN 1120-2386
IT
UDC 651.2
OFFICE FURNITURE. [Off. furnit.]. (1986)-. Periodical. Multiple languages. One time a year. L6000.00 Italy (surface mail); L150000.00 Europe, L200000.00 Africa and Asia and America, L250000.00 other (airmail). Alberto Greco Editore, Via Del Fusaro 8, 20146 Milan Italy. **Tel** 011 39 2 4819086 or 4691895, FAX 011 39 2 4819091, telex 315367.

ISSN 0273-964X
US
OFFICE GUIDE. See Occupations and Careers.

ISSN 0733-1266
US
OFFICE GUIDE TO ORLANDO. [Off. guide Orlando]. Vol. 1, No. 1 (Spring 1982)-. Trade Publication. English. Four times a year (Jan., Apr., July, Oct.). $30.00. Zink Media Group Ltd., 701 East Washington Street, Orlando FL 32801. **Tel** (407)628-3880, (407)426-9446. **ED** Carey A. Jasa and Warren Miller. **Ad Acc. Circ:** 12,093 (ctrl).
Desc: A complete guide to office space, products and services for the greater Orlando area.

ISSN 1120-012X
IT
UDC 651.2
OFFICE LAYOUT. [Off. Layout]. (1985)-. Periodical. Italian. Six times a year. L100000 Italy; L240000 other. Soiel International, Via Martiri Oscuri 3, 20125 Milan Italy. **Tel** 011 39 2 26148855.

LC HF5548 .O518 **ISSN** 0197-4602
DD 680 US
OFFICE PRODUCTS ANALYST, THE. (THE OFFICE PRODUCTS ANALYST : OPA.). [Off. prod. anal.]. **Added/Corp** Martin Simpson Research Associates. **VFOAT** OPA; O.P.A. Vol. 1, No. 1 (Feb. 1977)-. English. Twelve times a year. $195.00. Industry Analysts Inc., 50 Chestnut Street, Rochester NY 14604. **Tel** (716)232-5320, FAX (716)454-5760. **ED** Louis E. Slawetsky. Index available. **Circ:** 1,000 (ctrl).
Desc: Source of analysis for users of office equipment such as copier duplicators, mini-computer office systems, electronic typewriters, PBX, LANs, facsimile equipment, and laser printers.
Ind/Abst Comput. Bus. (19??-19??).

ISSN 1184-0536
DD 381/.456512/002571 CN
OFFICE PRODUCTS GOLD BOOK. [Off. prod. gold book]. **VFOAT** Gold Book. Vol. 3, Edition 1 (Feb. 1990)-. English (summaries and/or abstracts in French). Irregular. Free to subscribers of The Office Supplies Business Magazine. Abaco Communications Ltd., 44 Carlton Road, Unionville Ontario L3R 1Z5 Canada.

LC HF5548 .O52 **ISSN** 0163-9935
DD 381/.45/6512002573 US
OFFICE PRODUCTS, MASTER CATALOG & BUYING GUIDE. VAT Office Products, Master Catalog and Buying Guide. (1972)-. Catalog. English. Twelve times a year. $62.55. Hitchcock Publishing Company, 191 South Gary Avenue, Carol Stream IL 60188. **Tel** (708)665-1000. ***Continues*** *Office Products Buying Guide.*

ISSN 1034-6686
AT
CODEN OPNED2
OFFICE PRODUCTS NEWS (DARLINGHURST). (OFFICE PRODUCTS NEWS.). [Off. prod. news]. (1989)-. Periodical. English. Twelve times a year. Office Products News, 67-72 Wentworth Avenue, Darlinghurst Sydney, NSW 2010 Australia. ***Continues*** *Modern Office, 0810-9451.*

ISSN 0739-3156
US
CCC
OFFICE PROFESSIONAL, THE. (Oct. 1981)-. Bulletin. English. Twelve times a year. $48.00. Professional Training Associates, 210 Commerce Boulevard, Round Rock TX 78664. **Tel** (512)255-6006, (800)424-2112. **ED** Marilyn Johnson. Index available (free). cum. index. **Bk Rev**, (Qty: 3/yr). **Circ:** 20,000 (ctrl).
Desc: A training bulletin for administrative assistants, secretaries, and other support staff. Tips on grammar, language, getting along with people, career development and secretarial skills.

US
CEASED
OFFICE SKILLS WORKSHOP. Added/Corp Bureau of Business Practice. (19??)-(19??). Periodical. English. Bureau of Business Practice, 24 Rope Ferry Road, Waterford CT 06386. **Tel** (800)243-0876, (203)442-4365, (800)876-9105, FAX (203)443-1123. **ED** Miyo-Alida Amaral. **Circ:** 25,000.
Desc: Devoted to developing and improving basic office skills such as word processing, business writing, time management and techniques for good client relations.

LC HF5001 .O2 **ISSN** 0030-0128
DD 651.205 US
CCC
CODEN OFISAD
TITLE CHANGE
OFFICE (STAMFORD. 1936), THE. (THE OFFICE.). [Office]. (1936)-(Nov. 1993). Trade Publication. English. Office Publications, Inc., PO Box 120031, Stamford CT 06912-0031. **Tel** (203)972-4155. **ED** William R. Schulhof. **Ad Acc. Circ:** 165,000. available on microfilm and microfiche from University Microfilms International (UMI). Documents available from Ask*IEEE, UMI Article Clearinghouse. ***Continues*** *Office Economics.* ***Absorbed by*** *Managing Office Technology.*
Desc: Magazine for the office, administrative, EDP, MIS, systems, executives. Extensive editorial coverage of office related subjects. Introduces over 1,000 new products annually.
Ind/Abst ABI/INFORM Glob. Ed.; ABI/INFORM [Computer File] (Dec. 1971-1993); Abstr. Bull. Inst. Pap. Sci. Tech.; Acad. Abstr.; Acad. Search; Account. Art.; Bus. Index (1985-1993); Bus. Period. Index; Bus. Source Plus; Bus. Source; Comput. Database; Comput. Lit. Index; Consum. Index Prod. Eval. Inf. Source; EP Collect.; Gen. BusinessFile (1985-1993); Gen. Period. Index (1985-1993); Health Plan. Adminis.; Homework Help.; INFO-SOUTH Abstr.; INSPEC (Sept. 1981-1993); Mag. Index Plus (1992-1993); Mag. Search; Manage. Contents; MasterFile FullTEXT 1000; MasterFile FullTEXT 350; MasterFile FullTEXT 650; MasterFile FullTEXT (July 1993-Oct. 1993); Newsp. Period. Abstr. (1989-1993); OCLC; Pub. Lib. FullTEXT; Telebase; Vocat. Search; Wilson Bus. Abstr.; Work Relat. Abstr.; World Publ. Monit.

ISSN 1184-0528
DD 381/.456512/0097105 CN
OFFICE SUPPLIES BUSINESS MAGAZINE, THE. [Off. supplies bus. mag.]. Vol. 1, No. 1 (Apr. 1990)-. Periodical. English. Four times a year. Free. Abaco Communications Ltd., 44 Carlton Road, Unionville Ontario L3R 1Z5 Canada.

LC HF5548 .O523 **ISSN** 8750-3441
DD 651.8/05 US
CCC
CODEN OFSYEH
OFFICE SYSTEMS (GEORGETOWN, CONN.). (OFFICE SYSTEMS : THE MAGAZINE FOR SMALL AND MEDIUM OFFICES.). [Off. syst.]. Vol. 1, No. 1 (July-Aug. 1984)-. Periodical. English. Twelve times a year. Free on request. Office Systems Magazine Inc., 1111 Bethlehem Pike, Cappucio, Springhouse PA 19477. **Tel** (215)628-7716, FAX (215)540-8041. **ED** William M Hogan (editor's phone number: (203)544-9526). **Bk Rev. Ad Acc. Circ:** 100,000 (ctrl). available on microfilm and microfiche from University Microfilms International (UMI).
Desc: Represents the fastest growing segment of the office products field: small- to medium-size companies (50-500 employees).
Ind/Abst Bus. Educ. Index; F&S Index Plus Text, Int. [Select. Cov.]; Law Office Inf. Serv.; PROMT.

ISSN 0164-5951
DD 651 US
CCC
CODEN OWNEEH
OFFICE WORLD NEWS. [Off. world news]. **VFOAT** Office World News OWN; OWN. (197?)-. Trade Publication. English. Twelve times a year. $50.00. FM Business Publications, 342 Madison Avenue, 22nd Floor, New York NY 10173. **Tel** (212)867-2350. available on microfilm and microfiche from University Microfilms International (UMI). Documents available from Ask*IEEE.
Ind/Abst INSPEC (1985-).

LC HF5548 .O525 **ISSN** 0733-2564
DD 651.8/05 US
OFFICEMATION PRODUCT REPORTS. [Officemation prod. rep.]. **Added/Corp** Management Information Corporation. (1977)-. Periodical. English. Twelve times a year. $721.00 US; $796.00 other. Management Information Corporation, 1111 Marlkress Road, Cherry Hill NJ 08003. **Tel** (609)424-1100. **ED** David Axner. Index available. ***Continues*** *Officemation Reports, 0161-8768.*
Desc: Objective evaluations of office automation products.

ISSN 1070-938X
DD 651 US
OFFICIAL OFFICE MACHINES & BUSINESS EQUIPMENT USED PRICES GUIDE BLUE BOOK, THE. [Off. off. mach. bus. equip. used prices guide blue book]. **VFOAT** Official Office Machines and Business Equipment Used Prices Guide Blue Book; Office Machines and Business Equipment Used Prices Guide Blue Book; Blue Book; Office Machines & Business Equipment Used Prices Guide Blue Book; Used Prices Guide Blue Book. (19??)-. English. One time a year. $222.00. Asay Publishing Company, PO Box 670, Joplin MO 64802. **Tel** (417)781-9317, FAX (417)781-0427, (800)825-9633. **ED** Gail Evans (phone: (800)947-0225).

LC HF5541.T9 O3
DD 684.1/0068/8 US
CEASED
OPD. VFOAT Office Products Distribution; Office Products Dealer. Vol. 120, No. 2 (Feb. 1992)-Vol. 121, No. 11 (Nov. 1993). Periodical. English. Hitchcock Publishing Company, 191 South Gary Avenue, Carol Stream IL 60188. **Tel** (708)665-1000. ***Continues*** *Office Products Dealer, 0199-1329.*

LC HD9795.U6 C87 **ISSN** 0739-8271
DD 380.1/456816 US
PENS, PENCILS, AND MARKING DEVICES. (CURRENT INDUSTRIAL REPORTS. MA39A, PENS, PENCILS, AND MARKING DEVICES.). **Added/Corp** United States. Bureau of the Census. **VFOAT** Pens, Pencils, and Marking Devices. (1981)-. Government Publication. English. One time a year. $1.00. US Department of Commerce / Bureau of the Census, Data User Services Division, Customer Services, Washington DC 20233-0800. **Tel** (301)763-4100. **(Subscription address:** Superintendent of Documents, US Government Printing Office, Washington DC 20402. **)**
Desc: Presents data on the quantity and value of shipments of pens, mechanical pencils and parts, nonmechanical pencils, crayons and chalk, along with hand stamps, stencils, and other marketing devices.

ISSN 1054-7576
DD 004 US
PORTABLE OFFICE. BUYER'S GUIDE ... . [Portable off., Buyer's guide]. **VFOAT** Buyer's Guide ...; Portable Office Buyer's Guide; Buyer's Guide to ... . (1991)-. English. Six times a year. Portable Office, 80 Elm Street, Peterborough NH 03458.

ISSN 0965-4739
UK
PREMISES & FACILITIES MANAGEMENT. [Premises facil. manag.]. **VFOAT** Premises and Facilities Management. (1991)-. Trade Publication. English. Ten times a year. $188.23. IML Group, Blair House, 184-186 High Street, Tonbridge Kent, TN9 1BQ United Kingdom. **Tel** 011 44 1732 359990, FAX 011 44 1732 770049. **ED** Richard Byatt. **Ad Acc, Adv Mgr:** Mark Wiles. ***Continues*** *Premises Management & Facility Planning.*

LC HF5718.22 .P747 **ISSN** 1072-7531
DD 658 US
CCC
•PRESENTATIONS (MINNEAPOLIS, MINN.). (PRESENTATIONS.). [Presentations]. **VFOAT** Presentations Magazine. (1993)-. Periodical. English. Twelve times a year. $50.00. Lakewood Publications, 50 South Ninth Street, Minneapolis MN 55402. **Tel** (612)333-0471, (800)328-4329, FAX (612)333-6526. ***Continues*** *Presentation Products, 1070-6089.*

IT
SUSPENDED
PROGETTO UFFICIO. (19??)-(Dec. 1992). Italian. Irregular. Rima Srl, via V Da Filicaia 7, 20162 Milan Italy. **Tel** 011 39 2 66013539.

ISSN 0317-6339
DD 658.8/38/65120971 CN
PURCHASING PREFERENCE SURVEY : OFFICE EQUIPMENT AND SUPPLIES. (1975)-. English. One time a year. Maclean Hunter Canada / Montreal, 1001 bvd. de Maisonneuve W., Montreal Quebec H3A 3E1 Canada. **Tel** (514)845-5141, FAX (514)845-4302, telex 055-60604.

Business and Economics —Personnel Management

ISSN 0701-7898
DD 380.1/456841/00971 CN

QUARTERLY SHIPMENTS OF OFFICE FURNITURE PRODUCTS. [Q. shipm. off. furnit. prod.]. **Added/Corp** Statistics Canada. Manufacturing and Primary Industries Division. **VFOAT** Livraisons Trimestrielles des Produits du Meuble de Bureau. Vol. 1, No. 1 (Mar. 1972)-. Periodical. English (French). Four times a year. 32.00Can$ Canada; $39.60 US; $45.00 other. Statistics Canada Publications Sales and Services, R.H. Coats Building 6th Floor, Ottawa Ontario K1A 0T6 Canada. **Tel** (613)951-5078, (800)267-6677, FAX (613)951-1584, telex 053-3585.
Desc: Provides detailed information on office furniture products.

ISSN 8755-4038
DD 651 US

SECRETARIAL SERVICES TODAY. [Secr. serv. today]. Vol. 1, No. 1 (Dec. 1984)-. Periodical. English. Twelve times a year. $18.00. Secretarial Services Today, PO Box 29203, Shreveport LA 71149-9203.

LC HF5547.A2 S395 **ISSN** 0037-0622
DD 651.06273 US
 CCC

SECRETARY (KANSAS CITY, MO.), THE. (THE SECRETARY.). [Secretary]. **Added/Corp** National Secretaries Association (U.S.) Professional Secretaries International. National Secretaries Association (International). (1942)-. Periodical. English. Nine times a year. $16.00 US; $20.00 (surface mail); $42.00 (airmail) other. Professional Secretaries International, 10502 Northwest Ambassador Drive, Kansas City MO 64195. **Tel** (816)891-6600. **ED** Debra Stratton. Index Available in first issue of next volume--attached. **Bk Rev. Ad Acc. Circ:** 45,000 (ctrl). available on microfilm and microfiche from University Microfilms International (UMI). **Continues** National Secretary.
Desc: Articles directed to the professional secretary on office technology, management skills, career development and future trends.
Ind/Abst Bus. Educ. Index; Bus. Source Plus; Bus. Source; EP Collect.; Homework Help.; Mag. Search; MasterFile FullTEXT 1000; MasterFile FullTEXT 350; MasterFile FullTEXT 650; MasterFile FullTEXT (July 1993-); OCLC; Telebase; Vocat. Search.

US
CEASED
SECRETARY'S IMPROVEMENT PROGRAM. See Occupations and Careers.

ISSN 0738-6516
 US
SIZZLE SHEET, THE. See Business and Economics-Marketing and Purchasing.

LC PG3242 .S686 **ISSN** 0207-7698
 RU
SOVREMENNAIA DRAMATURGIIA. **Added/Corp** Soviet Union. Ministerstvo Kultury. Soiuz Pisatelei SSSR. (1982)-. Periodical. Russian. Twelve times a year. $109.95. (**Subscription address:** East View Publications Inc., 3020 Harbor Lane North, Suite 110, Minneapolis MN 55447. **Tel** (800)477-1005, (612)550-0961, FAX (612)559-2931.)

ISSN 0951-7820
DD 338.4767628230941 UK
STATIONERY TRADE NEWS. [Stationery trade news]. (1983)-. Periodical. English. Twelve times a year. £40.00 UK; £60.00 other. Trade Media Ltd. / UK, Brookmead House, Two Rivers, Station Lane, Witney Oxfordshire OX8 6BH United Kingdom. **Tel** 011 44 1993 775545, FAX 011 44 1993 778884. **ED** Ian Boughton. **Ad Acc, Adv Mgr:** Paula Sandmann. **Circ:** 8,187 (ctrl).
Desc: Product and market information for the office supplies industry.

LC HD9801.A1 T43 **ISSN** 8755-4526
DD 001.64 US
TECHNICAL OFFICE, THE. See Business and Economics-Computer Applications.

ISSN 1066-0011
DD 680 US
TONER TECHNOLOGY MONTHLY. [Toner technol. mon.]. **Added/Corp** Toner Technology, Inc. (1984)-. Periodical. English. Twelve times a year. $950.00 US and Canada; $1,050.00 other. Toner Research Services, 3495 Mustafa Drive, Sharonville OH 45241. **Tel** (513)733-4407, FAX (513)733-4744. **ED** John F. Cooper. **Circ:** 80.
Desc: Consists of six to eight sections providing current technical information related to copier, printer, toner and developer materials.

US
SUSPENDED
TRANSCRIPT, THE. VOL. 1 (1944)-Suspended Vol. 43, No. 3. Periodical. English. Four times a year. $15.00. New York Shorthand Reporters, 427 Kenwood Avenue, Delmar NY 12054. **Tel** (518)439-0981. Index available in last issue of volume--attached. **Bk Rev. Ad Acc. Circ:** 900.

Desc: Informative and educational articles of interest to shorthand reporters, especially members of their professional association.

ISSN 0897-0939
 US
UPDATE (HACKENSACK, N.J.). (UPDATE: THE EXECUTIVE'S PURCHASING ADVISOR.). [Update]. **Added/Corp** Buyers Laboratory. (19??)-. Periodical. English. Twelve times a year. $115.00. Buyers Laboratory Inc., 20 Railroad Avenue, Hackensack NJ 07601. **Tel** (201)488-0404. **ED** Daria Hoffman. Index available. **Circ:** 3,000.
Desc: Provides advice, analysis and information to purchasers of office equipment, including copiers, fax machines, typewriters, printers, furniture, mailing equipment, supplies, and etc.

ISSN 0042-3327
DD 658.8 US
VENDING TIMES. [Vend. times]. Vol. 1 (1961)-. Periodical. English. Twelve times a year. $35.00. Vending Times Inc, 545 8th Avenue, New York NY 10018. **Tel** (212)714-0101, FAX (212)564-0196. **ED** Arthur E Yohalem. **Bk Rev. Ad Acc. Circ:** 15,000 (ctrl). available on microfilm and microfiche from University Microfilms International (UMI). **Absorbed** Vend; V/T Music & Games.
Desc: Covers vending, coin-operated music and amusement machines, and coffee service fields.
Ind/Abst Bus. Index (Jan. 1985-Dec. 1985); EP Collect.; F&S Index Plus Text, Int. [Select. Cov.]; Foods Adlibra; Gen. BusinessFile (Jan. 1985-Dec. 1985); Gen. Period. Index (Jan. 1985-Dec. 1985); Homework Help.; Mag. Search; MasterFile FullTEXT 1000; MasterFile FullTEXT 350; MasterFile FullTEXT 650; MasterFile FullTEXT (July 1993-); OCLC; PROMT; Stat. Ref. Index; Telebase; Trade Ind. Index (1981-?); Vocat. Search.

US
VENDING TIMES, CENSUS OF THE INDUSTRY. English. One time a year. $25.00. Vending Times Inc, 545 8th Avenue, New York NY 10018. **Tel** (212)714-0101, FAX (212)564-0196.
Ind/Abst Predicasts Forecasts.

US
VENDING TIMES. INTERNATIONAL BUYERS GUIDE ISSUE. **VFOAT** International Buyers Guide Issue; Vending Times Buyers Guide Issue; V/T Buyers Guide. (1988)-. Consumer Publication. English. One time a year (August). $25.00. Vending Times Inc, 545 8th Avenue, New York NY 10018. **Tel** (212)714-0101, FAX (212)564-0196. **Continues** Vending Times. International Buyers Guide and Directory.

UK
WHAT TO BUY. English. Twelve times a year. £105.00 UK; £170.00 North America; £130.00 Europe. What to Buy, Quadrant House, The Quadrant, Sutton Surrey SM2 5AS, United Kingdom. **Tel** 011 44 181 6618700, FAX 011 44 181 7701284. **ED** Sarah Frater. Index available. cum. index. **Circ:** 10,000. **Continues** Copier User.
Desc: Independent business consumer report covering office equipment and services. Articles and charts covering everything from fax to finance, copiers to computers, typewriters to telephone systems and software stationary.

ISSN 0265-296X
DD 651.200294 UK
WHAT TO BUY FOR BUSINESS. [What buy bus.]. **VFOAT** What to Buy. (1980)-. Trade Publication. English. Twelve times a year. $205.35. Garrard House, 2 6 Homesdale Road, Bromley Kent, BR2 9WL United Kingdom. **Tel** 011 44 181 4028493, FAX 011 44 181 4029502.
Ind/Abst Curr. Cit.

LC HF5548 .W45 **ISSN** 0886-6163
DD 381./45/00029473 US
WHAT TO BUY FOR BUSINESS (U.S. ED.). (WHAT TO BUY FOR BUSINESS.). [What buy bus.]. (1981)-. Periodical. English. Ten times a year (published monthly with Jul./Aug. and Dec./Jan. issues combined). $125.00. What to Buy for Business, 924 Anacapa Street, Suite 4G, Santa Barbara CA 93101. **Tel** (805)963-3539, FAX (805)963-3740. **(Subscription address:** Palm Coast Data, PO Box 420163, Agency Department, Palm Coast FL 32142. **Tel** (904)445-4662 ext. 669, (800)829-5475.) Documents available from Ask*IEEE.
Ind/Abst Acad. Abstr.; Acad. Search; Bus. Source Plus; Bus. Source; EP Collect.; HILITES; Homework Help.; Inf. Manage. Technol.; INSPEC (June 1983-); Mag. Artic. Summar. Elite; Mag. Artic. Summar. Select; Mag. Artic. Summar. CD-ROM; Manage. Market. Abstr.; MasterFile FullTEXT 1000; MasterFile FullTEXT 350; MasterFile FullTEXT 650; MasterFile FullTEXT (July 1994-); OCLC; Print. Abstr.; Pub. Lib. FullTEXT; Telebase; Vocat. Search; World Ceram. Abstr.; World Publ. Monit.

ISSN 1068-9699
DD 651 US
 CODEN WOCREX
●**WORKGROUP COMPUTING REPORT.** [Workgr. comput. rep.]. **Added/Corp** Patricia Seybold Group. Vol. 16, No. 2 (Feb. 1993)-. Periodical. English. Twelve times a year. $440.00. Patricia Seybolds Office Computing Group, 148 State Street, Suite 700, Boston MA 02109. **Tel** (617)742-5200, (800)826-2424, FAX (617)742-1028. Documents available from Ask*IEEE. **Continues** Office Computing Report, 1057-8889.
Ind/Abst INSPEC; Print. Abstr.

LC HD9803.U6 W67 **ISSN** 1062-7650
DD 684 US
WORKSTATION REPORT'S ... BUYER' GUIDE TO OFFICE FURNITURE, THE. [Workstn. rep. buy. guide off. furnit.]. **Added/Corp** ZigZag Corporation. **VFOAT** Buyer' Guide to Office Furniture. (199?)-. Periodical. English. One time a year. $79.00. Design Network International Ltd., PO Box 638, Highland Park IL 60035. **Tel** (708)831-0300.
Desc: Analytical publications in the contract furniture industry. The Workstation Report combines insightful reviews, along with pricing comparisons and current industry news. This dynamic combination allows the reader to make informed decisions when purchasing or specifying office furniture products.

LC HF5001 .Z4 **ISSN** 0722-7485
DD 650/.05 GW
 CODEN ZFORET
ZEITSCHRIFT FUEHRUNG + ORGANISATION. See Business and Economics-Management.

PERSONNEL MANAGEMENT

ISSN 0922-2928
 NE
UDC 651
AANSPRAAK AMSTERDAM. (AANSPRAAK.). (1988)-. Periodical. Dutch. Eleven times a year. $143.88. Uitgeverij Imp, Molenweg 28, Postbus 69, 7213 ZH Gorssel Netherlands. **Tel** 011 31 5751 4288.

LC HF5549.5.C67 A23 **ISSN** 1068-0918
DD 331 US
Pr Rev.
ACA JOURNAL / AMERICAN COMPENSATION ASSOCIATION. [ACA j. - Am. Compens. Assoc.]. **Added/Corp** American Compensation Association. **VAT** American Compensation Association Journal. (1992)-. Trade Publication. English. Four times a year. $65.00. American Compensation Association, 14040 North Northsight Boulevard, Scottsdale AZ 85260. **Tel** (602)951-9191, FAX (602)483-8352.
Desc: Provides readers with compensation and benefits information that serves as an educational resource with respect to trends and contemporary issues, for the purpose of advancing total-compensation management, theory, knowledge and practice.

LC HD5650 .A327 **ISSN** 0885-3339
DD 658.3/152/05 US
ADVANCES IN THE ECONOMIC ANALYSIS OF PARTICIPATORY AND LABOR-MANAGED FIRMS. See Business and Economics-Labor.

LC KF5130 HF5549 **ISSN** 1080-2487
DD 347.73 658.3 US
●**ALTERNATIVE DISPUTE RESOLUTION ALERT.** See Law.

LC HM134 .A55 **ISSN** 1046-333X
DD 658.3 US
NLM W1; AN749T
 TITLE CHANGE
... ANNUAL, DEVELOPING HUMAN RESOURCES, THE. [Annu. dev. human resour.]. **Added/Corp** University Associates. **VFOAT** Developing Human Resources. (1984)-(1994). English. Pfeiffer & Company International Publishers, Roggestraat 15, 2153 GC Nieuw Venn Netherlands. **Tel** 011 31 2526 89840, FAX 011 31 2526 86885. **(Subscription address:** Pfeiffer and Company International Publ., 2780 Circleport Drive, Erlanger KY 41018. **Tel** (800)274-4434.)
Continues Annual for Facilitators, Trainers, and Consultants, 0732-037X. **Split into** Annual. Volume 1, Training **and** Annual. Volume 2, Consulting.
Ind/Abst Curr. Cit.

LC HD6948.M3 E48A
DD 658.3/006/06897 MW
ANNUAL REPORT AND REVIEW OF ACTIVITIES FOR THE YEAR / THE EMPLOYERS' CONSULTATIVE ASSOCIATION OF MALAWI. **Main/Corp** Employers' Consultative Association of Malawi. English.

Business and Economics —Personnel Management

One time a year. Employers' Consultative Association of Malawi, Dalveen House, Haile Selassie Road, PO Box 950, Blantyre Malawi. **Continues** ECAM Annual Report.

UK

ANNUAL REPORT ON TRAINING RESEARCH / EMPLOYMENT DEPARTMENT. Main/Corp Great Britain. Dept. of Employment. **VFOAT** Training Research Annual Report. (1991)-. Periodical. English.

LC WMLC 91/1385

US

ANNUAL REPORT / SOUTH CAROLINA, HUMAN SERVICES COORDINATING COUNCIL. Main/Corp South Carolina. Human Services Coordinating Council. (1989/1990)-. English.

LC HF5549.5.T7 A66

US

●**... ANNUAL. VOLUME 1, TRAINING, THE.** Added/Corp Pfeiffer & Company. **VFOAT** Training. (1995)-. English. Pfeiffer & Company International Publishers, Roggestraat 15, 2153 GC Nieuw Venn Netherlands. **Tel** 011 31 2526 89840, FAX 011 31 2526 86885. **(Subscription address:** Pfeiffer and Company International Publ., 2780 Circleport Drive, Erlanger KY 41018. **Tel** (800)274-4434.) **Continues in part** Annual, Developing Human Resources, 1046-333X.

LC HD58.8 .A66

US

●**... ANNUAL. VOLUME 2, CONSULTING, THE.** Added/Corp Pfeiffer & Company. **VFOAT** Consulting. (1995)-. English. Pfeiffer & Company International Publishers, Roggestraat 15, 2153 GC Nieuw Venn Netherlands. **Tel** 011 31 2526 89840, FAX 011 31 2526 86885. **(Subscription address:** Pfeiffer and Company International Publ., 2780 Circleport Drive, Erlanger KY 41018. **Tel** (800)274-4434.) **Continues in part** Annual, Developing Human Resources, 1046-333X.

LC HF5549.2.B7 A58
DD 658.3/00981

BL

ANUARIO BRASILEIRO DE RECURSOS HUMANOS. 1984-. Periodical. Portuguese. One time a year. Embranews Publicacoes Especializadas Ltda, Av Sao Luis 258 1O Andar Conj 101, CEP 01046 Sao Paulo SP Brazil.

LC NX399.I5 I53a

II

ANUDANOM KI MANGEM, MANAVA-SAMSADHANA VIKASA MANTRALAYA = DEMANDS FOR GRANTS OF MINISTRY OF HUMAN RESOURCE DEVELOPMENT. Main/Corp India. Ministry of Human Resource Development. **VFOAT** Demands for Grants of Ministry of Human Resource Development; Anudanom ki Mangem. (1987)-. English (Hindi). Government of India Press Department of Culture, Minto Road, New Delhi India. **Continues** India. Dept. of Culture. Anudanom ki Mangem.

ISSN 1055-9094
DD 658

US

APPLIED H.R.M. RESEARCH. [Appl. H.R.M. res.]. Added/Corp Association of I/O Graduates. **VAT** Applied Human Resources Management Research. Vol. 1, No. 1 (1990)-. English. Two times a year. $40.00. Micheal A Surrette, Department of Psychology, University of Rhode Island, Kingston RI.
Ind/Abst Person. Manage. Abstr.

ISSN 0889-8227
DD 658

US

APPLIED MANAGEMENT NEWSLETTER. [Appl. manage. newsl.]. Added/Corp National Association for Management (U.S.). (19??)-. Newsletter. English. Twelve times a year. $39.00. National Association for Management, 5920 East Central, Suite 205, Wichita KS 67208. **Tel** (316)688-0763, FAX (316)686-6702. Index available. **Ad Acc, Adv Mgr:** Eric J. Steele.
Desc: Management training into company training programs to help prepare individual managers for advancement, increase leadership effectiveness and assist in improving company profits.

NE

ARBO KNIPSELKRANT. See Sociology-Social Services and Welfare.

LC HF5549.A2 H85
ISSN 1038-4111

AT

Pr Rev.

ASIA PACIFIC JOURNAL OF HUMAN RESOURCES. [Asia Pac. j. hum. resour.]. Added/Corp Australian Human Resources Institute. Institute of Personnel Management New Zealand. Institute of Personnel Management Papua New Guinea. Vol. 30, No. 1 (Autumn 1992)-. Periodical. English. Three times a year. 59.20Au$. Institute of Personnel Management Australia, PO Box 461, Mulgrave North Vicotria 3170 Australia. **Tel** 011 61 3 3444481, FAX 011

61 3 3444122. **ED** Stephen Deery. **Bk Rev**, (Qty: 18).
Ad Acc, Adv Mgr: Ros Makris. **Circ:** 12,500 (ctrl).
Continues Asia Pacific HRM, 1032-3627.
Ind/Abst APAIS, Aust. Public Aff. Inf. Ser. (1992-).

ISSN 8750-2763
DD 338

US

ATTORNEYS PERSONNEL REPORT. See Law.

ISSN 0268-764X

UK

Pr Rev.

BENEFITS & COMPENSATION INTERNATIONAL. See Insurance.

ISSN 1069-1707

US

●**BENEFITS & COMPENSATION SOLUTIONS.** [Benefits compens. solut.]. **VFOAT** Benefits and Compensation Solutions; Solutions. Vol. 14, No. 4 (Apr. 1993)-. English. Eleven times a year. $50.00. AMR International Inc., 10 Valley Drive, Suite 9, Greenwich CT 06803. **Tel** (203)661-0101. **Continues** Payroll Exchange, 0194-6196; Benefits, 1062-1148.

ISSN 0703-7732
DD 658.32/5/0971

CN
CCC

BENEFITS CANADA. (1976)-. English. Eleven times a year. 60.03Can$. MacLean Hunter Ltd. Business Publishers / Canada, Box 9100, Station A, Toronto Ontario M5W 1A5 Canada. **Tel** (416)596-5000, , FAX (416)596-5552. **(Subscription address:** Indas Customer Service, 35 Riviera Drive, Building 17, Markham Ontario L3R 8N4 Canada. **Tel** (905)946-0406.) **ED** John Milne. **Bk Rev. Ad Acc. Circ:** 14,000 (ctrl). available on microfilm and microfiche from University Microfilms International (UMI). Documents available from UMI Article Clearinghouse.
Desc: Reaches Canada's top 5,000 companies and covers compensation, benefits, and pension fund investments. Directories on consultants, group insurance and money managers for pension funds.
Ind/Abst ABI/INFORM Glob. Ed.; Ins. Period. Index.

ISSN 1062-1148
DD 658

US
CODEN BENEEK
TITLE CHANGE

BENEFITS (CLEARWATER, FLA.). See Business and Economics-Labor.

ISSN 0341-1044

GW
UDC 658.3:349.2/.3
CCC
CODEN 658:351

BETRIEB UND PERSONAL. **VFOAT** B + P. Betrieb + Personal; B + P. Betriebe und Personal; Betrieb + Personal; Betrieb und Personal Aktuell. (1970)-. Periodical. German. Twelve times a year. Stollfuss Verlag Bonn GmbH, Postfach 2428, Dechenstrasse 7, D-53014 Bonn Germany. **Tel** 011 49 228 724257, FAX 011 49 228 7249266, telex 841 08869477.
Ind/Abst Selec. Coop. Index Manage. Period.

US

BETTER SUPERVISION. Added/Corp Economic Press. (19??)-. Periodical. English. Twenty-six times a year. $44.20. Economics Press Inc, 12 Daniel Road, Fairfield NJ 07004. **Tel** (201)227-1224, (800)526-2554, FAX (201)227-9742. **ED** Bob Guder. **Circ:** 43,000 (ctrl).
Desc: Deals with the art of managing people and work.

US

BETTER-WORK SUPERVISOR, THE. (May 7, 1979)-. Periodical. English. Twenty-four times a year. Price varies. Clement Communications Inc., Concord Industrial Park, Concordville PA 19331. **Tel** (800)345-8101, (610)459-4200. **ED** Carl Heyel. **Circ:** 40,000.
Desc: Designed to help supervisors do a better job.

ISSN 0005-3228

US
CCC

BNA POLICY AND PRACTICE SERIES. Main/Corp Bureau of National Affairs (Washington, D.C.). **VAT** Bureau of National Affairs Policy and Practice Series. (19??)-. Monographic series. English. Irregular. $1,295.00. Bureau of National Affairs Inc., 9435 Key West Avenue, Rockville MD 20850. **Tel** (800)372-1033, (301)258-1033, FAX (301)948-5823. **ED** Bill L Manville. available on an online database from Human Resources Information Network.
Desc: A reference and advisory service on the control of air pollution, designed to meet the information needs of individuals responsible for complying with EPA and state air pollution control regulations.

ISSN 1051-208X
DD 331

US

BNAC COMMUNICATOR. See Communications.

UK

BRITISH PERSONNEL MANAGEMENT. English. CCH Editions Ltd., Telford Road Bicester, Oxfordshire OX6 0XD United Kingdom. **Tel** 011 44 1869 253300, FAX 011 44 1869 245814.

ISSN 0525-2156
CCC

BULLETIN TO MANAGEMENT. Added/Corp Bureau of National Affairs (Washington, D.C.). (1968)-. Bulletin. English. One time a week. $254.00. Bureau of National Affairs Inc., 9435 Key West Avenue, Rockville MD 20850. **Tel** (800)372-1033, (301)258-1033, FAX (301)948-5823. **ED** Bill L. Manville. available on an online database from Human Resources Information Network.
Continues Labor Policy and Practice Bulletin to Management.
Desc: Summaries of current developments, discussions of real-life job situations, statistical charts and graphs, and ready-to-use policy guides.

US

BUREAU OF NAVAL PERSONNEL MANUAL. Main/Corp United States. Bureau of Naval Personnel. English. US Department of Defense Department of the Navy, Pentagon, Room 4E686, Washington DC 20350. **Tel** (703)695-0911.

ISSN 0736-4415
US

BUSINESS CURRENTS. TECHNICAL REPORT. Added/Corp National Alliance of Business. (1983)-. English. Irregular. $160.00. National Alliance of Business, 1201 New York Avenue Northwest, Suite 700, Washington DC 20005. **Tel** (202)289-2888. **ED** Alan Vannerman. **Ad Acc. Circ:** 2,300. **Continues** Business Currents in Employment Policy. Technical Supplement.
Desc: Job training programs involving the private sector that aid the poor.

ISSN 0397-2143
FR
UDC 65

CAHIERS D'INFORMATION DU DIRECTEUR DE PERSONNEL, LES. (1976)-. Periodical. French. Four times a year. 284.91F. Ste Contact CIDP, 156 rue du Faubourg St. Denis, 75010 Paris France. **Tel** 011 33 1 42068228.
Ind/Abst LABORDOC.

ISSN 0838-228X
DD 658.3/00971

CN

CANADIAN HR REPORTER. [Can. HR report.]. **VAT** Canadian Human Resource Reporter. Vol. 1, No. 1 (Sept. 21, 1987)-. Periodical. English. Twenty-two times a year. 36.81Can$. MPL Communications, 133 Richard Street West, Suite 700, Toronto Ontario M5H 3M8 Canada. **Tel** (416)869-1177, FAX (416)869-0456. **Bk Rev. Ad Acc. Circ:** 5,500. Documents available from UMI Article Clearinghouse.
Desc: Provides HR managers with timely news and advice on HR methods and techniques as well as insight into industry developments, trends, products and services.
Ind/Abst ABI/INFORM Glob. Ed.

NE

CAO'S IN NEDERLAND. Main/Corp Netherlands (Kingdom, 1815-) Loonbureau. **VFOAT** C. A. O.'s in Nederland. **VAT** Collectieve Arbeidsovereenkomsten en Nederland. 1970-. Periodical. Dutch. Two times a year. SDU Uitgeverij, Postbus 20014, Christoffel Plantijnstraat, 2500 EA Den Haag Netherlands. **Tel** 011 31 70 3789911.

ISSN 0888-3548
DD 331

US

CARTA-LEON DESDE WASHINGTON SOBRE ADMINISTRACION DE RECURSOS HUMANOS. (CARTA-LEON DESDE WASHINGTON SOBRE ADMINISTRACION DE RECURSOS HUMANOS / LEON DEVELOPING WORLD PUBLICATIONS, INC.). [Carta-Leon Wash. adm. recur. hum.]. Added/Corp Leon Developing World Publications, Inc. **VFOAT** Carta Leon Desde Washington. Vol. 1, No. 1 (June 1982)-. Periodical. Spanish. Twelve times a year. $39.00. Leon Developing World Publishing, PO Box 3932, Langley Park MD 20787. **Tel** (301)434-2431. **ED** F. L. Leon. Index available. cum. index. **Circ:** 300.
Desc: Spanish analyses and recommendations on adoption or adaptation of human resources technologies as they affect economic and social stages of development.

ISSN 1061-5997
US
TITLE CHANGE

CEO'S REPORT ON COST CUTTING. Added/Corp Institute of Management & Administration. **VFOAT** Report on Cost Cutting. (1992)-(19??). Periodical. English. Institute of Management and

Business and Economics —Personnel Management

Administration, 29 West 35th Street, 5th Floor, New York NY 10001-2299. **Tel** (212)244-0360, FAX (212)564-0465. **Continued by** Financial Manager's Report on Cost Cutting, 1070-2210.

IT
CLASS (MILAN, ITALY). (CLASS.). (May 1986)-. Periodical. Italian. Twelve times a year. L62400 Italy; L250000 The Americas and Asia; L142000 Europe; L226000 Africa; L334000 other. Class Editori, Via Burigozzo 5, 20122 Milan Italy. **Tel** 011 39 2 582191.

ISSN 0820-7658
DD 354.71001/7   CN
COMMUNICATIONS - INSTITUT PROFESSIONNEL DE LA FONCTION PUBLIQUE DU CANADA. (COMMUNICATIONS.). [Commun. - Inst. prof. Serv. public Can.]. **Added/Corp** Institut Professionnel de la Fonction Publique du Canada. Vol. 3, No. 8 (July 15, 1977)-. Periodical. French. Irregular. Free to members. Communications, a/s Institut Professionnel de la Fonction Publique de Canada, 786 Avenue Bronson, Ottawa Ontario K1S 4G4 Canada. **Continues** Communications (Institut Professionnel de la Fonction Publique du Canada). Francais, 0318-0646.

ISSN 0589-5014
UK
CONTACT. (Jan. 1969). Periodical. English. Four times a year. Free on request. EETPU, Editorial Office, Hayes Court, West Common Road, Bromley Kent United Kingdom. **ED** P. Gallageher. **Ad Acc, Adv Mgr:** M. Thompson. **Circ:** 330,000.
Desc: Matters pertaining to or involving AEEV members and the industries in which they work.

LC HD28 .C644
BL
CONTEXTO BOLETIM. Year 1- May/August 1974-. Bulletin. Portuguese (summaries and/or abstracts in English). Banco da Amazonia Centro de Documentacao e Biblioteca, Av Presidente Vargas 800 - 160 Andar, Belem Brazil. **Tel** (091)223-2657.

LC HF5601   **ISSN** 0745-0877
DD 657   US
CPA PERSONNEL REPORT. [CPA pers. rep.]. **VFOAT** C.P.A. Personnel Report; Certified Public Accountant Personnel Report. **VAT** Certified Public Accountant Personnel Report. (1982)-. Newsletter. English. Twelve times a year. $197.00. Strafford Publications Inc., 590 Dutch Valley Road Northeast, Atlanta GA 30324. **Tel** (404)881-1141, (800)926-7926, FAX (404)881-0074. **ED** Julie Tamminen. Index available. **Bk Rev**.
Desc: Newsletter detailing the latest trends and techniques in firm personnel management and accounting services.
Ind/Abst Account. Index Suppl. (1986-); Account. Tax Datab. (1986-).

LC HF5549 LC1660
DD 658.3 374   UK
●**CPD LINK.** (1994)-. Newsletter. English. Twelve times a year. Free. Continuing Professional Development Forum, Engineering Council, 10 Maltravers Street, London WC2R 3ER United Kingdom. **Tel** 011 44 171 2407891, FAX 011 44 171 3795586. **ED** John Lorriman. **Circ:** 60,000.
Desc: Looks at continuing development programs in the area of engineering.

ISSN 1053-170X
DD 331   US
CCC
CODEN CTTEEU
CREATIVE TRAINING TECHNIQUES. [Creat. train. tech.]. **VFOAT** Creative Training Techniques Newsletter. (1988)-. Newsletter. English. Twelve times a year. $99.00. Lakewood Publications, 50 South Ninth Street, Minneapolis MN 55402. **Tel** (612)333-0471, (800)328-4329, FAX (612)333-6526. **Bk Rev. Circ:** 8,000.
Desc: Tips, tactics and how-to's for delivering effective training. For managers, training professionals, supervisors, executives, or anyone who trains.

LC HG1501   **ISSN** 0143-5329
DD 332.1   UK
CREDIT CONTROL. See Business and Economics-Banks and Banking.

ISSN 0070-1580
UK
CRONER'S REFERENCE BOOK FOR EMPLOYERS. **VFOAT** Reference Book for Employers. (1???)-. English. Twelve times a year. £256.58. Croner Publ Ltd., Croner House London Road, Kingston Upon Thames, Surrey KT2 6SR United Kingdom. **Tel** 011 44 181 5473333, FAX 011 44 181 5472637.

LC LB2335.5.A1 C6   **ISSN** 1046-9508
DD 378.1005   US
CUPA JOURNAL (WASHINGTON, D.C.: 1987). (CUPA JOURNAL.). [CUPA j.]. **Added/Corp** College and University Personnel Association. **VAT** College and University Personnel Association Journal. Vol. 38, No. 1 (Fall 1987)-. Periodical. English. Four times a year. $90.00. College & University Personnel Association, 1233 20th Street Northwest, Suite 301, Washington DC 20036-1250. **Tel** (202)429-0311, FAX (202)429-0149. **ED** Stephanie L. Jones, David J. Uchie (Managing Editor). Index available (bound in last issue). cum. index. **Bk Rev. Ad Acc, Adv Mgr:** Robert Kruhm. ctrl circ. **Continues** Journal of the College & University Personnel Association, 0010-0935.
Desc: Articles focus on human resource themes such as benefits, EEO, early retirement and employee recruitment.
Ind/Abst Contents Pages Educ.; Curr. Index J. Educ. (March 1990); Educ. Index; High. Educ. Abstr.; Int. Labour Doc.

US
DIGEST OF DECISIONS. English. Irregular (once every 1 1/2 to 2 years). $14.30 (digest), $7.40 (supplement). State Personnel Commission, 121 East Wilson Street/2nd Floor, Madison WI 53702. **Circ:** 200 (ctrl).
Desc: The digest covers decisions issued by the Wisconsin Personnel Commission from its inception on Feb. 16, 1978 through June 30. 1988. The supplemental digest of decisions covers July 1, 1988 through May 31, 1992.

LC KF5372.A59 D53   **ISSN** 0276-3567
DD 342.73/0686/02638 347.30268602638   US
CEASED
DIGEST OF SIGNIFICANT CLASSIFICATION DECISIONS AND OPINIONS. [Dig. signif. classif. decis. opin.]. **Main/Corp** United States. Office of Personnel Management. (1981)-(Aug. 1994). Government Publication. English. Office of Personnel Management, 1900 East Street Northwest, OELR Room 7429, Washington DC 20415. **Tel** (202)632-6256. **(Subscription address:** Superintendent of Documents, US Government Printing Office, Washington DC 20402.)
Desc: Presents decisions and opinions made by Office of Personnel Management which have, in their opinion, Government-wide impact.

ISSN 0090-6484
DD 658   US
DIRECTORY OF EXECUTIVE RECRUITERS. (THE DIRECTORY OF EXECUTIVE RECRUITERS.). [Dir. exec. recruit.]. (1988/89)-. Directory. English. One time a year. $79.00. Kennedy Publications, Templeton Road, Fitzwilliam NH 03447. **Tel** (603)585-6544, (800)531-0007, FAX (603)585-9555.
Desc: Hardcover version for clients/users of search firms with more detailed information. Provides 100 pages of useful text on using executive recruiters.

LC HD38.25.U6 D57   **ISSN** 1059-163X
DD 338.7/61658407111/02573   US
DIRECTORY OF EXECUTIVE RECRUITERS (CORPORATE ED.), THE. (THE DIRECTORY OF EXECUTIVE RECRUITERS.). [Dir. exec. recruit.]. 1st Ed. (1988/1989)-. Directory. English. Every 2 years. $99.00. Kennedy Publications, Templeton Road, Fitzwilliam NH 03447. **Tel** (603)585-6544, (800)531-0007, FAX (603)585-9555.
Desc: Aimed especially at corporate buyers of search services who need more information about search firms. Provides expanded descriptions, staff and revenue information, telephone and fax numbers.

LC HF5549.5.R44 D58   **ISSN** 0090-6484
DD 658.31/11   US
DIRECTORY OF EXECUTIVE RECRUITERS (STANDARD ED.). (DIRECTORY OF EXECUTIVE RECRUITERS.). [Dir. exec. recruit.]. (1971)-. Directory. English. One time a year. $44.95. Kennedy Publications, Templeton Road, Fitzwilliam NH 03447. **Tel** (603)585-6544, (800)531-0007, FAX (603)585-9555. **ED** James H. Kennedy. Index available. **Bk Rev**.
Desc: Identifies executive recruiters throughout North America - heavily cross indexed by function, industry, geography and key principals. Lists salary minimum, professional affiliation and a 5-10 word description.

LC HF5549.5.D55 D57   **ISSN** 0735-3707
DD 331.12/8/02573   US
DIRECTORY OF OUTPLACEMENT FIRMS. [Dir. outplace. firms]. (Summer 1980)-. Directory. English. Every 2 years. $74.95. Kennedy Publications, Templeton Road, Fitzwilliam NH 03447. **Tel** (603)585-6544, (800)531-0007, FAX (603)585-9555.
Desc: Full-page profiles of over 230 firms: staff size, annual reviews, fee schedules, names of 750 key principals and where they work, plus 35-page overview of $500 million outplacement industry.

LC Z5055.I754 B47A LG341.B4
DD 016.3785694   IS
DIRECTORY OF RESEARCH PERSONNEL. **Main/Corp** Universitat Ben-Guryon Ba-Negev. Directory. English. Research and Development Authority, Universitat Ben-Guryon Ba-Negu, PO Box 1025, Beer-Sheva Israel.

IT
DIREZIONE DEL PERSONALE. Italian. Two times a year. L45000.00 Italy. AIDP / ASSN Ital Direz Personale, Via Cornalia 19, 20124 Milan Italy. **Tel** 02 6709558. **Bk Rev. Ad Acc, Adv Mgr:** Brevi Melania, **Tel** 02 6709558. **Circ:** 2,500 (ctrl).

US
DISCIPLINE & GRIEVANCES FOR SUPERVISORS, LOCAL, STATE, AND FEDERAL GOVERNMENT. **VFOAT** Discipline & Grievances. (198?)-. Periodical. English. Twelve times a year. $91.92 (US); $111.36 (Canada) (renewals only). Bureau of Business Practice, 24 Rope Ferry Road, Waterford CT 06386. **Tel** (800)243-0876, (203)442-4365, (800)876-9105, FAX (203)443-1123. **Continues** Discipline & Grievance Report.

LC HF5549.A2 D57   **ISSN** 0271-3462
DD 658.3/005   US
TITLE CHANGE
DISCIPLINE AND GRIEVANCES. WHITE COLLAR EDITION. (DISCIPLINE AND GRIEVANCES.). **Added/Corp** Bureau of Business Practice. (19??)-(1993). Periodical. English. Bureau of Business Practice, 24 Rope Ferry Road, Waterford CT 06386. **Tel** (800)243-0876, (203)442-4365, (800)876-9105, FAX (203)443-1123. **ED** Lori Michaelson. **Circ:** 8,200. **Supersedes in part** Discipline and Grievances, 0012-351X. **Continued by** Labor Relations Bulletin, 1080-3211.
Desc: Tells how to handle everyday employee relations problems. Based on actual grievances that have arisen in companies.

LC HF5549.5 .E42 E36   **ISSN** 0273-8910
DD 658.3/8/05   US
CODEN EAPDEW
EAP DIGEST. **VFOAT** E.A.P. Digest. **VAT** Employee Assistance Programs Digest. (Nov./Dec. 1980)-. Trade Publication. English. Six times a year. $36.00. Performance Resource Press, Inc., 1863 Technology Drive, Suite 200, Troy MI 48083. **Tel** (810)588-7733, (800)453-7733, FAX (810)588-6633. **(Subscription address:** EAP Digest, PO Box 6112, Syracuse NY 13217. **Tel** (800)825-0061.) **ED** Brent Chartier. Index available (bound in Nov. issue). **Ad Acc**. **Circ:** 16,000 (ctrl). available in reprints from the publisher.
Desc: Dedicated to reducing alcohol and other drug problems in the workplace through employee assistance programs.
Ind/Abst Soc. Work Abstr. (1988-?).

US
EMPLOYEE ASSISTANCE. See Business and Economics-Labor.

LC HD4928.N62 U63   **ISSN** 0277-1276
DD 331.2/0421381/0973   US
EMPLOYEE BENEFITS AND PERSONNEL PRACTICES SURVEY. SAN FRANCISCO BAY AREA, NORTHWEST, COLORADO, ARIZONA, AND TEXAS. **VFOAT** Employee Benefits Survey. English. One time a year. American Electronics Association, 5201 Great America Parkway, Santa Clara CA 95054. **Tel** (415)327-9300.

ISSN 0273-768X
US
CCC
EMPLOYEE BENEFITS COMPLIANCE COORDINATOR. **Added/Corp** Tax Research Institute of America, Inc. Research Institute of America, Inc. **VFOAT** RIA Employee Benefits Compliance Coordinator. (1979)-. Periodical. English. Twelve times a year. Research Institute of America, 117 East Stevens Avenue, Valhalla NY 10595. **Tel** (800)431-9025, FAX (800)820-3135 (914)749-5300. **ED** James E. Cheeks. **Supersedes** Pension Coordinator.
Desc: Provides everything you need to insure timely compliance for all types of employee benefit plans.

US
EMPLOYEE BENEFITS HANDBOOK. UPDATE WITH CUMULATIVE INDEX. (1983)-. English. Irregular. $129.00 US; $167.70 other. Warren Gorham & Lamont Inc., Park Square Building, 31 St. James Avenue, Boston MA 02116-4112. **Tel** (617)423-2020, (800)950-1207, FAX (617)423-2026.

US
EMPLOYEE BENEFITS MANAGEMENT DIRECTIONS. **Added/Corp** Commerce Clearing House. **VFOAT** Directions; CCH Employee Benefits Management Directions. (Jan. 1990)-. Periodical. English.

Business and Economics — Personnel Management

Twenty-four times a year. $155.00. Commerce Clearing House Inc., 4025 West Peterson Avenue, Chicago IL 60646-6085. **Tel** (312)583-8500, FAX (708)940-4600.

ISSN 0885-7202
DD 658 US
EMPLOYEE COMMUNICATION. [Empl. commun.]. (19??)-. Periodical. English. Twelve times a year. $95.00. Management Resources Inc, 861 LaFayette Road, Suite 5, Hampton NH 03842. **Tel** (603)929-1600. **ED** Robert Carpenter. **Bk Rev**, (Qty: 2-10).

LC HF ISSN 1351-055X
DD 658.311 UK
EMPLOYEE DEVELOPMENT BULLETIN. [Empl. dev. bull.]. (19??)-. Periodical. English. Twelve times a year. £125.00 UK; £135.00 other. Eclipse Publications Ltd., 18 20 Highbury Place, London N5 1QP United Kingdom. **Tel** 011 44 171 3545858.
Continues Recruitment and Development Report, 0959-146X.

UK
EMPLOYEE DEVELOPMENT BULLETIN. (19??)-. Bulletin. English. £120.00 UK; £130.00 other. Eclipse Publications Ltd., 18 20 Highbury Place, London N5 1QP United Kingdom. **Tel** 011 44 171 3545858.

ISSN 0142-5455
UK
CCC
CODEN EMREDQ
EMPLOYEE RELATIONS. [Empl. relat.]. Vol. 1 (1979)-. Periodical. English. Eight times a year. $3849.00. MCB University Press, 60 62 Toller Lane, Bradford, West Yorkshire BD8 9BY United Kingdom. **Tel** 011 44 1274 785280, FAX 011 44 1274 785200, telex 51317-MCBUNI-G. **(Subscription address:** MCB University Press / US and Canada Subscriptions, PO Box 10812, Birmingham AL 35201-0812. **Tel** (205)995-1567, (800)633-4931, FAX (205)995-1588.) **ED** John Berridge.
Bk Rev, available on an online database (file 15/Full-Text) from DIALOG. Documents available from UMI Article Clearinghouse.
Desc: Aims to help all those involved in the management of organisations to find and compare alternative strategies for improving employment conditions. Endeavours to cover all the main issues within the broad context of industrial relations. Each subject is given in-depth coverage while special issues take a critical overview of specific situations and high interest areas.
Ind/Abst ABI/INFORM Glob. Ed.; ABI/INFORM [Computer File] (1983-); Acad. Search; Anbar Account. Finan. Abstr. [Full Txt.]; Anbar Mark. Distr. Abstr. [Full Txt.]; Appl. Soc. Sci. Index Abstr.; Bus. Source Plus; Bus. Source; Contents Pages Manage.; Curr. Cit.; Curr. Index J. Educ.; EP Collect.; Gen. BusinessFile (1992-); Homework Help.; Hum. Resour. Abstr.; INFO-SOUTH Abstr.; Int. Bibliogr. Sociol.; Int. Labour Doc.; LABORDOC; Mag. Search; Manage. Market. Abstr.; Manage. Bibliogr. Rev.; MasterFile FullTEXT 1000; MasterFile FullTEXT 350; MasterFile FullTEXT 650; MasterFile FullTEXT (Jan. 1993-); OCLC; Oper. Prod. Manage. Abstr. [Full Txt.]; Person. Train. Abstr. [Full Txt.]; Person. Manage. Abstr.; Pub. Lib. FullTEXT; Tech. Educ. Train. Abstr.; Telebase; Vocat. Search; Women Manage. Rev. [Full Txt.].

ISSN 8756-3231
DD 331 US
EMPLOYEE RELATIONS BULLETIN (NEW YORK, N.Y.). See Business and Economics-Labor.

ISSN 0894-2080
DD 658 US
EMPLOYEE SECURITY CONNECTION. [Empl. secur. connect.]. **Added/Corp** National Security Institute (Westborough, Mass.). Vol. 1, No. 1 (Summer 1987)-. Periodical. English. Four times a year. $595.00. National Security Institute, 57 East Main Street, Suite 217, Westborough MA 01581. **Tel** (508)366-5800, FAX (508)898-0132. **ED** David A. Marston.
Desc: Security awareness for employees of large companies dealing with security and DoD procedures.

AT
●**EMPLOYER PLUS T&D.** (1995)-. English. Twenty-six times a year. 267.21Aus$. T & D Newsletter, PO Box 1480, Crowsnest NSW 2065 Australia. **Tel** 011 61 2 9061949. **Continues** T&D.

US
EMPLOYER'S GUIDE TO AUDITING PERSONNEL AND EMPLOYMENT PRACTICES. (19??)-. English. One time a year. $195.00 (basic 2 volumes). Business Laws Inc., 11630 Chillicothe Road, Chesterland OH 44026. **Tel** (216)729-7996, (800)759-0929, FAX (216)729-0645.

US
EMPLOYMENT COORDINATOR. VFOAT RIA Employment Coordinator. (1984)-. Periodical. English. Research Institute of America, 117 East Stevens Avenue, Valhalla NY 10595. **Tel** (800)431-9025, FAX (800)820-3135 (914)749-5300.

Desc: Covers benefits, compensation, employment practices, labor relations, personnel policy and workplace safety.

LC HF5549.2.U5 E47 ISSN 0886-8565
DD 338.7/616583/002573 US
EMPLOYMENT MARKETPLACE RESOURCE DIRECTORY. [Employ. marketpl. resour. dir.]. **Added/Corp** Employment Marketplace (Firm). VFOAT Employment Market Place Resource Directory. (1986)-. English. Four times a year. $15.00. Employment Marketplace, 12015 Robyn Park Drive, St. Louis MD 63131. **Tel** (314)569-3095, FAX (314)569-3095.

LC TD180 .U544A ISSN 0747-8186
DD 363.7/0023/73 US
EMPLOYMENT OPPORTUNITIES / UNITED STATES ENVIRONMENTAL PROTECTION AGENCY, PERSONNEL MANAGEMENT DIVISION. **Main/Corp** United States. Environmental Protection Agency. Personnel Management Division. (19??)-. English. One time a year. US Environmental Protection Agency, Personnel Management Division (PM 212), Washington DC 20460.

ISSN 0271-0781
US
ERN. EXECUTIVE RECRUITER NEWS. VFOAT Executive Recruiter News. (1980)-. Periodical. English. Twelve times a year. $187.00. Kennedy Publications, Templeton Road, Fitzwilliam NH 03447. **Tel** (603)585-6544, (800)531-0007, FAX (603)585-9555. **ED** James H Kennedy. Index available. cum. index. **Bk Rev**.
Desc: Lively newsletter covering trends and developments: key personnel changes, fees, mergers, defections, legal questions, exposes, ethics, association news.

LC HD8380.5.A5 E96 ISSN 0309-7234
DD 331/.094 UK
EUROPEAN INDUSTRIAL RELATIONS REVIEW. See Business and Economics-Labor.

ISSN 0738-6982
US
EXECUTIVE COMPENSATION REPORTS (ALEXANDRIA, VA.). (EXECUTIVE COMPENSATION REPORTS.). [Exec. compens. rep.]. VFOAT E.C.R.; ECR. (1987)-. Periodical. English. Twenty-four times a year. $439.00. DP Publications Company, PO Box 7188, Fairfax Station VA 22039. **Tel** (703)425-1322, FAX (703)425-7911, telex 263 128 CTOUR. **ED** Carol Bowie. **Circ:** 800.
Desc: Reports on executive compensation programs in the US and Canada. Analysis of executive compensation trends and new developments.

ISSN 0898-9753
DD 338 US
CCC
EXECUTIVE REPORT ON MANAGED CARE, THE. [Exec. rep. manag. care]. (1988)-. Periodical. English. Twelve times a year. $177.00. Health Resources Publishing, 3100 Highway 138, Wall Township NJ 07719-1442. **Tel** (908)681-1133, FAX (908)681-0490. **ED** Robert K Jenkins. Index available. **Bk Rev**. **Ad Acc**.
Desc: A report giving news of how major employers are implementing managed care programs. Helps companies prepare to evaluate and monitor various managed care proposals in terms of their cost effectiveness, quality, and liability to the employer.

ISSN 1050-9003
DD 331 US
EXECUTIVE SEARCH REVIEW. [Exec. search rev.]. Vol. 1, No. 1 (Oct. 1989)-. Periodical. English. Twelve times a year. $39.00. Hunt-Scanlon Publishing Company, Two Pickwick Plaza, Greenwich CT 06830. **Tel** (203)629-3629, FAX (203)629-3701.

LC HD
DD 658
EXPATRIATE OBSERVER. (19??)-. English. Four times a year. $50.00. Organization Resources Counselors, Inc., 1211 Avenue of the Americas, Rockefeller Center, New York NY 10036. **Tel** (212)852-0363, FAX (212)398-1358, (212)719-5625. **ED** Nancy Carter, (212)852-0313. ctrl circ.
Ind/Abst Person. Manage. Abstr.

ISSN 1053-2331
DD 658 US
FACT FINDER (JAMESTOWN, N.Y.), THE. (THE FACT FINDER.). [Fact finder]. **Added/Corp** Jamestown Area Labor Management Committee (Jamestown, N.Y.) Jamestown Community College Business and Industry Center (Jamestown, N.Y.). (19??)-. Periodical. English. Twelve times a year. $89.00. Jamestown Area Labor Management Committee Inc, PO Box 819, Jamestown NY 14702. **Tel** (800)542-7869, (716)665-3654, FAX (716)665-8060. **ED** Karen France. Index available. cum. index. **Circ:** 4,000.
Desc: A monthly source of information, tips and how-to's for people managing human resources.

LC HD4801 ISSN 1081-2717
DD 331 US
FAXNEWZ (DALLAS, TEX.). (FAXNEWZ.). [Faxnewz]. **Added/Corp** Integrity Center (Dallas, Tex.). (1992)-. Periodical. English. Irregular (every 6 weeks). Free. Integrity Center Inc., 2828 Forest Lane, Suite 1008, Dallas TX 75234. **Tel** (214)484-6140, (800)456-1811, FAX (214)484-6381. available via Internet (http://www.integctr.com/).
Desc: Covers topics relavent to personnel security and pre-employment screening.

US
FEDERAL LABOR AND EMPLOYEE RELATIONS UPDATE. See Business and Economics-Labor.

US
FEDERAL PERSONNEL MANUAL. See Public Administration-Civil Service.

US
FEDERAL PERSONNEL MANUAL SYSTEM. FPM SUPPLEMENT 271-1. DEVELOPMENT OF QUALIFICATION STANDARDS. See Public Administration-Civil Service.

US
FEDERAL PERSONNEL MANUAL SYSTEM. FPM SUPPLEMENT 293-31. BASIC PERSONNEL RECORDS AND FILES SYSTEM. See Public Administration-Civil Service.

US
FEDERAL PERSONNEL MANUAL SYSTEM. FPM SUPPLEMENT 752-1. ADVERSE ACTIONS BY AGENCIES. See Public Administration-Civil Service.

US
FEDERAL PERSONNEL MANUAL SYSTEM. FPM SUPPLEMENT 910-1. NATIONAL EMERGENCY READINESS OF FEDERAL PERSONNEL MANAGEMENT. See Public Administration-Civil Service.

US
FEDERAL PERSONNEL MANUAL SYSTEM. FPM SUPPLEMENT 990-2. HOURS OF DUTY, PAY, AND LEAVE, ANNOTATED. See Public Administration-Civil Service.

ISSN 1070-2210
DD 332 US
CCC
●**FINANCIAL MANAGER'S REPORT ON COST CUTTING, THE.** [Financ. manag. rep. cost cut.]. **Added/Corp** Institute of Management and Administration. Issue 93-8 (Aug. 1993)-. Periodical. English. Twelve times a year. $175.00. Institute of Management and Administration, 29 West 35th Street, 5th Floor, New York NY 10001-2299. **Tel** (212)244-0360, FAX (212)564-0465. **Continues** CEO's Report on Cost Cutting, 1061-5997.

LC HV8138 .F455 ISSN 0164-6397
DD 350.74/0973 US
FIRE AND POLICE PERSONNEL REPORTER. (FIRE AND POLICE PERSONNEL REPORTER : A MONTHLY PUBLICATION OF THE PUBLIC SAFETY PERSONNEL RESEARCH INSTITUTE.). **Added/Corp** Public Safety Personnel Research Institute (South San Francisco, Calif.). (19??)-. Periodical. English. Twelve times a year. $178.00. Public Safety Personnel Res In, 5519 North Cumberland, Suite 1008, Chicago IL 60656-1471. **Tel** (312)763-2800, FAX (312)763-3225. **ED** Wayne W. Schmidt (phone: (312)763-5259). Index available. cum. index. **Circ:** 1,300. **Continues** Fire Department Personnel Reporter.
Desc: Contains information on disciplinary problems, contested terminations, wrongful dismissal and labor problems in police, fire sheriff and corrections services.
Ind/Abst Crim. Justice Period. Index (-1989).

LC HF550.2 ISSN 0016-1616
DD 651.3 US
CCC
FROM NINE TO FIVE. (1960)-. Newsletter. English. Twenty-six times a year. $66.75. Dartnell Corporation, 4660 North Ravenswood Avenue, Chicago IL 60640. **Tel** (312)561-4000, (800)621-5463, FAX (312)561-3801. **ED** Kim Anderson. **Bk Rev**. **Circ:** 31,000. available with illustrations; available in Loose-leaf; available on microfilm and microfiche from University Microfilms International (UMI). Documents available from UMI Article Clearinghouse.
Desc: Presents office support staff tips on developing

skills to overcome problems, working better with other team members, and ways to increase company success thorough their own.

ISSN 1053-1726
DD 338 US
CODEN FLSEE2

FRONT-LINE SERVICE. [Front-line serv.]. (1989)-. Periodical. English. Twelve times a year. $69.00. Lakewood Publications, 50 South Ninth Street, Minneapolis MN 55402. **Tel** (612)333-0471, (800)328-4329, FAX (612)333-6526.

US

FRONT LINE SUPERVISOR'S BULLETIN. Bulletin. English. Twenty-four times a year. $63.60 (add $16.92 shipping and handling). Bureau of Business Practice, 24 Rope Ferry Road, Waterford CT 06386. **Tel** (800)243-0876, (203)442-4365, (800)876-9105, FAX (203)443-1123. Index available. **Bk Rev**. ctrl circ.
Desc: Emphasis is on the role of first-line supervisors and how supervisors can become more effective in their current positions by following guidelines and steps to success.

US

GETTING ALONG. (19??)-. Bulletin. English. Twenty-six times a year. $66.75. Dartnell Corporation, 4660 North Ravenswood Avenue, Chicago IL 60640. **Tel** (312)561-4000, (800)621-5463, FAX (312)561-3801. **ED** Douglas Leland.
Desc: Guide to building productive work relationships.

LC HF5549.2.N4 G56 **ISSN** 0165-0289
NE

GIDS VOOR PERSONEELSMANAGEMENT. Vol. 66, No. 4 (April 1987)-. Trade Publication. Dutch. Twelve times a year. $122.64. Kluwer Berdijfswetenschappen, Postbus 4, 2400 Alphen Rijn Netherlands. **Tel** 011 31 01720 66855. **(Subscription address:** Intermedia BV, Postbus 4, 2400 MA Alphen AD Rijn Netherlands. **Tel** 011 31 1720 66481.**)** ***Continues*** *Gids Personeelsbeleid, Arbeidsvraagstukken, Sociale Verzekering.*

ISSN 0148-7949
US
CCC
CEASED

GOVERNMENT MANAGER, THE. See Public Administration-Civil Service.

LC HJ275 .U525A **ISSN** 0095-6171
DD 336.1/85 US

GRANT AWARDS - UNITED STATES CIVIL SERVICE COMMISSION, BUREAU OF INTERGOVERNMENTAL PERSONNEL PROGRAMS. See Public Administration-Civil Service.

ISSN 1060-9873
DD 650 US
TITLE CHANGE

GREENWICH REGISTER: THE DIRECTORY OF PERSONNEL MANAGERS, HUMAN RESOURCE EXECUTIVES AND CORPORATE RECRUITERS, THE. [Greenwich regist.]. (1992)-(199?). Directory. English. Hunt-Scanlon Publishing Company, Two Pickwick Plaza, Greenwich CT 06830. **Tel** (203)629-3629, FAX (203)629-3701. ***Continued by*** *Hunt Scanlons Directory of Human Resource Executives.*

NE

HANDBOEK PERSOONLIJKE BESCHERMINGSMIDDELEN. (19??)-. Dutch. Irregular. Samsom Bedrijfsinformatie BV, Postbus 4, 2400 MA Alphen Rij Netherlands. **Tel** 011 31 1720 66633. **(Subscription address:** Intermedia BV, Postbus 4, 2400 MA Alphen AD Rijn Netherlands. **Tel** 011 31 1720 66481.**)**

LC HD28 **ISSN** 1353-5161
DD 658.4080941 UK

●**HEALTH & SAFETY MANAGER'S YEARBOOK, THE.** See Occupations and Careers.

ISSN 1080-1847
DD 658 US

●**HR BRIEFING.** [HR brief.]. **Added/Corp** Bureau of Business Practice. Issue No. 2223 (Dec. 1994)-. Newsletter. English. Twenty-six times a year. $162.00. Bureau of Business Practice, 24 Rope Ferry Road, Waterford CT 06386. **Tel** (800)243-0876, (203)442-4365, (800)876-9105, FAX (203)443-1123. ***Continues*** *Personnel Manager's Letter, 0885-3037.*

LC HF5549.2.U5 H74 **ISSN** 1072-0243
DD 658.3/005 US
CODEN HREREZ

HR EXECUTIVE REVIEW. [HR exec. rev.]. **Added/Corp** Conference Board. **VFOAT** Human Resources Executive Review. Vol. 1, No. 1 (19??)-. Periodical. English. Four times a year. $85.00. Conference Board, 845 Third Avenue, New York NY 10022. **Tel** (212)759-0900 ext. 582, (800)872-6273, FAX (212)980-7014. ***Absorbed*** *Human Resources Briefing, 1051-3760.*

LC HF5549.A2 P38 **ISSN** 1059-6038
DD 658.3/005 US
CCC
NLM W1; HR81G

HR FOCUS. (HR FOCUS : AMERICAN MANAGEMENT ASSOCIATION'S HUMAN RESOURCES PUBLICATION.). [HR focus]. **Added/Corp** American Management Association. **VFOAT** HRFocus; Human Resources Focus. **VAT** Human Resources Focus. Vol. 68, No. 11 (Nov. 1991)-. Academic Scholarly Publication. English. Twelve times a year. $78.75. American Management Association, 135 West 50th Street, New York NY 10020-1201. **Tel** (212)586-8100, (212)903-8375 (periodicals), FAX (212)903-8168, (212)903-8083 (periodicals). **(Subscription address:** Neodata / Colorado, PO Box 2606, Boulder CO 80322. **)** available on microfilm and microfiche from University Microfilms International (UMI). Documents available from UMI Article Clearinghouse. ***Continues*** *Personnel (Orange, N.J.), 0031-5702.*
Ind/Abst ABI/INFORM Glob. Ed.; ABI/INFORM [Computer File] (Sept. 1971-); Acad. Ind. [Computer File]; Bus. ASAP (1991-) [Full Txt.]; Bus. Index (1991-); Bus. Period. Index; Comput. Lit. Index; EMBASE; Expand. Acad. Index (1991-); Gen. BusinessFile (1991-); Gen. Period. Index (1991-); Hosp. Health Admin. Index (1977-1989); INFO-SOUTH Abstr.; Mag. Search; Manage. Contents; MasterFile FullTEXT (July 1993-) [Full Txt.]; Newsp. Period. Abstr. (1989-); Trade Ind. ASAP [Full Txt.]; Trade Ind. Index [Full Txt.]; UMI ABI/Inform--Bus. Period. Ondisc (Jan. 1987-) [Full Txt.]; Wilson Bus. Abstr.; Work Relat. Abstr.

LC HF5549.A2 H72 **ISSN** 1053-3656
DD 658.3/005 US
CCC
CEASED

HR HORIZONS. [HR horiz.]. **VFOAT** Horizons. **VAT** Human Resources Horizons. Issue 101 (Summer 1990)-(Jan. 1994). Periodical. English. Business & Legal Reports, 39 Academy Street, Madison CT 06443. **Tel** (203)245-7448, (800)727-5257, FAX (203)245-2559.

ISSN 1193-2449
DD 658.300971 CN

HR MANAGER'S SOURCEBOOK & BUYER'S GUIDE. [HR manag. sourceb. buy. guide]. **VFOAT** Human Resource Manager's Sourcebook and Buyer's Guide; Human Resource Sourcebook; HR Sourcebook. (1991)-. English. One time a year. 19.95Can$. MPL Communications, 133 Richard Street West, Suite 700, Toronto Ontario M5H 3M8 Canada. **Tel** (416)869-1177, FAX (416)869-0456.

LC HD9696.C63 U5183437 **ISSN** 0884-9129
DD 004 US

HR/PC. [HR/PC]. **VFOAT** HR PC. **VAT** Human Resources, Personal Computing. Vol. 1.1 (Nov. 1985)-. Trade Publication. English. Eight times a year. $115.00. DGM Associates, PO Box 10639, Marina del Rey CA 90292. **Tel** (310)578-1428. **ED** David G. Mahal. Index available. cum. index. **Bk Rev**. **Ad Acc**.
Desc: Computer technology for human resource management.

ISSN 0741-6997
US
CCC

HR REPORTER. [HR report.]. **VFOAT** H.R. Reporter. Vol. 1, Issue 1 (April 2, 1984)-. Periodical. English. Twelve times a year. $295.00. Buraff Publications Inc., 714 Church Street, Alexandria VA 22314. **Tel** (800)333-1291, (703)739-8500. **ED** Tessa Jolls.
Desc: Aimed at senior human resource managers. Covers issues, trends, how-to's. Includes four sections: Reporter includes interviews, case studies, profiles; Update covers trends, meetings, news and tips; Special Reports; and Index.

LC HF5549
DD 658.3/02/0971 CN

●**HR TODAY.** (1995)-. English. Twelve times a year. 96.00Can$. Institute of Professional Management, 2 Walton Court, Ottawa Ontario K1V 9T1 Canada. **Tel** (613)523-5957, FAX (613)523-8505. ***Continues*** *Recruiting and Supervision Today.*

ISSN 0847-5407
DD 658.31/05 CN

HRD TREND REPORT. [HRD trend rep.]. **Added/Corp** Glen Douglas Group. **VFOAT** Human Resources Development Trend Report. Vol. 1, Issue 1 (1990)-. Periodical. English. Twelve times a year. $187.00. Glen Douglas Group, PO Box 460, Thornhill Ontario L3T 4A2 Canada.

US

HRM DOWNSIZING STRATEGIES. **VFOAT** Downsizing Strategies. **VAT** Human Resource Management Downsizing Strategies. Feb. (1992)-. Periodical. English. Remy Publications Company, 350 Hubbard Street, Suite 400, Chicago IL 60610.

ISSN 1047-3149
DD 658 US
CCC
NLM W1; HR817

HRMAGAZINE (ALEXANDRIA, VA.). (HRMAGAZINE.). [HRMagazine]. **Added/Corp** Society for Human Resource Management (U.S.). **VFOAT** HR Magazine. **VAT** Human Resource Magazine. Vol. 35, No. 1 (Jan. 1990)-. Periodical. English. Twelve times a year. $60.00 (one-year), $90.00 (two-year), $130.00 (three-year) North America; $105.00 (one-year), $165.00 (two-year), $225.00 (three-year) other. Society for Human Resource Management, 606 North Washington Street, Alexandria VA 22314. **Tel** (703)548-3440, FAX (703)836-0367, telex 6503902491. available on microfilm and microfiche from University Microfilms International (UMI). Documents available from UMI Article Clearinghouse. ***Continues*** *Personnel Administrator, 0031-5729.*
Desc: Provides human resource management professionals with articles on a full range of human resource topics, from the latest trends in benefits and compensation to new technology, training techniques and labor issues.
Ind/Abst ABI/INFORM Glob. Ed.; ABI/INFORM Ondisc: Expr. Ed.; ABI/INFORM [Computer File] (Nov. 1971-); Acad. Search; Bus. ASAP (1992-) [Full Txt.]; Bus. Index (1990-); Bus. Period. Index; Bus. Source Plus; Bus. Source; Curr. Cit.; Curr. Index J. Educ.; EP Collect.; Gen. BusinessFile (1990-); Gen. Period. Index (1990-); Health Plan. Adminis.; Homework Help.; Hosp. Health Admin. Index (1990-); INFO-SOUTH Abstr.; Mag. Search; Manage. Market. Abstr.; MasterFile FullTEXT 1000; MasterFile FullTEXT 350; MasterFile FullTEXT 650; MasterFile FullTEXT (Jan. 1994-); OCLC; PAIS Int. Print (1991-); Telebase; Trade Ind. ASAP [Full Txt.]; Trade Ind. Index [Full Txt.]; UMI ABI/Inform--Bus. Period. Ondisc (Dec. 1987-) [Full Txt.]; Wilson Bus. Abstr.; Work Relat. Abstr.

ISSN 1047-3157
DD 331 US
CCC

HRNEWS (ALEXANDRIA, VA.). (HRNEWS.). [HRNews]. **Added/Corp** Society for Human Resource Management (U.S.). **VFOAT** Society for Human Resource Management's HRnews; HR News; Resource. **VAT** Human Resources News. Vol. 8, No. 1 (Jan. 1990)-. Periodical. English. Thirteen times a year (monthly with one special issue "Conference Wrap-Up"). $44.00. Society for Human Resource Management, 606 North Washington Street, Alexandria VA 22314. **Tel** (703)548-3440, FAX (703)836-0367, telex 6503902491. ***Continues*** *Resource (Berea, Ohio), 0746-7850.*
Desc: Offers business news that affects the workplace and the HR profession. As the monthly newspaper of the Society for Human Resource Management, HRNews reports on court decisions, legislative actions including government regulations and provides special coverage of speeches, surveys and trends and commentary.

ISSN 0733-0332
US
CCC
Pr Rev.

HRPLANNING NEWSLETTER, THE. **VFOAT** HRP Planning Newsletter; H.R.P. Planning Newsletter. **VAT** Human Resources Planning Newsletter. Vol. 4, No. 2 (1981)-. Newsletter. English. Ten times a year. $200.00. HR Planning Newsletter, 100 East Wisconsin Avenue, Suite 1750, Milwaukee WI 53202. **Tel** (414)347-7733, FAX (414)347-7740. **ED** James Peters (Editor's telephone: (414)347-7750). **Bk Rev**, (Qty: 10). **Circ:** 800 (ctrl). ***Continues*** *Manpower Planning, 0364-7358.*
Desc: Information pertaining to the acquisition development and deployment of organizations human resources.

LC HF5549.15 .H86 **ISSN** 1044-8004
DD 658.3/005 US
Pr Rev.

HUMAN RESOURCE DEVELOPMENT QUARTERLY. [Hum. resour. dev. q.]. **Added/Corp** American Society for Training and Development. Vol. 1, No. 1 (Spring 1990)-. Periodical. English. Four times a year. $88.00. Jossey Bass Inc., 350 Sansome Street, San Francisco CA 94104. **Tel** (415)433-1767, FAX (415)433-0499. **ED** Richard A. Swanson. Index available. **Bk Rev. Circ:** 1,700. available on microfilm and microfiche from University Microfilms International (UMI).
Desc: Assembles the work of scholars and practitioners from a range of disciplines, including training, management, industrial psychology, organizational behavior, economics, and vocational education to present advances in human resource development theory and research.
Ind/Abst Hum. Resour. Abstr.

ISSN 1040-0443
DD 658 US
CCC

HUMAN RESOURCE EXECUTIVE. [Hum. resour. exec.]. Vol. 1, No. 1 (May 1987)-. Trade Publication. English. Twelve times a year. $64.95. Axon Magazine Group, 747 Dresher Road, Department AA, PO Box 980, Horsham PA 19044. **Tel** (215)784-0860. **Bk Rev**. **Ad Acc**. **Circ:** 43,000 (ctrl).

Desc: Focuses on the people, organizations and issues affecting professionals in the field of human resources. Features cover policies in such areas as training, compensation and benefits, employee relations, career counseling, health and security.

ISSN 1010-8092
SA

HUMAN RESOURCE MANAGEMENT. [Hum. resour. manage.Durb.]. (1985)-. Periodical. English. Ten times a year. $82.00. Richard Havenga & Associates, PO Box 2239, Northcliff, 2115 Johannesburg South Africa. **Tel** 011 27 11 8886188, FAX 011 27 11 8882281. **ED** Richard Havenga. **Bk Rev**, (Qty: 15). **Ad Acc, Adv Mgr:** Richard Havenga. **Circ:** 12,000 (ctrl).
Desc: Covers the strategic importance of human resources to business organizations.

LC HF5549.A2 M3 **ISSN** 0090-4848
DD 658.3/005
US
CCC
Pr Rev.

HUMAN RESOURCE MANAGEMENT. [Hum. resour. manageme.]. Vol. 11 (Spring 1972)-. Trade Publication. English. Four times a year. $198.00. John Wiley & Sons, Inc., 605 Third Avenue, New York NY 10158-0012. **Tel** (212)850-6000, (212)850-6645, FAX (212)850-6088, telex 12-7063. **(Subscription address:** John Wiley & Sons Inc / New Jersey John Wiley & Sons Inc / New Jersey, PO Box 2575, PO Box 2575, Secaucus Secaucus NJ NJ 07096-2575 07096-2575. **Tel** , , FAX , , telex , .) **ED** David O. Ulrich. **Circ:** 2,500 (ctrl). available on microfilm and microfiche from University Microfilms International (UMI). Documents available from The Genuine Article, UMI Article Clearinghouse. ***Continues*** *Management of Personnel Quarterly, 0025-1852.*
Desc: Provides practicing managers and academics with the latest concepts, tools and information for effective problem solving and decision making fields. It explores issues of societal, organizational and individual relevance. Articles discuss new theories, new techniques, case studies, models and research trends of particular significance to practicing managers.
Ind/Abst Acad. Search; Bus. Source Plus; Bus. Source; Curr. Cit.; Curr. Contents Soc. Behav. Sci.; EP Collect.; Homework Help.; Mag. Search; MasterFile FullTEXT 1000; MasterFile FullTEXT 350; MasterFile FullTEXT 650; MasterFile FullTEXT (Jan. 1994-); OCLC; Res. Alert [Full Cov.]; Soc. Sci. Cit. Index [Full Cov.]; Telebase.

LC HF5549.A2 H857 **ISSN** 0967-0734
DD 658.3/005
UK

•**HUMAN RESOURCE MANAGEMENT INTERNATIONAL DIGEST.** **VFOAT** Human Resource Management. Vol. 1, No. 1 (1993)-. Periodical. English. Six times a year. $869.00. MCB University Press, 60 62 Toller Lane, Bradford, West Yorkshire BD8 9BY United Kingdom. **Tel** 011 44 1274 785280, FAX 011 44 1274 785200, telex 51317-MCBUNI-G.

ISSN 0954-5395
UK

HUMAN RESOURCE MANAGEMENT JOURNAL. **Added/Corp** Industrial Relations Services. Vol. 1, No. 1 (Autumn 1990)-. Periodical. English. Four times a year (Jan., Apr., July, Oct.). $222.45. Eclipse Publications Ltd., 18 20 Highbury Place, London N5 1QP United Kingdom. **Tel** 011 44 171 3545858. **(Subscription address:** Industrial Relations Services, 18-20 Highbury Place, London N5 1QP United Kingdom.)
Ind/Abst Curr. Cit.

US

HUMAN RESOURCE MANAGEMENT NEWS. **VFOAT** HRM Human Resource Management News. (June 2, 1984)-. English. One time a week (48 issues). $240.00. Remy Publishing Company, 350 Hubbard Street, Suite 440, Chicago IL 60610. **Tel** (312)464-0300, FAX (312)464-0166. **ED** Regina Ann Ludes. Index available (published separately). cum. index. **Bk Rev.** ctrl circ. ***Continues*** *Industrial Relations News, 0019-8714.*
Desc: Newsletter reporting trends and new ideas in the human resource field.

LC HF5549.2.U5 H83 **ISSN** 1053-4822
DD 658.3/005
US
CCC
CODEN HRMRE7

HUMAN RESOURCE MANAGEMENT REVIEW. [Hum. resour. manage. rev.]. Vol. 1, No. 1 (Spring 1991)-. Trade Publication. English. Four times a year. $165.00. JAI Press Inc., 55 Old Post Road, Suite 2, PO Box 1678, Greenwich CT 06836-1678. **Tel** (203)661-7602, FAX (203)661-0792. **ED** Jeffrey Kane and John Bernadin.
Desc: Covers conceptual/theoretical articles pertaining to human resource management and allied fields. It focuses primarily on issues of function. Its purpose is to provide a forum for ideas that will promote and lead research, as well as for the critical examination of existing concepts, models, and frameworks.
Ind/Abst Person. Manage. Abstr.; Soc. Plann. Policy Dev. Abstr.

LC HF5549.A2 P393
UK

HUMAN RESOURCE MANAGEMENT YEARBOOK, THE. **Added/Corp** Institute of Personnel Management. (1989)-. Periodical. English. One time a year (March). $76.57. AP Information Services, Roman House, 296 Golders Green Road, London NW11 9PZ United Kingdom. **Tel** 011 44 181 4554550, FAX 011 44 181 4556381. **ED** Michael Armstrong. Index available. **Ad Acc.** ***Continues*** *Personnel Yearbook.*
Desc: Geared toward the busy personnel professional. Contains articles on areas of current interest, plus a guide to employment and trade union legislation, as well as lists of major suppliers to this sector.

LC HD5701 .H8x **ISSN** 0199-8986
DD 658
US

HUMAN RESOURCE PLANNING. (HUMAN RESOURCE PLANNING : HR.). [Hum. resour. plann.]. **Added/Corp** Human Resource Planning Society. **VFOAT** HR. Vol. 1, No. 1 (Spring 1978)-. Trade Publication. English. Four times a year. $100.00. Human Resource Planning Society, 41 East 42nd Street, Suite 1509, New York NY 10017. **Tel** (212)490-6387, FAX (212)682-6851. **ED** David Schweiger. **Circ:** 2,700 (ctrl). available on microfilm and microfiche from University Microfilms International (UMI); available on an online database (file 15/Full-Text) from DIALOG. Documents available from UMI Article Clearinghouse.
Desc: Analytical and application oriented examples covering the range of human resource planning activities.
Ind/Abst ABI/INFORM Glob. Ed.; ABI/INFORM [Computer File] (1983-); Acad. Search; Bus. ASAP (1992-) [Full Txt.]; Bus. Index (1985-); Bus. Period. Index; Bus. Source Plus; Bus. Source; Contents Pages Manage.; Curr. Cit.; EP Collect.; Gen. BusinessFile (1985-); Gen. Period. Index (1985-); Homework Help.; Mag. Search; MasterFile FullTEXT 1000; MasterFile FullTEXT 350; MasterFile FullTEXT 650; MasterFile FullTEXT (Jan. 1992-); OCLC; Person. Manage. Abstr.; Telebase; UMI ABI/Inform--Bus. Period. Ondisc (1987-) [Full Txt.]; Wilson Bus. Abstr.

AT

HUMAN RESOURCE REPORT. (19??)-. English. Twenty-four times a year. 330.00Aus$. Newsletter Information Service, PO Box 693, Manly New South Wales 2095 Australia. **Tel** 011 61 2 9777500, FAX 011 61 2 9773310.

LC HD4904.7 .M36 **ISSN** 1051-3760
DD 658
US
CCC
CODEN HRBREK
TITLE CHANGE

HUMAN RESOURCES BRIEFING. [Hum. resour. brief.]. **Added/Corp** Conference Board. Vol. 6, No. 2 (Mar. 1990)-(19??). Periodical. English. Conference Board, 845 Third Avenue, New York NY 10022. **Tel** (212)759-0900 ext. 582, (800)872-6273, FAX (212)980-7014. ***Continues*** *Conference Board's Management Briefing. Human Resources, 0896-257X.* ***Merged into*** *HR Executive Review.*

LC HD5723 .H86 **ISSN** 1066-2758
DD 658.3/128
US

•**HUMAN RESOURCES FORECAST.** (HUMAN RESOURCES FORECAST / UCLA INSTITUTE OF INDUSTRIAL RELATIONS.). [Human resour. forecast]. **Added/Corp** University of California, Los Angeles. Instiute of Industrial Relations. (1993)-. English. One time a year. $25.00. Audrey Freedman & Associates, 111 Broadway, 5th Floor, New York NY 10006. **Tel** (212)406-2148, FAX (212)587-1929.

US

HUMAN RESOURCES FORUM / AMERICAN MANAGEMENT ASSOCIATION. **Added/Corp** American Management Association. (1989)-. Periodical. English. Twelve times a year. Comes with membership. American Management Association, 135 West 50th Street, New York NY 10020-1201. **Tel** (212)586-8100, (212)903-8375 (periodicals), FAX (212)903-8168, (212)903-8083 (periodicals).

ISSN 0791-847X
IE

HUMAN RESOURCES INTERNATIONAL. English. Ten times a year. $785.00. Lafferty Publications Ltd., Tower Ida Centre Pearse Street, Dublin 2 Ireland. **Tel** 011 353 1 6718022, FAX 011 353 1 718520.

UK

HUMAN RESOURCES; MANAGEMENT AND STRATEGY. (19??)-. Periodical. English. Irregular. £217.75. Croner Publ Ltd., Croner House London Road, Kingston Upon Thames, Surrey KT2 6SR United Kingdom. **Tel** 011 44 181 5473333, FAX 011 44 181 5472637.

UK

HUMAN RESOURCES MANAGEMENT INTERNATIONAL DIGEST. English. Six times a year. $644.00. MCB University Press, 60 62 Toller Lane, Bradford, West Yorkshire BD8 9BY United Kingdom. **Tel** 011 44 1274 785280, FAX 011 44 1274 785200, telex 51317-MCBUNI-G. **(Subscription address:** MCB University Press / US and Canada Subscriptions, PO Box 10812, Birmingham AL 35201-0812. **Tel** (205)995-1567, (800)633-4931, FAX (205)995-1588.)

ISSN 0745-0621
US

HUMAN RESOURCES MANAGEMENT. PERSONNEL PRACTICES/COMMUNICATIONS. [Hum. resour. manage., pers. pract. commun.]. **Added/Corp** Commerce Clearing House. **VFOAT** Personnel Practices/Communications. (19??)-. Periodical. English. Twelve times a year. $265.00. Commerce Clearing House Inc., 4025 West Peterson Avenue, Chicago IL 60646-6085. **Tel** (312)583-8500, FAX (708)940-4600. **ED** A.E. Schechter.
Desc: Supplies practical new personnel policies and ways to communicate them to employees, performance and productivity programs of top firms; studies, surveys, etc.

AT

HUMAN RESOURCES NEWS. (19??)-. English. Eleven times a year. 147.00Aus$. Ian Huntley Publishers Pty Limited, PO Box 99, Cremorne NSW 2090 Australia. **Tel** 011 61 2 9535788, FAX 011 61 2 9532280. **ED** Patricia Huntley. Index available. **Bk Rev**, (Qty: 6-8). **Circ:** 1,000.
Desc: Issues to improve productivity and efficiency via employee involvement and co-operation and reviews of consultancies who have special services in these areas.

ISSN 1075-8321
DD 658
US

•**HUMAN RESOURCES PRACTICE IDEAS.** (HUMAN RESOURCES PRACTICE IDEAS : HR.). [Hum. resour. pract. ideas]. **VFOAT** HR Practice Ideas. Vol. 9, No. 7 (March 1994)-. Periodical. English. Twelve times a year. $138.25. Warren Gorham & Lamont Inc., Park Square Building, 31 St. James Avenue, Boston MA 02116-4112. **Tel** (617)423-2020, (800)950-1207, FAX (617)423-2026. ***Continues*** *Personnel Practice Ideas, 0896-985X.*

ISSN 0847-9453
DD 658.3/00971
CN
CCC

HUMAN RESOURCES PROFESSIONAL. [Hum. resour. prof.]. **Added/Corp** Personnel Association of Ontario. Vol. 5, No. 1 (Jan. 1989)-. Periodical. English. Twelve times a year. 36.02Can$. HR Professional Association Ontario, 2nd Floor Street W, Suite 1902, Toronto Ontario M4W 3E2 Canada. **Tel** (416)923-2324, FAX (416)923-7264. **ED** Joanne Eidinger (editor's telephone: (416)923-2324, ext. 324). **Ad Acc, Adv Mgr:** Marta Pawych. ***Continues*** *HR Professional, 0833-8892.*
Desc: Magazine for Canadian human resources professionals.

LC HF5549.A2 H8 **ISSN** 1040-5232
DD 658
US
CCC
CODEN HRPREM

HUMAN RESOURCES PROFESSIONAL (NEW YORK, N.Y.), THE. (THE HUMAN RESOURCES PROFESSIONAL.). [Human resour. prof.]. Vol. 1, No. 1 (Nov./Dec. 1988)-. Periodical. English. Four times a year. $115.00. Faulkner & Gray Inc., 11 Penn Plaza, 17th Floor, New York NY 10001. **Tel** (212)967-7000, (800)535-8403. **ED** Pamela Goett. **Bk Rev. Ad Acc. Circ:** 1,500 (ctrl). available on microfilm and microfiche from University Microfilms International (UMI). ***Absorbed*** *Journal of Staffing & Recruitment, 1044-0038.*

LC HF5549.2.U5 H85 **ISSN** 0887-5316
DD 658.3/00973
US

HUMAN RESOURCES YEARBOOK. [Hum. resour. yearb.]. (1986)-. English. One time a year. $79.95. Macmillan Publishing Company / New Jersey, 100 Front Street, Box 500, Riverside NJ 08075-7500. **Tel** (800)257-5755, (609)461-6500, FAX (609)461-7070.

ISSN 1077-4335
DD 658
US

HUMAN SIDE, THE. [Human side]. **Added/Corp** National Foremen's Institute. **VFOAT** Human Side of Supervision. (1992)-. Periodical. English. Twenty-four times a year. $54.24. Bureau of Business Practice, 24 Rope Ferry Road, Waterford CT 06386. **Tel** (800)243-0876, (203)442-4365, (800)876-9105, FAX (203)443-1123. ***Continues*** *Human Side of Supervision.*

US

ICMA REPORTS ON PERSONNEL. (19??)-. Monographic series. English. Irregular. Price varies per volume. International City Management Association, 777 North Capitol Street NE, Suite 500, Washington DC 20002. **Tel** (202)289-4262, (800)745-8780, FAX (202)962-3500.

ISSN 0265-6019
DD 331.29410212
UK

IDS PAY DIRECTORY. **See** Business and Economics-Labor.

Business and Economics —Personnel Management

ISSN 0394-3690
IT
UDC 659.235
INCONTRI CEF. [Incontri CEF]. **VFOAT** Incontri Concorde Europenne Formation. (1985)-. Periodical. Italian. Two times a year. Free on request. Inst Europeo Studi Formazione Dir, Via Cosimo Del Fante 16, 20122 Milan Italy.

LC Z1223.C58 U49 JK765 **ISSN** 0882-2204
DD 353.001/05 US
INDEX TO INFORMATION (WASHINGTON, D.C.). (INDEX TO INFORMATION.). [Index inf.]. **Added/Corp** United States. Office of Personnel Management. Library. (19??)-. English. One time a year (with quarterly supplements). US Office of Personnel Management / Internal Distribution, Subunit Room B443, 1900 E Street NW, Washington DC 20415.

ISSN 0019-7858
UK
CCC
CODEN ILCTAU
INDUSTRIAL AND COMMERCIAL TRAINING. [Ind. commer. train.]. (Nov. 1969)-. Periodical. English. Eleven times a year. $3199.00. MCB University Press, 60 62 Toller Lane, Bradford, West Yorkshire BD8 9BY United Kingdom. **Tel** 011 44 1274 785280, FAX 011 44 1274 785200, telex 51317-MCBUNI-G. **(Subscription address:** MCB University Press / US and Canada Subscriptions, PO Box 10812, Birmingham AL 35201-0812. **Tel** (205)995-1567, (800)633-4931, FAX (205)995-1588.) **ED** Bryan Smith. **Bk Rev.** Documents available from UMI Article Clearinghouse, Ask*IEEE.
Desc: Provides information and news on the national context for training.
Ind/Abst ABI/INFORM Glob. Ed.; ABI/INFORM [Computer File] (Jan. 1978-Sept. 1981); Anbar Account. Finan. Abstr. [Full Txt.]; Anbar Mark. Distr. Abstr. [Full Txt.]; Anbar Top Manage. Abstr. [Full Txt.]; Curr. Cit.; INSPEC (July 1983-); Manage. Market. Abstr.; Manage. Bibliogr. Rev.; Oper. Prod. Manage. Abstr. [Full Txt.]; Person. Train. Abstr. [Full Txt.]; Res. High. Educ. Abstr.; Saf. Health Work; Tech. Educ. Train. Abstr.; Women Manage. Rev. [Full Txt.]; Work Relat. Abstr.

LC HD8690.5 .A18a
DD 331/.09549/1 PK
INDUSTRIAL RELATIONS JOURNAL (KARACHI, PAKISTAN). See Business and Economics-Labor.

ISSN 0749-2162
DD 331 US
INDUSTRIAL RELATIONS RESEARCH ASSOCIATION SERIES NEWSLETTER. See Business and Economics-Labor.

LC HD4965.5.U6 I54 **ISSN** 1041-908X
DD 331.2/81658302/0973021 US
INDUSTRY REPORT ON SUPERVISORY MANAGEMENT COMPENSATION. (INDUSTRY REPORT ON SUPERVISORY MANAGEMENT COMPENSATION / ECS.). [Ind. rep. superv. manage. compens.]. **Added/Corp** Executive Compensation Service (U.S.). 1st Ed. (1988/89)-. Trade Publication. English. One time a year. $490.00. ECS, Executive Compensation Service, Wyatt Data Services, 218 Route 17 North, Roselle Park NJ 07662-9832. **Tel** (201)843-1177, FAX (201)843-0101. available with charts.

LC TA158 .I47 **ISSN** 1063-0058
DD 331.2/973/021 US
INDUSTRY REPORT ON TECHNICIAN AND SKILLED TRADES PERSONNEL COMPENSATION. See Business and Economics-Labor.

ISSN 0165-0041
NE
UDC 658.8
TITLE CHANGE
INFORMATIE VOOR DE BUITENDIENST. [Inf. buitend.]. (1973)-(1994). Periodical. Dutch. Samsom Bedrijfsinformatie BV, Postbus 4, 2400 MA Alphen Rij Netherlands. **Tel** 011 31 1720 66633. **(Subscription address:** Intermedia BV, Postbus 4, 2400 MA Alphen AD Rijn Netherlands. **Tel** 011 31 1720 66481.) Continued by Professioneel Verkopen, 1380-6815.

LC HF5549.2.G7 I544 **ISSN** 0951-0524
DD 658.3/00941 UK
INFORMATION SERVICE NEWS AND ABSTRACTS. Added/Corp Great Britain. Work Research Unit. No. 78 (Jan./Feb. 1986)-. Periodical. English. Six times a year. Free on request. ACAS, Work Research Unit, St. Vincent House, 30 Orange Street, London WC2H 7HH United Kingdom. **Tel** 011 44 71 839 9289. **ED** A. Blandy. **Bk Rev. Circ:** 2,000. Continues Information System News and Abstracts, 0267-873X.
Ind/Abst Ergon. Abstr.; Manage. Market. Abstr.

US
TITLE CHANGE
INNOVATIONS IN INTERNATIONAL COMPENSATION. (19??)-(1995). English. Organization Resources Counselors, Inc., 1211 Avenue of the Americas, Rockefeller Center, New York NY 10036. **Tel** (212)852-0363, FAX (212)398-1358, (212)719-5625. **ED** Nancy Carter (Editor's telephone: (212)719-0313). Continued by Innovations in International HR.
Ind/Abst Person. Manage. Abstr.

US
●**INNOVATIONS IN INTERNATIONAL HR.** (1995)-. English. Four times a year. $50.00. Organization Resources Counselors, Inc., 1211 Avenue of the Americas, Rockefeller Center, New York NY 10036. **Tel** (212)852-0363, FAX (212)398-1358, (212)719-5625. Continues Innovations in International Compensation.

ISSN 0145-1049
US
INTERAGENCY TRAINING CALENDAR OF COURSES. (INTERAGENCY TRAINING CALENDAR OF COURSES : TRAINING COURSE PRESENTED BY OFFICE OF PERSONNEL MANAGEMENT.). **Main/Corp** United States. Office of Personnel Management. Apr., May, June 1979-. English. Four times a year. Office of Personnel Management, 1900 East Street Northwest, OELR Room 7429, Washington DC 20415. **Tel** (202)632-6256. Continues Interagency Training Calendar of Courses, 0145-1049.

LC HB501.5 .I57 **ISSN** 0958-5192
UK
CCC
CODEN IHMGEH
INTERNATIONAL JOURNAL OF HUMAN RESOURCE MANAGEMENT, THE. Vol. 1, No. 1 (June 1990)-. Trade Publication. English. Four times a year (Mar., Jun., Sep., Dec.). $170.00. Routledge, 11 New Fetter Lane, London EC4P 4EE United Kingdom. **Tel** 011 44 171 5839855, FAX 011 44 171 5830701. **(Subscription address:** Kinokuniya Company Ltd., 38-1 Sakuragaoka 5, chome Setagaya-ku, Tokyo 156 Japan. **Tel** FAX 011 03 3439 0136.) Documents available from UMI Article Clearinghouse.
Ind/Abst ABI/INFORM Glob. Ed.; Curr. Cit.; Int. Labour Doc.; LABORDOC; Person. Manage. Abstr.; Soc. Plann. Policy Dev. Abstr.

LC HD4805 .I76 **ISSN** 0143-7720
DD 331/.05 UK
CCC
INTERNATIONAL JOURNAL OF MANPOWER. See Business and Economics-Labor.

LC HF5549.5.S38 I57 **ISSN** 0965-075X
DD 658.3/112/05 UK
CCC
●**INTERNATIONAL JOURNAL OF SELECTION AND ASSESSMENT. VFOAT** Selection and Assessment; IJSA. Vol. 1, No. 1 (Jan. 1993)-. Academic Scholarly Publication. English. Four times a year. $160.00. Basil Blackwell Publishers Ltd., 108 Cowley Road, Oxford OX4 1JF United Kingdom. **Tel** 011 44 1235 465500, FAX 011 44 1235 465556, telex 837022 OXBOOK G. **(Subscription address:** Blackwell Publishers / UK, 108 Cowley Road, Oxford OX4 1JF United Kingdom. **Tel** 011 44 1865 791100, FAX 011 44 1865 791347.)
Desc: Contains information on employee selection, employee interviewing and predictions of occupational success.

ISSN 1067-5361
DD 658 US
CCC
●**IOMA'S REPORT ON MANAGING FLEXIBLE BENEFITS PLANS.** See Business and Economics-Labor.

US
IPMA ASSESSMENT COUNCIL MONOGRAPH SERIES. See Public Administration-Civil Service.

US
IPMA MONOGRAPH SERIES. See Public Administration-Civil Service.

US
IPMA NEWS / INTERNATIONAL PERSONNEL MANAGEMENT ASSOCIATION. See Public Administration-Civil Service.

UK
CODEN IISME4
IS : INDUSTRIAL SOCIETY MAGAZINE.
VFOAT Industrial Society Magazine; IS Magazine. (198?)-. Periodical. English. Four times a year. Industrial Society, International Department, Robert Hyde House, 48 Bryanston Square, London W1H 7LN United Kingdom.

Tel 011 44 171 2622401. Documents available from Ask*IEEE. Continues Industrial Society, 0019-8781.
Ind/Abst INSPEC (1987-1988).

US
ISSUES IN HR. Added/Corp Society for Human Resource Management (U.S.). **VFOAT** Issues in Human Resources. (199?)-. Periodical. English. Six times a year (Jan., Mar., May, July, Sept., Nov.). $89.00. Society for Human Resource Management, 606 North Washington Street, Alexandria VA 22314. **Tel** (703)548-3440, FAX (703)836-0367, telex 6503902491.

ISSN 0801-5988
DD 069 NO
IT BERGEN. [It Bergen]. **VFOAT** Comite International pour la Formation du Personnel ICOM Bulletin d'Information; ICOM International Committee on the Training of Personnel Newsletter. (1983)-. Bulletin. English. Two times a year.
Ind/Abst Museum Abstr.

US
JOINT TRAVEL REGULATIONS. VOLUME 2, DEPARTMENT OF DEFENSE CIVILIAN PERSONNEL.
Main/Corp United States. Dept. of Defense. **Added/Corp** United States. Per Diem, Travel, and Transportation Allowance Committee. **VFOAT** Department of Defense Civilian Personnel. (19??)-. Government Publication. English. Irregular (manual and supplements). $123.00 US; $153.75 other. US Department of Defense, The Pentagon, Washington DC 20301. **Tel** (703)545-6700. **(Subscription address:** Superintendent of Documents, US Government Printing Office, Washington DC 20402.)
Desc: This publication sets forth uniform per diem, travel, and transportation allowance regulations for civilian personnel of the Department of Defense. Includes the booklet "Commuted Rates Schedule for Transportation of Household Goods," which is issued periodically.

LC HD5701 .J6 **ISSN** 0022-166X
DD 331.1/1/0973 US
CCC
NLM W1 JO673W **CODEN** JHREA9
Pr Rev.
JOURNAL OF HUMAN RESOURCES, THE. [J. hum. resour.]. **Added/Corp** University of Wisconsin--Madison. Industrial Relations Research Institute. University of Wisconsin. Industrial Relations Research Institute. Vol. 1 (Summer 1966)-. Periodical. English. Four times a year. $86.00. University of Wisconsin Press, Journal Division, 114 North Murray Street, Madison WI 53715. **Tel** (608)262-4952, FAX (608)262-8909. **ED** Eugene Smolensky. Index available. **Bk Rev. Ad Acc. Circ:** 2,400. available on microfilm and microfiche from University Microfilms International (UMI). Documents available from The Genuine Article, UMI Article Clearinghouse.
Desc: Examines labor, health, education, and retirement issues with econometric tools. Focuses on policy implications. For scholars, policy makers, and practitioners in the human resources fields.
Ind/Abst ABI/INFORM Glob. Ed.; ABI/INFORM [Computer File] (Fall 1971-); Abstr. Soc. Gerontol.; Acad. Abstr.; Acad. Search; AGRICOLA; Appl. Soc. Sci. Index Abstr.; BioBusiness (1986-Nov. 1989); Bus. ASAP (1992-) [Full Txt.]; Bus. Index (1985-); Cumul. Index Nurs. Allied Health Lit.; Curr. Cit.; Curr. Contents Soc. Behav. Sci.; Curr. Index J. Educ.; Econ. Lit. Index; EP Collect.; Expand. Acad. Index (1984-); Gen. BusinessFile (1985-); Gen. Period. Index (1985-); High. Educ. Abstr. (1968-); Homework Help.; Hum. Resour. Abstr.; INFO-SOUTH Abstr.; Int. Bibliogr. Sociol.; Int. Labour Doc.; J. Econ. Lit.; J. Plan. Lit.; LABORDOC; Leis., Rec., Tour. Abstr.; Mag. Search; Manage. Contents; MasterFile FullTEXT 1000; MasterFile FullTEXT 350; MasterFile FullTEXT 650; MasterFile FullTEXT (Jan. 1992-); Middle East Abstr. Index; Newsp. Period. Abstr. (1991-); OCLC; Person. Manage. Abstr.; Pub. Lib. FullTEXT; Res. Alert [Full Cov.]; Rural Dev. Abstr.; Sage Fam. Stud. Abstr.; Sage Urban Stud. Abstr (?-?); Soc. Sci. Source; Soc. Sci. Cit. Index [Full Cov.]; Soc. Sci. Index; Soc. Sci. Index Fulltext (Fall 1988-) [Full Txt.]; Soc. Work Abstr. [Select. Cov.]; Sociol. Educ. Abstr.; Spec. Educ. Needs Abstr.; SportSearch; Stud. Women Abstr.; Telebase; UMI ABI/Inform--Bus. Period. Ondisc (Fall 1987-) [Full Txt.]; Women Stud. Abstr.; Work Relat. Abstr.; World Agric. Econ. Rural Sociol. Abstr.

LC HF5549.5.T7 J595 **ISSN** 0262-1711
DD 658.4/07124/05 UK
CCC
JOURNAL OF MANAGEMENT DEVELOPMENT, THE. [J. manage. dev.]. **VFOAT** J.M.D.; JMD. Vol. 1, No. 1 (1982)-. Periodical. English. Nine times a year. $3499.00. MCB University Press, 60 62 Toller Lane, Bradford, West Yorkshire BD8 9BY United Kingdom. **Tel** 011 44 1274 785280, FAX 011 44 1274 785200, telex 51317-MCBUNI-G. **(Subscription address:** MCB University Press / US and Canada Subscriptions, PO Box 10812, Birmingham AL 35201-0812. **Tel** (205)995-1567, (800)633-4931, FAX (205)995-1588.) **ED** Bernard Keys. Documents available from UMI Article Clearinghouse.
Desc: This specialized journal is devoted to the methods and processes involved in successful management development. It is targeted to management executives,

teachers and students of management.
Ind/Abst ABI/INFORM Glob. Ed.; ABI/INFORM [Computer File] (1983-); Anbar Account. Finan. Abstr. [Full Txt.]; Anbar Mark. Distr. Abstr. [Full Txt.]; Anbar Top Manage. Abstr. [Full Txt.]; Bus. Index (1986-); Curr. Cit.; Gen. BusinessFile (1986-); Gen. Period. Index (1985-); Hum. Resour. Abstr. (?-?); Manage. Market. Abstr.; Manage. Bibliogr. Rev.; Oper. Prod. Manage. Abstr. [Full Txt.]; Person. Train. Abstr. [Full Txt.]; Person. Manage. Abstr.; Psychol. Abstr. (1984-); PsycINFO; PsycLit; School Organ. Manage. Abstr. (1982-); Sociol. Educ. Abstr. (1983-); Women Manage. Rev. [Full Txt.].

LC HD31 .J68 **ISSN** 1041-2808
DD 658 US
Pr Rev.
JOURNAL OF MANAGEMENT SYSTEMS, THE. (THE JOURNAL OF MANAGEMENT SYSTEMS : THE FLAGSHIP OF HRMOB.). [J. manage. syst.]. **Added/Corp** Association of Human Resources Management and Organizational Behavior. Association of Management (Virginia Beach, Va.). **VFOAT** JMS. Vol. 1, No. 1 (1989)-. Periodical. English. Four times a year. $165.00. Association of Management, Route 17 George Washington Highway, PO Box 1301, Grafton VA 23692. **Tel** (804)479-5363, FAX (804)479-0656. **ED** W. H. Hamel Ph.D (editor's address: PO Box 64841, Virginia Beach, VA 23464-0841). **Bk Rev**, (Qty: 8). **Ad Acc. Circ:** 3,800 (ctrl).
Desc: Calls attention to the popularity, multiplicity, diversity and utility of systems approaches to organizations. Provides a holistic perspective. Promotes interdependencies and reciprocol connections between managerial, technical, information, and social subsystems of contemporary organizations. Stimulates contributions and interdisciplinary exchange between scientists and practitioners of human resources management, organizational behavior and management information systems.

LC HD7255.A2 J67 **ISSN** 0148-3846
US
NLM W1 JO866RE
JOURNAL OF REHABILITATION ADMINISTRATION. **See** Physically Impaired.

ISSN 0264-7265
UK
JOURNAL OF THE NATIONAL ASSOCIATION FOR STAFF DEVELOPMENT. [J. Natl. Assoc. Staff Dev.]. **VFOAT** NASD Journal; Journal - NASD. (1979)-. Periodical. English. Four times a year.
Ind/Abst Curr. Cit.

ISSN 1076-3309
DD 658 US
●**KEEP UP TO DATE ON PAYROLL.** [Keep date payr.]. (1994)-. Periodical. English. Twenty-three times a year. $230.00. Progressive Business Publications, 370 Technology Drive, PO Box 3019, Malvern PA 19355. **Tel** (617)527-8600, (800)220-5000, FAX (617)647-8089.

LC HF5549.2.J3 K45
DD 658.3 JA
KEIEI ROMU NO SHISHIN. **Added/Corp** Nihon Keieisha Dantai Renmei. (1972)-. Japanese. One time a year. ¥2300. Nihon Keieisha Dantai Remmei Kohobu, 2-1 Marunouchi 1-chome Chiyoda-ku, Tokyo Japan.

LC JQ1601 .K5
JA
KIKAN JINJI GYOSEI. **See** Public Administration-Civil Service.

LC HF5549.2.J3 A25
JA
KOYO KANRI CHOSA HOKOKU. **Main/Corp** Japan. Rodosho. Tokei Johobu. (19??)-. Periodical. Japanese. Daijin Kanbo, 7-3, Ichigaya Honmuracho, Shinjuku-ku Tokyo 162 Japan. ***Continues*** *Koyo Kanri Chosa Hokoku.*

LC Z7164.C81 U4568 HD8005. D8005.6.U5 **ISSN** 0730-5486
DD 016.353001 S 016.33189/041353 US
LABOR-MANAGEMENT RELATIONS IN THE PUBLIC SERVICE. **See** Business and Economics-Labor.

ISSN 1080-3211
DD 331 US
●**LABOR RELATIONS BULLETIN (WATERFORD, CONN.).** (LABOR RELATIONS BULLETIN.). [Labor relat. bull. (Waterf. Conn.)]. **Added/Corp** National Foremen's Institute. No. 631 (Oct. 1993)-. Bulletin. English. Twelve times a year. $92.80. Bureau of Business Practice, 24 Rope Ferry Road, Waterford CT 06386. **Tel** (800)243-0876, (203)442-4365, (800)876-9105, FAX (203)443-1123. ***Continues*** *Discipline and Grievances, 0271-3462.*
Desc: Tells how to handle everyday employee relations problems. Based on actual grievances that have arisen in companies.

LC HD8072 .L2553 **ISSN** 0023-6659
US
LABOR TRENDS (SOUTHFIELD, MICH.). **See** Business and Economics-Labor.

LC HF5549 **ISSN** 0969-6474
DD 658.3 UK
●**LEARNING ORGANIZATION, THE.** **Added/Corp** MCB University Press. (1994)-. Periodical. English. Four times a year. $274.00. MCB University Press, 60 62 Toller Lane, Bradford, West Yorkshire BD8 9BY United Kingdom. **Tel** 011 44 1274 785280, FAX 011 44 1274 785200, telex 51317-MCBUNI-G. **ED** John Peters.

GW
LEITENDE ANGESTELLTE. **Added/Corp** Union der Leitenden Angestellten. (1951)-. Periodical. German. Six times a year. $46.06. MSK Verlag GmbH, Schlehenstrasse 45, D-59063 Hamm Germany.
Ind/Abst Coal Abstr.

LC Z681.5 .L535 **ISSN** 0891-2742
DD 023 US
CCC
LIBRARY PERSONNEL NEWS. [Libr. pers. news]. **Added/Corp** American Library Association. Office for Library Personnel Resources. Vol. 1, No. 1 (Winter 1987)-. Trade Publication. English. Six times a year (Jan., Mar., May, July, Sept., Nov.). $20.00. American Library Association, 50 East Huron Street, Chicago IL 60611. **Tel** (312)944-6780, (800)545-2433, FAX (312)337-6787. **(Subscription address:** American Library Association, Subscription Department, 434 West Downer, Aurora IL 60506-9936. **Tel** (708)892-7465, FAX (708)892-7466.) **ED** Margaret Myers and Jeniece Guy. Index available. **Bk Rev. Circ:** 1,017. available on microfilm and microfiche from University Microfilms International (UMI).
Desc: Information on the field of personnel as it applies to libraries.
Ind/Abst Libr. Lit.

LC HF5549.5.T7 L527 **ISSN** 1064-234X
DD 338 US
LINTON TRAINER'S RESOURCE DIRECTORY, THE. [Linton train. resour. dir.]. 2nd Ed. (1992)-. English. Every 2 years. $395.00. Linton Publishing, 1011 First Street South, Hopkins MN 55343. **Tel** (612)936-2288. ***Continues*** *Linton Register, 1050-6454.*

US
MAKING, SERVING, AND KEEPING CUSTOMERS. (19??)-. Bulletin. English. Twenty-six times a year. $53.23. Dartnell Corporation, 4660 North Ravenswood Avenue, Chicago IL 60640. **Tel** (312)561-4000, (800)621-5463, FAX (312)561-3801.

LC HD28 .M3413 **ISSN** 0258-042X
DD 658/.005 II
MANAGEMENT AND LABOUR STUDIES. [Manage. labour stud.]. **Added/Corp** Xavier Labour Relations Institute. Vol. 1 (June 1975)-. English. Four times a year. $20.00. Xavier Labour Relations Institute, Jamshedpur 831001 India. **(Subscription address:** Prints India, 11 Darya Ganj, New Delhi 110002 India. **Tel** 011 91 11 3268645, FAX 011 91 11 3275542, telex 31-61087 PRIN-IN.)
Ind/Abst Person. Manage. Abstr.

ISSN 0315-5420
DD 331.2/81/658420971 CN
MANAGEMENT COMPENSATION IN CANADA. [Manage. compens. Can.]. **Added/Corp** Chapman (H.V.) & Associates. Compensation Division. Sobeco Group. **VFOAT** Sobeco Report. (1???)-. English. One time a year. HV Chapman and Associates, 2 Bloor Street West/Suite 700, Toronto Ontario M4W 1B1 Canada. **Tel** (416)961-3000. ***Continued in part by*** *Management Compensation in Canadian Finance and Insurance, 0383-7874.*

ISSN 1054-4275
DD 650 US
MANAGEMENT MATTERS (PLANTATION, FLA.). (MANAGEMENT MATTERS [COMPUTER FILE].). [Manage. matters]. (Oct. 1990)-. Periodical. English. Twelve times a year. $249.00 US; $269.00 Canada; $309.00 (surface), $349.00 (air) other. Merton Allen Associates, PO Box 15640, Plantation FL 33318-5640. available on an online database (file 636/Full-Text) from DIALOG; NEWSNET; and DATA-STAR.
Desc: Available through NewsNet, PROMPT (on DIALOG), and DATA-STAR (Europe).
Ind/Abst PTS Newsl. Database [Full Txt.].

ISSN 0745-4880
US
CCC
MANAGEMENT REPORT (NEW YORK, N.Y.). (MANAGEMENT REPORT.). [Manage. rep.]. **Added/Corp** Executive Enterprises Publications Co. Vol. 6, No. 2 (Feb. 1983)-. Periodical. English. Twelve times a year. $248.00. John Wiley & Sons, Inc., 605 Third Avenue, New York NY 10158-0012. **Tel** (212)850-6000, (212)850-6645, FAX (212)850-6088, telex 12-7063. **(Subscription address:** John Wiley & Sons Inc / New Jersey, PO Box 2575, Secaucus NJ 07096-2575. **) ED** Jane G. Bensahel. Index available. **Ad Acc.** available on microfilm; available on microfiche. ***Continues*** *Hughes Report, 0732-7919.*
Desc: Covers how-tos of preventing and counteracting union organization drives. Contains information on tools and techniques to maintain non-union status.

LC T58.A2 M37 **ISSN** 0025-1895
DD 658/.005 US
CCC
NLM W1 MA58
MANAGEMENT REVIEW (SARANAC LAKE). (MANAGEMENT REVIEW.). [Manage. rev.]. **Added/Corp** Amacom. American Management Association. Vol. 15, No. 1 (Jan. 1926)-. Periodical. English. Twelve times a year. $45.00. American Management Association, 135 West 50th Street, New York NY 10020-1201. **Tel** (212)586-8100, (212)903-8375 (periodicals), FAX (212)903-8168, (212)903-8083 (periodicals). **(Subscription address:** Neodata / Colorado, PO Box 2606, Boulder Boulder CO 80322. **) ED** Martha H. Peak. **Circ:** 75,000. available on microfilm and microfiche from University Microfilms International (UMI). Documents available from UMI Article Clearinghouse. ***Continues American Management Review.***
Desc: Monthly membership magazine of the American Management Association. Aimed at departmental managers, division heads, vice presidents and CEOs. Includes articles on current management trends, techniques and issue--angled wherever possible to the "how-to," non-theoretical side of management.
Ind/Abst ABI/INFORM Glob. Ed.; ABI/INFORM Ondisc: Expr. Ed.; ABI/INFORM [Computer File] (Oct. 1971-April 1977); Acad. Search; Account. Art.; Bus. ASAP (1990-) [Full Txt.]; Bus. Index (1985-); Bus. Period. Index; Bus. Source Plus; Bus. Source; Comput. Lit. Index; Comput. Rev. (Dec. 1977-Dec. 1989); Curr. Cit.; EP Collect.; Fed. Tax Artic.; Gen. BusinessFile (1985-); Gen. Period. Index (1985-); Homework Help.; Hosp. Health Admin. Index; INFO-SOUTH Abstr.; Int. Aerosp. Abstr. (1974-); Int. Exec.; Law Office Inf. Serv.; Lotus Notes; Mag. Search; Manage. Market. Abstr.; MasterFile FullTEXT 1000; MasterFile FullTEXT 350; MasterFile FullTEXT 650; MasterFile FullTEXT (July 1993-) [Full Txt.]; OCLC; PAIS Int. Print (1991-); Person. Manage. Abstr.; Selec. Coop. Index Manage. Period.; Telebase; Trade Ind. ASAP [Full Txt.]; Trade Ind. Index [Full Txt.]; UMI ABI/Inform--Bus. Period. Ondisc (Jan. 1987-) [Full Txt.]; Wilson Bus. Abstr.

US
MANAGEMENT SCIENCES TRAINING CENTER. **Main/Corp** United States. Office of Personnel Management. Workforce Effectiveness and Development Group. English. One time a year. Office of Personnel Management, 1900 East Street Northwest, OELR Room 7429, Washington DC 20415. **Tel** (202)632-6256.

DD 658.3/02 US
MANAGER'S TROUBLESHOOTER, THE. (19??)-. English. Irregular. $39.95. Prentice-Hall Law and Business, 270 Sylvan Avenue, Englewood Cliffs NJ 07632. **Tel** (800)223-0231, (201)894-8538, FAX (201)894-8666. **ED** Clay Carr and Mary Fletcher.
Desc: Offers solutions to people problems on the job.

LC HD28 **ISSN** 1355-1515
DD 658 UK
●**MANAGING BEST PRACTICE.** [Manag. best pract.]. (1994)-. Trade Publication. English. Irregular. Industrial Society, International Department, Robert Hyde House, 48 Bryanston Square, London W1H 7LN United Kingdom. **Tel** 011 44 171 2622401. **Bk Rev.**

US
MANAGING LEAVE & ATTENDANCE PROBLEMS - A GUIDE FOR THE FEDERAL SUPERVISOR. English. Irregular. $8.95 (US); $12.45 (Canada). FPMI Communications Inc., 707 Fiber Street, Huntsville AL 35801. **Tel** (205)539-1850, FAX (205)539-0911, .

US
MANNERING REPORT, THE. (19??)-. English. Six times a year (Jan., March, May, July, Sept., Nov.). $20.00. Options Unlimited Inc., 617 Sunrise Lane, Green Bay WI 54301. **Tel** (414)339-0011, FAX (414)339-0012. **ED** Wendy Mannering. **Bk Rev**, (Qty: 6). **Circ:** 100 (ctrl). ***Continues*** *The Rising Sun.*
Desc: News and views from experts in human resource development.

ISSN 0149-080X
US
MANPOWER AND HUMAN RESOURCES STUDIES. **See** Business and Economics-Labor.

LC UB357 .U54A **ISSN** 0094-4106
DD 353.001 US
MANPOWER PLANNING DATA (WASHINGTON). (MANPOWER PLANNING DATA.). **Main/Corp** United States. Veterans Administration. (19??)-. Periodical. English. US Veterans Administration / Washington DC, 810 Vermont Avenue Southwest, Washington DC 20420. **Tel** (202)393-2124.

Business and Economics —Personnel Management

ISSN 0792-0970
IS

UDC 331
MASABEY 'ENWS. See Business and Economics-Labor.

ISSN 0743-3832
US
MEETING PLANNERS ALERT. [Meet. plann. alert]. **Added/Corp** Practice Management Associates. Vol. 1, No. 1 (Mar. 1984)-. Periodical. English. Twelve times a year. $97.50. MPA Communications Inc., PO Box 24, Prudential Station, Boston MA 02199. **Tel** (603)432-0084. **ED** Joan Mather, (phone: (617)267-7151). Index available (Bound in next iss., in Dec.). cum. index. **Bk Rev**. **Circ**: 3,000 (ctrl).
Desc: The alert to teach meeting planners, tradeshow managers, and suppliers how to run better events.

LC HF5549.5.C67 A43a
DD 658.32/06/273
US
MEMBERSHIP DIRECTORY - AMERICAN COMPENSATION ASSOCIATION. Main/Corp American Compensation Association. (19??)-. Directory. English. American Compensation Association, 14040 North Northsight Boulevard, Scottsdale AZ 85260. **Tel** (602)951-9191, FAX (602)483-8352.

LC HD4965.5.U6 M53
ISSN 0741-5443
DD 331.2/8165843/0973
US
MIDDLE MANAGEMENT PERSONNEL. 1st Ed. (1981/1982)-. English. One time a year. Executive Compensation Service, American Management Association, 135 West 50th Street, New York NY 10020.

NE
MODELLENBOEK VOOR PERSONEELSWERK EN ORGANISATIE. (19??)-. Dutch. Irregular. Intermedia BV, Postbus 4, 2400 MA Alphen AD Rijn Netherlands. **Tel** 011 31 1720 66855, FAX 011 31 1720 94714.

LC HD28 .M6
DD 658/.005
UK
CODEN MODMEF
MODERN MANAGEMENT : JOURNAL OF THE INSTITUTE OF SUPERVISORY MANAGEMENT AND INSTITUTION OF INDUSTRIAL MANAGERS. Added/Corp Institute of Supervisory Management. Institution of Industrial Managers. Vol. 1, No. 1 (Winter 1986)-. Periodical. English. Five times a year. $41.07. Institute of Supervisory Management, Mansell House, 22 Bore Street, Lichfield Staffordshire WS13 6LP United Kingdom. **Tel** 011 44 1543 251346, FAX 011 44 1543 415804. **Continues** Supervisory Management (Lichfield, Staffs).
Ind/Abst Curr. Cit.

DD 331/.05
ISSN 0708-9945
CN
MONOGRAPHIE - ECOLE DE RELATIONS INDUSTRIELLES, UNIVERSITE DE MONTREAL. Main/Corp Universite de Montreal. Ecole de Relations Industrielles. No. 1 (1978)-. Monographic series. French. Price varies per volume. Service de Publication Ecole de Relations Industrielles, Universite de Montreal, CP 6128, Montreal Quebec H3T 1J4 Canada. **Tel** (514)343-7312. **ED** Gilles Trudeau. cum. index. **Circ**: 500.
Desc: Our collection is dealing with personnel management, labor law, labor economics and collective bargaining.

DD 338.88941
ISSN 0953-7929
UK
MULTINATIONAL EMPLOYER. [Multinatl. empl.]. (1988)-. Periodical. English. Eleven times a year. $290.00. Multinational Employer, 2 High Street Manningtree, Essex CO11 1AE United Kingdom. **Tel** 011 44 1376 397190, FAX 011 44 1376 397190. Index available. **Bk Rev**, (Qty: 10-15). **Continues** Corporate Expatriate, 0267-2324.

LC HD62.15 .N38
US
●**NATIONAL RESEARCH PANEL.** See Business and Economics-Management.

NE
NEDLLOYD PARADE. See Business and Economics-Office Equipment and Services.

LC HF5549.A2 N49
US
NEW APPROACHES TO EMPLOYEE MANAGEMENT. VFOAT Employment Management; New Approaches to Employment Management. Vol. 1 (1992)-. English. One time a year. $73.25. JAI Press Inc., 55 Old Post Road, Suite 2, PO Box 1678, Greenwich CT 06836-1678. **Tel** (203)661-7602, FAX (203)661-0792. **ED** David M. Saunders.

DD 658.31/52/0971
ISSN 0703-5861
CN
NEWSLETTER - CANADIANS FOR A DEMOCRATIC WORKPLACE. See Business and Economics-Labor.

LC LB2335.885.U6 N48
ISSN 0737-9285
DD 331.88/041378/120973
US
NEWSLETTER - NATIONAL CENTER FOR THE STUDY OF COLLECTIVE BARGAINING IN HIGHER EDUCATION AND THE PROFESSIONS (U.S.). See Education-Higher Education.

JA
NIKKEI OFFICE. (19??)-. Periodical. Japanese. Twelve times a year. $260.00. Nihon Keizai Shimbun Inc., 9-5 Otemachi 1 Chome, Chiyoda-ku Tokyo 100 Japan. **Tel** 011 81 3 32700251, 011 81 3 52108502 (Nikkei Business Publications Inc.), FAX 011 81 3 52552661, 011 81 3 52108119 (Nikkei Business Publications Inc.). **(Subscription address:** Maruzen Company Ltd., PO Box 5050, Import & Export Department, Tokyo 100 31 Japan. **Tel** 011 81 3 32789224.)

LC HD4928.N62 U653
ISSN 0740-7971
DD 331.25/5/0973
US
NUTSHELL (SNOWMASS VILLAGE, COLO.). (NUTSHELL.). [Nutshell]. (19??)-. Periodical. English. Twelve times a year. $156.00. The Country Press Inc. / Nutshell, Box 5880, Snowmass Village CO 81615. **Tel** (303)923-3210. **ED** Nanette Mosiman. Index available. cum. index. **Bk Rev**: **Circ**: 500.
Desc: News and information on pensions, health care cost and other related articles.

LC Discard
ISSN 0746-5122
US
OFFICE TOPICS. (19??)-. Periodical. English. Twenty-six times a year. $41.81. Economics Press Inc, 12 Daniel Road, Fairfield NJ 07004. **Tel** (201)227-1224, (800)526-2554, FAX (201)227-9742. **ED** Bob Guder. **Circ**: 18,500 (ctrl).
Desc: Booklets that improve job performance of office support staff.

DD 658
ISSN 1053-1580
US
ON Q (MILWAUKEE, WIS.). (ON Q : THE OFFICIAL NEWSLETTER OF THE AMERICAN SOCIETY FOR QUALITY CONTROL.). [On Q]. **Added/Corp** American Society for Quality Control. **VAT** On Quality. (1986)-. Newsletter. English. Twelve times a year. Free to members of the American Society for Quality Control. American Society for Quality Control, 611 East Wisconsin Avenue, PO Box 3005, Milwaukee WI 53201. **Tel** (414)272-8575, (800)248-1946, FAX (414)272-1734, telex 316567.
Desc: Informs about upcoming events, introduces new developments within the Society, and presents members' opinions on current quality issues.

LC HF5549
ISSN 0946-9834
DD 658.3
GW
●**ORGANISATIONSBERATUNG, SUPERVISION, CLINICAL MANAGEMENT.** (1994)-. Academic Scholarly Publication. English. Four times a year. DM81.00. Leske Verlag & Budrich GmbH, Postfach 300551, D-51334 Leverkusen Germany. **Tel** 011 49 21712079, FAX 011 49 217141209.

LC HD45
DD 658.3
XV
●**ORGANIZACIJA.** (1995)-. Periodical. Slovenian (summaries and/or abstracts in English). Twelve times a year. Moderna Organizacija, 64001 Kranj, Tomsiceva 7 Slovenia. **Tel** 011 064 211560, FAX 011 064 214458. **Continues** Organizacija in Kadri, 0350-1531.

LC HD28 .O75
YU
ORGANIZACIJA POSLOVANJA. **Added/Corp** Zavod za Organizaciju Poslovanja i Obrazovanje Kadrova. (19??)-. Serbo-Croatian (Roman). Irregular. 500.00Din. Zavod za Organizaciju i Upravljanje Poslovnim Sistgemom u Organizicijama Udruzenog Rada, Ul 29 Novembra Br 48/III, Belgrad Yugoslavia.

DD 331.2941
ISSN 0143-8328
UK
PAY & BENEFITS BULLETIN. [Pay benefits bull.]. **VFOAT** Pay and Benefits Bulletin; PABB. Pay & Benefits Bulletin. (1979)-. Bulletin. English. Twenty-four times a year. $301.17. Eclipse Publications Ltd., 18 20 Highbury Place, London N5 1QP United Kingdom. **Tel** 011 44 171 3545858.
Ind/Abst Leg. Resour. Index; LegalTrac (1988-).

DD 658.320941
ISSN 0950-8147
UK
PAYROLL MANAGER'S REVIEW. [Payr. manag. rev.]. (1986)-. Periodical. English. Twelve times a year. $133.48. Tolley Publishing Company Ltd., Tolley House, 2 Addiscombe Road, Croydon, Surrey CR9 5AF United Kingdom. **Tel** 011 44 181 6869141, FAX 011 44 181 6863155.
Desc: Provides a comprehensive news summary and detailed analysis of everything happening in payroll.

LC HD5715 .P43
MX
PEDAGOGIA PARA EL ADIESTRAMIENTO. (19??)-. Periodical. Spanish. Four times a year. Servicio Nacional Adiestramiento, Atzcapotzalco la Villa 209, Mexico 16 DF Mexico. Index available (Free).

US
PENSIONS MANAGEMENT. Periodical. English. Financial Times Business Information Ltd, Greystoke Place, Fetter Lane, London EC4A 1ND United Kingdom. **Tel** 011 44 171 4056969, FAX 011 44 171 2420347.

ISSN 1019-6196
SA
PEOPLE DYNAMICS. Added/Corp Institute of Personnel Management (South Africa). (19??)-. English. Twelve times a year. $80.52. South African Institute of Personnel Management, PO Box 31390, Braamfontein 2017, South Africa. **Tel** 011 27 11 6427263. **ED** Helene de Villiers & Linda Brims. Index Available Published separately--free--upon request. **Ad Acc, Adv Mgr:** Barbara Spence, **Tel** 011 886-5954. **Continues** IPM Journal, 1011-4149.
Desc: Official publication of the Institute of Personnel Management, whose aim it is to promote and develop the highest standards of competence and ethical conduct amongst its members and to influence and assist in the development and optimum utilisation of human resources in the interests of the South African community as a whole.

LC HF5549.A2 P36
UK
●**PEOPLE MANAGEMENT. Added/Corp** Institute of Personnel and Development. Vol. 1, No. 1 (Jan. 1995)-. Periodical. English. Twenty-five times a year. £72.00 UK; £110.00 Europe; £120.00 (surface mail), £170.00 (airmail) other. Personnel Publications Ltd., 17 Britton Street, London EC1M 5NQ United Kingdom. **Tel** 011 44 171 3367646, FAX 011 44 171 3367637. **(Subscription address:** Customer Interface Ltd., Charnwood House Marsh Road, Bristol BS3 2NA United Kingdom. **Tel** 011 44 117 9620090.) **Formed by the union of** Personnel Management, 0031-5761; Personnel Management Plus; Training & Development **and** Transition (London, England), 0267-8950.
Ind/Abst Curr. Cit.

US
PERFORMANCE APPRAISALS : THE LATEST LEGAL NIGHTMARE. (1989)-. English. Irregular (Publishes 2 or 3 times per year). $63.50 (latest edition). Alexander Hamilton Institute, 70 Hilltop Road, Ramsey NJ 07446-1119. **Tel** (201)825-8161, (800)879-2441, FAX (201)825-8696.
Desc: Manual to help modernize employee evaluations and performance review programs.

ISSN 0710-2895
DD 658.3/124/09714
CN
PERFORMANCE (MONTREAL, QUEBEC). (PERFORMANCE.). [Performance]. Vol. 5, No. 1 (Jan/Feb. 1981)-. Periodical. French. Six times a year. Free to members. Association Quebecoise Pour La Formation Et La Performance, En Milieu De Travail, CP 526, Tour De La Bourse, Montreal Quebec H4Z 1J8. **Continues** Format D, 0710-2909.

GW
PERSONAL; MENSCH UND ARBEIT IM BETRIEB. See Business and Economics-Labor.

LC HD28
ISSN 0031-5605
DD 658
GW
PERSONAL (MUENCHEN). (PERSONAL.). [Personal]. (Jan. 15, 1968)-. Trade Publication. German. Twelve times a year. DM298.00. Wirtschaftsverlag Bachem GmBH, Ursulaplatz 1, D-50668 Cologne Germany. **Tel** 011 49 221 1619224, FAX 011 49 221 1619205. **ED** Hans J. Schneider. Index available. cum. index. **Bk Rev**. **Ad Acc. Circ**: 4,500. available with charts; available with illustrations. **Continues** Mensch und Arbeit.
Ind/Abst Saf. Health Work; Selec. Coop. Index Manage. Period.

ISSN 0723-3868
GW
UDC 658.3
PERSONALFEUHRUNG. [Personalfuhrung]. (19??)-. Trade Publication. German. Twelve times a year. DM223.20. Deutsche Gesellschaft fuer Personalfuhrung, Dusseldorf Germany.

ISSN 0031-5656
NE
UDC 658.3
PERSONEELSBELEID. [Personeelsbeleid].
VFOAT Personeelbeleid. (19??)-. Periodical. Dutch. Eleven times a year. $133.61. NVP, Postbus 19124, 3501 DC Utrecht Netherlands. **Tel** 011 31 30 364720. Index available (bound in Dec. issue).

LC HF5549 **ISSN** 1044-2189
DD 658.38 US
TITLE CHANGE
PERSONNEL ALERT (MAYWOOD, N.J.), THE. (THE PERSONNEL ALERT.). **Added/Corp** Alexander Hamilton Institute (U.S.). Vol. 1, No. 1 (June 23, 1989)-(19??). Periodical. English. Alexander Hamilton Institute, 70 Hilltop Road, Ramsey NJ 07446-1119. **Tel** (201)825-8161, (800)879-2441, FAX (201)825-8696. ***Continued by*** *Personnel Legal Alert, 1084-6913.*

US
PERSONNEL ASSISTANT. (19??)-. English. Twelve times a year. $119.00 one-year; $199.00 two-year. Borgman Associates, 321 Lennon Lane, Walnut Creek CA 94598. **Tel** (510)944-5544, FAX (510)988-1888. **ED** Denise Daigle. **Circ:** 1,100.
Desc: We carry practical information on new developments in hiring, recordkeeping, benefits administration, legal compliance and related issues.

ISSN 1351-0614
UK
•**PERSONNEL ASSISTANT'S HANDBOOK.** (1993)-. Periodical. English. Twelve times a year. £88.25. Croner Publ Ltd., Croner House London Road, Kingston Upon Thames, Surrey KT2 6SR United Kingdom. **Tel** 011 44 181 5473333, FAX 011 44 181 5472637.

ISSN 0161-2425
US
SUSPENDED
PERSONNEL CONSULTANT. [Pers. consult.]. **VFOAT** PC. Personnel Consultant. Vol. 1 (Apr. 1978)-(19??). Periodical. English. Twelve times a year. $45.00. National Association of Personnel Consultants, 3133 Mt. Vernon Avenue, Alexandria VA 22305. **Tel** (703)684-0180. ***Supersedes*** *Placement Age.*

LC HF5549.2.U5 P43 **ISSN** 1068-4751
DD 658 US
•**PERSONNEL EXECUTIVES CONTACTBOOK.** [Pers. exec. contactb.]. **Added/Corp** Gale Research Inc. **VFOAT** Personnel Executives Contact Book. 1st Ed. (1993)-. English. $149.00. Gale Research Inc., 835 Penobscot Building, 645 Griswold Street, Detroit MI 48226. **Tel** (800)877-GALE, (313)961-2242, FAX (313)961-6083, (800)414-5043, telex TWX 810-221-7086. **ED** Cindy Spomer. available on magnetic tape; available on diskette.
Desc: Allows you to find the right person to contact regarding employment opportunities. Offers complete contact information for 30,000 key personnel officers at companies across the US.

LC HF5549.A2 P45 **ISSN** 0146-597X
DD 658.3/005 US
PERSONNEL FORUM. (19??)-. English. B Hodes Associates, 711 Fifth Avenue, New York NY 10022.

UK
PERSONNEL IN PRACTICE. (19??)-. English. £223.00. Croner Publ Ltd., Croner House London Road, Kingston Upon Thames, Surrey KT2 6SR United Kingdom. **Tel** 011 44 181 5473333, FAX 011 44 181 5472637. ***Absorbed*** *Employment Digest, 0309-4995.*

LC HF5549.A2 P5 **ISSN** 0031-5745
DD 658.3/005 US
CCC
CODEN PEJOAA
Pr Rev.
PERSONNEL JOURNAL. [Pers. j.]. **Added/Corp** Personnel Research Federation (U.S.). Vol. 6, No. 1 (June 1927)-. Trade Publication. English. Twelve times a year. $55.00. ACC Communications Inc., 245 Fischer Avenue B-2, Costa Mesa CA 92626. **Tel** (714)751-1883, FAX (714)751-4106. **(Subscription address:** Neodata / Colorado, PO Box 2606, Boulder Boulder CO 80322.) **ED** Alan Halcrow. Index available (bound in Dec. issue). cum. index. **Ad Acc. Circ:** 28,000. available on microfilm and microfiche from University Microfilms International (UMI). Documents available from The Genuine Article, UMI Article Clearinghouse. ***Continues*** *Journal of Personnel Research, 0886-750X.*
Desc: The management magazine for personnel executives. Covers labor relations, compensation, benefits, training, development, recruitment, employee assistance, testing, relocation and related topics.
Ind/Abst ABI/INFORM Glob. Ed.; ABI/INFORM Ondisc: Expr. Ed. (Vol. 56, No. 12 1977-Vol. 68, No. 12 1989); ABI/INFORM [Computer File] (Sept. 1971-); Acad. Abstr. Full Text Elite; Acad. Abstr.; Acad. Ind. [Computer File] (1984-); Acad. Search; AGRICOLA [Select. Cov.]; Anbar Account. Finan. Abstr. [Full Txt.]; Anbar Mark. Distr. Abstr. [Full Txt.]; Anbar Top Manage. Abstr. [Full Txt.]; Book Rev. Index (?-Jan. 1989); Bus. ASAP (1992-) [Full Txt.]; Bus. Index (1985-); Bus. Period. Index; Bus. Source Plus; Bus. Source; Chicano Index; Commun. Abstr.; Comput. Lit. Index; Contents Pages Manage.; Cumul. Index Nurs. Allied Health Lit.; Curr. Cit.; Curr. Contents Soc. Behav. Sci.; Curr. Index J. Educ.; EP Collect.; Expand. Acad. Index (1984-); Gen. BusinessFile (1985-); Gen. Period. Index (1985-); Homework Help.; Hosp. Health Admin. Index (Vol. 56 No. 12, 1977-Vol. 68 No. 12, 1989); Hum. Resour. Abstr.; INFO-SOUTH Abstr.; Law Office Inf. Serv.; Mag. Artic. Summar. Elite; Mag. Artic. Summar. Select; Mag. Artic. Summar. CD-ROM; Mag. Search; Manage. Market. Abstr.; Manage. Bibliogr. Rev.; Manage. Contents; MasterFile FullTEXT 1000; MasterFile FullTEXT 350; MasterFile FullTEXT 650; MasterFile FullTEXT (Jan. 1990-) [Full Txt.]; Newsp. Period. Abstr. (1986-); OCLC; Oper. Prod. Manage. Abstr. [Full Txt.]; PAIS Int. Print (1991-); Person. Train. Abstr. [Full Txt.]; Person. Manage. Abstr.; Psychol. Abstr. (1927-); PsycINFO; PsycLit; Pub. Lib. FullTEXT; Res. Alert [Full Cov.]; Saf. Health Work; Sage Fam. Stud. Abstr.; Selec. Coop. Index Manage. Period.; Soc. Sci. Cit. Index [Full Cov.]; Telebase; UMI ABI/Inform--Bus. Period. Ondisc (Jan. 1987-) [Full Txt.]; Vocat. Search; Wilson Bus. Abstr.; Women Manage. Rev. [Full Txt.]; Women Stud. Abstr.; Work Relat. Abstr.

LC HF5549 **ISSN** 1084-6913
DD 658.38 US
PERSONNEL LEGAL ALERT, THE. [Pers. leg. alert]. **Added/Corp** Alexander Hamilton Institute (U.S.). (19??)-. Periodical. English. Twenty-four times a year. Alexander Hamilton Institute, 70 Hilltop Road, Ramsey NJ 07446-1119. **Tel** (201)825-8161, (800)879-2441, FAX (201)825-8696. ***Continues*** *Personnel Alert (Maywood, N.J.), 1044-2189.*

ISSN 0149-2675
US
CCC
PERSONNEL MANAGEMENT. **Added/Corp** Bureau of National Affairs (Washington, D.C.). (19??)-. Periodical. English. Twenty-six times a year. $650.00. Bureau of National Affairs Inc., 9435 Key West Avenue, Rockville MD 20850. **Tel** (800)372-1033, (301)258-1033, FAX (301)948-5823. **ED** Bill L. Manville. available on an online database from Human Resources Information Network. Documents available from Ask*IEEE.
Desc: A loose-leaf, practical guide to handling non-legal employee relations problems in areas such as hiring, termination, workplace safety, grievances, training, and productivity.
Ind/Abst Bus. Period. Index; Contents Pages Manage.; INSPEC (May 1983-); Women Manage. Rev. [Full Txt.]; Work Relat. Abstr.

LC HF5549 .P452 **ISSN** 0031-577X
DD 658.3082 US
PERSONNEL MANAGEMENT ABSTRACTS. **See** Business and Economics-Abstracting, Bibliographies and Statistics.

ISSN 1355-8587
DD 658.3 UK
PERSONNEL MANAGEMENT AND EUROPE. [Pers. manag. Eur.]. **VFOAT** IPD Executive Brief. Personnel Management and Europe; IPD Brief. (?994)-. English. Four times a year (Jan., Apr., July, Nov.). $77.01. Institute of Personnel Management, IPM House Camp Road, Wimbledon London SW19 4UX United Kingdom. **Tel** 011 44 181 9469100 ext. 214, FAX 011 44 181 9472570. ***Continues*** *Single European Market and Personnel Management, 1351-6434.*

US
PERSONNEL MANAGEMENT IN STATE AND LOCAL GOVERNMENTS / OFFICE OF PERSONNEL MANAGEMENT. **Main/Corp** United States. Office of Personnel Management. Library. (1979)-. English. One time a year. Office of Personnel Management, 1900 East Street Northwest, OELR Room 7429, Washington DC 20415. **Tel** (202)632-6256. ***Continues*** *Personnel Management in State and Local Governments.*

LC HF5549.A2 P52 **ISSN** 0031-5761
DD 658.3/005 UK
CCC
CODEN PERMEEPTMABL
TITLE CHANGE
PERSONNEL MANAGEMENT (LONDON. 1969). (PERSONNEL MANAGEMENT.). [Pers. manage.]. **Added/Corp** Institute of Personnel Management. Vol. 1 (May 1969)-(199?). Trade Publication. English. Personnel Publications Ltd., 17 Britton Street, London EC1M 5NQ United Kingdom. **Tel** 011 44 171 3367646, FAX 011 44 171 3367637. **(Subscription address:** Customer Interface Ltd., Charnwood House Marsh Road, Bristol BS3 2NA United Kingdom. **Tel** 011 44 117 9620090.) **ED** Susanne Lawrence. Index available. cum. index. **Bk Rev. Ad Acc. Circ:** 48,000. available on microfilm and microfiche from University Microfilms International (UMI). Documents available from Ask*IEEE, UMI Article Clearinghouse. ***Formed by the union of*** *Personnel and Training Management.* ***Merged into*** *People Management.*

Desc: News and features on theory and practice in recruitment, selection, training, development, pay, benefits, labour law, work practice and all aspects of human resource management.
Ind/Abst ABI/INFORM Glob. Ed.; ABI/INFORM [Computer File] (Sept. 1972-1994); Acad. Search; Br. Humanit. Index; Bus. ASAP (1992-1994) [Full Txt.]; Bus. Index (1985-1994); Bus. Period. Index; Bus. Source Plus; Bus. Source; Contents Pages Manage.; Curr. Cit.; EP Collect.; Gen. BusinessFile (1985-1994); Gen. Period. Index (1985-1994); Homework Help.; INFO-SOUTH Abstr.; INSPEC (May 1983-1994); Int. Labour Doc.; Mag. Search; Manage. Market. Abstr.; Manage. Contents; MasterFile FullTEXT 1000; MasterFile FullTEXT 350; MasterFile FullTEXT 650; MasterFile FullTEXT (July 1993-1994); OCLC; Person. Manage. Abstr.; Saf. Health Work; Stud. Women Abstr.; Tech. Educ. Train. Abstr.; Telebase; UMI ABI/Inform--Bus. Period. Ondisc (Nov. 1987-1994) [Full Txt.]; Wilson Bus. Abstr.

LC HF5549.A2 P6
UK
TITLE CHANGE
PERSONNEL MANAGEMENT PLUS. **Added/Corp** Institute of Personnel Management. Vol. 4, No. 6 (June 1993)-(199?). Periodical. English. Personnel Publications Ltd., 17 Britton Street, London EC1M 5NQ United Kingdom. **Tel** 011 44 171 3367646, FAX 011 44 171 3367637. ***Continues*** *PM Plus, 0961-2777.* ***Merged into*** *People Management.*

US
PERSONNEL MANAGEMENT PROGRAM. English. $191.28 (US); $231.48 (Canada). Bureau of Business Practice, 24 Rope Ferry Road, Waterford CT 06386. **Tel** (800)243-0876, (203)442-4365, (800)876-9105, FAX (203)443-1123.

US
PERSONNEL MANAGEMENT REFORM. Vol. 1, No. 1 (Sept. 1979)-. Periodical. English. Four times a year. United States Office of Personnel Management, Office of Intergovernmental Personnel Programs, 1900 E Street NW, Washington DC 20415.

LC JK765 **ISSN** 0498-935X
DD 351 US
PERSONNEL MANAGEMENT SERIES (WASHINGTON). **See** Public Administration-Civil Service.

ISSN 0885-3037
DD 658 US
TITLE CHANGE
PERSONNEL MANAGER'S LETTER. (PERSONNEL MANAGER'S LETTER / EXECUTIVE REPORTS CORPORATION.). [Pers. manager's lett.]. **Added/Corp** Executive Reports Corporation. Prentice Hall Professional Newsletters. Bureau of Business Practice. (1985)-(1994). Newsletter. English. Bureau of Business Practice, 24 Rope Ferry Road, Waterford CT 06386. **Tel** (800)243-0876, (203)442-4365, (800)876-9105, FAX (203)443-1123. ***Continued by*** *HR Briefing, 1080-1847.*

US
PERSONNEL POLICY MANUAL. (19??)-. English. Twelve times a year. $387.00. Personnel Policy Service Inc., PO Box 7697, Louisville KY 40257. **Tel** (502)897-6782, (800)437-3735, FAX (502)896-4162. **ED** J.C. Norman Jr. Index available. cum. index. **Circ:** 6,000 (ctrl).
Desc: Contains adaptable personnel policies for management use.

ISSN 0896-985X
DD 658 US
TITLE CHANGE
PERSONNEL PRACTICE IDEAS. [Pers. pract. ideas]. (198?)-(19??)-. Periodical. English. Warren Gorham & Lamont Inc., Park Square Building, 31 St. James Avenue, Boston MA 02116-4112. **Tel** (617)423-2020, (800)950-1207, FAX (617)423-2026. ***Continued by*** *Human Resources Practice Ideas, 1075-8321.*

ISSN 0738-9914
US
PERSONNEL PRACTICES NEWSLETTER. **VFOAT** Personnel Practices. Vol. 1, No. 1 (May 1983)-. Newsletter. English. Twelve times a year. AC Croft Inc, 245 Fischer Avenue B 2, Costa Mesa CA 92626. **Tel** (714)751-1883. ***Continues*** *Human Resources Management Newsletter, 0731-4647.*

LC HF5549.A2 P53 **ISSN** 0031-5826
DD 658.305 US
CCC
NLM W1 PE8702 **CODEN** PPSYAQ
Pr Rev.
PERSONNEL PSYCHOLOGY. [Pers. psychol.]. Vol. 1 (Spring 1948)-. Academic Scholarly Publication. English. Four times a year (Mar., Jun., Sept., Dec.). $60.00. Personnel Psychology Inc., 745 Haskins Road, Suite A, Bowling Green OH 43402. **Tel** (419)352-1562, FAX (419)352-2645. Index available (bound in Dec. issue). **Bk Rev**, (Qty: 100). **Ad Acc. Circ:** 3,300. available on microfilm and microfiche from

University Microfilms International (UMI). Documents available from The Genuine Article, UMI Article Clearinghouse.
Desc: Publishes articles about applied research in personnel. Read by personnel managers, teachers and students in business schools and psychology departments.
Ind/Abst ABI/INFORM Glob. Ed.; ABI/INFORM [Computer File] (Fall 1971-); Acad. Search; Book Rev. Index; Bus. Index (1985-); Bus. Period. Index; Bus. Source Plus; Bus. Source; Contents Pages Manage.; Curr. Cit.; Curr. Contents Soc. Behav. Sci.; Curr. Index J. Educ.; EP Collect.; Gen. BusinessFile (1985-); Gen. Period. Index (1985-); Homework Help.; Hum. Resour. Abstr. (?-?); INFO-SOUTH Abstr.; J. Plan. Lit.; Mag. Search; Manage. Market. Abstr.; Manage. Contents; MasterFile FullTEXT 1000; MasterFile FullTEXT 350; MasterFile FullTEXT 650; MasterFile FullTEXT (July 1993-); OCLC; Person. Manage. Abstr.; Psychol. Abstr. (1949-); PsycINFO; PsycLit; PsycScan: Appl. Psych.; Res. Alert [Full Cov.]; Risk Abstr.; Selec. Coop. Index Manage. Period.; Soc. Sci. Cit. Index [Full Cov.]; Telebase; UMI ABI/Inform--Bus. Period. Ondisc (Winter 1987-) [Full Txt.]; Wilson Bus. Abstr.; Women Stud. Abstr.; Work Relat. Abstr.

LC JF1601 .P85 **ISSN** 0095-0394
DD 350/.1/008 US

PERSONNEL REPORT. English. International Personnel Management Association / Illinois, 1313 East 60th Street, Chicago IL 60637. ***Continues*** *Public Personnel Association. Personnel Report.*

ISSN 0148-6977
US

PERSONNEL RESEARCH AND DEVELOPMENT CENTER OF THE U. S. CIVIL SERVICE COMMISSION, THE. See Public Administration-Civil Service.

LC HF5549.A2 P54 **ISSN** 0048-3486
DD 658.3/005 UK
CCC

Pr Rev.

PERSONNEL REVIEW. [Pers. rev.]. **Added/Corp** Institute of Personnel Management. Vol. 1 (Autumn 1971)-. Periodical. English. Eight times a year. $3215.36. MCB University Press, 60 62 Toller Lane, Bradford, West Yorkshire BD8 9BY United Kingdom. **Tel** 011 44 1274 785280, FAX 011 44 1274 785200, telex 51317-MCBUNI-G. **(Subscription address:** MCB University Press / US and Canada Subscriptions, PO Box 10812, Birmingham AL 35201-0812. **Tel** (205)995-1567, (800)633-4931, FAX (205)995-1588.**) ED** Margaret Reid. available on an online database (file 15/Full-Text) from DIALOG. Documents available from The Genuine Article, UMI Article Clearinghouse.
Desc: Seeks to present the latest research and developments in all disciplines of relevance to the personnel specialist.
Ind/Abst ABI/INFORM Glob. Ed.; ABI/INFORM [Computer File] (Winter 1979-); Acad. Search; Anbar Account. Finan. Abstr. [Full Txt.]; Anbar Mark. Distr. Abstr. [Full Txt.]; Anbar Top Manage. Abstr. [Full Txt.]; Bus. Source Plus; Bus. Source; Contents Pages Manage.; Curr. Cit.; EP Collect.; Gen. BusinessFile (1992-); Gen. Period. Index (1985-); Homework Help.; INFO-SOUTH Abstr.; Mag. Search; Manage. Market. Abstr.; Manage. Bibliogr. Rev.; Manage. Contents; MasterFile FullTEXT 1000; MasterFile FullTEXT 350; MasterFile FullTEXT 650; MasterFile FullTEXT (Jan. 1993-); OCLC; Oper. Prod. Manage. Abstr. [Full Txt.]; Person. Train. Abstr. [Full Txt.]; Person. Manage. Abstr.; Res. Alert [Full Cov.]; School Organ. Manage. Abstr.; Selec. Coop. Index Manage. Period.; Soc. Sci. Cit. Index [Full Cov.]; Stud. Women Abstr.; Tech. Educ. Train. Abstr.; Telebase; Women Manage. Rev. [Full Txt.]; Work Relat. Abstr. (-19??).

LC HF5549.A2 A545 **ISSN** 0305-067X
DD 016.6583 UK

PERSONNEL + TRAINING ABSTRACTS. See Business and Economics-Abstracting, Bibliographies and Statistics.

UK

PERSONNEL TRAINING BULLETIN. [AUDIO CASSETTE]. (19??)-. Bulletin. English. Twelve times a year. £97.50. Didasko Ltd., Didasko House, Wennington Huntingdon, Cambridgeshire PE17 2LX United Kingdom. **Tel** 011 44 48 373232.

LC HF5549.A2 P6

UK
CODEN PMPLEN
Pr Rev. **TITLE CHANGE**

PM PLUS. Added/Corp Institute of Personnel Management. **VFOAT** Personnel Management Plus. Vol. 1, No. 1 (July 1990)-(1993). Periodical. English. Personnel Publications Ltd., 17 Britton Street, London EC1M 5NQ United Kingdom. **Tel** 011 44 171 3367646, FAX 011 44 171 3367637. **ED** Susanne Lawrence. Index available. **Bk Rev. Ad Acc. Circ:** 55,000. ***Continues*** *IPM Digest.* ***Continued by*** *Personnel Management Plus, 0031-5761.*
Desc: Personnel management carries in-depth analysis of all aspects of managing people at work.

US

POSITIVE ATTITUDE POSTERS. English (Spanish). Twenty-six times a year. $89.31. Economics Press Inc, 12 Daniel Road, Fairfield NJ 07004. **Tel** (201)227-1224, (800)526-2554, FAX (201)227-9742. **Bk Rev. Ad Acc. Circ:** 23,000 (ctrl).
Desc: Subjects emphasized are: quality production, punctuality, reliability, teamwork, other work-related habits and attitudes.

LC HF5549.A2 P526 **ISSN** 0361-7467
DD 658.3/008 US
CCC

PPF SURVEY. Added/Corp Bureau of National Affairs (Washington, D.C.). **VFOAT** Personnel Policies Forum Survey. No. 99 (Nov. 1972)-. English. Irregular. $40.00 (4 issues). Bureau of National Affairs Inc., 9435 Key West Avenue, Rockville MD 20850. **Tel** (800)372-1033, (301)258-1033, FAX (301)948-5823. **ED** Michael J. Reidy. available on microfilm from Xerox. ***Continues*** *Personnel Policies Forum.*
Desc: In-depth reports on human resources-topics derived from responses to questionnaires sent to BNA's Personnel Policies Forum. Topics included recruiting and selection policies, promotion and transfer procedures, wage and salary administration, employee benefits and services, communication programs, grievance procedures, performance evaluation and motivation programs.

ISSN 0742-7859
DD 658 US
CCC

PRACTICAL SUPERVISION. [Pract. superv.]. **Added/Corp** Professional Training Associates. No. 1 (Mar. 1, 1984)-. Periodical. English. Twelve times a year. $48.00. Professional Training Associates, 210 Commerce Boulevard, Round Rock TX 78664. **Tel** (512)255-6006, (800)424-2112. **ED** Judith Rappold. Index available (free). **Bk Rev.** ctrl circ.
Desc: How to solve the daily problems of supervising people and how to become an effective supervisor.

ISSN 0921-2442
NE

UDC 331.1

PRAKTIJKBLAD VOOR MEDEZEGGENSCHAP. [Praktijkbl. medezeggensch.]. (1987)-. Periodical. Dutch. Eleven times a year. $89.01. Welboombladen BV, OZ Voorburgwal 103, 1012 EM Amsterdam Netherlands. **Tel** 011 31 20 6267811. Index available. **Ad Acc.** ctrl circ. ***Continues*** *O.R. Blad, 0920-492X.*

LC KF3464.A15 P47
DD 344.73/01133/05 US

PRI REPORT. VAT Personnel Research Inc. Report. Vol. 4, No. 2 (July 1985)-. English. Four times a year. Free. PRI Associates Inc, 1905 Chapel Hill Road, Durham NC 27707. **Tel** (919)493-7534. **ED** Peter R Skalak. Index available. cum. index. **Circ:** 4,000 (ctrl). ***Continues*** *Personnel Research Report (Durham, N.C.), 0736-8224.*
Desc: Contains articles on all aspects on the use of statistics in litigation. Its emphasis is on personnel management and employment discrimination issues.

IT

PROCEDURE DI AMMINISTRAZIONE DEL PERSONALE. (19??)-. Periodical. Italian. Three times a year (April, Aug. and Dec.). IPSOA Editore SRL, Casella Postale 12055, Mastrangelo, 20120 Milan Italy. **Tel** 011 39 2 82476248. Index available (Included).

ISSN 1059-356X
US

PROCEEDINGS OF THE FIRST BIANNUAL INTERNATIONAL CONFERENCE ON ADVANCES IN MANAGEMENT. See Business and Economics-Management.

ISSN 0733-0898
US

PROCEEDINGS OF THE ... SPRING MEETING (INDUSTRIAL RELATIONS RESEARCH ASSOCIATION : 1979). See Business and Economics-Labor.

US

PRODUCTIVITY RESEARCH PROGRAM FOR FY ..., THE. Main/Corp United States. Office of Personnel Management. Productivity Research Division. 1981-. English. One time a year. Office of Personnel Management, 1900 East Street Northwest, OELR Room 7429, Washington DC 20415. **Tel** (202)632-6256.

ISSN 1380-6815
NE

UDC 658.85

•**PROFESSIONEEL VERKOPEN.** [Prof. verkopen]. (1994)-. Periodical. Dutch. Twenty-six times a year. $153.47. Samsom Bedrijfsinformatie BV, Postbus 4, 2400 MA Alphen Rij Netherlands. **Tel** 011 31 1720 66633. **(Subscription address:** Intermedia BV, Postbus 4, 2400 MA Alphen AD Rijn Netherlands. **Tel** 011 31 1720 66481.**)** ***Continues*** *Informatie voor de Buitendienst, 0165-0041.*

US

PUBLIC EMPLOYEE RELATIONS LIBRARY. See Public Administration-Civil Service.

LC HF5549.A2 P388 **ISSN** 0091-0260
DD 658.3/005 US
CCC

NLM W1 PU629 **CODEN** PPMNCX
Pr Rev.

PUBLIC PERSONNEL MANAGEMENT. [Public pers. manage.]. **Added/Corp** International Personnel Management Association. Vol. 2 (Jan./Feb. 1973)-. Periodical. English. Four times a year. $50.00. International Personnel Management Association, 1617 Duke Street, Alexandria VA 22314. **Tel** (703)549-7100, FAX (703)684-0948. **ED** Sarah Shiffert. Index available. **Ad Acc. Circ:** 9,000. available on microfilm and microfiche from University Microfilms International (UMI); available on an online database (file 648/Full-Text) from DIALOG. Documents available from The Genuine Article, UMI Article Clearinghouse. ***Continues*** *Personnel Administration and Public Personnel Review, 0885-6591.*
Desc: Articles on public sector human resource management - labor relations, assessment issues, comparative personnel policies, and governmental reform.
Ind/Abst ABC POL SCI; ABI/INFORM Glob. Ed.; ABI/INFORM [Computer File] (May 1973-); Acad. Search; Account. Index Suppl.; Anbar Account. Finan. Abstr. [Full Txt.]; Anbar Mark. Distr. Abstr. (1973-1981,1986-) [Full Txt.]; Anbar Top Manage. Abstr. [Full Txt.]; Book Rev. Index (19??-Oct. 1989); Bus. ASAP (1992-) [Full Txt.]; Bus. Index (1985-); Bus. Period. Index; Bus. Source Plus; Bus. Source; Curr. Cit.; Curr. Contents Soc. Behav. Sci.; Curr. Index J. Educ.; Educ. Adm. Abstr.; EP Collect.; Gen. BusinessFile (1985-); Gen. Period. Index (1985-); Homework Help.; INFO-SOUTH Abstr.; Int. Labour Doc.; LABORDOC; Mag. Search; Manage. Bibliogr. Rev. (1973-); MasterFile FullTEXT 1000; MasterFile FullTEXT 350; MasterFile FullTEXT 650; MasterFile FullTEXT (July 1993-); Middle East Abstr. Index; OCLC; Oper. Prod. Manage. Abstr. [Full Txt.]; PAIS Int. Print (1991-); Person. Train. Abstr. [Full Txt.]; Person. Manage. Abstr.; Psychol. Abstr. (1973-); PsycINFO; PsycLit; PsycScan: Appl. Psych.; Res. Alert [Full Cov.]; Soc. Sci. Cit. Index [Full Cov.]; Telebase; Wilson Bus. Abstr.; Women Manage. Rev. (May 1973-) [Full Txt.]; Work Relat. Abstr.

LC HD66 .Q333 **ISSN** 1049-8699
DD 658.4/036 US
CCC

QUALITY DIGEST. See Business and Economics-Labor.

LC HD62.15 .Q362 **ISSN** 1068-6967
DD 658.5/62/05 US
CCC

•**QUALITY MANAGEMENT JOURNAL, THE.** [Qual. manag. j.]. **Added/Corp** American Society for Quality Control. Vol. 1, Issue 1 (Oct. 1993)-. Periodical. English. Four times a year. $130.00. American Society for Quality Control, 611 East Wisconsin Avenue, PO Box 3005, Milwaukee WI 53201. **Tel** (414)272-8575, (800)248-1946, FAX (414)272-1734, telex 316567.
Desc: Links the efforts of academic researchers and quality management practitioners. Encourages pioneering research in the field of quality management by providing a forum for communication and discussing research findings.

UK

QWL NEWS & ABSTRACTS / WORK RESEARCH UNIT. Added/Corp Great Britain. Work Research Unit. **VFOAT** Quality of Working Life News & Abstracts. **VAT** QWL News and Abstracts. No. 110 (Spring 1992)-. Periodical. English. Four times a year. ACAS, Work Research Unit, St. Vincent House, 30 Orange Street, London WC2H 7HH United Kingdom. **Tel** 011 44 71 839 9289. **Bk Rev**, (Qty: 10). ctrl circ. ***Continues*** *WRU News & Abstracts, 0960-2615.*
Desc: News, notes and research on quality of working life issues. Includes book reviews, journal abstracts and a listing of future conferences.

ISSN 0033-7315
US

RACE RELATIONS & INDUSTRY. Added/Corp D. Parke Gibson International. D. Parke Gibson Associates. **VAT** Race Relations and Industry. (196?)-. Periodical. English. Twelve times a year. $100.00. Gibson Parke Association Inc, 475 5th Avenue, New York NY 10017. available on microfilm.

Business and Economics — Personnel Management

DD 658.3/02/0971
ISSN 1187-9378
CN
TITLE CHANGE
RECRUITING & SUPERVISION TODAY.
[Recruit. superv. today]. **Added/Corp** Institute of Professional Management. **VFOAT** Recruiting and Supervision Today. (1991)-(1995). Periodical. English. Institute of Professional Management, 2 Walton Court, Ottawa Ontario K1V 9T1 Canada. **Tel** (613)523-5957, FAX (613)523-8505. **Ad Acc**. *Formed by the union of Recruiting Today., 0845-2512 and Supervision Today., 1187-936X. Continued by HR Today.*
Desc: Strives to assist management professionals in developing management plans and strategies for today's human resources.

UK
TITLE CHANGE
RECRUITMENT SELECTION AND RETENTION. (19??)-(1994). English. MCB University Press, 60 62 Toller Lane, Bradford, West Yorkshire BD8 9BY United Kingdom. **Tel** 011 44 1274 785280, FAX 011 44 1274 785200, telex 51317-MCBUNI-G. *Merged into International Journal of Career Management, 0955-6214.*
Ind/Abst Ergon. Abstr.

LC HD28 .R2 **ISSN** 0033-6874
GW
CCC
CODEN REFNA9
REFA NACHRICHTEN. [REFA-Nachr.].
Main/Corp Verband fuer Arbeitsstudien. **Added/Corp** Verband fuer Arbeitsstudien. Nachrichten. **VAT** Reichsausschuss fuer Arbeitsstudien Nachrichten. (Feb. 1948)-. Trade Publication. German. Six times a year. $82.36. Beuth Verlag GmbH, Burggrafenstrasse 6, D-10787 Berlin Germany. **Tel** 011 49 30 260112573, FAX 011 49 30 24399926. Documents available from UMI Article Clearinghouse.
Ind/Abst ABI/INFORM Glob. Ed.; ABI/INFORM [Computer File] (Feb. 1981-); Saf. Health Work.

FR
RELOCALISER : LA LETRE DE LA MOBILITE-DEMOSCOOP. French. Eleven times a year. 2565.00F. Sofrexper, 3 rue de la Boetie, 75008 Paris France. **Tel** 011 33 1 44515959. Index available. cum. index. ctrl circ. *Continues Demoscoop l'Echo de Sofrexper.*
Desc: Features information on personnel management: legal, fiscal, economical information, staff management, and relocation assistance, worldwide.

DD 338 **ISSN** 1074-0686
US
RELOCATION UPDATE. [Relocat. update]. (19??)-. Periodical. English. Twelve times a year. $48.00 US; $65.00 other. Feasibility Inc., 8000 Glenbrittle Way, Raleigh NC 27615. **Tel** (919)676-2327, FAX (919)676-1865. **ED** Connie Ledicotte. **Bk Rev**, (Qty: 1-2). **Ad Acc**. **Circ**: 5,100 (ctrl). *Continues Relocation/RealtyUpdate.*

LC HF5549.2.U5 R46 **ISSN** 1063-1968
DD 331.2/816583/00973021 US
REPORT ON HUMAN RESOURCES COMPENSATION. [Rep. human resour. compens.]. **Added/Corp** Executive Compensation Service (U.S.). **VFOAT** Human Resources Compensation. (1992)-. Trade Publication. English. One time a year. $190.00. ECS, Executive Compensation Service, Wyatt Data Services, 218 Route 17 North, Roselle Park NJ 07662-9832. **Tel** (201)843-1177, FAX (201)843-0101.

ISSN 0360-7119
US
REPORTER. [Reporter]. Vol. 1, (Oct. 6, 1975)-. Periodical. English. Twelve times a year. $15.00. Concordia Publishing House, 3558 South Jefferson Avenue, St Louis MO 63118. **Tel** (314)268-1000, (800)325-3381, FAX (314)268-1329. **ED** Rev. David Mahsman. **Circ**: 65,000 (ctrl). *Absorbed Advance, 0001-8570.*
Desc: News of the church at large and the Lutheran church, Missouri Synod. Also includes ideas and resources for congregation leaders.
Ind/Abst Am. Hist. Life (1955-1957).

LC HF5549.A2 R49 **ISSN** 0742-7301
DD 658.3/005 US
CCC
RESEARCH IN PERSONNEL AND HUMAN RESOURCES MANAGEMENT. [Res. pers. hum. resour. manage.]. Vol. 1 (1983)-. English. One time a year. $73.25. JAI Press Inc., 55 Old Post Road, Suite 2, PO Box 1678, Greenwich CT 06836-1678. **Tel** (203)661-7602, FAX (203)661-0792. **ED** Gerald R. Ferris.
Desc: Includes monograph length conceptual papers designed to promote theory and research on substantive and methodological topics in the field of human resources management. Although each volume contains papers on a variety of topics and are not designed to be theme-oriented, a number of papers (across the several published volumes) share common themes.

FR
REVUE RESSOURCES HUMAINES.
French. Four times a year. 353.00F. Revue Ressources Humaines, 82 BD Sebastopol, F-75003 Paris France. **Tel** 011 33 1 42712929.

JA
ROMU KENKYU. (1948)-. Periodical. Japanese. Twelve times a year. $132.50. **(Subscription address:** Japan Publications Trading Company Ltd., PO Box 5030, Tokyo International, Tokyo 100-31 Japan. **Tel** 011 81 3 3292 3753.**)**

LC HD4965.3.E372 U57 **ISSN** 0276-4822
DD 331.2/8165843/0973 US
SALARY SURVEY OF MIDDLE MANAGEMENT AND SUPERVISORY PERSONNEL. SOUTHERN CALIFORNIA.
See Business and Economics-Labor.

ISSN 0363-4922
US
SECURITY LETTER. (197?)-. Periodical. English. Twenty-three times a year. $187.00. Security Letter Inc, 166 East 96th Street, New York NY 10128. **Tel** (212)348-1553, FAX (212)534-2957. **ED** Robert D McCrie. Index available. **Bk Rev**, (Qty: 3/yr). available on microfilm and microfiche from University Microfilms International (UMI).
Desc: Management newsletter concerned with protection of assets from loss. Reports on physical security, information protection, and computer crime.
Ind/Abst Crim. Justice Period. Index.

ISSN 0344-8746
UDC 65.012.7 GW
CCC
SICHERHEITS-BERATER. (1974)-. Periodical. German. Twenty-four times a year. $377.69. Handelsblatt GmbH, Postfach 102716, D-40018 Duesseldorf Germany. **Tel** 011 49 211 8871730, FAX 011 49 211 133523, telex 172114489.

DD 338 **ISSN** 1060-8184
US
CEASED
SMALL BUSINESS EMPLOYEE ASSISTANCE. [Small bus. empl. assist.].
Added/Corp First Health Group. (Nov. 1991)-(Jan. 1994). Periodical. English. First Health Group, 5305 Tractor Lane, Fairfax VA 22030. **Tel** (800)626-4327, (703)558-6188, FAX (703)836-7810. **ED** Richard Bickerton (editor's address: 3305 Carolina Place, Alexandria, VA 22305; phone(703)836-1096). Index available. **Circ**: 1,000 (ctrl).
Desc: Addresses drug-free work place issues and employee assistance issues in small business.

LC Z7164.C81 S7777 HF5549.A2 **ISSN** 1052-4819
DD 016.6583 US
STERN'S SOURCEFINDER. (STERN'S SOURCEFINDER : HUMAN RESOURCE MANAGEMENT.). [Stern's sourcefinder]. **VFOAT** Stern's Source Finder. (1991)-. English. $179.95. Michael Daniels Publishers, PO Box 3233, Culver City CA 90231-3233.

US
STRESS IN THE AMERICAN WORKPLACE. (19??)-. English. $23.45. LRP Publications, 747 Dresher Road, Suite 500, Horsham PA 19044. **Tel** (800)341-7874, (215)784-0941, FAX (215)784-9639, (215)784-0870.

US
SUCCESSFUL SUPERVISOR. (19??)-.
English. Twenty-six times a year. $66.75. Dartnell Corporation, 4660 North Ravenswood Avenue, Chicago IL 60640. **Tel** (312)561-4000, (800)621-5463, FAX (312)561-3801. **ED** Linda Segall.
Desc: Shows supervisors how to manage, motivate, and boost employee morale.

LC TS155.A1 S8 **ISSN** 0039-5854
DD 658.3/02/05 US
CCC
CODEN SUPRAO
SUPERVISION (BURLINGTON).
(SUPERVISION.). [Supervision]. **Added/Corp** National Association of Foremen. (Feb. 1939)-. Trade Publication. English. Twelve times a year. $87.20. National Research Bureau Inc. / Iowa, 200 North Fourth, PO Box 1, Burlington IA 52601. **Tel** (319)752-5415, FAX (319)752-3421. **(Subscription address:** National Research Bureau Inc., PO Box 1, Burlington IA 52601.**)** **ED** Barbara Boeding. **Circ**: 5,402 (ctrl). available on microfilm and microfiche from University Microfilms International (UMI). Documents available from UMI Article Clearinghouse. *Supersedes Foreman.*
Ind/Abst ABI/INFORM Glob. Ed.; ABI/INFORM [Computer File] (Feb. 1976-); Acad. Search; Bus. ASAP (1990-) [Full Txt.]; Bus. Index (1985-); Bus. Period.; Bus. Source Plus; Bus. Source; Curr. Cit.; EP Collect.; Gen. BusinessFile (1985-); Gen. Period. Index (1988-); Homework Help.; INFO-SOUTH Abstr.; Mag. Search; MasterFile FullTEXT 1000; MasterFile FullTEXT 350; MasterFile FullTEXT 650; MasterFile FullTEXT (Jan. 1993-); OCLC; Telebase; UMI ABI/Inform--Bus. Period. Ondisc (Dec. 1987-) [Full Txt.]; Vocat. Search; Wilson Bus. Abstr.

LC TS155.A1 S86 **ISSN** 0039-5889
US
CODEN SUPBEE
TITLE CHANGE
SUPERVISOR'S BULLETIN. **Added/Corp** National Foremen's Institute. (19??)-(199?). Bulletin. English. Bureau of Business Practice, 24 Rope Ferry Road, Waterford CT 06386. **Tel** (800)243-0876, (203)442-4365, (800)876-9105, FAX (203)443-1123. **ED** Bob Ellal. *Continued by Today's Leader, 1079-9850.*

LC HD4903.5.U58 S94 **ISSN** 0362-5826
DD 658.3/005 US
SUPERVISOR'S EEO REVIEW, THE. See Business and Economics-Labor.

LC HF5549.A2 S85 **ISSN** 1045-263X
DD 658.3/005 US
CCC
SUPERVISORY MANAGEMENT (1989).
(SUPERVISORY MANAGEMENT.). [Superv. manage.]. **Added/Corp** American Management Association. Periodicals Division. Vol. 34, No. 1 (Jan. 1989)-. Periodical. English. Twelve times a year. $65.00. American Management Association, 135 West 50th Street, New York NY 10020-1201. **Tel** (212)586-8100, (212)903-8375 (periodicals), FAX (212)903-8168, (212)903-8083 (periodicals). **(Subscription address:** Neodata / Colorado, PO Box 2606, Boulder Boulder CO 80322.**)** **ED** Florence Stone. Index available (bound in Dec. issue). available on microfilm and microfiche from University Microfilms International (UMI). Documents available from UMI Article Clearinghouse. *Continues Management Solutions, 0889-0226.*
Desc: Articles and departments help managers oversee others' work, speed up their employees' and own professional development, and strengthen their awareness of the importance of their functions as manager.
Ind/Abst Acad. Search; AGRICOLA [Select. Cov.]; Bus. Source Plus; Bus. Source; Curr. Cit.; EP Collect.; Gen. Period. Index (1985-); Homework Help.; INFO-SOUTH Abstr.; Lotus Notes; Mag. Search; Manage. Contents; MasterFile FullTEXT 1000; MasterFile FullTEXT 350; MasterFile FullTEXT 650; MasterFile FullTEXT (July 1993-) [Full Txt.]; Newsp. Period. Abstr. (1989-); OCLC; Telebase; UMI ABI/Inform--Bus. Period. Ondisc (Jan. 1987-) [Full Txt.]; Vocat. Search; Work Relat. Abstr.

ISSN 0274-645X
US
CCC
CEASED
SUPERVISORY SENSE. **Added/Corp** American Management Association. (19??)-(June 1994). Periodical. English. American Management Association, 135 West 50th Street, New York NY 10020-1201. **Tel** (212)586-8100, (212)903-8375 (periodicals), FAX (212)903-8168, (212)903-8083 (periodicals). **ED** Florence Stone. **Circ**: 13,700.
Desc: A problem solving aid for all those who supervise others. Covers supervisory and management skills situations to help first-line managers become aware of their responsibilities to their companies and employees, develop new or refine existing skills, and handle their jobs more efficiently and effectively.

LC HD4965.2 .R46
DD 331.2/16 US
SURVEY REPORT ON VARIABLE PAY PROGRAMS / WYATT DATA SERVICES, ECS. See Business and Economics-Labor.

ISSN 1037-9681
DD 658.30099405 AT
TITLE CHANGE
T AND D. (T & D.). [T D]. **VFOAT** T & D.; T and D. (1991)-(1995). Periodical. English. T & D Newsletter, PO Box 1480, Crowsnest NSW 2065 Australia. **Tel** 011 61 2 9061949. **ED** Kieran B. Smith. **Bk Rev**, (Qty: 26). *Continued by Employer Plus T & D.*

AT
TAFE AWARD COURSE HANDBOOK.
(199?)-. English. One time a year. 5.00Aus$. Department of Employment Training & Further Education, GPO Box 2352, Adelaide 5001 Australia. **Tel** 011 61 08 226 3409.

US
TAKE CHARGE ASSISTANT. (19??)-. Periodical. English. Twelve times a year. $75.00. American Management Association, 135 West 50th

Street, New York NY 10020-1201. **Tel** (212)586-8100, (212)903-8375 (periodicals), FAX (212)903-8168, (212)903-8083 (periodicals).

UK

TEAM LEADER'S BRIEFING. (19??)-. English. £44.50. Croner Publ Ltd., Croner House London Road, Kingston Upon Thames, Surrey KT2 6SR United Kingdom. **Tel** 011 44 181 5473333, FAX 011 44 181 5472637.

LC HD28 **ISSN** 1352-7592
DD 658 UK

•**TEAM PERFORMANCE MANAGEMENT: AN INTERNATIONAL JOURNAL.** (1994)-. Trade Publication. English. Four times a year. $149.00. MCB University Press, 60 62 Toller Lane, Bradford, West Yorkshire BD8 9BY United Kingdom. **Tel** 011 44 1274 785280, FAX 011 44 1274 785200, telex 51317-MCBUNI-G.

US

TECHNICAL EMPLOYMENT NEWS. (19??)-. Periodical. English. One time a week. $55.00 US; $88.00 Canada and Mexico; $152.00 Europe; $175.00 Japan, Australia and New Zealand; $160.00 other (includes the Directory of Technical Service Firms). Publications & Communications, 12416 Hymeadow Drive, Austin TX 78750. **Tel** (512)250-9023, (800)678-9724, FAX (512)331-3900, telex 384303. **(Subscription address:** Publications & Communications, PO Box 399, Cedar Park TX 78630. **)** ***Continues** PD News, 0478-9997.*
Desc: Serves the contract technical employment industry.

ISSN 0169-2216
NE
UDC 331

TIJDSCHRIFT VOOR ARBEIDSVRAAGSTUKKEN. [Tijdschr. arb.vraagst.]. (1985)-. Periodical. Dutch (summaries and/or abstracts in English). Four times a year. $91.13. Uitgeverij de Tijdstroom BV, Postbus 19135, 3501 DC Utrecht Netherlands. **Tel** 011 31 030 5869000, FAX 011 31 030 586950.

ISSN 0319-3845
DD 331 CN

TIRE A PART - ECOLE DE RELATIONS INDUSTRIELLES, UNIVERSITE DE MONTREAL. [Tire part -Ec. relat. ind., Univ. Montr.]. **Main/Corp** Universite de Montreal. Ecole de Relations Industrielles. 1- 1975-. Monographic series. French. Price varies per volume. Presses de l'Universite de Montreal, PO Box 6128 Station A, Montreal Quebec H3C 3J7 Canada. **Tel** (514)343-6933.
Desc: A reprint serial dealing with personnel management and labor law, collective bargaining and labor economics.

ISSN 1079-9850
DD 658.302/05 US
CEASED

TODAY'S LEADER. (TODAY'S LEADER : GUIDING YOUR PEOPLE TO SUCCESS.). [Today's lead.]. **Added/Corp** National Foremen's Institute. Issue No. 935 (Oct. 1994)-(July 1995). Periodical. English. Bureau of Business Practice, 24 Rope Ferry Road, Waterford CT 06386. **Tel** (800)243-0876, (203)442-4365, (800)876-9105, FAX (203)443-1123. ***Continues** Supervisor's Bulletin, 0039-5889.*

LC HD7260 .N345 **ISSN** 0734-3302
DD 658.3/02/05 US

TODAY'S SUPERVISOR. **See** Industrial Health and Safety.

LC HG4028.P5 T65
UK

TOLLEY'S PAYROLL HANDBOOK. **VFOAT** Payroll Handbook. (1987)-. English. £41.95. Tolley Publishing Company Ltd., Tolley House, 2 Addiscombe Road, Croydon, Surrey CR9 5AF United Kingdom. **Tel** 011 44 181 6869141, FAX 011 44 181 6863155.
Desc: Covers the whole range of payroll activities including income tax, national insurance, types of payment, administration, and dealings with the Inland Revenue and DSS.

ISSN 0888-5893
US
CEASED

TRAINER'S WORKSHOP. [Trainer's workshop]. **Added/Corp** American Management Association. Periodicals Division. Vol. 1, No. 1 (July 1986)-Vol. 9 (Mar. 1995). Periodical. English. American Management Association, 135 West 50th Street, New York NY 10020-1201. **Tel** (212)586-8100, (212)903-8375 (periodicals), FAX (212)903-8168, (212)903-8083 (periodicals). **(Subscription address:** American Management Association, PO Box 408, Saranac Lake NY 12983. **Tel** (800)262-9699, FAX (518)891-1500.**) ED** Barbara Parker.
Desc: A practical aid for trainers in business government and not-for-profit organizations. In each issue; a complete training module including course content, discussion questions, individual and group exercises, handouts and visuals.

ISSN 0264-1739
DD 331.25920941 UK

TRAINING & DEVELOPMENT. [Train. dev.]. **VFOAT** Training and Development. (1982)-. Periodical. English. Twelve times a year.
Ind/Abst Curr. Cit.

ISSN 0192-0596
DD 658 US
CCC
SUSPENDED

TRAINING AND DEVELOPMENT ALERT. **See** Business and Economics-Abstracting, Bibliographies and Statistics.

LC HF5549.5.T7 A6 HF5549.5.T7 T72 **ISSN** 1055-9760
DD 331 US
CCC
CODEN TRDEEL

TRAINING & DEVELOPMENT (ALEXANDRIA, VA.). (TRAINING & DEVELOPMENT.). [Train. dev.]. **Added/Corp** American Society for Training and Development. **VFOAT** Training and Development. Vol. 45, No. 5 (May 1991)-. Periodical. English. Twelve times a year. $85.00. American Society for Training and Development, 1640 King Strreet, PO Box 1443, Department 840, Alexandria VA 22313. **Tel** (703)683-8100, (703)683-8129, FAX (703)683-8103. Index available (bound in Dec. issue). available on microfilm and microfiche from University Microfilms International (UMI). Documents available from The Genuine Article, Ask*IEEE, UMI Article Clearinghouse. ***Continues** Training and Development Journal, 0041-0861.*
Desc: Reports on current training and human resource practices, shared new theories and their applications, and covers controversial issues. Content addresses the needs of both the new practitioner and the executive.
Ind/Abst ABI/INFORM Glob. Ed.; ABI/INFORM Ondisc: Expr. Ed.; ABI/INFORM [Computer File] (Sept. 1971-); Acad. Search; AGRICOLA; Bus. ASAP (199?-) [Full Txt.]; Bus. Index (1991-); Bus. Period. Index; Bus. Source Plus; Contents Pages Educ.; Curr. Cit.; Curr. Contents Soc. Behav. Sci.; EP Collect.; Gen. BusinessFile (1991-); Gen. Period. Index (1991-); Homework Help.; INSPEC (May 1991-); Manage. Contents; MasterFile FullTEXT 1000; MasterFile FullTEXT 350; MasterFile FullTEXT 650; MasterFile FullTEXT (July 1994-); Newsp. Period. Abstr. (1988-); Psychol. Abstr. (1969-); Res. Alert [Full Cov.]; Soc. Plann. Policy Dev. Abstr.; Soc. Sci. Cit. Index [Full Cov.]; Sociol. Abstr.; Telebase; Trade Ind. ASAP [Full Txt.]; Trade Ind. Index [Full Txt.]; UMI ABI/Inform--Bus. Period. Ondisc (Jan. 1987-) [Full Txt.]; Wilson Bus. Abstr.

LC Z5814.T4 T68 HF5549.5.T7 **ISSN** 0895-1748
DD 016.6583/124 US
CEASED

TRAINING AND DEVELOPMENT LITERATURE INDEX. [Train. dev. lit. index]. **Added/Corp** American Society for Training and Development. Information Center. Vol. 1, No. 1 (Spring 1988)-(Dec. 1993). English. American Society for Training and Development, 1640 King Strreet, PO Box 1443, Department 840, Alexandria VA 22313. **Tel** (703)683-8100, (703)683-8129, FAX (703)683-8103. Index available.

LC HF5549.5.T7 T6653 **ISSN** 1049-3875
DD 658.3/124/05 US

TRAINING AND DEVELOPMENT YEARBOOK. **See** Business and Economics-Abstracting, Bibliographies and Statistics.

ISSN 0141-7134
UK

TRAINING DIGEST. [Train. dig.]. (1978)-. Periodical. English. Twenty times a year. $1289.00. MCB University Press, 60 62 Toller Lane, Bradford, West Yorkshire BD8 9BY United Kingdom. **Tel** 011 44 1274 785280, FAX 011 44 1274 785200, telex 51317-MCBUNI-G. **(Subscription address:** MCB University Press / US and Canada Subscriptions, PO Box 10812, Birmingham AL 35201-0812. **Tel** (205)995-1567, (800)633-4931, FAX (205)995-1588.**) ED** Christie Quinn. Index available. **Bk Rev. Circ:** 1,000.
Desc: Covers the world of training issues.

ISSN 1050-6160
DD 658 US

TRAINING DIRECTORS' FORUM NEWSLETTER. [Train. directors' forum newsl.]. **VFOAT** Directors' Forum Newsletter; Training Directors' Forum; TDF Newsletter. Vol. 1, No. 1 (Nov./Dec. 1985)-. Newsletter. English. Twelve times a year. $118.00. Lakewood Publications, 50 South Ninth Street, Minneapolis MN 55402. **Tel** (612)333-0471, (800)328-4329, FAX (612)333-6526.
Desc: Designed to keep training executives abreast of how their peers successfully manage training. It helps them perform with the skills, confidence and the business competence required to earn the respect and authority necessary for training to achieve and maintain a role of strategic importance in an organization.

UK

TRAINING DIRECTORY, THE. **Added/Corp** British Association for Commercial and Industrial Education. (1989)-. Directory. English. One time a year. $47.06. Kogan Page Ltd., 120 Pentonville Road, London N1 9BR United Kingdom. **Tel** 011 44 171 2780433, FAX 011 44 171 8376348, telex 263088 KOGAN G. **Ad Acc. Circ:** 3,000. ***Continues** Directory of Trainer Support Services.*
Desc: Directory of providers of training, equipment and services to the training industry. Information on the latest government initiatives and incentives on training.

ISSN 0968-4875
UK

TRAINING FOR QUALITY. (19??)-. English. Three times a year. $649.00. MCB University Press, 60 62 Toller Lane, Bradford, West Yorkshire BD8 9BY United Kingdom. **Tel** 011 44 1274 785280, FAX 011 44 1274 785200, telex 51317-MCBUNI-G. **(Subscription address:** MCB University Press / US and Canada Subscriptions, PO Box 10812, Birmingham AL 35201-0812. **Tel** (205)995-1567, (800)633-4931, FAX (205)995-1588.**)**

LC HF5549.5.T7 T67 **ISSN** 0095-5892
DD 658.31/24/0405 US
CCC
CODEN TRNGB6

TRAINING (MINNEAPOLIS). (TRAINING.). [Training]. Vol. 11 No. 7 (July 1974)-. Periodical. English. Twelve times a year. $78.00. Lakewood Publications, 50 South Ninth Street, Minneapolis MN 55402. **Tel** (612)333-0471, (800)328-4329, FAX (612)333-6526. **ED** Jack Gordon. **Bk Rev. Ad Acc. Circ:** 50,000. available on microfilm and microfiche from University Microfilms International (UMI). Documents available from UMI Article Clearinghouse. ***Continues** Training in Business and Industry, 0041-0896.*
Desc: Provides a blend of how-tos, trend stories, research reviews, case studies, profiles and interviews covering aspects and types of training, management and organizational development, adult learning, instructional design and delivery, motivation and performance improvement.
Ind/Abst ABI/INFORM Glob. Ed.; ABI/INFORM [Computer File] (July 1974-); Acad. Search; AGRICOLA [Select. Cov.]; Bus. ASAP (199?-) [Full Txt.]; Bus. Index (1991-); Bus. Period. Index; Bus. Source Plus; Bus. Source; Curr. Cit.; Curr. Index J. Educ.; Curr. Lit. Fam. Plan. (July 1974-199?); EP Collect.; GATFWORLD (1989); Gen. BusinessFile (1991-); Gen. Period. Index (1991-); Homework Help.; INFO-SOUTH Abstr.; Inf. Instruc. Technol.; Mag. Search; Manage. Contents; MasterFile FullTEXT 1000; MasterFile FullTEXT 350; MasterFile FullTEXT 650; MasterFile FullTEXT (Jan. 1993-); OCLC; Telebase; Trade Ind. ASAP [Full Txt.]; Trade Ind. Index [Full Txt.]; UMI ABI/Inform--Bus. Period. Ondisc (Jan. 1987-) [Full Txt.]; Vocat. Search; Wilson Bus. Abstr.; Work Relat. Abstr.

UK

TRAINING NETWORK. English. Nine times a year. $259.00. MCB University Press, 60 62 Toller Lane, Bradford, West Yorkshire BD8 9BY United Kingdom. **Tel** 011 44 1274 785280, FAX 011 44 1274 785200, telex 51317-MCBUNI-G. **(Subscription address:** MCB University Press / US and Canada Subscriptions, PO Box 10812, Birmingham AL 35201-0812. **Tel** (205)995-1567, (800)633-4931, FAX (205)995-1588.**)**

ISSN 0041-090X
UK

TRAINING OFFICER, THE. [Train. off.]. **VFOAT** Training Officer Monthly. (Autumn 1965)-. Trade Publication. English. Ten times a year. $128.34. Marylebone Press Ltd, Lloyds House, 18 Lloyd Street, Manchester M2 5WA United Kingdom. **Tel** 011 44 161 8326541, FAX 011 44 161 8328129, telex 669362. **ED** Pat Rose. Index available. **Bk Rev. Ad Acc. Circ:** 2,400. available on microfilm from University Microfilms International (UMI). Documents available from Ask*IEEE.
Desc: A journal devoted entirely to training in industry, commerce and HE. Presents articles, news, training films, packages, diary dates and book reviews.
Ind/Abst Anbar Account. Finan. Abstr. [Full Txt.]; Anbar Mark. Distr. Abstr. [Full Txt.]; Anbar Top Manage. Abstr. [Full Txt.]; Br. Educ. Index; Curr. Cit.; INSPEC (July 1983-); Manage. Market. Abstr.; Manage. Bibliogr. Rev.; Oper. Prod. Manage. Abstr. [Full Txt.]; Person. Train. Abstr. [Full Txt.]; Women Manage. Rev. [Full Txt.].

ISSN 1081-2393
US

•**TRAINING RESEARCH JOURNAL.** (1995)-. English. Irregular. $60.00. Educational Technology Publications Inc., 700 Palisade Avenue, Englewood Cliffs NJ 07632. **Tel** (201)871-4007, (800)952-2665.

ISSN 0883-8402
US
CEASED

UTILITY SUPERVISION (1985). (UTILITY SUPERVISION.). **Added/Corp** National Foremen's Institute. Vol. 20, No. 7, (Apr. 15, 1985)-(19??).

Business and Economics —Personnel Management

Periodical. English. Bureau of Business Practice, 24 Rope Ferry Road, Waterford CT 06386. **Tel** (800)243-0876, (203)442-4365, (800)876-9105, FAX (203)443-1123. *Continues Utility Supervision and Safety Letter, 0744-7175.*

US

WHAT TO DO ABOUT PERSONNEL PROBLEMS IN NEW YORK STATE. (198?)-. English. Twelve times a year. $329.00. Business & Legal Reports, 39 Academy Street, Madison CT 06443. **Tel** (203)245-7448, (800)727-5257, FAX (203)245-2559. **ED** Leonard N Persson and Robert L Brady. Index available.
Desc: Covers federal and state employment regulations.

ISSN 1076-0466
DD 331 US

WHAT'S NEW IN BENEFITS & COMPENSATION. [What's new benefits compens.]. **VFOAT** What's New in Benefits and Compensation. (199?)-. Periodical. English. Twenty-three times a year. $299.00. Progressive Business Publications, 370 Technology Drive, PO Box 3019, Malvern PA 19355. **Tel** (617)527-8600, (800)220-5000, FAX (617)647-8089.

LC HF5549.2.U5 W49   ISSN 1047-3130
DD 658   US

WHO'S WHO IN HR. See Biographies.

LC HF5549.A2 I58a   ISSN 1064-1653
DD 658.3/006/21   US

WHO'S WHO IN THE INTERNATIONAL PERSONNEL MANAGEMENT ASSOCIATION. See Public Administration-Civil Service.

LC HF5549.5.T7 A58   ISSN 0092-4598
DD 658.31/24/02573   US
                          CCC

WHO'S WHO IN TRAINING AND DEVELOPMENT. **Added/Corp** American Society for Training and Development. (1970)-. English. One time a year (Apr. or May). $40.00. American Society for Training and Development, 1640 King Street, PO Box 1443, Department 840, Alexandria VA 22313. **Tel** (703)683-8100, (703)683-8129, FAX (703)683-8103. **Ad Acc.** **Circ:** 26,000 (ctrl). *Continues American Society for Training and Development. Membership Directory.*
Desc: A membership directory that allows members to keep in touch with colleagues.

ISSN 0272-4022
UK

WILEY SERIES ON STUDIES IN ENVIRONMENTAL MANAGEMENT AND RESOURCE DEVELOPMENT. [Wiley ser. stud. environ. manage. resour. dev.]. (1980)-. Monographic series. English. Price varies per volume. John Wiley & Sons Ltd., Baffins Lane, Chichester, West Sussex PO19 1UD United Kingdom. **Tel** 011 44 1243 779777, FAX 011 44 1243 776128 BTG:JWP001, telex 86290 WIBOOKG. **(Subscription address:** John Wiley & Sons Inc / New Jersey, PO Box 2575, Secaucus NJ 07096-2575.)

ISSN 1075-8550
DD 658   US
                          CODEN WILRE2
Pr Rev.

WILLIAMS REPORT. See Communications.

DD 658.3/12   US

WORK & FAMILY SOURCEBOOK, THE. See Family and Marriage.

LC HF5549.A2 W65   ISSN 0312-455X
DD 658.3/00994   AT
                          CCC

WORK AND PEOPLE. [Work & people]. **Added/Corp** Australia. Dept. of Labor and Immigration. Human Relations Branch. Vol. 1 (Autumn 1975)-. Government Publication. English. Three times a year. 21.00Aus$. Australian Government Publishing Service, GPO Box 84, Canberra ACT 2601 Australia. **Tel** 011 61 6 2954411, FAX 011 61 6 2954455. cum. index. Documents available from UMI Article Clearinghouse, Ask*IEEE. **Supersedes** *Personnel Practice Bulletin, 0031-5818.*
Ind/Abst ABI/INFORM Glob. Ed.; ABI/INFORM [Computer File] (Fall 1978-); Anbar Account. Finan. Abstr. [Full Txt.]; Anbar Mark. Distr. Abstr. [Full Txt.]; Anbar Top Manage. Abstr. [Full Txt.]; APAIS, Aust. Public Aff. Inf. Ser. (1976-); Aust. Educ. Index; INSPEC (1983-); Int. Labour Doc.; Manage. Bibliogr. Rev.; Oper. Prod. Manage. Abstr. [Full Txt.]; Person. Train. Abstr. [Full Txt.]; Saf. Health Work; Women Manage. Rev. [Full Txt.]; Work Relat. Abstr.

ISSN 0892-5488
DD 658   US
                          CEASED

WORK IN AMERICA. [Work Am.]. Vol. 12, No. 1 (Jan. 1987)-Vol. 20, No. 12 (1995). Periodical. English. Twelve times a year. $297.00. Work in America Institute Inc, 700 White Plains Road, Scarsdale NY 10583. **Tel** (914) 472-9600, FAX (914) 472-9606. *Continues World of Work Report, 0361-6959.*
Desc: Newsletter which provides reports on national work force policies, labor legislation, employee involvement programs, work and family, training for new technology, flexible work schedules, employee benefits and profit sharing, city and state productivity programs, and other issues of interest.
Ind/Abst Work Relat. Abstr. (-19??).

ISSN 1062-8991
DD 331   US
                          CCC

WORKFORCE STRATEGIES. (WORKFORCE STRATEGIES : A SUPPLEMENT TO BNA'S EMPLOYEE RELATIONS WEEKLY.). [Workforce strateg.]. **Added/Corp** Bureau of National Affairs (Washington, D.C.). **VFOAT** Work Force Strategies. (Sept. 24, 1990)-. Periodical. English. Twelve times a year. $148.00. Bureau of National Affairs Inc., 9435 Key West Avenue, Rockville MD 20850. **Tel** (800)372-1033, (301)258-1033, FAX (301)948-5823. *Continues Bulletin on Training.*

ISSN 1047-4447
DD 658   US
                          CCC

WORKPLACE TRENDS. [Workplace trends]. (Jan./Feb. 1990)-. Periodical. English. Six times a year. $48.00 North America; $54.00 other. Lacey and Company, PO Box 16619, Rocky River OH 44116. **Tel** (216) 835-1884. **ED** Dan Lacey. Index available. **Circ:** 500.
Desc: The newsletter for people who manage people.

LC HD5725.W9 W97
DD 331.1/09787/021   US
                          TITLE CHANGE

WYOMING INCOME AND EMPLOYMENT REPORT. See Business and Economics-Labor.

US

•**WYOMING INCOME, EMPLOYMENT, AND GROSS STATE PRODUCT REPORT.** See Business and Economics-Labor.

RETAIL

ISSN 0938-7927
GW
UDC 33

ACQUISA. [Acquisa]. (1989)-. Trade Publication. German. Twelve times a year. $59.87. Max Schimmel Verlag GmbH & Company, Robert Koch Str 34 36, D-Wuerzburg Germany. *Continues Der Industrie- und Handelsvertreter, 0019-9214.*

ISSN 1072-9291
DD 381   US

•**ACTION SPORTS RETAILER (1993).** (ACTION SPORTS RETAILER.). [Action sports retail.]. (1993)-. Periodical. English. Twelve times a year. $25.00. Miller Freeman Inc., 600 Harrison Street, San Francisco CA 94107. **Tel** (415)905-2337, (415)905-2200, FAX (415)905-2240, telex 278273. **ED** Brad Bonhall. **Ad Acc. Circ:** 15,900. *Continues Action Sports (South Laguna, Calif.), 1068-2619.*

LC HF5429.27 .A56   ISSN 0743-5460
DD 658.8/7   US

ANNUAL SECURITY AND SHRINKAGE STUDY. See Business and Economics-Management.

ISSN 0312-5327
DD 658.870994   AT

AUSTRALIAN GIFTGUIDE. See Gifts, Toys.

ISSN 0890-9768
DD 658   US
                          CCC
                          CODEN AIDNEE

AUTOMATIC I.D. NEWS. See Computers-Automation.

US

AUTOMATIC I.D. NEWS EUROPE. See Computers-Automation.

LC HD9710.A1 A78   ISSN 0746-2077
DD 380.1/456292/068   US

AUTOMOTIVE CHAIN STORE (NEW YORK, N.Y.). See Transportation-Automobiles.

MX

AVANCE DE INFORMACION ECONOMICA. ENCUESTA SOBRE ESTABLECIMIENTOS COMERCIALES (CIUDAD DE MEXICO, GUADALAJARA Y MONTERREY). **Added/Corp** Instituto Nacional de Estadistica, Geografia e Informatica (Mexico). **VFOAT** Encuesta Sobre Establecimientos Comerciales (Ciudad de Mexico, Guadalajara y Monterrey). (1992)-. Spanish. Twelve times a year. $83.30. INEGI / Instituto Nacional de Estadistica, Geografia e Informatica, Avenida Patriotismo 711 Segundo Piso, 03730 Mexico DF Mexico. **Tel** 011 52 5 5639935, 011 52 5 5988935, FAX 011 52 55987941. **(Subscription address:** INEGI / Instituto Nacional de Estadistica, Geografia e Informatica, Avenida Heroe de Nacozari 2301 Sur, Fracc. Jardines del Parque, CP 20270, Aguascalientes Mexico. **Tel** 011 52 49 182998.**)** *Continues Avance de Informacion Economica. Encuesta Sobre Establecimientos Comerciales.*

ISSN 1186-9208
DD 381   CN

B.C. RETAILER. [B.C. retail.]. **VFOAT** British Columbia Retailer. (1991)-. Periodical. English. Six times a year. $17.12 per year. RMABC Publishing Ltd., 205-1525 West 8th Avenue, Vancouver British Columbia V6J 1T5 Canada.

BILLBOARD ... RECORD RETAILING DIRECTORY. See Music.

US

BOB CARR'S INSIDE SPORTING GOODS. See Sports and Games.

ISSN 0291-0764
FR
UDC 677

BOUTIQUES DE FRANCE. [Boutiques Fr.]. (1953)-. Periodical. French. Irregular (22 issues). $118.11. Boutiques de France, 16 boulevard Saint Denis, F-75010 Paris France. **Tel** 011 33 1 42467212.

LC TX335 .B83   ISSN 0742-5589
DD 381/.029/474811   US

BUY BLACK. English. One time a year. Zicom Systems Inc, 1218 Chestnut Street, Philadelphia PA 19107.

ISSN 0822-7799
DD 381/.1/02571   CN

CANADIAN DIRECTORY OF SHOPPING CENTRES. [Can. dir. shopp. cent.]. (197?)-. Directory. English. One time a year (June). 280.12Can$. MacLean Hunter Publ. Limited / Toronto, 777 Bay Street, 8th Floor Agency Control, Toronto Ontario M5W 1A7 Canada. **Tel** (416)596-6045, , FAX (416)596-2510.
Desc: Includes owner/developer, list of tenants, number of stores, sizes, rents and common area costs.

ISSN 0226-9864
DD 381/.1/0971   CN

CANADIAN RETAILER. [Cah. retail.]. **Added/Corp** Retail Council of Canada. (Jan. 1973)-. Trade Publication. English. Six times a year. 28.01Can$. Retail Council of Canada, 210 Dundas Street West/Suite 600, Toronto Ontario M5G 2E8 Canada. **Tel** (416)598-4684.

ISSN 0889-2288
DD 381   US
                          CCC

CARLSONREPORT. [Carlsonreport]. **Added/Corp** Harold J. Carlson Associates (Mount Prospect, Ill.) Stillerman Jones & Company (Indianapolis, Ind.). **VFOAT** Carlson Report; Carlsonreport for Shopping Center Management. (198?)-. Periodical. English. Twelve times a year. $125.00. Carlsonreport Inc., PO Box 502830, Indianapolis IN 46250. **Tel** (317)576-9889, (800)546-9889, FAX (317)576-0441. **ED** William R. Wilburn. **Bk Rev,** (Qty: 12). **Ad Acc. Circ:** 1,300.
Desc: Covers all aspects of managing shopping centers. Provides information on renovation, security leasing personnel, and financing. Also prints results of annual food court survey, and the December issue is devoted to salary survey results.

ISSN 0742-4035
US

CATALOG SHOPPER. **Added/Corp** EGW International Corporation. (19??)-. Catalog. English. Four times a year. $7.00. EGW Publishing Company, 1041 Shary Circle, Concord CA 94518. **Tel** (510)671-9852, (800)777-1164, FAX (510)671-0692.

LC HF5429.3 U535
DD 381   US

CENSUS OF RETAIL TRADE. **Main/Corp** United States. Bureau of the Census. (1972)-. Government Publication. English. Irregular. Price varies. US Department of Commerce / Bureau of the Census, Data User Services Division, Customer Services, Washington DC 20233-0800. **Tel** (301)763-4100. **(Subscription address:** Superintendent of Documents, US Government Printing Office, Washington DC 20402. **)** *Continues Census of Business; Retail Trade.*

ISSN 0009-0921
DD 658   US

CHAIN MERCHANDISER. [Chain merch.]. (19??)-. Trade Publication. English. Six times a year. $12.00. Chain Merchandiser, 65 Crocker Avenue, Piedmont CA 94611. **Tel** (415)547-4545. **ED** Henry von Morpurgo. **Bk Rev. Ad Acc. Circ:** 14,000 (ctrl).
Desc: Devoted to improved merchandising methods at

every level of the distribution process, from field and factory to retail sales personnel, to provide better customer values, lower costs and greater profits.

US

•CHAIN STORE AGE. (1995)-. English. Twelve times a year. $99.00. Lebhar Friedman Inc., PO Box 31203, Tampa FL 33633. **Tel** (800)944-4676, (813)664-6707. ***Continues*** *Chain Store Age Executive with Shopping Center Age.*

US

CHAIN STORE AGE EXECUTIVE. (1975)-. Periodical. English. Twelve times a year. FREE (architects, real estate, retailers, and shopping center within US); $99.00 (US one-year); $125.00 (Canada one-year); $165.00 (other). Lebhar Friedman Inc., PO Box 31203, Tampa FL 33633. **Tel** (800)944-4676, (813)664-6707. available on an online database (files 16,648/Full-Text) from DIALOG.
Ind/Abst Bus. ASAP (1990-) [Full Txt.]; Bus. Index (1985-); F&S Index Plus Text, Int. [Full Txt.] [Select. Cov.]; Gen. BusinessFile (1985-); Gen. Period. Index (1985-); PROMT; Trade Ind. ASAP [Full Txt.]; Trade Ind. Index [Full Txt.].

US
TITLE CHANGE

CHAIN STORE AGE EXECUTIVE WITH SHOPPING CENTER AGE. [Chain store age exec. Shopp. cent. age]. **Added/Corp** Gesellschaft fuer Allergie- und Immunitaetsforschung der Deutschen Demokratischen Republik. Gesellschaft fuer Klinische und Experimentelle Immunologie der Deutschen Demokratischen Republik. **VFOAT** Shopping Center Age. Vol. 51 (Jan. 1975)-(Aug. 1995). Periodical. English. Lebhar Friedman Inc., PO Box 31203, Tampa FL 33633. **Tel** (800)944-4676, (813)664-6707. available on microfilm and microfiche from University Microfilms International (UMI). Documents available from Ask*IEEE, UMI Article Clearinghouse. ***Continues*** *Chain Store Age, Executives Edition Combined with Shopping Center Age, 0375-8443.* ***Continued by*** *Chain Store Age.*
Ind/Abst ABI/INFORM Glob. Ed.; ABI/INFORM [Computer File] (Jan. 1975-); Bus. Period. Index; Chicano Index; INSPEC (1986-); Mag. Search; MasterFile FullTEXT (July 1993-); Stat. Ref. Index; Wilson Bus. Abstr.

LC BV2369 .C53 **ISSN** 0892-0281
DD 206/.8/8 US

CHRISTIAN RETAILING. [Christ. retail.]. Vol. 32, No. 11 (Dec. 15, 1986)-. Periodical. English. Eighteen times a year. $45.00. Strang Communications Company, 600 Rinehart Road, Lake Mary FL 32746. **Tel** (407)333-0600, FAX (407)333-7100. **ED** Carol Chapman Stertzer. **Bk Rev**. **Ad Acc, Adv Mgr:** Bob Minotti, **Tel** (407)333-0600. **Circ:** 11,000 (ctrl). ***Continues*** *Christian Bookseller (Wheaton, Ill. : 1983), 0749-2510.*
Desc: Publishes articles on management, industry information and book reviews.

LC HF5429.4.C6 C66 **ISSN** 0732-071X
DD 381/.1/09788 US

COLORADO CITY RETAIL SALES BY STANDARD INDUSTRIAL CLASSIFICATION (ANNUAL). (COLORADO CITY RETAIL SALES BY STANDARD INDUSTRIAL CLASSIFICATION.). **Added/Corp** University of Colorado, Boulder. Business Research Division. (19??)-. English. One time a year. $75.00 US; $90.00 other. Business Research Division, University of Colorado, Campus Box 420, Boulder CO 80309-0420. **Tel** (303)492-8227, FAX (303)492-3620. ***Separated from*** *Colorado County and City Retail Sales by Standard Industrial Classification, 0091-4789.*

US

COLORADO STATE AND COUNTY RETAIL SALES BY STANDARD INDUSTRIAL CLASSIFICATION. **Main/Corp** Colorado. University. Business Research Division. **Added/Corp** First National Bank of Denver. (1977)-. Periodical. English. Four times a year. $75.00 US; $90.00 other. Business Research Division, University of Colorado, Campus Box 420, Boulder CO 80309-0420. **Tel** (303)492-8227, FAX (303)492-3620. ***Continues in part*** *Colorado County and City Retail Sales by Standard Industrial Classification.*

US

COMMERCIAL BUYERS GUIDE FOR ALASKA. (1991)-. Consumer Publication. English. Commercial Buyers Guide USA, Inc., PO Box 112955, Anchorage AK 99511.

US

COMPUTER & OFFICE ELECTRONICS RETAILER. (19??)-. English. Six times a year. $30.00 US, Canada and Mexico; $35.00 (surface mail), $69.00 (airmail) other. Gordon Publications Inc., A Subsidiary of Cahners Publishing Company, 301 Gibraltar Drive, Box 650, Morris Plains NJ 07950. **Tel** (201)292-5100, (800)637-6081.
Desc: Strives to help retailers boost customer satisfaction. Product descriptions, availability, price and distribution information help computer and office retailers in new product decision making.

ISSN 0893-8377
DD 381 US
CCC

COMPUTER RESELLER NEWS. **See** Computers-Computer Sales, Service and Supply.

UK

CONVENIENCE STORE. Trade Publication. English. Irregular. £40.00 UK; £50.00 rest of Europe; £80.00 other. William Reed Publishing Ltd., Broadfield Park, Crawley, West Sussex RH11 9RJ United Kingdom. **Tel** 011 44 1293 613400, FAX 011 44 1293 613156. available on an online database (file 648/Full-Text) from DIALOG.

ISSN 0190-5988
US

CURRENT BUSINESS REPORTS. ADVANCE MONTHLY RETAIL SALES. (CURRENT BUSINESS REPORTS. CB, ADVANCE MONTHLY RETAIL SALES.). [Curr. bus. rep., Adv. mon. retail sales]. **Added/Corp** United States. Bureau of the Census. **VFOAT** Advance Monthly Retail Sales. (19??)-. Government Publication. English. Twelve times a year. $67.00. US Department of Commerce / Bureau of the Census, Data User Services Division, Customer Services, Washington DC 20233-0800. **Tel** (301)763-4100. **(Subscription address:** Superintendent of Documents, US Government Printing Office, Washington DC 20402. **)** available in microform; available on an online database from CENDATA. Documents available from Documents on Demand.
Desc: Estimated monthly retail sales for the United States.
Ind/Abst Am. Stat. Index.

LC HF5429.3 .C85
DD 381/.1/0973021 US

CURRENT BUSINESS REPORTS. COMBINED ANNUAL AND REVISED MONTHLY RETAIL TRADE. [Curr. bus. rep., Retail trade annu. sales year-end inventories purch. gross margin acc. receiv. kind retail store]. **Added/Corp** United States. Bureau of the Census. **VFOAT** Combined Annual and Revised Monthly Retail Trade. (1992)-. Government Publication. English. Irregular. $2.00. US Department of Commerce / Bureau of the Census, Data User Services Division, Customer Services, Washington DC 20233-0800. **Tel** (301)763-4100. **(Subscription address:** Superintendent of Documents, US Government Printing Office, Washington DC 20402. **)** ***Formed by the union of*** *Current Business Reports. Revised Monthly Retail Sales and Inventories, 0272-443X* ***and*** *Current Business Reports. Retail Trade, Annual Sales, Year-End Inventories, Purchases, Gross Margin, and Accounts Receivable, by Kind of Retail Store, 0899-028X.*
Desc: Presents seasonally adjusted and unadjusted data, by kind of business, on revised estimates of monthly retail sales and on estimated end-of-month inventories.
Ind/Abst Predicasts Forecasts (?-?).

LC HF5429.3 .U535b **ISSN** 0739-5361
DD 381/.1/0973 US

CURRENT BUSINESS REPORTS. MONTHLY RETAIL TRADE, SALES AND INVENTORIES. (CURRENT BUSINESS REPORTS. BR, MONTHLY RETAIL TRADE, SALES AND INVENTORIES.). [Curr. bus. rep., Mon. retail trade sales invent.]. **Added/Corp** United States. Bureau of the Census. **VFOAT** Monthly Retail Trade, Sales and Inventories. (Jan. 1981)-. Government Publication. English. Twelve times a year. $65.00. US Department of Commerce / Bureau of the Census, Data User Services Division, Customer Services, Washington DC 20233-0800. **Tel** (301)763-4100. **(Subscription address:** Superintendent of Documents, US Government Printing Office, Washington DC 20402. **)** Documents available from Documents on Demand. ***Continues*** *Current Business Reports. BR, Monthly Retail Trade, Sales, Accounts Receivable, and Inventories, 0193-9769.*
Desc: Shows data at the United States level for estimates of monthly retail sales by major kind-of-business groups and selected kinds of business.
Ind/Abst Am. Stat. Index; Predicasts Forecasts.

LC HD9971.U6 D4
DD 381/.4568383/0973 US

•DEALERSCOPE CONSUMER ELECTRONIC MARKETPLACE. (1995)-. English. Twelve times a year. $65.00. North American Publishing Company, 401 North Broad Street, Philadelphia PA 19108. **Tel** (215)238-5300, (800)777-8074, FAX (215)238-5283. ***Continues*** *Dealerscope Merchandising.*

LC HD9971.U6 D4 **ISSN** 0888-4501
DD 381/.4568383/0973 US
CCC
TITLE CHANGE

DEALERSCOPE MERCHANDISING. [Dealerscope merch.]. **VFOAT** Dealerscope. (1986)-(1995). Trade Publication. English. North American Publishing Company, 401 North Broad Street, Philadelphia PA 19108. **Tel** (215)238-5300, (800)777-8074, FAX (215)238-5283. **ED** Neil Spann and Anne Fisher. **Ad Acc. Circ:** 61,500 (ctrl). available on microfilm and microfiche from University Microfilms International (UMI); available on an online database (files 15,648/Full-Text) from DIALOG. ***Formed by the union of*** *Dealerscope, 0011-7218* ***and*** *Merchandising, 0362-3920.* ***Continued by*** *Dealerscope Consumer Electronic Marketplace.*
Desc: Edited for retailers and distributors that sell consumer electronics and major appliances. Each issues advises retailers on how to market and merchandise appliances, audio and video components and home office equipment for maximum sales.
Ind/Abst Bus. Period. Index; Bus. Source Plus; Bus. Source; EP Collect.; F&S Index Plus Text, Int. [Select. Cov.]; Homework Help.; Mag. Search; MasterFile FullTEXT 1000; MasterFile FullTEXT 350; MasterFile FullTEXT 650; MasterFile FullTEXT (Jan. 1993-); OCLC; PROMT; Telebase; Vocat. Search; Wilson Bus. Abstr.

ISSN 1055-0771
DD 333 US

DEALMAKERS (BELLE MEAD, N.J.), THE. **See** Real Estate.

LC HF5465.U4 F55 **ISSN** 1058-5990
DD 381 US
TITLE CHANGE

DEPARTMENT AND SPECIALTY STORES FINANCIAL AND OPERATING RESULTS. (DEPARTMENT AND SPECIALTY STORES FINANCIAL AND OPERATING RESULTS, FISCAL ...). [Dep. spec. stores financ. oper. results]. **Added/Corp** National Retail Federation (U.S.). Financial Executives Division. **VFOAT** Financial & Operating Results of Retail Stores in ...; Financial and Operating Results of Retail Stores in ...; FOR of Department & Specialty Stores in ...; FOR of Department and Specialty Stores in ...; Financial and Operating Results. 66th Ed. (1991)-68th Ed. (1993). English. John Wiley & Sons Inc / New Jersey, 1 Wiley Drive, Somerset NJ 08875. **Tel** (800)225-5945, (908)469-4400. ***Continues*** *Financial and Operating Results of Department and Specialty Stores, 0547-8804.* ***Continued by*** *Financial & Operating Results of Retail Stores in ... .*

ISSN 0498-7284
DD 338.5 US

DEPARTMENT STORE INVENTORY PRICE INDEXES / U.S. DEPARTMENT OF LABOR, BUREAU OF LABOR STATISTICS. **Main/Corp** United States. Bureau of Labor Statistics. **Added/Corp** United States. Bureau of Labor Statistics. (19??)-. English. Two times a year. Free on request. US Department of Labor / Bureau of Labor Statistics, 441 G Street Northwest, Washington DC 20212. **Tel** (202)606-7800, FAX (202)606-7797. **ED** Douglas Robertson. **Circ:** 1,000. Documents available from Documents on Demand.
Desc: Price indexes for department store inventory groupings. Uses Consumer Price Index data and department store inventory weights.
Ind/Abst Am. Stat. Index.

ISSN 1183-7888
DD 381./141/0971 CN

DEPARTMENT STORE MONTHLY SALES, BY PROVINCE AND METROPOLITAN AREA (ENGLISH EDITION 1991). (DEPARTMENT STORE MONTHLY SALES, BY PROVINCE AND METROPOLITAN AREA.). [Dep. store mon. sales prov. metrop. area]. **Added/Corp** Statistics Canada. Industry Division. **VFOAT** Ventes Mensuelles des Grands Magasins, par Province et Region Metropolitaine. Vol. 6, No. 2 (Feb. 1991)-. Periodical. English (French). Twelve times a year. 27.00Can$ Canada; $32.00 US; $38.00 other. Statistics Canada Publications Sales and Services, R.H. Coats Building 6th Floor, Ottawa Ontario K1A 0T6 Canada. **Tel** (613)951-5078, (800)267-6677, FAX (613)951-1584, telex 053-3585. ***Continues*** *Department Store Monthly Sales, Including Concessions, by Province and Metropolitan Area., 1181-7747.*

ISSN 1183-7888
DD 381./141/0971 CN

DEPARTMENT STORE MONTHLY SALES, BY PROVINCE AND METROPOLITAN AREA (FRENCH EDITION 1991). (DEPARTMENT STORE MONTHLY SALES, BY PROVINCE AND METROPOLITAN AREA.). [Dep. store mon. sales prov. metrop. area]. **Added/Corp** Statistique Canada. Division de l'Industrie. **VFOAT** Ventes Mensuelles des Grands Magasins, par Province et Region Metropolitaine. Vol. 6, No. 2 (Feb. 1991)-. Periodical. French (English). Twelve times a year. 27.00Can$ Canada; $32.00 US; $38.00 other. Statistics Canada Publications Sales and Services, R.H. Coats Building 6th Floor, Ottawa Ontario K1A 0T6 Canada. **Tel** (613)951-5078, (800)267-6677, FAX (613)951-1584, telex 053-3585. ***Continues*** *Department Store Monthly Sales, Including Concessions, by Province and Metropolitan Area., 1181-7747.*

LC HF5465.C3 A315 ISSN 0380-7045
DD 381/.1/0971021 CN
DEPARTMENT STORE SALES AND STOCKS. [Dep. store sales stocks]. **Added/Corp** Canada. Dominion Bureau of Statistics. Merchandising and Services Section. Canada. Dominion Bureau of Statistics. Retail and Trade Section. Canada. Dominion Bureau of Statistics. Industry and Merchandising Division. Canada. Dominion Bureau of Statistics. Merchandising and Services Division. Statistics Canada. Merchandising and Services Division. Statistics Canada. Retail Trade Section. **VFOAT** Ventes et Stocks des Grands Magasins. Vol. 37 (1949)-. English (French). Twelve times a year. 192.00Can$. Statistics Canada Publications Sales and Services, R.H. Coats Building 6th Floor, Ottawa Ontario K1A 0T6 Canada. **Tel** (613)951-5078, (800)267-6677, FAX (613)951-1584, telex 053-3585. ***Continues*** *Department Store Sales and Inventories.*
Desc: Total sales and number of outlets, by province and selected metropolitan areas, and sales and inventories by departments in Canada.

ISSN 0419-2508
US
DIRECTORY OF DEPARTMENT STORES. **VFOAT** Department Store Guide Directory. (1955)-. Directory. English. One time a year. $244.00 continental US; $254.00 other US; $269.00 other. Lebhar Friedman Inc., PO Box 31203, Tampa FL 33633. **Tel** (800)944-4676, (813)664-6707. **ED** Barbara Brown.
Desc: Provides company profiles on 1,300 companies operating 9,000 stores. Separate sections feature listings on resident buying offices, 1,000 apparel and general merchandise mail order firms.

US
DIRECTORY OF DEPARTMENT STORES, MAIL ORDER FIRMS. **VFOAT** Directory of Department Stores; Chain Store Guide Directory. (19??)-. Directory. English. One time a year. $239.00. Lebhar Friedman Inc., PO Box 31203, Tampa FL 33633. **Tel** (800)944-4676, (813)664-6707.

LC HF5429.215.U6 .D58 ISSN 1084-533X
US
•**DIRECTORY OF DISCOUNT & GENERAL MERCHANDISE STORES.** **VFOAT** Directory of Discount and General Merchandise Stores. (1995)-. Directory. English. One time a year. Lebhar Friedman Inc., PO Box 31203, Tampa FL 33633. **Tel** (800)944-4676, (813)664-6707. ***Formed by the union of*** *Directory of Discount Department Stores (New York, N.Y. : 1988), 0897-5442* ***and*** *Directory of General Merchandise Variety Chains & Specialty Stores.*

ISSN 0897-5442
DD 381 US
TITLE CHANGE
DIRECTORY OF DISCOUNT DEPARTMENT STORES (1988). (DIRECTORY OF DISCOUNT DEPARTMENT STORES.). [Dir. discount dep. stores]. **VFOAT** Discount Department Stores. (1988)-(1994). Directory. English. Lebhar Friedman Inc., PO Box 31203, Tampa FL 33633. **Tel** (800)944-4676, (813)664-6707. ***Continues*** *Directory of Discount Department Stores/Catalog Showrooms, 0897-1765.* ***Merged with*** *Directory of General Merchandise Variety Chains & Specialty Stores* ***to form*** *Directory of Discount & General Merchandise Stores.*

LC HF54.G7 S8
DD 381/.1/025 UK
DIRECTORY OF EUROPEAN RETAILERS. 14th Ed. (1986/1987)-. Directory. English. Every 2 years. $239.57. Newman Publishing Company, 32 Vauxhall Bridge Road, London SW1V 2YY United Kingdom. **Tel** 011 44 171 9736402, FAX 011 44 171 2335081. **ED** Karen Rasmussen. **Bk Rev. Ad Acc.** available on labels (and mailing lists). ***Continues*** *Stores of the World Directory, 0081-5829.*
Desc: Details of over 3,000 major European retailers and 700 buying agents worldwide.

LC HF5429 .D5 ISSN 0070-556X
DD 650 US
DIRECTORY OF FRANCHISING ORGANIZATIONS. [Dir. franch. org.]. (19??)-. English. One time a year (January). $6.95. Pilot Books, 103 Cooper Street, Babylon NY 11702-2319. **Tel** (516)422-2225, FAX (516)422-2227. **ED** Sam Small. ***Continues*** *Directory of Franchising Organizations and a Guide to Franchising.*
Desc: A comprehensive listing of the top money-making franchises with concise description and approximate investment. Includes important facts about franchising and an evaluation checklist.

LC HF5468 .D57 ISSN 0741-6903
DD 381/.12/02273 US
TITLE CHANGE
DIRECTORY OF GENERAL MERCHANDISE VARIETY CHAINS & SPECIALTY STORES. **VFOAT** Directory of General Merchandise/Variety Chains & Specialty stores; General Merchandise Variety Chains & Specialty Stores; General Merchandise Variety Chains and Specialty Stores; Gen Mdse/Variety Chains and Specialty Stores; General Mdse/Variety Chains and Specialty Stores; General Merchandise/Variety Stores; Gen Mdse/Variety Chains & Specialty Stores; Directory of General Merchandise/Variety & Specialty Stores. **VAT** Directory of General Merchandise Variety Chains and Specialty Stores. (1983)-(1994). Directory. English. Lebhar Friedman Inc., PO Box 31203, Tampa FL 33633. **Tel** (800)944-4676, (813)664-6707. **ED** Barbara Brown. ***Continues*** *Directory of Gen Mdse/Variety Chains & Specialty Stores, 0731-6925.* ***Merged with*** *Directory of Discount Department Stores (New York, N.Y. : 1988)* ***to form*** *Directory of Discount & General Merchandise Stores.*
Desc: Provides company profiles on 700 GM/Variety store companies operating 18,200 stores. Separate sections are featured on various specialty stores.

LC HF5477.U5 D57
DD 381/.18 US
DIRECTORY OF LICENSED AUCTIONEERS, APPRENTICE AUCTIONEERS, AND FIRMS ENGAGED IN THE AUCTION BUSINESS IN NORTH CAROLINA. Directory. English. North Carolina Auctioneer Licensing Board, 3509 Haworth Drive, Raleigh NC 27609. **Tel** (607)722-2493, (800)3-HAWORTH, FAX (607)722-1424.

LC HF5430.3 .D54 ISSN 0732-5983
DD 381/.1/02573 US
CCC
DIRECTORY OF MAJOR MALLS. [Dir. major malls]. (19??)-. Directory. English. One time a year (Jan.). $399.00. Jomurpa Publishing Corporation, PO Box 1708, 7 South Myrtle Avenue, Spring Valley NY 10977. **Tel** (914)426-0040, FAX (914)426-0802. **ED** Murray Shor and Tama J. Shor. Index available. **Ad Acc. Circ:** 3,000. available on diskette.
Desc: Provides information on those shopping centers larger than 250,000 sq. ft. in the U.S. and Canada. Included are portfolios of developers, maps of 32 markets with malls pinpointed, tenant lists, and future projects to open within the next three years, with names, addresses, and telephone numbers.

ISSN 0225-9443
DD 381/.12/02571 CN
DIRECTORY OF RETAIL CHAINS IN CANADA. [Dir. retail chains Can.]. **VAT** Monday Report on Retailers. Directory Retail Chains in Canada. (1976)-. Directory. English. One time a year. $210.00. Maclean Hunter Canada / Montreal, 1001 bvd. de Maisonneuve W., Montreal Quebec H3A 3E1 Canada. **Tel** (514)845-5141, FAX (514)845-4302, telex 055-60604. ctrl circ.
Desc: A listing of retail chains including their head office address, management, number of stores, expansion plans, and the type of retailer they are.

LC HF5001 .D2 ISSN 0012-3579
DD 658.8/79/0973 US
CODEN DISMAD
DISCOUNT MERCHANDISER, THE. (THE DISCOUNT MERCHANDISER : DM.). [Discount merch.]. **VFOAT** DM. Vol. 1, No. 1 (June 1961)-. Trade Publication. English. Twelve times a year. $55.00. Sterling Macfadden, 233 Park Avenue South, New York NY 10003. **Tel** (212)979-4800. Index available. **Ad Acc. Circ:** 50,000 (ctrl). available on microfilm and microfiche from University Microfilms International (UMI); available on an online database (file 15/Full-Text) from DIALOG. Documents available from UMI Article Clearinghouse.
Desc: The publication for discount retailing in all its manifestations. The magazine has special appeal for executives of discount stores, supermarkets, drug stores, catalog showrooms, wholesale clubs, hyper markets, etc.
Ind/Abst ABI/INFORM Glob. Ed.; ABI/INFORM [Computer File] (Nov. 1972-); Bus. Period. Index; Bus. Source Plus; Bus. Source; EP Collect.; F&S Index Plus Text, Int. [Select. Cov.]; Homework Help.; Mag. Search; Mark. Advert. Ref. Serv.; MasterFile FullTEXT 1000; MasterFile FullTEXT 350; MasterFile FullTEXT 650; MasterFile FullTEXT (Jan. 1993-); OCLC; PAIS Int. Print; Predicasts Forecasts; Stat. Ref. Index; Telebase; Trade Ind. ASAP [Full Txt.]; Trade Ind. Index; UMI ABI/Inform--Bus. Period. Ondisc [Full Txt.]; Vocat. Search; Wilson Bus. Abstr.

LC HF5001 .D5 ISSN 0012-3587
DD 658.8/79/0973 US
CCC
DISCOUNT STORE NEWS. [Discount store news]. Vol. 1 (Jan. 1, 1962)-. Trade Publication. English. Twenty-three times a year. $99.00 US; $105.00 Canada; $195.00 other. Lebhar Friedman Inc., PO Box 31203, Tampa FL 33633. **Tel** (800)944-4676, (813)664-6707. available on microfilm and microfiche from University Microfilms International (UMI); available on an online database (files 16,570,648/Full-Text) from DIALOG. ***Continues*** *Apparel Merchandising, 0746-889X.*
Desc: Provides the latest news affecting the retailing industry, presents latest "spot" news as well as overall trends in every aspect of merchandising and management.
Ind/Abst Abstr. Engl. Stud.; Annu. Bibliogr. Engl. Lang. Lit.; Bus. ASAP (1990-) [Full Txt.]; Bus. Index (1985-); Bus. Source Plus; Bus. Source; EP Collect.; F&S Index Plus Text, Int. [Full Txt.] [Select. Cov.]; Gen. BusinessFile (1985-); Gen. Period. Index (1985-); Homework Help.; Mag. Search; Mark. Advert. Ref. Serv. [Full Txt.]; MasterFile FullTEXT 1000; MasterFile FullTEXT 350; MasterFile FullTEXT 650; MasterFile FullTEXT (July 1993-); MLA Int. Bibl. Books Artic. Mod. Lang. Lit.; OCLC; PROMT [Full Txt.]; Stat. Ref. Index; Telebase; Trade Ind. ASAP [Full Txt.]; Trade Ind. Index [Full Txt.]; Vocat. Search.

ISSN 0953-7147
DD 658.7880941 UK
DISTRIBUTION BUSINESS. [Distrib. bus.]. (1988)-. Trade Publication. English. Six times a year. $68.45. Landor Holdings Ltd, Quadrant House, 250 Kennington Lane, London SE11 5RD United Kingdom. **Tel** 011 44 71 735 5058, FAX 011 44 71 587 0497.
Desc: Probes issues of current interest to retail business and industrial users of distribution services; features articles on the crucial factors affecting them.

LC HD9666.3 .D78 ISSN 0277-3716
DD 381/.456151/02573 US
DRUG STORE MARKET GUIDE. **See** Pharmacy and Pharmacology.

LC HF5429.6.N4 E26D
NE
EIM MEDEDELINGEN, DE. **Main/Corp** Economisch Instituut voor het Midden- en Kleinbedrijf. **VAT** De Economisch Instituut voor het Midden- en Kleinbedrijf Mededelingen. Periodical. Dutch. Twelve times a year. Economisch Instituut voor het Midden- en Kleinbedrijf, Talielaan 33, Postbus 7001, 2701 AA Zoetermeer Netherlands.

ISSN 1074-9195
US
•**ELECTRONIC RETAILING.** (1994)-. Periodical. English. Twelve times a year. $39.95. Creative Age Publications, 7628 Densmore Avenue, Van Nuys CA 91406. **Tel** (800)624-4196.

US
ELECTRONIC RETAILING : IT'S NOT JUST HOME SHOPPING ANYMORE. (19??)-. English. One time a year. $495.00. Paul Kagan Associates Inc., 126 Clock Tower Place, Carmel CA 93923-8734. **Tel** (408)624-1536, FAX (408)625-3225, telex ITT 4938124 PKA UI.

LC HD9696.A1 E37 ISSN 0898-7149
DD 381/.45621381/0973 US
CEASED
ELECTRONICS DISTRIBUTION TODAY. See Electronics.

ISSN 1182-6371
DD 658.2/05 CN
ENERMARK NEWS. [EnerMark news]. **Added/Corp** Ontario Hydro. Commercial Programs Dept. **VFOAT** Retail Stores. Vol. 1, No. 1 (Feb. 1990)-. Periodical. English. Ontario Hydro, 700 University Avenue, Toronto Ontario M5G 1X6 Canada. **Tel** (416)592-5111.

LC AG ISSN 1079-0977
DD 028 US
•**ENVOY (ROUND ROCK, TEX.).** (ENVOY : NEWS ABOUT CENTRAL TEXAS WRITERS, ARTISTS AND BOOKSELLERS.). [Envoy]. Vol. 1, No. 1 (Oct. 1994)-. Periodical. English. Six times a year. Envoy, PO Box 564, Round Rock TX 78680-0564. available via Internet (ftp://io.com/pub/usr/envoy/).
Desc: Source of information the strives to facilitate cooperation between creators and those who sell their creations.

ISSN 1055-2839
DD 384 US
EUROPEAN HOME VIDEO. **See** Communications-Video.

UK
EUROPEAN RETAIL. (19??)-. English. Twenty-four times a year. $562.50 (schools and educational libraries), $750.00 (other) North America. The Economist Intelligence Unit, 40 Duke Street, London W1A 1DW United Kingdom. **Tel** 011 44 171 8301000. **(Subscription address:** Economist Intelligence Unit / North America Subscriptions, 111 West 57th Street, New York NY 10019. **Tel** 800 938-4685, (212)554-0600, FAX (212)586-1181, (212)586-1182.)

ISSN 1058-577X
US
EXCLUSIVELY MALLS : CHICAGO'S METROPOLITAN MALL RESOURCE AND REFERENCE DIRECTORY. (1991)-. Directory. English. Three times a year. $14.85. Alliance Publications, Inc., PO Box 179, Mokena IL 60448.

US
EXECUTIVE COMPENSATION IN RETAILING. (19??)-. English. Every 3 years (every three years). $650.00 members; $750.00 nonmembers. National Retail Federation, 325 7th Street NW Suite

1000, Washington DC 20004. **Tel** (202)626-8146.
Desc: An executive survey of information on retailing companies.

LC HF5429.3 .D66A **ISSN** 0161-2581
DD 381 US
EXPANSION SURVEY, RETAIL TRADE INDUSTRY. **Main/Corp** Donaldson, Lufkin & Jenrette Securities Corporation. 1975/77-. English. One time a year. Donaldson Lufkin & Jenrette Securities Corporation, 140 Broadway, New York NY 10005.

LC HF5421 .F33 **ISSN** 0146-2873
US
FACTORY OUTLET SHOPPING GUIDE. WASHINGTON, D.C., MARYLAND-DELAWARE-VIRGINIA. (1975)-. English. One time a year. Factory Outlet Shopping Guide / F.O.S.G. Publications, PO Box 256L, Oradell NJ 07649.

LC HF5429.3 .F35
US
FAIRCHILD'S RETAIL STORES FINANCIAL DIRECTORY. **Added/Corp** Fairchild Books and Visuals. 64th Ed. (1991/1992)-. Directory. English. Fairchild Publications Inc., 7 West 34th Street, 4th Floor, New York NY 10001-8191. **Tel** (212)630-4230, (800)247-6622. ***Continues*** *Fairchild's Financial Manual of Retail Stores, 0071-3716.*

LC S677 **ISSN** 1072-9038
DD 381 US
FARM SUPPLY RETAILING. **See** Agriculture-Agricultural Equipment.

LC HF5341 .T4 **ISSN** 1068-641X
DD 380.1/45/0002944 US
•**FIELDING'S SHOPPING EUROPE.** [Fielding's shopp. Eur.]. **VFOAT** Shopping Europe. 37th Ed. (1993)-. English. Fielding Worldwide, 308 South Catalina Avenue, Redondo Beach CA 90277. **Tel** (800)843-9389, (310)372-4474, FAX (212)261-6549. ***Continues*** *Fielding's Selective Shopping Guide to Europe, 0071-478X.*

LC HF5465.5 .F53 **ISSN** 0741-8892
DD 381/.14/02573 US
FIFTY BILLION DOLLAR DIRECTORY, THE. **VFOAT** 50 Billion Dollar Directory. (1984)-. Directory. English. Irregular. $65.00 US; $76.00 other. Publishers Services, 6318 Vesper Avenue, Van Nuys CA 91411. **Tel** (818)785-8039.

LC HF5465.U3 F56 **ISSN** 1082-1767
DD 381/1/0973021 US
•**FINANCIAL & OPERATING RESULTS OF RETAIL STORES IN ... .** (FINANCIAL & OPERATING RESULTS OF RETAIL STORES IN ... : FOR.). [Financ. oper. results retail stores]. **Added/Corp** Industry Insights, Inc. National Retail Federation (U.S.). **VFOAT** FOR; Financial and Operating Results of Retail Stores in ...; FOR of Department and Specialty Stores in ...; FOR of Department & Specialty Stores in ... . 69th Ed. (1994)-. English. One time a year (Nov.). $150.00 (nonmembers), $75.00 (members). John Wiley & Sons Inc / New Jersey, 1 Wiley Drive, Somerset NJ 08875. **Tel** (800)225-5945, (908)469-4400. ***Continues*** *Department and Specialty Stores Financial and Operating Results, 1058-5990.*

US
FRANCHISE ANNUAL HANDBOOK AND DIRECTORY. Directory. English. One time a year. $39.95 US; $49.95 other. Info Franchise News, 728 Center Street, Box 550, Lewiston NY 14092. **Tel** (716)754-4669, FAX (905)688-7728. **ED** Edward Dixon. Index available. **Ad Acc**, **Adv Mgr:** Denise Muir. **Circ:** 10,000.

LC HF5429.235.U5 F7 **ISSN** 0882-5505
DD 658.8/708/05 US
FRANCHISE HANDBOOK, THE. [Franch. handb.]. **Added/Corp** Enterprise Magazines, Inc. (1985)-. English. Four times a year (Jan., Apr., July and Oct.). $19.95. Enterprise Magazines Inc., 1020 North Broadway, Suite 111, Milwaukee WI 53202. **Tel** (414)272-9977, FAX (414)272-9973. **ED** Michael J. McDermott. Index available. **Ad Acc**, **Adv Mgr:** Barbara Monfeli, **Tel** (414)272-9977. **Circ:** 55,000.
Desc: Contains all pertinent information about all known franchises available to the public. It is indexed both alphabetically by business category and alphabetically by company name. It contains information on over 1,700 available franchises. The magazine features success stories and analytic articles for persons interested in the possible purchase of a franchised business.

LC HF5429.3 .U53a **ISSN** 0193-9017
DD 381/.13/0973021 US
FRANCHISING IN THE ECONOMY. [Franch. econ.]. **Added/Corp** United States. International Trade Administration. Office of Service Industries. United States. International Trade Administration. United States. Bureau of Industrial Economics. United States. Dept. of Commerce. United States. Industry and Trade Administration. United States. Bureau of Domestic Commerce. United States. Bureau of Competitive Assessment and Business Policy. (19??)-. Government Publication. English. One time a year. $9.75. Superintendent of Documents, US Government Printing Office, Washington DC 20402. **Tel** (202)275-3328, FAX (202)786-2377. **ED** Prepared by: Andrew Kostecka, 1972/74- with the assistance of Jacob Benison and Dorothy J. Miller, 1972/74-1974/76.
Ind/Abst Predicasts Forecasts.

LC KF2023.Z9 F68
DD 343.73/0887 347.303887 US
FRANCHISING (NEW YORK, N.Y.). (FRANCHISING : BUSINESS STRATEGIES AND LEGAL COMPLIANCE.). **Added/Corp** Practising Law Institute. (198?)-. English. One time a year. Practising Law Institute, 810 Seventh Avenue, New York NY 10019-5818. **Tel** (212)765-5700, FAX (212)581-4670 general correspondence, (212)265-4742 orders and billing inquiries.

LC TS840 .N28 **ISSN** 1047-4676
DD 338.4/7684/0097305 US
TITLE CHANGE
FURNITURE RETAILER (GREENSBORO, N.C.). **See** Interior Design and Decoration-Home Furnishings.

ISSN 1061-2106
DD 332 US
GUIDE TO RETAIL SHOPS. [Guide retail shops]. (1992)-. Periodical. English. Practitioners Publishing Company, PO Box 966, Fort Worth TX 76101-0966. **Tel** (800)332-3709.

ISSN 1074-293X
DD 338 US
HIGH POINTS FOR THE FURNITURE RETAILER. [High points furnit. retail.]. **VFOAT** High Points. (19??)-. Periodical. English. Twelve times a year. $30.00. Fairchild Publications Inc., 7 West 34th Street, 4th Floor, New York NY 10001-8191. **Tel** (212)630-4230, (800)247-6622.

ISSN 0848-8312
DD 338.4/7684/00971 CN
HOME GOODS RETAILING. **See** Interior Design and Decoration-Home Furnishings.

LC HF5429.7 .I375
US
ICSC RESEARCH BULLETIN. **Added/Corp** International Council of Shopping Centers. (June 1990)-. Bulletin. English. Four times a year. Free. International Council of Shopping Centers, 665 Fifth Avenue, New York NY 10022. **Tel** (212)421-8181, FAX (212)486-0849. ***Continues*** *ICSC Research Quarterly, 1043-5395.*

LC HF6146.P7 I49
DD 658.8/2/0941 UK
INCENTIVE MARKETING AND SALES PROMOTION: ANNUAL REVIEW AND BUYERS' GUIDE. **See** Business and Economics-Advertising and Public Relations.

LC HF6146.P7 I48 **ISSN** 0019-3348
DD 381 US
INCENTIVE (NEW YORK). (INCENTIVE.). Trade Publication. English. Twelve times a year. $4.00. Premium, 1515 Broadway, New York NY 10036. ***Continues*** *Premium Buyers' Guide.*

ISSN 0147-5924
US
INFO FRANCHISE NEWSLETTER, THE. **See** Business and Economics-Commerce.

US
INSIDE RETAILING. (19??)-. Periodical. English. Thirty-five times a year. $199.00. Lebhar Friedman Inc., PO Box 31203, Tampa FL 33633. **Tel** (800)944-4676, (813)664-6707.
Desc: Focuses on retailing decisions, reports trends, regrowth strategies, marketing shifts, what works and what doesn't.

ISSN 0310-5660
DD 658.870994 AT
INSIDE RETAILING. [Inside retail.]. (1971)-. Periodical. English. One time a week. 318.18Aus$. Ian Huntley Publishers Pty Limited, PO Box 99, Cremorne NSW 2090 Australia. **Tel** 011 61 2 9535788, FAX 011 61 2 9532280.

LC HF5429 .I548 **ISSN** 0959-0552
DD 658.8/7/005 UK
CCC
CODEN IRDMEQ
INTERNATIONAL JOURNAL OF RETAIL & DISTRIBUTION MANAGEMENT. [Int. j. retail distrib. manag.]. **VFOAT** International Journal of Retail and Distribution Management; IJR and DM; IJR & DM. Vol. 18, No. 1 (Jan./Feb. 1990)-. Periodical. English. Eight times a year. $2789.00. MCB University Press, 60 62 Toller Lane, Bradford, West Yorkshire BD8 9BY United Kingdom. **Tel** 011 44 1274 785280, FAX 011 44 1274 785200, telex 51317-MCBUNI-G. **(Subscription address:** MCB University Press / US and Canada Subscriptions, PO Box 10812, Birmingham AL 35201-0812. **Tel** (205)995-1567, (800)633-4931, FAX (205)995-1588.**)** **ED** John Fernie. available on an online database (file 15/Full-Text) from DIALOG. Documents available from UMI Article Clearinghouse, Ask*IEEE. ***Formed by the union of*** *International Journal of Retailing, 0268-3903* ***and*** *Retail & Distribution Management, 0307-2363.*
Desc: Aims to present the full picture of retail and distribution management with insights into areas of greatest concern. It is in no way beholden to advertisers thereby remaining fully independent. This means that, unlike other publications in the field, controversial or special issues can be covered fully and freely.
Ind/Abst ABI/INFORM Glob. Ed.; Bus. Index (1990-); Curr. Cit.; Gen. BusinessFile (1992-); INSPEC (Jan./Feb. 1990-); Trade Ind. ASAP [Full Txt.]; Trade Ind. Index [Full Txt.].

LC HF5428 .I6 **ISSN** 0959-3969
UK
CCC
INTERNATIONAL REVIEW OF RETAIL DISTRIBUTION CONSUMER RESEARCH. **VFOAT** Retail, Distribution and Consumer Research. Vol. 1, No. 1 (Oct. 1990)-. Periodical. English. Four times a year. $205.00. Routledge, 11 New Fetter Lane, London EC4P 4EE United Kingdom. **Tel** 011 44 171 5839855, FAX 011 44 171 5830701. **(Subscription address:** Kinokuniya Company Ltd., 38-1 Sakuragaoka 5, chome Setagaya-ku, Tokyo 156 Japan. **Tel** FAX 011 03 3439 0136.**)**
Ind/Abst Int. Bibliogr. Sociol.

ISSN 0273-7485
US
IS. INTER SERVICE. (INTER SERVICE : IS : THE JOURNAL OF THE AMERICAN LOGISTICS ASSOCIATION.). [IS. Inter serv.]. **Added/Corp** American Logistics Association. **VFOAT** IS; Interservice. Vol. 1, No. 1 (Fall 1980)-. Trade Publication. English. Four times a year (Jan., Apr., June, Sept.). $20.00. American Logistics Association, 1133 15th Street Northwest, Suite 640, Washington DC 20005. **Tel** (202)466-2520, FAX (202)296-4419. **ED** Herman O. Marshall. **Ad Acc. Circ:** 10,000 (ctrl). ***Continues*** *Review, 0034-6322.*
Desc: For sales and marketing executives who sell to or otherwise supply or operate the military's commissaries, exchanges, clubs, and other retail customer outlets.
Ind/Abst Air Univ. Libr. Index Mil. Period.

LC HF5001 .J65 **ISSN** 0022-4359
DD 380 US
CCC
CODEN JRLEA3
Pr Rev.
JOURNAL OF RETAILING. [J. retail.]. **Added/Corp** New York University. Institute of Retail Management. New York University. School of Retailing. Vol. 1 (April 1925)-. Periodical. English. Four times a year. $160.00. JAI Press Inc., 55 Old Post Road, Suite 2, PO Box 1678, Greenwich CT 06836-1678. **Tel** (203)661-7602, FAX (203)661-0792. **ED** Charles Ingene. **Bk Rev**. **Ad Acc**. **Circ:** 3,000 (ctrl). available on microfilm and microfiche from University Microfilms International (UMI). Documents available from The Genuine Article, UMI Article Clearinghouse.
Desc: Devoted to the studies of retailing practice.
Ind/Abst ABI/INFORM Glob. Ed.; ABI/INFORM Ondisc: Expr. Ed.; ABI/INFORM [Computer File] (Fall 1971-); Acad. Search; Account. Art.; Anbar Account. Finan. Abstr. [Full Txt.]; Anbar Mark. Distr. Abstr. [Full Txt.]; Anbar Top Manage. Abstr. [Full Txt.]; Bus. ASAP (1990-) [Full Txt.]; Bus. Index (1985-); Bus. Period. Index; Bus. Source Plus; Bus. Source; Comput. Lit. Index; Contents Pages Manage.; Curr. Cit.; Curr. Contents Soc. Behav. Sci.; EP Collect.; Gen. BusinessFile (1985-); Gen. Period. Index (1985-); Homework Help.; INFO-SOUTH Abstr.; Infobank (1979-); Mag. Search; Manage. Market. Abstr.; Manage. Bibliogr. Rev.; Mark. Advert. Ref. Serv.; MasterFile FullTEXT 1000; MasterFile FullTEXT 350; MasterFile FullTEXT 650; MasterFile FullTEXT (July 1993-); OCLC; Oper. Prod. Manage. Abstr. [Full Txt.]; Person. Train. Abstr. [Full Txt.]; Psychol. Abstr. (1982-); PsycINFO; PsycLit; Res. Alert [Full Cov.]; Soc. Sci. Cit. Index [Full Cov.]; Telebase; Trade Ind. ASAP [Full Txt.]; Trade Ind. Index [Full Txt.]; UMI ABI/Inform--Bus. Period. Ondisc (Winter 1987-) [Full Txt.]; Wilson Bus. Abstr.; Women Manage. Rev. [Full Txt.].

LC HF5428 .J68 **ISSN** 0969-6989
DD 381/.1/094105 UK
Pr Rev.
•**JOURNAL OF RETAILING AND CONSUMER SERVICES.** (1994)-. Academic Scholarly Publication. English. Four times a year. $248.00 The Americas; £166.00 other. Butterworth Heinemann Publishers, Linacre House Jordan Hill, Oxford OX2 8DP United Kingdom. **Tel** 011 44 1865 310366, FAX 011 44 1865 310898. **(Subscription address:** Elsevier Science Ltd. / Oxford Fulfillment Centre, PO Box 800, Kidlington OX5 1DX United Kingdom. **Tel** 011 44 865 843355.**)** available on an online database from Elsevier Electronic Subscriptions (EES).

Business and Economics —Retail

LC S677 **ISSN** 1199-1836
DD 381.4563151/0971 CN
KEEPING TRACK (BURLINGTON). See Agriculture-Agricultural Equipment.

LC HF5429.6.H8 K57
HU
KISKERESKEDELEM ES A FOGYASZTASI SZOLGALTATASOK ... BAN / KOZPONTI STATISZTIKAI HIVATAL, A. Hungarian. One time a year.

 ISSN 1079-6339
DD 346 US
●**LEADER'S FRANCHISING BUSINESS & LAW ALERT.** [Leader's franch. bus. law alert]. **Added/Corp** Leader Publications, Inc. **VFOAT** Leader's Franchising Business and Law Alert; Franchising Business & Law Alert; Franchising Business and Law Alert. Vol. 1, No. 1 (Oct. 1994)-. Periodical. English. Twelve times a year. $125.00. Leader Publications, 345 Park Avenue South, New York NY 10010. **Tel** (800)888-8300 ext. 6170, (212)545-6170, FAX (212)696-1848.

LC HF5430.3 .L42 **ISSN** 0732-9237
DD 381/.1/02573 US
LEASING OPPORTUNITIES (1983). (LEASING OPPORTUNITIES.). [Leas. oppor.]. **Added/Corp** International Council of Shopping Centers. (1983)-. English. One time a year. International Council of Shopping Centers, 665 Fifth Avenue, New York NY 10022. **Tel** (212)421-8181, FAX (212)486-0849. *Formed by the union of* Retail Expansion Plans, 0736-8275 *and* Directory of New and Expanding Shopping Centers, 0736-7856.

LC HD9666.4 .L55
DD 615.1065 US
LILLY DIGEST OF THE ... STATEMENTS OF ... RETAIL DRUG STORES. See Pharmacy and Pharmacology.

 ISSN 0068-9955
DD 338.4/7/688 CN
 CEASED
LLOYD'S CANADIAN VARIETY MERCHANDISE DIRECTORY. **VFOAT** Canadian Variety Merchandise Directory. (1967)-(1993). Directory. English. Sentinel Business Publications, 7575 Trans Canada Highway, Suite 500, St. Laurent Quebec H4T 1V6 Canada. **Tel** (514)333-1116, FAX (514)631-8858. **ED** Keith Fredericks. **Ad Acc, Adv Mgr:** P. Young. **Circ:** 3,500 (ctrl). *Continues* Lloyd's Canadian Toy, Notion and Stationery Directory, 0381-5757.
 Desc: A directory of product listings and suppliers of general merchandise for retailers.

US
LOEB RETAIL LETTER. (19??)-. Newsletter. English (English). Eleven times a year. $300.00. Loeb Associates Inc., PO Box 1155, New York NY 10018. **Tel** (212)536-4034, FAX (212)596-4642.

LC HF5429.6.B7 L63
BL
LOJAS & I.E. E LOJISTAS. Periodical. Portuguese. Sindicato dos Lojistas do Comercio de Sao Paulo, rua Xavier de Toledo 99 - 2 Andar, Sao Paulo Brazil.

 ISSN 0024-2632
UDC 65 FR
LSA. LIBRE SERVICE ACTUALITES. [LSA. Libre serv. actual.]. **VFOAT** Libre Service Actualites (Angouleme). (1958)-. Periodical. French. Forty-eight times a year. $300.74. CEP Communications Groupe LSA, 6 rue Marius Aufan, 92300 Levallois Perret France. **Tel** 011 33 1 47 582000, FAX 011 33 1 47 586070. **Ind/Abst** Infomat Int. Bus.; PROMT.

 ISSN 0743-5258
DD 381 US
 TITLE CHANGE
MASS MARKET RETAILERS. [Mass mark. retail.]. **VFOAT** ChainSigns; MMR. Vol. 1, No. 10 (Mar. 19, 1984)-(1994). Periodical. English. Racher Press, 220 Fifth Avenue, New York NY 10001. **Tel** (212)213-6000, FAX (212)213-6106. *Continues* ChainSigns, 0739-3776. *Continued by* MMR, 1080-0794.

 ISSN 1187-3469
DD 381/.456292/025711 CN
MEMBERSHIP ROSTER - AUTOMOTIVE RETAILERS ASSOCIATION (WINNIPEG). See Transportation-Automobiles.

 ISSN 0279-8999
 US
MEN'S AD REVIEW. See Business and Economics-Advertising and Public Relations.

AT
MINGAY'S ELECTRICAL RETAILER. See Engineering-Electrical Engineering.

AT
MINGAY'S RETAIL GUIDE. (19??)-. English. Two times a year. 158.00Aus$ Australia; 168.00Aus$ New Zealand, Papua New Guinea; 51.00Aus$ Malaysia, Indonesia, Fiji, Japan, India, Hong Kong; 171.00Aus$ US, Canada, Lebanon; 175.00Aus$ Europe, Africa, former USSR. Thomson Publications / Australia, 47 Chippen Street, Chippendale New South Wales 2008 Australia. **Tel** 011 61 2 6992411, FAX 011 61 2 6991184, telex 122226. **(Subscription address:** Thomson Publications Australia, PO Box 815, Strawberry Hills, New South Wales, 2012 Australia. **Tel** 011 61 2 6992411.**)** *Continues* Mingay's Product Service.

 ISSN 1080-0794
DD 381 US
●**MMR (NEW YORK, N.Y.).** (MMR : THE NEWSPAPER FOR DRUG, DISCOUNT, AND SUPERMARKET CHAINS.). [MMR]. (1994)-. Periodical. English. Twenty-four times a year. $99.00. Racher Press, 220 Fifth Avenue, New York NY 10001. **Tel** (212)213-6000, FAX (212)213-6106. *Continues* Mass Market Retailers, 0743-5258.

LC WMLC L 83/7270 **ISSN** 0191-6904
DD 381 US
MODEL RETAILER (CLIFTON, VA.). See Hobbies.

 ISSN 0700-3528
DD 381/.45/6588700971 CN
MONDAY REPORT ON RETAILERS. (1974)-. Periodical. English. One time a week. 316.13Can$. MacLean Hunter Publ. Limited / Toronto, 777 Bay Street, 8th Floor Agency Control, Toronto Ontario M5W 1A7 Canada. **Tel** (416)596-6045, , FAX (416)596-2510.
 Desc: Reports on Canadian chain retailers with an emphasis on store expansion plans, merchandise and policy changes, important staff changes and financial data.

 US
●**MOR : MERCHANDISING & OPERATING RESULTS OF RETAIL STORES IN ... . Added/Corp** National Retail Merchants Association. **VFOAT** MOR ... Merchandising and Operating Results of Retail Stores in ...; Merchandising and Operating Results of Retail Stores in ... . 69th Ed. (1994)-. English. Irregular. National Retail Federation, 325 7th Street NW Suite 1000, Washington DC 20004. **Tel** (202)626-8146. *Continues* Department and Specialty Store Merchandising and Operating Results, 0271-5015.

LC WMLC 93/994 **ISSN** 1049-6726
DD 381 US
MR (NORWALK, CONN.). (MR : THE MAGAZINE OF MENSWEAR RETAILING.). [MR]. **VFOAT** Menswear Retailing. Vol. 1, No. 1 (Mar. 1990)-. Trade Publication. English. Eight times a year. $24.00. Business Journals Inc, PO Box 5550, Norwalk CT 06856. **Tel** (203)853-6015, FAX (203)852-8175, telex 353706.

LC ML3790 .M75 **ISSN** 1051-1822
DD 381/.4780266/097305 US
 CEASED
MUSIC RETAILING. See Music.

LC HF5469.7 **ISSN** 1055-8268
DD 381.17 US
●**NATIONAL AUCTIONS & SALES.** See Consumer Education and Protection.

LC HD9773.U4 N37
DD 380.1/025/73 US
NATIONWIDE DIRECTORY, GIFT, HOUSEWARES & HOME TEXTILES BUYERS. Added/Corp Salesman's Guide, Inc. **VFOAT** Nationwide Directory, Gift, Housewares, and Home Textiles Buyers; Gift, Housewares, and Home Textiles Buyers; Salesman's Guide Gift, Housewares, and Home Textiles Buyers Nationwide Directory; Gift, Housewares & Home Textiles Buyers; Nationwide Directory of Gift, Housewares & Home Textiles Buyers; Salesman's Guide Gift, Housewares & Home Textiles Buyers Nationwide Directory. (198?)-. Directory. English. One time a year (May). $186.03. Salesman's Guide, A Reed Reference Publishing Company, Part of Reed International PLC, 121 Chanlon Road, New Providence NJ 07974. **Tel** (800)223-1797, (908)464-6800, FAX (908)665-3560, telex 138755. Index Available Published separately--free--upon request. *Continues* Salesman's Guide Nationwide Directory. Gift, Housewares & Stationery Buyers, 0734-8932.

 ISSN 0028-1948
 US
NEBRASKA RETAILER. See Food and Food Industry.

LC WMLC 91/746
 US
NEW YORK RETAILER, THE. Added/Corp College of the City of New York (1926-1961). City College. School of Business and Civic Administration. (19??)-. Periodical. English. Twelve times a year. City College of New York / New York Retailer, Convent Avenue and 138 St., New York NY 21114.

LC WMLC 93/1816 **ISSN** 1064-0347
DD 338 US
NICHE (BALTIMORE, MD.). (NICHE : THE MAGAZINE FOR PROGRESSIVE RETAILERS.). [Niche]. Vol. 1, No. 1 (Winter 1988)-. Periodical. English. Four times a year. $25.00. Niche Magazine Incorporated, 3000 Chestnut Avenue, Suite 300, Baltimore MD 21211. **Tel** (301)889-2933. **ED** Laura Rosen. **Bk Rev**, (Qty: 12). **Ad Acc. Circ:** 20,000 (ctrl).
 Desc: Targeted specifically to retailers of American contemporary crafts such as galleries, craft stores, and gift stores.

 ISSN 0748-8327
DD 659 US
NRMA AD/PRO. See Business and Economics-Advertising and Public Relations.

LC HF5429.215.U6 O36 **ISSN** 0748-917X
DD 381/.1 US
OFF-PRICE NEWS, THE. (THE OFF-PRICE NEWS OF ...). (19??)-. English. One time a year. The Off-Price News, PO Box 7870, St Petersburg FL 33734.

LC HD1393.25 .O33 **ISSN** 0748-9153
DD 381/.1 US
OFF-PRICE NEWS. THE BOOK ON OUTLET & OFF-PRICE LEASING, THE. VFOAT Book on Outlet & Off-Price Leasing; Book on Outlet and Off-Price Leasing. (19??)-. English. One time a year. The Off-Price News, PO Box 7870, St Petersburg FL 33734.

LC S677 .O34 **ISSN** 0162-6809
DD 381/.45/681763102573 US
OFFICIAL GUIDE, TRACTORS AND FARM EQUIPMENT. See Agriculture-Agricultural Equipment.

 ISSN 0030-1841
 US
OKLAHOMA RETAILER. (1961)-. Trade Publication. English. Twelve times a year. $12.00. Oklahoma Retailer Publishing Company, 4500 North Sewell, Oklahoma City OK 73118. **Tel** (405)528-0903. **ED** Fred Singleton. **Ad Acc. Circ:** 4,300 (ctrl), available on microfilm from University Microfilms International (UMI).
 Desc: Published for Oklahoma's appliance dealers; includes TV, plumbing, heating, air conditioning, lumber and building material, hardware-housewares, and furniture and home furnishings.

 ISSN 0824-6769
 CN
OPERATING SURVEY OF CANADIAN RETAILING. [Oper. surv. Can. retail.]. English. One time a year. 48.02Can$. Retail Council of Canada, 210 Dundas Street West/Suite 600, Toronto Ontario M5G 2E8 Canada. **Tel** (416)598-4684. **Bk Rev**.
 Desc: Comparative statistical- financial operating data for a number of different kinds of stores. Used for productivity improvement.

LC WMLC L 83/7287 **ISSN** 0279-8107
 US
 CCC
OUTDOOR RETAILER. Vol. 1, No. 1 (Mar./Apr. 1981)-. Periodical. English. Twelve times a year. $40.00. Miller Freeman Inc., 600 Harrison Street, San Francisco CA 94107. **Tel** (415)905-2337, (415)905-2200, FAX (415)905-2240, telex 278273. **(Subscription address:** Sunbelt Fulfillment Services, PO Box 5039, Brentwood TN 37024. **Tel** (800)685-3435.**) ED** Pam Montgomery. **Circ:** 8,500.

LC HF3790.5 .A15 **ISSN** 0250-4340
DD 380.1/029/45491 PK
PAKISTAN BUSINESS & SHOPPING GUIDE. VFOAT Pakistan Business and Shopping Guide. (197?)-. English. One time a year. Syed Wali Ahmad Maulai, J-12 Al-Naseer, Sharifabad, Karachi 19 Pakistan. *Continues* Business & Shopping Guide, Pakistan.

 ISSN 0299-4690
UDC 658.871.6 (058) FR
PANORAMA (LEVALLOIS). (PANORAMA.). [Panorama Levallois]. (1977)-. French. One time a year. $393.37. Liaisons & Convergence, 1 Avenue East Belin, F-92856 Rueil Mal France. **Tel** 011 33 1 41299872, FAX

011 33 1 47575420, telex 613128. **Ad Acc. Circ:** 6,500. available on magnetic tape; available on labels; available on diskette.

DD 658
ISSN 0899-6008
US
PARTY & PAPER RETAILER. [Party pap. retail.]. **VFOAT** Party and Paper Retailer; PPR. (198?)-. Trade Publication. English. Twelve times a year. $36.00. 4ward Corporation, 70 New Canaan Avenue, Norwalk CT 06850. **Tel** (203)845-8020, FAX (203)845-8022. available on an online database (file 648/Full-Text) from DIALOG.
Ind/Abst Trade Ind. ASAP [Full Txt.]; Trade Ind. Index [Full Txt.].

DD 338.528
ISSN 1300-1035
TU
PERAKENDE FIYAT ISTATISTIKLERI. [Perakende fiyat istat.]. **VFOAT** Retail Price Statistics. (1972)-. Periodical. Multiple languages. One time a year. $45.00. Turkish State Institute of Statistics, Necatibey Cadessi 114, Ankara 016100 Turkey. **Tel** 011 90 4 1188719, FAX 011 90 4 1253387, telex 46347 DIETR. Index available. cum. index. **Circ:** 600.

LC HF5035 .P48
DD 381/.1
US
Pr Rev.
PHELON'S DISCOUNT & JOBBING TRADE. **VFOAT** Phelon's Discount and Jobbing Trade; Discount & Jobbing Trade. (1991)-. English. Every 2 years (August). $140.00. Phelon Sheldon & Marsar Inc, 15 Industrial Avenue, PO Box 517, Fairview NJ 07022. **Tel** (201)941-8804, (800)234-8804, FAX (201)941-5515. **ED** Kenneth W. Phelon Jr. Index available. **Circ:** 3,000 (ctrl)
Continues Phelon's ... Directory of Discount Stores.

LC HD9940.U3 P5
DD 381/.45687/02573
ISSN 0737-3430
US
Pr Rev.
PHELON'S WOMEN'S APPAREL SHOPS. See Clothing Industry and Fashion.

UK
POST NEWS. See Electronics.

ISSN 0742-4183
US
PRIME SOURCE MINI REFERENCE DIRECTORY. MOST WANTED NAMES AND ADDRESSES OF : CHAIN STORES AND DEPARTMENT STORES. **VFOAT** Most Wanted Names and Addresses of: Chain Stores and Department Stores; Chain Stores and Department Stores. 1983-. Directory. English. One time a year. $19.95 US; $24.95 other. EGW Publishing Company, 1041 Shary Circle, Concord CA 94518. **Tel** (510)671-9852, (800)777-1164, FAX (510)671-0692.

LC HF5635 .P96
DD 657/.839
ISSN 0278-6486
US
PRINCIPLES AND PRESENTATION. RETAILING. [Princ. present., Retail.]. **Added/Corp** Peat, Marwick, Mitchell & Co. (19??)-. English. One time a year. $50.00. KPMG, Lock Box 23331, Newark NJ 07189. **Tel** (201)307-7752.

US
PROFESSIONAL SELLING. (19??)-. English. Twenty-four times a year. $111.96 (US); $136.08 (Canada). Bureau of Business Practice, 24 Rope Ferry Road, Waterford CT 06386. **Tel** (800)243-0876, (203)442-4365, (800)876-9105, FAX (203)443-1123.

US
PROFESSIONAL SELLING SERVICE. (19??)-. English. $177.36 (US); $216.96 (Canada) Includes: Selling Service Quarterly Report, Professional Selling, and Sales Memory Jogger. Bureau of Business Practice, 24 Rope Ferry Road, Waterford CT 06386. **Tel** (800)243-0876, (203)442-4365, (800)876-9105, FAX (203)443-1123.

LC HF5469.25 .D57
DD 381/.147/02573
ISSN 1046-5332
US
PROGRESSIVE GROCER'S DIRECTORY OF CONVENIENCE STORES. [Progress. groc. dir. conven. stores]. **VFOAT** Directory of Convenience Stores; Progressive Grocer ... Directory of Convenience Stores. (198?)-. English. One time a year. $220.00. Progressive Grocer, 263 Tresser Boulevard, Stamford CT 06901. **Tel** (203)977-7640, FAX (203)977-7645. **Continues** Directory of Convenience Store Companies and Profile of the Industry, 0278-9698.

LC HF5429.3 .P77
DD 381/.1/02573
ISSN 0890-7986
US
PROGRESSIVE GROCER'S ... DIRECTORY OF MASS MERCHANDISERS. [Progress. Groc. dir. mass merch.]. **VFOAT** Directory of Mass Merchandisers. (1987)-. English. One time a year. $220.00. Progressive Grocer, 263 Tresser Boulevard, Stamford CT 06901. **Tel** (203)977-7640, FAX (203)977-7645. **(Subscription address:** Progressive Grocer, PO Box 10246, Stamford CT 06913.) cum. index.
Desc: Profiles over 800 companies, including drug stores, discount/variety chains, department stores, 5- and 10s, club type stores. Features company data, corporate plans, key personnel and buyers.

UK
RETAIL. English. McCaughan Dyson Capel Cure, 65 Holborn Viaduct, London EC1A 2EU United Kingdom.

LC HF5429.3 .R48
DD 381
ISSN 0034-6004
US
RETAIL & BUSINESS REVIEW. **VFOAT** Retailer's Review. **VAT** Retail and Business Review. (19??)-. Trade Publication. English. Six times a year. Electrical Information Publications, Inc., 2132 Fordem Avenue, Madison WI 53707. **Tel** (608)244-3528.
Ind/Abst Account. Art.

DD 381.10941
ISSN 1352-9153
UK
RETAIL & CONSUMER PRODUCTS RETAIL TRADE REVIEW. [Retail consum. prod., Retail trade rev.]. **VFOAT** Retail and Consumer Products. Retail Trade Review; Retail & Consumer. Retail Trade Review. (1993)-. Periodical. English. Four times a year. The Economist Intelligence Unit, 40 Duke Street, London W1A 1DW United Kingdom. **Tel** 011 44 171 8301000. **Continues** Retail Business. Retail Trade Reviews, 0951-9742.
Ind/Abst Curr. Cit.

UK
RETAIL BREAKTHROUGHS INTERNATIONAL. (19??)-. English. Twelve times a year. £254.00 UK; $445.00 US. World Business Publications Ltd., 960 High Road, Britannia 4th Floor, London N12 9RY United Kingdom. **Tel** 011 44 181 4465141, FAX 011 44 181 4463659, telex 9419208.

LC HF5429.6.G7 R43
UK
TITLE CHANGE
RETAIL BUSINESS. MARKET REPORTS. **Added/Corp** Economist Intelligence Unit (Great Britain). **VFOAT** Market Reports. No. 347 (Jan. 1987)-(1993). Periodical. English. The Economist Intelligence Unit, 40 Duke Street, London W1A 1DW United Kingdom. **Tel** 011 44 171 8301000. **(Subscription address:** Economist Intelligence Unit / North America Subscriptions, 111 West 57th Street, New York NY 10019. **Tel** 800 938-4685, (212)554-0600, FAX (212)586-1181, (212)586-1182.) available on microfilm from World Microfilm Publications Ltd. **Continues in part** Retail Business, 0034-6012. **Continued by** Retail Business. Market Surveys.
Ind/Abst Trade Ind. Index.

LC HF5429.6.G7 R43
ISSN 0951-9734
UK
●**RETAIL BUSINESS. MARKET SURVEYS.** **Added/Corp** Economist Intelligence Unit (Great Britain). **VFOAT** Market Surveys; Retail & Consumer; Retail and Consumer; EIU Retail Business. No. 425 (July 1993)-. Periodical. English. Twelve times a year. $750.00. The Economist Intelligence Unit, 40 Duke Street, London W1A 1DW United Kingdom. **Tel** 011 44 171 8301000.
Continues Retail Business. Market Reports.
Ind/Abst Curr. Cit.

LC HF5429.6.G7 R47
DD 381.1
UK
RETAIL BUSINESS. RETAIL TRADE REVIEWS. **Added/Corp** Economist Intelligence Unit (Great Britain). **VFOAT** Retail Trade Reviews; Quarterly Retail Trade Reviews. (March 1987)-. Trade Publication. English. Four times a year. $375.00. The Economist Intelligence Unit, 40 Duke Street, London W1A 1DW United Kingdom. **Tel** 011 44 171 8301000. **(Subscription address:** Economist Intelligence Unit / North America Subscriptions, 111 West 57th Street, New York NY 10019. **Tel** 800 938-4685, (212)554-0600, FAX (212)586-1181, (212)586-1182.) available on microfilm from World Microfilm Publications Ltd. **Continues in part** Retail Business, 0034-6012.
Ind/Abst Trade Ind. Index.

LC HF5468 .R47
DD 381/.12/0971
ISSN 0227-017X
CN
RETAIL CHAIN AND DEPARTMENT STORES. (RETAIL CHAIN AND DEPARTMENT STORES = MAGASINS DE DETAIL A SUCCURSALES ET LES GRANDS MAGASINS.). [Retail chain dep. stores]. **Added/Corp** Statistics Canada. Merchandising and Services Division. Statistics Canada. Retail Trade Section. **VFOAT** Magasins de Detail A Succursales et les Grands Magasins. (1979)-. English (French). One time a year. 37.00Can$ Canada; $45.00 US; $52.00 other. Statistics Canada Publications Sales and Services, R.H. Coats Building 6th Floor, Ottawa Ontario K1A 0T6 Canada. **Tel** (613)951-5078, (800)267-6677, FAX (613)951-1584, telex 053-3585. **Circ:** 600. **Continues** Statistics Canada. Merchandising and Sevices Division. Retail Chain Stores, 0380-7878.
Desc: Fifty-five tables document the retail sales of chain and department stores in terms of kind of business, province, selected locality, number of stores and annual sales volume. Includes statistics about stocks on hand at year-end, cost of goods sold, gross margins and the correlation between sales volume and physical size of a store. Useful for calculating market share and evaluating store performance vs averages.

US
RETAIL CHALLENGE. (19??)-. English. Four times a year. $249.95 (nonmembers); $195.00 (members). International Council of Shopping Centers, 665 Fifth Avenue, New York NY 10022. **Tel** (212)421-8181, FAX (212)486-0849. **ED** Bena Green. **Circ:** 65,000.

UK
SUSPENDED
RETAIL DESIGN INTERNATIONAL. (19??)-(19??). English. Four times a year. £45.00. Pennington Press Ltd, Carlton House, 15 Church Road, Kent TN4 0RX United Kingdom. **Tel** 011 44 1892 36685.

UK
RETAIL DIRECTORY. 41st Ed. (1987)-. Directory. English. One time a year. £86.00 UK; £94.00 other. Newman Publishing Company, 32 Vauxhall Bridge Road, London SW1V 2YY United Kingdom. **Tel** 011 44 171 9736402, FAX 011 44 171 2335081. **ED** Karen Rasmussen. **Bk Rev. Ad Acc. Circ:** 4,200. **Continues** Stores, Shops, Hypermarkets Retail Directory.
Desc: Lists retailing firms throughout the UK. Company details include senior executives and buying personnel.

DD 004
ISSN 1060-3808
US
RETAIL INFO SYSTEMS NEWS. (RETAIL INFO SYSTEMS NEWS : RIS.). [Retail info syst. news]. **VFOAT** RIS; RIS News. (19??)-. Periodical. English. Ten times a year. Free to retailers; $50.00 other. Edgell Communications Inc, 10 West Hanover Avenue, Suite 107, Randolph NJ 07869. **Tel** (201)895-3300, FAX (201)895-7711. **Continues** RIS (Brookside, N.J.), 1044-6796.

UK
RETAIL INTELLIGENCE. English. Six times a year. £195.00. Mintel International Group Ltd., 18-19 Long Lane, London EC1A 9HE United Kingdom. **Tel** 011 44 171 6064533, FAX 011 44 171 6065932, telex 21405.

DD 381.1094
ISSN 0968-8234
UK
RETAIL MONITOR INTERNATIONAL. [Retail monit. int.]. (1992)-. Trade Publication. English. Twelve times a year. $790.00 US; £490.00 other. Euromonitor Publications Ltd., 60-61 Britton Street, London EC1M 5NA United Kingdom. **Tel** 011 44 171 2518024, FAX 011 44 171 6083149, telex 21120. **Continues** Retail Monitor, 0952-9594.
Desc: Provides reports and company profiles, plus a monthly news digest and sector reviews.

UDC 381.511
ISSN 1017-785X
FR
RETAIL NEWS LETTER ED. FRANCAISE. [Retail news lett.Ed. fr.]. (19??)-. Periodical. French (English). Twelve times a year. 170.00F. International Association of Department Stores, 72 boulevard Haussman, 75008 Paris France. **Tel** 011 33 1 43872580, FAX 011 33 1 43876684. **ED** Maarten de Groot van Embden. Index available. cum. index. **Bk Rev,** (Qty: 20). **Circ:** 900.
Desc: A selection of some 35 news items and covers retailing business worldwide.

LC HD9390.U62 D48
DD 381/.45/663500973
ISSN 0416-0525
US
RETAIL OUTLETS FOR THE SALE OF DISTILLED SPIRITS. **Main/Corp** Distilled Spirits Council of the U.S. English. Distilled Spirits Council of the United States, 1250 Eye Street Northwest, Suite 900, Washington DC 20005. **Tel** (202)628-3544. **Continues** Retail Outlets for the Sale of Distilled Spirits.

US
RETAIL POWER MONTHLY. (19??)-. English. Twelve times a year. $245.00. Cogen Publications, PO Box 2303, Falls Church VA 22042. **Tel** (703)641-0613. **Continues** Demand Side Monthly.

ISSN 1057-7033
US
RETAIL PROFIT FORUM. (1992)-. Periodical. English. Twelve times a year. $50.00. Retail Profit Planners, Inc., 100 Woodside Avenue, Narberth PA 19072.

US
RETAIL SALES OUTLOOK. (19??)-. English. Four times a year. $95.00. National Retail Federation, 325 7th Street NW Suite 1000, Washington DC 20004. **Tel** (202)626-8146.

LC KF2005.A15 R48
DD 345.73/0268 347.305268
ISSN 0735-8520
US
RETAIL SECURITY DIGEST. See Law.

Business and Economics —Retail

ISSN 0883-2234
DD 381 US
RETAIL SECURITY MANAGEMENT LETTER. [Retail secur. manage. lett.]. **VFOAT** Retail Security Management. (19??)-. Periodical. English. Twelve times a year. $127.00 (one-year), $227.00 (two-year). Strafford Publications Inc., 590 Dutch Valley Road Northeast, Atlanta GA 30324. **Tel** (404)881-1141, (800)926-7926, FAX (404)881-0074. **ED** M. M. Sweet and Jennifer Fogleman. **Bk Rev**.
Desc: A news and information monthly edited exclusively for the executive with security and loss prevention responsibility in the retail and shopping center environments.

ISSN 1047-8841
DD 658 US
 CCC
RETAIL STORE IMAGE. See Interior Design and Decoration.

ISSN 0898-8439
DD 338 US
RETAIL SYSTEMS ALERT. [Retail syst. alert]. Vol. 1, No. 1 (June 1988)-. Periodical. English. Twelve times a year. $295.00. Ardea Research Corporation, PO Box 312, Newton MA 02161. **Tel** (617)527-4626, FAX (517)527-8102. **ED** Thomas H. Friedman. cum. index. **Bk Rev**. ctrl circ.

LC HF5428 .R47 **ISSN 0731-1303**
DD 658.8/7/002854 US
RETAIL TECHNOLOGY. [Retail technol.]. Periodical. English. Four times a year. $20.00 US / $21.00 Canada. Lebhar Friedman Inc., PO Box 31203, Tampa FL 33633. **Tel** (800)944-4676, (813)664-6707. **(Subscription address:** CSG Information Services, 3922 Coconut Palm Drive, Tampa FL 33619. **)**
Ind/Abst Infomat Int. Bus.

LC HF5429.3 .N29 **ISSN 0887-0470**
DD 381/.1/02573 US
RETAIL TENANT DIRECTORY. [Retail tenant dir.]. (198?)-. Directory. English. One time a year. $325.00. Monitor CT, 4 Stamford Forum, Stamford CT 06901. **Tel** (203) 325-3500, (203) 977-2900. **ED** Donna Wetmore. **Ad Acc. Circ:** 2,000. available on diskette. **Continues** National Mall Monitor Inc.'s Retail Tenant Directory, 0277-9331.
Desc: Comprehensive listing of prospective retail tenants for shopping centers, including geographical areas of interest, space requirements, and key contact names.

UK
RETAIL TRADE INTERNATIONAL. (1977/78)-. Periodical. English. Irregular. $1,300 US; £650.00 other. Euromonitor Publications Ltd., 60-61 Britton Street, London EC1M 5NA United Kingdom. **Tel** 011 44 171 2518024, FAX 011 44 171 6083149, telex 21120. **Continues** Retail Trade Europe.
Desc: Contains information on consumer expenditure, structure of the retail trade and trade by form of organisation, food and non-food distribution trends, and retail forecasts the year 2000.

LC HF5429.6.C3 R44 **ISSN 0380-6146**
DD 381/.1/0971021 CN
RETAIL TRADE (MONTHLY ED.). (RETAIL TRADE.). [Retail trade]. **Added/Corp** Canada. Dominion Bureau of Statistics. Merchandising and Services Section. Canada. Dominion Bureau of Statistics. Retail Trade Section. Canada. Dominion Bureau of Statistics. Industry and Merchandising Division. Canada. Dominion Bureau of Statistics. Merchandising and Services Division. Statistics Canada. Merchandising and Services Division. Statistics Canada. Industry Division. Statistics Canada. Retail Trade Section. **VFOAT** Commerce de Detail. Vol. 21, Nos. 1 & 2 (Feb. 1949)-. Periodical. English (French). Twelve times a year. 240.00Can$. Statistics Canada Publications Sales and Services, R.H. Coats Building 6th Floor, Ottawa Ontario K1A 0T6 Canada. **Tel** (613)951-5078, (800)267-6677, FAX (613)951-1584, telex 053-3585. **Absorbed in part** Chain Store Sales and Stocks, 0840-3279; **Continues** Retail Sales (Ottawa, Ont.).
Desc: Total retail sales by provinces and kind of business for chain and independent stores; seasonally adjusted sales.

UK
RETAIL WEEK. (19??)-. English. Twelve times a year. £60.00 UK; £100.00 Europe; £150.00 other. EMAP Readerlink, Audit House, 260 Field End Road, Ruislip Middlesex HA4 9LT United Kingdom. **Tel** 011 44 1773 63100, FAX 011 44 1733 87367.
Ind/Abst Infomat Int. Bus.

AT
RETAIL WORLD. **Added/Corp** National Association of Retail Grocers of Australia. Vol. 25, No. 18 (Aug. 1972)-. Periodical. English. Twenty-four times a year. 168.55Aus$. Retail World Pty Ltd, PO Box 278, Rozelle New South Wales 2039 Australia. **Tel** 011 61 2 5551577, FAX 011 61 28108004. **ED** Barry Flanagan. **Bk Rev. Ad Acc. Circ:** 16,500 (ctrl).
Ind/Abst Infomat Int. Bus.

ISSN 8750-4391
DD 381 US
RETAILER NEWS. [Retail. news]. **VFOAT** Retailer News-S. Periodical. English. Twelve times a year. $18.00. Retailer News, 3821 W 226th Street, Torrance CA 90505. **Tel** (714)921-0600. **ED** Martin Barksy. **Circ:** 52,000.
Absorbed in part Consumer Electronics & Appliance News. Southern California., 0898-9559.

ISSN 0161-5688
US
RETAILER (RALEIGH), THE. (THE RETAILER.). Periodical. English. Twenty-four times a year. $5.00. North Carolina Merchants Association, 2400 Glenwood Avenue, Raleigh NC 27608.

ISSN 1038-5002
DD 381.10994 AT
RETAILERS DIGEST, THE. [Retail. dig]. (1992)-. Periodical. English. Six times a year. 24.67Aus$. Retailers Digest, PO Box 7905, Gold Coast Mail Ct., Queensland 4217 Australia. **Tel** 011 61 75 5920477.

LC HF5429.4.T2 T46A **ISSN 0361-0020**
DD 381 US
RETAILING IN TENNESSEE. Main/Corp Tennessee. Sales and Use Tax Division. English. Department of Revenue / Tennessee, 500 Deaderick Street, Nashville TN 37242. **Tel** (615)741-2461.

LC HD9940.U4 R89 **ISSN 0887-3003**
DD 746 US
Pr Rev.
RTW REVIEW. See Clothing Industry and Fashion.

ISSN 0033-7196
US
RWDSU RECORD. See Business and Economics-Labor.

LC HD9390.U6 S24 **ISSN 0741-6288**
DD 381/.456635/00973 US
SALES OF DISTILLED SPIRITS. See Food and Food Industry-Beverage Industry.

ISSN 0890-1252
DD 338 US
SATELLITE RETAILER. [Satell. retail.]. **VFOAT** Retailer. (1985)-. Trade Publication. English. Twelve times a year. $29.00. Triple D Publications, PO Box 2384, Shelby NC 28151. **Tel** (800)234-0021. **ED** David B. Melton. **Bk Rev. Ad Acc. Adv Mgr Tel** (704)482-9673. **Circ:** 12,000 (ctrl).

LC HF5421 .E44 **ISSN 0276-6701**
DD 381/.1 US
SAVE ON SHOPPING DIRECTORY. **VFOAT** S.O.S. 7th Ed.-. Directory. English. SOS Inc, 9109 San Jose Boulevard, Jacksonville FL 32217-5014. **Continues** Save on Shopping, 0092-8003.

ISSN 0843-1507
DD 381/.1/0971 CN
SCN : THE SHOPPING CENTRE NEWSLETTER. [SCN, Shopp. cent. newsl.]. **VFOAT** Shopping Centre Newsletter. Vol. 8, No. 3 (Feb. 1, 1988). Newsletter. English. Twenty-four times a year. $330.00. Maclean Hunter Canada / Montreal, 1001 bvd. de Maisonneuve W., Montreal Quebec H3A 3E1 Canada. **Tel** (514)845-5141, FAX (514)845-4302, telex 055-60604. **Continues** Shopping Centre News & Construction Update, 0712-1245.

US
SELLING. English. Ten times a year (July/Aug. and Dec./Jan. combined). $50.00. Selling Communications Assoc., 1225 Michigan Ave., Evanston IL 60202. **Tel** (708)866-9887.

US
SELLING KNACKS. Main/Corp National Sales Development Institute. English. Twenty-four times a year. $51.24 US; $66.84 Canada. Bureau of Business Practice, 24 Rope Ferry Road, Waterford CT 06386. **Tel** (800)243-0876, (203)442-4365, (800)876-9105, FAX (203)443-1123.

US
Pr Rev.
SHELDON'S MAJOR STORES AND CHAINS. English. One time a year (Mar.). $140.00. Phelon Sheldon & Marsar Inc, 15 Industrial Avenue, PO Box 517, Fairview NJ 07022. **Tel** (201)941-8804, (800)234-8804, FAX (201)941-5515. **ED** Kenneth W. Phelon Jr. Index available. **Circ:** 5,000 (ctrl).
Desc: Lists all executives and buyers of merchandise being sold in major retail stores and chains in the US and Canada.

LC HF5429.3 .S52 **ISSN 0094-0453**
DD 381 US
SHELDON'S RETAIL DIRECTORY OF THE UNITED STATES AND CANADA AND PHELON'S RESIDENT BUYERS AND MERCHANDISE BROKERS. [Sheldon's retail dir. U. S. Can. Phelon's resid. buy. merch. brok.]. **VFOAT** Sheldon's Retail and Phelon's Resident Buyers. (19??)-. Directory. English. One time a year. $125.00. Phelon Sheldon & Marsar Inc, 15 Industrial Avenue, PO Box 517, Fairview NJ 07022. **Tel** (201)941-8804, (800)234-8804, FAX (201)941-5515. **ED** Kenneth W Phelon. **Circ:** 5,000 (ctrl). **Formed by the union of** Sheldon's Retail Directory of the United States and Canada **and** Phelon's Resident Buyers and Merchandise Brokers of Department Store Merchandise, Ready to Wear, Millinery.
Desc: Directory of executives and buyers of the major department stores, women's apparel stores and specialty stores in the US and Canada. Provides addresses, phone numbers, executives, sales volume and more.

ISSN 0887-9397
US
SHOOTING SPORTS RETAILER. [Shoot. sports retail.]. (198?)-. Periodical. English. Six times a year (five issues per year). $24.00 US; $35.00 other. Shooting Sports Retailer, 130 West 42nd Street, New York NY 10036. **Tel** (212)840-0660, FAX (212)994-1884. **ED** John Bartimole. Index available. **Bk Rev. Ad Acc. Circ:** 16,000 (ctrl). **Continues** Shooting Sports Retailer Magazine, 0745-3779.
Desc: Contains management and merchandising articles aimed at retail and wholesale sellers of shooting sports equipment. Special editorial features inform and instruct retailers and wholesalers on sales techniques and problems.

ISSN 0885-209X
DD 381 US
SHOPPING CENTER DIGEST. [Shopp. cent. dig.]. Vol. 1 (1971)-. Periodical. English. Twenty-four times a year. $189.00. Jomurpa Publishing Corporation, PO Box 1708, 7 South Myrtle Avenue, Spring Valley NY 10977. **Tel** (914)426-0040, FAX (914)426-0802. **ED** Murray Shor. **Ad Acc**.

ISSN 0049-0393
US
 CCC
SHOPPING CENTER WORLD. Vol. 1 (Feb. 1972)-. Trade Publication. English. Twelve times a year. $74.00. Argus Business, 6151 Powers Ferry Road Northwest, Atlanta GA 30339. **Tel** (404)995-2500, FAX (404)995-0400. **(Subscription address:** Hallmark Data Systems, PO Box 1147, Skokie IL 60076. **Tel** (708)647-6933.) available on microfilm and microfiche from University Microfilms International (UMI).

LC HF5429.7 .S56 **ISSN 0885-9841**
DD 338 US
SHOPPING CENTERS TODAY. (SHOPPING CENTERS TODAY : A PUBLICATION OF INTERNATIONAL COUNCIL OF SHOPPING CENTERS.). [Shopp. cent. today]. **Added/Corp** International Council of Shopping Centers. (19??)-. Periodical. English. Twelve times a year. $70.00. International Council of Shopping Centers, 665 Fifth Avenue, New York NY 10022. **Tel** (212)421-8181, FAX (212)486-0849. **ED** James Pauia. **Ad Acc. Circ:** 26,000 (ctrl).

ISSN 0226-7551
DD 381/.0971 CN
SHOPPING CENTRE CANADA. [Shopp. cent. Can.]. Vol. 1 (May 1979)-. Periodical. English. Irregular. 15.00Can$. Maclean Hunter Canada / Montreal, 1001 bvd. de Maisonneuve W., Montreal Quebec H3A 3E1 Canada. **Tel** (514)845-5141, FAX (514)845-4302, telex 055-60604.
Desc: A publication written for retailers, developers, financial institutions and suppliers to the Canadian shopping centre industry.

ISSN 1035-915X
DD 381.45688760994 AT
TITLE CHANGE
SPORTS & LEISURE RETAILER. [Sports leis. retail.]. (1990)-(199?). Periodical. English. Yaffa Publishing Group Pty Ltd., GPO Box 606, Sydney New South Wales 2001 Australia. **Tel** 011 61 2 2812333, FAX 011 61 2 2812750. **Continues in part** Australasian Sportsgoods and Toy Retailer, 0004-8488. **Continued by** Sports Retailer.
Ind/Abst SPORT Discus.

ISSN 0830-1921
DD 381/.4568876/0971 CN
Pr Rev.
SPORTS BUSINESS. [Sports bus.]. Vol. 14, No. 1 (Feb. 1986)-. Trade Publication. English. Eight times a year. 44.02Can$. Laurentian Media Inc, 501 Oakdale Road, Downsview Ontario M3N 1W7 Canada. **Tel** (416)746-7300, (800)565-4007, FAX (416)746-1421. **ED** Melanie Lozinski. **Ad Acc. Circ:** 10,000 (ctrl).
Desc: Trade publication to Canadian sporting goods retailers.
Ind/Abst SportSearch (May 1987-).

AT
SPORTS RETAILER. (199?)-. English. Six times a year. 38.00Aus$ Australia; 105.00Aus$ other. Yaffa Publishing Group Pty Ltd., GPO Box 606, Sydney New South Wales 2001 Australia. **Tel** 011 61 2 2812333, FAX 011 61 2 2812750. **Continues** Sports & Leisure Retailer.

Business and Economics — Small Business

DD 381   **ISSN** 0890-8745
   US
   CCC

SPORTS TREND. [Sports trend]. Vol. 18, No. 9 (Sept. 1986)-. Trade Publication. English. Twelve times a year. $67.00. Shore Communications Inc., 6255 Barfield Road, Suite 200, Atlanta GA 30328. **Tel** (404)252-8831, (800)241-9034, FAX (404)252-4436. available on microfilm from University Microfilms International (UMI). **Continues** Sports Merchandiser, 0049-1985.

   US

STORE WINDOWS. **Added/Corp** Retail Reporting Corporation. (19??)-. Periodical. English. Irregular. Price varies. Retail Reporting Corporation, 302 Fifth Avenue, New York NY 10001. **Tel** (212)279-7000, (800)251-4545, FAX (221)279-7014. **Continues** Store Windows that Sell.

   US
   TITLE CHANGE

STORE WINDOWS THAT SELL. **Added/Corp** Retail Reporting Corporation. (19??)-(Aug. 5, 1995). Periodical. English. Retail Reporting Corporation, 302 Fifth Avenue, New York NY 10001. **Tel** (212)279-7000, (800)251-4545, FAX (221)279-7014. **Continued by** Store Windows.

LC HD9951 .N36
DD 658.97706273   **ISSN** 0039-1867
   US

STORES. (STORES : THE BULLETIN OF THE N.R.D.G.A.). [Stores]. **Added/Corp** National Retail Dry Goods Association. National Retail Merchants Association. Vol. 29, No. 1 (Jan. 1947)-. Bulletin. English. Twelve times a year. $49.00. National Retail Federation, 325 7th Street NW Suite 1000, Washington DC 20004. **Tel** (202)626-8146. **ED** Joan Bergmann. Bk Rev. Ad Acc. Circ: 31,560. available on microfilm and microfiche from University Microfilms International (UMI). Documents available from UMI Article Clearinghouse. **Continues** Bulletin of the National Retail Dry Good Association.
Desc: Investigates retail issues and concerns in areas such as MDSG, operations, credit, personnel. Special features include travel and retailing around the world.
Ind/Abst ABI/INFORM Glob. Ed.; ABI/INFORM [Computer File] (Jan 1991-); Biogr. Index; Bus. Index (1985-); Bus. Period. Index; EP Collect.; Gen. BusinessFile (1985-); Gen. Period. Index (1985-); Homework Help.; Infobank (1979-); Mag. Search; Mark. Advert. Ref. Serv.; MasterFile FullTEXT 1000; MasterFile FullTEXT 350; MasterFile FullTEXT 650; MasterFile FullTEXT (Jan. 1993-); OCLC; Telebase; Trade Ind. Index; UMI ABI/Inform--Bus. Period. Ondisc (Jan. 1991-) [Full Txt.]; Vocat. Search; Wilson Bus. Abstr.

DD 338   **ISSN** 1050-1789
   US

SULLIVAN'S RETAIL PERFORMANCE MONITOR. [Sullivan's retail perform. monit.]. **VFOAT** RPM; Retail Performance Monitor. (1990)-. Trade Publication. English. Twenty-six times a year. $357.00. Catalog Showroom Merchandiser, 195 Smithtown Boulevard, Nesconset NY 11767. **Tel** (516)265-3900. **Continues** Upscale Discounting, 1041-3219.

LC HF5469.23.U6 S86
DD 381/.148/02573   **ISSN** 1075-6892
   US

●**SUPERMARKET NEWS RETAILERS & WHOLESALERS.** [Supermark. news retail. wholes.]. **VFOAT** Supermarket News Retailers and Wholesalers; Retailers & Wholesalers; Retailers and Wholesalers; SN Retailers and Wholesalers; SN Retailers and Wholesalers Directory; SN; SN Directory; SN Retailers & Wholesalers Directory; SN Retailers & Wholesalers. (1994-). Directory. English. One time a year. $309.95. Fairchild Publications Inc., 7 West 34th Street, 4th Floor, New York NY 10001-8191. **Tel** (212)630-4230, (800)247-6622. **(Subscription address:** Fairchild Publications Inc., PO Box 7711, Riverton NJ 08077. **)**

   ISSN 0962-2225
   UK

SUPERSTORE MANAGEMENT INTERNATIONAL. [Superst. manag. int.]. (19??)-. Periodical. English. Twelve times a year. £44.00 UK; £59.00 all other except US and Canada. Faversham House Group Ltd, Faversham House, 111 Saint James Road, Croydon Surrey CR9 2TH United Kingdom. **Tel** 011 44 81 684 4082. **Continues** Superstore Management, 0950-9658.
Ind/Abst Infomat Int. Bus.

LC HF5429.6.F45 S87
DD 381/.0996/11021   FJ

SURVEY OF DISTRIBUTIVE TRADE. **Added/Corp** Fiji. Bureau of Statistics. (19??)-. English. Irregular. 5.50Fij$. Government of Fiji / Bureau of Statistics, Box 2221, Suva Fiji Islands. **Tel** 011 679 315144. **(Subscription address:** Government Printer / Fiji, PO Box 98, Suva Fiji. **)** Ad Acc. Circ: 80.
Desc: Employment, gross output and gross fixed capital formation.

LC HF5429.6.P33 P35B
DD 381/.0995/3   PP

SURVEY OF RETAIL SALES AND SELECTED SERVICES. **Main/Corp** Papua New Guinea. Bureau of Statistics. English. Bureau of Statistics / Papua New Guinea, PO Box 2032, Konedobu Papua New Guinea.

LC HF5429.6.P3 S87
DD 381/.09549/1   PK

SURVEY OF WHOLESALE & RETAIL TRADE & RESTAURANTS. **VFOAT** Survey of Wholesale and Retail Trade and Restaurants. 1975/76-. English. One time a year. NGM Communication, 3-D-1 Gulberg III, Near TP Exchange, Lahore 54660 Pakistan. **Tel** 011 92 21 428625, FAX 011 92 21 613854.

LC HF5429.6.E3 T54
   UA

TIJARAT AL-TAJZIAH FI AL-QUITA AL-KHASS, KHAMSAT MUSHTAGHILIN FA-AKTHAR, ADA AL-SHARIKAT AL-MUSAHIMAH WA-DHAT AL-MASULIYAH AL-MAHDUDAH WA-AL-TAWSIYAH BI-AL-ASHUM WA-FURU AL-SHARIKAT AL-AJNABIYAH. Arabic. Jihaz Al-Markazi Lil-Tabiah Al-Ammah Wa-Al-Ihsa, Tariq Salah Salim Madinatnasr, Al-Qahirah Egypt.

   ISSN 0950-365X
   UK

TOLLEY'S JOURNAL OF INTERNATIONAL FRANCHISING & DISTRIBUTION LAW. See Law.

DD 381.45688720994   **ISSN** 1035-9176
   AT

TOY & HOBBY RETAILER. See Gifts, Toys.

   US
Pr Rev.   CEASED

TOY & HOBBY WORLD. WEEKLY MARKET REPORT. See Gifts, Toys.

LC TX335 .U46   **ISSN** 0191-3549
DD 380.1/45/00097471   US

UNDERGROUND SHOPPER. NEW YORK CITY, THE. (1979)-. English. Susann Publications Inc, Route 2 PO Box 176 H, Roanoke TX 76262.

   ISSN 0742-3675
DD 380   US

UNITED STATES TRADE FAIR. See Business and Economics-Marketing and Purchasing.

LC HF5429.215.U6 V34
   US

VALUE RETAIL NEWS : THE JOURNAL OF VALUE-ORIENTED RETAILING & DEVELOPMENT. (19??)-. Trade Publication. English. Twelve times a year. $144.00. Value Retail News, 15950 Bay Vista Drive, Suite 250, Clearwater FL 34620. **Tel** (800)669-1020, (813)536-4047, FAX (813)545-2715. **ED** Kris Hundley. Ad Acc, Adv Mgr: Fran Tolson. ctrl circ.
Desc: Information on discount houses, retail trade, and outlet stores.

LC HF5483 .C35   **ISSN** 0527-6411
DD 338.4/7/629820971   CN

VENDING MACHINE OPERATORS. [Vend. mach. oper.]. **Added/Corp** Canada. Dominion Bureau of Statistics. Industry and Merchandising Division. Canada. Dominion Bureau of Statistics. Merchandising and Services Division. Statistics Canada. Merchandising and Services Division. Statistics Canada. Retail Trade Section. **VFOAT** Exploitants de Distributeurs Automatiques. (1958)-. Periodical. English (French). One time a year. 24.00Can$ Canada; $29.00 US; $34.00 other. Statistics Canada Publications Sales and Services, R.H. Coats Building 6th Floor, Ottawa Ontario K1A 0T6 Canada. **Tel** (613)951-5078, (800)267-6677, FAX (613)951-1584, telex 053-3585.
Desc: Sales of merchandise by vending machine operators through automatic vending machines, type of machine and by location; Canada and the provinces.

LC HF5801 .D55   **ISSN** 1072-9666
DD 659.1/05   US

VM & SD. (VM & SD : VISUAL MERCHANDISING AND STORE DESIGN.). [VM SD]. **VFOAT** VM and SD; Visual Merchandising and Store Design. (198?)-. Trade Publication. English. Twelve times a year. $39.00. Signs of the Times Publishing Company, 407 Gilbert Avenue, Cincinnati OH 45202. **Tel** (513)421-2050, (800)925-1110, FAX (513)421-5144. **ED** Janet Groeber. Index available. Bk Rev. Ad Acc. Circ: 21,000. Documents available from The UnCover Company, UMI Article Clearinghouse. **Continues** Visual Merchandising & Store Design, 0745-4295.
Desc: Examines display approaches used in stores thoroughout the country. Contains listings of products used for window and store decorating.

   IO

WARTA GPEI. See Business and Economics-Commerce.

   ISSN 0882-4207
DD 381   US

WASHINGTON RETAIL REPORT. [Wash. retail rep.]. **VFOAT** NRMA Washington Retail Report. (1975)-. Periodical. English. Six times a year. NRMA, 100 West 31st Street, New York NY 10001. **Tel** (212)244-8780, telex 220 883 TAUR. **Continues** NRMA Washington News Letter.

   ISSN 1058-4757
DD 380   US

WASHINGTON RETAIL WEEKLY. [Wash. retail wkly.]. **Added/Corp** American Retail Federation. Vol. 18, No. 1 (Jan. 14, 1991)-. Periodical. English. One time a week. included with membership. National Retail Federation, 325 7th Street NW Suite 1000, Washington DC 20004. **Tel** (202)626-8146. **Continues** Washington Report (American Retail Association), 0891-0219.

   ISSN 1044-7768
DD 658   US

WESTERN RETAILER. [West. retail.]. **Added/Corp** Western Association. (198?)-. Trade Publication. English. Twelve times a year. $12.00. Western Retail Implement and Hardware Association, Box 19264, Kansas City MO 64141. **Tel** (816)561-5323, FAX (816)561-1249. **Continues** Hardware & Farm Equipment, 0017-7679.

   ISSN 0279-2311
   US

WESTERN RETAILER NEWS. **VFOAT** Western Retailer. Vol. 1, No. 1 (Aug. 1981)-. Periodical. English. Twelve times a year. Southern California Retailer, Inc., 440 South Anaheim Blvd., Anaheim CA 92805.

LC HF1401   **ISSN** 1201-0588
DD 381/.0971/021   CN

●**WHOLESALING AND RETAILING IN CANADA.** [Wholes. retail. Can.]. **Added/Corp** Statistics Canada. Wholesale Trade Section. Statistics Canada. Retail Trade Section. **VFOAT** Commerces de Gros et de Detail au Canada. (1993)-. English (French). Statistics Canada Publications Sales and Services, R.H. Coats Building 6th Floor, Ottawa Ontario K1A 0T6 Canada. **Tel** (613)951-5078, (800)267-6677, FAX (613)951-1584, telex 053-3585. **Formed by the union of** Wholesale Trade Statistics, Wholesale Merchants, Agents and Brokers, 0823-1214 **and** Annual Retail Trade, 0843-557X.

LC HF5429.23 .W67   **ISSN** 1056-456X
DD 381/.13/025   US
   CEASED

WORLDWIDE FRANCHISE DIRECTORY. [Worldw. franch. dir.]. 1st Ed. (19??)-(19??). Directory. English. Gale Research Inc., 835 Penobscot Building, 645 Griswold Street, Detroit MI 48226. **Tel** (800)877-GALE, (313)961-2242, FAX (313)961-6083, (800)414-5043, telex TWX 810-221-7086. **ED** Susan Boyles.

SMALL BUSINESS

LC KF6369.8.E9 A14   **ISSN** 0191-8249
DD 343/.73/068   US

ALI-ABA COURSE OF STUDY. ABA SECTION OF TAXATION, ADVANCED STUDY SESSIONS, ESTATE AND INCOME TAX PLANNING FOR EXECUTIVES AND SMALL BUSINESS OWNERS : MATERIALS. See Law-Estate Planning.

LC KF6491.Z9 A18   **ISSN** 0190-9355
DD 343/.73/068   US

ALI-ABA COURSE OF STUDY. TAX AND BUSINESS PLANNING FOR THE SMALL BUT GROWING BUSINESS: MATERIALS. See Law-Taxation Law.

LC HD2346.I52 G834A
DD 354/.54/750082   II

ANNUAL REPORT AND ACCOUNTS - GUJARAT SMALL INDUSTRIES CORPORATION. **Main/Corp** Gujarat Small Industries Corporation. (19??)-. Multiple languages (English and Gujarati). Gufarat Small Industries Corporation, Bhagwati Chambers Ashram Road, Ahmedabad -13 India.

LC HG3729.U5 C24A   **ISSN** 0092-4253
DD 353.9/794/0082   US

ANNUAL REPORT - CALIFORNIA JOB DEVELOPMENT CORPORATION LAW EXECUTIVE BOARD. (ANNUAL REPORT.). **Main/Corp** California Job Development Corporation Law Executive Board. English. One time a year. California Job Development Corporation, Law Executive Board, 915 Capitol Mall Room 200, Sacramento CA 95814.

Business and Economics — Small Business

LC HG4949 .M35A
DD 338.9741/005　US
ANNUAL REPORT / FINANCE AUTHORITY OF MAINE. See Business and Economics-Banks and Banking.

LC HC106.5 .A27813　**ISSN** 0083-3274
DD 353.008/2　US
ANNUAL REPORT / SMALL BUSINESS ADMINISTRATION. [Annu. rep. - Small Bus. Administr.]. **Main/Corp** United States. Small Business Administration. **Added/Corp** United States. Small Business Administration. SBA Annual Report. **VFOAT** SBA Annual Report; Report; Annual Report for the U.S. Small Business Administration; A.US Small Business Administration annual report. (1966)-. English. Two times a year. $19.00. Small Business Administration, 1030 15th Street, Washington DC 20417. **Tel** (202)653-6963. **(Subscription address:** Superintendent of Documents, US Government Printing Office, Washington DC 20402. **)** available on microfiche (Vols. for (1985-) distributed to depository libraries). **Continues** United States. Small Business Administration. Annual Report to the President and Congress, 0502-5125.

　US
ATLANTA SMALL BUSINESS MONTHLY, THE. VFOAT Small Business Monthly. Periodical. English. Twelve times a year. $15.00. Atlanta Small Business Monthly, 2342 Perimeter Park Drive, Suite 200, Atlanta GA 30341. **Tel** (404)986-0447. **ED** Millan Travis Funk. **Bk Rev**. **Ad Acc**. **Circ**: 28,000 (ctrl). **Desc:** Business information for small business owners.

ISSN 1183-0069
DD 338.9715/05　CN
ATLANTIC JOURNAL OF OPPORTUNITY. [Atl. j. oppor.]. **Added/Corp** Atlantic Canada Opportunities Agency. **VFOAT** Journal des Perspectives de l'Atlantique. Vol. 1, No. 1 (Fall Quarter, 1990)-. Periodical. English (French). Four times a year.

LC HG450
DD 332.6　AT
　TITLE CHANGE
AUSTRALIAN SMALL BUSINESS & INVESTING. (19??)-(19??). Periodical. English. Federal Publishing Co Pty Ltd., PO Box 199, 180 Bourke Road, Alexandria New South Wales 2015 Australia. **Tel** 011 61 2 3539992, **FAX** 011 61 2 66923059935. **(Subscription address:** Federal Publishing Co. Pty Ltd., PO Box 199, Alexandria NSW 2015 Australia. **Tel** 011 61 2 3530666.**)** **Continues** Australian Small Business Review. **Continued by** Australian Small Business and Portfolio.

LC TP368 HD321
DD 664.752 338　US
●**BAKERY - DELI OPERATIONS.** See Food and Food Industry.

LC HF5001　**ISSN** 1198-8819
DD 650.1/05　CN
●**BIG DREAMS.** [Big dreams]. Vol. 1, No. 1 (July 1994)-. Periodical. English. Twelve times a year. Free. Dare to Dream Enterprises, 2515 Burian Drive, Coquitlam British Columbia V3K 5W8 Canada. **Tel** (604)760-1631, **FAX** (604)931-2198. available via Internet (http://www.wimsey.com/~duncans/). **Desc:** Newsletter covering topics related to small businesses.

ISSN 0823-289X
DD 381/.1/060714　CN
BULLETIN DU MOUVEMENT TRI-ACTION, LE. [Bull. Mouv. tri-action]. Vol. 5, No. 2 (Oct./Nov. 1982). Bulletin. French. Irregular. Free to members, $2.00 other. Agence De Promotion Et De Courtages, 462 boulevard Sainte-Foy, Longueuil Quebec J4J 1Y2 Canada. **Continues** Bulletin du Mouvement V.U.Q., 0712-6220.

LC HF5001 .S625　**ISSN** 0893-8326
DD 658/.022/05　US
BULLETIN - SMALL BUSINESS SERVICE BUREAU. (BULLETIN / SMALL BUSINESS SERVICE BUREAU INC.). [Bull. - Small Bus. Serv. Bur.]. **Added/Corp** Small Business Service Bureau. **VFOAT** Small Business Service Bureau Inc. Bulletin; SBSB Bulletin. (1982)-. Periodical. English. Six times a year. comes with Small Business Services Bureau membership. Small Business Services Bureau, 544 Main Street, PO Box 1441, Worchester MA 01615. **Tel** (508)756-3513. **Continues** Small Business Bulletin (Worcester, Mass.), 0195-2404.

ISSN 0824-3735
DD 338.6/42/0971　CN
BULLETIN SUR LA PME. [Bull. PME]. **VAT** Bulletin sur la Petite et Moyenne Entreprise. Bulletin. French. Free. Bulletin sur la PME, c/o Nouveau Parti Democratique, Chambre de Communes, Ottawa Ontario K1A 0A6 Canada.

ISSN 0823-9665
DD 338.6/42/0971　CN
BUSINESS ADVISORY REVIEW. [Bus. advis. rev.]. Vol. 3, No. 4 (Nov. 1983)-. Periodical. English. Irregular. Free. Editor of Business Advisory Review, Thorne Riddell & Company, PO Box 262 Toronto-Dominion Centre, Toronto Ontario M5K 1J9 Canada. ctrl circ. **Continues** Small Business Review, 0823-9657.

LC HF5001 .B846　**ISSN** 0190-4914
DD 650.05　US
BUSINESS OWNER (HICKSVILLE, N.Y.), THE. See Business and Economics-Banks and Banking.

ISSN 1045-232X
DD 338　US
BUSINESS PROFITABILITY DATA. (BUSINESS PROFITABILITY DATA / JOHN B. WALTON.). [Bus. profitab. data]. (1980)-. English. One time a year. $40.00. Weybridge Publishing Company, 16911 Brushfield Drive, Dallas TX 75248. **Tel** (214)931-7770. **ED** John Walton. Index available (published in September).

LC HB241
DD 338　UK
●**BUSINESS SERVICES RESEARCH MONOGRAPH.** (1994)-. Monographic series. English. Irregular. The Open University, Walton Hall, Milton Keynes MK7 6AA United Kingdom. **Tel** 011 44 1908 655831, **FAX** 011 44 1908 655898.

ISSN 0739-1994
　US
CHARLES FARRELL'S DANCE BUSINESS NEWSLETTER. See Dance.

LC HC466 .C4736
DD 330.9519/5043　KO
CHOSA WOLBO (KUNGMIN UNHAENG). (CHOSA WOLBO.). Periodical. English (Korean). Twelve times a year. Kungmin Unhaeng, 9-1 12-ka Namdaemun-no, Chung-ku, Seoul South Korea.

LC HD2341 .C57
DD 338.642　KO
CHUNGSO KIOP. HAEOE KYONGGONGOP. Added/Corp Chungso Kiop Unhaeng. **VFOAT** Haeoe Kyonggongop. (19??)-. Periodical. Korean. Twelve times a year. Chung so Kiop Unhaeng, 36-1 2-ka Oljiro, Chung-ku, Seoul Korea. **Absorbed** Haeoe Kyonggongop Chongbo41.

LC HD62.7 .C4793
　KO
CHUNGSO KIOP KYONGYONG KISUL CHONGBO. 1983-. Periodical. Korean. Chungso Kiop Chinhung Kongdan, 1-1040 Youido-dong Yongdungpo-ku, Seoul 150 Korea. **Formed by the union of** Chungso Kiop Kyongyong Chongbo **and** Chungso Kiop Kisul Chongbo.

LC HD2346.K6 C519
　KO
CHUNGSO KIOP SONGGONG SARYEJIP. 1 (1982)-. Korean. Chungso Kiop Hyoptong Chohap Chunganghoe, 138-1 Kongpyong-dong Chongno-ku, Seoul Korea.

LC Z7146.C81 C526 HD2341
　JA
CHUSHO KIGYO KANKEI BUNKEN SAKUIN. Added/Corp Chusho Kigyo Joho Senta. (19??)-. Japanese. Chusho Kigyo Joho Senta, (Small Business Information Centre), Sankaido Building, 1-9-13 Akasaka, Minatoku Tokyo Japan.

LC HD2346.J3 C35327
　JA
CHUSHO KIGYO KANKEI SHIRYO RISUTO. HOKOKUSHO HEN. Added/Corp Chusho Kigyo Joho Senta. (19??)-. Japanese. Chusho Kigyo Jigyodan Chusho Kigyo Joho Senta, (Small Business Information Center, Japan Small Business Corporation), Toranomon 37, Mori Building 5-1 Toranomon 3-chome, Minatoku Tokyo 105 Japan.

LC HD5077.Z9 A332a
　JA
CHUSHO KIGYO NO CHINGIN JIJO. See Business and Economics-Labor.

LC HG1501
DD 332.1　US
CODE OF FEDERAL REGULATIONS. 13, BUSINESS CREDIT AND ASSISTANCE. See Business and Economics-Banks and Banking.

ISSN 0825-2696
DD 338.6/42/09713　CN
CONNECTIONS (WILLOWDALE). (CONNECTIONS.). [Connections]. Vol. 1, No. 1 (Feb. 1984)-. Periodical. English. Four times a year. Free to members. Small Business Network, 52 Sheppard Avenue West, Willowdale Ontario M2N 1M2 Canada.

　US
DIGEST OF STATE LEGISLATION AND RULE MAKING ACTIVITIES. Added/Corp New York (State). Dept. of Commerce. New York (State). Dept. of State. (19??)-. Periodical. English.

ISSN 0225-9583
DD 338.6/42/025711　CN
DIRECTORY - INDEPENDENT CANADIAN BUSINESSMEN ASSOCIATION OF BRITISH COLUMBIA. [Dir. - Indep. Can. Bus. Assoc. B.C.]. **Main/Corp** Independent Canadian Businessmen Association of British Columbia. **VFOAT** I.C.B.A. Directory. **VAT** ICBA Directory (1979) Independent Canadian Businessmen Association of British Columbia Directory. 1979-. Directory. English. One time a year. Independent Canadian Businessmen Association of British Columbia, 12202B-86th Avenue, Surrey British Columbia V3W 3H7 Canada. **Continues** Independent Contractors & Businessmen Association of British Columbia. Directory, 0225-9575.

LC HG3729.U49 D57　**ISSN** 0736-2129
DD 332.6/722　US
DIRECTORY OF OPERATING SMALL BUSINESS INVESTMENT COMPANIES. See Industry and Production-Trade and Industrial Directories.

LC HD2346.I52 H354　**ISSN** 0376-8570
DD 338.6/42/02554558　II
DIRECTORY OF SMALL SCALE INDUSTRIAL UNITS EMPLOYING FIVE OR MORE PERSONS IN THE UNORGANISED SECTOR IN HARYANA. See Business and Economics-Labor.

LC HA1631 .A33 HD2346.Y8
DD 314.971　YU
DRUSTVENE ZANATSKE ORGANIZACIJE. See Business and Economics-Abstracting, Bibliographies and Statistics.

LC HC267.C7 A365
　CI
DRUSTVENI PROIZVOD I NARODNI DOHODAK NEPOLJOPRIVREDNIH DJELATNOSTI INDIVIDUALNOG SEKTORA PRIVREDE. (1977)-. Serbo-Croatian (Roman). One time a year. 70.00. Republicki Zavod za Statistiku, Central Bureau of Statistics of the Republic of Croatia, Ilica 3, Zagreb Croatia. **Tel** 011 385 41 45 44 22, **FAX** 011 385 41 42 94 13, 011 385 41 42 37 11, telex 21130 DZSTAT RH. **Continues** Republicki Zavod za Statistiku SR Hrvatske. Harodni Dohodak Nepoljoprivredni Privatnih Djelatnosti.

ISSN 0709-6828
DD 338.6/42/0971384　CN
ENTERPRISER OTTAWA. [Enterpriser]. Vol. 7, No. 1 (Jan. 1984)-. Periodical. English. Twelve times a year. $24.00. Brandy Publishing, 49 George Street, Ottawa Ontario K1N 8W5. **Continues** Enterpriser, 0709-6828.

LC HF5001 .I6744　**ISSN** 0163-3341
DD 338/.005　US
ENTREPRENEUR (SANTA MONICA, CALIF.). (ENTREPRENEUR.). [Entrepreneur] **VFOAT** Entrepreneur Magazine. Vol. 6, No. 5 (May 1978)-. Periodical. English. Twelve times a year. $19.97. Entrepreneur Inc., 2392 Morse Avenue, Irvine CA 92714. **Tel** (714)261-2393. **(Subscription address:** Neodata / Colorado, PO Box 2606, Boulder CO 80322. **) ED** R. Lesonsky. **Bk Rev**. **Ad Acc**. **Circ**: 250,000. available on microfilm and microfiche from University Microfilms International (UMI). **Continues** International Entrepreneurs'. **Superseded in part by** Hottest New Business Ideas, 0273-0618. **Desc:** America's 'how to' magazine for small businesses, offering inspiration and information to millions of Americans who already are, or want to become, business owners. **Ind/Abst** Acad. Search; Bus. Source Plus; Bus. Source; EP Collect.; Foods Adlibra; Homework Help.; Mag. Search; MasterFile FullTEXT 1000; MasterFile FullTEXT 350; MasterFile FullTEXT 650; MasterFile FullTEXT (July 1993-); OCLC; PAIS Int. Print (1991-); Pub. Lib. FullTEXT; Telebase; Vocat. Search.

LC HD2346.U5 A75　**ISSN** 1042-2587
DD 658.02/2/05　US
　CCC
ENTREPRENEURSHIP THEORY AND PRACTICE. (ENTREPRENEURSHIP THEORY AND PRACTICE : ET&P.). [Entrep. theory pract.].

Added/Corp United States Association for Small Business and Entrepreneurship. John F. Baugh Center for Entrepreneurship. **VFOAT** ET&P; ET and P. Vol. 13, No. 1 (Fall 1988)-. Periodical. English. Four times a year (Mar., June, Sept., Dec.). $80.00. Entrepreneurship Theory & Practice, Baylor University, Box 98011, Waco TX 76798. **Tel** (817)755-2265, FAX (817)755-2271. **ED** Sarah Downs. available on microfilm and microfiche from University Microfilms International (UMI). Documents available from UMI Article Clearinghouse, Ask*IEEE. ***Continues** American Journal of Small Business, 0363-9428.*
Desc: Publishes original, conceptual and empirical articles of interest to scholars, consultants and public policy makers. Topics include studies of enterprise creation, small business management, family firms, minorities in small business, research methodologies and case studies. Teaching notes to accompany cases are available.
Ind/Abst ABI/INFORM Glob. Ed. (July 1979-); ABI/INFORM Ondisc: Expr. Ed. (Spring 1987-); ABI/INFORM [Computer File] (July 1979-); Acad. Search; Account. Art.; Bus. ASAP (1992-) [Full Txt.]; Bus. Index (1988-); Bus. Period. Index; Bus. Source Plus; Bus. Source; Contents Pages Manage.; Curr. Cit.; EP Collect.; Gen. BusinessFile (1988-); Gen. Period. Index (1988-); Homework Help.; INFO-SOUTH Abstr.; INSPEC (Jan.-March 1982-1986); Leg. Resour. Index (1980-?); Mag. Search; Manage. Contents; MasterFile FullTEXT 1000; MasterFile FullTEXT 350; MasterFile FullTEXT 650; MasterFile FullTEXT (Jan. 1994-); OCLC; PAIS Int. Print (1991-); Telebase; UMI ABI/Inform--Bus. Period. Ondisc [Full Txt.]; Vocat. Search; Wilson Bus. Abstr.

LC HD4965.5.U6 C66b **ISSN** 0270-1561
DD 331.2/81658022/0973 US

EXECUTIVE COMPENSATION REPORT FOR SMALL TO MEDIUM SIZED COMPANIES. [Exec. compens. rep. small medium sized co.]. **Main/Corp** Compensation Institute. (19??)-. English. Compensation Institute, 3250 Wilshire Boulevard, Suite 900, Los Angeles CA 90010.

ISSN 1047-255X
DD 650 US
CCC

FAMILY BUSINESS. [Fam. bus.]. **VFOAT** Family Business, The Heart of American Business. Vol. 1, No. 1 (1989)-. Periodical. English. Four times a year. $95.00. Family Business, 229 South 18th Street, 3rd Floor, Philadelphia PA 19103. **Tel** (800)637-4464, (215)790-7000.
Desc: Devoted to the management issues affecting family owned businesses.

LC WMLC 93/338 **ISSN** 0894-4865
DD 330 US

FAMILY BUSINESS REVIEW. (FAMILY BUSINESS REVIEW : JOURNAL OF THE FAMILY FIRM INSTITUTE.). [Fam. bus. rev.]. **Added/Corp** Family Firm Institute. Vol. 1, No. 1 (Spring 1988)-. Periodical. English. Four times a year. $84.00. Jossey Bass Inc., 350 Sansome Street, San Francisco CA 94104. **Tel** (415)433-1767, FAX (415)433-0499. **ED** Ivan Lansberg and Kelin Gersick. **Bk Rev. Circ:** 1,200. available on microfilm and microfiche from University Microfilms International (UMI).
Desc: Exploring the dynamics of America's family-owned firms. Includes interviews with family business owners. Includes ideas and strategies for answering the needs of today's family-run businesses.

LC HD2346.U5 F55a **ISSN** 0363-8987
DD 658.1/5904 US

FINANCIAL STUDIES OF THE SMALL BUSINESS. See Business and Economics-Banks and Banking.

LC HD2346.U5 U57B **ISSN** 0195-5411
DD 338.6/422/02573 US

FIRMS IN THE 8(A) BUSINESS DEVELOPMENT PROGRAM. VAT Firms in the Eight(A) Business Development Program. English. Small Business Administration, 1030 15th Street, Washington DC 20417. **Tel** (202)653-6963.

LC HD2346.U52 F67
US

FLORIDA SMALL BUSINESS DIRECTORY / FLORIDA ECONOMIC DEVELOPMENT CENTER, FLORIDA STATE UNIVERSITY. Added/Corp Florida Economic Development Center. **VFOAT** Small Business Directory. (19??)-. Directory. English. Irregular. $19.95. Florida Economic Development Center, Florida State University, 119 College of Business, Tallahassee FL 32306. **Tel** (904)644-1044.

LC UB357.52 .F67
DD 353.88 US

FORECAST OF CONTRACTING OPPORTUNITIES / PREPARED BY OFFICE OF SMALL AND DISADVANTAGED BUSINESS UTILIZATION. Added/Corp United States. Dept. of Veterans Affairs. Office of Small and Disadvantaged Business Utilization.a40. (1991)-. English.

ISSN 0711-2335
DD 658/.022/0971 CN

FREELANCE (VANCOUVER). (THE FREELANCER.). [Freelancer]. Vol. 1, No. 1 (Apr. 1980)-. Periodical. English. Six times a year. $9.00. The Freelancer, 1225 Cardero Street/Suite 1805, Vancouver British Columbia V6G 2H8 Canada.

ISSN 0830-8535
DD 658/.022/05 CN

GREATER WINNIPEG BUSINESS. [Gt. Winn. bus.]. **VFOAT** Business. (Sept. 1983)-. Periodical. English. Twelve times a year. 24.00Can$. Harvard Publishing Company, 315 Queenston Street, Winnipeg Manitoba R3N 0W9 Canada. **Tel** (204)488-6419. **ED** Guy Rochon. **Bk Rev. Ad Acc. Circ:** 15,500 (ctrl). ***Continued in part by** Greater Winnipeg Business. Commercial Source Book., 0842-9731.*

LC HD2346.J3 C368c
JA

GYOKAI JITTAI CHOSA HOKOKUSHO. Main/Corp Chusho Kigyo Shinko Jigyodan. **Added/Corp** Chusho Kigyo Joho Senta. (19??)-. Periodical. Japanese. Twenty-four times a year. Chusho Kigyo Joho Senta, (Small Business Information Centre), Sankaido Building, 1-9-13 Akasaka, Minatoku Tokyo Japan.

LC HG3729.J3 A16a
JA

GYOMU HOKOKUSHO. Main/Corp Chusho Kigyo Kinyu Koko. (1954)-. Periodical. Japanese. Chusho Kigyo Kinkyu Koko Chosabu, 9-3 Otemachi 1-chome Chiyoda-ku, Tokyo Japan.

LC HD2346.G32 N68 **ISSN** 0300-1059
GW

HANDWERK IM LANDE NORDRHEIN-WESTFALEN, DAS. (DAS HANDWERK IM LANDE NORDRHEIN-WESTFALEN : ERGEBNISSE DER HANDWERKSSTATISTIK.). **Main/Corp** Westdeutscher Handwerkskammertag. German. One time a year. Free. Westdeutscher Hamdwekskammertag, Auf'm Tetelberg 7, W-4000 Dusseldorf 1 Germany. **Tel** (0211)30 10 8-0, telex 858 714 O HAWE D. **Circ:** 500 (ctrl).

LC HC466 .H214
KO

HAN'GUK CHUNGSO KIOPCHE CHONGNAM. VFOAT Prospectus of Korean Medium Enterprises. 1970-. Korean. Chongso Kiop Hyptong Chohap Chunganghoe, 138-1 Kongpyong-Dong, Chongno-ku, Seoul South Korea.

ISSN 1067-7739
DD 338 US

HOME-BASED & SMALL BUSINESS NETWORK. [Home-based small bus. netw.]. **Added/Corp** Graphics Plus Midwest (Cambridge, Minn.). **VFOAT** Home Based & Small Business Network; Home-Based and Small Business Network. Vol. 2, No. 2 (Apr/May/June, 1988)-. Periodical. English. Four times a year (Feb., May, Aug., Nov.). $12.00. Graphics Plus Midwest, PO Box 232, Cambridge MN 55008. **Tel** (612)689-1630. **ED** Joanne Frank, (phone: (612)444-6430). Index available ($10.00). **Bk Rev**, (Qty: 4). **Ad Acc. Circ:** 6,000 (ctrl). ***Continues** Home Business Network (Cambridge, Minn.).*
Desc: This magazine focuses on issues that is the home-based and small business.

LC TT950 **ISSN** 0277-0334
DD 646.724 US
Pr Rev.

HOW TO DOUBLE YOUR INCOME. See Beauty and Cosmetics.

LC HD9736.J33 H966
JA

HYOGO-KEN NO TOKUSAN KOGYO. Main/Corp Hyogo, Japan. Shokobu. (19??)-. Periodical. Japanese. Hyogo-ken Shokobu, 1 Shimo Yamatedori Ikuta-ku 650, Kobe Japan.

ISSN 0822-7187
DD 338.6/42/09711 CN

ICBA. INDEPENDENT CANADIAN BUSINESS ASSOCIATION OF BRITISH COLUMBIA. See Industry and Production.

LC HF5001 .I35 **ISSN** 0190-2458
DD 658/.022/05 US
CCC
CODEN INBSD5

IN BUSINESS. [In bus.]. (1979)-. Periodical. English. Six times a year. $29.00. The JG Press Inc, 419 State Avenue, Emmaus PA 18049. **Tel** (610)967-4135. **ED** Jerome Goldstein. Index available. **Bk Rev. Ad Acc. Circ:** 65,000. available on microfilm and microfiche from University Microfilms International (UMI). Documents available from Ask*IEEE, UMI Article Clearinghouse.
Desc: Covers environmental entrepreneuring.
Ind/Abst ABI/INFORM Glob. Ed.; ABI/INFORM [Computer File] (Nov. 1980-Aug. 1981); Bus. Index (1979-?); Bus. Source Plus; Environ. Period. Bibliogr.; EP Collect.; Homework Help.; INSPEC (Sept.-Oct. 1982-); MasterFile FullTEXT 1000; MasterFile FullTEXT 350; MasterFile FullTEXT 650; MasterFile FullTEXT; OCLC; Person. Manage. Abstr.; Telebase.

LC HD2346.U5 I55 **ISSN** 0162-8968
DD 658/.022 US
CCC
CODEN INCCDU

INC. (BOSTON, MASS.). (INC.). [Inc.]. **VAT** Incorporated. Vol. 1 (April 1979)-. Periodical. English. Eighteen times a year. $19.00. Inc. Publishing Corporation, 38 Commercial Wharf, Boston MA 02110. **Tel** (617)248-8000. **(Subscription address:** Neodata / Colorado, PO Box 2606, Boulder CO 80322. **) ED** George Gendron. available on microfilm and microfiche from University Microfilms International (UMI); available on an online database from NEXIS; and DIALOG. Documents available from UMI Article Clearinghouse, Ask*IEEE, Documents on Demand.
Desc: Provides information and ideas that can be used in running a small business. Each issue contains articles on financing, the law, marketing, taxes, and managing people. Plus, advice from consultants, facts on computers, and interviews with successful small company executives.
Ind/Abst ABI/INFORM Glob. Ed.; ABI/INFORM Ondisc: Expr. Ed.; ABI/INFORM [Computer File] (Aug. 1979-); Acad. Abstr. Full Text Elite; Acad. Abstr.; Acad. Search; AGRICOLA [Select. Cov.]; BioBusiness; Book Rev. Index; Bus. ASAP (1990-) [Full Txt.]; Bus. Index (1985-); Bus. Period. Index; Bus. Source Plus; Bus. Source; Environ. Abstr.; EP Collect.; F&S Index Plus Text, Int. [Select. Cov.]; Foods Adlibra; Gen. BusinessFile (1985-); Gen. Period. Index (1985-); Homework Help.; INFO-SOUTH Abstr.; INSPEC (May 1983-); Law Office Inf. Serv.; Mag. Artic. Summar. Elite; Mag. Artic. Summar. Select; Mag. Artic. Summar. CD-ROM; Mag. ASAP Plus [Full Txt.]; Mag. ASAP Sel. [Full Txt.]; Mag. Express (1986-) [Full Txt.]; Mag. Index Plus (1989-); Mag. Index. Sel. (1986-); Mag. Search; MasterFile FullTEXT 1000; MasterFile FullTEXT 350; MasterFile FullTEXT 650; MasterFile FullTEXT (Feb. 1984-) [Full Txt.]; Newsp. Period. Abstr. (1986-); OCLC; PROMT; Pub. Lib. FullTEXT; Resource/One Ondisc; Stat. Ref. Index; Telebase; Mag. Index (1979-); TOM Gen. Index (1992-) [Full Txt.]; Trade Ind. ASAP [Full Txt.]; Trade Ind. Index (1981-) [Full Txt.]; UMI ABI/Inform--Bus. Period. Ondisc (Dec. 1987-) [Full Txt.]; Vocat. Search; Wilson Bus. Abstr.; Work Relat. Abstr.

ISSN 0710-0531
DD 658/.022/09711 CN

INDEPENDENT BUSINESS FORUM. [Indep. bus. forum]. Vol. 1, Issue 1 (July 1980)-. Periodical. English. Twelve times a year. $1.00 per issue. Reid Communications Inc., 1500-1176 West Georgia Street, Vancouver BC V6E 4A2 Canada.

LC HD62.7 .I53 **ISSN** 1047-2347
DD 658.02/2/097305 US

INDEPENDENT BUSINESS : IB. [Indep. bus.]. **Added/Corp** National Federation of Independent Business. **VFOAT** IB; Independent Business Magazine. (1989)-. Periodical. English. Six times a year. comes with membership. National Federation of Independent Business, 53 Century Boulevard, Suite 300, Nashville TN 37214. **Tel** (615)872-5800. **ED** Daniel Kehren. ctrl circ. ***Continues** IB Magazine, L'Informatique en Marche.*
Desc: Provides practical information for the hands-on business owner and operator.

PE

INFORMAL : ORGANO INDEPENDIENTE DE LA PEQUENA, MICROEMPRESA Y DEL SECTOR INFORMAL, EL. VFOAT Formal. Vol. 1, No. 1 (Jan/Feb 1992)-. Periodical. Spanish. Grupo Alfa, Avenue Arenales 1080, Of. 1003, Santa Beatriz, Lima Peru.

LC HD2341 .I67 **ISSN** 0266-2426
DD 334 UK
Pr Rev.

INTERNATIONAL SMALL BUSINESS JOURNAL. [Int. small bus. j.]. Vol. 2, No. 1 (Autumn 1983)-. Periodical. English (summaries and/or abstracts in French, German and Spanish). Four times a year (Feb., May, Aug., Nov.). $143.75. Woodcock Publications Ltd., PO Box 1, Macclesfield Cheshire, SK10 4YQ United Kingdom. **Tel** 011 44 1625 828712, 011 44 1625 528516, FAX 011 44 1625 532644. **ED** Clive Woodcock. (bound in all issues). cum. index. **Bk Rev. Ad Acc.** available on an online database (file 15/Full-Text) from DIALOG. Documents available from UMI Article Clearinghouse. ***Continues** European Small Business Journal, 0264-6560.*
Desc: Refereed papers on empirical studies, theoretical developments and practical applications in the field of small business and entrepreneurship. Issues are aimed at both academics and policymakers in business and government.
Ind/Abst ABI/INFORM Glob. Ed.; Contents Pages Manage.; Curr. Cit.; Manage. Market. Abstr.; PAIS Int. Print (1991-); Selec. Coop. Index Manage. Period.

Business and Economics — Small Business

LC HD62.7 .J684
DD 338
Pr Rev.
ISSN 1042-6337
US
JOURNAL OF BUSINESS & ENTREPRENEURSHIP. (JOURNAL OF BUSINESS & ENTREPRENEURSHIP : JBE : A PUBLICATION OF THE SOUTHWESTERN SMALL BUSINESS INSTITUTE ASSOCIATION AND THE SCHOOL OF BUSINESS AT NORTHWESTERN STATE UNIVERSITY.). [J. bus. entrep.]. **Added/Corp** Northwestern State University of Louisiana. School of Business. Southwestern Small Business Institute Association (U.S.) California State University, San Bernardino. **VFOAT** Journal of Business and Entrepreneurship; JBE. Vol. 1, No. 1 (Mar. 1989)-. Periodical. English. Two times a year (Mar., Oct.). $45.00. Southwestern Small Business Institute Association, Northwestern State University of Louisiana, Natchitoches LA 71497. **Tel** (318)357-5708. **ED** Drs. S. Durlabhji and Norton Marks. **Circ:** 400.
Desc: Empirical and theoretical articles of interest to academists and practitioners in small business.

LC HD62.7 .J68
DD 658.02/2/05
ISSN 0218-4958
SI
●**JOURNAL OF ENTERPRISING CULTURE.** **Added/Corp** Nanyang Technological University. School of Accountancy & Business. (1993)-. Periodical. English. Four times a year. $96.00. World Scientific Publishing Company, PO Box 128, Farrer Road, Singapore 9128 Singapore. **Tel** 011 65 3825663, FAX 011 65 3825919, telex RS 28561 WSPC. (**Subscription address:** World Scientific Publishing Company, Inc., 1060 Main Street, Suite 1 B, River Edge NJ 07661. **Tel** (800)227-7562, (201)487-9655.)
Desc: Covers research and conceptual development in entrepreneurship, enterprising culture, and entrepreneurship development.

LC HF5601 .J76
DD 657/.0973/05
ISSN 1056-8662
US
TITLE CHANGE
JOURNAL OF PROFESSIONAL BOOKKEEPING AND MANAGEMENT, THE. See Business and Economics-Accounting.

DD 658/.022/0971
ISSN 0827-6331
CN
CCC
JOURNAL OF SMALL BUSINESS AND ENTREPRENEURSHIP. [J. small bus entrep.]. **Added/Corp** International Council for Small Business-Canada. Vol. 3, No. 1 (Summer 1985)-. Periodical. English (French; summaries and/or abstracts in French). Four times a year (Jan., Apr., July, Sept.). 48.02Can$. Centennial College, Center of Entrepreneurship, PO Box 651 Station A, Scarborough Ontario M1K 5E9 Canada. **Tel** FAX (416)439-0219.
Continues Journal of Small Business Canada, 0820-957X.

LC HG4027.7 .J68
DD 658.15/92/05
ISSN 1057-2287
US
CCC
JOURNAL OF SMALL BUSINESS FINANCE, THE. [J. small bus. finance]. Vol. 1, No. 1 (1991)-. Periodical. English. Three times a year. $160.00. JAI Press Inc., 55 Old Post Road, Suite 2, PO Box 1678, Greenwich CT 06836-1678. **Tel** (203)661-7602, FAX (203)661-0792.

LC HD69.S6 J67
DD 658/.022/05
Pr Rev.
ISSN 0047-2778
US
CODEN JSBMAU
JOURNAL OF SMALL BUSINESS MANAGEMENT. See Business and Economics-Management.

DD 658
ISSN 1068-2422
US
KANSAS CITY SMALL BUSINESS MONTHLY. [Kan. City small bus. mon.]. (Feb. 1992)-. Periodical. English. Twelve times a year. $15.00. DBH Communications Inc., 4747 Troost Avenue, #114, Kansas City MO 64110. **Tel** (816)753-7771, FAX (816)753-7791. **ED** David Byrne. **Ad Acc, Adv Mgr:** John Holson. ctrl circ.
Desc: Offers the small business community information on business strategies and techniques.

LC HD2346.I5 K45
DD 338.642
ISSN 0023-1029
II
KHADI GRAMODYOG. [Khadi gramodyog]. **Added/Corp** India. Khadi and Village Industries Commission. All India Khadi and Village Industries Board. Vol. 1, No. 1 (Oct. 1954)-. Periodical. English. Twelve times a year. Khadi and Village Industries Commission, Gramodaya Irla Road Vile Parle West, Bombay 400 056 India.
Ind/Abst Int. Labour Doc.; Maize Abstr.

LC HD2346.K6 K58
KO
KIUN CHOSA WOLBO. Periodical. Korean. Twelve times a year. Chungso Kiop Unhaeng, 36-1 2-ka Ulchi-ro, Chung-ku, Seoul South Korea. **Continues** Chosa Wolbo (Chungso Kiop Unhaeng).

LC HD2346.J3 J38a
JA
KOJIN KIGYO EIGYO CHOSA HOKOKU. **Main/Corp** Japan. Sorifu. Tokeikyoku. (19??)-. Japanese. Somucho Tokeikyoku, (Statistics Bureau Management & Coordination Agency), 19-1 Wakamatsucho Shinjukuku, Tokyo 162 Japan.

LC HD2346.G32 N65
GW
KONJUNKTUR IM HANDWERK, DIE. **Main/Corp** Rheinisch-Westfalisches Institut fur Wirtschaftsforschung Essen. German. One time a year. Duncker und Humblot Verlag, Postfach 410329, D-12113 Berlin Germany. **Tel** 011 49 30 79000612, 011 49 30 79000613. **Continues** Konjunkturberichte uber das Handwerk.

ISSN 1048-2822
US
LAFAYETTE BUSINESS DIGEST. Vol. 1, No. 1 Jan. (1983)-. Periodical. English. Forty-eight times a year. $43.50. Laurendeau Communications, PO Box 587, Lafayette IN 47902. **Tel** (317)742-6918, (800)521-0600, FAX (317)423-8134. **ED** Gwen Rodenberger. cum. index (from 1983-1989). **Ad Acc. Circ:** 9,000. available on microfilm from CMI; available on an online database from CMI. Documents available from UMI Article Clearinghouse.
Ind/Abst Bus. Dateline (Jan. 6, 1992-) [Full Txt.].

LC KF1659.A152 L56
DD 346.73/0652 347.306652
ISSN 0739-1889
US
LIMITED OFFERING EXEMPTIONS: REGULATION D. See Law-Corporation Law.

LC T176
DD 607.273
US
LIST OF SMALL BUSINESS CONCERNS INTERESTED IN PERFORMING RESEARCH AND DEVELOPMENT, A. **Main/Corp** United States. Small Business Administration. 1958-. English. Small Business Administration, 1030 15th Street, Washington DC 20417. **Tel** (202)653-6963.

DD 330.971/064/05
ISSN 1187-4619
CN
MANDAT (WILLOWDALE. 1991). (MANDAT / LA FEDERATION CANADIENNE DE L'ENTREPRISE INDEPENDANTE.). [Mandat]. **Added/Corp** Federation Canadienne de l'Entreprise Independante. **VFOAT** Actualites PME. (1991)-. Periodical. French. Six times a year. Limited Free Distribution. Federation Canadienne de L'Entreprise Independante, 4141 rue Yonge, Toronto Ontario M2P 2A6 Canada. **Continues** Quoi de Neuf? (Willowdale, Ont.)., 0849-2875.

DD 380
ISSN 0888-3327
US
MARKETERS FORUM MAGAZINE. [Mark. forum mag.]. (1984)-. Trade Publication. English. Twelve times a year. $30.00. Forum Publishers Company, 383 East Main Street, Centerpoint NY 11721-1538. **Tel** (516)754-5000, telex 804294. **ED** Martin Stevens. **Bk Rev. Ad Acc. Circ:** 70,000.

DD 650/.09714
ISSN 0848-0877
US
MEMO (QUEBEC). (MEMO.). [Memo]. Vol. 1, No. 1 (Oct. 1989)-. Periodical. French. Six times a year (Feb., Apr., June, Aug., Oct., Dec.). 12.01Can$. Editions du Rineva, 3715 Avenue Lacombe, Bureau 200, Montreal Quebec Canada, H3T 1M3. **Tel** (514)341-7916, FAX (514)341-2644. **ED** Michel Guenard. **Bk Rev. Ad Acc, Adv Mgr:** Maire-Claire Dupre. ctrl circ.

DD 658/.024/0285416
ISSN 0836-3587
CN
MICRO-GAZETTE. [Micro-gaz.]. (1986)-. Periodical. French. Irregular (6 to 10 per year). 29.96Can$ Canada; 46.96Can$ other. Micro-Gazette Inc., 434 A rue Isabey Street, St. Laurent QUE H4T 1V3 Canada. **Tel** (514)735-2992, FAX (514)735-1269. **ED** Gerald Gauthier. **Bk Rev. Ad Acc. Circ:** 12,000.
Desc: Specializing in computer and telecommunications applications related to business.

DD 650
ISSN 1078-1846
US
MINORITY TIMES & SMALL BUSINESS NEWS. [Minor. times & small bus. news]. (199?)-. Periodical. English. Twelve times a year. $20.00. Minority Business Times, 40 Underhill Blvd. Ste. 2D, Syosset NY 11791. **Tel** (516)921-9264. **ED** Trevor Pearson. **Bk Rev,** (Qty: 3). **Ad Acc. Circ:** 15,000. available on an online database. **Continues** Minority Business Times, 1071-8877.

LC JK6188.A1 M55a
DD 353.97760071/2/05
US
MN SMALL BUSINESS PROCUREMENT PROGRAM FOR SOCIALLY OR ECONOMICALLY DISADVANTAGED VENDORS F.Y. ... ANNUAL REPORT. **Main/Corp** Minnesota. Dept. of Administration. Division of Procurement. **VFOAT** M.N. Small Business Procurement Program for Socially or Economically Disadvantaged Vendors F.Y. ... Annual Report; Annual Report on Small Business Procurement Act Fiscal Year ... . **VAT** Minnesota Small Business Procurement Program for Socially or Economically Disadvantaged Vendors F.Y. ... Annual Report. (1982)-. English. One time a year. **Continues** Minnesota. Dept. of Administration. Division of Procurement. Annual Report to the Legislature on the Small Business Procurement Act.

LC HC107.N3 N387
DD 330.9793/005
US
NEVADA BUSINESS & ECONOMIC INDICATORS / NEVADA SMALL BUSINESS CENTER [AND] BUREAU OF BUSINESS AND ECONOMIC RESEARCH, COLLEGE OF BUSINESS ADMINISTRATION, UNIVERSITY OF NEVADA, RENO. **Added/Corp** Nevada Small Business Center. University of Nevada, Reno. Bureau of Business and Economic Research. **VFOAT** Nevada Business and Economic Indicators; Nevada Review of Business and Economics; Nevada Review of Business & Economics. (Winter 1991/1992)-. Periodical. English. Four times a year. $5.00. Bureau of Business & Economic Research / Nevada, University of Nevada, Business Building/Room 415, Reno NV 89557. **Tel** (702)784-6877. **Continues** Nevada Review of Business and Economics.

DD 338
ISSN 1056-0289
US
NEWSINDEX FOR SMALL BUSINESS ENTREPRENEURS, THE. [NewsINDEX small bus. entrep.]. **VFOAT** News Index for Small Business Entrepreneurs. Vol. 1, No. 1 (1991)-. Periodical. English. Twelve times a year. $24.97 US; $34.97 Canada. Newsindex, Box 1045, Clackamas OR 97015.

DD 338
ISSN 0289-6516
JA
NIKKEI BENCHA. [Nikkei bencha]. **VFOAT** Nikkei Venture. (1984)-. Trade Publication. Japanese. Twelve times a year. ¥12200. Nihon Keizai Shimbun Inc., 9-5 Otemachi 1 Chome, Chiyoda-ku Tokyo 100 Japan. **Tel** 011 81 3 32700251, 011 81 3 52108502 (Nikkei Business Publications Inc.), FAX 011 81 3 52552661, 011 81 3 52108119 (Nikkei Business Publications Inc.). **ED** Hiroto Suzuki.
Desc: Information and advice for risk-taking, management, growth, etc.

DD 338.6/42/0971
ISSN 0708-6148
CN
NOUVELLES DE LA PETITE ENTREPRISE. Jan. 1974-. Periodical. French. Four times a year. Banque Federale de Developpement, Services de Gestions-Conseil, CP 6021, Montreal Quebec H3C 3C3 Canada.

DD 343.71306/7/0263
ISSN 0225-1795
CN
ONTARIO CORPORATION AND INCOME TAX LEGISLATION INCLUDING MINING TAXES AND SMALL BUSINESS DEVELOPMENT CORPORATIONS. See Finance-Taxation.

DD 338.6/42/09714
ISSN 0705-0674
CN
P M E : REVUE DE LA PETITE ET MOYENNE ENTREPRISE. **VFOAT** Revue de la Petite et Moyenne Entreprise. **VAT** Petite et Moyenne Entreprise; Revue P.M.E. No. 1 (June 1977)-. Periodical. French. Twelve times a year. $40.00 Canada; $50.00 other. La Revue P M E, Place du Commerce, Suite E 1610 Provencher, Brossard Quebec J4W 2T9 Canada.

LC HC470.T4 P35
KO
PALCHON UL WIHAN TOJON. Vol. 1 (1982)-. Periodical. Korean. Hanguk Sanop Kyongje Kisul Yonguwon, 206-9 Chongnyangni-dong Tongdaemun-ku, Seoul Korea.

LC HD2346.I6 I548A
IO
PERKEMBANGAN PROYEK BIPIK. **Main/Corp** Proyek Bipik (Indonesia). **VAT** Perkembangan Proyek Bimbingan Dan Pengambangan Industri Kecil. Indonesian. Proyek Bipik, Jl Kebon Sirih No 36, Jakarta Indonesia.

DD 381/.45/3333309714
ISSN 0380-6766
CN
PHOTO COMMERCE EXPRESS. See Business and Economics-Commerce.

LC HD62.7 .P5
DD 658.562 IT
PICCOLA IMPRESA = SMALL BUSINESS. **Added/Corp** Universita di Urbino. Facolta di Economia e Commercio. **VFOAT** Small Business. (1987)-. Periodical. Italian (English). Three times a year. L30660. INS Edit Snc, Via Scarsellini 22, 16149 Genoa Italy. **Tel** 011 39 10 6457775.

ISSN 0828-8089
DD 338.6/42/09714 CN
PME (LAVAL). (PME : LE GUIDE OFFICIEL DU SALON DE LA PME.). [PME]. **VAT** Petites et Moyennes Entreprises (Laval). Vol. 1, No. 1 (Oct. 1984)-. Periodical. French. Ten times a year. 18.07Can$. Publications Transcontinental Inc, 1100 Rene-Levesque, 24Fl boulevard West, Montreal Quebec H3B 4X9 Canada. **Tel** (514)392-9000, FAX (514)392-4724. **ED** Claude Beauchamp and Christian Bellavance. **Ad Acc.**
Desc: Edited for small business owners and managers, as well as would-be entrepreneurs. Focuses on practical recipes for success of the small firm.
Ind/Abst Int. Labour Doc.; Repere.

ISSN 1183-188X
DD 657/.9042/0971405 CN
POUR MIEUX ENTREPRENDRE. (POUR MIEUX ENTREPRENDRE : LE BULLETIN DU COMITE DE LA PME.). [Pour mieux entrep.]. **Added/Corp** Ordre des Comptables Agrees du Quebec. Comite de la PME. Vol. 1, No 1 (Jan. 1991)-. Bulletin. French. Four times a year. Limited Free Distribution. Comite de la PME, Ordre des Compatables Agrees du Quebec, A/S P Normandin, 7E Etage, 680 Ouest rue Sherbrooke, Montreal Quebec H3A 2S3 Canada.

ISSN 1183-1898
DD 657/.9042/0971405 CN
POUR MIEUX ENTREPRENDRE : A PUBLICATION OF THE COMMITTEE ON SMALL BUSINESS. [Pour mieux entrep.]. **Added/Corp** Order of Chartered Accountants of Quebec. Committee on Small Business. Vol. 1, No. 1 (Jan. 1991)-. Periodical. English. Four times a year. Limited free distribution. Committee on Small Business, Order of Chartered Accountants of Quebec, 7th Floor, 680 West Sherbrooke Street, Montreal Quebec H3A 2S3 Canada.

ISSN 1183-1324
DD 338.6/42/0971 CN
PROFIT (TORONTO). (PROFIT.). [Profit]. Vol. 9, No. 11 (Nov. 1990)-. Trade Publication. English. Four times a year. 11.96Can$. CB Media Ltd., 777 Bay Street, Toronto Ontario M5W 1A7 Canada. **Tel** (416)596-5100, (416)596-5999, FAX (416)364-2783, (416)362-4505. **(Subscription address:** Indas Customer Service, 35 Riviera Drive, Building 17, Markham Ontario L3R 8N4 Canada. **Tel** (905)946-0406.) **ED** Rick Spence. **Ad Acc. Circ:** 100,000 (ctrl). ***Continues*** *Small Business (Toronto, Ont.), 0833-2223.*
Desc: Magazine for Canadian entrepreneurs.
Ind/Abst Can. Index; Can. Period. Index (19??-).

US
PUBLICATIONS - SMALL BUSINESS ADMINISTRATION. **Main/Corp** United States. Small Business Administration. **VFOAT** Small Business Administration Publications. 1958-. Periodical. English. Small Business Administration, 1030 15th Street, Washington DC 20417. **Tel** (202)653-6963.

ISSN 1076-7452
DD 338 US
●**QUICK-SOLUTIONS (FORT WASHINGTON, MD.).** (QUICK SOLUTIONS: THE SMALL BUSINESS INFORMATION AND COMPUTER GUIDE.). [Quick-solut.]. **VFOAT** Quick Solutions. (July 1994)-. Trade Publication. English. Four times a year (Published seasonally). $6.95 US; $9.95 other. Vincent Shelton, 8621 Trumps Hill Road, Upper Marlboro MD 20772. **Tel** (301)952-9774, FAX (301)699-0193. **ED** Vincent Shelton and B.C. Chancey. **Circ:** 5,000.

LC HT690.B4 B44a
BE
RAPPORT ANNUEL / CONSEIL SUPERIEUR DES CLASSES MOYENNES. **Main/Corp** Belgium. Conseil Superieur des Classes Moyennes. (19??)-. French (Dutch). One time a year. Hoge Raad voor de Middenstand, Liefdadigheidsstraat 24, 1040 Brussels Belgium. **Tel** 02/217.91.43, FAX 02/218.21.44. ctrl circ. ***Continues*** *Belgium. Conseil Superieur des Classes Moyennes. Rapport Annuel du Secretaire General.*

ISSN 1057-1930
DD 338 US
SUSPENDED
RURAL ENTERPRISE (MENOMONEE FALLS, WIS.). (RURAL ENTERPRISE.). [Rural enterp.]. Vol. 1, No. 1, (Summer 1986)-. English. Four times a year. $8.95 (U.S.), $12.95 (Canada). Rural Enterprise, PO Box 878, Menomonee Falls WI 53051.
Ind/Abst AGRICOLA [Full Cov.].

LC HG3729.U5 A3392C **ISSN** 0149-2500
DD 332.6/725 US
SBIC DIGEST. **VFOAT** S.B.I.C. Digest. **VAT** Small Business Investment Companies Digest. Periodical. English. Two times a year. Small Business Administration, 1030 15th Street, Washington DC 20417. **Tel** (202)653-6963. available on microfiche (Vols. for (1983-) distributed to depository libraries). ***Absorbed*** *SBIC Industry Review, 0083-3282.*

LC HD69.S6 S4
DD 658/.022 II
SEDME. **Added/Corp** Small Industry Extension Training Institute (India). **VFOAT** Small Enterprises Development, Management and Extension. Vol. 1 (June 1974)-. Periodical. English. Four times a year. $8.00 US. National Institute of Small Industry Extension Training, Yousufguda, Hyderabad 500 045 India. **ED** C. S. Raman. **Circ:** 425.
Desc: Small enterprises development, management and extension journal.

US
SELECTED ABSTRACTS OF COMPLETED RESEARCH STUDIES / U.S. SMALL BUSINESS ADMINISTRATION, ECONOMIC RESEARCH DIVISION, OFFICE OF ADVOCACY. Fiscal Years 1979-80-. English. Every 2 years. US Small Business Administration, Office of Advocacy, Economic Research Division, 1441 L Street NW, Washington DC 20416.

LC HD2346.U5 U57C **ISSN** 0742-3802
DD 353.9982/048/06 US
SEMI-ANNUAL REPORT OF THE INSPECTOR GENERAL, U.S. SMALL BUSINESS ADMINISTRATION. (SEMI-ANNUAL REPORT OF THE INSPECTOR GENERAL, U.S. SMALL BUSINESS ADMINISTRATION : PURSUANT TO PUBLIC LAW 95-452.). **Main/Corp** United States. Small Business Administration. Office of Inspector General. (April/Sept. 1979)-. English. Two times a year. Office of Inspector General, United States Small Business Administration, 409 Third Street SW, 7th Floor, Washington DC 20416. **Tel** (202)205-6580. **Circ:** 500 (ctrl). available on microfiche (Vols. for (April 1-Sept. 30, 1986-) distributed to depository libraries).

US
●**SERIOUS ABOUT SMALL BUSINESS.** (Summer 1995)-. English. **Bk Rev.**
Desc: Filled with ideas and sound business insights for small business owners.

ISSN 1081-2253
DD 338 US
SET-ASIDE CONTRACT OPPORTUNITIES. **VFOAT** Set Aside Contract Opportunities. (19??)-. Periodical. English. Twenty-four times a year. $187.00. Pasha Publications Inc., 1616 North Fort Myer Drive, Suite 1000, Arlington VA 22209. **Tel** (800)424-2908, (703)528-1244, FAX (703)528-3742, (703)528-1253.

LC HF5421.5.J3 S439
JA
SHOKIGYO NO KEIEI SHIHYO / KOKUMIN KINYU KOKO CHOSABU HEN. **See** Business and Economics-Commerce.

ISSN 0383-719X
DD 016.3386/42/0971 CN
SMALL BUSINESS, A CANADIAN VIEWPOINT. June 1972-. Periodical. English. Metropolitan Toronto Library Board, 789 Yonge Street, Toronto Ontario M4W 2G8 Canada. **Tel** (416)393-7134, telex 06-22232.

LC KF1659 .A297 **ISSN** 0502-2150
DD 346/.73/0652 US
SMALL BUSINESS ADMINISTRATION AND INVESTMENT ACT WITH AMENDMENTS. **Main/Corp** United States. (1953/61)-. English. $1.75 single issue. Small Business Administration, 1030 15th Street, Washington DC 20417. **Tel** (202)653-6963.

US
SMALL BUSINESS CHRONICLE. (1988)-. Trade Publication. English. Twelve times a year. $18.00. Philadelphia Small Business Chronicle, 426 Pennsylvania Avenue, Suite 3, Ft Washington PA 19034. **Tel** (215)540-9440, FAX (215)540-9442. **ED** John Hayes. **Bk Rev. Ad Acc. Circ:** 35,000 (ctrl).
Desc: How-to articles for businesses.

ISSN 0736-6957
DD 004 US
CODEN SBCNDL
SMALL BUSINESS COMPUTER NEWS. **See** Business and Economics-Computer Applications.

ISSN 1081-2245
DD 338 US
SMALL BUSINESS CONTRACT OPPORTUNITIES. [Small bus. contract oppor.]. (19??)-. Periodical. English. Twenty-four times a year. $187.00. Pasha Publications Inc., 1616 North Fort Myer Drive, Suite 1000, Arlington VA 22209. **Tel** (800)424-2908, (703)528-1244, FAX (703)528-3742, (703)528-1253.

LC HG4001 .F56 **ISSN** 1053-766X
DD 658.15/92/05 US
SMALL BUSINESS CONTROLLER, THE. [Small bus. control.]. **Added/Corp** Warren, Gorham & Lamont, Inc. Vol. 3, No. 4 (Fall 1990)-. Trade Publication. English. Four times a year. $95.98. Warren Gorham & Lamont Inc., Park Square Building, 31 St. James Avenue, Boston MA 02116-4112. **Tel** (617)423-2020, (800)950-1207, FAX (617)423-2026. available on microfilm and microfiche from University Microfilms International (UMI). ***Continues*** *Financial Manager, 1040-0842.*
Ind/Abst Account. Art.

ISSN 1080-0816
DD 338 US
●**SMALL BUSINESS ECONOMIC TRENDS.** [Small bus. econ. trends]. **Added/Corp** NFIB Education Foundation. **VFOAT** NFIB Quarterly Economic Report for Small Business. (1993)-. Periodical. English. Twelve times a year. $150.00. NFIB Education Foundation, 600 Maryland Avenue Southwest, Suite 700, Washington DC 20024. **Tel** (202)554-9000. ***Continues*** *Quarterly Economic Report for Small Business (San Mateo, Calif. : 1986), 1080-0913.*

LC HD2341 .S57 **ISSN** 0921-898X
DD 338.6/42/05 NE
CCC
CODEN SBECEX
SMALL BUSINESS ECONOMICS. [Small bus. econ.]. Vol. 1, No. 1 (1989)-. Periodical. English. Six times a year. $390.00. Kluwer Academic Publishers, Postbus 322, 3300 AH Dordrecht The Netherlands. **Tel** 011 31 78 524400, FAX 011 31 78 183273, telex 20083. **ED** Zoltan Acs. **Bk Rev. Ad Acc. Acid Free.** available on microfilm and microfiche from University Microfilms International (UMI). Documents available from The Genuine Article, UMI Article Clearinghouse.
Desc: Forum for economic analysis of the role of small business. Contains research employing theoretical or quantitative analysis from both a national and international perspective.
Ind/Abst ABI/INFORM Glob. Ed.; Curr. Cit.; Curr. Contents Soc. Behav. Sci.; Econ. Lit. Index; Res. Alert [Full Cov.]; Soc. Sci. Cit. Index [Full Cov.].

ISSN 1060-8184
DD 338 US
CEASED
SMALL BUSINESS EMPLOYEE ASSISTANCE. **See** Business and Economics-Personnel Management.

ISSN 0892-5992
US
SMALL BUSINESS EXCHANGE. (SMALL BUSINESS EXCHANGE : SBE.). [Small bus. exch.]. **VFOAT** SBE. (198?)-. Periodical. English. One time a week. $300.00. SBE / Small Business Exchange, 926 Natoma Street, San Francisco CA 94103. **Tel** (415)255-6411, FAX (415)255-6416. **(Subscription address:** SBE / Small Business Exchange, PO Box 422609, San Francisco CA 94142-2609. **Tel** (415)255-6411, (213)688-2848, (916)422-4942.) **ED** Gerald Johnson. **Ad Acc, Adv Mgr:** Robert Kratz. ***Continues*** *Minority Business Exchange.*
Desc: Products and services outreach reporting sub-bid requests and public/legal notices throughout California.

ISSN 1053-4695
DD 338 US
Pr Rev.
SMALL BUSINESS FORUM. (SMALL BUSINESS FORUM : THE JOURNAL OF THE ASSOCIATION OF SMALL BUSINESS DEVELOPMENT CENTERS.). [Small bus. forum]. **Added/Corp** University of Wisconsin Small Business Development Center. Association of Small Business Development Centers. **VFOAT** Journal of the Association of Small Business Development Centers. Vol. 8, No. 1 (Spring 1990)-. Trade Publication. English. Three times a year (Apr., July, Nov.). $40.00. Small Business Development Center, 432 North Lake Street, 425 Ext. Building, Madison WI 53706. **Tel** (608)263-7843, FAX (608)262-3878. **ED** Catherine Stover. Index available (published separately). cum. index. **Bk Rev**, (Qty: 9). **Circ:** 2,500. ***Continues*** *Wisconsin Small Business Forum, 0737-3597.*
Desc: The forum helps owners of small and growing businesses and their advisors with current, practical and theoretically-sound management information.

ISSN 1076-4488
US
●**SMALL BUSINESS HEALTH REFORM WATCH.** (1994)-. Periodical. English. Twelve times a year. $196.00. Aspen Publishers Inc., 7201 McKinney

Business and Economics — Small Business

Circle, Frederick MD 21701. **Tel** (800)234-1660, (301)698-7100, FAX (301)251-5784, telex 5106014543. **(Subscription address:** Aspen Publishers Inc., PO Box 990, Frederick MD 21701. **Tel** (800)901-9074, (301)698-7100.**)**

US
SMALL BUSINESS INVESTMENT COMPANY DIRECTORY AND HANDBOOK. **See** Industry and Production-Trade and Industrial Directories.

US
SMALL BUSINESS JOURNAL. (19??)-.
English. National Small Business Benefits Association, 2276 East Reservoir, Springfield IL 62702.

ISSN 1059-6550
DD 338 US
SMALL BUSINESS LETTER, THE. [Small bus. lett.]. Vol. 1, No. 1 (1991)-. Periodical. English. Twelve times a year. $20.00. Small Business Publishing Co., 200 West El Norte Parkway, Suite 260, Escondido CA 92026.

AT
SMALL BUSINESS LETTER. (19??)-.
Periodical. English. Twenty-three times a year. 102.77Aus$. Ian Huntley Publishers Pty Limited, PO Box 99, Cremorne NSW 2090 Australia. **Tel** 011 61 2 9535788, FAX 011 61 2 9532280.

ISSN 0887-4050
DD 658 US
SMALL BUSINESS PREFERENTIAL SUBCONTRACT OPPORTUNITIES MONTHLY. [Small bus. prefer. subcontract oppor. mon.]. **Added/Corp** Government Data Publications (Firm). (198?)-. Periodical. English. Twelve times a year. $84.00. Government Data Publications / New York, GDP Building, 1661 McDonald Avenue, Brooklyn NY 11230. **Tel** (718)627-0819.

US
SMALL BUSINESS REGISTER. **Added/Corp** Ohio. Office of Small Business. (1985)-. Periodical. English. One time a week. Ohio Department of Economic and Community Development, PO Box 1001, Columbus OH 43266. **Tel** (614)466-2285.

LC HD2346.U5 S64 ISSN 0164-5382
DD 658/.022/0973 US
CEASED
SMALL BUSINESS REPORT (MONTEREY, CALIF.). (SMALL BUSINESS REPORT.). [Small bus. rep.]. **Added/Corp** American Management Association. **VFOAT** Small Business Reports. (1976)-(1995). Periodical. English. American Management Association, 135 West 50th Street, New York NY 10020-1201. **Tel** (212)586-8100, (212)903-8375 (periodicals), FAX (212)903-8168, (212)903-8083 (periodicals). **ED** Tom Owens. Index available (bound in March issue). cum. index. **Bk Rev. Ad Acc. Circ:** 60,000. available on microfilm and microfiche from University Microfilms International (UMI). Documents available from UMI Article Clearinghouse.
Desc: Intelligence summaries and strategy tools for business decision makers.
Ind/Abst ABI/INFORM Glob. Ed.; ABI/INFORM Ondisc: Expr. Ed.; ABI/INFORM [Computer File] (1979-); Acad. Search; Bus. ASAP (1992-) [Full Txt.]; Bus. Index (1985-); Bus. Period. Index; Bus. Source Plus; Bus. Source; Curr. Cit.; EP Collect.; Gen. BusinessFile (1985-); Gen. Period. Index (1985-); Homework Help.; INFO-SOUTH Abstr.; Mag. Search; MasterFile FullTEXT 1000; MasterFile FullTEXT 350; MasterFile FullTEXT 650; MasterFile FullTEXT (July 1994-Nov. 1994) [Full Txt.]; OCLC; Pub. Lib. FullTEXT; Telebase; Trade Ind. Index [Full Txt.]; UMI ABI/Inform--Bus. Period. Ondisc (Jan. 1987-) [Full Txt.]; Vocat. Search; Wilson Bus. Abstr.; Work Relat. Abstr.

ISSN 0824-3719
DD 338.6/42/0971 CN
SMALL BUSINESS REPORT (OTTAWA). (SMALL BUSINESS REPORT.). [Small bus. rep.]. **Added/Corp** New Democratic Party. (1982)-. Periodical. English. Free. New Democratic Party, House of Commons, Ottawa Ontario K1A 0A6 Canada.

US
SMALL BUSINESS REVIEW. English. Four times a year. $98.50. Antitrust Law and Economic Review Inc., PO Box 3532, Vero Beach FL 32964. **Tel** FAX (407)461-6007. **ED** Charles E. Mueller.

LC HD2346.U5 S66 ISSN 0883-3397
DD 658/.022/07073 US
SMALL BUSINESS SOURCEBOOK. [Small bus. sourceb.]. **Added/Corp** Gale Research Company. 1st Ed. (1983)-. English. $235.00. Gale Research Inc., 835 Penobscot Building, 645 Griswold Street, Detroit MI 48226. **Tel** (800)877-GALE, (313)961-2242, FAX (313)961-6083, (800)414-5043, telex TWX 810-221-7086. **ED** Kathleen Maki. available on magnetic tape; available on diskette.
Desc: Provides the resources that help small business owners and entrepreneurs compete. A small business profile is provided for each small business, including a variety of retail, service, and manufacturing operations. Each profile contains listings for key sources of assistance, training, expertise, supplies, trade statistics, and more.

ISSN 1063-0252
US
SMALL BUSINESS SPOTLIGHT NEWS.
(1992)-. Periodical. English. Twelve times a year. $25.00. ML Publishing, PO Box 310815, Flint MI 31085.

LC HG4057 .A474 ISSN 0741-4811
DD 338.6/42/02573 US
SMALL BUSINESS SUBCONTRACTING DIRECTORY. (19??)-. Directory. English. Small Business Administration, 1030 15th Street, Washington DC 20417. **Tel** (202)653-6963.

LC KF6491.A15 S63 ISSN 0276-5322
DD 343.7306/8 347.30368 US
SMALL BUSINESS TAX REVIEW, THE.
See Finance-Taxation.

ISSN 0732-5525
US
SMALL BUSINESS TAX SAVER. Vol. 1, No. 1 (Sept. 1982)-. Periodical. English. Twelve times a year. $72.00. Enterprise Publishing Inc, 725 North Market Street, Wilmington DE 19801.

US
SMALL BUSINESS TODAY. Newspaper. English. Twelve times a year. $15.00. Small Business News, 20800 Center Ridge Road, Rocky River OH 44116. **Tel** (216)331-6397, FAX (216)333-4969. **ED** Lou Reyes Jr. **Bk Rev. Ad Acc. Adv Mgr:** Lena, **Tel** (216)331-6397. **Circ:** 32,000 (ctrl).
Desc: News and information on the small business of today.

ISSN 0835-4251
DD 051 CN
SUSPENDED
SMALL BUSINESS WORLD MAGAZINE.
[Small bus. world mag.]. Vol. 1, No. 1 (Summer 1987)-?. Periodical. English. Six times a year. 10.00Can$ (one-year), 18.00Can$ (two-year). Small Business World Magazine, PO Box 228, Station A, Ottawa Ontario K1N 8V2 Canada. **Tel** (613)733-4260.

LC HD28 ISSN 0968-1000
DD 658.022 UK
SMALL BUSINESSES AND SMALL BUSINESS DEVELOPMENT. [Small bus. small bus. develop.]. (1991)-. Trade Publication. English. Three times a year. $135.00. John Wiley & Sons Ltd., Baffins Lane, Chichester, West Sussex PO19 1UD United Kingdom. **Tel** 011 44 1243 779777, FAX 011 44 1243 776128 BTG:JWP001, telex 86290 WIBOOKG. **ED** Bill Richardson. **Bk Rev.** Documents available from BLDSC.
Desc: Concentrates on the creation and management of small businesses.

ISSN 0094-2464
US
SMALL BUSINESSMAN'S CLINIC. (19??)-.
Periodical. English. Twelve times a year. $28.00. Austin M. Elliott PE, 113 Vista del Largo, Scotts Valley CA 95066. **Tel** (408)438-1411. **ED** Austin M. Elliott. Index available. cum. index. **Circ:** 300 (ctrl).

ISSN 0957-1329
UK
SMALL ENTERPRISE DEVELOPMENT.
(1990)-. Periodical. English. Four times a year. $102.67. Intermediate Technology Publications Ltd., 103-104 Southampton Row, London WC1B 4HH United Kingdom. **Tel** 011 44 171 436 9761, FAX 011 44 171 436 2013, telex 268312. **ED** Clare Tawney. **Bk Rev. Ad Acc. Circ:** 600.
Desc: For everyone involved in the design and implementation of small business development programs, especially in developing countries. Contains detailed articles reporting original research, program evaluations and significant new approaches. Also case studies of projects, and grants from international and local agencies.
Ind/Abst Geogr. Abstr. Human Geogr.; Int. Bibliogr. Sociol.; Int. Dev. Abstr.; Int. Labour Doc.; LABORDOC; Person. Manage. Abstr.

LC HD2346.U5 U57a ISSN 0362-417X
DD 338.6/42/0973 US
SMALL ENTERPRISE IN THE ECONOMY. **Main/Corp** United States. Small Business Administration. Office of Advocacy, Planning, and Research. (19??)-. Periodical. English. Four times a year. Small Business Administration, 1030 15th Street, Washington DC 20417. **Tel** (202)653-6963.

LC HD2346.A744 U5a ISSN 0252-3426
DD 338.6/42/09505 US
UDC 6:(5)(5):6
SMALL INDUSTRY BULLETIN FOR ASIA AND THE PACIFIC. [Small ind. bull. Asia Pac.].
Main/Corp United Nations. Economic and Social Commission for Asia and the Pacific. **Added/Corp** United Nations. Economic and Social Commission for Asia and the Pacific. No. 12 (1974)-. Bulletin. English (summaries and/or abstracts in French). One time a year. $12.00. United Nations Publications, 2 United Nations Plaza, Room DC2 0853, Department 007C, New York NY 10017. **Tel** (212)963-8303, (800)253-9646. **Continues** Small Industry Bulletin for Asia and the Far East, 0081-0150.
Desc: Covers credit and financing facilities, management and problems or difficulties facing small industries, and the promotion of small-scale industry in developing countries.

ISSN 1184-602X
DD 658.15/92/0971 CN
SOURCES FOR SUCCESSFUL SMALL BUSINESS FINANCING IN CANADA.
[Sources success. small bus. financ. Can.]. **Added/Corp** Entrepreneurial Business Consultants of Canada. (1989/1990)-. English. One time a year. 244.10Can$. Productive Publications, PO Box 7200, Station A, Toronto Ontario M5W 1X8 Canada. **Tel** (416)483-0634. **Continues** Williamson, Iain. Successful Small Business Financing in Canada., 0834-3004.
Desc: Provides specific details on over 680 government programs and sub-programs, informal investors and network addresses, venture capital, and more.

LC HD70.U5 S617 ISSN 1055-0119
DD 658.02/2/097305 US
SOUTHWEST BUSINESS REVIEW (SAN MARCOS, TEX.). (SOUTHWEST BUSINESS REVIEW.). **Added/Corp** Southwest Texas State University. School of Business. Vol. 1, No. 1 (Spring 1991)-. Periodical. English. Two times a year. $30.00 (institutions), $12.00 (individuals) US; $15.00 (individuals) Canada. Southwest Texas State University / Business, School of Business, San Marcos TX 78666.

LC HD2346.U5 S78 ISSN 0735-1437
DD 338.6/42/0973 US
STATE OF SMALL BUSINESS, THE. (THE STATE OF SMALL BUSINESS : A REPORT OF THE PRESIDENT TRANSMITTED TO THE CONGRESS.). [State small bus.]. **Added/Corp** United States. President. United States. Small Business Administration. United States. Small Business Administration. Annual Report on Small Business and Competition of the U.S. Small Business Administration. **VFOAT** AAnnual Report on Small Business and Competition of the U.S. Small Business Administration. (1982)-. Periodical. English. One time a year. Small Business Administration, 1030 15th Street, Washington DC 20417. **Tel** (202)653-6963.

LC HD2346.U5 D57 ISSN 0742-843X
DD 353.9/382048/025 US
STATES AND SMALL BUSINESS, THE.
(THE STATES AND SMALL BUSINESS : PROGRAMS AND ACTIVITIES.). [States small bus.]. Oct. 1983-. English. One time a year. Small Business Administration, 1030 15th Street, Washington DC 20417. **Tel** (202)653-6963. **Continues** Directory of State Small Business Offices and Activities, 0736-7546.

LC KF6491.Z9 P73
DD 343.7306/8 US
SUBCHAPTER S ELECTION FOR "SMALL BUSINESS CORPORATIONS.",
THE. **Main/Corp** Prentice-Hall, Inc. (19??)-. English. $1.60. Prentice-Hall Law and Business, 270 Sylvan Avenue, Englewood Cliffs NJ 07632. **Tel** (800)223-0231, (201)894-8538, FAX (201)894-8666.

LC HF5001 .S77 ISSN 0161-2042
DD 658/.022/05 US
SUCCESSFUL BUSINESS. [Success. bus.].
Vol. 1 (Winter 1978)-. Periodical. English. Four times a year. $6.00. 13-30 Corporation, 505 Market Street, Knoxville TN 37902. **Tel** (615)521-0600. available on an online database (file 635/Full-Text) from DIALOG. Documents available from UMI Article Clearinghouse.
Ind/Abst Bus. Dateline (June 9, 1987-) [Full Txt.].

LC HD2346.U5 S94 ISSN 0743-6998
DD 338.6/42/0973 US
SUMMARY OF RESEARCH AWARDS.
English. US Small Business Administration, Office of Advocacy, Economic Research Division, 1441 L Street NW, Washington DC 20416.

LC KF6491.A73 I5 ISSN 0083-1484
DD 336.2 US
TAX GUIDE FOR SMALL BUSINESS. **See** Finance-Taxation.

ISSN 0746-0384
US
CCC
TAX UPDATE FOR BUSINESS OWNERS. **See** Finance-Taxation.

LC HD2346.J3 T634 JA
TOKUTEI SANGYO SHOKIBO KIGYO RODO JOKEN JITTAI CHOSA HOKOKU. **See** Business and Economics-Labor.

LC HF5601
DD 657 UK
VERY SMALL COMPANY AUDIT SYSTEM. **See** Business and Economics-Accounting.

ISSN 0824-4472
DD 338.6/42/0971134 CN
VICTORIA BUSINESS REVIEW. [Vic. bus. rev.]. Vol. 1, No. 1 (Feb. 1983)-. Periodical. English. Twelve times a year. 0.75Can$ each number. Victoria Business Review, 1157 Newport Avenue, Victoria British Columbia V8S 5E6 Canada.

ISSN 0037-7198
US
VOICE OF SMALL BUSINESS, THE. **Added/Corp** National Small Business Association. Vol. 33, No. 8 (Aug. 1970)-. Periodical. English. Twelve times a year. $50.00. National Small Businessmens Association, 1155 15th Street Northwest, Washington DC 20005. **Tel** (202)293-8830. **Circ:** 50,000 (ctrl). ***Continues*** *Small Business Bulletin (National Small Business Association).*
Desc: Information on the spectrum of small business interest from a national viewpoint, the majority of which is basically legislative.

ISSN 0897-5116
DD 322 US
WISCONSIN SMALL BUSINESS COUNSELOR. [Wisc. small bus. couns.]. **VFOAT** Counselor. (198?)-. Trade Publication. English. Ten times a year (Sept.- May, & July). $54.00. Counselor Magazine, PO Box 1896, Green Bay WI 54305. **Tel** (414)435-0808, FAX (414)432-8581. **ED** Phillip C. Hauck. cum. index. **Bk Rev**, (Qty: 12). **Ad Acc. Circ:** 3,000.
Desc: Information and tips to help Wisconsin independent business people manage their assets better.

LC HG4027.7 .Y68 **ISSN** 0736-4865
DD 332.024/005 US
YOU AND YOUR BUSINESS. **Added/Corp** Central Fidelity Bank (Tysons Corner, Va.). Vol. 1, No. 1 (1982)-. Periodical. English. Twelve times a year. Thomas J. Martin, 383 South Broadway, Hicksville NY 11801. **Tel** (516)681-2111.

CHEMISTRY AND CHEMICALS

UK
100 MODERN REAGENTS. (19??)-. English. £24.00. Royal Society of Chemistry, Thomas Graham House, Science Park, Cambridge CB4 4WF United Kingdom. **Tel** 011 44 1223 420066, FAX 011 44 1223 423623, telex 818293 ROYAL. **(Subscription address:** Royal Society of Chemistry, Turpin Distribution Services Ltd., Blackhorse Road, Letchworth, Hertfordshire SG6 1HN United Kingdom. **Tel** 011 44 1462 672555, FAX 011 44 1462 480947.**)** **ED** N. S. Simpkins.
Desc: Includes the following data on each reagent listed: name, structure, molecular formula, molecular weight, physical properties, preparation and/or suppliers, price range and safety precautions needed. The reagents area arranged in alphabetical order and cover two pages each, with the second page providing three reaction schemes highlighting the uses of the reagent.

ISSN 0065-7727
US
CCC
NLM W1 AB884 **CODEN** ACSRAL
ABSTRACTS OF PAPERS - AMERICAN CHEMICAL SOCIETY. [Abstr. pap. - Am. Chem. Soc.]. **Added/Corp** American Chemical Society. 93rd Ed. (1937)-. English. Two times a year. $49.00. American Chemical Society, 1155 Sixteenth Street Northwest, Washington DC 20036. **Tel** (800)333-9511, (800)227-5558, (614)447-3776, FAX (202)447-3671. **(Subscription address:** American Chemical Society / Washington D.C., PO Box 57136, West End Station, Washington DC 20037. **Tel** (800)227-5558.**)** Documents available from The Genuine Article, BIOSIS Document Express, CASDDS.
Ind/Abst Biodeter. Abstr.; Biol. Abstr.; Chem. Abstr. (1937-1985); GeoRef; Lit. Pat. Abstr., Oilfield Chem. (1958-); Lit. Abstr., Catal. Zeol.; Lit. Abstr., Health Environ.; Lit. Abstr., Pet. Refin. Petrochem.; Lit. Abstr., Pet. Substit.; Lit. Abstr., Transp. Storage; Mass Spect. Bull.; PESTDOC; Res. Alert [Full Cov.]; Sci. Cit. Index; SCISEARCH; Soc. Sci. Cit. Index [Select. Cov.]; Text. Technol. Dig.; Vitis Vitic. Enol. Abstr.; World Surf. Coat. Abstr.; World Text. Abstr.

ISSN 0705-5560
DD 540/.5 CN
ACADIAN LETTERS. **Added/Corp** Acadia Chemistry Club. (1977)-. Periodical. English. Six times a year. 5.00Can$ recommended donation. Acadian Letters, Chemistry Department, Acadia University, Wolfville Nova Scotia B0P 1X0 Canada. **Tel** (902)542-2201. **ED** C R Eisnor. Index available. cum. index. **Bk Rev. Ad Acc. Circ:** 750.
Desc: A communication among those interested in education in chemistry and related fields, generally junior high through senior high school.

LC QD1 .A275 **ISSN** 0001-4842
DD 540/.5 US
CCC
NLM W1 AC728 **CODEN** ACHRE4
Pr Rev.
ACCOUNTS OF CHEMICAL RESEARCH. [Acc. chem. res.]. **Added/Corp** American Chemical Society. Vol. 1 (Jan. 1968)-. Periodical. English. Twelve times a year. $237.00. American Chemical Society, 1155 Sixteenth Street Northwest, Washington DC 20036. **Tel** (800)333-9511, (800)227-5558, (614)447-3776, FAX (202)447-3671. **(Subscription address:** American Chemical Society / Ohio, Department L 0011, Columbus OH 43268-0011. **)** **ED** F. W. McLafferty. **Acid Free. Circ:** 7,000. available on microfilm and microfiche from University Microfilms International (UMI); available on an online database from STN International. Documents available from The Genuine Article, CASDDS, Documents on Demand.
Desc: A publication offering short, critical reviews written by scientists active in the research described.
Ind/Abst Abstr. Bull. Inst. Pap. Sci. Tech.; Chem. Abstr.; Chem. Titles; Coal Abstr.; Curr. Chem. React.; Curr. Cit.; Curr. Contents Life Sci.; Curr. Contents Phys. Chem. Earth Sci.; Dairy Sci. Abstr.; EMBASE; Energy Inf. Abstr.; Energy Res. Abstr.; Environ. Abstr.; GeoRef; Index Sci. Rev. [Full Cov.]; INIS Atomindex [Micro.]; Int. Aerosp. Abstr.; Leadscan; Mass Spect. Bull.; Methods Organ. Synth.; Nat. Prod. Updates; Life Sci. Collect.; Ref. Upd. Deluxe Ed.; Res. Alert [Full Cov.]; Sci. Cit. Index; SCISEARCH.

LC QD1 .M33 **ISSN** 1217-8969
DD 540/.5 HU
CCC
NLM W1; AC7289 **CODEN** ACMCEI
•ACH, MODELS IN CHEMISTRY. **Added/Corp** Magyar Tudomanyos Akademia. **VFOAT** Models in Chemistry; Acta Chimica Hungarica Models in Chemistry. Vol. 131, No. 1 (Feb. 1994)-. Academic Scholarly Publication. English. Six times a year. $164.00. Akademiai Kiado, Publishing House of the Hungarian Academy of Sciences, Prielle Kornelia u. 19-35, H-1117 Budapest Hungary. **Tel** 011 36 1 1811991, FAX 011 36 1 1811991, telex 22-6228 AKNYO H. ***Continues*** *Acta Chimica Hungarica, 0231-3146.*
Ind/Abst Chem. Abstr.; Curr. Cit.

US
ACS MONOGRAPH. **Main/Corp** American Chemical Society. **VAT** American Chemical Society Monograph. No. 164 (1968)-. Monographic series. English. Irregular. Price varies per volume. American Chemical Society, 1155 Sixteenth Street Northwest, Washington DC 20036. **Tel** (800)333-9511, (800)227-5558, (614)447-3776, FAX (202)447-3671. **(Subscription address:** American Chemical Society / Washington D.C., PO Box 57136, West End Station, Washington DC 20037. **Tel** (800)227-5558.**)** Documents available from BIOSIS Document Express, CASDDS. ***Continues*** *American Chemical Society. Monograph.*
Ind/Abst Biol. Abstr.; Chem. Abstr.

ISSN 0097-6156
DD 540 US
CCC
CODEN ACSMC8
Pr Rev.
ACS SYMPOSIUM SERIES. [ACS symp. ser.]. **Main/Corp** American Chemical Society. No. 1 (1974)-. Monographic series. English. Irregular. Price varies per volume. American Chemical Society, 1155 Sixteenth Street Northwest, Washington DC 20036. **Tel** (800)333-9511, (800)227-5558, (614)447-3776, FAX (202)447-3671. **(Subscription address:** American Chemical Society / Washington D.C., PO Box 57136, West End Station, Washington DC 20037. **Tel** (800)227-5558.**)** Documents available from Article Express International, The Genuine Article, BIOSIS Document Express, UMI Article Clearinghouse, Ask*IEEE, CASDDS.
Ind/Abst AGRICOLA [Select. Cov.]; Anim. Breed. Abstr.; Biocont. News Inf.; Biodeter. Abstr. (1991-); Bioeng. Abstr.; Biol. Abstr.; Ceram. Abstr. (19??-); Chem Inform; Chem. Abstr.; Coal Abstr.; Crop Physiol. Abstr.; Curr. Biotechnol.; Curr. Cit.; Dairy Sci. Abstr.; Ei Page One; Eng. Index Annu.; Field Crop Abstr.; Food Sci. Technol. Abstr.; For. Prod. Abstr. (1991-); GeoRef; Grass. Forage Abstr.; Hortic. Abstr.; Index Sci. Rev. [Full Cov.]; Index Vet.; INIS Atomindex [Micro.]; INSPEC (1986-); Lit. Pat. Abstr., Oilfield Chem. (1977-); Lit. Abstr., Catal. Zeol.; Lit. Abstr., Health Environ.; Lit. Abstr., Pet. Refin. Petrochem.; Lit. Abstr., Pet. Substit.; Lit. Abstr., Transp. Storage; Nematol. Abstr.; Plant Grow. Reg. Abstr.; Polymer Contents; Postharvest News Inf.; Res. Alert [Full Cov.]; Rev. Agric. Entomol.; Rev. Med. Vet. Entomol.; Rev. Plant Pathol.; Sci. Cit. Index; SCISEARCH; Soc. Sci. Cit. Index [Select. Cov.]; Soils Fert.; Soyabean Abstr.; Sug. Indus. Abstr.; Weed Abstr.

LC QD1 .M33 **ISSN** 0231-3146
DD 540/.5 HU
CCC
NLM W1; AC775R **CODEN** ACHUDC
Pr Rev. **TITLE CHANGE**
ACTA CHIMICA HUNGARICA. [Acta chim. Hun.]. **Added/Corp** Magyar Tudomanyos Akademia. Vol. 112, No. 1 (Jan. 1983)-(1993). Academic Scholarly Publication. English. Akademiai Kiado, Publishing House of the Hungarian Academy of Sciences, Prielle Kornelia u. 19-35, H-1117 Budapest Hungary. **Tel** 011 36 1 1811991, FAX 011 36 1 1811991, telex 22-6228 AKNYO H. **ED** Ferenc Marta and Gyula Deak (editorial address: Acta Chimica Hungarica, PO Box 67, H-1450 Budapest Hungary). **Ad Acc.** Documents available from The Genuine Article, BIOSIS Document Express, CASDDS. ***Continues*** *Acta Chemica Academiae Scientiarun Hungaricae, 0001-5407.* ***Continued by*** *ACH, Models in Chemistry, 1217-8969.*
Desc: Publishes original articles in the field of general, analytical, physical, inorganic and organic chemistry, macromolecular science, medicinal chemistry, and chemical technology.
Ind/Abst Alum. Ind. Abstr.; Anal. Abstr.; Biol. Abstr.; Chem Inform; Chem. Abstr. (1983-); Chem. Titles; Curr. Biotechnol.; Curr. Chem. React.; Curr. Cit.; Curr. Contents Phys. Chem. Earth Sci.; EMBASE; Food Sci. Technol. Abstr.; Index Chem.; Maize Abstr.; Mass Spect. Bull.; Met. Abstr.; Methods Organ. Synth.; Nat. Prod. Updates; Life Sci. Collect. (1985-); PESTDOC; Res. Alert [Full Cov.]; Sci. Cit. Index; SCISEARCH; Soyabean Abstr.

LC QD1 .V57 **ISSN** 1318-0207
DD 540/.5 XV
CODEN ACSLE7
•ACTA CHIMICA SLOVENICA. **Added/Corp** Slovensko Kemijsko Drustvo. (1993)-. Periodical. English (Slovenian). Four times a year. Slovenian Chemical Society, Hajdrihova 19, 61115 Ljubljana Slovenia. ***Continues*** *Vestnik Slovenskega Kemijskega Drustva, 0560-3110.*
Ind/Abst Chem. Abstr.; Curr. Cit.

LC QD1 .A3293 **ISSN** 0253-7338
DD 540/.5 II
CODEN ACICDV
ACTA CIENCIA INDICA. CHEMISTRY. [Acta cienc. indica, Chem.]. **Added/Corp** Society for the Progress of Science (India). **VFOAT** Chemistry. Vol. 5, No. 1 (1979)-. Academic Scholarly Publication. English. Four times a year. $50.00. Pragati Prakashan, PO Box 62, Begum Bridge, 250001 Meerut India. **Tel** 73022. **(Subscription address:** Prints India, 11 Darya Ganj, New Delhi 110002 India. **Tel** 011 91 11 3268645, FAX 011 91 11 3275542, telex 31-61087 PRIN-IN.**)** **ED** V.P. Kudesia. cum. index. **Bk Rev. Ad Acc. Circ:** 1,000. Documents available from Ask*IEEE, CASDDS. ***Continues in part*** *Acta Ciencia Indica, 0379-5411.*
Desc: Covers analytical chemistry, physical chemistry, kinetics of the oxidation of organic chemistry, studies on chromosomes, and physico-organic chemical oxidation of hippuric acid.
Ind/Abst Chem. Abstr.; Curr. Cit.; INSPEC (1979-); Math. Rev.

LC QC **ISSN** 0567-7947
DD 530 HU
CODEN APDBAN
ACTA PHYSICA ET CHIMICA DEBRECINA. **See** Physics.

LC QD1 .A34 **ISSN** 0208-6182
DD 540/.5 PL
ACTA UNIVERSITATIS LODZIENSIS. FOLIA CHIMICA. **Added/Corp** Uniwersytet Lodzki. **VFOAT** Folia Chimica. (1982)-. Academic Scholarly Publication. English (summaries and/or abstracts in Polish). Irregular. Price varies per volume. Wydawnictwo Uniwersytetu Lodzkiego, Ul. Jaracza 34, Lodz Poland. **Tel** 011 48 42 331671, 011 48 42 336541. **(Subscription address:** Ars Polona-Ruch, PO Box 1001, Krakowskie Przedmiescie 7, 00-068 Warsaw Poland. **Tel** 011 48 22 261201.**)** Documents available from CASDDS. ***Continues in part*** *Acta Universitatis Lodziensis. Seria II, Nauki Matematyczno-Przyrodnicze, 0137-4605.*
Desc: Research in physical, organic, inorganic and general chemistry.
Ind/Abst Chem. Abstr.

ISSN 0151-9093
FR
CODEN ACCHDG
ACTUALITE CHIMIQUE, L'. [Actual. chim.]. **Added/Corp** Societe Chimique de France. Societe de Chimie Industrielle (France). (1973)-. Academic Scholarly Publication. French (English). Seven times a year. $275.59. Dunod Gauthier Villars, 15 rue Gossin, 92543 Montrouge Cedex France. **Tel** 011 33 1 46565266, 011 33 1 40926527, FAX 011 33 1 40926597. **(Subscription address:** Centrale des Revues, 11 rue Gossin, 92543 Montrouge Cedex France. **Tel** 011 33 1 46565266.**)** Index available. **Bk Rev. Ad Acc. Circ:** 3,636 (ctrl). Documents available from The Genuine Article, CASDDS.
Desc: Contains scientific information, research in the chemical and pharmaceutical industry, articles and compositions.

Chemistry and Chemicals

Ind/Abst Chem Inform; Chem. Abstr.; Coal Abstr.; Curr. Biotechnol.; Curr. Cit.; EMBASE; Energy Res. Abstr. (April 1976-); Res. Alert; Soc. Sci. Cit. Index [Select. Cov.].

ISSN 0373-9805
BE
UDC 54
NLM W1 AC991G CODEN ACABDM
ACTUALITES DE CHIMIE ANALYTIQUE, ORGANIQUE, PHARMACEUTIQUE ET BROMATOLOGIQUE. See Pharmacy and Pharmacology.

ISSN 0320-7218
UN
ADSORBCIJA I ADSORBENTY. See Physics.

ISSN 0929-5607
NE
CCC
ADSORPTION. (19??)-. English. Four times a year. $319.00. Kluwer Academic Publishers, Postbus 322, 3300 AH Dordrecht The Netherlands. Tel 011 31 78 524400, FAX 011 31 78 183273, telex 20083.

ISSN 1068-8382
US
CCC
CODEN AAABE9
●**ADVANCE ACS ABSTRACTS.** See Chemistry and Chemicals-Abstracting, Bibliographies and Statistics.
LC QE516.3 .A38
DD 551.9
US
CODEN AANGEL
●**ADVANCES IN ANALYTICAL GEOCHEMISTRY.** See Earth Sciences-Geology.
US
ADVANCES IN ANTIVIRAL AGENT DESIGN. (19??)-. Periodical. English. $90.25. JAI Press Inc., 55 Old Post Road, Suite 2, PO Box 1678, Greenwich CT 06836-1678. Tel (203)661-7602, FAX (203)661-0792. ED Erik De Clercq.
US
ADVANCES IN CARBENE CHEMISTRY. (19??)-. Periodical. English. $90.25. JAI Press Inc., 55 Old Post Road, Suite 2, PO Box 1678, Greenwich CT 06836-1678. Tel (203)661-7602, FAX (203)661-0792. ED Udo H. Brinker.
Desc: Contributions addressing carbene chemistry.
LC QD1 .A355
ISSN 0065-2393
US
CCC
CODEN ADCSAJ
Pr Rev.
ADVANCES IN CHEMISTRY SERIES. [Adv. chem. ser.]. **Added/Corp** American Chemical Society. No. 1 (1950)-. Monographic series. English. Irregular. $139.95 (latest volume). American Chemical Society, 1155 Sixteenth Street Northwest, Washington DC 20036. Tel (800)333-9511, (800)227-5558, (614)447-3776, FAX (202)447-3671. (Subscription address: American Chemical Society / Washington D.C., PO Box 57136, West End Station, Washington DC 20037. Tel (800)227-5558.) Documents available from Article Express International, The Genuine Article, BIOSIS Document Express, CASDDS.
Ind/Abst AGRICOLA [Select. Cov.]; Bioeng. Abstr.; Biol. Abstr.; Chem Inform; Chem. Abstr.; Coal Abstr.; Curr. Cit.; Dairy Sci. Abstr.; Ei Page One; EMBASE; Energy Res. Abstr.; Eng. Index Annu.; Food Sci. Technol. Abstr.; GeoRef; Index Sci. Rev. [Full Cov.]; INIS Atomindex [Micro.]; Lit. Pat. Abstr., Oilfield Chem. (1972-); Lit. Abstr., Catal. Zeol.; Lit. Abstr., Health Environ.; Lit. Abstr., Pet. Refin. Petrochem.; Lit. Abstr., Pet. Substit.; Lit. Abstr., Transp. Storage; Life Sci. Collect.; Polymer Contents; Res. Alert [Full Cov.]; Sci. Cit. Index; SCISEARCH.
LC RB1 .A2
ISSN 0065-2423
DD 616.0756
US
UDC 616-098
CCC
NLM W1 AD54
CODEN ACLCA9
Pr Rev.
ADVANCES IN CLINICAL CHEMISTRY. [Adv. clin. chem.]. Vol. 1 (1958)-. Academic Scholarly Publication. English. Irregular. Price varies per volume. Academic Press Inc., 6277 Sea Harbor Drive, Orlando FL 32887. Tel (800)543-9534, (407)345-4100, FAX (407)352-3445. cum. index. Documents available from The Genuine Article, CASDDS.
Desc: Information on clinical chemistry, biochemistry, pathology and laboratory diagnosis.
Ind/Abst Chem. Abstr.; Curr. Aware. Biol. Sci.; CABS; Curr. Cit.; Energy Res. Abstr. (Aug. 1982-); Health Plan. Adminis.; Index Med.; Index Sci. Rev. [Full Cov.]; Res. Alert [Full Cov.]; Sci. Cit. Index; SCISEARCH.
US
●**ADVANCES IN DENDRITIC MACROMOLECULES.** (19??)-. Periodical. English. $90.25. JAI Press Inc., 55 Old Post Road, Suite 2, PO Box 1678, Greenwich CT 06836-1678. Tel (203)661-7602, FAX (203)661-0792. ED George R. Newkome.
US
ADVANCES IN NEAR-INFRARED MEASUREMENT. (19??)-. Periodical. English. $90.25. JAI Press Inc., 55 Old Post Road, Suite 2, PO Box 1678, Greenwich CT 06836-1678. Tel (203)661-7602, FAX (203)661-0792. ED Gabor Patonay.
LC QD181.S1 A38
US
CODEN ASLCEN
●**ADVANCES IN SULFUR CHEMISTRY.** Vol. 1 (1994)-. Monographic series. English. Irregular. Price varies per volume. JAI Press Inc., 55 Old Post Road, Suite 2, PO Box 1678, Greenwich CT 06836-1678. Tel (203)661-7602, FAX (203)661-0792.
Ind/Abst Chem. Abstr.
US
CODEN ASRTE2
ADVANCES IN THE SYNTHESIS AND REACTIVITY OF SOLIDS. Vol. 1 (1991)-. Academic Scholarly Publication. English. One time a year. $90.25. JAI Press Inc., 55 Old Post Road, Suite 2, PO Box 1678, Greenwich CT 06836-1678. Tel (203)661-7602, FAX (203)661-0792. ED Thomas E. Mallouk. Documents available from CASDDS.
Desc: Reviews of recent work on the preparation, characterization, structure, and reaction of chemistry of solid materials. Reviews research conducted in the authors' laboratories on a variety of synthetic problems. Covers other topics for physical scientists who make and use solid state compounds.
Ind/Abst Chem. Abstr.
ISSN 1064-3788
DD 536
US
CODEN ATHEEG
ADVANCES IN THERMODYNAMICS. See Physics-Heat.
US
●**ADVANCES IN URETHANE IONOMERS.** (July 1995)-. English. Irregular. $65.00. Technomic Publishing Company, Inc., 851 New Holland Avenue, Box 3535, Lancaster PA 17604. Tel (717)291-5609, (800)233-9936, FAX (717)295-4538. ED Dr. H.X. Xiao and Dr. Kurt C. Frisch.
Desc: Reports on important recent advances in the chemistry, development and applications of polyurethane ionomers as environmentally safe water-based, solvent-free adhesives and coatings.
LC TP1 .B35
ISSN 0001-9704
SP
CCC
CODEN AFINAE
Pr Rev.
AFINIDAD. (AFINIDAD : ORGANO DE LA ASOCIACION DE QUIMICOS DEL INSTITUTO QUIMICO DE SARRIA.). [Afinidad]. **Added/Corp** Instituto Quimico de Sarria. Asociacion de Quimicos. (1921)-. Academic Scholarly Publication. Spanish (English and Spanish; summaries and/or abstracts in Catalan). Six times a year. $80.00. Asociacion de Quimicos del IQS Sarria, S/N 08017 Barcelona Spain. Tel 011 34 3 2038900, FAX 011 34 3 2056266. ED Rafael Queralt Teixido. Index available. Bk Rev. Ad Acc. Circ: 2,500. Documents available from The Genuine Article, CASDDS.
Desc: Articles of general interest related to chemistry. Review papers and original scientific articles.
Ind/Abst Anal. Abstr.; Art Archaeol. Tech. Abstr.; Chem. Abstr.; Chem. Titles; Coal Abstr.; Curr. Biotechnol.; Curr. Cit.; Curr. Contents Phys. Chem. Earth Sci.; GeoRef; Leadscan; Mass Spect. Bull.; Res. Alert [Full Cov.]; SCISEARCH; World Surf. Coat. Abstr.
LC S
ISSN 0002-1849
DD 630
PL
CODEN AGROD4
AGROCHEMIA. See Agriculture.
LC S583 .A42
ISSN 0002-1857
DD 631.4/1/05
IT
CODEN AGRCAX
Pr Rev.
AGROCHIMICA. See Agriculture.
LC S583 .A43
ISSN 0002-1881
DD 630
RU
CCC
CODEN AGKYAU
AGROHIMIJA. See Agriculture.
LC S590
ISSN 0002-1873
DD 631.4
HU
CODEN AKTLAUAKTLUA
AGROKEMIA ES TALAJTAN. See Agriculture-Crop Production and Soils.

ISSN 1065-8033
US
ALCHEMIST JOURNAL, THE. (1992)-. Periodical. English. Four times a year. $16.00. The Alchemist Journal, B3 Starnes Avenue, Ft. Meyers FL 33916.
LC QD1 .A3529a
ISSN 0002-5100
DD 540/.5
US
NLM W1 AL315E
CODEN ALACBI
ALDRICHIMICA ACTA. [Aldrichimica acta]. **Main/Corp** Aldrich Chemical Company. Vol. 1 (1968)-. Academic Scholarly Publication. English (English). Irregular. Free on request. Aldrich Chemical Company Inc, PO Box 355, Milwaukee WI 53201. Tel (414)273-3850, FAX (414)273-4979, telex 26-843. Bk Rev. Circ: 250,000 (ctrl). Documents available from CASDDS. **Supersedes** Kardinex Sheets.
Desc: Contains chemical reviews, laboratory notes, and product applications.
Ind/Abst Chem Inform; Chem. Abstr.; Chem. Hazards Ind.; Lab. Hazards Bull.; Methods Organ. Synth.
LC TP1 .R357
SP
SUSPENDED
ALERTA INFORMATIVA. SERIA A: QUIMICA INDUSTRIAL. **Added/Corp** Instituto de Informacion y Documentacion en Ciencia y Tecnologia (Spain). (Jan. 1979)-(1991). Periodical. Spanish. Twelve times a year. Instituto de Informacion y Documentacion, Cientifica (CINDOC), Joaquin Costa 22, 28002 Madrid Spain. Tel 011 34 1 563-5482 87, FAX (91)564 26 44, telex 22628 CIDMD E. **Continues** Resumenes de Articulos Cientificos y Tecnicos. Serie A: Quimica Industrial.
LC QD1 .A385
ISSN 0002-6980
UK
NLM W1 AM105
CODEN AMBXAO
AMBIX. (AMBIX : THE JOURNAL OF THE SOCIETY FOR THE STUDY OF ALCHEMY AND EARLY CHEMISTRY.). [Ambix]. **Added/Corp** Society for the Study of Alchemy and Early Chemistry. Society for the History of Alchemy and Chemistry. Vol. 1, No. 1 (May 1937)-. Academic Scholarly Publication. English. Three times a year. $78.00. Black Bear Press Ltd, King's Hedges Road, Cambridge CB4 2PQ United Kingdom. Tel 011 44 1223 424571. ED W. H. Brock. cum. index. Bk Rev. Ad Acc. Circ: 550 (ctrl). Documents available from CASDDS.
Desc: Scholarly articles on the history of alchemy and chemistry from earliest times to the present.
Ind/Abst Am. Hist. Life (1967-); Chem. Abstr.
LC Q184 .A54
ISSN 0044-7749
DD 502/.8
US
NLM W1 AM533K
CODEN ALBYBL
Pr Rev.
AMERICAN LABORATORY (FAIRFIELD). (AMERICAN LABORATORY.). [Am. lab.]. **Added/Corp** International Scientific Communications, Inc. Vol. 1 (Jan. 1969)-. Trade Publication. English. Nineteen times a year. $210.00. International Scientific Communications Inc, PO Box 870, 30 Controls Drive, Shelton CT 06484-0870. Tel (203)926-9300, FAX (203)926-9310, telex 964292. ED Brian Howard. Index available. Bk Rev. Ad Acc. Circ: 130,000 (ctrl). Documents available from Article Express International, The Genuine Article, BIOSIS Document Express, Ask*IEEE, CASDDS, Documents on Demand.
Desc: For chemists and biologists who have a professional interest in all aspects of modern laboratory practice and basic research.
Ind/Abst Abstr. Bull. Inst. Pap. Sci. Tech.; AGRICOLA [Select. Cov.]; Art Archaeol. Tech. Abstr.; Biol. Abstr.; Ceram. Abstr.; Chem. Abstr.; Chem. Hazards Ind.; Coal Abstr.; Cumul. Index Nurs. Allied Health Lit.; Curr. Biotechnol.; Curr. Cit.; Curr. Contents Phys. Chem. Earth Sci.; Dairy Sci. Abstr.; EMBASE; Eng. Index Annu. [Select. Cov.]; Environ. Abstr.; Food Sci. Technol. Abstr.; Ind. Hyg. Dig. (199?-); INSPEC (Jan. 1974-); Lab. Hazards Abstr.; Mass Spect. Bull.; Nutr. Abstr. Rev., Ser. B, Live Feeds and Feed.; Nutr. Abstr. Rev., Ser. A, Hum. Exp.; Qual. Control Appl. Stat.; Res. Alert [Full Cov.]; Sci. Cit. Index; SCISEARCH.

ISSN 0939-4451
AU
NLM W1; AM884N
CODEN AACIE6
AMINO ACIDS. Vol. 1, No. 1 (1991)-. Academic Scholarly Publication. English. Eight times a year. $591.00. Springer-Verlag Vienna, Sachsenplatz 4 6, PO Box 89, A-1201 Vienna Austria. Tel 011 43 1 33024150, FAX 011 43 1 330242665. (Subscription address: Springer-Verlag New York Inc. / North America, PO Box 2485, Journal Fulfillment, Secaucus NJ 07096. Tel (201)348-4033, (800)777-4643, FAX (201)348-4505.) Documents available from BIOSIS Document Express, CASDDS, ADONIS.
Ind/Abst ADONIS; Biol. Abstr. (1991-); Chem. Abstr.; Curr. Aware. Biol. Sci.; CABS; Curr. Cit.

LC QD431.A1 A4
DD 541 UK
CODEN AAPPFP

•AMINO ACIDS, PEPTIDES, AND PROTEINS (CAMBRIDGE, ENGLAND). **Added/Corp** Royal Society of Chemistry (Great Britain). Vol. 25 (1992)-. English. Irregular. £105.00 (1993 volume). Royal Society of Chemistry, Thomas Graham House, Science Park, Cambridge CB4 4WF United Kingdom. **Tel** 011 44 1223 420066, FAX 011 44 1223 423623, telex 818293 ROYAL. **(Subscription address:** Royal Society of Chemistry, Turpin Distribution Services Ltd., Blackhorse Road, Letchworth, Hertfordshire SG6 1HN United Kingdom. **Tel** 011 44 1462 672555, FAX 011 44 1462 480947.) **ED** G.G. Briggs. ***Continues*** *Amino Acids and Peptides, 0269-7521.*
Desc: Provides a review of literature on amino acid and peptide chemistry.
Ind/Abst Biol. Abstr. (1994-); Chem. Abstr. (1994-).

ISSN 1011-4025
RM
CODEN AUFAEZ

ANALELE UNIVERSITATII DIN GALATI. FASCICULA VI, TEHNOLOGIA SI CHIMIA PRODUSELOR ALIMENTARE. **See** Science and Technology.

LC QA1 .T55 ISSN 0082-4453
RM
CODEN ATFCBV

ANALELE UNIVERSITATII DIN TIMISOARA. SERIA STINTE FIZICE-CHIMICE. **See** Physics.

LC Q65 .M87a ISSN 0213-5469
DD 540/.5 SP
CODEN ANCIET

ANALES DE CIENCIAS - UNIVERSIDAD DE MURCIA. (ANALES DE CIENCIAS.). [An. cienc. - Univ. Murcia]. **Main/Corp** Universidad de Murcia. **Added/Corp** Universidad de Murcia. Facultad de Ciencias (Quimicas y Matematicas). (19??)_. Academic Scholarly Publication. Spanish (English and French). Four times a year. 1000ptas Spain; $10.00 other. Universidad de Murcia / Servicio de Publicaciones, Calle Santo Cristo 1, 30001 Murcia Spain. **Tel** 011 34 68 363012, FAX 011 34 68 363414. **Bk Rev. Circ:** 300 (ctrl). Documents available from CASDDS. ***Continues*** *Anales de la Universidad de Murcia: Ciencias, 0463-9847.*
Desc: Publishes full papers, short communications, reviews on all aspects of the theory and practice of chemistry, chemical engineering and mathematics.
Ind/Abst Am. Hist. Life (1965-1978); Chem. Abstr. (1985-).

ISSN 0365-0375
AG
CODEN AAQAAE

ANALES DE LA ASOCIACION QUIMICA ARGENTINA. **Main/Corp** Asociacion Quimica Argentina. (1921)-. Periodical. English. Six times a year (Jan., Mar., May, July, Sept., Nov.,). $65.00. Fernando Garcia Cambeiro / Miami, 7331 Northwest 35th Street, Box 014 Skyway US, Miami FL 33122. Documents available from The Genuine Article, CASDDS. ***Continues*** *Sociedad Quimica Argentina. Anales de la Sociedad Quimica Argentina.*
Ind/Abst Ceram. Abstr. (19??-); Chem. Abstr.; Curr. Chem. React.; Curr. Cit.; Curr. Contents Phys. Chem. Earth Sci.; Food Sci. Technol. Abstr.; Index Chem.; Res. Alert [Full Cov.]; Sci. Cit. Index; SCISEARCH.

ISSN 1130-2283
SP
CCC
CODEN ANQUEX

ANALES DE QUIMICA (MADRID. 1990). (ANALES DE QUIMICA.). [An. quim.]. **Added/Corp** Real Sociedad Espanola de Quimica. Vol. 86, No. 1 (1990)-. Periodical. English (Spanish). Eight times a year. $285.00. Real Sociedad Espanola de Quimica, Facultad de Fisica y Quimicas, Ciudad Universitaria, 28040 Madrid Spain. **Tel** 011 34 1 2433879. Index available. Documents available from BIOSIS Document Express, CASDDS. ***Formed by the union of*** *Anales de Quimica. Serie A, Quimica Fisica y Quimica Tecnica, 0211-1330* ***and*** *Anales de Quimica. Serie B, Quimica Inorganica y Quimica Analitica, 0211-1349 Anales de Quimica. Serie C, Quimica Organica y Bioquimica, 0211-1357.*
Ind/Abst Biol. Abstr. (1991-); Chem. Abstr.; Curr. Cit.; Soc. Sci. Cit. Index [Select. Cov.].

ISSN 1017-317X
SA

UDC 542

ANALYTICAL REPORTER. [Anal. report.]. **VFOAT** Analytical Reporter Incorporating Laboratory. (1988)-. Periodical. English. Five times a year. $26.84. Analytical Reporter, PO Box 41897, Craighall 2024 South Africa. **Tel** 011 27 11 7284515.

ISSN 1191-4025
DD 665 CN

ANCIENNE USINE A GAZ DE LA RUE VERDUN A QUEBEC, L'. [Anc. usine gaz rue Verdun Que.]. **Added/Corp** Hydro-Quebec. Bulletin 1 (Mar. 1992)-. Periodical. French.

LC QD1 .A67 ISSN 0570-0833
DD 540/.5 GW
CCC
NLM W1 AN223J CODEN ACIEAY
Pr Rev.

ANGEWANDTE CHEMIE. INTERNATIONAL EDITION IN ENGLISH. (ANGEWANDTE CHEMIE.). [Angew. Chem., Int. ed. Eng.]. **Added/Corp** Gesellschaft Deutscher Chemiker. Vol. 1 (Jan. 1962)-. Periodical. English. Twenty-four times a year. $1448.00. VCH Verlagsgesellschaft GmbH, Postfach 101161, D-69451 Weinheim Germany. **Tel** 011 49 6201 606459, FAX 011 49 6201 606184. **(Subscription address:** VCH Publishers Inc., 303 Northwest 12th Avenue, Journals Department, Deerfield FL 33442. **Tel** (800)367-8249, (305)428-5566.) Documents available from Article Express International, The Genuine Article, BIOSIS Document Express, CASDDS. ***Formed by the union of*** *Zeitschrift fuer Chemie.*
Ind/Abst Abstr. Bull. Inst. Pap. Sci. Tech.; Alum. Ind. Abstr.; Anal. Abstr.; Bioeng. Abstr.; Biol. Abstr.; Chem. Abstr.; Coal Abstr.; Curr. Aware. Biol. Sci., CABS; Curr. Chem. React.; Curr. Cit.; Curr. Contents Life Sci.; Curr. Contents Phys. Chem. Earth Sci.; Ei Page One; EMBASE; Eng. Index Annu.; GeoRef; Index Chem.; Index Med.; Int. Aerosp. Abstr.; Mass Spect. Bull.; Met. Abstr.; Methods Organ. Synth.; NAPRALERT; Nat. Prod. Updates; Nutr. Abstr. Rev., Ser. B, Live Feeds and Feed.; Nutr. Abstr. Rev., Ser. A, Hum. Exp.; Life Sci. Collect.; PESTDOC; Ref. Upd. Deluxe Ed.; Res. Alert [Full Cov.]; Sci. Cit. Index; SCISEARCH; Soc. Sci. Cit. Index [Select. Cov.].

LC QD1 .C6883 ISSN 0044-8249
DD 540/.5 GW
CCC
CODEN ANCEAD

ANGEWANDTE CHEMIE (WEINHEIM AN DER BERGSTRASSE, GERMANY). (ANGEWANDTE CHEMIE.). [Angew. Chem.]. **Added/Corp** Gesellschaft Deutscher Chemiker. Vol. 61 (1949)-. Academic Scholarly Publication. German (summaries and/or abstracts in English and French). Twenty-four times a year. $1448.00. VCH Gesellschaft GmbH, Postfach 101161, D-69451 Weinheim Germany. **Tel** 011 49 6201 606459, FAX 011 49 6201 606184. **(Subscription address:** VCH Publishers Inc., 303 Northwest 12th Avenue, Journals Department, Deerfield FL 33442. **Tel** (800)367-8249, (305)428-5566.) available on microfilm; available on an online database from STN International. Documents available from CASDDS. ***Continues*** *Angewandte Chemie. Wissenschaftlicher Teil.*
Desc: Strives to have a stimulating mixture of review articles and short communications. Its review articles are always written by experts and cover all fields of chemistry. They summarize the important results of recent research on topical subjects, point to unresolved problems, and discuss possible developments.
Ind/Abst Chem Inform; Chem. Abstr.; Coal Abstr.; Curr. Biotechnol.; Curr. Cit.; EMBASE; Energy Res. Abstr.; GeoRef; Health Plan. Adminis.; Leadscan; Mass Spect. Bull.; NAPRALERT.

LC QD1 .S785 ISSN 0066-1961
FI
CODEN AAFCAX

ANNALES ACADEMIAE SCIENTIARUM FENNICAE. SERIES A2: CHEMICA. [Ann. Acad. Sci. Fenn. Ser. A2]. **Added/Corp** Suomalainen Tiedeakatemia. **VFOAT** Chemica. Vol. 106 (1961)-. Academic Scholarly Publication. English (German). Irregular. Price varies per volume. Bookstore Tiedekirja, Kirkkokatu 14, Helsinki 00170 Finland. **Tel** 011 358 0 635177. Documents available from Ask*IEEE, CASDDS. ***Continues*** *Suomalaisen Tiedeakatemian Toimituksia. Sarja A.2, Chemica.*
Ind/Abst Ceram. Abstr.; Chem. Abstr.; EMBASE; Energy Res. Abstr.; GeoRef; INSPEC (1968-).

LC QD1 .A715 ISSN 0151-9107
DD 540/.5 FR
CCC
CODEN ANCPAC

ANNALES DE CHIMIE (PARIS. 1914). (ANNALES DE CHIMIE--SCIENCE DES MATERIAUX.). [Ann. chim.]. Vol. 3 (1978)-. Academic Scholarly Publication. French (summaries and/or abstracts in English). Eight times a year. $343.39. Masson Editeur, BP 22, 41354 Vineuil Cedex France. **Tel** 011 33 54 504612, FAX 011 33 54 504611. Documents available from The Genuine Article, Ask*IEEE, CASDDS. ***Continues*** *Annales de Chimie, 0151-9107.*
Ind/Abst Chem Inform; Chem. Abstr.; Curr. Chem. React.; Curr. Cit.; Curr. Contents Phys. Chem. Earth Sci.; EMBASE; Eng. Mater. Abstr.; Index Chem.; INSPEC (1991-); Leadscan; Res. Alert [Full Cov.]; SCISEARCH.

LC QC1 .L793 ISSN 0137-6853
DD 540/.5 PL
CODEN AUMCD7

ANNALES UNIVERSITATIS MARIAE CURIE-SKLODOWSKA. SECTIO AA. CHEMIA. [Ann. Univ. Mariae Curie-Sktodowska, Sect. AA, Chem.]. **Added/Corp** Uniwersytet Marii Curie-Sklodowskiej. **VFOAT** Chemia. Vol. 31/32 (1977)-. Academic Scholarly Publication. English (Polish; summaries and/or abstracts in Russian). One time a year. Price varies per volume. Uniwersytet Marii Curie-Sklodowskiej, Biuro Wydawnictwo, Pl. Marii Curie-Sklodowskiej 5, 20-031 Lublin Poland. **Tel** 011 48 81 375304, FAX 011 48 81 336699, telex 0643223. Documents available from CASDDS. ***Continues in part*** *Annales Universitatis Mariae Curie-Sklodowska. Sectio AA. Physica et Chemia.*
Ind/Abst Chem. Abstr.

ISSN 0003-4592
IT
NLM W1 AN488 CODEN ANCRAI
Pr Rev.

ANNALI DI CHIMICA. [Ann. chim.]. **Added/Corp** Societa Chimica Italiana. Vol. 40 (1950)-. Periodical. English (Italian and English). Six times a year. L183740. Societa Chimica Italiana, Viale Liegi 48, 00198 Rome Italy. **Tel** (06)8549691. Documents available from The Genuine Article, BIOSIS Document Express, CASDDS. ***Continues*** *Annali di Chimica Applicata.*
Ind/Abst Anal. Abstr.; Biol. Abstr.; Ceram. Abstr.; Chem Inform; Chem. Abstr.; Curr. Chem. React.; Curr. Cit.; Curr. Contents Phys. Chem. Earth Sci.; EMBASE; Index Chem.; Leadscan; Mass Spect. Bull.; Life Sci. Collect.; PESTDOC; Pollut. Abstr. Indexes; Res. Alert [Full Cov.]; Sci. Cit. Index; SCISEARCH; Surf. Treat. Technol. Abstr.

LC QD49.F72 P373
DD 540/.7/2044 FR

ANNUAIRE : CHIMIE. **Added/Corp** Centre National de la Recherche Scientifique (France). (19??)-. French. One time a year. 150.00F. Editions du CNRS, 22 rue Saint Armand, F 75015 Paris France. **Tel** 011 33 1 45075050, telex 200 356 F.
Desc: Describes research activities of laboratories and foundations associated with the National Center for Scientific Research.

LC TP149 .A57
US
TITLE CHANGE

ANNUAL QUALITY CONGRESS / ASQC. **Added/Corp** American Society for Quality Control. **VFOAT** ASQC Presents the ... Annual Quality Congress Transactions; ASQC Quality Congress Transactions. (1992)-(1993). English. American Society for Quality Control, 611 East Wisconsin Avenue, PO Box 3005, Milwaukee WI 53201. **Tel** (414)272-8575, (800)248-1946, FAX (414)272-1734, telex 316567. ***Continues*** *Quality Congress. Annual Quality Congress Transactions.* ***Continued by*** *Quality Congress. ASQC ... Annual Quality Congress Proceedings.*

LC QD1 .C568 ISSN 0306-4875
DD 540/.6/2421 UK

ANNUAL REPORT OF COUNCIL AND ACCOUNTS - CHEMICAL SOCIETY. (ANNUAL REPORT OF COUNCIL AND ACCOUNTS.). **Main/Corp** Chemical Society (Great Britain). (19??)-. English. One time a year. Royal Society of Chemistry, Thomas Graham House, Science Park, Cambridge CB4 4WF United Kingdom. **Tel** 011 44 1223 420066, FAX 011 44 1223 423623, telex 818293 ROYAL. **(Subscription address:** Royal Society of Chemistry, Turpin Distribution Services Ltd., Blackhorse Road, Letchworth, Hertfordshire SG6 1HN United Kingdom. **Tel** 011 44 1462 672555, FAX 011 44 1462 480947.)

LC RS402 .A65 ISSN 0065-7743
DD 615.08 US
UDC 615.31 CCC
NLM W1 AN769G CODEN ARMCBI
Pr Rev.

ANNUAL REPORTS IN MEDICINAL CHEMISTRY. **See** Pharmacy and Pharmacology.

US
TITLE CHANGE

APPLIED POLYMER SYMPOSIA. (19??)-(19??). English. John Wiley & Sons, Inc., 605 Third Avenue, New York NY 10158-0012. **Tel** (212)850-6000, (212)850-6645, FAX (212)850-6088, telex 12-7063. **(Subscription address:** John Wiley & Sons / UK, Baffins Lane, Chichester, West Sussex PO19 1UD United Kingdom. **Tel** 011 44 1243 779777, FAX 011 44 243 776128, telex 86290 WIBOOKG.) ***Continued by*** *Journal of Applied Polymer Science, 0021-8995.*
Ind/Abst Abstr. Bull. Inst. Pap. Sci. Tech.; Curr. Cit.

LC GB855 .A645 ISSN 1380-6165
NE
CCC
CODEN AQGEFP

•AQUATIC GEOCHEMISTRY. **See** Earth Sciences-Geology.

LC QD1 .A733
CL

AREA QUIMICA. Added/Corp Universidad Tecnica del Estado (Chile). Direccion de Investigaciones Cientificas y Tecnologicas. (19??)-. Periodical. Spanish (English; summaries and/or abstracts in English). Editorial Universidad Tecnica del Estado, Avda Ecuador 3469, Santiago Chile.

LC QD1.A3515 A3 **ISSN** 0515-9628
AI
CODEN AYKZAN

ARMJANSKIJ HIMICESKIJ ZURNAL. (ARMIANSKII KHIMICHESKII ZHURNAL.). [Arm. him. z.]. **Added/Corp** Haykakan SSR Gitutyunneri Akademia. (1966)-. Academic Scholarly Publication. Armenian (Russian). Twelve times a year. $37.00. **(Subscription address:** Victor Kamkin, 4956 Boiling Brook Parkway, Rockville MD 20852. **Tel** (301)881-5973.**)** Documents available from CASDDS. ***Continues** Akademiia Nauk Armianskoi SSR. Izvestiia. Khimicheskie Nauki.*
Ind/Abst Alum. Ind. Abstr.; Art Archaeol. Tech. Abstr.; Chem. Abstr.; Energy Res. Abstr.; Mass Spect. Bull.; Met. Abstr.; Life Sci. Collect.

ISSN 0365-6187
JA
CODEN AROMBO

AROMATIKKUSU. (AROMATIKKUSU; AROMATICS.). [Aromatikkusu]. **Added/Corp** Nihon Taru Kyokai. Nihon Hokozoku Kogyokai. **VFOAT** Aromatics. Vol. 19 (1967)-. Periodical. Japanese. Six times a year. $74.00. Nihon Hokozoku Kogyokai, (Japan Aromatic Industry Association Inc.), 5-2 Nihonbashi Kayabacho 3 Chome, Chuoku Tokyo 103 Japan. **(Subscription address:** Japan Publications Trading Company Ltd., PO Box 5030, Tokyo International, Tokyo 100-31 Japan. **Tel** 011 81 3 3292 3753.) cum. index. Documents available from CASDDS. ***Continues** Koru Taru.*
Ind/Abst Chem. Abstr.

II
CODEN AJCHEW

ASIAN JOURNAL OF CHEMISTRY. Vol. 1, No. 1 (Jan. 1989)-. Academic Scholarly Publication. English. Four times a year. $100.00. Chemical Publishing Company / India, Sahibabad Ghaziabad India. **(Subscription address:** Prints India, 11 Darya Ganj, New Delhi 110002 India. **Tel** 011 91 11 3268645, FAX 011 91 11 3275542, telex 31-61087 PRIN-IN.**)** Documents available from CASDDS.
Ind/Abst Chem. Abstr.

ISSN 0971-0523
II
CODEN AJCRES

ASIAN JOURNAL OF CHEMISTRY REVIEWS. VFOAT Asian J. Chem. Revs. Vol. 1, No. 1 (Jan. 1990)-. Periodical. English. Two times a year. $65.00. Chemical Publishing Company / India, Sahibabad Ghaziabad India. **(Subscription address:** Prints India, 11 Darya Ganj, New Delhi 110002 India. **Tel** 011 91 11 3268645, FAX 011 91 11 3275542, telex 31-61087 PRIN-IN.**)** Documents available from CASDDS.
Ind/Abst Chem. Abstr.; Curr. Cit.

LC TP149 .A57 **ISSN** 1080-7764
DD 338.476 US

•**ASQC ... ANNUAL QUALITY CONGRESS PROCEEDINGS. Added/Corp** American Society for Quality Control. **VFOAT** Annual Quality Congress Proceedings. (1994)-. Proceedings. English. One time a year (May). $51.25. American Society for Quality Control, 611 East Wisconsin Avenue, PO Box 3005, Milwaukee WI 53201. **Tel** (414)272-8575, (800)248-1946, FAX (414)272-1734, telex 316567. **(Subscription address:** American Society for Quality Control, PO Box 3066, Milwaukee WI 35201. **)** ***Continues** Quality Congress. Annual Quality Congress.*
Ind/Abst Curr. Cit.; Eng. Index Annu.

NE

ASSOCIATION OF EXPLORATION GEOCHEMISTS SPECIAL PUBLICATION. See Earth Sciences-Geology.

RU

ATLAS SPEKTROV KHIMICHESKIKH PRODUKTOV. Added/Corp Novosibirskii Institut Organicheskoi Khimii. Nauchno-Informatsionnyi Tsentr po Molekuliarnoi Spektroskopii (Akademiia Nauk SSSR) NIIPM NPO "Plastmassy." Nauchno-Issledovatelskii Institut Rezinovoi Promyshlennosti (Moscow, R.S.F.S.R.). (19??)-. Monographic series. Russian. Price varies per volume.

LC QD1 .A85 **ISSN** 0004-9425
DD 540/.5 AT
CCC
NLM W1 AU558 **CODEN** AJCHAS
Pr Rev.

AUSTRALIAN JOURNAL OF CHEMISTRY. [Aust. j. chem.]. **Added/Corp** Commonwealth Scientific and Industrial Research Organization (Australia) Institute of Physics (Great Britain). Australian Branch. Australian National Research Council. Australian Academy of Science. Vol. 6, (Feb. 1953)-. Periodical. English. Twelve times a year. 530.00Aus$. CSIRO Publications, PO Box 89, 314 Albert Street, East Melborne Victoria 3002 Australia. **Tel** 011 61 3 4187333, 4187217, FAX 011 61 3 4190459, telex AA 30236. **ED** J. R. Zdysiewicz. **Ad Acc. Acid Free. Circ:** 790. available on microfilm and microfiche from University Microfilms International (UMI). Documents available from The Genuine Article, BIOSIS Document Express, CASDDS. ***Continues in part** Australian Journal of Scientific Research. Series A: Physical Science.*
Desc: Publishes articles which are considered to make an original contribution to any branch of experimental or theoretical chemistry and chemical technology. It has an international reputation, and is of interest to research workers in academic, government and industrial/commercial laboratories.
Ind/Abst Abstr. Bull. Inst. Pap. Sci. Tech.; Alum. Ind. Abstr.; Biol. Abstr. (-1992); Ceram. Abstr.; Chem Inform; Chem. Abstr.; Chem. Titles; Curr. Chem. React.; Curr. Cit.; Curr. Contents Phys. Chem. Earth Sci.; Dairy Sci. Abstr.; EMBASE; Eng. Mater. Abstr.; For. Prod. Abstr. (1991-); For. Abstr.; Hortic. Abstr.; Index Chem.; Index Vet.; Int. Aerosp. Abstr.; Leadscan; Mass Spect. Bull.; Met. Abstr.; Methods Organ. Synth.; Microbiol. Abstr. Sect. C; NAPRALERT; Nat. Prod. Updates; Life Sci. Collect.; PESTDOC; Protozoolog. Abstr.; Res. Alert [Full Cov.]; Sci. Cit. Index; SCISEARCH; Soils Fert.; Surf. Treat. Technol. Abstr.; Text. Technol. Dig.; World Text. Abstr.

ISSN 0005-2531
AJ

AZERBAIDZHANSKII KHIMICHESKII ZHURNAL / AKADEMIIA NAUK AZERBAIDZHANSKOI SSR. Added/Corp Azarbaijan SSR Elmlar Akademiiasy. **VFOAT** Azarbaijan Kimja Zhurnaly. (1959)-. Academic Scholarly Publication. Russian (Azerbaijani; summaries and/or abstracts in Azerbaijani). Six times a year. $38.00. **(Subscription address:** Victor Kamkin, 4956 Boiling Brook Parkway, Rockville MD 20852. **Tel** (301)881-5973.**)** Documents available from CASDDS.
Ind/Abst Art Archaeol. Tech. Abstr.; Chem. Abstr.

LC QD42 .B27a **ISSN** 0147-7374
DD 540 US

BARRON'S REGENTS EXAMS AND ANSWERS: CHEMISTRY. [Barron's regents exams answ., Chem.]. **Main/Corp** Barron's Educational Series, Inc. **Added/Corp** Barron's Educational Series, Inc. Regents Exams and Answers: Chemistry. (19??)-. English. Barrons Educational Series, 250 Wireless Boulevard, Hauppauge NY 11788. **Tel** (516)434-3311, (800)645-3476.

ISSN 0748-7169
DD 540 US

BERKELEY NEWSLETTER (BERKELEY, CALIF.). (BERKELEY NEWSLETTER, ANALYSIS OF MOLECULAR SPECTRA.). [Berkeley newsl.]. **Added/Corp** University of California, Berkeley. No. 105 (Sept. 1976)-. Newsletter. English. Six times a year. $30.00. University of California / Astronomy Department, 601 Campbell Hall, Berkeley CA 94720. **Tel** (415)642-1952. **ED** John Phillips. **Circ:** 150. ***Continues** Newsletter, Analysis of Molecular Spectra, 0893-9985.*
Ind/Abst Philos. Index.

ISSN 0366-0265
UK
CODEN BHTNAQ
CEASED

BIBLIOGRAPHY ON THE HIGH TEMPERATURE CHEMISTRY AND PHYSICS OF MATERIALS LONDON. (MATTER IN THE CONDENSED STATE.). [Bibliogr. High temp. Chem. phys. mater.Lond.]. **VFOAT** Bibliography on the High Temperature Chemistry and Physics of Materials (Washington). (1968)-(Sept. 1993). English. IUPAC High Temperature Bibliography, Imperial College / Metallurgy Department, London SW7 2BP United Kingdom. ***Continues** Bibliography on the High Temperature Chemistry and Physics of Gases and Plasmas, International Union of Pure and Applied Chemistry, Commission on High Temperatures in Gases and on Plasma Chemistry, 0539-1156 **and** Bibliography on the High Temperature Chemistry and Physics of Materials in the Condensed State, International Union of Pure and Applied Chemistry, Commission on High Temperatures and Refractories, 0539-1164.*

ISSN 0314-254X
AT

BIENNIAL REPORT / DIVISION OF PROTEIN CHEMISTRY, INSTITUTE OF INDUSTRIAL TECHNOLOGY. Main/Corp Commonwealth Scientific and Industrial Research Organization (Australia). Division of Protein Chemistry. (1986)-. English. Every 2 years. CSIRO Publications, PO Box 89, 314 Albert Street, East Melborne Victoria 3002 Australia. **Tel** 011 61 3 4187333, 4187217, FAX 011 61 3 4190459, telex AA 30236. ***Continues** Commonwealth Scientific and Industrial Research Organization (Austrlalia). Division of Protein Chemistry. Annual Report.*

LC QD1 .B55 **ISSN** 0304-4157
NE
CCC
Pr Rev.

BIOCHIMICA ET BIOPHYSICA ACTA (MR). REVIEWS ON BIOMEMBRANES. (REVIEWS ON BIOMEMBRANES.). [Biochim. biophys. acta (MR)]. Vol. MR1, No. 1 (1972)-. Academic Scholarly Publication. English. Three times a year (1 volume). $281.00. Elsevier Science Publishers BV, PO Box 211, 1000 AE Amsterdam Netherlands. **Tel** 011 31 20 4853641, 011 31 20 4853642, FAX 011 31 20 4853598. **ED** P. Borst, P. Cohen, K. van Dam, L.L.M. van Deenen, E. P. Kennedy, G.K. Radda, and E.C. Slater. available on microfilm and microfiche from University Microfilms International (UMI); available on an online database from Elsevier Electronic Subscriptions (EES). Documents available from ADONIS.
Ind/Abst ADONIS; Curr. Aware. Biol. Sci., CABS; EMBASE; PESTDOC; Protozoolog. Abstr.; Ref. Upd. Basic Ed.; Ref. Upd. Deluxe Ed.

NE

BIOMEDICAL AND CLINICAL ASPECTS OF COENZYME Q : PROCEEDINGS OF THE ... INTERNATIONAL SYMPOSIUM ON THE BIOMEDICAL AND CLINICAL ASPECTS OF COENZYME Q. Vol. 5 (Oct. 1985)-. Proceedings. English. Elsevier Science Publishers BV, PO Box 211, 1000 AE Amsterdam Netherlands. **Tel** 011 31 20 4853641, 011 31 20 4853642, FAX 011 31 20 4853598. Documents available from CASDDS. ***Continues** International Symposium on Coenzyme Q. Biomedical and Clinical Aspects of Coenzyme Q, 0167-8450.*
Ind/Abst Chem. Abstr.

LC QD **ISSN** 0968-0896
DD 574.192 UK
CCC
NLM W1; BI876E

•**BIOORGANIC & MEDICINAL CHEMISTRY. See** Biology-Biological Chemistry.

ISSN 0164-5315
US
CEASED

BIWEEKLY LIST OF PAPERS ON RADIATION CHEMISTRY AND PHOTOCHEMISTRY. Added/Corp University of Notre Dame. Radiation Chemistry Data Center. University of Notre Dame. Radiation Laboratory. Vol. 12 (Jan. 5, 1979)-Vol. 28 (1995). Abstracting/Indexing Service. English. Radiation Chemistry Data Center, University of Notre Dame, Notre Dame IN 46556. **Tel** (219)631-6527. Index available. **Circ:** 400. available on an online database from the publisher. ***Continues** Biweekly List of Papers on Radiation Chemistry, 0164-6370.*
Desc: Current Awareness service on photochemistry and radiation chemistry on solution kinetics involving free radical and excited states.

ISSN 0870-1180
PO
CODEN BSPQES

BOLETIM / SOCIEDADE PORTUGUESA DE QUIMICA. [Bol. - Soc. Port. Quim.]. **Added/Corp** Sociedade Portuguesa de Quimica. **VFOAT** Boletim da Sociedade Portuguesa de Quimica. (19??)-. Bulletin. Portuguese. Four times a year. Sociedade Portuguesa de Quimica, Ave da Republica 37-4, 1000 Lisbon Portugal. Documents available from CASDDS.
Ind/Abst Chem. Abstr.

ISSN 0366-1644
CL
UDC 54
CODEN BOCQAX

BOLETIN DE LA SOCIEDAD CHILENA DE QUIMICA. [Bol. Soc. Chil. Quim.]. (1949)-. Bulletin. Multiple languages (summaries and/or abstracts in English and Spanish). Four times a year. $70.00 Chile; $80.00 other. Sociedad Chilena de Quimica, Casilla 2613, Concepcion Chile. **Tel** 011 56 41 23581919. Index available. cum. index. **Bk Rev. Ad Acc. Circ:** 600. available with illustrations; available with charts. Documents available from The Genuine Article, CASDDS.
Ind/Abst Biol. Abstr.; Chem. Abstr.; Curr. Cit.; Res. Alert [Full Cov.]; Sci. Cit. Index; SCISEARCH; Soc. Sci. Cit. Index [Select. Cov.].

ISSN 0037-8623
PE
CODEN BSQPAQ
Pr Rev.

BOLETIN DE LA SOCIEDAD QUIMICA DEL PERU. [Bol. Soc. Quim. Peru]. (1934)-. Spanish (English). Four times a year (Mar., June, Sept., Dec.). $50.00. Sociedad Quimica del Peru, Apartado 891, 100 Lima Peru. Index available. cum. index. **Bk Rev. Ad Acc. Circ:** 1,000 (ctrl). Documents available from CASDDS.
Ind/Abst Chem. Abstr.

LC QD1 .B59
DD 540/.5 IT
CODEN BCISEN

BOLLETTINO DEI CHIMICI IGIENISTI. PARTE SCIENTIFICA. **Added/Corp** Unione Italiana Chimici Igienisti. Vol. 35, S1 (Jan. 1984)-. Academic Scholarly Publication. Italian (summaries and/or abstracts in English, French and German). L465000. Societa Editorial Farmaceutico, Via Ausonio 12, 20123 Milan Italy. **Tel** 011 39 2 89404545. Documents available from CASDDS. ***Continues in part*** *Bollettino dei Chimici dell'Unione Italiana dei Laboratori Provinciali.*
Ind/Abst Chem. Abstr.

ISSN 0006-7652
HU
CODEN BOPCAM

BOR- ES CIPOTECHNIKA. [Bor- es cipotechn,]. **Added/Corp** Bor- Cipo- es Borfeldolgozo Ipari Tudomanyos Egyesulet. (Feb. 1951)-. Periodical. Hungarian (summaries and/or abstracts in English, German and Russian; table of contents in English, German and Russian). Six times a year. $35.00. **(Subscription address:** Kultura, PO Box 143, H-1300 Budapest 3 Hungary. **Tel** 011 36 1 2500194.) Documents available from CASDDS.
Ind/Abst Chem. Abstr.

UK

BRITISH SULPHUR AMONIA QUARTERLY MARKET REPORT. (19??)-. English. Four times a year. £2050.00. British Sulphur Corporation Ltd, 31 Mount Pleasant, London WC1X 0AD United Kingdom. **Tel** 011 44 171 8375600, FAX 011 44 171 8370292, telex 918918 SULFEX G.

LC QD1 .B8185
DD 540/.5 RM

BULETIN STIINTIFIC. CHEMISTRY AND MATERIALS SCIENCE. **Added/Corp** Institutul Politehnic Bucuresti. **VFOAT** Chemistry and Materials Science; Scientific Bulletin. Chemistry and Materials Science. Vol. 52, No. 1 (1990)-. Bulletin. English (French, Romanian and Spanish). Four times a year. **(Subscription address:** Rompresfilatelia, PO Box 12 201, Bucharest Romania. **Tel** 011 40 0 10376.) ***Continues in part*** *Buletinul Institutului Politehnic Bucuresti. Seria Chimie, 1012-3229* ***and*** *Buletinul Institutului Politehnic Bucuresti. Seria Metalurgie, 1012-3210.*

LC QD1 .B833 **ISSN** 0324-1130
BU

BULGARIAN CHEMICAL COMMUNICATIONS. **Added/Corp** Bulgarska Akademiia na Naukite. Bulgarsko Khimichesko Druzhestvo. (19??)-. Periodical. English (summaries and/or abstracts in Bulgarian; table of contents in Bulgarian). Four times a year. DM453.00. **(Subscription address:** Kubon & Sagner, ABT Zeitschriftenimport, D 80328 Munich Germany. **Tel** 011 49 89 54218130.) ***Continues*** *Izvestiia po Khimiia, 0324-0401.*

LC QD1 .S309a
DD 540 SI

BULLETIN. **Main/Corp** Singapore National Institute of Chemistry. **VFOAT** SNIC Bulletin. Vol. 1 (1972)-. Bulletin. English. One time a year. Singapore National Institute of Chemistry, Singapore 5 Republic Singapore. Documents available from CASDDS.
Ind/Abst Chem. Abstr.

UK

BULLETIN. **Main/Corp** Society of Chemical Industry (Great Britain). **VFOAT** SCI Bulletin. (1991)-. Bulletin. English. Twelve times a year. Society of Chemical Industry, 14-15 Belgrave Square, London SW1X 8PS United Kingdom. **Tel** 011 44 171 2353681, FAX 011 44 171 8231698. ***Continues*** *Society of Chemical Industry (Great Britain). SCI Bulletin of News & Events of the Society of Chemical Industry.*

ISSN 0037-8968
FR
CCC
CODEN BSCFAS
Pr Rev.

BULLETIN DE LA SOCIETE CHIMIQUE DE FRANCE (PARIS, FRANCE : 1985). (BULLETIN DE LA SOCIETE CHIMIQUE DE FRANCE.). [Bull. Soc. chim. Fr.]. **Added/Corp** Societe Chimique de France. Societe Francaise de Chimie. (Jan./Feb. 1985)-. Bulletin. French. Eleven times a year. $827.00. Editions Scientifique Elsevier, 141 rue de Javel, 75747 Paris Cedex 15 France. **Tel** 011 33 1 45589067, FAX 011 33 1 45589424. **(Subscription address:** Editions Scientifiques Elsevier / for North America, PO Box 7247-7576, Philadelphia PA 19170-7576. **) ED** F. Mathey. available on microfilm and microfiche from University Microfilms International (UMI); available on an online database from Elsevier Electronic Subscriptions (EES). Documents available from The Genuine Article, BIOSIS Document Express, CASDDS. ***Formed by the union of*** *Bulletin de la Societe Chimique de France. Ptie 1, Physicochimie des Systemes Liquides, Electrochimie, Catalyse, Genie Chimique, 0037-8968* ***and*** *Bulletin de la Societe Chimique de France. Ptie 2, Chimie Moleculaire, Organique et Biologique, 0037-8968.*
Desc: Focuses on all aspects of molecular chemistry.
Ind/Abst Anal. Abstr.; Biol. Abstr.; Chem. Abstr.; Curr. Chem. React.; Curr. Cit.; Curr. Contents Phys. Chem. Earth Sci.; Eng. Mater. Abstr.; GeoRef; Index Chem.; Leadscan; Lit. Pat. Abstr., Oilfield Chem. (1954-1991); Lit. Abstr., Catal. Zeol.; Lit. Abstr., Health Environ.; Lit. Abstr., Pet. Refin. Petrochem.; Lit. Abstr., Pet. Substit.; Lit. Abstr., Transp. Storage; Mass Spect. Bull.; Methods Organ. Synth.; Nat. Prod. Updates; PESTDOC; Res. Alert [Full Cov.]; Sci. Cit. Index; SCISEARCH; Surf. Treat. Technol. Abstr.

ISSN 0242-8466
FR
UDC 66

BULLETIN DE LIAISON - GROUPE POLYPHENOLS. (1970)-. Periodical. French. One time a year. Documents available from CASDDS.
Ind/Abst Chem. Abstr.

LC QD1 .S35 **ISSN** 0037-9646
DD 540.62493 BE
CCC
NLM W1 BU609 **CODEN** BSCBAG
Pr Rev.

BULLETIN DES SOCIETES CHIMIQUES BELGES. [Bull. soc. chim. belg.]. **Added/Corp** Fondation Universitaire de Belgique. Belgium. Ministere de l'Education Nationale et de la Culture. Vlaamse Chemische Vereniging. Societe Chimique de Belgique. (1945)-. Bulletin. English (Dutch, French and German). Twelve times a year. 5,000F. Office Internationale des Periodiques, Kouterveld 14, B 1831 Diegem Belgium. **Tel** 011 32 2 7231158. **ED** Harry Paul Thun. cum. index. **Bk Rev. Ad Acc. Circ:** 1,500 (ctrl). Documents available from The Genuine Article, BIOSIS Document Express, CASDDS. ***Continues*** *Bulletin de la Societe Chimique de Belgique.*
Desc: Manuscripts submitted should represent original and unpublished research or critical reviews on chemistry.
Ind/Abst Alum. Ind. Abstr.; Anal. Abstr.; Art Archaeol. Tech. Abstr.; Biol. Abstr.; Chem Inform; Chem. Abstr.; Curr. Chem. React.; Curr. Cit.; Curr. Contents Phys. Chem. Earth Sci.; Dairy Sci. Abstr.; EMBASE; Eng. Mater. Abstr.; GeoRef; Index Chem.; Leadscan; Mass Spect. Bull.; Met. Abstr.; Life Sci. Collect.; PESTDOC; Res. Alert [Full Cov.]; Sci. Cit. Index; SCISEARCH; Surf. Treat. Technol. Abstr.

LC QD11 .B9 **ISSN** 1053-4385
DD 540/.9 US

BULLETIN FOR THE HISTORY OF CHEMISTRY. [Bull. hist. chem.]. **Added/Corp** American Chemical Society. Division of the History of Chemistry. University of Cincinnati. Oesper Collection in the History of Chemistry. Beckman Center for the History of Chemistry. **VFOAT** Bull. hist. chem. No. 1 (Spring 1988)-. Bulletin. English. Three times a year (Winter, Spring, Fall). $10.00 (ACS members), $12.00 (nonmembers), $15.00 (libraries). American Chemical Society / Ohio, University of Cincinnati, Department of Chemistry, Cincinnati OH 45221. **Tel** (513)556-9308. ***Continues*** *History of Chemistry Newsletter.*

LC QD1 .B837
DD 540/.5 II

BULLETIN OF PURE & APPLIED SCIENCES. SECTION C, CHEMISTRY. **VFOAT** Bulletin of Pure and Applied Sciences. Section C, Chemistry; Chemistry. Vol. 4, No. 1/2 (1985)-. Bulletin. English. One time a year. $24.00. Dr Ajay Kumar Sharma, PO Box 38, Modinagar 201204 India. **(Subscription address:** Prints India, 11 Darya Ganj, New Delhi 110002 India. **Tel** 011 91 11 3268645, FAX 011 91 11 3275542, telex 31-61087 PRIN-IN.) ***Continues*** *Bulletin of Pure & Applied Sciences. Section C, Physical Sciences, 0970-4620.*

LC QD1 .T63 **ISSN** 0009-2673
JA
CCC
NLM W1 BU8442 **CODEN** BCSJA8
Pr Rev.

BULLETIN OF THE CHEMICAL SOCIETY OF JAPAN. [Bull. Chem. Soc. Jpn.]. **Main/Corp** Nippon Kagakukai. Vol. 1 (Jan. 1926)-. Bulletin. English (French and German). Twelve times a year. $645.00. Nippon Kagakkai, (Chemical Society of Japan), 1-5 Kanda Surugadai, Chiyodaky Tokyo 101 Japan. **(Subscription address:** Maruzen Company Ltd., PO Box 5050, Import & Export Department, Tokyo 100 31 Japan. **Tel** 011 81 3 32789224.) **ED** Nobuyuki Tanaka. Index available in last issue of volume--attached. **Ad Acc. Circ:** 8,000 (ctrl). available on microfilm and microfiche from University Microfilms International (UMI). Documents available from Article Express International, The Genuine Article, Petroleum Abstracts Document Delivery Service, CASDDS.
Desc: Journal of dissertation about fundamental chemistry, chemical technology and industrial chemistry.
Ind/Abst Abstr. Bull. Inst. Pap. Sci. Tech.; Anal. Abstr.; Biodeter. Abstr.; Bioeng. Abstr.; Ceram. Abstr.; Chem Inform; Chem. Abstr.; Chem. Titles; Coal Abstr.; Curr. Biotechnol.; Curr. Chem. React.; Curr. Cit.; Curr. Contents Phys. Chem. Earth Sci.; Dairy Sci. Abstr.; Ei Page One; EMBASE; Energy Res. Abstr.; Eng. Index Annu.; Index Chem.; Int. Aerosp. Abstr.; Leadscan; Lit. Pat. Abstr., Oilfield Chem. (1964-); Lit. Abstr., Catal. Zeol.; Lit. Abstr., Health Environ.; Lit. Abstr., Pet. Refin. Petrochem.; Lit. Abstr., Pet. Substit.; Lit. Abstr., Transp. Storage; Mass Spect. Bull.; Methods Organ. Synth.; MINPROC; NAPRALERT; Nat. Prod. Updates; PESTDOC; Pet. Abstr.; Res. Alert [Full Cov.]; Sci. Cit. Index; SCISEARCH; Soc. Sci. Cit. Index [Select. Cov.]; Soils Fert.; Surf. Treat. Technol. Abstr.; World Surf. Coat. Abstr.

ISSN 0023-6071
JA
NLM W1 BU852I **CODEN** BICRAS

BULLETIN OF THE INSTITUTE FOR CHEMICAL RESEARCH, KYOTO UNIVERSITY. [Bull. inst. chem. res., Kyoto univ.]. **Main/Corp** Kyoto Daigaku. Kagaku Kenkyujo. (1950)-. Bulletin. English (Japanese and French). Six times a year. Kyoto University / Research Reactor Institute, Kumatori-cho Sonnan-gun, Osaka 590-04 Japan. Documents available from BIOSIS Document Express, Ask*IEEE, CASDDS. ***Continues*** *Kyoto Daigaku. Kagaku Kenkyujo. Reports of the Institute for Chemical Research.*
Ind/Abst Anal. Abstr.; Biol. Abstr. (-1988); Ceram. Abstr. (19??-); Chem. Abstr.; Curr. Cit.; INSPEC (1968-); Leadscan; Mass Spect. Bull.; Methods Organ. Synth.; Nat. Prod. Updates.

ISSN 0366-0370
CH
NLM W1 BU852P **CODEN** BICMAD
Pr Rev.

BULLETIN OF THE INSTITUTE OF CHEMISTRY. ACADEMIA SINICA. [Bull. inst. chem., acad. sin.]. **Main/Corp** Chung Yang Yen Chiu Yuan. Hua Hsueh Uen Chiu So. **Added/Corp** Chung Yang Yen Chiu Yuan. Hua Hsueh Yen Chiu So. Chi Kan. **VFOAT** Chi Kan. No. 1 (July 1959)-. Bulletin. English (summaries and/or abstracts in Chinese). One time a year (Mar.). Free on request. National Acacemy, Institute of Chemistry, Academia Sinica, Taipei 11529 Taiwan. **Tel** 011 886 2 7821889. **ED** Shu-Hun Chien. **Circ:** 300 (ctrl). Documents available from CASDDS.
Desc: Part A of the bulletin publishes original articles covering all fields in chemistry and closely related disciplines.
Ind/Abst Chem. Abstr.

LC QD1 .B84 **ISSN** 0253-2964
DD 540/.5 KO
UDC 54
CODEN BKCSDE

BULLETIN OF THE KOREAN CHEMICAL SOCIETY. [Bull. Korean Chem. Soc.]. Vol. 1, No. 1 (Mar. 30, 1980)-. Bulletin. English. Six times a year. $95.00. Korean Chemical Society, 335 5 Ka Anam Dong Sungbuk Ku, Seoul 136 075 Korea. **Tel** 011 82 2 926 5457, FAX 011 82 2 923 5589. **ED** Sae Hee Chang. Index available. cum. index. **Bk Rev. Circ:** 3,000. Documents available from The Genuine Article, CASDDS.
Desc: Reporting both experimental and theoretical research dealing with fundamental aspects of chemistry.
Ind/Abst Chem. Abstr.; Chem. Titles; Curr. Cit.; Curr. Contents Phys. Chem. Earth Sci.; Res. Alert [Full Cov.]; Sci. Cit. Index; SCISEARCH.

LC QD1 .P578 **ISSN** 0239-7285
DD 540 PL
NLM W1; BU886Q **CODEN** BPACEQ

BULLETIN OF THE POLISH ACADEMY OF SCIENCES. CHEMISTRY. [Bull. Pol. Acad. Sci., Chem.]. **Added/Corp** Polska Akademia Nauk. **VFOAT** Chemistry. Vol. 31, No. 1/2 (1983)-. Bulletin. English (French, German and Russian; summaries and/or abstracts in French, German, Russian and English). Four times a year. $100.00. **(Subscription address:** Ars Polona-Ruch, PO Box 1001, Krakowskie Przedmiescie 7, 00-068 Warsaw Poland. **Tel** 011 48 22 261201.) Documents available from The Genuine Article, CASDDS. ***Continues*** *Polska Akademia Nauk. Bulletin de l'Academie Polonaise des Sciences. Serie des Sciences Chimiques.*
Ind/Abst Alum. Ind. Abstr. (1983-); Chem. Abstr. (1983-); Chem. Titles (1983-); Curr. Contents Phys. Chem. Earth Sci.; Leadscan; Mass Spect. Bull.; Met. Abstr. (1983-); Methods Organ. Synth.; Nat. Prod. Updates; Res. Alert [Full Cov.]; SCISEARCH.

LC QD1 .A38143 **ISSN** 1063-5211
DD 540/.5 US
CCC
CODEN BADSEI
TITLE CHANGE

BULLETIN OF THE RUSSIAN ACADEMY OF SCIENCES, DIVISION OF CHEMICAL SCIENCE. [Bull. Russ. Acad. Sci. Div. Chem. Sci.]. **Added/Corp** Rossiiskaia Akademiia Nauk. **VFOAT** Seriia Khimicheskaia; Izvestiia Akademii Nauk. Seriia Khimicheskaia. Vol. 41, No. 1, Pt. 1 (Jan. 1992)-(1993). Bulletin. English (translations available in Russian). Consultants Bureau, A Division of Plenum Publishing Corporation, 233 Spring Street, New York NY 10013. **Tel** (212)620-8000, (212)620-8466, FAX

Chemistry and Chemicals

(212)463-0742, telex 23/421139. **Continues** Bulletin of the Academy of Sciences of the USSR, Division of Chemical Science, 0568-5230. **Continued by** Russian Chemical Bulletin, 1066-5285.
Ind/Abst Coal Abstr.; Curr. Contents Phys. Chem. Earth Sci.; Energy Res. Abstr.; GeoRef; Leadscan; Sci. Cit. Index (1992-1992).

LC QA
DD 510.5/6
Pr Rev.
ISSN 1220-9414
RM
BULLETIN OF THE TRANSYLVANIA UNIVERSITY OF BRASOV, SERIA C. MATEMATICA, FIZICA, CHIMIE. See Mathematics.

FR
BULLETIN SIGNALETIQUE. 170, CHIMIE / CENTRE NATIONAL DE LA RECHERCHE SCIENTIFIQUE. Added/Corp Centre de la Recherche Scientifique (France). Centre de Documentation. **VFOAT** Chimie. Vol. 32, No. 1 (1971)-. Bulletin. French. Twelve times a year. Centre National de la Recherche Scientifique Informascience, 15 Auai Anatole-Frnace, 75700 Paris France. **Continues** Bulletin Signaletique. 170, Chimie: Chimie Generale, Chimie Physique, Chimie Minerale, Chimie Analytique, Chimie Organique.

FR
CEASED
BULLETIN SIGNALETIQUE CHEMIE GENERALE ANALYTIQUE MINERALE ORGANIQUE SECT 917. See Mines and Mining-Mineralogy.

LC QD
DD 540
ISSN 0919-7087
JA
●**BUSHITSU KOGAKU KOGYO GIJUTSU KENKYUJO HOKOKU. VFOAT** Journal of the National Institute of Materials and Chemical Research. (1993)-. Academic Scholarly Publication. Japanese (summaries and/or abstracts in English). Six times a year. Free to academic institutions. National Chemical Laboratory for Industry Library, 1-1 Yatabemachi/Higash, Tsukubagun Ibaraki 305 Japan. **ED** Masanori Tachiya. Documents available from BLDSC, CASDDS. **Formed by the union of** Kagaku Gijutsu Kenkyujo Hokoku, 0388-3213 **and** Sen'i Kobunshi Zairyo Kenkyujo Kenkyu Hokoku, 0371-0807; **Continues** Seihin Kagaku Kenkyujo Kenkyu Hokoku, 0389-9659.

LC TP105 .B88
DD 338.4/7/661002551
JA
BUYERS GUIDE TO JAPAN'S INORGANIC CHEMICALS. See Industry and Production-Trade and Industrial Directories.

DD 547
ISSN 1049-1295
US
C2C ABSTRACTS JAPAN. HYDROCARBONS. See Chemistry and Chemicals-Abstracting, Bibliographies and Statistics.

DD 547
ISSN 1049-135X
US
C2C ABSTRACTS JAPAN. POLYMER CHEMISTRY. See Chemistry and Chemicals-Abstracting, Bibliographies and Statistics.

DD 541
ISSN 1049-1368
US
C2C ABSTRACTS JAPAN. SURFACE CHEMISTRY. See Chemistry and Chemicals-Abstracting, Bibliographies and Statistics.

DD 662
ISSN 0885-0097
US
CODEN CSRAEZ
CA SELECTS: ACID RAIN & ACID AIR. See Chemistry and Chemicals-Abstracting, Bibliographies and Statistics.

ISSN 0162-7686
US
CODEN CSADDQ
CA SELECTS: ADHESIVES. See Chemistry and Chemicals-Abstracting, Bibliographies and Statistics.

DD 629
ISSN 1066-1166
US
CODEN CSLCEB
●**CA SELECTS: ALUMINUM-LITHIUM & ALUMINUM-CERIUM ALLOYS.** See Chemistry and Chemicals-Abstracting, Bibliographies and Statistics.

DD 589
ISSN 1045-8522
US
CODEN CAAAES
CA SELECTS: ANTIBACTERIAL AGENTS. See Chemistry and Chemicals-Abstracting, Bibliographies and Statistics.

ISSN 0275-7028
US
CODEN CAAODZ
CA SELECTS: ANTIOXIDANTS. See Chemistry and Chemicals-Abstracting, Bibliographies and Statistics.

DD 541
ISSN 0890-183X
US
CODEN CSIDEX
CA SELECTS: ASYMMETRIC SYNTHESIS & INDUCTION. See Chemistry and Chemicals-Abstracting, Bibliographies and Statistics.

ISSN 0195-4911
US
CODEN CAASDD
CA SELECTS: ATOMIC SPECTROSCOPY. See Chemistry and Chemicals-Abstracting, Bibliographies and Statistics.

DD 543
ISSN 0740-0683
US
CODEN CSAAEI
CA SELECTS: AUTOMATED CHEMICAL ANALYSIS. See Chemistry and Chemicals-Abstracting, Bibliographies and Statistics.

ISSN 0162-7708
US
CODEN CBFCDV
CA SELECTS: BATTERIES & FUEL CELLS. See Chemistry and Chemicals-Abstracting, Bibliographies and Statistics.

DD 616
ISSN 0162-7716
US
CODEN CBASDK
CA SELECTS: BIOGENIC AMINES & THE NERVOUS SYSTEM. See Chemistry and Chemicals-Abstracting, Bibliographies and Statistics.

ISSN 1061-5342
US
CODEN CABCE5
CA SELECTS: BISMUTH CHEMISTRY. See Chemistry and Chemicals-Abstracting, Bibliographies and Statistics.

ISSN 0734-8851
US
CODEN CASPER
CA SELECTS: BLOCK & GRAFT POLYMERS. See Chemistry and Chemicals-Abstracting, Bibliographies and Statistics.

DD 547
ISSN 0740-0756
US
CODEN CSCAES
CA SELECTS: CARBOHYDRATES (CHEMICAL ASPECTS). See Chemistry and Chemicals-Abstracting, Bibliographies and Statistics.

DD 620
ISSN 0890-1856
US
CODEN CSCFE9
CA SELECTS: CARBON & GRAPHITE FIBERS. See Chemistry and Chemicals-Abstracting, Bibliographies and Statistics.

ISSN 0190-9401
US
CODEN CSHNDN
CA SELECTS: CARBON & HETEROATOM NMR. See Chemistry and Chemicals-Abstracting, Bibliographies and Statistics.

ISSN 0146-440X
US
CODEN CCARDO
CA SELECTS: CATALYSIS (APPLIED AND PHYSICAL ASPECTS). See Chemistry and Chemicals-Abstracting, Bibliographies and Statistics.

ISSN 0734-8800
US
CODEN CASREX
CA SELECTS: CATALYST REGENERATION. See Chemistry and Chemicals-Abstracting, Bibliographies and Statistics.

DD 543
ISSN 0890-1864
US
CODEN CSKAEY
CA SELECTS: CATALYTIC & KINETIC ANALYSIS. See Chemistry and Chemicals-Abstracting, Bibliographies and Statistics.

DD 666
ISSN 0885-0100
US
CODEN CSCPE5
CA SELECTS: CERAMIC MATERIALS (PATENTS). See Chemistry and Chemicals-Abstracting, Bibliographies and Statistics.

ISSN 0734-8797
US
CODEN CASAEG
CA SELECTS: CHELATING AGENTS. See Chemistry and Chemicals-Abstracting, Bibliographies and Statistics.

ISSN 0190-9398
US
CODEN CSCSDD
CA SELECTS: CHEMICAL HAZARDS, HEALTH, & SAFETY. See Chemistry and Chemicals-Abstracting, Bibliographies and Statistics.

ISSN 0195-4938
US
CODEN CCHIDW
CA SELECTS: CHEMICAL INSTRUMENTATION. See Chemistry and Chemicals-Abstracting, Bibliographies and Statistics.

ISSN 0195-4946
US
CODEN CACAD3
CA SELECTS: CHEMICAL PROCESSING APPARATUS. See Chemistry and Chemicals-Abstracting, Bibliographies and Statistics.

DD 671
ISSN 0885-0119
US
CODEN CSCDE3
CA SELECTS. CHEMICAL VAPOR DEPOSITION. See Chemistry and Chemicals-Abstracting, Bibliographies and Statistics.

DD 546
ISSN 1040-7146
US
CODEN CSIRE7
CA SELECTS: CHEMISTRY OF IR, OS, RH, & RU. See Chemistry and Chemicals-Abstracting, Bibliographies and Statistics.

ISSN 0146-4426
US
CODEN CSCCDX
CA SELECTS: COAL SCIENCE & PROCESS CHEMISTRY. See Chemistry and Chemicals-Abstracting, Bibliographies and Statistics.

ISSN 0190-9444
US
CODEN CCMADX
CA SELECTS: COLLOIDS (MACROMOLECULAR ASPECTS). See Chemistry and Chemicals-Abstracting, Bibliographies and Statistics.

ISSN 0160-8975
US
CODEN CCPADE
CA SELECTS: COLLOIDS (PHYSICOCHEMICAL ASPECTS). See Chemistry and Chemicals-Abstracting, Bibliographies and Statistics.

DD 535
ISSN 0885-0127
US
CODEN CSCSEE
CA SELECTS: COLOR SCIENCE. See Chemistry and Chemicals-Abstracting, Bibliographies and Statistics.

ISSN 0734-8789
US
CODEN CASDEP
CA SELECTS: COLORANTS & DYES. See Chemistry and Chemicals-Abstracting, Bibliographies and Statistics.

DD 620
ISSN 1066-114X
US
CODEN CSMPEL
●**CA SELECTS: COMPOSITE MATERIALS (METALLIC).** See Chemistry and Chemicals-Abstracting, Bibliographies and Statistics.

DD 668
ISSN 1040-7154
US
CODEN CAMTE9
CA SELECTS: COMPOSITE MATERIALS (POLYMERIC). See Chemistry and Chemicals-Abstracting, Bibliographies and Statistics.

DD 547
ISSN 0885-0135
US
CODEN CACPEF
CA SELECTS: CONDUCTIVE POLYMERS. See Chemistry and Chemicals-Abstracting, Bibliographies and Statistics.

Chemistry and Chemicals

DD 615

ISSN 0740-0748
US
CODEN CSCTEH

CA SELECTS: CONTROLLED RELEASE TECHNOLOGY. See Chemistry and Chemicals-Abstracting, Bibliographies and Statistics.

DD 620

ISSN 0749-7296
US
CODEN CASCEM

CA SELECTS: CORROSION-INHIBITING COATINGS. See Chemistry and Chemicals-Abstracting, Bibliographies and Statistics.

ISSN 0275-7044
US
CODEN CACCD9

CA SELECTS: COSMETIC CHEMICALS. See Chemistry and Chemicals-Abstracting, Bibliographies and Statistics.

DD 547

ISSN 0740-0721
US
CODEN CSCREB

CA SELECTS: CROSSLINKING REACTIONS. See Chemistry and Chemicals-Abstracting, Bibliographies and Statistics.

ISSN 0162-7740
US
CODEN CSCGDB

CA SELECTS: CRYSTAL GROWTH. See Chemistry and Chemicals-Abstracting, Bibliographies and Statistics.

ISSN 0162-7767
US
CODEN CSDSDI

CA SELECTS: DETERGENTS, SOAPS, & SURFACTANTS. See Chemistry and Chemicals-Abstracting, Bibliographies and Statistics.

ISSN 0275-7052
US
CODEN CDITD9

CA SELECTS: DISTILLATION TECHNOLOGY. See Chemistry and Chemicals-Abstracting, Bibliographies and Statistics.

DD 622

ISSN 0749-730X
US
CODEN CADMEB

CA SELECTS: DRILLING MUDS. See Chemistry and Chemicals-Abstracting, Bibliographies and Statistics.

ISSN 0162-7775
US
CODEN CSDTDL

CA SELECTS: DRUG & COSMETIC TOXICITY. See Chemistry and Chemicals-Abstracting, Bibliographies and Statistics.

DD 547

ISSN 0885-0143
US
CODEN CSEOEC

CA SELECTS: ELECTRICALLY CONDUCTIVE ORGANICS. See Chemistry and Chemicals-Abstracting, Bibliographies and Statistics.

ISSN 0734-8770
US
CODEN CAESEY

CA SELECTS: ELECTROCHEMICAL ORGANIC SYNTHESIS. See Chemistry and Chemicals-Abstracting, Bibliographies and Statistics.

ISSN 0146-4442
US
CODEN CSERDK

CA SELECTS: ELECTROCHEMICAL REACTIONS. See Chemistry and Chemicals-Abstracting, Bibliographies and Statistics.

ISSN 0162-7783
US
CODEN CSELD2

CA SELECTS: ELECTRODEPOSITION. See Chemistry and Chemicals-Abstracting, Bibliographies and Statistics.

ISSN 0146-4450
US
CODEN CSESDN

CA SELECTS: ELECTRON & AUGER SPECTROSCOPY. See Chemistry and Chemicals-Abstracting, Bibliographies and Statistics.

ISSN 0146-4469
US
CODEN CSEAD3

CA SELECTS: ELECTRON SPIN RESONANCE (CHEMICAL ASPECTS). See Chemistry and Chemicals-Abstracting, Bibliographies and Statistics.

DD 541

ISSN 0885-0151
US
CODEN CSEME6

CA SELECTS: ELECTRONIC CHEMICALS & MATERIALS. See Chemistry and Chemicals-Abstracting, Bibliographies and Statistics.

ISSN 0195-4962
US
CODEN CAELDC

CA SELECTS: ELECTROPHORESIS. See Chemistry and Chemicals-Abstracting, Bibliographies and Statistics.

ISSN 0734-8754
US
CODEN CAEDEN

CA SELECTS: EMULSIFIERS & DEMULSIFIERS. See Chemistry and Chemicals-Abstracting, Bibliographies and Statistics.

ISSN 0195-4970
US
CODEN CEPOD2

CA SELECTS: EMULSION POLYMERIZATION. See Chemistry and Chemicals-Abstracting, Bibliographies and Statistics.

ISSN 0162-7791
US
CODEN CSEBD6

CA SELECTS: ENERGY REVIEWS & BOOKS. See Chemistry and Chemicals-Abstracting, Bibliographies and Statistics.

ISSN 0734-8746
US
CODEN CAEREV

CA SELECTS: ENHANCED PETROLEUM RECOVERY. See Chemistry and Chemicals-Abstracting, Bibliographies and Statistics.

ISSN 0160-9041
US
CODEN CSPODW

CA SELECTS: ENVIRONMENTAL POLLUTION. See Chemistry and Chemicals-Abstracting, Bibliographies and Statistics.

ISSN 0275-7060
US
CODEN CEPRDB

CA SELECTS: EPOXY RESINS. See Chemistry and Chemicals-Abstracting, Bibliographies and Statistics.

ISSN 0275-7079
US
CODEN CSFODG

CA SELECTS: FATS & OILS. See Chemistry and Chemicals-Abstracting, Bibliographies and Statistics.

ISSN 0740-0713
US
CODEN CSFCEF

CA SELECTS: FERMENTATION CHEMICALS. See Chemistry and Chemicals-Abstracting, Bibliographies and Statistics.

DD 621

ISSN 0890-1872
US
CODEN CSOCEQ

CA SELECTS: FIBER OPTICS & OPTICAL COMMUNICATION. See Chemistry and Chemicals-Abstracting, Bibliographies and Statistics.

ISSN 0734-869X
US
CODEN CAFPEU

CA SELECTS: FIBER-REINFORCED PLASTICS. See Chemistry and Chemicals-Abstracting, Bibliographies and Statistics.

ISSN 0162-7805
US
CODEN CSFLD7

CA SELECTS: FLAMMABILITY. See Chemistry and Chemicals-Abstracting, Bibliographies and Statistics.

ISSN 0148-2327
US
CODEN CASFDU

CA SELECTS: FLAVORS & FRAGRANCES. See Chemistry and Chemicals-Abstracting, Bibliographies and Statistics.

ISSN 0195-4989
US
CODEN CFSTD5

CA SELECTS: FLUIDIZED SOLIDS TECHNOLOGY. See Chemistry and Chemicals-Abstracting, Bibliographies and Statistics.

ISSN 0362-9880
US
CODEN CSFCDE

CA SELECTS: FORENSIC CHEMISTRY. See Chemistry and Chemicals-Abstracting, Bibliographies and Statistics.

DD 660

ISSN 0890-1880
US
CODEN CAFCEP

CA SELECTS: FORMULATION CHEMISTRY. See Chemistry and Chemicals-Abstracting, Bibliographies and Statistics.

ISSN 0195-4997
US
CODEN CSFAD8

CA SELECTS: FUEL & LUBRICANT ADDITIVES. See Chemistry and Chemicals-Abstracting, Bibliographies and Statistics.

LC SB950.9
DD 632.952

ISSN 0160-9068
US
CODEN CSFNDD

CA SELECTS: FUNGICIDES. See Chemistry and Chemicals-Abstracting, Bibliographies and Statistics.

ISSN 0146-4477
US
CODEN CSGCDJ

CA SELECTS: GAS CHROMATOGRAPHY. See Chemistry and Chemicals-Abstracting, Bibliographies and Statistics.

ISSN 0160-9076
US
CODEN CSGTD2

CA SELECTS: GASEOUS WASTE TREATMENT. See Chemistry and Chemicals-Abstracting, Bibliographies and Statistics.

ISSN 0146-4485
US
CODEN CGPCDE

CA SELECTS: GEL PERMEATION CHROMATOGRAPHY. See Chemistry and Chemicals-Abstracting, Bibliographies and Statistics.

ISSN 1066-5730
US

●**CA SELECTS: GEOCHEMISTRY.** See Chemistry and Chemicals-Abstracting, Bibliographies and Statistics.

ISSN 0162-7821
US
CODEN CSHPDT

CA SELECTS: HEAT-RESISTANT & ABLATIVE POLYMERS. See Chemistry and Chemicals-Abstracting, Bibliographies and Statistics.

LC SB950.9
DD 632.954

ISSN 0160-9084
US
CODEN CSHEDU

CA SELECTS: HERBICIDES. See Chemistry and Chemicals-Abstracting, Bibliographies and Statistics.

DD 620

ISSN 0895-5891
US
CODEN CSHAEJ

CA SELECTS: HOT-MELT ADHESIVES. See Chemistry and Chemicals-Abstracting, Bibliographies and Statistics.

ISSN 0190-9436
US
CODEN CISAD3

CA SELECTS: INFRARED SPECTROSCOPY (PHYSICOCHEMICAL ASPECTS). See Chemistry and Chemicals-Abstracting, Bibliographies and Statistics.

ISSN 0734-8843
US
CODEN CAIPEB

CA SELECTS: INITIATION OF POLYMERIZATION. See Chemistry and Chemicals-Abstracting, Bibliographies and Statistics.

ISSN 0275-7087
US
CODEN CSACDN

CA SELECTS: INORGANIC ANALYTICAL CHEMISTRY. See Chemistry and Chemicals-Abstracting, Bibliographies and Statistics.

ISSN 0195-5012
US
CODEN CIOMDJ

CA SELECTS: INORGANIC & ORGANOMETALLIC REACTION MECHANISMS. See Chemistry and Chemicals-Abstracting, Bibliographies and Statistics.

Chemistry and Chemicals

LC SB951.145
DD 632.951
CA SELECTS: INSECTICIDES. See Chemistry and Chemicals-Abstracting, Bibliographies and Statistics.

ISSN 0195-5020
US
CODEN CSIPDY
CA SELECTS: ION-CONTAINING POLYMERS. See Chemistry and Chemicals-Abstracting, Bibliographies and Statistics.

ISSN 0146-4493
US
CODEN CSIODV
CA SELECTS: ION EXCHANGE. See Chemistry and Chemicals-Abstracting, Bibliographies and Statistics.

ISSN 0195-5039
US
CODEN CLAPDD
CA SELECTS: LASER APPLICATIONS. See Chemistry and Chemicals-Abstracting, Bibliographies and Statistics.

ISSN 0885-0178
DD 541
US
CODEN CSLREM
CA SELECTS: LASER-INDUCED CHEMICAL REACTIONS. See Chemistry and Chemicals-Abstracting, Bibliographies and Statistics.

ISSN 0160-9106
US
CODEN CSLTDR
CA SELECTS: LIQUID WASTE TREATMENT. See Chemistry and Chemicals-Abstracting, Bibliographies and Statistics.

ISSN 0734-8738
US
CODEN CASLEF
CA SELECTS: LUBRICANTS, GREASES & LUBRICATION. See Chemistry and Chemicals-Abstracting, Bibliographies and Statistics.

ISSN 0362-9872
US
CODEN CASSDZ
CA SELECTS: MASS SPECTROMETRY. See Chemistry and Chemicals-Abstracting, Bibliographies and Statistics.

ISSN 1062-8681
US
CA SELECTS: METALLIC GLASSES. See Chemistry and Chemicals-Abstracting, Bibliographies and Statistics.

ISSN 0160-9114
US
CODEN CSMCDF
CA SELECTS: METALLO ENZYMES & METALLO COENZYMES. See Chemistry and Chemicals-Abstracting, Bibliographies and Statistics.

ISSN 0740-0691
DD 547
US
CODEN CSNSEZ
CA SELECTS: NATURAL PRODUCT SYNTHESIS. See Chemistry and Chemicals-Abstracting, Bibliographies and Statistics.

ISSN 0148-2416
US
CODEN CSBCDS
CA SELECTS: NEW BOOKS IN CHEMISTRY. See Chemistry and Chemicals-Abstracting, Bibliographies and Statistics.

ISSN 0734-8673
US
CODEN CANPE2
CA SELECTS: NEW PLASTICS. See Chemistry and Chemicals-Abstracting, Bibliographies and Statistics.

ISSN 0734-872X
US
CODEN CAPREI
CA SELECTS: NOVEL NATURAL PRODUCTS. See Chemistry and Chemicals-Abstracting, Bibliographies and Statistics.

ISSN 0734-8819
US
CODEN CAPPEC
CA SELECTS: NOVEL POLYMERS FROM PATENTS. See Chemistry and Chemicals-Abstracting, Bibliographies and Statistics.

ISSN 0275-7109
US
CODEN COACDT
CA SELECTS: NOVEL SULFUR HETEROCYCLES. See Chemistry and Chemicals-Abstracting, Bibliographies and Statistics.

ISSN 1052-1984
US
CODEN CSONEP
CA SELECTS: OMEGA THREE FATTY ACIDS & FISH OIL. See Chemistry and Chemicals-Abstracting, Bibliographies and Statistics.

ISSN 0195-5063
US
CODEN COPMDW
CA SELECTS: OPTICAL & PHOTOSENSITIVE MATERIALS. See Chemistry and Chemicals-Abstracting, Bibliographies and Statistics.

ISSN 0195-5071
US
CODEN COORD8
CA SELECTS: OPTIMIZATION OF ORGANIC REACTIONS. See Chemistry and Chemicals-Abstracting, Bibliographies and Statistics.

ISSN 0275-7117
US
CODEN COACDT
CA SELECTS: ORGANIC ANALYTICAL CHEMISTRY. See Chemistry and Chemicals-Abstracting, Bibliographies and Statistics.

ISSN 0162-7848
US
CODEN CSOMDL
CA SELECTS: ORGANIC REACTION MECHANISMS. See Chemistry and Chemicals-Abstracting, Bibliographies and Statistics.

ISSN 0195-508X
US
CODEN CORSDQ
CA SELECTS: ORGANIC STEREOCHEMISTRY. See Chemistry and Chemicals-Abstracting, Bibliographies and Statistics.

ISSN 0160-9130
US
CODEN COMCDL
CA SELECTS: ORGANO-TRANSITION METAL COMPLEXES. See Chemistry and Chemicals-Abstracting, Bibliographies and Statistics.

ISSN 0160-905X
US
CODEN CORCDC
CA SELECTS: ORGANOFLUORINE CHEMISTRY. See Chemistry and Chemicals-Abstracting, Bibliographies and Statistics.

ISSN 0162-783X
DD 547
US
CODEN CAOCDZ
CA SELECTS: ORGANOPHOSPHORUS CHEMISTRY. See Chemistry and Chemicals-Abstracting, Bibliographies and Statistics.

ISSN 0362-9899
US
CODEN CSOCDP
CA SELECTS: ORGANOSILICON CHEMISTRY. See Chemistry and Chemicals-Abstracting, Bibliographies and Statistics.

ISSN 1040-7189
DD 547
US
CODEN CAOCE2
CA SELECTS: ORGANOSULFUR CHEMISTRY (JOURNALS). See Chemistry and Chemicals-Abstracting, Bibliographies and Statistics.

ISSN 0195-5101
US
CODEN COGCDP
CA SELECTS: ORGANOTIN CHEMISTRY. See Chemistry and Chemicals-Abstracting, Bibliographies and Statistics.

ISSN 1040-7170
DD 547
US
CODEN COXCE9
CA SELECTS: OXIDATION CATALYSTS. See Chemistry and Chemicals-Abstracting, Bibliographies and Statistics.

ISSN 0734-8711
US
CODEN CSPAEP
CA SELECTS: PAPER ADDITIVES. See Chemistry and Chemicals-Abstracting, Bibliographies and Statistics.

ISSN 0146-4515
US
CODEN CSPCDU
CA SELECTS: PAPER & THIN-LAYER CHROMATOGRAPHY. See Chemistry and Chemicals-Abstracting, Bibliographies and Statistics.

ISSN 0885-0194
DD 541
US
CODEN CSPCEV
CA SELECTS: PHASE TRANSFER CATALYSIS. See Chemistry and Chemicals-Abstracting, Bibliographies and Statistics.

ISSN 0362-9856
US
CODEN CAPHDL
CA SELECTS: PHOTOCHEMISTRY. See Chemistry and Chemicals-Abstracting, Bibliographies and Statistics.

ISSN 0885-0216
DD 541
US
CODEN CSPHEC
CA SELECTS: PHOTORESISTS. See Chemistry and Chemicals-Abstracting, Bibliographies and Statistics.

ISSN 0749-7326
DD 668
US
CODEN CSPPE2
CA SELECTS: PHOTOSENSITIVE POLYMERS. See Chemistry and Chemicals-Abstracting, Bibliographies and Statistics.

ISSN 0749-7334
DD 621
US
CODEN CSPEE3
CA SELECTS: PLASMA & REACTIVE ION ETCHING. See Chemistry and Chemicals-Abstracting, Bibliographies and Statistics.

ISSN 0195-511X
US
CODEN CSPFD5
CA SELECTS: PLASTIC FILMS. See Chemistry and Chemicals-Abstracting, Bibliographies and Statistics.

ISSN 0734-8681
US
CODEN CAADE3
CA SELECTS: PLASTICS ADDITIVES. See Chemistry and Chemicals-Abstracting, Bibliographies and Statistics.

ISSN 0275-7125
US
CODEN CPFUDD
CA SELECTS: PLASTICS FABRICATION & USES. See Chemistry and Chemicals-Abstracting, Bibliographies and Statistics.

ISSN 0275-7133
US
CODEN CSPPDZ
CA SELECTS: PLASTICS MANUFACTURING & PROCESSING. See Chemistry and Chemicals-Abstracting, Bibliographies and Statistics.

ISSN 0890-1937
DD 546
US
CODEN CPCHES
CA SELECTS: PLATINUM & PALLADIUM CHEMISTRY. See Chemistry and Chemicals-Abstracting, Bibliographies and Statistics.

ISSN 0160-9149
US
CODEN CSPMDQ
CA SELECTS: POLLUTION MONITORING. See Chemistry and Chemicals-Abstracting, Bibliographies and Statistics.

ISSN 0890-1945
DD 661
US
CODEN CSPJEI
CA SELECTS: POLYACRYLATES (JOURNALS). See Chemistry and Chemicals-Abstracting, Bibliographies and Statistics.

ISSN 0734-8703
US
CODEN CAPOE9
CA SELECTS: POLYESTERS. See Chemistry and Chemicals-Abstracting, Bibliographies and Statistics.

Chemistry and Chemicals

CA SELECTS: POLYMER BLENDS. See Chemistry and Chemicals-Abstracting, Bibliographies and Statistics.
ISSN 0734-8827 US CODEN CAPBE4

CA SELECTS: POLYMER DEGRADATION. See Chemistry and Chemicals-Abstracting, Bibliographies and Statistics.
ISSN 0734-8835 US CODEN CAPDEA

CA SELECTS: POLYMER MORPHOLOGY. See Chemistry and Chemicals-Abstracting, Bibliographies and Statistics.
ISSN 0195-5128 US CODEN CAPMD2

CA SELECTS: POLYMERIZATION KINETICS & PROCESS CONTROL. See Chemistry and Chemicals-Abstracting, Bibliographies and Statistics.
DD 668 ISSN 0885-0224 US CODEN CPKCEJ

CA SELECTS: POLYURETHANES. See Chemistry and Chemicals-Abstracting, Bibliographies and Statistics.
DD 547 ISSN 0740-0705 US CODEN CSPOEX

CA SELECTS: PORPHYRINS. See Chemistry and Chemicals-Abstracting, Bibliographies and Statistics.
ISSN 0195-5136 US CODEN CLPODH

CA SELECTS: PROSTAGLANDINS. See Chemistry and Chemicals-Abstracting, Bibliographies and Statistics.
ISSN 0148-2343 US CODEN CSEPDE

CA SELECTS: PROTON MAGNETIC RESONANCE. See Chemistry and Chemicals-Abstracting, Bibliographies and Statistics.
ISSN 0190-941X US CODEN CPMRD5

CA SELECTS: QUATERNARY AMMONIUM COMPOUNDS. See Chemistry and Chemicals-Abstracting, Bibliographies and Statistics.
DD 669 ISSN 0890-1953 US CODEN CSQPE7

CA SELECTS: RADIATION CHEMISTRY. See Chemistry and Chemicals-Abstracting, Bibliographies and Statistics.
ISSN 0146-4523 US CODEN CSRCD6

CA SELECTS: RADIATION CURING. See Chemistry and Chemicals-Abstracting, Bibliographies and Statistics.
DD 668 ISSN 0749-7342 US CODEN CSRCE7

CA SELECTS: RAMAN SPECTROSCOPY. See Chemistry and Chemicals-Abstracting, Bibliographies and Statistics.
ISSN 0148-2432 US CODEN CARSDU

CA SELECTS: RECOVERY & RECYCLING OF WASTES. See Chemistry and Chemicals-Abstracting, Bibliographies and Statistics.
ISSN 0160-9157 US CODEN CSRWDW

CA SELECTS: SELENIUM & TELLURIUM CHEMISTRY. See Chemistry and Chemicals-Abstracting, Bibliographies and Statistics.
DD 546 ISSN 0749-7350 US CODEN CSSCEC

CA SELECTS: SHAPE MEMORY ALLOYS. See Chemistry and Chemicals-Abstracting, Bibliographies and Statistics.
DD 669 ISSN 1062-869X US CODEN CSSLE5

CA SELECTS: SILICAS & SILICATES. See Chemistry and Chemicals-Abstracting, Bibliographies and Statistics.
DD 546 ISSN 0890-1961 US CODEN CSSSEQ

CA SELECTS: SILVER CHEMISTRY. See Chemistry and Chemicals-Abstracting, Bibliographies and Statistics.
ISSN 0148-2440 US CODEN CSCMDT

CA SELECTS: SOLAR ENERGY. See Chemistry and Chemicals-Abstracting, Bibliographies and Statistics.
ISSN 0148-236X US CODEN CASEDR

CA SELECTS: SOLID & RADIOACTIVE WASTE TREATMENT. See Chemistry and Chemicals-Abstracting, Bibliographies and Statistics.
ISSN 0160-9165 US CODEN CSSTDS

CA SELECTS: SOLVENT EXTRACTION. See Chemistry and Chemicals-Abstracting, Bibliographies and Statistics.
ISSN 0146-4531 US CODEN CSSEDH

CA SELECTS: SPECTROCHEMICAL ANALYSIS. See Chemistry and Chemicals-Abstracting, Bibliographies and Statistics.
DD 544 ISSN 0885-0232 US CODEN CSANEN

CA SELECTS: STEROIDS (CHEMICAL ASPECTS). See Chemistry and Chemicals-Abstracting, Bibliographies and Statistics.
ISSN 0160-9181 US CODEN CSASD3

CA SELECTS: SURFACE CHEMISTRY (PHYSICOCHEMICAL ASPECTS). See Chemistry and Chemicals-Abstracting, Bibliographies and Statistics.
ISSN 0146-454X US CODEN CSSAD5

CA SELECTS: SYNFUELS. See Chemistry and Chemicals-Abstracting, Bibliographies and Statistics.
ISSN 0195-5160 US CODEN CSSYD9

CA SELECTS: SYNTHETIC HIGH POLYMERS. See Chemistry and Chemicals-Abstracting, Bibliographies and Statistics.
ISSN 0275-7168 US CODEN CSYPDC

CA SELECTS: SYNTHETIC MACROCYCLIC COMPOUNDS. See Chemistry and Chemicals-Abstracting, Bibliographies and Statistics.
ISSN 0195-5179 US CODEN CSCPD4

CA SELECTS: TECHNICAL CERAMICS. See Chemistry and Chemicals-Abstracting, Bibliographies and Statistics.
DD 666 ISSN 1062-8703 US CODEN CATCER

CA SELECTS: THERMAL ANALYSIS. See Chemistry and Chemicals-Abstracting, Bibliographies and Statistics.
ISSN 0195-5187 US CODEN CSANDM

CA SELECTS: THERMOCHEMISTRY. See Chemistry and Chemicals-Abstracting, Bibliographies and Statistics.
ISSN 0162-7864 US CODEN CSTHDV

CA SELECTS: TRACE ELEMENT ANALYSIS. See Chemistry and Chemicals-Abstracting, Bibliographies and Statistics.
ISSN 0160-919X US CODEN CSTADA

CA SELECTS: ULTRAFILTRATION. See Chemistry and Chemicals-Abstracting, Bibliographies and Statistics.
ISSN 0195-5195 US CODEN CSULDE

CA SELECTS: ULTRAVIOLET & VISIBLE SPECTROSCOPY. See Chemistry and Chemicals-Abstracting, Bibliographies and Statistics.
ISSN 0195-5209 US CODEN CUVSDK

CA SELECTS: WATER-BASED COATINGS. See Chemistry and Chemicals-Abstracting, Bibliographies and Statistics.
DD 667 ISSN 0749-7369 US CODEN CSWCEW

CA SELECTS: WATER TREATMENT. See Chemistry and Chemicals-Abstracting, Bibliographies and Statistics.
DD 628 ISSN 0740-073X US CODEN CSWTEF

CA SELECTS: X-RAY ANALYSIS & SPECTROSCOPY. See Chemistry and Chemicals-Abstracting, Bibliographies and Statistics.
ISSN 0162-7872 US CODEN CSXSDG

CA SELECTS: ZEOLITES. See Chemistry and Chemicals-Abstracting, Bibliographies and Statistics.
ISSN 0190-4949 US CODEN CASZDM

CAHIERS BIBLIOGRAPHIQUES DE CHIMIE ORGANOMETALLIQUE.
FR
Added/Corp Universite de Rennes. VFOAT Bibliographic Notebooks for Organometallic Chemistry. (19??)-. French. Eight times a year. $240.60. Denis Neibecker, 205 Rte de Narbonne, F 31077 Toulouse Cedex France. Tel 011 31 61 553188, FAX 011 33 61 553003. Index available. Ad Acc. Circ: 200.
Desc: Graphical abstracts of selected recent publications in the field of organometallic chemistry, the applications of organometallic compounds in organic synthesis and homogeneous catalysis.

CAHIERS DE CHROMOTOGRAPHIE. See Photography.
FR

CAILIAO BAOHU. VFOAT Materials Protection. (1960)-. Periodical. Chinese. Six times a year. Documents available from CASDDS.
DD 620.11 ISSN 1001-1560 CC
Ind/Abst Chem. Abstr.

CAMFORD CHEMICAL REPORT. [Camford chem. rep.]. Added/Corp Camford Information Services. Vol. 24, No. 2 (Jan. 20, 1992)-. Periodical. English. One time a week. 599.45Can$. Camford Information Services, Suite 201, 801 York Mills Road, Don Mills Ontario M3B 1X7 Canada. Continues Corpus Chemical Report., 0228-653X.
DD 338.4/766/0097105 ISSN 1187-8746 CN

●**CANADA'S EXPORT STRATEGY, THE INTERNATIONAL TRADE BUSINESS PLAN. 7, CHEMICALS, PLASTICS AND ADVANCED MATERIALS.** See Plastics.
DD 382 ISSN 1190-9803 CN

CANADIAN JOURNAL OF CHEMISTRY.
LC QD1 .C285 ISSN 0008-4042
DD 540.5 CN
NLM W1 CA585 CODEN CJCHAG
Pr Rev.
[Can. j. chem.]. Added/Corp National Research Council of Canada. National Research Council Canada. VFOAT Journal Canadien de Chimie. Vol. 29, No. 1 (Jan. 1951)-. Academic Scholarly Publication. English (French). Twelve times a year. 545.00Can$. National Research Council of Canada, Receiver General for Canada, Ottawa Ontario K1A 0R6 Canada. Tel (613)993-0362, FAX (613)952-7656. ED B. Kratochvill and E. Schamedatus. Ad Acc. Circ: 2,300 (ctrl) available on microfilm from Princeton Microfilms; available on microfilm and microfiche from University Microfilms International (UMI); available on microfiche from Micromedia Limited. Documents available from The Genuine Article, BIOSIS Document Express, Ask*IEEE, CASDDS, Petroleum Abstracts Document Delivery Service. Continues Canadian Journal of Research. Section B, Chemical Sciences, 0366-7391.

Desc: Publishes papers and communications containing the results of original research in all areas of chemistry. Receives and publishes manuscripts from authors in more than 25 countries.
Ind/Abst Abstr. Bull. Inst. Pap. Sci. Tech.; Alum. Ind. Abstr.; Anal. Abstr.; Art Archaeol. Tech. Abstr.; Biocont. News Inf. (1991-); Biol. Abstr.; Ceram. Abstr.; Chem Inform; Chem. Abstr.; Chem. Titles; CSA Neuro. Abstr. (?-?); Curr. Chem. React.; Curr. Cit.; Curr. Contents Phys. Chem. Earth Sci.; Curr. Titles Electrochem.; Dairy Sci. Abstr.; EMBASE; Eng. Mater. Abstr.; GeoRef; Hortic. Abstr.; Index Chem.; Index Vet.; INSPEC (1968-); Int. Aerosp. Abstr.; Leadscan; Mass Spect. Bull.; Met. Abstr.; Methods Organ. Synth.; NAPRALERT; Nat. Prod. Updates; PESTDOC; Pet. Abstr.; Pig News Inf.; Plant Grow. Reg. Abstr.; Protozoolog. Abstr.; Ref. Upd. Deluxe Ed.; Res. Alert [Full Cov.]; Rev. Agric. Entomol.; Rev. Med. Vet. Entomol.; Rev. Plant Pathol.; Sci. Cit. Index; SCISEARCH; Soils Fert.; Surf. Treat. Technol. Abstr.; Vet. Bull.

ISSN 0411-0080
US

CAPITAL CHEMIST, THE. [Cap. chem.]. (Jan. 1951)-. Periodical. English. Ten times a year (monthly except July and Aug.). $5.00. Chemical Society of Washington. **Tel** (202)331-1305. **ED** James D and Nadine Adams. **Ad Acc. Circ:** 4,000.
Desc: The official publication of the Chemical Society of Washington, DC, the local section of the American Chemical Society.

ISSN 0748-0466
DD 540 US
UDC 54

CAROLINA CHEMTIPS. [Carol. chemtips]. **VFOAT** Carolina Chem Tips. Vol. 1, No. 1 (Spring 1984)-. Periodical. English. Three times a year. Free to chemistry teachers. Carolina Biological Supply Co, 2700 York Road, Burlington NC 27215. **Tel** (919)584-0381, FAX (919)584-3399, telex 574-354. **ED** Harry Shoffner. **Bk Rev**. ctrl circ.
Desc: Articles for chemistry teachers.

ISSN 0162-7112
DD 540 US
NLM W1 C135P **CODEN** CASRCV

CAS REPORT (COLUMBUS). (CAS REPORT / CHEMICAL ABSTRACTS SERVICE, A DIVISION OF THE AMERICAN CHEMICAL SOCIETY.). [CAS rep.]. **Main/Corp** American Chemical Society. Chemical Abstracts Service. **VAT** Chemical Abstracts Service Report (Columbus). No. 1 (Oct. 1972)-. English. Four times a year. Free on request. Chemical Abstracts Service, (Subsidiary of The American Chemical Society), 2540 Olentangy River Road, PO Box 3012, Columbus OH 43210-0012. **Tel** (614)447-3731, (800)753-4227, FAX (614)447-3751. **(Subscription address:** Chemical Abstracts Service, Customer Service Department, PO Box 3012, Columbus OH 43210. **Tel** (800)848-6538, (614)447-3600.) ***Continues*** *Castings.*

ISSN 1071-8796
US

•**CASURVEYOR. FOOD AND FEED CHEMISTRY.** See Food and Food Industry.

LC HD9657.I5 I54a
IO

CATALOGUE P. P2 S, PERUM. P2 S, P.T. P2 S INDUSTRI KIMIA. See Industry and Production.

ISSN 0920-4652
NE
CODEN CMCOES

CATALYSIS BY METAL COMPLEXES. [Catal. met. complexes]. (1979)-. Monographic series. English. Kluwer Academic Publishers, 101 Philip Drive, Norwell MA 02061. **Tel** (617)871-6600. **(Subscription address:** Kluwer Academic Publishers / US Subscriptions, PO Box 253, Accord Station, Hingham MA 02018. **Tel** (617)871-6600.) ***Continues*** *Homogeneous Catalysis in Organic and Inorganic Chemistry.*
Ind/Abst Chem. Abstr.; Curr. Cit.

ISSN 0920-5861
NE
CCC
Pr Rev.

CATALYSIS TODAY. Vol. 1, No. 1/2 (Feb. 1987)-. Academic Scholarly Publication. English. Twenty times a year. $2195.00. Elsevier Science Publishers BV, PO Box 211, 1000 AE Amsterdam Netherlands. **Tel** 011 31 20 4853641, 011 31 20 4853642, FAX 011 31 20 4853598. **ED** J.R.H. Ross. Index available. **Ad Acc.** available on microfilm and microfiche from University Microfilms International (UMI); available on an online database from Elsevier Electronic Subscriptions (EES). Documents available from Article Express International, The Genuine Article, CASDDS.
Desc: Devoted to currently important themes in catalysis and related subjects. Consists of separate issues, each covering a distinct topic as occurring in proceedings of short symposia and workshops, single (or multi-) author monographs, as well as collections of reviews of inter-related research papers.
Ind/Abst Chem. Abstr.; Coal Abstr.; Curr. Cit.; Curr. Contents Phys. Chem. Earth Sci.; Eng. Index Annu.; Lit. Pat. Abstr., Oilfield Chem. (1990-); Lit. Abstr., Catal. Zeol.; Lit. Abstr., Health Environ.; Lit. Abstr., Pet. Refin. Petrochem.; Lit. Abstr., Pet. Substit.; Lit. Abstr., Transp. Storage; Proc. Chem. Eng.; Res. Alert [Full Cov.]; Theor. Chem. Eng.

LC QD1 .C33 **ISSN** 0008-767X
US
CODEN CATLAG

CATALYST (PHILADELPHIA), THE. (CATALYST.). **Added/Corp** American Chemical Society. Philadelphia Section. Vol. 1 (1916)-. Periodical. English. Nine times a year. $4.25. American Chemical Society / Philadelphia Section, Department of Chemistry, University of Pennsylvania, Philadelphia PA 19104-6323. **Tel** (215)382-1589. **ED** Deborah Kilmartin. **Ad Acc. Circ:** 5,200 (ctrl).
Ind/Abst Soc. Work Abstr. (?-?).

ISSN 0309-5770
UK
CCC
CODEN CACHDO

CATALYSTS IN CHEMISTRY. See Literature-Abstracting, Bibliographies and Statistics.

ISSN 1057-1981
DD 338 US

CCPS/AICHE DIRECTORY OF CHEMICAL PROCESS SAFETY SERVICES. See Industrial Health and Safety.

LC HD9651.3 .C18 **ISSN** 0190-4760
DD 381/.45/66002573 US

CEC CENSUS OF BUYERS IN THE CHEMICAL PROCESS INDUSTRIES. **VFOAT** Chemical Engineering Catalog Census; Census of Buyers in the Chemical Process Industries. (19??)-. English. One time a year. $60.00. Penton Publishing, 1100 Superior Avenue, Cleveland OH 44114-2543. **Tel** (216)696-7000, FAX (216)696-0836. Full Page (Color) $6290.00.

ISSN 0576-9787
RM
CODEN CECTAH
Pr Rev.

CELLULOSE CHEMISTRY AND TECHNOLOGY. [Cellul. chem. technol.]. **Added/Corp** Academia Republicii Socialiste Romania. (Jan./Feb. 1967)-. Academic Scholarly Publication. English (French, German and Russian). Six times a year. $251.00. **(Subscription address:** Orion Press SRL, SPL Independentei 202-A, Bucharest 6 Romania. **Tel** 011 401 3122425.) Documents available from The Genuine Article, CASDDS.
Desc: International journal for physics, chemistry and technology of cellulose.
Ind/Abst Abstr. Bull. Inst. Pap. Sci. Tech.; AGRICOLA; Chem. Abstr.; Curr. Biotechnol.; Curr. Cit.; Curr. Contents Eng. Comput. Technol.; Pap. Board Abstr.; PESTDOC; Res. Alert [Full Cov.]; Rice Abstr.; Sci. Cit. Index; SCISEARCH; Sug. Indus. Abstr.; Text. Technol. Dig.; World Text. Abstr.

LC QD43 .C2 **ISSN** 0340-3335
DD 542 GW
UDC 542; 37.02:54
CODEN CHEDC2

CHED, CHEMIE EXPERIMENT + DIDAKTIK. **VFOAT** Chemie Experiment + I.E. und Didaktik. **VAT** CHED. Chemie, Experiment und Didaktik. (1975)-. Academic Scholarly Publication. German. DM48.00. Georg Thieme Verlag Stuttgart, Postfach 301120, D-70451 Stuttgart Germany. **Tel** 011 49 711 89310, FAX 011 49 711 8931298, telex 7 252 275 GTVD. **(Subscription address:** Thieme Medical Publishers Inc., 381 Park Avenue South, New York NY 10016. **Tel** (212)683-5088.) available on microfilm and microfiche from University Microfilms International (UMI). Documents available from CASDDS.
Ind/Abst Chem. Abstr.

ISSN 0703-1157
CN

CHEM 13 NEWS. CHEM 12 NEWS. See Education-Teaching and Curriculum.

UK

CHEM-FACTS: AMMONIA. English. £185.00 UK; $310.00 US; £190.00 Europe; £195.00 other. Chemical Intelligence Services, 39A Bowling Green Lane, London EC1R 0BJ United Kingdom. **Tel** 011 44 171 833812, 011 44 171 8331563, FAX 011 44 171 8831563, telex 28339 CPLCDP G. **Bk Rev**.
Desc: Worldwide survey of manufacturing and trade of ammonia.

UK

CHEM-FACTS: BELGIUM. English. £185.00 UK; £190.00 Europe; $310.00 US; £195.00 other. Chemical Intelligence Services, 39A Bowling Green Lane, London EC1R 0BJ United Kingdom. **Tel** 011 44 171 833812, 011 44 171 8331563, FAX 011 44 171 8831563, telex 28339 CPLCDP G. **Bk Rev**.
Desc: Detailed survey of the Belgium chemical industry.

UK

CHEM-FACTS: CANADA. English. Chemical Intelligence Services, 39A Bowling Green Lane, London EC1R 0BJ United Kingdom. **Tel** 011 44 171 833812, 011 44 171 8331563, FAX 011 44 171 8831563, telex 28339 CPLCDP G. **Bk Rev**.
Desc: Detailed survey of the Canadian chemical industry.

UK

CHEM-FACTS: FEDERAL REPUBLIC OF GERMANY. (19??)-. English. Irregular. £155.00 UK; $265.00 US; £160.00 Europe; $165.00 other. Chemical Intelligence Services, 39A Bowling Green Lane, London EC1R 0BJ United Kingdom. **Tel** 011 44 171 833812, 011 44 171 8331563, FAX 011 44 171 8831563, telex 28339 CPLCDP G. **(Subscription address:** Reed Telepublishing Ltd, 39A Bowling Green Lane, London EC1R 0BJ United Kingdom. **Tel** 011 44 171 8333812.) **Bk Rev**.
Desc: Detailed survey of West German chemical research.

UK

CHEM-FACTS: FRANCE. English. £200.00 UK; £205.00 Europe; $335.00 US; £210.00 other. Chemical Intelligence Services, 39A Bowling Green Lane, London EC1R 0BJ United Kingdom. **Tel** 011 44 171 833812, 011 44 171 8331563, FAX 011 44 171 8831563, telex 28339 CPLCDP G. **Bk Rev**.
Desc: Detailed survey of the French chemical industry.

UK

CHEM-FACTS: ITALY. English. Chemical Intelligence Services, 39A Bowling Green Lane, London EC1R 0BJ United Kingdom. **Tel** 011 44 171 833812, 011 44 171 8331563, FAX 011 44 171 8831563, telex 28339 CPLCDP G. **Bk Rev**.
Desc: Detailed survey of the Italian chemical industry.

UK

CHEM-FACTS: JAPAN. (19??)-. English. Chemical Intelligence Services, 39A Bowling Green Lane, London EC1R 0BJ United Kingdom. **Tel** 011 44 171 833812, 011 44 171 8331563, FAX 011 44 171 8831563, telex 28339 CPLCDP G. **Bk Rev**.
Desc: Detailed survey of the Japan chemical industry.

UK

CHEM-FACTS METHANOL. **VFOAT** Chemical-Facts: Methanol. (19??)-. English. £155.00 UK; $265.00 US; £160.00 Europe; £165.00 other. Chemical Intelligence Services, 39A Bowling Green Lane, London EC1R 0BJ United Kingdom. **Tel** 011 44 171 833812, 011 44 171 8331563, FAX 011 44 171 8831563, telex 28339 CPLCDP G. **Bk Rev**.
Desc: Worldwide survey of the manufacturing and trade of methanol.

UK

CHEM-FACTS: NETHERLANDS. English. £185.00 UK; £190.00 UK; $310.00 US; £195.00 other. Chemical Intelligence Services, 39A Bowling Green Lane, London EC1R 0BJ United Kingdom. **Tel** 011 44 171 833812, 011 44 171 8331563, FAX 011 44 171 8831563, telex 28339 CPLCDP G. **Bk Rev**.
Desc: Detailed survey of the Netherlands chemical industry.

UK

CHEM-FACTS: POLYETHYLENE. **VFOAT** Chemical-Facts: Polyethylene. English. £250.00 UK; £260.00 Europe; $430.00 US; £270.00 other. Chemical Intelligence Services, 39A Bowling Green Lane, London EC1R 0BJ United Kingdom. **Tel** 011 44 171 833812, 011 44 171 8331563, FAX 011 44 171 8831563, telex 28339 CPLCDP G. **Bk Rev**.
Desc: Worldwide survey of manufacture and trade of polyethylene.

UK

CHEM-FACTS: POLYPROPYLENE. **VFOAT** Chemical-Facts: Polypropylene. English. £250.00 UK; £260.00; $430.00 US; £270.00 other. Chemical Intelligence Services, 39A Bowling Green Lane, London EC1R 0BJ United Kingdom. **Tel** 011 44 171 833812, 011 44 171 8331563, FAX 011 44 171 8831563, telex 28339 CPLCDP G. **Bk Rev**.
Desc: Worldwide survey of manufacture and trade of polypropylene.

UK

CHEM-FACTS: SCANDINAVIA. (19??)-. English. Chemical Intelligence Services, 39A Bowling Green Lane, London EC1R 0BJ United Kingdom. **Tel** 011 44 171 833812, 011 44 171 8331563, FAX 011 44 171 8831563, telex 28339 CPLCDP G.
Desc: Detailed survey of the Scandinavia chemical industry.

UK

CHEM-FACTS: SPAIN. English. £200.00 UK; £205.00 Europe; $335.00 US; £210.00 other. Chemical Intelligence Services, 39A Bowling Green Lane, London EC1R 0BJ United Kingdom. **Tel** 011 44 171 833812, 011

Chemistry and Chemicals

44 171 8331563, FAX 011 44 171 8831563, telex 28339 CPLCDP G. **Bk Rev.**
Desc: Detailed survey of the Spain chemical industry.

UK

CHEM-FACTS: UNITED KINGDOM.
(19??)-. English. Irregular. £225.00 UK; $470.00 US; £230.00 Europe; £235.00 other. Chemical Intelligence Services, 39A Bowling Green Lane, London EC1R 0BJ United Kingdom. **Tel** 011 44 171 833812, 011 44 171 8331563, FAX 011 44 171 8831563, telex 28339 CPLCDP G. **Bk Rev.**
Desc: Detailed survey of the chemical industry in the United Kingdom.

LC QD1 .C695 ISSN 0931-7597
DD 540 GW
CCC

CHEM INFORM. See Chemistry and Chemicals-Abstracting, Bibliographies and Statistics.

LC TP12 .C443 ISSN 0094-6567
DD 660/.029/473 US
UDC 661
NLM TP 12 C516

CHEM SOURCES U.S.A. See Chemistry and Chemicals-Abstracting, Bibliographies and Statistics.

ISSN 0711-3447
DD 540/.5 CN

CHEM TRENDS. [Chem trends]. Added/Corp
University of Guelph. Dept. of Chemistry. **VFOAT** Chemtrends. (Fall 1980)-. Periodical. English. Irregular. Free. Chem Trends, Department of Chemistry, University of Guelph, Guelph Ontario Canada.

LC QD1 .C457 ISSN 0324-9034
DD 540 PL
CODEN ZWSCDK

CHEMIA. Added/Corp Wyzsza Szkola Pedagogiczna
im. Powstancow Slaskich w Opulu. (19??)-. Academic Scholarly Publication. Polish (summaries and/or abstracts in English). Irregular. Price varies per volume. Wyzsza Szkola Pedagogiczna, Opole, Ul. Oleska 48, 45-951 Opole Poland. **Tel** 011 48 77 38387. (**Subscription address:** Ars Polona-Ruch, PO Box 1001, Krakowskie Przedmiescie 7, 00-068 Warsaw Poland. **Tel** 011 48 22 261201.) Documents available from CASDDS.
Ind/Abst Chem. Abstr.

LC QD1 .A51 ISSN 0009-2258
DD 540/.05 US
NLM Z 5524 C517 CODEN CHABA8

CHEMICAL ABSTRACTS. See Chemistry and Chemicals-Abstracting, Bibliographies and Statistics.

LC QD ISSN 0009-2258
DD 540 US
CODEN CHABA8

CHEMICAL ABSTRACTS. See Business and Economics-Abstracting, Bibliographies and Statistics.

LC Z5521 ISSN 0090-8363
DD 016.54 US
CODEN CAAEA2

CHEMICAL ABSTRACTS. APPLIED CHEMISTRY AND CHEMICAL ENGINEERING SECTIONS. See Chemistry and Chemicals-Abstracting, Bibliographies and Statistics.

LC Z5521 ISSN 0093-5719
DD 016.54 US
CODEN CHABAB

CHEMICAL ABSTRACTS. INDEX GUIDE.
See Chemistry and Chemicals-Abstracting, Bibliographies and Statistics.

LC QD380 ISSN 0009-2274
DD 547.7 US
CODEN CAMLAF

CHEMICAL ABSTRACTS. MACROMOLECULAR SECTION. See
Chemistry and Chemicals-Abstracting, Bibliographies and Statistics.

ISSN 0278-1832
US
CODEN CAISDJ

CHEMICAL ABSTRACTS. PHYSICAL, INORGANIC, AND ANALYTICAL CHEMISTRY SECTIONS. See Business and Economics-Abstracting, Bibliographies and Statistics.

LC TP1 .C318 ISSN 0009-2320
DD 660.5 II
CCC
CODEN CHAIAT

CHEMICAL AGE OF INDIA. [Chem. age India].
(1953)-. Academic Scholarly Publication. English. Twelve times a year. $125.00. Technical Press Publications, 5-1 Convent Street, Colaba, Bombay 400 039 India. **Tel** 2021156, 2021446, 2026361, 3479 CHEM IN, telex 11-3479 CHEM IN. (**Subscription address:** Prints India, 11 Darya Ganj, New Delhi 110002 India. **Tel** 011 91 11 3268645, FAX 011 91 11 3275542, telex 31-61087 PRIN-IN.) **ED** Vatsala de Sousa. Index available (Bound in Dec. iss.). cum. index. **Bk Rev**, (Qty: 12). **Ad Acc.**

Circ: 6,500 (ctrl). available on microfilm, microfiche, and CD-ROM from University Microfilms International (UMI). Documents available from CASDDS. **Continues** Chemical Age (Bombay, India).
Desc: Serves a wide spectrum of chemical and allied process industries. The editorial contents reflect newer developments world-wide.
Ind/Abst Anal. Abstr.; Bioeng. Abstr.; Chem. Abstr.; Chem. Hazards Ind.; Coal Abstr.; Curr. Biotechnol.; Ei Page One; Fluid Abstr.; Civil Eng.; Fluid Abstr. Proc. Eng.; FLUIDEX; Lab. Hazards Bull.; Proc. Chem. Eng.; SEA Abstr.; Soils Fert.; Theor. Chem. Eng.

ISSN 0009-2401
US
CODEN CHEBAS
TITLE CHANGE

CHEMICAL BULLETIN, THE. (CHEMICAL BULLETIN; PUB. BY THE CHICAGO SECTION OF THE AMERICAN CHEMICAL SOCIETY, WITH THE COOPERATION OF THE MILWAUKEE, WISCONSIN, MINNESOTA, IOWA, AMES AND LOUISVILLE [ETC.] SECTIONS.). [Chem. bull.]. Added/Corp American
Chemical Society. Chicago Section. (Oct. 1914)-(19??). Bulletin. English. Chemical Bulletin, 7173 North Austin Avenue, Niles IL 60714. **Tel** (708)647-8405. **Continued by** Chicago Chemical Bulletin.
Ind/Abst Chem. Abstr.

LC TP1 .C332 ISSN 0731-8774
DD 338.4/766/005 US
CCC
CODEN CHBUD5
CEASED

CHEMICAL BUSINESS. [Chem. bus.]. (Oct.
1979)-(April 1994). Periodical. English. Schnell Publishing Company Inc., 80 Broad Street, New York NY 10004. **Tel** (212)248-4177, telex 226113 CMR UR. **ED** J Robert Warren. **Ad Acc. Circ:** 45,000 (ctrl). available on an online database; available on microfilm and microfiche from University Microfilms International (UMI). Documents available from CASDDS.
Desc: Feature magazine covering US and world developments in the chemical industry: markets, management, sales, research, engineering, production, shipping, legislation and equipment.
Ind/Abst Abstr. Bull. Inst. Pap. Sci. Tech.; AGRICOLA [Select. Cov.]; BioBusiness (1989-); Chem. Abstr.; Chem. Ind. Notes (1984-); Curr. Cit.; F&S Index Plus Text, Int. [Full Txt.] [Select. Cov.]; PROMT [Full Txt.]; Trade Ind. ASAP [Full Txt.]; Trade Ind. Index (1981-) [Full Txt.].

ISSN 0267-5889
UK

CHEMICAL BUSINESS BULLETIN. SPECIALITY CHEMICALS. [Chem. bus. bull., Spec. chem.]. VFOAT Speciality Chemicals (Nottingham).
(1985)-. English. Irregular.
Ind/Abst Biodeter. Abstr.

UK

CHEMICAL BUSINESS BULLETINS. See
Business and Economics-Abstracting, Bibliographies and Statistics.

UK

●CHEMICAL BUSINESS NEWSBASE [ONLINE DATABASE]. See Business and Economics-Abstracting, Bibliographies and Statistics.

ISSN 0950-6144
DD 016.3384766 UK

CHEMICAL BUSINESS UPDATE. See
Chemistry and Chemicals-Abstracting, Bibliographies and Statistics.

ISSN 0366-5607
SW
CODEN CCUSBN

CHEMICAL COMMUNICATIONS.
Added/Corp Stockholms Universitet. (1970)-. Academic Scholarly Publication. English. Irregular. Price varies per volume. University of Stockholm Institute of Inorganic and Physical Chemistry, 106 91 Stockholm Sweden. **Tel** 011 46 8 1622369, FAX 011 46 8 152187. **ED** Lars Kihlborg. ctrl circ. Documents available from CASDDS.
Ind/Abst Agrofor. Abstr.; Chem. Abstr.; For. Prod. Abstr.

JA

CHEMICAL CORRESPONDENCE. (198?)-.
Periodical. English. Twenty-four times a year. $950.00. Sumika Technical Information Service Inc., 5-15 Kitahama Higashiku, Osakashi Osakafu 541 Japan. **Tel** 06-220-3366. **Ad Acc. Circ:** 200 (ctrl).
Desc: Covering news in the high tech field: research and development, news of Japanese firms and governmental institutions, also covers news related to technology transfer.

ISSN 0970-9525
II
UDC 54

CHEMICAL DIGEST DELHI. [Chem. Dig.Delhi].
(1971)-. Periodical. English. Twelve times a year. $30.00. (**Subscription address:** Prints India, 11 Darya Ganj, New Delhi 110002 India. **Tel** 011 91 11 3268645, FAX 011 91 11 3275542, telex 31-61087 PRIN-IN.)

GW

CHEMICAL FIBERS INTERNATIONAL.
See Fabrics and Textile Industries.

ISSN 1066-5315
DD 540 US
CODEN CHHEEM

●CHEMICAL HERITAGE. [Chem. herit.].
Added/Corp Chemical Heritage Foundation. American Chemical Society. American Institute of Chemical Engineers. Vol. 10, No. 1 (Winter 1993)-. Periodical. English. Two times a year. $25.00. Chemical Heritage Foundation, 3401 Walnut Street, Philadelphia PA 19104. **Tel** (215)898-4896, FAX (215)898-3327. **Continues** News (Beckman Center for the History of Chemistry), 1052-0414.

LC TP12 .C57 ISSN 0591-1230
DD 338.4/7/66005 II

CHEMICAL INDUSTRIAL UNDERTAKINGS LICENSED. See Industry
and Production.

ISSN 0737-8025
US
CODEN CHEIDI

CHEMICAL INDUSTRIES (NEW YORK, N.Y. : 1979). (CHEMICAL INDUSTRIES.). [Chem. ind.]. Vol. 1 (1979)-. Academic Scholarly Publication.
English. Irregular. Price varies per volume. Marcel Dekker Inc., 270 Madison Avenue, New York NY 10016. **Tel** (212)696-9000, (800)228-1160, FAX (212)685-4540, telex 421419. (**Subscription address:** Marcel Dekker Inc., PO Box 5017, Monticello NY 12701. **Tel** (800)228-1160.) Documents available from CASDDS.
Desc: Analyzes areas relevant to the chemical industry. Includes topics such as solids handling and catalyst manufacture.
Ind/Abst Chem. Abstr.; Curr. Cit.; Ei Page One.

ISSN 1051-9041
DD 338 US

CHEMICAL INDUSTRIES NEWSLETTER. [Chem. ind. newsl.]. Added/Corp
SRI International. Chemical Industries Centers. (May/June 1985)-. Newsletter. English. Six times a year. Free on request. SRI, 333 Ravenswood Avenue, AE210, Menlo Park CA 94025. **Tel** (415)326-6200, (415)859-3715. **Continues** Chemical Industries Division Newsletter.

LC HD9658.S6 C5 ISSN 0304-1174
DD 380.1/45/66002568 SA

CHEMICAL INDUSTRY BUYER'S GUIDE FOR SOUTHERN AFRICA. See Industry and
Production-Trade and Industrial Directories.

LC TP1 .C34 ISSN 0960-2992
DD 660.58 UK

CHEMICAL INDUSTRY EUROPE. (1991)-.
English. One time a year. $148.87. Miller Freeman Technical Ltd., Riverbank House, Angel Lane, Tonbridge Kent TN9 1SE United Kingdom. **Tel** 011 44 1732 362666, FAX 011 44 1732 770483, telex 95454 BBIS. **ED** Gillian Bates and Kathy Tutt. **Circ:** 2,800. **Continues** Chemical Industry Directory.
Desc: Index by country of manufacturers and traders of chemicals, plant and laboratory equipment, plus chemical and oil storage depots, brand names and professional and trade organisations.

ISSN 0045-639X
US
CCC
CODEN CINTAW

CHEMICAL INDUSTRY NOTES. See
Chemistry and Chemicals-Abstracting, Bibliographies and Statistics.

ISSN 1064-4601
DD 363 US

CHEMICAL INFORMATION ALERT. [Chem.
inf. alert]. (1992)-. Periodical. English. Twelve times a year. $147.00. M. Lee Smith Publishers and Printers, PO Box 198867, Nashville TN 37219. **Tel** (615)242-7395, (800)274-6774, FAX (615)256-6601.

ISSN 0364-1910
US
NLM W1 CH25M

CHEMICAL INFORMATION BULLETIN.
[Chem. inf. bull.]. **Added/Corp** American Chemical Society. Division of Chemical Information. Vol. 27 No. 2 (Fall 1975)-. Bulletin. English. Three times a year (seasonal). $30.00. American Chemical Society Division of Chemical Information, PO Box 904, Spring House PA 19477. **Tel** (215)641-7820. **ED** Marge Matthews Institute for Scientific Information, 3501 Market Street,

Philadelphia, PA 19101. **Bk Rev. Ad Acc.** ***Continues*** *Chemical Literature, 0364-1929.*
Desc: A publication of the Division of Chemical Information of the American Chemical Society.

LC QD1 .C465 **ISSN** 0947-0662
US

●**CHEMICAL INTELLIGENCER.** (Jan. 1995)-. Periodical. English. Four times a year (quarterly). $69.00. Springer-Verlag New York Inc., 175 Fifth Avenue, New York NY 10010. **Tel** (212)460-1500 ext 256, FAX (212)533-3503, telex 232 235 SPB UR. **(Subscription address:** Springer-Verlag / Heidelberg, Electronic Media, Tiergartenstrasse 17, D-69121 Heidelberg Germany. **Tel** 011 49 6221 487457, FAX 011 49 6221 487366.**) ED** Istvan Hargittai (editor's address: Institute of General and Analytical Chemistry, Budapest Technical University, Szt. Gellert ter 4, H-1521 Budapest, Hungary; e-mail: hargittai@ch.bme.hu). **Ad Acc, Adv Mgr:** Brian Skepton, **Tel** (212)460-1575. **Acid Free.**
Desc: Devoted to the history and culture of chemistry. Intended to inform and entertain a broad audience of chemists including non-specialists.

GW

CHEMICAL PAPERS. (19??)-. German. Six times a year. Translibris Gmbh, PO Box 301373, D 50783 Cologne Germany. **Tel** 011 49 221 542085, 011 49 221 542086. Documents available from The Genuine Article, CASDDS.
Ind/Abst Ceram. Abstr. (19??-); Chem. Abstr.; Nat. Prod. Updates; Res. Alert [Full Cov.]; Sci. Cit. Index; SCISEARCH.

UK

CHEMICAL PATENTS INDEX. See Chemistry and Chemicals-Abstracting, Bibliographies and Statistics.

UK

CHEMICAL PATENTS INDEX. PLASTICS AND POLYMERS. See Chemistry and Chemicals-Abstracting, Bibliographies and Statistics.

LC QC176.8.E4 S87 **ISSN** 0142-3401
DD 530.4/1/05 UK
CODEN CPSSD4

CHEMICAL PHYSICS OF SOLIDS AND THEIR SURFACES. See Physics.

LC TP1 .C367 **ISSN** 0009-2630
DD 660 US
CCC

CHEMICAL PROCESSING (CHICAGO, ILL.). (CHEMICAL PROCESSING.). [Chem. process.]. Vol. 13 (Jan. 1950)-. Academic Scholarly Publication. English. Twelve times a year. $58.00. Putnam Publishing Company, 301 East Erie Street, Chicago IL 60611. **Tel** (312)644-2020 ext. 454, FAX (312)644-1131. available on microfilm and microfiche from University Microfilms International (UMI). Documents available from CASDDS, Documents on Demand. ***Continues*** *Chemical Processing Preview, 0069-3014.*
Ind/Abst Ceram. Abstr.; Chem. Abstr.; Coal Abstr.; Corros. Abstr. (-199?); Curr. Cit.; Energy Inf. Abstr.; Energy Res. Abstr.; Environ. Abstr.; Fluid Abstr., Civil Eng.; Fluid Abstr. Proc. Eng.; FLUIDEX; Gas Abstr.; INIS Atomindex [Micro.]; Ocean. Abstr.; Pollut. Abstr. Indexes; Proc. Chem. Eng.; Theor. Chem. Eng.

LC QD77 .M13a **ISSN** 0094-6249
DD 540/.21/2 US

CHEMICAL REFERENCE MANUAL. Main/Corp MC/B Manufacturing Chemists (Firm). Vol. 1 (1973)-. English. Irregular. Chemical Reference Manual, 2909 Highland Avenue, Norwood OH 45212.

LC KF3958.A15 B87 **ISSN** 0148-7973
DD 344/.73/042 US
CCC

CHEMICAL REGULATION REPORTER. See Law.

CH
CODEN CRCUED

CHEMICAL RESEARCH IN CHINESE UNIVERSITIES. Added/Corp China. Kuo Chia Chiao yu wei Yuan Hui. Vol. 7, No. 1 (Mar. 1991)-. Academic Scholarly Publication. English. Four times a year. Chemical Research in Chinese Universities, Editorial Department, Jilin University, Changchun 130021, People's Republic of China. Documents available from The Genuine Article, CASDDS. ***Continues*** *Kao Teng Hsueh Hsiao hua Hsueh Hsueh pao. English. Chemical Journal of Chinese Universities.*
Ind/Abst Chem. Abstr.; Res. Alert [Full Cov.].

LC QD **ISSN** 0009-2665
DD 540 US
CCC
NLM W1 CH263 **CODEN** CHREAY
Pr Rev.

CHEMICAL REVIEWS. [Chem. rev.]. **Added/Corp** American Chemical Society. Vol. 1 (April 1924)-. Academic Scholarly Publication. English. Eight times a year. $488.00. American Chemical Society, 1155 Sixteenth Street Northwest, Washington DC 20036. **Tel** (800)333-9511, (800)227-5558, (614)447-3776, FAX (202)447-3671. **(Subscription address:** American Chemical Society / Ohio, Department L 0011, Columbus OH 43268-0011.**) ED** Josef Michl. (free). cum. index. **Bk Rev. Ad Acc. Acid Free. Circ:** 5,054 (ctrl). available on microfilm and microfiche from University Microfilms International (UMI); available on an online database from STN International; available with charts; available with illustrations; available in microform; available on microfilm and microform. Documents available from The Genuine Article, UMI Article Clearinghouse, CASDDS, Documents on Demand, BLDSC, FAXON Xpress, The UnCover Company, SWETS.
Desc: Reviews of research in various areas of chemistry that eliminate the need to scan scores of articles concerning particular fields.
Ind/Abst Abstr. Bull. Inst. Pap. Sci. Tech.; Appl. Sci. Technol. Index; Chem Inform; Chem. Abstr.; Coal Abstr.; Curr. Chem. React.; Curr. Cit.; Curr. Contents Phys. Chem. Earth Sci.; Dairy Sci. Abstr.; Ei Page One; EMBASE; Energy Inf. Abstr.; Environ. Abstr.; Expand. Acad. Index (1992-); GeoRef; Index Sci. Rev. [Full Cov.]; INIS Atomindex [Micro.]; Int. Aerosp. Abstr.; Leadscan; Methods Organ. Synth.; Newsp. Period. Abstr. (1992-); Life Sci. Collect.; PESTDOC; Res. Alert [Full Cov.]; Sci. Cit. Index; SCISEARCH; Soils Fert.; Surf. Treat. Technol. Abstr.; World Surf. Coat. Abstr.; World Text. Abstr.

LC QD47 .C48 **ISSN** 1058-1227
DD 540/.71/173 US
CCC

CHEMICAL SCIENCES GRADUATE SCHOOL FINDER. [Chem. sci. grad. sch. finder]. **Added/Corp** American Chemical Society. (1992)-. English. One time a year. $59.95. American Chemical Society, 1155 Sixteenth Street Northwest, Washington DC 20036. **Tel** (800)333-9511, (800)227-5558, (614)447-3776, FAX (202)447-3671.

LC QD1 .C624 **ISSN** 0306-0012
DD 540/.5 UK
CCC
NLM W1 CH271D **CODEN** CSRVBR
Pr Rev.

CHEMICAL SOCIETY REVIEWS. [Chem. Soc. rev.]. **Main/Corp** Chemical Society (Great Britain). Vol. 1 (1972)-. Periodical. English. Six times a year. $225.00. Royal Society of Chemistry, Thomas Graham House, Science Park, Cambridge CB4 4WF United Kingdom. **Tel** 011 44 1223 420066, FAX 011 44 1223 423623, telex 818293 ROYAL. **(Subscription address:** Royal Society of Chemistry, Turpin Distribution Services Ltd., Blackhorse Road, Letchworth, Hertfordshire SG6 1HN United Kingdom. **Tel** 011 44 1462 672555, FAX 011 44 1462 480947.**)** available on microfilm and microfiche from University Microfilms International (UMI). Documents available from The Genuine Article, BIOSIS Document Express, CASDDS. ***Formed by the union of*** *Quarterly Reviews, Chemical Society, 0009-2681* ***and*** *RIC Reviews, 0035-8940.*
Desc: Provides review articles ranging over the whole of chemistry and its interfaces. There is a conscious attempt to provide consistency of depth and treatment, so that each article is of interest to chemists in general and not merely to the specialist.
Ind/Abst Biol. Abstr.; Chem Inform; Chem. Abstr.; Chem. Titles; Curr. Chem. React.; Curr. Cit.; Curr. Contents Phys. Chem. Earth Sci.; Dairy Sci. Abstr.; EMBASE; Food Sci. Technol. Abstr.; Index Sci. Rev. [Full Cov.]; Leadscan; Life Sci. Collect.; PESTDOC; Ref. Upd. Deluxe Ed.; Res. Alert [Full Cov.]; Sci. Cit. Index; SCISEARCH; World Ceram. Abstr.; World Surf. Coat. Abstr.; World Text. Abstr.

LC TD196.C45 C484 **ISSN** 0954-2299
DD 628.5/2 UK
CCC
CODEN CHSBEY

CHEMICAL SPECIATION AND BIOAVAILABILITY. See Environmental Issues.

ISSN 0271-1478
US
CCC

CHEMICAL SUBSTANCES CONTROL. [Chem. subst. control]. **Added/Corp** Bureau of National Affairs (Washington, D.C.). (1980)-. Periodical. English. Twenty-six times a year. $680.00. Bureau of National Affairs Inc., 9435 Key West Avenue, Rockville MD 20850. **Tel** (800)372-1033, (301)258-1033, FAX (301)948-5823. **ED** Eileen Z Joseph. available on an online database from Human Resources Information Network.
Desc: A reference and advisory service on the management of chemicals from premanufacture through use and disposal.

AU

CHEMICAL THERMODYNAMICS OF ACTINIDE ELEMENTS AND COMPOUNDS. (19??)-. Monographic series. English. Irregular. Price varies per volume. International Atomic Energy Agency / IAEA, Wagramerstrasse 5, PO Box 100, A-1400 Vienna Austria. **Tel** 011 43 1 206021270, FAX 011 43 1 20607. **(Subscription address:** UNIPUB, 4611 F Assembly Drive, Lanham MD 20706. **Tel** (800)274-4888, (301)459-7666.**)**
Desc: Series consisting of 10 parts, comprising a critical assessment of the chemical thermodynamic properties of the actinide elements and compounds.

LC TP1 .C345 **ISSN** 0149-2381
DD 338.4/7/66 US
CODEN CTTRDY

CHEMICAL TIMES & TRENDS. [Chem. times trends]. **Added/Corp** Chemical Specialties Manufacturers Association. **VAT** Chemical Times and Trends. Vol. 1 (Oct. 1977)-. Trade Publication. English. Four times a year. $27.00. Allen Press Inc., 810 East 10th Street, PO Box 1897, Lawrence KS 66044-8897. **Tel** (913)843-1221, (800)627-0629, FAX (913)843-1274. **Ad Acc.** Documents available from CASDDS.
Desc: Technical, regulatory and management review of industries producing pesticides, antimicrobials, detergents, polishes, automotives, industrial products, aerosols.
Ind/Abst BioBusiness; Chem. Abstr. (1989-); Curr. Cit.; Life Sci. Collect.

LC QD **ISSN** 0009-2711
DD 540 US
CCC
NLM Z 5524 C519 **CODEN** CHTIAM

CHEMICAL TITLES. See Chemistry and Chemicals-Abstracting, Bibliographies and Statistics.

LC TP1 .C37 **ISSN** 0009-272X
DD 660.2/05 US
CCC
NLM W1 CH271V **CODEN** CHWKA9

CHEMICAL WEEK. See Industry and Production.

ISSN 0162-637X
US

CHEMICAL WORKER, THE. See Business and Economics-Labor.

ISSN 0009-2770
XR
CCC
NLM W1 CH29 **CODEN** CHLSAC
Pr Rev.

CHEMICKE LISTY. [Chem. listy]. **Added/Corp** Ustredni Ustav Chemicky (Prague, Czechoslovakia) Ceskoslovenska Spolecnost Chemicka. Ceskoslovenska Akademie Ved. **VFOAT** Casopis Pro Prumysl Chemicky; Listy Chemicke. (1907)-. Periodical. Czech (English). Twelve times a year. $348.97. **(Subscription address:** Kubon & Sagner, ABT Zeitschriftenimport, D 80328 Munich Germany. **Tel** 011 49 89 54218130.**) ED** Jiri Gut. Index Available, published separately, free-automatically sent. **Bk Rev. Ad Acc. Circ:** 1,900 (ctrl). available on microfilm from University Microfilms International (UMI). Documents available from The Genuine Article, CASDDS. ***Continues*** *Chemicke Listy Pro Vedu a Prumysl.*
Desc: Articles on laboratory techniques, progresses in chemical science and industry, results in research. Information about congresses and symposia in all chemical fields as well as original papers.
Ind/Abst Alum. Ind. Abstr.; Anal. Abstr.; Art Archaeol. Tech. Abstr.; Ceram. Abstr. (19??-); Chem. Abstr.; Chem. Titles; Curr. Biotechnol.; Curr. Cit.; Curr. Contents Phys. Chem. Earth Sci.; Eng. Mater. Abstr.; Food Sci. Technol. Abstr.; Hortic. Abstr.; Leadscan; Met. Abstr.; Life Sci. Collect.; Res. Alert [Full Cov.]; Saf. Health Work; Sci. Cit. Index; SCISEARCH; Soc. Sci. Cit. Index [Select. Cov.]; Sug. Indus. Abstr.; Surf. Treat. Technol. Abstr.; World Surf. Coat. Abstr.

ISSN 0009-2789
DD 660 540 XR
CODEN CHPUA4

CHEMICKY PRUMYSL. [Chem. pr.-um.]. (1951)-. Academic Scholarly Publication. English. Six times a year. $53.50. **(Subscription address:** Kubon & Sagner, ABT Zeitschriftenimport, D 80328 Munich Germany. **Tel** 011 49 89 54218130.**)** Documents available from Article Express International, CASDDS. ***Supersedes*** *Chemicke Listy Pro Vedu a Prumysl* ***and*** *Chemicky Obzor;* ***Absorbed*** *Chemie. Mesicnek Pro Uzitou Vedu a Praxi.*
Ind/Abst Abstr. Bull. Inst. Pap. Sci. Tech.; Alum. Ind. Abstr.; Anal. Abstr.; Ceram. Abstr.; Chem. Abstr.; Coal Abstr.; Curr. Biotechnol.; Eng. Index Annu. [Select. Cov.]; Int. Polym. Sci. Tech.; Met. Abstr.; Life Sci. Collect. (1985-); Proc. Chem. Eng.; Saf. Health Work; Theor. Chem. Eng.; World Surf. Coat. Abstr.

GW

CHEMIE IN DER SCHULE. (1954)-. Periodical. German. Irregular. DM71.50. Paedagogischer Zeitschriftenverlag GmbH, Postfach 269, D-10107 Berlin Germany. **Tel** 011 49 30 20343431, FAX 011 49 30 20343432. **(Subscription address:** Cornelsen Velhagen & Klasing, Postfach 100271 Zeitschriften, D-33502 Bielefeld Germany. **Tel** 011 49 521 7872290.**)**

ISSN 0009-2851
DD 540 GW
CCC
CODEN CUNZAW
Pr Rev.

CHEMIE IN UNSERER ZEIT. [Chem. unserer Zeit]. **Added/Corp** Gesellschaft Deutscher Chemiker. Vol. 1 (March 1967)-. Periodical. German. Six times a year. $123.00. VCH Gesellschaft GmbH, Postfach 101161, D-69451 Weinheim Germany. **Tel** 011 49 6201 606459, FAX 011 49 6201 606184. **(Subscription address:** VCH Publishers Inc., 303 Northwest 12th

Avenue, Journals Department, Deerfield FL 33442. **Tel** (800)367-8249, (305)428-5566.) Documents available from The Genuine Article, CASDDS.
Ind/Abst Art Archaeol. Tech. Abstr.; Chem. Abstr.; Coal Abstr.; Curr. Biotechnol.; Curr. Cit.; Curr. Contents Phys. Chem. Earth Sci.; Energy Res. Abstr.; Food Sci. Technol. Abstr.; Leadscan; Res. Alert [Full Cov.]; Risk Abstr. (19??-19??); Sci. Cit. Index; SCISEARCH.

ISSN 0379-7651
BE
UDC 66
CODEN 541

CHEMIE MAGAZINE. (1974)-. Periodical. Dutch. Twelve times a year. 1300F. Technipress, Stationsstraat 30 bus 1, 1702 Groot-Bijgaarden Belgium. **Tel** 011 32 2 4818100, FAX 011 32 2 4818182.
Ind/Abst Curr. Cit.

BE
CODEN CHMADY

CHEMIE MAGAZINE : MAANDBLAD VAN DE VLAAMSE CHEMISCHE VERENIGING. **Added/Corp** Vlaamse Chemische Vereniging. **VFOAT** Chemie. (197?)-. Academic Scholarly Publication. Dutch. Twelve times a year. 1800F. KVCV, Groot Begijnhof 6, B 3000 Leuven Belgium. **Tel** 016 29 32 14, FAX 016 22 68 92. Index available. cum. index. **Bk Rev. Ad Acc. Circ:** 4,000 (ctrl). Documents available from CASDDS.
Ind/Abst Chem. Abstr.

ISSN 0235-7216
LI
CODEN CHMJES

CHEMIJA = KHIMIIA = CHEMISTRY. **Added/Corp** Lietuvos Mokslu Akademija. Chemijos ir Chemines Technologijos Institutas (Lietuvos TSR Mokslu Akademija). **VFOAT** Khimiia; Chemistry. (1990)-. Periodical. English (Russian; summaries and/or abstracts in Lithuanian). Four times a year. **(Subscription address:** Victor Kamkin, 4956 Boiling Brook Parkway, Rockville MD 20852. **Tel** (301)881-5973.) Documents available from CASDDS. ***Continues in part*** *Lietuvos TSR Mokslu Akademijos Darbai. Serija B, 0132-2729.*
Ind/Abst Chem. Abstr.

ISSN 0366-5526
GR
CODEN CCGEAC

CHEMIKA CHRONIKA. GENIKE EKDOSIS. (CHEMIKA CHRONIKA. CHIMIKA CHRONIKA. GENIKE EKDOSIS.). [Chem. chron., Gen. ekd.]. **Added/Corp** Henosis Hellenon Chemikon. **VFOAT** Chimika Chronika. Genike Ekdosis. Vol. 34 (Jan. 1969)-. Academic Scholarly Publication. Greek, Modern. Twelve times a year. $100.00. Association of Greek Chemists, 27 Kaningos Street, Athens 10682 Greece. **Tel** 011 30 1 3621524. Documents available from CASDDS. ***Supersedes in part*** *Chemika Chronika. Chimika Chronika.*
Ind/Abst Alum. Ind. Abstr.; Chem. Abstr.; Curr. Biotechnol.; Met. Abstr.

LC QD1 .N353
DD 540.(5/6) NE

CHEMISCH JAARBOEK. **Added/Corp** Koninklijke Nederlandse Chemische Vereniging. **VFOAT** Kncv Chemisch Jaarboek. (19??)-. Dutch. Secretariaat En Ledenadministratie KNCV, Burnierstraat 1 Postbus 90613, Den Haag 250G LP Denhaag Netherlands. **Tel** 070-469406. **Ad Acc.** ctrl circ. ***Continues*** *Chemisch Jaarboekje.*

ISSN 0167-2746
NE
NLM W1 CH307P **CODEN** CMAGDR

CHEMISCH MAGAZINE. [Chem. mag.]. (Feb. 1980)-. Academic Scholarly Publication. Dutch. Twelve times a year. Fl300.00. Ten Hagen and Stam BV, Postbus 34, 2501 AG The Hague Netherlands. **Tel** 011 31 70 3045700. Documents available from CASDDS. ***Continues*** *Chemisch Weekblad Magazine, 0378-1895.*
Ind/Abst Anal. Abstr.; Chem. Abstr.; Chem. Bus. Bull.; Chem. Bus. NewsBase (1985-); Chem. Bus. Update; Curr. Biotechnol.; Curr. Cit.; EMBASE; PESTDOC.

LC QD1 **ISSN** 0378-1887
NE
UDC 54

CHEMISCH WEEKBLAD. CHEMISCHE COURANT. (CHEMISCHE COURANT/CHEMISCH WEEKBLAD.). [Chem. weekbl., Chem. courant]. Vol. 72 (Jan. 1976)-. Periodical. Dutch. One time a week. Stam Tijdschriften BV, Postbus 235, 2280 AE Rijswijk Netherlands. **Tel** 011 31 70 3988100, FAX 011 31 70 3988276, telex 33702 STAM NL. ***Formed by the union of*** *Chemische Courant* ***and*** *Chemisch Weekblad, 0009-2932.*
Ind/Abst Anal. Abstr.; EMBASE; Saf. Health Work.

ISSN 0009-2940
GW
CCC
NLM W1 CH311 **CODEN** CHBEAM
Pr Rev. **TITLE CHANGE**

CHEMISCHE BERICHTE. [Chem. Ber.]. **Added/Corp** Gesellschaft Deutscher Chemiker. Deutsche Chemische Gesellschaft. **VFOAT** Chemische Berichte : Inorganic and Organometallic Chemistry,; Inorganic and Organometallic Chemistry. Vol. 80 (1947)-(1994). Periodical. German (English). VCH Gesellschaft GmbH, Postfach 101161, D-69451 Weinheim Germany. **Tel** 011 49 6201 606459, FAX 011 49 6201 606184. **(Subscription address:** VCH Publishers Inc., 303 Northwest 12th Avenue, Journals Department, Deerfield FL 33442. **Tel** (800)367-8249, (305)428-5566.) cum. index. Documents available from The Genuine Article, BIOSIS Document Express, CASDDS. ***Continues*** *Deutsche Chemische Gesellschaft. Berichte der Deutschen Chemischen Gesellschaft.* ***Merged with*** *Liebigs Annalen der Chemie, 0170-2041* ***to form*** *Liebigs Annalen, 0947-3440.*
Ind/Abst Abstr. Bull. Inst. Pap. Sci. Tech.; Biol. Abstr.; Ceram. Abstr.; Chem Inform; Chem. Abstr.; Curr. Chem. React.; Curr. Cit.; Curr. Contents Phys. Chem. Earth Sci.; Ei Page One; EMBASE; Energy Res. Abstr.; Index Chem.; Leadscan; Mass Spect. Bull.; Methods Organ. Synth.; Nat. Prod. Updates; Life Sci. Collect.; PESTDOC; Res. Alert [Full Cov.]; Sci. Cit. Index; SCISEARCH.

LC TP1 .C438 **ISSN** 0009-2959
GW
CCC
CODEN CHIUA3

CHEMISCHE INDUSTRIE (DUSSELDORF). (CHEMISCHE INDUSTRIE : ZEITSCHRIFT FUER DIE DEUTSCHE CHEMIEWIRTSCHAFT.). [Chem. Ind.]. **Added/Corp** Arbeitsgemeinschaft Chemische Industrie (Germany) Verband der Chemischen Industrie (Germany). Vol. 1, No. 1 (July 1949)-. Trade Publication. German (summaries and/or abstracts in English and French; table of contents in English and French). Twelve times a year. $303.99. Handelsblatt GmbH, Postfach 102716, D-40018 Duesseldorf Germany. **Tel** 011 49 211 8871730, FAX 011 49 211 133523, telex 172114489. **ED** Ernst Koch. Index Available, published separately, free-automatically sent. **Bk Rev. Ad Acc. Circ:** 5,000 (ctrl). Documents available from CASDDS. ***Continues*** *Chemische Industrie.*
Desc: Technical and economic aspects of developments, individual branches of chemical manufacture, advanced news of all major projects, comments on important new plants and equipment.
Ind/Abst Chem Inform; Chem. Abstr.; Chem. Bus. Bull.; Chem. Bus. NewsBase (1985-); Chem. Bus. Update; Chem. Ind. Notes; Coal Abstr.; Curr. Biotechnol.; Curr. Cit.; EMBASE; Energy Res. Abstr. (April 1976-); F&S Index Plus Text, Int. [Select. Cov.]; GeoRef; Infomat Int. Bus.; PESTDOC; PROMT; World Surf. Coat. Abstr.

ISSN 0009-2983
SZ
CCC
CODEN CHRUAE

CHEMISCHE RUNDSCHAU. [Chem. Rundsch.]. (1949)-. Periodical. German. One time a week. $127.30. Vogt Schild AG, Druck Verlag, Postfach 748 Zuchwilserstr 21, CH-4501 Solothurn Switzerland. **Tel** 011 41 65 247247. available on microfilm. Documents available from CASDDS. ***Continues*** *Chemisch-Technische Rundschau.*
Ind/Abst Alum. Ind. Abstr.; Chem. Abstr.; Chem. Bus. Bull.; Chem. Bus. NewsBase (1985-); Chem. Bus. Update; Chem. Ind. Notes; Energy Res. Abstr.; F&S Index Plus Text, Int. [Select. Cov.]; Met. Abstr.; PROMT; Saf. Health Work.

ISSN 0009-3025
US
CCC
NLM W1 CH314E **CODEN** CHESAB

CHEMIST (NEW YORK), THE. (CHEMIST.). [Chemist]. **Added/Corp** American Institute of Chemists. (1923)-. Trade Publication. English. Nine times a year. $30.00. American Institute of Chemists, 7315 Wisconsin Avenue, Suite 518 E, Bethesda MD 20814. **Tel** (301)652-2447. **ED** Sharon Dobson. **Bk Rev. Ad Acc. Circ:** 6,000. available on microfilm and microfiche from University Microfilms International (UMI).
Desc: Publishes articles on topics of professional and personal interest to chemists including major award acceptance, addresses, economic surveys, and news of the American Institute of Chemists activities and events.
Ind/Abst Abstr. Bull. Inst. Pap. Sci. Tech.

US

CHEMIST NEWS, THE. **Added/Corp** American Institute of Chemists. (19??)-. Periodical. English. Six times a year. American Institute of Chemists, 7315 Wisconsin Avenue, Suite 518 E, Bethesda MD 20814. **Tel** (301)652-2447.

LC QD1 .A67 **ISSN** 0947-6539
GW

•**CHEMISTRY : A EUROPEAN JOURNAL.** **Added/Corp** Gesellschaft Deutscher Chemiker. (1995)-. Periodical. English. Twelve times a year. VCH Gesellschaft GmbH, Postfach 101161, D-69451 Weinheim Germany. **Tel** 011 49 6201 606459, FAX 011 49 6201 606184.

LC QP501.C43 **ISSN** 1074-5521
DD 574.19/2/05 US
NLM W1; CH359

•**CHEMISTRY & BIOLOGY.** **See** Biology.

LC QP501
DD 574.19/2/ US

CHEMISTRY AND BIOLOGY OF MINERALIZED TISSUES : PROCEEDINGS OF THE SECOND INTERNATIONAL CONFERENCE ON THE CHEMISTRY AND BIOLOGY OF MINERALIZED TISSUES, THE. (1985)-. Proceedings. English. $55.00. Gordon & Breach Science Publishers, Inc., PO Box 786, Cooper Station, New York NY 10276. **Tel** (212)206-8900, FAX (212)645-2459. **ED** William Butler.

ISSN 0009-3068
UK
NLM W1 CH36 **CODEN** CHINAG
Pr Rev.

CHEMISTRY AND INDUSTRY (LONDON). (CHEMISTRY AND INDUSTRY.). [Chem. ind.]. **Added/Corp** Society of Chemical Industry (Great Britain). **VFOAT** Chemistry & Industry. (1932)-. Academic Scholarly Publication. English. Twenty-four times a year. $396.00. Society of Chemical Industry, 14-15 Belgrave Square, London SW1X 8PS United Kingdom. **Tel** 011 44 171 2353681, FAX 011 44 171 8231698. **(Subscription address:** American Chemical Society / Ohio, Department L 0011, Columbus OH 43268-0011. **) ED** Andrew Miller. Index available. **Bk Rev. Ad Acc. Circ:** 7,000. available on microfilm and microfiche from University Microfilms International (UMI); available on an online database (file 648/Full-Text) from DIALOG. Documents available from Article Express International, The Genuine Article, CASDDS, Documents on Demand. ***Continues*** *Chemistry and Industry Review.*
Desc: A news/review journal on the application of chemistry and related sciences.
Ind/Abst Abstr. BioCommer.; AgBiotech News Inf.; Agric. Eng. Abstr.; Alum. Ind. Abstr.; Anal. Abstr.; Appl. Sci. Technol. Index; Arts Humanit. Citation Index [Select. Cov.]; BioBusiness (1973-); Biocont. News Inf.; Biodeter. Abstr. (1991-); Ceram. Abstr.; Chem Inform; Chem. Abstr.; Chem. Bus. Bull.; Chem. Bus. NewsBase (1987-); Chem. Bus. Update; Chem. Hazards Ind.; Chem. Ind. Notes; Coal Abstr.; Curr. Biotechnol.; Curr. Chem. React.; Curr. Cit.; Curr. Technol. Index; Dairy Sci. Abstr.; EMBASE; Energy Inf. Abstr.; Eng. Mater. Abstr.; Eng. Index Annu.; Environ. Abstr.; F&S Index Plus Text, Int. [Select. Cov.]; Field Crop Abstr.; Fluid Abstr., Civil Eng.; Fluid Abstr. Proc. Eng.; FLUIDEX (1973-1989); Foods Adlibra; Grass. Forage Abstr.; Hortic. Abstr. (1989-); HTFS Dig.; Index Chem.; Index Vet.; Infomat Int. Bus.; Int. Packag. Abstr.; Lab. Hazards Bull.; Leadscan; Lit. Pat. Abstr., Oilfield Chem. (1954-); Lit. Abstr., Catal. Zeol.; Lit. Abstr., Health Environ.; Lit. Abstr., Pet. Refin. Petrochem.; Lit. Abstr., Pet. Substit.; Lit. Abstr., Transp. Storage; Maize Abstr.; Met. Abstr.; MINPROC; Mintec, Min. Technol. Abstr.; Nematol. Abstr.; Nutr. Abstr. Rev., Ser. B, Live Feeds and Feed.; Nutr. Abstr. Rev., Ser. A, Hum. Exp.; PESTDOC; Plant Breed. Abstr.; Potato Abstr.; Res. Alert [Full Cov.]; Res. High. Educ. Abstr.; Rev. Agric. Entomol.; Rev. Med. Vet. Entomol.; Rev. Plant Pathol.; Saf. Health Work; Sci. Cit. Index; SCISEARCH; Soc. Sci. Cit. Index [Select. Cov.]; Soils Fert.; Vet. Bull.; Trade Ind. ASAP [Full Txt.]; Trade Ind. Index [Full Txt.]; Weed Abstr.; Wheat Barley Trit. Abstr.; World Agric. Econ. Rural Sociol. Abstr.; World Surf. Coat. Abstr.; World Text. Abstr.

UK

CHEMISTRY AND INDUSTRY [MICROFORM]. **Added/Corp** Society of Chemical Industry (Great Britain). (19??)-. English. One time a year. $396.00. Society of Chemical Industry, 14-15 Belgrave Square, London SW1X 8PS United Kingdom. **Tel** 011 44 171 2353681, FAX 011 44 171 8231698.

ISSN 0737-8033
US
NLM W1 CH36D **CODEN** CPHDD6

CHEMISTRY AND PHARMACOLOGY OF DRUGS. **See** Pharmacy and Pharmacology.

ISSN 1057-6088
DD 016 US

CHEMISTRY CITATION INDEX. **See** Chemistry and Chemicals-Abstracting, Bibliographies and Statistics.

JA
CODEN CHEXEU

CHEMISTRY EXPRESS : JOURNAL OF KINKI CHEMICAL SOCIETY, JAPAN. **Added/Corp** Kinki Chemical Society. Vol. 1, No. 1 (1986)-. Academic Scholarly Publication. English. Twelve times a year. $50.00. Kinki Chemical Society, 1 8 4 Utsubo Honmachi Nishi Ku, Osaka 550 Japan. Documents available from The Genuine Article, CASDDS.

Ind/Abst Abstr. Bull. Inst. Pap. Sci. Tech.; Ceram. Abstr. (19??-); Chem. Abstr. (1986-); Curr. Biotechnol.; For. Prod. Abstr. (1991-); For. Abstr.; Hortic. Abstr.; Plant Breed. Abstr.; Plant Grow. Reg. Abstr.; Res. Alert [Full Cov.]; Rice Abstr.; Soyabean Abstr.; Sug. Indus. Abstr.; Weed Abstr.

LC TP1 .R62 **ISSN** 0314-4240
DD 660.2/094 AT
CCC
CODEN CHAUDY

CHEMISTRY IN AUSTRALIA. [Chem. Aust.]. **Main/Corp** Royal Australian Chemical Institute. Vol. 44, No. 7 (July 1977)-. Academic Scholarly Publication. English. Twelve times a year. 92.91Aus$. Royal Australian Chemical Institute, 1/21 Vale Street North Melbourne, Victoria 3051 Australia. **Tel** 011 61 3 3282033, FAX 011 61 3 3282670. **ED** Bruce Guise. Index available. **Bk Rev**. **Ad Acc**. **Circ:** 8,000 (ctrl). Documents available from CASDDS. ***Continues*** *PRACI, Proceedings of the Royal Australian Chemical Institute.*
Desc: Publishes material of interest and value to chemists, chemical technologists, chemical engineers, biochemists, biotechnologist and others associated with the practice of these professions.
Ind/Abst Art Archaeol. Tech. Abstr.; Ceram. Abstr.; Chem. Abstr.; Curr. Cit.; Food Sci. Technol. Abstr.; Leadscan; Res. High. Educ. Abstr.; Text. Technol. Dig.

LC QD1 .C743 **ISSN** 0009-3106
UK
CCC
NLM W1 CH36P **CODEN** CHMBAY
Pr Rev.

CHEMISTRY IN BRITAIN. [Chem. Brit.]. **Added/Corp** Chemical Society (Great Britain) Royal Institute of Chemistry. Vol. 1 (1965)-. Periodical. English. Twelve times a year. $464.00. Royal Society of Chemistry, Thomas Graham House, Science Park, Cambridge CB4 4WF United Kingdom. **Tel** 011 44 1223 420066, FAX 011 44 1223 423623, telex 818293 ROYAL. **(Subscription address:** Royal Society of Chemistry, Turpin Distribution Services Ltd., Blackhorse Road, Letchworth, Hertfordshire SG6 1HN United Kingdom. **Tel** 011 44 1462 672555, FAX 011 44 1462 480947.**)** Index available. **Bk Rev**. available on microfilm and microfiche from University Microfilms International (UMI). Documents available from Article Express International, The Genuine Article, BIOSIS Document Express, CASDDS. ***Formed by the union of*** *Chemical Society (Great Britain). Proceedings of the Chemical Society* ***and*** *Journal (Royal Institute of Chemistry).*
Desc: Contains important scientific articles of general chemical interest and keeps the scientist up to date on economic, political, and social factors and their effect on the scientific community. It also contains a wide range of articles on professional and industrial matters, news and announcements, book reviews, and details of conferences, exhibitions and meetings.
Ind/Abst Abstr. BioCommer.; Alum. Ind. Abstr.; Anal. Abstr.; Art Archaeol. Tech. Abstr.; Biol. Abstr.; Chem Inform; Chem. Abstr.; Chem. Bus. Bull.; Chem. Bus. NewsBase (1986-); Chem. Bus. Update; Chem. Hazards Ind.; Chem. Ind. Notes; Chem. Titles; Coal Abstr.; Curr. Biotechnol.; Curr. Cit.; Curr. Contents Phys. Chem. Earth Sci.; Curr. Technol. Index; Dairy Sci. Abstr.; EMBASE; Eng. Mater. Abstr.; Eng. Index Annu. [Select. Cov.]; GeoRef; Int. Aerosp. Abstr.; Lab. Hazards Bull.; Leadscan; Met. Abstr.; Methods Organ. Synth.; Nat. Prod. Updates; PESTDOC; Res. Alert [Full Cov.]; Res. High. Educ. Abstr.; Risk Abstr. (19??-19??); Saf. Health Work; Sci. Cit. Index; SCISEARCH; Soc. Sci. Cit. Index [Select. Cov.]; Soils Fert.; Trop. Dis. Bull.; World Ceram. Abstr.; World Surf. Coat. Abstr.

LC QD1 .N742 **ISSN** 0110-5566
DD 540/.9931 NZ
CODEN CMNZAA

CHEMISTRY IN NEW ZEALAND. [Chem. N. Z.]. **Added/Corp** New Zealand Institute of Chemistry. (1967)-. English. Six times a year. $35.82. Chemistry in New Zealand, PO Box 12 347, Wellington New Zealand. **Tel** 011 64 4 4739444. **ED** Bruce Graham. **Bk Rev**. **Ad Acc**. **Circ:** 2,500. Documents available from CASDDS. ***Continues*** *Journal of the New Zealand Institute of Chemistry, 0028-8225.*
Desc: Information of scientific papers submitted by members of New Zealand Institute of Chemistry, (NZIC) branch and national news and new product news.
Ind/Abst Chem. Abstr.; Curr. Cit.

ISSN 1012-8999
CE
CODEN CSLAE5

CHEMISTRY IN SRI LANKA. [Chem. Sri Lanka]. **Added/Corp** Institute of Chemistry, Ceylon. Vol. 1 (1984)-. Periodical. English. Two times a year. Documents available from CASDDS.
Ind/Abst Chem. Abstr.

LC QD1 .C7434 **ISSN** 0193-6484
DD 540/.5 UK
CCC
NLM W1 CH36V **CODEN** CINRDT

CHEMISTRY INTERNATIONAL. [Chem. int.]. **Added/Corp** International Union of Pure and Applied Chemistry. No. 3 (1979)-. Academic Scholarly Publication. English. Six times a year. $106.00. Blackwell Scientific Publications Ltd, Marston Book Services, PO Box 88, Oxford OX2 ONE United Kingdom. **Tel** 011 44 1865 206206, FAX 011 44 1865 206219, telex 837 515 MARDIS G. **ED** M. Freemantle. **Bk Rev**. **Ad Acc**. **Circ:** 2,600. available on microfilm and microfiche from University Microfilms International (UMI). Documents available from CASDDS, ADONIS. ***Continues*** *International Union of Pure and Applied Chemistry. Information Bulletin - International Union of Pure and Applied Chemistry, 0145-5672.*
Desc: Progress reports on IUPAC activities, letters, conference details and calendar, feature articles, details of IUPAC and other publications and reports.
Ind/Abst ADONIS; Art Archaeol. Tech. Abstr.; Chem. Abstr.; Coal Abstr.; EMBASE; World Surf. Coat. Abstr.

ISSN 0069-3154
US
CODEN CHECAV

CHEMISTRY OF HETEROCYCLIC COMPOUNDS, THE. (CHEMISTRY OF HETEROCYCLIC COMPOUNDS.). [Chem. heterocycl. compounds]. (1950)-. Academic Scholarly Publication. English. Irregular. Price varies per volume. John Wiley & Sons, Inc., 605 Third Avenue, New York NY 10158-0012. **Tel** (212)850-6000, (212)850-6645, FAX (212)850-6088, telex 12-7063. **(Subscription address:** John Wiley & Sons / UK, Baffins Lane, Chichester, West Sussex PO19 1UD United Kingdom. **Tel** 011 44 1243 779777, FAX 011 44 243 776128, telex 86290 WIBOOKG.) Documents available from CASDDS.
Ind/Abst Chem. Abstr.; INIS Atomindex [Micro.]; Mass Spect. Bull. (?-?).

LC QD1 .C7448 **ISSN** 0897-4756
DD 620.1/1 US
CCC
CODEN CMATEX

CHEMISTRY OF MATERIALS. **See** Engineering-Materials Science.

US

CHEMISTRY OF NUCLEOSIDES AND NUCLEOTIDES. (19??)-. English. Irregular. Plenum Press, 233 Spring Street, New York NY 10013-1578. **Tel** (212)620-8000, (800)221-9369, FAX (212)463-0742, (212)807-1047, telex 23/421139.

ISSN 0959-8464
UK
CCC

CHEMISTRY REVIEW DEDDINGTON. (CHEMISTRY REVIEW.). [Chem. Rev. Deddington]. (1991)-. Periodical. English. Five times a year. £19.50 UK; £29.00 Europe; £34.00 other. Philip Allan Publishers Ltd., Market Place, Deddington, Oxfordshire OX15 0SE United Kingdom. **Tel** 011 44 1869 338652, FAX 011 44 1869 338803.
Ind/Abst NAPRALERT.

ISSN 1071-6114
SZ

●**CHEMISTRY REVIEWS.** (1993)-. Periodical. English. Irregular. $463.00 universities, hospital and libraries; $723.00 other. Harwood Academic Publishers, PO Box 90, Reading RG1 8JL United Kingdom. **Tel** 011 44 1734 560080, FAX 011 44 1734 568211. ***Continues*** *Soviet Scientific Reviews. Section B, Chemistry Reviews, 0143-0408.*

LC QD **ISSN** 0944-5846
DD 540 GW

●**CHEMKON - CHEMIE KONKRET.** (1994)-. Academic Scholarly Publication. German. Four times a year. $55.00. VCH Verlagsgesellschaft MBH, Postfach 101161, 69451 Weinheim Germany. **Tel** 011 06201 606147, FAX 011 06201 606117.

ISSN 0736-4687
US

CHEMMATTERS. **Added/Corp** American Chemical Society. **VFOAT** Chem Matters. Vol. 1, No. 1 (Feb. 1983)-. Periodical. English. Four times a year. $7.75. American Chemical Society, 1155 Sixteenth Street Northwest, Washington DC 20036. **Tel** (800)333-9511, (800)227-5558, (614)447-3776, FAX (202)447-3671. **(Subscription address:** American Chemical Society / Ohio, Department L 0011, Columbus OH 43268-0011.)

ISSN 0937-7409
GW
CCC
CODEN CHMOE9

CHEMOECOLOGY. **See** Environmental Issues-Ecology.

ISSN 0009-3173
NE
UDC 54

CHEMPRESS. [Chempress]. (1967)-. Periodical. Dutch. Twenty-six times a year. $266.25. Misset Uitgeverij BV / Doetinchem, Postbus 4, 7000 BA Doetinchem Netherlands. **Tel** 011 31 8340 49911, 011 31 8340 49562, FAX 011 31 8340 43839, 011 31 8340 40515.

ISSN 0743-9806
DD 540 US

CHEMUNITY. [Chemunity]. **Added/Corp** American Chemical Society. Office of High School Chemistry. (19??)-. Periodical. English. Three times a year. Free on request. American Chemical Society, 1155 Sixteenth Street Northwest, Washington DC 20036. **Tel** (800)333-9511, (800)227-5558, (614)447-3776, FAX (202)447-3671. **ED** David P. Robson. **Circ:** 50,000.
Desc: A chemistry magazine for high school students. Brings chemistry to life with articles on modern applications of technology in the fields of interest to teens.

LC QD43 .C2 **ISSN** 0342-6696
GW

CHET, CHEMIE EXPERIMENT + TECHNOLOGIE. (CHET, CHEMIE EXPERIMENT + I.E. UND TECHNOLOGIE.). [ChET, Chem. exp. + technol.]. **VFOAT** Chemie Experiment + I.E. und Technologie. **VAT** Chemie Experiment Technologie, Chemie Experiment+ I.E. und Technology. (1977)-. Periodical. German. Twelve times a year. Georg Thieme Verlag Stuttgart, Postfach 301120, D-70451 Stuttgart Germany. **Tel** 011 49 711 89310, FAX 011 49 711 8931298, telex 7 252 275 GTVD. **(Subscription address:** Thieme Medical Publishers Inc., 381 Park Avenue South, New York NY 10016. **Tel** (212)683-5088.**)** ***Continues*** *CHED, Chemie Experiment Didaktik.*

US

CHICAGO CHEMICAL BULLETIN. (19??)-. Bulletin. English. Ten times a year. $15.00. Chemical Bulletin, 7173 North Austin Avenue, Niles IL 60714. **Tel** (708)647-8405. ***Continues*** *Chemical Bulletin, 0009-2401.*

LC TP1 .C64 **ISSN** 0009-4293
SZ
CODEN CHIMAD
Pr Rev.

CHIMIA. (CHIMIA; CHEMIE REPORT.). [Chimia]. **Added/Corp** Schweizerischer Chemiker-Verband. (Jan. 15, 1947)-. Academic Scholarly Publication. German (French). Twelve times a year. $254.59. Verlag Helvetica Chimica Acta, Postfach 313, CH-4010 Basel Switzerland. **Tel** 011 41 61 2724973, FAX 011 41 61 2724113. cum. index. Documents available from CASDDS. ***Supersedes*** *Schweizer Chemiker-Zeitung.*
Ind/Abst Alum. Ind. Abstr.; Chem Inform; Chem. Abstr.; Curr. Biotechnol.; Curr. Cit.; EMBASE; Energy Res. Abstr.; Met. Abstr.; Life Sci. Collect.; PESTDOC; Proc. Chem. Eng.; Saf. Health Work; Theor. Chem. Eng.

CK

CHIMIA. (1965)-. Periodical. Spanish. Documents available from The Genuine Article.
Ind/Abst Anal. Abstr.; Curr. Chem. React.; Curr. Contents Phys. Chem. Earth Sci.; Food Sci. Technol. Abstr.; Index Chem.; Methods Organ. Synth.; Nat. Prod. Updates; Res. Alert [Full Cov.]; Sci. Cit. Index; SCISEARCH; Soc. Sci. Cit. Index [Select. Cov.].

ISSN 0379-5896
TU
CODEN CATUA9

CHIMICA ACTA TURCICA. [Chim. acta Turc.]. **Added/Corp** Istanbul Universitesi. Kimya Fakultesi Dekanligi. Istanbul Universitesi. Muhendislik Fakultesi Dekanligi. Kimya Muhendisligi Bolumu. (1973)-. Academic Scholarly Publication. English (French and German). Irregular. Istanbul University / Engineering, Faculty of Engineering, Department of Chemical Engineering, Istanbul Turkey. Documents available from CASDDS.
Ind/Abst Anal. Abstr.; Chem. Abstr.; Curr. Cit.

ISSN 0009-4315
IT
CODEN CINMAB

CHIMICA E L'INDUSTRIA, LA. [Chim. ind.]. **Added/Corp** Societa Chimica Italiana. (1935)-. Academic Scholarly Publication. Italian. Eleven times a year. L150.000. Editrice Chimica SRL, Viale Liegi 48 C, 00198 Rome Italy. **Tel** 011 39 6 8549691. **ED** Domenico Giusto. Index Available, published separately, free-automatically sent. **Ad Acc**. **Circ:** 6,000. Documents available from CASDDS. ***Continues*** *L'Industria Chimica;* ***Absorbed*** *Giornale di Chimica Industriale Ed Applicata* ***and*** *Rich Mac Magazine.*
Desc: Official organ of the Italian Chemical Society. Covers research and development, processes, legislation, economics and education in pure and applied industrial chemistry fields.
Ind/Abst Alum. Ind. Abstr.; Ceram. Abstr.; Chem Inform; Chem. Abstr.; Chem. Bus. Bull.; Chem. Bus. NewsBase (1985-); Chem. Bus. Update; Chem. Hazards Ind.; Coal Abstr.; Curr. Biotechnol.; Curr. Cit.; Eng. Mater. Abstr.; Lab. Hazards Bull.; Leadscan; Met. Abstr.; Life Sci. Collect.; Proc. Chem. Eng.; Saf. Health Work; SCISEARCH; Theor. Chem. Eng.; Vitis Vitic. Enol. Abstr.; World Surf. Coat. Abstr.

IT

CHIMICA : SOCIETA MERCATI PAESI. SERVIZI DOCUMONT. Italian. Twelve times a year. Enichem, Cas Postale 10020, 20110 Milan Italy. **Tel** 011 39 2 62703388.

ISSN 0771-341X
BE

CHIMIE. (1983)-. Periodical. French. Nine times a year. $36.56. De Sikkel Media, Krijgslaan 281 512, 9000 Gent Belgium. **Tel** 011 32 3 3124761.
Ind/Abst Chem. Bus. Bull.; Chem. Bus. NewsBase (1986-); Chem. Bus. Update.

ISSN 0009-4323
FR
UDC 338.4:661 **CCC**
CODEN CHIABC

CHIMIE ACTUALITES. [Chim. actual.]. No. 1382 (1969)-. Periodical. French. Forty-Five times a year (43 issues with 2 special issues). $623.35. Soc Publications Specialisees, BP Paris Bourse 939, 75073 Paris Cedex 02 France. **Tel** 011 33 1 40268321 ext. 133, FAX 011 33 1 40399752, telex 220528. **ED** Cyrienne Clerc. **Bk Rev. Ad Acc. Circ:** 1,000. Documents available from CASDDS. ***Continues** Revue des Produits Chimiques.*
Desc: Informs weekly on the chemical industries in France, the companies involved, their results, perspectives and investments. Presents the current economic and industrial picture and analyzes different markets. Publishes 2 special numbers on eminent chemists world-wide and French chemists among them each year.
Ind/Abst Chem. Abstr.; Chem. Bus. Bull.; Chem. Bus. NewsBase (1985-); Chem. Bus. Update; Chem. Ind. Notes; Energy Res. Abstr. (Aug. 1978-); F&S Index Plus Text, Int. [Select. Cov.]; PROMT.

ISSN 0245-940X
FR
CCC

CHIMIE MAGAZINE. [Chim. mag.]. No. 1 (Jan. 1982)-. Periodical. French. Ten times a year. $146.54. Soc. Publications Specialisees, 142 rue Montmartre, 75073 Paris Cedex 02 France. **Tel** 011 33 1 40268321 ext.133, FAX 011 33 1 40399752, telex 220528F. **Ad Acc.** ctrl circ.
Desc: Each month devoted to an aspect of the chemical industry in France and its current concerns, such as security, environment, biotechnology, new markets and materials. Includes interviews, business management articles, and reports on latest lab proceedings.

ISSN 0771-730X
BE
UDC 66

CHIMIE NOUVELLE. (1983)-. Periodical. French (English). Four times a year. $88.03. Societe Royale de Chimie, ULB Campus, Plaine CP 206 4 boulevard du Triomphee, 1050 Brussels Belgium. **Tel** 011 32 2 6505208, FAX 011 32 2 6505184. **ED** D. Daloze. **Bk Rev. Ad Acc.** Documents available from CASDDS.
Desc: General articles or reviews in any field of chemistry.
Ind/Abst Chem. Abstr.

LC QD1 .C688492 **ISSN** 0366-693X
DD 540/.5 GR
CODEN CMCRCZ

CHIMIKA CHRONIKA (INTERNATIONAL EDITION). (CHEMIKA CHRONIKA.). **Added/Corp** Henosis Hellenon Chemikon. Epistemonike Epitrope. Henosis Hellenon Chemikon. **VFOAT** Chimika Chronika. Vol. 1, No. 1 (Jan./Feb. 1972)-. Periodical. English (French, German, Greek and Modern, Italian). Six times a year. Greek Chemists Association, 27 Kaningos Street, Athens 147 Greece. Documents available from CASDDS. ***Continues** Chemika Chronika. Chimika Chronika. Epistimonike Ekdosis.*
Ind/Abst Abstr. Bull. Inst. Pap. Sci. Tech.; Chem. Abstr.

LC QD1 .C782 **ISSN** 1001-604X
DD 540/.5 CC
CODEN CJOCEV
Pr Rev.

CHINESE JOURNAL OF CHEMISTRY. **Added/Corp** Chung-Kuo Hua Hsueh Hui (Peking, China). **VFOAT** Chung-Kuo Hua Hsueh. No. 1 (1990)-. Academic Scholarly Publication. English. Six times a year. $315.00. Science Press, 16 Donghuangchenggen North Street, Beijing 100707, People's Republic of China. **Tel** 011 86 1 4019821, 011 86 1 4010642, FAX 011 86 1 4012180, 011 86 1 4019810, telex 210147. **(Subscription address:** VSP International Science Publishers, PO Box 346, 3700 AH Zeist Netherlands. **Tel** 011 31 30 6925790, FAX 011 31 30 6932081.**) ED** Lu Xi-Yan. Documents available from The Genuine Article, CASDDS.
Desc: Mainly covers organic chemistry, physical chemistry, inorganic chemistry and analytical chemistry.
Ind/Abst Chem. Abstr.; Curr. Cit.; Res. Alert [Full Cov.].

ISSN 0256-7679
CC
CODEN CJPSEG
Pr Rev.

CHINESE JOURNAL OF POLYMER SCIENCE. [Chin. j. polym. sci.]. **Added/Corp** Chung-kuo Hua Hsueh Hui (Peking, China). **VFOAT** Kao Fen Tzu Kao Hsueh. (198?)-. Academic Scholarly Publication. English. Four times a year. $210.00. Science Press, 16 Donghuangchenggen North Street, Beijing 100707, People's Republic of China. **Tel** 011 86 1 4019821, 011 86 1 4010642, FAX 011 86 1 4012180, 011 86 1 4019810, telex 210147. **(Subscription address:** VSP International Science Publishers, PO Box 346, 3700 AH Zeist Netherlands. **Tel** 011 31 30 6925790, FAX 011 31 30 6932081.**) ED** Feng Xinde. Documents available from Article Express International, The Genuine Article, BIOSIS Document Express, CASDDS. ***Continues** Polymer Communications.*
Desc: Covers all branches of polymer science, including polymer synthesis, polymer chemistry, polymer physics, specialty polymers and polymer science applications. Papers originate from academic and industrial sources, mainly reporting recent progress and results of the fundamental research in the fields. Special attention is paid to the current topics, especially in functional polymers. Also contains occasional invited review articles for the introduction of the recent development and achievements of polymer research on specific topics by both Chinese and foreign scientists.
Ind/Abst Biol. Abstr.; Chem. Abstr.; Curr. Cit.; Eng. Mater. Abstr.; Eng. Index Annu.; Met. Abstr.; Res. Alert [Full Cov.].

US

CHLOR-ALKALI MARKETWIRE. (19??)-. English. One time a week. $1300.00. Chemical Week Association, 888 Seventh Avenue, 26th Floor, New York NY 10106. **Tel** (212)621-4900.
Desc: Includes latest contracts and spot prices for chlorine, caustic soda, and soda ash.
Ind/Abst PROMT; PTS Newsl. Database [Full Txt.].

LC S **ISSN** 0578-1736
DD 631.9 CH
CODEN CKNHAA

CHUNG-KUO NUNG YEH HUA HSUEH. HUI CHIH. See Agriculture.

LC S **ISSN** 0100-3267
DD 630 BL
CODEN CPRADD

CIENCIA E PRATICA. See Agriculture.

ISSN 0254-5403
TU
CODEN CBULDV

CIMENTO BULTENI. [Cimento bul.]. (1981)-. Periodical. Turkish. Turkiye Cimento Mustahsilleri, P K 2, 06582 Anakara Turkey. Documents available from CASDDS. ***Continues** Turkiye Cimento Mustahsilleri Bulteni, 0376-4621.*
Ind/Abst Chem. Abstr.

US

CLAIMS TERM LISTS. (19??)-. Periodical. English. Every 2 years. $325.00. IFI / Plenum Data Corporation / Delaware, 3202 Kirkwood Highway Suite 203, Wilmington DE 19808. **Tel** (302)998-0478, (800)331-4955, FAX (302)998-0733.

ISSN 0358-4879
FI
NLM W1 AC954NM no.33 etc.

CLINICAL CHEMICA (OULU). (CLINICA CHEMICA.). **Added/Corp** Oulun Yliopisto. No. 1 (1978)-. Monographic series. English (Finnish). Irregular. Price varies per volume. Professor Sakari Piha, University of Oulu, 90100 Oulu 10 Finland. **Tel** 358-81-332133. **ED** Leo Hirvonen. **Ad Acc. Circ:** 500 (ctrl).
Desc: Monographs, reviews and dissertations in the field of clinical chemistry.

ISSN 0892-2187
DD 611 SZ
CCC
NLM W1; CL685K **CODEN** CCECEY

CLINICAL CHEMISTRY AND ENZYMOLOGY COMMUNICATIONS. [Clin. chem. enzymol. commun.]. Vol. 1, No. 1 (June 1988)-. Periodical. English. Six times a year. $384.00 (universities, hospitals, and libraries), $599.00 other. Harwood Academic Publishers, PO Box 90, Reading RG1 8JL United Kingdom. **Tel** 011 44 1734 560080, FAX 011 44 1734 568211. **ED** Giorgio Federici.
Ind/Abst CSA Neuro. Abstr. (?-?); Curr. Aware. Biol. Sci., CABS; Curr. Cit.; EMBASE.

ISSN 1056-599X
DD 616 US

CLINICAL CHEMISTRY (CHICAGO, ILL.). (CLINICAL CHEMISTRY.). [Clin. chem.]. **Added/Corp** American Society of Clinical Pathologists. (19??)-. Periodical. English. Ten times a year. $130.00. American Society of Clinical Pathologists, 2100 West Harrison Street, Chicago IL 60612. **Tel** (312)738-1336, (800)621-4142, FAX (312)738-1619.
Ind/Abst Ref. Upd. Basic Ed.; Ref. Upd. Deluxe Ed.

LC RC **ISSN** 0161-9640
DD 616 US
CCC
TITLE CHANGE

CLINICAL CHEMISTRY NEWS. **Added/Corp** American Association for Clinical Chemistry. (19??)-(19??). Periodical. English. American Association of Clinical Chemistry, 2101 L Street, Suite 202, Washington DC 20037-1526. **Tel** (800)892-1400, (202)857-0717, FAX (202)887-5093, telex 251925 AACC UR. available on microfilm from University Microfilms International (UMI). ***Continued by** Clinical Laboratory News.*
Ind/Abst Abstr. BioCommer.

ISSN 0392-5803
IT
CODEN CLNRDG

CLINICAL CHEMISTRY NEWSLETTER. [Clin. chem. newsl.]. **VFOAT** Bulletin de Chimie Clinique. (19??)-. Newsletter. English. Twelve times a year. Dolphin Publishers S R L, POB 12110, Via Calvacanti 14, Milan Italy 20127. Documents available from CASDDS.
Ind/Abst Chem. Abstr.

ISSN 0009-9147
US
CCC
Pr Rev. **TITLE CHANGE**

CLINICAL CHEMISTRY (REFERENCE EDITION). (CLINICAL CHEMISTRY.). **Added/Corp** American Association for Clinical Chemistry. Vol. 29, No. 1 (Jan. 1983)-(1995). Academic Scholarly Publication. English. American Association of Clinical Chemistry, 2101 L Street, Suite 202, Washington DC 20037-1526. **Tel** (800)892-1400, (202)857-0717, FAX (202)887-5093, telex 251925 AACC UR. **Ad Acc.** available on microfilm and microfiche from University Microfilms International (UMI). Documents available from The Genuine Article, BIOSIS Document Express, CASDDS. ***Merged into** Clinical Chemistry, 0009-9147.*
Desc: Study text with 700 multiple-choice questions with answers explained reflect advances in the fields of molecular biology, toxiology, immunology, recombinant DNA, as well as others. Prepares students for board exams in pathology, toxiology and clinical chemistry.
Ind/Abst AgBiotech News Inf.; Anal. Abstr.; Biol. Abstr.; Chem. Abstr.; Curr. Biotechnol.; Curr. Cit.; Curr. Contents Life Sci.; Dairy Sci. Abstr.; EMBASE; Health Devices Alerts; Health Plan. Adminis.; IDIS; Index Vet.; Int. Aerosp. Abstr.; Mass Spect. Bull.; Nutr. Abstr. Rev., Ser. B, Live Feeds and Feed.; Nutr. Abstr. Rev., Ser. A, Hum. Exp.; Life Sci. Collect.; PESTDOC; Physic. Medline Plus; Res. Alert [Full Cov.]; Rev. Med. Vet. Mycology; Saf. Health Work; Sci. Cit. Index; SCISEARCH; Soc. Sci. Cit. Index [Select. Cov.]; Vet. Bull.

US

CLINICAL LABORATORY NEWS. **Added/Corp** American Association for Clinical Chemistry. (19??)-. Periodical. English. Twelve times a year. $30.00 US; $65.00 other. American Association of Clinical Chemistry, 2101 L Street, Suite 202, Washington DC 20037-1526. **Tel** (800)892-1400, (202)857-0717, FAX (202)887-5093, telex 251925 AACC UR. available on microfilm from University Microfilms International (UMI). ***Continues** Clinical Chemistry News, 0161-9640.*
Ind/Abst Abstr. BioCommer.

ISSN 0779-4762
BE
UDC 66
CEASED

CM MAGAZINE NEDERLANDSE ED. **VFOAT** Chemie Magazine (Nederlandse ed.). (1992)-(May/June 1995). Periodical. Dutch. Technipress, Stationsstraat 30 bus 1, 1702 Groot-Bijgaarden Belgium. **Tel** 011 32 2 4818100, FAX 011 32 2 4818182.
Ind/Abst Curr. Cit.

IT

CODICE DEGLI ALCOLI. Italian. Guido Scialpe Editore, Via Seneca 10, 00136 Rome Italy.

ISSN 1068-364X
DD 338 US
CCC

COKE AND CHEMISTRY (NEW YORK, N.Y.). (COKE AND CHEMISTRY.). [Coke chem.]. (19??)-. Periodical. English (translations available in Russian). Twelve times a year. $970.00. Allerton Press Inc., 150 Fifth Avenue, New York NY 10011. **Tel** (212)924-3950, FAX (212)463-9684, telex 427441 ALPRES. ***Continues** Coke and Chemistry U.S.S.R., 0010-0501.*
Ind/Abst Bioeng. Abstr.; Chem. Abstr.; Coal Abstr.; Curr. Cit.; Energy Inf. Abstr.; Energy Res. Abstr.; Eng. Index Annu.; Environ. Abstr.

LC QD1 .C8 **ISSN** 0010-0765
DD 540/.5 UK
CCC
CODEN CCCCAK
Pr Rev.

COLLECTION OF CZECHOSLOVAK CHEMICAL COMMUNICATIONS. [Collect. Czech. chem. commun.]. **Added/Corp** Ceskoslovenska Akademie Ved. **VFOAT** Sbornik Chekhoslovatskikh Khimicheskikh Rabot. Vol. 22 (Feb. 1957)-. Academic Scholarly Publication. English (French, German and Russian). Twelve times a year. $704.00. Academic Press Ltd., A Division of Harcourt Brace & Company Ltd., 24-28 Oval Road, London NW1 7DX United Kingdom. **Tel** 011 44 171 2674466, FAX 011 44 171 4822293, 011 44 171 4854752, telex 25775 ACPRES G. **(Subscription address:** Harcourt Brace & Company, Ltd., Foots Cray High Street, Sidcup Kent DA14 5HP United Kingdom. **Tel** 011 44 181 3003322, FAX 011 44 181 3090807, telex 896 377 ACADEM.**) ED** M Lebl. Index Available in last issue

Chemistry and Chemicals

of each volume--loose separately paged. Documents available from The Genuine Article, CASDDS. **Continues** Sbornik Chekhoslovatskikh Khimicheskikh Rabot. **Desc:** Publishes primary papers, invited reviews, and proceedings of scientific meetings held in Czechoslovakia. Also provides a unique view of the results of Czechoslovak research in topics ranging from border areas of chemical engineering to biochemistry. **Ind/Abst** Abstr. Bull. Inst. Pap. Sci. Tech.; AGRICOLA; Alum. Ind. Abstr.; Anal. Abstr.; Ceram. Abstr.; Chem Inform; Chem. Abstr.; Curr. Chem. React.; Curr. Cit.; Curr. Titles Electrochem.; EMBASE; Eng. Mater. Abstr.; Field Crop Abstr.; Food Sci. Technol. Abstr.; GeoRef; Grass. Forage Abstr.; Hortic. Abstr.; Index Chem.; Leadscan; Mass Spect. Bull.; Met. Abstr.; NAPRALERT; Nutr. Abstr. Rev., Ser. B, Live Feeds and Feed.; Nutr. Abstr. Rev., Ser. A, Hum. Exp.; Ornamental Hort. (1991-); Life Sci. Collect.; PESTDOC; Protozoolog. Abstr.; Res. Alert [Full Cov.]; Saf. Health Work; Sci. Cit. Index; SCISEARCH; Soils Fert.; Weed Abstr.; World Surf. Coat. Abstr.; World Text. Abstr.

LC QD47 .C64   **ISSN** 0588-2699
DD 540/.7/117   US
    CCC

COLLEGE CHEMISTRY FACULTIES.
(COLLEGE CHEMISTRY FACULTIES / AMERICAN CHEMICAL SOCIETY.). [Coll. chem. fac.]. **Added/Corp** American Chemical Society. No. 1 (1965)-. Monographic series. English. Irregular. $74.95 (latest edition). American Chemical Society, 1155 Sixteenth Street Northwest, Washington DC 20036. **Tel** (800)333-9511, (800)227-5558, (614)447-3776, FAX (202)447-3671. **(Subscription address:** American Chemical Society / Washington D.C., PO Box 57136, West End Station, Washington DC 20037. **Tel** (800)227-5558.**)**

    GW

COLLOQUIUM - GESELLSCHAFT FUER BIOLOGISCHE CHEMIE. Main/Corp
Gesellschaft fuer Biologische Chemie. **Added/Corp** Deutsche Gesellschaft fuer Physiologische Chemie. Gesellschaft fuer Physiologische Chemie. (19??)-. Monographic series. Multiple languages (English and German). Price varies per volume. Springer-Verlag GmbH & Company KG, Heidelberger Platz 3, D-14197 Berlin Germany. **Tel** 011 49 30 8207223, FAX 011 49 30 8214091, telex 183 319 SPBLN D.

    TU
    CODEN CFBEEC

COMMUNICATIONS DE LA FACULTE DES SCIENCES DE L'UNIVERSITE D'ANKARA. SERIES B, CHEMISTRY AND CHEMICAL ENGINEERING.
Added/Corp Ankara Universitesi. Fen Fakultesi. **VFOAT** Chemistry and Chemical Engineering. (198?)-. Academic Scholarly Publication. English. Three times a year. Faculty of Sciences, University of Ankara 06 100, Ankara Turkey. **Tel** (4)212-6720. Documents available from CASDDS. **Continues** Ankara Universitesi. Fen Fakultesi. Communications de la Faculte des Sciences de l'Universite d'Ankara. Serie B, Chimie. **Ind/Abst** Chem. Abstr.

    GW

COMPENDIUM OF SAFETY DATA SHEETS FOR RESEARCH AND INDUSTRIAL CHEMICALS. (19??)-. English.
Irregular. VCH Gesellschaft GmbH, Postfach 101161, D-69451 Weinheim Germany. **Tel** 011 49 6201 606459, FAX 011 49 6201 606184. **(Subscription address:** VCH Publishers Inc., 303 Northwest 12th Avenue, Journals Department, Deerfield FL 33442. **Tel** (800)367-8249, (305)428-5566.**)**

    ISSN 0927-6440
    NE
Pr Rev.

COMPOSITE INTERFACES. (1992)-. English.
Six times a year. DM480.00. VSP International Science Publishers, Godfried van Seystlaan 47, 3703 BR Zeist Netherlands. **Tel** 011 31 3404 25790, FAX 011 31 3404 32081, telex 40217 USP NL. **(Subscription address:** VSP International Science Publishers, PO Box 346, 3700 AH Zeist Netherlands. **Tel** 011 31 30 6925790, FAX 011 31 30 6932081.**) ED** H. Ishida.
Desc: Provides a forum for interdisciplinary scientific and engineering research on composite interfaces/interphases and their related phenomena. Presents new concepts and approaches for composite interface study. Balances interest in chemistry, physical properties, mechanical properties, molecular structures, characterization techniques and theories.
Ind/Abst Alum. Ind. Abstr.; Chem. Abstr.; Corros. Abstr.; Eng. Mater. Abstr.; Met. Abstr.; RAPRA Abstr.

    NE
    CODEN CMTSEN

COMPOSITE MATERIALS SERIES.
(1986)-. Monographic series. English. Irregular. Price varies per volume. Elsevier Science Publishers BV, PO Box 211, 1000 AE Amsterdam Netherlands. **Tel** 011 31 20 4853641, 011 31 20 4853642, FAX 011 31 20 4853598. Documents available from CASDDS.

Desc: Series covering polymers, ceramics and composite materials.
Ind/Abst Chem. Abstr.; Curr. Cit.

    ISSN 0069-8040
    NE
Pr Rev.

COMPREHENSIVE CHEMICAL KINETICS. [Compr. chem.kinet.]. (1969)-.
Monographic series. English. Four times a year. Price varies per volume. Elsevier Science Publishers BV, PO Box 211, 1000 AE Amsterdam Netherlands. **Tel** 011 31 20 4853641, 011 31 20 4853642, FAX 011 31 20 4853598.
Ind/Abst Math. Rev.

    US

COMPREHENSIVE DATABASE OF US CHEMICAL PATENTS TAPES. See
Chemistry and Chemicals-Abstracting, Bibliographies and Statistics.

LC QD1 .I8815   **ISSN** 0074-9508
    SP
UDC 54+66(063)

COMPTES RENDUS DE LA CONFERENCE - UNION INTERNATIONALE DE CHIMIE PURE ET APPLIQUE. (COMPTES RENDUS DE LA CONFERENCE.). Main/Corp International Union of Pure
and Applied Chemistry. 1.- 1920-. English. Every 2 years. Pergamon Press, An Imprint of Elsevier Science Ltd., The Boulevard, Langford Lane, Kidlington, Oxford OX5 1GB United Kingdom. **Tel** 011 44 1865 843000, 011 44 1865 843699, FAX 011 44 1865 843010.

LC TP12 .A83   **ISSN** 1064-2811
DD 660.2/025   US

CONSULTING SERVICES. [Consult. serv.].
Main/Corp Association of Consulting Chemists and Chemical Engineers. (1949)-. Directory. English. Every 2 years. $60.00 US; $75.00 (includes postage) other. Association of Consulting Chemists, 295 Madison Avenue, 27th Floor, New York NY 10017. **Tel** (212)983-3160, FAX (212)983-3161. **Continues** Association of Consulting Chemists and Chemical Engineers. Classified Directory.

    ISSN 1058-1936
DD 550   US
    CEASED

CORE ANALYTE. [Core anal.]. Added/Corp
American Society of Clinical Pathologists. Vol. 8, No. 2 (1992)-(19??). Periodical. English. American Society of Clinical Pathologists, 2100 West Harrison Street, Chicago IL 60612. **Tel** (312)738-1336, (800)621-4142, FAX (312)738-1619. **Continues** Core Chemistry, 1056-5914.

    ISSN 0891-1886
DD 660   US
    CCC

CPI DIGEST. (CPI DIGEST : SURVEY OF NEW MARKETING & TECHNICAL DEVELOPMENTS IN THE CHEMICAL PROCESS INDUSTRIES.). [CPI dig.]. VAT
Chemical Process Industries Digest. (198?)-. Periodical. English. Twelve times a year. $297.00. CPI Information Services, 2117 Cherokee Parkway, Louisville KY 40204. **Tel** (502)456-6288. **ED** George S. Mattingly. **Continues** Coatings Adlibra, 0146-9290.
Desc: World literature - serving coating plastic, fibers, adhesives and related industries.

    US

CRC HANDBOOK OF CHEMICAL SYNONYMS AND TRADE NAMES. VFOAT
Handbook of Chemical Synonyms and Trade Names.; Chemical Synonyms and Trade Names. 8th Ed. (1978)-. English. Irregular. Price varies per volume. CRC Press Inc., 2000 Corporate Boulevard Northwest, Boca Raton FL 33431. **Tel** (407)994-0555, (800)272-7737, FAX (407)998-9784, (800)374-3401, telex 568689. **(Subscription address:** CRC Press Inc. / New York, PO Box 750, Pearl River NY 10965. **) Continues** Chemical Synonyms and Trade Names.

LC QD65 .H3   **ISSN** 0147-6262
DD 540/.2/02   US
    CCC
NLM QD 65 H236

CRC HANDBOOK OF CHEMISTRY AND PHYSICS. VFOAT Handbook of Chemistry and
Physics. **VAT** Chemical Rubber Company Handbook of Chemistry and Physics. 58th Ed. (1977/1978)-. English. One time a year (June). $110.00 US; $132.00 other. CRC Press Inc., 2000 Corporate Boulevard Northwest, Boca Raton FL 33431. **Tel** (407)994-0555, (800)272-7737, FAX (407)998-9784, (800)374-3401, telex 568689. **(Subscription address:** CRC Press Inc. / New York, PO Box 750, Pearl River NY 10965. **) ED** Robert C. Weast.
Continues Handbook of Chemistry and Physics, 0363-3055.

    ISSN 0011-1643
    CI
NLM W1 CR218T   **CODEN** CCACAA
Pr Rev.

CROATICA CHEMICA ACTA. [Croat. chem. acta]. VFOAT Arhiv za Kemiju. (1956)-. Academic
Scholarly Publication. Serbo-Croatian (Roman) (English and German). Twelve times a year. $50.00. Hrvatsko Kemijsko Drustvo / Croatian Chemical Society, Marulicev Trg 19, 410000 Zagreb Croatia. **Tel** 011 385 41 446528. **(Subscription address:** Mladost Export Import, Borongajska 69, 41000 Zagreb Croatia. **Tel** 011 385 1 221488, 011 385 1 215853.**)** Index Available in last issue of each volume--loose separately paged. cum. index. available on microfilm and microfiche from University Microfilms International (UMI). Documents available from The Genuine Article, BIOSIS Document Express, CASDDS. **Continues** Arhiv za Kemiju, 0365-3730.
Ind/Abst Anal. Abstr.; Biol. Abstr.; Chem Inform; Chem. Abstr.; Curr. Cit.; Curr. Contents Phys. Chem. Earth Sci.; Leadscan; Nat. Prod. Updates; Life Sci. Collect.; Pollut. Abstr. Indexes; Res. Alert [Full Cov.]; Sci. Cit. Index; SCISEARCH.

    ISSN 0574-4741
    IT
    CODEN CROCBG

CRONACHE DI CHIMICA. [Cron. chim.].
(1963)-. Academic Scholarly Publication. Italian. Four times a year. Free. Farmitalia Carlo Erba, Via Imbonatii 24, 20159 Milan Italy. Documents available from CASDDS.
Ind/Abst Chem. Abstr. (1963-1982).

    ISSN 0826-1024
DD 616.07/56   CN

CSCC NEWS. [CSCC news]. Main/Corp Canadian
Society of Clinical Chemists. **VAT** Canadian Society of Clinical Chemists News. (1976)-. Periodical. English. Six times a year. comes with Canadian Society of Clinical Chemists membership. Canadian Society of Clinical Chemists, PO Box 1570, 190 Railway Street, Kingston Ontario K7K 5C8 Canada. **Tel** (613)531-9210, FAX (613)545-0806. **ED** E. Young. **Ad Acc**. **Circ:** 600 (ctrl). **Continues** Canadian Society of Clinical Chemists. Newsletter, 0826-1016.

    ISSN 0885-1980
DD 616   UK
    CCC

CURRENT ADVANCES IN CLINICAL CHEMISTRY. See Chemistry and
Chemicals-Abstracting, Bibliographies and Statistics.

    ISSN 0145-6814
    US

CURRENT AWARENESS PROFILE ON QUANTUM CHEMISTRY. Added/Corp Indiana
University. Department of Chemistry. Quantum Chemistry Program Exchange. **VFOAT** QCPE Current Awareness Profile on Quantum Chemistry. (19??)-. Periodical. English. Twenty-six times a year (Fri.). $75.00. Quantum Chemistry Program Exchange, Indiana University, Department of Chemistry, Bloomington IN 47405. **Tel** (812)855-4784.

    ISSN 0163-6278
DD 547   US
NLM Z 5524 C9742

CURRENT CHEMICAL REACTIONS. See
Chemistry and Chemicals-Abstracting, Bibliographies and Statistics.

    ISSN 0929-8673
    NE
    CCC

●CURRENT MEDICINAL CHEMISTRY. See
Medical Sciences.

LC QD1 .C984   **ISSN** 0732-4391
DD 540/.5   US

CURRENT TOPICS IN CHINESE SCIENCE. SECTION B, CHEMISTRY.
[Curr. top. Chin. sci, Sect. B, Chem.]. **VFOAT** Chemistry. Vol. 1 (1982)-. Periodical. English. One time a year. Gordon & Breach Science Publishers, Inc., PO Box 786, Cooper Station, New York NY 10276. **Tel** (212)206-8900, FAX (212)645-2459.

    UK

CUSTOM CHEMICAL SYNTHESIS SERVICES IN OTHER EUROPEAN COUNTRIES. (19??)-. Trade Publication. English.
Irregular. £150.00. IAL Consultants Ltd, 14 Buckingham Palace Road, London SW1W 0QP United Kingdom. **Tel** 011 44 171 8285036, FAX 011 44 171 8289318, telex 918666 CRECON G. **Bk Rev.**
Desc: Prepared to assist companies considering the use of outside custom manufacturing services or seeking technical or commercial links with companies in Europe

Chemistry and Chemicals

(for instance, through licensing or joint venture agreements). Each company is indexed by major products and preparative techniques.

US
CUSTOM PROCESSING SERVICES GUIDE. (19??)-. English. Irregular. $300.00 (latest editon). Custom Guide Company, PO Box 358, Closter NJ 07624. **Tel** (201)768-6126, FAX (201)768-6126. **ED** Lee Hanower.
Desc: A purchasing reference resource for the chemical industries looking for companies to perform customized services.

ISSN 0011-6335
DK
CODEN DAKEAT
DANSK KEMI. [Dan. kemi]. Vol. 43, No. 1 (1962)-. Academic Scholarly Publication. Danish. Eleven times a year. $99.78. Dansk Kemi, Kongstrupvej 3, Box 15, DK 4390 Vipperod Denmark. **Tel** 011 45 53482800, FAX 011 45 53482205. **Ad Acc**. Documents available from CASDDS. **Continues** Kemisk Maanedsblad Og Nordisk Handelsblad for Kemisk Industri.
Ind/Abst Chem. Abstr.; Chem. Bus. Bull.; Chem. Bus. NewsBase (1987-); Chem. Bus. Update; Curr. Biotechnol.; Energy Res. Abstr.; INIS Atomindex [Micro.]; Saf. Health Work.

ISSN 1000-8438
CC
CODEN DAHUEW
Pr Rev.
DAXUE HUAXUE. (TA HSUEH HUA HSUEH.). [Daxue huaxue]. **Added/Corp** Chung-Kuo Hua Hsueh Hui. Kao Teng Hsueh Hsiao Hua Hsueh Chiao Yu Yen Chiu Chung Hsin. **VFOAT** University Chemistry. (1986)-. Academic Scholarly Publication. Chinese. Six times a year. $30.00. China Chemistry Society, Beijing University Chemistry Building, Editorial Office, Haidian-qu Beijing 100871, People's Republic of China. **Tel** 861 250 1721. **ED** H. Tongwen. Documents available from CASDDS, BLDSC, CASDDS.
Ind/Abst Chem. Abstr.

ISSN 0070-315X
GW
UDC 54+66
CCC
CODEN DMDGAG
DECHEMA MONOGRAPHIEN. **VAT** Deutsche Gesellschaft fur Chemisches Apparatewesen Monographien. Vol. 1 (1930)-. German. Irregular. VCH Publishers Inc., 220 East 23rd Street, New York NY 10010. **Tel** (212)683-8333, FAX (212)481-0897. **(Subscription address:** VCH Publishers Inc., 303 Northwest 12th Avenue, Journals Department, Deerfield FL 33442. **Tel** (800)367-8249, (305)428-5566.) cum. index. Documents available from Article Express International, CASDDS.
Ind/Abst Bioeng. Abstr.; Chem. Abstr.; Ei Page One; Eng. Index Annu.; Food Sci. Technol. Abstr.

LC QD1 .A528
ISSN 0095-8387
DD 540/.6/2751
US
UDC 54(751)
CODEN DCBUAC
DEL-CHEM BULLETIN, THE. [Del-chem bull.]. **Main/Corp** American Chemical Society. Delaware Section. Bulletin. English. Twelve times a year. $2.00. Delaware Section of the American Chemical Society, PO Box 47, Wilmington DE 19877. **ED** Ann Moffett.

LC QE514
ISSN 0921-3198
DD 551.9
NE
CODEN DEVEEE
Pr Rev.
DEVELOPMENTS IN GEOCHEMISTRY. See Earth Sciences-Geology.

ISSN 0260-4337
UK
CODEN DEPODD
DEVELOPMENTS IN POLYMERISATION. [Dev. polym.]. (1979)-. Academic Scholarly Publication. English. Elsevier Science Publishers Ltd., Crown House, Linton Road, Barking Essex IG11 8JU United Kingdom. **Tel** 011 44 181 5947272, FAX 011 44 181 5945942, telex 896950. **ED** Robert Nobbs Haward. Documents available from CASDDS.
Ind/Abst Chem. Abstr.

ISSN 0198-6627
US
NLM W1 DI258F
DIAGNOSTIC DIALOG. **Added/Corp** Bio-Dynamics/Bmc. Vol. 1 (Mar. 1979)-. Periodical. English. Six times a year. Bio-Dynamics/BMC, Indianapolis IN 46250.

LC QD
DD 540
UK
●**DIALOG ONDISC CHEMICAL BUSINESS NEWSBASE.** (1994)-. Academic Scholarly Publication. English. Six times a year (bimonthly updates). £2,495.00. Royal Society of Chemistry, Thomas Graham House, Science Park, Cambridge CB4 4WF United Kingdom. **Tel** 011 44 1223 420066, FAX 011 44 1223 423623, telex 818293 ROYAL. **(Subscription address:** Turpin Distribution Services Limited, Blackhorse Road, Letchworth, Hertfordshire SH6 1HN United Kingdom. **Tel** 011 44 1462 672555, FAX 011 44 1462 480947.)

ISSN 0836-5369
DD 352.0714/55/05
CN
DIFFUSION BECANCOUR. [Diffus. Becancour]. **Added/Corp** Becancour (Quebec). **VFOAT** Diffusion. (1987)-. Periodical. French. Distribution Gratuite Restreinte. Vie Municipale, Ville de Becancour, Hotel de Ville, 1295 Perinot Nerrot, Becancour Quebec G0X 1B0 Canada. **Continues** Vie Municipale., 0713-6846.

LC WMLC 93/2179

US
DIRECTORY / ALUMNI ASSOCIATION, JEFFERSON MEDICAL COLLEGE, THOMAS JEFFERSON UNIVERSITY. **Main/Corp** Jefferson Medical College. Alumni Association. **VFOAT** Jefferson Medical College Alumni Directory. (19??)-. Trade Publication. English. One time a year. $60.00. American Chemical Society, 1155 Sixteenth Street Northwest, Washington DC 20036. **Tel** (800)333-9511, (800)227-5558, (614)447-3776, FAX (202)447-3671. **(Subscription address:** American Chemical Society / Ohio, Department L 0011, Columbus OH 43268-0011.)

LC HD9651.3 .D57
ISSN 0012-3277
DD 338.4/7/66002573
US
DIRECTORY OF CHEMICAL PRODUCERS : UNITED STATES OF AMERICA. See Industry and Production-Trade and Industrial Directories.

ISSN 0193-5011
US
NLM Z 5525.U5 A512
CODEN ACDGA
DIRECTORY OF GRADUATE RESEARCH. **Added/Corp** American Chemical Society. Committee on Professional Training. **VFOAT** ACS Directory of Graduate Research. **VAT** American Chemical Society Directory of Graduate Research. (1953)-. Directory. English. Every 2 years (every two years). $63.00. American Chemical Society, 1155 Sixteenth Street Northwest, Washington DC 20036. **Tel** (800)333-9511, (800)227-5558, (614)447-3776, FAX (202)447-3671. **(Subscription address:** American Chemical Society / Washington D.C., PO Box 57136, West End Station, Washington DC 20037. **Tel** (800)227-5558.) **Circ:** 5,000. **Continues** Faculties, Publications, and Doctoral Theses in Chemistry, and Chemical Engineering at United States Universities.
Desc: Listing of US and Canadian schools with master's and doctoral programs in chemistry, chemical engineering, and related fields.

LC QD1 .D63
ISSN 1010-7614
DD 540/.5
TU
CODEN DKSEE7
DOGA. TURKISH JOURNAL OF CHEMISTRY. **Added/Corp** Turkiye Bilimsel ve Teknik Arastrma Kurumu. **VFOAT** Turkish Journal of Chemistry. (19??)-. Academic Scholarly Publication. English (Turkish). Four times a year. $200.00. Tubitak, Ataturk Bulvari, No: 221, 06100 Kavaklidere Ankara Turkey. **(Subscription address:** Tubitak, Bilimsel Dergiler, Yazi Isleri Mudurlugu, PO Box 5, Kizilay 06420 Ankara Turkey. **Tel** 011 90 312 4685300 ext. 1122, 011 90 312 4270493, FAX 011 90 312 4271336.) **ED** Bahattin M. Baysal. **Circ:** 700. **Continues** Doga. Turk Kimya Dergisi, 1010-7614.
Desc: Covers all field of chemistry and chemical engineering.
Ind/Abst Chem. Abstr. (1986-); Chem. Cit. Index (1992-); Curr. Cit.; Res. Alert (1992-).

LC QD1 .A35953
ISSN 0012-5008
DD 540
US
NLM W1 DO64C
CODEN DKCHAY
DOKLADY. CHEMISTRY. [Doklady, Chem.]. **Main/Corp** Akademiia Nauk SSSR. **Added/Corp** Akademiia Nauk SSSR. Consultants Bureau. Consultants Bureau Enterprises. **VFOAT** Chemistry. (Jan./Feb. 1963)-. Periodical. English (Russian; translations available in Russian). Twelve times a year. $1195.00. MAIK Nauka / Interperiodica, Ulitsa Profsoyuznaia 90, Moscow 117864 Russia. **ED** AA Baev. Index available. available on microfilm and microfiche from University Microfilms International (UMI). **Continues** Proceedings of the Academy of Sciences of the USSR. Chemistry Section, 0197-8217.
Desc: Publishes articles on the chemistry of polymers, uranium complexes, semiconductors, and metallo-organics. Complete coverage on mass spectrometry, election diffraction and gas chromatography.
Ind/Abst Biochem. Abstr.; Eng. Mater. Abstr.; INIS Atomindex [Micro.]; Mass Spect. Bull.; Methods Organ. Synth.; NAPRALERT; Nat. Prod. Updates; Proc. Chem. Eng.; Theor. Chem. Eng.

UK
CEASED
EASTERN BLOC CHEMICALS. (19??)-(19??). English. Eastern Bloc Research Ltd., Newton Kyme, Tadcaster, North Yorkshire LS24 9LS United Kingdom. **Tel** 011 44 1937 835691, FAX 011 44 1937 835756. **ED** David Cameron Wilson. **Ad Acc**. **Circ:** 160.
Desc: Developments in the chemicals and petrochemical sectors of the USSR and Eastern Europe.

ISSN 0100-4670
BL
CODEN ECQUDX
ECLETICA QUIMICA. [Eclectica quimica]. **Added/Corp** Universidade Estadual Paulista. Departamento de Quimica. Universidade Estadual Paulista. Instituto de Quimica. Vol. 1 (1976)-. Portuguese (summaries and/or abstracts in English; translations available in English). Documents available from CASDDS.
Ind/Abst Chem. Abstr.; Soils Fert.; Sug. Indus. Abstr.

ISSN 0952-8377
UK
CCC
ECN CHEMSCOPE. [ECN chemscope]. **VFOAT** E.C.N. Chemscope. **VAT** European Chemical News Chemscope. (19??)-. Trade Publication. English. Irregular. Free to ECN subscribers. Reed Business Publishing / West Sussex, England, Perrymount Road, Haywards Heath, West Sussex RH16 3DH United Kingdom. **Tel** 011 44 1444 441212, FAX 011 44 1444 445447. Documents available from Documents on Demand.
Ind/Abst Bus. Index (1985-); Environ. Abstr.; F&S Index Plus Text, Int. [Select. Cov.]; Gen. BusinessFile (1985-); Gen. Period. Index (1985-); PROMT; Text. Technol. Dig.; Trade Ind. Index (1981-).

LC HD9650.1 .E22
ISSN 0014-2875
UK
CCC
CODEN ECHNAW
ECN. EUROPEAN CHEMICAL NEWS. See Industry and Production.

ISSN 0963-9292
DD 363.73
UK
CCC
●**ECOTOXICOLOGY LONDON.** See Environmental Issues-Ecology.

ISSN 0444-0013
UK
CODEN EPICDU
EDITED PROCEEDINGS ... INTERNATIONAL GALVANIZING CONFERENCE. **Added/Corp** Zinc Development Association. **VFOAT** Intergalvo. (1976)-. Proceedings. English. Every 3 years. Documents available from CASDDS. **Continues** International Conference on Hot Dip Galvanizing. Edited Proceedings.
Ind/Abst Chem. Abstr.

ISSN 0013-1350
UK
CCC
NLM W1 ED85
CODEN EDCHAU
EDUCATION IN CHEMISTRY. [Educ. chem.]. **Added/Corp** Royal Society of Chemistry (Great Britain) Royal Institute of Chemistry. Vol. 1 (1964)-. Periodical. English. Six times a year. $203.00. Royal Society of Chemistry, Thomas Graham House, Science Park, Cambridge CB4 4WF United Kingdom. **Tel** 011 44 1223 420066, FAX 011 44 1223 423623, telex 818293 ROYAL. **(Subscription address:** Royal Society of Chemistry, Turpin Distribution Services Ltd., Blackhorse Road, Letchworth, Hertfordshire SG6 1HN United Kingdom. **Tel** 011 44 1462 672555, FAX 011 44 1462 480947.) Index available (bound in last issue). available on microfilm and microfiche from University Microfilms International (UMI). Documents available from CASDDS.
Desc: Describes the latest methods of teaching and examining, reviews, books and developments in equipment, and provides information on courses and conferences of interest to teachers.
Ind/Abst Br. Educ. Index; Chem. Abstr.; Chem. Hazards Ind.; Curr. Biotechnol.; Curr. Cit.; Curr. Index J. Educ.; Educ. Technol. Abstr.; EMBASE; Lab. Hazards Bull.; Med. Rev. Dig.; Res. High. Educ. Abstr.; Tech. Educ. Train. Abstr.

LC QD1 .E24a
ER
CODEN ETAKE9
EESTI TEADUSTE AKADEEMIA TOIMETISED. **Added/Corp** Eesti Teaduste Akadeemia. **VFOAT** Keemia; Khimiia; Chemistry; Izvestiia Akademii Nauk Estonii. Khimiia; Proceedings of the Estonian Academy of Sciences. Chemistry. (1990)-. Academic Scholarly Publication. English (Estonian, French, German and Russian). Four times a year. Kirjastus Periodika, Pk 107, Parnu Mnt 8, Tallinn EE0090 Estonia. **Tel** 011 372 2 441365, FAX 011 372 2 442484. Documents available from CASDDS. **Continues**

Chemistry and Chemicals

Eesti NSV Teaduste Akadeemia. Eesti NSV Teaduste Akadeemia Toimetised. Keemia, 0201-8128.
Ind/Abst Chem. Abstr.

LC QD1 .J943 **ISSN** 0367-0422
DD 540/.5 UA
NLM W1 EG913KJ **CODEN** EGJCA3
EGYPTIAN JOURNAL OF CHEMISTRY.
[Egypt. j. chem.]. **Added/Corp** Jamiyah al-Kimiyaiyah al-Misriyah. **VFOAT** Majallah Al-Misriyah Lil-Kimiya. Vol. 15 (1972)-. Academic Scholarly Publication. English (summaries and/or abstracts in Arabic). Six times a year. $157.00. National Information & Documentation Center, A1-Tahrir St Dokki Awqaf PO, Cairo Egypt. **Tel** 011 20 2 701696, telex 93069. Documents available from CASDDS. **Continues** *United Arab Republic Journal of Chemistry.*
Ind/Abst Ceram. Abstr.; Chem Inform; Chem. Abstr.; Field Crop Abstr.; GeoRef; Grass. Forage Abstr.; Hortic. Abstr.

UK
Pr Rev.
EIGHT PEAK INDEX OF MASS SPECTRA.
(19??)-. English. One time a year. £1,295.00. Royal Society of Chemistry, Thomas Graham House, Science Park, Cambridge CB4 4WF United Kingdom. **Tel** 011 44 1223 420066, FAX 011 44 1223 423623, telex 818293 ROYAL. **(Subscription address:** Royal Society of Chemistry, Turpin Distribution Services Ltd., Blackhorse Road, Letchworth, Hertfordshire SG6 1HN United Kingdom. **Tel** 011 44 1462 672555, FAX 011 44 1462 480947.) Index available. cum. index.
Desc: Contains 81,123 mass spectra with a unique index for rapid location and easy identification of unknowns.

ISSN 0886-5671
DD 621 US
  CCC
ELECTRONIC CHEMICALS NEWS.
[Electron. chem. news]. Vol. 1, No. 1 (Jan. 6, 1986)-. Periodical. English. Twenty-six times a year. $452.00. Chemical Week Association, 888 Seventh Avenue, 26th Floor, New York NY 10106. **Tel** (212)621-4900. **ED** Deborah Hairston and Maurice Martorella. available on an online database (files 16,636/Full-Text) from DIALOG. **Continues** *Electronic Chemicals & Materials News, 0984-9757.*
Desc: Covers the electronic chemicals and materials business, including acquisitions, marketing strategies, new products and price data. Covers patent activity in Europe, Japan, and U.S.
Ind/Abst PTS Newsl. Database [Full Txt.].

ISSN 0276-9700
UK
ELLIS HORWOOD SERIES IN CHEMICAL SCIENCE.
[Ellis Horwood ser. chem. sci.]. (1980)-. Monographic series. English. Irregular. Price varies per volume. John Wiley & Sons Ltd., Baffins Lane, Chichester, West Sussex PO19 1UD United Kingdom. **Tel** 011 44 1243 779777, FAX 011 44 1243 776128 BTG:JWP001, telex 86290 WIBOOKG. **(Subscription address:** John Wiley & Sons Inc / New Jersey, PO Box 2575, Secaucus NJ 07096-2575.)

ISSN 0143-7151
UK
  CODEN EMPODC
  TITLE CHANGE
EMULSION POLYMERISATION.
(EMULSION POLYMERIZATION.). [Emuls. polym.]. (19??)-(19??). Academic Scholarly Publication. English. Solihull Chemical Services, 284 Warwich Road Solihull, West Midlands B9S 7AF United Kingdom. **Tel** 021-706-0904. Documents available from CASDDS. **Continued by** *Emulsion Polymerisation and Polymer Emulsions, 0955-2804.*
Ind/Abst Chem. Abstr.

US
ENCYCLOPEDIA OF INDUSTRIAL CHEMICAL ANALYSIS.
(1966)-. English. Irregular. John Wiley & Sons, Inc., 605 Third Avenue, New York NY 10158-0012. **Tel** (212)850-6000, (212)850-6645, FAX (212)850-6088, telex 12-7063. **(Subscription address:** John Wiley & Sons / UK, Baffins Lane, Chichester, West Sussex PO19 1UD United Kingdom. **Tel** 011 44 1243 779777, FAX 011 44 1243 776128, telex 86290 WIBOOKG.)

LC QD1 .E56 **ISSN** 0305-7712
DD 574.5/2 UK
  CCC
  CODEN ENCHDZ
ENVIRONMENTAL CHEMISTRY. See Environmental Issues-Ecology.

ISSN 1077-4009
DD 540 US
●**EURO CHEMICALS REPORT.** [Euro chem. rep.]. **Added/Corp** Ariel Research Corporation. (1994)-. Periodical. English. Twelve times a year. $595.00. Ariel Research Corp, 7910 Woodmont Avenue, Suite 902, Bethesda MD 20814. **Tel** (301)907-7771.

LC HD9650 **ISSN** 0014-2484
DD 338.4766 GW
  CCC
NLM W1 EU583L **CODEN** EUCHAD
EUROPA CHEMIE. [Eur.-Chem.]. No. 1 (1963)-.
Trade Publication. German. Thirty-six times a year. $200.36. Handelsblatt GmbH, Postfach 102716, D-40018 Duesseldorf Germany. **Tel** 011 49 211 8871730, FAX 011 49 211 133523, telex 172114489. **ED** H. Seidel. **Ad Acc.** Circ: 5,000 (ctrl). Documents available from CASDDS. **Continues** *Chemie Markt.*
Desc: Topical news service for the European chemical industry. Provides comprehensive summary of events in Europe's chemical markets.
Ind/Abst Biodeter. Abstr. (1991-); Chem. Abstr.; Chem. Bus. Bull.; Chem. Bus. NewsBase (1985-); Chem. Bus. Update; Chem. Ind. Notes; F&S Index Plus Text, Int. [Select. Cov.]; Infomat Int. Bus.; PROMT; World Surf. Coat. Abstr.

ISSN 1358-3120
UK
●**EUROPEAN DANGEROUS CHEMICALS LAW.** See Law.

FR
EUROPEAN ETHYLENE CRACKER REPORT.
(19??)-. English. Twelve times a year. $1709.50. ICIS Lor Group Ltd., 6 Spring Gardens, Citadel Place Tinworth, London SE11 5EH United Kingdom. **Tel** 011 44 171 8151100.

ISSN 0223-5234
FR
  CCC
NLM W1 EU72DI **CODEN** EJMCA5
Pr Rev.
EUROPEAN JOURNAL OF MEDICINAL CHEMISTRY. See Pharmacy and Pharmacology.

IT
NLM W1; FA826F **CODEN** FRMCE8
FARMACO (SOCIETA CHIMICA ITALIANA : 1989). See Pharmacy and Pharmacology.

LC HD9483.A1F47
DD 331.7 UK
FERTILIZER FOCUS. See Agriculture-Crop Production and Soils.

ISSN 0014-5920
DD 540 US
FLACS. (FLACS : PUBLICATION OF THE FLORIDA SECTION, AMERICAN CHEMICAL SOCIETY.).
[FLACS]. **Added/Corp** American Chemical Society. Florida Section. **VFOAT** F.L.A.C.S. **VAT** Florida American Chemical Society. (19??)-. Periodical. English. Four times a year. FLACS, PO Box 584, Lake Alfred FL 33850. **Continues** *American Chemical Society. Florida Section. News.*

LC QD501 **ISSN** 1351-4180
DD 541.39 UK
●**FOCUS ON CATALYSTS.** (1994)-. Newsletter. English. Twelve times a year. £165.00. Royal Society of Chemistry, Thomas Graham House, Science Park, Cambridge CB4 4WF United Kingdom. **Tel** 011 44 1223 420066, FAX 011 44 1223 423623, telex 818293 ROYAL. **(Subscription address:** Royal Society of Chemistry, Turpin Distribution Services Ltd., Blackhorse Road, Letchworth, Hertfordshire SG6 1HN United Kingdom. **Tel** 011 44 1462 672555, FAX 011 44 1462 480947.) **ED** Alan Comyns.
Desc: Monitors all key developments for catalysts and chemical processing.

UK
FOCUS ON CHEMICALS. English. Twenty-six times a year. £400.00. Stuart H Wamsley, Burwash Weald, East Sussex TN19 7LQ United Kingdom. **Tel** 011 44 1435 882957, FAX 011 44 1436 882965. **ED** Stuart Wamsley. Index available. cum. index. ctrl circ.
Desc: A commentary on the international chemical industry.

LC QD415 **ISSN** 0969-6229
DD 338.47616075 UK
●**FOCUS ON DIAGNOSTICS.** [Focus diagn.]. (1993)-. Newsletter. English. Twelve times a year. $300.00 US; £150.00 EC and other. Royal Society of Chemistry, Thomas Graham House, Science Park, Cambridge CB4 4WF United Kingdom. **Tel** 011 44 1223 420066, FAX 011 44 1223 423623, telex 818293 ROYAL. **(Subscription address:** Royal Society of Chemistry, Turpin Distribution Services Ltd., Blackhorse Road, Letchworth, Hertfordshire SG6 1HN United Kingdom. **Tel** 011 44 1462 672555, FAX 011 44 1462 480947.) **ED** Richard Clayton.
Desc: Covers all end-use sectors for diagnostics: human health, animal health and agriculture. Enables cross-fertilising of ideas.

LC QD273 **ISSN** 0969-6202
DD 541.37 UK
●**FOCUS ON ELECTRONICS CHEMICALS.** [Focus electron. chem.]. (1993)-. Newsletter. English. Twelve times a year. $282.35. Royal Society of Chemistry, Thomas Graham House, Science Park, Cambridge CB4 4WF United Kingdom. **Tel** 011 44 1223 420066, FAX 011 44 1223 423623, telex 818293 ROYAL. **(Subscription address:** Royal Society of Chemistry, Turpin Distribution Services Ltd., Blackhorse Road, Letchworth, Hertfordshire SG6 1HN United Kingdom. **Tel** 011 44 1462 672555, FAX 011 44 1462 480947.) **ED** Alan Comyns.
Desc: Covers new technologies and applications for diagnostics.

LC TP155 **ISSN** 1352-3538
DD 660 UK
●**FOCUS ON INTERMEDIATES AND CONTRACT CHEMICALS.** [Focus Intermed. Contract Chem.]. **VFOAT** Focus on Intermediates and Contract Chemicals. (1994)-. Newsletter. English. Twelve times a year. $300.00 US; £150.00 EC and other. Royal Society of Chemistry, Thomas Graham House, Science Park, Cambridge CB4 4WF United Kingdom. **Tel** 011 44 1223 420066, FAX 011 44 1223 423623, telex 818293 ROYAL. **(Subscription address:** Royal Society of Chemistry, Turpin Distribution Services Ltd., Blackhorse Road, Letchworth, Hertfordshire SG6 1HN United Kingdom. **Tel** 011 44 1462 672555, FAX 011 44 1462 480947.) **ED** Jill Dawson.
Desc: All contract chemical production is covered, from toll production to custom synthesis.

LC TP934 **ISSN** 0969-6210
DD 667.6 UK
●**FOCUS ON PIGMENTS.** See Paints and Painting.

US
FRONTIERS IN CARBOHYDRATE RESEARCH.
(1992)-. Academic Scholarly Publication. English. Elsevier Science Publishing Company Inc, Madison Square Station, PO Box 882, New York NY 10159-0882. **Tel** (212)633-3950, FAX (212)633-3990.

LC QC30 .F95
  DK
FYSIK-KEMI. See Physics.

LC TR692 .K36 **ISSN** 1000-3231
  CC
  CODEN GKKHE9
GANGUANG KEXUE YU GUANGHUAXUE. See Photography.

LC QD1 .K27 **ISSN** 0251-0790
DD 540/.5 CC
UDC 54
  CODEN KTHPDM
GAODENG XUEXIAO HUAXUE XUEBAO.
(KAO TENG HSUEH HSIAO HUA HEUSH HSUEH PAO.). [Gaodeng xuexiao huaxue xuebao]. **VFOAT** Chemical Journal of Chinese Universities. Vol. 1 (July 1980)-. Academic Scholarly Publication. Chinese (summaries and/or abstracts in English). Twelve times a year. $57.29. **(Subscription address:** China International Book Trading Corporation, PO Box 399, Library Service Department, Beijing 100044 People's Republic of China. **Tel** 011 86 1 8414284, FAX 011 86 1 8412023, telex 22496 CIBTC CN.) Documents available from CASDDS.
Desc: Contains information on chemistry in Chinese universities.
Ind/Abst Chem. Abstr.; Chem. Titles; Curr. Biotechnol.; Curr. Cit.; NAPRALERT.

LC TP935 **ISSN** 1000-7555
DD 668.9/05 CC
GAOFENZI CAILIAO KEXUE YU GONGCHENG. **VFOAT** Polymeric Materials Science & Engineering. (1985)-. Periodical. Chinese. Six times a year. Chengdu Keji Daxue, Xuebao Bianjibu Chengdu, Sichuan 610065, People's Republic of China. **Tel** 581554. Documents available from CASDDS.
Ind/Abst Chem. Abstr.

LC QD1 .G2 **ISSN** 0016-5603
  IT
NLM W1 GA78 **CODEN** GCITA9
Pr Rev.
GAZZETTA CHIMICA ITALIANA. [Gazz. chim. Ital.]. **Added/Corp** Societa Chimica Italiana. Vol. 1 (1871)-. Periodical. Italian. Twelve times a year. L258600. Societa Chimica Italiana, Viale Liegi 48, 00198 Rome Italy. **Tel** (06)8549691. cum. index. Documents available from The Genuine Article, CASDDS.
Ind/Abst Abstr. Bull. Inst. Pap. Sci. Tech.; AGRICOLA; Anal. Abstr.; Chem. Abstr.; Curr. Chem. React.; Curr. Cit.; Curr. Contents Phys. Chem. Earth Sci.; Index Chem.; Leadscan; Mass Spect. Bull.; Methods Organ. Synth.; NAPRALERT; Nat. Prod. Updates; PESTDOC; Res. Alert [Full Cov.]; Sci. Cit. Index; SCISEARCH.

Chemistry and Chemicals

LC QD1 .G45
DD 540.5
JA
CODEN GNKGAN

GENDAI KAGAKU. CHEMISTRY TODAY.
VFOAT Chemistry Today. (19??)-. Academic Scholarly Publication. Japanese. Twelve times a year. $148.00. Tokyo Kagaku Dojin, (Tokyo Kagaku Dojin Co. Ltd.), 36-7 Sengoku 3 Chome, Bunkyoku Tokyo 112 Japan. **Tel** 011 81 3 9465311, FAX 011 81 3 9465316. Index available. cum. index. **Bk Rev. Ad Acc. Circ:** 16,000. Documents available from CASDDS.
Ind/Abst Chem. Abstr.

ISSN 0910-4747
DD 540
JA

GENDAI KAGAKU. ZOKAN. [Gendai kagaku. Zokan]. (1984)-. Periodical. Japanese. Tokyo Kagaku Dojin, (Tokyo Kagaku Dojin Co. Ltd.), 36-7 Sengoku 3 Chome, Bunkyoku Tokyo 112 Japan. **Tel** 011 81 3 9465311, FAX 011 81 3 9465316. Documents available from CASDDS.
Ind/Abst Chem. Abstr.

ISSN 0363-8626
US
CODEN GHCSDE

GENERAL HETEROCYCLIC CHEMISTRY SERIES. [Gen. heterocycl. chem. ser.]. Vol. 1 (1971)-. Academic Scholarly Publication. English. Irregular. Price varies per volume. John Wiley & Sons Inc / New Jersey, 1 Wiley Drive, Somerset NJ 08875. **Tel** (800)225-5945, (908)469-4400. Documents available from CASDDS.
Ind/Abst Chem. Abstr.

FR

GENIE CHIMIQUE INDUSTRIES CHIMIQUE ET PARACHIMIQUE. F23.
(19??)-. French. Irregular. 883.17F France; 920.00F other. Institut de l'Information Scientique et Technique (INIST), 2 Allee du Parc de Brabois, 54514 Vandoeuvre Nancy Cedex France. **Tel** 011 33 83 504600, FAX 011 33 83 504650. **Continues** Pascal Folio. F23: Genie Chimique Industrie Chimique et Parachimique.

ISSN 1056-7518
US

GEOCHEMISTRY AND COSMOCHEMISTRY. See Earth Sciences-Geology.

LC QE514 .G443
DD 551.9
ISSN 0102-9800
BL
CODEN GEBREK

GEOCHIMICA BRASILIENSIS. See Earth Sciences-Geology.

LC QD1 .L44a
DD 540
RU

GERTSENOVSKIE CHTENIIA; KHIMIIA.
Main/Corp Leningradskii Gosudarstvennyi Pedagogicheskii Institut Imeni A. I. Gertsena. **VFOAT** Khimiia. (19??)-. Russian. Leningradskii Gosudarstvennyi Pedagogicheskii Institut Imeni, 191186 Moika 48, St. Petersburg Russia.

ISSN 0855-0484
GH
Pr Rev.

GHANA JOURNAL OF CHEMISTRY.
[Ghana J. Chem.]. (1989)-. Periodical. English. Two times a year. $85.00. University of Cape Coast Department of Chemistry, Cape Coast Ghana. **Tel** 011 9 233 4232446, telex 2552 UCC GH. **ED** V.P.Y. Gadzekpo. **Circ:** 40. Documents available from CASDDS.
Desc: Provides articles on pure and applied chemistry.
Ind/Abst Chem. Abstr.

ISSN 0367-4665
RU
CODEN GKMAAS

GIDROHIMICESKIE MATERIALY. See Earth Sciences-Hydrology.

ISSN 0392-2227
IT
NLM W1 GI769D
CODEN GICCD7

GIORNALE ITALIANO DI CHIMICA CLINICA. (GIORNALE ITALIANO DI CHIMICA CLINICA : ORGANO UFFICIALE DELLA SOCIETA ITALIANA DI BIOCHIMICA CLINICA.). [G. ital. chim. chin.]. **Added/Corp** Societa Italiana di Biochimica Clinica. (1976)-. Academic Scholarly Publication. English (English). Six times a year. L125000. Piccin Editore, Via Altinate 107, 35121 Padua Italy. **Tel** 011 39 49 655566, FAX 011 39 49 8750693. **ED** Giovanni Ceriotti. Index available. cum. index. **Bk Rev. Ad Acc. Circ:** 7,000. Documents available from BIOSIS Document Express, CASDDS.
Ind/Abst Anal. Abstr.; Biol. Abstr. (1984-); Chem. Abstr.; EMBASE.

LC TP845 .F5813
DD 666/.1/05
RU
CODEN GPHCEE

●**GLASS PHYSICS AND CHEMISTRY = FIZIKA I KHIMIYA STEKLA. See** Glass and Ceramics.

LC QD1.S74 G6
BU

GODISHNIK NA SOFIISKIIA UNIVERSITET "SV. KLIMENT OKHRIDSKI," KHIMICHESKI FAKULTET / ANNUAIRE DE L'UNIVERSITE DE SOFIA "ST. KLIMENT OHRIDSKI," FACULTE DE CHIMIE. Added/Corp Sofiiski Universitet "Kliment Okhridski." Khimicheski Fakultet. **VFOAT** Annuaire de l'Universite de Sofia "St. Kliment Ohridski," Faculte de Chimie. (1992)-. Bulgarian (English; summaries and/or abstracts in Russian). Izdatelstvo na Bulgarskata Akademiia na Naukite, 6 Rouski Boulevard, Sofia Bulgaria. **Tel** FAX 011 359 2 801341, telex 22267 HEMKIK. **Continues** Godishnik na Sofiiskiia Universitet "Kliment Okhridski," Khimicheski Fakultet, 0584-0317.

ISSN 0911-1166
JA
CODEN GOSKEI

GOSEI SENZAI KENKYUKAISHI. (GOSEI SENZAI KENKYUKAISHI = ANNUAL REPORT OF THE JAPANESE RESEARCH SOCIETY FOR SYNTHETIC DETERGENTS.). [Gosei Senzai Kenkyukaishi]. **Added/Corp** Gosei Senzai Kenkyukai. **VFOAT** Annual Report of the Japanese Research Society for Synthetic Detergents. (1977)-. Japanese. One time a year. Gosei Senzai Kenkyukai, Tokyo Japan. Documents available from CASDDS.
Ind/Abst Chem. Abstr.

ISSN 0171-4546
GW
UDC 539.1
CODEN GSIRDG

GSI-REPORT. [GSI-Rep.]. **VFOAT** Gesellschaft-fur-Schwerionenforschung-Report; GSI. (1979)-. Monographic series. German. Irregular. Price varies per volume. Documents available from CASDDS. **Formed by the union of** GSI-Bericht. A, 0171-4562; GSI-Bericht. J, 0171-4570; GSI-Bericht. M, 0171-4589; GSI-Bericht. P, 0171-192X; GSI-Bericht. Pa, 0171-4597; GSI-Bericht. PB, 0171-4600; GSI-Bericht. Pk, 0171-4619; GSI-Bericht. T, 0171-4627 **and** GSI-Bericht. Tr, 0171-4635.
Ind/Abst Chem. Abstr.

LC TP12 .G85
DD 660/.029/44
FR

GUIDE DE LA CHIMIE INTERNATIONAL.
(19??)-. French. One time a year. 490.00F. S. E. P. Edition, 194-196 rue Marcadet, 75018 Paris France. **Continues** Guide de la Chimie.

LC S583 .H36
DD 631
ISSN 0368-2897
KO
CODEN JKACA7

HAN'GUK NONGHWA HAKHOE CHI. See Agriculture.

UK

HEALTH AND SAFETY EXECUTIVE GUIDANCE NOTES. CHEMICAL SAFETY. See Public Health and Safety.

ISSN 0440-6826
YU
CODEN HMPGAI

HEMIJSKI PREGLED. [Hem. pregl.].
Added/Corp Srpsko Hemijsko Drustvo. **VFOAT** Chemical Review. (1950)-. Periodical. Serbo-Croatian (Cyrillic). Six times a year. Srpsko Hemijsko Drustvo, Karnegijeva 4, Belgrad Yugoslavia. Documents available from CASDDS.
Ind/Abst Chem. Abstr.

LC QD40 .H39
DD 540/.5
ISSN 0720-9428
GW

HENKEL-REFERATE : EXCERPTS OF HENKEL RESEARCH PAPERS.
Added/Corp Henkel KGaA. **VFOAT** Henkel Referate; Excerpts of Henkel Research Papers. Vol. 16 (1980)-. Periodical. English (English). One time a year. Free on request. Henkel Referate, Henkel KGAA, D-40191 Dusseldorf Germany. **Tel** 011 49 211 797 2787. **(Subscription address:** Henkel Referate Corporation, 2330 Circadian Way, Santa Rosa CA 95407. **Tel** (707)575-7155.) **ED** Marianne Reinhardt (editor's address: Henkel KGaA, Postfach 1100, 4000 Dusseldorf 1 West Germany). **Circ:** 5,000 (ctrl).
Desc: Excerpts of a selection of Henkel Research Papers which have been published in journals or presented at conferences.

ISSN 0191-1775
US
CODEN HEMIAL

HERCULES MIXER, THE. Added/Corp Hercules Powder Company. (19??)-. Periodical. English. Twelve times a year. Free on request. Hercules Inc., 910 Market Street, Hercules Tower, Wilmington DE 19899. **Tel** (302)575-5000. Documents available from CASDDS.
Ind/Abst Chem. Abstr.

LC QD
DD 540
UDC 615
ISSN 0793-0283
IS

●**HETEROCYCLIC COMMUNICATIONS.**
[Heterocycl. commun.]. (1994)-. Academic Scholarly Publication. English. Six times a year. $240.00. Freund Publishing House Ltd., PO Box 35010, 61 Nachmani Street, Tel Aviv 61350 Israel. **Tel** 011 972 3 5628540, FAX 011 972 3 5628538. **(Subscription address:** Freund Publishing House Ltd., Suite 500, Chesham House 150 Regent Street, London W1R 5FA United Kingdom. **Tel** 011 44 178 172811, FAX 011 972 3 615335.) **ED** R.R. Gupta. Documents available from CASDDS.

LC QD380 .H54
ISSN 0954-0083
UK
CCC
CODEN HPPOEX

HIGH PERFORMANCE POLYMERS. [High perform. polym.]. (1989)-. Academic Scholarly Publication. English. Four times a year. $338.00. Institute of Physics, Techno House, Redcliffe Way, Bristol BS1 6NX United Kingdom. **Tel** 011 44 117 9297481, FAX 011 44 117 9294318, telex 449149 INSTP G. **(Subscription address:** American Institute of Physics, Publishing Sales, 500 Sunnyside Blvd., Woodbury NY 11797. **Tel** (516)576-2200.) **ED** D. Wilson. Index available (bound in Dec. issue). Documents available from Ask*IEEE, CASDDS.
Desc: Presents original research in high performance polymer science and technology, primarily applications-driven, with a major focus on molecular structure/ processability/property relationship with regard to the specified applications.
Ind/Abst Chem. Abstr. (1989-); Curr. Cit.; INSPEC (1989-).

LC TP200 .V97
DD 540/.5
ISSN 0897-4403
US
CCC
CODEN HPSUEW
CEASED

HIGH-PURITY SUBSTANCES. [High-purity subst.]. **Added/Corp** Consultants Bureau. **VFOAT** Vysokochistye Veshchestva. **VAT** High Purity Substances. (1988)-Vol. 7, No. 6. Academic Scholarly Publication. English (translations available in Russian). Consultants Bureau, A Division of Plenum Publishing Corporation, 233 Spring Street, New York NY 10013. **Tel** (212)620-8000, (212)620-8466, FAX (212)463-0742, telex 23/421139. available on microfilm and microfiche from University Microfilms International (UMI). Documents available from CASDDS.
Ind/Abst Chem. Abstr.

ISSN 0018-1811
JA
CODEN HIKAAF

HIKAKU KAGAKU. See Leather and Fur Industry.

ISSN 0023-110X
RU
CCC
CODEN KPRMAW

HIMICESKAJ PROMYSLENNOST.
(KHIMICHESKAIA PROMYSHLENOST.). [Khim. prom.]. (1944)-. Periodical. Russian. Twelve times a year. $139.95. **(Subscription address:** East View Publications Inc., 3020 Harbor Lane North, Suite 110, Minneapolis MN 55447. **Tel** (800)477-1005, (612)550-0961, FAX (612)559-2931.) Documents available from The Genuine Article, CASDDS. **Continues** Zhurnal Khimicheskoi Promyshlennosti.
Ind/Abst Abstr. Bull. Inst. Pap. Sci. Tech.; Chem Inform; Chem. Abstr.; Leadscan; Res. Alert [Full Cov.].

ISSN 0368-556X
UN
CODEN KHMTA6

HIMICESKAJA TEHNOLOGIJA (KIEV. 1971). (KHIMICHESKAIA TEKHNOLOGIIA). [Him. tehnol.]. **Added/Corp** Akademiia nauk URSR, Kiev. Viddil Khimii ta Khimchnoi Tekhnolohii. Vsesoiuznoe Khimicheskoe Obshchestvo Imeni D. I. Mendeleeva. Ukrainskoe Respublikanskoe Pravlenie. (Jan./Feb. 1971)-. Academic Scholarly Publication. Russian. Six times a year. $99.95. Izdatelstvo Naukova Dumka / Ukrainian Academy of Sciences, Yu. A. Khramov, Dir., Ul. Repina 3, 252 601 Kiev Ukraine. **Tel** 011 7 44 4303441, 011 7 44 2254182, telex 131376. **(Subscription address:** East View Publications Inc., 3020 Harbor Lane North, Suite 110, Minneapolis MN 55447. **Tel** (800)477-1005, (612)550-0961, FAX (612)559-2931.) Documents available from CASDDS.
Ind/Abst Abstr. Bull. Inst. Pap. Sci. Tech.; AGRICOLA; Art Archaeol. Tech. Abstr.; Chem. Abstr.; Coal Abstr.

Chemistry and Chemicals

ISSN 0132-6244
LV
CCC
NLM W1 KH391 **CODEN** KGSSAQ
HIMIJA GETEROCIKLICESKIH SOEDINENIJ. (KHIMIIA GETEROTSIKLICHESKIKH SOEDINENII.). [Him. geterocikl. soedin.]. **Added/Corp** Organiskas Sintezes Instituts (Latvijas PSR Zinatnu Akademija). (1965)-. Academic Scholarly Publication. Russian (summaries and/or abstracts in English). Twelve times a year. $179.95. **(Subscription address:** East View Publications Inc., 3020 Harbor Lane North, Suite 110, Minneapolis MN 55447. **Tel** (800)477-1005, (612)550-0961, FAX (612)559-2931.) Documents available from The Genuine Article, CASDDS.
Ind/Abst Chem. Abstr.; Curr. Chem. React.; Index Chem.; PESTDOC; Res. Alert [Full Cov.]; Sci. Cit. Index; SCISEARCH.

ISSN 0454-8833
RU
CODEN KTDRA5
HIMIJA I TERMODINAMIKA RASTVOROV. (KHIMIIA I TERMODINAMIKA RASTVOROV / LENINGRADSKII ORDENA LENINA GOSUDARSTVENNYI UNIVERSITET IMENI A.A. ZHDANOVA.). [Him. termodin. rastvorov]. **Added/Corp** Leningradskii Gosudarstvennyi Universitet Imeni A.A. Zhdanova. (1964)-. Periodical. Russian. St. Petersburg State University / Izdatelstvo Leningradskogo Universiteta, Universitetskaia Nab 7/9, 199034 St. Petersburg Russia. **Tel** 011 7 812 2189788, FAX 011 7 812 2185152, telex 121481. Documents available from CASDDS.
Ind/Abst Chem. Abstr.

ISSN 0137-0340
RU
CODEN KTTEDF
HIMIJA TVERDOGO TELA. (KHIMIIA TVERDOGO TELA / MINISTERSTVO VYSSHEGOE I SREDNEGO SPETSIALNOGO OBRAZOVANIIA RSFSR, URALSKII ORDENA TRUDOVOGO KRASNOGO ZNAMENI POLITEKHNICHESKII INSTITUT IM. S.M. KIROVA.). [Him. tverd. tela]. **Added/Corp** Uralskii Politekhnicheskii Institut im. S.M. Kirova. Vol. 1 (1977)-. Periodical. Russian. Documents available from CASDDS.
Ind/Abst Chem. Abstr.

UK
HMSO CHEMICAL SAFETY SERIES. (19??)-. English. Irregular. Price varies per volume. Her Majesty's Stationery Office, 51 Nine Elms Lane, London SW8 5DR United Kingdom. **Tel** 011 44 171 8738459, 011 44 171 8738499, 011 44 171 8738499, 011 44 171 8738456, telex 297138. **(Subscription address:** Her Majesty's Stationery Office, PO Box 276, Public Centre, London SW8 5DT United Kingdom. **Tel** 011 44 171 8738499, 011 44 171 8738456.)

ISSN 0441-3768
DD 540 CH
HUA HSUEH. CHEMISTRY. VFOAT Chemistry. (Sept./Dec. 1954)-. Periodical. Chinese (summaries and/or abstracts in English). Four times a year. $6.00. Chinese Chemical Society, Room 903 9th Floor, 7 Chun Chin S Road, PO Box 609, Taipei Taiwan. **Tel** 886 -2-3118464, FAX 886-2-3118464. Documents available from CASDDS.
Ind/Abst Chem. Abstr.

LC QD1 .C7853 **ISSN** 0567-7351
CC
CODEN HHHPA4
Pr Rev.
HUA HSUEH HSUEH PAO. [Hua hsueh hsueh pao]. **Added/Corp** Chung-kuo Hua Hsueh Hui (Peking, China) Chung-kuo ko Hsueh Yuan. **VFOAT** Acta Chimica Sinica. Vol. 19, No. 3 (1953)-. Academic Scholarly Publication. Chinese (summaries and/or abstracts in English). Twelve times a year. $94.00. Science Press, 16 Donghuangchenggen North Street, Beijing 100707, People's Republic of China. **Tel** 011 86 1 4019821, 011 86 1 4010642, FAX 011 86 1 4012180, 011 86 1 4019810, telex 210147. **(Subscription address:** China International Book Trading Corporation, PO Box 399, Library Service Department, Beijing 100044 People's Republic of China. **Tel** 011 86 1 8414284, FAX 011 86 1 8412023, telex 22496 CIBTC CN.) **ED** Wang Yu. Documents available from CASDDS. **Continues** Journal. Chinese Chemical Society.
Desc: Papers included cover the following areas: organic chemistry, pharmaceutical chemistry, organometallic chemistry, and physical chemistry.
Ind/Abst Alum. Ind. Abstr.; Chem. Abstr.; Curr. Biotechnol.; Curr. Cit.; EMBASE; INIS Atomindex [Micro.]; Mass Spect. Bull. (?-?); Met. Abstr.

LC QD1 .H77 **ISSN** 0367-6358
DD 540 CC
HUA HSUEH SHIH CHIEH. (HUA HSUEH SHIH CHIEH = CHEMICAL WORLD.). [Hua Hsueh Shih Chieh]. **Added/Corp** Shang-hai Shih Hua Hsueh Hua Kung Hsueh Hui. **VFOAT** Chemical World; Huaxue Shijie. (May 1946)-. Periodical. Chinese. Shang-hai Shih Hua Hsueh Hua Kung Hsueh Hui, Shanghai, People's Republic of China. Documents available from CASDDS.
Ind/Abst Chem. Abstr.; Curr. Cit.

LC QD1 .H78 **ISSN** 0441-3776
DD 540/.3 CC
CODEN HHTPAU
HUA HSUEH TUNG PAO / CHUNG-KUO HUA HSUEH HUI = CHEMISTRY / CHINESE CHEMICAL SOCIETY.
Added/Corp Chung-Kuo Hua Hsueh Hui (Nan-Ching Shih, China). **VFOAT** Chemistry; Huaxue Tongbao. (1950)-. Academic Scholarly Publication. Chinese. Twelve times a year. $104.40. Science Press, 16 Donghuangchenggen North Street, Beijing 100707, People's Republic of China. **Tel** 011 86 1 4019821, 011 86 1 4010642, FAX 011 86 1 4012180, 011 86 1 4019810, telex 210147. **(Subscription address:** China International Book Trading Corporation, PO Box 399, Library Service Department, Beijing 100044 People's Republic of China. **Tel** 011 86 1 8414284, FAX 011 86 1 8412023, telex 22496 CIBTC CN.) Documents available from CASDDS.
Ind/Abst Chem. Abstr.; Curr. Cit.

ISSN 0254-0010
CH
CODEN HPHUDA
HUANJING BAOHU (TAIBEI). (HUAN CHING PAO HU.). [Huanjing baohu]. **Added/Corp** Chung-hua min kuo Huan Ching pao hu Hsueh hui. (1978)-. Periodical. Chinese (English). Irregular. Chung-hua min kuo Huan Ching pao hu Hsueh hui, Chung Li Hsi Lu, 1 Tuan 39 Hao, Taipei Shih Taiwan. Documents available from CASDDS.
Ind/Abst Chem. Abstr.

LC QD49.K8 H9 **ISSN** 0304-5277
KO
CODEN HWKYDI
HWAHAK KYOYUK. CHEMICAL EDUCATION. **Added/Corp** Daehan Hwahakhwoe. **VFOAT** Chemical Education. (19??)-. Academic Scholarly Publication. Korean. Four times a year. $43.00. Korean Chemical Society, 335 5 Ka Anam Dong Sungbuk Ku, Seoul 136 075 Korea. **Tel** 011 82 2 926 5457, FAX 011 82 2 923 5589. **ED** Hwa-Kuk Lee. Index available. cum. index. **Bk Rev. Circ:** 1,000. Documents available from CASDDS.
Desc: Reviews and reports on both experimental and theoretical research dealing with chemical education.
Ind/Abst Chem. Abstr.

LC QD1 .H85 KO
HWAHAK SEGYE: CHEMWORLD.
Added/Corp Taehan Hwahakhoe. **VFOAT** Chem World; Chemworld. (1992)-. Periodical. Korean. Taehan Hwahakhoe, 35 5-KA Anam-Dong, Songbuk-KU Soeul 136-075. **Continues** Hwahak Kwa Kongop ui Chinbo, 0439-9838.

ISSN 0142-0143
UK
NLM W1 I226
IFCC NEWS. [IFCC news]. **Added/Corp** International Federation of Clinical Chemistry. **VAT** International Federation of Clinical Chemistry News. No. 18 (Oct. 1977)-. Periodical. English. Six times a year. International Federation of Clinical Chemistry, University of Oulu, Dr. Rk Vihko, SF-90220 Oulu 22 Finland. **Tel** 011 358 81 254464. **Continues** Newsletter - International Federation of Clinical Chemistry.

LC WMLC L 83/4328 **ISSN** 0369-4178
XV
CODEN IPORDD
IJS POROCILO. INSTITUT JOZEF STEFAN. (IJS POROCILO.). [IJS Porocilo, Inst. Jozef Stefan]. **Added/Corp** Institut "Jozef Stefan". **VFOAT** I.J.S. Porocilo. (19??)-. Academic Scholarly Publication. Slovenian. Irregular. Univerza v Ljubljani / Institut Jozef Stefan, Ljubljana, Slovenia. Documents available from CASDDS. **Continues** NIJS Porocilo.
Ind/Abst Chem. Abstr. (1970-1983).

ISSN 0926-2067
NE
CCC
NLM QY 26; I33
Pr Rev.
IMMUNOASSAY KIT DIRECTORY. SERIES A, CLINICAL CHEMISTRY, THE.
VFOAT Clinical Chemistry; IKAD. Series A, Clinical Chemistry. Vol. 1, Pt. 1 (May 1991)-. Directory. English. Five times a year (5 issues per year). $560.00. Kluwer Academic Publishers, Postbus 322, 3300 AH Dordrecht The Netherlands. **Tel** 011 31 78 524400, FAX 011 31 78 183273, telex 20083. **ED** John Seth. **Acid Free.** available on microfilm and microfiche from University Microfilms International (UMI).
Desc: Provides clinical chemists with comparative aspects of over 1500 commercially available kits on peptide, steroid and thyroid hormones, proteins, tumor markers, therapeutic drugs.

LC Z5524.R25 I5 **ISSN** 0096-1345
DD 016.541/38 US
INDEX AND CUMULATIVE LIST OF PAPERS ON RADIATION CHEMISTRY.
See Chemistry and Chemicals-Abstracting, Bibliographies and Statistics.

ISSN 0891-6055
DD 540 US
NLM Z 5524; C9722
INDEX CHEMICUS (1987). **See** Chemistry and Chemicals-Abstracting, Bibliographies and Statistics.

ISSN 0253-6838
II
CODEN ICABD8
INDIAN CHEMICAL ABSTRACTS. (INDIAN CHEMICAL ABSTRACTS : ICA.). [Indian chem. abstr.]. **VFOAT** ICA. (1979)-. Academic Scholarly Publication. English. Twelve times a year. Techno-Doc Publications, Arya Building/3rd Floor, 209 P Demello Road, Bombay-400 001 India. Documents available from CASDDS.
Ind/Abst Chem. Abstr.

ISSN 0971-1627
II
INDIAN JOURNAL OF HETEROCYCLIC CHEMISTRY / PUBLISHED IN ASSOCIATION WITH NATIONAL ACADEMY OF CHEMISTRY AND BIOLOGY (INDIA). **Added/Corp** National Academy of Chemistry and Biology (India). **VAT** Indian j. heterocyclic chem. Vol. 1, No. 1 (June 1991)-. Periodical. English. Four times a year. $150.00. National Academy of Chemistry and Biology, Lucknow India. **(Subscription address:** Prints India, 11 Darya Ganj, New Delhi 110002 India. **Tel** 011 91 11 3268645, FAX 011 91 11 3275542, telex 31-61087 PRIN-IN.) Documents available from The Genuine Article.
Ind/Abst Res. Alert [Full Cov.].

ISSN 0019-6924
US
INDICATOR, THE. **Added/Corp** American Chemical Society. New Jersey Section. American Chemical Society. New York Section. (19??)-. Periodical. English. Ten times a year (monthly except July and Aug.). $20.00. American Chemical Society / New York and New Jersey Section, 43 Reservoir Place, Section 43, Cedar Grove NJ 07009. **Tel** (201)239-1975, (201)335-0912, FAX (201)785-4865. **ED** Lilian H. Sello. **Ad Acc, Adv Mgr:** Herman Burwasser, **Tel** (201)335-0912. **Circ:** 13,000 (ctrl).
Desc: Meeting information for Metropolitan New York and North New Jersey members of the American Chemical Society.

AG
Pr Rev.
INDUSTRIA Y QUIMICA. **Added/Corp** Asociacion Quimica Argentina. Vol. 1 (August 1935)-. Periodical. Spanish. Four times a year (Mar., June, Sept., Dec.). $35.00. Carlos Hirsch SRL, 4 Piso ESC 453/465, 1333 Buenos Aires Argentina. **Tel** 011 54 1 331 1787, FAX 011 54 1 331 1787, telex 21112 UAPE AR. **ED** Jaime Mazar Barnett. Index available. **Bk Rev. Ad Acc. Circ:** 4,000.
Desc: Up-to-date information in the various fields of chemistry.
Ind/Abst Ceram. Abstr.

ISSN 0020-045X
FR
CCC
CODEN INFCA8
INFORMATIONS CHIMIE (EDITION FRANCAISE). (INFORMATIONS CHIMIE). [Inf. chim.]. **Main/Corp** Societe d'Expansion Technique et Economique (France). (1963)-. Academic Scholarly Publication. French. Twelve times a year. $294.17. Soc Expansion Technique et Economique, 4 rue De Seze, 75009 Paris France. **Tel** 011 33 16 44945060. Documents available from CASDDS.
Ind/Abst Alum. Ind. Abstr.; Art Archaeol. Tech. Abstr.; Chem Inform; Chem. Abstr.; Chem. Bus. Bull.; Chem. Bus. NewsBase (1985-); Chem. Bus. Update; Coal Abstr.; Curr. Biotechnol.; Curr. Cit.; EMBASE; Energy Res. Abstr. (Aug. 1976-); F&S Index Plus Text, Int. [Select. Cov.]; Infomat Int. Bus.; Lit. Pat. Abstr., Oilfield Chem. (1978-); Lit. Abstr., Catal. Zeol.; Lit. Abstr., Health Environ.; Lit. Abstr., Pet. Refin. Petrochem.; Lit. Abstr., Pet. Substit.; Lit. Abstr., Transp. Storage; Met. Abstr.; PROMT.

ISSN 0339-6045
FR
CODEN ICHEDI
INFORMATIONS CHIMIE HEBDO. [Inf. chim. hebdo]. **Added/Corp** Societe d'Expansion Technique et Economique (France). **VFOAT** Info Chimie Hebdo. (1975)-. Periodical. French. One time a week. Society Expansion Tech. & Econ., 5 rue Jules Lefebvre, 75009 Paris France. **Tel** 011 33 1 48745370. Documents available from CASDDS. **Continues** Information Chimie. Supplement Hebdomadaire.

Chemistry and Chemicals

ISSN 0883-7201
DD 540 US
CODEN INRSEI

INSTRUMENTATION-RESEARCH.
[Instrum.-res.]. **Added/Corp** Perkin-Elmer Corporation. **VFOAT** Instrumentation Research. (March 1985)-. Academic Scholarly Publication. English. Four times a year. International Scientific Communications Inc, PO Box 870, 30 Controls Drive, Shelton CT 06484-0870. **Tel** (203)926-9300, FAX (203)926-9310, telex 964292. Documents available from CASDDS.
Ind/Abst Chem. Abstr. (1985-).

LC QD53 .C47
DD 542 US
ISSN 1073-9149
CCC
NLM W1; IN631AP **CODEN** ISCTEF

●INSTRUMENTATION SCIENCE AND TECHNOLOGY.
[Instrum. sci. technolog.]. **VFOAT** Instrumentation Science and Technology. (1994)-. Academic Scholarly Publication. English. Four times a year. $395.00. Marcel Dekker Inc., 270 Madison Avenue, New York NY 10016. **Tel** (212)696-9000, (800)228-1160, FAX (212)685-4540, telex 421419. **(Subscription address:** Marcel Dekker Inc., PO Box 5017, Monticello NY 12701. **Tel** (800)228-1160.) **Continues** Analytical Instrumentation, 0743-5797.
Ind/Abst Abstr. Bull. Inst. Paper Chem.; Air Pollut. Titles; Bioeng. Abstr.; Chem. Abstr.; Curr. Cit.; Curr. Contents Phys. Chem. Sci.; EMBASE; Energy Res. Abstr.; Eng. Index Annu.; Sci. Cit. Index.

LC TA455.P58 I58
DD 620.1/92/05
ISSN 0091-4037 US
CCC
CODEN IJPMCS
Pr Rev.

INTERNATIONAL JOURNAL OF POLYMERIC MATERIALS. See Plastics.

LC Q
DD 502 US
ISSN 0010-2164
NLM W1 IN805L **CODEN** ILBYA6

INTERNATIONAL LABORATORY. EUROPEAN ED.
[Int. lab., Eur. ed.]. (Jan./Feb. 1971)-. Trade Publication. English. Twelve times a year. $282.35. International Scientific Communications Ltd, 5 Whittle Parkway, Progress Business Center, Slough SL1 6DQ United Kingdom. **Tel** 011 44 1628 668881, FAX 011 44 1628 669199. **ED** Gabor B. Levy. **Ad Acc. Circ:** 55,000 (ctrl). Documents available from BIOSIS Document Express, CASDDS.
Desc: Articles for chemists and biologists working in the research laboratory.
Ind/Abst Abstr. BioCommer.; Alum. Ind. Abstr.; Anal. Abstr.; Art Archaeol. Tech. Abstr.; Biol. Abstr.; Chem. Abstr. (1971-1982); Chem. Hazards Ind.; Coal Abstr.; Curr. Biotechnol.; Curr. Cit.; EMBASE; HTFS Dig.; Lab. Hazards Bull.; Mass Spect. Bull.; Met. Abstr.; Saf. Health Work; Trop. Dis. Bull.; World Text. Abstr.

ISSN 0733-009X US

INTERNATIONAL PETROCHEMICAL REPORT, THE. See Petroleum and Natural Gas.

ISSN 0074-7866 US

INTERNATIONAL SCIENCE REVIEW SERIES. See Physics.

ISSN 0958-661X UK
CODEN ISMCEE

INTERNATIONAL SERIES OF MONOGRAPHS ON CHEMISTRY.
[Int. ser. monogr. chem.]. (1977)-. Monographic series. English. Clarendon Press, PO Box 1110, Clarendon TX 79226. **Tel** (806)874-2259, FAX (806)874-3124.
Ind/Abst Biol. Abstr. (1985-); Curr. Cit.

ISSN 0368-0827 PL
CODEN IZACAX

INZYNIERIA I APARATURA CHEMICZNA.
[Inz. apar. chem.]. (1970)-. Academic Scholarly Publication. Polish (summaries and/or abstracts in English, German and Russian). Four times a year. $78.00. **(Subscription address:** Ars Polona-Ruch, PO Box 1001, Krakowskie Przedmiescie 7, 00-068 Warsaw Poland. **Tel** 011 48 22 261201.) Documents available from CASDDS. **Continues** Aparatura Chemiczna.
Ind/Abst Chem. Abstr.; Proc. Chem. Eng.; Theor. Chem. Eng.

ISSN 1065-6081 US

NLM W1; IS52

●ISOLATION AND PURIFICATION.
(1993)-. Periodical. English. Four times a year. $323.00 (academic institutions), $504.00 (corporate institutions). Gordon & Breach Science Publishers, Inc., PO Box 786, Cooper Station, New York NY 10276. **Tel** (212)206-8900, FAX (212)645-2459. **Continues** Preparative Chromatography, 0890-9075.

LC QD1 .I927
ISSN 0021-2148 IS
CCC
NLM W1 IS63R **CODEN** ISJCAT
Pr Rev.

ISRAEL JOURNAL OF CHEMISTRY.
[Isr. j. chem.]. **Added/Corp** Moatsah Ha-Leumit Le-Mehkar Ule-Fituah (Israel). Vol. 1, No. 1 (July 1963)-. Periodical. English. Four times a year. $295.00. Laser Pages Publishing Ltd., PO Box 50257, Jerusalem 91502 Israel. **Tel** 011 972 2 829770, 011 972 2 370699, FAX 011 972 2 818782. **ED** H. Levanon. **Ad Acc. Circ:** 1,000. Documents available from The Genuine Article, BIOSIS Document Express, Ask*IEEE, CASDDS. **Continues** Moatsah Ha-Leumit Le-Mehkar Ule-Fituah (Israel). Bulletin of the Research Council of Israel. Section A. Chemistry.
Desc: Issues contain invited papers in a single field of current interest by internationally renowned scientists.
Ind/Abst AGRICOLA; Biol. Abstr.; Ceram. Abstr. (19??-); Chem Inform; Chem. Abstr.; Chem. Titles; Curr. Chem. React.; Curr. Cit.; Curr. Contents Phys. Chem. Earth Sci.; Dairy Sci. Abstr.; GeoRef; Index Chem.; INSPEC (1972-); Int. Aerosp. Abstr.; Leadscan; Mass Spect. Bull.; Methods Organ. Synth.; NAPRALERT; Nat. Prod. Updates; Life Sci. Collect.; PESTDOC; Res. Alert [Full Cov.]; Sci. Index; SCISEARCH.

ISSN 0132-7070 RU
CODEN IOKIDR

ISSLEDOVANIIA V OBLASTI KHIMII I TEKHNOLOGII PRODUKTOV PERERABOTKI GORIUCHIKH ISKOPAEMYKH.
Added/Corp Leningradskii Tekhnologicheskii Institut Imeni Lensoveta. (1974)-. Academic Scholarly Publication. Russian. St. Petersburg State University / Izdatelstvo Leningradskogo Universiteta, Universitetskaia Nab 7/9, 199034 St. Petersburg Russia. **Tel** 011 7 812 2189788, FAX 011 7 812 2185152, telex 121481. Documents available from CASDDS.
Ind/Abst Chem. Abstr.

LC QD380 .I8
ISSN
RU
CODEN IKTVAC

ITOGI NAUKI I TEKHNIKI. SERIIA KHIMIIA I TEKHNOLOGIIA VYSOKOMOLEKULIARNYKH SOEDINENII.
Added/Corp Vsesoiuznyi Institut Nauchnoi i Tekhnicheskoi Informatsii (Soviet Union). **VFOAT** Khimiia i Tekhnologiia Vysokomoliarnykh Soedinenii; Itogi Nauki i Tekhniki: Khimiia i Tekhnologiia Vysokomolekuliarnykh Soedinenii. (1973)-. Russian. VINITI - Vsesoyuznyi Institut Nauchno-Tekhnicheskoi Informatsii, All-Union Scientific and Technical Information Institute, Baltiiskaia ulitsa 14, 125219 Moscow Russia. **Tel** 011 7 95 2384600, FAX 011 7 95 9430060, telex 411160. Documents available from CASDDS. **Continues** Itogi Nauki: Khimiia i Tekhnologiia Vysokomolekuliarnykh Soedinenii.
Ind/Abst Chem. Abstr.

LC QD502 .I85
ISSN 0202-7968 RU
CODEN ITKKDY

ITOGI NAUKI I TEKHNIKI. SERIIA KINETIKA I KATALIZ / GOSUDARSTVENNYI KOMITET SSSR PO NAUKE I TEKHNIKE, AKADEMIIA NAUK SSSR, VSESOIUZNYI INSTITUT NAUCHNOI I TEKHNICHESKOI INFORMATSII.
Added/Corp Vsesoiuznyi Institut Nauchnoi i Tekhnicheskoi Informatsii (Soviet Union). **VFOAT** Seriia Kinetika i Kataliz; Kinetika i Kataliz; Itogi Nauki i Tekhniki. Kinetika i Kataliz. (1979)-. Monographic series. Russian. Price varies per volume. VINITI - Vsesoyuznyi Institut Nauchno-Tekhnicheskoi Informatsii, All-Union Scientific and Technical Information Institute, Baltiiskaia ulitsa 14, 125219 Moscow Russia. **Tel** 011 7 95 2384600, FAX 011 7 95 9430060, telex 411160. Documents available from CASDDS. **Continues** Itogi Nauki i Tekhniki. Kinetika i Kataliz.
Ind/Abst Chem. Abstr.

RU

ITOGI NAUKI I TEKHNIKI. SERIIA RASTVORY, RASPLAVY.
(19??)-. Russian. VINITI - Vsesoyuznyi Institut Nauchno-Tekhnicheskoi Informatsii, All-Union Scientific and Technical Information Institute, Baltiiskaia ulitsa 14, 125219 Moscow Russia. **Tel** 011 7 95 2384600, FAX 011 7 95 9430060, telex 411160.

ISSN 0275-0910 UK
CODEN DSEDC

IUPAC CHEMICAL DATA SERIES.
(IUPAC CHEMICAL DATA SERIES / INTERNATIONAL UNION OF PURE AND APPLIED CHEMISTRY.). [IUPAC chem. data ser.]. **VFOAT** Chemical Data Series. **VAT** International Union of Pure and Applied Chemistry Chemical Data Series. Academic Scholarly Publication. English. Irregular. Price varies per volume. Pergamon Press, An Imprint of Elsevier Science Ltd., The Boulevard, Langford Lane, Kidlington, Oxford OX5 1GB United Kingdom. **Tel** 011 44 1865 843000, 011 44 1865 843699, FAX 011 44 1865 843010. Documents available from CASDDS.
Ind/Abst Chem. Abstr.

LC QD1 .I98

GS
CODEN IANKEJ

IZVESTIIA AKADEMII NAUK GRUZII. SERIIA KHIMICHESKAIA / SAKARTVELOS MECNIEREBATA AKADEMIA MACNE. KIMIIS SIRIA.
Added/Corp Sakartvelos Mecnierebata Akademia. **VFOAT** Seriia Khimicheskaia; Sakartvelos Mecnierebata Akademia Macne. Kimiis Siria; Kimiis Siria; Proceedings of the Academy of Sciences of Georgia. Chemical Series; Chemical Series. (1991)-. Academic Scholarly Publication. Russian (English and Georgian). Four times a year. Izdatelstvo Metsniereba / Akademiya Nauk Gruzii, (Georgian Academy of Sciences), Ulitsa Kutuzova 19, 380060 Tbilisi 60 Georgia (Republic). **(Subscription address:** East View Publications Inc., 3020 Harbor Lane North, Suite 110, Minneapolis MN 55447. **Tel** (800)477-1005, (612)550-0961, FAX (612)559-2931.) **Continues** Izvestiia Akademii Nauk Gruzinskoi SSR. Seriia Khimicheskaia.
Ind/Abst Anal. Abstr.; Chem. Abstr.

ISSN 0002-3205 KZ
TITLE CHANGE

IZVESTIIA AKADEMII NAUK KAZAKHSKOI SSR. SERIIA KHIMICHESKAIA.
Added/Corp Qazaq SSR Ghylym Akademiiasy. **VFOAT** Qazaq SSR Ghylym Akademiiasynyng Khabarlary. Seriia Khimicheskaia; Seriia Khimicheskaia. (1966)-(199?). Periodical. Russian (summaries and/or abstracts in Kazakh; table of contents in Kazakh and Russian). Documents available from CASDDS. **Continues** Izvestiia Akademii Nauk Kazakhskoi SSR. Seriia Khimicheskikh Nauk. **Continued by** Izvestiia Akademii Nauk Respubliki Kazakstan. Seriia Khimicheskaia.
Ind/Abst Chem. Abstr. (?-?).

LC QD1 .A35833

KZ

IZVESTIIA AKADEMII NAUK RESPUBLIKI KAZAKHSTAN. SERIIA KHIMICHESKAIA.
Added/Corp Qazaqstan Respublikasy Ghylym Akademiiasy. **VFOAT** Seriia Khimicheskaia. (199?)-. Periodical. Russian (summaries and/or abstracts in Kazakh). Six times a year. **Continues** Izvestiia Akademii Nauk Kazakhskoi SSR. Seriia Khimicheskaia (1966).

RU
CODEN IASKEA

IZVESTIIA AKADEMII NAUK. SERIIA KHIMICHESKAIA / ROSSIISKAIA AKADEMIIA NAUK.
Added/Corp Rossiiskaia Akademiia Nauk. **VFOAT** Seriia Khimicheskaia. (Feb. 1992)-. Academic Scholarly Publication. Russian (summaries and/or abstracts in English; table of contents in English). Twelve times a year. Izdatelstvo Nauka / Akademiia Nauk, (Publishing House of the Russian Academy of Sciences), Leninskii Porspekt 14, 117901 Moscow Russia. **Tel** 011 95 9542153, FAX 011 95 9382144, telex 411964. **Continues** Izvestiia Akademii Nauk SSSR. Seriia Khimicheskaia, 0002-3353.
Ind/Abst Chem. Abstr.

LC QH301 .A332a
DD 574.05 MV
CODEN IAMNEN

IZVESTIIA AKADEMII NAUK SSR MOLDOVA. BIOLOGICHESKIE I KHIMICHESKIE NAUKI. See Biology.

LC QC1 .A42823

TK

IZVESTIIA AKADEMII NAUK TURKMENISTANA. SERIIA FIZIKO-MATEMATICHESKIKH, TEKHNICHESKIKH, KHIMICHESKIKH I GEOLOGICHESKIKH NAUK. See Physics.

TK
TITLE CHANGE
IZVESTIIA AKADEMII NAUK TURKMENSKOI SSR. SERIIA FIZIKO-MATEMATICHESKIKH, TEKHNICHESKIKH, KHIMICHESKIKH I GEOLOGICHESKIKH NAUK. **See** Physics.

ISSN 0869-2793
RU
TITLE CHANGE
IZVESTIIA SORAN. SIBIRSKII KHIMICHESKII ZHURNAL. **Added/Corp** Rossiiskaia Akademiia Nauk SSSR. Sibirskoe Otdelenie. **VFOAT** Sibirskii Khimicheskii Zhurnal; Izvestiia SO RAN. Sibirskii Khimicheskii Zhurnal; Siberian Journal of Chemistry; Izvestiia Sibirskogo Otdeleniia Rossiiskoi Akademii Nauk. Sibirskii Khimicheskii Zhurnal. (1992)-(1993). Academic Scholarly Publication. Russian (summaries and/or abstracts in English; table of contents in English). Documents available from The Genuine Article, CASDDS. ***Continues*** *Izvestiia So An SSSR. Sibirskii Khimicheskii Zhurnal.* ***Continued by*** *Khimiia v Interesakh Ustoichivogo Razvitiia.*
Ind/Abst Chem. Abstr.; Curr. Contents Phys. Chem. Earth Sci.; Res. Alert [Full Cov.]; Sci. Cit. Index; SCISEARCH.

LC QD1 .R852 **ISSN** 0579-2991
DD 540.(5/6) RU
CCC
CODEN IVUKAR
Pr Rev.
IZVESTIJA VYSSIH UCEBNYH ZAVEDENIJ. HIMIJA I HIMICESKAJA TEHNOLOGIJA. (IZVESTIIA VYSSHIKH UCHEBNYKH ZAVEDENII. KHIMIIA I KHIMICHESKAIA TEKHNOLOGIIA.). [Izv. vyss. ucebn. zaved., Him. him. tehnol.]. **Added/Corp** Soviet Union. Ministerstvo Vysshego Obrazovaniia. Soviet Union. Ministerstvo Vysshego i Srednego Spetsialnogo Obrazovaniia. Ivanovskii Khimiko-Tekhnologicheskii Institut. Soviet Union. Gosudarstvennyi Komitet po Narodnomu Obrazovaniiu. **VFOAT** Khimiia i Khimicheskaia Tekhnologiia; Izvestiia Vysshikh Uchebnykh Zavedenii Ministerstva Vysshego; Azovaniia SSSR. Khimiia i Khimicheskaiia Tekhnologiia. Vol. 1 (1958)-. Academic Scholarly Publication. Russian. Twelve times a year. **(Subscription address:** East View Publications Inc., 3020 Harbor Lane North, Suite 110, Minneapolis MN 55447. **Tel** (800)477-1005, (612)550-0961, FAX (612)559-2931.**)** Documents available from The Genuine Article, CASDDS. ***Absorbed*** *Nauchnye Doklady Vysshei Shkoly. Khnimiia i Khimicheskaia Tekhnologiia.*
Ind/Abst Abstr. Bull. Inst. Pap. Sci. Tech.; Anal. Abstr.; Chem. Abstr.; Res. Alert [Full Cov.]; Sci. Cit. Index; SCISEARCH.

LC QD1 **ISSN** 0579-2991
DD 540 RU
CCC
CODEN IVUKAR
IZVESTIJA VYSSIH UCEBNYH ZAVEDENIJ. HIMIJA I HIMICESKAJA TEHNOLOGIJA. (IZVESTIIA VYSSHIKH UCHEBNYKH ZAVEDENII. KHIMIIA I KHIMICHESKAIA TEKNOLOGIIA.). [Izv. vyss. uĉebn. zaved., Him. him. tehnol.]. (1958)-. Periodical. Russian. Twelve times a year. $129.95. **(Subscription address:** East View Publications Inc., 3020 Harbor Lane North, Suite 110, Minneapolis MN 55447. **Tel** (800)477-1005, (612)550-0961, FAX (612)559-2931.**)** Documents available from CASDDS.
Ind/Abst Abstr. Bull. Inst. Pap. Sci. Tech.; Ceram. Abstr. (19??-); Chem. Abstr.; Curr. Biotechnol.; Sug. Indus. Abstr.

LC TP1 .J17
DD 660/.05 GW
JAHRBUCH FUER DEN PRAKTIKER. **VFOAT** Chemieprodukte, Haushalt, Gewerbe, Industrie. Vol. 29 (1986)-. Trade Publication. German. One time a year. Verlag fuer Chemische Industrie, H Ziolkowsky, Postfach 102565, D-86015 Augsburg 1 Germany. **Tel** 011 49 821 519345, 011 49 821 519346, FAX 0821/51 79 53. ***Continues*** *Jahrbuch fur den Praktiker aus der Ol-, Fett-, Seifen- und Waschmittel-, Korperflegemittel-, Wachs- und Sonstigen Chem.-Techn. Industrie.*

LC TP733.G32 B453a
GW
JAHRESBERICHT. **Main/Corp** Berliner Gaswerke. (19??)-. German. Berliner Gaswerke, Kurfurstendamm 203-205 15, Berlin Germany.

ISSN 0771-4602
BE
UDC 541
JANSSEN CHIMICA ACTA. [Janssen Chim. Acta]. (1983)-. Periodical. English. Four times a year. Janssen Pharmaceutica, 501 George Street, New Brunswick NJ 08903. Documents available from CASDDS.
Ind/Abst Chem. Abstr.; Curr. Cit.

LC HD9657.J3 J29
DD 338.4/7/6600952 JA
CODEN JCANBJ
JAPAN CHEMICAL ANNUAL. (19??)-. Periodical. English. One time a year. $136.00. Chemical Daily Company Ltd, 3 16 8 Nihonbashi Hama Cho, Chuo Ku Tokyo 103 Japan. **Tel** 011 81 3 36637932, FAX 03 6632550, telex 2422362 NIPPO J. **(Subscription address:** Tekno Info Corporation, 500 Trotwood Place, Louisville KY 40245. **Tel** (502)254-5728.**)** **Ad Acc.**
Desc: Contents include the general outline of the Japanese chemical industry, MITI White Paper on international trade, explanation and statistical data on particular industrial fields.

LC TP12 .J28 **ISSN** 0075-3203
DD 660/.025/52 JA
JAPAN CHEMICAL DIRECTORY. **See** Industry and Production-Trade and Industrial Directories.

LC QD415 **ISSN** 0075-3696
DD 574.192 IS
NLM W3 JE56 **CODEN** JSQCA7
JERUSALEM SYMPOSIA ON QUANTUM CHEMISTRY AND BIOCHEMISTRY, THE. **See** Biology-Biological Chemistry.

ISSN 0254-5861
CC
CODEN JHUADF
JIEGOU HUAXUE. (CHIEH KOU HUA HSUEH.). [Jiegou huaxue]. **Added/Corp** Chung-Kuo Ko Hsueh Yuan. Fu Chien Wu Chih Chieh Kou Yen Chiu So. **VFOAT** Journal of Structural Chemistry. Vol. 1, No. 1 (August 1982)-. Academic Scholarly Publication. English (Chinese; summaries and/or abstracts in English). Six times a year. $98.00. Chinese Academy of Sciences, Fujian Institute of Research, Box 143, Fuzhou Fujian 350002 China. **Tel** 011 86 591 37113682151, FAX 011 86 591 714946. Index available (bound in last issue). available on microfilm and microfiche. Documents available from CASDDS.
Ind/Abst Chem. Abstr.

LC S583 .A7
DD 630/.24 US
JOURNAL - ASSOCIATION OF OFFICIAL ANALYTICAL CHEMISTS. **See** Agriculture.

ISSN 0253-1208
TI
CODEN JSCTDP
JOURNAL DE LA SOCIETE CHIMIQUE DE TUNISIE. [J. Soc. chim. Tunisie]. **Added/Corp** Societe Chimique de Tunisie. **VFOAT** Majallat Al-Jamiyah Al-Kimiyaiyah Al-Tunisiyah. No 1 (May 1979)-. Periodical. French (summaries and/or abstracts in English and Arabic). Documents available from CASDDS.
Ind/Abst Chem. Abstr.

LC QD1 .J75 **ISSN** 0941-1216
GW
CODEN JPCCEMJPCEAO
JOURNAL FUER PRAKTISCHE CHEMIE, CHEMIKER-ZEITUNG. **VFOAT** Journal fuer Praktische Chemie, Chemiker Zeitung. Vol. 334 (1992)-. Academic Scholarly Publication. German (English). Eight times a year. $343.00. Johann Ambrosius Barth, Prager Strasse 16 B, D-04103 Leipzig Germany. **Tel** 011 49 341 9781570, FAX 011 49 341 9781575. **(Subscription address:** Huethig Publishing Inc., 29 Macintosh Drive, Oxford CT 06478. **Tel** (203)881-2647.**)** Documents available from The Genuine Article, CASDDS, Documents on Demand. ***Formed by the union of*** *Journal fuer Praktische Chemie, 0021-8383* ***and*** *Chemiker Zeitung (1970), 0009-2894.*
Ind/Abst AGRICOLA; Chem. Abstr.; Coal Abstr.; Curr. Contents Eng. Comput. Technol.; Curr. Contents Phys. Chem. Earth Sci.; EMBASE; Energy Inf. Abstr.; Energy Res. Abstr.; Environ. Abstr.; GeoRef; Index Chem.; Nucl. Sci. Abstr.; Life Sci. Collect.; PESTDOC; Res. Alert [Full Cov.]; Saf. Health Work; Sci. Cit. Index; SCISEARCH.

LC S583 .J6 **ISSN** 0021-8561
DD 630.2405 US
CCC
NLM W1 JO534D **CODEN** JAFCAU
Pr Rev.
JOURNAL OF AGRICULTURAL AND FOOD CHEMISTRY. **See** Agriculture-Crop Production and Soils.

LC TP1 **ISSN** 0021-888X
DD 660.5 US
UDC 66.0 CCC
CODEN JAPUAW
TITLE CHANGE
JOURNAL OF APPLIED CHEMISTRY OF THE USSR. [J. appl. chem. USSR]. **VAT** Journal of Applied Chemistry of the Union of Soviet Socialist Republics. Vol. 23 (1950)-(199?). Academic Scholarly Publication. English (Russian). Plenum Press, 233 Spring Street, New York NY 10013-1578. **Tel** (212)620-8000, (800)221-9369, FAX (212)463-0742, (212)807-1047, telex 23/421139. **ED** V S Shpak. Index available. available on microfilm and microfiche from University Microfilms International (UMI). Documents available from Article Express International, The Genuine Article, CASDDS. ***Continued by*** *Russian Journal of Applied Chemistry.*
Desc: Reports on recent advances in all aspects of applied chemistry. Covers soil chemistry, inorganic chemistry, on-exchange electrochemistry, reversible reactions, chemistry of plastics, cracking reactions and organic and hydrocarbon chemistry.
Ind/Abst Chem. Abstr.; Coal Abstr.; Curr. Cit.; Curr. Contents Phys. Chem. Earth Sci.; Ei Page One; EMBASE; Energy Res. Abstr.; Eng. Index Annu.; GeoRef; HTFS Dig.; Pollut. Abstr. Indexes; Proc. Chem. Eng.; Res. Alert [Full Cov.]; Sci. Cit. Index; SCISEARCH; Soils Fert.; Theor. Chem. Eng.

LC QC879.6 .J68 **ISSN** 0167-7764
DD 551.5/11/05 NE
CCC
CODEN JATCE2
Pr Rev.
JOURNAL OF ATMOSPHERIC CHEMISTRY. **See** Earth Sciences-Meteorology.

LC WMLC 93/1865 **ISSN** 0883-9115
DD 547 US
CCC
NLM W1; JO561K **CODEN** JBCPEV
JOURNAL OF BIOACTIVE AND COMPATIBLE POLYMERS. [J. bioact. compat. polym.]. Vol. 1, No. 1 (Jan. 1986)-. Academic Scholarly Publication. English. Four times a year. $315.00. Technomic Publishing Company, Inc., 851 New Holland Avenue, Box 3535, Lancaster PA 17604. **Tel** (717)291-5609, (800)233-9936, FAX (717)295-4538. **ED** Raphael M. Ottenbrite. cum. index. **Circ:** 225. available on microfilm from University Microfilms International (UMI). Documents available from Article Express International, The Genuine Article, BIOSIS Document Express, CASDDS.
Desc: Intended to serve the community of scientists who are actively researching polymers for human, animal and botanical application, refereed research papers and short communications of interest to biological scientists and polymer chemists are provided. Contains reviews of frontier areas, listings of publications, patents, and current literature citations. Emphasis is placed on unusual polymers and the methods, applications, and problems related to biological systems. Preparations, modifications and characterizations of the polymers play a major role along with the biological evaluations and applications in medicinal, pharmaceutical, agricultural and other biologically related areas.
Ind/Abst Biol. Abstr. (1990-); Chem. Abstr. (1986-); Curr. Cit.; Curr. Contents Eng. Comput. Technol.; Ei Page One; EMBASE; Eng. Index Annu.; Res. Alert [Full Cov.]; SCISEARCH.

LC QD1 .J926 **ISSN** 0098-0331
DD 574.5/01/54 US
CCC
NLM W1 JO58P **CODEN** JCECD8
Pr Rev.
JOURNAL OF CHEMICAL ECOLOGY. **See** Environmental Issues-Ecology.

LC QD1 .J93 **ISSN** 0021-9584
DD 540/.7 US
CCC
NLM W1 JO581 **CODEN** JCEDA8
Pr Rev.
JOURNAL OF CHEMICAL EDUCATION. [J. chem. educ.]. **Added/Corp** American Chemical Society. Division of Chemical Education. American Chemical Society. Section of Chemical Education. Pacific Southwest Association of Chemistry Teachers. Proceedings. New England Association of Chemistry Teachers. Report. Vol. 1, No. 1 (Jan. 1924)-. Academic Scholarly Publication. English. Twelve times a year. $64.00 (institutions), $32.00 (individuals) US; $80.00 (institutions), $40.00 (individuals) other. Journal of Chemical Education, 1991 Northampton Street, Easton PA 18042-3189. **Tel** (610)250-7264. **ED** Joseph J. Lagowski. Index available. cum. index. **Bk Rev.** **Ad Acc.** **Circ:** 20,000. available on microfilm and microfiche from University Microfilms International (UMI). Documents available from The Genuine Article, Ask*IEEE, UMI Article Clearinghouse, CASDDS.
Desc: A textbook for the teacher, student, and chemist in industry.
Ind/Abst Abstr. Bull. Inst. Paper Chem.; Abstr. Bull. Inst. Pap. Sci. Tech.; Acad. Abstr.; Acad. Ind. [Computer File] (1992-); Acad. Search; Art Archaeol. Tech. Abstr.; Ceram. Abstr.; Chem Inform; Chem. Abstr.; Chem. Hazards Ind.; Chem. Titles; Coal Abstr.; Curr. Cit.; Curr. Contents Phys. Chem. Earth Sci.; Curr. Index J. Educ.; Educ. Index; Educ. Technol. Abstr.; EMBASE; EP Collect.; Expand. Acad. Index (1989-); Gen. Sci. Index; Gen. Sci. Source; GeoRef; Health Source Plus; Health Source; Homework Help.; INFO-SOUTH Abstr.; INIS Atomindex [Micro.]; INSPEC (1968-);; Int. Aerosp. Abstr.; Lab. Hazards Bull.; Mass Spect. Bull.; MasterFile FullTEXT 1000; MasterFile FullTEXT 350; MasterFile FullTEXT 650; MasterFile FullTEXT (Jan. 1992-); MINPROC; Newsp. Period. Abstr. (1989-); Nucl. Sci. Abstr.; OCLC; Ref. Sources; Res. Alert [Full Cov.]; Res. High. Educ. Abstr.; Sci. Cit. Index;

SCISEARCH; Sel. Water Resour. Abstr.; Soc. Sci. Cit. Index [Select. Cov.]; Surf. Treat. Technol. Abstr.; Tech. Educ. Train. Abstr.; Telebase.

LC QD40 .J64c
DD 540 UK

JOURNAL OF CHEMICAL RESEARCH. INDEXES. **Added/Corp** Chemical Society (Great Britain) Gesellschaft Deutscher Chemiker. Societe Chimique de France. (1977)-. English. One time a year. Journal of Chemical Research, London.

UK

JOURNAL OF CHEMICAL RESEARCH. MICROFICHE. (JOURNAL OF CHEMICAL RESEARCH.). (19??)-. English. Twelve times a year. £52.00 EC; $96.00 US; £55.00 other. Royal Society of Chemistry, Thomas Graham House, Science Park, Cambridge CB4 4WF United Kingdom. **Tel** 011 44 1223 420066, FAX 011 44 1223 423623, telex 818293 ROYAL. **(Subscription address:** Royal Society of Chemistry, Turpin Distribution Services Ltd., Blackhorse Road, Letchworth, Hertfordshire SG6 1HN United Kingdom. **Tel** 011 44 1462 672555, FAX 011 44 1462 480947.**)**

LC QD40 .J64b **ISSN** 0308-2350
DD 540 UK
NLM W1 JO581R **CODEN** JRMPDM
Pr Rev.

JOURNAL OF CHEMICAL RESEARCH. MINIPRINT. (JOURNAL OF CHEMICAL RESEARCH.). [J. chem. research (M)]. **Added/Corp** Chemical Society. Gesellschaft Deutscher Chemiker. Societe Chimique de France. (Jan. 1977)-. Periodical. English (French and German). Twelve times a year (plus index). $111.00. Royal Society of Chemistry, Thomas Graham House, Science Park, Cambridge CB4 4WF United Kingdom. **Tel** 011 44 1223 420066, FAX 011 44 1223 423623, telex 818293 ROYAL. **(Subscription address:** Royal Society of Chemistry, Turpin Distribution Services Ltd., Blackhorse Road, Letchworth, Hertfordshire SG6 1HN United Kingdom. **Tel** 011 44 1462 672555, FAX 011 44 1462 480947.**) ED** M. P. Ennis. Index available. cum. index. **Ad Acc.** available on microfiche. Documents available from CASDDS.
Desc: Publishes reports of original research in all branches of chemistry.
Ind/Abst Chem. Abstr.; GeoRef; Mass Spect. Bull. (?-?); NAPRALERT.

LC QD40 .J64a **ISSN** 0308-2342
DD 540/.5 UK
CCC
NLM W1 JO581S **CODEN** JRPSDC
Pr Rev.

JOURNAL OF CHEMICAL RESEARCH. SYNOPSES. (JOURNAL OF CHEMICAL RESEARCH.). [J. Chem. Research (S)]. **Added/Corp** Royal Society of Chemistry (Great Britain) Chemical Society (Great Britain) Gesellschaft Deutscher Chemiker. Societe Chimique de France. Issue 1 (Jan. 1977)-. Academic Scholarly Publication. English. Twelve times a year (plus index). $764.00. Royal Society of Chemistry, Thomas Graham House, Science Park, Cambridge CB4 4WF United Kingdom. **Tel** 011 44 1223 420066, FAX 011 44 1223 423623, telex 818293 ROYAL. **(Subscription address:** Royal Society of Chemistry, Turpin Distribution Services Ltd., Blackhorse Road, Letchworth, Hertfordshire SG6 1HN United Kingdom. **Tel** 011 44 1462 672555, FAX 011 44 1462 480947.**) ED** Marcus Ennis. Index available (free). cum. index. **Ad Acc.** available on microfiche; available on an online database from STN International. Documents available from The Genuine Article, BIOSIS Document Express, CASDDS, BLDSC, FAXON Xpress, SWETS.
Desc: Covers all areas of chemistry.
Ind/Abst Biol. Abstr.; Chem Inform; Chem. Abstr.; Chem. Titles; Curr. Chem. React.; Curr. Contents Phys. Chem. Earth Sci.; Leadscan; Mass Spect. Bull.; Methods Organ. Synth.; NAPRALERT; Nat. Prod. Updates; Refer. Z.; Res. Alert [Full Cov.]; Sci. Cit. Index; SCISEARCH.

ISSN 0377-8444
II
CODEN JCHSD3

JOURNAL OF CHEMICAL SCIENCES. [J. chem. sci.]. **Added/Corp** Guru Nanak Dev University. Vol. 1, No. 1 (Sept. 30, 1975)-. Periodical. English. One time a year. $15.00. Amritsar, Guru Nanak Dev University, India. **(Subscription address:** Prints India, 11 Darya Ganj, New Delhi 110002 India. **Tel** 011 91 11 3268645, FAX 011 91 11 3275542, telex 31-61087 PRIN-IN.**)**

LC TS695 .J68 **ISSN** 1056-7860
DD 671.7/35/05 US
CCC
CODEN JCVDET

JOURNAL OF CHEMICAL VAPOR DEPOSITION. [J. chem. vapor depos.]. (1992)-. Periodical. English. Four times a year (Jan., Apr., July and Oct.). $195.00. Technomic Publishing Company, Inc., 851 New Holland Avenue, Box 3535, Lancaster PA 17604. **Tel** (717)291-5609, (800)233-9936, FAX (717)295-4538.
Desc: Publishes the results of current research and development in the theory, practice, and applications of chemical vapor deposition. Representation from all countries active in this technology provides readers with information on major advances from around the world.

LC QD39.3.M3 J68 **ISSN** 0886-9383
DD 540.72 UK
CCC
CODEN JOCHEU

JOURNAL OF CHEMOMETRICS. [J. chemom.]. **Added/Corp** Chemometrics Society. Vol. 1, No. 1 (Jan. 1987)-. Academic Scholarly Publication. English. Six times a year. $545.00. John Wiley & Sons Ltd., Baffins Lane, Chichester, West Sussex PO19 1UD United Kingdom. **Tel** 011 44 1243 779777, FAX 011 44 1243 776128 BTG:JWP001, telex 86290 WIBOOKG. **(Subscription address:** John Wiley & Sons, Inc. / Philadelphia, PO Box 7247, Philadelphia PA 19170. **Tel** (212)850-6645, (800)225-5945.**) ED** Bruce R. Kowalski, P. Geladi, S. D. Brown, and P. Brown. available on microfilm and microfiche from University Microfilms International (UMI). Documents available from The Genuine Article, BIOSIS Document Express, CASDDS, ADONIS.
Desc: Contains papers on fundamental and applied aspects of chemometrics and provides a forum for the exchange of information on meetings, etc. for the international chemometrics research community.
Ind/Abst ADONIS; Anal. Abstr.; Biol. Abstr. (1987-); Chem. Abstr. (1987-); Curr. Aware. Biol. Sci., CABS; Curr. Cit.; Curr. Contents Phys. Chem. Earth Sci.; Food Sci. Technol. Abstr.; Mass Spect. Bull. (?-?); Res. Alert [Full Cov.]; SCISEARCH.

ISSN 0301-4770
NE
CCC
NLM W1 JO5846 **CODEN** JCLIDR
Pr Rev.

JOURNAL OF CHROMATOGRAPHY LIBRARY. [J. chromatogr. libr.]. Vol. 1 (1973)-. Monographic series. English. Irregular. Price varies per volume. Elsevier Science Publishers BV, PO Box 211, 1000 AE Amsterdam Netherlands. **Tel** 011 31 20 4853641, 011 31 20 4853642, FAX 011 31 20 4853598. Each issue contains an index to its own contents (no volume index)--loose. Documents available from BIOSIS Document Express, CASDDS.
Desc: Series focusing on chromatographic analysis.
Ind/Abst Biol. Abstr.; Chem. Abstr.; Curr. Cit.; Postharvest News Inf.; Seed Abstr.

LC QD39.3.E46 J68 **ISSN** 0192-8651
DD 542/.8/05 US
CCC
CODEN JCCHDD
Pr Rev.

JOURNAL OF COMPUTATIONAL CHEMISTRY. [J. comput. chem.]. Vol. 1 (Spring 1980)-. Academic Scholarly Publication. English. Twelve times a year. $896.00. John Wiley & Sons, Inc., 605 Third Avenue, New York NY 10158-0012. **Tel** (212)850-6000, (212)850-6645, FAX (212)850-6088, telex 12-7063. **(Subscription address:** John Wiley & Sons / UK, Baffins Lane, Chichester, West Sussex PO19 1UD United Kingdom. **Tel** 011 44 1243 779777, FAX 011 44 243 776128, telex 86290 WIBOOKG.**) ED** Norman L. Allinger and Paul von R. Schleyer. **Ad Acc. Circ:** 700. available on microfilm and microfiche from University Microfilms International (UMI). Documents available from The Genuine Article, Ask*IEEE, CASDDS, ADONIS.
Desc: Publishes articles concerned with all aspects of computational chemistry: organic, inorganic, physical, analytical and biological. Other topics explored are quantum chemistry and molecular mechanics.
Ind/Abst Abstr. Bull. Inst. Pap. Sci. Tech.; ACM Guide Comput. Lit.; ADONIS; Chem. Abstr.; Chem. Titles; Comput. Rev.; Curr. Cit.; Curr. Contents Phys. Chem. Earth Sci.; INSPEC (Spring 1980-); Leadscan; Math. Rev.; Ref. Upd. Deluxe Ed.; Res. Alert [Full Cov.]; Sci. Cit. Index; SCISEARCH.

LC QP801.P64 J68 **ISSN** 1064-7546
DD 620.1/9204223 US
CCC
CODEN JEPDED

•**JOURNAL OF ENVIRONMENTAL POLYMER DEGRADATION.** **See** Environmental Issues.

LC TX553.L5 J68 **ISSN** 1065-7258
DD 613.2/8 US
CODEN JFFLES

•**JOURNAL OF FOOD LIPIDS.** **See** Food and Food Industry.

LC QD1 **ISSN** 0022-1279
DD 540.5 US
UDC 54 CCC
NLM W1 JO666 **CODEN** JGCHA4
TITLE CHANGE

JOURNAL OF GENERAL CHEMISTRY OF THE USSR. (JOURNAL OF GENERAL CHEMISTRY OF THE U.S.S.R. IN ENGLISH TRANSLATION.). [J. gen. chem. USSR]. **VAT** Journal of General Chemistry of the Union of Soviet Socialist Republics. (1949)-(199?). Periodical. English (translations available in Russian). Plenum Press, 233 Spring Street, New York NY 10013-1578. **Tel** (212)620-8000, (800)221-9369, FAX (212)463-0742, (212)807-1047, telex 23/421139. **ED** B V Gidaspov. Index available. available on microfilm and microfiche from University Microfilms International (UMI). Documents available from CASDDS. ***Continued by*** *Russian Journal of General Chemistry.*
Desc: This important journal publishes original papers on experimental and theoretical work done by outstanding Soviet chemists in organic and inorganic chemistry and on research information.
Ind/Abst Ceram. Abstr.; Chem. Abstr.; Mass Spect. Bull.; Methods Organ. Synth.

LC TA401 .J68 **ISSN** 0959-9428
UK
CCC
CODEN JMACEP
Pr Rev.

JOURNAL OF MATERIALS CHEMISTRY. [J. mater. chem.]. **Added/Corp** Royal Society of Chemistry (Great Britain). **VFOAT** JMACEP. Vol. 1, No. 1 (Jan. 1991)-. Academic Scholarly Publication. English. Twelve times a year. $984.00. Royal Society of Chemistry, Thomas Graham House, Science Park, Cambridge CB4 4WF United Kingdom. **Tel** 011 44 1223 420066, FAX 011 44 1223 423623, telex 818293 ROYAL. **(Subscription address:** Royal Society of Chemistry, Turpin Distribution Services Ltd., Blackhorse Road, Letchworth, Hertfordshire SG6 1HN United Kingdom. **Tel** 011 44 1462 672555, FAX 011 44 1462 480947.**) ED** J. M. Leader. Index available. cum. index (author index). **Bk Rev. Circ:** 1,000 (ctrl). available on an online database. Documents available from The Genuine Article, CASDDS.
Desc: Focuses on areas of chemistry materials particularly associated with advanced technology, and papers covering the modelling of materials, their synthesis and structural characterization, physicochemical aspects of their fabrication, properties and applications. Contains original research reports of both full-length papers and short communication, occasional review articles, book reviews, details of forthcoming conferences and a cumulative author index, together with color photographs and diagrams where appropriate.
Ind/Abst Chem. Abstr.; Curr. Cit.; Curr. Contents Phys. Chem. Earth Sci.; Res. Alert [Full Cov.]; Sci. Cit. Index; SCISEARCH.

ISSN 1005-0302
US

JOURNAL OF MATERIALS SCIENCE & TECHNOLOGY. (199?)-. English. Six times a year. $415.00. Allerton Press Inc., 150 Fifth Avenue, New York NY 10011. **Tel** (212)924-3950, FAX (212)463-9684, telex 427441 ALPRES. ***Continues*** *Chinese Journal of Metal Science & Technology, 1000-3029.*

LC QD39.3.M3 J7 **ISSN** 0259-9791
DD 540/.151 NE
CCC
CODEN JMCHEG

JOURNAL OF MATHEMATICAL CHEMISTRY. Vol. 1, No. 1 (Jan. 1987)-. Periodical. English. Eight times a year. $938.80. Baltzer Science Publishers BV, Asterweg 1A, 1031 HL Amsterdam Netherlands. **Tel** 011 31 20 6370061, FAX 011 31 20 6323651. Documents available from The Genuine Article, CASDDS.
Ind/Abst Chem. Abstr.; Curr. Cit.; Curr. Contents Phys. Chem. Earth Sci.; Math. Rev. (1987-); Res. Alert [Full Cov.]; SCISEARCH.

LC QD505 .J673 **ISSN** 1381-1169
DD 621.3/95/05 NE
CCC
NLM W1; JO773EM **CODEN** JMCCF2

•**JOURNAL OF MOLECULAR CATALYSIS. A, CHEMICAL.** **VFOAT** Chemical. (1995)-. Periodical. English. Thirty times a year. $2964.00. Elsevier Science Publishers BV, PO Box 211, 1000 AE Amsterdam Netherlands. **Tel** 011 31 20 4853641, 011 31 20 4853642, FAX 011 31 20 4853598. available on an online database from Elsevier Electronic Subscriptions (EES). ***Continues in part*** *Journal of Molecular Catalysis, 0304-5102.*
Ind/Abst Curr. Cit.

LC QH366.A1 J68 **ISSN** 0022-2844
DD 575 GW
CCC
NLM W1 JO773K **CODEN** JMEVAU
Pr Rev.

JOURNAL OF MOLECULAR EVOLUTION. **See** Biology-Genetics.

LC QC173 .A2544 **ISSN** 0167-7322
DD 530.4/2 NE
CCC
CODEN JMLIDT
Pr Rev.

JOURNAL OF MOLECULAR LIQUIDS. **See** Physics.

ISSN 1012-8611
NP
CODEN JNCSEM

JOURNAL OF NEPAL CHEMICAL SOCIETY, NEPAL CHEMICAL SOCIETY. **Added/Corp** Nepal Chemical Society. (1981)-. Periodical. English. Nepal Chemical Society, c/o Dept of Chemistry, Kirtipur, Multiple Tribhuvan University, Kirtipur Kathmandu Nepal. Documents available from CASDDS.
Ind/Abst Chem. Abstr.

LC QH515 .J68 **ISSN** 1011-1344
DD 574.19/152 SZ
CCC
NLM W1; JO832BH **CODEN** JPPBEG
Pr Rev.

JOURNAL OF PHOTOCHEMISTRY AND PHOTOBIOLOGY. B, BIOLOGY. See Biology.

ISSN 0914-9244
DD 660 JA

JOURNAL OF PHOTOPOLYMER SCIENCE AND TECHNOLOGY. See Science and Technology.

LC Q199 .J68 **ISSN** 0047-2689
DD 530/.021/2 US
CCC
NLM W1 JO832K **CODEN** JPCRBU
Pr Rev.

JOURNAL OF PHYSICAL AND CHEMICAL REFERENCE DATA. See Physics.

LC QC176.A1 J6 **ISSN** 0022-3697
UK
CCC
NLM W1 JO836S **CODEN** JPCSAW

JOURNAL OF PHYSICS AND CHEMISTRY OF SOLIDS, THE. See Physics.

LC QD380 .J7 **ISSN** 0970-0838
DD 668.9/05 II
CCC
CODEN JOPME8

JOURNAL OF POLYMER MATERIALS. [J. polym. mater.]. Vol. 1, No. 1 (April 1984)-. Academic Scholarly Publication. English. Four times a year. $133.61. AA Balkema, Box 1675, 3000 BR Rotterdam Netherlands. **Tel** 011 31 10 4145822, FAX 011 31 10 4135947, telex 41605. **(Subscription address:** Prints India, 11 Darya Ganj, New Delhi 110002 India. **Tel** 011 91 11 3268645, FAX 011 91 11 3275542, telex 31-61087 PRIN-IN.) Documents available from CASDDS.
Ind/Abst Biodeter. Abstr. (1991-); Chem. Abstr. (1984-); Curr. Cit.; Curr. Titles Electrochem.

LC QC1 .H56 **ISSN** 0386-3034
DD 530/.05 JA
CODEN JHPCAR

JOURNAL OF SCIENCE OF THE HIROSHIMA UNIVERSITY. SERIES A. PHYSICS AND CHEMISTRY (1971). See Physics.

LC QD1 .A5 **ISSN** 0002-7863
DD 540/.5 US
CCC
NLM W1 JO908G **CODEN** JACSAT
Pr Rev.

JOURNAL OF THE AMERICAN CHEMICAL SOCIETY. [J. Am. Chem. Soc.]. **Main/Corp** American Chemical Society. **Added/Corp** American Chemical Society. Proceedings. Vol. 1 (1879)-. Academic Scholarly Publication. English. One time a week (51 issues). $1624.00. American Chemical Society, 1155 Sixteenth Street Northwest, Washington DC 20036. **Tel** (800)333-9511, (800)227-5558, (614)447-3776, FAX (202)447-3671. **(Subscription address:** American Chemical Society / Ohio, Department L 0011, Columbus OH 43268-0011. **) ED** Allen J. Bard. (free). cum. index. **Bk Rev. Ad Acc. Acid Free. Circ:** 13,758. available on microfilm from University Microfilms International (UMI); available with charts; available with illustrations; available on an online database from STN International. Documents available from Article Express International, The Genuine Article, BIOSIS Document Express, Ask*IEEE, UMI Article Clearinghouse, CASDDS. ***Absorbed*** *Journal of Analytic and Applied Chemistry* **and** *American Chemical Journal, 0096-4085.*
Desc: Each issue contains approximately 40 definitive articles and 25 communications reviewed by references prominent in respective fields. Publishes research of interest to all fields of chemistry.
Ind/Abst Abstr. Bull. Inst. Pap. Sci. Tech.; Acad. Ind. [Computer File] (1992-); Acad. Search; AGRICOLA; Appl. Sci. Technol. Index; Biol. Abstr.; Ceram. Abstr.; Chem Inform; Chem. Abstr.; Chem. Titles; Coal Abstr.; Curr. Aware. Biol. Sci., CABS; Curr. Biotechnol.; Curr. Chem. React.; Curr. Cit.; Curr. Contents Life Sci.; Curr. Contents Phys. Chem. Earth Sci.; Curr. Titles Electrochem.; Dairy Sci. Abstr.; Ei Page One; EMBASE [Select. Cov.]; Energy Res. Abstr.; Eng. Index Annu. [Select. Cov.]; EP Collect.; Expand. Acad. Index (1992-); Gen. Sci. Index; Gen. Sci. Source; Helminthol. Abstr. (1991-); Homework Help.; Hortic. Abstr. (1968-); Index Chem.; Index Vet.; INIS Atomindex [Micro.]; INSPEC (1968-); Int. Aerosp. Abstr.; Leadscan; Mag. Search; Mass Spect. Bull.; MasterFile FullTEXT 1000; MasterFile FullTEXT 350; MasterFile FullTEXT 650; MasterFile FullTEXT (Jan. 1993-); Methods Organ. Synth.; NAPRALERT; Nat. Prod. Updates; Newsp. Period. Abstr. (1992-); Nucl. Acids Abstr.; Nutr. Res. Newsl.; OCLC; Life Sci. Collect.; PESTDOC; Ref. Upd. Basic Ed.; Ref. Upd. Deluxe Ed.; Res. Alert [Full Cov.]; Rev. Agric. Entomol.; Rev. Med. Vet. Entomol.; Rev. Med. Vet. Mycology; Rev. Plant Pathol.; Sci. Cit. Index; SCISEARCH; Soils Fert.; Surf. Treat. Technol. Abstr.; Telebase; World Ceram. Abstr. (1968-).

LC QD1 .J94555
DD 540/.5 BG
CODEN JBLSEH

JOURNAL OF THE BANGLADESH CHEMICAL SOCIETY. **Added/Corp** Bangladesh Chemical Society. **VFOAT** JBCS. Vol. 1, No. 1 (1988)-. English. Two times a year. Bangladesh Chemical Society, Dept of Chemistry, University of Dhaka, Dhaka 1000 Bangladesh. Documents available from CASDDS.
Ind/Abst Chem. Abstr.

LC QD1 .J9456 **ISSN** 0103-5053
DD 540/.5 BL
CODEN JOCSET
Pr Rev.

JOURNAL OF THE BRAZILIAN CHEMICAL SOCIETY. **Added/Corp** Sociedade Brasileira de Quimica. Vol. 1, No. 1 (Jan./Apr. 1990)-. Academic Scholarly Publication. English. Three times a year. Sociedade Brasileira de Quimica- SBQ, Caixa Postal 26.037, CEP 005599-970 Sao Paulo SP Brasil. **Tel** 011 55 11 2102299, FAX 011 55 11 8143602. Index available. **Ad Acc, Adv Mgr:** Sueli Murakami, **Tel** 011 55 11 2102299. Full Page (B&W) $600.00. Half Page (B&W) $400.00. **Acid Free. Circ:** 500 (ctrl). Documents available from The Genuine Article.
Ind/Abst Res. Alert.

LC QD1 **ISSN** 0022-4936
DD 540/.5 UK
CCC
NLM W1 JO916G **CODEN** JCCCAT
Pr Rev.

JOURNAL OF THE CHEMICAL SOCIETY, CHEMICAL COMMUNICATIONS. (JOURNAL OF THE CHEMICAL SOCIETY. CHEMICAL COMMUNICATIONS.). [J. Chem. Soc., Chem. commun.]. **Added/Corp** Chemical Society (Great Britain) Royal Society of Chemistry (Great Britain). **VFOAT** Chemical Communications. No. 1 (Jan. 5, 1972)-. Academic Scholarly Publication. English. Twenty-four times a year (plus annual index). $1032.00. Royal Society of Chemistry, Thomas Graham House, Science Park, Cambridge CB4 4WF United Kingdom. **Tel** 011 44 1223 420066, FAX 011 44 1223 423623, telex 818293 ROYAL. **(Subscription address:** Royal Society of Chemistry, Turpin Distribution Services Ltd., Blackhorse Road, Letchworth, Hertfordshire SG6 1HN United Kingdom. **Tel** 011 44 1462 672555, FAX 011 44 1462 480947.) Index available. cum. index. **Bk Rev. Circ:** 3,987. available on microfilm and microfiche from University Microfilms International (UMI); available on an online database from STN International; available with charts; available with illustrations; available in microform. Documents available from The Genuine Article, BIOSIS Document Express, CASDDS, ADONIS, BLDSC, FAXON Xpress, The UnCover Company, SWETS, UMI Article Clearinghouse. ***Continues*** *Chemical Communications (1970).*
Desc: Reports on new developments in all branches of chemistry.
Ind/Abst Abstr. Bull. Inst. Pap. Sci. Tech.; ADONIS; Anal. Abstr.; Biol. Abstr.; Chem Inform; Chem. Abstr.; Curr. Biotechnol.; Curr. Chem. React.; Curr. Cit.; Curr. Contents Phys. Chem. Earth Sci.; Curr. Titles Electrochem.; EMBASE [Select. Cov.]; GeoRef; Index Chem.; Int. Aerosp. Abstr.; Mass Spect. Bull.; Methods Organ. Synth.; NAPRALERT; Nat. Prod. Updates; Life Sci. Collect.; PESTDOC; Ref. Upd. Deluxe Ed.; Res. Alert [Full Cov.]; Sci. Cit. Index; SCISEARCH.

LC QD1 .C674a **ISSN** 0253-5106
DD 540/.5 PK
CODEN JCSPDF
Pr Rev.

JOURNAL OF THE CHEMICAL SOCIETY OF PAKISTAN. [J. Chem. Soc. Pak.]. **Main/Corp** Chemical Society of Pakistan. Vol. 1 (Sept. 1979)-. Academic Scholarly Publication. English (French and German). Four times a year (Mar., June, Sept., Dec.). $58.00. Chemical Society of Pakistan, University of Karachi, Department of Physics, HEJ Res Institute of Chemistry, Karachi 32 Pakistan. **Tel** 011 92 21 463414. **ED** Atta-Ur-Rahman. **Circ:** 1,000. Documents available from The Genuine Article, CASDDS.
Desc: Research papers on subjects and topics in physical and biological sciences.
Ind/Abst Chem. Abstr.; Chem. Titles; Curr. Chem. React.; Curr. Cit.; Curr. Contents Phys. Chem. Earth Sci.; Food Sci. Technol. Abstr.; Index Chem.; Res. Alert [Full Cov.]; Sci. Cit. Index; SCISEARCH; Soils Fert.

LC QD1 .J685 **ISSN** 0009-4536
DD 540 CH
NLM W1 CH988A **CODEN** JCCTAC

JOURNAL OF THE CHINESE CHEMICAL SOCIETY (TAIPEI). (JOURNAL OF THE CHINESE CHEMICAL SOCIETY.). [J. Chin. Chem. Soc.]. **Main/Corp** Chung-Kuo Hua Hsueh Hui, Taipei. **Added/Corp** Chung-Kuo Hua Hsueh Hui (Taipei, Taiwan). **VFOAT** Chung-kuo Hua Hsueh Hui Hui Chih. Vol. 2, 1 (Dec. 1954)-. Academic Scholarly Publication. English. Six times a year (Feb., Apr., June, Aug., Oct., Dec.). $42.00 Hong Kong: $45.00 other. Chinese Chemical Society, Room 903 9th Floor, 7 Chun Chin S Road, PO Box 609, Taipei Taiwan. **Tel** 886 -2-3118464, FAX 886-2-3118464. **ED** Ho-Hsiang Wei. Index available. **Circ:** 1,600 (ctrl). Documents available from The Genuine Article, CASDDS.
Ind/Abst Chem. Abstr.; Chem. Titles; Curr. Cit.; Curr. Contents Phys. Chem. Earth Sci.; Mass Spect. Bull.; Methods Organ. Synth.; Nat. Prod. Updates; Res. Alert [Full Cov.]; Sci. Cit. Index; SCISEARCH; SEA Abstr.

LC QD1 .I57 **ISSN** 0019-4522
DD 540.5 II
NLM W1 JO93S **CODEN** JICSAH
Pr Rev.

JOURNAL OF THE INDIAN CHEMICAL SOCIETY. [J. Indian Chem. Soc.]. **Added/Corp** Indian Chemical Society. Vol. 5 (1928)-. Academic Scholarly Publication. English. Twelve times a year. $200.00. Indian Chemical Society, 92 Acharya Chandra Road, Calcutta 9 India. **Tel** 35-3478. **(Subscription address:** Prints India, 11 Darya Ganj, New Delhi 110002 India. **Tel** 011 91 11 3268645, FAX 011 91 11 3275542, telex 31-61087 PRIN-IN.) **ED** M M Chakrabarty, K C Joshi, and H L Nigam. Index Available, published separately, free-automatically sent. **Bk Rev. Ad Acc. Circ:** 2,000 (ctrl). available on microfilm and microfiche from University Microfilms International (UMI). Documents available from The Genuine Article, CASDDS. ***Continues*** *Quarterly Journal - Indian Chemical Society.*
Desc: Original contributions to new chemical knowledge, both experimental and theoretical, in all areas of chemistry: inorganic, physical, organic, analytical, biochemistry, industrial chemistry/chemical engineering, etc.
Ind/Abst Anal. Abstr.; Ceram. Abstr.; Chem Inform; Chem. Abstr.; Chem. Titles; Curr. Chem. React.; Curr. Cit.; Curr. Contents Phys. Chem. Earth Sci.; Curr. Titles Electrochem.; Dairy Sci. Abstr.; EMBASE; Food Sci. Technol. Abstr.; Index Chem.; Leadscan; Mass Spect. Bull.; Methods Organ. Synth.; NAPRALERT; Nat. Prod. Updates; PESTDOC; Protozoolog. Abstr.; Res. Alert; SCISEARCH; SEA Abstr.; Surf. Treat. Technol. Abstr.

LC TP1 .I735 **ISSN** 0020-3254
DD 660.0(5/6) II
NLM W1 JO931N

JOURNAL OF THE INSTITUTION OF CHEMISTS, CALCUTTA. (JOURNAL OF THE INSTITUTION OF CHEMISTS (INDIA).). [J. Inst. Chem., Calcutta]. **Added/Corp** Institution of Chemists (India). Vol. 39, Pt. 1 (Jan. 1967)-. Academic Scholarly Publication. English. Six times a year. $22.00. Institution of Chemists, 11/4 Dr Biresh Guha Road, Calcutta 700 017 India. **Tel** 433832. **(Subscription address:** Prints India, 11 Darya Ganj, New Delhi 110002 India. **Tel** 011 91 11 3268645, FAX 011 91 11 3275542, telex 31-61087 PRIN-IN.) **ED** Debi Chakravarti. Index available. **Bk Rev. Ad Acc. Circ:** 1,500. available on microfiche. Documents available from CASDDS. ***Continues*** *Journal and Proceedings of the Institution of Chemists (India).*
Desc: Original papers on results of research in chemistry, editorials, special articles and lectures, book reviews, and indexes.
Ind/Abst Anal. Abstr.; Chem. Abstr.; Curr. Cit.; Dairy Sci. Abstr.; EMBASE; Food Sci. Technol. Abstr.

LC QD1 .S673 **ISSN** 0352-5139
DD 540 YU
CODEN JSCSEN

JOURNAL OF THE SERBIAN CHEMICAL SOCIETY. [J. Serb. Chem. Soc.]. **Added/Corp** Srpsko Hemijsko Drustvo. Vol. 50, No. 1 (1985)-. Periodical. English (summaries and/or abstracts in Serbo-Croatian (Cyrillic)). Twelve times a year. $70.00. **(Subscription address:** Jugoslovenska Knjiga, PO Box 36, YU 11001 Belgrade Yugoslovia. **Tel** 011 38 11 621055, FAX 011 38 11 325970.) Documents available from BIOSIS Document Express, CASDDS. ***Continues*** *Glasnik Hemijskog Drustva Beograd, 0017-0941.*
Ind/Abst AGRICOLA; Alum. Ind. Abstr. (1985-); Anal. Abstr. (1985-); Biol. Abstr. (1986-1989); Chem. Abstr. (1985-); Corros. Abstr. (199?-); Curr. Biotechnol.; Curr. Cit.; Food Sci. Technol. Abstr.; Met. Abstr. (1985-); Nat. Prod. Updates.

LC QD **ISSN** 0388-3213
DD 540 JA
CODEN KGKHEP
TITLE CHANGE

KAGAKU GIJUTSU KENKYUSHO HOKOKU. (KAGAKU GIJUTSU KENKYUJO HOKOKU = JOURNAL OF THE NATIONAL CHEMICAL LABORATORY FOR INDUSTRY.). [Kagaku Gijutsu Kenkyusho hokoku]. **Added/Corp** Tokyo Kogyo Shikenjo.

Chemistry and Chemicals

Kagaku Gijutsu Kenkyujo (Japan). **VFOAT** Journal of the National Chemical Laboratory for Industry. (1979)-(1992). Academic Scholarly Publication. Japanese (summaries and/or abstracts in English; table of contents in English). National Chemical Laboratory for Industry Library, 1-1 Yatabemachi/Higash, Tsukubagun Ibaraki 305 Japan. Documents available from CASDDS. *Continues Tokyo Kogyo Shikenjo Hokoku, 0371-8808.* **Merged with** *Kenkyu Hokoku (Seni Kobunshi Zairyo Kenkyujo (Japan)), 0371-0807* **and** *Seihin Kagaku Kenkyujo Kenkyu Hokoku, 0389-9659* **to form** *Busshitsu Kogaku Kogyo Gijutsu Kenkyujo Hokoku, 0919-7087.*
Ind/Abst Abstr. Bull. Inst. Pap. Sci. Tech.; Ceram. Abstr.; Chem. Abstr.; Coal Abstr.; Energy Res. Abstr. (Oct. 1972-).

ISSN 0288-8882
JA
CODEN KKSHEP

KAGAKU KOGYO SHIRYO / KOGYO GIJUTSUIN ; KAGAKU GIJUTSU KENKYUJO. Added/Corp Kogyo Gijutsuin (Japan)
Kagaku Gijutsu Kenkyujo (Japan). (1983)-. Periodical. Japanese. Kogyo Gijutsuin Kagaku Gijutsu Kenkyujo, (National Chemical Lab. for Industry Agency of Industrial Science & Technology), 1-4 Higashi 1 Chome, Tsukubashi Ibarakiken 305 Japan. Documents available from CASDDS. *Continues in part Kagiken Nyusu, Kagaku Kogyo Shiryo, 0388-3744.*
Ind/Abst Chem. Abstr.

JA
CODEN KAKYDX

KAGAKU KYOIKU. [Kagaku kyoiku]. Added/Corp
Nihon Kagakkai. **VFOAT** Chemical Education. (1953)-. Academic Scholarly Publication. Japanese. Six times a year. $170.00. Nippon Kagakkai, (Chemical Society of Japan), 1-5 Kanda Surugadai, Chiyodaky Tokyo 101 Japan. **(Subscription address:** Japan Publications Trading Company Ltd., PO Box 5030, Tokyo International, Tokyo 100-31 Japan. **Tel** 011 81 3 3292 3753.) Documents available from CASDDS. *Continues Kagaku Kyoiku Shinpojiumu.*
Ind/Abst Chem. Abstr.

LC TP1 .K24
ISSN 0451-1964
JA
NLM W1 KA343J
CODEN KAKYAU

KAGAKU (KYOTO). (KAGAKU.). [Kagaku].
VFOAT Chemistry. (1946)-. Academic Scholarly Publication. Japanese. Twelve times a year. $171.50. Kagaku Dojin, 5-4 Nishino Noirocho, Yamashinaku, Kyoto 607 Japan. **(Subscription address:** Japan Publications Trading Company Ltd., PO Box 5030, Tokyo International, Tokyo 100-31 Japan. **Tel** 011 81 3 3292 3753.) Documents available from CASDDS. *Continues Kagaku Kogyo Jijo.*
Ind/Abst Chem. Abstr.; Coal Abstr.

LC QD1 .K24
DD 540

KAGAKU SHOHO. Added/Corp Kagaku Joho
Kyogikai. (19??)-. Periodical. Multiple languages (Japanese and English). Twenty-four times a year. $656.00. Kagaku Joho Kyokai, (Japan Assoc. for International Chemical Information), Gakkai Senta Biru, 4-16 Yayoi 2 Chome, Bunkyoku Tokyo 113 Japan. **(Subscription address:** Japan Publications Trading Company Ltd., PO Box 5030, Tokyo International, Tokyo 100-31 Japan. **Tel** 011 81 3 3292 3753.)

ISSN 0022-7684
JA
CCC
CODEN KAKTAF

KAGAKU TO KOGYO (TOKYO). (KAGAKU TO KOGYO.). [Kagaku to kogyo].
VFOAT Chemistry and Chemical Industry. (1948)-. Academic Scholarly Publication. Japanese. Twelve times a year. $321.00. Nippon Kagakkai, (Chemical Society of Japan), 1-5 Kanda Surugadai, Chiyodaky Tokyo 101 Japan. Documents available from CASDDS.
Ind/Abst Chem. Abstr.; Coal Abstr.; Curr. Biotechnol.

ISSN 0368-5470
JA
CODEN KGZKA3

KAGAKU, ZOKAN. [Kagaku, Zokan]. (1???)-.
Japanese. Irregular. Kagaku Dojin, 5-4 Nishino Noirocho, Yamashinaku Kyotoshi, Kyotofu 607 Japan. Documents available from CASDDS.
Ind/Abst Chem. Abstr.

LC HD9657.J3 K35
JA

KAGAKUHIN TORIHIKI YORAN. See Industry and Production.

ISSN 0286-1933
DD 540
JA

KANZEI CHUO BUNSEKISHOHO. [Kanzei Chuo Bunsekishoho]. VFOAT Reports of the Central Customs Laboratory. (1965)-. Periodical. Multiple languages. Two times a year. Okurasho Kanzei Chuo Bunsekijo, (Central Customs Lab. Ministry of Finance), 531 Iwase Matsudano, Chibaken 271 Japan. Documents available from CASDDS.
Ind/Abst Chem. Abstr.

LC QD380 .K36
ISSN 1000-3304
CC
CODEN GAXUE9

KAO FEN TZU HSUEH PAO = ACTA POLYMERICA SINICA. Added/Corp Chung-Kuo
Hua Hsueh Hui (Peking, China). "Kao Fen Tzu Hsueh Pao" Pien Wei Hui. **VFOAT** Acta Polymerica Sinica. (1987)-. Periodical. Chinese (summaries and/or abstracts in English; table of contents in English). Six times a year. $106.20. **(Subscription address:** Science Press / China, Marketing and Sales Department, 16 Donghuangchenggen North Street, Beijing 100717 People's Republic of China. **Tel** 4010642, FAX 4019810.) *Continues Kao Fen Tzu Tung Hsun.*

ISSN 0915-8847
DD 574.19 612
JA

KASSEI SANSO, FURI RAJIKARU. VFOAT
Journal of Active Oxygens & Free Radicals. (1990)-. Periodical. Multiple languages. Six times a year. Documents available from CASDDS.
Ind/Abst Chem. Abstr.

LC TP1 .K33
ISSN 0355-1628
DD 660
FI
CODEN KMKMAA

KEMIA. (KEMIA. KEMI.). [Kemia]. Added/Corp
Suomen Kemian Seura. Kemian Keskusliitto. **VFOAT** Kemi. (Jan. 1974)-. Academic Scholarly Publication. Finnish (English). Ten times a year (monthly except Jan., July). $153.52. Kemian Kustannus Oy, Hietaniemenkatu 2, Fin 00100 Helsinki Finland. **Tel** 011 358 0 490647, 011 358 0 490505, FAX 011 358 0 407091. **ED** Marjatta Kivimaki-Majanen. **Bk Rev** (Qty: 4). **Ad Acc, Adv Mgr:** Irja Marttila, **Tel,** 011 358 0 490641. **Circ:** 5,200 (ctrl). Documents available from Article Express International, CASDDS. *Formed by the union of Kemian Teollisuus; Suomen Kemistilehti, 0039-5536 and Finska Kemistsamfundets Meddelanden, 0015-2498.*
Desc: Subjects of articles range from chemistry and biochemistry to chemical process technologies and chemical industries including biochemical, pharmaceutical and food industries as well as chemical pulping. Environmental matters are one of our main issues. Chemical analytics and education are also covered.
Ind/Abst Anal. Abstr.; Bioeng. Abstr.; Chem. Abstr.; Chem. Bus. Bull.; Chem. Bus. NewsBase (1985-); Chem. Bus. Update; Chem. Hazards Ind.; Coal Abstr.; Curr. Biotechnol.; Curr. Cit.; Ei Page One; Energy Res. Abstr. (May 1974-); Eng. Index Annu.; Food Sci. Technol. Abstr.; Lab. Hazards Bull.; Proc. Chem. Eng.; Selec. Coop. Index Manage. Period.; Theor. Chem. Eng.

LC QD1 .K38
ISSN 0075-5397
HU
CODEN KUERDK

KEMIA UJABB EREDMENYEI, A. (19??)-.
Academic Scholarly Publication. Hungarian. Irregular. Price varies. Akademiai Kiado, Publishing House of the Hungarian Academy of Sciences, Prielle Kornelia u. 19-35, H-1117 Budapest Hungary. **Tel** 011 36 1 1811991, FAX 011 36 1 1811991, telex 22-6228 AKNYO H. **ED** Bela Csakvari. Documents available from CASDDS.
Ind/Abst Chem. Abstr.

LC QD1 .M35
ISSN 0022-9814
HU
CODEN KEKOAS

KEMIAI KOEZLEMENYEK. (KEMIAI KOEZLEMENYEK : A MAGYAR TUDOMANYOS AKADEMIA KEMIAI TUDOMANYOK OSZTALYANAK KOEZLEMENYEI.). [Kem. kozl.]. Added/Corp Magyar
Tudomanyos Akademia. Kemiai Tudomanyok Osztalya. Vol. 26 (1966)-. Academic Scholarly Publication. Hungarian. Two times a year. $18.00. Akademiai Kiado, Publishing House of the Hungarian Academy of Sciences, Prielle Kornelia u. 19-35, H-1117 Budapest Hungary. **Tel** 011 36 1 1811991, FAX 011 36 1 1811991, telex 22-6228 AKNYO H. **Bk Rev**. **Ad Acc**. Documents available from CASDDS. *Continues Magyar Tudomanyos Akademia. Kemiai Tudomanyok Osztalya. Magyar Tudomanyos Akademia Kemiai Tudomanyok Osztalyanak Koezlemenyei, 0369-0067.*
Ind/Abst Chem. Abstr.; Coal Abstr.

LC HD9656.F5 K46
ISSN 0786-0048
FI

KEMIAN TEOLLISUUS (FINLAND. TILASTOKESKUS). See Industry and Production.

LC TP1 .K36
ISSN 0022-9830
Pr Rev.
CI

KEMIJA U INDUSTRIJI. Added/Corp Drustvo
Kemicare-Tehnologa NR Hrvatske. (19??)-. Periodical. Serbo-Croatian (Roman) (summaries and/or abstracts in English, French and German). Twelve times a year. $80.00. Croatian Society of Chemical Engineers, Berislavicevaul 61, Zagreb Croatia. **Tel** 011 38 41 422931, FAX 011 38 41 422931. **ED** Professor Ivan Butula. Index available. **Bk Rev**. **Ad Acc**. **Circ:** 3,000. Documents available from CASDDS.
Desc: This features scientific papers, reviews, news, and professional papers.
Ind/Abst Anal. Abstr.; Chem Inform; Chem. Abstr.; Curr. Biotechnol.; Curr. Cit.; Proc. Chem. Eng.; Refer. Z.; Surf. Treat. Technol. Abstr.; Theor. Chem. Eng.

LC QD1 .S9
ISSN 0039-6605
DD 540
SW
NLM W1 KE565
CODEN KETIAL
Pr Rev.

KEMISK TIDSKRIFT. [Kem. tidskr.]. Added/Corp
Svenska Kemistsamfundet. Svenska Kemiingenjorers Riksforening. (1969)-. Academic Scholarly Publication. Multiple languages (English and Swedish). Fourteen times a year. Kr545.00 Nordic Countries; Kr690.00 other. Arbor Publishing AB, Box 26212, S 100 41 Stockholm Sweden. **Tel** 011 46 8 6799011, FAX 011 46 8 6643005. Documents available from The Genuine Article, CASDDS. *Continues Svensk Kemisk Tidskrift.*
Ind/Abst AGRICOLA; Chem Inform; Chem. Abstr.; Chem. Bus. Bull.; Chem. Bus. Inform; Chem. Bus. NewsBase (1986-); Chem. Bus. Update; Coal Abstr.; Curr. Cit.; Curr. Contents Eng. Comput. Technol.; Energy Res. Abstr.; Food Sci. Technol. Abstr.; GeoRef; Infomat Int. Bus.; Res. Alert [Full Cov.]; SCISEARCH.

ISSN 0250-8265
KE
CODEN KJSSDG

KENYA JOURNAL OF SCIENCE AND TECHNOLOGY. SERIES A, PHYSICAL AND CHEMICAL SCIENCES. See Physics.

ISSN 0303-4003
GW
CODEN KKBRAY

KERNFORSCHUNGSZENTRUM KARLSRUHE. (KFK / KERNFORSCHUNGSZENTRUM KARLSRUHE.). [Kernforschungszent. Karlsr.]. Added/Corp
Kernforschungszentrum Karlsruhe. **VFOAT** K.f.K.; Kf. K. (19??)-. Monographic series. German (summaries and/or abstracts in English). Kernforschungszentrum Karlsruhe, Postfach 3640, 7500 Karlsruhe F R Germany. **Tel** 011 49 721 7820.

LC QD1 .O23
BW
CODEN KKTEDK

KHIMIIA I KHIMICHESKAIA TEKHNOLOGIIA. Added/Corp Belaruski
Tekhnalahichny Instytut Imia S.M. Kirava. Vol. 7 (1974)-. Academic Scholarly Publication. Russian. 1.34rub. Vyshcha Shkola, Ulitsa Universitetskaia 16, Kharkov Ukraine. Documents available from CASDDS. *Continues Obshchaia I Prikladnaia Khimiia.*
Ind/Abst Chem. Abstr.; Int. Polym. Sci. Tech.

LC QD581 .K5
RU
CODEN KHPLDY

KHIMIIA PLAZMY. Vol. 1 (1974)-. Russian.
Atomizdat, Ulitsa Zhdanova 5, 103031 Moscow K-31 Russia. **(Subscription address:** East View Publications Inc., 3020 Harbor Lane North, Suite 110, Minneapolis MN 55447. **Tel** (800)477-1005, (612)550-0961, FAX (612)559-2931.) **ED** B.M. Smirnov. Documents available from CASDDS.
Ind/Abst Chem. Abstr.

LC QD
DD 540
RU

●KHIMIIA V INTERESAKH USTOICHIVOGO RAZVITIIA. (1993)-.
Academic Scholarly Publication. Russian. Six times a year. Rossiiskaya Akademiia Nauk, Sibirskoe Otdelenie, Pr. Akademika Lavrenteva 17, 630090 Novosibirsk Russia. *Continues Sibirskii Khimicheskii Zhurnal.*

ISSN 0368-5632
RU
CODEN KHSHAY

KHIMIIA V SHKOLE. (1937)-. Periodical. Russian.
Six times a year. $99.95. Uchpedgiz, Moscow Russia. **(Subscription address:** East View Publications Inc., 3020 Harbor Lane North, Suite 110, Minneapolis MN 55447. **Tel** (800)477-1005, (612)550-0961, FAX (612)559-2931.) *Continues in part Biologiia i Khimiia v Shkole.*

ISSN 0348-7199
SW
CODEN RKORD9

KI RAPPORT. (RAPPORT / KORROSIONSINSTITUTET.). [KI rapp.]. Added/Corp
Korrosionsinstitutet (Sweden). **VFOAT** KI Rapport. (19??)-. Academic Scholarly Publication. Swedish (English and Swedish). Korrosionsinstitutet, Box 5607, 114 86 Stockholm, Sweden. Documents available from CASDDS.
Ind/Abst Alum. Ind. Abstr.; Chem. Abstr.; Met. Abstr.

JA

KIKAN KAGAKU SOSETSU. Added/Corp
Nihon Kagakkai. No. 1 (1988)-. Periodical. Japanese (summaries and/or abstracts in English). Four times a year. ¥3500 (single issue). Gakkai Shuppan Senta, 6-2-10 Hongo, Bunkyo-ku, Tokyo-to 113 Japan. Documents available from CASDDS. *Continues Kagaku Sosetsu.*
Ind/Abst Chem. Abstr.

Chemistry and Chemicals

LC QD1 .K57   **ISSN** 0126-9070
DD 540/.5   MY
   CODEN KMIADZ
KIMIA. [Kimia]. **Added/Corp** Institiut Kimia Malaysia. No. 1 (1970)-. Academic Scholarly Publication. English. Malaysian Institute of Chemistry, 260 Jalan Ampang, 50450 Kuala Lumpur Malaysia. Documents available from CASDDS.
   Ind/Abst Chem. Abstr. (1970, 1977, 1979-).

   ISSN 0368-7163
   TU
   CODEN KVESAR
KIMYA VE SANAYI. [Kim. Sanayi]. **VFOAT** Chymia et Industria. (1950)-. Academic Scholarly Publication. Turkish. Four times a year. Turkiye Kimya Dernegi, Turkish Chemical Society, Halaskargazi Caddesi 53, Uzay Apt. D8, PK 829 Harbiye Istanbul Turkey. **ED** Ali Riza Berkem. **Ad Acc. Circ:** 5,000. available with illustrations. Documents available from CASDDS. *Continues Kimya Annali, 0023-1428.*
   Ind/Abst Chem. Abstr.

LC RB1 .L3   **ISSN** 0869-2084
   RU
NLM W1; KL186   **CODEN** KLDIES
KLINICHESKAIA LABORATORNAIA DIAGNOSTIKA. See Medical Sciences-Pathology.

   ISSN 0176-4829
   GW
NLM W1 KL437
KLINISCHE CHEMIE IN EINZELDARSTELLUNGEN. (1973)-. Monographic series. German. Irregular. Price varies per volume. Georg Thieme Verlag Stuttgart, Postfach 301120, D-70451 Stuttgart Germany. **Tel** 011 49 711 89310, FAX 011 49 711 8931298, telex 7 252 275 GTVD. **(Subscription address:** Thieme Medical Publishers Inc., 381 Park Avenue South, New York NY 10016. **Tel** (212)683-5088.) **ED** H. Breuer.

   ISSN 0270-4986
   US
   CODEN KLCBDZ
KODAK LABORATORY CHEMICALS BULLETIN. [Kodak lab. chem. bull.]. Bulletin. English. Free. Eastman Kodak Company, 343 State Street, Department 412 L, Rochester NY 14650. **Tel** (716)724-4000, (800)242-2424. Documents available from CASDDS.
   Ind/Abst Chem. Abstr.

   ISSN 0286-6943
   JA
   CODEN KTOSDW
KOGYO TOSO. [Kogyo toso]. **VFOAT** Industrial Coating. (1971)-. Periodical. Japanese. Six times a year. $146.00. Toryo Hochi Shinbunsha, Tokyo-to Japan. **(Subscription address:** Maruzen Company Ltd., PO Box 5050, Import & Export Department, Tokyo 100 31 Japan. **Tel** 011 81 3 32789224.) Documents available from CASDDS.
   Ind/Abst Chem. Abstr.

LC TP1 .K6   **ISSN** 0023-2815
   RU
   CODEN KOKKAI
KOKS I HIMIJA. (KOKS I KHIMIIA.). [Koks him.]. **VFOAT** Koks und Chemie; Coke and Chemistry. (1931)-. Academic Scholarly Publication. Russian. Twelve times a year. Free. Izdatelstvo Metallurgiia, 2-I Obydenskii Per. 14 G-34, Moscow Russia. **(Subscription address:** East View Publications Inc., 3020 Harbor Lane North, Suite 110, Minneapolis MN 55447. **Tel** (800)477-1005, (612)550-0961, FAX (612)559-2931.) Index available. **Bk Rev.** Documents available from Article Express International, CASDDS.
   Ind/Abst Alum. Ind. Abstr.; Chem. Abstr.; Coal Abstr.; Ei Page One; EMBASE; Energy Res. Abstr. (May 1980-); Eng. Index Annu.; Met. Abstr.; World Alum. Abstr.

   ISSN 0288-4534
   JA
   CODEN KONAE7
KONA. [Kona]. **Added/Corp** Funtai Gijutsu Danwakai (Japan). No. 1 (1983)-. Periodical. English. Party of Powder Technology, c/o Hoskawa Micrometrics Laboratory, 9 Shodai-Taijika 1-Chome Hirakata, Oasaka 573 Japan. Documents available from CASDDS.
   Ind/Abst Ceram. Abstr. (19??-); Chem. Abstr. (1983-).

LC S583   **ISSN** 0023-334X
DD 631   JA
UDC 632.95
   CODEN KONODE
KONGETSU NO NOYAKU. [Kongetsu no noyaku]. (1957)-. Academic Scholarly Publication. Japanese. Twelve times a year. $62.00. Kagaku Kogyo Nipposha, (Chemical Daily Co. Ltd.), 16-8 Nihonbashi Hamacho, 3 Chome Chuoku Tokyo 103 Japan. **(Subscription address:** Maruzen Company Ltd., PO Box 5050, Import & Export Department, Tokyo 100 31 Japan. **Tel** 011 81 3 32789224.) ctrl circ. Documents available from CASDDS.
   Desc: Explanation book of agricultural chemicals.
   Ind/Abst Chem. Abstr.

   GW
KORROSION. (1970)-. Academic Scholarly Publication. German. Six times a year. Deutscher Judo Verband, Redaktion Ippon Segewaldweg 40, D-12557 Berlin Germany. **Tel** 011 49 711 210770, telex 051 678. Documents available from CASDDS.
   Ind/Abst Biodeter. Abstr. (1991-); Chem. Abstr.; Corros. Abstr.; Eng. Mater. Abstr.; Surf. Treat. Technol. Abstr.

   JA
   CODEN KTSSDI
KYOZOME TO SEIREN SENSHOKU. [Kyozome to seiren senshoku]. **Added/Corp** Kyozome Kenkyukai (Kyoto, Japan) Seiren Senshoku Kenkyukai (Kyoto, Japan) Kyoto-Shi Senshoku Shikenjo. (1950)-. Periodical. Japanese. Four times a year. Kyozome Kenkyukai, (Kyozome Dyeing Assoc.), Kyotoshi Senshoku Shikenjo, Kamidachuri Agaru Karasuma, Doori Kamigyoku Kyotoshi, Kyotofu 602 Japan. Documents available from CASDDS.
   Ind/Abst Chem. Abstr.

   IT
LABORATORIO 2000 : RIVISTA DEL RICERCATORE CHEMICO E BIOCHIMICO. Italian. Morgan SRL, Piazzale Archinto 9, 20159 Milan Italy.

LC TP151 .H25   **ISSN** 0748-4585
DD 540/.5   US
LANGE'S HANDBOOK OF CHEMISTRY. [Lange's handb. chem.]. **VFOAT** Handbook of Chemistry. (1973)-. English. Irregular. McGraw Hill Publishing Company, Inc., 1221 Avenue of the Americas, New York NY 10020. **Tel** (212)512-6410, (800)525-5003, FAX (212)512-6111. *Continues Handbook of Chemistry, 0190-4035.*

LC HD9657.I5 I53A   IO
LAPORAN DIREKTORAT JENDERAL INDUSTRI KIMIA. **Main/Corp** Indonesia. Sirektorat Jenderal Industri Kimia. (19??)-. Indonesian. Departemen Perindustrian Direktorat Jenderal, Industri Kimia Indonesia, Jl Kebon Sirih 31, Jakarta Indonesia.

LC QD701 .L35   **ISSN** 0278-6273
DD 542   SZ
   CCC
   CODEN LSCHDB
Pr Rev.
LASER CHEMISTRY. [Laser chem.]. Vol. 1, No. 1 (Oct. 1982)-. Academic Scholarly Publication. English. Four times a year (1 volume). $543.00 (academic institutions), $847.00 (corporate institutions). Harwood Academic Publishers, PO Box 90, Reading RG1 8JL United Kingdom. **Tel** 011 44 1734 560080, FAX 011 44 1734 568211. **ED** Paul Dagdigian and William C Stwalley. Index available. **Bk Rev**. **Ad Acc.** Documents available from Article Express International, The Genuine Article, Ask*IEEE, CASDDS.
   Desc: Intended to bridge the gap between physics and chemistry laser-related research.
   Ind/Abst Chem. Abstr.; Chem. Titles; Curr. Cit.; Curr. Contents Phys. Chem. Earth Sci.; Ei Page One; Eng. Index Annu.; INSPEC (1983-); Mass Spect. Bull.; Res. Alert [Full Cov.]; Sci. Cit. Index; SCISEARCH.

LC QD1 .L34   **ISSN** 0868-8249
   LV
   CODEN LKZUE8
LATVIJAS KIMIJAS ZURNALS. **VFOAT** Latviiskii Khimicheskii Zhurnal; Latvian Journal of Chemistry. No. 1 (1991)-. Academic Scholarly Publication. Russian (summaries and/or abstracts in English and Latin). Six times a year. Zinatne / Science Publishing House, Turgeneva Iela 19, Riga Latvia 1530. **Tel** 3712 212 797. Documents available from CASDDS. *Continues Latvijas PSR Zinatnu Akademijas Vestis. Kimijas Serija, 0002-3248.*
   Ind/Abst Abstr. Bull. Inst. Pap. Sci. Tech.; Chem. Abstr.

LC QD79.C454   **ISSN** 0888-9090
DD 543/.0894   US
   CCC
NLM W1; LC433E   **CODEN** LCGCE7
Pr Rev.
LC GC. (LC GC : MAGAZINE OF LIQUID AND GAS CHROMATOGRAPHY.). [LC GC]. **VFOAT** LC-GC; LC GC Magazine. **VAT** Liquid Chromatography, Gas Chromatography. Vol. 4, No. 4 (April 1986)-. Academic Scholarly Publication. English. Twelve times a year. $64.00. Advanstar Communications Inc., 131 West First Street, Duluth MN 55802. **Tel** (218)723-9477, (800)346-0085, FAX (218)723-9437. **ED** Kari Hallenburg. Index available. cum. index. **Bk Rev**. **Ad Acc. Circ:** 60,000 (ctrl). available on microfilm from University Microfilms International (UMI). Documents available from The Genuine Article, CASDDS. *Continues LC, 0746-0252.*
   Desc: Devoted to the use of chromatography and capillary electrophoresis instrumentation in industry and academia. Includes articles on new applications, method improvements, equipment modifications and creative solutions to analytical problems.
   Ind/Abst Abstr. Bull. Inst. Pap. Sci. Tech.; Anal. Abstr.; Chem. Abstr.; Curr. Cit.; Mass Spect. Bull. (?-?); Res. Alert [Full Cov.]; Sci. Cit. Index; SCISEARCH.

   ISSN 0342-4901
   GW
   CCC
   CODEN LNCHDA
LECTURE NOTES IN CHEMISTRY. [Lect. notes chem.]. (1976)-. Academic Scholarly Publication. English. Irregular. Price varies per volume. Springer-Verlag GmbH & Company KG, Heidelberger Platz 3, D-14197 Berlin Germany. **Tel** 011 49 30 8207223, FAX 011 49 30 8214091, telex 183 319 SPBLN D. **(Subscription address:** Springer-Verlag New York Inc. / North America, PO Box 2485, Journal Fulfillment, Secaucus NJ 07096. **Tel** (201)348-4033, (800)777-4643, FAX (201)348-4505.) Documents available from Ask*IEEE, CASDDS.
   Desc: Articles on wavefunctions and mechanisms from electron scattering processes, and perspectives in theoretical stereochemistry.
   Ind/Abst Chem. Abstr.; INSPEC; Math. Rev.

   ISSN 0075-8515
   US
LECTURES ON GAS CHROMATOGRAPHY. (1962)-. Monographic series. English. Irregular. Price varies per volume. Plenum Press, 233 Spring Street, New York NY 10013-1578. **Tel** (212)620-8000, (800)221-9369, FAX (212)463-0742, (212)807-1047, telex 23/421139.

LC QD1 .L73   **ISSN** 0459-3391
   LI
   CODEN LAMCAJ
LIETUVOS TSR AUKSTUJU MOKYKLU MOKSLO DARBAI, CHEMIJA IR CHEMINIS TECHNOLOGIJA. (LIETUVOS TSR AUKSTUJU MOKYKLU MOKSLO DARBAI: CHEMIJA IR CHEMINE TECHNOLOGIJA.). [Liet. TSR auks. mokyklu moksio darb. Chem. ir chem. technol.]. **Added/Corp** Lithuania. Valstybinis Aukstojo ir Specialiojo Vidurinio Mokslo Komitetas. **VFOAT** Chemija ir Chemine Technologija; Nauchnye Trudy Vysshikh Uchebnykh Zavedenii Litovskoi SSR: Khimiia i Khimicheskaia Technilogiia; Khimiia i Khimicheskaia Tekhnologiia. (1961)-. Lithuanian (Russian; summaries and/or abstracts in Russian). Mintis / Idea, Z Sierakausko 15, Vilnius 2600 Lithuania. **Tel** 011 7 3702 632943. Documents available from CASDDS.
   Ind/Abst Ceram. Abstr. (19??-); Chem. Abstr. (1961-1980).

   ISSN 0956-666X
   UK
   CCC
LIPID TECHNOLOGY. [Lipid technol.]. Vol. 1, No. 1 (Aug. 1989)-. Periodical. English. Six times a year. $213.90. Elsevier Advanced Technology, An Imprint of Elsevier Science Ltd., The Boulevard, Langford Lane, Kidlington, Oxford OX5 1GB United Kingdom. **Tel** 011 44 1865 843000, 011 44 1865 843699, FAX 011 44 1865 843010. **(Subscription address:** Elsevier Science Ltd. / Oxford Fulfillment Centre, PO Box 800, Kidlington OX5 1DX United Kingdom. **Tel** 011 44 865 843355.) available on an online database from Elsevier Electronic Subscriptions (EES).
   Ind/Abst Dairy Sci. Abstr.; Food Sci. Technol. Abstr.; Soyabean Abstr.

   ISSN 0951-5836
   UK
LIQUID CHEMICALS. **Added/Corp** Drewry Shipping Consultants. (May 1987)-. English. Every 2 years. Drewry Shipping Consultants Ltd, 11 Heron Quay, London E14 4JF United Kingdom. **Tel** 011 44 171 5380191, FAX 011 44 171 9879396, telex 21167 HPDLDG.

LC Discard   **ISSN** 0262-4168
   UK
NLM Z 5524.C55; L7675
LIQUID CHROMATOGRAPHY MASS SPECTROMETRY ABSTRACTS. [Liq. chromatogr. mass spectrom. abstr.]. **VFOAT** Liquid Chromatography Mass Spectrometry Abstracts. Vol. 1, No. 1 (Nov. 1981)-. Periodical. English. Three times a year. $45.98. PRM Science & Technology Agency Ltd, 261A Finchley Road Hampstead, London NW3 6LV United Kingdom. **Tel** 011 44 171 4310372.

LC QP501 .M24   **ISSN** 0963-6986
DD 574.8/8   UK
NLM ZQU 55; M174
MACROMOLECULAR STRUCTURES. **VFOAT** MS. (1991)-. English. One time a year. $298.00. Current Science / England, Middlesex House, 34-42 Cleveland Street, London W1P 6LB United Kingdom. **Tel** 011 44 171 5808393, 011 44 171 3230323, FAX 011 44 171 5805646. **(Subscription address:** Current Science, 20 North 3rd Street, Philadelphia PA 19106. **Tel** (800)552-5866.)

Chemistry and Chemicals

LC QD1 .J62A **ISSN** 0379-8321
IQ
UDC 54
CODEN JICSDK
MAGALLAT AL-GAMIYYAT AL-KIMYAWIYAAT AL-IRAQIWAT.
(JOURNAL OF THE IRAQI CHEMICAL SOCIETY.). [Magallat al-Gamiyyat al-kimyawiyaat aliraqiwat]. **Main/Corp** Jamiyah Al-Kimawiyah Al-Iraqiyah. **VFOAT** Majallat Al-Jamiyah Al-Kimawiyah. Vol. 1 (Dec. 1976)-. Academic Scholarly Publication. English (summaries and/or abstracts in Arabic). Two times a year. Iraqi Chemical Society, PO Box 8011 Salihiyah, Baghdad Iraq. Documents available from BIOSIS Document Express, CASDDS.
Ind/Abst Biol. Abstr. (1986-); Chem. Abstr.; GeoRef; Soils Fert.

ISSN 0913-4867
DD 612 JA
MAGUNESHUMU KYOTO.
[MaguneshumuKyoto]. **VFOAT** Journal of Japanese Society of Magnesium Research. (1982)-. Periodical. Multiple languages. One time a year. Nihon Maguneshumu Kenkyukai, (Japanese Soc. for Magnesium Research), Kyoto Daigaku Igakubu Eiseigaku, Kyoshitsu Yoshida Konoecho, Sakyoku Kyotoshi Kyotofu 606, Japan. Documents available from CASDDS.
Ind/Abst Chem. Abstr.

LC QD1 .M3 **ISSN** 0025-0155
HU
CODEN MGKFA3
MAGYAR KEMIAI FOLYOIRAT. [M. kem. foly.].
Added/Corp Magyar Kemikusok Egyesuelete. Magyar Termeszettudomanyi Tarsulat, Budapest. Chemiai & Zakosztaly. **VFOAT** Hungarian Journal of Chemistry. Vol. 1 (Jan. 1895)-. Periodical. Hungarian. Twelve times a year. $76.00. **(Subscription address:** Kultura, PO Box 143, H-1300 Budapest 3 Hungary. **Tel** 011 36 1 2500194.) Documents available from The Genuine Article, BIOSIS Document Express, CASDDS.
Ind/Abst Alum. Ind. Abstr.; Anal. Abstr.; Biol. Abstr.; Chem Inform; Chem. Abstr.; Chem. Titles; Curr. Biotechnol.; Curr. Chem. React.; Curr. Cit.; Curr. Contents Phys. Chem. Earth Sci.; Eng. Mater. Abstr.; Index Chem.; Mass Spect. Bull.; Met. Abstr.; Nat. Prod. Updates; Res. Alert [Full Cov.]; Sci. Cit. Index; SCISEARCH; Surf. Treat. Technol. Abstr.

LC QD1 .M32 **ISSN** 0025-0163
HU
CODEN MGKLAL
MAGYAR KEMIKUSOK LAPJA. [Magy. kemikusok l.].
Added/Corp Magyar Kemikusok Egyesulete. Vol. 1 (1946)-. Academic Scholarly Publication. Hungarian. Twelve times a year. $58.00. **(Subscription address:** Kultura, PO Box 143, H-1300 Budapest 3 Hungary. **Tel** 011 36 1 2500194.) Documents available from CASDDS.
Ind/Abst Anal. Abstr.; Chem Inform; Chem. Abstr.; Coal Abstr.; Curr. Biotechnol.; EMBASE; Surf. Treat. Technol. Abstr.

LC TP1 .M26 **ISSN** 0262-4230
DD 338.4/76602/05 UK
CCC
MANUFACTURING CHEMIST (LONDON: 1981). (MANUFACTURING CHEMIST.). [Manuf. chem.].
Vol. 54 No. 9 (Sept. 1983)-. Academic Scholarly Publication. English. Twelve times a year. $175.00. Morgan Grampian, 40 Beresford Street Woolwich, London SE18 6BQ United Kingdom. **Tel** 011 44 181 8557777, FAX 011 44 181 8555548, telex 896238. **ED** Neil Eisberg. **Bk Rev**. **Ad Acc**. **Circ**: 5,500. available on microfilm and microfiche from University Microfilms International (UMI); available on an online database (files 16,648/Full-Text) from DIALOG. Documents available from The Genuine Article, Ask*IEEE, CASDDS.
Continues Manufacturing Chemist Incorporating Chemical Age, 0262-4230.
Desc: Journal for top and middle management in all sectors of the international chemical industry responsible for all aspects of the industry from research and development to production and packaging and distribution.
Ind/Abst Abstr. BioCommer.; BioBusiness (1984-); Biodeter. Abstr.; Chem. Abstr.; Chem. Bus. Bull.; Chem. Bus. NewsBase (1985-); Chem. Bus. Update; Chem. Hazards Ind.; Chem. Ind. Notes; Coal Abstr.; Curr. Biotechnol.; Curr. Cit.; Curr. Contents Eng. Comput. Technol.; Curr. Technol. Index; EMBASE; EP Collect.; F&S Index Plus Text, Int. [Select. Cov.]; Homework Help.; Infomat Int. Bus.; INSPEC (March 1984-); Int. Packag. Abstr.; Int. Pharm. Abstr. (19??-19??); Lab. Hazards Bull.; Leadscan; MasterFile FullTEXT 1000; MasterFile FullTEXT 350; MasterFile FullTEXT 650; MasterFile FullTEXT; OCLC; Life Sci. Collect.; PESTDOC; Proc. Chem. Eng.; PROMT [Full Txt.]; Res. Alert [Full Cov.]; Saf. Health Work; SCISEARCH; Soc. Sci. Cit. Index [Select. Cov.]; Telebase; Theor. Chem. Eng.; Trade Ind. ASAP [Full Txt.]; Trade Ind. Index [Full Txt.]; World Surf. Coat. Abstr.

LC QD39.3.M3 M367 **ISSN** 0340-6253
DD 540/.1/51 GW
CODEN MATCDY
MATCH (MUELHEIM). (MATCH.). [Match].
Added/Corp Max-Planck-Institut fuer Kohlenforschung. Institut fuer Strahlenchemie. Max-Planck-Institut fuer Strahlenchemie. (Oct. 1975)-. Academic Scholarly Publication. English (French and German). Irregular. Price varies per volume. Institut fur Strahlenchemie, PO Box 101365, Mrs. R. Wolf, D-45413 Muelheim Ruhr Germany. **Tel** 011 49 208 3043609, telex 856741 MPSTR D. **ED** A.T. Balaban, A. Dreiding, A. Kerber, O.E. Polansky. Index available. **Bk Rev**. **Circ**: 150 (ctrl). Documents available from The Genuine Article, CASDDS.
Desc: Chemical aspects of graphs, groups, topology, molecular and crystal structure; phase transitions; enumerations; information theory; differential equations, etc.
Ind/Abst Chem. Abstr.; Math. Rev.; Res. Alert [Full Cov.]; Zentralbl. Math. Ihre Grenzgeb.

LC QD **ISSN** 1049-2801
DD 540 US
MATHEMATICAL CHEMISTRY. [Math. chem.].
VFOAT Mathematical Chemistry Series. Vol. 1 (1991)-. Monographic series. English. Gordon & Breach Science Publishers, Inc., PO Box 786, Cooper Station, New York NY 10276. **Tel** (212)206-8900, FAX (212)645-2459.

LC TP202 .M23 **ISSN** 0145-6911
DD 660 US
MCCUTCHEON'S DETERGENTS & EMULSIFIERS : FUNCTIONAL MATERIALS.
VFOAT Functional Materials; McCutcheon's Functional Materials. **VAT** McCutcheon's Detergents and Emulsifiers. Functional Materials. (19??)-. English. One time a year. MC Publishing Company, 175 Rock Road, Glen Rock NJ 07452.

LC RS400 .M44 **ISSN** 1054-2523
DD 615/.19/005 US
CCC
NLM W1; M64B **CODEN** MCREEB
MEDICINAL CHEMISTRY RESEARCH.
See Pharmacy and Pharmacology.

LC TP200 **ISSN** 0958-2118
DD 660.284/24 UK
CCC
NLM W1; ME8937L
Pr Rev.
MEMBRANE TECHNOLOGY. See
Engineering-Chemical Engineering.

LC QD1 .K576 **ISSN** 0389-0279
JA
CODEN KDRKDD
MEMOIRS OF THE FACULTY OF SCIENCE, KOCHI UNIVERSITY. SERIES C, CHEMISTRY. (KOCHI DAIGAKU RIGAKUBU KIYO. KAGAKU.). [Mem. Fac. Sci., Kochi Univ., Ser.es C, Chem.].
Added/Corp Kochi Daigaku. Rigakubu. Kochi Daigaku. Rigakubu. Kagaku Kyoshitsu. **VFOAT** Memoirs of the Faculty of Science, Kochi University. Series C, Chemistry. Vol. 1 (1980)-. Academic Scholarly Publication. English (Japanese). Kochi Daigaku Rigakubu, (Faculty of Science Kochi University), 5-1 Akebonocho 2 chome, Kochishi Kochiken 780 Japan. Documents available from CASDDS.
Ind/Abst Chem. Abstr.

LC QD1 .K965 **ISSN** 0085-2635
JA
CODEN MFKCAL
MEMOIRS OF THE FACULTY OF SCIENCE, KYUSHU UNIVERSITY. SERIES C. CHEMISTRY. [Mem. Fac. Sci., Kyushu Univ., Ser. C].
Main/Corp Kyushu Daigaku. Rigakubu. **VFOAT** Kyushu Daigaku Rigakubu Kiyo. Vol. 1 (Mar. 1948)-. English. Kyushu University / Faculty of Science, 10-1 Hakozaki 6 Chome Higasiku, Fukuokasi Fukuokaken 812 Japan. Documents available from Ask*IEEE, CASDDS.
Ind/Abst Alum. Ind. Abstr.; Ceram. Abstr. (19??-); Chem. Abstr.; INSPEC (March 1968-); Mass Spect. Bull.; Met. Abstr.

LC T4 .W32 **ISSN** 0369-1950
JA
CODEN MSEWA6
MEMOIRS OF THE SCHOOL OF SCIENCE AND ENGINEERING. WASEDA UNIVERSITY. See Engineering-Chemical
Engineering.

LC QD1 .M378 **ISSN** 0025-925X
US
CCC
NLM W1 ME908T
MENDELEEV CHEMISTRY JOURNAL.
[Mendeleev chem. j.]. Vol. 11 (1966)-. Periodical. English (Russian). Six times a year. $995.00. Allerton Press Inc., 150 Fifth Avenue, New York NY 10011. **Tel** (212)924-3950, FAX (212)463-9684, telex 427441 ALPRES.
Ind/Abst AGRICOLA; Ceram. Abstr. (19??-); EMBASE.

LC QD1 .M379 **ISSN** 0959-9436
DD 540/.5 CCC
CODEN MENCEX
MENDELEEV COMMUNICATIONS / ROYAL SOCIETY OF CHEMISTRY, [AKADEMIIA NAUK SSSR].
Added/Corp Royal Society of Chemistry (Great Britain) Akademiia Nauk SSSR. No. 1 (Feb. 1991)-. Periodical. English. Six times a year. $325.00. Royal Society of Chemistry, Thomas Graham House, Science Park, Cambridge CB4 4WF United Kingdom. **Tel** 011 44 1223 420066, FAX 011 44 1223 423623, telex 818293 ROYAL. **(Subscription address:** Royal Society of Chemistry, Turpin Distribution Services Ltd., Blackhorse Road, Letchworth, Hertfordshire SG6 1HN United Kingdom. **Tel** 011 44 1462 672555, FAX 011 44 1462 480947.) **ED** O. M. Nefedov, H. M. Frey, Irina V. Makhova and S. Jane Davies. Documents available from The Genuine Article, CASDDS.
Desc: Provides international chemical community with access to preliminary accounts of results and covers all branches of chemistry.
Ind/Abst Chem. Abstr.; Curr. Cit.; Curr. Contents Phys. Chem. Earth Sci.; Res. Alert [Full Cov.]; Sci. Cit. Index.

UK
METHANOL MONTHLY NEWSLETTER.
(19??)-. Newsletter. English. Twelve times a year. £2100.00 (5 copies). Tecnon Ltd., 12 Calico House, Plantation Wharf, York Place Battersea, London SW11 3TN United Kingdom. **Tel** 011 44 171 9243955, FAX 011 44 171 9785307, telex 28521.

ISSN 0026-265X
DD 542 US
CCC
NLM W1 MI297 **CODEN** MICJAN
Pr Rev.
MICROCHEMICAL JOURNAL. [Mirochem. j.].
Added/Corp American Microchemical Society. Metropolitan Microchemical Society. Vol. 1 (1957)-. Academic Scholarly Publication. English. Eight times a year. $440.00. Academic Press Inc., 6277 Sea Harbor Drive, Orlando FL 32887. **Tel** (800)543-9534, (407)345-4100, FAX (407)352-3445. **ED** Joseph Sneddon and Donald R. Bobbitt. Documents available from The Genuine Article, BIOSIS Document Express, CASDDS.
Desc: Focuses on microscale chemical analysis including clinically significant methods and procedures. Covers innovations in techniques down to the finest possible limits.
Ind/Abst Abstr. Bull. Inst. Pap. Sci. Tech.; AGRICOLA; Anal. Abstr.; Biol. Abstr.; Chem. Abstr.; Chem. Titles; Coal Abstr.; Curr. Biotechnol.; Curr. Cit.; Curr. Contents Phys. Chem. Earth Sci.; EMBASE; Food Sci. Technol. Abstr.; GeoRef; Int. Aerosp. Abstr.; Leadscan; Maize Abstr.; Life Sci. Collect.; Postharvest News Inf.; Protozoolog. Abstr.; Res. Alert [Full Cov.]; Rev. Agric. Entomol.; Rev. Med. Vet. Entomol.; Sci. Cit. Index; SCISEARCH; Vitis Vitic. Enol. Abstr.

ISSN 0026-5411
DD 540 US
MINNESOTA CHEMIST, THE. [Minn. chem.].
Main/Corp American Chemical Society. Minnesota Section. (19??)-. Periodical. English. Twelve times a year. Minnesota Secretary of American Chemical Society, 11 Oak Street, Minneapolis MN 55414.

LC QD **ISSN** 0934-8506
DD 540 GW
NLM W1; MI9583 **CODEN** MGDCEV
MITTEILUNGEN. Added/Corp Gesellschaft
Deutscher Chemiker. Fachgruppe Geschichte der Chemie. (1988)-. Periodical. German.

ISSN 0411-8987
UDC 54 GW
CODEN CGDMBG
MITTEILUNGSBLATT / CHEMISCHE GESELLSCHAFT DER DEUTSCHEN DEMOKRATISCHEN REPUBLIK.
[Mitteilungsbl. Chem. Ges. D. D. R.]. (1954)-. Academic Scholarly Publication. German. Twelve times a year. Chemische Gesellschaft der DDR, Redaktionskollegium Mitteilungsblatt, Clara-Zetkin Str. 105, Postfach 1327, 1086 Berlin Germany. **Tel** 2291554. Documents available from CASDDS.
Ind/Abst Chem. Abstr.; Curr. Biotechnol.; Energy Res. Abstr. (Oct. 1981-).

ISSN 0178-4927
GW
CODEN MGDIEF
MITTEILUNGSBLATT / GESELLSCHAFT DEUTSCHER CHEMIKER, FACHGRUPPE CHEMIE-INFORMATION. [Mitt.bl. - Ges. Dtsch. Chem. Fachgr. Chem.-Inf.].
Added/Corp GDCh-Fachgruppe Chemie-Information. Nr. 1 (1982)-.

Chemistry and Chemicals

Academic Scholarly Publication. German. Price varies per volume. Documents available from CASDDS.
Ind/Abst Chem. Abstr.

ISSN 0195-3966
US
CCC
CODEN MPSSDC
MMI PRESS SYMPOSIUM SERIES. [MMI Press symp. ser.]. **VAT** Michigan Molecular Institute Press Symposium Series. (1980)-. Monographic series. English. Irregular. Price varies per volume. Harwood Academic Publishers / New York, PO Box 786, Cooper Station, New York NY 10276. **Tel** (212)206-8900, (201)643-7500. **ED** E G Elias. Documents available from Ask*IEEE. **Continues** Midland Macromolecular Monographs, 0141-0342.
Ind/Abst INSPEC.

ISSN 1065-3074
DD 574
US
CCC
NLM W1; MO194UK
●**MOLECULAR AND CELLULAR DIFFERENTIATION.** See Biology.

ISSN 1046-5219
DD 539
US
MOLECULAR DYNAMICS NEWS. [Mol. dyn. news]. **VFOAT** MDN. (19??)-. Periodical. English. Six times a year. $15.00. Molecular Dynamics News, University of California, Chemistry Department, Santa Cruz CA 95064. **Tel** (408)459-2854. **ED** Roger Anderson, Vincenzo Aquilanti (editor's address): Dipartimento de Chimica dell'Universita, 06123 Perugia Italy). **Ad Acc**.
Circ: 550.
Desc: Informal newsletter of coming attractions and current events in the world of reaction dynamics and associated phenomena.

ISSN 1056-1935
US
MOLECULAR MATERIAL. (1991)-. Periodical. English. Four times a year. Gordon & Breach Science Publishers, PO Box 90, Reading, Berkshire RG1 8JL United Kingdom. **Tel** 011 44 1734 560080, FAX 011 44 1734 568211.

LC QD142 .M675
RU
NLM W1 MO198J
MOLEKULIARNAIA FIZIKA I BIOFIZIKA VODNYKH SISTEM. **Added/Corp** Leningradskii Gosudarstvennyi Universitet Imeni A.A. Zhdanova. **VFOAT** Molecular Physics and Biophysics of Water Systems. Vol. 1 (1973)-. Academic Scholarly Publication. Russian. Irregular. St. Petersburg State University / Izdatelstvo Leningradskogo Universiteta, Universitetskaia Nab 7/9, 199034 St. Petersburg Russia. **Tel** 011 7 812 2189788, FAX 011 7 812 2185152, telex 121481. Documents available from CASDDS. **Continues** Struktura i Pol Vody v Zhivom Organizme.
Ind/Abst Chem. Abstr.

ISSN 0026-9247
US
UDC 54
CCC
NLM W1 MO343
CODEN MOCMB7
Pr Rev.
MONATSHEFTE FUER CHEMIE. [Monatsh. Chem.]. **VFOAT** Chemical Monthly. Vol. 99, (1968)-. Academic Scholarly Publication. German. Twelve times a year. $1037.00. Springer-Verlag Vienna, Sachsenplatz 4 6, PO Box 89, A-1201 Vienna Austria. **Tel** 011 43 1 33024150, FAX 011 43 1 330242665. (**Subscription address:** Springer-Verlag New York Inc. / North America, PO Box 2485, Journal Department, Secaucus NJ 07096. **Tel** (201)348-4033, (800)777-4643, FAX (201)348-4505.) **ED** H Brunner, H H Emons, R Noyori, E Vogel, and O Vogl. available on microfilm and microfiche from University Microfilms International (UMI). Documents available from The Genuine Article, BIOSIS Document Express, CASDDS, ADONIS. **Continues** Monatshefte fur Chemie und Verwandte Teile Anderer Wissenschaften, 0343-7329.
Desc: Features the most recent research results in inorganic, structural, physical, theoretical and organic chemistry as well as biochemistry.
Ind/Abst ADONIS; AGRICOLA; Alum. Ind. Abstr.; Anal. Abstr.; Biol. Abstr.; Ceram. Abstr. (19??-); Chem Inform; Chem. Abstr.; Chem. Titles; Coal Abstr.; Curr. Biotechnol.; Curr. Chem. React.; Curr. Cit.; Curr. Contents Phys. Chem. Earth Sci.; EMBASE; Energy Res. Abstr.; Eng. Abstr.; Index Chem.; Int. Aerosp. Abstr.; Mass Spect. Bull.; Met. Abstr.; Methods Organ. Synth.; NAPRALERT; Nat. Prod. Updates; Life Sci. Collect.; PESTDOC; Polymer Contents; Res. Alert [Full Cov.]; Sci. Cit. Index; Surf. Treat. Technol. Abstr.

LC QD1 .R6785
DD 540/.8
UK
MONOGRAPHS FOR TEACHERS. **Added/Corp** Chemical Society (Great Britain). (19??)-. Monographic series. English. Irregular. Price varies per volume. Royal Society of Chemistry, Thomas Graham House, Science Park, Cambridge CB4 4WF United Kingdom. **Tel** 011 44 1223 420066, FAX 011 44 1223 423623, telex 818293 ROYAL. (**Subscription address:** Royal Society of Chemistry, Turpin Distribution Services Ltd., Blackhorse Road, Letchworth, Hertfordshire SG6 1HN United Kingdom. **Tel** 011 44 1462 672555, FAX 011 44 1462 480947.) **Continues** Royal Institute of Chemistry. Monographs for Teachers.
Desc: Presents accounts of topics in chemistry for the guidance of teachers and students in further and higher education.

US
MONOGRAPHS IN ELECTROANALYTICAL CHEMISTRY AND ELECTROCHEMISTRY SERIES.
Monographic series. English. Irregular. Price varies per volume. Marcel Dekker Inc., 270 Madison Avenue, New York NY 10016. **Tel** (212)696-9000, (800)228-1160, FAX (212)685-4540, telex 421419. (**Subscription address:** Marcel Dekker Inc., PO Box 5017, Monticello NY 12701. **Tel** (800)228-1160.)
Desc: Topics covered have included the electrochemistry of metals and semiconductors, laboratory techniques in electroanalytical chemistry, and standard potentials in aqueous solution.

LC QD1 .M759
DD 540/.5
ISSN 0027-1314
US
CCC
NLM W1 MO931Q
MOSCOW UNIVERSITY CHEMISTRY BULLETIN. [Mosc. Univ. chem. bull.]. **Main/Corp** Moskovskii Gosudarstvennyi Universitet Im. M.V. Lomonosova. (19??)-. Bulletin. English (Russian). Six times a year. $845.00. Allerton Press Inc., 150 Fifth Avenue, New York NY 10011. **Tel** (212)924-3950, FAX (212)463-9684, telex 427441 ALPRES.

LC QD1 .N22
DD 540/.5
ISSN 0341-5163
GW
CCC
CODEN NCTLDI
NACHRICHTEN AUS CHEMIE, TECHNIK UND LABORATORIUM. (NACHRICHTEN AUS CHEMIE, TECHNIK UND LABORATORIUM / HERAUSGEGEBEN VON DER GESELLSCHAFT DEUTSCHER CHEMIKER.). [Nachr. Chem., Tech. Lab.]. **Added/Corp** Gesellschaft Deutscher Chemiker. Vol. 25 (1977)-. Academic Scholarly Publication. German. Twelve times a year. $263.00. VCH Gesellschaft GmbH, Postfach 101161, D-69451 Weinheim Germany. **Tel** 011 49 6201 606459, FAX 011 49 6201 606184. (**Subscription address:** VCH Publishers Inc., 303 Northwest 12th Avenue, Journals Department, Deerfield FL 33442. **Tel** (800)367-8249, (305)428-5566.) Documents available from The Genuine Article, CASDDS. **Continues** Nachrichten aus Chemie und Technik.
Ind/Abst Chem Inform; Chem. Abstr.; Coal Abstr.; Curr. Biotechnol.; Curr. Cit.; EMBASE; Energy Res. Abstr. (April 1978-); Res. Alert [Full Cov.]; Soc. Sci. Index [Select. Cov.].

ISSN 1011-3509
IR
CODEN IJCEE9
NASHRIYYAH-I SHIMI VA-MUHANDISI-I SHIMI-I IRAN. (IRANIAN JOURNAL OF CHEMISTRY & CHEMICAL ENGINEERING.). [Nashriyyah-i shimi va-muhandisi-i shimi-i Iran]. **VFOAT** Iranian Journal of Chemistry and Chemical Engineering. (19??)-. Periodical. Iranian. Documents available from CASDDS.
Ind/Abst Chem. Abstr.

ISSN 0270-3009
US
CODEN NMACDY
NATIONAL MEETING - AMERICAN CHEMICAL SOCIETY, DIVISION OF ENVIRONMENTAL CHEMISTRY. [Natl. meet. - Am. Chem. Soc., Div. Environ. Chem.]. **Main/Corp** American Chemical Society. Division of Environmental Chemistry. (1979)-. Academic Scholarly Publication. English. American Chemical Society, 1155 Sixteenth Street Northwest, Washington DC 20036. **Tel** (800)333-9511, (800)227-5558, (614)447-3776, FAX (202)447-3671. Documents available from Article Express International, CASDDS.
Ind/Abst Bioeng. Abstr.; Chem. Abstr.; Ei Page One; Eng. Index Annu.

LC TP977 .S3
DD 668/.372/05
ISSN 0164-4580
US
CODEN NSTRED
NAVAL STORES REVIEW (1979). See Forests and Forestry-Lumber and Wood.

NE
●**NEDERLANDS TIJDSCHRIFT VOOR KLINISCHE CHEMIE.** (1995)-. Dutch. Six times a year. $109.63. Bureau NVKC, Vredenburg 139 A, 3511 BG Utrecht Netherlands. **Tel** 011 31 30 328623, FAX 011 31 30 3111178. **Continues** Tijdschrift van de Nederlandse Vereniging voor Klinische Chemie.
Ind/Abst Curr. Cit.

LC HD9650.1 .N4
UDC 66(492)543.226
NLM W1 NE1907
ISSN 0470-6021
NE
CODEN NEDCAO
NEDERLANDSE CHEMISCHE INDUSTRIE. [Ned. chem. ind.]. Vol. 1 (Jan. 1959)-. Academic Scholarly Publication. Dutch. Twenty-six times a year. Fl125.00. Haagse Druk-En Uitg Mij, Postbus 30111, 2500 GC Den Haag Netherlands. **Tel** 011 31 70 209233. Index available. cum. index. **Ad Acc**. available on an online database. Documents available from CASDDS. **Supersedes** Chemische en Pharmaceutische Techniek; Vereniging van de Nederlandse Chemische Industrie. Mededelingen.
Ind/Abst Chem. Abstr.; Chem. Bus. Bull.; Chem. Bus. NewsBase (1985-); Chem. Bus. Update; Chem. Ind. Notes; F&S Index Plus Text, Int. [Select. Cov.]; PROMT; Saf. Health Work.

ISSN 0320-0094
RU
CODEN NENKDX
NEFTEPERERABOTKA I NEFTEHIMIJA (KAZAN). (NEFTEPERERABOTKA I NEFTEKHIMIIA.). [Neftepererab. neftehim.]. **Added/Corp** Kazanskii Khimiko-Tekhnologicheskii Institut. (1972)-. Academic Scholarly Publication. Russian. Irregular. $129.95. Izdatelstvo Naukova Dumka / Ukrainian Academy of Sciences, Yu. A. Khramov, Dir., Ul. Repina 3, 252 601 Kiev Ukraine. **Tel** 011 7 44 4303441, 011 7 44 2254182, telex 131376. (**Subscription address:** East View Publications Inc., 3020 Harbor Lane North, Suite 110, Minneapolis MN 55447. **Tel** (800)477-1005, (612)550-0961, FAX (612)559-2931.) Documents available from CASDDS.
Ind/Abst Chem. Abstr.

LC QD1 .N848
ISSN 1144-0546
FR
CCC
NLM W1; NE455E
CODEN NJCHE5
NEW JOURNAL OF CHEMISTRY (1987). (NEW JOURNAL OF CHEMISTRY.). [Nouv. j. chim.]. **Added/Corp** Centre National de la Recherche Scientifique (France) Societe Francaise de Chimie. **VFOAT** Nouveau Journal de Chimie. Vol. 11, No. 1 (Jan. 1987)-. Academic Scholarly Publication. English (French and German). Eleven times a year. $662.72. Gauthier-Villars, 15 rue Gossin, 92543 Montrouge Cedex France. **Tel** 33 1 40 92 65 00, FAX 33 1 40 92 65 97. (**Subscription address:** Centrale des Revues, 11 rue Gossin, 92543 Montrouge Cedex France. **Tel** 011 33 1 46565266.) Documents available from The Genuine Article, Ask*IEEE, CASDDS. **Continues** Nouveau Journal de Chimie, 0398-9836.
Ind/Abst Anal. Abstr.; Chem. Abstr.; Curr. Biotechnol.; Curr. Chem. React.; Curr. Cit.; Index Chem.; INSPEC (1987-); Mass Spect. Bull.; Methods Organ. Synth.; Nat. Prod. Updates; Res. Alert; Sci. Cit. Index; SCISEARCH.

ISSN 0169-6424
NE
NLM W1; NE484K
NEW POLYMERIC MATERIALS. Vol. 1, No. 1 (1988)-. Academic Scholarly Publication. English. Four times a year. DM280.00. VSP International Science Publishers, Godfried van Seystlaan 47, 3703 BR Zeist Netherlands. **Tel** 011 31 3404 25790, FAX 011 31 3404 32081, telex 40217 USP NL. (**Subscription address:** VSP International Science Publishers, PO Box 346, 3700 AH Zeist Netherlands. **Tel** 011 31 30 6925790, FAX 011 31 30 6932081.) **ED** F. E. Karasz. **Ad Acc**. Documents available from Article Express International, The Genuine Article, CASDDS.
Desc: Publishes original research on the chemistry, physics and biochemistry of macromolecules and oligomers. Covers conductivity in polymers, ionic and electronic properties of polymers, polymeric materials for communication and computer technologies, polymer membranes, thermostable polymers, reactive processing, biomedical applications of polymers and composites.
Ind/Abst Chem. Abstr.; Curr. Cit.; Ei Page One; Eng. Mater. Abstr.; Eng. Index Annu.; Polymer Contents; Res. Alert [Full Cov.].

LC Z5854 .N542
DD 016.6
ISSN 0028-6869
US
CODEN NTBOAJ
CEASED
NEW TECHNICAL BOOKS. See Chemistry and Chemicals-Abstracting, Bibliographies and Statistics.

LC QD40 .N37
DD 540/.7
FR
NLM W1 NE513E
NEW TRENDS IN CHEMISTRY TEACHING. **Added/Corp** Unesco. **VFOAT** Tendances Nouvelles de l'Enseignement de la Chimie. (1965)-. Periodical. Multiple languages (English and French). Every 2 years. UNIPUB, 4611-F Assembly Drive, Lanham MD 20706-4391. **Tel** (800)274-4888, FAX (301)459-0056, telex 28787 GATT CH.

LC WMLC L 83/4685
AT
NEWS BULLETIN (SYDNEY, AUSTRALIA). See College and School Publications.

Chemistry and Chemicals

ISSN 0288-7878
JA
NLM W1; NI426WCP
NIHON RINSHO KAGAKKAI NENKAI KIROKU = PROCEEDINGS OF THE ... ANNUAL MEETING OF JAPAN SOCIETY OF CLINICAL CHEMISTRY. **Main/Corp** Nihon Rinsho Kagakkai. Nenkai. **VFOAT** Nihon Rinsho Kagakukai Nenkai Kiroku; Proceedings of the ... Annual Meeting of the Japan Society of Clinical Chemistry. (1982)-. Proceedings. Japanese (summaries and/or abstracts in English). One time a year. Nihon Rinsho Kagakkai, (Japan Soc. of Clinical Chemistry), Osaka Daigaku Igakubu Fuzoku, Byoin 1-50 Fukushima 1 Chome, Fukushimaku Osakashi, Osaka 553 Japan. Documents available from CASDDS. **Continues** Rinsho Kagaku Shinpojiumu, 0301-0880.
Ind/Abst Chem. Abstr.

JA
CODEN NIRID7
NIIGATA RIKAGAKU : THE JOURNAL OF PHYSICS AND CHEMISTRY OF NIIGATA. See Physics.

ISSN 0029-0483
JA
CODEN NIGEB6
NIKKAKYO GEPPO. [NikkakyÂo geppÂo].
Added/Corp Nihon Kagaku Kogyo Kyokai. **VFOAT** Japan Chemical Industry Association Monthly. (1948)-. Academic Scholarly Publication. Japanese. Twelve times a year. Nihon Kagaku Kogyo Kyokai, (Japan Chemical Industry Assoc.), 2-6 Kasumigaseki 3 Chome, Chiyodaku Tokyo 100 Japan. Documents available from CASDDS.
Ind/Abst Chem. Abstr.

LC QD1 .N77
ISSN 0369-4577
JA
CCC
CODEN NKAKB8
Pr Rev.
NIPPON KAGAKUKAI (1972). (NIPPON KAGAKUKAI SHI.). [Nippon Kagakukai shi]. **Main/Corp** Nippon Kagakukai. **Added/Corp** Nihon Kagakkai. **VFOAT** Nippon Kagaku Kaishi. No. 1 (Jan. 1972)-. Academic Scholarly Publication. Japanese (summaries and/or abstracts in English; table of contents in English). Twelve times a year. $276.00. Nippon Kagakkai, (Chemical Society of Japan), 1-5 Kanda Surugadai, Chiyodaku Tokyo 101 Japan. **(Subscription address:** Maruzen Company Ltd., PO Box 5050, Import & Export Department, Tokyo 100 31 Japan. **Tel** 011 81 3 32789224.**)** Index available in last issue of volume--attached. available on microfilm from University Microfilms International (UMI). Documents available from The Genuine Article, CASDDS. **Formed by the union of** Nihon Kagaku Zasshi and Kogyo Kagaku Zasshi.
Ind/Abst AGRICOLA; Alum. Ind. Abstr.; Anal. Abstr.; Ceram. Abstr. (19??-); Chem Inform; Chem. Abstr.; Coal Abstr.; Curr. Biotechnol.; Curr. Chem. React.; Curr. Cit.; Curr. Contents Phys. Chem. Earth Sci.; Index Chem.; Leadscan; Lit. Pat. Abstr., Oilfield Chem. (1966-); Lit. Abstr., Catal. Zeol.; Lit. Abstr., Health Environ.; Lit. Abstr., Pet. Refin. Petrochem.; Lit. Abstr., Pet. Substit.; Lit. Abstr., Transp. Storage; Met. Abstr.; Life Sci. Collect.; Res. Alert [Full Cov.]; Sci. Cit. Index; SCISEARCH.

ISSN 1351-525X
UK
●**NITRIC OXIDE.** (1994)-. English. Irregular. £105.00. SUBIS, Mansion House 19 Kingfield Road, Sheffield S11 9AS United Kingdom. **Tel** 011 44 114 2554433, FAX 011 44 114 255 4626.

LC TP245.N8 N5
ISSN 0029-0777
UK
UDC 546.17; 661.5
CODEN NNNNAY
NITROGEN. [Nitrogen]. No. 1 (Feb. 1959)-. Academic Scholarly Publication. English. Six times a year. $495.00. British Sulphur Corporation Ltd, 31 Mount Pleasant, London WC1X 0AD United Kingdom. **Tel** 011 44 171 8375600, FAX 011 44 171 8375600 telex 918918 SULFEX G. **(Subscription address:** CRU International Ltd., 31 Mount Pleasant, London WC1X 0AD United Kingdom. **Tel** 011 44 171 8375600, FAX 011 44 171 8370292.**)** **ED** Nessa Keogh. **Ad Acc.** available on microfilm and microfiche from University Microfilms International (UMI); available on an online database (file 648/Full-Text) from DIALOG. Documents available from CASDDS.
Desc: Reporting on commerical and technical developments as they affect world nitrogen and methanol industries.
Ind/Abst Chem. Abstr.; Chem. Bus. Bull.; Chem. Bus. NewsBase (1984-); Chem. Bus. Update; Chem. Ind. Notes; Coal Abstr.; Curr. Cit.; F&S Index Plus Text, Int. [Select. Cov.]; PROMT; Soils Fert.; Trade Ind. ASAP [Full Txt.]; Trade Ind. Index [Full Txt.].

ISSN 0369-5131
JA
CODEN NOGUAR
NOGUCHI KENKYUJO JIHO. [Noguchi Kenkyujo jiho]. **Added/Corp** Noguchi Kenkyujo (Tokyo, Japan). (1951)-. Academic Scholarly Publication.

Japanese (summaries and/or abstracts in English). Noguchi Kenkyujo, (Noguchi Inst.), 8-1 Kaga 1 Chome, Itabashiku Tokyo 173 Japan. Documents available from CASDDS.
Ind/Abst Chem. Abstr.; Coal Abstr.

ISSN 0733-2092
US
NORG NEWS BULLETIN. [NORG news bull.]. **Added/Corp** NORG. **VFOAT** N.O.R.G. News Bulletin. VAT Neighborhood Organization Research Group News Bulletin. Vol. 3, No. 1 (Feb. 1980)-. Bulletin. English. Four times a year. $6.00. Indiana University Chemical Information Center, 814 East Third Street, Bloomington IN 47405. **Tel** (812)337-0441. **Continues** News Bulletin (NORG), 0733-0790.

ISSN 0550-1156
IT
NLM W1 NO813G
NOTIZIARIO CHIMICO E FARMACEUTICO. See Pharmacy and Pharmacology.

LC QD1 .N9
ISSN 0362-0026
DD 540.5
US
CODEN NCLUA2
NUCLEUS (CAMBRIDGE), THE. (THE NUCLEUS.). [Nucleus (Cambridge)]. **Added/Corp** American Chemical Society. Northeastern Section. Vol. 1 (Feb. 1924)-. Academic Scholarly Publication. English. Twelve times a year. $15.00. Union of Concerned Scientists, 26 Church Street, Cambridge MA 02238. **Tel** (617)546-5552, FAX (617)864-9405. **ED** G. W. Harris and W. G. Bullard. Documents available from The Genuine Article, CASDDS.
Ind/Abst Chem. Abstr.; Res. Alert [Select. Cov.]; SCISEARCH.

LC RA773
ISSN 0167-4587
DD 613.2
US
NLM W3 NU776
CODEN NUSYD8
Pr Rev.
NUTRICIA SYMPOSIUM. See Biology.

LC QE371 .O24
ISSN 0320-6386
RU
CODEN OFKPAE
OCHERKI FIZIKO-KHIMICHESKOI PETROLOGII. See Mines and Mining-Mineralogy.

LC QD1 .V5615
DD 540/.5
AU
CODEN OCMZAX
OESTERREICHISCHE CHEMIE-ZEITSCHRIFT. **Added/Corp** Verein Osterreichischer Chemiker. (19??)-. Academic Scholarly Publication. German. Six times a year. S720.00. Verlag Lorenz, Ebendorferstrasse 10, A-1010 Vienna Austria. **Tel** 011 43 222 426695, FAX 011 43 222 438693. Documents available from CASDDS.
Ind/Abst Chem. Abstr.; Surf. Treat. Technol. Abstr.

ISSN 0970-020X
II
UDC 54
CODEN OJCHEG
ORIENTAL JOURNAL OF CHEMISTRY. [Orient. j. chem.]. Vol. 1, No. 1 (Jan. 1985)-. Periodical. English. Four times a year. $100.00. **(Subscription address:** Prints India, 11 Darya Ganj, New Delhi 110002 India. **Tel** 011 91 11 3268645, FAX 011 91 11 3275542, telex 31-61087 PRIN-IN.**)**
Ind/Abst Curr. Cit.

LC T178.O75 O7B
UDC 54
UK
OSAKA KOGYO GIJUTSU SHIKENJO NEMPO. **Main/Corp** Osaka Kogyo Gijutsu Shikenjo. Japanese. Osaka Kogyo Gijutsu Shikenjo, 8-31 Midorigaoka, 1-chome 563, Ikeda Japan. **Tel** 0727-52-8351.
Desc: Covers inorganic chemistry, organic chemistry, glass and ceramic chemistry, applied chemistry, and physics.

UK
OXFORD CHEMISTRY SERIES. (1973)-. Monographic series. English. Irregular. Price varies per volume. Oxford University Press / New York, 200 Madison Avenue, New York NY 10016. **Tel** (212)679-7300, (919)677-0977, (800)451-7556, (800)445-9714, FAX (919)677-1303.

LC TA418.78 .P34
ISSN 0934-0866
DD 620/.43
GW
CCC
CODEN PPCHEZ
Pr Rev.
TITLE CHANGE
PARTICLE & PARTICLE SYSTEMS CHARACTERIZATION. (PARTICLE & PARTICLE SYSTEMS CHARACTERIZATION : MEASUREMENT AND DESCRIPTION OF PARTICLE PROPERTIES AND BEHAVIOR IN POWDERS AND OTHER DISPERSE SYSTEMS.). [Part. part. syst. charact.]. **VFOAT** A.Particle and particle systems

characterization. Vol. 5, No. 1, (March 1988)-(1995). Academic Scholarly Publication. English. VCH Gesellschaft GmbH, Postfach 101161, D-69451 Weinheim Germany. **Tel** 011 49 6201 606459, FAX 011 49 6201 606184. **(Subscription address:** VCH Publishers Inc., 303 Northwest 12th Avenue, Journals Department, Deerfield FL 33442. **Tel** (800)367-8249, (305)428-5566.**)** **ED** Kurt Leschonski. Documents available from Article Express International, The Genuine Article, CASDDS. **Continues** Particle Characterization, 0176-2265. **Continued by** Particle Science and Technologies.
Ind/Abst Chem. Abstr.; Coal Abstr.; Curr. Cit.; Curr. Contents Eng. Comput. Technol.; Ei Page One; Eng. Index Annu.; Fluid Abstr., Civil Eng.; Fluid Abstr. Proc. Eng.; FLUIDEX (19??-); Res. Alert [Full Cov.]; SCISEARCH.

GW
●**PARTICLE SCIENCE AND TECHNOLOGIES.** (1995)-. English. Six times a year. $459.00. VCH Gesellschaft GmbH, Postfach 101161, D-69451 Weinheim Germany. **Tel** 011 49 6201 606459, FAX 011 49 6201 606184. **(Subscription address:** VCH Publishers Inc., 303 Northwest 12th Avenue, Journals Department, Deerfield FL 33442. **Tel** (800)367-8249, (305)428-5566.**)** **Continues** Particle and Particle Systems Characterization.

ISSN 1146-5344
FR
UDC 011/016
PASCAL. E 18, CHROMATOGRAPHIE. **VFOAT** PASCAL. E Dix-Huit, Chromatographie; PASCAL. E 18, Chromatography; PASCAL. 18, Chromatographie. (1990)-. Periodical. Multiple languages. Ten times a year. 865.00F France; 915.00F other. CNRS / Institut d'Information Scientifique et Technique, (Centre National de la Recherche Scientifique), 15 Quai Anatole France, 75700 Paris France. **Tel** 011 33 1 47531515, FAX 011 33 1 45517307, telex 260034. **(Subscription address:** Institut d'Information Scientifique et Technique Diffusion, 2 Allee du Parc de Brabois, 54514 Vandoeuvre Nancy France. **Tel** 011 33 83 504664, FAX 011 33 83 504666, telex 961942.**)**

ISSN 1146-5123
FR
UDC 011
PASCAL. F 17, CHIMIE GENERALE MINERALE ET ORGANIQUE. **VFOAT** PASCAL. F 17, General Inorganic and Organic Chemistry; PASCAL. F Dix-Sept, Chimie Generale Minerale et Organique. (1990)-. Periodical. French. Ten times a year. 2355.00F France; 2495.00F other. CNRS / Institut National de la Recherche Scientifique), 15 Quai Anatole France, 75700 Paris France. **Tel** 011 33 1 47531515, FAX 011 33 1 45517307, telex 260034. **Continues** Pascal Folio: F17. Chimie Generale et Organique., 0761-1757.

ISSN 1065-2167
DD 665
US
PATENT ABSTRACTS. POLYMERS. See Chemistry and Chemicals-Abstracting, Bibliographies and Statistics.

ISSN 0388-3698
JA
UDC 577.112.6
NLM W3; SY451D
CODEN PECHDP
PEPTIDE CHEMISTRY : PROCEEDINGS OF THE ... SYMPOSIUM OF PEPTIDE CHEMISTRY. [Pept. chem.]. **Main/Conf** Symposium of Peptide Chemistry. **VFOAT** Proceedings of the Japanese Symposium on Peptide Chemistry. (1976)-. Academic Scholarly Publication. English. One time a year. $120.00. Protein Research Foundation, 4-1-2 Ina Minoh-Shi, Osaka 562 Japan. **Tel** 011 81 7 27294121, FAX 011 81 7 27294124, telex 5324111 PHOSA J. **ED** Noboru Yanaihara. **Circ:** 500. Documents available from CASDDS.
Ind/Abst Chem. Abstr.; Curr. Biotechnol.; Curr. Cit.

ISSN 1069-2630
US
TITLE CHANGE
PEPTIDE SCIENCES. (1993)-(Jan. 1995). Periodical. English. John Wiley & Sons, Inc., 605 Third Avenue, New York NY 10158-0012. **Tel** (212)850-6000, (212)850-6645, FAX (212)850-6088, telex 12-7063. **(Subscription address:** John Wiley & Sons / UK, Baffins Lane, Chichester, West Sussex PO19 1UD United Kingdom. **Tel** 011 44 1243 779777, FAX 011 44 1243 776128, telex 86290 WIBOOKG.**)** **ED** Dr. Murray Goodman. **Continued by** Biopolymers, 0006-3525.
Desc: Provides in-depth analysis and timely information needed by researchers and students. Correlates research results between the subdisciplines of peptide sciences.

US
PEPTIDES. SUPPLEMENTS. (19??)-. English. Irregular. Pergamon Press, An Imprint of Elsevier Science Ltd., The Boulevard, Langford Lane, Kidlington, Oxford OX5 1GB United Kingdom. **Tel** 011 44 1865 843000, 011 44 1865 843699, FAX 011 44 1865 843010.

Chemistry and Chemicals

UDC 615
Pr Rev.
PHARMA SELECTA. See Pharmacy and Pharmacology.

ISSN 0169-6882
NE

ISSN 0165-7208
NE
CCC
NLM W1 PH272L   **CODEN** PHLIDQ
PHARMACOCHEMISTRY LIBRARY. See Pharmacy and Pharmacology.

LC TP245.P5 P5   **ISSN** 0031-8426
UK
CODEN POPOA8
PHOSPHORUS AND POTASSIUM. [Phosphorus potassium]. **Added/Corp** British Sulphur Corporation, ltd. **VFOAT** Phosphorus & Potassium. No. 1 (April 1962)-. Trade Publication. English. Six times a year. $495.00. British Sulphur Corporation Ltd, 31 Mount Pleasant, London WC1X 0AD United Kingdom. **Tel** 011 44 171 8375600, FAX 011 44 171 8370292, telex 918918 SULFEX G. **(Subscription address:** CRU International Ltd., 31 Mount Pleasant, London WC1X 0AD United Kingdom. **Tel** 011 44 171 8375600, FAX 011 44 171 8370292.) **ED** Roger Manser. **Ad Acc.** available on microfilm and microfiche from University Microfilms International (UMI); available on an online database (file 648/Full-Text) from DIALOG.
Desc: Reporting on commerical and technical developments as they affect world potash and phosphates industries.
Ind/Abst AGRICOLA; Chem. Bus. Bull.; Chem. Bus. NewsBase (1985-); Chem. Bus. Update; Chem. Ind. Notes; Curr. Cit.; F&S Index Plus Text, Int. [Select. Cov.]; GeoRef; PROMT; Soils Fert.

LC QC801 .P46   **ISSN** 0079-1938
GW
CODEN PCSPDD
PHYSICS AND CHEMISTRY IN SPACE. See Physics.

LC QD541 .P53   **ISSN** 0031-9104
DD 530.4/2/05   US
CCC
CODEN PCLQAC
Pr Rev.
PHYSICS AND CHEMISTRY OF LIQUIDS. See Physics.

LC QD1 .P6   **ISSN** 0137-5083
DD 540/.5   PL
CCC
NLM W1 PO23C   **CODEN** PJCHDQ
POLISH JOURNAL OF CHEMISTRY. [Pol. j. chem.]. **Added/Corp** Polska Akademia Nauk. Komitet Nauk Chemicznej. Polskie Towarzystwo Chemiczne. Vol. 52 (1978)-. Academic Scholarly Publication. English. Twelve times a year. $300.00. **(Subscription address:** Ars Polona-Ruch, PO Box 1001, Krakowskie Przedmiescie 7, 00-068 Warsaw Poland. **Tel** 011 48 22 261201.) Documents available from CASDDS.
Continues Roczniki Chemii.
Ind/Abst Alum. Ind. Abstr.; Chem Inform; Chem. Abstr.; Chem. Titles; Curr. Cit.; Leadscan; Mass Spect. Bull.; Met. Abstr.; Methods Organ. Synth.; NAPRALERT; Nat. Prod. Updates; Life Sci. Collect.; Sci. Cit. Index; SCISEARCH.

DD 668   **ISSN** 0893-6684
US
CCC
POLYMER BLENDS, ALLOYS, AND INTERPENETRATING POLYMER NETWORKS ABSTRACTS. See Chemistry and Chemicals-Abstracting, Bibliographies and Statistics.

LC QD380 .P637   **ISSN** 0141-3910
DD 620.1/920422   UK
CCC
CODEN PDSTDW
Pr Rev.
POLYMER DEGRADATION AND STABILITY. See Plastics.

ISSN 0032-3934
US
CODEN ACPPAY
POLYMER PREPRINTS, AMERICAN CHEMICAL SOCIETY, DIVISION OF POLYMER CHEMISTRY. (POLYMER PREPRINTS.). [Polym. Prepr. Am. Chem. Soc., Div. Polym. Chem.]. **VFOAT** American Chemical Society, Division of Polymer Chemistry, Preprints. (1960)-. Proceedings. English. Two times a year (Apr. and Sept.). $90.00. Division Polymer Chemistry ACS, PO Box 20453, Newark NJ 07101. **Tel** (201)482-5744. **ED** Professor B. M. Culbertson, (editor's address: Ohio State University, Columbus, Ohio). Index Bound in First Issue (all issues). **Ad Acc. Circ:** 10,000 twice a year (ctrl).

Desc: Full texts of all papers presented before the Division of Polymer Chemistry.
Ind/Abst Curr. Cit.

JA
POLYMER PREPRINTS: JAPAN. English. Two times a year. ¥55600.00. The Society of Polymer Science, Nagaoka Building 2 4 2, Chuo Ku Tokyo 104 Japan. **Tel** 011 81 3 35433765.

LC QD471 .V913 QD380 .V9623   **ISSN** 0965-545X
RU
POLYMER SCIENCE. **Added/Corp** Rossiiskaia Akademia Nauk. **VFOAT** Polymer Science USSR; Polymer Science. Series A. Vol. 33, No. 2 (1991)-. Periodical. English (translations available in Russian). Twelve times a year. $1889.00. MAIK Nauka / Interperiodica, Ulitsa Profsoyuznaia 90, Moscow 117864 Russia. **(Subscription address:** Interperiodica Publishing, Subscription Office, PO Box 1831, Birmingham AL 35201-1831. **Tel** (800)633-4931, (205)995-1567 (outside US and Canada), FAX (205)995-1588.) Documents available from Article Express International. **Continues** Polymer Science U.S.S.R., 0032-3950.
Desc: Offers a view of theoretical and experimental polymer research and application.
Ind/Abst Eng. Index Annu.

LC QD380 .V9633
RU
●**POLYMER SCIENCE. SERIES B.**
Added/Corp Rossiiskaia Akademia Nauk. Vol. 35, No. 1 (1993)-. Periodical. English (translations available in Russian). Six times a year. $1889.00. MAIK Nauka / Interperiodica, Ulitsa Profsoyuznaia 90, Moscow 117864 Russia. **(Subscription address:** Interperiodica Publishing, Subscription Office, PO Box 1831, Birmingham AL 35201-1831. **Tel** (800)633-4931, (205)995-1567 (outside US and Canada), FAX (205)995-1588.)

LC QC173.4.S94 P48   **ISSN** 0734-1520
DD 530.4   US
CCC
CODEN PCMSER
POVERKHNOST. See Physics.

ISSN 0509-6790
PL
CODEN PIPSAC
PRACE INSTYTUTU PRZEMYSU SKORZANEGO. [Pr. Inst. Przem. Skorz.]. **Added/Corp** Instytut Przemysu Skorzanego w odzi. (1955)-. Academic Scholarly Publication. Polish (Polish; summaries and/or abstracts in English, French, German and Russian). Irregular. Instytut Przemyslu Skorzanego, Ul. Zgierska 73 Pl, Lodz Poland. Documents available from CASDDS.
Ind/Abst Chem. Abstr.

ISSN 0177-9516
GW
UDC 372.854
PRAXIS DER NATURWISSENSCHAFTEN CHEMIE. (1980)-. Periodical. German. Twelve times a year. $117.30. Aulis Verlag Deubner & Company, Antwerpenerstrasse 6 12, 50672 Cologne Germany. **Tel** 011 49 221 518051, FAX 011 49 221 518443.
Ind/Abst Curr. Cit.

LC QD1 .A536   **ISSN** 0740-0667
DD 540   US
Pr Rev.
PREPRINT EXTENDED ABSTRACT - AMERICAN CHEMICAL SOCIETY. DIVISION OF ENVIRONMENTAL CHEMISTRY. See Chemistry and Chemicals-Abstracting, Bibliographies and Statistics.

LC TP315 .A54   **ISSN** 0569-3772
DD 662/.6/05   US
CODEN ACFPAI
PREPRINTS OF PAPERS PRESENTED - AMERICAN CHEMICAL SOCIETY. DIVISION OF FUEL CHEMISTRY. See Petroleum and Natural Gas.

FR
PROCEEDINGS. 6th (1971)-. Academic Scholarly Publication. English (French). One time a year. Editions Frontieres, BP 33, 91192 Gif-sur-Yvette France. **Tel** 011 33 1 69285135. **ED** Tran Thanh Van. Documents available from CASDDS. **Continues** Rencontre de Moriond. Comptes Rendus.
Ind/Abst Chem. Abstr.

LC QD50I .I633
DD 541.39   NE
PROCEEDINGS - INTERNATIONAL CONGRESS ON CATALYSIS. **Main/Conf** International Congress on Catalysis. (1960)-. Proceedings. English (French and German). Irregular. Price varies per volume.

LC QD1 .N24a   **ISSN** 0896-2367
DD 540/.5   US
CODEN PRNOEN
PROCEEDINGS, NOBCCHE. (PROCEEDINGS, NOBCCHE / ANNUAL NATIONAL CONFERENCE OF THE NATIONAL ORGANIZATION FOR BLACK CHEMISTS AND CHEMICAL ENGINEERS.). [Proc. NOBCChE]. **Main/Corp** National Organization for Black Chemists and Chemical Engineers. National Conference. (19??)-. Proceedings. English. One time a year. $50.00. NOBCChE, National Executive Secretary, PO Box 1768, Pleasanton CA 94566. Documents available from CASDDS.
Ind/Abst Chem. Abstr.

LC QD1 .P76   **ISSN** 0253-4134
DD 540/.5   II
NLM W1 PR583JM   **CODEN** PIAADM
Pr Rev.
PROCEEDINGS OF THE INDIAN ACADEMY OF SCIENCES. CHEMICAL SCIENCES. (PROCEEDINGS. CHEMICAL SCIENCES.). [Proc. Indian Acad. Sci., Chem. sci.]. **Added/Corp** Indian Academy of Sciences. **VFOAT** Chemical Sciences; Proceedings of the Indian Academy of Sciences. Chemical Sciences. Vol. 89, No. 1 (Feb. 1980)-. Academic Scholarly Publication. English. Six times a year. $125.00. Indian Academy of Sciences Circulation, PO Box 8005, Department of Sadashivanagar, Bangalore 560 080 India. **Tel** 011 91 812 342546, 342310, telex 0845-2178 ACAD IN. **(Subscription address:** Prints India, 11 Darya Ganj, New Delhi 110002 India. **Tel** 011 91 11 3268645, FAX 011 91 11 3275542, telex 31-61087 PRIN-IN.) **ED** C N R Rao. Index available. **Circ:** 800. available on microfilm from University Microfilms International (UMI). Documents available from The Genuine Article, BIOSIS Document Express, Ask*IEEE, CASDDS. **Continues** Proceedings. A, Chemical Sciences, 0370-0089.
Desc: Contains original contributions in the areas of inorganic and analytical chemistry, organic chemistry, physical and theoretical chemistry, structural and surface chemistry.
Ind/Abst Alum. Ind. Abstr.; Anal. Abstr.; Biol. Abstr.; Chem. Abstr.; Chem. Titles; Curr. Cit.; Curr. Titles Electrochem.; Energy Inf. Abstr.; Energy Res. Abstr. (June 1981-); Eng. Mater. Abstr.; Field Crop Abstr.; Indian Geosci. Abstr.; INSPEC (Feb. 1980-); Math. Rev.; Met. Abstr.; Refer. Z.; Res. Alert [Full Cov.]; Rev. Plant Pathol.; Sci. Cit. Index; SCISEARCH.

ISSN 0145-7594
US
CODEN PSHMDR
PROCEEDINGS OF THE INTERNATIONAL SCHOOL OF HYDROCARBON MEASUREMENT. [Proc. Int. Sch. Hydrocarbon Meas.]. **Main/Conf** International School of Hydrocarbon Measurement. (19??)-. Academic Scholarly Publication. English. One time a year (May). $35.00. University of Oklahoma / Norman, F 339 / 100 East Boyd, Norman OK 73109. **Tel** (405)325-4394. Documents available from Article Express International, CASDDS.
Ind/Abst Chem. Abstr.; Curr. Cit.; Eng. Index Annu.

LC Q57 .P762   **ISSN** 0924-8323
NE
CODEN PKNSEK
PROCEEDINGS OF THE KONINKLIJKE NEDERLANDSE AKADEMIE VAN WETENSCHAPPEN (1990). See Biology.

ISSN 0557-1588
US
CODEN PRAWAC
PROCEEDINGS OF THE ROBERT A. WELCH FOUNDATION CONFERENCES ON CHEMICAL RESEARCH. [Proc. Robert A. Welch Found. Conf. Chem. Res.]. **Added/Corp** Robert A. Welch Foundation. (1957)-. Academic Scholarly Publication. English. One time a year. Robert A. Welch Foundation, 4605 Post Oak Place, Suite 200, Houston TX 77027. **Tel** (713)961-9884. Documents available from CASDDS.
Ind/Abst Chem. Abstr.

LC TP1180.P8 S66a   **ISSN** 0740-8897
DD 668.4/239/05   US
CODEN PSACEV
PROCEEDINGS OF THE SPI ... ANNUAL TECHNICAL/MARKETING CONFERENCE. [Proc. SPI annu. Tech./mark. Conf.]. **Added/Corp** Society of the Plastics Industry. Polyurethane Division. **VFOAT** Proceedings of the S.P.I. Annual Technical/Marketing Conference. **VAT** Proceedings of the Society of the Plastics Industry Annual Technical Marketing Conference. 27th (Oct. 20-22, 1982)-. Academic Scholarly Publication. English. One time a year. Technomic Pub. Co., PO Box 913, 265 Post Road West, Westport CT 06881. Documents available from CASDDS. **Continues** Society of the Plastics Industry. Urethane Division. Technical Conference.

Chemistry and Chemicals

Proceedings of the Annual Urethane Division, Technical Conference, 0271-1109.
Ind/Abst Chem. Abstr.

ISSN 0093-450X
US
NLM W3 PH51   **CODEN** PPMSDF
PROCEEDINGS - PHILIP MORRIS SCIENCE SYMPOSIUM. See Science and Technology.

ISSN 0032-9673
IT
SUSPENDED
PRODOTTO CHIMICO & AEROSOL SELEZIONE. [Prod. chim. aerosol sel.]. VFOAT
Prodotto Chimico e Aerosol Selezione; Prodotto Chimico. (19??)-(Dec. 1992). Academic Scholarly Publication. Italian. Twelve times a year. Athena, Via Dei Ciclamini 11, 20147 Milan Italy. Documents available from CASDDS.
Continues Prodotto Chimico.
Ind/Abst Chem. Abstr.; Curr. Biotechnol.

ISSN 0084-6376
US
UDC 54(060.21)(73)
PROFESSIONAL DIRECTORY / THE AMERICAN INSTITUTE OF CHEMISTS.
Main/Corp American Institute of Chemists. 1981-. Directory. English. One time a year. $35.00. American Institute of Chemists, 7315 Wisconsin Avenue, Suite 518 E, Bethesda MD 20814. **Tel** (301)652-2447. **ED** David A H Roethel. **Ad Acc. Circ:** 7,000. **Continues** Membership Directory / American Institute of Chemists.
Desc: Comprehensive listing of members of American Institute of Chemists by name, address, telephone, employer, position title, job responsibility, field of chemistry and highest degree.

ISSN 1047-8329
US
DD 540   CCC
PROFILES, PATHWAYS, AND DREAMS. See Biographies.

LC QD399 .P76
UK
CODEN PRHCEP
PROGRESS IN HETEROCYCLIC CHEMISTRY. Added/Corp International Society of Heterocyclic Chemistry. VFOAT
Heterocyclic Chemistry. Vol. 1 (1989)-. Academic Scholarly Publication. English. One time a year. $128.00. Pergamon Press, An Imprint of Elsevier Science Ltd., The Boulevard, Langford Lane, Kidlington, Oxford OX5 1GB United Kingdom. **Tel** 011 44 1865 843000, 011 44 1865 843699, FAX 011 44 1865 843010. Documents available from CASDDS.
Ind/Abst Chem. Abstr.; Curr. Cit.

ISSN 0920-9832
NE
NLM W1; PR67GR   **CODEN** PRHPEU
PROGRESS IN HPLC. [Prog. HPLC]. VAT
Progress in High Performance Liquid Chromatography. Vol. 1 (1985)-. Academic Scholarly Publication. English. Irregular. Price varies per volume. VSP International Science Publishers, Godfried van Seystlaan 47, 3703 BR Zeist Netherlands. **Tel** 011 31 3404 25700, FAX 011 31 3404 32081, telex 40217 USP NL. **(Subscription address:** Books International Inc., PO Box 605, Herndon VA 22070. **Tel** (703)435-7064.**)** Documents available from CASDDS.
Ind/Abst Chem. Abstr. (1985-).

LC RM30 .P7   **ISSN** 0079-6468
DD 615.19082
NE
CCC
NLM W1 PR6717   **CODEN** PMDCAY
Pr Rev.
PROGRESS IN MEDICINAL CHEMISTRY. See Pharmacy and Pharmacology.

LC QP552.L5 P76   **ISSN** 0168-9614
DD 574.19/2454
NE
NLM W1; PR678C   **CODEN** PPLIEF
PROGRESS IN PROTEIN-LIPID INTERACTIONS. [Prog. protein-lipid interact.]. VFOAT
Progress in Protein Lipid Interactions. Vol. 1 (1985)-. Academic Scholarly Publication. English. Irregular. Price varies per volume. Elsevier Science Publishing Company Inc, Madison Square Station, PO Box 882, New York NY 10159-0882. **Tel** (212)633-3950, FAX (212)633-3990. Documents available from CASDDS.
Ind/Abst Chem. Abstr. (1985-).

LC QD1 .I88152   **ISSN** 0033-4545
UK
CCC
NLM W1 PU963   **CODEN** PACHAS
Pr Rev.
PURE AND APPLIED CHEMISTRY. [Pure appl. chem.]. Added/Corp International Union of Pure and Applied Chemistry. VFOAT
Chimie Pure et Appliquee. Vol. 1 (1960)-. Academic Scholarly Publication. English (French and German). Twelve times a year. $950.00. Blackwell Scientific Publications Ltd, Marston Book Services, PO Box 88, Oxford OX2 ONE United Kingdom. **Tel** 011 44 1865 206206, FAX 011 44 1865 206219, telex 837 515 MARDIS G. **ED** P. D. Gujral. Index available (bound in last issue). cum. index. **Ad Acc. Circ:** 1,550 (ctrl). available on microfilm and microfiche from University Microfilms International (UMI). Documents available from The Genuine Article, BIOSIS Document Express, Ask*IEEE, CASDDS, ADONIS.
Desc: An interdisciplinary journal which presents the results of major research in all areas of chemistry.
Ind/Abst ADONIS; AGRICOLA; Anal. Abstr.; Art Archaeol. Tech. Abstr.; Biol. Abstr.; Ceram. Abstr. (19??-); Chem Inform; Chem. Abstr.; Coal Abstr.; Curr. Biotechnol.; Curr. Cit.; Curr. Contents Phys. Chem. Earth Sci.; EMBASE; GeoRef; Hortic. Abstr.; HTFS Dig.; INSPEC (1971-); Int. Aerosp. Abstr.; Leadscan; Methods Organ. Synth.; NAPRALERT; Nat. Prod. Updates; Polymer Contents; Res. Alert [Full Cov.]; Risk Abstr.; Sci. Cit. Index; SCISEARCH; Wheat Barley Trit. Abstr.

ISSN 0285-192X
JA
DD 615
PURE CHEMICALS DAIICHI. [Pure chem. Daiichi]. (1970)-. Academic Scholarly Publication.
Japanese. Four times a year. Daiichi Kagaku Yakuhin K.K., (Daiichi Pure Chemicals Co. Ltd.), 13-5 Nihonbashi 3 Chome, Chuoku Tokyo 103 Japan. Documents available from CASDDS.
Ind/Abst Chem. Abstr.

LC RM301.42 Q35   **ISSN** 0931-8771
DD 615/.7
GW
CCC
NLM W1; QU158MGF
Pr Rev.
QUANTITATIVE STRUCTURE-ACTIVITY RELATIONSHIPS. See Pharmacy and Pharmacology.

ISSN 0213-4152
SP
UDC 66
QUIMICA 2000. [Quimica 2000]. VFOAT Quimica Dos Mil. (1985)-. Periodical. Spanish. Twelve times a year. $100.00. Ediciones Tecnicas Izaro, Mazustegui 21, 48006 Bilbao Spain. **Tel** 011 34 94 415-9022.

ISSN 0213-7828
SP
UDC 54
QUIMICA HOY. (1984)-. Periodical. Spanish.
Eleven times a year. $100.00 Europe (except Spain); $115.00 other. Quimica Hoy, Santiago de Compostela 64, 28034 Madrid Spain. **Tel** 011 34 1 7305801, 011 34 1 7306601, FAX 011 34 1 2019358.

LC QD1 .Q55   **ISSN** 0100-4042
DD 540/.5
BL
CODEN QUNODK
QUIMICA NOVA. [Quim. nova]. Added/Corp Sociedade Brasileira de Quimica. (1978)-. Academic Scholarly Publication. Portuguese (English). Four times a year. Sociedade Brasileira de Quimica, CP 20 780 SBQ, Insti Quim USP, 01000 Sao Paulo, SP Brazil. Documents available from CASDDS.
Ind/Abst Chem. Abstr.

LC QD601.A1 I54   **ISSN** 0969-806X
UK
CCC
●RADIATION PHYSICS AND CHEMISTRY. See Physics-Light, Optics, Radiation.

ISSN 1066-3622
US
CCC
NLM W1; RA265P
●RADIOCHEMISTRY (NEW YORK, N.Y.). (RADIOCHEMISTRY.). (1993)-. Periodical. English. Six times a year. $1375.00. Consultants Bureau, A Division of Plenum Publishing Corporation, 233 Spring Street, New York NY 10013. **Tel** (212)620-8000, (212)620-8466, FAX (212)463-0742, telex 23/421139. **Continues** Soviet Radiochemistry, 0038-576X.
Ind/Abst Curr. Cit.; Sci. Cit. Index.

LC TP315   **ISSN** 0253-2409
DD 662/.6/05
CC
UDC 662.7
CODEN RHXUD8
RANLIAO HUAXUE XUEBAO. See Energy.

LC QD49.F7 F73A
DD 540/.7/2044
FR
UDC 54(047.31)(44)
RAPPORT NATIONAL DE CONJONCTURE SCIENTIFIQUE : CHIMIE. Main/Corp France. Centre National de la Recherche Scientifique. Comite National de la Recherche Scientifique. (19??)-. French. CNRS / Institut d'Information Scientifique et Technique, (Centre National de la Recherche Scientifique), 15 Quai Anatole France, 75700 Paris France. **Tel** 011 33 1 47531515, FAX 011 33 1 45517307, telex 260034.

LC QD1 .R225   **ISSN** 0379-7635
II
UDC 54
CODEN RSSKAR
RASAYANA SAMIKSHA. Vol. 1 (March 1974)-.
Academic Scholarly Publication. Hindi (summaries and/or abstracts in English). Rs40.00. Rajasthana Hindi Grantha Akadamy, A-26/2 Vidyalaya Marg Tilak Nagay, Jaipur 302004 India. **Tel** 46210. **ED** Emeritus R C Mehrotra and R K Mehrotra. **Ad Acc. Circ:** 200. Documents available from CASDDS.
Desc: Presents review articles on the latest developments in chemistry through the medium of Hindi (the national language of India).
Ind/Abst Chem. Abstr.

LC TP1 .R34   **ISSN** 0033-9334
IT
CODEN RACHAG
RASSEGNA CHIMICA. Added/Corp Unione Nazionale Chimici Italiani. Vol. 1 (Jan. 1949)-. Academic Scholarly Publication. Italian (English). Six times a year. L102190. Tecnindustria SRL, Via Crescenzio 43, 00193 Rome Italy. **Tel** 011 39 6 6875657. **ED** Dott M. Ragno. cum. index. **Bk Rev. Ad Acc. Circ:** 2,000 (ctrl). Documents available from CASDDS.
Desc: Experimental papers and updated articles on analytical and instrumental techniques, new products and materials, ecology, chemistry, and society news on materials, plants, processes, equipments, events. etc.
Ind/Abst Chem. Abstr.; Curr. Biotechnol.; Dairy Sci. Abstr.; Food Sci. Technol. Abstr.

ISSN 1353-1190
UK
DD 507.1241
●REACTION! DEDDINGTON. (REACTION!). [Reaction! Deddington]. (1994)-. English. Three times a year (Sept., Jan., Apr.). $35.68. Philip Allan Publishers Ltd., Market Place, Deddington, Oxfordshire OX15 0SE United Kingdom. **Tel** 011 44 1869 338652, FAX 011 44 1869 338803. **Continues** Eureka! (Deddington), 0968-6495.

US
REAGENT CHEMICALS : AMERICAN CHEMICAL SOCIETY SPECIFICATIONS.
Main/Corp American Chemical Society Committee on Analytical Reagents. **Added/Corp** American Chemical Society. 1st Edition (1950)-. English. Irregular (published every 5 years). $98.95. American Chemical Society, 1155 Sixteenth Street Northwest, Washington DC 20036. **Tel** (800)333-9511, (800)227-5558, (614)447-3776, FAX (202)447-3671. **(Subscription address:** American Chemical Society / Ohio, Department L 0011, Columbus OH 43268-0011. **)**

LC QP   **ISSN** 1060-6823
DD 612
SZ
CCC
NLM W1; RE107KT   **CODEN** RCHAE4
●RECEPTORS & CHANNELS. [Recept. channels]. VFOAT Receptors and Channels. Vol. 1, Issue 1 (1993)-. Periodical. English. Four times a year. $588.00 (university and hospital libraries), $916.00 (all except university and hospital libraries). Harwood Academic Publishers, PO Box 90, Reading RG1 8JL United Kingdom. **Tel** 011 44 1734 560080, FAX 011 44 1734 568211.
Desc: Covers research on receptors and ion channels. Brings together studies on these and the related signaling elements at the levels of molecular biology and genetics, biochemistry, physical analysis, molecular modeling, immunology, molecular pharmacology and eletrophysiology.
Ind/Abst Index Med.

ISSN 0776-3093
BE
UDC 543.54
RECORDER WEVELGEM. (RECORDER.). [Recorder Wevelgem]. (Feb. 1987)-. Periodical. English. Twelve times a year. $460.59. Recorder BVBA, PO Box 42, 8820 Torhout, Belgium. **Tel** 011 32 50 222626. FAX 011 32 50 222626. **ED** Dr. G. Redant. Index available (Included in Dec. issue). cum. index. ctrl circ.

LC QD1 .R3   **ISSN** 0165-0513
DD 540/.5
NE
CCC
NLM W1; RE115M   **CODEN** RJRSDK
Pr Rev.
RECUEIL DES TRAVAUX CHIMIQUES DES PAYS-BAS (1920). (RECUEIL : JOURNAL OF THE ROYAL NETHERLANDS CHEMICAL SOCIETY.). [Recl. trav. chim. Pays-Bas]. Added/Corp Koninklijke Nederlandse Chemische Vereniging. VFOAT
Recueil des Travaux Chimiques des Pays-Bas; Journal of the Royal Netherlands Chemical Society. Vol. 93, No. 1 (1974)-. Academic Scholarly Publication. English (French and German; summaries and/or abstracts in French and German). Twelve times a year (1 volume). Fl829.00. Elsevier Science Publishers BV, PO Box 211, 1000 AE Amsterdam Netherlands. **Tel** 011 31 20 4853641, 011 31 20 4853642, FAX 011 31 20 4853598. **ED** J. Reedijk. Index available. **Bk Rev. Ad Acc.** available in microform from University Microfilms International (UMI); available on microfilm from University Microfilms International

(UMI); available on an online database from Elsevier Electronic Subscriptions (EES). Documents available from CASDDS. ***Continues*** *Recueil des Travaux Chimiques des Pays-Bas (Leiden, Netherlands : 1920), 0165-0513.*
Desc: Contains exclusively English language papers on organic chemistry and related fields such as organometallic and bioorganic chemistry.
Ind/Abst Abstr. Bull. Inst. Pap. Sci. Tech.; Anal. Abstr.; Chem. Abstr. (1980-1984); Leadscan; Methods Organ. Synth.; Nat. Prod. Updates; PESTDOC (1980-1984).

LC QD1 .A3763 **ISSN** 0486-2325
RU
NLM ZQD 1 R332 **CODEN** RZKHAR
REFERATIVNYI ZHURNAL. KHIMIIA / AKADEMIIA NAUK SSSR, INSTITUT NAUCHNOI INFORMATSII. **Added/Corp** Institut Nauchnoi Informatsii (Akademiia Nauk SSSR) Vsesoiuznyi Institut Nauchnoi i Tekhnicheskoi Informatsii (Soviet Union). **VFOAT** Khimiia. (Oct. 1953)-. Abstracting/Indexing Service. Russian. Twenty-four times a year. VINITI - Vsesoyuznyi Institut Nauchno-Tekhnicheskoi Informatsii, All-Union Scientific and Technical Information Institute, Baltiiskaia ulitsa 14, 125219 Moscow Russia. **Tel** 011 7 95 2384600, FAX 011 7 95 9430060, telex 411160. Documents available from CASDDS.
Ind/Abst Chem. Abstr.

US
REGISTRY HANDBOOK. COMMON NAMES. MICROFORM. **Added/Corp** American Chemical Society. Chemical Abstracts Service. **VFOAT** CAS Registry Handbook. Common Names; CAS Registry Handbook-Common Names. (19??)-. English. $1110.00. Chemical Abstracts Service, (Subsidiary of The American Chemical Society), 2540 Olentangy River Road, PO Box 3012, Columbus OH 43210-0012. **Tel** (614)447-3731, (800)753-4227, FAX (614)447-3751. **(Subscription address:** Chemical Abstracts Service, Customer Service Department, PO Box 3012, Columbus OH 43210. **Tel** (800)848-6538, (614)447-3600.**)** available on microfilm.

US
REGISTRY HANDBOOK: NUMBER SECTION. SUPPLEMENT. **Main/Corp** Chemical Abstracts Service. **Added/Corp** American Chemical Society. (1972)-. Periodical. English. One time a year. $480.00. Chemical Abstracts Service, (Subsidiary of The American Chemical Society), 2540 Olentangy River Road, PO Box 3012, Columbus OH 43210-0012. **Tel** (614)447-3731, (800)753-4227, FAX (614)447-3751. **(Subscription address:** Chemical Abstracts Service, Customer Service Department, PO Box 3012, Columbus OH 43210. **Tel** (800)848-6538, (614)447-3600.**)** **ED** David W Weisgerber. **Bk Rev.**
Desc: Current-awareness bulletins on 164 separately-subscribed-to topics. Contains CA abstracts and associated bibliographic information.

ISSN 1058-1707
DD 540 US
REGULATED CHEMICALS DIRECTORY. [Regul. chem. dir.]. **Added/Corp** ChemADVISOR, Inc. (1992)-. Directory. English. One time a year. $375.00. Routledge Chapman & Hall Inc., 29 West 35th Street, New York NY 10001. **Tel** (212)244-3336, (212)244-6412.

LC TP12 .N86
DD 660/.25/45 IT
UDC 338.3:661
REPERTORIO CHIMICO ITALIANO. Trade Publication. Italian. Irregular (every four years). L390000. Dott M Ragno, Tecnindustria SRL, Via Crescenzio, 43 - 00193 Rome Italy. **Tel** 06/6875657. **ED** M Ragno. Index available. **Ad Acc. Circ:** 3,000 (ctrl). ***Continues*** *Repertorio della Produzione Chimica Italiana e del Commercio Chimico.*
Desc: Concerned with Italian and foreign chemical products and equipment; firms producing and trading chemical products; firms supplying chemical and ecology equipment; analysis, control and research laboratories; and consultation offices.

ISSN 0557-4048
UK
REPORT OF THE COUNCIL. **Main/Corp** Royal Institute of Chemistry, London. (19??)-. English. One time a year. Royal Institue of Chemistry, London.

LC TP193.G7 L7
DD 542.0942 UK
REPORT OF THE GOVERNMENT CHEMIST. **Main/Corp** London. Laboratory of the Government Chemist. **Added/Corp** London. Laboratory of the Government Chemist. Report of the Principal Chemist of the Government Laboratory upon the Work of the Laboratory. London. Laboratory of the Government Chemist. Report upon the Work. (19??)-. English. One time a year. Her Majesty's Stationery Office, 51 Nine Elms Lane, London SW8 5DR United Kingdom. **Tel** 011 44 171 8738459, 011 44 171 8738499, FAX 011 44 171 8738499, 011 44 171 8738456, telex 297138. **(Subscription address:** Her Majesty's Stationery Office, PO Box 276, Public Centre, London SW8 5DT United Kingdom. **Tel** 011 44 171 87384998456.**)**
Ind/Abst Food Sci. Technol. Abstr.

LC TP690.A1 A7418 **ISSN** 0190-8715
DD 665.5/05 US
REPORTS ON RESEARCH ASSISTED BY THE PETROLEUM RESEARCH FUND. See Petroleum and Natural Gas.

LC Q
DD 500 US
RESEARCH IN PROGRESS. PHYSICS, CHEMISTRY, BIOLOGICAL SCIENCES, MATHEMATICS, ENGINEERING SCIENCES, METALLURGY AND MATERIALS SCIENCE, GEOSCIENCES, ELECTRONICS, EUROPEAN RESEARCH PROGRAM / U.S. ARMY RESEARCH OFFICE. See Physics.

LC TP196 .A95a **ISSN** 0814-9992
DD 660/.05 AT
CODEN RACCE5
RESEARCH REVIEW / DIVISION OF CHEMICAL AND WOOD TECHNOLOGY. [Res. rev. - Div. Chem. Wood Technol.]. **Main/Corp** Commonwealth Scientific and Industrial Research Organization (Australia). Division of Chemical and Wood Technology. **Added/Corp** Commonwealth Scientific and Industrial Research Organization (Australia). Institute of Industrial Technology. (1983)-. English. One time a year. Free. CSIRO Publications, PO Box 89, 314 Albert Street, East Melborne Victoria 3002 Australia. **Tel** 011 61 3 4187333, 4187217, FAX 011 61 3 4190459, telex AA 30236. **ED** Kevin F. Jeans. **Circ:** 3,000. Documents available from BIOSIS Document Express. ***Continues*** *Commonwealth Scientific and Industrial Research Organization (Australia). Division of Chemical Technology. Research Review, 0312-9225.*
Desc: Outlines current research undertaken by the division in biotechnology, water purification, chemistry and forestry, including development of cellulose for a variety of products.
Ind/Abst Abstr. Bull. Inst. Pap. Sci. Tech.; AGRICOLA; Biol. Abstr.

ISSN 0250-5460
BO
CODEN RBQUDX
REVISTA BOLIVIANA DE QUIMICA. [Rev. boliv. quim.]. **Added/Corp** Universidad Boliviana (System). (1977)-. Periodical. Spanish. Universidad Mayor de San Andres, Centro Nacional de Documentation Cientifica y Tecnologica, Casilla 3283, La Paz Bolivia. Documents available from CASDDS.
Ind/Abst Chem. Abstr.

LC TP1 .R36 **ISSN** 0370-3797
DD 660.05 BL
CODEN RBQSAO
REVISTA BRASILEIRA DE QUIMICA. (REVISTA BRASILEIRA DE CHIMICA (SCIENCIA & INDUSTRIA).). [Rev. bras. quim.]. **VFOAT** Revista Brasileira de Quimica (Ciencia & Industria); Revista Brasileira de Chimica; Revista Brasileira de Quimica. Vol. 1, No. 1 (Jan. 1936)-. Periodical. Portuguese. Twelve times a year. Documents available from CASDDS.
Ind/Abst Ceram. Abstr.; Chem. Abstr. (1936-1979).

ISSN 1015-8553
CU
SUSPENDED
REVISTA CENIC. [Rev. CENIC, Cienc. quim.]. **VFOAT** Ciencias Quimicas. Vol. 17, No. 1-2 (1986)-?. Periodical. Spanish (Spanish). Three times a year. Ediciones Cubanas, Obispo 527 Altos ESQ Bernaza, CP 10100 Havana Cuba. Documents available from BIOSIS Document Express. ***Continues*** *Revista de Ciencias Quimicas.*
Ind/Abst Biol. Abstr.

LC RS402 .R47 **ISSN** 0034-7418
CK
NLM W1 RE356E **CODEN** RCQFAQ
REVISTA COLOMBIANA DE CIENCIAS QUIMICO-FARMACEUTICAS. See Pharmacy and Pharmacology.

LC QD1 .R327 **ISSN** 0120-2804
DD 540 CK
CODEN RCLQAY
REVISTA COLOMBIANA DE QUIMICA. [Rev. Colomb. quim.]. **Added/Corp** Colombia. Universidad, Bogota. Departamento de Quimica. Vol. 1 (1971)-. Periodical. Spanish. Documents available from CASDDS. ***Continues*** *Universidad Nacional de Colombia. Departamento de Quimica. Revista - Universidad Nacional de Colombia. Departamento de Quimica, 0120-2154.*
Ind/Abst Chem. Abstr.

ISSN 0258-5995
CU
CODEN RCQUE7
REVISTA CUBANA DE QUIMICA. [Rev. cuba. quim.]. Academic Scholarly Publication. Spanish. Four times a year. $15.00. Ediciones Cubanas, Obispo 527 Altos ESQ Bernaza, CP 10100 Havana Cuba. Documents available from CASDDS.
Ind/Abst Chem. Abstr. (1985-).

ISSN 0034-7752
RM
CODEN RCBUAU
Pr Rev.
REVISTA DE CHIMIE. **Added/Corp** Asociatia Stiintifica a Inginerilor si Tehnicienilor din Republica Populara Romana. Romania. Ministerul Industriei Metalurgice si Industriei Chimice. Romania. Ministerul Industriei Chimice. Romania. Ministerul Industriei Petrolului si Chimiei. Vol. 1 (1950)-. Periodical. Romanian. Twelve times a year. $169.00. **(Subscription address:** Orion Press SRL, SPL Independentei 202-A, Bucharest 6 Romania. **Tel** 011 401 3122425.**)** Documents available from The Genuine Article, CASDDS.
Desc: Publishes articles on all the matters relative to the chemical industry.
Ind/Abst Anal. Abstr.; Ceram. Abstr.; Chem. Abstr.; Chem. Hazards Ind.; Coal Abstr.; Curr. Biotechnol.; Curr. Cit.; Curr. Contents Eng. Comput. Technol.; Lab. Hazards Bull.; Res. Alert [Full Cov.]; Saf. Health Work; Soc. Sci. Cit. Index [Select. Cov.]; Surf. Treat. Technol. Abstr.

LC QC1 .R417
RM
REVISTA DE FIZICA SI CHIMIE. See Physics.

LC QD1 .S31153 **ISSN** 0583-7693
DD 540/.5 MX
NLM W1 RE415R **CODEN** RSQMAN
REVISTA DE LA SOCIEDAD QUIMICA DE MEXICO. [Rev. Soc. Quim. Mex.]. **Main/Corp** Sociedad Quimica de Mexico. Vol. 1 (Mar. 1957)-. Periodical. Spanish. Six times a year. $60.00. Sociedad Quimica de Mexico, Mar del Notre 5 Col S Alvaro, 02090 Mexico 4 DF Mexico. **Tel** 011 52 3862905 or, 3860255. Documents available from CASDDS.
Ind/Abst Chem. Abstr.

ISSN 0035-0419
UDC 54 PO
CODEN RPTQAT
REVISTA PORTUGUESA DE QUIMICA. [Rev. port. quim.]. (March 1958)-. Academic Scholarly Publication. Portuguese (English, Spanish and French). Four times a year. $18.00. Sociedade Portuguesa de Quimica, Ave da Republica 37-4, 1000 Lisbon Portugal. **ED** M A V Ribeiro da Silva. Index available. cum. index (annual). **Ad Acc. Circ:** 4,000. Documents available from CASDDS. ***Continues*** *Revista de Quimica Pura e Aplicada.*
Desc: Original papers, research notes and review articles in all subjects of chemistry.
Ind/Abst Art Archaeol. Tech. Abstr.; Chem. Abstr.

LC QD1 .R43 **ISSN** 0035-3930
RM
Pr Rev.
REVUE ROUMAINE DE CHIMIE. **Added/Corp** Academia Republicii Populare Romine. Academia Republicii Socialiste Romania. Vol. 1 (1956)-. Periodical. English (French, German, Russian, Spanish and English). Twelve times a year. $242.00. Editions de l'Academie Republique Popul., Bucharest Romania. **(Subscription address:** Orion Press SRL, SPL Independentei 202-A, Bucharest 6 Romania. **Tel** 011 401 3122425.**)** Documents available from The Genuine Article, CASDDS. ***Continues*** *Revue de Chimie.*
Desc: Publishes studies on chemistry.
Ind/Abst Abstr. Bull. Inst. Pap. Sci. Tech.; Anal. Abstr.; Ceram. Abstr.; Chem Inform; Chem. Abstr.; Chem. Titles; Curr. Chem. React.; Curr. Cit.; Curr. Contents Phys. Chem. Earth Sci.; Curr. Titles Electrochem.; Index Chem.; Leadscan; Methods Organ. Synth.; Nat. Prod. Updates; Res. Alert [Full Cov.]; Sci. Cit. Index; SCISEARCH; World Surf. Coat. Abstr.

IT
TITLE CHANGE
RICH MAC MAGAZINE. (19??)-(1995). English (Italian). Editrice Bias, Viale Premuda 2, 20129 Milan Italy. **Tel** 011 39 2 55181842. ***Merged into*** *La Chimica e l'Industria.*

ISSN 0370-5633
JA
NLM W1 RI2164K **CODEN** RIKAAN
RINSHO KAGAKU. (RINSHO KAGAKU. JAPANESE JOURNAL OF CLINICAL CHEMISTRY.). [Rinsho kagaku]. **Added/Corp** Nippon Rinsho Kagaku Kenkyukai. **VFOAT** Japanese Journal of Clinical Chemistry. (197?)-. Academic Scholarly Publication. Japanese (table of contents in English). Twelve times a year. $376.50. Japanese Journal of Clinical Chemistry, 1-50 Fukushima 1-chome, Fukushima-ku 545 Osaka Japan. **(Subscription address:** Japan Publications Trading Company Ltd., PO Box 5030, Tokyo

Chemistry and Chemicals

International, Tokyo 100-31 Japan. **Tel** 011 81 3 3292 3753.) Documents available from CASDDS.
Ind/Abst Chem. Abstr.; EMBASE.

IT
RIVISTA DI CHIMICA. Italian. Twelve times a year. L86000 Italy; L138000 other. Fabbri Rizzoli Edizioni Periodiche s.r.l., Via Mecenate 87-6, 20138 Milan Italy. **Tel** 011 39 2 5095222, FAX 011 39 2 5062865.

LC HD9656.R8 R64   ISSN 0370-6273
DD 338.4/7/66   RM
ROMANIAN JOURNAL OF CHEMISTRY. [Rom. j. chem.]. **Added/Corp** Camera de Comert a Republicii Socialiste Romania. (1971)-. Periodical. English. Four times a year. DM236.00. **(Subscription address:** Kubon & Sagner, ABT Zeitschriftenimport, D 80328 Munich Germany. **Tel** 011 49 89 54218130.)
Desc: Includes articles concerning the production and trading of chemical products equipment.
Ind/Abst Predicasts.

UK
RSC ANALYTICAL SPECTROSCOPY MONOGRAPHS. (19??)-. Monographic series. English. Irregular. Price varies per volume. Royal Society of Chemistry, Thomas Graham House, Science Park, Cambridge CB4 4WF United Kingdom. **Tel** 011 44 1223 420066, FAX 011 44 1223 423623, telex 818293 ROYAL. **(Subscription address:** Royal Society of Chemistry, Turpin Distribution Services Ltd., Blackhorse Road, Letchworth, Hertfordshire SG6 1HN United Kingdom. **Tel** 011 44 1462 672555, FAX 011 44 1462 480947.)

LC TS1870 .R75   ISSN 0035-9475
    US
    CODEN RCTEA4
Pr Rev.
RUBBER CHEMISTRY AND TECHNOLOGY. See Rubber.

LC QD1 .A38143   ISSN 1066-5285
DD 540/.5   US
    CCC
    CODEN RCBUEY
●**RUSSIAN CHEMICAL BULLETIN.** [Russ. chem. bull.]. **Added/Corp** Consultants Bureau. **VFOAT** Izvestiia Akademii Nauk. Seriia Khimicheskaia. Vol. 42, No. 1 (Jan. 1993)-. Bulletin. English (translations available in Russian). Twelve times a year. $1595.00. Consultants Bureau, A Division of Plenum Publishing Corporation, 233 Spring Street, New York NY 10013. **Tel** (212)620-8000, (212)620-8466, FAX (212)463-0742, telex 23/421139. Index available (bound in last issue). **Continues** Bulletin of the Russian Academy of Sciences, Division of Chemical Science, 1063-5211.
Ind/Abst Curr. Cit.; Sci. Cit. Index.

LC QD1 .U713   ISSN 0036-021X
    UK
NLM W1 RU813   CODEN RCRVAB
RUSSIAN CHEMICAL REVIEWS. [Russ. chem. rev.]. **Added/Corp** British Library Lending Division. Chemical Society (Great Britain) Royal Society of Chemistry (Great Britain). (Vol. 29, 1960)-. Academic Scholarly Publication. English (Russian). Twelve times a year. $1090.00. British Library Translated Journals, Boston Spa, Wetherby West Yorkshire LS23 7BQ United Kingdom. **Tel** 011 44 1937 546078, FAX 011 44 1462 480947. **(Subscription address:** Turpin Distribution Services Limited, Blackhorse Road, Letchworth, Hertfordshire SH6 1HN United Kingdom. **Tel** 011 44 1462 672555, FAX 011 44 1462 480947.)
Desc: A cover-to-cover English translation of Uspekhi Khimii. Published in Russia by the Academy of Sciences of the USSR.
Ind/Abst Curr. Cit.; EMBASE; GeoRef; Int. Aerosp. Abstr.; Mass Spect. Bull.; World Surf. Coat. Abstr.; World Text. Abstr.

    ISSN 1070-4272
    US
    CCC
●**RUSSIAN JOURNAL OF APPLIED CHEMISTRY. Added/Corp** Consultants Bureau. (1993)-. Academic Scholarly Publication. English (Russian). Twenty-four times a year. $1565.00. Consultants Bureau, A Division of Plenum Publishing Corporation, 233 Spring Street, New York NY 10013. **Tel** (212)620-8000, (212)620-8466, FAX (212)463-0742, telex 23/421139. Documents available from CASDDS. **Continues** Journal of Applied Chemistry of the USSR, 0021-888X.
Ind/Abst Chem. Abstr.; Coal Abstr.; Curr. Cit.; Energy Res. Abstr.; GeoRef; Pollut. Abstr. Indexes.

    ISSN 1070-3284
    US
    CCC
    CODEN RJCCEY
●**RUSSIAN JOURNAL OF COORDINATION CHEMISTRY. Added/Corp** Consultants Bureau. (1993)-. Periodical. English (translations available in Russian). Twelve times a year. $1025.00. Plenum Press, 233 Spring Street, New York NY 10013-1578. **Tel** (212)620-8000, (212)620-8466, FAX (212)463-0742, (212)807-1047, telex 23/421139. **(Subscription address:** Plenum Press Subscription Department, PO Box 730, Canal Street, Station NY 10013-1578. **Tel** (212)620-8000, (212)620-8466.) **Continues** Koordinatsionnaia Khimiia. English. Soviet Journal of Coordination Chemistry, 0364-4626.
Ind/Abst Curr. Cit.

    ISSN 1070-3632
    US
    CCC
●**RUSSIAN JOURNAL OF GENERAL CHEMISTRY.** (1993)-. Periodical. English. Twenty-four times a year. $1595.00. Consultants Bureau, A Division of Plenum Publishing Corporation, 233 Spring Street, New York NY 10013. **Tel** (212)620-8000, (212)620-8466, FAX (212)463-0742, telex 23/421139. **Continues** Journal of General Chemistry of the USSR, 0022-1279.
Ind/Abst Curr. Cit.

    ISSN 0100-6223
    BL
    CODEN SACCDF
SACCHARUM STAB. (SACCHARUM STAB : REVISTA TRIMESTRAL DA SOCIEDADE DOS TECNICOS ACUCAREIROS DO BRASIL.). [Saccharum STAB]. **Added/Corp** Sociedade dos Tecnicos Acucareiros do Brasil. **VFOAT** Saccharum S.T.A.B. (1978)-. Academic Scholarly Publication. Portuguese. Four times a year. APC Avenida Brigadeiro Luis Antonio 402 7, Andar Caixa Postal 5390, Sao Paulo Brazil. Documents available from CASDDS.
Ind/Abst Biodeter. Abstr. (1991-); Chem. Abstr. (1978-1982); Field Crop Abstr.; Sug. Indus. Abstr.

US
SAFETY IN THE CHEMICAL LABORATORY. (19??)-. Monographic series. English. Irregular. Price varies per volume. Journal of Chemical Education, 1991 Northampton Street, Easton PA 18042-3189. **Tel** (610)250-7264.

    ISSN 1062-936X
DD 600   UK
    CCC
NLM W1; SA9419   CODEN SQERED
●**SAR AND QSAR IN ENVIRONMENTAL RESEARCH.** [SAR QSAR environ. res.]. Vol. 1, No. 1 (1993)-. Periodical. Four times a year. $252.00 (academic institutions), $392.00 (corporate institutions). Gordon & Breach Science Publishers, PO Box 90, Reading, Berkshire RG1 8JL United Kingdom. **Tel** 011 44 1734 560080, FAX 011 44 1734 568211.
Desc: Covers SAR and QSAR models in environmental sciences, agrochemistry, toxicology, pharmacology and applied chemistry.

UN
    CODEN SNTVEB
SBORNIK NAUCHNYKH TRUDOV / VSESOIUZNYI NAUCHNO-ISSLEDOVATELSKII INSTITUT MONOKRISTALLOV, STSINTILLIATSIONNYKH MATERIALOV I OSOBO CHISTYKH KHIMICHESKIKH VESHCHESTV (VNII MONOKRISTALLOV). **Added/Corp** Vsesoiuznyi Nauchno-Issledovatelskii Institut Monokristallov,stsintilliatsionnykh Materialov i Osobo Chistykh Khimicheskikh Veshchestv (Soviet Union). (1978)-. Monographic series. Russian. Documents available from CASDDS.
Ind/Abst Chem. Abstr.

LC TP245.S5 .P73a   ISSN 0139-9683
    XR
SBORNIK VYSOKE SKOLY CHEMICKO-TECHNOLOGICKE V PRAZE. A. Added/Corp Vysoka Skola Chemicko-Technologicka v Praze. **VFOAT** Sbornik VSCHT v Praze. A. (198?)-. Czech (Slovak). Statni Pedagogicke Nakladatelstvi, Ostrovni 30, 113 01 Prague 1 Czech Republic. **Tel** (2)203787, FAX (2)293883. **Continues** Sbornik Vysoke Skoly Chemicko-Technologicke v Praze. Chemie a Technologie Silikatu.

    ISSN 0966-114X
    UK
SCICAT SCIENCE REFERENCE AND INFORMATION SERVICE. See Chemistry and Chemicals-Abstracting, Bibliographies and Statistics.

CC
SCIENCE IN CHINA. SERIES B, CHEMISTRY. English. Six times a year. $240.00. Science Press, 16 Donghuangchenggen North Street, Beijing 100707, People's Republic of China. **Tel** 011 86 1 4019821, 011 86 1 4010642, FAX 011 86 1 4012180, 011 86 1 4019810, telex 210147. **Separated from** Science in China. Series B, Chemistry, Life Sciences & Earth Sciences.

LC QD1 .S26   ISSN 1001-652X
DD 540   CC
NLM W1; SC72P   CODEN SCBSE5
    TITLE CHANGE
SCIENCE IN CHINA. SERIES B, CHEMISTRY, LIFE SCIENCES & EARTH SCIENCES. [Sci. China, Ser. B Chem. life sci. earth sci.]. **Added/Corp** Chung-Kuo ko Hsueh Yuan. **VFOAT** Chemistry, Life Sciences & Earth Sciences; Chemistry, Life Sciences and Earth Sciences. (Jan. 1989)-(1995). Periodical. English. Science Press, 16 Donghuangchenggen North Street, Beijing 100707, People's Republic of China. **Tel** 011 86 1 4019821, 011 86 1 4010642, FAX 011 86 1 4012180, 011 86 1 4019810, telex 210147. **(Subscription address:** Elsevier Science Ltd. / Oxford Fulfillment Centre, PO Box 800, Kidlington OX5 1DX United Kingdom. **Tel** 011 44 865 843355.) **ED** Yan Dongsheng. available on microfilm and microfiche from University Microfilms International (UMI). Documents available from The Genuine Article, BIOSIS Document Express, CASDDS. **Continues** Scientia Sinica. Series B, Chemical, Biological, Agricultural, Medical & Earth Sciences, 0253-5823. **Split into** Science in China. Series B, Chemistry; Science in China. Series C, Life Sciences **and** Science in China. Series D, Earth Sciences.
Desc: Provides regular and rapid reviews of current important developments in scientific research in China for scientific workers in both China and other countries. Includes academic papers in chemistry, life sciences and earth sciences.
Ind/Abst AgBiotech News Inf.; Biol. Abstr.; Chem. Abstr.; Curr. Cit.; Curr. Contents Life Sci.; Ecol. Abstr.; Geogr. Abstr. Phys. Geogr.; GeoRef; Helminthol. Abstr. (1991-); Index Med. (Jan. 1989-); Leadscan; Meteorol. Geoastrophys. Abstr. (199?-); Plant Grow. Reg. Abstr.; Protozoolog. Abstr.; Res. Alert [Full Cov.]; Sci. Cit. Index; SCISEARCH; SEA Abstr.; Soc. Sci. Cit. Index [Select. Cov.]; Soils Fert.; Soyabean Abstr.; Weed Abstr.

LC Q77.T55 A32   ISSN 0040-8808
DD 530.72   JA
    CODEN SRTAA6
SCIENCE REPORTS OF THE RESEARCH INSTITUTES. SERIES A, PHYSICS, CHEMISTRY, AND METALLURGY. See Physics.

LC QD   ISSN 0389-9659
DD 540   JA
    TITLE CHANGE
SEIHIN KAGAKU KENKYUJO KENKYU HOKOKU = BULLETIN OF THE INDUSTRIAL PRODUCTS RESEARCH INSTITUTE. Added/Corp Seihin Kagaku Kenkyujo (Japan). **VFOAT** Bulletin of the Industrial Products Research Institute. (1969)-(1992). Periodical. Japanese (summaries and/or abstracts in English). National Chemical Laboratory for Industry Library, 1-1 Yatabemachi/Higash, Tsukubagun Ibaraki 305 Japan. **Continues** Sangyo Kogei Shikenjo Hokoku. **Merged with** Kagaku Gijyutsu Kenkyujo Hokoku, 0388-3213 **and** Kenkyu Hokoku (Seni Kobunshi Zairyo Kenkyujo (Japan)), 0371-0807 **to form** Busshitsu Kogaku Kogyo Gijyutsu Kenkyujo Hokoku, 0919-7087.

LC S   ISSN 0395-8930
DD 630   FR
UDC 631.52
SEMENCES ET PROGRES. See Agriculture.

LC QA1 .P682   PL
DD 510.(5/6)   CODEN SCUCDH
SERIA CHEMIA. Added/Corp Uniwersytet Im. Adama Mickiewicza W Poznaniu. Wydzia Matematyki, Fizyki I Chemii. No. 11 (1971)-. Academic Scholarly Publication. Polish (summaries and/or abstracts in English). Ul Krakowski Azedmiescie 7, 00-068 Warszawa Poland. Documents available from CASDDS. **Continues** Uniwersytet Im. Adama Mickiewicza W Poznaniu. Wydzia Matematyki, Fizyki I Chemii. Prace Wydziau Matematyki, Fizyki I Chemii. Seria Chemia.
Ind/Abst Chem. Abstr.

    ISSN 0341-1990
    GW
UDC 331.823 613.62/.65 614.8-027
SICHERE CHEMIEARBEIT. [Sich. Chemiearb.]. (1963)-. Periodical. German. Twelve times a year. Free on request. Berufsgenossenschaft Chemischen Industrie, Kurfuersten Anlage 62, D-69115 Heidelberg Germany. **Tel** 011 49 6221 523423, FAX 011 49 6221 523323.
Ind/Abst Chem. Hazards Ind.; Lab. Hazards Bull.

    ISSN 0720-1370
    GW
    CODEN SIUMDL
SICHERHEIT IN CHEMIE UND UMWELT. [Sicherh. Chem. Umwelt]. (1981)-. Academic Scholarly Publication. German. Six times a year. Verlag Umwelt Energiewirtschaf, Hannover 1 Germany. Documents available from CASDDS.
Ind/Abst Chem. Abstr.; EMBASE; Energy Res. Abstr. (March 1982-).

Chemistry and Chemicals

ISSN 0234-968X
RU
SIGNALNAYA INFORMATSIYA KHIMIYA VYSOKIKH ENERGII. Russian. Six times a year. VINITI - Vsesoyuznyi Institut Nauchno-Tekhnicheskoi Informatsii, All-Union Scientific and Technical Information Institute, Baltiiskaia ulitsa 14, 125219 Moscow Russia. **Tel** 011 7 95 2384600, FAX 011 7 95 9430060, telex 411160. **Ad Acc. Circ:** 150 (ctrl).

ISSN 0234-971X
RU
SIGNALNAYA INFORMATSIYA NAPOLNENNYE I ARMIROVANNYE PLASTIKI. (19??)-. Russian. Six times a year. 1.44rub. VINITI - Vsesoyuznyi Institut Nauchno-Tekhnicheskoi Informatsii, All-Union Scientific and Technical Information Institute, Baltiiskaia ulitsa 14, 125219 Moscow Russia. **Tel** 011 7 95 2384600, FAX 011 7 95 9430060, telex 411160. **Ad Acc. Circ:** 385 (ctrl).

ISSN 0234-9701
RU
SIGNALNAYA INFORMATSIYA OCHISTKA I UTILIZATSIYA OTKHODOV KHIMICHESKIK PROIZVODSTV. Russian. Six times a year. VINITI - Vsesoyuznyi Institut Nauchno-Tekhnicheskoi Informatsii, All-Union Scientific and Technical Information Institute, Baltiiskaia ulitsa 14, 125219 Moscow Russia. **Tel** 011 7 95 2384600, FAX 011 7 95 9430060, telex 411160. **Ad Acc. Circ:** 860 (ctrl).

ISSN 0234-9698
RU
SIGNALNAYA INFORMATSIYA SORBENTY POVERKHNOSTNO-AKTIVNYE VESHCHESTVA. Russian. Six times a year. VINITI - Vsesoyuznyi Institut Nauchno-Tekhnicheskoi Informatsii, All-Union Scientific and Technical Information Institute, Baltiiskaia ulitsa 14, 125219 Moscow Russia. **Tel** 011 7 95 2384600, FAX 011 7 95 9430060, telex 411160. **Ad Acc. Circ:** 560 (ctrl).

ISSN 0258-6886
RM
CODEN LSBCDP
... SIMPOZION DE BIODETERIORARE SI CLIMATIZARE, AL. (AL ... SIMPOZION DE BIODETERIORARE SI CLIMATIZARE : COMUNICARI STIINIFICE.). [Simp. biodeterior. clim.]. **Added/Corp** Institutul de Cercetari Pentru Industria Electrotehnica (Romania). **VFOAT** Lucrarile Celui de al ... Simpozion de Biodeteriorare si Climatizare. (19??)-. Academic Scholarly Publication. Romanian. Price varies per volume. Documents available from CASDDS.
Ind/Abst Chem. Abstr.

LC QC176.A1 S615
DD 530.4/1
ISSN 0167-2738
NE
CCC
CODEN SSIOD3
Pr Rev.
SOLID STATE IONICS. See Physics.

LC QD1 .S53
DD 540/.5
ISSN 0379-4350
SA
CCC
CODEN SAJCDG
Pr Rev.
SOUTH AFRICAN JOURNAL OF CHEMISTRY. [S. Afr. j. chem.]. **VFOAT** Suid-Afrikaanse Tydskrif vir Chemie. Vol. 30 (1977)-. Academic Scholarly Publication. English (summaries and/or abstracts in Afrikaans). Four times a year. $42.64. Foundation for Education Science & Technology, PO Box 1758, Pretoria 0001 South Africa. **Tel** 011 27 12 3226404, FAX 011 27 12 3207803. **ED** J. R. Bull. Index available. **Bk Rev. Circ:** 1,800 (ctrl). available on microfilm from University Microfilms International (UMI). Documents available from The Genuine Article, CASDDS. **Continues** South African Chemical Institute. Journal of the South African Chemical Institute.
Desc: Original research articles on any field of chemistry.
Ind/Abst AGRICOLA; Anal. Abstr.; Chem. Abstr.; Chem. Titles; Curr. Cit.; Curr. Contents Phys. Chem. Earth Sci.; EP Collect.; Homework Help.; Mass Spect. Bull.; MasterFile FullTEXT 1000; MasterFile FullTEXT 350; MasterFile FullTEXT 650; MasterFile FullTEXT; OCLC; Pollut. Abstr. Indexes; Res. Alert [Full Cov.]; Sci. Cit. Index; SCISEARCH; Telebase.

ISSN 0306-4352
UK
CODEN SPBAD7
SPECIAL PUBLICATION - BRITISH CARBONIZATION RESEARCH ASSOCIATION. (SPECIAL PUBLICATION.). [Spec. publ. - Br. Carboniz. Res. Assoc.]. **Added/Corp** British Carbonization Research Association. (19??)-. Academic Scholarly Publication. English. Irregular. Price varies per volume. British Carbonization Research Association, Wingerworth Derbyshire. Documents available from CASDDS. **Continues** Special Publication (British Coke Research Association).
Ind/Abst Chem. Abstr. (1975-1982).

LC QD
DD 540
ISSN 0260-6291
UK
CODEN SROCDO
SPECIAL PUBLICATION / ROYAL SOCIETY OF CHEMISTRY. [Spec. publ. - R. Soc. Chem.]. **Added/Corp** Royal Society of Chemistry (Great Britain). No. 37 (1980)-. Academic Scholarly Publication. English. Irregular (publishes four or five times per year). Price varies per volume. Royal Society of Chemistry, Thomas Graham House, Science Park, Cambridge CB4 4WF United Kingdom. **Tel** 011 44 1223 420066, FAX 011 44 1223 423623, telex 818293 ROYAL. (**Subscription address:** Royal Society of Chemistry, Turpin Distribution Services Ltd., Blackhorse Road, Letchworth, Hertfordshire SG6 1HN United Kingdom. **Tel** 011 44 1462 672555, FAX 011 44 1462 480947.) Documents available from BIOSIS Document Express, CASDDS. **Continues** Special Publication (Chemical Society (Great Britain)), 0577-618X.
Ind/Abst Bioeng. Abstr.; Biol. Abstr.; Chem. Abstr.; Curr. Cit.; GeoRef; Nutr. Abstr. Rev., Ser. A, Hum. Exp.

UK
SPECIALIST PERIODICAL REPORTS. (19??)-. Academic Scholarly Publication. English. Irregular. Price varies. Royal Society of Chemistry, Thomas Graham House, Science Park, Cambridge CB4 4WF United Kingdom. **Tel** 011 44 1223 420066, FAX 011 44 1223 423623, telex 818293 ROYAL. (**Subscription address:** Royal Society of Chemistry, Turpin Distribution Services Ltd., Blackhorse Road, Letchworth, Hertfordshire SG6 1HN United Kingdom. **Tel** 011 44 1462 672555, FAX 011 44 1462 480947.)
Desc: Provides reviews of the literature in different chemical subject areas.

ISSN 0262-2262
UK
CODEN SPCHEY
SPECIALTY CHEMICALS (REDHILL). (SPECIALTY CHEMICALS.). [Spec. chem.]. (1981)-. Academic Scholarly Publication. English. Six times a year. $218.75. Argus Press Group, Queensway House, 2 Queensway Redhill, Surrey RH1 1QS United Kingdom. **Tel** 011 44 1737 768611, 011 44 1737 761685, FAX 011 44 1737 760510, telex 948669 TOPJNL G. **ED** Thomas Mulligan. Index available. cum. index. **Bk Rev. Ad Acc** available on an online database (file16/Full-Text) from DIALOG. Documents available from CASDDS.
Desc: Essential reading for all involved in the production, marketing and application of high-cost low volume specialty chemicals.
Ind/Abst Chem. Abstr.; Chem. Bus. Bull.; Chem. Bus. NewsBase (1985-); Chem. Bus. Update; Curr. Biotechnol.; Curr. Cit.; EMBASE; F&S Index Plus Text, Int. [Full Txt.] [Select. Cov.]; Infomat Int. Bus.; PROMT [Full Txt.]; World Surf. Coat. Abstr.

LC QD71
DD 543/.0858/05
ISSN 0712-4813
NE
CODEN SPIJDZ
Pr Rev.
SPECTROSCOPY (OTTAWA, ONT.). See Physics-Light, Optics, Radiation.

GW
SPEZIALINFORMATION DETERGENTIEN. German. Fachinformationszentrum Chemie, Steinplatz 2, D-10623 Berlin Germany. **Tel** 011 49 30 3190030.

GW
SPEZIALINFORMATION KATALYSE. (19??)-. German. Twenty-six times a year. Fachinformationszentrum Chemie, Steinplatz 2, D-10623 Berlin Germany. **Tel** 011 49 30 3190030.

ISSN 0172-6218
GW
CCC
CODEN SSCPDA
SPRINGER SERIES IN CHEMICAL PHYSICS. See Physics.

ISSN 0171-1873
GW
CCC
CODEN SSSSDV
SPRINGER SERIES IN SOLID-STATE SCIENCES. See Physics.

LC QD
DD 540
ISSN 0945-2737
GW
●**STANDORT CHEMIE.** (1994)-. Newspaper. German. Twenty-four times a year. $57.58. VCH Gesellschaft GmbH, Postfach 101161, D-69451 Weinheim Germany. **Tel** 011 49 6201 606459, FAX 011 49 6201 606184. (**Subscription address:** VCH Publishers Inc., 303 Northwest 12th Avenue, Journals Department, Deerfield FL 33442. **Tel** (800)367-8249,

(305)428-5566.) **ED** Ewald Schlueter.
Desc: Covers recent developments in the chemical industry.

LC TP186 .F65a
DD 660
GW
STATISTICHE UUBERSICHTEN : BESTAND UND BEDARF AN CHEMIKERN IN DER CHEMISCHEN INDUSTRIE DER BUNDESREPUBLIK DEUTSCHLAND. See Chemistry and Chemicals-Abstracting, Bibliographies and Statistics.

LC QD49.G3 F66a
DD 540/.7/1143
GW
STATISTISCHE UBERSICHTEN : CHEMIE AN DER HOCHSCHULEN DER BUNDESREPUBLIK DEUTSCHLAND. See Chemistry and Chemicals-Abstracting, Bibliographies and Statistics.

ISSN 1190-9811
DD 382
CN
●**STRATEGIE D'EXPORTATION DU CANADA, PLAN DE PROMOTION DU COMMERCE EXTERIEUR. 7, PRODUITS CHIMIQUES ET PLASTIQUES ET MATERIAUX DE POINTE.** See Plastics.

ISSN 0160-8614
US
CODEN SCKRA9
STREM CHEMIKER, THE. [Strem chem.]. **Added/Corp** Strem Chemicals. (1973)-. Academic Scholarly Publication. English. Irregular. Strem Chemicals Inc, 7 Mulliken Way, Newburyport MA 01950. **Tel** (508)462-3191, FAX (508)465-3191. **Circ:** 35,000. Documents available from CASDDS.
Desc: Short articles in a significant field of chemistry that can be read by people not necessarily in that field.
Ind/Abst Chem. Abstr.

LC Q111 .A28 QD1
DD 505 S 540/.5
UDC 54
SP
STUDIA CHEMICA. 1- 1965-. Spanish. Irregular. 1000ptas Spain and Portugal; 1100ptas Europe; 1200ptas other. Secretariado de Publicaciones E Intercambio, Universidad de Salamanca Cientifico Apartado 2, Salamanca Spain. **Tel** 34-23-231454. **ED** Juhio Casoho Linarejos. Index available. **Circ:** 500 (ctrl).
Desc: Covers studies in chemistry.
Ind/Abst Anal. Abstr.

LC QD1 .C789
DD 540/.5
ISSN 0039-3401
RM
CODEN SUBCAB
Pr Rev.
STUDIA UNIVERSITATIS BABES-BOLYAI. CHEMIA. Main/Corp Universitatea Babes-Bolyai. **Added/Corp** Universitatea "Babes-Bolyai.". Vol. 19, No. 2 (1974)-. Academic Scholarly Publication. English (Romanian, French and German). Two times a year. DM230.00. Biblioteca Centrala Universitara, Str. Clinicilor Nr. 2, 3400 Cluj Napoca Romania. **Tel** 95 117092, FAX 95 117633. (**Subscription address:** Kubon & Sagner, ABT Zeitschriftenimport, D 80328 Munich Germany. **Tel** 011 49 89 54218130.) **Circ:** 300. Documents available from CASDDS. **Continues** Studia Universitatis Babes-Bolyai. Series Chemia, 0039-3401.
Ind/Abst Anal. Abstr.; Chem. Abstr.

US
STUDIES IN NATURAL PRODUCTS CHEMISTRY. (19??)-. Monographic series. English. Price varies per volume. Elsevier Science Publishing Company Inc, Madison Square Station, PO Box 882, New York NY 10159-0882. **Tel** (212)633-3950, FAX (212)633-3990.
Ind/Abst Curr. Cit.

ISSN 0922-5579
NE
CODEN SPLSEA
STUDIES IN POLYMER SCIENCE. [Stud. polym. sci.]. Vol. 1, (1988)-. Academic Scholarly Publication. English. Price varies per volume. Elsevier Science Publishers BV, PO Box 211, 1000 AE Amsterdam Netherlands. **Tel** 011 31 20 4853641, 011 31 20 4853642, FAX 011 31 20 4853598. Documents available from BIOSIS Document Express, CASDDS.
Ind/Abst Biol. Abstr. (1991-); Chem. Abstr.; Curr. Cit.

ISSN 0371-4020
FR
CODEN SUFRA8
SUCRERIE FRANCAISE. (1949)-. Academic Scholarly Publication. French. Irregular. SEPAIC, 42 rue du Louvre, 75001 Paris France. **Tel** 233-61-32, telex 212 646F. Documents available from CASDDS. **Continues** Journal des Fabricants du Sucre.
Ind/Abst Chem. Abstr. (1949-1983); Curr. Cit.; Food Sci.

Chemistry and Chemicals

Technol. Abstr.; Maize Abstr.; Nutr. Abstr. Rev., Ser. A, Hum. Exp.; Soils Fert.; Sug. Indus. Abstr.; Weed Abstr.; World Agric. Econ. Rural Sociol. Abstr.

JA
CODEN SKAADZ
SUMITOMO KAGAKU. [Sumitomo kagaku]. **Added/Corp** Sumitomo Kagaku Kogyo. (1981)-. Academic Scholarly Publication. Japanese. Sumitomo Kagaku Kogyo K.K., (Sumitomo Chemical Co. Ltd.), Shinsumitomo Biru, 5-15 Kitahama Higashiku, Osakashi Osakafu 541, Japan. Documents available from CASDDS.
Ind/Abst Chem. Abstr.

ISSN 0251-1703
SZ
CODEN SCHEDQ
SWISS CHEM. [Swiss chem]. (1979)-. Academic Scholarly Publication. German (French, Italian and English). Twelve times a year. $188.58. Verlag Dr Felix Wuest AG, Seestrasse 5 Postfach, CH-8700 Kuesnacht Switzerland. **Tel** 011 41 1 9110055, FAX 011 41 1 9106080, telex 825705. Index available. ctrl circ. Documents available from CASDDS.
Ind/Abst Biodeter. Abstr. (1991-); Chem. Abstr.; Chem. Bus. Bull.; Chem. Bus. NewsBase (1985-); Chem. Bus. Update; Coal Abstr.; Curr. Cit.; EMBASE; Proc. Chem. Eng.; Theor. Chem. Eng.; World Surf. Coat. Abstr.

ISSN 0348-7180
SW
UDC 54
SYMPOSIUM ON CHEMICAL PROBLEMS CONNECTED WITH THE STABILITY OF EXPLOSIVES. [Symp. chem. probl. connect. stab. explos.]. **VFOAT** Chemical Problems Connected with the Stability of Explosives. (1967)-. English. Every 3 years. Documents available from CASDDS.
Ind/Abst Chem. Abstr.

LC QD1 .A5266
ISSN 0039-792X
DD 540.5
US
SYRACUSE CHEMIST, THE. Added/Corp American Chemical Society. Syracuse Section. (1908)-. Periodical. English. Nine times a year (monthly Sept. through May). $1.50. Bristol Laboratories Inc, Box 657, Syracuse NY 13201.

ISSN 0939-5148
GW
UDC 52/53
TAETIGKEITSBERICHT - MAX-PLANCK-INSTITUT FUER QUANTENOPTIK. See Physics-Light, Optics, Radiation.

LC TP
ISSN 0371-5345
DD 662
JA
UDC 66
TANSO. [Tanso]. **VFOAT** Carbons (Tokyo). (1949)-. Periodical. Japanese. Five times a year. $243.00. Tanso Zairyo Gakkai, (Carbon Soc. of Japan), 32-5 Hongo 3 Chome, Bunkyoku Tokyo 113 Japan. **(Subscription address:** Japan Publications Trading Company Ltd., PO Box 5030, Tokyo International, Tokyo 100-31 Japan. **Tel** 011 81 3 3292 3753.**)** Documents available from CASDDS.
Ind/Abst Ceram. Abstr. (19??-); Chem. Abstr.

US
CODEN TETDE7
TECHNICIANS TODAY. Added/Corp American Chemical Society. Vol. 1, No. 1 (Oct. 1989)-. Periodical. English. Two times a year. ACS, American Chemical Society, 1155 16th Street NW, Washington DC 20036.

ISSN 0245-9639
FR
UDC 54
TECHNIQUES DE L'INGENIEUR. ANALYSE CHIMIQUE ET CARACTERISATION. [Tech. ing., Anal. chim. caracter.]. (1976)-. French. Four times a year. Editions Dussart, rue Colonel Chaltin 103, 1180 Brussels Belgium. **Tel** 011 32 2 3745556. **Continues** Techniques de L'Ingenieur. Mesures et Analyse, 0399-4155.

LC QD61 .T4
ISSN 0082-2531
DD 542
US
CCC
NLM W1 TE197K
CODEN TQCMAT
TECHNIQUES OF CHEMISTRY. [Tech. chem.]. Vol. 1, Pt. 1A (1971)-. Academic Scholarly Publication. English. Irregular. Price varies per volume. John Wiley & Sons, Inc., 605 Third Avenue, New York NY 10158-0012. **Tel** (212)850-6000, (212)850-6645, FAX (212)850-6088, telex 12-7063. **(Subscription address:** John Wiley & Sons / UK, Baffins Lane, Chichester, West Sussex PO19 1UD United Kingdom. **Tel** 011 44 1243 779777, FAX 011 44 243 776128, telex 86290 WIBOOKG.**) ED** A. Weissberger. Documents available from CASDDS. **Formed by the union of** Technique of Inorganic Chemistry **and** Technique of Organic Chemistry.
Ind/Abst Chem. Abstr.

ISSN 0497-2627
UN
CCC
NLM W1 TE42
CODEN TEKHA4
Pr Rev.
TEORETICESKAJA I EKSPERIMENTALNAJA HIMIJA. (TEORETICHESKAIA I EKSPERIMENTALNAIA KHIMIIA.). [Teor. eksp. him.]. **Added/Corp** Akademiia Nauk Ukrainskoi RSR. Viddil Khimii i Khimichnoi Tekhnolohii. Vol. 1 (1965)-. Periodical. Russian (table of contents in English). Six times a year. $109.95. **(Subscription address:** East View Publications Inc., 3020 Harbor Lane North, Suite 110, Minneapolis MN 55447. **Tel** (800)477-1005, (612)550-0961, FAX (612)559-2931.**)** Documents available from The Genuine Article, Ask*IEEE, CASDDS.
Ind/Abst Chem. Abstr.; INSPEC (1968-); Res. Alert [Full Cov.]; Sci. Cit. Index; SCISEARCH.

ISSN 0168-8472
NE
CODEN TNVCE9
TIJDSCHRIFT VAN DE NEDERLANDSE VERENIGING VOOR KLINISCHE CHEMIE. [Tijdschr. Ned. Ver. Klin. Chem.]. **Added/Corp** Nederlandse Vereniging voor Klinische Chemie. (19??)-(Jan. 1995). Periodical. Dutch. Bureau NVKC, Vredenburg 139 A, 3511 BG Utrecht Netherlands. **Tel** 011 31 30 328623, FAX 011 31 30 3111178. **ED** Dr. ir. P.S.H. Kuppens (phone: 00 04950 72630). Documents available from CASDDS. **Continued by** Nederlands Tijdschrift voor Klinische Chemie.
Ind/Abst Chem. Abstr.; Curr. Cit.; EMBASE.

LC QD1 .T59
ISSN 1062-094X
DD 540/.5
US
CCC
CODEN TCWOE7
TODAY'S CHEMIST AT WORK. [Today's chem. work]. **Added/Corp** American Chemical Society. Vol. 1, No. 1 (Apr. 1992)-. Periodical. English. Eleven times a year. $95.00. American Chemical Society, 1155 Sixteenth Street Northwest, Washington DC 20036. **Tel** (800)333-9511, (800)227-5558, (614)447-3776, FAX (202)447-3671. **(Subscription address:** American Chemical Society / New Jersey, PO Box 1781, Riverton NJ 08077.**) ED** Patrick P. McCurdy (editor's telephone: (202)872-6280). **Bk Rev. Ad Acc, Adv Mgr:** Dean Baldwin, **Tel** (908)738-8200. **Acid Free. Circ:** 100,000 (ctrl). **Continues** Today's Chemist, 0896-7067.
Desc: Contains information for the industrial chemist.

NE
TOPICS IN CATALYSIS. (19??)-. English. Four times a year. 271.50F (includes distribution costs). Baltzer Science Publishers BV, Asterweg 1A, 1031 HL Amsterdam Netherlands. **Tel** 011 31 20 6370061, FAX 011 31 20 6323651.

ISSN 1022-5528
NE
CCC
Pr Rev.
●**TOPICS IN CATALYSIS.** (1994)-. Academic Scholarly Publication. English. Four times a year. Baltzer Science Publishers BV, Asterweg 1A, 1031 HL Amsterdam Netherlands. **Tel** 011 31 20 6370061, FAX 011 31 20 6323651.

LC QD1 .F58
ISSN 0340-1022
DD 540.8
GW
CCC
NLM W1 TO539LK
CODEN TPCCAQ
TOPICS IN CURRENT CHEMISTRY. [Top. curr. chem.]. (1973)-. Academic Scholarly Publication. English. $89.50 North America. Springer-Verlag GmbH & Company KG, Heidelberger Platz 3, D-14197 Berlin Germany. **Tel** 011 49 30 8207223, FAX 011 49 30 8214091, telex 183 319 SPBLN D. **(Subscription address:** Springer-Verlag New York Inc. / North America, PO Box 2485, Journal Fulfillment, Secaucus NJ 07096. **Tel** (201)348-4033, (800)777-4643, FAX (201)348-4505.**)** Documents available from The Genuine Article, CASDDS. **Continues** Fortschritte der Chemischen Forschung, 0071-7894.
Ind/Abst Chem Inform; Chem. Abstr.; Curr. Chem. React.; Curr. Cit.; Energy Res. Abstr. (March 1982-); GeoRef; Index Sci. Rev. [Full Cov.]; Int. Aerosp. Abstr.; Res. Alert [Full Cov.]; Sci. Cit. Index; SCISEARCH.

LC QC173.4.P67 T73
ISSN 0169-3913
DD 530.4/75
NE
CCC
CODEN TPMEEI
Pr Rev.
TRANSPORT IN POROUS MEDIA. [Transp. porous media]. **Added/Corp** Kluwer Academic Publishers. **VFOAT** TIPM. Vol. 1, No. 1 (1986)-. Periodical. English. Twelve times a year. $898.00. Kluwer Academic Publishers, Postbus 322, 3300 AH Dordrecht The Netherlands. **Tel** 011 31 78 524400, FAX 011 31 78 183273, telex 20083. **ED** Jacob Bear. **Acid Free.** available on microfilm and microfiche from University Microfilms International (UMI). Documents available from Article Express International, The Genuine Article, Petroleum Abstracts Document Delivery Service, CASDDS.
Desc: Devoted to the presentation of original basic and applied research work on the physical and chemical aspects of transport of extensive quantities such as mass of a fluid phase, mass of a component of a phase, momentum and energy, in single and multiphase flow in a (possibly deformable) porous medium domain, as encountered in a variety of scientific and engineering disciplines: chemical, civil, agricultural, petroleum and mechanical, to mention a few.
Ind/Abst Abstr. Bull. Inst. Pap. Sci. Tech.; Agric. Eng. Abstr. (1991-); Chem. Abstr.; Curr. Cit.; Curr. Contents Eng. Comput. Technol.; Ei Page One; Eng. Index Annu.; Fluid Abstr., Civil Eng.; Fluid Abstr. Proc. (199?-); GeoRef; Geotech. Abstr.; Irr. Drain. Abstr.; Mech. Eng. Abstr.; Pet. Abstr. (1986); Proc. Chem. Eng.; Res. Alert [Full Cov.]; Soils Fert.; Theor. Chem. Eng.

US
TSCA CHEMICALS IN PROGRESS BULLETIN. (1980)-. Bulletin. English. Six times a year. Free. Industry Assistance Office, PS 700 USEPA, Washington DC 20460.
Ind/Abst Chem. Bus. Bull.; Chem. Bus. NewsBase (1988-); Chem. Bus. Update; Ind. Hyg. Dig.

US
TSI JOURNAL OF PARTICLE INSTRUMENTATION. Vol. 1, No. 1 (Jan.-June 1986)-. Periodical. English. Two times a year. TSI Inc, POB 64394, St Paul MN 55164. Documents available from Article Express International. **Continues in part** TSI Quarterly. TSI Incorporated.
Ind/Abst Ei Page One; Eng. Index Annu.

ISSN 1300-0527
DD 546
TU
Pr Rev.
●**TURKISH JOURNAL OF CHEMISTRY.** [Turk. j. chem.]. (1994)-. Periodical. English. Four times a year. $100.00. Scientific and Technical Research Council of Turkey, No. 221, Kavaklidere, 06100 Anakara Turkey. **Tel** 011 90 312 4685300, FAX 011 90 312 4271336. **ED** Bahattin Baysal. **Continues** Doga. Turk Kimya Dergisi, 1010-7614.
Ind/Abst Curr. Cit.

LC QD1 .U4513
ISSN 1063-4568
DD 540
US
CCC
UKRAINIAN CHEMISTRY JOURNAL. [Ukr. chem. j.]. **VFOAT** Ukrainskii Khimicheskii Zhurnal. Vol. 58, 1 (1992)-. Periodical. English (translations available in Russian). Twelve times a year. $995.00. Allerton Press Inc., 150 Fifth Avenue, New York NY 10011. **Tel** (212)924-3950, FAX (212)463-9684, telex 427441 ALPRES. **Continues** Soviet Progress in Chemistry, 0038-5743.
Ind/Abst Curr. Cit.

LC QD1 .U45
ISSN 0041-6045
UN
CCC
Pr Rev.
UKRAINSKII KHIMICHESKII ZHURNAL. [Ukr. him. z.]. **Added/Corp** Akademiia Nauk Ukrainskoi RSR. Otdelenie Khimicheskikh i Geologicheskikh Nauk. Vol. 14 (1948)-. Academic Scholarly Publication. Russian (Ukrainian; summaries and/or abstracts in French and German; table of contents in English). Twelve times a year. $112.95. **(Subscription address:** East View Publications Inc., 3020 Harbor Lane North, Suite 110, Minneapolis MN 55447. **Tel** (800)477-1005, (612)550-0961, FAX (612)559-2931.**)** Documents available from Article Express International, The Genuine Article, CASDDS. **Continues** Ukrainskyi Khemichnyi Zhurnal.
Ind/Abst Abstr. Bull. Inst. Pap. Sci. Tech.; Alum. Ind. Abstr.; Ceram. Abstr.; Chem Inform; Chem. Abstr.; Coal Abstr.; Curr. Contents Phys. Chem. Earth Sci.; Ei Page One; Eng. Index Annu.; Met. Abstr.; Life Sci. Collect.; Potato Abstr.; Res. Alert [Full Cov.]; Sci. Cit. Index; SCISEARCH.

ISSN 1040-3396
DD 540
US
CODEN UNCHE8
UNDERGRADUATE CHEMISTRY. [Undergrad. chem.]. Vol. 1 (1973)-. Monographic series. English. Irregular. Price varies per volume. Marcel Dekker Inc., 270 Madison Avenue, New York NY 10016. **Tel** (212)696-9000, (800)228-1160, FAX (212)685-4540, telex 421419. **(Subscription address:** Marcel Dekker Inc., PO Box 5017, Monticello NY 12701. **Tel** (800)228-1160.**)**
Desc: A series of textbooks covering all aspects of chemistry.

ISSN 1011-2693
AU
UDC 661.879.1
CODEN NU063
URANIUM NEWSLETTER. [Uranium newsl.]. (1987)-. Periodical. English. Irregular. International Atomic Energy Agency / IAEA, Wagramerstrasse 5, PO Box 100, A-1400 Vienna Austria. **Tel** 011 43 1 206021270, FAX 011 43 1 20607. **(Subscription

Chemistry and Chemicals

address: UNIPUB, 4611 F Assembly Drive, Lanham MD 20706. **Tel** (800)274-4888, (301)459-7666.)
Ind/Abst AESIS Q.

LC QD1 .U7 **ISSN** 0042-1308
RU
CCC
NLM W1 US868 **CODEN** USKHAB
Pr Rev.
USPEKHI KHIMII. [Usp. him.]. **Added/Corp** Russian S.F.S.R. Narodnyi Komissariat Prosveshcheniia. Soviet Union. Narodnyi Komissariat Tiazheloi Promyshlennosti. Nauchno-Issledovatelskii Sektor. Upravlenie Vysshei Shkoly Narkomprosa RSFSR. Vsesoiuznoe Khimicheskoe Obshchestvo Im. D.I. Mendeleeva. AAkademiia Nauk SSSR. **VFOAT** Khimicheskii Zhurnal, Seriia G. Vol. 1, (1932)-. Academic Scholarly Publication. Russian. Twelve times a year. $194.00. Izdatelstvo Nauka / Akademiia Nauk, (Publishing House of the Russian Academy of Sciences), Leninskii Porspekt 14, 117901 Moscow Russia. **Tel** 011 95 9542153, FAX 011 95 9382144, telex 411964. **(Subscription address:** Victor Kamkin, 4956 Boiling Brook Parkway, Rockville MD 20852. **Tel** (301)881-5973.) Index available. cum. index. **Circ:** 4,225. Documents available from The Genuine Article, CASDDS.
Ind/Abst Alum. Ind. Abstr.; Ceram. Abstr.; Chem. Abstr.; Chem. Titles; Curr. Biotechnol.; Curr. Contents Phys. Chem. Earth Sci.; Energy Res. Abstr.; Eng. Mater. Abstr.; GeoRef; Index Sci. Rev. [Full Cov.]; Met. Abstr.; Life Sci. Collect.; Res. Alert [Full Cov.]; Sci. Cit. Index; SCISEARCH; Surf. Treat. Technol. Abstr.; World Alum. Abstr.

LC QD1 .U85 **ISSN** 0042-1707
UZ
NLM W1 UZ93N **CODEN** UZKZAC
UZBEKSKII KHIMICHESKII ZHURNAL.
[Uzb. khim. z.]. **Added/Corp** Uzbekiston SSR Fanlar Akademiiasi. (1958)-. Academic Scholarly Publication. Russian (Uzbek). Six times a year. $20.00. Akademiia Nauk Uzbekskoi, Ulitsa Gogolya 70, K 105, 700000 Tashkent Uzbekistan. **(Subscription address:** Victor Kamkin, 4956 Boiling Brook Parkway, Rockville MD 20852. **Tel** (301)881-5973.) Documents available from CASDDS.
Ind/Abst Abstr. Bull. Inst. Pap. Sci. Tech.; AGRICOLA; Chem. Abstr.; Chem. Titles; GeoRef.

ISSN 0231-0775
HU
VEGYIPARI SZAKIRODALMI TAJEKOZTATO MUANYAG- ES GUMIIPARI KULONLENYOMATA. (19??)-. Hungarian. Twelve times a year. Orszagos Muszaki Informacios Kozpont es Konyvtar (O.M.I.K.K.), National Technical Information Centre and Library Museum, Muzeum u. 17, PO Box 12, 1428 Budapest Hungary. **Tel** 011 36 1 1181994, FAX 011 36 1 1382414, telex 22-4944 OMIKK H. **ED** Eszter Molnar. Index available. cum. index. **Bk Rev. Ad Acc. Circ:** 150 (ctrl).
Desc: Information on analytical, inorganic, organic chemistry, physical and theoretical chemistry, and chemical engineering.

LC QD1 .A384925
BW
CODEN VAKNEK
VESCI AKADEMII NAVUK BELARUSI. SERYA HIMICNYH NAVUK. (VESTSI AKADEMII NAVUK BELARUSI. SERYIA KHIMICHNYKH NAVUK.). **Added/Corp** Akademiia Navuk Belarusi. **VFOAT** Seryia Khimichnykh Nauk; Seriia Khimicheskikh Nauk; Izvestiia Akademii Nauk SSSR. Seriia Khimicheskikh Nauk. (1992)-. Academic Scholarly Publication. Byelorussian (summaries and/or abstracts in English). Four times a year. $99.50. Vydavetstvo Navuka i Tekhnika, Zhodzinskaya 18, 220067 Minsk 67 Byelarus. **(Subscription address:** East View Publications Inc., 3020 Harbor Lane North, Suite 110, Minneapolis MN 55447. **Tel** (800)477-1005, (612)550-0961, FAX (612)559-2931.) Documents available from CASDDS.
Continues Vestsi Akademii Navuk BSSR. Seryia Khimichnykh Navuk, 0002-3590.
Desc: Papers on analytical, physical, organic, bioorganic chemistry, high-molecular compound chemistry, applied chemistry and chemical technology.
Ind/Abst Abstr. Bull. Inst. Pap. Sci. Tech.; Alum. Ind. Abstr.; Chem. Abstr.; Coal Abstr.; Energy Res. Abstr.; Int. Aerosp. Abstr.; Met. Abstr.

LC QD1 .K566a **ISSN** 0207-5288
DD 540 UN
VESTNIK KIEVSKOGO UNIVERSITETA. KHIMIIA. **Added/Corp** Kyivskyi Derzhavnyi Universytet im. T.H. Shevchenka. Ukraine. Ministerstvo Vyshchoi i Serednoi Spetsialnoi Osvity. **VFOAT** Khimiia. (19??)-. Russian. Tarasivska 11, Kiev Ukraine.
Continues Kyivskyi Derzhavnyi Universytet im. T.H. Shevchenka. Visnyk Kyivskoho Universytetu. Seriia Khimii, 0372-6088.

ISSN 0579-9384
RU
NLM W1 VE839C **CODEN** VMUKA5
VESTNIK MOSKOVSKOGO UNIVERSITETA. SERIIA II. KHIMIIA.
[Vestn. Mosk. univ. Ser. II]. **Main/Corp** Moskovskii Gosudarstvennyi Universitet Im. M. V. Lomonosova. (1960)-. Academic Scholarly Publication. Russian. Six times a year. $89.95. Izdatelstvo Moskovskogo Universiteta, K-9 Ulitsa Gertsena 5/7, 103009 Moscow Russia. **Tel** (301)881-5973. **(Subscription address:** East View Publications Inc., 3020 Harbor Lane North, Suite 110, Minneapolis MN 55447. **Tel** (800)477-1005, (612)550-0961, FAX (612)559-2931.) Documents available from The Genuine Article, CASDDS.
Supersedes in part Moskovskii Gosudarstvennyi Universitet im. M.V. Lomonosova. Vestnik. Seriia Matematiki, Mekhaniki, Astronomii, Fiziki, Khimii.
Ind/Abst Abstr. Bull. Inst. Pap. Sci. Tech.; AGRICOLA; Alum. Ind. Abstr.; Anal. Abstr.; Ceram. Abstr. (19??-); Chem. Abstr.; Curr. Biotechnol.; Energy Res. Abstr.; Eng. Mater. Abstr.; GeoRef; Int. Aerosp. Abstr.; Met. Abstr.; Res. Alert [Full Cov.]; Sci. Cit. Index; SCISEARCH.

LC QD1 .V57 **ISSN** 0560-3110
DD 540/.5 XV
CODEN VSKDAA
TITLE CHANGE
VESTNIK SLOVENSKEGA KEMIJSKEGA DRUSTVA. **Added/Corp** Slovensko Kemijsko Drustvo. **VFOAT** Bulletin of the Slovenian Chemical Society; Bulletin de la Societe Chimique Slovene. (1954)-(199?). Academic Scholarly Publication. English (German, Serbo-Croatian (Roman) and Slovenian). Drustvo Vestnik SKD, Hajdrihova 19, 61115 Ljubljana Slovenia. Documents available from CASDDS. **Continued by** Acta Chimica Slovenica, 1318-0207.
Ind/Abst Chem. Abstr.

ISSN 0460-0509
UN
NLM W1 VI899K
VISNYK L'VIVS'KOHO ORDENA LENINA DERZHAVNOHO UNIVERSYTETU IM IVANA FRANKA. SERIIA KHIMICHNA.
Added/Corp Lvivskyi Derzhavnyi Universytet im. Iv. Franka. (1960)-. Periodical. Ukrainian (summaries and/or abstracts in English).

LC TP200 .V95 **ISSN** 0235-0122
RU
VYSOKOCHISTYE VESHCHESTVA / AKADEMIIA NAUK SSSR. **Added/Corp** Akademiia Nauk SSSR. (Jan./Feb. 1987)-. Academic Scholarly Publication. Russian. Six times a year. $119.95. Izdatelstvo Nauka / Akademiia Nauk, (Publishing House of the Russian Academy of Sciences), Leninskii Porspekt 14, 117901 Moscow Russia. **Tel** 011 95 9542153, FAX 011 95 9382144, telex 411964. **(Subscription address:** East View Publications Inc., 3020 Harbor Lane North, Suite 110, Minneapolis MN 55447. **Tel** (800)477-1005, (612)550-0961, FAX (612)559-2931.)

RU
● **VYSOKOMOLEKULIARNYE SOEDINENIIA. SERIIA A I SERIIA B.**
Added/Corp Rossiiskaia Akademiia Nauk. Vol. 35, No. 1, (1993)-. Periodical. Russian (summaries and/or abstracts in English; table of contents in English). Twelve times a year. Rossiiskaya Akademiia Nauk, Sibirskoe Otdelenie, Pr. Akademika Lavrenteva 17, 630090 Novosibirsk Russia. **Formed by the union of** Vysokomolekuliarnye Soedineniia. Seriia A, 0507-5475 **and** Vysokomolekuliarnye Soedineniia. Seriia B, Kratkie Soobshcheniia, 0507-5483.
Ind/Abst Sci. Cit. Index.

LC HD9657.J3 J27a
JA
WAGA KUNI NO KOKOGYO: KAGAKU KOGYO HEN, GOMU SEIHIN HEN, PURASUCHIKKU SEIHIN HEN, YOGYO KENZAI HEN. See Industry and Production.

ISSN 0043-2989
DD 574.1/92/05 NR
NLM W1 WE329 **CODEN** WAJBAK
WEST AFRICAN JOURNAL OF BIOLOGICAL AND APPLIED CHEMISTRY. See Biology-Biological Chemistry.

ISSN 0308-0021
UK
WHERE TO BUY CHEMICALS AND CHEMICAL PLANT. (Dec. 1990)-. English. One time a year. £74.20 UK; $126.00 other. Argus Press Group, Queensway House, 2 Queensway Redhill, Surrey RH1 1QS United Kingdom. **Tel** 011 44 1737 768611, 011 44 1737 761685, FAX 011 44 1737 760510, telex 948669 TOPJNL G.

LC HD9652.3 .W48 **ISSN** 0308-0021
DD 381/.45/66002541 UK
TITLE CHANGE
WHERE TO BUY CHEMICALS AND CHEMICAL PLANT. [Where buy chem. chem. plant]. **Added/Corp** British Chemical Distributors & Traders Association. (19??)-(199?). English. Argus Press Group, Queensway House, 2 Queensway Redhill, Surrey RH1 1QS United Kingdom. **Tel** 011 44 1737 768611, 011 44 1737 761685, FAX 011 44 1737 760510, telex 948669 TOPJNL G. **Continues** Where to Buy; an Index to the Principal Sources of Supply of Chemicals, Chemical Plant & Apparatus. **Continued by** Where to Buy Chemicals, Plant, and Services.

LC HD9652.3 .W48
DD 381.45/66002541 UK
WHERE TO BUY CHEMICALS, PLANT, AND SERVICES. **Added/Corp** British Chemical Distributors & Traders Association. (199?)-. English. One time a year. $130.65. Argus Press Group, Queensway House, 2 Queensway Redhill, Surrey RH1 1QS United Kingdom. **Tel** 011 44 1737 768611, 011 44 1737 761685, FAX 011 44 1737 760510, telex 948669 TOPJNL G. **Continues** Where to Buy Chemicals and Chemical Plant, 0308-0021.

ISSN 0043-5104
PL
WIADOMOSCI CHEMICZNE. **Added/Corp** Komitet Studenckich Ko Chemicznych w Polsce. Polskie Towarzystwo Chemiczne. Vol. 1, (1947)-. Periodical. Polish. Twelve times a year. $75.00. **(Subscription address:** Ars Polona-Ruch, PO Box 1001, Krakowskie Przedmiescie 7, 00-068 Warsaw Poland. **Tel** 011 48 22 261201.)

LC QD96.P62 W56a **ISSN** 1042-0363
DD 543/.0858 US
WINTER CONFERENCE ON PLASMA SPECTROCHEMISTRY. **See** Physics-Light, Optics, Radiation.

ISSN 0941-9950
GW
UDC 62
WISSENSCHAFTLICHE ZEITSCHRIFT DER TECHNISCHEN UNIVERSITAET CHEMNITZ. [Wiss. Z. Tech. Univ. Chemnitz]. (1990)-. Academic Scholarly Publication. German. Six times a year. Documents available from CASDDS. **Continues** Wissenschaftliche Zeitschrift der Technischen Universitat Karl-Marx-Stadt, 0863-0615.
Ind/Abst Chem. Abstr.; Zentralbl. Math. Ihre Grenzgeb.

LC QD39.5 .W65
US
WOMEN CHEMISTS : A SUPPLEMENTARY REPORT TO THE AMERICAN CHEMICAL SOCIETY'S ... SURVEY OF MEMBER'S SALARY AND EMPLOYMENT. **Added/Corp** American Chemical Society. ACS Office of Statistical Services. (1980)-. English. $39.95 per issue. American Chemical Society, 1155 Sixteenth Street Northwest, Washington DC 20036. **Tel** (800)333-9511, (800)227-5558, (614)447-3776, FAX (202)447-3671.

ISSN 1000-6818
CC
CODEN WHXUEU
WULI HUAXUE XUEBAO. (WU LI HUA XUEH HSUEH PAO = ACTA PHYSICO-CHIMICA SINICA.). [Wuli huaxue xuebao]. **Added/Corp** Chung-Kuo Hua Hsueh Hui, (People's China). **VFOAT** Acta Physico-Chimica Sinica. (1985)-. Periodical. Chinese. Six times a year. **(Subscription address:** China International Book Trading Corporation, PO Box 399, Library Service Department, Beijing 100044 People's Republic of China. **Tel** 011 86 1 8414284, FAX 011 86 1 8412023, telex 22496 CIBTC CN.) Documents available from CASDDS.
Ind/Abst Chem. Abstr.; Curr. Cit.

LC QD1 .Y56
DD 540/.5 CC
YING YUNG HUA HSUEH (CHANG-CHUN SHIH, CHINA). (YING YUNG HUA HSUEH.). **VFOAT** Chinese Journal of Applied Chemistry; Yingyong Huaxue. (19??)-. Periodical. Chinese (summaries and/or abstracts in English). Four times a year. RMBY0.80. Ying Yung Hua Hsueh Pien Chi Wei Yuan Hui, Post Office, Chang-Chun Shih, People's Republic of China. Documents available from CASDDS.
Ind/Abst Chem. Abstr.; Curr. Titles Electrochem.

LC QD95 .Y66
KO
YONGU NONMUNJIP. **See** Physics.

LC T178.O75 O7a
JA
YORAN - KOGYO GIJUTSUIN OSAKA KOGYO GIJUTSU SHIKENJO. **Main/Corp** Osaka Kogyo Gijutsu Shikenjo. (19??)-. Periodical. Japanese. Osaka Kogyo Gijutsu Shikenjo, 8-31 Midorigaoka, 1-chome 563, Ikeda Japan. **Tel** 0727-52-8351. **ED** Ryozo Hayami. **Circ:** 3,000.
Desc: Covers inorganic chemistry, organic chemistry, glass and ceramic chemistry, applied chemistry and physics.

ISSN 0289-422X
JA
CODEN YOGIEE

YOSHA GIJUTSU. [Yosha gijutsu]. **Added/Corp** Nihon Yosha Kyokai. (1979)-. Periodical. Japanese. Nihon Yosha Kyokai, (Thermal Spraying Soc. of Japan), 2-29 Eiwa 2 Chome, Higashiosakashi Osakafu 577, Japan. Documents available from CASDDS.
Ind/Abst Chem. Abstr.

ISSN 0916-1589
DD 660
JA

YOYUEN OYOBI KOON KAGAKU. VFOAT Molten Salts (1989). (1989)-. Periodical. Multiple languages. Three times a year. Documents available from CASDDS. ***Continues** Yoyuen, 0387-138X.*
Ind/Abst Chem. Abstr.

LC QD1 .Z429 **ISSN** 0932-0776
DD 540/.5 GW
UDC 54 **CCC**
CODEN ZNBSEN

Pr Rev.

ZEITSCHRIFT FUR NATURFORSCHUNG. (ZEITSCHRIFT FUER NATURFORSCHUNG. B, A JOURNAL OF CHEMICAL SCIENCES.). [Z. Nat.forsch., B, J. chem. sci.]. **VFOAT** Journal of Chemical Sciences; Chemical Sciences. Vol. 42, No. 1 (Jan. 1987)-. Academic Scholarly Publication. English (German). Twelve times a year. DM737.00 (add DM45.00 for postage). Verlag der Zeitschrift fuer Naturforschung Tubingen, PO Box 2645, D-72016 Tuebingen Germany. **Tel** 011 49 7071 31555, FAX 07032/75465. **ED** H P Fritz, R Gompper, and H Schmidbaur. **Ad Acc. Circ:** 1,000 (ctrl). Documents available from The Genuine Article, BIOSIS Document Express, CASDDS. ***Continues** Zeitschrift fur Naturforschung. Teil B, Anorganische Chemie, Organische Chemie.*
Ind/Abst Anal. Abstr.; Biol. Abstr. (1987-); Chem Inform; Chem. Abstr. (1987-); Curr. Chem. React.; Curr. Cit.; Curr. Contents Phys. Chem. Earth Sci.; Field Crop Abstr.; Index Chem.; Mass Spect. Bull.; NAPRALERT; Protozoolog. Abstr.; Ref. Upd. Deluxe Ed.; Res. Alert [Full Cov.]; Rev. Agric. Entomol.; Rev. Med. Vet. Entomol.; Sci. Cit. Index; SCISEARCH; Seed Abstr.; Wheat Barley Trit. Abstr.

ISSN 0208-6360
PL
CODEN CTCHEM

ZESZYTY NAUKOWE - AKADEMIA TECHNICZNO-ROLNICZA IM. JANA I JEDRZEJA SNIADECKICH W BYDGOSZCZY. CHEMIA I TECHNOLOGIA CHEMICZNA. (CHEMIA I TECHNOLOGIA CHEMICZNA.). [Zesz. nauk. - Akad. Tech.-Rol. im. Jana Jedrzeja Sniadeckich Bydg., Chem. technol. chem.]. **Added/Corp** Akademia Techniczno-Rolnicza im. Jana i Jedrzeja Sniadeckich w Bydgoszczy. (1975)-. Periodical. Polish. Wydawnictwo Uczelniane Akademii Techniczno-Rolniczej w Bydgoszczy, Bydgoszcz Poland. Documents available from CASDDS.
Ind/Abst Chem. Abstr.

LC QD1 .Z48 **ISSN** 0860-1100
PL
CODEN ZNACE4
CEASED

ZESZYTY NAUKOWE AKADEMII GORNICZO-HUTNICZEJ IM. STANISLAWA STASZICA. CHEMIA. **Added/Corp** Akademia Gorniczo-Hutnicza im. S. Staszica w Krakowie. **VFOAT** Chemia; Scientific Bulletins of the Stanislaw Staszic University of Mining and Metallurgy. Chemistry. (1985)-(1994). Academic Scholarly Publication. Polish (summaries and/or abstracts in English). Wydawnictwo AGH / Wydawnictwo Akademia Gorniczo-Hutnicza im. S. Staszica, Al. Mickiewicza 30, 30-059 Krakow Poland. **Tel** 011 48 12 338100, FAX 011 48 12 3311014. **(Subscription address:** Ars Polona-Ruch, PO Box 1001, Krakowskie Przedmiescie 7, 00-068 Warsaw Poland. **Tel** 011 48 22 261201.) Documents available from CASDDS. ***Continues in part** Zeszyty Naukowe Akademii Gorniczo-Hutniczej im. Stanislawa Staszica. Matematyka, Fizyka, Chemia, 0372-8838.*
Ind/Abst Chem. Abstr.

LC QD1 .G57 **ISSN** 0372-9494
PL

ZESZYTY NAUKOWE - POLITECHNIKA SLASKA. CHEMIA. (ZESZYTY NAUKOWE POLITECHNIKI SLASKIEJ. CHEMIA.). [Zesz. nauk. - Politech. Sl., Chem.]. **Added/Corp** Politechnika Slaska im. W. Pstrowskiego. **VFOAT** Chemia; Zeszyty Naukowe. Chemia. (1954)-. Academic Scholarly Publication. Polish (summaries and/or abstracts in English and Russian). Irregular. Price varies per volume. Politechnika Slaska, Ul. Katowicka 7, 44-100 Gliwice Poland. **Tel** FAX 011 48 32 371655. **(Subscription address:** Ars Polona-Ruch, PO Box 1001, Krakowskie Przedmiescie 7, 00-068 Warsaw Poland. **Tel** 011 48 22 261201.) Documents available from CASDDS.
Ind/Abst Alum. Ind. Abstr.; Chem. Abstr.; Met. Abstr.

ISSN 0416-7341
PL
CODEN ZNGCAU

ZESZYTY NAUKOWE POLITECHNIKI GDANSKIEJ. CHEMIA. [Zesz. nauk. Politech. Gdan., Chem.]. **Added/Corp** Politechnika Gdanska. **VFOAT** Chemia. (1955)-. Monographic series. Polish (summaries and/or abstracts in English, German and Russian). Irregular. Price varies per volume. Politechnika Gdanska, Ul. G. Narutowicza 11-12, 80-952 Gdansk 6 Poland. Documents available from CASDDS.
Desc: Physical, organic, and analytic chemistry, along with corrosion protection technology, fats, food technology, etc.
Ind/Abst Chem. Abstr. (1955-1980)(19??-); Energy Res. Abstr. (July 1982-).

ISSN 0867-1095
PL
UDC 54

ZESZYTY NAUKOWE UNIWERSYTETU JAGIELLONSKIEGE. UNIVERSITATIS IAGELLONICAE ACTA CHIMICA. [Zesz. Nauk. Uniw. Jagiell., Univ. Iagell. Acta Chim.]. **VFOAT** Universitas Iagellonica Acta Scientiarum Litterarumque. Universitatis Iagellonicae Acta Chimica; Universitatis Iagellonicae Acta Chimica. (1990)-. Monographic series. Multiple languages. Irregular. Price varies per volume. Uniwersytet Jagiellonski, Ul. Golebia 24, 31-007 Krakow Poland. **(Subscription address:** Ars Polona-Ruch, PO Box 1001, Krakowskie Przedmiescie 7, 00-068 Warsaw Poland. **Tel** 011 48 22 261201.) Documents available from CASDDS. ***Continues** Zeszyty Naukowe Uniwersytetu Jagiellonskiego. Prace Chemiczne, 0083-4319.*
Ind/Abst Chem. Abstr.

ISSN 0373-0247
RU
CODEN ZVKOA6

ZHURNAL VSESOIUZNOGO KHIMICHESKOGO OBSHCHESTVA IM. D.I. MENDELEEVA. [Z. Vses. him. obscestva im. D. I. Mendeleeva]. **Main/Corp** Vsesoiuznoe Khimicheskoe Obshchestvo im. D.I. Mendeleeva. (1960)-. Periodical. Russian. Six times a year. $200.00. **(Subscription address:** Victor Kamkin, 4956 Boiling Brook Parkway, Rockville MD 20852. **Tel** (301)881-5973.) Documents available from BIOSIS Document Express, CASDDS. ***Continues** Khimicheskaia Nauka i Promyshlennost.*
Ind/Abst Biol. Abstr.; Ceram. Abstr. (19??-); Chem. Abstr.; Coal Abstr.; Curr. Biotechnol.; Energy Res. Abstr.; Food Sci. Technol. Abstr.

ISSN 0044-460X
RU
CCC
NLM W1 ZH423G **CODEN** ZOKHA4

ZURNAL OBSEJ HIMII. (ZHURNAL OBSHCHEI KHIMII.). [Z. obsc. him.]. **Added/Corp** Akademiia Nauk SSSR. **VFOAT** Khimicheskii Zhurnal. Seriia A, Zhurnal Obshchei Khimii. (1931)-. Academic Scholarly Publication. Russian (summaries and/or abstracts in English; table of contents in English and French). Twelve times a year. $364.00. **(Subscription address:** East View Publications Inc., 3020 Harbor Lane North, Suite 110, Minneapolis MN 55447. **Tel** (800)477-1005, (612)550-0961, FAX (612)559-2931.) available on micro-opaque. Documents available from The Genuine Article, CASDDS. ***Continues** Russkoe Fiziko-Khimicheskoe Obshchestvo, Leningrad. Zhurnal.*
Ind/Abst Abstr. Bull. Inst. Pap. Sci. Tech.; Chem Inform; Chem. Abstr.; Chem. Titles; Curr. Chem. React.; Curr. Contents Phys. Chem. Earth Sci.; EMBASE; Energy Res. Abstr.; GeoRef; Index Chem.; Life Sci. Collect.; PESTDOC; Res. Alert [Full Cov.]; Sci. Cit. Index; SCISEARCH.

LC TP1 .Z63 **ISSN** 0044-4618
RU
CCC
CODEN ZPKHAB

ZURNAL PRIKLADNOI HIMII. (ZHURNAL PRIKLADNOI KHIMII.). [Z. prikl. him.]. **Added/Corp** Russkoe Fiziko-Khimicheskoe Obshchestvo. Akademiia Nauk SSSR. **VFOAT** Khimicheskii Zhurnal. Seriia B; Journal of Applied Chemistry; Journal of Chimie Appliquee. Vol. 1, No. 1 (March 1928)-. Academic Scholarly Publication. Russian (summaries and/or abstracts in English, French and German; table of contents in English, French and German). Twelve times a year. $442.50. Izdatelstvo Nauka / Akademiia Nauk, (Publishing House of the Russian Academy of Sciences), Leninskii Porspekt 14, 117901 Moscow Russia. **Tel** 011 95 9542153, FAX 011 95 9382144, telex 411964. **(Subscription address:** East View Publications Inc., 3020 Harbor Lane North, Suite 110, Minneapolis MN 55447. **Tel** (800)477-1005, (612)550-0961, FAX (612)559-2931.) Documents available from CASDDS.
Ind/Abst Abstr. Bull. Inst. Pap. Sci. Tech.; Anal. Abstr.; Ceram. Abstr. (19??-); Chem Inform; Chem. Abstr.; Coal Abstr.; Curr. Biotechnol.; Energy Res. Abstr.; GeoRef; Int. Aerosp. Abstr.; Surf. Treat. Technol. Abstr.; World Text. Abstr.

ABSTRACTING, BIBLIOGRAPHIES AND STATISTICS

LC TP967 .A49 **ISSN** 0891-7760
DD 668/.3 UK

ADHESIVES ABSTRACTS. [Adhes. abstr.]. **Added/Corp** Rapra Technology Limited. Vol. 1, No. 1 (Jan. 1988)-. English. Twelve times a year. $370.00. RAPRA Technology Ltd., Shawbury Shrewsbury, Shropshire SY4 4NR United Kingdom. **Tel** 011 44 1939 250383, FAX 011 44 1939 251118, telex 35134 RAPRA G. **ED** Rebecca Meredith. available on an online database from STN International; Orbit Search Service; DIALOG; DATA-STAR; and (through via Pergamon ORBIT InfoLine as part of the Rapra Abstracts file); available on microfilm and microfiche from University Microfilms International (UMI). Documents available from UMI Article Clearinghouse.
Desc: Comprehensive guide to current literature on adhesives, sealants and adhesion science. Approximately 250 entries appear in each issue gathered from journals, conference proceedings, books, trade literature, standards and government publications. Each entry gives a concise summary of the content and a full reference so that the original document may be easily traced.

ISSN 1068-8382
US
CCC
CODEN AAABE9

●ADVANCE ACS ABSTRACTS. **Added/Corp** American Chemical Society. **VAT** Advance American Chemical Society Abstracts. (1993)-. English. Twenty-four times a year. $260.00. American Chemical Society, 1155 Sixteenth Street Northwest, Washington DC 20036. **Tel** (800)333-9511, (800)227-5558, (614)447-3776, FAX (202)447-3671. **(Subscription address:** American Chemical Society / Washington D.C., PO Box 57136, West End Station, Washington DC 20037. **Tel** (800)227-5558.) **Ad Acc, Adv Mgr Tel** (203)256-8211.
Desc: Previews 500-600 author abstracts for complete papers accepted for publication in 22 journals, up to eight weeks before they are published. Titles and authors of journal communications and notes are also included. Back issues and rental use of mailing list are available.

US

●ADVANCED POLYMERS ABSTRACTS. (1995)-. Abstracting/Indexing Service. English. One time a year. $595.00. American Society for Metals International, Materials Park OH 44073-0002. **Tel** (216)338-5151, FAX (216)338-4634, telex 980-619. ***Separated from** Engineered Materials Abstracts.*
Desc: Covers the development, production and processing of polymeric materials intended for engineering use. Each issue contains subject, trade name, materials, author and corporate author indexes.

LC QD71 .A49 **ISSN** 0003-2689
DD 016.543 UK
CCC
NLM ZQD 1 A532 **CODEN** AABSAR

ANALYTICAL ABSTRACTS. [Anal. abstr.]. **Added/Corp** Royal Society of Chemistry (Great Britain) Society for Analytical Chemistry. Chemical Society (Great Britain). Vol. 1 (Jan. 1954)-. Abstracting/Indexing Service. English. Twelve times a year. $1067.00. Royal Society of Chemistry, Thomas Graham House, Science Park, Cambridge CB4 4WF United Kingdom. **Tel** 011 44 1223 420066, FAX 011 44 1223 423623, telex 818293 ROYAL. **(Subscription address:** Royal Society of Chemistry, Turpin Distribution Services Ltd., Blackhorse Road, Letchworth, Hertfordshire SG6 1HN United Kingdom. **Tel** 011 44 1462 672555, FAX 011 44 1462 480947.) **ED** Janice Gordon. Index Available, published separately, free-automatically sent. cum. index. **Bk Rev. Ad Acc. Circ:** 3,800 (ctrl). available on microfilm and microfiche from University Microfilms International (UMI); available on an online database from STN International; Orbit Search Service; (File no.305) DIALOG; and DATA-STAR; available on CD-ROM from SilverPlatter (UK). Documents available from BLDSC, UMI Article Clearinghouse. ***Continues** British Abstracts. Section C, Analysis and Apparatus.*
Desc: Covers the whole field of analytical chemistry. Provides abstracts of papers and books considered to be of importance and interest to analytical chemistry.
Ind/Abst Abstr. Bull. Inst. Pap. Sci. Tech.; Dairy Sci. Abstr.; Field Crop Abstr.; Grass. Forage Abstr.; Hortic. Abstr.; Index Vet.; Int. Packag. Abstr.; Vet. Bull.; Weed Abstr.; World Ceram. Abstr.; World Surf. Coat. Abstr.; World Text. Abstr.

LC Z5524.C55 B53 QD79.C6 **ISSN** 0300-631X
DD 016.544/92 NE
UDC 543.544.42(048.3)

BIBLIOGRAPHY OF PAPER AND THIN-LAYER CHROMATOGRAPHY, AND SURVEY OF APPLICATIONS. 1961/65-. Bibliography. English. Irregular. Elsevier Science Publishers BV, PO Box 211, 1000 AE Amsterdam Netherlands. **Tel** 011 31 20 4853641, 011 31 20 4853642, FAX 011 31 20 4853598.

LC Z5524.C8 B9 QD905.2 **ISSN** 0304-1298
DD 016.548 FR
BULLETIN SIGNALETIQUE. 161, STRUCTURE DE L'ETAT CONDENSE, CRISTALLOGRAPHIE / CENTRE NATIONAL DE LA RECHERCHE SCIENTIFIQUE. **Added/Corp** Informascience (Centre National de la Recherche Scientifique) CNRS - PASCAL (Center). **VFOAT** Structure de l'Etat Condense, Cristallographie. (1976)-. Bulletin. French. Four times a year. 565.00F. Service des Abonnements du CDSH, 54 Bd Raspail, 75270 Paris Cedex 06 France. **Tel** 45 48 10 18, telex MSH 203 104F. ***Continues*** *Bulletin Signaletique. 161, Cristallographie.*

LC Z5523 .B84 QD31.2 **ISSN** 0240-8465
DD 016.54 FR
BULLETIN SIGNALETIQUE. 171, CHIMIE GENERALE ET CHIMIE PHYSIQUE / CENTRE NATIONAL DE LA RECHERCHE SCIENTIFIQUE. **Added/Corp** Centre National de la Recherche Scientifique (France). Centre de Documentation Scientifique et Technique. **VFOAT** Chimie Generale et Chimie Physique. Vol. 42, No. 1 (1981)-. Bulletin. French. Twelve times a year. 650.00F. Informascience, Centre de Documentation Scientifique et Technique Service des Abonnements, 26 rue Boyer, 75971 Paris Cedex 20 France. ***Continues*** *Bulletin Signaletique. 170, Chimie, 007-5396.*

LC Z5523 .B83 QD75.2 **ISSN** 0240-8473
DD 016.543 FR
BULLETIN SIGNALETIQUE. 172, CHIMIE ANALYTIQUE. **Added/Corp** France. Centre National de la Recherche Scientifique. Centre de Documentation Scientifique et Technique. **VFOAT** Chimie Analytique. Vol. 42, No. 1 (1981)-. Bulletin. French. Twelve times a year. 460.00F. Centre National de la Recherche Scientifique, Informascience, 26 rue Boyer, 75971 Paris France. **Tel** 011 33 1 61411105, telex CNRSDOC 220880 F. ***Continues in part*** *Bulletin Signaletique. 170, Chimie, 0007-5396.*

ISSN 1049-1279
DD 660 US
C2C ABSTRACTS JAPAN. CHEMICAL ENGINEERING. [C2C abstr. Jap., Chem. eng.]. **VFOAT** Chemical Engineering. Vol. 1, No. 1 (Feb. 1990)-. English. Twelve times a year. $200.00. SCAN C2C Inc., 500 E Street Southwest, Suite 800 8th Floor, Washington DC 20024. **Tel** (202)863-3850, (800)525-3865, FAX (202)863-3855. Index available. cum. index. available on CD-ROM from DIALOG; available on an online database from ORBIT; DATA-STAR; and DIALOG.
Desc: English abstracts of over 500 Japanese science, technical and business journals in the field of Chemical Engineering.

ISSN 1049-1287
DD 548 US
C2C ABSTRACTS JAPAN. CRYSTALLOGRAPHY. [C2C abstr. Jap., Crystallogr.]. **VFOAT** Crystallography. Vol. 1, No. 1 (Feb. 1990)-. English. Twelve times a year. $200.00. SCAN C2C Inc., 500 E Street Southwest, Suite 800 8th Floor, Washington DC 20024. **Tel** (202)863-3850, (800)525-3865, FAX (202)863-3855. Index available. cum. index. available on CD-ROM from DIALOG; available on an online database from ORBIT; DATA-STAR; and DIALOG.
Desc: English abstracts of over 500 Japanese science, technical and business journals in the field of Crystals and Crystallography.

ISSN 1049-1295
DD 547 US
C2C ABSTRACTS JAPAN. HYDROCARBONS. [C2C abstr. Jap., Hyrocarb.]. **VFOAT** Hydrocarbons. Vol. 1, No. 1 (Feb. 1990)-. English. Twelve times a year. $200.00. SCAN C2C Inc., 500 E Street Southwest, Suite 800 8th Floor, Washington DC 20024. **Tel** (202)863-3850, (800)525-3865, FAX (202)863-3855. Index available. cum. index. available on CD-ROM from DIALOG; available on an online database from ORBIT; DATA-STAR; and DIALOG.
Desc: English abstracts of over 500 Japanese science, technical and business journals in the field of Hydrocarbon Chemistry.

ISSN 1049-1309
DD 546 US
C2C ABSTRACTS JAPAN. INORGANIC CHEMISTRY. [C2C abstr. Jap., Inorg. chem.]. **VFOAT** Inorganic Chemistry. Vol. 1, No. 1 (Feb. 1990)-. English. Twelve times a year. $200.00. SCAN C2C Inc., 500 E Street Southwest, Suite 800 8th Floor, Washington DC 20024. **Tel** (202)863-3850, (800)525-3865, FAX (202)863-3855. Index available. cum. index. available on CD-ROM from DIALOG; available on an online database from DATA-STAR; and DIALOG.
Desc: English abstracts of over 500 Japanese science, technical and business journals in the field of inorganic chemistry.

ISSN 1049-1333
DD 541 US
C2C ABSTRACTS JAPAN. PHYSICAL CHEMISTRY. [C2C abstr. Jap., Phys. chem.]. **VFOAT** Physical Chemistry. Vol. 1, No. 1 (Feb. 1990)-. English. Twelve times a year. $200.00. SCAN C2C Inc., 500 E Street Southwest, Suite 800 8th Floor, Washington DC 20024. **Tel** (202)863-3850, (800)525-3865, FAX (202)863-3855. Index available. cum. index. available on CD-ROM from DIALOG; available on an online database from ORBIT; DATA-STAR; and DIALOG.
Desc: English abstracts of over 500 Japanese science, technical and business journals in the field of physical chemsitry.

ISSN 1049-135X
DD 547 US
C2C ABSTRACTS JAPAN. POLYMER CHEMISTRY. [C2C abstr. Jap., Polym. chem.]. **VFOAT** Polymer Chemistry. Vol. 1, No. 1 (Feb. 1990)-. English. Twelve times a year. $200.00. SCAN C2C Inc., 500 E Street Southwest, Suite 800 8th Floor, Washington DC 20024. **Tel** (202)863-3850, (800)525-3865, FAX (202)863-3855. Index available. cum. index. available on CD-ROM from DIALOG; available on an online database from ORBIT; DATA-STAR; and DIALOG.
Desc: English abstracts of over 500 Japanese science, technical and business journals in the field of Polymer chemistry.

ISSN 1049-1368
DD 541 US
C2C ABSTRACTS JAPAN. SURFACE CHEMISTRY. [C2C abstr. Jap., Surf. chem.]. **VFOAT** Surface Chemistry. Vol. 1, No. 1 (Feb. 1990)-. English. Twelve times a year. $100.00. SCAN C2C Inc., 500 E Street Southwest, Suite 800 8th Floor, Washington DC 20024. **Tel** (202)863-3850, (800)525-3865, FAX (202)863-3855. Index available. cum. index. available on CD-ROM from DIALOG; available on an online database from ORBIT; DATA-STAR; and DIALOG.
Desc: English content listings of Japanese science, technical and business journals in the field of surface chemsitry.

ISSN 0885-0097
DD 662 US
CODEN CSRAEZ
CA SELECTS: ACID RAIN & ACID AIR. [CA sel., Acid rain acid air]. **Added/Corp** American Chemical Society. Chemical Abstracts Service. **VFOAT** CA Selects. Acid Rain and Acid Air; Acid Rain and Acid Air; Acid Rain & Acid Air. **VAT** Chemical Abstracts Selects. Acid Rain and Acid Air. Iss. 1 (Jan. 13, 1986)-. Abstracting/Indexing Service. English. Twenty-six times a year. $220.00. Chemical Abstracts Service, (Subsidiary of The American Chemical Society), 2540 Olentangy River Road, PO Box 3012, Columbus OH 43210-0012. **Tel** (614)447-3731, (800)753-4227, FAX (614)447-3751. **(Subscription address:** Chemical Abstracts Service, Customer Service Department, PO Box 3012, Columbus OH 43210. **Tel** (800)848-6538, (614)447-3600.**)** **Bk Rev**.
Desc: Covers documents on the occurrence causes and effects of acidity in the atmosphere and in precipitation.

ISSN 0162-7686
US
CODEN CSADDQ
CA SELECTS: ADHESIVES. **Added/Corp** American Chemical Society. Chemical Abstracts Service. **VFOAT** Adhesives. **VAT** Chemical Abstracts Selects. Adhesives. (Jan. 8, 1979)-. Abstracting/Indexing Service. English. Twenty-six times a year. $220.00. Chemical Abstracts Service, (Subsidiary of The American Chemical Society), 2540 Olentangy River Road, PO Box 3012, Columbus OH 43210-0012. **Tel** (614)447-3731, (800)753-4227, FAX (614)447-3751. **(Subscription address:** Chemical Abstracts Service, Customer Service Department, PO Box 3012, Columbus OH 43210. **Tel** (800)848-6538, (614)447-3600.**)** **ED** David W. Weisgerber.
Desc: Covers adhesives, binders, glues, caulks, sealants, mastics and grouts.

ISSN 1040-7111
DD 616 US
CODEN CAISEK
CA SELECTS: AIDS & RELATED IMMUNODEFICIENCIES. [CA sel., AIDS relat. immunodefic.]. **Added/Corp** American Chemical Society. Chemical Abstracts Service. **VFOAT** CA Selects. AIDS and Related Immunodeficiencies; AIDS and Related Immunodeficiencies. **VAT** Chemical Abstracts Selects. AIDS & Related Immunodeficiencies. (Jan. 9, 1989)-. Abstracting/Indexing Service. English. Twenty-six times a year. $220.00. Chemical Abstracts Service, (Subsidiary of The American Chemical Society), 2540 Olentangy River Road, PO Box 3012, Columbus OH 43210-0012. **Tel** (614)447-3731, (800)753-4227, FAX (614)447-3751. **(Subscription address:** Chemical Abstracts Service, Customer Service Department, PO Box 3012, Columbus OH 43210. **Tel** (800)848-6538, (614)447-3600.**)** **ED** David Weisgerber.
Desc: Covers etiology, pathophysiology, clinical manifestations, diagnosis, and therapy of AIDS and other immunodeficiencies.

ISSN 0895-5980
DD 363 US
CODEN CSAPET
CA SELECTS: AIR POLLUTION (BOOKS & REVIEWS). [CA sel., Air pollut. books rev.]. **Added/Corp** American Chemical Society. Chemical Abstracts Service. **VFOAT** Air Pollution (Books & Reviews); Air Pollution (Books and Reviews). **VAT** Chemical Abstracts Selects. Air Pollution (Books & Reviews). (Jan. 11, 1988)-. Abstracting/Indexing Service. English. Twenty-six times a year. $220.00. Chemical Abstracts Service, (Subsidiary of The American Chemical Society), 2540 Olentangy River Road, PO Box 3012, Columbus OH 43210-0012. **Tel** (614)447-3731, (800)753-4227, FAX (614)447-3751. **(Subscription address:** Chemical Abstracts Service, Customer Service Department, PO Box 3012, Columbus OH 43210. **Tel** (800)848-6538, (614)447-3600.**)**
Desc: Covers pollution of the atmosphere by fixed and mobile sources, effects of air pollution on animals and vegetation and pollution-abatement procedures.

ISSN 0895-5964
DD 547 US
CODEN CSACEO
CA SELECTS: ALKYLATION & CATALYSTS. **Added/Corp** American Chemical Society. Chemical Abstracts Service. **VFOAT** CA Selects. Alkylation & Catalysts; Alkylation and Catalysts. **VAT** Chemical Abstracts Selects. Alkylation & Catalysts. (Jan. 11, 1988)-. Abstracting/Indexing Service. English. Twenty-six times a year. $220.00. Chemical Abstracts Service, (Subsidiary of The American Chemical Society), 2540 Olentangy River Road, PO Box 3012, Columbus OH 43210-0012. **Tel** (614)447-3731, (800)753-4227, FAX (614)447-3751. **(Subscription address:** Chemical Abstracts Service, Customer Service Department, PO Box 3012, Columbus OH 43210. **Tel** (800)848-6538, (614)447-3600.**)**
Desc: Covers alkylation of such compounds as alkanes, alkenes, benzenes and amines with agents such as alcohols and olefins; and catalysts used to effect alkylations.

ISSN 1066-1166
DD 629 US
CODEN CSLCEB
•**CA SELECTS: ALUMINUM-LITHIUM & ALUMINUM-CERIUM ALLOYS.** **Added/Corp** American Chemical Society. Chemical Abstracts Service. **VFOAT** Aluminum-Lithium & Aluminum-Cerium Alloys; Aluminum-Lithium and Aluminum-Cerium Alloys; Aluminum Lithium & Aluminum Cerium Alloys. **VAT** Chemical Abstracts Selects. Aluminum-Lithium & Aluminum-Cerium Alloys. (Jan. 11, 1993)-. Abstracting/Indexing Service. English. Twenty-six times a year. $215.00 US; $234.00 Canada, Mexico, Central and South America; $247.00 other. Chemical Abstracts Service, (Subsidiary of The American Chemical Society), 2540 Olentangy River Road, PO Box 3012, Columbus OH 43210-0012. **Tel** (614)447-3731, (800)753-4227, FAX (614)447-3751. **(Subscription address:** Chemical Abstracts Service, Customer Service Department, PO Box 3012, Columbus OH 43210. **Tel** (800)848-6538, (614)447-3600.**)**
Desc: Researches applications of alloys.

ISSN 1047-8183
DD 618 US
CODEN CSDDE8
CA SELECTS: ALZHEIMER'S DISEASE & RELATED MEMORY DYSFUNCTIONS. [CA sel., Alzheimer's dis. relat. mem. dysfunct.]. **Added/Corp** American Chemical Society. Chemical Abstracts Service. **VFOAT** Alzheimer's Disease & Related Memory Dysfunctions; Alzheimer's Disease and Related Memory Dysfunctions. **VAT** Chemical Abstracts Selects. Alzheimer's Disease & Related Memory Dysfunctions. Issue 1 (Jan. 8, 1990)-. Abstracting/Indexing Service. English. Twenty-six times a year. $220.00. Chemical Abstracts Service, (Subsidiary of The American Chemical Society), 2540 Olentangy River Road, PO Box 3012, Columbus OH 43210-0012. **Tel** (614)447-3731, (800)753-4227, FAX (614)447-3751. **(Subscription address:** Chemical Abstracts Service, Customer Service Department, PO Box 3012, Columbus OH 43210. **Tel** (800)848-6538, (614)447-3600.**)**
Desc: Covers Alzheimer's disease and other related illnesses, pathogenesis, diagnosis and biochemistry of the disease, and studies on drugs that control such dementias.

ISSN 0275-701X
US
CODEN CSAPDS
CA SELECTS: AMINO ACIDS, PEPTIDES & PROTEINS. **Added/Corp** American Chemical Society. Chemical Abstracts Service. **VFOAT** Amino Acids, Peptides & Proteins. **VAT** Chemical Abstracts Selects. Amino Acids, Peptides, and Proteins. (1981)-. Abstracting/Indexing Service. English. Twenty-six times a year. $220.00. Chemical Abstracts Service, (Subsidiary of The American Chemical Society), 2540 Olentangy River Road, PO Box 3012, Columbus OH 43210-0012. **Tel** (614)447-3731, (800)753-4227, FAX (614)447-3751. **(Subscription address:** Chemical Abstracts Service, Customer Service Department, PO Box 3012, Columbus

OH 43210. **Tel** (800)848-6538, (614)447-3600.) **ED** David W Weisgerber. Documents available from CASDDS.
Desc: Covers synthesis and chemistry of amino acids, peptides, and proteins.
Ind/Abst Chem. Abstr.

ISSN 0160-8959
US
CODEN CSAEDT

CA SELECTS: ANALYTICAL ELECTROCHEMISTRY. **Added/Corp** American Chemical Society. Chemical Abstracts Service. **VFOAT** Analytical Electrochemistry. **VAT** Chemical Abstracts Selects. Analytical Electrochemistry. (Jan. 8, 1979)-. Abstracting/Indexing Service. English. Twenty-six times a year. $220.00. Chemical Abstracts Service, (Subsidiary of The American Chemical Society), 2540 Olentangy River Road, PO Box 3012, Columbus OH 43210-0012. **Tel** (614)447-3731, (800)753-4227, FAX (614)447-3751. **(Subscription address:** Chemical Abstracts Service, Customer Service Department, PO Box 3012, Columbus OH 43210. **Tel** (800)848-6538, (614)447-3600.) **ED** David W Weisgerber.
Desc: Covers analytical electrochemistry involving organic and inorganic compounds. Also includes electroanalysis using ion-specific electrodes.

ISSN 0162-7694
US
CODEN CSLAD4

CA SELECTS: ANIMAL LONGEVITY & AGING. **Added/Corp** American Chemical Society. Chemical Abstracts Service. **VFOAT** Animal Longevity & Aging. **VAT** Chemical Abstracts Selects. Animal Longevity and Aging. (Jan. 8, 1979)-. Abstracting/Indexing Service. English. Twenty-six times a year. $220.00. Chemical Abstracts Service, (Subsidiary of The American Chemical Society), 2540 Olentangy River Road, PO Box 3012, Columbus OH 43210-0012. **Tel** (614)447-3731, (800)753-4227, FAX (614)447-3751. **(Subscription address:** Chemical Abstracts Service, Customer Service Department, PO Box 3012, Columbus OH 43210. **Tel** (800)848-6538, (614)447-3600.) **ED** David W Weisgerber.
Desc: Covers animal longevity and senescence, senility, limb regeneration, geriatrics and gerontology.

ISSN 0148-2394
US
CODEN CSARDY

CA SELECTS: ANTI-INFLAMMATORY AGENTS & ARTHRITIS. **Added/Corp** American Chemical Society. Chemical Abstracts Service. **VFOAT** Anti-Inflammatory Agents & Arthritis. **VAT** Chemical Abstracts Selects. Anti-Inflammatory Agents and Arthritis. (Jan. 9 1978)-. Abstracting/Indexing Service. English. Twenty-six times a year. $220.00. Chemical Abstracts Service, (Subsidiary of The American Chemical Society), 2540 Olentangy River Road, PO Box 3012, Columbus OH 43210-0012. **Tel** (614)447-3731, (800)753-4227, FAX (614)447-3751. **(Subscription address:** Chemical Abstracts Service, Customer Service Department, PO Box 3012, Columbus OH 43210. **Tel** (800)848-6538, (614)447-3600.) **ED** David W. Weisgerber.
Desc: Covers biochemistry of arthritis and rheumatism; effects and mechanism of action of inflammation inhibitors; synthesis and structure-activity relationships of drugs with potential anti-inflammatory activity.

ISSN 1045-8522
DD 589 US
CODEN CAAAES

CA SELECTS: ANTIBACTERIAL AGENTS. [CA sel., Antibact. agents]. **Added/Corp** American Chemical Society. Chemical Abstracts Service. **VFOAT** Antibacterial Agents. **VAT** Chemical Abstracts Selects. Antibacterial Agents. (Jan. 8, 1990)-. Abstracting/Indexing Service. English. Twenty-six times a year. $220.00. Chemical Abstracts Service, (Subsidiary of The American Chemical Society), 2540 Olentangy River Road, PO Box 3012, Columbus OH 43210-0012. **Tel** (614)447-3731, (800)753-4227, FAX (614)447-3751. **(Subscription address:** Chemical Abstracts Service, Customer Service Department, PO Box 3012, Columbus OH 43210. **Tel** (800)848-6538, (614)447-3600.)
***Continues** CA Selects. Bactericides, Disinfectants & Antiseptics, 0890-1848.*
Desc: Design, synthesis, therapeutic use, mode of action, structure-activity and relationships of antibacterial agents.

ISSN 0275-7028
US
CODEN CAAODZ

CA SELECTS: ANTIOXIDANTS. [CA sel., antioxid.]. **Added/Corp** American Chemical Society. Chemical Abstracts Service. **VFOAT** Antioxidants. **VAT** Chemical Abstracts Selects. Antioxidants. (1981)-. Abstracting/Indexing Service. English. Twenty-six times a year. $220.00. Chemical Abstracts Service, (Subsidiary of The American Chemical Society), 2540 Olentangy River Road, PO Box 3012, Columbus OH 43210-0012. **Tel** (614)447-3731, (800)753-4227, FAX (614)447-3751. **(Subscription address:** Chemical Abstracts Service, Customer Service Department, PO Box 3012, Columbus OH 43210. **Tel** (800)848-6538, (614)447-3600.) **ED** David W Weigerber. Documents available from CASDDS.
Desc: Covers chemistry of oxidation prevention, manufacture and new uses of antioxidants.
Ind/Abst Chem. Abstr.

ISSN 0148-2386
US
CODEN CSAADH

CA SELECTS: ANTITUMOR AGENTS. **Added/Corp** American Chemical Society. Chemical Abstracts Service. **VFOAT** Antitumor Agents. **VAT** Chemical Abstracts Selects. Antitumor Agents. (Jan. 9, 1978)-. Abstracting/Indexing Service. English. Twenty-six times a year. $220.00. Chemical Abstracts Service, (Subsidiary of The American Chemical Society), 2540 Olentangy River Road, PO Box 3012, Columbus OH 43210-0012. **Tel** (614)447-3731, (800)753-4227, FAX (614)447-3751. **(Subscription address:** Chemical Abstracts Service, Customer Service Department, PO Box 3012, Columbus OH 43210. **Tel** (800)848-6538, (614)447-3600.) **ED** David W Weisgerber.
Desc: Covers cytotoxic agents, antimetabolites, alkylating agents, neoplasm inhibitors, effect and mechanism of action, synthesis and structure-activity relationships of drugs with potential antitumor activity.

ISSN 0890-1813
DD 664 US
CODEN CSSWE4

CA SELECTS: ARTIFICIAL SWEETENERS. [CA sel., Artif. sweeten.]. **Added/Corp** American Chemical Society. Chemical Abstracts Service. **VFOAT** Artificial Sweeteners. **VAT** Chemical Abstracts Selects. Artificial Sweeteners. Issue 1 (Jan. 12, 1987)-. Abstracting/Indexing Service. English. Twenty-six times a year. $220.00. Chemical Abstracts Service, (Subsidiary of The American Chemical Society), 2540 Olentangy River Road, PO Box 3012, Columbus OH 43210-0012. **Tel** (614)447-3731, (800)753-4227, FAX (614)447-3751. **(Subscription address:** Chemical Abstracts Service, Customer Service Department, PO Box 3012, Columbus OH 43210. **Tel** (800)848-6538, (614)447-3600.)
Desc: Preparation, properties, reactions, and uses of synthetic substances developed as sugar substitutes or supplements.

ISSN 0890-183X
DD 541 US
CODEN CSIDEX

CA SELECTS: ASYMMETRIC SYNTHESIS & INDUCTION. **Added/Corp** American Chemical Society. Chemical Abstracts Service. **VFOAT** CA Selects. **VAT** Chemical Abstracts Selects. Asymmetric Synthesis and Induction. Issue 1 (Jan. 12, 1987)-. Abstracting/Indexing Service. English. Twenty-six times a year. $220.00. Chemical Abstracts Service, (Subsidiary of The American Chemical Society), 2540 Olentangy River Road, PO Box 3012, Columbus OH 43210-0012. **Tel** (614)447-3731, (800)753-4227, FAX (614)447-3751. **(Subscription address:** Chemical Abstracts Service, Customer Service Department, PO Box 3012, Columbus OH 43210. **Tel** (800)848-6538, (614)447-3600.)
Desc: Synthetic methods for enantiomeric enrichment of compounds that contain one or more asymmetric centers.

ISSN 0148-2378
US
CODEN CASDDO

CA SELECTS: ATHEROSCLEROSIS & HEART DISEASE. **Added/Corp** American Chemical Society. Chemical Abstracts Service. **VFOAT** Atherosclerosis & Heart Disease. **VAT** Chemical Abstracts Selects. Atherosclerosis and Heart Disease. (Jan. 9, 1978)-. Abstracting/Indexing Service. English. Twenty-six times a year. $220.00. Chemical Abstracts Service, (Subsidiary of The American Chemical Society), 2540 Olentangy River Road, PO Box 3012, Columbus OH 43210-0012. **Tel** (614)447-3731, (800)753-4227, FAX (614)447-3751. **(Subscription address:** Chemical Abstracts Service, Customer Service Department, PO Box 3012, Columbus OH 43210. **Tel** (800)848-6538, (614)447-3600.) **ED** David W. Weisgerber.
Desc: Covers atherosclerosis, arteriosclerosis, heart disease, hypertension, hypotension, embolic and thrombotic disorders, shock, pharmacology and treatment of cardiovascular disease.

ISSN 0195-4911
US
CODEN CAASDD

CA SELECTS: ATOMIC SPECTROSCOPY. [CA sel., At. spectrosc.]. **Added/Corp** American Chemical Society. Chemical Abstracts Service. **VFOAT** Atomic Spectroscopy. **VAT** Chemical Abstracts Selects. Atomic Spectroscopy. (Jan. 14, 1980)-. Abstracting/Indexing Service. English. Twenty-six times a year. $220.00. Chemical Abstracts Service, (Subsidiary of The American Chemical Society), 2540 Olentangy River Road, PO Box 3012, Columbus OH 43210-0012. **Tel** (614)447-3731, (800)753-4227, FAX (614)447-3751. **(Subscription address:** Chemical Abstracts Service, Customer Service Department, PO Box 3012, Columbus OH 43210. **Tel** (800)848-6538, (614)447-3600.) **ED** David W Weisgerber.
Desc: Covers atomic absorption, emission, and fluorescence in optical regions, i.e., infrared, visible, and ultraviolet.

ISSN 0740-0683
DD 543 US
CODEN CSAAEI

CA SELECTS: AUTOMATED CHEMICAL ANALYSIS. [CA sel., Autom. chem. anal.]. **Added/Corp** American Chemical Society. Chemical Abstracts Service. **VFOAT** Automated Chemical Analysis. **VAT** Chemical Abstracts Selects. Automated Chemical Analysis. (19??)-. Abstracting/Indexing Service. English. Twenty-six times a year. $220.00. Chemical Abstracts Service, (Subsidiary of The American Chemical Society), 2540 Olentangy River Road, PO Box 3012, Columbus OH 43210-0012. **Tel** (614)447-3731, (800)753-4227, FAX (614)447-3751. **(Subscription address:** Chemical Abstracts Service, Customer Service Department, PO Box 3012, Columbus OH 43210. **Tel** (800)848-6538, (614)447-3600.) **ED** David W Weisgerber.
Desc: Covers chemical analysis automated by computer control or mechanical means and automatic sampling analysis procedures.

ISSN 0148-2459
US
CODEN CSBADM

CA SELECTS: B-LACTAM ANTIBIOTICS. **Added/Corp** American Chemical Society. Chemical Abstracts Service. **VFOAT** b-Lactam Antibiotics. **VAT** Chemical Abstracts Selects. Beta-Lactam Antibiotics. (Jan. 9, 1978)-. Abstracting/Indexing Service. English. Twenty-six times a year. $220.00. Chemical Abstracts Service, (Subsidiary of The American Chemical Society), 2540 Olentangy River Road, PO Box 3012, Columbus OH 43210-0012. **Tel** (614)447-3731, (800)753-4227, FAX (614)447-3751. **(Subscription address:** Chemical Abstracts Service, Customer Service Department, PO Box 3012, Columbus OH 43210. **Tel** (800)848-6538, (614)447-3600.) **ED** David W Weisgerber.
Desc: Covers synthesis, biosynthesis, chemical reactivity, antimicrobial activity, pharmacodynamics, metabolism, toxicology, analysis and formulation.

ISSN 0162-7708
US
CODEN CBFCDV

CA SELECTS: BATTERIES & FUEL CELLS. **Added/Corp** American Chemical Society. Chemical Abstracts Service. **VFOAT** Batteries & Fuel Cells. **VAT** Chemical Abstracts Selects. Batteries and Fuel Cells. (Jan. 8, 1979)-. Abstracting/Indexing Service. English. Twenty-six times a year. $220.00. Chemical Abstracts Service, (Subsidiary of The American Chemical Society), 2540 Olentangy River Road, PO Box 3012, Columbus OH 43210-0012. **Tel** (614)447-3731, (800)753-4227, FAX (614)447-3751. **(Subscription address:** Chemical Abstracts Service, Customer Service Department, PO Box 3012, Columbus OH 43210. **Tel** (800)848-6538, (614)447-3600.) **ED** David W Weisgerber.
Desc: Covers design, manufacture, properties, and use of primary and secondary batteries; fuel cells; materials-related and electrochemical aspects; reclamation of materials from spent batteries and electrodes for batteries and fuel cells.

ISSN 0162-7716
DD 616 US
CODEN CBASDK

CA SELECTS: BIOGENIC AMINES & THE NERVOUS SYSTEM. [C A sel., Biogen. amines nerv. syst.]. **Added/Corp** American Chemical Society. Chemical Abstracts Service. **VFOAT** Biogenic Amines & the Nervous System. **VAT** Chemical Abstracts Selects. Biogenic Amines and the Nervous System. (Jan. 8, 1979)-. Abstracting/Indexing Service. English. Twenty-six times a year. $220.00. Chemical Abstracts Service, (Subsidiary of The American Chemical Society), 2540 Olentangy River Road, PO Box 3012, Columbus OH 43210-0012. **Tel** (614)447-3731, (800)753-4227, FAX (614)447-3751. **(Subscription address:** Chemical Abstracts Service, Customer Service Department, PO Box 3012, Columbus OH 43210. **Tel** (800)848-6538, (614)447-3600.) **ED** David W Weisgerber.
Desc: Covers involvement of biogenic amines in the nervous system and neurotransmission: monoamines, catecholamines, indoleamines, neurotransmitters, histamine and antihistaminics, enzymes in the metabolism of biogenic amines.

ISSN 1061-5342
US
CODEN CABCE5

CA SELECTS: BISMUTH CHEMISTRY. **Added/Corp** American Chemical Society. Chemical Abstracts Service. **VFOAT** Bismuth Chemistry. **VAT** Chemical Abstracts Selects. Bismuth Chemistry. (1992)-. Abstracting/Indexing Service. English. Twenty-six times a year. $215.00 US; $234.00 Canada, Mexico, Central and South America; $247.00 other. Chemical Abstracts Service, (Subsidiary of The American Chemical Society), 2540 Olentangy River Road, PO Box 3012, Columbus OH 43210-0012. **Tel** (614)447-3731, (800)753-4227, FAX (614)447-3751. **(Subscription address:** Chemical Abstracts Service, Customer Service Department, PO

Box 3012, Columbus OH 43210. **Tel** (800)848-6538, (614)447-3600.)
Desc: Information on the bismuth chemistry.

ISSN 0734-8851
US
CODEN CASPER

CA SELECTS: BLOCK & GRAFT POLYMERS.
[CA sel., Block graft polym.]. **Added/Corp** American Chemical Society. Chemical Abstracts Service. **VFOAT** Block & Graft Polymers; Block and Graft Polymers. **VAT** Chemical Abstracts Selects. Block and Graft Polymers. (19??)-. Abstracting/Indexing Service. English. Twenty-six times a year. $220.00. Chemical Abstracts Service, (Subsidiary of The American Chemical Society), 2540 Olentangy River Road, PO Box 3012, Columbus OH 43210-0012. **Tel** (614)447-3731, (800)753-4227, FAX (614)447-3751. **(Subscription address:** Chemical Abstracts Service, Customer Service Department, PO Box 3012, Columbus OH 43210. **Tel** (800)848-6538, (614)447-3600.) **ED** David W Weisgerber.
Desc: Coverage includes preparation, properties, uses of block or segmented polymers, synthesis of graft copolymers: catalytic, mechanistic, kinetic aspects with properties of resultant polymers and commercial manufacture.

ISSN 0162-7732
US
CODEN CBCODI

CA SELECTS: BLOOD COAGULATION.
Added/Corp American Chemical Society. Chemical Abstracts Service. **VFOAT** Blood Coagulation. **VAT** Chemical Abstracts Selects. Blood Coagulation. (Jan. 8, 1979)-. Abstracting/Indexing Service. English. Twenty-six times a year. $220.00. Chemical Abstracts Service, (Subsidiary of The American Chemical Society), 2540 Olentangy River Road, PO Box 3012, Columbus OH 43210-0012. **Tel** (614)447-3731, (800)753-4227, FAX (614)447-3751. **(Subscription address:** Chemical Abstracts Service, Customer Service Department, PO Box 3012, Columbus OH 43210. **Tel** (800)848-6538, (614)447-3600.) **ED** David W Weisgerber.
Desc: Covers blood-coagulation factors, vitamin K, anticoagulants, blood preservation and preservatives and blood platelet biochemistry.

DD 547
ISSN 0740-0756
US
CODEN CSCAES

CA SELECTS: CARBOHYDRATES (CHEMICAL ASPECTS).
[CA sel., Carbohydr. (chem. asp.)]. **Added/Corp** American Chemical Society. Chemical Abstracts Service. **VFOAT** Carbohydrates (Chemical Aspects). **VAT** Chemical Abstracts Selects. Carbohydrates (Chemical Aspects). (19??)-. Abstracting/Indexing Service. English. Twenty-six times a year. $220.00. Chemical Abstracts Service, (Subsidiary of The American Chemical Society), 2540 Olentangy River Road, PO Box 3012, Columbus OH 43210-0012. **Tel** (614)447-3731, (800)753-4227, FAX (614)447-3751. **(Subscription address:** Chemical Abstracts Service, Customer Service Department, PO Box 3012, Columbus OH 43210. **Tel** (800)848-6538, (614)447-3600.) **ED** David W Weisgerber.
Desc: Covers characterization, reactions, structure analysis, and nonindustrial synthesis of carbohydrates and their derivatives and polymers.

DD 620
ISSN 0890-1856
US
CODEN CSCFE9

CA SELECTS: CARBON & GRAPHITE FIBERS.
Added/Corp American Chemical Society. Chemical Abstracts Service. **VFOAT** CA Selects. Carbon and Graphite Fibers; Carbon and Graphite Fibers; Carbon & Graphite Fibers. **VAT** Chemical Abstracts Selects. Carbon and Graphite Fibers. Issue 1 (Jan. 12, 1987)-. Abstracting/Indexing Service. English. Twenty-six times a year. $220.00. Chemical Abstracts Service, (Subsidiary of The American Chemical Society), 2540 Olentangy River Road, PO Box 3012, Columbus OH 43210-0012. **Tel** (614)447-3731, (800)753-4227, FAX (614)447-3751. **(Subscription address:** Chemical Abstracts Service, Customer Service Department, PO Box 3012, Columbus OH 43210. **Tel** (800)848-6538, (614)447-3600.)
Desc: Preparation, properties, and uses of carbon fibers. Includes highly carbonized fibers called graphite fibers.

ISSN 0190-9401
US
CODEN CSHNDN

CA SELECTS: CARBON & HETEROATOM NMR.
Added/Corp American Chemical Society. Chemical Abstracts Service. **VFOAT** Carbon & Heteroatom NMR. **VAT** Chemical Abstracts Selects. Carbon and Heteroatom Nuclear Magnetic Resonance. (July 9, 1979)-. Abstracting/Indexing Service. English. Twenty-six times a year. $220.00. Chemical Abstracts Service, (Subsidiary of The American Chemical Society), 2540 Olentangy River Road, PO Box 3012, Columbus OH 43210-0012. **Tel** (614)447-3731, (800)753-4227, FAX (614)447-3751. **(Subscription address:** Chemical Abstracts Service, Customer Service Department, PO Box 3012, Columbus OH 43210. **Tel** (800)848-6538, (614)447-3600.) **ED** David W Weisgerber. ***Continues in part*** *CA Selects. Nuclear Magnetic Resonance, Chemical Aspects, 0146-4507.*
Desc: Covers chemical aspects of nuclear magnetic resonance of carbon, fluorine, phosphorus, and other heteroatoms with chemically-induced dynamic nuclear polarization, internuclear double resonance and nuclear quadrupole resonance.

DD 547
ISSN 0895-5956
US
CODEN CSCCEY

CA SELECTS: CARBON FIBER COMPOSITES.
[CA sel., Carbon fiber compos.]. **Added/Corp** American Chemical Society. Chemical Abstracts Service. **VFOAT** Carbon Fiber Composites. **VAT** Chemical Abstracts Selects. Carbon Fiber Composites. (Jan. 11, 1988)-. Abstracting/Indexing Service. English. Twenty-six times a year. $220.00. Chemical Abstracts Service, (Subsidiary of The American Chemical Society), 2540 Olentangy River Road, PO Box 3012, Columbus OH 43210-0012. **Tel** (614)447-3731, (800)753-4227, FAX (614)447-3751. **(Subscription address:** Chemical Abstracts Service, Customer Service Department, PO Box 3012, Columbus OH 43210. **Tel** (800)848-6538, (614)447-3600.)
Desc: Covers the chemistry, production and use of carbon fiber-reinforced composites with ceramic, metallic and polymeric matrixes.

LC QD
DD 574.192
ISSN 0148-2408
US
CODEN CSCTDG

CA SELECTS: CARCINOGENS, MUTAGENS & TERATOGENS.
Added/Corp American Chemical Society. Chemical Abstracts Service. **VFOAT** Carcinogens, Mutagens, & Teratogens. **VAT** Chemical Abstracts Selects. Carcinogens, Mutagens and Teratogens. (Jan. 9, 1978)-. Abstracting/Indexing Service. English. Twenty-six times a year. $220.00. Chemical Abstracts Service, (Subsidiary of The American Chemical Society), 2540 Olentangy River Road, PO Box 3012, Columbus OH 43210-0012. **Tel** (614)447-3731, (800)753-4227, FAX (614)447-3751. **(Subscription address:** Chemical Abstracts Service, Customer Service Department, PO Box 3012, Columbus OH 43210. **Tel** (800)848-6538, (614)447-3600.) **ED** David W. Weisgerber.
Desc: Biological response to carcinogens, mutagens, and teratogens. Also includes mechanism of action and structural requirements for activity, and detection and quantitation in feed and food material.

ISSN 0146-440X
US
CODEN CCARDO

CA SELECTS: CATALYSIS (APPLIED AND PHYSICAL ASPECTS).
Added/Corp American Chemical Society. Chemical Abstracts Service. **VFOAT** Catalysis (Applied and Physical Aspects). **VAT** Chemical Abstracts Selects. Catalysis, Applied and Physical Aspects. (July 11, 1977)-. Abstracting/Indexing Service. English. Twenty-six times a year. $220.00. Chemical Abstracts Service, (Subsidiary of The American Chemical Society), 2540 Olentangy River Road, PO Box 3012, Columbus OH 43210-0012. **Tel** (614)447-3731, (800)753-4227, FAX (614)447-3751. **(Subscription address:** Chemical Abstracts Service, Customer Service Department, PO Box 3012, Columbus OH 43210. **Tel** (800)848-6538, (614)447-3600.) **ED** David W. Weisgerber.
Desc: Theory and applications of heterogeneous and homogeneous catalysis and catalysts. Also covers effect of catalysts on reaction kinetics.

ISSN 0146-4396
US
CODEN CSCRDA

CA SELECTS: CATALYSIS (ORGANIC REACTIONS).
Added/Corp American Chemical Society. Chemical Abstracts Service. **VFOAT** Catalysis (Organic Reactions). **VAT** Chemical Abstracts Selects. Catalysis, Organic Reactions. (July 11, 1977)-. Abstracting/Indexing Service. English. Twenty-six times a year. $220.00. Chemical Abstracts Service, (Subsidiary of The American Chemical Society), 2540 Olentangy River Road, PO Box 3012, Columbus OH 43210-0012. **Tel** (614)447-3731, (800)753-4227, FAX (614)447-3751. **(Subscription address:** Chemical Abstracts Service, Customer Service Department, PO Box 3012, Columbus OH 43210. **Tel** (800)848-6538, (614)447-3600.) **ED** David W Weisgerber.
Desc: Covers theory and applications of heterogeneous and homogeneous catalysis and catalysts in organic chemistry.

ISSN 0734-8800
US
CODEN CASREX

CA SELECTS: CATALYST REGENERATION.
[CA sel., Catal. regen.]. **Added/Corp** American Chemical Society. Chemical Abstracts Service. **VFOAT** Catalyst Regeneration. **VAT** Chemical Abstracts Selects. Catalyst Regeneration. (19??)-. Abstracting/Indexing Service. English. Twenty-six times a year. $220.00. Chemical Abstracts Service, (Subsidiary of The American Chemical Society), 2540 Olentangy River Road, PO Box 3012, Columbus OH 43210-0012. **Tel** (614)447-3731, (800)753-4227, FAX (614)447-3751. **(Subscription address:** Chemical Abstracts Service, Customer Service Department, PO Box 3012, Columbus OH 43210. **Tel** (800)848-6538, (614)447-3600.) **ED** David W Weisgerber.
Desc: Covers regeneration and reactivation of catalysts in laboratory processes and industrial applications with reclamation and recovery of active components and reprocessing of used catalysts.

DD 543
ISSN 0890-1864
US
CODEN CSKAEY

CA SELECTS: CATALYTIC & KINETIC ANALYSIS.
[CA sel., Catal. kinet. anal.]. **Added/Corp** American Chemical Society. Chemical Abstracts Service. **VFOAT** CA Selects. Catalytic and Kinetic Analysis; Catalytic and Kinetic Analysis; Catalytic & Kinetic Analysis. **VAT** Chemical Abstracts Selects. Catalytic and Kinetic Analysis. Issue 1 (Jan. 12, 1987)-. Abstracting/Indexing Service. English. Twenty-six times a year. $220.00. Chemical Abstracts Service, (Subsidiary of The American Chemical Society), 2540 Olentangy River Road, PO Box 3012, Columbus OH 43210-0012. **Tel** (614)447-3731, (800)753-4227, FAX (614)447-3751. **(Subscription address:** Chemical Abstracts Service, Customer Service Department, PO Box 3012, Columbus OH 43210. **Tel** (800)848-6538, (614)447-3600.)
Desc: Covers analytic methods involving kinetic and catalytic procedures, and catalytic thermometric titration, reaction rate titration and analysis involving Landolt reactions.

DD 666
ISSN 0895-5948
US
CODEN CSCMEU

CA SELECTS: CERAMIC MATERIALS (JOURNALS).
[CA sel., Ceram. mater. j.]. **Added/Corp** American Chemical Society. Chemical Abstracts Service. **VFOAT** Ceramic Materials (Journals). **VAT** Chemical Abstracts Selects. Ceramic Materials (Journals). (Jan. 11, 1988)-. Abstracting/Indexing Service. English. Twenty-six times a year. $220.00. Chemical Abstracts Service, (Subsidiary of The American Chemical Society), 2540 Olentangy River Road, PO Box 3012, Columbus OH 43210-0012. **Tel** (614)447-3731, (800)753-4227, FAX (614)447-3751. **(Subscription address:** Chemical Abstracts Service, Customer Service Department, PO Box 3012, Columbus OH 43210. **Tel** (800)848-6538, (614)447-3600.)
Desc: Covers the chemistry, production and use of oxide and nonoxide ceramics and glass ceramics as structural and building materials, refractories, thermal and electric insulators, membranes, solid electrolytes, cutting tools and dishware. Also covers the chemistry, production and use of cements. Patents are not covered.

DD 666
ISSN 0885-0100
US
CODEN CSCPE5

CA SELECTS: CERAMIC MATERIALS (PATENTS).
[CA sel., Ceram. meter. pat.]. **Added/Corp** American Chemical Society. Chemical Abstracts Service. **VFOAT** Ceramic Materials (Patents); Ceramic Materials. **VAT** Chemical Abstracts Selects. Ceramic Materials (Patents). Issue 1 (Jan. 13, 1986)-. Abstracting/Indexing Service. English. Twenty-six times a year. $220.00. Chemical Abstracts Service, (Subsidiary of The American Chemical Society), 2540 Olentangy River Road, PO Box 3012, Columbus OH 43210-0012. **Tel** (614)447-3731, (800)753-4227, FAX (614)447-3751. **(Subscription address:** Chemical Abstracts Service, Customer Service Department, PO Box 3012, Columbus OH 43210. **Tel** (800)848-6538, (614)447-3600.) **Bk Rev.**
Desc: Covers patents on the chemistry and technology of the ceramics industry, including cermets.

ISSN 0734-8797
US
CODEN CASAEG

CA SELECTS: CHELATING AGENTS.
[CA sel., Chelating agents]. **Added/Corp** American Chemical Society. Chemical Abstracts Service. **VFOAT** Chelating Agents. **VAT** Chemical Abstracts Selects. Chelating Agents. (19??)-. Abstracting/Indexing Service. English. Twenty-six times a year. $220.00. Chemical Abstracts Service, (Subsidiary of The American Chemical Society), 2540 Olentangy River Road, PO Box 3012, Columbus OH 43210-0012. **Tel** (614)447-3731, (800)753-4227, FAX (614)447-3751. **(Subscription address:** Chemical Abstracts Service, Customer Service Department, PO Box 3012, Columbus OH 43210. **Tel** (800)848-6538, (614)447-3600.)
Desc: Covers chelating agents and complexing agents in analytical procedures, separation processes, isolation of metals and industrial processes.

ISSN 0190-9398
US
CODEN CSCSDD

CA SELECTS: CHEMICAL HAZARDS, HEALTH, & SAFETY.
Added/Corp American Chemical Society. Chemical Abstracts Service. **VFOAT** Chemical Hazards, Health, & Safety. **VAT** Chemical Abstracts Selects. Chemical Hazards, Health, and Safety. (July 9, 1979)-. Abstracting/Indexing Service. English. Twenty-six times a year. $220.00. Chemical Abstracts Service, (Subsidiary of The American Chemical Society), 2540 Olentangy River Road, PO Box 3012, Columbus OH 43210-0012. **Tel** (614)447-3731, (800)753-4227,

FAX (614)447-3751. **(Subscription address:** Chemical Abstracts Service, Customer Service Department, PO Box 3012, Columbus OH 43210. **Tel** (800)848-6538, (614)447-3600.**)** **ED** David W Weisgerber. ***Continues*** *CA Selects. Chemical Hazards, 0146-4418.*
Desc: Information on safety in chemical laboratories and in the chemical and nuclear industries with effects of human exposure to hazardous substances and includes hazardous properties of chemical substances and reactions.

ISSN 0195-4938
US
CODEN CCHIDW

CA SELECTS: CHEMICAL INSTRUMENTATION. [CA sel., Chem. instrum.]. **Added/Corp** American Chemical Society. Chemical Abstracts Service. **VFOAT** Chemical Instrumentation. **VAT** Chemical Abstracts Selects. Chemical Instrumentation. (Jan. 14, 1980)-. Abstracting/Indexing Service. English. Twenty-six times a year. $220.00. Chemical Abstracts Service, (Subsidiary of The American Chemical Society), 2540 Olentangy River Road, PO Box 3012, Columbus OH 43210-0012. **Tel** (614)447-3731, (800)753-4227, FAX (614)447-3751. **(Subscription address:** Chemical Abstracts Service, Customer Service Department, PO Box 3012, Columbus OH 43210. **Tel** (800)848-6538, (614)447-3600.**)** **ED** David W Weisgerber.
Desc: Covers use of analyzers, detectors, and meters in chemistry and related areas. Also covers construction and modification of such instrumentation.

ISSN 0195-4946
US
CODEN CACAD3

CA SELECTS: CHEMICAL PROCESSING APPARATUS. [CA sel., Chem. process. appar.]. **Added/Corp** American Chemical Society. Chemical Abstracts Service. **VFOAT** Chemical Processing Apparatus. **VAT** Chemical Abstracts Selects. Chemical Processing Apparatus. (Jan. 14, 1980)-. Abstracting/Indexing Service. English. Twenty-six times a year. $220.00. Chemical Abstracts Service, (Subsidiary of The American Chemical Society), 2540 Olentangy River Road, PO Box 3012, Columbus OH 43210-0012. **Tel** (614)447-3731, (800)753-4227, FAX (614)447-3751. **(Subscription address:** Chemical Abstracts Service, Customer Service Department, PO Box 3012, Columbus OH 43210. **Tel** (800)848-6538, (614)447-3600.**)** **ED** David W Weisgerber.
Desc: Covers apparatus for absorption, crystallization, distillation, extraction, filtration, purification, separation and chemical processing.

ISSN 0885-0119
DD 671 US
CODEN CSCDE3

CA SELECTS. CHEMICAL VAPOR DEPOSITION. (CA SELECTS: CHEMICAL VAPOR DEPOSITION : CVD.). [CA sel., Chem. vapor depos.]. **Added/Corp** American Chemical Society. Chemical Abstracts Service. **VFOAT** Chemical Vapor Deposition; CVD. **VAT** Chemical Abstracts Selects. Chemical Vapor Deposition. Issue 1 (Jan. 13, 1986)-. Abstracting/Indexing Service. English. Twenty-six times a year. $220.00. Chemical Abstracts Service, (Subsidiary of The American Chemical Society), 2540 Olentangy River Road, PO Box 3012, Columbus OH 43210-0012. **Tel** (614)447-3731, (800)753-4227, FAX (614)447-3751. **(Subscription address:** Chemical Abstracts Service, Customer Service Department, PO Box 3012, Columbus OH 43210. **Tel** (800)848-6538, (614)447-3600.**)** **Bk Rev**.
Desc: Covers documents on CVD processes, with emphasis on device fabrications.

ISSN 1040-7138
DD 541 US
CODEN CSCHEF

CA SELECTS: CHEMILUMINESCENCE. [CA sel., Chemilumin.]. **Added/Corp** American Chemical Society. Chemical Abstracts Service. **VFOAT** Chemiluminescence. **VAT** Chemical Abstracts Selects. Chemiluminescence. (Jan. 9, 1989)-. Abstracting/Indexing Service. English. Twenty-six times a year. $220.00. Chemical Abstracts Service, (Subsidiary of The American Chemical Society), 2540 Olentangy River Road, PO Box 3012, Columbus OH 43210-0012. **Tel** (614)447-3731, (800)753-4227, FAX (614)447-3751. **(Subscription address:** Chemical Abstracts Service, Customer Service Department, PO Box 3012, Columbus OH 43210. **Tel** (800)848-6538, (614)447-3600.**)**
Desc: Covers the phenomenon of chemiluminescence and the chemistry of compounds showing chemiluminescence.

ISSN 1040-7146
DD 546 US
CODEN CSIRE7

CA SELECTS: CHEMISTRY OF IR, OS, RH, & RU. [CA sel., Chem. Ir Os Rh Ru]. **Added/Corp** American Chemical Society. Chemical Abstracts Service. **VFOAT** Chemistry of IR, OS, RH, & RU. **VAT** Chemical Abstracts Selects. Chemistry of Iridium, Osmium, Rhodium, and Ruthenium. (Jan. 9, 1989)-. Abstracting/Indexing Service. English. Twenty-six times a year. $215.00 US; $234.00 Canada, Mexico, Central and South America; $247.00 other. Chemical Abstracts Service, (Subsidiary of The American Chemical Society), 2540 Olentangy River Road, PO Box 3012, Columbus OH 43210-0012. **Tel** (614)447-3731, (800)753-4227, FAX (614)447-3751. **(Subscription address:** Chemical Abstracts Service, Customer Service Department, PO Box 3012, Columbus OH 43210. **Tel** (800)848-6538, (614)447-3600.**)** ctrl circ.
Desc: Covers preparation, properties, uses and characterization of compounds containing iridium, osmium, rhodium, and ruthenium.

ISSN 0146-4426
US
CODEN CSCCDX

CA SELECTS: COAL SCIENCE & PROCESS CHEMISTRY. **Added/Corp** American Chemical Society. Chemical Abstracts Service. **VFOAT** Coal Science & Process Chemistry. **VAT** Chemical Abstracts Selects. Coal Science and Process Chemistry. (July 11, 1977)-. Abstracting/Indexing Service. English. Twenty-six times a year. $220.00. Chemical Abstracts Service, (Subsidiary of The American Chemical Society), 2540 Olentangy River Road, PO Box 3012, Columbus OH 43210-0012. **Tel** (614)447-3731, (800)753-4227, FAX (614)447-3751. **(Subscription address:** Chemical Abstracts Service, Customer Service Department, PO Box 3012, Columbus OH 43210. **Tel** (800)848-6538, (614)447-3600.**)** **ED** David W Weisgerber.
Desc: Covers coal liquefaction, coal gasification and coal combustion, coal mine gases, brown coal, fossil fuel energy, synthetic fuels derived from coal and coke by-products.

ISSN 0275-7036
US
CODEN CCIPDO

CA SELECTS: COATINGS, INKS, & RELATED PRODUCTS. [CA sel., Coat., inks, relat. prod.]. **Added/Corp** American Chemical Society. Chemical Abstracts Service. **VFOAT** Chemical Abstracts Selects. Coatings, Inks, and Related Products; Coatings, Inks, & Related Products. (1981)-. Abstracting/Indexing Service. English. Twenty-six times a year. $220.00. Chemical Abstracts Service, (Subsidiary of The American Chemical Society), 2540 Olentangy River Road, PO Box 3012, Columbus OH 43210-0012. **Tel** (614)447-3731, (800)753-4227, FAX (614)447-3751. **(Subscription address:** Chemical Abstracts Service, Customer Service Department, PO Box 3012, Columbus OH 43210. **Tel** (800)848-6538, (614)447-3600.**)** **ED** David W Weisgerber. Documents available from CASDDS.
Desc: Covers chemistry, chemical and physical properties, and analysis of decorative and protective coatings: paints, lacquers, varnishes, organic enamels, ink vehicles, drying oils, pigments and other components.
Ind/Abst Chem. Abstr.

ISSN 0190-9444
US
CODEN CCMADX

CA SELECTS: COLLOIDS (MACROMOLECULAR ASPECTS). [CA sel.. colloids (macromol. asp.)]. **Added/Corp** American Chemical Society. Chemical Abstracts Service. **VFOAT** Colloids (Macromolecular Aspects). **VAT** Chemical Abstracts Selects. Colloids (Macromolecular Aspects). (July 9, 1979)-. Abstracting/Indexing Service. English. Twenty-six times a year. $220.00. Chemical Abstracts Service, (Subsidiary of The American Chemical Society), 2540 Olentangy River Road, PO Box 3012, Columbus OH 43210-0012. **Tel** (614)447-3731, (800)753-4227, FAX (614)447-3751. **(Subscription address:** Chemical Abstracts Service, Customer Service Department, PO Box 3012, Columbus OH 43210. **Tel** (800)848-6538, (614)447-3600.**)** **ED** David W Weisgerber. ***Supersedes in part*** *CA Selects. Colloids (Applied Aspects), 0160-8967.*
Desc: Covers macromolecular emulsions, gels, latexes, micellar solutions, sols, other forms of colloidal dispersions and the uses in coatings, elastomers, plastics, textiles and other industries.

ISSN 0160-8975
US
CODEN CCPADE

CA SELECTS: COLLOIDS (PHYSICOCHEMICAL ASPECTS). **Added/Corp** American Chemical Society. Chemical Abstracts Service. **VFOAT** Colloids (Physicochemical Aspects). **VAT** Chemical Abstracts Selects. Colloids (Physicochemical Aspects). (July 10, 1978)-. Abstracting/Indexing Service. English. Twenty-six times a year. $220.00. Chemical Abstracts Service, (Subsidiary of The American Chemical Society), 2540 Olentangy River Road, PO Box 3012, Columbus OH 43210-0012. **Tel** (614)447-3731, (800)753-4227, FAX (614)447-3751. **(Subscription address:** Chemical Abstracts Service, Customer Service Department, PO Box 3012, Columbus OH 43210. **Tel** (800)848-6538, (614)447-3600.**)** **ED** David W Weisgerber.
Desc: Covers physical chemistry of colloids, suspensions, dispersions, sols, gels, emulsions, foams, micellar solutions and particles of near-colloidal size.

ISSN 0885-0127
DD 535 US
CODEN CSCSEE

CA SELECTS: COLOR SCIENCE. [CA sel., color sci.]. **Added/Corp** American Chemical Society. Chemical Abstracts Service. **VFOAT** Color Science. **VAT** Chemical Abstracts Selects. Color Science. Issue 1 (Jan. 13, 1986)-. Abstracting/Indexing Service. English. Twenty-six times a year. $220.00. Chemical Abstracts Service, (Subsidiary of The American Chemical Society), 2540 Olentangy River Road, PO Box 3012, Columbus OH 43210-0012. **Tel** (614)447-3731, (800)753-4227, FAX (614)447-3751. **(Subscription address:** Chemical Abstracts Service, Customer Service Department, PO Box 3012, Columbus OH 43210. **Tel** (800)848-6538, (614)447-3600.**)** **Bk Rev**.
Desc: Covers documents on photochromic materials, phosphors, and light-emitting substances with respect to color.

ISSN 0734-8789
US
CODEN CASDEP

CA SELECTS: COLORANTS & DYES. [CA sel., Color. dyes]. **Added/Corp** American Chemical Society. Chemical Abstracts Service. **VFOAT** Colorants & Dyes; Colorants and Dyes. **VAT** Chemical Abstracts Selects. Colorants and Dyes. (19??)-. Abstracting/Indexing Service. English. Twenty-six times a year. $220.00. Chemical Abstracts Service, (Subsidiary of The American Chemical Society), 2540 Olentangy River Road, PO Box 3012, Columbus OH 43210-0012. **Tel** (614)447-3731, (800)753-4227, FAX (614)447-3751. **(Subscription address:** Chemical Abstracts Service, Customer Service Department, PO Box 3012, Columbus OH 43210. **Tel** (800)848-6538, (614)447-3600.**)** **ED** David W Weisgerber.
Desc: Covers isolation, identification, processing, use of natural dyes and pigments, synthesis, manufacturing, properties, and use of synthetic dyes and pigments.

ISSN 1066-1158
DD 620 US
CODEN CSCEE6

•**CA SELECTS: COMPOSITE MATERIALS (CERAMIC).** [CA sel., Compos. mater. (ceram.)]. **Added/Corp** American Chemical Society. Chemical Abstracts Service. **VFOAT** Composite Materials (Ceramic). **VAT** Chemical Abstracts Selects. Composite Materials (Ceramic). (Jan. 11, 1993)-. Abstracting/Indexing Service. English. Twenty-six times a year. $215.00 US; $234.00 Canada, Mexico, Central and South America; $247.00 other. Chemical Abstracts Service, (Subsidiary of The American Chemical Society), 2540 Olentangy River Road, PO Box 3012, Columbus OH 43210-0012. **Tel** (614)447-3731, (800)753-4227, FAX (614)447-3751. **(Subscription address:** Chemical Abstracts Service, Customer Service Department, PO Box 3012, Columbus OH 43210. **Tel** (800)848-6538, (614)447-3600.**)**
Desc: Researches the composition, properties and use of oxide and non-oxide ceramic matrixes.

ISSN 1066-114X
DD 620 US
CODEN CSMPEL

•**CA SELECTS: COMPOSITE MATERIALS (METALLIC).** [CA sel., Compos. mater. (met.)]. **Added/Corp** American Chemical Society. Chemical Abstracts Service. **VFOAT** Composite Materials (Metallic). **VAT** Chemical Abstracts Selects. Composite Materials (Metallic). (Jan. 11, 1993)-. Abstracting/Indexing Service. English. Twenty-six times a year. $215.00 US; $234.00 Canada, Mexico, Central and South America; $247.00 other. Chemical Abstracts Service, (Subsidiary of The American Chemical Society), 2540 Olentangy River Road, PO Box 3012, Columbus OH 43210-0012. **Tel** (614)447-3731, (800)753-4227, FAX (614)447-3751. **(Subscription address:** Chemical Abstracts Service, Customer Service Department, PO Box 3012, Columbus OH 43210. **Tel** (800)848-6538, (614)447-3600.**)**
Desc: Covers the chemistry, properties, composition and use of composite materials.

ISSN 1040-7154
DD 668 US
CODEN CAMTE9

CA SELECTS: COMPOSITE MATERIALS (POLYMERIC). [CA sel., Compos. mater. (polym.)]. **Added/Corp** American Chemical Society. Chemical Abstracts Service. **VFOAT** Composite Materials (Polymeric). **VAT** Chemical Abstracts Selects. Composite Materials (Polymeric). (Jan. 9, 1989)-. Abstracting/Indexing Service. English. Twenty-six times a year. $220.00. Chemical Abstracts Service, (Subsidiary of The American Chemical Society), 2540 Olentangy River Road, PO Box 3012, Columbus OH 43210-0012. **Tel** (614)447-3731, (800)753-4227, FAX (614)447-3751. **(Subscription address:** Chemical Abstracts Service, Customer Service Department, PO Box 3012, Columbus OH 43210. **Tel** (800)848-6538, (614)447-3600.**)** ctrl circ.
Desc: Covers chemistry, manufacture and use of composites with plastic (polymeric) matrixes and fibrous, granular, or spherical fillers; laminated plastics and reinforced elastomers.

ISSN 0160-9025
US
CODEN CCOCDF

CA SELECTS: COMPUTERS IN CHEMISTRY. See Chemistry and Chemicals-Computer Applications.

ISSN 0885-0135
DD 547
US
CODEN CACPEF

CA SELECTS: CONDUCTIVE POLYMERS. [CA sel., Conduct. polym.]. **Added/Corp** American Chemical Society. Chemical Abstracts Service. **VFOAT** Conductive Polymers. **VAT** Chemical Abstracts Selects. Conductive Polymers. Issue 1 (Jan. 13, 1986)-. Abstracting/Indexing Service. English. Twenty-six times a year. $220.00. Chemical Abstracts Service, (Subsidiary of The American Chemical Society), 2540 Olentangy River Road, PO Box 3012, Columbus OH 43210-0012. **Tel** (614)447-3731, (800)753-4227, FAX (614)447-3751. **(Subscription address:** Chemical Abstracts Service, Customer Service Department, PO Box 3012, Columbus OH 43210. **Tel** (800)848-6538, (614)447-3600.) **Bk Rev**.
Desc: Covers documents on the preparation, properties, and uses of polymers with sufficient electrical conductivity to be classified as conductors or semiconductors.

ISSN 0740-0748
DD 615
US
CODEN CSCTEH

CA SELECTS: CONTROLLED RELEASE TECHNOLOGY. [CA sel., Control. release technol.]. **Added/Corp** American Chemical Society. Chemical Abstracts Service. **VFOAT** Controlled Release Technology. **VAT** Chemical Abstracts Selects. Controlled Release Technology. (19??)-. Abstracting/Indexing Service. English. Twenty-six times a year. $220.00. Chemical Abstracts Service, (Subsidiary of The American Chemical Society), 2540 Olentangy River Road, PO Box 3012, Columbus OH 43210-0012. **Tel** (614)447-3731, (800)753-4227, FAX (614)447-3751. **(Subscription address:** Chemical Abstracts Service, Customer Service Department, PO Box 3012, Columbus OH 43210. **Tel** (800)848-6538, (614)447-3600.) **ED** David W Weisgerber. **Bk Rev**.
Desc: Covers science and technology of controlled release of biologically active materials (drugs, agrochemicals). Also, information on polymeric delivery systems.

ISSN 0749-7296
DD 620
US
CODEN CASCEM

CA SELECTS: CORROSION-INHIBITING COATINGS. [CA sel., Corros.-inhib. coat.]. **Added/Corp** American Chemical Society. Chemical Abstracts Service. **VFOAT** Corrosion-Inhibiting Coatings; Corrosion Inhibiting Coatings. Issue 1 (Jan. 14, 1985)-. Abstracting/Indexing Service. English. Twenty-six times a year. $220.00. Chemical Abstracts Service, (Subsidiary of The American Chemical Society), 2540 Olentangy River Road, PO Box 3012, Columbus OH 43210-0012. **Tel** (614)447-3731, (800)753-4227, FAX (614)447-3751. **(Subscription address:** Chemical Abstracts Service, Customer Service Department, PO Box 3012, Columbus OH 43210. **Tel** (800)848-6538, (614)447-3600.)
Desc: Covers documents on the formulation and application of coating compositions intended to prevent corrosion of the metallic surfaces to which they are applied.

ISSN 0275-7044
US
CODEN CACCD9

CA SELECTS: COSMETIC CHEMICALS. [CA sel., Cosmet. chem.]. **Added/Corp** American Chemical Society. Chemical Abstracts Service. **VFOAT** Cosmetic Chemicals. **VAT** Chemical Abstracts Selects. Cosmetic Chemicals. (1981)-. Abstracting/Indexing Service. English. Twenty-six times a year. $220.00. Chemical Abstracts Service, (Subsidiary of The American Chemical Society), 2540 Olentangy River Road, PO Box 3012, Columbus OH 43210-0012. **Tel** (614)447-3731, (800)753-4227, FAX (614)447-3751. **(Subscription address:** Chemical Abstracts Service, Customer Service Department, PO Box 3012, Columbus OH 43210. **Tel** (800)848-6538, (614)447-3600.) **ED** David W Weisgerber. Documents available from CASDDS.
Desc: Covers synthesis or manufacturing of chemical substances of use in cosmetics and formulation of cosmetic preparations.
Ind/Abst Chem. Abstr.

ISSN 0740-0721
DD 547
US
CODEN CSCREB

CA SELECTS: CROSSLINKING REACTIONS. [CA sel., Crosslink. react.]. **Added/Corp** American Chemical Society. Chemical Abstracts Service. **VFOAT** Crosslinking Reactions. **VAT** Chemical Abstracts Selects. Crosslinking Reactions. (19??)-. Abstracting/Indexing Service. English. Twenty-six times a year. $220.00. Chemical Abstracts Service, (Subsidiary of The American Chemical Society), 2540 Olentangy River Road, PO Box 3012, Columbus OH 43210-0012. **Tel** (614)447-3731, (800)753-4227, FAX (614)447-3751. **(Subscription address:** Chemical Abstracts Service, Customer Service Department, PO Box 3012, Columbus OH 43210. **Tel** (800)848-6538, (614)447-3600.) **ED** David W Weisgerber.
Desc: Covers formation of three dimensional polymer networks by various means, e.g., polymerization of monomers with functionality greater than two, reaction of functional linear polymers with multifunctional agents.

ISSN 0162-7740
US
CODEN CSCGDB

CA SELECTS: CRYSTAL GROWTH. **Added/Corp** American Chemical Society. Chemical Abstracts Service. **VFOAT** Crystal Growth. **VAT** Chemical Abstracts Selects. Crystal Growth. (Jan. 8, 1979)-. Abstracting/Indexing Service. English. Twenty-six times a year. $220.00. Chemical Abstracts Service, (Subsidiary of The American Chemical Society), 2540 Olentangy River Road, PO Box 3012, Columbus OH 43210-0012. **Tel** (614)447-3731, (800)753-4227, FAX (614)447-3751. **(Subscription address:** Chemical Abstracts Service, Customer Service Department, PO Box 3012, Columbus OH 43210. **Tel** (800)848-6538, (614)447-3600.) **ED** David W Weisgerber.
Desc: Covers growth of crystals, dendrites, whiskers, crystallites with devitrification of glasses, epitaxial processes, and zone refining.

ISSN 0162-7767
US
CODEN CSDSDI

CA SELECTS: DETERGENTS, SOAPS, & SURFACTANTS. **Added/Corp** American Chemical Society. Chemical Abstracts Service. **VFOAT** Detergents, Soaps, & Surfactants. **VAT** Chemical Abstracts Selects. Detergents, Soaps, and Surfactants. (Jan. 8, 1979)-. Abstracting/Indexing Service. English. Twenty-six times a year. $220.00. Chemical Abstracts Service, (Subsidiary of The American Chemical Society), 2540 Olentangy River Road, PO Box 3012, Columbus OH 43210-0012. **Tel** (614)447-3731, (800)753-4227, FAX (614)447-3751. **(Subscription address:** Chemical Abstracts Service, Customer Service Department, PO Box 3012, Columbus OH 43210. **Tel** (800)848-6538, (614)447-3600.) **ED** David W Weisgerber.
Desc: Covers preparation, properties and uses of soaps and synthetic detergents, formulations, dry-cleaning solvents, and use of surfactants in petroleum recovery.

ISSN 0275-7052
US
CODEN CDITD9

CA SELECTS: DISTILLATION TECHNOLOGY. [CA sel., Distill. technol.]. **Added/Corp** American Chemical Society. Chemical Abstracts Service. **VFOAT** Distillation Technology. **VAT** Chemical Abstracts Selects. Distillation Technology. (1981)-. Abstracting/Indexing Service. English. Twenty-six times a year. $220.00. Chemical Abstracts Service, (Subsidiary of The American Chemical Society), 2540 Olentangy River Road, PO Box 3012, Columbus OH 43210-0012. **Tel** (614)447-3731, (800)753-4227, FAX (614)447-3751. **(Subscription address:** Chemical Abstracts Service, Customer Service Department, PO Box 3012, Columbus OH 43210. **Tel** (800)848-6538, (614)447-3600.) **ED** David W Weisgerber. Documents available from CASDDS.
Desc: Covers distillation as a unit process, design of distillation equipment, extractive distillation, molecular distillation, and applications of distillation technology.
Ind/Abst Chem. Abstr.

ISSN 0749-730X
DD 622
US
CODEN CADMEB

CA SELECTS: DRILLING MUDS. [CA sel., Drill. muds]. **Added/Corp** American Chemical Society. Chemical Abstracts Service. **VFOAT** Drilling Muds. Issue 1 (Jan. 14, 1985)-. Abstracting/Indexing Service. English. Twenty-six times a year. $220.00. Chemical Abstracts Service, (Subsidiary of The American Chemical Society), 2540 Olentangy River Road, PO Box 3012, Columbus OH 43210-0012. **Tel** (614)447-3731, (800)753-4227, FAX (614)447-3751. **(Subscription address:** Chemical Abstracts Service, Customer Service Department, PO Box 3012, Columbus OH 43210. **Tel** (800)848-6538, (614)447-3600.)
Desc: Covers documents on the formulation, properties, and performance of aqueous suspensions used in the drilling of oil and gas wells.

ISSN 0162-7775
US
CODEN CSDTDL

CA SELECTS: DRUG & COSMETIC TOXICITY. **Added/Corp** American Chemical Society. Chemical Abstracts Service. **VFOAT** Drug & Cosmetic Toxicity. **VAT** Chemical Abstracts Selects. Drug and Cosmetic Toxicity. (Jan. 8, 1979)-. Abstracting/Indexing Service. English. Twenty-six times a year. $220.00. Chemical Abstracts Service, (Subsidiary of The American Chemical Society), 2540 Olentangy River Road, PO Box 3012, Columbus OH 43210-0012. **Tel** (614)447-3731, (800)753-4227, FAX (614)447-3751. **(Subscription address:** Chemical Abstracts Service, Customer Service Department, PO Box 3012, Columbus OH 43210. **Tel** (800)848-6538, (614)447-3600.) **ED** David W Weisgerber.
Desc: Covers toxic manifestations of drugs, cosmetics, and ingredients of drug and cosmetic preparations, health hazards, side effects, and safety of drugs, cosmetics, and their ingredients, poisoning and treatment.

ISSN 1040-7162
DD 615
US
CODEN CSDSEJ

CA SELECTS: DRUG DELIVERY SYSTEMS & DOSAGE FORMS. [CA sel., Drug deliv. syst. dos. forms]. **Added/Corp** American Chemical Society. Chemical Abstracts Service. **VFOAT** Drug Delivery Systems & Dosage Forms; Drug Delivery Systems and Dosage Forms. **VAT** Chemical Abstracts Selects. Drug Delivery Systems & Dosage Forms. (Jan. 9, 1989)-. Abstracting/Indexing Service. English. Twenty-six times a year. $220.00. Chemical Abstracts Service, (Subsidiary of The American Chemical Society), 2540 Olentangy River Road, PO Box 3012, Columbus OH 43210-0012. **Tel** (614)447-3731, (800)753-4227, FAX (614)447-3751. **(Subscription address:** Chemical Abstracts Service, Customer Service Department, PO Box 3012, Columbus OH 43210. **Tel** (800)848-6538, (614)447-3600.)
Desc: Covers pharmaceutical dosage forms, and newer delivery systems and forms such as controlled-release devices, transdermal systems, ocular inserts, osmotic devices, antibody conjugates and liposomes. Pharmacological studies of drugs themselves with no formulation interest are excluded.

ISSN 0885-0143
DD 547
US
CODEN CSEOEC

CA SELECTS: ELECTRICALLY CONDUCTIVE ORGANICS. [CA sel., Electr. conduct. org.]. **Added/Corp** American Chemical Society. Chemical Abstracts Service. **VFOAT** Electrically Conductive Organics. **VAT** Chemical Abstracts Selects. Electrically Conductive Organics. Issue 1 (Jan. 13, 1986)-. Abstracting/Indexing Service. English. Twenty-six times a year. $220.00. Chemical Abstracts Service, (Subsidiary of The American Chemical Society), 2540 Olentangy River Road, PO Box 3012, Columbus OH 43210-0012. **Tel** (614)447-3731, (800)753-4227, FAX (614)447-3751. **(Subscription address:** Chemical Abstracts Service, Customer Service Department, PO Box 3012, Columbus OH 43210. **Tel** (800)848-6538, (614)447-3600.) **Bk Rev**.
Desc: Covers documents on electrical conductors and superconductors based on organic compounds e.g. TCNQ and TMTSF complexes.

ISSN 0734-8770
US
CODEN CAESEY

CA SELECTS: ELECTROCHEMICAL ORGANIC SYNTHESIS. [CA sel., Electrochem. org. synth.]. **Added/Corp** American Chemical Society. Chemical Abstracts Service. **VFOAT** Electrochemical Organic Synthesis. **VAT** Chemical Abstracts Selects. Electrochemical Organic Synthesis. (19??)-. Abstracting/Indexing Service. English. Twenty-six times a year. $220.00. Chemical Abstracts Service, (Subsidiary of The American Chemical Society), 2540 Olentangy River Road, PO Box 3012, Columbus OH 43210-0012. **Tel** (614)447-3731, (800)753-4227, FAX (614)447-3751. **(Subscription address:** Chemical Abstracts Service, Customer Service Department, PO Box 3012, Columbus OH 43210. **Tel** (800)848-6538, (614)447-3600.) **ED** David W Weisgerber.
Desc: Covers organic synthesis in which the starting material, one or more intermediates, or the final product is prepared by a specific electrochemical process.

ISSN 0146-4442
US
CODEN CSERDK

CA SELECTS: ELECTROCHEMICAL REACTIONS. **Added/Corp** American Chemical Society. Chemical Abstracts Service. **VFOAT** Electrochemical Reactions. **VAT** Chemical Abstracts Selects. Electrochemical Reactions. (July 11, 1977)-. Abstracting/Indexing Service. English. Twenty-six times a year. $220.00. Chemical Abstracts Service, (Subsidiary of The American Chemical Society), 2540 Olentangy River Road, PO Box 3012, Columbus OH 43210-0012. **Tel** (614)447-3731, (800)753-4227, FAX (614)447-3751. **(Subscription address:** Chemical Abstracts Service, Customer Service Department, PO Box 3012, Columbus OH 43210. **Tel** (800)848-6538, (614)447-3600.) **ED** David W Weisgerber.
Desc: Covers electrolysis, electro-oxidation, electroreduction, polarography, electrochemical reactions in biochemistry, organic, macromolecular, applied, and inorganic chemistry.

ISSN 0162-7783
US
CODEN CSELD2

CA SELECTS: ELECTRODEPOSITION. **Added/Corp** American Chemical Society. Chemical Abstracts Service. **VFOAT** Electrodeposition. **VAT** Chemical Abstracts Selects. Electrodeposition. (Jan. 8, 1979)-. Abstracting/Indexing Service. English. Twenty-six times a year. $220.00. Chemical Abstracts Service, (Subsidiary of The American Chemical Society), 2540

Olentangy River Road, PO Box 3012, Columbus OH 43210-0012. **Tel** (614)447-3731, (800)753-4227, FAX (614)447-3751. **(Subscription address:** Chemical Abstracts Service, Customer Service Department, PO Box 3012, Columbus OH 43210. **Tel** (800)848-6538, (614)447-3600.**)** **ED** David W Weisgerber.
Desc: Covers electroplating and electroforming, electrorefining, electrowinning, and electrolytic recovery, anodization and passivation, electrophoretic and electrostatic coating, and plasma coating, sputtering film deposition.

ISSN 0146-4450
US
CODEN CSESDN

CA SELECTS: ELECTRON & AUGER SPECTROSCOPY.

Added/Corp American Chemical Society. Chemical Abstracts Service. **VFOAT** Electron & Auger Spectroscopy. **VAT** Chemical Abstracts Selects. Electron and Auger Spectroscopy. (July 11, 1977)-. Abstracting/Indexing Service. English. Twenty-six times a year. $220.00. Chemical Abstracts Service, (Subsidiary of The American Chemical Society), 2540 Olentangy River Road, PO Box 3012, Columbus OH 43210-0012. **Tel** (614)447-3731, (800)753-4227, FAX (614)447-3751. **(Subscription address:** Chemical Abstracts Service, Customer Service Department, PO Box 3012, Columbus OH 43210. **Tel** (800)848-6538, (614)447-3600.**)** **ED** David W Weisgerber.
Desc: Covers electron spectroscopy, auger electron spectroscopy, ESCA, x-ray photoelectron spectroscopy, photoexcitation spectroscopy, and photoemission spectroscopy.

ISSN 0146-4469
US
CODEN CSEAD3

CA SELECTS: ELECTRON SPIN RESONANCE (CHEMICAL ASPECTS).

Added/Corp American Chemical Society. Chemical Abstracts Service. **VFOAT** Electron Spin Resonance (Chemical Aspects). **VAT** Chemical Abstracts Selects. Electron Spin Resonance, Chemical Aspects. (July 11, 1977)-. Abstracting/Indexing Service. English. Twenty-six times a year. $220.00. Chemical Abstracts Service, (Subsidiary of The American Chemical Society), 2540 Olentangy River Road, PO Box 3012, Columbus OH 43210-0012. **Tel** (614)447-3731, (800)753-4227, FAX (614)447-3751. **(Subscription address:** Chemical Abstracts Service, Customer Service Department, PO Box 3012, Columbus OH 43210. **Tel** (800)848-6538, (614)447-3600.**)** **ED** David W Weisgerber.
Desc: Covers chemical aspects of electron spin resonance, electron nuclear double resonance, and electron paramagnetic resonance.

ISSN 0885-0151
DD 541 US
CODEN CSEME6

CA SELECTS: ELECTRONIC CHEMICALS & MATERIALS.

[CA sel., Electron. chem. mater.]. **Added/Corp** American Chemical Society. Chemical Abstracts Service. **VFOAT** CA Selects. Electronic Chemicals and Materials; Electronic Chemicals & Materials; Electronic Chemicals and Materials. **VAT** Chemical Abstracts Selects. Electronic Chemicals & Materials. Iss 1 (Jan. 13, 1986)-. Abstracting/Indexing Service. English. Twenty-six times a year. $220.00. Chemical Abstracts Service, (Subsidiary of The American Chemical Society), 2540 Olentangy River Road, PO Box 3012, Columbus OH 43210-0012. **Tel** (614)447-3731, (800)753-4227, FAX (614)447-3751. **(Subscription address:** Chemical Abstracts Service, Customer Service Department, PO Box 3012, Columbus OH 43210. **Tel** (800)848-6538, (614)447-3600.**)** **Bk Rev.**
Desc: Covers documents on specialty chemicals, materials, and processes involved in the field of solid-state electronic device fabrication.

ISSN 0195-4962
US
CODEN CAELDC

CA SELECTS: ELECTROPHORESIS.

[CA sel., Electrophor.]. **Added/Corp** American Chemical Society. Chemical Abstracts Service. **VFOAT** Electrophoresis. **VAT** Chemical Abstracts Selects. Electrophoresis. (Jan. 14, 1980)-. Abstracting/Indexing Service. English. Twenty-six times a year. $220.00. Chemical Abstracts Service, (Subsidiary of The American Chemical Society), 2540 Olentangy River Road, PO Box 3012, Columbus OH 43210-0012. **Tel** (614)447-3731, (800)753-4227, FAX (614)447-3751. **(Subscription address:** Chemical Abstracts Service, Customer Service Department, PO Box 3012, Columbus OH 43210. **Tel** (800)848-6538, (614)447-3600.**)** **ED** David W Weisgerber.
Desc: Covers techniques of electrophoretic processes, and cataphoresis, ionophoresis, isoelectric focusing.

ISSN 0734-8754
US
CODEN CAEDEN

CA SELECTS: EMULSIFIERS & DEMULSIFIERS.

Added/Corp American Chemical Society. Chemical Abstracts Service. **VFOAT** Emulsifiers & Demulsifiers; Emulsifiers and Demulsifiers. **VAT** Chemical Abstracts Selects. Emulsifiers and Demulsifiers. (19??)-. Abstracting/Indexing Service. English. Twenty-six times a year. $220.00. Chemical Abstracts Service, (Subsidiary of The American Chemical Society), 2540 Olentangy River Road, PO Box 3012, Columbus OH 43210-0012. **Tel** (614)447-3731, (800)753-4227, FAX (614)447-3751. **(Subscription address:** Chemical Abstracts Service, Customer Service Department, PO Box 3012, Columbus OH 43210. **Tel** (800)848-6538, (614)447-3600.**)** **ED** David W Weisgerber.
Desc: Covers preparation, properties, uses of surface-active agents in formation, stabilization, or de-stabilization of emulsions, aqueous and nonaqueous emulsions, and applications in cosmetics, food, petroleum, and polymer industries.

ISSN 0195-4970
US
CODEN CEPOD2

CA SELECTS: EMULSION POLYMERIZATION.

[CA sel., Emuls. polym.]. **Added/Corp** American Chemical Society. Chemical Abstracts Service. **VFOAT** Emulsion Polymerization. **VAT** Chemical Abstracts Selects. Emulsion Polymerization. (Jan. 14, 1980)-. Abstracting/Indexing Service. English. Twenty-six times a year. $220.00. Chemical Abstracts Service, (Subsidiary of The American Chemical Society), 2540 Olentangy River Road, PO Box 3012, Columbus OH 43210-0012. **Tel** (614)447-3731, (800)753-4227, FAX (614)447-3751. **(Subscription address:** Chemical Abstracts Service, Customer Service Department, PO Box 3012, Columbus OH 43210. **Tel** (800)848-6538, (614)447-3600.**)** **ED** David W Weisgerber.
Desc: Covers polymerizations carried out in emulsion to produce plastics, elastomers, coating materials, and preparation of emulsifiers for use in such polymerizations.

ISSN 0162-7791
US
CODEN CSEBD6

CA SELECTS: ENERGY REVIEWS & BOOKS.

Added/Corp American Chemical Society. Chemical Abstracts Service. **VFOAT** Energy Reviews & Books. **VAT** Chemical Abstracts Selects. Energy Reviews and Books. (Jan. 8, 1979)-. Abstracting/Indexing Service. English. Twenty-six times a year. $220.00. Chemical Abstracts Service, (Subsidiary of The American Chemical Society), 2540 Olentangy River Road, PO Box 3012, Columbus OH 43210-0012. **Tel** (614)447-3731, (800)753-4227, FAX (614)447-3751. **(Subscription address:** Chemical Abstracts Service, Customer Service Department, PO Box 3012, Columbus OH 43210. **Tel** (800)848-6538, (614)447-3600.**)** **ED** David W Weisgerber.
Desc: Covers chemical aspects of energy and heat, primarily commercial and industrial applications, energy production, usage, storage, conservation, electrical and thermal power, fuels and propellants, heat transfer, nuclear fission and fusion.

ISSN 0734-8746
US
CODEN CAEREV

CA SELECTS: ENHANCED PETROLEUM RECOVERY.

Added/Corp American Chemical Society. Chemical Abstracts Service. **VFOAT** Enhanced Petroleum Recovery. **VAT** Chemical Abstracts Selects. Enhanced Petroleum Recovery. (19??)-. Abstracting/Indexing Service. English. Twenty-six times a year. $220.00. Chemical Abstracts Service, (Subsidiary of The American Chemical Society), 2540 Olentangy River Road, PO Box 3012, Columbus OH 43210-0012. **Tel** (614)447-3731, (800)753-4227, FAX (614)447-3751. **(Subscription address:** Chemical Abstracts Service, Customer Service Department, PO Box 3012, Columbus OH 43210. **Tel** (800)848-6538, (614)447-3600.**)** **ED** David W Weisgerber.
Desc: Covers means for stimulating production of oil wells, secondary and tertiary recovery techniques, and in-situ retorting of oil shales and tar sands.

ISSN 0160-9041
US
CODEN CSPODW

CA SELECTS: ENVIRONMENTAL POLLUTION.

Added/Corp American Chemical Society. Chemical Abstracts Service. **VFOAT** Environmental Pollution. **VAT** Chemical Abstracts Selects. Environmental Pollution. (July 10, 1978)-. Abstracting/Indexing Service. English. Twenty-six times a year. $220.00. Chemical Abstracts Service, (Subsidiary of The American Chemical Society), 2540 Olentangy River Road, PO Box 3012, Columbus OH 43210-0012. **Tel** (614)447-3731, (800)753-4227, FAX (614)447-3751. **(Subscription address:** Chemical Abstracts Service, Customer Service Department, PO Box 3012, Columbus OH 43210. **Tel** (800)848-6538, (614)447-3600.**)** **ED** David W Weisgerber.
Desc: Covers pollution of the environment by gaseous, liquid, solid and radioactive wastes, oil spills, nuclear fallout, runoff containing fertilizers from agricultural lands, and eutrophication of bodies of water.

ISSN 0895-593X
DD 547 US
CODEN CAEAEE

CA SELECTS: ENZYME APPLICATIONS.

[CA sel., Enzym. appl.]. **Added/Corp** American Chemical Society. Chemical Abstracts Service. **VFOAT** Enzyme Applications. **VAT** Chemical Abstracts Selects. Enzyme Applications. (Jan. 11, 1988)-. Abstracting/Indexing Service. English. Twenty-six times a year. $220.00. Chemical Abstracts Service, (Subsidiary of The American Chemical Society), 2540 Olentangy River Road, PO Box 3012, Columbus OH 43210-0012. **Tel** (614)447-3731, (800)753-4227, FAX (614)447-3751. **(Subscription address:** Chemical Abstracts Service, Customer Service Department, PO Box 3012, Columbus OH 43210. **Tel** (800)848-6538, (614)447-3600.**)**
Desc: Analyzes studies in which enzymes are used as catalytic agents for the synthesis of organic compounds and covers how enzymes are used in a single step of a multistep organic synthesis.

ISSN 0895-5808
DD 574 US
CODEN CSEAE4

CA SELECTS: ENZYME ASSAYS.

[CA sel., Enzym. assays]. **Added/Corp** American Chemical Society. Chemical Abstracts Service. **VFOAT** Enzyme Assays. **VAT** Chemical Abstracts Selects. Enzyme Assays. (Jan. 11, 1988)-. Abstracting/Indexing Service. English. Twenty-six times a year. $220.00. Chemical Abstracts Service, (Subsidiary of The American Chemical Society), 2540 Olentangy River Road, PO Box 3012, Columbus OH 43210-0012. **Tel** (614)447-3731, (800)753-4227, FAX (614)447-3751. **(Subscription address:** Chemical Abstracts Service, Customer Service Department, PO Box 3012, Columbus OH 43210. **Tel** (800)848-6538, (614)447-3600.**)**
Desc: Studies the quantitative and qualitative methods for the determination of enzymes and for the use of enzymes in laboratory or clinical analysis.

ISSN 0275-7060
US
CODEN CEPRDB

CA SELECTS: EPOXY RESINS.

[CA sel., Epoxy resins]. **Added/Corp** American Chemical Society. Chemical Abstracts Service. **VFOAT** Epoxy Resins; C.A. Selects. Epoxy Resins. **VAT** Chemical Abstracts Selects. Epoxy Resins. (1981)-. Abstracting/Indexing Service. English. Twenty-six times a year. $220.00. Chemical Abstracts Service, (Subsidiary of The American Chemical Society), 2540 Olentangy River Road, PO Box 3012, Columbus OH 43210-0012. **Tel** (614)447-3731, (800)753-4227, FAX (614)447-3751. **(Subscription address:** Chemical Abstracts Service, Customer Service Department, PO Box 3012, Columbus OH 43210. **Tel** (800)848-6538, (614)447-3600.**)** Documents available from CASDDS.
Desc: Covers synthesis, curing, properties, uses of macromolecular compounds rings.
Ind/Abst Chem. Abstr.

ISSN 0275-7079
US
CODEN CSFODG

CA SELECTS: FATS & OILS.

[CA sel., Fats oils]. **Added/Corp** American Chemical Society. Chemical Abstracts Service. **VFOAT** Fats & Oils; C.A. Selects. Fats and Oils. **VAT** Chemical Abstracts Selects. Fats and Oils. (1981)-. Abstracting/Indexing Service. English. Twenty-six times a year. $220.00. Chemical Abstracts Service, (Subsidiary of The American Chemical Society), 2540 Olentangy River Road, PO Box 3012, Columbus OH 43210-0012. **Tel** (614)447-3731, (800)753-4227, FAX (614)447-3751. **(Subscription address:** Chemical Abstracts Service, Customer Service Department, PO Box 3012, Columbus OH 43210. **Tel** (800)848-6538, (614)447-3600.**)** **ED** David W Weisgerber. Documents available from CASDDS.
Desc: Covers extraction, analysis, properties and uses of fats and oils.
Ind/Abst Chem. Abstr.

ISSN 0740-0713
DD 547 US
CODEN CSFCEF

CA SELECTS: FERMENTATION CHEMICALS.

[CA sel., Ferment. chem.]. **Added/Corp** American Chemical Society. Chemical Abstracts Service. **VFOAT** Fermentation Chemicals. **VAT** Chemical Abstracts Selects. Fermentation Chemicals. (19??)-. Abstracting/Indexing Service. English. Twenty-six times a year. $220.00. Chemical Abstracts Service, (Subsidiary of The American Chemical Society), 2540 Olentangy River Road, PO Box 3012, Columbus OH 43210-0012. **Tel** (614)447-3731, (800)753-4227, FAX (614)447-3751. **(Subscription address:** Chemical Abstracts Service, Customer Service Department, PO Box 3012, Columbus OH 43210. **Tel** (800)848-6538, (614)447-3600.**)** **ED** David W Weisgerber.
Desc: Covers compounds prepared by fermentation processes and compounds routinely used in fermentation processes.

ISSN 0890-1872
DD 621 US
CODEN CSOCEQ

CA SELECTS: FIBER OPTICS & OPTICAL COMMUNICATION.

[CA sel., Fiber opt. opt. commun.]. **Added/Corp** American Chemical Society. Chemical Abstracts Service. **VFOAT** CA Selects. Fiber Optics and Optical Communication. **VAT** Chemical Abstracts Selects. Fiber Optics & Optical Communication. Issue 1 (Jan. 12, 1987)-. Abstracting/Indexing Service.

English. Twenty-six times a year. $220.00. Chemical Abstracts Service, (Subsidiary of The American Chemical Society), 2540 Olentangy River Road, PO Box 3012, Columbus OH 43210-0012. **Tel** (614)447-3731, (800)753-4227, FAX (614)447-3751. **(Subscription address:** Chemical Abstracts Service, Customer Service Department, PO Box 3012, Columbus OH 43210. **Tel** (800)848-6538, (614)447-3600.**)**
Desc: Materials used for fiber optics and optical communications.

ISSN 0734-869X
US
CODEN CAFPEU

CA SELECTS: FIBER-REINFORCED PLASTICS. **Added/Corp** American Chemical Society. Chemical Abstracts Service. **VFOAT** Fiber-Reinforced Plastics. **VAT** Chemical Abstracts Selects. Fiber-Reinforced Plastics. (19??)-. Abstracting/Indexing Service. English. Twenty-six times a year. $220.00. Chemical Abstracts Service, (Subsidiary of The American Chemical Society), 2540 Olentangy River Road, PO Box 3012, Columbus OH 43210-0012. **Tel** (614)447-3731, (800)753-4227, FAX (614)447-3751. **(Subscription address:** Chemical Abstracts Service, Customer Service Department, PO Box 3012, Columbus OH 43210. **Tel** (800)848-6538, (614)447-3600.**)** **ED** David W Weisgerber.
Desc: Covers properties, processing and use of thermoplastics and thermosetting resins reinforced by natural or synthetic fibers.

ISSN 0162-7805
US
CODEN CSFLD7

CA SELECTS: FLAMMABILITY. **Added/Corp** American Chemical Society. Chemical Abstracts Service. **VFOAT** Flammability. **VAT** Chemical Abstracts Selects. Flammability. (Jan. 8, 1979)-. Abstracting/Indexing Service. English. Twenty-six times a year. $220.00. Chemical Abstracts Service, (Subsidiary of The American Chemical Society), 2540 Olentangy River Road, PO Box 3012, Columbus OH 43210-0012. **Tel** (614)447-3731, (800)753-4227, FAX (614)447-3751. **(Subscription address:** Chemical Abstracts Service, Customer Service Department, PO Box 3012, Columbus OH 43210. **Tel** (800)848-6538, (614)447-3600.**)** **ED** David W Weisgerber.
Desc: Covers flammability of materials and test methods for determining it, relationship of chemical structure to flammability and synthesis and use of flame retardants and fireproofing agents.

ISSN 0148-2327
US
CODEN CASFDU

CA SELECTS: FLAVORS & FRAGRANCES. **Added/Corp** American Chemical Society. Chemical Abstracts Service. **VFOAT** Flavors & Fragrances. **VAT** Chemical Abstracts Selects. Flavors and Fragrances. (Jan. 9, 1978)-. Abstracting/Indexing Service. English. Twenty-six times a year. $220.00. Chemical Abstracts Service, (Subsidiary of The American Chemical Society), 2540 Olentangy River Road, PO Box 3012, Columbus OH 43210-0012. **Tel** (614)447-3731, (800)753-4227, FAX (614)447-3751. **(Subscription address:** Chemical Abstracts Service, Customer Service Department, PO Box 3012, Columbus OH 43210. **Tel** (800)848-6538, (614)447-3600.**)** **ED** David W Weisgerber.
Desc: Covers substances affecting senses of smell and taste, synthetic methods for these compounds, olfaction and gustation.

ISSN 0195-4989
US
CODEN CFSTD5

CA SELECTS: FLUIDIZED SOLIDS TECHNOLOGY. [CA sel., Fluid. solids technol.]. **Added/Corp** American Chemical Society. Chemical Abstracts Service. **VFOAT** Fluidized Solids Technology. **VAT** Chemical Abstracts Selects. Fluidized Solids Technology. (Jan. 14, 1980)-. Abstracting/Indexing Service. English. Twenty-six times a year. $220.00. Chemical Abstracts Service, (Subsidiary of The American Chemical Society), 2540 Olentangy River Road, PO Box 3012, Columbus OH 43210-0012. **Tel** (614)447-3731, (800)753-4227, FAX (614)447-3751. **(Subscription address:** Chemical Abstracts Service, Customer Service Department, PO Box 3012, Columbus OH 43210. **Tel** (800)848-6538, (614)447-3600.**)** **ED** David W Weisgerber.
Desc: Covers apparatus design and engineering, fluidized combustion for energy production and waste disposal, and fluidized-bed drying.

DD 547 **ISSN** 0895-5921
US
CODEN CASFEV

CA SELECTS: FLUOROPOLYMERS. **Added/Corp** American Chemical Society. Chemical Abstracts Service. **VFOAT** Fluoropolymers. **VAT** Chemical Abstracts Selects. Fluoropolymers. (Jan. 11, 1988)-. Abstracting/Indexing Service. English. Twenty-six times a year. $220.00. Chemical Abstracts Service, (Subsidiary of The American Chemical Society), 2540 Olentangy River Road, PO Box 3012, Columbus OH 43210-0012. **Tel** (614)447-3731, (800)753-4227, FAX (614)447-3751. **(Subscription address:** Chemical Abstracts Service, Customer Service Department, PO Box 3012, Columbus OH 43210. **Tel** (800)848-6538, (614)447-3600.**)**
Desc: Covers the preparation, properties and uses of organic polymeric substances with a substantial flourine content.

DD 544 **ISSN** 0895-5913
US
CODEN CSFAE9

CA SELECTS: FOOD & FEED ANALYSIS. [CA sel., Food feed anal.]. **Added/Corp** American Chemical Society. Chemical Abstracts Service. **VFOAT** Food & Feed Analysis; Food and Feed Analysis CA Selects. **VAT** Chemical Abstracts Selects. Food & Feed Analysis. (Jan. 11, 1988)-. Abstracting/Indexing Service. English. Twenty-six times a year. $220.00. Chemical Abstracts Service, (Subsidiary of The American Chemical Society), 2540 Olentangy River Road, PO Box 3012, Columbus OH 43210-0012. **Tel** (614)447-3731, (800)753-4227, FAX (614)447-3751. **(Subscription address:** Chemical Abstracts Service, Customer Service Department, PO Box 3012, Columbus OH 43210. **Tel** (800)848-6538, (614)447-3600.**)**
Desc: Studies the methodology for determining natural components, additives and contaminants in food and feed, analysis of alcoholic and nonalcoholic beverages and determination of impurities.

DD 615 **ISSN** 1051-3914
US
CODEN CAFAEJ

CA SELECTS. FOOD, DRUGS, & COSMETICS. (CA SELECTS: FOOD, DRUGS, & COSMETICS : LEGISLATIVE & REGULATORY ASPECTS.). [Chem. Abstr. sel. Food drugs cosmet.]. **Added/Corp** American Chemical Society. Chemical Abstracts Service. **VFOAT** Food, Drugs, & Cosmetics. **VAT** Chemical Abstracts Selects. Food, Drugs, & Cosmetics. Issue 21 (Oct. 15, 1990)-. Abstracting/Indexing Service. English. Twenty-six times a year. $220.00. Chemical Abstracts Service, (Subsidiary of The American Chemical Society), 2540 Olentangy River Road, PO Box 3012, Columbus OH 43210-0012. **Tel** (614)447-3731, (800)753-4227, FAX (614)447-3751. **(Subscription address:** Chemical Abstracts Service, Customer Service Department, PO Box 3012, Columbus OH 43210. **Tel** (800)848-6538, (614)447-3600.**)** **ED** David Weisgerber. ctrl circ.
Desc: Abstracts from Chemical Abstracts and extracts from Chemical Industry Notes on the title subject.

ISSN 0162-7813
US
CODEN CSFTDV

CA SELECTS: FOOD TOXICITY. **Added/Corp** American Chemical Society. Chemical Abstracts Service. **VFOAT** Food Toxicity. **VAT** Chemical Abstracts Selects. Food Toxicity. (Jan. 8, 1979)-. Abstracting/Indexing Service. English. Twenty-six times a year. $220.00. Chemical Abstracts Service, (Subsidiary of The American Chemical Society), 2540 Olentangy River Road, PO Box 3012, Columbus OH 43210-0012. **Tel** (614)447-3731, (800)753-4227, FAX (614)447-3751. **(Subscription address:** Chemical Abstracts Service, Customer Service Department, PO Box 3012, Columbus OH 43210. **Tel** (800)848-6538, (614)447-3600.**)** **ED** David W Weisgerber.
Desc: Covers mutagenicity, teratogenicity, carcinogenicity, toxic side effects, and health hazards of foods and food additives.

ISSN 0362-9880
US
CODEN CSFCDE

CA SELECTS: FORENSIC CHEMISTRY. **Added/Corp** American Chemical Society. Chemical Abstracts Service. **VFOAT** Forensic Chemistry. **VAT** Chemical Abstracts Selects. Forensic Chemistry. (Oct. 18, 1976)-. Abstracting/Indexing Service. English. Twenty-six times a year. $220.00. Chemical Abstracts Service, (Subsidiary of The American Chemical Society), 2540 Olentangy River Road, PO Box 3012, Columbus OH 43210-0012. **Tel** (614)447-3731, (800)753-4227, FAX (614)447-3751. **(Subscription address:** Chemical Abstracts Service, Customer Service Department, PO Box 3012, Columbus OH 43210. **Tel** (800)848-6538, (614)447-3600.**)** **ED** David W Weisgerber.
Desc: Covers chemistry of investigative science, analytical techniques in forensic science, blood chemistry, biological fluid analysis and identification, chemical analysis of explosives and gunshot wounds.

DD 660 **ISSN** 0890-1880
US
CODEN CAFCEP

CA SELECTS: FORMULATION CHEMISTRY. **Added/Corp** American Chemical Society. Chemical Abstracts Service. **VFOAT** Formulation Chemistry. **VAT** Chemical Abstracts Selects. Formulation Chemistry. Issue 1 (Jan. 12, 1987)-. Abstracting/Indexing Service. English. Twenty-six times a year. $220.00. Chemical Abstracts Service, (Subsidiary of The American Chemical Society), 2540 Olentangy River Road, PO Box 3012, Columbus OH 43210-0012. **Tel** (614)447-3731, (800)753-4227, FAX (614)447-3751. **(Subscription address:** Chemical Abstracts Service, Customer Service Department, PO Box 3012, Columbus OH 43210. **Tel** (800)848-6538, (614)447-3600.**)**
Desc: Covers materials used as fillers and inactive agents in processed materials and drugs, cleaning agents, paints and cosmetics.

LC QD **ISSN** 0895-5905
DD 574 US
CODEN CAFRE2

CA SELECTS: FREE RADICALS (BIOCHEMICAL ASPECTS). [CA sel., Free radic. biomed. asp.]. **Added/Corp** American Chemical Society. Chemical Abstracts Service. **VFOAT** Free Radicals (Biochemical Aspects). **VAT** Chemical Abstracts Selects. Free Radicals (Biochemical Aspects). (Jan. 11, 1988)-. Abstracting/Indexing Service. English. Twenty-six times a year. $220.00. Chemical Abstracts Service, (Subsidiary of The American Chemical Society), 2540 Olentangy River Road, PO Box 3012, Columbus OH 43210-0012. **Tel** (614)447-3731, (800)753-4227, FAX (614)447-3751. **(Subscription address:** Chemical Abstracts Service, Customer Service Department, PO Box 3012, Columbus OH 43210. **Tel** (800)848-6538, (614)447-3600.**)**
Desc: Contains reactions and interactions of free radicals, including activated oxygen species in biological systems and the formation, metabolic aspects and toxicity of free radicals in intact organisms, isolated organs, tissues and cells and subcellular systems, as well as in model biological systems.

DD 541 **ISSN** 0895-5972
US
CODEN CFRAEC

CA SELECTS: FREE RADICALS (ORGANIC ASPECTS). [CA sel., Free radic. (Org. asp.)]. **Added/Corp** American Chemical Society. Chemical Abstracts Service. **VFOAT** Free Radicals (Organic Aspects). **VAT** Chemical Abstracts Selects. Free Radicals (Organic Aspects). (1988)-. Abstracting/Indexing Service. English. Twenty-six times a year. $215.00 US; $234.00 Canada, Mexico, Central and South America; $247.00 other. Chemical Abstracts Service, (Subsidiary of The American Chemical Society), 2540 Olentangy River Road, PO Box 3012, Columbus OH 43210-0012. **Tel** (614)447-3731, (800)753-4227, FAX (614)447-3751. **(Subscription address:** Chemical Abstracts Service, Customer Service Department, PO Box 3012, Columbus OH 43210. **Tel** (800)848-6538, (614)447-3600.**)** ***Continues*** *CA Selects. Free Radicals, 0885-016X.*
Desc: Contains information on formation, chemical reactions and reactivities of organic free radicals and spectral and other physical properties.

ISSN 0195-4997
US
CODEN CSFAD8

CA SELECTS: FUEL & LUBRICANT ADDITIVES. [CA sel., Fuel lubr. addit.]. **Added/Corp** American Chemical Society. Chemical Abstracts Service. **VFOAT** Fuel & Lubricant Additives. **VAT** Chemical Abstracts Selects. Fuel and Lubricant Additives. (Jan. 14, 1980)-. Abstracting/Indexing Service. English. Twenty-six times a year. $220.00. Chemical Abstracts Service, (Subsidiary of The American Chemical Society), 2540 Olentangy River Road, PO Box 3012, Columbus OH 43210-0012. **Tel** (614)447-3731, (800)753-4227, FAX (614)447-3751. **(Subscription address:** Chemical Abstracts Service, Customer Service Department, PO Box 3012, Columbus OH 43210. **Tel** (800)848-6538, (614)447-3600.**)** **ED** David W Weisgerber.
Desc: Covers manufacture, development, and use of additives for fuels and lubricants.

LC SB950.9 **ISSN** 0160-9068
DD 632.952 US
CODEN CSFNDD

CA SELECTS: FUNGICIDES. **Added/Corp** American Chemical Society. Chemical Abstracts Service. **VFOAT** Fungicides. **VAT** Chemical Abstracts Selects. Fungicides. (July 10, 1978)-. Abstracting/Indexing Service. English. Twenty-six times a year. $220.00. Chemical Abstracts Service, (Subsidiary of The American Chemical Society), 2540 Olentangy River Road, PO Box 3012, Columbus OH 43210-0012. **Tel** (614)447-3731, (800)753-4227, FAX (614)447-3751. **(Subscription address:** Chemical Abstracts Service, Customer Service Department, PO Box 3012, Columbus OH 43210. **Tel** (800)848-6538, (614)447-3600.**)** **ED** David W Weisgerber.
Desc: Covers preparation, mechanism of action, and effects of antifungal agents.

ISSN 0146-4477
US
CODEN CSGCDJ

CA SELECTS: GAS CHROMATOGRAPHY. **Added/Corp** American Chemical Society. Chemical Abstracts Service. **VFOAT** Gas Chromatography. **VAT** Chemical Abstracts Selects. Gas Chromatography. (July 11, 1977)-. Abstracting/Indexing Service. English. Twenty-six times a year. $220.00. Chemical Abstracts Service, (Subsidiary of The American Chemical Society), 2540 Olentangy River Road, PO Box 3012, Columbus OH 43210-0012. **Tel** (614)447-3731, (800)753-4227, FAX (614)447-3751. **(Subscription address:** Chemical Abstracts Service,

Customer Service Department, PO Box 3012, Columbus OH 43210. **Tel** (800)848-6538, (614)447-3600.) **ED** David W Weisgerber.
Desc: Covers gas chromatography in chemical analysis, gas-liquid chromatography, vapor phase chromatography, instrumentation and apparatus for gas chromatography, flame and ionization detectors.

ISSN 0160-9076
US
CODEN CSGTD2

CA SELECTS: GASEOUS WASTE TREATMENT.
Added/Corp American Chemical Society. Chemical Abstracts Service. **VFOAT** Gaseous Waste Treatment. **VAT** Chemical Abstracts Selects. Gaseous Waste Treatment. (July 10, 1978)-. Abstracting/Indexing Service. English. Twenty-six times a year. $220.00. Chemical Abstracts Service, (Subsidiary of The American Chemical Society), 2540 Olentangy River Road, PO Box 3012, Columbus OH 43210-0012. **Tel** (614)447-3731, (800)753-4227, FAX (614)447-3751. **(Subscription address:** Chemical Abstracts Service, Customer Service Department, PO Box 3012, Columbus OH 43210. **Tel** (800)848-6538, (614)447-3600.) **ED** David W Weisgerber.
Desc: Covers treatment and control of gaseous waste products from stationary sources, primarily industrial.

ISSN 0146-4485
US
CODEN CGPCDE

CA SELECTS: GEL PERMEATION CHROMATOGRAPHY.
Added/Corp American Chemical Society. Chemical Abstracts Service. **VFOAT** Gel Permeation Chromatography. **VAT** Chemical Abstracts Selects. Gel Permeation Chromatography. July 11, 1977-. Abstracting/Indexing Service. English. Twenty-six times a year. $220.00. Chemical Abstracts Service, (Subsidiary of The American Chemical Society), 2540 Olentangy River Road, PO Box 3012, Columbus OH 43210-0012. **Tel** (614)447-3731, (800)753-4227, FAX (614)447-3751. **(Subscription address:** Chemical Abstracts Service, Customer Service Department, PO Box 3012, Columbus OH 43210. **Tel** (800)848-6538, (614)447-3600.) **ED** David W Weisgerber.
Desc: Covers theory and applications of gel permeation chromatography, high-speed gel chromatography, size exclusion chromatographic techniques and affinity chromatography.

ISSN 1066-5730
US

•CA SELECTS: GEOCHEMISTRY.
Added/Corp American Chemical Society. Chemical Abstracts Service. **VFOAT** Geochemistry. **VAT** Chemical Abstracts Selects. Geochemistry. (1993)-. Abstracting/Indexing Service. English. Twenty-six times a year. $220.00. Chemical Abstracts Service, (Subsidiary of The American Chemical Society), 2540 Olentangy River Road, PO Box 3012, Columbus OH 43210-0012. **Tel** (614)447-3731, (800)753-4227, FAX (614)447-3751. **(Subscription address:** Chemical Abstracts Service, Customer Service Department, PO Box 3012, Columbus OH 43210. **Tel** (800)848-6538, (614)447-3600.)
Desc: Provides information on various aspects of geochemistry.

ISSN 0162-7821
US
CODEN CSHPDT

CA SELECTS: HEAT-RESISTANT & ABLATIVE POLYMERS.
Added/Corp American Chemical Society. Chemical Abstracts Service. **VFOAT** Heat-Resistant & Ablative Polymers. **VAT** Chemical Abstracts Selects. Heat Resistant and Ablative Polymers. (Jan. 8, 1979)-. Abstracting/Indexing Service. English. Twenty-six times a year. $220.00. Chemical Abstracts Service, (Subsidiary of The American Chemical Society), 2540 Olentangy River Road, PO Box 3012, Columbus OH 43210-0012. **Tel** (614)447-3731, (800)753-4227, FAX (614)447-3751. **(Subscription address:** Chemical Abstracts Service, Customer Service Department, PO Box 3012, Columbus OH 43210. **Tel** (800)848-6538, (614)447-3600.) **ED** David W Weisgerber. **Bk Rev. Ad Acc.** ctrl circ.
Desc: Covers polymers which are stable at high temperatures, e.g. plastics, fibers, rubbers, coatings and polymeric ablative materials.

LC SB950.9 **ISSN** 0160-9084
DD 632.954 US
CODEN CSHEDU

CA SELECTS: HERBICIDES.
Added/Corp American Chemical Society. Chemical Abstracts Service. **VFOAT** Herbicides. **VAT** Chemical Abstracts Selects. Herbicides. (July 10, 1978)-. Abstracting/Indexing Service. English. Twenty-six times a year. $220.00. Chemical Abstracts Service, (Subsidiary of The American Chemical Society), 2540 Olentangy River Road, PO Box 3012, Columbus OH 43210-0012. **Tel** (614)447-3731, (800)753-4227, FAX (614)447-3751. **(Subscription address:** Chemical Abstracts Service, Customer Service Department, PO Box 3012, Columbus OH 43210. **Tel** (800)848-6538, (614)447-3600.) **ED** David W Weisgerber.
Desc: Covers preparation, mechanism of action, and effects of herbicides.

LC QD **ISSN** 0195-5217
DD 540 US
CODEN CSHCDO

CA SELECTS: HIGH PERFORMANCE LIQUID CHROMATOGRAPHY.
[CA sel. High perform. liq. chromatogr.]. **Added/Corp** American Chemical Society. Chemical Abstracts Service. **VFOAT** High Performance Liquid Chromatography. **VAT** Chemical Abstracts Selects: High Performance Liquid Chromatography. (Jan. 14, 1980)-. Abstracting/Indexing Service. English. Twenty-six times a year. $220.00. Chemical Abstracts Service, (Subsidiary of The American Chemical Society), 2540 Olentangy River Road, PO Box 3012, Columbus OH 43210-0012. **Tel** (614)447-3731, (800)753-4227, FAX (614)447-3751. **(Subscription address:** Chemical Abstracts Service, Customer Service Department, PO Box 3012, Columbus OH 43210. **Tel** (800)848-6538, (614)447-3600.) **ED** David W. Weisgerber. ***Continues*** *CA Selects. High Speed Liquid Chromatography, 0362-9864.*
Desc: Covers high speed liquid chromatography, high pressure, high performance, high resolution liquid chromatography, solid-liquid column chromatography, and ion-exchange chromatography.

ISSN 0895-5891
DD 620 US
CODEN CSHAEJ

CA SELECTS: HOT-MELT ADHESIVES.
[CA sel., Hot-melt adhes.]. **Added/Corp** American Chemical Society. Chemical Abstracts Service. **VFOAT** Hot-Melt Adhesives; Hot Melt Adhesives. **VAT** Chemical Abstracts Selects. Hot-Melt Adhesives. (Jan. 11, 1988)-. Abstracting/Indexing Service. English. Twenty-six times a year. $220.00. Chemical Abstracts Service, (Subsidiary of The American Chemical Society), 2540 Olentangy River Road, PO Box 3012, Columbus OH 43210-0012. **Tel** (614)447-3731, (800)753-4227, FAX (614)447-3751. **(Subscription address:** Chemical Abstracts Service, Customer Service Department, PO Box 3012, Columbus OH 43210. **Tel** (800)848-6538, (614)447-3600.)
Desc: Contains information on preparation, composition, properties and uses of hot-melt adhesives and sealants.

ISSN 1051-3922
DD 616 US
CODEN CAHAET

CA SELECTS: HYPERTENSION & ANTIHYPERTENSIVES.
[Chem. Abstr. sel. Hypertens. antihypertens.]. **Added/Corp** American Chemical Society. Chemical Abstracts Service. **VFOAT** Hypertension & Antihypertensives; Hypertension and Antihypertensives. **VAT** Chemical Abstracts Selects. Hypertension & Antihypertensives. Issue 21 (Oct. 15, 1990)-. Abstracting/Indexing Service. English. Twenty-six times a year. $220.00. Chemical Abstracts Service, (Subsidiary of The American Chemical Society), 2540 Olentangy River Road, PO Box 3012, Columbus OH 43210-0012. **Tel** (614)447-3731, (800)753-4227, FAX (614)447-3751. **(Subscription address:** Chemical Abstracts Service, Customer Service Department, PO Box 3012, Columbus OH 43210. **Tel** (800)848-6538, (614)447-3600.)
Desc: Contains information on etiology, pathophysiology, clinical manifestations and diagnosis of hypertension and the chemistry, biochemistry and pharmacology of antihypertensive agents.

LC QD142 **ISSN** 0190-9428
DD 543.0858 US
CODEN CSIADN

CA SELECTS: INFRARED SPECTROSCOPY (ORGANIC ASPECTS).
Added/Corp American Chemical Society. Chemical Abstracts Service. **VFOAT** Infrared Spectroscopy (Organic Aspects). **VAT** Chemical Abstracts Selects. Infrared Spectroscopy (Organic Aspects). (July 9, 1979)-. Abstracting/Indexing Service. English. Twenty-six times a year. $220.00. Chemical Abstracts Service, (Subsidiary of The American Chemical Society), 2540 Olentangy River Road, PO Box 3012, Columbus OH 43210-0012. **Tel** (614)447-3731, (800)753-4227, FAX (614)447-3751. **(Subscription address:** Chemical Abstracts Service, Customer Service Department, PO Box 3012, Columbus OH 43210. **Tel** (800)848-6538, (614)447-3600.) **ED** David W Weisgerber. ***Continues in part*** *CA Selects. Infrared Spectroscopy, 0148-2424.*
Desc: Covers organic, macromolecular, and biochemical aspects of infrared spectroscopy.

ISSN 0190-9436
US
CODEN CISAD3

CA SELECTS: INFRARED SPECTROSCOPY (PHYSICOCHEMICAL ASPECTS).
Added/Corp American Chemical Society. Chemical Abstracts Service. **VFOAT** Infrared Spectroscopy (Physicochemical Aspects). **VAT** Chemical Abstracts Selects. Infrared Spectroscopy (Physicochemical Aspects). (July 9, 1979)-. Abstracting/Indexing Service. English. Twenty-six times a year. $220.00. Chemical Abstracts Service, (Subsidiary of The American Chemical Society), 2540 Olentangy River Road, PO Box 3012, Columbus OH 43210-0012. **Tel** (614)447-3731, (800)753-4227, FAX (614)447-3751. **(Subscription address:** Chemical Abstracts Service, Customer Service Department, PO Box 3012, Columbus OH 43210. **Tel** (800)848-6538, (614)447-3600.) **ED** David W Weisgerber. ***Continues in part*** *CA Selects. Infrared Spectroscopy, 0148-2424.*
Desc: Covers applied and physicochemical aspects of infrared spectroscopy, infrared lasers and infrared spectroscopic determination of organic and inorganic substances.

ISSN 0734-8843
US
CODEN CAIPEB

CA SELECTS: INITIATION OF POLYMERIZATION.
Added/Corp American Chemical Society. Chemical Abstracts Service. **VFOAT** Initiation of Polymerization. **VAT** Chemical Abstracts Selects. Initiation of Polymerization. (19??)-. Abstracting/Indexing Service. English. Twenty-six times a year. $220.00. Chemical Abstracts Service, (Subsidiary of The American Chemical Society), 2540 Olentangy River Road, PO Box 3012, Columbus OH 43210-0012. **Tel** (614)447-3731, (800)753-4227, FAX (614)447-3751. **(Subscription address:** Chemical Abstracts Service, Customer Service Department, PO Box 3012, Columbus OH 43210. **Tel** (800)848-6538, (614)447-3600.) **ED** David W Weisgerber.
Desc: Covers preparation of polymerization catalysts of initiators, characterization and use in polymerization.

ISSN 0275-7087
US
CODEN CSACDN

CA SELECTS: INORGANIC ANALYTICAL CHEMISTRY.
[CA sel., Inorg. anal. chem.]. **Added/Corp** American Chemical Society. Chemical Abstracts Service. **VFOAT** Inorganic Analytical Chemistry. **VAT** Chemical Abstracts Selects. Inorganic Analytical Chemistry. (1981)-. Abstracting/Indexing Service. English. Twenty-six times a year. $220.00. Chemical Abstracts Service, (Subsidiary of The American Chemical Society), 2540 Olentangy River Road, PO Box 3012, Columbus OH 43210-0012. **Tel** (614)447-3731, (800)753-4227, FAX (614)447-3751. **(Subscription address:** Chemical Abstracts Service, Customer Service Department, PO Box 3012, Columbus OH 43210. **Tel** (800)848-6538, (614)447-3600.) **ED** David W Weisgerber. Documents available from CASDDS.
Desc: Covers methods and reagents and detection and determination of elements, radicals, and compounds in inorganic materials.
Ind/Abst Chem. Abstr.

ISSN 0195-5012
US
CODEN CIOMDJ

CA SELECTS: INORGANIC & ORGANOMETALLIC REACTION MECHANISMS.
Added/Corp American Chemical Society. Chemical Abstracts Service. **VFOAT** Inorganic & Organometallic Reaction Mechanisms. **VAT** Chemical Abstracts Selects. Inorganic and Organometallic Reaction Mechanisms. (Jan. 14, 1980)-. Abstracting/Indexing Service. English. Twenty-six times a year. $220.00. Chemical Abstracts Service, (Subsidiary of The American Chemical Society), 2540 Olentangy River Road, PO Box 3012, Columbus OH 43210-0012. **Tel** (614)447-3731, (800)753-4227, FAX (614)447-3751. **(Subscription address:** Chemical Abstracts Service, Customer Service Department, PO Box 3012, Columbus OH 43210. **Tel** (800)848-6538, (614)447-3600.) **ED** David W Weisgerber.
Desc: Covers mechanistic and kinetic aspects of reaction of inorganic compounds, organometallic and organometalloidal compounds.

ISSN 0275-7095
US
CODEN CIRCD4

CA SELECTS: INORGANIC CHEMICALS & REACTIONS.
[CA sel., Inorg. chem. react.]. **Added/Corp** American Chemical Society. Chemical Abstracts Service. **VFOAT** Inorganic Chemicals & Reactions; C.A. Selects. Inorganic Chemicals & Reactions. **VAT** Chemical Abstracts Selects. Inorganic Chemicals and Reactions. (1981)-. Abstracting/Indexing Service. English. Twenty-six times a year. $220.00. Chemical Abstracts Service, (Subsidiary of The American Chemical Society), 2540 Olentangy River Road, PO Box 3012, Columbus OH 43210-0012. **Tel** (614)447-3731, (800)753-4227, FAX (614)447-3751. **(Subscription address:** Chemical Abstracts Service, Customer Service Department, PO Box 3012, Columbus OH 43210. **Tel** (800)848-6538, (614)447-3600.) **ED** David W Weisgerber. Documents available from CASDDS.
Desc: Covers synthesis, chemical properties, reactions, nonindustrial preparation and applications of inorganic compounds.
Ind/Abst Chem. Abstr.

LC SB951.145 **ISSN** 0160-9092
DD 632.951 US
CODEN CSEIDR

CA SELECTS: INSECTICIDES.
Added/Corp American Chemical Society. Chemical Abstracts Service. **VFOAT** Insecticides. **VAT** Chemical Abstracts Selects. Insecticides. (July 10, 1978)-. Abstracting/Indexing Service. English. Twenty-six times a year. $220.00.

Chemical Abstracts Service, (Subsidiary of The American Chemical Society), 2540 Olentangy River Road, PO Box 3012, Columbus OH 43210-0012. **Tel** (614)447-3731, (800)753-4227, FAX (614)447-3751. **(Subscription address:** Chemical Abstracts Service, Customer Service Department, PO Box 3012, Columbus OH 43210. **Tel** (800)848-6538, (614)447-3600.) **ED** David W Weisgerber.
Desc: Covers preparation, mechanism of action, and effects of insecticides.

ISSN 0890-1899
DD 543 US
CODEN CSICEU

CA SELECTS: ION CHROMATOGRAPHY.
[CA sel., Ion chromatogr.]. **Added/Corp** American Chemical Society. Chemical Abstracts Service. **VFOAT** Ion Chromatography. **VAT** Chemical Abstracts Selects. Ion Chromatography. Issue 1 (Jan. 12, 1987)-. Abstracting/Indexing Service. English. Twenty-six times a year. $220.00. Chemical Abstracts Service, (Subsidiary of The American Chemical Society), 2540 Olentangy River Road, PO Box 3012, Columbus OH 43210-0012. **Tel** (614)447-3731, (800)753-4227, FAX (614)447-3751. **(Subscription address:** Chemical Abstracts Service, Customer Service Department, PO Box 3012, Columbus OH 43210. **Tel** (800)848-6538, (614)447-3600.)
Desc: Contains principle and application of ion chromatography in analytical procedures.

ISSN 0195-5020
US
CODEN CSIPDY

CA SELECTS: ION-CONTAINING POLYMERS.
Added/Corp American Chemical Society. Chemical Abstracts Service. **VFOAT** Ion-Containing Polymers. **VAT** Chemical Abstracts Selects. Ion-Containing Polymers. (Jan. 14, 1980)-. Abstracting/Indexing Service. English. Twenty-six times a year. $220.00. Chemical Abstracts Service, (Subsidiary of The American Chemical Society), 2540 Olentangy River Road, PO Box 3012, Columbus OH 43210-0012. **Tel** (614)447-3731, (800)753-4227, FAX (614)447-3751. **(Subscription address:** Chemical Abstracts Service, Customer Service Department, PO Box 3012, Columbus OH 43210. **Tel** (800)848-6538, (614)447-3600.) **ED** David W Weisgerber.
Desc: Cover theoretical and practical aspects, polyelectrolytes, polymers with ions in the main chain, i.e. ionene polymers, and polymers with ions in side groups, i.e. ionomers.

ISSN 0146-4493
US
CODEN CSIODV

CA SELECTS: ION EXCHANGE.
Added/Corp American Chemical Society. Chemical Abstracts Service. **VFOAT** Ion Exchange. **VAT** Chemical Abstracts Selects. Ion Exchange. (July 11, 1977)-. Abstracting/Indexing Service. English. Twenty-six times a year. $220.00. Chemical Abstracts Service, (Subsidiary of The American Chemical Society), 2540 Olentangy River Road, PO Box 3012, Columbus OH 43210-0012. **Tel** (614)447-3731, (800)753-4227, FAX (614)447-3751. **(Subscription address:** Chemical Abstracts Service, Customer Service Department, PO Box 3012, Columbus OH 43210. **Tel** (800)848-6538, (614)447-3600.) **ED** David W Weisgerber.
Desc: Covers theory and applications including materials and equipment for ion exchange, ion-exchange chromatography, and ion-exchange processes, techniques and procedures.

ISSN 0895-5883
DD 547 US
CODEN CAICE6

CA SELECTS: ISOMERIZATION & CATALYSTS.
Added/Corp American Chemical Society. Chemical Abstracts Service. **VFOAT** Isomerization & Catalysts; CA Selects. Isomerization and Catalysts. **VAT** Chemical Abstracts Selects. Isomerization & Catalysts. (Jan. 11, 1988)-. Abstracting/Indexing Service. English. Twenty-six times a year. $220.00. Chemical Abstracts Service, (Subsidiary of The American Chemical Society), 2540 Olentangy River Road, PO Box 3012, Columbus OH 43210-0012. **Tel** (614)447-3731, (800)753-4227, FAX (614)447-3751. **(Subscription address:** Chemical Abstracts Service, Customer Service Department, PO Box 3012, Columbus OH 43210. **Tel** (800)848-6538, (614)447-3600.)
Desc: Contains information on organic isomerizations and the agents used for effecting them.

ISSN 0195-5039
US
CODEN CLAPDD

CA SELECTS: LASER APPLICATIONS.
Added/Corp American Chemical Society. Chemical Abstracts Service. **VFOAT** Laser Applications. **VAT** Chemical Abstracts Selects. Laser Applications. (Jan. 14, 1980)-. Abstracting/Indexing Service. English. Twenty-six times a year. $220.00. Chemical Abstracts Service, (Subsidiary of The American Chemical Society), 2540 Olentangy River Road, PO Box 3012, Columbus OH 43210-0012. **Tel** (614)447-3731, (800)753-4227, FAX (614)447-3751. **(Subscription address:** Chemical Abstracts Service, Customer Service Department, PO Box 3012, Columbus OH 43210. **Tel** (800)848-6538, (614)447-3600.) **ED** David W Weisgerber.
Desc: Covers interactions of laser radiation with materials, physicochemical and biochemical effects of laser radiation.

ISSN 0885-0178
DD 541 US
CODEN CSLREM

CA SELECTS: LASER-INDUCED CHEMICAL REACTIONS.
[CA sel., Laser induc. chem. react.]. **Added/Corp** American Chemical Society. Chemical Abstracts Service. **VFOAT** CA Selects. Laser Induced Chemical Reactions; Laser-Induced Chemical Reactions; Laser Induced Chemical Reactions. **VAT** Chemical Abstracts Selects. Laser-Induced Chemical Reactions. Iss 1 (Jan. 13, 1986)-. Abstracting/Indexing Service. English. Twenty-six times a year. $220.00. Chemical Abstracts Service, (Subsidiary of The American Chemical Society), 2540 Olentangy River Road, PO Box 3012, Columbus OH 43210-0012. **Tel** (614)447-3731, (800)753-4227, FAX (614)447-3751. **(Subscription address:** Chemical Abstracts Service, Customer Service Department, PO Box 3012, Columbus OH 43210. **Tel** (800)848-6538, (614)447-3600.) **Bk Rev.**
Desc: Coverage includes photochemical reactions initiated by laser radiation, thermal reactions induced by laser heating, and laser-induced ionization and plasma.

ISSN 0148-2351
US
CODEN CSLCDA

CA SELECTS: LIQUID CRYSTALS.
Added/Corp American Chemical Society. Chemical Abstracts Service. **VFOAT** Liquid Crystals. **VAT** Chemical Abstracts Selects. Liquid Crystals. (Jan. 9, 1978)-. Abstracting/Indexing Service. English. Twenty-six times a year. $220.00. Chemical Abstracts Service, (Subsidiary of The American Chemical Society), 2540 Olentangy River Road, PO Box 3012, Columbus OH 43210-0012. **Tel** (614)447-3731, (800)753-4227, FAX (614)447-3751. **(Subscription address:** Chemical Abstracts Service, Customer Service Department, PO Box 3012, Columbus OH 43210. **Tel** (800)848-6538, (614)447-3600.) **ED** David W Weisgerber.
Desc: Covers applications, preparation, properties, and structure of liquid crystals.

ISSN 0160-9106
US
CODEN CSLTDR

CA SELECTS: LIQUID WASTE TREATMENT.
Added/Corp American Chemical Society. Chemical Abstracts Service. **VFOAT** Liquid Waste Treatment. **VAT** Chemical Abstracts Selects. Liquid Waste Treatment. (July 10, 1978)-. Abstracting/Indexing Service. English. Twenty-six times a year. $220.00. Chemical Abstracts Service, (Subsidiary of The American Chemical Society), 2540 Olentangy River Road, PO Box 3012, Columbus OH 43210-0012. **Tel** (614)447-3731, (800)753-4227, FAX (614)447-3751. **(Subscription address:** Chemical Abstracts Service, Customer Service Department, PO Box 3012, Columbus OH 43210. **Tel** (800)848-6538, (614)447-3600.) **ED** David W Weisgerber.
Desc: Covers treatment and disposal by physical, chemical, and biological methods.

ISSN 0734-8738
US
CODEN CASLEF

CA SELECTS: LUBRICANTS, GREASES & LUBRICATION.
Added/Corp American Chemical Society. Chemical Abstracts Service. **VFOAT** Lubricants, Greases and Lubrication; Lubricants, Greases & Lubrication. **VAT** Chemical Abstracts Selects. Lubricants, Greases and Lubrication. (19??)-. Abstracting/Indexing Service. English. Twenty-six times a year. $220.00. Chemical Abstracts Service, (Subsidiary of The American Chemical Society), 2540 Olentangy River Road, PO Box 3012, Columbus OH 43210-0012. **Tel** (614)447-3731, (800)753-4227, FAX (614)447-3751. **(Subscription address:** Chemical Abstracts Service, Customer Service Department, PO Box 3012, Columbus OH 43210. **Tel** (800)848-6538, (614)447-3600.) **ED** David W Weisgerber.
Desc: Covers manufacture, properties, and uses of lubricants, oils, emulsions, greases, solid lubricants, and additives for lubricants.

ISSN 0362-9872
US
CODEN CASSDZ

CA SELECTS: MASS SPECTROMETRY.
Added/Corp American Chemical Society. Chemical Abstracts Service. **VFOAT** Mass Spectrometry. **VAT** Chemical Abstracts Selects. Mass Spectrometry. (Oct. 18, 1976)-. Abstracting/Indexing Service. English. Twenty-six times a year. $220.00. Chemical Abstracts Service, (Subsidiary of The American Chemical Society), 2540 Olentangy River Road, PO Box 3012, Columbus OH 43210-0012. **Tel** (614)447-3731, (800)753-4227, FAX (614)447-3751. **(Subscription address:** Chemical Abstracts Service, Customer Service Department, PO Box 3012, Columbus OH 43210. **Tel** (800)848-6538, (614)447-3600.) **ED** David W Weisgerber.
Desc: Covers methodology, apparatus, and experimental results obtained by various spectrometric techniques.

ISSN 1040-7197
DD 660 US
CODEN CAMSE6

CA SELECTS: MEMBRANE SEPARATION.
[CA sel., Membr. sep.]. **Added/Corp** American Chemical Society. Chemical Abstracts Service. **VFOAT** Membrane Separation. **VAT** Chemical Abstracts Selects. Membrane Separation. (Jan. 9, 1989)-. Abstracting/Indexing Service. English. Twenty-six times a year. $220.00. Chemical Abstracts Service, (Subsidiary of The American Chemical Society), 2540 Olentangy River Road, PO Box 3012, Columbus OH 43210-0012. **Tel** (614)447-3731, (800)753-4227, FAX (614)447-3751. **(Subscription address:** Chemical Abstracts Service, Customer Service Department, PO Box 3012, Columbus OH 43210. **Tel** (800)848-6538, (614)447-3600.)
Desc: Contains information on the theory and technology of dialysis, electrodialysis, electro-osmosis and gas separation by membrane permeation and pervaporation. Filtration, ultrafiltration and reverse osmosis are excluded.

ISSN 0890-1821
DD 621 US
CODEN CSMMEC

CA SELECTS: MEMORY & RECORDING DEVICES & MATERIALS.
[CA sel., Mem. rec. devices mater.]. **Added/Corp** American Chemical Society. Chemical Abstracts Service. **VFOAT** CA Selects. Memory and Recording Devices and Materials; Memory and Recording Devices and Materials; Memory & Recording Devices & Materials. **VAT** Chemical Abstracts Selects. Memory and Recording Devices and Materials. Issue 1 (Jan. 12, 1987)-. Abstracting/Indexing Service. English. Twenty-six times a year. $220.00. Chemical Abstracts Service, (Subsidiary of The American Chemical Society), 2540 Olentangy River Road, PO Box 3012, Columbus OH 43210-0012. **Tel** (614)447-3731, (800)753-4227, FAX (614)447-3751. **(Subscription address:** Chemical Abstracts Service, Customer Service Department, PO Box 3012, Columbus OH 43210. **Tel** (800)848-6538, (614)447-3600.)
Desc: Contains information on materials used for information storage and recording tapes/disks, optical disks and computer memories.

ISSN 1062-8681
US

CA SELECTS: METALLIC GLASSES.
Added/Corp American Chemical Society. Chemical Abstracts Service. **VFOAT** Metallic Glasses. **VAT** Chemical Abstracts Selects. Metallic Glasses. (1992)-. Abstracting/Indexing Service. English. Twenty-six times a year. $215.00 US; $234.00 Canada, Mexico, Central and South America; $247.00 other. Chemical Abstracts Service, (Subsidiary of The American Chemical Society), 2540 Olentangy River Road, PO Box 3012, Columbus OH 43210-0012. **Tel** (614)447-3731, (800)753-4227, FAX (614)447-3751. **(Subscription address:** Chemical Abstracts Service, Customer Service Department, PO Box 3012, Columbus OH 43210. **Tel** (800)848-6538, (614)447-3600.)

ISSN 0160-9114
US
CODEN CSMCDF

CA SELECTS: METALLO ENZYMES & METALLO COENZYMES.
Added/Corp American Chemical Society. Chemical Abstracts Service. **VFOAT** Metallo Enzymes & Metallo Coenzymes. **VAT** Chemical Abstracts Selects. Metallo Enzymes and Metallo Coenzymes. (July 10, 1978)-. Abstracting/Indexing Service. English. Twenty-six times a year. $220.00. Chemical Abstracts Service, (Subsidiary of The American Chemical Society), 2540 Olentangy River Road, PO Box 3012, Columbus OH 43210-0012. **Tel** (614)447-3731, (800)753-4227, FAX (614)447-3751. **(Subscription address:** Chemical Abstracts Service, Customer Service Department, PO Box 3012, Columbus OH 43210. **Tel** (800)848-6538, (614)447-3600.) **ED** David W Weisgerber.
Desc: Covers preparation, analysis, and biochemical effects of enzymes and coenzymes that contain metals (cobalt, copper, iron, zinc, and molybdenum), metalloproteins, metal-containing vitamins.

LC QD **ISSN** 1059-2784
DD 574.192 US

CA SELECTS: MOLECULAR MODELING (BIOCHEMICAL ASPECTS).
Added/Corp American Chemical Society. Chemical Abstracts Service. **VFOAT** Molecular Modeling; CA Selects. Molecular Modeling; Molecular Modeling (Biochemical Aspects). **VAT** Chemical Abstracts Selects. Molecular Modeling (Biochemical Aspects). (1992)-. Abstracting/Indexing Service. English. Twenty-six times a year. $220.00. Chemical Abstracts Service, (Subsidiary of The American Chemical Society), 2540 Olentangy River Road, PO Box 3012, Columbus OH 43210-0012. **Tel** (614)447-3731, (800)753-4227, FAX (614)447-3751. **(Subscription address:** Chemical Abstracts Service, Customer Service Department, PO Box 3012, Columbus OH 43210. **Tel** (800)848-6538, (614)447-3600.)

Desc: Contains information on the design of pharmaceuticals, agrochemicals and other bioactive agents, modeling studies on structures of macromolecules, pharmacophores and quantitative structure activity relationships.

DD 547 **ISSN** 0740-0691 US **CODEN** CSNSEZ

CA SELECTS: NATURAL PRODUCT SYNTHESIS. [CA sel., Nat. prod. synth.]. **Added/Corp** American Chemical Society. Chemical Abstracts Service. **VFOAT** Natural Product Synthesis. **VAT** Chemical Abstracts Selects. Natural Product Synthesis. (19??)-. Abstracting/Indexing Service. English. Twenty-six times a year. $220.00. Chemical Abstracts Service, (Subsidiary of The American Chemical Society), 2540 Olentangy River Road, PO Box 3012, Columbus OH 43210-0012. **Tel** (614)447-3731, (800)753-4227, FAX (614)447-3751. **(Subscription address:** Chemical Abstracts Service, Customer Service Department, PO Box 3012, Columbus OH 43210. **Tel** (800)848-6538, (614)447-3600.**)** **ED** David W Weisgerber.
Desc: Covers laboratory synthesis of known natural products, partial and total synthesis and unsuccessful attempts at synthesis.

DD 547 **ISSN** 0895-5875 US **CODEN** CSNAEF

CA SELECTS: NEW ANTIBIOTICS. [CA sel., New antibiot.]. **Added/Corp** American Chemical Society. Chemical Abstracts Service. **VFOAT** New Antibiotics. **VAT** Chemical Abstracts Selects. New Antibiotics. Issue 1 (Jan. 11, 1988)-. Abstracting/Indexing Service. English. Twenty-six times a year. $220.00. Chemical Abstracts Service, (Subsidiary of The American Chemical Society), 2540 Olentangy River Road, PO Box 3012, Columbus OH 43210-0012. **Tel** (614)447-3731, (800)753-4227, FAX (614)447-3751. **(Subscription address:** Chemical Abstracts Service, Customer Service Department, PO Box 3012, Columbus OH 43210. **Tel** (800)848-6538, (614)447-3600.**)**
Desc: Contains information on production, isolation, characterization, structure determination and antimicrobial activity of antibiotics, both natural and synthetic. Antiseptics, bactericides and disinfectants that are strictly synthetic compounds are not covered.

ISSN 0148-2416 US **CODEN** CSBCDS

CA SELECTS: NEW BOOKS IN CHEMISTRY. **Added/Corp** American Chemical Society. Chemical Abstracts Service. **VFOAT** New Books in Chemistry. **VAT** Chemical Abstracts Selects. New Books in Chemistry. (Jan. 9, 1978)-. Abstracting/Indexing Service. English. Twenty-six times a year. $220.00. Chemical Abstracts Service, (Subsidiary of The American Chemical Society), 2540 Olentangy River Road, PO Box 3012, Columbus OH 43210-0012. **Tel** (614)447-3731, (800)753-4227, FAX (614)447-3751. **(Subscription address:** Chemical Abstracts Service, Customer Service Department, PO Box 3012, Columbus OH 43210. **Tel** (800)848-6538, (614)447-3600.**)** **ED** David W Weisgerber.
Desc: Covers all new books in chemistry and chemical engineering cited in CA.

ISSN 0734-8673 US **CODEN** CANPE2

CA SELECTS: NEW PLASTICS. [CA sel., New plast.]. **Added/Corp** American Chemical Society. Chemical Abstracts Service. **VFOAT** New Plastics. **VAT** Chemical Abstracts Selects. New Plastics. (19??)-. Abstracting/Indexing Service. English. Twenty-six times a year. $220.00. Chemical Abstracts Service, (Subsidiary of The American Chemical Society), 2540 Olentangy River Road, PO Box 3012, Columbus OH 43210-0012. **Tel** (614)447-3731, (800)753-4227, FAX (614)447-3751. **(Subscription address:** Chemical Abstracts Service, Customer Service Department, PO Box 3012, Columbus OH 43210. **Tel** (800)848-6538, (614)447-3600.**)** **ED** David W Weisgerber.
Desc: Covers newly synthesized or newly reported thermoplastics and thermosetting resins.

LC QK **ISSN** 1047-8108
DD 581 US **CODEN** CSNFEU

CA SELECTS: NITROGEN FIXATION. [CA sel., Nitrogen fixat.]. **Added/Corp** American Chemical Society. Chemical Abstracts Service. **VFOAT** Nitrogen Fixation. **VAT** Chemical Abstracts Selects. Nitrogen Fixation. Issue 1 (Jan. 8, 1990)-. Abstracting/Indexing Service. English. Twenty-six times a year. $220.00. Chemical Abstracts Service, (Subsidiary of The American Chemical Society), 2540 Olentangy River Road, PO Box 3012, Columbus OH 43210-0012. **Tel** (614)447-3731, (800)753-4227, FAX (614)447-3751. **(Subscription address:** Chemical Abstracts Service, Customer Service Department, PO Box 3012, Columbus OH 43210. **Tel** (800)848-6538, (614)447-3600.**)** **ED** David W. Weisgerber. ctrl circ.

DD 660 **ISSN** 0895-5867 US **CODEN** CSNMEH

CA SELECTS: NONLINEAR OPTICAL MATERIALS. [CA sel., Nonlinear opt. mater.]. **Added/Corp** American Chemical Society. Chemical Abstracts Service. **VFOAT** Nonlinear Optical Materials. **VAT** Chemical Abstracts Selects. Nonlinear Optical Materials. (Jan. 11, 1988)-. Abstracting/Indexing Service. English. Twenty-six times a year. $220.00. Chemical Abstracts Service, (Subsidiary of The American Chemical Society), 2540 Olentangy River Road, PO Box 3012, Columbus OH 43210-0012. **Tel** (614)447-3731, (800)753-4227, FAX (614)447-3751. **(Subscription address:** Chemical Abstracts Service, Customer Service Department, PO Box 3012, Columbus OH 43210. **Tel** (800)848-6538, (614)447-3600.**)**
Desc: Covers materials with nonlinear optical properties and applications of these materials in optical communications, lasers, waveguides, electro-optical devices and photoelectric devices.

ISSN 0734-872X US **CODEN** CAPREI

CA SELECTS: NOVEL NATURAL PRODUCTS. [CA sel., Novel nat. prod.]. **Added/Corp** American Chemical Society. Chemical Abstracts Service. **VFOAT** Novel Natural Products. **VAT** Chemical Abstracts Selects. Novel Natural Products. (19??)-. Abstracting/Indexing Service. English. Twenty-six times a year. $220.00. Chemical Abstracts Service, (Subsidiary of The American Chemical Society), 2540 Olentangy River Road, PO Box 3012, Columbus OH 43210-0012. **Tel** (614)447-3731, (800)753-4227, FAX (614)447-3751. **(Subscription address:** Chemical Abstracts Service, Customer Service Department, PO Box 3012, Columbus OH 43210. **Tel** (800)848-6538, (614)447-3600.**)** **ED** David W Weisgerber.
Desc: Isolation, detection, or discovery of previously unknown natural products, synthesis of new derivatives or compounds of new or known natural products, synthesis of analogs of known natural products.

LC QD241 **ISSN** 0749-7318
DD 547 US **CODEN** CASHE3

CA SELECTS: NOVEL PESTICIDES & HERBICIDES. [CA sel., Nov. pestic. herbic.]. **Added/Corp** American Chemical Society. Chemical Abstracts Service. **VFOAT** Novel Pesticides & Herbicides; Novel Pesticides and Herbicides. (Jan. 14, 1985)-. Abstracting/Indexing Service. English. Twenty-six times a year. $220.00. Chemical Abstracts Service, (Subsidiary of The American Chemical Society), 2540 Olentangy River Road, PO Box 3012, Columbus OH 43210-0012. **Tel** (614)447-3731, (800)753-4227, FAX (614)447-3751. **(Subscription address:** Chemical Abstracts Service, Customer Service Department, PO Box 3012, Columbus OH 43210. **Tel** (800)848-6538, (614)447-3600.**)**
Desc: Covers documents describing newly prepared or published compounds that have activity, are being tested, or are to be tested as pesticides, e.g. antibacterials, fungicides, acaricides, herbicides.

ISSN 0734-8819 US **CODEN** CAPPEC

CA SELECTS: NOVEL POLYMERS FROM PATENTS. [CA sel., Novel polym. pat.]. **Added/Corp** American Chemical Society. Chemical Abstracts Service. **VFOAT** Novel Polymers from Patents. **VAT** Chemical Abstracts Selects. Novel Polymers from Patents. (19??)-. Abstracting/Indexing Service. English. Twenty-six times a year. $220.00. Chemical Abstracts Service, (Subsidiary of The American Chemical Society), 2540 Olentangy River Road, PO Box 3012, Columbus OH 43210-0012. **Tel** (614)447-3731, (800)753-4227, FAX (614)447-3751. **(Subscription address:** Chemical Abstracts Service, Customer Service Department, PO Box 3012, Columbus OH 43210. **Tel** (800)848-6538, (614)447-3600.**)** **ED** David W Weisgerber.
Desc: Patents mentioning newly reported polymeric materials.

ISSN 0275-7109 US **CODEN** COACDT

CA SELECTS: NOVEL SULFUR HETEROCYCLES. [CA sel., Novel sulfur heterocycl.]. **Added/Corp** American Chemical Society. Chemical Abstracts Service. **VFOAT** Novel Sulfur Heterocycles; C.A. Selects. Novel Sulfur Heterocycles. **VAT** Chemical Abstracts Selects. Novel Sulfur Heterocycles. (1981)-. Abstracting/Indexing Service. English. Twenty-six times a year. $220.00. Chemical Abstracts Service, (Subsidiary of The American Chemical Society), 2540 Olentangy River Road, PO Box 3012, Columbus OH 43210-0012. **Tel** (614)447-3731, (800)753-4227, FAX (614)447-3751. **(Subscription address:** Chemical Abstracts Service, Customer Service Department, PO Box 3012, Columbus OH 43210. **Tel** (800)848-6538, (614)447-3600.**)** **ED** David W Weisgerber. Documents available from CASDDS.
Desc: Synthesis of new sulfur-containing ring systems and new compounds containing known sulfur heterocycles.
Ind/Abst Chem. Abstr.

ISSN 1052-1984 US **CODEN** CSONEP

CA SELECTS: OMEGA THREE FATTY ACIDS & FISH OIL. **VFOAT** Omega Three Fatty Acids & Fish Oil; CA Selects. Omega-3 Fatty Acids and Fish Oil; Omega-3 Fatty Acids & Fish Oil. **VAT** Chemical Abstract Selects. Omega-3 Fatty Acids & Fish Oil. (1990)-. Abstracting/Indexing Service. English. Twenty-six times a year. $220.00. Chemical Abstracts Service, (Subsidiary of The American Chemical Society), 2540 Olentangy River Road, PO Box 3012, Columbus OH 43210-0012. **Tel** (614)447-3731, (800)753-4227, FAX (614)447-3751. **(Subscription address:** Chemical Abstracts Service, Customer Service Department, PO Box 3012, Columbus OH 43210. **Tel** (800)848-6538, (614)447-3600.**)** **ED** David Weisgerber. ctrl circ.
Desc: Abstracts from Chemical Abstracts on title subject.

ISSN 0195-5063 US **CODEN** COPMDW

CA SELECTS: OPTICAL & PHOTOSENSITIVE MATERIALS. [CA sel., Opt. photosensit. mater.]. **Added/Corp** American Chemical Society. Chemical Abstracts Service. **VFOAT** Optical & Photosensitive Materials. **VAT** Chemical Abstracts Selects. Optical and Photosensitive Materials. (Jan. 14, 1980)-. Abstracting/Indexing Service. English. Twenty-six times a year. $220.00. Chemical Abstracts Service, (Subsidiary of The American Chemical Society), 2540 Olentangy River Road, PO Box 3012, Columbus OH 43210-0012. **Tel** (614)447-3731, (800)753-4227, FAX (614)447-3751. **(Subscription address:** Chemical Abstracts Service, Customer Service Department, PO Box 3012, Columbus OH 43210. **Tel** (800)848-6538, (614)447-3600.**)** **ED** David W Weisgerber.
Desc: Covers light absorbing, transmitting, and reflective materials: films, coating, glasses, fibers, mirrors, polarizers and solar collectors.

ISSN 0195-5071 US **CODEN** COORD8

CA SELECTS: OPTIMIZATION OF ORGANIC REACTIONS. [CA sel., Optimiz. org. react.]. **Added/Corp** American Chemical Society. Chemical Abstracts Service. **VFOAT** Optimization of Organic Reactions. **VAT** Chemical Abstracts Selects. Optimization of Organic Reactions. (Jan. 14, 1980)-. Abstracting/Indexing Service. English. Twenty-six times a year. $220.00. Chemical Abstracts Service, (Subsidiary of The American Chemical Society), 2540 Olentangy River Road, PO Box 3012, Columbus OH 43210-0012. **Tel** (614)447-3731, (800)753-4227, FAX (614)447-3751. **(Subscription address:** Chemical Abstracts Service, Customer Service Department, PO Box 3012, Columbus OH 43210. **Tel** (800)848-6538, (614)447-3600.**)** **ED** David W Weisgerber.
Desc: Parameters and variables that affect reaction selectivity, product yield, and product quality.

ISSN 0275-7117 US **CODEN** COACDT

CA SELECTS: ORGANIC ANALYTICAL CHEMISTRY. [CA sel., Org. anal. chem.]. **Added/Corp** American Chemical Society. Chemical Abstracts Service.a41. **VFOAT** Organic Analytical Chemistry; C.A. Selects. Organic Analytical Chemistry. **VAT** Chemical Abstracts Selects. Organic Analytical Chemistry. (1981)-. Abstracting/Indexing Service. English. Twenty-six times a year. $220.00. Chemical Abstracts Service, (Subsidiary of The American Chemical Society), 2540 Olentangy River Road, PO Box 3012, Columbus OH 43210-0012. **Tel** (614)447-3731, (800)753-4227, FAX (614)447-3751. **(Subscription address:** Chemical Abstracts Service, Customer Service Department, PO Box 3012, Columbus OH 43210. **Tel** (800)848-6538, (614)447-3600.**)** **ED** David W Weisgerber. Documents available from CASDDS.
Desc: Detection and determination of elements, radicals, and compounds in organic materials and analysis of organometallic compounds.
Ind/Abst Chem. Abstr.

DD 547 **ISSN** 0885-0186 US **CODEN** CSOMEM

CA SELECTS: ORGANIC OPTICAL MATERIALS. [CA sel., Org. opt. meter.]. **Added/Corp** American Chemical Society. Chemical Abstracts Service. **VFOAT** Organic Optical Materials. **VAT** Chemical Abstracts Selects. Organic Optical Materials. Issue 1 (Jan. 13, 1986)-. Abstracting/Indexing Service. English. Twenty-six times a year. $220.00. Chemical Abstracts Service, (Subsidiary of The American Chemical Society), 2540 Olentangy River Road, PO Box 3012, Columbus OH 43210-0012. **Tel** (614)447-3731, (800)753-4227, FAX (614)447-3751. **(Subscription address:** Chemical Abstracts Service, Customer Service Department, PO Box 3012, Columbus OH 43210. **Tel**

(800)848-6538, (614)447-3600.) **Bk Rev**.
Desc: Covers documents on optical materials that are based on organic compounds.

ISSN 0162-7848
US
CODEN CSOMDL

CA SELECTS: ORGANIC REACTION MECHANISMS. **Added/Corp** American Chemical Society. Chemical Abstracts Service. **VFOAT** Organic Reaction Mechanisms. **VAT** Chemical Abstracts Selects. Organic Reaction Mechanisms. (Jan. 8, 1979)-. Abstracting/Indexing Service. English. Twenty-six times a year. $220.00. Chemical Abstracts Service, (Subsidiary of The American Chemical Society), 2540 Olentangy River Road, PO Box 3012, Columbus OH 43210-0012. **Tel** (614)447-3731, (800)753-4227, FAX (614)447-3751. **(Subscription address:** Chemical Abstracts Service, Customer Service Department, PO Box 3012, Columbus OH 43210. **Tel** (800)848-6538, (614)447-3600.**)** **ED** David W Weisgerber. **Bk Rev. Ad Acc.** ctrl circ.
Desc: Covers organic reaction pathways and organic reaction intermediates.

ISSN 0195-508X
US
CODEN CORSDQ

CA SELECTS: ORGANIC STEREOCHEMISTRY. [CA sel., Org. stereochem.]. **Added/Corp** American Chemical Society. Chemical Abstracts Service. **VFOAT** Organic Stereochemistry. **VAT** Chemical Abstracts Selects. Organic Stereochemistry. (Jan. 14, 1980)-. Abstracting/Indexing Service. English. Twenty-six times a year. $220.00. Chemical Abstracts Service, (Subsidiary of The American Chemical Society), 2540 Olentangy River Road, PO Box 3012, Columbus OH 43210-0012. **Tel** (614)447-3731, (800)753-4227, FAX (614)447-3751. **(Subscription address:** Chemical Abstracts Service, Customer Service Department, PO Box 3012, Columbus OH 43210. **Tel** (800)848-6538, (614)447-3600.**)** **ED** David W Weisgerber.
Desc: Covers conformational and configurational analysis, steric factors in organic reactions and properties of organic compounds.

ISSN 0160-9130
US
CODEN COMCDL

CA SELECTS: ORGANO-TRANSITION METAL COMPLEXES. **Added/Corp** American Chemical Society. Chemical Abstracts Service. **VFOAT** Organo-Transition Metal Complexes. **VAT** Chemical Abstracts Selects. Organo-Transition Metal Complexes. (July 10, 1978)-. Abstracting/Indexing Service. English. Twenty-six times a year. $220.00. Chemical Abstracts Service, (Subsidiary of The American Chemical Society), 2540 Olentangy River Road, PO Box 3012, Columbus OH 43210-0012. **Tel** (614)447-3731, (800)753-4227, FAX (614)447-3751. **(Subscription address:** Chemical Abstracts Service, Customer Service Department, PO Box 3012, Columbus OH 43210. **Tel** (800)848-6538, (614)447-3600.**)** **ED** David W Weisgerber.
Desc: Covers organic complexes of copper, silver, gold, titanium, zirconium, hafnium, vanadium, niobium, tantalum, chromium, manganese, molybdenum, tungsten, technetium, rhenium, iron, cobalt, nickel, ruthenium, rhodium, platinum, palladium, osmium, and iridium.

ISSN 0160-905X
US
CODEN CORCDC

CA SELECTS: ORGANOFLUORINE CHEMISTRY. **Added/Corp** American Chemical Society. Chemical Abstracts Service. **VFOAT** Organofluorine Chemistry. **VAT** Chemical Abstracts Selects. Organofluorine Chemistry. (July 10, 1978)-. Abstracting/Indexing Service. English. Twenty-six times a year. $220.00. Chemical Abstracts Service, (Subsidiary of The American Chemical Society), 2540 Olentangy River Road, PO Box 3012, Columbus OH 43210-0012. **Tel** (614)447-3731, (800)753-4227, FAX (614)447-3751. **(Subscription address:** Chemical Abstracts Service, Customer Service Department, PO Box 3012, Columbus OH 43210. **Tel** (800)848-6538, (614)447-3600.**)** **ED** David W Weisgerber.
Desc: Synthesis and manufacture of organofluorine compounds and properties, reactions, and uses of compounds containing a carbon-fluorine bond.

ISSN 0895-5859
DD 547
US
CODEN COOSEC

CA SELECTS: ORGANOMETALLICS IN ORGANIC SYNTHESIS. [CA sel., Organomet. org. synth.]. **Added/Corp** American Chemical Society. Chemical Abstracts Service. **VFOAT** Organometallics in Organic Synthesis. **VAT** Chemical Abstracts Selects. Organometallics in Organic Synthesis. (Jan. 11, 1988)-. Abstracting/Indexing Service. English. Twenty-six times a year. $220.00. Chemical Abstracts Service, (Subsidiary of The American Chemical Society), 2540 Olentangy River Road, PO Box 3012, Columbus OH 43210-0012. **Tel** (614)447-3731, (800)753-4227, FAX (614)447-3751. **(Subscription address:** Chemical Abstracts Service, Customer Service Department, PO Box 3012, Columbus OH 43210. **Tel** (800)848-6538, (614)447-3600.**)**
Desc: Contains information on the uses of organometallic compounds and complexes in the synthesis of organic compounds, generally those containing no carbon-metal bonds.

ISSN 0162-783X
DD 547
US
CODEN CAOCDZ

CA SELECTS: ORGANOPHOSPHORUS CHEMISTRY. **Added/Corp** American Chemical Society. Chemical Abstracts Service. **VFOAT** Organophosphorus Chemistry. **VAT** Chemical Abstracts Selects. Organophosphorus Chemistry. (Jan. 8, 1979)-. Abstracting/Indexing Service. English. Twenty-six times a year. $220.00. Chemical Abstracts Service, (Subsidiary of The American Chemical Society), 2540 Olentangy River Road, PO Box 3012, Columbus OH 43210-0012. **Tel** (614)447-3731, (800)753-4227, FAX (614)447-3751. **(Subscription address:** Chemical Abstracts Service, Customer Service Department, PO Box 3012, Columbus OH 43210. **Tel** (800)848-6538, (614)447-3600.**)** **ED** David W Weisgerber. **Bk Rev. Ad Acc.** ctrl circ.
Desc: Preparation of organophosphorus compounds, reactions and applications of organophosphorus compounds.

ISSN 0362-9899
US
CODEN CSOCDP

CA SELECTS: ORGANOSILICON CHEMISTRY. **Added/Corp** American Chemical Society. Chemical Abstracts Service. **VFOAT** Organosilicon Chemistry; Chemistry. **VAT** Chemical Abstracts Selects. Organosilicon Chemistry. (Oct. 18, 1976)-. Abstracting/Indexing Service. English. Twenty-six times a year. $220.00. Chemical Abstracts Service, (Subsidiary of The American Chemical Society), 2540 Olentangy River Road, PO Box 3012, Columbus OH 43210-0012. **Tel** (614)447-3731, (800)753-4227, FAX (614)447-3751. **(Subscription address:** Chemical Abstracts Service, Customer Service Department, PO Box 3012, Columbus OH 43210. **Tel** (800)848-6538, (614)447-3600.**)** **ED** David W Weisgerber.
Desc: Covers compounds containing a silicon-carbon bond: silanes, siloxanes, silocarboranes.

ISSN 1040-7189
DD 547
US
CODEN CAOCE2

CA SELECTS: ORGANOSULFUR CHEMISTRY (JOURNALS). **Added/Corp** American Chemical Society. Chemical Abstracts Service. **VFOAT** Organosulfur Chemistry (Journals). **VAT** Chemical Abstracts Selects. Organosulfur Chemistry (Journals). (Jan. 9, 1989)-. Abstracting/Indexing Service. English. Twenty-six times a year. $220.00. Chemical Abstracts Service, (Subsidiary of The American Chemical Society), 2540 Olentangy River Road, PO Box 3012, Columbus OH 43210-0012. **Tel** (614)447-3731, (800)753-4227, FAX (614)447-3751. **(Subscription address:** Chemical Abstracts Service, Customer Service Department, PO Box 3012, Columbus OH 43210. **Tel** (800)848-6538, (614)447-3600.**)** ctrl circ.
Desc: Journal literature on the chemistry of organic compounds containing sulfur.

ISSN 0195-5101
US
CODEN COGCDP

CA SELECTS: ORGANOTIN CHEMISTRY. **Added/Corp** American Chemical Society. Chemical Abstracts Service. **VFOAT** Organotin Chemistry. **VAT** Chemical Abstracts Selects. Organotin Chemistry. (Jan. 14, 1980)-. Abstracting/Indexing Service. English. Twenty-six times a year. $220.00. Chemical Abstracts Service, (Subsidiary of The American Chemical Society), 2540 Olentangy River Road, PO Box 3012, Columbus OH 43210-0012. **Tel** (614)447-3731, (800)753-4227, FAX (614)447-3751. **(Subscription address:** Chemical Abstracts Service, Customer Service Department, PO Box 3012, Columbus OH 43210. **Tel** (800)848-6538, (614)447-3600.**)** **ED** David W Weisgerber.
Desc: Preparation, properties, chemical behavior, and uses of compounds containing one or more carbon-tin bonds.

ISSN 1040-7170
DD 547
US
CODEN COXCE9

CA SELECTS: OXIDATION CATALYSTS. [CA sel., Oxid. catal.]. **Added/Corp** American Chemical Society. Chemical Abstracts Service. **VFOAT** Oxidation Catalysts. **VAT** Chemical Abstracts Selects. Oxidation Catalysts. (Jan. 9, 1989)-. Abstracting/Indexing Service. English. Twenty-six times a year. $220.00. Chemical Abstracts Service, (Subsidiary of The American Chemical Society), 2540 Olentangy River Road, PO Box 3012, Columbus OH 43210-0012. **Tel** (614)447-3731, (800)753-4227, FAX (614)447-3751. **(Subscription address:** Chemical Abstracts Service, Customer Service Department, PO Box 3012, Columbus OH 43210. **Tel** (800)848-6538, (614)447-3600.**)**
Desc: Covers new catalysts for known oxidation processes as well as catalysts for new oxidations.

ISSN 1040-7219
DD 547
US
CODEN CAOSEG

CA SELECTS: OXIDE SUPERCONDUCTORS. [CA sel., Oxide supercond.]. **Added/Corp** American Chemical Society. Chemical Abstracts Service. **VFOAT** Oxide Superconductors. **VAT** Chemical Abstracts Selects. Oxide Superconductors. (Jan. 9, 1989)-. Abstracting/Indexing Service. English. Twenty-six times a year. $220.00. Chemical Abstracts Service, (Subsidiary of The American Chemical Society), 2540 Olentangy River Road, PO Box 3012, Columbus OH 43210-0012. **Tel** (614)447-3731, (800)753-4227, FAX (614)447-3751. **(Subscription address:** Chemical Abstracts Service, Customer Service Department, PO Box 3012, Columbus OH 43210. **Tel** (800)848-6538, (614)447-3600.**)**
Desc: Covers oxides that are used or suitable for superconductors; materials such as the perovskites and the bismuth and thallium containing oxides of interest to the area of superconductivity.

ISSN 0734-8762
US
CODEN CAPADY

CA SELECTS: PAINT ADDITIVES. [CA sel., paint addit.]. **Added/Corp** American Chemical Society. Chemical Abstracts Service. **VFOAT** Paint Additives. **VAT** Chemical Abstracts Selects. Paint Additives. (19??)-. Abstracting/Indexing Service. English. Twenty-six times a year. $220.00. Chemical Abstracts Service, (Subsidiary of The American Chemical Society), 2540 Olentangy River Road, PO Box 3012, Columbus OH 43210-0012. **Tel** (614)447-3731, (800)753-4227, FAX (614)447-3751. **(Subscription address:** Chemical Abstracts Service, Customer Service Department, PO Box 3012, Columbus OH 43210. **Tel** (800)848-6538, (614)447-3600.**)** **ED** David W Weisgerber.
Desc: Covers materials added to paints (pigmented coatings) other than the basic polymeric binder, solvents and pigments.

ISSN 0734-8711
US
CODEN CSPAEP

CA SELECTS: PAPER ADDITIVES. [CA sel., Paper addit.]. **Added/Corp** American Chemical Society. Chemical Abstracts Service. **VFOAT** Paper Additives. **VAT** Chemical Abstracts Selects. Paper Additives. (19??)-. Abstracting/Indexing Service. English. Twenty-six times a year. $220.00. Chemical Abstracts Service, (Subsidiary of The American Chemical Society), 2540 Olentangy River Road, PO Box 3012, Columbus OH 43210-0012. **Tel** (614)447-3731, (800)753-4227, FAX (614)447-3751. **(Subscription address:** Chemical Abstracts Service, Customer Service Department, PO Box 3012, Columbus OH 43210. **Tel** (800)848-6538, (614)447-3600.**)** **ED** David W Weisgerber.
Desc: Covers noncellulosic materials added during papermaking and chemicals used for treating freshly formed sheets.

ISSN 0146-4515
US
CODEN CSPCDU

CA SELECTS: PAPER & THIN-LAYER CHROMATOGRAPHY. **Added/Corp** American Chemical Society. Chemical Abstracts Service. **VFOAT** Paper & Thin-Layer Chromatography. **VAT** Chemical Abstracts Selects. Paper and Thin-Layer Chromatography. July 11, 1977-. Abstracting/Indexing Service. English. Twenty-six times a year. $220.00. Chemical Abstracts Service, (Subsidiary of The American Chemical Society), 2540 Olentangy River Road, PO Box 3012, Columbus OH 43210-0012. **Tel** (614)447-3731, (800)753-4227, FAX (614)447-3751. **(Subscription address:** Chemical Abstracts Service, Customer Service Department, PO Box 3012, Columbus OH 43210. **Tel** (800)848-6538, (614)447-3600.**)** **ED** David W Weisgerber.
Desc: Covers theory and applications, paper chromatography, plate chromatography, thin-layer chromatography, equipment and materials.

ISSN 1040-7200
DD 676
US
CODEN CPCME9

CA SELECTS: PAPER CHEMISTRY. [CA sel., Pap. chem.]. **Added/Corp** American Chemical Society. Chemical Abstracts Service. **VFOAT** Paper Chemistry. **VAT** Chemical Abstracts Selects. Paper Chemistry. (Jan. 9, 1989)-. Abstracting/Indexing Service. English. Twenty-six times a year. $220.00. Chemical Abstracts Service, (Subsidiary of The American Chemical Society), 2540 Olentangy River Road, PO Box 3012, Columbus OH 43210-0012. **Tel** (614)447-3731, (800)753-4227, FAX (614)447-3751. **(Subscription address:** Chemical Abstracts Service, Customer Service Department, PO Box 3012, Columbus OH 43210. **Tel** (800)848-6538, (614)447-3600.**)**
Desc: Contains information on the chemical aspects of paper manufacture and stock preparation, various additives, sizing and coating.

ISSN 0890-1902
DD 615 US
CODEN CPHAEW

CA SELECTS: PHARMACEUTICAL ANALYSIS. [CA sel., Pharm. anal.]. **Added/Corp** American Chemical Society. Chemical Abstracts Service. **VFOAT** Pharmaceutical Analysis. **VAT** Chemical Abstracts Selects. Pharmaceutical Analysis. Issue 1 (Jan. 12, 1987)-. Abstracting/Indexing Service. English. Twenty-six times a year. $220.00. Chemical Abstracts Service, (Subsidiary of The American Chemical Society), 2540 Olentangy River Road, PO Box 3012, Columbus OH 43210-0012. **Tel** (614)447-3731, (800)753-4227, FAX (614)447-3751. **(Subscription address:** Chemical Abstracts Service, Customer Service Department, PO Box 3012, Columbus OH 43210. **Tel** (800)848-6538, (614)447-3600.)
Desc: Contains information on analysis of drugs in pure form or in pharmaceutical preparations.

ISSN 0890-1910
DD 615 US
CODEN CAPCE7

CA SELECTS: PHARMACEUTICAL CHEMISTRY (JOURNALS). [CA sel., Pharm. chem. (j.)]. **Added/Corp** American Chemical Society. Chemical Abstracts Service. **VFOAT** Pharmaceutical Chemistry (Journals). **VAT** Chemical Abstracts Selects. Pharmaceutical Chemistry (Journals). Issue 1 (Jan. 12, 1987)-. Abstracting/Indexing Service. English. Twenty-six times a year. $220.00. Chemical Abstracts Service, (Subsidiary of The American Chemical Society), 2540 Olentangy River Road, PO Box 3012, Columbus OH 43210-0012. **Tel** (614)447-3731, (800)753-4227, FAX (614)447-3751. **(Subscription address:** Chemical Abstracts Service, Customer Service Department, PO Box 3012, Columbus OH 43210. **Tel** (800)848-6538, (614)447-3600.)
Desc: Contains information on all aspects of pharmaceutical chemistry.

ISSN 0890-1929
DD 615 US
CODEN CPCPEI

CA SELECTS: PHARMACEUTICAL CHEMISTRY (PATENTS). [CA sel., Pharm. chem. (pat.)]. **Added/Corp** American Chemical Society. Chemical Abstracts Service. **VFOAT** Pharmaceutical Chemistry (Patents). **VAT** Chemical Abstracts Selects. Pharmaceutical Chemistry (Patents). Issue 1 (Jan. 12, 1987)-. Abstracting/Indexing Service. English. Twenty-six times a year. $220.00. Chemical Abstracts Service, (Subsidiary of The American Chemical Society), 2540 Olentangy River Road, PO Box 3012, Columbus OH 43210-0012. **Tel** (614)447-3731, (800)753-4227, FAX (614)447-3751. **(Subscription address:** Chemical Abstracts Service, Customer Service Department, PO Box 3012, Columbus OH 43210. **Tel** (800)848-6538, (614)447-3600.)
Desc: Contains information on patents in all aspects of pharmaceutical chemistry, formulations, prosthetic materials and surgical goods.

ISSN 0885-0194
DD 541 US
CODEN CSPCEV

CA SELECTS: PHASE TRANSFER CATALYSIS. [CA sel., Phase transf. catal.]. **Added/Corp** American Chemical Society. Chemical Abstracts Service. **VFOAT** Phase Transfer Catalysis. **VAT** Chemical Abstracts Selects. Phase Transfer Catalysis. Issue 1 (Jan. 13, 1986)-. Abstracting/Indexing Service. English. Twenty-six times a year. $220.00. Chemical Abstracts Service, (Subsidiary of The American Chemical Society), 2540 Olentangy River Road, PO Box 3012, Columbus OH 43210-0012. **Tel** (614)447-3731, (800)753-4227, FAX (614)447-3751. **(Subscription address:** Chemical Abstracts Service, Customer Service Department, PO Box 3012, Columbus OH 43210. **Tel** (800)848-6538, (614)447-3600.) **Bk Rev.**
Desc: Covers documents on reactions deliberately carried out in systems containing two or more phases, in the presence of agents that promote contact of materials in the phases.

ISSN 0148-2335
US
CODEN CSPHDB

CA SELECTS: PHOTOBIOCHEMISTRY. **Added/Corp** American Chemical Society. Chemical Abstracts Service. **VFOAT** Photobiochemistry. **VAT** Chemical Abstracts Selects. Photobiochemistry. (Jan. 9, 1978)-. Abstracting/Indexing Service. English. Twenty-six times a year. $220.00. Chemical Abstracts Service, (Subsidiary of The American Chemical Society), 2540 Olentangy River Road, PO Box 3012, Columbus OH 43210-0012. **Tel** (614)447-3731, (800)753-4227, FAX (614)447-3751. **(Subscription address:** Chemical Abstracts Service, Customer Service Department, PO Box 3012, Columbus OH 43210. **Tel** (800)848-6538, (614)447-3600.) **ED** David W Weisgerber.
Desc: Covers photochemistry of biological materials, their constituents, and molecules of biological interest.

ISSN 0885-0208
DD 547 US
CODEN CSPSEB

CA SELECTS: PHOTOCHEMICAL ORGANIC SYNTHESIS. [CA sel., Photochem. org. synth.]. **Added/Corp** American Chemical Society. Chemical Abstracts Service. **VFOAT** Photochemical Organic Synthesis. **VAT** Chemical Abstracts Selects. Photochemical Organic Synthesis. Issue 1 (Jan. 13, 1986)-. Abstracting/Indexing Service. English. Twenty-six times a year. $215.00 US; $234.00 Canada, Mexico, Central and South America; $247.00 other. Chemical Abstracts Service, (Subsidiary of The American Chemical Society), 2540 Olentangy River Road, PO Box 3012, Columbus OH 43210-0012. **Tel** (614)447-3731, (800)753-4227, FAX (614)447-3751. **(Subscription address:** Chemical Abstracts Service, Customer Service Department, PO Box 3012, Columbus OH 43210. **Tel** (800)848-6538, (614)447-3600.) **Bk Rev.**
Desc: Covers documents describing the preparation and reactions of organic compounds under irradiation, especially ultraviolet irradiation.

ISSN 0362-9856
US
CODEN CAPHDL

CA SELECTS: PHOTOCHEMISTRY. **Added/Corp** American Chemical Society. Chemical Abstracts Service. **VFOAT** Photochemistry. **VAT** Chemical Abstracts Selects. Photochemistry. (Oct. 18, 1976)-. Abstracting/Indexing Service. English. Twenty-six times a year. $220.00. Chemical Abstracts Service, (Subsidiary of The American Chemical Society), 2540 Olentangy River Road, PO Box 3012, Columbus OH 43210-0012. **Tel** (614)447-3731, (800)753-4227, FAX (614)447-3751. **(Subscription address:** Chemical Abstracts Service, Customer Service Department, PO Box 3012, Columbus OH 43210. **Tel** (800)848-6538, (614)447-3600.) **ED** David W Weisgerber.
Desc: Covers fluorescence, luminescence, phosphorescence, photochromism, phosphors, light-induced excited state interactions, photochemical mechanisms. Also includes photochemical reactions of molecules in theoretical, mechanistic and synthetic aspects.

ISSN 0885-0216
DD 541 US
CODEN CSPHEC

CA SELECTS: PHOTORESISTS. **Added/Corp** American Chemical Society. Chemical Abstracts Service. **VFOAT** Photoresists. **VAT** Chemical Abstracts Selects. Photoresists. (Jan. 13, 1986)-. Abstracting/Indexing Service. English. Twenty-six times a year. $220.00. Chemical Abstracts Service, (Subsidiary of The American Chemical Society), 2540 Olentangy River Road, PO Box 3012, Columbus OH 43210-0012. **Tel** (614)447-3731, (800)753-4227, FAX (614)447-3751. **(Subscription address:** Chemical Abstracts Service, Customer Service Department, PO Box 3012, Columbus OH 43210. **Tel** (800)848-6538, (614)447-3600.) **Bk Rev.**
Desc: Covers documents on materials and technology for the fabrication and development of photoresists.

ISSN 0749-7326
DD 668 US
CODEN CSPPE2

CA SELECTS: PHOTOSENSITIVE POLYMERS. [CA sel., Photosensit. polym.]. **Added/Corp** American Chemical Society. Chemical Abstracts Service. **VFOAT** Photosensitive Polymers. Issue 1 (Jan. 14, 1985)-. Abstracting/Indexing Service. English. Twenty-six times a year. $220.00. Chemical Abstracts Service, (Subsidiary of The American Chemical Society), 2540 Olentangy River Road, PO Box 3012, Columbus OH 43210-0012. **Tel** (614)447-3731, (800)753-4227, FAX (614)447-3751. **(Subscription address:** Chemical Abstracts Service, Customer Service Department, PO Box 3012, Columbus OH 43210. **Tel** (800)848-6538, (614)447-3600.)
Desc: Covers documents on the preparation, properties, and uses of light-sensitive polymers. Also, coverage includes plastics sensitized for degradation by light after disposal.

ISSN 0749-7334
DD 621 US
CODEN CSPEE3

CA SELECTS: PLASMA & REACTIVE ION ETCHING. **Added/Corp** American Chemical Society. Chemical Abstracts Service. **VFOAT** Plasma & Reactive Ion Etching; Plasma and Reactive Ion Etching. (Jan. 14, 1985)-. Abstracting/Indexing Service. English. Twenty-six times a year. $220.00. Chemical Abstracts Service, (Subsidiary of The American Chemical Society), 2540 Olentangy River Road, PO Box 3012, Columbus OH 43210-0012. **Tel** (614)447-3731, (800)753-4227, FAX (614)447-3751. **(Subscription address:** Chemical Abstracts Service, Customer Service Department, PO Box 3012, Columbus OH 43210. **Tel** (800)848-6538, (614)447-3600.) **ED** David W Weisgerber.
Desc: Covers documents on etching processes used in semiconductor and integrated circuit fabrication. Coverage includes laser etching in the fabrication of electronic devices.

ISSN 0195-511X
US
CODEN CSPFD5

CA SELECTS: PLASTIC FILMS. [CA sel., Plast. films]. **Added/Corp** American Chemical Society. Chemical Abstracts Service. **VFOAT** Plastic Films. **VAT** Chemical Abstracts Selects. Plastic Films. (Jan. 14, 1980)-. Abstracting/Indexing Service. English. Twenty-six times a year. $220.00. Chemical Abstracts Service, (Subsidiary of The American Chemical Society), 2540 Olentangy River Road, PO Box 3012, Columbus OH 43210-0012. **Tel** (614)447-3731, (800)753-4227, FAX (614)447-3751. **(Subscription address:** Chemical Abstracts Service, Customer Service Department, PO Box 3012, Columbus OH 43210. **Tel** (800)848-6538, (614)447-3600.) **ED** David W Weisgerber.
Desc: Covers manufacture, properties, fabrication, and applications of polymeric films.

ISSN 0734-8681
US
CODEN CAADE3

CA SELECTS: PLASTICS ADDITIVES. [CA sel., Plast. addit.]. **Added/Corp** American Chemical Society. Chemical Abstracts Service. **VFOAT** Plastics Additives. **VAT** Chemical Abstracts Selects. Plastics Additives. (19??)-. Abstracting/Indexing Service. English. Twenty-six times a year. $220.00. Chemical Abstracts Service, (Subsidiary of The American Chemical Society), 2540 Olentangy River Road, PO Box 3012, Columbus OH 43210-0012. **Tel** (614)447-3731, (800)753-4227, FAX (614)447-3751. **(Subscription address:** Chemical Abstracts Service, Customer Service Department, PO Box 3012, Columbus OH 43210. **Tel** (800)848-6538, (614)447-3600.) **ED** David W Weisgerber.
Desc: Covers material added to thermoplastic and thermosetting resins to modify properties.

ISSN 0275-7125
US
CODEN CPFUDD

CA SELECTS: PLASTICS FABRICATION & USES. [CA sel., Plast. fabr. uses]. **Added/Corp** American Chemical Society. Chemical Abstracts Service. **VFOAT** Plastics Fabrication and Uses; C.A. Selects. Plastics Fabrication and Uses. **VAT** Chemical Abstracts Selects. Plastics Fabrication and Uses. (1981)-. Abstracting/Indexing Service. English. Twenty-six times a year. $220.00. Chemical Abstracts Service, (Subsidiary of The American Chemical Society), 2540 Olentangy River Road, PO Box 3012, Columbus OH 43210-0012. **Tel** (614)447-3731, (800)753-4227, FAX (614)447-3751. **(Subscription address:** Chemical Abstracts Service, Customer Service Department, PO Box 3012, Columbus OH 43210. **Tel** (800)848-6538, (614)447-3600.) **ED** David W Weisgerber. Documents available from CASDDS.
Desc: Covers processes of chemical or chemical engineering interest for fabricating polymers or compositions containing them.
Ind/Abst Chem. Abstr.

ISSN 0275-7133
US
CODEN CSPPDZ

CA SELECTS: PLASTICS MANUFACTURING & PROCESSING. [CA sel., Plast. manuf. process.]. **Added/Corp** American Chemical Society. Chemical Abstracts Service. **VFOAT** Plastics Manufacturing & Processing; C.A. Selects. Plastics Manufacturing and Processing. **VAT** Chemical Abstracts Selects. Plastics Manufacturing and Processing. (1981)-. Abstracting/Indexing Service. English. Twenty-six times a year. $220.00. Chemical Abstracts Service, (Subsidiary of The American Chemical Society), 2540 Olentangy River Road, PO Box 3012, Columbus OH 43210-0012. **Tel** (614)447-3731, (800)753-4227, FAX (614)447-3751. **(Subscription address:** Chemical Abstracts Service, Customer Service Department, PO Box 3012, Columbus OH 43210. **Tel** (800)848-6538, (614)447-3600.) **ED** David W Weisgerber. Documents available from CASDDS.
Desc: Manufacture, testing, compounding, and processing of polymeric material for use as resin or unsupported films.
Ind/Abst Chem. Abstr.

ISSN 0890-1937
DD 546 US
CODEN CPCHES

CA SELECTS: PLATINUM & PALLADIUM CHEMISTRY. **Added/Corp** American Chemical Society. Chemical Abstracts Service. **VFOAT** CA Selects. Platinum and Palladium Chemistry; Platinum and Palladium Chemistry; Platinum & Palladium Chemistry. **VAT** Chemical Abstracts Selects. Platinum and Palladium Chemistry. Issue 1 (Jan. 12, 1987)-. Abstracting/Indexing Service. English. Twenty-six times a year. $220.00. Chemical Abstracts Service, (Subsidiary of The American Chemical Society), 2540 Olentangy River Road, PO Box 3012, Columbus OH 43210-0012. **Tel** (614)447-3731, (800)753-4227, FAX (614)447-3751. **(Subscription address:** Chemical Abstracts Service, Customer Service Department, PO Box 3012, Columbus OH 43210. **Tel** (800)848-6538, (614)447-3600.)
Desc: Contains information on the preparation, properties, reactions, uses and characterization of compounds that contain platinum or palladium. Alloys are excluded.

ISSN 0160-9149
US
CODEN CSPMDQ

CA SELECTS: POLLUTION MONITORING.

Added/Corp American Chemical Society. Chemical Abstracts Service. **VFOAT** Pollution Monitoring. **VAT** Chemical Abstracts Selects. Pollution Monitoring. (July 10, 1978)-. Abstracting/Indexing Service. English. Twenty-six times a year. $220.00. Chemical Abstracts Service, (Subsidiary of The American Chemical Society), 2540 Olentangy River Road, PO Box 3012, Columbus OH 43210-0012. **Tel** (614)447-3731, (800)753-4227, FAX (614)447-3751. **(Subscription address:** Chemical Abstracts Service, Customer Service Department, PO Box 3012, Columbus OH 43210. **Tel** (800)848-6538, (614)447-3600.) **ED** David W Weisgerber.
Desc: Analytical techniques and equipment related to monitoring pollution of land, water, and atmosphere by solid, liquid, and gaseous waste products.

ISSN 0890-1945
DD 661 US
CODEN CSPJEI

CA SELECTS: POLYACRYLATES (JOURNALS).

Added/Corp American Chemical Society. Chemical Abstracts Service. **VFOAT** Polyacrylates (Journals). **VAT** Chemical Abstracts Selects. Polyacrylates (Journals). Issue 1 (Jan. 12, 1987)-. Abstracting/Indexing Service. English. Twenty-six times a year. $220.00. Chemical Abstracts Service, (Subsidiary of The American Chemical Society), 2540 Olentangy River Road, PO Box 3012, Columbus OH 43210-0012. **Tel** (614)447-3731, (800)753-4227, FAX (614)447-3751. **(Subscription address:** Chemical Abstracts Service, Customer Service Department, PO Box 3012, Columbus OH 43210. **Tel** (800)848-6538, (614)447-3600.)
Desc: Polymers prepared from acrylic and/or methacrylic acid esters. Homopolymers and copolymers of acrylates with each other and with other unsaturated monomers.

ISSN 0734-8703
US
CODEN CAPOE9

CA SELECTS: POLYESTERS.

Added/Corp American Chemical Society. Chemical Abstracts Service. **VFOAT** Polyesters. **VAT** Chemical Abstracts Selects. Polyesters. (19??)-. Abstracting/Indexing Service. English. Twenty-six times a year. $220.00. Chemical Abstracts Service, (Subsidiary of The American Chemical Society), 2540 Olentangy River Road, PO Box 3012, Columbus OH 43210-0012. **Tel** (614)447-3731, (800)753-4227, FAX (614)447-3751. **(Subscription address:** Chemical Abstracts Service, Customer Service Department, PO Box 3012, Columbus OH 43210. **Tel** (800)848-6538, (614)447-3600.) **ED** David W Weisgerber.
Desc: Covers preparation, properties, formulation and use of polyesters. Also includes monomer solution of unsaturated polyesters use in fiber-reinforced plastics and laminates.

ISSN 0895-5840
DD 620 US
CODEN CSEPEF

CA SELECTS: POLYIMIDES.

Added/Corp American Chemical Society. Chemical Abstracts Service. **VFOAT** Polyimides. **VAT** Chemical Abstracts Selects. Polyimides. (Jan. 11, 1988)-. Abstracting/Indexing Service. English. Twenty-six times a year. $220.00. Chemical Abstracts Service, (Subsidiary of The American Chemical Society), 2540 Olentangy River Road, PO Box 3012, Columbus OH 43210-0012. **Tel** (614)447-3731, (800)753-4227, FAX (614)447-3751. **(Subscription address:** Chemical Abstracts Service, Customer Service Department, PO Box 3012, Columbus OH 43210. **Tel** (800)848-6538, (614)447-3600.)
Desc: Contains information on preparation, properties and uses of polymers that contain imide linkages in the main chain.

ISSN 0734-8827
US
CODEN CAPBE4

CA SELECTS: POLYMER BLENDS.

[CA sel., Polym. blends]. **Added/Corp** American Chemical Society. Chemical Abstracts Service. **VFOAT** Polymer Blends. **VAT** Chemical Abstracts Selects. Polymer Blends. (19??)-. Abstracting/Indexing Service. English. Twenty-six times a year. $220.00. Chemical Abstracts Service, (Subsidiary of The American Chemical Society), 2540 Olentangy River Road, PO Box 3012, Columbus OH 43210-0012. **Tel** (614)447-3731, (800)753-4227, FAX (614)447-3751. **(Subscription address:** Chemical Abstracts Service, Customer Service Department, PO Box 3012, Columbus OH 43210. **Tel** (800)848-6538, (614)447-3600.) **ED** David W Weisgerber.
Desc: Morphology, physical and mechanical properties of mixtures of polymers. Also includes factors affecting compatibility of polymers.

ISSN 0734-8835
US
CODEN CAPDEA

CA SELECTS: POLYMER DEGRADATION.

[CA sel., Polym. degrad.]. **Added/Corp** American Chemical Society. Chemical Abstracts Service. **VFOAT** Polymer Degradation. **VAT** Chemical Abstracts Selects. Polymer Degradation. (19??)-. Abstracting/Indexing Service. English. Twenty-six times a year. $220.00. Chemical Abstracts Service, (Subsidiary of The American Chemical Society), 2540 Olentangy River Road, PO Box 3012, Columbus OH 43210-0012. **Tel** (614)447-3731, (800)753-4227, FAX (614)447-3751. **(Subscription address:** Chemical Abstracts Service, Customer Service Department, PO Box 3012, Columbus OH 43210. **Tel** (800)848-6538, (614)447-3600.) **ED** David W Weisgerber.
Desc: Covers chemical, photochemical, radiochemical, mechanical, thermal, and oxidative degradation of polymers. Also includes kinetics and mechanisms of degradative reactions.

ISSN 0195-5128
US
CODEN CAPMD2

CA SELECTS: POLYMER MORPHOLOGY.

[CA sel., Polym. morphol.]. **Added/Corp** American Chemical Society. Chemical Abstracts Service. **VFOAT** Polymer Morphology. **VAT** Chemical Abstracts Selects. Polymer Morphology. (Jan. 14, 1980)-. Abstracting/Indexing Service. English. Twenty-six times a year. $220.00. Chemical Abstracts Service, (Subsidiary of The American Chemical Society), 2540 Olentangy River Road, PO Box 3012, Columbus OH 43210-0012. **Tel** (614)447-3731, (800)753-4227, FAX (614)447-3751. **(Subscription address:** Chemical Abstracts Service, Customer Service Department, PO Box 3012, Columbus OH 43210. **Tel** (800)848-6538, (614)447-3600.) **ED** David W Weisgerber.
Desc: Crystallinity and noncrystalline ordering on a supramolecular level in polymeric materials and their effect on physical and chemical properties of natural and synthetic polymers.

ISSN 0885-0224
DD 668 US
CODEN CPKCEJ

CA SELECTS: POLYMERIZATION KINETICS & PROCESS CONTROL.

[CA sel., Polym. kinet. process control]. **Added/Corp** American Chemical Society. Chemical Abstracts Service. **VFOAT** CA Selects. Polymerization Kinetics & Process Control; Polymerization Kinetics & Process Control; Polymerization Kinetics and Process Control. **VAT** Chemical Abstracts Selects. Polymerization Kinetics and Process Control. Iss 1 (Jan. 13, 1986)-. Abstracting/Indexing Service. English. Twenty-six times a year. $220.00. Chemical Abstracts Service, (Subsidiary of The American Chemical Society), 2540 Olentangy River Road, PO Box 3012, Columbus OH 43210-0012. **Tel** (614)447-3731, (800)753-4227, FAX (614)447-3751. **(Subscription address:** Chemical Abstracts Service, Customer Service Department, PO Box 3012, Columbus OH 43210. **Tel** (800)848-6538, (614)447-3600.) **Bk Rev.**
Desc: Covers documents on (a) kinetics studies on addition, condensation and other types of polymerization, and (b) the engineering of polymerization processes.

ISSN 0740-0705
DD 547 US
CODEN CSPOEX

CA SELECTS: POLYURETHANES.

[CA sel. Polyurethanes]. **Added/Corp** American Chemical Society. Chemical Abstracts Service. **VFOAT** Polyurethanes. **VAT** Chemical Abstracts Selects. Polyurethanes. (19??)-. Abstracting/Indexing Service. English. Twenty-six times a year. $220.00. Chemical Abstracts Service, (Subsidiary of The American Chemical Society), 2540 Olentangy River Road, PO Box 3012, Columbus OH 43210-0012. **Tel** (614)447-3731, (800)753-4227, FAX (614)447-3751. **(Subscription address:** Chemical Abstracts Service, Customer Service Department, PO Box 3012, Columbus OH 43210. **Tel** (800)848-6538, (614)447-3600.) **ED** David W Weisgerber.
Desc: Covers preparation, properties, reactions, uses of urethane polymers, i.e., derived from polyisocyanates and polyols.

ISSN 0195-5136
US
CODEN CLPODH

CA SELECTS: PORPHYRINS.

[CA sel., Porphyr.]. **Added/Corp** American Chemical Society. Chemical Abstracts Service. **VFOAT** Porphyrins. **VAT** Chemical Abstracts Selects. Porphyrins. (Jan. 14, 1980)-. Abstracting/Indexing Service. English. Twenty-six times a year. $220.00. Chemical Abstracts Service, (Subsidiary of The American Chemical Society), 2540 Olentangy River Road, PO Box 3012, Columbus OH 43210-0012. **Tel** (614)447-3731, (800)753-4227, FAX (614)447-3751. **(Subscription address:** Chemical Abstracts Service, Customer Service Department, PO Box 3012, Columbus OH 43210. **Tel** (800)848-6538, (614)447-3600.) **ED** David W Weisgerber.
Desc: Covers chemical and biochemical aspects of porophyrins.

ISSN 0148-2343
US
CODEN CSEPDE

CA SELECTS: PROSTAGLANDINS.

Added/Corp American Chemical Society. Chemical Abstracts Service. **VFOAT** Prostaglandins. **VAT** Chemical Abstracts Selects. Prostaglandins. Issue 1 (Jan. 9, 1978)-. Abstracting/Indexing Service. English. Twenty-six times a year. $220.00. Chemical Abstracts Service, (Subsidiary of The American Chemical Society), 2540 Olentangy River Road, PO Box 3012, Columbus OH 43210-0012. **Tel** (614)447-3731, (800)753-4227, FAX (614)447-3751. **(Subscription address:** Chemical Abstracts Service, Customer Service Department, PO Box 3012, Columbus OH 43210. **Tel** (800)848-6538, (614)447-3600.) **ED** David W Weisgerber.
Desc: Covers chemistry of prostaglandins, prostacyclins, thromboxanes, leukotrienes and enzymes of prostaglandin metabolism.

ISSN 0190-941X
US
CODEN CPMRD5

CA SELECTS: PROTON MAGNETIC RESONANCE.

Added/Corp American Chemical Society. Chemical Abstracts Service. **VFOAT** Proton Magnetic Resonance. **VAT** Chemical Abstracts Selects. Proton Magnetic Resonance. (July 9, 1979)-. Abstracting/Indexing Service. English. Twenty-six times a year. $220.00. Chemical Abstracts Service, (Subsidiary of The American Chemical Society), 2540 Olentangy River Road, PO Box 3012, Columbus OH 43210-0012. **Tel** (614)447-3731, (800)753-4227, FAX (614)447-3751. **(Subscription address:** Chemical Abstracts Service, Customer Service Department, PO Box 3012, Columbus OH 43210. **Tel** (800)848-6538, (614)447-3600.) **ED** David W Weisgerber. ***Continues in part*** *CA Selects. Nuclear Magnetic Resonance, Chemical Aspects, 0146-4507.*
Desc: Chemical aspects of nuclear magnetic resonance of hydrogen, deuterium, and tritium. Also covers internuclear double resonance, hydrogen spin coupling, nuclear magnetic relaxation, nuclear spin relaxation and spin-lattice relaxation.

ISSN 0362-9848
US
CODEN CASPDQ

CA SELECTS: PSYCHOBIOCHEMISTRY.

Added/Corp American Chemical Society. Chemical Abstracts Service. **VFOAT** Psychobiochemistry. **VAT** Chemical Abstracts Selects. Psychobiochemistry. (Oct. 18, 1976)-. Abstracting/Indexing Service. English. Twenty-six times a year. $220.00. Chemical Abstracts Service, (Subsidiary of The American Chemical Society), 2540 Olentangy River Road, PO Box 3012, Columbus OH 43210-0012. **Tel** (614)447-3731, (800)753-4227, FAX (614)447-3751. **(Subscription address:** Chemical Abstracts Service, Customer Service Department, PO Box 3012, Columbus OH 43210. **Tel** (800)848-6538, (614)447-3600.) **ED** David W Weisgerber.
Desc: Pathological and pharmacological aspects of mental function, human and animal behavior, and emotion.

ISSN 0890-1953
DD 669 US
CODEN CSQPE7

CA SELECTS: QUATERNARY AMMONIUM COMPOUNDS.

Added/Corp American Chemical Society. Chemical Abstracts Service. **VFOAT** Quaternary Ammonium Compounds. **VAT** Chemical Abstracts Selects. Quaternary Ammonium Compounds. Issue 1 (Jan. 12, 1987)-. Abstracting/Indexing Service. English. Twenty-six times a year. $220.00. Chemical Abstracts Service, (Subsidiary of The American Chemical Society), 2540 Olentangy River Road, PO Box 3012, Columbus OH 43210-0012. **Tel** (614)447-3731, (800)753-4227, FAX (614)447-3751. **(Subscription address:** Chemical Abstracts Service, Customer Service Department, PO Box 3012, Columbus OH 43210. **Tel** (800)848-6538, (614)447-3600.)
Desc: Preparation, properties, reactions, and uses of compounds that contain at least one nitrogen atom covalently bonded to four non-hydrogen atoms.

ISSN 0146-4523
US
CODEN CSRCD6

CA SELECTS: RADIATION CHEMISTRY.

Added/Corp American Chemical Society. Chemical Abstracts Service. **VFOAT** Radiation Chemistry. **VAT** Chemical Abstracts Selects. Radiation Chemistry. (July 11 1977)-. Abstracting/Indexing Service. English. Twenty-six times a year. $220.00. Chemical Abstracts Service, (Subsidiary of The American Chemical Society), 2540 Olentangy River Road, PO Box 3012, Columbus OH 43210-0012. **Tel** (614)447-3731, (800)753-4227, FAX (614)447-3751. **(Subscription address:** Chemical Abstracts Service, Customer Service Department, PO Box 3012, Columbus OH 43210. **Tel** (800)848-6538, (614)447-3600.) **ED** David W Weisgerber.
Desc: Covers radiation chemistry and biochemistry, radiation chemistry in aqueous and nonaqueous systems, energy transfer and ionic reactions.

ISSN 0749-7342
DD 668 US
CODEN CSRCE7

CA SELECTS: RADIATION CURING.

[CA sel., Radiat. curing]. **Added/Corp** American Chemical Society. Chemical Abstracts Service. **VFOAT** Radiation Curing. (Jan. 14, 1985)-. Abstracting/Indexing Service.

English. Twenty-six times a year. $220.00. Chemical Abstracts Service, (Subsidiary of The American Chemical Society), 2540 Olentangy River Road, PO Box 3012, Columbus OH 43210-0012. **Tel** (614)447-3731, (800)753-4227, FAX (614)447-3751. **(Subscription address:** Chemical Abstracts Service, Customer Service Department, PO Box 3012, Columbus OH 43210. **Tel** (800)848-6538, (614)447-3600.**)** **ED** David W Weisgerber.
Desc: Covers documents on the treatment of polymers with electron beams, gamma rays, and other forms of ionizing radiation.

ISSN 0148-2432
US
CODEN CARSDU

CA SELECTS: RAMAN SPECTROSCOPY. **Added/Corp** American Chemical Society. Chemical Abstracts Service. **VFOAT** Raman Spectroscopy. **VAT** Chemical Abstracts Selects. Raman Spectroscopy. (Jan. 9, 1978)-. Abstracting/Indexing Service. English. Twenty-six times a year. $220.00. Chemical Abstracts Service, (Subsidiary of The American Chemical Society), 2540 Olentangy River Road, PO Box 3012, Columbus OH 43210-0012. **Tel** (614)447-3731, (800)753-4227, FAX (614)447-3751. **(Subscription address:** Chemical Abstracts Service, Customer Service Department, PO Box 3012, Columbus OH 43210. **Tel** (800)848-6538, (614)447-3600.**)** **ED** David W Weisgerber.
Desc: All aspects of Raman spectroscopy: methodology, apparatus, experimental results, theoretical treatments, books and reviews.

ISSN 0160-9157
US
CODEN CSRWDW

CA SELECTS: RECOVERY & RECYCLING OF WASTES. **Added/Corp** American Chemical Society. Chemical Abstracts Service. **VFOAT** Recovery & Recycling of Wastes. **VAT** Chemical Abstracts Selects. Recovery and Recycling of Wastes. (1978)-. Abstracting/Indexing Service. English. Twenty-six times a year. $220.00. Chemical Abstracts Service, (Subsidiary of The American Chemical Society), 2540 Olentangy River Road, PO Box 3012, Columbus OH 43210-0012. **Tel** (614)447-3731, (800)753-4227, FAX (614)447-3751. **(Subscription address:** Chemical Abstracts Service, Customer Service Department, PO Box 3012, Columbus OH 43210. **Tel** (800)848-6538, (614)447-3600.**)** **ED** David W Weisgerber.
Desc: Processes and equipment used for recycling or recovery of all types of waste materials.

DD 546
ISSN 0749-7350
US
CODEN CSSCEC

CA SELECTS: SELENIUM & TELLURIUM CHEMISTRY. **Added/Corp** American Chemical Society. Chemical Abstracts Service. **VFOAT** Selenium & Tellurium Chemistry; Selenium and Tellurium Chemistry. Issue 1 (Jan. 14, 1985)-. Abstracting/Indexing Service. English. Twenty-six times a year. $220.00. Chemical Abstracts Service, (Subsidiary of The American Chemical Society), 2540 Olentangy River Road, PO Box 3012, Columbus OH 43210-0012. **Tel** (614)447-3731, (800)753-4227, FAX (614)447-3751. **(Subscription address:** Chemical Abstracts Service, Customer Service Department, PO Box 3012, Columbus OH 43210. **Tel** (800)848-6538, (614)447-3600.**)** **ED** David W Weisgerber. ***Absorbed*** *Selenium and Tellurium Abstracts, 0037-1467.*
Desc: Covers documents on all aspects of selenium and tellurium chemistry.

DD 669
ISSN 1062-869X
US
CODEN CSSLE5

CA SELECTS: SHAPE MEMORY ALLOYS. [CA sel., Shape mem. alloys]. **Added/Corp** American Chemical Society. Chemical Abstracts Service. **VFOAT** Shape Memory Alloys. **VAT** Chemical Abstracts Selects. Shape Memory Alloys. Issue 14 (July 13, 1992)-. Abstracting/Indexing Service. English. Twenty-six times a year. $215.00 US; $234.00 Canada, Mexico, Central and South America; $247.00 other. Chemical Abstracts Service, (Subsidiary of The American Chemical Society), 2540 Olentangy River Road, PO Box 3012, Columbus OH 43210-0012. **Tel** (614)447-3731, (800)753-4227, FAX (614)447-3751. **(Subscription address:** Chemical Abstracts Service, Customer Service Department, PO Box 3012, Columbus OH 43210. **Tel** (800)848-6538, (614)447-3600.**)**
Desc: Contains information on fabrication, testing, properties, applications and fundamental studies, including phase transformations, crystallography and modeling of the title alloys.

DD 546
ISSN 0890-1961
US
CODEN CSSSEQ

CA SELECTS: SILICAS & SILICATES. **Added/Corp** American Chemical Society. Chemical Abstracts Service. **VFOAT** CA Selects. Silicas and Silicates; Silicas and Silicates; Silicas & Silicates. **VAT** Chemical Abstracts Selects. Silicas and Silicates. Issue 1 (Jan. 12, 1987)-. Abstracting/Indexing Service. English. Twenty-six times a year. $220.00. Chemical Abstracts Service, (Subsidiary of The American Chemical Society), 2540 Olentangy River Road, PO Box 3012, Columbus OH 43210-0012. **Tel** (614)447-3731, (800)753-4227, FAX (614)447-3751. **(Subscription address:** Chemical Abstracts Service, Customer Service Department, PO Box 3012, Columbus OH 43210. **Tel** (800)848-6538, (614)447-3600.**)**
Desc: Preparation, properties, reactions, and uses of synthetic and naturally occurring inorganic compounds that contain silicon tetrahedrally bonded to oxygen oxygen. Silica minerals and polysilicates.

DD 547
ISSN 0895-5832
US
CODEN CSISEA

CA SELECTS: SILOXANES & SILICONES. **Added/Corp** American Chemical Society. Chemical Abstracts Service. **VFOAT** Siloxanes & Silicones; CA Selects. Siloxanes and Silicones. **VAT** Chemical Abstracts Selects. Siloxanes & Silicones. (Jan. 11, 1988)-. Abstracting/Indexing Service. English. Twenty-six times a year. $220.00. Chemical Abstracts Service, (Subsidiary of The American Chemical Society), 2540 Olentangy River Road, PO Box 3012, Columbus OH 43210-0012. **Tel** (614)447-3731, (800)753-4227, FAX (614)447-3751. **(Subscription address:** Chemical Abstracts Service, Customer Service Department, PO Box 3012, Columbus OH 43210. **Tel** (800)848-6538, (614)447-3600.**)**
Desc: Contains information on preparation, properties, reactions and uses of monomeric, oligomeric and polymeric compounds, the basic structure of which consists of alternating silicon and oxygen atoms.

ISSN 0148-2440
US
CODEN CSCMDT

CA SELECTS: SILVER CHEMISTRY. **Added/Corp** American Chemical Society. Chemical Abstracts Service. **VFOAT** Silver Chemistry. **VAT** Chemical Abstracts Selects. Silver Chemistry. (Jan. 9, 1978)-. Abstracting/Indexing Service. English. Twenty-six times a year. $220.00. Chemical Abstracts Service, (Subsidiary of The American Chemical Society), 2540 Olentangy River Road, PO Box 3012, Columbus OH 43210-0012. **Tel** (614)447-3731, (800)753-4227, FAX (614)447-3751. **(Subscription address:** Chemical Abstracts Service, Customer Service Department, PO Box 3012, Columbus OH 43210. **Tel** (800)848-6538, (614)447-3600.**)** **ED** David W Weisgerber.
Desc: Chemistry and chemical technology of silver and silver-containing compounds. Also includes uses of silver and silver compounds in meteorology, pharmacology, medicine, photography, electronics and dental materials.

ISSN 0148-236X
US
CODEN CASEDR

CA SELECTS: SOLAR ENERGY. **Added/Corp** American Chemical Society. Chemical Abstracts Service. **VFOAT** Solar Energy. **VAT** Chemical Abstracts Selects. Solar Energy. (Jan. 9, 1978)-. Abstracting/Indexing Service. English. Twenty-six times a year. $220.00. Chemical Abstracts Service, (Subsidiary of The American Chemical Society), 2540 Olentangy River Road, PO Box 3012, Columbus OH 43210-0012. **Tel** (614)447-3731, (800)753-4227, FAX (614)447-3751. **(Subscription address:** Chemical Abstracts Service, Customer Service Department, PO Box 3012, Columbus OH 43210. **Tel** (800)848-6538, (614)447-3600.**)** **ED** David W Weisgerber.
Desc: Covers solar-energy conversion devices materials and processes, biosolar energy processes and solar sea thermal energy conversion systems, photoelectric solar cells, photoelectrochemical cells, and photogalvanic cells.

ISSN 0160-9165
US
CODEN CSSTDS

CA SELECTS: SOLID & RADIOACTIVE WASTE TREATMENT. **Added/Corp** American Chemical Society. Chemical Abstracts Service. **VFOAT** Solid & Radioactive Waste Treatment. **VAT** Chemical Abstracts Selects. Solid and Radioactive Waste Treatment. (July 10, 1978)-. Abstracting/Indexing Service. English. Twenty-six times a year. $220.00. Chemical Abstracts Service, (Subsidiary of The American Chemical Society), 2540 Olentangy River Road, PO Box 3012, Columbus OH 43210-0012. **Tel** (614)447-3731, (800)753-4227, FAX (614)447-3751. **(Subscription address:** Chemical Abstracts Service, Customer Service Department, PO Box 3012, Columbus OH 43210. **Tel** (800)848-6538, (614)447-3600.**)** **ED** David W Weisgerber.
Desc: Chemical and chemical engineering aspects of treatment and disposal: municipal, industrial, laboratory wastes, sludges and slurries, nuclear fuel reprocessing wastes, combustion, incineration, biodegradation, hydrolysis, and chemical techniques.

DD 538
ISSN 0895-5824
US
CODEN CSSNEB

CA SELECTS: SOLID STATE NMR. [CA sel., Solid state NMR]. **Added/Corp** American Chemical Society. Chemical Abstracts Service. **VFOAT** Solid State NMR. **VAT** Chemical Abstracts Selects. Solid State Nuclear Magnetic Resonance. (Jan. 11, 1988)-. Abstracting/Indexing Service. English. Twenty-six times a year. $220.00. Chemical Abstracts Service, (Subsidiary of The American Chemical Society), 2540 Olentangy River Road, PO Box 3012, Columbus OH 43210-0012. **Tel** (614)447-3731, (800)753-4227, FAX (614)447-3751. **(Subscription address:** Chemical Abstracts Service, Customer Service Department, PO Box 3012, Columbus OH 43210. **Tel** (800)848-6538, (614)447-3600.**)**
Desc: Covers methodology and apparatus for solid-state NMR studies and NMR studies of organic and inorganic compounds in the solid state, as well as experimental results.

ISSN 0146-4531
US
CODEN CSSEDH

CA SELECTS: SOLVENT EXTRACTION. **Added/Corp** American Chemical Society. Chemical Abstracts Service. **VFOAT** Solvent Extraction. **VAT** Chemical Abstracts Selects. Solvent Extraction. (July 11, 1977)-. Abstracting/Indexing Service. English. Twenty-six times a year. $220.00. Chemical Abstracts Service, (Subsidiary of The American Chemical Society), 2540 Olentangy River Road, PO Box 3012, Columbus OH 43210-0012. **Tel** (614)447-3731, (800)753-4227, FAX (614)447-3751. **(Subscription address:** Chemical Abstracts Service, Customer Service Department, PO Box 3012, Columbus OH 43210. **Tel** (800)848-6538, (614)447-3600.**)** **ED** David W Weisgerber.
Desc: Covers chemical applications of solvent extraction, solvent properties, solvent recovery and fuel reprocessing.

DD 544
ISSN 0885-0232
US
CODEN CSANEN

CA SELECTS: SPECTROCHEMICAL ANALYSIS. [CA sel., Spectrochem. anal.]. **Added/Corp** American Chemical Society. Chemical Abstracts Service. **VFOAT** Spectrochemical Analysis. **VAT** Chemical Abstracts Selects. Spectrochemical Analysis. Iss 1 (Jan. 13, 1986)-. Abstracting/Indexing Service. English. Twenty-six times a year. $220.00. Chemical Abstracts Service, (Subsidiary of The American Chemical Society), 2540 Olentangy River Road, PO Box 3012, Columbus OH 43210-0012. **Tel** (614)447-3731, (800)753-4227, FAX (614)447-3751. **(Subscription address:** Chemical Abstracts Service, Customer Service Department, PO Box 3012, Columbus OH 43210. **Tel** (800)848-6538, (614)447-3600.**)** **Bk Rev.**
Desc: Covers documents on spectroscopic techniques used in chemical analysis.

ISSN 0160-9173
US
CODEN CSBSDB

CA SELECTS: STEROIDS (BIOCHEMICAL ASPECTS). **Added/Corp** American Chemical Society. Chemical Abstracts Service. **VFOAT** Steroids (Biochemical Aspects). **VAT** Chemical Abstracts Selects. Steroids (Biochemical Aspects). (July 10, 1978)-. Abstracting/Indexing Service. English. Twenty-six times a year. $220.00. Chemical Abstracts Service, (Subsidiary of The American Chemical Society), 2540 Olentangy River Road, PO Box 3012, Columbus OH 43210-0012. **Tel** (614)447-3731, (800)753-4227, FAX (614)447-3751. **(Subscription address:** Chemical Abstracts Service, Customer Service Department, PO Box 3012, Columbus OH 43210. **Tel** (800)848-6538, (614)447-3600.**)** **ED** David W Weisgerber.
Desc: Covers pharmacology, toxicology, general biochemistry, and nutritional uses of steroids.

ISSN 0160-9181
US
CODEN CSASD3

CA SELECTS: STEROIDS (CHEMICAL ASPECTS). **Added/Corp** American Chemical Society. Chemical Abstracts Service. **VFOAT** Steroids (Chemical Aspects). **VAT** Chemical Abstracts Selects. Steroids (Chemical Aspects). (July 10, 1978)-. Abstracting/Indexing Service. English. Twenty-six times a year. $220.00. Chemical Abstracts Service, (Subsidiary of The American Chemical Society), 2540 Olentangy River Road, PO Box 3012, Columbus OH 43210-0012. **Tel** (614)447-3731, (800)753-4227, FAX (614)447-3751. **(Subscription address:** Chemical Abstracts Service, Customer Service Department, PO Box 3012, Columbus OH 43210. **Tel** (800)848-6538, (614)447-3600.**)** **ED** David W Weisgerber.
Desc: Covers isolation and synthesis of steroids and their chemical reactions and transformations.

DD 620
ISSN 1066-1174
US
CODEN CSSTET

●**CA SELECTS: STRESS CORROSION - METALS.** [CA sel., Stress corros. - met.]. **Added/Corp** American Chemical Society. Chemical Abstracts Service. **VFOAT** Stress Corrosion - Metals. **VAT** Chemical Abstracts Selects. Stress Corrosion - Metals. (Jan. 11, 1993)-. Abstracting/Indexing Service. English. Twenty-six times a year. $215.00 US; $234 00 Canada, Mexico, Central and South America; $247.00 other. Chemical Abstracts Service, (Subsidiary of The American Chemical Society), 2540 Olentangy River Road, PO Box 3012, Columbus OH 43210-0012. **Tel**

(614)447-3731, (800)753-4227, FAX (614)447-3751. **(Subscription address:** Chemical Abstracts Service, Customer Service Department, PO Box 3012, Columbus OH 43210. **Tel** (800)848-6538, (614)447-3600.)
Desc: Contains information on such topics as corrosion mechanisms, hydrogen embrittlement and hydrogen sulfide cracking of structural metal and alloys.

ISSN 0895-5816
DD 546 US
CODEN CSSREN

CA SELECTS: STRUCTURE-ACTIVITY RELATIONSHIPS. [CA sel., Struct.-act. relatsh.]. **Added/Corp** American Chemical Society. Chemical Abstracts Service. **VFOAT** Structure-Activity Relationships. **VAT** Chemical Abstracts Selects. Structure-Activity Relationships. (Jan. 11, 1988)-. Abstracting/Indexing Service. English. Twenty-six times a year. $220.00. Chemical Abstracts Service, (Subsidiary of The American Chemical Society), 2540 Olentangy River Road, PO Box 3012, Columbus OH 43210-0012. **Tel** (614)447-3731, (800)753-4227, FAX (614)447-3751. **(Subscription address:** Chemical Abstracts Service, Customer Service Department, PO Box 3012, Columbus OH 43210. **Tel** (800)848-6538, (614)447-3600.)
Desc: Contains information on structure activity relationships of therapeutic agents and compounds that have potential therapeutic use and more.

ISSN 0195-5152
US
CODEN CSUADF

CA SELECTS: SURFACE ANALYSIS. [CA sel., surf. anal.]. **Added/Corp** American Chemical Society. Chemical Abstracts Service. **VFOAT** Surface Analysis. **VAT** Chemical Abstracts Selects. Surface Analysis. (Jan. 14, 1980)-. Abstracting/Indexing Service. English. Twenty-six times a year. $220.00. Chemical Abstracts Service, (Subsidiary of The American Chemical Society), 2540 Olentangy River Road, PO Box 3012, Columbus OH 43210-0012. **Tel** (614)447-3731, (800)753-4227, FAX (614)447-3751. **(Subscription address:** Chemical Abstracts Service, Customer Service Department, PO Box 3012, Columbus OH 43210. **Tel** (800)848-6538, (614)447-3600.) **ED** David W Weisgerber.
Desc: Covers analytical chemistry of surfaces technology and analytical use of ESCA, Auger spectroscopy and photoelectron spectroscopy.

ISSN 0146-454X
US
CODEN CSSAD5

CA SELECTS: SURFACE CHEMISTRY (PHYSICOCHEMICAL ASPECTS). **Added/Corp** American Chemical Society. Chemical Abstracts Service. **VFOAT** Surface Chemistry (Physicochemical Aspects). **VAT** Chemical Abstracts Selects. Surface Chemistry, Physicochemical Aspects. (July 11, 1977)-. Abstracting/Indexing Service. English. Twenty-six times a year. $215.00 US; $234.00 Canada, Mexico, Central and South America; $247.00 other. Chemical Abstracts Service, (Subsidiary of The American Chemical Society), 2540 Olentangy River Road, PO Box 3012, Columbus OH 43210-0012. **Tel** (614)447-3731, (800)753-4227, FAX (614)447-3751. **(Subscription address:** Chemical Abstracts Service, Customer Service Department, PO Box 3012, Columbus OH 43210. **Tel** (800)848-6538, (614)447-3600.) **ED** David W Weisgerber.
Desc: Covers physical chemistry and properties of solid surfaces, absorption, desorption, adhesion, surface defects and surface interactions.

ISSN 0195-5160
US
CODEN CSSYD9

CA SELECTS: SYNFUELS. [CA sel., Synfuels]. **Added/Corp** American Chemical Society. Chemical Abstracts Service. **VFOAT** Synfuels. **VAT** Chemical Abstracts Selects. Synfuels. (Jan. 14, 1980)-. Abstracting/Indexing Service. English. Twenty-six times a year. $220.00. Chemical Abstracts Service, (Subsidiary of The American Chemical Society), 2540 Olentangy River Road, PO Box 3012, Columbus OH 43210-0012. **Tel** (614)447-3731, (800)753-4227, FAX (614)447-3751. **(Subscription address:** Chemical Abstracts Service, Customer Service Department, PO Box 3012, Columbus OH 43210. **Tel** (800)848-6538, (614)447-3600.) **ED** David W Weisgerber.
Desc: Covers production of fuels from new sources, gasohol, gasification of coal, oil shale, tar sands, biomass, processes and equipment for synfuel production.

ISSN 0275-7168
US
CODEN CSYPDC

CA SELECTS: SYNTHETIC HIGH POLYMERS. [CA sel., Synth. high polym.]. **Added/Corp** American Chemical Society. Chemical Abstracts Service. **VFOAT** Synthetic High Polymers. **VAT** Chemical Abstracts Selects. Synthetic High Polymers. (1981)-. Abstracting/Indexing Service. English. Twenty-six times a year. $220.00. Chemical Abstracts Service, (Subsidiary of The American Chemical Society), 2540 Olentangy River Road, PO Box 3012, Columbus OH 43210-0012. **Tel** (614)447-3731, (800)753-4227, FAX (614)447-3751. **(Subscription address:** Chemical Abstracts Service, Customer Service Department, PO Box 3012, Columbus OH 43210. **Tel** (800)848-6538, (614)447-3600.) **ED** David W Weisgerber. Documents available from CASDDS.
Desc: Covers organic and physical chemistry of linear and branched synthetic organic and inorganic polymers.
Ind/Abst Chem. Abstr.

ISSN 0195-5179
US
CODEN CSCPD4

CA SELECTS: SYNTHETIC MACROCYCLIC COMPOUNDS. **Added/Corp** American Chemical Society. Chemical Abstracts Service. **VFOAT** Synthetic Macrocyclic Compounds; C.A. Selects. Synthetic Macrocyclic Compounds. **VAT** Chemical Abstracts Selects. Synthetic Macrocyclic Compounds. (Jan. 14, 1980)-. Abstracting/Indexing Service. English. Twenty-six times a year. $220.00. Chemical Abstracts Service, (Subsidiary of The American Chemical Society), 2540 Olentangy River Road, PO Box 3012, Columbus OH 43210-0012. **Tel** (614)447-3731, (800)753-4227, FAX (614)447-3751. **(Subscription address:** Chemical Abstracts Service, Customer Service Department, PO Box 3012, Columbus OH 43210. **Tel** (800)848-6538, (614)447-3600.) **ED** David W Weisgerber.
Desc: Synthesis and applications of macrocyclic compounds and ligands, e.g., crown ethers, macrocyclic tetramines.

ISSN 1062-8703
DD 666 US
CODEN CATCER

CA SELECTS: TECHNICAL CERAMICS. [CA sel., Tech. ceram.]. **Added/Corp** American Chemical Society. Chemical Abstracts Service. **VFOAT** Technical Ceramics. **VAT** Chemical Abstracts Selects. Technical Ceramics. Issue 14 (July 13, 1992)-. Abstracting/Indexing Service. English. Twenty-six times a year. $215.00 US; $234.00 Canada, Mexico, Central and South America; $247.00 other. Chemical Abstracts Service, (Subsidiary of The American Chemical Society), 2540 Olentangy River Road, PO Box 3012, Columbus OH 43210-0012. **Tel** (614)447-3731, (800)753-4227, FAX (614)447-3751. **(Subscription address:** Chemical Abstracts Service, Customer Service Department, PO Box 3012, Columbus OH 43210. **Tel** (800)848-6538, (614)447-3600.)

ISSN 0195-5187
US
CODEN CSANDM

CA SELECTS: THERMAL ANALYSIS. [CA sel., Therm. anal.]. **Added/Corp** American Chemical Society. Chemical Abstracts Service. **VFOAT** Thermal Analysis. **VAT** Chemical Abstracts Selects. Thermal Analysis. (Jan. 14, 1980)-. Abstracting/Indexing Service. English. Twenty-six times a year. $220.00. Chemical Abstracts Service, (Subsidiary of The American Chemical Society), 2540 Olentangy River Road, PO Box 3012, Columbus OH 43210-0012. **Tel** (614)447-3731, (800)753-4227, FAX (614)447-3751. **(Subscription address:** Chemical Abstracts Service, Customer Service Department, PO Box 3012, Columbus OH 43210. **Tel** (800)848-6538, (614)447-3600.) **ED** David W Weisgerber.
Desc: Covers DTA, thermogravimetry, differential scanning calorimetry, evolved-gas analysis, thermodilatometry, thermoelectrometry, thermomagnetometry and thermosonimetry.

ISSN 0162-7864
US
CODEN CSTHDV

CA SELECTS: THERMOCHEMISTRY. **Added/Corp** American Chemical Society. Chemical Abstracts Service. **VFOAT** Thermochemistry. **VAT** Chemical Abstracts Selects. Thermochemistry. (Jan. 8, 1979)-. Abstracting/Indexing Service. English. Twenty-six times a year. $220.00. Chemical Abstracts Service, (Subsidiary of The American Chemical Society), 2540 Olentangy River Road, PO Box 3012, Columbus OH 43210-0012. **Tel** (614)447-3731, (800)753-4227, FAX (614)447-3751. **(Subscription address:** Chemical Abstracts Service, Customer Service Department, PO Box 3012, Columbus OH 43210. **Tel** (800)848-6538, (614)447-3600.) **ED** David W Weisgerber. **Bk Rev. Ad Acc.** ctrl circ.
Desc: Covers chemical thermodynamics: heat capacities and thermodynamic functions such as enthalpies, free energies, and entropies for physicochemical and biochemical processes.

ISSN 0160-919X
US
CODEN CSTADA

CA SELECTS: TRACE ELEMENT ANALYSIS. **Added/Corp** American Chemical Society. Chemical Abstracts Service. **VFOAT** Trace Element Analysis. **VAT** Chemical Abstracts Selects. Trace Element Analysis. (July 10, 1978)-. Abstracting/Indexing Service. English. Twenty-six times a year. $220.00. Chemical Abstracts Service, (Subsidiary of The American Chemical Society), 2540 Olentangy River Road, PO Box 3012, Columbus OH 43210-0012. **Tel** (614)447-3731, (800)753-4227, FAX (614)447-3751. **(Subscription address:** Chemical Abstracts Service, Customer Service Department, PO Box 3012, Columbus OH 43210. **Tel** (800)848-6538, (614)447-3600.) **ED** David W Weisgerber.
Desc: Detection and determination of trace elements found in solid, liquid, or gaseous environments (food, rocks, soils, petroleum products, sewage).

ISSN 0195-5195
US
CODEN CSULDE

CA SELECTS: ULTRAFILTRATION. **Added/Corp** American Chemical Society. Chemical Abstracts Service. **VFOAT** Ultrafiltration. **VAT** Chemical Abstracts Selects. Ultrafiltration. (Jan. 14, 1980)-. Abstracting/Indexing Service. English. Twenty-six times a year. $220.00. Chemical Abstracts Service, (Subsidiary of The American Chemical Society), 2540 Olentangy River Road, PO Box 3012, Columbus OH 43210-0012. **Tel** (614)447-3731, (800)753-4227, FAX (614)447-3751. **(Subscription address:** Chemical Abstracts Service, Customer Service Department, PO Box 3012, Columbus OH 43210. **Tel** (800)848-6538, (614)447-3600.) **ED** David W Weisgerber.
Desc: Covers technology and use of hyperfiltration and ultrafiltration. Also includes reverse osmosis and manufacturing of ultrafiltration membranes.

ISSN 0195-5209
US
CODEN CUVSDK

CA SELECTS: ULTRAVIOLET & VISIBLE SPECTROSCOPY. **Added/Corp** American Chemical Society. Chemical Abstracts Service. **VFOAT** Ultraviolet & Visible Spectroscopy. **VAT** Chemical Abstracts Selects. Ultraviolet and Visible Spectroscopy. (Jan. 14, 1980)-. Abstracting/Indexing Service. English. Twenty-six times a year. $220.00. Chemical Abstracts Service, (Subsidiary of The American Chemical Society), 2540 Olentangy River Road, PO Box 3012, Columbus OH 43210-0012. **Tel** (614)447-3731, (800)753-4227, FAX (614)447-3751. **(Subscription address:** Chemical Abstracts Service, Customer Service Department, PO Box 3012, Columbus OH 43210. **Tel** (800)848-6538, (614)447-3600.) **ED** David W Weisgerber.
Desc: Covers methodology and experimental measurement of absorption and emission spectroscopy for UV and visible regions.

ISSN 0749-7369
DD 667 US
CODEN CSWCEW

CA SELECTS: WATER-BASED COATINGS. **Added/Corp** American Chemical Society. Chemical Abstracts Service. **VFOAT** Water Based Coatings. (Jan. 14, 1985)-. Abstracting/Indexing Service. English. Twenty-six times a year. $220.00. Chemical Abstracts Service, (Subsidiary of The American Chemical Society), 2540 Olentangy River Road, PO Box 3012, Columbus OH 43210-0012. **Tel** (614)447-3731, (800)753-4227, FAX (614)447-3751. **(Subscription address:** Chemical Abstracts Service, Customer Service Department, PO Box 3012, Columbus OH 43210. **Tel** (800)848-6538, (614)447-3600.) **ED** David W Weisgerber.
Desc: Covers documents on the formulation, application, and performance of water-borne coatings, e.g., water-soluble coatings, latex coatings, aqueous coatings.

ISSN 0740-073X
DD 628 US
CODEN CSWTEF

CA SELECTS: WATER TREATMENT. [CA sel., Water treat.]. **Added/Corp** American Chemical Society. Chemical Abstracts Service. **VFOAT** Water Treatment. **VAT** Chemical Abstracts Selects. Water Treatment. (19??)-. Abstracting/Indexing Service. English. Twenty-six times a year. $220.00. Chemical Abstracts Service, (Subsidiary of The American Chemical Society), 2540 Olentangy River Road, PO Box 3012, Columbus OH 43210-0012. **Tel** (614)447-3731, (800)753-4227, FAX (614)447-3751. **(Subscription address:** Chemical Abstracts Service, Customer Service Department, PO Box 3012, Columbus OH 43210. **Tel** (800)848-6538, (614)447-3600.) **ED** David W Weisgerber.
Desc: Covers chemical and physical purification of water for home and industrial use.

ISSN 0162-7872
US
CODEN CSXSDG

CA SELECTS: X-RAY ANALYSIS & SPECTROSCOPY. **Added/Corp** American Chemical Society. Chemical Abstracts Service. **VFOAT** X-Ray Analysis & Spectroscopy. **VAT** Chemical Abstracts Selects. X-Ray Analysis and Spectroscopy. (Jan. 8, 1979)-. Abstracting/Indexing Service. English. Twenty-six times a year. $220.00. Chemical Abstracts Service, (Subsidiary of The American Chemical Society), 2540 Olentangy River Road, PO Box 3012, Columbus OH 43210-0012. **Tel** (614)447-3731, (800)753-4227, FAX (614)447-3751. **(Subscription address:** Chemical Abstracts Service, Customer Service Department, PO Box 3012, Columbus OH 43210. **Tel** (800)848-6538, (614)447-3600.) **ED** David W Weisgerber.
Desc: Covers X-ray techniques in chemical analysis, x-ray emission and absorption spectra.

ISSN 0190-4949
US
CODEN CASZDM

CA SELECTS: ZEOLITES.

Added/Corp American Chemical Society. Chemical Abstracts Service. **VFOAT** Zeolites. **VAT** Chemical Abstracts Selects. Zeolites. (July 9, 1979)-. Abstracting/Indexing Service. English. Twenty-six times a year. $220.00. Chemical Abstracts Service, (Subsidiary of The American Chemical Society), 2540 Olentangy River Road, PO Box 3012, Columbus OH 43210-0012. **Tel** (614)447-3731, (800)753-4227, FAX (614)447-3751. **(Subscription address:** Chemical Abstracts Service, Customer Service Department, PO Box 3012, Columbus OH 43210. **Tel** (800)848-6538, (614)447-3600.) **ED** David W Weisgerber.
Desc: Covers use of synthetic and natural zeolites and molecular sieves in absorption and drying, catalysis, ion exchange, and separation by molecular size.

LC QD1 .C695 **ISSN** 0931-7597
DD 540 GW
CCC

CHEM INFORM.

Added/Corp Fachinformationszentrum Chemie. Gesellschaft Deutscher Chemiker. Farbenfabriken Bayer Aktiengesellschaft. **VFOAT** Cheminform. Vol. 1 (1987)-. Abstracting/Indexing Service. English (German). One time a week. $2803.00. VCH Gesellschaft GmbH, Postfach 101161, D-69451 Weinheim Germany. **Tel** 011 49 6201 606459, FAX 011 49 6201 606184. **(Subscription address:** VCH Publishers Inc., 303 Northwest 12th Avenue, Journals Department, Deerfield FL 33442. **Tel** (800)367-8249, (305)428-5566.) cum. index. **Circ:** 1,150. ***Continues*** *Chemischer Informationsdienst.*

LC TP12 .C443 **ISSN** 0094-6567
DD 660/.029/473 US
UDC 661
NLM TP 12 C516

CHEM SOURCES U.S.A.

[Chem sources, U.S.A.]. **VFOAT** Chem Sources USA; C.S.U. Chem Sources U.S.A.; CSU Chem Sources U.S.A. **VAT** Chem Sources, United States of America. 14th Ed. (1973)-. English. One time a year. $275.00. Chemical Sources International, Inc., PO Box 1824, Clemson SC 29633. **Tel** (803)646-7840, FAX (803)646-9938. **ED** Dale Krohn. Index available. cum. index. **Circ:** 5,000 (ctrl). available on microfiche; available on an online database from STN International. ***Continues*** *Chem Sources.*
Desc: Provides source information on 125,000 chemical products of all classes. Gives contact information for 900 chemical firms. Also includes a classified/trade name section of 6,000 trade names.

LC QD1 .A51 **ISSN** 0009-2258
DD 540/.05 US
NLM Z 5524 C517 **CODEN** CHABA8

CHEMICAL ABSTRACTS.

[Chem. abstr.]. **Added/Corp** American Chemical Society. Chemical Abstracts Service. **VFOAT** Chem Abstracts. Vol. 1 (Jan. 1, 1907)-. Abstracting/Indexing Service. English. One time a week. $10700.00. Chemical Abstracts Service, (Subsidiary of The American Chemical Society), 2540 Olentangy River Road, PO Box 3012, Columbus OH 43210-0012. **Tel** (614)447-3731, (800)753-4227, FAX (614)447-3751. **(Subscription address:** Chemical Abstracts Service, Customer Service Department, PO Box 3012, Columbus OH 43210. **Tel** (800)848-6538, (614)447-3600.) cum. index. **Bk Rev.** available in microform from STN International; available on CD-ROM; available on an online database from Orbit Search Service; European Space Agency; DIALOG; DATA-STAR; CISTI; BRS; and STN International. Documents available from BLDSC. ***Supersedes*** *Review of American Chemical Research.*
Desc: Provides summaries and extensive indexes of the major disclosures in recently published scientific documents and gives the information needed to determine whether or not you need to see the original document. Processes, substances, equipment, bibliographic information, and more are included in CA's comprehensive coverage. Provides bibliographic data, patent references, summaries of chemical information, structure diagrams, and commonly used chemical substance names or molecular formulas.
Ind/Abst Abstr. Bull. Inst. Pap. Sci. Tech.; Alum. Ind. Abstr.; Anal. Abstr.; Fluid Abstr., Civil Eng.; Fluid Abstr. Proc. Eng.; FLUIDEX (1973-1990)(1973-); Lit. Pat. Abstr., Oilfield Chem.; Met. Abstr.; MINPROC; Surf. Treat. Technol. Abstr.; Weed Abstr.

LC Z5521 **ISSN** 0090-8363
DD 016.54 US
CODEN CAAEA2

CHEMICAL ABSTRACTS. APPLIED CHEMISTRY AND CHEMICAL ENGINEERING SECTIONS.

Added/Corp American Chemical Society. Chemical Abstracts Service. (19??)-. Abstracting/Indexing Service. English. Twenty-six times a year. $2240.00. Chemical Abstracts Service, (Subsidiary of The American Chemical Society), 2540 Olentangy River Road, PO Box 3012, Columbus OH 43210-0012. **Tel** (614)447-3731, (800)753-4227, FAX (614)447-3751. **(Subscription address:** Chemical Abstracts Service, Customer Service Department, PO Box 3012, Columbus OH 43210. **Tel** (800)848-6538, (614)447-3600.) **ED** David W. Weisgerber. available on an online database from STN International.

ISSN 0097-6474
DD 540 US
CODEN CACICQ

CHEMICAL ABSTRACTS. COLLECTIVE INDEX.

[Chem. abstr., Collect. index]. **Added/Corp** American Chemical Society. Chemical Abstracts Service. (1961)-. English. Irregular. $10,300.00. Chemical Abstracts Service, (Subsidiary of The American Chemical Society), 2540 Olentangy River Road, PO Box 3012, Columbus OH 43210-0012. **Tel** (614)447-3731, (800)753-4227, FAX (614)447-3751. **(Subscription address:** Chemical Abstracts Service, Customer Service Department, PO Box 3012, Columbus OH 43210. **Tel** (800)848-6538, (614)447-3600.) **ED** David W Weisgerber. available on microfilm and microfiche. ***Continues*** *Decennial Index to Chemical Abstracts, 0894-2048.*
Desc: Current-awareness bulletins on 164 separately-subscribed-to topics. Contains CA abstracts and associated bibliographic information.

LC Z5521 **ISSN** 0093-5719
DD 016.54 US
CODEN CHABAB

CHEMICAL ABSTRACTS. INDEX GUIDE.

Added/Corp American Chemical Society. Chemical Abstracts Service. Vol. 69 (1968)-. English. Irregular (published every 5 years, with annual cumulative supplements). $70.00 13th Edition. Chemical Abstracts Service, (Subsidiary of The American Chemical Society), 2540 Olentangy River Road, PO Box 3012, Columbus OH 43210-0012. **Tel** (614)447-3731, (800)753-4227, FAX (614)447-3751. **(Subscription address:** Chemical Abstracts Service, Customer Service Department, PO Box 3012, Columbus OH 43210. **Tel** (800)848-6538, (614)447-3600.) **ED** David W Weisgerber. ***Continues in part*** *Chemical Abstracts. Subject Index.*
Desc: A reference for searching chemical substances. Links names used in the literature for chemical substances and general subject terms with the controlled terminology of CA volume indexes.

LC QD380 **ISSN** 0009-2274
DD 547.7 US
CODEN CAMLAF

CHEMICAL ABSTRACTS. MACROMOLECULAR SECTION.

[Chem. abstr., Macromol. sect.]. **Added/Corp** American Chemical Society. (1963)-. Abstracting/Indexing Service. English. One time a week. $2240.00. Chemical Abstracts Service, (Subsidiary of The American Chemical Society), 2540 Olentangy River Road, PO Box 3012, Columbus OH 43210-0012. **Tel** (614)447-3731, (800)753-4227, FAX (614)447-3751. **(Subscription address:** Chemical Abstracts Service, Customer Service Department, PO Box 3012, Columbus OH 43210. **Tel** (800)848-6538, (614)447-3600.) **ED** Dr. David W. Weisgerber. available on an online database from STN International; available with illustrations; available with charts.
Ind/Abst World Text. Abstr.

ISSN 0009-2282
US
CODEN CAOCAW

CHEMICAL ABSTRACTS. ORGANIC CHEMISTRY SECTIONS.

Added/Corp American Chemical Society. (1963)-. Periodical. English. Twenty-six times a year. $2240.00. Chemical Abstracts Service, (Subsidiary of The American Chemical Society), 2540 Olentangy River Road, PO Box 3012, Columbus OH 43210-0012. **Tel** (614)447-3731, (800)753-4227, FAX (614)447-3751. **(Subscription address:** Chemical Abstracts Service, Customer Service Department, PO Box 3012, Columbus OH 43210. **Tel** (800)848-6538, (614)447-3600.) available on an online database from STN International.

LC Z5523 .A52 QD1 **ISSN** 0001-0634
DD 016.54/05 US
CCC
NLM Z 5524 C517A **CODEN** CASSI6

CHEMICAL ABSTRACTS SERVICE SOURCE INDEX.

Main/Corp American Chemical Society. Chemical Abstracts Service. **Added/Corp** American Chemical Society. Chemical Abstracts Service. Source Index. **VFOAT** CASSI. (1969)-. English (Multiple languages). Irregular. $990.00. Chemical Abstracts Service, (Subsidiary of The American Chemical Society), 2540 Olentangy River Road, PO Box 3012, Columbus OH 43210-0012. **Tel** (614)447-3731, (800)753-4227, FAX (614)447-3751. **(Subscription address:** Chemical Abstracts Service, Customer Service Department, PO Box 3012, Columbus OH 43210. **Tel** (800)848-6538, (614)447-3600.) available on an online database from STN International; and Orbit Search Service.

ISSN 0950-6144
DD 016.3384766 UK

CHEMICAL BUSINESS UPDATE.

[Chem. bus. update]. (1987)-. Abstracting/Indexing Service. English. Twelve times a year. £645.00 EC; $1,420.00 US; £710.00 other. Royal Society of Chemistry, Thomas Graham House, Science Park, Cambridge CB4 4WF United Kingdom. **Tel** 011 44 1223 420066, FAX 011 44 1223 423623, telex 818293 ROYAL. **(Subscription address:** Royal Society of Chemistry, Turpin Distribution Services Ltd., Blackhorse Road, Letchworth, Hertfordshire SG6 1HN United Kingdom. **Tel** 011 44 1462 672555, FAX 011 44 1462 480947.) **ED** Kate Pearce. available on an online database from Textline; DIALOG; and DATA-STAR.
Desc: A printed monthly alert containing abstracts drawn from the grey literature on important business areas relating to the chemical and allied industries, with emphasis on the European market. Designed to provide the current and difficult to locate information required for the purpose of strategic planning, competitor monitoring, forecasting and general market awareness. It is a supplement to regular journal scanning, as it covers materials such as company reports, press releases, stockbroker reports and market research reports.

ISSN 0045-639X
US
CCC
CODEN CINTAW

CHEMICAL INDUSTRY NOTES.

[Chem. ind. notes]. **Added/Corp** American Chemical Society. Chemical Abstracts Service. (Dec. 6, 1971)-. Abstracting/Indexing Service. English. One time a week. $930.00. Chemical Abstracts Service, (Subsidiary of The American Chemical Society), 2540 Olentangy River Road, PO Box 3012, Columbus OH 43210-0012. **Tel** (614)447-3731, (800)753-4227, FAX (614)447-3751. **(Subscription address:** Chemical Abstracts Service, Customer Service Department, PO Box 3012, Columbus OH 43210. **Tel** (800)848-6538, (614)447-3600.) **ED** David W Weisgerber. Each issue contains an index to its own contents (no volume index)--loose. **Bk Rev.** available on an online database from STN International; Orbit Search Service; DIALOG; and DATA-STAR. ***Supersedes*** *Plastics Industry Notes, 0032-1214.*
Desc: Covers worldwide news in the chemical business industry and gives you the essential data from approximately 80 national and international business and trade journals. Divided into eight sections for easy reference, CIN covers news of corporate activities, production, pricing, sales, facilities, products and processes, government activities, and people in the chemical industry.

UK

CHEMICAL PATENTS INDEX.

(19??)-. English. One time a week. Derwent Publications Ltd., Derwent House 14, Great Queen Street, London WC2B 5DF United Kingdom. **Tel** 011 44 171 3442800, FAX 011 44 171 3442899.

UK

CHEMICAL PATENTS INDEX. PLASTICS AND POLYMERS.

English. One time a week. Derwent Publications Ltd., Derwent House 14, Great Queen Street, London WC2B 5DF United Kingdom. **Tel** 011 44 171 3442800, FAX 011 44 171 3442899.

LC QD **ISSN** 0009-2711
DD 540 US
CCC
NLM Z 5524 C519 **CODEN** CHTIAM

CHEMICAL TITLES.

[Chem. titles]. **Added/Corp** American Chemical Society. (Apr. 1960)-. Abstracting/Indexing Service. English. Twenty-six times a year. $540.00. Chemical Abstracts Service, (Subsidiary of The American Chemical Society), 2540 Olentangy River Road, PO Box 3012, Columbus OH 43210-0012. **Tel** (614)447-3731, (800)753-4227, FAX (614)447-3751. **(Subscription address:** Chemical Abstracts Service, Customer Service Department, PO Box 3012, Columbus OH 43210. **Tel** (800)848-6538, (614)447-3600.) **ED** Dr. David W. Weisgerber. available on an online database from CISTI.
Desc: Provides information needed to obtain the original document. Contains complete bibliographic information from each journal, arranged alphabetically by CODEN, including abbreviated journal titles, full titles, and page numbers of the articles. The keyword-in-context index identifies titles of recent articles by subject terms. The author index is included.

ISSN 1057-6088
DD 016 US

CHEMISTRY CITATION INDEX.

(CHEMISTRY CITATION INDEX. [COMPUTER FILE].). [Chem. cit. index]. **Added/Corp** Institute for Scientific Information. (July-Aug. 1991)-. English. Six times a year. $1969.00. Institute for Scientific Information, 3501 Market Street, Philadelphia PA 19104. **Tel** (215)386-0100, (800)523-1850, FAX (215)386-6362, telex 84-5305. **(Subscription address:** Institute for Scientific Information, PO Box 71416, Chicago IL 60694.)
Desc: Covers current literature on chemistry.

LC QD146 .C44 **ISSN** 1051-7227
DD 546/.05 US
CCC
CODEN CICHED

CHEMTRACTS. INORGANIC CHEMISTRY.

[Chemtracts Inorg. chem.]. **VFOAT** Inorganic Chemistry. Vol. 3, No. 1 (Jan./Feb. 1991)-. Academic Scholarly Publication. English. Four times a year. $290.00. Data Trace Publishing Group, PO Box

1239, Brooklandville MD 21022. **Tel** (410)494-4994, (800)342-0454, FAX (410)494-0515. **(Subscription address:** Data Trace Chemistry Publishers, Inc., PO Box 1239, Brooklandville MD 21022. **Tel** (410)494-4994, FAX (410)494-0515.) Documents available from CASDDS. ***Continues*** *Chemtracts. Analytical, Physical, and Inorganic Chemistry, 1048-7840.*
Desc: Provides insightful analysis of key current literature. Leading authorities contribute invited primary feature and prospectus articles. Topics include: organometallic, bioorganic, solid state, main group, coordination chemistry, etc.
Ind/Abst Chem. Abstr.

LC QD380 .C47 **ISSN** 0899-7829
DD 547.7 US
CCC
CODEN CMMCE8
CEASED

CHEMTRACTS. MACROMOLECULAR CHEMISTRY.
[Chemtracts, Macromol. chem.]. **VFOAT** Macromolecular Chemistry. Vol. 1, No. 1 (Jan./Feb. 1990)-Vol. 4, No. 2 (1994). Academic Scholarly Publication. English. Data Trace Publishing Group, PO Box 1239, Brooklandville MD 21022. **Tel** (410)494-4994, (800)342-0454, FAX (410)494-0515. **ED** Samuel Danishefsky. Documents available from CASDDS.
Desc: Provides critical, concise summaries of key papers that have appeared in current issues of research journals. Each issue includes up to 40 detailed research summaries with expert commentary ranging from the purpose of the study and its approach, to the reviewer's observations on the research and its implications.
Ind/Abst Chem. Abstr.

US

CHEMTRACTS. MACROMOLECULAR CHEMISTRY AND MATERIALS SCIENCE.
VFOAT Macromolecular Chemistry and Materials Science. (1991)-. Periodical. English. Six times a year. Data Trace Publishing Group, PO Box 1239, Brooklandville MD 21022. **Tel** (410)494-4994, (800)342-0454, FAX (410)494-0515. ***Continues*** *Chemtracts. Macromolecular Chemistry, 0899-7829.*

LC QD241 .C48 **ISSN** 0895-4445
DD 547/.005 US
CCC
NLM W1; CH41H **CODEN** CMOCEI

CHEMTRACTS. ORGANIC CHEMISTRY.
[Chemtracts, Org. chem.]. **VFOAT** Organic Chemistry. Vol. 1, No. 1 (Feb. 1988)-. Academic Scholarly Publication. English. Six times a year. $295.00. Data Trace Publishing Group, PO Box 1239, Brooklandville MD 21022. **Tel** (410)494-4994, (800)342-0454, FAX (410)494-0515. **(Subscription address:** Data Trace Chemistry Publishers, Inc., PO Box 1239, Brooklandville MD 21022. **Tel** (410)494-4994, FAX (410)494-0515.) Documents available from CASDDS.
Desc: Focuses on bringing to light the types of molecules that are biologically active in order to stimulate new research. Seeding ground between academic research and research at pharmaceutical houses.
Ind/Abst Chem. Abstr.

US

COMPREHENSIVE DATABASE OF US CHEMICAL PATENTS TAPES.
(19??)-. Periodical. English. Twelve times a year. $71,712.00. IFI / Plenum Data Corporation / Delaware, 3202 Kirkwood Highway Suite 203, Wilmington DE 19808. **Tel** (302)998-0478, (800)331-4955, FAX (302)998-0733.

ISSN 0885-1980
DD 616 UK
CCC

CURRENT ADVANCES IN CLINICAL CHEMISTRY.
[Curr. adv. clin. chem.]. **Added/Corp** Association of Clinical Biochemists. Vol. 13, No. 1, (Jan. 1986)-. Abstracting/Indexing Service. English. Twelve times a year. $756.00. Elsevier Geo Abstracts, An Imprint of Elsevier Science Ltd., The Boulevard, Langford Lane, Kidlington, Oxford OX5 1GB United Kingdom. **Tel** 011 44 1865 843000, 011 44 1865 843699, FAX 011 44 1865 843010. **(Subscription address:** Elsevier Science Ltd. / Oxford Fulfillment Centre, PO Box 800, Kidlington OX5 1DX United Kingdom. **Tel** 011 44 865 843355.) **ED** Harry Smith (editor's address: Department of Botany, University of Leicester, University Road, Leicester LE1 7QQ UK) and Peter N Campbell (editor's address: Department of Biochemistry, University College, London WC1E 6BT UK). **Bk Rev. Ad Acc.** available on microfilm and microfiche from University Microfilms International (UMI); available on an online database from Elsevier Electronic Subscriptions (EES); and BRS. Documents available from BLDSC, UMI Article Clearinghouse. ***Continues*** *Current Clinical Chemistry, 0305-0165.*
Desc: More than 1,000 biological journals are scanned by a team of editors to provide a subject-categorized listing of titles, authors, bibliographic details and authors' addresses. Titles are presented under 29 major subject headings with full cross-referencing.

ISSN 0163-6278
DD 547 US
NLM Z 5524 C9742

CURRENT CHEMICAL REACTIONS.
[Curr. chem. react.]. **Added/Corp** Institute for Scientific Information. **VFOAT** CCR. Vol. 1 (Jan. 1979)-. Abstracting/Indexing Service. English (Multiple languages). Twelve times a year. $1137.00. Institute for Scientific Information, 3501 Market Street, Philadelphia PA 19104. **Tel** (215)386-0100, (800)523-1850, FAX (215)386-6362, telex 84-5305. **(Subscription address:** Institute for Scientific Information, PO Box 71416, Chicago IL 60694.) cum. index. available on magnetic tape (as Current Chemical Reactions Database).
Desc: Presents graphic representations and bibliographic data for synthetic reactions and methods reported in organic chemistry journals.

ISSN 0300-4376
II

CURRENT TITLES IN ELECTROCHEMISTRY.
Added/Corp Society for Advancement of Electrochemical Science and Technology. (1969)-. Abstracting/Indexing Service. English. Twelve times a year. $135.00. Society for Advancement of Electrochemical Science and Technology, Karaikudi 623 006 India. **Tel** 2368, telex 0443-211 ECRI IN. **(Subscription address:** Prints India, 11 Darya Ganj, New Delhi 110002 India. **Tel** 011 91 11 3268645, FAX 011 91 11 3275542, telex 31-61087 PRIN-IN.) **ED** N S Rengaswamy. Index available. cum. index. **Ad Acc. Circ:** 850 (ctrl). ***Absorbed*** *Electrochemical News.*
Desc: Contains journals covering electrochemical science and technology including advance content pages of journals in well-documented subtitles.

US

DICTIONARY OF ORGANIC COMPOUNDS.
(1934)-. Periodical. English. Irregular. Routledge Chapman & Hall Inc., 29 West 35th Street, New York NY 10001. **Tel** (212)244-3336, (212)244-6412. **ED** J.B. Buckingham. available on an online database (file 303/Full-Text) from DIALOG.
Desc: An index of information on all the important organic chemical substances.

LC Z5320 **ISSN** 0300-5372
DD 016.57 NE
CCC
NLM ZW 1 E978I **CODEN** CLBIDV

EXCERPTA MEDICA. SECTION 29. CLINICAL BIOCHEMISTRY.
See Biology-Abstracting, Bibliographies and Statistics.

ISSN 0160-7464
US
CODEN EAPCDS

EXTENDED ABSTRACTS AND PROGRAM - BIENNIAL CONFERENCE ON CARBON.
[Ext. abstr. prog. - Bienn. Conf. Carbon]. **Added/Corp** American Carbon Society. University of Pittsburgh. School of Engineering. (19??)-. English. Every 2 years. $62.50. American Carbon Society / Stackpole Corporation, University of Pittsburgh, School of Engineering, St.Marys PA 15857. Documents available from Article Express International, CASDDS.
Ind/Abst Bioeng. Abstr.; Chem. Abstr. (-1985); Ei Page One; Eng. Index Annu.

LC QD79.C45 G35 **ISSN** 1059-3160
DD 543/.089 US

GAS & LIQUID CHROMATOGRAPHY LITERATURE, ABSTRACTS & INDEX.
[Gas liq. chromatogr. lit. abstr. index]. **VFOAT** Gas and Liquid Chromatography Literature Abstracts & Index. Vol. 1, No. 1 (Jan. 1992)-. English. Six times a year. $595.00. Preston Publications Inc., 7800 Merrimac Avenue, PO Box 48312, Niles IL 60714. **Tel** (708)965-0566, (708)967-1810, FAX (708)965-7639, telex 910-223-1780 PRESTON NILE. available on CD-ROM. ***Formed by the union of*** *Gas Chromatography Literature, Abstracts & Index, 0016-4895* ***and*** *Liquid Chromatography Literature, Abstracts & Index, 0147-328X.*

ISSN 0261-4707
DD 016.5430894 UK
CCC

HIGH PERFORMANCE LIQUID CHROMATOGRAPHY SHEFFIELD.
[High perform. liq. chromatogr.Sheff.]. (1982)-. English. Twenty-four times a year. $188.23. SUBIS, Mansion House 19 Kingfield Road, Sheffield S11 9AS United Kingdom. **Tel** 011 44 114 2554433, FAX 011 44 114 255 4626.

LC Z5524.R25 I5 **ISSN** 0096-1345
DD 016.541/38 US

INDEX AND CUMULATIVE LIST OF PAPERS ON RADIATION CHEMISTRY.
Added/Corp National Measurement Laboratory (U.S.). Office of Standard Reference Data. (19??)-. English. Two times a year. National Bureau of Standards, Room 120, Voice of Z39, Washington DC 20234.

ISSN 0891-6055
DD 540 US
NLM Z 5524; C9722

INDEX CHEMICUS (1987).
(INDEX CHEMICUS : IC.). [Index chem.]. **Added/Corp** Institute for Scientific Information. **VFOAT** IC. Vol. 104, No. 1 (Jan. 7, 1987)-. Abstracting/Indexing Service. English. One time a week (with cumulated indexes). $3945.00. Institute for Scientific Information, 3501 Market Street, Philadelphia PA 19104. **Tel** (215)386-0100, (800)523-1850, FAX (215)386-6362, telex 84-5305. **(Subscription address:** Institute for Scientific Information, PO Box 71416, Chicago IL 60694.) cum. index. ***Continues*** *Current Abstracts of Chemistry and Index Chemicus (Philadelphia, Pa. : 1978), 0161-455X.*
Desc: Presents graphic representations and complete bibliographic data on the new organic compounds reported in organic chemistry journals.

LC QD380 .I56 **ISSN** 0307-174X
DD 547/.84/05 UK

INTERNATIONAL POLYMER SCIENCE AND TECHNOLOGY.
[Int. polym. sci. tech.]. **Added/Corp** Rubber and Plastics Research Association of Great Britain. Vol. 1 (1974)-. Abstracting/Indexing Service. English. Twelve times a year. $1450.00. RAPRA Technology Ltd., Shawbury Shrewsbury, Shropshire SY4 4NR United Kingdom. **Tel** 011 44 1939 250383, FAX 011 44 1939 251118, telex 35134 RAPRA G. Index available. **Circ:** 350. ***Formed by the union of*** *Soviet Plastics* ***and*** *Soviet Rubber Technology.*
Desc: Contains English translations selected from ten rubber and plastics technical journals, five Russian, one Polish, one German, one Hungarian and two Japanese. Provides access to technical developments in these countries.
Ind/Abst Art Archaeol. Tech. Abstr.; Curr. Cit.; EMBASE; Eng. Mater. Abstr.; Fluid Abstr., Civil Eng.; Fluid Abstr. Proc. Eng.; FLUIDEX (1974-); World Surf. Coat. Abstr.

LC LC741 .J47 **ISSN** 0276-6310
DD 370/.89924073 US

JEWISH EDUCATION DIRECTORY.
Added/Corp American Association for Jewish Education. Dept. of Statistical Research and Information. (1971)-. Directory. English. Irregular. $8.50. Jewish Education Service of North America Inc., 730 Broadway, New York NY 10003. **Tel** (212)529-2000. ***Continues*** *Jewish Education Register and Directory.*

LC QC451 .M38 **ISSN** 0025-4738
DD 539 UK
CODEN MSPBBX

MASS SPECTROMETRY BULLETIN.
[Mass spectrom. bull.]. **Added/Corp** Mass Spectrometry Data Centre. Royal Society of Chemistry (Great Britain). Vol. 1 (Nov. 1966)-. Bulletin. English. Twelve times a year. $1019.00. Royal Society of Chemistry, Thomas Graham House, Science Park, Cambridge CB4 4WF United Kingdom. **Tel** 011 44 1223 420066, FAX 011 44 1223 423623, telex 818293 ROYAL. **(Subscription address:** Royal Society of Chemistry, Turpin Distribution Services Ltd., Blackhorse Road, Letchworth, Hertfordshire SG6 1HN United Kingdom. **Tel** 011 44 1462 672555, FAX 011 44 1462 480947.) **ED** S. Down. Index available. **Ad Acc. Circ:** 500 (ctrl). available on an online database from ESA-IRS.
Desc: Current awareness bulletin containing references to papers on mass spectrometry in organic, physical and analytical chemistry, instrumentation, medicine, biochemistry and geochemistry.
Ind/Abst Energy Res. Abstr.

ISSN 0265-4245
UK
CCC
CODEN MOSYDN

METHODS IN ORGANIC SYNTHESIS.
[Methods org. synth.]. **Added/Corp** Royal Society of Chemistry (Great Britain). No. 1 (Jan. 1984)-. Abstracting/Indexing Service. English. Twelve times a year (plus annual index). $437.00. Royal Society of Chemistry, Thomas Graham House, Science Park, Cambridge CB4 4WF United Kingdom. **Tel** 011 44 1223 420066, FAX 011 44 1223 423623, telex 818293 ROYAL. **(Subscription address:** Royal Society of Chemistry, Turpin Distribution Services Ltd., Blackhorse Road, Letchworth, Hertfordshire SG6 1HN United Kingdom. **Tel** 011 44 1462 672555, FAX 011 44 1462 480947.) Index available (free). **Ad Acc. Circ:** 700.
Desc: Full coverage of new synthetic methods, including such topics as asymmetric synthesis, protective groups, new reagents and synthons, functional group changes, bond forming reactions, hazards, new laboratory techniques and biotechnical methods.

LC QD98.E4 M5 **ISSN** 0278-1727
DD 543/.08586 US
CODEN MBANDD
Pr Rev.

MICROBEAM ANALYSIS.
[Microbeam anal.]. **Added/Corp** Microbeam Analysis Society. (1979)-. Academic Scholarly Publication. English. One time a year (Aug.). $84.00. San Francisco Press Inc., PO Box 426800, San Francisco CA 94142. **Tel** (510)524-1000. Index available. **Circ:** 600. Documents available from Article Express International, CASDDS. ***Continues*** *Microbeam Analysis Society. Proceedings, 0146-6275.*

Desc: Extended abstracts of papers presented at annual meeting of Microbeam Analysis Society; profusely illustrated, including high-quality micrographs.
Ind/Abst Chem. Abstr.; Eng. Index Annu.; Mass Spect. Bull. (?-?).

ISSN 0272-2755
US
CODEN MOHADW
MOSSBAUER HANDBOOK. [Mossbauer handb.]. **Added/Corp** University of North Carolina. Mossbauer Effect Data Center. (Sept. 1, 1980)-. Monographic series. English. Irregular. Price varies per volume. Mossbauer Effect Data Center / North Carolina, University of North Carolina, Asheville NC 28804-3299. **Tel** (704)251-6617, FAX (704)251-6002. **ED** John G. Stevens. **Bk Rev. Ad Acc.**
Desc: A series of handbooks on selected topics related to Mossbauer spectroscopy. Included in each are bibliographic references, abstracted data, subject and author indexes.

LC Z5521 **ISSN** 0950-1711
DD 016.54 UK
NLM ZQV 752; N285 **CODEN** NPUPEP
NATURAL PRODUCT UPDATES. [Nat. prod. updates]. **Added/Corp** Royal Society of Chemistry (Great Britain). No. 1 (Jan. 1987)-. Abstracting/Indexing Service. English. Twelve times a year (plus annual index). $472.00. Royal Society of Chemistry, Thomas Graham House, Science Park, Cambridge CB4 4WF United Kingdom. **Tel** 011 44 1223 420066, FAX 011 44 1223 423623, telex 818293 ROYAL. **(Subscription address:** Royal Society of Chemistry, Turpin Distribution Services Ltd., Blackhorse Road, Letchworth, Hertfordshire SG6 1HN United Kingdom. **Tel** 011 44 1462 672555, FAX 011 44 1462 480947.) Index available (free).
Desc: An alerting service giving worldwide and highly current coverage of developments in the field of natural product structure and biosynthesis, including such topics as isolation studies of new compounds and of known compounds from new sources; structure determination, including x-ray studies; total syntheses of natural products, covering key steps; and biosyntheses: incorporation studies.

LC Z5854 .N542 **ISSN** 0028-6869
DD 016.6 US
CODEN NTBOAJ
CEASED
NEW TECHNICAL BOOKS. [New tech. books]. **Main/Corp** New York (City). Public Library. **VFOAT** New York Public Library New Technical Books. Vol. 1 (June/Aug. 1915)-(1994). Periodical. English. New York Public Library Science and Technology Division, Room 120, 5th Avenue and 42nd Street, New York NY 10018. **Tel** (212)930-0574, (212)930-0576. **ED** Barbara A. List. **Bk Rev. Circ:** 1,500. Documents available from CASDDS.
Desc: Selective list of English language books giving annotations, listing books' full or abridged contents, bibliographic details and short descriptive notes, subjects: pure and applied physical sciences, mathematics, engineering, technology. Works for general readers, professional reference guides, selected college research monographs, conference proceedings.
Ind/Abst Abstr. Bull. Inst. Pap. Sci. Tech.; Book Rev. Index (1985-); Chem. Abstr.

LC Z5524.C8 M6 QD921
DD 016.548/81/08 S 016.548/81 NE
ORGANIC AND ORGANOMETALLIC CRYSTAL STRUCTURES; BIBLIOGRAPHY. **Added/Corp** Crystallographic Data Centre. International Union of Crystallography. (1969/71)-. Bibliography. English. Irregular. Kluwer Academic Publishers, Postbus 322, 3300 AH Dordrecht The Netherlands. **Tel** 011 31 78 524400, FAX 011 31 78 183273, telex 20083. **(Subscription address:** Kluwer Academic Publishers / US Subscriptions, PO Box 253, Accord Station, Hingham MA 02018. **Tel** (617)871-6600.)

LC QD241 .O684 **ISSN** 0445-3611
DD 547 US
ORGANIC SEMINAR ABSTRACTS. [Org. semin. abstr.]. **Added/Corp** University of Illinois (Urbana-Champaign Campus) Dept. of Chemistry and Chemical Engineering. University of Illinois at Urbana-Champaign. Dept. of Chemistry. (1963)-. English. Two times a year. $15.00. University of Illinois / Organic Chemistry, Box 68, R. Adams Laboratory, 1209 West Cal Street, Urbana IL 61801. **Tel** (217)333-2255. **Circ:** 100 (ctrl).
Desc: Organic chemistry seminar abstracts.

ISSN 1065-0474
DD 665 US
PATENT ABSTRACTS. CHEMICAL PRODUCTS. **See** Copyright, Intellectual Property-Abstracting, Bibliographies and Statistics.

ISSN 1065-2167
DD 665 US
PATENT ABSTRACTS. POLYMERS. [Pat. abstr., Polym.]. **Added/Corp** American Petroleum Institute. Central Abstracting & Information Services. **VFOAT** Polymers. (Jan. 6, 1992)-. English. One time a week. American Petroleum Institute, 275 Seventh Avenue, New York NY 10001. **Tel** (212)366-4040, FAX (212)366-4298.

ISSN 0385-8847
JA
PEPTIDE INFORMATION. **Added/Corp** Protein Research Foundation Peptide Institute. (197?)-. Periodical. English. Twenty-four times a year (plus 1 index). $450.00. Protein Research Foundation, 4-1-2 Ina Minoh-Shi, Osaka 562 Japan. **Tel** 011 81 7 27294121, FAX 011 81 7 27294124, telex 5324111 PHOSA J. **ED** Masaharu Isoyama. Index available. cum. index. **Circ:** 300 (ctrl). available on diskette.
Desc: Abstracts journal for retrieval of peptide literature in the field of the life sciences. Each article is abstracted in telegraphic form.

ISSN 0893-6684
DD 668 US
CCC
POLYMER BLENDS, ALLOYS, AND INTERPENETRATING POLYMER NETWORKS ABSTRACTS. (POLYMER BLENDS, ALLOYS, AND IPN'S - ABSTRACTS.). [Polym. blends alloys interpenetrat. polym. netw. abstr.]. (1987)-. Periodical. English. Twelve times a year. $385.00. Technomic Publishing Company, Inc., 851 New Holland Avenue, Box 3535, Lancaster PA 17604. **Tel** (717)291-5609, (800)233-9936, FAX (717)295-4538. **ED** John W. DeGroot. **Circ:** 200 (ctrl). available on microfilm from University Microfilms International (UMI).
Desc: Survey and summary of the growing literature and patents in this new area of plastics technology. Provides new information on chemistry, properties and performance, testing and analysis, processing, and applications. Designed to enable practitioners and researchers to follow developments and identify new opportunities.

LC QD1 .A536 **ISSN** 0740-0667
DD 540 US
Pr Rev.
PREPRINT EXTENDED ABSTRACT - AMERICAN CHEMICAL SOCIETY. DIVISION OF ENVIRONMENTAL CHEMISTRY. (PREPRINT EXTENDED ABSTRACT : PRESENTED BEFORE THE DIVISION OF ENVIRONMENTAL CHEMISTRY, AMERICAN CHEMICAL SOCIETY.). [Prepr. ext. abstr. - Am. Chem. Soc., Div. Environ. Chem.]. **Main/Corp** American Chemical Society. Division of Environmental Chemistry. English. Two times a year. $24.00. National Sanitation Foundation, PO Box 1468, Ann Arbor MI 48106. **Tel** (313)769-8010. Index available. **Circ:** 4,000. ***Continues*** *American Chemical Society. Division of Environmental Chemistry. Preprints of Papers.*
Ind/Abst Coal Abstr.

ISSN 0776-3093
BE
UDC 543.54
RECORDER WEVELGEM. **See** Chemistry and Chemicals.

LC Z5071- **ISSN** 0141-0164
DD 016.63 UK
RICE ABSTRACTS. **Added/Corp** Commonwealth Agricultural Bureaux. International Food Information Service. (1977)-. Abstracting/Indexing Service. English. Four times a year. $315.00. CAB International Centre, Wallingford, Oxfordshire OX10 8DE United Kingdom. **Tel** 011 44 1491 832111, FAX 011 44 1491 833508, telex 847964 COMAGG G. **Ad Acc. Circ:** 450. available on magnetic tape and CD-ROM; available on an online database from Tsukuba Daigaku; CAN/OLE; STN International; JICST; DATA-STAR; DIMDI; ESA-IRS; CISTI; BRS; and DIALOG.

ISSN 0966-114X
UK
SCICAT SCIENCE REFERENCE AND INFORMATION SERVICE. (SCICAT SCIENCE REFERENCE AND INFORMATION SERVICE CATALOGUE ON MICROFICHE.). [SCICAT Sci. Ref. Inf. Serv.]. **VFOAT** Science Reference and Information Service Catalogue. (19??)-. English. Four times a year. £240.00 UK; £245.00 other. British Library Science Reference Information Service, 25 Southampton Building, London WC21 1AW United Kingdom. **Tel** 011 44 181 6361544. **(Subscription address:** Turpin Distribution Services Limited, Blackhorse Road, Letchworth, Hertfordshire SH6 1HN United Kingdom. **Tel** 011 44 1462 672555, FAX 011 44 1462 480947.) ***Continues*** *SRIS Microfiche Catalogue, 0957-2422.*

LC TP186 .F65a
DD 660 GW
STATISTICHE UUBERSICHTEN : BESTAND UND BEDARF AN CHEMIKERN IN DER CHEMISCHEN INDUSTRIE DER BUNDESREPUBLIK DEUTSCHLAND. **Main/Corp** Fonds der Chemischen Industrie zur Forderung von Forschung, Wissenschaft und Lehre. (19??)-. German. Fonds der Chemischen Industrie, Frankfurt AM Main Germany.

LC QD49.G3 F66a
DD 540/.7/1143 GW
STATISTISCHE UBERSICHTEN : CHEMIE AN DER HOCHSCHULEN DER BUNDESREPUBLIK DEUTSCHLAND. **Main/Corp** Fonds der Chemischen Industrie (Germany). (19??)-. German. Fonds der Chemischen Industrie, Frankfurt AM Main Germany.

ANALYTICAL CHEMISTRY

LC QD606 .A253 **ISSN** 0307-9945
DD 543/.088 UK
ACTIVATION ANALYSIS ABSTRACTS. [Act. anal. abstr.]. **Added/Corp** Science & Technology Agency. (1971)-. English. Four times a year. £30.00. PRM Science & Technology Agency Ltd, 261A Finchley Road Hampstead, London NW3 6LV United Kingdom. **Tel** 011 44 171 4310372.

LC QD96.M65 A38
DD 543/.0858 SI
CODEN AMPSEF
ADVANCES IN MULTI-PHOTON PROCESSES AND SPECTROSCOPY. **VFOAT** Multi-Photon Processes and Spectroscopy. Vol. 1 (1984)-. English. Irregular. $77.00 (per copy). World Scientific Publishing Company, PO Box 128, Farrer Road, Singapore 9128 Singapore. **Tel** 011 65 3825663, FAX 011 65 3825919, telex RS 28561 WSPC. **(Subscription address:** World Scientific Publishing Company, Inc., 1060 Main Street, Suite 1 B, River Edge NJ 07661. **Tel** (800)227-7562, (201)487-9655.) Documents available from CASDDS.
Ind/Abst Chem. Abstr.

ISSN 1058-4382
DD 543 US
CODEN AMLUEZ
ADVANCES IN MULTIDIMENSIONAL LUMINESCENCE. [Adv. multidimens. lumin.]. Vol. 1 (1991)-. Periodical. English. One time a year. $90.25. JAI Press Inc., 55 Old Post Road, Suite 2, PO Box 1678, Greenwich CT 06836-1678. **Tel** (203)661-7602, FAX (203)661-0792. **ED** Isiah M. Warner and Linda B. McGowan.

IT
ALAMBICCO DELL ANCHID. (19??)-. Italian. Six times a year. L100000 Italy; L150000 other. Assn Naz Chimici Dogane, Via della Luce 35, 00153 Rome Italy. **Tel** 011 39 6 5800551.

LC QD71 .A42 **ISSN** 0365-4877
DD 543/.005 FR
CCC
NLM W1 AN1906 **CODEN** ANLSCY
Pr Rev.
ANALUSIS. [Analusis]. Vol. 1 (April/May 1972)-. Academic Scholarly Publication. French (summaries and/or abstracts in English). Ten times a year. $630.00. Editions Scientifique Elsevier, 141 rue de Javel, 75747 Paris Cedex 15 France. **Tel** 011 33 1 45589067, FAX 011 33 1 45589424. **(Subscription address:** Editions Scientifiques Elsevier / for North America, PO Box 7247-7576, Philadelphia PA 19170-7576.) **ED** N.Q. Dao. cum. index. **Bk Rev. Ad Acc. Circ:** 3,000 (ctrl). available on microfilm and microfiche from University Microfilms International (UMI); available on an online database from Elsevier Electronic Subscriptions (EES). Documents available from The Genuine Article, BIOSIS Document Express, CASDDS. ***Formed by the union of*** *Chimie Analytique* ***and*** *Methodes Physiques d'Analyse.*
Desc: Analytical chemistry, chemical analysis, instrumentation chromatography, spectrometry, and electroanalytical chemistry.
Ind/Abst Alum. Ind. Abstr.; Anal. Abstr.; Aquat. Sci. Fish. Abstr. [CD-ROM Ed.]; Biol. Abstr.; Chem. Abstr.; Chem. Titles; Curr. Cit.; Curr. Contents Phys. Chem. Earth Sci.; Dairy Sci. Abstr.; EMBASE; Energy Res. Abstr. (Jan. 1973-); Eng. Mater. Abstr.; Food Sci. Technol. Abstr.; GeoRef; Mass Spect. Bull.; Met. Abstr.; Res. Alert [Full Cov.]; Sci. Cit. Index; SCISEARCH.

LC QD71 .A45 **ISSN** 0003-2654
DD 543/.005 UK
CCC
NLM W1 AN191 **CODEN** ANALAO
Pr Rev.
ANALYST (LONDON). (THE ANALYST.). **Added/Corp** oyal Society of Chemistry (Great Britain) Society of Public Analysts (Great Britain) Society of Public Analysts and Other Analytical Chemists (Great Britain) Society for Analytical Chemistry. Chemical Society (Great Britain) Society of Public Analysts (Great Britain). Proceedings. Society of Public Analysts and Other Analytical Chemists (Great Britain). Proceedings. Society for Analytical Chemistry. Proceedings. Vol. 1, No. 1 (1876)-. Periodical. English. Twelve times a year (includes 1 index). $923.00. Royal Society of Chemistry, Thomas Graham House, Science Park, Cambridge CB4 4WF United Kingdom. **Tel** 011 44 1223 420066, FAX 011 44 1223 423623, telex 818293 ROYAL. **(Subscription address:** Royal Society of Chemistry, Turpin Distribution

Services Ltd., Blackhorse Road, Letchworth, Hertfordshire SG6 1HN United Kingdom. **Tel** 011 44 1462 672555, FAX 011 44 1462 480947.**)** Index available (free). cum. index. **Bk Rev**. **Ad Acc**. available on microfilm and microfiche from University Microfilms International (UMI); available on an online database from STN International. Documents available from The Genuine Article, Ask*IEEE, CASDDS, BLDSC, FAXON Xpress, SWETS, The UnCover Company, UMI Article Clearinghouse.
Desc: Contains original papers on the theory and practice of all aspects of analytical chemistry drawn from a wide range of sources.
Ind/Abst Abstr. Bull. Inst. Pap. Sci. Tech.; AgBiotech News Inf.; AGRICOLA; Alum. Ind. Abstr.; Anal. Abstr.; Art Archaeol. Tech. Abstr.; Biodeter. Abstr.; Ceram. Abstr.; Chem. Abstr.; Chem. Titles; Coal Abstr.; Crop Physiol. Abstr.; Curr. Aware. Biol. Sci., CABS; Curr. Biotechnol.; Curr. Cit.; Curr. Contents Life Sci.; Curr. Contents Phys. Chem. Earth Sci.; Curr. Technol. Index; Curr. Titles Electrochem.; Dairy Sci. Abstr.; EMBASE; Field Crop Abstr.; Food Sci. Technol. Abstr.; For. Prod. Abstr.; Geol. Abstr.; GeoRef; Health Plan. Adminis.; Hortic. Abstr.; Index Med.; Index Vet.; INSPEC (Nov. 1969); Int. Packag. Abstr.; Int. Pharm. Abstr.; Irr. Drain. Abstr.; Maize Abstr.; Mass Spect. Bull.; Met. Abstr.; Nutr. Abstr. Rev., Ser. B, Live Feeds and Feed.; Nutr. Abstr. Rev., Ser. A, Hum. Exp.; Pap. Board Abstr.; PESTDOC; Pig News Inf.; Plant Breed. Abstr.; Postharvest News Inf.; Potato Abstr.; Protozoolog. Abstr.; Ref. Upd. Deluxe Ed.; Res. Alert [Full Cov.]; Rev. Agric. Entomol.; Rev. Med. Vet. Mycology; Rice Abstr.; Saf. Health Work; Sci. Cit. Index; SCISEARCH; Soils Fert.; Vet. Bull.; Vitis Vitic. Enol. Abstr.; Weed Abstr.; Wheat Barley Trit. Abstr.; World Surf. Coat. Abstr.

LC QD71 .A47 **ISSN** 0003-2670
DD 543.05 NE
CCC
NLM W1 AN191L **CODEN** ACACAM
Pr Rev.

ANALYTICA CHIMICA ACTA. [Anal. chim. acta]. **Added/Corp** International Union of Pure and Applied Chemistry. Section of Analytical Chemistry. Vol. 1 (Jan. 1947)-. Academic Scholarly Publication. English (French and German). Sixty times a year. $4611.00. Elsevier Science Publishers BV, PO Box 211, 1000 AE Amsterdam Netherlands. **Tel** 011 31 20 4853641, 011 31 20 4853642, FAX 011 31 20 4853598. **ED** HL Pardue, A Townshend, JT Clerc, WE van der Linden, PJ Worsfold. Index available. cum. index. **Bk Rev**. available on microfilm and microfiche from University Microfilms International (UMI); available with charts; available with illustrations; available on an online database from Elsevier Electronic Subscriptions (EES); and STN International. Documents available from The Genuine Article, BIOSIS Document Express, CASDDS, Documents on Demand, ADONIS. ***Continued in part by*** *Vibrational Spectroscopy.*
Desc: Publishes original papers, short communications, and reviews dealing with every aspect of modern chemical analysis, both fundamental and applied.
Ind/Abst Abstr. Bull. Inst. Pap. Sci. Tech.; ADONIS; AgBiotech News Inf.; AGRICOLA; Alum. Ind. Abstr.; Anal. Abstr.; AQUAREF; Art Archaeol. Tech. Abstr.; Biodeter. Abstr. (1991-); Biol. Abstr.; Ceram. Abstr.; Chem. Abstr.; Chem. Titles; Coal Abstr.; Curr. Biotechnol.; Curr. Cit.; Curr. Contents Life Sci.; Curr. Contents Phys. Chem. Earth Sci.; Curr. Titles Electrochem.; Dairy Sci. Abstr.; Ei Page One; EMBASE; Energy Inf. Abstr.; Environ. Abstr.; Food Sci. Technol. Abstr.; For. Abstr.; GeoRef; Health Plan. Adminis.; Hortic. Abstr.; Index Med.; Int. Aerosp. Abstr.; Irr. Drain. Abstr.; Leadscan; Maize Abstr.; Met. Abstr.; Microbiol. Abstr. Sect. A; NAPRALERT; Nutr. Abstr. Rev., Ser. B, Live Feeds and Feed.; Nutr. Abstr. Rev., Ser. A, Hum. Exp.; Life Sci. Collect.; PESTDOC; Plant Grow. Reg. Abstr.; Pollut. Abstr. Indexes; Potato Abstr.; Protozoolog. Abstr.; Ref. Upd. Deluxe Ed.; Res. Alert [Full Cov.]; Rev. Agric. Entomol.; Rev. Med. Vet. Entomol.; Rev. Med. Vet. Mycology; Rev. Plant Pathol.; Rice Abstr.; Sci. Cit. Index; SCISEARCH; Soils Fert.; Sug. Indus. Abstr.; Surf. Treat. Technol. Abstr.; Vitis Vitic. Enol. Abstr.; Weed Abstr.; World Ceram. Abstr.

LC QD71 .A49 **ISSN** 0003-2689
DD 016.543 UK
CCC
NLM ZQD 1 A532 **CODEN** AABSAR

ANALYTICAL ABSTRACTS. **See** Chemistry and Chemicals-Abstracting, Bibliographies and Statistics.

ISSN 0167-6350
NE
NLM W3 AN54 **CODEN** ACSSDR

ANALYTICAL CHEMISTRY SYMPOSIA SERIES. [Anal. chem. symp. ser.]. (1980)-. Academic Scholarly Publication. English. Irregular. Price varies per volume. Elsevier Science Publishing Company Inc, Madison Square Station, PO Box 882, New York NY 10159-0882. **Tel** (212)633-3950, FAX (212)633-3990. Documents available from BIOSIS Document Express, CASDDS. ***Continues*** *Chromatography Symposia Series, 0166-2732.*
Ind/Abst Biol. Abstr.; Chem. Abstr.; GeoRef.

LC TP1 .I615 **ISSN** 0003-2700
US
CCC
NLM W1 AN1917 **CODEN** ANCHAM
Pr Rev.

ANALYTICAL CHEMISTRY (WASHINGTON). (ANALYTICAL CHEMISTRY.). [Anal. chem.]. **Added/Corp** American Chemical Society. American Chemical Society. Lab guide. Vol. 19, No. 1 (Jan. 1947)-. Academic Scholarly Publication. English. Twenty-four times a year. $685.00. American Chemical Society, 1155 Sixteenth Street Northwest, Washington DC 20036. **Tel** (800)333-9511, (800)227-5558, (614)447-3776, FAX (202)447-3671. **(Subscription address:** American Chemical Society / Ohio, Department L 0011, Columbus OH 43268-0011. **) ED** George H. Morrison. Index available (bound in last issue). **Bk Rev**. **Ad Acc**. **Acid Free. Circ:** 27,500 (ctrl). available on microfilm and microfiche from University Microfilms International (UMI); available on an online database from STN International. Documents available from The Genuine Article, BIOSIS Document Express, Ask*IEEE, UMI Article Clearinghouse, Petroleum Abstracts Document Delivery Service, CASDDS, BLDSC, SWETS, FAXON Xpress, The UnCover Company. ***Continues*** *Industrial and Engineering Chemistry. Analytical Edition, 0096-4484.*
Desc: Scientific articles on theoretical and applied aspects of analysis, laboratory aids, modern instrumentation, timely feature articles, advances in chemical instrumentation, news, meetings, new products, and chemicals.
Ind/Abst Abstr. Bull. Inst. Pap. Sci. Tech.; Acad. Ind. [Computer File] (1992-); Acad. Search; Alum. Ind. Abstr.; Anal. Abstr.; Appl. Sci. Technol. Index; Art Archaeol. Tech. Abstr.; Biodeter. Abstr.; Biol. Abstr.; Ceram. Abstr.; Chem. Abstr.; Chem. Hazards Ind.; Chem. Titles; Coal Abstr.; Comput. Abstr.; Crop Physiol. Abstr.; CSA Neuro. Abstr. (?-?); Curr. Biotechnol.; Curr. Cit.; Curr. Index J. Educ.; Curr. Titles Electrochem.; Ei Page One; EMBASE [Select. Cov.]; Energy Res. Abstr.; Eng. Mater. Abstr.; EP Collect.; Expand. Acad. Index (1992-); Field Crop Abstr.; Food Sci. Technol. Abstr.; Foods Adlibra; For. Prod. Abstr.; Gas Abstr.; Gen. Sci. Index; Gen. Sci. Source; GeoRef; Health Plan. Adminis.; Homework Help.; Index Med.; Ind. Hyg. Dig. (19??-19??); INFO-SOUTH Abstr.; INIS Atomindex [Micro.]; INSPEC (1968-); Lab. Hazards Bull.; Leadscan; Lit. Pat. Abstr., Oilfield Chem. (1954-); Lit. Abstr., Catal. Zeol.; Lit. Abstr., Health Environ.; Lit. Abstr., Pet. Refin. Petrochem.; Lit. Abstr., Pet. Substit.; Lit. Abstr., Transp. Storage; Mass Spect. Bull.; MasterFile FullTEXT 1000; MasterFile FullTEXT 350; MasterFile FullTEXT 650; MasterFile FullTEXT (July 1993-); Met. Abstr.; Nematol. Abstr.; Newsp. Period. Abstr. (1992-); Nutr. Abstr. Rev., Ser. B, Live Feeds and Feed.; Nutr. Abstr. Rev., Ser. A, Hum. Exp.; Ocean. Abstr.; OCLC; PESTDOC; Pet. Abstr.; Pollut. Abstr. Indexes; Polymer Contents; Ref. Upd. Basic Ed.; Ref. Upd. Deluxe Ed.; Res. Alert [Full Cov.]; Rev. Agric. Entomol.; Rev. Med. Vet. Entomol.; Rev. Plant Pathol.; Saf. Health Work; Sci. Cit. Index; SCISEARCH; Soc. Sci. Cit. Index [Select. Cov.]; Soils Fert.; Sorghum Mill. Abstr.; Stat. Theory Method Abstr. (1959-1963); Sug. Indus. Abstr.; Telebase; Text. Technol. Dig.; Weed Abstr.; World Ceram. Abstr.; World Surf. Coat. Abstr.

UK

•ANALYTICAL COMMUNICATIONS. (Jan. 1996)-. English. Twelve times a year. $361.00. Royal Society of Chemistry, Thomas Graham House, Science Park, Cambridge CB4 4WF United Kingdom. **Tel** 011 44 1223 420066, FAX 011 44 1223 423623, telex 818293 ROYAL. **(Subscription address:** Royal Society of Chemistry, Turpin Distribution Services Ltd., Blackhorse Road, Letchworth, Hertfordshire SG6 1HN United Kingdom. **Tel** 011 44 1462 672555, FAX 011 44 1462 480947.**)** ***Continues*** *Analytical Proceedings Including Analytical Communications.*

ISSN 0003-2719
DD 543 US
CCC
NLM W1 AN1917K **CODEN** ANALBP
Pr Rev.

ANALYTICAL LETTERS. [Anal. lett.]. **VFOAT** Chemical Analysis; Clinical and Biochemical Analysis. Vol. 1 (Oct. 1967)-. Periodical. English (French and German; summaries and/or abstracts in French and German). Fifteen times a year. $1695.00. Marcel Dekker Inc., 270 Madison Avenue, New York NY 10016. **Tel** (212)696-9000, (800)228-1160, FAX (212)685-4540, telex 421419. **(Subscription address:** Marcel Dekker Inc., PO Box 5017, Monticello NY 12701. **Tel** (800)228-1160.**) ED** George G. Guilbault, Ronald F. Evilia, James W. Munson, W. Purdy, Bruce Kowalski. cum. index. available on microfiche. Documents available from The Genuine Article, BIOSIS Document Express, CASDDS.
Desc: This rapid communication journal provides transmittal of recent advances in all areas of analytical chemistry. Presenting short papers, original ideas, observations, and analytical discoveries, this international journal furnishes scientists with new results to apply in their own research in the briefest time possible.
Ind/Abst Anal. Abstr.; AQUAREF; Biodeter. Abstr. (1991-); Biol. Abstr.; Chem. Abstr.; Chem. Titles; Coal Abstr.; Curr. Aware. Biol. Sci., CABS; Curr. Biotechnol.; Curr. Cit.; Curr. Contents Life Sci.; Curr. Contents Phys. Chem. Earth Sci.; Dairy Sci. Abstr.; EMBASE; Energy Res. Abstr.; Food Sci. Technol. Abstr.; GeoRef; Helminthol. Abstr. (1991-); Leadscan; Mass Spect. Bull.; Nutr. Abstr. Rev., Ser. B, Live Feeds and Feed.; Nutr. Abstr. Rev., Ser. A, Hum. Exp.; Phys. Briefs; Postharvest News Inf.; Ref. Upd. Deluxe Ed.; Res. Alert [Full Cov.]; Rev. Agric. Entomol.; Rev. Med. Vet. Entomol.; Rev. Med. Vet. Mycology; Rev. Plant Pathol.; Sci. Cit. Index; SCISEARCH; Soils Fert.; Sug. Indus. Abstr.; Vitis Vitic. Enol. Abstr.; Weed Abstr.

ISSN 0144-557X
UK
CCC
NLM W1 AN1918P **CODEN** ANPRDI
TITLE CHANGE

ANALYTICAL PROCEEDINGS. [Anal. proc.]. **Added/Corp** Chemical Society (Great Britain) Royal Society of Chemistry (Great Britain). Vol. 17, No. 1 (Jan. 1980)-Vol. 30, No. 12 (Dec. 1993). Academic Scholarly Publication. English. Royal Society of Chemistry, Thomas Graham House, Science Park, Cambridge CB4 4WF United Kingdom. **Tel** 011 44 1223 420066, FAX 011 44 1223 423623, telex 818293 ROYAL. **(Subscription address:** Royal Society of Chemistry, Turpin Distribution Services Ltd., Blackhorse Road, Letchworth, Hertfordshire SG6 1HN United Kingdom. **Tel** 011 44 1462 672555, FAX 011 44 1462 480947.**)** Index available (free). available on microfilm and microfiche from University Microfilms International (UMI). Documents available from The Genuine Article, BIOSIS Document Express, CASDDS. ***Continues*** *Proceedings of the Analytical Division of the Chemical Society, 0306-1396.* ***Continued by*** *Analytical Proceedings Including Analytical Communications.*
Desc: Contains special articles, reports of meetings, extended summaries of original papers, safety articles, details of recent legislation, surveys of equipment, and many other items of general interest to analytical chemists both in Britain and overseas.
Ind/Abst Abstr. Bull. Inst. Pap. Sci. Tech.; Alum. Ind. Abstr.; Anal. Abstr.; Biodeter. Abstr.; Biol. Abstr.; Chem. Abstr.; Chem. Hazards Ind.; Coal Abstr.; Curr. Biotechnol.; Curr. Cit.; Dairy Sci. Abstr.; EMBASE; GeoRef; Int. Pharm. Abstr.; Lab. Hazards Bull.; Leadscan; Mass Spect. Bull.; Met. Abstr.; Nutr. Abstr. Rev., Ser. B, Live Feeds and Feed.; PESTDOC; Res. Alert [Full Cov.]; Soils Fert.; Sug. Indus. Abstr.; World Ceram. Abstr.; World Surf. Coat. Abstr.

UK
CODEN ANPRDI
TITLE CHANGE

ANALYTICAL PROCEEDINGS INCLUDING ANALYTICAL COMMUNICATIONS. **Added/Corp** Royal Society of Chemistry (Great Britain) Royal Society of Chemistry (Great Britain). Analytical Division. **VFOAT** Analytical Communications. Vol. 31, No. 1 (Jan. 1994)-(Jan. 1996). Academic Scholarly Publication. English. Royal Society of Chemistry, Thomas Graham House, Science Park, Cambridge CB4 4WF United Kingdom. **Tel** 011 44 1223 420066, FAX 011 44 1223 423623, telex 818293 ROYAL. **(Subscription address:** Royal Society of Chemistry, Turpin Distribution Services Ltd., Blackhorse Road, Letchworth, Hertfordshire SG6 1HN United Kingdom. **Tel** 011 44 1462 672555, FAX 011 44 1462 480947.**)** ***Continues*** *Analytical Proceedings, 0144-557x.* ***Continued by*** *Analytical Communications.*
Ind/Abst Abstr. Bull. Inst. Pap. Sci. Tech.; Alum. Ind. Abstr.; Anal. Abstr.; Biodeter. Abstr.; Biol. Abstr.; Chem. Abstr.; Chem. Hazards Ind.; Coal Abstr.; Curr. Biotechnol.; Dairy Sci. Abstr.; EMBASE; GeoRef; Int. Pharm. Abstr.; Lab. Hazards Bull.; Leadscan; Mass Spect. Bull.; Met. Abstr.; Nutr. Abstr. Rev., Ser. B, Live Feeds and Feed.; PESTDOC; Res. Alert; Soils Fert.; Sug. Indus. Abstr.; World Ceram. Abstr.; World Surf. Coat. Abstr.

ISSN 0910-6340
JA
CCC
NLM W1; AN1918T **CODEN** ANSCEN
Pr Rev.

ANALYTICAL SCIENCES : THE INTERNATIONAL JOURNAL OF THE JAPAN SOCIETY FOR ANALYTICAL CHEMISTRY. **Added/Corp** Nihon Bunseki Kagakkai. Vol. 1, No. 1 (April 1985)-. Academic Scholarly Publication. English. Six times a year. $129.00. Royal Society of Chemistry, Thomas Graham House, Science Park, Cambridge CB4 4WF United Kingdom. **Tel** 011 44 1223 420066, FAX 011 44 1223 423623, telex 818293 ROYAL. **(Subscription address:** Royal Society of Chemistry, Turpin Distribution Services Ltd., Blackhorse Road, Letchworth, Hertfordshire SG6 1HN United Kingdom. **Tel** 011 44 1462 672555, FAX 011 44 1462 480947.**) ED** Mitsugi Senda. Index available. cum. index. **Ad Acc**. **Circ:** 3,500. Documents available from The Genuine Article, CASDDS.
Desc: Deals with fundamental and applied aspects of analytical chemistry.
Ind/Abst Anal. Abstr.; Chem. Abstr. (1985-); Chem. Titles; Curr. Cit.; Curr. Contents Phys. Chem. Earth Sci.; Mass Spect. Bull.; Res. Alert [Full Cov.]; Sci. Cit. Index.

Chemistry and Chemicals —Analytical Chemistry

ISSN 0926-4345
NE
CODEN ASLIE7

ANALYTICAL SPECTROSCOPY LIBRARY. [Anal. spectrosc. libr.]. (198?)-. Monographic series. English. Irregular. Price varies per volume. Elsevier Science Publishers BV, PO Box 211, 1000 AE Amsterdam Netherlands. **Tel** 011 31 20 4853641, 011 31 20 4853642, FAX 011 31 20 4853598. Documents available from BIOSIS Document Express, CASDDS.
Ind/Abst Biol. Abstr.; Chem. Abstr.; Curr. Cit.

UDC 543(047.31)(73)
US

ANNUAL REPORT ... CENTER FOR ANALYTICAL CHEMISTRY. Main/Corp Center for Analytical Chemistry (U.S.). 1981-. English. One time a year. Center for Analytical Chemistry, National Bureau of Standards, Washington DC 20234. **Continues** Technical Activities ... Center for Analytical Chemistry.

LC QD79.E44 A65 ISSN 0954-6642
UK
NLM W1; AP511 CODEN ATELEM
Pr Rev.

APPLIED AND THEORETICAL ELECTROPHORESIS. (APPLIED AND THEORETICAL ELECTROPHORESIS : THE OFFICIAL JOURNAL OF THE INTERNATIONAL ELECTROPHORESIS SOCIETY.). [Appl. theor. electrophor.]. **Added/Corp** International Electrophoresis Society. Vol. 1, No. 1 (1988)-. Academic Scholarly Publication. English. Six times a year. $168.00. Electrophoresis Society. **(Subscription address:** Applied and Theoretical Electrophoresis, PO Box 1897, Lawrence KS 66044-8897.) **ED** Carl R. Merril. **Bk Rev** available on microfilm and microfiche from University Microfilms International (UMI). Documents available from The Genuine Article, BIOSIS Document Express, CASDDS.
Desc: Aims to facilitate communications between researchers employing electrophoretic methods and those using the methods in a variety of applied settings.
Ind/Abst Biol. Abstr. (1991-); Chem. Abstr.; Curr. Cit.; Index Med.; Res. Alert [Full Cov.].

LC QD95 .A7 ISSN 0309-1813
DD 543/.085 UK
UDC 535.34(048.3); 543.42(048.3)

ATOMIC ABSORPTION AND EMISSION SPECTROMETRY ABSTRACTS. [At. absorpt. emiss. spectrom. abstr.]. Vol. 6 (Jan./Feb. 1974)-. English. Six times a year. PRM Science & Technology Agency Ltd, 261A Finchley Road Hampstead, London NW3 6LV United Kingdom. **Tel** 011 44 171 4310372. **Continues** Atomic Absorption and Flame Emission Spectroscopy Abstracts.
Ind/Abst GeoRef.

LC QC454.A8 A84 ISSN 0195-5373
DD 543/.0858 US
NLM W1 AT725J CODEN ASPND7
Pr Rev.

ATOMIC SPECTROSCOPY. [At. spectr.]. Vol. 1 (Jan./Feb. 1980)-. Academic Scholarly Publication. English. Six times a year. $45.00. Atomic Spectroscopy, PO Box 57, Florham Park NJ 07932. **Tel** (203)762-6023, (201)822-9162, FAX (201)822-9162, (203)762-4997. **ED** The Perkin-Elmer Corporation, 761 Main Avenue, Norwalk, CT 06859-0105 USA; Telephone: (203)762-6023; Fax: (203)762-6307. **Circ:** 4,500. available on microfilm and microfiche from University Microfilms International (UMI). Documents available from The Genuine Article, BIOSIS Document Express, Ask*IEEE, CASDDS, Documents on Demand.
Supersedes Atomic Absorption Newsletter, 0044-9954.
Desc: Purpose is to disseminate general information as well as new applications and analytical data in atomic spectrophotometry, atomic fluorescence, atomic emission and ICP-mass spectrometry by workers in the field.
Ind/Abst Bull. Inst. Pap. Sci. Tech.; Alum. Ind. Abstr.; Anal. Abstr. (Jan./Feb. 1980-); Biol. Abstr. (1986-); Chem. Abstr.; Coal Abstr.; Curr. Cit.; Curr. Contents Phys. Chem. Earth Sci.; EMBASE; Energy Inf. Abstr.; Eng. Mater. Abstr.; Environ. Abstr.; Geol. Abstr.; GeoRef; INSPEC (Jan./Feb. 1980-); Leadscan; Mass Spect. Bull.; Res. Alert [Full Cov.]; Sci. Cit. Index; SCISEARCH; Sel. Water Resour. Abstr.; Soils Fert.; World Alum. Abstr.; World Ceram. Abstr.; World Surf. Coat. Abstr.

ISSN 0737-4186
US
TITLE CHANGE

BENCH SHEET, THE. [Bench sheet].
Added/Corp Water Environment Federation. (19??)-(1993). Periodical. English. The Bench Sheet, Water Environment Federation, 601 Wythe Street, Alexandria VA 22314. **Tel** (703)684-2400, FAX (703)684-2492. **ED** John W Carnegie. **Bk Rev. Circ:** 1,000. **Continued by** Water Environment Laboratory Solutions, 1074-2972.
Desc: National publication devoted to water analysis. A valuable resource for sharpening analytical skills, expanding technical knowledge and improving communications among lab analysts.

ISSN 0145-5338
US
NLM W1 BE512

BENCHMARK PAPERS IN ANALYTICAL CHEMISTRY. Vol. 1 (1976)-. Monographic series. English. Irregular. Price varies per volume. Academic Press Inc., 6277 Sea Harbor Drive, Orlando FL 32887. **Tel** (800)543-9534, (407)345-4100, FAX (407)352-3445.

LC QD71 ISSN 0269-3879
DD 543 UK
CCC
NLM W1; BI854C CODEN BICHE2

BMC. BIOMEDICAL CHROMATOGRAPHY. (BIOMEDICAL CHROMATOGRAPHY : BMC.). [BMC, Biomed. chromatogr.]. **VFOAT** BMC. Vol. 1, No. 1 (Feb. 1986)-. Academic Scholarly Publication. English. Six times a year. $645.00. John Wiley & Sons Ltd., Baffins Lane, Chichester, West Sussex PO19 1UD United Kingdom. **Tel** 011 44 1243 779777, FAX 011 44 1243 776128 BTG:JWP001, telex 86290 WIBOOKG. **(Subscription address:** John Wiley & Sons, Inc. / Philadelphia, PO Box 7247, Philadelphia PA 19170. **Tel** (212)850-6645, (800)225-5945.) **ED** E.F. Hounsell, C.K. Lim. available on microfilm and microfiche from University Microfilms International (UMI). Documents available from The Genuine Article, CASDDS.
Desc: An international journal devoted to research in chromatographic methodologies and their applications in the biosciences.
Ind/Abst Anal. Abstr.; Chem. Abstr.; Curr. Aware. Biol. Sci.; CABS; Curr. Biotechnol.; Curr. Cit.; Curr. Contents Life Sci.; Curr. Contents Phys. Chem. Earth Sci.; EMBASE; Life Sci. Collect.; Res. Alert [Full Cov.]; Rev. Agric. Entomol.; Rev. Med. Vet. Entomol.; Rev. Med. Vet. Mycology; Sci. Cit. Index; SCISEARCH.

LC Z5523 .B83 QD75.2 ISSN 0240-8473
DD 016.543 FR

BULLETIN SIGNALETIQUE. 172, CHIMIE ANALYTIQUE. See Chemistry and Chemicals-Abstracting, Bibliographies and Statistics.

ISSN 0386-2178
JA
CODEN BUNSD3

BUNSEKI. (BUNSEKI. ANALYSIS.). [Bunseki]. **Added/Corp** Nihon Bunseki Kagakukai. (Jan. 1975)-. Periodical. Japanese. Twelve times a year. $250.00. Nihon Bunseki Kagakkai, (Japan Soc. for Analytical Chemistry), 26-2 Nishigotanda 1 chome, Shinagawaku Tokyo 114 Japan. **(Subscription address:** Maruzen Company Ltd., PO Box 5050, Import & Export Department, Tokyo 100 31 Japan. **Tel** 011 81 3 32789224.) Documents available from CASDDS.
Ind/Abst Chem. Abstr.

LC QD71 .B85
JA

BUNSEKI. Added/Corp Nihon Bunseki Kagakkai. Issue 46 (1978)-. Periodical. Japanese. Twelve times a year. ¥1,000. Nihon Bunseki Kagakkai, (Japan Soc. for Analytical Chemistry), 26-2 Nishigotanda 1 chome, Shinagawaku Tokyo 114 Japan. **ED** Kikuo Terada. Index available. **Bk Rev. Ad Acc. Circ:** 9,100 (ctrl).
Desc: Scientific journal concerned with analytical chemistry.
Ind/Abst Coal Abstr.; Curr. Biotechnol.

LC QD71 .B87 ISSN 0525-1931
DD 540 JA
CCC
NLM W1 BU944N CODEN BNSKAK
Pr Rev.

BUNSEKI KAGAKU. [Bunseki kagaku]. **Added/Corp** Nihon Bunseki Kagakkai. **VFOAT** Japan Analyst; Nihon Bunseki Kagakkai Shi. (1952)-. Academic Scholarly Publication. Japanese. Twelve times a year. $320.00. Nihon Bunseki Kagakukai, c/o Gotanda San Haitsu, 26-2 Nishigotanda 1-chome, Shinagawa-ku Tokyo-to 141 Japan. **Tel** 011 81 3 4903351, FAX 011 81 3 4903572, telex 03-490-3572. **(Subscription address:** Maruzen Company Ltd., PO Box 5050, Import & Export Department, Tokyo 100 31 Japan. **Tel** 011 81 3 32789224.) **ED** Shin Tsuge. Index available. **Ad Acc. Circ:** 4,300. Documents available from The Genuine Article, CASDDS.
Desc: Academic monographs concerned with analytical chemistry.
Ind/Abst Anal. Abstr.; Art Archaeol. Tech. Abstr.; Chem. Abstr.; Chem. Titles; Coal Abstr.; Curr. Contents Phys. Chem. Earth Sci.; Curr. Cit.; Dairy Sci. Abstr.; Food Sci. Technol. Abstr.; GeoRef; Leadscan; Mass Spect. Bull.; Res. Alert [Full Cov.]; Sci. Cit. Index; SCISEARCH; SEA Abstr.; Soils Fert.; Soyabean Abstr.; Vitis Vitic. Enol. Abstr.

ISSN 0160-8959
US
CODEN CSAEDT

CA SELECTS: ANALYTICAL ELECTROCHEMISTRY. See Chemistry and Chemicals-Abstracting, Bibliographies and Statistics.

LC QD142 ISSN 0190-9428
DD 543.0858 US
CODEN CSIADN

CA SELECTS: INFRARED SPECTROSCOPY (ORGANIC ASPECTS). See Chemistry and Chemicals-Abstracting, Bibliographies and Statistics.

ISSN 0890-1899
DD 543 US
CODEN CSICEU

CA SELECTS: ION CHROMATOGRAPHY. See Chemistry and Chemicals-Abstracting, Bibliographies and Statistics.

ISSN 0195-5152
US
CODEN CSUADF

CA SELECTS: SURFACE ANALYSIS. See Chemistry and Chemicals-Abstracting, Bibliographies and Statistics.

ISSN 0009-2223
PL
NLM W1 CH236 CODEN CANWAJ
Pr Rev.

CHEMIA ANALITYCZNA. [Chem. anal.]. **Added/Corp** Polska Akademia Nauk. Komitet Nauk Chemicznych. Polska Akademia Nauk. Komisja Chemii Analityczneh. Vol. 1 (1956)-. Academic Scholarly Publication. Polish (summaries available in English, German and Russian). Six times a year. $96.00. **(Subscription address:** Ars Polona-Ruch, PO Box 1001, Krakowskie Przedmiescie 7, 00-068 Warsaw Poland. **Tel** 011 48 22 261201.) Documents available from The Genuine Article, CASDDS.
Ind/Abst Anal. Abstr.; Ceram. Abstr. (19??-); Chem. Abstr.; Curr. Cit.; Curr. Contents Phys. Chem. Earth Sci.; Dairy Sci. Abstr.; Food Sci. Technol. Abstr.; Leadscan; Res. Alert [Full Cov.]; Sci. Cit. Index; SCISEARCH.

ISSN 0069-2883
DD 543 US
CODEN CAMCBN

CHEMICAL ANALYSIS. (CHEMICAL ANALYSIS : A SERIES OF MONOGRAPHS ON ANALYTICAL CHEMISTRY AND ITS APPLICATION.). [Chem. anal.]. Vol. 1 (1941)-. Monographic series. English. Irregular. Price varies per volume. John Wiley & Sons, Inc., 605 Third Avenue, New York NY 10158-0012. **Tel** (212)850-6000, (212)850-6645, FAX (212)850-6088, telex 12-7063. **(Subscription address:** John Wiley & Sons / UK, Baffins Lane, Chichester, West Sussex PO19 1UD United Kingdom. **Tel** 011 44 1243 779777, FAX 011 44 1243 776128, telex 86290 WIBOOKG.) Documents available from BIOSIS Document Express, CASDDS.
Ind/Abst Biol. Abstr.; Chem. Abstr.; Curr. Cit.; GeoRef.

LC RS1.N56 A15 ISSN 0009-2363
DD 543 615 JA
CCC
NLM W1 CH245N CODEN CPBTAL

CHEMICAL & PHARMACEUTICAL BULLETIN. See Pharmacy and Pharmacology.

LC QD415 ISSN 0722-6764
DD 543 GW
NLM W1; CL122E CODEN CCLBEW

CHEMIE IN LABOR UND BIOTECHNIK : CLB. VFOAT CLB. Vol. 1 No. 1 (Jan. 1990)-. Periodical. German. Twelve times a year. Umschau Verlag, Postfach 110262, D-60037 Frankfurt Germany. **Tel** 011 49 69 2600692, FAX 011 49 69 2600223, telex 411964. Documents available from CASDDS. **Continues** Chemie fur Labor und Betrieb.
Ind/Abst Chem. Abstr.; Curr. Cit.

LC QD71
DD 543 GW

CHEMISCHE ANALYSE. SAMMLUNG VON EINZELDARSTELLUNGEN AUF DEM GEBIETE DER CHEMISCHEN, TECHNISCH-CHEMISCHEN UND PHYSIKALISCH-CHEMISCHEN ANALYSE ..., DIE. Vol. 1 (1907)-. Periodical. German. Ferdinand Enke Verlag, Ruedigerstrasse 14, D-70469 Stuttgart Germany. **Tel** 011 49 711 8931124, 011 49 711 893123, FAX 011 49 711 8931419.

LC QD71 .C4 ISSN 0095-8484
US
NLM W1 CH314N

CHEMIST-ANALYST. Added/Corp Baker (J. T.) Chemical Company. (1911)-. Periodical. English. Editor Chemist-Analyst, J T Baker Chemical Company, Phillipsburg NJ 08865.

ISSN 0925-5281
NE
CCC
Pr Rev. TITLE CHANGE

CHEMOMETRICS AND INTELLIGENT LABORATORY SYSTEMS : LABORATORY INFORMATION MANAGEMENT. Vol. 1 (1991)-(199?). Academic Scholarly Publication. English. Elsevier Science

Publishers BV, PO Box 211, 1000 AE Amsterdam Netherlands. **Tel** 011 31 20 4853641, 011 31 20 4853642, FAX 011 31 20 4853598. **ED** R.D. McDowall and R.R. Mahaffey. Index available. **Bk Rev. Ad Acc. Circ:** 500. Documents available from Ask*IEEE. ***Continued by*** *Laboratory Automation and Information Management.*
Desc: The journal covers all aspects of information management in a laboratory environment, such as information technology, storage, processing, and flow of data.
Ind/Abst EMBASE; INSPEC (Sep. 1991-).

ISSN 1053-8097
DD 543 US
CODEN CHROEY

CHROMATOGRAM (SAN RAMON, CALIF.). (CHROMATOGRAM.). [Chromatogram]. **Added/Corp** Beckman Instruments, Inc. Altex Division. **VFOAT** Chromatogram HPLC Newsletter. **VAT** Chromatogram High Performance Liquid Chromatography Newsletter. (198?)-. Academic Scholarly Publication. English. Beckman Instruments, Altex Div., 2350 Camino Roma, Box 5101, San Ramon CA. Documents available from CASDDS. ***Continues*** *Altex Chromatogram, 0275-6234.*
Ind/Abst Chem. Abstr.; Curr. Biotechnol.

ISSN 0009-5893
DD 543 GW
CCC
NLM W1 CH94 **CODEN** CHRGB7
Pr Rev.

CHROMATOGRAPHIA. [Chromatographia]. Vol. 1 (1968)-. Academic Scholarly Publication. English (French and German; summaries and/or abstracts in French and German). Twenty-four times a year. $866.00. Pergamon Press, An Imprint of Elsevier Science Ltd., The Boulevard, Langford Lane, Kidlington, Oxford OX5 1GB United Kingdom. **Tel** 011 44 1865 843000, 011 44 1865 843699, FAX 011 44 1865 843010. **(Subscription address:** Elsevier Science Ltd. / Oxford Fulfillment Centre, PO Box 800, Kidlington OX5 1DX United Kingdom. **Tel** 011 44 865 843355.**) ED** T.A. Berger, H. Engelhardt. cum. index. available on microfilm and microfiche from University Microfilms International (UMI); available on an online database from Elsevier Electronic Subscriptions (EES). Documents available from The Genuine Article, BIOSIS Document Express, CASDDS, ADONIS.
Desc: Strives to meet the demand for the quick spread of accurate, concise information concerning chromatography and related fields.
Ind/Abst ADONIS; Anal. Abstr.; Aqualine Abstr.; Biodeter. Abstr.; Biol. Abstr.; Chem. Abstr.; Chem. Titles; Coal Abstr.; CSA Neuro. Abstr. (?-?); Curr. Aware. Biol. Sci., CABS; Curr. Cit.; Curr. Contents Life Sci.; Curr. Contents Phys. Chem. Earth Sci.; Dairy Sci. Abstr.; EMBASE; Energy Res. Abstr.; Field Crop Abstr.; Food Sci. Technol. Abstr.; For. Abstr.; GeoRef; Hortic. Abstr.; Index Vet.; Leadscan; Maize Abstr.; Mass Spect. Bull.; NAPRALERT; Nematol. Abstr.; Nutr. Abstr. Rev., Ser. B, Live Feeds and Feed.; Nutr. Abstr. Rev., Ser. A, Hum. Exp.; Life Sci. Collect.; Plant Breed. Abstr.; Postharvest News Inf.; Res. Alert [Full Cov.]; Rev. Agric. Entomol.; Rev. Med. Vet. Mycology; Sci. Cit. Index; SCISEARCH; Soyabean Abstr.; Sug. Indus. Abstr.; Vet. Bull.; Vitis Vitic. Enol. Abstr.

LC QD117.C5 G34 **ISSN** 0268-6287
DD 543/.089 UK
CCC
NLM Z 5524.O8; G246

CHROMATOGRAPHY ABSTRACTS. [Chromatogr. abstr.]. **Added/Corp** Chromatographic Society (Great Britain). Vol. 29, No. 1 (1986)-. English. Twelve times a year (1 volume). $830.00. Royal Society of Chemistry, Thomas Graham House, Science Park, Cambridge CB4 4WF United Kingdom. **Tel** 011 44 1223 420066, FAX 011 44 1223 423623, telex 818293 ROYAL. **(Subscription address:** Royal Society of Chemistry, Turpin Distribution Services Ltd., Blackhorse Road, Letchworth, Hertfordshire SG6 1HN United Kingdom. **Tel** 011 44 1462 672555, FAX 011 44 1462 480947.**) ED** E. R. Adlard and P. A. Sewell. available on microfilm and microfiche from University Microfilms International (UMI). ***Continues*** *Gas and Liquid Chromatography Abstracts, 0301-388X.*
Desc: Designed to provide an essential service to chromatographers throughout the world. A team of well-qualified abstractors continuously scans all the major world journals for papers reporting advances in chromatographic techniques and their application to specific problems.

LC QD415 **ISSN** 0095-4861
DD 574.192 US
NLM W1 CL654 **CODEN** CBAND5
Pr Rev.

CLINICAL AND BIOCHEMICAL ANALYSIS. **See** Biology-Biological Chemistry.

LC QD71 .C39 **ISSN** 1040-8347
DD 543/.005 US
CCC
NLM W1; C555 **CODEN** CCACBB
Pr Rev.

CRITICAL REVIEWS IN ANALYTICAL CHEMISTRY. [Crit. rev. anal. chem.]. **VFOAT** CRC Critical Reviews in Analytical Chemistry. **VAT** Chemical Rubber Company Critical Reviews in Analytical Chemistry. Vol. 9, Issue 2 (1980)-. Academic Scholarly Publication. English. Four times a year. $300.00. CRC Press Inc., 2000 Corporate Boulevard Northwest, Boca Raton FL 33431. **Tel** (407)994-0555, (800)272-7737, FAX (407)998-9784, (800)374-3401, telex 568689. **(Subscription address:** CRC Press Inc. / New York, PO Box 750, Pearl River NY 10965. **) ED** David M. Coleman & Patricia B. Coleman. Documents available from Article Express International, The Genuine Article, CASDDS. ***Continues*** *CRC Critical Reviews in Analytical Chemistry, 0007-8980.*
Desc: Provides scholarly reviews of topics within the discipline of analytical chemistry. Review articles teach the relevant underlying science, evaluates the field's status by putting developments into perspective and context, and speculates on possible future developments.
Ind/Abst Anal. Abstr.; Chem. Abstr.; Curr. Cit.; Curr. Contents Phys. Chem. Earth Sci.; Eng. Index Annu. [Select. Cov.]; Index Sci. Rev. [Full Cov.]; Res. Alert [Full Cov.]; Sci. Cit. Index; SCISEARCH.

LC QD **ISSN** 0385-1516
DD 543 JA
NLM W1 DO609 **CODEN** DONED9

DOJIN NYUSU. [Dojin nyusu]. **Added/Corp** Dojin Yakkagaku Kenkyusho. Dojin Kagaku Kenkyusho. **VFOAT** Dojin News. No. 1 (1976)-. Academic Scholarly Publication. Japanese. Four times a year. Dojin Kagaku Denkyujo, (Dojindo Lab.), 2861 Kengunmachi, Kumamotoshi Kumamotoken 862 Japan. Documents available from CASDDS. ***Formed by the union of*** *DBC Nyusu* ***and*** *Dotaito Nyusu Reta.*
Ind/Abst Chem. Abstr.

LC QC454.M3 D95 **ISSN** 0367-0007
DD 543/.0873 UK
UDC 543.51
CODEN DYMSAB

DYNAMIC MASS SPECTROMETRY. Vol. 1 (1970)-. Periodical. English. Irregular. $84.00. Heyden & Son Ltd, Spectrum House, Hillview Gardens, London NW4 2JQ United Kingdom. Documents available from CASDDS.
Desc: Papers presented at the International Dynamic Mass Spectrometry Symposium.
Ind/Abst Chem. Abstr.

LC QD115 .E499 **ISSN** 0070-9778
DD 545.3 US
CCC
NLM W1 EL31 **CODEN** ELCHAI

ELECTROANALYTICAL CHEMISTRY. (ELECTROANALYTICAL CHEMISTRY; A SERIES OF ADVANCES.). [Electroanal. chem.]. Vol. 1 (1966)-. Monographic series. English. Irregular. Price varies per volume. Marcel Dekker Inc., 270 Madison Avenue, New York NY 10016. **Tel** (212)696-9000, (800)228-1160, FAX (212)685-4540, telex 421419. **(Subscription address:** Marcel Dekker Inc., PO Box 5017, Monticello NY 12701. **Tel** (800)228-1160.**)** Documents available from The Genuine Article, CASDDS.
Desc: Each title covers a different topic in electroanalytical chemistry.
Ind/Abst Chem. Abstr.; Index Sci. Rev. [Full Cov.]; Res. Alert [Full Cov.]; Sci. Cit. Index (19??-19??); SCISEARCH.

LC QD79.E44 E44 **ISSN** 0173-0835
DD 543/.0871 GW
CCC
NLM W1 EL451T **CODEN** ELCTDN
Pr Rev.

ELECTROPHORESIS. [Electrophoresis]. **Added/Corp** Electrophoresis Society. International Electrophoresis Society. Vol. 1, No. 1 (April 1980)-. Academic Scholarly Publication. English (German and French). Twelve times a year. $640.00. VCH Gesellschaft GmbH, Postfach 101161, D-69451 Weinheim Germany. **Tel** 011 49 6201 606459, FAX 011 49 6201 606184. **(Subscription address:** VCH Publishers Inc., 303 Northwest 12th Avenue, Journals Department, Deerfield FL 33442. **Tel** (800)367-8249, (305)428-5566.**) ED** V Neuhoff. available on microfilm. Documents available from The Genuine Article, BIOSIS Document Express, CASDDS.
Desc: Contains information about new advances in general, about methods and applications of two-dimensional electrophoresis, and about applications of electrophoretic techniques in clinical and genetic research.
Ind/Abst AgBiotech News Inf.; Anal. Abstr.; Biol. Abstr.; Chem. Abstr.; Chem. Titles; CSA Neuro. Abstr. (?-?); Curr. Cit.; Curr. Contents Life Sci.; Dairy Sci. Abstr.; EMBASE; Food Sci. Technol. Abstr.; Genet. Abstr.; Health Plan. Adminis.; Hum. Genome Abstr.; Index Med.; Life Sci. Collect.; Plant Breed. Abstr.; Ref. Upd. Deluxe Ed.; Res. Alert [Full Cov.]; Rice Abstr.; Sci. Cit. Index; SCISEARCH; Sug. Indus. Abstr.; Wheat Barley Trit. Abstr.

ISSN 0272-6467
UK

ELLIS HORWOOD SERIES IN ANALYTICAL CHEMISTRY. [Ellis Horwood ser. anal. chem.]. (19??)-. Monographic series. English. Irregular. Price varies per volume. John Wiley & Sons Ltd., Baffins Lane, Chichester, West Sussex PO19 1UD United Kingdom. **Tel** 011 44 1243 779777, FAX 011 44 1243 776128 BTG:JWP001, telex 86290 WIBOOKG. **(Subscription address:** John Wiley & Sons Inc / New Jersey, PO Box 2575, Secaucus NJ 07096-2575. **)**
Ind/Abst Math. Rev. (1988-).

LC QD101 **ISSN** 1356-1049
DD 545 UK
Pr Rev.

•EUROPEAN MASS SPECTROSCOPY. (1995)-. Academic Scholarly Publication. English. Six times a year. $463.50. IM Publications, 6 Charlton Mill, Charlton, Chichester, West Sussex PO18 0HY United Kingdom. **Tel** 011 44 1243 811334, FAX 011 44 1243 811711. **ED** P.J. Derrick. Documents available from BLDSC, CASDDS.
Desc: Concerned with the mass spectrometry of atomic and molecular species.

LC QD71 .F47 **ISSN** 1000-0720
DD 543/.005 CC
CODEN FENSE4

FEN HSI SHIH YEN SHIH = ANALYTICAL LABORATORY. **Added/Corp** Chung-Kuo Yu Se Chin Shu Kung Yeh Tsung Kung Ssu. Chung-Kuo Yu Se Chin Shu Hsueh Hui. **VFOAT** Analytical Laboratory; Fenxi Shiyanshi. (19??)-. Periodical. Chinese. Twelve times a year. Documents available from CASDDS.
Ind/Abst Chem. Abstr.; Curr. Cit.

LC QD71 .F43 **ISSN** 0253-3820
CC
CODEN FHHHDT

FENXI HUAXUE. (FEN HSI HUA HSUEH.). [Fenxi huaxue]. (1973)-. Academic Scholarly Publication. Chinese. Twelve times a year. $1.30 per issue. Chinese Academy of Sciences, (Zhongguo Kexueyuan), Changchun Institute of Applied Chemistry, 109 Stalin Street, Changchun, Jilin 130022, People's Republic of China. **ED** Wang Erkang. **Ad Acc, Adv Mgr:** Shi Youlin. Full Page (B&W) $750.00. **Circ:** 8,000. Documents available from CASDDS.
Desc: Co-sponsored by the Chinese Chemical Society.
Ind/Abst Chem. Abstr.; NAPRALERT; Postharvest News Inf.; Soyabean Abstr.

LC QD71
DD 543.00(5/6) US

•FIELD ANALYTICAL CHEMISTRY & TECHNOLOGY. **VFOAT** Field Analytical Chemistry and Technology. (1996)-. English. Six times a year. $195.00 (US); $231.00 (other). Wiley Liss, 605 3rd Avenue, New York NY 10158. **Tel** (212)850-8800, (212)850-6645.

LC QD139.G5 F59 **ISSN** 0134-7071
LV
CODEN FKSID6

FIZIKA I KHIMIIA STEKLOOBRAZUIUSHCHIKH SISTEM. **Added/Corp** Latvia. Augstakas un Videjas Specialas Izglitbas Ministrija. Petera Stuckas Latvijas Valsts Universitate. Pusvaditaju Fizikas Problemu Laboratorija. Rigas Politehniskais Instituts. (1973)-. Academic Scholarly Publication. Russian. Latviiskii Gosudarstvennyi Universitet / University of Latvia, Bulvar Raina 19, 1586 Riga Latvia. **Tel** 22-90-76, FAX 22-50-39, telex 116172. Documents available from CASDDS.
Ind/Abst Ceram. Abstr.; Chem. Abstr.

ISSN 0937-0633
GW
CCC
NLM W1; FR839M **CODEN** FJACES
Pr Rev.

FRESENIUS' JOURNAL OF ANALYTICAL CHEMISTRY. [Fresenius' j. anal. chem.]. **Added/Corp** Gesellschaft Deutscher Chemiker. Fachgruppe Analytische Chemie. **VFOAT** Journal of Analytical Chemistry; Analytical Chemistry. Vol. 336, No. 1 (Jan. 1990)-. Academic Scholarly Publication. English (German; summaries and/or abstracts in English). Twenty-four times a year. $2187.00. Springer-Verlag GmbH & Company KG, Heidelberger Platz 3, D-14197 Berlin Germany. **Tel** 011 49 30 8207223, FAX 011 49 30 8214091, telex 183 319 SPBLN D. **(Subscription address:** Springer-Verlag New York Inc. / North America, PO Box 2485, Journal Fulfillment, Secaucus NJ 07096. **Tel** (201)348-4033, (800)777-4643, FAX (201)348-4505.**)** available on microfilm and microfiche from University Microfilms International (UMI). Documents available from The Genuine Article, BIOSIS Document Express, CASDDS. ***Continues*** *Fresenius' Zeitschrift fuer Analytische Chemie, 0016-1152.*
Ind/Abst Biol. Abstr.; Chem. Abstr. (1990-); Coal Abstr.; Curr. Cit.; Curr. Contents Phys. Chem. Earth Sci.; EMBASE; Energy Res. Abstr.; GeoRef; Met. Abstr.; Life

Sci. Collect.; PESTDOC; Postharvest News Inf.; Res. Alert [Full Cov.]; Rev. Agric. Entomol.; Rev. Med. Vet. Entomol.; Sci. Cit. Index; SCISEARCH; Sel. Water Resour. Abstr.; Soc. Sci. Cit. Index [Select. Cov.]; Vitis Vitic. Enol. Abstr.; World Alum. Abstr.

LC QD79.C45 G35 **ISSN** 1059-3160
DD 543/.089 US

GAS & LIQUID CHROMATOGRAPHY LITERATURE, ABSTRACTS & INDEX.
See Chemistry and Chemicals-Abstracting, Bibliographies and Statistics.

ISSN 0046-5461
UK

GAS CHROMATOGRAPHY-MASS SPECTROMETRY ABSTRACTS.
Added/Corp Science & Technology Agency. **VFOAT** Mass Spectrometry Abstracts. Vol. 1 (Jan./Mar. 1970)-. Periodical. English. Six times a year. PRM Science & Technology Agency Ltd, 261A Finchley Road Hampstead, London NW3 6LV United Kingdom. **Tel** 011 44 171 4310372.

LC QD79.C4 G58 **ISSN** 0940-032X
DD 543/.089 GW
NLM W1; GI96E

GIT SPEZIAL. CHROMATOGRAPHIE.
Added/Corp GIT Verlag. **VFOAT** Chromatographie. (19??)-. Academic Scholarly Publication. German (summaries and/or abstracts in English). Two times a year. DM35.00. GIT Verlag GmbH, Roblerstrabe 90, Postfach 110564, D-64220 Darmstadt Germany. **Tel** 011 49 6151 80900, FAX 011 49 6151 809045. ***Continues in part*** *Supplement (GIT Verlag), 0930-4061.*
Ind/Abst Curr. Cit.

NE
NLM W1; HA51J
Pr Rev.

HANDBOOK OF CHEMICAL NEUROANATOMY. Vol. 1 (1983)-. Monographic series. English. Irregular. Price varies per volume. Elsevier Science Publishers BV, PO Box 211, 1000 AE Amsterdam Netherlands. **Tel** 011 31 20 4853641, 011 31 20 4853642, FAX 011 31 20 4853598. **ED** A. Bjorklund and T. Hokfelt.
Desc: Contains information for those interested in the localization and function of putative transmitter substances in the nervous system. Series focuses on scholarly reviews, complete and theoretical backgrounds of the methods, discussions of their advantages and limitations as well as detailed recipes.

ISSN 0018-019X
SZ
CCC
NLM W1 HE848 **CODEN** HCACAV
Pr Rev.

HELVETICA CHIMICA ACTA. [Helv. chim. acta]. **Added/Corp** Schweizerische Chemische Gesellschaft. Vol. 1 (1918)-. Academic Scholarly Publication. Multiple languages (English, French and German). Eight times a year. $698.00. Verlag Helvetica Chimica Acta, Postfach 313, CH-4010 Basel Switzerland. **Tel** 011 41 61 2724973, FAX 011 41 61 2724113. **(Subscription address:** VCH Publishers Inc., 303 Northwest 12th Avenue, Journals Department, Deerfield FL 33442. **Tel** (800)367-8249, (305)428-5566.**) ED** E. Heilbronner. Index available. cum. index. **Ad Acc. Circ:** 2,400. Documents available from The Genuine Article, BIOSIS Document Express, CASDDS.
Desc: Concerns physical, organic and biological chemistry.
Ind/Abst Abstr. Bull. Inst. Pap. Sci. Tech.; AGRICOLA; BioBusiness (-1990); Biol. Abstr.; Ceram. Abstr.; Chem Inform; Chem. Abstr.; Chem. Titles; Curr. Biotechnol.; Curr. Chem. React.; Curr. Cit.; Curr. Contents Life Sci.; Curr. Contents Phys. Chem. Earth Sci.; Dairy Sci. Abstr.; EMBASE; Food Sci. Technol. Abstr.; GeoRef; Index Chem.; Index Med.; Int. Aerosp. Abstr.; Methods Organ. Synth.; NAPRALERT; Nat. Prod. Updates; Nutr. Abstr. Rev., Ser. B, Live Feeds and Feed.; Nutr. Abstr. Rev., Ser. A, Hum. Exp.; Life Sci. Collect.; PESTDOC; Protozoolog. Abstr.; Ref. Upd. Deluxe Ed.; Res. Alert [Full Cov.]; Sci. Cit. Index; SCISEARCH; Soc. Sci. Cit. Index [Select. Cov.]; Soils Fert.; Surf. Treat. Technol. Abstr.

ISSN 1046-039X
DD 544 US
NLM W1; HI22T

HIGH TECH SEPARATIONS NEWS. [High technol. sep. news]. (June 1988)-. Periodical. English. Twelve times a year. $365.00. Business Communications Inc., 25 Van Zant Street, Suite 13, Norwalk CT 06855. **Tel** (203)853-4266, FAX (203)853-0348. available on an online database (file 636/Full-Text) from DIALOG.
Ind/Abst PTS Newsl. Database [Full Txt.].

ISSN 0376-4710
II
CODEN ICACEC

INDIAN JOURNAL OF CHEMISTRY. SECTION A, INORGANIC, BIO-INORGANIC, PHYSICAL, THEORETICAL & ANALYTICAL CHEMISTRY. [Indian j. chem., Sect. A]. **Added/Corp** Council of Scientific & Industrial Research (India) Indian National Science Academy. **VFOAT** Inorganic, Bio-Inorganic, Physical, Theoretical & Analytical Chemistry. Vol. 29, No.3 (Mar. 1990)-. Periodical. English. Twelve times a year. $400.00. Publishers and Information Directorate, Hillside Road, New Delhi 110012 India. **Tel** 586301. **(Subscription address:** Prints India, 11 Darya Ganj, New Delhi 110002 India. **Tel** 011 91 11 3268645, FAX 011 91 11 3275542, telex 31-61087 PRIN-IN.**)** ***Continues*** *Indian Journal of Chemistry. Section A, Inorganic, Physical, Theoretical & Analytical, 0376-4710.*
Ind/Abst Curr. Cit.; Sci. Cit. Index.

LC TA401 .Z313 **ISSN** 0019-8447
DD 607.2 US
CCC
CODEN INDLAP

INDUSTRIAL LABORATORY. [Ind. lab.]. **Added/Corp** Consultants Bureau. Instrument Society of America. Consultants Bureau Enterprises. Vol. 24 (Feb. 1958)-. Periodical. English (Russian). Twelve times a year. $1295.00. Consultants Bureau, A Division of Plenum Publishing Corporation, 233 Spring Street, New York NY 10013. **Tel** (212)620-8000, (212)620-8466, FAX (212)463-0742, telex 23/421139. **ED** N. P. Lyakishev. available on microfilm and microfiche from University Microfilms International (UMI). Documents available from Article Express International, The Genuine Article, Ask*IEEE, CASDDS.
Desc: This journal presents the most recent developments in instrumentation for analytical chemistry and physical and mechanical methods for material research and testing.
Ind/Abst Alum. Ind. Abstr.; Appl. Mech. Rev.; Ceram. Abstr.; Chem. Abstr.; Coal Abstr.; Curr. Cit.; Curr. Contents Phys. Chem. Earth Sci.; Ei Page One; Eng. Index Annu.; Fluid Abstr., Civil Eng.; Fluid Abstr. Proc. Eng.; FLUIDEX (1973-); GeoRef; INIS Atomindex [Micro.]; INSPEC (March 1969-); Int. Aerosp. Abstr.; Leadscan; Met. Abstr.; Res. Alert [Full Cov.]; Sci. Cit. Index; SCISEARCH.

LC TP983 .A233 **ISSN** 0142-5463
DD 668/.55/05 UK
CCC
NLM W1 IN766F **CODEN** IJCMDW
Pr Rev.

INTERNATIONAL JOURNAL OF COSMETIC SCIENCE. **See** Beauty and Cosmetics.

LC QD71 .I55 **ISSN** 0306-7319
DD 543 US
CCC
NLM W1 IN766GK **CODEN** IJEAA3
Pr Rev.

INTERNATIONAL JOURNAL OF ENVIRONMENTAL ANALYTICAL CHEMISTRY. [Int. j. environ. anal. chem.]. Vol. 1 (Aug. 1971)-. Academic Scholarly Publication. English. Irregular. $746.00 (academic institutions), $1164.00 (corporate institutions). Gordon & Breach Science Publishers, Inc., PO Box 786, Cooper Station, New York NY 10276. **Tel** (212)206-8900, FAX (212)645-2459. **ED** R. W. Frei. **Bk Rev. Ad Acc.** Documents available from Article Express International, The Genuine Article, BIOSIS Document Express, CASDDS, Documents on Demand.
Ind/Abst AGRICOLA [Select. Cov.]; Anal. Abstr.; AQUAREF; Biodeter. Abstr. (19??-19??); Bioeng. Abstr.; Biol. Abstr. (-1984); Chem. Abstr.; Chem. Hazards Ind.; Chem. Titles; Coal Abstr.; Crop Physiol. Abstr.; Curr. Cit.; Curr. Contents Agric. Biol. Environ. Sci.; Dairy Sci. Abstr.; Ei Page One; EMBASE; Eng. Index Annu.; Environ. Abstr.; Environ. Period. Bibliogr.; Field Crop Abstr.; Food Sci. Technol. Abstr.; For. Abstr.; Hortic. Abstr.; Index Med. (Vol. 1, No. 1, 1971-Vol. 29, No. 4, 1987); Irr. Drain. Abstr.; Lab. Hazards Bull.; Leadscan; Nematol. Abstr.; Life Sci. Collect.; Plant Grow. Reg. Abstr.; Pollut. Abstr. Indexes; Res. Alert [Full Cov.]; Rev. Agric. Entomol.; Rev. Med. Vet. Entomol.; Rev. Plant Pathol.; Sci. Cit. Index; SCISEARCH; Soils Fert.; Weed Abstr.

ISSN 0143-5140
UK
Pr Rev.

INTERNATIONAL LABMATE. [Int. labmate]. (19??)-. Trade Publication. English. Seven times a year. $94.11. International Labmate Limited, Newgate Sandpit Lane, St. Albans Hertfordshire AL4 0BS United Kingdom. **Tel** 011 44 1727 851993, 011 44 1727 831337, FAX 011 44 1727 841694. **Bk Rev. Ad Acc. Circ:** 45,000 (ctrl). ***Continues*** *Separation.*
Desc: Latest news and information on laboratory equipment and chemicals.
Ind/Abst Curr. Cit.

US

INTERNATIONAL SERIES IN ANALYTICAL CHEMISTRY. Vol. 57 (1975)-. Monographic series. English. Irregular. Price varies per volume. Pergamon Press, An Imprint of Elsevier Science Ltd., The Boulevard, Langford Lane, Kidlington, Oxford OX5 1GB United Kingdom. **Tel** 011 44 1865 843000, 011 44 1865 843699, FAX 011 44 1865 843010. ***Continues*** *International Series of Monographs in Analytical Chemistry.*

ISSN 0144-6789
UK

INTERNATIONAL X-RAY EMISSION SPECTROMETRY. Vol. 1, No. 2 (1979)-. Periodical. English. Four times a year. Technical Media Abstracts, Media House, PO Box 188, London NW6 5LF United Kingdom. ***Continues*** *International X-Ray Fluorescence Spectrometry.*

LC QD79.C4 I87

RU
CODEN INTKD3

ITOGI NAUKI I TEKHNIKI : KHROMATOGRAFIA. **Added/Corp** Vsesoiuznyi Institut Nauchnoi i Tekhnicheskoi Informatsii (Soviet Union). **VFOAT** Khromatografia; Itogi Nauki I Tekhniki: Seriia Khromatografiia. Vol. 1 (1974)-. Academic Scholarly Publication. Russian. 6.60rub. VINITI - Vsesoyuznyi Institut Nauchno-Tekhnicheskoi Informatsii, All-Union Scientific and Technical Information Institute, Baltiiskaia ulitsa 14, 125219 Moscow Russia. **Tel** 011 7 95 2384600, FAX 011 7 95 9430060, telex 411160. Documents available from CASDDS.
Ind/Abst Chem. Abstr. (1974-1980).

LC QD71 .J58
DD 543/.005 US
UDC 543

SUSPENDED

JOURNAL OF ANALYSIS AND PURIFICATION. **VFOAT** Analysis and Purification. Vol. 1, No. 1 (March 1986)-?. Periodical. English. Four times a year. Journal of Analysis & Purification, PO Box 2931, Woburn MA 01888.

LC TP156.P9 J59 **ISSN** 0165-2370
DD 547.3/02 NE
CCC
NLM W1 JO535Q **CODEN** JAAPDD
Pr Rev.

JOURNAL OF ANALYTICAL AND APPLIED PYROLYSIS. [J. anal. appl. pyrolysis]. Vol. 1 (June 1979)-. Academic Scholarly Publication. English. Ten times a year (5 volumes). $1464.00. Elsevier Science Publishers BV, PO Box 211, 1000 AE Amsterdam Netherlands. **Tel** 011 31 20 4853641, 011 31 20 4853642, FAX 011 31 20 4853598. **ED** H.R. Schulten and R.P. Lattimer. **Bk Rev. Ad Acc.** ctrl circ. available on microfilm and microfiche from University Microfilms International (UMI); available on an online database from Elsevier Electronic Subscriptions (EES). Documents available from Article Express International, The Genuine Article, BIOSIS Document Express, CASDDS.
Desc: Devoted to the publication of qualitative and quantitative results relating to pyrolysis.
Ind/Abst Anal. Abstr.; Bioeng. Abstr.; Biol. Abstr.; Chem. Abstr.; Chem. Titles; Coal Abstr.; Curr. Cit.; Curr. Contents Phys. Chem. Earth Sci.; Ei Page One; Energy Res. Abstr. (March 1981-); Eng. Index Annu. [Select. Cov.]; Gas Abstr.; GeoRef; Mass Spect. Bull.; Res. Alert [Full Cov.]; Sci. Cit. Index; SCISEARCH.

ISSN 0267-9477
UK
CCC
NLM W1; JO535QD **CODEN** JASPE2
Pr Rev.

JOURNAL OF ANALYTICAL ATOMIC SPECTROMETRY. [J. anal. at. spectrom.]. **Added/Corp** Royal Society of Chemistry (Great Britain). **VFOAT** JAAS. Vol. 1, No. 1 (Feb. 1986)-. Academic Scholarly Publication. English. Thirteen times a year. $1136.00. Royal Society of Chemistry, Thomas Graham House, Science Park, Cambridge CB4 4WF United Kingdom. **Tel** 011 44 1223 420066, FAX 011 44 1223 423623, telex 818293 ROYAL. **(Subscription address:** Royal Society of Chemistry, Turpin Distribution Services Ltd., Blackhorse Road, Letchworth, Hertfordshire SG6 1HN United Kingdom. **Tel** 011 44 1462 672555, FAX 011 44 1462 480947.**)** Index available (free). available on microfilm and microfiche from University Microfilms International (UMI); available on an online database from STN International. Documents available from Article Express International, The Genuine Article, BIOSIS Document Express, CASDDS, BLDSC, FAXON Xpress, The UnCover Company, SWETS, UMI Article Clearinghouse.
Desc: Covers all aspects of the development and analytical applications of atomic spectrometric techniques, providing a forum for communication between research scientists and manufacturers and users of atomic spectrometric equipment.
Ind/Abst Anal. Abstr.; Biol. Abstr. (1987-); Chem. Abstr. (1986-); Chem. Titles; Coal Abstr.; Curr. Cit.; Curr. Contents Phys. Chem. Earth Sci.; Dairy Sci. Abstr.; Ei Page One; Eng. Index Annu. [Select. Cov.]; Food Sci. Technol. Abstr.; Hortic. Abstr.; Mass Spect. Bull. (?-?); Nutr. Abstr. Rev., Ser. B, Live Feeds and Feed.; Nutr. Abstr. Rev., Ser. A, Hum. Exp.; Res. Alert [Full Cov.]; Rev. Plant Pathol.; Sci. Cit. Index; SCISEARCH; Soils Fert.; Wheat Barley Trit. Abstr.

LC QD71 .J6 **ISSN** 1061-9348
DD 543.05 US
CCC
CODEN JACTE2

JOURNAL OF ANALYTICAL CHEMISTRY (NEW YORK, N.Y.). (JOURNAL OF ANALYTICAL CHEMISTRY.). [J. anal. chem.]. **Added/Corp** Consultants Bureau. Rossiiskaia Akademiia nauk. **VFOAT** Zhurnal Analiticheskoi Khimi. Vol. 46, No. 11, Pt. 2 (Nov. 1991)-. Academic Scholarly Publication. English (translations available in Russian). Twelve times a year. $1495.00. MAIK Nauka / Interperiodica, Ulitsa Profsoyuznaia 90, Moscow 117864 Russia. Documents available from CASDDS. ***Continues*** *Journal of Analytical Chemistry of the USSR, 0021-8766.*
Ind/Abst Chem. Abstr.; Curr. Cit.; Curr. Contents; Curr. Contents Phys. Chem. Earth Sci.; EMBASE; GeoRef; INIS Atomindex [Micro.]; Leadscan; Sel. Water Resour. Abstr.

US

JOURNAL OF ANALYTICAL CHEMISTRY = ZHURNAL ANALITICHESKOY. KHIMII. **Added/Corp** United States. Dept. of Commerce. Office of Technical Services. **VFOAT** Zhurnal Analiticheskoy Khimii. (19??)-. English. US Department of Commerce, 14th Street & Constitution Avenue NW, Washington DC 20230. **Tel** (202)482-2000, FAX (202)482-3772.

LC S583 .A7 **ISSN** 1060-3271
DD 630.24 US
CCC
CODEN JAINEE

JOURNAL OF AOAC INTERNATIONAL. [J. AOAC Int.]. **Added/Corp** AOAC International. Vol. 75, No. 1 (Jan./Feb. 1992)-. Academic Scholarly Publication. English. Six times a year. $208.00 North America, $254.00 other. AOAC International, 2200 Wilson Boulevard, Suite 400, Arlington VA 22201. **Tel** (703)522-3032, (800)379-2622, FAX (703)522-5468. available on an online database (CJAOAC) from STI International. Documents available from The Genuine Article, BIOSIS Document Express, CASDDS, Documents on Demand. ***Continues*** *Journal of the Association of Official Analytical Chemists, 0004-5756.*
Desc: An analytical methodology journal for chemists, biologists, microbiologists and other scientists working in food, drug, pesticides, fertilizer, feed water, environmental and other analysis for purposes of quality control, regulatory compliances, research, production control, etc. Publishes original papers on developing, improving and testing analytical methods, and newly adopted AOAC official methods.
Ind/Abst Abstr. Bull. Inst. Pap. Sci. Tech.; AGRICOLA; AQUAREF; Biol. Agric. Index (1992-); Biol. Abstr.; Chem. Abstr.; Curr. Cit.; Curr. Contents Agric. Biol. Environ. Sci.; Curr. Contents Life Sci.; EMBASE; Energy Res. Abstr.; Environ. Abstr.; Food Sci. Technol. Abstr.; Foods Adlibra (1992-); GeoRef; Index Med.; INIS Atomindex [Micro.]; Int. Packag. Abstr.; Leadscan; Life Sci. Collect.; PESTDOC (?-?); Res. Alert [Full Cov.]; Sci. Cit. Index; SCISEARCH; Soc. Sci. Cit. Index [Select. Cov.].

LC QD95 .Z513 **ISSN** 0021-9037
DD 621 US
CCC
NLM W1 JO544K **CODEN** JASYAP

JOURNAL OF APPLIED SPECTROSCOPY. [J. appl. spectrosc.]. **Added/Corp** Consultants Bureau. **VFOAT** Zhurnal Prikladnoi Spektroskopii. Vol. 2 (Jan. 1965)-. Periodical. English (translations available in Russian). Twelve times a year. $1295.00. Consultants Bureau, A Division of Plenum Publishing Corporation, 233 Spring Street, New York NY 10013. **Tel** (212)620-8000, (212)620-8466, FAX (212)463-0742, telex 23/421139. **ED** V. S. Burakov. Index available. cum. index. available on microfilm and microfiche from University Microfilms International (UMI). Documents available from Article Express International, Ask*IEEE, CASDDS.
Ind/Abst Appl. Mech. Rev.; Bioeng. Abstr.; Ceram. Abstr.; Chem. Abstr.; Coal Abstr.; Curr. Cit.; Ei Page One; Eng. Index Annu.; GeoRef; INIS Atomindex [Micro.]; INSPEC (Jan. 1970-); Pollut. Abstr. Indexes.

LC QD75.4.A8 J68 **ISSN** 0142-0453
DD 543/.0028/5 UK
CCC
NLM W1 JO547NM **CODEN** JAUCD6
Pr Rev.

JOURNAL OF AUTOMATIC CHEMISTRY, THE. [J. automat. chem.]. (Oct. 1978)-. Academic Scholarly Publication. English (summaries and/or abstracts in French and German). Six times a year. $255.00. Taylor & Francis Ltd. / UK, Rankine Road, Basingstoke, Hampshire RG24 8PR United Kingdom. **Tel** 011 44 1256 840366, FAX 011 44 1256 479438, telex 858540. **(Subscription address:** Taylor & Francis Inc., 1900 Frost Road, Suite 101, Bristol PA 19007-1598. **Tel** (215)785-5800, (800)821-8312, FAX (215)785-5515.) **ED** P. B. Stockwell (editor's address: Arthur House, B4 Chaucer Business Park, Watery Lane, Kemsing, Sevenoaks, Kent TN15 6QY United Kingdom). **Bk Rev.** available on microfilm and microfiche from University Microfilms International (UMI). Documents available from The Genuine Article, Ask*IEEE, CASDDS, ADONIS. ***Absorbed*** *Journal of Clinical Laboratory Automation, 0276-8860.*
Desc: Covers all aspects of automation and mechanization in analytical, clinical and industrial environments. The journal publishes original research papers, short communications on innovations, techniques and instrumentation or research in progress, reports on recent commercial development, and meeting reports, book reviews and information on forthcoming events.
Ind/Abst ADONIS; Anal. Abstr.; Chem. Abstr.; Curr. Biotechnol.; Curr. Cit.; Curr. Contents Life Sci.; Dairy Sci. Abstr.; Electron. Commun. Abstr. J.; EMBASE; Food Sci. Technol. Abstr.; INSPEC (Oct. 1979-); ISMEC Bull.; Pollut. Abstr. Indexes; Res. Alert [Full Cov.]; Saf. Sci. Abstr. J.; Sci. Cit. Index; SCISEARCH.

LC QD271 .J66 **ISSN** 0021-9665
DD 543/.08 US
CCC
NLM W1 JO5844 **CODEN** JCHSBZ
Pr Rev.

JOURNAL OF CHROMATOGRAPHIC SCIENCE. [J. chromatogr. sci.]. Vol. 7 (Jan. 1969)-. Academic Scholarly Publication. English. Twelve times a year. $220.00. Preston Publications Inc., 7800 Merrimac Avenue, PO Box 48312, Niles IL 60714. **Tel** (708)965-0566, (708)967-1810, FAX (708)965-7639, telex 910-223-1780 PRESTON NILE. **ED** Bert M. Gordon and John Q. Walker. Index available. **Bk Rev. Ad Acc. Circ:** 5,000. available on microfilm; available on microfiche. Documents available from Article Express International, The Genuine Article, BIOSIS Document Express, CASDDS. ***Continues*** *Journal of Gas Chromatography, 0096-2686.*
Desc: International scientific journal on theory and practice of chromatography.
Ind/Abst Abstr. Bull. Inst. Pap. Sci. Tech.; AGRICOLA; Art Archaeol. Tech. Abstr.; Bioeng. Abstr.; Biol. Abstr.; Chem. Abstr.; Chem. Titles; Coal Abstr.; Comput. Inf. Syst. Abstr. J. [Full Cov.]; Curr. Cit.; Curr. Contents Life Sci.; Curr. Contents Phys. Chem. Earth Sci.; Dairy Sci. Abstr.; Ei Page One; Elect. Comm. Abstr.; EMBASE; Energy Inf. Abstr.; Energy Res. Abstr. (March 1972-); Eng. Index Annu.; Environ. Eng. Abstr.; Food Sci. Technol. Abstr.; Foods Adlibra; Gas Abstr.; GeoRef; Hortic. Abstr.; Index Med.; INIS Atomindex [Micro.]; Int. Aerosp. Abstr.; Lit. Pat. Abstr., Oilfield Chem. (1969-); Lit. Abstr., Catal. Zeol.; Lit. Abstr., Health Environ.; Lit. Abstr., Pet. Refin. Petrochem.; Lit. Abstr., Pet. Substit.; Lit. Abstr., Transp. Storage; Mech. Eng. Abstr.; NAPRALERT; Nutr. Abstr. Rev., Ser. B, Live Feeds and Feed.; Nutr. Abstr. Rev., Ser. A, Hum. Exp.; Life Sci. Collect.; PESTDOC; Ref. Upd. Deluxe Ed.; Res. Alert [Full Cov.]; Rev. Agric. Entomol.; Rev. Med. Vet. Entomol.; Rev. Plant Pathol.; Sci. Cit. Index; SCISEARCH; Soils Fert.; Weed Abstr.; World Surf. Coat. Abstr.

LC QD271 .J65 **ISSN** 0021-9673
DD 544.9205 NE
CCC
NLM W1 JO5845 **CODEN** JOCRAM
Pr Rev. **TITLE CHANGE**

JOURNAL OF CHROMATOGRAPHY. [J. chromatogr.]. **VFOAT** Journal of Chromatography. Bibliography Section; Journal of Chromatography. Chromatographic Reviews; Journal of Chromatography. Biomedical Applications; Journal of Chromatography. Symposium Volumes. Vol. 1, No. 1 (Jan. 1958)-(1994). Academic Scholarly Publication. English (French and German; summaries and/or abstracts in French and German). Elsevier Science Publishers BV, PO Box 211, 1000 AE Amsterdam Netherlands. **Tel** 011 31 20 4853641, 011 31 20 4853642, FAX 011 31 20 4853598. **ED** M. Lederer, K. Macek and E. Heftmann. cum. index. available on microfilm and microfiche from University Microfilms International (UMI). Documents available from The Genuine Article, BIOSIS Document Express, CASDDS. ***Split into*** *Journal of Chromatography. A* ***and*** *Journal of Chromatography. B, Biomedical Applications.*
Desc: Journal on chromatography, electrophoresis and related methods. Contributions are primarily research papers dealing with chromatographic theory, instrumental development and their application in analysis and pure chemistry.
Ind/Abst Abstr. Bull. Inst. Pap. Sci. Tech.; AgBiotech News Inf.; AGRICOLA [Select. Cov.]; Agrofor. Abstr.; Anal. Abstr.; Art Archaeol. Tech. Abstr.; Biodeter. Abstr. (19??-19??); Biol. Abstr.; Chem. Abstr.; Chem. Titles; Coal Abstr.; Cot. Trop. Fibr. Abstr. Bibliogr.; Crop Physiol. Abstr.; CSA Neuro. Abstr. (?-?); Curr. Aware. Biol. Sci., CABS; Curr. Biotechnol.; Curr. Cit.; Curr. Contents Life Sci.; Curr. Contents Phys. Chem. Earth Sci.; Dairy Sci. Abstr.; Ei Page One; EMBASE; Field Crop Abstr.; Food Sci. Technol. Abstr.; Foods Adlibra; For. Prod. Abstr. (19??-19??); For. Abstr.; GeoRef; Grass. Forage Abstr.; Helminthol. Abstr. (1991-); Hortic. Abstr.; Immunol. Abstr.; Index Med.; Index Vet.; Int. Aerosp. Abstr.; Leadscan; Maize Abstr.; Mass Spect. Bull.; Microbiol. Abstr. Sect. B (19??-19??); Microbiol. Abstr. Sect. A; Microbiol. Abstr. Sect. C; NAPRALERT; Nat. Prod. Updates; Nematol. Abstr.; Nutr. Abstr. Rev., Ser. B, Live Feeds and Feed.; Nutr. Abstr. Rev., Ser. A, Hum. Exp.; Oceanogr. Lit. Rev.; Ornamental Hort.; Life Sci. Collect.; PESTDOC; Pig News Inf.; Plant Grow. Reg. Abstr.; Potato Abstr.; Poult. Abstr.; Protozoolog. Abstr.; Refer. Z.; Res. Alert [Full Cov.]; Rev. Med. Vet. Entomol.; Rev. Med. Vet. Mycology; Rev. Plant Pathol.; Rice Abstr.; Saf. Health Work; Sci. Cit. Index; SCISEARCH; Soc. Sci. Cit. Index [Select. Cov.]; Soils Fert.; Soyabean Abstr.; SPORT Discus; Sug. Indus. Abstr.; Vet. Bull.; Vitis Vitic. Enol. Abstr.; Weed Abstr.; Wheat Barley Trit. Abstr.

NE
NLM W1; JO5845M **CODEN** JCRAEY
Pr Rev.

•JOURNAL OF CHROMATOGRAPHY. A. **VFOAT** Journal of Chromatography. A, Symposium Volumes. Vol. 652, No. 1 (Oct. 15, 1993)-. Academic Scholarly Publication. English (French and German). Irregular (68 issues). $6519.00. Elsevier Science Publishers BV, PO Box 211, 1000 AE Amsterdam Netherlands. **Tel** 011 31 20 4853641, 011 31 20 4853642, FAX 011 31 20 4853598. **ED** U.A. Th. Brinkman, R.W. Giese, J.K. Haken, L.R. Snyder. available on an online database from Elsevier Electronic Subscriptions (EES). Documents available from ADONIS. ***Continues in part*** *Journal of Chromatography, 0021-9673.*
Desc: All aspects of chromatography, electrophoresis and related separation methods are covered in research papers dealing with theory, developments in instruments and applications.
Ind/Abst ADONIS; Curr. Cit.; Index Med.

LC QD480 .J68 **ISSN** 0920-654X
DD 541 NE
CCC
NLM W1; JO595KR **CODEN** JCADEQ
Pr Rev.

JOURNAL OF COMPUTER-AIDED MOLECULAR DESIGN. [J. comput.-aided mol. des.]. **VFOAT** Journal of Computer Aided Molecular Design; Computer-Aided Molecular Design; Computer Aided Molecular Design. Vol. 1, No. 1 (April 1987)-. Periodical. English. Six times a year. $933.00. ESCOM Science Publishers BV, PO Box 214, 2300 AE Leiden The Netherlands. **Tel** 011 31 71 127052. **ED** G. R. Marshall, J. G. Vinter, and H. D. Holtje. **Ad Acc. Circ:** 800. available on diskette. Documents available from The Genuine Article, BIOSIS Document Express.
Desc: Provides a forum for disseminating information on both the theory and the application of computer based methods in the analysis and design of molecules. Contributions on computer aided molecular modeling studies in pharmaceutical, polymer, materials and surface sciences, as well as other molecular based disciplines, are particularly welcome.
Ind/Abst Biol. Abstr. (1988-); Curr. Cit.; Food Sci. Technol. Abstr.; Index Med. (Vol.1 No 1, 1987-); Res. Alert [Full Cov.]; SCISEARCH.

LC QD79.C4 J65 **ISSN** 0935-6304
GW
CCC
NLM W1; JO6703F **CODEN** JHRCE7
Pr Rev.

JOURNAL OF HIGH RESOLUTION CHROMATOGRAPHY : HRC. [HRC, J. high resolut. chromatogr.]. **VFOAT** HRC. Vol. 12, No. 1 (Jan. 1989)-. Periodical. English. Twelve times a year. $394.00. Dr. Alfred Huethig Verlag GmbH, Postfach 102869, D-69018 Heidelberg Germany. **Tel** 011 49 6221 489281, FAX 011 49 6221 489279. **(Subscription address:** Huethig Publishing Inc., 29 Macintosh Drive, Oxford CT 06478. **Tel** (203)881-2647.) **ED** P. Sandra, W. Bertsch, W. Blum, F. Everaets, W. Jennings, V. Pretorius and S. Tsuge. Index available. **Bk Rev. Ad Acc. Circ:** 5,000. available on microfiche. Documents available from The Genuine Article, BIOSIS Document Express, CASDDS. ***Continues*** *HRC & CC. Journal of High Resolution Chromatography & Chromatography Communications, 0344-7138.*
Desc: An international journal for micro-separations and hyphenated techniques published in English.
Ind/Abst Biodeter. Abstr. (1991-); Biol. Abstr. (1989-); Chem. Abstr.; Curr. Cit.; Curr. Contents Phys. Chem. Earth Sci.; Ei Page One; Field Crop Abstr.; Hortic. Abstr.; Index Vet.; Mass Spect. Bull.; Postharvest News Inf.; Res. Alert [Full Cov.]; Rev. Agric. Entomol.; Rev. Med. Vet. Entomol.; Rev. Med. Vet. Mycology; Sci. Cit. Index; SCISEARCH; Vitis Vitic. Enol. Abstr.; Weed Abstr.; Wheat Barley Trit. Abstr.

LC QD79.C454 J68 **ISSN** 0148-3919
DD 544/.924/05 US
CCC
NLM W1 JO745P **CODEN** JLCHD8
Pr Rev. **TITLE CHANGE**

JOURNAL OF LIQUID CHROMATOGRAPHY. [J. liq. chromatogr.]. Vol. 1 (1978)-(Jan. 1996). Academic Scholarly Publication. English. Marcel Dekker Inc., 270 Madison Avenue, New York NY 10016. **Tel** (212)696-9000, (800)228-1160, FAX (212)685-4540, telex 421419. **(Subscription address:** Marcel Dekker Inc., PO Box 5017, Monticello NY 12701. **Tel** (800)228-1160.) **ED** Jack Cazes, Haleem J. Issaq and Steven H. Wong. available on microfiche. Documents available from Article Express International, The Genuine Article, BIOSIS Document Express, CASDDS, ADONIS. ***Continued by*** *Journal of Liquid Chromatography and Related Technologies.*
Desc: Contains an outstanding selection of critical, analytical, and preparative papers involving the application of liquid chromatography to the solution of problems in all areas of science and technology, as well as papers that deal specifically with liquid

chromatography as a science within itself. The coverage spans such areas as paper and thin layer chromatography and all modes of liquid column chromatography, including classical and HPLC. On a regular basis, entire issues are devoted to special topics on liquid chromatography, including an annual directory of LC manufacturers, suppliers, and services. In addition, each issue offers book reviews, liquid chromatography news, and a calendar of meetings and exhibitions.
Ind/Abst Abstr. Bull. Inst. Pap. Sci. Tech.; ADONIS; AGRICOLA; Anal. Abstr.; Biodeter. Abstr. (1991-); Bioeng. Abstr.; Biol. Abstr.; Chem. Abstr.; Chem. Titles; Coal Abstr.; Crop Physiol. Abstr.; Curr. Aware. Biol. Sci., CABS; Curr. Biotechnol.; Curr. Cit.; Curr. Contents Life Sci.; Curr. Contents Phys. Chem. Earth Sci.; Dairy Sci. Abstr.; Ei Page One; Elect. Comm. Abstr.; EMBASE; Energy Res. Abstr. (March 1979-); Eng. Index Annu.; Environ. Eng. Abstr.; Food Sci. Technol. Abstr.; For. Abstr.; Helminthol. Abstr. (1991-); Hortic. Abstr.; Index Vet.; INIS Atomindex [Micro.]; Int. Aerosp. Abstr.; Maize Abstr.; Mater. Sci. Eng. Abstr.; Mech. Eng. Abstr.; NAPRALERT; Nematol. Abstr.; Nutr. Abstr. Rev., Ser. B, Live Feeds and Feed.; Nutr. Abstr. Rev., Ser. A, Hum. Exp.; Ornamental Hort. (1991-); Life Sci. Collect.; Phys. Briefs; Pig News Inf.; Plant Grow. Reg. Abstr.; Postharvest News Inf.; Potato Abstr.; Poult. Abstr.; Protozoolog. Abstr.; Ref. Upd. Deluxe Ed.; Res. Alert [Full Cov.]; Rev. Med. Vet. Entomol.; Rev. Med. Vet. Mycology; Sci. Cit. Index; SCISEARCH; Soils Fert.; Solid State Supercond. Abstr.; Soyabean Abstr.; Sug. Indus. Abstr.; Vet. Bull.; Weed Abstr.

ISSN 1082-6076
US

•JOURNAL OF LIQUID CHROMATOGRAPHY & RELATED TECHNOLOGIES.
VFOAT Journal of Liquid Chromatography and Related Technologies. (1996)-. Periodical. English. Twenty times a year. $1595.00. Marcel Dekker Inc., 270 Madison Avenue, New York NY 10016. **Tel** (212)696-9000, (800)228-1160, FAX (212)685-4540, telex 421419. **(Subscription address:** Marcel Dekker Inc., PO Box 5017, Monticello NY 12701. **Tel** (800)228-1160.) ***Continues*** *Journal of Liquid Chromatography, 0148-3919.*

ISSN 1076-5174
UK
CCC
NLM W1; JO748P

•JOURNAL OF MASS SPECTROMETRY. PART A.
(1995)-. Periodical. English. Twelve times a year. $2195.00. John Wiley & Sons Ltd., Baffins Lane, Chichester, West Sussex PO19 1UD United Kingdom. **Tel** 011 44 1243 779777, FAX 011 44 1243 776128 BTG:JWP001, telex 86290 WIBOOKG. **(Subscription address:** John Wiley & Sons, Inc. / Philadelphia, PO Box 7247, Philadelphia PA 19170. **Tel** (212)850-6645, (800)225-5945.)
Ind/Abst Curr. Cit.

LC QD **ISSN** 1040-7685
DD 543
US
CCC
CODEN JMSEEJ

JOURNAL OF MICROCOLUMN SEPARATIONS, THE.
Vol. 1, No. 1 (Jan./Feb. 1989)-. Academic Scholarly Publication. English. Eight times a year. $328.00. John Wiley & Sons, Inc., 605 Third Avenue, New York NY 10158-0012. **Tel** (212)850-6000, (212)850-6645, FAX (212)850-6088, telex 12-7063. Index available. cum. index. **Bk Rev. Ad Acc.** Documents available from The Genuine Article, CASDDS.
Desc: An international publication dedicated to the advancement of all aspects of microcolumn separation methods, including microcolumn supercritical fluid chromatography and capillary gas chromatography.
Ind/Abst Chem. Abstr. (1989-); Curr. Cit.; Res. Alert [Full Cov.]; SCISEARCH.

ISSN 0236-5731
SZ
CCC

JOURNAL OF RADIOANALYTICAL AND NUCLEAR CHEMISTRY.
(JOURNAL OF RADIOANALYTICAL AND NUCLEAR CHEMISTRY. ARTICLES.). [J. radioanal. nucl. chem.]. Vol. 81, No. 1 (Jan. 1984)-. Periodical. English (French and German). Elsevier Sequoia SA, PO Box 564, CH-1001 Lausanne 1 Switzerland. **Tel** 011 41 21 3207381, FAX 011 41 21 3235444. ***Formed by the union of*** *Journal of Radioanalytical Chemistry* ***and*** *Radiochemical and Radioanalytical Letters.*
Ind/Abst Life Sci. Collect. (1984-); Sci. Cit. Index.

LC QD605 .J63 **ISSN** 0236-5731
DD 543/.088
SZ
CCC
NLM W1; JO864M **CODEN** JRNCDM
Pr Rev.

JOURNAL OF RADIOANALYTICAL AND NUCLEAR CHEMISTRY.
[J. radioanal. nucl. chem.]. **VFOAT** Radioanalytical and Nuclear Chemistry. Vol. 81, No. 1 (Jan. 1984)-. Academic Scholarly Publication. English (French and German). Thirty-nine times a year (13 vols.). 4940.00F. Elsevier Sequoia SA, PO Box 564, CH-1001 Lausanne 1 Switzerland. **Tel** 011 41 21 3207381, FAX 011 41 21 3235444. **ED** Tibor Braun (editor's address: Institute of Inorganic and Analytical Chemistry, L Eotvos University, PO Box 123, H-1443 Budapest Hungary) and Erno Bujdoso. available on microfilm and microfiche from University Microfilms International (UMI); available on an online database from Elsevier Electronic Subscriptions (EES). Documents available from The Genuine Article, BIOSIS Document Express, Ask*IEEE, CASDDS. ***Formed by the union of*** *Journal of Radioanalytical Chemistry* ***and*** *Radiochemical and Radioanalytical Letters.*
Desc: Publishes original papers, review papers and short communications on nuclear chemistry.
Ind/Abst Alum. Ind. Abstr.; Anal. Abstr.; Art Archaeol. Tech. Abstr.; Biol. Abstr.; Chem. Abstr. (1984-); Chem. Titles; Coal Abstr.; Curr. Cit.; Curr. Contents Phys. Chem. Earth Sci.; Dairy Sci. Abstr.; EMBASE; Field Crop Abstr.; Food Sci. Technol. Abstr.; For. Abstr.; GeoRef; Grass. Forage Abstr.; INSPEC (Jan. 1984-); Irr. Drain. Abstr.; Maize Abstr.; Mass Spect. Bull.; Met. Abstr.; Nutr. Abstr. Rev., Ser. A, Hum. Exp.; Life Sci. Collect.; Phys. Briefs; Poult. Abstr.; Res. Alert [Full Cov.]; Rev. Med. Vet. Mycology; Rice Abstr.; Sci. Cit. Index (19??-19??); SCISEARCH; Soc. Sci. Cit. Index [Select. Cov.]; Soils Fert.; Soyabean Abstr.

ISSN 0236-5731
SZ
CCC
Pr Rev.

JOURNAL OF RADIOANALYTICAL AND NUCLEAR CHEMISTRY. LETTERS.
Vol. 85, No. 1 (Jan. 20, 1984)-. Periodical. English. $4422.00. Elsevier Sequoia SA, PO Box 564, CH-1001 Lausanne 1 Switzerland. **Tel** 011 41 21 3207381, FAX 011 41 21 3235444. ***Formed by the union of*** *Journal of Radioanalytical Chemistry* ***and*** *Radiochemical and Radioanalytical Letters.*
Ind/Abst Sci. Cit. Index.

LC QC **ISSN** 1340-8097
DD 545
JA

•JOURNAL OF THE MASS SPECTROMETRY SOCIETY OF JAPAN.
[J. Mass Spectrom. Soc. Jpn.]. **VFOAT** Shitsuryo Bunseki. (1993)-. Periodical. Multiple languages. Six times a year. $150.00. Nihon Shitsuryo Bunseki Gakkai, (Mass Spectroscopy Soc. of Japan), 18-10 Koraku 2 Chome, Bunkyoku Tokyo 112 Japan. **(Subscription address:** Maruzen Company Ltd., PO Box 5050, Import & Export Department, Tokyo 100 31 Japan. **Tel** 011 81 3 32789224.) ***Continues*** *Shitsuryo Bunseki, 0542-8645.*
Ind/Abst Curr. Cit.

LC QD139.T7 J68 **ISSN** 0733-4680
DD 543
US
CCC
NLM W1 JO966KDL **CODEN** JTMTDE

JOURNAL OF TRACE AND MICROPROBE TECHNIQUES.
[J. trace microprobe tech.]. **VFOAT** Trace and Microprobe Techniques. Vol. 1, No. 1 (1982)-. Academic Scholarly Publication. English. Four times a year. $425.00. Marcel Dekker Inc., 270 Madison Avenue, New York NY 10016. **Tel** (212)696-9000, (800)228-1160, FAX (212)685-4540, telex 421419. **(Subscription address:** Marcel Dekker Inc., PO Box 5017, Monticello NY 12701. **Tel** (800)228-1160.) **ED** E. A. Schweikert, F. Adams, H. L. Rook, P. F. Kane, G. Tolg. **Bk Rev. Ad Acc.** ctrl circ. Documents available from CASDDS.
Desc: This journal provides investigators with a centralized, comprehensive source of information covering current findings. Covering aspects of trace and microprobe analysis - techniques, methods, and applications. Each issue features papers on topics in these areas by specialists in their respective fields, as well as reviews and symposia.
Ind/Abst Anal. Abstr.; Chem. Abstr.; Curr. Aware. Biol. Sci., CABS; Curr. Cit.; GeoRef; Mass Spect. Bull.

LC QD79.C8 J68 **ISSN** 0933-4173
DD 543/.08956
GW
CCC
NLM W1; JO837AJ **CODEN** JPCTE5

JPC. JOURNAL OF PLANAR CHROMATOGRAPHY, MODERN TLC.
(JOURNAL OF PLANAR CHROMATOGRAPHY--MODERN TLC : JPC.). [JPC, J. planar chromatogr. mod. TLC]. **VFOAT** JPC; Journal of Planar Chromatography. **VAT** Journal of Planar Chromatography--Modern Thin Layer Chromatography. Vol. 1 (Feb. 1988)-. Trade Publication. English. Six times a year. $264.00. Research Institute for Medicinal Plants, PO Box 11, H 2011 Budaklasz Hungary. **Tel** 011 36 1 1688042. **(Subscription address:** Springer-Hungarica, PO Box 142, H 1410 Budapest Hungary.) Index available. cum. index. **Bk Rev. Ad Acc. Circ:** 5,200. available on microfiche. Documents available from The Genuine Article, BIOSIS Document Express, CASDDS.
Desc: Devoted to all analytical and preparative methods embraced by the collective term planar chromatography, on all kinds of stationary phase (paper, gel, layer) and with various modes of migration.
Ind/Abst Anal. Abstr.; Biol. Abstr. (1990-); Chem. Abstr.; Curr. Cit.; Ei Page One; Index Vet.; Res. Alert [Full Cov.]; Rev. Agric. Entomol.; Rev. Plant Pathol.; Vet. Bull.; Weed Abstr.

ISSN 0895-5441
DD 543
US
CCC

LC GC INTERNATIONAL.
[LC GC int.]. **VFOAT** LCGC International. **VAT** Liquid Chromatography, Gas Chromatography International. Vol. 1 (Nov./Dec. 1987)-. Trade Publication. English. Twelve times a year. $174.55. Advanstar Communications Inc., 131 West First Street, Duluth MN 55802. **Tel** (218)723-9477, (800)346-0085, FAX (218)723-9437. **(Subscription address:** Advanstar Communications / UK Subscriptions, Park West Sealand Road, Chester CH1 4RN United Kingdom. **Tel** 011 44 1244 378888.) **ED** Kari Hallenburg. Index available. cum. index. **Bk Rev. Ad Acc. Circ:** 20,000 (ctrl). available on microfilm from University Microfilms International (UMI).
Desc: Targeted for users and specifiers of chromatographic equipment in Western Europe.
Ind/Abst Food Sci. Technol. Abstr.; Mass Spect. Bull. (?-?).

LC QD79.C454 L55 **ISSN** 0306-2104
DD 544/.924
UK
NLM Z 5524 C55 L767

LIQUID CHROMATOGRAPHY ABSTRACTS.
[Liq. chromatogr. abstr.]. Vol. 1 (July/Sept. 1973)-. English. Six times a year. PRM Science & Technology Agency Ltd, 261A Finchley Road Hampstead, London NW3 6LV United Kingdom. **Tel** 011 44 171 4310372.

ISSN 1001-5493
DD 543.0893
CH

LIZI JIAOHUAN YU XIFU.
VFOAT Ion Exchange and Absorption. (1985)-. Periodical. Chinese. Six times a year. Documents available from Article Express International, CASDDS.
Ind/Abst Chem. Abstr.; Ei Page One; Eng. Index Annu.

LC QD476 .O2 **ISSN** 0749-1581
DD 543/.0877
UK
CCC
CODEN MRCHEG
Pr Rev.

MAGNETIC RESONANCE IN CHEMISTRY : MRC.
[Magn. reson. chem.]. **VFOAT** MRC; M.R.C. Vol. 23, No. 1 (Jan. 1985)-. Academic Scholarly Publication. English. Thirteen times a year (monthly plus 1 special issue). $2245.00. John Wiley & Sons Ltd., Baffins Lane, Chichester, West Sussex PO19 1UD United Kingdom. **Tel** 011 44 1243 779777, FAX 011 44 1243 776128 BTG:JWP001, telex 86290 WIBOOKG. **(Subscription address:** John Wiley & Sons, Inc. / Philadelphia, PO Box 7247, Philadelphia PA 19170. **Tel** (212)850-6645, (800)225-5945.) **ED** H. Gunther. **Bk Rev. Ad Acc. Circ:** 1,200. available on microfilm and microfiche from University Microfilms International (UMI). Documents available from The Genuine Article, BIOSIS Document Express, CASDDS, ADONIS. ***Continues*** *OMR. Organic Magnetic Resonance, 0030-4921.*
Desc: Provides comprehensive coverage of magnetic resonance in all branches of chemistry. It also covers ESR and NQR, and papers dealing with new practical techniques.
Ind/Abst Abstr. Bull. Inst. Pap. Sci. Tech.; ADONIS; Anal. Abstr.; Biol. Abstr. (1991-); Chem. Abstr. (1985-); Chem. Titles; Curr. Aware. Biol. Sci., CABS; Curr. Chem. React.; Curr. Cit.; Curr. Contents Phys. Chem. Earth Sci.; Index Chem.; Mass Spect. Bull.; Nat. Prod. Updates; Ref. Upd. Deluxe Ed.; Res. Alert [Full Cov.]; Sci. Cit. Index; SCISEARCH.

LC QD95 .M29 **ISSN** 0305-9987
DD 545/.33
UK
CCC
NLM W1 MA827 **CODEN** MSSYBF
Pr Rev.

MASS SPECTROMETRY.
Added/Corp Chemical Society (Great Britain). Vol. 1 (June 1970)-. English. Irregular. Price varies per volume. Royal Society of Chemistry, Thomas Graham House, Science Park, Cambridge CB4 4WF United Kingdom. **Tel** 011 44 1223 420066, FAX 011 44 1223 423623, telex 818293 ROYAL. **(Subscription address:** Royal Society of Chemistry, Turpin Distribution Services Ltd., Blackhorse Road, Letchworth, Hertfordshire SG6 1HN United Kingdom. **Tel** 011 44 1462 672555, FAX 011 44 1462 480947.) **ED** M. E. Rose. Documents available from CASDDS.
Ind/Abst Chem. Abstr.

LC QC451 .M38 **ISSN** 0025-4738
DD 539
UK
CODEN MSPBBX

MASS SPECTROMETRY BULLETIN.
See Chemistry and Chemicals-Abstracting, Bibliographies and Statistics.

LC QC454.M3 M365 **ISSN** 0277-7037
DD 543/.0873
US
CCC
NLM W1 MA827M **CODEN** MSRVD3
Pr Rev.

MASS SPECTROMETRY REVIEWS.
[Mass spectrom. rev.]. Vol. 1, No. 1 (Spring 1982)-. Academic Scholarly Publication. English. Six times a year. $396.00. John Wiley & Sons, Inc., 605 Third Avenue, New York NY 10158-0012. **Tel** (212)850-6000, (212)850-6645, FAX (212)850-6088, telex 12-7063. **(Subscription address:** John Wiley & Sons / UK, Baffins Lane, Chichester, West

Sussex PO19 1UD United Kingdom. **Tel** 011 44 1243 779777, FAX 011 44 243 776128, telex 86290 WIBOOKG.) **ED** Maurice M Bursey and Nicco N M Nibbering. **Ad Acc. Circ:** 500. available on microfilm and microfiche from University Microfilms International (UMI). Documents available from The Genuine Article, BIOSIS Document Express, CASDDS, ADONIS.
Desc: Presents review articles on current research literature on mass spectrometry instrumentation and application in chemistry, biology, environmental science, medicine, agriculture, engineering, and physics.
Ind/Abst ADONIS; Anal. Abstr.; Biol. Abstr.; Chem. Abstr.; Curr. Cit.; Curr. Contents Phys. Chem. Earth Sci.; GeoRef; Index Sci. Rev. [Full Cov.]; Mass Spect. Bull.; Res. Alert [Full Cov.]; Sci. Cit. Index; SCISEARCH.

ISSN 0025-5270
GW
CCC
CODEN MOBHAK

MATERIAL UND ORGANISMEN; BEIHEFT. Vol. 1 (1966)-. Periodical. German. Four times a year. Price varies. Duncker und Humblot Verlag, Postfach 410329, D-12113 Berlin Germany. **Tel** 011 49 30 79000612, 011 49 30 79000613. **ED** J.N.R. Ruddick. **Bk Rev. Ad Acc. Circ:** 500. Documents available from CASDDS.
Ind/Abst Chem. Abstr.

LC QD271 .M46 **ISSN** 0076-6941
DD 543.8
US
CCC
NLM W1 ME9617 **CODEN** MBANAA

METHODS OF BIOCHEMICAL ANALYSIS. [Methods biochem. anal.]. Vol. 1 (1954)-. English. Irregular. $79.95. John Wiley & Sons Inc / New Jersey, 1 Wiley Drive, Somerset NJ 08875. **Tel** (800)225-5945, (908)469-4400. **(Subscription address:** John Wiley & Sons / UK, Baffins Lane, Chichester, West Sussex PO19 1UD United Kingdom. **Tel** 011 44 1243 779777, FAX 011 44 243 776128, telex 86290 WIBOOKG.) **ED** D Glick. cum. index. Documents available from The Genuine Article, BIOSIS Document Express, CASDDS.
Ind/Abst Biol. Abstr.; Chem. Abstr.; Curr. Aware. Biol. Sci., CABS; Curr. Cit.; Energy Res. Abstr. (March 1972-); Index Med.; Index Sci. Rev. [Full Cov.]; PESTDOC; Res. Alert [Full Cov.]; Sci. Cit. Index (19??-19??); SCISEARCH; Trop. Dis. Bull.

LC QD98.E4 M5 **ISSN** 0278-1727
DD 543/.08586
US
CODEN MBANDD
Pr Rev.

MICROBEAM ANALYSIS. **See** Chemistry and Chemicals-Abstracting, Bibliographies and Statistics.

LC QD71 .M53 **ISSN** 0026-3672
DD 543/.0813
AU
CCC
NLM W1 MI411 **CODEN** MIACAQ
Pr Rev.

MIKROCHIMICA ACTA (1966). (MIKROCHIMICA ACTA.). [Mikrochim. acta]. (1966)-. Academic Scholarly Publication. German (English, French and Spanish). Twelve times a year. $1209.00. Springer-Verlag Vienna, Sachsenplatz 4 6, PO Box 89, A-1201 Vienna Austria. **Tel** 011 43 1 33024150, FAX 011 43 1 330242665. **(Subscription address:** Springer-Verlag New York Inc. / North America, PO Box 2485, Journal Fulfillment, Secaucus NJ 07096. **Tel** (201)348-4033, (800)777-4643, FAX (201)348-4505.) **ED** M. Grasserbauer, F. M. Hawkridge, D. E. Leyden, A. Mizuike, T. A. Nieman, W. Simon, G. Tolg and W. Wegscheider. available on microfilm and microfiche from University Microfilms International (UMI). Documents available from The Genuine Article, BIOSIS Document Express, CASDDS. ***Continues*** *Mikrochimica et Ichnoanalytica Acta, 0369-0504.*
Desc: Covers elemental analysis, organic analysis, trace analysis, surface characterization, chromatographic analysis, molecular and atomic spectroscopic techniques, computer applications in analysis, electrochemical analysis and much more.
Ind/Abst AGRICOLA; Alum. Ind. Abstr.; Anal. Abstr.; Art Archaeol. Tech. Abstr.; Biol. Abstr.; Chem. Abstr.; Chem. Titles; Coal Abstr.; Curr. Biotechnol.; Curr. Cit.; Curr. Contents Phys. Chem. Earth Sci.; EMBASE; Eng. Mater. Abstr.; Food Sci. Technol. Abstr.; Int. Aerosp. Abstr.; Leadscan; Met. Abstr.; MINPROC; NAPRALERT; Numis. Lit.; Life Sci. Collect.; Res. Alert [Full Cov.]; Sci. Cit. Index; SCISEARCH; Soc. Sci. Cit. Index [Select. Cov.]; Vitis Vitic. Enol. Abstr.

ISSN 0076-8642
GW
UDC 543
CCC
NLM W1 MI411A **CODEN** MKASAK

MIKROCHIMICA ACTA. SUPPLEMENTUM (1966). (MIKROCHIMICA ACTA. SUPPLEMENTUM.). 1-. Academic Scholarly Publication. German (English and French). Irregular. Springer-Verlag GmbH & Company KG, Heidelberger Platz 3, D-14197 Berlin Germany. **Tel** 011 49 30 8207223, FAX 011 49 30 8214091, telex 183 319 SPBLN D. **(Subscription address:** Springer-Verlag New York Inc. / North America, PO Box 2485, Journal Fulfillment, Secaucus NJ 07096. **Tel** (201)348-4033, (800)777-4643, FAX (201)348-4505.) **ED** W Wegscheider, E S Etz, M Grasserbauer, D E Leyden, T S Ma, A Mizuike, W Simon and G Tolg. available on microfilm from University Microfilms International (UMI). Documents available from CASDDS.
Desc: Covers such topics as: elemental analysis, organic analysis, trace analysis, surface characterization, chromatographic analysis, molecular and atomic spectroscopic techniques, computer applications in analysis, and much more.
Ind/Abst Chem. Abstr.

US

MODERN MONOGRAPHS IN ANALYTICAL CHEMISTRY. (1981)-. Monographic series. English. Price varies per volume. Marcel Dekker Inc., 270 Madison Avenue, New York NY 10016. **Tel** (212)696-9000, (800)228-1160, FAX (212)685-4540, telex 421419. **(Subscription address:** Marcel Dekker Inc., PO Box 5017, Monticello NY 12701. **Tel** (800)228-1160.)
Desc: Presents topics such as analytical uses of immobilized enzymes and practical fluorescence.

LC QD79.T38 N48 **ISSN** 0386-2615
JA
CODEN NESOD2

NETSUSOKUTEI. **VFOAT** Calorimetry and Thermal Analysis. Academic Scholarly Publication. Japanese (summaries and/or abstracts in English). Four times a year. $75.00. Nihon Netsusokutei Gakkai, Saito Building, 2-16-13 Yushima, Bunkyo-ku Tokyo-to 113 Japan. **Tel** 011 81 3 8158514, FAX 011 81 3 8158939. **ED** Yusuke Matsuo. **Bk Rev. Ad Acc. Circ:** 1,000. Documents available from Ask*IEEE, CASDDS.
Desc: Original papers, notes, reviews, book review, and miscellaneous information of calorimetry and thermal analysis on various materials ranging organic to inorganic compounds and mixtures.
Ind/Abst Chem. Abstr.; INSPEC (Jan. 1985-).

ISSN 0916-085X
DD 545.33
JA

NIHON IYO MASU SUPEKUTORU GAKKAI KOENSHU. **VFOAT** Proceedings of the Japanese Society for Biomedical Mass Spectrometry2. (1988)-. Academic Scholarly Publication. Multiple languages. One time a year. Documents available from CASDDS. ***Continues*** *Iyo Masu Kenkyukai Koenshu, 0910-870X.*
Ind/Abst Chem. Abstr.

ISSN 0105-791X
DK
UDC 543.7/.8
CODEN NMRVD6

NYT FRA MILJSTYRELSENS REFERENCELABORAFORIUM. (NYT FRA MILJSTYRELSENS REFERENCELABORAFORIUM PA DET KEMISKE VANDANALYSEOMRADE.). [Nyt Miljstyr. referencelab.]. (197?)-. Academic Scholarly Publication. Danish (English). Irregular. Vandkvalitetsinstituttet ATV, Agern Alle 11, 2970 Hrsholm Denmark. **Tel** 45-2865211. Documents available from CASDDS.
Desc: Covers inorganic-organic analysis, water chemistry, and pollution control.
Ind/Abst Chem. Abstr.

LC S587 .O38 **ISSN** 0066-961X
DD 630/.2/43
US
CCC
NLM S 587 O32

OFFICIAL METHODS OF ANALYSIS OF THE ASSOCIATION OF OFFICIAL ANALYTICAL CHEMISTS. **Added/Corp** Association of Official Analytical Chemists. **VFOAT** Methods of Analysis, A.O.A.C.; Methods of Analysis, AOAC; AOAC Official Methods of Analysis; A.O.A.C. Official Methods of Analysis; Official Methods of Analysis. 11th Ed. (1970)-. English. Irregular (every 5-6 years). $359.00 North America; $399.00 other. AOAC International, 2200 Wilson Boulevard, Suite 400, Arlington VA 22201. **Tel** (703)522-3032, (800)379-2622, FAX (703)522-5468. **ED** Sidney Williams. Index available. **Circ:** 20,000. ***Continues*** *Official Methods of Analysis of the Association of Official Agricultural Chemists, 0884-0474.*
Desc: Methods of analysis for foods, drugs, cosmetics, disinfectants, pesticides, feeds, plants, fertilizers, preservatives, flavors, beverages, nutritional adjuncts, additives, residues, and hazardous substances, adulteration and contamination.

ISSN 0761-1749
FR
UDC 543/547

PASCAL FOLIO. F16, CHIMIE ANALYTIQUE, MINERALE ET ORGANIQUE. [PASCAL folio. F 16 Chim. anal. miner. org.]. **VFOAT** Inorganic and Organic Analytical Chemistry; Chimie Analytique Minerale et Organique. No. 1- (1986). Periodical. French (English). Ten times a year. 625.00F, 690.00F (airmail). Centre de Documentation Scientifique et Technique, Centre National de la Recherche Scientifique, 26 rue Boyer, 75971 Paris Cedex 20 France. **Tel** (1) 43 58 35 59, telex CNRSDOC 220880F. ***Continues*** *Bulletin Signaletique. 172, Chimie Analytique, 0240-8473.*

ISSN 0148-9054
US
CCC
CODEN PSPED9

PRACTICAL SPECTROSCOPY. [Pract. spectrosc.]. (1976)-. Academic Scholarly Publication. English. Irregular. Price varies per volume. Marcel Dekker Inc., 270 Madison Avenue, New York NY 10016. **Tel** (212)696-9000, (800)228-1160, FAX (212)685-4540, telex 421419. **(Subscription address:** Marcel Dekker Inc., PO Box 5017, Monticello NY 12701. **Tel** (800)228-1160.) **ED** E. Roland Menzel. Documents available from CASDDS.
Desc: Covers various aspects of spectroscopy. Topics include x-ray spectrometry and mass spectrometry.
Ind/Abst Chem. Abstr.; Curr. Cit.; GeoRef.

ISSN 0370-2677
RU
CODEN PYAKAP

PROBLEMY ANALITICHESKOI KHIMII. [Probl. anal. him.]. **Added/Corp** Nauchnyi Sovet po Analiticheskoi Khimii (Akademiia Nauk SSSR) Institut Geokhimii i Analiticheskoi Khimii im. V.I. Vernadskogo. (1970)-. Academic Scholarly Publication. Russian. Irregular. Price varies per volume. Izdatelstvo Nauka / Akademiia Nauk, (Publishing House of the Russian Academy of Sciences), Leninskii Porspekt 14, 117901 Moscow Russia. **Tel** 011 95 9542153, FAX 011 95 9382144, telex 411964. Documents available from CASDDS. ***Continues*** *Trudy Komissii po Analiticheskoi Khimii.*
Ind/Abst Chem. Abstr. (1970-1979).

LC QD71 .P76 **ISSN** 0136-8079
RU
CODEN PSAKDK

PROBLEMY SOVREMENNOJ ANALITICESKOJ KHIMII. (PROBLEMY SOVREMENNOI ANALITICHESKOI KHIMII / LENINGRADSKII GOSUDARSTVENNYI UNIVERSITET IMENI A.A. ZHDANOVA.). [Probl. sovrem. anal. him.]. **Added/Corp** Leningradskii Gosudarstvennyi Universitet Imeni A.A. Zhdanova. (19??)-. Academic Scholarly Publication. Russian. St. Petersburg State University / Izdatelstvo Leningradskogo Universiteta, Universitetskaia Nab 7/9, 199034 St. Petersburg Russia. **Tel** 011 7 812 2189788, FAX 011 7 812 2185152, telex 121481. Documents available from CASDDS.
Ind/Abst Chem. Abstr. (1976-1983).

US

PROCEEDINGS OF THE ... ASMS CONFERENCE ON MASS SPECTROMETRY AND ALLIED TOPICS. **Main/Conf** AMS Conference on Mass Spectrometry and Allied Topics. **Added/Corp** American Society for Mass Spectrometry. 36th (June 5-10, 1988)-. English. ***Continues*** *ASMS Conference on Mass Spectrometry and Allied Topics. ASMS Conference on Mass Spectrometry and Allied Topics.*
Ind/Abst Curr. Cit.

LC QD130 .C44
DD 546.3
UK
CODEN PCCODW

PROCEEDINGS OF THE ... CHEMISTS' CONFERENCE. **Added/Corp** British Iron and Steel Research Association. (19??)-. Academic Scholarly Publication. English. One time a year. Documents available from CASDDS.
Ind/Abst Bioeng. Abstr.; Chem. Abstr.

ISSN 1063-0708
US

PROCESS ANALYTICAL CHEMISTRY SOURCE BOOK. (PROCESS ANALYTICAL CHEMISTRY SOURCE BOOK: THE PACS BOOK.). **Added/Corp** InfoScience Services, Inc. **VFOAT** PACS Book. (1992)-. Periodical. English. Two times a year. $40.00. Infoscience Services, Inc., 3000 Dundee Road, Suite 313, Northbrook IL 60062.

LC QD71 .P86 **ISSN** 0555-781X
KN
CODEN PUHWAY

PUNSOK HWAHAK. [Punsok hwahak]. **VFOAT** Analytical Chemistry. (19??)-. Academic Scholarly Publication. Korean. W0.50. Kwahak, Paekkwa Sajon Chulpansa, Changgyong 2-dong Sosong-kuyok, Pyongyang-si North Korea. Documents available from CASDDS.
Ind/Abst Chem. Abstr. (1962-1982).

ISSN 0212-0569
SP

QUIMICA ANALITICA SALAMANCA. [Quim. anal. Salamanca]. **VFOAT** Quimica Analitica (Bellaterra, Barcelona). (1982)-. Periodical. Multiple languages. Four times a year. $119.85. Springer-Verlag Iberica SA, Avinguda Diagonal 468 4 C, 08006 Barcelona Spain. **Tel** 011 34 3 4157620, 011 34 3 4157621. **(Subscription address:** Springer-Verlag New York Inc. /

North America, PO Box 2485, Journal Fulfillment, Secaucus NJ 07096. **Tel** (201)348-4033, (800)777-4643, FAX (201)348-4505.)
Ind/Abst Curr. Cit.

LC QD96.M3 R36 **ISSN** 0951-4198
DD 543/.0873/05 UK
CCC
NLM W1; RA485H **CODEN** RCMSEF

RAPID COMMUNICATIONS IN MASS SPECTROMETRY. (RAPID COMMUNICATIONS IN MASS SPECTROMETRY : RCM.). [Rapid commun. mass spectrom.]. **VFOAT** RCM. Vol. 1, No. 1 (May 1987)-. Academic Scholarly Publication. English. Fifteen times a year. $1395.00. John Wiley & Sons Ltd., Baffins Lane, Chichester, West Sussex PO19 1UD United Kingdom. **Tel** 011 44 1243 779777, FAX 011 44 1243 776128 BTG:JWP001, telex 86290 WIBOOKG. **(Subscription address:** John Wiley & Sons, Inc. / Philadelphia, PO Box 7247, Philadelphia PA 19170. **Tel** (212)850-6645, (800)225-5945.) **ED** J. H. Beynon, G. Brenton, and A. G. Marshall. available on microfilm and microfiche from University Microfilms International (UMI). Documents available from The Genuine Article, Ask*IEEE, CASDDS.
Desc: Publishes original research ideas and results on all aspects of the science of gas-phase ions. Contributions may be theoretical or practical in nature. Also provides a forum for discussion and news. Regular items include letters, information on events, manufacturers announcements and book reviews.
Ind/Abst Anal. Abstr.; Chem. Abstr.; Curr. Aware. Biol. Sci., CABS; Curr. Cit.; Curr. Contents Phys. Chem. Earth Sci.; Index Med. (May 1987-); INSPEC (Oct. 1990-); Mass Spect. Bull. (?-?); Res. Alert [Full Cov.]; SCISEARCH.

ISSN 0896-7695
DD 543 US
CCC

REFEREE (ARLINGTON, VA.), THE. (THE REFEREE.). [Referee]. **Added/Corp** Association of Official Analytical Chemists. (19??)-. Periodical. English. Twelve times a year. Comes with Association of Official Analytical Chemists membership. AOAC International, 2200 Wilson Boulevard, Suite 400, Arlington VA 22201. **Tel** (703)522-3032, (800)379-2622, FAX (703)522-5468.

ISSN 0511-7003
DD 542 AT

REPORT OF THE GOVERNMENT CHEMICAL LABORATORIES. **Main/Corp** Government Chemical Laboratories (Western Australia). **VFOAT** Annual Report of the Government Chemical Laboratories. (19??)-. English. Government Printer / Chemical Laboratories, Harvest Terra, Perth Western Australia, 6000 Australia. **Tel** 011 61 9 3255544. ctrl circ.
Desc: Covers applied analytical chemistry.

LC QD71 .R44 **ISSN** 0048-752X
DD 543/.005 IS
CODEN RACYAX

REVIEWS IN ANALYTICAL CHEMISTRY. [Rev. anal. chem.]. Vol. 1 (1971)-. Periodical. English. Irregular. $230.00. Freund Publishing House Ltd., PO Box 35010, 61 Nachmani Street, Tel Aviv 61350 Israel. **Tel** 011 972 3 5628540, FAX 011 972 3 5628538. **(Subscription address:** Freund Publishing House Ltd., Suite 500, Chesham House 150 Regent Street, London W1R 5FA United Kingdom. **Tel** 011 44 178 172811, FAX 011 972 3 615335.) **ED** M. Zangen. Documents available from CASDDS.
Ind/Abst Alum. Ind. Abstr.; Anal. Abstr.; Chem. Abstr.; EMBASE; GeoRef; Mass Spect. Bull.; Met. Abstr.

LC TP1 .R372 **ISSN** 0370-694X
BL
CODEN RQIRAI

REVISTA DE QUIMICA INDUSTRIAL. **VFOAT** Quimica Industrial. (1932)-. Periodical. Portuguese. Twelve times a year. Documents available from CASDDS.
Ind/Abst Chem. Abstr.; Chem. Bus. Bull.; Chem. Bus. NewsBase (1986-); Chem. Bus. Update.

US

SADTLER STANDARD CARBON-13 NMR SPECTRA. **Main/Corp** Sadtler Research Laboratories. **VFOAT** Sadtler Standard Spectra. 1976-. Monographic series. English. Two times a year. Price varies per volume. Sadtler Research Laboratories Inc., 3316 Spring Garden Street, Philadelphia PA 19104. **Tel** (215)382-7800. **ED** Marie Scandone. Index available. available on microfilm; available on microfiche.
Desc: Continuing and expanding collection of carbon-13 NMR reference spectra used for identifying unknown chemical compounds. Throughly indexed for rapid location of data.

US

SADTLER ULTRA VIOLET STANDARD SPECTRA. **Main/Corp** Sadtler Research Laboratories. (19??)-. English. One time a year. $958.50. Sadtler Research Laboratories Inc., 3316 Spring Garden Street, Philadelphia PA 19104. **Tel** (215)382-7800. **ED** Marie Scandone. available on microfilm.
Desc: Continuing and expanding collection of ultraviolet reference spectra used for identifying unknown chemical compounds. Throughly indexed for rapid location of data.

LC QD71 .S37 **ISSN** 0300-9963
DD 543/.005 UK
NLM W1 SE32N

SELECTED ANNUAL REVIEWS OF THE ANALYTICAL SCIENCES. [Sel. annu. rev. anal. sci.]. **Added/Corp** Society for Analytical Chemistry. Vol. 1 (1971)-(19??). English. Irregular. Royal Society of Chemistry, Thomas Graham House, Science Park, Cambridge CB4 4WF United Kingdom. **Tel** 011 44 1223 420066, FAX 011 44 1223 423623, telex 818293 ROYAL. **(Subscription address:** Royal Society of Chemistry, Turpin Distribution Services Ltd., Blackhorse Road, Letchworth, Hertfordshire SG6 1HN United Kingdom. **Tel** 011 44 1462 672555, FAX 011 44 1462 480947.)

LC QD71
DD 543 US
Pr Rev.

•**SELECTED TOPICS IN MASS SPECTROMETRY.** (1994)-. Monographic series. English. Irregular. Price varies. Plenum Press, 233 Spring Street, New York NY 10013-1578. **Tel** (212)620-8000, (800)221-9369, FAX (212)463-0742, (212)807-1047, telex 23/421139. **ED** David H. Russell.

LC QD79.C4 S39 **ISSN** 1000-8713
DD 543/.089 CC
NLM W1; SE122 **CODEN** SEPUER

SEPU. (SE PU.). [Sepu]. **Added/Corp** Chung-Kuo Hua Hsueh Hui (Peking, China). **VFOAT** Chinese Journal of Chromatography. (19??)-. Academic Scholarly Publication. Chinese. Six times a year. $70.00. Zhongguo Kexueyuan / Dalian Huaxue Wuli Yanjiusuo, Chinese Academy of Sciences, Dalian Institute of Chemical Physics, 161 Zhongshan Lu Dalian, Liaoning 116012 People's Republic of China. **Tel** 3631841. **ED** Lu Peichang. **Circ:** 5,000. Documents available from BLDSC, CASDDS.
Desc: Contains information from chromatographic analysis.
Ind/Abst Chem. Abstr. (1985-); Curr. Cit.; Nutr. Abstr. Rev., Ser. B, Live Feeds and Feed.; Nutr. Abstr. Rev., Ser. A, Hum. Exp.; Plant Grow. Reg. Abstr.; Rev. Agric. Entomol.; Sug. Indus. Abstr.

ISSN 0542-8645
JA
CODEN SHIBAK
TITLE CHANGE

SHITSURYO BUNSEKI. (SHITSURYO BUNSEKI = MASS SPECTROSCOPY.). [Shitsuryo bunseki]. **Added/Corp** Nihon Shitsuryo Bunseki Gakkai. Shitsuryo Bunseki Gakkai. **VFOAT** Mass Spectroscopy. (1953)-(1993). Academic Scholarly Publication. Japanese (English). Nihon Shitsuryo Bunseki Gakkai, (Mass Spectroscopy Soc. of Japan), 18-10 Koraku 2 Chome, Bunkyoku Tokyo 112 Japan. **(Subscription address:** Maruzen Company Ltd., PO Box 5050, Import & Export Department, Tokyo 100 31 Japan. **Tel** 011 81 3 32789224.) Documents available from Ask*IEEE, CASDDS. ***Continued by*** *Journal of the Mass Spectrometry Society of Japan, 1340-8097.*
Ind/Abst Anal. Abstr.; Art Archaeol. Tech. Abstr.; Chem. Abstr.; Energy Res. Abstr.; INSPEC (1968-); Mass Spect. Bull.

LC QD63.E88 S65 **ISSN** 0736-6299
DD 660/.284248 US
CCC
CODEN SEIEDB
Pr Rev.

SOLVENT EXTRACTION AND ION EXCHANGE. [Solv. extr. ion exch.]. **VFOAT** Solvent Extraction & Ion Exchange. Vol. 1, No. 1 (1983)-. Academic Scholarly Publication. English. Six times a year. $750.00. Marcel Dekker Inc., 270 Madison Avenue, New York NY 10016. **Tel** (212)696-9000, (800)228-1160, FAX (212)685-4540, telex 421419. **(Subscription address:** Marcel Dekker Inc., PO Box 5017, Monticello NY 12701. **Tel** (800)228-1160.) **ED** E. Philip Horwitz, James R. Fair, David J. Pruett. available on microfiche. Documents available from Article Express International, The Genuine Article, CASDDS.
Desc: An international journal that provides current, comprehensive coverage of advances and developments in all areas of solvent extraction and ion exchange studies. Publishes original research articles, notes of work in progress, critical reviews, letters to the editor, as well as reviews of new books, a bibliography section, and notices of meetings. This journal offers readers the information they need to keep at the forefront of their specialty. Major topics discussed include absorption and extraction chromatography, separations using liquid membranes and related techniques, separation materials, and underlying principles.
Ind/Abst Alum. Ind. Abstr.; Anal. Abstr.; Chem. Abstr (1983-); Chem. Titles; Curr. Cit.; Curr. Contents Phys. Chem. Earth Sci.; Ei Page One; Eng. Index Annu.; Met. Abstr.; Pollut. Abstr. Indexes; Proc. Chem. Eng.; Res. Alert [Full Cov.]; Sci. Cit. Index; SCISEARCH; Soils Fert.; Theor. Chem. Eng.

LC QD95 .S636 **ISSN** 0584-8555
DD 544/.6 UK
CCC
NLM W1 SP316 **CODEN** SPIOAD
Pr Rev.

SPECTROSCOPIC PROPERTIES OF INORGANIC AND ORGANOMETALLIC COMPOUNDS. **Added/Corp** Chemical Society (Great Britain). **VFOAT** Inorganic and Organometallic Compounds. Vol. 1 (1967)-. English. Irregular. £167.50. Royal Society of Chemistry, Thomas Graham House, Science Park, Cambridge CB4 4WF United Kingdom. **Tel** 011 44 1223 420066, FAX 011 44 1223 423623, telex 818293 ROYAL. **(Subscription address:** Royal Society of Chemistry, Turpin Distribution Services Ltd., Blackhorse Road, Letchworth, Hertfordshire SG6 1HN United Kingdom. **Tel** 011 44 1462 672555, FAX 011 44 1462 480947.) **ED** G. Davidson. Documents available from CASDDS.
Desc: Includes nuclear magnetic resonance spectroscopy; nuclear quadruple resonance spectroscopy; rotational spectroscopy; characteristic vibrations of compounds of main-group elements; vibrational spectra of transition element compounds; vibrational spectra of some co-ordinated ligands; mossbauer spectroscopy; gas-phase molecular structures determined by electron diffraction.
Ind/Abst Chem. Abstr.; Curr. Cit.; GeoRef.

US

STANDARD GRATING SPECTRA. **Main/Corp** Sadtler Research Laboratories. **VFOAT** Standard Infrared Grating Spectra. Vol. 1; 1966-. English. One time a year. Sadtler Research Laboratories Inc., 3316 Spring Garden Street, Philadelphia PA 19104. **Tel** (215)382-7800. **ED** Marie Scandone. Index available. available on microfilm; available on microfiche.
Desc: Continuing and expanding collection of infrared grating reference spectra used for identifying unknown chemical compounds. Thoroughly indexed for rapid location of data.

US

STANDARD INFRARED PRISM SPECTRA. **Main/Corp** Sadtler Research Laboratories. **VFOAT** Sadtler Standard Spectra; Infrared Prism Spectra. (1956)-. Periodical. English. Irregular. Sadtler Research Laboratories Inc., 3316 Spring Garden Street, Philadelphia PA 19104. **Tel** (215)382-7800. **ED** Marie Scandone. Index available. available on microfilm.
Desc: Continuing and expanding collection of infrared prism spectra used for identifying unknown chemical compounds.

LC QD71 .T3 **ISSN** 0039-9140
DD 543.05 UK
CCC
NLM W1 TA472 **CODEN** TLNTA2
Pr Rev.

TALANTA (OXFORD). (TALANTA.). [Talanta]. Vol. 1 (July 1958)-. Academic Scholarly Publication. English (Greek, Modern). Twelve times a year. $1111.00 The Americas; £745.00 other. Pergamon Press, An Imprint of Elsevier Science Ltd., The Boulevard, Langford Lane, Kidlington, Oxford OX5 1GB United Kingdom. **Tel** 011 44 1865 843000, 011 44 1865 843699, FAX 011 44 1865 843010. **(Subscription address:** Elsevier Science Ltd. / Oxford Fulfillment Centre, PO Box 800, Kidlington OX5 1DX United Kingdom. **Tel** 011 44 865 843355.) **ED** G. Christian, E. Hansen. available on microfilm and microfiche from University Microfilms International (UMI); available on microfiche from the publisher; available on an online database from Elsevier Electronic Subscriptions (EES). Documents available from The Genuine Article, BIOSIS Document Express, Ask*IEEE, CASDDS.
Desc: Provides a forum for the publication of original research papers, preliminary communications, and reviews in all branches of pure and applied analytical chemistry.
Ind/Abst AGRICOLA; Alum. Ind. Abstr.; Anal. Abstr.; Aqualine Abstr.; AQUAREF; Biol. Abstr.; Chem. Abstr.; Chem. Titles; Coal Abstr.; Curr. Aware. Biol. Sci., CABS; Curr. Cit.; Curr. Contents Phys. Chem. Earth Sci.; Curr. Titles Electrochem.; Dairy Sci. Abstr.; EMBASE; Eng. Mater. Abstr.; Food Sci. Technol. Abstr.; GeoRef; INSPEC (Oct. 1969-); Met. Abstr.; MINPROC; Nutr. Abstr. Rev., Ser. B, Live Feeds and Feed.; Nutr. Abstr. Rev., Ser. A, Hum. Exp.; Life Sci. Collect.; Res. Alert [Full Cov.]; Rev. Agric. Entomol.; Rev. Plant Pathol.; Rice Abstr.; Sci. Cit. Index; SCISEARCH; Soils Fert.; Sug. Indus. Abstr.; Surf. Treat. Technol. Abstr.

ISSN 0167-9244
NE
CODEN TIACD4

TECHNIQUES AND INSTRUMENTATION IN ANALYTICAL CHEMISTRY. [Tech. instrum. anal. chem.]. (1978)-. Academic Scholarly Publication. English. Irregular. Price varies per volume. Elsevier Science Publishers BV, PO Box 211, 1000 AE Amsterdam Netherlands. **Tel** 011 31 20 4853641, 011 31 20 4853642, FAX 011 31 20 4853598. Documents available from BIOSIS Document Express, CASDDS.
Ind/Abst Biol. Abstr.; Chem. Abstr.; Curr. Cit.

ISSN 0163-9595
US
CODEN TASYD2
THERMAL ANALYSIS APPLICATION STUDY. [Therm. anal. appl. study]. **Added/Corp** Perkin-Elmer Corporation. (1972)-. Academic Scholarly Publication. English. Irregular. Price varies per volume. The Perkin-Elmer Corporation, Main Avenue MS 131, Norwalk CT 06856. **Tel** (203)762-1000, FAX (203)762-6037. Documents available from CASDDS.
Ind/Abst Chem. Abstr.

LC QD272.S6 T66 **ISSN** 0093-2221
DD 543/.08 US
NLM W1 TO539L **CODEN** TCNSD7
TOPICS IN CARBON-13 NMR SPECTROSCOPY. **VAT** Topics in Carbon-13 Nuclear Magnetic Resonance Spectroscopy. (1974)-. Academic Scholarly Publication. English. John Wiley & Sons, Inc., 605 Third Avenue, New York NY 10158-0012. **Tel** (212)850-6000, (212)850-6645, FAX (212)850-6088, telex 12-7063. **(Subscription address:** John Wiley & Sons / UK, Baffins Lane, Chichester, West Sussex PO19 1UD United Kingdom. **Tel** 011 44 1243 779777, FAX 011 44 243 776128, telex 86290 WIBOOKG.) **ED** G C Levy. Documents available from CASDDS.
Ind/Abst Chem. Abstr.

LC QD71 .T75 **ISSN** 0167-2940
DD 543/.005 NE
CCC
TRAC, TRENDS IN ANALYTICAL CHEMISTRY. (TRENDS IN ANALYTICAL CHEMISTRY : TRAC.). [TrAC, Trends anal. chem.]. **VFOAT** TRAC. Vol. 1 (1981/82)-. Academic Scholarly Publication. English. Ten times a year (1 volume, includes Library compendium). Fl804.00 (add Fl111.00 for postage). Elsevier Science Publishers BV, PO Box 211, 1000 AE Amsterdam Netherlands. **Tel** 011 31 20 4853641, 011 31 20 4853642, FAX 011 31 20 4853598. **ED** D. Coleman. Documents available from The Genuine Article, CASDDS.
Desc: Articles are concise overviews of new developments in analytical chemistry, and are aimed at helping analytical chemists and other users of analytical techniques explore and orient themselves in fields outside of their particular specialization.
Ind/Abst Chem. Abstr.; Res. Alert [Full Cov.]; Sci. Cit. Index; SCISEARCH.

LC QD71 **ISSN** 0165-9936
DD 543/.005 NE
UDC 543 **CCC**
NLM W1 TR3402M **CODEN** TTAEDJ
Pr Rev.
TRAC, TRENDS IN ANALYTICAL CHEMISTRY (PERSONAL EDITION). (TRENDS IN ANALYTICAL CHEMISTRY (PERSONAL EDITION).). [TrAC, Trends anal. chem.]. **VFOAT** TrAC. (1981)-. Academic Scholarly Publication. English. Eleven times a year (1 volume). $761.00. Elsevier Science Publishers BV, PO Box 211, 1000 AE Amsterdam Netherlands. **Tel** 011 31 20 4853641, 011 31 20 4853642, FAX 011 31 20 4853598. Index available. cum. index. **Bk Rev. Ad Acc.** available on microfilm and microfiche from University Microfilms International (UMI); available on an online database from Elsevier Electronic Subscriptions (EES). Documents available from Article Express International, BIOSIS Document Express, Ask*IEEE, CASDDS, ADONIS.
Desc: A publication comprising short critical reviews and news highlighting current trends and developments in all areas of analytical chemistry.
Ind/Abst ADONIS; Alum. Ind. Abstr.; Anal. Abstr.; Art Archaeol. Tech. Abstr.; Bioeng. Abstr.; Biol. Abstr.; Chem. Abstr.; Curr. Biotechnol.; Curr. Cit.; Curr. Contents Phys. Chem. Earth Sci.; Ei Page One; EMBASE; Eng. Mater. Abstr.; Eng. Index Annu. [Select. Cov.]; Food Sci. Technol. Abstr.; GeoRef; INSPEC (Nov. 1981-); Int. Pharm. Abstr. (199?-); Mass Spect. Bull.; Met. Abstr.; World Ceram. Abstr.

US
TRC SPECTRAL DATA--INFRARED. English. $499.00. TRC - Thermodynamics Research Center Data Distribution, Texas A&M University, Tees Business Office, College Station TX 77843-3124. **Tel** (409)845-5981, FAX (409)847-8590, telex 510-892-7689 TXINTLPRO COSN. Index available. cum. index. **Circ:** 150.
Desc: Collection of spectroscopic data.

US
TRC SPECTRAL DATA--ULTRAVIOLET. English. One time a year. $499.00. TRC - Thermodynamics Research Center Data Distribution, Texas A&M University, Tees Business Office, College Station TX 77843-3124. **Tel** (409)845-5981, FAX (409)847-8590, telex 510-892-7689 TXINTLPRO COSN. Index available. cum. index. **Circ:** 150.
Desc: Collection of spectroscopic data.

DD 543.082 NE
Pr Rev.
WILSON AND WILSON'S COMPREHENSIVE ANALYTICAL CHEMISTRY. **VFOAT** Comprehensive Analytical Chemistry. Vol. 3 (1975)-. Academic Scholarly Publication. English. Irregular. Elsevier Science Publishers BV, PO Box 211, 1000 AE Amsterdam Netherlands. **Tel** 011 31 20 4853641, 011 31 20 4853642, FAX 011 31 20 4853598. **ED** G Svehla. ***Continues*** *Comprehensive Analytical Chemistry, 0069-8024.*

LC QC481 .X16 **ISSN** 0049-8246
DD 543/.085 UK
CCC
CODEN XRSPAX
Pr Rev.
X-RAY SPECTROMETRY. (X-RAY SPECTROMETRY : XRS.). [X-ray spectrom.]. **Added/Corp** Microbeam Analysis Society. **VFOAT** XRS. Vol. 1, No. 1 (Jan. 1972)-. Periodical. Multiple languages (English, French and German). Six times a year (Feb., Apr., June, Aug., Oct., Dec.). $995.00. John Wiley & Sons Ltd., Baffins Lane, Chichester, West Sussex PO19 1UD United Kingdom. **Tel** 011 44 1243 779777, FAX 011 44 1243 776128 BTG:JWP001, telex 86290 WIBOOKG. **(Subscription address:** John Wiley & Sons, Inc. / Philadelphia, PO Box 7247, Philadelphia PA 19170. **Tel** (212)850-6645, (800)225-5945.) **ED** John V. Gilfrich. **Ad Acc. Circ:** 1,500. available on microfilm and microfiche from University Microfilms International (UMI). Documents available from The Genuine Article, Ask*IEEE, CASDDS.
Desc: The forum for the rapid publication of papers dealing with the theory and application of x-ray spectrometry. It covers advances in techniques, methods and equipment, news and events, and provides a platform for the discussion of more sophisticated x-ray analytical methods.
Ind/Abst Alum. Ind. Abstr.; Anal. Abstr.; Ceram. Abstr. (19??-); Chem. Abstr.; Chem. Titles; Coal Abstr.; Curr. Cit.; Curr. Contents Phys. Chem. Earth Sci.; Dairy Sci. Abstr.; GeoRef; INSPEC (April 1979-); Met. Abstr.; Res. Alert [Full Cov.]; Sci. Cit. Index; SCISEARCH; Soc. Sci. Cit. Index [Select. Cov.]; World Ceram. Abstr.

LC TA401 .Z3 **ISSN** 0321-4265
RU
CODEN ZVDLAU
ZAVODSKAJA LABORATORIJA. (ZAVODSKAIA LABORATORIIA.). [Zavod. lab.]. **Added/Corp** Soviet Union. Narodnyi Komissariat Chernoi Metallurgii. Soviet Union. Ministerstvo Chernoi Metallurgii. Soviet Union. Gosudarstvennyi Nauchno-Tekhnicheskii Komitet. Soviet Union. Gosudarstvennyi Komitet po Koordinatsii Nauchno-Issledovatelskikh Rabot. Soviet Union. Gosudarstvennyi Komitet po Chernoi i Tsvetnoi Metallurgii. Soviet Union. Ministerstvo Tsvetnoi Metallurgii. Nauchno-Tekhnicheskoe Obshchestvo Chernoi Metallurgii. Tsentralnoe Pravlenie. Vol. 1, (Jan. 1932)-. Periodical. Russian (summaries and/or abstracts in English and German; table of contents in English and German). Twelve times a year. $133.00. Izdatelstvo Metallurgiia, 2-I Obydenskii Per. 14 G-34, Moscow Russia. **(Subscription address:** Victor Kamkin, 4956 Boiling Brook Parkway, Rockville MD 20852. **Tel** (301)881-5973.) Index available. cum. index. **Bk Rev. Ad Acc.** Documents available from Ask*IEEE, CASDDS.
Ind/Abst Acoust. Abstr.; Alum. Ind. Abstr.; Anal. Abstr.; Chem. Abstr.; Eng. Mater. Abstr.; INSPEC (1969-); Met. Abstr.; World Alum. Abstr.

LC QD71 .Z5 **ISSN** 0044-4502
RU
CCC
NLM W1 ZH414 **CODEN** ZAKHA8
ZURNAL ANALITICHESKOI HIMII. (ZHURNAL ANALITICHESKOI KHIMII.). [Z. anal. him.]. **Added/Corp** Akademiia Nauk SSSR. **VFOAT** Journal of Analytical Chemistry. Vol. 1 (1946)-. Academic Scholarly Publication. Russian (summaries and/or abstracts in English; table of contents in English). Twelve times a year. $299.00. Izdatelstvo Nauka / Akademiia Nauk, (Publishing House of the Russian Academy of Sciences), Leninskii Porspekt 14, 117901 Moscow Russia. **Tel** 011 95 9542153, FAX 011 95 9382144, telex 411964. **(Subscription address:** East View Publications Inc., 3020 Harbor Lane North, Suite 110, Minneapolis MN 55447. **Tel** (800)477-1005, (612)550-0961, FAX (612)559-2931.) cum. index. available on microfiche (from Microcard Editions). Documents available from CASDDS.
Ind/Abst Abstr. Bull. Inst. Pap. Sci. Tech.; Anal. Abstr.; Ceram. Abstr.; Chem. Abstr.; Coal Abstr.; Curr. Biotechnol.; EMBASE; Energy Res. Abstr.; Food Sci. Technol. Abstr.; GeoRef; Life Sci. Collect.; Vitis Vitic. Enol. Abstr.

CHEMICAL TECHNOLOGY

LC HS9650 **ISSN** 1356-5389
DD 338.4766095 UK
•**ACN. ASIAN CHEMICAL NEWS.** [ACN, Asian chem. news]. **VFOAT** Asian Chemical News. (1994)-. Trade Publication. English. Fifty-two times a year. $677.64. Reed Business Publishing / West Sussex, England, Perrymount Road, Haywards Heath, West Sussex RH16 3DH United Kingdom. **Tel** 011 44 1444 441212, FAX 011 44 1444 445447. **(Subscription address:** ACN International Subscription Office, PO Box 302, Haywards Heath, West Sussex RH16 3YY United Kingdom.) **ED** Mary Heathcote.
Desc: Covers prices on bulk chemicals as well as market forecasts for the industry.

LC TS1300 .F34 **ISSN** 0323-7648
DD 668.9/05 GW
CCC
CODEN ACPODY
Pr Rev.
ACTA POLYMERICA. **See** Fabrics and Textile Industries.

ISSN 1070-9592
US
CCC
•**ADHESIVES & SEALANTS INDUSTRY.** **VFOAT** Adhesives and Sealants Industry. (1994)-. Trade Publication. English. Six times a year. $27.00. Business News Publishing Company, 755 West Big Beaver Road, Suite 1000, Troy MI 48084. **Tel** (810)362-3700, FAX (810)362-0317, telex 230295.
Desc: Serves manufacturers, applicators and suppliers of adhesives and sealants. Comprehensive coverage includes new technologies, new classes and derivatives of adhesives, new self-curing polyurethanes and bonding of new materials.

ISSN 0896-422X
DD 667 US
CCC
ADVANCED COATINGS & SURFACE TECHNOLOGY. [Adv. coat. surf. technol.]. **VFOAT** Advanced Coatings and Surface Technology. Vol. 1, No. 1 (Jan. 1988)-. Periodical. English. Twelve times a year. $590.00. Technical Insights Inc., PO Box 1304, Fort Lee NJ 07024-9967. **Tel** (201)568-4744, FAX (201)568-8247, telex 425900 SWIFT UI. **ED** Irv Schwartz. available on an online database from DIALOG; available on diskette.
Desc: Interprets developments ranging from traditional coatings processes to chemical vapor deposition and ion beam methods. Offers comprehensive, interdisciplinary analysis of those that have true commercial potential.
Ind/Abst PTS Newsl. Database [Full Txt.]; World Surf. Coat. Abstr.

ISSN 0270-773X
US
NLM W3 AD241 **CODEN** ACMGBR
ADVANCES IN CHROMATOGRAPHY (HOUSTON). (ADVANCES IN CHROMATOGRAPHY.). [Adv. chromatogr.]. **Added/Corp** University of Houston. Chromatography Symposium. (19??)-. Monographic series. English. Price varies per volume. Marcel Dekker Inc., 270 Madison Avenue, New York NY 10016. **Tel** (212)696-9000, (800)228-1160, FAX (212)685-4540, telex 421419. **(Subscription address:** Marcel Dekker Inc., PO Box 5017, Monticello NY 12701. **Tel** (800)228-1160.) Documents available from CASDDS. ***Continues*** *Advances in Gas Chromatography.*
Desc: This is an ongoing series. Each title has a different subject.
Ind/Abst Chem. Abstr.

ISSN 0360-4446
US
AEROSOL AND PRESSURIZED PRODUCTS SURVEY. **Added/Corp** Chemical Specialties Manufacturers Association. (195?)-. English. Chemical Specialties Manufacturers Association, 1001 Connecticut Avenue, Washington DC 20036.
Ind/Abst Predicasts Forecasts.

LC TP244.A3 A335 **ISSN** 0278-6826
DD 660.2/94515 US
CCC
CODEN ASTYDQ
Pr Rev.
AEROSOL SCIENCE AND TECHNOLOGY. (AEROSOL SCIENCE AND TECHNOLOGY : THE JOURNAL OF THE AMERICAN ASSOCIATION FOR AEROSOL RESEARCH.). [Aerosol sci. tech.]. **Added/Corp** American Association for Aerosol Research. Vol. 1, No. 1 (1982)-. Academic Scholarly Publication. English. Eight times a year (2 volumes). $716.00. Elsevier Science Publishing Company Inc, Madison Square Station, PO Box 882, New York NY 10159-0882. **Tel** (212)633-3950, FAX (212)633-3990. **ED** P. Hopke. **Bk Rev. Ad Acc. Circ:** 1,000. available on microfilm and microfiche from University Microfilms International (UMI); available on an online database from Elsevier Electronic Subscriptions (EES). Documents available from Article Express International, The Genuine Article, Ask*IEEE, CASDDS, Documents on Demand. ***Absorbed*** *Atomisation and Spray Technology, 0266-3481.*
Desc: Covers theoretical and experimental investigations of aerosol and closely related phenomena.
Ind/Abst Air Pollut. Titles; Anal. Abstr. (1983-); Chem. Abstr.; Chem. Hazards Ind.; Coal Abstr.; Curr. Cit.; Curr. Contents Eng. Comput. Technol.; Ei Page One; EMBASE; Energy Inf. Abstr.; Eng. Index Annu.; Environ. Abstr.; Environ. Period. Bibliogr. (?-?); Fluid Abstr., Civil Eng.; Fluid Abstr. Proc. Eng.; FLUIDEX; Geogr. Abstr. Phys. Geogr.; Health Saf. Sci. Abstr.; INIS Atomindex [Micro.]; INSPEC (1983-); Int. Aerosp. Abstr. (1983-); Lab. Hazards Bull.; Life Sci. Collect.; Pollut. Abstr. Indexes;

Chemistry and Chemicals —Chemical Technology

Proc. Chem. Eng.; Res. Alert [Full Cov.]; Sci. Cit. Index; SCISEARCH; Theor. Chem. Eng.; World Surf. Coat. Abstr.

LC TP244.A3 A32   **ISSN** 0941-0295
DD 660/.294515   GW
   CCC
AEROSOL SPRAY REPORT : INTERNATIONAL PERIODICAL FOR THE AEROSOL AND SPRAY INDUSTRY.
Added/Corp FEA. Vol. 30, No. 7 (July 1991)-. Trade Publication. English (French and German). Eleven times a year. $246.00. Dr. Alfred Huethig Verlag GmbH, Postfach 102869, D-69018 Heidelberg Germany. **Tel** 011 49 6221 489281, FAX 011 49 6221 489279. **(Subscription address:** Huethig Publishing Inc., 29 Macintosh Drive, Oxford CT 06478. **Tel** (203)881-2647.**)** Documents available from Article Express International. **Continues** Aerosol Report, 0001-9313.
Ind/Abst Curr. Cit.; Ei Page One; Eng. Index Annu. [Select. Cov.].

LC HD9482 .U6A45   **ISSN** 1053-0673
DD 338.7/66/02573   US
ALLIANCE ALERT. CHEMICALS/MATERIALS/ AGRICULTURE. [Alliance alert, Chem./mater./agric.]. **Added/Corp** Venture Economics, Inc. **VFOAT** Chemicals/Materials/Agriculture; Chemicals/Materials/Agriculture, Industry Alliances. **VAT** Chemicals, Materials, Agriculture, Industry Alliances. Vol. 1, Issue 1 (Apr. 1990)-. Periodical. English. Four times a year. $395.00 (1 industry), $635.00 (2 industries), $855.00 (3 industries), $975.00 (4 industries), $1095.00 (5 industries). Securities Data Company, 40 West 57th Street, 11th Floor, New York NY 10019. **Tel** (212)765-5311. available on an online database (files 16,636/Full-Text) from DIALOG.
Ind/Abst PROMT [Full Txt.]; PTS Newsl. Database [Full Txt.].

   SP
ANALES DE QUIMICA. SERIE A, QUIMICA FISICA Y QUIMICA TECNICA.
See Chemistry and Chemicals-Physical and Theoretical Chemistry.

   ISSN 1063-5246
   UK
ANALYTICAL METHODS AND INSTRUMENTATION. (1993)-. English. Six times a year. $345.00. John Wiley & Sons Ltd., Baffins Lane, Chichester, West Sussex PO19 1UD United Kingdom. **Tel** 011 44 1243 779777, FAX 011 44 1243 776128 BTG:JWP001, telex 86290 WIBOOKG. **(Subscription address:** John Wiley & Sons, Inc. / Philadelphia, PO Box 7247, Philadelphia PA 19170. **Tel** (212)850-6645, (800)225-5945.**) ED** H. Michael Widmer.
Desc: International attempt to unite relevant academic research with real-life problem-solving. Stresses the interrelationship between these two pillars of modern analytical science and technology.

LC HD9650.1 .U54a
DD 382/.45/6600212   US
ANNUAL BULLETIN OF TRADE IN CHEMICAL PRODUCTS. BULLETIN ANNUEL DU COMMERCE DES PRODUITS CHIMIQUES. EZHEGODNYI BIULLETEN EVROPEISKOI TORGOVLI KHIMICHESKMI PRODUKTAMI. See Industry and Production.

LC HD9576.I4 I53a
DD 354.540082/42   II
ANNUAL REPORT / GOVERNMENT OF INDIA, MINISTRY OF PETROLEUM AND CHEMICALS, DEPARTMENT OF CHEMICALS & PETROCHEMICALS. See Petroleum and Natural Gas.

   ISSN 0960-2739
DD 338.47660959   UK
   CCC
ASIA-PACIFIC CHEMICALS. [Asia-Pac. chem.]. (19??)-. Periodical. English. Ten times a year. $135.00 US and Canada; £75.00 other. Reed Business Publishing / West Sussex, England, Perrymount Road, Haywards Heath, West Sussex RH16 3DH United Kingdom. **Tel** 011 44 1444 441212, FAX 011 44 1444 445447.
Ind/Abst Infomat Int. Bus.

   AT
AVCA DIRECTORY : MEMBERS, OFFICERS, ACTIVITIES, AND SECRETARIAT. Main/Corp Agricultural & Veterinary Chemicals Association of Australia. **VAT** Agricultural & Veterinary Chemicals Association of Australia Directory. (19??)-. Directory. English. One time a year. Agricultural and Veterinary Chemicals Association of Australia Ltd, Private Bag 938, Sydney New South Wales 2059 Australia. **Tel** 011 61 02 9637 690.

   ISSN 1000-5668
DD 660   CC
BEIJING HUAGONG XUEYUAN XUEBAO ZIRAN KEXUE BAN. (BEIJING HUAGONG XUEYUAN XUEBAO.). **VFOAT** Journal of Beijing Institute of Chemical Technology. (1974)-. Periodical. Chinese. Four times a year. Beijing Huagong Xueyuan / Beijing Institute of Chemical Technology, Xuebao Bianjibu, 15 Beisanhuan Donglu, Beijing 100029, People's Republic of China. **ED** Fu Jufu. Documents available from CASDDS.
Ind/Abst Chem. Abstr.

LC TJ163.25.A8 I57a
DD 621.042/072094   AT
BIENNIAL RESEARCH REPORT. See Energy.

LC QR97.X46 B56   **ISSN** 0923-9820
DD 628.4   NE
   CCC
NLM W1; BI662S   **CODEN** BIODEG
Pr Rev.
BIODEGRADATION (DORDRECHT). See Environmental Issues-Pollution and Waste Management.

   ISSN 1081-8693
DD 660   US
●BIOPHOTONICS INTERNATIONAL.
[Bioiphoton. int.]. (Jan./Feb. 1995)-. Periodical. English. Six times a year. $57.00. Laurin Publishing Company Inc, PO Box 4949, Pittsfield MA 01202. **Tel** (413)499-0514, FAX (413)442-3180, telex 232-055 ASAS. **Continues** Biophotonics.

LC QH301
DD 574   NE
Pr Rev.
BIOTECHNOLOGIE. See Biology.

LC TP670 .I636a   **ISSN** 0304-5196
   PO
BOLETIM - INSTITUTO DO AZEITE E PRODUTOS OLEAGINOSOS. See Food and Food Industry.

   ISSN 0778-5097
   BE
UDC 662.6/.9
BRANDSTOFFEN BRUSSEL. [Brandstoffen Bruss.]. **VFOAT** Vakblad van de Belgische Federatie der Handelaars in Brandstoffen. (1990)-. Periodical. Dutch (French). Ten times a year. $89.18. Belgium Federatie der Brandstoffenhandelaar, Leon Lepage STR 4, B-1000 Brussels Belgium. **Tel** 011 32 2 5024200, FAX 011 32 2 5025446. **Ad Acc**. ctrl circ.
Desc: A journal on combustibles.

LC QD1 .B82
DD 540/.5   RM
BULETINUL STIINTIFIC SI TEHNIC AL INSTITUTULUI POLITEHNIC TRAIAN VUIA TIMISOARA. SERIA CHIMIE.
Added/Corp Institutul Politehnic "Traian Vuia" Timisoara. **VFOAT** Buletinul Stiintific Si Technic Al Institutului Politehnic Traian Vuia Timisoara. Chimie; Seria Chimie. (19??)-. Periodical. English (French, German and Romanian). **(Subscription address:** Ilexim Press Department, PO Box 1, 136-1-137, Bucharest, Romania. **Tel** 011 40 1 173836.**)** Documents available from Ask*IEEE.
Ind/Abst INSPEC (1978-).

   ISSN 1011-3924
   ET
BULLETIN OF THE CHEMICAL SOCIETY OF ETHIOPIA. [Bull. Chem. Soc. Ethiop.]. (1987)-. Bulletin. English. Two times a year. Chemical Society of Ethiopia, PO Box 32934, Addis Ababa Ethiopia. **Tel** 011 251 1 121201, FAX 011 251 1 551241. Documents available from The Genuine Article, CASDDS.
Ind/Abst Chem. Abstr.; NAPRALERT; Res. Alert.

LC TP156.C8 B89
DD 660.2/84   US
BUYER'S GUIDE TO REACTIVE CURE SYSTEMS, UV-IR-EB. VFOAT Reactive Cure Systems, UV-IR-EB. (19??)-. Directory. English. One time a year (with monthly newsletters). $166.00 US; $186.00 other. CAPTAN Associates Inc, PO Box 504, Brick NJ 08724. **Tel** (908)840-1244. **ED** C Bluestein and J Salser. Index available. **Bk Rev. Ad Acc. Circ:** 500. **Continues** Buyer's Guide to Reactive Cure Systems, UV-IR-EB, 0734-7200.
Desc: Buyer's guide to radiation processing: equipment, materials and services - commercial services.

   ISSN 0890-1813
DD 664   US
   CODEN CSSWE4
CA SELECTS: ARTIFICIAL SWEETENERS. See Chemistry and Chemicals-Abstracting, Bibliographies and Statistics.

   ISSN 1040-7197
DD 660   US
   CODEN CAMSE6
CA SELECTS: MEMBRANE SEPARATION. See Chemistry and Chemicals-Abstracting, Bibliographies and Statistics.

   ISSN 0895-5867
DD 660   US
   CODEN CSNMEH
CA SELECTS: NONLINEAR OPTICAL MATERIALS. See Chemistry and Chemicals-Abstracting, Bibliographies and Statistics.

   ISSN 0778-645X
   BE
UDC 663.4
CAFE REVUE (NEDERLANDSE ED.).
[Cafe Rev. Ned. ed.]. (1991)-. Periodical. Dutch. Six times a year. $41.05. Evolution Media Group, Vlasstraat 17, 8710 Wielsbeke Belgium. **Tel** 011 32 56 607333.
Continues Buitenwipper, 0771-9442.

LC TP1 .C615   **ISSN** 0823-5228
DD 660/.05   CN
   CCC
   CODEN CCHNEE
CANADIAN CHEMICAL NEWS. [Can. chem. news]. **Added/Corp** Chemical Institute of Canada. Chemical Society for Chemical Engineering. Chemical Society for Chemical and Biochemical Technology. **VFOAT** Actualite Chimique Canadienne; CCN/ACC; CCN ACC. Vol. 36, No. 1 (Jan. 1984)-. Academic Scholarly Publication. English (French). Ten times a year. 40.01Can$. Chemical Institute of Canada, 130 Slater Street/Suite 550, Ottawa Ontario K1P 6E2 Canada. **Tel** (613)232-6252, FAX (613)235-5862. available on an online database (file 648/Full-Text) from DIALOG. Documents available from CASDDS, Documents on Demand. **Continues** Chemistry in Canada, 0009-3114.
Ind/Abst AQUAREF; Chem. Abstr. (1984-); Coal Abstr.; Curr. Cit.; EMBASE; Energy Inf. Abstr.; Environ. Abstr.; F&S Index Plus Text, Int. [Select. Cov.]; INIS Atomindex [Micro.]; MINPROC; PROMT; Trade Ind. ASAP [Full Txt.]; Trade Ind. Index [Full Txt.].

   ISSN 1045-8565
DD 661   US
   CODEN CBUFEE
CAS BIOTECH UPDATES. COMMERCIAL FERMENTATION. [CAS biotechnol. updates, Commer. ferment.]. **Added/Corp** American Chemical Society. Chemical Abstracts Service. **VFOAT** Commercial Fermentation. **VAT** Chemical Abstracts Service Biotech Updates. Commercial Fermentation. (Jan. 8, 1990)-. English. Twenty-six times a year. $220.00. Chemical Abstracts Service, (Subsidiary of The American Chemical Society), 2540 Olentangy River Road, PO Box 3012, Columbus OH 43210-0012. **Tel** (614)447-3731, (800)753-4227, FAX (614)447-3751. **(Subscription address:** Chemical Abstracts Service, Customer Service Department, PO Box 3012, Columbus OH 43210. **Tel** (800)848-6538, (614)447-3600.**)**

   ISSN 1040-7103
DD 660   US
   CODEN CUPSEP
CAS BIOTECH UPDATES. PRODUCT PURIFICATION & SEPARATION. [CAS biotech updates, Prod. purif. sep.]. **Added/Corp** American Chemical Society. Chemical Abstracts Service. **VFOAT** CAS Biotech Updates. Product Purification and Separation; Product Purification and Separation; Product Purification & Separation. **VAT** Chemical Abstracts Service Biotech Updates. Product Purification & Separation. (Jan. 9, 1989)-. English. Twenty-six times a year. $220.00. Chemical Abstracts Service, (Subsidiary of The American Chemical Society), 2540 Olentangy River Road, PO Box 3012, Columbus OH 43210-0012. **Tel** (614)447-3731, (800)753-4227, FAX (614)447-3751. **(Subscription address:** Chemical Abstracts Service, Customer Service Department, PO Box 3012, Columbus OH 43210. **Tel** (800)848-6538, (614)447-3600.**)**

LC TP1 .C317   **ISSN** 0009-0352
DD 641.631   US
   CCC
   CODEN CECHAF
Pr Rev.
CEREAL CHEMISTRY. [Cereal chem.]. **Added/Corp** American Association of Cereal Chemists. Vol. 1 (Jan. 1924)-. Periodical. English. Six times a year. $225.00. American Association of Cereal Chemists, 3340 Pilot Knob Road, St. Paul MN 55121. **Tel** (612)454-7250, FAX (612)454-0766, telex 6502439657. **ED** Vladimir Rasper. cum. index. **Circ:** 3,000. available on microfilm and microfiche from University Microfilms International (UMI). Documents available from The Genuine Article, BIOSIS Document Express, CASDDS. **Continues** Journal of the American Association of Cereal Chemists, 0095-9847.
Desc: Contains scientific research papers dealing with raw materials, processes, and products with cereals, oil seeds and pulses. Articles discuss analytical procedures, technological tests and fundamental research in these industries.
Ind/Abst AgBiotech News Inf.; AGRICOLA [Full Cov.];

Agric. Eng. Abstr. (1991-); Anal. Abstr.; Bibliogr. Agric.; BioBusiness; Biodeter. Abstr. (1991-); Biol. Agric. Index; Biol. Abstr.; Chem. Abstr.; Crop Physiol. Abstr.; Curr. Aware. Biol. Sci., CABS; Curr. Biotechnol.; Curr. Cit.; Curr. Contents Agric. Biol. Environ. Sci.; Dairy Sci. Abstr.; EMBASE; Field Crop Abstr.; Food Sci. Technol. Abstr.; Foods Adlibra; Grass. Forage Abstr.; Irr. Drain. Abstr.; Leadscan; Maize Abstr.; Nutr. Abstr. Rev., Ser. B, Live Feeds and Feed.; Nutr. Abstr. Rev., Ser. A, Hum. Exp.; Nutr. Res. Newsl.; Life Sci. Collect.; Plant Breed. Abstr.; Plant Genet. Resour. Abstr.; Postharvest News Inf.; Poult. Abstr.; Res. Alert [Full Cov.]; Rev. Med. Vet. Mycology; Rev. Plant Pathol.; Rice Abstr.; Sci. Cit. Index; SCISEARCH; Seed Abstr.; Soils Fert.; Sorghum Mill. Abstr.; Soyabean Abstr.; Sug. Indus. Abstr.; Weed Abstr.; Wheat Barley Trit. Abstr.

LC TP12 .C4425
DD 660/.029/4 US

CHEM SOURCES INTERNATIONAL. **Added/Corp** Directories Publishing Company. **VFOAT** CSI. (1986)-. English. Every 2 years. $255.00. Chemical Sources International, Inc., PO Box 1824, Clemson SC 29633. **Tel** (803)646-7840, FAX (803)646-9938. **ED** Dale Krohn. Index available (free). cum. index. **Circ:** 500 (ctrl). available on an online database from STN International (Math) Database.
Desc: Provides chemical source information of the world chemical industry to chemical buyers world-wide. Lists 100,000 chemicals of all classifications produced or supplied by over 800 chemical firms from 60 countries.

LC TP202 .C494 **ISSN** 0736-6019
DD 660/.029/4 US
CCC

CHEMCYCLOPEDIA. [Chemcyclopedia]. **Added/Corp** American Chemical Society. **VFOAT** Chemcyclopedia of Chemicals. Vol. 1 (1982-83)-. English. One time a year. $60.00. American Chemical Society, 1155 Sixteenth Street Northwest, Washington DC 20036. **Tel** (800)333-9511, (800)227-5558, (614)447-3776, FAX (202)447-3671. **(Subscription address:** American Chemical Society / Ohio, Department L 0011, Columbus OH 43268-0011. **)**
Desc: Provides users and purchasers of chemicals with a unique source of information helpful in making buying decisions.

ISSN 0835-0183
DD 338.4/7661/00971 CN

CHEMICAL AND CHEMICAL PRODUCTS INDUSTRIES (1986). (CHEMICAL AND CHEMICAL PRODUCTS INDUSTRIES = INDUSTRIES CHIMIQUES.). [Chem. chem. prod. ind.]. **Added/Corp** Statistique Canada. Section du Recensement des Manufactures. Statistique Canada. Division de l'Industrie. Statistique Canada. Section de l'Enquete Annuelle des Manufactures. **VFOAT** Industries Chimiques; Autres Industries Chimiques. (1985)-. French (English). One time a year. 38.00Can$ Canada; $46.00 US; $54.00 other. Statistics Canada Publications Sales and Services, R.H. Coats Building 6th Floor, Ottawa Ontario K1A 0T6 Canada. **Tel** (613)951-5078, (800)267-6677, FAX (613)951-1584, telex 053-3585. ***Formed by the union of*** *Paint and Varnish Industry, 0833-7489; Miscellaneous Chemical Industries (Final), 0700-0464; Pharmaceuticals, Cleaning Compounds and Toilet Preparations, 0319-9061* ***and*** *Industrial and Agricultural Chemical Products, 0319-907X.*

LC TP1 .C35 **ISSN** 0009-2347
DD 660.5 US
CCC
NLM W1 CH245 **CODEN** CENEAR
Pr Rev.

CHEMICAL & ENGINEERING NEWS. (CHEMICAL AND ENGINEERING NEWS : "NEWS EDITION" OF THE AMERICAN CHEMICAL SOCIETY.). [Chem. eng. news]. **Added/Corp** American Chemical Society. **VFOAT** Chemical & Engineering News; Chemical and Engineering News; C & E News; C and E News; C & EN. Vol. 20, No. 1 (Jan. 1, 1942)-. Periodical. English. Fifty-one times per year. $132.00. American Chemical Society, 1155 Sixteenth Street Northwest, Washington DC 20036. **Tel** (800)333-9511, (800)227-5558, (614)447-3776, FAX (202)447-3671. **(Subscription address:** American Chemical Society / Ohio, Department L 0011, Columbus OH 43268-0011. **)** **ED** Michael Heylin. Index Available Received separately--bound from publisher. **Bk Rev. Ad Acc. Circ:** 139,000 (ctrl). available on microfiche from the publisher; available on microfilm and microfiche from University Microfilms International (UMI). Documents available from The Genuine Article, BIOSIS Document Express, UMI Article Clearinghouse, CASDDS, Documents on Demand. ***Continues*** *News Edition (American Chemical Society), 0097-6415.*
Desc: Covers chemical news through short articles, longer trend articles and features on topics of broad interest. ACS policies and activities are also presented.
Ind/Abst ABI/INFORM Glob. Ed.; ABI/INFORM [Computer File] (June 1973-Dec. 1978); Abstr. Bull. Inst. Pap. Sci. Tech.; Abstr. BioCommer.; Acad. Ind. [Computer File] (1992-); Acad. Search; ACM Guide Comput. Lit.; AGRICOLA [Select. Cov.]; Alum. Ind. Abstr.; Anal. Abstr.; Appl. Sci. Technol. Index; Art Archaeol. Tech. Abstr.; BioBusiness (1988-); Biol. Abstr.; Bus. Index (1985-); Bus. Period. Index; Bus. Source Plus; Bus. Source; Ceram. Abstr. (19??-); Chem. Abstr.; Chem. Bus. Bull.; Chem. Bus. NewsBase (1985-); Chem. Bus. Update; Chem. Hazards Ind.; Chem. Ind. Notes; Coal Abstr.; Comput. Rev.; Curr. Biotechnol.; Curr. Chem. React.; Curr. Cit.; Curr. Index J. Educ.; Curr. Titles Electrochem.; Ei Page One; Energy Inf. Abstr.; Eng. Mater. Abstr.; Environ. Abstr.; EP Collect.; Expand. Acad. Index (1992-); F&S Index Plus Text, Int. [Select. Cov.]; Foods Adlibra; Gas Abstr.; Gen. BusinessFile (1985-); Gen. Period. Index (1985-); Homework Help.; Ind. Hyg. Dig.; INFO-SOUTH Abstr.; Lab. Hazards Bull.; Lit. Pat. Abstr., Oilfield Chem. (1954-); Lit. Abstr., Catal. Zeol.; Lit. Abstr., Health Environ.; Lit. Abstr., Pet. Refin. Petrochem.; Lit. Abstr., Pet. Substit.; Lit. Abstr., Transp. Storage; MasterFile FullTEXT 1000; MasterFile FullTEXT 350; MasterFile FullTEXT 650; MasterFile FullTEXT (July 1993-); Met. Abstr.; Methods Organ. Synth.; NAPRALERT; Newsp. Period. Abstr. (1986-); OCLC; PESTDOC; Proc. Chem. Eng.; PROMT; Res. Alert [Full Cov.]; Risk Abstr.; Saf. Health Work; Sci. Cit. Index; SCISEARCH; Soc. Sci. Cit. Index [Select. Cov.]; Soils Fert.; Stat. Ref. Index; Telebase; Theor. Chem. Eng.; Trade Ind. Index (1981-); Vocat. Search; Wilson Bus. Abstr.; World Surf. Coat. Abstr.

LC TP1 .A6 **ISSN** 0360-7275
DD 660.6273 US
CCC
NLM W1 C264 **CODEN** CEPRA8
Pr Rev.

CHEMICAL ENGINEERING PROGRESS. [Chem. eng. prog.]. **Added/Corp** American Institute of Chemical Engineers. **VFOAT** CEP. Vol. 43, No. 1 (Jan. 1947)-. Trade Publication. English. Twelve times a year. $85.00. American Institute of Chemical Engineers, 345 East 47th Street, New York NY 10017. **Tel** (212)705-7663, (800)242-4363, FAX (212)705-8400. **ED** Agnes Dubberly. Index available (bound in Dec. issue). **Ad Acc. Circ:** 58,037. available on microfilm and microfiche from University Microfilms International (UMI). Documents available from Article Express International, The Genuine Article, Ask*IEEE, Petroleum Abstracts Document Delivery Service, CASDDS, Documents on Demand. ***Continues*** *American Institute of Chemical Engineers. Transactions of the American Institute of Chemical Engineers, 0096-7408.*
Desc: Contains up-to-date information on the latest advances in the chemical process and related industries.
Ind/Abst Abstr. Bull. Inst. Pap. Sci. Tech.; Abstr. BioCommer. (1973-); AGRICOLA [Select. Cov.]; Agric. Eng. Abstr. (1991-); Alum. Ind. Abstr.; Appl. Sci. Technol. Index; BioBusiness; Bioeng. Abstr.; Chem Inform; Chem. Abstr.; Chem. Bus. Bull.; Chem. Bus. NewsBase (1986-); Chem. Bus. Update; Chem. Hazards Ind.; Coal Abstr.; Curr. Biotechnol.; Curr. Cit.; Curr. Contents Eng. Comput. Technol.; Ei Page One (1984-); EMBASE; Energy Res. Abstr.; Eng. Index Annu.; Environ. Abstr.; F&S Index Plus Text, Int. [Select. Cov.]; Fluid Abstr., Civil Eng.; Fluid Abstr. Proc. Eng.; FLUIDEX (1973-); Gas Abstr.; Health Saf. Sci. Abstr.; Hortic. Abstr.; HTFS Dig.; INIS Atomindex [Micro.]; INSPEC (1968-); Int. Aerosp. Abstr.; Lab. Hazards Bull.; Lit. Pat. Abstr., Oilfield Chem. (1954-); Lit. Abstr., Catal. Zeol.; Lit. Abstr., Health Environ.; Lit. Abstr., Pet. Refin. Petrochem.; Lit. Abstr., Pet. Substit.; Lit. Abstr., Transp. Storage; Met. Abstr.; MINPROC; PESTDOC; Pet. Abstr.; Pollut. Abstr. Indexes; Postharvest News Inf.; PROMT; Res. Alert [Full Cov.]; Risk Abstr.; Saf. Health Work; Sci. Cit. Index; SCISEARCH; Soc. Sci. Cit. Index [Select. Cov.]; Soils Fert. (1988-).

ISSN 0009-2533
II
CODEN CHERDB

CHEMICAL ERA. [Chem. era]. Vol. 9, No. 10 (Nov. 1974)-. Periodical. English. Pandeya Publications, Block F 105C New Alipore, Calcutta 700053 India. Documents available from CASDDS.
Ind/Abst Chem. Abstr.

LC TP151 .B35
DD 660.831 US

CHEMICAL FORMULARY : A COLLECTION OF VALUABLE, TIMELY, PRACTICAL COMMERCIAL FORMULAE AND RECIPES FOR MAKING THOUSANDS OF PRODUCTS IN MANY FIELDS OF INDUSTRY, THE. Vol. 1 (1933)-. English. Chemical Publishing Company / New York, 80 Eighth Avenue, Room 1101, New York NY 10011. **Tel** (212)555-1950. **ED** Irene Ash and Harry Bennett. Index available. cum. index. **Bk Rev. Circ:** 5,000.

JA

CHEMICAL INDUSTRY. Vol. 1 (March 1950)-. Periodical. English. Twelve times a year. $206.00. Kagaku Kogyosha Inc., 5-9 Sendagaya 4 Chome, Shibuyaku Tokyo 151 Japan. **(Subscription address:** Maruzen Company Ltd., PO Box 5050, Import & Export Department, Tokyo 100 31 Japan. **Tel** 011 81 3 32789224.**)** **Ad Acc. Circ:** 32,000 (ctrl).
Desc: Primarily covers ultramodern techniques of petroleum, electronics, chemical technology. It reports wide divisions of special articles, from iron and steel to atomic energy.

ISSN 0045-6403
UK

CHEMICAL INSIGHT. [Chem. insight]. **VFOAT** Mike Hyde's Chemical Insight. (1972)-. English. Twenty-four times a year. $941.16. Reed Business Publishing / West Sussex, England, Perrymount Road, Haywards Heath, West Sussex RH16 3DH United Kingdom. **Tel** 011 44 1444 441212, FAX 011 44 1444 445447. **ED** M C Hyde and Nigel Davis. Index available. **Bk Rev.** ctrl circ.

UK

CHEMICAL MATTERS. **Added/Corp** World Petrochemicals Analysis Limited. **VFOAT** FertEcon Chemical Matters. (Jan. 1982)-. Newsletter. English. Twenty-six times a year. $752.93. Chem Matters Ltd. / England, 7 Schoolbell Mews, Arbery Road, London E3 5BZ United Kingdom. **Tel** 011 44 181 9813309, FAX 011 44 181 9834559. **ED** Hilfra Tandy. **Bk Rev**, (Qty: 5-6). ctrl circ. Documents available from BLDSC. ***Continues*** *World Petrochemicals, 0263-9122.*
Desc: Independent analysis reporting on international mainstream chemical industries, projects, markets, company results, and reviews; plus all major announcements.
Ind/Abst MasterFile FullTEXT (Sept. 1994-).

ISSN 1049-1015
DD 540 US

CHEMICAL MONITOR, THE. (THE CHEMICAL MONITOR : A MONTHLY NEWSLETTER DEDICATED TO CHEMICAL INSTRUMENTATION.). [Chem. monit.]. Vol. 1, No. 1 (Sept. 1985)-. Newsletter. English. Twelve times a year. $95.00. Chemical Monitor, Box 314, Lindenhurst NY 11757. **Tel** (516)669-8147. **ED** Angelo Tulumello. available on an online database from NEWSNET; (file 636/Full-Text) DIALOG; and DATA-STAR.
Ind/Abst PTS Newsl. Database [Full Txt.].

LC HD9650.3 .C49 **ISSN** 0160-6360
DD 381/.45/66002573 US

CHEMICAL NEW PRODUCT DIRECTORY, THE. **Added/Corp** Marketing Development (Firm). (1977)-. Directory. English. Marketing Development, 402 Border Road, Concord MA 01742.

LC TP159.C46 C45
DD 681/.2 JA
CODEN CSETER

CHEMICAL SENSOR TECHNOLOGY. Vol. 1 (1988)-. Monographic series. English. One time a year. Price varies per volume. Elsevier Science Publishing Company Inc, Madison Square Station, PO Box 882, New York NY 10159-0882. **Tel** (212)633-3950, FAX (212)633-3990. Documents available from CASDDS.
Desc: Series providing information on chemical detectors.
Ind/Abst Chem. Abstr.

ISSN 0945-9618
GW

•CHEMICAL TECHNOLOGY EUROPE. (1994)-. English. Six times a year. $78.00. VCH Gesellschaft GmbH, Postfach 101161, D-69451 Weinheim Germany. **Tel** 011 49 6201 606459, FAX 011 49 6201 606184. **(Subscription address:** VCH Publishers Inc., 303 Northwest 12th Avenue, Journals Department, Deerfield FL 33442. **Tel** (800)367-8249, (305)428-5566.**)**

ISSN 0009-2886
PL
CODEN CHGLAY

CHEMIK. **Added/Corp** Stowarzyszenie Inzynierow i Technikow Przemyslu Chemicznego. Poland. Ministerstwo Przemyslu Chemicznego. (1948)-. Academic Scholarly Publication. Polish (summaries and/or abstracts in English, Polish and Russian). Twelve times a year. Price on request. **(Subscription address:** Ars Polona-Ruch, PO Box 1001, Krakowskie Przedmiescie 7, 00-068 Warsaw Poland. **Tel** 011 48 22 261201.**)** Documents available from CASDDS.
Ind/Abst Chem. Abstr.

GW

•CHEMKON : CHEMIE KONKRET, FORUM FUER UNTERRICHT UND DIDAKTIK. Vol. 1 (1994)-. German. Four times a year. $55.00. VCH Gesellschaft GmbH, Postfach 101161, D-69451 Weinheim Germany. **Tel** 011 49 6201 606459, FAX 011 49 6201 606184. **(Subscription address:** VCH Publishers Inc., 303 Northwest 12th Avenue, Journals Department, Deerfield FL 33442. **Tel** (800)367-8249, (305)428-5566.**)**

LC TP1 .I612 **ISSN** 0009-2703
DD 660/.05 US
CCC
CODEN CHTEDD
Pr Rev.

CHEMTECH. [Chemtech]. **Added/Corp** American Chemical Society. **VFOAT** Chemical Technology; Chem Tech. Vol. 1 (Jan. 1971)-. Periodical. English. Twelve times a year. $430.00. American Chemical Society, 1155 Sixteenth Street Northwest, Washington DC 20036. **Tel**

(800)333-9511, (800)227-5558, (614)447-3776, FAX (202)447-3671. **(Subscription address:** American Chemical Society / Ohio, Department L 0011, Columbus OH 43268-0011. **) ED** Benjamin Luberoff. Index available (free). **Bk Rev. Ad Acc, Adv Mgr Tel** (203)256-8211. **Acid Free. Circ:** 11,000. available on microfilm and microfiche from University Microfilms International (UMI). Documents available from Article Express International, The Genuine Article, Ask*IEEE, UMI Article Clearinghouse, CASDDS, Documents on Demand. ***Continues*** *Industrial & Engineering Chemistry, 0019-7866.*
Desc: Designed to help chemists and engineers with innovative solutions to real problems. It covers many chemical specialties, from energy and materials to professional growth and catalysis.
Ind/Abst Abstr. Bull. Inst. Pap. Sci. Tech.; Acad. Search; Appl. Sci. Technol. Index; Art Archaeol. Tech. Abstr.; BioBusiness (1984-); Bioeng. Abstr.; Ceram. Abstr.; Chem Inform; Chem. Abstr.; Chem. Titles; Coal Abstr.; Curr. Biotechnol.; Curr. Cit.; Curr. Contents Eng. Comput. Technol.; Curr. Contents Phys. Chem. Earth Sci.; Curr. Titles Electrochem.; Ei Page One; EMBASE; Energy Inf. Abstr.; Energy Res. Abstr. (Sept. 1976-); Eng. Mater. Abstr.; Eng. Index Annu.; Environ. Abstr. (1984-?); EP Collect.; Expand. Acad. Index (1989-); Fluid Abstr., Civil Eng.; Fluid Abstr. Proc. Eng.; FLUIDEX (1973-); Foods Adlibra; Gen. Sci. Index; Gen. Sci. Source; Homework Help.; HTFS Dig.; INFO-SOUTH Abstr.; INSPEC (Dec. 1977-); Int. Aerosp. Abstr.; Mass Spect. Bull.; MasterFile FullTEXT 1000; MasterFile FullTEXT 350; MasterFile FullTEXT 650; MasterFile FullTEXT (July 1993-); Newsp. Period. Abstr. (1989-); OCLC; Proc. Chem. Eng.; Res. Alert [Full Cov.]; Risk Abstr. (1973-19??); Sci. Cit. Index; SCISEARCH; Soc. Sci. Cit. Index [Select. Cov.]; Soils Fert.; Telebase; Text. Technol. Dig.; Theor. Chem. Eng.; World Surf. Coat. Abstr.; World Text. Abstr.

ISSN 1001-8417
CH

CHINESE CHEMICAL LETTERS. (19??)-. English. Twelve times a year. $460.00. Chinese Chemical Society, Room 903 9th Floor, 7 Chun Chin S Road, PO Box 609, Taipei Taiwan. **Tel** 886 -2-3118464, FAX 886-2-3118464.
Ind/Abst Curr. Cit.

ISSN 0896-517X
DD 662 US
CEASED

CLEAN COAL TECHNOLOGIES. See Energy-Abstracting, Bibliographies and Statistics.

LC TP352 .U53b **ISSN** 0195-413X
DD 662.6/25 US

COAL CONVERSION. [Coal convers.]. **Added/Corp** United States. Division of Coal Conversion. United States. Dept. of Energy. Division of Fossil Fuel Processing. Cameron Engineers. Pace Company Consultants & Engineers. Rocky Mountain Division. (19??)-. Government Publication. English. One time a year. US Department of Energy, 1000 Independence Avenue SW, Washington DC 20585. **Tel** (202)586-5000, FAX (202)586-4073.

UK

COLOUR INDEX. ADDITIONS & AMENDMENTS. English. Four times a year. £72.00. Society of Dyers and Colourists, PO Box 244, 82 Gratton Road, Bradford West Yorkshire BD1 2JB United Kingdom. **Tel** 011 44 1274 725138, FAX 011 44 1274 392888, telex 51449 CHACOM G.

ISSN 0888-1227
DD 668 US
CCC

COMPOSITES & ADHESIVES NEWSLETTER, THE. [Compos. adhes. newsl.]. **VFOAT** Composites and Adhesives Newsletter. (1984)-. Newsletter. English. Four times a year (Jan., April, July, Oct.). $150.00. T/C Press, PO Box 36006, Los Angeles CA 90036. **Tel** (213)938-6923, FAX (213)938-6923. **ED** George Epstein. **Bk Rev**, (Qty: 3). **Ad Acc, Adv Mgr:** I. Stone. **Circ:** 250 (ctrl). available on an online database (files 16,636/Full-Text) from DIALOG; and DATA-STAR. Documents available from BLDSC.
Desc: Recent developments and advances composites in adhesives, applications, events, special features, alerts, and special reports.
Ind/Abst PROMT [Full Txt.]; PTS Newsl. Database [Full Txt.].

US

COMPOSITES FABRICATION. See Engineering-Materials Science.

ISSN 0074-7491
SZ
CODEN PCPIA8

COMPTE RENDU DU COLLOQUE DE L'INSTITUT INTERNATIONAL DE LA POTASSE. (PROCEEDINGS OF THE ... COLLOQUIUM OF THE INTERNATIONAL POTASH INSTITUTE.). [C. r. Colloq. Inst. int. potasse]. **Added/Corp** International Potash Institute. **VFOAT** Compte Rendu du ... Colloque de l'Institut International de la Potasse. (1967)-. Academic Scholarly Publication. English. One time a year. Documents available from BIOSIS Document Express, CASDDS. ***Continues*** *Compte Rendu du Colloque Regionale de l'Institut International de la Potasse.*
Ind/Abst Biol. Abstr. (?-1984); Chem. Abstr.; GeoRef.

ISSN 0212-7466
SP
CCC
CODEN CJCDD7

COMUNICACIONES PRESENTADAS A LAS ... JORNADAS DEL COMITE ESPANOL DE LA DETERGENCIA. [Comun. present. Jorn. Com. Esp. Deterg.]. **Added/Corp** Comite Espanol de la Detergencia. Asociacion de Investigacion de Detergentes, Tensioactivos y Afines. (19??)-. Academic Scholarly Publication. Spanish (English). One time a year. 14000ptas. Asociacion Investigaciones de Detergentes, C Jorge Girona Salgado 18-26, 08034 Barcelona Spain. **Tel** 011 34 3 2040212. Documents available from CASDDS.
Ind/Abst Chem. Abstr. (1983-); Curr. Cit.

LC TP882 .I44a **ISSN** 1079-9931
DD 666 US

•CONFERENCE RECORD / IEEE CEMENT INDUSTRY TECHNICAL CONFERENCE. [Conf. rec. - IEEE Cem. Ind. Tech. Conf.]. **Added/Corp** IEEE Industry Applications Society. Cement Industry Committee. 36th (May 29-June 2, 1994)-. English. IEEE, Institute of Electrical and Electronics Engineers Inc., 445 Hoes Lane, Piscataway NJ 08855. **Tel** (908)981-0060. ***Continues*** *IEEE Cement Industry Technical Conference. Record of Conference Papers, 1050-3854.*
Ind/Abst Curr. Cit.

LC TP200 .C67 **ISSN** 0746-9012
DD 660/.05 US
CCC
CODEN CPIPEE
CEASED

CPI PURCHASING. [CPI purch.]. **VAT** Chemical Process Industries Purchasing. (Jan. 1984)-(Dec. 1994). Trade Publication. English. Cahners Publishing Company, 249 West 17th Street, New York NY 10011. **Tel** (212)645-0067, FAX (212)242-6987. **(Subscription address:** Cahners Publishing Company / Colorado, Paid Subscription Service Center, PO Box 7610, Highlands Ranch CO 80126-7610. **Tel** (303)470-4466, FAX (303)470-4691.**)** available on microfilm and microfiche from University Microfilms International (UMI); available on an online database (file 648/Full-Text) from DIALOG. ***Formed by the union of*** *Purchasing (CPI Edition), 0746-9020* ***and*** *Chemical Purchasing, 0009-2657.*
Desc: About buying in the chemical and process industries. It provides those responsible for buying with the information most important to them: pricing, quality improvement ideas, leadtimes, price/availability forecasts, how professional purchasing departments buy and exclusive reader generated data.
Ind/Abst Chem. Bus. Bull.; Chem. Bus. NewsBase (1988-); Chem. Bus. Update; Chem. Hazards Ind.; F&S Index Plus Text, Int. [Select. Cov.]; Lab. Hazards Bull.; PROMT.

LC HD9660.G37 C79 **ISSN** 1052-0139
DD 338.4/7621564/05 US

CRYOGAS INTERNATIONAL. [CryoGas int.]. Vol. 28, No. 7 (Aug./Sept. 1990)-. Periodical. English. Ten times a year (June/July and Aug./Sept. issues combined). $150.00. J. R. Campbell and Associates Inc., 5 Militia Drive, Lexington MA 02173. **Tel** (617)862-0624, FAX (617)863-9411. **ED** Linda Grant. **Ad Acc, Adv Mgr:** Lori Frieling. **Circ:** 500. ***Continues*** *Cryogenic Information Report, 0011-2259.*
Desc: Reports advances in technology, market development and new products for the industrial gases and cryogenic equipment industries. Each issue contains articles about new gas plants, mergers and acquisitions, contract awards, organizational changes, financial results and industry statistics. Special sections feature new technology, international patent applications and US patent awards. Applications, market reports, and new products and services are highlighted. Feature articles cover topical issues and include interviews of industry executives.

LC TP873.5.D5 D5 **ISSN** 1051-9084
DD 666/.88 US
CODEN DDSTE3

DIAMOND DEPOSITIONS, SCIENCE AND TECHNOLOGY. [Diam. depos. sci. technol.]. **VFOAT** Diamond Depositions; DD:S and T; DDS&T; DD:S&T. (1990)-. Periodical. English. Twelve times a year. $177.00. Superconductivity Publications Inc., 828 Livingston Avenue, North Brunswick NJ 08902-2356. **Tel** (908)846-2002, FAX (908)846-2050. **ED** C. Jim Russell. Index available. cum. index. **Bk Rev**, (Qty: 6). **Ad Acc. Circ:** 400 (ctrl). available on diskette.
Desc: Covers the industrial synthetic diamond industry. Synthesis of diamond by low pressure and high pressure and temperature. Applications, markets, government activities and funding. Covers related materials including cubic boron nitride, SiC Si3N4 and others.

LC HD9655.C2 D57 **ISSN** 1045-5256
DD 338.7/66/002947 US

DIRECTORY OF CHEMICAL PRODUCERS, CANADA. [Dir. chem. prod. Can.]. **Added/Corp** SRI International. (19??)-. Directory. English. One time a year. SRI, 333 Ravenswood Avenue, AE210, Menlo Park CA 94025. **Tel** (415)326-6200, (415)859-3715.

LC TP1112 .D57 **ISSN** 0882-6021
DD 668.4/025/73 US

DIRECTORY OF CONSULTANTS IN PLASTICS AND CHEMICALS, THE. See Plastics.

LC TP789 .P7
DD 338.4/7/6667202573 US

DIRECTORY OF THE REFRACTORIES INDUSTRY. Added/Corp Refractories Institute. **VFOAT** Refractories Institute's Directory. (19??)-. English. Irregular. $35.00 (institute members), $75.00 (nonmembers). Refractories Institute, 301 5th Avenue 326, Pittsburgh PA 15222-2408. **Tel** (412)281-6787, FAX (412)281-6881. **ED** Paul Rozmus. ***Continues*** *Product Directory of the Refractories Industry in the United States, 0196-2388.*
Desc: Lists American, Canadian and Mexican refractories manufacturers, corporate officers, plant and sales office locations by state, and brand name by company.

US
CODEN DCHTA5

DOKLADY AKADEMII NAUK. Main/Corp Akademiia Nauk SSSR. **Added/Corp** Consultants Bureau. Consultants Bureau Enterprises. (1991)-. Periodical. English (Russian; translations available in Russian). Two times a year. $435.00 US; $510.00 other. MAIK Nauka / Interperiodica, Ulitsa Profsoyuznaia 90, Moscow 117864 Russia. **ED** A.A. Baev. available on microfilm and microfiche from University Microfilms International (UMI). Documents available from Article Express International. ***Continues*** *Akademiia Nauk SSSR, 0012-4990.*
Ind/Abst Ei Page One; Energy Res. Abstr. (July 1974-); Eng. Index Annu.; INIS Atomindex [Micro.]; Mass Spect. Bull.; Proc. Chem. Eng.; Theor. Chem. Eng.

US
CODEN DCHTA5

DOKLADY. CHEMICAL TECHNOLOGY : PROCEEDINGS OF THE ACADEMY OF SCIENCES, CHEMICAL TECHNOLOGY SECTION, DOKLADY AKADEMII NAUK. Added/Corp Consultants Bureau. Rossiiskaia Akademiia Nauk. **VFOAT** Chemical Technology. (July-Dec. 1991)-. Periodical. English (translations available in Russian). Twelve times a year. $475.00. Consultants Bureau, A Division of Plenum Publishing Corporation, 233 Spring Street, New York NY 10013. **Tel** (212)620-8000, (212)620-8466, FAX (212)463-0742, telex 23/421139. **(Subscription address:** Plenum Press Subscription Department, PO Box 730, Canal Street, Station NY 10013-1578. **Tel** (212)620-8000, (212)620-8466.**)** ***Continues*** *Akademiia Nauk SSSR. Doklady. Chemical Technology, 0012-4990.*
Ind/Abst Chem. Titles; Coal Abstr.; Energy Res. Abstr.; Eng. Index Annu.; Nucl. Sci. Abstr.

LC TP363 .D795 **ISSN** 0737-3937
DD 660.2/8426 US
CCC
CODEN DRTEDQ

Pr Rev.

DRYING TECHNOLOGY. [Dry. technol.]. Vol. 1, No. 1 (1983)-. Periodical. English. Nine times a year. $895.00. Marcel Dekker Inc., 270 Madison Avenue, New York NY 10016. **Tel** (212)696-9000, (800)228-1160, FAX (212)685-4540, telex 421419. **(Subscription address:** Marcel Dekker Inc., PO Box 5017, Monticello NY 12701. **Tel** (800)228-1160.**) ED** Arun S. Mujumdar and Masanabu Hasatani. available on microfiche. Documents available from Article Express International, The Genuine Article.
Desc: This multidisciplinary journal explores the science, technology, and engineering of drying, dewatering, and related topics. Articles cover transport phenomena in porous media, heat and mass transfer in single or multiphase systems, evaporation, membrane separation, solid/liquid separation, powder technology, fluidization, agglomeration, gas-solid systems, humidity and solid moisture content measurements/control, solids mixing, handling, transport, and more.
Ind/Abst Abstr. Bull. Inst. Pap. Sci. Tech.; AGRICOLA [Select. Cov.]; Agric. Eng. Abstr. (1991-); BioBusiness; Curr. Cit.; Curr. Contents Eng. Comput. Technol.; Eng. Index Annu.; Food Sci. Technol. Abstr.; Foods Adlibra; Proc. Chem. Eng.; Res. Alert [Full Cov.]; Rice Abstr.; SCISEARCH; Soyabean Abstr.; Sug. Indus. Abstr.; Theor. Chem. Eng.

ISSN 0095-8808
DD 660 US

DU PONT MAGAZINE. [Du Pont mag.]. **Added/Corp** E.I. du Pont de Nemours & Company. **VFOAT** Du Pont; Dupont. Vol. 1 (1913)-. Periodical. English. Six times a year (Jan., Mar., May, July, Sept.,

Chemistry and Chemicals —Chemical Technology

Nov.). Free on request. Dupont Company, Room N 9942, Wilmington DE 19898. **Tel** (302)774-6671, FAX (302)774-2370. **ED** Jack Murphy. Circ: 200,000 (ctrl). *Continues Agricultural Blaster.*
Desc: Covers Dupont products put to interesting uses by the Dupont customers.
Ind/Abst Abstr. Bull. Inst. Pap. Sci. Tech.; Art Archaeol. Tech. Abstr.; Eng. Mater. Abstr.; Fluid Abstr., Civil Eng.; Fluid Abstr. Proc. Eng.; FLUIDEX (199?-); Surf. Treat. Technol. Abstr.; Text. Technol. Dig.; World Ceram. Abstr.; World Text. Abstr.

ISSN 0191-782X
US

ELECTROCHEMICAL INDUSTRIES AND TECHNOLOGY. **Added/Corp** International Electrochemical Institute. Vol. 1 (1978)-. Monographic series. English. Irregular. Price varies per volume. International Electrochemical Institute, PO Box 285, Millburn NJ 07041. **Tel** (201)273-1088.

LC TP200 .F28
JA
CODEN FNKMAU

FAIN KEMIKARU. [Fain kemikaru]. **VFOAT** Fine Chemical. Academic Scholarly Publication. Japanese. Twenty-four times a year. ¥65000. Shi Emu Shi, (CMC Co. Ltd.), Miyako Biru, 5-4 Uchikanda 1 Chome, Chiyodaku Tokyo 101 Japan. Documents available from CASDDS.
Ind/Abst Chem. Abstr.

LC TP1 .F47   ISSN 0931-5985
DD 665/.3   GW
  CCC
CODEN FWTEEG

FETT. (FETT WISSENSCHAFT TECHNOLOGIE : ORGAN DER DEUTSCHEN GESELLSCHAFT FUER FETTWISSENSCHAFT E.V. = FAT SCIENCE TECHNOLOGY.). [Fett]. **Added/Corp** Deutsche Gesellschaft fuer Fettwissenschaft. **VFOAT** Fett; Fat; Fat Science Technology. Vol. 89, No. 1 (Jan. 1987)-. Academic Scholarly Publication. German (English; summaries and/or abstracts in English and German; table of contents in English and German). Fourteen times a year. $392.28. Konradin Verlagsgruppe, Robert Kohlhammer GmbH, D70765 Leinfelden Germany. **Tel** 011 49 711 7594370, 011 49 711 7594229. available on microfilm from University Microfilms International (UMI). Documents available from The Genuine Article, BIOSIS Document Express, CASDDS. *Continues Fette, Seifen, Anstrichmittel, 0015-038X.*
Ind/Abst AGRICOLA; Anal. Abstr.; BioBusiness; Biodeter. Abstr. (1991-); Biol. Abstr. (1987-); Chem. Abstr. (1987-); Chem. Titles; Crop Physiol. Abstr.; Curr. Cit.; Curr. Contents Agric. Biol. Environ. Sci.; Dairy Sci. Abstr.; Field Crop Abstr.; Food Sci. Technol. Abstr.; Hortic. Abstr.; Leadscan; Nutr. Abstr. Rev., Ser. B, Live Feeds and Feed; Nutr. Abstr. Rev., Ser. A, Hum. Exp.; PESTDOC; Pig News Inf.; Plant Breed. Abstr.; Plant Grow. Reg. Abstr.; Postharvest News Inf.; Poult. Abstr.; Res. Alert [Full Cov.]; Sci. Cit. Index; Seed Abstr.; Soyabean Abstr.; Wheat Barley Trit. Abstr.

LC TS1548.5 .F514   ISSN 0015-0541
  US
  CCC
CODEN FICYAP

FIBRE CHEMISTRY. See Fabrics and Textile Industries.

ISSN 1065-2841
DD 338   UK

FINANCIAL TIMES INDUSTRIAL COMPANIES. CHEMICALS. VFOAT Industrial Companies. Chemicals. (1990)-. English. $246.00. Longman Group Ltd., Fourth Avenue, Longman House, Harlow Essex CM19 5SR United Kingdom. **Tel** 011 44 1279 429655, FAX 011 44 1279 431067, telex 81259. (**Subscription address:** Gale Research Co., 835 Penobscot Building, Detroit MI 48226. **Tel** (800)347-4253.) *Continues Financial Times Industrial Companies. Volume II, Chemicals.*
Desc: Contains entries on the top 500 international companies involved in the chemical, petrochemical, and pharmaceutical industries.

ISSN 0264-729X
UK

FIZIKA I KHIMIIA OBRABOTKI MATERIALOV. See Engineering-Materials Science.

ISSN 1051-0281
DD 664   US

FLAVOR AND FRAGRANCE MATERIALS. (FLAVOR AND FRAGRANCE MATERIALS : WORLDWIDE REFERENCE LIST OF MATERIALS USED IN COMPOUNDING FLAVORS AND FRAGRANCES.). [Flavor fragr. mater.]. **Added/Corp** Chemical Sources Association. **VFOAT** Flavor & Fragrance Materials. (19??)-. English. Every 2 years (every two years). $115.00. Allured Publishing Corporation, 362 South Schmale Road, Carol Stream IL 60188-2787. **Tel** (708)653-2155, FAX (708)653-2192.

LC TP156.S45 F483   ISSN 1043-2558
DD 660/.2842/05   US
  CODEN FSJOE2

FLUID / PARTICLE SEPARATION JOURNAL. (FLUID / PARTICLE SEPARATION JOURNAL : A PUBLICATION OF THE AMERICAN FILTRATION SOCIETY.). [Fluid/part. sep. j.]. **Added/Corp** American Filtration Society. **VFOAT** Fluid Particle Separation Journal; F/PSJ. **VAT** F PSJ. Vol. 1, No. 1 (Sept. 1988)-. Periodical. English. Four times a year. $75.00. American Filtration Society, PO Box 6269, Kingwood TX 77325. **Tel** (713)441-7789.
Ind/Abst Curr. Cit.

LC TS1080   ISSN 1351-4199
DD 676   UK

●**FOCUS ON PAPER CHEMICALS.** See Paper and Pulp Industry.

LC TP155   ISSN 1351-4210
DD 660   UK

●**FOCUS ON SURFACTANTS.** [Focus Surfactants]. (1993)-. Newsletter. English. Twelve times a year. £165.00. Royal Society of Chemistry, Thomas Graham House, Science Park, Cambridge CB4 4WF United Kingdom. **Tel** 011 44 1223 420066, FAX 011 44 1223 423623, telex 818293 ROYAL. (**Subscription address:** Royal Society of Chemistry, Turpin Distribution Services Ltd., Blackhorse Road, Letchworth, Hertfordshire SG6 1HN United Kingdom. **Tel** 011 44 1462 672555, FAX 011 44 1462 480947.) **ED** Gordon Hollis.
Desc: Covers developments in this diversified sector of the chemical industry.

ISSN 0887-3895
DD 664   US
  TITLE CHANGE

FOOD PLANT EQUIPMENT : FPE. See Food and Food Industry.

LC QD415.A1 F67   ISSN 0887-736X
DD 660   US
NLM W1; FO555   CCC
Pr Rev.   CODEN FCINEI

FOR FORMULATION CHEMISTS ONLY. [For formul. chem. only]. **VFOAT** Fb2CO. (1991)-. Trade Publication. English. Three times a year. $285.00. CITA International, Industrial Publ Division, PO Box 70, Phoenix AZ 85001. **Tel** (602)447-0480, FAX (602)447-0305. **ED** E. Morsy. Index available. cum. index. Ad Acc. Circ: 5,500. *Absorbed Erde International, 0735-2840 and Technitrivia, 0892-4651.*
Desc: Covers applied chemical industrial technology, formulation, chemistry, raw materials for technicians in the chemical specialty and consumer product industries.

LC TP315 .F815   ISSN 0378-3820
DD 662/.6/05   NE
  CCC
CODEN FPTEDY

FUEL PROCESSING TECHNOLOGY. See Energy.

JA
CODEN FUJAD7

FUREGURANSU JANARU : FJ = FRAGRANCE JOURNAL. [Fureguransu janaru]. **VFOAT** Fragrance Journal; FJ; F.J. (19??)-. Academic Scholarly Publication. Japanese (summaries and/or abstracts in English). Six times a year. $376.00. Fureguransu Janarusha, (Fragrance Journal Ltd.), 9-10 Iidabashi 2 Chome, Chiyodaku Tokyo 102 Japan. (**Subscription address:** Maruzen Company Ltd., PO Box 5050, Import & Export Department, Tokyo 100 31 Japan. **Tel** 011 81 3 32789224.) **ED** Fumio Shigetoshi. Circ: 7,000 (ctrl). Documents available from CASDDS.
Desc: A special journal about fragrant goods.
Ind/Abst Chem. Abstr.; Curr. Cit.

US

GAAS NEWS. (19??)-. English. Twelve times a year. GaAs News, Gallium Arsenide, 101 First Street 335, Los Altos CA 94022. **Tel** (415)948-8171.
Ind/Abst Infomat Int. Bus.

ISSN 0913-283X
DD 338.4   JA

GAS & CHEMICAL REPORTER. See Petroleum and Natural Gas.

LC WMLC 93/325   ISSN 0950-4214
  UK
  CCC

GAS SEPARATION & PURIFICATION. See Petroleum and Natural Gas.

LC TP201 .G5   ISSN 0770-920X
DD 660.6/05   BE

GIFAP BULLETIN. Bulletin. English. Four times a year. Free. GIFAP, 79A Avenue Albert Lancaster, 1180 Brussels Belgium. **Tel** 011 32 2 3756860, FAX 011 32 2 3752793, telex 62120 GIFAP B.
Desc: Published for its members, interested universities, governments and research institutes, national and international regulatory and scientific bodies and involved in topics related to agrochemicals.

LC QH   ISSN 0282-0080
DD 574.192   UK
NLM W1; GL365   CCC
Pr Rev.   CODEN GLJOEW

GLYCOCONJUGATE JOURNAL. [Glycoconjugate j.]. Vol. 1, No. 1 (1984)-. Academic Scholarly Publication. English. Six times a year. $515.00. Chapman & Hall, 2-6 Boundary Row, London SE1 8HN United Kingdom. **Tel** 011 44 171 8650066, FAX 011 44 171 5229623, telex 290164 CHAPMA G. **ED** Alan Chester, Kenneth Lloyd, Toshiaki Osawa. Documents available from The Genuine Article, CASDDS, ADONIS. *Absorbed Glycosylation and Disease.*
Desc: Publishes papers and reviews on all aspects of glycoconjugate research and glycobiology. Emphasis is on the metabolism and function of glycolipids, glycoproteins, oligo- and polysaccharides and proteoglycans. This includes the mechanisms of biosynthesis and biodegradation of glycoconjugates, their roles in health and disease and their interactions with other molecules.
Ind/Abst ADONIS; Chem. Abstr. (1984-); Curr. Aware. Biol. Sci.; CABS; Curr. Cit.; Curr. Contents Life Sci.; EMBASE; Index Med.; Ref. Upd. Deluxe Ed.; Res. Alert [Full Cov.]; Sci. Cit. Index.

ISSN 0432-0905
DD 661 668   US

GOODYEAR CHEMICAL REVIEW. Vol. 1 (?)-. English. Goodyear Tire & Rubber Company, 1144 East Market Street, Akron OH 44316. **Tel** (216)796-4143.

ISSN 1251-3865
FR
UDC 677(44)

HEBDO TEX BLANCHISSERIE, L'. See Fabrics and Textile Industries.

ISSN 0989-4985
FR
UDC 677 : 331   TITLE CHANGE

HEBDO-TEX BOULOGNE-BILLANCOURT, L'. See Fabrics and Textile Industries.

ISSN 1251-3873
FR
UDC 677(44)   TITLE CHANGE

HEBDO TEX PRESSING, LAVERIE, LIBRE-SERVCE, L'. See Fabrics and Textile Industries.

LC TP500 .H44
DD 663/.13/05   CC

HEI-LUNG-CHIANG FA HSIAO. **Added/Corp** Hei-Lung-Chiang Sheng fa Hsiao Kung Yeh ko Chi Ching Pao Chan. Hei-Lung-Chiang Sheng Ching Kung Yeh Yen Chiu So. (19??)-. Periodical. Chinese. RMB¥0.50. Hei-Lung-Chiang Sheng Ching Kung Yeh Yen Chiu So, Harbin, People's Republic of China.

ISSN 1080-1278
US

●**HIGH TEMPERATURE AND MATERIALS SCIENCE.** See Engineering-Materials Science.

ISSN 0970-1281
II
CODEN HCPBE5

HIMALAYAN CHEMICAL AND PHARMACEUTICAL BULLETIN : HCPB. [Himal. chem. pharm. bull.]. **Added/Corp** Garhwal University. **VFOAT** HCPB. Vol. 1, No. 1 (Dec. 1984)-. Bulletin. English (Hindi). One time a year. $140.00. Pauri Garhwal - Garhwal University Campus. (**Subscription address:** Prints India, 11 Darya Ganj, New Delhi 110002 India. **Tel** 011 91 11 3268645, FAX 011 91 11 3275542, telex 31-61087 PRIN-IN.) Documents available from CASDDS.
Ind/Abst Chem. Abstr. (1984-).

ISSN 0204-3998
RU
CODEN KSFPD5

HIMICESKAJA PROMYSLENNOST. SERIJA, FOSFORNAJA PROMYSLENNOST. (KHIMICHESKAIA PROMYSHLENNOST. SERIIA, FOSFORNAIA PROMYSHLENNOST.). [Him. prom., Ser. Fosforn. prom.]. **Added/Corp** Nauchno-Issledovatelskii Institut Tekhniko-Ekonomicheskikh Issledovanii (Moscow, R.S.F.S.R.) Leningradskii Gosudarstvennyi Nauchno-Issledovatelskii i Proektnyi Institut Osnovnoi Khimicheskoi Promyslennosti. **VFOAT** Seria, Fosfornaia Promyslennost; Fosfornaia Promyshlennosti. (1979)-. Academic Scholarly Publication. Russian. Six times a year. Nauchno-Issledovatelskii Institut Tekhniko-Ekonomicheskikh Issledovanii, Moscow Russia. Documents available from CASDDS. *Continues Fosfornaia Promyshlenosti.*
Ind/Abst Chem. Abstr. (1979-1981); Gas Abstr.; Int. Labour Doc.

LC TP1 .K4145a ISSN 0023-1126
RU
CODEN KHNMAO

HIMICESKOE I NEFTJANOE MASINOSTROENIE. (KHIMICHESKOE I NEFTIANOE MASHINOSTROENIE.). [Him. neft. masinostr.]. **Added/Corp** Soviet Union. GosudarstvennyÊi Komitet Khimicheskogo i Neftianogo Mashinostroeniia. (1964)-. Academic Scholarly Publication. Russian. Twelve times a year. $129.95. **(Subscription address:** East View Publications Inc., 3020 Harbor Lane North, Suite 110, Minneapolis MN 55447. **Tel** (800)477-1005, (612)550-0961, FAX (612)559-2931.**)** Documents available from CASDDS. ***Continues*** *Khimicheskoe Mashinostroenie, 0451-8314.*
Ind/Abst Alum. Ind. Abstr.; Chem. Abstr.; Energy Res. Abstr.; Met. Abstr.

ISSN 0132-7046
RU
CODEN KTTSDN

HIMIJA I TEHNOLOGIJA CELLJULOZY.
See Paper and Pulp Industry.

LC HD9579.C3 H57
US

Pr Rev.
HISTORICAL PRICING--PETROCHEMICALS.
Added/Corp DeWitt & Company. **VFOAT** HPP. (19??)-. English. One time a year (May). $850.00. Dewitt & Company Inc, 16800 Greenspoint Park, #120 N, Houston TX 77060. **Tel** (713)875-5525, (713)875-0296, FAX (713)875-0175, telex 762-854. **ED** Ed Gartner, (phone: (713)875-6620). ctrl circ.
Desc: Historical pricing for over 140 energy, petrochemical, polymer products covering markets in Western Europe, the Far East, and the United States.

LC TP1 .H845 ISSN 0253-9683
DD 660/.05 CC
CODEN HHKPDM
TITLE CHANGE

HUADONG HUAGONG XUEYUAN XUEBAO. (HUA TUNG HUA KUNG HSUEH YUAN HSUEH PAO.). [Huadong huagong xueyuan xuebao]. **Added/Corp** Hua Tung Hua Kung Hsueh Yuan. **VFOAT** Huadong Huagong Xueyuan Xuebao; Journal of East China Institute of Chemical Technology. (1957)-(1994). Academic Scholarly Publication. Chinese (summaries and/or abstracts in English). Huadong Kexue Jishu Daxue, Xuebao Bianjibu, (East China Institute of Chemical Technology), 130 Meilong lu, Shanghai 200237, People's Republic of China. **Tel** 4394280, FAX 4700834. **ED** Chen Minheng. Documents available from Article Express International, CASDDS. ***Continued by*** *Huadong Ligong Daxue Xuebao.*
Desc: Covers the latest in chemical technology.
Ind/Abst Chem. Abstr.; Ei Page One; Eng. Index Annu.; NAPRALERT.

ISSN 0952-1399
DD 661.81 UK

HYDROCARBON TECHNOLOGY INTERNATIONAL. [Hydrocarb. technol. int.]. (1987)-. Periodical. English. Four times a year (within the seasons). £55.00. Sterling Publications Ltd., 57 North Wharf Road, London W2 1XR United Kingdom. **Tel** 011 44 171 9159660, FAX 011 44 171 3338155, telex 295819. **(Subscription address:** Sterling Publications Ltd., PO Box 799, Brunel House, London W2 1XR United Kingdom. **Tel** 011 44 181 9159660.**)**
Ind/Abst Curr. Cit.

ISSN 0367-648X
JA
CODEN HYMNB7

HYOMEN. [Hyomen]. **Added/Corp** Koroido Konwakai (Japan) Hyomen Danwakai (Japan). **VFOAT** Surface. (1963)-. Periodical. Japanese. Twelve times a year. Documents available from CASDDS.
Ind/Abst Chem. Abstr.

ISSN 0915-1869
JA
CCC

HYOMEN GIJUTSU. **Added/Corp** Hyomen Gijutsu Kyokai (Japan). **VFOAT** Journal of the Surface Finishing Society of Japan. Voll. 40, No. 1 (Jan. 1989)-. Periodical. Japanese (summaries and/or abstracts in English; table of contents in English). Twelve times a year. $334.01. Hyomen Gijutsu Kyokai, c/o Kyodo Building, 2 Kanda Iwamoto-cho, Chiyoda-ku, Tokyo-to 101 Japan. Documents available from CASDDS. ***Continues*** *Kinzoku Hyomen Gijutsu, 0026-0614.*
Ind/Abst Chem. Abstr.; Curr. Cit.

ISSN 0388-5321
JA
CODEN HYKAET

HYOMEN KAGAKU. (HYOMEN KAGAKU = JOURNAL OF THE SURFACE SCIENCE SOCIETY OF JAPAN.). [Hyomen kagaku]. **Added/Corp** Nihon Hyomen Kagakkai. **VFOAT** Journal of the Surface Science Society of Japan. (1980)-. Periodical. Japanese. Four times a year. Nihon Hyomen Kagakkai, (Surface Science Society of Japan), 40-13-402 Hongo 2 Chome, Bunkyoku Tokyo 113 Japan. Documents available from CASDDS.
Ind/Abst Chem. Abstr.

ISSN 0971-457X
II
CODEN ICHTEU

•INDIAN JOURNAL OF CHEMICAL TECHNOLOGY. **Added/Corp** Council of Scientific & Industrial Research (India). Publications & Information Directorate. Indian National Science Academy. Vol. 1, No. 1 (Jan. 1994)-. Periodical. English. Six times a year. $800.00. Council of Scientific & Industrial Research, Publications & Information Director, Hillside Road, New Delhi 110012 India. **Tel** FAX 011 91 11 5731353. **(Subscription address:** Prints India, 11 Darya Ganj, New Delhi 110002 India. **Tel** 011 91 11 3268645, FAX 011 91 11 3275542, telex 31-61087 PRIN-IN.**)** ***Continues in part*** *Indian Journal of Technology, 0019-5669.*
Ind/Abst Curr. Cit.

ISSN 0712-8592
DD 338.4/7661/00971 CN

INDUSTRIAL CHEMICALS AND SYNTHETIC RESINS. [Ind. chem. synth. resins]. **Added/Corp** Statistics Canada. Manufacturing and Primary Industries Division. Statistics Canada. Industry Division. **VFOAT** Produits Chimiques Industriels et Resines Synthetiques. Vol. 25, No. 1 (Jan. 1982)-. Periodical. English (French). Twelve times a year. 72.00Can$. Statistics Canada Publications Sales and Services, R.H. Coats Building 6th Floor, Ottawa Ontario K1A 0T6 Canada. **Tel** (613)951-5078, (800)267-6677, FAX (613)951-1584, telex 053-3585. ***Continues*** *Statistics Canada. Manufacturing and Primary Industries Division. Specified Chemicals, 0410-5893.*

LC T ISSN 0300-757X
DD 600 US
CCC

INSIDE R & D : THE WEEKLY REPORT ON TECHNICAL INNOVATION. [Inside R D]. **VFOAT** Inside R and D. (1972)-. Newsletter. English. One time a week. $790.00. Technical Insights Inc., PO Box 1304, Fort Lee NJ 07024-9967. **Tel** (201)568-4744, FAX (201)568-8247, telex 425900 SWIFT UI. **ED** Charles Joslin. available on an online database from NEXIS; and (files 16,636/Full-Text) DIALOG. Documents available from BLDSC.
Desc: Research and development breakthroughs in industry, government and academic labs, with emphasis on technology transfer.
Ind/Abst Predicasts F&S Index, U. S. Annu. Ed.; PROMT [Full Txt.]; PTS Newsl. Database [Full Txt.].

LC TP669 .I58 ISSN 0897-8026
DD 665 US
CCC

NLM W1; IN8255 CODEN IFRMEC

INTERNATIONAL NEWS ON FATS, OILS AND RELATED MATERIALS. (INTERNATIONAL NEWS ON FATS, OILS, AND RELATED MATERIALS : INFORM.). [Int. news fats oils relat. mater.]. **Added/Corp** American Oil Chemists' Society. **VFOAT** INFORM. Vol. 1, No. 1 (Jan. 1990)-. Trade Publication. English. Twelve times a year. $110.00. American Oil Chemists Society, PO Box 3489, Champaign IL 61826-3489. **Tel** (217)359-2344, FAX (217)351-8091, telex 4938651 AOCS UI. **ED** Tom H. Applewhite. Index available. cum. index. **Bk Rev. Ad Acc. Circ:** 7,000. available on microfilm and microfiche from University Microfilms International (UMI); available on CD-ROM. ***Continues in part*** *Journal of the American Oil Chemists' Society, 0003-021X.*
Desc: Devoted to fundamental and practical research, production, processing, packaging and distribution in the field of fats, oils, cleaning products and related materials.
Ind/Abst AGRICOLA [Select. Cov.]; Biodeter. Abstr. (1991-); Crop Physiol. Abstr.; Curr. Cit.; Dairy Sci. Abstr.; Ei Page One; Field Crop Abstr.; Food Sci. Technol. Abstr.; Foods Adlibra (1990-); Nutr. Abstr. Rev., Ser. A, Hum. Exp.; PAIS Int. Print (1991-); Postharvest News Inf.; PROMT; Seed Abstr.; Sug. Indus. Abstr.; Weed Abstr.

LC TP500 .I9A
JA

IWATE-KEN JOZO SHOKUHIN SHIKENJO HOKOKU. **Main/Corp** Iwate-Ken Jozo Shokuhin Shikenjo. (19??)-. Japanese. Iwateken Jozo Shokuhin Shikenjo, (Iwate Brewing & Food Manufacturing Research Inst.), 26 Tsushida Tonanmura, Shiwagun Iwateken 020 Japan.

LC Q
DD 500 KG
CODEN INRNE3

IZVESTIIA AKADEMII NAUK RESPUBLIKI KYRGYZSTAN. KHIMIKO-TEKHNOLOGICHESKIE I BIOLOGICHESKIE NAUKI = KYRGYZ RESPUBLIKASY ILIMDER AKADEMIIASYNYN KABARLARY. KHIMIIA-TEKHNOLOGIIA ZHANA BIOLOGIIA ILIMDERI. **Added/Corp** Kyrgyz Respublikasy Ilimder Akademiiasy. **VFOAT** Khimiko-Tekhnologicheskie i Biologicheskie Nauki; Khimiia-Tekhnologiia Zhana Biologiia Ilimderi; Chemical-Technological and Biological Sciences; Kyrgyz Respublikasy Ilimder Akademiiasynyn Kabarlary. Khimiia-Tekhnologiia Zhana Biologiia Ilimderi; Proceedings of the Kyrghyzstan Academy of the Sciences. Chemical-Technological and Biological Sciences. (1991)-. Periodical. Russian (summaries and/or abstracts in English and Kirghiz). Six times a year. Izdatelstvo Ilim, Leninsky Pr 265-A, Bishkek 720071 Kyrgyzstan. **Tel** 011 7 3312 253874. **ED** K. Sylaimankulov. ***Continues*** *Izvestiia Akademii Nauk Kirgizskoi SSR. Khimiko-Tekhnologicheskie i Biologicheskie Nauki (1989).*
Ind/Abst Chem. Abstr.

BL

JORNAL DO BRASIL. (1992)-. Periodical. English. Jornal do Brasil, Rio de Janeiro Brazil.
Ind/Abst Chem. Bus. Bull.; Chem. Bus. NewsBase (1986-); Chem. Bus. Update; PROMT.

LC TP248.13 .J68 ISSN 0268-2575
DD 660/.6/05 UK
CCC

NLM W1; JO581SU CODEN JCTBED

JOURNAL OF CHEMICAL TECHNOLOGY AND BIOTECHNOLOGY (1986). (JOURNAL OF CHEMICAL TECHNOLOGY AND BIOTECHNOLOGY.). [J. chem. technol. biotechnol.]. **Added/Corp** Society of Chemical Industry (Great Britain). Vol. 36, No. 1 (Jan. 1986)-. Academic Scholarly Publication. English. Twelve times a year. $745.00. John Wiley & Sons Ltd., Baffins Lane, Chichester, West Sussex PO19 1UD United Kingdom. **Tel** 011 44 1243 779777, FAX 011 44 1243 776128 BTG:JWP001, telex 86290 WIBOOKG. **(Subscription address:** John Wiley & Sons, Inc. / Philadelphia, PO Box 7247, Philadelphia PA 19170. **Tel** (212)850-6645, (800)225-5945.**)** **ED** J. Melling. **Bk Rev.** available in microform from University Microfilms International (UMI). Documents available from Article Express International, The Genuine Article, BIOSIS Document Express, CASDDS. ***Formed by the union of*** *Journal of Chemical Technology and Biotechnology. Chemical Technology, 0264-3413* ***and*** *Journal of Chemical Technology and Biotechnology. Biotechnology, 0264-3421.*
Desc: Publishes papers on all aspects of original research or technological achievement in biotechnical and chemical processes.
Ind/Abst AGRICOLA [Select. Cov.]; Anal. Abstr.; Appl. Sci. Technol. Index; BioBusiness; Biol. Abstr. (1986-); Biotechnol. Res. Abstr.; Ceram. Abstr.; Chem Inform; Chem. Abstr. (1986-); Curr. Aware. Biol. Sci., CABS; Curr. Biotechnol.; Curr. Cit.; Curr. Titles Electrochem.; Ei Page One; EMBASE; Eng. Index Annu.; HTFS Dig.; Leadscan; Lit. Pat. Abstr., Oilfield Chem. (1979-1991); Lit. Abstr., Catal. Zeol.; Lit. Abstr., Health Environ.; Lit. Abstr., Pet. Refin. Petrochem.; Lit. Abstr., Pet. Substit.; Lit. Abstr., Transp. Storage; Microbiol. Abstr. Sect. A; Microbiol. Abstr. Sect. C; Proc. Chem. Eng.; Res. Alert [Full Cov.]; Sci. Cit. Index; SCISEARCH; Theor. Chem. Eng.; World Ceram. Abstr.

LC TP201 .J68 ISSN 1045-0637
DD 660 US

JOURNAL OF CHEMICAL TRANSPORT & INDUSTRIAL HISTORY. [J. chem, transp. ind. hist.]. **Added/Corp** Society of Freight Car Historians. **VFOAT** Journal of Chemical Transport and Industrial History; Chemical Transport. (1990)-. Periodical. English. Two times a year. $5.00. David G Casdorph, POB 2480, Monrovia CA 91017.

LC QP958 .J68 ISSN 1041-2905
DD 668 US
CCC
CODEN JEOREG

JOURNAL OF ESSENTIAL OIL RESEARCH, THE. [J. essent. oil res.]. **VFOAT** JEOR. Vol. 1, No. 1 (Jan./Feb. 1989)-. Periodical. English. Six times a year. $230.00. Allured Publishing Corporation, 362 South Schmale Road, Carol Stream IL 60188-2787. **Tel** (708)653-2155, FAX (708)653-2192. **ED** Stanley Allured and Brian Lawrence. Index available. **Bk Rev. Ad Acc. Circ:** 300. Documents available from CASDDS.
Desc: Technical journal dealing with essential oils.
Ind/Abst AGRICOLA [Full Cov.]; Chem. Abstr.; Curr. Cit.; Food Sci. Technol. Abstr.; Plant Genet. Resour. Abstr.

ISSN 0387-5253
DD 668.55 JA

JOURNAL OF S C C J. [J. S C C J]. **VFOAT** Nihon Keshohin Gijutsushakai Kaishi. (1976)-. Periodical. Multiple languages. Four times a year. ¥6000. Nihon Keshohin Gijutsushakai, (Soc. of Cosmetic Chemists of Japan), c/o Shiseido 5-5 Ginza 7 Chome, Chuoku Tokyo 104 Japan. Documents available from CASDDS. ***Continues*** *Journal of JCCA, 0289-1379.*
Ind/Abst Chem. Abstr.; Curr. Cit.

Chemistry and Chemicals — Chemical Technology

LC TA418.9.C6 J65   ISSN 0892-7057
DD 620.1/18   US
    CCC
    CODEN JTMAEQ

JOURNAL OF THERMOPLASTIC COMPOSITE MATERIALS. [J. thermoplast. compos. mater.]. **Added/Corp** Technomic Publishing Company. American Society for Composites. **VFOAT** Thermoplastic Composite Materials. (1988)-. Periodical. English. Four times a year. $265.00. Technomic Publishing Company, Inc., 851 New Holland Avenue, Box 3535, Lancaster PA 17604. **Tel** (717)291-5609, (800)233-9936, FAX (717)295-4538. **ED** Selcuk Guceri. cum. index. **Circ**: 250 (ctrl) available on microfilm and microfiche from University Microfilms International (UMI). Documents available from Article Express International, The Genuine Article, CASDDS.
    Desc: Provides an international forum for the presentation of new advances in the technology of this class of materials.
    Ind/Abst Chem. Abstr.; Civ. Struct. Eng. Abstr.; Curr. Cit.; Ei Page One; Elect. Comm. Abstr.; Eng. Index Annu.; Int. Aerosp. Abstr.; Mater. Sci. Eng. Abstr.; Nonwovens Abstr.; Res. Alert [Full Cov.]; Solid State Supercond. Abstr.

LC TP194.J3 T64b
    JA

KAGAKU GIJUTSU KENKYUJO NENPO. Main/Corp Kagaku Gijutsu Kenkyujo (Japan). (1949)-. Japanese. One time a year. Kogyo Gijutsuin Kagaku Gijutsu Kenkyujo, (National Chemical Lab. for Industry Agency of Industrial Science & Technology), 1-4 Higashi 1 Chome, Tsukubashi Ibarakiken 305 Japan. **Continues** Tokyo Kogyo Shikenjo Nempo.

    ISSN 0453-0683
    JA
    CODEN KAKZAX

KAGAKU KEIZAI. [Kagaku keizai]. **Added/Corp** Kagaku Keizai Kenkyujo (Tokyo, Japan). (1953)-. Academic Scholarly Publication. Japanese. Twelve times a year. $192.50. Kagaku Keizai Kenkyujo, (Chemical Economy Research Inst.), 13-7 Uchikanda 1 Chome, Chiyodaku Tokyo 101 Japan. Documents available from CASDDS.
    Ind/Abst Chem. Abstr.

LC TP157 .K265   ISSN 0368-4849
    JA
    CODEN KASOB7

KAGAKU SOCHI. (KAGAKU SOCHI = PLANT AND PROCESS.). [Kagaku sochi]. **Added/Corp** Kogyo Chosakai. **VFOAT** Plant and Process. (1959)-. Academic Scholarly Publication. Japanese. Twelve times a year. $202.00. Kigyo Chosakai, (Kogyo Chosakai Publishing Co. Ltd.), 14-7 Hongo 2 Chome, Bunkyoku Tokyo 113 Japan. ctrl circ. Documents available from CASDDS.
    Desc: Technical subscription about chemical industry.
    Ind/Abst Chem. Abstr.; Coal Abstr.; Curr. Biotechnol.

    ISSN 1340-2781
    JA

●**KAYAKU GAKKAISHI = JOURNAL OF THE JAPAN EXPLOSIVES SOCIETY. See** Engineering-Chemical Engineering.

LC QD1 .T47   ISSN 0023-1983
    NO
    CODEN KJEMAR

KJEMI. See Metals and Metallurgy.

    ISSN 1065-0547
DD 665   US
    CEASED

LITERATURE & PATENT ABSTRACTS. OILFIELD CHEMICALS. See Petroleum and Natural Gas-Abstracting, Bibliographies and Statistics.

LC HD9650.1 .U54b
DD 382/.4566/0094021   US

MARKET TRENDS FOR SELECTED CHEMICAL PRODUCTS ... AND PROSPECTS TO ... / ECONOMIC COMMISSION FOR EUROPE. Added/Corp nited Nations. Economic Commission for Europe. (1989)-. Government Publication. English. Irregular. Price varies per volume. United Nations Publications, 2 United Nations Plaza, Room DC2 0853, Department 007C, New York NY 10017. **Tel** (212)963-8303, (800)253-9646. **Continues** Market Trends for Chemical Products ... and Prospects to ... .

LC TP157 .M29
    RU

MASHINY I APPARATY KHIMICHESKOI TEKHNOLOGII. Added/Corp Kazanskii Khimiko-Teknologicheskii Institut Im. S.M. Kirova. (1973)-. Russian. Redaktsionno-Izdatelskii / Kazakhstan, K Marksa 68, Kazakhstan.

LC TP992.5 .M23   ISSN 0734-0567
DD 660.2/94514/0294   US
    CODEN MCDEE9

MCCUTCHEON'S EMULSIFIERS & DETERGENTS (INTERNATIONAL EDITION). (MCCUTCHEON'S EMULSIFIERS & DETERGENTS). [McCutcheon's emuls. deterg., Int. ed.]. **VFOAT** Mccutcheon's Emulsifiers and Detergents; Emulsifiers and Detergents/International; Emulsifiers & Detergents/International. (1981)-. English. One time a year. $66.00. MC - Manufacturing Confectioner Publishing Company Inc, 175 Rock Road, Glen Rock NJ 07452. **Tel** (201)652-2655. **ED** Michael Allured. **Ad Acc**. **Continues** McCutcheon's Detergents & Emulsifiers (International Edition), 0145-7063.
    Desc: A formulator's reference guide comprehensively compiled and edited for users of surface active agents. This edition lists surfactants manufactured outside Canada and the United States.

LC TP202 .M24   ISSN 0734-0559
DD 660   US
    CODEN MMNEER

MCCUTCHEON'S FUNCTIONAL MATERIALS. NORTH AMERICAN EDITION. (MCCUTCHEON'S FUNCTIONAL MATERIALS.). [McCutcheon's funct. mater., North Am. ed.]. **VFOAT** Functional Materials. (198?)-. English. One time a year. $55.00. MC - Manufacturing Confectioner Publishing Company Inc, 175 Rock Road, Glen Rock NJ 07452. **Tel** (201)652-2655. **ED** Michael Allured. **Ad Acc**. **Continues** McCutcheon's Detergents & Emulsifiers. Functional Materials (North American Ed.).
    Desc: A formulator's reference guide comprehensively compiled and edited for users of functional materials in conjunction with surface active agents. This edition lists products manufactured in Canada and the United States.

    ISSN 1052-0953
DD 660   US

MEMBRANE QUARTERLY. (MEMBRANE QUARTERLY : NEWSLETTER OF THE NORTH AMERICAN MEMBRANE SOCIETY.). [Membr. q.]. **Added/Corp** North American Membrane Society. (198?)-. Newsletter. English. Four times a year (Jan., Apr., July, Oct.). $50.00 (one-year), $135.00 (three-year) comes with membership. North American Membrane Society, University of Texas at Austin, Department of Chemical Engineering, Austin TX 78712-1062. **Tel** (512)471-4033, FAX (512)471-9643. **ED** Bill Koros (phone: (512)471-5866). **Ad Acc, Adv Mgr**: V. Totten, **Tel** (512)471-4033. **Circ**: 600 (ctrl).

    AU

MITTEILUNGEN DER VERSUCHSSTATION FUER DAS GARUNGSGEWERBE IN WIEN. Main/Corp Vienna. Versuchsstation fuer das Garungsgewerbe. **Added/Corp** Vienna. Versuchsanstalt fuer das Garungsgewerbe. Bund Osterreichischer Braumeister und Brauereitechniker. Verband der Brauereien. Verbande der Hefe- und Spiritusindustrie. Universitat fuer Bodenkultur in Wien. Institut fuer Angewandte Mikrobiologie. Universitat fuer Bodenkultur in Wien. Lehrkanzel fuer Lehrkanzel fuer Biochemische Technologie. Vienna. Hochschule fuer Bodenkultur. Institut fuer Angewandte Mikrobiologie. Vienna. Hochschule fuer Bodenkultur. Lehrkanzel fuer Bodenkultur. Lehrkanzel fuer Biochemische Technologie. (1947)-. Periodical. German. Six times a year. Oesterreichisches Getraenke Institut, Michaelerstr 25, A 1182 Vienna Austria. **Tel** 011 43 1 4796924, FAX 011 43 1 692477. **ED** J. Puspok. **Circ**: 1,000.
    Desc: Transmits information from scientists to the technology industry for practical application.

    ISSN 0176-7615
    SZ
    CCC
    CODEN MSMEDT

MODERN SYNTHETIC METHODS. See Chemistry and Chemicals-Organic Chemistry.

    ISSN 0860-097X
    PL

UDC 62
MONOGRAFIA - POLITECHNIKA KRAKOWSKA IM. TADEUSZA KOSCIUSZKI. See Science and Technology.

LC QE390.2   ISSN 1340-7899
DD 553.6   JA

●**MUKI MATERIARU = INORGANIC MATERIALS. Added/Corp** Sekko Sekkai Gakkai (Tokyo, Japan). **VFOAT** Inorganic Materials. (1994)-. Periodical. Japanese (English). Sekko Sekkai Gakkai, (Soc. of Gypsum & Lime), 13-5 Nishishinjuku 7 Chome, Shinjukuku Tokyo 160 Japan. **Continues** Sekko to Sekkai, 0559-331X.

    UK

N. P. K. S. PROCESS & PLANT SUPPLIERS WORLD DIRECTORY. Directory. English. Irregular. £145.00. British Sulphur Corporation Ltd, 31 Mount Pleasant, London WC1X 0AD United Kingdom. **Tel** 011 44 171 8375600, FAX 011 44 171 8370292, telex 918918 SULFEX G. **(Subscription address**: CRU International Ltd., 31 Mount Pleasant, London WC1X 0AD United Kingdom. **Tel** 011 44 171 8375600, FAX 011 44 171 8370292.)
    Desc: The international directory for buyers and users of nitrogen, phosphorus, potassium and sulphur process technology and equipment.

LC Z5521   ISSN 0950-1711
DD 016.54   UK
NLM ZQV 752; N285
    CODEN NPUPEP

NATURAL PRODUCT UPDATES. See Chemistry and Chemicals-Abstracting, Bibliographies and Statistics.

    ISSN 0959-6062
DD 667.9   UK

NEW COATINGS & SURFACES. [New coat. surf.]. **VFOAT** New Coatings and Surfaces. (19??)-. Periodical. English. Twelve times a year. $470.00. World Business Publications Ltd., 960 High Road, Britannia 4th Floor, London N12 9RY United Kingdom. **Tel** 011 44 181 4465141, FAX 011 44 181 4463659, telex 9419208.

    ISSN 0225-2643
DD 661/.63   CN

NEW USES FOR SULPHUR TECHNOLOGY SERIES. [New uses sulphur technol. ser.]. **Added/Corp** Sulphur Development Institute of Canada. No. 1 (1977)-. Monographic series. English. Free. Sulphur Development Institute of Canada, Suite 830 202 6th Avenue SW, Calgary Alta T2P 2W6. ctrl circ.

LC TP967 .N55   ISSN 0916-4812
    JA

NIHON SETCHAKU GAKKAI SHI. Added/Corp Nihon Setchaku Gakkai. **VFOAT** Journal of the Adhesion Society of Japan; Adhesion. (1990)-. Academic Scholarly Publication. Japanese (summaries and/or abstracts in English). Twelve times a year. Nihon Setchaku Kyokai, (Adhesion Soc. of Japan), 8-29-908 Nishinakajima 5 Chome, Yodogawaku Osakashi, Osakafu 532 Japan. Documents available from CASDDS. **Continues** Nihon Setchaku Kyokai Shi, 0001-8201.
    Ind/Abst Chem. Abstr.

LC TP684.P3 P67   ISSN 0127-2209
DD 665/.3   MY

OCCASIONAL PAPER - PORIM. (PORIM OCCASIONAL PAPER.). [Occas. pap. - PORIM]. **Added/Corp** Institiut Penyelidikan Minyak Kelapa Sawit Malaysia. **VFOAT** Occasional Paper. **VAT** Palm Oil Research Institute of Malaysia Occasional Paper. No. 1 (1981)-. Monographic series. English. Irregular. Price varies per volume. Palm Oil Research Institute of Malaysia, PO Box 10620, 50720 Kuala Lumpur Malaysia. **Tel** 011 60 3 8259155.
    Ind/Abst Biocont. News Inf.; Hortic. Abstr.

    ISSN 1153-4664
    FR

OLEOSCOPE (PARIS). (OLEOSCOPE : LE BULLETIN DU CETIOM.). **Added/Corp** Centre technique Interprofessionnel des Oleagineux Metropolitains (France). (1991)-. Periodical. French. Six times a year. $85.30. CETIOM, 174 Avenue Victor Hugo, 75116 Paris France. **Tel** 011 33 1 44347200, 011 33 1 44347239. **Continues** Bulletin du C.E.T.I.O.M., 0373-1443.

    ISSN 0156-949X
    AT

PACE. PROCESS AND CHEMICAL ENGINEERING. (PACE: THOMSON'S PROCESS AND CHEMICAL ENGINEERING.). [PACE. Process chem. eng.]. **VFOAT** Thomson's Process and Chemical Engineering; Process and Chemical Engineering. Vol. 26, No. 3 (Mar. 1973)-. Periodical. English. Twelve times a year. 75.00Aus$ Australia; 104.00Aus$ New Zealand, Papua New Guinea; 109.00Aus$ Malaysia, Indonesia, Fiji; 110.00Aus$ Japan, India, Hong Kong; 124.00Aus$ US, Canada, Lebanon; 134.00Can$ Europe, Africa, former USSR. Thomson Publications / Australia, 47 Chippen Street, Chippendale New South Wales 2008 Australia. **Tel** 011 61 2 6992411, FAX 011 61 2 6991184, telex 122226. **(Subscription address**: Thomson Publications Australia, PO Box 815, Strawberry Hills, New South Wales, 2012 Australia. **Tel** 011 61 2 6992411.) **Continues** Australian Chemical Processing and Engineering.
    Ind/Abst Art Archaeol. Tech. Abstr.

    ISSN 0255-7177
    II
    CODEN PAFJDI

PAFAI JOURNAL. (PAFAI JOURNAL : OFFICIAL ORGAN OF THE PERFUMES AND FLAVOURS ASSOCIATION OF INDIA.). [PAFAI j.]. **Added/Corp** Perfumes and Flavours Association of India. Perfumes and Flavours Association of India Journal. **VFOAT** A.P.A.F.A.I. Journal. **VAT** Perfumes and Flavours Association of India Journal. (19??)-. Periodical. English. Four times a year. $25.00. Shaski Walavalkar, Bombay India. **(Subscription address**: Prints India, 11 Darya

Ganj, New Delhi 110002 India. **Tel** 011 91 11 3268645, FAX 011 91 11 3275542, telex 31-61087 PRIN-IN.)
Ind/Abst Curr. Cit.

UK

PERFORMANCE CHEMICALS. Vol. 1, No. 1 (May 1986)-. Periodical. English. Four times a year. $145.00. Reed Business Publishing / West Sussex, England, Perrymount Road, Haywards Heath, West Sussex RH16 3DH United Kingdom. **Tel** 011 44 1444 441212, FAX 011 44 1444 445447.
Ind/Abst Curr. Cit.; F&S Index Plus Text, Int. [Select. Cov.]; PROMT; World Surf. Coat. Abstr.

UK
CEASED

PERFORMANCE MATERIALS TECHNOLOGY. (19??)-(April 1994). English. World Business Publications Ltd., 960 High Road, Britannia 4th Floor, London N12 9RY United Kingdom. **Tel** 011 44 181 4465141, FAX 011 44 181 4463659, telex 9419208. ***Continues*** *New Materials World.*

ISSN 0031-6598
AG
UDC 665.6
CODEN PETOA

PETROTECNIA. [Petrotecnia]. (1960)-. Periodical. Spanish. Six times a year. $135.00. Instituto Argentino Petroleo, Maipu 645 3ER Piso, 1006 Buenos Aires Argentina. **Tel** 011 54 1 3935494. ***Continues*** *Instituto Argentino del Petroleo.*

ISSN 0892-6352
DD 660 US
Pr Rev.

PLASMA NEWS REPORT. [Plasma news rep.]. **Added/Corp** Research Institute of Plasma Chemistry and Technology (Carlsbad, Calif.). (19??)-. Periodical. English. Six times a year (Feb., Apr., June, Aug., Oct., Dec.). $450.00. Research Institute Plasma Chemical/Technology, PO Box 1653, Carlsbad CA 92008. **Tel** (619)729-7692. **ED** Professor H. V. Boenig Ph.D. Index available. **Bk Rev**, (Qty: 6).
Desc: Reviews all published papers, meetings, lectures, patents and patent applications in the field of low-temperature plasma chemistry and technology.

LC TP1101 **ISSN** 0969-5990
DD 668.4 UK

●**POLYMER RECYCLING.** [Polym. recycl.]. (1993)-. Trade Publication. English. Four times a year. $400.00. RAPRA Technology Ltd., Shawbury Shrewsbury, Shropshire SY4 4NR United Kingdom. **Tel** 011 44 1939 250383, FAX 011 44 1939 251118, telex 35134 RAPRA G. **ED** Michael Henstock. Documents available from BLDSC, CASDDS.
Desc: Covers developments in plastic and rubber recycling.

LC TP1080 .P66 **ISSN** 1042-7147
DD 668.9/05 UK
CCC
CODEN PADTE5

POLYMERS FOR ADVANCED TECHNOLOGIES. [Polym. adv. technol.]. **VFOAT** PAT. Vol. 1, No. 1 (Feb. 1990)-. Academic Scholarly Publication. English. Twelve times a year. $995.00. John Wiley & Sons Ltd., Baffins Lane, Chichester, West Sussex PO19 1UD United Kingdom. **Tel** 011 44 1243 779777, FAX 011 44 1243 776128 BTG:JWP001, telex 86290 WIBOOKG. **(Subscription address:** John Wiley & Sons, Inc. / Philadelphia, PO Box 7247, Philadelphia PA 19170. **Tel** (212)850-6645, (800)225-5945.**)** **ED** M. Lewin. available on microfilm and microfiche from University Microfilms International (UMI). Documents available from The Genuine Article, CASDDS.
Desc: Focuses on the interest of scientists and engineers who are participating in new areas of polymer research and development related to advanced technologies. Journal aims at encouraging innovation, invention, imagination and creativity by providing a broad interdisciplinary platform for the presentation of new research and development concepts, theories and results which reflect the changing image and pace of modern polymer science and technology.
Ind/Abst Chem. Abstr.; Curr. Cit.; Res. Alert [Full Cov.].

LC TP156.P6 P55 **ISSN** 0379-153X
KO
CODEN POLLDG

PORRIMER (SENUR). (POLLIMO.). [Porrimer]. **VFOAT** Polymer (Korea); Hanguk Kobunja Hakhoe Chi. Academic Scholarly Publication. Korean (summaries and/or abstracts in English). Six times a year. Hanguk Kobunja Akhoe, 146-2 Sangnim-Dong, Chung-Ku Seoul. Documents available from CASDDS.
Ind/Abst Chem. Abstr.; Curr. Cit.; Energy Res. Abstr. (May 1980-).

LC TP156.P3 P63 **ISSN** 0032-5910
SZ
CCC
CODEN POTEBX
Pr Rev.

POWDER TECHNOLOGY. [Powder technol.]. Vol. 1 (Feb. 1967)-. Periodical. English (French and German). Twelve times a year (4 vols.). $1475.00. Elsevier Sequoia SA, PO Box 564, CH-1001 Lausanne 1 Switzerland. **Tel** 011 41 21 3207381, FAX 011 41 21 3235444. **ED** R. Clift. **Ad Acc, Adv Mgr:** W. van Cattenburch (Amsterdam). available on microfilm and microfiche from University Microfilms International (UMI); available on an online database from Elsevier Electronic Subscriptions (EES). Documents available from Article Express International, The Genuine Article, Ask*IEEE, CASDDS.
Desc: An international journal on the science and technology of wet and dry particulate systems. It publishes papers on all aspects of the formation of particles and their characterization and on the study of systems containing particulate solids.
Ind/Abst Alum. Ind. Abstr.; Anal. Abstr.; Bioeng. Abstr.; Ceram. Abstr.; Chem. Abstr.; Chem. Hazards Ind.; Civ. Struct. Eng. Abstr.; Coal Abstr.; Comput. Inf. Syst. Abstr. J. [Full Cov.]; Curr. Cit.; Curr. Contents Agric. Biol. Environ. Sci.; Dairy Sci. Abstr.; Ei Page One; Energy Res. Abstr.; Eng. Mater. Abstr.; Eng. Index Annu.; Environ. Eng. Abstr.; Fluid Abstr., Civil Eng.; Fluid Abstr. Proc. Eng.; FLUIDEX (1973-); Gas Abstr.; GeoRef; HTFS Dig.; INSPEC (Sept. 1969-); Int. Aerosp. Abstr.; Lab. Hazards Bull.; Manuf. Process Eng. Abstr.; Mater. Sci. Eng. Abstr.; Mech. Eng. Abstr.; Met. Abstr.; MINPROC; Phys. Briefs; Proc. Chem. Eng.; Res. Alert [Full Cov.]; Sci. Cit. Index; SCISEARCH; Solid State Supercond. Abstr.; Sug. Indus. Abstr.; Theor. Chem. Eng.; World Ceram. Abstr.; World Surf. Coat. Abstr.

LC TS191 .P7 **ISSN** 1068-6037
DD 658.2/7/0288 US

●**PRECISION CLEANING.** [Prec. clean.]. Vol. 1, No. 1 (Nov./Dec. 1993)-. Trade Publication. English. Eleven times a year. Free (qualified persons), $99.00 (other). Witter Publishing Company Inc., 84 Park Avenue, Flemington NJ 08822. **Tel** (908)788-0343.
Desc: Critical cleaning for industrial applications.

US

PRELIMINARY REPORT ON U.S. PRODUCTION OF SYNTHETIC ORGANIC CHEMICALS. **Added/Corp** United States International Trade Commission. **VFOAT** Preliminary Report on US Production of Synthetic Organic Chemicals. (19??)-. Periodical. English. Four times a year (Also annual issue). $18.50. United States International Trade Commission, 500 E Street Southwest, Washington DC 20436. **Tel** (202)205-1806. **(Subscription address:** Superintendent of Documents, US Government Printing Office, Washington DC 20402. **)** **Circ:** 2,700. Documents available from Documents on Demand.
Ind/Abst Am. Stat. Index.

ISSN 1253-8736
FR
UDC 677(44)

●**PRESSING, LAVERIE, LIBRE-SERVICE.**
See Fabrics and Textile Industries.

LC TP325 .I6795a **ISSN** 0740-5162
DD 662 US
CODEN PITCEM

PROCEEDINGS OF THE ... CONFERENCE / INTERNATIONAL COAL TESTING CONFERENCE. [Proc. Conf. - Int. Coal Test. Conf.]. **Main/Conf** International Coal Testing Conference. 3rd (Oct. 24-26, 1983)-. Academic Scholarly Publication. English. One time a year. $100.00 US; $105.00 Canada; $110.00 other. Vanguard Solutions Inc., PO Box 1970, Ashland KY 41105-1970. **Tel** (606)325-1970, FAX (606)325-2689. Index available. **Circ:** 350-450. Documents available from CASDDS. ***Continues*** *Coal Testing Conference. Proceedings of the ... Conference, 0737-8041.*
Ind/Abst Chem. Abstr. (1984); Curr. Cit.

NE

PROCEEDINGS OF THE INTERNATIONAL CONGRESS ON CATALYSIS. 3rd (1964)-. Proceedings. English (French and German). Elsevier Science Publishers BV, PO Box 211, 1000 AE Amsterdam Netherlands. **Tel** 011 31 20 4853641, 011 31 20 4853642, FAX 011 31 20 4853598. ***Continues*** *International Congress on Catalysis. Actes.*
Ind/Abst Lit. Pat. Abstr., Oilfield Chem.; Lit. Abstr., Catal. Zeol.; Lit. Abstr., Health Environ.; Lit. Abstr., Pet. Refin. Petrochem.; Lit. Abstr., Pet. Substit.; Lit. Abstr., Transp. Storage.

SZ

PROCEEDINGS OF THE ... IPI-CONGRESS. **Main/Corp** International Potash Institute. **VFOAT** Proceedings of the ... I.P.I.-Congress. **VAT** Proceedings of the ... International Potash Institute -Congress. (1982)-. Academic Scholarly Publication. English. Documents available from CASDDS. ***Continues*** *International Potash Institute. Proceedings of the ... Congress of the International Potash Institute.*
Ind/Abst Chem. Abstr.

LC TP157 .T4 **ISSN** 0738-3231
DD 660.2/81 US
CCC

PROCEEDINGS - SYMPOSIUM ON INSTRUMENTATION FOR THE PROCESS INDUSTRIES (TEXAS A & M UNIVERSITY). (PROCEEDINGS / SYMPOSIUM ON INSTRUMENTATION FOR THE PROCESS INDUSTRIES.). **Main/Conf** Annual Symposium on Instrumentation for the Process Industries. **Added/Corp** Texas A & M University. Dept. of Chemical Engineering. **VFOAT** Texas A & M Symposium Proceedings ... Instrumentation for the Process Industries; Proceedings of the ... Annual Symposium; Annual Instrumentation for the Process Industries Symposium Proceedings. 25th (1970)-. Proceedings. English. One time a year. $42.50. Instrument Society of America, 67 Alexander Drive, Research Triangle NC 27709. **Tel** (919)549-8411, FAX (919)549-8288, telex 802 540. ***Continues*** *Texas A & M Symposium on Instrumentation for the Process Industries. Proceedings.*
Desc: Offers the current thinking and writings in the field of instrumentation. Proceedings of annual conference sponsored by Texas A & M University.

DD 660.2/83/02571 CN

PROCESS EQUIPMENT GUIDE. **VFOAT** Buyers Guide to Process Equipment, Controls, and Instrumentation. (1975)-. English. One time a year. Free to subscribers of Canadian Chemical Processing. Southam Business Communications Inc, 1450 Don Mills Road, Don Mills Ontario M3B 2X7 Canada. **Tel** (416)445-6641.

LC TP155.6 .P56 **ISSN** 1066-8527
DD 660.2/8/0068 US
CCC
CODEN PSAPE2

●**PROCESS SAFETY PROGRESS.** (PROCESS SAFETY PROGRESS : A PUBLICATION OF THE AMERICAN INSTITUTE OF CHEMICAL ENGINEERS.). [Process saf. prog.]. **Added/Corp** American Institute of Chemical Engineers. Vol. 12, No. 1 (Jan. 1993)-. Academic Scholarly Publication. English. Four times a year. $185.00. American Institute of Chemical Engineers, 345 East 47th Street, New York NY 10017. **Tel** (212)705-7663, (800)242-4363, FAX (212)705-8400. Documents available from CASDDS. ***Continues*** *Plant/Operations Progress, 0278-4513.*
Ind/Abst Chem. Abstr.; Curr. Cit.

ISSN 0896-8659
DD 661 US
CCC

PROCESSING (CHICAGO ILL.). (PROCESSING.). [Processing]. (Oct. 1987)-. Periodical. English. Thirteen times a year. $49.00. Putnam Publishing Company, 301 East Erie Street, Chicago IL 60611. **Tel** (312)644-2020 ext. 454, FAX (312)644-1131. available on microfilm from University Microfilms International (UMI). ***Continues*** *Chemical Product News, 0747-0398.*

ISSN 1220-8698
RM
UDC 665.6/7

PROGRESS IN CATALYSIS. [Progr. Catal.]. (1992)-. Periodical. English. Two times a year. $105.00. **(Subscription address:** Orion Press SRL, SPL Independentei 202-A, Bucharest 6 Romania. **Tel** 011 401 3122425.**)**

LC TP270.A1 P76 **ISSN** 0721-3115
DD 662/.26/05 GW
CCC
CODEN PEPYD5

PROPELLANTS, EXPLOSIVES, PYROTECHNICS. [Propellants, explos., pyrotech.]. **Added/Corp** International Pyrotechnics Society. Vol. 7, No. 1 (Feb. 1982)-. Academic Scholarly Publication. English (summaries and/or abstracts in French and German). Six times a year. $609.00. VCH Gesellschaft GmbH, Postfach 101161, D-69451 Weinheim Germany. **Tel** 011 49 6201 606459, FAX 011 49 6201 606184. **(Subscription address:** VCH Publishers Inc., 303 Northwest 12th Avenue, Journals Department, Deerfield FL 33442. **Tel** (800)367-8249, (305)428-5566.**)** Documents available from Article Express International, CASDDS. ***Continues*** *Propellants and Explosives, 0340-7462.*
Ind/Abst Bioeng. Abstr.; Chem. Abstr.; Chem. Titles; Curr. Cit.; Ei Page One; Energy Res. Abstr. (May 1983-); Eng. Index Annu.; Int. Aerosp. Abstr.; Soils Fert.

SP

PROYECTOS QUIMICOS. Spanish. One time a week. $320.00. Technipublicaciones SA, C/ Fernando VI No 27, 28004 Madrid Spain. **Tel** 011 34 1 3197889.

LC TP1 .P77 **ISSN** 0033-2496
PL
NLM W1 PR945 **CODEN** PRCHAB
Pr Rev.

PRZEMYS CHEMICZNY. [Przem. chem.]. **Added/Corp** Poland. Ministerstwo Wyznan Religijnych i Oswiecenia Publicznego. Wydzia Nauki. Chemiczny Instytut Badawczy (Warsaw, Poland) Polskie

Chemistry and Chemicals —Chemical Technology

Towarzystwo Chemiczne. (1920)-. Periodical. Polish. Twelve times a year. $144.00. **(Subscription address:** Ars Polona-Ruch, PO Box 1001, Krakowskie Przedmiescie 7, 00-068 Warsaw Poland. **Tel** 011 48 22 261201.**)** Documents available from Article Express International, The Genuine Article, CASDDS. *Continues Methan.*
Ind/Abst Bioeng. Abstr.; Ceram. Abstr.; Chem Inform; Chem. Abstr.; Chem. Titles; Coal Abstr.; Curr. Biotechnol.; Curr. Chem. React.; Curr. Cit.; Ei Page One; Eng. Index Annu.; Index Chem.; Leadscan; Proc. Chem. Eng.; Res. Alert [Full Cov.]; Soc. Sci. Cit. Index [Select. Cov.]; Surf. Treat. Technol. Abstr.; Theor. Chem. Eng.; World Surf. Coat. Abstr.

LC TP300 .P95
DD 662/.1/05
ISSN 0272-6521
US
CODEN PYROEO

PYROTECHNICA. [Pyrotechnica]. VFOAT
Pyrotechnica. (Oct. 1977)-. Academic Scholarly Publication. English (German and Japanese). Irregular. Price varies per volume. Pyrotechnica Publications, 2302 Tower Drive, Austin TX 78703. **Tel** (512)476-4062. **ED** Robert G. Cardwell, K. L. Kosanke, B. E. Douda and R. Lancaster. **Bk Rev. Ad Acc.** Documents available from CASDDS.
Desc: Devoted to technical and craft-oriented articles covering subjects of pyrotechnology and pyrochemistry and physics at length. Also publishes articles on historical, economic and legal aspects of fireworks, reviews and literature about pyrotechnics.
Ind/Abst Chem. Abstr.

LC TP994 .Q37
DD 660.2/9/45308
UK

QUARTERLY LITERATURE REPORTS : SURFACE ACTIVITY.
(1968)-. English. Four times a year. Kogan Page Ltd., 120 Pentonville Road, London N1 9BR United Kingdom. **Tel** 011 44 171 2780433, FAX 011 44 171 8376348, telex 263088 KOGAN G.

ISSN 0033-6521
SP
CCC
CODEN QUIBAL

QUIMICA E INDUSTRIA (MADRID).
(QUIMICA E INDUSTRIA.). [Quim. ind.]. **Added/Corp** Asociacion Nacional de Quimicos de Espana. Colegio Oficial de Quimicos. (1970)-. Academic Scholarly Publication. Spanish. Twelve times a year. $124.34. Quimica e Industria, C Lagasca 87, 28006 Madrid Spain. **Tel** 11 34 1 5767443. Documents available from CASDDS. *Continues Quimica e Industria (Bilbao), 0375-9695.*
Ind/Abst Chem. Abstr.; Coal Abstr.

ISSN 1045-845X
DD 660
US
CODEN RARAE6
Pr Rev.

RADIOACTIVITY & RADIOCHEMISTRY.
[Radioact. radiochem.]. **VFOAT** Radioactivity and Radiochemistry; R&R. Vol. 1, No. 1 (Winter 1990)-. Academic Scholarly Publication. English. Four times a year. $118.00. Caretaker Technology, PO Box 19656, Atlanta GA 30325. **Tel** (404)352-4620, FAX (404)352-0515. **ED** Thetis S. McFarland (editor's address: 1380 Seaboard Industrial Blvd, Atlanta, GA 30318). **Bk Rev. Ad Acc. Adv Mgr:** Laura Roop, **Tel** (404)352-4620. **Circ:** 1,500. Documents available from CASDDS.
Desc: A journal dedicated to providing practical information promoting the safe use of radioactive materials.
Ind/Abst Chem. Abstr.; Curr. Cit.; GeoRef.

LC TP155.5 .R43
RU

REFERATIVNYI ZHURNAL: KHIMICHESKOE, NEFTEPERERABATYVAIUSHCHEE I POLIMERNOE MASHINOSTROENIE. See
Petroleum and Natural Gas.

AT

REPORT. Main/Corp Chemical Research
Laboratories (Australia). English. One time a year.

ISSN 0035-6808
IT
CODEN RISGAD
Pr Rev.

RIVISTA ITALIANA DELLE SOSTANZE GRASSE.
[Riv. ital. sostanze grasse]. Vol.38 (1961)-. Periodical. Italian (English and French). Twelve times a year. L122490. Stazione Sperimentale Industrie Oli E Grassi, Via Giuseppe Colombo 79, 20133 Milan MI Italy. **Tel** (02)2361051, telex 340129 SSOG I. **Bk Rev. Ad Acc, Adv Mgr:** L. Cariboni. **Circ:** 5,000. Documents available from CASDDS. *Continues Rivista Italiana delle Sostanze Grasse Olii Minerali, Grassi e Saponi, Colori e Vernici.*
Desc: Covers chemistry, vegetable and animal oils, fats, vegetable proteins, paints, colours, detergents, soaps and cosmetics. Normalisation on same subjects in Italy and technology-processing.

Ind/Abst Anal. Abstr.; Art Archaeol. Tech. Abstr.; Chem. Abstr.; Curr. Cit.; Food Sci. Technol. Abstr.; Life Sci. Collect.; Soyabean Abstr.

ISSN 1001-1803
DD 668.1
CC

RIYONG HUAXUE GONGYE. VFOAT China
Surfactant, Detergent and Cosmetics. (1979)-. Periodical. Chinese. Six times a year. Documents available from CASDDS.
Ind/Abst Chem. Abstr.

ISSN 1068-3704
US
CCC

●RUSSIAN CHEMICAL INDUSTRY. (1993)-.
Periodical. English (translations available in Russian). Twelve times a year. $865.00. Allerton Press Inc., 150 Fifth Avenue, New York NY 10011. **Tel** (212)924-3950, FAX (212)463-9684, telex 427441 ALPRES. Index available (bound in Dec. issue). *Continues Soviet Chemical Industry, 0038-5344.*
Ind/Abst Curr. Cit.

ISSN 0370-8047
JA
CODEN RYUSAZ

RYUSAN TO KOGYO. [Ryusan to kogyo].
Added/Corp Ryusan Kyokai (Japan). **VFOAT** Sulphuric Acid and Industry. (1968)-. Periodical. Japanese. Twelve times a year. Ryusan Kyokai, (Sulphuric Acid Assoc. of Japan), 21-1 Shinbashi 2 Chome, Minatoku Tokyo 105 Japan. Documents available from CASDDS. *Continues Ryusan; Absorbed Ryusan Jiho.*
Ind/Abst Chem. Abstr.

ISSN 0553-2124
XR
CODEN SVPVA9

SBORNIK VEDECKYCH PRACI / VYSOKA SKOLA CHEMICKO-TECHNOLOGICKA PARDUBICE.
[Sb. ved. pr. - Vyso. sk. chemickotechnol. Pardubice]. **Added/Corp** Vysoka Skola Technicka Pardubice. **VFOAT** Scientific Papers. (1950)-. Czech (summaries and/or abstracts in English, German and Russian). Documents available from CASDDS.
Ind/Abst Chem. Abstr.

LC TP7 .B25
GW

SCHRIFTENREIHE. Main/Corp Badische Anilin-
und Soda-Fabrik. Unternehmensarchiv. German.

LC TJ1320
DD 621.885
ISSN 1350-4789
UK
CCC
Pr Rev.

●SEALING TECHNOLOGY. [Seal. Technol.].
(1994)-. Newsletter. English. Twelve times a year. $433.00. Elsevier Advanced Technology, An Imprint of Elsevier Science Ltd., The Boulevard, Langford Lane, Kidlington, Oxford OX5 1GB United Kingdom. **Tel** 011 44 1865 843000, 011 44 1865 843699, FAX 011 44 1865 843010. **(Subscription address:** Elsevier Science Ltd. / Oxford Fulfillment Centre, PO Box 800, Kidlington OX5 1DX United Kingdom. **Tel** 011 44 865 843355.**) ED** P. Ray. available on an online database from University Microfilms International (UMI).
Desc: Presents the recent developments in the design and production of seals.

LC QE390.2
DD 553.6
ISSN 0559-331X
JA
CODEN GYLIDC
TITLE CHANGE

SEKKO TO SEKKAI. (SEKKO TO SEKKAI =
GYPSUM & LIME.). [Sekko to sekkai]. **Added/Corp** Sekko Sekkai Kenkyukai (Tokyo, Japan) Sekko Sekkai Gakkai (Tokyo, Japan). **VFOAT** Gypsum and Lime; Gypsum & Lime. (1953)-(1994). Academic Scholarly Publication. Japanese (English; summaries and/or abstracts in English). Sekko Sekkai Gakkai, (Soc. of Gypsum & Lime.), 13-5 Nishishinjuku 7 Chome, Shinjukuku Tokyo 160 Japan. ctrl circ. Documents available from CASDDS. *Continues Sekko. Continued by Muki Materiaru, 1340-7899.*
Desc: Contributed treaties about chemistry and technology.
Ind/Abst Chem. Abstr.; Coal Abstr.

UK

SELF ADHESIVE MATERIALS & MARKETS BULLETIN. See Packaging.

LC TP890
DD 667
ISSN 0370-9671
JA

SENRYO TO YAKUHIN (TOKYO. 1956).
[Senryo to yakuhin Tokyo. 1956]. **VFOAT** Dyestuffs & Chemicals. (1956)-. Periodical. Japanese. Twelve times a year. Kaseihin Kogyo Kyokai, (Japan Dyestuff Industry Assoc.), 18-17 Roppongi 5 Chome, Minatoku Tokyo 106 Japan. Documents available from CASDDS.
Ind/Abst Chem. Abstr.

ISSN 0389-6277
JA
CODEN SEKEDL

SENSHOKU KENKYU. (SENSHOKU KENKYU =
DYEING RESEARCH.). [Senshoku kenkyu]. **Added/Corp** Kyoto-Shi Senshoku Shikenjo. Kyoto Senshoku Kenkyukai. **VFOAT** Dyeing Research. (1957)-. Periodical. Japanese. Four times a year. Kyoto Senshoku Kenkyukai, (Soc. of Kyoto Dyeing Research), Kyotoshi Senshoku Shikenjo, Kamidachuri Agaru Karasuma, Doori Kamigyoku Kyotoshi, Kyotofu 602 Japan. Documents available from CASDDS.
Ind/Abst Chem. Abstr.

ISSN 0370-9574
JA
CODEN SEKOBF

SENSHOKU KOGYO. (SENSHOKU KOGYO =
DYEING INDUSTRY.). [Senshoku kogyo]. **VFOAT** Dyeing Industry. (1953)-. Periodical. Japanese. Twelve times a year. $188.00. Shikisensha, (Shikisensha Co. Ltd.), 1-10 Tenjinbashi 7 Chome, Oyodoku Osakashi, Osakafu 531 Japan. Documents available from CASDDS.
Ind/Abst Chem. Abstr.

LC TP156.S45 P722
DD 660.2/842
ISSN 0360-2540
US
CCC
CODEN SPMHBD
Pr Rev.

SEPARATION AND PURIFICATION METHODS.
[Sep. purif. methods]. Vol. 1 (1972)-. Periodical. English. Two times a year. $350.00. Marcel Dekker Inc., 270 Madison Avenue, New York NY 10016. **Tel** (212)696-9000, (800)228-1160, FAX (212)685-4540, telex 421419. **(Subscription address:** Marcel Dekker Inc., PO Box 5017, Monticello NY 12701. **Tel** (800)228-1160.**) ED** Phillip C. Wankat, Eli Grushka, Carel J. Van Oss, Joseph D. Henry, Jr. **Bk Rev. Ad Acc.** ctrl circ. available on microfiche. Documents available from Article Express International, The Genuine Article, BIOSIS Document Express, CASDDS. *Supersedes Progress in Separation and Purification, 0079-676X.*
Desc: Provides summaries of significant novel developments in this constantly evolving field, including evaluations of methods, apparatus, and techniques. Discusses such topics as chromatography, crystallization, extraction, distillation, ultrafiltration, magnetic separation, sedimentation, electrodialysis, and more.
Ind/Abst Anal. Abstr.; Bioeng. Abstr.; Biol. Abstr.; Chem. Abstr.; Curr. Biotechnol.; Curr. Cit.; Curr. Contents Phys. Chem. Earth Sci.; Ei Page One; Energy Res. Abstr. (June 1973-); Eng. Index Annu.; Life Sci. Collect.; Pollut. Abstr. Indexes; Proc. Chem. Eng.; Res. Alert [Full Cov.]; Sci. Cit. Index; SCISEARCH; Theor. Chem. Eng.

LC TP156.S45 S4
DD 660.2/842
ISSN 0149-6395
US
CCC

NLM W1 SE67M
CODEN SSTEDS

SEPARATION SCIENCE AND TECHNOLOGY.
[Sep. sci. technol.]. Vol. 13 (Jan. 1978)-. Academic Scholarly Publication. English. Twenty times a year. $1825.00. Marcel Dekker Inc., 270 Madison Avenue, New York NY 10016. **Tel** (212)696-9000, (800)228-1160, FAX (212)685-4540, telex 421419. **(Subscription address:** Marcel Dekker Inc., PO Box 5017, Monticello NY 12701. **Tel** (800)228-1160.**) ED** J. Calvin Giddings, Jimmy T. Bell and J. A. Watson. **Bk Rev. Ad Acc.** ctrl circ. available on microfiche. Documents available from Article Express International, The Genuine Article, BIOSIS Document Express, CASDDS. *Continues Separation Science, 0037-2366.*
Desc: Explores the area separation phenomena. Reviews concepts and techniques for dealing with problems encountered by professionals. Includes articles, notes, and reviews on the aspects of separation, including separation theory, ultrafiltration, chromatography, electrophoresis, foam fractionation, and ion-exchange.
Ind/Abst Abstr. Bull. Inst. Pap. Sci. Tech.; AGRICOLA; Alum. Ind. Abstr.; Anal. Abstr.; Biol. Abstr.; Ceram. Abstr. (19??-); Chem. Abstr.; Chem. Titles; Coal Abstr.; Curr. Biotechnol.; Curr. Cit.; Curr. Contents Life Sci.; Curr. Contents Phys. Chem. Earth Sci.; EMBASE; Energy Res. Abstr. (April 1978-); Eng. Mater. Abstr.; Eng. Index Annu.; Fluid Abstr., Civil Eng.; Fluid Abstr. Proc. Eng.; FLUIDEX (1978-); GeoRef; Met. Abstr.; MINPROC; Life Sci. Collect.; Pollut. Abstr. Indexes; Proc. Chem. Eng.; Res. Alert [Full Cov.]; Sci. Cit. Index; SCISEARCH; Theor. Chem. Eng.

ISSN 0037-0495
JA
CODEN STHKAO

SETCHAKU. [Secchaku]. Added/Corp Kobunshi
Kankokai (Kyoto, Japan). **VFOAT** Technology on Adhesion & Sealing; Technology on Adhesion and Sealing; Adhesion and Sealing. (1957)-. Academic Scholarly Publication. Japanese. Twelve times a year. $179.00. Kobunshi Kankokai, Chiekoin Marutacho Sagaru, Kamigyoku Kyotoshi, Kyotofu 602 Japan. Documents available from CASDDS.
Ind/Abst Chem. Abstr.

ISSN 0010-180X
JA
CODEN SKYOAO

SHIKIZAI KYOKAISHI. [Shikizai Kyokaishi]. **Added/Corp** Shikizai Kyokai. **VFOAT** Journal of the Japan Society of Colour Material; Shikizai; Shikizai Kyokai Shi. (1927)-. Academic Scholarly Publication. Japanese (summaries and/or abstracts in English). Twelve times a year. $181.50. Shikizai Kyokai, (Japan Soc. of Color Material), 9-12 Iwamotocho 2 Chome, Chiyodaku Tokyo 101 Japan. **(Subscription address:** Japan Publications Trading Company Ltd., PO Box 5030, Tokyo International, Tokyo 100-31 Japan. **Tel** 011 81 3 3292 3753.**)** Documents available from CASDDS.
Ind/Abst Biodeter. Abstr.; Chem. Abstr.; Chem. Titles; Print. Abstr.; World Surf. Coat. Abstr.

ISSN 0379-5608
II
CODEN SDTRDU

SOAPS, DETERGENTS & TOILETRIES REVIEW. [Soaps deterg. toiletries rev.]. **VFOAT** Soaps, Detergents and Toiletries Review. (1971)-. Academic Scholarly Publication. English. Twelve times a year. $50.00. Wadhera Publications, 232 Dr D N Road, Bombay 400001 India. **Tel** 011 91 22 2046918, 231244. Documents available from CASDDS.
Ind/Abst Chem. Abstr.

LC TP1 .S5
GW

SOFW JOURNAL. **Added/Corp** Vereinigung der Seifen-, Parfum- und Waschmittelfachleute. **VFOAT** SOFW. 92/1 (Jan. 1992)-. Periodical. German (summaries and/or abstracts in English). Sixteen times a year. $331.62. Verlag fuer Chemische Industrie, H Ziolkowsky, Postfach 102565, D-86015 Augsburg 1 Germany. **Tel** 011 49 821 519345, 011 49 821 519346, FAX 0821/51 79 53. ***Continues** SOFW.*
Ind/Abst Curr. Cit.; Infomat Int. Bus.; PROMT.

ISSN 0038-9056
GW
CCC
CODEN STARDD
Pr Rev.

STAERKE, DIE. (STARCH. STAERKE.). [Staerke]. **VFOAT** Staerke. (1978)-. Periodical. English (French and German). Twelve times a year (monthly). $538.00. VCH Gesellschaft GmbH, Postfach 101161, D-69451 Weinheim Germany. **Tel** 011 49 6201 606459, FAX 011 49 6201 606184. **(Subscription address:** VCH Publishers Inc., 303 Northwest 12th Avenue, Journals Department, Deerfield FL 33442. **Tel** (800)367-8249, (305)428-5566.**)** Documents available from The Genuine Article, BIOSIS Document Express, CASDDS. ***Continues** Staerke, 0038-9056.*
Desc: Publishes contributions dealing with fundamental and applied research and with technological developments in the carbohydrate field. Informs about newly developed starches, modified starches, starch derivatives and products of starch saccharification. Of interest to the food, paper, adhesive, textile, chemical and pharmaceutical industries.
Ind/Abst Abstr. Bull. Inst. Pap. Sci. Tech.; Biodeter. Abstr.; Biol. Abstr.; Chem. Abstr.; Curr. Biotechnol.; Curr. Cit.; EMBASE; Energy Res. Abstr. (Sept. 1979-); Field Crop Abstr.; Food Sci. Technol. Abstr.; Maize Abstr.; Life Sci. Collect.; PESTDOC; Plant Breed. Abstr.; Potato Abstr.; Res. Alert [Full Cov.]; Sci. Cit. Index; SCISEARCH; Sug. Indus. Abstr.; Wheat Barley Trit. Abstr.; World Text. Abstr.

NE
TITLE CHANGE

STAINLESS STEEL EUROPE. (19??)-(Sept. 1995). English. KCI Media BV, PO Box 396, 7200 AJ Zutpheb The Netherlands. **ED** Sjef Roymans. Index available. **Bk Rev. Ad Acc, Adv Mgr:** Gert-Jan Kloos. **Circ:** 7500 (ctrl). ***Continued by** Stainless Steel World.*
Desc: Caters mainly to the major consumers of stainless steels and superalloys in the processing industry. The editorial program contains technical as well as techno-commercial articles from users and suppliers in application areas such as chemical and petrochemical industry, energy, oil, gas, food, dairy and the pulp and paper industry.
Ind/Abst Corros. Abstr. (199?-).

NE

•**STAINLESS STEEL WORLD.** (1995)-. English. Ten times a year. $252.15. KCI Media BV, PO Box 396, 7200 AJ Zutpheb The Netherlands. ***Continues** Stainless Steel Europe.*

ISSN 0039-4890
UK
CODEN SULPAW

SULPHUR. [Sulphur]. **Added/Corp** British Sulphur Corporation. No. 19 (Dec. 1957)-. Academic Scholarly Publication. English. Six times a year. $581.81. British Sulphur Corporation Ltd, 31 Mount Pleasant, London WC1X 0AD United Kingdom. **Tel** 011 44 171 8375600, FAX 011 44 171 8370292, telex 918918 SULFEX G. **(Subscription address:** CRU International Ltd., 31 Mount Pleasant, London WC1X 0AD United Kingdom. **Tel** 011 44 171 8375600, FAX 011 44 171 8370292.**)** **ED** Roger Manser. **Ad Acc.** available on microfilm and microfiche from University Microfilms International (UMI); available on an online database (file 648/Full-Text) from DIALOG. Documents available from CASDDS. ***Continues** British Sulphur Corporation. Quarterly Bulletin.*
Desc: Reporting on commerical and technical developments as they affect world sulphur and sulphuric acid markets.
Ind/Abst AGRICOLA; Chem. Abstr.; Chem. Bus. Bull.; Chem. Bus. NewsBase (1985-); Chem. Bus. Update; Chem. Ind. Notes; F&S Index Plus Text, Int. [Select. Cov.]; GeoRef; PROMT; Soils Fert.; Trade Ind. ASAP [Full Txt.]; Trade Ind. Index [Full Txt.].

LC QC173.4.S94 S96 ISSN 0142-2421
DD 660
UK
CCC
CODEN SIANDQ
Pr Rev.

SURFACE AND INTERFACE ANALYSIS : SIA. [Surf. interface anal.]. **VFOAT** SIA. (1979)-. Academic Scholarly Publication. English. Thirteen times a year (Mmonthly plus one special issue). $1945.00. John Wiley & Sons Ltd., Baffins Lane, Chichester, West Sussex PO19 1UD United Kingdom. **Tel** 011 44 1243 779777, FAX 011 44 1243 776128 BTG:JWP001, telex 86290 WIBOOKG. **(Subscription address:** John Wiley & Sons, Inc. / Philadelphia, PO Box 7247, Philadelphia PA 19170. **Tel** (212)850-6645, (800)225-5945.**)** **ED** David Briggs, J. T. Grant, and M. .P Seah. **Ad Acc. Circ:** 850. available on microfilm and microfiche from University Microfilms International (UMI). Documents available from Article Express International, The Genuine Article, Ask*IEEE, CASDDS.
Desc: Publishes papers on the development and application of characterization techniques for surfaces, interfaces and thin films. Includes papers dealing with standardization, quantification, applications to industrial problems.
Ind/Abst Acoust. Abstr.; Alum. Ind. Abstr.; Anal. Abstr.; Bioeng. Abstr.; Ceram. Abstr. (19??-); Chem. Abstr.; Civ. Struct. Eng. Abstr.; Coal Abstr.; Curr. Cit.; Curr. Contents Phys. Chem. Earth Sci.; Ei Page One; Elect. Comm. Abstr.; Eng. Mater. Abstr.; Eng. Index Annu.; Fluid Abstr., Civil Eng.; Fluid Abstr. Proc. Eng.; FLUIDEX (1979-); INSPEC (Feb. 1979-); Manuf. Process Eng. Abstr.; Mass Spect. Bull.; Mater. Sci. Eng. Abstr.; Mech. Eng. Abstr.; Met. Abstr.; Res. Alert [Full Cov.]; Sci. Cit. Index; SCISEARCH; Solid State Supercond. Abstr.; Soyabean Abstr.

ISSN 0815-709X
AT
CODEN SCAUE6

SURFACE COATINGS AUSTRALIA. **Added/Corp** Oil and Colour Chemists' Association, Australia. Vol. 21, No. 1/2 (Jan./Feb. 1984)-. Trade Publication. English. Eleven times a year (monthly with Jan./Feb. issues combined). 65.78Aus$. Surface Coatings Association of Australia, 443 High Street, Prahran Victoria 3181 Australia. **Tel** 011 61 3 5106238, FAX 011 61 3 5296069. **ED** Dick Harris. Index available. cum. index. **Ad Acc, Adv Mgr:** G. Goullet. **Circ:** 1,530 (ctrl). Documents available from CASDDS. ***Continues** Proceedings and News (Oil & Colour Chemists' Association, Australia).*
Desc: The aim is to report the proceedings of the five Australia sections and the two New Zealand Sections together with the activities of Council. Also reports news and technical papers of interest and relevance to the Surface Coatings Industries of Australia and New Zealand.
Ind/Abst Biodeter. Abstr. (1991-); Chem. Abstr. (1984-); Corros. Abstr. (1984-); Curr. Cit.; World Surf. Coat. Abstr. (1984-).

ISSN 1058-093X
DD 666
US
TITLE CHANGE

SURFACE MODIFICATION TECHNOLOGY NEWS. [Surf. modif. technol. news]. (Jan. 1991)-(1995). Periodical. English. Business Communications Inc., 25 Van Zant Street, Suite 13, Norwalk CT 06855. **Tel** (203)853-4266, FAX (203)853-0348. available on an online database (files 16,636/Full-Text) from DIALOG. ***Merged into** Thin Film / Diamond Technology News.*
Ind/Abst PROMT [Full Txt.]; PTS Newsl. Database [Full Txt.].

ISSN 0218-625X
SI

•**SURFACE REVIEW AND LETTERS.** Vol. 1, No. 1 (June 1994)-. Periodical. English. Four times a year. $425.00. World Scientific Publishing Company, PO Box 128, Farrer Road, Singapore 9128 Singapore. **Tel** 011 65 3825663, FAX 011 65 3825919, telex RS 28561 WSPC.

ISSN 0893-7044
DD 363
US

SUSPECT CHEMICALS SOURCEBOOK. UPDATE SERVICE. [Suspect chem. sourceb., Update serv.]. **Added/Corp** Roytech Publications. Vol. 1, No. 1 (Apr. 1987)-. Periodical. English. Four times a year. $515.00. Roytech Publications, 7910 Woodmont Avenue, #902, Bethesda MD 20814. **Tel** (301)654-4281, FAX (301)907-7773. **ED** Kenneth Clansky. Index available. cum. index. **Ad Acc, Adv Mgr:** Karen Winstedt.

UK
CODEN JSLUE6

SYNTHETIC LUBRICATION. [J. synth. lubr.]. **VFOAT** Synthetic Lubrication. (1988)-. Periodical. English. Four times a year. $185.00 US; £105.00 (surface mail) other. Leaf Coppin Publishing Ltd., 6 Coppin Street, Deal, Kent CT14 6JL United Kingdom. **Tel** 011 44 1304 360241, FAX 011 44 3321 872521, telex 96118 ANZEEC G LEAFCO.
Ind/Abst Chem. Abstr. (1984-); Ei Page One; Eng. Index Annu.; Fluid Abstr., Civil Eng.; Fluid Abstr. Proc. Eng.; FLUIDEX (1984-1991).

LC TP875 .S95 ISSN 0586-3791
HU

SZILIKATTECHNIKA. [Szilikattechnika]. **Added/Corp** Hungary. Epitesugyi es Varosfejlesztesi Miniszterium. (19??)-. Academic Scholarly Publication. Hungarian. Six times a year. Akademiai Kiado, Publishing House of the Hungarian Academy of Sciences, Prielle Kornelia u. 19-35, H-1117 Budapest Hungary. **Tel** 011 36 1 1811991, FAX 011 36 1 1811991, telex 22-6228 AKNYO H.
Ind/Abst Coal Abstr.

ISSN 0892-4651
US
CODEN TCINE2
TITLE CHANGE

TECHNITRIVIA (PHOENIX, ARIZ.). (TECHNITRIVIA.). **VFOAT** Trivia Chimicus. (1991)-(199?). Periodical. English. CITA International, Industrial Publ Division, PO Box 70, Phoenix AZ 85001. **Tel** (602)447-0480, FAX (602)447-0305. ***Absorbed by** For Formulation Chemists Only, 0887-736X.*

ISSN 0392-3452
IT
CODEN TECCDK

TECNOLOGIE CHIMICHE. [Tecnol. chim.]. (1981)-. Periodical. Italian. Eleven times a year. L68130. Stammer Spa, Via della Liberazione 1, 20068 Peschiera Borromeo Italy. **Tel** 011 39 2 55302606, FAX 011 39 2 55302700, telex 321083. Documents available from CASDDS.
Ind/Abst Chem. Abstr.; Curr. Cit.

LC TP692.4.T6 H93a ISSN 0271-2660
DD 661/.816
US
Pr Rev.

TOLUENE XYLENES ANNUAL. (19??)-. English. One time a week. $7,000.00 Comes with Toluene Xylenes Newsletter Full Service. Dewitt & Company Inc, 16800 Greenspoint Park, #120 N, Houston TX 77060. **Tel** (713)875-5525, (713)875-0296, FAX (713)875-0175, telex 762-854. ctrl circ. ***Continues** Toluene-Xylenes Annual World Survey, 0160-0192.*
Desc: Information on international market pricing review on TOL, XYL, OX, PY, Plastic anityoxide, DM7 and PTA.

LC HD9651.1 .U17 ISSN 1061-9143
DD 338.4/766/00973021
US

U.S. CHEMICAL INDUSTRY STATISTICAL HANDBOOK. [U.S. chem. ind. stat. handb.]. **Added/Corp** Chemical Manufacturers Association (U.S.). **VFOAT** US Chemical Industry Statistical Handbook; Chemical Industry Statistical Handbook. (1990)-. Statistical Publication. English. Chemical Manufacturers Association, 2501 M Street Northwest, Washington DC 20037. **Tel** (202)887-1100.
Ind/Abst PROMT.

GW

ULLMANN'S ENCYCLOPEDIA OF INDUSTRIAL CHEMISTRY. (19??)-. English. Irregular. VCH Gesellschaft GmbH, Postfach 101161, D-69451 Weinheim Germany. **Tel** 011 49 6201 606459, FAX 011 49 6201 606184. **(Subscription address:** VCH Publishers Inc., 303 Northwest 12th Avenue, Journals Department, Deerfield FL 33442. **Tel** (800)367-8249, (305)428-5566.**)**

GW

VWD CHEMIE KAUTSCHUK. Trade Publication. German. Five times a week (260 issues). DM2769.60 Germany; DM3152.40 Europe; DM3404.40 other. Vereinigte Wirtschaftsdienste, Postfach 6105, D-65735 Eschborn Germany. **Tel** 011 49 6196 405208.

LC TP270 .V8 ISSN 0372-7009
RU
CODEN VZDEAR

VZRYVNOE DELO. [Vzryvnoe delo]. **Added/Corp** Vsesoiuznyi Trest po Proizvodstvu Burovykh i Vzryvnykh Rabot. Nauchno-Tekhnicheskoe Gornoe Obshchestvo (Soviet Union). (1930)-. Academic Scholarly Publication. Russian. Price varies per volume. Documents available from CASDDS.
Ind/Abst Chem. Abstr.; GeoRef.

ISSN 0950-8686
UK
CODEN WCNSD6

WATER CHEMISTRY OF NUCLEAR REACTOR SYSTEMS. [Water chem. nucl. react. syst.]. **Added/Corp** British Nuclear Energy Society. Institution of Chemical Engineers (Great Britain) Royal Society of Chemistry (Great Britain). (Oct. 24-27 1977)-.

Chemistry and Chemicals — Chemical Technology

Academic Scholarly Publication. English. Every 3 years. British Nuclear Reactor Society, London United Kingdom. Documents available from CASDDS.
Ind/Abst Chem. Abstr.; Curr. Cit.

ISSN 0049-741X
US
WESTERN CLEANER & LAUNDERER.
VAT Western Cleaner and Launderer. (19??)-. Periodical. English. Twelve times a year. $490.00. Wakefield Publishing Company, 100 North Hill Avenue Suite C, Pasadena CA 91106. **Tel** (310)254-2320. **ED** D. Ballard. **Ad Acc. Circ:** 11,500 (ctrl).

ISSN 0208-7499
PL
CODEN WLCHDF
WLOKNA CHEMICZNE. [Wlok. chem.].
Added/Corp Instytut Wlokien Chemicznych. Instytut, Branzowy Osrodek Informacji Naukowej, Technicznej i Ekonomicznej Premyslu Wlokien Chemicznych. (1975)-. Academic Scholarly Publication. Polish. Four times a year. Premyslu Wlokien Chemicznych, Instytut Branzowy Osrodek Informacji Naukowej, Technicznej i Ekonomicznej, Lodz Poland. (**Subscription address:** Ars Polona-Ruch, PO Box 1001, Krakowskie Przedmiescie 7, 00-068 Warsaw Poland. **Tel** 011 48 22 261201.) Documents available from CASDDS. *Continues* Wlokna Sztuczne.
Ind/Abst Abstr. Bull. Inst. Pap. Sci. Tech.; Chem. Abstr.

LC S
DD 630
UK
WORLD DIRECTORY OF FERTILIZER PRODUCTS. See Agriculture.

LC TP692.4.N3 W68
DD 338.4/7/6655382409047
US
WORLD NAPHTHA SURVEY : REGIONAL ANALYSIS, THE. See Industry and Production.

UK
WORLD SULPHUR AND SULPHURIC ACID PLANT LIST. 6th Edition (March 1993)-.
Directory. English. Irregular. £235.00. British Sulphur Corporation Ltd, 31 Mount Pleasant, London WC1X 0AD United Kingdom. **Tel** 011 44 171 8375600, FAX 011 44 171 8370292, telex 918918 SULFEX G. **ED** Kevin Cunningham.
Desc: Lists maps showing the locations of all plants and mines. Details of sulphuric acid plants, recovered sulphur plants and mines. Information on operating plants, project plants, and capacity expansion.

LC TP155 .H75
DD 660.2/05
ISSN 0253-4320
CH
CODEN HTKUDJ
XIANDAI HUAGONG. See Engineering-Chemical Engineering.

ISSN 0916-6076
DD 671.7
JA
YOSHA. VFOAT Journal of Japan Thermal Spraying Society (1990). (1990)-. Periodical. Multiple languages. Four times a year. Documents available from CASDDS. *Continues* Nihon Yosha Kyokaishi, 0288-5522.
Ind/Abst Chem. Abstr.

LC TP669 .Y87
ISSN 0513-398X
JA
CCC
CODEN YKGKAM
YUKAGAKU. [Yukagaku]. Added/Corp Nihon Yushi Kagaku Kyokai. Nihon Yukagaku Kyokai. VFOAT Abura Kagaku; Journal of Japan Oil Chemists' Society; Journal of the Japan Oil Chemists' Society. Vol. 5, No. 1 (1956/1-Gatsu)-. Periodical. Japanese (summaries and/or abstracts in English). Twelve times a year. $290.00. Nihon Yukagaku Kyokai, (Japan Oil Chemists' Society), Yushi Kogyo Kaikan, 13-11 Nihonbashi 3 Chome, Chuoku Tokyo 103 Japan. Documents available from BIOSIS Document Express, CASDDS. *Continues* Yushi Kagaku Kyokai Shi.
Ind/Abst Biol. Abstr. (1991-); Chem. Abstr.; Curr. Cit.; Food Sci. Technol. Abstr.; Sug. Indus. Abstr.

JA
CODEN YUSHB8
YUSHI. [Yushi]. (1948)-. Periodical. Japanese. Twelve times a year. $409.00. Nihon Yushi Shobo, (Saiwai Shobo Co. Ltd.), 57-1 Kanda Jinbocho 1 Chome, Chiyodaku Tokyo 101 Japan. (**Subscription address:** Japan Publications Trading Company Ltd., PO Box 5030, Tokyo International, Tokyo 100-31 Japan. **Tel** 011 81 3 3292 3753.) Documents available from CASDDS.
Ind/Abst Chem. Abstr.

ISSN 0867-7735
PL
UDC 66
ZESZYT NAUKOWY - POLITECHNIKA KRAKOWSKA. INZYNIERIA I TECHNOLOGIA CHEMICZNA. See Engineering-Chemical Engineering.

ISSN 0209-0600
PL
CODEN ZPLSDI
ZESZYTY NAUKOWE - POLITECHNIKA LODZKA. TECHNOLOGIA I CHEMIA SPOZYWCZA. (ZESZYTY NAUKOWE. TECHNOLOGIA I CHEMIA SPOZYWCZA.). [Zesz. nauk. - Politech. Lodz., Technol. chem. spozyw.]. Added/Corp Politechnika Lodka. VFOAT Technologia i Chemia Spozywcza. No. 34 (1980)-. Monographic series. Polish. Irregular. Price varies per volume. Wydawnictwo Politechniki Lodzkiej, Ul. Wolczanska 223, 93-005 Lodz Poland. (Subscription address: Ars Polona-Ruch, PO Box 1001, Krakowskie Przedmiescie 7, 00-068 Warsaw Poland. Tel 011 48 22 261201.) Circ: 200. Documents available from CASDDS. *Continues* Chemia Spozywcza, 0528-9254.
Desc: Chemical technology of food, fermentation, bio-inorganic and analytical chemistry.
Ind/Abst Chem. Abstr.; Sug. Indus. Abstr.

COMPUTER APPLICATIONS

ISSN 0939-7698
GW
BEILSTEIN CURRENT FACTS IN CHEMISTRY [COMPUTER FILE].
Added/Corp Beilstein Institut fuer Literatur der Organischen Chemie. **VFOAT** Current Facts in Chemistry. Vol. 1-4 (1990)-. English. Four times a year. $1490.00. Beilstein Informationssysteme, C Bosch Haus Varrentrappstrasse 40, D-60486 Frankfurt Germany. **Tel** 011 49 69 7917411, 011 49 69 7917507, FAX 011 49 69 7917321, 011 49 69 7917669. (**Subscription address:** Beilstein Informations Systems / US, 15 Inverness Way East, Inverness Business Park, Englewood CO 80112. **Tel** (708)778-6900.)
Desc: Combines factual and structural searching with browsing capabilities to be ideally suited for current awareness and daily informational needs.

ISSN 0160-9025
US
CODEN CCOCDF
CA SELECTS: COMPUTERS IN CHEMISTRY. Added/Corp American Chemical Society. Chemical Abstracts Service. VFOAT Computers in Chemistry. VAT Chemical Abstracts Selects. Computers in Chemistry. (July 10, 1978)-. Abstracting/Indexing Service. English. Twenty-six times a year. $220.00. Chemical Abstracts Service, (Subsidiary of The American Chemical Society), 2540 Olentangy River Road, PO Box 3012, Columbus OH 43210-0012. Tel (614)447-3731, (800)753-4227, FAX (614)447-3751. (Subscription address: Chemical Abstracts Service, Customer Service Department, PO Box 3012, Columbus OH 43210. Tel (800)848-6538, (614)447-3600.) ED David W Weisgerber.
Desc: Covers online and offline uses of computers in chemistry. Information on data processing, information retrieval, process control, programmed calculations and computer simulation models.

ISSN 0886-6716
DD 540
US
CCC
CODEN CDANEK
CHEMICAL DESIGN AUTOMATION NEWS. [Chem. des. autom. news]. VFOAT CDA News. Vol. 1, No. 1 (April 1986)-. Periodical. English. Twelve times a year. $250.00. Butterworth Heinemann / Woburn, MA, 225 Wildwood Avenue, Unit B, Woburn MA 01801. Tel (800)366-2665, FAX (617)928-2620, telex 880052. (Subscription address: Elsevier Science Inc. / New York Books, 655 Avenue of the Americas, New York NY 10010. Tel (212)633-3650.) Index available. Bk Rev. Ad Acc.
Desc: Computer-assisted molecular and materials design.

ISSN 0169-7439
NE
CCC
NLM W1; CH375
CODEN CILSEN
Pr Rev.
CHEMOMETRICS AND INTELLIGENT LABORATORY SYSTEMS. (CHEMOMETRICS AND INTELLIGENT LABORATORY SYSTEMS : AN INTERNATIONAL JOURNAL SPONSORED BY THE CHEMOMETRICS SOCIETY.). [Chemom. intell. lab. syst.]. Added/Corp Chemometrics Society. VFOAT Chemometrics and Intelligent Laboratory Systems. Laboratory Information Management; Laboratory Information Management. Vol. 1, No. 1 (1986)-. Academic Scholarly Publication. English. Eight times a year (4 vols.). $1139.00. Elsevier Science Publishers BV, PO Box 211, 1000 AE Amsterdam Netherlands. Tel 011 31 20 4853641, 011 31 20 4853642, FAX 011 31 20 4853598. ED D.L. Massart. available on microfilm and microfiche from University Microfilms International (UMI). available on an online database from Elsevier Electronic Subscriptions (EES). Documents available from The Genuine Article, BIOSIS Document Express, Ask*IEEE,

CASDDS.
Desc: Publishes articles about new developments on laboratory techniques in chemistry and related disciplines which are characterized by the application of statistical and computer methods.
Ind/Abst Anal. Abstr.; Biol. Abstr. (1986-); Chem. Abstr. (1986-); CompuMath Cit. Index [Full Cov.]; Comput. Rev.; Curr. Cit.; Curr. Contents Eng. Comput. Technol.; Curr. Contents Phys. Chem. Earth Sci.; Curr. Index Stat.; Ei Page One; EMBASE; GeoRef; Health Saf. Sci. Abstr.; INSPEC (1986-); Mass Spect. Bull. (?-?); Res. Alert [Full Cov.]; Sci. Cit. Index; SCISEARCH.

LC QD39.3.E46 C43
DD 540
US
CHEMPUTER BUYERS' GUIDE.
Added/Corp American Chemical Society. Vol. 1 (1991-1992)-. Periodical. English. One time a year. $50.00. American Chemical Society, 1155 Sixteenth Street Northwest, Washington DC 20036. Tel (800)333-9511, (800)227-5558, (614)447-3776, FAX (202)447-3671. ED Stacy Diamond. Ad Acc. Circ: 65,000.
Desc: Contains articles of interest to computer specifiers and buyers in the chemical industries.

LC QD39.3.E46 C647
DD 542/.8
ISSN 0097-8485
UK
CCC
NLM W1 CO457RI
CODEN COCHDK
Pr Rev.
COMPUTERS & CHEMISTRY. [Comput. chem.]. VFOAT Computers and Chemistry. Vol. 1, No. 1 (1976)-. Periodical. English. Four times a year. $703.00. Pergamon Press, An Imprint of Elsevier Science Ltd., The Boulevard, Langford Lane, Kidlington, Oxford OX5 1GB United Kingdom. Tel 011 44 1865 843000, 011 44 1865 843699, FAX 011 44 1865 843010. (Subscription address: Elsevier Science Ltd. / Oxford Fulfillment Centre, PO Box 800, Kidlington OX5 1DX United Kingdom. Tel 011 44 865 843355.) ED David Edelson. available on microfilm and microfiche from University Microfilms International (UMI); available on an online database from Elsevier Electronic Subscriptions (EES). Documents available from Article Express International, The Genuine Article, BIOSIS Document Express, Ask*IEEE, CASDDS, ADONIS.
Desc: Publishes papers on applications of computer techniques to chemistry and biochemistry. Articles discuss both the development of original algorithms (software) and the development of original techniques of interfacing (hardware). Also featured are reviews evaluating the relative merits of existing software/hardware and brief comments on a topic of significance about the performance of such.
Ind/Abst Abstr. Bull. Inst. Pap. Sci. Tech.; ADONIS; Bioeng. Abstr.; Biol. Abstr.; Chem. Abstr.; Chem. Titles; CompuMath Cit. Index [Full Cov.]; Comput. Abstr.; Comput. Rev.; Curr. Biotechnol.; Curr. Cit.; Curr. Contents Phys. Chem. Earth Sci.; Ei Page One; Eng. Index Annu.; Inf. Sci. Abstr.; INSPEC (1976-); Leadscan; Mass Spect. Bull.; Pollut. Abstr. Indexes; Res. Alert [Full Cov.]; Sci. Cit. Index; SCISEARCH; Zentralbl. Math. Ihre Grenzgeb.

LC QD40 .C6
DD 373
ISSN 8756-8829
US
COMPUTERS IN CHEMICAL EDUCATION NEWSLETTER. [Comput. chem. educ. newsl.]. VFOAT Newsletter. (19??)-. Newsletter. English. Four times a year. $2.50. Dr Rosenthal, Department of Chemistry, Clarkson University, Potsdam NY 13676.

LC QD
DD 540
ISSN 0146-7115
US
CODEN CPCIBS
COMPUTERS IN CHEMISTRY AND INSTRUMENTATION. [Comput. chem. instrum.]. (1971)-. Academic Scholarly Publication. English. Price varies per volume. Marcel Dekker Inc., 270 Madison Avenue, New York NY 10016. Tel (212)696-9000, (800)228-1160, FAX (212)685-4540, telex 421419. (Subscription address: Marcel Dekker Inc., PO Box 5017, Monticello NY 12701. Tel (800)228-1160.) Documents available from CASDDS.
Desc: Covers topics such as laboratory systems and spectroscopy and computers in polymer sciences.
Ind/Abst Chem. Abstr.

ISSN 1070-9924
DD 004
US
CCC
CODEN ISCEE4
•IEEE COMPUTATIONAL SCIENCE AND ENGINEERING. See Engineering-Computer Applications.

LC QA75.5 .C543
DD 004/.05
ISSN 1001-4160
CC
CODEN JYYHE6
Pr Rev.
JISUANJI YU YINGYONG HUAXUE. (CHI SUAN CHI YU YING YUNG HUA HSUEH.). [Jisuanji yu yingyong huaxue]. Added/Corp Chung-Kuo Hua Kung Hsueh Hui. Chi Suan Chi Hua Kung Ying Yung Chuan Yeh Wei Yuan Hui. VFOAT Computers and Applied Chemistry, China; Computers and Applied Chemistry.

Chemistry and Chemicals —Crystallography

(1984)-. Academic Scholarly Publication. Chinese (summaries and/or abstracts in English). Four times a year. $52.80. Science Press, 16 Donghuangchenggen North Street, Beijing 100707, People's Republic of China. **Tel** 011 86 1 4019821, 011 86 1 4010642, FAX 011 86 1 4012180, 011 86 1 4019810, telex 210147. **Ad Acc. Circ:** 4,200. Documents available from CASDDS, BLDSC, CASDDS.
Ind/Abst Chem. Abstr.

ISSN 1050-4281
DD 540 US
CODEN JCECE9
CEASED

JOURNAL OF CHEMICAL EDUCATION. SOFTWARE, A. (JOURNAL OF CHEMICAL EDUCATION. A SOFTWARE. [COMPUTER FILE].). [J. chem. educ., Softw. A]. **Added/Corp** American Chemical Society. Division of Chemical Education. **VFOAT** Software. A; JCE. Software; JCE Software. A; JCE. A Software. Vol. 1A, No. 1 (Aug. 1988)-(19??). Academic Scholarly Publication. English. Journal of Chemical Education Software, 1101 University Avenue, UWM Chemistry Department, Madison WI 53706. **Tel** (608)262-5153. Documents available from CASDDS.
Ind/Abst Chem. Abstr.

ISSN 1050-429X
DD 540 US

JOURNAL OF CHEMICAL EDUCATION. SOFTWARE, B. (JOURNAL OF CHEMICAL EDUCATION. SOFTWARE. B [COMPUTER FILE].). [J. chem. educ., Softw. B]. **Added/Corp** American Chemical Society. Division of Chemical Education. **VFOAT** Software. B; JCE. Software; JCE. B Software. Vol. 1B, No. 1 (Oct. 1988)-. Periodical. English. Two times a year. $100.00. Eastern Michigan University / Chemistry Dept., Department of Chemistry, I Wojeik-Andrews, Ypsilanti MI 48197. **Tel** (313)487-0150.
Desc: System requirements: IBM PC or compatible computer; 512K RAM; MS-DOS 3.0; disk drive; color monitor; color graphics adapter; mouse.

ISSN 1050-4303
DD 540 US

JOURNAL OF CHEMICAL EDUCATION. SOFTWARE, C. (JOURNAL OF CHEMICAL EDUCATION. SOFTWARE. C [COMPUTER FILE].). [J. chem. educ., Softw. C]. **Added/Corp** American Chemical Society. Division of Chemical Education. **VFOAT** Software. C; JCE. Software; JCE Software C; JCE. C Software. Vol. 1C, No. 1 (Dec. 1989)-. Periodical. English. Two times a year. $100.00. Journal of Chemical Education Software, 1101 University Avenue, UWM Chemistry Department, Madison WI 53706. **Tel** (608)262-5153.
Desc: System requirements: Macintosh compatible; 3 1/2" diskette drive.

ISSN 1066-4157
US
Pr Rev.

•JOURNAL OF CHEMICAL EDUCATION. SOFTWARE. D. (JOURNAL OF CHEMICAL EDUCATION. D SOFTWARE. [COMPUTER FILE].). **Added/Corp** American Chemical Society. Division of Chemical Education. **VFOAT** Software. D; JCE. Software; JCE Software. D; JCE. D Software. (1993)-. Periodical. English. Two times a year. Journal of Chemical Education Software, 1101 University Avenue, UWM Chemistry Department, Madison WI 53706. **Tel** (608)262-5153.

LC QD1 .A495 **ISSN** 0095-2338
DD 029/.9/54 US
CCC
NLM Z 1007 J85 **CODEN** JCISD8

JOURNAL OF CHEMICAL INFORMATION AND COMPUTER SCIENCES. [J. chem. inf. comput. sci.]. **Added/Corp** American Chemical Society. Vol. 15 (Feb. 1975)-. Academic Scholarly Publication. English. Six times a year. $276.00. American Chemical Society, 1155 Sixteenth Street Northwest, Washington DC 20036. **Tel** (800)333-9511, (800)227-5558, (614)447-3776, FAX (202)447-3671. **(Subscription address:** American Chemical Society / Ohio, Department L 0011, Columbus OH 43268-0011. **)** **ED** George W. A. Milne. Index available (bound in Nov. issue). **Bk Rev. Ad Acc. Acid Free. Circ:** 2,600 (ctrl). available on microfilm and microfiche from University Microfilms International (UMI). Documents available from Article Express International, The Genuine Article, BIOSIS Document Express, Ask*IEEE, CASDDS. **Continues** Journal of Chemical Documentation, 0021-9576.
Desc: Publishes high-quality papers on new research and development, concepts, systems and programs in all areas of information science and computer science relevant to chemistry and chemical technology.
Ind/Abst Abstr. Bull. Inst. Pap. Sci. Tech.; ACM Guide Comput. Lit.; Biol. Abstr.; Chem. Abstr.; Chem. Titles; Coal Abstr.; CompuMath Cit. Index [Full Cov.]; Comput. Abstr.; Comput. Rev.; Curr. Cit.; Curr. Contents Phys. Chem. Earth Sci.; Ei Page One; EMBASE; Energy Res. Abstr. (Feb. 1980)-; Eng. Index Annu.; GeoRef; Index Med.; Inf. Sci. Abstr. [Full Cov.]; INSPEC (Feb. 1975)-;

Libr. Inf. Sci. Abstr.; Proc. Chem. Eng.; Res. Alert [Full Cov.]; Sci. Cit. Index; SCISEARCH; Soc. Sci. Cit. Index [Select. Cov.]; Theor. Chem. Eng.

ISSN 0928-1045
NE
UDC 681.3 CCC

JOURNAL OF COMPUTER-AIDED MATERIALS DESIGN. [J. comput.-aided mater. des.]. (1993)-. Periodical. English. Three times a year. $293.00. ESCOM Science Publishers BV, PO Box 214, 2300 AE Leiden The Netherlands. **Tel** 011 31 71 127052.
Desc: Deals with recent advances in material design with special emphasis on the use of computers in these developments. Covers theoretical and other approaches to materials design and applications in chemistry, biochemistry, biotechnolgy, catalysis, superconductors as well as in electronics.

LC QD461 **ISSN** 0263-7855
DD 541.2/2/028566 UK
CCC
NLM W1; MO773Q **CODEN** JMGRDV
Pr Rev.

JOURNAL OF MOLECULAR GRAPHICS. [J. mol. graph.]. **VFOAT** Molecular Graphics. Vol. 1, No. 1 (March 1983)-. Academic Scholarly Publication. English. Six times a year. $525.00. Butterworth Heinemann / Woburn, MA, 225 Wildwood Avenue, Unit B, Woburn MA 01801. **Tel** (800)366-2665, FAX (617)928-2620, telex 880052. **(Subscription address:** Elsevier Science Inc. / New York Books, 655 Avenue of the Americas, New York NY 10010. **Tel** (212)633-3650.**) ED** W G Richards (editor's address: University of Oxford, UK). Index available. **Bk Rev. Ad Acc.** available on microfilm and microfiche from University Microfilms International (UMI). Documents available from Article Express International, The Genuine Article, CASDDS, ADONIS.
Desc: Provides a multidisciplinary forum for the publication of original papers and short communications and review articles on hardware and software of molecular graphics systems, new algorithms and procedures, useful parametric plots, new representations of molecular structures, results of projects using molecular graphics and molecular modelling using computer graphics.
Ind/Abst ACM Guide Comput. Lit.; ADONIS; Chem. Abstr. (1983-); Comput. Rev.; Curr. Aware. Biol. Sci., CABS; Curr. Cit.; Curr. Contents Phys. Chem. Earth Sci.; Ei Page One; EMBASE; Eng. Index Annu. [Select. Cov.]; Health Plan. Adminis.; Index Med.; Ref. Upd. Deluxe Ed.; Res. Alert [Full Cov.]; Sci. Cit. Index; SCISEARCH.

ISSN 0966-9086
UK

WINDOW ON CHEMETRICS. (1993)-. English. Twelve times a year. $192.00. Royal Society of Chemistry, Thomas Graham House, Science Park, Cambridge CB4 4WF United Kingdom. **Tel** 011 44 1223 420066, FAX 011 44 1223 423623, telex 818293 ROYAL. **(Subscription address:** Royal Society of Chemistry, Turpin Distribution Services Ltd., Blackhorse Road, Letchworth, Hertfordshire SG6 1HN United Kingdom. **Tel** 011 44 1462 672555, FAX 011 44 1462 480947.**)**

CRYSTALLOGRAPHY

ISSN 0896-1654
DD 548 US

AACG NEWSLETTER. [AACG newsl.]. **Added/Corp** American Association for Crystal Growth. **VAT** American Association for Crystal Growth Newsletter. (Oct. 1971)-. Newsletter. English. Four times a year. $50.00 Comes with American Association for Crystal Growth membership. American Association for Crystal Growth, 1617 Cole Boulevard, Golden CO 80401. **Tel** (303)231-1371. Documents available from The Genuine Article.
Ind/Abst Res. Alert [Full Cov.].

ISSN 0514-8863
US

ACA MONOGRAPHS. **Main/Corp** American Crystallographic Association. (1953)-. Monographic series. English. American Crystallographic Association, PO Box 96 Ellicott Station, Buffalo NY 14205. **Tel** (716)856-9600.

LC QD901 .A25
DK
CODEN ACACEQ

•ACTA CRYSTALLOGRAPHICA. SECTION A, FUNDAMENTALS OF CRYSTALLOGRAPHY. [Acta crystallogr., Sect. A]. **Added/Corp** International Union of Crystallography. **VFOAT** Fundamentals of Crystallography. Vol. A50, Pt. 1 (Jan. 1, 1994)-. Periodical. English. Six times a year. $434.55. Munksgaard International Publishers Ltd, PO Box 2148, DK-1016 Copenhagen K Denmark. **Tel** 011 45 33 127030, FAX 011 45 33 129387, telex 19431 MUNKS

DK. **Continues** Acta Crystallographica. Section A, Foundations of Crystallography, 0108-7673.
Ind/Abst Curr. Cit.; Index Med.

LC QD901 **ISSN** 0108-7681
DD 548/.05 DK
UDC 548 CCC
NLM W1; AC7838BA **CODEN** ASBSDK
Pr Rev.

ACTA CRYSTALLOGRAPHICA. SECTION B, STRUCTURAL SCIENCE. [Acta crystallogr., Sec. B]. **VFOAT** Structural Science. Vol. B39, Pt. 1 (Feb. 1983)-. Academic Scholarly Publication. English (French and German). Six times a year. $434.55. Munksgaard International Publishers Ltd, PO Box 2148, DK-1016 Copenhagen K Denmark. **Tel** 011 45 33 127030, FAX 011 45 33 129387, telex 19431 MUNKS DK. **ED** C E Bugg. Documents available from Article Express International, The Genuine Article, BIOSIS Document Express, Ask*IEEE, CASDDS. **Continues** ACTA Crystallographica. Section B, Structural Crystallography and Crystal Chemistry, 0567-7408.
Ind/Abst Abstr. Bull. Inst. Pap. Sci. Tech.; Alum. Ind. Abstr.; Biol. Abstr. (1987-); Ceram. Abstr.; Chem. Abstr. (1983-); Chem. Titles; Curr. Aware. Biol. Sci., CABS; Curr. Cit.; Curr. Contents Phys. Chem. Earth Sci.; Ei Page One; Energy Res. Abstr. (1983-); Eng. Index Annu. [Select. Cov.]; GeoRef (1983-); Index Med.; INSPEC (April 1983-); Leadscan; Met. Abstr. (1983-); NAPRALERT; Life Sci. Collect.; Res. Alert [Full Cov.]; Sci. Cit. Index; SCISEARCH.

LC QD901 **ISSN** 0108-2701
DD 548/.05 DK
UDC 548 CCC
CODEN ACSCEE
Pr Rev.

ACTA CRYSTALLOGRAPHICA. SECTION C, CRYSTAL STRUCTURE COMMUNICATIONS. [Acta crystallogr., Sec. C, cryst. struct. commun.]. Vol. C39, Pt. 1 (Jan. 15, 1983)-. Academic Scholarly Publication. English (French and German). Twelve times a year. $1050.81. Munksgaard International Publishers Ltd, PO Box 2148, DK-1016 Copenhagen K Denmark. **Tel** 011 45 33 127030, FAX 011 45 33 129387, telex 19431 MUNKS DK. **ED** C E Bugg. Documents available from Article Express International, The Genuine Article, BIOSIS Document Express, Ask*IEEE, CASDDS. **Continues** Crystal Structure Communications, 0302-1742.
Ind/Abst Biol. Abstr. (1987-); Chem. Abstr.; Chem. Titles; Curr. Aware. Biol. Sci., CABS; Curr. Cit.; Curr. Contents Phys. Chem. Earth Sci.; Ei Page One; Eng. Index Annu. [Select. Cov.]; GeoRef; Index Med.; INSPEC (Jan. 1983-); Nat. Prod. Updates; Life Sci. Collect.; Res. Alert [Full Cov.]; Sci. Cit. Index; SCISEARCH; Soils Fert.

ISSN 0907-4449
DK
CCC
NLM W1; AC7838CD

•ACTA CRYSTALLOGRAPHICA. SECTION D, BIOLOGICAL CRYSTALLOGRAPHY. **Added/Corp** International Union of Crystallography. **VFOAT** Biological Crystallography. Vol. D49, Pt. 1 (Jan. 1993)-. Periodical. English. Six times a year. $434.55. Munksgaard International Publishers Ltd, PO Box 2148, DK-1016 Copenhagen K Denmark. **Tel** 011 45 33 127030, FAX 011 45 33 129387, telex 19431 MUNKS DK.
Ind/Abst Sci. Cit. Index.

LC Z5524.C8 B9 QD905.2 **ISSN** 0304-1298
DD 016.548 FR

BULLETIN SIGNALETIQUE. 161, STRUCTURE DE L'ETAT CONDENSE, CRISTALLOGRAPHIE / CENTRE NATIONAL DE LA RECHERCHE SCIENTIFIQUE. See Chemistry and Chemicals-Abstracting, Bibliographies and Statistics.

ISSN 1049-1287
DD 548 US

C2C ABSTRACTS JAPAN. CRYSTALLOGRAPHY. See Chemistry and Chemicals-Abstracting, Bibliographies and Statistics.

ISSN 0162-7740
US
CODEN CSCGDB

CA SELECTS: CRYSTAL GROWTH. See Chemistry and Chemicals-Abstracting, Bibliographies and Statistics.

ISSN 0148-2351
US
CODEN CSLCDA

CA SELECTS: LIQUID CRYSTALS. See Chemistry and Chemicals-Abstracting, Bibliographies and Statistics.

ISSN 0208-8584
PL
CODEN PRCCDX

CONFERENCE ON APPLIED CRYSTALLOGRAPHY. PROCEEDINGS. (PROCEEDINGS / CONFERENCE ON APPLIED CRYSTALLOGRAPHY; SILESIAN UNIVERSITY IN KATOWICE; INSTITUTE OF FERROUS METALLURGY IN GLIWICE.). [Conf. Appl. Crystallogr., Proc.]. **Added/Corp** Uniwersytet Slaski w Katowicach. Institute of Ferrous Metallurgy in Gliwice. (19??)-. Proceedings. English. Every 2 years. Institute of Ferrous Metallurgy / Instytut Metalurgii Zelaza, Ul. K. Miarki 12, 44-100 Gliwice Poland. **Tel** 011 48 32 314051, FAX 011 48 32 313594. Documents available from CASDDS. ***Continues*** *Konferencja Naukowo-Techniczna. Rentgenografia Stosowana.*
Ind/Abst Chem. Abstr.

LC QD901 .K665 **ISSN** 0232-1300
DD 548/.05
GW
CCC
CODEN CRTEDF
Pr Rev.

CRYSTAL RESEARCH AND TECHNOLOGY (1979). (CRYSTAL RESEARCH AND TECHNOLOGY.). [Cryst. res. technol.]. Vol. 16, No. 1 (1981)-. Academic Scholarly Publication. English (French and German). Eight times a year. $645.00. Akademie-Verlag GmbH, Postfach, D-13162 Berlin Germany. **Tel** 011 49 30 47889300, FAX 011 49 30 47889357. **(Subscription address:** VCH Publishers Inc., 303 Northwest 12th Avenue, Journals Department, Deerfield FL 33442. **Tel** (800)367-8249, (305)428-5566.**)** Documents available from The Genuine Article, Ask*IEEE, CASDDS. ***Continues*** *Kristall und Technik, 0023-4753.*
Ind/Abst Alum. Ind. Abstr.; Chem. Abstr.; Chem. Titles; Curr. Cit.; Curr. Contents Phys. Chem. Earth Sci.; Ei Page One; Energy Res. Abstr. (Feb. 1982-); Eng. Mater. Abstr.; INSPEC (1981-); Leadscan; Met. Abstr.; Res. Alert [Full Cov.]; Sci. Cit. Index; SCISEARCH; Soils Fert.

LC QD901 .K7135 **ISSN** 1063-7745
DD 548
US
CCC

•CRYSTALLOGRAPHY REPORTS. [Crystallogr. rep.]. **Added/Corp** American Institute of Physics. **VFOAT** Crystallography. Vol. 38, No. 1 (Jan./Feb. 1993)-. Periodical. English (translations available in Russian). Six times a year. $1350.00. American Institute of Physics, 500 Sunnyside Boulevard, Woodbury NY 11797-2999. **Tel** (516)576-2270, (800)344-6902, FAX (516)349-9704, telex 960983. Index available (bound in last issue). Documents available from Ask*IEEE. ***Continues*** *Soviet Physics, Crystallography, 0038-5638.*
Ind/Abst Alum. Ind. Abstr.; Curr. Cit.; Curr. Phys. Index; Energy Res. Abstr.; GeoRef; INSPEC; Int. Aerosp. Abstr.; Math. Rev.; Met. Abstr.; SPIN.

LC QD901 .C78 **ISSN** 0889-311X
DD 548/.05
US
CCC
CODEN CCRVEN

CRYSTALLOGRAPHY REVIEWS. [Crystallogr. rev.]. Vol. 1, No. 1 (1987)-. Periodical. English. Irregular. $339.00 University and Hospital Libraries; 529.00*other. Gordon & Breach Science Publishers, Inc., PO Box 786, Cooper Station, New York NY 10276. **Tel** (212)206-8900, FAX (212)645-2459. Documents available from Article Express International.
Ind/Abst Eng. Index Annu.

LC QD921 .C8 **ISSN** 0172-5076
DD 548/.05
GW
CCC
CODEN CGPAD8

CRYSTALS. [Cryst.]. (1978)-. Academic Scholarly Publication. English. Irregular. Price varies per volume. Springer-Verlag GmbH & Company KG, Heidelberger Platz 3, D-14197 Berlin Germany. **Tel** 011 49 30 8207223, FAX 011 49 30 8214091, telex 183 319 SPBLN D. **(Subscription address:** Springer-Verlag New York Inc. / North America, PO Box 2485, Journal Fulfillment, Secaucus NJ 07096. **Tel** (201)348-4033, (800)777-4643, FAX (201)348-4505.**) ED** Herbert Freyhardt, Georg Mueller. Documents available from Ask*IEEE, CASDDS.
Desc: Contains articles on modern theory of crystal growth, and growth and defect structures.
Ind/Abst Ceram. Abstr.; Chem. Abstr.; Ei Page One; INSPEC.

LC QD382.C78 D48 **ISSN** 0263-6204
DD 668.9
UK

DEVELOPMENTS IN CRYSTALLINE POLYMERS. [Dev. cryst. polym.]. (1982)-. Academic Scholarly Publication. English. Elsevier Science Publishers Ltd., Crown House, Linton Road, Barking Essex IG11 8JU United Kingdom. **Tel** 011 44 181 5947272, FAX 011 44 181 5945942, telex 896950. Documents available from CASDDS.
Ind/Abst Chem. Abstr.

ISSN 0275-9608
UK

FERROELECTRICS AND RELATED PHENOMENA. [Ferroelectr. relat. phenom.]. Vol. 2-. Monographic series. English. Price varies per volume. Gordon & Breach Science Publishers, PO Box 90, Reading, Berkshire RG1 8JL United Kingdom. **Tel** 011 44 1734 560080, FAX 011 44 1734 568211. ***Continues*** *Ferroelectricity and Related Phenomena.*

LC QD548 .F537
RU

FIZIKA KRISTALLIZATSII. Added/Corp Kalininskii Gosudarstvennyi Universitet. (19??)-. Russian. Kaliningradskii Gosudarstvennyi Universitet / Kaliningrad State University, Ulitsa A Nevskogo 14, 236041 Kaliningrad Russia. **Tel** 011 7 465917, FAX 011 7 465813, telex 262116.

US

GROWTH OF CRYSTALS. Added/Corp Institut Kristallografii im. A.V. Shubnikova. Consultants Bureau. (1956)-. Monographic series. English (Russian). Irregular. Price varies per volume. Plenum Press, 233 Spring Street, New York NY 10013-1578. **Tel** (212)620-8000, (800)221-9369, FAX (212)463-0742, (212)807-1047, telex 23/421139. **ED** A.V. Shubnikov and N.N. Sheftal.

ISSN 0202-7984
RU

IGOTI NAUKI I TEKHNIKI. SERIIA KRISTALLOKHIMIIA. Added/Corp Vsesoiuznyi Institut Nauchnoi i Tekhnicheskoi Informatsii (Soviet Union). **VFOAT** Seriia Kristallokhimia; Kristallokhomiia; Itogi Nauki i Tekhniki. Kristallokhimiia. (19??)-. Monographic series. Russian. VINITI - Vsesoyuznyi Institut Nauchno-Tekhnicheskoi Informatsii, All-Union Scientific and Technical Information Institute, Baltiiskaia ulitsa 14, 125219 Moscow Russia. **Tel** 011 7 95 2384600, FAX 011 7 95 9430060, telex 411160. Documents available from CASDDS. ***Continues*** *Itogi Nauki i Tekhniki. Kristallokhimiia.*
Ind/Abst Chem. Abstr.

LC QD951 .I8
RU
CODEN INKKBO

ITOGI NAUKI I TEKHNIKI : KRISTALLOKHIMIIA. Added/Corp Vsesoiuznyi Institut Nauchnoi i Tekhnicheskoi i Tekhnicheskoi Informatsii. **VFOAT** Itogi Nauki i Tekhniki: Seriia Kristallokhimiia; Itogi Nauki i Tekhniki: Seriia Kristallokhimiia. (1972)-. Academic Scholarly Publication. Russian. VINITI - Vsesoyuznyi Institut Nauchno-Tekhnicheskoi Informatsii, All-Union Scientific and Technical Information Institute, Baltiiskaia ulitsa 14, 125219 Moscow Russia. **Tel** 011 7 95 2384600, FAX 011 7 95 9430060, telex 411160. Documents available from CASDDS. ***Continues*** *Itogi Nauki: Kristallokhimiia.*
Ind/Abst Chem. Abstr.

LC QD901 **ISSN** 0021-8898
DD 548/.05
DK
UDC 548
CCC
CODEN JACGAR
Pr Rev.

JOURNAL OF APPLIED CRYSTALLOGRAPHY. [J. appl. crystallogr.]. Vol. 1 (Apr. 1968)-. Periodical. English (French). Six times a year. $406.90. Munksgaard International Publishers Ltd, PO Box 2148, DK-1016 Copenhagen K Denmark. **Tel** 011 45 33 127030, FAX 011 45 33 129387, telex 19431 MUNKS DK. **ED** M Schlenker. **Bk Rev. Ad Acc. Circ:** 1,200 (ctrl). Documents available from Article Express International, The Genuine Article, Ask*IEEE, CASDDS.
Desc: Methods, apparatus, problems, and discoveries in applied crystallography.
Ind/Abst Abstr. Bull. Inst. Pap. Sci. Tech.; Alum. Ind. Abstr.; Ceram. Abstr.; Chem. Abstr.; Chem. Titles; Civ. Struct. Eng. Abstr.; Comput. Inf. Syst. Abstr. J. [Full Cov.]; Curr. Aware. Biol. Sci., CABS; Curr. Cit.; Curr. Contents Phys. Chem. Earth Sci.; Ei Page One; Elect. Comm. Abstr.; Energy Res. Abstr.; Eng. Mater. Abstr.; Eng. Index Annu.; GeoRef; INSPEC (1968-); Leadscan; Mater. Sci. Eng. Abstr.; Mech. Eng. Abstr.; Met. Abstr.; Res. Alert [Full Cov.]; Sci. Cit. Index; SCISEARCH; Solid State Supercond. Abstr.; World Ceram. Abstr.; World Text. Abstr.

LC QD901 .J62 **ISSN** 1074-1542
DD 548
US
CODEN JCCYEV

•JOURNAL OF CHEMICAL CRYSTALLOGRAPHY. [J. chem. crystallogr.]. Vol. 24, No. 1 (Jan. 1994)-. Periodical. English. Twelve times a year. $525.00. Plenum Press, 233 Spring Street, New York NY 10013-1578. **Tel** (212)620-8000, (800)221-9369, FAX (212)463-0742, (212)807-1047, telex 23/421139. ***Continues*** *Journal of Crystallographic and Spectroscopic Research, 0277-8068.*
Ind/Abst Curr. Cit.

LC QD921 .J6 **ISSN** 0022-0248
NE
CCC
CODEN JCRGAE
Pr Rev.

JOURNAL OF CRYSTAL GROWTH. [J. cryst. growth]. Vol. 1 (Jan. 1967)-. Academic Scholarly Publication. English (French and German; summaries and/or abstracts in French and German). Forty-eight times a year (12 volumes). $6207.00. Elsevier Science Publishers BV, PO Box 211, 1000 AE Amsterdam Netherlands. **Tel** 011 31 20 4853641, 011 31 20 4853642, FAX 011 31 20 4853598. **ED** M. Schieber. cum. index. available on microfilm and microfiche from University Microfilms International (UMI); available on an online database from Elsevier Electronic Subscriptions (EES). Documents available from Article Express International, The Genuine Article, Ask*IEEE, CASDDS.
Desc: Offers a common reference and publication source for workers engaged in research and the experimental and theoretical aspects of crystal growth and its applications, e.g. in devices.
Ind/Abst Alum. Ind. Abstr.; Ceram. Abstr. (1968-); Chem. Abstr.; Chem. Titles; Civ. Struct. Eng. Abstr.; Comput. Inf. Syst. Abstr. J. [Full Cov.]; Curr. Cit.; Curr. Contents Phys. Chem. Earth Sci.; Ei Page One; Elect. Comm. Abstr.; Eng. Mater. Abstr. (1968-); Eng. Index Annu.; Environ. Eng. Abstr.; GeoRef; HTFS Dig.; INSPEC (1968-); Int. Aerosp. Abstr.; Leadscan; Manuf. Process Eng. Abstr.; Mater. Sci. Eng. Abstr.; Mech. Eng. Abstr.; Met. Abstr.; Phys. Briefs; Pollut. Abstr. Indexes; Proc. Chem. Eng.; Res. Alert [Full Cov.]; Sci. Cit. Index; SCISEARCH; Soils Fert.; Solid State Supercond. Abstr. (1968-); Theor. Chem. Eng.

LC QD901 .J62 **ISSN** 0277-8068
DD 548
US
CCC
NLM W1 JO612DE **CODEN** JCREDB
Pr Rev. **TITLE CHANGE**

JOURNAL OF CRYSTALLOGRAPHIC AND SPECTROSCOPIC RESEARCH. [J. crystallogr. spectrosc. res.]. Vol. 12, No. 1 (Feb. 1982)-(1994). Academic Scholarly Publication. English. Plenum Press, 233 Spring Street, New York NY 10013-1578. **Tel** (212)620-8000, (800)221-9369, FAX (212)463-0742, (212)807-1047, telex 23/421139. **ED** M.F.C Ladd, J.L. Atwood, S.F.A. Kettle. Index available. available on microfilm and microfiche from University Microfilms International (UMI). Documents available from The Genuine Article, Ask*IEEE, CASDDS. ***Continues*** *Journal of Crystal and Molecular Structure, 0308-4086.* ***Continued by*** *Journal of Chemical Crystallography, 1074-1542.*
Desc: International interdisciplinary medium for the rapid publication of research results in the general areas of crystallography and spectroscopy reporting on new research in crystal chemistry and physics.
Ind/Abst Chem. Abstr.; Chem. Titles; Curr. Cit.; Curr. Contents Phys. Chem. Earth Sci.; GeoRef; INIS Atomindex [Micro.]; INSPEC (Feb. 1982-); Res. Alert [Full Cov.]; Sci. Cit. Index; SCISEARCH; Sug. Indus. Abstr.

LC QD901 .K67
RU
CODEN KSKRD2

KRISTALLIZATSIIA I SVOISTVA KRISTALLOV; MEZHVUZOVSKII SBORNIK. Added/Corp Novocherkask, Russia. Politekhnicheskii Institut. **VFOAT** Mezhvuzovskii Sbornik Nauchnykh Trudov Kristallizatsiia I Svoistva Kristallov. Vol. 1 (1974)-. Academic Scholarly Publication. Russian. Politekhnicheskii Institut, Novocherkask Russia. Documents available from CASDDS.
Ind/Abst Chem. Abstr. (?-1976);(-1976).

LC QD901 .K7 **ISSN** 0023-4761
RU
CCC
CODEN KRISAJ
Pr Rev.

KRISTALLOGRAFIJA. (KRISTALLOGRAFIIA.). [Kristallografija]. **Added/Corp** Akademiia Nauk SSSR. (1956)-. Academic Scholarly Publication. Russian. Six times a year. $149.00. Izdatelstvo Nauka / Akademiia Nauk, (Publishing House of the Russian Academy of Sciences), Leninskii Porspekt 14, 117901 Moscow Russia. **Tel** 011 95 9542153, FAX 011 95 9382144, telex 411964. **(Subscription address:** East View Publications Inc., 3020 Harbor Lane North, Suite 110, Minneapolis MN 55447. **Tel** (800)477-1005, (612)550-0961, FAX (612)559-2931.**)** cum. index. Documents available from The Genuine Article, Ask*IEEE, CASDDS.
Ind/Abst Acoust. Abstr.; Alum. Ind. Abstr.; Ceram. Abstr.; Chem. Abstr.; Chem. Titles; Eng. Mater. Abstr.; GeoRef; INSPEC (1968-); Int. Aerosp. Abstr.; Leadscan; Math. Rev.; Met. Abstr.; Res. Alert [Full Cov.]; Sci. Cit. Index; SCISEARCH; World Alum. Abstr.; Zentralbl. Math. Ihre Grenzgeb.

LC QD923 .L543 **ISSN** 0267-8292
DD 548/.9
UK
CCC
CODEN LICRE6
Pr Rev.

LIQUID CRYSTALS. [Liq. cryst.]. Vol. 1, No. 1 (Jan./Feb. 1986)-. Academic Scholarly Publication. English. Twelve times a year. $1790.00. Taylor & Francis

Ltd. / UK, Rankine Road, Basingstoke, Hampshire RG24 8PR United Kingdom. **Tel** 011 44 1256 840366, FAX 011 44 1256 479438, telex 858540. **(Subscription address:** Taylor & Francis Inc., 1900 Frost Road, Suite 101, Bristol PA 19007-1598. **Tel** (215)785-5800, (800)821-8312, FAX (215)785-5515.**) ED** Professor George Gray, Professor E. T. Samulski and Mr. I. D. Fletcher, assistant editor. available on microfilm and microfiche from University Microfilms International (UMI). Documents available from The Genuine Article, Ask*IEEE, CASDDS.
Desc: Publishes accounts of original research concerned with all aspects of liquid crystal science and technology. Included in these are experimental and theoretical studies of liquid crystals together with their synthesis and applications. The journal provides the scientific community, in both academia and industry, with a publication of standing, guaranteed by the editors and the editorial board who are active scientists in the liquid crystal community.
Ind/Abst Chem. Abstr. (1986-); Chem. Titles; Curr. Cit.; Curr. Contents Phys. Chem. Earth Sci. (1986-); INSPEC (1986); Res. Alert [Full Cov.]; Sci. Cit. Index; SCISEARCH.

LC QD923 .L56 **ISSN** 0146-5597
DD 548/.9 US
CODEN LCOFDL

LIQUID CRYSTALS AND ORDERED FLUIDS. [Liq. cryst. ordered fluids]. **Main/Conf** Symposium on Ordered Fluids and Liquid Crystals. **Added/Corp** American Chemical Society. Division of Colloid and Surface Chemistry. Vol. 1 (1969)-. Academic Scholarly Publication. English. Irregular. Price varies per volume. Plenum Press, 233 Spring Street, New York NY 10013-1578. **Tel** (212)620-8000, (800)221-9369, FAX (212)463-0742, (212)807-1047, telex 23/421139. Documents available from Ask*IEEE, CASDDS.
Ind/Abst Chem. Abstr.; INSPEC.

LC QH201 .M585 **ISSN** 0026-282X
DD 502/.8/2 US
CCC
NLM W1; MI309H **CODEN** MICRAD
Pr Rev.

MICROSCOPE (LONDON). See Biology-Microscopy.

LC QD901
DD 548 US

MOLECULAR CRYSTALS AND LIQUID CRYSTALS. LETTERS SECTION (NEW YORK, N.Y. : 1991). (19??)-. Academic Scholarly Publication. English. Gordon & Breach Science Publishers, Inc., PO Box 786, Cooper Station, New York NY 10276. **Tel** (212)206-8900, FAX (212)645-2459. **ED** MM Labes. **Ad Acc.** available with charts; available with illustrations. Documents available from BLDSC, FAXON Xpress, SWETS.

LC QD901 .M64 **ISSN** 1058-725X
DD 548/.08 US
CCC
CODEN MCLCE9

MOLECULAR CRYSTALS AND LIQUID CRYSTALS SCIENCE AND TECHNOLOGY: SECTION A, MOLECULAR CRYSTALS AND LIQUID CRYSTALS. [Mol. cryst. liq. cryst. sci. technol., A Mol. cryst. liq. cryst.]. **VFOAT** Molecular Crystals and Liquid Crystals; MCLC. Vol. 210 (Jan. 1992)-. Periodical. English. Twelve times a year. $736.00 (academic institutions), $1148.00 (corporate institutions). Gordon & Breach Science Publishers, Inc., PO Box 786, Cooper Station, New York NY 10276. **Tel** (212)206-8900, FAX (212)645-2459. Documents available from Article Express International. ***Continues in part*** *Molecular Crystals and Liquid Crystals (New York, N.Y. : 1991), 1056-8816; Nonlinear Optics, 1055-5218.*
Ind/Abst Ei Page One; Eng. Index Annu.; Leadscan.

LC QC446.15 .N68 **ISSN** 1058-7268
DD 535.2/05 US
CCC
CODEN MCLOEB

MOLECULAR CRYSTALS AND LIQUID CRYSTALS SCIENCE AND TECHNOLOGY SECTION B, NONLINEAR OPTICS. [Mol. cryst. liq. cryst. sci. technol., B, Nonlinear opt.]. **VFOAT** Nonlinear Optics. Vol. 2, No. 1 (1992)-. Periodical. English. Four times a year (3 volumes). $375.00 (academic institutions), $588.00 (corporate institutions). Gordon & Breach Science Publishers, Inc., PO Box 786, Cooper Station, New York NY 10276. **Tel** (212)206-8900, FAX (212)645-2459. ***Continues*** *Nonlinear Optics, 1053-3729.*

ISSN 1058-7276
DD 548 US
CCC
CODEN MOMAEO

MOLECULAR CRYSTALS AND LIQUID CRYSTALS SCIENCE AND TECHNOLOGY SECTION C, MOLECULAR MATERIALS. [Mol. cryst. liq. cryst. sci. technol., C, Mol. mater.]. **VFOAT** Molecular Materials. Vol. 1, No. 1 (1992)-. Periodical. English. Four times a year. $373.00 (academic institutions), $582.00 (corporate institutions). Gordon & Breach Science Publishers, Inc., PO Box 786, Cooper Station, New York NY 10276. **Tel** (212)206-8900, FAX (212)645-2459. ***Continues in part*** *Molecular Crystals and Liquid Crystals (New York, N.Y. : 1991), 1056-8816.*

ISSN 1058-7284
US
CCC

•MOLECULAR CRYSTALS AND LIQUID CRYSTALS SCIENCE AND TECHNOLOGY SECTION D, DISPLAY AND IMAGING. **VFOAT** Display and Imaging. (1994)-. Periodical. English. Six times a year (1 volume). $457.00 (academic institutions), $713.00 (corporate institutions). Gordon & Breach Science Publishers, Inc., PO Box 786, Cooper Station, New York NY 10276. **Tel** (212)206-8900, FAX (212)645-2459. ***Continues in part*** *Molecular Crystals and Liquid Crystals (New York, N.Y. : 1991), 1056-8816; Nonlinear Optics.*

ISSN 0731-7689
DD 548 UK
UDC 532.783
CODEN MCLSDM

MOLECULAR CRYSTALS AND LIQUID CRYSTALS. SUPPLEMENT SERIES. [Mol. cryst. liq. cryst., Suppl. ser.]. Suppl. 1-. Academic Scholarly Publication. English. Price varies per volume. Gordon & Breach Science Publishers, PO Box 90, Reading, Berkshire RG1 8JL United Kingdom. **Tel** 011 44 1734 560080, FAX 011 44 1734 568211. **ED** M M Labes. Documents available from Ask*IEEE, CASDDS.
Ind/Abst Chem. Abstr. (1982); Curr. Contents Phys. Chem. Earth Sci.; INSPEC (1982-).

ISSN 0369-4585
JA
CODEN NKEGAF

NIHON KESSHO GAKKAI SHI. [Nihon Kessho Gakkaishi]. **Added/Corp** Nihon Kessho Gakkai. **VFOAT** Nihon Kessho Gakkai-Shi; Journal of the Crystallographic Society of Japan. Vol. 1, No. 1,2 (Nov. 1959)-. Academic Scholarly Publication. Japanese (summaries and/or abstracts in English). Six times a year. $177.00. Nihon Kessho Gakkai, (Crystallographic Soc. of Japan), Nihon Gakkai Jimu Senta, 4-16 Yayoi 2 Chome, Bunkyoku Tokyo 113 Japan. **(Subscription address:** Japan Publications Trading Company Ltd., PO Box 5030, Tokyo International, Tokyo 100-31 Japan. **Tel** 011 81 3 3292 3753.**)** available on an online database from CISTI; STN International; ORBIT; OCLC EPIC; DIALOG; and (GEOREF) BRS. Documents available from CASDDS.
Ind/Abst Chem. Abstr.; GeoRef.

LC QD921 .N53 **ISSN** 0385-6275
JA
UDC 548.2
CODEN NKSGDK

NIHON KESSHO SEICHO GAKKAI SHI. [Nihon Kessho Seicho Gakkai shi]. **VFOAT** Journal of the Japanese Association of Crystal Growth. Vol. 1, No. 1 (Nov. 1974)-. Academic Scholarly Publication. Japanese. Four times a year. 5000. Do Gakkai, Keto Tsushin 19-ban 30-go Mita, 2-chome Minato-ku, Tokyo 108 Japan. Documents available from CASDDS.
Ind/Abst Chem. Abstr.

LC Z5524.C8 M6 QD921
DD 016.548/81/08 S 016.548/81 NE

ORGANIC AND ORGANOMETALLIC CRYSTAL STRUCTURES; BIBLIOGRAPHY. See Chemistry and Chemicals-Abstracting, Bibliographies and Statistics.

LC QC482.D5 P643 **ISSN** 8756-0127
DD 548/.83 US

POWDER DIFFRACTION FILE ALPHABETICAL INDEX. INORGANIC PHASES. (POWDER DIFFRACTION FILE ALPHABETICAL INDEX.). [Powder diffr. file alph. index, Inorg. phases]. **Added/Corp** JCPDS--International Centre for Diffraction Data. **VFOAT** Powder Diffraction File Alphabetical Indexes. Inorganic Phases; Powder Diffraction File; Alphabetical Index. Inorganic Phases; Alphabetical Indexes. Inorganic Phases; Inorganic Phases; Powder Diffraction File Inorganic Phases Alphabetical Index (Chemical and Mineral name); Powder Diffraction File Inorganic Phases Alphabetical Indexes. (1980)-. English. One time a year. $300.00 soft cover book. Joint Committee on Powder Diffraction Standards / JCPDS, International Centre for Diffraction Data, 12 Campus Boulevard, Newton Square PA 19073. **Tel** (610)325-9810, FAX (610)325-9823, telex 847170. ***Continues*** *Powder Diffraction File Alphabetical Index: Inorganic Materials.*
Desc: List phases by chemical name and by portions of chemical name. Minerals are listed by mineralogical name and by groups.

LC QD901 .P77
RU
CODEN PRKREH

PROBLEMY KRISTALLOKHIMII. **Added/Corp** Nauchnyi Sovet po Khimicheskoi Kinetike i Stroeniiu (Akademiia Nauk SSSR) Institut Obshchei i Neorganicheskoi Khimii im. N.S. Kurnakova. (1984)-. Academic Scholarly Publication. Russian. One time a year. Izdatelstvo Nauka / Akademiia Nauk, (Publishing House of the Russian Academy of Sciences), Leninskii Porspekt 14, 117901 Moscow Russia. **Tel** 011 95 9542153, FAX 011 95 9382144, telex 411964. Documents available from CASDDS.
Ind/Abst Chem. Abstr.

LC QD921 .P747 **ISSN** 0960-8974
DD 548/.5 UK
CCC
CODEN PCGMED

PROGRESS IN CRYSTAL GROWTH AND CHARACTERIZATION OF MATERIALS. [Prog. cryst. growth charact. mater.]. **VFOAT** Prog. Crystal Growth and Charact. Vol. 20 No. 1/2 (1990)-. Academic Scholarly Publication. English. Eight times a year. $1431.00. Pergamon Press, An Imprint of Elsevier Science Ltd., The Boulevard, Langford Lane, Kidlington, Oxford OX5 1GB United Kingdom. **Tel** 011 44 1865 843000, 011 44 1865 843699, FAX 011 44 1865 843010. **(Subscription address:** Elsevier Science Ltd. / Oxford Fulfillment Centre, PO Box 800, Kidlington OX5 1DX United Kingdom. **Tel** 011 44 865 843355.**) ED** Brian Mullin, Claude Schwab, P. Krishna, and N. Singh. available on an online database from Elsevier Electronic Subscriptions (EES). Documents available from Article Express International, The Genuine Article, Ask*IEEE, CASDDS. ***Continues*** *Progress in Crystal Growth and Characterization, 0146-3535.*
Desc: Articles cover crystal growth and all aspects of related processing and characterization which are key technologies in the commercial exploitation of an extensive range of important advanced materials through organics to biomolecular crystals.
Ind/Abst Alum. Ind. Abstr.; Bioeng. Abstr. (1990-); Chem. Abstr. (1990-); Curr. Cit.; Curr. Contents Phys. Chem. Earth Sci.; Ei Page One (1990-); Eng. Index Annu.; Eng. Index Energy Abstr. (1990-); INSPEC (1990-); Met. Abstr. (1990-); Res. Alert [Full Cov.]; Sci. Cit. Index; SCISEARCH.

ISSN 1000-985X
DD 666.8 CC

RENGONG JINGTI XUEBAO. **VFOAT** Journal of Synthetic Crystals. (1989)-. Academic Scholarly Publication. Chinese. Four times a year. Documents available from CASDDS. ***Continues*** *Rengong Jingti, 1001-0904.*
Ind/Abst Chem. Abstr.

FR

ROCHES CRISTALLINES. F42. French. 627.92F France; 650.00F other. CNRS / Institut d'Information Scientifique et Technique, (Centre National de la Recherche Scientifique), 15 Quai Anatole France, 75700 Paris France. **Tel** 011 33 1 47531515, FAX 011 33 1 45517307, telex 260034. ***Continues*** *Pascal Folio. F42, Roches Cristallines, 0761-1838.*

LC QD921 .R628 **ISSN** 0485-4802
RU
CODEN RKANAQ

ROST KRISTALLOV . **Added/Corp** Institut Kristallografii im. A.V. Shubnikova. (1957)-. Russian. Izdatelstvo Nauka / Akademiia Nauk, (Publishing House of the Russian Academy of Sciences), Leninskii Porspekt 14, 117901 Moscow Russia. **Tel** 011 95 9542153, FAX 011 95 9382144, telex 411964. Documents available from CASDDS.
Ind/Abst Chem. Abstr.

LC QD901 .K7135 **ISSN** 0038-5638
DD 548.05 US
CCC
CODEN SPHCA6
TITLE CHANGE

SOVIET PHYSICS-CRYSTALLOGRAPHY. [Sov. phys. Crystallogr.]. **Added/Corp** American Institute of Physics. American Crystallographic Association. Vol. 1 (Jan./Feb. 1956)-(1993). Periodical. English (Russian). American Institute of Physics, 500 Sunnyside Boulevard, Woodbury NY 11797-2999. **Tel** (516)576-2270, (800)344-6902, FAX (516)349-9704, telex 960983. Documents available from Ask*IEEE. ***Continued by*** *Crystallography Reports.*
Ind/Abst Acoust. Abstr.; Alum. Ind. Abstr.; Curr. Phys. Index; Energy Res. Abstr.; Eng. Mater. Abstr.; Geol. Abstr.; GeoRef; INSPEC (1968-); Int. Aerosp. Abstr.; Math. Rev.; Met. Abstr.; SPIN (1970-); Zentralbl. Math. Ihre Grenzgeb.

FR

STRUCTURE DES LIQUIDES ET DES SOLIDES CRISTALLOGRAPHIE, E13. (19??)-. French. Irregular. 1271.15F France; 1320.00F other. CNRS / Institut d'Information Scientifique et Technique, (Centre National de la Recherche Scientifique), 15 Quai Anatole France, 75700 Paris

Chemistry and Chemicals — Crystallography

France. **Tel** 011 33 1 47531515, FAX 011 33 1 45517307, telex 260034. **Continues** Pascal Explore E13, Structure des Liquides et des Solides Cristallographique.
LC QD901 .S8
NE
CEASED

STRUCTURE REPORTS. Added/Corp International Union of Crystallography. Commision on Structure Reports. (1913/28)-(1985/1993). English. Kluwer Academic Publishers, Postbus 322, 3300 AH Dordrecht The Netherlands. **Tel** 011 31 78 524400, FAX 011 31 78 183273, telex 20083. **(Subscription address:** Kluwer Academic Publishers / US Subscriptions, PO Box 253, Accord Station, Hingham MA 02018. **Tel** (617)871-6600.) **ED** G. Ferguson. cum. index. **Circ:** 500.
Desc: Collation of all published crystal structure determinations.

ISSN 0309-8133
UK

SYNTHETIC CRYSTALS NEWSLETTER. [Synth. cryst. newsl.]. (1974)-. Newsletter. English. Ten times a year (Oct. thru July; academic year). $11.98. Michael Odonoghue Gemmologists, 7 Hillingdon Avenue, Sevenoak Kent, TN13 3RB United Kingdom. **Tel** 011 44 1732 453503, FAX 011 44 1732 740904. **ED** Michael O'Donoghue. **Bk Rev**, (Qty: 6).
Desc: Current awareness newsletter on man-made crystalline substances.
LC QD431.A1 K48
ISSN 0916-1554
JA
CODEN TKKDE4

TANPAKUSHITSU KOGAKU KISO KENKYU SENTA DAYORI. Added/Corp Osaka Daigaku. Tanpakushitsu Kogaku Kiso Kenkyu Senta. No. 10 (1989)-. Periodical. Japanese. Osaka Daigaku Tanpakushitsu Kenkyusho, Fuzoku Tanpakushitsu Kogaku Kiso Kenkyu, Senta, Yamadaoka Suita-shi Osaka Japan. **Continues** Kessho Kaiseki Kenkyu Senta Dayori, 0388-6409.
LC QD901 .T48
DD 548/.05
ISSN 0730-3300
US
CCC
CODEN TEMIDK

Pr Rev.
TEXTURES AND MICROSTRUCTURES. [Textures microstruct.]. Vol. 4, No. 4 (March 1982)-. Academic Scholarly Publication. English. Four times a year. Price varies. Gordon & Breach Science Publishers, Inc., PO Box 786, Cooper Station, New York NY 10276. **Tel** (212)206-8900, FAX (212)645-2459. **(Subscription address:** Gordon & Breach Science Publishers / England, PO Box 90 Reading, Berkshire RG1 8JL United Kingdom. **Tel** 011 44 734 560080.) **ED** S. H. White. **Bk Rev**. **Ad Acc**. Documents available from Article Express International, The Genuine Article, Ask*IEEE, CASDDS. **Continues** Texture of Crystalline Solids, 0309-7951.
Ind/Abst Alum. Ind. Abstr.; Annu. Bibliogr. Engl. Lang. Lit.; Bioeng. Abstr.; Chem. Abstr.; Curr. Cit.; Curr. Contents Eng. Comput. Technol.; Eng Index Eng. Mater. Abstr.; Eng. Index Annu.; GeoRef; INSPEC (1982-); Met. Abstr.; Res. Alert [Full Cov.].
LC QD901 .A7
DD 548/.05
ISSN 0065-8006
US
CCC
CODEN TACAAH

TRANSACTIONS OF THE AMERICAN CRYSTALLOGRAPHIC ASSOCIATION. [Trans. Am. Crystallogr. Assoc.]. **Added/Corp** American Crystallographic Association. Vol. 1, (1965)-. Monographic series. English. Irregular. $26.50. Polycrystal Book Service, PO Box 3439, Dayton OH 45401. **Tel** (513)223-9070. **Ad Acc**, **Adv Mgr:** American Crystallographic Association, **Tel** (716)856-9600. **Circ:** 3,500. Documents available from Article Express International, CASDDS.
Desc: Proceedings of the annual meeting of the American Crystallographic Association.
Ind/Abst Chem. Abstr.; Ei Page One; Energy Res. Abstr.; Eng. Index Annu.; GeoRef (1980-); SPIN.

ISSN 0277-2507
US

WILEY MONOGRAPHS IN CRYSTALLOGRAPHY. [Wiley monogr. crystallogr.]. (19??)-. Monographic series. English. Irregular. Price varies per volume. John Wiley & Sons, Inc., 605 Third Avenue, New York NY 10158-0012. **Tel** (212)850-6000, (212)850-6645, FAX (212)850-6088, telex 12-7063. **(Subscription address:** John Wiley & Sons / UK, Baffins Lane, Chichester, West Sussex PO19 1UD United Kingdom. **Tel** 011 44 1243 779777, FAX 011 44 243 776128, telex 86290 WIBOOKG.)
LC QD901 .Z5
DD 548/.05
GW
CODEN ZEKRDZ

Pr Rev.
ZEITSCHRIFT FUER KRISTALLOGRAPHIE. [Z. Kristallogr.]. Vol. 147 (1978)-. Academic Scholarly Publication. English (German). Twelve times a year. $1423.08. R Oldenbourg Verlag, Postfach 801360, D-81613 Munich Germany. **Tel** 011 49 89 450190, FAX 011 49 89 45019305. **Bk Rev**. **Ad Acc**. **Circ:** 1,000. available on microfilm from University Microfilms International (UMI). Documents available from The Genuine Article, Ask*IEEE, CASDDS. **Continues** Zeitschrift fur Kristallographie, Kristallgeometrie, Kristallphysik, Kristallchemie, 0044-2968.
Desc: Contains original research articles from the fields of crystal geometry, physics and chemistry.
Ind/Abst Ceram. Abstr. (19??-); Chem. Abstr.; Curr. Cit.; Curr. Contents Phys. Chem. Earth Sci.; Energy Res. Abstr.; Geol. Abstr.; GeoRef; INSPEC (1978-); Res. Alert [Full Cov.]; Sci. Cit. Index; SCISEARCH; World Ceram. Abstr.; Zentralbl. Math. Ihre Grenzgeb.
LC TP159.M6 Z46
DD 660.2/82
UDC 549.67
ISSN 0144-2449
US
CCC
CODEN ZEOLD3

Pr Rev.
ZEOLITES. See Chemistry and Chemicals-Inorganic Chemistry.

ELECTROCHEMISTRY

LC QD552 .A28
DD 541.3/7
ISSN 0938-5193
GW
CCC
CODEN AESEEY

ADVANCES IN ELECTROCHEMICAL SCIENCE AND ENGINEERING. Vol. 1 (1990)-. Academic Scholarly Publication. English. Irregular. Price varies. VCH Gesellschaft GmbH, Postfach 101161, D-69451 Weinheim Germany. **Tel** 011 49 6201 606459, FAX 011 49 6201 606184. **(Subscription address:** VCH Publishers Inc., 303 Northwest 12th Avenue, Journals Department, Deerfield FL 33442. **Tel** (800)367-8249, (305)428-5566.) Documents available from CASDDS. **Continues** Advances in Electrochemistry and Electrochemical Engineering, 0567-9907.
Ind/Abst Chem. Abstr. (1990-).
LC QP517.B53 B5
ISSN 0302-4598
SZ
CCC

BIOELECTROCHEMISTRY AND BIOENERGETICS. Vol. 28, No. 3 (Oct. 1992)-. Periodical. English. Six times a year (3 volumes). 1200.00F. Elsevier Sequoia SA, PO Box 564, CH-1001 Lausanne 1 Switzerland. **Tel** 011 41 21 3207381, FAX 011 41 21 3235444. **ED** H. Berg, M. Blank. available on an online database from Elsevier Electronic Subscriptions (EES). **Separated from** Journal of Electroanalytical Chemistry (Lausanne, Switzerland), 0022-0728.
Desc: Provides an international forum where life scientists and electrochemists interested in biological problems can find ideas and results originating from scientists of different basic backgrounds and education.

ISSN 0256-1654
II
CCC
CODEN BUELE6

BULLETIN OF ELECTROCHEMISTRY. [Bull. electrochem.]. **Added/Corp** Central Electrochemical Research Institute (India). Vol. 1, No. 1 (Jan./Feb. 1985)-. Bulletin. English. Twelve times a year. $300.00. Scientific Publishers, PO Box 91, Ratanada Road, Jodhpur 342011 India. **(Subscription address:** Prints India, 11 Darya Ganj, New Delhi 110002 India. **Tel** 011 91 11 3268645, FAX 011 91 11 3275542, telex 31-61087 PRIN-IN.) **ED** R Viswanathan. **Bk Rev**. **Circ:** 800 (ctrl). Documents available from The Genuine Article, CASDDS. **Formed by the union of** Corrosion Bulletin, 0253-7109; Electrometallurgy Bulletin; Electrochemicals Bulletin, 0255-7185 **and** Batteries Bulletin.
Ind/Abst Anal. Abstr.; Biodeter. Abstr.; Chem. Abstr. (1985-); Corros. Abstr.; Curr. Cit.; Curr. Titles Electrochem.; Gas Abstr.; Res. Alert [Full Cov.]; Soils Fert.; Surf. Treat. Technol. Abstr.; World Surf. Coat. Abstr.

ISSN 0160-8959
CODEN CSAEDT

CA SELECTS: ANALYTICAL ELECTROCHEMISTRY. See Chemistry and Chemicals-Abstracting, Bibliographies and Statistics.

ISSN 1146-1497
FR
TITLE CHANGE

CFE INDUSTRIE. VFOAT Cahiers Francais d'Electricite Industrie; Industrie. Vol. 3, No. 1 (Jan. 1992)-(1995). Periodical. French. Edicom, 21 rue Tournefort, F 75005 Paris France. **Tel** 011 33 1 47072929, FAX 011 33 1 47073066, 011 33 1 4703129. **ED** Marique Hemy. **Bk Rev**. **Ad Acc**. **Continues** Industrie Cfe; **Separated from** Journal Francias de l'Electrogenie Industrie, 0758-9735. **Continued by** Industrie Relation Elec.
Desc: Contains applications of electricity.

LC TN1 .M45
DD 660.5
ISSN 0009-2460
US
CCC
CODEN CHEEA3

NLM W1 CH248
Pr Rev.
CHEMICAL ENGINEERING (NEW YORK). See Engineering-Chemical Engineering.

ISSN 0300-4376
II

CURRENT TITLES IN ELECTROCHEMISTRY. See Chemistry and Chemicals-Abstracting, Bibliographies and Statistics.

LC QD551 .D46
DD 541
ISSN 0366-9297
JA
CCC
CODEN DNKKA2

Pr Rev.
DENKI KAGAKU OYOBI KOGYO BUTSURI KAGAKU. Added/Corp Denki Kagaku Kyokai (Japan). **VFOAT** Denki Kagaku. Vol. 29 No. 6 (1961)-. Periodical. Japanese. Twelve times a year. $210.00. **(Subscription address:** Maruzen Company Ltd., PO Box 5050, Import & Export Department, Tokyo 100 31 Japan. **Tel** 011 81 3 32789224.) Documents available from Ask*IEEE, CASDDS. **Absorbed** D.K. Newsletter; **Continues** Denki Kagaku.
Ind/Abst Chem. Abstr.; Coal Abstr.; Curr. Biotechnol.; Curr. Cit.; INSPEC; Sug. Indus. Abstr.
LC QD115 .E496
DD 543/.0871
ISSN 1040-0397
US
CCC
CODEN ELANEU

NLM W1; EL29
Pr Rev.
ELECTROANALYSIS (NEW YORK, N.Y.). (ELECTROANALYSIS.). [Electroanalysis]. Vol. 1, No. 1 (1989)-. Academic Scholarly Publication. English. Twelve times a year. $698.00. VCH Publishers Inc, 220 East 23rd Street, New York NY 10010. **Tel** (212)683-8333, FAX (212)481-0897. **(Subscription address:** VCH Publishers Inc., 303 Northwest 12th Avenue, Journals Department, Deerfield FL 33442. **Tel** (800)367-8249, (305)428-5566.) **ED** Joesph Wang. Documents available from The Genuine Article, BIOSIS Document Express, CASDDS.
Desc: International journal that contains original research papers, short papers, rapid communications and reviews concerned with the development and applications of electroanalytical techniques.
Ind/Abst Biol. Abstr. (1989-); Chem. Abstr. (1989-); Curr. Cit.; Curr. Contents Phys. Chem. Earth Sci.; Res. Alert [Full Cov.]; Sci. Cit. Index; SCISEARCH; Sug. Indus. Abstr.

ISSN 0963-5637
UK

ELECTROCHEMICAL SCIENCE AND TECHNOLOGY OF POLYMERS. [Electrochem. sci. technol. polym.]. (1987)-. Monographic series. English. Irregular. Elsevier Science Publishers Ltd., Crown House, Linton Road, Barking Essex IG11 8JU United Kingdom. **Tel** 011 44 181 5947272, FAX 011 44 181 5945942, telex 896950. Documents available from CASDDS.
Ind/Abst Chem. Abstr.
LC TP250 .E595
DD 660/.297
ISSN 1064-8208
US
CCC
CODEN ELSIE3

ELECTROCHEMICAL SOCIETY INTERFACE, THE. [Electrochem. Soc. interface]. **Added/Corp** Electrochemical Society. **VFOAT** Interface. Vol. 1, No. 1 (Winter 1992)-. Periodical. English. Four times a year. $40.00. Electrochemical Society, 10 South Main Street, Pennington NJ 08534. **Tel** (609)737-1902. **Separated from** Journal of the Electrochemical Society, 0013-4651.
Desc: Information on industrial electrochemistry.
Ind/Abst Acad. Search; Bus. Source Plus; Bus. Source; EP Collect.; Homework Help.; Int. Aerosp. Abstr.; MasterFile FullTEXT 1000; MasterFile FullTEXT 350; MasterFile FullTEXT 650; MasterFile FullTEXT (July 1993-); OCLC; Telebase.

ISSN 0733-6691
US

ELECTROCHEMISTRY & ELECTROCHEMICAL ENGINEERING. (ELECTROCHEMISTRY & ELECTROCHEMICAL ENGINEERING MICROFORM.). [Electrochem. electrochem. eng.]. **Added/Corp** Comtex Scientific Corporation. **VFOAT** Electrochemistry and Electrochemical Engineering. Vol. 1, No. 1 (1982)-. Monographic series. English. Irregular. Price varies per volume. Comtex, 850 3rd Avenue, New York NY 10017.

LC TP250 .E63
ISSN 0013-4686
UK
CCC
CODEN ELCAAV

Pr Rev.
ELECTROCHIMICA ACTA. [Electrochim. acta]. **Added/Corp** International Society of Electrochemistry. Vol. 1 (April 1959)-. Periodical. English (French and German; summaries and/or abstracts in French, German

and English). Eighteen times a year. $2093.00. Pergamon Press, An Imprint of Elsevier Science Ltd., The Boulevard, Langford Lane, Kidlington, Oxford OX5 1GB United Kingdom. **Tel** 011 44 1865 843000, 011 44 1865 843699, FAX 011 44 1865 843010. **(Subscription address:** Elsevier Science Ltd. / Oxford Fulfillment Centre, PO Box 800, Kidlington OX5 1DX United Kingdom. **Tel** 011 44 865 843355.**) ED** R. D. Armsrong and E. J. Cairns. available on microfilm and microfiche from University Microfilms International (UMI); available on an online database from Elsevier Electronic Subscriptions (EES). Documents available from Article Express International, The Genuine Article, Ask*IEEE, CASDDS.
Desc: Publishes original papers and critical reviews in the field of pure and applied electrochemistry by both members and nonmembers of the society. The areas covered include: fundamental interfacial electrochemistry, electrode and electrolyte materials, analytical and molecular electrochemistry, electrochemical energy conversion, corrosion, electrodeposition and surface treatment.
Ind/Abst Alum. Ind. Abstr.; Art Archaeol. Tech. Abstr.; Bioeng. Abstr.; Ceram. Abstr. (19??-); Chem Inform; Chem. Abstr.; Chem. Titles; Curr. Aware. Biol. Sci., CABS; Curr. Cit.; Curr. Contents Phys. Chem. Earth Sci.; Curr. Technol. Index; Curr. Titles Electrochem.; Ei Page One; Energy Res. Abstr.; Eng. Index Annu. [Select. Cov.]; Environ. Period. Bibliogr. (?-?); INIS Atomindex [Micro.]; INSPEC (Aug. 1969-); Int. Aerosp. Abstr.; Leadscan; Met. Abstr.; MINPROC; Proc. Chem. Eng.; Res. Alert [Full Cov.]; Sci. Cit. Index; SCISEARCH; Theor. Chem. Eng.

ISSN 0424-8570
RU
CCC
CODEN ELKKAX

ELEKTROHIMIA. (ELEKTROKHIMIIA.). [Elektrohimia]. **Added/Corp** Akademiia Nauk SSSR. (1965)-. Academic Scholarly Publication. Russian. Twelve times a year. $279.95. Izdatelstvo Nauka / Akademiia Nauk, (Publishing House of the Russian Academy of Sciences), Leninskii Porspekt 14, 117901 Moscow Russia. **Tel** 011 95 9542153, FAX 011 95 9382144, telex 411964. **(Subscription address:** East View Publications Inc., 3020 Harbor Lane North, Suite 110, Minneapolis MN 55447. **Tel** (800)477-1005, (612)550-0961, FAX (612)559-2931.) available on microfilm. Documents available from Ask*IEEE, CASDDS.
Ind/Abst Alum. Ind. Abstr.; Chem. Abstr.; Curr. Titles Electrochem.; Energy Res. Abstr.; Eng. Mater. Abstr.; INSPEC (1971-); Int. Aerosp. Abstr.; Met. Abstr.; World Alum. Abstr.

ISSN 0160-7464
US
CODEN EAPCDS

EXTENDED ABSTRACTS AND PROGRAM - BIENNIAL CONFERENCE ON CARBON. **See** Chemistry and Chemicals-Abstracting, Bibliographies and Statistics.

LC QD551 .E4914 **ISSN** 0160-4619
DD 541/.37/05 US
CCC

EXTENDED ABSTRACTS - ELECTROCHEMICAL SOCIETY. (EXTENDED ABSTRACTS.). [Ext. abstr. - Electrochem. Soc.]. **Main/Corp** Electrochemical Society. (19??)-. English. Two times a year (May & Oct.). $154.00. Electrochemical Society, 10 South Main Street, Pennington NJ 08534. **Tel** (609)737-1902. available on microfilm and microfiche from University Microfilms International (UMI). Documents available from Ask*IEEE.
Ind/Abst INSPEC.

LC QD551 .I84 **ISSN** 0202-8093
DD 541.3/7/05 RU

ITOGI NAUKI I TEKHNIKI. SERIIA ELEKTROKHIMIIA. **Added/Corp** Vsesoiuznyi Institut Nauchnoi i Tekhnicheskoi Informatsii (Soviet Union). **VFOAT** Seriia Elektrokhimiia; Elektrokhimiia; Itogi Nauki i Tekhniki. Elektrokhimiia. (1980)-. Periodical. Russian. 3.10rub (single issue). VINITI - Vsesoiuznyi Institut Nauchno-Tekhnicheskoi Informatsii, All-Union Scientific and Technical Information Institute, Baltiiskaia ulitsa 14, 125219 Moscow Russia. **Tel** 011 7 95 2384600, FAX 011 7 95 9430060, telex 411160. Documents available from CASDDS. ***Continues*** *Itogi Nauki i Tekhniki. Elektrokhimiia.*
Ind/Abst Chem. Abstr.

US

JEC BATTERY NEWSLETTER. (19??)-. Newsletter. English. Six times a year. $250.00. Robert Morey Associates, PO Box 30, Cooperstown NY 13326. **Tel** (607)547-5314, FAX (607)547-5314. **ED** A. Kozawa. **Ad Acc, Adv Mgr:** Robert Morey, **Tel** same as publisher.
Desc: Contains a new summary of developments, both marketing and technical, occurring in the battery and electrochemical fields of Japan and other industrialized countries.

LC TP250 .J68 **ISSN** 0021-891X
DD 660/.29/705 UK
CCC
CODEN JAELBJ
Pr Rev.

JOURNAL OF APPLIED ELECTROCHEMISTRY. [J. appl. electrochem.]. **VFOAT** Applied Electrochemistry. Vol. 1 (Feb. 1971)-. Academic Scholarly Publication. English (French and German). Twelve times a year. $849.00. Chapman & Hall, 2-6 Boundary Row, London SE1 8HN United Kingdom. **Tel** 011 44 171 8650066, FAX 011 44 171 5229623, telex 290164 CHAPMA G. **ED** A. A. Wragg. Index available. **Bk Rev. Ad Acc. Circ:** 750. available on microfilm and microfiche from University Microfilms International (UMI). Documents available from Article Express International, The Genuine Article, Ask*IEEE, CASDDS.
Desc: Concentrates on the interdisciplinary and technological aspects of electrochemistry. Broadly based and well established. Publishes articles in such fields as cell design, corrosion, electrochemical reaction engineering, the electrochemical treatment of effluents, hydrometallurgy, molten salt and solid state electrochemistry, new battery systems, solar cells and surface finishing.
Ind/Abst Alum. Ind. Abstr.; Appl. Sci. Technol. Index; Bioeng. Abstr.; Ceram. Abstr. (19??-); Chem. Abstr.; Chem. Titles; Curr. Cit.; Curr. Contents Phys. Chem. Earth Sci.; Curr. Titles Electrochem.; Ei Page One; Elect. Comm. Abstr.; EMBASE; Energy Res. Abstr. (April 1973-); Eng. Mater. Abstr.; Eng. Index Annu.; INSPEC (Aug. 1971-); Leadscan; Manuf. Process Eng. Abstr.; Mater. Sci. Eng. Abstr.; Mech. Eng. Abstr.; Met. Abstr.; MINPROC; Pollut. Abstr. Indexes; Res. Alert [Full Cov.]; Sci. Cit. Index; SCISEARCH; Solid State Supercond. Abstr.

LC QD551 .J6
SZ
CODEN JECHES

JOURNAL OF ELECTROANALYTICAL CHEMISTRY. Vol. 323, No. 1 and 2 (Jan. 24, 1992)-. Academic Scholarly Publication. English. Forty times a year (20 volumes). 7300.00F; 7935.00F combined subscription with Bioelectrochemistry and Bioenergetics. Elsevier Sequoia SA, PO Box 564, CH-1001 Lausanne 1 Switzerland. **Tel** 011 41 21 3207381, FAX 011 41 21 3235444. **ED** R. Parsons. available on an online database from Elsevier Electronic Subscriptions (EES). Documents available from The Genuine Article, Ask*IEEE, CASDDS. ***Continues*** *Journal of Electroanalytical Chemistry and Interfacial Electrochemistry, 0022-0728.* ***Continued in part by*** *Bioelectrochemistry and Bioenergetics (Lausanne, Switzerland), 0302-4598.*
Desc: Devoted to the interdisciplinary subject of electrochemistry in all its aspects, theoretical as well as applied.
Ind/Abst Chem. Abstr.; Curr. Contents Phys. Chem. Earth Sci.; INSPEC (1992-); Res. Alert [Full Cov.]; Sci. Cit. Index; SCISEARCH.

LC TP250 .E542 **ISSN** 0013-4651
DD 541.3705 US
CCC
NLM W1 JO92K **CODEN** JESOAN
Pr Rev.

JOURNAL OF THE ELECTROCHEMICAL SOCIETY. [J. Electrochem. Soc.]. **Added/Corp** Electrochemical Society. Vol. 93, No. 1 (Jan. 1948)-. Periodical. English. Twelve times a year. $425.00. Electrochemical Society, 10 South Main Street, Pennington NJ 08534. **Tel** (609)737-1902. **ED** Barry Miller. Index available. cum. index. **Ad Acc. Circ:** 8,600 (ctrl). available on microfilm and microfiche from University Microfilms International (UMI). Documents available from Article Express International, The Genuine Article, Ask*IEEE, CASDDS. ***Formed by the union of*** *Bulletin of the Electrochemical Society, 0898-1388* ***and*** *Electrochemical Society. Preprint- Electrochemical Society, 0898-1396;* ***Absorbed*** *Transactions of the Electrochemical Society, 0096-4743.* ***Continued in part by*** *Electrochemical Society Interface, 1064-8208.*
Desc: Electrochemical science and technology. Solid state science and technology.
Ind/Abst Abstr. Bull. Inst. Pap. Sci. Tech.; Acad. Search; Anal. Abstr.; Appl. Sci. Technol. Index; Art Archaeol. Tech. Abstr.; Ceram. Abstr.; Chem Inform; Chem. Abstr.; Chem. Titles; Civ. Struct. Eng. Abstr.; Coal Abstr.; Corros. Abstr. (199?-); Curr. Cit.; Curr. Contents Eng. Comput. Technol.; Curr. Contents Phys. Chem. Earth Sci.; Curr. Titles Electrochem.; Ei Page One; Elect. Comm. Abstr.; Energy Res. Abstr.; Eng. Mater. Abstr.; Eng. Index Annu.; Environ. Eng. Abstr.; EP Collect.; Gas Abstr. (?-?); Gen. Sci. Source; Homework Help.; HTFS Dig.; INFO-SOUTH Abstr.; INIS Atomindex [Micro.]; INSPEC (1968-); Int. Aerosp. Abstr.; Leadscan; Manuf. Process Eng. Abstr.; MasterFile FullTEXT 1000; MasterFile FullTEXT 350; MasterFile FullTEXT 650; MasterFile FullTEXT (July 1993-); Mater. Sci. Eng. Abstr.; Mech. Eng. Abstr.; Met. Abstr.; MINPROC; OCLC; Life Sci. Collect.; Res. Alert [Full Cov.]; Sci. Cit. Index; SCISEARCH; Soils Fert.; Solid State Supercond. Abstr.; Surf. Treat. Technol. Abstr.; Telebase; World Ceram. Abstr.

LC TP250 .E5425 **ISSN** 0013-466X
DD 660.2/97/05 II
CCC
CODEN JESIA5
Pr Rev.

JOURNAL OF THE ELECTROCHEMICAL SOCIETY OF INDIA. [J. electrochem. Soc. India]. **Added/Corp** Electrochemical Society of India. Vol. 13, No. 1 (Jan. 1964)-. Periodical. English. Four times a year. $80.00. Electrochemical Society of India, Indian Institute of Science, Bangalore 560012 India. **Tel** 340977, telex 0846-8349 BG ECSI. **(Subscription address:** Prints India, 11 Darya Ganj, New Delhi 110002 India. **Tel** 011 91 11 3268645, FAX 011 91 11 3275542, telex 31-61087 PRIN-IN.) **ED** S K Vijayalakshamma. Index available. **Bk Rev. Ad Acc. Circ:** 500. Documents available from Article Express International, Ask*IEEE, CASDDS. ***Continues*** *Bulletin of the India Section, The Electrochemical Society.*
Desc: Devoted to the science and technology of electrochemistry, electrohydrometallurgy, electrothermics, electronics, semiconductors, batteries, metal finishing, anodizing, corrosion surface treatment and allied subjects.
Ind/Abst Alum. Ind. Abstr.; Anal. Abstr.; Bioeng. Abstr.; Chem. Abstr.; Curr. Cit.; Curr. Titles Electrochem.; Ei Page One; Eng. Mater. Abstr.; Eng. Index Annu.; INSPEC (Oct. 1971-); Leadscan; Met. Abstr.; Soils Fert.

LC QD552 .M6 **ISSN** 0076-9924
DD 541/.37/05 US
CCC
NLM W1 MO124 **CODEN** MAECAO

MODERN ASPECTS OF ELECTROCHEMISTRY. [Mod. aspects electrochem.]. No. 1 (1954)-. Monographic series. English. Irregular. Price varies per volume. Plenum Press, 233 Spring Street, New York NY 10013-1578. **Tel** (212)620-8000, (800)221-9369, FAX (212)463-0742, (212)807-1047, telex 23/421139. Documents available from CASDDS.
Ind/Abst Chem. Abstr.; Energy Res. Abstr. (Sept. 1977-).

LC TP245.C5 M6 **ISSN** 0747-7406
DD 661/.0732 US

MODERN CHLOR-ALKALI TECHNOLOGY. **Added/Corp** Society of Chemical Industry (Great Britain). Vol. 1 (1980)-. Academic Scholarly Publication. English. Halsted Press, 605 Third Avenue, New York NY 10016. **Tel** (718)658-0888. Documents available from CASDDS.
Ind/Abst Chem. Abstr.

FR

MOLTEN SALTS BULLETIN / SELS FONDUS. (19??)-. Academic Scholarly Publication. English (French). Irregular (3-4 per year). $98.43. IUSTI / Institut Universitaire des Systemes Thermiques Industriels, Universite de Provence / SETT, UA 1168, Centre de Saint-Jerome, 13397 Marseille Cedex 20 France. **Tel** 011 33 91 288216. **ED** Marcelle Gaune-Escard. available on diskette; available with illustrations.

ISSN 0161-6374
US
CCC
CODEN PESODO

PROCEEDINGS - ELECTROCHEMICAL SOCIETY. (PROCEEDINGS.). [Proc., Electrochem. Soc.]. **Added/Corp** Electrochemical Society. (19??)-. Academic Scholarly Publication. English. Electrochemical Society, 10 South Main Street, Pennington NJ 08534. **Tel** (609)737-1902. Documents available from CASDDS.
Ind/Abst Bioeng. Abstr.; Chem. Abstr.

LC QD552 **ISSN** 0067-1827
DD 541.37082 UK

PROCEEDINGS OF THE AUSTRALIAN CONFERENCE ON ELECTROCHEMISTRY. **Main/Conf** Australian Conference on Electrochemistry. 1st- 1963-. Proceedings. English. Pergamon Press, An Imprint of Elsevier Science Ltd., The Boulevard, Langford Lane, Kidlington, Oxford OX5 1GB United Kingdom. **Tel** 011 44 1865 843000, 011 44 1865 843699, FAX 011 44 1865 843010. **ED** J A Friend, F Gutmann and J W Hayes.

ISSN 1070-3276
DD 541 US
CODEN RUELEC
TITLE CHANGE

RUSSIAN ELECTROCHEMISTRY. [Russ. electrochem.]. **Added/Corp** Consultants Bureau. (1993)-(1993). Academic Scholarly Publication. English. MAIK Nauka / Interperiodica, Ulitsa Profsoyuznaia 90, Moscow 117864 Russia. Documents available from CASDDS. ***Continues*** *Soviet Electrochemistry, 0038-5387.* ***Continued by*** *Elektrokhimia. English. Russian Journal of Electrochemistry.*
Ind/Abst Bioeng. Abstr.; Chem. Abstr.; Curr. Cit.; Int. Aerosp. Abstr.

Chemistry and Chemicals —Electrochemistry

LC QD551 .E5513
US

● **RUSSIAN JOURNAL OF ELECTROCHEMISTRY. Added/Corp** Interperiodica Publishing. (1993)-. Periodical. English (translations available in Russian). Twelve times a year. $1380.00 US; $1610.00 other. Plenum Press, 233 Spring Street, New York NY 10013-1578. **Tel** (212)620-8000, (800)221-9369, FAX (212)463-0742, (212)807-1047, telex 23/421139. **(Subscription address:** Plenum Press Subscription Department, PO Box 730, Canal Street, Station NY 10013-1578. **Tel** (212)620-8000, (212)620-8466.) **Continues** Elektrokhimia. English. *Russian Electrochemistry, 1070-3276.*
Ind/Abst Curr. Cit.

LC QD551 .E5513 **ISSN** 0038-5387
DD 541 US
CCC
CODEN SOECAI
Pr Rev. **TITLE CHANGE**

SOVIET ELECTROCHEMISTRY. [Sov. electrochem.]. **Added/Corp** Consultants Bureau Enterprises. Consultants Bureau. Vol. 1 (Jan. 1965)-(199?). Periodical. English. English (Russian). MAIK Nauka / Interperiodica, Ulitsa Profsoyuznaia 90, Moscow 117864 Russia. **ED** Ya M Kolotyrkin. Index available. available on microfilm and microfiche from University Microfilms International (UMI). Documents available from Article Express International, The Genuine Article, Ask*IEEE, CASDDS. **Continued by** *Russian Electrochemistry*.
Desc: This journal publishes articles on theoretical and applied electrochemistry. Reports Soviet developments in fuel cells, electrochemical controlling devices, electrochemical methods of processing materials.
Ind/Abst Anal. Abstr.; Bioeng. Abstr.; Chem. Abstr.; Curr. Contents Phys. Chem. Earth Sci.; Ei Page One; Eng. Index Annu. [Select. Cov.]; INSPEC (Jan. 1971-); Int. Aerosp. Abstr.; Res. Alert [Full Cov.]; Sci. Cit. Index; SCISEARCH; Soc. Sci. Cit. Index [Select. Cov.].

LC TK7881 .E46 **ISSN** 8756-7008
DD 660.2/97/05 US
CCC
TITLE CHANGE

SOVIET SURFACE ENGINEERING & APPLIED ELECTROCHEMISTRY. [Sov. surf. eng. appl. electrochem.]. **VFOAT** Elektronnaia Obrabotka Materialov. No. 1 (1984)-(1993). Periodical. English. Allerton Press Inc., 150 Fifth Avenue, New York NY 10011. **Tel** (212)924-3950, FAX (212)463-9684, telex 427441 ALPRES. **Continues** Electrochemistry in Industrial Processing & Biology. **Continued by** *Surface Engineering and Applied Electrochemistry*.
Ind/Abst Curr. Cit.

ISSN 1068-3755
US
CCC

● **SURFACE ENGINEERING AND APPLIED ELECTROCHEMISTRY. See** Engineering.

LC QD415 **ISSN** 0160-3183
DD 574.192 UK
UDC 577.23
NLM W1 TO539H **CODEN** TBBIDC

TOPICS IN BIOELECTROCHEMISTRY AND BIOENERGETICS. See Biology-Biological Chemistry.

ISSN 0036-0678
II
CCC
CODEN TSETA6

TRANSACTIONS OF THE SAEST. (TRANSACTIONS OF THE SAEST.). [Trans. SAEST]. **Added/Corp** Society for Advancement of Electrochemical Science and Technology. **VFOAT** Transactions of SAEST. **VAT** Transactions of the Society for Advancement of Electrochemical Science and Technology. Vol. 4, No. 1 (Jan./Mar. 1969). Academic Scholarly Publication. English. Four times a year. $30.00. Society for Advancement of Electrochemical Science and Technology, Karaikudi 623 006 India. **Tel** 2368, telex 0443-211 ECRI IN. **(Subscription address:** Prints India, 11 Darya Ganj, New Delhi 110002 India. **Tel** 011 91 11 3268645, FAX 011 91 11 3275542, telex 31-61087 PRIN-IN.) **ED** N S Rengaswamy. Index available. **Bk Rev. Ad Acc. Circ:** 1,300 (ctrl). Documents available from Article Express International, Ask*IEEE, CASDDS. **Continues** *Transactions of the Society for Advancement of Electrochemical Science and Technology, 0258-1779*.
Desc: Contains communications on power sources, electrometallurgy, corrosion, engineering, electroplating, metal finishing, electrochemicals, material science, solid state electrochemistry and basic electrochemistry.
Ind/Abst Alum. Ind. Abstr.; Bioeng. Abstr.; Chem. Abstr.; Curr. Cit.; Curr. Titles Electrochem.; Ei Page One; Eng. Mater. Abstr.; Eng. Index Annu.; INSPEC (Jan.-March 1972-1986); Met. Abstr.

INORGANIC CHEMISTRY

UDC 546.18(063)
FR
CODEN PCPCDR

ACTES - INTERNATIONAL CONGRESS ON PHOSPHORUS COMPOUNDS. Main/Conf International Congress on Phosphorus Compounds. **VFOAT** Proceedings; Actes du ... Congres International sur les Composes Phosphores. 1st- Oct. 1977-. Academic Scholarly Publication. French (English). Documents available from CASDDS.
Ind/Abst Chem. Abstr.; GeoRef.

LC QP501 .A37 **ISSN** 0190-0218
DD 574.19/214 US
NLM W1 AD648L **CODEN** AIBIDM

ADVANCES IN INORGANIC BIOCHEMISTRY. See Biology-Biological Chemistry.

LC QD151 **ISSN** 0898-8838
DD 546/.05 US
UDC 546 CCC
NLM W1; AD648Q **CODEN** AICHEP

ADVANCES IN INORGANIC CHEMISTRY. [Adv. inorg. chem.]. **VFOAT** Inorganic Chemistry. Vol. 31 (1987)-. Academic Scholarly Publication. English. Irregular. $95.00 (Vol. 40). Academic Press Inc., 6277 Sea Harbor Drive, Orlando FL 32887. **Tel** (800)543-9534, (407)345-4100, FAX (407)352-3445. **ED** A. G. Sykes. Documents available from The Genuine Article, BIOSIS Document Express, CASDDS. **Continues** *Advances in Inorganic Chemistry and Radiochemistry, 0065-2792.*
Ind/Abst Biol. Abstr.; Chem. Abstr.; Energy Res. Abstr.; GeoRef; Res. Alert [Full Cov.]; Sci. Cit. Index; SCISEARCH.

LC QD189 .A33 **ISSN** 0065-2954
DD 546/.34 US
CCC
CODEN AMSCCE
Pr Rev.

ADVANCES IN MOLTEN SALT CHEMISTRY. [Adv. molten salt chem.]. Vol. 1 (1971)-. Monographic series. English. Irregular. Price varies per volume. Elsevier Science Publishing Company Inc, Madison Square Station, PO Box 882, New York NY 10159-0882. **Tel** (212)633-3950, FAX (212)633-3990. Documents available from Ask*IEEE, CASDDS.
Desc: Series providing information on fused salts.
Ind/Abst Chem. Abstr.; Ei Page One; INSPEC.

LC QD181.S6 A385 **ISSN** 1059-4256
DD 546/.683 US
CODEN ADSDEO

ADVANCES IN SILICON CHEMISTRY. [Adv. silicon chem.]. Vol. 1 (1991)-. Academic Scholarly Publication. English. Irregular. $90.25. JAI Press Inc., 55 Old Post Road, Suite 2, PO Box 1678, Greenwich CT 06836-1678. **Tel** (203)661-7602, FAX (203)661-0792. Documents available from CASDDS.
Ind/Abst Chem. Abstr. (1991-).

LC QD1 .C57 **ISSN** 0260-1818
DD 546/.05 UK
CCC
NLM W1 AN769GS **CODEN** APCCDO

ANNUAL REPORTS ON THE PROGRESS OF CHEMISTRY. SECTION A, INORGANIC CHEMISTRY. [Annu. rep. progr. chem., A, Inorg. chem.]. **Added/Corp** Royal Society of Chemistry (Great Britain). **VFOAT** Inorganic Chemistry; Annual Reports. A. Vol. 76 (1979)-. Academic Scholarly Publication. English. One time a year (Oct. of following year). $215.00. Royal Society of Chemistry, Thomas Graham House, Science Park, Cambridge CB4 4WF United Kingdom. **Tel** 011 44 1223 420066, FAX 011 44 1223 423623, telex 818293 ROYAL. **(Subscription address:** Royal Society of Chemistry, Turpin Distribution Services Ltd., Blackhorse Road, Letchworth, Hertfordshire SG6 1HN United Kingdom. **Tel** 011 44 1462 672555, FAX 011 44 1462 480947.) Index available. cum. index. Documents available from BIOSIS Document Express, CASDDS. **Continues in part** *Annual Reports on the Progress of Chemistry. Section A, Physical and Inorganic Chemistry, 0308-6003*.
Desc: Devoted solely to inorganic chemistry.
Ind/Abst Biol. Abstr. (1985-); Chem. Abstr.

US

BENCHMARK PAPERS IN INORGANIC CHEMISTRY. (19??)-. Monographic series. English. Irregular. Price varies per volume. Academic Press Inc., 6277 Sea Harbor Drive, Orlando FL 32887. **Tel** (800)543-9534, (407)345-4100, FAX (407)352-3445.

LC QD241 .C12 **ISSN** 0275-7567
DD 546/.681 SZ
CCC
CODEN CMCHD6
CEASED

C1 MOLECULE CHEMISTRY. (C B 1 S MOLECULE CHEMISTRY.). [Cb1s mol. chem.]. **VFOAT** C One Molecule Chemistry; Molecule Chemistry. Vol. 1, No. 1 (April 1984)-Vol. 2 No. 1 (19??). Academic Scholarly Publication. English. Harwood Academic Publishers, PO Box 90, Reading RG1 8JL United Kingdom. **Tel** 011 44 1734 560080, FAX 011 44 1734 568211. **ED** Igor B. Tkatchenko. **Bk Rev. Ad Acc.** Documents available from CASDDS.
Ind/Abst Chem. Abstr. (1984-).

ISSN 1049-1309
DD 546 US

C2C ABSTRACTS JAPAN. INORGANIC CHEMISTRY. See Chemistry and Chemicals-Abstracting, Bibliographies and Statistics.

ISSN 1051-3906
DD 546 US
CODEN CASBEJ

CA SELECTS. CALCIUM CHANNEL BLOCKERS. Added/Corp American Chemical Society. Chemical Abstracts Service. **VFOAT** Calcium Channel Blockers. **VAT** Chemical Abstracts Selects. Calcium Channel Blockers. Issue 21 (Oct. 15, 1990)-. Abstracting/Indexing Service. English. Twenty-six times a year. $220.00. Chemical Abstracts Service, (Subsidiary of The American Chemical Society), 2540 Olentangy River Road, PO Box 3012, Columbus OH 43210-0012. **Tel** (614)447-3731, (800)753-4227, FAX (614)447-3751.

ISSN 0275-7095
US
CODEN CIRCD4

CA SELECTS: INORGANIC CHEMICALS & REACTIONS. See Chemistry and Chemicals-Abstracting, Bibliographies and Statistics.

ISSN 0895-5816
DD 546 US
CODEN CSSREN

CA SELECTS: STRUCTURE-ACTIVITY RELATIONSHIPS. See Chemistry and Chemicals-Abstracting, Bibliographies and Statistics.

LC QD181.C1 C3 **ISSN** 0008-6223
DD 546.68105 US
CCC
CODEN CRBNAH
Pr Rev.

CARBON (NEW YORK). (CARBON.). [Carbon]. **Added/Corp** American Carbon Committee. Vol. 1 (Oct. 1963)-. Periodical. English. Twelve times a year. $1424.00. Pergamon Press, An Imprint of Elsevier Science Ltd., The Boulevard, Langford Lane, Kidlington, Oxford OX5 1GB United Kingdom. **Tel** 011 44 1865 843000, 011 44 1865 843699, FAX 011 44 1865 843010. **(Subscription address:** Elsevier Science Ltd. / Oxford Fulfillment Centre, PO Box 800, Kidlington OX5 1DX United Kingdom. **Tel** 011 44 865 843355.) **ED** Peter A. Thrower. available on microfilm and microfiche from University Microfilms International (UMI); available on an online database from Elsevier Electronic Subscriptions (EES). Documents available from Article Express International, The Genuine Article, Ask*IEEE, CASDDS, Documents on Demand.
Desc: Publishes research devoted to the physics, chemistry and technology of those organic substances which are precursors for aromatically or tetrahedrally bounded carbonaceous solids, and of the materials produced from them.
Ind/Abst Alum. Ind. Abstr.; Bioeng. Abstr.; Ceram. Abstr.; Chem. Abstr.; Coal Abstr.; Curr. Aware. Biol. Sci., CABS; Curr. Biotechnol.; Curr. Cit.; Curr. Contents Phys. Chem. Earth Sci.; Ei Page One; Energy Inf. Abstr.; Energy Res. Abstr. (June 1980-); Eng. Index Annu.; Environ. Abstr.; INIS Atomindex [Micro.]; INSPEC (1968-); Int. Aerosp. Abstr.; Mass Spect. Bull.; Met. Abstr.; Res. Alert [Full Cov.]; Sci. Cit. Index; SCISEARCH; Sug. Indus. Abstr.

LC QD181.C1 C44 **ISSN** 0069-3138
DD 546.681 US
CCC
CODEN CPHCAY

CHEMISTRY AND PHYSICS OF CARBON. [Chem. phys. carbon]. Vol. 1 (1965)-. Monographic series. English. Irregular. Price varies per volume. Marcel Dekker Inc., 270 Madison Avenue, New York NY 10016. **Tel** (212)696-9000, (800)228-1160, FAX (212)685-4540, telex 421419. **(Subscription address:** Marcel Dekker Inc., PO Box 5017, Monticello NY 12701. **Tel** (800)228-1160.) **ED** Walker Thrower. Documents available from The Genuine Article, CASDDS.
Desc: This is an ongoing series. Each title has a different subject.
Ind/Abst Chem. Abstr.; GeoRef; Index Sci. Rev. [Full Cov.]; Res. Alert [Full Cov.]; Sci. Cit. Index (19??-19??); SCISEARCH.

LC QD146 .C44 **ISSN** 1051-7227
DD 546/.05 US
CCC
CODEN CICHED

CHEMTRACTS. INORGANIC CHEMISTRY. **See** Chemistry and Chemicals-Abstracting, Bibliographies and Statistics.

IT

CHIMICA INORGANICA. SERVIZI DOCUMONT. Italian. Twelve times a year. Enichem, Cas Postale 10020, 20110 Milan Italy. **Tel** 011 39 2 62703388.

LC QD146 .C65 **ISSN** 0260-3594
DD 546/.05 UK
CCC
CODEN COICDZ

COMMENTS ON MODERN CHEMISTRY. PART A, COMMENTS ON INORGANIC CHEMISTRY. [Comments mod. chem., A, Comments inorg. chem.]. **VFOAT** Comments on Inorganic Chemistry. Vol. 1, No. 1 (April 1981)-. Academic Scholarly Publication. English. Six times a year (1 volume). $425.00 (academic institutions), $662.00 (corporate institutions). Gordon & Breach Science Publishers, PO Box 90, Reading, Berkshire RG1 8JL United Kingdom. **Tel** 011 44 1734 560080, FAX 011 44 1734 568211. **ED** N. Sutin. **Bk Rev. Ad Acc.** Documents available from BIOSIS Document Express, CASDDS.
Ind/Abst Biol. Abstr. (?-1984); Chem. Abstr.; Curr. Cit.

LC QD146 **ISSN** 0300-9246
DD 546 UK
CCC
NLM W1 JO916GD **CODEN** JCDTBI
Pr Rev.

DALTON TRANSACTIONS. (JOURNAL OF THE CHEMICAL SOCIETY. DALTON TRANSACTIONS.). [Dalton trans.]. **Added/Corp** Chemical Society (Great Britain). **VFOAT** Dalton Transactions; Dalton Transactions: Inorganic Chemistry; J. C. S. Dalton. (1972)-. Academic Scholarly Publication. English. Twenty-four times a year. $1848.00. Royal Society of Chemistry, Thomas Graham House, Science Park, Cambridge CB4 4WF United Kingdom. **Tel** 011 44 1223 420066, FAX 011 44 1223 423623, telex 818293 ROYAL. **(Subscription address:** Royal Society of Chemistry, Turpin Distribution Services Ltd., Blackhorse Road, Letchworth, Hertfordshire SG6 1HN United Kingdom. **Tel** 011 44 1462 672555, FAX 011 44 1462 480947.**)** Index available (free). available on microfilm and microfiche from University Microfilms International (UMI); available on an online database from STN International. Documents available from The Genuine Article, BIOSIS Document Express, CASDDS, BLDSC, FAXON Xpress, The UnCover Company, SWETS, UMI Article Clearinghouse. ***Supersedes in part*** *Journal of the Chemical Society. A: Inorganic, Physical, Theoretical, 0022-4944.*
Desc: This publication contains papers on all aspects of the chemistry of inorganic and organometallic compounds, including bioinorganic and solid state inorganic chemistry. Also covers the applications of physicochemical techniques to the study of their structures, properties, and reactions, including kinetics and mechanism.
Ind/Abst Abstr. Bull. Inst. Pap. Sci. Tech.; Appl. Sci. Technol. Index; Biol. Abstr.; Chem Inform; Chem. Abstr.; Chem. Titles; Curr. Cit.; Curr. Contents Phys. Chem. Earth Sci.; GeoRef; Leadscan; Mass Spect. Bull.; Nucl. Sci. Abstr.; PESTDOC; Res. Alert [Full Cov.]; Sci. Cit. Index; SCISEARCH; World Ceram. Abstr.

LC QD1 .R3295 **ISSN** 0992-4361
DD 546/.05 FR
CCC
CODEN EJSCE5
Pr Rev.

EUROPEAN JOURNAL OF SOLID STATE AND INORGANIC CHEMISTRY. [Eur. j. solid state inorg. chem.]. Vol. 25, No. 1 (1988)-. Academic Scholarly Publication. French (summaries and/or abstracts in English). Eleven times a year. $448.38. Gauthier-Villars, 15 rue Gossin, 92543 Montrouge Cedex France. **Tel** 33 1 40 92 65 00, FAX 33 1 40 92 65 97. **(Subscription address:** Centrale des Revues, 11 rue Gossin, 92543 Montrouge Cedex France. **Tel** 011 33 1 46565266.**)** Documents available from The Genuine Article, Ask*IEEE, CASDDS. ***Continues*** *Revue de Chimie Minerale, 0035-1032.*
Ind/Abst Chem Inform; Chem. Abstr.; Curr. Cit.; Curr. Contents Phys. Chem. Earth Sci.; INSPEC (1988-); Leadscan; Res. Alert; Sci. Cit. Index; SCISEARCH; Soils Fert.

ISSN 1064-122X
DD 546 US
CCC
CODEN FTECEG
Pr Rev.

•**FULLERENE SCIENCE AND TECHNOLOGY.** Vol. 1, No. 1 (Feb. 1993)-. Periodical. English. Six times a year. $455.00. Marcel Dekker Inc., 270 Madison Avenue, New York NY 10016. **Tel** (212)696-9000, (800)228-1160, FAX (212)685-4540, telex 421419. **(Subscription address:** Marcel Dekker Inc., PO Box 5017, Monticello NY 12701. **Tel** (800)228-1160.**)**
Desc: Publishes original papers from all fields of scientific inquiry related to fullerene compounds. Provides a worldwide forum for investigators interested in fundamental and applied fullerene science issues. Discussing theoretical, experimental and applicatory aspects of fullerenes, it covers various topics.

GW

GMELIN HANDBOOK OF INORGANIC AND ORGANOMETALLIC CHEMISTRY. (19??)-. Monographic series. English. Irregular. Price varies per volume. Springer-Verlag GmbH & Company KG, Heidelberger Platz 3, D-14197 Berlin Germany. **Tel** 011 49 30 8207223, FAX 011 49 30 8214091, telex 183 319 SPBLN D. **(Subscription address:** Springer-Verlag New York Inc. / North America, PO Box 2485, Journal Fulfillment, Secaucus NJ 07096. **Tel** (201)348-4033, (800)777-4643, FAX (201)348-4505.**)** ***Continues*** *Gmelin Handbuch der Anorganischen Chemie.*

LC QE389.62 .K76 **ISSN** 1001-1625
DD 549/.6/05 CC
CODEN GUTOE9

GUISUANYAN TONGBAO. (KUEI SUAN YEN TUNG PAO.). [Guisuanyan tongbao]. **Added/Corp** Chung-kuo Kuei Suan Yen Hsueh Hui. Tien-chin Kuei Suan Yen Hsueh Hui. **VFOAT** Bulletin of the Chinese Silicate Society. (1979)-. Academic Scholarly Publication. Chinese. Six times a year. RMBY1.00. Tianjin Guisuanyan Xuehui, Tianjin Silicate Society, 26 Qudian Jie Hongqiao-qu, Tianjin 300230 People's Republic of China. **Tel** 250852. Documents available from CASDDS.
Ind/Abst Ceram. Abstr. (19??-); Chem. Abstr. (1985-).

ISSN 0376-4710
II
CODEN ICACEC

INDIAN JOURNAL OF CHEMISTRY. SECTION A, INORGANIC, BIO-INORGANIC, PHYSICAL, THEORETICAL & ANALYTICAL CHEMISTRY. **See** Chemistry and Chemicals-Analytical Chemistry.

US

INORGANIC CHEMICALS AND GASES. (19??)-. English. Twelve times a year. $225.00. Predicasts Inc., A Ziff Communications Company, 11001 Cedar Avenue, Cleveland OH 44106. **Tel** (800)321-6388, (216)795-3000, FAX (216)229-9944, telex 985 604. **(Subscription address:** Information Access Company, PO Box 61000, Department 1851, San Francisco CA 94161. **Tel** (800)321-6388.**)**

LC QD1 .I615 **ISSN** 0020-1669
DD 546/.05 US
CCC
NLM W1 IN455R **CODEN** INOCAJ
Pr Rev.

INORGANIC CHEMISTRY. [Inorg. chem.]. **Added/Corp** American Chemical Society. Vol. 1 (Feb. 1962)-. Academic Scholarly Publication. English. Twenty-six times a year. $1303.00. American Chemical Society, 1155 Sixteenth Street Northwest, Washington DC 20036. **Tel** (800)333-9511, (800)227-5558, (614)447-3776, FAX (202)447-3671. **(Subscription address:** American Chemical Society / Ohio, Department L 0011, Columbus OH 43268-0011.**)** **ED** M. Frederick Hawthorne. Index available (free). **Bk Rev. Ad Acc. Acid Free. Circ:** 4,331 (ctrl). available on microfilm and microfiche from University Microfilms International (UMI). Documents available from The Genuine Article, UMI Article Clearinghouse, CASDDS.
Desc: Experimental and theoretical studies, synthesis and properties of new compounds; quantitative studies of structure and thermodynamics; kinetics of inorganic reactions; bioinorganic chemistry; and solid state phenomena.
Ind/Abst Acad. Search; Ceram. Abstr.; Chem Inform; Chem. Abstr.; Chem. Titles; Coal Abstr.; Curr. Cit.; Curr. Contents Phys. Chem. Earth Sci.; Curr. Titles Electrochem.; EMBASE; Energy Inf. Abstr.; Energy Res. Abstr.; EP Collect.; Expand. Acad. Index (1992-); Gen. Sci. Index; Gen. Sci. Source; GeoRef; Homework Help.; INIS Atomindex [Micro.]; Int. Aerosp. Abstr.; Leadscan; Mass Spect. Bull.; MasterFile FullTEXT 1000; MasterFile FullTEXT 350; MasterFile FullTEXT 650; MasterFile FullTEXT (July 1993-); Newsp. Period. Abstr. (1992-); OCLC; Res. Alert [Full Cov.]; Sci. Cit. Index; SCISEARCH; Soils Fert.; Telebase; World Ceram. Abstr.

ISSN 0172-7966
GW

INORGANIC CHEMISTRY CONCEPTS. Vol. 1 (1977)-. Monographic series. English. Irregular. Price varies per volume. Springer-Verlag GmbH & Company KG, Heidelberger Platz 3, D-14197 Berlin Germany. **Tel** 011 49 30 8207223, FAX 011 49 30 8214091, telex 183 319 SPBLN D. **(Subscription address:** Springer-Verlag New York Inc. / North America, PO Box 2485, Journal Fulfillment, Secaucus NJ 07096. **Tel** (201)348-4033, (800)777-4643, FAX (201)348-4505.**)** ***Supersedes*** *Anorganische und Allgemeine Chemie in Einzeldarstellungen.*
Desc: This series covers concepts of inorganic chemistry.

LC TN4 .A334643 **ISSN** 0020-1685
DD 546/.3 US
CCC
CODEN INOMAF
Pr Rev.

INORGANIC MATERIALS. [Inorg. mater.]. **Added/Corp** Consultants Bureau. Consultants Bureau Enterprises. Vol. 1 (Jan. 1965)-. Academic Scholarly Publication. English (Russian). Twelve times a year. $1595.00. Plenum Press, 233 Spring Street, New York NY 10013-1578. **Tel** (212)620-8000, (800)221-9369, FAX (212)463-0742, (212)807-1047, telex 23/421139. **(Subscription address:** Plenum Press Subscription Department, PO Box 730, Canal Street, Station NY 10013-1578. **Tel** (212)620-8000, (212)620-8466.**)** **ED** V. B. Lazarev. Index available. available on microfilm and microfiche from University Microfilms International (UMI). Documents available from The Genuine Article, Ask*IEEE.
Desc: This journal publishes original research on the preparation and problems of new materials stable at high temperatures and with a complex of special physical properties.
Ind/Abst Coal Abstr.; Curr. Cit.; Curr. Contents Phys. Chem. Earth Sci.; INIS Atomindex [Micro.]; INSPEC (June 1971-); Int. Aerosp. Abstr.; Leadscan; Mass Spect. Bull.; Pollut. Abstr. Indexes; Res. Alert [Full Cov.]; Sci. Cit. Index; SCISEARCH.

GW

INORGANIC REACTIONS & METHODS. Monographic series. English. Irregular. Price varies per volume. VCH Gesellschaft GmbH, Postfach 101161, D-69451 Weinheim Germany. **Tel** 011 49 6201 606459, FAX 011 49 6201 606184. **(Subscription address:** VCH Publishers Inc., 303 Northwest 12th Avenue, Journals Department, Deerfield FL 33442. **Tel** (800)367-8249, (305)428-5566.**)**

LC QD156 .I56 **ISSN** 0073-8077
DD 541/.39 US
CODEN INSYA3

INORGANIC SYNTHESES. **Added/Corp** American Chemical Society. Vol. 1 (1939)-. Academic Scholarly Publication. English. Irregular. Price varies per volume. John Wiley & Sons, Inc., 605 Third Avenue, New York NY 10158-0012. **Tel** (212)850-6000, (212)850-6645, FAX (212)850-6088, telex 12-7063. **(Subscription address:** John Wiley & Sons / UK, Baffins Lane, Chichester, West Sussex PO19 1UD United Kingdom. **Tel** 011 44 1243 779777, FAX 011 44 243 776128, telex 86290 WIBOOKG.**)** Documents available from The Genuine Article, CASDDS.
Ind/Abst Chem. Abstr.; Curr. Cit.; Res. Alert [Full Cov.]; Sci. Cit. Index (19??-19??); SCISEARCH.

ISSN 0020-1693
SZ
CCC
Pr Rev.

INORGANICA CHIMICA ACTA : BIOINORGANIC CHEMISTRY ARTICLES AND LETTERS. Vol. 46B1 (Feb. 1980)-. Academic Scholarly Publication. English. Twenty-six times a year (13 vols.). $4476.00. Elsevier Sequoia SA, PO Box 564, CH-1001 Lausanne 1 Switzerland. **Tel** 011 41 21 3207381, FAX 011 41 21 3235444. **ED** U. Belluco. available on microfilm and microfiche from University Microfilms International (UMI); available on an online database from Elsevier Electronic Subscriptions (EES). Documents available from The Genuine Article, CASDDS. ***Continues in part*** *Inorganica Chimica Acta, 0020-1693.*
Desc: This scholarly publication contains original, high-level scientific information concerning important developments and research in bioinorganic chemistry. Subjects range from known bioinorganic and coordination compounds to interactions of compounds with biological systems.
Ind/Abst Acoust. Abstr.; Anal. Abstr.; Chem Inform; Chem. Abstr.; Chem. Titles; Curr. Cit.; Curr. Contents Phys. Chem. Earth Sci.; GeoRef; Mass Spect. Bull.; Phys. Briefs; Res. Alert [Full Cov.]; Sci. Cit. Index; SCISEARCH.

LC QD189 .I59 **ISSN** 0130-6359
RU
CODEN IORAD4

IONNYE RASPLAVY. [Ionnye Radplavy]. **Added/Corp** Nauchnyi Sovet po Fizicheskoi Khimii Ionnykh Rasplavov i Tverdykh Elektrolitov (Akademiia Nauk SSSR) Instytut Zahalnoi ta Neorhanichnoi Khimii (Akademiia Nauk Ukrainskoi RSR). Vol. 1 (1974)-. Academic Scholarly Publication. Russian. Izdatelstvo Naukova Dumka / Ukrainian Academy of Sciences, Yu. A. Khramov, Dir., Ul. Repina 3, 252 601 Kiev Ukraine. **Tel** 011 7 44 4303441, 011 7 44 2254182, telex 131376. Documents available from CASDDS.
Ind/Abst Chem. Abstr.

LC QD172.R2 I86
RU

ISSLEDOVANIIA V OBLASTI KHIMII REDKOZEMELNYKH ELEMENTOV.
Added/Corp Saratovskii Gosudarstvennyi Universitet Im. N.G. Chernyshevskogo. Vol. 1 (1969)-. Russian. Irregular. 0.55rub single issue. Saratov N.G. Chernyshevskii State University, Astrakhanskaya Ulitsa 83, 410071 Saratov Russia. **Tel** 011 7 241696, FAX 011 7 240446, telex 241125.

LC QD151 .I85
DD 546
RU
CODEN ITNKAC

ITOGI NAUKI I TEKHNIKI : NEORGANICHESKAIA KHIMIIA.
Added/Corp Vsesoiuznyi Institut Nauchnoi i Tekhnicheskoi Informatsii. **VFOAT** Neorganicheskaia Knimiia; Itogi Nauki i Tekhniki: Seriia Neorganicheskaia Khimiia. (1972)-. Periodical. Russian. One time a year. $12.00. VINITI - Vsesoyuznyi Institut Nauchno-Tekhnicheskoi Informatsii, All-Union Scientific and Technical Information Institute, Baltiiskaia ulitsa 14, 125219 Moscow Russia. **Tel** 011 7 95 2384600, FAX 011 7 95 9430060, telex 411160. Documents available from CASDDS. ***Continues*** *Itogi Nauki: Neorganicheskaia Khimiia.*
Ind/Abst Chem. Abstr.

ISSN 0002-337X
RU
CODEN IVNMAW

IZVESTIJA. AKADEMIJA NAUK SSSR. NEORGANICESKIE MATERIALY.
(IZVESTIIA. NEORGANICHESKIE MATERIALY.). [Izv. Akad. nauk SSSR. Neorg. mater.]. **Main/Corp** Akademiia Nauk SSSR. **VFOAT** Neorganicheskie Materialy. Vol. 1 (1965)-. Periodical. Russian. Twelve times a year. $288.00. Izdatelstvo Nauka / Akademiia Nauk, (Publishing House of the Russian Academy of Sciences), Leninskii Porspekt 14, 117901 Moscow Russia. **Tel** 011 95 9542153, FAX 011 95 9382144, telex 411964. **(Subscription address:** Victor Kamkin, 4956 Boiling Brook Parkway, Rockville MD 20852. **Tel** (301)881-5973.**)** Documents available from Article Express International, Ask*IEEE, CASDDS.
Ind/Abst Alum. Ind. Abstr.; Bioeng. Abstr.; Ceram. Abstr. (19??-); Chem. Abstr.; Ei Page One; Energy Res. Abstr.; Eng. Index Annu.; GeoRef; INSPEC (Aug. 1971-); Int. Aerosp. Abstr.; Met. Abstr.

LC QD146
DD 546
GW

•**JOURNAL OF BIOLOGICAL INORGANIC CHEMISTRY.** (1996)-. Academic Scholarly Publication. English. Six times a year. DM.590.00. Springer-Verlag GmbH & Company KG, Heidelberger Platz 3, D-14197 Berlin Germany. **Tel** 011 49 30 8207223, FAX 011 49 30 8214091, telex 183 319 SPBLN D. **(Subscription address:** Springer-Verlag New York Inc. / North America, PO Box 2485, Journal Fulfillment, Secaucus NJ 07096. **Tel** (201)348-4033, (800)777-4643, FAX (201)348-4505.**) ED** I. Bertini.

LC QD181.F1 J66
DD 546/.731/05
ISSN 0022-1139
SZ
CCC
NLM W1 JO65P
CODEN JFLCAR
Pr Rev.

JOURNAL OF FLUORINE CHEMISTRY.
[J. fluorine chem.]. **VFOAT** Fluorine Chemistry. Vol. 1 (July 1971)-. Periodical. English (French and German). Twelve times a year (6 volumes). $2115.00. Elsevier Sequoia SA, PO Box 564, CH-1001 Lausanne 1 Switzerland. **Tel** 011 41 21 3207381, FAX 011 41 21 3235444. **ED** D.W.A. Sharp and J.C. Tatlow. Index available. **Bk Rev. Ad Acc, Adv Mgr:** W. van Cattenburch (Amsterdam). available on microfilm and microfiche from University Microfilms International (UMI); available on an online database from Elsevier Electronic Subscriptions (EES). Documents available from The Genuine Article, CASDDS.
Desc: Contains original papers and preliminary communications describing research on the chemistry of fluorine and of compounds where that halogen is a dominant element. Theoretical, structural or mechanistic aspects of the subject are discussed as well as the normal types of preparative and physico-chemical investigation.
Ind/Abst Chem Inform; Chem. Abstr.; Chem. Titles; Curr. Biotechnol.; Curr. Chem. React.; Curr. Cit.; Curr. Contents Phys. Chem. Earth Sci.; Curr. Titles Electrochem.; Energy Res. Abstr. (April 1978-); Index Chem.; Int. Aerosp. Abstr.; Methods Organ. Synth.; Life Sci. Collect.; Phys. Briefs; Res. Alert [Full Cov.]; Sci. Cit. Index; SCISEARCH.

LC QD196 .J68
DD 547.7
ISSN 1053-0495
US
CCC
CODEN JIOPE4
Pr Rev.

JOURNAL OF INORGANIC AND ORGANOMETALLIC POLYMERS. **See** Chemistry and Chemicals-Organic Chemistry.

LC QD172.R2 C472
DD 546/.41/05
ISSN 1002-0721
CC
CODEN JREAE6

JOURNAL OF RARE EARTHS.
Added/Corp Chung-kuo Hsi Tu Hsueh Hui. Vol. 9, No. 1 (March 1991)-. Periodical. English. Four times a year. $140.00. International Academic Publishers, 137 Chaonei Dajie, Beijing 100010, People's Republic of China. **Tel** 011 86 4035533 217, FAX 011 86 10 5063101. ***Continues*** *Chung-kuo Hsi Tu Hsueh Pao. English. Journal of the Chinese Rare Earth Society, 1001-6503.*
Ind/Abst Chem. Abstr.

LC QD515 .J65
DD 546/.086/05
ISSN 0368-4466
UK
CCC
CODEN JTHEA9
Pr Rev.

JOURNAL OF THERMAL ANALYSIS. [J. therm. anal.]. **Added/Corp** kademiai Kiado. (19??)-. Periodical. English (French and German; summaries and/or abstracts in French, German and Russian). Twelve times a year. $2495.00. John Wiley & Sons Ltd., Baffins Lane, Chichester, West Sussex PO19 1UD United Kingdom. **Tel** 011 44 1243 779777, FAX 011 44 1243 776128 BTG:JWP001, telex 86290 WIBOOKG. **(Subscription address:** John Wiley & Sons, Inc. / Philadelphia, PO Box 7247, Philadelphia PA 19170. **Tel** (212)850-6645, (800)225-5945.**) ED** J. Simon. available on microfilm and microfiche from University Microfilms International (UMI). Documents available from Article Express International, The Genuine Article, Ask*IEEE, CASDDS, Documents on Demand.
Desc: Publishes high quality papers covering all aspects of thermal investigations. Much emphasis is on principles of thermal analysis in which experimental material is initially evaluated.
Ind/Abst Alum. Ind. Abstr.; Anal. Abstr.; Bioeng. Abstr.; Ceram. Abstr.; Chem. Abstr.; Chem. Titles; Coal Abstr.; Curr. Cit.; Curr. Contents Phys. Chem. Earth Sci.; Ei Page One; Energy Inf. Abstr.; Energy Res. Abstr. (Jan. 1971-); Eng. Index Annu.; Environ. Abstr.; Food Sci. Technol. Abstr.; GeoRef; INSPEC (1971-); Leadscan; Mass Spect. Bull.; Met. Abstr.; Polymer Contents; Res. Alert [Full Cov.]; Sci. Cit. Index; SCISEARCH.

LC TP785 .K83
DD 681/.7666/05
ISSN 0454-5648
CC
CODEN KSYHA5
Pr Rev.

KUEI SUAN YEN HSUEH PAO. [Kuei suan yen hsueh pao]. **Added/Corp** Chung-kuo Kuei Suan Yen Hsueh Hui. **VFOAT** Journal of the Chinese Ceramic Society; Journal of the Chinese Silicate Society; Guisuanyan Xuebao. (1962)-. Academic Scholarly Publication. Chinese (summaries and/or abstracts in English). Six times a year. $8.00 (per issue). Chinese Ceramic Society, Guojia Jiancaiju Nei, Baiwanzhuang Beijing 100831, People's Republic of China. **Tel** 861-8311144, FAX 861-8313364. **ED** G. Fuxi. **Ad Acc, Adv Mgr:** Shi Keshun. Documents available from BLDSC, CASDDS.
Desc: Contains information from the latest research, production and design of glass, ceramics, artificial crystal and nonmetal mine.
Ind/Abst Art Archaeol. Tech. Abstr.; Chem. Abstr.

LC QD501 .M425
DD 541.3/9/05
ISSN 0740-8900
US
CCC
CODEN MIORD8

MECHANISMS OF INORGANIC AND ORGANOMETALLIC REACTIONS. [Mech. inorg. organomet. react.]. (1983)-. Academic Scholarly Publication. English. Irregular. Price varies per volume. Plenum Press, 233 Spring Street, New York NY 10013-1578. **Tel** (212)620-8000, (800)221-9369, FAX (212)463-0742, (212)807-1047, telex 23/421139. **ED** M. V. Twigg. Documents available from CASDDS.
Ind/Abst Chem. Abstr. (1983-).

UK

OUTLOOK SULPHUR. English. Four times a year. £1750.00 UK; $3250.00 North America; 3750.00Can$ Canada. Fertecon Limited, 25 Copperfield Street, Suite B, London SE1 0EN United Kingdom. **Tel** 011 44 171 2619998, FAX 011 44 171 9287911. ***Continues*** *Fertecon Quarterly Sulphur Report.*
Desc: Supply and demand report.

LC QD181.O1 O97
DD 546/.721
ISSN 0191-9512
US
CCC
CODEN OZSEDS
Pr Rev.

OZONE : SCIENCE & ENGINEERING.
[Ozone: sci. eng.]. **Added/Corp** International Ozone Association. **VFOAT** Ozone: Science and Engineering; Ozone; Ob3szone Science & Engineering; Ob3szone; OS & E. **VAT** Ozone: Science and Engineering. Vol. 1 (1979)-. Academic Scholarly Publication. English. Six times a year. $275.00. CRC Press Inc., 2000 Corporate Boulevard Northwest, Boca Raton FL 33431. **Tel** (407)994-0555, (800)272-7737, FAX (407)998-9784, (800)374-3401, telex 568689. **(Subscription address:** CRC Press Inc. / New York, PO Box 750, Pearl River NY 10965. **) ED** Rip G. Rice. Documents available from Article Express International, The Genuine Article, BIOSIS Document Express, CASDDS, Documents on Demand.
Desc: This publication focuses on the technologies of ozone.
Ind/Abst AGRICOLA; Bioeng. Abstr.; Biol. Abstr. (1991-); Chem. Abstr.; Curr. Aware. Biol. Sci., CABS; Curr. Cit.; Curr. Contents Agric. Biol. Environ. Sci.; Curr. Ref. Fish Res.; Ei Page One; Energy Inf. Abstr.; Eng. Index Annu. [Select. Cov.]; Environ. Abstr.; Environ. Period. Bibliogr. (?-?); Life Sci. Collect.; Res. Alert [Full Cov.]; Sci. Cit. Index; SCISEARCH.

ISSN 0761-1749
FR
UDC 543/547

PASCAL FOLIO. F16, CHIMIE ANALYTIQUE, MINERALE ET ORGANIQUE. **See** Chemistry and Chemicals-Analytical Chemistry.

LC QD181.S1 P47
DD 546/.723
ISSN 1042-6507
US
CCC
CODEN PREEDF

PHOSPHORUS, SULFUR, AND SILICON AND THE RELATED ELEMENTS.
[Phosphorus sulfur silicon relat. elem.]. **VFOAT** Phosphorus, Sulfur, and Silicon. Vol. 41, No. 1/2 (Jan. 1989)-. Academic Scholarly Publication. English. Twelve times a year. Price varies. Gordon & Breach Science Publishers, Inc., PO Box 786, Cooper Station, New York NY 10276. **Tel** (212)206-8900, FAX (212)645-2459. **(Subscription address:** Gordon & Breach Science Publishers / US, 820 Town Center Drive, Langhorne PA 19047. **Tel** (215)750-2642.**)** Documents available from The Genuine Article, CASDDS. ***Continues*** *Phosphorus and Sulfur and the Related Elements, 0308-664X.*
Ind/Abst Chem. Abstr.; Curr. Chem. React.; Curr. Cit.; Curr. Contents Phys. Chem. Earth Sci.; Index Chem.; Leadscan; Res. Alert [Full Cov.]; Sci. Cit. Index; SCISEARCH; Soils Fert.

ISSN 0032-2725
PL
CODEN POLIA4

POLIMERY. [Polimery]. **Added/Corp** Instytut Chemii Przemysowej (Warsaw, Poland). (1961)-. Academic Scholarly Publication. Polish. Twelve times a year. Price on request. **(Subscription address:** Ars Polona-Ruch, PO Box 1001, Krakowskie Przedmiescie 7, 00-068 Warsaw Poland. **Tel** 011 48 22 261201.**)** Documents available from Article Express International, Ask*IEEE, CASDDS. ***Continues*** *Tworzywa Wielkoczasteczkowe.*
Ind/Abst Abstr. Bull. Inst. Pap. Sci. Tech.; Bioeng. Abstr.; Chem. Abstr.; Coal Abstr.; Curr. Cit.; Ei Page One; Eng. Mater. Abstr.; Eng. Index Annu.; INSPEC (1968-); Text. Technol. Dig.; World Surf. Coat. Abstr.

LC QD1 .P64
DD 546/.05
ISSN 0277-5387
UK
CCC
CODEN PLYHDE
Pr Rev.

POLYHEDRON. [Polyhedron]. Vol. 1, No. 1 (1928)-. Academic Scholarly Publication. English. Twenty-four times a year. $2939.00. Pergamon Press, An Imprint of Elsevier Science Ltd., The Boulevard, Langford Lane, Kidlington, Oxford OX5 1GB United Kingdom. **Tel** 011 44 1865 843000, 011 44 1865 843699, FAX 011 44 1865 843010. **(Subscription address:** Elsevier Science Ltd. / Oxford Fulfillment Centre, PO Box 800, Kidlington OX5 1DX United Kingdom. **Tel** 011 44 865 843355.**) ED** Geoffrey Wilkinson, D. C. Bradley, and M. H. Chisholm. **Bk Rev. Ad Acc.** available on microfilm and microfiche from University Microfilms International (UMI); available on microfiche from the publisher; available on an online database from Elsevier Electronic Subscriptions (EES). Documents available from The Genuine Article, BIOSIS Document Express, Ask*IEEE, CASDDS. ***Formed by the union of*** *Journal of Inorganic and Nuclear Chemistry, 0022-1902* ***and*** *Inorganic and Nuclear Chemistry Letters, 0020-1650.*
Desc: Publishes original, fundamental, experimental and theoretical work in areas of synthetic and reaction chemistry, photochemistry, and the use of metal and organometallic compounds in stoichiometric and catalytic syntheses of organic compounds.
Ind/Abst Biol. Abstr.; Chem. Abstr.; Chem. Titles; Curr. Chem. React.; Curr. Cit.; Curr. Contents Phys. Chem. Earth Sci.; EMBASE; Index Chem.; INSPEC (1982-); Leadscan; Mass Spect. Bull.; MINPROC; Res. Alert [Full Cov.]; Sci. Cit. Index; SCISEARCH.

US

POWDER DIFFRACTION FILE. Main/Corp American Society for Testing and Materials. (19??)-. Monographic series. English. One time a year. Joint Committee on Powder Diffraction Standards / JCPDS, International Centre for Diffraction Data, 12 Campus Boulevard, Newton Square PA 19073. **Tel** (610)325-9810, FAX (610)325-9823, telex 847170.

LC QC482.D5 P645
DD 543/.085 US
UDC 548.734.3

POWDER DIFFRACTION FILE ALPHABETICAL INDEX : INORGANIC COMPOUNDS. (19??)-. English. One time a year. Joint Committee on Powder Diffraction Standards / JCPDS, International Centre for Diffraction Data, 12 Campus Boulevard, Newton Square PA 19073. **Tel** (610)325-9810, FAX (610)325-9823, telex 847170. available on CD-ROM. ***Continues** Powder Diffraction File Search Manual Alphabetical Listing : Inorganic Compounds, 0092-0509.*

LC QC482.D5 P633 **ISSN** 1084-3124
DD 548/.83 US

POWDER DIFFRACTION FILE. HANAWALT SEARCH MANUAL. INORGANIC PHASES. [Powder diffr. file, Hanawalt search man., Inorg. phases]. **Added/Corp** JCPDS--International Centre for Diffraction Data. **VFOAT** Hanawalt Search Manual. Inorganic Phases; Powder Diffraction File; Inorganic Phases; Hanawalt Search Manual. Inorganic Phases. Sets 1-42 (1992)-. English. One time a year. $325.00. Joint Committee on Powder Diffraction Standards / JCPDS, International Centre for Diffraction Data, 12 Campus Boulevard, Newton Square PA 19073. **Tel** (610)325-9810, FAX (610)325-9823, telex 847170. available in hardback. ***Continues** Powder Diffraction File Search Manual, Hanawalt Method. Inorganic, 0092-1319.*

LC QD151 .P76 **ISSN** 0079-6379
DD 546.082 US
NLM W1 PR67P **CODEN** PIOCAR
Pr Rev.

PROGRESS IN INORGANIC CHEMISTRY. [Prog. inorg. chem.]. (1959)-. Monographic series. English. Irregular. Price varies per volume. John Wiley & Sons, Inc., 605 Third Avenue, New York NY 10158-0012. **Tel** (212)850-6000, (212)850-6645, FAX (212)850-6088, telex 12-7063. **(Subscription address:** John Wiley & Sons / UK, Baffins Lane, Chichester, West Sussex PO19 1UD United Kingdom. **Tel** 011 44 1243 779777, FAX 011 44 243 776128, telex 86290 WIBOOKG.) cum. index. Documents available from The Genuine Article, CASDDS.
Ind/Abst Chem. Abstr.; Index Sci. Rev. [Full Cov.]; Res. Alert [Full Cov.]; Sci. Cit. Index (19??-19??); SCISEARCH.

LC TP785 .R48
DD 666/.028 CC

RESEARCH IN INORGANIC MATERIALS. **Added/Corp** Shanghai Institute of Ceramics. (19??)-. Periodical. English.
Ind/Abst Ceram. Abstr. (19??-).

ISSN 0193-4929
UK
CCC
CODEN RICHD7
Pr Rev.

REVIEWS IN INORGANIC CHEMISTRY (LONDON, ENGLAND). (REVIEWS IN INORGANIC CHEMISTRY.). [Rev. inorgan. chem.]. Vol. 1 (Jan./Feb. 1979)-. Academic Scholarly Publication. English. Irregular. $250.00. Freund Publishing House Ltd., PO Box 35010, 61 Nachmani Street, Tel Aviv 61350 Israel. **Tel** 011 972 3 5628540, FAX 011 972 3 5628538. **(Subscription address:** Freund Publishing House Ltd., Suite 500, Chesham House 150 Regent Street, London W1R 5FA United Kingdom. **Tel** 011 44 178 172811, FAX 011 972 3 615335.) **ED** M. Zangen and H.D.B. Jenkins. **Bk Rev. Ad Acc.** Documents available from CASDDS.
Desc: Informs research chemists and students on developments in pure and applied inorganic chemistry.
Ind/Abst Chem. Abstr.; Curr. Cit.

LC QD1 .A37532 **ISSN** 0036-0236
DD 546.05 UK
NLM W1 RU814E **CODEN** RJICAQ

RUSSIAN JOURNAL OF INORGANIC CHEMISTRY. [Russ. j. inorg. chem.]. **Added/Corp** British Library. Lending Division. Royal Society of Chemistry (Great Britain) Chemical Society (Great Britain). (Jan. 1959)-. Periodical. English (translations available in Russian). Twelve times a year. $1955.00. MAIK Nauka / Interperiodica, Ulitsa Profsoyuznaia 90, Moscow 117864 Russia. **(Subscription address:** Interperiodica Publishing, Subscription Office, PO Box 1831, Birmingham AL 35201-1831. **Tel** (800)633-4931, (205)995-1567 (outside US and Canada), FAX (205)995-1588.) Documents available from Ask*IEEE. ***Continues** Journal of Inorganic Chemistry.*
Desc: Original papers on the synthesis and investigation of physiochemical analysis and materials science.
Ind/Abst Ceram. Abstr. (19??-); Curr. Cit.; GeoRef; INSPEC (Jan. 1987-); Int. Aerosp. Abstr. (1987-); Mass Spect. Bull.; MINPROC (1987-); Soils Fert.

LC QD146 .S26 **ISSN** 0551-8393
XR
CODEN SVACBE

SBORNIK VYSOKE SKOLY CHEMICKO-TECHNOLOGICKE V PRAZE. B, ANORGANICKA CHEMIE A TECHNOLOGIE. [Sb. Vys. sk. chem.-technol. Praze, Anorg. chem. technol.]. **Added/Corp** Vysoka Skola Chemicko-Technologicka v Praze. **VFOAT** Anorganicka Chemie a Technologie; Neorganicheskaia Khimiia i Tekhnologiia; Inorganic Chemistry and Technology; Sbornik Prazhskogo Khimiko-Tekhnologicheskogo Instituta. B, Neorganicheskaia Khimiia i Tekhnologiia; Scientific Papers of the Prague Institute of Chemical Technology. B, Inorganic Chemistry and Technology. (1966)-. Czech (English, French, German and Russian). Statni Pedagogicke Nakladatelstvi, Ostrovni 30, 113 01 Prague 1 Czech Republic. **Tel** (2)203787, FAX (2)293883. Documents available from CASDDS.
Ind/Abst Chem. Abstr.

LC TP1 .Z6134 **ISSN** 0038-5344
DD 660/.05 US
UDC 66.0(47+57) **CCC**
CODEN SVCIA7
TITLE CHANGE

SOVIET CHEMICAL INDUSTRY, THE. [Sov. chem. ind.]. (July 1969)-(1993). Periodical. English. Allerton Press Inc., 150 Fifth Avenue, New York NY 10011. **Tel** (212)924-3950, FAX (212)463-9684, telex 427441 ALPRES. **ED** Bill Bown. **Circ:** 350. ***Continued by** Russian Chemical Industry.*
Desc: Organic and inorganic chemistry technology covers such subjects as monomer synthesis, plant problems, coking or scaling in reactors, heavy chemicals, mineral acids, fertilizers, etc.
Ind/Abst Coal Abstr.; Curr. Biotechnol.; Curr. Cit.; EMBASE; Energy Res. Abstr. (April 1977-); Nutr. Abstr. Rev., Ser. B, Live Feeds and Feed.; Proc. Chem. Eng.; Soils Fert.; Theor. Chem. Eng.

LC QD461 .S92 **ISSN** 0081-5993
DD 541.22 GW
CCC
NLM W1 ST82K **CODEN** STBGAG

STRUCTURE AND BONDING (BERLIN). (STRUCTURE AND BONDING.). [Struct. bond.]. Vol. 1 (1966)-. Monographic series. English. Irregular. Price varies per volume. Springer-Verlag GmbH & Company KG, Heidelberger Platz 3, D-14197 Berlin Germany. **Tel** 011 49 30 8207223, FAX 011 49 30 8214091, telex 183 319 SPBLN D. **(Subscription address:** Springer-Verlag New York Inc. / North America, PO Box 2485, Journal Fulfillment, Secaucus NJ 07096. **Tel** (201)348-4033, (800)777-4643, FAX (201)348-4505.) **ED** M. J. Clarke. **Circ:** 300. Documents available from The Genuine Article, BIOSIS Document Express, CASDDS.
Desc: Offers reviews from chemistry-associated fields where the general subject of chemical bonding is of central concern.
Ind/Abst Biol. Abstr. (-1972); Chem. Abstr.; Curr. Cit.; Ei Page One; Energy Res. Abstr. (March 1982-); Index Sci. Rev. [Full Cov.]; Res. Alert [Full Cov.]; Sci. Cit. Index; SCISEARCH.

ISSN 0169-3158
NE
CCC
CODEN SICHEJSINCDO

STUDIES IN INORGANIC CHEMISTRY. [Stud. inorg. chem.]. (1979)-. Academic Scholarly Publication. English. Irregular. Price varies per volume. Elsevier Science Publishers BV, PO Box 211, 1000 AE Amsterdam Netherlands. **Tel** 011 31 20 4853641, 011 31 20 4853642, FAX 011 31 20 4853598. **(Subscription address:** Elsevier Science Inc. / New York Books, 655 Avenue of the Americas, New York NY 10010. **Tel** (212)633-3650.) Documents available from BIOSIS Document Express, CASDDS.
Ind/Abst Biol. Abstr. (?-1985); Chem. Abstr.; Curr. Cit.

LC QD181.S1 S94 **ISSN** 0278-6117
DD 546/.723/05 UK
CCC
CODEN SULED2

SULFUR LETTERS. [Sulfur lett.]. Vol. 1, No. 1 (May 1982)-. Academic Scholarly Publication. English. Six times a year. $463.00 university and hospital libraries;, $723.00 other. Harwood Academic Publishers, PO Box 90, Reading RG1 8JL United Kingdom. **Tel** 011 44 1734 560080, FAX 011 44 1734 568211. **ED** Alexander Senning. **Bk Rev. Ad Acc.** Documents available from CASDDS.
Ind/Abst Chem. Abstr.; Chem. Titles; Curr. Cit.; Mass Spect. Bull.

LC QD181.S1 S95 **ISSN** 0196-1772
DD 546/.723 SZ
CCC
CODEN SUREDW

SULFUR REPORTS. [Sulfur rep.]. Vol. 1, No. 1 (May 1980)-. Academic Scholarly Publication. English. Four times a year. $543.00 (academic institutions), $847.00 (corporate institutions). Harwood Academic Publishers, PO Box 90, Reading RG1 8JL United Kingdom. **Tel** 011 44 1734 560080, FAX 011 44 1734 568211. **ED** Alexander Senning. **Bk Rev. Ad Acc.** Documents available from CASDDS.
Ind/Abst Chem. Abstr.; Curr. Cit.

ISSN 0082-495X
NE
Pr Rev.

TOPICS IN INORGANIC AND GENERAL CHEMISTRY. (1964)-. Monographic series. English. Irregular. Price varies per volume. Elsevier Science Publishers BV, PO Box 211, 1000 AE Amsterdam Netherlands. **Tel** 011 31 20 4853641, 011 31 20 4853642, FAX 011 31 20 4853598.

LC QD181.H1 K37 **ISSN** 0287-1408
JA
CODEN KTDSDB

TOYAMA DAIGAKU TORICHIUMU KAGAKU SENTA KENKYU HOKOKO. (KENKYU HOKOKU.). [Toyama Daigaku Torichiumu Kagaku Senta kenkyu hokoku]. Vol. 1, No. 1 (1981)-. Academic Scholarly Publication. Japanese (summaries and/or abstracts in English). One time a year. ¥120. Toyama Daigaku Torichiumu Kagaku Senta, 3190 Gofuku, Toyama-shi 930 Japan. **Tel** 0764-41-1271. **Circ:** 200. Documents available from CASDDS.
Ind/Abst Chem. Abstr.

LC GB855 .W38 **ISSN** 0266-4615
DD 546/.22/05 UK
CCC
CODEN WSCRER
CEASED

WATER SCIENCE REVIEWS. (1985)-Series complete (19??). Academic Scholarly Publication. English. Cambridge University Press, The Edinburgh Building, Shaftesbury Road, Cambridge CB2 2RU United Kingdom. **Tel** 011 44 1223 312393, FAX 011 44 1223 315052, telex 851-817256. **ED** F. Franks. Documents available from CASDDS.
Ind/Abst Chem. Abstr. (?-?); GeoRef (?-?); Index Sci. Rev. (?-?) [Full Cov.].

LC QD146-197 **ISSN** 1001-4861
DD 546 CC

WUJI HUAXUE XUEBAO. **VFOAT** Journal of Inorganic Chemistry. (1988)-. Periodical. Chinese. Four times a year. Nanjing Gai Kan Bianjibu, People's Republic of China. Documents available from CASDDS.
Ind/Abst Chem. Abstr.

ISSN 0044-2313
GW
CCC
NLM W1 ZE233 **CODEN** ZAACAB
Pr Rev.

ZEITSCHRIFT FUER ANORGANISCHE UND ALLGEMEINE CHEMIE. Vol. 264 (1950)-. Periodical. German (English). Twelve times a year. $674.00. Johann Ambrosius Barth, Prager Strasse 16 B, D-04103 Leipzig Germany. **Tel** 011 49 341 9781570, FAX 011 49 341 9781575. **(Subscription address:** Huethig Publishing Inc., 29 Macintosh Drive, Oxford CT 06478. **Tel** (203)881-2647.) cum. index. available on microfilm from University Microfilms International (UMI). Documents available from The Genuine Article, CASDDS. ***Continues** Zeitschrift fuer Anorganische Chemie.*
Ind/Abst Alum. Ind. Abstr.; Ceram. Abstr. (19??-); Chem. Abstr.; Curr. Cit.; Curr. Contents Phys. Chem. Earth Sci.; Energy Res. Abstr.; Eng. Mater. Abstr.; GeoRef; Int. Aerosp. Abstr.; Mass Spect. Bull.; Met. Abstr.; Res. Alert [Full Cov.]; Sci. Cit. Index; SCISEARCH; World Ceram. Abstr.

LC TP159.M6 Z46 **ISSN** 0144-2449
DD 660.2/82 US
UDC 549.67 **CCC**
CODEN ZEOLD3
Pr Rev.

ZEOLITES. (ZEOLITES : THE INTERNATIONAL JOURNAL OF MOLECULAR SIEVES.). [Zeolites]. Vol. 1, No. 1 (April 1981)-. Academic Scholarly Publication. English. Twelve times a year. $994.00. Butterworth Heinemann / Woburn, MA, 225 Wildwood Avenue, Unit B, Woburn MA 01801. **Tel** (800)366-2665, FAX (617)928-2620, telex 880052. **(Subscription address:** Elsevier Science Inc. / New York Books, 655 Avenue of the Americas, New York NY 10010. **Tel** (212)633-3650.) **ED** L V C Rees. Index available. **Bk Rev. Ad Acc. Circ:** 600. available on microfilm and microfiche from University Microfilms International (UMI). Documents available from Article Express International, The Genuine Article, CASDDS.
Desc: Brings together the different and diverse aspects of zeolite science and technology from research workers studying the structure, synthesis, properties and applications of both natural and synthetic zeolites. It publishes research papers and shorter communications as well as review articles, book reviews, conference reports, patent reports, and a calendar of meetings.
Ind/Abst Ceram. Abstr. (19??-); Chem. Abstr.; Chem. Titles; Curr. Cit.; Ei Page One; Eng. Index Annu.; Geol. Abstr.; GeoRef; Lit. Pat. Abstr., Oilfield Chem. (1983-); Lit. Abstr., Catal. Zeol.; Lit. Abstr., Health Environ.; Lit. Abstr., Pet. Refin. Petrochem.; Lit. Abstr., Pet. Substit.; Lit. Abstr., Transp. Storage; Res. Alert [Full Cov.]; Sci. Cit. Index; SCISEARCH.

ISSN 0044-457X
RU
CCC
CODEN ZNOKAQ
Pr Rev.
ZHURNAL NEORGANICHESKOI KHIMII. [Z. neorg. khim.]. **Added/Corp** Akademiia Nauk SSSR. Vol. 1 (1956)-. Academic Scholarly Publication. Russian. Twelve times a year. $439.95. Izdatelstvo Nauka / Akademiia Nauk, (Publishing House of the Russian Academy of Sciences), Leninskii Porspekt 14, 117901 Moscow Russia. **Tel** 011 95 9542153, FAX 011 95 9382144, telex 411964. **(Subscription address:** East View Publications Inc., 3020 Harbor Lane North, Suite 110, Minneapolis MN 55447. **Tel** (800)477-1005, (612)550-0961, FAX (612)559-2931.**)** **ED** V.I. Spitjin. Documents available from The Genuine Article, Ask*IEEE, CASDDS.
Ind/Abst Alum. Ind. Abstr.; Ceram. Abstr.; Chem Inform; Chem. Abstr.; Curr. Contents Phys. Chem. Earth Sci.; Energy Res. Abstr.; GeoRef; INSPEC (Jan. 1987-); Met. Abstr.; Res. Alert [Full Cov.]; Sci. Cit. Index; SCISEARCH; Sug. Indus. Abstr.; World Alum. Abstr.

ORGANIC CHEMISTRY

LC QC457 .A33
DD 547/.308/5 UK
ABSORPTION SPECTRA IN THE INFRARED REGION. (1974)-. English. Two times a year. Butterworth Heinemann Publishers, Linacre House Jordan Hill, Oxford OX2 8DP United Kingdom. **Tel** 011 44 1865 310366, FAX 011 44 1865 310898.

ISSN 0306-3747
UK
CCC
ADDITIVES FOR POLYMERS. [Addit polym.]. (1971)-. Periodical. English. Twelve times a year. $589.00. Elsevier Advanced Technology, An Imprint of Elsevier Science Ltd., The Boulevard, Langford Lane, Kidlington, Oxford OX5 1GB United Kingdom. **Tel** 011 44 1865 843000, 011 44 1865 843699, FAX 011 44 1865 843010. **(Subscription address:** Elsevier Science Ltd. / Oxford Fulfillment Centre, PO Box 800, Kidlington OX5 1DX United Kingdom. **Tel** 011 44 865 843355.**)** **ED** J. Shelton. available on an online database from Elsevier Electronic Subscriptions (EES).
Desc: Comprehensive summary of information concerning polymer additives. The newsletter covers developments around the world focusing on North America, Europe and Japan. It provides an insight into the latest developments in markets and products, helping today's professional to readily access the news as it occurs.

LC QD305.C3 A38 **ISSN** 1047-3645
DD 547.1/39 US
CODEN ADCCE9
ADVANCES IN CARBOCATION CHEMISTRY. (ADVANCES IN CARBOCATION CHEMISTRY : A RESEARCH ANNUAL.). Vol. 1 (1989)-. English. One time a year. Price varies. JAI Press Inc., 55 Old Post Road, Suite 2, PO Box 1678, Greenwich CT 06836-1678. **Tel** (203)661-7602, FAX (203)661-0792. Documents available from CASDDS.
Ind/Abst Chem. Abstr.

LC QD320 .A34 **ISSN** 1062-0044
DD 547.7/8/05 UK
CODEN ACANEP
ADVANCES IN CARBOHYDRATE ANALYSIS. [Adv. carbohydr. anal.]. Vol. 1 (1991)-. Academic Scholarly Publication. English. Irregular. Price varies. JAI Press Inc., 55 Old Post Road, Suite 2, PO Box 1678, Greenwich CT 06836-1678. **Tel** (203)661-7602, FAX (203)661-0792. Documents available from CASDDS.
Ind/Abst Chem. Abstr.

LC QD271 .A23 **ISSN** 0065-2415
DD 544.92 US
CCC
NLM W1 AD53U **CODEN** ADCYA3
Pr Rev.
ADVANCES IN CHROMATOGRAPHY (NEW YORK, N.Y.). (ADVANCES IN CHROMATOGRAPHY.). [Adv. chromatogr.]. Vol. 1 (1965)-. Monographic series. English. Irregular. Price varies per volume. Marcel Dekker Inc., 270 Madison Avenue, New York NY 10016. **Tel** (212)696-9000, (800)228-1160, FAX (212)685-4540, telex 421419. **(Subscription address:** Marcel Dekker Inc., PO Box 5017, Monticello NY 12701. **Tel** (800)228-1160.**)** **ED** J. C. Giddings and R. A. Keller. cum. index. **Bk Rev.** Documents available from Article Express International, The Genuine Article, CASDDS.
Desc: Provides reviews of the recent research in chromatographic science.
Ind/Abst AGRICOLA [Select. Cov.]; Chem. Abstr.; Curr. Biotechnol.; Curr. Cit.; Eng. Index Annu.; Food Sci. Technol. Abstr.; GeoRef; Health Plan. Adminis.; Index Med.; Index Sci. Rev. [Full Cov.]; Res. Alert [Full Cov.]; Sci. Cit. Index; SCISEARCH.

LC QD281.R5 A35 **ISSN** 1052-2077
DD 547/.2 US
CODEN ADCYE7
ADVANCES IN CYCLOADDITION. [Adv. cycloaddit.]. Vol. 1 (1988)-. English. One time a year. $90.25. JAI Press Inc., 55 Old Post Road, Suite 2, PO Box 1678, Greenwich CT 06836-1678. **Tel** (203)661-7602, FAX (203)661-0792. **ED** Dennis P. Curran. Documents available from CASDDS.
Ind/Abst Chem. Abstr.

LC QD501 .A345 **ISSN** 1063-0619
DD 547.1/394 US
CODEN ADRMEC
ADVANCES IN DETAILED REACTION MECHANISMS. [Adv. detail. react. mech.]. Vol. 1 (1991)-. Periodical. English. Irregular. $90.25. JAI Press Inc., 55 Old Post Road, Suite 2, PO Box 1678, Greenwich CT 06836-1678. **Tel** (203)661-7602, FAX (203)661-0792. **ED** James M. Coxon.
Desc: Study of detailed reaction mechanisms, of how and why molecular change occurs. Intended to highlight selected approaches which have led to advances.

LC QD400 .A18 **ISSN** 0065-2725
DD 547.59 US
UDC 547.7/.8 CCC
NLM W1 AD633 **CODEN** AHTCAG
ADVANCES IN HETEROCYCLIC CHEMISTRY. [Adv. heterocycl. chem.]. Vol. 1 (1963)-. Academic Scholarly Publication. English. Irregular. $105.00 (Vol. 59). Academic Press Inc., 6277 Sea Harbor Drive, Orlando FL 32887. **Tel** (800)543-9534, (407)345-4100, FAX (407)352-3445. **ED** A. R. Katritzky. Documents available from The Genuine Article, BIOSIS Document Express, CASDDS.
Ind/Abst Biol. Abstr.; Chem Inform; Chem. Abstr.; Curr. Chem. React.; Curr. Cit.; Index Sci. Rev. [Full Cov.]; Res. Alert [Full Cov.]; Sci. Cit. Index; SCISEARCH.

LC RS400 .A4 **ISSN** 1067-571X
DD 615/.19 US
NLM W1; AD634 **CODEN** AHNSE4
ADVANCES IN HETEROCYCLIC NATURAL PRODUCT SYNTHESIS. [Adv. heterocycl. nat. prod. synth.]. Vol. 1 (1990)-. Academic Scholarly Publication. English. One time a year. $90.25. JAI Press Inc., 55 Old Post Road, Suite 2, PO Box 1678, Greenwich CT 06836-1678. **Tel** (203)661-7602, FAX (203)661-0792. **ED** William Pearson. Documents available from CASDDS.
Desc: Heterocyclic compounds represent a majority of the important medicinal agents discovered in nature. The development of new synthetic methodology for the preparation of such heterocycles, and the application of these methods to the synthesis of heterocyclic natural products; recent progress in this area of organic chemistry.
Ind/Abst Chem. Abstr.

LC QD382.P67 A39 **ISSN** 1068-3550
DD 547.7 US
ADVANCES IN INTERPENETRATING POLYMER NETWORKS. [Adv. interpenetr. polym. netw.]. **VFOAT** Advances in IPNs. Vol. 1 (1989)-. English. Irregular. $75.00 (vol. 4). Technomic Publishing Company, Inc., 851 New Holland Avenue, Box 3535, Lancaster PA 17604. **Tel** (717)291-5609, (800)233-9936, FAX (717)295-4538. **ED** Daniel Klempner and Kurt C. Frisch.
Desc: A major presentation of IPN science and technology from around the world covering in-depth reports in IPN chemistry, synthesis, properties, and R&D activity. Details of new IPN materials using a variety of polymers.

LC RS400 .A424 **ISSN** 1067-5698
DD 615/.19/005 US
NLM W1; AD679PT **CODEN** ADCHEO
ADVANCES IN MEDICINAL CHEMISTRY. See Biology-Bioengineering.

LC QD410 .A38 **ISSN** 1045-0688
DD 547/.05 US
CODEN ADMCEP
ADVANCES IN METAL-ORGANIC CHEMISTRY. [Adv. metal-org. chem.]. **VFOAT** Advances in Metal Organic Chemistry. Vol. 1 (1989)-. English. Irregular. $90.25. JAI Press Inc., 55 Old Post Road, Suite 2, PO Box 1678, Greenwich CT 06836-1678. **Tel** (203)661-7602, FAX (203)661-0792. **ED** Lanny S. Liebeskind. Documents available from CASDDS.
Desc: Accounts of emerging synthetic organic methods and of concepts that highlight the attributes of organometallic chemistry applied to problems in organic synthesis.
Ind/Abst Chem. Abstr.

LC QD411 .A35 **ISSN** 0065-3055
DD 547 US
UDC 547.25 CCC
NLM W1 AD695 **CODEN** AOMCAU
Pr Rev.
ADVANCES IN ORGANOMETALLIC CHEMISTRY. [Adv. organomet. chem.]. Vol. 1 (1964)-. Academic Scholarly Publication. English. Irregular. $105.00 (Vol. 36). Academic Press Inc., 6277 Sea Harbor Drive, Orlando FL 32887. **Tel** (800)543-9534, (407)345-4100, FAX (407)352-3445. **ED** F. G. A. Stone and R. West. Documents available from The Genuine Article, BIOSIS Document Express, CASDDS.
Ind/Abst Biol. Abstr. (1985-); Chem Inform; Chem. Abstr.; Curr. Chem. React.; Curr. Cit.; Index Sci. Rev. [Full Cov.]; Mass Spect. Bull.; Res. Alert [Full Cov.]; Sci. Cit. Index; SCISEARCH.

LC QD476 .A4 **ISSN** 0065-3160
DD 547.1082 UK
UDC 547
NLM W1 AD782 **CODEN** APORAO
Pr Rev.
ADVANCES IN PHYSICAL ORGANIC CHEMISTRY. See Chemistry and Chemicals-Physical and Theoretical Chemistry.

LC QD281.P6 F6 **ISSN** 0065-3195
DD 547.7 GW
CCC
CODEN APSIDK
Pr Rev.
ADVANCES IN POLYMER SCIENCE. [Adv. polym. sci.]. **VFOAT** Fortschritte der Hochpolymeren-Forschung. Vol. 8 (1971)-. Academic Scholarly Publication. English. Irregular. Price varies per volume. Springer-Verlag GmbH & Company KG, Heidelberger Platz 3, D-14197 Berlin Germany. **Tel** 011 49 30 8207223, FAX 011 49 30 8214091, telex 183 319 SPBLN D. **(Subscription address:** Springer-Verlag New York Inc. / North America, PO Box 2485, Journal Fulfillment, Secaucus NJ 07096. **Tel** (201)348-4033, (800)777-4643, FAX (201)348-4505.**)** **ED** A. Abe, H. Benoit, H.J. Cantow, P. Corradini, K. Dusek, S. Edwards, H. Fujita, G. Glockner, H. Hocker, H.H. Horhold, H.H. Kausch, J.P. Kennedy, J.L. Koenig, A. Ledwith, J.E. McGrath, L. Monnerie, S. Okamura, C.G. Overberger, H. Ringsdorf, T. Saegusa, J.C. Salamone, J.L. Schrag, J.K. Stille, G. Wegner, G. Henrici-Olive, G. Heublein, S. Olive, W.P. Slichter. Documents available from Article Express International, The Genuine Article, BIOSIS Document Express, Ask*IEEE, CASDDS. ***Continues*** *Fortschritte der Hochpolymeren-Forschung.*
Desc: Series covering polymers and polymerization.
Ind/Abst Bioeng. Abstr.; Biol. Abstr. (-1976); Chem. Abstr.; Curr. Cit.; Ei Page One; Energy Res. Abstr. (1982-); Eng. Index Annu.; Index Sci. Rev. [Full Cov.]; INSPEC; Int. Aerosp. Abstr.; Res. Alert [Full Cov.]; Sci. Cit. Index; SCISEARCH; World Text. Abstr.

LC QD431 .A3 **ISSN** 0065-3233
DD 547.8 US
UDC 547.82/.85 CCC
NLM W1 AD79 **CODEN** APCHA2
ADVANCES IN PROTEIN CHEMISTRY. [Adv. protein chem.]. Vol. 1 (1944)-. Academic Scholarly Publication. English. Irregular. $90.00 (Vol. 45). Academic Press Inc., 6277 Sea Harbor Drive, Orlando FL 32887. **Tel** (800)543-9534, (407)345-4100, FAX (407)352-3445. **ED** M. L. Anson and John T. Edsall. cum. index. Documents available from The Genuine Article, CASDDS.
Ind/Abst Chem. Abstr.; Curr. Aware. Biol. Sci., CABS; Dairy Sci. Abstr.; EMBASE; Energy Res. Abstr. (Aug. 1982-); Food Sci. Technol. Abstr.; Index Med.; Index Sci. Rev. [Full Cov.]; Nutr. Abstr. Rev., Ser. B, Live Feeds and Feed.; Nutr. Abstr. Rev., Ser. A, Hum. Exp.; Life Sci. Collect.; Ref. Upd. Basic Ed.; Ref. Upd. Deluxe Ed.; Res. Alert [Full Cov.]; Sci. Cit. Index; SCISEARCH; Vitis Vitic. Enol. Abstr.

LC QD461 .A33 **ISSN** 1061-8902
DD 547 UK
CODEN AOCEEO
ADVANCES IN STRAIN IN ORGANIC CHEMISTRY. [Adv. strain org. chem.]. Vol. 1 (1991)-. Academic Scholarly Publication. English. Irregular. $90.25. JAI Press Inc., 55 Old Post Road, Suite 2, PO Box 1678, Greenwich CT 06836-1678. **Tel** (203)661-7602, FAX (203)661-0792. **ED** Brian Halton. Documents available from CASDDS.
Desc: Essays on the facets of strained organic molecules.
Ind/Abst Chem. Abstr.

LC QD380 .A23 **ISSN** 1068-7459
DD 547.7/05 US
CODEN ASUCEY
ADVANCES IN SUPRAMOLECULAR CHEMISTRY. [Adv. supramol. chem.]. **VFOAT** Supramolecular Chemistry. Vol. 1 (1990)-. Periodical. English. Irregular. $90.25. JAI Press Inc., 55 Old Post Road, Suite 2, PO Box 1678, Greenwich CT 06836-1678. **Tel** (203)661-7602, FAX (203)661-0792. **ED** George W. Gokel.

ISSN 1075-2099
DD 547 US
CODEN AUSCE4
•**ADVANCES IN THE USE OF SYNTHONS IN ORGANIC CHEMISTRY.** **VFOAT** Use of Synthons in Organic Chemistry. Vol. 1 (1993)-. Periodical. English. Irregular. $90.25. JAI Press Inc., 55 Old Post Road, Suite 2, PO Box 1678, Greenwich CT 06836-1678. **Tel** (203)661-7602, FAX (203)661-0792. **ED** Alessandro Dondoni.

Chemistry and Chemicals —Organic Chemistry

LC QD255.4 .A38
DD 547/.005
ISSN 1046-5766
US
CODEN ATIMEB
ADVANCES IN THEORETICALLY INTERESTING MOLECULES. [Adv. theor. interest. mol.] Vol. 1 (1989)-. Academic Scholarly Publication. English. One time a year. $90.25. JAI Press Inc., 55 Old Post Road, Suite 2, PO Box 1678, Greenwich CT 06836-1678. **Tel** (203)661-7602, FAX (203)661-0792. Documents available from CASDDS.
Ind/Abst Chem. Abstr.

LC QD421.A1 A43
DD 547.7/2/05
UDC 547.94
NLM W1 AL43
ISSN 0099-9598
US
CCC
CODEN ALKAAR
ALKALOIDS. CHEMISTRY AND PHARMACOLOGY, THE. [Alkaloids]. **VFOAT** Chemistry and Pharmacology. (1983)-. Academic Scholarly Publication. English. Irregular. $120.00 (Vol. 45). Academic Press Inc., 6277 Sea Harbor Drive, Orlando FL 32887. **Tel** (800)543-9534, (407)345-4100, FAX (407)352-3445. **ED** Arnold Brossi. Documents available from BIOSIS Document Express, CASDDS. **Continues** Alkaloids. Chemistry and Physiology, 0099-9598.
Ind/Abst AGRICOLA; Biol. Abstr.; Chem. Abstr.

LC QD262 .A558
DD 547/.2/08
NLM Z 5524.08 A615
ISSN 0066-409X
US
CCC
CODEN ARSYEF
ANNUAL REPORTS IN ORGANIC SYNTHESIS. [Annu. rep. org. synth.]. (1970)-. Academic Scholarly Publication. English. Irregular. $65.00 (latest edition). Academic Press Inc., 6277 Sea Harbor Drive, Orlando FL 32887. **Tel** (800)543-9534, (407)345-4100, FAX (407)352-3445. **ED** L. G. Wade and Martin J. O'Donnell. Documents available from BIOSIS Document Express.
Ind/Abst Biol. Abstr. (1990-).

LC QD1 .C57
DD 547/.005
NLM W1 CH266B
ISSN 0069-3030
UK
CCC
CODEN CACBB4
ANNUAL REPORTS ON THE PROGRESS OF CHEMISTRY. SECTION B, ORGANIC CHEMISTRY. [Annu. rep. prog. chem., Sect. B.]. **Added/Corp** Chemical Society (Great Britain) Royal Society of Chemistry (Great Britain). **VFOAT** Organic Chemistry; Annual Reports. B. Vol. 64 (1967)-. English. One time a year (Oct. of following year). $205.00. Royal Society of Chemistry, Thomas Graham House, Science Park, Cambridge CB4 4WF United Kingdom. **Tel** 011 44 1223 420066, FAX 011 44 1223 423623, telex 818293 ROYAL. **(Subscription address:** Royal Society of Chemistry, Turpin Distribution Services Ltd., Blackhorse Road, Letchworth, Hertfordshire SG6 1HN United Kingdom. **Tel** 011 44 1462 672555, FAX 011 44 1462 480947.) Index available. cum. index. Documents available from BIOSIS Document Express, CASDDS. **Continues in part** Annual Reports on the Progress of Chemistry.
Desc: Covers organic chemistry.
Ind/Abst Biol. Abstr. (1985-); Chem. Abstr.

LC QD410 .A66
DD 547/.05
ISSN 0268-2605
UK
CCC
CODEN AOCHEX
APPLIED ORGANOMETALLIC CHEMISTRY. [Appl. organomet. chem.]. Vol. 1 (1987)-. Academic Scholarly Publication. English. Eight times a year. $695.00. John Wiley & Sons Ltd., Baffins Lane, Chichester, West Sussex PO19 1UD United Kingdom. **Tel** 011 44 1243 779777, FAX 011 44 1243 776128 BTG:JWP801, telex 86290 WIBOOKG.
(Subscription address: John Wiley & Sons, Inc. / Philadelphia, PO Box 7247, Philadelphia PA 19170. **Tel** (212)850-6645, (800)225-5945.) **ED** P. J. Craig. **Bk Rev. Ad Acc.** available on microfilm and microfiche from University Microfilms International (UMI). Documents available from The Genuine Article, CASDDS.
Desc: Provides an effective outlet to applied work in the organometallic field. It contains original papers, short communications, reviews, and reports of relevant conferences. Coverage includes: catalysis and synthesis using organometallics; electronic applications with organometallics; molecular electronics; diffusion studies with organometallics in plastics, food, etc.
Ind/Abst Chem. Abstr.; Mass Spect. Bull.; Curr. Cit.; Curr. Contents Phys. Chem. Earth Sci.; Lab. Hazards Bull.; Mass Spect. Bull. (?-?); Res. Alert [Full Cov.]; SCISEARCH.

LC QD501 .A83
NE
CEASED
ASPECTS OF HOMOGENEOUS CATALYSIS. (1970)-Series complete with Vol. 7. Academic Scholarly Publication. English. Kluwer Academic Publishers, Postbus 322, 3300 AH Dordrecht The Netherlands. **Tel** 011 31 78 524400, FAX 011 31 78 183273, telex 20083. **ED** Renato Ugo. **Circ:** 500. Documents available from CASDDS.

Desc: Special and well-defined review articles in the field of homogeneous catalysis.
Ind/Abst Chem. Abstr. (1970-1984).

GW
BEILSTEINS HANDBUCH DER ORGANISCHEN CHEMIE. HRSG. VON BEILSTEIN-INSTITUT FUER LITERATURE DER ORGANISCHEN CHEMIE, FRANKFORT AM MAIN. 4. AUFL. DRITTES UND VIERTES ERGANZUNGSWERK; DIE LITERATUR VON 1930 BIS 1959 UMFASSEND. Vol. 17 (1974)-. Periodical. German. Springer-Verlag GmbH & Company KG, Heidelberger Platz 3, D-14197 Berlin Germany. **Tel** 011 49 30 8207223, FAX 011 49 30 8214091, telex 183 319 SPBLN D. **(Subscription address:** Springer-Verlag New York Inc. / North America, PO Box 2485, Journal Fulfillment, Secaucus NJ 07096. **Tel** (201)348-4033, (800)777-4643, FAX (201)348-4505.) available on an online database (File no. 390) from DIALOG. **Formed by the union of** Beilsteins Handbuch der Organischen Chemie. 4. Aufl. Drittes Erganzungswerk **and** Beilsteins Handbuch der Organischen Chemie. 4. Aufl. Viertes Erganzungswerk.

LC QP501 .B58
DD 574.1/924/05
NLM W1 BI876K
Pr Rev.
ISSN 0045-2068
US
CCC
CODEN BOCMBM
BIOORGANIC CHEMISTRY. See Biology-Biological Chemistry.

LC QP550 .B562
DD 574.19/2/05
NLM W1; BI89S
GW
CODEN BCFRE5
BIOORGANIC CHEMISTRY FRONTIERS. See Biology-Biological Chemistry.

LC QD415.A1 B55
ISSN 0132-3423
RU
CCC
NLM W1 BI876M
Pr Rev.
CODEN BIKHD7
BIOORGANICHESKAIA KHIMIIA.
Added/Corp Akademiia Nauk SSSR. Vol. 1, (Jan. 1975)-. Academic Scholarly Publication. Russian (summaries and/or abstracts in English). Twelve times a year. $420.00. **(Subscription address:** East View Publications Inc., 3020 Harbor Lane North, Suite 110, Minneapolis MN 55447. **Tel** (800)477-1005, (612)550-0961, FAX (612)559-2931.) Documents available from The Genuine Article, BIOSIS Document Express, CASDDS.
Ind/Abst AGRICOLA; Biol. Abstr.; Chem. Abstr.; Chem. Titles; Chemorecept. Abstr.; CSA Neuro. Abstr. (?-?); Curr. Biotechnol.; Energy Res. Abstr. (April 1978-);;; Index Med. (1983-); Index Vet.; Mass Spect. Bull.; Microbiol. Abstr. Sect. B; NAPRALERT; Life Sci. Collect.; PESTDOC; Plant Breed. Abstr.; Postharvest News Inf.; Res. Alert [Full Cov.]; Rev. Med. Vet. Entomol.; Sci. Cit. Index; SCISEARCH; Vet. Bull.

ISSN 0397-7730
FR
BULLETIN SIGNALETIQUE 780: POLYMERES, PEINTURES, BOIS, CUIRS. Added/Corp France. Centre National de la Recherche Scientifique. Centre de Documentation Scientifique et Technique. **VFOAT** Polymeres, Peintures, Bois, Cuirs. Vol. 38 (1977)-. Bulletin. French. Irregular. $150.99. Editions du CNRS, 22 rue Saint Armand, F 75015 Paris France. **Tel** 011 33 1 45075050, telex 200 356 F. **Continues** Bulletin Signaletique 780: Polymeres, Chimie et Technologie.

DD 547
ISSN 1049-1325
US
C2C ABSTRACTS JAPAN. ORGANIC CHEMISTRY. [C2C abstr. Jap., Org. chem.]. **VFOAT** Organic Chemistry. Vol. 1, No. 1 (Feb. 1990)-. English. Twelve times a year. $200.00. SCAN C2C Inc., 500 E Street Southwest, Suite 800 8th Floor, Washington DC 20024. **Tel** (202)863-3850, (800)525-3865, FAX (202)863-3855. Index available. cum. index. available on CD-ROM from DIALOG; available on an online database from ORBIT; DATA-STAR; and DIALOG.
Desc: English abstracts of over 500 Japanese science, technical and business journals in the field of organic chemistry.

DD 547
ISSN 0895-5964
US
CODEN CSACEO
CA SELECTS: ALKYLATION & CATALYSTS. See Chemistry and Chemicals-Abstracting, Bibliographies and Statistics.

DD 547
ISSN 0275-701X
US
CODEN CSAPDS
CA SELECTS: AMINO ACIDS, PEPTIDES & PROTEINS. See Chemistry and Chemicals-Abstracting, Bibliographies and Statistics.

DD 547
ISSN 0895-5956
US
CODEN CSCCEY
CA SELECTS: CARBON FIBER COMPOSITES. See Chemistry and Chemicals-Abstracting, Bibliographies and Statistics.

ISSN 0146-4396
US
CODEN CSCRDA
CA SELECTS: CATALYSIS (ORGANIC REACTIONS). See Chemistry and Chemicals-Abstracting, Bibliographies and Statistics.

ISSN 0190-9444
US
CODEN CCMADX
CA SELECTS: COLLOIDS (MACROMOLECULAR ASPECTS). See Chemistry and Chemicals-Abstracting, Bibliographies and Statistics.

DD 547
ISSN 0895-593X
US
CODEN CAEAEE
CA SELECTS: ENZYME APPLICATIONS. See Chemistry and Chemicals-Abstracting, Bibliographies and Statistics.

DD 547
ISSN 0895-5921
US
CODEN CASFEV
CA SELECTS: FLUOROPOLYMERS. See Chemistry and Chemicals-Abstracting, Bibliographies and Statistics.

DD 547
ISSN 0895-5883
US
CODEN CAICE6
CA SELECTS: ISOMERIZATION & CATALYSTS. See Chemistry and Chemicals-Abstracting, Bibliographies and Statistics.

DD 547
ISSN 0885-0186
US
CODEN CSOMEM
CA SELECTS: ORGANIC OPTICAL MATERIALS. See Chemistry and Chemicals-Abstracting, Bibliographies and Statistics.

DD 547
ISSN 0895-5859
US
CODEN COOSEC
CA SELECTS: ORGANOMETALLICS IN ORGANIC SYNTHESIS. See Chemistry and Chemicals-Abstracting, Bibliographies and Statistics.

DD 547
ISSN 1040-7219
US
CODEN CAOSEG
CA SELECTS: OXIDE SUPERCONDUCTORS. See Chemistry and Chemicals-Abstracting, Bibliographies and Statistics.

DD 547
ISSN 0885-0208
US
CODEN CSPSEB
CA SELECTS: PHOTOCHEMICAL ORGANIC SYNTHESIS. See Chemistry and Chemicals-Abstracting, Bibliographies and Statistics.

DD 547
ISSN 0895-5832
US
CODEN CSISEA
CA SELECTS: SILOXANES & SILICONES. See Chemistry and Chemicals-Abstracting, Bibliographies and Statistics.

LC QD241
DD 547
Pr Rev.
ISSN 0007-9510
FR
CODEN CACAAY
TITLE CHANGE
CAFE, CACAO, THE. [Cafe, cacao, the].
Added/Corp Institut Francais du Cafe et du Cacao. (1957)-(1994). Academic Scholarly Publication. French (summaries and/or abstracts in English, German and Spanish). Centre de Cooperation International en Recherche Agronomique pour le Developpement CP - CIRAD CP, Department des Cultures Perennes, 12 Square Petrarque, 75116 Paris France. **Tel** 011 33 1 53702000, telex 620871. **ED** J. Collot. Index available. cum. index. **Bk Rev. Ad Acc. Circ:** 150. Documents available from The Genuine Article, BIOSIS Document Express, CASDDS. **Merged into** Plantations, Recherche, Developpement, 1254-7670.
Desc: Agronomy, chemistry and technology on coffee, cocoa, tea, and cola.
Ind/Abst AgBiotech News Inf.; Agrofor. Abstr.; BioBusiness; Biol. Abstr.; Chem. Abstr.; Chemorecept. Abstr.; Crop Physiol. Abstr.; Curr. Aware. Biol. Sci.; CABS; Curr. Cit.; Curr. Contents Agric. Biol. Environ. Sci.; Food Sci. Technol. Abstr.; Hortic. Abstr.; Life Sci. Collect.; PESTDOC; Plant Breed. Abstr.; Plant Genet. Resour. Abstr.; Plant Grow. Reg. Abstr.; Postharvest News Inf.; Res. Alert [Select. Cov.]; Rev. Agric. Entomol.; Rev. Med.

Vet. Mycology; Rev. Plant Pathol.; SCISEARCH; Seed Abstr.; Soc. Sci. Cit. Index [Select. Cov.]; Soils Fert.; Weed Abstr.

LC QD305.H7 C35
DD 547'.412 US
CARBENES. Vol. 1 (1973)-. Monographic series. English. Irregular. Price varies per volume. John Wiley & Sons, Inc., 605 Third Avenue, New York NY 10158-0012. **Tel** (212)850-6000, (212)850-6645, FAX (212)850-6088, telex 12-7063. **(Subscription address:** John Wiley & Sons / UK, Baffins Lane, Chichester, West Sussex PO19 1UD United Kingdom. **Tel** 011 44 1243 779777, FAX 011 44 243 776128, telex 86290 WIBOOKG.)

LC QD321 .C26 **ISSN** 0576-7172
DD 547/.01 UK
CCC
NLM W1 CA762K **CODEN** CBHCA4
CARBOHYDRATE CHEMISTRY. [Carbohydr. chem.]. **Added/Corp** Chemical Society (Great Britain). Vol. 1 (1967)-. English. One time a year. £120.00. Royal Society of Chemistry, Thomas Graham House, Science Park, Cambridge CB4 4WF United Kingdom. **Tel** 011 44 1223 420066, FAX 011 44 1223 423623, telex 818293 ROYAL. **(Subscription address:** Royal Society of Chemistry, Turpin Distribution Services Ltd., Blackhorse Road, Letchworth, Hertfordshire SG6 1HN United Kingdom. **Tel** 011 44 1462 672555, FAX 011 44 1462 480947.) Documents available from CASDDS.
Desc: Covers general methods; plant and algal polysaccharides; microbial polysaccharides; glycoproteins, glycopeptides, proteoglycans, and animal polysaccharides; enzymes; glycolipids and gangliosides; chemical synthesis and modification of oligosaccharides, polysaccharides, glycoproteins, enzymes, and glycolipids.
Ind/Abst Chem. Abstr.

LC QD320 .C35 **ISSN** 0144-8617
DD 547.7/8/05 UK
CCC
CODEN CAPOD8
Pr Rev.
CARBOHYDRATE POLYMERS. [Carbohydr. polym.]. Vol. 1, No. 1 (Sept. 1981)-. Academic Scholarly Publication. English. Twelve times a year. $1257.00. Elsevier Applied Science, An Imprint of Elsevier Science Ltd., The Boulevard, Langford Lane, Kidlington, Oxford OX5 1GB United Kingdom. **Tel** 011 44 1865 843000, 011 44 1865 843699, FAX 011 44 1865 843010. **(Subscription address:** Elsevier Science Ltd. / Oxford Fulfillment Centre, PO Box 800, Kidlington OX5 1DX United Kingdom. **Tel** 011 44 865 843355.) **ED** J. F. Kennedy, J. R. Mitchell and P. A. Sandford. **Bk Rev. Ad Acc.** available on microfilm and microfiche from University Microfilms International (UMI); available on an online database from Elsevier Electronic Subscriptions (EES). Documents available from Article Express International, The Genuine Article, BIOSIS Document Express, CASDDS.
Desc: Provides a forum for publications relating to the scientific study and technological exploitation of polymers which have, or potentially offer, industrial applications in fields such as foods, textiles, paper, wood, adhesives, pharmaceuticals and industrial chemistry.
Ind/Abst Abstr. Bull. Inst. Pap. Sci. Tech.; AGRICOLA; Biol. Abstr. (1988-); Chem. Abstr.; Chem. Titles; Curr. Cit.; Curr. Contents Agric. Biol. Environ. Sci.; Curr. Contents Life Sci.; Curr. Contents Phys. Chem. Earth Sci.; Dairy Sci. Abstr.; Ei Page One; Eng. Index Annu.; Field Crop Abstr.; Food Sci. Technol. Abstr.; Foods Adlibra; Index Vet.; Life Sci. Collect.; Polymer Contents; Res. Alert [Full Cov.]; Sci. Cit. Index; SCISEARCH; Seed Abstr.; Sug. Indus. Abstr.; Vet. Bull.; Wheat Barley Trit. Abstr.

LC QD321 .C3 **ISSN** 0008-6215
DD 547.7805 NE
CCC
NLM W1 CA762N **CODEN** CRBRAT
Pr Rev.
CARBOHYDRATE RESEARCH. [Carbohydr. res.]. Vol. 1 No. 1 (July/Aug. 1965)-. Academic Scholarly Publication. English (French and German). Thirty-four times a year. $4128.00. Elsevier Science Publishers BV, PO Box 211, 1000 AE Amsterdam Netherlands. **Tel** 011 31 20 4853641, 011 31 20 4853642, FAX 011 31 20 4853598. **ED** L Anderson, DC Baker, JG Buchanan, J Defaye, D Horton, EF Hounsell, AS Serianni, JM Webber. Index available. **Bk Rev. Ad Acc.** available on microfilm and microfiche from University Microfilms International (UMI); available on an online database from Elsevier Electronic Subscriptions (EES); and STN International. Documents available from Article Express International, The Genuine Article, BIOSIS Document Express, CASDDS, ADONIS.
Desc: Includes all aspects of carbohydrate chemistry and biochemistry. Articles cover sugars and their derivatives: oleo and polysaccharides, nucleotides and glycoconjugates.
Ind/Abst Abstr. Bull. Inst. Pap. Sci. Tech.; ADONIS; AGRICOLA [Select. Cov.]; Anal. Abstr.; Biol. Abstr.; Chem Inform; Chem. Abstr.; Chem. Titles; Comput. Inf. Syst. Abstr. J. [Full Cov.]; Cot. Trop. Fibr. Abstr. Bibliogr.; Crop Physiol. Abstr.; Curr. Aware. Biol. Sci., CABS; Curr. Biotechnol.; Curr. Chem. React.; Curr. Cit.; Curr. Contents Agric. Biol. Environ. Sci.; Curr. Contents Life Sci.; Curr. Contents Phys. Chem. Earth Sci.; Dairy Sci. Abstr.; EMBASE; Energy Res. Abstr. (Jan. 1971-); Eng. Index Annu.; Environ. Eng. Abstr.; Field Crop Abstr.; Food Sci. Technol. Abstr.; Foods Adlibra; For. Prod. Abstr. (19??-19??); For. Abstr.; Health Plan. Adminis.; Hortic. Abstr.; Index Chem.; Index Med.; Index Vet.; Int. Aerosp. Abstr.; Mass Spect. Bull.; Methods Organ. Synth.; NAPRALERT; Nat. Prod. Updates; Nutr. Abstr. Rev., Ser. B, Live Feeds and Feed.; Nutr. Abstr. Rev., Ser. A, Hum. Exp.; Life Sci. Collect.; PESTDOC; Potato Abstr.; Protozoolog. Abstr.; Ref. Upd. Deluxe Ed.; Res. Alert [Full Cov.]; Rev. Med. Vet. Mycology; Rev. Plant Pathol.; Rice Abstr.; Sci. Cit. Index; SCISEARCH; Soils Fert.; Solid State Supercond. Abstr.; Soyabean Abstr.; Sug. Indus. Abstr.; Vet. Bull.; Vitis Vitic. Enol. Abstr.; Wheat Barley Trit. Abstr.

LC QD262 .C562A **ISSN** 0197-534X
DD 547/.2/05 US
UDC 541.128:547.057
CODEN CAOSDF
CATALYSIS IN ORGANIC SYNTHESES. [Catal. org. synth.]. **Main/Conf** Conference On Catalysis In Organic Syntheses. (19??)-. Academic Scholarly Publication. English. Irregular. Price varies per volume. Academic Press Inc., 6277 Sea Harbor Drive, Orlando FL 32887. **Tel** (800)543-9534, (407)345-4100, FAX (407)352-3445. **ED** William H. Jones. Documents available from CASDDS.
Ind/Abst Chem. Abstr. (1975-1978).

ISSN 0009-2282
US
CODEN CAOCAW
CHEMICAL ABSTRACTS. ORGANIC CHEMISTRY SECTIONS. See Chemistry and Chemicals-Abstracting, Bibliographies and Statistics.

ISSN 0009-255X
US
CHEMICAL HIGHLIGHTS. **Added/Corp** Columbia University. Dept. of Chemistry. Vol. 1 (1969)-. Periodical. English. Six times a year (Jan., Mar., May, July, Sept., Nov.). $135.00. Columbia University / NY, Box 666, Havemeyer Hall, New York NY 10027. **Tel** (212)854-2176. Index available. cum. index. **Circ:** 500.
Desc: Emphasizes fast "visual retrieval" of material from the current chemical literature which is of special interest to those concerned with organic synthesis.

LC QD1 .C744 **ISSN** 0366-7022
DD 540/.8 JA
CCC
NLM W1 CH362 **CODEN** CMLTAG
Pr Rev.
CHEMISTRY LETTERS. [Chem. lett.]. **Added/Corp** Nihon Kagakkai. No. 1 (1972)-. Periodical. English (French, German and Japanese). Twelve times a year. $348.00. Nippon Kagakkai, (Chemical Society of Japan), 1-5 Kanda Surugadai, Chiyodaky Tokyo 101 Japan. **(Subscription address:** Maruzen Company Ltd., PO Box 5050, Import & Export Department, Tokyo 100 31 Japan. **Tel** 011 81 3 32789224.) available on microfilm and microfiche from University Microfilms International (UMI). Documents available from The Genuine Article, CASDDS.
Ind/Abst Anal. Abstr.; Chem Inform; Chem. Abstr.; Chem. Titles; Coal Abstr.; Curr. Biotechnol.; Curr. Chem. React.; Curr. Cit.; Curr. Contents Phys. Chem. Earth Sci.; Dairy Sci. Abstr.; EMBASE; GeoRef; Index Chem.; Leadscan; Mass Spect. Bull.; Methods Organ. Synth.; Nat. Prod. Updates; Ornamental Hort.; Life Sci. Collect.; PESTDOC; Ref. Upd. Deluxe Ed.; Res. Alert [Full Cov.]; Rev. Plant Pathol.; Sci. Cit. Index; SCISEARCH.

US
Pr Rev.
CHEMISTRY OF FUNCTIONAL GROUPS, THE. (1964)-. Monographic series. English. Irregular. Price varies per volume. John Wiley & Sons, Inc., 605 Third Avenue, New York NY 10158-0012. **Tel** (212)850-6000, (212)850-6645, FAX (212)850-6088, telex 12-7063. **(Subscription address:** John Wiley & Sons / UK, Baffins Lane, Chichester, West Sussex PO19 1UD United Kingdom. **Tel** 011 44 1243 779777, FAX 011 44 243 776128, telex 86290 WIBOOKG.) **ED** Saul Patai.

LC QD400 .K513 **ISSN** 0009-3122
DD 547/.59/05 US
CCC
NLM W1 CH364H
CHEMISTRY OF HETEROCYCLIC COMPOUNDS (NEW YORK. 1965). (CHEMISTRY OF HETEROCYCLIC COMPOUNDS.). [Chem. heterocycl. compd.]. **VFOAT** Khimiia Geterotsiklicheskikh Soedinenii. Vol. 1 (Jan./Feb. 1965)-. English (Russian). Twelve times a year. $1425.00. Consultants Bureau, A Division of Plenum Publishing Corporation, 233 Spring Street, New York NY 10013. **Tel** (212)620-8000, (212)620-8466, FAX (212)463-0742, telex 23/421139. **ED** E. Ya Lukevits. available in microform.
Ind/Abst Curr. Cit.; PESTDOC (?-?).

ISSN 0723-6271
GW
CODEN CHPPER
CHEMISTRY OF PEPTIDES AND PROTEINS. (CHEMISTRY OF PEPTIDES AND PROTEINS : PROCEEDINGS OF THE ... USSR-FRG SYMPOSIUM ...). [Chem. pept. proteins]. Vol. 1 (Oct. 2-6, 1980)-. Proceedings. English. Every 2 years. Walter de Gruyter Inc., PO Box 303421, D-10728 Berlin Germany. **Tel** 011 49 30 260050, FAX 011 49 30 26005251, telex 184027. Documents available from CASDDS.
Ind/Abst Chem. Abstr.

LC QD380 .C47 **ISSN** 0899-7829
DD 547.7 US
CCC
CODEN CMMCE8
CEASED
CHEMTRACTS. MACROMOLECULAR CHEMISTRY. See Chemistry and Chemicals-Abstracting, Bibliographies and Statistics.

US
CHEMTRACTS. MACROMOLECULAR CHEMISTRY AND MATERIALS SCIENCE. See Chemistry and Chemicals-Abstracting, Bibliographies and Statistics.

LC QD241 .C48 **ISSN** 0895-4445
DD 547/.005 US
CCC
NLM W1; CH41H **CODEN** CMOCEI
CHEMTRACTS. ORGANIC CHEMISTRY. See Chemistry and Chemicals-Abstracting, Bibliographies and Statistics.

ISSN 0892-256X
DD 547 US
CODEN COECEG
COENZYMES AND COFACTORS. Vol. 1 (1986)-. Academic Scholarly Publication. English. Irregular. Price varies per volume. John Wiley & Sons, Inc., 605 Third Avenue, New York NY 10158-0012. **Tel** (212)850-6000, (212)850-6645, FAX (212)850-6088, telex 12-7063. **(Subscription address:** John Wiley & Sons / UK, Baffins Lane, Chichester, West Sussex PO19 1UD United Kingdom. **Tel** 011 44 1243 779777, FAX 011 44 243 776128, telex 86290 WIBOOKG.) Documents available from CASDDS.
Ind/Abst Chem. Abstr. (1986-).

ISSN 0892-2101
DD 547 UK
CCC
CODEN CACHEP
COMMENTS ON MODERN CHEMISTRY. PART B, COMMENTS ON AGRICULTURAL AND FOOD CHEMISTRY. [Comments mod. chem., B, Comments agric. food chem.]. **VFOAT** Comments on Agricultural and Food Chemistry. Vol. 1, No. 1 (1987)-. Periodical. English. Six times a year (1 volume). $407.00 (academic institutions), $635.00 (corporate institutions). Gordon & Breach Science Publishers, PO Box 90, Reading, Berkshire RG1 8JL United Kingdom. **Tel** 011 44 1734 560080, FAX 011 44 1734 568211. Documents available from CASDDS.
Ind/Abst Chem. Abstr.; Curr. Cit.; Food Sci. Technol. Abstr.; Rev. Plant Pathol.

LC QD262 .C53 **ISSN** 0149-9378
DD 547/.2 US
COMPENDIUM OF ORGANIC SYNTHETIC METHODS. [Compend. org. synth. methods]. (1971)-. Monographic series. English. Irregular. Price varies per volume. John Wiley & Sons, Inc., 605 Third Avenue, New York NY 10158-0012. **Tel** (212)850-6000, (212)850-6645, FAX (212)850-6088, telex 12-7063. **(Subscription address:** John Wiley & Sons / UK, Baffins Lane, Chichester, West Sussex PO19 1UD United Kingdom. **Tel** 011 44 1243 779777, FAX 011 44 243 776128, telex 86290 WIBOOKG.)

LC QD262 .C565 **ISSN** 1350-4894
DD 547.3 UK
CCC
CODEN COGSE6
●**CONTEMPORARY ORGANIC SYNTHESIS.** **Added/Corp** Royal Society of Chemistry (Great Britain). **VFOAT** COS. Vol. 1, No. 1 (Feb. 1994)-. Academic Scholarly Publication. English. Six times a year. $350.00. Royal Society of Chemistry, Thomas Graham House, Science Park, Cambridge CB4 4WF United Kingdom. **Tel** 011 44 1223 420066, FAX 011 44 1223 423623, telex 818293 ROYAL. **(Subscription address:** Royal Society of Chemistry, Turpin Distribution Services Ltd., Blackhorse Road, Letchworth, Hertfordshire SG6 1HN United Kingdom. **Tel** 011 44 1462 672555, FAX 011 44 1462 480947.) **ED** Board. Documents available from BLDSC, CASDDS, SWETS.
Continues *General and Synthetic Methods.*

LC QD380 .C63 **ISSN** 0160-6727
DD 547/.84/08 US
CCC
CODEN CTPSDH
CONTEMPORARY TOPICS IN POLYMER SCIENCE. [Contemp. top. polym. sci.]. Vol. 1 (1977)-. Academic Scholarly Publication. English. Irregular. Price varies per volume. Plenum Press, 233 Spring Street, New York NY 10013-1578. **Tel** (212)620-8000,

(800)221-9369, FAX (212)463-0742, (212)807-1047, telex 23/421139. Documents available from CASDDS.
Ind/Abst Chem. Abstr.; Polymer Contents.

UK
CREATIVITY IN ORGANIC SYNTHESIS. Vol. 1 (1975)-. Monographic series. English. Irregular. Price varies per volume. Academic Press Inc., 6277 Sea Harbor Drive, Orlando FL 32887. **Tel** (800)543-9534, (407)345-4100, FAX (407)352-3445. **ED** Jasjit S. Bindra and Ranjna Bindra.

ISSN 0163-6278
DD 547 US
NLM Z 5524 C9742
CURRENT CHEMICAL REACTIONS. See Chemistry and Chemicals-Abstracting, Bibliographies and Statistics.

ISSN 0951-256X
DD 547.7815 HU
CYCLODEXTRIN NEWS. [Cyclodext. news]. **VFOAT** CD News. (1986)-. Periodical. English. Twelve times a year. $225.00. Cyclolab, PO Box 435, H 1525 Budapest Hungary. **Tel** 011 36 1 1151669, FAX 011 36 1 1352112. **ED** L. Szejtli. Index available. **Bk Rev**. **Ad Acc, Adv Mgr:** G. Szejtli, **Tel** (361)1-115-1669.

LC QD382.B5 D48 **ISSN** 0264-8393
DD 547.7/05 UK
CODEN DBCODT
DEVELOPMENTS IN BLOCK COPOLYMERS. [Dev. block copolym.]. (1982)-. Academic Scholarly Publication. English. Elsevier Science Publishers BV, PO Box 211, 1000 AE Amsterdam Netherlands. **Tel** 011 31 20 4853641, 011 31 20 4853642, FAX 011 31 20 4853598. Documents available from CASDDS.
Ind/Abst Chem. Abstr.

LC QD380 .D478 **ISSN** 0264-7982
DD 547.8/4 UK
CODEN DEIPDF
DEVELOPMENTS IN IONIC POLYMERS. [Dev. ionic polym.]. (1983)-. Academic Scholarly Publication. English. Elsevier Science Publishers BV, PO Box 211, 1000 AE Amsterdam Netherlands. **Tel** 011 31 20 4853641, 011 31 20 4853642, FAX 011 31 20 4853598. Documents available from CASDDS.
Ind/Abst Chem. Abstr. (1983-).

LC QD380 .D49 **ISSN** 0264-3022
DD 547.7 UK
CODEN DOPODF
Pr Rev.
DEVELOPMENTS IN ORIENTED POLYMERS. [Dev. oriented polym.]. Vol. 1 (1982)-. Academic Scholarly Publication. English. Irregular. Price varies per volume. Elsevier Science Publishing Company Inc, Madison Square Station, PO Box 882, New York NY 10159-0882. **Tel** (212)633-3950, FAX (212)633-3990. Documents available from CASDDS.
Ind/Abst Chem. Abstr.

LC QD381.8 .D483 **ISSN** 0260-4310
DD 668.9 UK
UDC 678
DEVELOPMENTS IN POLYMER DEGRADATION. [Dev. polym. degrad.]. (1977)-. Monographic series. English. Price varies per volume. Chapman & Hall, 2-6 Boundary Row, London SE1 8HN United Kingdom. **Tel** 011 44 171 8650066, FAX 011 44 171 5229623, telex 290164 CHAPMA G. Documents available from CASDDS.
Ind/Abst Art Archaeol. Tech. Abstr.; Chem. Abstr.

US
DICTIONARY OF ORGANIC COMPOUNDS. See Chemistry and Chemicals-Abstracting, Bibliographies and Statistics.

ISSN 0096-221X
US
CODEN EOCBAL
EASTMAN ORGANIC CHEMICAL BULLETIN. [Eastman org. chem. bull.]. Bulletin. English. Irregular. Eastman Kodak Company, 343 State Street, Department 412 L, Rochester NY 14650. **Tel** (716)724-4000, (800)242-2424. available on microfilm from University Microfilms International (UMI). Documents available from CASDDS. ***Continues** Synthetic Organic Chemicals.*
Ind/Abst Chem. Abstr.

LC QD281.P6 E8 **ISSN** 0014-3057
DD 547/.84/05 UK
CCC
CODEN EUPJAG
Pr Rev.
EUROPEAN POLYMER JOURNAL. [Eur. polym. j.]. Vol. 1 (Feb. 1965)-. Periodical. English. Twelve times a year. $1514.00. Pergamon Press, An Imprint of Elsevier Science Ltd., The Boulevard, Langford Lane, Kidlington, Oxford OX5 1GB United Kingdom. **Tel** 011 44 1865 843000, 011 44 1865 843699, FAX 011 44 1865 843010. **(Subscription address:** Elsevier Science Ltd. / Oxford Fulfillment Centre, PO Box 800, Kidlington OX5 1DX United Kingdom. **Tel** 011 44 865 843355.**) ED** M. Stacey, J. C. Bevington, and J. V. Dawkins. available on microfilm and microfiche from University Microfilms International (UMI); available on an online database from Elsevier Electronic Subscriptions (EES). Documents available from Article Express International, The Genuine Article, Ask*IEEE, CASDDS.
Desc: Acts as a medium for the exchange of research in the area of macromolecular substances, both synthetic and natural, and publishes results bearing on the physics or chemistry of polymers.
Ind/Abst Art Archaeol. Tech. Abstr.; Chem. Abstr.; Chem. Titles; Curr. Cit.; Curr. Contents Phys. Chem. Earth Sci.; Ei Page One; EMBASE; Eng. Mater. Abstr.; Eng. Index Annu.; INSPEC (1979-); Int. Aerosp. Abstr.; Mass Spect. Bull.; Life Sci. Collect.; Polymer Contents; RAPRA Abstr.; Res. Alert [Full Cov.]; Sci. Cit. Index; SCISEARCH; Text. Technol. Dig.; World Surf. Coat. Abstr.

LC QD262 .R33 **ISSN** 0271-616X
DD 547.2 US
FIESER AND FIESER'S REAGENTS FOR ORGANIC SYNTHESIS. [Fieser Fieser's reag. org. synth.]. **VFOAT** Reagents for Organic Synthesis; Fiesers' Reagents for Organic Synthesis. Vol. 8 (1980)-. Monographic series. English. Irregular. Price varies per volume. John Wiley & Sons, Inc., 605 Third Avenue, New York NY 10158-0012. **Tel** (212)850-6000, (212)850-6645, FAX (212)850-6088, telex 12-7063. **(Subscription address:** John Wiley & Sons / UK, Baffins Lane, Chichester, West Sussex PO19 1UD United Kingdom. **Tel** 011 44 1243 779777, FAX 011 44 243 776128, telex 86290 WIBOOKG.**)** ***Continues** Reagents for Organic Synthesis, 0271-6747.*

LC TP365 **ISSN** 1351-4202
DD 660.29482 UK
●**FOCUS ON SOLVENTS.** [Focus Solvents]. (1993)-. Newsletter. English. Twelve times a year. £165.00. Royal Society of Chemistry, Thomas Graham House, Science Park, Cambridge CB4 4WF United Kingdom. **Tel** 011 44 1223 420066, FAX 011 44 1223 423623, telex 818293 ROYAL. **(Subscription address:** Royal Society of Chemistry, Turpin Distribution Services Ltd., Blackhorse Road, Letchworth, Hertfordshire SG6 1HN United Kingdom. **Tel** 011 44 1462 672555, FAX 011 44 1462 480947.**) ED** Bob Gladding.
Desc: Covers the issues that concern the suppliers and users of solvents.

LC TP453.C65 F69 **ISSN** 0268-005X
DD 664 UK
CCC
NLM W1; FO456F **CODEN** FOHYES
FOOD HYDROCOLLOIDS. [Food hydrocoll.]. Vol. 1, No. 1 (Sept. 1986)-. Academic Scholarly Publication. English. Six times a year. $295.00. Oxford University Press / UK, Walton Street, Oxford OX2 6DP United Kingdom. **Tel** 011 44 1865 56767, FAX 011 44 1865 267773, telex 851/837330 OXPRES G. **(Subscription address:** Oxford University Press / USA, Journals Marketing Department, Oxford University Press, 2001 Evans Road, Cary NC 27513. **Tel** (800)451-7556, (919)677-0977, FAX (919)677-1714.**) ED** G. O. Phillips, P. A. Williams, D. J. Wedlock. available on microfilm and microfiche from University Microfilms International (UMI). Documents available from The Genuine Article, BIOSIS Document Express, CASDDS.
Desc: Analytical techniques for identification and essay of hydrocolloids in food systems; novel procedures for extraction and work-up of hydrocolloids; structural characterization of both existing and new hydrocolloids; use of cell culture and bacterial fermentation technology; physio-chemical properties of solutions including rheological characterization, organoleptic evaluation, etc.
Ind/Abst AGRICOLA [Full Cov.]; Biodeter. Abstr. (1991-); Biol. Abstr. (1986-); Chem. Abstr. (1986-); Crop Physiol. Abstr.; Curr. Aware. Biol. Sci., CABS; Curr. Cit.; Curr. Contents Agric. Biol. Environ. Sci.; Dairy Sci. Abstr.; Ei Page One; Field Crop Abstr.; Food Sci. Technol. Abstr.; Foods Adlibra; Grass. Forage Abstr.; Hortic. Abstr.; Nutr. Abstr. Rev., Ser. A, Hum. Exp.; Potato Abstr.; Res. Alert [Full Cov.]; Rev. Med. Vet. Mycology; Sci. Cit. Index; SCISEARCH; Sug. Indus. Abstr.

LC QD241 .F6 **ISSN** 0071-7886
DD 547/.005 AU
CCC
NLM W1 FO834 **CODEN** FCONAA
FORTSCHRITTE DER CHEMIE ORGANISCHER NATURSTOFFE. (FORTSCHRITTE DER CHEMIE ORGANISCHER NATURSTOFFE. PROGRESS IN THE CHEMISTRY OF ORGANIC NATURAL PRODUCTS.). [Fortschr. Chem. org. Naturst.]. **VFOAT** Progress in the Chemistry of Organic Natural Products. Vol. 1 (1938)-. Academic Scholarly Publication. English (French and German). Irregular. Price varies per volume. Springer-Verlag Vienna, Sachsenplatz 4 6, PO Box 89, A-1201 Vienna Austria. **Tel** 011 43 1 33024150, FAX 011 43 1 330242665. **(Subscription address:** Springer-Verlag New York Inc. / North America, PO Box 2485, Journal Fulfillment, Secaucus NJ 07096. **Tel** (201)348-4033, (800)777-4643, FAX (201)348-4505.**) ED** W. Herz, G.W. Kirby, R.E. Moore, W. Steglich, C. Tamm. cum. index. Documents available from BIOSIS Document Express, CASDDS.
Desc: Contains contributions on the origin, distribution, chemistry, synthesis, biochemistry, function or use of naturally occurring substances.
Ind/Abst AGRICOLA [Select. Cov.]; Biol. Abstr.; Chem Inform; Chem. Abstr.; EMBASE; Index Med.; Life Sci. Collect.; PESTDOC; Vitis Vitic. Enol. Abstr.

LC QD262 .G45 **ISSN** 0141-2140
DD 547/.2/05 UK
UDC 547.057 **CCC**
NLM W1 GE231M **CODEN** GSMEDV
CEASED
GENERAL AND SYNTHETIC METHODS. [Gen. synth. methods]. Vol. 1 (1976)-Vol. 16 (1994). Academic Scholarly Publication. English. Royal Society of Chemistry, Thomas Graham House, Science Park, Cambridge CB4 4WF United Kingdom. **Tel** 011 44 1223 420066, FAX 011 44 1223 423623, telex 818293 ROYAL. **(Subscription address:** Royal Society of Chemistry, Turpin Distribution Services Ltd., Blackhorse Road, Letchworth, Hertfordshire SG6 1HN United Kingdom. **Tel** 011 44 1462 672555, FAX 011 44 1462 480947.**) ED** G Pattenden. Index Available in last issue of each volume--loose separately paged. Documents available from BIOSIS Document Express, CASDDS. ***Supersedes in part** Aliphatic Chemistry, 0305-618X.*
Desc: This series nicely complements other compilations of methodology which consists solely of formulas with little or no discussion of scope or limitations of specific procedures. As such it will prove to be a useful resource to practitioners of organic sythesis.
Ind/Abst Biol. Abstr.; Chem. Abstr.; Curr. Cit.

US
●**GENOME RESEARCH. VFOAT** Polymerase Chain Reaction Methods and Applications. **VAT** Polymerase Chain Reaction Methods and Applications. Vol. 5 (Aug. 1995)-. Academic Scholarly Publication. English. Twelve times a year. $276.00 US; $292.00 others. Cold Spring Harbor Laboratory, 10 Skyline Drive, Plainview NY 11803. **Tel** (516)349-1930, (800)843-4388, FAX (516)349-1946. **Ad Acc**. Documents available from The Genuine Article, CASDDS. ***Absorbed** PCR Methods and Applications, 1054-9803.*
Desc: Publishes research papers detailing improvements in PCR methodology and new application of these techniques, as well as papers describing the application of these methods to a wide variety of research problems.
Ind/Abst Ceram. Abstr.; Chem. Abstr.; Curr. Aware. Biol. Sci., CABS; Genet. Abstr.; Index Med.; Res. Alert [Full Cov.].

LC QP751 .H33 **ISSN** 0163-9102
US
CODEN HLREDI
HANDBOOK OF LIPID RESEARCH. [Handb. lipid res.]. (1978)-. Academic Scholarly Publication. English. Irregular. Price varies per volume. Plenum Press, 233 Spring Street, New York NY 10013-1578. **Tel** (212)620-8000, (800)221-9369, FAX (212)463-0742, (212)807-1047, telex 23/421139. Documents available from CASDDS.
Ind/Abst Chem. Abstr. (1978-1983).

LC QD399 .H62 **ISSN** 1042-7163
DD 547/.59 US
CCC
CODEN HETCE8
HETEROATOM CHEMISTRY. Vol. 1 No. 1 (Jan. 1990)-. Academic Scholarly Publication. English. Six times a year. $475.00. VCH Publishers Inc, 220 East 23rd Street, New York NY 10010. **Tel** (212)683-8333, FAX (212)481-0897. **(Subscription address:** VCH Publishers Inc., 303 Northwest 12th Avenue, Journals Department, Deerfield FL 33442. **Tel** (800)367-8249, (305)428-5566.**)** Documents available from The Genuine Article, CASDDS.
Desc: Brings together a broad, interdisciplinary group of chemists who work with compounds containing main-group elements of groups 13 through 17 of the Periodic Table and certain other related elements. For any chemist who works within these limits.
Ind/Abst Chem. Abstr.; Curr. Cit.; Curr. Contents Phys. Chem. Earth Sci.; Res. Alert [Full Cov.]; SCISEARCH.

LC QD399 .H63 **ISSN** 0385-5414
DD 547/.51/05 JA
CCC
NLM W1 HE995 **CODEN** HTCYAM
Pr Rev.
HETEROCYCLES. [Heterocycles]. **Added/Corp** Sendai Fukusokan Kagaku Kenkyujo. (Oct. 1973)-. Academic Scholarly Publication. English. Fourteen times a year. $2052.00. Elsevier Science Publishers BV, PO Box 211, 1000 AE Amsterdam Netherlands. **Tel** 011 31 20 4853641, 011 31 20 4853642, FAX 011 31 20 4853598. **ED** K. Fukumoto. **Ad Acc.** available on microfilm and microfiche from University Microfilms International (UMI); available on an online database from Elsevier Electronic Subscriptions (EES). Documents available from The Genuine Article, BIOSIS Document Express, CASDDS.
Desc: Provides a platform for rapid exchange of research in the areas of organic, pharmaceutical, analytical, and medicinal chemistry of heterocyclic compounds.
Ind/Abst Biol. Abstr.; Chem Inform; Chem. Abstr.; Chem. Titles; Curr. Biotechnol.; Curr. Chem. React.; Curr. Cit.; Curr. Contents Phys. Chem. Earth Sci.; Index Chem.;

Mass Spect. Bull.; Methods Organ. Synth.; NAPRALERT; Nat. Prod. Updates; Res. Alert [Full Cov.]; Sci. Cit. Index; SCISEARCH; Soc. Sci. Cit. Index [Select. Cov.].

ISSN 1068-6983
DD 547 UK
CCC
CODEN HCREEO

•HETEROGENEOUS CHEMISTRY REVIEWS. [Heterogeneous chem. rev.]. (1994)-. Periodical. English. Four times a year. $325.00. John Wiley & Sons Ltd., Baffins Lane, Chichester, West Sussex PO19 1UD United Kingdom. **Tel** 011 44 1243 779777, FAX 011 44 1243 776128 BTG:JWP001, telex 86290 WIBOOKG. **(Subscription address:** John Wiley & Sons, Inc. / Philadelphia, PO Box 7247, Philadelphia PA 19170. **Tel** (212)850-6645, (800)225-5945.**)** **ED** D. Avnir and M. Asscher (associate editor).
Desc: Aimed at facilitating information flow between diverse scientific fields, which commonly deal with chemistry in multiphase environments. Offers various types of summaries suitable for a variety of information needs.

ISSN 0387-4141
DD 547.75 JA

HISSU AMINOSAN KENKYU. [Hissu aminosan kenkyu]. **VFOAT** Reports of the Research Committee of Essential Amino Acids (Japan). (1958)-. Periodical. Japanese. Four times a year. Hissu Aminosan Kenku linkai, (Research Committee of Essential Amino Acids), Kokuritsu Koshu Eiseiin Eiyo, Seikagakubu 6-1 Shirokanedai, 4 Chome Minatoku, Tokyo 108 Japan. Documents available from CASDDS.
Ind/Abst Chem. Abstr.

LC QD241 **ISSN** 0161-6951
DD 547 US
CODEN ICPNDH
Pr Rev.

ICP INFORMATION NEWSLETTER. [ICP inf. newsl.]. **Added/Corp** University of Massachusetts at Amherst. Dept. of Chemistry. **VAT** Inductively Coupled Plasma Information Newsletter. Vol. 1, No. 1 (June 1975)-. Newsletter. English. Twelve times a year. $65.00. University of Massachusetts / Department of Chemistry, Lederle GRC Towers, PO Box 34510, Amherst MA 01003-4510. **Tel** (413)545-2294, FAX (413)545-4490, (413)545-3757, telex 955491. **ED** Ramon M. Barnes. Index available. **Bk Rev. Ad Acc. Circ:** 700 (ctrl). Documents available from CASDDS.
Desc: Devoted exclusively to the dissemination of news and literature information related to the development and application of plasma sources for spectrochemical analysis.
Ind/Abst Chem. Abstr.; Curr. Cit.; GeoRef; Mass Spect. Bull. (?-?).

ISSN 0376-4699
II
NLM W1 IN206PX **CODEN** IJSBDB

INDIAN JOURNAL OF CHEMISTRY. SECTION B : ORGANIC INCLUDING MEDICINAL. [Indian j. chem., Sect. B]. **Added/Corp** Indian National Science Academy. Council of Scientific & Industrial Research (India). Vol. 14B (Jan. 1976)-. Academic Scholarly Publication. English. Twelve times a year. $400.00. Council of Scientific & Industrial Research, Publications & Information Director, Hillside Road, New Delhi 110012 India. **Tel** FAX 011 91 11 5731353. **(Subscription address:** Prints India, 11 Darya Ganj, New Delhi 110002 India. **Tel** 011 91 11 3268645, FAX 011 91 11 3275542, telex 31-61087 PRIN-IN.) Documents available from The Genuine Article, BIOSIS Document Express, Ask*IEEE, CASDDS. ***Continues in part*** *Indian Journal of Chemistry, 0019-5103.*
Ind/Abst AGRICOLA; Biol. Abstr.; Chem Inform; Chem. Abstr.; Chem. Titles; Curr. Chem. React.; Curr. Cit.; Curr. Contents Phys. Chem. Earth Sci.; Curr. Titles Electrochem.; Hortic. Abstr.; Index Chem.; INSPEC (Jan. 1976-); Mass Spect. Bull.; Methods Organ. Synth.; NAPRALERT; Nat. Prod. Updates; Nutr. Abstr. Rev., Ser. B, Live Feeds and Feed.; Nutr. Abstr. Rev., Ser. A, Hum. Exp.; Life Sci. Collect.; Protozoolog. Abstr.; Res. Alert [Full Cov.]; Sci. Cit. Index; SCISEARCH; Soc. Sci. Cit. Index [Select. Cov.]; World Text. Abstr.

ISSN 0367-8377
DK
CCC
NLM W1 IN771R **CODEN** IJPPC3

INTERNATIONAL JOURNAL OF PEPTIDE AND PROTEIN RESEARCH. [Int. j. pept. protein res.]. Vol. 4, No. 2 (1972)-. Academic Scholarly Publication. English. Twelve times a year. $770.34. Munksgaard International Publishers Ltd, PO Box 2148, DK-1016 Copenhagen K Denmark. **Tel** 011 45 33 127030, FAX 011 45 33 129387, telex 19431 MUNKS DK. **ED** Victor J Hruby. Index available. **Bk Rev. Ad Acc. Circ:** 1,200 (ctrl). Documents available from The Genuine Article, BIOSIS Document Express, CASDDS, ADONIS. ***Continues*** *International Journal of Protein Research, 0020-7551.*
Desc: Proteins, peptide and amino acids.
Ind/Abst ADONIS; AGRICOLA; Anim. Breed. Abstr.; Biol. Abstr.; Chem. Abstr.; Chem. Titles; CSA Neuro. Abstr. (?-?); Curr. Aware. Biol. Sci., CABS; Curr. Chem. React.; Curr. Cit.; Curr. Contents Life Sci.; Dairy Sci. Abstr.; EMBASE; Energy Res. Abstr. (April 1978-); Field Crop Abstr.; Index Chem.; Index Med.; Index Vet.; Int. Aerosp. Abstr.; Life Sci. Collect.; PESTDOC; Protozoolog. Abstr.; Ref. Upd. Deluxe Ed.; Res. Alert [Full Cov.]; Rev. Agric. Entomol.; Rev. Med. Vet. Entomol.; Rev. Med. Vet. Mycology; Sci. Cit. Index; SCISEARCH; Seed Abstr.; Vet. Bull.; Trop. Dis. Bull.

LC QD380 .I56 **ISSN** 0307-174X
DD 547/.84/05 UK

INTERNATIONAL POLYMER SCIENCE AND TECHNOLOGY. **See** Chemistry and Chemicals-Abstracting, Bibliographies and Statistics.

NE
Pr Rev.

ISOTOPES IN ORGANIC CHEMISTRY. Vol. 1 (1975)-. Monographic series. English. Irregular. Price varies per volume. Elsevier Science Publishers BV, PO Box 211, 1000 AE Amsterdam Netherlands. **Tel** 011 31 20 4853641, 011 31 20 4853642, FAX 011 31 20 4853598. **ED** E. Buncel, C.C. Lee. Documents available from CASDDS.
Ind/Abst Chem. Abstr.

LC QD245 .I86 **ISSN** 0137-0251
RU

ITOGI NAUKI I TEKHNIKI. SERIIA ORGANICHESKAIA KHIMIIA. **Added/Corp** Vsesoiuznyi Institut Nauchnoi i Tekhnicheskoi Informatsii (Soviet Union). **VFOAT** Seriia Organicheskaia Khimiia; Organicheskaia Khimiia; Itogi Nauki i Tekhniki. Organicheskaia Khimiia. (1984)-. Monographic series. Russian. Price varies per volume. VINITI - Vsesoyuznyi Institut Nauchno-Tekhnicheskoi Informatsii, All-Union Scientific and Technical Information Institute, Baltiiskaia ulitsa 14, 125219 Moscow Russia. **Tel** 011 7 95 2384600, FAX 011 7 95 9430060, telex 411160. Documents available from CASDDS. ***Continues*** *Itogi Nauki i Tekhniki. Organicheskaia Khimiia.*
Ind/Abst Chem. Abstr.

LC TP1 .I86 **ISSN** 0202-8042
DD 547/.005 RU

ITOGI NAUKI I TEKHNIKI. SERIIA TEKHNOLOGIIA ORGANICHESKIKH VESHCHESTV. **Added/Corp** Vsesoiuznyi Institut Nauchnoi i Tekhnicheskoi Informatsii (Soviet Union). **VFOAT** Seriia Tekhnologiia Organicheskikh Veshchestv; Itogi Nauki i Tekhniki. Tekhnologiia Organicheskikh Veshchestv. (1981)-. Monographic series. Russian. Price varies per volume. VINITI - Vsesoyuznyi Institut Nauchno-Tekhnicheskoi Informatsii, All-Union Scientific and Technical Information Institute, Baltiiskaia ulitsa 14, 125219 Moscow Russia. **Tel** 011 7 95 2384600, FAX 011 7 95 9430060, telex 411160. Documents available from CASDDS. ***Continues*** *Itogi Nauki I Tekhniki. Tekhnologiia Organicheskikh Veshchestv.*
Ind/Abst Chem. Abstr.

ISSN 0271-9460
US
CCC
CODEN JPSSDD

JOURNAL OF APPLIED POLYMER SCIENCE. APPLIED POLYMER SYMPOSIUM. [J. appl. polym. sci., Appl. polym. symp.]. (1977)-. Academic Scholarly Publication. English. One time a week. $5,772.00 US; $6,292.00 Canada and Mexico; $6,487.00 other. John Wiley & Sons, Inc., 605 Third Avenue, New York NY 10158-0012. **Tel** (212)850-6000, (212)850-6645, FAX (212)850-6088, telex 12-7063. **(Subscription address:** John Wiley & Sons / UK, Baffins Lane, Chichester, West Sussex PO19 1UD United Kingdom. **Tel** 011 44 1243 779777, FAX 011 44 243 776128, telex 86290 WIBOOKG.) available in microform. Documents available from Article Express International, CASDDS. ***Continues*** *Applied Polymer Symposia, 0570-4898.*
Ind/Abst Abstr. Bull. Inst. Pap. Sci. Tech.; Chem. Abstr.; Chem. Titles; Ei Page One; Eng. Index Annu.; Text. Technol. Dig.; World Surf. Coat. Abstr.; World Text. Abstr.

LC QD320 .J65 **ISSN** 0732-8303
DD 547.7/8/05 US
CCC
NLM W1 JO574G **CODEN** JCACDM
Pr Rev.

JOURNAL OF CARBOHYDRATE CHEMISTRY. [J. carbohydr. chem.]. Vol. 1, No. 1 (1982)-. Academic Scholarly Publication. English (French and German). Nine times a year. $795.00. Marcel Dekker Inc., 270 Madison Avenue, New York NY 10016. **Tel** (212)696-9000, (800)228-1160, FAX (212)685-4540, telex 421419. **(Subscription address:** Marcel Dekker Inc., PO Box 5017, Monticello NY 12701. **Tel** (800)228-1160.**)** **ED** Donald E. Kiely. **Bk Rev. Ad Acc.** ctrl circ. Documents available from The Genuine Article, BIOSIS Document Express, CASDDS. ***Continues in part*** *Journal of Carbohydrates, Nucleosides, Nucleotides, 0094-0585.*
Desc: Serves as a convenient, international forum for novel synthetic methods for carbohydrates; mechanistic carbohydrate chemistry; uses of carbohydrates in national products, drugs, carbohydrate antibiotics, saccharides, and oligosaccharide syntheses; saccharide interconversions; carbohydrates as synthetic reagents; separation methods as applied to carbohydrate reactions and synthesis; and spectroscopic and crystallographic structure studies of carbohydrates.
Ind/Abst Abstr. Bull. Inst. Pap. Sci. Tech.; AGRICOLA [Select. Cov.]; Biol. Abstr.; Chem Inform; Chem. Abstr.; Chem. Titles; Curr. Aware. Biol. Sci., CABS; Curr. Chem. React.; Curr. Cit.; Curr. Contents Life Sci.; EMBASE; Index Chem.; Mass Spect. Bull.; Nat. Prod. Updates; Ref. Upd. Deluxe Ed.; Res. Alert [Full Cov.]; Sci. Cit. Index; SCISEARCH; Sug. Indus. Abstr.

LC QD271 .J652 **ISSN** 0378-4347
DD 574.19 NE
CCC
NLM W1; JO5845P
Pr Rev.

•JOURNAL OF CHROMATOGRAPHY. B, BIOMEDICAL APPLICATIONS. **VFOAT** Biomedical Applications; Chromatography B. Vol. 652, No. 1 (Jan. 14, 1994)-. Academic Scholarly Publication. English. Twenty-six times a year. $2830.00. Elsevier Science Publishers BV, PO Box 211, 1000 AE Amsterdam Netherlands. **Tel** 011 31 20 4853641, 011 31 20 4853642, FAX 011 31 20 4853598. **ED** K. Macek, I.W. Wainer. available on an online database from Elsevier Electronic Subscriptions (EES). ***Continues in part*** *Journal of Chromatography, 0021-9673.*
Desc: Publishes papers on all aspects of chromatography, electrophoresis and related methods in the biomedical disciplines.
Ind/Abst Curr. Cit.; Index Med.; Key Abstr., Adv. Mater.; Sci. Cit. Index.

LC QD921 .J59 **ISSN** 1040-7278
DD 547/.05 US
CCC
CODEN JCSCEB

JOURNAL OF CLUSTER SCIENCE. [J. clust. sci.]. Vol. 1, No. 1 (Mar. 1990)-. Academic Scholarly Publication. English. Four times a year. $245.00. Plenum Press, 233 Spring Street, New York NY 10013-1578. **Tel** (212)620-8000, (800)221-9369, FAX (212)463-0742, (212)807-1047, telex 23/421139. **ED** David H. Russell and Boon K. Teo. available on microfilm and microfiche from University Microfilms International (UMI). Documents available from Ask*IEEE, CASDDS.
Desc: An interdisciplinary exploration of the chemical and physical properties, bonding and structure, mathematics, and molecular biology of clusters.
Ind/Abst Chem. Abstr. (1990-); INSPEC (Mar. 1990-).

LC QD400 .J6 **ISSN** 0022-152X
US
CCC
NLM W1 JO67P **CODEN** JHTCAD
Pr Rev.

JOURNAL OF HETEROCYCLIC CHEMISTRY. [J. heterocycl. chem.]. Vol. 1 (Feb. 1964)-. Academic Scholarly Publication. English (French and German). Six times a year (Jan., Mar., May, July, Sept., Nov.). $460.00. Hetero Corporation, PO Box 41743, St. Petersburg FL 33743-1743. **Tel** (813)974-3161. **(Subscription address:** HeteroCorporation, PO Box 20285, Tampa FL 33622-0285. **)** **ED** Raymond N. Castle. cum. index. **Bk Rev. Circ:** 1,600. Documents available from The Genuine Article, BIOSIS Document Express, CASDDS. ***Absorbed*** *Lectures in Heterocyclic Chemistry, 0090-2268.*
Desc: Original international research in heterocyclic chemistry for anti-cancer and other drugs, with methodology, new ring systems, etc.
Ind/Abst AGRICOLA; Biol. Abstr.; Chem Inform; Chem. Abstr.; Chem. Titles; Coal Abstr.; Curr. Chem. React.; Curr. Cit.; Curr. Contents Phys. Chem. Earth Sci.; EMBASE [Select. Cov.]; Index Chem.; Int. Aerosp. Abstr.; Methods Organ. Synth.; NAPRALERT; Nat. Prod. Updates; Nucl. Sci. Abstr.; Life Sci. Collect.; PESTDOC; Res. Alert [Full Cov.]; Sci. Cit. Index; SCISEARCH.

LC QD196 .J68 **ISSN** 1053-0495
DD 547.7 US
CCC
CODEN JIOPE4
Pr Rev.

JOURNAL OF INORGANIC AND ORGANOMETALLIC POLYMERS. [J. inorg. organomet. polym.]. Vol. 1, No. 1 (Mar. 1991)-. Periodical. English. Four times a year. $195.00 (institutions), $45.00 (individuals) US; $230.00 (institutions), $53.00 (individuals) other. Plenum Press, 233 Spring Street, New York NY 10013-1578. **Tel** (212)620-8000, (800)221-9369, FAX (212)463-0742, (212)807-1047, telex 23/421139. **ED** Martel Zeldin. **Bk Rev.** Documents available from The Genuine Article.
Desc: Publishes peer-reviewed papers and short communications on synthesis characterization, evaluation, and phenomena in inorganic and organometallic polymers.
Ind/Abst Alum. Ind. Abstr.; Curr. Cit.; Eng. Mater. Abstr.; Met. Abstr.; Res. Alert [Full Cov.].

ISSN 0921-8319
NE
NLM W1; JO745K **CODEN** JLMEEG
Pr Rev. **TITLE CHANGE**
JOURNAL OF LIPID MEDIATORS. [J. lipid mediat.]. **VFOAT** JLM. Vol. 1 No. 1 (Jan. 1989)-(199?). Academic Scholarly Publication. English. Elsevier Science Publishers BV, PO Box 211, 1000 AE Amsterdam Netherlands. **Tel** 011 31 20 4853641, 011 31 20 4853642, FAX 011 31 20 4853598. available on microfilm and microfiche from University Microfilms International (UMI). Documents available from The Genuine Article, BIOSIS Document Express, CASDDS, ADONIS. ***Continued by*** *Journal of Lipid Mediators and Cell Signalling.*
Ind/Abst ADONIS; Biol. Abstr.; Chem. Abstr.; Curr. Aware. Biol. Sci., CABS; Curr. Contents Life Sci.; EMBASE; PESTDOC; Ref. Upd. Deluxe Ed.; Res. Alert [Full Cov.]; Sci. Cit. Index; SCISEARCH.

ISSN 0929-7855
NE
CCC
NLM W1; JO745KM
Pr Rev.
●**JOURNAL OF LIPID MEDIATORS AND CELL SIGNALLING.** Vol. 9, No. 1 (Feb. 1994)-. Academic Scholarly Publication. English. Six times a year. $694.00. Elsevier Science Publishers BV, PO Box 211, 1000 AE Amsterdam Netherlands. **Tel** 011 31 20 4853641, 011 31 20 4853642, FAX 011 31 20 4853598. **ED** B.B. Vargaftig. available on an online database from Elsevier Electronic Subscriptions (EES). ***Continues*** *Journal of Lipid Mediators, 0921-8319.*
Desc: Publishes articles on the chemistry, biophysics, biochemistry, pharmacology, toxicology, pathology, immunology and clinical aspects of lipid mediators in general.
Ind/Abst Curr. Cit.; Index Med.

LC QD380 .J67 **ISSN** 1060-1325
DD 547.7/05 US
CCC
CODEN JSPCE6
JOURNAL OF MACROMOLECULAR SCIENCE. PURE AND APPLIED CHEMISTRY. [J. macromol. sci., Pure appl. chem.]. **VFOAT** Pure and Applied Chemistry; J.M.S. Pure Appl. Chem.; J.M.S. Pure and Applies Chemistry. Vol. A29, No. 1 (Jan. 1992)-. Academic Scholarly Publication. English. Twelve times a year. $2395.00. Marcel Dekker Inc., 270 Madison Avenue, New York NY 10016. **Tel** (212)696-9000, (800)228-1160, FAX (212)685-4540, telex 421419. **(Subscription address:** Marcel Dekker Inc., PO Box 5017, Monticello NY 12701. **Tel** (800)228-1160.**)** Documents available from Article Express International, BIOSIS Document Express, CASDDS. ***Continues*** *Journal of Macromolecular Science. Chemistry, 0022-233X.*
Desc: Information on polymerization and polymers.
Ind/Abst Art Archaeol. Tech. Abstr. (1992-); Bioeng. Abstr. (1992-); Biol. Abstr. (1992-); Chem. Abstr. (1992-); Curr. Contents Phys. Chem. Earth Sci.; Ei Page One (1992-); Eng. Index Annu.; Int. Aerosp. Abstr. (1992-); Life Sci. Collect. (1992-); Sci. Cit. Index; World Surf. Coat. Abstr. (1992-).

LC QD380 .J69 **ISSN** 0022-2356
DD 547/.84/05 US
CCC
CODEN JMRMBZ
JOURNAL OF MACROMOLECULAR SCIENCE. REVIEWS IN MACROMOLECULAR CHEMISTRY. (JOURNAL OF MACROMOLECULAR SCIENCE. [PART C]: REVIEWS IN MACROMOLECULAR CHEMISTRY.). [J. macromol. sci. Rev. macromol. chem.]. Vol. 1, (1966)-. Periodical. English. Two times a year. $575.00. Marcel Dekker Inc., 270 Madison Avenue, New York NY 10016. **Tel** (212)696-9000, (800)228-1160, FAX (212)685-4540, telex 421419. **(Subscription address:** Marcel Dekker Inc., PO Box 5017, Monticello NY 12701. **Tel** (800)228-1160.**)** **ED** George B. Butler, Kenneth F. O'Driscoll and Garth L. Wilkes. **Bk Rev**. **Ad Acc.** ctrl circ. Documents available from CASDDS.
Desc: Exemplary source of specialized reviews in high polymer chemistry and physics.
Ind/Abst Chem. Abstr.; Chem. Titles.

LC QD380 .J69 **ISSN** 0736-6574
DD 547.7/05 US
CCC
NLM W1; JO748DE **CODEN** JMSPDH
JOURNAL OF MACROMOLECULAR SCIENCE. REVIEWS IN MACROMOLECULAR CHEMISTRY AND PHYSICS. [J. macromol. sci., Rev. macromol. chem. phys.]. **VFOAT** Reviews in Macromolecular Chemistry and Physics. Vol. C22, No. 1 (1983)-. Academic Scholarly Publication. English. Four times a year. $695.00. Marcel Dekker Inc., 270 Madison Avenue, New York NY 10016. **Tel** (212)696-9000, (800)228-1160, FAX (212)685-4540, telex 421419. **(Subscription address:** Marcel Dekker Inc., PO Box 5017, Monticello NY 12701. **Tel** (800)228-1160.**)** **ED** George B. Butler, Kenneth F. O'Driscoll, and Garth L. Wilkes. available on microfiche. Documents available from Article Express International, The Genuine Article, BIOSIS Document Express, Ask*IEEE, CASDDS. ***Continues*** *Journal of Macromolecular Science. Reviews in Macromolecular Chemistry, 0022-2356.*
Desc: Reviews of timely topics in high polymer chemistry and physics that offer readers a large amount of scientific and technical information presented in a concise, concentrated, and organized manner. These reviews permit scientists to concentrate on special areas of interest while becoming informed in the broad areas of macromolecular science and technology.
Ind/Abst Biol. Abstr. (1985-); Chem. Abstr.; Curr. Chem. React.; Curr. Cit.; Curr. Contents Phys. Chem. Earth Sci.; Ei Page One; Eng. Index Annu.; Index Sci. Rev. [Full Cov.]; INSPEC (1988-); Life Sci. Collect. (1988-); Polymer Contents (1988-); Res. Alert [Full Cov.]; Sci. Cit. Index; SCISEARCH.

ISSN 1076-5174
UK
CCC
NLM W1; JO748P
●**JOURNAL OF MASS SPECTROMETRY. PART A.** **See** Chemistry and Chemicals-Analytical Chemistry.

LC QH1 .L94 **ISSN** 0163-3864
DD 547.7/05 US
NLM W1 JO777T **CODEN** JNPRDF
Pr Rev.
JOURNAL OF NATURAL PRODUCTS. [J. nat. prod.]. **Added/Corp** American Society of Pharmacognosy. Lloyd Library and Museum. Vol. 42 (Jan./Feb. 1979)-. Academic Scholarly Publication. English (French). Twelve times a year. $290.00. American Society of Pharmacognosy, College of Pharmacy, 555 31st Street, Downers Grove IL 60515. **Tel** (708)971-6417, FAX (708)971-6097. **ED** James E. Robbers. Index available (bound in Dec. issue). **Bk Rev**. **Circ:** 1,800. Documents available from The Genuine Article, BIOSIS Document Express, CASDDS. ***Continues*** *Lloydia, 0024-5461.*
Desc: All aspects of natural product research; chemistry and/or biochemistry of naturally occurring compounds or the biology of living systems from which they are obtained.
Ind/Abst AgBiotech News Inf.; AGRICOLA [Full Cov.]; Agrofor. Abstr. (19??-19??); Anal. Abstr.; Biocont. News Inf. (1991-); Biol. Agric. Index; Biol. Abstr.; Chem Inform; Chem. Abstr.; Chem. Titles; Crop Physiol. Abstr.; Curr. Aware. Biol. Sci., CABS; Curr. Biotechnol.; Curr. Chem. React.; Curr. Cit.; Curr. Contents Agric. Biol. Environ. Sci.; Curr. Contents Life Sci.; Dairy Sci. Abstr.; EMBASE; Field Crop Abstr.; For. Prod. Abstr. (19??-19??); For. Abstr.; Grass. Forage Abstr.; Helminthol. Abstr. (19??-19??); Hortic. Abstr.; Index Chem.; Index Med.; Index Vet.; Int. Pharm. Abstr.; Mass Spect. Bull.; NAPRALERT; Nat. Prod. Updates; Nematol. Abstr.; Nutr. Abstr. Rev., Ser. B, Live Feeds and Feed.; Nutr. Abstr. Rev., Ser. A, Hum. Exp.; Ornamental Hort. (1991-); Life Sci. Collect.; PESTDOC; Plant Breed. Abstr.; Plant Grow. Reg. Abstr.; Protozoolog. Abstr.; Ref. Upd. Deluxe Ed.; Res. Alert [Full Cov.]; Rev. Agric. Entomol.; Rev. Med. Vet. Entomol.; Rev. Med. Vet. Mycology; Rev. Plant Pathol.; Sci. Cit. Index; SCISEARCH; Seed Abstr.; Vet. Bull.; Weed Abstr.

LC QD241 .J6 **ISSN** 0022-3263
DD 547.05 US
CCC
NLM W1 JO804H **CODEN** JOCEAH
Pr Rev.
JOURNAL OF ORGANIC CHEMISTRY. [J. org. chem.]. **Added/Corp** American Chemical Society. Vol. 1 (Mar. 1936)-. Academic Scholarly Publication. English. Twenty-six times a year. $1058.00. American Chemical Society, 1155 Sixteenth Street Northwest, Washington DC 20036. **Tel** (800)333-9511, (800)227-5558, (614)447-3776, FAX (202)447-3671. **(Subscription address:** American Chemical Society / Ohio, Department L 0011, Columbus OH 43268-0011. **)** **ED** Clayton H. Heathcock. Index available (free). **Ad Acc. Acid Free. Circ:** 10,199. available on microfilm and microfiche from University Microfilms International (UMI). Documents available from The Genuine Article, BIOSIS Document Express, UMI Article Clearinghouse, CASDDS.
Desc: Critical accounts of work in a given field, reviews of existing data and new viewpoints, including organic reactions, natural products, mechanism studies, bioorganic chemistry, theoretical organic chemistry and spectroscopy.
Ind/Abst Abstr. Bull. Inst. Pap. Sci. Tech.; Acad. Ind. [Computer File] (1992-); Acad. Search; AGRICOLA; Agrofor. Abstr.; Biol. Abstr.; Chem Inform; Chem. Abstr.; Chem. Titles; Chemorecept. Abstr.; Coal Abstr.; Curr. Biotechnol.; Curr. Chem. React.; Curr. Cit.; Curr. Contents Life Sci.; Curr. Contents Phys. Chem. Earth Sci.; Curr. Titles Electrochem.; EMBASE [Select. Cov.]; Energy Res. Abstr.; EP Collect.; Expand. Acad. Index (1992-); Food Sci. Technol. Abstr.; For. Prod. Abstr. (1991-); Gen. Sci. Index; Gen. Sci. Source; Helminthol. Abstr. (1991-); Homework Help.; Index Chem.; INFO-SOUTH Abstr.; Int. Aerosp. Abstr.; MasterFile FullTEXT 1000; MasterFile FullTEXT 350; MasterFile FullTEXT 650; MasterFile FullTEXT (July 1993-); Methods Organ. Synth.; NAPRALERT; Nat. Prod. Updates; Newsp. Period. Abstr. (1992-); OCLC; Life Sci. Collect.; PESTDOC; Postharvest News Inf.; Ref. Upd. Deluxe Ed.; Res. Alert [Full Cov.]; Rev. Agric. Entomol.; Rev. Med. Vet. Mycology; Rev. Plant Pathol.; Rice Abstr.; Sci. Cit. Index; SCISEARCH; Soyabean Abstr.; Sug. Indus. Abstr.; Telebase.

LC QD241 **ISSN** 0022-3271
DD 547/.005 US
UDC 547 **CCC**
NLM W1 JO804L **CODEN** JOCYA9
TITLE CHANGE
JOURNAL OF ORGANIC CHEMISTRY OF THE USSR. **VAT** Journal of Organic Chemistry of the Union of Soviet Socialist Republics. Vol. 1 (Jan. 1965)-(199?). Periodical. English. Plenum Press, 233 Spring Street, New York NY 10013-1578. **Tel** (212)620-8000, (800)221-9369, FAX (212)463-0742, (212)807-1047, telex 23/421139. **ED** N S Zefirov. Index available. available on microfilm and microfiche from University Microfilms International (UMI). Documents available from CASDDS. ***Continued by*** *Russian Journal of Organic Chemistry.*
Desc: Featuring continuing reports on research from outstanding Soviet lands and institutes. This journal covers advanced work in organic chemistry.
Ind/Abst Chem. Abstr.; Curr. Cit.; Mass Spect. Bull.; Methods Organ. Synth.; NAPRALERT; Nat. Prod. Updates.

ISSN 1070-4280
US
CCC
●**JOURNAL OF ORGANIC CHEMISTRY OF THE USSR.** (RUSSIAN JOURNAL OF ORGANIC CHEMISTRY.). **Added/Corp** Consultants Bureau. (1993)-. Academic Scholarly Publication. English (translations available in Russian). Twenty-four times a year. $1625.00. Consultants Bureau, A Division of Plenum Publishing Corporation, 233 Spring Street, New York NY 10013. **Tel** (212)620-8000, (212)620-8466, FAX (212)463-0742, telex 23/421139. Documents available from CASDDS. ***Continues*** *Zhurnal Organicheskoi Khimii. English. Journal of Organic Chemistry of the USSR, 0022-3271.*
Ind/Abst Chem. Abstr.; Curr. Cit.

LC QD411 .J65 **ISSN** 0022-328X
DD 547 SZ
CCC
NLM W1 JO804M **CODEN** JORCAI
Pr Rev.
JOURNAL OF ORGANOMETALLIC CHEMISTRY. [J. organomet. chem.]. Vol. 1 (Oct. 1963)-. Periodical. English (French and German). Forty-two times a year. $5968.00. Elsevier Sequoia SA, PO Box 564, CH-1001 Lausanne 1 Switzerland. **Tel** 011 41 21 3207381, FAX 011 41 21 3235444. **(Subscription address:** Elsevier Science Ltd., PO Box 7247, Philadelphia PA 19170. **)** **ED** C Eaborn, WA Herman, RB King, A Nakamura, OA Reutov. **Ad Acc.** available on microfilm and microfiche from University Microfilms International (UMI); available on an online database from Elsevier Electronic Subscriptions (EES); and STN International. Documents available from The Genuine Article, CASDDS. ***Absorbed*** *Organometallic Chemistry Reviews, Section A: Subject Reviews* ***and*** *Organometallic Chemistry Reviews, Section B, Annual Surveys.*
Desc: Publishes full papers, preliminary communications, subject reviews and annual surveys on theoretical aspects, structural chemistry, synthesis and physical and chemical properties including reaction mechanisms and practical applications of organoelement compounds in a sense corresponding essentially to Section 29 of Chemical Abstracts (Organometallic and Organometalloidal Compounds).
Ind/Abst AGRICOLA; Chem Inform; Chem. Abstr.; Chem. Titles; Curr. Chem. React.; Curr. Cit.; Curr. Contents Phys. Chem. Earth Sci.; Index Chem.; Int. Aerosp. Abstr.; Mass Spect. Bull.; Methods Organ. Synth.; Res. Alert [Full Cov.]; Sci. Cit. Index; SCISEARCH.

ISSN 0378-5203
NE
CCC
NLM W1 JO804MB **CODEN** JOCLD7
Pr Rev.
JOURNAL OF ORGANOMETALLIC CHEMISTRY LIBRARY. [J. organomet. chem. libr.]. (1976)-. Academic Scholarly Publication. English. Irregular. Price varies per volume. Elsevier Science Publishers BV, PO Box 211, 1000 AE Amsterdam Netherlands. **Tel** 011 31 20 4853641, 011 31 20 4853642, FAX 011 31 20 4853598. Documents available from CASDDS.
Desc: Provides information on organometallic compounds and organic chemistry.
Ind/Abst Chem Inform; Chem. Abstr.

LC QP901 **ISSN** 1075-2617
DD 612.015 UK
NLM W1; JO828HK
●**JOURNAL OF PEPTIDE SCIENCE.** (1994)-. Academic Scholarly Publication. English. Six times a year. $295.00. John Wiley & Sons Ltd., Baffins Lane, Chichester, West Sussex PO19 1UD United Kingdom. **Tel** 011 44 1243 779777, FAX 011 44 1243 776128 BTG:JWP001, telex 86290 WIBOOKG. **(Subscription address:** John Wiley & Sons, Inc. / Philadelphia, PO Box 7247, Philadelphia PA 19170. **Tel** (212)850-6645,

(800)225-5945.) **ED** Conrad H. Schneider. **Ad Acc, Adv Mgr:** Michael J. Levermore.
Desc: Official publication of the European Peptide Society.

LC QD476 .J64 **ISSN** 0894-3230
DD 547.1/3 UK
CCC
CODEN JPOCEE
Pr Rev.

JOURNAL OF PHYSICAL ORGANIC CHEMISTRY.
[J. phys. org. chem.]. **VFOAT** Physical Organic Chemistry. Vol. 1 (1988)-. Academic Scholarly Publication. English. Twelve times a year. $745.00. John Wiley & Sons Ltd., Baffins Lane, Chichester, West Sussex PO19 1UD United Kingdom. **Tel** 011 44 1243 779777, FAX 011 44 1243 776128 BTG:JWP001, telex 86290 WIBOOKG. **(Subscription address:** John Wiley & Sons, Inc. / Philadelphia, PO Box 7247, Philadelphia PA 19170. **Tel** (212)850-6645, (800)225-5945.) **ED** J. B. Lambert, F. D. Lewis, W. Ando, P. Laszlo and H. J. Schneider. available on microfilm and microfiche from University Microfilms International (UMI). Documents available from The Genuine Article, Ask*IEEE, CASDDS.
Desc: Provides an international forum for the rapid publication of original scientific papers dealing with physical organic chemistry in its broadest sense. Devotes attention to the following fields: organic chemistry; bio-organic chemistry; organometallic chemistry; theoretical chemistry; catalytic chemistry; photochemistry; and supramolecular chemistry.
Ind/Abst Chem. Abstr.; Curr. Aware. Biol. Sci., CABS; Curr. Cit.; Curr. Contents Phys. Chem. Earth Sci.; INSPEC (March/April 1988-); Mass Spect. Bull. (?-?); Res. Alert [Full Cov.]; Sci. Cit. Index; SCISEARCH.

LC QD471 .J6425 **ISSN** 0887-624X
DD 547.7 US
CCC
NLM W1; JO837NAL **CODEN** JPACEC
Pr Rev.

JOURNAL OF POLYMER SCIENCE. PART A, POLYMER CHEMISTRY.
[J. polym. sci., A, Polym. chem.]. **VFOAT** Polymer Chemistry. Vol. 24, No. 2 (Feb. 1986)-. Academic Scholarly Publication. English. Seventeen times a year. $2,540 (includes part B) US; $2,800 (includes part B) Canada and Mexico; $2,897.50 (includes part B) other. John Wiley & Sons, Inc., 605 Third Avenue, New York NY 10158-0012. **Tel** (212)850-6000, (212)850-6645, FAX (212)850-6088, telex 12-7063. **(Subscription address:** John Wiley & Sons / UK, Baffins Lane, Chichester, West Sussex PO19 1UD United Kingdom. **Tel** 011 44 1243 779777, FAX 011 44 243 776128, telex 86290 WIBOOKG.) **ED** Charles G. Overberger, Eli M. Pearce, David A. Tirrell, Eric J. Amis. available on microfilm and microfiche from University Microfilms International (UMI). Documents available from Article Express International, The Genuine Article, Ask*IEEE, CASDDS. ***Continues*** *Journal of Polymer Science. Polymer Chemistry Edition, 0360-6376;* ***Absorbed in part*** *Journal of Polymer Science. Part C. Polymer Letters, 0887-6258.*
Desc: Covers results of fundamental research in all areas of high polymer chemistry and physics.
Ind/Abst Anal. Abstr.; Appl. Mech. Rev.; Art Archaeol. Tech. Abstr.; Chem. Abstr. (1986-); Chem. Titles; Curr. Cit.; Curr. Contents Phys. Chem. Earth Sci.; Ei Page One; Eng. Index Annu.; HTFS Dig.; INSPEC (May 1986-); Mass Spect. Bull. (?-?); RAPRA Abstr.; Res. Alert [Full Cov.]; Sci. Cit. Index; SCISEARCH.

LC QD471 .J6426 **ISSN** 0887-6266
DD 547.7 US
CCC
NLM W1; J0837PJ **CODEN** JPBPEM
Pr Rev.

JOURNAL OF POLYMER SCIENCE. PART B, POLYMER PHYSICS.
[J. polym. sci., B, Polym. phys.]. **VFOAT** Polymer Physics. Vol. 24, No. 2 (Feb. 1986)-. Academic Scholarly Publication. English. Thirteen times a year. $1,950 (includes Part A) US; $2,275 (includes Part A) other. John Wiley & Sons, Inc., 605 Third Avenue, New York NY 10158-0012. **Tel** (212)850-6000, (212)850-6645, FAX (212)850-6088, telex 12-7063. **(Subscription address:** John Wiley & Sons / UK, Baffins Lane, Chichester, West Sussex PO19 1UD United Kingdom. **Tel** 011 44 1243 779777, FAX 011 44 243 776128, telex 86290 WIBOOKG.) **ED** Edward F Casassa and Guy C Berry. available on microfilm and microfiche from University Microfilms International (UMI). Documents available from Article Express International, The Genuine Article, Ask*IEEE, CASDDS. ***Continues*** *Journal of Polymer Science. Polymer Physics Edition, 0098-1273;* ***Absorbed*** *Journal of Polymer Science. Part C, Polymer Letters, 0887-6258.*
Desc: Covers results of fundamental research in all areas of high polymer chemistry and physics.
Ind/Abst Appl. Mech. Rev.; Art Archaeol. Tech. Abstr.; Chem. Abstr. (1986-); Chem. Titles; Civ. Struct. Eng. Abstr.; Curr. Cit.; Curr. Contents Phys. Chem. Earth Sci.; Ei Page One; Elect. Comm. Abstr.; Eng. Index Annu.; INSPEC (May 1986-); Mater. Sci. Eng. Abstr.; Mech. Eng. Abstr.; RAPRA Abstr.; Res. Alert [Full Cov.]; Sci. Cit. Index; SCISEARCH; Solid State Supercond. Abstr.

ISSN 0260-8847
UK
UDC 547.057

JOURNAL OF SYNTHETIC METHODS.
[J. synth. methods]. Vol. 4 (1978)-. Periodical. English. Twelve times a year. Derwent Publications Ltd., Derwent House 14, Great Queen Street, London WC2B 5DF United Kingdom. **Tel** 011 44 171 3442800, FAX 011 44 171 3442899. cum. index. ***Continues*** *Abstracts Journal - Chemical Reactions Documentation Service.*
Desc: A fully indexed publication which provides the organic chemist with detailed abstracts for each month's new chemical reactions and forms part of the Chemical Reactions Documentation Service.

LC QD1 .A3585 QD380
KZ

KHIMIIA I FIZICHESKAIA KHIMIIA POLIMEROV.
(19??)-. Periodical. Russian. 4.40rub single issue. Izdatelstvo Kazahhstana / Kazakhstan Publishing House, Prospeky Abaya 143, 480124 Alma-Ata Kazakhstan. **Tel** 3272 42 29 29.

ISSN 0023-1150
UZ
NLM W1 KH47 **CODEN** KPSUAR
Pr Rev.

KHIMIIA PRIRODNYKH SOEDINENII.
[Khim. prir. soedin.]. **Added/Corp** Uzbekiston SSR Fanlar Akademiiasi. (1965)-. Academic Scholarly Publication. Russian. Six times a year. $84.00. **(Subscription address:** Victor Kamkin, 4956 Boiling Brook Parkway, Rockville MD 20852. **Tel** (301)881-5973.) Documents available from The Genuine Article, BIOSIS Document Express, CASDDS.
Ind/Abst Abstr. Bull. Inst. Pap. Sci. Tech.; AGRICOLA; Biol. Abstr.; Chem. Abstr.; Curr. Biotechnol.; Curr. Chem. React.; Index Chem.; NAPRALERT; Life Sci. Collect.; Res. Alert [Full Cov.]; Sci. Cit. Index; SCISEARCH.

ISSN 0454-1138
JA
NLM W1 KO282H **CODEN** KOBUA3

KOBUNSHI.
[Kobunshi]. (1952)-. Academic Scholarly Publication. English. Twelve times a year. $302.67. The Society of Polymer Science, Nagaoka Building 2 4 2, Chuo Ku Tokyo 104 Japan. **Tel** 011 81 3 35433765. Documents available from CASDDS.
Ind/Abst Chem. Abstr.; Coal Abstr.

LC TA418.9.C6 K615 **ISSN** 0203-3275
UN
CODEN KPMAD8

KOMPOZITSIONNYE POLIMERNYE MATERIALY.
[Kompoz. polim. mater.]. **Added/Corp** Instytut Khimii Vysokomolekuliarnykh Spoluk (Akademiia Nauk Ukrainskoi RSR). Vol. 1 (1979)-. Academic Scholarly Publication. Russian. Four times a year. Izdatelstvo Naukova Dumka / Ukrainian Academy of Sciences, Yu. A. Khramov, Dir., Ul. Repina 3, 252 601 Kiev Ukraine. **Tel** 011 7 44 4303441, 011 7 44 2254182, telex 131376. Documents available from CASDDS.
Ind/Abst Chem. Abstr.; Eng. Mater. Abstr.

LC QD241 **ISSN** 1120-8376
DD 547 IT
UDC 542.1

LABORATORIO 2000.
[Lab. 2000]. **VFOAT** Laboratorio Duemila. (1987)-. Periodical. Italian. Nine times a year. L68130. Morgan Edizioni Tecniche, Via E Oldofredi 39, 20124 Milan Italy. **Tel** 011 39 2 6900122730, FAX 011 39 2 6900122932. Index available. cum. index. **Bk Rev. Ad Acc, Adv Mgr:** Marcnesu Nibuca, **Tel** 02 69001267. **Circ:** 9,000 (ctrl). Documents available from CASDDS.
Desc: Information on non-clinical lab that conducts analysis and research in the fields of chemistry and biology.
Ind/Abst Chem. Abstr.; Curr. Cit.

LC QD415 **ISSN** 0929-5666
DD 574.192 NE
CCC

LETTERS IN PEPTIDE SCIENCE.
(1994)-. English. Six times a year. $539.00. ESCOM Science Publishers BV, PO Box 214, 2300 AE Leiden The Netherlands. **Tel** 011 31 71 127052.
Desc: Aimed at peptide and protein scientists as well as all chemists, biochemists and molecular biologists concerned with the isolation, structural characterization, synthesis and biological activity of peptides.

LC QD1 .L7 **ISSN** 0170-2041
DD 540.5/6 GW
CCC
NLM W1 LI26 **CODEN** LACHDL
Pr Rev. **TITLE CHANGE**

LIEBIGS ANNALEN DER CHEMIE.
[Liebigs Ann. Chem.]. **Added/Corp** Gesellschaft Deutscher Chemiker. **VFOAT** Annalen der Chemie. (Jan. 1979)-(Dec. 1994). Academic Scholarly Publication. German (English; summaries and/or abstracts in English). VCH Gesellschaft GmbH, Postfach 101161, D-69451 Weinheim Germany. **Tel** 011 49 6201 606459, FAX 011 49 6201 606184. **(Subscription address:** VCH Publishers Inc., 303 Northwest 12th Avenue, Journals Department, Deerfield FL 33442. **Tel** (800)367-8249, (305)428-5566.) cum. index. Documents available from The Genuine Article, BIOSIS Document Express, CASDDS. ***Continues*** *Justus Liebigs Annalen der Chemie.* ***Merged with*** *Chemische Berichte, 0009-2940* ***to form*** *Liebigs Annalen, 0947-3440.*
Ind/Abst AGRICOLA; Biol. Abstr.; Chem Inform; Chem. Abstr.; Chem. Titles; Chemorecept. Abstr.; CSA Neuro. Abstr. (?-?); Curr. Biotechnol.; Curr. Chem. React.; Curr. Cit.; Curr. Contents Life Sci.; Curr. Contents Phys. Chem. Earth Sci.; EMBASE; Energy Res. Abstr. (Jan. 1983-); For. Prod. Abstr. (1991-); For. Abstr.; Hortic. Abstr.; Index Chem.; Leadscan; Mass Spect. Bull.; Methods Organ. Synth.; NAPRALERT; Nat. Prod. Updates; Nematol. Abstr.; Life Sci. Collect.; PESTDOC; Postharvest News Inf.; Protozoolog. Abstr.; Res. Alert [Full Cov.]; Rev. Agric. Entomol.; Rev. Med. Vet. Entomol.; Rev. Med. Vet. Mycology; Sci. Cit. Index; SCISEARCH.

ISSN 0947-3440
GW
NLM W1; LI26
Pr Rev.

LIEBIGS ANNALEN : ORGANIC AND BIOORGANIC CHEMISTRY.
VFOAT Chemische Berichte : Inorganic and Organometallic Chemistry,; Inorganic and Organometallic Chemistry; Annalen der Chemie. (Jan. 1995)-. Academic Scholarly Publication. English (German; summaries and/or abstracts in English). Twelve times a year. $1300.00. VCH Gesellschaft GmbH, Postfach 101161, D-69451 Weinheim Germany. **Tel** 011 49 6201 606459, FAX 011 49 6201 606184. **(Subscription address:** VCH Publishers Inc., 303 Northwest 12th Avenue, Journals Department, Deerfield FL 33442. **Tel** (800)367-8249, (305)428-5566.) Index available. cum. index. Documents available from The Genuine Article, BIOSIS Document Express, CASDDS. ***Formed by the union of*** *Liebigs Annalen der Chemie, 0170-2041* ***and*** *Chemische Berichte, 0009-2940.*
Ind/Abst Abstr. Bull. Inst. Pap. Sci. Tech.; AGRICOLA; Bibliogr. Agric.; Biol. Abstr.; Ceram. Abstr.; Chem Inform; Chem. Abstr.; Chem. Titles; Chemorecept. Abstr.; CSA Neuro. Abstr.; Curr. Biotechnol.; Curr. Chem. React.; Curr. Cit.; Curr. Contents Life Sci.; Curr. Contents Phys. Chem. Earth Sci.; Ei Page One; EMBASE; Energy Res. Abstr.; For. Prod. Abstr.; For. Abstr.; Hortic. Abstr.; Index Chem.; Leadscan; Mass Spect. Bull.; Methods Organ. Synth.; NAPRALERT; Nat. Prod. Updates; Nematol. Abstr.; Life Sci. Collect.; PESTDOC; Postharvest News Inf.; Protozoolog. Abstr.; Res. Alert; Rev. Agric. Entomol.; Rev. Med. Vet. Entomol.; Rev. Med. Vet. Mycology; RINGDOC; Sci. Cit. Index; SCISEARCH; VETDOC.

GW

LIEBIGS ANNALEN - ORGANIC CHEMISTRY.
[Liebigs Ann. Chem.]. **VFOAT** Annalen der Chemie. (19??)-. Academic Scholarly Publication. German (summaries and/or abstracts in English). Twelve times a year. VCH Gesellschaft GmbH, Postfach 101161, D-69451 Weinheim Germany. **Tel** 011 49 6201 606459, FAX 011 49 6201 606184. **(Subscription address:** VCH Publishers Inc., 303 Northwest 12th Avenue, Journals Department, Deerfield FL 33442. **Tel** (800)367-8249, (305)428-5566.) cum. index. Documents available from The Genuine Article, BIOSIS Document Express, CASDDS. ***Continues*** *Liebigs Annalen der Chemie, 0170-2041.*
Ind/Abst AGRICOLA; Biol. Abstr.; Chem Inform; Chem. Abstr.; Chem. Titles; Chemorecept. Abstr.; CSA Neuro. Abstr. (?-?); Curr. Biotechnol.; Curr. Chem. React.; Curr. Contents Life Sci.; Curr. Contents Phys. Chem. Earth Sci.; EMBASE; Energy Res. Abstr. (Jan. 1983-); For. Prod. Abstr. (1991-); For. Abstr.; Hortic. Abstr.; Index Chem.; Leadscan; Mass Spect. Bull.; Methods Organ. Synth.; NAPRALERT; Nat. Prod. Updates; Nematol. Abstr.; Life Sci. Collect.; PESTDOC; Postharvest News Inf.; Protozoolog. Abstr.; Res. Alert [Full Cov.]; Rev. Agric. Entomol.; Rev. Med. Vet. Entomol.; Rev. Med. Vet. Mycology; Sci. Cit. Index; SCISEARCH.

LC QD380 .M26 **ISSN** 0144-2988
DD 547.8/4/05 UK
CODEN MCCHDC

MACROMOLECULAR CHEMISTRY (ROYAL SOCIETY OF CHEMISTRY (GREAT BRITAIN)).
(MACROMOLECULAR CHEMISTRY.). [Macromol. chem.]. **Added/Corp** Royal Society of Chemistry (Great Britain). Vol. 1 (1980)-. Academic Scholarly Publication. English. Irregular. £107.00. Royal Society of Chemistry, Thomas Graham House, Science Park, Cambridge CB4 4WF United Kingdom. **Tel** 011 44 1223 420066, FAX 011 44 1223 423623, telex 818293 ROYAL. **(Subscription address:** Royal Society of Chemistry, Turpin Distribution Services Ltd., Blackhorse Road, Letchworth, Hertfordshire SG6 1HN United Kingdom. **Tel** 011 44 1462 672555, FAX 011 44 1462 480947.) **ED** A. D. Jenkins and J. F. Kennedy. Documents available from BIOSIS Document Express, CASDDS.
Desc: Provides the professional with broad coverage and a thorough update of this rapidly growing field.
Ind/Abst Biol. Abstr.; Chem. Abstr. (1980-1984); Polymer Contents.

Chemistry and Chemicals —Organic Chemistry

LC QD380 .M33
DD 547.7/05
ISSN 1022-1336
SZ
CODEN MRCOE3
Pr Rev.

●**MACROMOLECULAR RAPID COMMUNICATIONS.** Vol. 15, No. 1 (Jan. 1994)-. Academic Scholarly Publication. English. Twelve times a year. $225.00. Huethig & Wepf Verlag, Neugasse 29, CH-6301 Zug Switzerland. **Tel** 011 41 42 222494, FAX 011 41 42 218360. Documents available from CASDDS. **Continues** Makromolekulare Chemie. Rapid Communications, 0173-2803.
  Ind/Abst Chem. Abstr.; Curr. Cit.

LC QD380 .M275
DD 547.7/05
ISSN 1060-278X
US
CCC
CODEN MREPEG

MACROMOLECULAR REPORTS. [Macromol. rep.]. Vol. A28, Suppl. 1 (Apr. 1991)-. Periodical. English. Eight times a year. $295.00. Marcel Dekker Inc., 270 Madison Avenue, New York NY 10016. **Tel** (212)696-9000, (800)228-1160, FAX (212)685-4540, telex 421419. **(Subscription address:** Marcel Dekker Inc., PO Box 5017, Monticello NY 12701. **Tel** (800)228-1160.)

LC QD380 .M328
DD 547.7
ISSN 1022-1360
GW
CODEN MSYMEC

●**MACROMOLECULAR SYMPOSIA.** (1994)-. Periodical. English. Twelve times a year. $740.00. Huethig & Wepf Verlag, Neugasse 29, CH-6301 Zug Switzerland. **Tel** 011 41 42 222494, FAX 011 41 42 218360. **Continues** Makromolekulare Chemie. Makromolekulare Symposia, 0258-0322.
  Desc: Contains presentations in the field of macromolecular chemistry and physics made at selected international meetings, especially those of the IUPAC.
  Ind/Abst Chem. Abstr.; Curr. Cit.

LC QD262 .M26
DD 547.28
ISSN 0076-2091
US
CCC
NLM W1 MA172S
CODEN MASYAO

MACROMOLECULAR SYNTHESES. [Macromol. synth.]. Vol. 1 (1963)-. Monographic series. English. One time a year (Summer). Price varies per volume. MRG Polymer Press, Southern Station, PO Box 10076, Hattiesburg MS 39406. **Tel** (601)266-4871, (601)266-4876. Documents available from CASDDS.
  Ind/Abst Chem. Abstr.

LC QD380 .M3
DD 547/.7/05
ISSN 0163-6189
US

MACROMOLECULAR SYNTHESES. COLLECTIVE VOLUME. (1977)-. English. Irregular. John Wiley & Sons, Inc., 605 Third Avenue, New York NY 10158-0012. **Tel** (212)850-6000, (212)850-6645, FAX (212)850-6088, telex 12-7063. **(Subscription address:** John Wiley & Sons / UK, Baffins Lane, Chichester, West Sussex PO19 1UD United Kingdom. **Tel** 011 44 1243 779777, FAX 011 44 243 776128, telex 86290 WIBOOKG.)

LC QD380 .M333
DD 547.7/05
ISSN 1022-1344
SZ
CODEN MTHSEK
Pr Rev.

●**MACROMOLECULAR THEORY AND SIMULATIONS.** Vol. 3, No. 1 (Jan. 1994)-. Academic Scholarly Publication. English. Six times a year. $213.00. Huethig & Wepf Verlag, Neugasse 29, CH-6301 Zug Switzerland. **Tel** 011 41 42 222494, FAX 011 41 42 218360. Documents available from CASDDS. **Continues** Makromolekulare Chemie. Theory and Simulations, 1018-5054.
  Ind/Abst Chem. Abstr.

LC QD380 .M32
DD 547/.84/05
ISSN 0024-9297
US
CCC
NLM W1 MA172V
CODEN MAMOBX
Pr Rev.

MACROMOLECULES. [Macromolecules]. **Added/Corp** American Chemical Society. Vol. 1 (Jan./Feb. 1968)-. Periodical. English. Twenty-six times a year. $1145.00 (institutions) US. American Chemical Society, 1155 Sixteenth Street Northwest, Washington DC 20036. **Tel** (800)333-9511, (800)227-5558, (614)447-3776, FAX (202)447-3671. **(Subscription address:** American Chemical Society / Ohio, Department L 0011, Columbus OH 43268-0011.) **ED** Field H. Winslow. Index available (free). **Bk Rev. Ad Acc. Acid Free. Circ:** 2,700 (ctrl). available on microfilm and microfiche from University Microfilms International (UMI). Documents available from Article Express International, The Genuine Article, CASDDS.
  Desc: Fundamental aspects of polymer chemistry including synthesis, polymerization mechanisms and kinetics, chemical reactions, solution characteristics, spectroscopy, and bulk properties of organic, inorganic, and biopolymers.
  Ind/Abst Abstr. Bull. Inst. Pap. Sci. Tech.; AGRICOLA; Chem. Abstr.; Chem. Titles; Comput. Inf. Syst. Abstr. J. [Full Cov.]; Curr. Biotechnol.; Curr. Chem. React.; Curr. Contents Phys. Chem. Earth Sci.; Curr. Titles Electrochem.; Ei Page One!; Elect. Comm. Abstr.; Eng. Mater. Abstr.; Eng.

Index Annu.; Food Sci. Technol. Abstr.; INIS Atomindex [Micro.]; Int. Aerosp. Abstr.; Mass Spect. Bull.; Mater. Sci. Eng. Abstr.; Mech. Eng. Abstr.; Life Sci. Collect.; Polymer Contents; Res. Alert [Full Cov.]; Sci. Cit. Index; SCISEARCH; Solid State Supercond. Abstr.; Text. Technol. Dig.; World Surf. Coat. Abstr.; World Text. Abstr.

LC QD476 .O2
DD 543/.0877
ISSN 0749-1581
UK
CCC
CODEN MRCHEG
Pr Rev.

MAGNETIC RESONANCE IN CHEMISTRY : MRC. See Chemistry and Chemicals-Analytical Chemistry.

LC QD410 .R48
DD 547/.05
IS

MAIN GROUP METAL CHEMISTRY. **VFOAT** MGMC. Vol. 10, No. 1 (1987)-. Periodical. English. Irregular. $410.00. Freund Publishing House Ltd., PO Box 35010, 61 Nachmani Street, Tel Aviv 61350 Israel. **Tel** 011 972 3 5628540, FAX 011 972 3 5628538. **(Subscription address:** Freund Publishing House Ltd., Suite 500, Chesham House 150 Regent Street, London W1R 5FA United Kingdom. **Tel** 011 44 178 172811, FAX 011 972 3 615353.) **ED** M. Gielen and B.F. Speilvogel. Index available. **Bk Rev. Ad Acc. Circ:** 200. Documents available from CASDDS. **Continues** Silicon, Germanium, Tin and Lead Compounds, 0334-7575.
  Desc: Information on organometallic compounds and metals.
  Ind/Abst Chem. Abstr.; Curr. Cit.

NLM W1 MA493CS
CODEN MACEAKMCPHD9
SZ
Pr Rev.
TITLE CHANGE

MAKROMOLEKULARE CHEMIE (BASEL, SWITZERLAND : 1981). (DIE MAKROMOLEKULARE CHEMIE.). [Makromol. Chem.]. **VFOAT** Macromolecular Chemistry and Physics. (Mar. 16, 1981)-(Dec. 1993). Academic Scholarly Publication. English (French and German). Huethig & Wepf Verlag, Neugasse 29, CH-6301 Zug Switzerland. **Tel** 011 41 42 222494, FAX 011 41 42 218360. **ED** H. Hoecker. Index available. cum. index. **Ad Acc.** Documents available from The Genuine Article, CASDDS. **Continues** Macromolecular Chemistry and Physics, 0025-116X. **Continued by** Macromolecular Chemistry and Physics, 1022-1352.
  Ind/Abst AGRICOLA; Art Archaeol. Tech. Abstr.; Chem. Abstr.; Curr. Biotechnol.; Curr. Chem. React.; Curr. Contents Phys. Chem. Earth Sci.; Index Chem.; Polymer Contents; Res. Alert [Full Cov.]; Sci. Cit. Index (19??-19??); SCISEARCH; World Surf. Coat. Abstr.

LC QD380 .M328
DD 547.7
ISSN 0258-0322
SZ
CCC
NLM W3; MA296
CODEN MCMSES
Pr Rev.
TITLE CHANGE

MAKROMOLEKULARE CHEMIE. MACROMOLECULAR SYMPOSIA, DIE. [Makromol. Chem., Macromol. symp.]. **VFOAT** Macromolecular Symposia. (Jan. 1986)-(Jan. 1994). Academic Scholarly Publication. English. Huethig & Wepf Verlag, Neugasse 29, CH-6301 Zug Switzerland. **Tel** 011 41 42 222494, FAX 011 41 42 218360. Documents available from The Genuine Article, CASDDS. **Continues** Makromolekulare Chemie. Supplement, 0253-5904. **Continued by** Macromolecular Symposia.
  Ind/Abst Chem. Abstr. (1986-); Curr. Contents Phys. Chem. Earth Sci.; Res. Alert [Full Cov.]; SCISEARCH; World Surf. Coat. Abstr.

LC QD380 .M33
DD 547.7/05
ISSN 0173-2803
SZ
CCC
NLM W1 MA493DC
CODEN MCRCD4
Pr Rev.
TITLE CHANGE

MAKROMOLEKULARE CHEMIE. RAPID COMMUNICATIONS, DIE. [Makromol. Chem., Rapid commun.]. **VFOAT** Rapid Communications. Vol. 1, No. 1 (Jan. 11, 1980)-Vol. 14, No. 12 (Dec. 1993). Academic Scholarly Publication. English (French and German). Huethig & Wepf Verlag, Neugasse 29, CH-6301 Zug Switzerland. **Tel** 011 41 42 222494, FAX 011 41 42 218360. **ED** Hartwig Hoecker. Index available. cum. index. **Ad Acc.** Documents available from The Genuine Article, CASDDS. **Continues in part** Makromolekulare Chemie, 0025-116X. **Continued by** Macromolecular Rapid Communications, 1022-1336.
  Ind/Abst Chem. Abstr.; Curr. Biotechnol.; Curr. Chem. React.; Curr. Contents Phys. Chem. Earth Sci.; Index Chem.; Polymer Contents; Res. Alert [Full Cov.]; Sci. Cit. Index (19??-19??); SCISEARCH; World Surf. Coat. Abstr.

LC QD380 .M333
DD 547.7/05
ISSN 1018-5054
SZ
CODEN MCTSET
TITLE CHANGE

MAKROMOLEKULARE CHEMIE: THEORY AND SIMULATIONS, DIE. **VFOAT** Theory and Simulations. Vol. 1, No. 1 (Jan. 1992)-Vol. 2, No. 6 (Nov. 1993). Academic Scholarly Publication.

English. Huethig & Wepf Verlag, Neugasse 29, CH-6301 Zug Switzerland. **Tel** 011 41 42 222494, FAX 011 41 42 218360. Documents available from CASDDS. **Continued by** Macromolecular Theory and Simulations, 1022-1344.
  Ind/Abst Chem. Abstr.; Curr. Contents Phys. Chem. Earth Sci.

LC TP992.5 .M24
DD 338.4/7/668140257
UDC 661.185
ISSN 0145-7055
US

MCCUTCHEON'S DETERGENTS & EMULSIFIERS. NORTH AMERICAN EDITION. (MCCUTCHEON'S DETERGENTS & EMULSIFIERS.). **VFOAT** Detergents & Emulsifiers: North American. **VAT** McCutcheon's Detergents and Emulsifiers. North American Edition. (1973)-. English. One time a year. $45.00. MC Publishing Company, 175 Rock Road, Glen Rock NJ 07452. **Ad Acc. Supersedes in part** McCutcheon's Detergents & Emulsifiers.

LC QD410 .M48
DD 547.05
ISSN 0235-0114
RU
CODEN MEKHEX
CEASED

METALLOORGANICHESKAIA KHIMIIA. **Added/Corp** Akademiia Nauk SSSR. Rossiiskaia Akademiia Nauk. **VFOAT** Metallo-Organicheskaia Khimiia. Vol. 1, No. 1 (Jan./Feb. 1988)-(1993). Academic Scholarly Publication. Russian (table of contents in English). Six times a year. Izdatelstvo Nauka / Akademiia Nauk, (Publishing House of the Russian Academy of Sciences), Leninskii Porspekt 14, 117901 Moscow Russia. **Tel** 011 95 9542153, FAX 011 95 9382144, telex 411964. Documents available from CASDDS.
  Ind/Abst Chem. Abstr.

ISSN 0265-4245
UK
CCC
CODEN MOSYDN

METHODS IN ORGANIC SYNTHESIS. See Chemistry and Chemicals-Abstracting, Bibliographies and Statistics.

ISSN 0275-7265
DD 547
US

MMI PRESS POLYMER MONOGRAPH SERIES. [MMI Press polym. monogr. ser.]. **VFOAT** M.M.I. Press Polymer Monograph Series. **VAT** Michigan Molecular Institute Press Polymer Monograph Series. Vol. 1 (1982)-. Monographic series. English. Price varies per volume. Harwood Academic Publishers / New York, PO Box 786, Cooper Station, New York NY 10276. **Tel** (212)206-8900, (201)643-7500. **ED** R. Breitmaier.

ISSN 0176-7615
SZ
CODEN MSMEDT

MODERN SYNTHETIC METHODS. (MODERN SYNTHETIC METHODS : CONFERENCE PAPER OF THE INTERNATIONAL SEMINAR ON MODERN SYNTHETIC METHODS / SPONSORED AND ORGANIZED BY THE ASSOCIATION OF SWISS CHEMISTS.). [Mod. synth. methods]. **Added/Corp** Schweizerischer Chemiker-Verband. Vol. 1 (1976)-. Academic Scholarly Publication. English. Every 3 years. Price varies per volume. Springer-Verlag New York Inc., 175 Fifth Avenue, New York NY 10010. **Tel** (212)460-1500 ext 256, FAX (212)533-3503, telex 232 235 SPB UR. **(Subscription address:** Springer-Verlag New York Inc. / North America, PO Box 2485, Journal Fulfillment, Secaucus NJ 07096. **Tel** (201)348-4033, (800)777-4643, FAX (201)348-4505.) Documents available from CASDDS.
  Desc: Reviews in organic synthesis, including experimental data.
  Ind/Abst Chem Inform; Chem. Abstr.

LC QD415.A1
DD 574.192
ISSN 0265-0568
UK
CCC
NLM W1; NA805H
CODEN NPRRDF
Pr Rev.

NATURAL PRODUCT REPORTS. See Biology-Biological Chemistry.

UDC 547.057
GW

NEW SYNTHETIC METHODS. Vol. 1 (1975)-. English. Irregular. VCH Publishers Inc, 220 East 23rd Street, New York NY 10010. **Tel** (212)683-8249, FAX (212)481-0897. **(Subscription address:** VCH Publishers Inc., 303 Northwest 12th Avenue, Journals Department, Deerfield FL 33442. **Tel** (800)367-8249, (305)428-5566.)

LC Z5524.C8 M6 QD921
DD 016.548/81/08 S 016.548/81
NE

ORGANIC AND ORGANOMETALLIC CRYSTAL STRUCTURES; BIBLIOGRAPHY. See Chemistry and Chemicals-Abstracting, Bibliographies and Statistics.

LC RS400 .O74 **ISSN** 8755-383X
DD 615/.19 US

ORGANIC CHEMISTRY OF DRUG SYNTHESIS, THE. **See** Pharmacy and Pharmacology.

UK

ORGANIC CHEMISTRY SERIES (PERGAMON PRESS). (ORGANIC CHEMISTRY SERIES.). (1982)-. Monographic series. English. Price varies per volume. Pergamon Press, An Imprint of Elsevier Science Ltd., The Boulevard, Langford Lane, Kidlington, Oxford OX5 1GB United Kingdom. **Tel** 011 44 1865 843000, 011 44 1865 843699, FAX 011 44 1865 843010.

LC QD262 .O632 **ISSN** 0092-6094
DD 547/.2 US

ORGANIC COMPOUNDS : REACTIONS AND METHODS. (19??)-. Monographic series. English (Russian). Irregular. Price varies per volume. Plenum Press, 233 Spring Street, New York NY 10013-1578. **Tel** (212)620-8000, (800)221-9369, FAX (212)463-0742, (212)807-1047, telex 23/421139.

LC QD271.A1 O18 **ISSN** 0030-493X
DD 547 UK
CCC
CODEN ORMSBGORMRBD
Pr Rev. **TITLE CHANGE**

ORGANIC MASS SPECTROMETRY. (OMS. ORGANIC MASS SPECTROMETRY.). [Org. mass spectrom.]. **VFOAT** Organic Mass Spectrometry. Vol. 1 (Feb. 1968)-(Jan. 1995). Periodical. English (German). John Wiley & Sons Ltd., Baffins Lane, Chichester, West Sussex PO19 1UD United Kingdom. **Tel** 011 44 1243 779777, FAX 011 44 1243 776128 BTG:JWP001, telex 86290 WIBOOKG. **ED** P J Derrick. cum. index. **Bk Rev.** **Ad Acc.** **Circ:** 1,400. available on microfilm and microfiche from University Microfilms International (UMI). Documents available from The Genuine Article, BIOSIS Document Express, CASDDS, ADONIS. ***Continued by*** *Journal of Mass Spectrometry, 1076-5174.*
Desc: Provides for the timely publication of reviews, papers and letters ranging from the application of mass spectrometry to problems in organic and gas phase ion chemistry.
Ind/Abst ADONIS; Anal. Abstr.; Biol. Abstr. (1989-); Chem. Abstr.; Chem. Titles; Coal Abstr.; Curr. Aware. Biol. Sci., CABS; Curr. Chem. React.; Curr. Cit.; Curr. Contents Phys. Chem. Earth Sci.; Index Chem.; Int. Aerosp. Abstr.; Mass Spect. Bull.; NAPRALERT; Res. Alert [Full Cov.]; Sci. Cit. Index; SCISEARCH; Sug. Indus. Abstr.; Weed Abstr.

LC QD601.A1 O7 **ISSN** 0078-6152
DD 547/.1/35 US
CCC
NLM W1 OR63K **CODEN** 0RPHAV

ORGANIC PHOTOCHEMISTRY (NEW YORK). (ORGANIC PHOTOCHEMISTRY.). [Org. photochem.]. Vol. 1 (1967)-. Monographic series. English. Irregular. Price varies per volume. Marcel Dekker Inc., 270 Madison Avenue, New York NY 10016. **Tel** (212)696-9000, (800)228-1160, FAX (212)685-4540, telex 421419. **(Subscription address:** Marcel Dekker Inc., PO Box 5017, Monticello NY 12701. **Tel** (800)228-1160.**)** Documents available from CASDDS.
Desc: Each title covers a different topic in organic photochemistry.
Ind/Abst Chem. Abstr.

LC QD262 .O67 **ISSN** 0030-4948
DD 547/.2 US
CODEN OPPIAK
Pr Rev.

ORGANIC PREPARATIONS AND PROCEDURES INTERNATIONAL. [Org. prep. proced. int.]. Vol. 3 (Feb. 1971)-. Academic Scholarly Publication. English. Six times a year. $250.00. Organic Preparations and Procedures Inc, PO Box 9, Newton Highlands MA 02161. **Tel** (617)929-7529. **ED** J. P. Anselme. Index available. **Bk Rev.** **Ad Acc.** Documents available from The Genuine Article, CASDDS. ***Continues*** *Organic Preparations and Procedures, 0885-6672.*
Ind/Abst Chem Inform; Chem. Abstr.; Chem. Titles; Curr. Chem. React.; Curr. Cit.; Curr. Contents Phys. Chem. Earth Sci.; Index Chem.; Int. Aerosp. Abstr.; Mass Spect. Bull. (?-?); Methods Organ. Synth.; Nat. Prod. Updates; Res. Alert [Full Cov.]; Sci. Cit. Index; SCISEARCH; Soc. Sci. Cit. Index [Select. Cov.].

LC QD258 .O82 **ISSN** 0474-4772
UK
UDC 541.14:547
CODEN ORRMAM

ORGANIC REACTION MECHANISMS. [Org. react. mech.]. (1965)-. English. Irregular. $350.00. Kreiger Publications, PO Box 9542, Melbourne FL 32901. **Tel** (407)724-9542. cum. index. Documents available from CASDDS.
Ind/Abst Chem. Abstr.

LC QD251 .O7 **ISSN** 0078-6179
DD 547 US
UDC 541.14:547
NLM W1 OR631 **CODEN** ORREAW

ORGANIC REACTIONS. [Org. react.]. Vol. 1 (1942)-. English. Irregular. $75.00. John Wiley & Sons, Inc., 605 Third Avenue, New York NY 10158-0012. **Tel** (212)850-6000, (212)850-6645, FAX (212)850-6088, telex 12-7063. **(Subscription address:** John Wiley & Sons / UK, Baffins Lane, Chichester, West Sussex PO19 1UD United Kingdom. **Tel** 011 44 1243 779777, FAX 011 44 243 776128, telex 86290 WIBOOKG.**)** Documents available from BIOSIS Document Express, CASDDS.
Ind/Abst Biol. Abstr.; Chem. Abstr.; Index Sci. Rev. [Full Cov.].

LC QD241 .O684 **ISSN** 0445-3611
DD 547 US

ORGANIC SEMINAR ABSTRACTS. **See** Chemistry and Chemicals-Abstracting, Bibliographies and Statistics.

LC QD262 .O7 **ISSN** 0078-6209
DD 547.058 US
CCC
NLM W1 OR649 **CODEN** ORSYAT

ORGANIC SYNTHESES. [Organic synth.]. Vol. 1 (1921)-. Monographic series. English. Irregular. Price varies per volume. John Wiley & Sons, Inc., 605 Third Avenue, New York NY 10158-0012. **Tel** (212)850-6000, (212)850-6645, FAX (212)850-6088, telex 12-7063. **(Subscription address:** John Wiley & Sons / UK, Baffins Lane, Chichester, West Sussex PO19 1UD United Kingdom. **Tel** 011 44 1243 779777, FAX 011 44 243 776128, telex 86290 WIBOOKG.**)** **ED** R. Adams, J. B. Conant, H. T. Clarke, and O. Kamm. cum. index. Documents available from The Genuine Article, CASDDS.
Ind/Abst Abstr. Bull. Inst. Pap. Sci. Tech.; Chem. Abstr.; Res. Alert [Full Cov.]; Sci. Cit. Index (19??-19??); SCISEARCH.

LC QD262 .O722 **ISSN** 0078-6217
US

ORGANIC SYNTHESES. COLLECTIVE VOLUME. [Org. synth., Collect. vol.]. (1932)-. English. Irregular. John Wiley & Sons, Inc., 605 Third Avenue, New York NY 10158-0012. **Tel** (212)850-6000, (212)850-6645, FAX (212)850-6088, telex 12-7063. **(Subscription address:** John Wiley & Sons / UK, Baffins Lane, Chichester, West Sussex PO19 1UD United Kingdom. **Tel** 011 44 1243 779777, FAX 011 44 243 776128, telex 86290 WIBOOKG.**)**

LC QD411 .W4
DD 547/.45 US

ORGANIC SYNTHESES VIA METAL CARBONYLS. Vol. 1 (1968)-. Periodical. English. Irregular. John Wiley & Sons, Inc., 605 Third Avenue, New York NY 10158-0012. **Tel** (212)850-6000, (212)850-6645, FAX (212)850-6088, telex 12-7063. **(Subscription address:** John Wiley & Sons / UK, Baffins Lane, Chichester, West Sussex PO19 1UD United Kingdom. **Tel** 011 44 1243 779777, FAX 011 44 243 776128, telex 86290 WIBOOKG.**)** **ED** I Wender and P Pino.

LC QD262 .O7245 **ISSN** 1047-773X
DD 547.2 US
CODEN OSTAE7

ORGANIC SYNTHESIS. (ORGANIC SYNTHESIS : THEORY AND APPLICATIONS.). [Org. synth.]. **VFOAT** Organic Synthesis, Theory and Applications. Vol. 1 (1989)-. Periodical. English. Irregular. $90.25. JAI Press Inc., 55 Old Post Road, Suite 2, PO Box 1678, Greenwich CT 06836-1678. **Tel** (203)661-7602, FAX (203)661-0792. **ED** Tomas Hudlicky.

ISSN 0078-6225
GW

ORGANISCHE CHEMIE IN EINZELDARSTELLUNGEN. (1940)-. Monographic series. German. Irregular. Price varies per volume. Springer-Verlag GmbH & Company KG, Heidelberger Platz 3, D-14197 Berlin Germany. **Tel** 011 49 30 8207223, FAX 011 49 30 8214091, telex 183 319 SPBLN D. **(Subscription address:** Springer-Verlag New York Inc. / North America, PO Box 2485, Journal Fulfillment, Secaucus NJ 07096. **Tel** (201)348-4033, (800)777-4643, FAX (201)348-4505.**)**

LC QD410 b .M482 **ISSN** 0955-8586
UK
Pr Rev. **CEASED**

ORGANOMETALLIC CHEMISTRY IN THE USSR. **Added/Corp** British Library. Document Supply Centre. Royal Society of Chemistry (Great Britain). (1988)-(1993). Periodical. English (translations available in Russian). British Library Translated Journals, Boston Spa, Wetherby West Yorkshire LS23 7BQ United Kingdom. **Tel** 011 44 1937 546078, FAX 011 44 1462 480947. **ED** M J Winter. **Circ:** 40. Documents available from The Genuine Article.
Desc: A cover to cover translation of Metalloorganicheskaya Khimiya.
Ind/Abst Res. Alert [Full Cov.].

LC QD410 .O73 **ISSN** 0301-0074
DD 547/.05 UK
CCC
NLM W1 OR663N **CODEN** OGMCAQ

ORGANOMETALLIC CHEMISTRY (LONDON. 1972). (ORGANOMETALLIC CHEMISTRY.). [Organomet. chem.]. **Added/Corp** Chemical Society (Great Britain) Royal Society of Chemistry (Great Britain). Vol. 1 (1971)-. English. One time a year. £165.00. Royal Society of Chemistry, Thomas Graham House, Science Park, Cambridge CB4 4WF United Kingdom. **Tel** 011 44 1223 420066, FAX 011 44 1223 423623, telex 818293 ROYAL. **(Subscription address:** Royal Society of Chemistry, Turpin Distribution Services Ltd., Blackhorse Road, Letchworth, Hertfordshire SG6 1HN United Kingdom. **Tel** 011 44 1462 672555, FAX 011 44 1462 480947.**)** **ED** E. W. Abel and F. G. A. Stone. Documents available from BIOSIS Document Express, CASDDS.
Ind/Abst Biol. Abstr.; Chem. Abstr.; Curr. Cit.

LC QD411 .O7 **ISSN** 0030-5138
DD 547.05 UK
CCC

ORGANOMETALLIC COMPOUNDS. **See** Literature-Abstracting, Bibliographies and Statistics.

LC QD410 .O733 **ISSN** 0276-7333
DD 547/.05/05 US
CCC
CODEN ORGND7
Pr Rev.

ORGANOMETALLICS. [Organometallics]. **Added/Corp** American Chemical Society. Vol. 1, No. 1 (Jan. 1982)-. Academic Scholarly Publication. English. Twenty-six times a year. $1230.00. American Chemical Society, 1155 Sixteenth Street Northwest, Washington DC 20036. **Tel** (800)333-9511, (800)227-5558, (614)447-3776, FAX (202)447-3671. **(Subscription address:** American Chemical Society / Ohio, Department L 0011, Columbus OH 43268-0011. **)** **ED** Dietmar Seyferth. Index available (free). **Bk Rev.** **Ad Acc.** **Acid Free.** **Circ:** 3,000 (ctrl). available on microfilm and microfiche from University Microfilms International (UMI). Documents available from Article Express International, The Genuine Article, CASDDS.
Desc: Journal with an interdisciplinary approach to organometallic chemistry-synthesis, structure, and bonding, reactivity, and mechanism, applications in organic, inorganic, polymer, solid state chemistry and materials science.
Ind/Abst Chem Inform; Chem. Abstr.; Chem. Titles; Coal Abstr.; Curr. Chem. React.; Curr. Cit.; Curr. Contents Phys. Chem. Earth Sci.; Curr. Titles Electrochem.; Eng. Index Annu. [Select. Cov.]; Index Chem.; Leadscan; Mass Spect. Bull.; Methods Organ. Synth.; Res. Alert [Full Cov.]; Sci. Cit. Index; SCISEARCH.

LC QD412.P1 O65 **ISSN** 0306-0713
UK
CCC
NLM W1 OR663U **CODEN** OPCMAZ

ORGANOPHOSPHORUS CHEMISTRY. **Added/Corp** Chemical Society (Great Britain). Vol. 1 (1969)-. English. Irregular. £152.50. Royal Society of Chemistry, Thomas Graham House, Science Park, Cambridge CB4 4WF United Kingdom. **Tel** 011 44 1223 420066, FAX 011 44 1223 423623, telex 818293 ROYAL. **(Subscription address:** Royal Society of Chemistry, Turpin Distribution Services Ltd., Blackhorse Road, Letchworth, Hertfordshire SG6 1HN United Kingdom. **Tel** 011 44 1462 672555, FAX 011 44 1462 480947.**)** **ED** E. W. Hutchinson and B. J. Walker. Documents available from CASDDS.
Desc: Includes phosphines and phosphonium salts; quinquecovalent phosphorus compounds; phosphine oxides and related compounds; tervalent phosphorus acids; quinquevalent phosphorus acids; phosphates and phosphonates biochemical interest; nucleotides and nucleic acids; ylides and related compounds; phosphazenes; physical methods.
Ind/Abst Chem. Abstr.; Curr. Cit.

UK

OUTLOOK CONCENTRATED PHOSPHATES. English. Four times a year. £1750.00 UK; $3250.00 North America; 3750.00Can$ Canada. Fertecon Limited, 25 Copperfield Street, Suite B, London SE1 0EN United Kingdom. **Tel** 011 44 171 2619998, FAX 011 44 171 9287911.
Desc: Supply and demand report.

LC QD281.O9 O97 **ISSN** 0209-4541
BU
CCC
NLM W1 OX621V **CODEN** OXCODW
Pr Rev.

OXIDATION COMMUNICATIONS. [Oxid. commun.]. Vol. 1, No. 1 (1979)-. Academic Scholarly Publication. English. Two times a year (published in four books included in two double issues). $195.00. Bulgarian Academy of Sciences, 1 rue 15 Noemvri, 1040 Sofia Bulgaria. **Tel** 011 359 2 803127. **(Subscription address:**

Professor Dr. Slavi Ivanov, PO Box 1369, Publishscieset Company Ltd., 1080 Sofia Bulgaria.) **ED** Dr. Slavi K. Ivanov. Index available. cum. index. **Bk Rev. Ad Acc, Adv Mgr:** M. Boneva. ctrl circ. Documents available from CASDDS.
Desc: Publishes papers reporting the results of experimental and theoretical research in physical and biological oxidation processes.
Ind/Abst Chem. Abstr.; Curr. Cit.; Life Sci. Collect.

ISSN 1017-0626
PK
UDC 54
PAKISTAN JOURNAL OF HYDROCARBON RESEARCH. [Pak. j. hydrocarb. res.]. (1989)-. Periodical. English. Two times a year. Islamabad Hydrocarbon Development Institute of Pakistan, 230 Nizamuddin Rd, PO Box 1308, Islambad, Pakistan.

LC QD281.P6 A53 **ISSN** 0569-3802
DD 547.7/05 US
CODEN ACPPAY
PAPERS PRESENTED AT THE MEETING. Main/Corp American Chemical Society. Division of Polymer Chemistry. **Added/Corp** American Chemical Society. Division of Polymer Chemistry. Polymer Preprints. **VFOAT** Polymer Preprints. Vol. 1 (Apr. 1960)-. English. Two times a year. American Chemical Society, 1155 Sixteenth Street Northwest, Washington DC 20036. **Tel** (800)333-9511, (800)227-5558, (614)447-3776, FAX (202)447-3671. Documents available from Article Express International, CASDDS.
Ind/Abst Bioeng. Abstr.; Chem. Abstr.; Ei Page One; Eng. Index Annu.; World Surf. Coat. Abstr.

ISSN 0761-1749
FR
UDC 543/547
PASCAL FOLIO. F16, CHIMIE ANALYTIQUE, MINERALE ET ORGANIQUE. See Chemistry and Chemicals-Analytical Chemistry.

LC QP606.D46 P34 **ISSN** 1054-9803
DD 547 US
CCC
NLM W1; PC11 **CODEN** PMAPES
TITLE CHANGE
PCR METHODS AND APPLICATIONS. [PCR methods appl.]. **VFOAT** Polymerase Chain Reaction Methods and Applications. **VAT** Polymerase Chain Reaction Methods and Applications. Vol. 1, No. 1 (Aug. 1991)-(1994). Academic Scholarly Publication. English. Cold Spring Harbor Laboratory, 10 Skyline Drive, Plainview NY 11803. **Tel** (516)349-1930, (800)843-4388, FAX (516)349-1946. **Ad Acc.** Documents available from The Genuine Article, CASDDS. ***Merged into** Genome Research.*
Desc: Publishes research papers detailing improvements in PCR methodology and new application of these techniques, as well as papers describing the application of these methods to a wide variety of research problems.
Ind/Abst Ceram. Abstr. (19??-19??); Chem. Abstr.; Curr. Aware. Biol. Sci., CABS; Curr. Cit.; Genet. Abstr.; Index Med. (Aug. 1991-); Res. Alert [Full Cov.].

ISSN 0385-8847
JA
PEPTIDE INFORMATION. See Chemistry and Chemicals-Abstracting, Bibliographies and Statistics.

ISSN 1040-5704
DD 547 US
CCC
NLM W1; PE769J **CODEN** PEREEO
Pr Rev.
PEPTIDE RESEARCH. [Pept. res.]. Vol. 1, No. 1 (Sept./Oct. 1988)-. Academic Scholarly Publication. English. Six times a year. $85.00. Eaton Publishing Company, 154 East Central Street, Natick MA 01760. **Tel** (508)655-8282, FAX (508)655-9910. **ED** Richard A. Houghten. Index available. cum. index. **Ad Acc. Circ:** 3,000. Documents available from The Genuine Article, BIOSIS Document Express, CASDDS.
Desc: Publishes science papers dealing with the application, synthesis and analysis of peptides.
Ind/Abst Abstr. BioCommer.; Biol. Abstr. (1989-); Chem. Abstr.; Curr. Aware. Biol. Sci., CABS; Curr. Cit.; Curr. Contents Life Sci.; Index Med. (Sept./Oct. 1988-); Ref. Upd. Deluxe Ed.; Res. Alert [Full Cov.]; Sci. Cit. Index; SCISEARCH.

LC QD241 **ISSN** 0300-922X
DD 547 UK
CCC
NLM W1 JO916GP **CODEN** JCPRB4
Pr Rev.
PERKIN TRANSACTIONS 1. (JOURNAL OF THE CHEMICAL SOCIETY. PERKIN TRANSACTIONS 1.). [Perkin trans., 1]. **Added/Corp** Chemical Society (Great Britain). **VFOAT** J. C. S. Perkin 1; Organic and Bio-Organic Chemistry; Perkin Transactions 1: Organic and Bio-Organic Chemistry. (1972)-. Periodical. English. Twenty-four times a year (plus an index). $1486.00. Royal Society of Chemistry, Thomas Graham House, Science Park, Cambridge CB4 4WF United Kingdom. **Tel** 011 44 1223 420066, FAX 011 44 1223 423623, telex 818293 ROYAL. **(Subscription address:** Royal Society of Chemistry, Turpin Distribution Services Ltd., Blackhorse Road, Letchworth, Hertfordshire SG6 1HN United Kingdom. **Tel** 011 44 1462 672555, FAX 011 44 1462 480947.) Index available (free). available on microfilm and microfiche from University Microfilms International (UMI); available on an online database from STN International. Documents available from The Genuine Article, BIOSIS Document Express, CASDDS, ADONIS, BLDSC, FAXON Xpress, The UnCover Company, SWETS, UMI Article Clearinghouse. ***Continues** Journal of the Chemical Society. C: Organic, 0022-4952.*
Desc: Contains papers on all aspects of organic and bioorganic chemistry.
Ind/Abst Abstr. Bull. Inst. Pap. Sci. Tech.; ADONIS; AgBiotech News Inf.; AGRICOLA; Biol. Abstr.; Chem. Abstr.; Curr. Aware. Biol. Sci., CABS; Curr. Chem. React.; Curr. Cit.; Curr. Contents Life Sci.; Curr. Contents Phys. Chem. Earth Sci.; Helminthol. Abstr. (1991-); Hortic. Abstr.; Index Chem.; Leadscan; Mass Spect. Bull.; Methods Organ. Synth.; NAPRALERT; Nat. Prod. Updates; Ornamental Hort.; Life Sci. Collect.; PESTDOC; Protozoolog. Abstr.; Ref. Upd. Deluxe Ed.; Res. Alert [Full Cov.]; Rev. Med. Vet. Entomol.; Rev. Med. Vet. Mycology; Rev. Plant Pathol.; Sci. Cit. Index; SCISEARCH; Seed Abstr.; Soils Fert.; Weed Abstr.

LC QD241 **ISSN** 0300-9580
DD 547 UK
CCC
NLM W1 JO916GQ **CODEN** JCPKBHJPCKBH
PERKIN TRANSACTIONS. 2. (JOURNAL OF THE CHEMICAL SOCIETY. PERKIN TRANSACTIONS 2.). [Perkin trans., 2]. **Added/Corp** Chemical Society (Great Britain). **VFOAT** J. C. S. Perkin 2; Perkin Transactions 2: Physical Organic Chemistry; Physical Organic Chemistry. (1972)-. Proceedings. English. Twelve times a year (plus an index). $1234.00. Royal Society of Chemistry, Thomas Graham House, Science Park, Cambridge CB4 4WF United Kingdom. **Tel** 011 44 1223 420066, FAX 011 44 1223 423623, telex 818293 ROYAL. **(Subscription address:** Royal Society of Chemistry, Turpin Distribution Services Ltd., Blackhorse Road, Letchworth, Hertfordshire SG6 1HN United Kingdom. **Tel** 011 44 1462 672555, FAX 011 44 1462 480947.) Index available (free). available on microfilm and microfiche from University Microfilms International (UMI); available on an online database from STN International. Documents available from The Genuine Article, CASDDS, BLDSC, FAXON Xpress, The UnCover Company, SWETS, UMI Article Clearinghouse. ***Continues** Journal of the Chemical Society. B: Physical Organic, 0045-6470.*
Ind/Abst Abstr. Bull. Inst. Pap. Sci. Tech.; Chem. Abstr.; Curr. Chem. React.; Curr. Cit.; Curr. Contents Life Sci.; Curr. Contents Phys. Chem. Earth Sci.; Index Chem.; Leadscan; Mass Spect. Bull.; Methods Organ. Synth.; NAPRALERT; Nat. Prod. Updates; Life Sci. Collect.; PESTDOC; Res. Alert [Full Cov.]; Sci. Cit. Index; SCISEARCH.

ISSN 0031-6342
US
CCC
PETROCHEMICAL NEWS. See Petroleum and Natural Gas.

US
PHYSICAL METHODS IN ORGANIC CHEMISTRY. (19??)-. Monographic series. English. Irregular. Price varies per volume. John Wiley & Sons, Inc., 605 Third Avenue, New York NY 10158-0012. **Tel** (212)850-6000, (212)850-6645, FAX (212)850-6088, telex 12-7063. **(Subscription address:** John Wiley & Sons / UK, Baffins Lane, Chichester, West Sussex PO19 1UD United Kingdom. **Tel** 011 44 1243 779777, FAX 011 44 243 776128, telex 86290 WIBOOKG.)

LC TP155
DD 660 US
●**PLASMAS AND POLYMERS : AN INTERNATIONAL JOURNAL.** (1996)-. Academic Scholarly Publication. English. Four times a year. $150.00 (institutions), $50.00 (individuals) US; $175.00 (institutions), $59.00 (individuals) other. Plenum Press, 233 Spring Street, New York NY 10013-1578. **Tel** (212)620-8000, (800)221-9369, FAX (212)463-0742, (212)807-1047, telex 23/421139. **ED** R. D'Agostino and B. Ratner. **Bk Rev. Ad Acc.** available on microfilm.

LC QD335 .P6 **ISSN** 1040-6638
DD 547/.6 US
CCC
NLM W1; PO31J **CODEN** PARCEO
POLYCYCLIC AROMATIC COMPOUNDS. [Polycycl. aromat. compd.]. Vol. 1, No. 1/2 (Feb. 1990)-. Academic Scholarly Publication. English. Four times a year. $480.00 (academic institutions), $749.00 (corporate institutions). Gordon & Breach Science Publishers, Inc., PO Box 786, Cooper Station, New York NY 10276. **Tel** (212)206-8900, FAX (212)645-2459. Documents available from CASDDS.
Ind/Abst Chem. Abstr.; Food Sci. Technol. Abstr.

LC QD380 .P6366 **ISSN** 0170-0839
DD 547.7 GW
CCC
CODEN POBUDR
Pr Rev.
POLYMER BULLETIN (BERLIN, WEST). (POLYMER BULLETIN.). [Polym. bull.]. Vol. 1, No. 1 (Aug. 1978)-. Bulletin. English. Twelve times a year. $999.00. Springer-Verlag GmbH & Company KG, Heidelberger Platz 3, D-14197 Berlin Germany. **Tel** 011 49 30 8207223, FAX 011 49 30 8214091, telex 183 319 SPBLN D. **(Subscription address:** Springer-Verlag New York Inc. / North America, PO Box 2485, Journal Fulfillment, Secaucus NJ 07096. **Tel** (201)348-4033, (800)777-4643, FAX (201)348-4505.) **ED** H J Cantow, J P Kennedy, and T Saegusa. **Ad Acc. Circ:** 510. available on microfilm and microfiche from University Microfilms International (UMI). Documents available from Article Express International, The Genuine Article, Ask*IEEE, CASDDS.
Desc: Provides rapid publications of significant advances in polymer science, including biopolymers and polymer engineering. Serves as a meeting ground for researchers, who daily, encounter problems related to polymers and biopolymers and welcome opportunities to share their discoveries in a most expeditious manner.
Ind/Abst Abstr. Bull. Inst. Pap. Sci. Tech.; AGRICOLA; Bioeng. Abstr.; Chem. Abstr.; Chem. Titles; Curr. Biotechnol.; Curr. Cit.; Curr. Contents Phys. Chem. Earth Sci.; Ei Page One; Energy Res. Abstr. (Feb. 1982-); Eng. Mater. Abstr.; Eng. Index Annu.; INSPEC (Nov. 1978-); Leadscan; Phys. Briefs; Polymer Contents; Protozoolog. Abstr.; Res. Alert [Full Cov.]; Sci. Cit. Index; SCISEARCH; Sug. Indus. Abstr.

LC QD549.2.P64 P65 **ISSN** 0966-7822
DD 547.7 UK
CCC
CODEN PGNEEI
Pr Rev.
●**POLYMER GELS AND NETWORKS.** Vol. 1, No. 1 (1993)-. Academic Scholarly Publication. English. Six times a year. $311.00. Elsevier Applied Science, An Imprint of Elsevier Science Ltd., The Boulevard, Langford Lane, Kidlington, Oxford OX5 1GB United Kingdom. **Tel** 011 44 1865 843000, 011 44 1865 843699, FAX 011 44 1865 843010. **(Subscription address:** Elsevier Science Ltd. / Oxford Fulfillment Centre, PO Box 800, Kidlington OX5 1DX United Kingdom. **Tel** 011 44 865 843355.) **ED** T. Tanaka. available on an online database from Elsevier Electronic Subscriptions (EES). Documents available from CASDDS.
Desc: Provides a venue for publication of research results dealing with the structure and properties of these materials.
Ind/Abst Chem. Abstr.

LC TP156.P6 P6 **ISSN** 0032-3861
DD 547.8405 UK
CCC
NLM W1 PO31P **CODEN** POLMAG
Pr Rev.
POLYMER (GUILFORD). (POLYMER.). [Polymer]. Vol. 1 (March 1960)-. Periodical. English. Twenty-six times a year. $2696.00. Butterworth Heinemann Publishers, Linacre House Jordan Hill, Oxford OX2 8DP United Kingdom. **Tel** 011 44 1865 310366, FAX 011 44 1865 310898. **(Subscription address:** Elsevier Science Ltd. / Oxford Fulfillment Centre, PO Box 800, Kidlington OX5 1DX United Kingdom. **Tel** 011 44 865 843355.) Index available. **Ad Acc.** available on microfilm and microfiche from University Microfilms International (UMI); available on an online database from Elsevier Electronic Subscriptions (EES). Documents available from Article Express International, The Genuine Article, Ask*IEEE, CASDDS. ***Absorbed** Polymer Communications, 0263-6476.*
Desc: International journal for the science and technology of polymers. The scope includes: synthesis, characterization, morphology and structure, physical and mechanical properties, polymer applications, reaction and kinetics, structural analysis, polymer engineering, and polymer processing.
Ind/Abst Abstr. Bull. Inst. Pap. Sci. Tech.; Acoust. Abstr.; AGRICOLA; Art Archaeol. Tech. Abstr.; Bioeng. Abstr.; Chem. Abstr.; Curr. Cit.; Curr. Contents Phys. Chem. Earth Sci.; Ei Page One; Eng. Index Annu.; INSPEC (Jan. 1971-); Polymer Contents; Res. Alert [Full Cov.]; Sci. Cit. Index; SCISEARCH; Text. Technol. Dig.; World Surf. Coat. Abstr.; World Text. Abstr.

LC QD380 .P64 **ISSN** 0032-3896
DD 547/.84/05 JA
CCC
CODEN POLJB8
Pr Rev.
POLYMER JOURNAL. [Polym. j.]. **Added/Corp** Kobunshi Gakkai. Vol. 1 (Jan. 1970)-. Periodical. English. Twelve times a year. $575.00. The Society of Polymer Science, Japan (SPSJ), Tsukiji Daisan Nagaoka Building, 2-4-2 Tsukiji Chuo-ku, Tokyo 03-3502-6471 Japan. **Tel** 011 81 3 35026471, FAX 011 81 3 35932709. **(Subscription address:** Maruzen Company Ltd., PO Box 5050, Import & Export Department, Tokyo 100 31 Japan. **Tel** 011 81 3 32789224.) **ED** T. Saegusa. **Ad Acc.** Documents available from Article Express International, The Genuine Article, CASDDS.
Desc: Published for the purpose of encouragement of

research by younger scientists in the field of polymer science.
Ind/Abst Abstr. Bull. Inst. Pap. Sci. Tech.; Bioeng. Abstr.; Chem. Abstr.; Chem. Titles; Curr. Cit.; Curr. Contents Phys. Chem. Earth Sci.; Ei Page One; EMBASE; Eng. Mater. Abstr.; Eng. Index Annu.; Polymer Contents; Res. Alert [Full Cov.]; Sci. Cit. Index; SCISEARCH; Text. Technol. Dig.

ISSN 0275-5777
US

POLYMER MONOGRAPHS (NEW YORK, N.Y. : 1981). (POLYMER MONOGRAPHS.). [Polym. monogr.]. (1981)-. Monographic series. English. Irregular. Price varies per volume. Gordon & Breach Science Publishers, Inc., PO Box 786, Cooper Station, New York NY 10276. **Tel** (212)206-8900, FAX (212)645-2459. Documents available from Ask*IEEE.

DD 547.7/05 **ISSN** 1181-9510
CN
CCC
CODEN PNBLES
Pr Rev.

POLYMER NETWORKS & BLENDS. [Polym. netw. blends]. **VFOAT** Polymer Networks and Blends. Vol. 1, No. 1 (1991)-. Periodical. English. Four times a year. 175.00Can$. Chemtec Publishing, 38 Earswick Drive, Toronto Ontario M1E 1C6 Canada. **Tel** (416)265-2603, FAX (416)265-1399. **ED** George Wypych. Index available. cum. index. **Bk Rev. Ad Acc.** Documents available from Article Express International, The Genuine Article.
Desc: Information regarding the fact that by the end of this century 90% of polymers will be processed in form of blends of composites. Includes papers which facilitate development of modern industry.
Ind/Abst Civ. Struct. Eng. Abstr.; Elect. Comm. Abstr.; Eng. Index Annu.; Mater. Sci. Eng. Abstr.; Mech. Eng. Abstr.; Res. Alert [Full Cov.].

LC QD380 .P654 **ISSN** 0738-1743
DD 547.7 SZ

POLYMER YEARBOOK. [Polym. yearb.]. 1st Ed. (1984)-. Periodical. English. Irregular. Harwood Academic Publishers / New York, PO Box 786, Cooper Station, New York NY 10276. **Tel** (212)206-8900, (201)643-7500. **ED** Richard A. Pethrick.
Desc: A desk-reference annual that helps keep the polymer scientist abreast of the latest developments by reporting current information.

LC QC482.D5 P644 **ISSN** 1084-3159
DD 547.3/08586 US

•**POWDER DIFFRACTION FILE. ORGANIC AND ORGANOMETALLIC PHASES SEARCH MANUAL. HANAWALT INDEX, ALPHABETICAL INDEX, AND ORGANIC FORMULA INDEX.** [Powder diffr. file, Org. organomet. phases search man., Hanawalt index alph. index org. formula index]. **Added/Corp** JCPDS--International Centre for Diffraction Data. American Ceramic Society. **VFOAT** Organic and Organometallic Phases. Hanawalt Numerical, Alphabetical Index, and Organic Formula Index, Powder Diffraction file; Organic and Organometallic Phases; Organic and Organometallic Phases Search Manual; Hanawalt Index, Alphabetical Index, and Organic Formula Index; Hanawalt Numerical, Alphabetical Index, and Organic Formula Index. (1994)-. English. Joint Committee on Powder Diffraction Standards / JCPDS, International Centre for Diffraction Data, 12 Campus Boulevard, Newton Square PA 19073. **Tel** (610)325-9810, FAX (610)325-9823, telex 847170. ***Continues*** *Powder Diffraction File Organic Phases Search Manual. Hanawalt, Alphabetical, Formulae, 0736-0851.*

LC QC482.D5 P644 **ISSN** 0736-0851
DD 547.3/08586 US
TITLE CHANGE

POWDER DIFFRACTION FILE ORGANIC PHASES SEARCH MANUAL. HANAWALT, ALPHABETICAL, FORMULAE. [Powder diffr. file org. phases search man., Hanawalt, alph., formulae]. **Added/Corp** JCPDS--International Centre for Diffraction Data. **VFOAT** Powder Diffraction File; Organic Phases Search Manual. Hanawalt, Alphabetical, Formulae; Hanawalt, Alphabetical, Formulae; Search Manual (Hanawalt). Alphabetical and Formulae Indexes; Alphabetical and Formulae Indexes; Organic and Organometallic Phases, Search Manual (Hanawalt), Alphabetical and Formulae Indexes; Search Manual (Hanawalt), Alphabetical and Formulae Indexes; Powder Diffraction File, Organic and Organometallic Phases Search Manual (Hanawalt) Alphabetical and Formulae Indexes. (1980)-(199?). English. Joint Committee on Powder Diffraction Standards / JCPDS, International Centre for Diffraction Data, 12 Campus Boulevard, Newton Square PA 19073. **Tel** (610)325-9810, FAX (610)325-9823, telex 847170. ***Continues*** *Powder Diffraction File Organic Materials Search Manual. Hanawalt, Alphabetical, Formulae.* ***Continued by*** *Powder Diffraction File. Organic and Organometallic Phases Search Manual. Hanawalt Index, Alphabetical Index, and Organic Formula Index, 1084-3159.*

LC QC482.D5 P65 **ISSN** 0092-0576
DD 547/.34/66 US
Pr Rev.

POWDER DIFFRACTION FILE SEARCH MANUAL : ORGANIC AND ORGANOMETALLIC. [Powder diff. file search man., Org.]. **Added/Corp** Joint Committee on Powder Diffraction Standards. **VFOAT** Powder Diffraction File Search Manual (Numerical, Alphabetical, Formulae). (19??)-. English. One time a year. $300.00. Joint Committee on Powder Diffraction Standards / JCPDS, International Centre for Diffraction Data, 12 Campus Boulevard, Newton Square PA 19073. **Tel** (610)325-9810, FAX (610)325-9823, telex 847170. **Acid Free.** available on magnetic tape and CD-ROM; available on microfilm.
Desc: Alphabetical listing - one entry for each phase in alphabetical order of the chemical name.

JA

PROCEEDINGS OF THE SYMPOSIUM ON SOLVENT EXTRACTION. (19??)-. Proceedings. English. One time a year. ¥6500.00. Japanese Association of Solvent Extraction, Nihon Yobai Chushutsu Gakkai, Shizuoka Daigaku Kogakubu Oyokagakka, 5-1 Johoku 3-chome, Hamamatsu-shi, Shizuoka-ken 432 Japan.
Ind/Abst Curr. Cit.

LC QD301 .P69 **ISSN** 0163-7827
DD 574.1/9247/05 UK
CCC
NLM W1 PR6705 **CODEN** PLIRDW
Pr Rev.

PROGRESS IN LIPID RESEARCH. [Prog. lipid res.]. Vol. 17 (1978)-. Academic Scholarly Publication. English. Four times a year. $605.00. Pergamon Press, An Imprint of Elsevier Science Ltd., The Boulevard, Langford Lane, Kidlington, Oxford OX5 1GB United Kingdom. **Tel** 011 44 1865 843000, 011 44 1865 843699, FAX 011 44 1865 843010. **(Subscription address:** Elsevier Science Ltd. / Oxford Fulfillment Centre, PO Box 800, Kidlington OX5 1DX United Kingdom. **Tel** 011 44 865 843355.) **ED** Ralph Holman. available on microfilm and microfiche from University Microfilms International (UMI); available on an online database from Elsevier Electronic Subscriptions (EES). Documents available from The Genuine Article, BIOSIS Document Express, CASDDS. ***Continues*** *Progress in the Chemistry of Fats and other Lipids, 0079-6832.*
Desc: Each volume contains surveys of special aspects of lipid research. Reviews are comprehensive enough to provide sufficient overview but concentrate on reporting and critically appraising the most recent data.
Ind/Abst AGRICOLA; Biol. Abstr.; Chem. Abstr.; Curr. Aware. Biol. Sci., CABS; Curr. Cit.; Curr. Contents Agric. Biol. Environ. Sci.; Curr. Contents Life Sci.; Dairy Sci. Abstr.; EMBASE; Food Sci. Technol. Abstr.; Index Med.; Index Sci. Rev. [Full Cov.]; NAPRALERT; Nutr. Abstr. Rev., Ser. A, Hum. Exp.; Ref. Upd. Deluxe Ed.; Res. Alert [Full Cov.]; Sci. Cit. Index; SCISEARCH.

LC QD330 .P76 **ISSN** 0195-4237
DD 547/.5/05 US
NLM W1 PR67087 **CODEN** PMCHDD

PROGRESS IN MACROCYCLIC CHEMISTRY. [Prog. macrocycl. chem.]. (1979)-. Academic Scholarly Publication. English. Irregular. Price varies per volume. John Wiley & Sons, Inc., 605 Third Avenue, New York NY 10158-0012. **Tel** (212)850-6000, (212)850-6645, FAX (212)850-6088, telex 12-7063. **(Subscription address:** John Wiley & Sons / UK, Baffins Lane, Chichester, West Sussex PO19 1UD United Kingdom. **Tel** 011 44 1243 779777, FAX 011 44 243 776128, telex 86290 WIBOOKG.) Documents available from CASDDS.
Ind/Abst Chem. Abstr.

LC QD476 .P74 **ISSN** 0079-6662
DD 547.1 US
NLM W1 PR677P **CODEN** PPOCA8

PROGRESS IN PHYSICAL ORGANIC CHEMISTRY. [Prog. phys. org. chem.]. **VFOAT** Physical Organic Chemistry. Vol. 1 (1963)-. English. Irregular. Price varies per volume. John Wiley & Sons, Inc., 605 Third Avenue, New York NY 10158-0012. **Tel** (212)850-6000, (212)850-6645, FAX (212)850-6088, telex 12-7063. **(Subscription address:** John Wiley & Sons / UK, Baffins Lane, Chichester, West Sussex PO19 1UD United Kingdom. **Tel** 011 44 1243 779777, FAX 011 44 243 776128, telex 86290 WIBOOKG.) **ED** S. G. Cohen, A. Streitwieser, and R. W. Taft. Documents available from CASDDS.
Ind/Abst Chem Inform; Chem. Abstr.; Index Sci. Rev. [Full Cov.].

LC QD281.P6 P75 **ISSN** 0079-6700
DD 547/.84/08 UK
CCC
NLM W1 PR677XK **CODEN** PRPSB8
Pr Rev.

PROGRESS IN POLYMER SCIENCE. [Prog. polym. sci.]. Vol. 1 (1967)-. English. Six times a year. $788.00. Pergamon Press, An Imprint of Elsevier Science Ltd., The Boulevard, Langford Lane, Kidlington, Oxford OX5 1GB United Kingdom. **Tel** 011 44 1865 843000, 011 44 1865 843699, FAX 011 44 1865 843010. **(Subscription address:** Elsevier Science Ltd. / Oxford Fulfillment Centre, PO Box 800, Kidlington OX5 1DX United Kingdom. **Tel** 011 44 865 843355.) **ED** O. Vogl. available on microfilm and microfiche from University Microfilms International (UMI); available on an online database from Elsevier Electronic Subscriptions (EES). Documents available from Article Express International, The Genuine Article, Ask*IEEE, CASDDS.
Desc: Publishes overview articles in polymer science and engineering.
Ind/Abst Bioeng. Abstr.; Chem. Abstr.; Curr. Cit.; Curr. Contents Phys. Chem. Earth Sci.; Ei Page One; Eng. Index Annu.; Highw. Res. Abstr.; INSPEC (1977-); Polymer Contents; Res. Alert [Full Cov.]; Sci. Cit. Index; SCISEARCH.

LC QD380 .P76 **ISSN** 0286-2999
DD 547 547/.84 JA
NLM W1 PR677XN **CODEN** PPSJBG

PROGRESS IN POLYMER SCIENCE, JAPAN. [Prog. polym. sci., Japan]. Vol. 1 (19??)-. Periodical. English. Irregular. Kodansha Ltd / Japan, 12-21 Otowa 2-chome, 112 Bunkyo-ku, Tokyo Japan. **Tel** 03 5395 3517, FAX 03 9466200, telex 22570. Documents available from CASDDS.
Ind/Abst Chem. Abstr.; Ei Page One.

ISSN 0165-2362
NE
CODEN PTOCD5
Pr Rev.

PROGRESS IN THEORETICAL ORGANIC CHEMISTRY. [Prog. theor. org. chem.]. (1976)-. Academic Scholarly Publication. English. Irregular. Price varies per volume. Elsevier Science Publishers BV, PO Box 211, 1000 AE Amsterdam Netherlands. **Tel** 011 31 20 4853641, 011 31 20 4853642, FAX 011 31 20 4853598. Documents available from Ask*IEEE, CASDDS.
Ind/Abst Chem. Abstr.; INSPEC.

LC QD415 **ISSN** 0929-8665
DD 574.192 NE
CCC
NLM W1; PR787H

•**PROTEIN AND PEPTIDE LETTERS.** Vol. 1, No. 1 (July 1994)-. Academic Scholarly Publication. English. Six times a year. $295.00. Bentham Science Publishers BV, PO Box 75676, 1118 Schiphol Netherlands. **Tel** 011 31 20 6720924.

LC QD380 .Q37 **ISSN** 0032-3977
DD 547/.84 UK
NLM Z 5524.P7 Q1

QUARTERLY LITERATURE REPORTS : POLYMERS. [Q. lit. rep., Polym.]. (1968)-. English. Four times a year. $20.00. Kogan Page Ltd., 120 Pentonville Road, London N1 9BR United Kingdom. **Tel** 011 44 171 2780433, FAX 011 44 171 8376348, telex 263088 KOGAN G.

NE

REACTIVE AND FUNCTIONAL POLYMERS. (199?)-. Academic Scholarly Publication. English. Nine times a year (3 vols.). Fl1335.00. Elsevier Science Publishers BV, PO Box 211, 1000 AE Amsterdam Netherlands. **Tel** 011 31 20 4853641, 011 31 20 4853642, FAX 011 31 20 4853598. available on an online database from Elsevier Electronic Subscriptions (EES). ***Continues*** *Reactive Polymers.*

LC QD380 **ISSN** 0923-1137
DD 547.7 NE
CCC
CODEN REPLEN
Pr Rev. **TITLE CHANGE**

REACTIVE POLYMERS. Vol. 10 No. 1 (March 1989)-(19??). Academic Scholarly Publication. English. Elsevier Science Publishers BV, PO Box 211, 1000 AE Amsterdam Netherlands. **Tel** 011 31 20 4853641, 011 31 20 4853642, FAX 011 31 20 4853598. **ED** A. Warshawsky. available on microfilm and microfiche from University Microfilms International (UMI). Documents available from Article Express International, The Genuine Article, CASDDS. ***Continues*** *Reactive Polymers, Ion Exchangers, Sorbents, 0167-6989.* ***Continued by*** *Reactive and Functional Polymers.*
Desc: Devoted to new ideas and developments in the science and technology of reactive and functioned polymers and ion-exchangers.
Ind/Abst Abstr. Bull. Inst. Pap. Sci. Tech.; Chem. Abstr.; Curr. Cit.; Curr. Contents Phys. Chem. Earth Sci.; Eng. Index Annu.; Res. Alert [Full Cov.]; Sci. Cit. Index; SCISEARCH.

ISSN 0341-2377
US
NLM W1 RE1J CODEN RSCCDS
REACTIVITY AND STRUCTURE. [React. struct.]. **VFOAT** Concepts in Organic Chemistry. Vol. 1 (1975)-. Academic Scholarly Publication. English. Irregular. Price varies per volume. Springer-Verlag New York Inc., 175 Fifth Avenue, New York NY 10010. **Tel** (212)460-1500 ext 256, FAX (212)533-3503, telex 232 235 SPB UR. **(Subscription address:** Springer-Verlag New York Inc. / North America, PO Box 2485, Journal Fulfillment, Secaucus NJ 07096. **Tel** (201)348-4033, (800)777-4643, FAX (201)348-4505.) Documents available from BIOSIS Document Express, CASDDS.
Desc: Contains topics on peptide synthesis, and organic synthesis.
Ind/Abst Biol. Abstr.; Chem. Abstr.

LC QD415.A1 R43 **ISSN** 0079-9947
HU
CODEN RDCCAM
RECENT DEVELOPMENTS IN THE CHEMISTRY OF NATURAL CARBON COMPOUNDS. [Recent dev. chem. nat. carbon compd.]. **Added/Corp** Magyar Tudomanyos Akademia. Kemiai Tudomanyok Osztalya. Vol. 1 (1965)-. Academic Scholarly Publication. English (Hungarian). Irregular. Price varies per volume. Akademiai Kiado, Publishing House of the Hungarian Academy of Sciences, Prielle Kornelia u. 19-35, H-1117 Budapest Hungary. **Tel** 011 36 1 1811991, FAX 011 36 1 1811991, telex 22-6228 AKNYO H. **(Subscription address:** Kultura, PO Box 143, H-1300 Budapest 3 Hungary. **Tel** 011 36 1 2500194.) Documents available from CASDDS.
Ind/Abst AGRICOLA; Chem. Abstr.

ISSN 0167-0115
NE
CCC
NLM W1 RE173JG **CODEN** REPPDY
Pr Rev.
REGULATORY PEPTIDES. [Regul. pept.]. Vol. 1, No. 1 (Aug. 1980)-. Academic Scholarly Publication. English. Twenty-one times a year. $1877.00. Elsevier Science Publishers BV, PO Box 211, 1000 AE Amsterdam Netherlands. **Tel** 011 31 20 4853641, 011 31 20 4853642, FAX 011 31 20 4853598. **ED** Floyd E Bloom, Rolf Hakanson, Marvin Brown, and Frank Sundler. available on microfilm and microfiche from University Microfilms International (UMI); available on an online database from Elsevier Electronic Subscriptions (EES). Documents available from The Genuine Article, BIOSIS Document Express, CASDDS, ADONIS.
Desc: Provides a medium for the rapid publication of interdisciplinary studies on the physiology and pathology of peptides of the gut, endocrine and nervous systems which regulate cell or tissue function.
Ind/Abst ADONIS; Biol. Abstr.; Chem. Abstr.; Chem. Titles; CSA Neuro. Abstr.; Curr. Aware. Biol. Sci., CABS; Curr. Cit.; Curr. Contents Life Sci.; Dairy Sci. Abstr.; EMBASE; Index Med.; Oncog. Growth Factors Abstr.; Life Sci. Collect.; Pig News Inf.; Ref. Upd. Basic Ed.; Ref. Upd. Deluxe Ed.; Res. Alert [Full Cov.]; Rev. Med. Vet. Entomol.; Sci. Cit. Index; SCISEARCH.

LC TP196 .A95b **ISSN** 0312-8466
DD 661/.8 AT
RESEARCH REPORT - DIVISION OF APPLIED ORGANIC CHEMISTRY.
Main/Corp Commonwealth Scientific and Industrial Research Organization. Division of Applied Organic Chemistry. (1974)-. English. Every 2 years. CSIRO Publications, PO Box 89, 314 Albert Street, East Melborne Victoria 3002 Australia. **Tel** 011 61 3 4187333, 4187217, FAX 011 61 3 4190459, telex AA 30236. ctrl circ.

LC QD1 .R32915 **ISSN** 0370-5943
DD 540.5/6 MX
CODEN RLAQA8
Pr Rev.
REVISTA LATINOAMERICANA DE QUIMICA. [Rev. latinoam. quim.]. **Added/Corp** Federacion Latinoamericana de Quimica. (1970)-. Periodical. Spanish (English; summaries and/or abstracts in English). Four times a year. $55.00. Federacion Latinoamericana de Quimica, Apartado 4606, Sucursal J, Monterrey NL Mexico. **Tel** 011 52 83 634926. **ED** Xorge A Dominguez. **Bk Rev. Ad Acc. Circ:** 2,000. Documents available from BIOSIS Document Express, CASDDS.
Desc: Original papers in organic chemistry, natural products, biochemistry, and chemotaxonomy.
Ind/Abst Biol. Abstr.; Chem. Abstr.; Curr. Cit.; Food Sci. Technol. Abstr.; Life Sci. Collect.

LC QD241 **ISSN** 0035-3000
DD 547 FR
CODEN RFCGAE
Pr Rev. **TITLE CHANGE**
REVUE FRANCAISE DES CORPS GRAS. [Rev. Fr. Corps Gras]. **Added/Corp** Institut des Corps Gras (Paris, France) Association Francaise pour l'Etude des Corps Gras. Federation Nationale des Industries de Corps Gras (France). (1954)-(19??). Academic Scholarly Publication. French (summaries and/or abstracts in English and German; table of contents in English). ETIG, 118 Avenue Achile Peretti, 92200 Neuilly Sur Seine France. **Tel** 011 33 1 46410544. Documents available from The Genuine Article, BIOSIS Document Express, CASDDS. ***Continues*** *Institut Technique d'Etudes et de Recherches des Corps Gras. Bulletin Mensuel de d'I.T.E.R.G., 0366-4449.* ***Merged with*** *Informations Techniques (Paris, France), 0374-1451* ***and*** *Oleagineux, 0030-2082* ***to form*** *OCL.*
Ind/Abst AGRICOLA (19??-); Biol. Abstr. (1989-); Chem. Abstr. (19??-); Curr. Cit.; Curr. Contents Agric. Biol. Environ. Sci. (19??-); EMBASE (19??-); Food Sci. Technol. Abstr. (19??-); Life Sci. Collect. (19??-); Res. Alert (19??-) [Select. Cov.]; Saf. Health Work (19??-); Soc. Sci. Cit. Index [Select. Cov.].

LC QD390 .R56 **ISSN** 0742-5996
DD 547/.5 US
CODEN RSHAEE
RING SYSTEMS HANDBOOK. [Ring syst. handb.]. **Added/Corp** American Chemical Society. Chemical Abstracts Service. **VFOAT** Ring Systems Hand Book. (1984)-. Periodical. English. Irregular. $670.00 (base book and supplements). Chemical Abstracts Service, (Subsidiary of The American Chemical Society), 2540 Olentangy River Road, PO Box 3012, Columbus OH 43210-0012. **Tel** (614)447-3731, (800)753-4227, FAX (614)447-3751. **(Subscription address:** Chemical Abstracts Service, Customer Service Department, PO Box 3012, Columbus OH 43210. **Tel** (800)848-6538, (614)447-3600.) **ED** David W Weisgerber. **Bk Rev.**
Desc: Current-awareness bulletins on 164 separately-subscribed-to topics. Contains CA abstracts and associated bibliographic information.

ISSN 8756-565X
US
CODEN RSHSEY
RING SYSTEMS HANDBOOK. SUPPLEMENT. [Ring syst handb., Suppl.]. **Added/Corp** American Chemical Society. Chemical Abstracts Service. No. 1 (1984)-. English. Two times a year. $330.00 (cumulative supplements only). Chemical Abstracts Service, (Subsidiary of The American Chemical Society), 2540 Olentangy River Road, PO Box 3012, Columbus OH 43210-0012. **Tel** (614)447-3731, (800)753-4227, FAX (614)447-3751. **(Subscription address:** Chemical Abstracts Service, Customer Service Department, PO Box 3012, Columbus OH 43210. **Tel** (800)848-6538, (614)447-3600.)

US
SADTLER STANDARD CARBON-13 NMR SPECTRA. **See** Chemistry and Chemicals-Analytical Chemistry.

US
SADTLER ULTRA VIOLET STANDARD SPECTRA. **See** Chemistry and Chemicals-Analytical Chemistry.

LC TP247 .S23 **ISSN** 0554-9728
XR
CODEN SVOCAF
SBORNIK VYSOKE SKOLY CHEMICKO-TECHNOLOGICKE V PRAZE. C, ORGANICKA CHEMIE A TECHNOLOGIE. [Sb. Vys. sk. chem.-technol. Praze, Org. chem. technol.]. **Added/Corp** Vysoka Skola Chemicko-Technologicka v Praze. **VFOAT** Organicka Chemie a Technologie; Organic Chemistry and Technology; Organicheskaia Khimiia; Scientific Papers of the Prague Institute of Chemical Technology. C, Organic Chemistry and Technology; Sbornik Prazhskogo Khimiko-Tekhnologicheskogo Instituta. C, Organicheskaia Khimiia. (1964)-. Periodical. Czech (English, French, German and Russian). Statni Pedagogicke Nakladatelstvi, Ostrovni 30, 113 01 Prague 1 Czech Republic. **Tel** (2)203787, FAX (2)293883. Documents available from CASDDS.
Ind/Abst Chem. Abstr.

LC QD380 .P72a **ISSN** 0139-908X
XR
CODEN SVSZD5
SBORNIK VYSOKE SKOLY CHEMICKO-TECHNOLOGICKE V PRAZE. POLYMERY-CHEMIE, VLASTNOSTI A ZPRACOVANI. [Sb. Vys. sk. chem.-technol. Praze, Polym.-chem. vlastn. zprac.]. **Main/Corp** Vysoka Skola Chemicko-Technologicka v Praze. **Added/Corp** Vysoka Skola Chemicko-Technologicka v Praze. Sbornik Prazhskogo khimiko-tekhnologicheskogo Instituta. Polimery-Khimiia, Svoista i Pererabotka. Vysoka Skola Chemicko-Technologicka v Praze. Scientific Papers of the Prague Institute of Chemical Technology. Polymers-Chemistry, Properties and Processing. **VFOAT** Sbornik Prazhskogo Khimiko-Tekhnologicheskogo Instituta. Polimery-Khimiia, Svoistva I Pererabotka; Scientific Papers of the Prague Institute of Chemical Technology. Technology. Polymers- Chemistry, Properties and Processing; Polymery-Chemie, Vlastnosti a Zpracovani. Vol. 1 (1978)-. Academic Scholarly Publication. Czech (English; summaries and/or abstracts in German). One time a year. kcs28.00. VSCHT, Suchbatarova 5, 166 28 Prague 6 Dejvice. **Tel** 1942 2 332 3221. **ED** J. Mostecky and J. Zachoval. **Ad Acc. Circ:** 300. Documents available from CASDDS.
Desc: Publishes original papers and reviews from the fields of polymer organic chemistry and physics, plastics and rubber processing, and polymer application in artistic work restoration.
Ind/Abst Chem. Abstr.

LC TP1 .Z6134 **ISSN** 0038-5344
DD 660/.05 US
UDC 66.0(47+57) **CCC**
CODEN SVCIA7
TITLE CHANGE
SOVIET CHEMICAL INDUSTRY, THE. **See** Chemistry and Chemicals-Inorganic Chemistry.

LC QD415.A1 **ISSN** 0360-4497
DD 547/.7/05 US
UDC 577.1 **CCC**
NLM W1 SO996JH **CODEN** SJBCD5
TITLE CHANGE
SOVIET JOURNAL OF BIOORGANIC CHEMISTRY. [Sov. j. bioorg. chem.]. Vol. 1 (Jan. 1975)-(199?). Academic Scholarly Publication. English (Russian). Plenum Press, 233 Spring Street, New York NY 10013-1578. **Tel** (212)620-8000, (800)221-9369, FAX (212)463-0742, (212)807-1047, telex 23/421139. **ED** V T Ivanov. Index available. available on microfilm and microfiche from University Microfilms International (UMI). Documents available from BIOSIS Document Express, CASDDS. ***Continued by*** *Russian Journal of Bioorganic Chemistry.*
Desc: Provides latest Soviet research in all areas and phases of bio-organic chemistry.
Ind/Abst AGRICOLA [Select. Cov.]; Biol. Abstr. (-1984); Chem. Abstr.; Curr. Biotechnol.; EMBASE; Mass Spect. Bull.

ISSN 0371-2192
RU
CODEN SPOKAV
SOVREMENNYE PROBLEMY ORGANICESKOJ HIMII. (SOVREMENNYE PROBLEMY ORGANICHESKOI KHIMII.). [Sovrem. probl. org. him.]. **Added/Corp** Leningradskii Gosudarstvennyi Universitet Imeni A.A. Zhdanova. (1969)-. Academic Scholarly Publication. Russian. Irregular. St. Petersburg State University / Izdatelstvo Leningradskogo Universiteta, Universitetskaia Nab 7/9, 199034 St. Petersburg Russia. **Tel** 011 7 812 2189788, FAX 011 7 812 2185152, telex 121481. Documents available from CASDDS.
Ind/Abst Chem. Abstr. (1969-1982).

US
STANDARD GRATING SPECTRA. **See** Chemistry and Chemicals-Analytical Chemistry.

GW
STEREOCHEMISTRY, FUNDAMENTALS AND METHODS. (1977)-. Monographic series. English. Irregular. Price varies per volume. Heyden & Son Ltd, Spectrum House, Hillview Gardens, London NW4 2JQ United Kingdom. **ED** Henri B Kagan.

ISSN 0165-3253
NE
CCC
NLM W1 ST931 **CODEN** SOCHDQ
Pr Rev.
STUDIES IN ORGANIC CHEMISTRY (AMSTERDAM). (STUDIES IN ORGANIC CHEMISTRY.). [Stud. org. chem.]. (1979)-. Monographic series. English. Irregular. Price varies per volume. Elsevier Science Publishers BV, PO Box 211, 1000 AE Amsterdam Netherlands. **Tel** 011 31 20 4853641, 011 31 20 4853642, FAX 011 31 20 4853598. **(Subscription address:** Elsevier Science Inc. / New York Books, 655 Avenue of the Americas, New York NY 10010. **Tel** (212)633-3650.) Documents available from BIOSIS Document Express, CASDDS.
Desc: Aims to publish books presenting information on organic chemistry. Previous volumes have covered polysaccharides, biocatalysis, photochromism, and much more.
Ind/Abst Biol. Abstr. (1987-); Chem. Abstr.; Curr. Cit.

LC QD380 .S85 **ISSN** 1061-0278
DD 547/.005 SW
CCC
CODEN SCHEER
•**SUPRAMOLECULAR CHEMISTRY.** [Supramol. chem.]. (1993)-. Academic Scholarly Publication. English. Irregular (four issues per volume). $265.00 (academic institutions), $413.00 (corporate institutions). Gordon & Breach Science Publishers, PO Box 90, Reading, Berkshire RG1 8JL United Kingdom. **Tel** 011 44 1734 560080, FAX 011 44 1734 568211. **(Subscription address:** Gordon & Breach Science Publishers / US, 820 Town Center Drive, Langhorne PA 19047. **Tel** (215)750-2642.)

Desc: Features contributions describing work that bridges the organic-inorganic, physical-organic or inorganic, bio-organic, bio-inorganic, biophysical, and biochemical fields where the emphasis remains chemical. Topics include macrocytes and more.

LC QD262 .S96 **ISSN** 0936-5214
GW
CCC
NLM W1; SY537 **CODEN** SYNLES

SYNLETT. [Synlett]. **VFOAT** Accounts and Rapid Communications in Synthetic Organic Chemistry. No. 1 (Jan. 1990)-. Academic Scholarly Publication. English. Twelve times a year. $365.00. Georg Thieme Verlag Stuttgart, Postfach 301120, D-70451 Stuttgart Germany. **Tel** 011 49 711 89310, FAX 011 49 711 8931298, telex 7 252 275 GTVD. **(Subscription address:** Thieme Medical Publishers Inc., 381 Park Avenue South, New York NY 10016. **Tel** (212)683-5088.) **ED** K P C Vollhardt, B Giese, S Ley, V A Snieckus, H Yamamoto. available on microfilm and microfiche from University Microfilms International (UMI). Documents available from The Genuine Article, BIOSIS Document Express, CASDDS, ADONIS.
Desc: Of interest to organic chemists, in general, and all chemists at universities, research institutions, and in industry who are engaged in the preparative aspects of organic, organoelement, organometallic, biological, and medicinal chemistry, as well as polymers and new materials.
Ind/Abst Abstr. Bull. Inst. Pap. Sci. Tech.; ADONIS; Biol. Abstr. (1990-); Chem. Abstr.; Curr. Chem. React.; Curr. Cit.; Curr. Contents Phys. Chem. Earth Sci.; Index Chem.; Res. Alert [Full Cov.]; Sci. Cit. Index; SCISEARCH.

LC QD262 .S93 **ISSN** 0039-7881
DD 547/.2/05 GW
CCC
NLM W1 SY66H **CODEN** SYNTBF
Pr Rev.

SYNTHESIS (STUTTGART). (SYNTHESIS.). [Synthesis]. (1969)-. Academic Scholarly Publication. English (German). Twelve times a year. $687.00. Georg Thieme Verlag Stuttgart, Postfach 301120, D-70451 Stuttgart Germany. **Tel** 011 49 711 89310, FAX 011 49 711 8931298, telex 7 252 275 GTVD. **(Subscription address:** Thieme Medical Publishers Inc., 381 Park Avenue South, New York NY 10016. **Tel** (212)683-5088.) **ED** M Regitz, D Enders, D Hoppe, P J Kocienski, I Kuwajima, P A Wender. **Circ:** 3,200. available on microfilm and microfiche from University Microfilms International (UMI). Documents available from The Genuine Article, BIOSIS Document Express, CASDDS, ADONIS.
Desc: Latest advances in synthetic organic chemistry both in original papers and abstracts.
Ind/Abst Abstr. Bull. Inst. Pap. Sci. Tech.; ADONIS; Biol. Abstr.; Chem. Abstr.; Curr. Chem. React.; Curr. Cit.; Curr. Contents Life Sci.; Curr. Contents Phys. Chem. Earth Sci.; EMBASE; Index Chem.; Int. Aerosp. Abstr.; Mass Spect. Bull.; Methods Organ. Synth.; Nat. Prod. Updates; Life Sci. Collect.; Res. Alert [Full Cov.]; Sci. Cit. Index; SCISEARCH.

LC QD262 .S935 **ISSN** 0039-7911
DD 547/.2/05 US
CCC
CODEN SYNCAV
Pr Rev.

SYNTHETIC COMMUNICATIONS. [Synth. commun.]. Vol. 1 (1971)-. Academic Scholarly Publication. English. Twenty-four times a year. $1335.00. Marcel Dekker Inc., 270 Madison Avenue, New York NY 10016. **Tel** (212)696-9000, (800)228-1160, FAX (212)685-4540, telex 421419. **(Subscription address:** Marcel Dekker Inc., PO Box 5017, Monticello NY 12701. **Tel** (800)228-1160.) **ED** James A. Marshall. **Bk Rev. Ad Acc.** ctrl circ. available on microfiche. Documents available from The Genuine Article, BIOSIS Document Express, CASDDS, ADONIS.
Desc: Presents timely and extensive coverage on a broad range of topics, ranging from the synthesis of natural products and related intermediates to the synthesis and utilization of new reagents for functional group interconversions. Featuring in-depth reporting on new experimental methods and reagents pertaining to synthetic organic chemistry, each paper in this journal is profusely illustrated, greatly simplifying the task of organizing and processing the new information presented in each issue.
Ind/Abst ADONIS; AGRICOLA; Biol. Abstr.; Chem Inform; Chem. Abstr.; Chem. Titles; Curr. Chem. React.; Curr. Cit.; Curr. Contents Phys. Chem. Earth Sci.; EMBASE; Index Chem.; Int. Aerosp. Abstr.; Mass Spect. Bull. (?-?); Methods Organ. Synth.; Nat. Prod. Updates; PESTDOC; Res. Alert [Full Cov.]; Sci. Cit. Index; SCISEARCH.

US

SYNTHETIC ORGANIC CHEMICALS; UNITED STATES PRODUCTION AND SALES OF CYCLIC INTERMEDIATES. PRELIMINARY. **Added/Corp** United States International Trade Commission. **VFOAT** Cyclic Intermediates. (19??)-. Periodical. English. United States International Trade Commission, 500 E Street Southwest, Washington DC 20436. **Tel** (202)205-1806.

US

TECHNIQUES AND APPLICATIONS IN ORGANIC SYNTHESIS SERIES.
Monographic series. English. Irregular. Price varies per volume. Marcel Dekker Inc., 270 Madison Avenue, New York NY 10016. **Tel** (212)696-9000, (800)228-1160, FAX (212)685-4540, telex 421419. **(Subscription address:** Marcel Dekker Inc., PO Box 5017, Monticello NY 12701. **Tel** (800)228-1160.)
Desc: Topics covered have included catalytic hydrogenation, oxidation, and organic electrochemistry.

ISSN 1080-8914
DD 547 US
NLM W1; TE197CM

TECHNIQUES IN PROTEIN CHEMISTRY. [Tech. protein chem.]. **Added/Corp** Protein Society. Meeting. 1st (1989)-. English. Academic Press Inc., 6277 Sea Harbor Drive, Orlando FL 32887. **Tel** (800)543-9534, (407)345-4100, FAX (407)352-3445.
Ind/Abst Curr. Cit.

LC QD504 .T77

RU
CODEN TOSOD2

TERMODINAMIKA ORGANICHESKIKH SOEDINENII. **Added/Corp** Gorkovskii Gosudarstvennyi Universitet Imeni N.I. Lobachevskogo. Vol. 5 (1976)-. Academic Scholarly Publication. Russian. Ministerstvo Vyshego I Srednego Spetsialnogo Obrazovaniia, Prospekt Gagarina, D 23 Korpus 5, Nizhni Novgorod Russia. Documents available from CASDDS. ***Continues*** *Trudy Po Khimii i Khimicheskoi Tekhnologii.*
Ind/Abst Chem. Abstr.

LC QD241 .T4 **ISSN** 0040-4020
DD 547.05 UK
CCC
NLM W1 TE636 **CODEN** TETRAB

TETRAHEDRON. [Tetrahedron]. Vol. 1 (April 1957)-. Academic Scholarly Publication. English (French and German). Sixty times a year. $7330.00. Pergamon Press, An Imprint of Elsevier Science Ltd., The Boulevard, Langford Lane, Kidlington, Oxford OX5 1GB United Kingdom. **Tel** 011 44 1865 843000, 011 44 1865 843699, FAX 011 44 1865 843010. **(Subscription address:** Elsevier Science Ltd. / Oxford Fulfillment Centre, PO Box 800, Kidlington OX5 1DX United Kingdom. **Tel** 011 44 865 843355.) **ED** Sir Robert Robinson, R. B. Woodward and Sir Derek Barton. cum. index. available on microfilm and microfiche from University Microfilms International (UMI); available on microfiche from the publisher; available on an online database from Elsevier Electronic Subscriptions (EES). Documents available from The Genuine Article, BIOSIS Document Express, CASDDS, ADONIS. ***Continued in part by*** *Tetrahedron Letters, 0040-4039.*
Desc: Publishes experimental and theoretical research results of outstanding significance and timeliness in the field of organic chemistry and its application to related disciplines especially bio-organic chemistry. Areas covered by the journal include the many facets of organic synthesis, organic reactions, natural products chemistry, studies of reaction mechanism and the various aspects of spectroscopy.
Ind/Abst ADONIS; AgBiotech News Inf.; AGRICOLA; Agrofor. Abstr. (19??-19??); Biol. Abstr.; Chem Inform; Chem. Abstr.; Chem. Titles; Curr. Aware. Biol. Sci., CABS; Curr. Biotechnol.; Curr. Chem. React.; Curr. Cit.; Curr. Contents Life Sci.; Curr. Contents Phys. Chem. Earth Sci.; EMBASE; For. Prod. Abstr. (19??-19??); For. Abstr.; Hortic. Abstr.; Index Chem.; Mass Spect. Bull.; Methods Organ. Synth.; NAPRALERT; Nat. Prod. Updates; Ornamental Hort.; Life Sci. Collect.; PESTDOC; Protozoolog. Abstr.; Ref. Upd. Deluxe Ed.; Res. Alert [Full Cov.]; Rev. Agric. Entomol.; Rev. Med. Vet. Entomol.; Rev. Med. Vet. Mycology; Rev. Plant Pathol.; Sci. Cit. Index; SCISEARCH.

LC QD241 .T42 **ISSN** 0040-4039
DD 547.05 UK
CCC
NLM W1 TE637 **CODEN** TELEAY
Pr Rev.

TETRAHEDRON LETTERS.
(TETRAHEDRON LETTERS; THE INTERNATIONAL ORGAN FOR THE RAPID PUBLICATION OF PRELIMINARY COMMUNICATIONS IN ORGANIC CHEMISTRY.). [Tetrahedron lett.]. No. 1 (March 1959)-. Academic Scholarly Publication. English (French and German). One time a week. $6003.00. Pergamon Press, An Imprint of Elsevier Science Ltd., The Boulevard, Langford Lane, Kidlington, Oxford OX5 1GB United Kingdom. **Tel** 011 44 1865 843000, 011 44 1865 843699, FAX 011 44 1865 843010. **(Subscription address:** Elsevier Science Ltd. / Oxford Fulfillment Centre, PO Box 800, Kidlington OX5 1DX United Kingdom. **Tel** 011 44 865 843355.) **ED** Sir Robert Robinson, R. B. Woodward and Sir Derek Barton. available on microfilm and microfiche from University Microfilms International (UMI); available on microfiche from the publisher; available on an online database from Elsevier Electronic Subscriptions (EES). Documents available from The Genuine Article, BIOSIS Document Express, CASDDS, ADONIS. ***Continues in part*** *Tetrahedron, 0040-4020.*
Desc: Provides maximum dissemination of outstanding developments in organic chemistry. Covers developments in techniques, structures, methods and conclusions in experimental and theoretical organic chemistry. Rapid publication of timely and significant research results enables researchers from all over the world to transmit quickly their new contributions to large, international audiences.
Ind/Abst Abstr. Bull. Inst. Pap. Sci. Tech.; ADONIS; AGRICOLA [Select. Cov.]; Agrofor. Abstr. (19??-19??); Biol. Abstr.; Chem Inform; Chem. Abstr.; Chem. Titles; Coal Abstr.; Crop Physiol. Abstr.; Curr. Aware. Biol. Sci., CABS; Curr. Biotechnol.; Curr. Chem. React.; Curr. Cit.; Curr. Contents Life Sci.; Curr. Contents Phys. Chem. Earth Sci.; EMBASE; For. Prod. Abstr. (19??-19??); For. Abstr.; Helminthol. Abstr. (1991-); Hortic. Abstr.; Index Chem.; Int. Aerosp. Abstr.; Methods Organ. Synth.; NAPRALERT; Nat. Prod. Updates; Ornamental Hort. (1991-); Life Sci. Collect.; PESTDOC; Protozoolog. Abstr.; Ref. Upd. Basic Ed.; Ref. Upd. Deluxe Ed.; Res. Alert [Full Cov.]; Rev. Agric. Entomol.; Rev. Med. Vet. Entomol.; Rev. Med. Vet. Mycology; Rev. Plant Pathol.; Rice Abstr.; Sci. Cit. Index; SCISEARCH.

LC QD241 **ISSN** 0040-4039
DD 547 UK
CCC
CODEN TELEAY

TETRAHEDRON LETTERS.
(TETRAHEDRON LETTERS [MICROFORM].). [Tetrahedron lett.]. (Mar. 1959)-. Periodical. English (French and German). One time a week. £2748.00 UK; £4096.00 Americas. Pergamon Press, An Imprint of Elsevier Science Ltd., The Boulevard, Langford Lane, Kidlington, Oxford OX5 1GB United Kingdom. **Tel** 011 44 1865 843000, 011 44 1865 843699, FAX 011 44 1865 843010. **(Subscription address:** Elsevier Science Ltd. / Oxford Fulfillment Centre, PO Box 800, Kidlington OX5 1DX United Kingdom. **Tel** 011 44 865 843355.) Documents available from BIOSIS Document Express, CASDDS. ***Continues in part*** *Tetrahedron, 0040-4020.*
Ind/Abst AGRICOLA; Biol. Abstr.; Chem. Abstr.

LC QD262 .S94 **ISSN** 0253-200X
DD 547.2/05 SZ
CCC
NLM W1; TH118S

THEILHEIMER'S SYNTHETIC METHODS OF ORGANIC CHEMISTRY.
[Theilheimer synth. meth. org. chem.]. **VFOAT** Synthetic Methods of Organic Chemistry; Synthetische Methoden der Organischen Chemie. Vol. 36 (1982)-. English (summaries and/or abstracts in German). One time a year. 800.00F (approx. per volume). S. Karger AG, Allschwilerstrasse 10, PO Box, CH-4009 Basel Switzerland. **Tel** 011 41 61 3061111, FAX 011 41 61 3061234, telex CH 962 652. **ED** A. F. Finch. available on microfilm; available on an online database from ORBIT. Documents available from BIOSIS Document Express. ***Continues*** *Synthetic Methods of Organic Chemistry, 0032-1136.*
Desc: Each yearbook presents abstracts published in major journals during the previous year, accompanied by brief structural representations depicting the starting materials and the product of the reaction, permitting a rapid visualization of the structural change achieved by the method.
Ind/Abst Biol. Abstr.; Ref. Upd. Deluxe Ed.

US
NLM W1 TO539R
CEASED

TOPICS IN LIPID CHEMISTRY. Vol. 1 (1970)-Completed series. English. John Wiley & Sons, Inc., 605 Third Avenue, New York NY 10158-0012. **Tel** (212)850-6000, (212)850-6645, FAX (212)850-6088, telex 12-7063. **(Subscription address:** John Wiley & Sons / UK, Baffins Lane, Chichester, West Sussex PO19 1UD United Kingdom. **Tel** 011 44 1243 779777, FAX 011 44 243 776128, telex 86290 WIBOOKG.) **ED** F.D. Gunstone.

UK
CEASED

TOPICS IN PHYSICAL ORGANOMETALLIC CHEMISTRY.
(1985)-Series completed with Vol. 4 (1993). Monographic series. English. Freund Publishing House Ltd., PO Box 35010, 61 Nachmani Street, Tel Aviv 61350 Israel. **Tel** 011 972 3 5628540, FAX 011 972 3 5628538. **ED** Marcel F. Gielen.

LC QD481 .T6 **ISSN** 0082-500X
DD 547/.1223 US
NLM W1 TO54U **CODEN** TOSTBF

TOPICS IN STEREOCHEMISTRY. [Top. stereochem.]. Vol. 1 (1967)-. Monographic series. English. Irregular. Price varies per volume. John Wiley & Sons, Inc., 605 Third Avenue, New York NY 10158-0012. **Tel** (212)850-6000, (212)850-6645, FAX (212)850-6088, telex 12-7063. **(Subscription address:** John Wiley & Sons / UK, Baffins Lane, Chichester, West Sussex PO19 1UD United Kingdom. **Tel** 011 44 1243 779777, FAX 011 44 243 776128, telex 86290 WIBOOKG.) cum. index. Documents available from The Genuine Article,

CASDDS.
Ind/Abst Chem. Abstr.; Res. Alert [Full Cov.]; Sci. Cit. Index (19??-19??); SCISEARCH.

ISSN 0915-7352
DD 547.78 664 JA

TRENDS IN GLYCOSCIENCE AND GLYCOTECHNOLOGY. [Trends glycosci. glycotechnol.]. **VFOAT** TIGG. Trends in Glycoscience and Glycotechnology. (1989)-. Periodical. Multiple languages. Six times a year. Comes with FCCA membership. FCCA, 3 10 1 Koufudai Fujishirocho, Ibaraki Ken 300 15 Japan. **Tel** 011 81 297837635.
Ind/Abst Curr. Cit.

ISSN 0966-4793
DD 547.7005 UK
CCC

TRENDS IN POLYMER SCIENCE REGULAR ED. (TRENDS IN POLYMER SCIENCE.). [Trends polym. sci. Regul. ed.]. Volume 1 (1993)-. Academic Scholarly Publication. English. Twelve times a year. $632.00. Elsevier Trends Journals, An Imprint of Elsevier Science Ltd., The Boulevard, Langford Lane, Kidlington, Oxford OX5 1GB United Kingdom. **Tel** 011 44 1865 843000, 011 44 1865 843699, FAX 011 44 1865 843010. **(Subscription address:** Elsevier Science Ltd. / Oxford Fulfillment Centre, PO Box 800, Kidlington OX5 1DX United Kingdom. **Tel** 011 44 865 843355.**) ED** W. Hawthorne. Index available. available on an online database from Elsevier Electronic Subscriptions (EES). Documents available from CASDDS.
Desc: Current awareness journal for polymer scientists.
Ind/Abst Chem. Abstr.; Res. Alert.

LC QD
DD 547 UK

WORLDWIDE DIRECTORY OF AGROBIOLOGICALS, THE. (1991)-. Directory. English. One time a year. £95.00. C P L Scientific Ltd., 43 Kingfisher Court, Hambridge Road, Newbury, Berkshire RG14 5SJ United Kingdom. **Tel** 011 44 1635 524064, FAX 011 44 1635 529322. **ED** S.G. Lisnasky and J.Coombs.
Desc: Contains listings for over 1,000 biological and nonsynthetic chemical products for use in agriculture, horticulture, forestry, and gardening

ISSN 0749-503X
DD 547 UK
CCC
NLM W1; YE463H **CODEN** YESTE3
Pr Rev.

YEAST CHICHESTER (WEST SUSSEX). (YEAST.). [Yeast]. Vol. 1, No. 1 (Sept. 1985)-. Academic Scholarly Publication. English. Sixteen times a year. $835.00. John Wiley & Sons Ltd., Baffins Lane, Chichester, West Sussex PO19 1UD United Kingdom. **Tel** 011 44 1243 779777, FAX 011 44 1243 776128 BTG:JWP001, telex 86290 WIBOOKG. **(Subscription address:** John Wiley & Sons, Inc. / Philadelphia, PO Box 7247, Philadelphia PA 19170. **Tel** (212)850-6645, (800)225-5945.**) ED** S. G. Oliver and R. Wickner. available on microfilm and microfiche from University Microfilms International (UMI). Documents available from BIOSIS Document Express, CASDDS, ADONIS.
Desc: Contains original research articles along with major and minor reviews and short communications on all aspects of saccharomyces and other yeast genera. By focusing on the most significant developments in this research area the journal is aimed at those wishing to keep up to date in the field.
Ind/Abst ADONIS; Biol. Abstr. (1989-); Chem. Abstr. (1985); Curr. Aware. Biol. Sci., CABS; Curr. Cit.; Curr. Contents Agric. Biol. Environ. Sci.; Curr. Contents Life Sci.; EMBASE; Food Sci. Technol. Abstr.; Index Med. (1985-); Nucl. Acids Abstr.; PESTDOC; Ref. Upd. Deluxe Ed.; Sci. Cit. Index; SCISEARCH.

ISSN 0253-2786
CC
CODEN YCHHDX

YOUJI HUAXUE. (YU CHI HUA HSUEH.). [Youji huaxue]. **Added/Corp** Shang-Hai Yu Chi Hua Hsueh Yen Chiu So. **VFOAT** Organic Chemistry; Yuji Huaxue. (19??)-. Periodical. Chinese (summaries and/or abstracts in English). Six times a year. $47.60. Science Press, 16 Donghuangchenggen North Street, Beijing 100707, People's Republic of China. **Tel** 011 86 1 4019821, 011 86 1 4010642, FAX 011 86 1 4012180, 011 86 1 4019810, telex 210147. **(Subscription address:** China International Book Trading Corporation, PO Box 399, Library Service Department, Beijing 100044 People's Republic of China. **Tel** 011 86 1 8414284, FAX 011 86 1 8412023, telex 22496 CIBTC CN.) Documents available from CASDDS.
Ind/Abst Chem. Abstr.

ISSN 0037-9980
JA
CCC
NLM W1 YU605 **CODEN** YGKKAE
Pr Rev.

YUKI GOSEI KAGAKU KYOKAISHI. **Main/Corp** Yuki Gosei Kagaku Kyokai. **VFOAT** Journal of Synthetic Organic Chemistry, Japan. (1943)-. Periodical. Japanese. Twelve times a year. $340.00. Yuki Gosei Kagaku Kyokai, (Society of Synthetic Organic Chemistry Japan), 2-12 Azabudai 2 Chome, Minatoku Tokyo 106 Japan. **(Subscription address:** Maruzen Company Ltd., PO Box 5050, Import & Export Department, Tokyo 100 31 Japan. **Tel** 011 81 3 32789224.) Documents available from Article Express International, The Genuine Article, CASDDS.
Ind/Abst Chem. Abstr.; Chem. Titles; Curr. Chem. React.; Curr. Cit.; Ei Page One; Eng. Index Annu. [Select. Cov.]; Index Chem.; Mass Spect. Bull.; Methods Organ. Synth.; Nat. Prod. Updates; Res. Alert [Full Cov.]; Sci. Cit. Index; SCISEARCH.

ISSN 0514-7492
RU
CCC
NLM W1 ZH423K **CODEN** ZORKAE
Pr Rev.

ZURNAL ORGANICESKOJ HIMII. (ZHURNAL ORGANICHESKOI KHIMII.). [Z. org. him.]. **Added/Corp** Akademiia Nauk SSSR. Vol. 1 (1965)-. Academic Scholarly Publication. Russian. Twelve times a year. $400.00. Izdatelstvo Nauka / Akademiia Nauk, (Publishing House of the Russian Academy of Sciences), Leninskii Porspekt 14, 117901 Moscow Russia. **Tel** 011 95 9542153, FAX 011 95 9382144, telex 411964. **(Subscription address:** East View Publications Inc., 3020 Harbor Lane North, Suite 110, Minneapolis MN 55447. **Tel** (800)477-1005, (612)550-0961, FAX (612)559-2931.) available on microfilm. Documents available from The Genuine Article, CASDDS.
Ind/Abst Chem. Abstr.; Curr. Chem. React.; Curr. Contents Phys. Chem. Earth Sci.; Energy Res. Abstr.; Index Chem.; NAPRALERT; PESTDOC; Res. Alert [Full Cov.]; Sci. Cit. Index; SCISEARCH; Soc. Sci. Cit. Index [Select. Cov.].

PHYSICAL AND THEORETICAL CHEMISTRY

ISSN 0904-213X
DK
UDC 54 CCC
NLM W1; AC776C **CODEN** ACHSE7
Pr Rev.

ACTA CHEMICA SCANDINAVICA (COPENHAGEN, DENMARK : 1989). (ACTA CHEMICA SCANDINAVICA.). Vol. 43, No. 1 (Jan. 1989)-. Academic Scholarly Publication. English (French and German). Twelve times a year. $610.15. Munksgaard International Publishers Ltd, PO Box 2148, DK-1016 Copenhagen K Denmark. **Tel** 011 45 33 127030, FAX 011 45 33 129387, telex 19431 MUNKS DK. **ED** Lauri Niinisto and Lennart Eberson. Documents available from The Genuine Article, BIOSIS Document Express, CASDDS, ADONIS. ***Formed by the union of*** *Acta Chemica Scandinavica. Series B, Organic Chemistry and Biochemistry, 0302-4369* ***and*** *Acta Chemica Scandinavica. Series A, Physical and Inorganic Chemistry, 0302-4377.*
Ind/Abst ADONIS; Biol. Abstr.; Chem Inform; Chem. Abstr. (1989-); Curr. Chem. React.; Curr. Cit.; Curr. Contents Phys. Chem. Earth Sci.; Index Chem.; Index Med.; INIS Atomindex [Micro.]; Leadscan; Res. Alert [Full Cov.]; Sci. Cit. Index; SCISEARCH.

LC TP968 .A24 **ISSN** 0260-4450
DD 668.3/05 UK
CCC
CODEN ADHED5
Pr Rev.

ADHESION (LONDON). (ADHESION.). [Adhesion]. Vol. 1 (1977)-. Academic Scholarly Publication. English. Irregular. Price varies per volume. Routledge Chapman & Hall Inc., 29 West 35th Street, New York NY 10001. **Tel** (212)244-3336, (212)244-6412. Documents available from CASDDS. ***Continues*** *Aspects of Adhesion.*
Ind/Abst Chem. Abstr.

LC TP967 .A49 **ISSN** 0891-7760
DD 668/.3 UK

ADHESIVES ABSTRACTS. **See** Chemistry and Chemicals-Abstracting, Bibliographies and Statistics.

ISSN 0890-0884
DD 338 US

ADHESIVES & SEALANTS NEWSLETTER. [Adhes. sealants newsl.]. **VFOAT** Adhesives and Sealants Newsletter. (197?)-. Newsletter. English. Twelve times a year. $180.00. Adhesives Information Service Inc., PO Box 1123, Mishawaka IN 46546. **Tel** (219)255-6749. **ED** W. F. Harrington. **Bk Rev.**
Desc: Analyzes and condenses research reports, new books, journal articles, trade publications and product announcements so that you know what it means, not just what it says.

UK

ADHESIVES DIRECTORY; A DIRECTORY FOR THE INDUSTRIAL USER OF ADHESIVES. **VFOAT** Ad Adhesives Directory. (1966)-. Directory. English. One time a year (Jan.). $56.47. Turret Group, 177 Hagden Lane, Watford Hertfordshire WD1 8LN United Kingdom. **Tel** 011 44 1923 228577, FAX 011 44 1923 221346.

LC QD547 .A3613 **ISSN** 0092-8089
DD 541/.3453 US

ADSORPTION AND ADSORBENTS. No. 1 (1973)-. English. Irregular. Price varies per volume. John Wiley & Sons, Inc., 605 Third Avenue, New York NY 10158-0012. **Tel** (212)850-6000, (212)850-6645, FAX (212)850-6088, telex 12-7063. **(Subscription address:** John Wiley & Sons / UK, Baffins Lane, Chichester, West Sussex PO19 1UD United Kingdom. **Tel** 011 44 1243 779777, FAX 011 44 243 776128, telex 86290 WIBOOKG.)

LC QD501 .A33 **ISSN** 0360-0564
DD 541/.395/05 US
CCC
NLM W1 AD53H
Pr Rev.

ADVANCES IN CATALYSIS. [Adv. catal.]. Vol. 22 (1972)-. Monographic series. English. Irregular. Price varies per volume. Academic Press Inc., 6277 Sea Harbor Drive, Orlando FL 32887. **Tel** (800)543-9534, (407)345-4100, FAX (407)352-3445. Documents available from The Genuine Article, BIOSIS Document Express, CASDDS. ***Continues*** *Advances in Catalysis and Related Subjects, 0065-2342.*
Ind/Abst Biol. Abstr.; Chem. Abstr.; Curr. Chem. React.; Curr. Cit.; Index Sci. Rev. [Full Cov.]; Res. Alert [Full Cov.]; Sci. Cit. Index; SCISEARCH.

LC QD453 .A27 **ISSN** 0065-2385
DD 541 US
CCC
NLM W1 AD53L **CODEN** ADCPAA
Pr Rev.

ADVANCES IN CHEMICAL PHYSICS. [Adv. chem. phys.]. Vol. 1 (1958)-. Monographic series. English. Irregular. Price varies per volume. John Wiley & Sons Inc / New Jersey, 1 Wiley Drive, Somerset NJ 08875. **Tel** (800)225-5945, (908)469-4400. **(Subscription address:** John Wiley & Sons, Inc. / Philadelphia, PO Box 7247, Philadelphia PA 19170. **Tel** (212)850-6645, (800)225-5945.**) ED** I Prigogine. Documents available from The Genuine Article, BIOSIS Document Express, CASDDS.
Ind/Abst Biol. Abstr. (-1975); Chem. Abstr.; Curr. Cit.; Energy Res. Abstr.; Index Sci. Rev. [Full Cov.]; Mass Spect. Bull.; Math. Rev. (1987-); Res. Alert [Full Cov.]; Sci. Cit. Index (19??-19??); SCISEARCH.

LC QD501 .A343 **ISSN** 1066-5005
DD 541.3/94 US
CODEN ATMEE7

ADVANCES IN CLASSICAL TRAJECTORY METHODS. [Adv. class. traject. methods]. **VFOAT** Classical Trajectory Methods. Vol. 1 (1992)-. Academic Scholarly Publication. English. One time a year. $90.25. JAI Press Inc., 55 Old Post Road, Suite 2, PO Box 1678, Greenwich CT 06836-1678. **Tel** (203)661-7602, FAX (203)661-0792. **ED** William Hase. Documents available from CASDDS.
Ind/Abst Chem. Abstr.

LC QD506 .A33 **ISSN** 0001-8686
DD 541.3/45/05 NE
CCC
NLM W1; AD547 **CODEN** ACISB9
Pr Rev.

ADVANCES IN COLLOID AND INTERFACE SCIENCE. [Adv. colloid interface sci.]. Vol. 1 (March 1967)-. Academic Scholarly Publication. English. Eighteen times a year (6 volumes). $1433.00. Elsevier Science Publishers BV, PO Box 211, 1000 AE Amsterdam Netherlands. **Tel** 011 31 20 4853641, 011 31 20 4853642, FAX 011 31 20 4853598. **ED** Th.F. Tadros, T.G.M. van de Ven. **Bk Rev. Ad Acc.** available on microfilm and microfiche from University Microfilms International (UMI); available on an online database from Elsevier Electronic Subscriptions (EES). Documents available from Article Express International, The Genuine Article, Ask*IEEE, CASDDS.
Desc: An international journal for experimental and theoretical developments in interfacial and colloidal phenomena; their implications in biology, chemistry, physics and technology.
Ind/Abst Abstr. Bull. Inst. Pap. Sci. Tech.; Acoust. Abstr. (Feb. 1974-Nov. 1983); Bioeng. Abstr.; Chem. Abstr.; Chem. Titles (Feb. 1974-Nov. 1983); Curr. Cit.; Curr. Contents Phys. Chem. Earth Sci.; Ei Page One; Eng. Mater. Abstr.; Eng. Index Annu.; Index Med.; INSPEC (Feb. 1974-Nov. 1983); Int. Aerosp. Abstr.; Polymer Contents; Res. Alert [Full Cov.]; Sci. Cit. Index; SCISEARCH; World Surf. Coat. Abstr.

LC QD501 .A345 **ISSN** 1063-0619
DD 547.1/394 US
CODEN ADRMEC

ADVANCES IN DETAILED REACTION MECHANISMS. **See** Chemistry and Chemicals-Organic Chemistry.

LC QD63.O9 A38 ISSN 1061-8937
DD 541.3/93 US
CODEN AETCEX

ADVANCES IN ELECTRON TRANSFER CHEMISTRY. [Adv. electron transf. chem.]. **VFOAT** Electron Transfer Chemistry. Vol. 1 (1991)-. Academic Scholarly Publication. English. One time a year. $90.25. JAI Press Inc., 55 Old Post Road, Suite 2, PO Box 1678, Greenwich CT 06836-1678. **Tel** (203)661-7602, FAX (203)661-0792. **ED** Patrick Mariano. Documents available from CASDDS.
Desc: Focuses on chemical and biochemical aspects of electron transfer chemistry. Coverage spans the areas of organic, physical, inorganic, and biological chemistry.
Ind/Abst Chem. Abstr.

LC QP519.9.E434 A38 ISSN 0932-3031
DD 541.3/72 GW
UDC 543.545 CCC
NLM W1; AD554 CODEN ADELEC

ADVANCES IN ELECTROPHORESIS. [Adv. electrophor.]. Vol. 1 (1987)-. Academic Scholarly Publication. English. One time a year. Price varies per volume. VCH Gesellschaft GmbH, Postfach 101161, D-69451 Weinheim Germany. **Tel** 011 49 6201 606459, FAX 011 49 6201 606184. **(Subscription address:** VCH Publishers Inc., 303 Northwest 12th Avenue, Journals Department, Deerfield FL 33442. **Tel** (800)367-8249, (305)428-5566.) Documents available from CASDDS.
Ind/Abst Chem. Abstr.; Curr. Cit.

LC QD581 .A335 ISSN 0887-6193
DD 541/.0424 US
CODEN ALPAEM

ADVANCES IN LOW-TEMPERATURE PLASMA CHEMISTRY, TECHNOLOGY, APPLICATIONS. [Adv. low-temp. plasma chem. technol. appl.]. **VFOAT** Advances in Low Temperature Plasma Chemistry, Technology, Applications. Vol. 1 (1984)-. Periodical. English. Technomic Publishing Company, Inc., 851 New Holland Avenue, Box 3535, Lancaster PA 17604. **Tel** (717)291-5609, (800)233-9936, FAX (717)295-4538. Documents available from CASDDS.
Ind/Abst Chem. Abstr.

LC QD461 .A29 ISSN 1057-8951
DD 541.2/2 US
CODEN AMETEV

ADVANCES IN MOLECULAR ELECTRONIC STRUCTURE THEORY. [Adv. mol. electron. struct. theory]. Vol. 1 (1990)-. Periodical. English. One time a year. $90.25. JAI Press Inc., 55 Old Post Road, Suite 2, PO Box 1678, Greenwich CT 06836-1678. **Tel** (203)661-7602, FAX (203)661-0792. Documents available from CASDDS.
Ind/Abst Chem. Abstr.

LC QD461.5 .A35 ISSN 1063-5467
DD 541.2/2 US
CODEN AMVDEY

ADVANCES IN MOLECULAR VIBRATIONS AND COLLISION DYNAMICS. [Adv. mol. vib. collis. dyn.]. Vol. 1A (1991)-. Periodical. English. One time a year. $90.25. JAI Press Inc., 55 Old Post Road, Suite 2, PO Box 1678, Greenwich CT 06836-1678. **Tel** (203)661-7602, FAX (203)661-0792. **ED** Joel M. Bowman.

LC QD601.A1 A28 ISSN 0065-3152
DD 541.35082 US
CCC
NLM W1 AD781T CODEN ADPCA2

ADVANCES IN PHOTOCHEMISTRY. [Adv. photochem.]. Vol. 1 (1963)-. Monographic series. English. Irregular. Price varies per volume. John Wiley & Sons Inc / New Jersey, 1 Wiley Drive, Somerset NJ 08875. **Tel** (800)225-5945, (908)469-4400. Documents available from CASDDS.
Ind/Abst Chem Inform; Chem. Abstr.

LC QD476 .A4 ISSN 0065-3160
DD 547.1082 UK
UDC 547
NLM W1 AD782 CODEN APORAO
Pr Rev.

ADVANCES IN PHYSICAL ORGANIC CHEMISTRY. [Adv. phys. org. chem.]. **VFOAT** Physical Organic Chemistry. Vol. 1 (1963)-. Academic Scholarly Publication. English. Irregular. $95.00 (Vol. 29). Academic Press Inc., 6277 Sea Harbor Drive, Orlando FL 32887. **Tel** (800)543-9534, (407)345-4100, FAX (407)352-3445. **ED** V. Gold. Documents available from The Genuine Article, CASDDS.
Ind/Abst Chem Inform; Chem. Abstr.; Index Sci. Rev. [Full Cov.]; Res. Alert [Full Cov.]; Sci. Cit. Index; SCISEARCH.

LC QD453 .A28 ISSN 0065-3276
DD 541.383082 US
CCC
CODEN AQCHA9

ADVANCES IN QUANTUM CHEMISTRY. [Adv. quantum chem.]. Vol. 1 (1964)-. Academic Scholarly Publication. English. One time a year. $75.00 (Vol. 25). Academic Press Inc., 6277 Sea Harbor Drive, Orlando FL 32887. **Tel** (800)543-9534, (407)345-4100, FAX (407)352-3445. **ED** Per-Olov Londin. Documents available from The Genuine Article, Ask*IEEE, CASDDS.
Ind/Abst Chem. Abstr.; Index Sci. Rev. [Full Cov.]; INSPEC; Res. Alert [Full Cov.]; Sci. Cit. Index; SCISEARCH.

LC QD478 .A37 ISSN 1046-5723
DD 541/.0421 US
CODEN ASCHER

ADVANCES IN SOLID-STATE CHEMISTRY. [Adv. solid-state chem.]. **VFOAT** Advances in Solid State Chemistry. Vol. 1 (1989)-. English. One time a year. $90.25. JAI Press Inc., 55 Old Post Road, Suite 2, PO Box 1678, Greenwich CT 06836-1678. **Tel** (203)661-7602, FAX (203)661-0792. **ED** C.R.A. Catlow. Documents available from CASDDS.
Ind/Abst Chem. Abstr.

LC QD801 .A38
DD 541.3 UK
CODEN ADSOEN

ADVANCES IN SONOCHEMISTRY. Vol. 1 (1990)-. English. One time a year. $90.25. JAI Press Inc., 55 Old Post Road, Suite 2, PO Box 1678, Greenwich CT 06836-1678. **Tel** (203)661-7602, FAX (203)661-0792. **ED** Timothy J. Mason. Documents available from CASDDS.
Ind/Abst Chem. Abstr.

LC TP365
DD 660.29 US

AEROSOL RELEASE AND TRANSPORT PROGRAM QUARTERLY PROGRESS REPORT. **Added/Corp** U.S. Nuclear Regulatory Commission. Office of Nuclear Regulatory Research. Oak Ridge National Laboratory. Engineering Technology Division. (Oct./Dec. 1981)-. Periodical. English. Two times a year. National Technical Information Service - NTIS, Room 2027S, 5285 Port Royal Road, Springfield VA 22161. **Tel** (703)487-4630, (703)487-4660, (703)487-4650, FAX (703)321-8547, telex 89-9405. available on microfiche. ***Continues*** *LMFRB Aerosol Release and Transport Program Quarterly Progress Report for ... .*

ISSN 0568-062X
UK

AEROSOL REVIEW. [Aerosol rev.]. (1966)-. English. One time a year (Aug.). £25.00. Morgan Grampian, 40 Beresford Street Woolwich, London SE18 6BQ United Kingdom. **Tel** 011 44 181 8557777, FAX 011 44 181 8555548, telex 896238. **(Subscription address:** Benn Business Information Services Ltd., 30 Calderwood Street Woolwich, London SE18 6QH United Kingdom. **Tel** 011 44 181 8557777.) ***Continues in part*** *Manufacturing Chemist and Aerosol News.*

SP

ANALES DE QUIMICA. SERIE A, QUIMICA FISICA Y QUIMICA TECNICA. Spanish. Facultad de Fisica y Quimica, Ciudad Universitaria, 28040 Madrid Spain.
Ind/Abst Ceram. Abstr. (19??-); Mass Spect. Bull.

LC QD1 .C57 ISSN 0260-1826
DD 541.3/05 UK
CCC
NLM W1 AN769GSB CODEN ACPCDW

ANNUAL REPORTS ON THE PROGRESS OF CHEMISTRY. SECTION C, PHYSICAL CHEMISTRY. [Annu. rep. prog. chem. Sect. C. Phys. chem.]. **Added/Corp** Royal Society of Chemistry (Great Britain). **VFOAT** Physical Chemistry; Annual Reports. C. Vol. 76 (1979)-. Academic Scholarly Publication. English. One time a year (Oct. of following year). $215.00. Royal Society of Chemistry, Thomas Graham House, Science Park, Cambridge CB4 4WF United Kingdom. **Tel** 011 44 1223 420066, FAX 011 44 1223 423623, telex 818293 ROYAL. **(Subscription address:** Royal Society of Chemistry, Turpin Distribution Services Ltd., Blackhorse Road, Letchworth, Hertfordshire SG6 1HN United Kingdom. **Tel** 011 44 1462 672555, FAX 011 44 1462 480947.) Index available. cum. index. Documents available from BIOSIS Document Express, CASDDS. ***Continues in part*** *Annual Reports on the Progress of Chemistry. Section A, Physical and Inorganic Chemistry, 0308-6003.*
Desc: Consisting critical accounts of progress in major areas by acknowledged experts.
Ind/Abst Biol. Abstr. (1985-); Chem. Abstr.

LC QD1 .A732 ISSN 0066-426X
DD 541.058 US
CCC
NLM W1 AN778P CODEN ARPLAP
Pr Rev.

ANNUAL REVIEW OF PHYSICAL CHEMISTRY. [Annu. rev. phys. chem.]. Vol. 1 (1950)-. English. One time a year (November). $56.00. Annual Reviews Inc., 4139 El Camino Way, PO Box 10139, Palo Alto CA 94303-0139. **Tel** (415)493-4400, (800)523-8635, FAX (415)855-9815. **ED** Herbert L. Strauss. Index available. cum. index. ctrl circ. available on microfilm and microfiche from University Microfilms International (UMI). Documents available from The Genuine Article, CASDDS.
Desc: Comprehensive, thorough coverage of latest advances in physical chemistry; written by acknowledged experts in the field. Extensive literature citations included.
Ind/Abst Abstr. Bull. Inst. Pap. Sci. Tech.; Chem. Abstr.; Curr. Cit.; Curr. Contents Phys. Chem. Earth Sci.; Ei Page One; Energy Res. Abstr.; GeoRef; Index Med.; Index Sci. Rev. [Full Cov.]; Int. Aerosp. Abstr.; Leadscan; Life Sci. Collect.; Polymer Contents; Res. Alert [Full Cov.]; Sci. Cit. Index; SCISEARCH; Surf. Treat. Technol. Abstr.; World Surf. Coat. Abstr.

ISSN 0277-4747
US

BENCHMARK PAPERS IN PHYSICAL CHEMISTRY AND CHEMICAL PHYSICS. [Benchmark pap. phys. chem. chem. phys.]. Vol. 1 (1978)-. Monographic series. English. Irregular. Price varies per volume. Academic Press Inc., 6277 Sea Harbor Drive, Orlando FL 32887. **Tel** (800)543-9534, (407)345-4100, FAX (407)352-3445.

LC TP250 .Z6 ISSN 0005-9021
DD 660.2/97/05 GW
CCC
CODEN BBPCAX
Pr Rev. TITLE CHANGE

BERICHTE DER BUNSEN-GESELLSCHAFT FUER PHYSIKALISCHE CHEMIE. [Ber. Bunsenges. Phys. Chem.]. **Added/Corp** Deutsche Bunsen-Gesellschaft fuer Physikalische Chemie. **VFOAT** Berichte der Bunsen-Gesellschaft; International Journal of Physical Chemistry. (1963)-(1994). Academic Scholarly Publication. English (German). VCH Gesellschaft GmbH, Postfach 101161, D-69451 Weinheim Germany. **Tel** 011 49 6201 606459, FAX 011 49 6201 606184. **(Subscription address:** VCH Publishers Inc., 303 Northwest 12th Avenue, Journals Department, Deerfield FL 33442. **Tel** (800)367-8249, (305)428-5566.) **ED** Konrad Georg Weil and Alarich Weiss. Index available. cum. index. **Bk Rev. Ad Acc. Circ:** 3,000 (ctrl). available on photocopies (reproduced and distributed by the Alien Property Custodian); available in microform. Documents available from Article Express International, The Genuine Article, BIOSIS Document Express, Ask*IEEE, CASDDS. ***Continues*** *Zeitschrift fuer Elektrochemie (Weinheim an der Bergstrasse, Germany).* ***Continued by*** *Berichte der Bunsen-Gesellschaft. Physical Chemistry, Chemical Physics.*
Ind/Abst Alum. Ind. Abstr.; Bioeng. Abstr.; Biol. Abstr. (-1990); Ceram. Abstr.; Chem. Abstr.; Coal Abstr.; Curr. Cit.; Curr. Contents Phys. Chem. Earth Sci.; Curr. Titles Electrochem.; Ei Page One; Energy Res. Abstr.; Eng. Index Annu.; GeoRef; INSPEC (1968-); Int. Aerosp. Abstr.; Lit. Pat. Abstr., Oilfield Chem. (1966-); Lit. Abstr., Catal. Zeol.; Lit. Abstr., Health Environ.; Lit. Abstr., Pet. Refin. Petrochem.; Lit. Abstr., Pet. Substit.; Lit. Abstr., Transp. Storage; Mass Spect. Bull. (1968-); Met. Abstr.; Res. Alert [Full Cov.]; Sci. Cit. Index; SCISEARCH.

LC TP250 .Z6
GW

●**BERICHTE DER BUNSEN-GESELLSCHAFT. PHYSICAL CHEMISTRY, CHEMICAL PHYSICS.** **Added/Corp** Deutsche Bunsen-Gesellschaft fuer Physikalische Chemie. **VFOAT** Berichte der Bunsen-Gesellschaft fuer Physikalische Chemie; Physical Chemistry, Chemical Physics. Vol. 99, No. 1 (Jan. 1995)-. Periodical. English. Twelve times a year. $735.00. VCH Gesellschaft GmbH, Postfach 101161, D-69451 Weinheim Germany. **Tel** 011 49 6201 606459, FAX 011 49 6201 606184. **(Subscription address:** VCH Publishers Inc., 303 Northwest 12th Avenue, Journals Department, Deerfield FL 33442. **Tel** (800)367-8249, (305)428-5566.) ***Continues*** *Berichte der Bunsen-Gesellschaft fuer Physikalische Chemie, 0005-9021.*

LC QA1 .L7813 ISSN 0460-2366
DD 510 PL
CODEN BLTMDK

BIULETYN LUBELSKIE TOWARZYSTWA NAUKOWEGO. MATEMATYKA, FIZYKA-CHEMIA. **See** Mathematics.

LC Z5523 .B84 QD31.2 ISSN 0240-8465
DD 016.54 FR

BULLETIN SIGNALETIQUE. 171, CHIMIE GENERALE ET CHIMIE PHYSIQUE. **See** Chemistry and Chemicals-Abstracting, Bibliographies and Statistics.

LC QC176.A1 T58A ISSN 0385-9843
JA
CODEN BUDADZ

BUSSEIKEN DAYORI (TOKYO). **See** Physics.

ISSN 1049-1333
DD 541 US

C2C ABSTRACTS JAPAN. PHYSICAL CHEMISTRY. **See** Chemistry and Chemicals-Abstracting, Bibliographies and Statistics.

ISSN 1040-7138
DD 541 US
CODEN CSCHEF

CA SELECTS: CHEMILUMINESCENCE. **See** Chemistry and Chemicals-Abstracting, Bibliographies and Statistics.

ISSN 0275-7036
US
CODEN CCIPDO

CA SELECTS: COATINGS, INKS, & RELATED PRODUCTS. See Chemistry and Chemicals-Abstracting, Bibliographies and Statistics.

ISSN 0895-5972
DD 541
US
CODEN CFRAEC

CA SELECTS: FREE RADICALS (ORGANIC ASPECTS). See Chemistry and Chemicals-Abstracting, Bibliographies and Statistics.

ISSN 0734-8762
US
CODEN CAPADY

CA SELECTS: PAINT ADDITIVES. See Chemistry and Chemicals-Abstracting, Bibliographies and Statistics.

LC QD503 .C2 **ISSN** 0364-5916
DD 669/.94
US
CCC
CODEN CCCTD6
Pr Rev.

CALPHAD. (CALPHAD : COMPUTER COUPLING OF PHASE DIAGRAMS AND THERMOCHEMISTRY.). [Calphad]. **VFOAT** Computer Coupling of Phase Diagrams and Thermochemistry. **VAT** Calculation of Phase Diagrams. Vol. 1 (1977)-. Academic Scholarly Publication. English. Four times a year. $692.00. Pergamon Press, An Imprint of Elsevier Science Ltd., The Boulevard, Langford Lane, Kidlington, Oxford OX5 1GB United Kingdom. **Tel** 011 44 1865 843000, 011 44 1865 843699, FAX 011 44 1865 843010. **(Subscription address:** Elsevier Science Ltd. / Oxford Fulfillment Centre, PO Box 800, Kidlington OX5 1DX United Kingdom. **Tel** 011 44 865 843355.) **ED** Larry Kaufman. Index available. available on microfilm and microfiche from University Microfilms International (UMI); available on an online database from Elsevier Electronic Subscriptions (EES). Documents available from Article Express International, The Genuine Article, BIOSIS Document Express, Ask*IEEE, CASDDS.
Desc: Covers phase diagrams and thermochemistry.
Ind/Abst Alum. Ind. Abstr.; Bioeng. Abstr.; Biol. Abstr.; Chem. Abstr.; Chem. Titles; Comput. Rev.; Curr. Aware. Biol. Sci., CABS; Curr. Cit.; Curr. Contents Eng. Comput. Technol.; Curr. Contents Phys. Chem. Earth Sci.; Ei Page One; Energy Res. Abstr.; Eng. Mater. Abstr.; Eng. Index Annu.; INIS Atomindex [Micro.]; INSPEC (1977-); Met. Abstr.; Pollut. Abstr. Indexes; Res. Alert [Full Cov.]; Sci. Cit. Index; SCISEARCH.

LC QD505 .C38 **ISSN** 0140-0568
DD 541.3/95/05
UK
CCC
CODEN CATADK
Pr Rev.

CATALYSIS. **Added/Corp** Chemical Society (Great Britain). Vol. 1, (1977)-. Academic Scholarly Publication. English. One time a year. £105.00 (1992 volume). Royal Society of Chemistry, Thomas Graham House, Science Park, Cambridge CB4 4WF United Kingdom. **Tel** 011 44 1223 420066, FAX 011 44 1223 423623, telex 818293 ROYAL. **(Subscription address:** Royal Society of Chemistry, Turpin Distribution Services Ltd., Blackhorse Road, Letchworth, Hertfordshire SG6 1HN United Kingdom. **Tel** 011 44 1462 672555, FAX 011 44 1462 480947.) **ED** G. C. Bond and G. Webb. Documents available from CASDDS.
Desc: Provides a review of recent literature in the subject of catalysis.
Ind/Abst Chem. Abstr.

ISSN 1011-372X
NE
CCC

CATALYSIS LETTERS. Vol. 1, No. 1/3 (1988)-. Periodical. English. Twenty-four times a year. $2047.24. Baltzer Science Publishers BV, Asterweg 1A, 1031 HL Amsterdam Netherlands. **Tel** 011 31 20 6370061, FAX 011 31 20 6323651. **ED** Gabor A. Somorjai. Documents available from Article Express International, The Genuine Article, CASDDS.
Ind/Abst Chem. Abstr.; Curr. Cit.; Curr. Contents Phys. Chem. Earth Sci.; Eng. Index Annu.; Lit. Pat. Abstr., Oilfield Chem. (1990-); Lit. Abstr., Catal. Zeol.; Lit. Abstr., Health Environ.; Lit. Abstr., Pet. Refin. Petrochem.; Lit. Abstr., Pet. Substit.; Lit. Abstr., Transp. Storage; Res. Alert [Full Cov.]; Sci. Cit. Index; SCISEARCH.

LC QD501 .C4457 **ISSN** 0161-4940
DD 541/.395/05
US
CCC
NLM W1 CA95J **CODEN** CRSEC9
Pr Rev.

CATALYSIS REVIEWS : SCIENCE AND ENGINEERING. [Catal. rev., Sci. eng.]. Vol. 9 (1974)-. Periodical. English. Four times a year. $535.00. Marcel Dekker Inc., 270 Madison Avenue, New York NY 10016. **Tel** (212)696-9000, (800)228-1160, FAX (212)685-4540, telex 421419. **(Subscription address:** Marcel Dekker Inc., PO Box 5017, Monticello NY 12701. **Tel** (800)228-1160.) **ED** Alexis T. Bell, Kamil Klier, Robert J. Madix, John B. Butt. **Bk Rev. Ad Acc.** available on microfiche. Documents available from Article Express International, The Genuine Article, CASDDS. ***Formed by the union of*** *Catalysis Reviews, 0360-2451* ***and*** *Catalysis Reviews, 0008-7645.*
Desc: This publication features an interdisciplinary view-point and is designed to stimulate progressive ideas throughout this broad science, offering articles in such areas as advances in technology and theory, engineering and chemical aspects of catalytic reactions, reactor design, computer models, analytical tools, and statistical evaluations.
Ind/Abst Alum. Ind. Abstr.; Bioeng. Abstr.; Chem Inform; Chem. Abstr.; Curr. Chem. React.; Curr. Cit.; Curr. Contents Phys. Chem. Earth Sci.; Ei Page One; Energy Res. Abstr. (Apr. 1977-); Eng. Mater. Abstr.; Eng. Index Annu.; Gas Abstr.; Index Sci. Rev. [Full Cov.]; INIS Atomindex [Micro.]; Lit. Pat. Abstr., Oilfield Chem. (1969-); Lit. Abstr., Catal. Zeol.; Lit. Abstr., Health Environ.; Lit. Abstr., Pet. Refin. Petrochem.; Lit. Abstr., Pet. Substit.; Lit. Abstr., Transp. Storage; Met. Abstr.; Phys. Briefs; Proc. Chem. Eng.; Res. Alert [Full Cov.]; Sci. Cit. Index; SCISEARCH; Theor. Chem. Eng.

ISSN 0898-3089
DD 541
US
Pr Rev.

CATALYST REVIEW NEWSLETTER, THE. [Catal. rev. newsl.]. **VFOAT** Catalyst Review. Vol. 1, No. 1 (1988)-. Newsletter. English. Twelve times a year. $590.00. Catalyst Consultants Publishing, PO Box 637, Spring House PA 19477. **Tel** (215)628-4447, FAX (215)628-2267. **ED** Mary Ann Jones.
Desc: Global overview of events impacting the catalyst industry.

FI

CHEMICA. **Added/Corp** Oulun Yliopisto. **VFOAT** Chemica. (1972)-. Monographic series. English (Finnish and German). Irregular. Price varies per volume. Professor Leo Hirvonen, University of Oulu, 90100 Oulu 10 Finland. **Tel** 358-81-332133. **ED** Seppo Lakovaara. cum. index. **Ad Acc. Circ:** 450 (ctrl).
Desc: Monographs, reviews and dissertations in the field of chemistry.

LC QD450 .C44 **ISSN** 0301-0104
DD 541/.05
NE
CCC
NLM W1 CH26P **CODEN** CMPHC2
Pr Rev.

CHEMICAL PHYSICS. [Chem. phys.]. Vol. 1 (Jan./Feb. 1973)-. Academic Scholarly Publication. English. Thirty-nine times a year (13 volumes). $4241.00. Elsevier Science Publishers BV, PO Box 211, 1000 AE Amsterdam Netherlands. **Tel** 011 31 20 4853641, 011 31 20 4853642, FAX 011 31 20 4853598. **ED** R.H. Hochstrasser, G.L. Hofacker. available on microfilm and microfiche from University Microfilms International (UMI); available on an online database from Elsevier Electronic Subscriptions (EES). Documents available from The Genuine Article, Ask*IEEE, CASDDS.
Desc: Covers experimental and theoretical research involving problems of both a chemical and physical nature. It publishes experimental and theoretical papers on all aspects of chemical physics.
Ind/Abst Chem. Abstr.; Chem. Titles; Curr. Cit.; Curr. Contents Phys. Chem. Earth Sci.; Ei Page One; INSPEC (Jan./Feb. 1973-); Int. Aerosp. Abstr.; Leadscan; Math. Rev. (?-199?); Life Sci. Collect.; Phys. Briefs; Res. Alert [Full Cov.]; Sci. Cit. Index; SCISEARCH.

ISSN 0009-2614
NE
CCC
CODEN CHPLBC
Pr Rev.

CHEMICAL PHYSICS LETTERS. [Chem. phys. lett.]. Vol. 1 (1967)-. Academic Scholarly Publication. English. Irregular (108 issues per year). $6569.00. Elsevier Science Publishers BV, PO Box 211, 1000 AE Amsterdam Netherlands. **Tel** 011 31 20 4853641, 011 31 20 4853642, FAX 011 31 20 4853598. **ED** A.D. Buckingham, D.A. King, A.H. Zewail. cum. index. available on microfilm from University Microfilms International (UMI); available on an online database from Elsevier Electronic Subscriptions (EES). Documents available from The Genuine Article, Ask*IEEE, CASDDS.
Desc: Devoted to the analysis of phenomena in the domain of chemical physics, with an emphasis on theoretical interpretation.
Ind/Abst Ceram. Abstr. (1968-); Chem. Abstr.; Chem. Titles (1968-); Curr. Cit.; Curr. Contents Phys. Chem. Earth Sci.; GeoRef; INSPEC (1968-); Int. Aerosp. Abstr.; Leadscan; Mass Spect. Bull. (1968-); Math. Rev. (-199?); Phys. Briefs; Res. Alert [Full Cov.]; Sci. Cit. Index; SCISEARCH.

LC QD1 .C744 **ISSN** 0366-7022
DD 540/.8
JA
CCC
NLM W1 CH362 **CODEN** CMLTAG
Pr Rev.

CHEMISTRY LETTERS. See Chemistry and Chemicals-Organic Chemistry.

LC QD505 .T78 **ISSN** 0253-9837
DD 541.3/95/05
CC
CODEN THHPD3
Pr Rev.

CHIHUA XUEBAO. (TSUI HUA HSUEH PAO.). [Chihua xuebao]. **Added/Corp** Chung-Kuo Ko Hsueh Yuan. **VFOAT** Journal of Catalysis; Cuihua Xuebao. (1980)-. Academic Scholarly Publication. Chinese (summaries and/or abstracts in English). Six times a year. $85.70. Science Press, 16 Donghuangchenggen North Street, Beijing 100707, People's Republic of China. **Tel** 011 86 1 4019821, 011 86 1 4010642, FAX 011 86 1 4012180, 011 86 1 4019810, telex 210147. **Ad Acc. Circ:** 6,100. Documents available from CASDDS, BLDSC, CASDDS.
Ind/Abst Chem. Abstr.

LC QD549 .K92 **ISSN** 0303-402X
DD 541/.3451
GW
CCC
NLM W1 CO212T **CODEN** CPMSB6CPMSBKZZPAF
Pr Rev.

COLLOID AND POLYMER SCIENCE. (COLLOID AND POLYMER SCIENCE. KOLLOID-ZEITSCHRIFT & ZEITSCHRIFT FUER POLYMERE.). [Colloid polym. sci.]. **Added/Corp** Kolloid-Gesellschaft. **VFOAT** Kolloid-Zeitschrift & Zeitschrift fuer Polymere. Vol. 252 (Jan. 1974)-. Periodical. Multiple languages (English, French and German). Twelve times a year. $1337.00. Dr Dietrich Steinkopff Verlag, PO Box 111442, D-64229 Darmstadt Germany. **Tel** 011 49 6151 17450, FAX 011 49 6151 174510. **(Subscription address:** Springer-Verlag New York Inc. / North America, PO Box 2485, Journal Fulfillment, Secaucus NJ 07096. **Tel** (201)348-4033, (800)777-4643, FAX (201)348-4505.) **ED** H.G. Kilian and A. Weiss. **Bk Rev. Ad Acc. Circ:** 3,000 (ctrl). Documents available from Article Express International, The Genuine Article, BIOSIS Document Express, Ask*IEEE, Petroleum Abstracts Document Delivery Service, CASDDS. ***Continues*** *Kolloid-Zeitschrift & Zeitschrift fuer Polymere, 0023-2904.*
Desc: Covers fields such as solid state physics, polymer chemistry, biophysics, biology, pharmacology and medicine.
Ind/Abst Abstr. Bull. Inst. Pap. Sci. Tech.; Art Archaeol. Tech. Abstr.; Bioeng. Abstr.; Biol. Abstr. (-1982); Ceram. Abstr.; Chem. Abstr.; Chem. Titles; Curr. Cit.; Curr. Contents Phys. Chem. Earth Sci.; Dairy Sci. Abstr.; Ei Page One; Energy Res. Abstr. (Jan. 1975-); Eng. Index Annu.; GeoRef; INSPEC (Jan. 1988-); Int. Packag. Abstr.; Life Sci. Collect.; Pet. Abstr.; Polymer Contents; Res. Alert [Full Cov.]; Sci. Cit. Index; SCISEARCH; Soils Fert.; World Surf. Coat. Abstr.; World Text. Abstr.

ISSN 1061-933X
DD 541
US
CCC
CODEN CJRSEQ

COLLOID JOURNAL OF THE RUSSIAN ACADEMY OF SCIENCES. (COLLOID JOURNAL OF THE RUSSIAN ACADEMY OF SCIENCES: KOLLOIDNYI ZHURNAL.). [Colloid j. Russ. Acad. Sci.]. **Added/Corp** Consultants Bureau. **VFOAT** Kolloidnyi Zhurnal. (1992)-. Academic Scholarly Publication. English (translations available in Russian). Six times a year. $1245.00. MAIK Nauka / Interperiodica, Ulitsa Profsoyuznaia 90, Moscow 117864 Russia. Documents available from Article Express International, The Genuine Article, Ask*IEEE, CASDDS. ***Continues*** *Colloid Journal of the USSR, 0010-1303.*
Ind/Abst AGRICOLA; Chem. Abstr. (1992-); Curr. Cit.; Curr. Contents Phys. Chem. Earth Sci.; Ei Page One (1992-); Eng. Index Annu.; INSPEC (1992-); MINPROC (1992-); Nucl. Sci. Abstr. (1992-); Res. Alert [Full Cov.]; World Surf. Coat. Abstr. (1992-).

LC QD549 .C63 **ISSN** 0166-6622
DD 541.3/451/05
NE
CCC
CODEN COSUD3
Pr Rev. **TITLE CHANGE**

COLLOIDS AND SURFACES. [Colloids surf.]. Vol. 1 (Jan. 1980)-(1993). Academic Scholarly Publication. English. Elsevier Science Publishers BV, PO Box 211, 1000 AE Amsterdam Netherlands. **Tel** 011 31 20 4853641, 011 31 20 4853642, FAX 011 31 20 4853598. **ED** P Somasundaran, E D Goddard, R J Hunter and Th F Tadros. available on microfilm and microfiche from University Microfilms International (UMI). Documents available from Article Express International, The Genuine Article, BIOSIS Document Express, Ask*IEEE, CASDDS. ***Split into*** *Colloids and Surfaces. A, Physicochemical and Engineering Aspects* ***and*** *Colloids and Surfaces. B, Biointerfaces.*
Desc: An international journal concerned with applications and principles of colloidal and interfacial phenomena.
Ind/Abst Abstr. Bull. Inst. Pap. Sci. Tech. (19??-19??); Alum. Ind. Abstr. (19??-19??); Bibliogr. Mission. (19??-19??); Bioeng. Abstr. (19??-19??); Biol. Abstr. (19??-19??); Ceram. Abstr. (19??-19??); Chem. Abstr. (19??-19??); Chem. Titles (19??-19??); Coal Abstr. (19??-19??); Curr. Biotechnol. (19??-19??); Curr. Contents Phys. Chem. Earth Sci. (19??-19??); Ei Page One (19??-19??); EMBASE (19??-19??); Eng. Mater. Abstr. (19??-19??); Eng. Index Annu. (19??-19??) [Select. Cov.]; Fluid Abstr., Civil Eng. (19??-19??); Fluid Abstr. Proc. Eng. (19??-19??); FLUIDEX (1980-1987); GeoRef (19??-19??); HTFS Dig. (19??-19??); INSPEC (Jan. 1980-19??); Met. Abstr. (19??-19??); Polymer Contents (1980-19??); Res. Alert (19??-19??) [Full Cov.]; Sci. Cit. Index (19??-19??); SCISEARCH (19??-19??); World Ceram. Abstr. (19??-19??); World Surf. Coat. Abstr. (19??-19??).

LC QD549 .C63 ISSN 0927-7757
NE
CCC

Pr Rev.
•COLLOIDS AND SURFACES. A, PHYSICOCHEMICAL AND ENGINEERING ASPECTS. VFOAT
Physicochemical and Engineering Aspects. Vol. 70, No. 1 (29 Jan. 1993)-. Academic Scholarly Publication. English. Thirty-six times a year (12 volumes). $3403.00. Elsevier Science Publishers BV, PO Box 211, 1000 AE Amsterdam Netherlands. **Tel** 011 31 20 4853641, 011 31 20 4853642, FAX 011 31 20 4853598. **ED** P. Somasundaran, Th.F. Tadros. available on an online database from Elsevier Electronic Subscriptions (EES). Documents available from BIOSIS Document Express, Ask*IEEE, CASDDS. ***Continues in part*** *Colloids and Surfaces, 0166-6622.*
Desc: Publishes original research papers and reviews on basic colloid and surface science, and in particular its application in engineering and applied science.
Ind/Abst Biol. Abstr.; Chem. Abstr.; Curr. Cit.; EMBASE; FLUIDEX; INSPEC; Met. Abstr.; Sci. Cit. Index; Soc. Sci. Cit. Index [Select. Cov.]; World Surf. Coat. Abstr.

LC QD549 .C632 ISSN 0927-7765
NE
CCC
NLM W1; CO2126 CODEN CSBBEQ
Pr Rev.
•COLLOIDS AND SURFACES B: BIOINTERFACES. VFOAT
Biointerfaces. Vol. 1, No. 1 (14 May 1993)-. Academic Scholarly Publication. English. Eighteen times a year. $860.00. Elsevier Science Publishers BV, PO Box 211, 1000 AE Amsterdam Netherlands. **Tel** 011 31 20 4853641, 011 31 20 4853642, FAX 011 31 20 4853598. **ED** J.L. Brash, H.J. Busscher, D.W. Osborne. available on an online database from Elsevier Electronic Subscriptions (EES). Documents available from CASDDS. ***Continues in part*** *Colloids and Surfaces, 0166-6622.*
Desc: International journal devoted to fundamental and applied research on colloid and interfacial phenomena in relation to systems of biological origin. Has particular relevance to the medical, pharmaceutical, biotechnological, food and cosmetic fields.
Ind/Abst Chem. Abstr.; Soc. Sci. Cit. Index [Select. Cov.].

LC QD516 .C613 ISSN 0010-2180
DD 541.36 US
CCC
CODEN CBFMAO
Pr Rev.
COMBUSTION AND FLAME.
[Combust. flame]. **Added/Corp** Combustion Institute (U.S.). Vol. 1 (March 1957)-. Academic Scholarly Publication. English. Sixteen times a year (4 volumes). $830.00. Elsevier Science Publishing Company Inc, Madison Square Station, PO Box 882, New York NY 10159-0882. **Tel** (212)633-3950, FAX (212)633-3990. **ED** D Bradley and R A Strehlow. available on microfilm and microfiche from University Microfilms International (UMI); available on an online database from Elsevier Electronic Subscriptions (EES). Documents available from Article Express International, The Genuine Article, Ask*IEEE, CASDDS, Documents on Demand.
Desc: Provides worldwide coverage of experimental and theoretical investigations into combustion phenomena.
Ind/Abst Bioeng. Abstr.; Ceram. Abstr.; Chem. Abstr.; Chem. Hazards Ind.; Chem. Titles; Coal Abstr.; Curr. Cit.; Curr. Contents Eng. Comput. Technol.; Curr. Technol. Index; Ei Page One; EMBASE; Energy Inf. Abstr.; Eng. Index Annu.; Environ. Abstr.; Fluid Abstr., Civil Eng.; Fluid Abstr. Proc. Eng.; FLUIDEX; Gas Abstr.; Health Saf. Sci. Abstr.; HTFS Dig.; INIS Atomindex [Micro.]; INSPEC (1968-); Int. Aerosp. Abstr.; Lab. Hazards Bull.; Lit. Pat. Abstr., Oilfield Chem. (1958-); Lit. Abstr., Catal. Zeol.; Lit. Abstr., Health Environ.; Lit. Abstr., Pet. Refin. Petrochem.; Lit. Abstr., Pet. Substit.; Lit. Abstr., Transp. Storage; Mass Spect. Bull.; Pollut. Abstr. Indexes; Proc. Chem. Eng.; Res. Alert [Full Cov.]; Saf. Health Work; Sci. Cit. Index; SCISEARCH; Theor. Chem. Eng.; World Ceram. Abstr.

LC QD516 .F5813 ISSN 0010-5082
US
CCC
CODEN CESWA4
Pr Rev.
COMBUSTION, EXPLOSION, AND SHOCK WAVES.
[Combust. explos. shock waves]. **Added/Corp** Consultants Bureau. Vol. 1 (1965)-. Periodical. English (Russian). Six times a year. $1145.00. Consultants Bureau, A Division of Plenum Publishing Corporation, 233 Spring Street, New York NY 10013. **Tel** (212)620-8000, (212)620-8466, FAX (212)463-0742, telex 23/421139. **ED** V. M. Titov. Index available. available on microfilm and microfiche from University Microfilms International (UMI). Documents available from Article Express International, The Genuine Article, Ask*IEEE, CASDDS.
Desc: Thoroughly investigates theoretical and applied problems in combustion and explosion.
Ind/Abst Acoust. Abstr.; Appl. Mech. Rev.; Bioeng. Abstr.; Chem. Abstr.; Coal Abstr.; Curr. Cit.; Curr. Contents Eng. Comput. Technol.; Ei Page One; Energy Res. Abstr. (Sept. 1977-); Eng. Index Annu.; INIS Atomindex [Micro.]; INSPEC (1968-); Int. Aerosp. Abstr.; Pollut. Abstr. Indexes; Res. Alert [Full Cov.]; Sci. Cit. Index; SCISEARCH.

LC QD516 .C616 ISSN 0010-2202
DD 541/.361/05 US
CCC
CODEN CBSTB9
Pr Rev.
COMBUSTION SCIENCE AND TECHNOLOGY.
[Combust. sci. technol.]. Vol. 1 (July 1969)-. Periodical. English. Twelve times a year. $441.00 (academic institutions), $688.00 (corporate institutions). Gordon & Breach Science Publishers, Inc., PO Box 786, Cooper Station, New York NY 10276. **Tel** (212)206-8900, FAX (212)645-2459. Index available. **Bk Rev. Ad Acc.** Documents available from Article Express International, The Genuine Article, CASDDS. ***Supersedes*** *Pyrodynamics, 0555-8344.*
Desc: International journal that provides for open discussion and prompt publication of new results, discoveries and developments in the various disciplines that constitute the field of combustion.
Ind/Abst Appl. Sci. Technol. Index; Bioeng. Abstr.; Chem. Abstr.; Chem. Titles; Coal Abstr.; Curr. Cit.; Curr. Contents Eng. Comput. Technol.; Ei Page One; EMBASE; Energy Res. Abstr. (June 1971-); Eng. Index Annu.; Gas Abstr.; HTFS Dig.; Int. Aerosp. Abstr.; Pollut. Abstr. Indexes; Proc. Chem. Eng.; Res. Alert [Full Cov.]; Sci. Cit. Index; SCISEARCH; Theor. Chem. Eng.

ISSN 0883-5519
DD 541 US
COMBUSTION SCIENCE AND TECHNOLOGY BOOK SERIES.
Vol. 2, (1975)-. Monographic series. English. Irregular. Price varies per volume. Gordon & Breach Science Publishers, Inc., PO Box 786, Cooper Station, New York NY 10276. **Tel** (212)206-8900, FAX (212)645-2459. **ED** I. Glassman. ***Continues*** *Combustion Science and Technology (Series).*

ISSN 1043-3996
DD 541 UK
CONTEMPORARY TOPICS IN PURE AND APPLIED CONDENSED MATTER SCIENCE.
[Contemp. topics pure appl. condens. matter sci.]. Periodical. English. Two times a year. Gordon & Breach Science Publishers, PO Box 90, Reading, Berkshire RG1 8JL United Kingdom. **Tel** 011 44 1734 560080, FAX 011 44 1734 568211.

LC QD475 .C63 ISSN 0010-8545
DD 541.2/242/05 SZ
CCC
NLM W1 CO825 CODEN CCHRAM
Pr Rev.
COORDINATION CHEMISTRY REVIEWS.
[Coord. chem. rev.]. (July 1966)-. Periodical. English. Nine times a year (9 volumes). $2930.00. Elsevier Sequoia SA, PO Box 564, CH-1001 Lausanne 1 Switzerland. **Tel** 011 41 21 3207381, FAX 011 41 21 3235444. **ED** A B P Lever. available on microfilm and microfiche from University Microfilms International (UMI); available on an online database from Elsevier Electronic Subscriptions (EES). Documents available from The Genuine Article, CASDDS.
Desc: Includes aspects of organometallic, theoretical and bioinorganic chemistry.
Ind/Abst Chem Inform; Chem. Abstr.; Chem. Titles; Coal Abstr.; Curr. Cit.; Curr. Contents Phys. Chem. Earth Sci.; Energy Res. Abstr.; Index Sci. Rev. [Full Cov.]; Life Sci. Collect.; Res. Alert [Full Cov.]; Sci. Cit. Index; SCISEARCH.

LC QD506.A1 C75 ISSN 1049-9407
DD 541.3/3 US
CCC
CODEN CRCYEP
CRITICAL REVIEWS IN SURFACE CHEMISTRY.
[Crit. rev. surf. chem.]. **VFOAT** Surface Chemistry. **VAT** Chemical Rubber Company Critical Reviews in Surface Chemistry. Vol. 1, Issue 1 (1990)-. Academic Scholarly Publication. English. Four times a year. $230.00. Begell House Inc., 79 Madison Avenue, New York NY 10016-7892. **Tel** (212)725-1999, FAX (212)213-8368. **(Subscription address:** Begell House Inc., PO Box 1109, Pearl River NY 10965. **Tel** (212)725-1999.**)** **ED** Peter M.A. Sherwood. Documents available from Article Express International, CASDDS.
Desc: Active areas include the investigation of structure-sensitive catalytic reactions, acid-base reactions on acidic, basic surfaces or oxide surfaces, oxidation and corrosion, material surface studies, and surface electron transfer reactions.
Ind/Abst Chem. Abstr.; Curr. Cit.; Eng. Index Annu. [Select. Cov.].

ISSN 0891-0006
DD 541 US
CODEN CUSEEW
CURRENT SEPARATIONS.
[Curr. sep.]. **Added/Corp** Bioanalytical Systems Inc. Vol. 1, No. 1 (1979)-. Periodical. English. Four times a year. $23.00. Bas Press, PO Box 2206, West Lafayette IN 47906. **Tel** (317)463-4527. Documents available from CASDDS.
Ind/Abst Chem. Abstr.

ISSN 0418-2472
KO
CODEN DHWHAB
Pr Rev.
DAEHAN HWAHAK HWOEJEE.
(TAEHAN HWAHAKHOE CHI.). [Daehan Hwahak hwoejee]. **Added/Corp** Taehan Hwahakhoe. **VFOAT** Journal of the Korean Chemical Society.; Taehan Hwahakhoe Chi. (1963)-. Academic Scholarly Publication. Korean (English). Twelve times a year. $80.00. Korean Chemical Society, 335 5 Ka Anam Dong Sungbuk Ku, Seoul 136 075 Korea. **Tel** 011 82 2 926 5457, FAX 011 82 2 923 5589. **ED** Chi-Sun Han. Index available. cum. index. **Circ:** 3,000. Documents available from CASDDS.
Desc: Covers experimental and theoretical chemistries.
Ind/Abst Art Archaeol. Tech. Abstr.; Chem. Abstr.; Curr. Cit.; Mass Spect. Bull.

LC QD461 .D53 ISSN 0137-1053
PL
CODEN DOAMD2
DIELEKTRYCZNE I OPTYCZNE ASPEKTY ODDZIAYWAN MIEDZYCZASTECZKOWYCH. VFOAT
Dielectric and Optical Aspects of Intermolecular Interactions. Vol. 1 (1974)-. Academic Scholarly Publication. Polish (summaries and/or abstracts in English). Panstwowe Wydawnictwo Naukowe / PWN, (Polish Scientific Publishers PWN Ltd.), Ul. Miodowa 10, PO Box 391, 00-251 Warsaw Poland. **Tel** 011 48 22 312738, FAX 011 48 22 267163. Documents available from CASDDS.

UK
DIFFERENTIAL THERMAL ANALYSIS.
Vol. 1 (1970)-. Monographic series. English. Irregular. Price varies per volume. Academic Press Inc., 6277 Sea Harbor Drive, Orlando FL 32887. **Tel** (800)543-9534, (407)345-4100, FAX (407)352-3445.

ISSN 1012-0386
SZ
CODEN DDAFE7
DIFFUSION AND DEFECT DATA. [PT. A], DEFECT AND DIFFUSION FORUM.
[Diffus. defect data, Solid state data, Pt. A Defect diffus. forum]. **VFOAT** Diffusion and Defect Data. Defect and Diffusion Forum; Defect and Diffusion Forum; DDF. Vol. A57-58 (1988)-. Academic Scholarly Publication. English. Twelve times a year. $1128.00. Scitec Publications Ltd., Trans Tech House, Hardstrasse 13, CH-4714 Aedermannsdorf Switzerland. **Tel** FAX 011 41 62 741058. **(Subscription address:** Scitec Publications Ltd., Credit Suisse, CH-6301 Zug Switzerland. **)** Documents available from Ask*IEEE, CASDDS. ***Continues in part*** *Diffusion and Defect Data, 0377-6883.*
Ind/Abst Chem. Abstr. (1988-); Curr. Cit.; INSPEC (1988-).

ISSN 1012-0394
LH
CODEN DDBPE8
DIFFUSION AND DEFECT DATA. [PT. B], SOLID STATE PHENOMENA : SSP.
[Diffus. defect data, Solid state data, Pt. B Solid state]. **VFOAT** Diffusion and Defect Data. Solid State Phenomena; Solid State Phenomena; SSP. Vols. B1 & 2 (1988)-. Academic Scholarly Publication. English. Six times a year. $564.00. Scitec Publications Ltd., Trans Tech House, Hardstrasse 13, CH-4714 Aedermannsdorf Switzerland. **Tel** FAX 011 41 62 741058. **(Subscription address:** Scitec Publications Ltd., Credit Suisse, CH-6301 Zug Switzerland. **)** Documents available from Ask*IEEE, CASDDS. ***Continues in part*** *Diffusion and Defect Data, 0377-6883.*
Ind/Abst Chem. Abstr. (1988-); INSPEC (1988-).

LC QD551 .E4913 ISSN 0735-8687
DD 541.3/7/0601 US
DIRECTORY OF MEMBERS - ELECTROCHEMICAL SOCIETY.
(DIRECTORY OF MEMBERS.). [Dir. memb. - Electrochem. Soc.]. **Main/Corp** Electrochemical Society. **VFOAT** Electrochemical Society Directory. (19??)-. English. Every 2 years. Electrochemical Society, 10 South Main Street, Pennington NJ 08534. **Tel** (609)737-1902.

ISSN 0012-5016
US
CCC
CODEN DKPCAG
DOKLADY. PHYSICAL CHEMISTRY.
(DOKLADY. PHYSICAL CHEMISTRY : PROCEEDINGS OF THE ACADEMY OF SCIENCES OF THE USSR.). [Dokl., Phys. chem.]. **Added/Corp** Akademiia Nauk SSSR. Consultants Bureau Enterprises. **VFOAT** Physical Chemistry. Vol. 148, No. 1-6 (Jan.-Feb. 1963)-. Periodical. English (Russian; translations available in Russian). Twelve times a year. $1525.00. MAIK Nauka / Interperiodica, Ulitsa Profsoyuznaia 90, Moscow 117864 Russia. Index available. available on microfilm and microfiche from University Microfilms International (UMI). ***Continues*** *Akademiia Nauk SSSR. Proceedings of the Academy of Sciences of the USSR. Physical Chemistry Section.*
Desc: This journal presents a comprehensive study of research in physical chemistry.

Ind/Abst Coal Abstr.; Curr. Cit.; Energy Res. Abstr. (June 1974-); Eng. Mater. Abstr.; GeoRef; INIS Atomindex [Micro.]; Mass Spect. Bull.

LC Z5524.I65 E36 QD561 **ISSN** 0132-2354
RU

EKSTRAKTSIIA, IONNYI OBMEN.
Added/Corp Gosudarstvennaia Publichnaia Nauchno-Tekhnicheskaia Biblioteka (Akademiia Nauk SSSR). (Mar. 1968)-. Russian (Multiple languages). Twelve times a year. Izdatelstvo Nauka / Akademiia Nauk, (Publishing House of the Russian Academy of Sciences), Leninskii Porspekt 14, 117901 Moscow Russia. **Tel** 011 95 9542153, FAX 011 95 9382144, telex 411964.

LC QD450 **ISSN** 1082-4928
DD 541 UK

•**ELECTRONIC JOURNAL OF THEORETICAL CHEMISTRY.** (1995)-. Academic Scholarly Publication. English. Fifty times a year. $150.00. John Wiley & Sons Ltd., Baffins Lane, Chichester, West Sussex PO19 1UD United Kingdom. **Tel** 011 44 1243 779777, FAX 011 44 1243 776128 BTG:JWP001, telex 86290 WIBOOKG. **(Subscription address:** John Wiley & Sons, Inc., 605 Third Avenue, New York NY 10158-0012. **Tel** (212)850-6645, FAX (212)850-6021.**)**

LC TP **ISSN** 0264-9047
DD 668.305 UK
UDC 66

EUROPEAN ADHESIVES & SEALANTS. [Eur. adhes. sealants]. **VFOAT** European Adhesives and Sealants. (1983)-. Periodical. English. Four times a year (Mar., June, Sept., Dec.). $165.74. Argus Press Group, Queensway House, 2 Queensway Redhill, Surrey RH1 1QS United Kingdom. **Tel** 011 44 1737 768611, 011 44 1737 761685, FAX 011 44 1737 760510, telex 948669 TOPJNL G. **(Subscription address:** FMJ International Publications Ltd., Queensway House 2 Queensway, Redhill Surrey RH1 1QS United Kingdom. **Tel** 011 44 1737 768611, FAX 011 44 1737 773993, telex 948669 TOPJNL G.**) ED** John Ward. Index available. **Ad Acc. Circ:** 3,200. available on an online database from DIALOG.
Desc: Technical articles on adhesives and sealant application, latest developments in raw materials, reviews on process applications equipment, general industry news and new product information.
Ind/Abst Chem. Bus. Bull.; Chem. Bus. NewsBase; Chem. Bus. Update; Curr. Cit.; F&S Index Plus Text, Int.; Infomat Int. Bus.; PROMT.

UK
NLM W1; FA459 **CODEN** FDISE6

FARADAY DISCUSSIONS. Added/Corp Royal Society of Chemistry (Great Britain). Faraday Division. No. 92 (1991)-. Monographic series. English. Three times a year. $437.00. Royal Society of Chemistry, Thomas Graham House, Science Park, Cambridge CB4 4WF United Kingdom. **Tel** 011 44 1223 420066, FAX 011 44 1223 423623, telex 818293 ROYAL. **(Subscription address:** Royal Society of Chemistry, Turpin Distribution Services Ltd., Blackhorse Road, Letchworth, Hertfordshire SG6 1HN United Kingdom. **Tel** 011 44 1462 672555, FAX 011 44 1462 480947.**)** Documents available from BIOSIS Document Express, Ask*IEEE, CASDDS. ***Continues*** *Faraday Discussions of the Chemical Society, 0301-1249.*
Ind/Abst Biol. Abstr.; Chem. Abstr.; Index Med. (1992-); INSPEC (1978-); Sci. Cit. Index; World Surf. Coat. Abstr.; World Text. Abstr.

LC QD450 .F65 **ISSN** 0378-4843
DD 541/.05 SP
CCC
CODEN FCTLDW

FCTL. FOLIA CHIMICA THEORETICA LATINA. (FOLIA CHIMICA THEORETICA LATINA : FCTL.). **Added/Corp** Instituto de Estructura de la Materia del C.S.I.C. Laboratorio de Quimica Cuantica. **VFOAT** FCTL. (19??)-. Academic Scholarly Publication. Spanish (Italian; summaries and/or abstracts in English, French and Spanish). Four times a year. $25.00. Folia Chimica Theoretica Latina, Calle Serrano 119, Professor Smeyers, 28006 Madrid Spain. **Tel** 011 34 1 2619800 ext. 299, FAX 011 34 1 5642431. Documents available from CASDDS.
Ind/Abst Chem. Abstr.

ISSN 1001-3555
DD 541.395 CC

FENZI CUIHUA. VFOAT Journal of Molecular Catalysis. (1987)-. Periodical. Chinese. Four times a year. Documents available from CASDDS.
Ind/Abst Chem. Abstr.

LC QD461 .F37 **ISSN** 0253-3677
DD 541.2/2/05 CC
CODEN FKXUDX

FENZI KEXUE YUEBAO. (FEN TZU KO HSUEH HSUEH PAO.). [Fenzi kexue xuebao]. **VFOAT** Journal of Molecular Science. Vol. 1 (Sept. 1981)-. Academic Scholarly Publication. Chinese (summaries and/or abstracts in English). Four times a year. RMBY0.80. Fen Tzu Ko Hsueh Hsueh Pao, Hua Chung Kung Hsueh Yuan, Wu-Han Shih, People's Republic of China. Documents available from Ask*IEEE, CASDDS.
Ind/Abst Chem. Abstr.; INSPEC (June 1984-).

LC QD450 .F59
RU
CODEN FIKHEI

FIZICHESKAIA KHIMIIA. (19??)-. Academic Scholarly Publication. Russian (summaries and/or abstracts in English). One time a year. Izdatelstvo Khimiia, Novaia Ploshchad. 10, K-12, Moscow Russia. Documents available from CASDDS.
Ind/Abst Chem. Abstr.

LC QD461 .F48 **ISSN** 0131-176X
UN
CODEN FIMODE

FIZIKA MOLEKUL (KIEV). (FIZIKA MOLEKUL.). [Fiz. mol. (Kiev)]. **Added/Corp** Institut Teoreticheskoi Fiziki (Akademiia Nauk Ukrainskoi RSR). (1975)-. Academic Scholarly Publication. Russian (summaries and/or abstracts in English). Izdatelstvo Naukova Dumka / Ukrainian Academy of Sciences, Yu. A. Khramov, Dir., Ul. Repina 3, 252 601 Kiev Ukraine. **Tel** 011 7 44 4303441, 011 7 44 2254182, telex 131376. Documents available from CASDDS.
Ind/Abst Chem. Abstr. (1975-1982); Int. Aerosp. Abstr.

LC TA405 .F514 **ISSN** 0204-5958
BU
CODEN FKMEDW

FIZIKO-HIMICESKA MEHANIKA. (FIZIKO-KHIMICHESKA MEKHANIKA.). **Added/Corp** Bulgarska Akademiia na Naukite. **VFOAT** Physico-Cchemical Mechanics. (1975)-. Multiple languages (Bulgarian, German and Russian; summaries and/or abstracts in English). Irregular. 1.50lv (single issue). Izdatelstvo na Bulgarskata Akademiia na Naukite, 6 Rouski Boulevard, Sofia Bulgaria. **Tel** FAX 011 359 2 801341, telex 22267 HEMKIK. **Circ:** 480. available with illustrations. Documents available from CASDDS.
Ind/Abst Chem. Abstr.

LC Z5524.C7 F54 QD549 **ISSN** 0367-2409
DD 016.54 UN
CODEN FKMLAG

FIZIKO-KHIMICHESKAIA MEKHANIKA I LIOFILNOST DISPERSNYKH SISTEM.
Added/Corp Instytut Koloidnoi Khimii i Khimii Vody (Akademiia Nauk Ukrainskoi RSR). (1968)-. Academic Scholarly Publication. Russian. One time a year. Vidavnitstvo Naukova Dumka, Vul. Tereshchnivska 3, 252601 Kiev Ukraine. **Tel** 011 7 44 2244068, FAX 011 7 44 2247060. **ED** F. D. Ovcharenko. Documents available from CASDDS.
Ind/Abst Chem. Abstr.

LC QD504 .F55 **ISSN** 0378-3812
DD 541/.369 NE
CCC
CODEN FPEQDT

Pr Rev.

FLUID PHASE EQUILIBRIA. [Fluid phase equilib.]. Vol. 1 (Sept. 1977)-. Academic Scholarly Publication. English. Twenty-six times a year. $3250.00. Elsevier Science Publishers BV, PO Box 211, 1000 AE Amsterdam Netherlands. **Tel** 011 31 20 4853641, 011 31 20 4853642, FAX 011 31 20 4853598. **ED** H Renon. **Bk Rev. Ad Acc.** available on microfilm and microfiche from University Microfilms International (UMI); available on an online database from Elsevier Electronic Subscriptions (EES). Documents available from Article Express International, The Genuine Article, Ask*IEEE, Petroleum Abstracts Document Delivery Service, CASDDS.
Desc: Embraces experimental and theoretical research studies together with their applications.
Ind/Abst Bioeng. Abstr.; Chem. Abstr.; Chem. Titles; Coal Abstr.; Curr. Biotechnol.; Curr. Cit.; Curr. Contents Eng. Comput. Technol.; Curr. Contents Phys. Chem. Earth Sci.; Ei Page One; Energy Res. Abstr. (March 1979-); Eng. Index Annu.; Fluid Abstr., Civil Eng.; Fluid Abstr. Proc. Eng.; FLUIDEX; Gas Abstr. (?-?); INSPEC (Sept. 1977-); Lit. Pat. Abstr., Oilfield Chem. (1993-); Lit. Abstr., Catal. Zeol.; Lit. Abstr., Health Environ.; Lit. Abstr., Pet. Refin. Petrochem.; Lit. Abstr., Pet. Substit.; Lit. Abstr., Transp. Storage; Pet. Abstr.; Proc. Chem. Eng.; Res. Alert [Full Cov.]; Sci. Cit. Index; SCISEARCH; Theor. Chem. Eng.

LC TP270.A1 S95a **ISSN** 0348-6613
SW
CODEN FOPYDX

FOREDRAG VID PYROTEKNIKDAGEN.
Main/Corp Svenska Nationalkommitten for Mekanik. Sektionen for Detonik och Forbranning. **VFOAT** Pyroteknikdagen. (1969)-. Academic Scholarly Publication. English (Swedish, German and French). Every 3 years. Swedish Match Industries AB, Solstickegatan 1, Box 607, S-551 18 Jonkoping Sweden. **Tel** 011 46 36 119900, FAX 011 46 36 122777, telex 70044 MATCH S. **ED** J Hansson. **Circ:** 250. Documents available from CASDDS.
Desc: Papers presented at pyrotechnical conferences concerning chemical, physical and technological aspects of the field.
Ind/Abst Chem. Abstr.

ISSN 0071-7924
GW

FORTSCHRITTE DER PHYSIKALISCHEN CHEMIE. Vol. 1 (1957)-. Monographic series. German. Irregular. Price varies per volume. Dr Dietrich Steinkopff Verlag, PO Box 111442, D-64229 Darmstadt Germany. **Tel** 011 49 6151 17450, FAX 011 49 6151 174510. **ED** W. Jost.
Desc: A serial about current topics in physical chemistry and related fields.

ISSN 1071-5762
US

•**FREE RADICAL RESEARCH.** (1993)-. Periodical. English. Six times a year. Harwood Academic Publishers, PO Box 90, Reading RG1 8JL United Kingdom. **Tel** 011 44 1734 560080, FAX 011 44 1734 568211. ***Continues*** *Free Radical Research Communications, 8755-0199.*
Ind/Abst Curr. Cit.; Index Med.

LC QD505 .F86 **ISSN** 0271-1842
US
CODEN FRHCDG

FUNDAMENTAL RESEARCH IN HOMOGENEOUS CATALYSIS. [Fundam. res. homog. catal.]. **VFOAT** Homogeneous Catalysis. Vol. 1 (1976)-. Academic Scholarly Publication. English. Irregular. Price varies per volume. Plenum Press, 233 Spring Street, New York NY 10013-1578. **Tel** (212)620-8000, (800)221-9369, FAX (212)463-0742, (212)807-1047, telex 23/421139. Documents available from CASDDS.
Ind/Abst Chem. Abstr. (1977-1984).

LC QD505 .I58a **ISSN** 0254-4946
DD 541.3/95 BU
CODEN GEKADD

GETEROGENNYJ KATALIZ. (GETEROGENNYI KATALIZ : TRUDY ... MEZHDUNARODNOGO SIMPOZIUMA PO GETEROGENNOMU KATALIZU = HETEROGENEOUS CATALYSIS : PROCEEDINGS OF THE ... INTERNATIONAL SYMPOSIUM ON HETEROGENOUS CATALYSIS..). [Geterogen. katal.]. **Added/Corp** Edinen Tsentur Po Khimiia (Bulgarska Akademiia na Naukite). **VFOAT** Heterogeneous Catalysis. (1967)-. Academic Scholarly Publication. English (Russian). Bulgarska Akademiia na Naukite, 7 Noemvri 1, Sofia Bulgaria. Documents available from CASDDS.
Ind/Abst Chem. Abstr.

LC QC770 .H59 **ISSN** 0253-9950
DD 541.3/8/05 CC
CODEN HHHHDH

HE HUAXUE YU FANGSHE HUAXUE. (HO HUA HSUEH YU FANG SHE HUA HSUEH / CHUNG-KUO HO HUA HSUEH YU FANG SHE HUA HSUEH HUI.). [He huaxue yu Fangshe huaxue]. **Added/Corp** Chung-kuo ho Hua Hsueh yu Fang She Hua Hsueh Hui. **VFOAT** Journal of Nuclear and Radiochemistry; He Huaxue yu Fangshe Huaxue. Vol. 1 (Nov. 1979)-. Academic Scholarly Publication. Chinese (summaries and/or abstracts in English). Four times a year. $1.50 (per issue). Yuanzineng Chubanshe / Atomic Energy Press, 43 Fucheng Road Haidian District, Beijing 100037 People's Republic of China. **(Subscription address:** China International Book Trading Corporation, PO Box 399, Library Service Department, Beijing 100044 People's Republic of China. **Tel** 011 86 1 8414284, FAX 011 86 1 8412023, telex 22496 CIBTC CN.**) ED** Wang De-Xi. **Bk Rev. Ad Acc. Circ:** 2,200. Documents available from Ask*IEEE, CASDDS.
Desc: Covers academic theses with creativeness in theoretical and experimental researches on nuclear and radiochemistry.
Ind/Abst Art Archaeol. Tech. Abstr.; Chem. Abstr.; Chem. Titles; INSPEC (Feb. 1981-); NAPRALERT.

LC QD601.A1 H53 **ISSN** 0018-1439
US
CCC
CODEN HIECAP

Pr Rev.

HIGH ENERGY CHEMISTRY. [High energy chem.]. **Added/Corp** Consultants Bureau. Vol. 1 (Jan./Feb. 1967)-. Periodical. English (Russian). Six times a year. $1345.00. MAIK Nauka / Interperiodica, Ulitsa Profsoyuznaia 90, Moscow 117864 Russia. **ED** A.K. Pikaev. Index available. available on microfilm and microfiche from University Microfilms International (UMI). Documents available from The Genuine Article, CASDDS.
Desc: Contains articles on radiation chemistry, plasma chemistry, and chemistry of the ionosphere. Also covers important aspects of chemistry, photochemistry and nuclear chemistry.
Ind/Abst Chem. Abstr.; Coal Abstr.; Curr. Cit.; Curr. Contents Phys. Chem. Earth Sci.; Energy Res. Abstr.; Leadscan; Phys. Briefs; Res. Alert [Full Cov.]; Sci. Cit. Index; SCISEARCH.

LC QD450 .K469 **ISSN** 0207-401X RU **CCC** **CODEN** KHFID9

HIMICESKAJA FIZIKA. (KHIMICHESKAIA FIZIKA.). [Him. fiz.]. **Added/Corp** Akademiia Nauk SSSR. No. 1 (1982)-. Academic Scholarly Publication. Russian. Twelve times a year. $259.00. Izdatelstvo Nauka / Akademiia Nauk, (Publishing House of the Russian Academy of Sciences), Leninskii Porspekt 14, 117901 Moscow Russia. **Tel** 011 95 9542153, FAX 011 95 9382144, telex 411964. **(Subscription address:** East View Publications Inc., 3020 Harbor Lane North, Suite 110, Minneapolis MN 55447. **Tel** (800)477-1005, (612)550-0961, FAX (612)559-2931.) Documents available from The Genuine Article, Ask*IEEE, CASDDS. **Ind/Abst** Chem. Abstr.; INSPEC (1982-); Res. Alert [Full Cov.]; Sci. Cit. Index; SCISEARCH.

LC QD510 .I76 **ISSN** 0302-9751 RU **CODEN** IKTRAY

HIMICESKAJA TERMODINAMIKA I RAVNOVESIJA. (ITOGI NAUKI I TEKHNIKI : KHIMICHESKAIA TERMODINAMIKA I RAVNOVESIIA.). [Him. termodin. ravnov.]. **Added/Corp** Vsesoiuznyi Institut Nauchnoi i Tekhnicheskoi Informatsii (Soviet Union). **VFOAT** Itogi Nauki Tekhniki: Seriia Khimicheskaia Termodinamika i Ravnovesiia; Khimicheskaia Termodinamika I Ravnovesiia; Seriia Khimicheskaia Termodinamika I Ravnovesiia. Vol. 2 (1972)-. Academic Scholarly Publication. Russian. Irregular. Price varies. VINITI - Vsesoyuznyi Institut Nauchno-Tekhnicheskoi Informatsii, All-Union Scientific and Technical Information Institute, Baltiiskaia ulitsa 14, 125219 Moscow Russia. **Tel** 011 7 95 2384600, FAX 011 7 95 9430060, telex 411160. Documents available from CASDDS. ***Continues in part*** *Itogi Nauki Fizicheskaia Khimiia.*
Ind/Abst Chem. Abstr. (1972-1978).

ISSN 0023-1193 RU **CODEN** KHVKAO

HIMIJA VYSOKIH ENERGIJ. (KHIMIIA VYSOKIKH ENERGII.). [Him. vys. energ.]. **Added/Corp** Akademiia Nauk SSSR. Vol. 1 (1967)-. Academic Scholarly Publication. Russian. Six times a year. $300.00. Izdatelstvo Nauka / Akademiia Nauk, (Publishing House of the Russian Academy of Sciences), Leninskii Porspekt 14, 117901 Moscow Russia. **Tel** 011 95 9542153, FAX 011 95 9382144, telex 411964. **(Subscription address:** East View Publications Inc., 3020 Harbor Lane North, Suite 110, Minneapolis MN 55447. **Tel** (800)477-1005, (612)550-0961, FAX (612)559-2931.) cum. index. Documents available from CASDDS.
Ind/Abst Chem. Abstr.; Coal Abstr.; Energy Res. Abstr.; Sug. Indus. Abstr.

LC QD450 .K9a **ISSN** 0917-1746 JA **CODEN** KDGHEI

HOBUNSHU. **Main/Corp** Kyoto Daigaku. Genshiro Jikkenjo. Gakujutsu Koenkai. **Added/Corp** Kyoto Daigaku. Genshiro Jikkenjo. Gakujutsu Kokai Iinkai. **VFOAT** Kyoto Daigaku Genshiro Jikkensho Gakujutsu Koenkai Houbunshu; Abstracts of Report at Scientific Meeting of the Research Reactor Institute, Kyoto University. Issue 25 (Jan 1991)-. Japanese (summaries and/or abstracts in English). Documents available from CASDDS. ***Continues*** *Koen Yoshishu, 0287-9131.*
Ind/Abst Chem. Abstr.

ISSN 0376-4710 II **CODEN** ICACEC

INDIAN JOURNAL OF CHEMISTRY. SECTION A, INORGANIC, BIO-INORGANIC, PHYSICAL, THEORETICAL & ANALYTICAL CHEMISTRY. **See** Chemistry and Chemicals-Analytical Chemistry.

ISSN 0143-7496 UK **CCC** **CODEN** IJAADK

Pr Rev.

INTERNATIONAL JOURNAL OF ADHESION AND ADHESIVES. [Int. j. adhes. adhes]. Vol. 1 (July 1980)-. Academic Scholarly Publication. English. Four times a year. $414.00. Butterworth Heinemann Publishers, Linacre House Jordan Hill, Oxford OX2 8DP United Kingdom. **Tel** 011 44 1865 310366, FAX 011 44 1865 310898. **(Subscription address:** Elsevier Science Ltd. / Oxford Fulfillment Centre, PO Box 800, Kidlington OX5 1DX United Kingdom. **Tel** 011 44 865 843355.) **ED** John Herriot. Index available. cum. index. **Bk Rev. Ad Acc.** available on microfilm and microfiche from University Microfilms International (UMI); available on an online database from Elsevier Electronic Subscriptions (EES). Documents available from Article Express International, The Genuine Article, CASDDS.
Desc: Provides a medium through which all those active in the field of adhesion science and adhesives technology, and those with an interest in the uses of adhesive bonding, can communicate results, identify requirements and review progress. Original research papers on the science of adhesion, structural applications of adhesives, news items, conference reports, book reviews and a calendar.
Ind/Abst Abstr. Bull. Inst. Pap. Sci. Tech.; Alum. Ind. Abstr.; Art Archaeol. Tech. Abstr.; Bioeng. Abstr.; Chem. Abstr.; Curr. Cit.; Curr. Contents Eng. Comput. Technol.; Ei Page One; Eng. Mater. Abstr.; Eng. Index Annu.; For. Prod. Abstr.; Highw. Res. Abstr.; Int. Aerosp. Abstr.; Int. Packag. Abstr.; Met. Abstr.; Pollut. Abstr. Indexes; Polymer Contents; RAPRA Abstr.; Res. Alert [Full Cov.]; SCISEARCH; World Surf. Coat. Abstr.

LC QD501 .I634 **ISSN** 0538-8066
DD 541/.39 US **CCC**
NLM W1 IN766D **CODEN** IJCKBO

Pr Rev.

INTERNATIONAL JOURNAL OF CHEMICAL KINETICS. [Int. j. chem. kinet.]. Vol. 1 (Jan. 1969)-. Periodical. English (French and German; summaries and/or abstracts in English, French and German). Twelve times a year. $1368.00. John Wiley & Sons, Inc., 605 Third Avenue, New York NY 10158-0012. **Tel** (212)850-6000, (212)850-6645, FAX (212)850-6088, telex 12-7063. **(Subscription address:** John Wiley & Sons / UK, Baffins Lane, Chichester, West Sussex PO19 1UD United Kingdom. **Tel** 011 44 1243 779777, FAX 011 44 243 776128, telex 86290 WIBOOKG.) **ED** David Mark Golden. available on microfilm and microfiche from University Microfilms International (UMI). Documents available from Article Express International, The Genuine Article, BIOSIS Document Express, CASDDS.
Desc: Covers quantitative relationships between molecular structure and chemical activity, organic/inorganic chemistry, biochemical kinetics, reaction mechanisms and surface kinetics.
Ind/Abst Biol. Abstr.; Chem Inform; Chem. Abstr.; Chem. Titles; Coal Abstr.; Curr. Cit.; Curr. Contents Phys. Chem. Earth Sci.; Ei Page One; Eng. Index Annu.; Int. Aerosp. Abstr. (1983-); Mass Spect. Bull.; Res. Alert [Full Cov.]; Sci. Cit. Index; SCISEARCH.

LC TP250 .Z6 QD450 .I54
DD 660.2/97/05 GW

INTERNATIONAL JOURNAL OF PHYSICAL CHEMISTRY : BERICHTE DER BUNSEN-GESELLSCHAFT, AN. **Added/Corp** Deutsche Bunsen-Gesellschaft fur Physikalische Chemie. **VFOAT** Physical Chemistry; Berichte der Bunsen-Gesellschaft; Berichte der Bunsen-Gesellschaft fuer Physikalische Chemie. Vol. 95, No. 1 (Jan. 1991)-. Periodical. English (German). Twelve times a year. $735.00. VCH Gesellschaft GmbH, Postfach 101161, D-69451 Weinheim Germany. **Tel** 011 49 6201 606459, FAX 011 49 6201 606184. **(Subscription address:** VCH Publishers Inc., 303 Northwest 12th Avenue, Journals Department, Deerfield FL 33442. **Tel** (800)367-8249, (305)428-5566.) ***Continues*** *Berichte der Bunsen-Gesellschaft fur Physikalische Chemie, 0005-9021.*

LC QD462 .I5 **ISSN** 0020-7608
DD 541/.286/05 US **CCC** **CODEN** IJQCB2

Pr Rev.

INTERNATIONAL JOURNAL OF QUANTUM CHEMISTRY. [Int. j. quant. chem.]. Vol. 1 (Jan. 1967)-. Periodical. Multiple languages (English, French and German). Twenty-six times a year (twice per month plus two symposia issues). $2,886.00 (US); $3,146.00 (Canada and Mexico); $3,243.50 (other). Uitj Kluwer Rechtswetenschappe, 2100Deurne Antwerp Belgium. **Tel** 011 32 3 3000353, FAX 011 32 3 3600467. **(Subscription address:** John Wiley & Sons / UK, Baffins Lane, Chichester, West Sussex PO19 1UD United Kingdom. **Tel** 011 44 1243 779777, FAX 011 44 243 776128, telex 86290 WIBOOKG.) **ED** Per-Olov Lowdin, Jean-Louis Calais, and N. Yngve Ohrn. available on microfilm and microfiche from University Microfilms International (UMI). Documents available from The Genuine Article, Ask*IEEE, CASDDS.
Desc: Covers a broad scope of advanced information on quantum mechanics, fundamental concepts, mathematical structure, and applications to atoms, molecules, crystals and molecular biology.
Ind/Abst Ceram. Abstr.; Chem. Abstr.; Chem. Titles; Curr. Cit.; Curr. Contents Phys. Chem. Earth Sci.; Energy Res. Abstr.; INIS Atomindex [Micro.]; INSPEC (1968-); Mass Spect. Bull.; Res. Alert [Full Cov.]; Sci. Cit. Index; SCISEARCH.

LC QD462 .I52 **ISSN** 0161-3642
DD 541/.28 US **CCC** **CODEN** IJQSDI

INTERNATIONAL JOURNAL OF QUANTUM CHEMISTRY. QUANTUM CHEMISTRY SYMPOSIUM. [Int. j. quantum chem., Quantum chem. symp.]. **VFOAT** Quantum Chemistry Symposium; Quantum Chemistry Symposia. No. 11 (1977)-. Academic Scholarly Publication. English. One time a year. John Wiley & Sons, Inc., 605 Third Avenue, New York NY 10158-0012. **Tel** (212)850-6000, (212)850-6645, FAX (212)850-6088, telex 12-7063. **(Subscription address:** John Wiley & Sons / UK, Baffins Lane, Chichester, West Sussex PO19 1UD United Kingdom. **Tel** 011 44 1243 779777, FAX 011 44 243 776128, telex 86290 WIBOOKG.) Documents available from Ask*IEEE, CASDDS. ***Continues*** *International Journal of Quantum Chemistry. Symposium, 0538-821X.*
Ind/Abst Chem. Abstr.; Chem. Titles; Energy Res. Abstr.; INSPEC (1980-); Math. Rev.

LC QD450 .I58 **ISSN** 0144-235X
DD 541.3/05 UK **CCC** **CODEN** IRPCDL

Pr Rev.

INTERNATIONAL REVIEWS IN PHYSICAL CHEMISTRY. [Int. rev. phys. chem.]. Vol. 1, No. 1 (Apr. 1981)-. Academic Scholarly Publication. English. Two times a year. $370.00. Taylor & Francis Ltd. / UK, Rankine Road, Basingstoke, Hampshire RG24 8PR United Kingdom. **Tel** 011 44 1256 840366, FAX 011 44 1256 479438, telex 858540. **(Subscription address:** Taylor & Francis Inc., 1900 Frost Road, Suite 101, Bristol PA 19007-1598. **Tel** (215)785-5800, (800)821-8312, FAX (215)785-5515.) **ED** D. C. Clary (editor's address: Dept. of Chemistry, University of Cambridge, Lensfield Road, Cambridge CB2 1EW United Kingdom). available on microfilm from University Microfilms International (UMI). Documents available from The Genuine Article, CASDDS.
Desc: Covers scholarly and critical reviews on important and developing aspects of modern physical chemistry and chemical physics, providing a means of assisting specialists and generalists in research, industry and teaching to keep abreast of advances in expanding subjects. Internationally renowned scientists describe their own research in the wider context of the field.
Ind/Abst Alum. Ind. Abstr.; Chem. Abstr.; Curr. Cit.; Curr. Contents Phys. Chem. Earth Sci.; Energy Res. Abstr. (Nov. 1981-); Eng. Mater. Abstr.; Index Sci. Rev. [Full Cov.]; Met. Abstr.; Res. Alert [Full Cov.]; Sci. Cit. Index; SCISEARCH; World Alum. Abstr.

LC QD561 .I59 **ISSN** 0091-0619
DD 541/.3723/05 US
NLM W1 IO112 **CODEN** IEXMBW

ION EXCHANGE AND MEMBRANES. [Ion exch. membranes]. (1972)-. English. $16.00 vol. of 4 issues. Gordon & Breach Science Publishers, Inc., PO Box 786, Cooper Station, New York NY 10276. **Tel** (212)206-8900, FAX (212)645-2459. Documents available from BIOSIS Document Express, Ask*IEEE, CASDDS.
Ind/Abst Biol. Abstr. (-1975); Chem. Abstr.; Energy Res. Abstr. (Feb. 1973-); INSPEC (Dec. 1972-).

LC QD561 .I58 **ISSN** 0092-0193
DD 541/.3723 US
NLM W1 IO1125 **CODEN** IESEBH

ION EXCHANGE AND SOLVENT EXTRACTION. [Ion exch. solvent extr.]. Vol. 3 (1973)-. Academic Scholarly Publication. English. Irregular. Price varies per volume. Marcel Dekker Inc., 270 Madison Avenue, New York NY 10016. **Tel** (212)696-9000, (800)228-1160, FAX (212)685-4540, telex 421419. **(Subscription address:** Marcel Dekker Inc., PO Box 5017, Monticello NY 12701. **Tel** (800)228-1160.) **ED** J. A. Marinsky and Y. Marcus. Documents available from CASDDS. ***Formed by the union of*** *Solvent Extraction Reviews, 0038-125X* ***and*** *Ion Exchange, 0075-0328.*
Ind/Abst Chem. Abstr.; Ei Page One; Energy Res. Abstr. (Mar. 1979-).

LC QD561 .I68
DD 541.3/723/05 RU **CODEN** IOIODZ

IONNYI OBMEN I IONOMETRIIA. **Added/Corp** Leningradskii Gosudarstvennyi Universitet Imeni A.A. Zhdanova. Vol. 1 (1976)-. Periodical. Russian. St. Petersburg State University / Izdatelstvo Leningradskogo Universiteta, Universitetskaia Nab 7/9, 199034 St. Petersburg Russia. **Tel** 011 7 812 2189788, FAX 011 7 812 2185152, telex 121481. Documents available from CASDDS.
Ind/Abst Chem. Abstr.

LC QD1 .J69 **ISSN** 0021-7689
DD 541.05 FR **CCC**
NLM W1 JO238 **CODEN** JCPBAN

Pr Rev.

JOURNAL DE CHIMIE PHYSIQUE ET DE PHYSICO-CHIMIE BIOLOGIQUE. [J. chim. phys. physicochim. biol.]. **Added/Corp** Societe de Chimie Physique. Vol. 36, (1939)-. Academic Scholarly Publication. French. Ten times a year (1 volume). $726.00. Editions Scientifique Elsevier, 141 rue de Javel, 75747 Paris Cedex 15 France. **Tel** 011 33 1 45589067, FAX 011 33 1 45589424. **(Subscription address:** Editions Scientifiques Elsevier / for North America, PO Box 7247-7576, Philadelphia PA 19170-7576.) **ED** R. Marx. available in microform from University Microfilms International (UMI); available on an online database from Elsevier Electronic Subscriptions (EES). Documents available from The Genuine Article, Ask*IEEE, CASDDS. ***Continues*** *Journal de Chemie Physique;* ***Absorbed*** *Revue Generale des Colloides.*
Desc: Covers all fields of physical chemistry and

chemical physics including biophysics, quantum and theoretical chemistry, physical chemistry of polymers, and computer science in physical chemistry.
Ind/Abst Chem. Abstr.; Chem. Titles; Coal Abstr.; Curr. Biotechnol.; Curr. Cit.; Curr. Contents Phys. Chem. Earth Sci.; Energy Res. Abstr.; INSPEC (1968-); Leadscan; Life Sci. Collect.; Res. Alert [Full Cov.]; Sci. Cit. Index; SCISEARCH.

LC QC183 .J63 **ISSN** 0021-8464
DD 541/.3453 UK
CCC
CODEN JADNAJ

Pr Rev.
JOURNAL OF ADHESION, THE. [J. adhes.]. **VFOAT** Adhesion. Vol. 1 (Jan. 1969)-. Periodical. English. Three times a year. Price varies. Gordon & Breach Science Publishers, PO Box 90, Reading, Berkshire RG1 8JL United Kingdom. **Tel** 011 44 1734 560080, FAX 011 44 1734 568211. **(Subscription address:** Gordon & Breach Science Publishers / US, 820 Town Center Drive, Langhorne PA 19047. **Tel** (215)750-2642.) **ED** L. H. Sharpe. **Bk Rev. Ad Acc.** Documents available from Article Express International, The Genuine Article, Ask*IEEE, CASDDS.
Ind/Abst Abstr. Bull. Inst. Pap. Sci. Tech.; Acoust. Abstr.; Art Archaeol. Tech. Abstr.; Bioeng. Abstr.; Chem. Abstr.; Curr. Cit.; Curr. Contents Eng. Comput. Technol.; Curr. Contents Phys. Chem. Earth Sci.; Ei Page One (1984); Eng. Index Annu. (1968); INSPEC (July 1972-); Int. Aerosp. Abstr.; Pollut. Abstr. Indexes; Res. Alert [Full Cov.]; Sci. Cit. Index; SCISEARCH; World Surf. Coat. Abstr.

LC TP967 .J685 **ISSN** 0169-4243
NE
CODEN JATEE8

Pr Rev.
JOURNAL OF ADHESION SCIENCE AND TECHNOLOGY. [J. adhes. sci. technol.]. Vol. 1, No. 1 (1987)-. Periodical. English. Twelve times a year. DM1150.00. VSP International Science Publishers, Godfried van Seystlaan 47, 3703 BR Zeist Netherlands. **Tel** 011 31 3404 25790, FAX 011 31 3404 32081, telex 40217 USP NL. **(Subscription address:** VSP International Science Publishers, PO Box 346, 3700 AH Zeist Netherlands. **Tel** 011 31 30 6925790, FAX 011 31 30 6932081.) **ED** K. L. Mittal, W. G. van Ooij. **Bk Rev. Ad Acc.** Documents available from Article Express International, The Genuine Article, Ask*IEEE, CASDDS.
Desc: Provides a forum for the basic aspects, theories and mechanisms of adhesion and deals with applications of adhesion principles in all areas of technology.
Ind/Abst Chem. Abstr.; Curr. Cit.; Curr. Contents Eng. Comput. Technol.; Ei Page One; Eng. Mater. Abstr.; Eng. Index Annu.; INSPEC (1988-); Mech. Eng. Abstr.; Met. Abstr.; Res. Alert [Full Cov.]; Sci. Cit. Index; SCISEARCH; Solid State Supercond. Abstr.; World Surf. Coat. Abstr.

LC QC882 .J68 **ISSN** 0021-8502
DD 541/.34515/05 UK
CCC
NLM W1 JO534AS **CODEN** JALSB7

Pr Rev.
JOURNAL OF AEROSOL SCIENCE. [J. aerosol sci.]. **Added/Corp** Gesellschaft fuer Aerosolforschung (Germany). **VFOAT** Aerosol Science. Vol. 1 (Feb. 1970)-. Academic Scholarly Publication. English (French and German). Eight times a year. $1144.00. Pergamon Press, An Imprint of Elsevier Science Ltd., The Boulevard, Langford Lane, Kidlington, Oxford OX5 1GB United Kingdom. **Tel** 011 44 1865 843000, 011 44 1865 843699, FAX 011 44 1865 843010. **(Subscription address:** Elsevier Science Ltd. / Oxford Fulfillment Centre, PO Box 800, Kidlington OX5 1DX United Kingdom. **Tel** 011 44 865 843355.) **ED** G. Kasper and J. H. Vincent. available on microfilm from Microfilms International Marketing Corp.; available on microfilm and microfiche from University Microfilms International (UMI); available on an online database from Elsevier Electronic Subscriptions (EES). Documents available from Article Express International, The Genuine Article, Ask*IEEE, CASDDS, Documents on Demand.
Desc: Sets out to encourage and foster all aspects of basic and applied aerosol research.
Ind/Abst Acoust. Abstr.; Air Pollut. Titles; Anal. Abstr.; Bioeng. Abstr.; Biogr. Index; Chem. Abstr.; Coal Abstr.; Curr. Cit.; Curr. Contents Eng. Comput. Technol.; Ei Page One; EMBASE; Eng. Index Annu.; Environ. Abstr.; Fluid Abstr., Civil Eng.; Fluid Abstr. Proc. Eng.; FLUIDEX (1973-); INIS Atomindex [Micro.]; INSPEC (May 1970-); Int. Aerosp. Abstr.; Leadscan; Life Sci. Collect.; PESTDOC; Pollut. Abstr. Indexes; Proc. Chem. Eng.; Res. Alert [Full Cov.]; Saf. Health Work; Sci. Cit. Index; SCISEARCH; Theor. Chem. Eng.

LC QD501 .J77 **ISSN** 0021-9517
DD 541/.395/05 US
CCC
NLM W1 JO578 **CODEN** JCTLA5

Pr Rev.
JOURNAL OF CATALYSIS. [J. catal.]. Vol. 1 (Mar. 1962)-. Academic Scholarly Publication. English. Fourteen times a year. $1726.00. Academic Press Inc., 6277 Sea Harbor Drive, Orlando FL 32887. **Tel** (800)543-9534, (407)345-4100, FAX (407)352-3445. **ED** Gary L. Haller and Frank S. Stone. Documents available from The Genuine Article, CASDDS.
Desc: Original studies in heterogeneous and homogeneous catalysis as well as studies relating catalytic properties with chemical processes at surfaces, studies of the chemistry of surfaces, and engineering studies related to catalysis.
Ind/Abst Appl. Sci. Technol. Index (1991-); Chem Inform; Chem. Abstr.; Chem. Titles; Coal Abstr.; Curr. Cit.; Curr. Contents Phys. Chem. Earth Sci.; EMBASE; Energy Res. Abstr.; Gas Abstr.; INIS Atomindex [Micro.]; Int. Aerosp. Abstr.; Lit. Pat. Abstr., Oilfield Chem. (1963-); Lit. Abstr., Catal. Zeol.; Lit. Abstr., Health Environ.; Lit. Abstr., Pet. Refin. Petrochem.; Lit. Abstr., Pet. Substit.; Lit. Abstr., Transp. Storage; Mass Spect. Bull.; Proc. Chem. Eng.; Res. Alert [Full Cov.]; Sci. Cit. Index; SCISEARCH; Theor. Chem. Eng.

LC QD502 .J68 **ISSN** 1058-5834
DD 541.3/94 US
CODEN JCBKEI

JOURNAL OF CHEMICAL AND BIOCHEMICAL KINETICS. [J. chem. biochem. kinet.]. Vol. 1, No. 1 (1991)-. Academic Scholarly Publication. English. Four times a year. $195.00. Nova Science Publishers Inc., 6080 Jericho Turnpike, Suite 207, Commack NY 11725-2808. **Tel** (516)499-3103, (516)499-3106, FAX (516)499-3146. Documents available from CASDDS.
Ind/Abst Chem. Abstr.

LC QD1 .J94 **ISSN** 0021-9606
DD 541.05 US
CCC
NLM W1 JO581J **CODEN** JCPSA6

Pr Rev.
JOURNAL OF CHEMICAL PHYSICS, THE. [J. chem. phys.]. **Added/Corp** American Institute of Physics. **VFOAT** Chemical Physics. Vol. 1 (Jan. 1933)-. Periodical. English. Irregular (48 issues). $2980.00. American Institute of Physics, 500 Sunnyside Boulevard, Woodbury NY 11797-2999. **Tel** (516)576-2270, (800)344-6902, FAX (516)349-9704, telex 960983. Index available (free). available on microfilm and microfiche (16mm or 35mm). Documents available from Article Express International, The Genuine Article, Ask*IEEE, Petroleum Abstracts Document Delivery Service, CASDDS.
Ind/Abst Abstr. Bull. Inst. Pap. Sci. Tech.; Acoust. Abstr.; AQUAREF; Ceram. Abstr.; Chem Inform; Chem. Abstr.; Chem. Titles; Curr. Cit.; Curr. Contents Phys. Chem. Earth Sci.; Curr. Phys. Index; Ei Page One; Energy Res. Abstr.; Eng. Index Annu. [Select. Cov.]; GeoRef; HTFS Dig.; INIS Atomindex [Micro.]; INSPEC (1968-); Int. Aerosp. Abstr.; Mass Spect. Bull.; Math. Rev.; Pet. Abstr.; Proc. Chem. Eng.; Ref. Upd. Deluxe Ed.; Res. Alert [Full Cov.]; Sci. Cit. Index; SCISEARCH; Soils Fert.; SPIN (1968-); Surf. Treat. Technol. Abstr.; Theor. Chem. Eng.; World Ceram. Abstr.

LC QD501 .J78 **ISSN** 0021-9614
DD 541/.369/05 UK
CCC
CODEN JCTDAF

Pr Rev.
JOURNAL OF CHEMICAL THERMODYNAMICS, THE. [J. chem. thermodyn.]. Vol. 1 (1969)-. Academic Scholarly Publication. English. Twelve times a year. $735.81. Academic Press Ltd., A Division of Harcourt Brace & Company Ltd., 24-28 Oval Road, London NW1 7DX United Kingdom. **Tel** 011 44 171 2674466, FAX 011 44 171 4822293, 011 44 171 4854752, telex 25775 ACPRES G. **(Subscription address:** Harcourt Brace & Company, Ltd., Foots Cray High Street, Sidcup Kent DA14 5HP United Kingdom. **Tel** 011 44 181 3003322, FAX 011 44 181 3090807, telex 896 377 ACADEM.) **ED** M. L. McGlashan and P. A. G. O'Hare. cum. index. Documents available from The Genuine Article, Ask*IEEE, CASDDS.
Desc: Publishes papers reporting the results of significant new measurements of thermochemical and equilibrium quantities for chemical reactions and of thermodynamic properties of pure substances and of mixtures, using calorimetric, pVT, spectroscopic, and other methods.
Ind/Abst Acoust. Abstr.; Alum. Ind. Abstr.; Ceram. Abstr. (Nov. 1971-); Chem Inform; Chem. Abstr.; Chem. Titles; Curr. Cit.; Curr. Contents Phys. Chem. Earth Sci.; Eng. Mater. Abstr.; Gas Abstr. (Nov. 1971-); GeoRef; HTFS Dig.; INSPEC (Nov. 1971-); Leadscan; Lit. Pat. Abstr., Oilfield Chem. (1972-); Lit. Abstr., Catal. Zeol.; Lit. Abstr., Health Environ.; Lit. Abstr., Pet. Refin. Petrochem.; Lit. Abstr., Pet. Substit.; Lit. Abstr., Transp. Storage; Mass Spect. Bull. (Nov. 1971-); Met. Abstr.; MINPROC; Res. Alert [Full Cov.]; Sci. Cit. Index; SCISEARCH.

LC QD549 .J67 **ISSN** 0021-9797
DD 541/.3451/05 US
CCC
NLM W1 JO593 **CODEN** JCISA5

Pr Rev.
JOURNAL OF COLLOID AND INTERFACE SCIENCE. [J. colloid interface sci.]. Vol. 21 (Jan. 1966)-. Academic Scholarly Publication. English. Sixteen times a year. $1766.00. Academic Press Inc., 6277 Sea Harbor Drive, Orlando FL 32887. **Tel** (800)543-9534, (407)345-4100, FAX (407)352-3445. **ED** Milton Kerker and Josip P. Kratohvil. **Bk Rev.** Documents available from Article Express International, The Genuine Article, BIOSIS Document Express, Ask*IEEE, Petroleum Abstracts Document Delivery Service, CASDDS.
Continues *Journal of Colloid Science, 0095-8522.*
Desc: Publishes original research on fundamental principles and their applications. Concerned with the work of investigators in relevant areas of chemistry, physics, engineering, biology, and applied mathematics. Features original research contributions from university, government, and industrial laboratories worldwide.
Ind/Abst Abstr. Bull. Inst. Pap. Sci. Tech.; AGRICOLA; Biol. Abstr.; Ceram. Abstr.; Chem. Abstr.; Chem. Titles; Coal Abstr.; Curr. Biotechnol.; Curr. Cit.; Curr. Contents Phys. Chem. Earth Sci.; Dairy Sci. Abstr.; Ei Page One; EMBASE; Eng. Index Annu.; Food Sci. Technol. Abstr.; GATFWORLD (1984); GeoRef; HTFS Dig.; INIS Atomindex [Micro.]; INSPEC (1968-); Int. Aerosp. Abstr.; Lit. Pat. Abstr., Oilfield Chem. (1954-); Lit. Abstr., Catal. Zeol.; Lit. Abstr., Health Environ.; Lit. Abstr., Pet. Refin. Petrochem.; Lit. Abstr., Pet. Substit.; Lit. Abstr., Transp. Storage; Math. Rev.; Life Sci. Collect.; Pet. Abstr.; Polymer Contents; Proc. Chem. Eng.; Res. Alert [Full Cov.]; Sci. Cit. Index; SCISEARCH; Soils Fert.; Theor. Chem. Eng.; World Ceram. Abstr.; World Surf. Coat. Abstr.

LC QD471 .J635 **ISSN** 0095-8972
DD 541/.2242/05 US
CCC
CODEN JCCMBQ

Pr Rev.
JOURNAL OF COORDINATION CHEMISTRY. [J. coord. chem.]. **VFOAT** Coordination Chemistry. Vol. 1, No. 1 (Aug. 1971)-. Periodical. English. Four times a year (3 volumes). Price varies. Gordon & Breach Science Publishers, Inc., PO Box 786, Cooper Station, New York NY 10276. **Tel** (212)206-8900, FAX (212)645-2459. **(Subscription address:** Gordon & Breach Science Publishers / England, PO Box 90 Reading, Berkshire RG1 8JL United Kingdom. **Tel** 011 44 734 560080.) Documents available from The Genuine Article, Ask*IEEE, CASDDS.
Ind/Abst Chem. Abstr. (May 1972-); Curr. Cit.; Curr. Contents Phys. Chem. Earth Sci.; Energy Res. Abstr. (May 1972-); INIS Atomindex [Micro.]; INSPEC (May 1972-); Leadscan; Res. Alert [Full Cov.]; Sci. Cit. Index; SCISEARCH.

LC QD549 .J68 **ISSN** 0193-2691
DD 541.3/451 US
CCC
CODEN JDTEDS

Pr Rev.
JOURNAL OF DISPERSION SCIENCE AND TECHNOLOGY. [J. dispers. sci. technol.]. Vol. 1 (1980)-. Academic Scholarly Publication. English. Six times a year. $585.00. Marcel Dekker Inc., 270 Madison Avenue, New York NY 10016. **Tel** (212)696-9000, (800)228-1160, FAX (212)685-4540, telex 421419. **(Subscription address:** Marcel Dekker Inc., PO Box 5017, Monticello NY 12701. **Tel** (800)228-1160.) **ED** Stig E. Friberg and Paul Becher. **Bk Rev. Ad Acc.** ctrl circ. available on microfiche; available on microfilm; available in microform. Documents available from Article Express International, The Genuine Article, CASDDS.
Desc: Deals with dispersions on the technological level. It demonstrates the power of colloid sciences in solving real-world dispersion problems, and serves as a source for researchers, educators, and all industry personnel working in this area. The journal emphasizes discussion and application of theoretical aspects, and includes both reviews of the latest findings and original research papers.
Ind/Abst Acoust. Abstr.; Bioeng. Abstr.; Chem. Abstr.; Chem. Titles; Curr. Cit.; Curr. Contents Phys. Chem. Earth Sci.; Dairy Sci. Abstr.; Ei Page One; Eng. Index Annu.; Food Sci. Technol. Abstr.; Int. Pharm. Abstr.; Lit. Pat. Abstr., Oilfield Chem. (1982-1990); Lit. Abstr., Catal. Zeol.; Lit. Abstr., Health Environ.; Lit. Abstr., Pet. Refin. Petrochem.; Lit. Abstr., Pet. Substit.; Lit. Abstr., Transp. Storage; Proc. Chem. Eng.; Res. Alert [Full Cov.]; Sci. Cit. Index; SCISEARCH; Theor. Chem. Eng.; World Surf. Coat. Abstr.

ISSN 0923-0750
NE
CCC
CODEN JIMCEN

Pr Rev.
JOURNAL OF INCLUSION PHENOMENA AND MOLECULAR RECOGNITION IN CHEMISTRY. [J. incl. phenom. mol. recognit. chem.]. **VFOAT** Journal of Inclusion Phonomena. Vol. 7, No. 1 (Feb. 1989)-. Academic Scholarly Publication. English. Twelve times a year. $682.00. Kluwer Academic Publishers, Postbus 322, 3300 AH Dordrecht The Netherlands. **Tel** 011 31 78 524400, FAX 011 31 78 183273, telex 20083. **ED** John Lamb and Eric Davies. **Acid Free.** Documents available from The Genuine Article, CASDDS. ***Continues*** *Journal of Inclusion Phenomena, 0167-7861.*
Desc: Interdisciplinary publication reporting on original research into aspects of host-guest systems. It publishes reports of original research and preliminary communications, provided the latter represent a significant advance in the advance in the understanding of inclusion science.
Ind/Abst Chem. Abstr.; Curr. Chem. React.; Curr. Cit.; Curr. Contents Phys. Chem. Earth Sci.; Res. Alert [Full Cov.]; Sci. Cit. Index; SCISEARCH.

LC QD466 .J59 **ISSN** 0362-4803
DD 541/.3884/5 UK
CCC
NLM W1 JO733N **CODEN** JLCRD4
Pr Rev.
JOURNAL OF LABELLED COMPOUNDS & RADIOPHARMACEUTICALS. [J. labelled compd. radiopharm.]. **VFOAT** A.Journal of labelled compounds and radiopharmaceuticals. **VAT** Journal of Labelled Compounds and Radiopharmaceuticals. Vol. 12 (Jan./March 1976)-. Academic Scholarly Publication. English (French and German). Thirteen times a year (includes special issue). $1295.00. John Wiley & Sons Ltd., Baffins Lane, Chichester, West Sussex PO19 1UD United Kingdom. **Tel** 011 44 1243 779777, FAX 011 44 1243 776128 BTG:JWP001, telex 86290 WIBOOKG. **(Subscription address:** John Wiley & Sons, Inc. / Philadelphia, PO Box 7247, Philadelphia PA 19170. **Tel** (212)850-6645, (800)225-5945.) **ED** J. R. Jones, A. P. Wolf, and L. Pichat. **Circ:** 750. available on microfilm and microfiche from University Microfilms International (UMI). Documents available from The Genuine Article, BIOSIS Document Express, CASDDS, ADONIS. ***Continues*** *Journal of Labelled Compounds, 0022-2135.*
Desc: Publishes scientific manuscripts dealing research and development in labelled compound preparation. Related areas, such as analytical control, self radiolysis, quality control handling and storage are also covered.
Ind/Abst ADONIS; Anal. Abstr.; Biol. Abstr.; Chem. Abstr.; Chem. Titles; CSA Neuro. Abstr. (?-?); Curr. Chem. React.; Curr. Cit.; Curr. Contents Life Sci.; Curr. Contents Phys. Chem. Earth Sci.; Dairy Sci. Abstr.; EMBASE; Health Saf. Sci. Abstr.; Index Chem.; Mass Spect. Bull.; Methods Organ. Synth.; Microbiol. Abstr. Sect. A; Nat. Prod. Updates; Life Sci. Collect.; PESTDOC; Plant Grow. Reg. Abstr.; Pollut. Abstr. Indexes; Protozoolog. Abstr.; Res. Alert [Full Cov.]; Rev. Agric. Entomol.; Rev. Med. Vet. Entomol.; Sci. Cit. Index; SCISEARCH; Virol. AIDS Abstr.

LC QD505 .J67 **ISSN** 0304-5102
DD 541/.395/05 NE
CCC
NLM W1 JO773D **CODEN** JMCADS
Pr Rev. **TITLE CHANGE**
JOURNAL OF MOLECULAR CATALYSIS. [J. molec. catal.]. Vol. 1 (Sept. 1975)-(1994). Academic Scholarly Publication. English. Elsevier Science Publishers BV, PO Box 211, 1000 AE Amsterdam Netherlands. **Tel** 011 31 20 4853641, 011 31 20 4853642, FAX 011 31 20 4853598. **ED** E.G. Derouane. available on microfilm and microfiche from University Microfilms International (UMI). Documents available from Article Express International, The Genuine Article, BIOSIS Document Express, CASDDS. ***Split into*** *Journal of Molecular Catalysis. A, Chemical, 1381-1169* ***and*** *Journal of Molecular Catalysis. B, Enzymatic, 1381-1177.*
Desc: International forum for discussion on all aspects of catalytic activation; published in three sections: biochemical catalysis, chemical catalysis and industrial catalysis.
Ind/Abst Bioeng. Abstr.; Biol. Abstr.; Chem. Abstr.; Chem. Titles; Coal Abstr.; Curr. Biotechnol.; Curr. Cit.; Curr. Contents Phys. Chem. Earth Sci.; Ei Page One; EMBASE; Eng. Index Annu.; Lit. Pat. Abstr., Oilfield Chem. (1990-); Lit. Abstr., Catal. Zeol.; Lit. Abstr., Health Environ.; Lit. Abstr., Pet. Refin. Petrochem.; Lit. Abstr., Pet. Substit.; Lit. Abstr., Transp. Storage; Life Sci. Collect.; Res. Alert [Full Cov.]; Sci. Cit. Index; SCISEARCH.

LC QD505 .J673 **ISSN** 1381-1177
DD 621.3/95/05 NE
JOURNAL OF MOLECULAR CATALYSIS B : ENZYMATIC. (19??)-. Academic Scholarly Publication. English. Four times a year. $296.00. Elsevier Science Publishers BV, PO Box 211, 1000 AE Amsterdam Netherlands. **Tel** 011 31 20 4853641, 011 31 20 4853642, FAX 011 31 20 4853598. available on an online database from Elsevier Electronic Subscriptions (EES). ***Continues in part*** *Journal of Molecualr Catalysis.*

LC QD461 **ISSN** 0263-7855
DD 541.2/2/028566 UK
CCC
NLM W1; MO773Q **CODEN** JMGRDV
Pr Rev.
JOURNAL OF MOLECULAR GRAPHICS. **See** Chemistry and Chemicals-Computer Applications.

LC QD471 .J638 **ISSN** 0022-2860
DD 541 NE
CCC
NLM W1 JO774F **CODEN** JMOSB4
Pr Rev.
JOURNAL OF MOLECULAR STRUCTURE. [J. mol. struct.]. Vol. 1 (Oct. 1967)-. Academic Scholarly Publication. English (French and German). Forty-two times a year. $3517.00. Elsevier Science Publishers BV, PO Box 211, 1000 AE Amsterdam Netherlands. **Tel** 011 31 20 4853641, 011 31 20 4853642, FAX 011 31 20 4853598. **ED** A. Barnes, W.J. Orville-Thomas, H. Ratajczak. **Bk Rev. Ad Acc.** ctrl circ. available on microfilm and microfiche from University Microfilms International (UMI); available on an online database from Elsevier Electronic Subscriptions (EES). Documents available from The Genuine Article, Ask*IEEE, CASDDS.
Desc: Brings together in a single publication papers which provide important new information on molecular structure, regardless of the physical method (or methods) used in the study.
Ind/Abst Chem Inform; Chem. Abstr.; Chem. Titles; Curr. Cit.; Curr. Contents Phys. Chem. Earth Sci.; INSPEC (May-June 1969-); Int. Aerosp. Abstr.; Leadscan; Mass Spect. Bull.; NAPRALERT; Life Sci. Collect.; Res. Alert [Full Cov.]; Sci. Cit. Index; SCISEARCH; Soils Fert.

LC QD471 .T52 **ISSN** 0166-1280
DD 541.2/05 NE
CCC
CODEN THEODJ
Pr Rev.
JOURNAL OF MOLECULAR STRUCTURE. THEOCHEM. (THEOCHEM.). [J. mol. struct., Theochem]. Vol. 1, No. 1 (Jan. 1981)-. Academic Scholarly Publication. English (French and German). Forty-Five times a year. $3769.00. Elsevier Science Publishers BV, PO Box 211, 1000 AE Amsterdam Netherlands. **Tel** 011 31 20 4853641, 011 31 20 4853642, FAX 011 31 20 4853598. **ED** I.G. Csizmadia, C.E. Dykstra, J.L. Rivail. available on microfilm from University Microfilms International (UMI); available on an online database from Elsevier Electronic Subscriptions (EES). Documents available from The Genuine Article, Ask*IEEE, CASDDS.
Desc: Devoted to the application of theoretical chemistry to organic, inorganic and biological molecules, including polymer, solid and liquid structures.
Ind/Abst Chem Inform; Chem. Abstr.; Curr. Contents Phys. Chem. Earth Sci.; GeoRef; INSPEC (Jan. 1981-); Res. Alert [Full Cov.]; Sci. Cit. Index; SCISEARCH.

LC QD701 .J68 **ISSN** 1010-6030
DD 541/.35/05 SZ
CCC
Pr Rev.
JOURNAL OF PHOTOCHEMISTRY AND PHOTOBIOLOGY. A, CHEMISTRY. **VFOAT** Chemistry. Vol. 40, No. 1 (Sept./Oct. 1987)-. Academic Scholarly Publication. English. Twenty-four times a year (8 volumes). $2988.00. Elsevier Sequoia SA, PO Box 564, CH-1001 Lausanne 1 Switzerland. **Tel** 011 41 21 3207381, FAX 011 41 21 3235444. **ED** R.P. Wayne. **Ad Acc, Adv Mgr:** W. van Cattenburch (Amsterdam). available on microfilm and microfiche from University Microfilms International (UMI); available on an online database from Elsevier Electronic Subscriptions (EES). Documents available from The Genuine Article, Ask*IEEE, CASDDS. ***Continues in part*** *Journal of Photochemistry, 0047-2670.*
Desc: Concerned with either quantitative or qualitative aspects of photochemistry. Papers related to applied photochemistry are also published.
Ind/Abst Chem. Abstr.; Curr. Cit.; Curr. Contents Phys. Chem. Earth Sci.; INSPEC; Met. Abstr.; Phys. Briefs; Polymer Contents; Res. Alert [Full Cov.]; Sci. Cit. Index; SCISEARCH.

ISSN 0022-3654
DD 541 US
CCC
NLM W1 JO833 **CODEN** JPCHAX
Pr Rev.
JOURNAL OF PHYSICAL CHEMISTRY (1952). (THE JOURNAL OF PHYSICAL CHEMISTRY.). [J. phys. chem.]. **Added/Corp** American Chemical Society. Vol. 56 (1952)-. Periodical. English. One time a week (51 issues). $1795.00. American Chemical Society, 1155 Sixteenth Street Northwest, Washington DC 20036. **Tel** (800)333-9511, (800)227-5558, (614)447-3776, FAX (202)447-3671. **(Subscription address:** American Chemical Society / Ohio, Department L 0011, Columbus OH 43268-0011.) **ED** Mostafa A. El-Sayed. Index available (bound in Nov. issue). **Ad Acc, Adv Mgr Tel** (203)256-8211. **Acid Free. Circ:** 4,528. available on microfilm and microfiche from University Microfilms International (UMI). Documents available from The Genuine Article, Ask*IEEE, Petroleum Abstracts Document Delivery Service, CASDDS. ***Continues*** *Journal of Physical & Colloid Chemistry, 0092-7023.*
Desc: Reports theoretical and experimental research dealing with fundamental aspects of physical chemistry and chemical physics including new concepts, techniques, interpretations, articles, communications and symposia proceedings.
Ind/Abst Abstr. Bull. Inst. Pap. Sci. Tech.; Acoust. Abstr.; Alum. Ind. Abstr.; Appl. Sci. Technol. Index; Ceram. Abstr.; Chem. Abstr.; Chem. Titles; Coal Abstr.; Curr. Cit.; Curr. Contents Phys. Chem. Earth Sci.; Curr. Titles Electrochem.; Ei Page One; Energy Res. Abstr.; Eng. Mater. Abstr.; GeoRef; INIS Atomindex [Micro.]; INSPEC (1968-); Int. Aerosp. Abstr.; Lit. Pat. Abstr., Oilfield Chem. (1954-); Lit. Abstr., Catal. Zeol.; Lit. Abstr., Health Environ.; Lit. Abstr., Pet. Refin. Petrochem.; Lit. Abstr., Pet. Substit.; Lit. Abstr., Transp. Storage; Mass Spect. Bull.; Met. Abstr.; Pet. Abstr.; Polymer Contents; Proc. Chem. Eng.; Ref. Upd. Deluxe Ed.; Res. Alert [Full Cov.]; Sci. Cit. Index; SCISEARCH; Soils Fert.; Theor. Chem. Eng.; World Ceram. Abstr.

LC QD1
US
JOURNAL OF PHYSICAL CHEMISTRY. SUPPLEMENTARY MATERIAL, THE. **Added/Corp** American Chemical Society. (1973)-. Periodical. English. Princeton Microfilm Corporation, Alexander Road, Princeton NJ 08540.

LC QD901 .J64 **ISSN** 0022-4596
DD 541 US
CCC
CODEN JSSCBI
Pr Rev.
JOURNAL OF SOLID STATE CHEMISTRY. [J. solid state chem.]. Vol. 1 (June 1969)-. Academic Scholarly Publication. English (French and German). Fourteen times a year. $1723.00. Academic Press Inc., 6277 Sea Harbor Drive, Orlando FL 32887. **Tel** (800)543-9534, (407)345-4100, FAX (407)352-3445. **ED** J. M. Honig and J. W. Richardson. Documents available from Article Express International, The Genuine Article, Ask*IEEE, CASDDS.
Desc: Covers major developments in the field of solid state chemistry. Features studies of chemical structural, thermodynamic, electronic, magnetic, and optical processes in solids. The systems covered include ionic solids, semiconductors, metals, thin films, and glasses, as well as nonstoichiometric compounds, ferroelectrics, superconductors, and defect structures.
Ind/Abst Bioeng. Abstr.; Ceram. Abstr.; Chem. Abstr.; Chem. Titles; Coal Abstr.; Curr. Cit.; Curr. Contents Phys. Chem. Earth Sci.; Ei Page One; Energy Res. Abstr.; Eng. Mater. Abstr.; Eng. Index Annu.; GeoRef; INSPEC (Nov. 1971-); Res. Alert [Full Cov.]; Sci. Cit. Index; SCISEARCH; Soc. Sci. Cit. Index [Select. Cov.]; Soils Fert.

LC QD541 .J8 **ISSN** 0095-9782
DD 541/.34/05 US
CCC
NLM W1 JO901D **CODEN** JSLCAG
Pr Rev.
JOURNAL OF SOLUTION CHEMISTRY. [J. solution chem.]. Vol. 1 (July 1972)-. Academic Scholarly Publication. English. Twelve times a year. $645.00. Plenum Press, 233 Spring Street, New York NY 10013-1578. **Tel** (212)620-8000, (800)221-9369, FAX (212)463-0742, (212)807-1047, telex 23/421139. **ED** Robert L. Kay. available on microfilm and microfiche from University Microfilms International (UMI). Documents available from The Genuine Article, BIOSIS Document Express, CASDDS.
Desc: This journal is a forum for research on the physical chemistry of liquid solutions covering such fields as: physical chemistry, chemical physics, molecular biology, biochemistry, and biophysics.
Ind/Abst AQUAREF; Biol. Abstr.; Chem. Abstr.; Chem. Titles; Curr. Cit.; Curr. Contents Phys. Chem. Earth Sci.; Curr. Titles Electrochem.; Energy Res. Abstr. (Jan. 1974-); GeoRef; Res. Alert [Full Cov.]; Sci. Cit. Index; SCISEARCH; Soils Fert.

LC QD1 .Z5312 **ISSN** 0022-4766
DD 541/.05 US
CCC
CODEN JSTCAM
JOURNAL OF STRUCTURAL CHEMISTRY. (JOURNAL OF STRUCTURAL CHEMISTRY. ZHURNAL STRUKTURNOI KHIMII.). [J. struct. chem.]. **Added/Corp** Consultants Bureau Enterprises. Consultants Bureau. **VFOAT** Zhurnal Strukturnoi Khimii. Vol. 1 (May/June 1960)-. Periodical. English (Russian). Six times a year. $1265.00. Consultants Bureau, A Division of Plenum Publishing Corporation, 233 Spring Street, New York NY 10013. **Tel** (212)620-8000, (212)620-8466, FAX (212)463-0742, telex 23/421139. **ED** L. N. Mazalov. Index available. available on microfilm and microfiche from University Microfilms International (UMI). Documents available from The Genuine Article, Ask*IEEE, CASDDS.
Ind/Abst Ceram. Abstr.; Chem. Abstr.; Chem. Titles; Curr. Cit.; Curr. Contents Phys. Chem. Earth Sci.; Energy Res. Abstr.; Eng. Mater. Abstr.; GeoRef; INIS Atomindex [Micro.]; INSPEC (Jan./Feb. 1972-); Mass Spect. Bull.; Res. Alert [Full Cov.]; Sci. Cit. Index; SCISEARCH.

ISSN 0956-5000
UK
CCC
NLM W1; JO916GF **CODEN** JCFTEV
JOURNAL OF THE CHEMICAL SOCIETY. FARADAY TRANSACTIONS. (JOURNAL OF THE CHEMICAL SOCIETY. FARADAY TRANSACTIONS.). [J. Chem. Soc., Faraday trans.]. **Added/Corp** Royal Society of Chemistry (Great Britain) Royal Society of Chemistry (Great Britain). Faraday Division. **VFOAT** Faraday Transactions. Vol. 86, No. 1 (Jan. 7, 1990)-. Academic Scholarly Publication. English. Twenty-four times a year (plus index). $1717.00. Royal Society of Chemistry, Thomas Graham House, Science Park, Cambridge CB4 4WF United Kingdom. **Tel** 011 44 1223 420066, FAX 011 44 1223 423623, telex 818293 ROYAL. **(Subscription address:** Royal Society of Chemistry, Turpin Distribution Services Ltd., Blackhorse Road, Letchworth, Hertfordshire SG6 1HN United Kingdom. **Tel** 011 44 1462 672555, FAX 011 44 1462 480947.) Index available (free). available on microfilm and microfiche from University Microfilms International

(UMI); available on an online database from STN International. Documents available from The Genuine Article, BIOSIS Document Express, Ask*IEEE, CASDDS, BLDSC, FAXON Xpress, SWETS, UMI Article Clearinghouse. ***Formed by the union of*** *Journal of the Chemical Society. Faraday Transactions I, Physical Chemistry in Condensed Phases* ***and*** *Journal of the Chemical Society. Faraday Transactions II, Molecular and Chemical Physics.*
Desc: Original work in physical chemistry and chemical physics. It covers topics such as gas-phase kinetics and dynamics, molecular beam kinetics and spectroscopy, photochemistry and quantum chemistry.
Ind/Abst Biol. Abstr.; Chem. Abstr. (1990-); Curr. Cit.; Ei Page One; HTFS Dig.; INSPEC (Jan. 1990-); Leadscan; Lit. Pat. Abstr., Oilfield Chem. (1954-); Lit. Abstr., Catal. Zeol.; Lit. Abstr., Health Environ.; Lit. Abstr., Pet. Refin. Petrochem.; Lit. Abstr., Pet. Substit.; Lit. Abstr., Transp. Storage; Res. Alert [Full Cov.]; Sci. Cit. Index; SCISEARCH; Soils Fert.

LC QC770 .T58A **ISSN** 0385-2105
DD 539.7/05 JA
CODEN TLNRBV
KAKURIKEN KEDKYU HOKOKU. See Physics-Nuclear Physics.

LC QD501 .K33
DD 541.39 UN
KATALIZ I KATALIZATORY; RESPUBLIKANSKII MEZHVEDOMSTVENNYI SBORNIK.
Added/Corp Akademiia Nauk Ukrainskoi RSR. (1965)-. Russian. Izdatelstvo Naukova Dumka / Ukrainian Academy of Sciences, Yu. A. Khramov, Dir., Ul. Repina 3, 252 601 Kiev Ukraine. **Tel** 011 7 44 4303441, 011 7 44 2254182, telex 131376. Documents available from CASDDS.
Ind/Abst Chem. Abstr.

ISSN 1102-6650
SW
KEMIVARLDEN. (1992)-. Trade Publication. Swedish. Sixteen times a year. Kr495.00 Sweden; Kr396.00 other Nordic countries; Kr673.00 other Europe; Kr752.00 other. Ekonomi och Teknik Foerlag AB, Klara Soedra Kyrkogata 1, 106 12 Stockholm Sweden. **Tel** 011 46 8 796-6652, 796-6661, 796-6500, FAX 46 8 21 76 11. **Ad Acc, Adv Mgr:** Ellinor Jenneholt.
Desc: Provides trade news for the chemical industry.

LC QD450 .K47 **ISSN** 0733-2831
DD 539 US
CCC
CODEN SJCPDF
KHIMICHESKAIA FIZIKA. (SOVIET JOURNAL OF CHEMICAL PHYSICS.). [Sov. j. chem. phys.]. No. 1 (Nov. 1983)-. Periodical. English (Russian). Twelve times a year. $2136.00 (academic institutions), $3332.00 (corporate institutions). Gordon & Breach Science Publishers, Inc., PO Box 786, Cooper Station, New York NY 10276. **Tel** (212)206-8900, FAX (212)645-2459. **ED** N. N. Semenov. **Bk Rev. Ad Acc.** Documents available from Article Express International, Ask*IEEE.
Ind/Abst Ei Page One; Eng. Index Annu.; INSPEC (1984-); Mass Spect. Bull.

LC QD501 **ISSN** 0023-1584
DD 541.3/95/05 US
UDC 541.124/.128 **CCC**
CODEN KICAA8
Pr Rev.
KINETICS AND CATALYSIS. [Kinet. catal.]. **VFOAT** Kinetika i Kataliz. Vol. 1 (May/June 1960)-. Periodical. English (Russian). Six times a year. $1475.00. Plenum Press, 233 Spring Street, New York NY 10013-1578. **Tel** (212)620-8000, (800)221-9369, FAX (212)463-0742, (212)807-1047, telex 23/421139. **(Subscription address:** Plenum Press Subscription Department, PO Box 730, Canal Street, Station NY 10013-1578. **Tel** (212)620-8000, (212)620-8466.**) ED** V. B. Kanzanskii. Index available. available on microfilm and microfiche from University Microfilms International (UMI). Documents available from The Genuine Article, CASDDS.
Desc: Contains reports on the latest research performed on various catalytic materials and on processes of autocatalysts, degradation of organic materials and the kinetics of reactions with or without catalysis.
Ind/Abst Chem. Abstr.; Coal Abstr.; Curr. Biotechnol.; Curr. Cit.; Curr. Contents Phys. Chem. Earth Sci.; Energy Res. Abstr.; INIS Atomindex [Micro.]; Mass Spect. Bull.; Proc. Chem. Eng.; Res. Alert [Full Cov.]; Sci. Cit. Index; SCISEARCH; Theor. Chem. Eng.

LC QD501 .K745 **ISSN** 0453-8811
RU
CODEN KNKTA4
KINETIKA I KATALIZ. [Kinet. katal.]. **Added/Corp** Akademiia Nauk SSSR. Vol. 1, (May/June 1960)-. Academic Scholarly Publication. Russian (table of contents in English). Six times a year. $277.50. Izdatelstvo Nauka / Akademiia Nauk, (Publishing House of the Russian Academy of Sciences), Leninskii Porspekt 14, 117901 Moscow Russia. **Tel** 011 95 9542153, FAX 011 95 9382144, telex 411964. **(Subscription address:** East View Publications Inc., 3020 Harbor Lane North, Suite 110, Minneapolis MN 55447. **Tel** (800)477-1005, (612)550-0961, FAX (612)559-2931.) available in microform from University Microfilms International (UMI). Documents available from CASDDS.
Ind/Abst Chem. Abstr.; Energy Res. Abstr.; Int. Aerosp. Abstr.; Lit. Pat. Abstr., Oilfield Chem. (1962, 1966-); Lit. Abstr., Catal. Zeol.; Lit. Abstr., Health Environ.; Lit. Abstr., Pet. Refin. Petrochem.; Lit. Abstr., Pet. Substit.; Lit. Abstr., Transp. Storage.

ISSN 0943-1454
GW
UDC 621.792.053
KLEBEN & DICHTEN. [Kleb. dicht.]. **VFOAT** Kleben und Dichten. (1992)-. Periodical. German. Ten times a year. $277.74. Vieweg Publishing, PO Box 5829, D-65048 Wiesbaden Germany. **Tel** 011 49 611 160230, FAX 011 49 611 534430. ***Continues*** *Adhaesion, 0001-8198.*
Ind/Abst Curr. Cit.

LC QD549 .K925 **ISSN** 0023-2912
RU
CODEN KOZHAG
KOLLOIDNYI ZHURNAL. [Kolloidn. z.]. **Added/Corp** Gosudarstvennyi n.-i. Institut Kolloidnoi Khimii (R.S.F.S.R.) Akademiia Nauk SSSR. Vol. 1, No. 1 (1935)-. Academic Scholarly Publication. Russian (summaries and/or abstracts in English; table of contents in English). Six times a year. $415.00. Izdatelstvo Nauka / Akademiia Nauk, (Publishing House of the Russian Academy of Sciences), Leninskii Porspekt 14, 117901 Moscow Russia. **Tel** 011 95 9542153, FAX 011 95 9382144, telex 411964. **(Subscription address:** East View Publications Inc., 3020 Harbor Lane North, Suite 110, Minneapolis MN 55447. **Tel** (800)477-1005, (612)550-0961, FAX (612)559-2931.) cum. index. Documents available from Article Express International, Ask*IEEE, CASDDS.
Ind/Abst Abstr. Bull. Inst. Pap. Sci. Tech.; Alum. Ind. Abstr.; Ceram. Abstr.; Chem. Abstr.; Chem. Titles; Coal Abstr.; Ei Page One; Energy Res. Abstr.; Eng. Index Annu.; GeoRef; INSPEC (Jan.-Feb. 1972-); Met. Abstr.; Life Sci. Collect.; Surf. Treat. Technol. Abstr.

LC TA418.9.C6 K615 **ISSN** 0203-3275
UN
CODEN KPMAD8
KOMPOZITSIONNYE POLIMERNYE MATERIALY. See Chemistry and Chemicals-Organic Chemistry.

LC QD474 .K67 **ISSN** 0132-344X
RU
CODEN KOKHDC
KOORDINACIONNAJA HIMIJA. (KOORDINATSIONNAIA KHIMIIA.). [Koord. him.]. **Added/Corp** Akademiia Nauk SSSR. Vol. 1 (1975)-. Academic Scholarly Publication. Russian. Twelve times a year. $177.50. **(Subscription address:** East View Publications Inc., 3020 Harbor Lane North, Suite 110, Minneapolis MN 55447. **Tel** (800)477-1005, (612)550-0961, FAX (612)559-2931.) Documents available from The Genuine Article, CASDDS.
Ind/Abst Chem. Abstr.; Energy Res. Abstr. (Jan. 1977-); Res. Alert [Full Cov.]; Sci. Cit. Index; SCISEARCH.

LC QD506.A1 L35 **ISSN** 0743-7463
DD 541.3/453/05 US
CCC
CODEN LANGD5
Pr Rev.
LANGMUIR. (LANGMUIR : THE ACS JOURNAL OF SURFACES AND COLLOIDS.). [Langmuir]. **Added/Corp** American Chemical Society. Vol. 1, No. 1 (Jan./Feb. 1985)-. Academic Scholarly Publication. English. Twenty-six times a year. $1093.00. American Chemical Society, 1155 Sixteenth Street Northwest, Washington DC 20036. **Tel** (800)333-9511, (800)227-5558, (614)447-3776, FAX (202)447-3671. **(Subscription address:** American Chemical Society / Ohio, Department L 0011, Columbus OH 43268-0011. **) ED** Arthur W. Adamson. **Bk Rev. Ad Acc. Acid Free. Circ:** 1,300 (ctrl). available on microfilm and microfiche from University Microfilms International (UMI). Documents available from Article Express International, The Genuine Article, CASDDS.
Desc: A journal of UHR surface chemistry and spectroscopy, heterogeneous catalysis and interface chemistry involving fluids and disperse systems.
Ind/Abst Abstr. Bull. Inst. Pap. Sci. Tech.; Ceram. Abstr. (19??-); Chem. Abstr. (1985-); Chem. Titles; Civ. Struct. Eng. Abstr.; Comput. Inf. Syst. Abstr. J. [Full Cov.]; Curr. Cit.; Curr. Contents Phys. Chem. Earth Sci.; Ei Page One; Elect. Comm. Abstr.; Eng. Index Annu.; Environ. Eng. Abstr.; HTFS Dig.; Lit. Pat. Abstr., Oilfield Chem. (1985-); Lit. Abstr., Catal. Zeol.; Lit. Abstr., Health Environ.; Lit. Abstr., Pet. Refin. Petrochem.; Lit. Abstr., Pet. Substit.; Lit. Abstr., Transp. Storage; Mater. Sci. Eng. Abstr.; Mech. Eng. Abstr.; Res. Alert [Full Cov.]; Sci. Cit. Index; SCISEARCH; Soils Fert.; Solid State Supercond. Abstr.; World Surf. Coat. Abstr.

LC QD471 .M3 **ISSN** 1022-1352
DD 541.7 SZ
CCC
Pr Rev.
•**MACROMOLECULAR CHEMISTRY AND PHYSICS.** Vol. 195, No. 1 (Jan. 1994)-. Periodical. English (French and German). Thirty times a year. $2255.00. Huethig & Wepf Verlag, Neugasse 29, CH-6301 Zug Switzerland. **Tel** 011 41 42 222494, FAX 011 41 42 218360. ***Continues*** *Makromolekulare Chemie, 0025-116X.*
Ind/Abst AGRICOLA; Art Archaeol. Tech. Abstr.; Chem. Abstr.; Curr. Biotechnol.; Curr. Chem. React.; Curr. Cit.; Curr. Contents Phys. Chem. Earth Sci.; Index Chem.; Polymer Contents; Res. Alert; Sci. Cit. Index; SCISEARCH; World Surf. Coat. Abstr.

LC QD380 .M328 **ISSN** 0258-0322
DD 547.7 SZ
CCC
NLM W3; MA296 **CODEN** MCMSES
Pr Rev. **TITLE CHANGE**
MAKROMOLEKULARE CHEMIE. MACROMOLECULAR SYMPOSIA, DIE. See Chemistry and Chemicals-Organic Chemistry.

ISSN 0254-0584
SZ
CCC
CODEN MCHPDR
Pr Rev.
MATERIALS CHEMISTRY AND PHYSICS. [Mater. chem. phys.]. Vol. 8, No. 1 (Jan. 1983)-. Academic Scholarly Publication. English. Sixteen times a year (4 vols.). $1344.00. Elsevier Sequoia SA, PO Box 564, CH-1001 Lausanne 1 Switzerland. **Tel** 011 41 21 3207381, FAX 011 41 21 3235444. **ED** L.J. Chen, K.N. Tu. available on microfilm and microfiche from University Microfilms International (UMI); available on an online database from Elsevier Electronic Subscriptions (EES). Documents available from Article Express International, The Genuine Article, Ask*IEEE, CASDDS. ***Continues*** *Materials Chemistry, 0390-6035.*
Desc: Publishes results on experimental and theoretical physical properties and behaviour of different classes of materials, as related to their structure, environment and fabrication processes.
Ind/Abst Alum. Ind. Abstr.; Ceram. Abstr.; Chem. Abstr. (1983-); Chem. Titles; Curr. Cit.; Curr. Contents Phys. Chem. Earth Sci.; Curr. Titles Electrochem.; Ei Page One; Eng. Mater. Abstr.; Eng. Index Annu.; GeoRef; INSPEC (Jan. 1983-); Leadscan; Met. Abstr.; Phys. Briefs; Pollut. Abstr. Indexes; Res. Alert [Full Cov.]; Sci. Cit. Index; SCISEARCH; Surf. Treat. Technol. Abstr.; World Ceram. Abstr.; World Surf. Coat. Abstr.

ISSN 0737-8483
US
CCC
NLM W1; ME8933
MEMBRANE & SEPARATION TECHNOLOGY NEWS. [Membr. sep. technol. news]. **VFOAT** Membrane and Separation Technology News. (198?)-. Periodical. English. Twelve times a year. $395.00. Business Communications Inc., 25 Van Zant Street, Suite 13, Norwalk CT 06855. **Tel** (203)853-4266, FAX (203)853-0348. available on an online database (file 636/Full-Text) from DIALOG.
Ind/Abst PTS Newsl. Database [Full Txt.].

US
MEMOIRS - HARVARD UNIVERSITY. UNIVERSITY LABORATORY OF PHYSICAL CHEMISTRY. Main/Corp Harvard University. University Laboratory of Physical Chemistry Related to Medicine and Public Health. (1951)-. Academic Scholarly Publication. English. Irregular. Academic Press Inc., 6277 Sea Harbor Drive, Orlando FL 32887. **Tel** (800)543-9534, (407)345-4100, FAX (407)352-3445.

FR
METROLOGIE ET APPAREILLAGE EN PHYSIQUE ET PHYSICOCHIMIE. E32. French. Institut de l'Information Scientique et Technique (INIST), 2 Allee du Parc de Brabois, 54514 Vandoeuvre Nancy Cedex France. **Tel** 011 33 83 504600, FAX 011 33 83 504650. ***Continues*** *Pascal Explore. E32: Metrologie et Appareillage en Physique et Physicochimie.*

LC QD474 .M64 **ISSN** 0091-0082
DD 541/.2242 US
MOLECULAR COMPLEXES. Vol. 1 (1973)-. Academic Scholarly Publication. English. Crane Russak & Company, 1900 Frost Road, Suite 101, Bristol PA 19007. **Tel** (800)821-8312.

LC QC173 .M57 **ISSN** 0026-8976
DD 539/.6/05 UK
CCC
CODEN MOPHAM
Pr Rev.
MOLECULAR PHYSICS. See Physics.

LC QD606 .N48
DD 545/.822 UK
NEUTRON ACTIVATION ANALYSIS ABSTRACTS. (July/Sept. 1971)-. English. Four times a year. $72.00. PRM Science & Technology Agency Ltd, 261A Finchley Road Hampstead, London NW3 6LV United Kingdom. **Tel** 011 44 171 4310372.
Desc: Covers radioactivation analysis.

LC QD1 .F58 ISSN 0340-1073
DD 540/.8 GW

NEW CONCEPTS. 1- 1973-. Periodical. English. Springer-Verlag GmbH & Company KG, Heidelberger Platz 3, D-14197 Berlin Germany. **Tel** 011 49 30 8207223, FAX 011 49 30 8214091, telex 183 319 SPBLN D. **(Subscription address:** Springer-Verlag New York Inc. / North America, PO Box 2485, Journal Fulfillment, Secaucus NJ 07096. **Tel** (201)348-4033, (800)777-4643, FAX (201)348-4505.)

ISSN 0392-6737
IT
CCC
CODEN NCSDDN
Pr Rev.

NUOVO CIMENTO DELLA SOCIETA ITALIANA DI FISICA, [SEZIONE] D. See Physics-Nuclear Physics.

US

OPTICAL PROPERTIES OF SOLIDS. (19??)-. Monographic series. English. Irregular. Price varies per volume. Plenum Press, 233 Spring Street, New York NY 10013-1578. **Tel** (212)620-8000, (800)221-9369, FAX (212)463-0742, (212)807-1047, telex 23/421139.

LC QD450 .P48 ISSN 0191-9059
UK
CCC
CODEN PPHYD8
TITLE CHANGE

PCH. PHYSICOCHEMICAL HYDRODYNAMICS. (PHYSICOCHEMICAL HYDRODYNAMICS : PCH.). [PCH. Physicochem. hydrodyn.]. **VFOAT** PCH. Vol. 1, No. 1 (1980)-(19??). Academic Scholarly Publication. English. Pergamon Press, An Imprint of Elsevier Science Ltd., The Boulevard, Langford Lane, Kidlington, Oxford OX5 1GB United Kingdom. **Tel** 011 44 1865 843000, 011 44 1865 843699, FAX 011 44 1865 843010. available on microfilm and microfiche from University Microfilms International (UMI). Documents available from Article Express International, CASDDS. ***Merged into*** *International Journal of Multiphase Flow., 0301-9322.*
Ind/Abst Abstr. Bull. Inst. Pap. Sci. Tech.; Bioeng. Abstr.; Chem. Abstr.; Chem. Titles (1980-); Ei Page One; Eng. Index Annu.; Fluid Abstr., Civil Eng.; Fluid Abstr. Proc. Eng.; FLUIDEX (1980-1989); GeoRef; Int. Aerosp. Abstr. (1980-1989).

LC QD601.A1 P46 ISSN 0556-3860
DD 541/.35 UK
CCC
NLM W1 PH655 CODEN PHCYAQ

PHOTOCHEMISTRY (LONDON). (PHOTOCHEMISTRY.). [Photochemistry]. Vol. 1 (July 1968/June 1969)-. English. One time a year. £160.00. Royal Society of Chemistry, Thomas Graham House, Science Park, Cambridge CB4 4WF United Kingdom. **Tel** 011 44 1223 420066, FAX 011 44 1223 423623, telex 818293 ROYAL. **(Subscription address:** Royal Society of Chemistry, Turpin Distribution Services Ltd., Blackhorse Road, Letchworth, Hertfordshire SG6 1HN United Kingdom. **Tel** 011 44 1462 672555, FAX 011 44 1462 480947.) **ED** D. Bryce-Smith. Documents available from BIOSIS Document Express, CASDDS.
Desc: Reviews the literature published between mid 1984 and mid 1985. Includes photophysical processes in condensed phases; gas-phase photoprocesses.
Ind/Abst Biol. Abstr.; Chem. Abstr.; Curr. Cit.

ISSN 0144-963X
US
CODEN PCFSBN

PHYSICAL CHEMISTRY OF FAST REACTIONS. [Phys. chem. fast react.]. (1973)-. Academic Scholarly Publication. English. Irregular. Price varies per volume. Plenum Press, 233 Spring Street, New York NY 10013-1578. **Tel** (212)620-8000, (800)221-9369, FAX (212)463-0742, (212)807-1047, telex 23/421139. Documents available from CASDDS.
Desc: Presents an account of the present state of knowledge in a particular field of physical chemistry.
Ind/Abst Chem. Abstr.

LC QD581 .P62 ISSN 0272-4324
DD 541/.0424 US
CCC
CODEN PCPPDW
Pr Rev.

PLASMA CHEMISTRY AND PLASMA PROCESSING. See Engineering-Chemical Engineering.

US

PLASTICS MATERIALS. ADHESIVES, SEALANTS, AND PRIMERS. (ADHESIVES, SEALANTS AND PRIMERS.). [Plast. mater. Adhes., sealants, prim.]. **Added/Corp** International Plastics Selector, Inc. **VFOAT** Adhesives; Plastic Materials; Plastics Materials. (1991)-. English. $180.00. DATA Business Publishing, PO Box 6510, 15 Inverness Way East, Englewood CO 80155. **Tel** (800)447-4666, (303)799-0381, FAX (303)799-4082. ***Continues*** *Plastics Materials. Adhesives.*

ISSN 0370-0305
RU
CODEN PKKAAF

PROBLEMY KINETIKI I KATALIZA. (PROBLEMY KINETIKI I KATALIZA / ADADEMIIA NAUK SSSR, ORDENA LENINA INSTITUT KHIMICHESKOI FIZIKI.). [Probl. kinet. katal.]. **Added/Corp** Institut Khimicheskoi Fiziki (Akademiia Nauk SSSR). (1935)-. Academic Scholarly Publication. Russian. Irregular. Price varies per volume. Izdatelstvo Nauka / Akademiia Nauk, (Publishing House of the Russian Academy of Sciences), Leninskii Porspekt 14, 117901 Moscow Russia. **Tel** 011 95 9542153, FAX 011 95 9382144, telex 411964. Documents available from CASDDS.
Ind/Abst Chem. Abstr.

LC QD475 .P7
RU

PROBLEMY SOVREMENNOI KHIMII KOORDINATSIONYKH SOEDINENII. **Added/Corp** Leningradskii Gosudarstvennyi Universitet, Imeni A.A. Zhdanova. Vol. 1 (1966)-. Academic Scholarly Publication. Russian. St. Petersburg State University / Izdatelstvo Leningradskogo Universiteta, Universitetskaia Nab 7/9, 199034 St. Petersburg Russia. **Tel** 011 7 812 2189788, FAX 011 7 812 2185152, telex 121481. Documents available from CASDDS.
Ind/Abst Chem. Abstr.

LC QD474 .K59a
DD 541.2/242 XO

PROCEEDINGS OF THE ... CONFERENCE ON COORDINATION CHEMISTRY. (19??)-. Academic Scholarly Publication. English. Irregular. Price varies. Slovenska Vysoka Skola Technicka, Janska 1, 812 37 Bratislava Slovakia. Documents available from CASDDS.
Desc: Information on coordination compounds.
Ind/Abst Chem. Abstr.

LC QD450 .P48
DD 541.3 S 541.3 UK

PROCEEDINGS OF THE ... INTERNATIONAL PHYSICOCHEMICAL HYDRODYNAMICS CONFERENCE. **Main/Conf** International Physicochemical Hydrodynamics Conference. Proceedings. English. Pergamon Press, An Imprint of Elsevier Science Ltd., The Boulevard, Langford Lane, Kidlington, Oxford OX5 1GB United Kingdom. **Tel** 011 44 1865 843000, 011 44 1865 843699, FAX 011 44 1865 843010.

LC QD625 .T53a ISSN 0134-126X
DD 541.3/82/05 HU
NLM W3 TI568 CODEN PTSCDP

PROCEEDINGS OF THE ... TIHANY SYMPOSIUM ON RADIATION CHEMISTRY. [Proc. Tihany Symp. Radiat. Chem.]. **Added/Corp** Hungary. Orszagos Atomenergia Bizottsag. Magyar Kemikusok Egyesulete. International Atomic Energy Agency. (1962)-. Academic Scholarly Publication. English. **ED** Editors: Peter Hedvig and, 2nd-3rd, Janos Dobo; and 4th- Robert Schiller. Documents available from CASDDS.
Ind/Abst Chem. Abstr.

LC QD549 .K922 ISSN 0340-255X
DD 541/.3451 GW
CCC
NLM W1 PR668HN CODEN PCPSD7

PROGRESS IN COLLOID & POLYMER SCIENCE. [Prog. colloid & polym. sci.]. **Added/Corp** Kolloid-Gesellschaft. **VFOAT** Forstchriffsberichte uber Kolloide und Polymere. **VAT** Progress in Colloid and Polymer Science. Vol. 56 (1975)-. Monographic series. English (French and German). Irregular. Price varies per volume. Dr Dietrich Steinkopff Verlag, PO Box 111442, D-64229 Darmstadt Germany. **Tel** 011 49 6151 17450, FAX 011 49 6151 174510. **ED** H G Kilian and A Weiss. Documents available from Article Express International, CASDDS. ***Continues*** *Fortschrittsberichte uber Kolloide & Polymere, 0071-8017.*
Desc: Published as supplement to our journal 'Colloid and Polymer Science'. Articles range from solid state physics, polymer and colloid chemistry, to biophysics, biology and medicine.
Ind/Abst Chem. Abstr.; Curr. Cit.; Energy Res. Abstr. (March 1982-); Eng. Index Annu.; Polymer Contents; World Surf. Coat. Abstr.; World Text. Abstr.

LC QD501 .P827 ISSN 0079-6743
DD 541.394 US
CCC
CODEN PRKNAZ

PROGRESS IN REACTION KINETICS. Vol. 1 (1961)-. Academic Scholarly Publication. English. Four times a year. $347.00. Pergamon Press, An Imprint of Elsevier Science Ltd., The Boulevard, Langford Lane, Kidlington, Oxford OX5 1GB United Kingdom. **Tel** 011 44 1865 843000, 011 44 1865 843699, FAX 011 44 1865 843010. **(Subscription address:** Elsevier Science Ltd. / Oxford Fulfillment Centre, PO Box 800, Kidlington OX5 1DX United Kingdom. **Tel** 011 44 865 843355.) **ED** R.B. Cundall, T.J. Kemp, M.A.J. Rodgers. cum. index. available on microfilm from Microfilms International Marketing Corp.; available on microfilm and microfiche from University Microfilms International (UMI); available on an online database from Elsevier Electronic Subscriptions (EES). Documents available from BIOSIS Document Express, CASDDS.
Desc: Publishes review articles and mini-reviews on chemical kinetics.
Ind/Abst Biol. Abstr.; Chem Inform; Chem. Abstr.; Curr. Aware. Biol. Sci., CABS.

LC QD473 .P7 ISSN 0079-6786
UK
CCC
CODEN PSSTAW
Pr Rev.

PROGRESS IN SOLID STATE CHEMISTRY. [Prog. solid state chem.]. **Added/Corp** Reiss, Howard. Vol. 1 (1964)-. Periodical. English. Four times a year. $422.00. Pergamon Press, An Imprint of Elsevier Science Ltd., The Boulevard, Langford Lane, Kidlington, Oxford OX5 1GB United Kingdom. **Tel** 011 44 1865 843000, 011 44 1865 843699, FAX 011 44 1865 843010. **(Subscription address:** Elsevier Science Ltd. / Oxford Fulfillment Centre, PO Box 800, Kidlington OX5 1DX United Kingdom. **Tel** 011 44 865 843355.) **ED** G. M. Rosenblatt and W. L. Worrell. available on microfilm and microfiche from University Microfilms International (UMI); available on an online database from Elsevier Electronic Subscriptions (EES). Documents available from Article Express International, The Genuine Article, Ask*IEEE, CASDDS.
Desc: Provides critical reviews written by authorities in the field, surveys of research progress and specialized articles on recent developments. Emphasis is given to relating physical properties and structural chemistry.
Ind/Abst Bioeng. Abstr.; Chem. Abstr.; Ei Page One; Eng. Index Annu.; Index Sci. Rev. [Full Cov.]; INSPEC (1975-); Mass Spect. Bull.; Res. Alert [Full Cov.]; Sci. Cit. Index; SCISEARCH.

LC QD506 .P76 ISSN 0079-6816
DD 541/.3453/05 UK
CCC
NLM W1 PR681LE CODEN PSSFBP
Pr Rev.

PROGRESS IN SURFACE SCIENCE. [Prog. surf. sci.]. Vol. 1 (1971)-. Periodical. English. Twelve times a year. $835.00. Pergamon Press, An Imprint of Elsevier Science Ltd., The Boulevard, Langford Lane, Kidlington, Oxford OX5 1GB United Kingdom. **Tel** 011 44 1865 843000, 011 44 1865 843699, FAX 011 44 1865 843010. **(Subscription address:** Elsevier Science Ltd. / Oxford Fulfillment Centre, PO Box 800, Kidlington OX5 1DX United Kingdom. **Tel** 011 44 865 843355.) **ED** Sydney Davison, W.K. Liu. available on microfilm and microfiche from University Microfilms International (UMI); available on an online database from Elsevier Electronic Subscriptions (EES). Documents available from Article Express International, The Genuine Article, Ask*IEEE, CASDDS.
Desc: Publishes review articles from invited authors of international stature and, on occasion, special issues devoted to conference proceedings, selected works and dedicated volumes.
Ind/Abst Alum. Ind. Abstr.; Bioeng. Abstr.; Chem. Abstr.; Curr. Cit.; Curr. Contents Phys. Chem. Earth Sci.; Ei Page One; Eng. Mater. Abstr.; Eng. Index Annu.; Index Sci. Rev. [Full Cov.]; INSPEC (1972-); Mass Spect. Bull.; Met. Abstr.; Res. Alert [Full Cov.]; Sci. Cit. Index; SCISEARCH.

ISSN 0889-7514
DD 541 US

QCPE BULLETIN. [QCEP bull.]. **Added/Corp** Quantum Chemistry Program Exchange. **VFOAT** Q.C.P.E. Bulletin. **VAT** Quantum Chemistry Exchange Program Bulletin. Vol. 1, No. 1 (Feb. 1981)-. Bulletin. English. Four times a year (Feb., May, Aug., Nov.). $20.00. Quantum Chemistry Program Exchange, Indiana University, Department of Chemistry, Bloomington IN 47405. **Tel** (812)855-4784. ***Continues*** *Newsletter of the Quantum Chemistry Program Exchange.*

LC QD601.A1 R29 ISSN 0033-8230
US
CCC
NLM W1 RA217 CODEN RAACAP
Pr Rev.

RADIOCHIMICA ACTA. [Radiochim. acta]. Vol. 1 (1962)-. Academic Scholarly Publication. English (French and German). Sixteen times a year. $1143.65. R Oldenbourg Verlag, Postfach 801360, D-81613 Munich Germany. **Tel** 011 49 89 450190, FAX 011 49 89 45019305. **ED** J.P. Adloff, K.H. Lieser, G.L. Stocklin, T. Tominaga, A.P. Wolf and R.G. Wymer. cum. index. **Ad Acc. Circ:** 450. Documents available from The Genuine Article, BIOSIS Document Express, CASDDS.
Desc: Covers all chemical aspects of nuclear science and technology: nuclear and radiochemistry, actinides, nuclear fuel cycle, hot atom chemistry, radionuclides in life sciences and environment and radioanalysis.
Ind/Abst Biol. Abstr.; Chem. Abstr.; Chem. Titles; Curr. Cit.; Curr. Contents Phys. Chem. Earth Sci.; EMBASE; Energy Res. Abstr.; GeoRef; Int. Aerosp. Abstr.; Res. Alert [Full Cov.]; Sci. Cit. Index; SCISEARCH.

LC QD502 .R4 ISSN 0304-4122
DD 541/.39/05 HU
CCC
CODEN RKCLAU
Pr Rev.
REACTION KINETICS AND CATALYSIS LETTERS. (REACTION KINETICS AND CATALYSIS LETTERS. SOOBSHCHENIIA PO KINETIKE I KATALIZU.). [React. kinet. catal. lett.]. **Added/Corp** Magyar Tudomanyos Akademia. Akademiia Nauk SSSR. **VFOAT** Soobshcheniia po Kinetike I Katalizu. Vol. 1 (1974)-. Academic Scholarly Publication. Multiple languages (English and Russian). Six times a year (3 vols.). $960.00. Elsevier Science Publishers BV, PO Box 211, 1000 AE Amsterdam Netherlands. **Tel** 011 31 20 4853641, 011 31 20 4853642, FAX 011 31 20 4853598. **ED** K I Zamaraev, Ferenc Nagy. available on microfilm from University Microfilms International (UMI); available on an online database from Elsevier Electronic Subscriptions (EES). Documents available from Article Express International, The Genuine Article, CASDDS.
Desc: A forum for rapid publication of new results in the field of kinetics of homogeneous reactions in gas, liquid and solid phase, homogeneous and heterogeneous catalysis, absorption in heterogeneous catalysis, transport processes related to reaction kinetics and catalysis, preparation and study of catalysts, reactors and apparatus.
Ind/Abst Chem. Abstr.; Coal Abstr.; Curr. Contents Phys. Chem. Earth Sci.; Eng. Index Annu.; Lit. Pat. Abstr., Oilfield Chem. (1990-); Lit. Abstr., Catal. Zeol.; Lit. Abstr., Health Environ.; Lit. Abstr., Pet. Refin. Petrochem.; Lit. Abstr., Pet. Substit.; Lit. Abstr., Transp. Storage; Res. Alert [Full Cov.].

LC QD476 .R42 ISSN 0320-2909
RU
CODEN RSMSDO
REAKCIONNAJA SPOSOBNOST I MEHANIZMY REAKCIJ ORGANICESKIH SOEDINENIJ. (REAKTSIONNAIA SPOSOBNOST I MEKHANIZMY REAKTSII ORGANICHESKIKH SOEDINENII.). **Added/Corp** Leningradskii Gosudarstvennyi Universitet, Imeni A.A. Zhdanova. Vol. 1 (1971)-. Academic Scholarly Publication. Russian. Price varies per volume. St. Petersburg State University / Izdatelstvo Leningradskogo Universiteta, Universitetskaia Nab 7/9, 199034 St. Petersburg Russia. **Tel** 011 7 812 2189788, FAX 011 7 812 2185152, telex 121481. Documents available from CASDDS.
Ind/Abst Chem. Abstr.

LC QD471 .R43 ISSN 0486-4476
JA
REPORTS ON PROGRESS IN POLYMER PHYSICS IN JAPAN. [Rep. prog. polym. phys. Jpn.]. **Added/Corp** Research Group of Polymer Physics in Japan. Research Group of Polymer Physics in Japan. Publication Committee. Gakujutsu Bunken Fukyukai. Vol. 1 (1958)-. Periodical. English. One time a year. $97.00. Kobunshi Butsuri Nenpo Kankokai, (Research Group of Polymer Physics in Japan), Tokyo Kogyo Daigaku, 2-12 Ookayama Meguroku, Tokyo 151 Japan. **(Subscription address:** Japan Publications Trading Company Ltd., PO Box 5030, Tokyo International, Tokyo 100-31 Japan. **Tel** 011 81 3 3292 3753.)
Ind/Abst Abstr. Bull. Inst. Pap. Sci. Tech.

ISSN 0922-6168
NE
CCC
CODEN RCINEE
Pr Rev.
RESEARCH ON CHEMICAL INTERMEDIATES. **VFOAT** Chemical Intermediates. Vol. 11, No. 1 (Jan. 1989)-. Academic Scholarly Publication. English. Nine times a year. DM820.00. VSP International Science Publishers, Godfried van Seystlaan 47, 3703 BR Zeist Netherlands. **Tel** 011 31 3404 25790, FAX 011 31 3404 32081, telex 40217 USP NL. **(Subscription address:** VSP International Science Publishers, PO Box 346, 3700 AH Zeist Netherlands. **Tel** 011 31 30 6925790, FAX 011 31 30 6932081.) **ED** M. Anpo, M.C. Depew and J.K.S. Wan. available on microfilm and microfiche from University Microfilms International (UMI). Documents available from The Genuine Article, CASDDS. ***Continues** Reviews of Chemical Intermediates, 0162-7546.*
Desc: Contains articles in related disciplines such as spectroscopy, molecular biology and biochemistry, atmospheric and environmental sciences, catalysis, photochemistry and photophysics.
Ind/Abst Chem. Abstr. (1989-); Curr. Chem. React.; Curr. Cit.; Curr. Contents Phys. Chem. Earth Sci.; Ei Page One; Index Chem.; Res. Alert [Full Cov.]; Sci. Cit. Index; SCISEARCH.

JA
CODEN RHCHEZ
REVIEWS ON HETEROATOM CHEMISTRY. Vol. 1 (1988)-. Academic Scholarly Publication. English. One time a year. $324.00. **(Subscription address:** Maruzen Company Ltd., PO Box 5050, Import & Export Department, Tokyo 100 31 Japan. **Tel** 011 81 3 32789224.) Each issue contains an index to its own contents (no volume index)--loose. Documents available from The Genuine Article, CASDDS.
Ind/Abst Chem. Abstr.; Res. Alert [Full Cov.].

LC QD1 .Z512 ISSN 0036-0244
DD 541.05 UK
CODEN RJPCAR
RUSSIAN JOURNAL OF PHYSICAL CHEMISTRY. [Russ. j. phys. chem.]. **Added/Corp** British Library. Lending Division. Chemical Society (Great Britain) Royal Society of Chemistry (Great Britain). Vol. 33 (July 1959)-. Periodical. English (Russian). Twelve times a year. $1955.00. MAIK Nauka / Interperiodica, Ulitsa Profsoyuznaia 90, Moscow 117864 Russia. **(Subscription address:** Interperiodica Publishing, Subscription Office, PO Box 1831, Birmingham AL 35201-1831. **Tel** (800)633-4931, (205)995-1567 (outside US and Canada), FAX (205)995-1588.) Documents available from Ask*IEEE.
Desc: Coverage of topics such as materials structure and quantum chemistry, chemical kinetics and catalysis, the physical chemistry of separation processes, and the methods and techniques of physiochemical investigations.
Ind/Abst Acoust. Abstr. (1987-); Alum. Ind. Abstr.; Ceram. Abstr. (19??-); Curr. Biotechnol.; Curr. Cit.; Eng. Mater. Abstr.; HTFS Dig.; INSPEC (Jan. 1987-); Int. Aerosp. Abstr. (1987-); Mass Spect. Bull.; Met. Abstr. (1987-); Proc. Chem. Eng.; Theor. Chem. Eng.

LC QD450 P73a ISSN 0139-682X
DD 541.0 XR
CODEN SPFCDX
SBORNIK VYSOKE SKOLY CHEMICKO-TECHNOLOGICKE V PRAZE. FIZIKALNI CHEMIE = SBORNIK PRAZHSKOGO KHIMIKO-TECHNOLOGICHESKOGO INSTITUTA. FIZICHESKAIA KHIMIIA = SCIENTIFIC PAPERS OF THE PRAGUE INSTITUTE OF CHEMICAL TECHNOLOGY. PHYSICAL CHEMISTRY. **Main/Corp** Vysoka Skola Chemicko-Technologicka v Praze. **Added/Corp** Vysoka Skola Chemicko-Technologicka v Praze. Sbornik Prazhskogo Khimiko- Technologicheskogo Instituta. Fizicheskaia Khimiia. Vysoka Skola Chemicko-Technologicka v Praze. Scientific Papers of the Prague Institute of Chemical Technology. Physical Chemistry. **VFOAT** Fizikalni Chemie; Fizicheskaia Khimiia; Scientific Papers of the Prague Institute of Chemical Technology. Physical Chemistry. No. 1 (1974)-. Periodical. Czech (English and German; summaries and/or abstracts in Russian). Statni Pedagogicke Nakladatelstvi, Ostrovni 30, 113 01 Prague 1 Czech Republic. **Tel** (2)203787, FAX (2)293883. Documents available from CASDDS.
Ind/Abst Chem. Abstr.

ISSN 0044-7595
DD 541 US
SCALACS. **Main/Corp** American Chemical Society. Southern California Section. **VAT** Southern California Section of the American Chemical Society. (19??)-. Newsletter. English. Seven times a year. American Chemical Society, Southern California Section, 14934 S. Figueroa Street, Gardena CA 90248. **Tel** (310) 327-1216, FAX (310) 538-9965. **ED** Paula Sandovai. **Ad Acc, Adv Mgr:** Myriam Easton. **Circ:** 3,000.
Desc: Editorial content is directed towards chemists and chemical engineers and includes information regarding the southern California section of The American Chemical Society events and other articles of interests to chemists.

LC QP501 ISSN 0031-9082
DD 612.015 JA
NLM W1 SE249NE CODEN SBBKA4
SEIBUTSU-BUTSURI-KAGAKU. **See** Biology-Biological Chemistry.

LC QD541 .S43 ISSN 0147-1503
US
CCC
CODEN ISDMAT
SELECTED DATA ON MIXTURES. SER. A. THERMODYNAMIC PROPERTIES OF NON-REACTING BINARY SYSTEMS OF ORGANIC SUBSTANCES. **Added/Corp** Texas A & M University. Thermodynamics Research Center. **VFOAT** Thermodynamic Properties of Non-Reacting Binary Systems of Organic Substances. **VAT** Selected Data on Mixtures. Series A. Thermodynamic Properties of Non-Reacting Binary Systems of Organic Substances. (1973)-. Academic Scholarly Publication. English. Four times a year (Jan., Apr., July, Oct.). $1000.00. TRC - Thermodynamics Research Center Data Distribution, Texas A&M University, Tees Business Office, College Station TX 77843-3124. **Tel** (409)845-5981, FAX (409)847-8590, telex 510-892-7689 TXINTLPRO COSN. **ED** Kenneth N. Marsh. Index available (Published in Oct.). cum. index. **Circ:** 150. Documents available from CASDDS.
Desc: Excess functions, gas liquid critical properties, liquid-liquid equilibrium, liquid-vapor equilibrium for hydrocarbons and other organic substances.
Ind/Abst Chem. Abstr.

LC QD461 .S423
JA
SENTA REPOTO. **Added/Corp** Bunshi Kagaku Kenkyujo. Denshi Keisanki Senta. No. 1 (Jan./March 1979)-. Japanese. Bunshi Kagaku Kenkyujo Denshi Keisanki Senta, 38 Saigo Naka Myodaijicho, Okazakishi Aichiken 444 Japan.

ISSN 0559-8958
JA
CODEN SHKUAJ
SHOKUBAI. (CATALYST : SHOKUBAI.). [Shokubai]. **VFOAT** Catalyst (Tokyo); Catalyst (Sapporo); Shokubai (Sapporo). (1946)-. Japanese. Eight times a year. $345.00. Shokubai Gakkai / Catalysis Society of Japan, 21-13-302 Higashigotanda 5 Chome, Shinagawaku Tokyo 141 Japan. Documents available from CASDDS.
Ind/Abst Chem. Abstr.

ISSN 0234-9736
RU
SIGNALNAYA INFORMATSIYA KATALIZ I KATALIZATORY. Russian. Six times a year. 11.76rub. VINITI - Vsesoyuznyi Institut Nauchno-Tekhnicheskoi Informatsii, All-Union Scientific and Technical Information Institute, Baltiiskaia ulitsa 14, 125219 Moscow Russia. **Tel** 011 7 95 2384600, FAX 011 7 95 9430060, telex 411160. **Ad Acc. Circ:** 240 (ctrl).

LC QD543 .S6629 ISSN 0191-5622
DD 541.3/42/05 UK
CCC
CODEN SDSEDK
SOLUBILITY DATA SERIES. Vol. 1 (1979)-. Academic Scholarly Publication. English. Four times a year. $395.00. Oxford University Press / UK, Walton Street, Oxford OX2 6DP United Kingdom. **Tel** 011 44 1865 56767, FAX 011 44 1865 267773, telex 851/837330 OXPRES G. **(Subscription address:** Oxford University Press / USA, Journals Marketing Department, Oxford University Press, 2001 Evans Road, Cary NC 27513. **Tel** (800)451-7556, (919)677-0977, FAX (919)677-1714.) **ED** A S Kertes. available in microform. Documents available from CASDDS.
Desc: Aimed at researchers and major reference libraries in chemistry, chemical engineering, materials science, medicine and biology, sciences.
Ind/Abst Chem. Abstr.; Curr. Cit.

LC QD474 ISSN 0364-4626
DD 541/.2242/05 US
UDC 541.572.5 CCC
CODEN SJCCDA
TITLE CHANGE
SOVIET JOURNAL OF COORDINATION CHEMISTRY. [Sov. j. coord. chem.]. Vol. 1 (Jan. 1975)-(199?). Periodical. English (Russian). MAIK Nauka / Interperiodica, Ulitsa Profsoyuznaia 90, Moscow 117864 Russia. Index available. available on microfilm and microfiche from University Microfilms International (UMI). Documents available from BIOSIS Document Express. ***Continued by** Russian Journal of Coordination Chemistry.*
Desc: This journal is devoted to topics such as syntheses and properties of new coordination compounds, bioinorganic coordination chemistry, spectrochemistry of coordination compounds and mechanisms of complexity reactions.
Ind/Abst Biol. Abstr. (-1984); Mass Spect. Bull.

LC QD481 .S763 ISSN 0924-3984
DD 541.2/23/05 NE
NLM W1; ST445 CODEN SOICE8
Pr Rev.
STEREOCHEMISTRY OF ORGANOMETALLIC AND INORGANIC COMPOUNDS. [Stereochem. organomet. inorg. compd.]. Vol. 1 (1986)-. Academic Scholarly Publication. English. Irregular. price varies per volume. Elsevier Science Publishers BV, PO Box 211, 1000 AE Amsterdam Netherlands. **Tel** 011 31 20 4853641, 011 31 20 4853642, FAX 011 31 20 4853598. Documents available from BIOSIS Document Express, CASDDS.
Ind/Abst Biol. Abstr. (1988-); Chem. Abstr.

LC QD471 .S833 ISSN 1040-0400
DD 541.2/05 US
CCC
CODEN STCHES
STRUCTURAL CHEMISTRY. [Struct. chem.]. Vol. 1, No. 1 (Jan. 1990)-. Academic Scholarly Publication. English. Six times a year. $325.00. Plenum Press, 233 Spring Street, New York NY 10013-1578. **Tel** (212)620-8000, (800)221-9369, FAX (212)463-0742, (212)807-1047, telex 23/421139. **ED** Istvan Hargittai and Arthur Greenberg. Documents available from The Genuine Article, BIOSIS Document Express, Ask*IEEE, CASDDS.
Desc: An international journal concerned with energy and structure, along with their physical and biological properties.
Ind/Abst Biol. Abstr. (1991-); Chem. Abstr.; Curr. Cit.; Curr. Contents Phys. Chem. Earth Sci.; INSPEC (Jan. 1991-); Res. Alert [Full Cov.]; Sci. Cit. Index; SCISEARCH.

ISSN 0081-6590
PL

STUDIA I MATERIALY Z DZIEJOW NAUKI POLSKIEJ. SERIA C : HISTORIA NAUK MATEMATYCZNYCH, FIZYKO-CHEMICZNYCH I GEOLOGICZNO-GEOGRAFICZNYCH.
See Mathematics.

ISSN 0167-6881
NE
CCC
CODEN SPTCDZ

STUDIES IN PHYSICAL AND THEORETICAL CHEMISTRY. [Stud. phys. theor. chem.]. (1979)-. Academic Scholarly Publication. English. Irregular. Price varies per volume. Elsevier Science Publishers BV, PO Box 211, 1000 AE Amsterdam Netherlands. **Tel** 011 31 20 4853641, 011 31 20 4853642, FAX 011 31 20 4853598. Documents available from BIOSIS Document Express, CASDDS.
Ind/Abst Bioeng. Abstr.; Biol. Abstr. (?-1983); Chem. Abstr.; Curr. Cit.; Math. Rev.

ISSN 0167-2991
NE
CCC
CODEN SSCTDM

STUDIES IN SURFACE SCIENCE AND CATALYSIS. [Stud. surf. sci. catal.]. (1976)-. Academic Scholarly Publication. English. Irregular. Price varies per volume. Elsevier Science Publishers BV, PO Box 211, 1000 AE Amsterdam Netherlands. **Tel** 011 31 20 4853641, 011 31 20 4853642, FAX 011 31 20 4853598. Documents available from Article Express International, Ask*IEEE, CASDDS.
Ind/Abst Bioeng. Abstr.; Chem. Abstr.; Curr. Cit.; Ei Page One; Eng. Index Annu.; INSPEC; Lit. Pat. Abstr., Oilfield Chem. (1992-); Lit. Abstr., Catal. Zeol.; Lit. Abstr., Health Environ.; Lit. Abstr., Pet. Refin. Petrochem.; Lit. Abstr., Pet. Substit.; Lit. Abstr., Transp. Storage; Sci. Cit. Index.

LC QD40 .U54A **ISSN** 0195-7341
DD 541.3/07/2073 US

SUMMARIES OF FY ... RESEARCH IN THE CHEMICAL SCIENCES. English. One time a year. National Technical Information Service - NTIS, Room 2027S, 5285 Port Royal Road, Springfield VA 22161. **Tel** (703)487-4630, (703)487-4660, (703)487-4650, FAX (703)321-8547, telex 89-9405. available on microfiche (Vols. for 1982- distributed to depository libraries).

LC QD506.A1 S85 **ISSN** 0081-9573
DD 541/.345/05 US
NLM W1 SU717 **CODEN** SCOSBX

SURFACE AND COLLOID SCIENCE. [Surface colloid sci.]. Vol. 1 (1969)-. Monographic series. English. Irregular. Price varies per volume. Plenum Press, 233 Spring Street, New York NY 10013-1578. **Tel** (212)620-8000, (800)221-9369, FAX (212)463-0742, (212)807-1047, telex 23/421139. Documents available from CASDDS.
Ind/Abst Chem. Abstr.

LC QD506 .S8 **ISSN** 0039-6028
NE
CCC
CODEN SUSCAS

Pr Rev.
SURFACE SCIENCE. [Surf. sci.]. Vol. 1 (Jan. 1964)-. Academic Scholarly Publication. English (French and German). Irregular (72 issues a year; 24 volumes). $7507.00. Elsevier Science Publishers BV, PO Box 211, 1000 AE Amsterdam Netherlands. **Tel** 011 31 20 4853641, 011 31 20 4853642, FAX 011 31 20 4853598. **ED** C.B. Duke. cum. index. available on microfilm and microfiche from University Microfilms International (UMI); available on an online database from Elsevier Electronic Subscriptions (EES). Documents available from Article Express International, The Genuine Article, Ask*IEEE, CASDDS.
Desc: Deals exclusively with fundamental theoretical and experimental studies in the physics and chemistry of surfaces. Covers topics contributing to a better understanding of basic phenomena occurring on surfaces; the word 'surface' being interpreted in include free surfaces as well as interfaces generally.
Ind/Abst Alum. Ind. Abstr.; Ceram. Abstr.; Chem. Abstr.; Chem. Titles; Curr. Cit.; Curr. Contents Phys. Chem. Earth Sci.; Ei Page One; Eng. Mater. Abstr.; Eng. Index Annu.; INSPEC (1968-); Int. Aerosp. Abstr.; Mass Spect. Bull.; Met. Abstr.; Phys. Briefs; Pollut. Abstr. Indexes; Res. Alert [Full Cov.]; Sci. Cit. Index; SCISEARCH; Soc. Sci. Cit. Index [Select. Cov.]; World Ceram. Abstr.

LC QD516 .S92 **ISSN** 0082-0784
DD 541.39 541.36* US
CODEN SYMCAQ

SYMPOSIUM (INTERNATIONAL) ON COMBUSTION. PAPERS. [Symp., Int., Combust.]. **Main/Conf** Symposium (International) on Combustion. **Added/Corp** Combustion Institute (U.S.) Symposium (International) on Combustion. Standing Committee on Combustion Symposia. **VFOAT** Combustion and Detonation Waves; Combustion in Engines and Combustion Kinetics. 4th (Sept. 1-5, 1952)-. English. Every 2 years. $225.00. The Combustion Institute, 5001 Baum Boulevard, Pittsburgh PA 15213. **Tel** (412)687-1366, FAX (412)687-0340. cum. index. **Circ:** 2,000 (ctrl). Documents available from Article Express International, CASDDS. ***Continues*** *Symposium on Combustions and Flame, and Explosion Phenomena, 1062-2896.*
Desc: Collection of research results on combustion.
Ind/Abst Bioeng. Abstr.; Chem. Abstr.; Coal Abstr.; Curr. Cit.; Ei Page One; Eng. Index Annu.; Lit. Pat. Abstr., Oilfield Chem.; Lit. Abstr., Catal. Zeol.; Lit. Abstr., Health Environ.; Lit. Abstr., Pet. Refin. Petrochem.; Lit. Abstr., Pet. Substit.; Lit. Abstr., Transp. Storage.

LC QD450 **ISSN** 0919-7621
DD 541 JA

•**SYMPOSIUM ON PLASMA SCIENCE FOR MATERIALS.** [Symp. plasma scie. mater.]. (1993)-. Periodical. English. One time a year. ***Continues*** *Proceedings of Japanese Symposium on Plasma Chemistry, 0915-1699.*

LC QD156 .S9 **ISSN** 0094-5714
DD 541/.39 US
CCC
CODEN SRIMCN

Pr Rev.
SYNTHESIS AND REACTIVITY IN INORGANIC AND METAL-ORGANIC CHEMISTRY. [Synth. react. inorg. met.-org. chem.]. Vol. 4 (1974)-. Academic Scholarly Publication. English. Ten times a year. $895.00. Marcel Dekker Inc., 270 Madison Avenue, New York NY 10016. **Tel** (212)696-9000, (800)228-1160, FAX (212)685-4540, telex 421419. **(Subscription address:** Marcel Dekker Inc., PO Box 5017, Monticello NY 12701. **Tel** (800)228-1160.**) ED** Kurt Moedritzer. **Bk Rev. Ad Acc.** available on microfiche. Documents available from The Genuine Article, CASDDS. ***Continues*** *Synthesis in Inorganic and Metal-Organic Chemistry.*
Desc: Provides rapid dissemination of important, original research papers as well as critical, in-depth reviews of reactions, techniques, and synthetic methods. Dealing with compounds of main-group elements and transition elements, this journal delivers penetrating up-to-the-minute coverage that includes: the synthesis, characterization, and reactivity of new compounds; new or improved synthetic procedures, physical-chemical data, and reactions for known compounds; and detailed descriptions of experimental work so that results can be reproduced and applied in readers' laboratory research.
Ind/Abst Chem. Abstr.; Curr. Chem. React.; Curr. Cit.; Curr. Contents Phys. Chem. Earth Sci.; Index Chem.; Phys. Briefs; Res. Alert [Full Cov.]; Sci. Cit. Index; SCISEARCH.

LC PT994 .T45
DD 668/.1/05 GW
CODEN TSDEES

TENSIDE, SURFACTANTS, DETERGENTS. **Added/Corp** Gesellschaft Deutscher Chemiker. Fachgruppe "Waschmittelchemie." Verband der Chemischen Industrie (Germany). Deutscher Ausschuss fuer Grenzflachenaktive Stoffe. **VFOAT** Tenside Detergents. Vol. 23, No. 1 (Jan./Feb. 1986)-. Academic Scholarly Publication. English (German). Six times a year. $364.33. Carl Hanser Verlag, Postfach 860420, D-81631 Munich Germany. **Tel** 011 49 89 998300, FAX 011 49 89 981264. Documents available from Article Express International, CASDDS. ***Continues*** *Tenside Detergents, 0040-3490.*
Ind/Abst Chem Inform; Chem. Abstr. (1986-); Curr. Cit.; Ei Page One; Eng. Index Annu.

LC QD481 .T43 **ISSN** 0957-4166
DD 541.2/23 UK
CCC
NLM W1; TE6361 **CODEN** TASYE3

TETRAHEDRON, ASYMMETRY. [Tetrahedron: asymmetry]. **VFOAT** Tetrahedron. Vol. 1, No. 1 (1990)-. Periodical. English. Twelve times a year. $1010.00. Pergamon Press, An Imprint of Elsevier Science Ltd., The Boulevard, Langford Lane, Kidlington, Oxford OX5 1GB United Kingdom. **Tel** 011 44 1865 843000, 011 44 1865 843699, FAX 011 44 1865 843010. **(Subscription address:** Elsevier Science Ltd. / Oxford Fulfillment Centre, PO Box 800, Kidlington OX5 1DX United Kingdom. **Tel** 011 44 865 843355.**) ED** Stephen G. Davies (editor's address: The Dyson Perrins Laboratory, South Parks Road, Oxford OX1 3QY United Kingdom). available on microfilm and microfiche from University Microfilms International (UMI); available on an online database from Elsevier Electronic Subscriptions (EES). Documents available from The Genuine Article, BIOSIS Document Express, CASDDS, ADONIS.
Desc: Presents experimental or theoretical research results of outstanding significance and timeliness on asymmetry in organic, inorganic, organometallic and physical chemistry, as well as its application to related disciplines, especially bio-organic chemistry. The journal publishes critical reviews, original research articles and preliminary communications dealing with all aspects of the chemical, physical and theoretical properties of nonracemic organic and inorganic materials and processes.
Ind/Abst ADONIS; Biol. Abstr.; Chem. Abstr.; Curr. Aware. Biol. Sci., CABS; Curr. Chem. React.; Curr. Cit.; Curr. Contents Phys. Chem. Earth Sci.; EMBASE; Index Chem.; PESTDOC; Ref. Upd. Deluxe Ed.; Res. Alert [Full Cov.]; Sci. Cit. Index; SCISEARCH.

LC QD1 .T43 **ISSN** 0040-5744
GW
CCC
CODEN TCHAAM

Pr Rev.
THEORETICA CHIMICA ACTA. [Theor. chim. acta]. Vol. 1 (Aug. 1962)-. Periodical. English (French, German and Latin; summaries and/or abstracts in German, English and French). Eighteen times a year. $2153.00. Springer-Verlag GmbH & Company KG, Heidelberger Platz 3, D-14197 Berlin Germany. **Tel** 011 49 30 8207223, FAX 011 49 30 8214091, telex 183 319 SPBLN D. **(Subscription address:** Springer-Verlag New York Inc. / North America, PO Box 2485, Journal Fulfillment, Secaucus NJ 07096. **Tel** (201)348-4033, (800)777-4643, FAX (201)348-4505.**) ED** K Ruedenberg, D Chandler, E R Davidson, N C Handy, J Jortner, W Kutzelnigg, J Michl, W H Miller, K Morokuma, B O Roos, H F Schaefer III, and D G Truhlar. available on microfilm and microfiche from University Microfilms International (UMI). Documents available from The Genuine Article, Ask*IEEE, CASDDS.
Desc: Covers theoretical chemistry, chemical physics, quantum chemistry, gas phase dynamics, structure and dynamics of condensed phases, statistical mechanics.
Ind/Abst Chem Inform; Chem. Abstr.; Chem. Titles; Curr. Cit.; Curr. Contents Phys. Chem. Earth Sci.; Energy Res. Abstr.; INSPEC (1972-); Int. Aerosp. Abstr.; Mass Spect. Bull.; Math. Rev.; Life Sci. Collect.; Phys. Briefs; Res. Alert [Full Cov.]; Sci. Cit. Index; SCISEARCH.

LC QD1 .T413 **ISSN** 0040-5760
US
CCC
NLM W1 TH12H **CODEN** TEXCAK

THEORETICAL AND EXPERIMENTAL CHEMISTRY. [Theor. exp. chem.]. **Added/Corp** Consultants Bureau. Vol. 1 (Jan./Feb. 1965)-. Periodical. English (Russian). Six times a year. $1245.00. Consultants Bureau, A Division of Plenum Publishing Corporation, 233 Spring Street, New York NY 10013. **Tel** (212)620-8000, (212)620-8466, FAX (212)463-0742, telex 23/421139. **ED** V. D. Pokhodenko. Index available. available on microfilm and microfiche from University Microfilms International (UMI). Documents available from Ask*IEEE, CASDDS.
Desc: Publishes English translation or original Russian research done by the Academy of Science of the USSR on numerous aspects of chemistry in theory.
Ind/Abst Ceram. Abstr. (19??-); Chem. Abstr.; INSPEC (1968-).

LC QD510 .T5 **ISSN** 0040-6031
NE
CCC
CODEN THACAS

Pr Rev.
THERMOCHIMICA ACTA. [Thermochim. acta]. Vol. 1 (March 1970)-. Academic Scholarly Publication. English. Forty-two times a year (21 volumes). $5250.00. Elsevier Science Publishers BV, PO Box 211, 1000 AE Amsterdam Netherlands. **Tel** 011 31 20 4853641, 011 31 20 4853642, FAX 011 31 20 4853598. **ED** J.N. Hay, W. Hemminger, L.F. Whiting. available on microfilm and microfiche from University Microfilms International (UMI); available on an online database from Elsevier Electronic Subscriptions (EES). Documents available from The Genuine Article, CASDDS, Documents on Demand.
Desc: Original research contributions in thermal analysis, thermochemistry, and chemical thermodynamics.
Ind/Abst Anal. Abstr.; Ceram. Abstr.; Chem Inform; Chem. Abstr.; Chem. Titles; Coal Abstr.; Crop Physiol. Abstr.; Curr. Cit.; Curr. Contents Phys. Chem. Earth Sci.; Energy Inf. Abstr.; Eng. Mater. Abstr.; Environ. Abstr.; For. Abstr.; Geol. Abstr.; GeoRef; Int. Aerosp. Abstr.; Mass Spect. Bull.; Life Sci. Collect.; Polymer Contents; Res. Alert [Full Cov.]; Rev. Agric. Entomol.; Rev. Med. Vet. Mycology; Sci. Cit. Index; SCISEARCH; Soils Fert.; Sug. Indus. Abstr.

LC TP968 .T67 **ISSN** 0082-6235
DD 668/.3 US

TREATISE ON ADHESION AND ADHESIVES. Vol. 1 (1967)-. Monographic series. English. Irregular. Price varies per volume. Marcel Dekker Inc., 270 Madison Avenue, New York NY 10016. **Tel** (212)696-9000, (800)228-1160, FAX (212)685-4540, telex 421419. **(Subscription address:** Marcel Dekker Inc., PO Box 5017, Monticello NY 12701. **Tel** (800)228-1160.**) ED** R. L. Patrick.
Desc: Presents information on adhesion and adhesives. Topics include structural adhesives and theory.

LC QC454.V5 V53 **ISSN** 0090-1911
DD 537.53/52 NE
NLM W1 VI169E **CODEN** VBSSBB
Pr Rev.
VIBRATIONAL SPECTRA AND STRUCTURE. **See** Physics-Light, Optics, Radiation.

LC QD502 .V66   ISSN 0320-0027 RU
CODEN VKKADG
VOPROSY KINETIKI I KATALIZA. [Vopr. kinet. katal.]. **Added/Corp** Ivanovskii Khimiko-Tekhnologicheskii Institut. Vol. 1 (1973)-. Academic Scholarly Publication. Russian. Price varies per volume. 153460 Ul Fridrikha Engelsa, Inanovo 7 Russia. Documents available from CASDDS.
Ind/Abst Chem. Abstr.

LC QC1 .Z42   ISSN 0932-0784
DD 530   GW
CCC
CODEN ZNASEI
ZEITSCHRIFT FUER NATURFORSCHUNG. See Physics.

LC QD1 .Z45   GW
ZEITSCHRIFT FUER PHYSIKALISCHE CHEMIE. (Feb. 1887)-. Periodical. German. cum. index.
Ind/Abst Ceram. Abstr. (19??-).

LC QD1 .Z46   ISSN 0044-3336
GW
CCC
NLM W1 ZE532U   CODEN ZPCFAX
ZEITSCHRIFT FUER PHYSIKALISCHE CHEMIE (NEUE FOLGE). (ZEITSCHRIFT FUER PHYSIKALISCHE CHEMIE.). [Z. phys. Chem.]. **VFOAT** Physikalische Chemie; Physical Chemistry & Chemical Physics; International Journal of Research in Physical Chemistry & Chemical Physics. No. 1 (April 1954)-. Periodical. German. Ten times a year. DM1423.00. R Oldenbourg Verlag, Postfach 801360, D-81613 Munich Germany. **Tel** 011 49 89 450190, FAX 011 49 89 45019305. **ED** E. Wicke, G. Briegleb, G. Ertl, F. Hensel, H.G. Hertz, W. Jaenicke, J Troe, H.G. Wagner and A. Weller. cum. index. **Ad Acc.** available on microfilm from University Microfilms International (UMI). Documents available from BIOSIS Document Express, Ask*IEEE, CASDDS. **Absorbed** Zeitschrift fuer Physikalische Chemie, 0323-4479.
Desc: Demonstrates the handling of current problems in science by modern methods of research in experiment and theory with particular emphasis on promising developments in future.
Ind/Abst Biol. Abstr.; Ceram. Abstr. (19??-); Chem Inform; Chem. Abstr.; Curr. Cit.; Curr. Contents Phys. Chem. Earth Sci.; Energy Res. Abstr.; GeoRef; INSPEC (1991-); Life Sci. Collect.

ISSN 0724-410X
GW
CODEN ZPCSD7
ZEITSCHRIFT FUER PHYSIKALISCHE CHEMIE. SUPPLEMENTHEFT (NEUE FOLGE). (ZEITSCHRIFT FUER PHYSIKALISCHE CHEMIE. SUPPLEMENTHEFT.). [Z. phys. Chem., Suppl.]. (1982)-. Academic Scholarly Publication. English (summaries and/or abstracts in German). R Oldenbourg Verlag, Postfach 801360, D-81613 Munich Germany. **Tel** 011 49 89 450190, FAX 011 49 89 45019305. Documents available from CASDDS.
Ind/Abst Chem. Abstr.

LC QD601.A1 Z45   ISSN 0323-8776
DD 541.3/8/05   GW
CODEN ZIMIDC
ZFI-MITTEILUNGEN. [Zfl-MiH.]. **Added/Corp** Zentralinstitut fuer Isotopen- und Strahlenforschung (Akademie der Wissenschaften der DDR). **VFOAT** Zfl Mitteilungen; Z.f.I.-Mitteilungen. **VAT** Zentralinstitut fuer Isotopen- und Strahlenforschung Mitteilungen. No. 1 (1975)-. Academic Scholarly Publication. German (English and Russian). Irregular. Free on request. Akademie der Wissenschaften Zentinst, Permoserstrasse 15, O-7010 Leipzig Germany. **ED** H. Huebner. cum. index. **Circ:** 250. available in microform. Documents available from BIOSIS Document Express, CASDDS.
Desc: Papers, reports, reviews, bibliographies, etc. concerning isotope and radiation research (including stable isotopes and their applications), radiochemistry and analytical chemistry, and information science.
Ind/Abst Anal. Abstr.; Biol. Abstr.; Chem. Abstr.; Ecol. Abstr. (?-?); Energy Res. Abstr. (July 1976-); Food Sci. Technol. Abstr.; Geol. Abstr.; GeoRef; Refer. Z.

LC QD1 .Z5   ISSN 0044-4537
RU
CCC
CODEN ZFKHA9
Pr Rev.
ZHURNAL FIZICHESKOI KHIMII. [Z. fiz. khim.]. **Added/Corp** Akademiia Nauk SSSR. **VFOAT** Khimicheskii Zhurnal. Seriia V, Zhurnal Fizicheskoi Khimii. Vol. 1 (1930)-. Academic Scholarly Publication. Russian (summaries and/or abstracts in English; table of contents in English). Twelve times a year. $576.25. Izdatelstvo Nauka / Akademiia Nauk (Publishing House of the Russian Academy of Sciences), Leninskii Porspekt 14, 117901 Moscow Russia. **Tel** 011 95 9542153, FAX 011 95 9382144, telex 411964. **(Subscription address:** East View Publications Inc., 3020 Harbor Lane North, Suite 110, Minneapolis MN 55447. **Tel** (800)477-1005, (612)550-0961, FAX (612)559-2931.) Index available. cum. index. **Bk Rev.** available on microfilm. Documents available from The Genuine Article, Ask*IEEE, CASDDS.
Ind/Abst Alum. Ind. Abstr.; Ceram. Abstr.; Chem Inform; Chem. Abstr.; Curr. Biotechnol.; Energy Res. Abstr.; Gas Abstr.; GeoRef; INSPEC (Jan. 1987-); Math. Rev.; Met. Abstr.; Res. Alert [Full Cov.]; Sci. Cit. Index; SCISEARCH; World Alum. Abstr.

RU
ZHURNAL FIZICHESKOI KHIMII. MICROFORM. Added/Corp Akademiia Nauk SSSR. (1930)-. Academic Scholarly Publication. Russian (Russian; summaries and/or abstracts in English; table of contents in English). Twelve times a year. $319.95 (print). Izdatelstvo Nauka / Akademiia Nauk, (Publishing House of the Russian Academy of Sciences), Leninskii Porspekt 14, 117901 Moscow Russia. **Tel** 011 95 9542153, FAX 011 95 9382144, telex 411964. **(Subscription address:** East View Publications Inc., 3020 Harbor Lane North, Suite 110, Minneapolis MN 55447. **Tel** (800)477-1005, (612)550-0961, FAX (612)559-2931.) cum. index. available in print.

LC QD1 .A3754   ISSN 0136-7463
DD 541   RU
CODEN ZSTKAI
ZHURNAL STRUKTURNOJ HIMII. (ZHURNAL STRUKTURNOI KHIMII.). [Z. strukt. him.]. **Added/Corp** Akademiia Nauk SSSR. Vol. 1, (May/June 1960)-. Academic Scholarly Publication. Russian. Six times a year. $129.95. Izdatelstvo Nauka / Akademiia Nauk, (Publishing House of the Russian Academy of Sciences), Leninskii Porspekt 14, 117901 Moscow Russia. **Tel** 011 95 9542153, FAX 011 95 9382144, telex 411964. **(Subscription address:** East View Publications Inc., 3020 Harbor Lane North, Suite 110, Minneapolis MN 55447. **Tel** (800)477-1005, (612)550-0961, FAX (612)559-2931.) Index available. Documents available from Ask*IEEE, CASDDS.
Ind/Abst Alum. Ind. Abstr.; Chem. Abstr.; Energy Res. Abstr.; INSPEC (1972-);; Math. Rev.; Met. Abstr.; Life Sci. Collect.; World Alum. Abstr.

CHILDREN AND YOUTH INTERESTS

DD J220.6/05   UK
1 TO ONE (MARKHAM, ONT.). See Religions and Theology.

ISSN 0195-4105
US
3-2-1 CONTACT. [3-2-1 contact]. **Added/Corp** Children's Television Workshop. **VFOAT** Contact. **VAT** Three Two One Contact; 3 2 1 Contact; (19??)-. Periodical. English. Ten times a year. $17.97. Children's Television Workshop, One Lincoln Plaza, Box TG, New York NY 10023. **Tel** (212)595-3456. **(Subscription address:** Neodata / Colorado, PO Box 2606, Boulder CO 80322.) **ED** Jonathan Rosenbloom. **Ad Acc. Circ:** 400,000. **Absorbed** Enter.
Desc: Articles about nature, science, and technology written for the young adult reader (ages 8 to 14 years). Contains projects, puzzles, experiments, and feature stories, and helps develop confidence in solving math problems.
Ind/Abst Child. Mag. Guide (1981-); Comput. Rev. Index (1986-); EP Collect.; Homework Help.; Mag. Artic. Summar. Elite; Mag. Artic. Summar. Select; Mag. Artic. Summar. CD-ROM; Mag. Search; MasterFile FullTEXT 1000; MasterFile FullTEXT 350; MasterFile FullTEXT 650; MasterFile FullTEXT (July 1989-); Mid. Search; OCLC; Prim. Search; Pub. Lib. FullTEXT; Res. Alert; Telebase.

US
4-H HAPPINESS. Added/Corp Cooperative Extension Association of Onondaga County. (19??)-. Periodical. English. **Continues** Onondaga County. 4-H Club News.

ISSN 0740-848X
US
4-H SOUNDER. Added/Corp Cornell University. Cooperative Extension. Cooperative Extension Association of Suffolk County. 4-H Division. **VFOAT** Four-H Sounder. **VAT** 4 H Sounder. (19??)-. Periodical. English. Twelve times a year. Free. Cooperation Extension of Suffolk County, 246 Griffing Avenue, Riverhead NY 11901. **Tel** (516)727-7850. **ED** Mary Louise B. Fisher. **Bk Rev. Ad Acc. Circ:** 2,300 (ctrl).
Desc: Publication for and about youth involved in 4-H programs in Suffolk County NY; calendar of events; advertising and reviews of current 4-H contributing educational events and activities.

DD 051   ISSN 0270-899X
US
TITLE CHANGE
16 MAGAZINE. [16 mag.]. **VFOAT** Sixteen Magazine. (19??)-(19??). Periodical. English. Sixteen Magazine Inc, 157 West 57th Street, New York NY 10019. **Tel** (212)489-7220. **ED** Randi Reisfeld and Hedy End. **Ad Acc. Circ:** 400,000. **Continued by** 16, 1075-3109.
Desc: Magazine dealing with teen-age entertainment, photos, interviews, contests, reader contributions, advice and give aways.

ISSN 1075-3109
DD 051   US
16 (NEW YORK, N.Y.). (16.). [16]. **VFOAT** Sixteen; Sixteen Magazine; 16 Magazine. (19??)-. Periodical. English. Twelve times a year. $19.95. Sterling Macfadden, 233 Park Avenue South, New York NY 10003. **Tel** (212)979-4800. **ED** Randi Reisfeld and Hedy End. **Ad Acc. Circ:** 400,000. **Continues** 16 Magazine, 0270-899X.
Desc: Magazine dealing with teen entertainment, photos, interviews, contests, reader contributions, advice and give aways.

ISSN 0246-2591
UDC 636   FR
30 MILLIONS D'AMIS, LA VIE DES BETES. [30 millions amis, Vie betes]. **VFOAT** Trente Millions d'Amis, la Vie des Betes. (1979)-. Periodical. French. Eleven times a year. $54.68. Dawson France SA, BP 40, 91121 Palaiseau Cedex France. **Tel** 011 33 1 69104700, FAX 011 33 1 64548326, telex 220064F. **Formed by the union of** 30 Millions d'Amis, 0181-6209 and La Vie des Betes, Betes et Nature, 0399-8592.

LC PN500   ISSN 1077-3878
DD 808   US
●**360 DEGREES : THE MAGAZINE WITH EVERY ANGLE. See** Sociology.

AU
1000 UND 1 BUCH. (19??)-. Periodical. German. Six times a year (Feb., Apr., Jun., Aug., Oct., Dec.). $32.73. Internationale Institut Jugendliteratur & Leseforschung Mayerhofgasse 6, Mayerhofgasse 6, A-1040 Vienna Austria. **Tel** 011 43 1 50503590, 011 43 1 50528310. Index available. **Bk Rev.** ctrl circ. **Continues** Jugend und Buch.

ISSN 1043-3635
DD 741   US
2000 AD PRESENTS. [2000 AD presents]. **VFOAT** 2000 AD; Two Thousand AD Presents. (198?)-. Periodical. English. One time a week. £51.00. World Wide Subscription Services, Unit 4, Gibbs Reed Farm, East Sussex TN5 7HE United Kingdom. **Tel** 011 44 1580 200657, FAX 011 44 1580 200616.

US
ACORN : STORIES, POEMS, ESSAYS, REVIEWS. See Literature.

ISSN 0229-2653
DD 649/.1/0971   CN
ACTION FOR CANADA'S CHILDREN. [Action - Can. Counc. Child. Youth]. **VFOAT** Action pour les Enfants du Canada. Vol. 1, No. 1 (1980)-. Periodical. English (French). Four times a year. $10.00. Canadian Council on Children and Youth, 55 Parkdale Avenue/3rd Floor, Ottawa Ontario K1Y 1E5 Canada. **Tel** (613)722-0133, FAX (613)722-4829. **Bk Rev. Ad Acc. Circ:** 1,000 (ctrl). **Continued in part by** Action pour les Enfants du Canada.

ISSN 0337-9566
UDC 37   FR
ACTUEL CIDJ. [Actuel CIDJ]. **VFOAT** Actuel Centre d'Information et de Documentation Jeunesse. (1975)-. Periodical. French. Twelve times a year. $813.64. CIDJ, 101 Quai Branly, 75740 Paris Cedex 15 France. **Tel** 011 33 1 45673585, FAX 011 33 1 40650261. Index available. **Bk Rev. Circ:** 5,500 (ctrl).
Desc: Information on every subject which could interest young people. Contains documents on studies, professional training, employment, daily life, leisure time, holidays, sports, and foreign countries.

LC HV701
DD 362.7   RM
●**ADOLESCENTA.** (1995)-. Russian. Twelve times a year. Grupul Salor Industrial Tractorul, Str. Turnului Nr. 3, 2200 Brasov Rumania.

LC SF   ISSN 1066-2324
DD 636   US
AHA HORSES FOR YOUNG HORSELOVERS. See Horses and Horsemanship.

LC Q4 .S487
UA
AL-SHABAB WA-ULUM AL-MUSTAQBAL. Added/Corp Muassasat Al-Ahram. **VFOAT** Youth, Science & Future. Vol. 1 (Aug.

Children and Youth Interests

1977)-. Periodical. Arabic (English). Twelve times a year. $15.00. Al Ahram, Al Ahram Building, Al Galaa Street, Cairo ARE Egypt. **Tel** 011 20 2 755500, 011 20 2 745666. **(Subscription address:** Al Ahram Newspaper, 405 Lexington Avenue, Chrysler Building, New York NY 10174. **Tel** (212)972-6440.)
  Desc: Scientific, social magazine. Satisfies the needs of youth in many fields.

ISSN 1200-4170
CN
DD 791.45/01/3
ALLIANCE INFO. See Communications-Television and Cable.

II
AMAR CHITRA KATHA. (19??)-. English (Hindi, Kannada, Bengali, French, Spanish and Dutch). Twelve times a year. India Book House Private Ltd, Eruchshaw BLD 3rd Floor, 249 DN Road, Bombay 4000 001 India. **Tel** 011 91 22 26 43 64 5. **ED** Anant Pai. **Ad Acc. Circ:** 70,000.
  Desc: All comics children's magazine to acquaint children with their cultural heritage.

ISSN 0745-6506
US
AMAZING HEROES. See Leisure and Recreation-Amusements.

ISSN 1062-7812
US
DD 051
●**AMERICAN GIRL (MIDDLETON, WIS.).** (AMERICAN GIRL). [Am. girl]. Vol. 1, No. 1 (Jan./Feb. 1993)-. Periodical. English. Six times a year (Jan., Mar., May, Jul., Sept., Nov.). $19.95. Pleasant Company, PO Box 620998, Middleton WI 53562. **Tel** (800)233-0264, (800)845-0005. **(Subscription address:** Palm Coast Data, PO Box 420163, Agency Department, Palm Coast FL 32142. **Tel** (904)445-4662 ext. 669, (800)829-5475.) **ED** Margo L. Clark.
  Desc: Literature and entertainment for girls age 7-12.
  Ind/Abst EP Collect.; Homework Help.; Mag. Artic. Summar. Elite; Mag. Artic. Summar. Select; Mag. Artic. Summar. FullTEXT 1000; MasterFile FullTEXT; MasterFile FullTEXT 350; MasterFile FullTEXT 650; MasterFile FullTEXT (July 1994-); Mid. Search; OCLC; Prim. Search; Pub. Lib. FullTEXT; Telebase; Mag. Index.

LC HQ796 .A675
ISSN 0003-1542
US
AMERICAN YOUTH. Vol. 1 (Jan./Feb. 1960)-. Periodical. English. Six times a year. General Motors Corporation, 3044 West Grand Boulevard, Detroit MD 48202. **Tel** (313)556-2054. available on microfilm from University Microfilms International (UMI).

ISSN 0318-5737
CN
CEASED
AMISOL. Added/Corp Service Mond-ami. Vol. 1 (Sept./Oct. 1973)-Vol. 22 No. 4 (19??). Periodical. French. Service Mond-Ami, 4055 Avenue Du Mont Royal Est., Montreal Quebec HIX 1Y5 Canada. **Tel** (514)251-2664, **Fax** (514)251-7449. **Circ:** 35,000.

ISSN 0934-9219
GW
UDC 371.8
AN-ALFABETEN, DIE. [An-Alfabeten]. (1983)-. Periodical. German. Ten times a year. Albrecht Durer Gymnasium, Emser Str 133, W-1000 Berlin 44 Germany.
  Desc: Interests of the pupils of Berliner Schools. Especially arts and expositions.

IT
ANDERSEN : IL MONDO DELL INFANZIA. (19??)-. Italian. Ten times a year. L55000.00 Italy; L100000.00 other. Feguagiskia Studios, Via Crosa Di Vergagni 3R, 16124 Genoa Italy. **Tel** 011 39 10 282654.

LC HV880 .G57a
DD 369.46
US
ANNUAL REPORT / GIRLS CLUBS OF AMERICA. Main/Corp Girls Clubs of America, Inc. (19??)-. English. One time a year. Girls Clubs of America, 30 East 33rd Street, New York NY 10016. **Tel** (212)689-3700.

ISSN 1062-502X
US
DD 793
APHELION (SANTA ANA, CALIF.). See Leisure and Recreation-Amusements.

LC Comics box 23a
US
●**ARCHIE'S CHRISTMAS STOCKING.** See Leisure and Recreation-Amusements.

ISSN 1042-9271
US
SUSPENDED
DD 028
ATLANTA KIDS MAGAZINE. [Atlanta kids mag.]. **VFOAT** Atlanta Kids. Vol. 1, No. 1 (May/June 1989)-Suspended. Periodical. English. Six times a year. $10.00. Atlanta Kids Magazine, PO Box 11549, Atlanta GA 30355.

LC Z1037 .C925 PN1009.A1
ISSN 1055-792X
US
DD 028.1/62/079
AWARD-WINNING BOOKS FOR CHILDREN AND YOUNG ADULTS. See Literature.

ISSN 1163-6262
FR
UDC 087.5(44)
BABAR PARIS. (BABAR.). (1991)-. Periodical. French. Twelve times a year. $64.52. Bayard Presse, Svc Client, 3 rue Bayard, Department 2, 75393 Paris Cedex 08 France. **Tel** 011 33 1 44355907, **FAX** 011 33 1 44356025. Continues La Semaine de Babar, 1154-4368.

LC PZ
ISSN 1077-1131
US
DD 808.83
●**BABYBUG (PERU, ILL.).** (BABYBUG.). **VFOAT** Babybug Magazine. (Nov. 1994)-. Consumer Publication. English. Nine times a year. $27.97. Open Court Publishing Company, 315 Fifth Street, PO Box 300, Peru IL 61354. **Tel** (800)435-6850, (815)223-1500, **FAX** (815)224-6675. **(Subscription address:** CDS / SIFD Agency Control, 1901 Bell Avenue, Des Moines IA 50315. **Tel** (515)246-6812.) **ED** Paula Morrow. **Circ:** 25,000. available with illustrations.
  Desc: Poems and stories made for toddlers.
  Ind/Abst EP Collect.; Homework Help.; MasterFile FullTEXT 1000; MasterFile FullTEXT 350; MasterFile FullTEXT 650; MasterFile FullTEXT (Jan. 1995-); OCLC; Telebase.

ISSN 0715-5182
CN
DD 051
BACKYARDS. [Backyards]. (1980)-. Newspaper. English. Twelve times a year. $0.35 per no. Backyards, 1235 Dresden Row, Halifax NS B3J 2K3 Canada.

LC AP
ISSN 0743-4898
US
DD 051
●**BARBIE (NEW YORK, N.Y. 1984).** (BARBIE.). [Barbie]. **VFOAT** Barbie Magazine. (Winter 1984)-. Periodical. English. Six times a year. $13.50. Welsh Publishing Group Inc., 300 Madison Avenue, New York NY 10017. **Tel** (212)687-0680, **FAX** (212)986-5849. **(Subscription address:** CDS Agency Hard Copy, PO Box 4966, Des Moines IA 50340. **Tel** (515)247-7569.) **Ad Acc, Adv Mgr:** Jacob Hill. **Circ:** 600,000.
  Desc: Celebrity interviews, fashion, and stories and features for fans of Barbie.

ISSN 0347-772X
SW
UDC 82
BARNBOKEN. [Barnboken]. (1978)-. Periodical. Swedish. Two times a year. Kr90.00. Svenska Barnboksinstitutet, Swedish Institute for Children's Books, 61 Odengatan, S-113 22 Stockholm Sweden. **Tel** 011 46 8 332323, **FAX** 011 46 8 332423. **ED** Eva Nordlinder. **Circ:** 1,000.
  Ind/Abst Child. Lit. Abstr. (19??-).

ISSN 1075-217X
US
●**BARNEY MAGAZINE.** (1994)-. Periodical. English. Five times a year. $12.50. Welsh Publishing Group Inc., 300 Madison Avenue, New York NY 10017. **Tel** (212)687-0680, **FAX** (212)986-5849.

ISSN 1045-6724
US
DD 028
Pr Rev.
BAYVIEWS (OAKLAND, CALIF.). See Library and Information Sciences.

ISSN 0745-6972
US
BEAGLE BUGLE. (BEAGLE BUGLE : QUARTERLY NEWSLETTER OF THE SNOOPY FAN CLUB.). Added/Corp Snoopy Fan Club. Vol. 1, No. 1 (Feb. 1993)-. Newsletter. English. Four times a year. Snoopy Fan Club, 9 Snoopy Place, Santa Rosa CA 95401.

ISSN 0334-973X
IS
UDC 82
Pr Rev.
BE'EMET?!. (1987)-. Periodical. Hebrew. One time a year. $10.00. Beit Berl College, Yemima Center 55 905, Israel. **ED** Sh Hariel. Index available. cum. index. Bk Rev. **Circ:** 1,000 (ctrl).
  Desc: Includes articles from writers, researchers and critics from all over Israel and from abroad.

ISSN 0991-8787
FR
UDC 084.12-053.5
BELLES HISTOIRES DE POMME D'API (PARIS. 1972), LES. **VFOAT** Belles Histoires de Pomme d'Api (Mensuel). (1972)-. Periodical. French. Twelve times a year. $108.27. Bayard Presse, Svc Client, 3 rue Bayard, Department 2, 75393 Paris Cedex 08 France. **Tel** 011 33 1 44355907, **FAX** 011 33 1 44356025.

ISSN 1076-433X
US
DD 790
●**BEST TOYS, BOOKS AND VIDEOS FOR KIDS, THE.** [Best Toys Books Videos Kids]. **VFOAT** Best Toys, Books & Videos for Kids. (1994)-. English. Irregular. $12.00. Harper Collins Publishers, Keystone Industrial Park, Scranton PA 18512. **Tel** (800)242-7737, (800)233-4727, **FAX** (800)822-4090.

ISSN 0895-4194
US
DD 741
BETTY AND VERONICA. See Leisure and Recreation-Amusements.

ISSN 1058-1596
US
CEASED
DD 791
BEVERLY HILLS 90210, THE OFFICIAL MAGAZINE. [Beverly Hills 90210 off. mag.]. **VFOAT** Official Beverly Hills 90210 Magazine; Beverly Hills 90210. No. 1 (1991)-(1993). Periodical. English. Welsh Publishing Group Inc., 300 Madison Avenue, New York NY 10017. **Tel** (212)687-0680, **FAX** (212)986-5849.

ISSN 1053-9212
US
TITLE CHANGE
DD 791
BIG BOPPER, THE. [Big bopper]. (198?)-(199?). Periodical. English. Laufer Publishing Co., 12711 Ventura Boulevard, Suite 220, Studio City CA 91604. **Tel** (818)508-2010, **FAX** (818)508-2030. Continued by Bop's BB, 1083-9356.
  Desc: Popular entertainment features for teens and youth. Picture-oriented with posters and pin-ups.

ISSN 0347-7096
SW
UDC 82
BILD & BUBBLA. See Literature.

LC AP211 .B54
AG
BILLIKEN. (1919)-. Periodical. Spanish. One time a week. $305.00. Interamerican Network, PO Box 364, Scarsdale NY 10583. **Tel** (914)793-9764, **FAX** (914)337-1273. **Bk Rev. Ad Acc. Circ:** 120,000 (ctrl).
  Desc: A magazine of science and general information for children and youth.

LC CT107 .B54
ISSN 1058-2347
US
DD 920/.009/04
Pr Rev.
BIOGRAPHY TODAY. See Biographies.

ISSN 0165-1196
NE
UDC 82-9
BOBO. [Bobo]. (1968)-. Periodical. Dutch. Twenty-six times a year. $63.02. Medianet BV, Postbus 6298, 2001 LN Haarlem Netherlands. **Tel** 011 31 23 173311.

ISSN 0773-0306
BE
UDC (024.7)
BONJOUR AVERBODE. [Bonjour Averbode]. (1960)-. Periodical. French. Fifty-one times per year. $80.97. Uitgeverij Averbode, BP 54, 3281 Averbode Belgium. **Tel** 011 32 13 780135. Index available.

LC Z1037 .N568 Z1037.A1
ISSN 0068-0192
US
DD 028.5
BOOKS FOR THE TEEN AGE. [Books teen age]. (195?)-. English. One time a year. $7.00. New York Public Library, Office of Branch Libraries, 455 Fifth Avenue, New York NY 10016. **Tel** (212)340-0909. **ED** Ruth Rausen. **Circ:** 10,000. Continues Books for Young People.
  Desc: List of recommended books for teenagers covering a variety of subject headings, mainly adult titles, some juvenile and all briefly annotated.

LC Z1037.A1 B59
ISSN 0006-7482
UK
DD 028.1
BOOKS FOR YOUR CHILDREN. See Literary and Political Reviews.

ISSN 1052-1682
US
DD 051
BOOMERANG! (SAN FRANCISCO, CALIF.). (BOOMERANG! [SOUND RECORDING].). [Boomerang!]. (1990)-. Periodical. English. Twelve times a year. $43.95. Listen & Learn, PO Box 261, La Honda CA 94020. **Tel** (415)747-0978. available on audiocassette.
  Desc: Audio magazine about big ideas. It teaches kids about worldwide events, history, literature, money and more. In a fun format that children can follow with the accompanying illustrated newsletters. It also contains games and quizzes.

ISSN 8750-7242
US
DD 051
BOP. [Bop]. (198?)-. Periodical. English. Twelve times a year. $22.00. Laufer Publishing Co., 12711 Ventura Boulevard, Suite 220, Studio City CA 91604. **Tel** (818)508-2010, **FAX** (818)508-2030.
  Desc: Popular entertainment features for teens and youth.

ISSN 1083-9356
DD 791 US
BOP'S BB. [Bop's BB]. **VFOAT** Bop's Big Bopper; BB. (19??)-. Periodical. English. Twelve times a year. $22.00 US; $25.00 Canada; $27.00 others. Laufer Publishing Co., 12711 Ventura Boulevard, Suite 220, Studio City CA 91604. **Tel** (818)508-2010, FAX (818)508-2030. ***Continues*** *Big Bopper, 1053-9212.*
Desc: Popular entertainment features for teens and youth. Picture-oriented with posters and pin-ups.

LC AP201 .B53 ISSN 0006-8608
DD 369.43/05 US
BOYS' LIFE. [Boy's life]. **Added/Corp** Boy Scouts of America. Vol. 1 (March 1, 1911)-. Periodical. English. Twelve times a year. $15.60. Boys' Life, 1325 Walnut Hill Lane, Irving TX 75062. **Tel** (214)580-2088. **ED** William McMorris. **Ad Acc**, **Adv Mgr Tel** (212)532-0985. **Circ:** 1,475,000. available on microfilm and microfiche from University Microfilms International (UMI); available on an online database (file 647/Full-Text) from DIALOG. Documents available from UMI Article Clearinghouse, Magazine Collection.
Desc: Features scouting, sports, careers, health, science, fiction, various hobbies and other subjects of interest to boys 7 to 17 years old.
Ind/Abst Access (1975-); Child. Mag. Guide (1981-); EP Collect.; Gen. Period. Index (1985-); Homework Help.; Index Inf. (1963-); Mag. Artic. Summar. Elite; Mag. Artic. Summar. Select; Mag. Artic. Summar. CD-ROM; Mag. Index Plus (1989-); Mag. Search; MasterFile FullTEXT 1000; MasterFile FullTEXT 350; MasterFile FullTEXT 650; MasterFile FullTEXT (July 1989-) [Full Txt.]; Mid. Search; Newsp. Period. Abstr. (1988-); OCLC; Prim. Search; Pub. Lib. FullTEXT; Telebase; Mag. Index (1977-); TOM Gen. Index (1985-).

ISSN 1078-9006
US
●**BOYS' QUEST.** (1995)-. Periodical. English. Six times a year (Jan., Mar., May, July, Sept., Nov.). $15.00. Hopscotch Inc., PO Box 164, Bluffton OH 45817. **Tel** (419)358-4610.
Ind/Abst EP Collect.; Homework Help.; MasterFile FullTEXT 1000; MasterFile FullTEXT 350; MasterFile FullTEXT 650; MasterFile FullTEXT (Jan. 1995-); OCLC; Telebase.

FR
BT (CANNES, FRANCE). (BT.). **VFOAT** B.T.; Bibliotheque de Travail. No. 970 (Sept. 1985)-. Periodical. French. Irregular. PEMF Publ de l Ecole Moderne Francaise, 06376 Mouans Sartoux CX France. **Tel** 011 33 92 921757. ***Continues*** *Bibliotheque de Travail, 0005-335X.*

ISSN 0195-1580
US
BUILDING BLOCKS. **See** Literature.

LC Z1037.A1 C4 ISSN 0008-9036
DD 810 US
CCC
BULLETIN OF THE CENTER FOR CHILDREN'S BOOKS. **See** Literature.

ISSN 0167-6520
NE
UDC 087.5
BUMPER. **See** Literature.

ISSN 0721-183X
GW
UDC 087.5
BUNTE HUND, DER. [Bunte Hund]. (1981)-. Periodical. German. Three times a year. $25.02. Julius Beltz GmbH & Co. KG, Postfach 100161, D-69441 Weinheim Germany. **Tel** 011 49 6201 703220.

ISSN 1043-0806
DD 051 US
SUSPENDED
BURIED TREASURE (WESTLAKE, OHIO). (BURIED TREASURE.). (1988)-(19??). Periodical. English. Twelve times a year. $15.00 US; $18.00 Canada. Learning Exchange, 25935 Detroit Road, Suite 331, Westlake OH 44145. **Tel** (216)331-8494. **Circ:** 1,000.
Desc: Newsletter for children 8-12, based on a theme of treasure maps, pirates, and high-seas adventure. Develops a variety of skills plus creativity.
Ind/Abst Genealogical Period. Annu. Index.

ISSN 1064-2609
DD 028 US
C.A.R.E. PACKAGE, THE. (THE C.A.R.E. PACKAGE : CHILDREN'S AUTHORS MAKE READING EXCITING! / THE APPLE PEDDLER, INC.). [C.A.R.E. package]. **VFOAT** CARE Package. Vol. 1, No. 1 (1990)-. Periodical. English. Six times a year. $19.95. Apple Peddler Inc., 25112 Woodfield School Road, Gaithersburg MD 20882. **Tel** (301)253-0694, FAX (301)253-0694. **ED** Kathy Rogers. **Bk Rev**, (Qty: 50). **Ad Acc. Circ:** 3,000.
Desc: Selected children literature used to entice children to read and help them write. The works of different authors are featured each issue.

ISSN 0335-6469
FR
UDC 08
Pr Rev.
CALAO. (1974)-. Periodical. French. Six times a year. $17.24. Segedo, 12 rue du Quatre Septembre, 75002 Paris France. **Tel** 011 33 1 42968607. **Ad Acc. Circ:** 180,000.

ISSN 1050-7086
DD 909 US
CALLIOPE (PETERBOROUGH, N.H.). (CALLIOPE : WORLD HISTORY FOR YOUNG PEOPLE.). [Calliope]. Vol. 1, No. 1 (Sept./Oct. 1990)-. Periodical. English. Five times a year (Jan., Mar., May, Sept., Nov.). $18.95. Cobblestone Publishing Inc., 7 School Street, Peterborough NH 03458. **Tel** (603)924-7209, FAX (603)924-7380. **Circ:** 5,000. ***Continues*** *Classical Calliope, 0271-1966.*
Desc: Covers the world history themes, which show readers that world history is a continuation of events, not a series of isolated, and unrelated occurrences. Packed with maps, time lines, activities, and photographs.
Ind/Abst EP Collect.; Homework Help.; MasterFile FullTEXT 1000; MasterFile FullTEXT 350; MasterFile FullTEXT 650; MasterFile FullTEXT (Jan. 1993-); Mid. Search; OCLC; Prim. Search; Pub. Lib. FullTEXT; Telebase.

LC BV3750 .Y6 ISSN 0008-2538
DD 269/.05 US
CAMPUS LIFE (WHEATON, ILL.). (CAMPUS LIFE.). [Campus life]. **Added/Corp** Youth for Christ International. Christianity Today, Inc. (1965)-. Periodical. English. Ten times a year (monthly with May/June and Jul./Aug. issues combined). $14.95. Christianity Today Inc., 465 Gundersen Drive, Carol Stream IL 60188. **Tel** (708)260-6200, FAX (708)261-0114. **(Subscription address:** CDS / SIFD Agency Control, 1901 Bell Avenue, Des Moines IA 50315. **Tel** (515)246-6812.**) ED** Jim Long. **Bk Rev. Ad Acc. Circ:** 140,000. available on microfilm from Xerox; available on microfilm and microfiche from University Microfilms International (UMI). ***Continues*** *Youth for Christ.*
Desc: Contains graphics, humor, fiction and inspiring true life stories written for teenagers. Speaks with enthusiasm and authority on creative wholesome activities, social problems, sports, hobbies, health and spiritual concerns.
Ind/Abst Acad. Abstr.; Acad. Search; Christ. Period. Index; EP Collect.; Homework Help.; Mag. Artic. Summar. Elite; Mag. Artic. Summar. Select; Mag. Artic. Summar. CD-ROM; MasterFile FullTEXT 1000; MasterFile FullTEXT 350; MasterFile FullTEXT 650; MasterFile FullTEXT (July 1994-) [Full Txt.]; OCLC; Pub. Lib. FullTEXT; Telebase; Vocat. Search.

LC PN1009.A1 C317 ISSN 0319-0080
DD C810/.9/928205 CN
Pr Rev.
CANADIAN CHILDREN'S LITERATURE. **See** Literary and Political Reviews.

ISSN 0708-594X
DD C810/.9/928205 CN
CANSCAIP NEWS. **See** Literature.

ISSN 0312-3502
DD 362.7099423 AT
CARING (ADELAIDE. 1975). [Caring Adel., 1975]. (1975)-. Periodical. English. Four times a year (Mar., June, Sept., Dec.). 6.16Aus$. Service to Youth Council Inc., 38 Waymouth Street, Adelaide South Australia, 5000 Australia. **Tel** 011 61 8 2118466.

ISSN 0311-0486
DD 372.05 AT
CHALLENGE MELBOURNE. [Challenge Melb.]. (1971)-. Periodical. English. Four times a year. 8.00Aus$ Victoria, Australia; 9.00Aus$ other. Marayanga Publications, Box 258, Prahran Victoria 3181 Australia. **Tel** 011 61 3 5251388. **ED** Meredith Costain. **Bk Rev**, (Qty: 64). **Circ:** 30,000.
Desc: Articles and stories of interest to students 10 to 12 years of age.

ISSN 0992-4698
FR
UDC 084.12-053.6
CHEVAUX DE PENNY (MONTFORT L'AMAURY), LES. (LES CHEVAUX DE PENNY.). (1988)-. Periodical. French. Twelve times a year. 150.00F France; 218.00F North America. Optipress, BP 60, 78490 Montfort L'Amaury France. **Tel** 011 33 1 34862922. **ED** Jerome Chehu. Index available. **Ad Acc.** ctrl circ.
Desc: Publication about horses and ponies for children 8 to 16 years of age.

ISSN 0707-4611
DD 051 CN
CHICKADEE. [Chicadee]. **Added/Corp** Young Naturalist Foundation. Vol. 1 (Jan. 1979)-. Periodical. English. Ten times a year. 17.00Can$. Young Naturalist Foundation, 179 John Street, Suite 500, Toronto Ontario M5T 3G5 Canada. **Tel** (416)971-5275. **(Subscription address:** Chickadee, 25 Boxwood Lane, Buffalo NY 14427. **Tel** (416)971-5275.**) ED** Janis Nostbakken. **Circ:** 100,000.
Desc: For three to nine year-olds. Each issue features photographs and illustrations, stories, games, puzzles, crafts and a monthly pull-out.
Ind/Abst Can. Index (?-?); Can. Period. Index (19??-); Child. Mag. Guide (1981-); EP Collect.; Homework Help.; Mag. Search; MasterFile FullTEXT 1000; MasterFile FullTEXT 350; MasterFile FullTEXT 650; MasterFile FullTEXT (July 1993-); Mid. Search; OCLC; Prim. Search; Pub. Lib. FullTEXT; Res. Alert; Telebase.

ISSN 0009-3971
US
CHILD LIFE (INDIANAPOLIS, IND. 1922). (CHILD LIFE.). **Added/Corp** Benjamin Franklin Literary & Medical Society. (1922)-. Periodical. English. Eight times a year. $15.95. Benjamin Franklin Literary and Medical Society, 1100 Waterway Boulevard, Indianapolis IN 46206. **Tel** (317)636-8881, FAX (317)637-0126. **(Subscription address:** CDS Agency Hard Copy, PO Box 4966, Des Moines IA 50340. **Tel** (515)247-7569.**) ED** Steve Charles. **Bk Rev. Ad Acc. Circ:** 80,000. available on microfilm and microfiche from University Microfilms International (UMI).
Desc: Entertaining puzzles and more for children ages 9 to 11. Emphasis is placed on developing good health habits with articles about nutrition, exercise and safety.
Ind/Abst Child. Mag. Guide; EP Collect.; Homework Help.; MasterFile FullTEXT 1000; MasterFile FullTEXT 350; MasterFile FullTEXT 650; MasterFile FullTEXT (July 1994-); Mid. Search; OCLC; Prim. Search; Pub. Lib. FullTEXT; Telebase.

TH
CHILD WORKERS IN ASIA. Vol. 1, No. 1 (July-Sept. 1985)-. Periodical. English. Four times a year. $12.00. Child Workers in Asia / CWA, 4 68 Vipawadi Rangsit Road, Bangkok 10900 Thailand.
Ind/Abst Hum. Rights Intern. Rep.

ISSN 0882-942X
DD 305 US
CEASED
CHILDREN & TEENS TODAY. **See** Psychology.

ISSN 0278-3746
US
CHILDREN'S BIBLE STUDIES. ELEMENTARY B. STUDENT BOOK. **VFOAT** Elementary B. Student. Vol. 1, No. 1 (Fall 1982)-. Periodical. English. Four times a year. $7.75. Graded Press, 201 Eighth Avenue South, Box 801, Nashville TN 37202. **Tel** (615)749-6417. ***Continues*** *Middle Elementary Student, 0149-774X.*

ISSN 0705-0038
DD 028.5/0971 CN
CHILDREN'S BOOK NEWS (TORONTO). (THE CHILDREN'S BOOK NEWS.). [Child. book news]. **Added/Corp** Children's Book Centre. **VFOAT** Book News. Vol. 1 (1978)-. Periodical. English (French). Four times a year (Mar., June, Sept., Dec.). Canadian Childrens Book Centre, 35 Spadina Road, Toronto Ontario M5R 2S9 Canada. **Tel** (416)597-1331.
Ind/Abst Book Rev. Index.

LC Z1037.A1 C475 ISSN 0147-5681
DD 028.52 US
CHILDREN'S BOOK REVIEW INDEX. **See** Literary and Political Reviews.

ISSN 1078-7879
US
●**CHILDREN'S BOOK REVIEW MAGAZINE.** **See** Literary and Political Reviews.

LC Z1037.A1 C476 ISSN 0090-7987
DD 028.1 US
CHILDREN'S BOOK REVIEW SERVICE. **See** Literary and Political Reviews.

LC Z1037.A2 C53a PN1009.A1 ISSN 0098-9371
DD 741.64/2 US
CHILDREN'S BOOK SHOWCASE, THE. (THE CHILDREN'S BOOK SHOWCASE. [CATALOG].). **Main/Corp** Children's Book Council (New York, N.Y.). (1972)-. Catalog. English. Children's Book Council, 568 Broadway, New York NY 10012. **Tel** (212)489-1638.

LC Z1037.A2 W47a ISSN 0069-3472
DD 028.52 US
CHILDREN'S BOOKS. AWARDS & PRIZES. **See** Literature.

ISSN 0272-7145
US
CHILDREN'S DIGEST (INDIANAPOLIS. : 1981). (CHILDREN'S DIGEST.). [Child. dig.]. **Added/Corp** Benjamin Franklin Literary and Medical Society. No. 302, (Dec. 1980)-. Periodical. English. Eight times a year. $15.95. Benjamin Franklin Literary and Medical Society, 1100 Waterway Boulevard, Indianapolis IN 46206. **Tel** (317)636-8881, FAX (317)637-0126. **(Subscription address:** CDS Agency Hard Copy, PO Box 4966, Des Moines IA 50340. **Tel** (515)247-7569.**) ED** Elizabeth Rinck. ***Continues*** *Children's Digest and Children's Playcraft, 0273-7582.*
Desc: Edited for the 8 to 10 year old and features health,

Children and Youth Interests

safety, exercise, and nutrition, along with stories, articles, and activities. Emphasis is placed on developing good health habits with articles about nutrition, exercise and safety.
 Ind/Abst Child. Mag. Guide (1981-); EP Collect.; Homework Help.; MasterFile FullTEXT 1000; MasterFile FullTEXT 350; MasterFile FullTEXT 650; MasterFile FullTEXT (July 1994-); Mid. Search; OCLC; Prim. Search; Pub. Lib. FullTEXT; Telebase.

ISSN 1350-4347
UK
CHILDREN'S FICTION ON FICHE. See Literature.

ISSN 0893-486X
US
CHILDREN'S FOCUS. (198?)-. Periodical. English. Twelve times a year. Children's Focus, PO Box 7196, Main Street, Flushing NY 11355. **Tel** (718)353-6008. **ED** Ndanu Consuela. **Bk Rev. Ad Acc.**

LC Z1037 .C5446 PN1009.A1   ISSN 0306-2015
DD 028.52   UK
CHILDREN'S LITERATURE ABSTRACTS. See Literature-Abstracting, Bibliographies and Statistics.

LC PN1009.A1 C5139   ISSN 0362-4145
DD 028.52   US
CHILDREN'S LITERATURE REVIEW. See Literary and Political Reviews.

LC AI3 .S83   ISSN 0743-9873
DD 051   CCC
CHILDREN'S MAGAZINE GUIDE. See Library and Information Sciences-Abstracting, Bibliographies and Statistics.

US
SUSPENDED
CHILDREN'S MAGIC WINDOW MAGAZINE. (19??)-Suspended with Vol. 2, No. 2 (19??). English. Six times a year. Finders Publications Inc, 3718 Macalaster Drive NE, Minneapolis MN 55421. **Tel** (612)788-7669.

LC Z479 .C45   ISSN 0734-8169
DD 070.5/025/73   US
CHILDREN'S MEDIA MARKET PLACE. See Communications.

ISSN 0705-3819
DD 793.7/3/05   CN
CHILDRENS' MYSTERY WORD. See Leisure and Recreation-Amusements.

LC AP201 .C572
DD 052   KE
CHILDREN'S OWN. Vol. 1 (Oct. 15, 1972)-. Periodical. English. Twenty-four times a year. Commercial Syndicate Ltd, PO Box 48057, Nairobi Kenya.

HK
SUSPENDED
CHILDREN'S PARADISE. (19??)-Suspended (Dec. 1994). Chinese. Twenty-four times a year. Union Press Ltd., 6 Victory Avenue, 3rd Floor, Homantin Kowloon Hong Kong.

ISSN 0009-4161
US
CHILDREN'S PLAYMATE MAGAZINE. [Child. playmate mag.]. **Added/Corp** Benjamin Franklin Literary and Medical Society. **VFOAT** Children's Playmate. **VAT** Children's Play Mate Magazine. (19??)-. Periodical. English. Eight times a year. $15.95. Benjamin Franklin Literary and Medical Society, 1100 Waterway Boulevard, Indianapolis IN 46206. **Tel** (317)636-8881, FAX (317)637-0126. **(Subscription address:** CDS Agency Hard Copy, PO Box 4966, Des Moines IA 50340. **Tel** (515)247-7569.) **ED** Elizabeth Rinck. Index available. **Ad Acc. Circ:** 120,000. available on microfilm and microfiche from University Microfilms International (UMI). **Continues** Play Mate.
 Desc: Edited for the 6 to 8 year old. Features easy-to-read and read-aloud stories that are full of humor and excitement. Plenty of things to make and do. Emphasis is on health, safety, exercise and nutrition.
 Ind/Abst Child. Mag. Guide (1981-); EP Collect.; Homework Help.; MasterFile FullTEXT 1000; MasterFile FullTEXT 350; MasterFile FullTEXT 650; MasterFile FullTEXT (July 1994-); Mid. Search; OCLC; Prim. Search; Pub. Lib. FullTEXT; Telebase.

ISSN 8750-1929
US
CHILDREN'S SERMONS SERVICE PLUS. See Religions and Theology-Protestantism.

ISSN 1069-9430
US
●**CHILDREN'S SOFTWARE REVUE.** See Education-Computer Applications.

US
CHILDREN'S SURPRISES. English. Six times a year. $14.95 (one-year), $24.95 (two-year), $31.95 (three-year). Surprises, 1200 North 7th Street, Minneapolis MN 55411. **Tel** 800 356-8899, (612)521-8090, FAX (612)522-1182. **Continues** Surprises.

ISSN 0883-6922
US
CHILDREN'S VIDEO REPORT. Added/Corp Great Mountain Productions (New York, N.Y.). Vol. 1, No. 1 (May 1985)-. Periodical. English. Eight times a year. $60.00. Children's Video Report, 370 Court Street, Suite 76, Brooklyn NY 11231. **Tel** (718)935-0600. **ED** Martha Dewing.
 Desc: Features articles written by various professionals in the field of children's media, as well as extensive reviews of new children's video releases.

ISSN 0895-2094
DD 791   US
CHILDREN'S VIDEO REVIEW NEWSLETTER. See Communications-Video.

II
CHILDREN'S WORLD. See Mathematics.

LC PN147.5 .C48   ISSN 0897-9790
DD 070.5/2 808   US
CHILDREN'S WRITER'S & ILLUSTRATOR'S MARKET. See Literature.

LC KD735.A13 C48   ISSN 0265-1459
DD 346.4101/35 344.106135   UK
CHILDRIGHT. See Political Science-Civil Rights.

ISSN 0185-1756
DD 028.55   MX
CHISPA. [Chispa]. (1980)-. Periodical. Spanish. Twelve times a year. $50.00. Innovacion y Comunicacion SA, Apdo Postal 19 456, 03910 Mexico df, Mexico. **Tel** 11 52 5 6626046.

ISSN 0564-478X
US
CHISPA. Added/Corp Tuolumne County Historical Society. Quarterly. Tuolumne County Historical Society. Vol. 1 (July/Sept. 1961)-. Periodical. English. Four times a year. Tuolumne County Historical Society, Rt 2 Box 159, Sonora CA 95370. **Tel** (303)669-0586.
 Desc: A science periodical published in Mexico for children and young adults. The goal is to interest readers in the wonders of nature and scientific discovery.

LC Z1039.S5 C47   ISSN 0735-6358
DD 011/.63   US
CHOICES (EVANSTON, ILL.). See Literature.

LC PZ10.831 .C63835   ISSN 0412-4154
DD 371.9 362.7   CC
CHUNG-KUO ERH TUNG. VFOAT Zhongguo Ertong. No. 1 (19??)-. Periodical. Chinese. Twelve times a year. $25.00. China Juvenile Press / Zhongguo Shaonian Ertong Chubanshe, 21 Dongsi Shi'er 12 Tiao, Beijing 100708 People's Republic of China. **Tel** 444761-225. **(Subscription address:** China Books & Periodicals Inc., 2929 24th Street, San Francisco CA 94110. **Tel** (415)282-2994.)
 Desc: Chinese literature for children.

ISSN 0214-4123
UDC 82.93   SP
CLIJ. See Literature.

ISSN 1071-4073
DD 268   US
CLUBHOUSE (BERRIEN SPRINGS, MICH.). See Religions and Theology.

LC E169.1 .C58   ISSN 0199-5197
DD 973/.05   US
COBBLESTONE. [Cobblestone]. Vol. 1 (Jan. 1980)-. Periodical. English. Nine times a year (monthly except June, July and Aug.) $24.95. Cobblestone Publishing Inc., 7 School Street, Peterborough NH 03458. **Tel** (603)924-7209, FAX (603)924-7380. **ED** Carolyn P. Yoder. Index available. cum. index. **Bk Rev. Circ:** 45,000. Documents available from UMI Article Clearinghouse.
 Desc: Presents American History through firsthand accounts, biographies, historical drawings and photographs, maps, stories, poems and games for the 8-14 year old.
 Ind/Abst Abstr. Engl. Stud.; Child. Mag. Guide (1981-); EP Collect.; Homework Help.; Mag. Artic. Summar. Elite; Mag. Artic. Summar. Select; Mag. Artic. Summar. CD-ROM; Mag. Search; MasterFile FullTEXT 1000; MasterFile FullTEXT 350; MasterFile FullTEXT 650; MasterFile FullTEXT (July 1989-) [Full Txt.]; Mid. Search; Newsp. Period. Abstr. (1989-); OCLC; Prim. Search; Pub. Lib. FullTEXT; Telebase.

ISSN 0747-3575
US
COMIC READER, THE. See Leisure and Recreation-Amusements.

ISSN 0748-2264
DD 741   US
COMIC TALE EASY READER. [Comic tale easy read.]. **VFOAT** Comic Tale. (19??)-. Periodical. English. Irregular. May Davenport Publishers, 26313 Purissima Road, Los Altos Hills CA 94022. **Tel** (415)948-6499. **ED** May Davenport. **Bk Rev. Ad Acc. Circ:** 3,000. (ctrl).
 Desc: Illustrations with humorous narratives to make children laugh, to encourage literary interest as well as visual comprehension, and to help TV oriented youth to read and write.

LC HV878 .C66   ISSN 0272-6513
US
CONNECTIONS (NEW YORK, N.Y.). (CONNECTIONS : THE QUARTERLY MAGAZINE OF BOYS CLUBS OF AMERICA.). [Connections]. **Added/Corp** Boys' Clubs of America. Vol. 1, No. 1 (Dec. 1980)-. Periodical. English. Four times a year (Jan., Apr., Jul., Oct.). $10.00. Boys Clubs of America, 771 First Avenue, New York NY 10017. **Tel** (212)557-8555. **ED** Daniel M. Fallon. **Bk Rev. Circ:** 3,000. **Continues** Keynote, 0047-3413.
 Desc: Provides pertinent and timely information to youth workers and boys club boards on issues effecting youth and the management of boys clubs.

US
CONQUISTA JUVENIL. (19??)-. Periodical. Spanish. Six times a year (bimonthly). $2.50. Casa Nazarena de Publicaciones, 6401 The Paseo, Kansas City MO 64131. **Tel** (816)333-7000. **Circ:** 3,300.
 Desc: Christian youth magazine.

ISSN 1032-1268
DD b820.809282   AT
CONTAGIOUS MAGAZINE. [Contag. mag.]. **VFOAT** Feeling Great is Contagious Magazine; Contagious. (1992)-. Periodical. English. Six times a year (Feb., Apr., June, Aug., Oct., Dec.). 22.00Aus$ Australia; 30.00Aus$ others. System House Pty. Ltd., PO Box 611, Unley South Australia 5061 Australia. **Tel** 011 61 8 2711024, FAX 011 61 8 2711024. **ED** Helen Marron (Editor's address: 2A Hannah Street Beecroft New South Wales, 2119 Australia; telephone: 011 61 2 4849650). **Bk Rev.** ctrl circ.
 Desc: Features articles of short stories, poems, puzzles, comic strips, cartoons, poster and other interesting facts for the kids and adults.

ISSN 0822-7098
DD 054/.1   CN
COULICOU. [Coulicou]. Vol. 1 No 1 (Jan. 1984)-. Periodical. French. Ten times a year. 15.97Can$. Les Editions Heritage Inc., 300 Avenue Arran, St. Lambert Quebec J4R 1K5 Canada. **Tel** (514)875-0327, (514)672-6710, FAX (514)672-1481, (514)672-5448. **(Subscription address:** Informatique Rive Sud Inc., 25 Taschereau Bur 201, Greenfield Park, Quebec J4V 2G8 Canada. **Tel** (514)875-4444.) **ED** M. C. Favreau. **Bk Rev. Ad Acc. Circ:** 25,000. (ctrl).
 Desc: A magazine for children, richly illustrated in full-color drawings of animals. Conservation and naturalism are introduced through cartoons, poems, and games.
 Ind/Abst Can. Period. Index.

ISSN 0892-9599
DD 051   US
CREATIVE KIDS. [Creat. kids]. Vol. 5, No. 1 (Oct. 1986)-. Periodical. English. Six times a year. $19.95. Prufrock Press, PO Box 8813, Waco TX 76714-8813. **Tel** (817)756-3337, FAX (817)756-3339. **ED** Fay L. Gold. **Bk Rev. Ad Acc. Circ:** 10,000. **Continues** Chart Your Course (Mobile, Ala.), 0744-3420.
 Desc: Ideas and activities to entertain, challenge, and stimulate creativity in children ages 8-14. Includes examples of student work, and art, photography, music, games, puzzles, contests, and stories.

LC AP201 .C8   ISSN 0090-6034
DD 808.8/99282   US
CRICKET (LA SALLE). (CRICKET.). [Cricket]. (Jan. 1973)-. Periodical. English. Twelve times a year. $27.97. Open Court Publishing Company, 315 Fifth Street, PO Box 300, Peru IL 61354. **Tel** (800)435-6850, (815)223-1500, FAX (815)224-6675. **(Subscription address:** Cricket Magazine, Box 387, Mt. Morris IL 61054.) **ED** Marianne Carus. Index available. cum. index. **Circ:** 111,050. available on magnetic tape (Kable News / 308 E Hitt Street, Mt. Morris, IL 61054); available on microfilm and microfiche from University Microfilms International (UMI).
 Desc: Includes folk and fairy tales, fantasy and science fiction, biographies; articles about history, nature and science, music and art, sports and travel; serious and humorous poetry, recipes, crafts, riddles, puzzles and jokes, and animal stories.
 Ind/Abst Child. Mag. Guide (1981-); EP Collect.; Homework Help.; Mag. Artic. Summar. Elite; Mag. Artic. Summar. Select; Mag. Artic. Summar. CD-ROM; Mag. Search; MasterFile FullTEXT 1000; MasterFile FullTEXT

Children and Youth Interests

350; MasterFile FullTEXT 650; MasterFile FullTEXT (July 1989-); Mid. Search; OCLC; Prim. Search; Pub. Lib. FullTEXT; Telebase.

DD 809/.89282/072
ISSN 0820-8247
CN

CRSCL NEWSLETTER. See Literature.

US

DABAU. English. Eight times a year. $16.50. Midwest European Publication, 8220 North Christiana Avenue, Skokie IL 60076. **Tel** (708)676-1196, FAX (800)433-9229, telex 256262.

ISSN 0773-0292
BE

DAUPHIN. [Dauphin]. (1978)-. Periodical. French. One time a week. $79.84. Uitgeverij Averbode, BP 54, 3281 Averbode Belgium. **Tel** 011 32 13 780135. Index available.
Desc: Discovering the world in time and space, looking at things from different angles, the fun of reading and more.

DD J505
ISSN 1187-8681
CN

DEBROUILLARDS (MONTREAL). (LES DEBROUILLARDS.). [Debrouillards]. **Added/Corp** Club des Debrouillards. Conseil de Developpement du Loisir Scientifique. No. 110 (Jan. 1992)-. Periodical. French. Ten times a year. 19.96Can$. Conseil de Developpement du Loisir Scientifique, 4545 Avenue Pierre de Coubertin, Montreal Quebec H1V 3R2 Canada. **Tel** (514)252-3027. (**Subscription address:** Abonnement Service, 25 Boulevard Taschereau, Bureau 201, Greenfield PK Quebec J4V 3P1 Canada. **Tel** (514)875-4444.) Continues *Je me Petitdebrouille, 0714-4067.*
Ind/Abst Repere (1992-).

DD 028.5
ISSN 0418-7946
RU

DETSKAIA LITERATURA. See Literature.

US

●**DIGITAL KIDS.** (1995)-. English. Twelve times a year. Jupiter Communications, 594 Broadway, Suite 1003, New York NY 10012. **Tel** (212)941-9252.

DD 264/.02/005
ISSN 0317-2198
CN

DIMANCHE ET FETE. No. 1 (Jan. 1975)-. French. Novalis, PO Box 990, Outremont Quebec H2V 4S7 Canada. **Tel** (514)948-1222.

ISSN 1060-4006
US

DINOSAUR REVIEW (BOULDER, COLO.), THE. See Paleontology.

LC HS3260.U5 D57
ISSN 1044-4440
DD 369.4/02573
US

DIRECTORY OF AMERICAN YOUTH ORGANIZATIONS. See Children and Youth Interests-Abstracting, Bibliographies and Statistics.

ISSN 1321-8093
AT

DISABLED CHILDREN'S JOURNAL, THE. See Physically Impaired.

ISSN 1050-2491
DD 051
US

DISNEY ADVENTURES. [Disney adv.]. **VFOAT** Disney Adventures Magazine; Adventures. Vol. 1, No. 1 (Nov. 12, 1990)-. Periodical. English. Fourteen times a year. $19.95. Walt Disney Publishing Inc., 500 South Buena Vista Street, Burbank CA 91521. **Tel** (212)807-5816. (**Subscription address:** Palm Coast Data, PO Box 420163, Agency Department, Palm Coast FL 32142. **Tel** (904)445-4662 ext. 669, (800)829-5475.) **ED** Tommi Lewis. **Ad Acc**.
Desc: Editorial includes comics, stories about real life heroes and articles on fashion and styles, science, electronic games, sports, movies and celebrities.

ISSN 1053-6272
DD 741
US

DISNEY BABIES OUT & AROUND / DISNEY. [Disney babies out around]. **Added/Corp** Walt Disney Company. **VFOAT** Disney Babies Out and Around. (1991)-. Monographic series. English. Disney Books by Mail / California, 500 South Buena Vista Street, Tower 3144, Burbank CA 91505.

US

DISNEY CATALOGUE. (19??)-. English. Four times a year. Free on request. Disney Corporation, 250 Park Avenue South, New York NY 10003. **Tel** (913)752-1000.

LC AP201 .D56a
ISSN 0362-1960
DD 051
US

DISNEY MAGAZINE. **Main/Corp** Walt Disney Productions. (May 1975)-. Periodical. English. Four times a year. $16.95. Disney Magazine, PO Box 4489, Anaheim CA 92803. **Tel** (714)520-2533. (**Subscription address:** Neodata / Colorado, PO Box 2606, Boulder CO 80322.) **ED** Anne P. Okey. **Ad Acc**, **Adv Mgr:** V. Barne. Continues *Disney News.*

ISSN 1050-2599
DD 741
US

DISNEY'S CHIP 'N' DALE RESCUE RANGERS. [Disney's Chip 'n' Dale rescue rangers]. **VFOAT** Chip 'N' Dale Rescue Rangers. No. 1 (June 1990)-. Periodical. English. Twelve times a year. Walt Disney Productions, 500 South Buena Vista, Burbank CA 91521.

ISSN 1055-4203
DD 741
US

DISNEY'S TALE SPIN. [Disney's tale spin]. **VFOAT** Tale Spin. (June 1991)-. Periodical. English. Twelve times a year. $18.00. W D Publications, 500 South Buena Vista, Burbank CA 91521.

ISSN 0273-1274
US

DISNEY'S YEAR BOOK. (1981)-. English. One time a year. Grolier Enterprises Inc, Sherman Turnpike, Danbury CT 06816. **Tel** (203)797-3500.

ISSN 1158-4270
FR

UDC 08-053.5/.6

DO RE MI PARIS. (DO RE MI.). (1990)-. Monographic series. French (Dutch and French). Twenty-four times a year. Editions Presse Europeenne, BP 54, 3281 Averbode Belgium. **Tel** 011 32 13 773311, FAX 011 32 13 777243, telex 39104. **ED** N Bruyr and J Lembrechts. Index available.
Desc: Everyday topics are presented in a variety of playful ways. Packed with things to make and do. Contains large brilliant illustrations.

ISSN 0811-7179
AT

DOLLY. (19??)-. English. Twelve times a year. 34.53Aus$. Australian Consolidated Press Ltd., Private Bag 92615 Symonds St, Auckland New Zealand. **Tel** 011 64 9 3735408, FAX 011 64 9 3022889.

ISSN 8756-6362
DD 574
US

DOLPHIN LOG. See Earth Sciences-Oceanography.

ISSN 1062-1385
US

DON THE BEAR SERIES. **VFOAT** Don the Bear; Don and Scooter too!. (1992)-. Monographic series. English. Price varies per volume. Bye Monthly Publishing, PO Box 762, Barre VT 05641.

ISSN 1062-3426
DD 248
US

DONKEY TALK. See Religions and Theology.

ISSN 0163-3562
US

DYNAMITE (NEW YORK). (DYNAMITE.). [Dynamite]. Periodical. English. Six times a year. $15.00. Scholastic Inc, 730 Broadway, New York NY 10003. **Tel** (416)883-5300, FAX (212)505-3653. available on microfilm and microfiche from University Microfilms International (UMI).
Ind/Abst Child. Mag. Guide (1981-).

LC GV750
ISSN 1070-566X
DD 797.5
US

●**EAA SPORT AVIATION FOR KIDS.** See Aeronautics, Astronautics.

ISSN 8755-2175
US

EARLITEEN (TEACHER'S ED.). See Religions and Theology.

UK

EDGE, THE. **Added/Corp** Oxfam. Youth & Education Dept. Issue No. 1 (Spring 1988)-. Periodical. English. Continues *Bother.*

ISSN 1191-2286
DD J054/.1
CN

EN PRIMEUR JEUNE S. See Communications-Video.

LC AP221 .E52
ISSN 0793-1891
DD 050
IS

●**ENAYIM.** **Added/Corp** Muzeon Yisrael (Jerusalem). Agaf ha-Noar. **VFOAT** Einayim. (1994)-. Consumer Publication. Hebrew. Four times a year. IL60.00. Einayim Publishers, PO Box 3211, Jerausalem 91031 Israel.

US

ENCOUNTER : THE CHALLENGING WORLD OF NEWS. (19??)-. Newsletter. English. Twelve times a year. $68.25. National Research Bureau Inc. / Iowa, 200 North Fourth, PO Box 1, Burlington IA 52601. **Tel** (319)752-5415, FAX (319)752-3421.
Desc: A publication for teenagers.

BE

NLM W1 EN569
CEASED

ENFANT. (1947)-(1993). Periodical. French. Office de la Naissance Enfance, 86 Avenue de la Toison D OR, 1060 Brussels Belgium. **Tel** 011 32 2 6520013. Continues *Revue Trimestrielle.*
Ind/Abst Repere (1983-).

ISSN 0397-4820
FR

UDC 61

ENFANTS MAGAZINE PARIS. [Enfants mag. Paris]. (1976)-. Periodical. French. Twelve times a year. $52.49. PGM, 5 rue des Morillons, 75015 Paris France. **Tel** 011 33 1 45300319.

ISSN 0274-8592
US

ENTERPRISE (NEW YORK). See Political Science.

ISSN 0196-0911
US

EQUIPPING YOUTH. **Added/Corp** Southern Baptist Convention. Sunday School Board. Vol. 1, No. 1 (Oct./Nov./Dec.) 1981)-. Periodical. English. Four times a year. $8.50 (one-year); $16.75 (two-year); $23.25 (three-year). Southern Baptist Convention, 901 Commerce, Suite 750, Nashville TN 37203. **Tel** (615)244-2355, FAX (615)742-8919. (**Subscription address:** Sunday School Board, Customer Service, 127 9th Avenue North, Nashville TN 37234. **Tel** (800)458-2772.) Continues *Care for Leaders, 0162-4539.*

LC Z1037.8.C5 E74
CH

ERH TUNG TU SHU YU CHIAO YU TSA CHIH = THE CHILDREN'S LITERATURE & EDUCATION MAGAZINE. **VFOAT** The Children's Literature & Education Magazine; Children's Literature and Education Magazine; Children's Literature & Education Magazine. (July 1981)-. Periodical. Chinese. Twelve times a year. Chi Yuan Wen Hua Shih Yeh, 96-2 Chung Hsiao E Rd 4 Sect, Taipei Taiwan.

ISSN 0891-3846
US

EVANGELIZING TODAY'S CHILD. See Religions and Theology.

LC GN301 .F33
ISSN 0749-1387
DD 392/.05
US

FACES (PETERBOROUGH, N.H.). (FACES.). [Faces]. **Added/Corp** American Museum of Natural History. Vol. 1, No. 1 (Oct. 1984)-. Periodical. English. Nine times a year (monthly except June, July, and Aug.). $23.95. Cobblestone Publishing Inc., 7 School Street, Peterborough NH 03458. **Tel** (603)924-7209, FAX (603)924-7380. **ED** C. Yoder. **Circ**: 12,000.
Desc: The magazine that shows its readers how the peoples of the world live, think, work and play. Packed with articles, activities, maps, games, and photos to provide intellectual as well as visual stimulation.
Ind/Abst Child. Mag. Guide; Consumer Index; Homework Help.; Mag. Search; MasterFile FullTEXT 1000; MasterFile FullTEXT 350; MasterFile FullTEXT 650; MasterFile FullTEXT (Jan. 1993-); Mid. Search; OCLC; Prim. Search; Pub. Lib. FullTEXT; Telebase.

ISSN 0827-1356
DD 520/.5
CN

FEUILLETS DU NATURALISTE, ASTRONOMIE, LES. See Astronomy.

LC Z1037.A1 F53
ISSN 0819-5358
DD 028.5/35
AT

FICTION FOCUS. See Literature.

ISSN 0426-1216
PL

UDC 304(438)

FILIPINKA WARSZAWA. (FILIPINKA.). [Filipinka Warsz.]. (1957)-. Periodical. Polish. Twenty-six times a year. $65.00. Filipinka, 00-236 Warsaw, Swietojerska 5/7 Poland. **Tel** (22)312221. (**Subscription address:** Ars Polona-Ruch, PO Box 1001, Krakowskie Przedmiescie 7, 00-068 Warsaw Poland. **Tel** 011 48 22 261201.) **ED** Hanna Jaworowska-Blonska. **Circ**: 125,600.

ISSN 0227-0315
DD 054/.1
CN

FILLES D'AUJOURD'HUI. Vol. 1, No 1 (1???)-. Periodical. French. Twelve times a year. 23.48Can$. Publications Quebecor le Nordais, 5800 rue St. Denis Bar 605, Montreal Quebec H2S 3L5 Canada. **Tel** (514)272-6330, FAX (514)270-7079. **ED** Marie Dufour. **Ad Acc**. **Circ**: 35,000 (ctrl). available on microfiche.
Desc: Geared to the female teens of Canada. Contains

Children and Youth Interests

articles on beauty, sex, music and more. Includes tear-out posters.
Ind/Abst Repere (Vol. 11, No. 3, Jan. 1991-).

US
FINGER PRINTS. (19??)-. English. Six times a year. $20.00. Children's Museum, 311 Main Street, Utica NY 13501. **Tel** (315)724-6128. **ED** Jeffrey Chard. **Circ:** 2,500.
LC WMLC 93/416   ISSN 0892-6735
DD 028   US
FIVE OWLS, THE. See Literary and Political Reviews.

UK
FIZZ. (19??)-. English. One time a week. £10.20. Scottish Braille Press, Craigmillar Park, Edinburgh EH16 5NB United Kingdom. **Tel** 011 44 131 6624445.
Desc: Braille magazine for teenagers, containing star interviews, the gossip on the music scene, as well as a star-scope. Also includes a question and answer problem page.

GW
FLOH KISTE. (19??)-. German. Twenty-six times a year. DM96.00 Germany; DM127.00 other. Domino Verlag Gunther Brinek GmbH, Hubertustrabe 22, D-80639 Munich Germany. **Tel** 011 49 89 179130.

ISSN 0895-1136
DD 071   US
FOCUS ON THE FAMILY CLUBHOUSE.
Added/Corp Focus on the Family (Organization). VFOAT Clubhouse; Family Clubhouse. Vol. 1, No. 1 (Feb. 1987)-. Periodical. English. Twelve times a year. $12.00. Focus on the Family, Colorado Springs CO 80995. **Tel** (800)232-6459. **ED** Ray Seldomridge and Beth Ann Deltoni. **Circ:** 125,000.
Desc: A Christian children's magazine.
LC Z5346.A2 F6   ISSN 0093-2825
DD 028.52/05   US
FOR YOUNGER READERS. See Physically Impaired.

US
FOTONOVELAS : CHILDREN'S SPANISH LANGUAGE POPULAR FICTION. (19??)-. Periodical. Spanish. Twelve times a year. $281.60. Hispanic Books Distributors Inc., 1665 West Grant Road, Tucson AZ 85745. **Tel** (520)882-9484, (800)634-2124, FAX (520)882-7696.

ISSN 0362-9066
US
FPS. (FPS; A MAGAZINE OF YOUNG PEOPLE'S LIBERATION.). Periodical. English. Twelve times a year. $10.00 general, $6.00 under the age of 18. Youth Liberation Press, 2007 Washtenaw Avenue, Ann Arbor MI 48104.
LC AG600 .F73   ISSN 1056-9693
DD 011   US
FREE STUFF FOR KIDS (DEEPHAVEN, MINN.). (FREE STUFF FOR KIDS.). **Added/Corp** Meadowbrook, Inc. (1976)-. English. One time a year. $4.95. Meadowbrook Press, 18318 Minnetonka Boulevard, Deephaven MN 55391. **Tel** (800)338-2232, (212)698-7000. **ED** Bruce Lansky. **Continues** Rainbow Book, 1057-7289.

SI
FRIDAY WEEKLY. (19??)-. Chinese. One time a week. $99.48. Singapore Press Holdings Ltd, 82 Genting Lane Level 7, Singapore 1334 Singapore. **Tel** 011 65 7438400, FAX 011 65 7444875, 011 65 7461925, telex 55959. **ED** Tom Yim Seong. **Ad Acc, Adv Mgr:** Lawrence Loh, **Tel** 740-2038. **Circ:** 40,000.
Desc: Targeted at students ranging from ages 12-16; contents include: general news, school news, sports, entertainment, fashion, and students' contributions.
LC LB1501   ISSN 1352-1942
DD 372.241   UK
•**FUN TO LEARN - PETER RABBIT AND FRIENDS.** (1994)-. Consumer Publication. English. Twelve times a year. £11.90. The Redan Company Ltd., Appleton House, 139 King Street, London W6 9JG United Kingdom. **Tel** 011 44 181 5631563, FAX 011 44 181 5631478. **(Subscription address:** MMC, Octagon House, White Hart Meadows, Ripley, Woking, Surrey GU23 6HR United Kingdom. **Tel** 011 44 1483 211731, FAX 011 44 1483 211731.) **ED** Diana Barton. **Ad Acc. Circ:** 140,000.
Desc: Directed at children between the ages of three and seven years old.

ISSN 0155-1019
DD 372.2109944   AT
GETTING TOGETHER. [Getting together]. (1978)-. Periodical. English. Three times a year.
Ind/Abst Aust. Educ. Index (1978-1982).

ISSN 1078-3326
DD 051   US
•**GIRLS' LIFE (BALTIMORE, MD.).** (GIRLS' LIFE.). [Girls' life]. Vol. 1, No.1 (Aug./Sept. 1994)-. Periodical. English. Six times a year. $19.95 US; $24.95 other. Monarch Avalon Inc., 4517 Harford Road, Baltimore MD 21214. **Tel** (410)254-9200, FAX (410)254-0991.

ISSN 1054-1837
US
GOD'S WORLD TODAY. (19??)-. Periodical. English. One time a week (weekly during school year). $19.00. God's World Publications, Box 2330, Asheville NC 28802. **Tel** (704)253-8063, (800)951-5437. **ED** Norm Bomer. **Circ:** 250,000.
Desc: News, features, and activities for kids from a Biblical perspective.
LC F621 .G63   ISSN 0278-0208
DD 977   US
    CCC
GOLDFINCH, THE. (THE GOLDFINCH. IOWA STATE HISTORICAL DEPARTMENT, DIVISION OF THE STATE HISTORICAL SOCIETY.). **Added/Corp** Iowa. Division of the State Historical Society. (1975)-. Periodical. English. Four times a year (Feb., Apr., Sept., Nov.). $10.00. State Historical Society of Iowa, 402 Iowa Avenue, Centennial Building, Iwoa City IA 52240. **Tel** (319)335-3916, FAX (319)335-3924. **ED** Deborah Gore Ohrn. cum. index. **Circ:** 5,000. available on CD-ROM.
Desc: A children's magazine about Iowa history. Included are articles, activities, historical photographs and primary sources.

ISSN 0046-8061
    CN
Pr Rev.
GOTUJS' (TORONTO). (HOTUJS'.). **Added/Corp** Plast. VFOAT Hotuys. (1???)-. Periodical. Ukrainian. Six times a year. 28.01Can$. Plast Publishing, 2199 Bloor Street West, Toronto Ontario M6S 1N2 Canada. **Tel** (416)769-7855, FAX (416)763-0185. **Circ:** 1,200.

GW
GRIMM & GRIPS. See Theater.

ISSN 0163-8971
DD 268   US
GROUP (LOVELAND, COLO.). See Religions and Theology.

ISSN 0017-5226
US
GUIDE (WASHINGTON). See Religions and Theology.

ISSN 0159-0340
DD 369.4630994   AT
GUIDING IN AUSTRALIA. [Guiding Aust.]. (1980)-. Periodical. English. Ten times a year (monthly except Jan./Dec.). 22.04Aus$. Girl Guides Association of Australia, PO Box 6, Strawberry Hills, NSW 2012 Australia. **Tel** 011 61 3197206, FAX 011 61 3197453. **ED** Nadene Cattell. **Ad Acc. Circ:** 7,000 (ctrl).

US
HAND TO HAND. See Museums and Galleries.

ISSN 0438-6019
    PL
UDC 329.78
HARCERSTWO WARSZAWA.
(HARCERSTWO.). [Harcerstwo Warsz.]. (1959)-. Periodical. Polish. Twelve times a year. $21.00. **(Subscription address:** Ars Polona-Ruch, PO Box 1001, Krakowskie Przedmiescie 7, 00-068 Warsaw Poland. **Tel** 011 48 22 261201.)

ISSN 1106-1405
    GR
UDC 740
HAROUMENES ISTORIES NTISNEY.
[Haroum. Ist. Ntisney]. (1992)-. Periodical. Greek, Modern. Twelve times a year. $39.00. Geniki Ekdotiki Attikis EPE, 7. Fragoklisias Street, GR 15125 Marousi Greece. **Tel** 011 30 1 689-6366, FAX 011 30 1 689-9162, 011 30 1 689-5360, telex TER GR 218063. **(Subscription address:** GEA Subscription Service, 7 Fragokisias ST, GR 151 25 Marousi Greece. **Tel** 011 30 1 6899149.) **ED** Stelios Nicolaou (editor.). **Tel** 011 30 1 689-6366). **Ad Acc, Adv Mgr:** R. Papadopoulou, **Tel** 011 30 1 689-9154 ext. 9. **Circ:** 17,000 (ctrl). **Continues** Tsip & Nteel, 1105-1620.
Desc: Selected Disney stories for young readers and pre-school children.

ISSN 0893-536X
DD 248   US
HEARTS AFLAME. Added/Corp Blue Army of Our Lady of Fatima. (June/July 1987)-. Periodical. English. Four times a year (published seasonally). $5.00. World Apostolate of Fatima, Box 976, Mountain View Road, Washington NJ 07882. **Tel** (201)689-1700, FAX (201)689-6279. **ED** Mary Celeste.
Desc: A Catholic teen magazine.

ISSN 0709-9177
    CN
DD 509.71
HIBOU (ST-LAMBERT). (HIBOU.). [Hibou]. Vol. 1 (Jan. 1980)-. Periodical. French. Ten times a year. 15.97Can$. Les Editions Heritage Inc., 300 Avenue Arran, St. Lambert Quebec J4R 1K5 Canada. **Tel** (514)875-0327, (514)672-6710, FAX (514)672-1481, (514)672-5448. **(Subscription address:** Abonnement Quebec, 25 Boulevard Taschereau, Bureau 201, Greenfield PK Quebec J4V 3P1 Canada. **Tel** (514)875-4444.) **ED** Dominique Chauveau and Marie-Claude Favreau. Index available. **Bk Rev. Ad Acc. Circ:** 26,500 (ctrl).
Desc: Participation magazine for eight to twelve year-olds. Includes articles on science and nature; an animal of the month; the answers to questions sent in by readers; brain teasers; detective games; the totally safe science experiments of Dr. Zed; the adventures of the incredible shrinking Mighty Mites; and contests.
Ind/Abst Can. Period. Index (19??-); Repere (1983-).

ISSN 0190-3802
    US
HIGH ADVENTURE. Added/Corp Royal Rangers. (19??)-. Periodical. English. Four times a year (Seasonally). $1.75. Assemblies of God Archives, 1445 Boonville Avenue, Springfield MO 65802-1894. **Tel** (417)862-2781, (417)862-1447, FAX (417)862-8558. **ED** Ken Hunt and Marshall Bruner. **Circ:** 86,000.
Desc: Challenges boys in narrative form to higher ideals and to perpetuate the spirit of the Royal Rangers program through stories, ideals, and illustrations.
LC AP201 .H45   ISSN 0018-165X
DD 051   US
HIGHLIGHTS FOR CHILDREN. [Highlights child.]. Vol. 1, No. 1 (June 1946)-. Periodical. English. Eleven times a year (monthly with combined July/Aug.). $26.04. Highlights for Children, PO Box 18275, 2300 West 5th Avenue, Columbus OH 43218-0275. **Tel** (614)486-0631, (800)255-9517. **ED** Kent L. Brown, Jr. Index available. **Circ:** 3,000,000. available on microfilm and microfiche from University Microfilms International (UMI). **Absorbed** Children's Activities.
Desc: Children's magazine which contains stories, articles, crafts, riddles, games, thinking and creating activities, geared toward developing thinking and reading skills. Content appeals to interests of children from ages 2-12.
Ind/Abst Child. Mag. Guide (1981-); EP Collect.; Homework Help.; Mag. Artic. Summar. File; Mag. Artic. Summar. Select; Mag. Artic. Summar. CD-ROM; Mag. Search; MasterFile FullTEXT 1000; MasterFile FullTEXT 350; MasterFile FullTEXT 650; MasterFile FullTEXT (July 1989-) [Full Txt.]; Mid. Search; OCLC; Prim. Search; Pub. Lib. FullTEXT; Res. Alert; Subj. Index Child. Mag. (1946-1981); Telebase.

ISSN 1044-0488
DD 051   US
HOPSCOTCH (SARATOGA SPRINGS, N.Y.). (HOPSCOTCH.). [Hopscotch]. Vol. 1, No. 1 (June/July 1989)-. Periodical. English. Six times a year. $15.00. Hopscotch Inc., PO Box 164, Bluffton OH 45817. **Tel** (419)358-4610. **ED** Donald P. Evans. Index available. cum. index. **Bk Rev. Ad Acc. Circ:** 4,000.
Desc: Magazine for girls of ages 6-12 that emphasizes traditional themes and values in its articles, fiction, poetry, crafts and puzzles.
Ind/Abst EP Collect.; Homework Help.; Mag. Search; MasterFile FullTEXT 1000; MasterFile FullTEXT 350; MasterFile FullTEXT 650; MasterFile FullTEXT (July 1993-) [Full Txt.]; Mid. Search; OCLC; Prim. Search; Pub. Lib. FullTEXT; Telebase.
LC Z1037 .H67   ISSN 1044-405X
DD 028   US
HORN BOOK GUIDE TO CHILDREN'S AND YOUNG ADULT BOOKS, THE. See Literary and Political Reviews.
LC Z1037.A1 A15   ISSN 0018-5078
DD 028   US
HORN BOOK MAGAZINE (1945), THE.
(THE HORN BOOK MAGAZINE.). [Horn book mag.]. Vol. 21 No. 3 (May/June 1945)-. Periodical. English. Six times a year (Jan., Mar., May, July, Sept., Nov.). $43.00. The Horn Book Inc., 11 Beacon Street, Suite 1000, Boston MA 02108-3704. **Tel** (617)227-1555, (800)325-1170, FAX (617)523-0299. **ED** Anita Silvey. Index available (In each issue). cum. index (In November issue). **Bk Rev. Ad Acc. Circ:** 24,000 (ctrl). available on microfilm and microfiche from University Microfilms International (UMI); available on CD-ROM; available on an online database (file 647/Full-Text) from DIALOG. Documents available from UMI Article Clearinghouse, Magazine Collection. **Continues** Horn Book (Boston, Mass. : 1944).
Desc: Combines an extensive book review section with articles and columns. Strives to explore all aspects of children's literature from different points of view, yet is devoted to discovering the best that is published for young people.
Ind/Abst Acad. Abstr.; Acad. Ind. [Computer File] (1984-); Acad. Search; Access (1980-); ARTbibliogr. Mod. (1981-); Book Rev. Digest; Book Rev. Index; Child. Lit. Abstr.; Child. Mag. Guide (1981-); Curr. Index J. Educ.; EP Collect.; Expand. Acad. Index (1984-); Gen. Period. Index (1985-); Homework Help.; Libr. Lit.; Mag.

Children and Youth Interests

Artic. Summar. Elite; Mag. Artic. Summar. Select; Mag. Artic. Summar. CD-ROM; Mag. Index Plus (1989-); Mag. Search; MasterFile FullTEXT 1000; MasterFile FullTEXT 350; MasterFile FullTEXT 650; MasterFile FullTEXT (July 1990-) [Full Txt.]; Med. Rev. Dig.; Mid. Search; Newsp. Period. Abstr. (1988-); OCLC; Prim. Search; Pub. Lib. FullTEXT; Res. Alert; Sci. Fict. Fantasy Book Rev. Index; Telebase; Mag. Index (1977-); World Mag. Bank.

LC PZ10.831 .H6634

CC

HSIAO HSI LIU = XIAO XI LIU. VFOAT Xiao Xi Liu. (19??)-. Periodical. Chinese. Six times a year. Science Press, 16 Donghuangchenggen North Street, Beijing 100707, People's Republic of China. **Tel** 011 86 1 4019821, 011 86 1 4010642, **FAX** 011 86 1 4012180, 011 86 1 4019810, telex 210147.

LC DLC   **ISSN** 0273-7590
US

HUMPTY DUMPTY'S MAGAZINE. [Humpty Dumpty's mag.]. Vol. 27, No. 272 (Nov. 1979)-. Periodical. English. Eight times a year. $15.95. Benjamin Franklin Literary and Medical Society, 1100 Waterway Boulevard, Indianapolis IN 46206. **Tel** (317)636-8881, **FAX** (317)637-0126. (**Subscription address:** CDS Agency Hard Copy, PO Box 4966, Des Moines IA 50340. **Tel** (515)247-7569.) **ED** Christine French Clark. **Bk Rev**. **Ad Acc. Circ:** 250,000. available on microfilm and microfiche from University Microfilms International (UMI). **Continues** Humpty Dumpty's Magazine for Little Children, 0018-7666.
   Desc: For ages 4 to 6 - stories, puzzles, etc. that promote good health. Emphasis is placed on developing good health habits with articles about nutrition, exercise and safety.
   Ind/Abst Child. Mag. Guide (1981-); EP Collect.; Homework Help.; Mag. Search; MasterFile FullTEXT 1000; MasterFile FullTEXT 350; MasterFile FullTEXT 650; MasterFile FullTEXT (July 1993-); Mid. Search; OCLC; Prim. Search; Pub. Lib. FullTEXT; Telebase.

UK

I-D MAGAZINE. (19??)-. English. Twelve times a year. £24.00 UK; £52.00 US; £32.00 Europe. Seven Dails Warehouse, 44 Earlham Street, London WC2M 9LA United Kingdom. **Tel** 071 240 3382, **FAX** 071 240 3250. **ED** Mattew Collin. **Bk Rev**, (Qty: 100/yr). **Ad Acc, Adv Mgr:** Jo Peters. **Circ:** 35,500.

ISSN 0738-2715
US

IDEAS (YOUTH SPECIALTIES (ORGANIZATIONS)). (IDEAS.). No. 1 (1968)-. Periodical. English. Four times a year. $35.80 (US); $42.80 (other). Youth Specialties Inc., 1224 Greenfield Drive, El Cajon CA 92021. **Tel** (619)440-2333. Index Available Received separately--bound from publisher.

ISSN 0019-3259
DD 028.5/0971   CN

IN REVIEW (TORONTO). (IN REVIEW; CANADIAN BOOKS FOR CHILDREN.). **Added/Corp** Ontario. Provincial Library Service. (1967)-. Periodical. English (French; summaries and/or abstracts in French). Four times a year. Free in Canada; $3.00 other. Provincial Library Service, 14th Floor/Mowat Block, Queen's Park, Toronto Ontario M7A 2R9 Canada.

ISSN 1024-6363
PE

●**INFANCIA Y SOCIEDAD.** (1994)-. Spanish. Irregular. Instituto de Estudios Peruanos, I E P Ediciones, Horacio Urteaga 694, Lima 11 Peru. **Tel** 011 51 14 323070, **FAX** 011 51 14 324981.

GW

INFO-INFOGETTABLE. (19??)-. German. Markus Poenitz, Barbaraosstr, 6 W-2800 Bremen 41 Germany. **Tel** 011 49 421 490637, **FAX** 011 49 421 493333. **ED** Markus Ponite. **Bk Rev**. **Ad Acc**. **Circ:** 10,000 (ctrl).
   Desc: Contains articles on business, youth and young people in Bremen. Includes film, music, book reviews and sports.

ISSN 1043-6057
DD 595   US

INSECT WORLD (LANSING, MICH.). (INSECT WORLD : A PUBLICATION OF THE YOUNG ENTOMOLOGISTS' SOCIETY.). [Insect world]. **Added/Corp** Young Entomologists' Society. Vol. 1, No 1 (Feb. 1979)-. Periodical. English. Four times a year. $18.00. Young Entomologists Society Inc, 1915 Peggy Place, Lansing MI 48910. **Tel** (517)887-0499. **ED** Gary A. Dunn. **Bk Rev**. **Circ:** 250 (ctrl).
   Desc: Factual articles, stories, poems, cartoons, games, puzzles, activities and project ideas on insects for 6-14 year olds.

LC HQ789 .I57   **ISSN** 0259-3696
DD 305.23/5   SZ

INTERNATIONAL CHILDREN'S RIGHTS MONITOR. See Political Science-Civil Rights.

ISSN 0269-0500
Pr Rev.   UK
     TITLE CHANGE

INTERNATIONAL REVIEW OF CHILDREN'S LITERATURE AND LIBRARIANSHIP. See Library and Information Sciences.

LC Z1037.A1 I795   **ISSN** 0146-5562
DD 011/.62   US

INTERRACIAL BOOKS FOR CHILDREN BULLETIN. [Interracial books child. bull.]. **Added/Corp** Council on Interracial Books for Children. Vol. 5 No. 7/8 (1975)-. Bulletin. English. Irregular (Eight issues combined mail 4 times per year). $18.00. Council on Interracial Books, 1841 Broadway, New York NY 10023. **Tel** (212)757-5339. **ED** Ruth Charnes. Index available. cum. index. **Bk Rev**. **Circ:** 5,000 (ctrl). available on microfilm and microfiche from University Microfilms International (UMI). **Continues** Interracial Books for Children, 0020-9708.
   Desc: Periodical focusing on the content value of children's books. Critical reading for raising children in a bias-free environment.
   Ind/Abst Altern. Press Index; Book Rev. Digest; Book Rev. Index; Child. Lit. Abstr. (19??-); Educ. Index; Libr. Lit.

ISSN 0316-6759
DD C810/.8/0928205   CN

JABBERWOCKY (TORONTO). (JABBERWOCKY.). (June 1973)-. English. Four times a year. $1.50 per no. Leslie Cowger, Apt 612 35 Charles Stret West, Toronto Ontario M4Y 1R6 Canada.

ISSN 0021-3829
US

JACK AND JILL. (JACK AND JILL; THE MAGAZINE FOR BOYS AND GIRLS.). [Jack Jill]. (1938)-. Periodical. English. Eight times a year. $15.95. Benjamin Franklin Literary and Medical Society, 1100 Waterway Boulevard, Indianapolis IN 46206. **Tel** (317)636-8881, **FAX** (317)637-0126. **ED** Steve Charles. **Bk Rev**. **Ad Acc. Circ:** 326,000. available on microfilm and microfiche from University Microfilms International (UMI).
   Desc: A variety of adventure and humorous stories, plus contemporary articles. Lists the craft projects and materials that can be use from around the home. Emphasis on health, safety, exercise and nutrition.
   Ind/Abst Child. Mag. Guide (1981-); EP Collect.; Homework Help.; Mag. Search; MasterFile FullTEXT 1000; MasterFile FullTEXT 350; MasterFile FullTEXT 650; MasterFile FullTEXT (July 1993-); Mid. Search; OCLC; Prim. Search; Pub. Lib. FullTEXT; Telebase.

ISSN 0835-7714
DD J843/.914/08   CN

J'AIME LIRE (SAINT-LAMBERT). (J'AIME LIRE.). [J'aime lire]. Vol.1 (Sept. 1987)-. Periodical. French. Ten times a year. 34.13Can$. Bayard Presse, Svc Client, 3 rue Bayard, Department 2, 75393 Paris Cedex 08 France. **Tel** 011 33 1 44355907, **FAX** 011 33 1 44356025.

LC Z1037.8.J3 J36 PN1009.J3
DD 011/.62   JA

JAPANESE CHILDREN'S BOOKS OF INTERNATIONAL INTEREST. **Added/Corp** Japanese Board on Books for Young People. (19??)-. English. Every 3 years. ¥500 (add ¥130 for postage). Japanese Board on Books for Young People, 2-8-7 Shibuya, Shibuyaku Tokyo 150 Japan. **Tel** 03 4984424. **Circ:** 2,000.

ISSN 0756-564X
UDC 087.5   FR

JE BOUQUINE. [Je bouquine]. (1983)-. Periodical. French. Twelve times a year. $132.33. Bayard Presse, Svc Client, 3 rue Bayard, Department 2, 75393 Paris Cedex 08 France. **Tel** 011 33 1 44355907, **FAX** 011 33 1 44356025.

LC PL2513 .J39
DD 895.1/08/005   CH

JEN MIN WEN HSUEH. See Literature.

ISSN 0757-0171
FR

JEUN. LIB. VFOAT Jeunesse Liberee. (1982)-. Periodical. French. Five times a year. 13.99. A S B L Hosanna Diffusion, 62 Cite Bellevue, 6481 Baileux Chimay Belgium. **Tel** 011 32 60 213824. **Continues** J.L. Jeunesse Liberee Magazine, 0757-0163.

ISSN 0984-760X
UDC 087.2-055.2   FR

JEUNE ET JOLIE (PARIS). (JEUNE ET JOLIE.). [1987)-. Periodical. French. Twelve times a year. $41.34. Publications Filipacchi, 149 rue Anatole, 92534 Levallois Perret France. **Tel** 011 33 1 41346456, telex 651-294. (**Subscription address:** CBA ILE de France, 128 rue Haxo, 75922 Paris Cedex 19 France. **Tel** 011 33 1 44846666, **FAX** 011 33 1 44846665.)

FR

JEUNES ANNEES. AGES 3 TO 6. French. Five times a year. 135.00F France; 165.00F other. Les Francas, 10/14 rue Tolain, 75020 Paris France. **Tel** 011 33 1 44642100, **FAX** 011 33 1 43672829, telex 680 086 F. **Continues** Juenes Annees., 0220-7303.

NE

JONGE KIND. See Education.

ISSN 0242-9225
UDC 084.12-053.5/.6   FR

JOURNAL DE MICKEY (1952), LE. (1952)-. Periodical. French. One time a week. $159.22. Edimonde Loisirs, 90 rue de Flandre, 75947 Paris Cedex 19 France. **Tel** 011 33 1 44894489. **Continues** Le Journal de Mickey et Hop-la Reunis, 1241-1027.

LC GV   **ISSN** 0986-9050
DD 790
UDC 07-053.2

JOURNAL DES ENFANTS (ED. NATIONALE), LE. (LE JOURNAL DES ENFANTS.). (19??)-. Periodical. French. One time a week. $74.36. Societe Alsacienne de Publications, BP 1489, 68072 Mulhouse Cedex France. **Tel** 011 33 89 327010, **FAX** 011 33 89 327091. **Bk Rev**, (Qty: 2-3). **Circ:** 160,000.
   Desc: Children's paper with three pages of world news and a fourth page with comics, jokes, contests and mail.

ISSN 0849-5734
DD 071/.1272   CN

JOURNAL DES JEUNES (SAINT-BONIFACE). (LE JOURNAL DES JEUNES.). [Journal des jeunes]. Vol. 1, No 1, 15/18 (Sept. 1989)-. Periodical. French. Twenty-one times a year (September to June). 10.40Can$. Journal Des Jeunes, PO Box 47007, St Boniface Man R2H 3G9 Canada. **Tel** (204)237-4823, **FAX** (2040231-1998. **ED** Laurent Gimenez. Index available. cum. index. **Circ:** 10,000.
   Desc: Canadian and international news and articles written for young people aged approximately 10 to 14.

ISSN 1182-2589
DD 369.43/09714/05   CN

JOURNAL PLUS, LE. See Societies and Clubs.

MX

●**JOVENES SONORENSES.** (1994)-. Spanish. ERA Comunicacion SA de C.V., Heriberto Aja 155, Hermosillo Sonora Mexico.

LC Z316 .J83   **ISSN** 0723-8991
DD 070.5/0943   GW

JUGENDBUCH HEUTE. Added/Corp Arbeitsgemeinschaft von Jugendbuchverlegern (Germany). (19??)-. Periodical. German (English). Verlag Heinrich Ellermann, Romanstrasse 16, W-8000 Munich 19 Germany. **Tel** 0711/21055-39.

ISSN 0022-5975
GW

UDC 253: [362.8+374.3]

JUGENDWOHL. [Jugendwohl]. (1912)-. Periodical. German. Twelve times a year. DM58.00. Lambertus-Verlag GmbH, Postfach 1026, 79010 Freiburg, Germany. **Tel** 011 49 761 3 68 25 0, **FAX** 011 49 761 3 70 64. Index available. cum. index. **Bk Rev**. **Ad Acc. Circ:** 2,200.

LC AP30 .J85
DD 053   GW

JUNGE WELT. Added/Corp Freie Deutsche Jugend. (Feb. 15, 1947)-. Periodical. German. One time a week. Verlag Junge Welt, Mauerstrasse 39 40, D-10117 Berlin Germany. **Tel** 011 49 30 22330.

ISSN 0170-5857
UDC 087.5   GW

JUNGE ZEIT. [Junge Zeit]. (1972)-. Periodical. German. Twelve times a year. $37.77. Weltbild Verlag, Postfach 100085, D-86135 Augsburg Germany. **Tel** 011 49 821 32570, **FAX** 011 49 821 3257157, 011 49 821 3257201. **Continues** Der Pflug (Munchen), 0170-5865.

LC Z1037.A1 J85   **ISSN** 0022-6505
DD 028.5   UK

JUNIOR BOOKSHELF, THE. [Jr. bookshelf]. Vol. 1 (Nov. 1936)-. Periodical. English. Six times a year. $35.00. Junior Bookshelf, Marsh Hall, Thurstonland, Huddersfield HD4 6XB United Kingdom. **Tel** 011 44 1484 661811, **FAX** 011 44 1484 510237. **ED** D. J. Morrell. Index available (Free with Dec. issue). **Bk Rev**. **Ad Acc**. available on microfilm and microfiche from University Microfilms International (UMI).
   Ind/Abst Annu. Bibliogr. Engl. Lang. Lit.; Book Rev. Index; Child. Lit. Abstr. (19??-); Ref. Sources.

Children and Youth Interests

LC AP201 .J68
DD 051
ISSN 0022-6688
US
JUNIOR SCHOLASTIC. [Jr. scholast.]. **VFOAT** JS. Junior Scholastic. Vol. 1, (Sept. 18, 1937)-. Periodical. English. Eighteen times a year. $24.00. Scholastic Inc., 2931 East McCarty Street, PO Box 3710, Jefferson City MO 65102-9957. **Tel** (314)636-5271, (800)631-1586. **ED** Lee Baier. Index available. **Bk Rev. Ad Acc. Circ:** 700,000 (ctrl). available on microfilm and microfiche from University Microfilms International (UMI).
 Desc: Current news, world cultures, U.S. history, geography, and social studies skills for students in grades 6-8 and ages 11-14, distributed primarily through schools.
 Ind/Abst Child. Mag. Guide (1981-); EP Collect.; Homework Help.; Mag. Search; MasterFile FullTEXT 1000; MasterFile FullTEXT 350; MasterFile FullTEXT 650; MasterFile FullTEXT (Jan. 1993-); Mid. Search; OCLC; Prim. Search; Pub. Lib. FullTEXT; Telebase.

US
JUNIOR TRAIL. See Religions and Theology-Protestantism.

LC AG
DD 028.7
II
●**KALIKKUDUKKA.** (1995)-. Malayalam. Twelve times a year. Rs72.00. M.M. Publications Pvt Ltd., PO Box 226, Erayilkadavu Kottayam 696 001 India. **Tel** 011 091 481 564393, **FAX** 011 091 481 564393. **ED** Bina Mathew. **Circ:** 75,000.

ISSN 0899-4293
DD 051
US
KID CITY. [Kid city]. **Added/Corp** Children's Television Workshop. No. 1 (Sept. 1988)-. Periodical. English. Ten times a year. $16.97. Children's Television Workshop, One Lincoln Plaza, Box TG, New York NY 10023. **Tel** (212)595-3456. **(Subscription address:** Neodata / Colorado, PO Box 2606, Boulder CO 80322. **)** *Continues* Electric Company Magazine, 0197-0062.
 Desc: Created for the beginning reader. Contains puzzles, stories, jokes and activities developed to make learning enjoyable.
 Ind/Abst Child. Mag. Guide (Sept. 1988-); EP Collect.; Homework Help.; Mag. Search; MasterFile FullTEXT 1000; MasterFile FullTEXT 350; MasterFile FullTEXT 650; MasterFile FullTEXT (July 1993-); Mid. Search; OCLC; Prim. Search; Pub. Lib. FullTEXT; Telebase.

ISSN 0843-0284
DD J051
CN
CEASED
KID PROOF. [Kid proof]. Issue No. 1 (Jan. 1988)-(1995). Periodical. English. Kid Proof, Box 709, Radville Saskatchewan S0C 2G0 Canada. **Tel** (306)869-2652. **ED** Lynn MacDonald, Lynne Hall and Geeta McLeod. **Bk Rev. Ad Acc. Circ:** 2,500 (ctrl).

ISSN 1057-3011
US
KIDDIE BAZAAR. (1992)-. Periodical. English. Twelve times a year. $3.50 (single issue). FFI Fashion Flair/McConneghey, PO Box 1746, New York NY 10027.

LC AP201 .K5
DD 810/.8/0520
ISSN 0023-1312
US
KIDS. [Kids]. No. 1 (1970)-. Periodical. English. Twelve times a year. $7.00. Childpub Management Corporation, 747 Third Avenue, New York NY 10017.
 Desc: Includes stories, poems, illustrations and cartoons.

US
KIDS CHAT. (19??)-. Newsletter. English. Twelve times a year. $8.00. Kids Chat, Rural Route 1 Box 257 A, Gerald MO 63037. **Tel** (317)764-4815. **ED** Keith Dunn.
 Desc: This newsletter features trivia, riddles, recipes, learning tips and other information for children. Contains story contributions from kids in 10 states.

ISSN 1048-8839
DD 051
US
KIDS CLUB MAGAZINE. [Kids club mag.]. (1985)-. Periodical. English. Twelve times a year. Kids Club Inc, 4264 Arsenal Street, St Louis MO 63116-1902. *Continues* Nine for Kids Club Magazine.

ISSN 1063-9659
US
KIDS COPY. [Kids copy]. (March 1992)-. Periodical. English. Ten times a year. $10.00. Kids Copy, PO Box 42, Wyncote PA 19095. **Tel** (215)635-3603.
 Desc: Designed for students in grades four through eight. Encourages a positive attitude toward reading and learning by making the process fun. Focuses on world and national news, sports and entertainment. Features puzzles and children's reviews and writing.

ISSN 1054-2868
DD 051
US
KIDS DISCOVER. [Kids discov.]. (1991)-. Periodical. English. Ten times a year. $17.95. Kids Discover, 170 5th Avenue, 6th Floor, New York NY 10160. **Tel** (212)242-5133. **(Subscription address:** Neodata / Colorado, PO Box 2606, Boulder CO 80322. **)** **Circ:** 167,000.
 Desc: Educational and entertainment publication for children ages 6-12.
 Ind/Abst Child. Mag. Guide; EP Collect.; Homework Help.; Mag. Search; MasterFile FullTEXT 1000; MasterFile FullTEXT 350; MasterFile FullTEXT 650; MasterFile FullTEXT (July 1993-); Mid. Search; OCLC; Prim. Search; Pub. Lib. FullTEXT; Telebase.

US
CEASED
KIDS' PUZZLE EXPRESS. (19??)-(Apr. 1993). English. (Jan., March, May, July, Sept., Nov.). Kids' Puzzle Express, PO Box 3083, Princeton NJ 08543-3083. **Tel** (609)466-2073. **ED** Helene Hovanee.
 Desc: A puzzle magazine filled with crosswords, word finds, fill-ins, visual puzzles, mazes and mind-stretching novelty puzzles. This magazine, for children ages 5 to 11, is published and edited by educators and puzzle experts.

ISSN 1053-2420
DD 649
US
KIDS' TIME OUT. [Kids' time out]. **VFOAT** Time Out. Vol. 1, No. 1 (Dec. 1990/Feb. 1991)-. Periodical. English. Four times a year. $2.50 (single issue). Kids' Time Out, Route 203, North Chatham NY 12132.

ISSN 0826-9696
DD 790.1/922/09713541
CN
TITLE CHANGE
KIDS TORONTO. See Leisure and Recreation-Amusements.

ISSN 0847-3935
DD 791.43/05
CN
KIDS TRIBUTE. [Kids tribut.]. Vol. 1, Issue 1 (Nov. 1989)-. Periodical. English. Four times a year. 12.00Can$. Tribute Publication, 900 A Don Mills Road, Suite 1000, Don Mills, Ontario M3C 1V6 Canada. **Tel** (416)445-0544, **FAX** (416)445-2894. **ED** Sandra I. Stewart.

ISSN 0842-4241
DD 917.11/33/0025
KIDS VANCOUVER DIRECTORY, THE. [Kids Vanc. dir.]. 1989-. Directory. English. One time a year. $3.95 (per volume). Kidscanada Publishing Corp, 542 Mt Pleasant Road/Suite 401, Toronto Ontario M4S 2M7 Canada.

ISSN 1194-9562
DD 051
CN
●**KIDS WORLD MAGAZINE.** [Kids world mag.]. Vol. 1, No. 1 (Mar./Apr. 1993)-. Periodical. English. Six times a year. 12.77Can$. MIR Communications Inc, 320 Danforth Avenue, Suite 204, Toronto Ontario, M4K 1N8 Canada. **Tel** (416)466-4956.

ISSN 0892-8991
US
KIDSART NEWS. **VFOAT** Kids Art News. (198?)-. Periodical. English. Four times a year. $10.00. Kidsart News, PO Box 274, Mt Shasta CA 96067. **Tel** (916)926-5076, **FAX** (916)926-3820. **ED** Kim Solga. Index available. cum. index. **Circ:** 1,500.
 Desc: Children's art education articles and activities.

LC HE
DD 384
ISSN 1064-1114
US
KIDSNET (WASHINGTON, D.C.). See Communications-Television and Cable.

ISSN 1054-7002
DD 796
US
CEASED
KIDSPORTS (ARLINGTON, VA.). (KIDSPORTS.). [KidSports]. **VFOAT** Kid Sports. (1989)-(1994). Periodical. English. Southern Media Corporation, 9625 West Sample Road, Coral Springs FL 33065. **Tel** (305)344-0332. **Bk Rev. Ad Acc.**
 Desc: Designed for children ages 6-12. Features instructional and inspirational articles written in the first person by professional and world class athletes. Includes games, puzzles and contests.
 Ind/Abst EP Collect.; Homework Help.; Mag. Search; MasterFile FullTEXT 1000; MasterFile FullTEXT 350; MasterFile FullTEXT (July 1993-Apr. 1994); Mid. Search; OCLC; Prim. Search; Pub. Lib. FullTEXT; Res. Alert; Telebase.

ISSN 1064-2056
US
●**KIDSTAR 1250.** **Added/Corp** Kidstar 1250 AM (Radio Station : Seattle, Wash.). **VFOAT** Kidstar Twelve Fifty; Kidstar; Kidstar 1250 Magazine. (Summer 1993)-. Periodical. English. Twelve times a year. $12.50. Kidstar 1250, 140 Lakeside Avenue, Suite 240, Seattle WA 98122.

ISSN 0278-632X
US
KIDSTUFF. **VFOAT** Kid Stuff. (1981)-. Periodical. English. Four times a year. $24.00. Guidelines Press, 1307 South Killian Drive, Lake Park FL 33403. **Tel** (407)842-9411.
 Desc: Includes fingerplays, craft ideas, songs, poetry, flannelboard stories and patterns, games, age grouped reading lists and more.
 Ind/Abst Foods Adlibra.

US
KIDZ MAGAZINE. (1988)-. English. Twelve times a year. $12.00. Kids Production Inc, Box 24032, Omaha NE 68124-0032. **Tel** (402)391-0441. **ED** Melanie Morrissey Clark. Index available. **Bk Rev. Ad Acc.** ctrl circ. *Continues* Kids, Kids, Kidz.
 Desc: Information for parents including a medical column, education column, and a spotlight on area events.

US
KIRKUS CHILDRENS. See Literary and Political Reviews.

ISSN 0271-1990
US
KOBRIN LETTER, THE. See Literary and Political Reviews.

LC Z1037.8.J3 K633 PN1009.J3
JA
KODOMO NO HONDANA. **Added/Corp** Nihon Kodomo no Hon Kenkyukai. (19??)-. Periodical. Japanese. Twelve times a year. ¥3000. Nihon Kodomo No Hon Kenkyukai, c/o Sakuradai Mai Kopo 105, 4-4 Toyotama Kita, Nerima-ku 176, Tokyo Japan.

LC PZ49.2 .K62
JA
KODOMO NO TOMO. See Literature.

ISSN 0023-3692
NE
UDC 922
KONTAKTO - UNIVERSALA ESPERANTO-ASOCIO. [Kontakto - Univers. Esperanto-Asoc.]. (1963)-. Periodical. Esperanto (Dutch). Six times a year. Fl38.68. Universala Esperanto-Asocio, Nieuwe Binnenweg 176, 3015 BJ Rotterdam Netherlands. **Tel** 011 31 10 4361044, **FAX** 011 31 10 4361751, telex 23721. **ED** F. Veuthey. **Bk Rev.** (Qty: 5). **Ad Acc, Adv Mgr:** O. Buller. **Circ:** 2,000.

LC HQ799.G53 K66
DD 305.2/35/09431
GW
KONTANT (BERLIN, GERMANY). (KONTAKT.). **Added/Corp** Freie Deutsche Jugend. Zentralrat. (19??)-. Periodical. English (French, Spanish, Arabic and Portuguese). Six times a year. Verlag Junge Welt, Mauerstrasse 39 40, D-10117 Berlin Germany. **Tel** 011 49 30 22330. **ED** Christel Manigk. **Bk Rev. Circ:** 50,000 (ctrl).

ISSN 0740-3437
US
L.A. PARENT. **VFOAT** LA Parent. **VAT** Los Angeles Parent. (198?)-. Periodical. English. Twelve times a year. $12.00. Los Angeles Parent, PO Box 3204, Burbank CA 91504. **Tel** (818) 846-0400. *Absorbed* Pony Ride, 0745-2314.

US
LA YOUTH. English (Spanish). Five times a year (published 5 times during school year). $10.00. Youth News Service, 6030 Wilshire Boulevard, Los Angeles CA 90036. **Tel** (213)938-9194. **Bk Rev.** (Qty: 4). **Ad Acc. Circ:** 100,000 (ctrl).

LC AP201 .L33
DD 808
ISSN 1051-4961
US
LADYBUG (PERU, ILL.). (LADYBUG.). [Ladybug]. Vol. 1, No. 1 (Sept. 1990)-. Periodical. English. Twelve times a year. $27.97. Open Court Publishing Company, 315 Fifth Street, PO Box 300, Peru IL 61354. **Tel** (800)435-6850, (815)223-1500, **FAX** (815)224-6675. **(Subscription address:** Ladybug Magazine, Box 592, Mt. Morris IL 61054. **) ED** Marianne Carus. **Circ:** 100,000. available on magnetic tape (Kable News / 308 E Hitt Street, Mt Morris, IL 61054).
 Desc: Published for toddlers, preschoolers and beginning readers. Includes a collection of stories, poems, songs, action games and adventures.
 Ind/Abst EP Collect.; Homework Help.; Mag. Search; MasterFile FullTEXT 1000; MasterFile FullTEXT 350; MasterFile FullTEXT 650; MasterFile FullTEXT (July 1993-); Mid. Search; OCLC; Prim. Search; Pub. Lib. FullTEXT; Telebase.

ISSN 0711-5377
DD 369.43/.0971
CN
LEADER (OTTAWA. 1976). (THE LEADER.). [Leader]. **VFOAT** Canadian Leader. **VAT** Canadian Leader (1976). Vol. 7, No. 1 (Aug./Sept. 1976)-. Periodical. English. Ten times a year (monthly with Jun/July & Aug/Sept issues combined). 8.00Can$. Canyouth Publications, PO Box 5112 Station F, Ottawa Ontario K2C 3H4 Canada. **Tel** (613)224-5131, **FAX** (613)224-3571. **ED** Allen Macartney. Index available. **Bk Rev. Ad Acc. Circ:** 45,000. *Continues* Canadian

Children and Youth Interests

Leader, 0036-9462.
Desc: A program and activity resource recommended to adult members of the Boy Scouts of Canada.

FR
LECTURE JEUNE. French. Four times a year. 150.00F France; 170.00F other. Lecture Jeunesse, 36 rue Emeriau, 75015 Paris France. **Tel** 011 33 1 45781389. *Continues* Lecture Jeunesse, 0152-8505.

LC HQ767.8 .L54   ISSN 0767-0303
FR
LIEUX DE L'ENFANCE. (1985)-. Periodical. French. Four times a year. Editions Privat, 14 rue des Arts, 31000 Toulouse Cedex France. **Tel** 011 33 61 230926.

LC PN1009.A1 L54   ISSN 0147-2593
DD 809/.89282   US
CCC
LION AND THE UNICORN (BROOKLYN), THE. See Literary and Political Reviews.

LC HV5285 .L65   ISSN 0024-435X
DD 178.05   US
LISTEN (MOUNTAIN VIEW, CALIF.). See Drug Abuse and Alcoholism.

ISSN 1060-8001
US
CEASED
LITTLE MERMAID MAGAZINE, THE. (1992)-(199?). Periodical. English. Welsh Publishing Group, Inc., PO Box 7556, Red Oak IA 51591.

LC Z2694.5 .L56 PC3902
SP
LLIBRES INFANTILS, JUVENILS I DIDACTICS EN CATALA. VFOAT Cataleg de Llibres Infantils, Juvenils i Didactics en Catala. (1979)-. Catalan. One time a year.

LC AP215.R6 L8
RM
CEASED
LUMINITA. (19??-19??). Romanian. **(Subscription address:** Ilexim Press Department, PO Box 1, 136-1-137, Bucharest, Romania. **Tel** 011 40 1 173836.)
Desc: Magazine for children.

ISSN 0705-6567
DD 028.5/05   CN
LURELU. [Lurelu]. Vol. 1 (Feb. 1978)-. Periodical. French. Three times a year. 10.40Can$. Lurelu, CP 220 Succ. E, Montreal Quebec H2T 3A7 Canada. **Tel** (514)723-6693. **ED** Daniel Sernine. **Bk Rev**, (Qty: 200). **Ad Acc. Circ:** 2,400.
Desc: Literature of Quebec for young readers.
Ind/Abst Can. Period. Index (19??-); Repere.

GW
MADCHEN. VFOAT Maedchen. (19??)-. German. Twenty-six times a year. DM120.00. Pegasus GmbH, Plieninger Strasse 100, D-70567 Stuttgart Germany. **(Subscription address:** DSB ABO Betreuung GmbH, Heiner Fleischmann Strasse 2, D-74168 Neckarsulm Germany. **Tel** 011 49 71329590.)

ISSN 1187-435X
DD 305.23   CN
MAGAZINE ENFANTS, LE. [Mag. enfants]. (1991)-. Periodical. French. Ten times a year. 14.40Can$. Magazine Enfants, 300 rue Arran, St. Lambert Quebec J4R 1K5 Canada. **Tel** (514)672-7027. **(Subscription address:** Maison Abonnements / Quebec, 25 Boulevard Taschereau, Bureau 201, Greenfield Park Quebec J4V 3P1 Canada. **Tel** (514)875-4444.) *Continues* Le Mensuel Enfants., 0835-5223.

ISSN 8756-4564
DD 051   US
CEASED
MAGAZINE FOR CHRISTIAN YOUTH, THE. [Mag. Christ. youth]. **Added/Corp** United Methodist Church (U.S.). Board of Discipleship. Curriculum Resources Committee. **VFOAT** Youth. (Sept. 1985)-(Aug. 1995). Periodical. English. Graded Press, 201 Eighth Avenue South, Box 801, Nashville TN 37202. **Tel** (615)749-6417. **ED** Christopher B. Hughes. **Bk Rev. Circ:** 50,000.
Desc: Purpose is to help teens develop Christian identity and live the Christian faith in their contemporary culture.

LC Z6944.C5 M34 PN4835   ISSN 0000-1368
DD 011.62   US
MAGAZINES FOR YOUNG PEOPLE. [Mag. young people]. **Added/Corp** R.R. Bowker Company. 2nd Ed. (1991)-. English. Irregular. $38.00. R.R. Bowker, A Reed Reference Publishing Company, Part of Reed International PLC, PO Box 31, 121 Chanlon Drive, New Providence NJ 07974. **Tel** (908)464-6800, (800)521-8110, FAX (908)665-6688, telex 138-755. *Continues* Magazines for School Libraries, 0000-0957.
Desc: Describes and evaluates over 1,100 magazines in 74 subjects.

LC Z286.C48 M37   ISSN 1045-4292
DD 028   US
MARTHA'S KIDLIT NEWSLETTER. See Literature.

ISSN 0309-7471
UK
MATERIAL MATTERS. See Library and Information Sciences.

ISSN 0025-6218
US
MAZPUTNINS. **Added/Corp** Latvian Youth Literary Society (U.S.) Latvian Institute. (19??)-. Periodical. Latin. Twelve times a year (Jan.). $30.00. Latvian Institute, 100 Cherry Hill Drive, Kalamazoo MI 49006. **Tel** (616)343-1838. **ED** L. Dindonis. **Bk Rev. Circ:** 1,100. available with illustrations.
Desc: Latvian children's magazine for ages 4-12.

ISSN 0891-1673
US
MCGUFFEY WRITER, THE. VFOAT McG Writer. (19??)-. Periodical. English. Three times a year (Mar., May, Dec.). $15.00. The McGuffey Writer, PO Box 502, Oxford OH 45056. **Tel** (513)529-6462.

ISSN 0882-2050
DD 810   US
MERLYN'S PEN. [Merlyn's pen]. (Oct./Nov. 1985)-. Periodical. English. Four times a year (during school year). $21.00. Merlyn's Pen, PO Box 1058, East Greenwich RI 02818. **Tel** (800)247-2027, (401)885-5175. **ED** R. James Stahl. **Bk Rev. Ad Acc. Circ:** 15,000.
Desc: Writing and art work by students in grades 7-10.
Ind/Abst EP Collect.; Homework Help.; Mag. Artic. Summar. Elite; Mag. Artic. Summar. Select; Mag. Artic. Summar. CD-ROM; MasterFile FullTEXT 1000; MasterFile FullTEXT 350; MasterFile FullTEXT 650; MasterFile FullTEXT (July 1994-); Mid. Search; Telebase.

GW
METAL MANIACS. See Music.
Pr Rev.
MICKY MAUS. (19??)-. German. One time a week. $90.00. Ehapa Verlag GmbH, Postfach 101245, D-7000 Stuttgart Germany. **Tel** 011 49 711 79711, FAX 011 49 711 7979929. **(Subscription address:** German Language Publications Inc., 153 South Dean Street, Englewood NJ 07631. **Tel** (201)871-1010, (800)457-4443.) **ED** Peter Schlecht. **Ad Acc. Circ:** 932,508 (ctrl).
Desc: Contains Disney comics, gimmicks, riddles, and games.

ISSN 1077-4483
US
●**MIGHTY MORPHIN POWER RANGERS.** [Mighty Morphin power rangers]. (1994)-. Periodical. English. Five times a year. $12.50. Welsh Publishing Group Inc., 300 Madison Avenue, New York NY 10017. **Tel** (212)687-0680, FAX (212)986-5849.

ISSN 1105-1426
GR
UDC 741.5
MIKU MAOUS. See Leisure and Recreation-Amusements.

ISSN 1105-1442
GR
UDC 741.5
MIKY. See Leisure and Recreation-Amusements.

SA
●**MINIMAG.** (1994)-. English. Twelve times a year. Elken Publishing, PO Box 72738, Lynnwood Ridge 0040 South Africa.

ISSN 1053-6280
DD 808   US
MINNIE 'N ME, THE BEST FRIENDS COLLECTION. [Minnie'n me]. VFOAT Minnie and Me, the Best Friends Collection; Minnie'n Me, the Best Friends Collection; Minnie 'n Me Best Friends Collection; Minnie 'n Me; Best Friends Collection. (1991)-. Monographic series. English. Disney Books by Mail / Iowa, PO Box 11440, Des Moines IA 50336.

ISSN 0137-7698
PL
UDC 82-93
MIS. [Mis]. (1957)-. Periodical. Polish. Twenty-four times a year. $36.00. **(Subscription address:** Ars Polona-Ruch, PO Box 1001, Krakowskie Przedmiescie 7, 00-068 Warsaw Poland. **Tel** 011 48 22 261201.)

RU
MISHA. (19??)-. Russian (English, French, German, Spanish, Italian and Hungarian). Twelve times a year. $99.95 US and Canada; $124.95 other. **(Subscription address:** East View Publications Inc., 3020 Harbor Lane North, Suite 110, Minneapolis MN 55447. **Tel** (800)477-1005, (612)550-0961, FAX (612)559-2931.)
Desc: Russian children's magazine published in various languages and dealing with the lives of Russian children. Carries stories, poems, tales, riddles and make-it-yourself hints for the youngest readers.

LC HQ799.C9 M53   ISSN 0323-2042
XR
MLADY SVET. [Mlady svet]. **Added/Corp** Socialisticky Svaz Mladeze. Ustredni Vybor. (1959)-. Periodical. Czech. One time a week. $156.00. **(Subscription address:** Kubon & Sagner, ABT Zeitschriftenimport, D 80328 Munich Germany. **Tel** 011 49 89 54218130.)

ISSN 0867-4329
PL
UDC 884
MOJE LEKTURY. [Moje Lekt.]. (1990)-. Monographic series. Polish. Six times a year. Price varies per volume. **(Subscription address:** Ars Polona-Ruch, PO Box 1001, Krakowskie Przedmiescie 7, 00-068 Warsaw Poland. **Tel** 011 48 22 261201.)

RU
MOLODEZHNAIA ESTRADA. (19??)-. Periodical. Russian. Four times a year. $69.95. Izdatelstvo Molodaia Gvardiia, Novodmitrovskaya Ulitsa 5A, 125015 Moscow Russia. **Tel** 011 95 285 1935. **(Subscription address:** East View Publications Inc., 3020 Harbor Lane North, Suite 110, Minneapolis MN 55447. **Tel** (800)477-1005, (612)550-0961, FAX (612)559-2931.)

ISSN 1071-8974
DD 051   US
SUSPENDED
●**MONEY MAGAZINE FOR KIDS.** [Money mag. kids]. VFOAT Money for Kids. (Spring 1993)-Suspended (1995). Periodical. English. Irregular. Free. Time Inc. / New York, Time & Life Building, Rockefeller Center, New York NY 10020. **(Subscription address:** Money for Kids, Janus Funds, PO Box 173375, Denver CO 80217. **Tel** (800)525-8983.)

ISSN 1065-5093
US
●**MORE FREE STUFF FOR KIDS.** (1993)-. Periodical. English. $5.00. Meadowbrook Press, 18318 Minnetonka Boulevard, Deephaven MN 55391. **Tel** (800)338-2232, (212)698-7000.

RU
MURZILKA. **Added/Corp** Vsesoiuznaia Pionerskaia Organizatsiia Imeni V. I. Lenina. (1925)-. Periodical. Russian. Twelve times a year. $99.95. **(Subscription address:** East View Publications Inc., 3020 Harbor Lane North, Suite 110, Minneapolis MN 55447. **Tel** (800)477-1005, (612)550-0961, FAX (612)559-2931.)

ISSN 0027-5387
US
MY DEVOTIONS. See Religions and Theology.

ISSN 1057-1558
DD 051   US
CEASED
MY FIRST MAGAZINE. [My first mag.]. (1991)-(May 1994). Periodical. English. Scholastic Inc., 2931 East McCarty Street, PO Box 3710, Jefferson City MO 65102-9957. **Tel** (314)636-5271, (800)631-1586.

LC L   ISSN 1050-7647
DD 370   US
UDC 37
MY WEEKLY READER. SUMMER EDITION A. VFOAT Summer Edition A. (1989)-. Periodical. English. Twenty-six times a year. Weekly Reader Corporation, 3001 Cindel Drive, Delran NJ 08370. **Tel** (609)786-1000, (800)446-3355, FAX (609)786-3360. *Continues* Weekly Reader. Summer Edition A, 0899-6091.

LC PZ7.K23 Nan
US
NANCY DREW MYSTERY STORIES. See Literature-Detective and Mystery.

ISSN 0867-4787
PL
UDC 304(438)
NASTOLATKI WARSZAWA. (NASTOLATKI.). [Nastolatki Warsz.]. (1991)-. Periodical. Polish. Six times a year. Price on request. **(Subscription address:** Ars Polona-Ruch, PO Box 1001, Krakowskie Przedmiescie 7, 00-068 Warsaw Poland. **Tel** 011 48 22 261201.)

LC G1 .N325   ISSN 0361-5499
DD 910/.5   US
Pr Rev.
NATIONAL GEOGRAPHIC WORLD. [Natl. geogr. world]. **Added/Corp** National Geographic Society (U.S.). VFOAT World. (Sept 1975)-. Periodical. English. Twelve times a year. $14.95. National Geographic Society, 11555 Darnestown, Gaithersburg MD 20878. **Tel** (202)857-7000, (800)638-4077, FAX (202)429-5727, telex 64194 NATGEO. **(Subscription address:** National Geographic Society, Attention: Agent Desk, PO Box 98035, Washington DC 20090-8035.) **ED** Pat Robbins. cum. index. **Circ:** 1,300,000 (ctrl). available on microfilm and microfiche from University Microfilms International

Children and Youth Interests

(UMI). Documents available from UMI Article Clearinghouse. **Supersedes** National Geographic School Bulletin.
 Desc: Features factual stories on outdoor adventure, natural history, geography, sports, science, and history for children ages 8 through 13.
 Ind/Abst Abr. Read. Guide Period. Lit.; Acad. Abstr. Full Text Elite; Acad. Abstr.; Can. Index (?-?); Can. Period. Index (1991-); Child. Mag. Guide (1981-); EP Collect.; Gen. Period. Index (1985-); Homework Help.; Mag. Artic. Summar. Elite; Mag. Artic. Summar. Select; Mag. Artic. Summar. CD-ROM; Mag. Index Plus (1989-); Mag. Index. Sel. (1986-); Mag. Search; MasterFile FullTEXT 1000; MasterFile FullTEXT 350; MasterFile FullTEXT 650; MasterFile FullTEXT (Dec. 1984-); Mid. Search; Newsp. Period. Abstr. (1988-); OCLC; Prim. Search; Pub. Lib. FullTEXT; Read. Guide Abstr. Select Ed.; Read. Guide Period. Lit.; Telebase; Mag. Index (1977-).

GR

NEOELLINIKI PAIDEIA. (19??)-. Greek, Modern. Twenty-four times a year. Dr400.00 Greece; Dr2000.00 US, Canada and Australia. Neoelliniki Paideia, Solonos 71, Athens 106 79 Greece. **Tel** 011 30 01 36 46 697.

ISSN 0270-2541
US
CEASED

NEW DESIGNS FOR YOUTH DEVELOPMENT. [New des. youth dev.]. **Added/Corp** Associates for Youth Development. **VFOAT** New Designs. Vol. 1, No. 1 (Nov./Dec. 1979)-Vol. 11, No. 4 (1994). Periodical. English. AYD - Associates Youth Development, PO Box 36748, Tucson AZ 85740. **Tel** (602)292-9767, FAX (602)297-5160. **ED** William A. Lofquist. Index available. **Bk Rev**, (Qty: 2-4). **Circ:** 1,000 (ctrl).
 Desc: Positive approaches to promoting the growth and development of young people with an emphasis on involving young people as resources.
 Ind/Abst AGRICOLA [Select. Cov.].

UK
Pr Rev.

●**NEW REVIEW OF CHILDREN'S LITERATURE AND LIBRARIANSHIP. See** Library and Information Sciences.

ISSN 0737-285X
US

NEW YOUTH CONNECTIONS. (NEW YOUTH CONNECTIONS : NYC.). **VFOAT** NYC; N.Y.C. (19??)-. Periodical. English. Eight times a year. $10.00. Youth Communications of the New York Center, 144 West 27th Street, 8 Rear, New York NY 10001. **Tel** (212)242-3270. **ED** Allyson Reid. **Bk Rev**. **Ad Acc**. **Circ:** 79,000 (ctrl).
 Desc: A teen-writing newsmagazine serving the area of New York City.

ISSN 1058-8795
DD 051 US

NEWS FOR KIDS. [News kids]. (Sept. 1991)-. Periodical. English. Twelve times a year. DM Publishing Inc., 19742 MacArthur Boulevard, Irvine CA 92715.

ISSN 0831-9197
DD 028.5/06/01 CN

NEWSLETTER - INTERNATIONAL BOARD ON BOOKS FOR YOUNG PEOPLE. CANADIAN SECTION (1980). (NEWSLETTER / BULLETIN.). [Newsl. - Int. Board Books Young People, Can. Sect.]. **Added/Corp** Union Internationale pour les Livres de Jeunesse. Section Canadienne. **VFOAT** Bulletin. **VAT** Bulletin - Union Internationale pour les Livres de Jeunesse. Section Canadienne (1980). (1980)-. Newsletter. French (English). Union Internationale Pour les Livres de Jeunesse, Section Canadienne, A/S Provincial Library Service, 7E Etage, 77 Ouest, Rue Bloor, Toronto, Ontario M7A 2R9 Canada. **Continues** IBBY Newsletter, 0828-847X.

KE

NEWSLETTER / ORTHODOX CHRISTIAN YOUTH ASSOCIATION OF KENYA. See Religions and Theology-Orthodox Eastern Churches.

ISSN 1073-7510
DD 051 US

●**NICKELODEON.** (1993)-. Periodical. English. Twelve times a year. $16.97. Nickelodeon Magazine, 1515 Broadway, 50th Floor, New York NY 10036. **Tel** (212)258-7500.

LC AP95.C4 N53

HK
CEASED

NIEN CHING JEN. VFOAT Teens. (Oct. 1973)-(19??). Chinese (Chinese). Teens' Magazine Publishing Company, No 1 on Ning Lane, Sai Ying Pun Hong Kong Hong Kong.

LC PN3159.J3 N52

JA

NIHON NO JIDO ENGEKI. See Theater.

ISSN 0757-1984
FR
UDC 78

NINETEEN. VFOAT Nineteen Magazine; Nineteen Going Loco. (1982)-. Periodical. French. Twelve times a year. $49.29. IPC Magazines Ltd., Perrymount Road, Haywards Heath, West Sussex RH16 3DH United Kingdom. **Tel** 011 44 1444 440421, FAX 011 44 1444 445599.

ISSN 0892-4945
DD 296 US

NOAH'S ARK. [Noah's ark]. **VFOAT** Noah's Ark, A Newspaper for Jewish Children. (197?)-. Periodical. English. Ten times a year (monthly except July & Aug.). $18.50. Noah's Ark, 8323 Southwest Freeway, Suite 250, Houston TX 77074. **Tel** (713)771-7144, (713)729-6221. **ED** Debbie Israel Dubin and Linda Freedman Block. **Bk Rev**, (Qty: 10-20). **Circ:** 200,000.
 Desc: Presents Jewish culture, history, holidays, and events in interesting and creative ways by using stories, games, puzzles, recipes, craft projects, Hebrew columns, facts, and more.

ISSN 0318-2835
DD C810/.8/0928205 CN

NOUS JOURNAL. Vol. 1 (Spring 1975)-. English. Irregular. $1.50. All About US/NOUS Autres, PO Box 1985, Ottawa K1P 5R5.

ISSN 0153-9027
FR
UDC 028
Pr Rev.

NOUS VOULONS LIRE PESSAC. See Literary and Political Reviews.

IT

NUOVO ALBERO A ELICA. (19??)-. Italian. Jonica Editrice, Via Figurella 1/5, 87011 Cassano Jonico Italy.

LC QB46 .O3a ISSN 0163-0946
DD 520/.5 US

ODYSSEY (PETERBOROUGH, N.H.). (ODYSSEY.). [Odyssey]. (Jan. 1979)-. Periodical. English. Nine times a year (monthly except June, July and Aug.). $24.95. Cobblestone Publishing Inc., 7 School Street, Peterborough NH 03458. **Tel** (603)924-7209, FAX (603)924-7380. **ED** Nancy Mack. **Bk Rev**. **Ad Acc**. **Circ:** 86,000. Documents available from UMI Article Clearinghouse.
 Desc: Written in a language for kids aged 8-14 that can understand and enjoy reading about outer space, space exploration, and astronomy. Packed with exciting articles, puzzles, contests, projects, and spectacular photographs to make science come alive for young people.
 Ind/Abst Child. Mag. Guide (1981-); EP Collect.; Homework Help.; Mag. Artic. Summar. Elite; Mag. Artic. Summar. Select; Mag. Artic. Summar. CD-ROM; Mag. Search; MasterFile FullTEXT 1000; MasterFile FullTEXT 350; MasterFile FullTEXT 650; MasterFile FullTEXT (July 1989-) [Full Txt.]; Mid. Search; Newsp. Period. Abstr. (1992-); OCLC; Prim. Search; Pub. Lib. FullTEXT; Telebase.

LC PZ5 .O3 ISSN 0000-1376
DD 808 US

OF CABBAGES AND KINGS. (OF CABBAGES AND KINGS : THE YEAR'S BEST MAGAZINE WRITINGS FOR KIDS.). [Of cabbages kings]. (1991)-. Periodical. English. Irregular. $29.95. R.R. Bowker, A Reed Reference Publishing Company, Part of Reed International PLC, PO Box 31, 121 Chanlon Drive, New Providence NJ 07974. **Tel** (908)464-6800, (800)521-8110, FAX (908)665-6688, telex 138-755.
 Desc: A potpourri of articles from over 400 issues of children's magazines.

ISSN 1059-3993
DD 028 US
CEASED

OFF THE SHELF (HUMBLE, TEX.). (OFF THE SHELF.). [Off shelf]. **Added/Corp** Progressive Educational Concepts. (1990)-(Spring 1994). Periodical. English. Progressive Educational Concepts Inc, PO Box 2761, Humble TX 77347. **Tel** (713)358-8027, FAX (713)852-6560. **ED** Kenneth Kowen, 1502 Chestnut Ridge, Humble, TX. **Bk Rev**, (Qty: 100). **Ad Acc**.

LC GV881.2 .L57a
DD 796.357/62 US

OFFICIAL REGULATIONS AND PLAYING RULES. LITTLE LEAGUE, SENIOR LEAGUE, BIG LEAGUE SOFTBALL. See Sports and Games.

ISSN 0021-566X
FR
TITLE CHANGE

OK AGE TENDRE. (19??)-(1993). French. Publications Filipacchi, 149 rue Anatole, 92534 Levallois Perret France. **Tel** 011 33 1 41346456, telex 651-294. **Absorbed by** Ok Podium.

NE

OKKI. (19??)-. Dutch. One time a week. F39.25 Netherlands; F67.35 other. Malmborg BV, PO Box 233 Leeghwaterlaan 16, 5223 BA Den Bosch Netherlands. **Tel** 011 31 73 288711, telex 50058.

ISSN 1061-0952

ON COURSE (SPRINGFIELD, MO.). See Religions and Theology.

ISSN 1071-2526
DD 808 US

ONCE UPON A TIME (ST. PAUL, MINN.). See Literature.

ISSN 0258-610X
US

ONE IN TEN. (1981)-. Periodical. English. Four times a year.
 Ind/Abst Hum. Rights Intern. Rep.

ISSN 1061-4796
DD 268 US

ONE TO ONE (UPPER DARBY, PA.). See Religions and Theology.

ISSN 1066-2952
US

●**ONLY FOR KIDS MINI MAG. VFOAT** Only for Kids. (1993)-. Periodical. English. Twelve times a year. $1.95 (single issue). A Wilson, 10707 Lee Avenue, Number 2, Cleveland OH 44106.

BE

OPINION JEUNESSE. (19??)-. Newspaper. English (French). Four times a year. Free. Forum Jeunesse, 120 rue Joseph 2, Jozef II Straat 120, B-1040 Brussels Belgium. **ED** Mary Creagh. **Acid Free. Circ:** 10,000 (ctrl).
 Desc: Looks at European issues and how they affect young people and their organizations. Also provides news of youth organization activities.

LC Z675.S3 O577 ISSN 0045-6705
DD 027.62/6/0994 AT

ORANA. See Library and Information Sciences.

ISSN 1071-233X
DD 618 US
Pr Rev.

ORIGINAL NEWS PEPPER, THE. See Medical Sciences-Pediatrics.

ISSN 1052-8415
DD 179 US
CEASED

OTTERWISE (PORTLAND, ME.). (OTTERWISE.). [Otterwise]. **VFOAT** Otherwise; Otter Wise. (1990)-(Sept. 1994). Newsletter. English. Otterwise, PO Box 1374, Portland ME 04104. **Tel** (207)883-4426. **ED** Marianne Matte. **Bk Rev**, (Qty: 4). **Circ:** 3,000.
 Desc: A newsletter for children from ages 8 to 13. Presents animal facts and issues in an upbeat style. Articles, stories, activities and puzzles to help a child develop a compassion for animals and the natural world around them.

US

OUR KID'S MAGAZINE. (19??)-. English. Two times a year. Alexander Graham Bell Association for the Deaf, 3417 Volta Place Northwest, Washington DC 20007. **Tel** (202)337-5220.

ISSN 1069-420X
US

●**OUTSIDE KIDS.** (1993)-. Periodical. English. Four times a year. $9.97. Outside, 400 Market Street, Santa Fe NM 87501. **Tel** (505)989-7100. **(Subscription address:** Neodata / Colorado, PO Box 2606, Boulder CO 80322. **)**
 Ind/Abst EP Collect.; Homework Help.; MasterFile FullTEXT 1000; MasterFile FullTEXT 350; MasterFile FullTEXT 650; MasterFile FullTEXT (Sept. 1994-); Mid. Search; Prim. Search; Pub. Lib. FullTEXT; Telebase.

ISSN 0382-6627
DD 500.9/71 CN

OWL (DON MILLS). (OWL.). [Owl] **Added/Corp** Young Naturalist Foundation. Vol. 1 (Jan. 1976)-. Periodical. English (French and Italian). Ten times a year. 17.00Can$. Young Naturalist Foundation, 179 John Street, Suite 500, Toronto Ontario M5T 3G5 Canada. **Tel** (416)971-5275. **(Subscription address:** Owl, 25 Boxwood Lane, Buffalo NY 14427. **Tel** (416)971-5275.**)** **ED** Sylvia Funston. Index available. **Bk Rev**. **Circ:** 160,000. Documents available from UMI Article Clearinghouse. **Supersedes** Young Naturalist, 0513-3009.
 Desc: Canada's discovery magazine for eight to twelve

Children and Youth Interests

year-olds; includes involving articles by top science writers, hands-on activities and photographs and illustrations. Together with its companion television series "OWL/TV," the magazine sparks children's curiosity about the world and encourages them to get involved in caring for the environment.
Ind/Abst Can. Period. Index (19??-); Child. Mag. Guide (1981-); EP Collect.; Homework Help.; Mag. Artic. Summar. Elite; Mag. Artic. Summar. Select; Mag. Artic. Summar. CD-ROM; Mag. Search; MasterFile FullTEXT 1000; MasterFile FullTEXT 350; MasterFile FullTEXT 650; MasterFile FullTEXT (July 1989-); Mid. Search; Newsp. Period. Abstr. (1992-); OCLC; Prim. Search; Pub. Lib. FullTEXT; Telebase.

ISSN 0176-4152
GW

UDC 001.92 :05
P. M. PETER MOOSLEITNERS INTERESSANTES MAGAZIN. [P. M. Peter Moosleitners interess. Mag.]. **VFOAT** Peter Moosleitners Interessantes Magazin. (1978)-. Periodical. German. Twelve times a year. $79.22. Gruner und Jahr Ag & Co, Abonnenten Service, D-20080 Hamburg Germany. **Tel** 011 49 40 37030, FAX 011 49 40 37035657.

ISSN 0030-901X
US
PACK-O-FUN. **VAT** Pack of Fun. (1951)-. Periodical. English. Six times a year (Jan., Mar., May, July, Sept., Nov.). $14.97. Clapper Communications, 2400 Devon, Suite 375, Des Plaines IL 60018. **Tel** (800)272-3871, (708)635-5800. **ED** Marie Petersen. **Bk Rev. Ad Acc. Circ:** 35,000. available on microfilm from University Microfilms International (UMI).
Desc: Scrap-craft magazine for children, featuring simple crafts, seasonal decorations, skits, and program ideas.

IT
PAGINE GIOVANI. (19??)-. Italian. Four times a year. L30000.00. Gr Serv Letterario Giovanile, P Za Card Ferrari 4, 00167 Rome Italy. **Tel** 011 39 6 66000998.

ISSN 1064-7589
US
●**PAINTBOX (LOS ANGELES, CALIF.).** (PAINTBOX : THE CHILDREN'S MAGAZINE.). **VFOAT** Paint Box. (1992)-. Periodical. English. Six times a year. $15.95 US; $22.95 Canada and Mexico. Paintbox, 23383 Livonia Avenue, Los Angeles CA 90034.

DD 809.89282
AT
Pr Rev.
PAPERS (VICTORIA PARK). (PAPERS.). [Pap. Vic. Park]. (1990)-. Periodical. English. Three times a year. 28.78Aus$. Centre of Research and Cultural Communications, Faculty of Arts, Deakin Uni 221 Burwood, Hyw Burwood 3125 Australia. **Tel** 011 3 92446487. **Bk Rev. Ad Acc. Circ:** 500.
Desc: Historical, comparative and evaluative studies into children's literature.
Ind/Abst Aust. Educ. Index; Child. Lit. Abstr. (19??-); EP Collect.; Homework Help.; MasterFile FullTEXT 1000; MasterFile FullTEXT 350; MasterFile FullTEXT 650; MasterFile FullTEXT (Sept. 1994-); Telebase; World Mag. Bank.

ISSN 0031-3777
IT
UDC 37.01
PEDAGOGIA E VITA. [Pedagog. vita]. (1952)-. Periodical. Italian. Six times a year. L40200. Editrice Scuola Spa, Via L Cadorna 11, 25186 Brescia Italy. **Tel** 011 39 30 2993246.

LC AC
DD 080
UDC 087.5(44)
ISSN 1164-9526
FR
PERLIN (1992). (PERLIN.). (1992)-. Periodical. French. Fifty-two times a year. $107.61. Fleurus Presse International, 21 rue Faubourg St. Antoine, 75550 Paris Cedex 11 France. **Tel** 011 33 1 40026300. **(Subscription address:** Fleurus Presse Service Abbonnements, BP 72, 77932 Perthes Cedex France. **Tel** 011 33 1 64380389.) **Continues** Perlin et Pinpin (1990), 1153-0308.

UDC 087.5(44)
ISSN 0249-8138
FR
PHOSPHORE PARIS. [Phosphore Paris]. (1981)-. Periodical. French. Twelve times a year. 102.51Can$. Bayard Presse, Svc Client, 3 rue Bayard, Department 2, 75393 Paris Cedex 08 France. **Tel** 011 33 1 44355907, FAX 011 33 1 44356025. **Continues** Record-Dossier, 0151-2404.

LC AP200
DD 051
ISSN 1056-0505
US
PHOTOPLAY PRESENTS TEEN BEAT ALL-STARS POP-OUTS!. [Photoplay Presents Teen Beat All-Stars Pop-Outs!]. **VFOAT** A.Pop-outs; Pop Outs; Teen Beat All-Stars Pop-Outs. (19??)-. Periodical. English. Four times a year. $21.95. Sterling Macfadden, 233 Park Avenue South, New York NY 10003. **Tel** (212)979-4800.

ISSN 0767-807X
FR
PICSOU MAGAZINE. [Picsou mag.]. (1972)-. Periodical. French. Twelve times a year. $52.49. Edimonde Loisirs, 90 rue de Flandre, 75947 Paris Cedex 19 France. **Tel** 011 33 1 44894489.

ISSN 0813-7846
DD 808.54305
AT
PIED PIPER. [Pied piper]. (1982)-. Periodical. English. Six times a year. Storytelling Guild of South Australia, 37 Fourth Avenue, St Peters SA 5069 Australia. **Continues** Newsletter - Storytelling Guild of South Australia, 0813-7838.
Ind/Abst Aust. Educ. Index.

LC AP215.R9 P5
RU
PIONER. (1924)-. Periodical. Russian. Twelve times a year. $99.95. Pioner, Bumazhnii Proezd 14, Moscow 101459 Russia. **(Subscription address:** East View Publications Inc., 3020 Harbor Lane North, Suite 110, Minneapolis MN 55447. **Tel** (800)477-1005, (612)550-0961, FAX (612)559-2931.)

LC AP215.R9 P53
RU
PIONERSKAIA PRAVDA. Added/Corp Vsesoiuznyi Leninskii Kommunisticheskii Soiuz Molodezhi. Tsentralnyi Komitet. Vsesoiuznyi Leninskii Kommunisticheskii Soiuz Molodezhi. Moskovskii Oblastnoi Komitet. Vsesoiuznaia Pionerskaia Organizatsiia Imeni V.I. Lenina. Tsentralnyi Sovet. (March 1925)-. Periodical. Russian. Forty-eight times a year. $129.95. **(Subscription address:** East View Publications Inc., 3020 Harbor Lane North, Suite 110, Minneapolis MN 55447. **Tel** (800)477-1005, (612)550-0961, FAX (612)559-2931.) available on microfilm.

LC HS3325.C9 P56
XR
PIONYRSKA STAFETA. Added/Corp Sdruzeni Pionyru CSSR. Vol. 1 (1969)-. Periodical. Czech. Twelve times a year. $15.40. Mlada Fronta, Radlicka 61, 150 02 Prague 5 Czech Republic. **Tel** 42 2 544941. **(Subscription address:** Artia Pegas Press Ltd., Palac Metro Narodni Trida 25, 11210 Prague 1 Czech Republic. **Tel** 011 42 2 24196265, 011 42 2 24196266.) **ED** Hynek Gregor.

ISSN 1062-6956
DD 791
US
SUSPENDED
PLAY (GAINESVILLE, FLA.). (PLAY MAGAZINE.). [Play]. **VFOAT** Play Magazine. Vol. 1, No. 1 (Winter 1992/1993)-Suspended (1994). Periodical. English. Four times a year. $12.00 US; $16.00 Canada and Mexico; $24.00 other. Meg Inc., 3620 Northwest 43rd Street, Suite D, Gainesville FL 32606. **Tel** (904)375-3705.

LC PN1601 .P6
DD 371.8952
ISSN 0032-1540
PLAYS (BOSTON). See Theater.

ISSN 0278-565X
US
POCKETS. Vol. 1, No. 1 (Nov./Dec. 1981)-. Periodical. English. Eleven times a year (monthly except Jan./Feb.). $16.95. Upper Room, 1908 Grand Avenue, PO Box 189, Nashville TN 37202. **Tel** (800)925-6847, FAX (615)340-7275. **ED** Janet McNish Bugg. **Circ:** 55,000.
Desc: Devotional magazine for children 6 to 12. Uses stories, games, family activities, scripture, and prayer to open the gospel's fullness to children.

ISSN 0137-8511
PL
UDC 82-93
POMYCZEK. [Pomyczek]. (1919)-. Periodical. Polish. Twelve times a year. **(Subscription address:** Ars Polona-Ruch, PO Box 1001, Krakowskie Przedmiescie 7, 00-068 Warsaw Poland. **Tel** 011 48 22 261201.)

ISSN 0299-3147
FR
UDC 087.5
POPI. (1986)-. Periodical. French. Twelve times a year. $88.58. Bayard Presse, Svc Client, 3 rue Bayard, Department 2, 75393 Paris Cedex 08 France. **Tel** 011 33 1 44355907, FAX 011 33 1 44356025. **(Subscription address:** Bayard Presse Notre Temps, BP2, 99505 Paris Enterprises France.)

DD 372
ISSN 0270-6288
US
PRIMARY-JUNIOR KID-CRAFTS. [Prim.-jr. kid-crafts]. **VFOAT** Primary Junior Kid Crafts. Vol. 17, No. 4 (Sept./Nov. 1980)-. Periodical. English. Four times a year. David C. Cook Foundation, 850 North Grove Avenue, Elgin IL 60120. **Tel** (800)323-7543. **Continues** Primary-Junior Read 'n Do Stories.

ISSN 0270-6318
US
PRIMARY KID-CRAFTS. VAT Primary Kid Crafts. (19??)-. Periodical. English. Four times a year. David C. Cook Foundation, 850 North Grove Avenue, Elgin IL 60120. **Tel** (800)323-7543. **Continues** Primary Color 'N' Do Stories.

ISSN 0032-8316
US
PRIMARY TREASURE. (19??)-. Periodical. English. One time a week. Pacific Press Publishing Association, 1350 Villa Street, Mountain View CA 94040.

ISSN 1012-7895
SZ
PRO JUVENTUTE. [Pro juv.]. (1920)-. Periodical. German. Four times a year. $34.70. Verlag Pro Juventute, Seehofstrasse 15, CH-8022 Zurich Switzerland. **Tel** 011 41 1 2520719.

LC HQ799.R9 K5847
ISSN 0236-0268
RU
PUL'S. Added/Corp Vsesoiuznyi Leninskii Kommunisticheskii Soiuz Molodezhi. Tsentralnyi Komitet. (1990)-. Periodical. Russian. Twelve times a year. $99.95. Izdatelstvo Molodaia Gvardiia, Novodmitrovskaya Ulitsa 5A, 125015 Moscow Russia. **Tel** 011 95 285 1935. **(Subscription address:** East View Publications Inc., 3020 Harbor Lane North, Suite 110, Minneapolis MN 55447. **Tel** (800)477-1005, (612)550-0961, FAX (612)559-2931.) **Continues** Komsomolskaia Zhizn, 0130-2469.

ISSN 1070-969X
US
SUSPENDED
●**QUAKE (NEW YORK, N.Y.).** (QUAKE.). **VFOAT** Quake Magazine. (1993)-Suspended (Aug. 1994). Periodical. English. Six times a year. $9.97. Welsh Publishing Group Inc., 300 Madison Avenue, New York NY 10017. **Tel** (212)687-0680, FAX (212)986-5849. **(Subscription address:** CDS Agency Hard Copy, PO Box 4966, Des Moines IA 50340. **Tel** (515)247-7569.) **ED** Brett Mirsky & Tucker Shaw.
Desc: Provides entertainment news concerning music, movies, and television of interest to youth from 15 to 20 years of age.

DD 796
ISSN 1056-7623
US
RACING FOR KIDS. [Racing Kids]. Vol. 1, No. 1 (Mar. 1990)-. Periodical. English. Twelve times a year. $25.00. Griggs Publishing Company Inc., PO Box 500, Concord NC 28026. **Tel** (704)786-7132, (800)883-7323, FAX (704)788-4420. **ED** Donna Cox. **Ad Acc, Adv Mgr:** Zeta Smith, **Tel** (704)786-7131. **Circ:** 10,000 (ctrl).
Desc: A children's magazine reviewing the motor sports world.

DD 051
ISSN 0708-9961
CN
RAINCOAST. (Jan. 1979)-. Periodical. English. Irregular. $6.00. Raincoast Chronicles, PO Box 91603, West Vancouver B.C. V7V 3P3. **Tel** (604)883-2730.

LC QH48 .R34
DD 591/.05
ISSN 0738-6656
US
RANGER RICK. [Ranger Rick]. **Added/Corp** National Wildlife Federation. Canadian Wildlife Federation. Vol. 17, No. 1 (Jan. 1983)-. Periodical. English. Twelve times a year. $15.00. National Wildlife Federation / Virginia, 8925 Leesburg Pike, Vienna VA 22184. **Tel** (703)790-4000, (800)822-9919, FAX (703)442-7332. **ED** Gerald Bishop. Index available. **Circ:** 1,000,000 (ctrl). available on microfilm and microfiche from University Microfilms International (UMI). **Continues** Ranger Rick's Nature Magazine, 0033-9229. **Continued in part by** Ranger Rick (Ottawa, Ont.), 0828-8739.
Desc: Children 6-12 learn to understand and appreciate nature through photographs and illustrations, nature and wildlife articles, fiction, games and crafts. A magazine for school and home.
Ind/Abst Child. Mag. Guide (1983-); EP Collect.; Homework Help.; Mag. Artic. Summar. Elite; Mag. Artic. Summar. Select; Mag. Artic. Summar. CD-ROM; Mag. Search; MasterFile FullTEXT 1000; MasterFile FullTEXT 350; MasterFile FullTEXT 650; MasterFile FullTEXT (July 1989-) [Full Txt.]; Mid. Search; OCLC; Prim. Search; Pub. Lib. FullTEXT; Telebase.

DD 054/.1
ISSN 0841-758X
CN
RAYON JEUNESSE. See Education.

DD 028
ISSN 1040-3558
US
READING EDGE (CROWNSVILLE, MD.), THE. See Literature.

US
READY. See Linguistics.

ISSN 0829-3724
DD 267/.61/0971372 CN
REPORT TO THE PEOPLE. See Religions and Theology.

BL
RESENHA DE LIVROS PARA A INFANCIA E JUVENTUDE. See Literature.

ISSN 0164-341X
US
REVIEWERS' CONSENSUS. See Literary and Political Reviews.

LC HQ799.S7 R48 ISSN 0211-4364
SP
REVISTA DE ESTUDIOS DE JUVENTUD. **Added/Corp** Spain. Direccion General de Juventud y Promocion Sociocultural. Subdireccion General de Estudios e Investigaciones. Centro Nacional de Informacion y Documentacion de Juventud (Spain). Vol. 13 (March 1984)-. Periodical. Spanish. Four times a year. Instituto de la Juventud Centro Nacional de Informacion y Documentacion de Juventud, Marques de Rical 16, 28010 Madrid Spain. ***Continues*** *De Juventud.*

LC PN1009.A1 B84
DD 028.52 FR
REVUE DES LIVRES POUR ENFANTS, LA. See Literary and Political Reviews.

ISSN 0399-0265
FR
UDC 36
REVUE SAMU, LA. [Rev. SAMU]. **VFOAT** Revue Services d'Aides Medicales Urgentes. (1977)-. Periodical. French. Six times a year. $109.36. Societe Francaise d'Editions Medecine, 22 rue du Chateau des Rentiers, 75013 Paris France. **Tel** 011 33 1 45835054.

ISSN 0048-8305
DD 781 US
RIGHT ON (HOLLYWOOD, CALIF.). (RIGHT ON!.). [Right on]. (197?)-. Periodical. English. Twelve times a year. $19.95. Sterling Macfadden, 233 Park Avenue South, New York NY 10003. **Tel** (212)979-4800.
Desc: Entertainment magazine for black teens.

ISSN 0747-5977
US
RIGHT ON POSTER BOOK. (RIGHT ON! POSTER BOOK.). **VFOAT** Right on Annual Poster Book. (198?)-. Periodical. English. One time a year. D S Magazines Inc., 1086 Teaneck Road, Teaneck NJ 07666. **Tel** (201)833-1800. **ED** Cynthia Horner. **Bk Rev. Ad Acc.**
Desc: Huge 16x22 inch posters with information of favorite TV and music stars. A must for every teenage dreamer's bedroom walls.

ISSN 8755-8661
DD 784 US
ROCK POSTER MAGAZINE. [Rock poster mag.]. (1983)-. Periodical. English. Four times a year. Rock Poster Magazine, 475 Park Avenue South, New York NY 10016.

ISSN 1050-2602
DD 741 US
ROGER RABBIT. [Roger Rabbit]. No. 1 (June 1990)-. Periodical. English. Twelve times a year. Walt Disney Productions, 500 South Buena Vista, Burbank CA 91521.

UK
ROUNDABOUT. (19??)-. English. Twelve times a year. £10.80. Royal National Institute for the Blind, PO Box 173, Peterborough PE2 6WS United Kingdom. **Tel** 011 44 1733 3730777, FAX 011 44 1733 371555.
Desc: Aimed at children aged seven to eleven, produced in braille. Takes information from popular children's magazines; produced in a widely spaced format to aid reading.

LC HQ796 .R74 ISSN 0485-5167
RU
ROVESNIK. **Added/Corp** Vsesoiuznyi Leninskii Kommunisticheskii Soiuz Molodezhi. Tsentralnyi Komitet. Komitet Molodezhnykh Organizatsii SSSR. Vol. 1, No. 1 (July 1962)-. Periodical. Russian. Twelve times a year. $129.95. **(Subscription address:** East View Publications Inc., 3020 Harbor Lane North, Suite 110, Minneapolis MN 55447. **Tel** (800)477-1005, (612)550-0961, FAX (612)559-2931.**)**

ISSN 0397-7854
FR
UDC 08
SALUT!... PARIS. (1976)-. Periodical. French. Twenty-six times a year. $64.52. EDI Presse, 13 rue de la Cerisaie, 75004 Paris France. **Tel** 011 33 1 42771810. ***Continues*** *Salut Les Copains (Paris. 1962), 0036-3650.*

LC WMLC 93/1290 ISSN 0899-9953
DD 646 US
SASSY (NEW YORK, N.Y. 1988). (SASSY.). [Sassy]. (March 1988)-. Periodical. English. Twelve times a year. $14.97. Lang Communications, 230 Park Avenue, New York NY 10169. **Tel** (212)551-9500, FAX (212)599-4597. **(Subscription address:** Neodata / Colorado, PO Box 2606, Boulder CO 80322.**)** **Ad Acc.**
Ind/Abst Abr. Read. Guide Period. Lit.; Read. Guide Period. Lit.

ISSN 1040-7707
DD 794 US
SCHOOL MATES. See Sports and Games.

ISSN 0147-3654
US
SCIENCELAND. (19??)-. Periodical. English. Eight times a year (monthly Sept. through May excluding Dec.). $42.00. Scienceland Inc., 501 Fifth Avenue/Suite 2108, New York NY 10017-6165. **Tel** (212)490-2180, FAX (212)490-2187. **ED** A. H. Matano. Index available. cum. index. **Circ:** 20,000. available on microfilm and microfiche from University Microfilms International (UMI).
Desc: Encourages children to read and learn about science with its photo features and illustrated stories.
Ind/Abst Child. Mag. Guide (1981-); EP Collect.; Gen. Sci. Source; Homework Help.; Mag. Search; MasterFile FullTEXT 1000; MasterFile FullTEXT 350; MasterFile FullTEXT 650; MasterFile FullTEXT; Mid. Search; OCLC; Prim. Search; Pub. Lib. FullTEXT; Res. Alert; Telebase.

NE
SCOUTING MAGAZINE. (19??)-. Dutch. Ten times a year. Fl50.00. Scouting Nederland, Larikslaan 5, 3833 AH Leusden Netherlands. **Tel** 31 033 960911. ***Continues*** *Scouting.*

IT
SCUOLA MATERNA. (19??)-. Italian. L67000 Italy; L97000 others. Editrice Scuola Spa, Via L Cadorna 11, 25186 Brescia Italy. **Tel** 011 39 30 2993246.

US
SUSPENDED
SEE WHAT'S HAPPENING. See Physically Impaired.

LC HQ799.J3 S3353
JA
SEISHONEN MONDAI CHOSA NENPO. **Added/Corp** Japan. Seishonen Taisaku Honbu. (1989)-. Japanese. Youth Affairs Administration, Management and Coordination, Agency, Prime Minister's Office, 1-1 Kasumigaseki 3-chome, Chiyoda-ku Tokyo 100 Japan. **Tel** 03-580-5367, telex 03-593-1620. ***Continues*** *Seishonen Mondai Kenkyu Chosa Kiho.*

LC HQ799.R9 S36
RU
SELSKAIA MOLODEZH. **Added/Corp** Vsesoiuznyi Leninskii Kommunisticheskii Soiuz Molodezhi. Tsentralnyi Komitet. Vol. 29, No. 1 (Jan. 1962)-. Periodical. Russian. Twelve times a year. $79.95. Izdatelstvo Molodaia Gvardiia, Novodmitrovskaya Ulitsa 5A, 125015 Moscow Russia. **Tel** 011 95 285 1935. **(Subscription address:** East View Publications Inc., 3020 Harbor Lane North, Suite 110, Minneapolis MN 55447. **Tel** (800)477-1005, (612)550-0961, FAX (612)559-2931.**)** ***Continues*** *Molodoi Kolkhoznik.*

ISSN 0503-8308
DD 833 VE
SERIE DE CUENTOS PARA LA JUVENTUD. **Main/Corp** Venezuela. Universidad Central, Caracas. Departamento de Aleman. (1956)-. Spanish. Irregular. Universidad Central de Venezuela / Serie de Cuentos para la Juventud, Apartado Postal 6622, Caracas 1010 A Venezuela. **Tel** 011 58 2 7523266.

ISSN 0049-0253
US
SESAME STREET MAGAZINE. **Added/Corp** Children's Television Workshop. (1970)-. Periodical. English (Spanish). Ten times a year. $19.90. Children's Television Workshop, One Lincoln Plaza, Box TG, New York NY 10023. **Tel** (212)595-3456. **(Subscription address:** Neodata / Colorado, PO Box 2606, Boulder Boulder CO 80322.**)** **ED** Marge Kennedy. **Ad Acc. Circ:** 1,000,000.
Desc: For pre-schoolers ages 2 to 6 year old. Contains stories, puzzles, and games involving the basic A-B-C's and 1-2-3's.
Ind/Abst Child. Mag. Guide; Mag. Search; MasterFile FullTEXT (July 1993-).

ISSN 0037-301X
US
SEVENTEEN. [Seventeen]. (Sept. 1944)-. Periodical. English. Twelve times a year. $17.00. K-III Magazine Corporation, 200 Madison Avenue, 8th Floor, New York NY 10016. **Tel** (212)447-4700, (212)447-4732. **(Subscription address:** Neodata / Colorado, PO Box 2606, Boulder Boulder CO 80322.**)** **Ad Acc.** available on microfilm and microfiche from University Microfilms International (UMI). Documents available from UMI Article Clearinghouse.
Ind/Abst Abr. Read. Guide Period. Lit.; Acad. Abstr. Full Text Elite; Acad. Abstr.; Biogr. Index; EP Collect.; Gen. Period. Index (1985-); Homework Help.; Mag. Artic. Summar. Elite; Mag. Artic. Summar. Select; Mag. Artic. Summar. CD-ROM; Mag. Express (1988-) [Full Txt.]; Mag. Index Plus (1989-); Mag. Index. Sel. (1986-); Mag. Search; MasterFile FullTEXT 1000; MasterFile FullTEXT 350; MasterFile FullTEXT 650; MasterFile FullTEXT (Jan. 1989-); Med. Rev. Dig.; Mid. Search; Newsp. Period. Abstr. (1988-); OCLC; Pub. Lib. FullTEXT; Read. Guide Abstr. Select Ed.; Read. Guide Period. Lit.; Resource/One Ondisc; Telebase; Mag. Index (1977-); TOM Gen. Index (1985-) [Full Txt.].

II
SHANKAR'S CHILDREN'S ART NUMBER. Vol. 35 (1985)-. English. One time a year. Price varies. Indraprastha Press, New Delhi India. **(Subscription address:** Prints India, 11 Darya Ganj, New Delhi 110002 India. **Tel** 011 91 11 3268645, FAX 011 91 11 3275542, telex 31-61087 PRIN-IN.**)** ***Continues*** *Shankar's Children's Number.*

ISSN 0748-9706
DD 296 US
SHOFAR (MELVILLE, N.Y.). (SHOFAR.). [Shofar]. Vol. 1, No. 1 (Mar. 1984)-. Periodical. English (Hebrew). Ten times a year (monthly with Dec./Jan. and Apr./May issues combined). $14.95. Senior Publ Limited, PO Box 852, Wheatley Heights NY 11798. **Tel** (516)643-4598, FAX (516)643-4598. **ED** Gerald H. Grayson. **Bk Rev**, (Qty: varies). **Ad Acc. Circ:** 10,000.
Desc: Presents stories, articles, news, sports, games, and puzzles to enhance and instill an American child's sense of Jewish identity and pride.

LC PN6010.5 .S55 ISSN 0732-5266
DD 808.83/1 US
SHORT STORY INTERNATIONAL. SEEDLING SERIES. **VFOAT** Seedling Series. (1981)-. Periodical. English. Four times a year (Mar., June, Sept., Dec.). $18.00. Short Story International, PO Box 405, Great Neck NY 11022. **Tel** (516)466-6091. **ED** Sylvia Tankel. **Circ:** 9,000.
Desc: Contemporary short stories from all lands geared to grades 4-7.
Ind/Abst Acad. Abstr.; Acad. Search; EP Collect.; Homework Help.; Mag. Artic. Summar. Elite; Mag. Artic. Summar. Select; Mag. Artic. Summar. CD-ROM; Mag. Search; MasterFile FullTEXT 1000; MasterFile FullTEXT 350; MasterFile FullTEXT 650; MasterFile FullTEXT (Jan. 1993-); Mid. Search; OCLC; Prim. Search; Pub. Lib. FullTEXT; Telebase.

LC PR9084.5 .S5 ISSN 0732-5274
DD 823/.01/08 US
SHORT STORY INTERNATIONAL. STUDENT SERIES. **VFOAT** Student Short Story International. (1981)-. Periodical. English. Four times a year (Mar., June, Sept., Dec.). $21.00. Short Story International, PO Box 405, Great Neck NY 11022. **Tel** (516)466-6091. **ED** Sylvia Tankel. **Circ:** 11,000.
Desc: Contemporary short stories from all lands geared to grades 8-12.
Ind/Abst Acad. Abstr.; Acad. Search; EP Collect.; Homework Help.; Mag. Artic. Summar. Elite; Mag. Artic. Summar. Select; Mag. Artic. Summar. CD-ROM; Mag. Search; MasterFile FullTEXT 1000; MasterFile FullTEXT 350; MasterFile FullTEXT 650; MasterFile FullTEXT (Jan. 1993-); Mid. Search; OCLC; Prim. Search; Pub. Lib. FullTEXT; Telebase.

LC PN1009.H4 S57
IS
SIFRUT YELADIM VA-NOAR. **Added/Corp** Israel. Misrad Ha-Hinukh Veha-Tarbut. Mador Le-Sifrut Yeladim. Vol. 1 (May 1974)-. Periodical. Hebrew. Four times a year. Misrad Ha-Hinukh Veha-Tarbut, Ha-Mador Le-Sifrut Yeladim, David Ha-Melekh 18, Yerushalayim Israel. **Tel** 02 238202/4. **ED** Gershon Bergson. Index available. cum. index. **Bk Rev. Circ:** 1,000 (ctrl).

ISSN 0899-529X
DD 305 US
SKIPPING STONES. **Added/Corp** Aprovecho Institute (Cottage Grove, Or.). Vol. 1, No. 1 (Fall/Winter 1988)-. Periodical. English. Five times a year. $30.00. Skipping Stones, PO Box 3939, Eugene OR 97403. **Tel** (503)342-4956. **ED** Arun Toke. Index available. cum. index. **Bk Rev**, (Qty: 20). **Circ:** 2,500.
Desc: Children's magazine encouraging cooperation, creativity and celebration of cultural and environmental richness.

ISSN 1060-9911
DD 796 US
SOCCER JR. [Soccer Jr.]. **VFOAT** Soccer Magazine for Kids. Vol. 1, No. 1 (July/Aug. 1992)-. Periodical. English. Six times a year (Jan., Mar., May, July, Sept., Nov.). $14.97. Triplepoint Inc., 27 Unquowa Road, Fairfield CT 06430. **Tel** (203)259-5766, (800)829-5382, FAX (203)256-1119. **(Subscription address:** Soccer Jr. Magazine, PO Box 420441, Palm Coast FL 32142.**)** **ED** Joseph R. Provey. **Bk Rev**, (Qty: 1-2). **Ad Acc, Adv Mgr:** M. Haisch, **Tel** (203)259-5766. **Circ:** 60,000.
Desc: Soccer magazine for kids. Contains news about the teams and the players.

CU
SOMOS. (1992)-. Periodical. Spanish. Twelve times a year. Ediciones Cubanas, Obispo 527 Altos ESQ Bernaza, CP 10100 Havana Cuba. ***Continues*** *Somos Jovenes.*

ISSN 1057-5227
DD 051 US
CEASED
SPARK (CINCINNATI, OHIO). (SPARK : CREATIVE FUN FOR KIDS.). [Spark]. Vol. 1, No. 1 (Sept. 1991)-(Dec. 1993). Periodical. English. F&W Publications, 1507 Dana Avenue, Cincinnati OH 45207.

Children and Youth Interests

Tel (513)531-2222, FAX (513)531-1843. **(Subscription address:** CDS Agency Hard Copy, PO Box 4966, Des Moines IA 50340. **Tel** (515)247-7569.)
Desc: The colorful magazine of creative fun for kids 3-12. Filled with unique, step-by-step art and writing projects that stimulate imagination and build self-esteem...drawing, painting, storytelling, work games, greeting cards and many more. Includes Spark! For Parents, a free pull-out guide offering ideas and activities that nuture creativity in children.

AU

SPATZENPOST. (19??)-. German. Ten times a year. Wagner Sche Univ Druckerei, Matthias Schmid Strasse 12, PF 478, A-6021 Innsbruck Austria. **Tel** 011 43 512 59140.

US

SPICE. (19??)-. Periodical. English. Eight times a year. $15.47 US; $23.47 other. Starlog Press Inc., 475 Park Avenue South, New York NY 10016. **Tel** (212)689-2830, FAX (212)889-7933. **(Subscription address:** Kable Publishers Aide / Illinois, 308 East Hitt Street, Subscription Department, Mt. Morris IL 61054-1473. **Tel** (815)734-1261.) *Continues Black Teen.*

ISSN 1070-2911
US

●**SPIDER (PERU, ILL.).** (SPIDER : THE MAGAZINE FOR CHILDREN.). (1994)-. Periodical. English. Twelve times a year. $27.97. Open Court Publishing Company, 315 Fifth Street, PO Box 300, Peru IL 61354. **Tel** (800)435-6850, (815)223-1500, FAX (815)224-6675. **(Subscription address:** Spider Magazine, Box 639, Mt. Morris IL 61054.) **ED** Lynn Gutknecht. available on magnetic tape (Kable News / 308 E Hitt Street, Mt. Morris, IL 61054).
Desc: Designed for children between the ages of six and nine.
Ind/Abst EP Collect.; Homework Help.; Mag. Artic. Summar. Elite; Mag. Artic. Summar. Select; Mag. Artic. Summar. CD-ROM; MasterFile FullTEXT 1000; MasterFile FullTEXT 350; MasterFile FullTEXT 650; MasterFile FullTEXT (July 1994-); Mid. Search; OCLC; Prim. Search; Pub. Lib. FullTEXT; Res. Alert; Telebase.

ISSN 1042-394X
DD 796   US

SPORTS ILLUSTRATED FOR KIDS.
[Sports illus. kids]. Vol. 1, No. 1 (Jan. 1989)-. Periodical. English. Twelve times a year. $23.95. Time Inc. / New York, Time & Life Building, Rockefeller Center, New York NY 10020. **(Subscription address:** Time Customer Service, PO Box 60050, Tampa FL 33609. **Tel** (800)541-9955.) **ED** John Papanck. **Ad Acc. Circ:** 600,000. available on microfilm and microfiche from University Microfilms International (UMI).
Desc: Provides innovative sports coverage for 8-12-year olds. Includes interviews with professionals and rising stars and coverage of sports events for kids.
Ind/Abst Child. Mag. Guide; EP Collect.; Homework Help.; Mag. Search; MasterFile FullTEXT 1000; MasterFile FullTEXT 350; MasterFile FullTEXT 650; MasterFile FullTEXT (July 1992-); Mid. Search; OCLC; Prim. Search; Pub. Lib. FullTEXT; Telebase.

ISSN 0938-0914
UDC 37   GW

STEPPKE. [Steppke]. (1990)-. Periodical. German. Eleven times a year. DM20.00 Germany; DM50.00 other. Doterner Verlags GmbH, Westfalenstr 98, W 4300 Essen 1 Germany. **Tel** 49 201 518521, FAX 149 201 519551. **ED** Bodo and Petra Schmischke. **Bk Rev. Ad Acc. Circ:** 10,000.
Desc: Magazine by and for parents with children to age ten.

LC PS508.C5 S76   ISSN 0094-579X
DD 810/.8/09282   US

STONE SOUP (SANTA CRUZ, CALIF.).
(STONE SOUP). [Stone soup]. (19??)-. Periodical. English. Five times a year. $24.00. Childrens Art Foundation, PO Box 83, Santa Cruz CA 95063. **Tel** (408)426-5557, (800)447-4569, FAX (408)426-1161. **ED** Gerry Mandel. Index available (bound in May issue). **Bk Rev. Ad Acc. Circ:** 13,000 (ctrl).
Desc: Stories, poems, book reviews, and art by children up to age 13. Activity guide bound into each issue.

ISSN 1063-1380
US

STORIES THAT RHYME EVERY TIME KIDS PAGES. (1992)-. English. Story Time Stories That Rhyme, Box 14, Denver CO 80201. **Tel** (803)575-5676.

ISSN 1045-5515
DD 811   US

STORY TIME STORIES THAT RHYME NEWSLETTER. (Jan. 1990)-. Newsletter. English. Four times a year. Story Time Stories That Rhyme, Box 14, Denver CO 80201. **Tel** (803)575-5676. **ED** A. C. Doyle. **Circ:** 5,000. available on videocassette; available on audiocassette.
Desc: Stories ranging from the inspirational, the educational and the informative to the purely entertaining.

ISSN 1062-0095
DD 305   US

STRAIGHT TALK (PLEASANTVILLE, N.Y.). (STRAIGHT TALK: A MAGAZINE FOR TEENS.). **Added/Corp** Learning Partnership. Monographic series. English. Four times a year. Price varies. The Learning Partnership, PO Box 199, Pleasantville NY 10570. **Tel** (914)769-0055, FAX (914)769-5676. *Continues Rodale's Straight Talk, 1057-9753.*

LC HS3325.R8 D43   ISSN 0869-0022
RU

STUPENI. Added/Corp Soiuz Pionerskikh Organizatsii (Federatsiia Detskikh Organizatsii) SSSR. TSentral'nyi Sovet. (1991)-. Periodical. Russian. Twelve times a year. Izdatelstvo Molodaia Gvardiia, Novodmitrovskaya Ulitsa 5A, 125015 Moscow Russia. **Tel** 011 95 285 1935. *Continues Vozhatyi, 0321-0642.*

ISSN 0821-3615
DD 051   CN

SUNRISE EXPRESS. [Sunr. express]. 1st Ed. (1983)-. Periodical. English. Twelve times a year. Pepper Wood, PO Box 185, West Hill Ontario M1E 4R4 Canada.

ISSN 1066-2898
DD 641   US

SUPER SNACK NEWS. See Home Economics.

ISSN 8750-1767
US

SUPER TEEN. (19??)-. Periodical. English. Six times a year. $11.95. Sterling Macfadden, 233 Park Avenue South, New York NY 10003. **Tel** (212)979-4800.

ISSN 0890-3573
DD 649   US
TITLE CHANGE

SURPRISES. [Surprises]. (198?)-(19??). Periodical. English. Surprises, 1200 North 7th Street, Minneapolis MN 55411. **Tel** 800 356-8899, (612)521-8090, FAX (612)522-1182. **ED** Jeanne Palmer and Peggy Simenson. **Ad Acc. Circ:** 100,000. *Continues Surprise Magazine. Continued by Children's Surprises.*
Desc: Includes activities, puzzles, games in reading, language arts, math, science and art. Non-fiction articles or stories about history, geography and animals are also included.

ISSN 1064-5977
DD 051   US

SWEET B'S PAD. (SWEET B'S PAD : GROWING FUN FOR AFRICAN AMERICAN CHILDREN.). [Sweet B's pad]. **VFOAT** Sweet Bee's Pad. Vol. 1, No. 1 (Jan. 1992)-. Periodical. English. Twelve times a year. $5.00. Sweet Bees' Pad, PO Box 30149, Washington DC 20030.

ISSN 0137-9321
UDC 329.78   PL

SWIAT MODYCH (WARSZAWA. 1949).
(SWIAT MODYCH.). [Swiat Mod. Warsz., 1949]. (1949)-. Newspaper. Polish. One time a week. $78.00. **(Subscription address:** Ars Polona-Ruch, PO Box 1001, Krakowskie Przedmiescie 7, 00-068 Warsaw Poland. **Tel** 011 48 22 261201.)

ISSN 0239-6653
UDC 51-8   PL

SZKIEKO I OKO. [Szkie. Oko]. (1983)-. Periodical. Polish. Twenty-four times a year. **(Subscription address:** Ars Polona-Ruch, PO Box 1001, Krakowskie Przedmiescie 7, 00-068 Warsaw Poland. **Tel** 011 48 22 261201.) *Continues Maa Delta, 0209-133X.*

ISSN 0557-9783
UDC 304(438)   PL
CODEN 327

SZTANDAR MODYCH. VFOAT SM. Sztandar Modych. (1950)-. Newspaper. Polish. Seven times a week. $130.00. **(Subscription address:** Ars Polona-Ruch, PO Box 1001, Krakowskie Przedmiescie 7, 00-068 Warsaw Poland. **Tel** 011 48 22 261201.)

ISSN 1043-4739
DD 741   US

TALES OF THE NINJA WARRIORS. [Tales Ninja warriors]. No. 1 (April 1988)-. Periodical. English. Twelve times a year. Kable News, 308 East Hitt Street, Mt Morris IL 61054. **Tel** (800)967-6572.

ISSN 0882-5424
DD 303   US

TAPORI (NEW YORK, N.Y.). (TAPORI.). [Tapori]. **Added/Corp** New, Int. International Movement ATD Fourth World. (19??)-. Newsletter. English (French). Twelve times a year. $7.00. Fourth World Movement, 7600 Willow Hill Drive, Landover MD 20785. **Tel** (301)336-9489, FAX (301)336-0092. **ED** S. Devins. **Circ:** 12,000 (ctrl).
Desc: Gives disadvantaged children a means of expression, and gives other children a means to learn about poverty, communicate and show their friendship.

NE

TAPTOE. (19??)-. Periodical. Dutch. Irregular (20 issues). FI34.55. Malmberg BV, PO Box 233 Leeghwaterlaan 16, 5223 BA Den Bosch Netherlands. **Tel** 011 31 73 288711, telex 50058.

LC AP   ISSN 0040-2001
DD 050   US

'TEEN. [Teen]. (1957)-. Periodical. English. Twelve times a year. $15.95. Petersen Publishing Company, 6420 Wilshire Boulevard, Los Angeles CA 90048. **Tel** (213)782-2485, FAX (213)782-2526. **(Subscription address:** Neodata / Colorado, PO Box 2606, Boulder CO 80322.) **ED** Robert MacLeod. **Ad Acc. Circ:** 338,500. available on microfilm and microfiche from University Microfilms International (UMI); available on an online database from DIALOG. Documents available from UMI Article Clearinghouse, Magazine Collection.
Desc: Covers the things girls want to know about -- guys, fashion, friends, movies, beauty tips, and more. Also featured are up-close looks at celebrities, horoscopes, quizzes, prizes, and more.
Ind/Abst Acad. Abstr. Full Text Elite; Acad. Abstr.; EP Collect.; Gen. Period. Index (1985-); Homework Help.; Mag. Artic. Summar. Elite; Mag. Artic. Summar. Select; Mag. Artic. Summar. CD-ROM; Mag. Index Plus (1989-); Mag. Index. Sel. (1986-); Mag. Search; MasterFile FullTEXT 1000; MasterFile FullTEXT 350; MasterFile FullTEXT 650; Mag. Search; Newsp. Period. Abstr. (1988-); OCLC; Pub. Lib. FullTEXT; Read. Guide Abstr. Select Ed.; Read. Guide Period. Lit.; Resource/One Ondisc (1988-); Telebase; Mag. Index (1959-); TOM Gen. Index (1985-) [Full Txt.].

LC NX   ISSN 1186-611X
DD 700/.835   CN

TEEN ARTS CONNECTION/TORONTO.
[Teen arts connect./Tor.]. **Added/Corp** Youth Communication/Toronto. (1990)-. English. Free. Youth Communication Toronto, Suite 208, 56 The Esplanade, Toronto Ontario M5V 2G9 Canada.

ISSN 0731-9991
US
SUSPENDED

TEEN BAG. (19??)-Suspended (199?). Periodical. English. Six times a year. Lopez Publications Inc., 152 Madison Avenue, Suite 905 & 906, New York NY 10016. **Tel** (212)689-3933.

ISSN 1056-0513
DD 051   US

TEEN BEAT. [Teen beat]. (19??)-. Periodical. English. Twelve times a year. $19.95. MacFadden Women's Group, 233 Park Avenue South, New York NY 10003. **Tel** (212)979-4800, (800)666-8783. **(Subscription address:** CDS Agency Hard Copy, PO Box 4966, Des Moines IA 50340. **Tel** (515)247-7569.)

ISSN 0747-4695
DD 791   US
CEASED

TEEN MACHINE. [Teen mach.]. (19??)-(Feb. 1994). Periodical. English. Sterling Macfadden, 233 Park Avenue South, New York NY 10003. **Tel** (212)979-4800.

ISSN 0735-6986
US

TEEN TIMES (WASHINGTON, D.C.).
(TEEN TIMES; MAGAZINE OF THE FUTURE HOMEMAKERS OF AMERICA.). **Added/Corp** Future Homemakers of America. (19??)-. Periodical. English. Four times a year (Jan., Mar., Sept., Nov.). $6.00. Future Homemakers of America, 1910 Association Drive, Reston VA 22091. **Tel** (703)476-4900.

ISSN 1074-7494
DD 305   US
Pr Rev.

●**TEEN VOICES.** [Teen voices]. **VFOAT** Teen Voices Magazine. (1993)-. Periodical. English. Four times a year (Mar., June, Sept., Dec.). $20.00. Women Express Inc., PO Box 6329, Boston MA 02114. **Tel** (617)262-2434, FAX (617)267-4653. **ED** Alison Amoroso (editor's address: 316 Huntington Avenue Boston MA 02115). Index available. cum. index. **Bk Rev**, (Qty: 2). **Ad Acc. Circ:** 30,000. *Continues Teen Voices Magazine.*
Desc: Addresses many issues such as sexism, racism, drug abuse and eating disorders through the voices of teenage girls around the country.

US
TITLE CHANGE

TEEN VOICES MAGAZINE. Added/Corp Women Express, Inc. **VFOAT** Teen Voices. (1992)-(199?). Periodical. English. Women Express Inc., PO Box 6329, Boston MA 02114. **Tel** (617)262-2434, FAX (617)267-4653. *Continues Teen Voices. Continued by Teen Voices (Boston, Mass. : 1993), 1074-7494.*

Children and Youth Interests

ISSN 1063-2492
US
CEASED
TEEN WORLD, THE MAGAZINE FOR TOMORROW'S LEADERS. (19??)-(19??).
English. Les and Joyce Lester, 299 Yates, Calumet City IL 60409. **Tel** (312)483-8808, FAX (312)874-0930. **ED** Les Lester. **Circ:** 1000 (ctrl).
Desc: Spotlights positive inner-city youth role models, acts as a self-help guide for teens and promotes a leadership mentality among youth.

US
TEENAGE CHRISTIAN. See Religions and Theology.

ISSN 0890-4006
DD 248 US
Pr Rev.
TEENQUEST. (TEENQUEST : TQ.). [Teenquest]. **VFOAT** Teen Quest; TQ. (198?)-. Periodical. English. Ten times a year (July/Aug. issues combined). $14.50. Shephard Ministries, 2845 West Airport Freeway, Suite 137, Irving TX 75062. **Tel** (214)570-7599. **ED** Chris Lyon. **Bk Rev**. **Ad Acc**, **Adv Mgr:** Mike Stephens, **Tel** (214)570-7597. **Circ:** 50,000. *Continues Young Ambassador, 0044-071X.*
Desc: A Bible centered magazine geared to reaching our teenagers.

ISSN 1059-3764
US
TEENSCOPE MAGAZINE. **VFOAT** Teenscope. (1992)-. Periodical. English. Twelve times a year. $12.00. Andre Gray, PO Box 06555, Chicago IL 60606-5555.

ISSN 0820-3334
DD 791.45/75 CN
TELE DES ENFANTS, LA. See Communications-Television and Cable.

ISSN 1058-7136
DD 808 US
TELLTALES (STERLING, VA.). (TELLTALES : A LITERARY JOURNAL WRITTEN BY KIDS FOR KIDS.). [Telltales]. Vol. 1, No. 1 (Fall 1991)-. Periodical. English. Four times a year. $15.95. Telltale Publishing, 3 Crisswell Court, Sterling VA 22170. **Tel** (800)322-8253.
Desc: Literary journal for children in grades 1-3, 85% of work published is childrens.

ISSN 1049-474X
DD 051 US
TEXAS TEEN!. [Tex. teen]. (Summer 1991)-. Periodical. English. Twelve times a year. $15.95. Texas Teen Inc., PO Box 5787, Denton TX 76203.

ISSN 1200-2305
DD 051 CN
TG MAGAZINE (1992). (TG MAGAZINE.). [TG mag.]. **VFOAT** Edge; Today's Generation Magazine; Contact Avenir. Vol. 52, No. 5 (Oct. 1992)-. Periodical. English (summaries and/or abstracts in French). Four times a year. 46.8Can$. TG, 347 Bay Street, Suite 800, Toronto Ontario M5H 2R3 Canada. **Tel** (416)777-2590. *Continues TG, 0843-4557.*

ISSN 1121-2357
IT
TGN. TUTTOGIOVANI NOTIZIE. [TGN, Tuttogiov. not.]. **VFOAT** Tuttogiovani Notizie. (1986)-. Periodical. Italian. Four times a year. L22490. Editrice Las, Piazza dell Ateneo Salesiano 1, 00139 Rome Italy. **Tel** 011 872 90 626, FAX 06 872 90 629.
Ind/Abst Soc. Plann. Policy Dev. Abstr.

ISSN 0342-7145
GW
UDC 37.013.42
THEORIE UND PRAXIS DER SOZIALPADAGOGIK. See Religions and Theology.

ISSN 0040-7380
US
TIGER BEAT. (1965)-. Periodical. English. Six times a year. $14.95. Sterling Macfadden, 233 Park Avenue South, New York NY 10003. **Tel** (212)979-4800. **Ad Acc**. *Continues Lloyd Thaxton's Tiger Beat.*

ISSN 0165-0890
NE
TIKKER. (19??)-. Periodical. Dutch. Four times a year. $21.49. Wolters Noordhoff BV, Postbus 567, 9700 AN Groningen Netherlands. **Tel** 011 31 50 226886, FAX 011 31 50 264866.
Desc: Magazine for youth literature.

II
TINKLE. (19??)-. English (Hindi and Assamese). Twenty-four times a year. Rs12.00 India. India Book House Pty Ltd, 412 Tulsiani Chambers, Nariman Point, Bombay 400 021 India. **Tel** (22)240606, telex 116297. **ED** Anant Pai. **Ad Acc**. **Circ:** 85,000.
Desc: To make education, particularly science, history and geography interesting to children.

ISSN 0256-6095
SA
UDC 57
TOKTOKKIE AFRIKAANSE ED. See Environmental Issues-Conservation and Natural Resources.

ISSN 1068-865X
DD 051 US
TOMORROW'S MORNING. [Tomorrow's morning]. (1992)-. Periodical. English. One time a week (published on Monday). $29.95. Tomorrow's Morning, 11466 San Vicente Boulevard, Los Angeles CA 90049. **Tel** (310)826-5187. **(Subscription address:** Neodata / Colorado, PO Box 2606, Boulder CO 80322. **)**

ISSN 0844-5818
DD 784.1/006/0713541 CN
TORONTO CHILDREN'S CHORUS. See Music.

LC G
DD 910 US
●**TRAILBLAZERS OF THE WILD WEST.** (1995)-. Monographic series. English. Irregular. $89.70. Enslow Publishers Inc., 44 Fadem Road, Box 699, Springfield NJ 07081-0699. **Tel** (201)379-8890, FAX (201)379-0699.
Desc: For teen readers. Covers information on groups who were important in American history.

US
TRANSCEND. (19??)-. English. Four times a year. $5.00. Paywoods Enterprises, 4 Daniels Farm Road, Suite 134, Trumbull CT 06611. **Tel** (203)372-1745. **ED** Quentin J Plair. **Ad Acc**. **Circ:** 5,000 (ctrl).
Desc: African American teens, motivational articles and entertainment news.

ISSN 0177-4719
GW
UDC 087.5
TREFF. [Treff]. **VFOAT** Treff-Schulermagazin. (1974)-. Academic Scholarly Publication. German. Twelve times a year. DM53.40 Germany; DM60.00 other. Velber Verlag GmbH, Im Brande 1, D-30926 Seelze Germany. **Tel** 011 49 5137 878602. **ED** Detlef Kersten.

ISSN 0041-2279
BE
UDC (024.7)
TREMPLIN AVERBODE. (1961)-. Periodical. French (Dutch). One time a week. $80.97. Editions Presse Europeenne, BP 54, 3281 Averbode Belgium. **Tel** 011 32 13 773311, FAX 011 32 13 777243, telex 39104. *Continues Petits Belges. Tremplin, 0773-0330.*

ISSN 1043-5999
US
TULSA KIDS. (1988)-. Periodical. English. Twelve times a year. Tulsa Kids, PO Box 52037, Tulsa OK 74152-0037.

ISSN 0191-3654
US
TURTLE MAGAZINE FOR PRESCHOOL KIDS. **VFOAT** Turtle. (Dec. 1979)-. Periodical. English. Irregular (8 times a year). $15.95. Benjamin Franklin Literary and Medical Society, 1100 Waterway Lane, Indianapolis IN 46206. **Tel** (317)636-8881, FAX (317)637-0126. **ED** Beth Wood Thomas. **Ad Acc**. **Circ:** 350,000.
Desc: For ages two to five. Entertaining stories, poems, games and activities to promote better health habits.
Ind/Abst EP Collect.; Homework Help.; MasterFile FullTEXT 1000; MasterFile FullTEXT 350; MasterFile FullTEXT 650; MasterFile FullTEXT (July 1994-); Prim. Search; Pub. Lib. FullTEXT; Telebase.

ISSN 1056-2567
DD 789 US
TUTTI FRUTTI. See Music.

ISSN 0895-9471
DD 051 bUS
U.S. KIDS. [U. S. kids]. **VFOAT** US Kids; USKids; U S Kids; U.S.Kids. (1987)-. Periodical. English. Eight times a year. $18.95. Benjamin Franklin Literary and Medical Society, 1100 Waterway Boulevard, Indianapolis IN 46206. **Tel** (317)636-8881, FAX (317)637-0126. **Ad Acc**.
Desc: Written for children between the ages of five and 12 years of age. Presents information about real people, places, and things.
Ind/Abst Child. Mag. Guide; EP Collect.; Homework Help.; Mag. Search; MasterFile FullTEXT 1000; MasterFile FullTEXT 350; MasterFile FullTEXT 650; MasterFile FullTEXT (July 1993-); Mid. Search; OCLC; Prim. Search; Pub. Lib. FullTEXT; Telebase.

ISSN 0044-1384
CN
Pr Rev.
UNAK (TORONTO). (IUNAK YUNAK.). [Unak]. **Added/Corp** Plast. **VFOAT** Yunak; Yunak Magazine. Vol. 1 (1963)-. Periodical. Ukrainian. Six times a year (Jan., Mar., May, July, Sept., Dec.). 28.01Can$. Plast Publishing, 2199 Bloor Street West, Toronto Ontario M6S 1N2 Canada. **Tel** (416)769-7855, FAX (416)763-0185. **ED** Mr. Yuri Monchak (phone: (514)725-8626). **Circ:** 1,200.
Desc: For children between the ages of 12 and 17.

ISSN 1065-5913
DD 289 US
UNITED YOUTH DIGEST. See Religions and Theology-Other Religions, Sects and Cults.

AG
VAMOS!. **VFOAT** Vamos al Tiempo Joven. (1976)-. Periodical. Spanish. Ediciones Tiempo Joven, Av Rivadavia 8836, Buenos Aires Argentina.

ISSN 0300-6379
US
CEASED
VESELKA. **Added/Corp** Ukrainian National Association. **VFOAT** Rainbow. (1954)-(June 1995). Periodical. Ukrainian. Svoboda, 30 Montgomery Street, PO Box 346, Jersey City NJ 07302. **Tel** (201)434-0237.

ISSN 0504-0523
RU
VESELYE KARTINKI. **Added/Corp** Vsesoiuznyi Leninskii Kommunisticheskii Soiuz Molodezhi. Tsentralnyi Komitet. (19??)-. Periodical. Russian. Twelve times a year. $89.95. Izdatelstvo Molodaia Gvardiia, Novodmitrovskaya Ulitsa 5A, 125015 Moscow Russia. **Tel** 011 95 285 1935. **(Subscription address:** East View Publications Inc., 3020 Harbor Lane North, Suite 110, Minneapolis MN 55447. **Tel** (800)477-1005, (612)550-0961, FAX (612)559-2931.**)**

ISSN 0315-3975
CN
SUSPENDED
VIDEO-PRESSE. [Video-presse]. (Oct. 1971)-Suspended (June 1995). Periodical. French. Ten times a year (publishes monthly except July and Aug.). Video Presse, 3965 boulevard Henri-Bourassa E, Montreal Quebec H1H 1L1 Canada. **Tel** (514)322-7341, FAX (514)322-4281. **ED** Pierre Claude. Index available. cum. index. **Bk Rev**. **Ad Acc**. **Circ:** 25,000.
Desc: A magazine of general information for youth.
Ind/Abst Can. Period. Index (19??-); Repere (1983-).

LC HQ799.V5 V53
DD 301.43/15/09597 VM
VIETNAM YOUTH. **Added/Corp** Hoi Lien Thanh Nien Viet Nam. Hoi Lien Hiep Sinh Vien Viet-Nam. (19??)-. English (French). Irregular. Vietnam Youth Federation, Vietnam National Union of Students, 64 Ba Trieu Street, Hanoi Vietnam.

LC E148.S65 V6
DD 325.243670973
ISSN 0042-8256
US
VOICE OF YOUTH (CHICAGO, ILL.), THE. (VOICE OF YOUTH.). [Voice youth]. **VFOAT** Mladinski List. (1922)-. Periodical. English. Eleven times a year (monthly except Jan. - Feb.). Slovene National Benefit Society, 166 Shore Drive, Burr Ridge IL 60521. **Tel** (312)887-7660. **ED** Louise Hegner. ctrl circ.
Desc: Composed of articles submitted by the Juvenile members of our organization in an effort to hold their interest during the younger years. Submissions include drawings, jokes, essays and other material suitable for publication.

LC Z718.5 .V65
DD 027.62/605
ISSN 0160-4201
US
VOICE OF YOUTH ADVOCATES. See Library and Information Sciences.

US
VOILA. (19??)-. English (French). Eight times a year. $16.50 US; $19.50 other. Midwest European Publication, 8220 North Christiana Avenue, Skokie IL 60076. **Tel** (708)676-1196, FAX (800)433-9229, telex 256262. available on audiocassette from the publisher.
Desc: Full color magazine for children grades K-2. Contains songs, puzzles, cartoons, and many more.

ISSN 1050-2580
DD 741 US
WALT DISNEY'S GOOFY ADVENTURES. [Walt Disney's Goofy adventures]. **VFOAT** Goofy Adventures. (June 1990)-. Periodical. English. Twelve times a year. $18.00. Walt Disney Publishing Inc., 500 South Buena Vista Street, Burbank CA 91521. **Tel** (212)807-5816.

ISSN 0895-285X
DD 052 US
WALT DISNEY'S MICKEY MOUSE MAGAZINE. [Walt Disney's Mickey Mouse mag.]. **VFOAT** Mickey Mouse Magazine. (Winter 1988)-. Periodical. English. Four times a year. $12.50. Welsh Publishing Group Inc., 300 Madison Avenue, New York NY 10017. **Tel** (212)687-0680, FAX (212)986-5849. **(Subscription address:** CDS Agency Hard Copy, PO Box 4966, Des Moines IA 50340. **Tel** (515)247-7569.**)** **Circ:** 450,000.

ISSN 1055-6907
DD 808 US
WEB (SANTA CRUZ, CALIF.), THE. See Literature.

ISSN 0899-6121
US
WEEKLY READER. SUMMER EDITION C. **VFOAT** Summer Edition C. (198?)-. Periodical. English. Twenty-six times a year. Field Publications, 4343

Children and Youth Interests

Equity Drive, Columbus OH 43216. **Tel** (800)456-8220. ***Continues*** Weekly Reader. Summer Edition, Gr. 3-5, 0894-7449.

CN

●**WILD.** (1995)-. Periodical. English. Eight times a year. 25.00Can$ Canada; 33.00Can$ other. Canadian Wildlife Federation, 2740 Queensview Drive, Ottawa Ontario K2B 1A2 Canada. **Tel** (514)323-6800, , **FAX** (514)327-0602. Index available. ***Continues*** Ranger Rick (Ottawa).

ISSN 0043-5937
US

WINNER (WASHINGTON, D.C.), THE. (THE WINNER.). [Winner]. **Added/Corp** Narcotics Education, inc. (19??)-. Periodical. English. Nine times a year. $8.97. Review and Herald Publishing Association, 55 West Oak Ridge Drive, Hagerstown MD 21740. **Tel** (301)791-7000 ext. 2534, **FAX** (301)790-9734. **ED** Barbara Wetherell. **Circ:** 30,000.
 Desc: Activity book for children in grades 4-8 which uses stories, games, and puzzles to try to teach drug prevention in a fun, positive way.

ISSN 0296-8576
FR

WINNIE. [Winnie]. (1985)-. Periodical. French. Twelve times a year. $70.86. Edimonde Loisirs, 90 rue de Flandre, 75947 Paris Cedex 19 France. **Tel** 011 33 1 44894489. **Circ:** 95,000.

ISSN 1072-4958
US

●**WINSOME WAY MAGAZINE FOR CHILDREN.** (WINSOME WAY MAGAZINE FOR CHILDREN : THE SMART WAY TO HAVE FUN.). **VFOAT** Winsome Way; Winsome Way, Children's Magazine. (1993)-. Periodical. English. Six times a year. $21.75. Winsome Way Children's Magazine, PO Box 769282, Holcombe Bridge Station, Atlanta GA 30076. **Tel** (404)551-9565.

ISSN 0279-361X
US
SUSPENDED

WOMBAT (ATHENS, GA.). (WOMBAT.). Vol. 1 (Sept./Oct. 1979)-Suspended (19??). Periodical. English. Eight times a year. Wombat, PO Box 8088, Athens GA 30603. **Tel** (706)549-4875. **ED** Jacquelin Howe. **Bk Rev. Ad Acc. Circ:** 1,000 (ctrl).
 Desc: Presents creative works (poetry, short stories, nonfiction, artwork, illustrations, cartoons, etc.) by and for young people aged 6-16. Intended to encourage reading, writing, drawing and painting.

US

WONDERSCIENCE : FUN PHYSICAL SCIENCE ACTIVITIES FOR CHILDREN AND ADULTS TO DO TOGETHER. See Science and Technology.

SZ

WORLD SCOUTING NEWS. (19??)-. English. Six times a year. 30.00F. World Scout Bureau, Box 241, 1211 Geneva 4 Switzerland. **Tel** 011 4122 204233, **FAX** 011 4122 7812053, telex 845-4281 39.

LC HQ793 .W7

US

WORLD YOUTH. Added/Corp World Federation of Democratic Youth. (1946)-. Periodical. English. Four times a year. $10.00. World Youth, PO Box 147, 1389 Budapest Hungary. **Tel** 011 36 1 1154095.

ISSN 0707-2279
CN
DD 248.8/2/05

WORLDWIND. Vol. 1 (Fall 1978)-. Periodical. English. Two times a year. Division of Communication, United Church of Canada, 85 Saint Clair Avenue East, Toronto Ontario M4T 1M5 Canada. **Tel** (416)925-5931. **ED** Rebekah Chevalier. **Circ:** 10,000 (ctrl).
 Desc: Children's magazine for ages 6 to 9.

ISSN 0701-8894
CN
DD 028.5

YA HOTLINE. (Y-A HOTLINE.). **Added/Corp** Dalhousie University. School of Library Service. **VFOAT** Y A Hotline. **VAT** Young Adult Hotline; Hotline (Halifax). (1977)-. Periodical. English. Irregular. 10.00Can$ Canada; 13.00Can$ US; 17.00Can$ other. Dalhousie University / School of Library & Information Studies, Halifax Nova Scotia B3H 4H8 Canada. **Tel** (902)494-3656, **FAX** (902)494-2451, telex 019-21863. **ED** Larry Amey. Index available. cum. index. **Bk Rev. Ad Acc. Circ:** 450 (ctrl).
 Desc: Literature and social issues of interest and applicability to young adults (teenagers).

LC AG103
DD 028

ISSN 0888-5745
US

YELLOW BRICK ROAD (ROCHESTER, N.Y.). See Library and Information Sciences.

LC AP201 .C18
DD 051

ISSN 0888-5842
US

YM. [YM]. **VFOAT** Young & Modern; Young and Modern. Vol. 34, No. 2 (March 1986)-. Periodical. English. Ten times a year. $18.00. Gruner & Jahr AG & Co. / US, 685 Third Avenue, 23rd Floor, New York NY 10017. **Tel** (212)599-4040. (**Subscription address:** CDS Agency Hard Copy, PO Box 4966, Des Moines IA 50340. **Tel** (515)247-7569.) **ED** Bonnie Hurowitz-Fuller. **Ad Acc. Circ:** 925,000. available on microfilm and microfiche from University Microfilms International (UMI). Documents available from UMI Article Clearinghouse. ***Continues*** Young Miss Magazine, 0886-7453.
 Desc: A beauty/fashion book for teen girls 12-19. It strives to help with the unique problems teenagers face.
 Ind/Abst Child. Mag. Guide (1986-); EP Collect.; Homework Help.; Mag. Artic. Summar. Elite; Mag. Artic. Summar. Select; Mag. Artic. Summar. CD-ROM; Mag. Search; MasterFile FullTEXT 1000; MasterFile FullTEXT 350; MasterFile FullTEXT 650; MasterFile FullTEXT (July 1989-); Mid. Search; Newsp. Period. Abstr. (1992-); OCLC; Pub. Lib. FullTEXT; Telebase; Vocat. Search.

ISSN 0897-7704
US
DD 793

YO YO TIMES. [Yo Yo times]. **VFOAT** YoYo Times; Yo-Yo Times. No. 1 (Spring 1988)-. Periodical. English. Four times a year. $12.00. Creative Communications, PO Box 1519-EBS, Herndon VA 22070. **Tel** (710)742-9696. **ED** Stuart Crump Jr. **Bk Rev. Ad Acc.** ctrl circ.

ISSN 1075-3656
US
DD 051

●**YOUNG ADULT PRESS.** (YOUNG ADULT PRESS : YAP.). [Young adult press]. **VFOAT** YAP. (March 1994)-. Periodical. English. Twelve times a year. Free. Young Adult Press, Box 21, Mound MN 55364. ***Continues*** Midwest Teen Scene.

SI
Pr Rev.

YOUNG GENERATION. (19??)-. English (Chinese). Twelve times a year. 19.20Sing$ Singapore; 36.60Sing$ Malaysia; 39.60Sing$ Thailand, Australia and Honk Kong; 46.80Sing$ other. EPB Publishers Pte. Ltd., Bukit Merah Central #043545, Singapore 0315 Singapore. **Tel** 011 65 2780881, **FAX** 011 65 278456. **ED** Jasmit Kaur & Koih Swee Yang. **Ad Acc. Circ:** 39,000.

LC AP222 .Y73
DD 296

ISSN 0044-0817
US

YOUNG JUDAEAN. See Religions and Theology-Judaism.

ISSN 0738-887X
US
SUSPENDED

YOUNG PEOPLE TODAY. Suspended with Vol. 7, No. 4 (Oct. 1989). Periodical. English. Six times a year. $9.95 US; $12.95 Canada. Young People Today, PO Box 3141, Culver City CA 90231.

ISSN 0300-3264
AT

YOUNG SOLDIER. (THE YOUNG SOLDIER.). **Added/Corp** Salvation Army. (1890)-. Periodical. English. One time a week. 30.00Aus$. Salvation Army / Australia, The Editorial Department, 1-9 Drill Street, PO Box 137, Hawthorn Victoria 3122 Australia. **Tel** (03)819 4864. **Bk Rev.** ctrl circ.
 Desc: A Christian newspaper for children.

ISSN 0162-2692
US

YOUNG SPARTACUS. (19??)-. Periodical. English. Twelve times a year. $2.00. Spartacus Youth Publishing Co., Box 825 Canal Street Station, New York NY 10013. available on microfilm from University Microfilms International (UMI).

ISSN 0196-092X
US

YOUNG SUPERSTARS. (1979)-. Periodical. English. Twelve times a year. Young Superstars, PO Box 36524, Grosse Pointe MI 48236.

ISSN 1046-8404
US
DD 372

YOUNG VOICES (OLYMPIA, WASH.). (YOUNG VOICES.). [Young voices]. (1988)-. Periodical. English. Six times a year (Jan., Mar., May, July, Sept., Nov.). $15.00. Young Voices, PO Box 2321, Olympia WA 98507. **Tel** (206)357-4683. **ED** Char Simons. **Bk Rev** (Qty: 10/year). **Ad Acc. Circ:** 3,000.
 Desc: Features stories, poems, essays and drawings by elementary through high school age children.

ISSN 0989-733X
FR
UDC 087.5

YOUPI PARIS. (YOUPI.). (1988)-. Periodical. French. Twelve times a year. $94.05. Bayard Presse, Svc Client, 3 rue Bayard, Department 2, 75393 Paris Cedex 08 France. **Tel** 011 33 1 44355907, **FAX** 011 33 1 44356025.

LC NOT IN LC
DD 639

ISSN 0886-5299
US

YOUR BIG BACKYARD. [Your big backyard]. **Added/Corp** National Wildlife Federation. (1980)-. Periodical. English. Twelve times a year. $14.00. National Wildlife Federation / Virginia, 8925 Leesburg Pike, Vienna VA 22184. **Tel** (703)790-4000, (800)822-9919, **FAX** (703)442-7332. **ED** Gerald Bishop and Sallie Luther.
 Circ: 600,000 (ctrl).
 Desc: Preschoolers and beginning readers 3-5 develop letter, number and conceptual skills while learning about animals, nature and conservation. Big up-close photos and illustrations accompany the stories, games, poetry, and simple crafts.
 Ind/Abst Child. Mag. Guide (1981-).

ISSN 0262-9798
UK

YOUTH AND POLICY. Vol. 1, No. 1 (1982)-. Periodical. English. Four times a year (Jan., Apr., July and Oct.). $78.72. Youth and Policy, 10 Lady Beatrice Terrace, Tyne and Wear DH4 4NE United Kingdom. **ED** M Banim. Index available. cum. index. **Bk Rev. Ad Acc. Circ:** 1,000 (ctrl).
 Ind/Abst Curr. Cit.; Sage Race Relat. Abstr.; Sociol. Educ. Abstr.; Stud. Women Abstr.; Tech. Educ. Train. Abstr.

ISSN 0190-4566
US

YOUTH LEADER (SPRINGFIELD, MO.), THE. See Religions and Theology.

LC HV
DD 362
UDC 362.8

ISSN 0294-7579
AT

YOUTH LINK. [Youth link]. **VFOAT** Youthlink. (1979)-. Newsletter. English (French). Four times a year. South Pacific Commission, PO Box D5, Noumea Cedex New Caledonia. **Tel** 011 687 262000, **FAX** 011 687 263818.
 Desc: Newsletter of the Youth & Adult Education programme reporting news from Youth Ministries, meetings, and agencies.

ISSN 0279-6651
US
DD 259

YOUTH (PASADENA, CALIF.). (YOUTH ...). [Youth]. **Added/Corp** Worldwide Church of God. (Jan. 1981)-. Periodical. English. Six times a year (Jan., Mar., May, Jul., Sept., Nov.). $9.95. Worldwide Church of God, 300 West Green Street, Pasadena CA 91123. **Tel** (818)304-6077, (800)309-4466, **FAX** (818)792-5106. **ED** Mike Bennett. **Photos. Circ:** 38,000.
 Desc: Dedicated to showing teenagers that God's way of life is relevant, interesting and helpful to today's teens.

ISSN 0894-4377
US
DD 796

YOUTH SPORTS. See Sports and Games.

LC GN301
DD 305.235

ISSN 1038-2569
AT

YOUTH STUDIES AUSTRALIA. Added/Corp National Clearinghouse for Youth Studies. (Autumn 1992)-. Periodical. English. Four times a year (Mar., June, Sept., Dec.). 60.00Aus$. National Clearinghouse for Youth Studies, GPO Box 252C, Center Education, Hobart Tasmania 7001 Australia. **Tel** 011 61 2 202591, **FAX** 011 61 2 202578. **ED** Sheila Allison. Index available. cum. index. **Circ:** 1,400. ***Continues*** Youth Studies.
 Desc: Interdisciplinary journal on youth related issues.
 Ind/Abst APAIS, Aust. Public Aff. Inf. Ser. (1992-); EP Collect.; Homework Help.; MasterFile FullTEXT 1000; MasterFile FullTEXT 350; MasterFile FullTEXT 650; MasterFile FullTEXT (Jan. 1994-); Telebase; World Mag. Bank.

LC PN3157 .Y68
DD 792/.0226/05
Pr Rev.

ISSN 0892-9092
US

YOUTH THEATRE JOURNAL. See Theater.

ISSN 0713-3634
CN
DD 268/.433/05

YOUTHS & ADULTS TOGETHER. See Religions and Theology.

HK

YOUTH'S WEEKLY. (19??)-. Newspaper. Chinese. One time a week. 172.10Can$.

US

YOUTHVIEWS. (19??)-. Newsletter. English. Ten times a year. $38.00. Gallup International Institute, 47 Hulfish Street, Princeton NJ 08542. **Tel** (609)921-6200, **FAX** (609)924-0228. **ED** Wendy Plump.
 Desc: Newsletter of the Gallup Youth Survey.

US

YOUTHWALK. (19??)-. Periodical. English. Twelve times a year. $15.00. Focus on the Family, Colorado Springs CO 80995. **Tel** (800)232-6459.

ISSN 0747-3486
US

YOUTHWORKER JOURNAL. See Religions and Theology.

LC HQ799.I5 Y85
DD 301.43/15/0954

II

YUVA BHARATI. Added/Corp Vivekananda Rock Memorial Committee. Vol. 1 (Aug. 1973)-. Periodical. English. Four times a year. Vivekananda Kendra Prakashan, 3 Singarachari Street, Triplicane Madras 600005 India.

Children and Youth Interests

LC TX336 .P46
DD 640/.73/05
ISSN 1050-8163
US
ZILLIONS (MOUNT VERNON, N.Y.). (ZILLIONS.). [Zillions]. **Added/Corp** Consumers Union of United States. Vol. 1, No. 1 (Aug./Sept. 1990)-. Periodical. English. Six times a year. $16.00. Consumers Union, 101 Truman Avenue, Yonkers NY 10703. **Tel** (800)288-7898, (914)378-2000, FAX (914)378-2900. **(Subscription address:** Neodata / Colorado, PO Box 2606, Boulder CO 80322.) available on microfilm and microfiche from University Microfilms International (UMI). **Continues** Penny Power, 0190-1966.
Desc: Magazine for 8-to-14-year-olds that evaluates toys, games, food and other products kids use, and provides advice on consumer and life-style problems kids face.
Ind/Abst Child. Mag. Guide (1990-); EP Collect.; Foods Adlibra; Homework Help.; Mag. Artic. Summar. Elite; Mag. Artic. Summar. Select; Mag. Artic. Summar. CD-ROM; Mag. Search; MasterFile FullTEXT 1000; MasterFile FullTEXT 350; MasterFile FullTEXT 650; MasterFile FullTEXT (July 1990-); Mid. Search; OCLC; Prim. Search; Pub. Lib. FullTEXT; Telebase.

ABSTRACTING, BIBLIOGRAPHIES AND STATISTICS

LC Z1037 .B545
DD 028.52
US
BEST BOOKS FOR CHILDREN : A CATALOG OF ... TITLES. 7th Ed. (1967)-. Catalog. English. One time a year. $48.00. R.R. Bowker, A Reed Reference Publishing Company, Part of Reed International PLC, PO Box 31, 121 Chanlon Drive, New Providence NJ 07974. **Tel** (908)464-6800, (800)521-8110, FAX (908)665-6688, telex 138-755. **ED** M. C. Turner. available on CD-ROM from R.R. Bowker. **Continues** Catalog of ... the Best Books for Children.
Desc: A listing of 15,000 titles, each with two or three recommendations from other journals.

DD 011
ISSN 1064-0541
US
CHILDREN'S BOOK BAG, THE. [Child. book bag]. **Added/Corp** Foundation for Children's Books. Vol. 1 (Summer 1985)-. Periodical. English. Four times a year. $25.00 (individual membership), $40.00 (institutional membership). Foundation for Children's Books, 30 Common Street, Watertown MA 02172. **Tel** (617)926-8190, FAX (617)965-8184. **Bk Rev**.
Desc: Up-to-date bibliography of quality childrens literature.

LC Z1037.A1 C482
DD 028.52
ISSN 0069-3480
US
CHILDREN'S BOOKS IN PRINT (NEW YORK). (CHILDREN'S BOOKS IN PRINT.). **Added/Corp** R.R. Bowker Company. (1969)-. English. One time a year. $145.00 (2 volume set). R.R. Bowker, A Reed Reference Publishing Company, Part of Reed International PLC, PO Box 31, 121 Chanlon Drive, New Providence NJ 07974. **Tel** (908)464-6800, (800)521-8110, FAX (908)665-6688, telex 138-755. available on magnetic tape and CD-ROM; available on an online database (File no.470) from DIALOG; and BRS. **Supersedes** Children's Books for Schools and Libraries.
Desc: Contains information on children's books that are indexed by title, author and illustrator.

LC Z1039
DD 013
US
CHILDREN'S BOOKS IN PRINT. SUBJECT GUIDE. See Literature-Abstracting, Bibliographies and Statistics.

LC Z
DD 028.5
UK
CHILDREN'S BOOKS OF THE YEAR. See Publishing-Books and Bookmaking.

LC HS3260.U5 D57
DD 369.4/02573
ISSN 1044-4440
US
DIRECTORY OF AMERICAN YOUTH ORGANIZATIONS. [Dir. Am. youth organ.]. (1983)-. Directory. English. Every 2 years. $18.95. Free Spirit Publishing Inc, 400 1st Avenue North, Suite 616, Minneapolis MN 55401-1724. **Tel** (612)338-2068, FAX (612)337-5207. **ED** Judith B Erickson. Index available. **Circ:** 5,000.
Desc: A guide to over 400 clubs, groups, troups, teams, societies, lodges and more for young people.

DD 051
ISSN 0822-8450
CN
GETTING THERE (BURLINGTON, ONT.). (GETTING THERE.). [Getting there]. Vol. 1, Issue 3 (Jan. 1983)-. English (French). Four times a year. Free. The Bank of Nova Scotia, PO Box 4071 Station A, Toronto Ontario M5W 1H8 Canada. **Tel** (416)866-5776. **Circ:** 160,000. **Continues** Getting There with Scotiabank, 0821-4018.
Desc: Valuable learning about participation in recreation, sports, the arts, the development of life skills and the key steps to financial responsibility for youths age six to sixteen.

DD 054/.1
ISSN 0822-8469
CN
HORIZON JEUNESSE. [Horiz. jeun.]. Vol. 1, No. 3 (Jan. 1983)-. Periodical. French. Twelve times a year. Banque de Nouvelle-Ecosse, 44 King Street West, Toronto Ontario M5H 1H1 Canada. **Continues** Horizon Jeunesse Bne, 0821-4026.

CIVIL DEFENSE

LC HV555.J3 A537
DD 363.34809
JA
AICHI-KEN CHIIKI BOSAI KEIKAKU. FUZOKU SHIRYO. Added/Corp Aichi Bosai Kaigi. (1963)-. Japanese. Aichi Bosai Kaigi, 1-ban 2-go Sannomaru, 3-chome Naku-ku, Nagoya Japan.

LC UA929.N2 A7
ISSN 0920-3168
NE
ALERT / REDACTIONELE VERANTWOORDELIJKHEID VAN HET MINISTERIE VAN BINNENLANDSE ZAKEN. Added/Corp Netherlands. Ministerie van Binnenlandse Zaken. (May/June 1984)-. Periodical. Dutch. Eleven times a year. F89.63. Haagse Drukkerij & Uitg Mij, PO Box 43250, 2504 AG Den Haag Netherlands. **Tel** 011 31 70 3218218.

LC HV555.U62 V53a
DD 353.97550075/4/06
US
ANNUAL REPORT / COMMONWEALTH OF VIRGINIA, DES, DEPARTMENT OF EMERGENCY SERVICES. Main/Corp Virginia. Dept. of Emergency Services. (1984/1985)-. English. Virginia Office of Emergency & Energy Service, Richmond VA 23219. **Continues** Annual Report.

DD 363
ISSN 0001-2165
US
Pr Rev.
APCO BULLETIN, THE. [APCO bull.]. **Added/Corp** Associated Public-Safety Communications Officers. **VFOAT** Journal of Public-Safety Communications. **VAT** Associated Public Safety Communications Officers Bulletin. (19??)-. Trade Publication. English. Twelve times a year. $100.00. Association of Public Safety Communications Officers, 2040 S Ridgewood Ave, Suite 104, South Daytona FL 32119-2257. **Tel** (904)322-2500. **ED** Alan Chase. Index available. cum. index. **Ad Acc. Circ:** 9,750 (ctrl). available on microfilm; available on microfiche; available on CD-ROM; available on an online database.
Desc: News and features on public safety communications, from law enforcement and fire departments, civil defense, 9-1-1- centers. Stories on power supplies, antennas, and recording devices.

US
AWARE. Added/Corp United States. National Weather Service. United States. National Oceanic and Atmospheric Administration. (Jan. 1990)-. Periodical. English. Four times a year. US Department of Commerce / National Weather Service, 1325 East-West Highway, Room 18130, Silver Spring MD 20912. **Tel** (301)713-0689, FAX (301)713-0610. **Continues** Disaster Preparedness Report.

LC UA926.A1 Z18
DD 363.3/5/0943
GW
BEVOELKERUNGSSCHUTZ : MAGAZIN FUER ZIVIL- UND KATASTROPHENSCHUTZ. Added/Corp Bundesverband fuer den Selbstschutz. Vol. 8 (1989)-. Periodical. German. Twelve times a year. DM32.80. Bundesverband Selbstschutz, Postfach 200161, D 53131 Bonn Germany. **Tel** 011 49 2289400, telex 812370. **(Subscription address:** Druckhaus Coburg GmBH, Postfach 1525, D 96045 Coburg Germany. **Tel** 011 49 9561 86350.) **Continues** Zivilschutz Magazin, 0173-7872.

LC UA928.M4 M37a
DD 353.9/744/00755
ISSN 0097-7543
US
BIENNIAL REPORT OF THE MASSACHUSETTS CIVIL DEFENSE AGENCY AND OFFICE OF EMERGENCY PREPAREDNESS TO THE GOVERNOR AND GENERAL COURT. Main/Corp Massachusetts. Civil Defense Agency and Office of Emergency Preparedness. (1974)-. English. Every 2 years. Civil Defense Agency and Office of Emergency Preparedness, 400 Worcester Road, Framingham MA 01701.

JA
BOSAI ROPPO. Main/Corp Japan. **Added/Corp** Japan. Shobocho. Bosai Kyukyuka. Japan. Shobocho. Bosaika. (19??)-. Periodical. Japanese. ¥2500. Zenkoku Kajo Horei Shuppan Company Ltd., Dai 1 Zenkoku Biru 18 Saneicho, Shinjukuku Tokyo 160 Japan.

ISSN 0253-9349
LE
NLM W1 RE156UQT
BULLETIN / CROIX-ROUGE LIBANAISE. [Bull. - Croix-Rouge liban.]. **Main/Corp** Croix-Rouge Libanaise. Bulletin. French. Twelve times a year. La Croix-Rouge, 95 Est rue Wellesley, Toronto Ontario M4Y 1H6.

ISSN 0847-947X
DD 363.3/48/0971
CN
Pr Rev.
CANADIAN EMERGENCY NEWS. [Can. emerg. news]. **VFOAT** Emergency News. Vol. 12, No. 1 (Jan./Feb. 1989)-. Periodical. English. Six times a year. 36.02Can$. Pendragon Publishing Ltd., PO Box 68010, 7750 Ranchview Drive Northwest, Calgary Alberta T3G 3N8 Canada. **Tel** (403)547-5748, (800)567-0911, FAX (403)547-5749. **(Subscription address:** Canadian Emergency News, PO Box 68010, Calgary Alberta T3G 3N8 Canada.) **ED** Lyle Blumhagen. **Bk Rev**, (Qty: varies). **Ad Acc, Adv Mgr:** Warren Whalen, **Tel** (514)426-7299. **Circ:** 5,000 (ctrl). Documents available. **Continues** Canadian Emergency Services News., 0706-9278.
Desc: Emergency response professionals give information on emergency medicine, firefighting, search and rescues, and more.

ISSN 0961-2564
UK
Pr Rev.
CIVIL PROTECTION. [Civ. prot.]. (1986)-. Periodical. English. Four times a year. Free on request. Home Office Police Research Group, Queen Anne's Gate, Room 137 Edit, London SW1H 9AT United Kingdom. **Tel** 011 44 171 2733762, 011 44 171 2733511, FAX 011 44 171 2732568. **ED** Bernard Smyth. **Bk Rev**, (Qty: 2-3). **Circ:** 43,000 (ctrl).
Desc: Provides a communication channel for people involved in planning for major emergencies in Britain. It goes to a wide spread of readers within the field and contains news as well as articles on the latest thinking and on examples of good practice. Open to letters and articles from activists in this area, either professional or volunteer.
Ind/Abst Chem. Hazards Ind.; Lab. Hazards Bull.

US
CODE OF FEDERAL REGULATIONS. 44, EMERGENCY MANAGEMENT AND ASSISTANCE. Added/Corp United States. Office of the Federal Register. **VFOAT** Emergency Management and Assistance; CFR. 30, Emergency Management and Assistance. (19??)-. English. One time a year. $37.00. Superintendent of Documents, US Government Printing Office, Washington DC 20402. **Tel** (202)275-3328, FAX (202)786-2377. available on microfiche.
Desc: Special edition of the Federal Register, containing a codification of documents.

US
DEM DIGEST. (19??)-. English. Five times a year (Jan., Apr., July, Sept., Oct.). Free on request. Texas Department of Public Safety, PO Box 4087, 5805 North Lamar Boulevard, Austin TX 78773. **Tel** (512)465-2138, FAX (512)465-2444. **ED** Jo Schweikhard Moss. ctrl circ.

LC HV553 . U16
DD 363.3/4526/05
SZ
●**DHA NEWS. Added/Corp** United Nations. Dept. of Humanitarian Affairs. **VFOAT** Complex Emergencies and Natural Disasters in 1992--An Overview. **VAT** Department of Humanitarian Affairs News. (Jan./Feb. 1993)-. Periodical. English. Six times a year. United Nations Publishers / Department of Humanitarian Affairs, Palais des Nations, CH-1211 Geneva 10 Switzerland. **Tel** 011 41 22 7988400. **Continues** DHA UNDRO News.

LC HV555.U6 D55
DD 361.5/025/73
US
DIRECTORY OF GOVERNORS AND STATE OFFICIALS RESPONSIBLE FOR DISASTER OPERATIONS. Government Publication. English. One time a year. US Department of Housing and Urban Development, 451 Seventh Street SW, Washington DC 20401. **Tel** (202)708-0980, FAX (202)708-0299. available on microfiche (Vols. for (1979) distributed to depository libraries).

ISSN 0961-1428
UK
TITLE CHANGE
DISASTER MANAGEMENT REDHILL. (DISASTER MANAGEMENT.). [Disaster manag. Redhill]. (1988)-(19??). Periodical. English. MCB University Press, 60 62 Toller Lane, Bradford, West Yorkshire BD8 9BY

United Kingdom. **Tel** 011 44 1274 785280, FAX 011 44 1274 785200, telex 51317-MCBUNI-G. ***Merged into*** *Disaster Prevention Management Incorporating Disaster Management.*
Desc: Analysis of disaster management and contingency planning.
Ind/Abst Curr. Cit.

ISSN 0251-4494
US
NLM W1; DI732
DISASTER PREPAREDNESS IN THE AMERICAS. AMERICAN SANITARY BUREAU. [Disaster prep. Am.]. **Added/Corp** Pan American Sanitary Bureau. Pan American Health Organization. Emergency Preparedness and Disaster Relief Coordination Office. Pan American Health Organization. Emergency Preparedness and Disaster Relief Coordination Program. (19??)-. Periodical. English (Spanish). Four times a year. Free on request. Pan American Health Organization, 525 23rd Street Northwest, Office District Sales, Washington DC 20037. **Tel** (202)293-8130, FAX (202)338-0869. **ED** Liz Stonaker. **Bk Rev**, (Qty: 12). **Circ:** 18,000 (ctrl). Documents available from Documents on Demand.
Desc: Contains articles on current topics related to emergency preparedness and disaster relief coordination; news from international organizations and member countries in the Americas; reviews current publications and audiovisual material on the subject.
Ind/Abst Environ. Abstr.

LC HV551.2 .D56 **ISSN** 0965-3562
DD 363.3/4/05 UK
CODEN DPMAEY
TITLE CHANGE
DISASTER PREVENTION AND MANAGEMENT. **Added/Corp** University of Bradford. Disaster Prevention and Limitation Unit. Vol. 1, No. 1 (1992)-(19??). Academic Scholarly Publication. English. MCB University Press, 60 62 Toller Lane, Bradford, West Yorkshire BD8 9BY United Kingdom. **Tel** 011 44 1274 785280, FAX 011 44 1274 785200, telex 51317-MCBUNI-G. **(Subscription address:** MCB University Press / US and Canada Subscriptions, PO Box 10812, Birmingham AL 35201-0812. **Tel** (205)995-1567, (800)633-4931, FAX (205)995-1588.**)** ***Absorbed*** *Disaster Management, 0961-1428.* ***Merged into*** *Disaster Prevention Management.*
Ind/Abst Curr. Cit.

LC HV551 **ISSN** 1079-736X
DD 363 US
CODEN DREJEZ
DISASTER RECOVERY JOURNAL. [Disaster recovery j.]. **VFOAT** DRJ. Vol. 1, No. 1 (1987)-. Periodical. English. Four times a year (Jan., Apr., July, Oct.). Free on request. Systems Support Inc., PO Box 510110, St. Louis MO 63151. **Tel** (314)894-0276, FAX (314)894-7474. **ED** Janette Ballman and Kevin J. Kraff. Index available (advertising index). **Ad Acc**, **Adv Mgr:** Patti Fitzgerald. **Circ:** 35,000.
Desc: The journal dedicated to business continuity.

LC HV5512 .D57 **ISSN** 1074-0112
DD 363.3/48/029473 US
DISASTER RECOVERY YELLOW PAGES. [Disaster Recovery Yellow Pages]. **Added/Corp** Systems Audit Group, Inc. (19??)-. Directory. English. Two times a year. $78.00. Systems Support Inc., PO Box 510110, St. Louis MO 63151. **Tel** (314)894-0276, FAX (314)894-7474.

LC HV553 .D57 **ISSN** 0361-3666
DD 361.5/05 UK
CCC
NLM W1 DI742T
Pr Rev.
DISASTERS. [Disasters]. **Added/Corp** London Technical Group. Relief and Development Institute (London, England). Vol. 1 (1977)-. Academic Scholarly Publication. English. Four times a year (Mar., June, Sept., Dec.). $172.00. Basil Blackwell Publishers Ltd., 108 Cowley Road, Oxford 0X4 1JF United Kingdom. **Tel** 011 44 1235 465500, FAX 011 44 1235 465556, telex 837022 OXBOOK G. **(Subscription address:** Blackwell Publishers / UK, 108 Cowley Road, Oxford OX4 1JF United Kingdom. **Tel** 011 44 1865 791100, FAX 011 44 1865 791347.**)** **ED** Charles Melville. Index available. **Bk Rev**. **Ad Acc**. **Circ:** 700. available on microfilm and microfiche from University Microfilms International (UMI). Documents available from The Genuine Article.
Desc: Multi-disciplinary journal covering all aspects of disasters, including sudden onset disasters, food emergencies, refugees, disasters and developments.
Ind/Abst Abstr. J. Earthq. Eng.; Archit. Period. Index; Commun. Abstr.; Curr. Cit.; Curr. Contents Soc. Behav. Sci.; EMBASE; Geogr. Abstr. Human Geogr.; Geol. Abstr.; GeoRef; Health Saf. Sci. Abstr.; Index Med.; Int. Bibliogr. Sociol.; Int. Civil Eng. Abstr.; Int. Dev. Abstr.; J. Plan. Lit.; Leis., Rec., Tour. Abstr.; Linguist. Lang. Behav. Abstr.; Nutr. Abstr. Rev., Ser. B, Live Feeds and Feed.; Nutr. Abstr. Rev., Ser. A, Hum. Exp.; PAIS Int. Print (1991-); Pollut. Abstr. Indexes; Res. Alert [Full Cov.]; Rice Abstr.; Risk Abstr. (19??-19??); Rural Dev. Abstr.; Soc. Plann. Policy Dev. Abstr.; Soc. Sci. Cit. Index [Full Cov.]; Sociol. Abstr.; Trop. Dis. Bull.; World Agric. Econ. Rural Sociol. Abstr.

IT
DOSSIER DI PROTEZIONE CIVILE E AMBIENTE. (19??)-. Italian. Four times a year. L90000.00 Italy; L150000.00 other. CESP, Via Modica 9, 20143 Milan Italy. **Tel** 011 39 2 8911761.

UK
●**EMERGENCY.** (1993)-. English. Four times a year. $103.63. Brodie Publishing Limited, 11 13 Victoria Street, Liverpool L2 5QQ United Kingdom. **Tel** 011 44 151 2367518. ***Continues*** *Journal of the Institute of Civil Defense and Disaster Studies.*

ISSN 0747-9085
DD 363 US
EMERGENCY MANAGEMENT TODAY : AN INFORMATION SERVICE OF EMERGENCY MANAGEMENT INFORMATION SERVICES. [Emerg. manage. today]. **Added/Corp** Emergency Management Information Services. (1983)-. Periodical. English. Twenty-six times a year. $132.00. Emergency Management Group, 1508 East 86th Street, Suite 315, Indianapolis IN 46240. **Tel** (317)255-4942. **ED** Douglas L Crichlow. Index available. cum. index. **Bk Rev**, (Qty: 15-20). **Circ:** 3,120.
Desc: Covers trends in management of major emergencies and disasters caused by natural, technological and human behavioral hazards from perspective of public and private sector organizations.

LC UA926.A1 E52 **ISSN** 0837-5771
DD 354.710075/4 CN
EMERGENCY PREPAREDNESS DIGEST. [Emerg. prep. dig.]. **VFOAT** Revue de la Protection Civile. Vol. 14, No. 1 (Jan./March 1987)-. Periodical. English (French). Four times a year (Mar., June, Sept., Dec.). 26.00Can$. Canada Communication Group Publishers, Order Processing, Ottawa Ontario K1A 0S9 Canada. **Tel** (819)956-4800, (819)956-4802. **ED** Joan Borsu. **Bk Rev**. **Circ:** 15,000 (ctrl). available on microfilm and microfiche from University Microfilms International (UMI). ***Continues*** *Emergency Planning Digest, 0317-3518.*
Desc: Provides current information and reference material on broad range of subjects involving emergency preparedness for natural and other disasters.
Ind/Abst Abstr. J. Earthq. Eng.

ISSN 0275-3782
US
CCC
EMERGENCY PREPAREDNESS NEWS. [Emerg. prep. news]. Vol. 1 (1976)-. Periodical. English. Twenty-six times a year. $314.00. Business Publishers Inc., 951 Pershing Drive, Silver Spring MD 20910-4464. **Tel** (301)587-6300, (800)274-0122, FAX (301)585-9075. **ED** Cathy Dombrowski.
Desc: Reports on coping with natural and man-made disasters, covering contingency planning, crises management and disaster relief for civil defense, floods, fires, riots, chemical spills, etc.

ISSN 0148-8104
US
GOODHUE COUNTY RURAL IDENTIFICATION DIRECTORY. [Goodhue Cty. rural identif. dir.]. (19??)-. Directory. English. Irregular. Public Safety Building, Goodhue County Civil Defense, Sixth Street, Red Wing MN 55066.

ISSN 1062-8096
DD 363 US
TITLE CHANGE
HAZARDOUS EMERGENCY RESPONSE. [Hazard. emerg. response]. Vol. 1, No. 1 (Feb. 1992)-(19??). Periodical. English. Stevens Publishing Corporation, 225 North New Road, Waco TX 76702-2604. **Tel** (800)727-7573, (817)776-9000, FAX (817)776-9018. ***Merged into*** *HAZMAT News.*
Ind/Abst Foods Adlibra (1992-).

LC UA927 .I48 **ISSN** 0740-3445
DD 363.3/5/0973 US
IMPACT (GREAT FALLS, MONT.). (IMPACT.). [Impact]. **Added/Corp** United States Civil Defense Council. Vol. 1, No. 1 (Fall 1982)-. Periodical. English. Four times a year. $12.00. United States Civil Defense Council, Box 6457, Great Falls MT 59406.

ISSN 0280-7270
SW
INTERNATIONAL JOURNAL OF MASS EMERGENCIES AND DISASTERS. **VFOAT** Mass Emergencies and Disasters. Vol. 1, No. 1 (March 1983)-. Periodical. English. Three times a year (Mar., Aug., Nov.). $48.00. Disaster Research Center, University of Delware, K. Tiernry, Newark DE 19716. **Tel** (302)451-6618, FAX (302)451-2828.
Ind/Abst Curr. Cit.; J. Plan. Lit.; Soc. Plann. Policy Dev. Abstr.; Sociol. Abstr. (1983-) [Full Cov.].

ISSN 1065-2302
DD 363 US
INTERNATIONAL SEARCH AND RESCUE TRADE ASSOCIATION (INSARTA). (INTERNATIONAL SEARCH AND RESCUE TRADE ASSOCIATION (INSARTA) : [NEWSLETTER].). [Int. Search Rescue Trade Assoc. (INSARTA)]. **Added/Corp** International Search and Rescue Trade Association. Emergency Response Institute (Tacoma, Wash.). **VFOAT** International Search and Rescue Trade Association (INSARTA) Newsletter; INSARTA Newsletter. Vol. 1, No. 1 (Spring 1992)-. Newsletter. English. Four times a year. $50.00 (agencies). INSARTA, 4537 Foxhall Drive NE, Olympia WA 98506.

LC UA926.A1 J68 **ISSN** 0740-5537
DD 363.3/5/05 US
JOURNAL OF CIVIL DEFENSE. [J. civ. def.]. **Added/Corp** Civil Defense Forum. Vol. 9 (Jan./Feb. 1976)-. Periodical. English. Four times a year. $18.00. Journal of Civil Defense, Box 910, Starke FL 32091. **Tel** (904)964-5397, FAX (904)964-9641. **ED** Walter Murphey. Index available. cum. index. **Bk Rev**, (Qty: 30). **Ad Acc**. **Circ:** 2,000. ***Continues*** *Survive, 0039-6354.*
Desc: Materials on practical peace initiatives through population protection measures and the resultant escalation of risk for potential aggressors.
Ind/Abst Urban Aff. Abstr.

JA
KYUKYU SHOROPPO. **Main/Corp** Japan. **Added/Corp** Japan. Shobocho. Bosai Kyukyuka. Japan. Shobocho. Anzen Kyukyuka. Japan. Shobocho. Yobo Kyukyuka. (19??)-. Japanese. ¥2300. Zenkoku Kajo Horei Shuppan Company Ltd., Dai 1 Zenkoku Biru 18 Saneicho, Shinjukuku Tokyo 160 Japan.

ISSN 0712-2462
DD 363.3/5 CN
LIFELINE (SORRENTO). (LIFELINE.). [Lifeline]. (1980)-. Periodical. English. Six times a year. $13.00. Lifeline Publications, PO Box 206, Sorrento BC V2E 2W0.

ISSN 0193-8355
US
CODEN NSOBD7
NATURAL HAZARDS OBSERVER. [Nat. hazards obs.]. **Added/Corp** University of Colorado, Boulder. Natural Hazards Research and Applications Information Center. Vol. 1, (Sept. 1976)-. Periodical. English. Six times a year (Jan., Mar., May, July, Sept., Nov.). Free on request. University of Colorado / Campus Box 482, Campus Box 482, Boulder CO 80309. **Tel** (303)492-6818, FAX (303)492-2151. **ED** Dane Butler. Index available. cum. index. **Bk Rev**. **Circ:** 9,600 (ctrl). Documents available from Documents on Demand.
Desc: The purpose of this magazine is to strengthen communication among researchers and the individuals and organizations, concerned with mitigating natural disasters.
Ind/Abst Environ. Abstr.; GeoRef; Health Saf. Sci. Abstr.; Meteorol. Geoastrophys. Abstr. (199?-); Pollut. Abstr. Indexes; Risk Abstr.

US
NEWS / OXFAM AMERICA. **Added/Corp** Oxfam America. (19??)-. Periodical. English. Four times a year. Oxfam America, 115 Broadway, Boston MA 02116.
Ind/Abst Hum. Rights Intern. Rep.

LC UA928.M8 M55a **ISSN** 0364-0337
DD 363.3/4/09778 US
NEWSLETTER - DISASTER OPERATIONS OFFICE, STATE OF MISSOURI. **Main/Corp** Missouri. Disaster Planning and Operations Office, Civil Defense. Vol. 21, No. 5 (Sept./Oct. 1974)-. Newsletter. English. Six times a year. Disaster Planning and Operations Office / Missouri, 1717 Industrial Drive, Jefferson City MO 65102. ***Continues*** *Missouri. Disaster Planning and Operations Office, Civil Defense. Missouri Disaster Planning and Operations Newsletter.*

LC UA926.A1 Z58 **ISSN** 0938-7390
GW
NOTFALLVORSORGE UND ZIVILE VERTEIDIGUNG. **VFOAT** Notfallvorsorge und Zivilverteidigung. (1990)-. Periodical. German. Four times a year (Feb., May, Aug., Nov.). $44.90. Osang Verlag Gmbh, Am Roemerlager 2, D-53117 Bonn 1 F R Germany. **Tel** 011 49 228 678383. ***Continues*** *Zivilverteidigung, 0044-4839.*

LC HV553 .U45a
DD 363.3/48/05 US
OFDA ANNUAL REPORT / OFFICE OF U.S. FOREIGN DISASTER ASSISTANCE, AGENCY FOR INTERNATIONAL DEVELOPMENT. **Main/Corp** United States. Agency for International Development. Office of U.S. Foreign Disaster Assistance. **VFOAT** Annual Report.

Civil Defense

(1986)-. English. *Continues* Annual Report / United States. Agency for International Development. Office of US Foreign Disaster Assistance.

IT
PROTEZIONE CIVILE E SOCIETA OGGI. (19??)-. Italian. Six times a year. L120000. Edisanitrix Medical Distr Srl, V Caduti per la Resistenza 183, 00128 Rome Italy. **Tel** 011 39 6 5081047.

IT
PROTEZIONE CIVILE ITALIANA, LA. (19??)-. Italian. Six times a year. L80000 Italy; L160000 other. Edizioni Nazionali Srl, Viale Faenza 26 5, 20142 Milan Italy. **Tel** 011 39 2 8135018.

LC UA929.9.P7 P78

PL
PRZEGLAD OC. Added/Corp Poland. Inspektorat Obrony Cywilnej. (19??)-. Periodical. Polish. Inspektorat Obrony Cywilnij, UL Wronia 23 Konto PK0 NR 1-6-100024, Warsaw Poland. **(Subscription address:** Ars Polona-Ruch, PO Box 1001, Krakowskie Przedmiescie 7, 00-068 Warsaw Poland. **Tel** 011 48 22 261201.**)**

LC UA929.Q3 B87A **ISSN** 0714-7805
DD 354.7140075/4 CN
RAPPORT ANNUEL / BUREAU DE LA PROTECTION CIVILE DU QUEBEC. [Rapp. annu. - Bur. prot. civ. Que.]. **Main/Corp** Bureau de la Protection Civile du Quebec. 1980-81-. French. One time a year. Editeur Officiel du Quebec, 1283 boulevard Charest Ouest, Quebec Quebec G1N 2C9 Canada. *Continues* Protection Civile du Quebec. Rapport d'Activities, 0229-849X.

LC UA18.U5 U48A **ISSN** 0094-1905
DD 355.2/6/02573 US
REGISTER OF PLANNED EMERGENCY PRODUCERS. (1975)-. English. One time a year. Defense Logistics Agency / Alexandria, Attn DLA-XPD, Cameron Station, Alexandria VA 22314. *Continues* Register Planned Emergency Producers, 0094-1905.

LC TA654.6 .C3A **ISSN** 0098-2717
DD 363.3/4 US
REPORT OF THE GOVERNOR'S EARTHQUAKE COUNCIL. [Rep. Gov. Earthq. Counc.]. **Main/Corp** California. Governor's Earthquake Council. English. Governor's Earthquake Council, Resources Building/Room 1115, 1416 9th Street, Sacramento CA 98517.
Ind/Abst GeoRef.

LC UA926.A1 R48
DD 363.3/5/05 SZ
REVUE INTERNATIONALE DE PROTECTION CIVILE. Added/Corp International Civil Defence Organization. **VFOAT** International Civil Defence Journal; Majallah Al-Dawliyah Lil-Himayah Al-Madaniyah; Revue de l'OIPC. **VAT** Revue de l'Organisation Internationale de Protection Civile. (Jan./Feb./March 1988)-. Periodical. Arabic (English, French and Spanish). Four times a year. $66.00. Organisation Internationale de Protection Civile, 10-12 Chemin de Surveille, 1213 Petit-Lancy Switzerland. **Tel** 011 32 22 7934433, FAX 011 32 22 7934428, telex 423786.

US
RIGHT-TO-KNOW PLANNING REPORT : CHEMICAL HAZARD COMMUNICATION AND EMERGENCY PLANNING. VFOAT Chemical Hazard Communication and Emergency Planning. (1987)-. Monographic series. English. Twenty-six times a year. Comes with Right to Know Planning Guide. Bureau of National Affairs Inc., 9435 Key West Avenue, Rockville MD 20850. **Tel** (800)372-1033, (301)258-1033, FAX (301)948-5823. **ED** Eileen Z Joseph.
Desc: A newsletter providing information on new community right-to-know and community emergency response programs.

ISSN 1183-5036
DD 363.3 CN
SARSCENE (OTTAWA). (SARSCENE.). [Sarscene]. **Added/Corp** National Search and Rescue Program (Canada). National Search and Rescue Secretariat. **VFOAT** Your Canadian Search and Rescue Newsletter; Sarscene. Vol. 1, No. 1 (Apr. 1991)-. Periodical. English (French). Four times a year (Jan., Apr., July, Oct.). Free on request. National Search and Rescue Secretariat, 275 Slater Street, Ottawa Ontario K1A 0K2 Canada. **Tel** (613)996-2642, FAX (613)996-3746. **ED** Carol O'Rourke-Elliott. Index available. cum. index. **Bk Rev. Circ:** 12,500 (ctrl).

ISSN 0222-559X
FR
UDC 33.
SECURITE CIVILE ET INDUSTRIELLE. (1979)-. Periodical. French (summaries and/or abstracts in English and Spanish). Eleven times a year (July/Aug. issues combined). $126.85. France Selection, 9-13 rue de la Nule, 93303 Aubervilliers Cedex France. **Tel** 011 33 14 48331818. *Continues* Protection Civile et Securite

Industrielle, 0033-1724.
Desc: Covers security from all points of view: fire, industry, home, traffic, etc.

LC HV555.A8 S57
DD 361.5/09944 AT
SITREP. Added/Corp New South Wales. State Emergency Services. Bush Fire Council of New South Wales. (19??)-. English. Four times a year. New South Wales St Emergency, Box 42, Queen Victoria Building, Sydney New South Wales 2000 Australia. *Formed by the union of* New South Wales. State Emergency Services. Bulletin *and* Bush Fire Council of New South Wales. Bulletin.

ISSN 0042-0468
US
UNSCHEDULED EVENTS. [Unsched. events]. **Added/Corp** Ohio State University. Disaster Research Center. Vol. 1 (Spring 1967)-. Periodical. English. Three times a year. $22.00. Disaster Research Center, University of Delware, K. Tierrny, Newark DE 19716. **Tel** (302)451-6618, FAX (302)451-2828. **ED** Joanne M Nigg. **Bk Rev. Circ:** 300.
Desc: News in the field of disasters and mass emergencies (mainly for members of the Committee of Disaster Research).

IT
VOCE DEI VIGILI URBANI, LA. Italian. Editrice Edipol Srl, Viale Tunisia 41, 20124 Milan Italy.

LC U4 .V874
RU
VOENNYE ZNANIIA. Vol. 8 (Jan. 1931)-. Periodical. Russian. Twelve times a year. $109.95. **(Subscription address:** East View Publications Inc., 3020 Harbor Lane North, Suite 110, Minneapolis MN 55447. **Tel** (800)477-1005, (612)550-0961, FAX (612)559-2931.**)** *Formed by the union of* Aviatsiia i Khimiia *and* Khimiia Trudiashchimsia.
Ind/Abst Curr. Mil. Pol. Lit.

LC UA929.A9 Z5
DD 363.3/5/09436 AU
ZIVILSCHUTZ AKTUELL. Added/Corp OEZSV (Association). (1987)-. Bulletin. German. Four times a year. S230.00. Oesterreichischer Zivilschutzverband, Bohmann Druck und Verlag GmbH & Co. KG, Leberstrasse, A-1110 Vienna Austria. **Tel** 011 43 222 740950, FAX 011 43 222 74095183. **Circ:** 41,000. *Continues* Zivilschutz (Vienna, Austria).

SZ
ZIVILSCHUTZ = PROTECTION CIVILE = PROTEZIONE CIVILE = PROTECZIUN CIVILA. Added/Corp Schweizerischer Bund fuer Zivilschutz. Zivilschutz-Fachverband der Stadte (Switzerland) Schweizerische Gesellschaft fuer Kulturgueterschutz. Schweizerischer Zivilschutzverband. **VFOAT** Protection Civile; Protezione Civile; Protecziun Civila. (195?)-. Periodical. German (French and Italian). Ten times a year. $56.58. Vogt Schild AG, Druck Verlag, Postfach 748 Zuchwilserstr 21, CH-4501 Solothurn Switzerland. **Tel** 011 41 65 247247. *Absorbed* Schutz und Wehr.

CLASSICAL STUDIES

GW
ABHANDLUNGEN - BAYERISCHE AKADEMIE DER WISSENSCHAFTEN, PHILOSOPHISCH-HISTORISCHE KLASSE. Main/Corp Akademie der Wissenschaften, Munich. Philosophisch-Historische KLA. **Added/Corp** Akademie der Wissenschaften, Munich. Philosophisch-Philologische Klasse. Akademie der Wissenschaften, Munich. Historische Klasse. Akademie der Wissenschaften, Munich. Philosophisch-Historische Abteilung. Vol. 1 (1835)-. German. Irregular. Bayerische Akademie der Wissenschaften, Marstallplatz 8, D-80539 Munich Germany. **Tel** 011 49 89 23031113. **Bk Rev.** Acid Free. ctrl circ.

LC AS182 .G812 **ISSN** 0930-4304
GW
ABHANDLUNGEN DER AKADEMIE DER WISSENSCHAFTEN IN GOTTINGEN. PHILOLOGISCH-HISTORISCHE KLASSE. Added/Corp Akademie der Wissenschaften in Gottingen. Philologisch-Historische Klasse. (194?)-. Monographic series. German. Irregular. Price varies per volume. Vandenhoeck & Ruprecht, Robert Bosch Breite 6, D-37079 Goettingen Germany. **Tel** 011 49 551 695911, FAX 011 49 551 695917, telex 965226 VAN d. **Bk Rev.** ctrl circ. *Continues* Abhandlungen der Gesellschaft der Wissenschaften Zu Gottingen. Philologisch-Historische Klasse.
Desc: Each fascicle contains a short piece of research in

the field of humanities.
Ind/Abst BHA : Biblio. Hist. Art; MLA Int. Bibl. Books Artic. Mod. Lang. Lit.

LC AS182 .H435 **ISSN** 0017-9574
GW
ABHANDLUNGEN DER HEIDELBERGER AKADEMIE DER WISSENSCHAFTEN, PHILOSOPHISCH-HISTORISCHE KLASSE. See History.

LC CC1 .A19 **ISSN** 0044-5975
HU
CCC
ACTA ANTIQUA ACADEMIAE SCIENTIARUM HUNGARICAE. See Linguistics.

LC PA25 .A2 **ISSN** 0065-1141
SA
CCC
ACTA CLASSICA. Added/Corp Classical Association of South Africa. Classical Association of South Africa. Verhandelinge. Classical Association of South Africa. Proceedings. Vol. 1 (1958)-. English (French, Afrikaans and Multiple languages). One time a year. $30.00. University of South Africa / Department of Classical Studies, PO Box 392, Pretoria 0001 South Africa. **Tel** 011 27 12 4296501.

ISSN 0196-2086
US
AMERICAN CLASSICAL LEAGUE NEWSLETTER. Added/Corp American Classical League. American Classical League. Newsletter. Vol. 1 (Sept. 1978)-. Newsletter. English. Two times a year. $25.00. American Classical League, Miami University / Ohio, Oxford OH 45056. **Tel** (513)529-7741, FAX (513)529-7742.

ISSN 0278-5943
US
AMERICAN CLASSICAL STUDIES. No. 1-. Monographic series. English. Irregular. Price varies per volume. Scholars Press / Georgia, PO Box 1589, Atlanta GA 30333-0399. **Tel** (404)636-4757, (404)727-2320, FAX (404)727-2348. **ED** Susan Treggiari.
Desc: Contains works dealing in detail with some limited aspect of the ancient world, ranging from literature to history, linguistics, and religion.

LC DE1 .A365 **ISSN** 0362-8914
DD 938/.005 US
AMERICAN JOURNAL OF ANCIENT HISTORY. Vol. 1 (Jan. 1976)-. Periodical. English (English, Greek and Modern, Latin). Two times a year. $22.00. American Journal of Ancient History, Harvard University, Robinson Hall, Room 201, Cambridge MA 02138. **Tel** (617)495-2545, FAX (617)496-3425. **ED** E. Badian. **Ad Acc, Adv Mgr:** Wendy Lurie. **Circ:** 600.
Desc: Publishes articles on all aspects of ancient Greek and Roman history, from the origins of Greek civilization to the fall of the Roman Empire, and on others in contact with Greece and Rome.
Ind/Abst Middle East Abstr. Index.

LC P1 .A5 **ISSN** 0002-9475
DD 405 US
CCC
AMERICAN JOURNAL OF PHILOLOGY. [Am. j. philol.]. Vol. 1 (Feb. 1880)-. Academic Scholarly Publication. English. Four times a year (March, June, September and December). $79.00. Johns Hopkins University Press, 2715 North Charles Street, Baltimore MD 21218-4319. **Tel** (410)516-6987, FAX (410)516-6968. **(Subscription address:** John Hopkins University Press, Journals Publishing Division, PO Box 19966, Baltimore MD 21211. **Tel** (800)516-6987, (800)548-1784, FAX (410)516-6968.**) ED** George Kennedy. Index available. **Bk Rev. Ad Acc. Circ:** 1,400. available on microfilm and microfiche from University Microfilms International (UMI). Documents available from The Genuine Article, UMI Article Clearinghouse.
Desc: Publishes articles concerned with literary interpretation and history, textual criticism, historical investigation, epigraphy, religion, linguistics and philosophy.
Ind/Abst Acad. Search; Annu. Bibliogr. Engl. Lang. Lit.; Arts Humanit. Citation Index [Full Cov.]; Book Rev. Index; Curr. Contents Arts Humanit.; EP Collect.; Expand. Acad. Index (1989-); Homework Help.; Humanit. Index; Humanit. Source; INFO-SOUTH Abstr.; Linguist. Lang. Behav. Abstr.; Lit. Crit. Regist.; Mag. Search; MasterFile FullTEXT 1000; MasterFile FullTEXT 350; MasterFile FullTEXT 650; MasterFile FullTEXT (July 1993-); Newsp. Period. Abstr. (1991-); Numis. Lit.; OCLC; Philos. Index; Res. Alert [Full Cov.]; Soc. Plann. Policy Dev. Abstr.; Soc. Sci. Cit. Index [Select. Cov.]; Soc. Sci. Index; Sociol. Abstr.; Telebase.

LC PA3339 .A5 **ISSN** 0569-8642
US
AMERICAN STUDIES IN PAPYROLOGY. Added/Corp American Society of Papyrologists. Vol. 1 (1966)-. Monographic series. English. Irregular. Price

varies per volume. Scholars Press / Georgia, PO Box 15399, Atlanta GA 30333-0399. **Tel** (404)636-4757, (404)727-2320, FAX (404)727-2348. **ED** Ludwig Koenen. **Bk Rev**. **Ad Acc**.
Desc: First editions of Papyri and Ostraka in American and Canadian collections and monographs or reference works in administrative, social and economic history, literary and Biblical Papyrology, and Epigraphy of Greek and Roman Egypt.

ISSN 1058-238X
US

AMS ANCIENT AND CLASSICAL STUDIES. **VFOAT** Studies in Ancient and Classical Cultures. (1992)-. Monographic series. English. Price varies per volume. AMS Press Inc., 56 East 13th Street, New York NY 10003. **Tel** (212)777-4700, FAX (212)995-5413, telex 710 581 2302.

ISSN 0835-3638
DD 930/.05 CN

ANCIENT HISTORY BULLETIN. (THE ANCIENT HISTORY BULLETIN.). [Anc. hist. bull.]. **Added/Corp** University of Calgary. Dept. of Classics. Loyola University of Chicago. Dept. of Classical Studies. Vol. 1, No. 1 (Jan. 1987)-. Bulletin. English (Greek, Ancient, French, German and Italian, Spanish; summaries and/or abstracts in Greek, Modern). Four times a year. 17.00Can$. Ancient History Bulletin, University of Calgary, Classics Department, 2500 University Drive Northwest, Calgary Alberta T2N 1N4 Canada. **Tel** (403)220-5537.
Desc: Provides a forum for scholarly discussion in ancient history and in the ancillary fields of epigraphy, papyrology and numismatics.

ISSN 0066-1619
BE

ANCIENT SOCIETY. **Added/Corp** Katholieke Universiteit te Leuven. Vol. 1 (1970)-. Multiple languages (English, French, German and Italian). One time a year (published in Nov.). 3000F. Editions Peeters SA, Bondgenotenlaan 153, BP 41, B-3000 Leuven Belgium. **Tel** 011 32 16 235170, FAX 011 32 16 228500, telex 65987 PUL B. **ED** H. Verdin and P. Van Dessel. Index available.
Desc: Journal of ancient history of the Greek, Hellenistic and Roman world.
Ind/Abst Numis. Lit.

LC DE1 .A375 **ISSN** 0160-9645
DD 930/.005 US
Pr Rev.

ANCIENT WORLD, THE. **See** Archaeology.

ISSN 0066-2348
FR
CCC

ANNEE EPIGRAPHIQUE, L'. (L'ANNEE EPIGRAPHIQUE; REVUE DES PUBLICATIONS EPIGRAPHIQUES RELATIVES A L'ANTIQUITE ROMAINE.). **Added/Corp** Academie des Inscriptions et Belles-Lettres, Paris. (1888)-. French. Irregular (1 issue). $98.43. Presses Universitaires de France, Department des Revues, 17 Rue Soufflot, 75005 Paris France. **Tel** 011 33 1 43267741, telex PUF 600 474 F. cum. index.
Desc: Ancient history, Latin literature and Roman civilization are reflected through publication of ancient inscriptions and scientific commentaries on them. Includes Latin inscriptions and Greek inscriptions of general interest.
Ind/Abst Br. Archaeol. Bibliogr.

IT

ANNUARIO PER GLI ANNI ACCADEMICI ... / UNIVERSITA DEGLI STUDI DI PADOVA. **Main/Corp** Universita di Padova. **VFOAT** Annuario. Italian. One time a year. ***Continues** Annuario della R. Universita Degli Studi di Padova.*

LC PA1 .A5 **ISSN** 0066-4774
DD 480/.05 AT
Pr Rev.

ANTICHTHON. [Antichthon]. **Added/Corp** Australian Society for Classical Studies. Vol. 1 (1967)-. English. One time a year. $30.00. Antichthon, University of New England, Armidale New South Wales 2351 Australia. **Tel** 011 61 67 728282. **ED** G.R. Stanton and N. O'Sullivan. **Ad Acc. Circ:** 450.
Ind/Abst APAIS, Aust. Public Aff. Inf. Ser. (1968-); Numis. Lit.

LC DE1 .A379

SP

ANTIGUEDAD Y CRISTIANISMO. **Added/Corp** Universidad de Murcia. Catedra de Historia Antigua. Fundacion Pastor de Estudios Clasicos. Universidad de Alcala de Henares. Catedra de Historia Antigua. (1984)-. Periodical. Spanish (Spanish). One time a year. Universidad de Murcia, Apartado 4021, 30380 Murcia Spain. **Tel** 011 34 68 363013, 011 34 68 363014.

LC PA3 .A55 **ISSN** 0003-5696
GW
CCC

ANTIKE UND ABENDLAND. (1945)-. Periodical. German. One time a year. $166.00. Walter de Gruyter Inc., PO Box 303421, D-10728 Berlin Germany. **Tel** 011 49 30 260050, FAX 011 49 30 26005251, telex 184027. Documents available from The Genuine Article.
Ind/Abst Arts Humanit. Citation Index (19??-19??) [Full Cov.]; BHA : Biblio. Hist. Art; Curr. Contents Arts Humanit.; Res. Alert [Full Cov.].

LC DE1 .A43 **ISSN** 0770-2817
BE

ANTIQUITE CLASSIQUE, L'. [Antiq. class.]. **Added/Corp** Belgium. Ministere de l'Education Nationale et de la Culture. Fondation Universitaire de Belgique. (Dec. 1932)-. Periodical. French (German, Spanish and English). One time a year (December). $125.00. Antiquite Classique Asbl, Avenue Leopold 28 A, B 1330 Bixensart Belgium. **Tel** 011 32 10 474880. **Bk Rev**. ctrl circ.
Desc: Greek and Latin, as well as contiguous domains, prehellenic, Italic and Etruscan: languages, history, archaeology, art history, up to Byzantine and Renaissance ramifications.
Ind/Abst BHA : Biblio. Hist. Art; Br. Archaeol. Bibliogr.; MLA Int. Bibl. Books Artic. Mod. Lang. Lit.; Numis. Lit.

ISSN 0003-6390
DD 180/.05 CN

APEIRON (CLAYTON). (APEIRON.). [Apeiron]. **Added/Corp** University of Alberta. Dept. of Classics. Monash University. Dept. of Classical Studies. Monash College. Dept. of Classical Studies. Vol. 1 (July 1966)-. Periodical. English. Four times a year (3 regular issues and plus special double issue). 82.00Can$. Academic Printing and Publishing, PO Box 4218, South Edmonton, Alberta T6E 4T2 Canada. **Tel** (403)435-5898, FAX (403)435-5852. **ED** Roger A. Shiner. Index available. **Bk Rev. Ad Acc. Circ:** 350. Documents available from Ask*IEEE.
Desc: A scholarly journal for ancient philosophy and science.
Ind/Abst INSPEC (Sept. 1987-); Philos. Index.

LC DE1 .A55

GR

ARCHAIOGNOSIA. Vol. 1, No. 1 (June 1980)-. Periodical. Greek, Modern (English, French, German and Italian). Two times a year. Archaiologikon Spoudastirion, Panepisth Athenon, 57 Solonos, 0679 Athens Greece.

LC DE1 .A65 **ISSN** 0391-8165
IT

ARCHEOLOGIA CLASSICA. **See** Archaeology.

ISSN 0391-6952
IT
UDC 9

ARCHIVIO DELLA SOCIETA ROMANA DI STORIA PATRIA (1947). [Arch. Soc. rom. stor. patria 1947]. (1947)-. Periodical. Multiple languages. One time a year. Societa Romana Storia Patria, P Za Chiesa Nuova 18 Vallicell, 00186 Rome Italy. **Tel** 011 39 6 68307513. ***Continues** Archivio Della Deputazione Romana di Storia Patria, 0393-6872.*
Ind/Abst BHA : Biblio. Hist. Art.

LC PA1 .A715 **ISSN** 0004-0975
DD 880 US
CCC
CODEN AETHEE

ARETHUSA. [Arethusa]. **Added/Corp** State University of New York at Buffalo. Dept. of Classics. Vol. 1 (Fall 1968)-. Periodical. English (French, German and Greek, Modern). Three times a year. $42.00. Johns Hopkins University Press, 2715 North Charles Street, Baltimore MD 21218-4319. **Tel** (410)516-6987, FAX (410)516-6968. **(Subscription address:** John Hopkins University Press, Journals Publishing Division, PO Box 19966, Baltimore MD 21211. **Tel** (410)516-6987, (800)548-1784, FAX (410)516-6968.**) ED** John Peradotto. Index available. cum. index. **Circ:** 505. available on microfilm and microfiche from University Microfilms International (UMI). Documents available from The Genuine Article.
Desc: Interdisciplinary studies in Greco-Roman antiquity.
Ind/Abst Arts Humanit. Citation Index [Full Cov.]; Curr. Contents Arts Humanit.; MLA Int. Bibl. Books Artic. Mod. Lang. Lit.; Numis. Lit.; Res. Alert [Full Cov.].

US

ARION. Third Series, Vol. 1, No. 1 (Winter 1990)-. Periodical. English. Three times a year. $35.00. Boston University / Brookline, MA, 10 Lenox Street, Boston MA 02146. **Tel** (617)353-6480. **(Subscription address:** Arion, Boston University, Office of Scholarly Publications, 985 Commonwealth Avenue, Boston MA 02215. **) ED** Herbert Golder. Index available (in last volume of series). cum. index. **Bk Rev**, (Qty: 18). **Ad Acc, Adv Mgr:** Julie Seeger. **Circ:** 750 controlled, 2500 printed (ctrl). available on microfilm and microfiche from University Microfilms International (UMI). Documents available from The Genuine Article. ***Continues** Arion, 0095-5809.*
Desc: Literary essays, translations and reviews of ancient Greek and Roman culture.
Ind/Abst Am. Humanit. Index; Arts Humanit. Citation Index (19??-19??); Curr. Contents Arts Humanit.; Index Am. Period. Verse; MLA Int. Bibl. Books Artic. Mod. Lang. Lit. [Select. Cov.]; Res. Alert [Full Cov.].

LC AS284 .L83 **ISSN** 0349-053X
SW

ARSBOK - VETENSKAPSSOCIETETEN I LUND. (ARSBOK - VETENSKAPS-SOCIETETEN I LUND. YEARBOOK OF THE NEW SOCIETY OF LETTERS AT LUND.). [Arsb. - Vetensk.soc. Lund]. **Main/Corp** Vetenskaps-Societeten i Lund. **Added/Corp** Vetenskaps-Societeten i Lund. Yearbook of the New Society of Letters at Lund. **VFOAT** Yearbook of the New Society of Letters at Lund. (1920)-. Swedish. One time a year. Kr82.50 (latest edition). New Society of Letters at Lund, University Library, Lund Sweden.
Ind/Abst BHA : Biblio. Hist. Art; MLA Int. Bibl. Books Artic. Mod. Lang. Lit.

LC AS911 .C2612 **ISSN** 0105-9858
DK

ARSSKRIFT - CARLSBERGFONDET, FREDERIKSBORGMUSEET, NY CARLSBERGFONDET. **Main/Corp** Carlsbergfondet (Copenhagen, Denmark). **Added/Corp** Nationalhistoriske Museum pa Frederiksborg. Ny Carlsbergfondet (Copenhagen, Denmark). (1???)-. Danish. One time a year.
Ind/Abst BHA : Biblio. Hist. Art.

ISSN 0004-6493
IT

ATENE E ROMA. **Added/Corp** Associazione Italiana di Cultura Classica. Societa Italiana per la Diffusione e l'Incoraggiamento Degli Studi Classici. Vol. 1-22, (1898-1919)-. Periodical. Italian. Four times a year. L18400. Editoriale Finanz le Monnier, PO Box 202, Via Meucci 2, 50015 Grassina Florence Italy. **Tel** 011 39 55 64910. **Circ:** 5,000. Documents available from The Genuine Article.
Ind/Abst Arts Humanit. Citation Index [Full Cov.]; Curr. Contents Arts Humanit.; Res. Alert [Full Cov.]; Soc. Sci. Cit. Index [Select. Cov.].

LC AS202 .A5 **ISSN** 1011-1557
DD 068.495 GR

ATHENA (ATHENI). (ATHENA : SYNGRAMMA PERIODIKON TES EN ATHENAIS EPISTEMONIKES HETAIREIAS.). [Athena]. **Added/Corp** En Athenais Epistemonike Hetaireia. (1889)-. Academic Scholarly Publication. Greek, Modern (English). One time a year. Athenais Epistimonike Hetaireia, 74 Eressou Street, 106 83 Athens Greece. **Tel** 011 30 1 3634069. **ED** N. Livadaras. **Bk Rev**.
Ind/Abst Am. Hist. Life; Hist. Abstr.; MLA Int. Bibl. Books Artic. Mod. Lang. Lit.

LC PA1.A1 T43 **ISSN** 0004-6574
DD 480/.05 IT

ATHENAEUM (PAVIA, ITALY). (ATHENAEUM.). [Athenaeum]. **Added/Corp** Universita di Pavia. (1913)-. Periodical. Italian (English and Italian). Two times a year. L78000. New Press di Marzio Botta, Via Cosenz 8, 21100 Como Italy. **Tel** 011 39 31 273281, FAX 011 39 31 241177. **ED** Emilio Gabba. Index available in last issue of volume--attached. **Circ:** 800 (ctrl). available on microfilm from University Microfilms International (UMI). Documents available from The Genuine Article.
Desc: Studies in history and literature of ancient Greeks and Romans.
Ind/Abst Arts Humanit. Citation Index [Full Cov.]; Curr. Contents Arts Humanit.; MLA Int. Bibl. Books Artic. Mod. Lang. Lit.; Numis. Lit.; Res. Alert [Full Cov.]; Soc. Sci. Cit. Index [Select. Cov.].

LC AS222 .N62
DD 05/.1 IT

ATTI DELLA ACCADEMIA PONTANIANA. **Main/Corp** Accademia Pontaniana (1825). Vol. 1 (1832)- Vol. 63 (1933); New Ser., Vol. 1 (1947)-. Italian. One time a year. ***Supersedes** Societa Pontaniana. Atti della Societa Pontaniana di Napoli.*
Ind/Abst BHA : Biblio. Hist. Art; Math. Rev. (1983-).

ISSN 0365-0081
IT

ATTI DELLA ACCADEMIA ROVERETANA DEGLI AGIATI. **Main/Corp** Accademia Roveretana degli Agiati. Vol. 1 (1826)-(18??); 2nd Ser., Vol. 1 (1883)- Vol. 12 (1894); 3rd Ser., Vol. 1 (1895)- Vol. 18 (1912); 4th Ser., Vol. 1 (1913)-. Italian.
Ind/Abst BHA : Biblio. Hist. Art.

ISSN 0394-297X
IT
UDC 008

AUFIDUS. [Aufidus]. (1987)-. Periodical. Italian. Three times a year. L47690. Kepos Srl, Via Prenestina 685, 00155 Rome Italy. **Tel** 011 39 6 2288448.

ISSN 0067-6055
GW

BERLINER BYZANTINISTISCHE ARBEITEN. **See** History-History of Europe.

ISSN 0067-7965
SZ
CCC

BIBLIOTHECA HELVETICA ROMANA. **Added/Corp** Istituto Svizzero di Roma. (1954)-. Periodical. Multiple languages. Irregular. 98.00F. Librairie Droz SA, 11 rue Massot BP 389, CH-1211 Geneva 12 Switzerland. **Tel** 011 41 22 3466666, FAX 011 41 22 472391.

NE

BIBLIOTHECA HUMANISTICA ET REFORMATORICA. (1971)-. Monographic series. Multiple languages (English, French, German and Dutch). Irregular. Price varies per volume. De Graaf Publishers, Zuideinde 40, PO Box 6, 2479 AA Nieuwkoop Netherlands. **Tel** 011 31 172571461. **Bk Rev.** ctrl circ.
Desc: Monographs in the field of renaissance, reformation, neolatinism.

DD 880 GW

BIBLIOTHEK DER GRIECHISCHEN LITERATUR. Vol. 1 (1971)-. Monographic series. German. Irregular. Price varies per volume. Anton Hiersemann Verlag, Rosenbergstrasse 113, D-70193 Stuttgart Germany. **Tel** 011 49 711 638264 5. **ED** P. Wirth, W. Gessel. **Circ:** 900.
Desc: Translations from old Greek texts into German with bibliography of author.

ISSN 0587-6060
PO

BOLETIM - COIMBRA. UNIVERSIDADE. CENTRO DE ESTUDOS GEOGRAFICOS. **Main/Corp** Coimbra. Universidade. Centro de Estudos Geograficos. No. 1- June 1950-. Bulletin. Portuguese. Instituto Estudos Classicos, Faculdade Letras, 3049 Coimbra Codex Portugal. **Tel** 25551/2. **Bk Rev. Circ:** 500.
Desc: Archaeology, Greek art, Greek literature, Latin literature humanism in Portugal.

LC AS88 .L34 **ISSN** 0459-410X
PE

BOLETIN DEL INSTITUTO RIVA-AGUERO. [Bol. Inst. Riva-Aguero]. **Main/Corp** Instituto Riva Aguero. **VFOAT** BIRA. No. 1 (1952)-. Periodical. Spanish. Pontificia Universidad Catolica del Peru, Fondo Editorial, Apartado 1761, Lima 1 Peru. **Tel** 011 51 14 622540.
Ind/Abst Am. Hist. Life (1953-1976).

ISSN 0391-8270
IT

BOLLETTINO DEI CLASSICI. **Added/Corp** Accademia Nazionale dei Lincei. Comitato per la Preparazione dell'Edizione Nazionale dei Classici Greci e Latini. Series 3A, No. 1 (1980)-. Monographic series. Italian (English, Spanish, French and German). Irregular. Price varies per volume. Accademia Nazionale dei Lincei, Via Lungara 10 Uff Diff Pubbl., 00165 Rome Italy. **Tel** 011 39 6 6838831. **(Subscription address:** Bardi Editore, Salita de Crescenzi 16, 00186 Rome Italy. **Tel** 011 39 6 68801490.**)** **ED** C.F. Golisano. **Circ:** 500. ***Continues*** *Bollettino del Comitato Per la Preparazione dell'Edizione Nazionale dei Classici Greci e Latini.*

LC DA145 .B88 **ISSN** 0068-113X
DD 936.1/03/05 UK

BRITANNIA (SOCIETY FOR THE PROMOTION OF ROMAN STUDIES). (BRITANNIA.). **Added/Corp** Society for the Promotion of Roman Studies. (1970)-. English. One time a year. £30.00; £60.00 combined with Journal of Roman Studies. Society for Promotion of Roman Studies, 31-34 Gordon Square, London WC1H 0PP United Kingdom. **Tel** 011 44 171 3878157. **ED** Prof. A.F. Wallace-Hadrill. Index available. cum. index. **Bk Rev**, (Qty: 25). **Ad Acc**, **Adv Mgr:** H.Cockle. **Circ:** 1,500.
Desc: Features articles and reviews on Roman Britain.
Ind/Abst Br. Archaeol. Bibliogr.; Numis. Lit.

LC PA1 .B78 **ISSN** 1055-7660
DD 880/.5 US

BRYN MAWR CLASSICAL REVIEW. [Bryn Mawr class. rev.]. **Added/Corp** Thomas Library (Bryn Mawr College). Vol. 1, No. 1 (Nov. 1990)-. Periodical. English. Eight times a year. $20.00. Bryn Mawr Commentaries, Bryn Mawr College, Thomas Library, Bryn Mawr PA 19010. **Tel** (610)526-5384, FAX (610)526-7475. **ED** Richard Hamilton, (editor's address: Department of Greek, Bryn Mawr College, Bryn Mawr, PA 19010, phone: (610)526-5384). **Bk Rev**, (Qty: 100). **Circ:** 300 paper, 1,800 electronic. available on an online database from Internet.
Desc: Contains reviews of books on classical subjects.

US

BULLETIN. **Main/Corp** Joint Association of Classical Teachers. **VFOAT** JACT Bulletin. No. 1 (1963)-. Bulletin. English. Three times a year. Free to members; $30.00 membership. Joint Association of Classical Teachers / Amherst, University of Massachusetts, Herter Hall 528, Amherst MA 01003. **Tel** (413)549-5780, FAX (413)549-6401. **Bk Rev. Ad Acc. Circ:** 4,000.

LC DE2 .V4 **ISSN** 0165-9367
NE

BULLETIN ANTIEKE BESCHAVING : BABESCH. **See** History.

ISSN 1148-7852
FR

UDC 061.7(449.3)

BULLETIN DE L'ACADEMIE DU VAR. [Bull. Acad. Var]. (1879)-. Periodical. French. One time a year. ***Continues*** *Bulletin de la Societe Academique du Var, 1149-4425.*
Ind/Abst BHA : Biblio. Hist. Art.

LC PA25 .L8 **ISSN** 0076-0730
DD 480/.05 UK

BULLETIN - INSTITUTE OF CLASSICAL STUDIES. **Main/Corp** University of London. Institute of Classical Studies. No. 1 (1954)-. Bulletin. English (Greek, Modern and Latin). One time a year. £25.00. University of London, 31-34 Gordon Square, London WC1H OPY United Kingdom. **Tel** 011 44 171 3877696. **ED** J. P. Barron. Index available. **Bk Rev. Circ:** 500 (ctrl). available in microform. Documents available from The Genuine Article.
Ind/Abst Arts Humanit. Citation Index (19??-19??) [Full Cov.]; Curr. Contents Arts Humanit.; Numis. Lit.; Res. Alert [Full Cov.].

LC DF503 .V97 **ISSN** 1105-0772
GR

BUZANTINA (THESSALONIKE). (VYZANTINA : EPISTEMONIKON ORGANON KENTROU VYZANTINON EREUNON PHILOSOPHIKES SCHOLES ARISTOTELEIOU PANEPISTEMIOU.). **Added/Corp** Aristoteleio Panepistemio Thessalonikes. Kentro Vyzantinon Ereunon. **VFOAT** Byzantina. (1969)-. English (French, German and Greek, Modern). Every 2 years. Byzantine Research Center, Aristoteleiou University, 54006 Thessaloniki Greece. **Tel** 011 30 31 278210. **(Subscription address:** Byzantina Pournaras Panagiotis, Kastritsiou 12, PO Box 11220, 54623 Thessaloniki Greece. **Tel** 011 30 31 270941.**)** **ED** Kas M. Grigori. Index available. **Bk Rev**.
Ind/Abst BHA : Biblio. Hist. Art.

LC CB231 .B9 **ISSN** 0007-7712
DD 990 XR

BYZANTINOSLAVICA. **See** Literature-Abstracting, Bibliographies and Statistics.

LC PA5000 .B9 **ISSN** 0378-2506
BE

BYZANTION (BRUXELLES). (BYZANTION; REVUE INTERNATIONALE DES ETUDIES BYZANTINES.). [Byzantion]. **Added/Corp** Societe Belge d'Etudes Byzantines. Centre National de Recherches Byzantines. Byzantine Institute of America. (1924)-. Periodical. English (French, German, Greek, Modern and Italian, Latin). Two times a year. $86.74. Universa, rue Hoender 24, 9200 Wetteren Belgium. **Tel** 011/32/91/691563.
Desc: Includes section "Comptes Rendus."
Ind/Abst BHA : Biblio. Hist. Art; MLA Int. Bibl. Books Artic. Mod. Lang. Lit.; Numis. Lit.

ISSN 0245-5196
FR

CAESARODUNUM : BULLETIN DE L'INSTITUT D'ETUDES LATINES DE LA FACULTE DES LETTRES ET SCIENCES HUMAINES D'ORLEANS-TOURS. **Added/Corp** Universite de Tours. Institut d'Etudes Latines. Centre de Recherches A. Piganiol. Centre Regional de Documentation Pedagogique d'Orleans. Universite de Tours. (1967)-. Bulletin. French. Irregular. Price varies per volume. Universite de Tours, Inst de Rech Piganiol, 3 rue Tanneurs, 37041 Tours France.

ISSN 0183-536X
FR

CAHIERS DE LA ROTONDE. [Cah. Rotonde]. **Added/Corp** Commission du Vieux Paris. (1978)-. Periodical. French. Irregular. Commission du Vieux Paris / Rotonde de la Villette, Place Bat Stalingrad, 75019 Paris France. **Tel** 011 33 1 40342358.
Ind/Abst Avery Index Archit. Period. Suppl. Colum. Univ. (1989); BHA : Biblio. Hist. Art.

ISSN 0244-6103
FR

CAHIERS D'ETUDES ROMANES : C.E.R. [Cah. etudes rom.]. **VFOAT** C.E.R. 1-. Periodical. French. Two times a year. Universite de Toulouse le Mirail, Service des Publications, 56 rue du Taur, 31000 Toulouse France.
Ind/Abst BHA : Biblio. Hist. Art; MLA Int. Bibl. Books Artic. Mod. Lang. Lit.

BL

CALIOPE. **Added/Corp** Universidade Federal do Rio de Janeiro. Departamento de Letras Clasicas. Ano 1, No. 1 (Julho/Dez. 1984)-. Periodical. Portuguese. Two times a year. Departamento de Letras Clasicas Faculdade de Letras, Rio de Janeiro Brazil.
Ind/Abst Mag. Search.

ISSN 0068-6638
UK

CAMBRIDGE CLASSICAL TEXTS AND COMMENTARIES. (1965)-. Monographic series. English. Irregular. Price varies per volume. Cambridge University Press, The Edinburgh Building, Shaftesbury Road, Cambridge CB2 2RU United Kingdom. **Tel** 011 44 1223 312393, FAX 011 44 1223 315052, telex 851-817256. **(Subscription address:** Cambridge University Press / North America, 110 Midland Avenue, Port Chester NY 10573. **Tel** (800)431-1580, (914)937-9600.**)**
Desc: Series of critical editions with introduction and commentary of works by Greek and Latin writers.

UK

CAMBRIDGE GREEK & LATIN CLASSICS. Academic Scholarly Publication. English. Irregular. Cambridge University Press, The Edinburgh Building, Shaftesbury Road, Cambridge CB2 2RU United Kingdom. **Tel** 011 44 1223 312393, FAX 011 44 1223 315052, telex 851-817256.

ISSN 0069-3715
DD 913 GW

CHIRON. **Added/Corp** Deutsches Archaologisches Institut. Kommission fuer Alte Geschichte und Epigraphik. Vol. 1 (1971)-. Monographic series. German. One time a year. Price varies per volume. CH Beck Verlagsbuchhandlung, D-80791 Munich Germany. **Tel** 011 49 89 381891. **Ad Acc. Circ:** 450.
Ind/Abst Numis. Lit.

LC PA9 .C5
DK

CLASSICA ET MEDIAEVALIA. **Added/Corp** Societe Danoise les Etudes Anciennes et Medievales. (1938)-. Periodical. English (French and German). One time a year. kr395.00. Museum Tusculanum Press, University of Copenhagen, Njalsgade 92, DK-2300 Copenhagen S Denmark. **Tel** 011 45 35 329109, FAX 011 45 35 329113. cum. index. available on CD-ROM.
Desc: International journal of philology and history. Includes studies on Greek and Latin language and literature from antiquity to the middle ages as well as ancient history and tradition.
Ind/Abst Annu. Bibliogr. Engl. Lang. Lit.

LC PN883 .C54 **ISSN** 0197-2227
DD 809 US
CCC

Pr Rev.

CLASSICAL AND MODERN LITERATURE. [Classical mod. lit.]. Vol. 1, No. 1 (Fall 1980)-. Academic Scholarly Publication. English. Four times a year. $24.00. Classical and Modern Literature, PO Box 629, Terre Haute IN 47808-0629. **Tel** (812)237-2362. **ED** James O. Loyd and Virginia Leon de Vivero. Index available. **Bk Rev. Ad Acc. Circ:** 500.
Desc: A scholarly journal which publishes articles on the interrelationships between classical and modern literatures.
Ind/Abst Annu. Bibliogr. Engl. Lang. Lit.; Book Rev. Index; Child. Lit. Abstr. (19??-); Lit. Crit. Regist.; MLA Int. Bibl. Books Artic. Mod. Lang. Lit.; Romant. Move.

LC DE1 .C64 **ISSN** 0278-6656
DD 938/.005 US
CCC

Pr Rev.

CLASSICAL ANTIQUITY. [Classical antiq.]. Vol. 1, No. 1 (April 1982)-. Academic Scholarly Publication. English. Two times a year (Apr., Oct.). $64.00. University of California Press, 2120 Berkeley Way, Berkeley CA 94720. **Tel** (510)642-4191, (510)642-3907, FAX (510)642-9917. **ED** Donald Mastronarde. **Bk Rev. Ad Acc. Circ:** 650 (ctrl). available on microfilm and microfiche from University Microfilms International (UMI). Documents available from The Genuine Article, UMI Article Clearinghouse. ***Continues*** *California Studies in Classical Antiquity.*
Desc: Articles on Greek and Roman literature, history, archaeology, art, philosophy, and philology from the Bronze Age through late Antiquity.
Ind/Abst Acad. Abstr.; Acad. Ind. [Computer File] (1987-); Acad. Search; Arts Humanit. Citation Index [Full Cov.]; Curr. Contents Arts Humanit.; EP Collect.; Expand. Acad. Index (1987-); Hist. Source (July 1990-); Homework Help.; Humanit. Index; Humanit. Source; INFO-SOUTH Abstr.; Mag. Search; MasterFile FullTEXT 1000; MasterFile FullTEXT 350; MasterFile FullTEXT 650; MasterFile FullTEXT (July 1990-); Newsp. Period. Abstr. (1991-); OCLC; Pub. Lib. FullTEXT; Res. Alert [Full Cov.]; Soc. Sci. Cit. Index [Select. Cov.]; Telebase.

LC PA1 .C33 **ISSN** 0009-8337
DD 913.38 US

CLASSICAL BULLETIN (ST. LOUIS, MO.), THE. (THE CLASSICAL BULLETIN.). [Classical bull.]. **Added/Corp** St. Louis University. Dept. of Classical Languages. **VFOAT** CB. (1925)-. Bulletin. English. Two times a year. $30.00. Bolchazy Carducci Publishers, 1000 Brown Street Unit 101, Wauconda IL 60084. **Tel** (708)526-4344, FAX (708)526-2867. **ED** Al N. Oikonomides. cum. index. **Bk Rev**, (Qty: 25). **Ad Acc**, **Adv Mgr:** L. Bolchazy. **Circ:** 500. available on microfilm and microfiche from University Microfilms International

(UMI). Documents available from The Genuine Article.
Desc: Articles, book reviews, and poetry in classical studies: literature, history, paleography, and pedagogy.
Ind/Abst Annu. Bibliogr. Engl. Lang. Lit.; Arts Humanit. Citation Index (19??-19??) [Full Cov.]; Cathol. Period. Index; Curr. Contents Arts Humanit.; Res. Alert [Full Cov.]; Soc. Sci. Cit. Index [Select. Cov.].

US
CLASSICAL FORUM. 1- June 1971-. Periodical. English. Classical America Inc, PO Box 821 Times Square Station, New York NY 10036.

LC PA1 .C4 **ISSN** 0009-8353
DD 880/.05 US
CLASSICAL JOURNAL (CLASSICAL ASSOCIATION OF THE MIDDLE WEST AND SOUTH), THE. (THE CLASSICAL JOURNAL.). [Class. j.]. **Added/Corp** Classical Association of the Middle West and South. Vol. 1, (Dec. 1905)-. Periodical. English. Four times a year (Feb., Apr., Oct., Dec.). $30.00. Brigham Young University / 118 Knight Magnum Building, John F. Hall, Provo UT 84602. **Tel** (801)378-2074. **ED** John F. Miller (editor's address: Department of Classics, 146 New Cabell Hall, University of Virginia, Charlottsville, VA 22903). cum. index. **Bk Rev**. **Ad Acc**. **Circ:** 2,700. available on microfilm and microfiche from University Microfilms International (UMI). Documents available from The Genuine Article.
Ind/Abst Annu. Bibliogr. Engl. Lang. Lit.; Arts Humanit. Citation Index [Full Cov.]; Book Rev. Index; Curr. Contents Arts Humanit.; Educ. Index; Index Book Rev. Humanit.; MLA Int. Bibl. Books Artic. Mod. Lang. Lit.; Numis. Lit.; Res. Alert [Full Cov.].

ISSN 0009-8361
US
CLASSICAL OUTLOOK, THE. [Classical outl.]. **Added/Corp** American Classical League. Vol. 14 (Oct. 1936)-. Periodical. English. Four times a year (Fall, Winter, Spring, Summer). $25.00. American Classical League, Miami University / Ohio, Oxford OH 45056. **Tel** (513)529-7741, FAX (513)529-7742. **ED** Richard A. LaFleur, (editor's address: Department of Classics, Park Hall, University of Georgia, Athens, GA 30602-6203). Index available. **Bk Rev**. **Ad Acc**. **Circ:** 4,350. available on microfilm and microfiche from University Microfilms International (UMI); available on photocopies from University Microfilms International (UMI). ***Continues** Latin Notes.*
Desc: Information on developments within the profession. Includes discussion and thinking about the educational aspects of teaching classical languages and humanities and the techniques and practices of actual classroom teaching.
Ind/Abst Book Rev. Index; Curr. Index J. Educ.

LC PA1 .C5 **ISSN** 0009-837X
DD 480/.05 US
CCC
CLASSICAL PHILOLOGY. [Classical philol.]. Vol. 1 (Jan. 1906)-. Periodical. English. Four times a year. $95.00. University of Chicago Press / Journals Division, PO Box 37005, 5720 South Woodlawn, Chicago IL 60637. **Tel** (312)753-3347, FAX (312)753-0811. **ED** Richard P. Saller. cum. index. **Acid Free.** available on microfilm and microfiche from University Microfilms International (UMI). Documents available from The Genuine Article, UMI Article Clearinghouse.
Desc: A journal for the study of life, language, and thought of classical antiquity. Devoted to increasing our understanding of the intellectual and spiritual heritage of Greek and Roman civilization. Presents papers in ancient history, philosophy, epigraphy, and religion as well as in language and literature.
Ind/Abst Acad. Search; Annu. Bibliogr. Engl. Lang. Lit.; Arts Humanit. Citation Index; EP Collect.; Expand. Acad. Index (1989-); Homework Help.; Humanit. Index; Humanit. Source; INFO-SOUTH Abstr.; Linguist. Lang. Behav. Abstr.; Mag. Search; MasterFile FullTEXT 1000; MasterFile FullTEXT 350; MasterFile FullTEXT 650; MasterFile FullTEXT (July 1993-); New Testam. Abstr.; Newsp. Period. Abstr. (1989-); Numis. Lit.; OCLC; Res. Alert [Full Cov.]; Soc. Plann. Policy Dev. Abstr.; Soc. Sci. Cit. Index [Select. Cov.]; Soc. Sci. Index; Sociol. Abstr.; Telebase.

LC PA1 .C6 **ISSN** 0009-8388
DD 480/.5 UK
CCC
CLASSICAL QUARTERLY. [Class. q.]. **Added/Corp** Classical Association (Great Britain). Vol. 1 (April 1907)-. Periodical. English. Two times a year. $76.00. Oxford University Press / UK, Walton Street, Oxford OX2 6DP United Kingdom. **Tel** 011 44 1865 56767, FAX 011 44 1865 267773, telex 851/837330 OXPRES G. **(Subscription address:** Oxford University Press / UK, PO Box 417, Oxford OX2 6YS United Kingdom. **Tel** 011 44 1865 56767.**) ED** D. N. Sedley and A. Hollis. Index available. cum. index. **Ad Acc. Circ:** 1,350. available on microfilm and microfiche from University Microfilms International (UMI). Documents available from The Genuine Article, UMI Article Clearinghouse.
Desc: Devoted to Greco-Roman antiquity in the English-speaking world. Includes research papers and short notes in the fields of language, literature, history and philosophy, normally in English but sometimes in other languages.
Ind/Abst Acad. Search; Arts Humanit. Citation Index (19??-19??) [Full Cov.]; Br. Archaeol. Bibliogr.; Br. Humanit. Index; Curr. Contents Arts Humanit.; EP Collect.; Expand. Acad. Index (1989-); Homework Help.; Humanit. Index; Humanit. Source; INFO-SOUTH Abstr.; Mag. Search; MasterFile FullTEXT 1000; MasterFile FullTEXT 350; MasterFile FullTEXT 650; MasterFile FullTEXT (Jan. 1993-); MLA Int. Bibl. Books Artic. Mod. Lang. Lit.; New Testam. Abstr.; Newsp. Period. Abstr. (1991-); OCLC; Philos. Index; Res. Alert [Full Cov.]; Soc. Sci. Cit. Index [Select. Cov.]; Telebase; World Mag. Bank.

LC PA1 .C7 **ISSN** 0009-840X
UK
CCC
NLM Z 7016 C615
CLASSICAL REVIEW. (THE CLASSICAL REVIEW.). [Class. rev.]. **Added/Corp** Classical Association (Great Britain). (1887)-. Periodical. English. Two times a year. $76.00. Oxford University Press / UK, Walton Street, Oxford OX2 6DP United Kingdom. **Tel** 011 44 1865 56767, FAX 011 44 1865 267773, telex 851/837330 OXPRES G. **(Subscription address:** Oxford University Press / USA, Journals Marketing Department, Oxford University Press, 2001 Evans Road, Cary NC 27513. **Tel** (800)451-7556, (919)677-0977, FAX (919)677-1714.**) ED** A. F. Garvie and H. M. Hine. Index available. cum. index. **Bk Rev**. **Ad Acc**. available on microfilm and microfiche from University Microfilms International (UMI). Documents available from The Genuine Article.
Desc: Critical reviews by experts of new publications in the fields of Graeco-Roman antiquity from all countries.
Ind/Abst Arts Humanit. Citation Index [Full Cov.]; Book Rev. Digest; Book Rev. Index; Curr. Contents Arts Humanit.; Humanit. Index; Index Book Rev. Relig.; Middle East Abstr. Index; MLA Int. Bibl. Books Artic. Mod. Lang. Lit.; Numis. Lit.; Res. Alert [Full Cov.]; Soc. Sci. Cit. Index [Select. Cov.].

ISSN 1070-9711
US
•**CLASSICAL RUSSIA.** (1994)-. Periodical. English. $30.00. University of Utah / Department of Languages and Literature, Salt Lake City UT 84112.

DK
CLASSICAL STUDIES (ODENSE). (CLASSICAL STUDIES.). **Main/Corp** Odense Universitet. Vol. 1 (1971)-. Monographic series. English (Danish and French). Irregular. Price varies per volume. Odense University Press, 55 Campusvej, DK-5230 Odense M Denmark. **Tel** 011 45 7 66157999, FAX 011 45 7 66158126. **Circ:** 30.
Desc: Greek and Roman history, Roman art textual transmission.

ISSN 0009-8418
US
Pr Rev.
CLASSICAL WORLD, THE. [Classical world]. **Added/Corp** Classical Association of the Atlantic States. Vol. 51, No. 1228 (Oct. 1957)-. Periodical. English. Six times a year (Jan., Mar., May, July, Sept., Nov.). $22.00. CAAS Classical World, Duquesne University Department of Classics, Pittsburgh PA 15282. **Tel** (412)396-6450, FAX (412)396-5197. **ED** Matthew Santirocco. Index available (bound in 6 issue, July/Aug.). **Bk Rev**, (Qty: 200-250). **Ad Acc**, **Adv Mgr:** Lawrence Gaichas. **Circ:** 3,000. available on microfilm and microfiche from University Microfilms International (UMI). Documents available from The Genuine Article. ***Continues** Classical Weekly.*
Desc: All phases of classical antiquity.
Ind/Abst Annu. Bibliogr. Engl. Lang. Lit.; Arts Humanit. Citation Index [Full Cov.]; Book Rev. Digest; Book Rev. Index; Curr. Contents Arts Humanit.; Middle East Abstr. Index; New Testam. Abstr.; Numis. Lit.; Res. Alert [Full Cov.]; Soc. Sci. Cit. Index [Select. Cov.].

LC DE1 .C53 **ISSN** 0791-9417
DD 930/.0 IE
•**CLASSICS IRELAND.** **Added/Corp** Classical Association of Ireland. Vol. 1 (1994)-. Academic Scholarly Publication. English. One time a year. University College Dublin, Department of Classics, Belfield Dublin 4 Ireland. **ED** Andrew Smith. available via Internet (gopher.ucd.ie). Documents available from BLDSC.
Desc: Publishes articles covering classical antiquities and classical philology.

ISSN 0755-1959
FR
CLASSIQUES FRANCAIS DU MOYEN-AGE. (LES CLASSIQUES FRANCAIS DU MOYEN AGE / PUBLIES SOUS LA DIRECTION DE MARIO ROQUES.). [Class. fr. m.-age]. No. 1 (1910)-. French (English). Irregular. 30.00F (latest volume). Slatkine Editions, PO Box 765, 1211 Geneva 3 Switzerland. **Tel** 011 41 22 762551.
Ind/Abst MLA Int. Bibl. Books Artic. Mod. Lang. Lit.

ISSN 0588-0777
DD 489 IT
COLLANA DI STUDI CLASSICI. Vol. 1 (1967)-. Periodical. Italian. Viale dell'Astronomia 30, 00144 Rome Italy.

LC DE1 .E25
IT
COLLECTION DE L'ECOLE FRANCAISE DE ROME. **Main/Corp** Ecole Francaise de Rome. **Added/Corp** Ecole Francaise de Rome. Vol. 8 (1972)-. Monographic series. French. Irregular. Price varies per volume. Diffusion de Boccard, 11 rue de Medicis, 75006 Paris France. **Tel** 011 33 1 43260037. ***Continues** Ecole Francaise de Rome. Melanges d'Archeologie et d'Histoire. Supplements.*

BE
COLLECTION LATOMUS. (1939)-. Monographic series. English (French, German, Spanish and Italian). Irregular. Price varies per volume. Collection Latomus, 18 Avenue van Cutsem, B-7500 Tournai Belgium.
Desc: All that concerns Latin studies-literature, philology, history and archaeology.
Ind/Abst Br. Archaeol. Bibliogr.

NE
COLUMBIA STUDIES IN THE CLASSICAL TRADITION. Vol. 1 (1976)-. Monographic series. English. Irregular. Price varies per volume. E.J. Brill, Postbus 9000, 2300 PA Leiden The Netherlands. **Tel** 011 31 71 312624, FAX 011 31 71 317532, telex 39296 BRILL NL.

US
CONTRIBUTIONS OF THE UCLA CENTER FOR MEDIEVAL AND RENAISSANCE STUDIES. **Main/Corp** University of California, Los Angeles. Center for Medieval and Renaissance Studies. (1965)-. Monographic series. English. Irregular. Price varies per volume. University of California Press, 2120 Berkeley Way, Berkeley CA 94720. **Tel** (510)642-4191, (510)642-3907, FAX (510)642-9917.
Desc: UCLA center for medieval and renaissance studies.

LC DF261.C65 A6
US
CORINTH : RESULTS OF EXCAVATIONS CONDUCTED BY THE AMERICAN SCHOOL OF CLASSICAL STUDIES AT ATHENS. **Main/Corp** American School of Classical Studies at Athens. (1929)-. Monographic series. English. Irregular. Price varies per volume. American School of Classical Studies, Institute of Advanced Study, Princeton NJ 08543. **Tel** (609)734-8387, FAX (609)924-0578.

LC PA227
DD 480 SP
CUADERNOS DE FILOLOGIA CLASICA. ESTUDIOS LATINOS. **See** Linguistics.

ISSN 0705-1085
DD 180 CN
DIONYSIUS. [Dionysius]. Vol. 1 (Dec. 1977)-. English (French). One time a year. $10.00 (individuals), $15.00 (institutions). Dalhousie University Department of Classics, Halifax Nova Scotia B3H 3J5 Canada. **Tel** (902)494-3468. **ED** A H Armstrong, R D Crouse and J A Doull. **Circ:** 300.
Desc: Articles on classics, ancient and medieval philosophy, theology, classical, Christian, and Jewish literature and religion.
Ind/Abst Philos. Index.

LC PA1.A1 E4 **ISSN** 1121-8819
IT
EIKASMOS : QUADERNI BOLOGNESI DI FILOLOGIA CLASSICA. **Added/Corp** Universita di Bologna. Dipartimento di Filologia Classica e Medioevale. (1990)-. Periodical. Italian (English and German). One time a year. L65.000 Italy; L90.000 other. Patron Editore, Via Badini 12, 40050 Quarto Inferiore, Bologna Italy. **Tel** 011 39 51 767003, FAX 011 39 51 768252.

LC PA1.A1 E5 **ISSN** 0046-1628
DD 230 XR
EIRENE; STUDIA GRAECA ET LATINA. **Added/Corp** Ceskoslovenska Akademie Ved. Kabinet Pro Studia Recka, Rimska a Latinska. Vol. 1 (1960)-. Multiple languages (English, French, German and Russian). One time a year. $94.00. John Benjamins BV, Amsteldijk 44, PO Box 75577, 1070 AN Amsterdam Netherlands. **Tel** 011 31 20 6738156, FAX 011 31 20 739773. **(Subscription address:** John Benjamins North America, PO Box 27519, Philadelphia PA 19118-0519. **Tel** (215)836-1200, FAX (215)836-1204.**) ED** Jan Janda.
Desc: Publishes monographical articles in classical studies, namely by scholars from socialist countries. Besides main features there are also discussions, book reviews and news.

LC PA9 .E5 **ISSN** 0013-6662
SP
EMERITA. (EMERITA / JUNTA PARA AMPLIACION DE ESTUDIOS, CENTRO DE ESTUDIOS HISTORICOS.). [Emerita]. **Added/Corp** Instituto Antonio de Nebrija. Centro de Estudios Historicos (Spain). Vol. 1

(1933)-. Periodical. Spanish. Two times a year. 5500ptas. Consejo Superior Investigacion Cientificas / CSIC, Vitruvio 8, 28006 Madrid Spain. **Tel** 011 34 1 5612833, FAX 011 34 1 4113077, telex 42182. **Bk Rev**.
Desc: Publishes contributions from classical scholars world-wide on the literature, culture, history, thought, religion, and languages of ancient Greece and Rome, with special attention to language and culture of ancient Spain.
Ind/Abst MLA Int. Bibl. Books Artic. Mod. Lang. Lit.

ISSN 0071-0822
SZ
CCC

ENTRETIENS SUR L'ANTIQUITE CLASSIQUE. **Added/Corp** Fondation Hardt pour l'Etude de l'Antiquite Classique. **VFOAT** Entretiens. Vol. 1 (1952)-. Monographic series. French. Irregular. Price varies per volume. Librairie Droz SA, 11 rue Massot BP 389, CH-1211 Geneva 12 Switzerland. **Tel** 011 41 22 3466666, FAX 011 41 22 472391.

LC DG89 .E64 **ISSN** 0071-0989
GW

EPIGRAPHISCHE STUDIEN. **Added/Corp** Rheinisches Landesmuseum Bonn Gesellschaft der Freunde und Forderer des Rheinischen Landesmuseums in Bonn. Vol. 1 (1967)-. Monographic series. German. Irregular. Price varies per volume. Dr. Rudolf Habelt GmbH, Postfach 150104, D-53040 Bonn Germany. **Tel** 011 49 228 232015. ctrl circ.
Ind/Abst Br. Archaeol. Bibliogr.

LC PA9 .E7 **ISSN** 0013-9947
SW

ERANOS. [Eranos]. Vol. 1 (1896)-. Periodical. Swedish (English and German). Two times a year. $83.00. Scandinavian University Press, PO Box 2959 Toeyen, N 0608 Oslo 6 Norway. **Tel** 011 47 2 2575400, FAX 011 47 2 2575353, telex 71896 UROR N. **(Subscription address:** Scandinavian University Press, 200 Meacham Ave., Elmont NY 11003. **Tel** (516)352-7300, FAX (516)352-7377.**)** **ED** Sten Eklund (editor's address: Department of Classical Philology, PO Box 513, S-751 Uppsala Sweden; editor's FAX: 4618 181421). cum. index. **Ad Acc. Circ:** 600.
Desc: Presents original papers on Greek and Latin philology, including medieval Latin, Byzantine Greek, and antiquity in general.
Ind/Abst MLA Int. Bibl. Books Artic. Mod. Lang. Lit.

LC B785.E64 A13 **ISSN** 0276-2854
DD 199/.492 US
Pr Rev.

ERASMUS OF ROTTERDAM SOCIETY YEARBOOK. [Erasmus Rotterdam Soc. yearb.]. **Added/Corp** Erasmus of Rotterdam Society. (1981)-. Academic Scholarly Publication. English. One time a year (December). $45.00. Erasmus of Rotterdam Society, University of Kentucky, Department of the Classics, Lexington KY 40506. **Tel** (606)257-5710, FAX (606)258-1073. **ED** Jane E. Phillips. **Bk Rev**, (Qty: 3-6). **Circ:** 350.
Desc: Contains scholarly articles and book reviews which deal with the life and works of Erasmus, a humanist of the Renaissance.

GW

ERGAENZUNGSBAENDE ZUM REALLEXIKON DER GERMANISCHEN ALTERTUMSKUNDE. **VFOAT** Reallexikon der Germanischen Altertumskunde. Ergaenzungsbaende. (1986)-. Monographic series. German. Irregular. Price varies per volume. Walter de Gruyter Inc. / Hawthorne, 200 Saw Mill River Road, Hawthorne NY 10532. **Tel** (914)747-0110, GERMANY: 011/49/30/260050, FAX (914)747-1326, telex 646677.

ISSN 0425-2268
GW

ERLANGER BEITRAEGE ZUR SPRACH UND KUNSTWISSENSCHAFT. [Erlanger Beitr. Sprach- Kunstwiss.]. Vol. 1 (1958)-. Monographic series. German (English). Price varies per volume. Verlag Hans Carl GmbH & Company KG, Andernacher Strasse 33A, D-90411 Nuernberg Germany. **Tel** 011 49 911 9528531, FAX 011 49 911 9528547. cum. index. **Bk Rev**. **Circ:** 1,000.
Desc: Scientific collection on studies of German, English and American philology, romance languages, classical philology and arts.
Ind/Abst MLA Int. Bibl. Books Artic. Mod. Lang. Lit.

ISSN 0014-1453
SP

ESTUDIOS CLASICOS (MADRID). (ESTUDIOS CLASICOS.). [Estud. clas.]. **Added/Corp** Sociedad Espanola de Estudios Clasicos. Patronato Marcelino Menendez y Pelayo. Instituto "San Jose de Calasanz.". (1950)-. Periodical. Spanish. Two times a year. 3000ptas. Sociedad Espanola Estudios Clasicos, Hortaleza 104 2DA IZQ, 28004 Madrid Spain. **Tel** 011 34 1 3081446. Documents available from The Genuine Article.
Ind/Abst Arts Humanit. Citation Index (19??-19??) [Full Cov.]; Curr. Contents Arts Humanit.; Res. Alert [Full Cov.]; Soc. Sci. Cit. Index [Select. Cov.].

LC AS241 .E8 **ISSN** 0014-200X
BE

ETUDES CLASSIQUES (NAMUR, BELGIUM). (LES ETUDES CLASSIQUES.). [Etud. class.]. Vol. 1, No. 1 (Jan. 1932)-. Periodical. French. Four times a year (Jan., Apr., July, Oct.). $52.24. Les Etudes Classiques, rue de Bruxelles 61, 5000 Namur Belgium. **Tel** 011 32 81 229061 ext. 2307, FAX 011 32 81 230391, telex 59222. **ED** P. Marchetti and L. Isebaert. Index available. cum. index. **Bk Rev**, (Qty: 150). **Ad Acc**. Documents available from The Genuine Article.
Desc: Covers classical studies, pedagogical and academic research, classical history and civilization and modern literature.
Ind/Abst Arts Humanit. Citation Index [Full Cov.]; Curr. Contents Arts Humanit.; MLA Int. Bibl. Books Artic. Mod. Lang. Lit.; Numis. Lit.; Res. Alert [Full Cov.]; Romant. Move.; Soc. Sci. Cit. Index [Select. Cov.].

SP

FAVENTIA. (1979)-. Catalan (French, English and Spanish). Two times a year. Departament de Classiques, Facultat de Lettre, Publicacions de la Universitat Autonoma de Barcelona, Barcelona Spain.

ISSN 1047-0212
DD 480 US

FAVONIUS SUPPLEMENTARY VOLUME. [Favonius suppl. vol.]. Vol. 1 (1987)-. Monographic series. English (Latin and Greek, Ancient). Irregular. Price varies per volume. University of California Department of Classics, 405 Hilgrade Avenue, Los Angeles CA 90024. **Tel** (213)825-4171.

ISSN 0071-495X
AG

FILOLOGIA. [Filologia]. **Added/Corp** Universidad de Buenos Aires. Instituto de Filologia. Buenos Aires. Universidad Nacional. Instituto de Filologia Romanica. (May/Aug. 1949)-. Periodical. Spanish. Two times a year. $35.00 (institutions); $20.00 (individuals). Universidad de Buenos Aires / Argentina, Facultdad Filosofia Letras Puan 470, Buenos Aires 1406, Argentina. **Tel** 011 54 1 4320537, 011 54 1 4328696.
Ind/Abst Am. Hist. Life (1968-1971); MLA Int. Bibl. Books Artic. Mod. Lang. Lit.

LC AP85 .P45 **ISSN** 1105-1000
DD 059.89 GR

FILOLOGIKE PROTOHRONIA. **See** Linguistics.

ISSN 0015-1815
PL
UDC 008

FILOMATA. [Filomata]. (1929)-. Periodical. Polish. Six times a year. $10.00. **(Subscription address:** Ars Polona-Ruch, PO Box 1001, Krakowskie Przedmiescie 7, 00-068 Warsaw Poland. **Tel** 011 48 22 261201.**)**

LC PA1000 .F64
DD 489/.3/05 NE

FOLIA NEOHELLENICA. **Added/Corp** Ruhr-Universitat Bochum. Vol. 1 (1975)-. English (French, German, Greek and Modern, Italian). Irregular. Adolf M. Hakkert Editore, Calle Alfambra 26, Las Palmas Gran Canaria Spain. **Tel** 011 34 28 277350, FAX 011 34 28 277350. **ED** AM Hakkert. **Ad Acc**.

LC B4 .G5 **ISSN** 0017-0089
DD 195/.05 IT

GIORNALE CRITICO DELLA FILOSOFIA ITALIANA. [G. crit. filos. ital.]. (1920)-. Periodical. Italian. Three times a year. L120000. Le Lettere, Costa San Giorgio 28, 50125 Florence Italy. **Tel** 011 39 55 2342710. **(Subscription address:** Licosa s.p.a., PO Box 552, 50125 Florence Italy. **Tel** 011 39 55 645415.**)** **ED** Eugenio Garin. cum. index. Documents available from The Genuine Article.
Desc: Aim is a historical investigation of the roots of 18th-19th century Italian thought, its ties with civilized society and the cultural world of Europe, often through reconstructions of significant people and trends of the past.
Ind/Abst Arts Humanit. Citation Index [Full Cov.]; Bibliogr. Mission.; Curr. Contents Arts Humanit.; MLA Int. Bibl. Books Artic. Mod. Lang. Lit.; Philos. Index; Res. Alert [Full Cov.]; Soc. Sci. Cit. Index [Select. Cov.].

LC DE1 .G7 **ISSN** 0017-3835
DD 913.38 UK
CCC

GREECE & ROME. [Greece Rome]. **Added/Corp** Classical Association (Great Britain). **VFOAT** Greece and Rome. (Oct. 1931)-. Periodical. English. Two times a year. $66.00. Oxford University Press / UK, Walton Street, Oxford OX2 6DP United Kingdom. **Tel** 011 44 1865 56767, FAX 011 44 1865 267773, telex 851/837330 OXPRES G. **(Subscription address:** Oxford University Press / USA, Journals Marketing Department, Oxford University Press, 2001 Evans Road, Cary NC 27513. **Tel** (800)451-7556, (919)677-0977, FAX (919)677-1714.**)** **ED** Ian McAuslan and P. Walcot. Index available. cum. index. **Bk Rev. Ad Acc. Circ:** 900. available on microfilm and microfiche from University Microfilms International (UMI). Documents available from The Genuine Article, UMI Article Clearinghouse.
Desc: Literary evaluation of the major Greek and Roman authors, and articles on ancient history, art, archaeology, the classical tradition, and on the teaching of classics at the tertiary level.
Ind/Abst Acad. Search; Arts Humanit. Citation Index [Full Cov.]; Br. Archaeol. Bibliogr.; Br. Humanit. Index; Curr. Contents Arts Humanit.; EP Collect.; Expand. Acad. Index (1989-); Homework Help.; Humanit. Index; Humanit. Source; INFO-SOUTH Abstr.; Mag. Search; MasterFile FullTEXT 1000; MasterFile FullTEXT 350; MasterFile FullTEXT 650; MasterFile FullTEXT (July 1993-); Newsp. Period. Abstr. (1991-); OCLC; Res. Alert [Full Cov.]; Telebase.

ISSN 0072-7474
DD 938 US

GREEK, ROMAN AND BYZANTINE MONOGRAPHS. Vol. 1 (1959)-. Monographic series. English. Irregular. Price varies per volume. Greek, Roman and Byzantine Studies, 329 Perkins Library, Duke University, Durham NC 27708-0199. **Tel** (919)684-6456, FAX (919)681-4262. **ED** D. Keith Stanley. **Circ:** 1,200.
Desc: Concerned with all aspects of the Greek world from prehistory through the Byzantine era.

LC DE1 .G73 **ISSN** 0017-3916
DD 938/.005 US
Pr Rev.

GREEK, ROMAN AND BYZANTINE STUDIES. **Added/Corp** Duke University. Vol. 2, No. 1 (Jan. 1959)-. Academic Scholarly Publication. English (French and German). Four times a year. $25.00. Greek, Roman and Byzantine Studies, 329 Perkins Library, Duke University, Durham NC 27708-0199. **Tel** (919)684-6456, FAX (919)681-4262. **ED** D. Keith Stanley and Kent J. Rigsby. Index available in last issue of volume--attached. **Circ:** 900 (ctrl). available in microform from Kraus Microform. Documents available from The Genuine Article, UMI Article Clearinghouse. ***Continues** Greek and Byzantine Studies, 0884-7304.*
Desc: Significant research articles on all aspects of the Greek world from prehistoric antiquity through the Hellenic, Roman and Byzantine periods. Includes stories of modern scholarship. Articles concerned primarily with Latin are excluded: the "Roman" in the title refers to the Greek world during the Roman period.
Ind/Abst Acad. Search; Arts Humanit. Citation Index [Full Cov.]; BHA : Biblio. Hist. Art; Curr. Contents Arts Humanit.; EP Collect.; Expand. Acad. Index (1989-); Hist. Source (July 1993-); Homework Help.; Humanit. Index; Humanit. Source; Index Book Rev. Relig.; INFO-SOUTH Abstr.; Mag. Search; MasterFile FullTEXT 1000; MasterFile FullTEXT 350; MasterFile FullTEXT 650; MasterFile FullTEXT (Jan. 1993-); Middle East Abstr. Index; New Testam. Abstr.; Newsp. Period. Abstr. (1990-); OCLC; Relig. Index One Period. (1959-); Res. Alert [Full Cov.]; SportSearch; Telebase.

ISSN 0072-7482
DD 800 US

GREEK, ROMAN AND BYZANTINE STUDIES. SCHOLARLY AIDS. Vol. 1 (1961)-. Monographic series. English. Irregular. Price varies per volume. Greek, Roman and Byzantine Studies, 329 Perkins Library, Duke University, Durham NC 27708-0199. **Tel** (919)684-6456, FAX (919)681-4262. **ED** D. Keith Stanley. **Circ:** 1,000.
Desc: Studies and teaching aids for modern classical scholarship.
Ind/Abst Curr. Contents Arts Humanit.

ISSN 0342-5231
GW

GYMNASIUM (HEIDELBERG). (GYMNASIUM.). [Gymnasium]. Vol. 19 (19??)-. Periodical. German. Six times a year. DM138.00 Germany; DM171.00 other. Universitatsverlag Carl Winter, POB 106140, D-69051 Heidelberg Germany. **Tel** 011 49 6221 770260. **ED** Franz Bomer. **Bk Rev. Ad Acc. Circ:** 2,700 (ctrl). Documents available from The Genuine Article. ***Continues** Humanistische Gymnasium.*
Desc: Classical philology, study of the cultures of antiquity and humanistic education.
Ind/Abst Arts Humanit. Citation Index [Full Cov.]; Curr. Contents Arts Humanit.; MLA Int. Bibl. Books Artic. Mod. Lang. Lit.; Res. Alert [Full Cov.].

SP

HABIS. **Added/Corp** Universidad de Sevilla. (1970)-. Periodical. Spanish. One time a year. 3000ptas Spain; 3330ptas other. Universidad de Sevilla / Servicio de Publicaciones, Valparaiso 5, 41013 Seville Spain. **Tel** 011 34 95 423-1958, 011 34 95 423-5976.
Ind/Abst BHA : Biblio. Hist. Art.

LC PA25 .H3 **ISSN** 0073-0688
US

HARVARD STUDIES IN CLASSICAL PHILOLOGY. **Added/Corp** Harvard University. Dept. of the Classics. Harvard University. Vol. 1 (1890)-. Monographic series. English. One time a year. Price varies per volume. Harvard University Press, 79 Garden Street, Cambridge MA 02138. **Tel** (617)496-1344, (800)448-2242. cum. index. Documents available from The Genuine Article.
Desc: Covers classical philology.
Ind/Abst Arts Humanit. Citation Index (19??-19??) [Full Cov.]; Res. Alert [Full Cov.].

ISSN 0930-1208
GW
UDC 931
HEIDELBERGER ALTHISTORISCHE BEITRAEGE UND EPIGRAPHISCHE STUDIEN.
[Heidelb. althist. Beitr. epigr. Stud.]. (1986)-. Monographic series. German. Irregular. Price varies per volume. Franz Steiner Verlag GmbH, Postfach 101061, D-70009 Stuttgart Germany. **Tel** 011 49 711 2582372, FAX 011 49 711 2582290, telex 723636 daz d. **ED** Geza Alfoldy.

ISSN 0017-9981
IT
HELIKON (ROMA).
(HELIKON; RIVISTA DI TRADIZIONE E CULTURA CLASSICA.). [Helikon]. **Added/Corp** Universita di Messina. Vol. 1 (1961)-. Italian. Irregular. Price varies. Herder Editrice e Libreria SRL, Piazza Montecitorio 117-120, 00186 Rome Italy. **Tel** 011 39 6 679 4628, FAX 011 39 6 678 4751.

LC PA1 .H44 **ISSN** 0160-0923
DD 880/.09 US
HELIOS (LUBBOCK).
(HELIOS : JOURNAL OF THE CLASSICAL ASSOCIATION OF THE SOUTHWEST.). (19??)-. Periodical. English. Two times a year. $32.00. Texas Tech University Press, Administrative Education Room 43, West Basement, Lubbock TX 79409-1037. **Tel** (800)832-4042, (806)742-2982. **ED** Stephen Oberhelman. **Bk Rev**. **Ad Acc**. **Circ:** 500. Documents available from The Genuine Article.
Desc: Publishes articles that explore innovative approaches to the study of classical culture, literature and society.
Ind/Abst Annu. Bibliogr. Engl. Lang. Lit.; Arts Humanit. Citation Index [Full Cov.]; Res. Alert [Full Cov.].

ISSN 0018-0114
SP
HELMANTICA.
Added/Corp Salamanca. Pontificia Universidad Eclesiastica. Agrupacion Humanistica Espanola. Vol. 1 No. 1 (Jan./Mar. 1950)-. Periodical. Spanish. Three times a year. $55.00. Universidad Pontificia de Salamanca, Apartado de Correos 541, 37080 Salamanca Spain. **Tel** 011 34 23 215140. **ED** Jose Oroz Reta. **Bk Rev**. **Circ:** 550.
Ind/Abst BHA : Biblio. Hist. Art.

GW
HERMES (1936).
(HERMES : EINZELSCHRIFTEN. ZEITSCHRIFT FUER KLASSISCHE PHILOLOGIE.). **VFOAT** Einzelschriften. (1936)-. Monographic series. German (English). Irregular. Price varies per volume. Franz Steiner Verlag GmbH, Postfach 101061, D-70009 Stuttgart Germany. **Tel** 011 49 711 2582372, FAX 011 49 711 2582290, telex 723636 daz d. **ED** J. Blansdorf, J. Bleicken, W. Kullmann. Index available. **Ad Acc**. Documents available from The Genuine Article.
Desc: Series of scholarly monographs published irregularly as supplements to the quarterly-published Hermes.
Ind/Abst Arts Humanit. Citation Index [Full Cov.]; Res. Alert [Full Cov.].

LC DF10 .H4 **ISSN** 0018-098X
DD 949.5/005 US
Pr Rev.
HESPERIA.
[Hesperia]. **Added/Corp** Institute for Advanced Study (Princeton, N.J.) American School of Classical Studies at Athens. Vol. 1 (1932)-. Periodical. English. Four times a year (Jan., Apr., July, Oct.). $55.00. American School of Classical Studies, Institute of Advanced Study, Princeton NJ 08543. **Tel** (609)734-8387, FAX (609)924-0578. **ED** Marian H. McAllister. cum. index. **Circ:** 1,013 (ctrl). Documents available from The Genuine Article.
Desc: News and information on the classical studies at Athens.
Ind/Abst Abstr. Anthropol.; Art Archaeol. Tech. Abstr.; Art Index; Arts Humanit. Citation Index [Full Cov.]; BHA : Biblio. Hist. Art; Curr. Contents Arts Humanit.; Curr. Contents Soc. Behav. Sci.; Numis. Lit.; Res. Alert [Full Cov.]; Soc. Sci. Cit. Index [Full Cov.].

UK
HISPANIC CLASSICS.
English (Spanish). £19.95. Humanities Press, 165 1st Avenue, Atlantic Highlands NJ 07716. **Tel** (908)872-1441, (800)221-3845, FAX (908)872-0717, telex 752233. Index available.

ISSN 0340-6849
GW
HOLDERLIN-JAHRBUCH.
See Literature.

UK
ILIAD.
(19??)-. Academic Scholarly Publication. English. Irregular. Price varies per volume. Cambridge University Press, The Edinburgh Building, Shaftesbury Road, Cambridge CB2 2RU United Kingdom. **Tel** 011 44 1223 312393, FAX 011 44 1223 315052, telex 851-817256. **(Subscription address:** Cambridge University Press / North America, 110 Midland Avenue, Port Chester NY 10573. **Tel** (800)431-1580, (914)937-9600.**)**

LC PA1 .I43 **ISSN** 0363-1923
DD 880/.05 US
ILLINOIS CLASSICAL STUDIES.
Added/Corp University of Illinois at Urbana-Champaign. University of Illinois at Chicago Circle. Classics Dept. Vol. 1 (1976)-. Academic Scholarly Publication. English. Two times a year. $30.00. Scholars Press / Georgia, PO Box 15399, Atlanta GA 30333-0399. **Tel** (404)636-4757, (404)727-2320, FAX (404)727-2348. **Circ:** 160.
Desc: Presents scholarly writing in the Classics.

ISSN 0073-5752
IT
INCUNABULA GRAECA.
Added/Corp Rome (City). Universit·a. Centro di Studi Micenei. Vol. 1 (1961)-. Monographic series. Multiple languages (French, Italian, English, Latin and German). Irregular. Price varies per volume. Edizioni dell'Ateno, Casella Postale 7216, 00100 Rome Italy. **Tel** 011 39 6 7593456.

GW
INSCHRIFTEN GRIECHISCHER STADTE AUS KLEINASIEN.
Added/Corp Cologne. Universitat. Institut fuer Altertumskunde. Osterreichische Akademie der Wissenschaften. Kommission fuer die Archaologische Erforschung Kleinasiens. Vol. 1 (1972)-. Monographic series. German. Irregular. Price varies per volume. Dr. Rudolf Habelt GmbH, Postfach 150104, D-53040 Bonn Germany. **Tel** 011 49 228 232015.

BE
INSTRUMENTA LEXICOLOGICA LATINA. SERIES B, ENUMERATIO LEMATUM, CONCORDANTIA LEMMATUM ET FORMARUM, INDEX FORMARUM ET LEMMATUM, INDEX LEMMATUM A TERGO ORDINATORUM, TABULA FREQUENTIARUM.
Added/Corp CETEDOC. **VFOAT** Instrumenta Lexicologica Latina. Series B, Lemmata; Corpus Christianorum. Instrumenta Lexicologica Latina. No. 1 (1982)-. Monographic series. Latin. Irregular. Price varies per volume. Brepols Publishers, Steenweg OP Tielen 68, B-2300 Turnhout Belgium. **Tel** 011 32 14 402500.

LC PN883 .I58 **ISSN** 1073-0508
DD 880 US
•INTERNATIONAL JOURNAL OF THE CLASSICAL TRADITION.
(INTERNATIONAL JOURNAL OF THE CLASSICAL TRADITION : THE OFFICIAL JOURNAL OF THE INTERNATIONAL SOCIETY FOR THE CLASSICAL TRADITION.). [Int. j. class. tradit.]. **Added/Corp** International Society for the Classical Tradition. **VFOAT** IJCT. Vol. 1, No. 1 (Summer 1994)-. Periodical. English (French, German, Italian and Spanish). Four times a year. $96.00. Transaction Publishers / Rutgers State University, Department 3091 or 3092, New Brunswick NJ 08903. **Tel** (908)932-2280 ext. 105, FAX (908)932-3138.
Ind/Abst EP Collect.; Homework Help.; Humanit. Source; MasterFile FullTEXT 1000; MasterFile FullTEXT 350; MasterFile FullTEXT 650; MasterFile FullTEXT; OCLC; Telebase.

ISSN 0310-9186
DD 880.09 AT
IRIS AND RES NOVISSIMAE.
[Iris res novis.]. **VFOAT** Iris. Res Novissimae. (1973)-. Periodical. English. Two times a year (June and Nov.). 12.00Aus$; comes also with Classical Association of Victoria membership. Classical Association of Victoria, University of Melbourne, Department of Classical Studies, Parkville Victoria 3052 Australia. **Tel** 011 61 3 344 5671.
Ind/Abst Aust. Educ. Index.

ISSN 0268-0181
DD 880.09 UK
JACT REVIEW.
See Education-Teaching and Curriculum.

LC DF501 .O3 **ISSN** 0378-8660
AU
JAHRBUCH DER OSTERREICHISCHEN BYZANTINISTIK.
[Jahrb. osterr. Byz.]. **Added/Corp** Universitat Wien. Institut fuer Byzantinistik. Osterreichische Akademie der Wissenschaften. Kommission fuer Byzantinistik. Universitat Wien. Institut fuer Byzantinistik und Neograzistik. Vol. 18 (1969)-. English (French, Greek and Modern, Italian). One time a year. S770.00 Austria; DM110.00 Germany. Oesterreichischen Akademie Wissenschaften, Dr. Ignaz Seipel Platz 2, A-1010 Vienna Austria. **Tel** 011 43 1 51581. Index available. **Circ:** 600. ***Continues*** *Jahrbuch der Osterreichischen Byzantinischen Gesellschaft.*
Desc: Literature and history of Byzantium.
Ind/Abst Art Archaeol. Tech. Abstr.; Avery Index Archit. Period. Suppl. Colum. Univ. (19??-199?); BHA : Biblio. Hist. Art; MLA Int. Bibl. Books Artic. Mod. Lang. Lit.

LC DF10 .J8 **ISSN** 0075-4269
UK
JOURNAL OF HELLENIC STUDIES.
(THE JOURNAL OF HELLENIC STUDIES / THE SOCIETY FOR THE PROMOTION OF HELLENIC STUDIES.). [J. Hell. stud.]. **Added/Corp** Society for the Promotion of Hellenic Studies (London, England). Vol. 1 (April/Oct. 1880)-. English. Irregular. $90.00. Society for the Promotion of Hellenic Studies, 31-34 Gordon Square, London WC1H 0PP United Kingdom. **Tel** 011 44 171 3877495. **ED** A. H. Sommerstein. cum. index. **Bk Rev**. **Ad Acc**. **Circ:** 3,000 (ctrl). available on microfilm from University Microfilms International (UMI). Documents available from The Genuine Article, UMI Article Clearinghouse.
Desc: Covers issues in history, art, archaeology, literature, and philosophy of the Hellenic world, particularly of Ancient Greece and the Byzantine Empire.
Ind/Abst Acad. Search; Anthropol. Index; Art Index; Arts Humanit. Citation Index (19??-19??) [Full Cov.]; Avery Index Archit. Period. Suppl. Colum. Univ. (19??-199?); Br. Humanit. Index; Curr. Contents Arts Humanit.; EP Collect.; Expand. Acad. Index (1989-); Homework Help.; Humanit. Index; Humanit. Source; INFO-SOUTH Abstr.; Mag. Search; MasterFile FullTEXT 1000; MasterFile FullTEXT 350; MasterFile FullTEXT 650; MasterFile FullTEXT (July 1993-); MLA Int. Bibl. Books Artic. Mod. Lang. Lit.; New Testam. Abstr.; Newsp. Period. Abstr. (1991-); Numis. Lit.; OCLC; Philos. Index; Res. Alert [Full Cov.]; Soc. Sci. Cit. Index [Select. Cov.]; Telebase; World Mag. Bank.

LC DG11 .J7 **ISSN** 0075-4358
UK
JOURNAL OF ROMAN STUDIES, THE.
[J. Rom. stud.]. Vol. 1 (1911)-. English (French, German and Latin). One time a year (Nov.). £25.00. Society for Promotion of Roman Studies, 31-34 Gordon Square, London WC1H 0PP United Kingdom. **Tel** 011 44 171 3878157. **ED** Andrew F. Wallace-Hadrill, (Department of Classics, Univ. of Reading). Index available (Bound in November.). **Bk Rev**, (Qty: 80/yr). **Ad Acc**, **Adv Mgr Tel** 071-387-8157. **Circ:** 2,700. available on microfilm; available on CD-ROM. Documents available from The Genuine Article, UMI Article Clearinghouse.
Desc: History, art, archaeology, literature of Italy and the Roman Empire down to about 700 AD.
Ind/Abst Acad. Search; Arts Humanit. Citation Index (19??-19??) [Full Cov.]; Br. Archaeol. Bibliogr.; Br. Humanit. Index; Curr. Contents Arts Humanit.; EP Collect.; Expand. Acad. Index (1989-); Homework Help.; Humanit. Index; Humanit. Source; INFO-SOUTH Abstr.; MasterFile FullTEXT 1000; MasterFile FullTEXT 350; MasterFile FullTEXT 650; MasterFile FullTEXT (July 1993-); Middle East Abstr. Index; New Testam. Abstr.; Newsp. Period. Abstr. (1991-); Numis. Lit.; OCLC; Res. Alert [Full Cov.]; Soc. Sci. Cit. Index [Select. Cov.]; Telebase; World Mag. Bank.

ISSN 0454-1596
IT
KOKALOS : STUDI PUBBLICATI DALL'ISTITUTO DI STORIA ANTICA DELL'UNIVERSITA DI PALERMO.
Added/Corp Universita di Palermo. Istituto di Storia Antica. (1955)-. Italian. Irregular. L320000. Dr Giorgio Bretschneider, Via Crescenzio 43, 00193 Rome Italy. **Tel** 011 39 6 6879361. Index available. **Ad Acc**.

ISSN 0221-5896
FR
KTEMA.
[Ktema]. (1976)-. French. One time a year. $88.58. AECR, Attn Edmond Frezouls, Box 350R9, 67009 Strasbourg Cedex France.

GW
KURZBERICHTE AUS DEN PAPYRUSSAMMLUNGEN = BIBLIOTHEK DER JUSTUS LIEBIG-HOCHSCHULE.
Main/Corp Giessen. Universitat Bibliothek. **Added/Corp** Universitaetsbibliothek Giessen. No. 1 (1956)-. Monographic series. German. Irregular. Price varies per volume. Universitatsbibliothek, Bismarckstrasse 37, D-35390 Giessen Germany. **ED** Manfred Landfester. **Circ:** 500.
Desc: Publications from and about the papyrus collections of the University Library of Gieben.

ISSN 0318-8450
DD 938/.005 CN
LABYRINTH (WATERLOO).
(LABYRINTH.). **Added/Corp** University of Waterloo. Classics Division. (Feb. 1975)-. Periodical. English. Three times a year. 4.80Can$. Labyrinth, University of Waterloo, Department of Classical Studies, Waterloo Ontario N2L 3G1 Canada. **Tel** (319)885-1211 Ext. 2428. **ED** P Y Forsyth. Index available. cum. index. **Bk Rev**. ctrl circ.
Desc: A journal of short articles on all aspects of the ancient world intended for the use of secondary school students.

ISSN 0891-4087
DD 880 US
LANG CLASSICAL STUDIES.
[Lang class. stud.]. English. One time a year. Peter Lang Publishing, 62 West 45th Street, 4th Floor, New York NY 10036. **Tel** (212)764-1471, (800)770-5264, FAX (212)302-7574, telex 6973364 PLNY.

LC PA9 .L5 **ISSN** 0024-4457
XR
LISTY FILOLOGICKE (PRAGUE, CZECHOSLOVAKIA : 1946).
See Linguistics.

Classical Studies

LC DP501 .L77   **ISSN** 0024-7413
DD 946.9/005   US
    CCC
LUSO-BRAZILIAN REVIEW. [Luso-Braz. rev.]. **Added/Corp** University of Wisconsin--Madison. Dept. of Spanish and Portuguese. Vol. 1 (June 1964)-. Academic Scholarly Publication. English (Portuguese and Spanish). Two times a year. $86.00. University of Wisconsin Press, Journal Division, 114 North Murray Street, Madison WI 53715. **Tel** (608)262-4952, FAX (608)262-8909. **ED** Stanley Payne and Mary Lou Daniel. **Bk Rev. Ad Acc. Circ:** 700. available on microfilm and microfiche from University Microfilms International (UMI).
Desc: Covers Portuguese and Brazilian culture, with special emphasis on scholarly work in the social sciences and literature.
Ind/Abst Am. Hist. Life (1964-); Hisp. Am. Period. Index, HAPI; MLA Int. Bibl. Books Artic. Mod. Lang. Lit.; Multicult. Educ. Abstr.; Soc. Plann. Policy Dev. Abstr.; Sociol. Educ. Abstr.

LC PA3 .L8   **ISSN** 0024-7421
DD 480   GW
    CCC
LUSTRUM. Vol. 1 (1956)-. Periodical. German (English and German). One time a year. DM140.00. Vandenhoeck & Ruprecht, Robert Bosch Breite 6, D-37079 Goettingen Germany. **Tel** 011 49 551 695911, FAX 011 49 551 695917, telex 965226 VAN d. **ED** H J Mette and A Thierfelder. **Bk Rev. Ad Acc. Circ:** 800. **Supersedes** Jahresbericht Uber die Fortschritte der Klassischen Altertumswissenschaft.

LC PA9 .M34   **ISSN** 0025-0538
    IT
MAIA. [Maia]. Vol. 1 (Jan./March 1948)-. Periodical. Italian (German, French, English and Greek, Modern). Three times a year. L60000. GEM Srl Nuova Cappelli, Via Farini 14, 40124 Bologna Italy. **Tel** 011 39 51 239060. **ED** F. Della Corte. Index available. cum. index. **Bk Rev. Circ:** 1,000 (ctrl). Documents available from The Genuine Article.
Desc: The review publishes articles about classical studies in Latin, Greek and other languages.
Ind/Abst Arts Humanit. Citation Index [Full Cov.]; MLA Int. Bibl. Books Artic. Mod. Lang. Lit.; Res. Alert [Full Cov.]; Soc. Sci. Cit. Index [Select. Cov.].

    ISSN 0392-6338
    IT
MATERIALI E DISCUSSIONI PER L'ANALISI DEI TESTI CLASSICI. [Mater. discuss. anal. testi class.]. **VFOAT** MD; Analisi Dei Testi Classici. (1978)-. Periodical. Italian. Two times a year. L60000. Giardini Editori Stampatori, Via Santa Bibbiana 28, 56127 Pisa Italy. **Tel** 011 39 50 934242.

LC DE71 .M4   **ISSN** 0025-6285
    PL
MEANDER. [Meander]. Vol. 1 (1945)-. Periodical. Polish. Twelve times a year. $54.00. **(Subscription address:** Ars Polona-Ruch, PO Box 1001, Krakowskie Przedmiescie 7, 00-068 Warsaw Poland. **Tel** 011 48 22 261201.)
Ind/Abst MLA Int. Bibl. Books Artic. Mod. Lang. Lit.

LC AS182 .M6   **ISSN** 1149-0349
    FR
MEMOIRES DE L'ACADEMIE DE METZ. (MEMOIRES DE L'ACADEMIE NATIONALE DE METZ.). [Mem. Acad. Metz]. **Added/Corp** Academie Nationale de Metz. (1920)-. Academic Scholarly Publication. French. One time a year. Academie Nationale de Metz, 20 en Nexirue, 57000 Metz France. **Tel** 011 33 1 87752973. cum. index. **Continues** Memoires de l'Academie de Metz, 1149-0349.
Ind/Abst BHA : Biblio. Hist. Art.

LC DG12 .A575   **ISSN** 0065-6801
    IT
MEMOIRS OF THE AMERICAN ACADEMY IN ROME. Main/Corp American Academy in Rome. Vol. 1 (1916)-. English. Irregular. Price varies per volume. Pennsylvania State University Press, 820 North University Drive, Suite C, University Park PA 16802-1003. **Tel** (814)865-1327, (800)326-9180, FAX (814)863-1408. **Continues in part** Supplementary Papers of the American School of Classical Studies in Rome.
Ind/Abst Numis. Lit.

LC PA9 .M56   **ISSN** 0213-9634
DD 480/.09/05   SP
MINERVA : REVISTA DE FILOLOGIA CLASICA. Added/Corp Universidad de Valladolid. Dpto. de Filologia Clasica. No. 1 (1987)-. Spanish. One time a year. 2546ptas Spain; 2603ptas other. Universidad Valladolid Secretariado Publicaciones, Juan Mambrillia 14, 47003 Valladolid Spain. **Tel** 011 34 83 294144, 011 34 82 294499. **(Subscription address:** L'Estaquirot S A, Nuestra Senora del Coll 53, 08023 Barcelona Spain. **Tel** 011 34 3 2850327.)

    ISSN 0959-0218
DD 930.05   UK
MINIBUS LONDON. (MINIBUS). [Minibus Lond.]. (1989)-. Periodical. English. Two times a year. £1.00 (per number). Joint Association of Classical Teachers / Cambridge, 19 Glisson Road, Cambridge CB1 2HA United Kingdom. **Tel** 0223-65762. **ED** Mrs J. Cohen. **Circ:** 5,000.
Desc: Magazine for junior high school students interested in Greek, Latin and classical civilization.

LC DF759 .M58   **ISSN** 1105-1019
    GR
MNEMOSUNE (ATHENAI). See History-History of Europe.

LC PA9 .M6   **ISSN** 0026-7074
    NE
    CCC
MNEMOSYNE. (MNEMOSYNE. BIBLIOTHECA CLASSICA BATAVA.). [Mnemosyne]. **VFOAT** Bibliotheca Classica Batava. Vol. 1 (1852)-. Periodical. English (French, German and Latin). Five times a year. $162.00. E.J. Brill, Postbus 9000, 2300 PA Leiden The Netherlands. **Tel** 011 31 71 312624, FAX 011 31 71 317532, telex 39296 BRILL NL. **ED** C. J. Ruijgh. **Circ:** 550. Documents available from UMI Article Clearinghouse.
Desc: First appeared as a journal of textual critism. It focuses on all aspects of the ancient world, including inscriptions, papyri, language, religion and philosophy.
Ind/Abst Acad. Search; EP Collect.; Homework Help.; Humanit. Index; Humanit. Source; INFO-SOUTH Abstr.; Mag. search; MasterFile FullTEXT 1000; MasterFile FullTEXT 350; MasterFile FullTEXT 650; MasterFile FullTEXT (July 1993-); MLA Int. Bibl. Books Artic. Mod. Lang. Lit.; Newsp. Period. Abstr. (1991-); OCLC; Telebase.

    ISSN 0169-8958
    NE
MNEMOSYNE. SUPPLEMENTUM. (MNEMOSYNE : SUPPLEMENTUM. BIBLIOTHECA CLASSICA BATAVA.). [Mnemosyne. Suppl.]. **VFOAT** Supplement to Mnemosyne. (1938)-. Monographic series. English (French). Irregular. Price varies per volume. E.J. Brill, Postbus 9000, 2300 PA Leiden The Netherlands. **Tel** 011 31 71 312624, FAX 011 31 71 317532, telex 39296 BRILL NL. **(Subscription address:** E.J. Brill / US and Canada, 24 Hudson Street, Kinderhook NY 12106. **Tel** (800)962-4406 ext. 11, FAX (518)758-1959.)
Desc: Devoted mainly to textual criticism on all aspects of the ancient world, including inscriptions, papyrology, language, religion and philosophy.
Ind/Abst MLA Int. Bibl. Books Artic. Mod. Lang. Lit.

LC DE1 .M79
DD 913/.03/05   NR
MUSEUM AFRICUM. Added/Corp West African Classical Association. University of Ibadan. Dept. of Classics. Vol. 1 (1972)-. English (Latin and Greek, Modern). One time a year (Dec.). N14.00. University of Ibadan Department of Classics, Oya State, Ibadan Nigeria. **Supersedes** Nigeria and the Classics.

LC PA3 .M73   **ISSN** 0027-4054
DD 480/.05   SZ
    CCC
MUSEUM HELVETICUM. See Archaeology.

    ISSN 0710-7331
DD 930/.06/07   CN
NEWSLETTER (ASSOCIATION OF ANCIENT HISTORIANS). (NEWSLETTER / THE ASSOCIATION OF ANCIENT HISTORIANS.). [Newsl. - Assoc. Anc. Hist.]. 1 (Nov. 1974)-. Newsletter. English. Irregular. Professor S Burstein, 7563 Midfield Avenue, Los Angeles CA 90045.

LC CB311 .O26   **ISSN** 0275-2158
DD 930/.05   US
    SUSPENDED
OCCASIONAL PUBLICATIONS IN CLASSICAL STUDIES. (OCCASIONAL PUBLICATIONS IN CLASSICAL STUDIES : OPCS.). [Occas. publ. classical stud.]. **VFOAT** OPCS. No. 1 (1978)-?. Periodical. English. One time a year. $3.50. Professor George E Fay, Editor Museum of Anthropology, University of Northern Colorado, Greeley CO 80639.

    ISSN 0261-507X
    UK
OMNIBUS (LONDON). (OMNIBUS). [Omnibus]. (1981)-. Periodical. English. Two times a year. £25.00 or $30.00. Joint Association of Classical Teachers (JACT), 16 Dunster Road, Nottingham NG2 6JF United Kingdom. **Tel** 011 44 171 6100849.

LC DE3 .O6   **ISSN** 0078-5520
    SW
OPUSCULA ATHENIENSIA. [Opusc. Athen.]. 1 (1953)-. English (French, German and Latin). Every 2 years. Kr400.00. Paul Astroms Forlag, V Hamngatan 3, S 41117 Goteborg Sweden. **Tel** 31-95 66 00. **ED** Brita Alroth. **Bk Rev. Circ:** 500 (ctrl).
Desc: Articles on Greek classical and prehistoric archaeology, ancient Greek history and civilization.
Ind/Abst Art Archaeol. Tech. Abstr.; Numis. Lit.

LC DG12 .S815   **ISSN** 0471-7309
    SW
OPUSCULA ROMANA. English (French, German, Latin and Italian). Irregular. Paul Astroms Forlag, V Hamngatan 3, S 41117 Goteborg Sweden. **Tel** 31-95 66 00. **ED** Brita Alroth. **Circ:** 500. **Continues** Opuscula Archaeologica.
Desc: Articles on Roman and Etruscan archaeology and history.

    ISSN 0078-5555
    GW
ORBIS ANTIQUUS. Added/Corp Munster. Universitat. Altertumswissenschaftliche Gesellschaft. No. 1 (1950)-. Monographic series. German. Irregular. Price varies per volume. Aschendorffsche Verlagsbuchhandlung, Postfach 1124, D-48135 Muenster Germany. **Tel** 011 49 251 690132, telex 08-92 830 WN MS D. **ED** Max Wegner.
Desc: Monograph series on Greek and Roman art and literature, government, religions, architecture, music and geography.

LC DG201
DD 937   IT
●**ORIENS GRAECOLATINUS.** (1994)-. Monographic series. Italian. Irregular. Istituto Ellenico di Studi Bizantini e Post-Bizantini, Castello 3412, 30122 Venice Italy. **Tel** 011 39 41 5238248.

    ISSN 0030-5790
    IT
ORPHEUS : RIVISTA DI UMANITA CLASSICA E CRISTIANA. Added/Corp Universita di Catania. Centro di Studi Sull'antico Cristianesimo. Vol. 1 No 1 (1954)- Vol. 25 (1978); New Ser. Vol. 1 No. 1 (1980)-. Periodical. English (French, German, Greek, Modern and Italian, Latin). Two times a year (Jan. & June). L27250. Univ Catania Centro Studies, Sullantico Cristianesimo, 95124 Catania Italy. **Tel** 011 39 95 7102659.
Ind/Abst MLA Int. Bibl. Books Artic. Mod. Lang. Lit.
    UK
Pr Rev.
PAPERS OF THE LEEDS INTERNATIONAL LATIN SEMINAR. 6th Vol. (1990)-. Monographic series. English. Irregular. Price varies. Francis Cairns, c/o Leeds University, Department of Classic Leeds, West Yorkshire LS2 9JT United Kingdom. **Tel** 011 44 1532 333538. **ED** Francis Cairns and Malcolm Heath. **Continues** Liverpool Latin Seminar. Papers of the Liverpool Latin Seminar.
Desc: University-level articles on Greek and Roman literature and related topics.
    IT
PARAGONE. LETTERATURA. No. 2 (Feb. 1950)-. Periodical. Italian. Six times a year. Licosa Spa, PO Box 552, 50125 Florence Italy. **Tel** 011 39 55 645415. **ED** Lucia Longhi.
Desc: Has outstanding contributors from the humanistic culture of today. Characterized by freedom of opinions and articles of enduring substance and quality.

LC CB351 .P32   **ISSN** 0313-6221
DD 914/.03/105   AT
Pr Rev.
PARERGON. [Parergon]. **Added/Corp** Australian and New Zealand Association for Medieval and Renaissance Studies. (Dec. 1971)-. Academic Scholarly Publication. English. Two times a year (July and Dec.). 41.11Aus$. University of Sydney / Department of English, Sydney New South Wales 2006 Australia. **Tel** 011 61 2 6922374, FAX 011 61 2 6924203. **ED** Diane Speed. **Bk Rev. Circ:** 350 (ctrl). Documents available from The Genuine Article. **Supersedes** Australian and New Zealand Association for Medieval and Renaissance Studies. ANZAMRS Bulletin.
Desc: Scholarly research articles on a wide range of medieval and Renaissance subjects, principally literature, languages, music, visual arts and history and politics.
Ind/Abst Annu. Bibliogr. Engl. Lang. Lit.; APAIS, Aust. Public Aff. Inf. Ser. (1972-); Arts Humanit. Citation Index (19??-19??) [Full Cov.]; Curr. Contents Arts Humanit.; MLA Int. Bibl. Books Artic. Mod. Lang. Lit.; Res. Alert [Full Cov.].

    ISSN 0031-2355
    IT
PAROLA DEL PASSATO, LA. Vol. 1, No. 1 (1946)-. Periodical. Italian (German, Greek, Modern, English and Latin, French). Six times a year. L68130. Gaetano Macchiaroli Editore, Via Michetti 11, 80127 Naples Italy. **Tel** 11 39 81 5783129, FAX 11 39 81 5780568. cum. index. **Bk Rev. Ad Acc.**
Desc: Covers ancient history, archaeology and philology.

LC DS54.A2 P5
    CY
PHILOLOGIKE KYPROS . See Linguistics.
    GR
Pr Rev.
PHILOLOGOS. (19??)-. Greek, Modern. Four times a year. $40.00. Philologos, PO Box 10836, 54110 Thessaloniki Greece. **Tel** 011 30 31 272735. **ED** A. Alexiades. Index available. cum. index. **Bk Rev,** (Qty: 10-20). **Ad Acc. Circ:** 3,000 (ctrl).
Desc: Covers classical studies, mainly to help teachers of Ancient Greek in High School. Main emphasis is on Ancient Greece, but articles on history, psychology and pedagogie are included.

LC PA1 .P48 ISSN 0031-8299
DD 480.5 CN
PHOENIX (TORONTO). (PHOENIX.). [Phoenix]. **Added/Corp** Ontario Classical Association. Classical Association of Canada. Vol. 1 (Jan. 1946)-. Periodical. English (French). Four times a year. 55.00Can$ (institutions), 50.00Can$ (individuals). Trinity College-Phoenix, University of Toronto, Larkin 339, Toronto Ontario M5S 1H8 Canada. **Tel** (416)978-3037. **ED** Catherine Rubincam. Index available. **Bk Rev**, (Qty: 50). **Ad Acc. Circ:** 1,150. Documents available from The Genuine Article.
Desc: Covers archaeology, history, poetry, drama, philosophy and other literature on the Greek and Roman period up to early Christianity.
Ind/Abst Arts Humanit. Citation Index (19??-19??) [Full Cov.]; Index Book Rev. Humanit.; MLA Int. Bibl. Books Artic. Mod. Lang. Lit.; Numis. Lit.; Philos. Index; Res. Alert [Full Cov.]; Soc. Plann. Policy Dev. Abstr.; Soc. Sci. Cit. Index [Select. Cov.]; Sociol. Abstr.

LC DF901.P46 P48
GR
PHTHIOTIKA CHRONIKA. (1980)-. Greek, Modern. Demetrios Th Natsios, Ath Bitsola 10, Lamia Greece.

LC PA19 .P53 ISSN 1105-073X
GR
PLATON. **Added/Corp** Hetaireia Hellenon Philologon. (1949)-. Greek, Modern (English, French, German and Latin). One time a year. $25.00. Societe des Philologues Grecs, PO Box 3373, Athens 102 10 Greece. **Tel** 30 1 3213363. **ED** P Georgountzos (editor's address: Euripidou 12 GR-105 59 Athens Greece). **Bk Rev**, (Qty: 1,000). **Circ:** 2,000 (ctrl).
Desc: On ancient Greek and Latin literature, ancient and modern philosophy, linguistics, ancient and medieval history, ancient mythology, archaeology with book reviews.

ISSN 1105-0969
GR
PRAKTIKA TES EN ATHENAIS ARCHAIOLOGIKES HETAIREIAS. See Archaeology.

LC DR301 .P7 ISSN 0555-1153
DD 939.8 BN
PRILOZI ZA ORIJENTALNU FILOLOGIJU = REVUE DE PHILOLOGIE ORIENTALE. **Added/Corp** Orijentalni Institut u Sarajevu. **VFOAT** Revue de Philologie Orientale. (1959)-. Serbo-Croatian (Roman) (Arabic and Turkish; summaries and/or abstracts in English, French and German). One time a year. ***Continues*** *Prilozi za Orijentalnu Filologiju i Istoriju Jugoslovenskih Naroda Pod Turskom Vladavinom.*
Ind/Abst Am. Hist. Life (1954-1975).

LC CC23 .C2 ISSN 0309-3603
UK
PROCEEDINGS OF THE CAMBRIDGE ANTIQUARIAN SOCIETY. See History.

LC BR140.5 .P37a ISSN 0272-8710
DD 940.1/05 US
Pr Rev.
PROCEEDINGS OF THE PMR CONFERENCE. [Proc. PMR Conf.]. **Main/Conf** Patristic, Mediaeval and Renaissance Conference. **Added/Corp** Augustinian Historical Institute. **VAT** Proceedings of the Patristic, Mediaeval and Renaissance Conference. Vol. 1 (1976)-. Proceedings. English. One time a year. $16.00. Augustinian Historical Institute, Villanova University, Villanova PA 19085. **Tel** (610)645-7590. **ED** Phillip Pulsiano. Index available. cum. index. **Circ:** 200 (ctrl).
Desc: Patristic, medieval and renaissance studies.
Ind/Abst MLA Int. Bibl. Books Artic. Mod. Lang. Lit.; Abr. Cathol. Period. Lit. Index; Cathol. Period. Lit. Index.

ISSN 0098-0900
US
PROTOCOL OF THE COLLOQUY OF THE CENTER FOR HERMENEUTICAL STUDIES IN HELLENISTIC AND MODERN CULTURE. **Main/Corp** Center for Hermeneutical Studies in Hellenistic and Modern Culture. No. 1 (April 25, 1970)-. Monographic series. English. Irregular. Price varies per volume. Center for Hermeneutical Studies, 2465 Leconte Avenue, Berkeley CA 94709. **Tel** (415)649-2749. **Circ:** 200 (ctrl).
Desc: Proceedings of scholarly colloquia on interpretive studies.

ISSN 0068-6344
US
PUBLICATIONS: CLASSICAL STUDIES. **Main/Corp** University of California, Berkeley. (1965)-. Monographic series. English. Irregular. Price varies per volume. University of California Press, 2120 Berkeley Way, Berkeley CA 94720. **Tel** (510)642-4191, (510)642-3907, FAX (510)642-9917. **Circ:** 850 (ctrl).

LC D1 .Q27
DD 905 IT
QUADERNI DI STORIA. See History.

ISSN 0033-4987
IT
QUADERNI URBINATI DI CULTURA CLASSICA. **Added/Corp** Universita di Urbino. Istituto di Filologia Classica. Universita di Urbino. Centro di Studi Sulla Lirica Greca e Sulla Metrica Greca e Latina. Italy. Consiglio Nazionale delle Ricerche. Gruppo di Ricerca per la Lirica Greca e la Metrica Greca e Latina. No. 1 (1966)-. Periodical. Multiple languages (English, French and Italian). Three times a year. L102190. Gruppo Editoriale Intern SRL, V S Bibiana 30, 56127 Pisa Italy. **Tel** 011 39 50 934242. **ED** Bruno Gentili. **Bk Rev. Circ:** 1,000.
Ind/Abst Arts Humanit. Citation Index (19??-19??) [Full Cov.].

LC PA1 .R35 ISSN 0048-671X
DD 880/.09 AT
CCC
Pr Rev.
RAMUS. (RAMUS, CRITICAL STUDIES IN GREEK AND ROMAN LITERATURE.). [Ramus]. **VFOAT** Ramus. Vol. 1 (1972)-. Periodical. English. Two times a year (June & Dec.). 38.23Aus$. Aureal Publications, PO Box 49, Bendigo North, Victoria 3550 Australia. **Tel** 011 61 54 447237, FAX 011 61 54 447777. **ED** A J Boyle and J L Penwill. Index available (In every 10th volume). **Bk Rev. Ad Acc. Circ:** 300. Documents available from The Genuine Article.
Desc: Essays of literary criticism on works of classical Greek and Roman literature.
Ind/Abst APAIS, Aust. Public Aff. Inf. Ser. (1974-); Arts Humanit. Citation Index [Full Cov.]; Res. Alert [Full Cov.].

LC PQ4001 .R3 ISSN 0033-9423
IT
RASSEGNA DELLA LETTURATURA ITALIANA, LA. [Rass. lett. ital.]. **Added/Corp** Istituto Universitario di Magistero (Genoa, Italy). Universita di Roma. Istituto di Filologia Moderna. Ser. 7, Vol. 57 (1953)-. Periodical. Italian. Three times a year. L160000 Italy; L210000 other. Le Lettere, Costa San Giorgio 28, 50125 Florence Italy. **Tel** 011 39 55 2342710. **ED** Walter Binni. Index Available, published separately, free-automatically sent. Documents available from The Genuine Article. ***Continues*** *Rassegna.*
Desc: Structure consists of essays and notes, and bibliographical - critical review by century. Its historical - critical methodology provides a link with current Italian studies and as an instrument for charting knowledge and criticism from scholars of Italian all over the world.
Ind/Abst Arts Humanit. Citation Index [Full Cov.]; Curr. Contents Arts Humanit.; MLA Int. Bibl. Books Artic. Mod. Lang. Lit.; Res. Alert [Full Cov.]; Soc. Sci. Cit. Index [Select. Cov.].

GW
REALLEXIKON ZUR BYZANTINISCHEN KUNST. (19??)-. German. Anton Hiersemann Verlag, Rosenbergstrasse 113, D-70193 Stuttgart Germany. **Tel** 011 49 711 638264 5. **Circ:** 1,500.
Desc: Encyclopedia on arts in the former Byzantine empire.

GW
RELIGIONSGESCHICHTLICHE VERSUCHE UND VORARBEITEN. See Religions and Theology.

LC CC ISSN 0330-843X
DD 930.1 TI
REPPAL. See Archaeology.

LC AS30 .R48 ISSN 0275-4304
DD 051 IT
Pr Rev.
RES PUBLICA LITTERARUM. [Res publica litterarum]. **Added/Corp** University of Kansas. (1978)-. English (Italian, German and French). One time a year. L50000. Res Publica Litterarum, Via dell'Abbazia 40, 61032 Fano PS Italy. **Tel** 39 721 802750, FAX 39 721 803726. **ED** Sesto Prete. **Bk Rev**, (Qty: 10). **Circ:** 500 (ctrl).
Desc: Contains articles concerning greco-latin antiquities and the traditions of the medieval and modern world.
Ind/Abst MLA Int. Bibl. Books Artic. Mod. Lang. Lit.

SP
REVISTA DE FILOLOGIA ROMANICA. **Added/Corp** Universidad Complutense de Madrid. Seccion de Filologia Romanica. (1983)-. Periodical. Spanish (French). One time a year. 1800ptas. Editorial Complutense, Donoso Cortes 65, Primera Planta, 28015 Madrid Spain. **Tel** 011 34 1 3946372, 011 34 1 3946373, 011 34 1 3946374.

LC PA12 .R4 ISSN 0035-2004
FR
REVUE DES ETUDES ANCIENNES. [Rev. etud. anc.]. Vol. 1 (Jan./March 1899)-. Periodical. French (summaries and/or abstracts in English). Two times a year (July, & Dec.). 450.00F. University de Bordeaux, Revue des Etudes, Anciennes Domaine University, Talence 33405 France. **Tel** 011 33 56 845171. ***Supersedes in part*** *Revue des Universites du Midi.*
Ind/Abst BHA : Biblio. Hist. Art; MLA Int. Bibl. Books Artic. Mod. Lang. Lit.; Numis. Lit.

LC PA ISSN 0947-0565
DD 480 GW
•**ROMANISTIK IN GESCHICHTE UND GEGEWART.** (1995)-. Academic Scholarly Publication. English. Two times a year. DM98.00. Helmut Buske Verlag Hamburg, Postfach 760244, D-22052 Hamburg Germany. **Tel** 011 49 40 2999580, FAX 011 49 40 2993614. **ED** J. Kramer and H.J. Niederehe.

LC DG504 .R65
DD 945 IT
ROMANOBARBARICA. (1976)-. Monographic series. English (French and Italian). One time a year. Price varies per volume. Herder Editrice e Libreria SRL, Piazza Montecitorio 117-120, 00186 Rome Italy. **Tel** 011 39 6 679 4628, FAX 011 39 6 678 4751. **ED** Bruno Luiselli and Manlio Simonetti.
Desc: Contributions to the study of cultural relations between the Latin world and barbarians; covers history, art and philology.
Ind/Abst BHA : Biblio. Hist. Art.

LC DG404 .R6 ISSN 0080-3790
AU
ROMISCHE HISTORISCHE MITTEILUNGEN. See History-History of Europe.

ISSN 0732-9814
US
RUTGERS UNIVERSITY STUDIES IN CLASSICAL HUMANITIES. [Rutgers Univ. stud. cl. humanit.]. Vol. 1 (1983)-. Monographic series. English. Every 2 years. $49.95 (cloth). Transaction Publishers / Rutgers State University, Department 3091 or 3092, New Brunswick NJ 08903. **Tel** (908)932-2280 ext. 105, FAX (908)932-3138. **ED** William W Fortenbaugh.
Desc: Authoritative and significant research and analysis in the field of classics. Contributions are by international experts and each volume has a particular focus: Arius Didymus, Theophrastus, Cicero.

ISSN 0080-6684
US
SATHER CLASSICAL LECTURES. **Added/Corp** University of California, Berkeley. Sather Classical Lectures. (1921)-. Monographic series. English. Irregular. Price varies per volume. University of California Press, 2120 Berkeley Way, Berkeley CA 94720. **Tel** (510)642-4191, (510)642-3907, FAX (510)642-9917. **(Subscription address:** California Princeton Fulfillment Service, 1445 Lower Ferry Road, Ewing NJ 08618. **Tel** (800)777-4726, (609)883-1759.**) ED** Doris Kretschmer.
Desc: Life and literature of the classics time.

ISSN 0080-696X
GW
SCHRIFTEN UND QUELLEN DER ALTEN WELT. **Added/Corp** Deutsche Akademie der Wissenschaften, Berlin. Sektion fuer Altertumswissenschaft. Vol. 1 (1956)-. Monographic series. German. Irregular. Price varies per volume. Akademie-Verlag GmbH, Postfach, D-13162 Berlin Germany. **Tel** 011 49 30 47889300, FAX 011 49 30 47889357. **(Subscription address:** VCH Publishers Inc., 303 Northwest 12th Avenue, Journals Department, Deerfield FL 33442. **Tel** (800)367-8249, (305)428-5566.**)**

IT
SCRIPTORIUM. Italian. Casa Editrice Leo S. Olschki, Viuzzo del Pozzetto, Casella Postale 66, 50126 Florence Italy. **Tel** 011 39 55 6530684, FAX 011 39 55 6530214.

ISSN 0211-464X
SP
UDC 8
SENARA. See Linguistics.

IT
SILENO. **VFOAT** Rivista di Studi Classici e Cristiani. (1975)-. Periodical. Italian (French). Four times a year. L128000 Italy; L162000 other. L'Erma di Bretschneider SPA, via Cassiodoro 19, 00193 Rome Italy. **Tel** 011 39 6 6874127, 011 39 6 6874129, FAX 011 39 6 6874129.

LC AS142 .V31 ISSN 0029-8832
DD 069.01 AU
SITZUNGSBERICHTE. See History.

LC AS182 .M823 ISSN 0342-5991
GW
SITZUNGSBERICHTE DER BAYERISCHEN AKADEMIE DER WISSENSCHAFTEN. PHILOSOPHISCH-HISTORISCHE KLASSE. [Sitzungsber. - Bayer. Akad. Wiss., Philos.-Hist. Kl.]. **Added/Corp** Bayerische Akademie der Wissenschaften. Philosophisch-Historische Klasse. **VFOAT** Sitzungsberichte. (1946)-. Monographic series. German. Irregular. DM11.00. CH Beck

Classical Studies

Verlagsbuchhandlung, D-80791 Munich Germany. **Tel** 011 49 89 381891. **Continues** *Sitzungsberichte der Bayerischen Akademie der Wissenschaften. Philosophisch-Historische Abteilung.*
Ind/Abst BHA : Biblio. Hist. Art.

LC PG1 .S637
DD 491.8/05
XO
SLOVAK REVIEW. See Literature.

JA
SOPHIA. Added/Corp Jochi Daigaku. Vol. 1, No. 1 (Spring l952)-. Periodical. Japanese (English). Four times a year.
Ind/Abst MLA Int. Bibl. Books Artic. Mod. Lang. Lit.

CY
STASINOS, DELTION TOU SYNDESMOU HELLENON PHILOLOGON KYPROU. (1963)-. Greek, Modern.

ISSN 0081-6124
IT
Pr Rev.
STUDI CLASSICI E ORIENTALI. Vol. 1 (1951)-. Italian (English and French). One time a year. L81750. Giardini Editori Stampatori, Via Santa Bibbiana 28, 56127 Pisa Italy. **Tel** 011 39 50 934242. **ED** Antonioni Carlini.

LC PQ4332 .S67   **ISSN** 0391-7835
DD 851.15
IT
STUDI DANTESCHI. [Studi dant.]. **Added/Corp** Societa Dantesca Italiana. Vol. 1 (1920)-. Periodical. Italian. Irregular. L100000 italy; L120000 other. Le Lettere, Costa San Giorgio 28, 50125 Florence Italy. **Tel** 011 39 55 2342710. **(Subscription address:** Licosa s.p.a., PO Box 552, 50125 Florence Italy. **Tel** 011 39 55 645415.) **ED** Francesco Mazzoni. **Continues** *Bullettino della Societa Dantesca Italiana.*
Desc: The most important and most qualified of the journals, Italian and foreign, devoted to the study of the times, the life, and the works of Dante. Examines cultural and historical influences on his thought and poetry.
Ind/Abst MLA Int. Bibl. Books Artic. Mod. Lang. Lit.

LC PA9 .S7   **ISSN** 0039-2987
DD 480/.05
IT
STUDI ITALIANI DI FILOLOGIA CLASSICA. See Linguistics.

LC DE3 .S78
DD 930
IT
STUDI MICENEI ED EGEO-ANATOLICI. Added/Corp Centro di Studi Micenei ed Egeo-Anatolici (Italy). Istituto per Gli Studi Micenei ed Egeo-Anatolici (Italy). No. 1 (1966)-. Italian (English, French and German). Irregular. Edizioni Ateneo and Bizzarri Srl, Via Ruggero Bonghi 11 B, 00184 Rome Italy. **Tel** 011 39 6 7593456. **(Subscription address:** Courier SAS, via l a de Bosis 25 27, 50145 Florence Italy. **Tel** 011 39 55 300010.)
Ind/Abst MLA Int. Bibl. Books Artic. Mod. Lang. Lit.

ISSN 0899-9929
DD 400
US
STUDIA CLASSICA. [Stud. class.]. English. One time a year. Peter Lang Publishing, 62 West 45th Street, 4th Floor, New York NY 10036. **Tel** (212)764-1471, (800)770-5264, FAX (212)302-7574, telex 6973364 PLNY.

IT
STUDIA OLIVERIANA. Vol. 1 (1953)-Vol. 19/20 (1975); New Series Vol. 1 (1981)-. Periodical. Italian. One time a year. cum. index.

ISSN 1100-8091
SW
STUDIA SEMINARII LATINI UPSALIENSIS. See Linguistics.

GW
STUDIEN ZUR PALEOGRAPHIE UND PAPYRUSKUNDE. German. Irregular. Adolf M. Hakkert Editore, Calle Alfambra 26, Las Palmas Gran Canaria Spain. **Tel** 011 34 28 277350, FAX 011 34 28 277350. **ED** A M Hakkert.

GW
STUDIENREIHE ROMANIA. Monographic series. German. Irregular. Price varies per volume. Erich Schmidt Verlag GmbH, Postfach 304240, D-10724 Berlin Germany. **Tel** 011 49 30 25008525. **ED** E Leube and L Schrader.
Desc: Roman literature studies.

ISSN 0897-7828
DD 487
US
STUDIES IN CLASSICAL GREEK. [Stud. Biblic. Greek]. (1989)-. Monographic series. English. Irregular. Price varies per volume. Peter Lang Publishing,

62 West 45th Street, 4th Floor, New York NY 10036. **Tel** (212)764-1471, (800)770-5264, FAX (212)302-7574, telex 6973364 PLNY.

NE
STUDIES IN GREEK AND ROMAN RELIGION. Vol. 1 (1980)-. Monographic series. English. Irregular. Price varies per volume. E.J. Brill, Postbus 9000, 2300 PA Leiden The Netherlands. **Tel** 011 31 71 312624, FAX 011 31 71 317532, telex 39296 BRILL NL.

LC PQ2105.A2 S8   **ISSN** 0435-2866
UK
STUDIES ON VOLTAIRE AND THE EIGHTEENTH CENTURY. [Stud. Voltaire eight. century]. **Added/Corp** Institut et Musee Voltaire. Voltaire Foundation. Vol. 2 (1956)-. Monographic series. English (French). Irregular. Price varies per volume. Voltaire Foundation, University of Oxford, 99 Banbury Road, Oxford OX2 7RB United Kingdom. **Tel** 011 44 1865 284600, FAX 011 44 1865 270740. **ED** Haydn Mason. Index available. cum. index. **Continues** *Travaux sur Voltaire et le Dix-Huitieme Siecle.*
Desc: All aspects of Eighteenth Century culture, literature and history, with particular emphasis upon the European Enlightenment.
Ind/Abst MLA Int. Bibl. Books Artic. Mod. Lang. Lit.; Romant. Move.

CN
SUBSIDIA MEDIAEVALIA. (1972)-. Monographic series. English (Latin). Irregular. Price varies per volume. Pontifical Institute of Mediaeval Studies, 59 Queens Park Crescent East, Toronto Ontario M5S 2C4 Canada. **Tel** (416)926-7144, FAX (416)926-7276.
Desc: Monograph series of reference books covering a wide range of topics pertaining to the Middle Ages.

LC AS284.A1 S85
SW
SVENSKLARARFORENINGENS ARSSKRIFT. Added/Corp Svensklarareforeningen. VFOAT SLA. (19??)-. Periodical. Swedish.
Ind/Abst MLA Int. Bibl. Books Artic. Mod. Lang. Lit.

LC PA1 .S95   **ISSN** 1040-3612
DD 880.9/0005
US
Pr Rev.
SYLLECTA CLASSICA. [Syllecta class.]. **Added/Corp** University of Iowa. Vol. 1 (1989)-. English. One time a year. $30.00. University of Iowa Syllecta Classical, 112 Shaeffer Hall, University of Iowa, Iowa City IA 52242. **Tel** (319)335-2323, FAX (319)335-2070. **ED** Helena Dettmer and E. B. Holtsmark, (phone: (319)335-2323). cum. index. **Bk Rev**. **Ad Acc**. **Circ**: 100 (ctrl).

LC PA19 .S8   **ISSN** 0039-7679
NO
SYMBOLAE OSLOENSES. See Linguistics.

ISSN 0173-4865
GW
TEXTE DER HETHITER. [Texte Hethit.]. No. 1 (1971)-. Periodical. German (English). Irregular. DM125.00 (cloth), DM98.00 (paper). Universitatsverlag Carl Winter, POB 106140, D-69051 Heidelberg Germany. **Tel** 011 49 6221 770260. **ED** A. Kammenhuber.
Desc: Texts of the Hittites.
Ind/Abst MLA Int. Bibl. Books Artic. Mod. Lang. Lit.

ISSN 0145-3203
US
TEXTS AND TRANSLATIONS. Added/Corp Society of Biblical Literature. VFOAT Texts and Translations Series; Texts & Translations. (19??)-. Monographic series. English. Irregular. Price varies per volume. Scholars Press / Georgia, PO Box 15399, Atlanta GA 30333-0399. **Tel** (404)636-4757, (404)727-2320, FAX (404)727-2348. **ED** H. Betz, E. O'Neil, W. Schoedel, J. Vanderkam and R. Wilken.
Desc: Texts, translations and critical analyses of ancient manuscripts related to early Western history and culture.

ISSN 0361-8641
US
THESAURUS LINGUAE GRAECAE; NEWSLETTER. VFOAT TLG Newsletter. No. 1- Apr. 1973-. Newsletter. English. Two times a year. University of California / Berkeley, Berkeley CA 94720. **ED** Theodore F Brunner, Thesaurus Linguae Graecae.
Desc: Progress and status report on Thesaurus Linguae Graecae data bank of ancient Greek texts.

GW
TRAGICORUM GRAECORUM FRAGMENTA. (19??)-. Monographic series. German. Irregular. Price varies per volume. Vandenhoeck

& Ruprecht, Robert Bosch Breite 6, D-37079 Goettingen Germany. **Tel** 011 49 551 695911, FAX 011 49 551 695917, telex 965226 VAN d.

US
TRANSFORMATION OF THE CLASSICAL HERITAGE, THE. (1981)-. Monographic series. English. Irregular. Price varies per volume. Regents University of California Press, 2120 Berkeley Way, Berkeley CA 94720. **Tel** (510)642-4191.

LC DF503 .C45
DD 949.5/02
FR
TRAVAUX ET MEMOIRES (CENTRE DE RECHERCHE D'HISTOIRE ET CIVILISATION DE BYZANCE (PARIS, FRANCE)). (TRAVAUX ET MEMOIRES / CENTRE DE RECHERCHE D'HISTOIRE ET CIVILISATION DE BYZANCE.). **Added/Corp** Centre de Recherche d'Histoire et Civilisation de Byzance (Paris, France). No. 5 (1973)-. Monographic series. French. Irregular. Price varies per volume. Diffusion de Boccard, 11 rue de Medicis, 75006 Paris France. **Tel** 011 33 1 43260037. **Continues** *Travaux et Memoires (Centre de Recherche d'Histoire et Civilisation Byzantines).*
Ind/Abst BHA : Biblio. Hist. Art.

US
UKRAINIAN CLASSICS IN TRANSLATION. No. 1 (1970)-. Monographic series. English. Irregular. Price varies per volume. Ukrainian Academic Press, Littleton CO.

LC PA6825.A2 V47   **ISSN** 0506-7294
DD 871/.01
US
Pr Rev.
VERGILIUS (1959). (VERGILIUS.). [Vergilius]. No. 5 (Fall 1959)-. English. One time a year (December). $25.00. Vergilian Society of America, PO Box 817, Robert Wilhelm, Oxford OH 45056. **Tel** (513)529-1482, FAX (513)529-1516. **ED** Ward Briggs. **Ad Acc**. **Circ**: 1,300. available on microfilm from University Microfilms International (UMI). **Continues** *Vergilian Digest,* 0272-3026.
Desc: Articles and book reviews on Roman poet Vergil; annual Vergilian bibliography.

ISSN 0568-4358
GW
VEROFFENTLICHUNGEN. Main/Corp Akademie der Wissenschaften, Munich. Kommission fur die Herausgabe Ungedruckter Texte aus der Mittelalterlichen Geisteswelt. (1965)-. Periodical. German. Irregular. Price varies per volume. CH Beck Verlagsbuchhandlung, D-80791 Munich Germany. **Tel** 011 49 89 381891. **Ad Acc**. **Circ**: 450 (ctrl).

LC CB3 .V53   **ISSN** 0083-5897
DD 914/.03/105
US
CCC
Pr Rev.
VIATOR (BERKELEY). (VIATOR.). [Viator]. Vol. 1 (1970)-. English. One time a year. $58.00. University of California Press, 2120 Berkeley Way, Berkeley CA 94720. **Tel** (510)642-4191, (510)642-3907, FAX (510)642-9917. **ED** Mary Rouse and Simon Varey. **Bk Rev**. **Ad Acc**. **Circ**: 400. available on microfilm from University Microfilms International (UMI). Documents available from The Genuine Article.
Desc: Intercultural and interdisciplinary study of the historical periods of late antiquity through the Northern Renaissance.
Ind/Abst Am. Hist. Life (1986-); Annu. Bibliogr. Engl. Lang. Lit.; Arts Humanit. Citation Index (19??-19??) [Full Cov.]; BHA : Biblio. Hist. Art; MLA Int. Bibl. Books Artic. Mod. Lang. Lit.; Res. Alert [Full Cov.].

LC PR1 .V5   **ISSN** 0042-5222
DD 820/.9/008
US
VICTORIAN STUDIES. See Literature.

ISSN 0743-927X
US
VOX MEDIAEVALIS. Added/Corp Western Michigan University. Medieval Institute. Kobenhavns Universitet. Center for Europaeiske Middelalderstudier. Vol. 1 (Spring 1984)-. English (English, French, German and Italian). One time a year. $4.00. Vox Mediavalis, c/o Medieval Institute Publications, Western Michigan University, Kalamazoo MI 49008. **Tel** (616)383-4980. **ED** Constance Nehile and Brian P. McGuire. **Circ**: 100.
Desc: International newsletter for the exchange of information among those interested in medieval studies.

ISSN 0083-9965
AU
WIENER HUMANISTISCHE BLATTER. Added/Corp Verein der Freunde des Humanistischen Gymnasiums. Mitteilungen. Reihe 2. Heft 3-. No. 1, (1958)-. German. Herrn Prof Dr Kraus, Institut fuer Klassische Philologie, Universitaet Vienna, Dr Karl Lueger-Ring 1, A-1010 Vienna Austria. **Tel** 0222/4300/2321. **Ad Acc**. **Circ**: 1,000 (ctrl). **Continues** *Verein der Freunde des Humanistischen Gymnasiums Mitteilungen.*

Desc: Provides instructional material and information for teachers of Greek and Latin through current scientific research findings.

LC PA25 .W85 ISSN 0342-5932
  GW

WUERZBURGER JAHRBUECHER FUER DIE ALTERTUMSWISSENSCHAFT.
[Wuerzbg. Jahrb. Altertumswiss.]. (1946)-. Periodical. German (English and Italian). One time a year. DM100.00. Ferdinand Schoeningh Komm Verlag, Postfach 110852, D-97034 Wuerzburg Germany. **Tel** 011 49 931 309810. **ED** Joachim Latacz and Gunter Neumann. **Ad Acc. Circ:** 600.

  US

YALE CLASSICAL MONOGRAPHS.
(1978)-. Monographic series. English. Irregular. Price varies per volume. Yale University Press, PO Box 209040, New Haven CT 06520. **Tel** (203)432-0940, (800)987-7323, FAX (203)432-0948.

  ISSN 0084-330X
  UK

YALE CLASSICAL STUDIES. Added/Corp
Yale University. Dept. of Classics. (1928)-. Academic Scholarly Publication. English. Irregular. Price varies per volume. Cambridge University Press, The Edinburgh Building, Shaftesbury Road, Cambridge CB2 2RU United Kingdom. **Tel** 011 44 1223 312393, FAX 011 44 1223 315052, telex 851-817256. **(Subscription address:** Cambridge University Press / North America, 110 Midland Avenue, Port Chester NY 10573. **Tel** (800)431-1580, (914)937-9600.)
Ind/Abst BHA : Biblio. Hist. Art.

LC PA9 .Z5 ISSN 0514-7727
  XN

ZIVA ANTIKA. Added/Corp Skopje, Yugoslavia.
Univerzitet. Filosofski Fakultet. Seminar na Klasicna Filologija. Drustvo za Anticki Studii na SRM. **VFOAT** Antiquite Vivante. Vol. 1 (1951)-. Periodical. English (French, German, Latin and Serbo-Croatian (Roman)). Two times a year. $25.00. Redakcita Ziva Antika, Seminar Za Klasicnu Filologiju, Skopje 91000 Macedonia. Documents available from The Genuine Article.
Ind/Abst Arts Humanit. Citation Index (19??-19??) [Full Cov.]; BHA : Biblio. Hist. Art; Curr. Contents Arts Humanit.; MLA Int. Bibl. Books Artic. Mod. Lang. Lit.; Res. Alert [Full Cov.].

ABSTRACTING, BIBLIOGRAPHIES AND STATISTICS

LC Z7016 .A46 ISSN 0044-7633
DD 016.91338 US
  SUSPENDED

AMERICAN CLASSICAL REVIEW. [Am. class. rev.]. Added/Corp City University of New York. Vol. 1, No. 1 (Feb. 1971)-Suspended. Periodical. English. Six times a year. City University of New York / Queen's College, Queen's College, Professor Ursula Schoenheim, Flushing NY 11367.

CLOTHING INDUSTRY AND FASHION

  ISSN 8750-2453
DD 380 US

ACCESSORIES. [Accessories]. VFOAT Fashion
Accessories Magazine; Accessories Magazine. (198?)-. Trade Publication. English. Twelve times a year. $35.00. Business Journals Inc, PO Box 5550, Norwalk CT 06856. **Tel** (203)853-6015, FAX (203)852-8175, telex 353706. **ED** Karen Alberg. **Circ:** 19,477. **Continues** Fashion Accessories Magazine, 0193-0915.
Ind/Abst Trade Ind. Index.

LC TT500 .A34 ISSN 0148-9135
DD 391/.005 US

AMBIANCE. Vol. 1 (Mar. 1978)-. Periodical. English.
Twelve times a year. $20.00. Lalinea USA Publications, PO Box 915, Radio City Station, New York NY 10019.
Desc: Fashion and beauty information.

LC TS945 .A6 ISSN 0146-6437
DD 338.4/7/685310257 US

AMERICAN SHOEMAKING DIRECTORY OF SHOE MANUFACTURERS. (1??)-.
English. One time a year. $42.00. Shoe Trades Publishing Company, 61 Massachusetts Avenue, Arlington MA 02174. **Tel** (617)648-8160, FAX (617)492-0126, telex 325736 SHOETRADE.

  ISSN 0003-1771
  FR
UDC 087.5

AMI COOP LIMOGES, L'. VFOAT Amis Coop
(Limoges). (1953)-. Periodical. French. Eleven times a year. 110.00F France; 150.00F other. Office Central de Cooperation, 101 Bis rue du Ranelagh, 75016 Paris France. **Tel** 45245950.

  ISSN 1120-4338
  IT
UDC 391
  CEASED

AMORE. (1990)-(1993). Periodical. Italian. RCS
Rizzoli Periodici, Via A Rizzoli 2, 20132 Milan Italy. **Tel** 011 39 2 27200720.

LC HD9940.I8 A54
  IT

ANNUARIO DELL'ABBIGLIAMENTO E DEL TEMPO LIBERO. See Industry and Production.

LC HD9940.I8 A55
DD 338.4/7687/02545 IT

ANNUARIO SEAT. VOL. F, ABBIGLIAMENTO ED ESTETICA. See
Industry and Production.

  ISSN 0914-7594
DD 646 JA

APN. APPAREL PRODUCTION NEWS.
[APN, Appar. prod. news]. **VFOAT** Apparel Production News. (1987)-. Periodical. English. Twelve times a year. $105.00. **(Subscription address:** Japan Publications Trading Company Ltd., PO Box 5030, Tokyo International, Tokyo 100-31 Japan. **Tel** 011 81 3 3292 3753.) **Continues** New Japan Sewing Machine News, 0545-1914.

  NZ

APPAREL. (19??)-. Periodical. English. Eleven times
a year (monthly except Jan.). $185.00. Apparel Publishing Limited, PO Box 56-071, Dominion Road, Auckland 3 New Zealand. **Tel** 011 64 9 6315685, FAX 011 64 9 6303706. **ED** Paul Blamfield. **Ad Acc. Circ:** 3,200 (ctrl).
Desc: Covers news, products, and people from the New Zealand apparel, textile, and footwear trade.

  ISSN 1041-5181
  US

APPAREL IMPORT DIGEST. Added/Corp
American Apparel Manufacturers Association. (19??)-. Trade Publication. English. One time a year. Free on request. American Apparel Manufacturers Association, 2500 Wilson Boulevard, Suite 301, Arlington VA 22201. **Tel** (703)524-1864.

LC HD9868.A8 A6
  AT

●APPAREL INDUSTRY. (1993)-. Trade
Publication. English. Six times a year. 28.78Aus$. Yaffa Publishing Group Pty Ltd., GPO Box 606, Sydney New South Wales 2001 Australia. **Tel** 011 61 2 2812333, FAX 011 61 2 2812750. **Continues** Australian Apparel Manufacturer.

LC HD9940.U3 A64 ISSN 0192-1878
DD 338.4/7687/0973 US
  CCC

APPAREL INDUSTRY MAGAZINE. [Appar.
ind. mag.]. (19??)-. Trade Publication. English. Twelve times a year. $57.00. Shore Communications Inc., 6255 Barfield Road, Suite 200, Atlanta GA 30328. **Tel** (404)252-8831, (800)241-9034, FAX (404)252-4436. **ED** Karen Schaffner, Karen Benning and Meg Thornton. Index available. **Ad Acc. Circ:** 18,600 (ctrl). available on an online database from Information Access Company; BRS; and (file 648/Full-Text) DIALOG. Documents available from BLDSC, The UnCover Company, UMI Article Clearinghouse.
Desc: Provides information on manufacturing, technology, management, finance, personal quality, design, merchandising and industry issues.
Ind/Abst Bus. Source Plus; Curr. Cit.; EP Collect.; Homework Help.; MasterFile FullTEXT 1000; MasterFile FullTEXT 350; MasterFile FullTEXT 650; MasterFile FullTEXT; OCLC; Telebase; Text. Technol. Dig.; Trade Ind. ASAP [Full Txt.]; Trade Ind. Index [Full Txt.]; World Text. Abstr.

  ISSN 0263-1008
  UK

APPAREL INTERNATIONAL. (APPAREL
INTERNATIONAL : THE JOURNAL OF THE CLOTHING AND FOOTWEAR INSTITUTE). [Apparel int.].
Added/Corp Clothing and Footwear Institute (Great Britain). Vol. 1, No. 1 (Jan. 1982)-. Trade Publication. English. Eleven times a year (July/Aug. issue combined). $75.00. Cowise International Publishing Group, White House, 60 High Street, Hertfordshire EN6 5AB United Kingdom. **Tel** 011 44 171 70756828, FAX 011 44 171 70745322. **ED** Kenneth Clark. Index available. **Bk Rev**. **Ad Acc. Circ:** 6,000 (ctrl). **Formed by the union of** Clothing & Footwear Journal **and** Clothing Research Journal.
Desc: Apparel manufacture, design, fabrics, marketing and management techniques.
Ind/Abst Curr. Technol. Index; Nonwovens Abstr.; Text. Technol. Dig.; World Text. Abstr.

  ISSN 0744-6403
DD 338 US

APPAREL NEWS SOUTH. [Appar. news south].
Vol. 4, No. 3 (May, 1982)-. Periodical. English. Five times a year. $20.00. Apparel News Group, 110 East 9th Street, Suite A-777 Road, Los Angeles CA 90079. **Tel** (213)627-3737, FAX (213)623-5707. **ED** Anne Harnagel. **Ad Acc. Circ:** 13,000 (ctrl). **Separated from** Atlanta Apparel News, 0273-785X; Apparel South, 0195-3168.

LC HD9940.U3 A655 ISSN 0191-1392
DD 381/.45/6870973 US

APPAREL OUTLOOK. Added/Corp Credit
Clearing House. (19??)-. Periodical. English. One time a year. Dun & Bradstreet / New York, 299 Park Avenue, 24th Floor, New York NY 10171. **Tel** (212)593-4173.

LC HD4966.C62 U623 ISSN 0275-8873
DD 331.2/87/0973 US

APPAREL PLANT WAGES SURVEY. See
Business and Economics-Labor.

  ISSN 1196-2283
  CN

APPAREL (SAINTE-ANNE-DE-BELLEVUE).
(APPAREL.). **VFOAT** Canadian Apparel Manufacturer; Fabricant du Vetement Canadien. (19??)-. Periodical. English (French). Six times a year. 35.00Can$. CTJ Inc., 1 rue Pacifique, Sainte-Anne-de-Bellevue, Quebec H9X 1C5 Canada. **Tel** (514)457-2347, FAX (514)457-2147. **ED** Gillian Crosby. Index available (bound in 6th issue). **Ad Acc, Adv Mgr:** Lumina Fillion. **Continues** Canadian Apparel Manufacturer, 0705-3010.
Desc: Contains features for everyone in the garment industry.

LC HF5439.7 .A53a ISSN 0731-3802
DD 331.2/8138145687/0973 US

APPAREL SALES MARKETING COMPENSATION SURVEY. See Business and
Economics-Marketing and Purchasing.

  US

APPAREL STRATEGIST. (19??)-. Periodical.
English. Twelve times a year. $375.00 (one-year), $675.00 (two-year), $950.00 (three-year). Apparel Information Resources, 101 East Locust Street, Fleetwood PA 19522. **Tel** (610)944-5995, FAX (610)944-0325. **ED** Philip Black. ctrl circ.
Desc: Business journal of the apparel and textile industry.

  ISSN 0160-7278
  US

ARMY/NAVY STORE & OUTDOOR MERCHANDISER. VAT Army Navy Store and
Outdoor Merchandiser. (19??)-. Periodical. English. Twelve times a year. $25.00. PTN Publishing Company, 445 Broad Hollow Road, Melville NY 11747. **Tel** (516)845-2700, FAX (516)845-7109. **Ad Acc. Circ:** 10,500.

LC NK8800 .A68
DD 746/.05 IT

ARTE TESSILE : RIVISTA-ANNUARIO DEL CENTRO ITALIANO PER LO STUDIO DELLA STORIA DEL TESSUTO. See Fabrics and Textile Industries.

  AT
  TITLE CHANGE

AUSTRALIAN APPAREL MANUFACTURER. See Fabrics and Textile
Industries.

  AT
  CEASED

AUSTRALIAN FASHION QUARTERLY.
(19??)-(Summer 1994). English. Australian Consolidated Press Ltd., Private Bag 92615 Symonds St, Auckland New Zealand. **Tel** 011 64 9 3735408, FAX 011 64 9 3022889.

  ISSN 0005-3554
  GW
UDC 687.13:338.45
  CODEN 688:381

B & J. BABY & JUNIOR. VFOAT Baby & Junior
(1976); B und J. Baby und Junior. (1976)-. Trade Publication. Multiple languages. Twelve times a year. $89.82. Meisenbach GmbH, Postfach 2069, D-96011 Bamberg Germany. **Tel** 011 49 951 861135, FAX 011 49 951 861161.

  IT

BAMBINO COLLEZIONI. (19??)-. Italian. Zanfi
Editori SRL, Via Emilia Ovest 954, CP 433, 41100 Modena Italy. **Tel** 011 39 59 891700, FAX 011 39 59 225719, telex 52 22 72.

Clothing Industry and Fashion

ISSN 0266-5794
UK
BEACHWEAR FORECAST INTERNATIONAL. (19??)-. Trade Publication. English. Two times a year. $72.00. International Textile Benjamin Dent Ltd., 23 Bloomsbury Square, London WC1 A2P United Kingdom. **Tel** 011 44 171 6372211, FAX 011 44 171 6372248, telex 8954884.
Desc: Concentrates on the professional needs of swim and beachwear buyers and producers throughout the world.

ISSN 0005-7487
US
BEAUTY FASHION. (19??)-. Trade Publication. English. Eleven times a year. $25.00. Beauty Fashion Inc, 530 5th Avenue, New York NY 10036. **Tel** (212)840-8800.

ISSN 1121-175X
IT
UDC 746.4
BENISSIMO MILANO. [Benissimo Milano]. (1982)-. Periodical. Italian. Twelve times a year. L31340. RCS Rizzoli Periodici, Via A Rizzoli 2, 20132 Milan Italy. **Tel** 011 39 2 27200720.

ISSN 0221-7996
FR
UDC 087.6
BIBA. (1980)-. Periodical. French. Twelve times a year. $62.56. Excelsior Publications, 1 rue du Colonel Pierre Avia, 75503 Paris Cedex 15 France. **Tel** 011 33 1 46484848, FAX 011 33 1 46484758.

ISSN 0192-5938
US
DD 646
BIG BEAUTIFUL WOMAN. [Big beautiful woman]. **VFOAT** BBW; BBW Magazine. (1979)-. Periodical. English. Six times a year. $9.95. LFP Inc., 8484 Wilshire Boulevard, Suite 900, Beverly Hills CA 90210. **Tel** (213)651-5400. **(Subscription address:** Kable Publishers Aide / Illinois, 308 East Hitt Street, Subscription Department, Mt. Morris IL 61054-1473. **Tel** (815)734-1261.) **ED** Carole Shaw. **Bk Rev**. **Ad Acc**.
Desc: Fashion and lifestyle magazine for the large-size woman.

US
BIG BOOK OF PATTERNS. (19??)-. Monographic series. English. Irregular. Price varies per volume. Education Center Inc, 1607 Battleground Avenue, Greensboro NC 27429. **Tel** (919)273-9409, (800)334-0298.

ISSN 1121-8320
IT
UDC 646
BIMBI DI ELEGANTISSIMA. [Bimbi elegantissima]. (1982)-. Periodical. Multiple languages. Two times a year. L80850. A Pieroni SRL, Viale Vittorio Veneto 28, 20124 Milan Italy. **Tel** 39 2 29000282, 29002876.

ISSN 1041-3936
US
DD 381
BLUE SWAN REVIEW : GUIDE TO WOMEN'S FASHION CATALOGS, THE. [Blue swan rev.]. **VFOAT** Blue Swan Review. (1990)-. English. One time a year. $6.00. Blue Swan Communications, POB 9925, San Diego CA 92109. **Tel** (619)272-5718. **ED** Randall Cornish, Kimberly Swan. **Ad Acc**. **Circ:** 3,000.
Desc: Directory of women's fashion catalogs with subject index, feature articles, photographs.

LC TT490 .B6
DD 677
ISSN 0896-3991
US
BOBBIN (1987). (BOBBIN.). [Bobbin]. **VFOAT** Bobbin Magazine. Vol. 28, No. 6 (Feb. 1987)-. Periodical. English. Twelve times a year. $48.00. Bobbin Blenheim Media Corporation, 1110 Shop Road, Columbia SC 29202. **Tel** (803)771-7500, (800)845-8820, FAX (803)799-1461. **ED** Susan Black. Index available. **Ad Acc**. **Continues** Bobbin Magazine, 0894-8259 **and** Apparel Manufacturer.
Desc: News and information source of the global sewn products industry.
Ind/Abst AGRICOLA (1987-); Curr. Cit.; Trade Ind. ASAP [Full Txt.]; Trade Ind. Index [Full Txt.]; World Text. Abstr. (1987-).

ISSN 0194-7249
US
CCC
BOBINA, LA. (19??)-. Periodical. Spanish. Twelve times a year. $70.00. Bobbin Blenheim Media Corporation, 1110 Shop Road, Columbia SC 29202. **Tel** (803)771-7500, (800)845-8820, FAX (803)799-1461.

LC TT490 .B62a
DD 658.8/09/68722
ISSN 0360-3520
US
CCC
BODY FASHIONS/INTIMATE APPAREL. [Body fashions-intim. appar.]. (1913)-. Trade Publication. English. Twelve times a year. $35.00. Advanstar Communications Inc., 131 West First Street, Duluth MN 55802. **Tel** (218)723-9477, (800)346-0085, FAX (218)723-9437. **ED** Jill Gerson. **Circ:** 10,407. available on microfilm and microfiche from University Microfilms International (UMI). **Absorbed** Hosiery and Underwear; **Formed by the union of** Body Fashions **and** Intimate Apparel.
Desc: Business publication for retailers and manufacturers of foundation garments, sleepwear, lingerie, robes, loungewear, hosiery, and underwear.
Ind/Abst Bus. Index (Jan. 1985-Dec. 1985); Gen. BusinessFile (Jan. 1985-Dec. 1985); Text. Technol. Dig.; Trade Ind. Index (1981-?); World Text. Abstr.

LC TT495 .C6
DD 338.4/7/6872502573
ISSN 0362-2452
US
BODY FASHIONS/INTIMATE APPAREL DIRECTORY. (1913)-. Trade Publication. English. One time a year. $20.00. Advanstar Communications Inc., 131 West First Street, Duluth MN 55802. **Tel** (218)723-9477, (800)346-0085, FAX (218)723-9437. **ED** Jill Gerson. **Continues** Body Fashions Directory.

IT
BOOK MODA-ALTA MODA. Italian. Two times a year. L80000. Moda Information Italia, Via Noto 10, 20141 Milan Italy. **Tel** 011 39 2 55213541.

US
BRIDAL APPAREL NEWS. English. Two times a year. $6.00 US; $11.00 Canada. Apparel News Group, 110 East 9th Street, Suite A-777 Road, Los Angeles CA 90079. **Tel** (213)627-3737, FAX (213)623-5707. **ED** Anne Harnagel. **Ad Acc**. **Circ:** 10,000 (ctrl).

ISSN 0957-3933
UK
BRIDES OF BERKSHIRE. See Women's Interests.

ISSN 0957-7432
UK
BRIDES OF BRISTOL BATH & AVON. See Women's Interests.

ISSN 0957-3941
UK
BRIDES OF DEVON & CORNWALL. See Women's Interests.

ISSN 0957-7270
UK
BRIDES OF EAST ANGLIA. See Women's Interests.

ISSN 0957-395X
UK
BRIDES OF HERTS, BUCKS & BEDS. See Women's Interests.

ISSN 0957-7440
UK
BRIDES OF NORTH EAST ENGLAND. See Women's Interests.

ISSN 0957-7289
UK
BRIDES OF SCOTLAND. See Women's Interests.

ISSN 0957-3968
UK
BRIDES OF SOMERSET. See Women's Interests.

ISSN 0957-3976
UK
BRIDES OF SURREY. See Women's Interests.

ISSN 0958-7039
UK
BRIDES OF THE NORTH WEST. See Women's Interests.

ISSN 0957-3984
UK
BRIDES OF YORKSHIRE & HUMBERSIDE. See Women's Interests.

GW
BRIGITTE. (197?)-. Periodical. German. Twenty-six times a year. $120.00. Gruner und Jahr Ag & Co, Abonnenten Service, D-20080 Hamburg Germany. **Tel** 011 49 40 37030, FAX 011 49 40 37035657. **ED** Gruner and Jagr Verlag. **Ad Acc**. available on microfilm from University Microfilms International (UMI).
Desc: Women-journal in German language, for young and modern women.

LC HD9940.G78 C56a
DD 687/.029/441
UK
BRITISH CLOTHING INDUSTRY YEAR BOOK. **Added/Corp** Clothing Export Council of Great Britain. 5th Ed. (1978)-. English. One time a year. £22.00. Kemps Publishing Ltd., 11 Swan Courtyard Yardley, Birmingham B26 1BU United Kingdom. **Tel** 011 44 121 7654144, FAX 011 44 121 7063941. **Ad Acc**. **Continues** Clothing Export Council of Great Britain's Directory for the Clothing Industry.
Desc: A comprehensive guide to the British clothing and textile industry containing sections covering suppliers of all types of made-up clothing, fabrics, equipment and many services to the "rag trade".

ISSN 0937-356X
GW
UDC 746
BURDA INTERNATIONAL AUSG. FUER DEUTSCHLAND. [Burda int. Ausg. Dtschl.]. (1967)-. Periodical. German. Four times a year. $40.00. Verlag Aenne Burda, Postfach 1185, D-77601 Offenburg Germany. **Tel** 011 49 781 843275. **(Subscription address:** German Language Publications Inc., 153 South Dean Street, Englewood NJ 07631. **Tel** (201)871-1010, (800)457-4443.)

ISSN 0007-6031
GW
CCC
BURDA-MODEN (1964). (BURDA MODEN.). [Burda-moden]. Trade Publication. German (English, Spanish, French, Italian, Arabic, Turkish, Portuguese, Dutch and Russian). Twelve times a year. $60.00. German Language Publications Inc., 560 Sylvan Avenue, Englewood Cliffs NJ 07632. **Tel** (201)871-1010.

GW
BURDA MODEN SONDERHEFT FUER MAEDCHEN UND JUNGEN. (19??)-. Trade Publication. German. Two times a year. Verlag Aenne Burda, Postfach 1185, D-77601 Offenburg Germany. **Tel** 011 49 781 843275.

LC HF5429.3 .D5
DD 381/.45687/02573
US
BUYING OFFICES & ACCOUNTS. **Added/Corp** Salesman's Guide, Inc. **VFOAT** Buying Offices and Accounts. (1988)-. English. One time a year. $98.86. Salesman's Guide, A Reed Reference Publishing Company, Part of Reed International PLC, 121 Chanlon Road, New Providence NJ 07974. **Tel** (800)223-1797, (908)464-6800, FAX (908)665-3560, telex 13755. **Continues** Directory of Buying Offices and Accounts.

ISSN 0008-0896
US
CALIFORNIA APPAREL NEWS. (19??)-. Periodical. English. One time a week. $36.00. Apparel News Group, 110 East 9th Street, Suite A-777 Road, Los Angeles CA 90079. **Tel** (213)627-3737, FAX (213)623-5707. **ED** Anne Harnagel. **Ad Acc**. **Circ:** 15,000 (ctrl).

MX
CALZADO Y TENERIA. (1???)-. Periodical. Spanish. Twelve times a year. $30.00. Editorial Elizondo, Apartado Postal 7103, CP 06000 Mexico 1 DF Mexico. **Tel** 557-63-96. **Bk Rev**. **Circ:** 3,500 (ctrl).
Desc: Technical and literary articles on the shoe industry. Presentation of fashion trends in shoe-manufacturing materials as well as in completed shoes. Photographs and reports on events.

ISSN 0008-3232
CN
SUSPENDED
CANADIAN CLOTHING JOURNAL. [Can. cloth. j.]. (1950)-Suspended. Periodical. English. Twelve times a year. $3.09. Julius Hayman Ltd, 77 Mowat Avenue, Suite 016, Toronto Ontario M6K 3E3 Canada. **Tel** (416)537-2696.
Ind/Abst World Text. Abstr.

ISSN 0705-1433
DD 338.4/7/68530971
CANADIAN FOOTWEAR JOURNAL. Vol. 91, No. 1 (Jan./Feb. 1978)-. Periodical. English. Nine times a year. 50.00Can$. Canadian Footwear Journal, 1 Pacifique Ste Anne de Bellevue, Quebec H9X 1C5 Canada. **Tel** (514)457-2423, FAX (514)457-2577, telex 055 61811 MGMSECT. **ED** Barbara McRush. **Ad Acc**, **Adv Mgr:** Brian Murphy. **Circ:** 9,000 (ctrl). available on microfiche from University Microfilms International (UMI). **Continues** Shoe and Leather Journal, 0037-4032; **Absorbed** Canadian Shoemaking, 1979, 0707-185X.
Desc: Features on fashion, business administration, efficient buying and stock control, store design and new developments in technology, materials and manufacturing processes.

ISSN 1196-1007
DD 391/.005
CN
●**CANADIAN IMAGES, BEAUTY, FASHION & STYLE.** [Can. images beauty fash. style]. **VFOAT** Canadian Images; Images Magazine. (1993)-. Periodical. English. Four times a year. 10.37Can$. Telemedia Publishing Inc., 25 Shephard Avenue West, Suite 100, North York Ontario M2N 6S7 Canada. **Tel** (604)877-7732. **Continues** Images (Toronto, Ont.)., 0826-5127.

ISSN 0068-9238
DD 338.4/7/68702571
CN
CANADIAN MERCHANDISE MART. (1956)-. English. One time a year. Byers Associates, 1885 Wilson Avenue, Weston Ontario M9M 1A2 Canada.

Clothing Industry and Fashion

LC NA7100 .C33
DD 728/.05
SP

CASA VOGUE ESPANA. **VFOAT** Casa Vogue. (198?)-. Periodical. Spanish. Twelve times a year. $120.00. Conde Nast Publications / Spain, Ediciones Ed, Serrano #3, 28001 Madrid Spain.

LC HD9787.B83 R52A
DD 338.4/768531/0098165
BL

CENSO DO CALCADO RS. **VFOAT** Censo do Calcado R.S. (19??)-. Portuguese. One time a year. Associacao Comercial e Industrial de Novo Hamburgo, rua Joaquim Pedro Soares 540, CP 468, Novo Hamburgo RS Brazil. **Tel** (0512)954044, telex (51)2507. Index available. cum. index. **Bk Rev**. **Ad Acc. Circ:** 100. *Continues Producao de Calcados No Rio Grande do Sul.*

LC GT500
DD 391/.005
ISSN 0823-7794
CN

C'EST MOI!. [C'est moi]. Vol. 1, No. 1 (Summer 1983)-. Periodical. French. Four times a year. Editions De l'Art Quebecois, 9922 boulevard, St Laurent Montreal Quebec H3L 3R2 Canada.

ISSN 0151-4040
FR

UDC 685.3

CHAUSSER (1968). **VFOAT** Chausser Magazine. (1968)-. Trade Publication. French. Eleven times a year. 445.00F France; 482.00F other. Societe des Publications le Cuir, 1 rue Garnier, 92200 Neuilly Seine France. **Tel** 011 33 1 47381107, FAX 011 33 1 46249924, telex 610-672. **ED** Gabrielle Masson. **Ad Acc, Adv Mgr:** Chantelat. **Circ:** 8,000 (ctrl). *Continues Le Nouveau Chausser, 0151-4032.*
Desc: Publication on shoes and boots.

ISSN 0195-0819
DD 338
US

CHICAGO APPAREL NEWS. [Chic. appar. news]. Vol. 1 (July 1979)-. Periodical. English. Five times a year. $20.00. Apparel News Group, 110 East 9th Street, Suite A-777 Road, Los Angeles CA 90079. **Tel** (213)627-3737, FAX (213)623-5707. **ED** Anne Harnagel. **Ad Acc. Circ:** 8,000 (ctrl).
Desc: Covers fashion and the garment industry in Chicago.

US

CHICAGO MANUAL OF STYLE, THE.
Added/Corp University of Chicago. Press. 13th Ed. (1982)-. Monographic series. English. Irregular. Price varies per volume. University of Chicago Press / Book Department, 11030 South Langley Avenue, Chicago IL 60628. **Tel** (800)621-2736, (312)568-1550, FAX (312)753-0811, telex 23933. *Continues Manual of Style.*

ISSN 0884-2280
DD 380
US
CCC

CHILDREN'S BUSINESS. [Child. bus.]. Vol. 1, No. 1 (Oct. 1985)-. Periodical. English. Twelve times a year. $39.00. Fairchild Publications Inc., 7 West 34th Street, 4th Floor, New York NY 10001-8191. **Tel** (212)630-4230, (800)247-6622. **(Subscription address:** Children's Business, PO Box 3094, Southeastern PA 19398.) available on an online database (files 16,570,648/Full-Text) from DIALOG.
Ind/Abst F&S Index Plus Text, Int. [Full Txt.] [Select. Cov.]; Mark. Advert. Ref. Serv. [Full Txt.]; PROMT [Full Txt.]; Trade Ind. ASAP [Full Txt.]; Trade Ind. Index [Full Txt.].

ISSN 0711-0340
DD 391/.005
CN

CLIN D'OEIL (VILLE MONT-ROYAL). See Beauty and Cosmetics.

UK
CEASED

CLOTH DIRECTORY. (19??)-(April 1995). Directory. English. International Thomas Business Publ, Greater London House, Hamstead Road, London NW1 7Q2 United Kingdom. **Tel** 011 44 171 387611, FAX 011 44 171 3837717. **(Subscription address:** EMAP Business Publishing, 4 Admiral House Cardinal Way, Middlesex HA3 5SQ United Kingdom. **Tel** 011 44 181 8684499.) **ED** Brenda Saunders. Index available. cum. index. **Ad Acc. Circ:** 2,500.
Desc: Includes style trend predictions, indexes, industry diary, news items.

LC TT507 .C6
DD 016.391
ISSN 0887-2937
US

CLOTHING AND TEXTILE ARTS INDEX, THE. [Cloth. text. arts index]. (1984)-. English. One time a year. $75.00. Clothing & Textile Arts Index, PO Box 1300, Monument CO 80132. **Tel** (719)488-3716. **ED** Sandra S Hutton. **Circ:** 150. available on CD-ROM. *Continues Clothing Index.*

ISSN 0887-302X
DD 646
US
CODEN CTRJEZ
Pr Rev.

CLOTHING AND TEXTILES RESEARCH JOURNAL. See Fabrics and Textile Industries.

LC HD9940.C18 C56
DD 338.4/7687/0971021
ISSN 0835-006X
CN

CLOTHING INDUSTRIES. (CLOTHING INDUSTRIES.). [Cloth. ind.]. **Added/Corp** Statistics Canada. Census of Manufactures Section. Statistics Canada. Industry Division. **VFOAT** Industries de l'Habillement. (1985)-. English (French). One time a year. 38.00Can$ Canada; $46.00 US; $54.00 other. Statistics Canada Publications Sales and Services, R.H. Coats Building 6th Floor, Ottawa Ontario K1A 0T6 Canada. **Tel** (613)951-5078, (800)267-6677, FAX (613)951-1584, telex 053-3585. *Formed by the union of Miscellaneous Clothing Industries (Statistics Canada : Final), 0384-3769; Women's and Children's Clothing Industries, 0384-4498 and Men's Clothing Industries, 0527-5679.*

LC HD9940.G78 C57a
DD 338.4/7/68706241
ISSN 0307-8515
UK

CLOTHING INSTITUTE YEAR BOOK & MEMBERSHIP REGISTER, THE. (YEAR BOOK & MEMBERSHIP REGISTER - CLOTHING INSTITUTE.). **Main/Corp** Clothing Institute. **VAT** Clothing Institute Year Book and Membership Register. (19??)-. English. One time a year. Sterling Publications Ltd., 57 North Wharf Road, London W2 1XR United Kingdom. **Tel** 011 44 171 9159660, FAX 011 44 171 3338155, telex 295819. *Continues Clothing Institute. Annual Report and Year Book.*

IT

COLLEZIONI DONNA. **VFOAT** Womens Fashion. (19??)-. Trade Publication. Italian. Six times a year. $287.00. Zanfi Editori SRL, Via Emilia Ovest 954, CP 433, 41100 Modena Italy. **Tel** 011 39 59 891700, FAX 011 39 59 225719, telex 52 22 72.

ISSN 0245-5781
FR

UDC 677

CONFECTION 2000 NOUVELLES TECHNIQUES DE L'HABILLEMENT. **VFOAT** Confection Deux Mille Nouvelles Techniques de l'Habillement. (1980)-. Periodical. French (summaries and/or abstracts in English). Twelve times a year. $148.73. Editions Techniques de l'Habillement, 14 rue des Reculettes, 75013 Paris France. **Tel** 011 33 1 44081900. Index available (bound in Dec. issue).

ISSN 0393-4888
IT

UDC 687

CONFEZIONE. [Confezione]. (1985)-. Periodical. Italian. Twelve times a year. L122630. Tecniche Nuove SPA, Via Ciro Menotti 14, 20129 Milan Italy. **Tel** 011 39 2 75701, FAX 011 39 2 7570205, telex 334647 TECHS I.

LC HF2651.T42 U53
DD 382/.45677/00973021
US

CORRELATION, TEXTILE, AND APPAREL CATEGORIES WITH TARIFF SCHEDULES OF THE UNITED STATES ANNOTATED / PREPARED BY INTERNATIONAL AGREEMENTS AND MONITORING DIVISION. See Fabrics and Textile Industries.

LC AP2 .H4
DD 051
ISSN 0010-9541
US

COSMOPOLITAN (1952). See Women's Interests.

LC AP2
DD 052
ISSN 0310-2076
AT

COSMOPOLITAN AUSTRALIAN EDITION. See Women's Interests.

LC WMLC L 83/4015
DD 391
ISSN 0590-8876
UK

COSTUME. [Costume]. **Added/Corp** Costume Society. Victoria and Albert Museum. (1967/68)-. English. One time a year. $37.64. Costume Society, 21 Oak Road, Woolston SO19 9BQ United Kingdom. **Tel** 011 44 1703 442011. **ED** Ann Saunders. Index available. cum. index. **Bk Rev. Circ:** 1,200 (ctrl).
Desc: The Costume Society exists to encourage the study of the history of clothing and the preservation of significant examples.
Ind/Abst Art Archaeol. Tech. Abstr.; ARTbibliogr. Mod.; BHA : Biblio. Hist. Art; Br. Archaeol. Bibliogr.; Br. Humanit. Index; RILA, Int. Rep. Lit. Art; World Text. Abstr.

ISSN 0336-7266
FR

UDC 66-69

CREATIONS LINGERIE. [Creat. lingerie]. (1970)-. Periodical. French. Four times a year. $109.36. Groupe Creations, 40 rue de Chabrol, 75010 Paris France. **Tel** 011 33 1 42464473, FAX 011 33 1 42461438. **ED** Philippe Maillot. **Ad Acc.** ctrl circ.

ISSN 0336-7274
FR

UDC 66-69

CREATIONS TISSUS. [Creat. tissus]. **VFOAT** Creations Tissus Lingerie. (1974)-. Periodical. French. Two times a year. 370.99F France; 550.00F other. Groupe Creations, 40 rue de Chabrol, 75010 Paris France. **Tel** 011 33 1 42464473, FAX 011 33 1 42461438.

LC HD9787.U4 C87
DD 338.4/76853F/0973
US

CURRENT INDUSTRIAL REPORTS. MA31A, FOOTWEAR. **Added/Corp** United States. Bureau of the Census. **VFOAT** Footwear. (1977)-. Government Publication. English. One time a year. US Department of Commerce / Bureau of the Census, Data User Services Division, Customer Services, Washington DC 20233-0800. **Tel** (301)763-4100. **(Subscription address:** Superintendent of Documents, US Government Printing Office, Washington DC 20402.)
Desc: Presents data on production, inventories, and orders.

ISSN 1071-1147
DD 338
US

CUSTOM TAILOR, THE. [Cust. tailor].
Added/Corp Merchant Tailors & Designers Association of America. (19??)-. Trade Publication. English. Three times a year (Mar., June, Oct.). $35.00. Custom Tailors & Designers Association, 17 East 45th Street, New York NY 10017. **Tel** (212)661-1960. **ED** Irma Blipkin. **Ad Acc. Circ:** 1,000 (ctrl).

ISSN 0162-2161
DD 338
US
CCC

DNR. DAILY NEWS RECORD. (DNR. DAILY NEWS RECORD.). [Dly. news rec.]. Vol. 5, No. 62 (Mar. 31, 1975)-. Periodical. English. Five times a week (daily except Sat. and Sun.). $69.00. Fairchild Publications Inc., 7 West 34th Street, 4th Floor, New York NY 10001-8191. **Tel** (212)630-4230, (800)247-6622. **ED** Michael Luther. **Bk Rev. Ad Acc. Circ:** 27,000. available on microfiche from University Microfilms International (UMI); available on an online database (files 570,648/Full-Text) from DIALOG. *Continues Daily News Record, 0162-2161.*
Desc: Coverage of international men's business wear; including retailers, manufacturers, mills and designers.

ISSN 1041-1119
DD 338
US
CCC

DAILY NEWS RECORD. [Dly. news rec.].
VFOAT DNR; DNR Monday. (Dec. 11, 1916)-. Newspaper. English. Seven times a week. $62.00 (retailers), $79.00 (finance and media), $72.00 other. Fairchild Publications Inc., 7 West 34th Street, 4th Floor, New York NY 10001-8191. **Tel** (212)630-4230, (800)247-6622. *Continues Daily Trade Record.*
Ind/Abst Acad. Search; EP Collect.; Homework Help.; MasterFile FullTEXT 1000; MasterFile FullTEXT 350; MasterFile FullTEXT 650; MasterFile FullTEXT (July 1993-); OCLC; Predicasts; Telebase; Trade Ind. Index (1981-).

ISSN 0279-4888
DD 338
US

DALLAS APPAREL NEWS. [Dallas appar. news]. Vol. 1 No. 1 (Oct. 1981)-. Periodical. English. Five times a year. $20.00. Apparel News Group, 110 East 9th Street, Suite A-777 Road, Los Angeles CA 90079. **Tel** (213)627-3737, FAX (213)623-5707. **ED** Anne Harnagel. **Ad Acc. Circ:** 17,000 (ctrl). *Absorbed Fashion Showcase Retailer.*

ISSN 0706-6449
DD 646/.34/05
CN

DAZZLE. See Beauty and Cosmetics.

FR

DECOLLETAGE. (19??)-. French. Imprimerie du Messager, 22 Av du Generale de Gaulle, F 74201 Thonon Cedex France.

FR

DEPECHE MODE GRAND PUBLIC. (19??)-. French. Editions Mondiales, 9 11 13 rue du Col Pierre Avia, 75754 Paris Cedex 15 France. **Tel** 011 33 1 46622162.

Clothing Industry and Fashion

ISSN 0981-1842
FR
UDC 087.2-055.2
DESSOUS MODE INTERNATIONAL.
(1987)-. Periodical. French. Four times a year. $87.49. Dessous Mode International, 175 boulevard Anatole France, BP 189, 93208 St. Denis France. **Tel** 011 33 1 4833858.

LC HD9940.U3 A58a **ISSN** 0738-520X
DD 687/.029/473
US
DIRECTORY, MEMBERS AND ASSOCIATE MEMBERS - AMERICAN APPAREL MANUFACTURERS ASSOCIATION (1983). (DIRECTORY, MEMBERS AND ASSOCIATE MEMBERS / AMERICAN APPAREL MANUFACTURERS ASSOCIATION.). [Dir., memb. assoc. memb. - Am. Apparel Manuf. Assoc.]. **Main/Corp** American Apparel Manufacturers Association. **VFOAT** Directory ... Members/Associate Members. (1983)-. English. One time a year. $100.00. American Apparel Manufacturers Association, 2500 Wilson Boulevard, Suite 301, Arlington VA 22201. **Tel** (703)524-1864. **Continues** AAMA Directory.

LC HD9787.U4 D58 **ISSN** 1057-7610
DD 685/.3/029473
US
DIRECTORY OF FOOTWEAR & RELATED ACCESSORIES BUYERS. [Dir. footwear relat. accessories buy.]. **Added/Corp** Salesman's Guide, Inc. **VFOAT** Directory of Footwear and Related Accessories Buyers; Footwear and Related Accessories Buyers; Directory of Footwear Buyers; Footwear & Related Accessories Buyers. (1991)-. Directory. English. Salesman's Guide, A Reed Reference Publishing Company, Part of Reed International PLC, 121 Chanlon Road, New Providence NJ 07974. **Tel** (800)223-1797, (908)464-6800, FAX (908)665-3560, telex 138755.

LC HD9940.U3 D48 **ISSN** 0277-9625
DD 687
US
DIRECTORY OF MEN'S & BOYS' WEAR SPECIALTY STORES. **VFOAT** Directory of Men's and Boy's Wear Specialty Stores; Men's and Boy's Specialty Stores; Men's and Boy's Wear Specialty Stores; Men's & Boy's Specialty Stores. (1982)-. Directory. English. One time a year. $185.00 continental US; $195.00 other US; $210.00 other. Lebhar Friedman Inc., PO Box 31203, Tampa FL 33633. **Tel** (800)944-4676, (813)664-6707. **Continues** Directory of Men's and Boy's Specialty Stores, 0272-1112.
Desc: Complete company profiles on 3,600 men and boys' wear specialty store companies and sport shops/activewear retailers operating 21,500 stores.

US
DIRECTORY OF RESOURCES. (19??)-. Directory. English. $22.50. Intimate Fashion News, 309 5th Avenue, New York NY 10016. **Tel** (212)679-6677, FAX (212)679-6374.

LC HD9940.U3 D46 **ISSN** 0277-9617
DD 687/.029/473
US
DIRECTORY OF WOMEN'S & CHILDREN'S WEAR SPECIALTY STORES. **VFOAT** Directory of Women's and Children's Wear Specialty Stores; Women's & Children's Specialty Stores; Women's and Children's Specialty Stores. (1982)-. Directory. English. One time a year. $195.00. Lebhar Friedman Inc., PO Box 31203, Tampa FL 33633. **Tel** (800)944-4676, (813)664-6707. **(Subscription address:** CSG Information Services, 3922 Coconut Palm Drive, Tampa FL 33619.) **ED** Barbara Brown and Elaine Kohlstein. **Continues** Directory of Apparel Specialty Stores, Women's & Children's, 0272-1104.
Desc: Complete company profiles on women's and children's wear specialty store companies and sport shops/activewear retailers.

DD 338
US
DNR : THE MAGAZINE. (19??)-. Periodical. English. Twelve times a year. Fairchild Publications Inc., 7 West 34th Street, 4th Floor, New York NY 10001-8191. **Tel** (212)630-4230, (800)247-6622.

ISSN 0393-7968
IT
UDC 391
DONNA & BAMBINI. **VFOAT** Donna e Bambini. (1983)-. Periodical. Italian. Two times a year. L12800 (Italy); L22000 (other). Rusconi Editore Spa, Servicio Abbonements, Viale Le Sarca 235, 20126 Milan Italy. **Tel** 011 39 2 66192634, FAX 011 39 2 66192206.

UK
DR : THE FASHION BUSINESS. (Sept. 24, 1988)-. English. One time a year. £45.00 UK; £136.00 (airmail) US. International Thomson Business Publications, 42 Bedford Square, London WC1B 3SC United Kingdom. **Tel** 011 44 171 3236986. **ED** Sally Bain. Index available. **Bk Rev. Ad Acc. Circ:** 19,683.

LC GT605 .D74 **ISSN** 0361-2112
DD 391/.00973
US
Pr Rev.
DRESS. [Dress]. Vol. 1, (1975)-. Periodical. English. One time a year. $55.00 individuals, $30.00 libraries, $85.00 institutions, $300.00 corporations (membership fees). Costume Society of America, 55 Edgewater Drive, PO Box 73, Earlville MD 21919. **Tel** (410)275-2329. **ED** Pat Trautman. **Bk Rev. Circ:** 1,500 (ctrl).
Desc: Covers subjects pertaining to all matters of dress and its ramifications emphasizing history and design.
Ind/Abst Art Archaeol. Tech. Abstr.; ARTbibliogr. Mod.; BHA : Biblio. Hist. Art.

ISSN 0012-611X
JA
DRESSMAKING. (1961)-. Periodical. Japanese. Twelve times a year. $150.50. **(Subscription address:** Japan Publications Trading Company Ltd., PO Box 5030, Tokyo International, Tokyo 100-31 Japan. **Tel** 011 81 3 3292 3753.)

LC TT635 .A15 **ISSN** 0161-2786
DD 658.89/687/13
US
EARNSHAW'S INFANTS-GIRLS-BOYS WEAR REVIEW. **VFOAT** Earnshaw's Infants Girls and Boy's Wear Review; Earnshaw's; Earnshaw's Review. **VAT** Earnshaw's Infants Girls Boys Wear Review. (July 1971)-. Trade Publication. English. Twelve times a year. $24.00. Earnshaw Publications Inc., 475 Fire Island Avenue, Babylon NY 11702. **Tel** (516)661-4637. **ED** Tom Hudson Sr. **Bk Rev. Ad Acc. Circ:** 10,000 (ctrl). **Continues** Earnshaw's Infants & Children's Review, 0012-8198.
Desc: News and information on the children's clothing and accessories trade.

CN
EGO KIDS MAGAZINE. English. 39.00Can$ (one-year), 64.00Can$ (two-year) Canada; 66.00Can$ (one-year), 94.00Can$ (two-year) North America; 100.00Can$ other. 430 rue St Helene/Suite 103, Montreal Quebec H2Y 2K7 Canada. **Tel** (514)987-9679. **ED** Chevonne Miller. **Bk Rev. Ad Acc. Circ:** 10,000 (ctrl).
Desc: Canada's national childrens fashion, business and trade publications. Features indepth industry reports, news and photo editorials.

LC AS30 .E34 **ISSN** 0148-5822
DD 051
US
EGO (SAN FRANCISCO). (EGO.). Vol. 1 (Jan. 1976)-. Periodical. English. Four times a year. $24.00. Harrison Fashion Publishing, 254 Brighton Drive, Beaconsfield Quebec H9W 2L4 Canada. **Tel** (514)426-1446.

SZ
ELEGANCE. (19??)-. Periodical. English (French and German). Two times a year. Elegance Publications SA, Gartenstrasse 14, CH 8039 Zurich Switzerland. **Tel** 011 41 1 2025719. **(Subscription address:** Mode Information Heinz Kramer, Pilgerstrasse 20, D 51491 Overath Germany. **Tel** 011 49 2206 60070.)

ISSN 0821-4182
CN
DD 391/.005
ELEGANT (MONTREAL). (ELEGANT.). [Elegant]. Vol. 1, No. 1 (Fall 1982)-. Periodical. Multiple languages (English and French). Four times a year. $20.00. Elegant Publishing, 1844 William Street, Montreal Quebec H3J 1R5 Canada.

LC TT950
DD 646.72
NE
ELLE. See Women's Interests.

LC TT500
DD 391
AT
ELLE (AUSTRALIAN EDITION). See Women's Interests.

LC TT950 **ISSN** 1120-4397
DD 646.72
IT
UDC 391 & B79
ELLE ED. ITALIANA. See Women's Interests.

LC TT500 .E44 **ISSN** 0935-462X
DD 391/.2/05
GW
ELLE (MUNICH, GERMANY). See Women's Interests.

ISSN 0013-6298
FR
ELLE (NEUILLY-SUR-SEINE, FRANCE). See Women's Interests.

LC TT500 .E44 **ISSN** 0888-0808
DD 391/.2/05
US
ELLE (NEW YORK, N.Y.). See Women's Interests.

ISSN 0046-1962
FR
UDC 677-053.2
ENFANCE ET LA MODE, L'. [Enfance mode]. (1961)-. Periodical. French. Four times a year. Soc Technique Art Realisation, 11 rue de Chateaudun, 75009 Paris France. **Tel** 011 33 1 48783743.

LC WMLC L 83/9100 **ISSN** 1054-9323
DD 687
US
EQUINE BUSINESS JOURNAL. (EQUINE BUSINESS JOURNAL : EBJ.). [Equine bus. j.]. **VFOAT** EBJ. Vol. 31, No. 10 (Oct. 1990)-. Periodical. English. Twelve times a year. Western & English Fashions, 2403 Champa Street, Denver CO 80205. **Tel** (303)296-1600, FAX (303)295-2159. **Continues** Western & English Fashions, 0747-0770.

ISSN 0139-8717
XO
UDC 646.7
EVA BRATISLAVA. [EvaBratisl.]. (1970)-. Periodical. Slovak. Twelve times a year. DM69.00. Euroscop Inc, Pribinova 25, 819 39 Bratislava, Slovakia. **Tel** 011 42 7 2103340, FAX 011 42 7 2103910. **(Subscription address:** Kubon & Sagner, ABT Zeitschriftenimport, D 80328 Munich Germany. **Tel** 011 49 89 54218130.)

ISSN 1075-2137
US
●**EXOTIC MAGAZINE (TAMPA, FLA.).** (EXOTIC MAGAZINE.). **VFOAT** Exotic Magazine for Todays and Tomorrows Woman in Fashion. (1996)-. Periodical. English. Twelve times a year. $15.95. Whitaker and Whitaker Publications, P.O. Box 23961, Tampa FL 33623-3961.

LC HD9787.U4 A43B **ISSN** 0362-3890
DD 338.4/7/68530973
US
FACTS AND FIGURES ON FOOTWEAR.
Main/Corp American Footwear Industries Association. Statistical Dept. English. $175.00. American Footwear Industries Association, 1420 K Street NW/#600, Washington DC 20005-2401. **Tel** (703)522-7275. **ED** Janet Treber. **Circ:** 300.
Desc: Footwear Industries of America's Footwear Manual. A comprehensive statistical study of the footwear industry, examining marketing, manufacturing, trade, labor, finance, and more.

ISSN 1067-7062
DD 338
US
FAIRCHILD'S TEXTILE & APPAREL FINANCIAL DIRECTORY. See Fabrics and Textile Industries.

LE
FAIRUZ. Arabic. Twelve times a year. $110.00 US; $130.00 Canada; $200.00 Australia. Dar Assayad Sal, PO Box 1038, Beirut Lebanon. **Tel** 011 1 452700387020.

IT
FASHION. (19??)-. Italian. Forty times a year. L195000 Italy; L350000 other. Edizioni Ecomarket Spa, C So Venezia 26, 20121 Milan Italy. **Tel** 011 39 2 76007371.

ISSN 0255-7290
HK
FASHION ACCESSORIES. [Fash. accessories]. **VFOAT** Asian Sources Fashion Accessories. (1984)-. Trade Publication. English. Twelve times a year. $70.00. Trade Media Ltd / Hong Kong, GPO Box 11411, Hong Kong Hong Kong. **Tel** 011 852 25554777, FAX 011 852 28700637. Index available. **Ad Acc. Circ:** 20,900 (ctrl). **Continues** Asian Sources Garments and Accessories.
Desc: Focuses on accessories such as purses and wallets, handbags, belts, footwear, gems, costume jewelry, luggage, hats and caps, and hosiery.

US
FASHION CALENDER. English. Twenty-six times a year. $393.87 New York; $365.00 other. Fashion Calendar, 153 East 87th Street, New York NY 10128. **Tel** (212)289-0420.
Desc: Listing of US and European fashion dates, designer and trade shows.

UK
FASHION FORECAST. (1946)-. Periodical. English. Twenty-four times a year (Mar. and Sept.). $72.00. International Textiles, Benjamin Dent Ltd, 33 Bedford Place, London WC1B 5JX United Kingdom. **Tel** 011 44 171 6372211, FAX 011 44 171 6372248, telex 8954884. **ED** Suzanne Turoner. **Ad Acc.**

ISSN 0952-701X
UK
FASHION FORECAST INTERNATIONAL. [Fash. forecast int.]. (1987)-. Trade Publication. Multiple languages. Two times a year. $72.00. International Textile Benjamin Dent Ltd., 23 Bloomsbury Square, London WC1 A2P United Kingdom. **Tel** 011 44 171 6372211, FAX 011 44 171 6372248, telex 8954884. **Continues** Fashion Forecast for International Buyers, 0014-8679.
Desc: Highlights the serious style directions to watch for at the start of each major international buying season.

Clothing Industry and Fashion

ISSN 0942-8151
GW
UDC 687.016
FASHION GUIDE DUSSELDORF. [Fash. guideDusseld.]. **VFOAT** German Fashion Guide. (19??)-. Periodical. Multiple languages (German and English). Two times a year (Feb. & Aug.). $63.56. W. Zerres GmbH & Co, Bekleidungswerke, Muelgaustr 322-324, 41238 Moenchengladbach, Postfach 35 01 40, 41223 Moenchengladbach, Germany. **Tel** 011 49 02166 919300, FAX 011 49 02166 1 81 05, telex 85 27 82. **ED** Marita Sonnenberg. **Ad Acc. Continues** German Fashion Guide, 0176-6112.
Desc: German magazine that covers fashion trends, designers, and the overall fashion industry.

LC TT500 ISSN 0228-829X
DD 391/.005 CN
FASHION IMAGES. [Fash. images]. Oct. 1979-. Periodical. English. Irregular. $3.00. Fashion Images, 10444-125th Street, Surrey British Columbia V3V 4Y8 Canada.

US
FASHION INTERNATIONAL. Trade Publication. English. Eight times a year. $100.00. Fashion Calendar, 153 East 87th Street, New York NY 10128. **Tel** (212)289-0420. **ED** Deborah Brumfield.
Desc: Features new or established designers entering into new markets, business features, and color and fabric forecasts.

ISSN 0300-7111
US
FASHION NEWSLETTER, THE. (1962)-. Newsletter. English. Eleven times a year. $179.00. Newsletter Services Inc., 9700 Philadelphia Court, Lanham MD 20706. **Tel** (800)345-2611. **ED** Peter S. Nagan.
Desc: Forecast of international fashions.

ISSN 1044-3568
DD 746 US
FASHION WATCH. [Fash. watch]. **Added/Corp** Retail Reporting Corporation. (19??)-. Periodical. English. Irregular. $323.00. Retail Reporting Corporation, 302 Fifth Avenue, New York NY 10001. **Tel** (212)279-7000, (800)251-4545, FAX (221)279-7014. **Continues** Retail News Fashion Merchandising Report.

ISSN 0892-5216
DD 391 US
FASHIONEWS (BURLINGAME, CALIF.). (FASHIONEWS). **VFOAT** Fashion News. (198?)-. Periodical. English. Four times a year. $15.00. Lois Day Limited, 699 8th Street, Suite 2238A, San Francisco CA 94103. **Tel** (415)864-6455, FAX (415)864-6747. **ED** Lois M. Day. Index available. **Bk Rev. Circ:** 1,500.
Continues Fashion News.
Desc: Seasonal fashion forecasts and ideas, shopping sources, cosmetic news and updates, and designer profiles.

ISSN 0014-9918
US
SUSPENDED
FEMME-LINES. **VAT** Femme Lines. (Feb. 1957)-. Suspended (19??). Periodical. English. Six times a year. Earl Barron Publ Inc, 225 East 36th Street, New York NY 10016. **Tel** (212)683-6593.

ISSN 0706-7534
DD 338.4/7/6853100971 CN
FOOTWEAR FORUM. Vol. 1, (Aug. 1978)-. Trade Publication. English. Twelve times a year (Published 7 issues of Forum and 5 issues of a Newsletter). 17.61Can$. Mackirk Publications, 1448 Lawrence Ave. East, Toronto Ontario M4A 2V6 Canada. **Tel** (416)775-6191, FAX (416)755-9123. **ED** Victoria Curran. **Ad Acc, Adv Mgr:** S. Boake, **Tel** (416)755-5799. **Circ:** 7,500 (ctrl).

LC HD9787.U45 U53A
DD 338.4/7/6853100973 US
FOOTWEAR INDUSTRY REVITALIZATION PROGRAM. (1978)-. English. One time a year. Footwear Industry Team, Department of Commerce, Washington DC 20230.

LC HD9787.U4 F657 ISSN 0095-1048
DD 338.4/768531/00973021 US
TITLE CHANGE
FOOTWEAR MANUAL. **Added/Corp** Footwear Industries of America. American Footwear Industries Association. (1974)-(1995). Trade Publication. English. Footwear Industries of America, 1420 K Street Northwest, Suite 600, Washington DC 20005. **Tel** (202)789-1420, FAX (202)789-4058. **ED** Elizabeth M. Forest. **Circ:** 400.
Continued by Shoestab.
Desc: Covers US footwear production, import/export market, international industry, and labor and raw materials.
Ind/Abst Stat. Ref. Index.

ISSN 0162-914X
DD 338 US
FOOTWEAR NEWS. [Footwear news]. **VFOAT** FN. Vol. 1 (Oct. 6, 1945)-. Trade Publication. English. One time a week. $51.00. Fairchild Publications Inc., 7 West 34th Street, 4th Floor, New York NY 10001-8191. **Tel** (212)630-4230, (800)247-6622. available on an online database (files 16,570,648/Full-Text) from DIALOG.
Ind/Abst Bus. ASAP (1990-) [Full Txt.]; Bus. Index (1985-); F&S Index Plus Text, Int. [Full Txt.] [Select. Cov.]; Gen. BusinessFile (1985-); Mark. Advert. Ref. Serv. [Full Txt.]; PROMT [Full Txt.]; Trade Ind. ASAP [Full Txt.]; Trade Ind. Index (1981-) [Full Txt.].

ISSN 0725-3362
AT
FOOTWEAR NEWS AUSTRALIA. (197?)-. Periodical. English. Eleven times a year (monthly except January). 39.46Aus$. V. Hatton, 70 Kingsway, Suite 7, Glen Waverley Victoria 3150 Australia. **Tel** 011 61 3 5605099, FAX 011 61 3 5600620. **Ad Acc.** ctrl circ.

LC HD9787.U4 F66 ISSN 0429-0208
DD 338.4/7/68530973 US
FOOTWEAR NEWS FACT BOOK. (1954)-. English. One time a week. $51.00 US; $240.00 other. Footwear News, 7 East 34th Street, New York NY 10001. **Ad Acc.**
Desc: Covers footwear.

ISSN 0888-2053
DD 338 US
FOOTWEAR NEWS MAGAZINE. [Footwear news mag.]. (197?)-. Periodical. English. Fairchild Publications Inc., 7 West 34th Street, 4th Floor, New York NY 10001-8191. **Tel** (212)630-4230, (800)247-6622. available on an online database (file 648/Full-Text) from DIALOG.
Ind/Abst Bus. ASAP (1992-) [Full Txt.]; Bus. Index (1985-); Gen. BusinessFile (1985-); Trade Ind. ASAP [Full Txt.]; Trade Ind. Index (1981-) [Full Txt.].

ISSN 1054-898X
DD 338 US
FOOTWEAR PLUS. [Footwear plus]. (Jan. 1991)-. Periodical. English. Ten times a year. $36.00. Earnshaw Footwear Plus, Inc., 475 Fire Island Avenue, Babylon NY 11702.

ISSN 0380-707X
DD 338.4/768531/00971 CN
FOOTWEAR STATISTICS. See Clothing Industry and Fashion-Abstracting, Bibliographies and Statistics.

ISSN 1083-0308
DD 051 US
●**FOREHEAD MAGAZINE.** [Forehead mag.]. (1994)-. Consumer Publication. English. Six times a year. $6.00. Forehead Magazine, 32 Gramercy Park South, #17D, New York NY 10003-1713. **Tel** (212)979-5106, FAX (212)460-5138. **ED** Alison M. McGonigal. **Bk Rev** (Qty: 6). **Photos. Ad Acc, Adv Mgr:** Christopher Sanderson, **Tel** (212)460-5095. **Pub. Size:** Standard. **Circ:** 15,000.
Desc: Presents the urban lifestyle of fashion, art, literature, music and culture. Provides features on a wide range of topics such as works of poets and graffiti artists, fashion coverage, and cafe reviews.

ISSN 0016-3252
IE
FUTURA. (19??)-. Trade Publication. English. Twelve times a year. 27.00p Ireland; 45.00p US; 35.00p other. Futura Communications Limited, Unit 9 Sandylord Office Park, Sandylord Dublin 18 Ireland. **Tel** (01)958119, FAX (01)958065. **ED** Pat Lehane. **Bk Rev. Ad Acc.** ctrl circ.
Desc: Ireland's trade magazine for the fashion and footwear industry.

ISSN 1065-1330
DD 338 US
GARMENT MANUFACTURERS INDEX. [Garment manuf. index]. **Added/Corp** Klevens Publications, Inc. (19??)-. English. One time a year. $42.50. Klevens Publications Inc., 7600 Avenue, Litterlock CA 93543. **Tel** (805)944-4111. **Ad Acc, Adv Mgr:** Edward Klevens. ctrl circ.

LC TT500 .G46 ISSN 0017-0747
DD 687.082 US
GLAMOUR. [Glamour]. (1941)-. Periodical. English. Twelve times a year. $15.00. Conde Nast Publications / New York, 350 Madison Avenue, New York NY 10017. **Tel** (212)880-8800, (800)777-0700, FAX (212)880-8331. (**Subscription address:** Neodata / Colorado, PO Box 2606, Boulder CO 80322.) **ED** Ruth Whitney. **Photos. Ad Acc.** available on microfilm and microfiche from University Microfilms International (UMI). Documents available from UMI Article Clearinghouse, Magazine Collection. **Continues** Glamour of Hollywood; **Absorbed** Charm.
Desc: A fashion/beauty monthly; how to use new fashion, look great, keep fit, give parties, travel stylishly, advance careers, enjoy life.
Ind/Abst Acad. Abstr. Full Text Elite; Acad. Abstr.; Consum. Health Nutr. Index (?-?); Consum. Index Prod. Eval. Inf. Source; EP Collect.; Gen. Period. Index (1985-); Health Ref. Cent. (1987-) [Select. Cov.]; Homework Help.; Mag. Artic. Summar. Elite; Mag. Artic. Summar. Select; Mag. Artic. Summar. CD-ROM; Mag. Index Plus (1989-); Mag. Index Sel. Microfiche (1990-) [Full Txt.]; Mag. Index. Sel. (1986-); Mag. Search; MasterFile FullTEXT 1000; MasterFile FullTEXT 350; MasterFile FullTEXT 650; MasterFile FullTEXT (Jan. 1989-); Med. Rev. Dig.; Newsp. Period. Abstr. (1988-); OCLC; Pub. Lib. FullTEXT; Read. Guide Abstr. Select Ed.; Read. Guide Period. Lit.; Telebase; Mag. Index (1977-); TOM Gen. Index (1985-) [Full Txt.]; Vocat. Search.

LC TT500 ISSN 0990-6479
DD 391 FR
UDC 087.2-055.2
TITLE CHANGE
GLAMOUR PARIS. See Women's Interests.

LC TT570 .A6 ISSN 0016-6979
DD 646/.32/05 US
GQ. See Men's Interests.

LC TX340 .H28a
DD 677 KO
HAN'GUK UIRYU HAKHOE CHI. JOURNAL OF THE KOREAN SOCIETY OF CLOTHING & TEXTILES. See Fabrics and Textile Industries.

LC TT500 .H3 ISSN 0017-7873
DD 646.05 US
HARPER'S BAZAAR. [Harper's bazaar]. Vol. 1, (Nov. 2, 1867)-. Periodical. English. Twelve times a year. $17.94. The Hearst Corporation, 250 West 55th Street, New York NY 10019. **Tel** (212)649-4014, (800)925-0485. (**Subscription address:** CDS Agency Hard Copy, PO Box 4966, Des Moines IA 50340. **Tel** (515)247-7569.) **Ad Acc.** available on microfilm and microfiche from University Microfilms International (UMI); available on an online database (file 647/Full-Text) from DIALOG. Documents available from UMI Article Clearinghouse, Magazine Collection.
Ind/Abst Acad. Abstr. Full Text Elite; Acad. Abstr.; EP Collect.; Gen. Period. Index (1985-); Homework Help.; Mag. Artic. Summar. Elite; Mag. Artic. Summar. Select; Mag. Artic. Summar. CD-ROM; Mag. Index Plus (1989-); Mag. Index Sel. Microfiche (1986-) [Full Txt.]; Mag. Index. Sel. (1986-); Mag. Search; MasterFile FullTEXT 1000; MasterFile FullTEXT 350; MasterFile FullTEXT 650; MasterFile FullTEXT (Jan. 1989-); Newsp. Period. Abstr. (1988-); OCLC; Pub. Lib. FullTEXT; Read. Guide Abstr. Select Ed.; Read. Guide Period. Lit.; Telebase; Mag. Index (1977-).

ISSN 0890-9598
DD 391 US
HARPER'S BAZAAR EN ESPANOL. [Harper's bazaar esp.]. (19??)-. Periodical. Spanish. Twelve times a year. $29.75. Editorial America SA, 6355 Northwest 36th Street, Miami FL 33166. **Tel** (305)871-6400. (**Subscription address:** CDS / SIFD Agency Control, 1901 Bell Avenue, Des Moines IA 50315. **Tel** (515)246-6812.)

ISSN 1121-7375
IT
UDC 659.152
HARPER'S BAZAAR ITALIA. [Harper's baazar Ital.]. (1970)-. Periodical. Italian. Six times a year. L100000. (**Subscription address:** Agenzia Italiana Esportazione, Via Manzoni 12, 20089 Rozzano Milan, Italy. **Tel** 011 39 2 57512575). **Photos. Ad Acc.**
Desc: Devoted to women's fashion and contains articles on beauty, news and subjects of general interest to the reader.

JA
HI-FASHION. (19??)-. Japanese. Twelve times a year. $222.00. Bunka Shuppankyoku, 3-22-1 Yoyogi Shibuyaku, Tokyo 151 Japan. (**Subscription address:** Japan Publications Trading Company Ltd., PO Box 5030, Tokyo International, Tokyo 100-31 Japan. **Tel** 011 81 3 3292 3753.)

LC WMLC 93/400 ISSN 1043-6839
DD 687 US
IMPRESSIONS (DALLAS, TEX.). (IMPRESSIONS : THE MAGAZINE FOR IMPRINTED SPORTSWEAR AND TEXTILE SCREEN PRINTING.). [Impressions]. (1977)-. Trade Publication. English. Fifteen times a year (monthly with double issues in Spring, Fall and mid-June). $36.00. Impressions / Texas, 13760 Noel Road, Suite 500, Dallas TX 75240. **Tel** (214)239-3060, FAX (214)419-7825. **ED** Laurie Gonz. **Ad Acc, Adv Mgr** **Tel** (214)239-3060.

LC WMLC 93/5129 ISSN 1066-7083
DD 381 US
IMPRINTING BUSINESS. [Impr. bus.]. Vol. 15, No. 10 (Oct./Nov. 1992)- Vol. 15 (Jan. 1993)-. Trade Publication. English. Eleven times a year (monthly with Oct./Nov. combined). $30.00. WFC Corporation, 3000 Hadley Road, South Plainfield NJ 07080. **Tel** (201)769-1160, FAX (201)769-1171. **ED** Bruce Shachensky. Index Bound in First Issue. **Bk Rev. Ad Acc. Circ:** 24,000. **Continues** Screen Printer & T-shirt

Clothing Industry and Fashion

Retailer Magazine, 1066-7083.
 Desc: Contains information for the imprinted garment industry.

GW

IMPULS MODA IN PELLE. VFOAT Shoes & Leatherwear. (19??)-. German. Four times a year. DM499.33. Mode Information Heinz Kramer, POB 1180, D-51491 Overath Germany. **Tel** 011 49 2206 60070.

ISSN 0883-6183
DD 391 US
SUSPENDED
IN FASHION. [In fash.]. (1990)-(1995). Periodical. English. Four times a year. $14.95 US; $38.95 Canada and Mexico; $59.95 other. Ideas & Trends, 29 West 38th Street, 15th Floor, New York NY 10018. **Tel** (212)768-8450, FAX (212)768-8472. (**Subscription address:** In Fashion, PO Box 377, Plainview NY 11803.) *Continues* In Fashion, 0883-6183.

LC HD9940.U3 I37
DD 381/.45687 US
INDEPENDENT WOMEN'S SPECIALTY STORES & BOUTIQUES. VFOAT Independent Women's Specialty Stores and Boutiques; Directory of Independent Women's Specialty Stores and Boutiques. (19??)-. English. One time a year. $179.69. Salesman's Guide, A Reed Reference Publishing Company, Part of Reed International PLC, 121 Chanlon Road, New Providence NJ 07974. **Tel** (800)223-1797, (908)464-6800, FAX (908)665-3560, telex 138755.

US
INDEX. (19??)-. Periodical. English. Four times a year. $19.99. Fairchild Publications Inc., 7 West 34th Street, 4th Floor, New York NY 10001-8191. **Tel** (212)630-4230, (800)247-6622.

LC HD9014.B8 F85A
BL
INQUERITO NACIONAL DE PRECOS : GENEROS ALIMENTICIOS E ARTIGOS DO VESTUARIO, COMERCIO ATACADISTA E VAREJISTA NAS UNIDADES DA FEDERACAO. Main/Corp Fundacao Instituto Brasileiro de Geografia e Estatistica. Departamento de Estatisticas Industriais, Comerciais e de Servicos. Periodical. Portuguese. Twelve times a year. *Continues* Inquerito Nacional de Precos: Generos Alimenticios e Artigos do Vestuario, Comercio Atacadista e Varejista Nas Unidades da Federacao.

LC NK1700
DD 747 UK
●**INTERNATIONAL COLOUR AUTHORITY. COLOUR FORECAST FOR CARPETS.** (1994)-. Trade Publication. English. One time a year. £170.00 Europe; £180.00 other. International Textile Benjamin Dent Ltd., 23 Bloomsbury Square, London WC1 A2P United Kingdom. **Tel** 011 44 171 6372211, FAX 011 44 171 6372248, telex 8954884. (**Subscription address:** International Colour Authority, PO Box 1897, Lawrence KS 66044-8897.)
 Desc: Previews the colors in style for the coming season and provides color samples.

LC NK1700
DD 747 UK
●**INTERNATIONAL COLOUR AUTHORITY. COLOUR FORECAST FOR INTERIOR TEXTILES.** (1994)-. Trade Publication. English. One time a year. £170.00 Europe; £180.00 other. International Textile Benjamin Dent Ltd., 23 Bloomsbury Square, London WC1 A2P United Kingdom. **Tel** 011 44 171 6372211, FAX 011 44 171 6372248, telex 8954884. (**Subscription address:** International Colour Authority, PO Box 1897, Lawrence KS 66044-8897.)
 Desc: Previews the colors in style for the coming season and provides color samples.

ISSN 0940-7278
GW
UDC 687.12
INTERNATIONAL FASHION TRENDS. [Int. fash. trends]. VFOAT Fashion Trends. (19??)-. English. Four times a year (Mar., June, Oct., Dec.). $402.26. Mode Information Heinz Kramer, POB 1180, D-51491 Overath Germany. **Tel** 011 49 2206 60070.

LC TS1300 .I683 ISSN 0955-6222
DD 687/.05 UK
CCC
CODEN ICSTEH
INTERNATIONAL JOURNAL OF CLOTHING SCIENCE AND TECHNOLOGY. VFOAT Clothing Science and Technology; IJCST. (1989)-. Periodical. English (French; summaries and/or abstracts in German). Five times a year. $1329.00. MCB University Press, 60 62 Toller Lane, Bradford, West Yorkshire BD8 9BY United Kingdom. **Tel** 011 44 1274 785280, FAX 011 44 1274 785200, telex 51317-MCBUNI-G. (**Subscription address:** MCB University Press / US and Canada Subscriptions, PO Box 10812, Birmingham AL 35201-0812. **Tel** (205)995-1567, (800)633-4931, FAX (205)995-1588.) **ED** George Stylios. Index available. cum. index. **Bk Rev.** Documents available from UMI Article Clearinghouse.
 Desc: Aims to promote the science and technology of clothing by publishing academic and industrial reserach findings. It takes only material based on sound technical foundation and is intended to satisfy the specialist knowledge to all academics and industrialists in the field.
 Ind/Abst ABI/INFORM Glob. Ed.; Curr. Cit.

ISSN 1061-5792
DD 338 US
Pr Rev.
INTIMATE FASHION NEWS. [Intim. fash. news]. VFOAT IFN. (1976)-. Periodical. English. Twenty-four times a year. $27.50. Intimate Fashion News, 309 5th Avenue, New York NY 10016. **Tel** (212)679-6677, FAX (212)679-6374. **ED** Nancy Meyer. **Bk Rev**, (Qty: 2-3). **Ad Acc, Adv Mgr:** E.A. Greenberg, **Tel** (212)679-6677. **Circ:** 8,000 (ctrl) *Continues* Corset, Bra & Lingerie Magazine.
 Desc: Covers the intimate apparel industry.

IT
INTIMO PIU MARE. (19??)-. Trade Publication. Italian (English, French and German). Six times a year. $119.50. Editoriale Moda SNC, Via Giardini 476, Scala N, 41100 Modena Italy. **Tel** 011 39 59 342001. **Ad Acc.** **Circ:** 20,000.
 Desc: Lingerie, corsetry, homewear and beachwear collections and previews.

ISSN 0279-6511
US
IT'S ME. Vol. 1, No. 1 (Spring/Summer 1981)-. Periodical. English. Six times a year. $12.00. It's Me Magazine, Inc., PO Box 10142, Des Moines IA 50340.

ISSN 0021-5457
FR
JARDIN DES MODES. (Aug. 1922)-. Periodical. French. Four times a year. $61.24. Jardin des Modes, Centre Gaite 80 Avenue du Maine, F-75014 Paris Cedex 1037 France. **Tel** 011 33 1 44108844, FAX 011 33 1 47233185, telex 615142. **Supersedes** L'Illustration; **Absorbed** Chic et Practique.

ISSN 1080-0352
US
●**KASHMIR TODAY (NEW YORK, N.Y.).** (KASHMIR TODAY.). (1994)-. Periodical. English. Six times a year. $20.00. Kashmir Solidarity USA, 1123 Broadway, Suite 305, New York NY 10010. **Tel** (212)627-2210. *Continues* Kashmir Update, 1079-5995.

ISSN 1357-1680
UK
●**KEY NOTE REPORT. CHILDRENSWEAR.** [Key note rep., childrenswear]. (1994)-. English. Key Note Publications Ltd., Field House, 72 Oldfield Road, Hampton Middlesex TW12 2HQ United Kingdom. **Tel** 011 0181 7830755, FAX 011 0181 7831940.

ISSN 1354-2133
UK
●**KEY NOTE REPORT. CLOTHING RETAILING.** (1994)-. English. Key Note Publications Ltd., Field House, 72 Oldfield Road, Hampton Middlesex TW12 2HQ United Kingdom. **Tel** 011 0181 7830755, FAX 011 0181 7831940.

ISSN 1055-680X
US
KIDDEE PALACE. (KIDDIE PALACE.). (1991)-. Periodical. English. Twelve times a year. $42.00. FFI Fashion Flair/McConneghey, PO Box 1746, New York NY 10027.

CN
KIDS CREATIONS. (19??)-. English. Four times a year. 30.00Can$ Canada; 31.20Can$ Quebec; 45.00Can$ other. Childrens Apparel Manufacturers Association, 8270 Mountain Sights, Suite 101, Montreal Quebec H4P 2B7 Canada. **Tel** (514)731-7774, FAX (514)731-7459. *Continues* Kids Parade, 1183-4501.

LC TT490 .K53 ISSN 0362-6660
DD 380.1/45/6871305 US
CEASED
KIDS FASHIONS MAGAZINE. VFOAT Kids Fashions. (March 1976)-(1995). Trade Publication. English. Larkin Group, 100 Wells Avenue, Newton MA 02159. **Tel** (617)964-5100, 800-869-7469, FAX (617)964-2752. **Ad Acc.** ctrl circ.

ISSN 0895-3465
US
CEASED
L.A. STYLE. [L.A. style]. VFOAT LA Style. (198?)-(April 1993). Periodical. English. American Express Publishing Company, 1120 Avenue of the Americas, New York NY 10036. **Tel** (212)382-5642. (**Subscription address:** CDS Agency Hard Copy, PO Box 4966, Des Moines IA 50340. **Tel** (515)247-7569.)
 Desc: Keeps pace with all the excitement and glamour that make Los Angeles the country's most dazzling city.

ISSN 8755-4313
DD 746 US
LC & YOU. See Beauty and Cosmetics.

IT
LINEA INTIMA ITALIA. (19??)-. Trade Publication. Italian (English). Six times a year. $125.00. Publitype SAS, Via G Watt 27 1, 20143 Milan Italy. **Tel** 011 39 2 89127117, FAX 011 39 2 89127095. (**Subscription address:** Agenzia Italiana Esportazione, Via Manzoni 12, 20089 Rozzano Milan, Italy. **Tel** 011 39 2 57512575.) **Ad Acc.** *Continues* Linea Intima.
 Desc: Publication of the industrial panorama for the lingerie, swimwear, hosiery and materials sectors. All the fashion and the trends of the sector, presented in an homogeneous and clear context and organized by topic and argument.

IT
LINEAPELLE. See Leather and Fur Industry.

ISSN 0344-5224
GW
UDC 687.21/.25
LINIE KOELN, DIE. [Linie Koln]. (1950)-. Trade Publication. German. Six times a year. $180.40. Rudolf Heber Verlag GmbH, Stadtwaldguertel 46, D-50931 Cologne Germany. **Tel** 011 49 221 2033166.

ISSN 0823-5635
DD 391/.005 CN
LOOK (MONTREAL). (LE LOOK.). [Look]. No 1-. Periodical. French. Twelve times a year. $2.95 per no. Look, 181 Est rue St. Paul, Montreal Quebec B2Y 1G8 Canada.

UK
MADAM. VFOAT z. (19??)-. English. Twelve times a year. £9.00. Scottish Braille Press, Craigmillar Park, Edinburgh EH16 5NB United Kingdom. **Tel** 011 44 131 6624445.
 Desc: Contains fiction, topical articles, features on beauty and fashion as well as knitting patterns and cookery recipes.

LC TP ISSN 0024-936X
DD 660 GW
UDC 646.4
MADAME. See Beauty and Cosmetics.

ISSN 0246-5205
FR
MADAME FIGARO. (Mar. 12, 1983)-. Periodical. French. One time a week. $166.22. Societe de Presse Jours de France, 12 rue du Mail, 75002 Paris France. **Tel** 011 33 1 42216200. (**Subscription address:** Societe de Presse Jours de France Service Abonnements, 99 rue d Amsterdam, 75008 Paris France. **Tel** 011 33 1 42806855.)

LC AP2 .M2334 ISSN 0024-9394
DD 051 US
MADEMOISELLE (NEW YORK, N.Y. 1935). See General Interest-General Interest-North America.

LC HQ799.P6 M315
PL
MAGAZYN MODZIEZY. (19??)-. Polish.

ISSN 0024-9947
IT
UDC 687
MAGLIE CALZE INDUSTRIA. [Magl. calze ind.]. (1967)-. Periodical. Italian. Six times a year. L54500. Gesto Srl, Via C Battisti 21, 20122 Milan Italy. **Tel** 011 39 2 55187581, FAX 011 39 2 5465310.

ISSN 0033-9067
IT
CEASED
MAGLIERIA. (1918)-(Dec. 1994). Periodical. Italian. Six times a year. G.B.P. Communications, Via N Battaglia 19, 20127 Milan Italy. **Tel** 011 39 2 2885901, FAX 011 39 2 2840224.

IT
MAGLIERIA ITALIANA. (19??)-. Trade Publication. Italian (English). Four times a year. L32.000 Italy; L72.000 other. Editoriale Moda SNC, Via Giardini 476, Scala N, 41100 Modena Italy. **Tel** 011 39 59 342001.

ISSN 1074-1682
US
MAJOR MASS MARKET MERCHANDISERS. VFOAT Directory of Major Mass Market Merchandisers. (1985)-. English. *Continues* Nationwide Directory. Major Mass Market Merchandisers, 0737-016X.

ISSN 0025-2565
UK
TITLE CHANGE
MANUFACTURING CLOTHIER (LONDON). (MANUFACTURING CLOTHIER.). [Manuf. cloth.]. ol. 55, No. 9 (Sept. 1974)-(19??). Periodical. English. International Textile Benjamin Dent Ltd., 23 Bloomsbury Square, London WC1 A2P United

Kingdom. **Tel** 011 44 171 6372211, FAX 011 44 171 6372248, telex 8954884. **ED** Sarah Wolff. **Bk Rev.** **Ad Acc.** **Circ:** 5,809 (ctrl). ***Continues*** *MC: Manufacturing Clothier;* ***Absorbed*** *Women's Wear Manufacturer.* ***Continued by*** *World Clothing Manufacturer.*
Ind/Abst Text. Technol. Dig.; World Text. Abstr.

LC TP890
DD 687 HK
●**MANUFACTURING SUPPLIES & FABRICS.** **VFOAT** Manufacturing Supplies and Fabrics. (1995)-. Trade Publication. English. Twelve times a year. $55.00. Asian Sources Media Group, GPO Box 12367, Hong Kong. **Tel** 011 852 25554777. **(Subscription address:** Wordright Enterprises Inc., PO Box 3062, Evanston IL 60204. **Tel** (708)475-1900.) **ED** Michael Hay. available on CD-ROM.
Desc: Deals with the clothing manufacturing industry, covers materials, supplies and machinery.

ISSN 0188-2724
DD 056. MX
MARIE CLAIRE EN ESPANOL. [Marie Claire esp.]. (1990)-. Periodical. Spanish. Twelve times a year. Societe Marie Claire, 11 Bis rue Boissy d'Anglas, F-75008 Paris France. **Tel** 011 33 1 42668888.

LC AP **ISSN** 0025-3057
DD 050 FR
UDC 087-055.2
CEASED
MARIE-FRANCE PARIS. [Marie-Fr. Paris]. (1973)-(1993). Periodical. French. Societe Bauer, 37 rue Bergere, 75009 Paris France. **Tel** 011 33 1 45235509, 011 33 1 05345486.

LC TS1023.A1 M3 **ISSN** 0275-1992
DD 685.31 US
MASTER SHOE REBUILDER, THE. Vol. 1 (Jan. 1941)-. Periodical. English. Twelve times a year. W C Hatch Publishing Company, 16 Stonybrook Drive, Levittown PA 19055. ***Absorbed*** *Shoe Repairer and Findings Dealer.*

IT
MAX (MILAN, ITALY). (MAX.). Vol. 1, No. 1 (March 1985)-. Periodical. Italian. Twelve times a year. L135000. RCS Rizzoli Periodici, Via A Rizzoli 2, 20132 Milan Italy. **Tel** 011 39 2 27200720. **(Subscription address:** Speedimpex USA, Inc., 35 02 48th Avenue, Long Island City NY 11101. **Tel** (718)392-7477.)

PO
MAXIMA. (19??)-. Periodical. Portuguese. Twelve times a year. 30000$00. Edimoda, Rua Victor Gordon 37-3, 1200 Lisbon Portugal. **Tel** 011 351 1 604003.

ISSN 0887-5219
DD 646 US
MEN'S GUIDE TO FASHION. (MEN'S GUIDE TO FASHION : MGF.). [Men's guide fash.]. **VFOAT** MGF. (198?)-. Periodical. English. Six times a year. MGF Publishing Corporation, 3 West 18th Street, New York NY 10018. **Tel** (815)734-6309.

ISSN 1079-6207
US
●**MEN'S STYLE.** See Men's Interests.

ISSN 0937-3543
GW
UDC 746
MISS B ENGLISH ED. [Miss B Engl. ed.]. (19??)-. Periodical. English (French). Four times a year. $33.00. German Canadian News Co Ltd, 25-29 Coldwater Road, Toronto Ontario M3B 1Y8 Canada. **Tel** (416)391-4192, FAX (416)391-4194.
Desc: Fashion magazine for young girls.

IT
MODA. (19??)-. Italian. Twelve times a year. L29300. Nuova Eri / Edizioni Rai, Via Arsenale 41, 10121 Turin Italy. **Tel** 011 39 11 8102238. **Ad Acc.** ***Continues*** *Moda Italia.*
Desc: Women's fashion magazine.

ISSN 1120-1967
IT
UDC 687
MODA IN. [Moda in]. (1975)-. Periodical. Multiple languages. Four times a year. L55000. Zanfi Editori SRL, Via Emilia Ovest 954, CP 433, 41100 Modena Italy. **Tel** 011 39 59 891700, FAX 011 39 59 225719, telex 52 22 72.

IT
MODA VIVA. Italian. Editrice Renoma Srl, Via Ippolito Nievo 33, 20145 Milan Italy.

IT
MODASPORT VACANZE. (19??)-. Italian. Four times a year. L65000.00 Italy; L135000.00 other. Acalifa Srl, Via San Rocco 17, 20135 Milan Italy. **Tel** 011 39 2 58315800, FAX 011 39 2 58316313. Index available. cum. index. **Bk Rev**, (Qty: 4). **Ad Acc.** **Circ:** 46,000 (ctrl).

ISSN 0155-4611
DD 746.920994 AT
MODE AUSTRALIA. [Mode Aust.]. (1977)-. Periodical. English. Eight times a year. 36.18Aus$. Australian Consolidated Press Ltd., Private Bag 92615 Symonds St, Auckland New Zealand. **Tel** 011 64 9 3735408, FAX 011 64 9 3022889.

FR
SUSPENDED
MODE EN PEINTURE. (19??)-(19??). French. Societe Assouline, 14 rue de la Faisanderie, 75116 Paris France.

JA
MODE ET MODE. (19??)-. Japanese. $72.00. Intercontinental Marketing Corporation, IPO Box 5056, Tokyo 100-31 Japan. **Tel** 011 81 3 36617458, FAX 011 81 3 36619646. **(Subscription address:** Maruzen Company Ltd., PO Box 5050, Import & Export Department, Tokyo 100 31 Japan. **Tel** 011 81 3 32789224.)

LC TT500 .M536 **ISSN** 0162-1378
DD 391/.005 US
MODE INTERNATIONAL. [Mode int.]. Oct. 1978-. Periodical. English. Six times a year (ten no. a year). $32.50. Mode International, Sherry Netherland Hotel, Suite 201/781 Fifth Avenue, New York NY 10022.

BE
MODE MAGAZINE TRIBUNE. French. Twenty-four times a year. Mode Magazine Tribune, Lakborslei 112, 2100 Deurne Belgium. **Tel** 03 324 3875.

GR
MODEHELLAS. HOME BEACH EDITION. (19??)-. Greek, Modern. Two times a year. $40.00. Modehellas Publishing Company, 84 Doiranis Street, 17672 Athens Greece.

ISSN 1061-4737
DD 338 US
MODEL CALL / RICHARD POIRIER MODEL & TALENT AGENCY. [Model call]. **Added/Corp** Richard Poirier Model and Talent Agency. Vol. 1, No. 1 (1991)-. Trade Publication. English. Four times a year. $14.00. Richard Poirier Model & Talent Agency, 3575 Cahuenga Boulevard West, #254, Los Angeles CA 90068-1341. **Tel** (213)969-9990, FAX (213)850-3382.

LC AP
DD 051 FR
MODELE MAGAZINE. See Beauty and Cosmetics.

ISSN 0723-7839
GW
UDC 687.4
MODELLHUT (1975). [Modellhut 1975]. (1975)-. Trade Publication. German. Seven times a year. $92.12. Verlag Neuer Merkur GmbH, Postfach 460805, D-80916 Munich Germany. **Tel** 011 49 89 3189050. ***Continues*** *Modellhut + Accessoires, 0723-788X.*

ISSN 1121-8290
IT
UDC 646
MODELLINA MILANO. (MODELLINA.). [Modellina Milano]. (1948)-. Periodical. Multiple languages. Three times a year. L39.400. A Pieroni SRL, Viale Vittorio Veneto 28, 20124 Milan Italy. **Tel** 39 2 29000282, 29002876.

ISSN 0992-5597
FR
UDC 687
MODES & TECHNIQUES INTERNATIONAL. **VFOAT** International Modes & Techniques; Modes et Techniques International. (1988)-. Periodical. French. Six times a year. $131.23. Editions Vauclair, 8 rue d Aboukir, 75002 Paris France. **Tel** 011 33 1 45085131.

FR
MODES & TECHNIQUES VETIR. **VFOAT** Modes et Techniques Vetir. No. 572 (June 1986)-. Periodical. French. Six times a year. Editions Vauclair, 8 rue d Aboukir, 75002 Paris France. **Tel** 011 33 1 45085131. ***Formed by the union of*** *Modes et Techniques* ***and*** *Vetir, 0030-0489.*

LC WMLC 93/994 **ISSN** 1049-6726
DD 381 US
MR (NORWALK, CONN.). See Business and Economics-Retail.

ISSN 0834-0064
DD 338.4/7687/0971 CN
MW : MEN'S WEAR OF CANADA. [MW, Men's wear Can.]. **VFOAT** Men's Wear of Canada. Vol. 76, No. 1 (Feb. 1985)-. Periodical. English. Irregular. 37.00Can$ Canada; $50.00 other. Men's Wear of Canada, 501 Oakdale Road, Downsview Ontario M3N 1W7 Canada. ***Continues*** *Men's Wear of Canada, 0025-9535.*

LC HD9940.U4 N47 **ISSN** 0737-061X
DD 381/.45687/02573 US
TITLE CHANGE
NATIONWIDE DIRECTORY. MAJOR MASS MARKET MERCHANDISERS. See Industry and Production-Trade and Industrial Directories.

US
NATIONWIDE WOMEN'S & CHILDREN'S WEAR DIRECTORY. (19??)-. Directory. English. One time a year (Nov). $137.00. Salesman's Guide, A Reed Reference Publishing Company, Part of Reed International PLC, 121 Chanlon Road, New Providence NJ 07974. **Tel** (800)223-1797, (908)464-6800, FAX (908)665-3560, telex 138755. Index available.

ISSN 0279-7844
US
NEW YORK APPAREL NEWS. [New York apparel news]. Vol. 1, No. 1 (Feb./March 1981)-. Periodical. English. Five times a year. $20.00. Apparel News Group, 110 East 9th Street, Suite A-777 Road, Los Angeles CA 90079. **Tel** (213)627-3737, FAX (213)623-5707. **Ad Acc.** **Circ:** 7,000 (ctrl).

FR
NEWLOOK. English. Twelve times a year. 200.00F France; 290.00F other. Newlook Svc Abonnements, 99 rue d'Amsterdam, F-75008 Paris France. **Tel** 011 33 1 42806855.

LC HD9787.U45 U55A **ISSN** 0196-4712
DD 338.4/768531/00973 US
NONRUBBER FOOTWEAR: ANNUAL SURVEY OF PRODUCERS AND IMPORTERS. See Business and Economics-Commerce.

LC HD9787.U4 U54A **ISSN** 0198-8417
DD 338.4/768531/00973 US
NONRUBBER FOOTWEAR : U.S. PRODUCTION, IMPORTS FOR CONSUMPTION, APPARENT U.S. CONSUMPTION, EMPLOYMENT, WHOLESALE PRICE INDEX, AND CONSUMER PRICE INDEX. **Main/Corp** United States International Trade Commission. **VAT** Nonrubber Footwear: United States Production, Imports for Consumption, Apparent United States Consumption, Employment, Wholesale Price Index, and Consumer Price Index. (19??)-. Periodical. English. Four times a year. US International Trade Commission, 701 E Street NW, Washington DC 20436. **Tel** (202)523-0235.

ISSN 0195-0827
US
NOTIVEST. (19??)-. Periodical. Spanish. Six times a year. Denyse & Company, 5170 Garden Grove Avenue, Tarzana CA 91356.

IT
OBIETTIVO MODA. (19??)-. Italian (English). Two times a year. L130000.00. Centro Promoz Pubblicita, Via Baldassare Francheschini 5, 50142 Florence Italy. **Tel** 011 39 55 700478, 011 39 55 7398754. **Bk Rev.** **Circ:** 10,000 (ctrl).

ISSN 0030-0403
FR
OFFICIEL DE LA COUTURE ET DE LA MODE DE PARIS. [Off. couture, mode Paris]. **VFOAT** Officiel. (192?)-. Periodical. French. Eight times a year. 150.00F North America; 244.86F France; 500.00F other. L Off Couture Mode de Paris, 202 Quai de Clichy, 92110 Clichy France. **Tel** 011 33 1 47393870.

FR
OFFICIEL DU PRET A PORTER, L'. **VFOAT** Pret a Porter; Officiel du Pret a Porter. No. 1 (4th Qtr. 1968)-. Periodical. French. Four times a year. 200.00F France; 280.00F Europe; 300.00F Mideast; 320.00F Western Hemisphere and Africa; 340.00F other. Publications Mandel, 43 BD Vauban, 78182 St. Quen Yvl Cedex France. **Tel** 011 33 1 34834230. ***Continues in part*** *Textiles Nouveautes.*

LC HD9940.C18 C35b **ISSN** 0829-7401
DD 381/.45/687110971 CN
OPERATING RESULTS. MEN'S RETAIL CLOTHING STORES. See Clothing Industry and Fashion-Abstracting, Bibliographies and Statistics.

LC NK7300 .B42 **ISSN** 0148-3897
DD 739.27/05 US
ORNAMENT (LOS ANGELES, CALIF.). See Jewelry.

LC GT500
DD 391 AT
OUR BABY. BURDA. (19??)-. Trade Publication. English (German). Two times a year. 23.00Aus$. Overseas Periodicals Australia Pty., PO Box 36,

Clothing Industry and Fashion

Bankstown NSW 2200 Australia. **Tel** 011 61 2 7074577, FAX 011 61 2 7086025, telex 25712.
Desc: Fashion and clothing information for babies.

ISSN 1055-1514
US

OUR FOUNDATION. (1991)-. Periodical. English. Twelve times a year. $3.25. FFI Fashion Flair/McConneghey, PO Box 1746, New York NY 10027.

IT
TITLE CHANGE

PANORAMA MODA & ABBIGLIAMENTO. (19??)-(1995). Italian. Editoriale Alfa Srl, Viale Marelli 19 3, 20099 Sesto S Giovanni Italy. **Tel** 011 39 2 2423566, FAX 011 39 2 22476521. Index available. cum. index. **Bk Rev**. **Ad Acc**. Continued by Panorama Moda and Marketing.

IT

●**PANORAMA MODA & MARKETING.** (1995)-. Italian. Twelve times a year. L60.000. Editoriale Alfa Srl, Viale Marelli 19 3, 20099 Sesto S Giovanni Italy. **Tel** 011 39 2 2423566, FAX 011 39 2 22476521. *Continues* Panorama Moda & Abbigliamento.

BE

PARIS SUCCESS. (19??)-. French (Dutch). Twenty-four times a year (2 issues). 1,400F. Paris Success, Avenue des Eglantiers 42, 1180 Brussels Belgium. **Tel** 011 32 2 374-5155. **ED** Gallet Marylyn. **Bk Rev**, (Qty: 2). **Circ:** F (ctrl).
Desc: Fashion models and patterns for ladies.

IT

PELLICCE MODA. See Leather and Fur Industry.

ISSN 0886-5302
US

PETITE. (1991)-. Periodical. English. Twelve times a year. $12.95. Dan Stanton, 5225-A 19th Street SW, Seattle WA 98106.

LC HD9940.U3 P5
DD 381/.45687/02573
Pr Rev.

ISSN 0737-3430
US

PHELON'S WOMEN'S APPAREL SHOPS. **VFOAT** Women's Apparel Shops. 8th Ed. (1983-84)-. English. Every 2 years. $140.00. Phelon Sheldon & Marsar Inc, 15 Industrial Avenue, PO Box 517, Fairview NJ 07022. **Tel** (201)941-8804, (800)234-8804, FAX (201)941-5515. **ED** Kenneth W. Phelon Jr. Index available. **Ad Acc**. **Circ:** 1,000 (ctrl). available on labels. *Continues* Phelon's Women's Specialty Stores.
Desc: Provides information on 16,000 women's apparel and accessory shops in the US. Includes address, phone number, merchandise price ranges, resident buying offices, buyers and store owners and lines carried; 400 pages.

LC TT498
DD 687
IT

●**PLUS.** (1994)-. Italian. Six times a year. L60.000. Leader Interservice s.r.l., Piazza Piemonte 8, 20145 Milan Italy. **Tel** 011 39 2 463462, FAX 011 39 2 4980526. **Ad Acc**.

GW

PLUS (BAIERSBRONN). (PLUS.). (19??)-. Periodical. English. Two times a year. DM297.00. Plus Verlag / Hueber Verlag GmbH, Bildstoeckleweg 10, Postfach 1308, D-72258 Baiersbronn Germany. **Tel** 011 49 7442 3969, FAX 011 49 7442 7784. **Ad Acc**.
Desc: Fashion guide for stylists and shoe-fabrics. Shows exclusive models created by the Plus Design studios.

ISSN 1052-6587
DD 746
US

PRESS (LITTLETON, COLO.). (THE PRESS.). [Press]. **VFOAT** Press Magazine. (19??)-. Periodical. English. Twelve times a year. $24.71 US; $34.12 Canada; $54.12 other. Intertec Publishing Corporation, 9800 Metcalf, Overland Park KS 66212. **Tel** (913)341-1300. *Continues* Press Magazine, 0744-3161.

GW

READYWEAR. INTERNATIONAL TRADE INFORMATION SERVICE FOR CLOTHING MANUFACTURERS. See Fabrics and Textile Industries.

US

REGIONAL CALENDAR. English. One time a year. $120.00. Fashion Calendar, 153 East 87th Street, New York NY 10128. **Tel** (212)289-0420.

ISSN 1010-2469
INT

UDC 687
CODEN NU051

REPORT - INTERNATIONAL LABOUR ORGANISATION, TECHNICAL TRIPARTITE MEETING FOR THE CLOTHING INDUSTRY. [Rep. - Int. Lab. Organ. Tech. Tripart. Meet. Cloth. Ind.]. (19??)-. Monographic series. English. Irregular. Price varies per volume.

International Labour Office - ILO, Publications Sales Service, CH-1211 Geneva 22 Switzerland. **Tel** 011 41 22 7996111, FAX 011 41 22 7986253, telex 415 647 ilo ch.

IT

RM1 : RIVISTA DELLA MAGLIERIA. Italian. Four times a year. L30000 Italy; L60000 other. Publitype SAS, Via G Watt 27 1, 20143 Milan Italy. **Tel** 011 39 2 89127117, FAX 011 39 2 89127095.

LC HD9940.U3 R5
DD 338.7/687/02573
US

RN & WPL ENCYCLOPEDIA / THE SALESMAN'S GUIDE, INC. See Fabrics and Textile Industries.

SZ

ROBES COUTURE. (19??)-. Trade Publication. French. Two times a year. 45.00F Europe; 50.00F other. Editions C. Weder, Rennweg 64, 4052 Basel Switzerland. **Tel** 011 41 61 3126263, FAX 011 41 61 3126266, telex 845/965920.

SZ

ROBES MANTEAUX. (19??)-. Trade Publication. French. Two times a year. 46.00F Europe; 503.00F other. Editions C. Weder, Rennweg 64, 4052 Basel Switzerland. **Tel** 011 41 61 3126263, FAX 011 41 61 3126266, telex 845/965920.

ISSN 1056-1056
US

ROY DEAN'S STYLE. **VFOAT** Style. (1991)-. Periodical. English. Six times a year. Beverly Hills Bluebook, 2801 4th Avenue, San Diego CA 92103.

LC HD9940.U4 R89
DD 746
Pr Rev.

ISSN 0887-3003
US

RTW REVIEW. [RTW rev.]. Added/Corp Danielle Consultants (Firm). **VFOAT** Ready-to-Wear Review; Ready to Wear Review. Vol. 1, No. 1 (April 1986)-. Periodical. English. Six times a year. $149.00. Danielle Consultants, PO Box 27688, Milwaukee WI 53227. **Tel** (414)425-5503, FAX (414)425-2501. **ED** Lauren Daniel-Falk. **Bk Rev**, (Qty: 150). **Ad Acc**. **Adv Mgr:** Jim Windler. **Circ:** 5,000 (ctrl).
Desc: Fashion coverage, merchandising strategies and emerging industry trends.

ISSN 0722-2858
GW

UDC 687.0/.4

RUNDSCHAU FUER INTERNATIONALE DAMENMODE MIT DOB- + HAKA-PRAXIS. [Rundsch. int. Damenmode DOB- + Haka-Prax.]. **VFOAT** Rundschau fuer Internationale Damenmode Mit DOB- + Haka- Praxis. (1982)-. Periodical. German. Twelve times a year. $171.80. Rundschau Verlag OG Koeniger GmbH, Postfach 401568, Ohmstrasse 15, W8000 Munich 40 Germany. **Tel** 011 49 89 38160532. *Formed by the union of* Rundschau fuer Internationale Damenmode, 0035-9912 *and* DOB- + Haka-Praxis, 0342-1627.

ISSN 0722-2866
GW

UDC 687.0/.4

RUNDSCHAU FUER INTERNATIONALE HERRENMODE MIT DOB- + HAKA-PRAXIS. [Rundsch. int. Herrenmode DOB- + Haka-Prax.]. **VFOAT** Rundschau fuer Internationale Herrenmode Mit DOB- + Haka- Praxis. (1982)-. Trade Publication. German. Twelve times a year. DM190.80. Rundschau Verlag OG Koeniger GmbH, Postfach 401568, Ohmstrasse 15, W8000 Munich 40 Germany. **Tel** 011 49 89 38160532. *Formed by the union of* Rundschau fuer Internationale Herrenmode, 0342-8850 *and* DOB- + Haka-Praxis, 0342-1627.
Desc: Trade journal for men's tailors, designers and the ready-to-wear industry.

JA

RYUKOSHOKU. FASHION COLORS. (19??)-. Periodical. Japanese. Twelve times a year. $255.00. (Subscription address: Maruzen Company Ltd., PO Box 5050, Import & Export Department, Tokyo 100 31 Japan. **Tel** 011 81 3 32789224.)

ISSN 1071-5606
DD 338
US

●**SALON NEWS.** [Salon news]. **VFOAT** Salonnews. (1993)-. Periodical. English. Twelve times a year. $24.00 US; $60.00 other. Fairchild Publications Inc., 7 West 34th Street, 4th Floor, New York NY 10001-8191. **Tel** (212)630-4230, (800)247-6622. (**Subscription address:** Salon News, PO Box 5035, Brentwood TN 37024-5030.)

GW

SANDRA : TOLLE STRICKMODE. See Home Economics-Sewing and Needlework.

LC HD9787.N35 N47A
NE

SCHOENINDUSTRIE. **VFOAT** Manufacture of Footwear. 1981-. Dutch (summaries and/or abstracts in English). One time a year. Fl9.25. Centraal Bureau voor de Statistiek, AFD ALG Zaken, Postbus 959, 2270 AZ Voorburg Netherlands. **Tel** 011 31 70 3373800, FAX 011 31 70 0387429, telex 32692 CBS NL. *Continues* Netherlands. Produktiestatieken: Schoenindustrie.

ISSN 0933-808X
GW

UDC 685.3
Pr Rev.

SCHUHTECHNIK (1987). [Schuhtechnik 1987]. **VFOAT** Technique de la Chaussure (1987); Shoe Techniques (1987); Tecnica della Calzatura (1987); Schuhtechnik + ABC (1987). (1987)-. Trade Publication. German (English). Twelve times a year. $124.00. Dr. Alfred Huethig Verlag GmbH, Postfach 102869, D-69018 Heidelberg Germany. **Tel** 011 49 6221 489281, FAX 011 49 6221 489279. (**Subscription address:** Huethig Publishing Inc., 29 Macintosh Drive, Oxford CT 06478. **Tel** (203)881-2647.) **ED** A. Wilhelm. Index available. cum. index. **Bk Rev**. **Ad Acc**. **Circ:** 7,000. *Continues* Schuhtechnik + ABC, 0341-8413.
Desc: International magazine for all producers of shoes.

US

SHELDON'S RETAIL DIRECTORY OF THE UNITED STATES AND CANADA. Directory. English. One time a year. $104.00 (library), $130.00. Phelon Sheldon & Marsar Inc, 15 Industrial Avenue, PO Box 517, Fairview NJ 07022. **Tel** (201)941-8804, (800)234-8804, FAX (201)941-5515. **ED** J R Marson, Jr. Index available. **Ad Acc**. **Circ:** 5000.
Desc: Contains information on department stores and chains, women's stores and chains, home furnishing chains, major retail chains, resident buying offices in the US and Canada, executives and buyers.

US

SHOE FACTORY BUYERS' GUIDE. (19??)-. Consumer Publication. English. Shoe Trades Publishing Company, 61 Massachusetts Avenue, Arlington MA 02174. **Tel** (617)648-8160, FAX (617)492-0126, telex 325736 SHOETRADE. **Ad Acc**. **Circ:** 2,500.
Desc: Buyers' guide for footwear manufacturing industry.

ISSN 0744-9259
US

SHOE SERVICE. TRADE EDITION. (SHOE SERVICE.). Vol. 61, No. 5 (May 1982)-. Trade Publication. English. Twelve times a year. $15.00. Shoe Service Institute of America, 5024-R Campbell Boulevard, Baltimore MD 21236.

US

●**SHOESTAB.** (1995)-. English. One time a year. $295.00. Footwear Industries of America, 1420 K Street Northwest, Suite 600, Washington DC 20005. **Tel** (202)789-1420, FAX (202)789-4058. **ED** John Burnham. **Circ:** 150. *Continues* Footwear Manual.

LC HD9787.B8 I57A
DD 338.4/7/6853100981
BL

SISTEMA DE INFORMACAO ESTATISTICA PARA A INDUSTRIA NACIONAL DE CALCADOS. Main/Corp Instituto Brasileiro do Couro, Calcados e Afins. No. 1- Jan./May 1973-. Portuguese. Rio Grande do Sul Instituto Brasileiro do Coura, Calcados E Afins, rua Gregorio Matos 111, Caixa Postal 48, Estancia Velha Brazil.

LC TS989
DD 685.31
US

●**SOLE SOURCE.** (1994)-. Directory. English. One time a year. $50.00. Footwear Industries of America, 1420 K Street Northwest, Suite 600, Washington DC 20005. **Tel** (202)789-1420, FAX (202)789-4058. **ED** Anita Lawson. **Ad Acc**. **Circ:** 2,000.
Desc: Provides a list of distributors and suppliers for the footwear industry.

IT

SOLOINTIMO SOLOMARE. (19??)-. Italian. L40000.00 Italy; L90000.00 other. Acalifa Srl, Via San Rocco 17, 20135 Milan Italy. **Tel** 011 39 2 58315800, FAX 011 39 2 58316313. Index available. cum. index. **Bk Rev**, (Qty: 4). **Ad Acc**. **Circ:** 31,000 (ctrl).
Desc: Covers lingerie and footwear for women, men and children.

LC TT495 .S64
DD 687/.029/473
US

SOURCING DIRECTORY. Added/Corp American Apparel Manufacturers Association. Apparel Contractor Relations Committee. (1988)-. Directory. English. One time a year. $10.00 (members), $20.00 (nonmembers). American Apparel Manufacturers Association, 2500 Wilson Boulevard, Suite 301, Arlington VA 22201. **Tel** (703)524-1864.

LC TT649 .S66
DD 687/.16
ISSN 0162-2242
US

SPORT STYLE. **VFOAT** Sportstyle. (Oct. 9, 1978)-. Trade Publication. English. Twenty times a year. $35.00 US; $41.00 Canada. Fairchild Publications Inc., 7 West 34th Street, 4th Floor, New York NY 10001-8191. **Tel** (212)630-4230, (800)247-6622. available on an online database (files 16,570/Full-Text) from DIALOG.

Clothing Industry and Fashion

LC TT649 .S67   **ISSN** 0743-1155
DD 687/.16   US
SPORTSWEAR INTERNATIONAL (U.S.A. ED.). (SPORTSWEAR INTERNATIONAL.). [Sportsw. int.]. **VFOAT** Sports Wear International; Sports Wear International, USA; Sportswear International, USA. (19??)-. Periodical. English. Eight times a year. $60.00. Ideas & Trends, 29 West 38th Street, 15th Floor, New York NY 10018. **Tel** (212)768-8450, FAX (212)768-8472.
Desc: In-depth features on international trade in the fashion industry and the latest trend in men and women's markets. Market report on increasing sales and prestige, merchandising techniques and more.

US
SPORTSWEAR INTERNATIONAL'S KIDS. (19??)-. Periodical. English. Four times a year. $1.95 per issue. Sportswear International, 29 West 38th Street, 15th Floor, New York NY 10018. **Tel** (212)768-8450, FAX (212)768-8472. **ED** Susan Carlucci. **Ad Acc**, **Adv Mgr:** Constantine Floris.
Desc: Fashion and lifestyle magazine for parents and kids.

ISSN 0394-3682
UDC 687   IT
SPOSABELLA. [Sposabella]. (1974)-. Periodical. Italian. Two times a year. L59870. Mode Information Heinz Kramer, POB 1180, D-51491 Overath Germany. **Tel** 011 49 2206 60070.

ISSN 0039-4246
CN
STYLE (TORONTO). (STYLE.). (1???)-. Trade Publication. English. Fifteen times a year. 26.41Can$. Style Communications, 1448 Lawrence Avenue East, Suite 302, Toronto Ontario M4A 2V6 Canada. **Tel** (416)755-5199, FAX (416)755-9123. **ED** Marilyn Bolton and Vivian Wilcox. **Ad Acc**, **Adv Mgr:** S. Swan, **Tel** (416)755-5799. **Circ:** 11,000. available on microfilm and microfiche from University Microfilms International (UMI).
Desc: Canada's fashion newspaper for women's clothing retailers, buyers, manufacturers, importers and their agents.

US
SWIM FASHION QUARTERLY. (19??)-. English. Six times a year. $66.00 Canada; $30.00 US; $95.00 other. Virgo Publishing Inc., 4141 North Scottsdale Road, Suite 316, Scottsdale AZ 85251. **Tel** (602)483-0014, (602)990-1101, FAX (602)990-0819.

ISSN 0194-2794
US
T-SHIRT TIMES, THE. VAT T Shirt Times. Vol. 1 (Aug. 1979)-. Periodical. English. Twelve times a year. $35.00 US; $45.00 other. Southwest Screen Print Ind, Inc., PO Box 423, Scottsdale AR 85252.

ISSN 1053-5578
US
TAILS (PADUCAH, KY.). (TAILS : MAGAZINE FOR THE FORMAL WEAR INDUSTRY.). (1991)-. Periodical. English. Four times a year. Free. Tails, Subscription, 2701 Wayne Sullivan Drive, Paducah KY 42003.

ISSN 1079-9443
DD 391   US
TATTOO FLASH. [Tattoo Flash]. **VFOAT** Flash. (199?)-. Periodical. English. Six times a year. $29.90. Paisano Publications Inc., 28210 Dorothy Drive, PO Box 1050, Agoura Hills CA 91301. **Tel** (818)889-8740, FAX (818)889-4726. **(Subscription address:** Tatoo Flash, PO Box 469064, Escondido CA 92046. **Tel** (619)738-8907.) **Continues** Flash (Agoura Hills, Calif.).

ISSN 1034-4837
DD 338.456770994   AT
TCF INDUSTRY ADVISOR. [TCF ind. advis.]. **VFOAT** Textiles Clothing and Footwear Industry Advisor. (1989)-. Periodical. English. Twenty times a year. 411.09Aus$. Business Communications Group, PO Box 250, Mawson ACT 2607 Australia. **Tel** 011 61 6 2864605, FAX 011 61 6 2863441. **ED** Trevor Thomas. Index available. cum. index. **Circ:** 500.

ISSN 0394-9796
UDC 685.3   IT
TECNICA CALZATURIERA. [Tec. calz.]. (1964)-. Trade Publication. Italian. Twelve times a year. L74940. Tecniche Nuove SPA, Via Ciro Menotti 14, 20129 Milan Italy. **Tel** 011 39 2 75701, FAX 011 39 2 7570205, telex 334647 TECHS I.

SP
TECNICA DEL CALZADO. Spanish. Six times a year. 3450.00ptas, $38.36 The Americas and Indonesia; 3950.00ptas, $43.92 Asia; 3350.00ptas, $37.25 other. Prensa Tecnica, Caspe 118, 120 Piso 6-1A, 08013 Barcelona Spain. **Tel** 011 34 3 2455190, 011 34 3 2455198, 011 34 3 2455199.

IT
TESSUTO COLLEZIONI. Italian. Zanfi Editori SRL, Via Emilia Ovest 954, CP 433, 41100 Modena Italy. **Tel** 011 39 59 891700, FAX 011 39 59 225719, telex 52 22 72.
Desc: Fabrics and yarns collections.

LC TS1300 .T219   **ISSN** 0810-574X
DD 338.4/7677/00994   AT
TITLE CHANGE
TEXTILE & APPAREL MANUFACTURER. [Text. apparel manuf.]. **VFOAT** Textile and Apparel Manufacturer; T.A.M.; TAM. Vol. 57, No. 5 (Aug./Sept. 1982)-. Periodical. English. Yaffa Publishing Group Pty Ltd., GPO Box 606, Sydney New South Wales 2001 Australia. **Tel** 011 61 2 2812333, FAX 011 61 2 2812750. **Continues** Textile Journal/Australia. **Continued by** Australian Apparel Manufacture.
Ind/Abst Text. Technol. Dig.; World Text. Abstr.

LC TS1399 .T44   **ISSN** 0049-3554
DD 338.4/7/677095   HK
CODEN TASIDM
Pr Rev.
TEXTILE ASIA. See Fabrics and Textile Industries.

NE
TEXTILE VIEW MAGAZINE. English (French, German, Italian, Spanish, Japanese and Chinese). Four times a year (Mar., June, Oct., Dec.). Fl224.00. Metropolitan Publications, PO Box 53261, David Shaw, 1007 RG Amsterdam Netherlands. **Tel** (20)6177624, FAX (201)6179357. **(Subscription address:** Mode Information Heinz Kramer, Pilgerstrasse 20, D 51491 Overath Germany. **Tel** 011 49 2206 60070.) **Bk Rev. Ad Acc. Circ:** 11,000.
Desc: Color, textiles, fabrics and fashion for men and women.

LC NK4700
DD 746.92   US
●**TOP MODEL.** (1994)-. Consumer Publication. English. Six times a year. Elle Publishing, 1633 Broadway, 41st Floor, New York NY 10019. **Tel** (212)787-5800. **Ad Acc.**

LC HD9969.K7 N47A   **ISSN** 0168-4469
NE
TRICOT- EN KOUSENINDUSTRIE. VFOAT Knitting and Hosiery Mills. (1981)-. Dutch (summaries and/or abstracts in English). One time a year. Fl8.00. Centraal Bureau voor de Statistiek, AFD ALG Zaken, Postbus 959, 2270 AZ Voorburg Netherlands. **Tel** 011 31 70 3373800, FAX 011 31 70 0387429, telex 32692 CBS NL. available on audiocassette. **Continues** Netherlands. Centrall Bureau Voor de Statistiek. Produktiestatistieken: Tricot- en Kouseindustrie.

FR
TRICOT SELECTION. (19??)-. French. Twelve times a year. 210.58F France; 297.00F other. Editions de Saxe, 20 rue Croix Barret, 69524 Lyon France. **Tel** 011 33 7 8729254.

LC TT490 .U39
KO
UIRYU KISUL. VFOAT Apparel Journal. (19??)-. Periodical. Korean (Korean). Four times a year. Hanguk Uiryu Shihom Komsaso, 232-22 Yongdu-dong Tongdaemun-ku, Seoul Korea.

IT
ULTIMISSIME PELLICCERIA. See Leather and Fur Industry.

IT
UOMO COLLEZIONI. (19??)-. Trade Publication. Italian. Two times a year. $110.00. Agenzia Italiana di Esportazione, Via Manzoni 12, 20089 Rozzano Milan Italy. **Tel** 011 39 2 57512575.

ISSN 1121-5496
IT
UOMO HARPER'S BAZAAR. (1984)-. Periodical. Italian. Four times a year. L50000. **(Subscription address:** Agenzia Italiana Esportazione, Via Manzoni 12, 20089 Rozzano Milan, Italy. **Tel** 011 39 2 57512575.) **Ad Acc. Continues** Men's Bazaar Italia, 1121-550X.
Desc: Devoted entirely to men's fashions. Due to its content, which proposes the latest creations of the stylists for man, the magazine is mainly addressed to young people. Besides fashion, one will find other sections dealing with news and subjects of general interest, with considerations and deepenings about materials, firms and trends.

LC TT570 .U57
DD 646/.32/06   IT
UOMO VOGUE, L'. (1968)-. Periodical. Italian. Eleven times a year. L82680. Edizioni Conde Nast Spa, Piazza Castello 27, 20121 Milan Italy. **Tel** 011 39 2 85611.

SP
VESTIRAMA. (19??)-. Spanish. Four times a year. 4.500ptas Spain; $82.00 US. Gamamoda, Caspe 116 5 3A, 13 Barcelona Spain. **ED** Eugenio Rodriguez. **Ad Acc. Circ:** 8,000 (ctrl).
Desc: Fashion for men, women, and children.

LC N6480 .V57   **ISSN** 1071-5266
DD 704.9/428/05   US
VISIONAIRE (NEW YORK, N.Y.). See The Arts-Art.

LC TT500 .V714   **ISSN** 0042-8027
DD 646/.34/05   IT
VOGUE. See Women's Interests.

LC TT500
DD 646/.34/05   UK
VOGUE. (BRITISH EDITION). See Women's Interests.

LC TT635 .V645
DD 391/.3/05   FR
VOGUE ENFANTS. No. 1 (Autumn-Winter 1987/88)-. Periodical. French. 30.00F single issue. Les Editions Conde Nast, Service Abonnements B620, 60732 S Genevieve Cedex 9 France. **Tel** 011 33 45 673505, 011 33 44 034400.

LC AP20 .V78   **ISSN** 0750-3628
DD 054/.1   FR
VOGUE HOMMES. (19??)-. Periodical. French. Ten times a year. $95.00. Les Editions Conde Nast, Service Abonnements B620, 60732 S Genevieve Cedex 9 France. **Tel** 011 33 45 673505, 011 33 44 034400. **(Subscription address:** International Subscriptions Inc., 30 Montgomery Street, 7th Floor, Jersey City NJ 07302. **Tel** (201)451-9420, (800)544-6748.)

LC TT635 .V65   **ISSN** 1120-7787
DD 391/.3/05   IT
VOGUE ITALIA. BAMBINI (MILAN, ITALY : 1982). (VOGUE ITALIA. BAMBINI.). **VFOAT** Vogue Bambini. No. 38 (Jan./Feb. 1982)-. Italian. Six times a year. L47570. Edizioni Conde Nast Spa, Piazza Castello 27, 20121 Milan Italy. **Tel** 011 39 2 85611. **(Subscription address:** Arnoldo Mondadori Editore, UFF Cont Abbonamenti, 20090 Segrate Mi Italy. **Tel** 011 39 2 75422753.) **Continues** Vogue Bambini.

LC TT500   **ISSN** 0176-6104
DD 646/.34/05   GW
UDC 391:687
VOGUE MUENCHEN. See Women's Interests.

LC TT500 .V7   **ISSN** 0042-8000
DD 646/.34/05   US
VOGUE (NEW YORK). See Women's Interests.

LC TT500 .V716
DD 391/.2/05   FR
VOGUE PARIS. See Women's Interests.

LC TT524 .V63   **ISSN** 1120-7795
DD 391/.2   IT
VOGUE PELLE. No. 2 (Feb. 1981)-. Periodical. Italian (English). Two times a year. L19930. Edizioni Conde Nast Spa, Piazza Castello 27, 20121 Milan Italy. **Tel** 011 39 2 85611. **(Subscription address:** Sodip Spa, Via Bettola 18, 20092 Cinisello Balsamo Italy. **Tel** 011 39 2 66030322.) **Continues** Vogue Italia. Pelle.

LC TT500 .W165   **ISSN** 0162-9115
DD 746.9/2/05   US
W. (1972)-. Periodical. English. Twenty-six times a year. $29.90. Fairchild Publications Inc., 7 West 34th Street, 4th Floor, New York NY 10001-8191. **Tel** (212)630-4230, (800)247-6622. **(Subscription address:** Neodata / Colorado, PO Box 2606, Boulder CO 80322.) **ED** John Fairchild. **Bk Rev. Ad Acc. Circ:** 226,323. available with illustrations; available in microform.
Desc: The fashion newspaper for the discerning woman. Features the heights of haute couture, whatever is new, fascinating and fun in the world of fashion.
Ind/Abst Access (1975-).

LC TT649 .W47   **ISSN** 0049-7487
DD 646/.47   US
WESTERN OUTFITTER. (19??)-. Periodical. English. Twelve times a year. $12.00 US; $13.50 other. Houston Business Journal, One West Loop South, Suite 650, Houston TX 77027. **Tel** (713)688-8811, FAX (713)963-0482.

Clothing Industry and Fashion

WHAT'S HOT. [What's hot]. (1987)-Suspended (19??). Periodical. English. Twelve times a year. $18.98. What's Hot, 82 Wall Street/Suite 1105, New York NY 10005. **Tel** (212)877-1780.
ISSN 0893-598X
US
SUSPENDED

WHO'S WHO IN FASHION. 1st Ed. (1982)-. English. Every 3 years. Who's Who in Italy SRL, CP 61, 20091 Bresso Milan Italy. **Tel** 011 39 2 6100237.
LC TT500 .W68
SZ

WOLGAN MOT. Added/Corp Tonga Ilbosa. VFOAT Mot. (1984)-. Periodical. Korean. Twelve times a year. $117.00. Tonga Ilbosa, PO Box 400, Kwanghwamun Ucheguk, Seoul 110 Korea. **(Subscription address:** Seoul Books and Records, 3450 West Peterson Avenue, Chicago IL 60659. **Tel** (312)463-7756.)
KO

LC HD9940.U3 N33
DD 381/.456871/062573
ISSN 0741-0735
US

WOMEN'S AND CHILDREN'S WEAR AND FASHION ACCESSORIES BUYERS. [Women's child. wear fash. accessories buy.]. **Added/Corp** Salesman's Guide, Inc. VFOAT Women's & Children's Wear & Fashion Accessories Buyers; Women's & Children's Wear and Fashion Accessories Buyers; Women's and Children's Wear & Fashion Accessories Buyers; National Directory of Women's & Children's Wear and Fashion Accessories; Salesman's Guide Women's and Children's Wear and Fashion Accessories Buyers Nationwide Directory; Nationwide Directory, Women's & Children's Wear Buyers. (19??)-. Trade Publication. English. One time a year. $95.00. Salesman's Guide, A Reed Reference Publishing Company, Part of Reed International PLC, 121 Chanlon Road, New Providence NJ 07974. **Tel** (800)223-1797, (908)464-6800, FAX (908)665-3560, telex 138755. **ED** Edward R. Blank. **Bk Rev. Ad Acc. Circ:** 4,000 (ctrl). **Continues** Women's and Children's Wear and Fashion Accessories Buyers, 0741-0735.
Desc: Lists over 6,000 major retail stores in the US with names of buyers and merchandising managers of women's and children's apparel and accessories.

LC HD9940.U3 W36
ISSN 0743-3972
US

WOMEN'S LARGE & HALF SIZE SPECIALTY STORES. VFOAT Women's Large and Half Size Specialty Stores. (19??)-. English. Salesman's Guide, A Reed Reference Publishing Company, Part of Reed International PLC, 121 Chanlon Road, New Providence NJ 07974. **Tel** (800)223-1797, (908)464-6800, FAX (908)665-3560, telex 138755. **ED** Edward R. Blank. **Bk Rev. Ad Acc. Circ:** 700 (ctrl).
Desc: Lists 4,000 women's clothing stores carrying extra large, large and half sizes, with buyer's name, address and phone number.

DD 687
ISSN 1350-6773
UK

WORLD CLOTHING MANUFACTURER. [World Cloth. Manuf.]. (1993)-. Periodical. English. Ten times a year. $190.00. International Textile Benjamin Dent Ltd., 23 Bloomsbury Square, London WC1 A2P United Kingdom. **Tel** 011 44 171 6372211, FAX 011 44 171 6372248, telex 8954884. **Continues** Manufacturing Clothier, 0025-2565.
Desc: Provides information on the clothing manufacturing industry internationally. Features articles on garment-making techniques, processes and developments.
Ind/Abst Curr. Cit.

DD 685
ISSN 0894-3079
US

WORLD FOOTWEAR. [World footwear]. Vol. 1, No. 1 (May 1987)-. Trade Publication. English. Six times a year. $60.00. Shoe Trades Publishing Company, 61 Massachusetts Avenue, Arlington MA 02174. **Tel** (617)648-8160, FAX (617)492-0126, telex 325736 SHOETRADE. **ED** Iain Howie. **Bk Rev. Ad Acc. Circ:** 15,000 (ctrl).

LC HD9940.U3 W4
DD 338.4/7/646
ISSN 0149-5380
US
CCC

WWD. [WWD]. **VAT** Women's Wear Daily. (197?)-. Newspaper. English. Five times a week (except Sat., Sun., and holidays). $89.00. Fairchild Publications Inc., 7 West 34th Street, 4th Floor, New York NY 10001-8191. **Tel** (212)630-4230, (800)247-6622. **(Subscription address:** Neodata / Colorado, PO Box 2606, Boulder CO 80322.**) Ad Acc. Pub. Size:** Tabloid. **Circ:** 56,249. available on microfilm and microfiche from University Microfilms International (UMI); available on an online database (file 648/Full-Text) from DIALOG; available with illustrations. **Continues** Women's Wear Daily, 0043-7581.
Ind/Abst EP Collect.; Homework Help.; Infobank (197?-)(197?-); MasterFile FullTEXT 1000; MasterFile FullTEXT 350; MasterFile FullTEXT 650; MasterFile FullTEXT (July 1993-); OCLC; Pub. Lib. FullTEXT; Telebase; Vocat. Search.

DD 051
ISSN 1189-4695
CN

YOU (TORONTO. 1990). (YOU LIVING WITH VERVE.). [You Tor., 1990]. VFOAT You. (1990)-. Periodical. English. Four times a year (Mar., June, Sept., Dec.). 14.95Can$ (two-year), 19.95Can$ (three-year) Canada; 28.00Can$ (two-year), 42.00Can$ (three-year) other. Family Communications Ltd., 37 Hanna Avenue Unit 1, Toronto Ontario, M6K 1X1 Canada. **Tel** (416)537-2604, FAX (416)538-1794. **Ad Acc, Adv Mgr:** Faye Gruenspan. **Circ:** 200,000. **Continues** You Verve, 0841-6648.

ABSTRACTING, BIBLIOGRAPHIES AND STATISTICS

BIBLIOGRAPHY - COSTUME SOCIETY OF AMERICA. Main/Corp Costume Society of America. VFOAT Bibliography of Recent Books Relating to Costume; Bibliography of Recent Books Relating to Fashion; Bibliography of Recent Publications Relating to Costume. 1- 1975-. Bibliography. English. **ED** A Filene.
US

DD 338.4/768531/00971
ISSN 0380-707X
CN

FOOTWEAR STATISTICS. [Footwear stat.]. **Added/Corp** Canada. Dominion Bureau of Statistics. Industry Division. Canada. Dominion Bureau of Statistics. Manufacturing and Primary Industries Division. Statistics Canada. Manufacturing and Primary Industries Division. Statistics Canada. Industry Division. VFOAT La Statistique de la Chaussure. Vol. 41, No. 10 (Oct. 1966)-. Statistical Publication. English (French). Twelve times a year. 24.00Can$ Canada; $29.00 US; $34.00 other. Statistics Canada Publications Sales and Services, R.H. Coats Building 6th Floor, Ottawa Ontario K1A 0T6 Canada. **Tel** (613)951-5078, (800)267-6677, FAX (613)951-1584, telex 053-3585. **Continues** Production of Leather Footwear, 0380-7088.
Desc: Covers production of footwear in Canada, by type of footwear.

LC HD9940.C18 C35b
DD 381/.45/687110971
ISSN 0829-7401
CN

OPERATING RESULTS. MEN'S RETAIL CLOTHING STORES. (OPERATING RESULTS, MEN'S RETAIL CLOTHING STORES = RESULTATS DE L'EXPLOITATION, MAGASINS DE VENTE AU DETAIL DE VETEMENTS POUR HOMMES.). [Oper. results, Mens retail cloth. stores]. **Added/Corp** Statistics Canada. Merchandising and Services Division. Statistics Canada. Merchandising and Services Division. Analysis and Development Section. Statistics Canada. Retail Trade Section. VFOAT Resultats de l'Exploitation, Magasins de Vente au Detail de Vetements Pour Hommes. (1974)-. English (French). Irregular. 15.00Can$ Canada; $16.00 other. Statistics Canada Publications Sales and Services, R.H. Coats Building 6th Floor, Ottawa Ontario K1A 0T6 Canada. **Tel** (613)951-5078, (800)267-6677, FAX (613)951-1584, telex 053-3585.

COLLEGE AND SCHOOL PUBLICATIONS

LC LH1 .E24
DD 373.1/8/0973
ISSN 0163-1640
US

18 ALMANAC. VAT Eighteen Almanac. (19??)-. Periodical. English. One time a year. Approach 13 30 Corporation, 505 Market Street, Knoxville TN 37902.

LC LH5 .A3
ISSN 0001-320X
UK

ABERDEEN UNIVERSITY REVIEW. [Aberd. Univ. rev.]. **Added/Corp** University of Aberdeen. Aberdeen University. Alumnus Association. Vol. 1 (Nov. 1913)-. Periodical. English. Two times a year (Apr., Oct.). $20.53. University of Aberdeen / Alumnus Association, Kings College High Street, Aberdeen AB9 2UB United Kingdom. **Tel** 011 44 224 40241, telex 73458 UNIABN G. **ED** Dr. Ian Olson. Index available (Bound in last issue). **Bk Rev, (Qty: 4-5). Circ:** 1,650 (ctrl).
Desc: Articles of general university interest, local archaeology, reviews and news of alumni.
Ind/Abst Abstr. Engl. Stud.; Annu. Bibliogr. Engl. Lang. Lit.

LC AP1 .A4
DD 052
ISSN 0001-8015
UK

ADAM INTERNATIONAL REVIEW. See Library and Information Sciences.

ADVOCATE. (19??)-. Periodical. English. Four times a year. Free on request. North Carolina State University / Adult Education, Department of Adult Community College Education, Box 7801, Raleigh NC 27695. **Tel** (919)515-6248.
US

LC U
DD 358
AIR UNIVERSITY CATALOG. Main/Corp Air University (U.S.). (19??)-. Catalog. English. Irregular. Air University, CADRE/PT, Building 1400, Maxwell Air Force Base AL 36112.
US

ALBANY : THE UNIVERSITY AT ALBANY MAGAZINE WITH THE CARILLON. Added/Corp State University of New York at Albany. VFOAT Carillon. (Fall 1991)-. Periodical. English. Two times a year. The University of New York at Albany, Department of English, Albany NY 12222. **Tel** (518)442-4091. **Formed by the union of** University at Albany Magazine **and** Researcher.
US

ISSN 0742-096X
US

ALLEGHENY REVIEW, THE. [Allegheny rev.]. **Added/Corp** Allegheny College (Meadville, Pa.). Vol. 1, No. 1 (1983)-. Academic Scholarly Publication. English. One time a year. $4.00. Allegheny Review, Allegheny College, PO Box 32, Meadville PA 16335. **Tel** (814)332-6553.

DD 051
ISSN 0712-4589
CN

ALPHA DELTA PHI LITERARY JOURNAL, THE. [Alpha Delta Phi lit. j.]. **Added/Corp** Alpha Delta hi. Alpha Delta Phi. Toronto Chapter. Vol. 1 (1980/1981)-. English. One time a year. Free. Alpha Delta Phi Literary Journal, 94 Prince Arthur Avenue, Toronto Ontario M5R 1B6 Canada. ctrl circ.

DD 378
ISSN 1066-3452
US

ALTERNATIVE ORANGE, THE. [Altern. orange]. (1991)-. Periodical. English. Seven times a year. Free to the Syracuse University community; $20.00 US; $25.00 Canada; $30.00 other. Alternative Orange, 126T Schine Student Center, Syracuse University, Syracuse NY 13340. **Continues** Alrternative Orange.

DD 674
ISSN 0187-6112
MX

AMATL. [Amatl]. VFOAT Boletin Informativo del Instituto de Madera Celulosa y Papel. (1987)-. Bulletin. Spanish. Four times a year. Universidad de Guadalajara, Apdo. Postal 4-120, 44400 Guadalajara Jal. Mexico.
Ind/Abst Abstr. Bull. Inst. Pap. Sci. Tech.

LC SD1 .A56
DD 634.9/05
US

AMES FORESTER. See Forests and Forestry.

LC DP302.C217 A54
DD 946/.88/005
SP

ANALES DE LA UNIVERSIDAD DE CADIZ. Added/Corp Universidad de Cadiz. Servicio de Publicaciones. (1984)-. Periodical. Spanish. Twelve times a year. $10.00 Spain; $22.50 Europe; $25.00 other. Fac de Ciencias Dep de Quimica, Apartado 40, Puerto Real Cadiz Spain. **Tel** 956-22-3808.

LC AS222 .N8
ISSN 0399-0389
FR

ANNALES DU CENTRE UNIVERSITAIRE MEDITERRANEEN. [Ann. Cent. univ. mediterr.]. **Main/Corp** Centre Universitaire Mediterraneen de Nice. (1946/47)-. French. One time a year. Societe des Amis du Centre Universitaire Mediterraneen, 06209 Nice France. cum. index.
Ind/Abst Am. Hist. Life (1952-).

SP

ANUARIO DE LA UNIVERSIDAD DE BARCELONA. Added/Corp Universidad de Barcelona. VFOAT Universidad de Barcelona. (1921)-. Spanish. Irregular. **Continues** Anuario del Curso Academico de ... .

DD 700
ISSN 0900-338X
DK

ARGOS (ODENSE). (ARGOS.). [Argos Odense]. (1985)-. Periodical. Danish. Two times a year. Kr78.40. Odense University Press, 55 Campusvej, DK-5230 Odense M Denmark. **Tel** 011 45 7 66157999, FAX 011 45 7 66158126.
Ind/Abst BHA : Biblio. Hist. Art.

LC AS552.A73 A73a
ISSN 0385-6844
JA
CODEN AKKKDJ

ARIAKE KOGYO KOTO SEMMON GAKKO KIYO. See Science and Technology.

ISSN 0004-1882
US

ARKA TECH. Main/Corp Arkansas Tech University. Periodical. English. One time a year. Arka Tech, Arkansas Tech University, Russelville AR 72801. **Tel** (501)968-0284. **Circ:** 2,879.

College and School Publications

LC LH5.A78 A78
DD 050
GR
ATHENAIOS. VFOAT Athenian. (Jan. 1929)-.
English (Greek, Modern). Kollegion Athenon, Athens Greece.

ISSN 1071-1279
US
AUBURN PLAINSMAN, THE. (19??)-.
Newspaper. English. Thirty-five times a year (Not published between quarters or on holidays of the university). $20.00. Auburn Plainsman, Basement Union Building, Auburn AL 36849. **Tel** (334)844-4130, FAX (334)844-9114. **ED** Jan Clifford, (Editor's address: B-100 Union Building, Auburn University, AL 36849-5343; telephone: (205)844-9021). **Ad Acc. Circ:** 19.500 (ctrl). available on microfiche from Ralph Draughon Library.
Continues Plainsman (Auburn, Ala.).

ISSN 0045-1304
US
BADGER HERALD. Added/Corp University of Wisconsin. (19??)-. Periodical. English. One time a week. $7.00. Badger Herald Inc, 638 State Street, Madison WI 53703. **Tel** (608)257-3005. **ED** Brenda Regeth. **Bk Rev. Ad Acc. Circ:** 20,000 (ctrl).
Desc: Independent student newspaper offering news, fine arts, sports and conservative editorials.

LC AS471 .B35
ISSN 0970-4825
II
BANASTHALI PATRIKA, THE. [Banasthali patrika]. **Added/Corp** Banasthali Vidyapith. (19??)-. Periodical. English. Four times a year. Banasthali Vidyapith, Jaipur Rajasthan India.
Ind/Abst MLA Int. Bibl. Books Artic. Mod. Lang. Lit.

ISSN 0005-6014
US
BARNARD BULLETIN. Bulletin. English. One time a week. Barnard College Womens Center, 3009 Broadway, New York NY 10027. **Tel** (212)280-2067.

ISSN 1055-4726
US
Pr Rev.
BATTALION (COLLEGE STATION, TEX. 1893), THE. (THE BATTALION.). VFOAT Texas A&M Battalion. (Oct. 1, 1893)-. Newspaper. English. (165 issues per year). $50.00. Texas A & M University / Battalion, The Battalion, Student Publications, College Station TX 77843-1111. **Tel** (409)845-2611, FAX (409)845-2647. **ED** Jay Robbins Summer (phone: (409)845-3313). **Bk Rev,** (Qty: 10). **Ad Acc, Adv Mgr:** Patricia Heck, **Tel** (409)845-2696. **Circ:** 21,500 (Fall), 11,500 (Summer) (ctrl). available on microfilm from Southwest Micropublishing International. **Continues** College Journal.

LC AS243 .B36
ISSN 0005-738X
NE
BEAKEN. (IT BEAKEN.). [Beaken]. **Added/Corp** Fryske Akademy. (Dec. 1938)-. Periodical. Dutch. Four times a year. $38.03. Fryske Akademy, Postbus 54, 8900 AB Leeuwarden Netherlands. **Tel** 011 31 58 131414.
Ind/Abst MLA Int. Bibl. Books Artic. Mod. Lang. Lit.

ISSN 0005-982X
US
BETHEL COLLEGE BULLETIN. Main/Corp Bethel College (North Newton, Kan.). Bulletin. English. Twelve times a year. Bethel College Bulletin, PO Drawer B, North Newton KS 67117.

US
BLACK AND MAGENTA, THE. (1902)-.
Newspaper. English. One time a week. $10.00. Muskingum College, New Concord OH 43762. **Tel** (614)826-8296. **Ad Acc. Circ:** 1,500. available with illustrations.

US
BLACK AND RED. (1897)-. Periodical. English. Twelve times a year. $4.00. Northwestern College, 1300 Western Avenue, Watertown WI 53094. **Tel** (414)261-4352. **ED** Board. Index available. **Bk Rev. Ad Acc. Circ:** 600. available with illustrations.

ISSN 0746-2557
US
BLUE & GOLD ILLUSTRATED. VFOAT Blue and Gold Illustrated. Vol. 3, Issue 1 (Aug. 29, 1983)-. Periodical. English. Twenty times a year. $34.95. Fan Action Inc., 3930 Edison Lakes Parkway, Suite 130, Mishawaka IN 46545. **Tel** (219)277-6332. **(Subscription address:** Blue and Gold Illustrated, PO Box 1007, Notre Dame IN 46556.) **Continues** Go Irish, 0744-950X.

LC LH7.U52 B58
IO
BM : BERITA MAHASISWA. VFOAT B.M.; Berita Mahasiswa. Periodical. Indonesian. Departemen Penerangan Sm-Feui, Salemba 4, Jakarta Indonesia.

ISSN 0186-3924
MX
DD 015
BOLETIN EDITORIAL - COLEGIO DE MEXICO. [Bol. ed. - Col. Mex.]. (1985)-. Bulletin. Spanish. Six times a year. Colegio de Mexico AC, Camino Al Ajusco No 20, 10740 Mexico DF Mexico. **Tel** 011 52 5 6455955 ext. 3138, telex 1777585 COLME.

ISSN 0543-7369
MX
BOLETIN SEMESTRAL - COLEGIO DE MEXICO. **Main/Corp** Colegio de Mexico. (1963)-. Periodical. Spanish. Six times a year. Free. Colegio de Mexico AC, Camino Al Ajusco No 20, 10740 Mexico DF Mexico. **Tel** 011 52 5 6455955 ext. 3138, telex 1777585 COLME. **ED** Angel Miquel. Index available. **Bk Rev. Ad Acc. Circ:** 4,000.
Desc: Contains advances of books soon to be published and describes editorial novelties.

ISSN 8750-989X
US
BOSTON UNIVERSITY TODAY (1984). (BOSTON UNIVERSITY TODAY.). **Added/Corp** Boston University. Vol. 1, No. 1 (Sept. 5, 1984)-. Periodical. English. Thirty-five times a year (weekly Sept.-June). $20.00. Boston University, 10 Lenox Street, Brookline MA 02146. **Tel** (617)353-3986. **Continues** World at Boston University.

ISSN 8750-5266
US
BRIDGE (LAFAYETTE, IND.). (BRIDGE.).
Added/Corp Eta Kappa Nu. (19??)-. Periodical. English. Four times a year. $7.50. Eta Kappa Nu, University of Missouri-Rolla, EE Department, Rolla MO 65401. **Tel** (314)341-4513. **Continues** Bridge of Eta Kappa Nu, 0006-9809.

LC LH1. L4 B7
US
BROWN AND WHITE, THE. Added/Corp Lehigh University. Vol. 1 (Jan. 16, 1894)-. Newspaper. English. Irregular (Tues. & Wed. during school year). $25.00. Brown & White, Lehigh University, University Center Room 29, Bethlehem PA 18015. **Tel** (610)758-4180. **ED** Lori Montemurro (Editor-in-Chief) and Paul Mare (Managing Editor). **Photos. Ad Acc, Adv Mgr:** Cameron Moltzman, **Tel** (610)758-4184. Full Page (B&W) $300.00. Half Page (B&W) $150.00. **Pub. Size:** Standard. available in microform.

ISSN 0745-1083
US
BULL GATOR. Periodical. English. One time a week. Bull Gator News, Po Box 13512, Gainesville FL 32604.

ISSN 0228-1252
CN
DD 378/.198974/09714
BULLETIN DE NOUVELLES - PRESSE ETUDIANTE DU QUEBEC. (BULLETIN DE NOUVELLES.). [Bull. nouv. - Presse etud. Que.]. **VAT** Bulletin de Nouvelles de la PEQ; Bulletin de Nouvelles de la Presse Etudiante du Quebec. Bulletin. French. Irregular. 24.01Can$. Presse Etudiante du Quebec, 1581 rue Dufresne, Montreal Quebec H2K 3J6 Canada. **Tel** (514)526-0235. **Bk Rev. Circ:** 90 (ctrl). **Continues** Bulletin de Nouvelles (Presse Etudiante Nationale (1975-1978)), 0714-3702.
Desc: Articles from and for student newspapers. Subjects that are talked about are: education, politics, arts, condition of youth.

ISSN 0822-9376
CN
DD 378.713/84
BULLETIN - FEDERATION DES ETUDIANTS DE L'U. DE O. (LE BULLETIN / FEDERATION DES ETUDIANTS DE L'U. DE O.). [Bull. - Fed. etud. Univ. Ottawa.]. **VFOAT** The Bulletin; Bulletin. **VAT** Bulletin - Federation des Etudiants de l'Universite d'Ottawa; Bulletin - Students Federation of the University of Ottawa. Vol. 1, No. 1 (Dec. 1982)-. Bulletin. English (French). Twelve times a year. Free. Students Federation of the University of Ottawa, 85 Hastet/Room 07, Ottawa Ontario K1N 6N5 Canada.

ISSN 0296-3698
FR
UDC 511.001
BUSEFAL. BULLETIN POUR LES SOUS ENSEMBLES FLOUS ET LEURS APPLICATIONS. [BUSEFAL, Bulletin pour les Sous Ensembles Flous et Leurs Applications]. **VFOAT** Bulletin for Studies and Exchanges on Fuzziness and Its Applications; BUSEFAL. Bulletin for Studies and Exchanges on Fuzziness and Its Applications; Bulletin pour les Sous Ensembles Flous et Leurs Applications. (198?)-. Bulletin. English. Universite Paul Sabatier LSI, Lab LSI, 118 Route de Narbonne, 31062 Toulouse Cedex France.

ISSN 0227-2822
CN
DD 001.3
CAHIERS DE CAP-ROUGE. [Cah. Cap-Rouge]. (1972)-. Periodical. French. Four times a year. 18.00Can$. Campus Notre Dame de Foy, 5000 rue Clement Lockquell, St Augustin Quebec, G3A 1B3 Canada. **Tel** (418)872-8041.
Ind/Abst Repere (1983-).

ISSN 0999-2413
FR
UDC 372.871/.878(443.61)
CAHIERS DE L'ACADEMIE ANQUETIN NEUILLY-SUR-SEINE, LES. [Cah. acad. Anquetin Neuilly-sur-Seine]. (1965)-. Periodical. French. Two times a year. $16.80. Cahiers de l Academie Anquetin, 15 rue Jacque Dulud, 92200 Neuilly Sur Seine France. **Tel** 011 33 1 47221610.
Ind/Abst BHA : Biblio. Hist. Art.

FR
CAHIERS DE L'IPC. French. Two times a year. 140.00F. Univ Paris VII / IPC, 13 rue Santeuil, F 75005 Paris France. **Tel** 011 33 1 45874118.

LC AP8 .C2
ISSN 0045-3846
II
DD 052
SUSPENDED
CALCUTTA REVIEW. [Calcutta rev.].
Added/Corp University of Calcutta. University of Calcutta. Dept. of English. (1844)-Suspended (1991). Periodical. English. Four times a year. Calcutta University / Business Affairs and Finance, Pro Vice Chanc, Calcutta 12 India. cum. index.
Ind/Abst MLA Int. Bibl. Books Artic. Mod. Lang. Lit.

ISSN 0313-4466
AT
DD 378.994
TITLE CHANGE
CALENDAR - UNIVERSITY OF SYDNEY.
[Cal - Univ. Syd.]. (1853)-(1994). Periodical. English. University of Student / Student Centre, Sydney New South Wales 2006, Australia. **Tel** 011 61 2 6923023, FAX 011 61 2 6923023. **Continued by** Statutes & Regulations / University of Sydney.

ISSN 0008-1302
US
CALIFORNIA MONTHLY. Added/Corp California Alumni Association. (19??)-. Periodical. English. Six times a year (Feb., Apr., June, Sept., Nov., Dec.). $40.00. California Alumni Association, University of California Alumni House, Berkeley CA 94720. **Tel** (415)642-7026. **ED** Russell Schoch (phone: (510)642-5782). **Bk Rev,** (Qty: 5-6). **Ad Acc, Adv Mgr:** Lora Dinga, **Tel** (510)526-4766. **Circ:** 90,000 (ctrl).
Desc: Reports the issues, discoveries and people of the University of California-Berkeley. Keeps its graduates informed and updated.

ISSN 0008-1582
US
CALIFORNIA TECH, THE. Periodical. English. One time a week. $9.00. The California Tech, 40-58 Student Activity Center, California Institute of Technology, Pasadena CA 91125. **Tel** (818)356-6154. **ED** Theodore H Rivette. **Bk Rev. Ad Acc. Circ:** 3,200.
Desc: News and features of interest to the Caltech community.

LC LH5 .C178
ISSN 0008-2007
UK
CCC
CAMBRIDGE REVIEW, THE. Vol. 1, No. 1 (Oct. 15, 1879)-. Academic Scholarly Publication. English. Two times a year. $69.00. Cambridge University Press, The Edinburgh Building, Shaftesbury Road, Cambridge CB2 2RU United Kingdom. **Tel** 011 44 1223 312393, FAX 011 44 1223 315052, telex 851-817256. **(Subscription address:** Cambridge University Press / North America, 110 Midland Avenue, Port Chester NY 10573. **Tel** (800)431-1580, (914)937-9600.) **ED** Ruth Morse and Stefan Collini. **Bk Rev. Ad Acc. Circ:** 1,000,000 (ctrl). available on microfilm from University Microfilms International (UMI).
Desc: This "journal of university life and thought" features poetry, essays, book reviews, biographies and articles to keep readers informed on matters of general intellectual interest. It contains writing on current intellectual developments and topical cultural themes as well as items of interest to all involved in higher education in general and Cambridge University in particular. Draws on a great wealth of talent both from within Cambridge and beyond in an attempt to match the right writers with the right topics.
Ind/Abst Annu. Bibliogr. Engl. Lang. Lit.; Archit. Period. Index; Romant. Move.

UK
CAMBRIDGE UNIVERSITY GUIDE TO COURSES. Added/Corp University of Cambridge. (1990/91)-. Academic Scholarly Publication. English. $14.95. Cambridge University Press, The Edinburgh Building, Shaftesbury Road, Cambridge CB2 2RU United Kingdom. **Tel** 011 44 1223 312393, FAX 011 44 1223 315052, telex 851-817256. **Ad Acc, Adv Mgr:** Nick Kelley, **Tel** 0223 325757. **Continues** Cambridge University Handbook.

College and School Publications

CAMBRIDGE UNIVERSITY REPORTER.
ISSN 0008-2015 UK
Main/Corp University of Cambridge. (1870)-. Academic Scholarly Publication. English. Irregular (70 per year). $76.75. Cambridge University Press, The Edinburgh Building, Shaftesbury Road, Cambridge CB2 2RU United Kingdom. **Tel** 011 44 1223 312393, **FAX** 011 44 1223 315052, telex 851-817256. **(Subscription address:** Cambridge University Press / Trinity - UK, 1 Trinity Street, Cambridge CB2 1S2 United Kingdom. **Tel** 011 44 1223 333333.)
LC WMLC 93/5185

CAMPUS. (19??)-. Italian. Ten times a year.
IT
L28000.00 Italy; L118000.00 The Americas and Asia; L68000.00 Europe; L107000.00 Africa; L156000.00 other. Class Editori CAM, Via Burigozzo 5, 20122 Milan Italy. **Tel** 011 39 2 582191.

CAMPUS CANADA (TORONTO, ONT.).
ISSN 0829-3309 CN
DD 378/.198/0971
(CAMPUS CANADA.). [Campus Can.]. Vol. 2, No. 4 (Feb./Mar. 1985)-. Periodical. English. Four times a year. 6.73Can$. CCMC / Canadian Controlled Media Communications, 287 MacPherson Avenue, Toronto Ontario M4V 1A4 Canada. **Tel** (416)928-2909, **FAX** (416)966-1181. **ED** Sarah Moore. **Ad Acc, Adv Mgr:** H.Wolfe. ctrl circ. **Continues** Campus Digest, 0823-4531.
Ind/Abst Can. Index.

CAMPUS DIGEST. [Campus dig.]. Vol. 1, No. 1
ISSN 0823-4531 CN
DD 378/.198/0971
(Oct. 1983)-. Periodical. English. Irregular. Free to Universities. Campus Digest, 487 King Street East, Toronto Ontario M5A 1L9 Canada.

CAMPUS REPORT (STANFORD).
ISSN 0049-2108 US
(CAMPUS REPORT.). **Main/Corp** Stanford University. Office of Public Affairs. (1968)-. Periodical. English. Forty-Four times a year. $50.00. Stanford University Press, Courtyard Santa Teresa Street, Stanford CA 94305. **Tel** (415)723-9434. **ED** Karen Bartholomew and Terry Johnston. **Bk Rev. Circ:** 16,000 (ctrl).
Desc: A newspaper of record for faculty and staff of Stanford University.
LC LH1 .C35

CAMPUS TIMES, THE. Vol. 1, No. 1 (Sept. 17,
US
1990)-. Periodical. English. Seven times a week. $24.00. The Campus Times, PO Box 7141, Athens GA 30604.

CAMPUSKRANT. (1990)-. French. Twenty-six
BE
times a year. Ku Leuven, Informatie Onthaal, Universiteitshal Oude Markt 13, 3000 Leuven Belgium.

CAPAHA ARROW, THE. (19??)-. Periodical.
ISSN 0008-5774 US
English. One time a week. Southeast Missouri State University, 400 North Pacific, Cape Girardeau MO 63701. **Tel** (314)651-2636.
LC LD3225 .A17
DD 378.748/56

CARONTAWAN. English. One time a year.
US
Mansfield State College, Belknap Hall, Mansfield PA 16933.

CHALLENGE FUND JOURNAL.
ISSN 0838-8334 CN
DD 378.713/84
(JOURNAL.). [Chall. Fund j.]. **Added/Corp** Carleton University. **VFOAT** Carleton University Challenge Fund Campaign Report. Vol. 1, No. 1 (Summer 1987)-. Periodical. English. Irregular. Carleton University / Administration Building, Room 510, Colonel By Drive, Ottawa Ontario K1S 5B6 Canada. **Continues** Carleton University News, 0319-3292.
LC LD3967 .A26
DD 378.784/13

CHIP OFF THE OLD BISON, A. Added/Corp
US
North Dakota. State University of Agriculture and Applied Science, Fargo. Board of Student Publications. (1978)-. English. One time a week. North Dakota State University / Publications, Board of Student Publications, Fargo ND 58102.
LC AP95.C4 C558

CHUNG HSUEH SHENG. VFOAT Student
HK
Magazine. First published in July 1975-. Multiple languages (English). $4.00. The Time Press, 17/F Flat B7, 15 Canal Road, Hsiang-Kang Hong Kong.

CIRCLE K. Periodical. English. Four times a year.
ISSN 0745-1962 US
Circle K International, 3636 Woodview Trace, Indianapolis IN 46268. **Continues** Circle K Magazine, 0578-3097.

CITY ON A HILL. Periodical. English. One time a
ISSN 0273-7736 US
week. City on a Hill Press, Stonehouse, University of California-Santa Cruz, Santa Cruz CA 95064. **Tel** (408)429-4359. **Circ:** 11,000.
LC LH5.S35

CIVITAS. Vol. 1 (Oct. 1945)-. Periodical. German
SZ
(French and Italian). Irregular. Schweizer Studentenverein, Ramistrasse 6, 8001 Zurich Switzerland. **Supersedes** Schweizerischer Studentenverein. Monatschrift.
Ind/Abst Am. Hist. Life (1973-1984).

CLAFLIN REVIEW, THE. [Claflin rev.].
ISSN 0895-5182 US
DD 051
Added/Corp Claflin College (Orangeburg, S.C.). (Spring 1986)-. Periodical. English. Four times a year. **Continues** Claflin College Review, 0191-216X.
Ind/Abst MLA Int. Bibl. Books Artic. Mod. Lang. Lit.

CLARION. Periodical. English. Bethel College
US
Clarion, PO Box 2381, Saint Paul MN 55112.
Ind/Abst Art Archaeol. Tech. Abstr.; Art Index.

COCKTAIL MOLOTOV, LE. Vol. 1, No. 2 (Oct.
ISSN 0228-9067 CN
DD 378.714/16
21, 1980)-. Periodical. French. Six times a year. Free. Le Cocktail Molotov, College de Jonquiere, 65 rue St. Hubert Canada. ctrl circ. **Continues** Journal Etudiant, 0228-9059.

COLLEGE HEIGHTS HERALD, THE. Vol. 1,
US
No. 1 (Jan. 29, 1925)-. Newspaper. English. Two times a week. $15.00. College Heights Herald, 109 Garrett Conference Center, West Kentucky University, Bowling Green KY 42101. **Tel** (502)745-2653.

COLLEGE NEWSPAPER DIRECTORY AND RATE BOOK. (1982/83)-. Directory. English.
US
One time a year. American Passage Media Corp, 500 Third Avenue West, Seattle WA 98119. **Tel** (202)282-8111, (800)426-5537.

COLLEGE UNION & ON-CAMPUS HOSPITALITY. [Coll. union on-campus hosp.].
ISSN 0887-431X US
DD 378
VFOAT College Union and On Campus Hospitality. Vol. 8, No. 2 (April 1986)-. Periodical. English. Seven times a year. $18.00. Executive Business Media, PO Box 1500, Westbury NY 11590. **Tel** (516)334-3030, **FAX** (516)334-3059. **ED** Robert Moran. **Ad Acc.** ctrl circ. **Continues** College Union, 0192-3307.
LC LD6051

COLONIAL ECHO. 1899-. English. One time a
US
year. $25.00. Yearbook Campus Center, College of William and Mary, Williamsburg VA 23185. **Tel** (804)253-4896. **ED** Mary Beth Straight. **Ad Acc. Circ:** 4,000 (ctrl).
Desc: Published by the student body of William and Mary College in Williamsburg Va. It depicts the year of the students' in whole.

COLUMBIA DAILY SPECTATOR. English.
US
Five times a week. $85.00. Columbia University Spectator Publishing Co., 1125 Amsterdam Avenue/2nd Floor, New York NY 10025. **Tel** (212)280-4771. **ED** Kirsten Davis. **Bk Rev. Ad Acc. Circ:** 10,000.
Desc: Campus newspaper.
LC LH1.C7 J3

COLUMBIA JESTER, THE. Added/Corp
US
Columbia University. (19??)-. Periodical. English. Two times a year. $20.00. Columbia University / Jester, 206 Ferris Booth Hall, New York NY 10027. **Tel** (212)854-3611. **Ad Acc. Circ:** 10,000. available with illustrations.
LC LD1237.5 .C6
DD 378.747/1

COLUMBIA (NEW YORK, N.Y. 1978).
ISSN 0162-3893 US
(COLUMBIA : THE MAGAZINE OF COLUMBIA UNIVERSITY.). [Columbia]. **Added/Corp** Columbia University. (Spring 1978)-. Periodical. English. Five times a year. $25.00. Columbia Magazine, 3 Claremont Avenue, New York NY 10027. **Tel** (212)280-3603. **ED** Meg Dooley. **Bk Rev. Ad Acc. Circ:** 66,000 (ctrl). **Continues** Columbia Today (New York, N.Y.), 0146-423X.
Desc: General interest feature magazine of Columbia University. Covers science, medicine, culture, history, and the arts. Also includes light pieces and fiction. Focus is on people.
Ind/Abst Art Archaeol. Tech. Abstr.; Index Am. Period. Verse.

COLUMNS (FAIRMONT), THE. (THE
ISSN 0010-2091 US
COLUMNS.). **Added/Corp** Fairmont State College. (19??)-. Periodical. English. One time a week. Free. Fairmont State College, Office of Publications, 121 Library Building, Locust Avenue, Fairmont WV 26554. **Circ:** 2,000. available with illustrations.
Desc: School publication providing information of interest to students and faculty of Fairmont State College.

COMMONS (HARRISONBURG, VA.), THE. (THE COMMONS : A WEEKLY PUBLICATION
ISSN 1059-5015 US
FOR THE PEOPLE OF JAMES MADISON UNIVERSITY.). **Added/Corp** James Madison University. Division of University Relations. (1991)-. Periodical. English. One time a week. JMU Division of University Relations, James Madison University, Harrisonburg VA 22807. **Continues** JMU News (Harrisonburg, Va. : 1990), 1054-5875.

COMMONWEALTH PAPERS. Main/Corp
ISSN 0076-0765 UK
London. University. Institute of Commonwealth Studies. No. 1/20, (1954/1976)-. Monographic series. English. Irregular. Price varies per volume. Humanities Press, 165 1st Avenue, Atlantic Highlands NJ 07716. **Tel** (908)872-1441, (800)221-3845, **FAX** (908)872-0717, telex 752233.
Ind/Abst Urban Aff. Abstr.

CONCORDIA UNIVERSITY MAGAZINE.
ISSN 0706-1005 CN
DD 378.714/281
VAT University Alumni Magazine. Vol. 2, No. 1 (Sept./Oct. 1976)-. Periodical. English. Six times a year. University Information Office, Concordia University, 1455 de Maisonneuve Boulevard West Canada. **Formed by the union of** Concordia University Magazine. Loyola Ed., 0708-0913 **and** Concordia University Magazine. Sir George Ed., 0708-0816.

CONCORDIAN, THE. Added/Corp Concordia
US
College (Moorhead, Minn.). (1909)-. Periodical. English. One time a week (Fridays, during academic year). The Concordian, Concordia College, 901 South 8th Street, FPO Box 104, Moorhead MN 56560. **Tel** (218)299-3826. **ED** Debra Morrill. **Ad Acc. Circ:** 3,500 (ctrl). available on microfilm.

CONNECTICUT COLLEGE MAGAZINE.
ISSN 1060-5134 US
Added/Corp Connecticut College. Connecticut College Alumni Association. **VFOAT** ConnecticutCollegeMagazine. (1991)-. Periodical. English. Six times a year. Connecticut College Magazine, 270 Mohegan Avenue, New London CT 06320. **Continues** Connecticut College Alumni Magazine.

●**CONNECTIONS (ASSOCIATION OF AMERICAN COLLEGES).** (CONNECTIONS.).
ISSN 1064-8755 US
Added/Corp Association of American Colleges. Periodical. English. Four times a year. $42.00 US, $49.00 Canada and Mexico, $54.00 other (nonmembers), $36.00 US, $43.00 Canada and Mexico, $48.00 other (members) Comes with Liberal Education membership. Association of American Colleges / Publications Desk, 1818 R Street Northwest, Washington DC 20009. **Tel** (202)387-3760, **FAX** (202)265-9532.

CORNELL CHRONICLE. Added/Corp Cornell
ISSN 0747-4628 US
University. (1970)-. Periodical. English. One time a week. Free (Cornell University faculty, students and staff). Cornell Chronicle, 110 Day Hall, Ithaca NY 14853. **Tel** (607)256-4206. available via Internet (silvia_hoisie@cornell.edu).

COUGAR REPORT, THE. Periodical. English.
ISSN 0747-3656 US
Twelve times a year. University of Houston Student Publications, Houston TX 77004. **Tel** (713)749-1212.

CPU REVIEW. Added/Corp Columbia Pacific
ISSN 1056-1838 US
University. **VAT** Columbia Pacific University Review. (1991)-. Periodical. English. Two times a year. $14.00. Columbia Pacific University Press, 1415 3rd Street, San Rafael CA 94901.
LC BR1 .C6965

CRITERION (CHICAGO). See Religions and
ISSN 0590-0980 US
Theology.

ISSN 1042-9220
DD 378 US
CWRU - CASE WESTERN RESERVE UNIVERSITY. (CWRU : THE MAGAZINE OF CASE WESTERN RESERVE UNIVERSITY.). [CWRU - Case West. Reserve Univ.]. Vol. 1, No. 1 (Fall 1988)-. Periodical. English. Four times a year. CWRU Office of Public Affairs, Case Western Reserve University, 2040 Adelbert Road, Cleveland OH 44106.

US
DAILY COUGAR, THE. Added/Corp University of Houston--University Park. University of Houston Central Campus. University of Houston. Vol. 32, No. 2 (Sept. 21, 1965)-. Newspaper. English. Five times a week. $55.00. University of Houston Student Publications, Houston TX 77004. **Tel** (713)749-1212. **ED** Debra Fitzgerald. **Circ:** 13,000. ***Continues** Cougar (Houston, Tex. : 1934).*

ISSN 0894-1599
US
DAILY EASTERN NEWS, THE. Added/Corp Eastern Illinois University. **VFOAT** Summer Eastern News; Eastern News. (1980)-. Newspaper. English. Seven times a week. $60.00. Daily Eastern News, Eastern Illinois University, Buzzard Building, Charleston IL 61920. **Tel** (217)581-2812. **ED** Stuart Tart. Index available. **Bk Rev. Ad Acc. Pub. Size:** Tabloid. **Circ:** 8,900. available on microfilm. ***Continues** Eastern News (Charleston, Ill.).*

ISSN 0011-5819
DD 378.716/22 CN
DALHOUSIE GAZETTE, THE. [Dalhous. gaz.]. **Added/Corp** Dalhousie University. (Nov. 18, 1871)-. Periodical. English. One time a week. 10.00Can$ (one-year), 20.00Can$ (two-year); 25.00Can$ (three-year). Dalhousie Gazette, Dalhousie University, Halifax Nova Scotia B3H 4J2 Canada. **Tel** (902)424-2507. **Bk Rev. Ad Acc. Circ:** 10,000 (ctrl). ***Continues** Dalhousie College Gazette.*

ISSN 0845-8677
DD 378.716/22 CN
DALHOUSIE NEWS (HALIFAX). (DALHOUSIE NEWS.). [Dalhous. news]. **Main/Corp** Dalhousie University. (1988)-. Periodical. English. Twenty-six times a year. Limited free distribution. DAL News, Public Relations Office, Dalhousie University, Halifax Nova Scotia B3H 3J5 Canada. **Tel** (902)424-3643. ***Continues** Dal News., 0826-0419.*

ISSN 0199-9931
US
DARTMOUTH, THE. (19??)-. Periodical. English. Irregular. $20.00 Hannover, New Hampshire, $27.00 all other in the US, $17.50 students. Dartmouth College / The Dartmouth, Hinman Box 6175, Hanover NH 03755.

US
DARTMOUTH REVIEW, THE. Vol. 1, No. 1 (June 7, 1980)-. Newspaper. English. One time a week (except Christmas, holidays, and spring break). $30.00. Dartmouth Review, PO Box 343, Hanover NH 03755. **Tel** (603)643-4370, FAX (603)643-3070. **ED** Oron Strauss. **Bk Rev. Ad Acc.** ctrl circ.

ISSN 0714-4032
DD 378.714/471 CN
DEFI-SCIENCE. (DEFI-SCIENCE : JOURNAL DE L'ASSOCIATION DES ETUDIANTS EN SCIENCES ET GENIE DE LAVAL.). [Defi-sci.]. **Added/Corp** Universite Laval. Association des Etudiants en Sciences et Genie. **VFOAT** Defiscience. Vol. 1, No. 1 (9 Nov. 1977)-. Periodical. French. Free to members. Defiscience, c/o l'Association des Etudiants en Sciences et Genie Porte, 0600 Pavillon Vachon, Universite Laval, Quebec Quebec G1K 7P4 Canada.

ISSN 0011-9210
DD 810 US
DESCANT (FORT WORTH, TEX.). (DESCANT : THE TEXAS CHRISTIAN UNIVERSITY LITERARY JOURNAL.). **Added/Corp** Texas Christian University. (Fall 1956)-. Periodical. English. Two times a year. $12.00. Texas Christian University / English, PO Box 32875, Fort Worth TX 76129. **Tel** (817)921-7221, FAX (817)921-7333. **ED** Betsy Colquitt and Stanley Trachtenberg. **Circ:** 500 (ctrl). Documents available from The Genuine Article. ***Absorbed** Quartet, 0033-586X.*
Desc: Fiction and poetry.
Ind/Abst Abstr. Engl. Stud.; Annu. Bibliogr. Engl. Lang. Lit.; Arts Humanit. Citation Index [Full Cov.]; MLA Int. Bibl. Books Artic. Mod. Lang. Lit.; Res. Alert [Full Cov.].

LC AS181 .D5
GW
DIAGONAL : ZEITSCHRIFT DER UNIVERSITAT-GESAMTHOCHSCHULE-SIEGEN. Added/Corp Universitat-Gesamthochschule-Siegen. No. 1 (1991)-. Periodical. German. Two times a year.

LC LH1.D7 A4 ISSN 0271-9134
DD 378.748/43 US
DICKINSON MAGAZINE. Added/Corp Dickinson College. Dickinson College. Dickinson College Magazine. **VFOAT** Dickinson College Magazine. (19??)-. Periodical. English. Four times a year. Free on request. Dickinson College, Carlisle PA 17013. **Tel** (717)245-1528. **ED** Nancy L. Winkelman. **Circ:** 22,500 (ctrl). ***Continues** Dickinson Alumnus.*
Desc: Contains research and creative articles from the college constituency.

ISSN 1080-0476
DD 658 US
•DIMENSIONS (RESTON, VA.). (DIMENSIONS : A PUBLICATION OF DECA, AN ASSOCIATION OF MARKETING STUDENTS.). [Dimensions]. **Added/Corp** Distributive Education Clubs of America. **VFOAT** DECA Dimensions. Vol. 14, No. 1 (Sept./Oct. 1994)-. Periodical. English. Four times a year. Distributive Education Clubs of America, 1908 Association Drive, Reston VA 22091. **Tel** (703)860-5000, FAX (703)860-4013. ***Continues** DECA Dimensions, 1060-6106.*

LC AS30 .D55 ISSN 0197-4947
DD 051 US
DISCOVERY (AUSTIN). (DISCOVERY.). [Discovery]. **VFOAT** Research and Scholarship at the University of Texas at Austin. Vol. 1 (Sept. 1976)-. Academic Scholarly Publication. English. Four times a year. The University of Texas at Austin, Main Building 201, Austin TX 78712. **Tel** (512)471-5056. **ED** Carol S. Hatfield. Index available. cum. index. **Circ:** 10,000 (ctrl).
Desc: A journal of research and scholarly activities at the University of Texas at Austin.

LC LH1.F5 D5 ISSN 0012-3889
DD 376.8759 US
DISTAFF, A CRITICAL-LITERARY QUARTERLY, THE. VFOAT Spinner of Yarns. Vol. 1 (1926)-. Periodical. English. Four times a year. Students of Florida State College for Women, Tallahassee FL 32306.

ISSN 0743-2860
DD 378 US
DORM. [Dorm]. **VFOAT** Dorm Magazine. Vols. 1, No. 1 (Fall 1984)-. Periodical. English. Two times a year. Campus Publishing Inc., 90 Knollwood Road, Upper Saddle River NJ 07458. **ED** Garvin Lally. **Bk Rev. Ad Acc. Circ:** 1,000,000 (ctrl).
Desc: A general interest and lifestyle magazine for on-campus residents, particularly freshmen and sophomores.

US
DRAKE UPDATE. English. Three times a year. Free. Drake University, Office of Marketing and University Communications, 200 Old Main, Des Moines IA 50311. **Tel** (515)271-2169, FAX (515)271-3977. **ED** Barbara Dietrich. **Bk Rev. Circ:** 43,000 (ctrl).
Desc: News and features on Drake University alumni, students, faculty, sports, and other campus developments.

UK
DUNELMIAN. (19??)-. English. Durham School, Quarry Heads Lane, Durham City United Kingdom.

ISSN 0012-7280
UK
DURHAM UNIVERSITY JOURNAL, THE. [Durham Univ. j.]. **Main/Corp** University of Durham. **Added/Corp** University of Durham Journal. Vol. 1 (1876)-. Periodical. English (French). Two times a year (Jan., & July). $46.21. The Senate / University of Durham, Department of English Studies, Elvet Riverside, Durham DH1 3JT United Kingdom. **Tel** 011 44 191 3742000 ext 2744, FAX 011 44 191 3743740. **ED** Peter Lewis. Index available. cum. index. **Bk Rev. Ad Acc. Circ:** 500. available on microfilm from Xerox; available on microfilm and microfiche from University Microfilms International (UMI). Documents available from The Genuine Article.
Desc: Academic journal publishing articles and reviews on literature, history, classics, photography, music, theology and church history.
Ind/Abst Abstr. Engl. Stud.; Am. Hist. Life (1954-); Annu. Bibliogr. Engl. Lang. Lit.; Arts Humanit. Citation Index [Full Cov.]; BHA : Biblio. Hist. Art; Br. Archaeol. Bibliogr.; Br. Humanit. Index; Curr. Cit.; Curr. Contents Arts Humanit.; Middle East Abstr. Index; MLA Int. Bibl. Books Artic. Mod. Lang. Lit.; Res. Alert [Full Cov.]; Romant. Move.

ISSN 1048-8596
US
EDWARDIAN (LEWISTON, N.Y.). (EDWARDIAN.). (1990)-. Periodical. English. $19.95 (paperbound), $29.95 (casebound). Edwin Mellen Press, 415 Ridge Street, PO Box 450, Lewiston NY 14092. **Tel** (716)754-2266, (716)754-2788, FAX (716)754-4056.

ISSN 0701-1709
DD 378.714/17 CN
ELAN (HAUTERIVE). (L'ELAN.). Vol. 1 (Nov. 19, 1975)-. Periodical. French. L'Elan Bibliotheque, 537 boulevard Blanche, Hauterive Quebec G5C 2B2 Canada.

ISSN 0013-6727
US
EMORY MAGAZINE. Added/Corp Emory University. Office of Alumni Publications. Emory University. Office of University Periodicals. (19??)-. Periodical. English. Five times a year. $12.00. Emory University / Alumni Office, 1641 North Decatur Road, Atlanta GA 30322. **Tel** (404)727-7872.

ISSN 0381-1913
DD 370.7/3/09714471 CN
EXCELSIOR (QUEBEC). (EXCELSIOR.). Vol. 1 (Nov. 1970)-. Periodical. French. College Merici, 755 Chemin Saint-Louis, Quebec Quebec G1S 1C1 Canada. ***Supersedes** Piolet, 0381-1921.*

LC HF5001 .E915 ISSN 0146-4000
DD 658.4/005 US
EXCHANGE (PROVO). (EXCHANGE.). **Added/Corp** Brigham Young University, Provo, Utah. College of Business. Vol. 1 (Fall/Winter 1976)-. English. Two times a year. free. Brigham Young University / College of Business, 588 Tanner Building, Provo UT 84602. **Tel** (801)378-2182. **ED** Ed Nelson. **Bk Rev. Ad Acc. Circ:** 30,000 (ctrl).
Desc: Articles of a general management nature, involving both public and private sectors. Strong emphasis on ethics in the work place. Some faculty highlights.

LC LD7501.E9 P25 ISSN 0195-0207
DD 373.442/6 US
EXETER. (EXETER : THE BULLETIN OF THE PHILLIPS EXETER ACADEMY.). Bulletin. English. Four times a year. Free. Alumni Office / Phillips Exeter Academy, Jeremiah Smith Hall, Exeter NH 03833. **Tel** (603)772-4311. **ED** Paul Sadler Jr. **Bk Rev. Circ:** 24,500. ***Continues** Phillips Exeter Bulletin, 0031-7942.*
Desc: News about independent secondary education and news about Exeter alumni and alumnae.

US
FACCC BULLETIN. (19??)-. Bulletin. English. Four times a year. Free on request. Faculty Association of California Community Colleges, 926 J Street, Suite 211, Sacramento CA 95814.
Ind/Abst Calif. Period. Index (19??-); Calif. Period. Microfi. (19??-).

ISSN 1056-4276
DD 051 US
FIAT LUX. [Fiat lux]. **Added/Corp** University of California, Riverside. University Relations Office. Vol. 1, No. 1 (April 1991)-. Periodical. English. Six times a year. Fiat Lux, Subscription Services, University of California Riverside, 3148 Administration, Riverside CA 92521-0149. ***Formed by the union of** At UCR, **and** UC Riverside Magazine, 1049-3719.*

ISSN 0161-8350
US
FLETCHER. Main/Corp Fletcher School of Law and Diplomacy. Vol. 1 (Spring 1978)-. Periodical. English. Three times a year. Free. Fletcher School of Law and Diplomacy, Tufts University, Medford MA 02155. **Tel** (617)628-7010, telex 710 328-1128. **ED** R M Vitanye. **Circ:** 4,200 (ctrl).
Desc: Reports programs and activities of the nation's oldest graduate school of international relations.

ISSN 1057-9044
US
FLORIDA COLLEGE COMMUNIQUE. Added/Corp Florida College (Temple Terrace, Fla.). Vol. 39, No. 4 (July 1991)-. Periodical. English. Four times a year. Florida College, 119 Glen Arven, Tampa FL 33617-5578. **Tel** (813)988-5131. ***Continues** News Bulletin (Florida College), 8750-751X.*

ISSN 0332-9666
DD 796.4 NO
CCC
FRIIDRETT. [Friidrett]. (1950)-. Periodical. Norwegian. Ten times a year. Kr315.00, $63.00. Scandinavian University Press, PO Box 2959 Toeyen, N 0608 Oslo 6 Norway. **Tel** 011 47 2 2575400, FAX 011 47 2 2575353, telex 71896 UROR N. **(Subscription address:** Scandinavian University Press, 200 Meacham Ave., Elmont NY 11003. **Tel** (516)352-7300, FAX (516)352-7377.)
Desc: Publication of the Norwegian Athletics Association.

GW
FU-NACHRICHTEN. VFOAT Freie Universitat-Nachrichten; Fun (Berlin); Universitat Berlin Freie Universitat : FU-Nachrichten. (1965)-. German (English). Ten times a year. DM30.00. Presse und Informationsstelle der Fu, Kaiserswerther Strasse 16-18, 14195 Berlin Germany. **Tel** 838 73 180, FAX 838 73 187. **ED** Christian Walther. **Ad Acc, Adv Mgr:** Gabriela Gast-Anhzith, **Tel** 49 30 838 73 185. Full Page (B&W) $1,200.00. Half Page (B&W) $600.00. **Acid Free. Circ:** 20,000. ***Continues** FU-Info, 0173-4105.*
Desc: News and information from inside the university. Research results made understandable for the public and includes alumni news.

College and School Publications

GAKUJUTSU KIYO. See Science and Technology.
LC HV2561.W18 W344
DD 371.91/2/09753
NLM W1 GA397K
JA
CODEN KKOCAK
ISSN 0016-4089
US

GALLAUDET TODAY. See Education-Special Education and Rehabilitation.

DD 378/.715/23
ISSN 0380-6774
CN
GAZETTE DE L'UNIVERSITE DE MONCTON. Main/Corp Universite de Moncton. (Mar. 1971)-. Newspaper. French. La Revue de l'Universite de Moncton, Moncton New Brunswick E1A 3E9 Canada. **Tel** (506)858-4062, **FAX** (506)858-4103.

AT
GAZETTE / THE UNIVERSITY OF SYDNEY, THE. Main/Corp University of Sydney. Vol. 4, No. 14 (Dec. 1985)-. Periodical. English. Four times a year. University of Sydney, 116 Darlington Road / H42, Sydney NSW 2006 Australia. **Tel** 011 61 2 6922666, **FAX** 011 61 2 6922666. **Continues** University of Sydney. Gazette and Letter to Graduates.
Ind/Abst Child. Lit. Abstr. (19??-).

ISSN 0895-1624
US
TITLE CHANGE
GEORGETOWN (WASHINGTON, D.C. : 1987). (GEORGETOWN.). Added/Corp Georgetown University. Office of University Relations. **VFOAT** Georgetown Magazine. Vol. 19, No. 1 (Winter 1987)-(19??). Periodical. English. Georgetown Magazine, Georgetown University, Office of University Relations, Washington DC 20057. **Tel** (202)687-4317, **FAX** (202)687-1670. **ED** Maura Griffin. **Bk Rev. Circ:** 85,000 (ctrl). **Continues** Georgetown Magazine (Washington, D.C.), 0745-9009. **Continued by** Georgetown Magazine (Washington, D.C. : 1993), 1074-8784.
Desc: Items of interest to Georgetown University and its graduates.

ISSN 1063-1127
US
GET A CLUE: GUIDE TO CORNELL & ITHACA, NY. Added/Corp Student Agencies, Inc. **VFOAT** Guide to Cornell & Ithaca, NY. (1992)-. English. $5.95. Clue Publications, C/O Student Agencies, 409 College Avenue, Ithaca NY 14850.

DD 378.714/575
ISSN 0712-337X
CN
GLOBULE ROUGE. [Globule rouge]. Added/Corp College de Thetford Mines. (19??)-. Periodical. French. Twelve times a year. Free. College de Thetford Mines, Local 4052, 671 Sud boulevard Smith, Thetford Mines Quebec G6G 1N1 Canada. ctrl circ.

LC LH1 .G64
DD 378.752/6
ISSN 0739-5795
US
GOUCHER. (GOUCHER : THE GOUCHER QUARTERLY.). Added/Corp Goucher College. **VFOAT** Goucher Quarterly. (198?)-. Periodical. English. Four times a year. $3.00. Goucher College, Baltimore MD 21204. **Tel** (410)337-6180. **ED** Karen Harrop. **Circ:** 15,000. **Continues** Goucher Quarterly, 0274-5046.
Desc: News and articles pertaining to the alumni, faculty and students of the college.

LC LH1 .G645
DD 051
ISSN 0098-3284
US
GRADUATE, THE. 1975-. English. One time a year. $2.00 single issue.

LC TX911.5 .G85
DD 647.94/071/173
US
GUIDE TO COLLEGE PROGRAMS IN HOSPITALITY AND TOURISM : A DIRECTORY OF CHRIE MEMBER COLLEGES AND UNIVERSITIES, A. See Travel and Tourism.

ISSN 0213-0610
SP
GUINIGUADA / UNIVERSIDAD DE LA LAGUNA. Added/Corp Universidad de La Laguna. Secretariado de Publicaciones. Universidad de Las Palmas de Gran Canaria. (19??)-. Periodical. Spanish. One time a year. Secretariado de Publicaciones de la Universidad de la Laguna, Tenerife Spain.

AT
H.A.C. JOURNAL. Added/Corp Hawkesbury Assembly of Convocation. Hawkesbury Union. **VFOAT** Hawkesbury Journal; Hawkesbury Journal. **VAT** Hawkesbury Assembly of Convocation Journal. Vol. 89, No. 4 (Aug. 1992)-. Newsletter. English. Six times a year. University of Western Sydney / Hawkesbury, Bourke Street, Richmond NSW 2753 Australia. **Tel** 011 61 45 784647, **FAX** 011 61 45 885612. **ED** Lynn Davie. **Ad Acc. Circ:** 2,000 (ctrl). **Continues** Journal (Hawkesbury Agricultural College. Old Boy's Union).
Desc: Contains letters from graduates, reunion reports, and information on the university.

US
HARVARD INDEPENDENT, THE. **VFOAT** Inde. Vol. 1, No. 1 (Oct. 9, 1969)-. Newspaper. English. Thirty-two times a year. $15.00 (one-year), $26.00 (two-year). Harvard Independent, Harvard University, Canaday G Basement, Cambridge MA 02138. **Tel** (617)495-3682. **ED** Kristin Amerling. **Bk Rev. Ad Acc. Circ:** 21,000.
Desc: Newspaper distributed to Harvard undergraduates and graduates. Contains news, features, commentary, arts, books and sports sections.

LC LH1.H3 L2
DD 378/.198/097444
US
HARVARD LAMPOON, THE. **VFOAT** Lampoon. Vol. 9 (June 1880); Series 2, Vol. 1 (Feb. 1881)-. Periodical. English. Four times a year. $15.00. Harvard Lampoon, 44 Bow Street, Cambridge MA 02138. **Tel** (617)495-7801. available on microfilm and microfiche from University Microfilms International (UMI).

LC LH1.H3 A5
DD 051
ISSN 0095-2427
US
HARVARD MAGAZINE. [Harv. mag.]. VOL. 76 (Sept. 1973)-. Periodical. English. Six times a year. $30.00. Harvard Magazine, 7 Ware Street, Cambridge MA 02138. **Tel** (617)495-5746, (800)648-4499. **ED** John Bethell. **Bk Rev. Ad Acc. Circ:** 198,000 (ctrl). Documents available from Documents on Demand. **Continues** Harvard Bulletin, 0361-669X.
Desc: A general interest magazine covering events both in and outside the Harvard community.
Ind/Abst Access (1981-); Art Archaeol. Tech. Abstr.; Environ. Abstr.; GeoRef; Index Period. Artic. Relat. Law.

LC LH1.H3 G3
ISSN 0364-7692
US
HARVARD UNIVERSITY GAZETTE. Added/Corp Harvard University. (1906)-. Periodical. English. One time a week (published weekly except one week in Jan. & Dec., and 2 weeks in July & Aug.). $20.00. Harvard University Gazette, Holyoke Center 1060, 1350 Massachusetts Avenue, Cambridge MA 02138. **Tel** (617)495-1585, **FAX** (617)495-0754. **ED** Laura Ferguson. **Circ:** 30,000. **Continues** Harvard University Calendar.
Desc: Official University publication/newspaper. Reports stories and news of interest to the Harvard University community.

LC PE9 .H37
DD 410/.5
UDC 802.0
BG
HARVEST (DACCA, BANGLADESH). (HARVEST : AN ANNUAL OF THE DEPARTMENT OF ENGLISH, JAHANGIRNAGAR UNIVERSITY.). Vol. 3 (1978-79)-. English. One time a year. Bulletin of the Department of English, Jahangirnagar University.

ISSN 1044-3851
US
HEIDELBERG BULLETIN, THE. **VFOAT** Heidelberg. (198?)-. Bulletin. English. Four times a year. Alumni Office/Heidelberg College, 67 Greenfield Street, Tiffin OH 44883-2461. **Tel** (419)438-2031. **ED** Jamie Abel and Cheryl Staib. **Circ:** 10,500 (ctrl). **Continues** Heidelberg, 8750-9822.
Desc: A newspaper of and for the alumni and friends of Heidelberg College. Contains news and editorials covering academics, achievements, sporting events and gatherings.

US
HERALD (FLORIDA SCHOOL FOR THE DEAF AND BLIND). (THE HERALD : NEWSLETTER OF THE FLORIDA SCHOOL FOR THE DEAF AND BLIND.). Added/Corp Florida School for the Deaf and Blind. **VFOAT** Florida School Herald. (Feb. 1987)-. Newsletter. English. Irregular (7 issues). $6.00. Florida School for the Deaf & Blind, 207 North San Marco Avenue, St. Augustine FL 32084. **Tel** (904)823-4000, (904)823-4019.

US
HILLSDALE MAGAZINE. English. Four times a year. Hillsdale College Press, 33 East College Street, Hillsdale MI 49242. **Tel** (517)437-7341, (517)439-1524. **ED** William J. Koshelnyk.

ISSN 0120-2537
CK
HUELLAS : REVISTA DE LA UNIVERSIDAD DEL NORTE. Added/Corp Universidad del Norte (Barranquilla, Colombia). (1980)-. Periodical. Spanish. Four times a year. Universidad del Norte, Apartado Aereo 1569, Barranquilla Colombia.
Ind/Abst Am. Hist. Life (1988-).

ISSN 1001-943X
CC
CODEN HDXUE7
HUNAN DAXUE XUEBAO. (HU-NAN TA HSUEH HSUEH PAO.). [Hunan daxue xuebao]. Added/Corp Hu-Nan ta Hsueh. **VFOAT** Hunandaxue Xuebao; Journal of Hunan University. (19??)-. Periodical. Chinese. Four times a year. Documents available from CASDDS.
Ind/Abst Chem. Abstr.

ISSN 0744-5806
US
ILLINOIS BENEDICTINE MAGAZINE, THE. Periodical. English. Four times a year. free. Illinois Benedictine College, 5700 College Road, Lisle IL 60532. **Tel** (312)960-1500. **ED** Gerald Czerak. **Circ:** 13,000 (ctrl).
Desc: News and features about the college or college life and educational articles written by persons affiliated with the college.

DD 760
ISSN 8756-6664
US
IMAGE WORLD. [Image world]. Added/Corp Rochester Institute of Technology. Technicial and Education Center of the Graphic Arts. **VFOAT** Imageworld. Vol. 1, No. 1 (Sept./Oct. 1986)-. Periodical. English. Five times a year. Free. Rochester Institute of Technology, Technology & Education Center, PO Box 9887, Rochester NY 14623. **Tel** (716)475-2737, **FAX** (716)475-7052. **ED** Sandy Richolson. **Circ:** 150,000 (ctrl).
Desc: Promotes careers in graphic communications, highlighting the variety of jobs available and the rapid technological changes now occurring. Audience is older college-bound high schoolers, and college students.

ISSN 0889-2423
US
INDEPENDENT FLORIDA ALLIGATOR, THE. **VFOAT** Alligator. (19??)-. Periodical. English. Irregular (180 issues). Campus Communications Inc, PO Box 14257, University of Florida, Gainesville FL 32604. **Continues** University of Florida. Florida Alligator.

ISSN 0740-9664
US
INDIANA DAILY STUDENT, THE. Added/Corp Indiana University. Indiana University, Bloomington. **VFOAT** IDS. (1914)-. Periodical. English. Five times a week (Mon.-Fri.). $64.32. Indiana Daily Student, Ernie Pyle Hall, Bloomington IN 47401. **Tel** (812)335-0768. **Circ:** 10,000. **Continues** Indiana Student (Bloomington, Ind. : 1912).

IT
INFORMATORE SCOLASTICO. (19??)-. Italian. Twenty-four times a year. L64040 Italy; L90000 other. Informatore Scolastico, Via Kerbaker 55, 80129 Naples Italy. **Tel** 011 39 81 5786814, **FAX** 011 39 81 5560617. **ED** Clara Franciosi. Index available. cum. index. **Bk Rev. Ad Acc.**

DD 373.714/221
ISSN 0705-0569
CN
JARGON (HULL). (JARGON). Vol. 1 (Feb. 1977)-. Periodical. English (French). Twelve times a year. 0.10Can$ per number. Jargon, d'Arcy McGee High School, 75 Booth Street, Hull Quebec J8Y 3H1 Canada.

ISSN 0744-7213
US
JOHN WESLEY COLLEGE CRUSADER. Added/Corp John Wesley College. **VFOAT** Crusader; JWC Crusader. (19??)-. Periodical. English. Four times a year. $2.00. John Wesley College, 2314 North Centennial, High Point NC 27260. **Tel** (919)889-2261. **ED** Kenneth E. Temple. **Circ:** 5,000 (ctrl).

DD 657/.07/11714281
ISSN 0822-8116
CN
JOURNAL L'ACTION. (LE JOURNAL L'ACTION : JOURNAL DES ETUDIANTS(E)S EN SCIENCES COMPTABLES DE L'UQAM.). [J. action]. Added/Corp **VFOAT** Journal des Etudiants (E)s en Sciences Comptables de l'Uqam; Action. **VAT** Action - Groupe Action (Montreal, Quebec). Vol. 1, No. 1 (12 Sept 1983)-. Periodical. French. Twenty-six times a year. Free. Journal des Etudiants(es) en Sciences Comptables de l'Universite du Quebec a Montreal, C P 8888 Succursale A, Montreal Quebec H3C 3P8 Canada.

DD 378.7123/3
ISSN 0823-1672
CN
JOURNALIST (EDMONTON). (THE JOURNALIST). [Journalist]. Added/Corp Grant MacEwan Community College. **VFOAT** MacEwan Journalist. (1983)-. Newspaper. English. Six times a year. Free. Grant MacEwan Community College, 10045-156 Street, Edmonton Alberta T5P 2P7 Canada. **Tel** (403)483-2365. **ED** John Brittain. **Bk Rev. Ad Acc, Adv Mgr:** Keith Borgess, **Tel** (403)497-5644. Full Page (B&W) $700.00. Half Page (B&W) $350.00. **Circ:** 2,500. **Continues** MacEwan Journal, 0229-3439.
Desc: General community news and sports.

DD 378.715/23
ISSN 0829-5476
CN
JURISTE (MONCTON). (LE JURISTE.). [Juriste]. Added/Corp Universite de Moncton. Ecole de Droit. No. 1 (Nov. 1985)-. Newsletter. French. Irregular. Universite de Moncton / Ecole de Droit, Moncton New Brunswick E1A 3E9 Canada. **Tel** (506)858-4145. **Circ:** 1,200.
Desc: Newsletter from the Law School to its alumni and friends and to members of the legal profession.

College and School Publications

CODEN TBDKDS JA
KENKYU KIYO. [Tokushima Bunri Daigaku kenkyu kiyo]. **Added/Corp** Tokushima Bunri Daigaku. **VFOAT** Tokushima Bunri Daigaku Kenkyu Kiyo. (1974)-. Japanese. Documents available from CASDDS. **Continues** Tokushima Bunri Daigaku Tanki Daigaku Kenkyu Kiyo.
Ind/Abst Chem. Abstr.

CODEN KDSHA6 JA
KENKYU KIYO. SHIZEN KAGAKU HEN / NATURAL SCIENCE. BULLETIN OF THE FACULTY OF EDUCATION, KAGOSHIMA UNIVERSITY. KAGOSHIMA DAIGAKU KYOIKUGAKUBU. See Science and Technology.

LC LJ85.P2 K4 **ISSN** 0023-0804
DD 371.852 US
KEY REPORTER, THE. [Key report.]. **Added/Corp** Phi Beta Kappa. Vol. 1 (Winter 1936)-. Academic Scholarly Publication. English. Four times a year. Phi Beta Kappa, 1811 Q Street Northwest, Washington DC 20009. **Tel** (202)265-3808. **ED** Priscilla S. Taylor. **Bk Rev. Circ:** 250,000 (ctrl). **Supersedes** Phi Beta Kappa Annals.
Desc: Scholarly newsletter containing one feature article and perhaps 50 brief book reviews of general interest.

ISSN 0285-5283 JA
CODEN KKKHDI
KITAKYUSHU KOGYO KOTO SENMON GAKKO KENKYU HOKOKU. See Science and Technology.

ISSN 0388-3647
DD 800 JA
KIYO - KYORITSU JOSHI TANKI DAIGAKU. BUNKA. See Literature.

ISSN 0389-0244 JA
CODEN KDGAAR
KOCHI DAIGAKU GAKUJUTSU KENKYU HOKOKU. SHIZEN KAGAKU. See Science and Technology.

LC AS **ISSN** 0386-4405
DD 060 JA
KONAN JOSHI DAIGAKU KENKYU KIYO. [Konan Joshi Daigaku kenkyu kiyo]. **VFOAT** Researches - Konan Women's University; Researches - Konan Women's College. (1965)-. Periodical. Japanese (summaries and/or abstracts in English). One time a year. Documents available from CASDDS.
Ind/Abst Chem. Abstr.

ISSN 0368-5837 JA
CODEN KJDGA4
KUMAMOTO JOSHI DAIGAKU GAKUJUTSU KIYO. [Kumamoto Joshi Daigaku gakujutsu kiyo]. **Added/Corp** Kumamoto Joshi Daigaku. **VFOAT** Journal of Kumamoto Women's University. (1950)-. Japanese (English). Documents available from CASDDS.
Ind/Abst Chem. Abstr.

LC WMLC L 83/5250 SW
KURSKATALOG. CIVILINGENJOERS- OCH ARKITEKTLINJER / CHALMERS TEKNISKA HOEGSKOLA = COURSE PROGRAMS. FACULTY OF ENGINEERING / CHALMERS UNIVERSITY OF TECHNOLOGY. See Engineering-Civil Engineering.

LC LH7.K86 K87
KWANDONG. Added/Corp Kwandong Taehak. Hakto Hoguktan. Munyebu. **VFOAT** Gwan Dong. (19??)-. Periodical. Japanese (Korean). Kwandong Taehak Hakto Hoguktan Kangnung-si, Korea.

JA
CODEN KKHGDY
KYOYOBU KENKYU HOKOKU / GIFU DAIGAKU. [Kyoyobu kenkyu hokoku - Gifu Daigaku]. **Added/Corp** Gifu Daigaku. Kyoyobu. **VFOAT** Bulletin of the Faculty of General Education, Gifu University. (1965)-. Bulletin. Japanese. Gifu Daigaku Kyoikugakubu, (Faculty of Education Gifu University), 1-1 Yanagido, Gifushi Gifuken 501-11 Japan. Documents available from CASDDS.
Ind/Abst Chem. Abstr.

US
LANTERN. Vol. 92, No. 20 (Sept. 27, 1972)-. Newspaper. English. Irregular (170 issues). $62.00. Ohio State Lantern, 242 West 18th Street, Room 281, Columbus OH 43210. **Tel** (614)292-3021, (614)292-2638, FAX (614)292-3722. **Bk Rev. Ad Acc, Adv Mgr:** Beth Renner. **Circ:** 30,000 (ctrl). **Continues** Ohio State Lantern.

US
LANTHORN (HOUGHTON COLLEGE). (THE LANTHORN.). **Added/Corp** Houghton College. Houghton College. English Dept. Vol. 1, No. 1 (May 1932)-. Periodical. English. Two times a year. Lanthorn Publication, Houghton College, Houghton NY 14744.

LC LH1.L28 A4 **ISSN** 0091-2034
DD 378.775/39 US
LAWRENCE. ALUMNI EDITION. (LAWRENCE.). (19??)-. English. Irregular. Lawrence University, Editor Office of Publications and Public Information, Appletown WI 54911. **Continues** Lawrence Alumnus.

ISSN 1075-8852
Pr Rev.
LEBANON LIGHT. (1919)-. Newspaper. English. Eight times a year. $5.00 (libraries), $10.00 (other) US; $10.00 (libraries), $15.00 (other) Canada; $15.00 (libraries), $20.00 (other) other. Lebanon Light, 160 Miller Road, Lebanon OH 45036-1299. **Tel** (513)932-6798, FAX (513)933-2150. **ED** Charles E. Zimkus. **Photos. Ad Acc, Adv Mgr:** David Little. Full Page (B&W) $125.00. Half Page (B&W) $60.00. **Acid Free. Circ:** 2,000.
Desc: General reporting of scholastic activity and interests of Lebanon High School and the community of Lebanon, Warren County, Ohio.

ISSN 0318-8418
CN
LIAISON (SHERBROOKE). (LIAISON.). **Added/Corp** Universite de Sherbrooke. Vol. 1 (Dec. 2, 1966)-. Periodical. French. Twenty times a year (bimonthly Sept. to April, monthly May to Aug.). Free on request. University Sherbrooke / Public Relations Service, 2500 boulevard Univ, Sherbrooke Quebec J1K 2R1 Canada. **Tel** (819)821-7388.
Ind/Abst Can. Index (?-?); Crim. Penol. Police Sci. Abstr.

SP
LINO. Spanish. One time a year. 3330ptas. Universidad de Oviedo, Arguelles 19, 33003 Oviedo Spain. **Tel** 011 34 8 5210160.

ISSN 0744-8074
US
LIONS MAGAZINE. Periodical. English. Six times a year. Zale and Associates, PO Box 509, Pontiac MI 48056.

US
MAINESTREAM. Periodical. English. University of Maine Student Center, Farmington ME 04938.

LC AS587.A1 R58a
SU
MAJALLAT KULLIYAT AL-ADAB, JAMIAT AL-MALIK SAUD. See The Arts-Art.

UK
Pr Rev.
MANCUNION : THE OFFICIAL NEWSPAPER OF MANCHESTER UNIVERSITY STUDENTS UNION. (19??)-. English. One time a week. free. University Union, Oxford Road, M13 9PP Manchester United Kingdom. **ED** Alex Cole. **Bk Rev. Ad Acc. Circ:** 20,000.
Desc: General news, sports, and features aimed at the students studying at Manchester University, Manchester Polytechnic and The University of Manchester Institute of Science and Technology.

ISSN 0025-2867
US
MARCOLIAN, THE. Periodical. English. One time a week. Marietta College, Box 17A, Marietta OH 45750.

ISSN 0890-0434
US
MASSACHUSETTS DAILY COLLEGIAN, THE. VFOAT Collegian. (1890)-. Newspaper. English. Seven times a week (Sept.-May). $100.00. The Massachusetts Daily, University of Massachusetts, 113 Campus Center, Amherst MA 01003. **Tel** (413)545-3500. **ED** Michelle Bayliss. cum. index. **Bk Rev. Ad Acc, Adv Mgr:** Danielle Yaniro, **Tel** (413)545-3500. **Circ:** 20,000 (ctrl). available on microfilm.

LC LH3.M2 M3 **ISSN** 0024-9068
DD 378.71 CN
MCGILL NEWS, THE. Vol. 1, No. 1 (Dec. 1919)-. Periodical. English. Four times a year. McGill University / Graduate Society, 3605 Mountain Street, Montreal Quebec Canada. **Tel** (514)392-4813. **Ad Acc. Circ:** 35,000.
Desc: Feature articles, and class notes for, and about, graduates, and other supporters of McGill University.

JA
MEMOIRS OF THE FACULTY OF SCIENCE KYUSHU UNIVERSITY. SERIES A. (1940)-. Periodical. English. Kyushu University / Faculty of Science, 10-1 Hakozaki 6 Chome Higasiku, Fukuokasi Fukuokaken 812 Japan.

ISSN 1055-0984
DD 051 US
METAPHOR (SAN JOSE, CALIF.). (METAPHOR : A PUBLICATION FOR STUDENT WRITERS.). [Metaphor]. Vol. 1, No. 1 (1991)-. Periodical. English. Twelve times a year. $49.00. Whitfield Publishing Co., PO Box 53617, San Jose CA 95153. **Continues** Scrolling Pen.

ISSN 0745-2454
US
MIDDLEBURY COLLEGE MAGAZINE. VFOAT Middlebury. Vol. 56, No. 10 (Autumn 1981)-. Periodical. English. Four times a year. Wilson House/Middlebury College, Middlebury VT 05753. **Tel** (802)388-3711. **ED** Tim Etchells. **Bk Rev. Circ:** 33,000 (ctrl). **Continues** Middlebury College Newsletter.
Desc: Information for and about Middlebury College students, faculty, staff, parents, and alumni.

ISSN 0711-5911
DD 905 CN
MIRROR (LONDON, ONT.). See History.

LC LF2405 .A16 **ISSN** 0723-0745
DD 378.431/55 GW
MITTEILUNGEN FU BERLIN : AMTSBLATT DER FREIEN UNIVERSITAET BERLIN. Added/Corp Freie Universitat Berlin. **VFOAT** F.U.-Mitteilungen; FU Mitteilungen; FU-Mitteilungen; Amtsblatt der Freien Universitat Berlin. (19??)-. German. Der President der Freien Universitat Berlin, Altensteinstrasse 40, 1000 Berlin Germany. **Continues** FU-Mitteilungen.

ISSN 0387-1150
JA
CODEN NKKOB2
NARA KOGYO KOTO SENMON GAKKO KENKYU KIYO. See Science and Technology.

LC LH1 .N24 **ISSN** 0883-2374
DD 810/.8 US
NASSAU LITERARY REVIEW, THE. [Nassau lit. rev.]. Periodical. English. Two times a year. Free on campus, $11.00 off campus. Princeton University / New Jersey, Room 401, University Place, Princeton NJ 08544. **ED** Lyric Wallwork, Melissa Sydeman and Allison Blyler. **Ad Acc. Circ:** 4,000. **Continues** Nassau Lit, 0360-2222.
Desc: Oldest undergraduate university literary magazine in the United States. Publishes prose, poetry, and visual arts produced by Princeton students. Also includes interviews with important literary figures.

US
NATIONAL RATE BOOK AND COLLEGE NEWSPAPER DIRECTORY. VFOAT College Newspaper Directory. Directory. English. One time a year. Cass Student Service Inc, 1633 West Central Street, Evanston IL 60201.

ISSN 1061-6993
DD 810 US
Pr Rev.
NEBRASKA ENGLISH JOURNAL. [Neb. Eng. j.]. **Added/Corp** Creighton University. Nebraska English Language Arts Council. (1992)-. Periodical. English. Two times a year. $20.00. Creighton University / English Department, 2500 California Plaza, Omaha NE 68178. **Tel** (402)280-2822. **Continues** Nebraska English and Language Arts Journal, 1051-9823.

ISSN 0270-4412
US
NEBRASKA REVIEW (FAIRBURY, NEB.). (NEBRASKA REVIEW.). **Added/Corp** Southeast Community College (Neb.). Fairbury Campus. No. 1 (1981)-. Periodical. English. One time a year. $2.00. Nebraska Review / Fairbury, Southeast Community College, Fairbury NE 68352.
Ind/Abst Am. Humanit. Index.

ISSN 0742-9347
DD 051 US
NEW HAMPSHIRE COLLEGE JOURNAL. [N. H. Coll. j.]. **Added/Corp** New Hampshire College. Vol. 1, No. 1 (Spring 1984)-. Periodical. English. One time a year. Free on request. New Hampshire College, 2500 North River Road, Manchester NH 03104. **Tel** (603)668-2211.

College and School Publications

NEW HAMPSHIRE MAGAZINE (DURHAM). (NEW HAMPSHIRE MAGAZINE.). Periodical. English. Twelve times a year. $22.00. New Hampshire Magazine, University of New Hampshire Memorial Union, Durham NH 03824. **Tel** (603)862-1490. **ED** Edmund Mander. **Bk Rev**. **Ad Acc**. **Circ**: 11,000.
Desc: A twice a week college newspaper covering campus and local news, features, and also national and international issues. Caters to students, staff, alumni and local residents.
ISSN 0199-0306 US

LC LH1 .N52
DD 378.1/98/795097468
ISSN 0028-6001 US
NEW JOURNAL (NEW HAVEN, CONN.), THE. (THE NEW JOURNAL.). [New j.]. Vol. 1 (Oct. 15, 1967)-. Periodical. English. Six times a year. $18.00. The New Journal, 3432 Yale Station, New Haven CT 06520. **Tel** (203)432-1957. **ED** Martha Brant. **Bk Rev**. **Ad Acc**. **Circ**: 11,000 (ctrl).
Desc: News and features magazine covering Yale and New Haven.

NEW SCHOOL OBSERVER, THE. **Added/Corp** New School for Social Research (New York, N.Y.). (June 1979)-. English. Ten times a year (monthly except combined Dec./Jan. and June/July issues). New School for Social Research Public Relations Office, 838 Broadway, 5th Floor, New York NY 10003. **Tel** (212)229-5600. **ED** Christine Van Horn. ctrl circ.
ISSN 0883-6248 US

NEW YORK TIMES SCHOOL WEEKLY, THE. [N. Y. times sch. wkly.]. **VFOAT** School Weekly. (19??)-. Periodical. English. One time a week. The New York Times, 229 West 43rd Street, New York NY 10036. **Tel** (800)631-2580, (212)556-1234, FAX (212)556-4603.
ISSN 0028-7830 US

NEWS, THE. Newsletter. English. Eleven times a year (published monthly with July/Aug. issue combined). free. Christian College Coalition, 329 8th Street Northeast, Washington DC 20002. **Tel** (202)546-8713, FAX (202)546-8913. **ED** Sandy Swartzentruber. **Circ**: 4,100.
Desc: Published by the Christian College Coalition as a service to its members.

LC WMLC L 83/4685
AT
NEWS BULLETIN (SYDNEY, AUSTRALIA). (NEWS BULLETIN / SYDNEY TECHNICAL COLLEGE CHEMICAL SOCIETY.). **Added/Corp** Sydney Technical College Chemical Society. (19??)-. Bulletin. English. Sydney Technical College Chemical Society, Sydney NSW Australia.

ISSN 8750-2216 US
NEWS (CLAREMONT GRADUATE SCHOOL). (NEWS / THE CLAREMONT GRADUATE SCHOOL.). **VFOAT** Claremont Graduate School Newsletter. Periodical. English. Four times a year. The Claremont Graduate School, Office of Public Information, 154 East 10th Street, Claremont CA 91711. **Continues** Claremont Graduate School Bulletin.

NEWS NOTES & QUOTES. **Added/Corp** Association of Records Managers and Administrators. **VFOAT** ARMA News Notes & Quotes. (19??)-. Periodical. English. Four times a year. comes with membership. Association of Records Managers and Administrators Inc., PO Box 8540, Prairie Village KS 66208. **Tel** (800)422-2762, (913)341-3808, FAX (913)341-3742.

US
NEWSLETTER - APPALACHIAN CENTER, BEREA COLLEGE. **Main/Corp** Berea College. Appalachian Center. (Winter 1972)-. Newsletter. English. Four times a year. Free on request. Berea College Appalachian Center, CPO 2336, Berea College, Berea KY 40404. **Tel** (606)986-9341. **ED** Loyal Jones and Thomas Parrish. **Bk Rev**. ctrl circ.

ISSN 0029-3032 US
NORTHEASTERN NEWS, THE. (19??)-. Periodical. English. One time a week. Northeastern University Press, 360 Huntington Avenue, Suite 272 HN, Boston MA 02115. **Tel** (617)373-5480, FAX (617)373-5483.

ISSN 1041-6900 US
NOVA QUARTERLY. **Added/Corp** University of Texas at El Paso. News and Publications Office. Vol. 22, No. 4 (June 1987)-. Periodical. English. Four times a year. News and Publications Office, University of Texas at El Paso, El Paso TX 79968-0522. **Tel** (915)747-5526. **Continues** Nova, 0029-4985.

ISSN 0029-7526
OBERLIN REVIEW, THE. Periodical. English. Two times a week. Oberlin College, Rice Hall, Oberlin OH 44074. **Tel** (216)775-8408, FAX (216) 775-8124.

LC AS633.A1 O25
DD 068/.669
ISSN 0536-2326 NR
CODEN OPASA9
OCCASIONAL PUBLICATION / INSTITUTE OF AFRICAN STUDIES, UNIVERSITY OF IBADAN. [Occas. publ. - Ibadan Univ., Inst. Afr. Stud.]. **Added/Corp** University of Ibadan. Institute of African Studies. No. 1 (1963)-. Monographic series. English.
Ind/Abst MLA Int. Bibl. Books Artic. Mod. Lang. Lit.

LC LJ75 .S3
DD 378/.198/5505
ISSN 0744-6969 US
OCTAGONIAN OF SIGMA ALPHA MU, THE. Periodical. English. Four times a year. Sigma Alpha Mu, 651 North Range Line Road, Carmel IN 46032. **Continues** Octagonian.

US
OHIO CHRONICLE, THE. (19??)-. Newspaper. English. Five times a year. $3.00. Ohio Chronicle, 500 Morse Road, Columbus OH 43214. **Tel** (614)888-1550, FAX (614)888-0583. **ED** Pam Brodie (editor-in-chief) and Kevin Skehan (managing editor). **Photos**. **Pub. Size**: Standard. **Circ**: 1,500 (ctrl).
Desc: School newspaper for the Ohio School for the Deaf.

ISSN 0030-1221 US
OHIO WESLEYAN MAGAZINE. **Added/Corp** Ohio Wesleyan University. (19??)-. Periodical. English. Four times a year. Free. The Ohio Wesleyan Magazine, Ohio Wesleyan University, Delaware OH 43015. **Tel** (614)369-4431. **ED** Pamela Besel. **Circ**: 24,000 (ctrl).
Desc: Contains feature articles, news of the university, alumni news, sports updates and a class notes section.

LC LH1.O7 O4
ISSN 8755-9536 US
OLD OREGON. (19??)-. Periodical. English. Four times a year. Old Oregon, University of Oregon, 101 Chapman Hall, Eugene OR 97403.

DD 378/.1543/09713
ISSN 0714-444X US
ONTARIO COLLEGE NEWSLETTER. [Ont. coll. newsl.]. Newsletter. English. Free. Association of Colleges of Applied Arts and Technology of Ontario, Suite 703, 2 Sheppard Avenue East, Willowdale Ontario M2N 2Y7. ctrl circ.

ISSN 0030-4069 US
OPTIMIST (ABILENE), THE. (THE OPTIMIST.). Periodical. English. Twenty-six times a year. $20.00. Abilene Christian College, ACC Station/Box 8203, Abilene TX 79601. **Tel** (915)677-1911. **ED** Cindy Patterson. **Bk Rev**. **Ad Acc**. **Circ**: 5,000 (ctrl).

US
ORACLE, THE. (19??)-. Newspaper. English. Five times a week (Mon.-Fri. except school holidays). $50.00. University of South Florida, CPR 472, Tampa FL 33620-5600. **Tel** (813)974-2617. **ED** Kevin Connolly (editor's address: CPR 469, Tampa, FL 33620). **Ad Acc**.

US
OSAMAYOR : GRADUATE STUDENT MAGAZINE / DEPT. OF HISPANIC L & L, UNIVERSITY OF PITTSBURGH. See Linguistics.

US
OUTLOOK. Periodical. English. Three times a year. Iowa State University at Ames, 16 G Hamilton Hall, Ames IA 50012. **Tel** (515)294-9388. **Ad Acc**. ctrl circ. **Continues** Outlook for Today's Woman.
Desc: For students in the college of Family and Consumer Sciences who are preparing for careers in the professions and related industries.

DD 810
Pr Rev.
ISSN 1069-2215 US
OWEN WISTER REVIEW. [Owen Wister rev.]. **Added/Corp** University of Wyoming. Student Publications Board. (1978)-. Periodical. English. Two times a year. $15.00. University of Wyoming Student Publications, Box 4233 / University Station, Laramie WY 82071. **Tel** (307)766-6190, 766-6191. **ED** Georgette Hartley. **Circ**: 500.
Desc: A literary/art magazine, student-produced at the University of Wyoming, containing poetry, prose, art and photography from a wide variety of genres.

LC LH5 .O75
DD 378.42
ISSN 0030-7645 UK
OXFORD. **Added/Corp** Oxford Society. (Summer 1934)-. Periodical. English. Two times a year. Oxford Society, c/o 8 Wellington Square, Oxford OX1 2AY United Kingdom. **ED** H.A. Hurren. **Circ**: 24,000.

US
OYEZ REVIEW. **Added/Corp** Roosevelt University (Chicago, Ill.). (19??)-. Periodical. English. Two times a year. $3.00. Roosevelt University, 430 South Michigan Avenue, Chicago IL 60605. **Tel** (312)341-3820. **ED** Helen Forsythe. **Circ**: 400 (ctrl). **Continues** Oyez Magazine.
Desc: Interested in poetry, short fiction, short drama, excerpts from longer works, and black/white art.

ISSN 0030-8994 US
PACIFICAN. Periodical. English. One time a week. University of the Pacific Holt Atherton Center, Western Studies, Stockton CA 95211. **Tel** (209)946-2404. **Circ**: 6,000.

ISSN 1056-4314 US
PATRIOT REVIEW, THE. **Added/Corp** Union County High School (Union County, Ind.). (1991)-. English. $2.00. Union City High School, Patriot Parkway, Liberty IN 47353.

LC PJ10 .P45
DD 495/.05
ISSN 0553-9536 US
CEASED
PHI THETA PAPERS. (PHI THETA PAPERS : PUBLICATION OF THE HONOR SOCIETY IN ORIENTAL LANGUAGES OF THE UNIVERSITY OF CALIFORNIA, BERKELEY.). [Phi Theta pap.]. **Added/Corp** Phi Theta (University of California, Berkeley) Oriental Languages Students Association (University of California, Berkeley). Vol. 6 (May 1961)-(19??). English. University of California Oriental Language Honor Society, Berkeley CA 94720. **Continues** Phi Theta Annual.

DD 281.9305
ISSN 0819-4920 AT
PHRONEMA. [Phronema]. (1986)-. English. Irregular. 16.44Aus$. St. Andrews Greek Orthodox Theological College, 242 Cleveland Street, Redfern New South Wales 2016 Australia. **Tel** 011 61 2 6985066, FAX 011 61 2 6985368. **ED** Dr. Guy Freeland. **Bk Rev**. **Circ**: 800.

DD 378.714/281
ISSN 0710-3522 CN
POLYSCOPE (MONTREAL). (LE POLYSCOPE.). [Polyscope]. **Added/Corp** Ecole Polytechnique (Montreal, Quebec). (1966)-. Newspaper. French. One time a week. Free on request. Association des Etudiants Polytechnique, Case Postal 6079 Succursale A, Montreal Quebec H3C 3A7 Canada. **Tel** (514)344-4645. **Ad Acc**. **Circ**: 5,000 (ctrl).
Desc: Student newspaper of L'Ecole Polytechnique de Montreal. Contains stories about engineering, education and news.

ISSN 0170-3722 GW
UDC 372 :373.3
PRAXIS GRUNDSCHULE. (1978)-. Periodical. German. Six times a year. $75.08. Westermann Schulbuchverlag GmbH, Postfach 4938, D-38039 Braunschweig Germany. **Tel** 011 49 531 708377. Index available. **Bk Rev**. **Ad Acc**. ctrl circ.
Desc: Copy material for teachers and students of all disciplines.

ISSN 0744-7515 US
PRINCETON MAGAZINE (PRINCETON, N.J. : 1982). (PRINCETON MAGAZINE.). **VFOAT** Princeton. Vol. 1, No. 1 (Apr. 1982)-. Periodical. English. Twelve times a year. Princeton Magazine, 1101 E State Road, Building 3, Princeton NJ 08540. available on microfilm from University Microfilms International (UMI).

US
PRINCETON WEEKLY BULLETIN. (19??)-. Bulletin. English. Thirty times a year (weekly Sept.-June except mid term semester breaks, Thanksgiving, Christmas). $22.00. Princeton University, Stanhope Hall, Princeton NJ 08544. **Tel** (609)258-3600. **ED** Sally Freedman.
Desc: Contains a weekly calendar and employment page.

LC Z5055.I8 M547 AS222.M63
ISSN 0300-1792 IT
PUBBLICAZIONI DELL'UNIVERSITA CATTOLICA DEL SACRO CUORE. [Pubbl. Univ. cattol. Sacro Cuore]. **Main/Corp** Universita Cattolica del Sacro Cuore. (19??)-. Italian. Universita Cattolica del Sacro Cuore, L GO F Vito 1 Cepsag, 00168 Rome Italy. **Tel** 011 39 6 3052469.

College and School Publications

LC Z3601 .S68a DT753
DD 015/.68
SA
PUBLICATIONS OF THE UNIVERSITY OF SOUTH AFRICA. PUBLIKASIES VAN DIE UNIVERSITEIT VAN SUID-AFRIKA. **Main/Corp** University of South Africa. **Added/Corp** University of South Africa Publikasies van die Universiteit van Suid-Afrika. **VFOAT** Publikasies van die Universiteit van Suid-Afrika. (19??)-. Afrikaans (English). Free on request. University of South Africa, PO Box 392, Pretoria 0001 South Africa. **Tel** 011 27 12 4293111, **FAX** 011 27 12 4293221. **Circ:** 2,500.
Desc: Catalogue of publications.

ISSN 1195-4353
DD 378.1
CN
●**QC. COLLEGE QUARTERLY.** (COLLEGE QUARTERLY : QC.). [QC, Coll. q.]. **Added/Corp** Seneca College of Applied Arts and Technology. Centre for Teaching and Learning. Seneca College of Applied Arts and Technology. **VFOAT** QC. Vol. 1, No. 1 (Fall 1993)-. Periodical. English. Four times a year. 16.01Can$. Seneca College / College of Applied Arts and Technology, 1750 Finch Avenue East, North York Ontario, M2J 2X5 Canada. **Tel** (416)491-5050 ext. 2080.

US
QUADRANGLE (NEW YORK, N.Y.). (THE QUADRANGLE.). **Added/Corp** Manhattan College. Vol. 1 (1924)-. Periodical. English. One time a week. Manhattan College, Bronx NY 10471.

ISSN 0382-8530
DD 378.714/281
CN
QUARTIER LATIN (MONTREAL. 1976). (LE QUARTIER LATIN.). [Quart. lat.]. Vol. 58, No. 24 (March 15, 1976)-. Periodical. French. One time a week. Universite du Quebec - Montreal / Service des Publications, CP 8888 Succursale Point A, Montreal Quebec H3C 3P8 Canada. **Tel** (514)987-7771, (514)987-4851, **FAX** (514)987-0307. **Continues** Volume ... du Quartier Latin, 0033-4804.

ISSN 0033-6556
US
QUINCY COLLEGE BULLETIN. Bulletin. English. Four times a year. Free. Quincy College Vice-President for Development, 1831 College Avenue, Quincy IL 62301. **Tel** (217)228-5275. **ED** Donald Werr. **Ad Acc. Circ:** 9,620 (ctrl).
Desc: Quincy College news as well as alumni and local news items and commentary on issues in higher education.

ISSN 0229-978X
DD 071/.1343
CN
"QUOTE UNQUOTE". (QUOTE UNQUOTE.). Vol. 1, Issue 1 (Oct. 1978)-. Periodical. English. Irregular. Quote Unquote, Room 264, University Centre, University of Guelph, Guelph Ontario N1G 2W1 Canada.

LC AS142 .J7
CI
RAD HRVATSKE AKADEMIJE ZNANOSTI I UMJETNOSTI. **Added/Corp** Hrvatska Akademija Znanosti i Umjetnosti. (1991)-. Serbo-Croatian (Roman) (English and German). **Continues** Jugoslavenske Akademije Znanosti i Umjetnosti. Rad Jugoslavenske Akademije Znanosti i Umjetnosti.

ISSN 0710-3638
DD 378.714
CN
REFLEXION (MONTREAL). (REFLEXION.). [Reflexion]. **VFOAT** Journal Reflexion. **VAT** Reflexions (Montreal). Vol. 2, No. 1 Spring. Periodical. French. Free. Reflexion, 1270 Avenue Lemoine, Sillery Quebec G1S 1A2 Canada. **Continues** Reflexions (Sillery, Quebec), 0712-9491.

ISSN 0413-8465
DD 301
US
REPORT. **Main/Corp** Columbia University. Conservation of Human Resources Project. (Oct. 1949/June 1950)-. Periodical. English. Columbia University. Conservation of Human Resources Project / Columbia University, 562 West 113th Street, New York NY 10025.

ISSN 0848-8533
DD 378.711/37
CN
REPORT - TRINITY WESTERN UNIVERSITY. (REPORT.). [Rep. - Trinity West. Univ.]. **Added/Corp** Trinity Western University. **VFOAT** Trinity Western University Report; Trinity Western Report. (Oct. 1989)-. Periodical. English. Three times a year. Free on request. Trinity Western University, 7600 Glover Road, Langley British Columbia V3A 4R9 Canada. **Tel** (604)888-7511. **Continues** Trinity Western World., 0710-5762.

LC AP63 .U625
ISSN 0120-2367
DD 056/.1
CK
REVISTA UNIVERSIDAD DE ANTIOQUIA. [Rev. Univ. Antioquia]. **Added/Corp** Universidad de Antioquia. Vol. 52, No. 202 (Oct./Dec. 1985)-. Periodical. Spanish. Four times a year. $60.00. Universidad de Antioquia / Departamento de Publicaciones, Apartado 1226, Medellin Colombia. **Tel** 011 57 4 2631311, 011 57 4 2630011, **FAX** 011 57 4 2638282. **Continues** Universidad de Antioquia.
Ind/Abst Am. Hist. Life (1985-).

ISSN 0891-6446
US
TITLE CHANGE
RHODES TODAY. **Added/Corp** Rhodes College. **VFOAT** Today. (1986)-(1993). Periodical. English. Rhodes Today, 2000 North Parkway, Memphis TN 38112. **Continues** Rhodes College Today, 0886-0971. **Continued by** Rhodes, 1075-3036.

ISSN 0035-7936
US
ROLLINS SANDSPUR. (19??)-. Periodical. English. One time a week. Rollins College Student Association, Rollins College, Box 2742, Winter Park FL 32789.

ISSN 0035-8606
UK
CCC
ROYAL AIR FORCE COLLEGE JOURNAL, THE. (19??)-. English. One time a year (March). £2.75 UK; £4.00 other. Royal Air Force College, Cranwell Sleaford, Lincolnshire NC34 8HB United Kingdom. **Tel** 011 44 1400 61201 ext 6250. **ED** Flight Lt. Martin Horton. **Ad Acc, Adv Mgr:** Martin Horton. **Circ:** 1800 (ctrl).
Desc: Records the events of the college and other departments at Royal Air Force-Cranwell.

LC AS30 .S2515
ISSN 0276-7643
DD 051
US
SACRED HEART UNIVERSITY REVIEW. **Added/Corp** Sacred Heart University (Bridgeport, Conn.). **VFOAT** Review. Vol. 1, No. 1 (Fall 1980)-. Periodical. English. Two times a year.
Ind/Abst MLA Int. Bibl. Books Artic. Mod. Lang. Lit.

LC AS284.G87 A32
ISSN 0586-5360
SW
SAGA OCH SED. (SAGA OCH SED; KUNGL. GUSTAV ADOLFS AKADEMIES AARSBOK.). [Saga sed]. **Added/Corp** Kungl. Gustav Adolfs Akademien (Uppsala, Sweden) Sagoforskarekongress. (19??)-. English (German and Swedish). One time a year.
Ind/Abst MLA Int. Bibl. Books Artic. Mod. Lang. Lit.

ISSN 0286-6250
JA
CODEN SJDKA2
SAGAMI JOSHI DAIGAKU KIYO. [Sagami Joshi Daigaku kiyo]. **Added/Corp** Sagami Joshi Daigaku. **VFOAT** Journal of Sagami Women's University. (1956)-. Japanese. One time a year. Sagami Joshi Daigaku, Kokubunka Dai 1 Kenkyushitsu 1-1 Bunkyo 2-chome, Sagamihara 228 Japan. Documents available from CASDDS.
Ind/Abst Chem. Abstr.

LC F26 .S22
ISSN 0160-7537
DD 974.1/04/05
US
SALT (KENNEBUNK). (SALT.). [Salt]. **Added/Corp** Kennebunk High School. **VFOAT** Salt Magazine. Vol. 1 (Jan. 1974)-. Periodical. English. Irregular. $24.00 (institutions); $16.00 (individuals). Salt / Center for Documentary Field Studies, PO Box 4077, 19 Pine Street, Portland ME 04102. **Tel** (207)761-0660. **ED** Pamela H. Wood. **Ad Acc. Circ:** 5,000.
Desc: A cultural journalism field project involving students and professionals using an interdisciplinary perspective in examining and documenting Maine and its people (their lives and work).

ISSN 0386-4391
JA
CODEN SKHODA
SASEBO KOGYO KOTO SENMON GAKKO KENKYU HOKOKU. **See** Science and Technology.

ISSN 0736-0533
DD 051
US
SCHOLASTIC NEWS (PILOT EDITION). (SCHOLASTIC NEWS.). [Scholast. news]. **VFOAT** Scholastic News Pilot; SN Pilot. (198?)-. Periodical. English. Thirty-two times a year. $6.50. Scholastic Inc., 2931 East McCarty Street, PO Box 3710, Jefferson City MO 65102-9957. **Tel** (314)636-5271, (800)631-1586. available on microfilm from Xerox. **Continues** Scholastic News Pilot, 0028-9329.

ISSN 0036-6412
DD 051
US
SCHOLASTIC SCOPE. [Scholast. scope]. (19??)-. Periodical. English. Irregular. $25.00. Scholastic Inc., 2931 East McCarty Street, PO Box 3710, Jefferson City MO 65102-9957. **Tel** (314)636-5271, (800)631-1586. available on microfilm and microfiche from University Microfilms International (UMI).

LC LH9 .S34
AT
SCHOOL MAGAZINE. Added/Corp New South Wales. Dept. of Education. (19??)-. Periodical. English. Ten times a year. 36.18Aus$. School Magazine, Department of School Education, Private Bag 3, Ryde 2112 Australia. **Tel** 011 61 2 8089444. **ED** Anna Fienberg. **Bk Rev. Circ:** 305,000.
Desc: Contains short stories, plays, poems, and articles for reading for children three to six years old in primary schools.

LC LH5 .S34
AU
SCHULERFRONT. No. 1 (Oct. 1974)-. German. Irregular. 35.00. **Supersedes** Contra.

LC LG341.J4 S3
IS
SCOPUS. Added/Corp Universitah ha-Ivrit bi-Yerushalayim. (Nov. 1946)-. Periodical. English. One time a year. Free on request. Hebrew University of Jerusalem / Centre for Research and Documentation in East European Jewry, Jerusalem 91904 Israel. **Tel** 011 972 2 584271, 584262. **ED** Vivian London. **Circ:** 20,000 (ctrl).
Desc: Higher education and research at the Hebrew University of Jerusalem in science, humanities, medicine, law, social sciences, agriculture, Jewish studies, student and faculty personalities.
Ind/Abst Key Word Index Wildl. Res.

ISSN 0286-6366
JA
CODEN KSTDD5
SEITOKU EIYO TANKI DAIGAKU KIYO. **See** Nutrition and Dietetics.

LC PS508.C6 S48
ISSN 0037-2420
DD 810/.8
US
SEQUOIA (STANFORD, CALIF.). **See** Literature.

ISSN 0037-3044
US
SEWANEE NEWS, THE. Periodical. English. Four times a year. University of the South Office of Public Relations, Sewanee TN 37375.

LC Q4 .S488
ISSN 0253-9942
DD 505
CC
CODEN SCTPDH
SHANGHAI JIAOTONG DAXUE XUEBAO. **See** Science and Technology.

ISSN 0892-6603
US
SHORTHORN, THE. (THE SHORTHORN / THE UNIVERSITY OF TEXAS AT ARLINGTON.). **Added/Corp** University of Texas at Arlington. (19??)-. Periodical. English. Irregular. $40.00. The Shorthorn, PO Box 19038, Student Publ, Arlington TX 76019. **Tel** (817)273-3661, **FAX** (817)794-5630. **ED** Lisa Garrison. cum. index. **Bk Rev. Ad Acc, Adv Mgr:** Arnie Phillips. **Circ:** 15,000 Fall, 12,000 Summer (ctrl).

US
SIGNATURES. Added/Corp Anderson College (Anderson, Ind.) Anderson University (Anderson, Ind.). **VFOAT** Anderson College Names and News; Anderson University Names and News. Vol. 69, No. 2 (Spring 1987)-. Periodical. English. Four times a year. Anderson College, 1100 East 5th Street, Anderson IN 46011. **Continues** Anderson College News, 0003-193X; **Absorbed** Anderson College (Anderson, Ind.). President's Report.

LC LH1.S45 R4
ISSN 0049-0512
DD 376.8744
US
SIMMONS REVIEW, THE. Added/Corp Simmons College. Simmons College. Alumnae Association. (19??)-. Periodical. English. Four times a year. Free on request. Simmons College, 300 The Fenway, Boston MA 02115. **Tel** (617)738-2124. **ED** Peggy Loeb. **Bk Rev. Circ:** 18,500. available with illustrations.

ISSN 8755-1322
US
SINTE GLESDA COLLEGE NEWS. Added/Corp Sinte Gleska College. Vol. 1, No. 1 (1978)-. Periodical. English. Twelve times a year. Free on request. Sinte Glesda College News, Library Media Center, Box 107, Mission SD 57555. **Continues** Sinte Gleska College Center. News Letter.

ISSN 0038-1497
US
SOONER, THE. (THE SOONER; YEARBOOK OF THE UNIVERSITY OF OKLAHOMA.). [Sooner]. **Added/Corp** University of Oklahoma. (19??)-. English. Six times a year. University Oklahoma Alumni Association, 900 Asp Avenue, Norman OK 73019. **Tel** (405)325-6478. **ED** Twila J. Smith. Index available. **Ad Acc. Circ:** 2,000.
Desc: Student publication covering academics, administration, housing, Greeks, sports, organizations and general campus life.

College and School Publications

SOUTHWESTERN. Periodical. English. One time a week. $3.00. Southwestern Oklahoma State University, University Campus, Weatherford OK 73096. **Tel** (405)772-6611. **ED** Dick Wilson. **Circ:** 2,900.

ISSN 0038-4852
US

ISSN 0037-0479
US

SPECTATOR (SEATTLE), THE. (THE SPECTATOR.). **Added/Corp** Seattle University. (19??)-. Periodical. English. One time a week. $20.00. Seattle University / Spectator, 825 10th Avenue, Seattle WA 98122. **ED** Jennifer Kampsula.

LC LH1.C224 S7
ISSN 0038-7061
US
Pr Rev.

SPECTRUM (SANTA BARBARA, CALIF.). (SPECTRUM.). **Added/Corp** Students Literary Association (University of California, Santa Barbara) University of California, Santa Barbara. Office of Public Information. University of California, Santa Barbara. Associated Students. Vol. 1 (Winter 1957)-. Periodical. English. One time a year (June). $10.00. Spectrum / California, Box 14800 UCSB, Santa Barbara CA 93107. **Tel** (805)893-2364. **ED** Rebecca Johnston. cum. index. **Ad Acc. Circ:** 500. available on microfilm and microfiche from University Microfilms International (UMI).

US

SPELMAN MESSENGER. **Added/Corp** Spelman College, Atlanta, Ga. (18??)-. Periodical. English. Four times a year. Spelman Messenger, 350 Spelman Lane, Spelman College, Atlanta GA 30314.

ISSN 0747-1025
US

ST. CLOUD STATE UNIVERSITY CHRONICLE. **Added/Corp** St. Cloud State University. **VFOAT** S.C.S. Chronicle; SCS Chronicle; Saint Cloud State University Chronicle; Chronicle. Vol. 52, No. 58 (Aug. 6, 1975)-. Periodical. English. Two times a week. $20.00. St. Cloud State University, 13 Stewart Hall, St Cloud MN 56301. **Tel** (612)255-4086. **ED** Heidi Everett. **Bk Rev. Ad Acc.** ctrl circ. available on microfilm. **Continues** *Chronicle (Saint Cloud State College).*
Desc: Publication of St. Cloud State University.

ISSN 1060-829X
US

ST. JOHN'S OBELISK, THE. **Added/Corp** St. John's College (Santa Fe, N.M.). **VFOAT** Obelisk. Vol. 1, No. 1 (Dec. 18, 1991)-. Periodical. English. Twenty-six times a year. Free (Santa Fe), $30.00 (other areas). The Obelisk, St. John's College, 1160 Camino de la Cruz Blanca, Santa Fe NM 87501-4599.

LC LH1.S77 S7
US

STANFORD CHAPARRAL, THE. **Added/Corp** Stanford University. Associated Students. Hammer and Coffin National Honorary Society. Chaparral Chapter. **VFOAT** Chaparral. (Oct. 5, 1899)-. Periodical. English. Four times a year (Mar., June, Sept., Dec.). $11.00. Hammer and Coffin Society, Box 8585, Stanford University, Stanford CA 94305. **Tel** (415)723-1468. **ED** Trey Ellis.

ISSN 0745-3981
US

STANFORD MAGAZINE, THE. [Stanford mag.]. **Added/Corp** Stanford Alumni Association. (Fall/Winter 1973)-. Periodical. English. Four times a year. $12.00. Stanford Alumni Association, Bowman Alumni House, Stanford University, Stanford CA 94305. **Tel** (415)723-2021. **ED** Debby Fife. Index available. cum. index. **Bk Rev. Ad Acc. Circ:** 120,000 (ctrl).
Desc: Gives a representation of the intellectual, cultural, and social diversity of the Stanford community through editorials based on the thinking and work of Stanford professors and the accomplishments and activities of Stanford graduates.

ISSN 0038-979X
US

STANFORD OBSERVER, THE. **Added/Corp** Stanford University. (19??)-. Periodical. English. Irregular (6 issues). Free on request. The Observer, News Service, Santa Teresa Street, Stanford CA 94305. **Tel** (415)723-2558. **ED** Harry Press. **Circ:** 160,000.

LC LJ75 .P87
DD 371.85
ISSN 0038-9854
US
TITLE CHANGE

STAR AND LAMP OF PI KAPPA PHI, THE. **Main/Corp** Pi Kappa Phi. (19??)-(19??). Periodical. English. Pi Kappa Phi Fraternity Publications Office, PO Box 240526, Charlotte NC 28224-0526. **Tel** (704)523-6000. **ED** Durward W Owen. **Ad Acc. Circ:** 35,000 (ctrl). **Continued by** *Pi Kappa Phi Star & Lamp, 1066-2073.*
Desc: A leadership/educational publication targeted towards members and alumni of Pi Kappa Phi fraternity and other friends of Pi Kappa Phi. Material relating to alumni and undergraduates.

US

STATESMAN (STONY BROOK, N.Y.). (STATESMAN.). (19??)-. Periodical. English. Two times a week. $18.00. Statesman, Suny Stony Brook, PO Box AE, Stony Brook NY 11790. **Tel** (516)632-6480. **ED** Ray Parish and George Bidermann. **Bk Rev. Ad Acc. Circ:** 148,000 (ctrl). **Continues** *Sucolian (Stony Brook, N.Y.).*
Desc: Student newspaper in existence since 1958, covers news, features, and sports as well as running viewpoints and letters.

AT

●**STATUTES & REGULATIONS.** [Cal - Univ. Syd.]. (1994/95)-. Periodical. English. One time a year. 14.79Aus$. University of Student / Student Centre, Sydney New South Wales 2006, Australia. **Tel** 011 61 2 6923023, FAX 011 61 2 6923023. ctrl circ. **Continues** *Calendar - University of Sydney, 0313-4466.*

US

STOUTONIA, THE. **Added/Corp** University of Wisconsin--Stout. Stout State University. (19??)-. Newspaper. English. One time a week (Thursdays). $25.00. The Stoutonia, University of Wisconsin - Stout, 149 Memorial Student Center, Menomonie WI 54751. **Tel** (715)232-2272, FAX (715)232-1432. **ED** Erica Kalkofen. **Bk Rev. Photos. Ad Acc. Pub. Size:** Tabloid. **Wire Svcs.:** AP. **Circ:** 5,500.

ISSN 0039-2804
US

STUDENT VOICE. Periodical. English. Irregular. $10.00. University of Wisconsin-River Falls, South Hall, River Falls WI 54022. **Tel** (715)425-3906. **ED** Dianne Keene. **Bk Rev. Ad Acc. Circ:** 4,000.
Desc: For students at the University of Wisconsin in River Falls Wisconsin.

LC LF2525 .A34
DD 378.1/98/09435514
GW

STUDIEREN IN KOELN. **Added/Corp** Kolner Studentenwerk. Universitat zu Koln. AStA. Vol. 1 (Oct. 1990)-. Periodical. English. Kolner Studentenwerk, Universitatsstrasse 16, 5000 Cologne 41 Germany.

ISSN 0745-4147
US

SUNY GENESCO COMPASS. **VFOAT** S.U.N.Y. Geneseo Compass; Geneseo Compass. Vol. 12, No. 1 (Sept. 11, 1981)-. Periodical. English. Twelve times a year. free. Geneseo Compass, Office of Communications and Development SUNY Geneseo, Geneseo NY 14454. **Tel** (716)245-5516, FAX (716)245-5514. **ED** Doug Lippincott, (address) Erwin 201, 1 College Circle, Suny Genesco, New York, NY 11454. **Acid Free. Circ:** 3,000 (ctrl).
Desc: News and features focusing on events and people of Suny Genesco.

ISSN 0890-3107
US

TARTAN, THE. (THE TARTAN / CARNEGIE MELLON UNIVERSITY.). **Added/Corp** Carnegie-Mellon University. (19??)-. Periodical. English. Twenty-four times a year. $25.00. Tartan, Skibo 103, Carnegie Mellon University, Pittsburgh PA 15213. **Tel** (412)268-2111.

US

TENNESSEE VOLUNTEERS MAGAZINE. (19??)-. English. Twenty-six times a year. $24.97. University of Tennessee Athletic Department, Box 15016, Knoxville TN 37901. **Tel** (615)974-1212. **ED** Thomas Mattingly. Index available. cum. index. **Bk Rev. Ad Acc. Continues** *Smokey's Tale.*

US

TORCH (BLOOMINGTON, MINN.). (THE TORCH.). **Added/Corp** John F. Kennedy Senior High School. (196?)-. Periodical. English. Twelve times a year. John F. Kennedy Senior High School, 9701 Nicollet Avenue South, Bloomington MN 55420.

ISSN 1183-2215
DD 332.024
CN

TRADITION D'AVENIR. (UNE TRADITION D'AVENIR.). [Tradit. avenir]. **Added/Corp** Universite d'Ottawa. Bureau des Anciens et du Developpement. Universite d'Ottawa. Responsable des Dons Planifies. **VFOAT** Tradition Lives On. Winter (1991)-. Periodical. French. Two times a year. Free. Responsable des Dons Planifies, Bureau des Anciens et du Developpement, Universite D'Ottawa, 190 Est Avenue Laurier, Ottawa Ontario K1N 6N5 Canada.

US
Pr Rev.

TRANS/FORMS : INSURGENT VOICES IN EDUCATION. **See** *Education-Educational Research.*

LC AS30 .T7
DD 081
ISSN 0736-2439
US

TRINITY PAPERS, THE. [Trinity pap.]. **Added/Corp** Trinity College (Hartford, Conn.). Vol. 1, No. 1 (Spring 1982)-. Periodical. English. One time a year. Trinity College, 300 Summit Street, Hartford CT 06106. **Tel** (203)527-3151.
Desc: A collection of academic papers produced by Trinity students during the year.

US

TUESDAY BULLETIN. (19??)-. Bulletin. English. Free on request. Michigan State University African Studies Center, East Lansing MI 48824. **Tel** (517)353-1700, FAX (517)353-7254, telex 650 277 3148.

ISSN 0041-4026
US

TULANIAN, THE. Periodical. English. Four times a year. Tulane University, 300 Herbert Hall, New Orleans LA 70118.

ISSN 0706-4713
CN

U-CHOOSE. (19??)-. Periodical. English. Every 3 years. $15.95. Moving Publications Ltd., 44 Upjohn Road, Suite 100, Don Mills Ontario M3B 2W1 Canada. **Tel** (416)441-1168, FAX (416)441-1641. **ED** Anne Dunlop. **Ad Acc, Adv Mgr:** Anita Wood, **Tel** (416)441-1168. **Circ:** 15,000.
Desc: An independent guide, giving objective comparable material on undergraduate programs at all major universities in Canada to help high school students select the university that suits their academic and social needs.

ISSN 0745-3213
US
SUSPENDED

UC CLIP SHEET. **VFOAT** U.C. Clip Sheet. **VAT** University of California Clip Sheet. (1920)-Suspended (Nov. 1990). Periodical. English. Irregular. $5.00. University of California Office of University Relations, 131 University Hall, Berkeley CA 94720. **Tel** (415)987-9197. **ED** Camille Parker. ctrl circ.
Desc: Designed to keep the media informed about research and activities going on throughout the campus system.

ISSN 0896-9299
US

UCI JOURNAL. [UCI j.]. **Added/Corp** University of California, Irvine. Communications Office. **VAT** University of California Journal. Periodical. English. Four times a year. Public Information Office / University, UCI Journal, University of California, Irvine CA 92717. **Tel** (714)856-6923. **Continues** *Journal - University of California, Irvine, 0745-3264.*

ISSN 0733-9712
US

UGAZINE. (UGAZINE : THE STUDENT MAGAZINE OF THE UNIVERSITY OF GEORGIA.). **VAT** University of Georgia Magazine. Vol. 1, No. 1 (Fall 1980)-. Periodical. English. Four times a year. University of Georgia Institute of Government, 201 North Milledge Avenue, Athens GA 30602. **Tel** (706)542-2736, FAX (706)542-9301.

LC LA2100 .U55
DD 370/.994
ISSN 0311-4775
AT

UNICORN (CARLTON, TAS.). (UNICORN : BULLETIN OF THE AUSTRALIAN COLLEGE OF EDUCATION.). **Added/Corp** Australian College of Education. (March 1975)-. Academic Scholarly Publication. English. Four times a year (Feb., May, Aug., Nov.). 32.88Aus$. Australian College of Education, PO Box 323, Curtin ACT 2605 Australia. **Tel** 011 61 62 811677. **ED** B. Pope. cum. index. **Bk Rev. Ad Acc. Circ:** 6,500 (ctrl).
Desc: Theme papers of scholarly content - education.
Ind/Abst APAIS, Aust. Public Aff. Inf. Ser.; Aust. Educ. Index; Educ. Technol. Abstr.; Sociol. Educ. Abstr.; Spec. Educ. Needs Abstr.; Stud. Women Abstr.; Tech. Educ. Train. Abstr.

AT
TITLE CHANGE

UNION RECORDER, THE. **Main/Corp** Sydney University. Sydney University Union. (1???)-(19??). Periodical. English. University of Sydney, 116 Darlington Road / H42, Sydney NSW 2006 Australia. **Tel** 011 61 2 6922666, FAX 011 61 2 6922666. **ED** M. Karpin, M. Swivel, J. Lipman and M. Hellyer. **Circ:** 6,000. **Continued by** *Union Recorder, 0041-7017.*
Desc: News, reviews and features of interest to university students along with poems and short stories written by students.

ISSN 0041-7017
AT

UNION RECORDER. **Added/Corp** University of Sydney Union. **VFOAT** Recorder. (1920)-. Periodical. English. Fifteen times a year. 10.00Aus$. University of Sydney, 116 Darlington Road / H42, Sydney NSW 2006 Australia. **Tel** 011 61 2 6922666, FAX 011 61 2 6922666. **Continues** *The Union Recorder.*

College and School Publications —Alumni

LC LH7.M28 U5   ISSN 0041-7149
PH
UNITAS (MANILA). (UNITAS.). [Unitas]. **Added/Corp** University of Santo Tomas. (1922)-. Periodical. English (Spanish). Four times a year. University of Santo Tomas / Manila, Manila Philippines. Documents available from UMI Article Clearinghouse. **Ind/Abst** ABI/INFORM Glob. Ed.; ABI/INFORM [Computer File] (1959-); Am. Hist. Life (1959-); Bibliogr. Mission. (1959-); Index Philip. Period. (1959-); MLA Int. Bibl. Books Artic. Mod. Lang. Lit.; PAIS Int. Print; Selec. Coop. Index Manage. Period.; UMI ABI/Inform--Bus. Period. Ondisc (1987-) [Full Txt.].

CN
UNIVERSITY CALENDAR SIMON FRASER. UNIVERSITY OF BC. (19??)-. English. One time a year. 5.00Can$ Canada; 7.00Can$ US; 12.00Can$ other. Simon Fraser University, University Bookstore, Burnaby BC V5A 1S6 Canada. **Tel** (604)291-3224, FAX (604)291-4969. Index available (Free). **Ad Acc. Circ:** 40,000.

LC LH1.C225 U55   ISSN 0147-6149
DD 378.794/32   US
UNIVERSITY JOURNAL, THE. (Spring 1974)-. Periodical. English. Two times a year. California State University - Chico / Center for Business & Economic Research, Graduate School, Chico CA 95929. **Tel** (916)895-5711.
Ind/Abst Zentralbl. Math. Ihre Grenzgeb.

LC AS30 .U53   ISSN 0041-9524
US
UNIVERSITY OF DAYTON REVIEW, THE. [Univ. Dayt. rev.]. **Main/Corp** University of Dayton. **Added/Corp** University of Dayton. Review. Vol. 1 (Spring 1964)-. Periodical. English. Irregular (3 issues per year). Free. University of Dayton Law Review, 300 College Park, Dayton OH 45469. **Tel** (513)229-3642. **ED** Robert Conard. Index available. **Circ:** 1,500.
Ind/Abst Abstr. Engl. Stud.; Am. Bibligr. Slavic East Europ. Stud.; Annu. Bibligr. Engl. Lang. Lit.; MLA Int. Bibl. Books Artic. Mod. Lang. Lit.

ISSN 0747-3028
US
UNIVERSITY OF HARTFORD OBSERVER. Periodical. English. Twelve times a year. University of Hartford, 200 Bloomfield Avenue, English Department, West Hartford CT 06117. **Tel** (203)768-4574.

ISSN 0041-9737
UK
UNIVERSITY OF LEEDS REVIEW, THE. [Univ. Leeds rev.]. **Added/Corp** University of Leeds. (1948-). Periodical. English. One time a year (Dec.). $31.75. Brotherton Library / University of Leeds, Publications Office, Leeds LS2 9JT United Kingdom. **Tel** 011 44 113 2335525, FAX 011 44 113 2335524, telex 556473. **ED** Gwyneth Pitt. Index available. **Circ:** 850 (ctrl).
Ind/Abst MLA Int. Bibl. Books Artic. Mod. Lang. Lit.

LC Z5055.U5 U538 AS36.U585
US
UNIVERSITY OF TENNESSEE PUBLICATIONS AND CREATIVE ACHIEVEMENTS : A CATALOG OF PUBLICATIONS AND CREATIVE ACHIEVEMENTS OF THE FACULTY AND STAFF. Main/Corp University of Tennessee (System). Office of the Vice President for Academic Affairs and Research. **VFOAT** University of Tennessee Publications & Creative Achievements; Publications and Creative Achievements. (1984-). Catalog. English. University of Tennessee Office of the Vice-President For Academic Affairs and Research, Knoxville TN 37916.
Continues University of Tennessee, Knoxville. Research, Publications and Creative Achievements, 0195-881X.

ISSN 0746-5149
US
UNIVERSITY OF VIRGINIA RECORD. **VFOAT** Record. Vol. 1-7 (Sept. 1907/June 1914)-. English. Six times a year. University of Virginia Printing Office, PO Box 1 Newcomb Hall Station, Charlottesville VA 22903.

ISSN 8750-7927
US
USC TROJAN FAMILY. VAT University of Southern California Trojan Family. Periodical. English. Nine times a year. University of Southern California / 357 Administration Building, Los Angeles CA 90007. **Tel** (310)743-2684. **ED** Susan Heitman. **Circ:** 180,000.
Continues Trojan Family, 0042-0085.
Desc: News and features about people and programs connected with the University of Southern California.

ISSN 0747-3672
US
VALLEY : LEBANON VALLEY COLLEGE MAGAZINE, THE. Vol. 1, No. 1 (Spring 1984)-. Periodical. English. Four times a year. Lebanon Valley College, Annville PA 17003.

ISSN 0042-2517
US
VANDERBILT HUSTLER, THE. Periodical. English. Two times a week. $12.00. Vanderbilt University / Student Communications, PO Box 1504 Station B, Nashville TN 37235.

ISSN 0042-2789
CN
VARSITY (TORONTO). (THE VARSITY.). [Varsity]. **Added/Corp** University of Toronto. **VFOAT** Summer Varsity. (1880)-. Periodical. English. Irregular. 48.02Can$. The Varsity, 44 Saint George Street, Toronto Ontario M5S 2E4 Canada. **Tel** (416)979-2856. **ED** Jeb Blount. **Bk Rev**. **Ad Acc. Circ:** 25,000 (ctrl). available on microfilm.
Desc: Official undergraduate paper of the University of Toronto providing news, reviews, entertainment and opinions.

ISSN 1102-4380
SW
VETSKAP. (19??)-. Swedish. Twenty times a year. $120.21. Univ i Linkoping, S 58183, Linkoping Sweden. **Tel** 011 46 13 281682, FAX 011 46 13 282825. **Ad Acc. Circ:** 1400 (ctrl).

LC LD1851 .V55   ISSN 0091-3456
DD 378.757/84   US
VIGNETTES. [Vignettes]. English. One time a year. $25.00. Francis Marion College, Box 100547, Florence SC 29501-0547. **Tel** (803)661-1223, FAX (803)661-1219. **Circ:** 900 (ctrl).
Desc: A yearbook which records the student activities and events of each academic year.

ISSN 1061-3498
US
VIKING (INKSTER, MICH.), THE. (THE VIKING / INKSTER HIGH SCHOOL.). **Added/Corp** Inkster High School. Vol. 1, Issue 1 (Nov. 6 1991)-. Periodical. English. Twelve times a year. Free. The Viking, 3250 Middlebelt Road, Inkster MI 48141.

ISSN 0733-9720
US
VISTAS (MIAMI, FLA.). (VISTAS.). (1979)-. Periodical. English. One time a week. $311.00. University Relations & Development, Florida International University, Tamiami Trail, Miami FL 33199.

JA
WAKAYAMA KOGYO KOTO SENMON GAKKO KENKYU KIYO. See Science and Technology.

US
WASATCH WAVE, THE. See Newspapers.

DD 917.13/72044/05   ISSN 0839-1483
CN
WELCOME BACK STUDENT GUIDE. [Welcome back stud. guide]. (Fall/Winter 1987)-. Periodical. English. Kingston Publications, PO Box 1352, Kingston Ontario K7L 5C6 Canada. **Tel** (613)549-8442.
Continues Welcome Back Magazine., 0828-6221.

ISSN 0279-3628
US
WESTERNER, THE. Vol. 1 (June 1980)-. English. Six times a year. Western Michigan University, 1921 West Michigan Avenue, Kalamazoo MI 49008. **Continues** University Magazine.

LC AS30 .W56
DD 051   US
WISCONSIN DIALOGUE : A FACULTY JOURNAL FOR THE UNIVERSITY OF WISCONSIN-EAU CLAIRE. No. 1 (Fall 1980)-. Periodical. English. One time a year. University of Wisconsin-Eau Claire, Department of English, Eau Claire WI 54702-4004. **Tel** (715)836-2639.

LC AS182 .H125   ISSN 0440-1298
GW
WISSENSCHAFTLICHE BEITRAEGE DER MARTIN-LUTHER-UNIVERSITAT HALLE-WITTENBERG. [Wiss. Beitr. - Martin-Luther-Univ. Halle-Wittenb.]. **Added/Corp** Martin-Luther-Universitat Halle-Wittenberg. **VFOAT** Wissenschaftliche Beitraege. (19??)-. Academic Scholarly Publication. German. Martin-Luther-Universitat Halle-Wittenberg, August-Bebel-Strasse 13, DDR-4010 Halle Germany. **Tel** 895 271, telex 04 353 UNI HAL DD. Documents available from CASDDS.
Ind/Abst Chem. Abstr.; GeoRef.

ISSN 1000-5900
CC
CODEN XDZXEW
XIANGTAN DAXUE ZIRAN KEXUE XUEBAO. See Science and Technology.

ISSN 0084-3318
US
YALE COLLEGE SERIES. Vol. 1 (1964)-. English. Irregular. Price varies per volume. Yale University Press, PO Box 209040, New Haven CT 06520. **Tel** (203)432-0940, (800)987-7323, FAX (203)432-0948.

LC PS501 .Y342
US
YALE LITERARY MAGAZINE, THE. VFOAT Excommunicate; Yale Lit. Vol. 1, Issue 1 (Spring 1989)-. Periodical. English. Two times a year. $35.00 (institutions), $15.00 (individuals). YLM Publishing Fund, Box 209087, Yale Station, New Haven CT 06520.
Continues Yale Literary Magazine, 0044-0108.
Desc: Contains writings by, and for, the students of Yale University.

ISSN 0740-0233
US
UDC 37
YALE WEEKLY BULLETIN AND CALENDAR. Added/Corp Yale University. **VFOAT** Weekly Bulletin and Calendar. Vol. 1 (Sept. 1972)-. Bulletin. English. One time a week (35 issues per year). $27.00. Yale Weekly Bulletin and Calendar, Box 2118 Yale Station, New Haven CT 06520. **Tel** (203)432-1333. **ED** Walter D. Littell and LuAnn Z. Bishop. **Circ:** 15,000. available on an online database. **Supersedes** Yale University. Yale University Bulletin; **Absorbed** Yale Staff News.
Desc: A comprehensive list of free events, lectures, workshops, debates, concerts, sports, art exhibits, films and theater. Special reports on research, recent publications, etc.

ISSN 0702-1755
CN
YOUNG. Vol. 1 (Nov. 1967)-. Periodical. English (French). Twelve times a year. 2.40Can$. Young Magazine, 241 Amherst, Winnipeg Manitoba R3J 1Y5 Canada. **Tel** (204)889-5255. **ED** Charles Colyer. **Ad Acc**.
Desc: By, for, and about secondary school students; prose, poetry, features, and pen pals.

ABSTRACTING, BIBLIOGRAPHIES AND STATISTICS

LC Z5055.U5 L8514   ISSN 0099-1457
DD 016.05   US
LOUISIANA TECH UNIVERSITY FACULTY PUBLICATIONS. ANNUAL SUPPLEMENT. (LOUISIANA TECH UNIVERSITY FACULTY PUBLICATIONS.). **Main/Corp** Louisiana Tech University. English. One time a year. Louisiana Tech University, Research Council, Baton Rouge LA 70803.

ALUMNI

US
AGUILA. Added/Corp Texas. North Texas State University, Denton. Alumni Association. Vol. 1, (Spring 1975)-. Periodical. English. Four times a year. North Texas State University / Alumni Association, PO Box 23557, NT Station, Denton TX 76203.

LC L51 .V42
RU
ALMA MATER. Added/Corp Soviet Union. Gosudarstvennyi Komitet po Narodnomu Obrazovaniiu. (1991)-. Periodical. Russian (table of contents in English). Six times a year. $69.95. Izdatelstvo Vysshaia Shkola, Neglinnaya Ulitsa, Dom 29-14, GSP-4, Moscow 101430 Russia. **(Subscription address:** East View Publications Inc., 3020 Harbor Lane North, Suite 110, Minneapolis MN 55447. **Tel** (800)477-1005, (612)550-0961, FAX (612)559-2931.) **Continues** Vestnik Vysshei Shkoly, 0321-0383.

ISSN 0065-6445
US
ALMA MATER. Added/Corp Baltimore College of Dental Surgery. Alumni Association. Vol. 1 (1959)-. Periodical. English.
Ind/Abst Health Plan. Adminis.

LC WMLC L 83/4321
US
ALUMNAE DIRECTORY / DELTA ZETA SORORITY. Main/Corp Delta Zeta Sorority. **VFOAT** Delta Zeta Sorority Alumnae Directory. Directory. English. Bernard C. Harris Publishing Company, 3 Barker Avenue, White Plains NY 10601. **Tel** (914)946-7500.

LC LD7096.3 .M68a
DD 378.744/23   US
●**ALUMNAE DIRECTORY / MOUNT HOLYOKE COLLEGE. Main/Corp** Mount Holyoke College. **Added/Corp** Alumnae Association of Mount Holyoke College. (1993)-. Directory. English.

College and School Publications —Alumni

Irregular. Alumnae Association, Mount Holyoke College, South Hadley MA 01075. **Continues** *Mount Holyoke College. Alumnae Register.*

LC LD3561.M868 A14
DD 378.753
US

ALUMNAE DIRECTORY / MOUNT VERNON COLLEGE. Main/Corp Mount Vernon College. **VFOAT** Mount Vernon College Alumnae Directory. Directory. English. College & University Press / Alabama, One Bell Road, PO Box 17940, Montgomery AL 36117.

LC WMLC L 83/7189
US

ALUMNAE DIRECTORY OF SWEET BRIAR COLLEGE. Main/Corp Sweet Briar College. **Added/Corp** Sweet Briar College Alumnae Association. **VFOAT** Alumnae Directory; Sweet Briar College Alumnae Directory. (1917)-. English. Four times a year (Jan., Apr., July, Oct.). Free. Sweet Briar College, Sweet Briar College Alumnae Association, Sweet Briar VA 24595. **Tel** (804)381-6131, **FAX** (804)381-6132. **ED** Nancy Baldwin. **Bk Rev**, (Qty: only books by alumnae). **Circ:** 12,000 (ctrl). **Continues** *Lifline.*
Desc: Keeps alumnae and friends informed about the state of the College and about the activities of the Alumnae Association and individual alumnae. Articles are written by mostly faculty, staff and alumnae of Sweet Briar College.

LC LD7251.L852 A3
DD 378.755/671
US

ALUMNAE DIRECTORY / RANDOLPH-MACON WOMAN'S COLLEGE. Main/Corp Randolph-Macon Woman's College. **VFOAT** Randolph-Macon Woman's College Alumnae Directory. Directory. English. College & University Press / Alabama, One Bell Road, PO Box 17940, Montgomery AL 36117.

LC WMLC 91/3202
US

ALUMNAE DIRECTORY / SIGMA SIGMA SIGMA. Main/Corp Sigma Sigma Sigma. **VFOAT** Sigma Sigma Sigma Alumnae Directory. 1st Ed. (1991)-. Directory. English. Bernard C. Harris Publishing Company, 3 Barker Avenue, White Plains NY 10601. **Tel** (914)946-7500.

LC LD5171.S524 A36A **ISSN** 0738-6842
DD 378.778/29
US

ALUMNAE DIRECTORY / STEPHENS COLLEGE. Main/Corp Stephens College. Directory. English. Bernard C. Harris Publishing Company, 3 Barker Avenue, White Plains NY 10601. **Tel** (914)946-7500.

LC LD7501.N494 A25 **ISSN** 0742-5007
DD 373.747/1
US

ALUMNAE DIRECTORY / THE BREARLEY SCHOOL. Main/Corp Brearley School. **VFOAT** Brearley School Alumnae Directory. Directory. English. Bernard C. Harris Publishing Company, 3 Barker Avenue, White Plains NY 10601. **Tel** (914)946-7500.

LC WMLC 91/3299
US

ALUMNAE/I DIRECTORY. Main/Corp Boston University. College of Engineering. **VFOAT** Alumni Directory; Boston University College of Engineering Alumnae/I Directory ... . (1991)-. Directory. English. Bernard C. Harris Publishing Company, 3 Barker Avenue, White Plains NY 10601. **Tel** (914)946-7500.

LC LD2897 .A15 **ISSN** 0738-2510
DD 378.771/334
US

ALUMNAE/I DIRECTORY / LAKE ERIE COLLEGE. Main/Corp Lake Erie College. **VFOAT** Lake Erie College Alumnae/I Directory. (19??)-. Directory. English. Bernard C. Harris Publishing Company, 3 Barker Avenue, White Plains NY 10601. **Tel** (914)946-7500.

LC KF292.R87 A837 **ISSN** 0738-6672
DD 340/.07/1174932
US

ALUMNAE/I DIRECTORY - RUTGERS LAW SCHOOL (NEWARK, N.J.). (ALUMNAE/I DIRECTORY / RUTGERS, THE STATE UNIVERSITY OF NEW JERSEY, CAMPUS AT NEWARK, SCHOOL OF LAW.). **Main/Corp** Rutgers Law School (Newark, N.J.). **VFOAT** Rutgers School of Law Newark Alumnae/I Directory. (19??)-. Directory. English. One time a year. Bernard C. Harris Publishing Company, 3 Barker Avenue, White Plains NY 10601. **Tel** (914)946-7500.

ISSN 0892-7839
US

ALUMNEWS (NORFOLK, VA.). (ALUMNEWS / OLD DOMINION UNIVERSITY.). **Added/Corp** Old Dominion University. Old Dominion University. Office of Alumni Relations. Old Dominion University. Alumni Office. (Summer 1977)-. Periodical. English. Six times a year. **Continues** *ODU Magazine.*

LC WMLC 91/265
US

ALUMNI/AE DIRECTORY. Main/Corp Archbishop Carroll High School. **VFOAT** Alumnae Directory; Archbishop Carroll High School Alumni/ae Directory. (1991)-. Directory. English. Bernard C. Harris Publishing Company, 3 Barker Avenue, White Plains NY 10601. **Tel** (914)946-7500.

LC WMLC 91/5114
US

ALUMNI/AE DIRECTORY / HARVARD DIVINITY SCHOOL. Main/Corp Harvard Divinity School. **VFOAT** Alumnae Directory; Harvard Divinity School Alumni/ae Directory. (1991/1992)-. Directory. English. Bernard C. Harris Publishing Company, 3 Barker Avenue, White Plains NY 10601. **Tel** (914)946-7500.

LC WMLC L 83/8167
US

ALUMNI AND ALUMNAE DIRECTORY. Main/Corp Hobart and William Smith Colleges. Directory. English. **Continues** *Alumni and Alumnae directory.*

LC WMLC 91/3318
US

ALUMNI DIRECTORY. Main/Corp University of Central Oklahoma. **VFOAT** University of Central Oklahoma Alumni Directory. (1992)-. Directory. English. Bernard C. Harris Publishing Company, 3 Barker Avenue, White Plains NY 10601. **Tel** (914)946-7500.

LC WMLC 91/3766
US

ALUMNI DIRECTORY. Main/Corp University of Illinois at Urbana-Champaign. College of Veterinary Medicine. **VFOAT** University of Illinois, College of Veterinary Medicine ... Alumni Directory. (1992)-. Directory. English. Bernard C. Harris Publishing Company, 3 Barker Avenue, White Plains NY 10601. **Tel** (914)946-7500.

LC WMLC 91/4581
US

ALUMNI DIRECTORY. Main/Corp Benjamin N. Cardozo School of Law. (1991)-. Directory. English. Bernard C. Harris Publishing Company, 3 Barker Avenue, White Plains NY 10601. **Tel** (914)946-7500.

LC WMLC 91/5164
US

ALUMNI DIRECTORY. Main/Corp North Dakota State College of Science. **VFOAT** North Dakota State College of Science Alumni Directory. (1992)-. Directory. English. Bernard C. Harris Publishing Company, 3 Barker Avenue, White Plains NY 10601. **Tel** (914)946-7500.

LC KF292.A52 A52
DD 340/.07/1174743
US

ALUMNI DIRECTORY / ALBANY LAW SCHOOL OF UNION UNIVERSITY. Main/Corp Albany Law School. **VFOAT** Albany Law School of Union University Alumni Directory. (1981)-. Directory. English. Bernard C. Harris Publishing Company, 3 Barker Avenue, White Plains NY 10601. **Tel** (914)946-7500.

LC LD91.A55 A14 **ISSN** 0740-1620
DD 378.747/43
US

ALUMNI DIRECTORY - ALBANY STATE COLLEGE. (ALUMNI DIRECTORY.). **Main/Corp** Albany State College. **VFOAT** Albany State College Alumni Directory. 1983-. Directory. English. Office of Alumni Affairs, Albany State College, Albany GA 31705.

LC WMLC 91/5126
US

ALUMNI DIRECTORY / ALLEN UNIVERSITY. Main/Corp Allen University. **VFOAT** Allen University Alumni Directory. (1992)-. Directory. English. Bernard C. Harris Publishing Company, 3 Barker Avenue, White Plains NY 10601. **Tel** (914)946-7500.

LC R747 .B6954 **ISSN** 0743-5533
DD 610/.7/1174461
US

ALUMNI DIRECTORY / ALUMNI ASSOCIATION, BOSTON UNIVERSITY SCHOOL OF MEDICINE. Main/Corp Boston University. School of Medicine. Alumni Association. (19??)-. Directory. English. Boston University / School of Medicine, 80 East Concord Street, Boston MA 02118. **Tel** (617)247-5000. **Circ:** 4,200 (ctrl).
Desc: A listing of doctors who have graduated form BUSM along with their present addresses. Comprised of four sections: Alpha, Class, Geographical, and Specialty.

LC LD2101.H662 A14 **ISSN** 0278-887X
DD 378.744/23
US

ALUMNI DIRECTORY (AMHERST, MASS.). (ALUMNI DIRECTORY / HAMPSHIRE COLLEGE.). **Added/Corp** Hampshire College. (19??)-. Directory. English. Free to alumni. Hampshire College, Amherst MA 01002.

LC QE23 .U56a
DD 550/.7/11756563
US

ALUMNI DIRECTORY AND NEWSLETTER - UNIVERSITY OF NORTH CAROLINA AT CHAPEL HILL. DEPT. OF GEOLOGY. Main/Corp University of North Carolina at Chapel Hill. Dept. of Geology. (19??)-. Directory. English. Irregular. University of North Carolina at Chapel Hill Department of Geology, Mitchell Hall 029 A, Chapel Hill NC 27514.

LC WMLC L 83/6170
US

ALUMNI DIRECTORY / ANTIOCH COLLEGE. Main/Corp Antioch College. (19??)-. Directory. English. Marquis Who's Who, A Reed Reference Publishing Company, Part of Reed International PLC, 121 Chanlon Road, New Providence NJ 07974. **Tel** (908)464-6800, (800)521-8110, **FAX** (908)665-6688, telex 138 755. **Continues** *Antioch Alumni Directory.*

LC LD371.B6651a B45a **ISSN** 0740-1752
DD 378.756/773
US

ALUMNI DIRECTORY / BELMONT ABBEY COLLEGE. Main/Corp Belmont Abbey College. **VFOAT** Belmont Abbey College Alumni Directory. (19??)-. Directory. English. Irregular. Belmont Abbey College, Belmont NC 28012.

LC WMLC 91/3304
DD 379
US

ALUMNI DIRECTORY / BETHEL COLLEGE. Main/Corp Bethel College (North Newton, Kan.). **VFOAT** Bethel College Alumni Directory. (19??)-. Directory. English. Bethel College / Alumni Directory, North Newton KS 67117.

LC LD451.B31A B47A **ISSN** 0731-4159
DD 378.768/25
US

ALUMNI DIRECTORY - BETHEL COLLEGE (MCKENZIE, TENN.). (ALUMNI DIRECTORY / BETHEL COLLEGE.). **Main/Corp** Bethel College (McKenzie, Tenn.). **VFOAT** Bethel College Alumni Directory. 1981-. Directory. English. College & University Press / Alabama, One Bell Road, PO Box 17940, Montgomery AL 36117.

LC WMLC 91/3275
US

ALUMNI DIRECTORY / BLACK HILLS STATE UNIVERSITY. Main/Corp Black Hills State University. **VFOAT** Black Hills State University ... Alumni Directory. (1992)-. Directory. English. Bernard C. Harris Publishing Company, 3 Barker Avenue, White Plains NY 10601. **Tel** (914)946-7500.

LC WMLC 90/0749
US

ALUMNI DIRECTORY / BOISE STATE UNIVERSITY. Main/Corp Boise State University. **VFOAT** Boise State University Alumni Directory. (1990)-. Directory. English. Bernard C. Harris Publishing Company, 3 Barker Avenue, White Plains NY 10601. **Tel** (914)946-7500.

LC WMLC 91/3297
US

ALUMNI DIRECTORY / BOSTON UNIVERSITY, COLLEGE OF BASIC STUDIES. Main/Corp Boston University. College of Basic Studies. **VFOAT** Boston University College of Basic Studies Alumni Directory ... . (1991)-. Directory. English. Bernard C. Harris Publishing Company, 3 Barker Avenue, White Plains NY 10601. **Tel** (914)946-7500.

LC WMLC 91/3298
US

ALUMNI DIRECTORY / BOSTON UNIVERSITY, GENERAL EDUCATION. Main/Corp Boston University. Division of General Education. **VFOAT** Boston University General Education Alumni Directory ... . (1991)-. Directory. English. Bernard C. Harris Publishing Company, 3 Barker Avenue, White Plains NY 10601. **Tel** (914)946-7500.

LC WMLC 91/1363
US

ALUMNI DIRECTORY / BRIGHAM YOUNG UNIVERSITY, COLLEGE OF ENGINEERING AND TECHNOLOGY. Main/Corp Brigham Young University. College of Engineering and Technology. **VFOAT** Brigham Young University College of Engineering and Technology ... Alumni Directory. (1991)-. Directory. English. Bernard C. Harris Publishing Company, 3 Barker Avenue, White Plains NY 10601. **Tel** (914)946-7500.

LC WMLC 91/3158
US

ALUMNI DIRECTORY / BROOKLYN COLLEGE, THE CITY UNIVERSITY OF NEW YORK. Main/Corp Brooklyn College. **VFOAT** Brooklyn College Alumni Directory. (1991)-. Directory. English. Bernard C. Harris Publishing Company, 3 Barker Avenue, White Plains NY 10601. **Tel** (914)946-7500.

College and School Publications —Alumni

LC LD649.8 .A125
DD 378.745/1
ISSN 0738-1158 US
ALUMNI DIRECTORY / BRYANT COLLEGE. Main/Corp Bryant College. VFOAT Bryant College Alumni Directory. Directory. English. Bernard C. Harris Publishing Company, 3 Barker Avenue, White Plains NY 10601. Tel (914)946-7500.

LC LD701.B31 B84A
DD 378.777/18 US
ALUMNI DIRECTORY / BUENA VISTA COLLEGE. Main/Corp Buena Vista College. VFOAT Buena Vista College Alumni Directory. Directory. English. College & University Press / Alabama, One Bell Road, PO Box 17940, Montgomery AL 36117.

LC N330.O352 C343A
DD 707/.1179466
ISSN 0731-8928 US
ALUMNI DIRECTORY - CALIFORNIA COLLEGE OF ARTS AND CRAFTS (OAKLAND, CALIF.). (ALUMNI DIRECTORY / CALIFORNIA COLLEGE OF ARTS AND CRAFTS.). Main/Corp California College of Arts and Crafts (Oakland, Calif.). VFOAT California College of Arts and Crafts Alumni Directory. 1981-. Directory. English. College & University Press / Alabama, One Bell Road, PO Box 17940, Montgomery AL 36117.

LC LD729.6.N6 A22
DD 378.794/94
ISSN 0736-6426 US
ALUMNI DIRECTORY / CALIFORNIA STATE UNIVERSITY, NORTHRIDGE. Main/Corp California State University, Northridge. VFOAT California State University, Northridge Alumni Directory. 1982-. Directory. English. College & University Press / Alabama, One Bell Road, PO Box 17940, Montgomery AL 36117.

LC LD791.C51A C36A
DD 378.747/97 US
ALUMNI DIRECTORY / CANISIUS COLLEGE. Main/Corp Canisius College. VFOAT Canisius College Alumni Directory. 1982-. Directory. English. College & University Press / Alabama, One Bell Road, PO Box 17940, Montgomery AL 36117.

LC WMLC 90/0665 US
ALUMNI DIRECTORY / CAPITAL UNIVERSITY LAW AND GRADUATE CENTER. Main/Corp Capital University. Law and Graduate Center. VFOAT Capital University Law and Graduate Center Alumni Directory. (1990)-. Directory. English. Bernard C. Harris Publishing Company, 3 Barker Avenue, White Plains NY 10601. Tel (914)946-7500.

LC WMLC 91/1543 US
ALUMNI DIRECTORY / CARROLL COLLEGE. Main/Corp Carroll College (Helena, Mont.). VFOAT Carroll College Alumni Directory. (1991)-. Directory. English. Bernard C. Harris Publishing Company, 3 Barker Avenue, White Plains NY 10601. Tel (914)946-7500.

LC LD801.C41 C37A
DD 378.756/71
ISSN 0732-345X US
ALUMNI DIRECTORY / CATAWBA COLLEGE. Main/Corp Catawba College. VFOAT Catawba College Alumni Directory. (19??)-. Directory. English. $27.45 Alumni and Staff. College & University Press / Alabama, One Bell Road, PO Box 17940, Montgomery AL 36117.

LC LD7501.W253 A15
DD 373.2/22/097467
ISSN 0738-680X US
ALUMNI DIRECTORY / CHOATE ROSEMARY HALL. Main/Corp Choate Rosemary Hall. VFOAT Choate Rosemary Hall Alumni Directory. Directory. English. Bernard C. Harris Publishing Company, 3 Barker Avenue, White Plains NY 10601. Tel (914)946-7500.

LC LD1061.C62 A25
DD 378.757/66
ALUMNI DIRECTORY / COKER COLLEGE. Main/Corp Coker College. VFOAT Coker College Alumni Directory. Directory. English. College & University Press / Alabama, One Bell Road, PO Box 17940, Montgomery AL 36117.

LC WMLC 91/5842 US
ALUMNI DIRECTORY / COLLEGE OF BUSINESS ADMINISTRATION. Main/Corp University of Illinois at Chicago. College of Business Administration. VFOAT CBA Alumni Directory; College of Business Administration UIC Alumni Directory. (1992)-. Directory. English. Bernard C. Harris Publishing Company, 3 Barker Avenue, White Plains NY 10601. Tel (914)946-7500.

LC WMLC L 83/6269 US
ALUMNI DIRECTORY / COLLEGE OF ENGINEERING, UNIVERSITY OF MASSACHUSETTS AT AMHERST. Main/Corp University of Massachusetts at Amherst. College of Engineering. VFOAT College of Engineering Alumni Directory. 1988-. Directory. English. Bernard C. Harris Publishing Company, 3 Barker Avenue, White Plains NY 10601. Tel (914)946-7500.

LC WMLC 91/965 US
ALUMNI DIRECTORY / COLLEGE OF LETTERS, ARTS AND SCIENCES, UNIVERSITY OF SOUTHERN CALIFORNIA. Main/Corp University of Southern California. College of Letters, Arts and Sciences. VFOAT College of Letters, Arts and Sciences, University of Southern California Alumni Directory. (1990)-. Directory. English. Bernard C. Harris Publishing Company, 3 Barker Avenue, White Plains NY 10601. Tel (914)946-7500.

LC WMLC 91/5852 US
ALUMNI DIRECTORY / COLLEGE OF LIBERAL ARTS, THE UNIVERSITY OF TEXAS AT AUSTIN. Main/Corp University of Texas at Austin. College of Liberal Arts. VFOAT College of Liberal Arts The University of Texas at Austin Alumni Directory. (1992)-. Directory. English. Bernard C. Harris Publishing Company, 3 Barker Avenue, White Plains NY 10601. Tel (914)946-7500.

LC LD7501.O657 .A15
DD 373.782/254
ISSN 0740-1787 US
ALUMNI DIRECTORY / CREIGHTON PREPARATORY SCHOOL. Main/Corp Creighton Preparatory School. VFOAT Creighton Preparatory School Alumni Directory. (19??)-. Directory. English. Alumni Directory Creighton Preparatory School, 7400 Western Avenue, Omaha NE 68114.

LC TX661 .C84a
DD 641.5/025/73
ISSN 0738-1557 US
ALUMNI DIRECTORY - CULINARY INSTITUTE OF AMERICA. (ALUMNI DIRECTORY.). Main/Corp Culinary Institute of America. VFOAT Culinary Institute of America Alumni Directory. (19??)-. Directory. English. Culinary Institute of America, Public Relations Department, Hyde Park NY 12538. Tel (914)452-9600.

LC WMLC 91/5382 US
ALUMNI DIRECTORY / DANIEL WEBSTER COLLEGE, NEAI. Main/Corp Daniel Webster College. VFOAT Daniel Webster College/NEAI Alumni Directory. (1992)-. Directory. English. Bernard C. Harris Publishing Company, 3 Barker Avenue, White Plains NY 10601. Tel (914)946-7500.

LC LD1662.3 .D5a
DD 378.748/43
ISSN 1071-6777 US
ALUMNI DIRECTORY / DICKINSON COLLEGE. [Alumni dir. - Dickinson Coll.]. Main/Corp Dickinson College. (199?)-. Directory. English. Bernard C. Harris Publishing Company, 3 Barker Avenue, White Plains NY 10601. Tel (914)946-7500. Continues Dickinson College. Directory of Alumni, 0738-1999.

LC WMLC 91/3441 US
ALUMNI DIRECTORY / DUKE, THE FUQUA SCHOOL OF BUSINESS. Main/Corp Fuqua School of Business (Duke University). VFOAT Fuqua School of Business Alumni Directory. (1991)-. Directory. English. Bernard C. Harris Publishing Company, 3 Barker Avenue, White Plains NY 10601. Tel (914)946-7500.

LC LD1751.E371A E45A
DD 378.755/725
ISSN 0738-3738 US
ALUMNI DIRECTORY / EMORY & HENRY COLLEGE. Main/Corp Emory and Henry College. VFOAT Emory and Henry College Alumni Directory; Emory & Henry College Alumni Directory. Directory. English. Bernard C. Harris Publishing Company, 3 Barker Avenue, White Plains NY 10601. Tel (914)946-7500.

LC WMLC 91/5401 US
ALUMNI DIRECTORY / FERRIS STATE UNIVERSITY, COLLEGE OF ALLIED HEALTH SCIENCES. Main/Corp Ferris State University. College of Allied Health Sciences. VFOAT Ferris State University, College of Allied Health Sciences Alumni Directory ... (1992)-. Directory. English. Bernard C. Harris Publishing Company, 3 Barker Avenue, White Plains NY 10601. Tel (914)946-7500.

LC LD1771.F81 F57A
DD 378.759/67 US
ALUMNI DIRECTORY - FLORIDA SOUTHERN COLLEGE. Main/Corp Florida Southern College. VFOAT Florida Southern College Alumni Directory. 1981-. Directory. English. College & University Press / Alabama, One Bell Road, PO Box 17940, Montgomery AL 36117.

LC LD2001.G43 A2
DD 378.754/27
ISSN 0732-040X US
ALUMNI DIRECTORY / GLENVILLE STATE COLLEGE. Main/Corp Glenville State College. VFOAT Glenville State College Alumni Directory. (19??)-. Directory. English. College & University Press / Alabama, One Bell Road, PO Box 17940, Montgomery AL 36117.

LC WMLC 91/4798 US
ALUMNI DIRECTORY / GOLDEN GATE BAPTIST THEOLOGICAL SEMINARY. Main/Corp Golden Gate Baptist Theological Seminary. VFOAT Golden Gate Baptist Theological Seminary Alumni Directory. (1992)-. Directory. English. Bernard C. Harris Publishing Company, 3 Barker Avenue, White Plains NY 10601. Tel (914)946-7500.

LC LD2072.3 .G76A
DD 378.748/95
ISSN 0743-4405 US
ALUMNI DIRECTORY / GROVE CITY COLLEGE. Main/Corp Grove City College. VFOAT Grove City College Alumni Directory. Directory. English. Bernard C. Harris Publishing Company, 3 Barker Avenue, White Plains NY 10601. Tel (914)946-7500.

LC LD7501.L97 A2
DD 373.771/31 US
ALUMNI DIRECTORY / HAWKEN SCHOOL. Main/Corp Hawken School (Lyndhurst, Ohio). VFOAT Hawken School Alumni Directory. Directory. English. College & University Press / Alabama, One Bell Road, PO Box 17940, Montgomery AL 36117.

LC WMLC 91/1288 US
ALUMNI DIRECTORY / HOLMES COMMUNITY COLLEGE. Main/Corp Holmes Community College. VFOAT Holmes Community College Alumni Directory. (1991)-. Directory. English. Bernard C. Harris Publishing Company, 3 Barker Avenue, White Plains NY 10601. Tel (914)946-7500.

LC WMLC 91/1460 US
ALUMNI DIRECTORY / INTERLOCHEN CENTER FOR THE ARTS. Main/Corp Interlochen Center for the Arts. VFOAT Interlochen Center for the Arts Alumni Directory. (1991)-. Directory. English. Bernard C. Harris Publishing Company, 3 Barker Avenue, White Plains NY 10601. Tel (914)946-7500.

LC LD2645 .A27
DD 378.756/76
ISSN 0738-2006 US
ALUMNI DIRECTORY / JOHNSON C. SMITH UNIVERSITY. Main/Corp Johnson C. Smith University. VFOAT Johnson C. Smith University Alumni Directory. 1983-. Directory. English. Bernard C. Harris Publishing Company, 3 Barker Avenue, White Plains NY 10601. Tel (914)946-7500.

LC LD7501.W75 A2
DD 373.746/2
ISSN 0738-5897 US
ALUMNI DIRECTORY - LOOMIS CHAFFEE SCHOOL. (ALUMNI DIRECTORY.). Main/Corp Loomis Chaffee School. VFOAT Loomis Chaffee School Alumni Directory. Directory. English. Bernard C. Harris Publishing Company, 3 Barker Avenue, White Plains NY 10601. Tel (914)946-7500.

LC WMLC 91/5128 US
ALUMNI DIRECTORY / LUTHERAN SCHOOL OF THEOLOGY AT CHICAGO. Main/Corp Lutheran School of Theology at Chicago. VFOAT Lutheran School of Theology at Chicago Alumni Directory. (1992)-. Directory. English. Bernard C. Harris Publishing Company, 3 Barker Avenue, White Plains NY 10601. Tel (914)946-7500.

LC LD3231.M631 M37A
DD 378.754/42 US
ALUMNI DIRECTORY / MARSHALL UNIVERSITY. Main/Corp Marshall University. VFOAT Marshall University Alumni Directory. Directory. English. College & University Press / Alabama, One Bell Road, PO Box 17940, Montgomery AL 36117.

LC WMLC 91/5524 US
ALUMNI DIRECTORY / MERCY COLLEGE. Main/Corp Mercy College. VFOAT Mercy College Alumni Directory. (1992)-. Directory. English. Bernard C. Harris Publishing Company, 3 Barker Avenue, White Plains NY 10601. Tel (914)946-7500.

College and School Publications —Alumni

LC S537.M716 M53a
DD 630/.7/1177427
ISSN 0739-6147
US
ALUMNI DIRECTORY / MICHIGAN STATE UNIVERSITY, COLLEGE OF AGRICULTURE AND NATURAL RESOURCES. Main/Corp Michigan State University. College of Agriculture and Natural Resources. (1983)-. Directory. English. Michigan State University / College of Agriculture and Natural Resources, Alumni Association, Agriculture Hall, East Lansing MI 48824.

LC WMLC 90/0630
US
ALUMNI DIRECTORY / MINNEAPOLIS COLLEGE OF ART AND DESIGN. Main/Corp Minneapolis College of Art and Design. (1990)-. Directory. English. Bernard C. Harris Publishing Company, 3 Barker Avenue, White Plains NY 10601. **Tel** (914)946-7500.

LC WMLC 91/5452
US
ALUMNI DIRECTORY / MONTANA STATE UNIVERSITY. Main/Corp Montana State University. **VFOAT** Montana State University Alumni Directory. (1992)-. Directory. English. Bernard C. Harris Publishing Company, 3 Barker Avenue, White Plains NY 10601. **Tel** (914)946-7500.

LC WMLC 91/4406
US
ALUMNI DIRECTORY / NEW MEXICO HIGHLANDS UNIVERSITY. Main/Corp New Mexico Highlands University. **VFOAT** New Mexico Highlands University ... Alumni Directory. (1991)-. Directory. English. Bernard C. Harris Publishing Company, 3 Barker Avenue, White Plains NY 10601. **Tel** (914)946-7500.

LC U430.N5 A2A
DD 378.789/43
ISSN 0738-8160
US
ALUMNI DIRECTORY / NEW MEXICO MILITARY INSTITUTE. Main/Corp New Mexico Military Institute. **VFOAT** Directory of Alumni; New Mexico Military Institute Alumni Directory. 1981-. Directory. English. Bernard C. Harris Publishing Company, 3 Barker Avenue, White Plains NY 10601. **Tel** (914)946-7500.

LC U430.N7 A2
DD 355/.007/1173
ISSN 8755-6952
US
ALUMNI DIRECTORY / NEW YORK MILITARY ACADEMY. Main/Corp New York Military Academy. **VFOAT** New York Military Academy Alumni Directory. (19??)-. English. Bernard C. Harris Publishing Company, 3 Barker Avenue, White Plains NY 10601. **Tel** (914)946-7500.

LC LD3914 .A3A
DD 373.747/97
ISSN 0732-0388
US
ALUMNI DIRECTORY - NICHOLS SCHOOL (BUFFALO, N.Y.). (ALUMNI DIRECTORY / NICHOLS SCHOOL.). **Main/Corp** Nichols School (Buffalo, N.Y.). **VFOAT** Nichols School Alumni Directory. Directory. English. College & University Press / Alabama, One Bell Road, PO Box 17940, Montgomery AL 36117.

LC WMLC 91/4638
US
ALUMNI DIRECTORY / NORTHWEST COLLEGE. Main/Corp Northwest College. **VFOAT** Northwest College Alumni Directory. (1991)-. Directory. English. Bernard C. Harris Publishing Company, 3 Barker Avenue, White Plains NY 10601. **Tel** (914)946-7500.

LC WMLC 91/1346
US
ALUMNI DIRECTORY / NORTHWESTERN. Main/Corp Northwestern State University of Louisiana. **VFOAT** Northwestern Alumni Directory; Northwestern State University Alumni Directory. (1991)-. Directory. English. Bernard C. Harris Publishing Company, 3 Barker Avenue, White Plains NY 10601. **Tel** (914)946-7500.

LC WMLC 91/264
CN
ALUMNI DIRECTORY / NOVA SCOTIA AGRICULTURAL COLLEGE. Main/Corp Nova Scotia Agricultural College. **VFOAT** Nova Scotia Agricultural College Alumni Directory. (1991)-. Directory. English. Bernard C. Harris Publishing Company, 3 Barker Avenue, White Plains NY 10601. **Tel** (914)946-7500.

LC WMLC 91/1689
US
ALUMNI DIRECTORY / PENNSTATE COLLEGE OF EARTH AND MINERAL SCIENCES. Main/Corp Pennsylvania State University. College of Earth and Mineral Sciences. **VFOAT** Alumni Directory ... Penn State, College of Earth and Mineral Sciences; Alumni Directory ... PennState, College of Earth and Mineral Sciences. (1991)-. Directory. English. Bernard C. Harris Publishing Company, 3 Barker Avenue, White Plains NY 10601. **Tel** (914)946-7500.

LC HB848 .P632B
DD 304.6/06
US
ALUMNI DIRECTORY - POPULATION COUNCIL. Main/Corp Population Council (New York, N.Y.). Directory. English. Four times a year. The Population Council, One Dag Hammarskjold Plaza, New York NY 10017. **Tel** (212)644-1614, (212)339-0500, FAX (212)755-6052, telex 9102900660 POPCO.

LC WMLC 91/1477
US
ALUMNI DIRECTORY / SAINT LEO COLLEGE. Main/Corp Saint Leo College (St. Leo, Fla.). **VFOAT** Centennial Alumni Directory; Saint Leo College Centennial Alumni Directory. (1991)-. Directory. English. Bernard C. Harris Publishing Company, 3 Barker Avenue, White Plains NY 10601. **Tel** (914)946-7500.

LC LD4819.S43 A2
DD 373.746/7
US
ALUMNI DIRECTORY / SAINT MARGARET'S-MCTERNAN. Main/Corp Saint Margaret's-McTernan (School). **VFOAT** Saint Margaret's-McTernan Alumni Directory. Directory. English. College & University Press / Alabama, One Bell Road, PO Box 17940, Montgomery AL 36117.

LC WMLC 91/3885
US
ALUMNI DIRECTORY / SCHOOL OF MUSIC, UNIVERSITY OF SOUTHERN CALIFORNIA. Main/Corp University of Southern California. School of Music. (1991)-. Directory. English. Bernard C. Harris Publishing Company, 3 Barker Avenue, White Plains NY 10601. **Tel** (914)946-7500.

LC LD4931.S37 A25A
DD 378.756/55
ISSN 0740-9362
US
ALUMNI DIRECTORY / SHAW UNIVERSITY. Main/Corp Shaw University. **VFOAT** Shaw University Alumni Directory. 1982-. Directory. English. College & University Press / Alabama, One Bell Road, PO Box 17940, Montgomery AL 36117.

LC LD4933 .A25
DD 378.747/42
ISSN 0738-8179
US
ALUMNI DIRECTORY / SIENA COLLEGE. Main/Corp Siena College. 1982-. Directory. English. Bernard C. Harris Publishing Company, 3 Barker Avenue, White Plains NY 10601. **Tel** (914)946-7500.

LC LD5101 .S3651a
DD 378.764/2812
ISSN 0738-1174
US
ALUMNI DIRECTORY / SOUTHERN METHODIST UNIVERSITY. Main/Corp Southern Methodist University. **VFOAT** S.M.U. Alumni Directory; SMU Alumni Directory. (1978)-. English. Irregular. Bernard C. Harris Publishing Company, 3 Barker Avenue, White Plains NY 10601. **Tel** (914)946-7500. **Continues** Southern Methodist University. SMU Alumni Directory.

LC LD5171.S48 A24
DD 378.744/26
US
ALUMNI DIRECTORY - SPRINGFIELD COLLEGE. Main/Corp Springfield College. Directory. English. College & University Press / Alabama, One Bell Road, PO Box 17940, Montgomery AL 36117.

LC WMLC 91/5277
ISSN 1065-5166
US
ALUMNI DIRECTORY / STOCKTON STATE COLLEGE. Main/Corp Stockton State College. **VFOAT** Stockton State College Alumni Directory. (1992)-. Directory. English. Bernard C. Harris Publishing Company, 3 Barker Avenue, White Plains NY 10601. **Tel** (914)946-7500.

LC WMLC L 90/0005
US
ALUMNI DIRECTORY / TEIKYO WESTMAR UNIVERSITY. Main/Corp Teikyo Westmar University. **VFOAT** Teikyo Westmar University Alumni Directory. (1990)-. Directory. English. Bernard C. Harris Publishing Company, 3 Barker Avenue, White Plains NY 10601. **Tel** (914)946-7500.

LC LD5308 .A22
DD 378.764/472
ISSN 0738-2219
US
ALUMNI DIRECTORY / TEXAS A & I UNIVERSITY. Main/Corp Texas A & I University. **VFOAT** Texas A and I University Alumni Directory; Texas A & I University Alumni Directory. Directory. English. College & University Press / Alabama, One Bell Road, PO Box 17940, Montgomery AL 36117.

LC LD5311 .T381A
DD 378.764/5315
ISSN 0147-4898
US
ALUMNI DIRECTORY - TEXAS CHRISTIAN UNIVERSITY, THE. Main/Corp Texas Christian University. Directory. English. Texas Christian University / Alumni, Office of Alumni, Fort Worth TX 76129.

LC LD5675.3 .U54A
DD 378.755/481
ISSN 0738-0852
US
ALUMNI DIRECTORY / THE ALUMNI ASSOCIATION OF THE UNIVERSITY OF VIRGINIA. Main/Corp University of Virginia. Alumni Association. **VFOAT** Alumni Association of the University of Virginia Alumni Directory. Directory. English. Bernard C. Harris Publishing Company, 3 Barker Avenue, White Plains NY 10601. **Tel** (914)946-7500.

LC WMLC 91/5575
US
ALUMNI DIRECTORY / THE CALIFORNIA CULINARY ACADEMY. Main/Corp California Culinary Academy. **VFOAT** California Culinary Academy Alumni Directory. (1992)-. Directory. English. Bernard C. Harris Publishing Company, 3 Barker Avenue, White Plains NY 10601. **Tel** (914)946-7500.

LC WMLC 91/5105
US
ALUMNI DIRECTORY / THE STATE UNIVERSITY OF NEW YORK COLLEGE AT BROCKPORT. Main/Corp State University of New York College at Brockport. **VFOAT** State University of New York College at Brockport Alumni Directory; SUNY College at Brockport Alumni Directory. (1992)-. Directory. English. Bernard C. Harris Publishing Company, 3 Barker Avenue, White Plains NY 10601. **Tel** (914)946-7500.

LC KF292.C45 A832
DD 340/.07/1177311
ISSN 0162-0371
US
ALUMNI DIRECTORY - THE UNIVERSITY OF CHICAGO LAW SCHOOL. Main/Corp University of Chicago. Law School. (19??)-. Directory. English. Irregular (every five years). $15.00. University of Chicago Legal Forum, 1111 East 60th Street, 4th Floor, Chicago IL 60637. **Tel** (312)702-9593. ctrl circ.
Desc: Directory of alumni of University of Chicago Law School.

LC WMLC 91/1692
US
ALUMNI DIRECTORY / THE UNIVERSITY OF HEALTH SCIENCES, COLLEGE OF OSTEOPATHIC MEDICINE. Main/Corp University of Health Sciences. College of Osteopathic Medicine. **VFOAT** University of Health Sciences, College of Osteopathic Medicine Alumni Directory. (1991)-. Directory. English. Bernard C. Harris Publishing Company, 3 Barker Avenue, White Plains NY 10601. **Tel** (914)946-7500.

LC WMLC 91/4142
US
ALUMNI DIRECTORY / THE UNIVERSITY OF MICHIGAN, SCHOOL OF INFORMATION AND LIBRARY STUDIES. Main/Corp University of Michigan. School of Information and Library Studies. **VFOAT** University of Michigan, School of Information and Library Studies Alumni Directory. (1991)-. Directory. English. Bernard C. Harris Publishing Company, 3 Barker Avenue, White Plains NY 10601. **Tel** (914)946-7500.

LC WMLC L 83/8092
US
ALUMNI DIRECTORY / THE UNIVERSITY OF NORTH CAROLINA AT CHARLOTTE. Main/Corp University of North Carolina at Charlotte. **VFOAT** University of North Carolina at Charlotte Alumni Directory. 1988-. Directory. English. Bernard C. Harris Publishing Company, 3 Barker Avenue, White Plains NY 10601. **Tel** (914)946-7500.

LC WMLC 91/2923
US
ALUMNI DIRECTORY / THOMAS COLLEGE, WATERVILLE, MAINE. Main/Corp Thomas College (Waterville, Maine). **VFOAT** Thomas College ... Alumni Directory. (1991)-. Directory. English. Bernard C. Harris Publishing Company, 3 Barker Avenue, White Plains NY 10601. **Tel** (914)946-7500.

LC LD5361.T31 T74A
DD 378.772/78
US
ALUMNI DIRECTORY / TRI-STATE UNIVERSITY. Main/Corp Tri-State University (U.S.). **VFOAT** Tri-State University Alumni Directory. Directory. English. College & University Press / Alabama, One Bell Road, PO Box 17940, Montgomery AL 36117.

College and School Publications —Alumni

LC LD5361.T41a T74a   **ISSN** 0740-1671
DD 378.746/3   US
ALUMNI DIRECTORY - TRINITY COLLEGE (HARTFORD, CONN.). (ALUMNI DIRECTORY / TRINITY COLLEGE.). **Main/Corp** Trinity College (Hartford, Conn.). **VFOAT** Trinity College Alumni Directory. (19??)-. English. Irregular. Trinity College, 300 Summit Street, Hartford CT 06106. **Tel** (203)527-3151. **ED** Gerald J. Hansen.

LC LD781.D3 A15   **ISSN** 0742-4345
DD 378.794/51   US
ALUMNI DIRECTORY / UNIVERSITY OF CALIFORNIA, DAVIS. **Main/Corp** University of California, Davis. **VFOAT** University of California Davis, Alumni Directory. Directory. English. Bernard C. Harris Publishing Company, 3 Barker Avenue, White Plains NY 10601. **Tel** (914)946-7500.

LC HD30.42.U5 U54A   **ISSN** 0738-1182
DD 658/.007/1179494   US
ALUMNI DIRECTORY - UNIVERSITY OF CALIFORNIA, LOS ANGELES. GRADUATE SCHOOL OF MANAGEMENT. (ALUMNI DIRECTORY / UCLA GRADUATE SCHOOL OF MANAGEMENT.). **Main/Corp** University of California, Los Angeles. Graduate School of Management. **VFOAT** U.C.L.A. G.S.M. Alumni Directory; UCLA GSM Alumni Directory. Directory. English. Bernard C. Harris Publishing Company, 3 Barker Avenue, White Plains NY 10601. **Tel** (914)946-7500.

LC HF1134.U54 U54A
DD 650/.07/1178863   US
ALUMNI DIRECTORY / UNIVERSITY OF COLORADO, BOULDER, COLLEGE OF BUSINESS AND ADMINISTRATION. **Main/Corp** University of Colorado, Boulder. College of Business and Administration. **VFOAT** University of Colorado, Boulder College of Business and Administration Alumni Directory. Directory. English. Bernard C. Harris Publishing Company, 3 Barker Avenue, White Plains NY 10601. **Tel** (914)946-7500.

LC LD1562.3 .U54A   **ISSN** 0738-3630
DD 378.788/83   US
ALUMNI DIRECTORY / UNIVERSITY OF DENVER. **Main/Corp** University of Denver. Directory. English. Bernard C. Harris Publishing Company, 3 Barker Avenue, White Plains NY 10601. **Tel** (914)946-7500.

LC LD1761.E61A U54A   **ISSN** 0738-078X
DD 378.772/33   US
ALUMNI DIRECTORY / UNIVERSITY OF EVANSVILLE. **Main/Corp** University of Evansville. **VFOAT** University of Evansville Alumni Directory. (19??)-. Directory. English. Bernard C. Harris Publishing Company, 3 Barker Avenue, White Plains NY 10601. **Tel** (914)946-7500.

DD 378.713/43   **ISSN** 1182-9877
   CN
ALUMNI DIRECTORY / UNIVERSITY OF GUELPH. [Alumni dir. - Univ. Guelph]. **Main/Corp** University of Guelph. **Added/Corp** University of Guelph. Alumni Association. University of Guelph. Alumni Affairs and Community Relations. **VFOAT** University of Guelph Alumni Directory. 1st Ed. (1990)-. English. Every 3 years. $35.00. University of Guelph Alumni House, Guelph Ontario N1G 2W1 Canada.

LC R747 .M7774   **ISSN** 0739-6899
DD 610/.7/11776579   US
ALUMNI DIRECTORY / UNIVERSITY OF MINNESOTA MEDICAL SCHOOL. **Main/Corp** University of Minnesota. Medical School. **VFOAT** University of Minnesota Medical School Alumni Directory. (19??)-. English. College & University Press / Alabama, One Bell Road, PO Box 17940, Montgomery AL 36117.

LC WMLC 90/0662
   US
ALUMNI DIRECTORY / UNIVERSITY OF NEBRASKA-LINCOLN ALUMNI ASSOCIATION. **Main/Corp** University of Nebraska--Lincoln Alumni Association. **Added/Corp** University of Nebraska--Lincoln. **VFOAT** University of Nebraska--Lincoln Alumni Directory. (1990)-. Directory. English.

LC LD3942.3 .U53A   **ISSN** 0146-7433
DD 378.756/565   US
ALUMNI DIRECTORY - UNIVERSITY OF NORTH CAROLINA AT CHAPEL HILL. (ALUMNI DIRECTORY - THE ALUMNI OFFICE OF THE GENERAL ALUMNI ASSOCIATION.). **Main/Corp** University of North Carolina at Chapel Hill. General Alumni Association. Alumni Office. Directory. English. University of North Carolina at Chapel Hill Alumni Office, Chapel Hill NC 27514.

LC LD4701.R6641A U54A   **ISSN** 0739-1366
DD 378.794/95   US
ALUMNI DIRECTORY / UNIVERSITY OF REDLANDS. **Main/Corp** University of Redlands. **VFOAT** University of Redlands Alumni Directory. Directory. English. Bernard C. Harris Publishing Company, 3 Barker Avenue, White Plains NY 10601. **Tel** (914)946-7500.

LC R747.U6838 U54a   **ISSN** 0736-6671
DD 610/.7/1174789   US
ALUMNI DIRECTORY - UNIVERSITY OF ROCHESTER. SCHOOL OF MEDICINE AND DENTISTRY. (ALUMNI DIRECTORY / UNIVERSITY OF ROCHESTER, SCHOOL OF MEDICINE & DENTISTRY.). **Main/Corp** University of Rochester. School of Medicine and Dentistry. **Added/Corp** College & University Press. **VFOAT** University of Rochester School of Medicine & Dentistry Alumni Directory. (19??)-. Directory. English. College & University Press / Alabama, One Bell Road, PO Box 17940, Montgomery AL 36117.

DD 378.713/541   **ISSN** 0225-2333
   CN
ALUMNI DIRECTORY - UNIVERSITY OF TORONTO. [Alumni dir. - Univ. Toronto]. **Main/Corp** University of Toronto. 1979/80-. Directory. English. Department of Alumni Affairs, Alumni House, 14 Willcocks Street, University of Toronto, Toronto Ontario M5S 1A1 Canada. **Continues** Directory, Alumni Officers, Varsity Fund Board, University of Toronto, 0381-999X.

LC WMLC 91/4396
   US
ALUMNI DIRECTORY / UNIVERSITY OF TORONTO, UNITED STATES ALUMNI. **Main/Corp** University of Toronto. United States Alumni. **VFOAT** University of Toronto United States Alumni Alumni Directory. (1991)-. Directory. English. Bernard C. Harris Publishing Company, 3 Barker Avenue, White Plains NY 10601. **Tel** (914)946-7500.

LC WMLC 91/1461
   CN
ALUMNI DIRECTORY / UNIVERSITY OF WESTERN ONTARIO. **Main/Corp** University of Western Ontario. **VFOAT** University of Western Ontario Alumni Directory. (1991)-. Directory. English. Bernard C. Harris Publishing Company, 3 Barker Avenue, White Plains NY 10601. **Tel** (914)946-7500.

LC LD7251.B7868 A2A   **ISSN** 0738-5250
DD 378.755/725   US
ALUMNI DIRECTORY / VIRGINIA INTERMONT COLLEGE. **Main/Corp** Virginia Intermont College. **VFOAT** Virginia Intermont College Alumni Directory. (19??)-. Directory. English. Bernard C. Harris Publishing Company, 3 Barker Avenue, White Plains NY 10601. **Tel** (914)946-7500.

LC LC2851.V7 A15   **ISSN** 0740-1795
DD 378.755/451   US
ALUMNI DIRECTORY - VIRGINIA UNION UNIVERSITY (RICHMOND, VA.). (ALUMNI DIRECTORY / VIRGINIA UNION UNIVERSITY.). **Main/Corp** Virginia Union University (Richmond, VA.). **VFOAT** Virginia Union University Alumni Directory. 1983-. Directory. English. Virginia Union University, 1500 North Lombardy Street, Richmond VA 23220.

LC LD5901.W49 A38A   **ISSN** 0732-0450
DD 378.754/14   US
ALUMNI DIRECTORY / WEST LIBRARY STATE COLLEGE. **Main/Corp** West Liberty State College. **VFOAT** West Liberty State College Alumni Directory. 1981-. Directory. English. College & University Press / Alabama, One Bell Road, PO Box 17940, Montgomery AL 36117.

LC WMLC 91/5521
   US
ALUMNI DIRECTORY / WESTCHESTER COMMUNITY COLLEGE. **Main/Corp** Westchester Community College. **VFOAT** Westchester Community College ... Alumni Directory. (1992)-. Directory. English. Bernard C. Harris Publishing Company, 3 Barker Avenue, White Plains NY 10601. **Tel** (914)946-7500.

LC WMLC 91/3292
   US
ALUMNI DIRECTORY / WESTFIELD STATE COLLEGE. **Main/Corp** Westfield State College. **VFOAT** Westfield State College Alumni Directory. (1991)-. Directory. English. Bernard C. Harris Publishing Company, 3 Barker Avenue, White Plains NY 10601. **Tel** (914)946-7500.

LC WMLC L 83/5920
   US
ALUMNI DIRECTORY / WHEELOCK COLLEGE. **Main/Corp** Wheelock College. **VFOAT** Centennial Alumni Directory; Wheelock College Centennial Alumni Directory. 1988/89-. Directory. English. Bernard C. Harris Publishing Company, 3 Barker Avenue, White Plains NY 10601. **Tel** (914)946-7500.

LC WMLC 91/4815
   US
ALUMNI DIRECTORY / WILLIAM E. SIMON GRADUATE SCHOOL OF BUSINESS ADMINISTRATION, UNIVERSITY OF ROCHESTER. **Main/Corp** William E. Simon Graduate School of Business Administration. **VFOAT** William E. Simon Graduate School of Business Administration Alumni Directory. (1992)-. Directory. English. Bernard C. Harris Publishing Company, 3 Barker Avenue, White Plains NY 10601. **Tel** (914)946-7500.

LC LD6072.3 .W54A   **ISSN** 0738-3517
DD 378.744/1   US
ALUMNI DIRECTORY / WILLIAMS COLLEGE. **Main/Corp** Williams College. Directory. English. Every 3 years. $9.00. Alumni Office / Williamstown, PO Box 38, Williamstown MA 01267.

LC S539.I5 M434
DD 630.72   IO
ALUMNI FAKULTAS PERTANIAN UNIVERSITAS SUMATERA UTARA. **Main/Corp** Medan, Indonesia. Universitas Sumatera Utara. Fakultas Pertanian. (1975)-. Indonesian. Fakultas Pertahian Usu, Jl Prof A Sofyan, Medan Indonesia.

   ISSN 0149-2608
   US
NLM W1 AL996V
ALUMNI MAGAZINE - ALUMNI ASSOCIATION OF THE JOHNS HOPKINS HOSPITAL SCHOOL OF NURSING, THE. See Medical Sciences-Nursing.

   ISSN 0898-4093
DD 610   US
NLM W1; AL996U
ALUMNI MAGAZINE / COLUMBIA UNIVERSITY-PRESBYTERIAN HOSPITAL SCHOOL OF NURSING ALUMNI ASSOCIATION, INC. [Alumni mag. - Columbia Univ.-Presbyt. Hosp. School Nurs. Alumni Assoc.]. **Added/Corp** Columbia University-Presbyterian Hospital School of Nursing Alumni Association. Vol. 80, No. 1 (Winter 1985)-. Periodical. English. Three times a year. Columbia University / Presbyterian Hospital Nursing Association, 179 Fort Washington, New York NY 10032. **Tel** (212)694-3193. **Continues** Alumnae Magazine (Columbia University-Presbyterian Hospital School of Nursing Alumnae Association), 0069-634X. **Ind/Abst** Int. Nurs. Index (Winter 1985-).

LC LH1.W5 W47
DD 378.754/53   US
ALUMNI MAGAZINE (MORGANTOWN, W. VA.). (ALUMNI MAGAZINE / WEST VIRGINIA UNIVERSITY.). **VFOAT** West Virginia University Alumni Magazine. (Summer 1979)-. Periodical. English. Three times a year. Free. Editors West Virginia University Alumni Magazine, Office of Communications Services, 102 Communications Building, Morgantown WV 26506. **Tel** (304)293-6368. **ED** John Luchok. **Bk Rev**. **Ad Acc**. **Circ:** 100,000 (ctrl). **Continues** West Virginia University Alumni Quarterly, 0163-366X.
Desc: Contains news of alumni of West Virginia University with feature stories such as; campus highlights, WVU Foundation News, book reviews, and news.

   US
ALUMNI NEWSLETTER / UNIVERSITY OF CALIFORNIA, LOS ANGELES, DEPARTMENT OF EARTH & SPACE SCIENCES. See Earth Sciences.

   US
ALUMNI UPDATE : PHILADELPHIA COLLEGE OF TEXTILES AND SCIENCE. (19??)-. English. Four times a year. Free. Philadelphia College of Textiles & Science, School House Lane and Henry Avenue, Philadelphia PA 19144-5497. **Tel** (215)951-2700, FAX (215)951-2615. **ED** Guy R Solomon Jr. **Circ:** 9,000 (ctrl).
Desc: Alumni newsletter.

   ISSN 0226-5389
DD 378.713/84   CN
ALUMNINEWS - CARLETON UNIVERSITY. (ALUMNINEWS.). [Alumninews - Carleton Univ.]. **VFOAT** Alumni News. **VAT** Alumni News - Carleton University. Vol. 1 (Apr. 1980)-. Periodical. English. Three times a year. Free. Carleton University / Alumni News, Room 510/Administration Building, Ottawa Ontario K1S 5B6 Canada. **Tel** (613)788-3636, FAX (613)788-4447, telex 0534232. **ED** Richard Austen. Index available. **Bk Rev**. **Ad Acc**. **Circ:** 40,000 (ctrl).
Supersedes Carleton Alumni News, 0319-6895.

College and School Publications —Alumni

Desc: To advance the excellence and prestige of Carleton University as a distinguished institution of higher learning in Canada.

ISSN 1055-5196
US
AMES HIGH ALUMNI NEWSLETTER.
(1990)-. Newsletter. English. Ames High Alumni Newsletter, 20th & Ridgewood, Ames IA 50010.

ISSN 0279-5183
US
ARIZONA STATESMAN OUTLOOK.
Added/Corp Arizona State University. Alumni Association. (19??)-. Periodical. English. Four times a year. Arizona State University Alumni Association, Alumni Center, Arizona State University, Tempe AZ 85287. **Continues** Arizona Statesman, 0195-2927.

DD 355
ISSN 1041-2581
US
ASSEMBLY (WEST POINT, N.Y.).
(ASSEMBLY / ASSOCIATION OF GRADUATES, U.S.M.A.). [Assembly]. **Main/Corp** United States Military Academy. Association of Graduates. Vol. 1, No. 1 (Apr. 1942)-. Periodical. English. Six times a year (Jan., Mar., May, June, Sept., Nov.). $35.00. Association of Graduates, United States Military Academy, West Point NY 10996. **Tel** (914)446-5800, FAX (914)446-6988. **Continues in part** Annual Report.

LC LH1.B35 A6
DD 378.769
ISSN 0005-8874
US
BEREA ALUMNUS, THE.
Added/Corp Berea College. Alumni Association. Vol. 1 (Apr. 1931)-. Periodical. English. Four times a year. $10.00. Berea College Appalachian Center, CPO 2336, Berea College, Berea KY 40404. **Tel** (606)986-9341. **ED** Claude Hammond. **Circ:** 30,000 (ctrl). available with illustrations.
Desc: Primary focus is feature articles on individual alumni, academic departments, college programs or special events. Secondary goals include section of brief discussion of alumni/college activities and class notes.

LC LD7501.M9275 A2
DD 378.758/35
ISSN 0741-9112
US
BERRY ALUMNI DIRECTORY.
(BERRY ALUMNI DIRECTORY / BERRY ALUMNI ASSOCIATION.). **Main/Corp** Berry Alumni Association. (1983)-. Directory. English. Bernard C. Harris Publishing Company, 3 Barker Avenue, White Plains NY 10601. **Tel** (914)946-7500.

LC LD451.B564
DD 378.794/93
US
BIOLA COLLEGE ALUMNI DIRECTORY.
Main/Corp Biola College. 1979-. Directory. English. Biola College, 13800 Biola Avenue, La Mirada CA 90639.

DD 305
ISSN 1040-7758
US
BLACK ALUMNI NETWORK NEWSLETTER.
[Black alumni netw. newsl.]. **VFOAT** Black Alumni Network. (198?)-. Newsletter. English. Twelve times a year. $20.00. Black Alumni Network Newsletter, 5 Hopewell Lane, Sicklerville NJ 08081. **Tel** (609)728-4062, (609)728-4001. **Continues** Letter (Columbia, MO.).
Desc: Offers career advice, journalism education, and media industry coverage.

LC PS501 .B76
DD 810/.8/0974723
ISSN 0883-2846
US
BROOKLYN LITERARY REVIEW. See
Literary and Political Reviews.

LC V437 .A32
DD 359.9/7/07117456
ISSN 0191-9814
US
BULLETIN - U.S. COAST GUARD ACADEMY ALUMNI ASSOCIATION.
Main/Corp United States. Coast Guard Academy, New London, Conn. Alumni Association. **VAT** Bulletin - United States Coast Guard Academy Alumni Association. Bulletin. English. Six times a year (plus October directory). $24.00 (regular alumni members), $18.00 (associate members) US. US Coast Guard Academy Alumni Association, United States Coast Guard Academy, New London CT 06320-4195. **Tel** (203)444-8320. **ED** James R Kelly. **Bk Rev. Ad Ac.:** **Circ:** 6,400 (ctrl). **Continues** Alumni Bulletin, 0094-744X.
Desc: Serves as a forum for the publication of professional material/discussion of matters pertaining to the entire spectrum of coast guard interests and activities.

LC LD2147 1913B
DD 378.744/4
ISSN 0092-122X
US
CLASS DIRECTORY - HARVARD. 1913.
(CLASS DIRECTORY.). **Main/Corp** Harvard University. Class of 1913. Directory. English. Harvard University Class of 1913, 79 Garden Street, Cambridge MA 02138.

DD 207/.71274
ISSN 0823-2725
CN
CMBC ALUMNI BULLETIN.
[CMBC alumni bull.]. **Added/Corp** Canadian Mennonite Bible College. Alumni Association. **VAT** Canadian Mennonite Bible College Alumni Bulletin (1978). Vol. 17, No. 1 (March 1978)-. Bulletin. English. Four times a year. Canadian Mennonite Bible College Alumni Association, 600 Shaftesbury Boulevard, Winnipeg Manitoba R3P 0M4 Canada. **Tel** (204)888-6781. **ED** Werner Kliewer. **Circ:** 1,000. **Continues** Canadian Mennonite Bible College. Alumni Bulletin, 0823-2733.

ISSN 0279-1862
US
COASTLINES (SANTA BARBARA, CALIF.).
(COASTLINES / UNIVERSITY OF CALIFORNIA, SANTA BARBARA.). **Added/Corp** University of California, Santa Barbara. Office of Alumni Affairs. Vol. 11, No. 6 (May/June 1981)-. Periodical. English. Six times a year. $20.00. League for Coastal Protection, PO Box 190812, San Francisco CA 94119. **Tel** (415)777-0220. **Continues** Alumnus.

LC WMLC 90/0643
DD 630
US
COLLEGE OF AGRICULTURE ALUMNI DIRECTORY.
Main/Corp University of Kentucky. College of Agriculture. **VFOAT** University of Kentucky, College of Agriculture Alumni Directory. (1990)-. Directory. English. Bernard C. Harris Publishing Company, 3 Barker Avenue, White Plains NY 10601. **Tel** (914)946-7500.

LC Q183.3.P43 P4613
DD 507/.11748/53
ISSN 0740-462X
US
COLLEGE OF SCIENCE ALUMNI DIRECTORY, THE PENNSYLVANIA STATE UNIVERSITY.
Main/Corp Pennsylvania State University. College of Science. (19??)-. Directory. English. Pennsylvania State Alumni Association, 105 Old Main, University Park PA 16802.

LC KF292.C6 A75
DD 340/.07/117471
US
COLUMBIA LAW ALUMNI BULLETIN (NEW YORK, N.Y. : 1980).
(COLUMBIA LAW ALUMNI BULLETIN.). **Added/Corp** Columbia Law School Alumni Association. Vol. 13, No. 4 (Fall 1980)-. Bulletin. English. Four times a year. Columbia University School of Law, 435 West 116th Street, New York NY 10027. **Tel** (212)854-4398, (212)854-3742. **Continues** Law Alumni Bulletin (Columbia Law School Alumni Association).

ISSN 1058-3467
US
TITLE CHANGE
CORNELL ALUMNI NEWS.
(THE CORNELL ALUMNI NEWS.). **Added/Corp** Cornell University. Cornell Alumni Federation. (1899)-(1993). Periodical. English. Cornell Alumni News, 626 Thurston Avenue, Ithaca NY 14853. **Tel** (607)255-4121, FAX (607)255-7533. **ED** Elsie McMillan and Mary Jaye Bruce. **Bk Rev. Ad Acc. Circ:** 35,000. English. **Continued by** Cornell Magazine (Ithaca, N.Y. : 1993), 1070-2733.
Desc: Covers news of Cornell University and its alumni.

LC LH1.C8 C583
DD 378.747/71
ISSN 1070-2733
US
●## CORNELL MAGAZINE.
Added/Corp Cornell Alumni Federation. (1993)-. Periodical. English. Twelve times a year. Cornell Alumni News, 626 Thurston Avenue, Ithaca NY 14853. **Tel** (607)255-4121, FAX (607)255-7533. **Continues** Cornell Alumni News, 1058-3467.
Desc: Covers news of Cornell University and its alumni.

US
DARTMOUTH ALUMNI MAGAZINE.
Vol. 1 (Oct. 1908)-. Periodical. English. Twelve times a year. $13.50. Dartmouth Alumni Magazine, 320 Blunt Alumni Center, Hanover NH 03755. **Tel** (603)646-2256. **ED** Douglas M Greenwood. Index Available, published separately, free-automatically sent. **Bk Rev. Ad Acc. Circ:** 43,000 (ctrl). **Continues** Dartmouth Bi-Monthly.
Desc: Reports news on the college and its alumni and provides a medium for the exchange of views concerning college affairs.

LC LD1522.3 .D46A
DD 378.771/54
US
DENISON UNIVERSITY ALUMNI DIRECTORY.
Main/Corp Denison University. Directory. English. Alumni Office / Granville, PO Box A, Granville OH 43023.

LC KF292.D47 A73
DD 340/.07/1177434
US
DETROIT COLLEGE OF LAW ALUMNI NEWS.
Main/Corp Detroit College of Law. **Added/Corp** Detroit College of Law. Alumni news. (19??)-. Periodical. English. Every 2 years. Detroit College of Law, 130 East Elizabeth Street, Detroit MI 48201. **Tel** (313)226-0100. **ED** Thomas E. Reynolds. **Bk Rev. Ad Acc. Circ:** 6,500 (ctrl).
Desc: Interpretation and analysis of current legal issues. Trends in education.

US
DIMENSIONS.
(19??)-. Periodical. English. Five times a year. Free. University of Dayton, Alumni Records, Dayton OH 45469. **Tel** (513)229-3241.

ISSN 0705-1875
CN
DD 634.9/07/11713541
DIRECTORY AND NEWSLETTER - FORESTRY ALUMNI ASSOCIATION, UNIVERSITY OF TORONTO.
Main/Corp University of Toronto. Forestry Alumni Association. (1962)-. Directory. English. Department of Alumni Affairs, Alumni House, 47 Willcocks Street, University of Toronto, Toronto Ontario M5S 1A1 Canada.

LC WMLC 93/3447
US
●## DIRECTORY / EASTERN KENTUCKY UNIVERSITY, NATIONAL ALUMNI ASSOCIATION.
Main/Corp Eastern Kentucky University. National Alumni Association. **VFOAT** Eastern Kentucky University Alumni Directory. (1993)-. Directory. English. Bernard C. Harris Publishing Company, 3 Barker Avenue, White Plains NY 10601. **Tel** (914)946-7500.
Continues Eastern Kentucky University. Eastern Kentucky University Alumni Directory.

LC L961.P4 N37A
DD 378.599/1
PH
DIRECTORY OF ALUMNI - NATIONAL SCHOLARSHIP CENTER (PHILIPPINES).
Main/Corp National Scholarship Center (Philippines). Directory. English. National Scholarship Center, Ministry of Education and Culture, Arroceros Street, Manila 2801 Philippines.

LC QE47.P42 P46A
DD 550/.7/1174853
ISSN 0739-1331
US
DIRECTORY OF ALUMNI / PENNSYLVANIA STATE UNIVERSITY, COLLEGE OF EARTH AND MINERAL SCIENCES.
Main/Corp Pennsylvania State University. College of Earth and Mineral Science. **VFOAT** Pennsylvania State University College of Earth and Mineral Sciences Directory of Alumni. 1980-. Directory. English. Bernard C. Harris Publishing Company, 3 Barker Avenue, White Plains NY 10601. **Tel** (914)946-7500.

ISSN 0736-637X
US
DIRECTORY OF CLUB OFFICERS.
Main/Corp Harvard Alumni Association. (19??)-. Directory. English. Harvard Alumni Association, Wadsworth House, Cambridge MA 02138. **Continues** Associated Harvard Alumni. Directory of Officers, 0736-8828.

LC V437 .A445
DD 359.9/7/07117465
US
DIRECTORY - U. S. COAST GUARD ACADEMY ALUMNI ASSOCIATION.
Main/Corp United States. Coast Guard Academy, New London, Conn. Alumni Association. (1978)-. Directory. English. One time a year. $24.00 (available to members only). US Coast Guard Academy Alumni Association, United States Coast Guard Academy, New London CT 06320-4195. **Tel** (203)444-8320. **ED** James R Kelly. **Ad Acc. Circ:** 5,800 (ctrl). **Continues** Annual Directory - U. S. Coast Guard Academy Alumni Association.
Desc: Listing of membership of the Coast Guard Academy Alumni Association.

ISSN 0162-5349
US
EMORY ALUMNUS, THE.
(19??)-. Periodical. English. Six times a year. $3.00. Office of Alumni Publications of Emory Publications, 709 Gatewood House, Atlanta GA 30322.

LC LD1871 .F71A
DD 378.757/27
ISSN 0148-2580
US
FURMAN UNIVERSITY ALUMNI DIRECTORY.
Main/Corp Furman University Association. 1976-. Directory. English. Furman University College & University Press, PO Box 28884, Greenville SC 29405.

US
GATEWAY.
(19??)-. English. Irregular. Golden Gate Baptist Theological Seminary, Mill Valley CA 94941.
Desc: An alumni newsletter for the Golden Gate Baptist Theological Seminary.
Ind/Abst South. Baptist Period. Index (1987-).

DD 378
ISSN 1074-8784
US
GEORGETOWN MAGAZINE (1993).
(GEORGETOWN MAGAZINE.). [Georget. mag.]. **Added/Corp** Georgetown University. Office of Alumni and University Relations. (19??)-. Periodical. English. Four times a year. Free (alumni). Georgetown Magazine, Georgetown University, Office of University Relations, Washington DC 20057. **Tel** (202)687-4317, FAX (202)687-1670. **ED** Nancy Freiberg Robertson. **Continues** Georgetown (Washington, D.C. : 1987), 0895-1624.
Desc: Alumni magazine of Georgetown University. Relates events and news at Georgetown.

College and School Publications —Alumni

ISSN 0016-8130
US
TITLE CHANGE
GEORGIA ALUMNI RECORD. Added/Corp Georgia Alumni Society. (1920)-(199?). Periodical. English. Alumni Society, University of Georgia, Athens GA 30601. Tel (706)542-2251. ED E Dianne Belch. **Ad Acc. Circ:** 18,000 (ctrl). *Continued by Georgia Magazine (Athens, Ga.), 1085-1402.*
Desc: Articles of interest to UGA alumni featuring graduates and campus departments and professors.

ISSN 1085-1402
US
GEORGIA MAGAZINE (ATHENS, GA.). (GEORGIA MAGAZINE.). Added/Corp University of Georgia. (199?)-. Periodical. English. Four times a year. Alumni Society, University of Georgia, Athens GA 30601. Tel (706)542-2251. *Continues Georgia Alumni Record, 0016-8130.*

ISSN 0276-1947
US
GRIFFIN (BUFFALO, N.Y.), THE. (THE GRIFFIN.). Added/Corp Canisius College. (19??)-. Periodical. English. Irregular. Canisius College, 2001 Main Street, Buffalo NY 14208. Tel (716)888-2822, (716)883-7000, FAX (716)888-2525.

LC LD2138 .H3 **ISSN 0895-1683**
DD 378 US
HARVARD ALUMNI DIRECTORY. (HARVARD ALUMNI DIRECTORY / COMPILED BY THE HARVARD ALUMNI DIRECTORY, AN OFFICE OF HARVARD UNIVERSITY.). [Harv. alumni dir.]. Added/Corp Harvard Alumni Directory (Office) Harvard Alumni Association. Harvard University. **VFOAT** 350th Anniversary Alumni Directory. (1919)-. Directory. English. Irregular (every 5 years). Harvard University Alumni Record Office, 1350 Massachusetts Avenue, Room 671, Cambridge MA 02138. Tel (617)495-2371. *Continues Harvard University Directory; Absorbed Quinquennial Catalog of the Officers and Graduates. Harvard University.*

LC R747 .H385 **ISSN 0191-7757**
DD 610 US
NLM W1 HA636
HARVARD MEDICAL ALUMNI BULLETIN. [Harv. med. alumni bull.]. Added/Corp Harvard Medical Alumni Association. **VFOAT** Harvard Medical Alumni/ae Bulletin. Vol. 6 (1931)-. Bulletin. English. Four times a year. Free on request. Harvard Medical School Alumni Association, 25 Shattuck Street, Boston MA 02115. Tel (617)732-1548. ED J. Gordon Scannell, Ellen Barlow. **Bk Rev. Ad Acc. Circ:** 15,000. *Continues Bulletin of the Harvard Medical Alumni Association, 1069-8345.*

ISSN 0017-8357
US
HATCHET. Periodical. English. Twenty-four times a year. Hatchet, George Washington University, 800 21st Street NW/Suite 434, Washington DC 20052.

US
IMVO = NEWS. See Education-Higher Education.

ISSN 0740-0071
US
INTERPRETE ALUMNOS, EL. Added/Corp Southern Baptist Convention. Sunday School Board. (19??)-. Periodical. Spanish. Four times a year. $5.75. Southern Baptist Convention, 901 Commerce, Suite 750, Nashville TN 37203. Tel (615)244-2355, FAX (615)742-8919. **(Subscription address:** Sunday School Board, Customer Service, 127 9th Avenue North, Nashville TN 37234. Tel (800)458-2772.**)** *Continues Adultos en la Escuela Dominical.*

ISSN 0021-3276
US
IVY LEAF (CHICAGO). (IVY LEAF.). Added/Corp Alpha Kappa Alpha Sorority. (19??)-. Periodical. English. Four times a year (Jan., Apr., July, Oct.). $12.00. Alpha Kappa Alpha Sorority Inc., 5656 South Stony Island Avenue, Chicago IL 60637. Tel (312)684-1282. ED Alison Harris Alexander & Vanessa Lovelace. **Ad Acc. Circ:** 35,000 (ctrl).

LC LH1.J7 J73 **ISSN 0021-7255**
US
JOHNS HOPKINS MAGAZINE. [Johns Hopkins mag.]. Added/Corp Johns Hopkins University. Vol. 1 (April 1950)-. Periodical. English. Five times a year (Feb., Apr., June, Sept., Nov.). $18.00. Johns Hopkins Magazine, John Hopkins University, 212 Whitehead Hall, Baltimore MD 21218. Tel (410)516-7645, (410)516-5251. ED Elise Hancock and Sue De Pasquale, (phone:(410)516-7645). **Ad Acc, Adv Mgr:** Susan Smart, Tel (410)532-2136. **Circ:** 95,000 (ctrl). available on microfilm and microfiche from University Microfilms International (UMI).
Desc: General information to interest alumni and friends of Johns Hopkins University and Hospital: Science, Literature, History, Art, Medicine, and Engineering, are also included.
Ind/Abst Peace Res. Abstr. J. (1963).

LC LJ75 .K2 **ISSN 0888-8868**
DD 371 US
KAPPA ALPHA JOURNAL, THE. See Societies and Clubs.

ISSN 0732-6297
US
KENTUCKY ALUMNUS. Periodical. English. Four times a year. $12.00. University of Kentucky Alumni Association, 400 Rose Street, Lexington KY 40506. Tel (606)257-8905. ED Liz Howard Demoran. **Bk Rev. Circ:** 18,500 (ctrl).
Desc: Features and news about the University of Kentucky and her alumni. Emphasis or people, programs, and services.

ISSN 0458-8428
DD 340 US
LAW ALUMNI JOURNAL (PHILADELPHIA, PA.), THE. (THE LAW ALUMNI JOURNAL.). [Law alumni journal]. Added/Corp Law Alumni Society (University of Pennsylvania). University of Pennsylvania. Law School. Annual Report of Giving. (Fall 1965)-. Periodical. English. Three times a year. University of Pennsylvania / Law Review, 3400 Chestnut Street / 14, Philadelphia PA 19104. Tel (215)898-7060. ED Joanna Charnes. **Circ:** 8,000.

LC LH1.M25 A6
DD 378.741/3 US
MAINE (ORONO, ME.). (MAINE.). Periodical. English. Four times a year. $10.00. University of Maine Alumni Association, Crossland Alumni Center, University of Maine, Orono ME 04469. ED Jim Frick. Index available. **Bk Rev. Ad Acc.** ctrl circ. *Continues Maine Alumnus.*
Desc: Includes feature stories on what is taking place at The University of Maine and its alumni body.

US
MAYO ALUMNI. (19??)-. Periodical. English. Four times a year. Free. Mayo Clinic, 200 First Street Southwest, Rochester MN 55905. Tel (800)633-4567. *Continues Mayo Alumnus, 0300-7456.*

ISSN 0300-7456
US
NLM W1 MA997U
MAYO ALUMNUS. Added/Corp Mayo Foundation for Medical Education and Research. Vol. 1 (1965)-. Periodical. English. Four times a year. Mayo Clinic, 200 First Street Southwest, Rochester MN 55905. Tel (800)633-4567.

ISSN 8750-7706
US
MILLIKIN QUARTERLY. Vol. 1, No. 1 (Winter 1985)-. Periodical. English. Four times a year. Millikin Quarterly, 1184 West Main Street, Decatur IL 62522-2084. Tel (217)424-6350. ED Reginald N Syrcle. **Circ:** 19,500. *Formed by the union of Bulletin (Millikin University); Focus Alumni and Notes & Quotes (Decatur, Ill.).*
Desc: Contains news and information about Millikin University and its alumni, and other material of interest to Millikin alumni and friends.

LC KF292.M57 A74 **ISSN 0540-2239**
DD 340.07/11776579 US
MINNESOTA LAW ALUMNI NEWS. Added/Corp Minnesota. University. Law Alumni Association. **VFOAT** Minnesota Law School News. Vol. 20, No. 2 (Spring 1970)-. Periodical. English. Four times a year. University of Minnesota / Law Building, 285 Law Building, 229 19th Avenue South, Minneapolis MN 55455. *Continues Law School News.*

LC LD3342 .M56 **ISSN 0164-9450**
DD 378.776579 US
MINNESOTA (ST. PAUL. 1978). (MINNESOTA.). Vol. 78, No. 1 (Sept. 1978)-. Periodical. English. Twelve times a year. $15.00. Minnesota Alumni Association, 100 Morrill Hall, 100 Church Street SE, Minneapolis MN 55455. *Continues Minnesota Alumni News, 0162-5209.*

LC LH1.M63 A5 **ISSN 0745-0583**
DD 378.778 US
MISSOURI ALUMNUS. Periodical. English. Four times a year. $25.00. University of Missouri Alumni Association, 132 Alumni Center. Tel (314)882-7357, FAX (314)882-7290. ED Karen Worley and Michelle Burke. **Ad Acc. Circ:** 118,000 (ctrl).
Desc: An alumni publication that includes features on the University, professors and students.

ISSN 1052-3634
US
MONTEVALLO TODAY. Added/Corp University of Montevallo. (19??)-. Periodical. English. Four times a year. University of Montevallo / Office of Alumni Affairs, Station 6215, Montevallo AL 35115-6000. Tel (205)665-6230, FAX (205)665-6224.

ISSN 0824-8125
DD 378.7123/3 CN
NEW TRAIL (1982). (NEW TRAIL / THE UNIVERSITY OF ALBERTA ALUMNI ASSOCIATION.). [New trail]. Added/Corp University of Alberta. Alumni Association. (1982)-. Periodical. English. Four times a year. Free to alumni; 15.00Can$ other. University of Alberta / Folio, 430 Athabasca Hall, University of Alberta, Edmonton Alberta T6G 2E8 Canada. Tel (403)432-2325. ED Richard Pilger. **Ad Acc. Circ:** 76,000 (ctrl). *Separated from Folio (University of Alberta, 0015-5764.*
Desc: The alumni magazine of the University of Alberta Alumni Association.

ISSN 0544-070X
US
NEWSLETTER OF THE MIDWEST CHINESE STUDENT & ALUMNI SERVICES. VFOAT Mei-Chung Tung Hsun; Newsletter of the Midwest Chinese Student and Alumni Services. (1957)-. Newsletter. English. Four times a year. Midwest Chinese Student & Alumni Services, PO Box 809, Chicago IL 60690.

ISSN 0161-987X
US
NOTRE DAME MAGAZINE. Added/Corp University of Notre Dame. **VFOAT** Notre Dame. (19??)-. Periodical. English. Four times a year. $15.00. Notre Dame Magazine, 415 Administration Building, Notre Dame IN 46556. Tel (219)239-6947, (800)231-6580. ED Walton R. Collins. **Circ:** 120,000 (ctrl).
Desc: Primarily for alumni of the University of Notre Dame. Continuing education material for college graduates.

LC WMLC 91/3193 US
OAKLAND UNIVERSITY ... ALUMNI DIRECTORY. Main/Corp Oakland University. **VFOAT** Alumni Directory. (1991)-. Directory. English. Bernard C. Harris Publishing Company, 3 Barker Avenue, White Plains NY 10601. Tel (914)946-7500.

UK
●**OLD BRADFIELDIAN.** (1994)-. English. Two times a year. Bradfield College Old Bradfiedian Society, Bradfield Berks, RG7 6AY United Kingdom. Tel 011 1734 744356, FAX 011 1734 744330.
Desc: For alumni of Bradfield College.

ISSN 0732-6319
US
OPEN DOOR (LEXINGTON, KY.), THE. (THE OPEN DOOR : A QUARTERLY PUBLICATION OF THE UNIVERSITY OF KENTUCKY ALUMNI ASSOCIATION.). (19??)-. Periodical. English. Four times a year. $6.00. University of Kentucky Alumni Association, 400 Rose Street, Lexington KY 40506. Tel (606)257-8905. ED Liz Howard Demoran. **Bk Rev. Circ:** 87,000 (ctrl).
Desc: News features about the University of Kentucky and the UK National Alumni Association.

ISSN 0268-1137
UK
CCC
OXFORD MAGAZINE. [Oxf. mag.]. No. 1 (1985)-. Academic Scholarly Publication. English. Twelve times a year. £14.00 UK; $27.00 US. Oxford University Press / UK, Walton Street, Oxford OX2 6DP United Kingdom. Tel 011 44 1865 56767, FAX 011 44 1865 267773, telex 851/837330 OXPRES G. **(Subscription address:** Oxford University Press / USA, Journals Marketing Department, Oxford University Press, 2001 Evans Road, Cary NC 27513. Tel (800)451-7556, (919)677-0977, FAX (919)677-1714.**)** ED T.J. Reed. available on microfilm and microfiche from University Microfilms International (UMI).

US
PITT MAGAZINE. Added/Corp University of Pittsburgh. Dept. of News and Publications. Vol. 1, No. 1 (March 1986)-. Periodical. English. Six times a year. $18.00. University of Pittsburgh Department of University Relations, 400 Craig Hall, Pittsburgh PA 15260. Tel (412)624-4147. ED Sally Ann Flecker. **Bk Rev. Ad Acc. Circ:** 125,000 (ctrl). available with charts; available with illustrations. *Formed by the union of Pitt and Alumni Times.*
Desc: School publication of the University of Pittsburgh.

LC LH1.P8 A4 **ISSN 0149-9270**
US
PRINCETON ALUMNI WEEKLY. Added/Corp Princeton University. Vol. 1, (Apr. 7, 1900)-. Periodical. English. Seventeen times a year. $22.00. Princeton Alumni Weekly, 194 Nassau Street, Princeton NJ 08542. Tel (609)258-4885, FAX (609)258-2247. ED J. I. Merritt. **Bk Rev,** (Qty: 17). **Ad Acc, Adv Mgr:** Lolly O'Brien, Tel (609)258-4886. **Circ:** 57,000.
Desc: To record news of alumni and review achievements and to discuss problems of the administration, faculty, and student body.

College and School Publications —Alumni

LC LH1.P9 A4 **ISSN** 0033-4502
US
PURDUE ALUMNUS, THE. Added/Corp Purdue Alumni Association. Vol. 1 (1914)-. English. Nine times a year (during school year). $20.00. Purdue University Alumni Association, Purdue University, Union Building, West Lafayette IN 47907. **Tel** (317)494-5184. **ED** Gay L. Totten. **Bk Rev. Ad Acc. Circ:** 70,000.
Desc: Alumni magazine focusing on news, events and issues of interest to alumni members-subscribers of Purdue University.

QUARTERLY LAW NOTES AND ALUMNI NEWS. See Law.

LC LD6053 .A32
DD 378.764/1411 US
RICE UNIVERSITY ALUMNI DIRECTORY. Main/Corp William Marsh Rice University, Houston, Tex. Office of Development. (19??)-. Periodical. English. Rice University, PO Box 1892, Houston TX 77251.

LC LH1.S5 S6
US
SMITH ALUMNAE QUARTERLY. Periodical. English. Four times a year. $30.00. Smith College, Alumnae House, Northampton MA 01063. **Tel** (413)584-2985. **ED** Helen R Haddad and Jacelyn W Franklin. **Bk Rev. Circ:** 40,000 (ctrl).
Desc: Articles and news items of interest to Smith College alumnae.

ISSN 0887-0934
US
SOUTHEASTERN OUTLOOK. See Religions and Theology-Protestantism.

US
SPIRE. (19??)-. Periodical. English. Four times a year. Free on request. Midwestern Baptist Theological Seminary, 5001 North Oak Street Traffic Way, Kansas City MO 64118. **Tel** (816)453-4600.
Desc: Alumni news publication for the Midwestern Baptist Theological Seminary.
Ind/Abst South. Baptist Period. Index (1991-).

ISSN 0890-4170
US
SPOTLIGHT (WAYNE, N.J.). (SPOTLIGHT / WPC ALUMNI ASSOCIATION, WILLIAM PATERSON COLLEGE.). **Added/Corp** William Paterson College of New Jersey. Alumni Association. **VFOAT** Spot Light. (19??)-. Periodical. English. Four times a year. William Patterson College, 300 Pompton Road, Alumni Association, Wayne JN 07470. **Tel** (201)595-2175.

LC KF292.S84 A836 **ISSN** 0196-318X
DD 340/.07/1174461 US
SUFFOLK UNIVERSITY LAW SCHOOL ALUMNI DIRECTORY. Main/Corp Suffolk University, Boston. Law School. Suffolk Law Alumni Association. **Added/Corp** Suffolk University. Law School. Alumni Association. Alumni Directory of Suffolk University Law School. **VFOAT** Alumni Directory of Suffolk University Law School. (19??)-. Directory. English. One time a year. Alumni Office / Suffolk University, Beacon Hill, 41 Temple Street, Boston MA 02114. **Tel** (617)573-8180.

LC LH1.S8
DD 378.747 US
SYRACUSE UNIVERSITY ALUMNI NEWS. VFOAT Alumni News. Periodical. English. Four times a year. Syracuse University / Alumni, Alumni Association, 343 H B Crouse Hall, Syracuse NY 13210.

ISSN 1061-561X
US
TEXAS ALCALDE. (TEXAS ALCALDE: UT AUSTIN ALUMNI MAGAZINE.). **Added/Corp** Ex-Students' Association of the University of Texas. **VFOAT** Alcalde. Vol. 80, No. 3 (Jan./Feb. 1992)-. Periodical. English. Six times a year. $8.50 (libraries), $40.00 other. Ex-Students' Association, University of Texas, PO Box 7278, University Station, Austin TX 78713. **Tel** (512)471-3799, FAX (512)471-8088. **ED** Ernestine Wheelock. **Ad Acc, Adv Mgr:** Amy Katz, **Tel** (512)471-8086. **Circ:** 53,000. **Continues** Alcalde, 0002-497X.
Desc: This publication contains informational and feature articles about the programs, research, events, faculty, students, alumni, projects, and members of The University of Texas at Austin and the University of Texas Ex-Students' Association. Some material of current general interest that relates to the university is also included as historical material.

ISSN 1075-2749
DD 378 US
UCLA MAGAZINE (1989). (UCLA MAGAZINE.). [UCLA mag.]. **Added/Corp** UCLA Alumni Association. Vol. 1, No. 1 (Spring 1989)-. Periodical. English. Four times a year. Free on request. UCLA Magazine, 405 Hilgard Avenue, Los Angeles CA 90024-1391. **Tel** (310)206-0686, FAX (310)206-5673. **ED** Mark Wheeler.

Bk Rev. Ad Acc. Circ: 225,000 (ctrl). **Continues** UCLA Monthly.
Desc: Explores issues of societal concern by drawing on the expertise of the faculty and alumni.

LC LH5.E4 U55 **ISSN** 0041-9567
DD 052 UK
UNIVERSITY OF EDINBURGH JOURNAL. Added/Corp University of Edinburgh. Graduates' Association. University of Edinburgh. Journal. (Autumn 1925)-. Periodical. English. Two times a year (June & Dec.). $14.12. University of Edinburgh / Graduate Association, 5 Buccleurgh Place, Edinburgh EH8 9LN United Kingdom. **Tel** 011 44 131 6671011 ext. 6395. **ED** Jean R. Guild. **Bk Rev. Ad Acc. Circ:** 3,500.
Desc: Articles on subjects likely to interest graduates of all faculties. Contains accounts of local events, and memories of undergraduate days.

LC LH1.F56 F53
US
UNIVERSITY OF FLORIDA TODAY : FLORIDA'S FIRST UNIVERSITY.
Added/Corp University of Florida National Alumni Association. **VFOAT** Today. Vol. 9, No. 4 (Fall 1984)-. Periodical. English. Four times a year (quarterly). $25.00. University of Florida Alumni Association, 355 Tiger Hall, Gainesville FL 32611. **Tel** (904)392-0186, FAX (904)392-3536. **Circ:** 25,000. **Continues** Florida's First University Today.

LC WMLC 91/1587
US
UNIVERSITY OF PENNSYLVANIA MEDICAL CENTER ALUMNI DIRECTORY. Main/Corp University of Pennsylvania. Medical Center. **VFOAT** Medical Center Alumni Directory; Alumni Directory. (1991)-. Directory. English. Bernard C. Harris Publishing Company, 3 Barker Avenue, White Plains NY 10601. **Tel** (914)946-7500.

LC LH1.V25 A4
DD 378.768 US
VANDERBILT MAGAZINE. Added/Corp Vanderbilt University. Alumni Association. Vol. 70, No. 4 (Winter 1986)-. Periodical. English. Four times a year. Free on request. Vanderbilt University / Office of Alumni Publications, PO Box 91 Peabody Station, Nashville TN 37203. **Tel** (615)322-7311. **ED** Jean B. Crawford. **Bk Rev. Circ:** 30,000 (ctrl). **Continues** Vanderbilt Alumnus.

LC R747.V36 A38 **ISSN** 0740-901X
DD 610/.7/1176147 US
VANDERBILT MEDICAL ALUMNI DIRECTORY. Main/Corp Vanderbilt University. School of Medicine. **Added/Corp** College & University Press. **VFOAT** Alumni Directory. (19??)-. Directory. English. One time a year. College & University Press / Alabama, One Bell Road, PO Box 17940, Montgomery AL 36117.

ISSN 0279-2540
US
VANDERBILT TODAY. Added/Corp Vanderbilt University. (1960)-. Periodical. English. Four times a year. Free to alumni and parents of undergraduates. Vanderbilt University / Office of Alumni Publications, PO Box 91 Peabody Station, Nashville TN 37203. **Tel** (615)322-7311. **Circ:** 70,000.
Desc: Features news about Vanderbilt University; distributed to alumni and parents of undergraduates.

LC KF292.W28 A838 **ISSN** 0278-7652
DD 340/.07/1178163 US
WASHBURN UNIVERSITY SCHOOL OF LAW ALUMNI DIRECTORY. Main/Corp Washburn University of Topeka. School of Law. Directory. English. Irregular. College & University Press / Alabama, One Bell Road, PO Box 17940, Montgomery AL 36117.

LC LD5901.W36 A15 **ISSN** 0148-4249
DD 378.746/6 US
WESLEYAN (MIDDLETOWN). (WESLEYAN; THE WESLEYAN UNIVERSITY ALUMNI MAGAZINE.). **Added/Corp** Wesleyan University (Middletown, Conn.). (19??)-. Periodical. English. Four times a year. free. Wesleyan University / Middletown, PO Box 2700, Middletown CT 06457. **Tel** (203)347-9411. **ED** Nancy Smith. **Bk Rev. Circ:** 27,500 (ctrl). **Continues** The Alumnus.
Desc: Articles and profiles of alumni, news about the institution, essays and class notes.

ISSN 8755-1519
DD 610 US
WISCONSIN MEDICAL ALUMNI QUARTERLY. [Wis. med. alumni q.]. **Added/Corp** Wisconsin Medical Alumni Association. (196?)-. Periodical. English. Four times a year. Free. 758 Warf Building, 610 North Walnut Street, Madison WI 53706. **Tel** (608)262-5363. **ED** Victor Falk. **Circ:** 10,000 (ctrl).
Desc: Faculty honors, research, department profiles, medical school news and alumni news.

ISSN 8750-409X
DD 378 US
YALE ALUMNI MAGAZINE (1984). (YALE ALUMNI MAGAZINE.). [Yale alumni mag.]. **VFOAT** Yale. Vol. 48, No. 1 (Oct. 1984)-. Periodical. English. Eight times a year (Monthly Oct.-Dec., Feb.-May). $19.50. Yale Alumni Publications Inc., 149 York Street, PO Box 1905, New Haven CT 06509. **Tel** (203)432-0645, FAX (203)432-0651. **ED** Carter Wiseman. Index available (published separately). **Bk Rev,** (Qty: 30-35). **Ad Acc, Adv Mgr:** Barbara Durland. **Circ:** 71,000. available on an online database (via Internet (Gopher Server Yale Info)). **Continues** Yale Alumni Magazine and Journal, 0164-9264.
Desc: Provides timely and candid reporting on matters relating to the University, and a forum for alumni comments.
Ind/Abst Am. Hist. Life (1974-1976).

COMMUNICATIONS

ISSN 0162-248X
US
2108 NEWS. See Business and Economics-Labor.

US
A P C O PUBLIC SAFETY COMMUNICATIONS. See Public Health and Safety.

LC TK6630.A1 A84 **ISSN** 0126-6209
DD 621.38/05 MY
ABU TECHNICAL REVIEW. [ABU tech. rev.]. **Main/Corp** Asia-Pacific Broadcasting Union. **Added/Corp** Asia-Pacific Broadcasting Union. Technical review. **VAT** Asia-Pacific Broadcasting Union Technical Review. No. 48 (Jan. 1977)-. Trade Publication. English. Six times a year (Jan., Mar., May, July, Sept., Nov.). $25.00. Asia Pacific Broadcasting Union, PO Box 1164, 59700 Kuala Lumpur Malaysia. **Tel** 11 60 3 2823108, FAX 11 60 3 2822592, telex MA 32227. **ED** Om P. Khushu. Index available. **Bk Rev. Ad Acc. Circ:** 1,000. available on an online database (INSP) from DATA-STAR. Documents available from Ask*IEEE. **Continues** Asian Broadcasting Union. ABU Technical Review.
Desc: Broadcast engineering journal of the Asian-Pacific Broadcasting Union, with articles by ABU member organizations, international news digest (technical), equipment trends, technical reviews, personalities and news from the countries of members.
Ind/Abst Ei Page One; INSPEC (1977-).

UK
ACTION. See Religions and Theology.

ISSN 0842-1854
DD 020/.6234/714 CN
ACTUALITES SDM. [Actual. SDM]. **Added/Corp** Services Documentaires Multimedia. **VAT** Actualites Services Documentaires Multimedia. No. 7 (May 1988)-. Bulletin. French. Four times a year. Free. Services Documentaires Multimedia Inc, 75 rue de Port-Royal, Suite 300, Montreal Quebec H3L 3T1 Canada. **Tel** (514)382-0895, FAX (514)384-9139. ctrl circ. **Continues** Actualites CB., 0835-0272.

LC F1001 .E55
DD 971/.005 CN
ADDRESSES. Main/Corp Empire Club of Canada. **VFOAT** Empire Club of Canada Addresses. English. Empire Club, Royal York Hotel, 100 Front Street West, Toronto Ontario M5J 1E3 Canada. **Tel** (416)364-2878. **Continues** Addresses Delivered to the Members During the Sessions of ... .

LC P88.8 .A34 **ISSN** 0925-2932
DD 070 NE
ADFOMEDIA HANDBOEK. No. 1 (Apr. 1991)-. Dutch. Two times a year. Samsom Bedrijfsinformatie BV, Postbus 4, 2400 MA Alphen Rij Netherlands. **Tel** 011 31 1720 66633.

ISSN 0192-4346
UK
CEASED
ADVANCES IN EXPERIENTIAL SOCIAL PROCESSES. See Social Sciences.

ISSN 0190-9703
DD 152 US
NLM W1 AD8801
ADVANCES IN THE STUDY OF COMMUNICATION AND AFFECT. See Psychology.

ISSN 0313-2382
DD 659.10994 AT
ADVERTISING EXPENDITURE IN MAIN MEDIA. [Adver. expend. main media]. (1960)-. Periodical. English. One time a year (Apr.). 490.00Aus$. Commercial Economic Advisors Service of Australia, PO

Communications

Box 104 St. Leonards, New South Wales 2065 Australia. **Tel** 011 61 2 4393790, 011 61 2 4393750, FAX 011 61 2 4383729. Index available. cum. index. **Ad Acc, Adv Mgr Tel** 02 439 3750. ctrl circ.

LC HE8461 .A37 — ISSN 1053-2897
DD 302.2/096/05 — US
AFRICA COMMUNICATIONS. [Afr. commun.].
(1990)-. Periodical. English. Six times a year (Jan., Mar., May, July, Sept., Nov.). $42.00. Africa Telecommunications, 1000 Connecticut Avenue, Suite #9, Washington DC 20036. **Tel** (202)667-2111.

LC WMLC 93/1938 — ISSN 0258-4913
DD 070 — KE
AFRICA MEDIA REVIEW. Added/Corp Institute
for Communication Development and Research (African Council on Communication Education). Vol. 1, No. 1 (June 1986)-. Periodical. English (summaries and/or abstracts in French). Three times a year. $60.00. African Council of Communication Education, PO Box 47495, Nairobi Kenya. **Tel** 011 254 2 215270 28328, FAX 011 254 2 216135.
Ind/Abst Abstr. Anthropol. (19??-); Film Lit. Index (19??-).

US
ALABAMA NEWS MEDIA DIRECTORY.
VFOAT News Media Directory. (19??)-. Directory. English. One time a year (Feb.). $45.00. News Media Directories, PO Box 316, Mount Dora FL 32757. **Tel** (904)383-3023, (800)749-6399.

ISSN 1058-126X
DD 621 — US
ALL IN COMMUNICATIONS. [All commun.].
Added/Corp Centour of Miami Corporation. **VFOAT** Todo en Comunicaciones. (1991)-. Periodical. English (Spanish). Twelve times a year. Free US; $40.00 Canada. All in Communications, 8250 NW 27th Street, Suite 301, Miami FL 33122-9920.

ISSN 1053-0657
DD 384 — US
ALLIANCE ALERT. COMMUNICATIONS.
[Alliance alert, Commun.]. **VFOAT** Communications. Vol. 1, Issue 1 (Apr. 1990)-. Periodical. English. Four times a year. $395.00 (1 industry), $635.00 (2 industries), $855.00 (3 industries), $975.00 (4 industries), $1095.00 (5 industries). Securities Data Company, 40 West 57th Street, 11th Floor, New York NY 10019. **Tel** (212)765-5311. available on an online database (files 16,636/Full-Text) from DIALOG.
Ind/Abst PROMT [Full Txt.]; PTS Newsl. Database [Full Txt.].

ISSN 0392-5692
UDC 621.39 — IT
ALTRIMEDIA. [Altrimedia]. (1976)-. Periodical.
Italian. Eleven times a year. Mass Media, Via Gaffurio 4, 20124 Milan Italy. **ED** Eduardo Fleischner. **Ad Acc. Circ:** 42,000.

ISSN 1078-5671
DD 808 — US
●AMERICAN SPEAKER. (AMERICAN SPEAKER :
YOUR GUIDE TO SUCCESSFUL SPEAKING.). [Am. speak.]. (1993)-. Periodical. English. Irregular. $307.00. Georgetown Publishing House, 1101 30th Street Northwest, Suite 130, Washington DC 20007. **Tel** (800)915-0022.

ISSN 0740-5111
US
AMERICAN UNIVERSITY STUDIES. SERIES XV, COMMUNICATIONS. [Am. Univ.
stud., Ser. XV, Commun.]. **VFOAT** Communications; American American University Studies. Series Fifteen, Communications; American University Studies. Series 15, Communications. (1984)-. Monographic series. English. Irregular. Price varies per volume. Peter Lang Publishing, 62 West 45th Street, 4th Floor, New York NY 10036. **Tel** (212)764-1471, (800)770-5264, FAX (212)302-7574, telex 6973364 PLNY.

BL
AMIGA. (1???)-. Periodical. Portuguese. Irregular.
$83.33. Bloch Editoras SA, Rua do Russell 766 804, 22210 Rio de Janeiro Brazil. **Tel** 011 51 21 2652012, 011 51 21 2850033.

ISSN 0211-2175
SP
ANALISI : QUADERNS DE COMUNICACIO I CULTURA. Added/Corp
Universidad Autonoma de Barcelona. Departement de Teoria de al Comunicacio. Vol. 1 (1980)-. Periodical. Catalan (Spanish; summaries and/or abstracts in English). Two times a year. Universitat Autonoma de Barcelona / Ciencies, Facultat de Ciencies de la Informacio, Departement de Teoria de la Comunicacio, Apartado Postal 20, Bellaterra 08193 Spain. **Tel** 011 34 3 5811022.

ISSN 0270-241X
US
ANDREW SEYBOLD'S REPORT ON MOBILE EMERGENCY COMMUNICATIONS. VFOAT Mobile Energy
Communications. Vol. 1 (1980)-. Periodical. English. Twelve times a year. $60.00. Emergency Communications Services, PO Box 208, Redondo Beach CA 90277.

LC P92.B4 A56
DD 302.23/09493/05 — BE
ANNUAIRE DE L'AUDIOVISUEL DE LA COMMUNAUTE FRANCAISE. Added/Corp
Belgium. Ministere de la Communaute Francaise. Direction d'Administration de l'Audiovisuel. (Sept. 1986)-. French. One time a year. 1000F Belgium and Luxembourg; 260F France; 1700F other. Edimedia ASBL, rue de la Constitution 22, 1030 Brussels Belgium. **Tel** 011 32 2 2180031. **Bk Rev. Ad Acc.**

LC J905 .L3 HE8699.A8 — ISSN 0728-8883
DD 300/.994 354.940087/4/06 — AT
ANNUAL REPORT - AUSTRALIAN BROADCASTING TRIBUNAL. Main/Corp
Australian Broadcasting Tribunal. (197?)-. English. One time a year. $11.50. Australian Government Publishing Service, GPO Box 84, Canberra ACT 2601 Australia. **Tel** 011 61 6 2954411, FAX 011 61 6 2954455. **Continues** Australian Broadcasting Control Board. Annual Report.

LC HE8677 — ISSN 0083-0585
DD 001.5 — US
ANNUAL REPORT / FEDERAL COMMUNICATIONS COMMISSION.
Main/Corp United States. Federal Communications Commission. **VFOAT** FCC Annual Report. (1935)-. Government Publication. English. One time a year. Superintendent of Documents, US Government Printing Office, Washington DC 20402. **Tel** (202)275-3328, FAX (202)786-2377. **Continues** Annual Report of the Federal Radio Commission to the Congress of the United States.
Ind/Abst Predicasts Forecasts.

LC P87 .A5
DD 001.55/025/81 — BL
ANUARIO BRASILEIRO DE MIDIA.
Portuguese. $350. Editora Meis S Meurageu Ltda, rua Caetes 139, CEP 05016 Sao Paulo SP Brazil. **Circ:** 10,000. **Continues** Anuario Brasileiro de Media.

SP
ANUARIO / LA VOZ DE GALICIA.
Added/Corp Voz de Galicia (Firm). (1984)-. Spanish. Seven times a week (daily and Sun.). 37300ptas Spain; 63790ptas Europe; 88219ptas other. La Voz de Galicia, Concepcion Arenas 11 13, 15006 La Coruna Spain. **Tel** 011 34 81 180180, FAX 011 34 81 180180.

LC PN4171 .A46a — ISSN 1051-1431
DD 808.5/1/05 — US
Pr Rev.
ARGUMENTATION AND ADVOCACY.
(ARGUMENTATION AND ADVOCACY : THE JOURNAL OF THE AMERICAN FORENSIC ASSOCIATION.). [Argum. advocacy]. **Added/Corp** American Forensic Association. **VFOAT** Journal of the American Forensic Association. Vol. 25, No. 1 (Summer 1988)-. Periodical. English. Four times a year (Jan., Apr., July, Oct.). $45.00. American Forensic Association, Box 256, River Falls WI 54022. **Tel** (715)425-3198, (800)228-5424, FAX (715)425-9533. Index available. cum. index. **Bk Rev**, (Qty: varies). **Ad Acc, Adv Mgr Tel** (800)228-5424. **Circ:** 1,000 (ctrl). available on microfilm and microfiche from University Microfilms International (UMI). Documents available from UMI Article Clearinghouse. **Continues** American Forensic Association. Journal of the American Forensic Association, 0002-8533.
Ind/Abst Acad. Ind. [Computer File] (1992-); Acad. Search; Curr. Index J. Educ. (March 1990); EP Collect.; Expand. Acad. Index (1989-); Homework Help.; Linguist. Lang. Behav. Abstr.; MasterFile FullTEXT 1000; MasterFile FullTEXT 350; MasterFile FullTEXT 650; MasterFile FullTEXT (July 1994-); Newsp. Period. Abstr. (1989-); Soc. Plann. Policy Dev. Abstr.; Sociol. Abstr.; Telebase.

ISSN 0840-478X
CN
ARGUS PROMOTIONNEL OFICHIER D'ORDINATEUR. (19??)-. French. Eight times a
year (one basic document and 7 updates). 234.50Can$. Argus Communications Inc, 1161 Lac Cache, CP 26, St. Alexis Quebec J0K 1V0 Canada. **Tel** (819)265-2072, FAX (819)265-3135.

LC DS432.B4 A74
DD 934 — II
ARITRA. Periodical. Bengali (Bengali). Twelve times a
year. 2.00. Binay Bandopadhyay, 23 Brindavan Basak Street, Calcutta 700012 India.

LC UA943 .A75 — ISSN 0362-5745
DD 358/.24/0973 — US
ARMY COMMUNICATOR, THE. See Military
and Defense.

ISSN 1084-0710
DD 384 — US
●ASIACOM (THOUSAND OAKS, CALIF.).
(ASIACOM.). (1995)-. Periodical. English. Twenty-four times a year. $695.00. Baskerville Communications, PO Box 5084, Thousand Oaks CA 91359. **Tel** (805)499-0721 ext. 289. **(Subscription address:** Nextech Customer Service, PO Box 303, Shrub Oak NY 10588-9904. **Tel** (914)962-6297, FAX (914)962-1338.**)**

ISSN 0952-7516
UK
ASIAN COMMUNICATIONS. [Asian commun.].
(1987)-. Trade Publication. English (Chinese). Twelve times a year. $110.00. ICOM Publications Ltd., Chancery House, St. Nicholas Way, Sutton Surrey SM1 1JB United Kingdom. **Tel** 011 44 181 6421117, FAX 011 44 181 6421941. **ED** David Shortland. **Bk Rev. Ad Acc. Circ:** 8,500 (ctrl).
Desc: Reports news and technical matters of relevance to professionals in the communications market in the Asia/Pacific market.

ISSN 0956-2931
UK
AUDIO VISUAL DIRECTORY. (19??)-.
English. One time a year. £25.00. Emap Vision, 19 Scarbrook Road, Croydon CR9 1QH United Kingdom. **Tel** 01-760 9690, FAX 01-681 1672, telex 946665. **ED** Milasy Jolmers. **Ad Acc. Circ:** 2,500.
Desc: Manufacturers and suppliers of audio visual and broadcasting products and services.

ISSN 1063-0244
DD 028 — US
Pr Rev.
AUDIOFILE (PORTLAND, ME.). (AUDIOFILE:
THE MONTHLY NEWSLETTER OF AUDIO REVIEWS.). [AudioFile]. **VFOAT** Audio File. Vol. 1, No. 1 (June 1992)-. Newsletter. English. Twelve times a year. $48.00. Audiofile, 37 Silver Street, PO Box 109, Portland ME 04112. **Tel** (207)774-7563, FAX (207)775-3744. **ED** Robin F Whitten. Index available (bound in May issue). cum. index. **Bk Rev**, (Qty: 550). **Ad Acc, Adv Mgr:** Merris Grohman, **Tel** (207)828-3994. **Circ:** 1,000 per month (ctrl).
Desc: A newsletter of audio reviews and information with over thirty reviews of audio books and spoken-word audio presentations plus publishers information.

ISSN 1045-5795
DD 384 — US
Pr Rev.
AUDIOTEX UPDATE. See
Computers-Simulation.

LC TK5102.5 .A785 — ISSN 0090-3590
DD 621.38/05 — US
AUERBACH DATA COMMUNICATIONS EQUIPMENT DIGEST. [Auerbach data commun.
equip. dig.]. Periodical. English. Two times a year. Auerbach Publishers Inc., Park Square Building, 31 St. James Avenue, Boston MA 02116. **Tel** (800)950-1207.

ISSN 0743-4618
DD 616 — US
— CCC
NLM W1; AU208 — CODEN AAACEC
AUGMENTATIVE AND ALTERNATIVE COMMUNICATION. See Physically Impaired.

ISSN 0726-3252
DD 302.206 — AT
— CEASED
AUSTRALIAN COMMUNICATION REVIEW. [ACA Aust. Commun. rev.]. Added/Corp
Australian Communication Association. **VFOAT** ACA. Australian Communication Association; ACA Australian Communication Review. (1981)-(Dec. 1994). Periodical. English. Communication Research Institution Australia, PO Box 8, Hackett ACT 2602 Australia. **Tel** 011 61 62 573155, FAX 011 61 62 2475056. **ED** Raymond Archee. Index available. cum. index. **Bk Rev. Ad Acc. Circ:** 250 (ctrl). **Continues** ACA Newsletter, 0157-8812.
Desc: Articles and new information concerning communication in Australia and overseas.

ISSN 0811-6202
AT
Pr Rev.
AUSTRALIAN JOURNAL OF COMMUNICATION. Added/Corp Australian
Communication Association. Queensland Institute of Technology. Communication Institute. No. 1-2, Jan./Dec. (1982)-. Periodical. English. Three times a year. 41.11Aus$. QLD University of Technology, GPO Box 2434, Brisbane Queensland 4001 Australia. **Tel** 011 61 7 8642111, FAX 011 61 7 8641510, telex 44699. **ED** Roslyn M Petelin. **Bk Rev. Ad Acc. Circ:** 400. **Continues** Australian Scan.
Desc: Information pertaining to public communication, mass communication and media studies, interpersonal communication, computer communication, and

Communications

organizational communication.
Ind/Abst APAIS, Aust. Public Aff. Inf. Ser.; Aust. Educ. Index.

AT
AUSTRALIAN MEDIA DIRECTORY.
(19??)-. Directory. English. Irregular (approximately 6 issues). 330.47Aus$. International Public Relations Pty Ltd., 33 Walsh Street, West Melbourne Victoria 3003 Australia. **Tel** 011 61 3 3299333, FAX 011 61 3 92099320.

ISSN 0237-9740
HU
UDC 371.333
AV KOMMUNIKACIO. **VFOAT** Audiovizualis
Kommunikacio. (1987)-. Periodical. Hungarian. Six times a year. $32.00. Omikk Technoinform, PO Box 12, H-1428 Budapest Hungary. **Tel** 011 36 1 137609, FAX 011 36 1 1382414, telex 22-4944 OMIKK H. **ED** Janos Duzs and Arkos Juan. Index available. cum. index. **Bk Rev**. **Ad Acc. Circ:** 830 (ctrl). *Continues Technical & Scientific Films.*
Desc: Articles on the information industry, educating media, video, computer techniques, and application of information bearers.

LC TS2301.A7 F472
DD 621.389/7
ISSN 1064-7112
US
TITLE CHANGE
AVC PRESENTATION FOR THE VISUAL COMMUNICATOR. See Business and Economics.

LC P92.B28 B35
DD 302.23/09496/05
ISSN 0861-5047
BU
BALKANMEDIA. **Added/Corp** Balkanmedia
Association. **VFOAT** Balkan Media. (Winter 1991/92)-. Periodical. English. Four times a year (Mar., June, Sept., Nov.). $60.00. Balkanmedia Association, 96 Lubotren Street, 1407 Sofia Bulgaria. **Tel** 11 3592 875975, 11 3592 871698, FAX 11 3592 875975. **ED** Rossen Milev. cum. index. **Bk Rev**, (Qty: 12-15). **Ad Acc. Circ:** 3,000 (ctrl).
Desc: This publication covers the problems of mass media, art, culture, and communications of the Balkan countries. Articles deal with television, cinema, radio, and traditional arts as well as theoretical materials on culture.

LC P88.8 .B48
ISSN 0968-4557
UK
●BENN'S MEDIA. 141st Ed. (1993)-. English. Miller
Freeman Technical Ltd., Riverbank House, Angel Lane, Tonbridge Kent TN9 1SE United Kingdom. **Tel** 011 44 1732 362666, FAX 011 44 1732 770483, telex 95454 BBIS. **(Subscription address:** Benn Business Information Services Ltd., 30 Calderwood Street Woolwich, London SE18 6QH United Kingdom. **Tel** 011 44 181 8557777.) *Continues Benn's Media Directory.*

UK
BENN'S MEDIA DIRECTORY. VOLUME 1, UNITED KINGDOM. (19??)-. English. One
time a year. £103.50. Miller Freeman Technical Ltd., Riverbank House, Angel Lane, Tonbridge Kent TN9 1SE United Kingdom. **Tel** 011 44 1732 362666, FAX 011 44 1732 770483, telex 95454 BBIS.

ISSN 0742-4027
US
BEST MEDIA. **Added/Corp** EGW International
Corporation. (1983)-. Periodical. English. Two times a year. EGW Publishing Company, 1041 Shary Circle, Concord CA 94518. **Tel** (510)671-9852, (800)777-1164, FAX (510)671-0692.

ISSN 0092-8607
US
NLM W1 BI854D
CEASED
BIOMEDICAL COMMUNICATIONS.
[Biomed. commun.]. Vol. 1 (Jan. 1973)-(19??). Periodical. English. Institut Torcuato di Tella, 11 de Septiembre 2139, 1423 Buenos Aires Argentina. **Tel** 781-5013, FAX 784 8225, telex 15 2817051. **(Subscription address:** Media Horzions Inc. / Circulation Department, 228 East 45th Street, New York NY 10017.) available on microfilm and microfiche from University Microfilms International (UMI).
Ind/Abst Health Plan. Adminis.; Hosp. Health Admin. Index; Int. Pharm. Abstr.; Pollut. Abstr. Indexes.

ISSN 1051-208X
DD 331
US
BNAC COMMUNICATOR. [BNAC commun.].
Added/Corp BNA Communications. **VAT** Bureau of National Affairs Communications Communicator; BNA Communications Communicator. Vol. 1, No. 1 (Fall 1980)-. Periodical. English. Three times a year (Jan., Apr., Sept.). Free. BNA Communications Inc., 9439 Key West Avenue, Rockville MD 20850. **Tel** (301)948-0540, FAX (301)948-2085. **ED** Tony Cornish (phone: (301)294-6771). **Bk Rev**. ctrl circ.
Desc: Trends and topics concerning training issues in the areas of the workforce diversity, sexual harassment, labor relations and safety.

ISSN 0103-9318
BL
BRAZILIAN COMMUNICATION RESEARCH YEARBOOK. **Added/Corp**
Universidade de Sao Paulo. Escola de Comunicacoes e Artes. (1992)-. English (summaries and/or abstracts in French, Portuguese and Spanish). One time a year. Universidade de Sao Paulo / School of Communications and Arts, Avenue Prof. Lucio Martins Rodrigues 443, Butana 05508 Sao Paulo SP Brazil. **Tel** 011 55 11 8133222, FAX 011 55 11 8154272, telex 80629 UVSI BR. **ED** Jose Marques de Melo.

ISSN 1183-0212
DD 070.1/025/711
CN
BRITISH COLUMBIA MEDIA GUIDE. [B.C.
media guide]. **Added/Corp** British Columbia. Public Affairs Bureau. Nov. (1990)-. English. *Continues Regional Media Guide., 0847-0022.*
Desc: Information on the mass media in British Columbia.

UK
NLM W1 BR526LM
BRITISH JOURNAL OF DISORDERS OF COMMUNICATION. MONOGRAPH. See
Physically Impaired.

US
BROADCAST ACTIONS. **Main/Corp** United
States. Federal Communications Commission. (19??)-. Periodical. English. FCC / Federal Communications Commission, 1919 M Street Northwest, Room 538, Washington DC 20554. **Tel** (202)632-6302.

ISSN 0889-2644
DD 384
US
BROADCAST BANKER/BROKER. See
Business and Economics-Banks and Banking.

ISSN 0882-5688
DD 621
US
BROADCAST EQUIPMENT BUYERS GUIDE (SHAWNEE MISSION, KAN.).
(BROADCAST EQUIPMENT BUYERS GUIDE.). **Added/Corp** Bill Daniels Co. **VFOAT** Broadcast Equipment Buyer's Guide. (1985)-. Consumer Publication. English. Daniels Publishing Group Inc, PO Box 2056, Shawnee Mission KS 66201. **Tel** (913)492-9900. **Bk Rev**. **Ad Acc. Circ:** 6,000. *Continues Illustrated Broadcast Equipment Encyclopedia, 0747-7694.*
Desc: Illustrated trade reference for broadcast equipment and services.

ISSN 0959-5813
DD 621.38
UK
TITLE CHANGE
BROADCAST SYSTEMS INTERNATIONAL. [Broadcast syst. int.].
(1989)-(19??). Periodical. English. Link House Magazines Ltd., Link House, Dingwall Avenue, Croydon, Surrey CR9 2TA United Kingdom. **Tel** 011 44 181 6862599, FAX 011 44 181 7600973, telex 947709. *Continues Broadcast Systems Engineering, 0267-565X. Merged into Studio Sound, 0144-5944.*

LC KF2801.A3 B76
DD 343.73/09945 347.3039945
ISSN 0737-3120
US
BROADCASTING AND GOVERNMENT.
[Broadcast. gov.]. **Added/Corp** National Association of Broadcasters. Legal Dept. National Association of Broadcasters. Government Relations Dept. (19??)-. English. Four times a year. Free. National Association of Broadcasters, 1771 N Street NW/Suite 600, Washington DC 20036.

LC HE8689.8 .U54b
DD 353.008/74/54
US
BUDGET - BOARD FOR INTERNATIONAL BROADCASTING.
Main/Corp United States. Board for International Broadcasting. (19??)-. English. One time a year. Board for International Broadcasting, Suite 400/1201 Connecticut Avenue NW, Washington DC 20036.

LC P92.E9 M42
ISSN 1021-5719
UK
BULLETIN - EUROPEAN INSTITUTE FOR THE MEDIA, THE. **Added/Corp** European
Institute for the Media. **VFOAT** The Bulletin of the European Institute for the Media. (19??)-. Bulletin. English. Four times a year. $115.15. European Institute for the Media, Kaistrasse 13, D-40221 Dusseldorf Germany. **Tel** 011 49 211 90104-0, FAX 011 49 211 90104-56. *Continues Media Bulletin, 0267-5382.*

ISSN 8756-1972
DD 658
US
TITLE CHANGE
BULLETIN OF THE ASSOCIATION FOR BUSINESS COMMUNICATION, THE. See
Business and Economics.

US
SUSPENDED
BURRELLE'S BLACK HISPANIC MEDIA DIRECTORY. (19??)-Suspended (1992). Directory.
English. Every 2 years. Burrelle's Media Directories, 75 East Northfield Road, Livingston NJ 07039. **Tel** (201)992-6600, (800)631-1160. *Absorbed Burrelle's Black Media Directory.*

LC P94.5.A37 B87
DD 001.51/08996073
ISSN 0748-4259
US
TITLE CHANGE
BURRELLE'S BLACK MEDIA DIRECTORY. [Burrelle's Black media dir.].
Added/Corp Burrelle's Media Directories (Firm). **VFOAT** Black Media Directory. (1984)-(19??). Directory. English. Burrelle's Media Directories, 75 East Northfield Road, Livingston NJ 07039. **Tel** (201)992-6600, (800)631-1160. *Continues in part Burrelle's Special Groups Media Directory. Merged into Burrelle's Black Hispanic Media Directory.*

ISSN 0883-9999
DD 071
US
BURRELLE'S NEW ENGLAND MEDIA DIRECTORY. [Burrelle's N. Engl. media dir.].
Added/Corp Burrelle's Media Directories (Firm). **VFOAT** Burrelle's Media Directory, New England; New England Media Directory. (1988)-. English. Burrelle's Media Directories, 75 East Northfield Road, Livingston NJ 07039. **Tel** (201)992-6600, (800)631-1160. *Continues New England Media Directory, 0195-7619.*

LC P88.8 .N484
DD 001.51/025749
ISSN 0883-9778
US
SUSPENDED
BURRELLE'S NEW JERSEY MEDIA DIRECTORY. [Burrelle's N.J. media dir.]. **VFOAT**
New Jersey Media Directory. (1981)-(19??). English. Irregular. Burrelle's Media Directories, 75 East Northfield Road, Livingston NJ 07039. **Tel** (201)992-6600, (800)631-1160. *Continues New Jersey Media Directory, 0195-6817.*

LC P88.8 .B87
DD 070.1/025/748
ISSN 0276-7872
US
BURRELLE'S ... PENNSYLVANIA MEDIA DIRECTORY. **Added/Corp** Burrelle's Media
Directories (Firm). **VFOAT** Pennsylvania Media Directory. (1981)-. Directory. English. One time a year. $89.00. Burrelle's Media Directories, 75 East Northfield Road, Livingston NJ 07039. **Tel** (201)992-6600, (800)631-1160.

LC P94.5.W652 U62
DD 001.51/088042
ISSN 0748-4240
US
BURRELLE'S WOMEN'S MEDIA DIRECTORY. [Burrelle's women's media dir.].
VFOAT Women's Media Directory. 1983-84. Directory. English. Irregular. $50.00. Burrelle's Media Directories, 75 East Northfield Road, Livingston NJ 07039. **Tel** (201)992-6600, (800)631-1160. *Continues in part Burrelle's Special Groups Media Directory.*

LC HD59 .B869
DD 302.2/34
ISSN 0270-3572
US
BUSINESS AND THE MEDIA. **Added/Corp**
Media Institute (Washington, D.C.). Vol. 2 (Spring 1980)-. Periodical. English. Four times a year. Moselio Schaechter, 855 Commonwealth Avenue, Newton Center MA 02159. **ED** Moselio Schaechter. **Bk Rev**. Circ: 400. *Continues Newsletter (Media Institute (Washington, D.C.), 0270-3564.*

ISSN 1080-5699
DD 658
US
●BUSINESS COMMUNICATION QUARTERLY : A PUBLICATION OF THE ASSOCIATON FOR BUSINESS COMMUNICATION. See Business and
Economics.

LC HF5717 .B87
DD 658.4/5/05
ISSN 0162-3885
US
CCC
CODEN BCORBD
BUSINESS COMMUNICATIONS REVIEW. See Business and
Economics-Management.

LC HF5001 .B837
DD 001.55/05
ISSN 8756-9639
US
BUSINESS MEDIA WEEK. See Business and
Economics.

US
C C U M C LEADER. See Education-Higher
Education.

ISSN 1073-3108
DD 621
US
●CABLING INSTALLATION & MAINTENANCE. [Cabling install. maint.]. **VFOAT**
Cabling Installation and Maintenance; Installation and Maintenance; A.Installation & maintenance. Vol. 1, No. 1

Communications

(Apr./May 1993)-. Trade Publication. English. Six times a year. $38.00. PennWell Publishing Company, 1421 South Sheridan, PO Box 1260, Tulsa OK 74101. **Tel** (918)835-3161, (800)331-4463, FAX (918)831-9497. **(Subscription address:** Cabling Installation & Maintenance, Publishing Services, PO Box 2520, Tulsa OK 74101. **Tel** (918)832-9349, FAX (918)832-9295.)
 Desc: Hands-on magazine devoted to specifying, installing, maintaining and troubleshooting today's complex voice, data and imaging communications systems.
 Ind/Abst EP Collect.; Homework Help.; MasterFile FullTEXT 1000; MasterFile FullTEXT 350; MasterFile FullTEXT 650; MasterFile FullTEXT (Jan. 1995-); OCLC; Telebase.

LC P92.C3 C37   ISSN 0705-3657
DD 302.23/0971/05   CN
   CCC

CANADIAN JOURNAL OF COMMUNICATION. [Can. j. commun.]. Vol. 4, No. 2 (Fall 1977)-. Periodical. English (French; summaries and/or abstracts in French). Four times a year (published within the seasons). 75.00Can$. Wilfrid Laurier University Press, 75 University Avenue West, Waterloo Ontario N2L 3C5 Canada. **Tel** (519)884-1970 ext. 6124, FAX (519)725-1399. **ED** G. J. Robinson. **Bk Rev**. **Ad Acc**. **Circ:** 400 (ctrl). available on microfiche from Micromedia Limited. Documents available from Ask*IEEE. **Continues** Media Probe, 0384-1618.
 Desc: Communication and journalism theory from Canadian scholars.
 Ind/Abst Can. Index; Can. Period. Index (19??-); Commun. Abstr.; Educ. Technol. Abstr.; Film Lit. Index (19??-); INSPEC (Winter 1983-).

   ISSN 0710-4340
DD 370.7/78/05   CN
Pr Rev.

CANADIAN JOURNAL OF EDUCATIONAL COMMUNICATION. [Can. j. educ. commun.]. **Added/Corp** Association for Media and Technology in Education in Canada. Vol. 11, No. 1 (Fall 1981)-. Periodical. English (summaries and/or abstracts in French). Three times a year (May, Sept., Dec.). 33.66Can$. Association for Communications and Technology in Education in Canada, 3-1750 The Queensway, Suite 1318, Etobicoke Ontario M9C 5H5 Canada. **Tel** (709)737-8624, (709)753-8626, FAX (709)737-2345. **ED** Mary F. Kennedy (editor's address: Faculty of Education, Memorial University, St. John's, Newfoundland, A1B 3X8 Canada; phone: (709)737-8624 or (709)753-8626; FAX: (709)737-2345). Index available in last issue of volume--attached. **Bk Rev**, **Cir:** (Qty: 6/year). **Circ:** 500. **Continues** Media Message, 0380-0199.
 Ind/Abst Curr. Cit.; Curr. Index J. Educ.; Educ. Technol. Abstr.; Inf. Sci. Abstr. (?-?); Tech. Educ. Train. Abstr.

   ISSN 0849-2883
DD 070.1/02571   CN

CANADIAN MEDIA LIST, THE. [Can. media list]. **Added/Corp** Canadian Book Information Centre. **VFOAT** For Immediate Release. (198?)-. Directory. English. One time a year (September). 240.10Can$. Canadian Book Information Centre, 2 Gloucester Street / Suite 301, Toronto Ontario M4Y 1L5 Canada. **Tel** (416)413-4930, FAX (416)361-0643. **ED** Patti McCabe. **Circ:** 150. available on labels.
 Desc: Media directory including information on newspapers, radio, TV, and magazines across Canada.

   ISSN 1188-5556
DD 338.4/7371334/05   CN

CANADIAN MULTI MEDIA MAGAZINE, THE. [Can. multi media mag.]. **VFOAT** Canadian MMM. (1992)-. Periodical. English. Six times a year. $68.00 per year. Alberta Communications Group, Suite 205, 10840-124th Street, Edmonton Alberta T5M 0H3 Canada.

LC F1001 .C287   ISSN 1191-0860
DD 971/.005   CN

CANADIAN SPEECHES, ISSUES OF THE DAY. [Can. speeches issues day]. **VFOAT** Canadian Speeches; Issues of the Day; Issues. Vol. 5, Issue 7 (Nov. 1991)-. Periodical. English. Ten times a year. 63.57Can$. Canadian Speeches, PO Box 250, Woodville Ontario K0M 2T0 Canada. **Tel** (705)439-2580, FAX (705)439-2646. **ED** A. Earle Gray. Index available. cum. index. **Bk Rev**. **Circ:** 1,000. available on microfilm; available on an online database. **Continues** Canadian Speeches/Issues, Informed Thought, 0849-9918.
 Desc: Source of information and views on current Canadian affairs. For writers, researchers, the news media, public affairs professionals, students.
 Ind/Abst Can. Index; Can. Period. Index (19??-).

   ISSN 0822-918X
DD 700/.29/471384   CN

CAPITAL REGION CREATIVE SERVICES DIRECTORY, THE. See The Arts.

   AT
   CEASED
CB ACTION. (19??)-(June 1995). English. Australian Consolidated Press Ltd., Private Bag 92615 Symonds St, Auckland New Zealand. **Tel** 011 64 9 3735408, FAX 011 64 9 3022889.

   ISSN 1122-6455
   IT
UDC 681.3
● **CD-ROM & MULTIMEDIA. See** Computers-Optical Storage, CD-ROM Applications.

   ISSN 0749-6001
DD 363   US
CENSORSHIP NEWS. (CENSORSHIP NEWS : A NEWSLETTER OF THE NATIONAL COALITION AGAINST CENSORSHIP.). [Censorsh. news]. **Added/Corp** National Coalition against Censorship (U.S.). (19??)-. Newsletter. English. Four times a year. $40.00 (Comes with National Coalition Against Censorship Friends membership). National Coalition Against Censorship, 275 7th Avenue, 20th Place, New York NY 10001. **Tel** (212)807-6222, FAX (212)807-6245. **ED** Roz Vdow. **Circ:** 5,000 (ctrl).
 Desc: Monitors and reports on censorship nationwide as it affects schools, libraries, literature and the arts, critical thinking and political life.

LC HM258 .C454
DD 302.2   EC
Pr Rev.
CHASQUI : REVISTA LATINOAMERICANA DE COMUNICACION. **Added/Corp** Centro Internacional de Estudios Superiores de Comunicacion para America Latina. (19??)-. Periodical. Spanish. Four times a year. $40.00. Ciespal, Apartado 584, Quito Ecuador. **Tel** 011 593 2 545831, 011 593 2 5446224. **Continues** Chasqui.

   ISSN 1058-4935
   US
CHICAGO MEDIA UPDATE. (1991)-. Periodical. English. $101.50. The Lavery Company, 15 Spinning Wheel Road, Suite 20, Hinsdale IL 60521.

   ISSN 1058-4927
   US
CHICAGO METRO MARKET MEDIA DIRECTORY. (1991)-. Directory. English. $101.50. The Lavery Company, 15 Spinning Wheel Road, Suite 20, Hinsdale IL 60521.

LC Z479 .C45   ISSN 0734-8169
DD 050.5/025/73   US
CHILDREN'S MEDIA MARKET PLACE. [Child. media mark. place]. **VFOAT** Children's Media Marketplace. (1978)-. Periodical. English. Irregular. $45.00 (3rd edition). Neal-Schuman Publishers Inc., 100 Varick Street, New York NY 10013. **Tel** (212)925-8650, FAX (212)219-8916. **ED** Delores Jones.
 Desc: A directory covering 25 areas, including publishers, AV and software producers and distributors, periodicals, agents, organizations, radio and television, examination and selecting centers.

   US
CHISPAS. **Added/Corp** California. University. Movimiento Estudiantil Chicano de Aztlan. (19??)-. Periodical. English. Three times a year. Free on request. Mecha Communications, University of California, 516 Eshleman Hall, Berkeley CA 94720.

   ISSN 0009-5303
   CN
CHRISTIAN COMMUNICATIONS. [Christ. commun.]. **Added/Corp** National Catholic Centre for Radio, Television, Film, and Press. St. Paul University (Ottawa, Ont.). St. Paul Society (Sherbrooke, Quebec). Christian Communication Service. St. Paul University (Ottawa, Ont.). School of Communications. Vol. 1 (Dec. 1962)-. Periodical. English. Four times a year. Saint Paul University, 223 Main Street, Ottawa Ontario K1S 1C4 Canada. **Tel** (613)236-1393 ext. 2332, FAX (613)782-3026. available on microfilm from University Microfilms International (UMI).

LC P91.5.U5 C56   ISSN 0742-3632
DD 001.51/07/1173   US
CINCOM. **Added/Corp** Communications Library (San Francisco, Calif.). **VFOAT** Courses in Communications. (19??)-. English. Every 2 years. $38.00. Communications Library, Lockbox 472139, Marina Station, San Francisco CA 94147. **Tel** (415)626-5050, FAX (415)346-4466. **ED** T.S. Connelly. **Circ:** 100,000.
 Desc: Contains Asian, Canadian, European, Mid-Eastern, and accredited United States IHEs offering courses and degree programs in communications.

LC TR   ISSN 1016-9660
DD 770   BE
UDC 77
CINE & MEDIA. (1988)-. Multiple languages (English, French and Spanish). Six times a year. $25.00. International Catholic Organization for Cinema and Audiovisual, 15 rue du Saphir, B-1040 Brussels Belgium. **Tel** 011 32 2 7344294, FAX 011 32 7343207, telex 0402 6105905 GMA LU. **ED** Robert Molhant. **Bk Rev**. **Ad Acc**. **Circ:** 12,500. **Continues** OCIC Newsletter.
 Desc: Covers film, festivals, filmprogrammes, people, institutions, events, and books which mark communication between men.
 Ind/Abst Film Lit. Index (19??-).

   ISSN 0821-1876
DD 418/.02/05   CN
● **CIRCUIT (MONTREAL). See** Linguistics.

LC PN4855 .C6
   US
CLIO AMONG THE MEDIA : NEWSLETTER OF THE AEJMC HISTORY DIVISION. See Journalism.

LC WMLC 93/3183   ISSN 1072-5393
DD 384   US
● **CNS OUTLOOK.** [CNS outlook]. Vol. 1, No. 1 (Oct. 15, 1993)-. Periodical. English. Twenty-five times a year. $495.00. Phillips Business Information Inc., 1201 Seven Locks Road, PO Box 61130, Potomac MD 20854. **Tel** (301)424-3338, (301)340-1520, (800)777-5005, FAX (301)424-4297, telex 358149. **ED** Damon Hart. **Ad Acc, Adv Mgr:** Jim Snyder.

   ISSN 0178-8728
UDC 681.3.02   GW
● **COGITO DARMSTADT. See** Computers.

   ISSN 1075-8496
DD 027   US
● **COLLEGE & UNIVERSITY MEDIA REVIEW.** [Coll. univ. med. rev.]. **Added/Corp** Consortium of College and University Media Centers. **VFOAT** College and University Media Review. Vol. 1, No. 1 (Summer 1994)-. Periodical. English. Four times a year. comes with Consortium of College and University Media Centers membership. Consortium of College and University Media Centers, Iowa State University, 121 Pearson Hall, Ames IA 50011. **Tel** (515)294-1811.

LC Z6944.S8 D57 LB3621.65   ISSN 1046-4255
DD 378.1/9897/02573   US
COLLEGE MEDIA DIRECTORY, THE. See Education-Higher Education.

   ISSN 1065-0296
DD 658   US
Pr Rev.
COLLEGIATE TRENDS (RIDGEWOOD, N.J.). See Education-Higher Education.

   US
COMMON CARRIER DOMESTIC FACILITIES APPLICATIONS. **Main/Corp** United States. Federal Communications Commission. (19??)-. English. FCC / Federal Communications Commission, 1919 M Street Northwest, Room 538, Washington DC 20554. **Tel** (202)632-6302.

   US
COMMON CARRIER PUBLIC MOBILE SERVICES INFORMATION. **Main/Corp** United States. Federal Communications Commission. (19??)-. English. FCC / Federal Communications Commission, 1919 M Street Northwest, Room 538, Washington DC 20554. **Tel** (202)632-6302.

   US
   TITLE CHANGE
COMMUNCIATIONS MANAGER. (19??)-(19??). Periodical. English. Communications Concepts Inc., 7481 Huntsman Boulevard, Suite 720, Springfield VA 22153. **Tel** (703)643-2200. **ED** Bill Londino, Carolyn Bulford, and Nancy Rathbun Scott. **Continues** Communications Concepts, 0741-0069. **Merged into** Writing Concepts Business Communications Report.

   ISSN 0846-5347
DD 378.714/565   CN
COMMUNIC-ACTION (VICTORIAVILLE). (COMMUNIC-ACTION.). [Communic-action]. **Added/Corp** Cegep de Victoriaville. (1989)-. Periodical. French. One time a week. Gratuit. Cegep de Victoriaville, 475 Est rue Notre-Dame, Victoriaville Quebec G6P 4B3 Canada. **Continues** Comunic., 0821-4646.

   ISSN 0700-5261
DD 001.5/05   CN
COMMUNICATEUR. (LE COMMUNICATEUR.). (1976)-. Periodical. French. Twelve times a year. Argus Communications Inc, 1161 Lac Cache, CP 26, St. Alexis Quebec J0K 1V0 Canada. **Tel** (819)265-2072, FAX (819)265-3135.

   ISSN 0771-7342
UDC 654.028   BE
Pr Rev.
COMMUNICATIE. [Communicatie]. (1975)-. Periodical. Dutch. Four times a year. $40.30. Centrum voor Communicatieweten, Schappen van Evenstraat 2A, B3000 Louvain Belgium. **Tel** 011 32 16 283220, FAX

016/28 32 10. **ED** L. Van Poecke. **Bk Rev. Ad Acc. Circ:** 1,000 (ctrl). ***Continues*** *Informatie Bulletin CE. CO. WE., 0771-7334.*
Desc: A specialist journal on mass media and culture.

NE

COMMUNICATIE TECHNIEK & MANAGEMENT. Dutch. Six times a year. AV Press BV, Postbus 155, 6500 AD Nijmegen Netherlands. **Tel** 011 31 80 787444.

NE
TITLE CHANGE

COMMUNICATIEF. (19??)-(19??). Dutch. Bohn Stafleu van Loghum BV, Postbus 246, 3990 GA Houten Netherlands. **Tel** 011 31 3403 95782. **(Subscription address:** Intermedia BV, Postbus 4, 2400 MA Alphen AD Rijn Netherlands. **Tel** 011 31 1720 66481.**)** ***Continued by*** *Tijdschrift over Communicatie.*

ISSN 0822-0638
DD 001.56 CN
COMMUNICATING TOGETHER. See Physically Impaired.

LC P87 .C595
DD 384 SA
COMMUNICATIO. Added/Corp University of Pretoria. Dept. of Communication. (19??)-. Periodical. Afrikaans (English). Two times a year. $5.23. University of South Africa, PO Box 392, Pretoria 0001 South Africa. **Tel** 011 27 12 4293111, FAX 011 27 12 4293221. **ED** Pieter Fourie. **Bk Rev. Circ:** 950.
Desc: Medium for practitioners in the fields of the press, radio, film, television, advertising, public relations media, science and diplomacy. Attention to semiological structuralism.

LC P87 .C5973 **ISSN** 0305-4233
DD 001.5/05 US
CCC
CEASED
COMMUNICATION. [Communication]. Vol. 1 (June 1974)-(1993). Periodical. English. Gordon & Breach Science Publishers, Inc., PO Box 786, Cooper Station, New York NY 10276. **Tel** (212)206-8900, FAX (212)645-2459. Documents available from The Genuine Article.
Desc: Provides a forum for the debate of current issues and critical work in the field of communications and media studies. Pays equal attention to social implications of mass media both inside the US and internationally.
Ind/Abst Commun. Abstr.; Curr. Contents Soc. Behav. Sci.; Int. Bibliogr. Sociol.; Psychol. Abstr. (1974-); PsycINFO (1990-); PsycLit; Res. Alert [Full Cov.]; Soc. Plann. Policy Dev. Abstr.; Soc. Sci. Cit. Index [Full Cov.]; Sociol. Abstr. (?-?).

LC P87 .C59733 **ISSN** 0162-2811
DD 001.5/05 US
CCC
COMMUNICATION ABSTRACTS. See Communications-Abstracting, Bibliographies and Statistics.

ISSN 0730-7799
DD 658 US
COMMUNICATION BRIEFINGS. [Commun. brief.]. **VFOAT** Ideas That Work. Vol. 1, No. 1 (1981)-. Periodical. English. Twelve times a year (monthly). $79.00. Encoders, Inc., (A division of Capitol Publications, Inc.), 700 Black Horse Pike, Suite 108, Blackwood NJ 08012. **Tel** (609)232-6380, FAX (609)232-8229. **(Subscription address:** Communication Briefings, 1101 King Street, Suite 110, Alexandria VA 22314. **Tel** (703)548-3800, FAX (703)684-2136.**) ED** Frank Grazian. Index available. **Bk Rev. Circ:** 29,000.
Desc: Communication ideas, techniques and research designed to help readers write, speak, present, persuade and motivate better.

US
COMMUNICATION (COMMUNICATION ASSOCIATION OF THE PACIFIC). (COMMUNICATION.). **Added/Corp** Communication Association of the Pacific. (19??)-. Periodical. English. Irregular. Communication Association of the Pacific, Department of Speech, University of Hawaii, Honolulu HI 96822.

BE
UDC 05
COMMUNICATION DIGEST. French. Six times a year. Editions PMB, rue de la Duchesse 13, 1040 Brussels Belgium.

ISSN 1053-0169
DD 658 US
COMMUNICATION EDGE, THE. See Business and Economics-Management.

LC PN4071 .S74 **ISSN** 0363-4523
DD 808.5 /05 US
Pr Rev.
COMMUNICATION EDUCATION. [Commun. educ.]. **Added/Corp** Speech Communication Association. Vol. 25 (Jan. 1976)-. Periodical. English. Four times a year (Jan., Apr., July and Oct.). $96.00. Speech Communication Association, 5105 Backlick Road, Suite E, Annandale VA 22003. **Tel** (703)750-0533, FAX (703)914-9471. Index available. cum. index. **Bk Rev. Ad Acc. Circ:** 5,000 (ctrl). available on microfilm and microfiche from University Microfilms International (UMI). Documents available from The Genuine Article, UMI Article Clearinghouse. ***Continues*** *Speech Teacher, 0038-7177.*
Desc: Publishes articles on topics related to communication in instructional settings. Articles include research, theory, and application oriented works.
Ind/Abst Acad. Abstr.; Acad. Ind. [Computer File] (1987-); Acad. Search; Annu. Bibliogr. Engl. Lang. Lit.; Commun. Abstr.; Contents Pages Educ.; Cumul. Index Nurs. Allied Health Lit.; Curr. Cit.; Curr. Contents Soc. Behav. Sci.; Curr. Index J. Educ.; Educ. Index; Educ. Adm. Abstr.; EP Collect.; Expand. Acad. Index (1987-); Homework Help.; Humanit. Source; INFO-SOUTH Abstr.; Lang. Lang. Behav. Abstr.; Linguist. Lang. Behav. Abstr.; Mag. Search; MasterFile FullTEXT 1000; MasterFile FullTEXT 350; MasterFile FullTEXT 650; MasterFile FullTEXT (July 1990-); Med. Rev. Dig.; MLA Int. Bibl. Books Artic. Mod. Lang. Lit.; Newsp. Period. Abstr. (1989-); OCLC; Psychol. Abstr. (1986-); PsycINFO; PsycLit; Pub. Lib. FullTEXT; Ref. Sources; Res. Alert [Full Cov.]; Soc. Plann. Policy Dev. Abstr.; Soc. Sci. Cit. Index [Full Cov.]; Sociol. Abstr.; Telebase.

ISSN 1081-1680
US
•COMMUNICATION LAW AND POLICY. See Law.

LC PN4077 .S6 **ISSN** 0363-7751
DD 001.54/2/05 US
NLM W1 CO4273
Pr Rev.
COMMUNICATION MONOGRAPHS. [Commun. monogr.]. **Added/Corp** Speech Communication Association. Vol. 43 (Mar. 1976)-. Periodical. English. Four times a year (Mar., June, Sept., Dec.). $96.00. Speech Communication Association, 5105 Backlick Road, Suite E, Annandale VA 22003. **Tel** (703)750-0533, FAX (703)914-9471. Index available. cum. index. **Bk Rev. Ad Acc. Circ:** 4,500 (ctrl). available on microfilm and microfiche from University Microfilms International (UMI). Documents available from The Genuine Article, UMI Article Clearinghouse. ***Continues*** *Speech Monographs, 0038-7169.*
Desc: Devoted mainly to scientific and empirical investigations of communication processes.
Ind/Abst Acad. Abstr.; Acad. Ind. [Computer File] (1987-); Acad. Search; Am. Hist. Life (1965-1988)(1976-); Annu. Bibliogr. Engl. Lang. Lit.; Arts Humanit. Citation Index [Select. Cov.]; Commun. Abstr.; Curr. Cit.; Curr. Contents Soc. Behav. Sci.; Curr. Index J. Educ.; Educ. Index; EP Collect.; Except. Child Educ. Abstr.; Except. Child Educ. Resour. (19??-19??); Expand. Acad. Index (1987-); Homework Help.; Humanit. Source; INFO-SOUTH Abstr.; Lang. Lang. Behav. Abstr.; Lang. Teach.; Linguist. Lang. Behav. Abstr.; Mag. Search; MasterFile FullTEXT 1000; MasterFile FullTEXT 350; MasterFile FullTEXT 650; MasterFile FullTEXT (July 1990-); Middle East Abstr. Index; MLA Int. Bibl. Books Artic. Mod. Lang. Lit.; Newsp. Period. Abstr. (1990-); OCLC; Psychol. Abstr. (1976-); PsycINFO; PsycLit; Recent. Publ. Artic.; Res. Alert [Full Cov.]; Soc. Plann. Policy Dev. Abstr.; Soc. Sci. Source; Soc. Sci. Cit. Index [Full Cov.]; Sociol. Abstr.; Telebase; Writ. Am. Hist.

ISSN 0819-9817
AT
COMMUNICATION NEWS. (1987)-. Periodical. English. Six times a year. 49.34Aus$. Communication Research Institution Australia, PO Box 8, Hackett ACT 2602 Australia. **Tel** 011 61 62 573155, FAX 011 61 62 2475056. ***Continues*** *CARE Newsletter (Canberra), 0818-3570.*

ISSN 0161-4126
DD 616 US
COMMUNICATION OUTLOOK. [Commun. outlook]. **Added/Corp** International Society for Augmentative and Alternative Communication. Trace Research and Development Center on Communication Control and Computer Access for Handicapped Individuals. Michigan State University. Artificial Language Laboratory. International Action Group for Communication Enhancement. University of Wisconsin--Madison. Trace Research and Development Center for the Severely Communicatively Handicapped. University of Wisconsin--Madison. Trace Research and Development Center on Communication, Control, and Computer Access for Handicapped Individuals. Vol. 1 (Spring 1978)-. Periodical. English. Four times a year (Mar., June, Sept., Dec.). $18.00. Michigan State University Artificial Language Laboratory, 405 Computer Center, East Lansing MI 48824-1042. **Tel** (517)353-0870, FAX (517)353-4766. **ED** Jessica Gifford. Index available. cum. index. **Bk Rev. Ad Acc, Adv Mgr:** Julie Warren. **Circ:** 2,649. available on audiocassette. Documents available from Ask*IEEE.
Desc: Focusing on communication aids and techniques: application of technology to the needs of persons who experience communication handicaps due to neurological and neuromuscular conditions.
Ind/Abst INSPEC (Winter 1984-).

ISSN 0993-9903
FR
UDC 629.11.012.5
COMMUNICATION PNEU : SAINT-CLOUD. (1988)-. Periodical. French. Twelve times a year. Francese Editions, 11 rue d'Orleans, F 92210 Saint Cloud France. **Tel** 011 33 1 47711468.

LC PN4071 .T6 **ISSN** 0146-3373
DD 001.5/05 US
Pr Rev.
COMMUNICATION QUARTERLY. [Commun. q.]. **Added/Corp** Eastern Communication Association. Vol. 24 (Winter 1976)-. Periodical. English. Four times a year (Spring, Summer, Fall, Winter). $25.00. Eastern Communciation Association, University of New Haven, Maxcy Hall Room 101, 300 Orange Avenue, West Haven CT 06516. **Tel** (203)932-7208, FAX (203)937-0756. **ED** Linda Lederman and Virginia P. Richmond. Index available. **Ad Acc. Circ:** 3,000 (ctrl). available on microfilm and microfiche from University Microfilms International (UMI). Documents available from UMI Article Clearinghouse. ***Continues*** *Today's Speech, 0040-8573.*
Desc: Rhetorical theory, broadcasting, oral interpretation, and other aspects of the communication arts field.
Ind/Abst Abstr. Anthropol.; Acad. Ind. [Computer File] (1992-); Acad. Search; Contents Pages Educ.; Curr. Cit.; Curr. Index J. Educ.; Educ. Index; EP Collect.; Expand. Acad. Index (1989-); Homework Help.; Humanit. Index; Humanit. Source; INFO-SOUTH Abstr.; Linguist. Lang. Behav. Abstr.; Mag. Search; MasterFile FullTEXT 1000; MasterFile FullTEXT 350; MasterFile FullTEXT 650; MasterFile FullTEXT (Jan. 1994-); Multicult. Educ. Abstr.; Newsp. Period. Abstr. (1991-); OCLC; Sage Fam. Stud. Abstr.; Soc. Plann. Policy Dev. Abstr.; Sociol. Abstr.; Spec. Educ. Needs Abstr.; Stud. Women Abstr.; Telebase.

LC P91.5.U5 C656 **ISSN** 0893-4215
DD 001 US
CCC
COMMUNICATION REPORTS (PULLMAN, WASH.). (COMMUNICATION REPORTS.). **Added/Corp** Western Speech Communication Association. Western States Communication Association. Vol. 1, No. 1 (Winter 1988)-. Periodical. English. Two times a year. Univerrsity of Utah, WSCA, Department of Communication, Salt Lake City UT 84112. **Tel** (801)581-6526. available on microfilm and microfiche from University Microfilms International (UMI). Documents available.
Ind/Abst Bus. Source Plus; Commun. Abstr.; EP Collect.; Homework Help.; Linguist. Lang. Behav. Abstr.; MasterFile FullTEXT 1000; MasterFile FullTEXT 350; MasterFile FullTEXT 650; MasterFile FullTEXT; OCLC; Soc. Plann. Policy Dev. Abstr.; Sociol. Abstr.; Telebase.

LC P91 .C56 **ISSN** 0093-6502
DD 001.5 US
CCC
CODEN CRESDG
Pr Rev.
COMMUNICATION RESEARCH. [Communic. res.]. Vol. 1 (Jan. 1974)-. Periodical. English. Six times a year (Feb., Apr., June, Aug., Oct., Dec.). $255.00. SAGE Periodical Press, 2455 Teller Road, Thousand Oaks CA 91320. **Tel** (805)499-0721, FAX (805)499-0871, telex 100799. **ED** Sandra J. Ball-Rokeach, Charles R. Berger. **Acid Free.** available on microfilm and microfiche from University Microfilms International (UMI). Documents available from The Genuine Article, UMI Article Clearinghouse.
Desc: Provides an interdisciplinary forum for scholars and professionals to present new research in communication. Encourages rigorous studies of mass and interpersonal communication.
Ind/Abst Acad. Search; Arts Humanit. Citation Index [Select. Cov.]; Commun. Abstr.; Curr. Cit.; Curr. Contents Soc. Behav. Sci.; Curr. Index J. Educ.; Educ. Technol. Abstr.; EP Collect.; Expand. Acad. Index (1989-); Film Lit. Index (19??-); Homework Help.; Humanit. Index; Humanit. Source; Index Period. Artic. Relat. Law; INFO-SOUTH Abstr.; Linguist. Lang. Behav. Abstr.; Mag. Search; MasterFile FullTEXT 1000; MasterFile FullTEXT 350; MasterFile FullTEXT 650; MasterFile FullTEXT (July 1993-); Newsp. Period. Abstr. (1991-); OCLC; Psychol. Abstr. (1974-); PsycINFO; PsycLit; Res. Alert [Full Cov.]; Sage Fam. Stud. Abstr. (?-?); Sage Urban Stud. Abstr (?-?); Soc. Plann. Policy Dev. Abstr.; Soc. Sci. Source; Soc. Sci. Cit. Index [Full Cov.]; Soc. Sci. Index; Soc. Sci. Index Fulltext (Oct. 1988-) [Full Txt.]; Sociol. Abstr.; Stud. Women Abstr.; Telebase.

ISSN 0882-4096
DD 302 US
COMMUNICATION RESEARCH REPORTS. (COMMUNICATION RESEARCH REPORTS : CCR.). [Commun. res. rep.]. **Added/Corp** World Communication Association. West Virginia University. Speech Communication Dept. **VFOAT** CRR. Vol. 1, No. 1 (Dec. 1984)-. English. Two times a year. Free to members of the World Communication Association. World Communication Association, Westfield State College, Westfield MA 01086. **Tel** (413)568-3311. **(Subscription address:** World Communications Association, 202 Lasher Hall, Ohio

University, Athens OH 45701. **Tel** (614)593-4831.) **ED** Michael Beatty. **Bk Rev. Ad Acc. Circ:** 500 (ctrl).
Desc: Publishes articles on all aspects of communication research and practice in nature. Prefers research on communication of all types although intercultural is preferred.
Ind/Abst Linguist. Lang. Behav. Abstr.; Psychol. Abstr. (1984-); PsycINFO; PsycLit; Soc. Plann. Policy Dev. Abstr.; Sociol. Abstr.

ISSN 0144-4646
US

COMMUNICATION RESEARCH TRENDS. [Commun. res. trends]. **Added/Corp** Centre for the Study of Communication and Culture (London, England). Vol. 1, No. 1 (Spring 1980)-. Periodical. English. Four times a year (quarterly). $30.00. Centre for the Study of Communication and Culture, 321 North Spring Avenue, St. Louis MO 63156. **Tel** (314)977-7290, FAX (314)977-7296. **(Subscription address:** Centre for the Study of Communication and Culture, PO Box 56907, St. Louis MO 63136. **Tel** (314)977-7290.) **ED** William E. Biernatzki, S.J. **Bk Rev. Circ:** 1,600. ***Continues*** *CSCC Newsletter.*
Desc: Surveys the state-of-the-art in selected communication research fields by reviewing recent publications and listing important additional bibliography and active researchers and centers.
Ind/Abst Film Lit. Index (1982-1985).

CN

COMMUNICATION REVUE QUEBECOISE DES RECHERCHES ET DES PRATIQUES EN COMMUNICATION. French. Two times a year (May, Nov.). 25.00Can$ (individuals), 40.00Can$ (institutions) US and Canada; 30.00Can$ (individuals), 45.00Can$ (institutions) other. Universite of Laval Pavillon Casault, Department of Information, B 5420, Sainte-Foy Quebec G1K 7P4 Canada. **Tel** (418)656-7588, 656-5212, FAX (418)651-3419.

LC Z5632 .C66 P87 **ISSN** 1041-7893
DD 016.3022/05 US
Pr Rev.

•**COMMUNICATION SERIALS. See** Communications-Abstracting, Bibliographies and Statistics.

LC PN4001 .C45 **ISSN** 1051-0974
DD 302.2/05 US
CODEN CSTDEK
Pr Rev.

COMMUNICATION STUDIES. [Commun. stud.]. **Added/Corp** Central States Communication Association (U.S.). Vol. 40, No. 1 (Spring 1989)-. Periodical. English. Four times a year. $40.00. Central States Communication Association, Box A-6 East Central University, Ada OK 74820-6899. **Tel** (405)332-8000 ext. 214 or 713, FAX (405)332-1623. **ED** Kevin Barge. Index available. cum. index. **Circ:** 2,700. available on microfilm and microfiche from University Microfilms International (UMI). Documents available from UMI Article Clearinghouse. ***Continues*** *Central States Speech Journal, 0008-9575.*
Desc: Research in areas of speech communication: interpersonal, small group, public, mass communication, and theatre communication education, and public relations.
Ind/Abst Commun. Abstr.; Curr. Index J. Educ.; Expand. Acad. Index (1989-); Newsp. Period. Abstr. (1989-); Soc. Plann. Policy Dev. Abstr.

LC P87 .C59737 **ISSN** 1050-3293
DD 302.2/05 US
CCC
CODEN CNTHEV
Pr Rev.

COMMUNICATION THEORY. (COMMUNICATION THEORY : CT : A JOURNAL OF THE INTERNATIONAL COMMUNICATION ASSOCIATION.). [Commun. theory]. **Added/Corp** International Communication Association. **VFOAT** CT. (Feb. 1991)-. Periodical. English. Four times a year. $90.00. Guilford Publications Inc., 72 Spring Street, New York NY 10012. **Tel** (212)431-9800, (800)365-7006, FAX (212)966-6708. **(Subscription address:** Turpin Distribution Services Limited, Blackhorse Road, Letchworth, Hertfordshire SH6 1HN United Kingdom. **Tel** 011 44 1462 672555, FAX 011 44 1462 480947.) **ED** Donald Ellis. **Bk Rev. Ad Acc.** available on microfilm and microfiche from University Microfilms International (UMI). Documents available from UMI Article Clearinghouse.
Desc: An international interdisciplinary forum for theory and theoretically oriented research on all aspects of communication.
Ind/Abst Commun. Abstr.; Int. Bibliogr. Sociol.; Linguist. Lang. Behav. Abstr.; Newsp. Period. Abstr. (1989-); Soc. Plann. Policy Dev. Abstr.; Sociol. Abstr.

DD 960 ZA

COMMUNICATION - UNIVERSITY OF ZAMBIA. INSTITUTE FOR AFRICAN STUDIES. Main/Corp University of Zambia. Institute for African Studies. (1971)-. Monographic series. English. Price varies per volume. University of Zambia / Institute for African Studies, The Library, PO Box 2379, Lusaka Zambia. ***Continues*** *University of Zambia. Institute for Social Research. Communication.*

LC HF5718 .C65x **ISSN** 0744-7612
DD 659 US
CCC

COMMUNICATION WORLD (SAN FRANCISCO, CALIF.). (COMMUNICATION WORLD.). [Commun. world]. **Added/Corp** International Association of Business Communicators. Vol. 1, No. 1 (Nov. 1983)-. Trade Publication. English. Eight times a year. $95.00. International Association of Business Communicators, One Hallidie Plaza, Suite 600, San Francisco CA 94102. **Tel** (415)433-3400, FAX (415)362-8762. **ED** Gloria Gordon. Index available. cum. index. **Bk Rev**, (Qty: 11). **Ad Acc, Adv Mgr:** T. Gradie. **Circ:** 12,500 (ctrl). available on microfilm and microfiche from University Microfilms International (UMI); available on an online database from Lexis-Nexis; and (files 15,648/Full-Text) DIALOG. Documents available from UMI Article Clearinghouse, BLDSC, The UnCover Company. ***Continues*** *Communication World (San Francisco, Calif. : 1981), 0744-7612.*
Desc: Reports on new ideas, people, issues and other information designed to keep communication and public relations professionals informed of what is happening in the industry.
Ind/Abst ABI/INFORM Glob. Ed.; ABI/INFORM [Computer File] (1983-); Acad. Search; Bus. ASAP (1990-) [Full Txt.]; Bus. Index (1985-); Bus. Source Plus; Bus. Source; Curr. Cit.; EP Collect.; Gen. BusinessFile (1985-); Gen. Period. Index (1985-); Homework Help.; Humanit. Source; INFO-SOUTH Abstr.; Lotus Notes; Mag. Search; Manage. Contents; MasterFile FullTEXT 1000; MasterFile FullTEXT 350; MasterFile FullTEXT 650; MasterFile FullTEXT (Jan. 1994-); OCLC; Telebase; Trade Ind. ASAP [Full Txt.]; Trade Ind. Index [Full Txt.]; UMI ABI/Inform--Bus. Period. Ondisc [Full Txt.].

LC P87 .C5974 **ISSN** 0147-4642
DD 001.5/05 US
NLM W1 CO4273M

COMMUNICATION YEARBOOK. Added/Corp International Communication Association. No. 1, (1977)-. English. Irregular. $69.95. SAGE Periodical Press, 2455 Teller Road, Thousand Oaks CA 91320. **Tel** (805)499-0721, FAX (805)499-0871, telex 100799. **Acid Free.**

UK

COMMUNICATIONS. English. £22.50 UK; £30.00 other. International Thomson Business Publications, 42 Bedford Square, London WC1B 3SC United Kingdom. **Tel** 011 44 171 3236986.

US

COMMUNICATIONS. (19??)-. English. Twelve times a year. $225.00. Predicasts Inc., A Ziff Communications Company, 11001 Cedar Avenue, Cleveland OH 44106. **Tel** (800)321-6388, (216)795-3000, FAX (216)229-9944, telex 985 604. **(Subscription address:** Information Access Company, PO Box 61000, Department 1851, San Francisco CA 94161. **Tel** (800)321-6388.)

UK

COMMUNICATIONS AFRICA. (19??)-. English (French). Six times a year. $75.00 US; £43.50 other. Alain Charles Publishing Ltd., 27 Wilfred Street, London SW1E 6PR United Kingdom. **Tel** 011 44 171 8347676, FAX 011 44 171 9730076, telex 297165.

LC P87 .C59 **ISSN** 0378-0880
DD 302.2/05 BE
CCC
Pr Rev.

COMMUNICATIONS & COGNITION. [Commun. cogn.]. **Added/Corp** Rijksuniversiteit te Gent. Werkgroep voor de Studie van Communicatieve en Cognitieve Processen. **VFOAT** Communication and Cognition. Vol. 4, No. 1 (1971)-. Periodical. English (Dutch, French and German). Three times a year. $70.89. Communication & Cognition, Blandijnberg 2, Dr Vandamme, B-9000 Ghent Belgium. **Tel** 11 32 91 643952, FAX (32) 91 24 16 21. **ED** F. Vandamme. Index available. cum. index. **Bk Rev. Ad Acc. Circ:** 1,000. ***Continues*** *Communicatie en Cognitie.*
Desc: Interdisciplinary oriented focus on linguistics, psychology, logic, methodology of science anthropology, aesthetics, culture, sociology, computer sciences and learning processes.
Ind/Abst Annu. Bibliogr. Engl. Lang. Lit.; J. Econ. Lit.; Linguist. Lang. Behav. Abstr.; Math. Rev.; Philos. Index; Psychol. Abstr. (1971-); PsycINFO; PsycLit; Soc. Plann. Policy Dev. Abstr.; Sociol. Abstr.

FR

COMMUNICATIONS D'ENTERPRISE. (19??)-. French. Twelve times a year. 561.34F France; 600.00F other. CEEPP, 120 Av des Champs Elysees, 75008 Paris France. **Tel** 011 33 1 45627642.

LC HE8123 .C65
DD 380.3/025/415 IE

COMMUNICATIONS DIRECTORY & YEARBOOK. (19??)-. Directory. English. Mount Salus Press, Tritonville Road Sandymount, Dublin 4 Ireland.

LC KF4774 .N48 **ISSN** 0898-2457
DD 343.73/0998 347.303998 US

COMMUNICATIONS LAW (1982). See Law.

LC KF2750.A15 C65 **ISSN** 0737-7622
DD 343.73/099 347.30399 US

COMMUNICATIONS LAWYER : PUBLICATION OF THE FORUM COMMITTEE ON COMMUNICATIONS LAW, AMERICAN BAR ASSOCIATION. See Law.

US

COMMUNICATIONS MANAGER. English. Twelve times a year. $99.00 US; $129.00 other. Communication Concepts Inc., 2100 National Press Building, Washington DC 20045. **ED** Bill Londino. ***Continues*** *Communications Concepts.*
Desc: Indexed newsletter written for publication, PR and desktop publishing managers and staff. It covers publication design and production, PR and marketing strategies, business writing and editing, publication productivity, communications resources and practical ideas that work in publication management.

LC HE **ISSN** 1356-3327
DD 384 UK

•**COMMUNICATIONS MARKETS ANALYSIS.** (1995)-. Trade Publication. English. One time a year. £595.00. MDIS Publications Limited, MDIS House, City Fields Business Park, City Fields Way, Chichester, West Sussex PO20 6FS United Kingdom. **Tel** 011 44 1243 533322, FAX 011 44 1243 533418. **ED** John Bennett. available on diskette; available on CD-ROM.

ISSN 0961-7590
DD 384 UK

COMMUNICATIONS MIDDLE EAST AFRICA. [Commun. Middle East Africa]. **VFOAT** Communications MEA. (1991)-. Trade Publication. English. Twelve times a year. $136.89. Information Technology Publishing Company, Angus House, 13 Tilehouse Street HITC, Hertfordshire SG5 2DU United Kingdom. **Tel** 011 44 1462 420785, FAX 011 44 1462 420786.

UK

COMMUNICATIONS NETWORK SERVICES. (19??)-. English. Irregular. $588.00. Datapro International, McGraw Hill House, Shoppenhangers Road, Maidenhead Berkshire SL6 2QL United Kingdom. **Tel** 011 44 1628 773277, FAX 011 44 1628 773628.

ISSN 0966-4882
DD 384 UK

COMMUNICATIONS NETWORKS. [Commun. netw.]. (1991)-. Trade Publication. English. Twelve times a year. $136.89. EMAP Readerlink, Audit House, 260 Field End Road, Ruislip Middlesex HA4 9LT United Kingdom. **Tel** 011 44 1773 63100, FAX 011 44 1733 87367. **(Subscription address:** EMAP Business Publishing, 4 Admiral House Cardinal Way, Middlesex HA3 5SQ United Kingdom. **Tel** 011 44 181 8684499.) Documents available from Ask*IEEE. ***Continues*** *Communications (London), 0266-8009.*
Ind/Abst Curr. Cit.; Infomat Int. Bus.; INSPEC.

LC TK5101.A1 C64 **ISSN** 0010-3632
DD 621 US
CCC

COMMUNICATIONS NEWS (GENEVA, ILL.). (COMMUNICATIONS NEWS.). [Commun. news]. Vol. 1, (Oct. 1964)-. Trade Publication. English. Twelve times a year. $60.00. Nelson Publishing, 2504 North Tamiami Trail, Nokomis FL 34275. **Tel** (813)966-9521, FAX (813)966-2590. **ED** Thomas L. Quigley. available on microfilm from University Microfilms International (UMI); available on an online database (files 15,16,648,675/Full-Text) from DIALOG. Documents available from Ask*IEEE, BLDSC, The UnCover Company, SWETS, UMI Article Clearinghouse. ***Absorbed*** *Wire & Radio Communications.*
Desc: For personnel in business and government responsible for the design, engineering, construction and maintenance of communications systems.
Ind/Abst Acad. Search; Bus. Index (1985-); Bus. Period. Index; Bus. Source Plus; Bus. Source; Comput. ASAP [Full Txt.]; Comput. Bus. (19??-19??); Comput. Database [Full Txt.]; Comput. Lit. Index; Curr. Cit.; Data Process. Dig.; Electron. Pub. Abstr.; EP Collect.; F&S Index Plus Text, Int. [Full Txt.] [Select. Cov.]; Gen. BusinessFile (1985-); Gen. Period. Index (1985-); HILITES; Homework Help.; Humanit. Source; INFO-SOUTH Abstr.; Infomat Int. Bus.; INSPEC (May 1985-); Lotus Notes; Mag. Search; Manage. Market. Abstr.; MasterFile FullTEXT 1000; MasterFile FullTEXT 350; MasterFile FullTEXT 650; MasterFile FullTEXT (July 1993-); OCLC; Predicasts;

Communications

PROMT [Full Txt.]; Telebase; Trade Ind. ASAP [Full Txt.]; Trade Ind. Index (1981-) [Full Txt.]; Wilson Bus. Abstr.; World Publ. Monit.

LC P87 .C6   ISSN 0588-8018
DD 384   FR
    CCC

COMMUNICATIONS (PARIS. 1962).
(COMMUNICATIONS / ECOLE PRATIQUE DES HAUTES ETUDES, CENTRE D'ETUDES DES COMMUNICATIONS DE MASSE.). [Communications]. **Added/Corp** Ecole Pratique des Hautes Etudes (France). Centre d'Etudes des Communications de Masse. Ecole Pratique des Hautes Etudes (France). Centre d'Etudes Transdisciplinaires (Sociologie, Anthropologie, Semiologie) Ecole des Hautes Etudes en Sciences Sociales. Centre d'Etudes Transdisciplinaires (Sociologie, Anthropologie, Semiologie). (1961)-. Periodical. French. Two times a year. $44.84. Bayard Services Informatique, 49 rue de la Vanne, 92120 Montrouge Cedex France. **Tel** 011 33 1 41171300.
  Ind/Abst Int. Polit. Sci. Abstr.; Linguist. Lang. Behav. Abstr.; Soc. Plann. Policy Dev. Abstr.; Sociol. Abstr.

    ISSN 1035-6959
    AT

COMMUNICATIONS REPORT. SYDNEY.
(1990)-. Periodical. English. Irregular (48 issues). 640.00Aus$ Australia; 690.00Aus$ other. C R Publishing, 515 Kent Street, 1st Floor, Sydney 2000 Australia. **Tel** 011/61/02/2612123, FAX 011/61/02/2672261. **ED** Martin Lim. Index available (bound in each issue). **Ad Acc.**

LC P87 .I56   ISSN 0341-2059
DD 001.51/05   GW

COMMUNICATIONS (SANKT AUGUSTIN). (COMMUNICATIONS.).
[Communications]. **Added/Corp** Deutsche Gesellschaft fuer Kommunikationsforschung. Internationale Vereinigung fuer Kommunikationswissenschaft. (1976)-. Periodical. German (English, French and German). Three times a year. $150.46. K.G. Saur Verlag KG, A Reed Reference Publishing Company, Part of Reed International PLC, Ortlerstrasse 8, D-81373 Munich Germany. **Tel** 011 49 89 769020, FAX 011 49 89 76902150, telex 5212067-SAUR-D. **Continues** *Internationale Zeitschrift fuer Kommunikationsforschung, 0340-0158.*
  Ind/Abst Infomat Int. Bus.; Linguist. Lang. Behav. Abstr.; Psychol. Abstr. (1976-); Soc. Plann. Policy Dev. Abstr.; Sociol. Abstr.

    ISSN 1064-3907
DD 384   US
    TITLE CHANGE

COMMUNICATIONS STANDARDS REVIEW.
[Commun. stand. rev.]. Vol. 1, No. 1 (Jan. 1990)-(1994). Periodical. English. Communications Standards Review, 757 Greer Road, Palo Alto CA 94303. **Tel** (415)856-9018, FAX (415)856-6591. **ED** Elanie Baskin. **Circ:** 175. available on diskette from MACPHUS. **Split into** *Communications Standard Reviews Telecommunications* **and** *Commmunications Standards Reviews Radiocommunications.*

    ISSN 1075-5721
DD 384   US
    TITLE CHANGE

COMMUNICATIONS STANDARDS SUMMARY.
[Commun. stand. summ.]. **VFOAT** CSS. Vol 1, No. 1 (Feb. 1994)-(1995). Periodical. English. Communications Standards Review, 757 Greer Road, Palo Alto CA 94303. **Tel** (415)856-9018, FAX (415)856-6591. **Continued by** *Fiber Optics Standards Summary.*
  Desc: Summarizes the status of all committee open projects and recently completed standards.

    ISSN 1042-6086
DD 384   US
    CCC

COMMUNICATIONSWEEK INTERNATIONAL.
[CommunicationsWeek int.]. **VFOAT** Communications Week International. (1988)-. Periodical. English. Irregular (20 issues). $150.00. CMP Publications Inc., One Jericho Plaza, Wing A, 2nd Floor, Jericho NY 11753. **Tel** (516)733-6700. **(Subscription address:** CommunicationsWeek International, Garrard House 2 6 Homesdale Road, Bromley BR2 9WL United Kingdom. **Tel** 011 44 181 4028181, FAX 011 44 181 4028383.) available on an online database (file 16/Full-Text) from DIALOG.
  Desc: Recognized leader in delivering news, analysis and solutions on this fast-changing world. Addresses networking and information technology around the world. Each issue goes deep into regional and national issues to pinpoint the policies, technologies, trends, applications and solutions as they emerge.
  Ind/Abst F&S Index Plus Text, Int. [Full Txt.] [Select. Cov.]; Infomat Int. Bus.; PROMT [Full Txt.].

LC HE271.5 .C65
DD 380   PK

COMMUNICATOR, THE. Added/Corp Pakistan.
Communications Information Cell. (1976)-. Periodical. English. Twelve times a year. Communications Information Cell, Ministry of Communications, 1st Floor/NSC Building, Karachi Pakistan.

    ISSN 0745-3671
    US

COMMUNICATOR (ALEXANDRIA, VA.).
(COMMUNICATOR.). [Communicator]. **Added/Corp** National Association of Government Communicators (U.S.). (19??)-. Periodical. English. Twelve times a year. National Association of Government Communicators, 80 South Early Street, Alexandria VA 22304. **Tel** (703)823-4821.

    ISSN 0953-3699
    UK
    CODEN CMMUES

COMMUNICATOR - INSTITUTE OF SCIENTIFIC AND TECHNICAL COMMUNICATORS. (THE COMMUNICATOR.).
[Communicator - Inst. Sci. Tech. Commun.]. **Added/Corp** Institute of Scientific and Technical Communicators. **VFOAT** Communicator of Scientific and Technical Information. No. 63 (April 1985)-. Periodical. English. Four times a year. $42.78. Institute of Scientific and Technical Communicators, Kings Court, 2 16 Goodge Street, London W1P 1FF United Kingdom. **Tel** 011 44 171 4364425, FAX 011 44 171 5800747. **ED** R. Webster. **Bk Rev. Ad Acc. Adv Mgr:** J.P. Hobart. **Circ:** 1,800 (ctrl). Documents available from Ask*IEEE. **Continues** *Communicator of Scientific and Technical Information, 0308-6925.*
  Ind/Abst Curr. Cit.; INSPEC (1987-).

    ISSN 0193-5437
    US

COMMUNICATOR (NORTHWEST COMMUNICATION ASSOCIATION), THE.
(THE COMMUNICATOR.). **Added/Corp** Northwest Communication Association. University of Idaho. School of Communication. (1969)-. Periodical. English. One time a year. Pacific Lutheran University, Department of Speech Communications, Tacoma WA 98447. **Tel** (406)994-0211.

LC P87 .C633   ISSN 0737-3244
DD 001.51/05   US

COMMUNICATOR'S JOURNAL. [Commun. j.].
Vol. 1, No. 1 (May/June 1983)-. Periodical. English. Six times a year. $42.00. Communicators Journal Inc., Kansas City MO 64193. **ED** James D. Fograty. **Circ:** 20,000.
  Desc: First independent trade publication for business communicators, featuring teleconferencing, language use communications, how-to, and book reviews.

    ISSN 0821-4379
DD 302.2/06/071   CN

COMMUNIQUE / CANADIAN COMMUNICATION ASSOCIATION.
[Commun. - Can. Commun. Assoc.]. **Main/Corp** Canadian Communication Association. Vol. 1, No. 1-. Periodical. English (French). Three times a year. Free. Canadian Communication Association, Mass Communication Program, Carleton University, School of Journalism, Ottawa K1S 5B6 Canada. **Tel** (613)788-7425. **ED** Paul Attallah. **Bk Rev. Circ:** 350 (ctrl).

    US

COMMUNIQUE / THE FREEDOM FORUM MEDIA STUDY CENTER.
English. Free on request. Freedom Forum Media Studies Center, Columbia University, Financial Department, 2950 Broadway, New York NY 10027. **Tel** (212)678-6600, FAX (212)678-6663.

    SA

●COMMUNITAS.
(1994)-. Academic Scholarly Publication. Afrikaans (English). One time a year. University of the Orange Free State Department of Communications, Postbus 339, Bloemfontein 9300 South Africa.

    ISSN 1074-9004
    US

●COMMUNITY MEDIA REVIEW.
(COMMUNITY MEDIA REVIEW : CMR.). **Added/Corp** Alliance for Community Media. **VFOAT** CMR. (1994)-. Periodical. English. Six times a year. (Jan., Mar., May, July, Sept., Nov.). $25.00. Alliance for Community Media, 666 11th Street Northwest, Suite 806, Washington DC 20001. **Tel** (202)393-2650, FAX (202)393-2653. Index available ($5.00). **Continues** *Community Television Review (DLC) sn 85024268.*

    ISSN 0010-3926
    FR
    CODEN CELCAB

COMMUTATION & ELECTRONIQUE.
[Commut. electron.]. No. 1 (Nov. 1961)-. Periodical. French. Socotel, 40 rue du Generale Leclerc, Issy les Moulineaux Seine France. Documents available from Article Express International, Ask*IEEE.
  Ind/Abst Ei Page One; Eng. Index Annu.; INSPEC (1968-).

    US

COMPETITION IN THE LOCAL LOOP.
(19??)-. English. One time a year. $495.00. Paul Kagan Associates Inc., 126 Clock Tower Place, Carmel CA 93923-8734. **Tel** (408)624-1536, FAX (408)625-3225, telex ITT 4938124 PKA UI.

    UK

COMPUTERS & COMMUNICATIONS. See Computers.

    ISSN 0954-7479
DD 004   UK

COMPUTING, COMMUNICATIONS & MEDIA TREND MONITOR. See Computers.

LC P87 .C637
DD 302.2   BL

COMUNICACAO. Added/Corp Faculdade de
Comunicacao Social Anhembi. (1976)-. Periodical. Portuguese. Universidade de Sao Paulo / Faculdade de Comunicacao Social Anhembi, rua Casa do Ator 90, Sao Paulo Brazil.

LC HM258 .C58924
DD 302.2/05   BL

COMUNICACAO E SOCIEDADE.
Added/Corp Instituto Metodista de Ensino Superior (Sao Paulo, Brazil). **VFOAT** Comunicacao & Sociedade. No. 1 (June 1979)-. Academic Scholarly Publication. Portuguese. Two times a year. $12.00. Instituto Metodista de Ensino Superior, Curso de Pos-Graduacao em Comunicacao Social, Rua do Sacramento 230, Rudge Ramos, 09735-460 Sao Bernardo do Campo SP Brazil. **Tel** 011 457 3733, FAX 011 455 3349. **ED** Onesimo de Oliveira Cardoso.

LC HM258 .C5894
DD 301.14   VE

COMUNICACION. Added/Corp Centro de
Comunicacion Social Jesus Maria Pellin. (1975)-. Periodical. Spanish. Four times a year. $19.00. Centro de Comunicacion Social Jesus Maria Pellin, Apartado 20133, Caracas Venezuela. **Tel** 563-50-96. **ED** Fundacion Centro Gumilla. **Ad Acc.** ctrl circ.
  Desc: Information pertaining to communications, press, and broadcasting.

    AG
    SUSPENDED

COMUNICACION Y CULTURA. Added/Corp
Argentina. Servicio Oficial de Radiodifusion. Ano 1, No. 1 (Enero/Feb. 1981)-?. Periodical. Spanish. Six times a year. Comunicacion Cultura Univ Auto, Metropol Calzada Hueso 1100, Mexico 22 DF Mexico. **Tel** 011 52 5 594-7833 ext.129.
  Ind/Abst Hisp. Am. Period. Index, HAPI (19??-).

LC HM258 .C5895
DD 302.2/34/098   MX

COMUNICACION Y CULTURA EN AMERICA LATINA. VFOAT Comunicacion y
Cultura. (19??)-. Periodical. Spanish. Four times a year. $15.00 (Latin America), $18.00 (US and Europe). Comunicacion Cultura Univ Auto, Metropol Calzada Hueso 1100, Mexico 22 DF Mexico. **Tel** 011 52 5 594-7833 ext.129. **Continues** *Comunicacion y Cultura.*

    ISSN 0214-0039
UDC 070   SP
Pr Rev.

COMUNICACION Y SOCIEDAD. [Comun.
soc.]. (1987)-. Periodical. Spanish (summaries and/or abstracts in English). Two times a year. $40.00. Universidad de Navarra Publicaciones, Apartado 41 FD, 31080 Pamplona Spain. **Tel** 011 34 48 252700 ext. 883, FAX 011 34 48 173650, telex 37917 UNAV E. **ED** Esteban Lopez-Escobar and Jose Javier Sanchez Arsuda. **Bk Rev. Circ:** 600.
  Desc: The journal covers a manifold field in the area of public communication.

LC P92.I8 C58   ISSN 0392-8667
DD 302.2/34/05   IT

COMUNICAZIONI SOCIALI. Added/Corp
Universita Cattolica del Sacro Cuore. Scuola Superiore delle Comunicazioni Sociali. (Jan./March 1979)-. Periodical. Italian. Four times a year. L64000. Vita e Pensiero Pubblic University, Largo Gemelli 1, 20123 Milan Italy. **Tel** 011 39 2 72342310, 011 39 2 72342370. **Continues** *Annali della Scuola Superiore delle Comunicazioni Sociali.*

    ISSN 0897-5973
DD 070   US
    CEASED

CONFETTI (ELK GROVE VILLAGE, ILL.).
(CONFETTI.). [Confetti]. **VFOAT** Confetti, Bits and Pieces for Creative Communicators. Vol. 1, No. 1 (Oct./Nov. 1988)-(Jan. 1994). Trade Publication. English. Randall Publishing Inc., 1425 Lunt Avenue, Elk Grove Village IL 60007. **Tel** (708)437-6604, FAX (708)437-6618. **ED** Peg Carmack Short. **Ad Acc. Circ:**

15,000.
Desc: Devoted to the interests of California communication arts pros. Innovative ideas, new techniques and technology for those writing, editing, designing, marketing, and producing creative communications.

US
•**CONNECT.** (1994)-. Periodical. English. Four times a year. $35.00. Center for Media Literacy, 1962 South Shenandoah Street, Los Angeles CA 90034. **Tel** (310)559-2944, FAX (310)559-9396. **ED** Jay Dover. **Circ:** 5,000 (ctrl). ***Continues*** *Media & Values, 0149-6980.*
Desc: An interfaith media education magazine prompting social analysis and practical local action on issues of contemporary media and new technology.
Ind/Abst MasterFile FullTEXT (July 1994-).

ISSN 1055-0666
DD 384 US
CONSUMER MEDIA TECH. **See** Business and Economics-Marketing and Purchasing.

ISSN 1067-7887
DD 338 US
CCC
CONSUMER MULTIMEDIA REPORT. [Consum. multimed. rep.]. Vol. 1, No. 1 (Oct. 1992)-. Periodical. English. Twenty-six times a year. $453.00. Warren Publishing, Inc., 2115 Ward Court Northwest, Washington DC 20037. **Tel** (202)872-9200, FAX (202)293-3435.

ISSN 0732-4456
US
CONTRIBUTIONS TO THE STUDY OF MASS MEDIA AND COMMUNICATIONS. [Contrib. study mass media commun.]. No. 1 (1983)-. Monographic series. English. Irregular. Price varies per volume. Greenwood Press Inc., PO Box 5007, Westport CT 06881-5007. **Tel** (203)226-3571, FAX (203)222-1502. **Bk Rev. Ad Acc.**
Desc: This series surveys the evolution of newspaper, journalism, radio, television, and other means of mass communications in the modern world.

LC HD28 **ISSN** 1356-3289
DD 658 UK
•**CORPORATE COMMUNICATIONS.** **See** Business and Economics-Management.

GW
CQ-DL. [Cq-DL]. (1972)-. German. Twelve times a year. DM72.00 (surface mail), DM130.00 (airmail). Darc Verlag GmbH, Postfach 1155, 34216 Baunatal Germany. **Tel** 011 49 5603 9333-0, FAX 011 49 5603 9333-20. **ED** Hans Schware and Thomas Kamp. **Bk Rev. Ad Acc. Circ:** 60,000 (ctrl). ***Continues*** *Das DL-QTC, 0011-4995.*
Desc: Equipment tests, circuit descriptions, amateur radio techniques and international affairs.

LC HE8689 .C664a **ISSN** 0271-4795
DD 384.54/05 US
CRI COMMUNICATIONS UPDATE SERVICE. **Main/Corp** CRI (Institute). **VFOAT** Communications Update Service. **VAT** Communications Research Institute Communications Update Service. (19??)-. English. Four times a year. $15.00. Communications Research Institute, 515 Madison Avenue 2100, New York NY 10022. **Tel** (212)752-9635. **ED** Scott H. Robb.
Desc: Provides information on broadcasting and telecommunications.

LC P92.S58 C74 **ISSN** 0256-0046
DD 016.00151/0968 SA
CRITICAL ARTS. [Crit. arts]. **Added/Corp** Critical Arts Study Group (South Africa). Vol. 1 No. 1 (Mar. 1980)-. Periodical. English. Two times a year. $60.00. Contemporary Cultural Studies, University of Natal, King George V Avenue, Durban 4001 South Africa. **Tel** 011 27 31 8162505, 8162298. **ED** K.G. Tomaselli. Index available. cum. index. **Bk Rev. Ad Acc. Circ:** 800.
Desc: Application of media, cultural analysis and political theories to cinema, performance, press and broadcasting in the third world.
Ind/Abst Altern. Press Index (199?-); Annu. Bibliogr. Engl. Lang. Lit.; EP Collect.; Film Lit. Index (1982-1991); Homework Help.; Hum. Rights Intern. Rep.; Humanit. Source; Linguist. Lang. Behav. Abstr.; MasterFile FullTEXT 1000; MasterFile FullTEXT 350; MasterFile FullTEXT 650; MasterFile FullTEXT; MLA Int. Bibl. Books Artic. Mod. Lang. Lit.; OCLC; Soc. Plann. Policy Dev. Abstr.; Sociol. Abstr.; Telebase; World Mag. Bank.

LC P87 .C73 **ISSN** 0739-3180
DD 302.23/05 US
Pr Rev.
CRITICAL STUDIES IN MASS COMMUNICATION. (CRITICAL STUDIES IN MASS COMMUNICATION : CSMC : A PUBLICATION OF THE SPEECH COMMUNICATION ASSOCIATION.). [Crit. stud. mass commun.]. **Added/Corp** Speech Communication Association. **VFOAT** CSMC. Vol. 1, No. 1 (March 1984)-. Periodical. English. Four times a year (Mar., June, Sept., Dec.). $96.00. Speech Communication Association, 5105 Backlick Road, Suite E, Annandale VA 22003. **Tel** (703)750-0533, FAX (703)914-9471. Index available. cum. index. **Bk Rev. Ad Acc. Circ:** 3,200 (ctrl). available on microfilm and microfiche from University Microfilms International (UMI). Documents available from The Genuine Article, UMI Article Clearinghouse.
Desc: Focus on the range of critical perspectives which help define the expanding area of mass communication research.
Ind/Abst Am. Hist. Life (1985-); Arts Humanit. Citation Index [Select. Cov.]; Commun. Abstr.; Curr. Cit.; Curr. Contents Soc. Behav. Sci.; Curr. Index J. Educ.; Expand. Acad. Index (1989-); Linguist. Lang. Behav. Abstr.; Newsp. Period. Abstr. (1992-); Res. Alert [Full Cov.]; Sage Fam. Stud. Abstr.; Soc. Plann. Policy Dev. Abstr.; Soc. Sci. Cit. Index [Full Cov.]; Sociol. Abstr.

LC P87 .C25 **ISSN** 0007-9219
DD 791.43/7 US
CTVD, CINEMA, TV DIGEST. **See** Communications-Television and Cable.

LC P87 .C77
DD 302/.2 PE
CUADERNOS DE COMUNICACION & INFORMACION. **Added/Corp** Cuadernos de Comunicacion e Informacion. (1979)-. Spanish. Irregular. Prolongacion Arenales, 183 San Isidro, Lima 27 Peru.

ISSN 0740-5405
US
CYRANO'S JOURNAL. [Cyrano's j.]. **Added/Corp** New England Communications Task Force. **VFOAT** Cyrano. Vol. 1 No. 1 (Fall 1982)-. Periodical. English. Four times a year. $18.00 individuals, $24.00 libraries. New England Communications Task Force, Box 68, Westport CT 06881.

US
DATAPRO BROADBAND NETWORKING. (19??)-. English. Twelve times a year. $499.00. Datapro Information Services Group, 600 Delran Parkway, Delran NJ 08075. **Tel** (609)764-0100, (800)328-2776, FAX (609)764-8953.

US
DATAPRO LAN INTERNETWORKING. (19??)-. English. Twelve times a year. $419.00. Datapro Information Services Group, 600 Delran Parkway, Delran NJ 08075. **Tel** (609)764-0100, (800)328-2776, FAX (609)764-8953.

US
DATAPRO LOCAL AREA NETWORKS. (19??)-. English. Twelve times a year. $740.00. Datapro Information Services Group, 600 Delran Parkway, Delran NJ 08075. **Tel** (609)764-0100, (800)328-2776, FAX (609)764-8953.

US
DATAPRO NETWORK MANAGEMENT. (19??)-. English. Irregular. $598.00. Datapro Information Services Group, 600 Delran Parkway, Delran NJ 08075. **Tel** (609)764-0100, (800)328-2776, FAX (609)764-8953.

US
DATAPRO NETWORK MANAGEMENT INFORMATION SERVICES. (19??)-. English. $961.00. Datapro Information Services Group, 600 Delran Parkway, Delran NJ 08075. **Tel** (609)764-0100, (800)328-2776, FAX (609)764-8953.

US
DATAPRO NETWORK MANAGEMENT SYSTEMS. (19??)-. English. Twelve times a year. $598.00. Datapro Information Services Group, 600 Delran Parkway, Delran NJ 08075. **Tel** (609)764-0100, (800)328-2776, FAX (609)764-8953.

UK
DATAPRO REPORTS ON INTERNATIONAL TELECOMMUNICATIONS. (19??)-. English. Twelve times a year. $626.00 (one-year), $1,157.00 (two-year). Datapro International, McGraw Hill House, Shoppenhangers Road, Maidenhead Berkshire SL6 2QL United Kingdom. **Tel** 011 44 1628 773277, FAX 011 44 1628 773628.

ISSN 0886-1803
US
DEBATE ISSUES. [Debate issues]. Vol. 9 (1975)-. Periodical. English. Six times a year (Feb.-April, Oct.-Dec.). $12.00. The Alan Company, PO Box 16250, Clayton MO 63105. **Tel** (314)531-1668. **ED** James E. Sayer. ***Continues*** *Issues (Skokie, Ill.).*
Desc: Contains articles on the current debate topic, as well as debate theory and practice.

ISSN 1165-8606
FR
•**DECISIONS MEDIAS.** (1993)-. French. Eleven times a year. 161.61F France; 495.00F Europe; 650.00F other. Decisions Medias, 44 rue Gabriel Peri, 92300 Levallois Perret France. **Tel** 011 33 1 47480808, FAX 011 33 1 47480814. **ED** Phillipe Larroque. Index available. cum. index. **Bk Rev. Ad Acc. Circ:** 10,000 (ctrl). ***Continues*** *DM. Decisions Medias, 0998-6553.*
Desc: The economic and strategic stakes of media in France and around the world.

LC T4 .D46 **ISSN** 0493-4253
JA
CODEN DTDRAU
DENKI TSUSHIN DAIGAKU GAKUHO. [Denki Tsushin Daigaku gakuho]. **VFOAT** Reports of the University of Electro-Communications. (1950)-. Academic Scholarly Publication. Japanese. One time a year. Free. University of Electro-Communications, 1-5-1 Ghofugaoka Chofu-shi, Tokyo 181 Japan. Documents available from Ask*IEEE, CASDDS.
Ind/Abst Chem. Abstr.; INSPEC (March 1971-); Math. Rev.

ISSN 0196-8491
US
DENVER METROPOLITAN MEDIA DIRECTORY. (1980)-. Directory. English. One time a year. $196.30. Kelly Communications, 9600 East Arapahoe Road, Suite 230, Englewood CO 80112. **Tel** (303)792-0025, FAX (303)792-0150.

FR
DEPECHE, LA. French. 150.00F. M le Professeur Farriaux, Service Pediatrie Hop Huriez, F 59037 Lille Cedex France. **Tel** 011 33 20 445962.

LC T10.5 .D48 **ISSN** 0970-8154
DD 601.4 II
DESIDOC BULLETIN. **Added/Corp** Defence Scientific Information and Documentation Centre (India). **VAT** Defence Scientific Information and Documentation Centre Bulletin. (198?)-. Bulletin. English. Six times a year.
Ind/Abst Indian Libr. Sci. Abstr.

LC HN980 .D48 **ISSN** 0192-1312
DD 307 US
CEASED
DEVELOPMENT COMMUNICATION REPORT. [Dev. commun. rep.]. **Added/Corp** Clearinghouse on Development Communication. No. 17 (Jan. 1977)-(19??). Periodical. English (Spanish and French). Clearinghouse Development Communication, 1815 North Fort Myer Drive, 6th Floor, Arlington VA 22209. **Tel** (703)527-5546, FAX (703)527-4661. **ED** Andrea Bosch. Index available. cum. index. **Bk Rev. Circ:** 6,500 (ctrl). available on an online database. ***Continues*** *ICIT Report.*
Desc: Examines the most recent applications of communication technologies and uses of different media in development projects in the developing countries of the world.
Ind/Abst Educ. Technol. Abstr.

ISSN 0985-3766
FR
UDC 159.9
DEVELOPPEMENT PERSONNEL. **VFOAT** Collection Developpement Personnel. (1981)-. Periodical. French. Twelve times a year. $128.60. Editeur Godefroy, BP 94, F 60505 Chantilly Cedex France. **Tel** 011 33 44 580029. cum. index. **Ad Acc.**

LC BF637.C45 D47
DD 153 US
DEVEREUX PAPERS, THE. **Added/Corp** Devereux Foundation. Vol. 1 (Fall 1972)-. Periodical. English. Devereux Foundation, Devon PA 19333.

LC AP2 .D49 **ISSN** 0272-7692
DD 051 US
DIALOGUE (WASHINGTON, D.C. : ENGLISH ED.). (DIALOGUE.). [Dialogue]. **Added/Corp** United States. International Communication Agency. United States Information Agency. (19??)-. Periodical. English. Four times a year. International Communication Agency, 1776 Pennsylvania Avenue, Washington DC 20547. ***Continues*** *Dialogue.*

US
DIRECTIONS (EVANSTON, ILL.). (DIRECTIONS.). (1983)-. Periodical. English. One time a year. $20.00. Directions / Evanston, 212 Speech Building, Northwestern University, Evanston IL 60208. **Tel** (708)491-2252, FAX (708)467-2389. **ED** Manjunath Pendakur (editor's address: Northwestern University, Department of Radio-TV-Film, Evanston, IL 60208-2270; phone: (708)491-7315). **Circ:** 1,500.

LC P92.M45 D55
MX
DIRECTORIO DE MEDIOS. (19??)-. Spanish. Four times a year. Medios Publicitarios Mexicanos, AV Mexico 99 303, Col Hip Conde, 06170 Mexico City DF Mexico. **Tel** 011 52 5 5742858.
Desc: Classified information of advertising agencies, their staffs, and the calculations they handle.

Communications

LC WMLC L 83/1191 **ISSN** 0577-098X
US

DIRECTORY OF MEMBERSHIP - CENTRAL STATES COMMUNICATION ASSOCIATION. **Main/Corp** Central States Communication Association (U.S.). (1968)-. Directory. English. Four times a year. Central States Communication Association, Box A-6 East Central University, Ada OK 74820-6899. **Tel** (405)332-8000 ext. 214 or 713, FAX (405)332-1623. Index available. cum. index. **Circ**: 2,000. **Continues in part** Central States Speech Journal, 0008-9575.

LC HE9761 **ISSN** 1055-5803
DD 387.7 US

DIRECTORY OF NORTH AMERICAN MILITARY AVIATION COMMUNICATIONS, VHF/UHF. SOUTHEASTERN. See Aeronautics, Astronautics.

LC Z7962 .I52 HQ1101 **ISSN** 1040-1156
DD 305.4/025/73 US

DIRECTORY OF WOMEN'S MEDIA. See Women's Interests.

LC P87 .D57 **ISSN** 0730-1081
DD 302.2/34/05 US
Pr Rev.

DISCOURSE (BERKELEY, CALIF.).
(DISCOURSE : JOURNAL FOR THEORETICAL STUDIES IN MEDIA AND CULTURE.). [Discourse]. **Added/Corp** University of Wisconsin–Milwaukee. Center for Twentieth Century Studies. No. 1 (Fall 1979)-. Periodical. English. Three times a year. $50.00. Indiana University Press, 601 North Morton Street, Bloomington IN 47404. **Tel** (812)855-3830, (800)842-6796. **ED** Roswitha Mueller and Kathleen Woodward. **Bk Rev**. **Ad Acc**. **Circ**: 700.
 Desc: Explores a variety of topics in continental philosophy, theories of media and literature and the politics of sexuality.
 Ind/Abst BHA : Biblio. Hist. Art; Curr. Cit.; Film Lit. Index; MLA Int. Bibl. Books Artic. Mod. Lang. Lit.

ISSN 0965-4364
DD 338.4778149 UK

DJ LONDON. [DJ Lond.]. **VFOAT** Disc Jockey. (1991)-. Periodical. English. Twenty-five times a year. $179.67. Nexus Business Communications, Warwick House Azalea Drive, Kent BR8 8HY United Kingdom. **Tel** 011 44 1322 660070, FAX 011 44 1322 667633. **(Subscription address:** NEXUS, Tower House Sovereign Park, Lathkill Street, Leicestershire LE16 9F United Kingdom. **Tel** 011 44 1858 435322, 011 44 1858 435344.) **Continues** Jocks, 0951-5143.

ISSN 0848-7642
DD 338.7/6165845/09713 CN

DRH COMMUNICATIONS QUARTERLY, THE. See Business and Economics.

BL

ECO : PUBLICACAO DA POS-GRADUACAO DA ESCOLA DE COMUNICACAO DA UNIVERSIDADE FEDERAL DO RIO DE JANEIRO.
Added/Corp Universidade Federal do Rio de Janeiro. Pos-Graduacao em Comunicacao e Cultura. (1992)-. Periodical. Portuguese. Two times a year. Universidade Federal de Rio de Janeiro, Escola de Comunicacao, Imago Editorial Ltda., Rua San Rodrigues 201-A, 20250 Rio de Janeiro RJ Brazil. **Tel** 293-1092.

LC HE **ISSN** 1083-5431
DD 384 US

●EDUCATIONAL TECHNOLOGY MARKETS. (EDUCATIONAL TECHNOLOGY MARKETS : THE HELLER REPORT.). [Educ. technol. mark.]. **VFOAT** Heller Report; Heller Report on Educational Technology Markets. Vol. 6, No. 8 (June 1995)-. Periodical. English. Twelve times a year. Nelson B Heller and Association, 1910 First Street, Suite 303, Highland Park IL 60035. **Tel** (708)441-2920, FAX (708)926-0202. **Continues** Heller Report on Educational Technology and Telecommunications Markets, 1047-5230.

ISSN 0745-0311
US
CCC

ELECTRONIC MEDIA. (Aug. 5, 1982)-. Periodical. English. One time a week. $93.00. Crain Communications Inc., 1400 Woodbridge, Detroit MI 48207-3187. **Tel** (313)446-6000, (800)992-9970. **Bk Rev**. **Ad Acc**. **Circ**: 28,000 (ctrl). available on microfilm and microfiche from University Microfilms International (UMI); available on an online database (file 16/Full-Text) from DIALOG. **Continues** Advertising Age. Electronic Media Edition, 0744-6675.
 Desc: Covers the broadcast industry covering television, radio, cable and satellite beats.
 Ind/Abst F&S Index Plus Text, Int. [Full Txt.] [Select. Cov.]; PROMT [Full Txt.]; Trade Ind. Index.

LC HE7742 .W45
DD 384/.025/73 US
SUSPENDED

ELECTRONIC MESSAGING DIRECTORY & BUYER'S GUIDE. **Added/Corp** American Telephone and Telegraph Company. **VFOAT** Electronic Messaging Directory and Buyer's Guide; Directory and Buyer's Guide. (1991)-(1991). Directory. English. AT&T Directory & Buyer's Guide, 3405 Hollenberg Drive, Bridgeton MO 63044. **Continues** Western Union Directory & Buyer's Guide, 0889-633X.

ISSN 1044-9892
DD 384 UK
CCC

ELECTRONIC MESSAGING NEWS.
[Electron. messaging news]. (July 20, 1989)-. Periodical. English. Twenty-five times a year (biweekly). $497.00. Omnicom PPI Limited, (A Phillips Business Information company), Forum Chambers, The Forum Stevenage Hertfordshire SG1 1EL United Kingdom. **Tel** 011 44 1438 742424, FAX 011 44 1438 740154. **ED** John Lilley, David Toll (US editor). available on an online database (file 636/Full-Text) from DIALOG. **Absorbed in part** Viewtext, 0275-0686.
 Desc: Information on various computer communication networks and software.
 Ind/Abst PTS Newsl. Database [Full Txt.].

ISSN 1130-6971
SP

UDC 621.3

ELECTRONICA & COMUNICACIONES MAGAZINE. [Electr–on. comun. mag.]. (1987)-. Periodical. Spanish. Eleven times a year (monthly except Aug.). $142.04. Cypsela Sl, Apartado de Correos 8054, 08010 Barcelona Spain. **Tel** 34 1 93 4123899, FAX 34 1 93 3182951. Index available. cum. index. **Ad Acc**, **Adv Mgr**: Corenzo Aulesa. **Circ**: 8,000. **Continues** Revista U.N.C.E.T. de Electronica, Informatica y Comunicaciones, 1130-698X.
 Desc: Contains communications & radio-communications interviews.

LC TK7800 .E4395 **ISSN** 0013-5194
DD 621.381/05 UK
CCC
CODEN ELLEAK

Pr Rev.

ELECTRONICS LETTERS. See Electronics.

ISSN 0374-3098
AU
CODEN EKITA9

ELEKTRON INTERNATIONAL. [Elektr. int.]. No. 1 (1967)-. Periodical. German. Twelve times a year. Elektron Verlag, Postfach 156, A-4010 Linz Austria. Documents available from Ask*IEEE. **Continues** Elektron.
 Ind/Abst Energy Res. Abstr. (Aug. 1976-); INSPEC (1969-).

ISSN 0258-9672
KU
NLM W1; NE998DE CODEN EMPNEA

EMP NEWSLETTER. (NEWSLETTER EMP : ENGLISH FOR MEDICAL, PARAMEDICAL PURPOSES.). [EMP newsl.]. **Added/Corp** Jamiat al-Kuwayt. Medical Study Skills Division. **VFOAT** English for Medical, Paramedical Purposes; EMP Newsletter. (198?)-. Newsletter. English.
 Ind/Abst Soc. Plann. Policy Dev. Abstr.

ISSN 0885-7202
DD 658 US

EMPLOYEE COMMUNICATION. See Business and Economics-Personnel Management.

ISSN 1355-0721
DD 420.71041 UK

●ENGLISH & MEDIA MAGAZINE, THE. See Linguistics.

ISSN 0896-7083
DD 551 US

EOSAT LANDSAT APPLICATION NOTES. (EOSAT LANDSAT APPLICATION NOTES / EARTH OBSERVATION SATELLITE CO.].).
Added/Corp Eosat. **VFOAT** Landsat Application Notes; EOSAT Application Notes. **VAT** Earth Observation Satellite Company Landsat Application Notes. Vol. 1, No. 1 (June 1986)-. Periodical. English. Irregular. Free on request. EOSAT Public Affairs Office, 4300 Forbes Boulevard, Lanham MD 20706. **Tel** (800)344-9933, (301)552-0567.

ISSN 0746-1550
US

ERIE & CHAUTAUQUA MAGAZINE.
VFOAT Erie and Chautauqua Magazine; Erie & Chautauqua. Vol. 1 No. 1 (Aug. 1983)-. Periodical. English. Two times a year. $8.00. Erie & Chautauqua Communications Corporation, 317 West 6th Street, Erie PA 16507. **Tel** (814)455-4772. **Continues** Erie Magazine, 0194-8636.

ISSN 1061-2874
DD 338 US
TITLE CHANGE

EUROMEDIA ACQUISITIONS. See Business and Economics.

US

●EUROMEDIA ACQUISITIONS AND FINANCE. See Business and Economics.

ISSN 1070-3233
DD 338 UK
TITLE CHANGE

EUROMEDIA FINANCE. See Business and Economics-Banks and Banking.

ISSN 0955-4041
DD 621.38094 UK

EUROPEAN COMMUNICATIONS. [Eur. commun.]. (1989)-. Trade Publication. English. Four times a year. $47.92. Harrington Kilbride Plc, Highbury Station Road, London N1 1SE United Kingdom. **Tel** 011 44 171 2262222, FAX 011 44 171 2201255. **ED** Andrew Maiden. **Ad Acc**.
 Desc: Deals with critical issues surrounding the growing communications industry throughout Europe; analyzes the developments in products, technology, and regulations.

LC P91.3 .E87 **ISSN** 0267-3231
DD 302.23/05 UK
CODEN EJCOET

Pr Rev.

EUROPEAN JOURNAL OF COMMUNICATION (LONDON).
(EUROPEAN JOURNAL OF COMMUNICATION.). [Eur. j. commun.]. Vol. 1, No. 1 (March 1986)-. Periodical. English. Four times a year. $176.00. Sage Publications Ltd., 6 Bonhill Street, London EC2A 4PU United Kingdom. **Tel** 011 44 181 3740645, FAX 011 44 181 3748741, telex 296207 SAGE G. **ED** Jay G. Blumler, Denis McQuail and Karl Erik Rosengren. **Bk Rev**. **Ad Acc**. Acid Free. **Circ**: 900.
 Desc: Represents the best of communication theory and research in Europe in all its diversity.
 Ind/Abst Arts Humanit. Citation Index [Select. Cov.]; Commun. Abstr.; Curr. Cit.; Educ. Adm. Abstr.; Int. Polit. Sci. Abstr.; Soc. Plann. Policy Dev. Abstr.; Soc. Sci. Cit. Index [Full Cov.].

ISSN 1071-1570
DD 332 US
CCC

EUROPEAN MEDIA BUSINESS & FINANCE. See Business and Economics.

LC QA76.575 .E97 **ISSN** 0966-7709
UK
TITLE CHANGE

EUROPEAN MULTIMEDIA YEARBOOK.
Added/Corp Multimedia Ventures (Firm). (19??)-(1995). English. Interactive Media Publications Ltd, 104A Saint John Street, London EC1M 4EH United Kingdom. **Tel** 011 44 171 4901185, FAX 011 44 171 4904706. **Continued by** Multimedia Yearbook.

US

EX PARTE PRESENTATIONS IN INFORMAL RULEMAKINGS. **Main/Corp** United States. Federal Communications Commission. (19??)-. English. FCC / Federal Communications Commission, 1919 M Street Northwest, Room 538, Washington DC 20554. **Tel** (202)632-6302.

ISSN 0163-7282
US

EXETASIS. Vol. 1 (197?)-. Academic Scholarly Publication. English. Irregular. California State University / Northridge, Dearby Annex 213, F. McMahon Ed., Northridge CA 91324. **Tel** (818)885-2853. **ED** Fred McMahon. **Circ**: 350.
 Desc: Scholarly essays about rhetoric used in major communications and events such as speeches, campaigns, movies and music.

US

FAULKNER COMMUNICATIONS INFODISK CD ROM. (19??)-. Periodical. English. Four times a year. $2067.00 US $2267.00 Canada; $2167.00 other. Faulkner Technical Reports, 7905 Browning Road, Suite 114, Pennsauken NJ 08109. **Tel** (800)843-0460.

US

FCC CALENDAR OF EVENTS FOR WEEK OF ... . **Main/Corp** United States. Federal Communications Commission. **VAT** Federal Communications Commission Calendar of Events for Week of ... . (19??)-. English. FCC / Federal

Communications

Communications Commission, 1919 M Street Northwest, Room 538, Washington DC 20554. **Tel** (202)632-6302. **Ind/Abst** PTS Newsl. Database [Full Txt.].

US

FCC NEWS REPORT. English. $195.00 US and Canada; $250.00 other; includes FCC Hot Line Report. R & B Enterprises, 20 Clipper Road, West Conshohocken PA 19428. **Tel** (610)825-1960, FAX (610)825-1684, (510)660-8120.

LC HE **ISSN** 1081-9541
DD 384 US
FCC REPORT. [FCC rep.]. **VFOAT** Federal Communications Commission Report. Vol. 11, No. 18 (May 4, 1992)-. Periodical. English. Twenty-four times a year. Telecom Publishing Group, 1101 King Street, Suite 444, Alexandria VA 22314. **Tel** (703)683-4100, (800)327-7205, FAX (703)739-6490. **Continues** F.C.C. Week, 0748-5714.

US

FEDERAL COMMUNICATIONS COMMISSION RULES AND REGULATIONS.--INDIVIDUAL PARTS. See Law.

LC 610 302.2 **ISSN** 0198-6635
DD R HM258 US
NLM W1 FE398E
FEEDBACK (MILLBRAE). See Medical Sciences-Medical Education.

ISSN 0015-010X
UDC 621.39 GW
CODEN FINGAQ
FERNMELDE-INGENIEUR. [Fernmelde-Ing.]. (1???)-. German. Twelve times a year. $115.15. Verlag Wissenschaft & Leben, PO Box 3566, D-91023 Erlangen Germany. **Tel** 011 49 9131 32162, FAX 011 49 9131 304144. Documents available from Ask*IEEE.
Ind/Abst Ei Page One; INSPEC (1968-).

LC TK **ISSN** 1081-6844
DD 621 US
●**FIBER OPTICS STANDARDS SUMMARY.** [Fiber opt. stand. summ.]. Vol. 1, No. 1 (Feb.-Apr. 1995)-. Periodical. English. Four times a year (Feb., May, July, Oct.). $250.00. Communications Standards Review, 757 Greer Road, Palo Alto CA 94303. **Tel** (415)856-9018, FAX (415)856-6591. **ED** Elaine Baskin. **Circ:** 100 (ctrl). **Continues** Communications Standards Summary.
 Desc: Summarizes all Telecommunications Industry Association (TIA) Fiber Optic (FO) Committee active standards projects and recently completed standards.

LC P88.8 .F5615 **ISSN** 0196-8548
DD 070 US
FINDER BINDER. ARIZONA'S UPDATED MEDIA DIRECTORY. (FINDERBINDER. STATE OF ARIZONA.). **Added/Corp** Rita Sanders Advertising & Public Relations Agency. **VFOAT** Arizona's Updated Media Directory; Finderbinder. **VAT** Finderbinder. Arizona's Updated Media Directory. (1980)-. English. Twelve times a year. $191.00. Arizona's Updated Media Directory, 432 East Southern Avenue, Tempe AZ 85282. **Tel** (602)967-8714, FAX (602)894-6216. **ED** Sandy Painter. **Circ:** 700 (ctrl).
 Desc: Media Directory

ISSN 1057-0888
US
FINDER BINDER. THE SACRAMENTO, STOCKTON AND NORTHERN CALIFORNIA UPDATED NEWS MEDIA DIRECTORY. **VFOAT** Sacramento, Stockton and Northern California Updated News Media directory; Finderbinder. 1st Ed. (1990)-. Directory. English. $95.00. California Publicom, Inc., 4679 Vista Street, San Diego CA 92116-4848.

LC PN4071 .F57 **ISSN** 1050-3366
DD 808.5/07/12 US
Pr Rev.
FLORIDA COMMUNICATION JOURNAL, THE. [Fla. commun. j.]. **Added/Corp** Florida Communication Association. Vol. 16, No. 1 (1988)-. Periodical. English. Two times a year. $25.00. Florida Communication Association, 275 Date Palm Road 305, PO Box 06210, Fort Meyers FL 33906. **Tel** (813)489-9478, (813)472-8937. **ED** Dr. Anthony J. Clark. **Circ:** 225 (ctrl). **Continues** Florida Speech Communication Journal, 0093-6138.
 Desc: This journal emphasizes articles relevant to communication education. It includes practical as well as theoretical articles from all aspects of the discipline.

US

FLORIDA MEDIA QUARTERLY : A PUBLICATION OF THE FLORIDA ASSOCIATION OF MEDIA IN EDUCATION. **Added/Corp** Florida Association for Media in Education. Vol. 1, No. 1 (Fall 1975)-. Periodical. English. Four times a year. $40.00. Florida Association Media in Education, PO Box 13119, Tallahassee FL 32317. **Tel** (904)893-5396. **ED** Pat Conlon (editor's phone: (904)620-7587). **Ad Acc, Adv Mgr:** Nancy Jackson, **Tel** (305)370-1617. **Circ:** 1,600 (ctrl). **Continues** Florida Association for Media in Education. FAME Newsletter.
 Ind/Abst Libr. Lit.

LC PN4844 .F56 **ISSN** 1063-2360
DD 071/.3/025 US
FLORIDA NEWS MEDIA & VALUABLE SOURCES GUIDE, THE. [Fla. News Media Valuab. Sources Guide]. **VFOAT** Florida News Media and Valuable Sources Guide. (1991)-. English. Irregular. Florida News Media & Valuable Sources Guide, Route 2, PO Box 380, Branford FL 32008.

US

FLORIDA NEWS MEDIA DIRECTORY. **VFOAT** News Media Directory. (1979)-. Directory. English. One time a year (Aug.). $50.00. News Media Directories, PO Box 316, Mount Dora FL 32757. **Tel** (904)383-3023, (800)749-6399. **Continues** Dahne's Florida News Media Directory, 0161-231X.

LC PN4177 .F6 **ISSN** 0015-735X
DD 808.5/1/05 US
Pr Rev.
FORENSIC OF PI KAPPA DELTA, THE. **Main/Corp** Pi Kappa Delta. **VFOAT** Forensic. (Oct. 1976)-. Periodical. English. Four times a year (June, Sept., Dec., Mar.). $20.00. Pi Kappa Delta / North Dakota State University, Box 5075, Fargo ND 58105. **Tel** (701)237-8721, FAX (701)237-7784. **ED** Steven Hunt, Communications Department, Lewis & Clark College, Portland, OR 97219 USA; Telephone: (503)768-7617. cum. index. **Bk Rev** (Qty: 5-10). **Circ:** 1,700. available on microfilm and microfiche from University Microfilms International (UMI). **Continues** Forensic, 0195-8216.
 Desc: Articles of competitive speech and debate topics.

ISSN 0196-304X
US
FORENSIC QUARTERLY, THE. **Added/Corp** National University Extension Association. Committee on Discussion and Debate. (1???)-. Monographic series. English. Four times a year. Price varies per volume. National Federation of State High School Associations, 11724 Northwest Plaza Circle, PO Box 20626, Kansas City MO 64195-0626. **Tel** (816)464-5400, FAX (816)464-5571. **ED** Richard E. Edwards.

ISSN 1051-9971
DD 384 US
CCC
TITLE CHANGE
FUTURE HOME TECHNOLOGY NEWS. [Future home technol. news]. (1990)-(19??). Periodical. English. Phillips Business Information, 1201 Seven Locks Road, PO Box 61130, Potomac MD 20854. **Tel** (301)424-3338, (301)340-1520, (800)777-5005, FAX (301)424-4297, telex 358149. **Absorbed in part** Viewtext, 0275-0686. **Continued by** Home Media Technology.
 Ind/Abst PTS Newsl. Database [Full Txt.].

LC Z6951 .A97 PN4867 **ISSN** 1048-7972
DD 302.23/025/73 US
GALE DIRECTORY OF PUBLICATIONS AND BROADCAST MEDIA. [Gale dir. publ. broadcast media]. **Added/Corp** Gale Research Inc. 122nd Ed. (1990)-. Directory. English. One time a year. $395.00. Gale Research Inc., 835 Penobscot Building, 645 Griswold Street, Detroit MI 48226. **Tel** (800)877-GALE, (313)961-2242, FAX (313)961-6083, (800)414-5043, telex TWX 810-221-7086. **ED** Karen Troshynski-Thomas, Deborah M. Burek. available on magnetic tape; available on diskette; available on an online database (File 469) from DIALOG. **Continues** Gale Directory of Publications, 0892-1636.
 Desc: Contains 38,000 entries, including listings for radio and television stations and cable companies.

LC PN4699 .G3 **ISSN** 0016-5492
DD 070.5 NE
CCC
Pr Rev.
GAZETTE. (GAZETTE: INTERNATIONAL JOURNAL FOR MASS COMMUNICATION STUDIES.). [Gazette]. **VFOAT** International Journal for Mass Communication Studies. Vol. 1 (Jan. 1955)-. Periodical. English (French and German). Six times a year. $307.00. Kluwer Academic Publishers, Postbus 322, 3300 AH Dordrecht The Netherlands. **Tel** 011 31 78 524400, FAX 011 31 78 183273, telex 20083. **ED** Wim Noomen, Harold De Bock, Ed Hollander, Jan Wieten. **Acid Free.** available on microfilm and microfiche from University Microfilms International (UMI). Documents available from UMI Article Clearinghouse.
 Desc: Provides a forum for the scientific discussion, exchange, and comparison of ideas on an international basis. Topics covered include: the role of communication in international relations and in international understanding; communication and development with special attention to research methods; legal and sociocultural aspects of innovative information technologies with special attention to integration; and communication policy and planning.
 Ind/Abst Am. Hist. Life (1973-); Commun. Abstr. (1973-); Curr. Cit.; Expand. Acad. Index (1992-); Int. Polit. Sci. Abstr.; Middle East Abstr. Index; Newsp. Period. Abstr. (1992-); PAIS Int. Print (1991-).

LC P88.8 .G4a **ISSN** 0097-8175
DD 301.16/1/02573 US
GEBBIE PRESS ALL-IN-ONE DIRECTORY. [Gebbie Press all-in-one dir.]. **Main/Corp** Gebbie Press. **VFOAT** All-in-One Directory. 1st Ed. (1972)-. Directory. English. One time a year. $88.25. Gebbie Press, Box 1000, New Paltz NY 12561. **Tel** (914)255-7560. **ED** Amalia Gebbie. Index available.
 Desc: Covers daily and weekly newspapers, radio and television stations, consumer magazines, business and financial papers, trade journals and magazines, farm publications, news syndicates and complete addresses, circulation figures, editors, publishers and other media information; 520 pages.

GW

GELBE SEITEN. 99, ORTSNETZ MUENCHEN. **VFOAT** Gelbe Seiten 99, Munchen; Munchen. (19??)-. German.

US

GEORGIA NEWS MEDIA DIRECTORY. **Added/Corp** News Media Directories (Firm). **VFOAT** Georgia Directory. (19??)-. Directory. English. One time a year (Jan.). $50.00. News Media Directories, PO Box 316, Mount Dora FL 32757. **Tel** (904)383-3023, (800)749-6399.

ISSN 1031-1211
DD 384.0994 AT
GERARD HENDERSON'S MEDIA WATCH. [Gerard Henderson's media watch]. **VFOAT** Media Watch. (1988)-. Periodical. English. Four times a year. 24.67Aus$. Sydney Institute, 41 Phillip Street, Sydney 2000 Australia. **Tel** 011 61 2 2523366, FAX 011 61 23 2523360. **ED** Gerard Henderson.

LI

GIMTOJI KALBA. See Linguistics.

LC TK6570.M6 G56 **ISSN** 0195-2250
DD 621.3841/65/05 US
CCC
CODEN GLCODU
SUSPENDED
GLOBAL COMMUNICATIONS. [Glob. commun.]. (Fall 1979)-Suspended(August 1994). Trade Publication. English. Four times a year. Cardiff Publishing Company, 6300 South Syracuse Way, Suite 650, Englewood CO 80111. **Tel** (303)220-0600, FAX (303)770-0253, telex 450726. (**Subscription address:** Sunbelt Fulfillment Services / Nashville, PO Box 41369, Nashville TN 37204. **Tel** (615)377-3322, (800)888-5139.) **ED** Cathy Chalmers. **Ad Acc. Circ:** 10,000 (ctrl). available on microfilm from University Microfilms International (UMI); available on an online database (file 648/Full-Text) from DIALOG. Documents available from Ask*IEEE.
 Desc: International trade journal for the mobile communications industry: two-way radio, cellular communications, paging, interconnect, new technology system design, etc.
 Ind/Abst INSPEC (Winter 1979-); Trade Ind. ASAP [Full Txt.]; Trade Ind. Index [Full Txt.].

LC P87 .G68 **ISSN** 0161-2077
DD 070/.05 US
GRADUATE COMMUNICATION STUDIES. **Added/Corp** Illinois. Southern Illinois University, Carbondale. Mass Communications Research Center. (Spring 1977)-. Periodical. English. One time a year. $2.00. Southern Illinois University / Carbondale - Communication Studies, Carbondale IL 62901.

US

●**GRADUATE DIRECTORY, SPEECH COMMUNICATION ASSOCIATION, MEMBER INSTITUTIONS.** **Added/Corp** Speech Communication Association. (1994)-. Directory. English. Speech Communication Association, 5105 Backlick Road, Suite E, Annandale VA 22003. **Tel** (703)750-0533, FAX (703)914-9471. **Continues** Directory of Graduate Programs in the Communication Arts and Sciences.

US

GRANTS FOR FILM, MEDIA & COMMUNICATIONS / THE FOUNDATION CENTER. See Philanthropy.

ISSN 0746-3626
DD 331 US
GRAPHICOMMUNICATOR. (GRAPHIC COMMUNICATOR : THE NEWSPAPER OF THE GRAPHIC COMMUNICATIONS UNION.). [GraphiCommunicator]. **Added/Corp** Graphic Communications International Union. **VFOAT** Graphiccommunicator. Vol. 1, No. 1 (Oct. 1983)-. Periodical. English. Eight times a year. $12.00. GraphiCommunicator, 1900 L Street Northwest,

Washington DC 20036. **Tel** (202)462-1400. **ED** Herald Grandstaff. ctrl circ. ***Continues*** *Union Tabloid, 0275-8342.*
Desc: To inform and educate readers on the news, activities, and programs of the union. News on the technological printing development and training for such new procedures.
Ind/Abst Abstr. Bull. Inst. Pap. Sci. Tech.; Graph. Arts Bull. Inst. Pap. Sci. Technol. (Feb. 1989, April 1989, Oct. 1989).

LC P88.8 .G73 **ISSN** 0275-8369
DD 302.2/3 US
GREATER BOSTON MEDIA DIRECTORY. (1981)-. Directory. English. Media Directories Division, New England Newsclip, 5 Auburn Street, Framingham MA 01701.

US
•GREGORY'S MEDIA DIRECTORY. (1995)-. Directory. English. Three times a year. $220.00. Gregory Communications, 1250 North Santa Anita Avenue, Arcadia CA 91006. **Tel** (818)449-3676, FAX (818)584-0907. ***Continues*** *Gregory's Media Watch.*

UY
GUIA COMERCIAL Y TELEFONICA DEL DEPARTAMENTO DE SORIANO. (19??)-. Periodical. Spanish. Talleres Graficos Moyano, Del Departamento de Soriano, Roosevelt 602 Al 610, Mercedes Uruguay.

AG
GUIA DE ABONADOS : PARANA, VICTORIA, GUALEGUAY. Main/Corp Compania Entrerriana de Telefonos. **VFOAT** Guia Telefonica: Parana, Gualeguay, Victoria. ?-. Spanish. Compania Entrerriana de Telefonos, Buenos Aires 156 Parana Argentina.

SP
TITLE CHANGE
GUIA DE LOS MEDIOS, LA. VFOAT Guia de los Medios Publicitarios Espanoles; GM. (19??)-(19??). Spanish. Remarca SA, Avd Alfonso XIII 15, 28002 Madrid Spain. **Tel** 011 34 1 5191799. ***Continued by*** *Guia de los Medios de Comunicacion de Espana, Portugal, Andorra y Gibraltar.*

LC P94.5.M552 A84 **ISSN** 0811-6636
DD 001.51/025/945 AT
GUIDE TO ETHNIC MEDIA IN VICTORIA. See Ethnic Interests.

LC HE **ISSN** 0955-4564
DD 384.09536 UK
GULF COMMS GUIDE. (THE GULF COMMS GUIDE.). [Gulf comms guide]. (1988)-. English. One time a year. £10.00. Information Technology Publishing Company, Angus House, 13 Tilehouse Street HITC, Hertfordshire SG5 2DU United Kingdom. **Tel** 011 44 1462 420785, FAX 011 44 1462 420786.

LC HN490.M3 G85
DD 361.945 IT
Pr Rev.
GULLIVER (BARI, ITALY). (GULLIVER.). Vol. 1, No. 1 (Jan. 1982)-. Periodical. Italian. Twelve times a year. L40000.00 Italy; L90000.00 other. Associazione Gulliver, Via Tor di Quinto 19/B, 00191 Rome Italy. **Tel** 011 39 6 3331718, FAX 011 39 6 3331716. Index available. **Bk Rev. Ad Acc. Circ:** 3,000.
Desc: Political analysis and documentation on mass media.

ISSN 0388-2306
DD 621.38 JA
HAM JOURNAL TOKYO. [Ham. j. Tokyo]. **VFOAT** CQ Ham Radio. Bessatsu. (1974)-. Periodical. Japanese. Twelve times a year. $121.41. Nippon IPS Co. Ltd., 11 6 3 Chome Iidabashi, Chiyodaku Tokyo 102 Japan. **Tel** 011 81 3 3238 0700.

ISSN 1081-180X
US
CCC
•HARVARD INTERNATIONAL JOURNAL OF PRESS/POLITICS. (1996)-. Periodical. English. Four times a year. $100.00. Massachusetts Institute of Technology (MIT) Press, 55 Hayward Street, Cambridge MA 02142. **Tel** (617)253-2889, (617)625-8481, FAX (617)258-6779.

LC HE **ISSN** 1047-5230
DD 384 US
CCC
TITLE CHANGE
HELLER REPORT ON EDUCATIONAL TECHNOLOGY AND TELECOMMUNICATIONS MARKETS, THE. [Heller rep. educ. technol. telecommun. mark.]. **VFOAT** Heller Report. (1989)-(199?). Periodical. English. Nelson B Heller and Association, 1910 First Street, Suite 303, Highland Park IL 60035. **Tel** (708)441-2920, FAX (708)926-0202. **ED** Anne Wujick (editor's phone: (703)548-1037). ***Continued by*** *Educational Technology Markets, 1083-5431.*

ISSN 0843-4441
DD 001.56 CN
HEUREUX QUI COMMUNIQUE. (HEUREUX QUI COMMUNIQUE. JOURNAL DU CENTRE DE COMMUNICATION.). [Heureux qui commun.]. **Added/Corp** Centre Quebecois de Communication Non Orale. Vol. 1 (Oct./Nov./Dec. 1987)-. Periodical. French. Four times a year (Mar., June, Sept., Dec.). $5.35 Canada; $7.35 other. Association Paralysie Cerebrale Quebec, 525 Blvd Hamel Est Bureau A-50, Quebec Quebec G1M 2S8 Canada. **Tel** (418)529-5371.

LC P87 .H68 **ISSN** 1064-6175
DD 302.2/05 US
CODEN HJCOES
Pr Rev.
HOWARD JOURNAL OF COMMUNICATIONS, THE. [Howard j. commun.]. **Added/Corp** Howard University. Center for Communications Research. **VFOAT** HJC. Vol. 1, No. 1 (Spring 1988)-. Periodical. English. Four times a year (Mar., June, Sept., Dec.). $109.00. Howard Journal of Communications, PO Box 1233, Howard University, Washington DC 20059. **Tel** (202)806-7690. **ED** William J. Starosta (editor's address: PO Box 471, Howard University, Washington, D.C. 20059; (202)806-4039). Index available (bound in last issue). cum. index. **Bk Rev**, (Qty: 8). **Ad Acc. Circ:** 500.
Desc: Offers interdisciplinary research on communication and culture or gender.

LC P88.8 .H83 **ISSN** 0885-1328
DD 001.51/025/73 US
HUDSON'S STATE CAPITALS NEWS MEDIA CONTACTS DIRECTORY. See Communications-Abstracting, Bibliographies and Statistics.

LC RC423.A1 H85 **ISSN** 1046-7599
DD 616.85/5/005 US
NLM W1; HU445FC
HUMAN COMMUNICATION AND ITS DISORDERS (NORWOOD, N.J.). See Physically Impaired.

LC P91.3 .H85 **ISSN** 0360-3989
DD 301.2/1 US
CCC
NLM W1 HU445H
Pr Rev.
HUMAN COMMUNICATION RESEARCH. [Human commun. res.]. **Added/Corp** International Communication Association. Vol. 1 (Fall 1974)-. Periodical. English. Four times a year (Mar., June, Sept., Dec.). $179.00. SAGE Periodical Press, 2455 Teller Road, Thousand Oaks CA 91320. **Tel** (805)499-0721, FAX (805)499-0871, telex 100799. **ED** Howard Giles (University of California, Santa Barbara). **Acid Free.** available on microfilm and microfiche from University Microfilms International (UMI). Documents available from The Genuine Article, UMI Article Clearinghouse.
Desc: Publishes important research and high-quality reports that contribute to the expanding body of knowledge about human communication.
Ind/Abst Abstr. Anthropol.; AGRICOLA [Select. Cov.]; Commun. Abstr.; Curr. Cit.; Curr. Contents Soc. Behav. Sci.; Curr. Index J. Educ.; EP Collect.; Expand. Acad. Index (1989-); Film Lit. Index; Homework Help.; Hum. Resour. Abstr.; MasterFile FullTEXT 1000; MasterFile FullTEXT 350; MasterFile FullTEXT 650; MasterFile FullTEXT (Jan. 1995-); Middle East Abstr. Index; Newsp. Period. Abstr. (1989-); OCLC; Psychol. Abstr. (1975-); PsycINFO; PsycLit; Res. Alert [Full Cov.]; Sage Fam. Stud. Abstr.; Sage Public Adm. Abstr. (?-?); School Organ. Manage. Abstr.; Soc. Plann. Policy Dev. Abstr.; Soc. Sci. Cit. Index [Full Cov.]; Sociol. Abstr.; Spec. Educ. Needs Abstr.; Telebase.

LC PN4003 .H9
DD 808.5 KO
HWASUL. Added/Corp Hanguk Hwasul Kyoyukhoe. (19??)-. Periodical. Korean. Six times a year. Hanguk Hwasul Kyoyukhoe, 462-2 Pyongchang-Dong Chongno-ku, Seoul 110 Korea.

LC Discard
US
IASCP BULLETIN : [A PUBLICATION OF IASCP], THE. Added/Corp University of Florida. Institute for Advanced Study of the Communication Processes. **VFOAT** I.A.S.C.P. Bulletin. (19??)-. Bulletin. English. Two times a year.
Ind/Abst Soc. Plann. Policy Dev. Abstr.

ISSN 0018-876X
US
ICA NEWSLETTER (AUSTIN). (ICA NEWSLETTER.). **Main/Corp** International Communication Association. **Added/Corp** International Communication Association. Newsletter. **VAT** International Communication Association Newsletter. (19??)-. Periodical. English. Four times a year. $10.00. International Communication Association, PO Box 9589, Austin TX 78766. **Tel** (512)454-8299. **ED** Robert L. Cox. **Ad Acc, Adv Mgr:** Sandra Ridings, **Tel** (512)454-8299. **Circ:** 2,700.
Desc: Covers activities of the Association and its members, as well as news of programs and people in communication studies all around the world.

LC TK5105.5 .I3 **ISSN** 1063-6692
DD 004.6/05 US
CODEN IEANEP
•IEEE/ACM TRANSACTIONS ON NETWORKING. See Computers-Computer Networks.

US
•IEEE PERSONAL COMMUNICATIONS MAGAZINE. Added/Corp Institute of Electrical and Electronics Engineers. (1994)-. English. Six times a year. $130.00. IEEE / Institute of Electrical and Electronics Engineers Inc., 345 East 47th Street, New York NY 10017-2394. **Tel** (908)981-1393, FAX (908)981-9667. **(Subscription address:** IEEE / Institute of Electrical and Electronics Engineers, 445 Hoes Lane, PO Box 1331, Piscataway NJ 08855-1331. **Tel** (800)701-IEEE, (908)981-0060, FAX (908)981-9667, telex 833233.**) ED** Hamid Ahmadi.
Desc: Covers all technical and policy issues related to personalized, location-independent communications in all media. Highlights such topics as portable telephones, communicating palmtop computers, protocols, messaging, communications, and personalized traffic filtering. Also covers such policy issues as spectrum allocation, industry structure and technology evolution.

LC TK7882.M6 I2 **ISSN** 0018-9545
DD 621.3841/65 US
CCC
CODEN ITUTAB
Pr Rev.
IEEE TRANSACTIONS ON VEHICULAR TECHNOLOGY. [IEEE trans. veh. technol.]. **Added/Corp** Vehicular Technology Society. Institute of Electrical and Electronics Engineers. IEEE Vehicular Technology Group. **VFOAT** Transactions on Vehicular Technology; Vehicular Technology. (Oct. 1967)-. Academic Scholarly Publication. English. Four times a year. $225.00. IEEE / Institute of Electrical and Electronics Engineers Inc., 345 East 47th Street, New York NY 10017-2394. **Tel** (908)981-1393, FAX (908)981-9667. **(Subscription address:** IEEE / Institute of Electrical and Electronics Engineers, 445 Hoes Lane, PO Box 1331, Piscataway NJ 08855-1331. **Tel** (800)701-IEEE, (908)981-0060, FAX (908)981-9667, telex 833233.**)** available on microfiche. Documents available from Article Express International, The Genuine Article, Ask*IEEE, CASDDS, Documents on Demand. ***Continues*** *IEEE Transactions on Vehicular Communications, 0096-2503.*
Desc: Covers land, airborne, and maritime mobile services; portable or hand carried and citizen's communications services, when used as an adjunct to a vehicular system; vehicular electrotechnology, equipment and systems ordinarily identified with the automotive industry, excluding systems associated with public transit.
Ind/Abst Acoust. Abstr.; Bioeng. Abstr.; Chem. Abstr.; Civ. Struct. Eng. Abstr.; Comput. Inf. Syst. Abstr. J. [Full Cov.]; Curr. Cit.; Curr. Contents Eng. Comput. Technol.; Ei Page One; Elect. Comm. Abstr.; EMBASE; Energy Inf. Abstr.; Energy Res. Abstr.; Eng. Index Annu.; Environ. Abstr.; Expand. Acad. Index (1992-); Highw. Res. Abstr.; Index IEEE Publ.; INIS Atomindex [Micro.]; INSPEC (1968-); Int. Aerosp. Abstr.; Leadscan; Mech. Eng. Abstr.; Pollut. Abstr. Indexes; Res. Alert [Full Cov.]; Sci. Cit. Index; SCISEARCH.

ISSN 0019-1744
IT
IKON. (IKON : RIVISTA DELL'ISTITUTO A. GEMELLI.). [Ikon]. **Added/Corp** Istituto Agostino Gemelli per lo Studio Sperimentale di Problemi Sociali dell'Informazione Visiva. (1982)-. Periodical. Italian (summaries and/or abstracts in English). Two times a year. L43550. Franco Angeli Riviste SRL, Viale Monza 106, 20127 Milan Italy. **Tel** 011 39 2 2827651, 011 39 2 289562, FAX 011 39 2 258004, telex 051-511650. ***Formed by the union of*** *Ikon, 0019-1744* ***and*** *Ricerche Sulla Comunicazione.*

ISSN 1058-7705
DD 384 US
CCC
IMAGING NEWS (ALEXANDRIA, VA.). (IMAGING NEWS.). [Imaging news]. Vol. 1, No. 1 (Aug. 14, 1991)-. Periodical. English. Twenty-four times a year. $380.00 (bulk subscriptions, additional mailed in same envelope) North America. Telecom Publishing Group, 1101 King Street, Suite 444, Alexandria VA 22314. **Tel** (703)683-4100, (800)327-7205, FAX (703)739-6490. available on an online database (file 636/Full-Text) from DIALOG.
Ind/Abst PTS Newsl. Database [Full Txt.].

ISSN 1048-2296
DD 384 US
IMAGING RETAIL NEWS. [Imaging retail news]. Vol. 1, No. 1 (Feb. 5, 1990)-. Periodical. English. Twenty-four times a year. Billboard Publications Inc., 1515 Broadway Billboard, New York NY 10036. **Tel** (212)764-7300, FAX (305)755-7048, telex WU TWX 710-581-6279.

Communications

ISSN 0953-7856
DD 004.33
UK
IMI. INTERACTIVE MEDIA INTERNATIONAL. [IMI, Interact. media int.]. **VFOAT** Interactive Media International; IMI Newsletter; Interactive Media International Newsletter. (1987)-. Periodical. English. Twelve times a year. £155.00 (EEC); £175.00 (outside EEC, inclusive of airmail). Interactive Media Publications Ltd, 104A Saint John Street, London EC1M 4EH United Kingdom. **Tel** 011 44 171 4901185, FAX 011 44 171 4904706.
Ind/Abst Inf. Manage. Technol.

US
IMMEDIATE IMPACT. (19??)-. English. Four times a year. $50.00 (institutions), $35.00 (individuals) comes with Media Network membership. Media Network, 39 West 14th Street, Suite 403, New York NY 10011. **Tel** (212)929-2663, FAX (212)929-2732. **ED** Ilana Navaro. **Circ:** 2,000 (ctrl).
Desc: Newsletter on alternative media.

LC PN1991.3.I4 I53
DD 808.822
II
INDIAN BROADCAST MEDIA YEAR BOOK. (1982)-. English. Irregular. Marwah Publications, H-39 Green Park Extension, New Delhi 110016 India. **(Subscription address:** Prints India, 11 Darya Ganj, New Delhi 110002 India. **Tel** 011 91 11 3268645, FAX 011 91 11 3275542, telex 31-61087 PRIN-IN.**)**

LC Z6958.I4 I46a
DD 016.07
II
INDIAN NEWSPAPER SOCIETY PRESS HANDBOOK. Added/Corp Indian Newspaper Society. **VFOAT** INS Press Handbook; Indian and Eastern Newspaper Society Press Handbook. (1988)-. English. IENS Buildings, Rafi Marg 110001, New Delhi India. **Continues** Indian & Eastern Newspaper Society Press Handbook.

BE
INDICATEUR PUBLICITAIRE MEDIA. (19??)-. Multiple languages (French and Dutch). Irregular. 7420.00F Belgium; 8300.00F other. Chambre Agences Conseils Publ, Avenue du Barbeau 28, 1160 Brussels Belgium.

ISSN 0737-0415
US
CCC
TITLE CHANGE
INDUSTRIAL COMMUNICATIONS. [Ind. commun.]. **Added/Corp** Washington Radio Reports (Firm). (19??)-(199?). Periodical. English. Phillips Business Information Inc., 1201 Seven Locks Road, PO Box 61130, Potomac MD 20854. **Tel** (301)424-3338, (301)340-1520, (800)777-5005, FAX (301)424-4297, telex 358149. available on an online database (files 636,648/Full-Text) from DIALOG. **Continues** Mobile Radio Reports. **Continued by** Land Mobile Radio News.
Ind/Abst F&S Index Plus Text, Int. [Select. Cov.]; PTS Newsl. Database [Full Txt.].

ISSN 0827-4711
CN
INFO PRESSE COMMUNICATIONS. (19??)-. French. Twelve times a year (Dec./Jan. combined). 39.22Can$. Editions Info Presse, 4316 boulevard Saint-Laurent, Bureau 400, Montreal Quebec H2W 1Z3 Canada. **Tel** (514)842-5873. **(Subscription address:** Express Magazine, 4011 Boulevard Robert, Montreal, Quebec H1Z 4H6 Canada. **Tel** (800)363-1310, (514)374-9811.**) Continues** Info Presse Canada l'Actualite de la Presse et des Medias, 1200-3638.
Ind/Abst Repere (1989-).

FR
INFO-VISU: BULLETIN D'INFORMATION ET DE LIAISON DU CLUB VISUALISATION. (19??)-. Bulletin. French. Four times a year. 100.00F. Club Visu / SID France, BP 105, F-19105 Brive La Gaillarde Cedex France. **Tel** 011 33 55 879491.

SA
CEASED
INFORMA. Added/Corp South Africa. Bureau for National and International Communications. Vol. 25, No. 12 (Dec. 1978)-(19??). Periodical. English (Afrikaans). Department of Development Planning, Private Bag X644, Pretoria 0001 South Africa. **Tel** (012)3412381. **ED** Andries le Roux. **Circ:** 45,000 (ctrl). **Continues** Progressus.

LC HE7 .C6
DD 385.1 384
MX
INFORMACION (MEXICO. SECRETARIA DE COMUNICACIONES Y TRANSPORTES). (INFORMACION.). **Added/Corp** Mexico. Secretaria de Comunicaciones y Transportes. **VFOAT** SCT Informacion. (Jan. 1977)-. Periodical. Spanish. Six times a year. Centro Scop Xola y Universidad. **Continues** Comunicaciones y Transportes.

ISSN 0716-0658
UDC 681.3
CL
Pr Rev.
INFORMATICA. REVISTA DE COMPUTACION Y SISTEMAS. See Computers-Computer Systems.

LC P87 .I536
DD 001.51/05
NLM P 87; I428
ISSN 0740-5502
US
INFORMATION AND BEHAVIOR. [Inf. behav.]. Vol. 1 (1985)-. Monographic series. English. Irregular. Price varies per volume. Transaction Publishers / Rutgers State University, Department 3091 or 3092, New Brunswick NJ 08903. **Tel** (908)932-2280 ext. 105, FAX (908)932-3138. **ED** Brent D. Ruben.
Desc: Examines the forms, technologies, organization, and uses of information and their impact on human behavior. Coverage includes the impact of new technology on office and home life, regulation and control of information, and the economics of information.
Ind/Abst Int. Polit. Sci. Abstr.

ISSN 1033-6273
AT
Pr Rev.
INFORMATION AND SOCIETY. See Sociology.

ISSN 0142-5471
UK
CCC
INFORMATION DESIGN JOURNAL. [Inf. des.]. (1979)-. Periodical. English. Three times a year. $90.00. Information Design Journal, PO Box 1978, Gerrards Cross, Buckinghamshire SL9 9BT United Kingdom. **Tel** 011 44 1753 892278.
Ind/Abst ARTbibliogr. Mod.; Ergon. Abstr.; HILITES; Libr. Inf. Sci. Abstr.; Print. Abstr.; World Publ. Monit.

ISSN 0167-6245
NE
CCC
Pr Rev.
INFORMATION ECONOMICS AND POLICY. [Inf. econ. policy]. Vol. 1, No. 1 (1983)-. Academic Scholarly Publication. English. Four times a year (1 volume). $249.00. Elsevier Science Publishers BV, PO Box 211, 1000 AE Amsterdam Netherlands. **Tel** 011 31 20 4853641, 011 31 20 4853642, FAX 011 31 20 4853598. **ED** R Noll. **Ad Acc.** available on microfilm and microfiche from University Microfilms International (UMI); available on an online database from Elsevier Electronic Subscriptions (EES). Documents available from UMI Article Clearinghouse, Ask*IEEE.
Desc: Provides an interdisciplinary and international forum for publications with telecommunications economics and policy as its core, including related issues on information economics and media policy.
Ind/Abst ABI/INFORM Glob. Ed.; ABI/INFORM [Computer File] (1983-); ACM Guide Comput. Lit.; Commun. Abstr.; Comput. Rev.; Contents Recent Econ. J.; Curr. Cit.; Econ. Lit. Index; Ei Page One; Gen. BusinessFile (1992-); Geogr. Abstr. Human Geogr.; INSPEC (1983-); Int. Polit. Sci. Abstr.; J. Econ. Lit. (1983-); J. Plan. Lit.; Soc. Plann. Policy Dev. Abstr.

LC Discard
UK
INFORMATION FROM THE VOLUNTEER CENTRE MEDIA PROJECT : THE ... YEAR REPORT OF THE MEDIA PROJECT. **Main/Corp** Volunteer Centre. **VFOAT** Year Report of the Media Project. 1st (1977-1978)-. English. Irregular. $22.98. The Volunteer Centre UK, Carriage Row 183 Eversholt Street, London NW1 1BU United Kingdom. **Tel** 011 44 171 3889888, FAX 011 44 171 3830448.

ISSN 1062-1059
DD 384
US
INFORMATION FUTURES. [Inf. futures]. Vol. 1, No. 1 (Mar. 14, 1992)-. Periodical. English. Four times a year. $195.00. Amirado Computer Technologies, PO Box 260472, Plano TX 75026-0472.

ISSN 1073-8126
DD 384
US
CCC
TITLE CHANGE
INFORMATION NETWORKS. [Inf. netw.]. Vol. 6 No. 4 (Apr. 1993)-(1995). Periodical. English. Telecom Publishing Group, 1101 King Street, Suite 444, Alexandria VA 22314. **Tel** (703)683-4100, (800)327-7205, FAX (703)739-6490. **ED** Dick Stirba. Index available. available on an online database (file 636/Full-Text) from DIALOG. **Continues** Enhanced Services Outlook, 0897-2915. **Merged into** Interactive TV Strategies.

ISSN 1043-3694
DD 384
US
CCC
TITLE CHANGE
INFOTEXT (IRVINE, CALIF.). (INFOTEXT.). **VFOAT** Info Text; InfoText Magazine. (1988)-(1993). Trade Publication. English. Advanstar Communications Inc., 131 West First Street, Duluth MN 55802. **Tel** (218)723-9477, (800)346-0085, FAX (218)723-9437. **Absorbed by** Voice Processing Magazine, 1042-0460.

UK
INSIDE MULTIMEDIA NEWS. (19??)-. Bulletin. English. Twenty-five times a year. $598.92. Omnicom PPI Limited, (A Phillips Business Information company), Forum Chambers, The Forum Stevenage Hertfordshire SG1 1EL United Kingdom. **Tel** 011 44 1438 742424, FAX 011 44 1438 740154. **Continues** European Multimedia Bulletin.

LC TK5105.875.I57 I53
DD 004.6/7
ISSN 1075-7902
US
●**INSIDE THE INTERNET.** See Computers-Computer Networks.

ISSN 1042-6930
DD 384
US
CCC
INTELLIGENT NETWORK NEWS. [Intell. netw. news]. Vol. 1, No. 1 (Feb. 1989)-. Periodical. English. Twelve times a year. $317.00. Telecom Publishing Group, 1101 King Street, Suite 444, Alexandria VA 22314. **Tel** (703)683-4100, (800)327-7205, FAX (703)739-6490. available on an online database (file 636/Full-Text) from DIALOG. **Continues** Enhanced Services Outlook, 0897-2915.
Ind/Abst PTS Newsl. Database [Full Txt.].

US
INTERACTIVE AGE. (199?)-. Trade Publication. English. Twenty-six times a year. $79.00 US. CMP Publications Inc., One Jericho Plaza, Wing A, 2nd Floor, Jericho NY 11753. **Tel** (516)733-6700. **(Subscription address:** CMP Publications, Inc. / Illinois, PO Box 5920, Department 100, Carol Stream IL 60197-5920. **)**
Desc: Devoted exclusively to covering and analyzing the rapid convergence of the communications, entertainment/media, cable, computer and information industries.

ISSN 1065-299X
DD 338
US
CCC
TITLE CHANGE
INTERACTIVE MEDIA BUSINESS. [Interact. media bus.]. Vol. 1, No. 1 (July 1992)-(19??). Periodical. English. Interactive Media Business, 701 Westchestger Avenue, White Plains NY 10604. **Continued by** Smartmedia Business.

LC HE
DD 384
ISSN 1068-9834
US
●**INTERACTIVE MULTIMEDIA INVESTOR.** [Interact. multimed. invest.]. **Added/Corp** Paul Kagan Associates. No. 1 (Mar. 22, 1993)-. Proceedings. English. Twenty-four times a year. $650.00. Paul Kagan Associates Inc., 126 Clock Tower Place, Carmel CA 93923-8734. **Tel** (408)624-1536, FAX (408)625-3225, telex ITT 4938124 PKA UI.
Desc: Follows the public stocks and private deals that influence media. Analyzes publicly-held interactive multimedia companies and tracks industry subgroups.

US
●**INTERACTIVE TV STRATEGIES.** (1995)-. English. Twenty-four times a year. $425.00. Telecom Publishing Group, 1101 King Street, Suite 444, Alexandria VA 22314. **Tel** (703)683-4100, (800)327-7205, FAX (703)739-6490. **Absorbed** Information Networks.

ISSN 1062-2098
DD 384
US
CEASED
INTERACTIVE WORLD. [Interact. world]. (199?)-(April 1993). Periodical. English. Virgo Publishing Inc., 4141 North Scottsdale Road, Suite 316, Scottsdale AZ 85251. **Tel** (602)483-0014, (602)990-1101, FAX (602)990-0819. **Continues** 4th Media Journal, 1053-6213.

LC H35 .I6
DD 808.85
US
... INTERCOLLEGIATE DEBATES. Vol. 1-22. Periodical. English.

ISSN 0164-6206
US
INTERCOM (WASHINGTON, D.C. 1968). (INTERCOM.). [Intercom]. **Added/Corp** Society for Technical Communication. **VFOAT** STC Intercom. (1968)-. Periodical. English. Six times a year. Society for Technical Communication, 901 Stuart Street, Suite 904, Arlington VA 22203. **Tel** (703)522-4114.

US
INTERCOM : WOMEN IN COMMUNICATIONS. (19??)-. English. Women in Communications Inc., Boston Professional Chapter, 67 Harlow Street, Boston MA 02174. **Tel** (617)868-0238. **Continues** Update : Newsletter of the Boston Professional Chapter, Women in Communications, Inc., 0893-3308.

LC HM132 **ISSN** 1057-7769
DD 302 US
Pr Rev.
INTERCULTURAL COMMUNICATION STUDIES. [Intercult. commun. stud.]. **Added/Corp** Institute for Cross-Cultural Research (U.S.). Vol. 1, No. 1 (Spring 1991)-. Periodical. English. Two times a year. $50.00. Institute for Cross-Cultural Research, Box 418, Trinity University, 715 Stadium Drive, San Antonio TX 78212. **Tel** (210)736-7369, FAX (210_494-4435. **ED** Bates Hoffer. **Bk Rev. Ad Acc. Circ:** 200.
Desc: A multi-disciplinary journal on cross-cultural communication.

LC HM258 .I528 **ISSN** 0270-6075
DD 303.4/82 US
INTERNATIONAL AND INTERCULTURAL COMMUNICATION ANNUAL. [Int. intercult. commun. annu.]. **Added/Corp** Speech Communication Association. Speech Communication Association. Commission on International and Intercultural Communication. Speech Communication Association. International and Intercultural Communication Division. **VFOAT** IIC Annual. (1974)-. English. One time a year. $48.00. SAGE Periodical Press, 2455 Teller Road, Thousand Oaks CA 91320. **Tel** (805)499-0721, FAX (805)499-0871, telex 100799. **Acid Free.**

II
INTERNATIONAL JOURNAL OF COMMUNICATION : IJC. VFOAT IJC. Vol. 1, No. 1 (Jan.-June 1991)-. Periodical. English. Two times a year. $40.00. Bahri Publications, PO Box 4453, 997A Street No 9, Gobindpuri Kalkaji, New Delhi 110019 India. **Tel** 011-6445710, 011-6448606. **(Subscription address:** Prints India, 11 Darya Ganj, New Delhi 110002 India. **Tel** 011 91 11 3268645, FAX 011 91 11 3275542, telex 31-61087 PRIN-IN.)

ISSN 0269-3615
UK
INTERSPACE FLEET. [InterspaceFleet]. (1983)-. Periodical. English. Forty-nine times a year. $682.77. European Satellite & Space News, The Counting House, 21 Market Street Alton, Hampshire GU34 1HA United Kingdom. **Tel** 011 44 1420 88558, 44 420 80142, FAX 011 44 1420 541544. **ED** Roger Stanyard. Index available. **Circ:** 600.
Desc: Newsletter on satellite communications, broadcasting, news analysis, special reports, and surveys.

US
Pr Rev.
IOWA JOURNAL OF COMMUNICATION. (19??)-. English. Two times a year (Apr. & Sept.). $15.00 (one-year); $29.00 (two-year); $42.00 (three-year). Department Communication Studies, M. Jensen, University of Iowa, Cedar Falls IA 50614. **Tel** (319) 266-7903, (319) 273-2593. **ED** Fred Antczak. cum. index. **Ad Acc. Circ:** 500.

LC PN4001 .T6 **ISSN** 0885-8063
DD 001.51/07 US
ITC COMMUNICATOR. [ITC commun.]. **Added/Corp** International Training in Communication (Organization). **VAT** International Training in Communication Communicator. Vol. 1, No. 1 (Sept./Oct. 1985)-. Periodical. English. Six times a year. $10.00. International Training in Communication, 2519 Woodland Drive, Anaheim CA 92801. **Tel** (714)995-3660, FAX 714-995-6974. **ED** Joann Levy. Index available. **Bk Rev. Circ:** 20,000 (ctrl). ***Continues*** *Toastmistress, 0279-4713.*
Desc: Features to amplify our four-point training program in communication skills, leadership development, organizational abilities, and personal development.

LC LB2341 .J67 **ISSN** 0360-0939
DD 808.5/07/1173 US
•**JACA : JOURNAL OF THE ASSOCIATION FOR COMMUNICATION ADMINISTRATION. Added/Corp** Association for Communication Administration. **VFOAT** Journal of the Association for Communication Administration. No. 1 (Jan. 1993)-. Periodical. English. Three times a year. $60.00. Association for Communication Administration, 5105 Backlick Road Building E, Annandale VA 22003. **Tel** (703)750-0533, FAX (703)914-9471. **ED** Ron Applbaum (Editor's address: Westfield State College, Westfield, MA 01086; telephone: (413)572-5200). **Bk Rev,** (Qty: 3-4). ctrl circ. ***Continues*** *Association for Communication Administration. ACA Bulletin, 0360-0939.*

ISSN 0749-4351
DD 808 US
JOKESMITH, THE. [Jokesmith]. Vol. 1, No. 1 (Spring 1984)-. Periodical. English. Four times a year. $40.00. The Jokesmith, 44 Queen's View Road, Marborough MA 01752. **Tel** (508)481-0591. **ED** Edward C. McManus. **Bk Rev,** (Qty: 6-8).
Desc: A comedy newsletter for business professionals, and their writers. Offers professional communicators jokes, comments, presentation ideas, and stories that make a point.

LC HM258 .J67 **ISSN** 0090-9882
DD 302.2/05 US
JOURNAL OF APPLIED COMMUNICATION RESEARCH : JACR. [J. appl. commun. res.]. **Added/Corp** Speech Communication Association. University of South Florida. Dept. of Communication. **VFOAT** JACR. Vol. 9, No. 1 (Spring 1981)-. Periodical. English. Four times a year (Feb., May, Aug., Nov.). $96.00. Speech Communication Association, 5105 Backlick Road, Suite E, Annandale VA 22003. **Tel** (703)750-0533, FAX (703)914-9471. **ED** Catherine C. Newman. Index available. **Bk Rev. Ad Acc. Circ:** 225. available on microfilm and microfiche from University Microfilms International (UMI). Documents available from UMI Article Clearinghouse. ***Continues*** *Journal of Applied Communications Research, 0090-9882.*
Desc: Research about solving and studying communication problems in organizational, management, employee, therapeutic, public, family and government settings.
Ind/Abst Commun. Abstr.; Curr. Index J. Educ.; Expand. Acad. Index (1992-); Lang. Lang. Behav. Abstr.; Newsp. Period. Abstr. (1992-); Soc. Plann. Policy Dev. Abstr.; Sociol. Abstr.

LC P92.P16 J68 **ISSN** 0957-6851
DD 302.2/091823/05 UK
CCC
CODEN JACNEI
Pr Rev.
JOURNAL OF ASIAN PACIFIC COMMUNICATION. VFOAT Asian Pacific Communication. Vol. 1 (1990)-. Trade Publication. English. Four times a year. $189.00. Multilingual Matters Ltd., Frankfurt Lodge, Clevedon Hall, Victoria Road, Clevedon Avon BS21 7SJ United Kingdom. **Tel** 011 44 1275 876519, FAX 011 44 1275 343096. **ED** H. Giles and H. Pierson. Index available. **Bk Rev.**
Desc: Papers on research into language issues and communication problems in the Asian Pacific.
Ind/Abst Curr. Index J. Educ.; Linguist. Lang. Behav. Abstr. (1990-) [Full Cov.]; Soc. Plann. Policy Dev. Abstr.

LC HF5717 .I595 **ISSN** 1050-6519
DD 658.4/5/05 US
CCC
CODEN JBTCE9
JOURNAL OF BUSINESS AND TECHNICAL COMMUNICATION. **See** Business and Economics.

LC HF5718 .J6 **ISSN** 0021-9436
DD 658 US
CODEN JBCOAO
JOURNAL OF BUSINESS COMMUNICATION (1973). (THE JOURNAL OF BUSINESS COMMUNICATION.). [J. bus. commun.]. **Added/Corp** American Business Communication Association. Association for Business Communication (U.S.). Vol. 11, No. 1 (Fall 1973)-. Periodical. English. Four times a year (Jan., Apr., July, Oct.). $40.00. Association of Business Communication, College of Business Administration, University of North Texas, Denton TX 76203. **Tel** (817)565-4332, FAX (817)565-4930. **ED** Dr. N. L. Reinsch (phone: (202)687-5125) Journal; Dr. Kitty O. Locker (phone: (614)292-6556) Bulletin. Index available. **Bk Rev. Ad Acc. Circ:** 2,700. available on microfilm and microfiche from University Microfilms International (UMI). Documents available from UMI Article Clearinghouse. ***Continues*** *ABCA Journal of Business Communication, 0886-7216.*
Desc: Contains major papers dealing with important areas and aspects of business communication.
Ind/Abst ABI/INFORM Glob. Ed.; ABI/INFORM [Computer File] (Fall 1973-); Acad. Search; Anbar Account. Finan. Abstr. [Full Txt.]; Anbar Mark. Distr. Abstr. [Full Txt.]; Anbar Top Manage. Abstr. [Full Txt.]; Bus. Educ. Index; Bus. Index (1985-); Bus. Period. Index; Bus. Source Plus; Bus. Source; Curr. Cit.; Curr. Index J. Educ.; EP Collect.; Gen. BusinessFile (1985-); Gen. Period. Index (1985-); Homework Help.; INFO-SOUTH Abstr.; Mag. Search; Manage. Bibliogr. Rev.; Manage. Contents; MasterFile FullTEXT 1000; MasterFile FullTEXT 350; MasterFile FullTEXT 650; MasterFile FullTEXT (July 1993-); OCLC; Oper. Prod. Manage. Abstr. [Full Txt.]; Person. Train. Abstr. [Full Txt.]; Soc. Plann. Policy Dev. Abstr.; Sociol. Abstr.; Telebase; UMI ABI/Inform--Bus. Period. Ondisc (Spring 1988-) [Full Txt.]; Wilson Bus. Abstr.; Women Manage. Rev. [Full Txt.].

LC TK6201
DD 621.38 CC
•**JOURNAL OF CHINA UNIVERSITIES OF POSTS AND TELECOMMUNICATIONS.** (1994)-. Academic Scholarly Publication. English. Two times a year. Beijing University of Posts and Telecommunications, 42 Xueyuan Lu, Beijing 100088, People's Republic of China. **Tel** 011 861 203388, FAX 011 861-2028643.

LC P87 .J6 **ISSN** 0021-9916
DD 001.5/05 US
CCC
NLM W1 JO593H
Pr Rev.
JOURNAL OF COMMUNICATION. [J. commun.]. **Added/Corp** National Society for the Study of Communication. International Communication Association. Annenberg School of Communications (University of Pennsylvania). Vol. 1 (May 1951)-. Periodical. English. Four times a year. $78.00 (institutions), $36.50 (individuals) US; $93.00 (institutions), $51.50 (individuals) other. Oxford University Press / New York, 200 Madison Avenue, New York NY 10016. **Tel** (212)679-7300, (919)677-0977, (800)451-7556, (800)445-9714, FAX (919)677-1303. **(Subscription address:** Oxford University Press / USA, Journals Marketing Department, Oxford University Press, 2001 Evans Road, Cary NC 27513. **Tel** (800)451-7556, (919)677-0977, FAX (919)677-1714.) **ED** George Gerbner and Marsh Siefert. cum. index. **Bk Rev. Ad Acc. Circ:** 6,500 (ctrl). available on microfilm from Xerox; available on microfilm and microfiche from University Microfilms International (UMI). Documents available from The Genuine Article, UMI Article Clearinghouse.
Desc: Devoted to communications theory, research, policy, and practice.
Ind/Abst ABI/INFORM Glob. Ed.; ABI/INFORM [Computer File] (Spring 1975-Spring 1976); Acad. Abstr. Full Text Elite; Acad. Abstr.; Acad. Ind. [Computer File] (1987-); Acad. Search; AGRICOLA [Select. Cov.]; Am. Hist. Life (1974-); Am. Bibliogr. Slavic East Europ. Stud.; Annu. Bibliogr. Engl. Lang. Lit.; Arts Humanit. Citation Index [Select. Cov.]; Book Rev. Index; Child. Lit. Abstr. (19??-); Commun. Abstr.; Curr. Cit.; Curr. Contents Soc. Behav. Sci.; Curr. Index J. Educ.; Educ. Index; EP Collect.; Expand. Acad. Index (1987-); Film Lit. Index; Homework Help.; Humanit. Index; Humanit. Source; Index Period. Artic. Relat. Law; INFO-SOUTH Abstr.; Infobank (1979-); Inf. Sci. Abstr.; Int. Bibliogr. Sociol.; Int. Polit. Sci. Abstr.; Mag. Search; Mark. Advert. Ref. Serv.; MasterFile FullTEXT 1000; MasterFile FullTEXT 350; MasterFile FullTEXT 650; MasterFile FullTEXT (July 1990-); Middle East Abstr. Index; MLA Int. Bibl. Books Artic. Mod. Lang. Lit.; Newsp. Period. Abstr. (1988-); OCLC; Psychol. Abstr. (1953-); PsycINFO; PsycLit; Pub. Lib. FullTEXT; Res. Alert [Full Cov.]; Risk Abstr. (19??-19??); Sage Fam. Stud. Abstr.; Sage Public Adm. Abstr.; Soc. Plann. Policy Dev. Abstr.; Soc. Sci. Source; Soc. Sci. Cit. Index [Full Cov.]; Soc. Sci. Index; Soc. Sci. Index Fulltext (Autumn 1988-) [Full Txt.]; Sociol. Abstr.; Telebase; Topicator; Women Stud. Abstr.

LC P87 .J62 **ISSN** 0196-8599
DD 302.2/05 US
Pr Rev.
JOURNAL OF COMMUNICATION INQUIRY, THE. [J. commun. inq.]. **Added/Corp** University of Iowa. School of Journalism. (1976)-. Periodical. English. Two times a year. $33.00. University of Iowa School of Journalism, 205 Communications Center, Iowa City IA 55242. **Tel** (319)335-5821. **Ad Acc. Circ:** 500. Documents available from UMI Article Clearinghouse.
Desc: Forum for humanistically oriented research into the philosophical, historical, legal and ethical dimensions of communications.
Ind/Abst Am. Hist. Life (1986-); Commun. Abstr.; Film Lit. Index; MLA Int. Bibl. Books Artic. Mod. Lang. Lit.; Newsp. Period. Abstr. (1992-); Soc. Plann. Policy Dev. Abstr.

LC TK7800 .R413 **ISSN** 1064-2269
DD 621.381/05 US
CODEN JTELEJ
•**JOURNAL OF COMMUNICATIONS TECHNOLOGY & ELECTRONICS.** [J. commun. technol. electron.]. **VFOAT** Journal of Communications Technology and Electronics. Vol. 38, No. 1 (1993)-. Periodical. English (translations available in Russian). Sixteen times a year. $1901.00. Scripta Technica, A Subsidiary of John Wiley & Sons Inc., 7961 Eastern Avenue, Silver Spring MD 20910. **Tel** (301)588-0484, FAX (301)588-5278. **(Subscription address:** John Wiley & Sons, Inc. / Philadelphia, PO Box 7247, Philadelphia PA 19170. **Tel** (212)850-6645, (800)225-5945.) **ED** Reuben Glass, City University, London. Documents available from Article Express International, Ask*IEEE. ***Continues*** *Radiotekhnika i Elektronika. English. Soviet Journal of Communications Technology & Electronics, 8756-6648.*
Desc: Devoted to the theory and physical fundamentals of communications and electronics engineering, this journal offers original work from research centers of the Russian Academy of Sciences, as well as frequent state-of-the-art reviews.
Ind/Abst Bioeng. Abstr.; Curr. Cit.; Ei Page One; Electron. Commun. Abstr. J.; Eng. Index Annu.; INSPEC; Int. Aerosp. Abstr.; ISMEC Bull.; Math. Rev.; Pollut. Abstr. Indexes; Saf. Sci. Abstr. J.

LC HM258 .J68 **ISSN** 0194-2158
DD 302.2/24 US
JOURNAL OF COMMUNITY COMMUNICATION, THE. (19??)-. Periodical. English. Four times a year. Village Design, PO Box 1220, Berkeley CA 94701.

Communications

LC P92.2 .J68
DD 302.2/09172405
ISSN 0128-3863
MY

JOURNAL OF DEVELOPMENT COMMUNICATION, THE. Added/Corp Asian Institute for Development Communication. Vol. 1, No. 1 (June 1990)-. Periodical. English. Two times a year (June, Dec.). $23.00 (developing countries); $42.00 other. Asian Institute of Development Communication / AIDCOM, 9th Floor APDC Building, Persiaran Duta, 50480 Kuala Lumpur Malaysia. **Tel** 011 60 3 2542558 2903, FAX 011 61 3 2543785, telex MA31533 ACTION. **(Subscription address:** AIDCOM, 9th Floor, APDC Building, Persiaran Duta, 50480 Kuala Lumpur, Malaysia. **) ED** Khairul Bashar. **Bk Rev. Ad Acc. Circ:** 3,000 (ctrl).
Desc: Scholarly articles on communication, journalism and other sectoral development issues, reviews, calendar of events, viewpoints, case studies, and reports.
Ind/Abst Commun. Abstr.

ISSN 1358-1651
UK
Pr Rev.

●JOURNAL OF EDUCATIONAL MEDIA. (1995)-. Periodical. English. Three times a year (Mar., June, Oct.). $438.00. Carfax Publishing Company, PO Box 25, Abingdon, Oxfordshire OX14 3UE United Kingdom. **Tel** 011 44 1235 555335, FAX 011 44 1235 553559, telex 817484. **ED** Maire Messenger Davies. **Bk Rev. Ad Acc.** available on microfiche. Documents available from The Genuine Article. **Continues** Journal of Educational Television, 0260-7417.
Ind/Abst Br. Educ. Index; Child. Lit. Abstr.; Commun. Abstr.; Curr. Contents Soc. Behav. Sci.; Curr. Index J. Educ.; Educ. Adm. Abstr.; Educ. Technol. Abstr.; Inf. Sci. Abstr.; Multicult. Educ. Abstr.; Res. Alert [Full Cov.]; Res. High. Educ. Abstr.; School Organ. Manage. Abstr.; Soc. Sci. Cit. Index [Full Cov.]; Sociol. Educ. Abstr.; Stud. Women Abstr.; Tech. Educ. Train. Abstr.

NR

JOURNAL OF LANGUAGE ARTS AND COMMUNICATION (J.L.A.C.). See Language Arts.

ISSN 1352-7266
UK

●JOURNAL OF MARKETING COMMUNICATIONS. See Business and Economics-Marketing and Purchasing.

LC P96.E252 U645
DD 380
ISSN 0899-7764
US
Pr Rev.

JOURNAL OF MEDIA ECONOMICS. [J. media econ.]. Added/Corp Emerson College. Vol. 1, No. 1 (Spring 1988)-. Periodical. English. Three times a year (June, Aug., and Dec.). $115.00. Lawrence Erlbaum Associates, Inc., 10 Industrial Avenue, Mahwah NJ 07430. **Tel** (201)236-9500, (800)926-6579, FAX (201)666-2394. **ED** Robert G. Picard. **Bk Rev.** (Qty: 4). **Ad Acc.** Full Page (B&W) $300.00. Half Page (B&W) $200.00. **Circ:** 400.
Desc: Covers the economic aspects of mass media and economic policy issues confronting media worldwide.
Ind/Abst Commun. Abstr.

LC BF353 .E55
DD 153.6
ISSN 0191-5886
US
CCC
NLM W1 JO795J
CODEN JNVBDV
Pr Rev.

JOURNAL OF NONVERBAL BEHAVIOR. See Psychology.

LC HD30.2 .J69
DD 658/.00285
ISSN 1054-1721
US
CODEN JORCEM
TITLE CHANGE

JOURNAL OF ORGANIZATIONAL COMPUTING. See Business and Economics-Management.

LC PN4073 .I5813
DD 808.5/08
ISSN 0145-5516
US
Pr Rev.

JOURNAL OF THE ILLINOIS SPEECH & THEATRE ASSOCIATION. Main/Corp Illinois Speech and Theatre Association. **VAT** Journal of the Illinois Speech and Theatre Association. (19??)-. English. One time a year. Free to members; $35.00 membership. Illinois Speech and Theatre Association, Bradley University, Central Office, Peoria IL 61625. **Tel** (309)677-2364, FAX (309)677-2330. **ED** Dr. Mary Pelias. **Circ:** 400 (ctrl).

US
Pr Rev.

JOURNAL OF THE INTERNATIONAL LISTENING ASSOCIATION : JILA. Added/Corp International Listening Association. **VFOAT** JILA; Journal of International Listening. Vol. 1, No. 1 (Spring 1987)-. Periodical. English. $10.00. Center for Information and Communication Sciences, Ball State University, Muncie IN 47306. **Tel** (317)285-1889, FAX (317)285-1516. **ED** Dr. William Arnold (Editor's Address: Department of Communication, Arizona State University, Tempe, AZ 85258-1205; Phone: (602)965-5559; **Circ:** 500.
Desc: Publishes peer reviewed research and theoretical articles pertaining to human listening processes.

LC P92.U5 K28
DD 302.23/0973/021
ISSN 0893-2700
US

KAGAN MEDIA INDEX, THE. See Communications-Abstracting, Bibliographies and Statistics.

LC P96.E252 U645
DD 384/.041/05/220
ISSN 1070-6917
US

KAGAN'S MEDIA TRENDS. [Kagan's media trends]. Added/Corp Paul Kagan Associates. **VFOAT** Media Trends. (19??)-. English. Irregular. $345.00. Paul Kagan Associates Inc., 126 Clock Tower Place, Carmel CA 93923-8734. **Tel** (408)624-1536, FAX (408)625-3225, telex ITT 4938124 PKA UI.
Desc: Analysis of media statistics, trends, technologies, consumer spending patterns, technology penetration rates, billing activity, economic indicators and private market value estimates for television, cable TV, pay TV, wireless cable, motion pictures, home video and newspaper.

LC P87 .K43
DD 001.51/05
ISSN 0388-7596
JA
Pr Rev.

KEIO COMMUNICATION REVIEW. Added/Corp Keio Gijuku Daigaku. Shinbun Kenkyujo. No. 1 (Mar. 1980)-. English. One time a year (Mar.). $14.00. Keio University, Institute of Communications Research, Minato Ku Tokyo 108 Japan. **Tel** 011 81 467 833045, FAX 011 81 467 580805. **ED** Youichi Ito. **Circ:** 600 (ctrl).

LC WMLC 93/5134
ISSN 0177-4565
GW
CCC
CODEN KZKEED

KES : ZEITSCHRIFT FUER KOMMUNIKATIONS UND EDV SICHERHEIT. [KES, Z. Kommun.- EDV-Sicherh.]. **VFOAT** Zeitschrift fuer Kommunikations-und EDV-Sicherheit; Kommunikations-und EDV-Sicherheit. (1985)-. Trade Publication. German. Six times a year. $199.59. Secumedia Verlags GmbH, Postfach 1234, D-55205 Ingelheim Germany. **Tel** 011 49 6725 5995, FAX 011 49 6725 5994. Documents available from Ask*IEEE.
Ind/Abst INSPEC (Feb. 1990-).

LC BF637.C45 K52
DD 153.6
ISSN 0193-1911
US

KINESIS REPORT, THE. See Psychology.

ISSN 0966-3371
UK

KNOWLEDGE, THE. (1986)-. English. One time a year. £62.50. Miller Freeman Technical Ltd., Riverbank House, Angel Lane, Tonbridge Kent TN9 1SE United Kingdom. **Tel** 011 44 1732 362666, FAX 011 44 1732 770483, telex 95454 BBIS. **ED** Douglas Marshall.

ISSN 0897-1986
US
CCC

KNOWLEDGE AND POLICY. Added/Corp Transaction Periodicals Consortium. University of Pittsburgh. School of Library and Information Science. (1991)-. Periodical. English. Four times a year. Fl209.00 (individuals), Fl362.50 (institutions). Transaction Publishers / Rutgers State University, Department 3091 or 3092, New Brunswick NJ 08903. **Tel** (908)932-2280 ext. 105, FAX (908)932-3138. **ED** Esther K. Hicks. **Circ:** 500. available on labels. **Continues** Knowledge in Society, 0897-1986.
Desc: An international journal devoted to the development of an interdisciplinary science of knowledge transfer. Combines, links, and applies insights and findings of scholars working in traditional disciplines with ideas from newer fields such as information science risk analysis and decision theory.
Ind/Abst Acad. Search; EP Collect.; Homework Help.; MasterFile FullTEXT 1000; MasterFile FullTEXT 350; MasterFile FullTEXT 650; MasterFile FullTEXT (July 1994-); Soc. Plann. Policy Dev. Abstr.; Soc. Sci. Source; Telebase.

US

KNOWLEDGE INDUSTRY PUBLICATIONS 200. Added/Corp Knowledge Industry Publications, Inc. **VFOAT** Knowledge Industry Publications Two Hundred. (19??)-. Knowledge Industry Publications Inc, 701 Westchester Avenue, White Plains NY 10604. **Tel** (914)328-9157, (800)800-5474, FAX (914)328-9093. **Continues** Knowledge Industry 200.

LC P87 .K56
DD 070
ISSN 0126-2491
IO

KOMUNIKA. Added/Corp Lembaga Ilmu Pengetahuan Indonesia. (19??)-. Periodical. Indonesian. Rp1800, Rp1500 (Students). Lembaga Ilmu Pengetahuan Indonesia, Biro Penerbitan Ilmiah Lipi, Medan Merdeka Selatan No. 11, Jakarta Indonesia.

LC P87 .K57
DD 070
KO

KOMYUUNIKEISYON KWAHAK. Added/Corp Koryo Taehakkyo. Pusol Sinmun Pangsong Yonguso. **VFOAT** Journal of Communication Science. (1976)-. Periodical. Korean. Koryo Taihakkyo Pusol Sinmun Pangsong Yonguso, 1 5-ka Anam-dong, Songbuk-ku, Seoul South Korea.

ISSN 0902-8099
DK
DD 700

KUNST & KOMMUNIKATION DANSK UDG. See The Arts-Art.

LC P88.8 .L35
DD 001.51/025/753
ISSN 0741-689X
US

LAMBERT'S COMMUNICATIONS DIRECTORY, WASHINGTON-BALTIMORE. **VFOAT** Communications Directory, Washington-Baltimore. Directory. English. $25.00. Lambert Publications Inc, PO Box 21008, Washington DC 20009.

LC P87 .L36
DD 001.51/05
ISSN 0271-5309
UK
CCC
CODEN LACOD8
Pr Rev.

LANGUAGE & COMMUNICATION. See Linguistics.

LC P1 .L32
DD 414.05
ISSN 0023-8309
UK
CCC
NLM W1 LA615
Pr Rev.

LANGUAGE AND SPEECH. See Linguistics.

UK

LANS & INTERNETWORKING. (19??)-. English. Twelve times a year. $1406.00. Datapro International, McGraw Hill House, Shoppenhangers Road, Maidenhead Berkshire SL6 2QL United Kingdom. **Tel** 011 44 1628 773277, FAX 011 44 1628 773628. **(Subscription address:** Datapro Research Corporation, 600 Delran Parkway, Delran NJ 08075. **) Absorbed** Datapro Reports on International Communications Software; **Separated from** Datapro Reports on Data Communications; Datapro Reports on International Networks and Services **and** Datapro Communication International.

US

LEARN TO SIGN SERIES. (19??)-. English. Irregular. Broadcast Productions Ltd, 6000 Carmel Stations Avenue, Charlotte NC 28226. **Tel** (704)544-1719.

ISSN 1145-9646
FR
UDC 69

LETTRE DE L'EDI PARIS, LA. (LA LETTRE DE L'EDI.). **VFOAT** Lettre des EDI (Paris). (198?)-. Periodical. French. Eleven times a year. $568.67. Edicom, 21 rue Tournefort, F 75005 Paris France. **Tel** 011 33 1 47072929, FAX 011 33 1 47073066, 011 33 1 4703129. **ED** Camille Elisabeth. **Bk Rev. Ad Acc.**

FR
CEASED

LETTRE DE LIAISON POUR LA RECHERCHE EUROPEENNE EN COMMUNICATION. (19??)-(19??). French. IDATE, BP 4167, 34092 Montpellier CED 5 France. **Tel** 011 33 67 144444, FAX 011 33 67 144400.

LC QA76.57.T44 L48
DD 384.3/5
ISSN 0766-5385
FR

LETTRE DE TELETEL, LA. Added/Corp France. Direction des Affaires Commerciales et Telematiques. France. Direction de Programme Teletel. (19??)-. French. Four times a year. Free on request. Telecom, 20 Avenue de Segur, 75700 Paris France. **Tel** 011 33 1 44440671, FAX 011 33 1 43216534. **ED** C. Fourgeot. Index available. **Bk Rev.**

ISSN 0823-3926
CN
DD 384/.09714

LETTRE DES COMMUNICATIONS - CLAUDE PICHE COMMUNICATIONS. (LA LETTRE DES COMMUNICATIONS.). [Lett. commun. - Claude Piche commun.]. Vol. 1, No. 1 (11 Jan. 1984)-. Periodical. French. Twenty-four times a year. $175.00.

LC Z5630 .U53A P90
DD 016.3022/3 FR
SUSPENDED

LIST OF DOCUMENTS AND PUBLICATIONS IN THE FIELD OF MASS COMMUNICATION. See Communications-Abstracting, Bibliographies and Statistics.

UK

LOOK HEAR. (19??)-. English. Three times a year. Comes with Professional Council for Religious Education membership. Christian Education Movement, Royal Buildings, Victoria Street, Derby DE1 1GW United Kingdom. **Tel** 011 44 1332 296655, FAX 011 44 1332 43253.
Ind/Abst Child. Lit. Abstr. (19??-).

LC P87 .L84
DD 302.2 BL

LUGAR EM COMUNICACAO. Vol. 1 (4th Quarter 1972)-. Periodical. Multiple languages (French and Portuguese). 15.00. Editora Rio, Avenida Paulo de Frontin 226/228 ZC-10, Rio de Janeiro Brazil.

US

MAJOR MATTERS BEFORE THE FEDERAL COMMUNICATIONS COMMISSION. **Main/Corp** United States. Federal Communications Commission. (1980)-. English. One time a year. FCC / Federal Communications Commission, 1919 M Street Northwest, Room 538, Washington DC 20554. **Tel** (202)632-6302. ***Continues*** *United States. Federal Communications Commission. Major Matters before the Commission.*

LC WMLC 93/1318 **ISSN** 0893-3189
DD 658 US
CCC

MANAGEMENT COMMUNICATION QUARTERLY. (MANAGEMENT COMMUNICATION QUARTERLY : MCQ.). [Manage. commun. q.]. **VFOAT** MCQ. Vol. 1, Issue 1 (Aug. 1987)-. Periodical. English. Four times a year (Feb., May, Aug., Nov.). $168.00. SAGE Periodical Press, 2455 Teller Road, Thousand Oaks CA 91320. **Tel** (805)499-0721, FAX (805)499-0871, telex 100799. **ED** Katherine I. Miller. Index available (fourth issue). **Bk Rev. Ad Acc. Acid Free. Circ:** 892. available on microfilm and microfiche from University Microfilms International (UMI).
Desc: Brings together communication research from a wide variety of fields, with a focus on managerial and organizational effectiveness.
Ind/Abst Commun. Abstr.; Contents Pages Manage.; Curr. Cit.; Curr. Index J. Educ. (March 1990); EP Collect.; Homework Help.; Hum. Resour. Abstr.; MasterFile FullTEXT 1000; MasterFile FullTEXT 350; MasterFile FullTEXT 650; MasterFile FullTEXT; OCLC; Person. Manage. Abstr.; Sage Fam. Stud. Abstr.; Soc. Plann. Policy Dev. Abstr.; Telebase; Work Relat. Abstr.

LC HE7710 .I6 **ISSN** 0076-4418
US

MARCONI'S INTERNATIONAL REGISTER. **Added/Corp** Marconi International Code Company, Inc. Telegraphic Cable and Radio Registrations, Inc. (1917)-. English. One time a year. $155.00. Telegraphic Cable & Radio Registrations, Inc., 19 Dogwood Lane, Larchmont NY 10538. **Tel** (914)632-8171, FAX (914)698-1804. **ED** C.G. Graham. Index available. **Ad Acc.**
Desc: A reference directory containing information on 40,000 firms throughout the world conducting commercial activities Internationally. Entries include mailing address, business description officers, telephone, FAX and telex numbers.

AT

MARGARET GEE'S MEDIA GUIDE. English. Information Australia Group Pty. Ltd., 45 Flinders Lane, Melbourne Victoria 3000 Australia. **Tel** 011 61 3 96542800, FAX 011 61 3 96505261.

LC HF5549.5.C6 M27
GW

MARKT KOMMUNIKATION. (19??)-. Monographic series. German. Irregular. Price varies per volume. Verlag Technik und Wirtschaft, Postfach 4026, D-55030 Mainz Germany. **Tel** 011 49 6131 99203.

US

MARTH'S FLORIDA GUIDE. **VFOAT** Florida Guide. (19??)-. English. One time a year. $34.95. Marth's 1995 Florida Guide, Route 2, Box 380, Branford FL 32008. **Tel** (904)935-2707, FAX (904)935-2707. **ED** Marty Marth. ***Continues*** *Guide.*
Desc: Information on newspapers, radio stations and television broadcasting.

LC Z5632 .M37 P87 P92.A7 M37 **ISSN** 0217-1287
DD 016.00151 SI

MASS COM PERIODICAL LITERATURE INDEX. **Added/Corp** Asian Mass Communication Research and Information Center. Documentation Unit. Vol. 2, No. 1 (June 1982)-. Periodical. English. Two times a year. Free on request. Asian Mass Communication Research and Information Center, 39 Newton Road, Singapore 1130 Singapore. **Tel** 011 65 2515106, FAX 2534535, telex AMICSI RS 55524. ***Continues*** *Mass Com Periodical Literature, 0217-1287.*

ISSN 0193-7707
US
Pr Rev.

MASS COMM REVIEW. [Mass comm rev.]. **Added/Corp** Association for Education in Journalism. Mass Communications and Society Division. **VFOAT** MCR. **VAT** Mass Communications Review. Vol. 1 (Aug. 1973)-. Periodical. English. Two times a year. $30.00 (one-year), $53.00 (two-year), $75.00 (three-year) US; $45.00 (one-year), $80.00 (two-year), $110.00 (three-year) other. Mass Comm Review, 1 Washington, San Jose State University, San Jose CA 95191. **Tel** (408)924-3240. **ED** Diana Tillinghast. Index available. cum. index. **Ad Acc.** ctrl circ. available on microfilm and microfiche from University Microfilms International (UMI). Documents available from UMI Article Clearinghouse.
Desc: A refereed journal publishing research from all mass communication subfields.
Ind/Abst Acad. Search; Commun. Abstr. (?-?); EP Collect.; Expand. Acad. Index (1987-); Homework Help.; Humanit. Index; Humanit. Source; INFO-SOUTH Abstr.; Mag. Search; Manage. Contents (1974-); MasterFile FullTEXT 1000; MasterFile FullTEXT 350; MasterFile FullTEXT 650; MasterFile FullTEXT (July 1993-); Newsp. Period. Abstr. (1990-); OCLC; Telebase.

LC P92.I7 M32
DD 302.2/3 II

MASS MEDIA IN INDIA. **Added/Corp** India. Ministry of Information and Broadcasting. Research and Reference Division. (1978)-. English. One time a year. Price varies. Ministry of Information and Broadcasting, Government of India, Patiala House, New Delhi 110 001 India. **Tel** 387983. **(Subscription address:** Prints India, 11 Darya Ganj, New Delhi 110002 India. **Tel** 011 91 11 3268645, FAX 011 91 11 3275542, telex 31-61087 PRIN-IN.)

LC WMLC 93/417
IT

MASS MEDIA : RIVISTA BIMESTRALE DELLA COMUNICAZIONE. (19??)-. Periodical. Italian. Six times a year. L32700. Capone Editore, Via Provinciale Lecce Cavallino, 73020 Cavallino Italy. **Tel** 011 39 832 612618, FAX 011 39 832 611877. **Bk Rev**, (Qty: 50). **Ad Acc. Circ:** 1,500.

NE

MASSACOMMUNICATIE. Dutch. Uitgeverij H Gianotten BV, Bredaseweg 61, 5038 NA Tilburg Netherlands.
Ind/Abst Soc. Res. Methodol. Abstr. (1990-).

RU

MASTERA KHUDOZHESTVENNOGO SLOVA. (1983)-. Russian. Irregular. Izdatel'stvo Iskusstvo, Vorotnikovskii Pereulok 11, 103009 Moscow Russia.

ISSN 0380-4437
CN
TITLE CHANGE

MATTHEWS' LIST. **Main/Corp** Syd Matthews & Partners Limited. **Added/Corp** Canadian Corporate News (Firm). Vol. 1 (Jan. 1957)-(19??). Periodical. English (French). Canadian Corporate News, 25 Adelaide Street East, Suite 500, Toronto Ontario M5C 3A1 Canada. **Tel** (416)362-5739, (800)363-9296, FAX (416)362-9693. **ED** Gordon Sova and Lisa Colliss. **Circ:** 1,200. ***Continued by*** *Matthews' Media Directory.*
Desc: Detailed listings covering all Canadian radio, TV, newspaper, business and consumer outlets.

ISSN 1193-9575
DD 070.1/02571 CN

MATTHEWS MEDIA DIRECTORY. [Matthews media dir.]. **Added/Corp** Canadian Corporate News (Firm). **VFOAT** Annuaire des Media Matthews. Vol. 36, No. 1 (Feb. 1992)-. Directory. English (French). Three times a year. 156.07Can$. Canadian Corporate News, 25 Adelaide Street East, Suite 500, Toronto Ontario M5C 3A1 Canada. **Tel** (416)362-5739, (800)363-9296, FAX (416)362-9693. ***Continues*** *Matthews' List., 0380-4437.*

LC PN1990 .M33 **ISSN** 0743-1279
DD 384.54/06/07471 US

MB NEWS (NEW YORK, N.Y.). (MB NEWS.). **Added/Corp** Museum of Broadcasting (New York, N.Y.). **VFOAT** M.B. News; Museum of Broadcasting Newsletter. (19??)-. English. Museum of Broadcasting, One East 53rd Street, New York NY 10022.

UK

MEDIA & MARKETING EUROPE. (19??)-. Periodical. English. Twelve times a year. £50.00 UK; £60.00 Europe; £75.00 other. Media Week Ltd., Wilmington House, Churchill Dar, Foxtrot Kent DA2 7ES United Kingdom. **(Subscription address:** EMAP Business Publishing, 4 Admiral House Cardinal Way, Middlesex HA3 5SQ United Kingdom. **Tel** 011 44 181 8684499.)

LC P94 .M35 **ISSN** 0149-6980
DD 302.2/34/05 US
TITLE CHANGE

MEDIA & VALUES. **Added/Corp** Media Action Research Center (U.S.) National Sisters Communications Service (U.S.) Center for Communications Ministry (Los Angeles, Calif.). **VFOAT** Media and Values. (1977)-(1993). Periodical. English. Center for Media Literacy, 1962 South Shenandoah Street, Los Angeles CA 90034. **Tel** (310)559-2944, FAX (310)559-9396. **ED** Elizabeth Thoman. **Circ:** 10,000 (ctrl). ***Continued by*** *Connect.*
Desc: An interfaith media education magazine prompting social analysis and practical local action on issues of contemporary media and new technology.
Ind/Abst Acad. Abstr.; Acad. Search; EP Collect.; Homework Help.; Mag. Artic. Summar. Elite; Mag. Artic. Summar. Select; Mag. Artic. Summar. CD-ROM; MasterFile FullTEXT 1000; MasterFile FullTEXT 350; MasterFile FullTEXT 650; MasterFile FullTEXT; OCLC; Pub. Lib. FullTEXT; Read. Guide Period. Lit.; Soc. Sci. Source; Telebase; Vocat. Search.

LC P92.A7 M43 **ISSN** 0129-6612
DD 301.16 SI

MEDIA ASIA. [Media Asia]. **Added/Corp** Asian Mass Communication Research and Information Centre. Vol. 1 (1974)-. Periodical. English. Four times a year. $40.00. Asian Mass Communication Research and Information Center, 39 Newton Road, Singapore 1130 Singapore. **Tel** 011 65 2515106, FAX 2534535, telex AMICSI RS 55524. Index available. cum. index. **Bk Rev.** ***Continues*** *Asian Mass Communication Research and Information Centre. Documentation List.*
Desc: Journal on contemporary issues in mass communication in Asia. Facilitates exchange of views between Asian countries and the North and South.
Ind/Abst Commun. Abstr.

LC P92.E9 M42 **ISSN** 0267-5382
DD 400 UK
TITLE CHANGE

MEDIA BULLETIN. **Added/Corp** European Institute for the Media. (19??)-(19??). Bulletin. English. European Institute for the Media, Kaistrasse 13, D-40221 Dusseldorf Germany. **Tel** 011 49 211 90104-0, FAX 011 49 211 90104-56. ***Continued by*** *Bulletin : European Institue for the Media, 1021-5719.*

ISSN 1045-716X
DD 380 US

MEDIA BUSINESS. [Media bus.]. (198?)-. Periodical. English. One time a week. $450.00. Transmedia Partners Inc, 1900 Grant Street 720, Denver CO 80203. **Tel** (303)355-2101, (800)325-0156, FAX (303)355-2144. ***Continues*** *Media Business News, 0898-283X.*

US

MEDIA CULTURE REVIEW. English. Six times a year (published Feb., Apr., June, Aug., Oct., Dec.). $36.00 institutions, $24.00 individuals. Institute for Alternative Journalism., 100 East 85th Street, New York NY 10028. **Tel** (212)799-4822. **ED** Don Hazen 2025 Eye Street Northwest Washington, DC 20009 (202)887-0022. **Bk Rev**, (Qty: 3).

GW

MEDIA DATEN. SCHWEIZ. German. Two times a year. DM376.00. Media Daten Verlagsgesellschaf GmbH, Postfach 4260, D-65032 Wiesbaden Germany. **Tel** 011 49 6123 7000, FAX 011 49 6123 700122.

LC BV4319 .W63a **ISSN** 0143-5558
DD 201/.41 UK
CCC

MEDIA DEVELOPMENT. [Media dev.]. **Added/Corp** World Association for Christian Communication. Vol. 27 (1980)-. Periodical. English (French, German and Spanish). Four times a year. $68.45. World Association for Christian Communication, 357 Kennington Lane, London SE11 5QY United Kingdom. **Tel** 011 44 171 5829139, FAX 011 44 171 7350340. **ED** Michael Traber and Philip Lee. **Bk Rev. Circ:** 1,800 (ctrl). ***Continues*** *WACC Journal, 0092-7821.*
Desc: Analysis of communication theory and practice from a Christian perspective with particular emphasis on socio-economic development.
Ind/Abst Christ. Period. Index (19??-); Commun. Abstr. (?-?).

ISSN 0146-2091
US

MEDIA DIGEST (FINKSBURG). (MEDIA DIGEST.). Vol. 1 (1972)-. Periodical. English. Four times a year. $6.00 US; $7.00 Canada. Charles H Slingluff, 137 West Patrick Street, Frederick MD 21701-5513. available on microfilm and microfiche from University Microfilms International (UMI).

CN

MEDIA IMPACT. **Main/Corp** Canada. Ministry of State, Science and Technology. (1973)-. Monographic series. English. Price varies per volume. Ministry of State, Science & Technology Building, 270 Albert Street, Ottawa Ontario K1A 1A1 Canada.

Communications

LC HF5801
DD 659.1
ISSN 0024-9793
US
CCC
MEDIA INDUSTRY NEWSLETTER. See Business and Economics-Advertising and Public Relations.

ISSN 0312-9616
AT
TITLE CHANGE
MEDIA INFORMATION AUSTRALIA. [Media inf. Aust.]. **Added/Corp** Australian Film and Television School. Vol. 1, No. 1 (July 1976)-(Aug. 1995). Periodical. English. (Feb., May, Aug., Nov.). Australian Film Television and Radio School, PO Box 126, North Ryde NSW 2113 Australia. **Tel** 011 61 2 8056454, FAX 011 61 2 8871030. **ED** Stuart Cunningham, Murray Goot, Elizabeth Jacka, Deena Shiff, John Sinclair, Rodney Tiffen and Peter B. White. Index available. cum. index. **Bk Rev. Ad Acc. Circ:** 1,200 (ctrl). *Continued by Media International Australia*.
Desc: Covers media and communications. Contains analyses of broadcasting telecommunications issues, research, reviews, news and abstracts of articles.
Ind/Abst APAIS, Aust. Public Aff. Inf. Ser. (1981-); Aust. Educ. Index (1979-); Commun. Abstr.; Film Lit. Index (19??-).

AT
●**MEDIA INTERNATIONAL AUSTRALIA.** (1995)-. English. Four times a year. 90.00Aus$ (institutions), 50.00Aus$ (individuals) Australia; 115.00Aus$ other. Australian Film Television and Radio School, PO Box 126, North Ryde NSW 2113 Australia. **Tel** 011 61 2 8056454, FAX 011 61 2 8871030. *Continues Media Information Australia*.

IT
MEDIA KEY SYNTHESIS. (19??)-. Trade Publication. Italian. Twenty-four times a year. L200000 Italy; L260000 other. Media Key Srl, Via Filippino Lippi 33 C, 20131 Milan Italy. **Tel** 011 39 2 70638348, FAX 011 39 2 2363662.

ISSN 1188-1577
DD 027
CN
MEDIA MANAGER : A PUBLICATION OF THE ASSOCIATION OF MEDIA MANAGERS, THE. [Media manag.]. **Added/Corp** Association of Media Managers. Vol. 1, No. 1 (Fall 1991)-. Periodical. English. Two times a year. Limited free distribution. Association of Media Managers, 211 Watline Avenue, Mississauga Ontario L4Z 1P3 Canada.

ISSN 0747-0908
US
CEASED
MEDIA MEMO (ENGLEWOOD, COLO.). (MEDIA MEMO.). (19??)-(19??). Periodical. English. Media Memo, 4585 Wolff Street, Denver CO 80212. **Tel** (303)455-9125. **ED** Tom Pade. **Circ:** 3,000.

ISSN 0895-4550
DD 336
US
MEDIA MERGERS & ACQUISITIONS. [Media mergers acquis.]. **Added/Corp** Paul Kagan Associates. **VFOAT** PK Media Mergers & Acquisitions; Media Mergers and Acquisitions. No. 1 (Aug. 26, 1987)-. Newsletter. English. Twelve times a year. $595.00. Paul Kagan Associates Inc., 126 Clock Tower Place, Carmel CA 93923-8734. **Tel** (408)624-1536, FAX (408)625-3225, telex ITT 4938124 PKA UI. available via fax.
Desc: Scorecard of deals done by media companies, including dollar amounts, multiples paid, trends captured in summaries of complex transactions.

ISSN 1061-9267
DD 028
US
MEDIA MONITOR (DANVILLE, CALIF.). (MEDIA MONITOR.). [Media monit.]. Issue No. 1 (Feb. 1992)-. Periodical. English. Four times a year. $20.00. Plastic Cow Productions, PO Box 3081, Danville CA 94526.

LC P96.C762 I425
DD 001.51/0954
II
MEDIA MONITOR (NEW DELHI, INDIA). (MEDIA MONITOR.). **Added/Corp** Living Media Research Foundation. Vol. 1, No. 1 (April 1986)-. Periodical. English. Twelve times a year. Living Media Research Foundation, 3rd Floor, Competent House F-14, Connaught Place, New Delhi 110001 India.
Desc: Newsletter of the center for media and public affairs. Each issue provides statistical analysis with user friendly charts and text of media coverage of current issues and events. Public policy leaders, executives, professors, students and journalists use the monitor as a scientific basis for judging media fairness and accuracy.

ISSN 0033-3913
US
CEASED
MEDIA NEWS KEYS. (19??)-(May 1993). Trade Publication. English. Television Index Inc, 40/29 27th Street/2nd Floor, Long Island City NY 11101. **Tel** (718)937-3990. *Absorbed Publicity Record*.

ISSN 0815-5615
AT
MEDIA PEOPLE (N.S.W./A.C.T. ED.). See Communications-Abstracting, Bibliographies and Statistics.

ISSN 0170-1754
GW
MEDIA PERSPEKTIVEN. Trade Publication. German. Twelve times a year. Arbeitsgemeinschaft Rundfunkwerbung, Am Steinernen Stock 1, W-6000 Frankfurt M1 Germany. **Tel** 069/155-2664. **ED** Klaus Berg, Marie-Luise Kiefer and Christa-Maria Ridder. Index available. **Circ:** 6,500.

ISSN 1120-5784
IT
UDC 681.84
MEDIA PRODUCTION. [Media prod.]. (1990)-. Periodical. Italian. Ten times a year. L42240. Production Publishing Co., Ripa di Porta Ticinese 93, 20143 Milan Italy.

LC HQ1402 .M44
DD 302.2/3
ISSN 0145-9651
US
CCC
Pr Rev.
MEDIA REPORT TO WOMEN. [Media rep. women]. **Added/Corp** Women's Institute for Freedom of the Press. Vol. 1 (June 1972)-. Periodical. English. Four times a year (Jan., April, July, Oct.). $55.00. Communication Research Associates Inc., 10606 Mantz Road, Silver Spring MD 20903-1228. **Tel** (301)445-3230, FAX (301)314-9981. **ED** Sheila J. Gibbons. **Bk Rev. Circ:** 1,600. Documents available from UMI Article Clearinghouse.
Desc: Deals with the role women are playing in the media and in P.R., advertising. Reports on how women are presented by the media.
Ind/Abst Expand. Acad. Index (1992-); Film Lit. Index (1977-1991); Hum. Rights Intern. Rep.; Newsp. Period. Abstr. (1992-); Women Stud. Abstr.

ISSN 1077-6818
DD 384
US
●**MEDIA REPORTER (ORLANDO, FLA.), THE.** (THE MEDIA REPORTER / FALCON COMMUNICATIONS.). [Media report.]. Vol. 1, Issue 1 (Sept. 1994)-. Periodical. English. Twelve times a year. $195.00. Falcon Communications, 8879 West Colonial Drive, Suite 138, Ocoee FL 34761. **Tel** (407)294-6750. **ED** Milo Falcon. Index available. cum. index. **Bk Rev**, (Qty: 5). ctrl circ.

LC P87 .M363
DD 302.23/05
ISSN 1115-4489
NR
MEDIA REVIEW. Vol. 1, No. 1 (April 1991)-. Periodical. English. Eleven times a year. $66.00. Diamond Publications, 9 James Robertson Street, Surulere Lagos Nigeria. **Tel** 011 234 1 842741, 011 234 1 833163.

LC P87 .G36
DD 001.51/05
ISSN 1057-7416
US
MEDIA STUDIES JOURNAL. [Media stud. j.]. **Added/Corp** Freedom Forum Media Studies Center. Vol. 5, No. 4 (Fall 1991)-. Periodical. English. Four times a year (published seasonally). $32.00. Freedom Forum Media Studies Center, Columbia University, Financial Department, 2950 Broadway, New York NY 10027. **Tel** (212)678-6600, FAX (212)678-6663. **ED** Everette Dennis. Documents available from UMI Article Clearinghouse. *Continues Gannett Center Journal, 0893-8342*.
Ind/Abst Newsp. Period. Abstr. (1992-); PAIS Int. Print; Soc. Sci. Cit. Index [Select. Cov.].

ISSN 0741-2983
US
TITLE CHANGE
MEDIA WATCH. LOS ANGELES/ORANGE COUNTY. **VFOAT** Los Angeles/Orange County Media Watch; Los Angeles, Orange County Media Watch. (1983)-(1995). Periodical. English. Gregory Communications, 1250 North Santa Anita Avenue, Arcadia CA 91006. **Tel** (818)449-3676, FAX (818)584-0907. **ED** John Gregory. Index available ($82.00). *Continued by Gregory's Media Directory*.

UK
MEDIA WEEK. English. One time a week. $120.00. EMAP Business Publishing Ltd., 260 Field End Road, Audit House, Ruislip Middlesex HA4 9LT United Kingdom. **Tel** 011 44 181 9563000, FAX 011 44 181 4293117.

ISSN 1054-6952
DD 384
US
MEDIA LETTER (CORAL GABLES, FLA.). (MEDIA LETTER.). [Media lett.]. (1990)-. Periodical. English. Twelve times a year. $245.00 (schools/non-profit organizations), $395.00 (other). The Winta Group, 44 Pleasant Street, Suite 200, Watertown MA 02172. **Tel** (617)926-5500, (617)926-2134, FAX (617)926-5222. **ED** Dr. Pamela Gray. **Bk Rev**, (Qty: 6). ctrl circ.
Desc: Provides analysis and information about trends, tools, projects and software relating to multi-media technology, both in the U.S. and international (Japanese & European) markets.

LC P92.N4 M42
NE
MEDIAMARKT. **VFOAT** Media Markt. (198?)-. Periodical. Dutch. Twelve times a year. Samsom Bedrijfsinformatie BV, Postbus 4, 2400 MA Alphen Rij Netherlands. **Tel** 011 31 1720 66633.

LC P88.8 .M42
NE
MEDIAMARKT. BIJLAGE. **VFOAT** Media Markt. (198?)-. Periodical. Dutch. Three times a year. Samsom Bedrijfsinformatie BV, Postbus 4, 2400 MA Alphen Rij Netherlands. **Tel** 011 31 1720 66633.

IT
MEDIAS. See Journalism.

ISSN 1192-330X
DD 302.23/025/714
CN
●**MEDIAS ET COMMUNICATIONS AU QUEBEC.** (REPERTOIRE DESCRIPTIF. MEDIAS ET COMMUNICATIONS AU QUEBEC.). [Medias commun. Que.]. **Added/Corp** Quebec Dans le Monde (Association). **VFOAT** Medias et Communications au Quebec. (1993)-. Periodical. French. Every 2 years. 46.95Can$. Quebec Dans Le Monde, CP 8503, Sainte-Foy Quebec G1V 4N5 Canada. **Tel** (418)659-5540, FAX (418)659-4143. *Continues Repertoire Descriptif. Le Monde des Medias et des Communications au Quebec., 1183-4838*.

LC WMLC 93/446
DD 384
ISSN 0762-5642
FR
MEDIASPOUVOIRS. (1985)-. Periodical. French. Four times a year. $109.36. Mediaspouvoirs, 9 Bis rue Abel Hovelacque, 75013 Paris France. **Tel** 011 33 1 44088400. **(Subscription address:** Com et Com, 383 Avenue General de Gaulle, 92140 Clamart France. **Tel** 011 33 1 46315063.) **ED** Vebret Joseph (editor's phone: 33 1 44088377). **Bk Rev**, (Qty: 4). **Ad Acc.** ctrl circ.
Ind/Abst PAIS Int. Print (1991-).

LC P92.U5 M535
DD 070
ISSN 1053-8321
US
MEDIAWATCH (ALEXANDRIA, VA.). (MEDIAWATCH.). [MediaWatch]. **Added/Corp** Media Research Center. **VFOAT** Media Watch; MW. (19??)-. Periodical. English. Twelve times a year. $29.00. Media Research Center, 113 Southwest Street, 2nd Floor, Alexandria VA 22314. **Tel** (703)683-9733, FAX (703)683-9736. **ED** Brent Baker, (phone: (703)683-9733). **Ad Acc.** ctrl circ.

CN
MEDIAWAVE. (19??)-. Periodical. English. Six times a year. 18.00Can$ (one-year), 28.00Can$ (two-year). Mediawave Magazine, 916 West Broadway #580, Vancouver British Columbia, V5Z 1K7 Canada. **Tel** (604)875-1942. *Continues Media West, 0228-1554*.

ISSN 0723-2128
GW
UDC 791.43
CODEN 654.19
MEDIEN-BULLETIN. (1982)-. Periodical. German. Twelve times a year. $178.87. Medien Bulletin Leserservice, Postfach 1111, Karlstrasse 41, W-7900 Ulm Germany. **Tel** 011 49 731 152022.

LC P87 .M375
DD 302.2/34/05
ISSN 0341-6860
GW
CCC
MEDIEN + ERZIEHUNG. (MEDIEN + ERZIEHUNG : MERZ.). [Medien + Erzieh.]. **VFOAT** Medien und Erziehung; MERZ. (1976)-. German. Six times a year. $39.91. Kopaed Verlag, Pfaelzer Wald Str 64, D-81539 Munich Germany. **Tel** 011 49 89 689 89200, FAX 011 49 89 689 89111. **ED** Martin Keilhacker, Edmund Budrich and Wilhelm Kogel. Index available. cum. index. **Bk Rev. Ad Acc.** ctrl circ.
Desc: Comments, analysis and reviews of movies and books on movies.
Ind/Abst Film Lit. Index.

ISSN 0931-9808
GW
UDC 791.43
Pr Rev.
MEDIEN KONKRET. [Medien konkret]. **VFOAT** Medien Concret. (1987)-. Periodical. German. Four times a year. DM28.00. Medienconcret, Postfach 101087 Judgendfilmclb, W-5000 Cologne 1 F R Germany. **Tel** 011 49 221 120093, FAX 011 49 221 132592. Index available. **Bk Rev. Ad Acc. Circ:** 3,000 (ctrl). *Continues Spektrum Film, 0176-4594*.

ISSN 0179-5724
GW
UDC 654.197 :33
MEDIENSPIEGEL. [Medienspiegel]. **VFOAT** Medienspiegel des Instituts der Deutschen Wirtschaft (1986). (1986)-. Periodical. German. One time a week. $439.96. Deutscher Instituts Verlag, Postfach 510670, W-5000 Cologne 51 Germany. **Tel** 011 49 221 370801. *Continues Medienspiegel des Instituts der Deutschen Wirtschaft, 0171-3930*.

Communications

LC P87 .M39
DD 302.23/05
ISSN 0176-4241
GW
CCC

MEDIENWISSENSCHAFT, REZENSIONEN. Added/Corp Philipps-Universitaet Marburg. Universitaet-Gesamthochschule-Siegen. **VFOAT** Medienwissenschaft. Vol. 1 (1984)-. Periodical. German. Four times a year. $84.44. Max Niemeyer Verlag, Postfach 2140, D-72011 Tuebingen Germany. **Tel** 011 49 7071 989494, FAX 011 49 7071 989450. **ED** Juergen Felix, Heinz Heller, Karl Riha.

LC P92.G4 M39
DD 302.23/0943/05
ISSN 0025-8350
GW

MEDIUM (FRANKFURT). (MEDIUM.). [Medium]. Periodical. German. Twelve times a year. Haus der Evangelischen Publizistik, Friedrichstr 34, 6 Frankfurt Mainz Germany. **Tel** (069)7151-105. **Bk Rev. Ad Acc. Circ:** 3,500. *Formed by the union of Medium (Witten) and Evangelischer Film-Beobachter.*
Desc: Journal for broadcasting, television, film and print media. Political and social sciences.
Ind/Abst Film Lit. Index.

UK

MEJ : MEDIA EDUCATION JOURNAL. (19??)-. Academic Scholarly Publication. English. Two times a year. £30.00 UK; £35.00 other. Ames / Scottish Film Council, Dowanhill 74 Victoria Crescent Road, Glasgow G12 9JN United Kingdom. **ED** Margaret Hubbard. Index Bound in First Issue. **Bk Rev. Ad Acc. Adv Mgr:** M. Hubbard.
Ind/Abst Br. Educ. Index.

ISSN 0364-8052
US

MEMORANDUM OPINION AND ORDER. **Main/Corp** United States. Federal Communications Commission. **VFOAT** Before the Federal Communications Commission. (19??). English. FCC / Federal Communications Commission, 1919 M Street Northwest, Room 538, Washington DC 20554. **Tel** (202)632-6302.

LC HM263 .C2
DD 302.2/34/025794
ISSN 0889-2776
US

METRO CALIFORNIA MEDIA. [Metro Calif. media]. (197?)-. English. Two times a year (June & Dec.). $149.50. Public Relations Plus Inc., PO Drawer 1197, New Milford CT 06776. **Tel** (800)-999-8448, FAX (203)355-8048. **ED** Harold D. Hansen (phone: (203)354-9361). *Continues California Publicity Outlets.*

US

Pr Rev.

MICHIGAN ASSOCIATION OF SPEECH COMMUNICATION JOURNAL, THE. **Added/Corp** Michigan Association of Speech Communication. **VFOAT** MASC. Vol. 19 (1984)-. Periodical. English. One time a year. $6.00. Michigan Association of Speech Communication, East Michigan University, Ypsilanti MI 48197. **Tel** (313)487-0064. **ED** David Ling. **Circ:** 250 (ctrl). *Continues Michigan Speech Association Journal, 0543-9965.*

DD 621.3805
ISSN 0269-9567
UK

MIDDLE EAST COMMUNICATIONS. [Middle East commun.]. (1986)-. Periodical. English. Eleven times a year (monthly except combined July/Aug.). ICOM Publications Ltd., Chancery House, St. Nicholas Way, Sutton Surrey SM1 1JB United Kingdom. **Tel** 011 44 181 6421117, FAX 011 44 181 6421941.

ISSN 0295-3943
FR

UDC 791(447)
CODEN 791(449)

MIDI MEDIA. (1986)-. Periodical. French. Twelve times a year. 390.00F France; 490.00F other. Midi Media, BP 27, 31012 Toulouse Cedex France. **Tel** 011 33 61 555494, FAX 011 33 61 250309. **ED** Jean-Paul Bobin. **Ad Acc, Adv Mgr:** Rebecca Arditti. **Circ:** 10,000.

ISSN 0196-8505
US

MILWAUKEE AREA MEDIA DIRECTORY. (1979)-. Directory. English. One time a year. Bishea Meili & Associates Inc, 220 Southeast 2nd Avenue, Fort Lauderdale FL 33301. **Tel** (305)276-7580. **ED** Constance J Bowman. **Circ:** 2,000.
Desc: Listing of all print and electronic media for 6 counties surrounding Milwaukee, Wisconsin and for Metro Madison, Wisconsin.

DD 001
ISSN 1057-3240
US

MINNESOTA MEDIA DIRECTORY (MIDWEST ED.). (MINNESOTA MEDIA DIRECTORY.). [Minn. media dir.]. **Added/Corp** Delmont Communications, Inc. (1991)-. Directory. English. Delmont Communications, Inc., 1700 Livingston Avenue, St. Paul MN 55118. *Continues Minnesota Media Directory (Greater Minnesota Ed.), 1046-8919.*

DD 001
ISSN 1056-6465
US

MINNESOTA MEDIA DIRECTORY (TWIN CITIES ED. 1991). (MINNESOTA MEDIA DIRECTORY.). [Minn. media dir.]. (1991)-. Directory. English. Delmont Communications, Inc., 1700 Livingston Avenue, St. Paul MN 55118. *Continues Twin Cities Media Directory (Saint Paul, Minn.), 1051-5704.*

LC P96.M5 M56
DD 001.51/025/73
ISSN 0730-5141
US

MINORITY/ETHNIC MEDIA GUIDE, USA. [Minority ethn. media guide, USA]. **VFOAT** Minority/Ethnic Media Guide U.S.A.; Minority/Ethnic Media Guide. **VAT** Minority Ethnic Media Guide United States of America. (1980)-. English. One time a year. $58.00. Directories International Inc, 118 21 Queens Boulevard, Room 417, Forest Hills NY 11375-7201. **Tel** (203)853-7880, FAX (203)853-7370. *Continues Minority Group Media Guide, USA, 0149-9572.*

US

MISSISSIPPI NEWS MEDIA DIRECTORY. (19??)-. Directory. English. One time a year (Feb.). $25.00. News Media Directories, PO Box 316, Mount Dora FL 32757. **Tel** (904)383-3023, (800)749-6399.

ISSN 0941-7494
GW

UDC 654

MOBILFUNK HEIDELBERG. [Mobilfunk Heidelb.]. **VFOAT** Mobil-Funk. Periodical. German. Irregular. DM24.00. Dr. Alfred Huethig Verlag GmbH, Postfach 102869, D-69018 Heidelberg Germany. **Tel** 011 49 6221 489281, FAX 011 49 6221 489279.
(Subscription address: Huethig Publishing Inc., 29 Macintosh Drive, Oxford CT 06478. **Tel** (203)881-2647.)

LC HM258
DD 302.2/244/0971405
ISSN 1183-515X
CN

MONDE ALPHABETIQUE, LE. [Monde alph.]. **Added/Corp** Regroupement des Groupes Populaires en Alphabetisation du Quebec. Spring (1991)-. Periodical. French. Two times a year (Dec., May). 10.00Can$. Le Regroupement des Groupes Populaires en Alphabetisation du Quebec, 5040 boulevard St-Laurent, Suite 1, Montreal Quebec H2T 1R7 Canada. **Tel** (514)277-9976, FAX (514)277-2044. **Bk Rev. Circ:** 500.

DD 363
ISSN 1058-3459
US

MORALITY IN MEDIA NEWSLETTER. [Moral. Media newsl.]. **Added/Corp** Morality in Media, Inc. **VFOAT** Morality in Media, Inc. Newsletter; MIM; Morality in Media. (19??)-. Newsletter. English. Six times a year. $20.00. Morality in Media Inc., 475 Riverside Drive, New York NY 10115. **Tel** (212)870-3222, FAX (212)870-2765. *Continues Morality in Media Inc. Newsletter, 0027-1004.*
Desc: Aims to combat obscenity and address issues of indecency in the media.

IT

MULTIMEDIA. (19??)-. Italian. Six times a year. L50000 Itlay; L80000 other. Edizioni Sonda, V Ciamarella 23 3, 10149 Turin Italy. **Tel** 011 39 11 211442. *Continues Quaderni di Comunicazione Audiovisiva e Nuove Tecnologie.*

DD 338
ISSN 1065-8300
US
CCC

MULTIMEDIA BUSINESS REPORT. [Multimed. bus. rep.]. **Added/Corp** Simba Information, Inc. (1992)-. Periodical. English. Twenty-four times a year. $479.00. SIMBA Information Inc., 213 Danbury Road, PO Box 7430, Wilton CT 06897-7430. **Tel** (203)834-0033 ext. 173, FAX (203)884-1771.
(Subscription address: Simba Information Inc., PO Box 7430, Wilton CT 06897. **Tel** (203)834-0033 ext. 160, FAX (203)834-1771.) *Continues New Media in Education and Entertainment; Multimedia Computing and Presentation.*

US

Pr Rev.

MULTIMEDIA TECHNOLOGIES AND SYSTEMS. (19??)-. English. One time a year. $490.00. Information Workstation Group, 501 Queens Street, Alexandria VA 22314. **Tel** (703)548-4320, FAX (703)838-9271. **ED** John Gale. Index available.
Desc: This 278 page report introduces the multimedia technologies -- the CD family; DVI, CDTV, CVD, Interactive Television, IVD, DAT, JPEG, MPEG, etc. Separate chapters address the CD family, digital video-interactive and digital audio tape. Video processors and systems are described in detail. Detail of computerized home entertainment is also described. Relevant bridging technologies and systems are also discussed.

DD 005
ISSN 1075-6612
US

●**MULTIMEDIA TODAY (VERO BEACH, FLA.).** (MULTIMEDIA TODAY.). [Multimed. today]. **Added/Corp** Redgate Communications Corporation. **VFOAT** Multimedia. (1993)-. English. Four times a year. $19.95. Redgate Communications Corporation, 660 Beachland Boulevard, Vero Beach FL 32963. **Tel** (407)231-6904, FAX (407)231-7872. **ED** Geoffrey R. Amthor. **Ad Acc, Adv Mgr:** Melissa McKee. **Tel** (407)231-6904. **Circ:** 70,000.

DD 338
ISSN 1064-6639
US
CCC
CODEN MUWEEQ

MULTIMEDIA WEEK. (MULTIMEDIA WEEK : THE EXECUTIVE REPORT ON BUSINESS OPPORTUNITIES IN THE MULTIMEDIA MARKETPLACE.). [Multimed. week]. Vol. 1, No. 1 (Aug. 17, 1992)-. Periodical. English. One time a week (50 issues). $597.00. Phillips Business Information Inc., 1201 Seven Locks Road, PO Box 61130, Potomac MD 20854. **Tel** (301)424-3338, (301)340-1520, (800)777-5005, FAX (301)424-4297, telex 358149. available on an online database (file 636/Full-Text) from DIALOG. *Absorbed The S. Klein Newsletter on Computer Graphics and Open Media Letter; Absorbed in part Home Media Technology News.*

DD 338
ISSN 1076-2442
US

●**MULTIMEDIA WIRE (FAX).** (MULTIMEDIA WIRE.). [Multimed. wire]. (1994)-. Periodical. English. Seven times a week. $495.00. Proactive Media Inc, 43 Randolph Road, Suite 128, Silver Springs MD 20904. **Tel** (301)890-7950.

UK

●**MULTIMEDIA YEARBOOK.** (1995)-. English. One time a year. $231.02. Interactive Media Publications Ltd, 104A Saint John Street, London EC1M 4EH United Kingdom. **Tel** 011 44 171 4901185, FAX 011 44 171 4904706. *Continues International Multimedia Yearbook.*

IT

MUSIC AND COMMUNICATION. See Music.

ISSN 0815-7441
AT

NAATI ANNUAL REPORT. (19??)-. Periodical. English. One time a year. 12.33Aus$. NAATI Executive Secretary, PO Box 349, Jamison Australian Capital Territory, 2614 Australia. **Tel** 011 61 62 514044, FAX 011 61 62 531575. **ED** S. Bell. **Circ:** 100.

LC WMLC 93/1529
DD 808
ISSN 0749-1042
US

NATIONAL FORENSIC JOURNAL. [Natl. forensic j.]. **Added/Corp** National Forensic Association. Vol. 1, No. 1 (Spring 1983)-. Periodical. English. Two times a year (Apr. and Oct.). $10.00. Suffolk University / Communications, Department of Communications, 41 Temple Street, Boston MA 02114. **Tel** (617)573-8504. **ED** Sheryl A. Freidley. **Bk Rev. Ad Acc. Circ:** 325 (ctrl).
Desc: Encourages contributions from authors who represent all aspects of forensics including readers' theatre and debate.

LC P87 .W56a
DD 001.5/025/73
ISSN 0360-3296
US

NATIONAL MEMBERSHIP DIRECTORY - WOMEN IN COMMUNICATIONS, INC. **Main/Corp** Women in Communications, Inc. (19??)-. Directory. English. Irregular. $49.95. Women in Communications Inc., 3717 Columbia Pike, Suite 310, Arlington VA 22204-4255. **Tel** (703)920-5555, FAX (703)920-5556.

IT

NELLA GALASSIA DELL'INFORMAZIONE. **Added/Corp** Federazione Nazionale Della Stampa Italiana. **VFOAT** Galassia. (July 1987)-. Trade Publication. Italian. Ten times a year (monthly except Aug. and Oct.). L76800. Federazione Nazionale Stampa, Corso Vitt Emanuele 349, 00186 Rome Italy. **Tel** 011 39 6 6833879. *Continues Numerozero.*

ISSN 0987-6014
FR

UDC 654:91

NETCOM ISSY-LES-MOULINEAUX. (NETCOM.). **VFOAT** Notes Etudes Travaux Communication. (1987)-. Periodical. French.
Ind/Abst Geogr. Abstr. Human Geogr.; Int. Dev. Abstr.

UK
TITLE CHANGE

NETWORK CONSULTANT QUARTERLY. (19??)-(1993). English. Telematics International, Isis House, Reading Road Chineham, Hampshire RG24 OTW United Kingdom. **Tel** 011 44 1256 467385. *Continued by Telematics Communications Quarterly.*

UK

NETWORK MANAGEMENT INFORMATION SERVICE. (19??)-. English. Twelve times a year. $2,411.00. Datapro International, McGraw Hill House, Shoppenhangers Road, Maidenhead Berkshire SL6 2QL United Kingdom. **Tel** 011 44 1628 773277, FAX 011 44 1628 773628.

ISSN 0278-6923
US

NETWORK NEWS (STANFORD, CALIF.). (NETWORK NEWS.). **Added/Corp** Cooperative Information Network of San Mateo, Santa Clara, Santa

Communications

Cruz, Monterey and San Benito Counties. (19??)-. Periodical. English. Six times a year. Free. Cin Green Library, West Stanford University, Stanford CA 94305.

ISSN 0734-8142
US

NEW BOOKS IN THE COMMUNICATIONS LIBRARY. See Communications-Abstracting, Bibliographies and Statistics.

ISSN 0915-3160
DD 384 JA
NEW BREEZE. [New breeze]. (1989)-. Periodical. English. Four times a year. $45.00. New ITU Association of Japan Inc, Kyodo Building 2-4-10, Iwamoto-Cho, Chiyoda Ku Tokyo 101 Japan. **Tel** 011 81 3 58205620, FAX 011 81 3 58205621. **ED** Makoto Endo. **Ad Acc, Adv Mgr:** A. Manabe. **Circ:** 8,000.

ISSN 1055-9345
US
NEW INFORMATION NEWS. (1991)-. Periodical. English. Six times a year. Media Concepts Plus, 60 John Street, Brooklyn NY 11201.

LC HM132 ISSN 1067-9154
DD 302 US
Pr Rev.

●**NEW JERSEY JOURNAL OF COMMUNICATION, THE.** [N.J. j. commun.]. **Added/Corp** William Paterson College of New Jersey. School of the Arts and Communication. **VFOAT** Journal of Communication. Vol. 1, No. 1 (Spring 1993)-. Academic Scholarly Publication. English. Two times a year (Apr., Nov.). $30.00 (libraries), $20.00 (individuals). William Paterson College of New Jersey, Department of Communication, Wayne NJ 07470. **Tel** (201)595-3342, FAX (201)595-2483. **ED** Gary P. Radford. **Ad Acc, Adv Mgr:** G. Radford, **Tel**, (201)595-3342.
 Desc: Concerned with the study of communication theory, practice and policy. Addresses those in every field who are interested in communication research, both academic and professional.

ISSN 1054-5190
DD 071 US
NEW JERSEY MEDIA GUIDE. [N. J. media guide]. **VFOAT** Media Guide. (1989)-. English. Every 2 years. $79.95 (single issue). Resource Communications Group, 3011 North Lamar Boulevard, Austin TX 78705. **Tel** (512)458-2021, FAX (512)458-2059. **ED** Jeanne Graves and Jack M. Bruner. Index available. cum. index. **Bk Rev. Circ:** 1,000. available on labels.
 Desc: Guide to daily and weekly newspapers, magazines, news services, radio, TV and cable stations, directories, newsletters and other inclusive media information.

ISSN 1035-8714
AT
CEASED
NEW ZEALAND MEDIA GUIDE. (1991)-(19??). Periodical. English. Information Australia Group Pty. Ltd., 45 Flinders Lane, Melbourne Victoria 3000 Australia. **Tel** 011 61 3 96542800, FAX 011 61 3 96505261.

ISSN 1083-415X
US
●**NEWAVES IN PERSONAL COMMUNICATION.** **VFOAT** Newaves. (1995)-. English. Twelve times a year. Free on request. PCIA, 1501 Duke Street, Suite 200, Alexandria VA 22314. **Tel** (703)739-0300.

LC QA76.575 .N48 ISSN 1060-7188
DD 006.6/05 US
NEWMEDIA (SAN MATEO, CALIF.). (NEWMEDIA.). [Newmedia]. **VFOAT** New Media. Vol. 1, No. 5 (July/Aug. 1991)-. Periodical. English. Twelve times a year. $38.00. HyperMedia Communications, 901 Mariner's Island Boulevard, Suite 365, San Mateo CA 94404. **Tel** (415)573-5170. **(Subscription address:** New Media Magazine, PO Box 1771, Riverton NJ 08077. **) Continues** Newmedia Age, 1058-0492.

LC Z6951 .N626 PN4841.A1 ISSN 1054-3791
DD 070.4/35/02573 US
CEASED
NEWS BUREAU CONTACTS. [News bur. contacts]. **Added/Corp** BPi Media Services. (1990)-(1993). English. BPi Media Services, 1515 Broadway, New York NY 10036. **Tel** (800)753-6675, (518)753-6675, FAX (518)374-7889. **ED** Mitch Tebo. **Continues** News Bureaus in the U.S. (New York, N.Y. : 1989), 1047-7616.
 Desc: Designed to aid publicist target print media. Contains information regarding those publications which maintain bureau systems including over 180 daily newspapers, 21 news services, 30+ consumer magazines, 90+ trade publications and over 1300 local bureaus. Focuses on comprehensive details of organization, staff and editorial content.

ISSN 1187-3493
DD 384.3 CN
NEWS CORPORATION. [News corp.]. No. 1 (1991)-. Periodical. English. Four times a year. Limited free distribution. News Corporation, 6th Floor, 366 Adelaide Street West, Toronto Ontario M5V 1R9 Canada. **Continues** PR Services., 1187-3507.

US
●**NEWS INC.** (Oct. 1993)-. English. Twenty-six times a year. $395.00. SIMBA Information Inc., 213 Danbury Road, PO Box 7430, Wilton CT 06897-7430. **Tel** (203)834-0033 ext. 173, FAX (203)884-1771. **(Subscription address:** Simba Information Inc., PO Box 7430, Wilton CT 06897. **Tel** (203)834-0033 ext. 160, FAX (203)834-1771.**)**

LC PN4899.W304 N49 ISSN 1071-8931
DD 302 US
●**NEWS MEDIA YELLOW BOOK.** [News media yellow book]. **Added/Corp** Monitor Leadership Directories, Inc. Vol. 5, No. 1 (Winter 1994)-. Directory. English. Four times a year. $250.00. Leadership Directories, Inc., 104 Fifth Avenue, Second Floor, New York NY 10011. **Tel** (212)627-4140, FAX (212)645-0931. Index available (included in each issue). **Acid Free.** available on CD-ROM from Chadwyck-Healey, Inc. **Continues** News Media Yellow Book of Washington and New York, 1043-2620.
 Desc: A national directory of over 2,700 news media organizations and those who report, write, edit and produce the news. Provides names, titles, addresses, direct-dial telephone and facsimile numbers of over 25,000 journalists. Indexed by name, assignment, Washington based regional assignment, media organization, geographical location, programs and periodicals by subject.

LC PN4899.W304 N49 ISSN 1043-2620
DD 302.23/025/7541 US
TITLE CHANGE
NEWS MEDIA YELLOW BOOK OF WASHINGTON AND NEW YORK, THE. [News media yellow book Wash. N. Y.]. **Added/Corp** Monitor Publishing Company. **VFOAT** Yellow Book. (Winter 1990)-(1993). Directory. English. Leadership Directories, Inc., 104 Fifth Avenue, Second Floor, New York NY 10011. **Tel** (212)627-4140, FAX (212)645-0931. **ED** David Hurvitz. Index available. **Continued by** News Media Yellow Book, 1071-8931.
 Desc: A directory of those who report, write, edit and produce the news in the nation's government and business capitals.

ISSN 1185-1821
DD 384 CN
NEWSLETTER / ATWATER INSTITUTE. [Newsl. - Atwater Inst.]. **Added/Corp** Atwater Institute. (Jan. 1990)-. Newsletter. English. Limited free distribution. Atwater Institute, Suite PH-211, 1625 de Maisonneuve West, Montreal Quebec H3H 2N4 Canada. **Continues** Atwater Newsletter., 1185-1813.

ISSN 0728-3717
DD 026.7914066094 AT
NEWSLETTER - AUSTRALIAN ASSOCIATION OF FILM AND VIDEO LIBRARIES. See Library and Information Sciences.

ISSN 0707-3062
DD 302.2/05 CN
NEWSLETTER - COMMUNICATION EFFECTIVENESS CENTRE. (NEWSLETTER / C.CEC.). [Newsl. - Commun. Eff. Cent.]. **Added/Corp** Communication Effectiveness Centre. **VFOAT** CEC Newsletter. **VAT** Communication Effectiveness Centre Newsletter. Vol. 1, No. 1 (Jan./Feb. 1977)-. Newsletter. English. Six times a year. $5.00. Communication Effectiveness Centre, 1502 Rebecca Street, Oakville Ontario L6L 1Z7 Canada. **ED** John A. Rush.

US
NICEM A-V MARC. (19??)-. English. Four times a year (1 disk with quarterly updates). $995.00. Library Corporation, PO Box 557, Winchester VA 22604. **Tel** (800)325-7759, (304)229-0100, FAX (304)229-0295.
 Desc: Bibliographic database of audio-visual materials from the National Information Center for Educational Media (NICEM).

NE
NIEUWSTRIBUNE. Dutch. Irregular. Nieuwstribune, AFD Abonnementen Wisselweg 1, 1314 CA Almere-Std Netherlands. **Tel** 011 31 03240/42020.

ISSN 1040-1598
US
NIGERIAN FRONTLINE NEWS. **VAT** Nigerian Front Line News. (1989)-. Periodical. English. Nigerian Frontline News Inc, 1511 K Street NW, Washington DC 20005.

LC P92.J3 N55
DD 302.2 JA
NIHON MASUKOMI SORAN. (19??)-. Periodical. Japanese. ¥6000. Bunka Tsushinsha, 1-12 Yushima 4-chome Bunkyo-ku, Tokyo 113 Japan.

ISSN 0916-7943
JA
NIKKEI DETAPURO KOMYUNIKESHON SOKUHO-BAN. **VFOAT** Nikkei Datapro Communications Sokuho-ban. (1990)-. Newsletter. Japanese. Twelve times a year. Nihon Keizai Shimbun Inc., 9-5 Otemachi 1 Chome, Chiyoda-ku Tokyo 100 Japan. **Tel** 011 81 3 32700251, 011 81 3 52108502 (Nikkei Business Publications Inc.), FAX 011 81 3 52552661, 011 81 3 52108119 (Nikkei Business Publications Inc.). **Formed by the union of** Nikkei Detapuro Deta Tsushin Hyojun, 0912-5914; Nikkei Detapuro Terekomu Sabisu, 0913-851X **and** Nikkei Detapuro Deta Komu, 0914-935X.

ISSN 0910-7215
DD 384 JA
NIKKEI KOMYUNIKESHON. [Nikkei komyunikeshon]. **VFOAT** Nikkei Communications. (1985)-. Trade Publication. Japanese. Twenty-four times a year. $408.00. Nihon Keizai Shimbun Inc., 9-5 Otemachi 1 Chome, Chiyoda-ku Tokyo 100 Japan. **Tel** 011 81 3 32700251, 011 81 3 52108502 (Nikkei Business Publications Inc.) FAX 011 81 3 52552661, 011 81 3 52108119 (Nikkei Business Publications Inc.). **(Subscription address:** Maruzen Company Ltd., PO Box 5050, Import & Export Department, Tokyo 100 31 Japan. **Tel** 011 81 3 32789224.**)**
 Desc: Communications industry updates, including information on equipment and regulations.

ISSN 0349-6244
SW
NORDICOM REVIEW OF NORDIC MASS COMMUNICATION RESEARCH, THE. [NORDICOM rev. Nord. mass commun. res.]. **Added/Corp** Nordicom. **VFOAT** N.O.R.D.I.C.O.M. Review of Nordic Mass Communication Research; Review of Nordic Mass Communication Research. No. 1 (1981)-. Periodical. English (Danish, Norwegian and Swedish). Two times a year (June and Dec.). Free on request. Nordicom Sprangkullsgatan 21, 411 23 Goteborg Sweden. **Tel** 011 46 31 631219. **Bk Rev. Circ:** 1,500. **Ind/Abst** Commun. Abstr.; Soc. Plann. Policy Dev. Abstr.; Sociol. Abstr.

US
NORTH CAROLINA NEWS MEDIA DIRECTORY. Directory. English. One time a year (in April). $50.00. News Media Directories, PO Box 316, Mount Dora FL 32757. **Tel** (904)383-3023, (800)749-6399.

ISSN 0833-0050
DD 017/.1 CN
CEASED
NOUVEAUTES DE LA BIBLIOTHEQUE ADMINISTRATIVE. See Public Administration.

LC HE
DD 384 US
NTIS ALERT. COMMUNICATION. **Added/Corp** United States. National Technical Information Service. (19??)-. Periodical. English. Twenty-four times a year. $145.00 US; $210.00 other. National Technical Information Service - NTIS, Room 2027S, 5285 Port Royal Road, Springfield VA 22161. **Tel** (703)487-4630, (703)487-4660, (703)487-4650, FAX (703)321-8547, telex 89-9405. Index available. **Continues** Communication / NTIS, 0364-4944.
 Desc: Provides information on common carrier and satellite communication and information theory, graphics, radio and television equipment, etc.

ISSN 0381-8632
DD 301.16/1/05 CN
O C S NOUVELLES. **Main/Corp** Office des Communications Sociales. No. 1, Aug. 30, 1971-. Periodical. French. Irregular (eight-ten issues per year). 20.01Can$. Office Des Communications Sociales, 1340 boulevard St. Joseph EST, Montreal Quebec H2J 1M3 Canada. **Tel** (514)524-8223, FAX (514)524-8522.
 Desc: Bulletin of news about mass media in Canada and elsewhere.

ISSN 0911-5943
DD 621.38 JA
O PLUS E. [O plus E]. (1979)-. Periodical. Japanese. Twelve times a year. $163.57. Shingijutsu Communication Co., No. 16-13 Hyakunincho 2-Chome, Shinjuku-ku Tokyo 169 Japan.

US
OHIO NEWS MEDIA DIRECTORY. (1980)-. Directory. English. One time a year (Oct.). $45.00. News Media Directories, PO Box 316, Mount Dora FL 32757. **Tel** (904)383-3023, (800)749-6399.

LC PN4071 .O35 ISSN 0078-4052
DD 001 US
Pr Rev.

OHIO SPEECH JOURNAL, THE. [Ohio speech j.]. **Added/Corp** Ohio Association of College Teachers of Speech. Ohio Speech Association. Speech Communication Association of Ohio. Vol. 1 (1962)-. Periodical. English. One time a year (Oct.). $20.00. University of Dayton / Deptartment of Communication,

Communications

C/O Dr. Robinson, Dayton OH 45469. **ED** K. German. **Ad Acc. Circ:** 300 (ctrl).
Desc: Research, theory, and practice of communication in education, business, medical, government, religious, and family contexts.
Ind/Abst Soc. Plann. Policy Dev. Abstr.; Sociol. Abstr.

LC P87 .O453
DD 070 KO
OLLON SAHOE MUNHWA. Added/Corp
Yonse Taehakkyo. Sinmun Pangsong Hakkwa. **VFOAT** Communication, Society, and Culture; Ollon Yongu Nonchong. Vol. 1 (1991)-. Periodical. Korean. Two times a year. Opera Lyra Ottawa, 2 Daly Avenue, Ottawa Ontario K1N 6E2 Canada.

ISSN 0840-612X
DD 320.971 CN
ON BALANCE (VANCOUVER). (ON BALANCE: MEDIA TREATMENT OF PUBLIC POLICY ISSUES.). [On balance]. **Added/Corp** Fraser Institute (Vancouver, B.C.). Vol. 1, No. 1 (Oct. 1988)-. Periodical. English. Ten times a year. 38.42Can$. The Fraser Institute, 626 Bute Street/2nd Floor, Vancouver British Columbia V63 3M1 Canada. **Tel** (604)688-0221, FAX (608)688-8539. **ED** Kristin McCahon. **Circ:** 5,000.
Desc: This serial collates research results from the National Media Archive, which monitors the primary newscasts of Canada's major networks to provide an analysis of the media's balance of reporting on public policy issues.

ISSN 1041-6234
DD 369 US
ON CUE. [On cue]. **Added/Corp** Cued Speech Association. National Cued Speech Association. (198?)-. Periodical. English. Four times a year. $20.00. National Cued Speech Association, PO Box 31345, Raleigh NC 27622. **Tel** (919)828-1218. **ED** Barbara Caldwell. **Bk Rev. Circ:** 500 (ctrl).

LC HE8700.7 .O5
DD 384.55/5/05 **ISSN** 1076-0334 US
●**ON DEMAND.** See Communications-Television and Cable.

LC P96.F672 .U626A **ISSN** 0737-8858
DD 001.51/0973 US
OUTLOOK FOR THE MEDIA. (OUTLOOK FOR THE MEDIA / PAINE WEBBER MITCHELL HUTCHINS, INC. ... ANNUAL CONFERENCE.). [Outlook media]. **Main/Corp** Paine, Webber, Mitchell, Hutchins. Conference. 10th (1983)-. English. One time a year. $85.00. Knowledge Industry Publications Inc, 701 Westchester Avenue, White Plains NY 10604. **Tel** (914)328-9157, (800)800-5474, FAX (914)328-9093. **Continues** Annual Conference on the Outlook for the Media.

ISSN 0747-8763 US
OUTSIDE PLANT. (19??)-. Trade Publication. English. Twelve times a year. $32.00. Practical Communications Inc, PO Box 183, Cary IL 60013. **Tel** (312)639-2200. **ED** Rick Hoelzer. Index available. **Bk Rev. Ad Acc.** ctrl circ.
Desc: Tutorial and on-the-job type articles for construction, maintenance, and engineering people employed by the phone companies and contractors.

ISSN 1066-3894
DD 384 US
PACIFIC TELECOMMUNICATIONS REVIEW. [Pac. telecommun. rev.]. **VFOAT** PTR. (1992)-. Periodical. English. Four times a year (Jan., Apr., July, Oct.). $35.00. Pacific Telecommunications Council, 2454 South Beretania Street, Suite 302, Honolulu HI 96826. **Tel** (808)941-3789, FAX (808)944-4874. **ED** James Savage. **Bk Rev.** (Qty: 4). **Ad Acc, Adv Mgr:** J. Savage. **Circ:** 2,500. **Continues** Pacific Telecommunications, 0899-434X.
Desc: A blend of information, analysis, and opinion. A resource for everyone involved in international telecommunications, focusing on communications in the Pacific hemisphere from Canada - India; Russia - Chile.

KO
PANGSONG PYOLLAM. Added/Corp
Pangsong Wiwonhoe (Korea) Pangsong Simui Wiwonhoe (Korea). (19??)-. Korean. Pangsong Wiwonhoe, 16F Boyung Building, 108 Phung-dong, Chongro-ku 110, Seoul South Korea.

US
PARTY LINE : THE MEDIA NEWSLETTER. (1993)-. Newsletter. English. One time a week. $175.00. Party Line Publishing, 35 Sutton Place, New York NY 10022. **Tel** (212)755-3487, FAX (212)755-3488, . **ED** Morton Yarmon. **Circ:** 1,200.
Desc: A weekly newsletter of media placement information, lists the newest information in printed media, radio and television.

II
PCI REVIEW / PRESS COUNCIL OF INDIA. Added/Corp Press Council of India. **VFOAT** Press Council of India Review. Vol. 1, No. 1 (Jan. 1980)-. Periodical. English. Four times a year. Press Council of India, Faridkot House/Ground Floor, Copernicus Marg, New Delhi 110 001 India. **Tel** 388 885. **Continues** P.C.I. Review.

US
PCS (ALEXANDRIA, VA.). (PCS : A REPORT ON PERSONAL COMMUNICATIONS SERVICES IN NORTH AMERICA.). [PCS]. **VAT** Personal Communications Services. 1st Ed.(1991)-. English. One time a year. $540.00. Telecom Publishing Group, 1101 King Street, Suite 444, Alexandria VA 22314. **Tel** (703)683-4100, (800)327-7205, FAX (703)739-6490.

LC HE **ISSN** 1051-3833
DD 384 US
CCC
TITLE CHANGE
PCS NEWS. [PCS news]. (199?)-(199?). Periodical. English. Phillips Business Information Inc., 1201 Seven Locks Road, PO Box 61130, Potomac MD 20854. **Tel** (301)424-3338, (301)340-1520, (800)777-5005, FAX (301)424-4297, telex 358149. available on an online database (file 636/Full-Text) from DIALOG. **Continues** PCN News, 1051-3833. **Continued by** Phillips Business Information's PCS Week, 1080-7187.

ISSN 1065-111X
US
PCS, THE REGULATORY CHALLENGE.
VFOAT PCS; Personal Communications Services, The Regulatory Challenge. (1992)-. English. $455.00. Telecom Publishing Group, 1101 King Street, Suite 444, Alexandria VA 22314. **Tel** (703)683-4100, (800)327-7205, FAX (703)739-6490.

LC P95 .P45 **ISSN** 0889-5570
DD 001.54/2 US
PENNSYLVANIA SPEECH COMMUNICATION ANNUAL, THE. [Pa. speech commun. annu.]. **Added/Corp** Speech Communication Association of Pennsylvania. Vol. 29 (1973)-. Academic Scholarly Publication. English. One time a year (published in Sept.). $5.00. Speech Communication Association of Pennsylvania, Slippery Rock University, Department of Communication, Slippery Rock PA 16057. **Tel** (412)738-2565. **ED** Herman Cohen. **Ad Acc. Circ:** 200 (ctrl). **Continues** Speech Communication Association of Pennsylvania Annual.
Desc: A scholarly journal concerned with all aspects of human communication including rhetoric, theatre, group communication, mass communication, intrapersonal communication and communication theory.

ISSN 0304-3053
SP
PERSPECTIVAS : REVISTA TRIMESTRAL DE EDUCACION. See Education.

ISSN 1080-7187
DD 384 US
●**PHILLIPS BUSINESS INFORMATION'S PCS WEEK.** (PCS WEEK.). [Phillips Bus. Inf. PCS week]. **VFOAT** PCS Week. (1995)-. Periodical. English. Two times a month. $697.00. Phillips Business Information Inc., 1201 Seven Locks Road, PO Box 61130, Potomac MD 20854. **Tel** (301)424-3338, (301)340-1520, (800)777-5005, FAX (301)424-4297, telex 358149. **Absorbed** Personal Communications Report, 1051-3833.

LC HE8801 .C65 **ISSN** 1053-7279
DD 384.6/025/73 US
PHONEFICHE, COMMUNITY CROSS-REFERENCE GUIDE. [Phonefiche community cross-ref. guide]. **Added/Corp** University Microfilms International. **VFOAT** Phonefiche, Community Cross Reference Guide; Community Cross Reference Guide; Community Cross-Reference Guide, Phonefiche; Community Cross-Reference Guide. (1986)-. English. One time a year. University Microfilms International, 300 North Zeeb Road, Ann Arbor MI 48106-1346. **Tel** (313)761-4700, (800)521-0600 Exts. 2490, 2491, FAX (313)973-1540. **Continues** Community Cross-Reference Guide To--Phonefiche, 0275-8172.
Desc: Examines phonefiche as an alternative form of communication.

LC P215 .P53 **ISSN** 0031-8388
DD 414 SZ
CCC
NLM W1 PH624 **CODEN** PHNTAW
Pr Rev.
PHONETICA. See Linguistics.

ISSN 0261-5169
DD 070.02541 UK
PIMS MEDIA DIRECTORY. (UNITED KINGDOM MEDIA DIRECTORY.). [PIMS media dir.]. **VFOAT** Press Information and Mailing Services Media Directory. (1981)-. Directory. English. Twelve times a year. £240.00. PIMS UK Ltd, Pims House Mildnay Avenue, London N1 4RS United Kingdom. **Tel** 011 44 171 2261000, FAX 011 44 171 7041360. **ED** J Turner. **Circ:** 1,200. available on an online database; available on labels. **Continues** PRADS Media Lists, 0144-3933.
Desc: Editorial contacts listing containing media contacts of all listed subjects.

ISSN 1055-9051
DD 384 US
PIPELINE (ST. PAUL, MINN.). (PIPELINE : NEWSLETTER OF THE INDEPENDENT MEDIA DISTRIBUTORS ALLIANCE.). [Pipeline]. **Added/Corp** Independent Media Distributors Alliance. (1990)-. Newsletter. English. Four times a year. Free. The Independent Media Alliance, c/o ArtBase, PO Box 2154, St Paul MN 55102.

LC JF1525.P8 P64 **ISSN** 1058-4609
DD 306/.2 US
CCC
CODEN PLCMEM
POLITICAL COMMUNICATION. See Political Science.

ISSN 1059-2164
DD 621 US
POPULAR COMMUNICATIONS COMMUNICATIONS GUIDE. [Pop. commun. commun. guide]. **VFOAT** Popular Communications Summer Communications Guide; Communications Guide; Pop'Comm ... Communications Guide. No. 1 (1992)-. Periodical. English. Two times a year. $4.95. CQ Communications Inc, 76 North Broadway, Hicksville NY 11801. **Tel** (516)681-2922, FAX (516)681-2926.

LC AI21 .P67 **ISSN** 1070-4930
DD 071 US
POST-TRIBUNE SUBJECT INDEX.
[Post-Trib. subj. index]. **Added/Corp** Lake County Public Library. **VFOAT** Post Tribune Subject Index; Subject Index; Post-Tribune. (1990)-. Periodical. English. Irregular. $100.00. Lake County Public Library, 1919 West 81st Avenue, Merrillville IN 46410.

LC P88.8 .P68 **ISSN** 1045-9545
DD 302.23/02573 US
POWER MEDIA SELECTS. [Power media sel.]. **Added/Corp** Broadcast Interview Source (Firm). 1st Ed. (Jan. 1989)-. English. One time a year. $166.50. Broadcast Interview Source, 2233 Wisconsin Avenue Northwest, Suite 540, Washington DC 20007-4104. **Tel** (800)955-0311, (202)333-4904, FAX (202)342-5411. **ED** Alan Caruba.
Desc: Approximately 500 entries of the nation's media elite. Covers newswire services, syndicates, syndicated columnists, national newspapers, Sunday supplements, daily newspapers, magazines, radio and television talk shows, and newsletters.

LC Z5630 .P18
GW
PRD. PUBLIZISTIKWISSENSCHAFTLICHER REFERATE-DIENST. See Communications-Abstracting, Bibliographies and Statistics.

LC P301 .P68 **ISSN** 0731-0714
DD 808/.005 US
Pr Rev.
PRE/TEXT. See Linguistics.

LC P88.8 .P73
DD 301.16/1/0994 AT
PRESS, RADIO AND TV GUIDE : AUSTRALIA, NEW ZEALAND AND THE PACIFIC ISLANDS. See Communications-Abstracting, Bibliographies and Statistics.

LC P92.U5 M46 **ISSN** 1045-1234
DD 302.23/0973/05 US
PREVUE (READING, PA.). (PREVUE.). [Prevue]. **VFOAT** Mediascene Prevue. Vol. 2, No. 29 (Aug./Oct. 1987)-. Periodical. English. Four times a year. $19.95. Supergraphics, PO Box 4489, Reading PA 19606. **Tel** (610)370-0666. **ED** J. Steranko. **Bk Rev. Ad Acc. Circ:** 250,000. **Continues** Mediascene Prevue, 0199-9257.
Desc: Interviews with stars and filmmakers. Features about film productions, celebrity stories and photos.

ISSN 0390-3311
IT
UDC 055.1
PRIMA COMUNICAZIONE. [Prima comun.]. (1973)-. Trade Publication. Italian. Eleven times a year. L102190. Nuova Societa Srl, Via A Saffi 12, 20123 Milan Italy. **Tel** 011 39 2 48194401, FAX 011 39 2 4818658. **Ad Acc, Adv Mgr:** Sig. Buonacasa. **Continues** Prima.

LC Q350 .P72 **ISSN** 0555-2923
RU
CODEN PPDIA5
PROBLEMY PEREDACI INFORMACII.
(PROBLEMY PEREDACHI INFORMATSII.). [Probl. pereda. inf.]. **Added/Corp** Akademiia Nauk SSSR. (1965)-. Academic Scholarly Publication. Russian. Six times a year. $100.00. Izdatelstvo Nauka / Akademiia Nauk, (Publishing House of the Russian Academy of

Sciences), Leninskii Porspekt 14, 117901 Moscow Russia. **Tel** 011 95 9542153, FAX 011 95 9382144, telex 411964. **(Subscription address:** East View Publications Inc., 3020 Harbor Lane North, Suite 110, Minneapolis MN 55447. **Tel** (800)477-1005, (612)550-0961, FAX (612)559-2931.) cum. index. Documents available from Article Express International, Ask*IEEE. *Supersedes Problemy Peredachi Informatsii.*
Ind/Abst Eng. Index Annu.; INSPEC (1968-); Math. Rev.; Zentralbl. Math. Ihre Grenzgeb.

LC P90.I55 A1
DD 659 808 808.066   US
PROCEEDINGS OF THE INSTITUTE IN TECHNICAL AND INDUSTRIAL COMMUNICATIONS. **Main/Corp** Institute in Technical and Industrial Communications, Colorado State University. 1st (1958)-. Proceedings. English. Institute in Technical & Industrial Communications, Room C 225/Social Science Building, Fort Collins CO 80521.

LC HE30.A3 P39a   ISSN 1189-2005
DD 380.3/0971   CN
PROCEEDINGS OF THE STANDING SENATE COMMITTEE ON TRANSPORT AND COMMUNICATIONS. **Main/Corp** Canada. Parliament. Senate. Standing Committee on Transport and Communications. **Added/Corp** Canada. Parliament. Senate. Standing Committee on Transport and Communications. Deliberations du Comite Senatorial Permanent des Transports et des Communications. **VFOAT** Deliberations du Comite Senatorial Permanent des Transports et des Communications. (Nov. 15, 1951)-. Periodical. English (French). Canada Communication Group Publishers, Order Processing, Ottawa Ontario K1A 0S9 Canada. **Tel** (819)956-4800, (819)956-4802.
Absorbed Canada. Parlement. Senat. Comite Permanent des Transports et des Communications. Deliberations du Comite Senatorial Permanent des Transports et des Communications.

    ISSN 1059-003X
DD 384   US
PROCEEDINGS - RF EXPO EAST. (PROCEEDINGS.). [Proc. - RF Expo East]. **VFOAT** RF Expo East. (19??)-. English. Cardiff Publishing Company, 6300 South Syracuse Way, Suite 650, Englewood CO 80111. **Tel** (303)220-0600, FAX (303)770-0253, telex 450726.
Ind/Abst Curr. Cit.

LC T10.5 .I57
DD 601.4   US
    CODEN PCNCEI
PROCEEDINGS / STC, SOCIETY FOR TECHNICAL COMMUNICATION ANNUAL CONFERENCE. **See** Science and Technology.

    ISSN 0891-1207
DD 384   US
PROFESSIONAL COMMUNICATOR, THE. [Prof. commun.]. **Added/Corp** Women in Communications, Inc. Vol. 5, No. 8/9 (Aug./Sept. 1985)- . Trade Publication. English. Five times a year. $18.50. Women in Communications Inc., 3717 Columbia Pike, Suite 310, Arlington VA 22204-4255. **Tel** (703)920-5555, FAX (703)920-5556. **ED** Leslie Sansom. **Bk Rev**, (Qty: 5/year). **Ad Acc**. **Circ**: 12,000 (ctrl). *Continues Pro/Comm, 0279-8255.*
Desc: Features communications management practices, how-to material, membership news, legislative updates, job networking ideas and information affecting communicators and the communications industry.
Ind/Abst Work Relat. Abstr. (-19??).

LC P87 .P74   ISSN 0163-5689
DD 001.5/05   US
PROGRESS IN COMMUNICATION SCIENCES. Vol. 1 (1979)-. Periodical. English. Irregular. Price varies per volume. Ablex Publishing Corporation, 355 Chestnut Street, Norwood NJ 07648. **Tel** (201)767-8450, (201)767-8455 (Customer Service), FAX (201)767-6717. **ED** Brenda Dervin and Melvin J. Voigt.
Desc: Book series bringing together research from many disciplines to better understand communications and information processing.

LC P92.F8 P76
DD 301.16/1   FR
PROSCOP MEDIA. **Added/Corp** Institut Proscop. (19??)-. French. Institut Proscop, 25 rue Marbœuf, Paris 75008 France.

LC P87 .P77   ISSN 0887-932X
DD 302.2/05   US
PUBLIC COMMUNICATION AND BEHAVIOR. [Public commun. behav.]. (1986)-. Monographic series. English. Irregular. Price varies per volume. Academic Press Inc., 6277 Sea Harbor Drive, Orlando FL 32887. **Tel** (800)543-9534, (407)345-4100, FAX (407)352-3445.

LC HE
DD 380   US
PUBLISHED SEARCH BIBLIOGRAPHIES FROM THE NTIS BIBLIOGRAPHIC DATA BASE. COMMUNICATION AND ELECTROTECHNOLOGY. **See** Communications-Abstracting, Bibliographies and Statistics.

LC P87 .E5
DD 400   SP
PUNTA, EN. (19??)-. Periodical. Spanish. Irregular. Investigaciones Y Estudios de la Comunicacion, Jardin San Federico 5 Bajo, Madrid Spain.

LC PN4071 .Q3   ISSN 0033-5630
DD 808.5   US
QUARTERLY JOURNAL OF SPEECH, THE. [Q. j. speech]. **Added/Corp** Speech Communication Association. National Association of Teachers of Speech (U.S.) Speech Association of America. Vol. 14, No. 1 (Feb. 1928)-. Periodical. English. Four times a year (Feb., May, Aug., Nov.). $96.00. Speech Communication Association, 5105 Backlick Road, Suite E, Annandale VA 22003. **Tel** (703)750-0533, FAX (703)914-9471. available on microfilm and microfiche from University Microfilms International (UMI). Documents available from The Genuine Article, UMI Article Clearinghouse. *Continues Quarterly Journal of Speech Education.*
Ind/Abst Abstr. Engl. Stud.; Acad. Abstr. Full Text Elite; Acad. Abstr.; Acad. Ind. [Computer File] (1987-); Acad. Search; Am. Hist. Life (1967-); Annu. Bibliogr. Engl. Lang. Lit.; ARTbibliogr. Mod.; Arts Humanit. Citation Index [Select. Cov.]; Biogr. Index; Book Rev. Index; Commun. Abstr.; Contents Pages Educ.; Curr. Cit.; Curr. Contents Soc. Behav. Sci.; Curr. Index J. Educ.; Educ. Index; EP Collect.; Expand. Acad. Index (1987-); Homework Help.; Humanit. Index (1964-); INFO-SOUTH Abstr.; Lang. Teach. (1966-); Mag. Search; MasterFile FullTEXT 1000; MasterFile FullTEXT 350; MasterFile FullTEXT 650; MasterFile FullTEXT (July 1990-); MLA Int. Bibl. Books Artic. Mod. Lang. Lit.; Newsp. Period. Abstr. (1988-); OCLC; Psychol. Abstr. (1966-); PsycINFO; PsycLit; Recent. Publ. Artic.; Res. Alert [Full Cov.]; Romant. Move.; Soc. Plann. Policy Abstr.; Soc. Sci. Cit. Index [Full Cov.]; Soc. Welf. Soc. Plan./Policy Soc. Dev.; Sociol. Abstr.; Telebase; Women Stud. Abstr.; Writ. Am. Hist.

LC PE1460.A2 Q37   ISSN 0735-5920
DD 427/.973/05   US
QUARTERLY REVIEW ON DOUBLESPEAK. **See** Linguistics.

    ISSN 0743-2933
    US
QUICKREPORT. **Added/Corp** Communications Concepts (Firm). **VFOAT** Quick Report. No. 1 (May 1984)-. Periodical. English. Six times a year. $99.00 US, Canada and Mexico; $119.00 other. Communications Concepts Inc., 7481 Huntsman Boulevard, Suite 720, Springfield VA 22153. **Tel** (703)643-2200. Index available (Free on request).

    ISSN 1062-9009
DD 384   US
    TITLE CHANGE
QUICKTIME FORUM, THE. [Quicktime forum]. **VFOAT** Quick Time Forum. (July 1991)-(199?). Periodical. English. Multi Facet Communications, 499 South Sunnyvale Avenue, Sunnyvale CA 94086. **Tel** (408)749-0549. *Continued by Converge, 1072-9224.*

LC PN6081 .Q65   ISSN 0273-6705
DD 081   US
QUOTE (ATLANTA, GA.). **See** Leisure and Recreation-Amusements.

    ISSN 0290-9693
    FR
UDC 621.398
R.C.M. RADIO COMMANDE MAGAZINE. [R.C.M. radio commande mag.]. **VFOAT** Radio Commande Magazine. (1981)-. Periodical. French. Twelve times a year. 220.00F France; 260.00F Europe; 300.00F other. Radio Commande Magazine, 1 place Mendes France, 91000 Evry France.

    UK
RADIO CONTROL MODEL WORLD. English. Twelve times a year. £36.00. Traplet Publications Ltd., Traplet House, Severn Drive, Upton-Upon-Severn, Worcestershire WR8 0JL United Kingdom. **Tel** 011 44 1684 594505, FAX 011 44 1684 594586.

    ISSN 0197-6060
DD 658   US
RAGAN REPORT, THE. **See** Business and Economics.

    ISSN 0033-9962
    SW
UDC 621.3
    TITLE CHANGE
RATEKO. [Rateko]. (1955)-(19??). Periodical. Swedish. *Continued by Rateko & Foto.*
Ind/Abst Infomat Int. Bus.

LC K4240.A12 N38   ISSN 0899-0883
DD 016.343/09945 016.34239945   US
RECENT TITLES IN LAW FOR THE SUBJECT SPECIALIST. COMMUNICATION LAW. **See** Law-Abstracting, Bibliographies and Statistics.

    ISSN 0932-1543
UDC 82.085   GW
REDEN-BERATER, DER. [Reden-Berat.]. (1987)-. German. Six times a year. DM200.00. Verlag Norman Rentrop, Theodor Heuss Strasse 4, D-53177 Bonn Germany. **Tel** 011 49 228 82050, FAX 011 49 228 364411, telex 17228309 TTX D. **ED** Norman Rentrop. Index available. **Bk Rev**.
Desc: A how-to loose leaf service on speech writing.

    RU
REFERATIVNYI ZHURNAL: RADIOTEKHNIKA. **Added/Corp** Akademiia Nauk SSSR. Institut Nauchnoi i Tekhnicheskoi Informatsii. **VFOAT** Radiotekhnika. (1967)-. Periodical. Russian. Twelve times a year. $699.95. VINITI - Vsesoyuznyi Institut Nauchno-Tekhnicheskoi Informatsii, All-Union Scientific and Technical Information Institute, Baltiiskaia ulitsa 14, 125219 Moscow Russia. **Tel** 011 7 95 2384600, FAX 011 7 95 9430060, telex 411160. **(Subscription address:** East View Publications Inc., 3020 Harbor Lane North, Suite 110, Minneapolis MN 55447. **Tel** (800)477-1005, (612)550-0961, FAX (612)559-2931.) *Supersedes in part Referativnyi Zhurnal: Radiotekhnika I Elektrosviaz.*

DD 808.53   US
REFERENCE SHELF, THE. Vol. 1, (1922)-. Monographic series. English. Six times a year. $62.00 US and Canada; $67.00 other. H W Wilson Company, 950 University Avenue, Bronx NY 10452. **Tel** (800)367-6770, (718)588-8400 ext. 2245, FAX (718)681-1511, telex 4990003 HWILSON.
Desc: Consisting of excerpts from a wide range of publications, each title is devoted to a single issue of contemporary importance.

    ISSN 0080-1356
DD 384   FR
REPORTS AND PAPERS ON MASS COMMUNICATION. **Main/Corp** United Nations Educational, Scientific and Cultural Organization. Dept. of Mass Communications. **Added/Corp** United Nations Educational, Scientific and Cultural Organization. Division of Free Flow of Information. United Nations Educational, Scientific and Cultural Organization. Dept. of Mass Communications. Press, Film, Radio. (1952)-. Monographic series. English (French and Spanish). Irregular. Price varies per volume. UNESCO / France, 31 rue Francois Bonvin, 75732 Paris Cedex 15 France. **Tel** 011 33 1 45684564, 011 33 1 45684565, FAX 011 33 1 45669270, telex 204461 Paris. **(Subscription address:** UNIPUB, 4611 F Assembly Drive, Lanham MD 20706. **Tel** (800)274-4888, (301)459-7666.)

    US
RESEARCH & DEVELOPMENT. TELEPHONE DIRECTORY. **See** Encyclopedias and General Reference Books.

LC P1 .P35   ISSN 0835-1813
DD 401/.9/05   CN
    CCC
RESEARCH ON LANGUAGE AND SOCIAL INTERACTION. **See** Linguistics.

    ISSN 1188-2522
DD 384/.05   CN
    CEASED
RESOURCES 2000. [Resour. 2000]. **VFOAT** Resources Two Thousand. Vol. 1, No. 1 (Nov. 1991)-(199?). Periodical. English. Resources 2000, Box 42043, 2200 Oak Bay Avenue, Victoria British Columbia V8R 1G0 Canada.

LC P87 .C584   ISSN 0102-0897
DD 001.51/05   BL
REVISTA COMUNICACOES E ARTES. **Added/Corp** Universidade de Sao Paulo. Escola de Comunicacoes e Artes. **VFOAT** Comunicacoes e Artes. (1981)-. Periodical. Portuguese (summaries and/or abstracts in English). Three times a year. Universidade de Sao Paulo, Cidade Universitaria CP 8191, Sao Paulo Brazil. **Tel** 011 55 11 8150899, FAX 011 55 11 8154272. *Continues Comunicacoes e Artes.*

    ISSN 0187-8190
    MX
REVISTA MEXICANA DE COMUNICACION. **VFOAT** Comunicacion; RMC. Vol. 1, No. 1 (Sept./Oct. 1988)-. Periodical. Spanish. Six times a year. $95.00. AGB Comunicacion, Guaymas 8-408 Col Roma, 06700 Mexico DF Mexico. **Tel** 011 52 5 2084261, FAX 011 52 5 2084261.

Communications

REVUE INTERNATIONALE DE C.F.A.O. ET D'INFOGRAPHIE. ISSN 0298-0924 FR. UDC 681.39:62. VFOAT Revue Internationale de Conception et Fabrication Assistees par Ordinateur. (1986)-. Periodical. French (summaries and/or abstracts in English). Six times a year. $433.07. Editions Hermes, 14 rue Lantiez, 75017 Paris France. **Tel** 11 33 1 42294466.

REVUE TUNISIENNE DE COMMUNICATION. LC P87 .R46. DD 001.51/05. ISSN 0330-8480 TI. **Added/Corp** Mahad al-Sihafah wa-Ulum al-Ikhbar (Tunis, Tunisia). VFOAT Majallah Al-Tunisiyah Li-Ulum Al-Ittisal. No. 1 (Jan./June 1982)-. Periodical. Arabic (French and English). Two times a year. 10.00TD. Institut de Presse et des Sciences de l'Information, 7 Impasse Mohamed Bachrouch, Montfleury 1008 Tunis Tunisia. **Tel** 011 216 1 335228, FAX 011 216 1 348596, telex 15254 TN. **Circ:** 2,000 (ctrl).

ROSTRUM, THE. US. **Added/Corp** National Forensic League. National Forensic League. Bulletin of the National Forensic League. Vol. 1 (Sept. 1926)-. Periodical. English. Ten times a year. $10.00. National Forensic League, PO Box 38, Ripon WI 54971. **Tel** (414)748-6206, FAX (414)748-9478. **ED** James M. Copeland. **Bk Rev**, (Qty: 2-3). **Ad Acc. Circ:** 11,000. **Desc:** Contains news of the National Forensic League, its activities, and members. Articles of interest to students and coaches involved in speech and debate activities.

RULES AND REGULATIONS. See Law.

S/N. SPEECHWRITER'S NEWSLETTER. ISSN 0272-8079 US. VFOAT Speechwriter's Newsletter. **VAT** Speech Writer's Newsletter. (19??)-. Newsletter. English. One time a week. $287.00. Ragan Communications Inc., 212 West Superior Street, Suite 200, Chicago IL 60610. **Tel** (312)335-0037, (800)878-5331, FAX (312)335-9583. **ED** Janine Ragan. **Bk Rev. Circ:** 2,000 (ctrl). **Desc:** Termed "The Voice of the Silent Profession", this newsletter highlights the newest tips, ideas and resources for those whose job it is to give others a voice.

SAGE ANNUAL REVIEWS OF COMMUNICATIONS RESEARCH. ISSN 0099-1414 US. VFOAT Annual Reviews of Communications Research. (19??)-. Monographic series. English. One time a year. $52.00. SAGE Periodical Press, 2455 Teller Road, Thousand Oaks CA 91320. **Tel** (805)499-0721, FAX (805)499-0871, telex 100799. Acid Free.

SANCARA MANTRALAYA KI ANUDANOM KI MANGEM. LC HE271 .I494a. DD 354/.54/00874 II. **Main/Corp** India. Ministry of Communications. VFOAT Demands for Grants of Ministry of Communication. (19??)-. Multiple languages (English and Hindi). Government of India Press Ministry of Communications, Minto Road, New Delhi India.

●SATELLITE INDUSTRY DIRECTORY. US. (1996)-. English. One time a year. $255.00. Phillips Business Information Inc., 1201 Seven Locks Road, PO Box 61130, Potomac MD 20854. **Tel** (301)424-3338, (301)340-1520, (800)777-5005, FAX (301)424-4297, telex 358149. **Continues** World Satellite Directory.

SATELLITE TV EUROPE. DD 384.554. ISSN 0268-8425 UK. [Satell. TV Eur.]. VFOAT Satellite Television Europe. (1986)-. Periodical. English. Twelve times a year. £24.00 UK; £42.00 other. 21st Century Publishing, 531-583 Kings Road, London SW10 0TZ United Kingdom. **Tel** 011 44 71 3513612. (**Subscription address:** Satellite TV Europe, Unit 5, Billet Lane, Berhamsted, Herts HP4 1HL United Kingdom. **Tel** 011 44 1442 876661.)

●SEMIOSFERA (GETAFE, MADRID). ISSN 1134-3974 SP. UDC 62/69 :008. See Humanities.

SHARING IDEAS. DD 001. ISSN 0886-1501 US. [Shar. ideas]. VFOAT Speakers & Meeting Planners Sharing Ideas; Speakers and Meeting Planners Sharing Ideas. (1978)-. Trade Publication. English. Six times a year. $95.00 (two-year). Royal Publishing, 18825 Hicrest Avenue, Box 1120, Glendora CA 91740. **Tel** (818)335-8069, FAX (818)335-6127. **ED** Dorothy Walters. **Bk Rev. Ad Acc.** **Circ:** 4,000 (ctrl). **Desc:** Articles by top speakers, meeting planners and bureaus.

SIGN LANGUAGE STUDIES. LC HV2350 .S58. DD 001.56. ISSN 0302-1475 US CCC. NLM W1 SI388. **Pr Rev.** See Linguistics.

SIGNAL (1950). LC UG1 .M65. DD 358/.24. ISSN 0037-4938 US CCC. CODEN SGNAAZ. See Military and Defense.

SIMBA'S INFORMATION MEDIA AND THE LAW. US. (19??)-. English. Two times a week. $327.00. Cowles Business Media Inc. / Connecticut, 6 River Bend Center, 911 Hope Street, Stamford CT 06907. **Tel** (203)358-9900, (800)775-3777, FAX (203)357-9014.

SINGLE MARKET COMMUNICATIONS LIMITED. UK. (19??)-. English. Four times a year. £55.00. Tempest Public Relations, PO Box 601, London SW12 9BU United Kingdom. **Tel** 011 44 181 6737744.

SITZUNGSBERICHTE. VEROEFFENTLICHUNGEN DER KOMMISSION FUER LINGUISTIK UND KOMMUNIKATIONSFORSCHUNG. LC AS142 .V31. DD 060 AU. See Linguistics.

SOCIOLOGIA DELLA COMUNICAZIONE. LC HM258 .S588. DD 302.2 IT. (1982)-. Periodical. Italian. Two times a year. L54440. Franco Angeli Riviste SRL, Viale Monza 106, 20127 Milan Italy. **Tel** 011 39 2 2827651, 011 39 2 289562, FAX 011 39 2 258004, telex 051-511650. **Ind/Abst** Int. Bibliogr. Sociol.

SOLUTIONS TELEMATIQUES PARIS. ISSN 1167-2501 FR. UDC 681.3:654. (SOLUTIONS TELEMATIQUES.). (1992)-. Periodical. French. Fifteen times a year. $171.69. A Jour, 11 rue du Marche St. Honore, 75001 Paris France. **Tel** 011 33 1 44553849. **Continues** Videotex & RNIS Magazine, 1143-6360.

SONOVISION PARIS. ISSN 0768-956X FR. UDC 654.19. CODEN 77. (1971)-. Periodical. French. Twelve times a year. $120.30. Liaisons & Convergence, 1 Avenue East Belin, F-92856 Rueil Mal France. **Tel** 011 33 1 41299872, FAX 011 33 1 47575420, telex 613128. **Ad Acc. Circ:** 15,000.

SOUND & COMMUNICATIONS. DD 621. ISSN 0038-1845 US. [Sound commun.]. **VAT** Sound and Communications. Vol. 15, No. 11 (March 1970)-. Trade Publication. English. Twelve times a year. $15.00. Sound and Communications Pub Inc, 25 Willowdale Avenue, Port Washington NY 11050. **Tel** (516)767-2500. **ED** Chris Foreman. **Bk Rev. Ad Acc. Circ:** 10,000 (ctrl). **Continues** Sound Merchandising/Modern Communications. **Desc:** Trade magazine covering telecommunications, engineered sound, and electro-acoustics. **Ind/Abst** Shock Vibr. Dig.

SOUND AND IMAGE. DEE WHY. DD 381.453883320994. ISSN 1032-3899 AT. (SOUND AND IMAGE.). [Sound Image Dee Why]. (1988)-. Periodical. English. Six times a year. 33.00Aus$ Australia; 38.00Aus$ (surface mail), 48.00Aus$ (airmail) other. Horwitz Publications Pty Ltd, 55 Chandos Street, St. Leonards 2065 Australia. **Tel** 011 61 2 9016100, FAX 011 61 2 9016166.

SOUTH CAROLINA NEWS MEDIA DIRECTORY. US. Directory. English. One time a year (Feb.). $40.00. News Media Directories, PO Box 316, Mount Dora FL 32757. **Tel** (904)383-3023, (800)749-6399.

SOUTHERN CALIFORNIA MEDIA DIRECTORY. US. Directory. English. One time a year. $120.00 (nonmembers), $60.00 (members). Publicity Club of Los Angeles Inc., 5000 Van Nuys Boulevard, Suite 300, Sherman Oaks CA 91403. **Tel** (213)872-0525. **Desc:** Covers the California area's media market.

SOUTHERN COMMUNICATION JOURNAL, THE. LC PN4071 .S65. DD 302.2/242/05. ISSN 1041-794X US. **Pr Rev.** [South. commun. j.]. **Added/Corp** Southern States Communication Association (U.S.). Vol. 54, No. 1 (Fall 1988)-. Periodical. English. Four times a year. $32.00. Southern States Communication Association, University of Southern Mississippi, Box 5131, Hattiesburg MS 39406. **Tel** (901)678-2350, FAX (901)678-5118. **ED** Andrew King (editor's phone:(504)388-4172). Index available. **Bk Rev. Ad Acc, Adv Mgr:** Jeff Dolan. **Circ:** 2,500 (ctrl). available on microfilm. Documents available from UMI Article Clearinghouse. **Continues** Southern Speech Communication Journal, 0361-8269. **Ind/Abst** Abstr. Engl. Stud. (1988-); Am. Hist. Life (1988-); Commun. Abstr.; Curr. Index J. Educ. (1988-); Expand. Acad. Index (1989-); Newsp. Period. Abstr. (1992-); Soc. Plann. Policy Dev. Abstr.; Sociol. Abstr. (1988-).

SOUTHWESTERN MASS COMMUNICATION JOURNAL. LC P87 .S81. DD 302. ISSN 0891-9186 US. **Pr Rev.** [Southwest. mass commun. j.]. **Added/Corp** Southwest Education Council for Journalism/Mass Communications (U.S.). Vol. 1, No. 1 (1985)-. Periodical. English. Two times a year (April and Oct.). $25.00. Arkansas State University, PO Box 1930, State University AR 72467. **ED** John Marlin Shipman (editor's phone: (501)972-3075). **Ad Acc, Adv Mgr:** Gil Fowlee, **Tel** (501)972-3075. **Circ:** 500. **Continues** Studies in Journalism and Mass Communication.

SPEAKER'S DIGEST. DD 808. ISSN 0883-8607 US CEASED. [Speak. dig.]. Vol. 1, No. 1 (Apr. 1985)-Vol. 9, No. 6. Periodical. English. Lime Rock Press, Inc., 200 Route 126, Falls Village CT 06031. **Tel** (203)824-1411, FAX (203)824-1210.

SPEAKER'S IDEA FILE. US. (19??)-. Newsletter. English. Twelve times a year. $119.00. Ragan Communications Inc., 212 West Superior Street, Suite 200, Chicago IL 60610. **Tel** (312)335-0037, (800)878-5331, FAX (312)335-9583. **Desc:** Publication to be used by anyone who does public speaking. It is filled with quotes, anecdotes, public speaking tips, and statistics that can be used to help spice up anyone's speech.

SPECTRA : A MONTHLY PUBLICATION OF THE SPEECH COMMUNICATION ASSOCIATION. US. **Added/Corp** Speech Communication Association. Vol. 1 (Oct. 1965)-. Periodical. English. Eleven times a year. $36.00. Speech Communication Association, 5105 Backlick Road, Suite E, Annandale VA 22003. **Tel** (703)750-0533, FAX (703)914-9471. **Ad Acc.**

SPECTRUM (BLOOMSBURG, PA.). ISSN 0892-9459 US. (SPECTRUM.). **Added/Corp** Bloomsburg University. Dept. of Mass Communications. Program in Journalism. VFOAT Spectrum for Columbia County, Pennsylvania. Vol. 1, No. 1 (Jan. 1987)-. Periodical. English. Two times a year. Bloomsburg University, Mass Communications Department, Bloomsburg PA 17815. **Tel** (717)389-4565. **ED** Walter Brascla. **Ad Acc. Circ:** 1,750. **Ind/Abst** Abstr. Bull. Inst. Pap. Sci. Tech.

SPECTRUM NEWSLETTER. ISSN 0738-9051 US. [Spectr. newsl.]. (19??)-. Newsletter. English. Three times a year. $15.00. Spectrum Composition Services, 225 West 39th Street, New York NY 10018. **Tel** (212)391-3940. **ED** R. N. Weltz. **Circ:** 3,000 (ctrl).

SPECTRUM REPORT : NEWS AND ANALYSIS ON THE GLOBAL FREQUENCY ALLOCATION BATTLE, THE. DD 384. ISSN 1053-993X US CCC TITLE CHANGE. [Spectr. rep.]. (1991)-(June 1993). Periodical. English. Phillips Business Information Inc., 1201 Seven Locks Road, PO Box 61130, Potomac MD 20854. **Tel** (301)424-3338, (301)340-1520, (800)777-5005, FAX (301)424-4297, telex 358149. **Merged with** Telephone News **and** Telecommunications Regulatory Monitor **to form** Washington Telecom News. **Ind/Abst** PTS Newsl. Database [Full Txt.].

Communications

ISSN 0167-6393
NE
CCC
CODEN SCOMDH
Pr Rev.
SPEECH COMMUNICATION. [Speech commun.]. **Added/Corp** European Association for Signal Processing. Vol. 1, No. 1 (May 1982)-. Academic Scholarly Publication. English. Twelve times a year. $777.00. Elsevier Science Publishers BV, PO Box 211, 1000 AE Amsterdam Netherlands. **Tel** 011 31 20 4853641, 011 31 20 4853642, FAX 011 31 20 4853598. **ED** M Wajskop and J P Koster. **Bk Rev. Ad Acc.** available on microfilm and microfiche from University Microfilms International (UMI); available on an online database from Elsevier Electronic Subscriptions (EES). Documents available from Article Express International, The Genuine Article, Ask*IEEE.
Desc: Incorporates all theoretical and experimental aspects of the speech communication processes.
Ind/Abst ACM Guide Comput. Lit.; Comput. Rev.; Curr. Cit.; Curr. Contents Soc. Behav. Sci.; Ei Page One; Eng. Index Annu.; Ergon. Abstr.; INSPEC (May 1982-); Pollut. Abstr. Indexes; Psychol. Abstr. (May 1982-); PsycINFO; PsycLit; Res. Alert [Full Cov.]; Soc. Plann. Policy Dev. Abstr.; Soc. Sci. Cit. Index [Full Cov.]; Sociol. Abstr.

US
SPEECH COMMUNICATION DIRECTORY. (19??)-. Directory. English. One time a year. Speech Communication Association, 5105 Backlick Road, Suite E, Annandale VA 22003. **Tel** (703)750-0533, FAX (703)914-9471.

ISSN 1060-9601
DD 302 US
SPEECH MAKERS NEWSLETTER. [Speech makers newsl.]. Vol. 1, No. 6 (Nov./Dec. 1991)-. Newsletter. English. Six times a year. $24.95 US; $26.95 Canada. Edward J Finn, Jr., PO Box 3182, Davenport IA 52808.

ISSN 0276-1726
US
ST. LOUIS METRO MEDIA GUIDE. VAT Saint Louis Metro Media Guide. 1st- Ed. English. Twelve times a year. $40.00. Drohlich Associates Inc., 1221 South Brentwood Blvd., St Louis MO 63117.

ISSN 0890-6688
DD 004 US
STARTEXT INK. [Startext ink]. (198?)-. Periodical. English. Twelve times a year. $128.04. Startext, PO Box 1870, Fort Worth TX 76101. **Tel** (817)390-7892. **ED** Mike Holland. **Bk Rev**, (Qty: 12/y). **Ad Acc, Adv Mgr:** Gerry Barker. **Circ:** 4,000 (ctrl).
Desc: Publication of Startext, the electronic information service of the Fort Worth Star-Telegram. It offers news, sports, weather and travel information and business reports.

US
SUSPENDED
STILL HERE : JOB/SCHOLARSHIP REFERRAL NEWSLETTER. Added/Corp Howard University. School of Communications. (1975)-Suspended (Aug. 1985). Newsletter. English. Twelve times a year (with Feb./March and July/Aug. issues combined). $15.00. Howard University School of Communication, Job Scholarship Referral Services, Washington DC 20059. **Tel** (202)636-7491. **ED** Lionel C. Barrow Jr. **Bk Rev. Ad Acc. Circ:** 6,000 (ctrl).
Desc: A communications, career-oriented newsletter focusing on minority employment opportunities in the communications industry.

LC P91.5.U5 S78 **ISSN** 0730-5117
DD 302.2/34/079 US
STUDENT GUIDE TO MASS MEDIA INTERNSHIPS, THE. Added/Corp University of Colorado, Boulder. School of Journalism. Intern Research Group. (19??)-. English. One time a year. $40.00. Internships Research Group, Regent Hall, PO Box 52, Boulder CO 80309.

NE
STUDIES IN ARGUMENTATION IN PRAGMATICS AND DISCOURSE ANALYSIS. VFOAT Pragmatics and Discourse Analysis; PDA. (1984)-. Monographic series. English. Price varies per volume. Foris Publications, PO Box 509, 3300 AM Dordrecht Netherlands. **Tel** 011 31 78 510454.

DD 384 US
STUDIES IN COMMUNICATION (NORWOOD, N.J.). (STUDIES IN COMMUNICATION.). Vol. 1 (1988)-. Monographic series. English. Irregular. Price varies per volume. Ablex Publishing Corporation, 355 Chestnut Street, Norwood NJ 07648. **Tel** (201)767-8450, (201)767-8455 (Customer Service), FAX (201)767-6717. **ED** Sari Thomas.

LC P87 .S68 **ISSN** 0275-7982
DD 001.51/05 US
STUDIES IN COMMUNICATIONS. [Stud. commun.]. Vol. 1 (1980)-. English. One time a year. $73.25. JAI Press Inc., 55 Old Post Road, Suite 2, PO Box 1678, Greenwich CT 06836-1678. **Tel** (203)661-7602, FAX (203)661-0792. **ED** Thelma McCormick.
Ind/Abst Soc. Plann. Policy Dev. Abstr.; Sociol. Abstr. [Full Cov.].

ISSN 0752-4757
UDC 7.097 FR
T.V. VIDEO JAQUETTES. VFOAT Television Video Jaquettes. (1982)-. Periodical. French. Twelve times a year. 300.00F France; 560.00F other. TV Video Jaquettes, 22 rue de Billancourt, 92100 Boulogne France.

LC T11 .T336 **ISSN** 1057-2252
DD 001 US
Pr Rev.
TECHNICAL COMMUNICATION QUARTERLY. (TECHNICAL COMMUNICATION QUARTERLY : TCQ.). [Tech. commun. q.]. **Added/Corp** University of Minnesota. Rhetoric Dept. Association of Teachers of Technical Writing. VFOAT TCQ. Vol. 1, No. 1 (Winter 1992)-. Periodical. English. Four times a year (Feb., May, Aug., Nov.). $30.00 (individuals); $50.00 (institutions). Association of Teachers of Technical Writing, University of Minnesota, 202 Haecker Hall, St Paul MN 55108. **Tel** (612)624-9729, FAX (612)624-3617. **ED** Mary M. Lay (phone: (612)624-2262) and Billie J. Wahlstrom (phone: (612)624-7750). **Bk Rev**, (Qty: 20). **Ad Acc, Adv Mgr:** Dr. B. Wahlstrom, **Tel** (612)624-7750. **Circ:** 1,100. available on microfilm from University Microfilms International (UMI); available on CD-ROM from University Microfilms International (UMI); available on an online database from University Microfilms International (UMI). **Continues** Technical Writing Teacher, 0888-4323.
Ind/Abst Acad. Search; Bus. Source Plus; Bus. Source; Curr. Index J. Educ.; Educ. Index; EP Collect.; Homework Help.; MasterFile FullTEXT 1000; MasterFile FullTEXT 350; MasterFile FullTEXT 650; MasterFile FullTEXT (July 1993-); OCLC; Telebase.

ISSN 1076-0326
DD 070 US
●**TECHNIQUE (HYATTSVILLE, MD.).** (TECHNIQUE.). (1994)-. Periodical. English. Twelve times a year. $39.00. In Print Publishing Inc., 10 Post Office Square 6005, Boston MA 02109. **Tel** (617)422-8650. **(Subscription address:** Technique, PO Box 9164, Hyattsville MD 20781. **Tel** (617)722-0960.) **ED** Jill Robbins Israel. **Ad Acc, Adv Mgr:** Lynn Wilczynski.

LC HE7601
DD 384.1 US
●**TECHNOLOGY FOR COMMUNICATIONS.** **See** Computers-Computer Networks.

ISSN 1017-9410
UDC 008(55) IR
TEHRAN TIMES TEHRAN. [Tehran times Tehran]. (1979)-. Newspaper. English. Seven times a week. $500.00 one-year. Publiink, PO Box 19395, 4443 Tehran Iran. **Tel** FAX 011 98 21 769432. **Circ:** 230,000.
Desc: News in various fields.

UK
TELECOMEUROPA'S COMMUNICATIONS NEWSLETTER. Newsletter. English. Twenty-six times a year. $450.00 (add $50.00 for postage). Telecomeuropa, 3 Princes Building, George Street, Bath BA1 2ED United Kingdom. **Tel** 011 44 1225 445282, FAX 011 44 1225 445283. **Continues** Communications Newsletter, 0950-5717.

ISSN 0958-398X
UK
TELECOMEUROPA'S COMMUNICATIONS NEWSLETTER. [Telecomeur. commun. newsl.]. (1989)-. Newsletter. English. Twenty-four times a year. Telecomeuropa, 3 Princes Building, George Street, Bath BA1 2ED United Kingdom. **Tel** 011 44 1225 445282, FAX 011 44 1225 445283. **Continues** Communications Newsletter (Bath), 0956-7771.

IT
TELEGRAPH AFFARI ESTEUROPA. (19??)-. Periodical. Italian. Irregular (48 issues). L650000 Italy. Agenz Giornalistica Telegraphs, Via Chelini 9, 00197 Rome Italy. **Tel** 011 39 6 8078113, FAX 011 39 6 8083607.

US
TELEMATICS COMMUNICATIONS QUARTERLY. (1988)-. Newsletter. English. Four times a year. Free. Telematics International, Isis House, Reading Road Chineham, Hampshire RG24 OTW United Kingdom. **Tel** 011 44 1256 467385. **ED** Philip Smith. **Bk Rev**, (Qty: 1). **Acid Free.** ctrl circ.

Desc: Informs and educates customers, consultants, and others on technology and relates it to Telematics products and market strategies.

LC G64
DD 910.25 US
TELEPHONE DIRECTORY / UNITED STATES DEPARTMENT OF THE INTERIOR, GEOLOGICAL SURVEY, CENTRAL REGION. Main/Corp Geological Survey (U.S.). Central Region. (19??)-. Directory. English. US Geological Survey / Denver, PO Box 25286, Denver CO 80225. **Tel** (303)493-8401.

ISSN 0040-2699
UDC 791 FR CCC
TELERAMA ED. PARISIENNE. (TELERAMA.). (1980)-. Periodical. French. One time a week. $129.05. Telerama, 129 Blvd Malesherbes, 75017 Paris France. **Tel** 011 33 1 48884500. **Continues** Telerama (1974), 1151-2075.

US
TELEVISION BUYER. (19??)-. Periodical. English. Twelve times a year. £52.00. EMAP Readerlink, Audit House, 260 Field End Road, Ruislip Middlesex HA4 9LT United Kingdom. **Tel** 011 44 1773 63100, FAX 011 44 1733 87367. **(Subscription address:** EMAP Business Publishing, 4 Admiral House Cardinal Way, Middlesex HA3 5SQ United Kingdom. **Tel** 011 44 181 8684499.)

ISSN 0797-6488
UY
TEMAS DE COMUNICACION. Added/Corp Universidad de la Rep,ublica (Uruguay). Ciencias de la Comunicacion. VFOAT Comunicacion. No. 1 (Sept. 1992)-. Periodical. Spanish. Four times a year. Licenciatura de Ciencias de la Comunicacion, Aduardo Acevedo 928, 11200 Montevideo Uruguay. **Tel** 5982-417995, FAX 5982-486796. **ED** Sergio Israel.

VE
TEMAS DE COMUNICACION. Added/Corp Universidad Cat,olica Andres Bello. Escuela de Comunicacion Social. VFOAT Comunicacion. No. 1 (1992)-. Periodical. Spanish. Three times a year. Universidad Catolica Andres Bello, Escuela de Comunicacion Social, Caracas Venezuela.

US
TENNESSEE NEWS MEDIA DIRECTORY. Directory. English. One time a year (June). $45.00. News Media Directories, PO Box 316, Mount Dora FL 32757. **Tel** (904)383-3023, (800)749-6399.

ISSN 0929-9971
NE
UDC 80
●**TERMINOLOGY AMSTERDAM.** (TERMINOLOGY.). [Terminology Amst.]. (1994)-. Periodical. English. Two times a year. $122.00. John Benjamins BV, Amsteldijk 44, PO Box 75577, 1070 AN Amsterdam Netherlands. **Tel** 011 31 20 6738156, FAX 011 31 20 739773. **(Subscription address:** John Benjamins North America, PO Box 27519, Philadelphia PA 19118-0519. **Tel** (215)836-1200, FAX (215)836-1204.) **ED** Helmi Sonneveld, Kurt Loenig.
Desc: Focuses on the discussion of solutions not only of language problems encountered in translation, but also, for example, of (monolingual) problems of ambiguity, reference and developments in multidisciplinary communication.

ISSN 0749-9949
US
TEXAS MEDIA GUIDE, THE. Added/Corp Ampersand Incorporated. (19??)-. English. One time a year. $80.00. Texas Media Guide, 1103 South Shepard Drive, Houston TX 77019. **Tel** (713)630-0651.

LC PN4071 .T48 **ISSN** 0363-8782
DD 808.5 US
TEXAS SPEECH COMMUNICATION JOURNAL. Added/Corp Texas Speech Communication Association. Vol. 1 (1976)-. English. One time a year (June or July). $10.00. Texas Speech Communication Association, University of Houston, 627 Arnall Hall, Houston TX 77204. **Tel** (713)749-3521.

NE
TIJDSCHRIFT OVER COMMUNICATIE. (19??)-. Dutch. Six times a year. Fl155.66. Bohn Stafleu van Loghum BV, Postbus 246, 3990 GA Houten Netherlands. **Tel** 011 31 3403 95782. **(Subscription address:** Intermedia BV, Postbus 4, 2400 MA Alphen AD Rijn Netherlands. **Tel** 011 31 1720 66481.) **Absorbed** Communicatief.

US
TJFR HEALTH NEWS REPORTER. See Medical Sciences.

Communications

LC PN4193.O4 T58
DD 808.5
ISSN 0040-8263
US
TOASTMASTER, THE. Added/Corp Toastmasters International. **VFOAT** Toastmaster Magazine. Vol. 1 (Apr. 1933)-. Periodical. English. Twelve times a year. Comes with Toastmasters International membership. Toastmasters International, PO Box 9052, Mission Viejo CA 92690. **Tel** (714)858-8255, FAX (714)858-1207. **ED** Suzanne Frey and Keith Bush. Index available. **Ad Acc. Circ:** 130,000 (ctrl). **Supersedes** *Gavel*.
Desc: A organization devoted to the improvement of listening, speaking and thinking skills and self-development.

LC K10 .O882
DD 343/.099/05 342.39905
UK
TOLLEY'S JOURNAL OF MEDIA LAW AND PRACTICE. See Law.

ISSN 0040-9340
US
TOPICATOR. See Communications-Abstracting, Bibliographies and Statistics.

ISSN 1072-3188
US
CCC
●**TRAINING MEDIA REVIEW.** (1993)-. English. Six times a year. $189.00. TMR Publications, PO Box 381822, Cambridge MA 02238. **Tel** (617)661-1095. **ED** Bill Ellet. **Bk Rev**, (Qty: 10).
Desc: Reviews training media, primarily video but including books and multimedia, for company and government trainers.

ISSN 0193-2136
US
TRAINING WORLD. (197?)-. Periodical. English. Six times a year. Fenn Co, 148 Kingside Road, Kingston Ontario L0G 1K0 Canada. **Continues** *Sales Training*, 0161-8229.

ISSN 1040-4848
DD 384
US
Pr Rev.
TRANSCRIPT (SAN FRANCISCO, CALIF.). (TRANSCRIPT.). [Transcript]. **Added/Corp** Communications Institute (San Francisco, Calif.). (198?)-. Periodical. English. Four times a year. Communications Institute / San Francisco, Lockbox 5891, San Francisco CA 94101-5891. **Tel** (415)626-5050. **ED** Theodore S Connelly. **Bk Rev. Circ:** 5,000 (ctrl).
Desc: Topical subjects for teachers and professors of communication arts and sciences.

ISSN 1033-9752
AT
TRANSPORT AND COMMUNICATIONS INDICATORS. See Transportation.

LC HE261.A15 T74
SP
TRANSPORTES Y LAS COMUNICACIONES, LOS. See Transportation-Roads and Traffic.

FR
TYPEX. French. Editions du Boisbaudry, BP 6359, 35036 Rennes Cedex France. **Tel** 011 33 99 322121.

ISSN 0893-3308
US
TITLE CHANGE
UPDATE - WOMEN IN COMMUNICATIONS, INC. BOSTON PROFESSIONAL CHAPTER. (UPDATE : NEWSLETTER OF THE BOSTON PROFESSIONAL CHAPTER, WOMEN IN COMMUNICATIONS, INC.). **Added/Corp** Women in Communications, Inc. Boston Professional Chapter. (Sept. 1986)-(19??). Newsletter. English. Women in Communications Inc., Boston Professional Chapter, 67 Harlow Street, Boston MA 02174. **Tel** (617)868-0238. **Continued by** *Intercom : Women in Communications*.

ISSN 0849-0805
DD 917.13/585/0025
CN
VERNON'S ... BELLEVILLE CITY DIRECTORY. [Vernon's Belleville city dir.]. **Added/Corp** Vernon Directories. **VFOAT** Vernon's Belleville City Directory; Belleville City Directory. (1990)-. Directory. English. Every 2 years. Vernon Directories Ltd., 111 Fried Street, Hamilton Ontario L8P 4M3 Canada. **Tel** (416)522-5066. **Continues** *Vernon's City of Belleville (Ontario) Directory.*, 0383-0063.

ISSN 0177-7505
GW
UDC 621.396.24
VHF COMMUNICATIONS. [VHF commun.]. **VFOAT** Very High Frequency Communications. (1969)-. Periodical. English. Four times a year. $27.37. KM Publications, 5 Ware Orchardbarby NR, Rugby Warwickshire CV23 Suffolk United Kingdom. Documents available from Ask*IEEE.
Ind/Abst INSPEC (Spring 1984-).

II
VIDURA. English. Four times a year. $50.00. Press Institute of India, Sapru House Annexe Barakhamba Road, New Delhi 110001 India. **Tel** 3318066 OR 3318646. **(Subscription address:** Prints India, 11 Darya Ganj, New Delhi 110002 India. **Tel** 011 91 11 3268645, FAX 011 91 11 3275542, telex 31-61087 PRIN-IN.**) Bk Rev. Ad Acc. Circ:** 1,000 (ctrl).
Desc: Disseminates improved techniques in editorial work and production of newspapers. Carries thought-provoking, research-oriented articles on the press, radio, television, cinema, advertising and public relations.
Ind/Abst Curr. Lit. Sci. Sci.

ISSN 1063-0325
DD 384
US
VIEW POINTS (FULLERTON, CALIF.). (VIEW POINTS: VP: NEWSLETTER OF THE VISUAL COMMUNICATION DIVISION OF THE ASSOCIATION FOR EDUCATION IN JOURNALISM AND MASS COMMUNICATION.). [View points]. **Added/Corp** Association for Education in Journalism and Mass Communication. Visual Communication Division. **VFOAT** VP; Viewpoints. Vol. 11, No. 2 (Feb. 1992)-. Newsletter. English. Four times a year. Free. California State University / School of Communications, Fullerton CA 92634. **Continues** *Visual Communications Newsletter*.

US
VISUAL COMMUNICATION QUARTERLY. (19??)-. English. Four times a year. Free on request. College of Journalism and Mass Communication, University of South Carolina, Columbia SC 29208. **Tel** (803)777-3302, FAX (803)777-4103. **ED** Keith R. Kenney.
Desc: Publishes applied research that has immediate relevance to visual communicators. Each issue will feature informed opinions about controversial and important images in the print and broadcast media.

LC P87 .V59
DD 302.23/05
ISSN 1053-6256
US
VIZIONS (CAMDEN, ME.). (VIZIONS.). [Vizions]. **Added/Corp** Camden New Media Institute. Vol. 1, No. 1 (Winter 1991)-. Periodical. English. Four times a year. $24.00 US; $36.00 Canada. Image Tech, 21 Elm Street 3rd Floor, Box 1347, Camden ME 04843. **Tel** (207)236-6267, FAX (207)236-6018.

LC HE
DD 384
UK
●**VOICE PLUS.** (1994)-. Trade Publication. English. Nine times a year. £102.00. Advanstar Communications, Advanstar House, Park West, Sealand Road, Chester CH1 4RN United Kingdom. **Tel** 011 44 1244 378888, FAX 011 44 1244 370512. **ED** Stuart Sharrock. **Ad Acc, Adv Mgr:** Jane Murphy. Full Page (B&W) £2,650.00. Full Page (Color) £3,450.00.
Desc: Concerned with the benefits of voice automation and computer telephony.

ISSN 1067-1323
DD 384
US
●**VOZ Y DATOS.** [Voz datos]. (1993)-. Periodical. Spanish. Four times a year. $28.00. Argus Business, 6151 Powers Ferry Road Northwest, Atlanta GA 30339. **Tel** (404)995-2500, FAX (404)995-0400.

ISSN 0196-8572
US
WASHINGTON STATE MEDIA DIRECTORY. 8th Ed. (1986). Directory. English. Twelve times a year. $85.00 US; $95.00 other. McConnell Company Public Relations, 200 West Mercer Street/Suite 201, Seattle WA 98119. **Tel** (206)285-0140. **ED** Jane B Mcconnell. Index available. **Circ:** 500. **Continues** *Puget Sound Media Directory*.
Desc: A publicist's guide to Washington state news media.

LC PN4071 .W45
DD 001.54/2/05
ISSN 1057-0314
US
CCC
CODEN WJSCDW
WESTERN JOURNAL OF COMMUNICATION. [West. j. commun.]. **Added/Corp** Western States Communication Association. Vol. 56, No. 1 (Winter 1992)-. Periodical. English. Four times a year. University of Utah Department of Communication, WSCA, Salt Lake City UT 84112. **Tel** (801)581-6526. Documents available from UMI Article Clearinghouse. **Continues** *Western Journal of Speech Communication*, 0193-6700.
Ind/Abst Commun. Abstr. (?-?); Curr. Index J. Educ.; EP Collect.; Homework Help.; Hum. Resour. Abstr.; MasterFile FullTEXT 1000; MasterFile FullTEXT 350; MasterFile FullTEXT 650; MasterFile FullTEXT; Newsp. Period. Abstr. (1992-); OCLC; Psychol. Abstr.; Soc. Plann. Policy Dev. Abstr.; Sociol. Abstr.; Telebase.

ISSN 0956-2362
UK
WHAT SATELLITE. [What satell.]. **VFOAT** What Satellite and Cable. (198?)-. Periodical. English. Twelve times a year. $99.25. WV Publications, 57-59 Rochester Place, London NW1 9JU United Kingdom. **Tel** 011 44 171 4850011. **(Subscription address:** WV Publications, Unit 5 Billet Lane, Berkhampstead, Hertfordshire HP4 1HL United Kingdom. **Tel** 011 44 1442 876661.**)**

UK
WIDE AREA COMMUNICATIONS. (19??)-. English. Irregular. $588.00. Datapro International, McGraw Hill House, Shoppenhangers Road, Maidenhead Berkshire SL6 2QL United Kingdom. **Tel** 011 44 1628 773277, FAX 011 44 1628 773628.

ISSN 1075-8550
DD 658
US
CODEN WILRE2
Pr Rev.
WILLIAMS REPORT. [Williams rep.]. (1989)-. Periodical. English. Twelve times a year. $137.00. Joe Williams Communication Inc., PO Box 924, Bartlesville OK 74005. **Tel** (918)336-2267, FAX (918)336-2733. **ED** Reba Payne. **Bk Rev**, (Qty: 4). **Circ:** 500 (ctrl). **Continues** *Communications Ideas, Plans & Strategies Report*.
Desc: Contains information on corporate employee communication.
Ind/Abst Chem. Abstr.

LC P96.S48 W66
DD 302.2/082
ISSN 0749-1409
US
WOMEN'S STUDIES IN COMMUNICATION. [Women's stud. commun.]. **Added/Corp** Organization for Research on Women and Communication (U.S.). Vol. 5, No. 1 (Spring 1982)-. Periodical. English. Two times a year (June & Dec.). Comes with Organization for Research on Women and Communication membership. Organization for Research on Women and Communication, Department of Speech, 1250 Bellflower Boulevard, Long Beach CA 90840. **Tel** (310)985-4301, (310)985-4314, FAX (310)985-4259. **ED** Sharon D. Downey. **Bk Rev.** Documents available from UMI Article Clearinghouse. **Continues** *ORWAC Bulletin*.
Desc: Provides a forum for research scholarship, reviews, and commentary concerning women and communication. It features critical, social scientific, and feminist perspectives on communication in areas such as interpersonal, small group, and organizational communication, rhetorical theory and criticism, and media studies. It also encourages the study of communication systems through alternate and nontraditional research methodologies and in contexts traditionally dominated by women--in the family, home, school, and social environment; with child bearing, artistic expressions, and labor practices.
Ind/Abst Commun. Abstr.; Expand. Acad. Index (1992-); Newsp. Period. Abstr. (1992-); Psychol. Abstr. (1987-); PsycINFO; PsycLit; Women Stud. Abstr.

LC NX1 .W64
DD 700/.5
ISSN 0266-6286
UK
CCC
WORD & IMAGE (LONDON. 1985). See The Arts.

US
WORKING COMMUNICATOR. (19??)-. Newsletter. English. Twelve times a year. $97.00. Ragan Communications Inc., 212 West Superior Street, Suite 200, Chicago IL 60610. **Tel** (312)335-0037, (800)878-5331, FAX (312)335-9583.
Desc: A newsletter that has something for everyone. From trends in the workplace, to tips on organization, funny quips, quotes and customer service or sales techniques.

LC Z6951 .W6
DD 071.47
ISSN 0084-1323
US
WORKING PRESS OF THE NATION, THE. See Journalism-Abstracting, Bibliographies and Statistics.

LC P87 .W63
DD 001.51/05
ISSN 0887-4182
US
WORLD MEDIA REPORT (WASHINGTON, D.C.). (WORLD MEDIA REPORT.). [World media rep.]. **Added/Corp** World Media Association. Vol. 1, No. 1 (Winter 1986)-. Periodical. English. Four times a year. $22.00 US; $28.00 other. World Media Association, 2550 M Street NW, Suite 475, Washington DC 20037.
Ind/Abst Hum. Rights Intern. Rep.

LC P211 .W737
DD 302.2/244/05
ISSN 0741-0883
US
CCC
Pr Rev.
WRITTEN COMMUNICATION. [Writ. commun.]. Vol. 1, No. 1 (Jan. 1984)-. Periodical. English. Four times a year (Jan., Apr., July, Oct.). $182.00. SAGE Periodical Press, 2455 Teller Road, Thousand Oaks CA 91320. **Tel** (805)499-0721, FAX (805)499-0871, telex 100799. **ED** Deborah Barndt, Martin Nystrand and Stephen P. Witte. **Acid Free.** available on microfilm and microfiche from University Microfilms International (UMI).

Documents available from The Genuine Article.
Desc: Provides a forum for free exchange of ideas, theoretical viewpoints, and methodological approaches that define and develop thought and practice in the study of the written word.
Ind/Abst Commun. Abstr.; Curr. Cit.; Curr. Contents Soc. Behav. Sci.; Curr. Index J. Educ.; Educ. Adm. Abstr.; EP Collect.; Homework Help.; Hum. Resour. Abstr.; MasterFile FullTEXT 1000; MasterFile FullTEXT 350; MasterFile FullTEXT 650; MasterFile FullTEXT; OCLC; Res. Alert [Full Cov.]; Soc. Plann. Policy Dev. Abstr.; Soc. Sci. Cit. Index [Full Cov.]; Telebase.

LC VK397 .S62A **ISSN** 0098-5910
DD 384.5/2/09 US
YEARBOOK - SOCIETY OF WIRELESS PIONEERS. (YEAR BOOK.). **Main/Corp** Society of Wireless Pioneers. English. One time a year. Society of Wireless Pioneers Inc, PO Box 530, Santa Rosa CA 95402.

ABSTRACTING, BIBLIOGRAPHIES AND STATISTICS

LC PN4888.T4 A34 **ISSN** 0891-8775
DD 070.1/9 US
ABC NEWS INDEX. [ABC news index]. **VAT** American Broadcasting Corporation News Index. (Jan.-Mar. 1986)-. Abstracting/Indexing Service. English. Four times a year (Jan., Apr., Jul., Dec.). $217.30. Primary Source Media, 12 Lunar Drive, Woodbridge CT 06525. **Tel** (800)444-0799, FAX (203)397-3893. **(Subscription address:** Research Publications Inc. / Microfilm, 12 Lunar Drive Drawer AB, Woodbridge CT 06525. **Tel** (800)444-0799, (203)397-2600, FAX (203)397-3893.**)**

LC HE7601 .A55
DD 384 SZ
ANNUAIRE STATISTIQUE DES TELECOMMUNICATIONS DU SECTEUR PUBLIC (GENEVA, SWITZERLAND: 1980). (ANNUAIRE STATISTIQUE DES TELECOMMUNICATIONS DU SECTEUR PUBLIC.). **Added/Corp** International Telecommunication Union. **VFOAT** Yearbook of Common Carrier Telecommunication Statistics. (1979)-. English (French and Spanish). One time a year. International Telecommunication Union, place des Nations, CH-1211 Geneva 20 Switzerland. **Tel** 011 41 22 7305111, FAX 011 41 22 7337256. ***Continues*** *Annuaire Statistique des Telecommunications du Secteur Public ... et Statistiques des Radiocommunciations.*

LC HE7125 .C643b
DD 383.49 PO
ANUARIO ESTATISTICO - CORREIOS E TELECOMUNICACOES DE PORTUGAL. **Main/Corp** Correios e Telecomunicacoes de Portugal. (19??)-. Portuguese. Correios e Telecomunicacoes de Portugal, rua Alexandre Herculano 100 - 2 Po S, Lisbon Portugal.

LC HE8700 **ISSN** 0742-4914
DD 384.554/6 US
Pr Rev.
BIBLIOGRAPHY ON CABLE TELEVISION : BCTV. **Added/Corp** Communications Library (San Francisco, Calif.). **VFOAT** BCTV. (19??)-. Periodical. English. One time a year. $40.00. Communications Library, Lockbox 472139, Marina Station, San Francisco CA 94147. **Tel** (415)626-5050, FAX (415)346-4466. **ED** T.S. Connelly. Index available. cum. index. **Circ:** 100,000 (ctrl).
Desc: Comprehensive list of published references on cable television: access, advertising, audience, broadcast radiation, business, education, finance, international, legislation, marketing, operations, programming, regulations, satellite transmission, social effects, subscribers, technology, telex, videotex. open-ended, non-cumulative.

ISSN 0749-2936
US
BROADCAST STATS. **Added/Corp** Paul Kagan Associates. No. 1 (Aug. 17, 1984)-. Newsletter. English. Twelve times a year. $575.00. Paul Kagan Associates Inc., 126 Clock Tower Place, Carmel CA 93923-8734. **Tel** (408)624-1536, FAX (408)625-3225, telex ITT 4938124 PKA UI. available via fax.
Desc: Newsletter containing new data on radio and television market billing, revenue and cash flow, with by-market history of station sales and a digest of financial data.

ISSN 0000-1511
US
CCC
•BROADCASTING & CABLE YEARBOOK. **VFOAT** Broadcasting and Cable Yearbook. (1993)-. English. One time a year. $180.66. R.R. Bowker, A Reed Reference Publishing Company, Part of Reed International PLC, PO Box 31, 121 Chanlon Drive, New Providence NJ 07974. **Tel** (908)464-6800, (800)521-8110, FAX (908)665-6688, telex 138-755.
Desc: Features include listings for all radio and TV stations in the US and Canada, indexes of radio and TV station call letters, vital details on ownership, FCC rules and regulations, and information on new and expanding industry services.

LC HE8700.7.C6 C3335
DD 384.55/47 US
CABLE TV FINANCIAL DATABOOK, THE. **Added/Corp** Paul Kagan Associates. **VFOAT** Cable Television Financial Databook. (June 1991)-. English. One time a year. $235.00. Paul Kagan Associates Inc., 126 Clock Tower Place, Carmel CA 93923-8734. **Tel** (408)624-1536, FAX (408)625-3225, telex ITT 4938124 PKA UI. ***Continues*** *Kagan Cable TV Financial Databook.*
Desc: Reference source of cable TV statistics - industry's financial condition, research on private and public markets, capital sources and service suppliers.

LC P87 .C59733 **ISSN** 0162-2811
DD 001.5/05 US
CCC
COMMUNICATION ABSTRACTS. [Commun. abstr.]. **Added/Corp** Temple University. School of Communications and Theater. Vol. 1 (March 1978)-. Abstracting/Indexing Service. English. Six times a year (Feb., Apr., June, Aug., Oct., Dec.). $474.00. SAGE Periodical Press, 2455 Teller Road, Thousand Oaks CA 91320. **Tel** (805)499-0721, FAX (805)499-0871, telex 100799. **ED** Thomas F. Gordon (Temple University). **Acid Free. Circ:** 1,200. available on CD-ROM; available on microfilm and microfiche from University Microfilms International (UMI).
Desc: Provides coverage of recent literature in all areas of communication studies (both mass and interpersonal). Includes expanded coverage of new communications technologies.

ISSN 0748-657X
US
COMMUNICATION BOOKNOTES. [Commun. booknotes]. **Added/Corp** George Washington University. Center for Telecommunications Studies. No. 140 (1982)-. Periodical. English. Six times a year. $95.00. Communication Booknotes, 4507 Airlie Way, Annandale VA 22003. **Tel** (202)994-6352. **ED** Chris Sterling (Editor's Address: Lisner Aud B-10, George Washington University, Washington, DC 20052). **Bk Rev. Circ:** 1,700 (ctrl). ***Continues*** *Mass Media Booknotes, 0740-6479.*
Desc: Covers recent titles in telecommunications, information, and media.

LC Z5632 .C66 P87 **ISSN** 1041-7893
DD 016.3022/05 US
Pr Rev.
•COMMUNICATION SERIALS. [Commun. ser.]. (1992/1993)-. English. Every 2 years. $133.50. SovaComm Inc, PO Box 64697, Virginia Beach VA 23464. **Tel** (804)420-3564, FAX (804)420-0840. **ED** Harry and Patricia Sova. Index available. **Circ:** 5,000.
Desc: 3,000 annotated communication serials for library, academic, and business research.

LC PN1993.5.U8 E83 **ISSN** 0737-0113
DD 384/.8/025797 US
EVERGREEN STATE FILM & VIDEO INDEX, THE. **VFOAT** Evergreen State Film and Video Index. (19??)-. Directory. English. One time a year. $15.00. Media Index Publishing, PO Box 24365, Seattle WA 98124-0365. **Tel** (206)382-9220. **ED** Richard K. Woltjer. **Ad Acc. Circ:** 5,000.
Desc: Directory of motion picture, video, sound, talent and multi-image resources in Washington state.

LC P88.8 .H83 **ISSN** 0885-1328
DD 001.51/025/73 US
HUDSON'S STATE CAPITALS NEWS MEDIA CONTACTS DIRECTORY. [Hudson's state cap. news media contacts dir.]. **VFOAT** State Capitals News Media Contacts Directory; Hudson's State Capitals Directory. (1985)-. Directory. English. One time a year. $75.00. Hudson's State Capitals, 44 Market Street Po Box 311, Rhinebeck NY 12572. **Tel** (301)340-2100. **ED** H P Hudson. Each issue contains an index to its own contents (no volume index)--loose. **Ad Acc.**
Desc: Complete guide to the state capitals press corps; contains information on publications, correspondents, wire services, news bureaus, newspapers, syndicates, radio, TV and other media representatives at each state capital.

LC P92.U5 K28 **ISSN** 0893-2700
DD 302.23/0973/021 US
KAGAN MEDIA INDEX, THE. [Kagan media index]. **Added/Corp** Paul Kagan Associates. No. 1 (Mar. 10, 1987)-. Newsletter. English. Twelve times a year. $575.00. Paul Kagan Associates Inc., 126 Clock Tower Place, Carmel CA 93923-8734. **Tel** (408)624-1536, FAX (408)625-3225, telex ITT 4938124 PKA UI. available via fax.
Desc: Reference publication featuring a collection of comprehensive statistics and data found in the 24 other Kagan newsletters, plus previously unpublished estimates and monthly updates.

LC TK5101.A1 K43 **ISSN** 0950-4877
DD 621.382/05 UK
KEY ABSTRACTS. TELECOMMUNICATIONS. **Added/Corp** INSPEC (Information Service) Institute of Electrical and Electronics Engineers. **VFOAT** Telecommunications. (1987)-. Abstracting/Indexing Service. English. Twelve times a year. $185.00. Institution of Electrical Engineers / IEE, Michael Faraday House, Six Hills Way, Stevenage Hertfordshire SG1 2AY United Kingdom. **Tel** 011 44 1438 313311, FAX 011 44 1438 742840, telex 825578 IEESTV G. **(Subscription address:** IEEE / Institute of Electrical and Electronics Engineers, 445 Hoes Lane, PO Box 1331, Piscataway NJ 08855-1331. **Tel** (800)701-IEEE, (908)981-0060, FAX (908)981-9667, telex 833233.**)** ***Continues*** *Key Abstracts. Communication Technology, 0306-5588.*
Desc: Covers articles on information theory, modulation, switching theory, applications of telecommunications, stations and equipment, switching centres, transmission line links, optical communications.

LC Z5630 .U53A P90
DD 016.3022/3 FR
SUSPENDED
LIST OF DOCUMENTS AND PUBLICATIONS IN THE FIELD OF MASS COMMUNICATION. **Main/Corp** United Nations Educational, Scientific and Cultural Organization. No. 1 (1976)-(19??). English. UNESCO / Communication Documentation, Division Free Flow Information Communication Polcie, 75700 Paris France.

LC Z5834.T4 I532a TK5101
DD 016.384 SZ
LIST OF PUBLICATIONS / INTERNATIONAL TELECOMMUNICATION UNION. **Main/Corp** International Telecommunication Union. (19??)-. English (French and Spanish). Two times a year. Free on request. International Telecommunication Union, place des Nations, CH-1211 Geneva 20 Switzerland. **Tel** 011 41 22 7305111, FAX 011 41 22 7337256. **Circ:** 10,000.
Desc: Detailed list of publications which are available from the international telecommunications union.

ISSN 0815-5615
DD 302.23402594 AT
MEDIA PEOPLE (N.S.W./A.C.T. ED.). [Media People (N.S.W./A.C.T. ed.)]. (1984)-. Periodical. English. Eleven times a year (monthly except Jan.). 386.42Aus$. Media Monitors, NJP Pty Limited, 36-75 Reservoir Street, Surry Hills NSW 2010 Australia. **Tel** 011 61 2 3103155. **(Subscription address:** Media Monitors, PO Box K527, Haymarket, New South Wales 2000 Australia. **Tel** 011 61 2 2124133, FAX 011 61 2 2124315, 011 61 2 2812846.**) ED** Gai LeRoy. **Bk Rev.** available on diskette.
Desc: Media guide listing information on press, radio, television, and magazines around Australia or by state.

ISSN 0734-8142
US
NEW BOOKS IN THE COMMUNICATIONS LIBRARY. **Main/Corp** University of Illinois at Urbana-Champaign. Communications Library. **Added/Corp** University of Illinois at Urbana-Champaign. College of Communications. (19??)-. Periodical. English. Four times a year. University of Illinois Urbana-Champaign, 119 Gregory Hall, Urbana IL 61801. **Tel** (217)333-2350. **ED** Diane Foxhill Carothers. **Bk Rev. Circ:** 500 (ctrl).
Desc: Entries consist of brief annotation of new books received in Communications Library and include full bibliographic information.

LC Z5630 .P18
GW
PRD. PUBLIZISTIKWISSENSCHAFTLICHER REFERATE-DIENST. **Added/Corp** Berlin. Freie Universitaet. Institut fuer Publizistik. **VFOAT** Publizistikwissenschaftlicher Referate-Dienst. Vol. 1, (Summer 1966)-. Periodical. German. Four times a year. K.G. Saur Verlag KG, A Reed Reference Publishing Company, Part of Reed International PLC, Ortlerstrasse 8, D-81373 Munich Germany. **Tel** 011 49 89 769020, FAX 011 49 89 76902150, telex 5212067-SAUR-D. **(Subscription address:** St. Martin's Press, 175 5th Avenue, New York NY 10010. **Tel** (800)221-7945.**)**

LC P88.8 .P73
DD 301.16/1/0994 AT
PRESS, RADIO AND TV GUIDE : AUSTRALIA, NEW ZEALAND AND THE PACIFIC ISLANDS. (19??)-. English. One time a year. 75.00Aus$. Media Monitors, NJP Pty Limited, 36-75 Reservoir Street, Surry Hills NSW 2010 Australia. **Tel** 011 61 2 3103155. **(Subscription address:** Media Monitors, PO Box K527, Haymarket, New South Wales 2000 Australia. **Tel** 011 61 2 2124133, FAX 011 61 2 2124315, 011 61 2 2812846.**) Ad Acc.**
Desc: Includes listings of all print and electronic media in Australia, New Zealand and the Pacific Islands. Also

covers the main media associations together with text explaining their roles, and a comprehensive listing of public relations companies and advertising agencies.

LC Discard
DD 380 US
PUBLISHED SEARCH BIBLIOGRAPHIES FROM THE NTIS BIBLIOGRAPHIC DATA BASE. COMMUNICATION AND ELECTROTECHNOLOGY. **Added/Corp** United States. National Technical Information Service. **VFOAT** Published Search Bibliographies from the N.T.I.S. Bibliographic Data Base. Communication and Electrotechnology; Communication and Electrotechnology. (19??)-. English. Irregular. Free on request. National Technical Information Service - NTIS, Room 2027S, 5285 Port Royal Road, Springfield VA 22161. **Tel** (703)487-4630, (703)487-4660, (703)487-4650, FAX (703)321-8547, telex 89-9405.

LC Z7403 .P85 Q158.5
DD 016.5 US
PUBLISHED SEARCH MASTER CATALOG. **Added/Corp** United States. National Technical Information Service. NERAC, Inc. (1988)-. Catalog. English. Irregular. Free on request. National Technical Information Service - NTIS, Room 2027S, 5285 Port Royal Road, Springfield VA 22161. **Tel** (703)487-4630, (703)487-4660, (703)487-4650, FAX (703)321-8547, telex 89-9405. ***Continues*** *Published Search Catalog.*

LC Z1223.Z7 S45 **ISSN** 0748-4836
DD 015.73/053 US
SELECTED AUDIOVISUAL MATERIALS PRODUCED BY THE UNITED STATES GOVERNMENT. [Sel. audiov. mater. prod. U.S. gov.]. **Added/Corp** National Audiovisual Center. (19??)-. English. Every 2 years. Free. National Audiovisual Center, 8700 Edgeworth Drive, Capitol Heights MD 20743. **Tel** (301)763-1896, (800)788-6282.

US
SPEECH INDEX. (1935)-. Abstracting/Indexing Service. English. Irregular. Price varies. VOYA Scarecrow, 4720 Boston Way, Lanham MD 20706. **Tel** (800)462-6420 ext. 7132. **ED** Compiler: 1935-66, Roberta Briggs Sutton; 1966/70, Roberta Briggs Sutton and Charity Mitchell, 1971/75- Charity Mitchell.
Desc: An index to collections of world famous orations and speeches for various occasions.

LC HE8801 .S7
DD 384.6/3 US
•**STATISTICAL REPORT. RURAL TELECOMMUNICATIONS BORROWERS.** **Added/Corp** United States. Rural Utilities Service. **VFOAT** Rural Telecommunications Borrowers. (1994)-. English. US Department of Agriculture, 14th Street and Independence Avenue SW, Washington DC 20250. **Tel** (202)720-5457. ***Continues*** *Statistical Report. Rural Telephone Borrowers, 0731-8251.*

LC HE8801 .S7 **ISSN** 0731-8251
DD 384.6/3 US
TITLE CHANGE
STATISTICAL REPORT. RURAL TELEPHONE BORROWERS. **Added/Corp** United States. Rural Electrification Administration. **VFOAT** Rural Telephone Borrowers. (1980)-(1993). Statistical Publication. English. US Department of Agriculture, 14th Street and Independence Avenue SW, Washington DC 20250. **Tel** (202)720-5457. available on microfiche (Vols. for (1981-) distributed to depository libraries). ***Continues*** *Annual Statistical Report. Rural Telephone Borrowers.* ***Continued by*** *Statistical Report. Rural Telecommunications Borrowers.*

ISSN 0161-5173
DD 384 US
STATISTICS OF COMMUNICATIONS COMMON CARRIERS. [Stat. commun. common carr.]. **Added/Corp** United States. Federal Communications Commission. **VFOAT** FCC Common Carrier Statistics. **VAT** Federal Communications Commission Common Carrier Statistics. (Dec. 31, 1957)-. Government Publication. English. Irregular. Superintendent of Documents, US Government Printing Office, Washington DC 20402. **Tel** (202)275-3328, FAX (202)786-2377. ***Continues*** *Statistics of the Communications Industry in the United States.*
Ind/Abst Predicasts Forecasts.

LC HE8801 .S73 **ISSN** 1054-7886
DD 384.6/0973/021 US
STATISTICS OF THE LOCAL EXCHANGE CARRIERS. (STATISTICS OF THE LOCAL EXCHANGE CARRIERS ... FOR THE YEAR ...). [Stat. local exch. carr.]. **Added/Corp** United States Telephone Association. (1989)-. English. One time a year (fall). $250.00. United States Telephone Association, 1401 H Street NW Suite 600, Washington DC 20005. **Tel** (202)326-7270, FAX (202)326-7333.
Formed by the union of *Annual Statistical Volume (United States Telephone Association)* ***and*** *Statistics of the Telephone Industry.*

LC HE6981 .M53A
DD 331.7/613803/0944 FR
STATISTIQUES DE PERSONNEL / MINISTERE DES PTT, DIRECTION DU PERSONNEL ET DES AFFAIRES SOCIALES. **Main/Corp** France. Ministere des P.T.T.. Direction du Personnel et des Affaires Sociales. French. One time a year.

LC HE7811 .A382 **ISSN** 0703-7252
DD 384/.0971 CN
CEASED
TELECOMMUNICATIONS STATISTICS. [Telecommun. stat.]. **Main/Corp** Statistics Canada. Communications Section. **Added/Corp** Statistics Canada. Communications Section. **VFOAT** Statistique des Telecommunications. (1972)-(19??). Statistical Publication. English (French). Statistics Canada Publications Sales and Services, R.H. Coats Building 6th Floor, Ottawa Ontario K1A 0T6 Canada. **Tel** (613)951-5078, (800)267-6677, FAX (613)951-1584, telex 053-3585. ***Continues*** *Statistics Canada. Public Utilities Section. Telegraph and Cable Statistics.*
Desc: Revenues, expenses, number of messages sent, mileage operated, employees, salaries, wages; by company.

LC HE8861 .S7b **ISSN** 0380-7843
DD 384.6/0971/021 CN
TELEPHONE STATISTICS. [Teleph. stat.]. **Main/Corp** Canada. Statistics Canada. Communications Section. **Added/Corp** Statistics Canada. Public Utilities Section. Statistics Canada. Communications Section. Statistics Canada. Communications and Information Section. Statistics Canada. Telecommunications Section. **VFOAT** Statistiques du Telephone. (1970)-. Statistical Publication. English (French). One time a year. 31.21Can$. Statistics Canada Publications Sales and Services, R.H. Coats Building 6th Floor, Ottawa Ontario K1A 0T6 Canada. **Tel** (613)951-5078, (800)267-6677, FAX (613)951-1584, telex 053-3585. ***Continues*** *Canada. Dominion Bureau of Statistics. Telephone Statistics.*
Desc: Number of telephone calls; telephones by type of service and organization; wire and pole-line mileage; employees, salaries and wages; assets, liabilities and net worth data; and revenue and expenditure by province.

ISSN 0707-9753
DD 384.6/0971 CN
TELEPHONE STATISTICS (MONTHLY ED.). (TELEPHONE STATISTICS.). [Teleph. stat.]. **Added/Corp** Statistics Canada. **VFOAT** Statistique du Telephone; Statistiques du Telephone. Vol. 1, No. 1 (Apr. 1977)-. Statistical Publication. English (French). Twelve times a year. 108.00Can$. Statistics Canada Publications Sales and Services, R.H. Coats Building 6th Floor, Ottawa Ontario K1A 0T6 Canada. **Tel** (613)951-5078, (800)267-6677, FAX (613)951-1584, telex 053-3585.

LC HE8805.W6 P8a **ISSN** 0097-9198
DD 385.6/3/09775 US
TELEPHONE STATISTICS : SELECTED FINANCIAL DATA FOR WISCONSIN TELEPHONE COMPANIES. **Main/Corp** Public Service Commission of Wisconsin. Accounts and Finance Division. (19??)-. English. Wisconsin Public Service Commission, PO Box 7854, Madison WI 53707. **Tel** FAX (608)266-3957. ***Continues*** *Telephone Statistics: Selected Financial Data for Wisconsin Telephone Companies, 0097-9198.*

LC AI3 .T44 **ISSN** 0085-7157
DD 011 US
TELEVISION NEWS INDEX AND ABSTRACTS. **Added/Corp** Vanderbilt Television News Archive. (Jan. 1972)-. Abstracting/Indexing Service. English. Twelve times a year. $550.00 (profit and non-academic organizations and government agencies); $330.00 other. Television News Archive, Vanderbilt University, 110 21st Avenue South, Suite 704, Nashville TN 37203. **Tel** (615)322-2927, FAX (615)343-8250. **ED** Andrew H. Pfeiffer. Index available. cum. index. **Circ:** 200. available on microfilm.
Desc: A research guide to the evening news broadcasts of ABC, CBS and NBC, videotapes of which are in the collection of the Vanderbilt TV News Archive.

ISSN 0085-7157
US
TELEVISION NEWS INDEX AND ABSTRACTS : ANNUAL INDEX. **Added/Corp** Vanderbilt Television News Archive. (Aug. 5, 1968)-. Abstracting/Indexing Service. English. One time a year. $550.00 (individuals), $330.00 (institutions). Television News Archive, Vanderbilt University, 110 21st Avenue South, Suite 704, Nashville TN 37203. **Tel** (615)322-2927, FAX (615)343-8250. **ED** Andrew H. Pfeiffer. Index available. **Circ:** 250. available on microfilm.

ISSN 0040-9340
US
TOPICATOR. [Topicator]. **Added/Corp** Thompson Bureau. (1965)-. Abstracting/Indexing Service. English. Six times a year (Jan., Mar., May, July, Sept., Nov.). $110.00. Topicator / Texas, 205 South Stewart Road. #229, Mission TX 78572. **Tel** (210)581-4197. **ED** Wendell Wolles. Index available (each bimonthly issue). **Circ:** 200 (ctrl). available on microfiche.
Desc: Classified article guide to the Advertising/Communications/Marketing Periodical Press. Features international news as one of the 88 main catagories. These, in turn, are broken into over 300 subheadings.

ISSN 1040-6123
DD 384 US
TV PROGRAM STATS. [TV program stats]. **Added/Corp** Paul Kagan Associates. **VAT** Television Program Stats. No. 1 (Sept. 1, 1988)-. Newsletter. English. Twelve times a year. $550.00. Paul Kagan Associates Inc., 126 Clock Tower Place, Carmel CA 93923-8734. **Tel** (408)624-1536, FAX (408)625-3225, telex ITT 4938124 PKA UI. available via fax.
Desc: A compendium of statistics that come from the world's most-watched TV shows.

COMPUTER APPLICATIONS

ISSN 1080-4056
US
•**ANDREW SEYBOLD'S OUTLOOK ON COMMUNICATIONS AND COMPUTING.** (1995)-. Periodical. English. Twelve times a year. $395.00. Pinecrest Press, PO Box 917, Brookdale CA 95007. **Tel** (408)338-7701, FAX (408)338-7806. Index available. cum. index. **Bk Rev.** available on CD-ROM and diskette from Ziff Communications. Documents available from Ask*IEEE. ***Formed by the union of*** *Andrew Seybold's Outlook on Professional Computing, 0895-3821* ***and*** *Andrew Seybold's Outlook on Mobile Computing, 1066-8845.*
Ind/Abst Comput. Bus.; INSPEC; SCISEARCH; World Publ. Monit.

LC HD9696.S64 A87 **ISSN** 1051-4163
DD 006.5/05 US
ASR NEWS : AUTOMATIC SPEECH RECOGNITON NEWS. [ASR News]. **Added/Corp** Voice Information Associates. **VFOAT** Automatic Speech Recogniton News; ASRNews. Vol. 1, No. 1 (July 1990)-. Periodical. English. Twelve times a year. $295.00. Voice Information Associates Inc., 1775 Massachusetts Avenue, PO Box 625, Lexington MA 02173. **Tel** (617)861-6680, FAX (617)861-2083. **ED** John A. Obenteuffer. Index available. cum. index. **Bk Rev**, (Qty: 3-4).
Desc: Update of the automatic speech recognition industry, including news on products, markets, applications, investments, and technology.

ISSN 1067-5221
US
ATM NEWSLETTER. **See** Computers-Electronic Data Processing.

ISSN 1043-6065
DD 070 US
TITLE CHANGE
BOVE & RHODES INSIDE REPORT ON DESKTOP PUBLISHING AND MULTIMEDIA. **See** Computers-Desktop Publishing.

ISSN 1055-4548
DD 004 US
BTN (BIRMINGHAM, ALA.). (BTN [COMPUTER FILE] : BIRMINGHAM TELECOMMUNICATIONS NEWS.). [BTN]. **VFOAT** Birmingham Telecommunications News. (1988)-. Periodical. English. Twelve times a year. Free. Birmingham Telecommunications News, 221 Chestnut Street, Birmingham AL 35210-3219.
Desc: Available on ExNet.

LC QA76.575 .C35 **ISSN** 1069-3009
DD 006.6 CN
•**CD-ROM MULTI MEDIA MAGAZINE.** [CD-ROM multi media mag.]. **VFOAT** CD ROM Multi Media Magazine; Multi Media Magazine; CDROM Multimedia. **VAT** Compact Disc Read Only Memory Media Magazine. (1993)-. Periodical. English. Six times a year. $19.95. Universal Multimedia, PO Box 2946, Plattsburgh NY 12901-9863.

LC TK5101.A1 C626 **ISSN** 1057-0071
DD 621.382 US
CEASED
COMMUNICATION & COMPUTER NEWS. (COMMUNICATION & COMPUTER NEWS : C&C NEWS.). [Commun. comput. news]. **VFOAT** Communication and Computer News; C&C News. Vol. 2 No. 3 (Mar 1991)-(1993). Periodical. English. Horizon House Publications, 1019 Stafford House, 5555

Communications — Computer Applications

Wissahicken Avenue, Philadelphia PA 19144. **Continues** Communication & Computer Products & Software News, 1059-5465.

LC HD9811.A1 I57a   **ISSN** 1051-2721
DD 621.388/332/025   US
COMPLETE MEMBERSHIP DIRECTORY OF THE INTERACTIVE MULTIMEDIA ASSOCIATION, THE. See Computers-Computer Industry and Industry Directories.

US
COMPU-MGR TELE-MGR. (19??)-. English. Four times a year. $20.00 North America; $40.00 other. James Publishing & Associates, 899 Presidential Drive, Suite 110, Richardson TX 75081. **Tel** (800)864-1155, FAX (214)238-1132. **ED** Sarah Klein. Index available. cum. index. **Ad Acc, Adv Mgr:** Jim Reilly. **Circ:** 40,000 (ctrl).
Desc: One section is directed towards purchasing managers seeking telecom equipment in the secondary market. The other section is directed towards purchasing managers seeking computer equipment in the secondary market.

LC TK5105.5 .C6373   **ISSN** 0140-3664
DD 384   UK
   CCC
   CODEN COCOD7
Pr Rev.
COMPUTER COMMUNICATIONS. See Computers-Computer Networks.

LC HM   **ISSN** 1076-027X
DD 302   US
●**COMPUTER-MEDIATED COMMUNICATION MAGAZINE.** (COMPUTER-MEDIATED COMMUNICATION MAGAZINE [COMPUTER FILE].). [Comput.-mediat. commun. mag.]. **VFOAT** Computer Mediated Communication Magazine; CMC Magazine. Vol. 1, No. 1 (May 1, 1994)-. Periodical. English. Twelve times a year. Free. John December, 154 Third Street, Troy NY 12180. **Tel** (518)271-8469. available via Internet (http://www.rpi.edu/~decemj/cmc/mag/current/toc.html).
Desc: Covers research related to computer-mediated communication (CMC).

   ISSN 1072-1711
   US
●**COMPUTER TELEPHONY.** (1993)-. Periodical. English. Twelve times a year. Free on request. Telecom Library Inc., 12 West 21st Street, New York NY 10010. **Tel** (212)691-8215, (800)542-7279. (**Subscription address:** Telecom Library, 1265 Industrial Highway, Southampton PA 18966. **Tel** (800)677-3435, (215)355-2886, FAX (215)355-1068.)

   ISSN 1069-7020
DD 006   US
●**COMPUTERVIDEO (VENTURA, CALIF.).** (COMPUTERVIDEO.). [ComputerVideo]. **VFOAT** Computer Video. Vol. 1, No. 1 (Spring 1993)-. Periodical. English. Four times a year. Miller Magazines Inc, 4880 Market Street, Ventura CA 93003. **Tel** (805)664-3824, FAX (805)664-3875.

UK
COMPUTING & COMMUNICATIONS DECISIONS. (19??)-. Trade Publication. English. One time a year. £65.00 UK; £70 other. Techgnosis Ltd., Blade House, Battersea Road, Cheshire SK4 3EA United Kingdom. **Tel** 011 44 161 4422639, FAX 011 44 161 4431162.

   ISSN 1188-3383
DD 004.6   CN
COMPUTING & COMMUNICATIONS NEWSLETTER. [Comput. commun. newsl.]. **Added/Corp** University of Toronto. Computing and Communications Dept. **VAT** Computing and Communications Newsletter (Toronto). (Fall 1991)-. Newsletter. English. Four times a year. Free. University of Toronto Planning and Coordination, 4th Floor, 215 Huron Street, Toronto Ontario M5S 1A1 Canada.

   ISSN 1184-7557
DD 004   CN
COMPUTING & COMMUNICATIONS NEWSLETTER. [Comput. commun. newsl.]. **Main/Corp** Memorial University of Newfoundland. Dept. of Computing and Communications. **VAT** Computing and Commmunications Newsletter. Vol. 5, No. 2 (Winter 1990/91)-. Newsletter. English. Four times a year. Memorial University of Newfoundland / Department of Computing and Communication, Newsletter Editor, Henrietta Harvey Building, St. John's Newfoundland A1C 5S7 Canada. **Continues** Computing Services Newsletter., 0843-2902.

   ISSN 0748-3104
DD 384   US
COMUNICACIONES (CORAL GABLES, FLA.). (COMUNICACIONES.). [Comunicaciones]. (19??)-. Trade Publication. Spanish. Four times a year. $30.00. Latcom Incorporated, 9200 South Dadeland Boulevard, Suite 309, Miami FL 33156. **Tel** (305)660-9444. **ED** Thomas E. Will. **Bk Rev**. **Ad Acc**. **Circ:** 12,000 (ctrl).
Desc: Telecommunication and computer magazine. Edited for senior level managers and engineers in Central and South America, and also the Caribbean.

   ISSN 1052-6226
DD 005   US
DATAPRO COMPETITIVE EDGE IN COMMUNICATIONS, THE. (THE DATAPRO COMPETITIVE EDGE IN COMMUNICATIONS [COMPUTER FILE].). [Datapro compet. edge commun.]. (1990)-. Periodical. English. Twelve times a year. $5,000.00. Datapro Information Services Group, 600 Delran Parkway, Delran NJ 08075. **Tel** (609)764-0100, (800)328-2776, FAX (609)764-8953.
Desc: System requirements: IBM AT, AT or compatible, 640K memory, 2MB hard disk, CD-ROM drive.

UK
TITLE CHANGE
DATAPRO REPORTS ON INTERNATIONAL COMMUNICATIONS SOFTWARE. (19??)-(19??). English. Datapro International, McGraw Hill House, Shoppenhangers Road, Maidenhead Berkshire SL6 2QL United Kingdom. **Tel** 011 44 1628 773277, FAX 011 44 1628 773628. (**Subscription address:** Datapro Research Corporation, 600 Delran Parkway, Delran NJ 08075.) **Merged into** LANs and Internetworking.

LC AI   **ISSN** 0838-3189
DD 016   CN
DSI. DIFFUSION SELECTIVE DE L'INFORMATION. (DSI, DIFFUSION SELECTIVE DE L'INFORMATION.). [DSI, Diffus. s,el. inf.]. **Added/Corp** Services Documentaires Multimedia. **VFOAT** Diffusion Selective de l'Information, DSI. (1988)-. Monographic series. French. Irregular. Services Documentaires Multimedia Inc, 75 rue de Port-Royal, Suite 300, Montreal Quebec H3L 3T1 Canada. **Tel** (514)382-0895, FAX (514)384-9139. **Continues** DSI/CB., 0825-5024.

LC P95.8   **ISSN** 1062-9424
DD 384   US
EFFECTOR ONLINE. (EFFECTOR ONLINE [COMPUTER FILE].). [Eff. online]. **Added/Corp** Electronic Frontier Foundation. (May 1, 1991)-. Periodical. English. Irregular (roughly biweekly). Free. Electronic Frontier Foundation, 1667 K Street Northwest, Suite 801, Washington DC 20006-1605. **Tel** (202)861-7700, FAX (202)861-1258. available via Internet (effector-online-request@eff.org). **Continues** EFF News.
Desc: Online publication of the Electronic Frontier Foundation.

   ISSN 1072-1959
   US
●**ELECTRONIC MESSAGING UPDATE.** (ELECTRONIC MESSAGING UPDATE : THE JOURNAL OF THE ELECTRONIC MESSAGING ASSOCIATION.). **Added/Corp** Electronic Messaging Association. **VFOAT** Journal of the Electronic Messaging Association. (1993)-. Periodical. English. Six times a year. $95.00. Electronic Messaging Association, 1655 North Fort Meyer Drive, Suite 850, Arlington VA 22209.

   ISSN 1069-9392
   US
●**ELECTRONIC SUPER-HIGHWAY.** **VFOAT** Electronic Super Highway. (1994)-. Periodical. English. Twelve times a year. $38.00. Donald F. Eddy & Stephen Kirk Boulter, 3377 Blake Street, No. 207, Denver CO 80205.

   ISSN 1074-1119
DD 384   UK
●**EUROPEAN INTERACTIVE MULTIMEDIA.** [Eur. interact. multimed.]. No. 1 (Nov. 17, 1993)-. Newsletter. English. Twelve times a year. $595.00. Kagan World Media Inc., 126 Clock Tower Place, Carmel CA 93923-8734. **Tel** (408)624-1536, FAX (408)625-3225. (**Subscription address:** Kagan World Media Ltd., 524 Fulham Road, London SW6 5NR United Kingdom. **Tel** 011 44 171 3718880, FAX 011 44 171 3718715.) available via fax.
Desc: Covers all facets of the convergence of computers, consumer electronics, communications, cable TV and content providers in Europe. Features exclusive growth projections, economic modeling and analysis of new technologies.

US
FAULKNER COMPUTER AND COMMUNICATIONS LIBRARY. (19??)-. Periodical. English. One time a year. $7240.00 US; $8270.00 Canada; $9230.00 other. Faulkner Technical Reports, 7905 Browning Road, Suite 114, Pennsauken NJ 08109. **Tel** (800)843-0460.

LC JK468.A8 F42   **ISSN** 1057-5804
DD 353.04/0285   US
FEDERAL ADP AND TELECOMMUNICATIONS STANDARDS INDEX. [Fed. ADP telecommun. stand. index]. **Added/Corp** United States. General Services Administration. Information Resources Management Service. **VAT** Federal automated data processing and telecommunications standards index. (19??)-. Government Publication. English. Two times a year. $19.00. Superintendent of Documents, US Government Printing Office, Washington DC 20402. **Tel** (202)275-3328, FAX (202)786-2377. **Continues** ADP and Telecommunication Standards Index.
Desc: Contains revised standards requirements statements that were formerly printed in the Federal Information Resources Management Regulations.

   ISSN 1062-4538
   US
FERRIS E-MAIL UPDATE. **Added/Corp** Ferris Networks. **VFOAT** Ferris E Mail Update. (1992)-. Periodical. English. Twelve times a year. $395.00. Ferris Networks, 353 Sacramento Street #600, San Francisco CA 94111. **Tel** (415)986-1414.

   ISSN 0255-030X
DD 001.64/05   CN
HANDI-COMMUNICATIONS. [Handi-commun.]. **Added/Corp** University of Western Ontario. Dept. of Computer Science. International Federation for Information Processing. International Computer Message Services. Vol. 1, No. 1 (Winter 1984)-. Periodical. English. Four times a year. Handi-Communications, Department of Computer Science Ontario, London Ontario N6A 5B7 Canada.

LC TK
DD 384.1   GW
●**INFO-SYS JOURNAL.** (1994)-. Trade Publication. English. Six times a year. Dekotec GmbH, Gasstrasse 18, Haus 1, 22761 Hamburg Germany. **Tel** 011 49 40 891027, FAX 011 49 40 896069. **ED** J. Fandrey. **Circ:** 10,000.

   ISSN 0924-3461
   FR
INFORMATION, COMPUTER, COMMUNICATIONS POLICY. See Computers.

   ISSN 1078-6589
DD 384   US
●**INFORMATION SUPERHIGHWAYS.** See Computers-Computer Networks.

US
INSIDE REPORT ON NEW MEDIA. (19??)-. English. Twelve times a year. $195.00. HyperMedia Communications, 901 Mariner's Island Boulevard, Suite 365, San Mateo CA 94404. **Tel** (415)573-5170. **Continues** Bove and Rhodes Report on Desktop Publishing & Multimedia.

LC TK6687 .I57   **ISSN** 1047-5265
DD 070.1/95   US
INTERACT JOURNAL. (INTERACT JOURNAL : CREATING A FORUM FOR INTERACTIVE VIDEO COMMUNICATION.). [Interact j.]. **Added/Corp** International Interactive Communications Society. **VFOAT** IICS Journal; IICS. Vol. 1 (Winter 1988/89)-. Periodical. English. Irregular. free to members of the International Interactive Communications Society. IICS National Headquarters, 2120 Steiner Street, San Francisco CA 94115.

   ISSN 1067-3156
DD 621   US
INTERACTIVE MULTIMEDIA NEWS. [Interact. multimed. news]. **Added/Corp** Interactive Multimedia Association. (1992)-. Periodical. English. Six times a year. IMA Compatibility Project Headquarters, 9 Randall Court, Annapolis MD 21401. **Continues** Interactive Industry News, 1051-273X.

   ISSN 1075-5276
DD 338   US
INTERNATIONAL ISDN YELLOW PAGES. See Computers-Computer Networks.

LC TK5105.5 .I5743   **ISSN** 1055-7148
DD 004.6/05   UK
   CCC
   CODEN INMTEU
INTERNATIONAL JOURNAL OF NETWORK MANAGEMENT. [Int. j. netw. manage.]. Vol. 1, No. 1 (Sept. 1991)-. Periodical. English. Six times a year. $335.00. John Wiley & Sons Ltd., Baffins Lane, Chichester, West Sussex PO19 1UD United Kingdom. **Tel** 011 44 1243 779777, FAX 011 44 1243 776128 BTG:JWP001, telex 86290 WIBOOKG. (**Subscription address:** John Wiley & Sons, Inc. / Philadelphia, PO Box 7247, Philadelphia PA 19170. **Tel** (212)850-6645, (800)225-5945.) **ED** Gilbert Held. **Ad Acc**. available on microfilm and microfiche from University Microfilms International (UMI).
Desc: Dedicated to the dissemination of practical information which enables readers to better manage, operate and maintain communications networks. Articles and columns for the journal are selected with the intent to facilitate the reader's evaluation of equipment and systems, to provide a detailed understanding of performance issues, and to discuss the advantages and disadvantages of a variety of networking approaches that

can be used to satisfy an organization's communications requirements.
Ind/Abst Curr. Cit.

US
●INTERNET CONNECTION, THE. Vol. 1, Issue 1 (Jan. 1995)-. Periodical. English. Ten times a year. $69.00. Bernan Associates, 4611-F Assembly Drive, Lanham MD 20706-4391. **Tel** (301)459-7666, (800)274-4447 US, (800)233-0504 CANADA, FAX (301)459-0056, telex 7108260418.

LC TK5105.875.I57 H34
DD 621.382 US
●INTERNET YELLOW PAGES, THE. (1994)-. Directory. English. One time a year. $27.95. Osborne and Associates Inc., 2600 Tenth Street, Berkeley CA 94710. **Tel** (800)227-0900, (800)262-4729, (510)548-4805.

LC QA75 **ISSN** 0735-1844
DD 004 US
CCC
ISDN (BROOKLINE, MASS.). See Computers-Computer Networks.

ISSN 1080-2991
DD 004 US
●ISDN FOR SMALL BUSINESS. See Computers-Computer Networks.

US
ISDN INFORMATION SOURCEBOOK. See Computers-Computer Networks.

ISSN 0899-9554
DD 384 UK
CCC
ISDN NEWS. See Computers-Computer Networks.

ISSN 1058-7470
DD 004 US
TITLE CHANGE
ISDN USER MAGAZINE. See Computers-Computer Networks.

ISSN 1078-1005
DD 004 US
ISDN USER NEWSLETTER. See Computers-Computer Networks.

LC QA75 **ISSN** 1058-7306
DD 004 SZ
CCC
JAPANESE TECHNOLOGY REVIEWS. SECTION B, COMPUTERS AND COMMUNICATION. [Jpn. technol. rev., Sect. B Comput. commun.]. **VFOAT** Computers and Communication. (19??)-. Periodical. English. Four times a year. $185.00 (academic institutions), $289.00 (corporate institutions). Gordon & Breach Science Publishers, Inc., PO Box 786, Cooper Station, New York NY 10276. **Tel** (212)206-8900, FAX (212)645-2459. ***Continues in part*** *Japanese Technology Reviews, 0898-5693.*

LC HE **ISSN** 1083-6101
DD 384 US
JOURNAL OF COMPUTER-MEDIATED COMMUNICATION. (JOURNAL OF COMPUTER-MEDIATED COMMUNICATION [COMPUTER FILE] : JCMC.). [J. comput.-mediat. commun.]. **Added/Corp** Annenberg School of Communications (University of Southern California). **VFOAT** JCMC; Journal of Computer Mediated Communication. Vol. 1, No. 1 (June 1995)-. Periodical. English. Four times a year. available via Internet (http://www.huji.ac.il/www_jcmc/jcmc.html).
Desc: Covers topics such as privacy, economics and social policy issues relevant to the use of computer-mediated communication.

CN
LIEN MULTIMEDIA. (19??)-. English. Irregular. 79.23Can$. Multimediadialog Inc, 1131 rue Rachel, Montreal Quebec H2J 2J6 Canada.

UK
MONITOR. See Computers-Online Computing and Information.

ISSN 1075-234X
US
CCC
●MULTIMEDIA AND TECHNOLOGY LICENSING LAW REPORT. (1994)-. Periodical. English. Twelve times a year. $203.25. Warren Gorham & Lamont Inc., Park Square Building, 31 St. James Avenue, Boston MA 02116-4112. **Tel** (617)423-2020, (800)950-1207, FAX (617)423-2026.

ISSN 0942-4962
GW
CCC
CODEN MUSYEW
●MULTIMEDIA SYSTEMS. Added/Corp Association for Computing Machinery. Vol. 1, No. 1 (June 1993)-. Periodical. English. Six times a year. $281.00. Springer-Verlag GmbH & Company KG, Heidelberger Platz 3, D-14197 Berlin Germany. **Tel** 011 49 30 8207223, FAX 011 49 30 8214091, telex 183 319 SPBLN D. **(Subscription address:** Springer-Verlag New York Inc. / North America, PO Box 2485, Journal Fulfillment, Secaucus NJ 07096. **Tel** (201)348-4033, (800)777-4643, FAX (201)348-4505.**)**

ISSN 1043-4143
DD 384 US
NATIONAL DIRECTORY OF ADDRESSES AND TELEPHONE NUMBERS (MARINA DEL REY, CALIF.), THE. (THE NATIONAL DIRECTORY OF ADDRESSES AND TELEPHONE NUMBERS [COMPUTER FILE].). [Natl. dir. addresses teleph. numbers]. **Added/Corp** Xiphias (Firm). (1989)-. Directory. English. One time a year. $198.50. Xiphias, Helms Hall, 8758 Venice Boulevard, Los Angeles CA 90034. **Tel** (310)841-2790, FAX (310)841-2559.
Desc: This CD-ROM includes over 120,000 listings of the most useful and important addresses, telephone numbers and FAX numbers throughout the world.

ISSN 1080-2681
US
●NET (GREENSBORO, N.C.), THE. (THE NET.). (1995)-. Periodical. English. Twelve times a year. $24.95. Imagine Publishing Inc., 1350 Old Bayshore Highway, Suite 210, Burlingame CA 94010. **Tel** (415)696-1688, FAX (415)696-1678.

ISSN 1080-3971
US
●NETWARE/INTERNET EXCHANGE. (1995)-. Periodical. English. Twelve times a year. $149.00. IDG Newsletter Corporation, 77 Franklin Street, Suite 310, Boston MA 02110. **Tel** (617)482-8470, (800)807-0771, FAX (617)338-0164. **(Subscription address:** IDG Newsletters, PO Box 145, Oxon Hill MD 20750. **Tel** (800)549-9494.**)**

LC Z278 **ISSN** 1356-5702
DD 070.5 UK
●OASIS. See Publishing.

US
●OFFICIAL INTERNET WORLD INTERNET YELLOW PAGES. (1995)-. English. One time a year. $39.99. Mecklermedia Corporation, 11 Ferry Lane West, Westport CT 06880. **Tel** (203)226-6967, (800)632-5537, FAX (203)454-5840. ***Continues*** *Internet Worlds on Internet.*

ISSN 1077-4696
DD 384 UK
CCC
●PHILLIPS BUSINESS INFORMATION'S COMMUNICATIONS STANDARDS NEWS. [Phillips Bus. Inf. commun. stand. news]. **Added/Corp** Phillips Business Information, Inc. **VFOAT** Communications Standards News. Transmission 179 (July 13, 1994)-. Periodical. English. Twenty-five times a year (biweekly). $497.00. Omnicom PPI Limited, (A Phillips Business Information company), Forum Chambers, The Forum Stevenage Hertfordshire SG1 1EL United Kingdom. **Tel** 011 44 1438 742424, FAX 011 44 1438 740154. **ED** John W. Lilley. ***Absorbed*** *Open Systems Communication, 0741-2851.*
Desc: Covers TCP/IP, LANs, WANs, multimedia, wireless, and open systems communication.

ISSN 1055-9051
DD 384 US
PIPELINE (ST. PAUL, MINN.). (PIPELINE [COMPUTER FILE] : THE NEWSLETTER OF THE INDEPENDENT MEDIA DISTRIBUTORS ALLIANCE.). [Pipeline]. **Added/Corp** Independent Media Distributors Alliance. Vol. 1, 1 (Fall 1990)-. Newsletter. English. Four times a year. Free. The Independent Media Alliance, c/o ArtBase, PO Box 2154, St Paul MN 55102.
Desc: Available from INTERNET.

LC TK5103.7 .I57a **ISSN** 1015-8057
DD 621.382 SZ
PROCEEDINGS / INTERNATIONAL ZURICH SEMINAR ON DIGITAL COMMUNICATIONS. [Proc. - Int. ZÈurich Semin. Digit. Commun.]. **Added/Corp** Eidgenossische Technische Hochschule. (Mar. 1974)-. Proceedings. English. Irregular. IEEE / Institute of Electrical and Electronics Engineers Inc., 345 East 47th Street, New York NY 10017-2394. **Tel** (908)981-1393, FAX (908)981-9667. ***Continues*** *International Zurich Seminar on Integrated Systems for Speech, Video, and Data Communications. Proceedings, 1015-8057.*
Desc: Information on digital communications and integrated services digital networks.

ISSN 1056-750X
DD 658 US
PURCHASING PERFORMANCE BENCHMARKS FOR THE U.S. COMPUTER AND TELECOMMUNICATIONS EQUIPMENT INDUSTRY. [Purch. perform. benchmarks U. S. comput. telecommun. equip. ind.]. **Added/Corp** Center for Advanced Purchasing Studies. (1991)-. Trade Publication. English. Free. Center for Advanced Purchasing Studies, PO Box 22160, Tempe AZ 85285. **Tel** (602)752-2277.

LC HE8220.2 .A3 **ISSN** 1077-4653
DD 384/.0947/05 US
●RUSSIA ONLINE AND WIRELESS. [Russ. online wirel.]. **VFOAT** Russia Online; ROL. Vol. 1, No. 1 (July 1994)-. Newsletter. English. Twelve times a year. $350.00. Gist, Inc., 2200 Wilson Boulevard, Suite 102-G, Arlington VA 22201. **Tel** (703)527-7459, FAX (703)528-1477. **ED** Michael Peil. Index available.

LC HE8081 **ISSN** 0775-2857
DD 384.094 BE
UDC 654
TECH-EUROPE ED. FRANCAISE. (19??)-. Periodical. French. Eleven times a year. 19300.00F. Europe Information Service, rue de Geneve 6, 1140 Brussels Belgium. **Tel** 011 32 2 242 6020, FAX 011 32 2 242 9549. **Bk Rev.** available on an online database from Lexis-Nexis; available on CD-ROM.
Desc: Provides information on European activities and decisions in the field of information and telecommunications technology.

NE
Pr Rev.
●TELETRAFFIC SCIENCE AND ENGINEERING. See Computers-Computer Networks.

NE
TELINDUS NEWS. (19??)-. Dutch. Four times a year. Free on request. Telindus BV Networks, Savannaweg 19, PO Box 9559, 3542 AW Utrecht Netherlands. **Tel** 011 31 30 477711, FAX 011 31 30 410560. ctrl circ.
Desc: Provides news on the latest developments in the telecom industry.

US
U.S. TELECOMMUNICATIONS. See Communications-Telecommunication.

US
VIDEODISC BOOK, THE. (1984)-. English. One time a year. John Wiley & Sons, Inc., 605 Third Avenue, New York NY 10158-0012. **Tel** (212)850-6000, (212)850-6645, FAX (212)850-6088, telex 12-7063. **(Subscription address:** John Wiley & Sons / UK, Baffins Lane, Chichester, West Sussex PO19 1UD United Kingdom. **Tel** 011 44 1243 779777, FAX 011 44 243 776128, telex 86290 WIBOOKG.**)**

ISSN 0886-2087
DD 006 US
VOICE NEWS. (VOICENEWS.). [Voice news]. **VFOAT** Voice News. **VAT** Voice News. (19??)-. Periodical. English. Twelve times a year. $297.00. Stoneridge Technical Services, PO Box 1891, Rockville MD 20849. **Tel** (301)424-0114, FAX (301)424-8971. **ED** Bill Creitz. Index available. cum. index.
Desc: Information on voice mail, response and speech synthesis.

LC WMLC 93/4041 TK7882.S65 .V65 **ISSN** 1042-0460
DD 006 US
CCC
TITLE CHANGE
VOICE PROCESSING MAGAZINE. [Voice process. mag.]. **VFOAT** Voice Processing; VPM; Information Publishing Corporation's Voice Processing Magazine. Vol. 1, No. 1 (1st. Quarter, 1989)-(199?). Trade Publication. English. Advanstar Communications Inc., 131 West First Street, Duluth MN 55802. **Tel** (218)723-9477, (800)346-0085, FAX (218)723-9437. **ED** Patrick Cassidy. **Ad Acc, Adv Mgr:** Webster. **Circ:** 25,000. ***Continues*** *InfoText, 1043-3694.* ***Continued by*** *Enterprise Communications.*
Desc: Covers applications of computer, telephone integration, and voice automation. It also covers products, services, applications and benefits of voice mail and messaging, voice response, call processing, voice recognition, speech synthesis, text to speech, voice/data networking, service bureaus, and more.

ISSN 1056-4977
US
WIRELESS COMPUTING. (1991)-. Periodical. English. Twenty-six times a year. $495.00. Waters Information Services, PO Box 2248, Binghamton NY 13902-2248. **Tel** (607)770-8535, FAX (607)798-1692.

US
●WIRELESS MEDIA & MESSAGING. (Jan. 1993)-. English. Twelve times a year. $347.00 US and Canada; $367.00 other. Probe Research Inc., Three Wing Drive, Suite 240, Cedar Knolls NJ 07927-1000. **Tel** (201)285-1500, FAX (201)285-1519.
Desc: Coverage of devices, networks and applications in the areas of personal communications, integration of voice, data, facsimile and video, WLANs, CPE, modems, and software. Also includes major players and market potential.

POSTAL COMMUNICATIONS

ADMINISTRATIVE SUPPORT MANUAL.
Main/Corp United States Postal Service. (June 1979)-. Government Publication. English. Irregular. Price varies. Superintendent of Documents, US Government Printing Office, Washington DC 20402. **Tel** (202)275-3328, FAX (202)786-2377. **Supersedes in part** United States Postal Service. Postal Service Manual.
Desc: Describes matters of internal administration in the Postal Service. Includes functional statements, and policies and requirements regarding security, communications (printing, directives, forms, records, newsletters), government relations, procurement and supply, data processing systems, maintenance and engineering.

LC HE6187 .A25   ISSN 0739-0939
US

AIRPOST JOURNAL, THE. Added/Corp
American Air Mail Society. Vol. 1 No. 1 (Nov. 20, 1929)-. Periodical. English. Twelve times a year. $20.00. American Airmail Society, PO Box 110, Mineola NY 11501. **Tel** (516)746-5543. **ED** James W. Grave, (editor's address: East 11911 Conner Road., Valleyford, WA 99036; (telephone: (509)924-4484). Index available. cum. index. **Bk Rev. Ad Acc, Adv Mgr:** S. Solart, **Tel** (215)949-1548. **Circ:** 2,000.
Desc: News and information on air mail stamps, flown covers and air mail history.

LC HE6499 .A64   ISSN 0044-7811
DD 331.881/1/3830973   US

AMERICAN POSTAL WORKER, THE. See
Business and Economics-Labor.

LC NC1870 .A53   ISSN 0145-3920
DD 741.68/3/075   US

AMERICAN POSTCARD JOURNAL.
VFOAT American Post Card Journal; APCJ. Vol. 1, No. 1 (Sept./Oct. 1975)-. Periodical. English. American Postcard Journal, PO Box 526, West Haven CT 06516.
Absorbed Picture Postcard News, 0884-1640.

CN
ANNUAL REPORT. English. Post Office Department, Sir Alexander Campbell Building, Confederation Heights, Ottawa Ontario K1A 0B1 Canada.

LC HE7183 .A25A   ISSN 0256-8535
DD 354.56450087/3/06   CY

ANNUAL REPORT OF THE DEPARTMENT OF POSTAL SERVICES (CYPRUS). Main/Corp Cyprus. Tmema Tachydromeion. English. One time a year. **Continues** Annual Report of the Department of Posts.

US
ANNUAL REPORT OF THE POSTMASTER GENERAL. Main/Corp United States Postal Service. Fiscal Year (1989)-. English. US Postal Service / Washington, 475 l'Enfant Plaza West SW, Washington DC 20260-0010. **Continues** United States Postal Service. Annual Report of the United States Postal Service.

LC HE6995 .A7   ISSN 0003-8989
DD 383.49   GW
TITLE CHANGE

ARCHIV FUER DEUTSCHE POSTGESCHICHTE. [Arch. dtsch. Postgesch.]. **Added/Corp** Gesellschaft fur Deutsche Postgeschichte. (1953)-(1994). Periodical. German. Gesellschaft fur Deutsche Postgeschichte, Schaumainkai 53, D-60596 Frankfurt Germany. **Tel** 011 49 69 611040. Index available. cum. index. **Circ:** 63,000. **Continued by** Post- und Telekommunikationsgeschichte.
Ind/Abst Am. Hist. Life (1989-).

LC HE6363.A6 A74
DD 383/.145   US

ARIZONA AND NEW MEXICO ZIP+4 STATE DIRECTORY. Added/Corp United States Postal Service. Address Information Systems Division. United States Postal Service. Office of Address Information Systems. United States Postal Service. Customer and Automation Services Dept. **VFOAT** Arizona, New Mexico Zip+4 State Directory; Zip+4 State Directory. Arizona, New Mexico. **VAT** Arizona, New Mexico Zip Plus Four State Directory. (1985)-. Directory. English. One time a year. St Louis PDC, Zip+4 State Directory Orders, PO Box 14921, St. Louis MO 63180-9988.

ISSN 0744-4540
DD 769   US

BARR'S POST CARD NEWS. [Barr's post card news]. **VFOAT** Barr's News. (19??)-. Trade Publication. English. One time a week. $29.00. Barr's Post Card News, 70 South Sixth Street, Lansing IA 52151. **Tel** (319)538-4500. **ED** Bill Cote. **Bk Rev. Ad Acc. Circ:** 5,000.

Desc: All the facts about post cards and other American paper. Includes post card news, articles, mail auctions, calendar of events, classified advertising and sales.

LC HE6811 .A47
DD 383   AG

BOLETIN DE LA SECRETARIA DE ESTADO DE COMUNICACIONES.
Main/Corp Argentine Republic. Secretaria de Estado de Comunicaciones. (19??)-. Spanish. Secretaria de Estado de Comunicaciones, Buenos Aires Argentina. **Continues** Argentine Republic. Subsecretaria de Comunicaciones. Boletin.

IT
BOLLETTINO UFFICIALE PT- PART 2.
(19??)-. Italian. Twenty-four times a year. L75000.00. AMM Ptd CPA Prov Abb, Pubbl Serv Vle Europa 175, 00144 Rome Italy.

ISSN 0701-0575
DD 331.88/11/38340971   CN

BULLETIN - C P A A C M P A. Main/Corp
Canadian Postmasters and Assistants Association. Vol. 1, No. 6 (May 1976)-. Bulletin. English (French). Twelve times a year. Free. Canadian Postmasters and Assistants Association, Suite 1204 130 Albert Street, Ottawa Ontario K1P 5AG4 Canada. ctrl circ. **Continues** Canadian Postmasters Association. Bulletin, 0701-0567.

ISSN 1240-2095
UDC 656   FR

●CAHIERS DE L'IREPP, LES. [Cah. IREPP].
VFOAT Cahiers de l'Institut de Recherche, d'Etudes et de Prospective Postales. (1992)-. Periodical. French. IREPP, 52 56 Avenue de la Croix Nivert, 75015 Paris France. **Tel** 011 33 1 45579686. **Continues** Bulletin de l'IREPP, 0994-3749.

US
CALIFORNIA ZIP+4 STATE DIRECTORY.
Added/Corp United States Postal Service. Address Information Systems Division. United States Postal Service. Office of Address Information Systems. United States Postal Service. Customer Service Support.
VFOAT California ZIP Plus Four State Directory; ZIP Plus Four State Directory. California; California State Directory; ZIP+4 State Directory. California. **VAT** California Zip Plus Four State Directory. (1985)-. English. One time a year. St Louis PDC, Zip+4 State Directory Orders, PO Box 14921, St. Louis MO 63180-9988.

CN
CANADA POSTAL GUIDE. Main/Corp
Canada. Post Office Department. English. Twelve times a year. 50.00Can$. National Philatelic Centre, Canada Postal Corporation, Station 1, Antigonish Nova Scotia B2G 2R8 Canada. **Tel** (902)863-6550, (800)565-4362, FAX (902)863-6796.

US
CL PACE REPORT. (19??)-. Newsletter. English. Twelve times a year. $75.00. CL Pace Associates, 36 Henry Austin Drive, Wilton CT 06897. **Tel** (203)834-0533, FAX (203)834-0207. **ED** Charles Pace. **Circ:** 300.
Desc: Postal affairs newsletter.

ISSN 1193-7238
DD 769.56971   CN

CMS BULLETIN (OTTAWA). (CMS BULLETIN / BULLETIN DU SMS.). [CMS bull.]. **Added/Corp** Canada Post Corporation. CMS Group. **VFOAT** Bulletin du SMS; Bulletin CMS/SMS. **VAT** Corporate Manual System Bulletin; Bulletin du Systeme du Manuel de la Societe. Vol. 71, No. 22 (Sept. 14, 1992)-. Periodical. English (French). Canada Post Corporation, 2701 Riverside Dr, Suite N0621, Ottawa Ontario K1A 0B1 Canada. **Tel** (613)734-7638. **Continues** Canada. Post Office Dept. Bulletin - Canada Post. Bulletin - Postes Canada., 0708-0646.

US
COLORADO ZIP+4 STATE DIRECTORY.
Added/Corp United States Postal Service. Address Information Systems Division. United States Postal Service. Office of Address Information Systems. United States Postal Service. Customer and Automation Services Dept. United States Postal Service. Customer Service Support. **VFOAT** Colorado ZIP Plus Four State Directory; ZIP Plus Four State Directory. Colorado; Colorado State Directory; ZIP+4 State Directory. Colorado. **VAT** Colorado Zip Plus Four State Directory. (1985)-. Directory. English. One time a year. St Louis PDC, Zip+4 State Directory Orders, PO Box 14921, St. Louis MO 63180-9988.

LC HE6311 .C65   ISSN 0882-8970
DD 383/.4973   US

COMPETITORS AND COMPETITION OF THE U.S. POSTAL SERVICE. [Compet. compet. U.S. Post. Serv.]. **Added/Corp** United States Postal Service. Marketing Dept. Marketing Services Branch. United States Postal Service. Marketing Services Division. **VAT** Competitors and Competition of the United States Postal Service. (19??)-. English. Every 2 years.

United States Postal Service Marketing Services Division, Office of Commercial Marketing Customer Services Department, Washington DC 20260.

ISSN 1140-7581
UDC 771   FR

COURRIER PROFESSIONNEL PARIS, LE. (1969)-. Periodical. French. Four times a year. 160.00F. Kodak Pathe M Labonde, 26 rue Villiot, 75594 Paris Cedex 12 France. **Tel** 011 33 1 40013714. **Continues** Courrier Professionnel Kodak (Paris), 1140-7573.

LC HE6009.I5 A32   ISSN 0011-5762
II

DAK TAR. (1???)-. Periodical. English. Twelve times a year. $6.00. Office of Director-General of Posts & Telegraphs, New Delhi India.

LC HE6723 .D57
DD 383/.025/7287   PN

DIRECTORIO POSTAL DE PANAMA.
Added/Corp Correo Nacional de Panama. (19??)-. Spanish. One time a year. El Cangrejo, Cl 59 San Felipe Urbanizacion Obarrio, Edificio Yasa, 2do piso Oficina 1, Apartado 9-103, Zona 9 Panama. **Tel** 63-5190. Index available. **Ad Acc. Circ:** 50,000 (ctrl).
Desc: An alphabetical and numerical list of subscribers to post boxes in the entire Republic of Panama. Lists with information and advertisements of the subscribers of commercial post boxes of Panama.

LC HE6656.O5 D5
DD 383/.14   CN

DIRECTORY : EASTERN ONTARIO, POSTAL CODE. VFOAT Repertoire: Est de l'Ontario, Code Postal; Eastern Ontario, Postal Code. Directory. Multiple languages (English and French). Information Canada, 171 Slater Street, Ottawa Ontario K1A 0S9 Canada. **Tel** (819)997-1095.

LC HE6656.O5 D53   ISSN 0317-4271
DD 383/.14   CN

DIRECTORY. ONTARIO POSTAL REGION. POSTAL CODE. (POSTAL CODE DIRECTORY: ONTARIO POSTAL REGION. CODE POSTAL, REPERTOIRE: REGION POSTALE DE L'ONTARIO.). **Added/Corp** Canada. Post Office Dept. **VFOAT** Code Postal, Repertoire : Region Postale de l'Ontario. (19??)-. English (French). One time a year (11.00Can$). Free. National Philatelic Centre, Canada Postal Corporation, Station 1, Antigonish Nova Scotia B2G 2R8 Canada. **Tel** (902)863-6550, (800)565-4362, FAX (902)863-6796.

LC HE6653 .C35   ISSN 0835-4693
CN

DIRECTORY. POSTAL CODE. (CANADA'S POSTAL CODE DIRECTORY.). **VFOAT** Repertoire des Codes Postaux au Canada; Postal Code Directory. (1987)-. Directory. English (French). One time a year (May). 11.20Can$. National Philatelic Centre, Canada Postal Corporation, Station 1, Antigonish Nova Scotia B2G 2R8 Canada. **Tel** (902)863-6550, (800)565-4362, FAX (902)863-6796. **Ad Acc. Circ:** 500,000. available on CD-ROM; available on microfiche.

LC HE6311 A312 HE6376.W3
DD 383/.145   US

DISTRICT OF COLUMBIA VIRGINIA ZIP+4 STATE DIRECTORY. VFOAT Zip Plus Four State Directory. **VAT** District of Columbia, Virginia Zip Plus Four State Directory. 1985-. Directory. English. One time a year. St Louis PDC, Zip+4 State Directory Orders, PO Box 14921, St. Louis MO 63180-9988. available on microfiche (Vols. for (1987-) distributed to depository libraries).

US
DOMESTIC AIR SERVICE INSTRUCTIONS. Main/Corp United States Postal Service. (1980)-. English. US Postal Service / Washington, 475 l'Enfant Plaza West SW, Washington DC 20260-0010.

LC Discard HE6311 .A355   ISSN 1058-0867
DD 383   US
CODEN DMUSD4

DOMESTIC MAIL MANUAL. [Domest. mail man.]. **Main/Corp** United States Postal Service. **VFOAT** DMM. July (1979)-. Government Publication. English. Four times a year. $47.00. US Postal Service / Washington, 475 l'Enfant Plaza West SW, Washington DC 20260-0010. **(Subscription address:** Superintendent of Documents, US Government Printing Office, Washington DC 20402.
Desc: Designed to assist customers in obtaining maximum benefits from domestic postal services. Includes applicable regulations and information about rates and postage, classes of mail, special services, wrapping and mailing requirements, and collection and delivery services.

Communications —Postal Communications

LC HE7351 .A25c
DD 354.680072/2253 SA
ESTIMATES OF ADDITIONAL EXPENDITURE - DEPARTMENT OF POSTS AND TELECOMMUNICATIONS.
Main/Corp South Africa. Dept. of Posts and Telecommunications. **Added/Corp** South Africa. Dept. of Posts and Telecommunications. Begroting van Addisionele Uitgawe. **VFOAT** Begroting van Addisionele Uitgawe - Departement van Pos- en Telekommunikasiewese. (19??)-. Afrikaans (English). Government Printer / South Africa, Bosman Street, Private Bag X85, Pretoria 0001 South Africa. **Tel** 011 27 12 3239731 ext. 262.

US
SUSPENDED
FINANCIAL MANAGEMENT MANUAL.
Main/Corp United States Postal Service. (Sept. 29, 1978)-(19??). English. Irregular (supplements). $27.00 US; $33.75 other. United States Postal Service, 475 l'Enfant Plaza SW, Washington DC 20260-0010. **Tel** (202)245-4000, FAX (202)268-4980, telex 892314. **Supersedes in part** United States Postal Service. Postal Service Manual.
Desc: Presents an overview of the financial activities of the Postal Service. It summarizes the following topics: general accounting, post office accounting, accounts receivable and accounts payable, budget and planning, payroll accounting and control of assets.

US
FLORIDA ZIP+4 STATE DIRECTORY.
Added/Corp United States Postal Service. Address Information Systems Division. United States Postal Service. Office of Address Information Systems. United States Postal Service. Customer and Automation Services Dept. United States Postal Service. Customer Service Support. **VFOAT** Florida ZIP Plus Four State Directory; ZIP Plus Four State Directory. Florida; Florida State Directory; ZIP+4 State Directory. Florida. **VAT** Florida Zip Plus Four State Directory. (1985)-. Directory. English. One time a year. St Louis PDC, Zip+4 State Directory Orders, PO Box 14921, St. Louis MO 63180-9988.

LC HE6971 .A94A
DD 354.4360087/4/06 AU
GESCHAFTSBERICHT. **Main/Corp** Austria.
Generaldirektion fur die Post und Telegraphenverwaltung. **VFOAT** Annual Report. English (English). One time a year.

LC HE7276.T6 T64a
JA
GYOMU GAIYO. **Main/Corp** Tokyo Chuo
Yubinkyoku. (19??)-. Academic Scholarly Publication. Japanese. One time a year. Miyazaki Prefectural Government / Environmental Health Division, 10-1 Tachibana doori Higashi, 2-chome Miyazakishi, Miyazakiken 880 Japan. **(Subscription address:** Japan Publications Trading Company Ltd., PO Box 5030, Tokyo International, Tokyo 100-31 Japan. **Tel** 011 81 3 3292 3753.) Documents available from CASDDS.
Ind/Abst Chem. Abstr.

LC HE7276.H63 J36a
JA
HOKURIKU YUSEIKYOKU TOKEI
NEMPO. Main/Corp Japan. Hokuriku Yuseikyoku. No. 24 Issue 47 (1972)-. Periodical. Japanese. Hokuriku Yuseikyoku, 1-1 Owaricho 1-chome, Kanazawa 920 Japan. **Continues** Kanazawa Yuseikyoku Tokei Nempo.

US
INDIANA ZIP+4 STATE DIRECTORY.
Added/Corp United States Postal Service. Address Information Systems Division. United States Postal Service. Office of Address Information Systems. United States Postal Service. Customer and Automation Services Dept. United States Postal Service. Customer Service Support. **VFOAT** Indiana ZIP Plus Four State Directory; ZIP Plus Four State Directory. Indiana; Indiana State Directory; ZIP+4 State Directory. Indiana. **VAT** Indiana Zip Plus Four State Directory. (1985)-. Directory. English. One time a year. St Louis PDC, Zip+4 State Directory Orders, PO Box 14921, St. Louis MO 63180-9988.

LC HE7033 .I5
DD 383/.49493 BE
INDICATEUR OFFICIEL DES POSTES
DE BELGIQUE. French. 220F. Government of Belgium, L'Administration Des Postes, Brussels Belgium.

US
INSTRUCTIONS FOR MAILERS. **Main/Corp**
United States Postal Service. (Oct. 1970)-. Periodical. English. US Postal Service / Washington, 475 l'Enfant Plaza West SW, Washington DC 20260-0010. **Continues in part** United States. Postal Office Dept. Postal Manual.

LC HE6237 .I58 **ISSN** 1043-7134
DD 383/.24 US
Pr Rev.
INTERNATIONAL JOURNAL OF RESEARCH AND ENGINEERING (POSTAL APPLICATION). [Int. j. res. eng. post. appl.]. **VFOAT** IJRE. **VAT** International Journal of Research & Engineering. (1989)-. Periodical. English (French and Russian; summaries and/or abstracts in German, Italian and Japanese). Four times a year (Mar., June, Sept., Dec.). $145.00. Technopost V Uzilevsky, 4 Maria Ulianova, 191025 St. Petersburg Russia. **ED** Gary P. Herring. **Bk Rev. Circ:** 10,000 (ctrl).

LC HE6445 .I58 **ISSN** 1058-0875
DD 383/.23/0973 US
CODEN IMAMEA
INTERNATIONAL MAIL MANUAL.
(INTERNATIONAL MAIL MANUAL.). [Int. mail man.]. **Added/Corp** United States Postal Service. United States Postal Service. Document Control Division. **VFOAT** Imm. (1981)-. Government Publication. English. Two times a year. $30.00. US Postal Service / Washington, 475 l'Enfant Plaza West SW, Washington DC 20260-0010. **(Subscription address:** Superintendent of Documents, US Government Printing Office, Washington DC 20402.) **Continues** International Mail.

US
INTERNATIONAL POSTAL
HANDBOOK. (1977)-. English. New Harbinger Publications, 5674 Shattuck Avenue, Oakland CA 94609-1662.

LC HE6995 .J29
DD 383/.0943 GW
JAHRBUCH DER DEUTSCHEN
BUNDESPOST. (1977)-. German (summaries and/or abstracts in English and French). **Formed by the union of** Jahrbuch des Elektrischen Fernmeldewesens **and** Jahrbuch des Postwesens.

US
KANSAS, NEBRASKA ZIP+4 STATE
DIRECTORY. VFOAT Zip Plus Four State Directory. Kansas, Nebraska; Zip+4 State Directory. Kansas, Nebraska. **VAT** Kansas, Nebraska Zip Plus Four State Directory. 1985-. Directory. English. One time a year. $12.00. Zip+4 State Directory Orders, Address Information Center, 6060 Primacy Parkway/Suite 101, Memphis TN 38188-9980. available on diskette.

LC HE7276.K35 J35a
JA
KANTO YUSEIKYOKU TOKEI NEMPO.
Main/Corp Japan. Kanto Yuseikyoku. (1972)-. Periodical. Japanese. Kanto Yuseikyoku, Otemachi Chiyoda-ku, Tokyo 100 Japan.

US
KENTUCKY, WEST VIRGINIA ZIP+4
STATE DIRECTORY. Added/Corp United States Postal Service. Address Information Systems Division. United States Postal Service. Office of Address Information Systems. United States Postal Service. Customer and Automation Services Dept. United States Postal Service. Customer Service Support. **VFOAT** Kentucky, West Virginia ZIP Plus Four State Directory; ZIP Plus Four State Directory. Kentucky, West Virginia; Kentucky, West Virginia State Directory; ZIP+4 State Directory. Kentucky, West Virginia. **VAT** Kentucky, West Virginia Zip Plus Four State Directory. (1985)-. Directory. English. One time a year. St Louis PDC, Zip+4 State Directory Orders, PO Box 14921, St. Louis MO 63180-9988.

LC HE7276.K95 J37a
JA
KYUSHU YUSEIKYOKU TOKEI NEMPO.
Main/Corp Japan. Kyushu Yuseikyoku. (1972)-. Periodical. Japanese. Kyushu Yuseikyoku, Jotocho, Kumamoto 860 Japan.

LC HE7123 .C67A
DD 383/.025/469 PO
LISTA DAS ESTACOES E POSTOS,
CORREIO. Main/Corp Correios e Telecomunicacoes de Portugal. Portuguese. One time a year.

LC HE6251.A1 L5
SZ
LISTE DES DISTANCES KILOMETRIQUES, AFFERENTES AUX PARCOURS TERRITORIAUX DES DEPECHES EN TRANSIT. **Main/Corp**
Universal Postal Union. International Bureau. **VFOAT** Distances Kilometriques. French.

UK
LONDON POSTAL HISTORY GROUP
NOTEBOOK. (19??)-. English. Irregular. £5.00. London Postal History Group, 24 Dover Court Road, Dulwich SE22 8ST United Kingdom.

US
Pr Rev.
LONG ISLAND POSTAL HISTORIAN.
(19??)-. English. Four times a year. $15.00 US; $20.00 Canada; $20.00 (surface mail), $30.00 (airmail) other. Long Island Postal History Society, 144 Hamilton Avenue, Clifton NJ 07011. **Tel** (201)772-1413. **ED** Brad Arch. **Circ:** 100.

LC HE6300 .M35 **ISSN** 1053-0703
DD 651.7/59/05
CODEN MJCDEG
MAIL (MILFORD, PA.). (MAIL.). (198?)-.
Periodical. English. Nine times a year. $31.00. Excelsior Publications / Milford, Millstone Road, Gold Key Box 2425, Milford PA 18337. **Tel** (717)686-2111.

ISSN 1079-7300
DD 658 US
MAILING & SHIPPING TECHNOLOGY.
(MAILING & SHIPPING TECHNOLOGY : MAST.). [Mail. ship. technol.]. **VFOAT** Mailing and Shipping Technology; MAST. (199?)-. Trade Publication. English. Six times a year. $27.00. RB Publishing Company, 2701 East Washington Avenue, Madison WI 53704. **Tel** (608)241-8777, FAX (608)241-8666. **Continues** MAST (Madison, Wis.), 1051-824X.

LC HF5863 .M34 **ISSN** 1043-4372
DD 381/.1 US
MAILING LIST COMPANIES AND CATAGORIES ... DIRECTORY. (1989)-.
Directory. English. One time a year. $22.50 US; $24.00 other. Enterprise Publishers, 3809 Hudee Drive, Mitchellville MD 20716-2432. **Tel** (301)464-2110. **ED** B J Russo. **Ad Acc.** ctrl circ.
Desc: An information resource directory which lists names, addresses, zip codes and local/toll-free/FAX numbers of over 2,100 list houses. Also includes over 3,000 categories of mailing lists offered by companies.

LC HE6363.M2 M34 **ISSN** 8756-9841
DD 383/.145 US
MAINE, NEW HAMPSHIRE, VERMONT ZIP+4 STATE DIRECTORY. (MAINE, NEW
HAMPSHIRE, VERMONT ZIP+4 STATE DIRECTORY / PREPARED BY THE ADDRESS INFORMATION SYSTEMS DIVISION, DELIVERY SERVICES DEPARTMENT.). [Me. N.H. Vt. ZIP+4 state dir.]. **Added/Corp** United States Postal Service. Address Information Systems Division. United States Postal Service. Office of Address Information Systems. United States Postal Service. Customer and Automation Services Dept. United States Postal Service. Customer Service Support. **VFOAT** Maine, New Hampshire, Vermont ZIP Plus Four State Directory; ZIP Plus Four State Directory. Maine, New Hampshire, Vermont; Maine, New Hampshire, Vermont Directory; ZIP+4 State Directory. Maine, New Hampshire, Vermont. **VAT** Maine, New Hampshire, Vermont Zip Plus Four State Directory. (1985)-. Directory. English. One time a year. St Louis PDC, Zip+4 State Directory Orders, PO Box 14921, St. Louis MO 63180-9988.

ISSN 1187-4147
DD 383 CN
MANAGER NEWSLETTER. [Manag. newsl.].
Added/Corp Canada Post Corporation. **VFOAT** Cadres, Bulletin d'Information. Vol. 1, No. 1 (June 1991)-. Newsletter. English (French). Irregular. **Continues** Manager (Ottawa, Ont.)., 0846-5843.

US
MASSACHUSETTS ZIP+4 STATE
DIRECTORY. Added/Corp United States Postal Service. Address Information Systems Division. United States Postal Service. Office of Address Information Systems. United States Postal Service. Customer and Automation Services Dept. **VFOAT** Zip Plus Four State Directory. **VAT** Massachusetts Zip Plus Four State Directory. (1985)-. Directory. English. One time a year. St Louis PDC, Zip+4 State Directory Orders, PO Box 14921, St. Louis MO 63180-9988.

LC HF5761 .M24 **ISSN** 1051-824X
DD 658.7 US
CODEN MSTTE8
TITLE CHANGE
MAST (MADISON, WIS.). (MAST : FOR
MAILING AND SHIPPING PROFESSIONALS.). [Mast]. (198?)-(199?). Trade Publication. English. RB Publishing Company, 2701 East Washington Avenue, Madison WI 53704. **Tel** (608)241-8777, FAX (608)241-8666. **ED** Ron Brent. **Ad Acc, Adv Mgr:** Ron Brent. **Circ:** 40,000 (ctrl). **Continued by** Mailing & Shipping Technology, 1079-7300.
Desc: Servicing the information needs of the mail services manager, providing coverage of the issues of concern. Each issue features the latest in equipment, technology and products, services designed to cut expenses, personnel management tips and reference guides and charts to manage mailing operations.

US
MEMO TO MAILERS. **Added/Corp** United States
Postal Service. Dept. of Public and Employee Communications. United States Postal Service. Communications Dept. (19??)-. Trade Publication.

Communications — Postal Communications

English. Twelve times a year. Free. US Postal Service / National Customer Support Center, 6060 Primacy Parkway, Suite 101, Memphis TN 38188-0001. **ED** Jim Quirk.
 Desc: Publication of interest to business mailers, mailroom managers and customers originating significant quanities of mail.

LC HE6187 .M56
DD 383.23
IT

MEMORIE DELL'ACCADEMIA ITALIANA DI STUDI FILATELICI E NUMISMATICI. **Added/Corp** Accademia Italiana di Studi Filatelici e Numismatici. (198?)-. Periodical. Italian. Accademia Italiana di Studi Filatelici e Numismatici, Palazzo Capitano del Popolo, Piazza C Battisti 1, Reggio Emilia Italy.

LC HE6005 .P67
DD 380.3/0944
FR

MESSAGES DES POSTES ET TELECOMMUNICATIONS. **Added/Corp** France. Secretariat d'Etat aux Postes et Telecommunications. Service de l'Information et des Relations Publiques. (1976)-. French. Twelve times a year. Secretariat d'Etat aux Postes et Telecommunications. Service de l'Information et des Relations Publiques, 20 Avenue de Segur, 75700 Paris France. **Continues** Postes et Telecommunications.

US

MISSOURI ZIP+4 STATE DIRECTORY. **Added/Corp** United States Postal Service. Address Information Systems Division. United States Postal Service. Office of Address Information Systems. **VFOAT** Missouri ZIP Plus Four State Directory; ZIP Plus Four State Directory. Missouri; Missouri State Directory; ZIP+4 State Directory. Missouri. 1985-. Directory. English. One time a year. Saint Louis PDC, Zip + 4 State Directory Orders, PO Box 14921.

LC HE6376.A1 M95 **ISSN** 0146-5368
DD 383/.09786
US

MONTANA POSTAL CACHE. **Added/Corp** Montana Postal History Society. (1975)-. Periodical. English. Four times a year. Montana Postal History Society, 1117 16th Street, Havre MT 59501.

ISSN 0194-536X
US

MOUNTAINEER POSTMASTER. (19??)-. Periodical. English. Six times a year. Mountaineer Postmaster, 416 Mansion Street, Hamlin WV 25523.

US

NATIONAL DIRECTORY OF MAILING LISTS, THE. (1990)-. Directory. English. $345.00. Oxbridge Communications Inc., 150 5th Avenue, Room 302, New York NY 10011. **Tel** (212)741-0231, FAX (212)633-2938. (**Subscription address:** Gale Research Co., 835 Penobscot Building, Detroit MI 48226. **Tel** (800)347-4253.)
 Desc: Organizes and describes more than 15,000 listings for magazines, journals, newsletters, catalogs, directories, newspapers, tabloids, looseleafs, bulletins, indices, etc. with available lists.

LC HE6361 .N37 **ISSN** 0731-9185
DD 383/.145
CODEN NFDDD3

NATIONAL FIVE DIGIT ZIP CODE AND POST OFFICE DIRECTORY. **Added/Corp** United States Postal Service. Retail Operations Division. United States Postal Service. Address Information Systems Division. United States Postal Service. Office of Address Information Systems. United States Postal Service. Customer and Automation Services Dept. **VFOAT** National five-digit zip code and post office directory; National five-digit zip code & post office directory. (1982)-. Directory. English. One time a year. $18.00. National Five-Digit Zip Code Directory Orders, National Customer Support Center, 6060 Primacy Parkway, Suite 101, Memphis TN 38188-0001. **Tel** (800)331-5746 ext. 640. **Continues** National Zip Code & Post Office Directory, 0191-6971.

LC HD6350.P77 N3 **ISSN** 0028-0089
DD 353
US

NATIONAL RURAL LETTER CARRIER, THE. [Natl. rural lett. carr.]. Trade Publication. English. Twelve times a year. National Rural Letter Carriers Association, 1750 Pennsylvania Avenue NW, Washington DC 20006. **Absorbed** RFD News.
 Ind/Abst Work Relat. Abstr.

ISSN 1054-9188
DD 383
US

NCPHS NEWSLETTER. (NCPHS NEWSLETTER / NORTH CAROLINA POSTAL HISTORY SOCIETY.). [NCPHS newsl.]. **Added/Corp** North Carolina Postal History Society. **VAT** North Carolina Postal History Society Newsletter. (Feb. 1982)- vol. 12 (1993)-. Newsletter. English. Four times a year (Jan., Apr., July, Oct.). $10.00. North Carolina Postal History Society, Route 2 Box 26, Trinity NC 27370. **Tel** (919)434-2403. **ED** Vernon Stroups and Tony Crumbley. **Bk Rev. Ad Acc. Circ:** 150.

US

NEW JERSEY ZIP+4 STATE DIRECTORY. **VFOAT** Zip Plus Four State Directory. New Jersey; Zip Plus Four State Directory. New Jersey. **VAT** New Jersey Zip Plus Four State Directory. (1985)-. Directory. English. One time a year. $12.00. Zip+4 State Directory Orders, Address Information Center, 6060 Primacy Parkway/Suite 101, Memphis TN 38188-9980.

US

NEW YORK ZIP+4 STATE DIRECTORY. **VFOAT** Zip Plus Four State Directory. **VAT** New York Zip Plus Four State Directory. 1985-. Directory. English. One time a year. $12.00. PDC Zip+4 State Directory Orders, PO Box 1492, St Louis MO 63180-9988. available on diskette.

LC HE6009.N6 N6
DD 383/.4948/05
SW

NORDISK POSTTIDSKRIFT. (19??)-. Periodical. Swedish. Irregular. Norkisk Posttidskrift, Postens Arkiv- Och Forlagstjanst, S-105 00 Stockholm Sweden. cum. index. **Continues** Tidskrift for Postvasendet.

US

NORTH CAROLINA ZIP+4 STATE DIRECTORY. **Added/Corp** United States Postal Service. Address Information Systems Division. United States Postal Service. Office of Address Information Systems. United States Postal Service. Customer and Automation Services Dept. United States Postal Service. Customer Service Support. **VFOAT** North Carolina ZIP Plus Four State Directory; ZIP Plus Four State Directory. North Carolina; North Carolina State Directory; ZIP+4 State Directory. North Carolina. **VAT** North Carolina Zip Plus Four State Directory. (1985)-. Directory. English. One time a year. St Louis PDC, Zip+4 State Directory Orders, PO Box 14921, St. Louis MO 63180-9988.

LC HE7276.O5 J36a
JA

OKINAWA YUSEI KANRI JIMUSHO TOKEI NEMPO. **Main/Corp** Japan. Okinawa Yusei Kanri Jimusho. (19??)-. Periodical. Japanese. Okinawa Yusie Kanri Jimusho, 26-5 Higashicho, Naha 900 Japan.

LC HE6993 .O73
GW

ORTSVERZEICHINIS II, VERZEICHNIS DER ORTE IM BEREICH DER DEUTSCHEN POSTVERWALTUNGEN. **Added/Corp** Germany (West). Bundesmininsterium feur das Post-und Fernmeldewesen. Deutsche Bundespost. **VFOAT** Verzeichnis der Orte Im Bereich der Deutschen Postverwaltungen. **VAT** Otsverzeichinis Zwei, Verzeichnis der Orte im Bereich der Deutschen Postverwaltungen. (19??)-. German. Postfach 80 01, 5300 Bonn 1 Germany.

LC HE6000 .P58a **ISSN** 1015-6844
DD 380.3/05
SZ

P.T.T.I. STUD. (P. T. T. I. STUDIES.). [P.T.T.I. studies]. **Main/Corp** Postal, Telegraph and Telephone Workers' International. (1973)-. Periodical. English. Four times a year. Postal Telegraph and Telephone Worker's International, S Nedzynski Piti 36 Avenue du Lignon, Geneva Switzerland.

LC HE7220.5 .A227
DD 383/.495491/05
PK

PAK POST : A PUBLICATION OF THE PAKISTAN POST OFFICE. **Added/Corp** Pakistan. Post Office Dept. **VFOAT** Pakpost. No. 1, Vol. 1 (Jan.-June 1991)-. Periodical. English. Two times a year. Postal Staff College, G- 8/4, Islamabad- 44000, Pakistan.

LC Al21.P36 P363
DD 079/.95/3
PP

PAPUA NEW GUINEA POST COURIER SELECTIVE INDEX. **Added/Corp** Institute of Applied Social and Economic Research. **VFOAT** Post Courier Selective Index; Post Courier Index. (19??)-. English. One time a year. The National Research Institute, PO Box 5854 Boroko, Boroko Papua New Guinea.

LC HE6300 **ISSN** 1081-4035
DD 383.4
US

●PARCEL SHIPPING & DISTRIBUTION. [Parcel shipp. distrib.]. **Added/Corp** RB Publishing (Madison, Wis.). **VFOAT** Parcel Shipping and Distribution. (March/Apr. 1994)-. Trade Publication. English. Four times a year. $20.00. RB Publishing Company, 2701 East Washington Avenue, Madison WI 53704. **Tel** (608)241-8777, FAX (608)241-8666. **Ad Acc.** Full Page (B&W) $3,255.00. Full Page (Color) $4,355.00.
 Desc: Information on parcel shipments.

US

PENNSYLVANIA ZIP+4 STATE DIRECTORY. **VFOAT** Zip Plus Four State Directory. Pennsylvania; Zip+4 State Directory. Pennsylvania. **VAT** Pennsylvania Zip Plus Four State Directory. 1985-. Directory. English. One time a year. St Louis PDC, Zip+4 State Directory Orders, PO Box 14921, St. Louis MO 63180-9988. available on microfiche (Vols. for (1987-) distributed to depository libraries).
 Desc: Provides a full nine-digit listing for street addresses, suite and apartment numbers, post office boxes, rural and star routes, general delivery and postmasters.

ISSN 0832-1213
DD 383/.49713/8405
CN

PERFORMANCE (OTTAWA). (PERFORMANCE : CANADA POST EMPLOYEE NEWSPAPER--HEAD OFFICE AND RIDEAU DIVISION.). [Performance]. **Main/Corp** Canada Post Corporation. **Added/Corp** Canada Post Corporation. Rideau Division. **VFOAT** Performance. Vol. 1, No. 1 (April 9, 1986)-. Periodical. English (French). Twelve times a year. Free on request. Canada Post Corporation, 2701 Riverside Dr, Suite N0621, Ottawa Ontario K1A OB1 Canada. **Tel** (613)734-7638. **ED** Barbara Leimsner. **Continues in part** Canada Post Corporation. Messages., 0821-0578 **and** Canada Post Corporation. Rideau Division. Rideau Press., 0832-1221.

ISSN 0031-7381
UK

PHILATELIC EXPORTER, THE. [Phil. export.]. (July 1950)-. Trade Publication. English. Twelve times a year. $41.41. The Philatelic Exporter Ltd., PO Box 137, Hatfield, Hertfordshire AL10 9DB United Kingdom. **Tel** 011 44 1707 266331. **ED** Graham Phillips. Index available. **Bk Rev. Ad Acc. Circ:** 4,000. **Absorbed** Philatelic Trader.
 Desc: News, comments, etc of interest to international postage stamp trade.

ISSN 0714-8305
DD 383/.4971
CN

PHSC JOURNAL. (PHSC JOURNAL / POSTAL HISTORY SOCIETY OF CANADA.). [PHSC j.]. **Added/Corp** Postal History Society of Canada. No. 29 (March 31, 1982)-. Periodical. English. Four times a year. Free to members. PHSC Journal, Box 3461 Station C, Ottawa Ontario K1Y 4J6 Canada. **Continues** Postal History Society of Canada Journal, 0703-5365.

LC HE7355.A4 S95a
DD 383/.0968/3
SQ

POST OFFICE GUIDE. **Main/Corp** Swaziland. Dept. of Posts and Telecommunications. **Added/Corp** Swaziland. Dept. of Posts and Telecommunications. Swaziland Post Office Guide. **VFOAT** Swaziland Post Office Guide. (19??)-. English. Posts and Telecommunications, PO Box 125, Mbabane Swaziland.

LC HE7131 .S37a
DD 383/.49494
SZ

POST-, TELEFON- UND TELEGRAFEN-AMTSBLATT. FEUILLE OFFICIELLE DES POSTES, TELEPHONES ET TELEGRAPHES. FOGLIO UFFICIALE DELLE POSTE, DEI TELEFONI E DEI TELEGRAFI. **Main/Corp** Schweizerische Post-, Telephon- und Telegraphenbetriebe. Generaldirektion. **Added/Corp** Schweizerische Post-, Telephon- und Telegraphenbetriebe. Generaldirektion. Feuille Officielle des Postes, Telephones et Telegraphes. Schweizerische Post-, Telephon- und Telegraphenbetriebe. Generaldirektion. Foglio Ufficiale delle Poste, dei Telefoni e dei Telegrafi. **VFOAT** Feuille Officielle des Postes, Telephones et Telegraphes; Foglio Ufficiale delle Poste, dei Telefoni e dei Telegrafi. (19??)-. French (German and Italian). One time a week. 26.00F. Generaldirektion, Postcheckkonto 30-6450, Ptt-Zeitschriften, 3030 Bern Switzerland. **Supersedes** Switzerland. Generaldirektion der Post-, Telegraphen- und Telephonverwaltung. Post-, Telegraphen- und Telephon-Amtsblatt.

LC HE6995 .A7 **ISSN** 0947-9945
DD 383.49
GW

●POST- UND TELEKOMMUNIKATIONSGESCHICHTE. **Added/Corp** Deutsche Gesellschaft fuer Post- und Telekommunikationsgeschichte. (1995)-. Periodical. German. Four times a year. Gesellschaft fur Deutsche Postgeschichte, Schaumainkai 53, D-60596 Frankfurt Germany. **Tel** 011 49 69 611040. **Continues** Archiv fuer Deutsche Postgeschichte.

LC HE6009.H9 P67
HU

POSTA. (19??)-. Periodical. Hungarian. Twelve times a year. $17.00. (**Subscription address:** Kultura, PO Box 143, H-1300 Budapest 3 Hungary. **Tel** 011 36 1 2500194.)

Communications —Postal Communications

LC HE6933 .P67
DD 383/.49/41
UK
POSTAL ADDRESSES AND INDEX TO POSTCODE DIRECTORIES. Added/Corp
Great Britain. Post Office. (Nov. 1974)-. English. British Post Office, 2 12 Gresham Street/Room 120, London EC2V 7A0 United Kingdom. **Formed by the union of** *Great Britain. Post Office. Postal Addresses, United Kingdom and the Irish Republic Excluding the London Postal Area* **and** *Index to Postcode Directories.*

LC HE6311 .P6
ISSN 0364-863X
US
POSTAL BULLETIN. (THE POSTAL
BULLETIN.). **Added/Corp** United States. Post Office Dept. United States Postal Service. Directives Control Division. United States Postal Service. Directives and Forms Division. United States Postal Service. Vol. 39, No. 11605 (Mar. 20, 1918)-. Bulletin. English. Twenty-six times a year. $86.00. US Postal Service / Washington, 475 l'Enfant Plaza West SW, Washington DC 20260-0010. (**Subscription address:** Superintendent of Documents, US Government Printing Office, Washington DC 20402.) **Continues** *Daily Bulletin of Orders Affecting the Postal Service. United States. Post Office Dept.;* **Absorbed** *USPS Stamp Poster.*
Desc: Contains current orders, instructions and information relating to the United States Postal Service, and Commemorative Stamp Posters.

US
POSTAL CONTRACTING MANUAL.
Main/Corp United States Postal Service. (Oct. 1971)-. Government Publication. English. Irregular. $62.00. Superintendent of Documents, US Government Printing Office, Washington DC 20402. **Tel** (202)275-3328, **FAX** (202)786-2377.
Desc: Consists of a basic manual and supplementary material for an indeterminate period.

CN
POSTAL GUIDE = LE GUIDE DES POSTES.
French. 50.00Can$. National Philatelic Centre, Canada Postal Corporation, Station 1, Antigonish Nova Scotia B2G 2R8 Canada. **Tel** (902)863-6550, (800)565-4362, **FAX** (902)863-6796.

LC HE6951 .P68
DD 383/.49411
UK
POSTAL HISTORY ANNUAL, THE. (19??)-.
English. One time a year. £5.50 UK; $12.00 US. James A Mackay, 11 Newall Terrace, Dumfries DG1 1LN United Kingdom. **Tel** 011 44 1387 55250. **ED** James A Mackay.
Bk Rev. Circ: 2,000.
Desc: Articles and shorter notes on aspects of British postal history, supplements to standard reference works on postal history.

LC HE6001 .P58
ISSN 0032-5341
DD 383/.49
US
POSTAL HISTORY JOURNAL. [Post. hist. j.].
Vol. 1, No. 1 (April 1957)-. Periodical. English. Three times a year (Feb., June, Oct.). $20.00. Postal History Society Inc, PO Box 61774, Virginia Beach VA 23462. **Tel** (804)495-6059. **ED** Harlan F Stone. Index available. cum. index. **Bk Rev. Ad Acc. Circ:** 700 (ctrl). available on microfilm from University Microfilms International (UMI).
Desc: Articles relate to the development of postal systems, ways of handling mail and treaties between countries relative to rates and distribution; covers censored, wrecked, disinfected and prisoner-of-war mail.

US
POSTAL OPERATIONS MANUAL.
Main/Corp United States Postal Service. **VFOAT** POM. (May 1979)-. English. Irregular. $47.00. United States Postal Service, 475 l'Enfant Plaza SW, Washington DC 20260-0010. **Tel** (202)245-4000, **FAX** (202)268-4980, telex 892314. (**Subscription address:** Superintendent of Documents, US Government Printing Office, Washington DC 20402.) **Supersedes in part** *Postal Service Manual.*

LC HD6350.P75 P7
ISSN 0032-5376
US
POSTAL RECORD, THE. Added/Corp National
Association of Letter Carriers (U.S.). (1888)-. Periodical. English. Twelve times a year. $16.00. National Association of Letter Carriers, 100 Indiana Avenue NW, Washington DC 20001. **Tel** (202)393-4695.

POSTAL SERVICE MANUAL. Main/Corp
United States Postal Service. (1970)-. Periodical. English. US Postal Service / Washington, 475 l'Enfant Plaza West SW, Washington DC 20260-0010. **Continues** *United States. Post Office Dept. Postal Manual.*

LC HE6001 .N25
ISSN 0032-5384
US
POSTAL SUPERVISOR, THE. Added/Corp
National Association of Postal Supervisors. (19??)-. Trade Publication. English. Twelve times a year. $4.00. National Association of Postal Supervisors, 490 l'Enfant Plaza, Suite 3200, Washington DC 20024. **Tel** (202)484-6070.
Ind/Abst Work Relat. Abstr.

DD 383
ISSN 1052-3944
US
CODEN POWAE5
POSTAL WATCH. [Post. watch]. Vol. 1, No. 1
(Aug. 3, 1990)-. Periodical. English. Twenty-four times a year. $283.53. Intertec Publishing Corporation, 9800 Metcalf, Overland Park KS 66212. **Tel** (913)341-1300. (**Subscription address:** Intertec Publishing Corporation, PO Box 2901, Overland Park KS 66282. **Tel** 800 441-0294.)

US
POSTAL WORLD. Added/Corp National Institute
for Public Services. (197?)-. Trade Publication. English. Twenty-five times a year. $367.00. United Communications Group, 11300 Rockville Pike, Suite 1100, Rockville MD 20852. **Tel** (301)816-8950 ext. 313, **FAX** (301)816-8945. **ED** Marcus Smith (editor's telephone: (301)961-8700).
Desc: The Washington newsletter for mail users.

ISSN 0390-5942
IT
UDC 621.39
POSTE E TELECOMUNICAZIONI NELLO SVILUPPO DELLA SOCIETA.
[Poste telecomun. sviluppo soc.]. (1968)-. Periodical. Italian. Six times a year. L70.000. Editore Fondazione Ego Bordoni 59, 00142 Rome Italy. **Tel** (06)54804504-5, telex 622539 FUB I. **Circ:** 4,000. **Continues** *Poste e Telecomunicazioni, 0390-5950.*

LC HE6001 .P8
ISSN 0032-5511
US
POSTMASTERS' ADVOCATE. Added/Corp
National League of Postmasters. Vol. 1 (1894)-. Periodical. English. Twelve times a year. $24.00. National League of Postmasters, 1023 North Royal Street, Alexandria VA 22314-1569. **Tel** (703)548-5922.
Ind/Abst Work Relat. Abstr.

LC HE6001 .N33
ISSN 0032-552X
US
POSTMASTERS GAZETTE. [Postmast. gaz.].
Added/Corp National Association of Postmasters. (19??)-. Periodical. English. Eleven times a year (Nov./Dec. issues combined). $10.00. National Association Postmasters of US, 8 Herbert Street, Alexandria VA 22305. **Tel** (703)683-9027.

LC HE6991 .P66
ISSN 0554-842X
GW
CCC
POSTPRAXIS, DIE. (1950)-. Periodical. German.
Twelve times a year. DM27.00. Josef Keller GmbH & Co. Verlags KG, Postfach 1455, D-82317 Starnberg Germany. **Tel** 011 49 (08151)771-0, **FAX** 011 49 (08151)771-152, telex 566438. **Bk Rev. Ad Acc. Circ:** 19,000.

LC R
ISSN 0269-1396
DD 610
UK
PRATIQUE LONDON. See Medical
Sciences-Communicable Diseases.

LC HE6187 .P76
ISSN 0273-5415
US
PRECANCEL FORUM. (1940)-. Periodical.
English. Twelve times a year. Precancel Stamp Society Inc., PO Box 1134, Wichita KS 67201-1134.

LC HE
ISSN 1053-0916
DD 383
US
PTT (CLARKSBURG, MD.). (PTT :
[COMPUTER FILE]. INTERNATIONAL GUIDE TO POSTS, TELEPHONE, TRANSPORTATION.). [PTT]. **VFOAT** International Guide to Posts, Telephone, Transportation. (1991)-. English. Four times a year. Performance Marketing, 24115 Clarksburg Road, Clarksburg MD 20871.

LC HE7131 .A46312
DD 384/.09490/05
SZ
PTT-GESCHAFTSBERICHT UND FINANZRECHNUNG. Main/Corp Schweizerische
Post-, Telefon- und Telegrafenbetriebe. **VFOAT** PTT Geschaftsbericht und Finanzrechnung. (198?)-. German. One time a year. **Continues** *Schweizerische Post-, Telefon- und Telgrafenbetriebe. PTT-Geschaftsbericht.*

US
RAND MCNALLY ZIP CODE FINDER.
(19??)-. Directory. English. One time a year. $6.95. Rand McNally & Company, PO Box 32, Skokie IL 60076. **Tel** (708)673-0813, (800)444-4062.
Desc: Includes ZIP codes for over 120,000 cities and towns, postal and private carrier rate information, and three-digit ZIP code maps of all 50 states and Washington, D.C.

IT
RASSEGNA POSTELEGRAFONICA.
(19??)-. Italian. Eleven times a year. L66000 Italy; L70000 other. Edizioni Margherita, Via Larga 2, 20122 Milan Italy. **Tel** 011 39 2 90784970.

ISSN 0983-1924
FR
UDC 656.80
REFERENCES DE LA POSTE PARIS.
[Ref. poste Paris]. **VFOAT** References la Poste (Paris). (1986)-. Periodical. French. Four times a year. 100.00F France; 120.00F other. Direction Generale de la Poste, Direction du Reseau, Piece 3206, 20 Avenue de Segur, 75700 Paris France. **Tel** 011 33 1 5641005. **Bk Rev. Ad Acc. Circ:** 27,000. **Continues** *References (Paris, 1983), 0756-967X.*

LC HE6656.M65 R45
DD 383/.14
CN
REPERTOIRE : MONTREAL METROPOLITAIN, CODE POSTAL. VFOAT
Directory Metropolitan Montreal, Postal Code. (19??)-. Multiple languages (English and French). One time a year. Sir Alexander Campbell Building, Klaobl, Ottawa Ontario Canada.

LC J961 .H835 HE7486.F5
DD 354/.96/1100873
FJ
REPORT - DEPT. OF POSTS AND TELECOMMUNICATIONS. Main/Corp Fiji.
Dept. of Posts and Telecommunications. (19??)-. English. 0.25. **Continues** *Fiji. Posts and Telegraph Dept. Report.*

LC HE7351 .A22a
DD 354.680072/32
SA
REPORT OF THE AUDITOR-GENERAL ON THE ACCOUNTS OF THE DEPARTMENT OF POSTS AND TELECOMMUNICATIONS. Main/Corp South
Africa. Controller and Auditor-General. **Added/Corp** South Africa. Dept. of the Auditor-General. Verslag van die Ouditeur-Generaal Oor Die Rekenings van die Departement van Pos- en Telekommunikasiewese. **VFOAT** Verlag van die Ouditeur-Generaal oor die Rekenings van die Department van Pos-en Telekommunikasiewese. (19??)-. Afrikaans (English). Government Printer / South Africa, Bosman Street, Private Bag X85, Pretoria 0001 South Africa. **Tel** 011 27 12 3239731 ext. 262.

LC HE7211 .A55
II
REPORT : UNION GOVERNMENT (POSTS AND TELEGRAPHS). Main/Corp
India. Comptroller and Auditor-General. (1971)-. English. Comptroller and Auditor-General Manager of Publications, Delhi-6, New Delhi India. **Continues** *India. Comptroller and Auditor-General. Audit Report, Posts and Telegraphs.*

SZ
●REVUE PTT. Added/Corp Schweizerische Post-,
Telefon- und Telegrafenbetriebe. **VFOAT** PTT Revue; Revue des PTT. (1993)-. Periodical. French (German and Italian). Twelve times a year. Hallwag AG, Nordring 4, CH-3001 Bern Switzerland. **Tel** 011 41 31 3323131, **FAX** 011 41 31 414133, telex 912661 HAWA CH. **Continues** *PTT-Zeitschrift.*

ISSN 0733-2297
SAN BERNARDINO STREET ATLAS. ZIP CODE EDITION. (19??)-. Periodical. English. One
time a year. $12.95. Thomas Brothers Maps, Lockbox PO Box 30845, Los Angeles CA 90030. **Tel** (714)863-1984, (800)899-6277, **FAX** (714)757-1564. **Ad Acc.**
Desc: Street maps and index for San Bernardino county in California with zip code overlay.

FR
SERVICES POSTE AERIENNE. French.
Sixteen times a year. 285.00F. Indicateur Universel des PTT, 6 rue le Goff, 75005 Paris France. **Tel** 011 33 1 43267942.

LC HE7276.S55 J37a
JA
SHIKOKU YUSEI TOKEI NEMPO.
Main/Corp Japan. Shikoku Yuseikyoku. (1972)-. Periodical. Japanese. Shikoku Yuseikyoku, 8-5 Miyatacho, Matsuyama Japan.

ISSN 0744-5644
US
SOONER POSTMASTER. Added/Corp
National Association of Postmasters of the United States. Oklahoma Chapter. (19??)-. Periodical. English. Six times a year. Sooner Postmaster, Fairfax OK 74637.

US
SOUTH CAROLINA ZIP+4 STATE DIRECTORY. Added/Corp United States Postal
Service. Address Information Systems Division. United States Postal Service. Office of Address Information Systems. United States Postal Service. Customer and Automation Services Dept. **VFOAT** South Carolina ZIP Plus Four State Directory; ZIP Plus Four State Directory. South Carolina; South Carolina State Directory; ZIP+4 State Directory. South Carolina. **VAT** South Carolina Zip

Communications —Radio

Plus Four State Directory. (1985)-. Directory. English. One time a year. St Louis PDC, Zip+4 State Directory Orders, PO Box 14921, St. Louis MO 63180-9988.

LC HE6184.S42 S68   **ISSN** 0738-2529
DD 769.5/7   US
SPRINGER'S HANDBOOK OF NORTH AMERICAN CINDERELLA STAMPS, INCLUDING TAXPAID REVENUES. VFOAT Catalogue of Various North American Cinderella Stamps. (19??)-. English. $6.00. Springer-Verlag New York Inc., 175 Fifth Avenue, New York NY 10010. **Tel** (212)460-1500 ext 256, FAX (212)533-3503, telex 232 235 SPB UR. **(Subscription address:** Springer-Verlag New York Inc. / North America, PO Box 2485, Journal Fulfillment, Secaucus NJ 07096. **Tel** (201)348-4033, (800)777-4643, FAX (201)348-4505.**)**

LC HE6981 .M53A
DD 331.7/613803/0944   FR
STATISTIQUES DE PERSONNEL See Communications-Abstracting, Bibliographies and Statistics.

US
TELEPHONE DIRECTORY / U.S. POSTAL SERVICE. Main/Corp United States Postal Service. (19??)-. Directory. English. US Postal Service / Washington, 475 l'Enfant Plaza West SW, Washington DC 20260-0010.

LC HE7276.T6 J36a
JA
TOKYO YUSEIKYOKU TOKEI NEMPO. Main/Corp Japan. Tokyo Yuseikyoku. (1949)-. Japanese. Tokyo Yuseikyoku, 3-ban 2-go Otemachi 2-chome Chiyoda-ku, Tokyo Japan.

LC HE7186 .T64
DD 383/.495694   IS
TOLDOT HA-DOAR SHEL ERETS YISRAEL. See Hobbies-Philately.

ISSN 0390-5187
IT
UDC 656
TRIBUNA POSTALE E DELLE TELECOMUNICAZIONI. [Trib. post. telecomun.]. (1973)-. Periodical. Italian. Six times a year. L25000. Tosco Editore, Viale Shakespeare 57, 00144 Rome Italy. **Tel** 011 39 6 5926489. **Continues** La Tribuna Postale, 0041-2791.

LC HE6251.A1 U5
DD 383/.05   SZ
UNION POSTALE. Added/Corp Universal Postal Union. International Bureau. (Oct. 1875)-. Periodical. French (English, German, Spanish, Arabic, Chinese and Russian). Four times a year. $19.81. Bureau International de l'Union Postale, Case Postale, CH-3000 Bern 15 Switzerland. **Tel** 011 41 31 3503111, FAX 011 41 31 3503110. **ED** F. Cacciatore and S. E-Doomun. Index available. cum. index. **Bk Rev. Ad Acc. Circ:** 4,000.
 Desc: Regulation planning, UPU activities, modernization, mechanization, international cooperation, standardization, and development of postal communication.

LC HE6187 .B8   **ISSN** 0164-923X
US
UNITED STATES SPECIALIST, THE. [U. S. spec.]. **Added/Corp** Bureau Issues Association. (1930)-. Periodical. English. Twelve times a year. $20.00. Bureau Issues Association / Illinois, PO Box 1047, Belleville IL 62223. **ED** Belmont Faries. **Ad Acc. Circ:** 2,200.
 Continues Bureau Specialist.
 Desc: Research papers on the entire field of U.S. postage and revenue stamped papers produced for use in the U.S. or U.S. administered areas.

ISSN 0192-4591
US
UNITED STATES ZIP CODE MARKETING BUSINESS MAP ATLAS. NATIONAL EDITION. (UNITED STATES ZIP CODE MARKETING BUSINESS MAP ATLAS.). **VFOAT** United States Zip Code Maps. (1979)-. English. Data Publications, 24 East Wesley Street, South Hackensack NJ 07606.

US
●**USPS PROCUREMENT MANUAL. Main/Corp** United States Postal Service. **VFOAT** United States Postal Service Procurement Manual; Procurement Manual. (June 30, 1993)-. Government Publication. English. Irregular. $62.00 US; $77.50 other. Superintendent of Documents, US Government Printing Office, Washington DC 20402. **Tel** (202)275-3328, FAX (202)786-2377. **Continues** United States Postal Service. Procurement Manual.
 Desc: Establishes uniform policies and procedures relating to procuring facilities, equipment, supplies and services under the authority of Chapter 4, Title 39, of the United States Code, and mail transportation services by contract under Part 5, Title 39, United States Code.

LC HE7343 .A386a
DD 383.49   SA
VERSLAG VAN DIE GEKOSE KOMITEE OOR POS- EN TELEKOMMUNIKASIEWESE. REPORT OF THE SELECT COMMITTEE ON POSTS AND TELECOMMUNICATIONS. Main/Corp South Africa. Parliament. House of Assembly. Select Committee on Posts and Telecommunications. **Added/Corp** South Africa. Parliament. House of Assembly. Select Committee on Posts and Telecommunications. Report of the Select Committee on Posts and Telecommunications. **VFOAT** Report of the Select Committee on Posts and Telecommunications. (19??)-. Afrikaans (English). R5.10. Government Printer / South Africa, Bosman Street, Private Bag X85, Pretoria 0001 South Africa. **Tel** 011 27 12 3239731 ext. 262.

ISSN 0744-2297
US
VIRGINIA POSTMASTER, THE. (THE VIRGINIA POSTMASTER : OFFICIAL PUBLICATION OF THE VIRGINIA CHAPTER OF THE NATIONAL ASSOCIATION OF POSTMASTERS.). **Added/Corp** National Association of Postmasters of the United States. Virginia Chapter. (19??)-. Periodical. English. Six times a year. Virginia Postmaster, 4212 King Street, Alexandria VA 22302-1595.

LC HE6376.A1 V88   **ISSN** 0273-3765
DD 383/.49755/05   US
WAY MARKINGS. Added/Corp Virginia Postal History Society. (Aug. 1971)-. Periodical. English. Four times a year. Virginia Postal Historical Society, 2703 Dellrose Avenue, Richmond VA 23228. **Tel** (804)262-2816.

ISSN 0841-6001
DD 769.56971   CN
WEBB'S POSTAL STATIONERY CATALOGUE OF CANADA AND NEWFOUNDLAND. [Webb's post. stationery cat. Can. Nfld.]. **VFOAT** Postal Stationery Catalogue of Canada and Newfoundland. 5th Ed (1988)-. English. J F Webb, Hornby Ontario L0P 1E0 Canada. **Continues** Canada & Newfoundland Postal Stationery Catalogue, 0705-7067.

US
WISCONSIN ZIP+4 STATE DIRECTORY. VFOAT Zip Plus Four State Directory. Wisconsin; Zip+4 State Directory. Wisconsin. **VAT** Wisconsin Zip Plus Four State Directory. 1985-. Directory. English. One time a year. $12.00. Zip+4 State Directory Orders, Address Information Center, 6060 Primacy Parkway/Suite 101, Memphis TN 38188-9980. available on diskette.

LC HE6237 .Y83
JA
YUBIN GAIMU NO KISO. Added/Corp Japan. Yuseisho. Yumukyoku. Gyomuka. (19??)-. Periodical. Japanese. ¥300. Hifuni Shobo, c/o Miyagi Kaikan, 3-10 Nishi Kanda 3-chome Chiyoda-ku, Tokyo 101 Japan.

JA
YUSEI GYOSEI ROPPO. Main/Corp Japan. **Added/Corp** Japan. Yuseisho. Bunshoka. (1985)-. Japanese. ¥3900. Yusei Gyosho Roppo, Takmura Biru 8-4, Toranomon 5, Tokyo-to 105 Japan. **Continues** Yusei Roppo.

LC HE6237 .Y87
JA
YUSEI SHIZAI. Added/Corp Japan. Yuseisho. Daijin Kambo. Shizaibu. (19??)-. Japanese. ¥80. Yusei Honsho Iigura Bunshitsu, Azabukyoku-Kunai 106 Minato-ku, Tokyo Japan.

US
ZIP + 4 CODE STATE DIRECTORY. (19??)-. Directory. English (Spanish). $15.00. US Postal Service / Tennessee, 6060 Primacy Parkway, Suite 101, Memphis TN 38188. **Tel** (800)233-0453.

RADIO

UK
3-FM. (19??)-. English. One time a week. £39.00. Royal National Institute for the Blind, PO Box 173, Peterborough PE2 6WS United Kingdom. **Tel** 011 44 1733 3730777, FAX 011 44 1733 371555.
 Desc: Contains information for BBC national radio 3 and CLASSIC FM.

LC TK9956 .S46   **ISSN** 1052-2522
DD 621.3841/66/05   US
CODEN ARTAEG
73 AMATEUR RADIO TODAY. [73 amat. radio today]. **VFOAT** 73; 73 Amateur Radio; Seventy-three Amateur Radio Today. Issue #361 (Oct. 1990)-. Periodical. English. Twelve times a year. $24.97. Wayne Green Enterprises, 70 Route 202 North, Peterborough NH 03458. **Tel** (603)924-0058. available on microfilm and microfiche from University Microfilms International (UMI). Documents available from Ask*IEEE. **Continues** 73 Amateur Radio, 0889-5309.
 Ind/Abst INSPEC (1990-).

LC PN1991.3.U6 A34   **ISSN** 0278-4467
DD 791.44/025/73   US
A.I.R. DIRECTORY OF RADIO PROGRAMMING. VFOAT AIR Directory of Radio Programming. **VAT** Association of Independent Radioproducers Directory of Radio Programming. Winter 1981-. Directory. English. $14.95. Association of Independent Radioproducers, Box 888, Universal City CA 91608. **Continues** Directory of Radio Programming.

LC TK6565.A6 A2   **ISSN** 1048-1699
DD 621.384135   US
A.R.R.L. ANTENNA BOOK, THE. [ARRL antenna book]. **Added/Corp** American Radio Relay League. **VFOAT** American Radio Relay League Antenna Book. 1st Ed. (1939)-. English. Irregular. $30.00. American Radio Relay League, 225 Main Street, Newington CT 06111. **Tel** (203)666-1541 ext. 253, FAX (203)665-7531. Index available (bound in all issues).

ISSN 0821-0209
DD 269/.2   CN
UDC 269; 286.3
ACCENT ON ARTS. See Religions and Theology-Protestantism.

LC VK397 .A35
DD 623.89/32   UK
ADMIRALTY LIST OF RADIO SIGNALS DIAGRAMS RELATING TO RADIOBEACONS. Added/Corp Great Britain. Hydrographic Dept. English. One time a year.

ISSN 1061-3730
US
●**AFRIKA MIX.** (AFRIKA MIX: RADIO AFRIKA REPORT.). **Added/Corp** Radio Afrika Foundation. **VFOAT** Afraka Mix. (1992)-. Periodical. English. Four times a year. $9.00. Radio Afrika Foundation, Inc., PO Box 123, New York NY 10027.

LC VK397 .A45   **ISSN** 8755-3422
DD 623.89/32/025798   US
ALASKA MARINE RADIO DIRECTORY. Added/Corp Alascom, Inc. (19??)-. Directory. English. One time a year. Free. ALASCOM Inc, Marketing Department, Marine Service, PO Box 196607, Anchorage AK 99519-6607. **Tel** (907)264-7394. **Ad Acc. Circ:** 11,000 (ctrl).

ISSN 0193-3671
US
AM-FM FACILITIES CHANGES ADDENDA. VFOAT Weekly AM-FM Addenda to Television Digest. **VAT** AM, FM Facilities Changes Addenda. Periodical. English. One time a week. Warren Publishing, Inc., 2115 Ward Court Northwest, Washington DC 20037. **Tel** (202)872-9200, FAX (202)293-3435.

ISSN 0160-8150
US
AM-FM RADIO GUIDE NEW YORK. VFOAT Radio Guide. Vol. 1 (May 1978)-. Periodical. English. Two times a year. $10.00. New york FM Radio Guide Inc., 40 Railroad Avenue, Glen Head NY 11545. **ED** Alicia A Dodd. **Ad Acc. Circ:** 20,000.
 Desc: Serves as a directory of radio programming in New Jersey. Lists radio programs, times and descriptions for 70 AM and FM stations, plus other station information.

LC VK397 .S62e   **ISSN** 0278-1379
DD 384.5/2/05   US
AMATEUR CALL BOOK, THE. [Amat. call book]. **Main/Corp** Society of Wireless Pioneers. **Added/Corp** Society of Wireless Pioneers. SOWP Amateur Radio Call Book. Society of Wireless Pioneers. S.O.W.P. Amateur Call Book. Society of Wireless Pioneers. S.O.W.P. Radio Amateur Call Book. Society of Wireless Pioneers. Amateur Radio Station Directory of S.O.W.P. Members. **VFOAT** S.O.W.P. Radio Amateur Call Book; Amateur Radio Station Directory of S.O.W.P. Members; SOWP Amateur Radio Call Book; S.O.W.P. Amateur Call Book. (19??)-. English. Free to members. Society of Wireless Pioneers Inc, PO Box 530, Santa Rosa CA 95402.

ISSN 0156-7071
DD 621.3841510994   AT
CEASED
AMATEUR RADIO ACTION. [Amat. radio action]. (1978)-Vol. 18 (June 1995). Periodical. English. Australian Consolidated Press Ltd., Private Bag 92615 Symonds St, Auckland New Zealand. **Tel** 011 64 9 3735408, FAX 011 64 9 3022889.

Communications —Radio

AMATEUR RADIO (BICESTER). (AMATEUR RADIO.). [Amat. radio]. (198?)-. Periodical. English. Twelve times a year. £26.50 UK; £32.40 Europe; £28.55 other. Goodhead Publications Ltd., 27 Murdock Road, Bicester Oxfordshire United Kingdom.
ISSN 0264-2557
UK
CODEN AMRDEE

LC TK6540 .A62

AMATEURFUNK-MAGAZIN. Periodical. German. 18.00. Verlag fur Technische Information, Winzerstr 82, 533 Konigswinter 1 Germany.
GW

LC HE8698 .A64
DD 384.54/025/73
ISSN 0738-8675
US

AMERICAN RADIO REPORT. [Am. radio rep.]. **Added/Corp** Duncan's American Radio, Inc. **VFOAT** American Radio. Small Market Ed.; American Radio. (Sept. 1976)-. English. Five times a year. $54.00. Duncans American Radio Inc., PO Box 90284, Indianapolis IN 46290. **Tel** (317)848-3223. **ED** James Duncan Jr. **Circ:** 2,500.
 Desc: Analysis of ratings and programming trends of over 250 markets. Additionally, comprehensive analysis of national radio trends.

LC HE8689.9.C3 C38a
DD 384.54/06/571
ISSN 0708-9392
CN

ANNUAL REPORT - CANADIAN BROADCASTING CORPORATION. See Communications-Television and Cable.

LC HE8690 .U56a
DD 353.0081/9
US

ANNUAL REPORT ON RADIO FREE EUROPE/RADIO LIBERTY. Main/Corp United States. Board for International Broadcasting. English. Board for International Broadcasting, Suite 400/1201 Connecticut Avenue NW, Washington DC 20036. **Continues** Annual Report.

ISSN 0208-7782
PL

UDC 7.097

ANTENA. (1981)-. Periodical. Polish. One time a week. $78.00. **(Subscription address:** Ars Polona-Ruch, PO Box 1001, Krakowskie Przedmiescie 7, 00-068 Warsaw Poland. **Tel** 011 48 22 261201.)

LC TK6550 .R18
DD 621.3841
ISSN 0890-3565
US

ARRL HANDBOOK FOR THE RADIO AMATEUR, THE. [ARRL handb. radio amat.]. **Added/Corp** American Radio Relay League. **VFOAT** ARRL Handbook for Radio Amateurs; Handbook for the Radio Amateur; American Radio Relay League Handbook for the Radio Amateur. 62nd Ed. (1985)-. English. One time a year (Nov.). $43.50. American Radio Relay League, 225 Main Street, Newington CT 06111. **Tel** (203)666-1541 ext. 253, FAX (203)665-7531. Each issue contains an index to its own contents (all volume index)--loose. **Continues** Radio Amateur's Handbook, 0079-9440.

ISSN 0190-3632
US

ARRL REPEATER DIRECTORY. Main/Corp American Radio Relay League. **VFOAT** Repeater Directory. **VAT** American Radio Relay League Directory. (19??)-. English. One time a year. $6.00. American Radio Relay League, 225 Main Street, Newington CT 06111. **Tel** (203)666-1541 ext. 253, FAX (203)665-7531. **ED** Bruce Jahnke. **Circ:** 50,000.
 Desc: Published in April of each year and lists over 9,000 amateur radio repeater stations in the US and Canada by location and frequency.

LC TK6554.5 .A78
DD 621.3841/6/076
ISSN 1056-6856
US

ARRL TECHNICIAN CLASS LICENSE MANUAL FOR THE RADIO AMATEUR, THE. (THE ARRL ... TECHNICIAN CLASS LICENSE MANUAL FOR THE RADIO AMATEUR.). [ARRL tech. class license man. radio amat.]. **Added/Corp** American Radio Relay League. **VFOAT** American Radio Relay League ... Technician Class License Manual for the Radio Amateur; Technician Class License Manual. (1992)-. English. Irregular. $6.00. ARRL Headquarters, 225 Main Street, Newington CT 06111.

ISSN 0162-5934
US

ASWLC. Main/Corp American Shortwave Listeners Club. **VFOAT** SWL. (1959)-. Periodical. English. Twelve times a year. $23.00. American Shortwave Listeners, 16182 Ballad Lane, Huntington Beach CA 92649-2272. **Tel** (714)846-1685. **Bk Rev. Ad Acc. Circ:** 450.

LC HE8689.9.B7 A93
BL

AUDIENCIA. See Communications-Television and Cable.

US

BACON'S RADIO TV CABLE DIRECTORY. (19??)-. English. One time a year (Nov.). $270.00 US; $293.63 Illinois; $290.00 Canada; $345.00 UK, Belgium, France, Holland and Honk Kong; $355.00 Sweden and Switzerland and Austria; $410.00 Saudi Arabia. Bacon's Publishing Co., 332 South Michigan Avenue, Chicago IL 60604. **Tel** (312)922-2400, (800)621-0561, FAX (312)922-3127. **Continues** Bacon's Radio TV Directory, 0891-0103.

LC HE8689.8 .B33
DD 384.54/02573
ISSN 0891-0103
US
TITLE CHANGE

BACON'S RADIO/TV DIRECTORY. See Communications-Television and Cable.

LC HE8699.A8 B7
DD 384.54/0994
AT

B&T YEAR BOOK. See Communications-Television and Cable.

LC HE8690
DD 384.54
UK

●**BBC AL-MUSHAHID.** (1995)-. Consumer Publication. Arabic. One time a week. $150.00. Media World Services Ltd., Awdry House, 11 Kingsway, London WC2B 6YE United Kingdom. **Tel** 011 44 171 2404550, FAX 011 44 171 2404607. **ED** Nasr al-Majali. **Ad Acc.**
 Desc: Provides Arabic-speaking persons with articles and television listings.

LC PN1991 .L84
DD 384.545
UK

BBC WORLDWIDE : THE BBC WORLD SERVICE MAGAZINE. Added/Corp BBC World Service. No. 1 (Nov. 1992)-. Periodical. English. Twelve times a year. BBC World Service, PO Box 76, Bush House Strand, London WC2B 4PH United Kingdom. **Tel** 011 44 171 2572906, FAX 011 44 171 3790519. **Continues** London Calling (London, England : 1981).

US

BILLBOARD BOOK OF NUMBER ONE HITS. (19??)-. English. Irregular. $7.95. Billboard Publications Inc., 1515 Broadway Billboard, New York NY 10036. **Tel** (212)764-7300, FAX (305)755-7048, telex WU TWX 710-581-6279.

US

BILLBOARD BOOK OF TOP 40 ALBUMS. (19??)-. English. Irregular. $7.95. Billboard Publications Inc., 1515 Broadway Billboard, New York NY 10036. **Tel** (212)764-7300, FAX (305)755-7048, telex WU TWX 710-581-6279.

LC TK6553 .P62a
PL

BIULETYN - POLSKI ZWIAZEK KROTKOFALOWCOW. Main/Corp Polski Zwiazek Krotkofalowcow. (19??)-. Polish. Irregular. $78.00. Zarzad Glowny Polskiego Zwiazku Krotkofalowcow, Ul. Nowy Pjazd 1, Warsaw Poland.

UK

BLUE BOOK OF BRITISH BROADCASTING, THE. (19??)-. Periodical. English. One time a year (Mar.). $77.01. Tellex Monitors Limited, Communications House 210 Old Street, London EC1V 9UN United Kingdom. **Tel** 011 44 171 4901447, 4908018.

LC HE8689.9.U8 B64
DD 384.54/09895
UY

BOLETIN DE ANDEBU. See Communications-Television and Cable.

UK

BRAILLE RADIO TIMES. (19??)-. English. One time a week. £57.20. Royal National Institute for the Blind, PO Box 173, Peterborough PE2 6WS United Kingdom. **Tel** 011 44 1733 3730777, FAX 011 44 1733 371555.
 Desc: Contains information about BBC national radios 1,2,4,5 live and VIRGIN 1215. Also has optional supplement giving details of the BBC's regional services in Scotland, Wales and Ulster.

LC ML3478 .B5
DD 780/.8996073
ISSN 1063-1011
US

BRE (HOLLYWOOD, CALIF.). (BRE : BLACK ENTERTAINMENT'S PREMIERE MAGAZINE). **VAT** Black Radio Exclusive. Vol. 13, No. 47 (Dec. 23, 1988)-. Periodical. English. Forty-seven times a year. $175.00 US; $250.00 Canada; $350.00 other. Black Radio Exclusive, PO Box 2694, Los Angeles CA 90078. **Tel** (213)469-7262, FAX (213)469-4121. **Continues** Black Radio Exclusive, 0745-5992.

ISSN 0040-2788
UK

BROADCAST (BORDON). See Communications-Television and Cable.

LC HG450
DD 332.6
ISSN 0146-0110
US

BROADCAST INVESTOR. See Communications-Television and Cable.

LC HG450
DD 332.6
ISSN 0736-9069
US

BROADCAST INVESTOR CHARTS. See Communications-Television and Cable.

ISSN 0749-2936
US

BROADCAST STATS. See Communications-Abstracting, Bibliographies and Statistics.

LC TK6540 .B846
DD 621.384
ISSN 0899-6725
US

BROADCAST TECHNICAL DATA AND APPLICATION INFORMATION MANUAL. See Communications-Television and Cable.

ISSN 0008-3038
CN

BROADCASTER (TORONTO). See Communications-Television and Cable.

DD 384.54/0971
ISSN 0709-0676
CN

BULLETIN - ASSOCIATION FOR THE STUDY OF CANADIAN RADIO AND TELEVISION. Main/Corp Association for the Study of Canadian Radio and Television. No. 3 (Jan. 1979)-. Bulletin. English (French). Three times a year. 40.00Can$. Association for the Study of Canadian Radio and Television, Radio Drama Project, Concordia University, 1455 Maissonneuve boulevard West, Montreal Quebec H3G 1M8 Canada. **ED** Frances Ennes. **Bk Rev. Circ:** 200. **Continues** A S C R T Newsletter, 0707-6002.
 Desc: Issues, news, reviews, on the subjects of broadcasting, broadcasting history, studies, and archives in Canada.

ISSN 1182-4573
CN

DD 791.44/7

BULLETIN DE RCI. [Bull. RCI]. **Main/Corp** Radio Canada International. **VAT** Bulletin de Radio Canada International. Vol. 1, No. 1 (Jan. 1990)-. Bulletin. French.

ISSN 0041-543X
BE

UDC 621.391
CODEN 654.

BULLETIN D'INFORMATION - URSI.
VFOAT Information Bulletin - International Union of Radio Science. (1938)-. Bulletin. Multiple languages. Four times a year. URSI Secretariat University of Ghent, Sint Pietersnieuwstraat 41, B 9000 Gent Belgium. **Tel** 011 32 92643320, FAX 011 32 92643593. **Bk Rev. Circ:** 1,700. **Ind/Abst** Int. Aerosp. Abstr.

LC TK6540 .A26
DD 384.5/3/05
ISSN 0746-8911
US
CEASED

BUSINESS RADIO. [Bus. radio]. **Added/Corp** National Association of Business and Educational Radio (U.S.). (198?)-(June 1995). Trade Publication. English. National Association Business Education Radio Inc., 1501 Duke Street, Suite 200, Alexandria VA 22314. **Tel** (703)739-0300, FAX (703)683-1608. **ED** A. E. Goeil. Index available (Dec. iss.). **Bk Rev. Ad Acc. Adv Mgr:** Robin Little, **Tel** (703)739-0300. **Circ:** 3,000 (ctrl).
 Continues Business Radio Action, 0093-0245.
 Desc: Non-profit trade association representing users of land mobile communications equipment, owners and operators of land mobile dealerships, specialized mobile radio operations, private carrier paging companies, manufacturers, and technicians.

DD 621.38
ISSN 0007-8964
JA

C.Q. HAM RADIO. [C.Q. Ham Radio]. (1946)-. Periodical. Japanese. Twelve times a year. $121.44. Nippon IPS Co. Ltd., 11 6 3 Chome Iidabashi, Chiyodaku Tokyo 102 Japan. **Tel** 011 81 3 3238 0700.

ISSN 0834-3977
CN

DD 621.3841/66/05

CANADIAN AMATEUR (1987). (THE CANADIAN AMATEUR.). [Can. amat.]. **Added/Corp** Canadian Amateur Radio Federation. Vol. 15, No. 2 (Feb. 1987)-. Periodical. English (French). Eleven times a year. 53.00Can$. Radio Amateurs of Canada Inc., PO Box 356, Kingston Ontario K7L 4W2 Canada. **Tel** (613)634-4184. **Bk Rev. Ad Acc. Circ:** 5,000 (ctrl). **Continues** TCA : the Canadian Amateur, 0228-6513.
 Desc: Covers amateur radio stations.

ISSN 0261-0361
UK

CB. CITIZENS BAND. [CB. Cit. band]. **VFOAT** Citizens Band. (1980)-. Periodical. English. Twelve times a year. $45.35. Argus Specialist Publications, Argus House, Boundary Way / Hemel, Hempstead Herts HP27ST United Kingdom. **Tel** 011 44 181 6671033, FAX 011 44 181 6889573, telex 948669 TOPJNL G.

Communications — Radio

Desc: Covers a wide range of topics, including the latest reviews on equipment; practical projects; national land and international band news; and the QSL pages, articles on shortwave listening, and reports on UHF CB.

LC TK6570.C5 M43   ISSN 0145-8167
DD 621.3845/4/05   US
CB RADIO JOURNAL. (MECHANIX ILLUSTRATED CB RADIO JOURNAL.). **VFOAT** CB Radio Journal. **VAT** Citizens Band Radio Journal. (19??)-. English. Mail Order Department, Fawcett Publications, 1 Fawcett Place, Greenwich CT 06830.

    BE
CCRM MARINE REPORTS. VAT Centre de Controle des Radiocommunications Services Mobiles Marine Reports. (19??)-. French (English). Twelve times a year. 3.000F. CCRM, rue des Belles Pierres 5, 1421 Ophain B S I Belgium. **Tel** 011 32 2 3844094, telex 69078 CCRM B. **Circ:** 50.
Desc: Contains information on radio monitoring and frequency measurements.

LC HD9696.R363 U617   ISSN 0741-6520
DD 384.5/3   US
    CCC
CELLULAR BUSINESS. [Cell. bus.]. Vol. 1, No. 1 (Jan./Feb. 1984)-. Trade Publication. English. Twelve times a year. $44.71. Intertec Publishing Corporation, 9800 Metcalf, Overland Park KS 66212. **Tel** (913)341-1300. (**Subscription address:** Intertec Publishing Corporation, PO Box 2901, Overland Park KS 66282. **Tel** 800 441-0294.) **ED** Rhonda L. Wickham and Kenda Richardson. **Bk Rev. Ad Acc. Circ:** 12,000 (ctrl). available on microfilm and microfiche from University Microfilms International (UMI); available on an online database (files 648/Full-Text) from DIALOG. Documents available from UMI Article Clearinghouse.
Desc: Devoted to the cellular radiotelephone industry, in editorial coverage and circulation. Discusses marketing, engineering and industry news. For cellular's primary participants: operators, dealers, agents, suppliers and consultants.
Ind/Abst ABI/INFORM Glob. Ed.; ABI/INFORM [Computer File] (July 1985); F&S Index Plus Text, Int. [Select. Cov.]; Infomat Int. Bus.; PROMT; Trade Ind. ASAP [Full Txt.]; Trade Ind. Index [Full Txt.]; UMI ABI/Inform--Bus. Period. Ondisc [Full Txt.].

    SZ
CERTITUDES. (19??)-. French. Five times a year (Jan., March, May, Aug., Nov.). 22.00F Switzerland; 27.00F other. Action Chretienne Radio Presse, Les Chapons 4, CH-2022 Bevaix Switzerland. **Tel** 011 41 38 461655.

LC HE8662 .A466
    SW
CIRCULAIRE HEBDOMADAIRE DE L'IFRB. Added/Corp International Frequency Registration Board. **VFOAT** Circulaire Hebdomadaire; IFRB Weekly Circular. **VAT** Circulaire Hebdomadaire de l'International Frequency Registration Board; International Frequency Registration Board Weekly Circular. (198?)-. English (French and Spanish). One time a week. Price varies. International Telecommunication Union, place des Nations, CH-1211 Geneva 20 Switzerland. **Tel** 011 41 22 7305111, FAX 011 41 22 7337356. **Continues** Circulaire de l'I.F.R.B.

LC DK266
DD 947   RU
CIS TODAY. Added/Corp Radio Liberty Monitoring. RFE/RL, Inc. (Jan. 1, 1992)-. Periodical. Russian. Radio Free Europe RL Res Publ, Oettingenstrasse 67, D-80538 Munich Germany. **Tel** 011 49 89 21022631. **Continues** CIS Today.

    UK
CITIZENS' BAND. English. Twelve times a year. £20.40 UK; $55.00 other. Argus Specialist Publications, Argus House, Boundary Way / Hemel, Hempstead Herts HP27ST United Kingdom. **Tel** 011 44 181 6671033, FAX 011 44 181 6889573, telex 948669 TOPJNL G.

    ISSN 1188-1518
DD 782.42164/0971/05   CN
CMJ CANADA. [CMJ Can.]. Issue 1 (Nov. 1, 1991)-. Periodical. English. One time a week. $95.00 per year. CMJ Canada, 61 Jefferson Avenue, Toronto Ontario M6K 1Y3 Canada.

    ISSN 1055-0461
DD 384   US
COLLEGE BROADCASTER. [Coll. broadcast.]. **Added/Corp** National Association of College Broadcasters. Vol. 1, No. 1 (Sept. 1988)-. Trade Publication. English. Four times a year (Feb., May, Sept., Nov.). $30.00 (associates and professionals); $75.00 (college stations, radio or TV); $20.00 (individuals, students, faculty) comes with membership. National Association of College Broadcast, 71 George Street, Providence RI 02912. **Tel** (401)863-2225, FAX (401)863-2221. **ED** JoAnne Forgit. Index available. cum. index. **Bk Rev**, (Qty: 4). **Ad Acc, Adv Mgr:** JoAnne Forgit, **Tel**, (401)863-2225. **Circ:** 4,000. available on an online database from Internet.
Desc: Covers legal issues, industry news, opinions, and record for student radio and television outlets.

LC HE8700.9.G7 C6   ISSN 0306-7718
DD 384.55/4/02541   UK
COMMERCIAL TELEVISION AND RADIO YEAR BOOK. See Communications-Television and Cable.

    ISSN 0988-3851
UDC 659   FR
    CODEN 654
COMMUNICATION & ... : LEVALLOIS-PERRET. (COMMUNICATION & ...). **VFOAT** Communication CB news; Communication et ... (Levallois-Perret). (1988)-. Periodical. French. Four times a year. Aguesseau Communication Presse, 175 177 rue d'Aguesseau, 92100 Boulogne France. **Tel** 011 33 1 46041212.

    US
●**COMMUNICATIONS STANDARDS REVIEWS RADIOCOMMUNICATIONS.** (Jan. 10, 1995)-. English. Irregular (6 to 8 issues per year). $595.00. Communications Standards Review, 757 Greer Road, Palo Alto CA 94303. **Tel** (415)856-9018, FAX (415)856-6591. **ED** Elanie Baskin. **Circ:** 175. available on diskette from MACPHUS. **Separated from** Communications Standards Review, 1064-3907.

    US
COMMUNITY RADIO NEWS. (19??)-. English. Twelve times a year. $75.00. National Federation of Community Broadcasters, 666 11th Street Northwest, Suite 805, Washington DC 20001. **Tel** (202)393-2355. **ED** Douglas Bostrom. **Bk Rev**, (Qty: 5 - 8). **Ad Acc. Circ:** 500.
Desc: Newsletter of the National Federation of Community Broadcasters. Provides updates on regulation and funding of public broadcasting.

LC HE8700   ISSN 1354-8565
DD 384.55   UK
●**CONVERGENCE : THE JOURNAL OF RESEARCH INTO NEW MEDIA TECHNOLOGIES. See** Communications-Television and Cable.

    US
    CEASED
CPB REPORT. See Communications-Television and Cable.

LC TK6540 .C18   ISSN 0007-893X
DD 621.38405   US
    CODEN CQCQAO
CQ. [CQ]. **VFOAT** Amateur Radio. Vol. 1 (Jan. 1945)-. Periodical. English. Twelve times a year. $24.95. CQ Communications Inc, 76 North Broadway, Hicksville NY 11801. **Tel** (516)681-2922, FAX (516)681-2926. cum. index. Documents available from Ask*IEEE. **Absorbed** Ham Radio.
Desc: America's fastest growing magazine for the active ham radio operator.
Ind/Abst Curr. Cit.; Index Inf.; INSPEC (July 1971-).

LC TK9956 .C788
DD 384.54   US
●**CQ ... AMATEUR RADIO ALMANAC, THE. Added/Corp** CQ Communications. **VFOAT** Amateur Radio Almanac. (1993)-. Periodical. English. One time a year. CQ Communications Inc, 76 North Broadway, Hicksville NY 11801. **Tel** (516)681-2922, FAX (516)681-2926.

    ISSN 1068-848X
DD 621   US
●**CQ AMATEUR RADIO ... BEGINNER'S GUIDE TO AMATEUR RADIO.** [CQ amat. radio begin. guide amat. radio]. **VFOAT** CQ's Beginner's Guide to Amateur Radio; Beginner's Guide to Amateur Radio; CQ Beginner's Guide to Amateur Radio. (1993)-. English. Irregular. $4.95. CQ Communications Inc, 76 North Broadway, Hicksville NY 11801. **Tel** (516)681-2922, FAX (516)681-2926. **Continues** CQ Amateur Radio ... Antenna Buyer's Guide, 1043-3201.

LC TK6560 .C67   ISSN 1040-1369
DD 621.3841/6   US
●**CQ AMATEUR RADIO ... BUYER'S GUIDE.** [CQ amat. radio buy. guide]. **VFOAT** Amateur Radio ... Buyer's Guide; CQ Buyer's Guide. Vol. 1 (1989)-. Periodical. English. Two times a year. $4.95. CQ Communications Inc, 76 North Broadway, Hicksville NY 11801. **Tel** (516)681-2922, FAX (516)681-2926.
Desc: Contains detailed model information on more than 600 amateur radio products, including high-frequency transceivers, antennas and computers, as well as "who's who" sections on sources and retailers.

LC HD9696.R363 U67
DD 338.4/76213841/0973   US
CURRENT INDUSTRIAL REPORTS. MA-36M, RADIO AND TELEVISION RECEIVERS, PHONOGRAPHS, AND RELATED EQUIPMENT. Added/Corp United States. Bureau of the Census. **VFOAT** Radio and Television Receivers, Phonographs and Related Equipment. (1978)-. Government Publication. English. One time a year. US Department of Commerce / Bureau of the Census, Data User Services Division, Customer Services, Washington DC 20233-0800. **Tel** (301)763-4100. (**Subscription address:** Superintendent of Documents, US Government Printing Office, Washington DC 20402.) **Continues** Radio Receivers and Television Sets, Phonographs and Record Players, Speakers and Related Equipment.
Desc: Presents data on production, inventories, and orders.

LC LB1044.8 .C87   ISSN 0739-991X
    US
CURRENT (WASHINGTON, D.C. : 1980). (CURRENT.). [Current]. **Added/Corp** National Association of Educational Broadcasters. Vol. 45, No. 2 (Mar. 15, 1980) ;New Series, Vol. 1, No. 14 (Nov. 12, 1982)-. Periodical. English. Twenty-three times a year (twice monthly except monthly July and Dec.). $70.00. Current Publishing Committee, 1612 K Street Northwest, Suite 704, Washington DC 20006. **Tel** (202)463-7055. **ED** J.J. Yore. **Circ:** 1,800. **Continues** Public Telecommunications Letter.
Ind/Abst Read. Guide Abstr. Select Ed.; Read. Guide Period. Lit.

LC ML5 .D275
DD 791.44/5   UK
DEE JAY AND RADIO MONTHLY. (Oct. 1972)-. Periodical. English. Twelve times a year. £0.20 single issue. B.C. Enterprises, New English Library / Magazine Division, Barnards Inn London WC2 United Kingdom.

LC WMLC 93/4078
    SZ
●**DIGITAL AUDIO BROADCASTING NEWSLETTER. Added/Corp** European Broadcasting Union. **VFOAT** DAB Newsletter. No. 1 (Summer 1993)-. Periodical. English. Four times a year. Free on request. European Broadcasting Union, Case Postale 67, CH-1218 Geneva Switzerland. **Tel** 011 41 22 7172111, FAX 011 41 22 7985897, telex 41 57 00 EBU CH.

LC HE8698 .D57   ISSN 0198-6422
DD 384.54/52   US
DIRECTORY OF FIELD CONTACTS FOR THE COORDINATION FOR THE USE OF RADIO FREQUENCIES. [Dir. field contacts coord. use radio freq.]. Directory. English. FCC / Federal Communications Commission, 1919 M Street Northwest, Room 538, Washington DC 20554. **Tel** (202)632-6302. available on microfiche (Vols. for (1978-) distributed to depository libraries).

    US
DIRECTORY OF MONTANA BROADCASTERS. See Communications-Television and Cable.

    ISSN 0702-892X
DD 791.44/3   CN
DISC JOKIES. Vol. 1, (Sept. 16/22, 1974)-. Periodical. English. One time a week. $80.00. WWJ-Folio Radio Services, 301 Davenport Road, Toronto Ontario M5R 1K5.

    ISSN 1045-9693
DD 781   US
DJ TIMES. [DJ times]. **VAT** Disk Jockey Times. (198?)-. Periodical. English. Twelve times a year. $30.00. Testa Communications, 25 Willowdale Avenue, Port Washington NY 11050. **Tel** (516)767-2500, FAX (516)767-9335. **ED** Jim Tremayme. **Ad Acc.** ctrl circ.
Desc: Dedicated to mobile and club disc jockeys. Focuses on recorded music and the latest sound and lighting products; also sponsors the International DJ Exposition.

LC HE8689 .I5713
DD 384.54/05   SZ
DOC. - C.C.I.R. Main/Corp International Radio Consultative Committee. **VAT** Document - Comite Consultatif International des Radio Communications. Multiple languages (English, French and Spanish). Irregular. International Telecommunication Union, place des Nations, CH-1211 Geneva 20 Switzerland. **Tel** 011 41 22 7305111, FAX 011 41 22 7337256.

    ISSN 1078-3784
DD 384   US
DOSSIER. ASIAN TELECOM SERVICE MARKETS. ASIAN CELLULAR OPERATORS. [Doss., Asian telecom serv. mark., Asian cell. oper.]. **VFOAT** Asian Telecom Service Markets. Asian Cellular Operators; Asian Cellular Operators. (19??)-. English. Irregular. Northern Business Information, 157 Chambers Street, 7th Floor, New York NY 10007-1015. **Tel** (212)732-0775, FAX (212)233-6231.

LC HF6146.R3 D786   ISSN 0743-7498
DD 384.54/3   US
DUNCAN'S RADIO MARKET GUIDE. (DUNCAN'S RADIO MARKET GUIDE / COMPILED AND EDITED BY JAMES H. DUNCAN.). **Added/Corp** Duncan

Communications —Radio

Media Enterprises. Duncan's American Radio. **VFOAT** Radio Market Guide. (1984)-. English. One time a year (Jan.). $275.00. Duncans American Radio Inc., PO Box 90284, Indianapolis IN 46290. **Tel** (317)848-3223. **ED** James H. Duncan Jr. **Circ:** 1,400.
 Desc: An economic analysis of over 170 markets with emphasis on the viability of radio in each market. Over 40 tables and rankings for each market.

ISSN 0279-8077
DD 384 US
DX BULLETIN, THE. [DX bull.]. (19??)-. Bulletin. English. One time a week. $42.00. The DX Bulletin, PO Box 50, Fulton CA 95439. **Tel** (707)523-1001, FAX (707)523-1001. **ED** Chad Harris. Index available. **Circ:** 8,000. *Continued in part by DX Magazine, 1043-4208.*
 Desc: Amateur radio, long-distance communications and DX news.

ISSN 1043-4208
DD 384 US
DX MAGAZINE (FULTON, CALIF.), THE. (THE DX MAGAZINE.). [DX mag.]. Vol. 1, No. 1 (Jan. 1989)-. Periodical. English. Twelve times a year. $15.00. The DX Magazine, PO Box 50, Fulton CA 95439. **Tel** (707)523-1001, FAX (707)523-1001. **ED** Chod Harris. Index available. cum. index. **Bk Rev**. **Ad Acc**. **Circ:** 10,000. *Separated from DX Bulletin, 0279-8077.*
 Desc: Amateur radio DX and contests.
 Ind/Abst Index Inf. (1990-).

ISSN 0737-1659
US
DX NEWS. (DX NEWS : THE MAGAZINE OF THE NATIONAL RADIO CLUB SINCE 1933 / NATIONAL RADIO CLUB.). **Added/Corp** National Radio Club (U.S.). (19??)-. Periodical. English. Irregular. $24.00. National Radio Club, PO Box 118, Poquonock CT 06064. **Tel** (608)423-4159. **ED** Mike Knitter. Index available. cum. index. **Bk Rev**. **Circ:** 750 (ctrl). available on audiocassette.
 Desc: The AM Broadcast Band Hobby magazine of the National Radio Club since 1933.

LC TK6540 .E22 **ISSN** 1019-6587
DD 621.3841/05 SZ
CODEN ETEREG
EBU TECHNICAL REVIEW. [EBU tech. rev.]. **Added/Corp** European Broadcasting Union. **VFOAT** European Broadcasting Union Technical Review. No. 251 (Spring 1992)-. Periodical. English. Four times a year. $150.86. European Broadcasting Union, Case Postale 67, CH-1218 Geneva Switzerland. **Tel** 011 41 22 7172111, FAX 011 41 22 7985897, telex 41 57 00 EBU CH. *Continues EBU Review, Technical, 1018-7391.*
 Ind/Abst INSPEC (1992-).

LC PN1991.3 .R8S6 **ISSN** 0131-694X
RU
EFIR. See Communications-Television and Cable.

LC TK6540 .B838 **ISSN** 0954-0695
DD 621.381/05 UK
CCC
CODEN ECEJE9
ELECTRONICS & COMMUNICATIONS ENGINEERING JOURNAL. See Electronics.

ISSN 1144-5742
FR
UDC 537
ELECTRONIQUE RADIO PLANS PARIS. (ELECTRONIQUE RADIO PLANS.). [Electron. radio plans Paris]. (1989)-. Periodical. French. Twelve times a year. $79.61. Les Publ Georges Ventillard, 2 A 12 rue de Bellevue, 75019 Paris Cedex 19 France. **Tel** 011 33 1 44848484. *Formed by the union of Electronique Applications (Paris), 0243-489X and Radio-Plans (Paris), 0033-7668.*

ISSN 0254-4318
AU
UDC 621.38
ES. ELEKTRONIKSCHAU. [ES, Elektron.schau]. **VFOAT** Elektronikschau. (1977)-. Periodical. German. Twelve times a year. S400.00. Technischer Verlag ERB, Eichenstrasse 38, A-1120 Vienna Austria. **Tel** 011 43 1 81120. *Continues Radio Elektronik Schau, 0374-4299.*
 Ind/Abst Curr. Cit.

LC PN1991.8.E84 S67a
DD 384.54/43 AT
ETHNIC BROADCASTING IN AUSTRALIA. Main/Corp Special Broadcasting Service (Australia). (19??)-. English. 5 Elizabeth Street, Sydney 2000 Australia.

BE
SUSPENDED
ETUDES DE RADIO TELEVISION. (19??)-(19??)-. French (English, German and Dutch). Irregular. 1400.00F Belgium; 1500.00F other. Etudes de Radio Television, boulevard Reyers 52, 1040 Brussels Belgium. **Tel** 011 32 2 7372534, FAX 011 32 2 7334020. Index available. cum. index.
 Desc: Covers media analysis and experiences.

LC PN1991.3.B4 E89 **ISSN** 0770-9994
BE
CEASED
ETUDES DE RADIO-TELEVISION - RTBF. See Communications-Television and Cable.

NE
EUROFILE RADIO INDUSTRY DIRECTORY. (19??)-. Directory. English. Two times a year. Fl135.00 Benelux; DM120.00 Germany, Austria, Switzerland; £40.00 UK; 420.00F France; $84.00 other. Music & Media, PO Box 9027, 1006 AA Amsterdam Netherlands. **Tel** 011 31 20 6691961, FAX 011 31 20 6691941. **ED** Cesco Van Gool. **Ad Acc, Adv Mgr:** Ron Betist. available on labels.
 Desc: Contains detailed information on thousands of national and local European radio stations. Provides address information, key contacts, and information on each station's major music programs, broadcasting hours, formats, frequencies and more.

ISSN 1050-0561
DD 384 US
EUROPEAN RADIO. [Eur. radio]. No. 1 (1990)-. Newsletter. English. Twelve times a year. $595.00. Kagan World Media Inc., 126 Clock Tower Place, Carmel CA 93923-8734. **Tel** (408)624-1536, FAX (408)625-3225. (Subscription address: Kagan World Media Ltd., 524 Fulham Road, London SW6 5NR United Kingdom. **Tel** 011 44 171 3718880, FAX 011 44 171 3718715.) available via fax.
 Desc: Covers and analyzes Europe's radio industry. Learn about regulatory changes, advertiser spending, station launches, demographics, ratings, market shares, ownership, etc.

UK
EUROPEAN RADIO DATABOOK. (19??)-. English. One time a year. $395.00. Kagan World Media Inc., 126 Clock Tower Place, Carmel CA 93923-8734. **Tel** (408)624-1536, FAX (408)625-3225. (Subscription address: Kagan World Media Ltd., 524 Fulham Road, London SW6 5NR United Kingdom. **Tel** 011 44 171 3718880, FAX 011 44 171 3718715.)
 Desc: A reference guide to the level of development in each market. Historic and projected revenues, country-by-country analysis of radio markets, lists of key contact names and direct dial numbers.

US
FM ATLAS. **VFOAT** Frequency Modulation Atlas. 13th Edition (1990)-. English. Irregular. $18.00. FM Atlas Publishing Company, PO Box 24, Adolph MN 55701. **Tel** (218)879-7676. *Continues FM Atlas and Station Directory.*

LC TK6555 .N73 **ISSN** 1061-8325
DD 384.54/53/0257 US
TITLE CHANGE
FM RADIO LOG. [FM radio log]. **VFOAT** FM Log. **VAT** Frequency Modulation Radio Log. (1992)-(1997)-. English. Dajja Enterprises, PO Box 24, Cambridge WI 53523-0024. *Continues NRC FM Radio Log, 1054-7444. Continued by FM Journal, 1068-0012.*

LC TK6555 .F57 **ISSN** 0899-5303
DD 384.54/53/02573 US
FM STATION ADDRESS BOOK. [FM stn. address book]. **Added/Corp** National Radio Club (U.S.). **VAT** Frequency modulation station address book. (1988)-. English. One time a year. $7.95. National Radio Club, PO Box 118, Poquonock CT 06064. **Tel** (608)423-4159.

ISSN 0274-4856
US
FOLIO (NORTH HOLLYWOOD). (FOLIO / PACIFICA RADIO, KPFK/FM 90.7.). **Main/Corp** KPFK (Radio Station : Los Angeles, California). **VFOAT** Folio KPFK-FM. (19??)-. Periodical. English. Six times a year. $50.00. KPFK-FM Radio PAC Foundation, 3729 Cahuenga Boulevard West, North Hollywood CA 91604. **Tel** (818)985-2711. *Continues KPFK (Radio Station : Los Angeles, Calif.) KPFK Folio.*

ISSN 0821-6681
DD 384.54/025/713541 CN
FRAME BY FRAME (TORONTO, ONT.). See Communications-Television and Cable.

ISSN 0160-1989
US
FRENDX. Added/Corp North American Short Wave Association. (19??)-. Periodical. English. Twelve times a year. $13.00. North American Short Wave Association, 52 South 17th Street, Richmond IN 47374-5647.

LC TK7800 .F86 **ISSN** 0016-2841
GW
CCC
CODEN FUSHA2
FUNKSCHAU. See Electronics.

LC TK7800 .F862 **ISSN** 0172-2778
DD 621.38/05 GW
FUNKSCHAU. SONDERHEFT. See Electronics.

LC PN1991.3.G5 G48A
DD 384.54/09667 GH
SUSPENDED
GBC RADIO AND TV TIMES. Main/Corp Ghana Broadcasting Corporation. **VAT** Ghana Broadcasting Corporation Radio and Television Times. (19??)-(19??). Periodical. English. 5.20. Ghana Broadcasting Corporation, Broadcasting House, PO Box 1633, Accra Ghana. *Continues Ghana Radio & Television Times.*

ISSN 1054-1071
DD 384 US
GREAT LAKES MONITOR. [Great Lakes monit.]. **Added/Corp** Michigan Area Radio Enthusiasts. Issue No. 37 (Jan. 1991)-. Periodical. English. Six times a year. $9.50 (membership included). Michigan Area Radio Enthusiasts, Inc., PO Box 311, Wixom MI 48393-0311. *Continues Member's Newsletter (Michigan Area Radio Enthusiasts), 1041-7559.*

US
HAM CALL. CD-ROM. (19??)-. Directory. English. Two times a year. $105.00. Buckmaster Publishing, Route 4 Box 1630, Mineral VA 23117. **Tel** (703)894-5777.

ISSN 0269-8269
UK
HAM RADIO TODAY. [Ham radio today]. (1983)-. Periodical. English. Twelve times a year. $53.00. Argus Specialist Publications, Argus House, Boundary Way / Hemel, Hempstead Herts HP27ST United Kingdom. **Tel** 011 44 181 6671033, FAX 011 44 181 6889573, telex 948669 TOPJNL G.
 Desc: Caters to the serious radio amateur; delivers in-depth reviews of products and features construction, conversions, pocket radio, club news, etc.

LC PN1993.5.A1 H54 **ISSN** 0143-9685
DD 791.4/05 UK
CCC
HISTORICAL JOURNAL OF FILM, RADIO, AND TELEVISION. See Motion Picture.

US
HITMAKERS. English. One time a week (50 issues). $150.00 radio stations; $295.00 other. Hot Sheet Publishing Inc., 22222 Sherman Way, Suite 205, Canoga Park CA 91303. **Tel** (818)887-3440, FAX (818)883-1097.

LC HE8663 .I47A
DD 384.54/52 GW
HORAIRE PROVISOIRE DE RADIODIFFUSION A ONDES DECAMETRIQUES. Main/Corp International Frequency Registration Board. **VFOAT** Tentative High Frequency Broadcasting Schedule; Horario Provisional de Radiodifusion por Ondas Decametricas. Multiple languages (English, French and Spanish). Four times a year. International Telecommunication Union, place des Nations, CH-1211 Geneva 20 Switzerland. **Tel** 011 41 22 7305111, FAX 011 41 22 7337256.

LC PN1992 .H67
JA
HOSOGAKU KENKYU. See Communications-Television and Cable.

LC PN1991.3.R8 H68
UN
HOVORYT I POKOZUIE UKRAINA. See Communications-Television and Cable.

LC TK9956 .I52A **ISSN** 0093-1926
DD 384.54/53 US
I.R.C.A. FOREIGN LOG. Main/Corp International Radio Club of America. (1971/72)-. English. One time a year. International Radio Club of America, 12536 Arabian Way, Poway CA 92064.

LC PN1991.3.U6 I3 **ISSN** 0748-0237
DD 384.54/025/796 US
IDAHO BROADCASTING GUIDE. (19??)-. English. Two times a year. Aden Frank E Jr, 5147 Morris Hill 133, Boise ID 83706-1638. **Tel** (208)377-5346. **ED** Frank Aden. **Circ:** 100.
 Desc: List and guide to the radio and TV stations licensed to and operating in the state of Idaho.

LC TK7800 .I2 **ISSN** 0018-926X
US
CCC
CODEN IETPAK
Pr Rev.
IEEE TRANSACTIONS ON ANTENNAS AND PROPAGATION. [IEEE trans. antennas propag.]. **Added/Corp** IEEE Antennas and Propagation Society. Institute of Electrical and Electronics Engineers. Antennas and Propagation Group. **VFOAT** Transactions on Antennas and Propagation; Antennas and Propagation. Vol. AP-11 (Jan. 1963)-. Periodical. English. Twelve times a year. $245.00. IEEE / Institute of Electrical and Electronics Engineers Inc., 345 East 47th Street, New York NY 10017-2394. **Tel** (908)981-1393, FAX (908)981-9667. (Subscription address: IEEE / Institute

Communications —Radio

of Electrical and Electronics Engineers, 445 Hoes Lane, PO Box 1331, Piscataway NJ 08855-1331. **Tel** (800)701-IEEE, (908)981-0060, FAX (908)981-9667, telex 833233.) cum. index. available in microform. Documents available from Article Express International, The Genuine Article, Ask*IEEE, CASDDS. *Continues IRE Transactions on Antennas and Propagation, 0096-1973.*
Ind/Abst Acoust. Abstr.; Appl. Sci. Technol. Index (1991-); Bioeng. Abstr.; Chem. Abstr.; Coal Abstr.; Comput. Abstr.; Curr. Cit.; Curr. Contents Eng. Comput. Technol.; Ei Page One; Energy Res. Abstr.; Eng. Index Annu.; Expand. Acad. Index (1992-); Index IEEE Publ.; INIS Atomindex [Micro.]; INSPEC (1968-); Int. Aerosp. Abstr.; Math. Rev.; Res. Alert [Full Cov.]; Sci. Cit. Index; SCISEARCH.

ISSN 0018-9316
DD 384 US
CCC
CODEN IETBAC

Pr Rev.
IEEE TRANSACTIONS ON BROADCASTING. See
Communications-Television and Cable.

ISSN 1042-4334
DD 384 US

IHN NEWS. [IHN news]. Added/Corp International Order of Handicapped Radio Amateurs. VFOAT International Handicappers' Net News. (1984)-. Periodical. English. Four times a year. Free. International Order of Handicapped Radio Amateurs, PO Box 1185, Ashland OR 97520.

LC HE8699.I4 I5
DD 384.54/0954 II

INDIA CALLING. Added/Corp All India Radio. (196?)-. Periodical. English. Irregular. Free. All India Radio, Akashvani Bhauan, Parliament Street, New Delhi 1 India. Tel 382249. ED S. K. Sundar. Bk Rev. Ad Acc. Circ: 10,000.

ISSN 0705-307X
DD 621.3845/4 CN

INFORMATION CB. (INFORMATION C B.). VAT Information Citizens Band. (1977)-. Periodical. French. Twelve times a year. Les Editions Unies, 5685 rue Fullum, Montreal Quebec H2G 2H6 Canada.

ISSN 0258-9494
UDC 061 (100) :621.39 BE

INFORMATIONS MONDIALES - UNDA.
See Communications-Television and Cable.

ISSN 0731-9312
US

INSIDE RADIO. (1975)-. Trade Publication. English. Six times a week (312 per year). $365.00. Inside Radio Inc., Executive Mews, 1930 East Marlton Pike, Suite S-93, Cherry Hill NJ 08003. Tel (609)424-6800, FAX (609)424-2301. ED Jerry del Colliano. Bk Rev. Ad Acc. ctrl circ. Continues Inside Radio; Absorbed Radio Only.
Desc: Weekly newsletter for radio executives and college communication majors. Contains articles covering the latest radio trends, features on new station ideas, syndication, programming, and radio rating analyses.

US

INSTANT BACKGROUND. Added/Corp Radio Advetising Bureau. VFOAT RAB Instant Background. (Spring 1990)-. English. One time a year (Spring). $25.00 (members of RAB). $30.00 (nonmembers). Radio Advertising Bureau, 304 Park Avenue South, New York NY 10010. Tel (212)387-2100, FAX (212)254-8713. ED Kenneth Coita (phone: 212)387-2185). Circ: 6,000. available on CD-ROM. Documents available from FAXON Xpress. Continues RAB Instant Background.

LC TK6540 .I562
DD 621.3841/05 ISSN 0957-4425
UK
CODEN IBSODS

INTERNATIONAL BROADCASTING. See
Communications-Television and Cable.

LC HE8696 .U53A
DD 384.54/05 US

INTERNATIONAL BROADCASTING OF ALL NATIONS; REPORT. Main/Corp United States. Information Agency. Office of Research and Evaluation. (1948)-. Periodical. English. One time a year. Information Agency, 1776 Pennsylvania Avenue NW, Washington DC 20547.

LC HE8698 .I56
DD 384.54/3 US

INVESTING IN RADIO. Added/Corp Broadcast Investment Analysts (Washington, D.C.). (19??)-. English. Irregular. $670.00. Broadcast Investment Analysts, PO Box 17307, Washington DC 20041. Tel (703)818-2425.

LC TK6540 .I854
RU

ITOGI NAUKI I TEKHNIKI. SERIIA RADIOTEKHNIKA. Added/Corp Vsesoiuznyi Institut Nauchnoi i Tekhnicheskoi Informatsii (Soviet Union). VFOAT Seriia Radiotekhnika; Radiotekhniki;

Itogi Nauki i Tekhniki. Radiotekhnika. (1980)-. Periodical. Russian. Irregular. Price varies per volume. VINITI - Vsesoyuznyi Institut Nauchno-Tekhnicheskoi Informatsii, All-Union Scientific and Technical Information Institute, Baltiiskaia ulitsa 14, 125219 Moscow Russia. **Tel** 011 7 95 2384600, FAX 011 7 95 9430060, telex 411160. *Continues Itogi Nauki i Tekhniki. Radiotekhnika, 0202-0769.*

US

ITV RESOURCES IN THE DEFINED MINIMUM PROGRAM. See
Communications-Television and Cable.

LC TK7800 .R8713
DD 621.38/05 ISSN 0735-2727
CCC
CODEN RCSYDS

IZVESTIIA VYSSHIKH UCHEBMYKH ZAVEDENII. RADIOELEKTRONIKA. See
Electronics.

LC TK6540 .R96 ISSN 0021-3470
UN
CODEN IVUZB5

Pr Rev.
IZVESTIJA VYSSIH UCEBNYH ZAVEDENIJ. RADIOELEKTRONIKA. See
Electronics.

LC QC 661 .R8 ISSN 0021-3462
RU
CCC
CODEN IVYRAY

Pr Rev.
IZVESTIJA VYSSIH UCEBNYH ZAVEDENIJ. RADIOFIZIKA. (IZVESTIIA VYSSHIKH UCHEBNYKH ZAVEDENII. RADIOFIZIKA.). [Izv. vyss. ucebn. zaved., Radiofiz.]. Added/Corp Gorkovskii Gosudarstvennyi Universitet Imeni N.I. Lobachevskogo. Nauchno-Issledovatelskii Radiofizicheskii Institut (Gorkii, R.S.F.S.R.) Gorkovskii Issledovatelskii Fiziko-Tekhnicheskii Institut. VFOAT Radiofizika. Vol. 1 (1958)-. Academic Scholarly Publication. Russian (summaries and/or abstracts in English; table of contents in English). Twelve times a year. $279.00. Izdatelstvo Vysshaia Shkola, Neglinnaya Ulitsa, Dom 29-14, GSP-4, Moscow 101430 Russia. (Subscription address: East View Publications Inc., 3020 Harbor Lane North, Suite 110, Minneapolis MN 55447. Tel (612)477-1005, (612)550-0961, FAX (612)559-2931.) Documents available from Article Express International, The Genuine Article, Ask*IEEE, CASDDS.
Ind/Abst Chem. Abstr.; Ei Page One; Eng. Index Annu.; GeoRef; INSPEC (1968-); Int. Aerosp. Abstr.; Math. Rev.; Res. Alert [Full Cov.]; Sci. Cit. Index; SCISEARCH.

LC PN1991.3.U6 J65
DD 384.54/0973/05 US

JOURNAL OF RADIO STUDIES : JRS.
VFOAT JRS. Vol. 1 (1992)-. English. Irregular. Journal of Radio Studies, Nassau Community College, Garden City NY 11530-6793.

LC HE8698 .R313
DD 384.54/06/573 US

● ### KAGAN'S RADIO DEAL RECORD.
Added/Corp Paul Kagan Associates. VFOAT Radio Deal Record. (1995)-. English. One time a year. $195.00. Paul Kagan Associates Inc., 126 Clock Tower Place, Carmel CA 93923-8734. **Tel** (408)624-1536, FAX (408)625-3225, telex ITT 4938124 PKA UI. *Continues Radio Deal Record, 1067-3032.*
Desc: Record of all radio station deals proposed and filed with the FCC in the last decade. Includes cash flow multiples, prior sale prices, terms of deals, seller financing values, etc.

LC HE ISSN 1064-1114
DD 384 US

KIDSNET (WASHINGTON, D.C.). See
Communications-Television and Cable.

US

KPFA PROGRAM FOLIO. Main/Corp Berkeley, California. Radio Station KPFA. VFOAT KPFA Folio. Vol.1 (June 1949)-. Periodical. English. Twelve times a year. $45.00. KPFA Program Folio, 2207 Shattuck Avenue, Berkeley CA 94704. Tel (415)848-6767. ED Ralph Steiner. Circ: 15,000 (ctrl).
Desc: Detailed program listing for KPFA-FM, Pacifica radio in Berkeley, with articles on programming, radio and other topics of interest to listeners.

ISSN 1070-6593
DD 384 US
CCC

LAND MOBILE RADIO NEWS. [Land mob. radio news]. (199?)-. Periodical. English. One time a week (50 issues). $597.00. Phillips Business Information Inc., 1201 Seven Locks Road, PO Box 61130, Potomac MD 20854. Tel (301)424-3338, (301)340-1520, (800)777-5005, FAX (301)424-4297, telex 358149. available on an online database (file 636/Full-Text) from DIALOG. Continues Industrial Communications, 0737-0415.

LC TK6570.C5 B84 ISSN 0148-0189
DD 384.5/3 US

LEN BUCKWALTER'S NORTH AMERICAN CB CHANNEL DIRECTORY.
VFOAT North American CB Channel Directory; CB Channel Directory. VAT Len Buckwalter's North American Citizen's Band Channel Directory. (1977)-. Directory. English. One time a year. Grosset & Dunlap, 51 Madison Avenue, New York NY 10010.

LC VK397 .I58b
DD 623.8561 SZ

LISTE DES INDICATIFS D'APPEL ET DES IDENTITES NUMERIQUES DES STATIONS UTILISEES DANS LES SERVICES MOBILE MARITIME ET MOBILE MARITIME PAR SATELLITE.
Added/Corp International Telecommunication Union. General Secretariat. VFOAT Call Signs and Numerical Identities; List of Call Signs and Numerical Identities of Stations Used; The Maritime Mobile and Maritime Mobile-Satellite Services; Indicatifs d'Appel et Identites Numeriques. (1985)-. Chinese (English, French, Russian and Spanish). Every 2 years. Service des Ventes de l'Union Internationale des Telecommunications, place des Nations, CH-1211 Geneva 20 Switzerland. *Continues International Telecommunication Union. General Secretariat. Liste Alphabetique des Indicatifs d'Appel des Stations Utilisees dans le Service Mobile Maritime, des Numeros ou Signaux d'Appel Selectif de Station de Navire et des Numeros ou Signaux d'Identification de Station Cotiere.*

ISSN 0110-5787
DD 791 NZ
CCC

LISTENER WELLINGTON. [Listener Wellingt.].
VFOAT Radio and Television Listener; NZ Listener. (1973)-. Periodical. English. Fifty-one times per year. $114.98. Listener, PO Box 100-741, North Shore Mail Centre, Auckland 1330 New Zealand. **Tel** 011 64 9 4430238, FAX 011 64 9 443-0249. *Continues New Zealand Listener, 0028-839X.*
Ind/Abst EP Collect.; Homework Help.; MasterFile FullTEXT 1000; MasterFile FullTEXT 350; MasterFile FullTEXT 650; MasterFile FullTEXT; Telebase; World Mag. Bank.

LC HE ISSN 1052-7109
DD 384 US

M STREET JOURNAL, THE. [M Str. j.].
Added/Corp M Street Corp. (1984)-. English. One time a week. $119.00. M Street Corporation, 340 Park Avenue South, 7th Floor, New York NY 10010. **Tel** (800)248-4242, FAX (212)473-4626. ED Robert Unmacht and Pat McCrummen. **Bk Rev. Ad Acc. Adv Mgr:** Pat McCrummen. Circ: 1,000.

LC HE8698 .M2 ISSN 1052-7117
DD 384.55/43/02573 US

M STREET RADIO DIRECTORY, THE. [M Str. radio dir.]. (1989)-. Directory. English. Irregular. $32.95. M Street Corporation, 340 Park Avenue South, 7th Floor, New York NY 10010. Tel (800)248-4242, FAX (212)473-4626. ED Robert Unmacht.

US

MANUAL OF REGULATIONS AND PROCEDURES FOR FEDERAL RADIO FREQUENCY MANAGEMENT. Main/Corp
United States. Interdepartment Radio Advisory Committee. (Jan. 1979)-. Government Publication. English. Irregular. $95.00 domestic; $118.75 other. US Department of Commerce, 14th Street & Constitution Avenue NW, Washington DC 20230. **Tel** (202)482-2000, FAX (202)482-3772. **(Subscription address:** Superintendent of Documents, US Government Printing Office, Washington DC 20402.) *Continues Manual of Regulations and Procedures for Radio Frequency Management.*
Desc: Covers the regulation of Federal interstate and foreign telecommunications.

US

MANUAL OF REGULATIONS AND PROCEDURES FOR RADIO FREQUENCY MANAGEMENT. Added/Corp
United States. Office of Telecommunications Policy. (19??)-. Government Publication. English. Irregular (manual and supplementary material). $72.00 US; $90.00 other. Superintendent of Documents, US Government Printing Office, Washington DC 20402. **Tel** (202)275-3328, FAX (202)786-2377.
Desc: Covers the regulation of Federal interstate and foreign telecommunications.

ISSN 1044-1190
DD 384 US
CCC

MOBILE PRODUCT NEWS. See
Communications-Telecommunication.

Communications — Radio

DD 621
ISSN 0745-7626
US
CCC
MOBILE RADIO TECHNOLOGY. [Mobil. radio technol.]. **VFOAT** Mobile Radio Technology Magazine. (198?)-. Trade Publication. English. Twelve times a year. $35.29. Intertec Publishing Corporation, 9800 Metcalf, Overland Park KS 66212. **Tel** (913)341-1300. **(Subscription address:** Intertec Publishing Corporation, PO Box 2901, Overland Park KS 66282. **Tel** 800 441-0294.)
Desc: Contains applications-oriented information on technology. Technical articles cover equipment, system maintenance and industry and regulatory news. Target audience is communications dealers, services providers and end-users in public safety and industry.

LC TK6553 .M636
DD 621.384/151
ISSN 0889-5341
US
MONITORING TIMES. [Monit. times]. **VFOAT** MT. (198?)-. Periodical. English. Twelve times a year. $23.95. Grove Enterprises, 140 Dog Branch Rd, Brasstown NC 28902. **Tel** (800)438-8155, (704)837-9200, FAX (704)837-2216. **ED** Rachel Baughn. Index available. **Bk Rev**. **Ad Acc**. **Circ:** 38,000. **Absorbed** International Radio.
Ind/Abst Access (1991-).

LC PN1991.67.M86 M87
DD 384.54/025/73
US
SUSPENDED
... MUSIC RADIO DIRECTORY, THE. See Music.

LC HD6350.B86 N18
ISSN 0027-5697
US
TITLE CHANGE
NABET NEWS. INTERNATIONAL EDITION. See Communications-Television and Cable.

LC PN1991.3.U6 N28
DD 384.54/0973
ISSN 0730-014X
US
NARA NEWS. (NARA NEWS / NORTH AMERICAN RADIO ARCHIVES.). **Added/Corp** North American Radio Archives. **VAT** North American Radio Archives News. Vol. 1 (1973)-. Periodical. English. Four times a year. comes with membership. North American Radio Archives, 134 Vincewood Drive, Nicholasville KY 40356. **Tel** (606)885-1031.

DD 791.44/7/0971
ISSN 0849-3952
CN
NATIONAL RADIO GUIDE. (NATIONAL RADIO GUIDE : ... LISTINGS FOR CBC RADIO AND CBC STEREO.). [Natl. radio guide]. **Added/Corp** Canadian Broadcasting Corporation. **VFOAT** Radio Guide. Vol. 8, No. 5 (May 1988)-. Periodical. English. Twelve times a year. 28.00Can$ (one-year) Canada; 50.00Can$ (one-year) other. Core Group Publishers Inc., PO Box 48417, Bentall Center, Vancouver BC V7X 1A2 Canada. **Tel** (604)688-0382, FAX (604)688-3105. **ED** Catherine Robertson. **Ad Acc**, **Adv Mgr:** Jane McIvor. **Circ:** 17,000 (ctrl). **Continues** Radio Guide, 0711-642X.

ISSN 0276-4520
US
NATIONAL RADIO PUBLICITY DIRECTORY. (19??)-. Directory. English. Six times a year. $95.00. PO Box 1197, 333 Whittlesey Avenue, New Milford CT 06776. **Tel** (800)223-1254. **ED** Ronald T Robinson. **Bk Rev**. **Ad Acc**. ctrl circ.
Desc: Comprehensive directory covering all of the 50 states as well as key Canadian cities, with special attention paid to major markets.

LC HE8664 .N38
DD 384.54/53/02573
ISSN 0889-2784
US
NATIONAL RADIO PUBLICITY OUTLETS. [Natl. radio public. outlets]. No. 1 (Jan. 1986)-. Periodical. English. Two times a year. $160.00. Morgan-Rand Publications Inc., 1800 Byberry Road 800, Huntingdon Valley PA 19006. **Tel** (215)938-5511, FAX (215)988-0402. **ED** Allan Priaulx. cum. index. **Circ:** 2,000. available on diskette.
Desc: Includes all stations arranged by market within each state, names of hosts and contacts for each program, programs that do telephone interviews, days and times programs air, advance booking requirements for guests, audience ratings, topics covered and format, programs that accept call-ins, specific tape and production requirements, details on network and syndicated shows, market data at-a-glance.

LC PN1990.9.T34 N48
DD 791.44/75/02574
ISSN 0741-7225
US
NEW ENGLAND TALK SHOW DIRECTORY. See Communications-Television and Cable.

LC TK6540 .N45
DD 791.405
NZ
TITLE CHANGE
NEW ZEALAND LISTENER. **Added/Corp** New Zealand Broadcasting Service. Vol. 1, No. 1 (June 30, 1939)-(1994). Periodical. English. Broadcasting Corp New Zealand, PO Box 3140, Wellington New Zealand.

Tel 64 4 741 200, FAX 64 4 741 231, telex NZ31031 BENZWEL. **ED** David Beatson and Peter Stewart. **Bk Rev**. **Ad Acc**. **Circ:** 281,000. **Absorbed** New Zealand Radio Record. **Continued by** Listener, 0110-5787.
Desc: Mass-circulation magazine featuring advance information on television and radio programmes and containing a wide range of general and special interest features.
Ind/Abst Annu. Bibliogr. Engl. Lang. Lit.

LC VK397 .N53
JA
NIHON SEMPAKU MUSEN DENSHINKYOKU KYOKUMEIROKU. **Added/Corp** Sempaku Tsushinshi Rodo Kumiai. Kyokumeiroku Henshu Iinkai. (19??)-. Japanese. ¥8000. Musen Tsushinsha, (Radio News Agency), 14-8 Shibaura 1 chome Minato-ku, Tokyo 105 Japan. **Tel** 03-451-4729. **ED** K. Seikiguchi. **Ad Acc**. **Circ:** 3,000 (ctrl).
Desc: A handbook for use by maritime radiocommunications service.

LC HE8698 .N345
DD 384.54/.43/02573
US
NORTH AMERICAN RADIO GUIDE. **Added/Corp** WF Innovations,. (1991)-. Periodical. English. Irregular. $7.95. WF Innovations Inc, PO Box 93142, Milwaukee WI 53203. **Continues** National Radio Guide (Milwaukee, Wis.), 1054-3244.

LC TK6555 .J6
DD 621.38416
ISSN 0078-1347
US
NORTH AMERICAN RADIO-TV STATION GUIDE. **VFOAT** Radio-TV Station Guide. **VAT** North American Radio, Television Station Guide. 1st Ed.(1963)-. Periodical. English. Irregular. Howard Sams & Company, Inc., 2647 Waterfront Parkway E Drive, Indianapolis IN 46214. **Tel** (800)428-7267, (317)298-5400.
Desc: Listing of all radio and television stations in U.S., Canada, Mexico and the West Indies. Indexed by location, call letters, and frequency.

LC CT120 .N77 PN4784.I6 N67
DD 070
ISSN 1078-0211
US
●**NPR INTERVIEWS, THE.** [NPR interviews]. **Added/Corp** National Public Radio (U.S.). **VFOAT** National Public Radio Interviews. (1994)-. English. One time a year. $24.95. Houghton Mifflin Company, Wayside Road, Burlington MA 01803. **Tel** (800)225-3362, (617)272-1500.

ISSN 0736-4237
US
NRBA RADIONEWTECH. [NRBA RadioNewTech]. **Added/Corp** National Radio Broadcasters Association (U.S.). **VFOAT** N.R.B.A. Radionewtech; Radionewtech; N.R.B.A. Radio New Tech; NRBA Radio New Tech. **VAT** National Radio Broadcasters Association Radionewtech. Vol. 1, No. 1 (Jan. 1983)-. Periodical. English. Twelve times a year. $10.00. National Radio Broadcasters Association, 1705 Desales Street NW/Suite 500, Washington DC 20036.

ISSN 0277-0245
US
NRBA SALES AND PROMOTION NEWS. [NRBA sales promot. news]. **Added/Corp** National Radio Broadcasters Association (U.S.). **VFOAT** Sales and Promotion News. **VAT** National Radio Broadcasters Association Sales and Promotion News. Vol. 1, No. 1 (July 15th, 1981)-. Periodical. English. Twenty-four times a year. $12.00. National Radio Broadcasters Association, 1705 Desales Street NW/Suite 500, Washington DC 20036.

ISSN 0027-6952
US
NRI JOURNAL. **Main/Corp** National Radio Institute. **VAT** National Radio Institute Journal. (19??)-. Periodical. English. Six times a year. $11.00 graduates; $6.00 other. National Radio Institute, 3939 Wisconsin Avenue, ATT Journal, Washington DC 20016. **Tel** (202)244-1600.

LC PN1995.9.C54 O36
DD 791.4/075/0973
ISSN 0748-7606
US
OFFICIAL PRICE GUIDE TO RADIO, TV & MOVIE MEMORABILIA, THE. See Communications-Television and Cable.

DD 791
ISSN 1057-9893
US
ON THE AIR MAGAZINE. [On air mag.]. Opus 1, No. 1 (Apr. 1990)-. Periodical. English. Twelve times a year. $23.00. Classical Guide Inc., PO Box 19600, Denver CO 80219. **Tel** (303)347-9752, FAX (303)988-1871.
Ind/Abst Music Artic. Guide.

ISSN 0739-5442
US
ONE TO ONE. **VFOAT** 1 to 1. (19??)-. Trade Publication. English. Fifty times a year. $95.00. CreeYadio Service, Box 9787, Fresno CA 93794. **Tel** (209)226-0558. **ED** Jay Trachman. cum. index. **Bk Rev**, (Qty: 5-10). **Ad Acc**. **Circ:** 1,251. available on online database (file 16/Full-Text) from DIALOG. **Continues**

Fruitbowl.
Desc: Preparation service for radio personalities. Contains humor, promotions, day to day calendars of history and events, artist information, "talent tips," and editorials.

ISSN 0958-6857
UK
OVERSEAS BROADCASTERS CIRCUIT. [Overseas broadcast. circuit]. **VFOAT** OB Circuit. (19??)-. Periodical. English. Free. OB Circuit, Attn Jocelyn Mayne, 24 Park Village East, London NW1 7PZ United Kingdom.

LC PN1990 .P35
KO
PANGSONG YONGU. See Communications-Television and Cable.

LC TK6555 .P37
DD 384.54/53/025
ISSN 0897-0157
US
PASSPORT TO WORLD BAND RADIO. [Passpt. world band radio]. **VFOAT** Radio Database International. (1988)-. English (French, Spanish and Japanese). One time a year (October). $19.90. International Broadcasting Service Ltd, PO Box 300, Penns Park PA 18943. **Tel** (215)794-3410, FAX (215)794-3396. **ED** Lawrence Magne, Tony Jones. **Ad Acc**. **Circ:** 50,000. **Continues** Radio Database International.
Desc: Provides information on world band and short wave radio newscasts, music and entertainment. Includes Buyers Guide to World Band Radios.

LC TK6570.C5 P18
DD 621.3845/4/05
ISSN 0363-1885
US
PC, PERSONAL COMMUNICATIONS SHOW DAILY. **VFOAT** Personal Communications Show Daily. Vol. 1 (March 30, 1976)-. English. St Regis Publications, 390 5th Avenue, New York NY 10018.
US
PIKE & FISCHER RADIO REGULATION. **VFOAT** Radio Regulation. (1947)-. English. One time a week. $3300.00. Pike & Fischer Inc., 4600 East-West Highway, Suite 200, Bethesda MD 20814-1438. **Tel** (301)654-6262, FAX (301)654-6297. **ED** Robert E. Emeritz, Jeffrey Tobias and Michael M. Eisenstadt. Index available. **Circ:** 450.
Desc: Provides research on telecommunications law and regulation; full text and digest of FCC and court decisions. FCC rules updated weekly.

US
PIKE FEE DIRECTORY. (19??)-. Directory. English. Irregular. $125.00. Pike & Fischer Inc., 4600 East-West Highway, Suite 200, Bethesda MD 20814-1438. **Tel** (301)654-6262, FAX (301)654-6297.
Desc: Covers information on fees for items in radio to be filed with the FCC.

DD 338.4/77914/0971
ISSN 0836-2114
CN
PLAYBACK (TORONTO). See Communications-Television and Cable.

LC TK6555 .P64
DD 621.3841/6
ISSN 0098-177X
US
POLICE CALL, FIRE EMERGENCY RADIO DIRECTORY. (19??)-. Directory. English. One time a year. $7.95 per volume. Hollins Radio Data, PO Box 35002, Los Angeles CA 90035. **Tel** (310)202-1418. **ED** Gene Hughes.
Desc: Data on radio systems used by police, fire fighters, rescue units, etc.

LC TK9956 .P59
DD 621.3841/51/05
ISSN 0733-3315
US
POPULAR COMMUNICATIONS. [Pop. commun.]. Vol. 1, No. 1 (Sept. 1982)-. Periodical. English. Twelve times a year. $22.95. CQ Communications Inc, 76 North Broadway, Hicksville NY 11801. **Tel** (516)681-2922, FAX (516)681-2926. **ED** Tom Kneitel. **Bk Rev**. **Ad Acc**. **Circ:** 100,000 (ctrl).
Desc: Exciting reading for the shortwave and scanner listener.
Ind/Abst Index Inf.

UK
PRACTICAL WIRELESS. Vol. 1, No. 1 (1932)-. English. Twelve times a year. PW Publishing Ltd, Arrowsmith Court, Bradstone, Dorset BH18 8PW United Kingdom. **Tel** 011 44 202659910.

US
PRIVATE RADIO RULES. (19??)-. English. Irregular (Master Volume with bimonthly looseleaf reports). $350.00. Pike & Fischer Inc., 4600 East-West Highway, Suite 200, Bethesda MD 20814-1438. **Tel** (301)654-6262, FAX (301)654-6297. available on diskette.

DD 384
ISSN 0033-779X
US
CODEN PRCAAO
PROCEEDINGS - THE RADIO CLUB OF AMERICA, INC. [Proc. Radio Club Am. Inc.]. **Main/Corp** Radio Club of America. Vol. 1 (1920)-.

Communications —Radio

Proceedings. English. Two times a year. $6.00. Radio Club of America Inc, 324 South 3rd Avenue, Highland Park NJ 08904. **Tel** (201)391-7664. **ED** John Morrisey. **Ad Acc. Circ:** 1,200. Documents available from Ask*IEEE.
 Desc: Articles by members on advances in the communications art; historical articles; news of the club.
 Ind/Abst INSPEC (March 1971-).

ISSN 0701-5887
CN

PROGRAM SCHEDULE - RADIO CANADA INTERNATIONAL. (RADIO CANADA INTERNATIONAL; PROGRAM SCHEDULE. RADIO CANADA INTERNATIONAL; PROGRAMME DES EMISSIONS.). **Main/Corp** Radio Canada International. **VFOAT** Radio Canada International; Programme des Emissions. (Fall 1970)-. Periodical. English (French, Portuguese, German, Spanish and Russian). Two times a year (Mar., & Sept.). Free. Radio Canada International Community, PO Box 6000, Montreal Quebec H3C 3A8 Canada. **Tel** (514)597-7555, FAX (514)284-0891, telex 05/267417. **Continues** Canadian Broadcasting Corporation. International Service. Program Schedule.
 Desc: Broadcast containing the schedule of the Radio Canada International programs and Canadian Broadcasting Corporation programs.

UY

PROHIBIDO. See Communications-Television and Cable.

LC PN1990.9.P82 P82 **ISSN** 0193-3663
DD 384.54/43 US
CCC

PUBLIC BROADCASTING REPORT, THE. [Public broadcast. rep.]. **Added/Corp** Television Digest, Inc. (19??)-. Periodical. English. Twenty-six times a year. $434.00. Warren Publishing, Inc., 2115 Ward Court Northwest, Washington DC 20037. **Tel** (202)872-9200, FAX (202)293-3435. **ED** Jeffrey Kole. available on an online database (files 16,636/Full-Text) from DIALOG.
 Desc: Covering all aspects of public broadcasting including personnel, policies, funding, regulation, etc.
 Ind/Abst PROMT [Full Txt.]; PTS Newsl. Database [Full Txt.].

US

PUBLIC NOTICE - FEDERAL COMMUNICATIONS COMMISSION. DOMESTIC PUBLIC LAND MOBILE RADIO SERVICE. Main/Corp United States. Federal Communications Commission. **VFOAT** Domestic Public Land Mobile Radio Service. (19??)-. Periodical. English. FCC / Federal Communications Commission, 1919 M Street Northwest, Room 538, Washington DC 20554. **Tel** (202)632-6302.

US

PUBLIC NOTICE - FEDERAL COMMUNICATIONS COMMISSION. SAFETY AND SPECIAL ACTIONS. See Communications-Telecommunication.

US

PUBLIC RADIO PROGRAMMING FISCAL YEAR ... . **Added/Corp** Corporation for Public Broadcasting. National Public Radio (U.S.). Office of Audience Research and Program Evaluation. (198?)-. Periodical. English. Corporation for Public Broadcasting, 901 E Street Northwest, Washington DC 20001. **Tel** (202)879-9600. **Continues** Katzman, Natan. Public Radio Programming, Content by Category.

ISSN 0886-8093
DD 621 US

QEX. [QEX]. **Added/Corp** American Radio Relay League. (19??)-. Periodical. English. Twelve times a year. $20.00. American Radio Relay League, 225 Main Street, Newington CT 06111. **Tel** (203)666-1541 ext. 253, FAX (203)665-7531.

ISSN 0744-8554
DD 384 US

QRZ DX. [QRZ DX]. (197?)-. Periodical. English. One time a week. QRZ DX, PO Box 832205, Richardson TX 75083-2205.

LC TK1 .Q2 **ISSN** 0033-4812
DD 621.3841/66/05 US

QST. [QST]. **Added/Corp** American Radio Relay League. Vol. 1 (Dec. 1915)-. Periodical. English. Twelve times a year. $31.00. American Radio Relay League, 225 Main Street, Newington CT 06111. **Tel** (203)666-1541 ext. 253, FAX (203)665-7531. **ED** Paul Rinaldo. Index available (bound in Dec. issue). **Bk Rev. Ad Acc. Circ:** 135,000.
 Desc: Electronic and amateur radio publication.
 Ind/Abst Appl. Sci. Technol. Index; Consum. Index Prod. Eval. Inf. Source.

DD 621.3841/66/0971 **ISSN** 0840-6170
CEASED

QST CANADA. (QST CANADA : OFFICIAL JOURNAL OF THE CANADIAN RADIO RELAY LEAGUE.). [QST Can.]. **VFOAT** Journal Officiel de la Ligue Canadienne de la Radio Amateur. (June 1988)-(June 1993). Periodical. English. Canadian Radio Relay League, PO Box 7009, Station E, London Ontario N5Y 4J9 Canada. **Ad Acc. Circ:** 5,800.

LC HE **ISSN** 1076-6502
DD 384 US

R & R (LOS ANGELES, CALIF.). (R & R) : [RADIO AND RECORDS] : THE INDUSTRY'S NEWSPAPER.). [R & R]. **VFOAT** Radio and Records; R and R. (199?)-. Trade Publication. English. One time a week (Fridays, except during the week of Christmas). $299.00. Radio & Records Inc., 10100 Santa Monica Boulevard, 5th Floor, Los Angeles CA 90067. **Tel** (310)788-1625, FAX (310)203-8727, telex 194561 LSA. **ED** Ken Barnes. **Ad Acc. Circ:** 9,000. **Continues** Radio & Records, 0277-4860.
 Desc: Trade newspaper for the radio and record industries; contains national airplay charts; FCC and industry news; and editorial for music, sales, management and programming.

LC TK6540 .R123 **ISSN** 0163-321X
DD 621.3841/05 CCC
CODEN RFDEDG

R.F. DESIGN. [R.F. des.]. **VFOAT** RF Design; RFDesign. Vol. 1 (Nov./Dec. 1978)-. Trade Publication. English. Twelve times a year. $48.00. Argus Business, 6151 Powers Ferry Road Northwest, Atlanta GA 30339. **Tel** (404)995-2500, FAX (404)995-0400. **(Subscription address:** Hallmark Data Systems, PO Box 1147, Skokie IL 60076. **Tel** (708)647-6933.) **Bk Rev. Ad Acc. Circ:** 33,382 (ctrl). available on microfilm and microfiche from University Microfilms International (UMI). Documents available from Ask*IEEE.
 Desc: Magazine for radio frequency engineers and design engineers.
 Ind/Abst Curr. Cit.; INSPEC (Sept./Oct. 1981-).

ISSN 0033-765X
RU

RADIO. **Added/Corp** Soviet Union. Ministerstvo Sviazi. DOSAAF SSSR. (1924)-. Periodical. Russian. Twelve times a year. $139.95. **(Subscription address:** East View Publications Inc., 3020 Harbor Lane North, Suite 110, Minneapolis MN 55447. **Tel** (800)477-1005, (612)550-0961, FAX (612)559-2931.) **Continues** Radiofront.

US

RADIO AAHS. (19??)-. English. Twelve times a year. $69.95. Warner Music Enterprises, 170 5th Avenue, New York NY 10010. **(Subscription address:** Warner Music Enterpises, PO Box 30616, Tampa FL 33630. **Tel** (800)274-7300.)

LC HF5905 .S74 **ISSN** 1071-4707
DD 659.1/42/02573 US

●**RADIO ADVERTISING SOURCE.** [Radio advert. source]. **Added/Corp** Standard Rate & Data Service. **VFOAT** SRDS Radio Advertising Source. Vol. 75, No. 10 (Oct. 1993)-. Trade Publication. English. Twelve times a year. $428.67. SRDS / Standard Rate & Data Service, 3004 Glenview Road, Wilmette IL 60091. **Tel** (708)375-5049, (800)851-7737, FAX (708)375-5003. **(Subscription address:** Neodata / Colorado, PO Box 2606, Boulder CO 80322.) **Continues** Spot Radio Rates and Data, 0038-9560; **Absorbed** Radio Local Markets Source.

ISSN 0892-6360
DD 621 US

RADIO AGE (AUGUSTA, GA.). (RADIO AGE.). [Radio age]. (19??)-. Periodical. English. Twelve times a year. $16.00 (one-year); $30.00 (two-year). Radio Age, 636 Cambridge Road, Augusta GA 30909. **Tel** (404)738-7227. Index available. **Bk Rev. Ad Acc.** ctrl circ.

LC TK6555 .R17 **ISSN** 0892-8002
DD 384.54/53/025 US

RADIO AMATEUR CALLBOOK. INTERNATIONAL LISTINGS, EXCLUSIVE OF NORTH AMERICA & HAWAII. [Radio amat. callbook, Int. list. exclus. North Am. Hawaii]. **VFOAT** Callbook; Radio Amateurs of the World; AWAII; Callbook-International Listings, Exclusive of North America. (1986)-. English. One time a year. $35.00. Radio Amateur Callbook Inc, 1695 Oak Street, Lakewood NJ 08701. **Tel** (908)905-2961, FAX (908)363-0338. **Continues** Radio Amateur Callbook. Foreign Listings.

LC TK6555 .R18
DD 384.54/53/0257 US

RADIO AMATEUR CALLBOOK. NORTH AMERICAN LISTINGS, INCLUDING HAWAII & US POSSESSIONS. **VFOAT** Radio Amateur Callbook. Radio Amateurs of North America; Radio Amateurs of North America, Including Hawaii and the U.S. Possessions; Callbook-North American Listings, Including Hawaii & U.S. Possessions. (1986)-. English. One time a year. $35.00. Radio Amateur Callbook Inc, 1695 Oak Street, Lakewood NJ 08701. **Tel** (908)905-2961, FAX (908)363-0338. **Continues** Radio Amateur Callbook. United States Listings.

LC PN1991.67.P67 R33 **ISSN** 0277-4860
DD 384.54/0973 US
TITLE CHANGE

RADIO & RECORDS. (RADIO & RECORDS : R & R.). [Radio rec.]. **VFOAT** Radio and Records; R and R; R & R. (197?)-(199?). Trade Publication. English. Radio & Records Inc., 10100 Santa Monica Boulevard, 5th Floor, Los Angeles CA 90067. **Tel** (310)788-1625, FAX (310)203-8727, telex 194561 LSA. **ED** Ken Barnes. **Ad Acc. Circ:** 10,000. **Continued by** R & R (Los Angeles, Calif.), 1076-6502.
 Desc: Trade newspaper for the radio and record industries; contains national airplay charts; FCC and industry news; and editorial for music, sales, management and programming.

ISSN 0575-9560
DD 384.54/0971/021 CN

RADIO AND TELEVISION BROADCASTING. [Radio telev. broadcast.]. **Added/Corp** Canada. Bureau Federal de la Statistique. Section des Services d'Utilite Publique. Canada. Bureau Federal de la Statistique. Section des Transports et des Services d'Utilite Publique. Statistique Canada. Section des Services d'Utilite Publique. Statistique Canada. Section des Communications. Statistique Canada. Section des Communications et des Informations. Statistique Canada. Section des Telecommunications. **VFOAT** Radio et Television; Radiodiffusion et Television. (1957)-(1991). French (English). One time a year. 39.00Can$. Statistics Canada Publications Sales and Services, R.H. Coats Building 6th Floor, Ottawa Ontario K1A 0T6 Canada. **Tel** (613)951-5078, (800)267-6677, FAX (613)951-1584, telex 053-3585. **Absorbed** Radio et Television, 0833-6792; **Continues** Radio and Television Broadcasting Statistics.

LC TK6555 .R19 **ISSN** 0812-2016
DD 384.54/53/02594 AT

RADIO AND TELEVISION BROADCASTING STATIONS. (1979)-. English. One time a year.

LC PN1990.55 .R33 **ISSN** 1062-0737
DD 384.54/02573 US

RADIO & TELEVISION CAREER DIRECTORY. See Communications-Television and Cable.

LC TK6553.A1 R25 **ISSN** 0307-3165
DD 621.38 UK

RADIO AND TELEVISION SERVICING. (195?)-. English. One time a year. MacDonald and Jane's Publishers, Paulton House, 8 Shepherdess Walk, London N1 7LW United Kingdom.

ISSN 0741-8469
US

RADIO BUSINESS REPORT. [Radio bus. rep.]. **VFOAT** R.B.R.; RBR. Vol. 1, Issue 1 (Jan. 1984)-. Periodical. English. Twelve times a year. Radio Business Report Inc, PO Box 782, Springfield VA 22150. **Tel** (703)866-9300, FAX (703)866-9306.

LC HE8698 .R27
US

●**RADIO BUSINESS REPORT. SOURCE GUIDE AND DIRECTORY.** **VFOAT** Source Guide and Directory; Source Guide; Source Guide & Directory; Radio Business Report Source Guide. (1993)-. English. Radio Business Report Inc, PO Box 782, Springfield VA 22150. **Tel** (703)866-9300, FAX (703)866-9306.

LC PN1991.3.U6 R327 **ISSN** 1044-9647
DD 384.54/09773/11 US
SUSPENDED

RADIO-CHICAGO. [Radio Chic.]. **VFOAT** Radio Chicago. (1989)-Suspended. Periodical. English. Four times a year. $12.00. Donna Walters, 332 South Michigan Avenue #1158, Chicago IL 60604. **Tel** (312)939-5480, FAX (312)341-0222. **ED** Linda Cain. **Ad Acc. Circ:** 20,000.
 Desc: Devoted entirely to radio (stations, guides, and personalities) in Chicago.

US

RADIO COMMON CARRIER RULES. (19??)-. English. Irregular (Master Volume with bimonthly looseleaf reports). $345.00. Pike & Fischer Inc., 4600 East-West Highway, Suite 200, Bethesda MD 20814-1438. **Tel** (301)654-6262, FAX (301)654-6297. available on diskette.

LC TK6540 .T15 **ISSN** 0033-7803
DD 621.3841/05 UK
CODEN RADCB7

RADIO COMMUNICATION. [Radio commun.]. Vol. 44 (Jan. 1968)-. Periodical. English. Twelve times a year. $54.76. Radio Society of Great Britain England, Cranbourne Road, Potters Bar, Hertfordshire EN6 3JW

Communications —Radio

United Kingdom. **Tel** 011 44 1707 59015, FAX 011 44 1707 45105, telex 25280. **ED** Mike Demison. Index available. **Bk Rev**. **Ad Acc**. **Circ**: 36,000 (ctrl). available on microfilm and microfiche from University Microfilms International (UMI). Documents available from Ask*IEEE.
Continues *R.S.G.B. Bulletin*.
Desc: Amateur radio journal of the radio society of Great Britain.
Ind/Abst Curr. Cit.; Curr. Technol. Index; INSPEC (Sept. 1971-).

DD 384
ISSN 0744-0618
US

RADIO COMMUNICATIONS REPORT.
(RADIO COMMUNICATIONS REPORT : RCR.). [Radio commun. rep.]. **VFOAT** RCR. Vol. 1, No. 1 (Dec. 15, 1981)-. Newspaper. English. Twenty-four times a year. $39.00. RCR Publications Inc., 777 East Speer Boulevard, Denver CO 80203-4214. **Tel** (303)733-2500, FAX (303)733-9941.

LC HE8698 .R28
DD 384.54/53/02573
ISSN 0146-6852
US
CEASED

RADIO CONTACTS. (19??)-(1993). English. BPi Media Services, 1515 Broadway, New York NY 10036. **Tel** (800)753-6675, (518)753-6675, FAX (518)374-7889. **ED** Michael M Smith.
Desc: Directory of radio stations including all programming data for local stations, networks, and syndicates.

LC HE8698 .R313
DD 384.54/06/573
ISSN 1067-3032
US
TITLE CHANGE

RADIO DEAL RECORD, THE. [Radio deal rec.]. **Added/Corp** Paul Kagan Associates. (19??)-(1994). English. Paul Kagan Associates Inc., 126 Clock Tower Place, Carmel CA 93923-8734. **Tel** (408)624-1536, FAX (408)625-3225, telex ITT 4938124 PKA UI. **Continued by** *Kagan's Radio Deal Record*.
Desc: Record of all radio station deals proposed and filed with the FCC in the last decade. Includes cash flow multiples, prior sale prices, terms of deals, seller financing values, etc.

AU

RADIO ELEKTRONIK SCHAU. (1971)-. German. Resch Media Mail Verlag GmbH, Postfach 1260, D-82166 Graefelfing Germany. **Tel** 011 49 89 8580710. **Continues** *Radioschau*.

LC TK6540 .R464
GW

RADIO-, FERNSEH-, PHONO-PRAXIS.
VFOAT RP. (19??)-. Periodical. German. Twelve times a year. Vogel Verlag, Postfach 6740, D-97064 Wuerzburg Germany. **Tel** 011 49 931 4182145, 011 49 931 4182483, FAX 011 49 931 4182670, telex 841 680131.

LC TK7800 .R37
ISSN 0033-7900
GW

RADIO, FERNSEHEN, ELEKTRONIK. See Communications-Telecommunication.

LC HE8698 .R314
DD 384.54/3
ISSN 1041-5017
US

RADIO FINANCIAL REPORT. [Radio financ. rep.]. **Added/Corp** National Association of Broadcasters. (19??)-. English. One time a year. National Association of Broadcasters, 1771 N Street NW/Suite 600, Washington DC 20036. **Continues** *NAB Radio Financial Report*.

ISSN 0148-0715
US

RADIO FREQUENCY PLAN. **VFOAT** U.S. Coast Guard Radio Frequency Plan. (19??)-. English. Irregular. US Coast Guard, 2100 2nd Street Southwest, Washington DC 20590. **Tel** (202)267-1408.

DD 384
ISSN 1055-887X
US

RADIO FUN. [Radio fun]. (Summer 1991)-. Periodical. English. Twelve times a year. $12.97. Radio Fun, PO Box 4926, Manchester NH 03108. **Tel** (603)625-1163.

ISSN 0199-6606
US

RADIO GUIDE (MADISON). (RADIO GUIDE). **Main/Corp** Wisconsin Educational Radio Network. (Sept. 1978)-. Periodical. English. Twelve times a year. Wisconsin Educational Communications Board, 732 North Midvale Boulevard, Madison WI 53705. **Continues** *Radio Guide & Broadcasting News*.

LC HE8698 .R316
DD 384.54/0973
ISSN 0740-2341
US

RADIO IN THE UNITED STATES. [Radio U. S.]. **Added/Corp** Duncan Media Enterprises. (1982)-. English. Irregular. $110.00. Duncans American Radio Inc., PO Box 90284, Indianapolis IN 46290. **Tel** (317)848-3223. **ED** James H. Duncan Jr. **Bk Rev**. **Ad Acc**. **Circ**: 2,000 (ctrl).
Desc: A statistical history of the commercial radio industry. It covers ratings and economic data for over 170 markets.

LC HE
DD 384
ISSN 1064-587X
US

RADIO INK. (RADIO INK : RADIO'S PREMIER MANAGEMENT & MARKETING MAGAZINE.). [Radio ink]. Vol. 7, No. 14 (July 13, 1992)-. Trade Publication. English. Twenty-five times a year. $125.00 US; $225.00 Canada; $199.00 other. Radio Ink, 224 Datura Street, 7th Floor, West Palm Beach FL 33401. **Tel** (407)655-/778, FAX (407)655-6164, (407)655-6134. **ED** Eric Rhoads. **Bk Rev**, (Qty: 25). **Ad Acc**, **Adv Mgr:** Yvonne Harmon. **Circ:** 4,500. **Continues** *Pulse of Radio, 1044-1603*.

ISSN 1071-4669
TITLE CHANGE

RADIO LOCAL MARKETS SOURCE.
Added/Corp Standard Rate & Data Service. (1993)-(1994). Trade Publication. English. SRDS / Standard Rate & Data Service, 3004 Glenview Road, Wilmette IL 60091. **Tel** (708)375-5049, (800)851-7737, FAX (708)375-5003. **Continues** *Spot Radio, 1066-2030*. **Merged into** *Radio Advertising Source, 1071-4707*.

DD 384.54/0971
ISSN 0709-552X
CN

RADIO (MONTREAL). (RADIO). **Main/Corp** Bureau Canadien de la Radio. **VFOAT** Radio Fact Book. French (English). One time a year. Bureau Canadien De La Radio, 1200 Ouest rue Sherbrooke, Montreal Quebec H3A 1H6 Canada.

SP

RADIO NACIONAL DE ESPANA. (19??)-. Spanish. Eight times a year. 12000ptas America and Africa; 10000ptas Europe, Argelia, Tunisia, Morocco; 8000ptas Spain; 14000ptas others. Radio Nacional de Espana CCI, Casa de la Radio Prado del Rey, 28023 Madrid Spain. **Tel** 011 34 1 3461406, 011 34 1 3461761.

ISSN 1053-1068
US

RADIO NEW YORK : LISTENER'S GUIDE TO RADIO PROGRAMMING IN THE GREATER NEW YORK AREA. (1991)-. English. $7.95. Want Publishing Company, 1511 K Street Northwest, Suite 635, Washington DC 20005. **Tel** (202)783-1887, FAX (202)393-5106.

LC HE8698 .R32
DD 384.54
US

RADIO ONLY. Vol. 11, No. 7 (Oct. 1992)-. Periodical. English. Twelve times a year. $150.00. Inside Radio Inc., Executive Mews, 1930 East Marlton Pike, Suite S-93, Cherry Hill NJ 08003. **Tel** (609)424-4600, FAX (609)424-2301. **Continues** *Radio (Cherry Hill, N.J.)*.

DD 384
ISSN 0742-5783
US

RADIO PC REPORT. [Radio PC rep.]. **VFOAT** Radio P.C. Report. Vol. 1, No. 1 (Apr. 1984)-. Periodical. English. Twelve times a year. $119.00. Waters & Company, Security Mutual Building/Suite 322, Binghamton NY 13901. **Tel** (607)770-1945. **ED** Dennis P Waters.
Desc: Features, news and reviews related to the use of the personal computer in managing radio stations.

DD 659
Pr Rev.
ISSN 1044-985X
US

RADIO PROMOTION BULLETIN. [Radio promot. bull.]. Vol. 1, No. 1 (May 1989)-. Bulletin. English. Twelve times a year. The Sullivan Co., PO Box 841002, Houston TX 77284. **Tel** (713)684-6914, FAX (713)855-3475. **ED** Jon Sullivan. **Circ:** 450.
Desc: Contains sales promotion ideas for commercial radio station sales managers, marketing managers and promotion executives. Only one subscriber per radio market accepted.

DD 384
ISSN 1061-6705
US

RADIO REGULARS. [Radio regul.]. (1991)-. Periodical. English. Four times a year. $5.00. Radio Regulars, 700 Washington Avenue NE, Suite 91, Minneapolis MN 55414.

ISSN 0963-0678
UK

RADIO TECHNOLOGY INTERNATIONAL. [Radio technol. int.]. (1991)-. English. Twelve times a year. $470.00. World Business Publications Ltd., 960 High Road, Britannia 4th Floor, London N12 9RY United Kingdom. **Tel** 011 44 181 4465141, FAX 011 44 181 4463659, telex 9419208.

LC TK6540 .B78
DD 791.4
ISSN 0033-8060
UK

RADIO TIMES. **Added/Corp** British Broadcasting Company Limited. British Broadcasting Corporation. (1923)-. Periodical. English. One time a week. $77.01. BBC Publications, 35 Marylebone High Street, London W1 United Kingdom. **Tel** 011 44 71 580 5577. **Absorbed** *World-Radio*.
Desc: Journal of the BBC containing full listings of the week's BBC TV and radio programmes with supporting illustrated feature articles.

US

RADIO TODAY. (1970)-. Periodical. English. National Association of Broadcasters, 1771 N Street NW/Suite 600, Washington DC 20036.

DD 384
ISSN 0883-640X
US

RADIO/TV HIGHLIGHTS. See Communications-Television and Cable.

DD 384
ISSN 0274-8541
US

RADIO WORLD (FALLS CHURCH, VA.).
(RADIO WORLD). [Radio world]. **VFOAT** RW; Radio World Newspaper. Vol. 4, No. 7 (July 1980)-. Trade Publication. English. Twenty-four times a year. Free on request. Industrial Marketing Advisory, PO Box 1214, Falls Church VA 22041. **Tel** (703)998-7600, FAX (703)998-2966. **ED** Judith Gross. **Ad Acc**. **Circ**: 18,000. **Continues** *Broadcast Equipment Exchange, 0194-2190*.

DD 384.5/3/097105
ISSN 1196-0809
CN
TITLE CHANGE

RADIOCOMM MAGAZINE. [RadioComm mag.]. **Added/Corp** RadioComm Association of Canada. **VFOAT** RadioComm. Vol. 11, No. 1 (1st Quarter 1993)-(19??). Trade Publication. English. Canadian Wireless Telecommunications Association, 275 Slater Street, Suite 2004, Ottawa Ontario K1P 5H9 Canada. **Tel** (613)233-4888, FAX (613)233-2032. **ED** Roger Poirier. **Ad Acc**. **Circ**: 3,000 (ctrl). **Continues** *Radiocomm in Canada., 0845-4531*. **Continued by** *Wireless Telecom*.
Desc: Official publication of the RadioComm Association of Canada.

DD 384
Pr Rev.
ISSN 1050-3641
US

RADIOSCAN MAGAZINE (SPANISH ED.). (RADIOSCAN MAGAZINE : LA REVISTA INTERNACIONAL DEL RADIOAFICIONADO.). [Radioscan mag.]. **VFOAT** Radio Scan Magazine; Radio Scan; RadioScan. Vol. 1 No. 1 (July 1989)-. Periodical. Spanish. Twelve times a year. $19.95. Radioscan Corporation, 8250 Northwest 27th Street, Suite 301, Miami FL 33122. **Tel** (305)594-7734, FAX (305)594-7677. **Bk Rev**. **Ad Acc**. **Circ**: 30,000.
Desc: Latest news about amateur radio communications. Equipment and book reviews, experiments and personal profiles.

ISSN 0485-8972
UN
CODEN RTKHAJ

RADIOTEHNIKA (HARKOV).
(RADIOTEKHNIKA.). [Radiotehnika]. **Added/Corp** Kharkovskii Institut Radioelektroniki Kharkivskyi Derzhavnyi Universytet. (1965)-. Periodical. Russian. Documents available from Ask*IEEE, CASDDS.
Ind/Abst Chem. Abstr. (1965-1981); INSPEC (1973-); Int. Aerosp. Abstr.; Math. Rev.

LC TK5700 .R32
ISSN 0033-8486
RU
CODEN RATEAO

RADIOTEHNIKA (MOSKVA).
(RADIOTEKHNIKA.). [Radiotehnika]. **Added/Corp** Vsesoiuznoe Nauchno-Tekhnicheskoe Obshchestvo Radiotekhniki i Elektrosviazi Im. A.S. Popova. Nauchno-Tekhnicheskoe Obshchestvo Radiotekhniki i Elektrosviazi Im. A.S. Popova. Nauchno-Tekhnicheskoe Obshchestvo Radiotekhniki, Elektroniki i Sviazi Im. A.S. Popova. Vol. 1, (1946)-. Academic Scholarly Publication. Russian (summaries and/or abstracts in English; table of contents in English). Twelve times a year. $185.95. **(Subscription address:** East View Publications Inc., 3020 Harbor Lane North, Suite 110, Minneapolis MN 55447. **Tel** (800)477-1005, (612)550-0961, FAX (612)559-2931.) Index available. **Bk Rev**. **Ad Acc**. Documents available from Article Express International, Ask*IEEE, CASDDS.
Ind/Abst Chem. Abstr. (-1973); Eng. Index Annu.; GeoRef; INSPEC (1968-); Int. Aerosp. Abstr.

LC TK7800 .R4
ISSN 0033-8494
RU
CCC
CODEN RAELA4
Pr Rev.

RADIOTEKHNIKA I ELEKTRONIKA. See Electronics.

DD 384
ISSN 1054-9048
US

RADIOWEEK. [RadioWeek]. **Added/Corp** National Association of Broadcasters. **VFOAT** Radio Week. (May 30, 1988)-. Periodical. English. One time a week. $52.00. National Association of Broadcasters, 1771 N Street NW/Suite 600, Washington DC 20036. **Formed by the union of** *RadioActive, 0747-4032* and *Radio Today*.

Communications —Radio

LC TK6555 .R27
DD 384.54/53/025796   US
RAID : RADIO AMATEUR IDAHO DIRECTORY. **VFOAT** Radio Amateur Idaho Directory. (1988)-. Directory. English. One time a year. RAID, PO Box 434, Nampa ID 83653-0434.

DD 384.5   SW
RATEKO & FOTO. (19??)-. Swedish. Twelve times a year. Radio- och Hemelektronikhandelns Riksfoerbund, Kungsgatan 19, 105 61 Stockholm Sweden. **ED** Jan Ljuhs. *Continues* Rateko.

ISSN 1182-4581
DD 791.44/7   CN
RCI NEWSLETTER. [RCI newsl.]. **Main/Corp** Radio Canada International. **VAT** Radio Canada International Newsletter. Vol. 1, No. 1 (Jan. 1990)-. Newsletter. English.

LC HE8811 .R35   ISSN 1060-0868
US
RCR'S CELLULAR HANDBOOK. [RCR's cell. handb.]. **VFOAT** Cellular Handbook. **VAT** Radio Communications Report's Cellular Handbook. (1991)-. English. Irregular. $69.00. RCR Publications Inc., 777 East Spear Boulevard, Denver CO 80203-4214. **Tel** (303)733-2500, FAX (303)733-9941.

RU
REFERATIVNYI ZHURNAL: RADIOTEKHNIKA. See Communications.

LC TK6552 .F4   ISSN 1066-2731
DD 621.38   US
REFERENCE DATA FOR ENGINEERS : RADIO, ELECTRONICS, COMPUTER, AND COMMUNICATIONS. [Ref. data eng.]. (1985)-. English. Irregular. $99.95. Howard Sams & Company, Inc., 2647 Waterfront Parkway E Drive, Indianapolis IN 46214. **Tel** (800)428-7267, (317)298-5400. **ED** E C Jordan. *Continues* Reference Data for Radio Engineers.
 Desc: Reference book containing charts, graphs, diagrams, tables, curves and illustrations.

LC BV655 .R45   ISSN 0034-4079
DD 260   US
RELIGIOUS BROADCASTING. See Religions and Theology.

LC HE8689.9.N45 B76a
DD 384.54/060931   NZ
REPORT OF THE BROADCASTING CORPORATION OF NEW ZEALAND. See Communications-Television and Cable.

LC HE8689.9.N45 B78A
DD 384.54/09931   NZ
REPORT OF THE BROADCASTING TRIBUNAL FOR THE YEAR ENDED 31 MARCH ... . See Communications-Television and Cable.

LC TK6563 .R428   ISSN 0742-9088
DD 621.3841/36/075   US
REPRODUCER, THE. (THE REPRODUCER : JOURNAL OF THE VINTAGE RADIO AND PHONOGRAPH SOCIETY, INC.). [Reproducer]. **Added/Corp** Vintage Radio and Phonograph Society (U.S.). (19??)-. Periodical. English. Four times a year. Free. VRPS Inc, POB 165345, Irving TX 75016. **ED** George J Potter and Ken Deibel. **Bk Rev. Ad Acc. Circ:** 450.
 Desc: Covers antique radio and phonograph collecting, restoration methods, historical documentation, collectors, ads, and articles on radio equipment.

ISSN 0149-9971
US
REVIEW OF INTERNATIONAL BROADCASTING. Issue No. 2 (Apr. 1977)-. Periodical. English. Four times a year. Review of International Broadcasting, PO Box 1684, Enid OK 73702-1684. **Tel** (405)237-3676. **ED** Glenn Hauser. **Bk Rev. Ad Acc. Circ:** 1,700. *Continues* Glenn Hauser's Independent Publication.
 Desc: Program and frequency schedules of international shortwave stations, reviews and recommendations by readers, equipment forum, CIA monitoring reports, station profiles, domestic information and associated listening.

LC DJK51 .R48   ISSN 0941-505X
GW
CEASED
RFE/RL RESEARCH REPORT. (RFE/RL RESEARCH REPORT : WEEKLY ANALYSES FROM THE RFE/RL RESEARCH INSTITUTE.). **Added/Corp** RFE/RL, Inc. Research Institute. **VFOAT** Radio Free Europe/Radio Liberty Research Report; Radio Free Europe Radio Liberty Research Report. Vol. 1, No. 1 (Jan. 1992)-Vol. 3. Periodical. English. Radio Free Europe RL Res Publ, Oettingenstrasse 67, D-8538 Munich Germany. **Tel** 011 49 89 21022631. Documents available from UMI Article Clearinghouse. *Formed by the union of* Report on Eastern Europe, 0937-7441 *and* Report on the USSR, 1042-7503.
 Ind/Abst Hum. Rights Intern. Rep.; Newsp. Period. Abstr. (1992-); PAIS Int. Print.

LC AP30 .R5
DD 053/.1   GW
RIAS QUARTAL. Added/Corp Rundfund im Amerikanischen Sektor (Berlin, Germany). Intendanz und Gesamtbetriebsrat. (19??)-. Periodical. German. Four times a year. Free. DeutschlandRadio / RIAS / Berlin, Kufsteiner Strabe 69, 1000 Berlin 62 Germany. **Tel** 0 30 85 03 0, telex 183 790. **Circ:** 2,600-2,800 (ctrl).
 Desc: Contains the contents of news about the radio station RIAS in Berlin, its programmes, activities and its personalities..

LC PN1991.3.M68 R16
DD 384/.54/05   MZ
RM MENSARIO: RADIO MOCAMBIQUE. Added/Corp Radio Clube de Mocambique. **VFOAT** Radio Mocambique. **VAT** Radio Mocambique Mensario: Radio Mocambique. (1935)-. Periodical. Portuguese. Twelve times a year. Radio Mocambique, Caixa Postal 2000, Lourenco Marques Mozambique.

LC PN1991.3.C9 N3
XR
ROZHLAS. See Communications-Television and Cable.

UK
RSGB AMATEUR RADIO CALL BOOK. (19??)-. Directory. English. One time a year. £9.50. Radio Society of Great Britain, Cranborne Road, Potter Bar Hertfordshire EN6 3JE United Kingdom. **Tel** 011 44 1707 659015, FAX 011 44 1707 645105. **ED** Brett Rider. **Ad Acc, Adv Mgr:** Victor Brand, **Tel** 0953 898422.

LC HE8690 .R8   ISSN 0035-9874
GW
CCC
RUNDFUNK UND FERNSEHEN. See Communications-Television and Cable.

ISSN 0035-9890
GW
CODEN RUMIA5
RUNDFUNKTECHNISCHE MITTEILUNGEN. See Communications-Television and Cable.

LC TK6570.C5 S15   ISSN 0193-7014
DD 621.3841/6   US
S9 HOBBY RADIO. VAT S Nine Hobby Radio. Vol. 19, No. 9 (Sept. 1979)-. English. Twelve times a year. $12.00. Cowan Publishing Corporation, 14 Devanventer Avenue, Port Washington NY 11050. *Continues* CB Radio S9, 0145-4560.

LC TK6570.A8 S29   ISSN 0163-3627
DD 629.2/77   US
SAMS AUTO RADIO SERVICE DATA.
Main/Corp Howard W. Sams and Co. **Added/Corp** Howard W. Sams & Co. Auto Radio Service Data. Vol. 267 (Oct. 1978)-. English. Howard Sams & Company, Inc., 2647 Waterfront Parkway E Drive, Indianapolis IN 46214. **Tel** (800)428-7267, (317)298-5400. **Bk Rev. Ad Acc.** *Continues* Sams Photofact Auto Radio Series.
 Desc: Full service documentation for repair of auto radios.

ISSN 0581-4693
US
SAMS PHOTOFACT CB RADIO SERIES. Added/Corp Howard W. Sams & Co. **VAT** Sams Photofact Citizens Band Radio Series. Vol. 4 (Sept. 1963)-. English. Twelve times a year. Howard Sams & Company, Inc., 2647 Waterfront Parkway E Drive, Indianapolis IN 46214. **Tel** (800)428-7267, (317)298-5400. *Continues* Sams Citizens Band Radio Manual.

LC TK6564.T7 S3
DD 621.3841/87   US
SAMS TRANSISTOR RADIO. Main/Corp Howard W. Sams & Co. **VFOAT** Transistor Radio. English. Twelve times a year. $3.50 (single issue). Howard Sams & Company, Inc., 2647 Waterfront Parkway E Drive, Indianapolis IN 46214. **Tel** (800)428-7267, (317)298-5400. **Bk Rev. Ad Acc.** *Continues* Sams Photofact Transistor Radio Series.
 Desc: Full service documentation for repair of popular transistor radios.

ISSN 0745-0923
US
SCAN MAGAZINE. [Scan mag.]. **Added/Corp** Scanner Association of North America. **VFOAT** Scan. (19??)-. Periodical. English. Six times a year. Scan, East Wacker Drive/Suite 1212/111, Chicago IL 60601.

LC TK9956 .S325   ISSN 1078-3164
DD 384.54/53/0257949   US
SCANFAN SOUTHERN CALIFORNIA.
[ScanFan South. Calif.]. **VFOAT** Southern California ScanFan. (19??)-. English. Irregular. ScanFan Publications, PO Box 544, San Marcos CA 92079.

LC TK9956 .S513   ISSN 0037-4261
DD 621.384   UK
SHORT WAVE MAGAZINE, THE. [Short wave mag.]. (1937)-. Periodical. English. Twelve times a year. $46.21. PW Publishing Ltd., Arrowsmith Court, Bradstone, Dorset BH18 8PW United Kingdom. **Tel** 011 44 202659910. Documents available from Ask*IEEE.
 Ind/Abst Curr. Cit.; INSPEC (Sept. 1983-).

US
SOUTH CAROLINA SCENE: ETV/RADIO GUIDE. Added/Corp South Carolina. Educational Television Commission. **VFOAT** ETV/Radio Guide. Vol. 11, No. 24 (Sept. 1978)-. English. Twelve times a year. Free to South Carolina schools; $30.00 other. ETV Endowment, 2712 Millwood Avenue, Drawer L, Columbia SC 29250. **Tel** (800)553-7752, (803)758-7285. *Continues* ETV Guide: South Carolina Educational Television and Radio Programs.

LC HE8689.9.G7 I528   ISSN 0962-1830
DD 384.55/4/0941   UK
SPECTRUM : THE QUARTERLY MAGAZINE OF THE INDEPENDENT TELEVISION COMMISSION. See Communications-Television and Cable.

ISSN 0882-8199
DD 384   US
SPEEDXGRAM. [Speedxgram]. **Added/Corp** Speedx. (19??)-. Periodical. English. Twelve times a year. Speedxgram, 7738 East Hampton Street, Tucson AZ 85715.

LC ML18 .Y8
US
SPOT! : YELLOW PAGES OF ROCK. Added/Corp Album Network. **VFOAT** Network Magazine Group; Album Network's Spot! Yellow Pages of Rock. (19??)-. English. Irregular. The Album Network Inc, 120 North Victory Boulevard, 3rd Floor, Burbank CA 91502.

US
STATUS REPORT OF PUBLIC BROADCASTING. See Communications-Television and Cable.

ISSN 0313-0797
DD 791.445   AT
STEREO FM RADIO. [Stereo FM radio]. **VFOAT** Stereo Frequency Modulated Radio. (1975)-. Periodical. English. Twelve times a year. 49.34Aus$. Music Broadcasting Society of NSW Cooperative, 76 Chandos Street, Saint Leonards New South Wales Australia. **Tel** 011 61 2 439 4777, FAX (612)439-4064. **ED** Virginia Lloyd. **Bk Rev.** (Qty: 4). **Ad Acc. Circ:** 7,000.

LC PN1992 .S85
DD 301.16/1   JA
STUDIES OF BROADCASTING. See Communications-Television and Cable.

LC HE8660   ISSN 1352-1438
DD 384.5   UK
●**SUMMARY OF WORLD BROADCASTS. MEDIA. WORLD BROADCASTING INFORMATION.** **VFOAT** World Broadcasting Information. (1994)-. Trade Publication. English. One time a week. £390.00 UK; £420.00 Europe; £435.00 other. BBC Monitoring, Caversham Park, Reading, Berkshire RG4 8TZ United Kingdom. **Tel** 011 44 1734 469289, FAX 011 44 1734 463823. **ED** Bob Eggington. **Circ:** 1,000. available on an online database from DATA-STAR.

LC HE8663 .S86
DD 384.53/52/025   SZ
SUPPLEMENT ... DE LA NOMENCLATURE DES STATIONS DE RADIOREPERAGE ET DES STATIONS EFFECTUANT DES SERVICES SPECIAUX. ADDITIONS / UNION INTERNATIONALE DES TELECOMMUNICATIONS. VFOAT Additions; Supplement of the List of Radiodetermination and Special Service Stations Additions. English (French and Spanish).

LC HE8660   ISSN 1352-1446
DD 384.5   UK
●**SWB. SUMMARY OF WORLD BROADCASTS. MEDIA, BROADCASTING SCHEDULES.** (1994)-. Trade Publication. English. One time a week. £105.00 UK; £130.00 Europe; £145.00 other. BBC Monitoring, Caversham Park, Reading, Berkshire RG4 8TZ United Kingdom. **Tel** 011 44 1734 469289, FAX 011 44 1734 463823. **ED** Bob Eggington. **Circ:** 1,000. available on an online database.
 Desc: Consists of operational program and frequency schedules.

Communications —Radio

TECHNICAL NOTES - RCA. [Tech. notes, RCA]. **Main/Corp** Radio Corporation of America. **VAT** Technical Notes - Radio Corporation of America. Periodical. English. Four times a year. Radio Corporation of America, PO Box 432, Technical Laboratories, Princeton NJ 08540. **Tel** (609)734-3223. Documents available from Article Express International, Ask*IEEE.
Ind/Abst Bioeng. Abstr.; Ei Page One; Eng. Index Annu.; INSPEC (April 1968-1971, 1975-).
LC PN1991.3.R8 S6
ISSN 0483-7495
US
CODEN RCTNAV

TELEVIDENIE, RADIOVESHCHANIE. See Communications-Television and Cable.
LC HE8689 .R62
DD 384.54/05
ISSN 0131-694X
RU

TELEVISION/RADIO AGE COMMUNICATIONS COURSEBOOK. See Communications-Television and Cable.
LC PN1992.3.B8 T18
ISSN 0271-4809
US

TELEVIZIIA, RADIO. **Added/Corp** Bulgarska Televiziia. Bulgarsko Radio. (19??)-. Periodical. Bulgarian. One time a week. DM165.00. **(Subscription address:** Kubon & Sagner, ABT Zeitschriftenimport, D 80328 Munich Germany. **Tel** 011 49 89 54218130.) Continues TR. Televiziia, Radio, 0302-7309.
LC TK6570.M6 T45
DD 384.5/3/05
ISSN 0193-1458
US
CCC
TITLE CHANGE

TELOCATOR. [Telocator]. **Added/Corp** Telocator Network of America. Vol. 1, No. 1 (Oct. 1977)-Vol. 18, No. 1 (Jan. 1994). Periodical. English. Business Word Inc., 5350 South Roslyn Street, Suite 400, Englewood CA 80111-2125. **Tel** (303)290-8500, FAX (303)290-9025. **ED** Catherine Baker. **Ad Acc.** ctrl circ. Continues Communicator. Continued by PCIA Journal, 1075-7821.
DD 354.710085
ISSN 1187-4848
CN

TETE-A-TETE (OTTAWA. 1991). (TETE-A-TETE : CRTC, COMMENTS, INQUIRIES AND COMPLAINTS.). [Tete-a-tete]. **Main/Corp** Canadian Radio-Television and Telecommunications Commission. **VFOAT** Tete-a-Tete. (1991)-. English (French). Canadian Radio-Television and Telecommunications Commission Information Services, 100 Metcalfe Street, Ottawa Ontario K1A 0N2 Canada.
DD 791.44/09713/84
ISSN 0704-478X
CN

TRANS FM. (TRANS F M.). [Trans FM]. **Added/Corp** C K C U (Radio station) Ottawa, Ont. (1979)-. Periodical. English. Ten times a year. Radio Carelton, Trans FM, Room 517/Unicentre, Carleton University, Ottawa Ontario K1S 5B6 Canada. **Tel** (613)788-2898. **Ad Acc.** ctrl circ.
LC HE8690 .T7
DD 384.54/43/023
ISSN 1062-9181
US

TRAVELER'S GUIDE TO WORLD RADIO. [Travel. guide world radio]. **Added/Corp** Billboard Books (Firm). **VFOAT** Guide to World Radio. (1991)-. Consumer Publication. English. One time a year. $9.95. Watson Guptill Publications, PO Box 2014, Lakewood NJ 08701. **Tel** (800)451-1741, (908)363-5679, FAX (908)363-0338. **ED** Andrew G. Sennitt.
Desc: Covers English-language radio broadcasts around the world and offers details on local AM-FM broadcasts, schedules of major shortwave broadcasters such as the BBC and Voice of America, and travel information.
LC HE8697.25.U6 T74
DD 384.54/43
US

TRI-S SPOT-LIGHT. **VFOAT** Tri-S Spotlight; Tri S Spotlight. (19??)-. Periodical. English. Twelve times a year. Soma Communications Inc, 3839 Alto, Carrollento TX 75007.
LC QC676 .D46
ISSN 0914-9279
JA
CODEN TSKKED

TSUSHIN SOGO KENKYUJO KIHO. See Communications-Telecommunication.
LC HE8698 .U18
DD 384.54/025/73
ISSN 1075-8208
US

●**U.S. RADIO STATIONS WITH AFRICAN AMERICAN LISTENERS.** [U.S. radio stations Afr. Am. listen.]. **VFOAT** US Radio Stations with African American Listeners. **VAT** United States Radio Stations with African American Listeners. (1994)-. Trade Publication. English. Irregular. St. Vincent Communications, PO Box 55735, Washington DC 20040-5735.

UK RADIO DATABOOK. (19??)-. English. One time a year. $445.00. Kagan World Media Inc., 126 Clock Tower Place, Carmel CA 93923-8734. **Tel** (408)624-1536, FAX (408)625-3225. **(Subscription address:** Kagan World Media Ltd., 524 Fulham Road, London SW6 5NR United Kingdom. **Tel** 011 44 171 3718880, FAX 011 44 171 3718715.)
ISSN 0049-5778
CN

VE6. (Jan. 1971)-. Periodical. English. Twelve times a year. Amateur Radio League of Alberta, JH Hunter Membership Secretary, 506-11th Avenue NE, CAlgary Alta. T2E 0Z5. Supersedes Alberta Amateur, 0002-4716.
US

WBAI FOLIO. **Main/Corp** WBAI (Radio Station) New York (City). (19??)-. English. Twelve times a year. $50.00. Pacifica WBAI-FM, PO Box 12345, Church Street Station, New York NY 10249. **Tel** (212)279-0707. **ED** Sharon Griffiths. **Bk Rev. Ad Acc. Circ:** 20,000.
Desc: Program guide for listener sponsored FM radio station. Includes articles on media, arts, politics and music.
LC PN1990 .C617
DD 384.54/06/01
UK

WHO'S WHO - COMMONWEALTH BROADCASTING ASSOCIATION. See Communications-Television and Cable.
LC VK397 .S62d
DD 384.5/35/025
ISSN 0277-2825
US

WIRELESS REGISTER. WORLD WIDE EDITION, THE. (THE WIRELESS REGISTER.). [Wirel. regist., world wide ed.]. **Main/Corp** Society of Wireless Pioneers. (19??)-. English. Free. Society of Wireless Pioneers Inc, PO Box 530, Santa Rosa CA 95402. ctrl circ.
CN

WIRELESS TELECOM. (19??)-. Trade Publication. English. Twelve times a year. $695.00. Canadian Wireless Telecommunications Association, 275 Slater Street, Suite 2004, Ottawa Ontario K1P 5H9 Canada. **Tel** (613)233-4888, FAX (613)233-2032. **ED** Catherine Hopwood (Managing Editor). **Ad Acc. Circ:** 3,000 (ctrl). Continues RadioComm Magazine, 1196-0809.
Desc: Official publication of the Canadian Wireless Telecommunications Association of Canada.
LC HE7601
DD 384
ISSN 1084-1180
US

●**WJCT IMAGINE MAGAZINE.** **Added/Corp** WJCT-TV/FM. **VFOAT** WJCT Imagine. (July 1995)-. Periodical. English. Twelve times a year. WJCT Magazine, 100 Festival Park Avenue, Jacksonville FL 32202. Continues WJCT Magazine, 1065-8564.
ISSN 1065-8564
US
TITLE CHANGE

WJCT MAGAZINE. **Added/Corp** WJCT-TV/FM. Vol. 1, No. 1 (Oct. 1992)-(199?). Periodical. English. WJCT Magazine, 100 Festival Park Avenue, Jacksonville FL 32202. Continues Public Broadcasting News. Continued by WJCT Imagine Magazine, 1084-1180.
LC PN1990.6.K6 W64
KO

WOLGAN PANGSONG. See Communications-Television and Cable.
DD 384
ISSN 0892-2640
US

WORLD RADIO REPORT. [World radio rep.]. **Added/Corp** Foundation for International Broadcasting. (1986)-. Periodical. English. Twelve times a year. $18.00. Miller, PO Box 360, Wagontown PA 19376-0360.
LC TK6540 .W67
DD 621.384
ISSN 0144-7750
UK

WORLD RADIO TV HANDBOOK. [World radio tv handb.]. **VFOAT** World Radio Television Handbook. **VAT** World Radio Television Handbook; World Radio and TV Handbook. 15th Ed. (1961)-. English. One time a year. $24.95. World Radio TV Handbook, Solljevej 44, DK 2650 Hvidovre Denmark. **Tel** 011 45 317 88508. **(Subscription address:** Watson Guptill Publications, PO Box 2014, Lakewood NJ 08101.) **Ad Acc. Circ:** 50,000. Continues World Radio Handbook; Absorbed Listen to the World.
Desc: Country-by-country listings of long, medium and short-wave broadcasters by frequency, time and language.
US

WORLDRADIO, INC. (19??)-. English. $14.00 US; $24.00 other. MHR Publishing Incorporated, 2122 28th Street, Sacramento CA 95818. **Tel** (916)457-8990, (800)366-9192. **ED** Robert Wortley. Index available. **Bk Rev. Ad Acc. Circ:** 30,000. available on audiocassette.

Desc: Special interest publication for amateur radio operators featuring public service, FCC updates, DX news, etc.
US

WORLDRADIO NEWS. English. Twelve times a year. $14.00 (one-year); $27.00 (two-year); $39.00 (three-year). Worldradio Inc., 2120 28th Street, Sacramento CA 95818. **Tel** (916)457-3655.
LC TK6540 .W88
DD 384.5
CH

WU HSIEN TIEN. **VFOAT** Wuxiandian. Periodical. Chinese. NT$0.25. Science Press, 16 Donghuangchenggen North Street, Beijing 100707, People's Republic of China. **Tel** 011 86 1 4019821, 011 86 1 4010642, FAX 011 86 1 4012180, 011 86 1 4019810, telex 210147.
LC TK7800 .W8
CH

WU HSIEN TIEN YUEH KAN. See Electronics.
ISSN 1055-2960
US

Pr Rev.
WXXI (ROCHESTER, N.Y.). (WXXI.). **Added/Corp** WXXI Public Broadcasting Council. **VFOAT** WXXI Magazine; WXXI Program Guide. Periodical. English. Twelve times a year. $36.00 (includes membership). WXXI Program Guide, 280 State Street, Rochester NY 14614. **Tel** (716)325-7500. **(Subscription address:** WXXI, PO Box 21, Rochester NY 14601.) **ED** Katherine Hartman. **Ad Acc, Adv Mgr:** Judith Lemoncelli, **Tel** (716)325-7500. **Circ:** 35,000 (ctrl). Continues WXXI Program Guide (Rochester, N.Y. : 1985), 0883-1106.
Desc: Program listings for WXXI-AM,FM, and TV plus information on station events and happenings. Articles on people and programs featured on our stations.
US

YELLOW PAGES OF ROCK. See Music.

TELECOMMUNICATION

LC TK5101
DD 621.382
US
411 NEWSLETTER. (19??)-. Newsletter. English. Twenty-four times a year. $359.00. United Communications Group, 11300 Rockville Pike, Suite 1100, Rockville MD 20852. **Tel** (301)816-8950 ext. 313, FAX (301)816-8945. Continues Telephone Angles.
US
TITLE CHANGE

800 900 REVIEW. English. Opus Research Incorporated, 345 Chenery Street, San Francisco CA 94131. **Tel** (800)428-6787, (415)239-0244, FAX (415)239-6932. available on an online database (files 16,636/Full-Text) from DIALOG. Absorbed Telemarketer, 8750-9067. Absorbed by Telemedia News and Views, 1071-135X.
JA
CEASED

ABSTRACTS OF SCIENCE AND TECHNOLOGY IN JAPAN. ELECTRONICS AND COMMUNICATION. See Electronics-Abstracting, Bibliographies and Statistics.
LC HE7761 .O42a
DD 353.008/74
ISSN 0363-8103
US

ACTIVITIES AND PROGRAMS - OFFICE OF TELECOMMUNICATIONS POLICY. (ACTIVITIES AND PROGRAMS.). **Main/Corp** United States. Office of Telecommunications Policy. (19??)-. English. One time a year. Office of Telecommunications, Washington DC 20504.
DD 384
ISSN 1058-7713
US
CCC
TITLE CHANGE

ADVANCED WIRELESS COMMUNICATIONS. [Adv. wireless commun.]. (Nov. 7, 1990)-(1995). Periodical. English. Telecom Publishing Group, 1101 King Street, Suite 444, Alexandria VA 22314. **Tel** (703)683-4100, (800)327-7205, FAX (703)739-6490. **(Subscription address:** Telecom Publishing Group, PO Box 1455, Alexandria VA 22313. **Tel** 800 327-7205, (703)683-4100.) available on an online database from Information Access Company; NEWSNET; and (file 636/Full-Text) DIALOG. Merged into PCS News.
Ind/Abst PTS Newsl. Database [Full Txt.].
LC HE7661 .A38
DD 384/.068
ISSN 1050-9291
US

ADVANCES IN TELECOMMUNICATIONS MANAGEMENT. [Adv. telecommun. manage.]. Vol. 1 (1990)-. English. One time a year. $73.25. JAI Press

Communications —Telecommunication

Inc., 55 Old Post Road, Suite 2, PO Box 1678, Greenwich CT 06836-1678. **Tel** (203)661-7602, FAX (203)661-0792. **ED** Jagdish Sheth and Gary L. Frazier.

LC TK5101.A1 A32   **ISSN** 1050-9496
DD 384   US
ADVANCES IN TELEMATICS. [Adv. telemat.].
Vol. 1 (1991)-. English. Irregular. Price varies per volume. Ablex Publishing Corporation, 355 Chestnut Street, Norwood NJ 07648. **Tel** (201)767-8450, (201)767-8455 (Customer Service), FAX (201)767-6717.

LC TK7800 .A22   **ISSN** 0001-1096
GW
CCC
CODEN AEUTAH
Pr Rev.
AEU. ARCHIV. FUER ELEKTRONIK UND UBERTRAGUNGSTECHNIK. (AEU.
ARCHIV FUER ELEKTRONIK UND UBERTRAGUNGSTECHNIK. ELECTRONICS AND COMMUNICATION.). [AEU, Arch. Elektron. Ubertragungstech.]. **VFOAT** Archiv fuer Elektronik und Ubertragungstechnik; Electronics and Communication. Vol. 25 (Jan. 1971)-. Periodical. German (English). Six times a year. $567.69. S. Hirzel Verlag Stuttgart, Postfach 101061, D-70009 Stuttgart Germany. **Tel** 011 49 711 25820, FAX 0711/2582 290, telex 723636 daz d. **ED** R. Pauli. Index available in last issue of volume--attached.
Bk Rev. **Ad Acc**. **Circ**: 1,000. Documents available from Article Express International, The Genuine Article, Ask*IEEE. Continues Archiv der Elektrischen Ubertragung.
Desc: International journal in the fields of antennas, propagation, information theory, microwaves, communications and networks, circuit and system theory, and optical communications.
Ind/Abst Acoust. Abstr.; Bioeng. Abstr.; Curr. Cit.; Curr. Contents Eng. Comput. Technol.; Ei Page One; Electron. Commun. Abstr. J.; EMBASE; Energy Res. Abstr. (July 1978-); Eng. Index Annu.; INSPEC (Dec. 1971-); Int. Aerosp. Abstr.; ISMEC Bull.; Math. Rev.; Pollut. Abstr. Indexes; Res. Alert [Select. Cov.]; Saf. Sci. Abstr. J.; Sci. Cit. Index (19??-19??); SCISEARCH.

ISSN 0890-5657
DD 384   US
AFRICA TELECOMMUNICATIONS REPORT. [Afr. telecommun. rep.]. Vol. 1, No. 9 (Sept. 1986)-. Periodical. English. Twelve times a year. $120.00 (universities and libraries); $350.00 (regular). Africa Telecommunications Report, 1000 Connecticut Avenue NW/Suite 9, Washington DC 20036. **Tel** (202)667-2111, FAX (203)866-5928. **ED** Imad Musa and Raymond Akwule.
Desc: Directed to the academic and policy making communities. News and feature articles about developments in African telecommunications.

ISSN 0044-7676
US
AFTRA. See Business and Economics-Labor.

LC HE9559 .A52
DD 384.6/025/6751   CG
AGENTS ECONOMIQUES DU ZAIRE : ANNUAIRE. (1976)-. French. Societe MYK Service, BP 5502, Kinshasa Gombe Zaire. Continues Annuaire des Petites et Moyennes Entreprises.

FR
●ALCATEL TELECOMMUNICATIONS REVIEW. (1995)-. English (French). Four times a year. Electrical Communication / Alcatel, 54 rue la Boetie, 75008 Paris Cedex 08 France. **Tel** 011 33 1 40761347, 011 33 1 40761349, FAX 011 33 1 40761426. Continues Electrical Communication.

ISSN 0889-6089
DD 384   US
AMATEUR SATELLITE REPORT. [Amat. satell. rep.]. **Added/Corp** AMSAT. AMSAT-NA (U.S.). **VFOAT** AMSAT ASR. (198?)-. Periodical. English. Twenty-six times a year. $30.00 US; $36.00 Canada and Mexico; $45.00 other Comes with AMSAT membership. AMSAT / Radio Amateur Satellite Corporationoration, PO Box 27, Washington DC 20044. **Tel** (301)589-6062. Continues Satellite Journal, 8750-7617.

LC HE7601 .A4   **ISSN** 1075-5292
DD 384/.05   US
CCC
●AMERICA'S NETWORK. (AMERICA'S NETWORK : TECHNOLOGY FOR THE INFORMATION HIGHWAY.). [Am. netw.]. Vol. 1, No. 1 (Feb. 15, 1994)-. Periodical. English. Twenty-four times a year. $44.00. Advanstar Communications Inc., 131 West First Street, Duluth MN 55802. **Tel** (218)723-9477, (800)346-0085, FAX (218)723-9437. available with illustrations; available on an online database from DIALOG. Continues Telephone Engineer & Management, 0040-263X.
Desc: Serves professionals responsible for design and operation of phone systems. Looks at technical, legislative and marketplace changes affecting the industry.
Ind/Abst Acad. Search; Bus. Source Plus; Curr. Cit.; EP Collect.; Homework Help.; MasterFile FullTEXT 1000;

MasterFile FullTEXT 350; MasterFile FullTEXT 650; MasterFile FullTEXT (Feb. 1994-); OCLC; Telebase; Vocat. Search.

US
AMERICA'S NETWORK DIRECTORY. (19??)-. Directory. English. One time a year. $130.00. Advanstar Communications Inc., 131 West First Street, Duluth MN 55802. **Tel** (218)723-9477, (800)346-0085, FAX (218)723-9437. Continues Telephone Engineer and Management Directory.

LC HE8153 .G47a
DD 387.1   GW
AMTLICHES VERZEICHNIS DER TEILNEHMER DES OEFFENTLICHEN BILDUBERTRAGUNGSNETZES.
Main/Corp Germany (West). Fernmeldetechnisches Zentralamt. (19??)-. German. Postfach 800, 61 Darmstadt Germany.

ISSN 1187-5046
DD 384.6/4/02571   CN
ANGUS TELEMANAGEMENT BUYERS' GUIDE TO LONG DISTANCE RESALE IN CANADA, THE. [Angus TeleManage. buy. guide long distance resale Can.]. **Added/Corp** Angus Telemanagement Group. **VFOAT** Buyers' Guide to Long Distance Resale in Canada; Long Distance Resale in Canada. 4th Ed. (Sept. 1991)-. Consumer Publication. English. Irregular. 42.42Can$. Angus Telemanagement Group Inc., 8 Old Kingston Road, Ajax Ontario L1T 2Z7 Canada. **Tel** (905)686-5050, FAX (905)686-2655.
Continues Who's Who in Long Distance Resale in Canada., 1186-8236.

LC TK2 .A57   **ISSN** 0003-4347
FR
CODEN ANTEAU
Pr Rev.
ANNALES DES TELECOMMUNICATIONS. [Ann. telecommun.]. (1946)-. Academic Scholarly Publication. French. Six times a year. $177.27. Centre National d'Etudes des Telecommunications, 38-40 rue du General LeClerc, 92131 Issy les Moulineaux France. **Tel** 011 33 1 45294312 or, 45295108. **Bk Rev**. **Circ**: 1,300 (ctrl). Documents available from Article Express International, The Genuine Article, Ask*IEEE, CASDDS.
Desc: Covers networks, telecommunications services, transmission, cable optical, fibre, satellite, switching, teletraffic, antennas, circuits, information theory, image speech processing and economical aspects.
Ind/Abst Acoust. Abstr.; Bioeng. Abstr.; Chem. Abstr.; Curr. Cit.; Curr. Contents Eng. Comput. Technol.; Ei Page One; Energy Res. Abstr.; Eng. Index Annu.; INSPEC (1968-); Int. Aerosp. Abstr.; Math. Rev.; Meteorol. Geoastrophys. Abstr.; Res. Alert [Full Cov.]; Sci. Cit. Index; SCISEARCH; Zentralbl. Math. Ihre Grenzgeb.

LC HE8313 .A56
BU
ANNUAIRE DES ABONNES AU SERVICE TELEX . **Added/Corp** Bulgaria. Ministere des Postes et Telecommunications. (19??)-. Bulgarian (French). One time a year. Durzhavno Izdatelstvo Tekhnika, Ruski 6, Sofia Bulgaria.

LC HE8501 .A52
DD 384.1/4   CG
ANNUAIRE OFFICIEL TELEX DU ZAIRE. **Added/Corp** Zaire. Office National des Postes et Telecommunications. **VFOAT** Annuaire Telex Officiel du Zaire. (1979)-. French. One time a year. Snat, B P 15.598, Kinshasa Zaire.

LC HE7601 .A55
DD 384   SZ
ANNUAIRE STATISTIQUE DES TELECOMMUNICATIONS DU SECTEUR PUBLIC (GENEVA, SWITZERLAND: 1980). See Communications-Abstracting, Bibliographies and Statistics.

ISSN 1189-3125
DD 384   CN
ANNUAL REPORT - CANADA. GOVERNMENT TELECOMMUNICATIONS AGENCY.
(RAPPORT ANNUEL / AGENCE DES TELECOMMUNICATIONS GOUVERNEMENTALES.). [Annu. rep. - Can., Gov. Telecomun. Agency]. **Main/Corp** Canada. Agence des Telecommunications Gouvernementales. (1990/91)-. French (English).

ISSN 1189-3125
DD 384   CN
ANNUAL REPORT - CANADA. GOVERNMENT TELECOMMUNICATIONS AGENCY.
(ANNUAL REPORT / GOVERNMENT TELECOMMUNICATIONS AGENCY.). [Annu. rep. - Can., Gov. Telecomun. Agency]. **Main/Corp** Canada.

Government Telecommunications Agency. **VFOAT** Rapport Annuel. **VAT** Rapport Annuel - Canada. Agence des Telecommunications. (1990/91)-. English (French).

LC TK7812.I5 I57A
DD 621.3/06/054   II
ANNUAL REPORT / IETE. See Electronics.

LC HE9719 .I59a   **ISSN** 1082-4510
DD 341.7/577   US
ANNUAL REPORT - INTERNATIONAL TELECOMMUNICATIONS SATELLITE ORGANIZATION (1992). See Law.

LC F1057 .O637   **ISSN** 0840-7193
DD 354.7130085   CN
ANNUAL REPORT - MINISTRY OF CULTURE AND COMMUNICATIONS (TORONTO). (ANNUAL REPORT / MINISTRY OF CULTURE AND COMMUNICATIONS.). [Ann. rep. - Minist. Cult. Commun.]. **Main/Corp** Ontario. Ministry of Culture and Comnnications. **VFOAT** Rapport Annuel. (1988)-. English (French). One time a year. Ministry of Culture and Communications, 77 Bloor Street West, 6th Floor, Toronto Ontario, M7A 2R9 Canada. *Formed by the union of* Ontario. Ministry of Transportation and Communications. Annual Report, 0703-6140 *and* Ontario. Ministry of Citizenship and Culture. Annual Report, 0823-504X.

US
ANNUAL REPORT OF THE BOARD OF DIRECTORS OF THE RURAL TELEPHONE BANK. **Main/Corp** Rural Telephone Bank. 12th (1983)-. Government Publication. English. US Department of Agriculture, 14th Street and Independence Avenue SW, Washington DC 20250. **Tel** (202)720-5457. Continues Annual Rural Telephone Bank Report.

LC HE7352 .A24a
DD 354.68910087/4/06   RH
ANNUAL REPORT / POSTS AND TELECOMMUNICATIONS CORPORATION. **Main/Corp** Posts and Telecommunications Corporation (Zimbabwe). (1970/1971)-. English. One time a year. Posts and Telecommunications Corporation, PO Box 8061, Causeway Zimbabwe Rhodesia. **Tel** 728811, telex 4281. **Circ**: 1,500 (ctrl).
Desc: Report on the functions of the posts and telecommunications corporation.

LC HE8261 .T45B
DD 354/.485/0087405   SW
ANNUAL REPORT - TELEVERKET. **Main/Corp** Sweden. Televerket. English. One time a year. Televerket, Ekonomiavdelningen Finanssektioner, 123 86 Farsta, Stockholm Sweden. **Tel** 468 713 1000. **Circ**: 2,000. Continues Annual Report - Board of Swedish Telecommunications.
Desc: Administration report on Swedish telecom's activities and radio communication. Financial statements and statistical summaries.

LC HE7791.N25 N43a
DD 384/09782/05   US
ANNUAL REPORT TO THE LEGISLATURE ON THE STATUS OF THE NEBRASKA TELECOMMUNICATIONS INDUSTRY. **Main/Corp** Nebraska. Public Service Commission. **VFOAT** Annual Rreport on Telecommunications to the Nebraska Legislature. (1988)-. Government Publication. English. Irregular. Nebraska Public Service Commission, 1342 M Street, Lincoln NE 68508.

LC TK5 .N37   **ISSN** 1073-0885
DD 621.38   US
ANNUAL REVIEW OF COMMUNICATIONS. (ANNUAL REVIEW OF COMMUNICATIONS / NATIONAL ENGINEERING CONSORTIUM.). [Annu. rev. commun.]. **Added/Corp** National Engineering Consortium. Vol. 46 (1992-1993)-. English. One time a year (Oct.). $205.00. Professional Education International, 303 East Wacker Drive, Suite 739, Chicago IL 60601. **Tel** (312)938-3500. Continues National Communications Forum. Proceedings of the National Communications Forum, 0886-229X.

LC HE7125 .C643b
DD 383.49   PO
ANUARIO ESTATISTICO - CORREIOS E TELECOMUNICACOES DE PORTUGAL. See Communications-Abstracting, Bibliographies and Statistics.

LC TK5101.A1 A22
TH
APT TELECOM JOURNAL : JOURNAL OF THE ASIA PACIFIC TELECOMMUNITY. **Added/Corp** Asia Pacific Telecommunity (Organization). **VFOAT** Telecom Journal; Asia Pacific Telecommunity Telecom Journal; APT

Journal. (19??)-. Periodical. English. Four times a year. $55.00. ICOM Publications Ltd., Chancery House, St. Nicholas Way, Sutton Surrey SM1 1JB United Kingdom. **Tel** 011 44 181 6421117, FAX 011 44 181 6421941.

LC HE8660 TK6001 **ISSN** 1353-0356
DD 384.5 621.38 UK

●**APT YEARBOOK.** (A P T YEARBOOK.). [APT yearb.]. (1994)-. English. One time a year. $185.00. ICOM Publications Ltd., Chancery House, St. Nicholas Way, Sutton Surrey SM1 1JB United Kingdom. **Tel** 011 44 181 6421117, FAX 011 44 181 6421941. **ED** A. Narayan. **Ad Acc, Adv Mgr:** Chris Ayres. Full Page (B&W) $5445.00. Full Page (Color) $4675.00.
Desc: Provides listings of Asia's communications services.

ISSN 0943-2337
GW

●**ARCHIV FUER POST UND TELEKOMMUNIKATION.** (1992)-. German. Four times a year. $42.99. Verieb Amtlicher Blaetter, Postamt 1 Postfach 109091, D-50482 Koeln Germany. **Tel** 011 49 221 1401256.

LC HE8689.9.G4 A75 **ISSN** 0066-5746
GW

ARD JAHRBUCH. Main/Corp Arbeitsgemeinschaft der Offentlich-Rechtlichen Rundfunkanstalten der Bundesrepublik Deutschland. **VFOAT** ARD-Jahrbuch; A.R.D. Jahrbuch. (1969)-. Trade Publication. German. One time a year. $12.89. Verlag Hans Bredow Institut, Heimhuderstrasse 21, D-20148 Hamburg Germany. **Tel** 011 040 447034, FAX 011 040 417870. **(Subscription address:** NOMOS Verlag, Postfach 610, 76484 Baden-Baden, Germany. **) ED** Horst Halefeldt.

LC HE8721 .A68 **ISSN** 1040-032X
DD 384.6/025/73 US

AREA CODE HANDBOOK. (AREA CODE HAND BOOK. AT & T.). [Area code handb.]. **Added/Corp** AT&T Customer Information Center. **VFOAT** Area Code Hand Book. (19??)-. English. Irregular. $2.95. AT&T Customer Information Center, PO Box 19901, Indianapolis IN 46219. **Tel** (800)432-6600.
Desc: Lists area codes for the United States, Canadian Provinces, and other locations. Provides numerical lists of area codes for the US, Canadian Provinces and other locations. Gives numerical listing of international country and city codes.

LC HE8261 .T46A
SW

ARSREDOVISNING - TELEVERKET. Main/Corp Sweden. Televerket. (19??)-. Swedish (English). One time a year. Televerket, Ekonomiavdelningen Finanssektioner, 123 86 Farsta, Stockholm Sweden. **Tel** 468 713 1000. **Circ:** 17,000.
Desc: Administration report on Swedish telecom's activities and radio communication. Financial statements and statistical summaries.

ISSN 1015-5473
SZ

ASCOM TECHNISCHE MITTEILUNGEN. [Ascom Tech. Mitt.]. **VFOAT** Technische Mitteilungen - Ascom. (1989)-. Periodical. German (English). Irregular (2-3 times per year). Free on request. Ascom Tech, Morgenstrasse 129, CH-3018 Bern Switzerland. **Tel** 011 41 31 9993806, FAX 011 41 31 9991835. **ED** Sebastian Vogler. **Circ:** 2,500 English, 6,000 German. ***Continues*** *Hasler-Mitteilungen, 0017-8306.*
Desc: Technical journal specializing in the field of telecommunication and service automation. Sent to customers and interested persons.

ISSN 1079-7831
DD 384 US

●**ASIA PACIFIC TELECOM INVESTOR.** [Asia Pac. telecom investor]. No. 1 (Aug. 5, 1994)-. Newsletter. English. Twelve times a year. $695.00. Kagan World Media Inc., 126 Clock Tower Place, Carmel CA 93923-8734. **Tel** (408)624-1536, FAX (408)625-3225. **(Subscription address:** Kagan World Media Ltd., 524 Fulham Road, London SW6 5NR United Kingdom. **Tel** 011 44 171 3718880, FAX 011 44 171 3718715.**)** available via fax.
Desc: Evaluations of deals and initial public offerings in the telecommunications market, projections of growth in fixed-line and wireless networks, updates of infrastructure buildouts and new services, network design and revenue forecasts, stock charts and performance tables for companies conducting business in Asia and the Pacific Rim.

LC WMLC 93/1528 **ISSN** 1041-2530
DD 384 US

AT&T DATALINE. [AT&T dataline]. **VFOAT** Dataline. **VAT** American Telephone & Telegraph Dataline. Vol. 1, No. 1 (Jan./Feb. 1989)-. Periodical. English. Six times a year. Free. Publications & Communications, 12416 Hymeadow Drive, Austin TX 78750. **Tel** (512)250-9023, (800)678-9724, FAX (512)331-3900, telex 384303. **ED** Mark Cappell. **Ad Acc.** ctrl circ.
Desc: Resource guide for AT&T computer owners to improve the use of their systems, keep up to date on new products and learn more about AT&T's products and long-range strategies.

LC TK1 .B425 **ISSN** 8756-2324
DD 621.38/05 US
CCC

NLM W1; AT205D

AT&T TECHNICAL JOURNAL. [ATT tech. j.]. **Added/Corp** American Telephone and Telegraph Company. **VFOAT** AT and T Technical Journal; Technical Journal. **VAT** American Telephone and Telegraph Company Technical Journal. Vol. 64, No. 1, Pt. 1 (Jan. 1985)-. Periodical. English. Six times a year (six issues per year). $61.00. AT&T Bell Laboratories, 600 Mountain Avenue, Room 3C 417, Murray Hill NJ 07974. **Tel** (908)582-4732, (908)582-4823, FAX (908)582-4430. **ED** Bert Vorchheimer. Index available. **Circ:** 35,000 (ctrl). available on microfilm and microfiche from University Microfilms International (UMI); available on photocopies. Documents available from Article Express International, The Genuine Article, Ask*IEEE. ***Continues*** *AT&T Bell Laboratories Technical Journal, 0748-612X.*
Desc: Information research, science, technology, computing technology and telecommunications technology.
Ind/Abst Acoust. Abstr.; Appl. Sci. Technol. Index; Bus. Source Plus; Comput. Database; Comput. Rev.; Curr. Cit.; Curr. Contents Eng. Comput. Technol.; Eng. Index Annu.; EP Collect.; Ergon. Abstr.; Expand. Acad. Index (1992-); HILITES; Homework Help.; Inf. Sci. Abstr. (?-?); INIS Atomindex [Micro.]; INSPEC (Jan. 1985-); Linguist. Lang. Behav. Abstr.; MasterFile FullTEXT 1000; MasterFile FullTEXT 350; MasterFile FullTEXT 650; MasterFile FullTEXT; Math. Rev. (1985-); OCLC; Res. Alert [Full Cov.]; Sci. Cit. Index; SCISEARCH; Soc. Plann. Policy Dev. Abstr.; Soc. Sci. Cit. Index [Select. Cov.]; Sociol. Abstr.; Telebase; Zentralbl. Math. Ihre Grenzgeb.

LC TK1 .B4 **ISSN** 0889-8979
DD 621.385 US

AT&T TECHNOLOGY. [AT&T technol.]. **Added/Corp** American Telephone and Telegraph Company. **VFOAT** AT and T Technology. **VAT** American Telephone and Telegraph Technology. Vol. 1, No. 1 (1986)-. Periodical. English. Four times a year. $48.00. AT&T Bell Laboratories, 600 Mountain Avenue, Room 3C 417, Murray Hill NJ 07974. **Tel** (908)582-4732, (908)582-4823, FAX (908)582-4430. **ED** R.D. Freed. available on microfilm and microfiche from University Microfilms International (UMI). Documents available from Article Express International, UMI Article Clearinghouse, Ask*IEEE. ***Continues*** *Record (AT & T Bell Laboratories), 0749-8152.*
Desc: Informs customers of the technologies underlying AT&T's products, systems and applications. Articles by experts from AT&T Bell laboratories and the AT&T Marketing organizations.
Ind/Abst ABI/INFORM Glob. Ed.; ABI/INFORM [Computer File] (1987); Appl. Sci. Technol. Index; Curr. Cit.; Eng. Index Annu.; EP Collect.; Homework Help.; INSPEC (1987-); MasterFile FullTEXT 1000; MasterFile FullTEXT 350; MasterFile FullTEXT 650; MasterFile FullTEXT; OCLC; Telebase; UMI ABI/Inform--Bus. Period. Ondisc (1988-) [Full Txt.].

US

AT&T TECHNOLOGY, PRODUCTS, SYSTEMS, AND SERVICES. (19??)-. English. Four times a year. $40.00 (one-year), $72.00 (two-year), $94.00 (three-year). Bell Telephone Laboratories, 101 JF Kennedy Parkway, Room 1E 335, Short Hills NJ 07078. **Tel** (201)564-2582.
Desc: Communications and computing technology for use by AT&T customers.

LC HE8811 .A53 **ISSN** 1075-5950
DD 384 US

●**AT&T TOLL-FREE NATIONAL 800 DIRECTORY (CONSUMER ED.).** (AT&T TOLL-FREE NATIONAL 800 DIRECTORY.). [AT&T toll-free natl. 800 dir.]. **Added/Corp** American Telephone and Telegraph Company. **VFOAT** AT&T Toll Free National Eight Hundred Directory; AT and T Toll Free National Eight Hundred Directory; Shopper's Guide; AT&T Toll-Free National 800 Directory. Shopper's Guide. (1994)-. Directory. English. One time a year. AT&T 800 Directory, 13100 East 39th Avenue, Denver CO 80239. **Tel** (800)426-8686. **(Subscription address:** US West Direct, 13100 East 39 Avenue, Unit U, Denver CO 80239. **) *Continues*** *AT&T Toll-Free 800 Directory (Consumer Ed.), 1064-962X.*

ISSN 0001-2777
AT
CODEN ATRABH

Pr Rev.

ATR; AUSTRALIAN TELECOMMUNICATION RESEARCH. [Aust. telecommun. res.]. **Added/Corp** Telecommunication Society of Australia. **VFOAT** Australian Telecommunication Research. Vol. 1 (1967)-. Periodical. English. Two times a year. 56.73Aus$. Telecomm Society of Australia, GPO Box 4050, Melbourne Victoria 3001 Australia. **Tel** 011 61 3 6390906, FAX 011 61 3 6391515. **ED** Carth Jenkinson. Index available. ctrl circ. available on microfilm and microfiche from University Microfilms International (UMI). Documents available from Article Express International, The Genuine Article, Ask*IEEE.
Ind/Abst Bioeng. Abstr.; Curr. Cit.; Curr. Contents Eng. Comput. Technol.; Ei Page One; Eng. Index Annu. [Select. Cov.]; INSPEC (Nov. 1968-); Int. Aerosp. Abstr. (1991-); Res. Alert [Select. Cov.]; SCISEARCH.

ISSN 1042-6329
DD 384 US

AUDIOTEX DIRECTORY & BUYER'S GUIDE. [Audiotex dir. buy. guide]. **VFOAT** Audiotex Directory and Buyer's Guide; ADBG. Vol. 1, No. 1 (Fall/Winter 1988-'89)-. Directory. English. Two times a year. $25.00 (single issue) US; $30.00 (single issue) Canada. ADBG Publishing, PO Box 25961, Los Angeles CA 90025.

ISSN 1063-1348
DD 384 US

AUDIOTEX NEWS. (AUDIOTEX NEWS : THE INFORMATION BY PHONE MARKETING NEWSLETTER.). [Audiotex news]. (1989)-. Newsletter. English. Twelve times a year. $249.00. Audiotex News, 2362 Hempstead Turnpike, East Meadow NY 11554. **Tel** (516)735-3398, (800)735-3398, FAX (516)735-3682. **ED** Carol Morse Ginsburg and Debra Velsmid. cum. index. **Bk Rev**, (Qty: 2). **Circ:** 500 (ctrl). Documents available from the publisher. ***Continues*** *Audiotex Ideal Dial.*
Desc: A newsletter providing analysis and information covering the audiotex industry. Includes news, trends and regulations about all 900-pay-per-call developments.

US
TITLE CHANGE

AUDIOTEX NOW. English. Opus Research Incorporated, 345 Chenery Street, San Francisco CA 94131. **Tel** (800)428-6787, (415)239-0244, FAX (415)239-6932. available on an online database (files 16,636/Full-Text) from DIALOG. ***Absorbed by*** *Telemedia News and Views, 1071-135X.*
Ind/Abst PROMT [Full Txt.]; PTS Newsl. Database [Full Txt.].

AT

●**AUSTRALASIAN TELECOMMUNICATIONS MARKETING AND MANAGEMENT NEWSLETTER.** (1995)-. Newsletter. English. Ten times a year. 242.54Aus$. Paul Budde Communication Pty Ltd, 2643 George Downes Drive, Bucketty NSW 2250 Australia. **Tel** 61 (0)49 988 144, FAX 61 (0)49 988 247. ***Continues*** *Telecommunications Management and Marketing Newsletter.*

ISSN 0849-6013
DD 340/.025/711 CN

B C LAWYERS' TELEPHONE, FAX AND SERVICES DIRECTORY. See Law.

ISSN 1040-2020
DD 384 US

BELLCORE EXCHANGE. [Bellcore exch.]. **Added/Corp** Bellcore (Firm). **VFOAT** Exchange. Vol. 4, Issue 1 (Jan./Feb. 1988)-. Periodical. English. Twenty-six times a year. $35.00. Bell Communications Research, 60 New England Avenue, Piscataway NJ 08854. **Tel** (908)699-5800, FAX (908)699-0936. **ED** Ruth Steinberg (phone: (201)699-2865). available on microfilm from University Microfilms International (UMI). ***Continues*** *Bell Communications Research Exchange, 0891-4877.*
Desc: Contains discussions of scientific inquiries that explore the vision of Bellcore's leading scientists in the field of telecommunications research. Provides research, technical support and services for the Bellcore client companies.

LC HE9290.F8 A3
DK

BERETNING OG REGNSKAB FOR ARET ... . Main/Corp Fyns Kommunale Telefonselskab. (19??)-. Corporate Report. Danish. Fyns Telefon, Telehojen 1, 5220 Odense SO Denmark. **Tel** 45 65 90 90 90, FAX 45 65 25 25. ***Continues*** *Fyns Kommunale Telefonselskab. Aarsberetning.*

LC HD9696.D38 B58
DD 621.382/35/029473 US

BLI FACSIMILE SPECIFICATIONS GUIDE. Added/Corp Buyers Laboratory. **VFOAT** Facsimile Specification Guide. **VAT** Buyers Laboratory Inc. Facsimile Specification Guide. (19??)-. English. Four times a year. $73.90. Buyers Laboratory Inc., 20 Railroad Avenue, Hackensack NJ 07601. **Tel** (201)488-0404.

LC HE8093 .B74A
DD 380.3/025/41 UK

BRITISH TELECOM GUIDE. Main/Corp British Telecom. Nov. 1980-. English. One time a year. Telecom Headquarters, 2-12 Gresham Street, London EC2V 7AG United Kingdom.

Communications —Telecommunication

LC TK5101.A1 B76
DD 621.38/05
ISSN 0262-401X
UK
CODEN BTEND4
Pr Rev.
BRITISH TELECOMMUNICATIONS ENGINEERING. [Br. telecommun. eng.].
Added/Corp Institution of British Telecommunications Engineers. Vol. 1, No. 1 (April 1982)-. Periodical. English. Four times a year (Jan., Apr., July, Oct.). $77.01. The Institution of British Telecommunications Engineers, Post Point GO12, 2-12 Gresham Street, London EC2V 7AG United Kingdom. **Tel** 011 44 171 3568050, FAX 011 44 171 3567942. Documents available from Article Express International, The Genuine Article, Ask*IEEE. *Continues Post Office Electrical Engineers' Journal.*
Desc: Source of reference for all aspects of telecommunications.
Ind/Abst Bioeng. Abstr.; Curr. Cit.; Curr. Contents Eng. Comput. Technol.; Curr. Technol. Index; Ei Page One; Eng. Index Annu.; INSPEC (April 1982-); Res. Alert [Full Cov.]; SCISEARCH; Soc. Sci. Cit. Index [Select. Cov.].

DD 384
ISSN 1059-0544
US
CCC
BROADBAND NETWORKING NEWS.
Vol. 1, No. 1 (Nov. 1991)-. Periodical. English. Twenty-five times a year (biweekly). $597.00. Phillips Business Information Inc., 1201 Seven Locks Road, PO Box 61130, Potomac MD 20854. **Tel** (301)424-3338, (301)340-1520, (800)777-5005, FAX (301)424-4297, telex 358149. **ED** Jennifer Whalen, John W. Lilley (European editor). available on an online database from NEWSNET; and (file 636/Full-Text) DIALOG. *Absorbed US Telecommunications.*
Desc: Published jointly between Phillips Business Information, Inc. and Omnicom PPI Ltd. Includes information on business news and analysis of ATM, frame relay, SMDS and B-ISDN.
Ind/Abst PTS Newsl. Database [Full Txt.].

US
BROADCAST ACTIONS. See
Communications.

DD 384/.029/471
ISSN 0841-2545
CN
BROADCAST PRODUCT NEWS. [Broadcast prod. news].
(1986)-. Periodical. English. Four times a year. $15.00. Broadcast Product News, 1645 Warden Avenue, Scarborough, Ontario M1R 5B3 Canada.

UK
CODEN BTJUEH
BT TECHNOLOGY JOURNAL. Added/Corp
British Telecom. Laboratories. **VFOAT** BT Technology. Vol. 9, No. 3 (July 1991)-. Periodical. English. Four times a year. $185.00. Chapman & Hall, 2-6 Boundary Row, London SE1 8HN United Kingdom. **Tel** 011 44 171 8650066, FAX 011 44 171 5229623, telex 290164 CHAPMA G. Documents available from The Genuine Article. *Continues British Telecom Technology Journal.*
Ind/Abst Curr. Cit.; HILITES; Res. Alert [Full Cov.]; Sci. Cit. Index.

SZ
BULLETIN DE TELECOMMUNICATION.
(19??)-. Bulletin. French. Twelve times a year. 90.00F. La Presse Technique SA, 3A rue du Vieux Billard, CH1205 Geneva Switzerland. **Tel** 011 41 22 995285.

ISSN 0007-5302
FR
BULLETIN SIGNALETIQUE DES TELECOMMUNICATIONS. Added/Corp
France. Centre National d'Etude des Telecommunications. Vol. 13 (Jan. 1958)-. Bulletin. French. Twelve times a year. $204.51. Centre National d'Etudes des Telecommunications, 38-40 rue du General LeClerc, 92131 Issy les Moulineaux France. **Tel** 011 33 1 45294312 or, 45295108. **Bk Rev. Circ:** 1,400.
Desc: Bibliographical journal publishing references (with abstracts) of books and articles on telecommunications, electronics and associate fields.

UDC 384
ISSN 0778-7588
BE
BUSINESS & TELECOM (NEDERLANDSE ED.). See Business and Economics.

UK
BUSINESS COMMUNICATIONS. See
Business and Economics.

LC TK6540 .A26
DD 384.5/3/05
ISSN 0746-8911
US
CEASED
BUSINESS RADIO. See Communications-Radio.

DD 384
ISSN 1041-6137
US
TITLE CHANGE
BUSINESS TELECOMMUNICATIONS DIRECTORY. [Bus. telecommun. dir.].
(1988)-(199?). Directory. English. Design Publishers, 800 Siesta Way, Sonoma CA 95476. **Tel** (707)939-9306, FAX (707)939-9235. **ED** Silvano Payne. Index available. cum. index. **Bk Rev. Ad Acc. Circ:** 5,000. available on diskette. *Continued by What's On Satellite, 1067-0793.*

LC GV742.3 .C33
DD 070.4/49796/0973
ISSN 1049-6009
US
CABLE MEDIA ADVERTISING. See Business and Economics-Advertising and Public Relations.

DD 384
ISSN 1050-0553
US
CABLE-TELCO REPORT, THE. [Cable-telco rep.].
VFOAT Cable Telco Report. (Apr. 1990)-. Trade Publication. English. Twelve times a year. $549.00. Telecommunications Reports, 1333 H Street Northwest, 2nd Floor West Tower, Washington DC 20005. **Tel** (202)842-0520, (800)822-6338, FAX (202)842-3047. **(Subscription address:** Telecommunications Reports, PO Box 675, Cooper Station, New York NY 10276.) available on an online database from NEWSNET.

DD 384
ISSN 1051-1938
US
CABLEOPTICS NEWSLETTER.
(CABLEOPTICS NEWSLETTER : COVERING WORLDWIDE DEVELOPMENTS IN THE APPLICATION OF FIBER OPTICS IN CATV SYSTEMS.). **VFOAT** Cable Optics Newsletter. (1990)-. Trade Publication. English. Twelve times a year. $575.00. Information Gatekeepers Inc., 214 Harvard Avenue, Boston MA 02134. **Tel** (617)232-3111, (617)738-8088, (800)323-1088, FAX (617)734-8562.

DD 384
ISSN 1064-5543
US
CALL CENTER MAGAZINE. [Call cent. mag.].
VFOAT Call Center. Vol. 1, No. 1 (July 1992)-. Trade Publication. English. Twelve times a year. $14.00. Telecom Library Inc., 12 West 21st Street, New York NY 10010. **Tel** (212)691-8215, (800)542-7279.
(Subscription address: Telecom Library, 1265 Industrial Highway, Southampton PA 18966. **Tel** (800)677-3435, (215)355-2886, FAX (215)355-1068.) *Continues Inbound/Outbound, 1042-6116.*

LC HE8731 .C34
DD 384.6/05
ISSN 0360-3539
US
CALLING THE WORLD. Added/Corp
American Telephone and Telegraph Company. Long Lines Dept. (1973)-. Periodical. English. One time a year. New York AT&T Long Line, Overseas Administration, 5 World Trade Center, New York NY 10048.

DD 382
ISSN 1190-996X
CN
●CANADA'S EXPORT STRATEGY, THE INTERNATIONAL TRADE BUSINESS PLAN. 15, INFORMATION TECHNOLOGIES AND TELECOMMUNICATIONS. [Can. export strategy int. trade bus. plan, 15 Inf. technol. telecommun.].
Added/Corp Canada. **VFOAT** Information Technologies and Telecommunications. (1996)-. Government Publication. English. Irregular. *Continues Canada's International Trade Business Plan. 16, Information Technologies, 1200-1368.*

DD 380.3/0971
ISSN 0825-3021
CN
CANADIAN COMMUNICATIONS NETWORK LETTER. [Can. commun. netw. lett.].
Added/Corp Evert Communications Ltd. **VAT** Network Letter (Ottawa). Vol. 4, No. 27 (Aug. 13, 1984)-. Periodical. English. Forty times a year. $775.00 (one issue), $1,150.00 (two issue), $1,395.00 (three issue). Evert Communications Ltd, 1296 Carling Avenue, Ottawa Ontario, K1Z 7K8 Canada. **Tel** (613)728-4621, FAX (613)728-0385. **ED** Gordan D. Hutchison. Index available. *Continues Communications Week, 0227-0382.*
Desc: Newsletter dealing with telecommunications. Focuses on regulated telecommunications carriers and competitive services suppliers. Coverage includes policies and practices of telecommunications carriers, activities of the relevant trade association, telecommunications / cable television and telecommunications commission, and the policy initiatives of the department of communications.

DD 354.710087/4/05
ISSN 0711-1967
CN
CANADIAN COMMUNICATIONS REGULATION & POLICY. [Can. commun. regul. policy]. Vol. 1, No. 1 (Oct. 14, 1981)-. Periodical. English. Forty times a year. Alex Dryden, 33 F Woodfield Drive, Nepean Ontario L2G 3Y6 Canada. **Tel** (613)238-2628.

DD 384/.065/71
ISSN 0828-0150
CN
CANADIAN INTERCONNECT DIRECTORY, THE. [Can. interconnect dir.].
Oct. 1981-. Directory. English. One time a year. $35.00 per vol. Northern Business Information, 157 Chambers Street, 7th Floor, New York NY 10007-1015. **Tel** (212)732-0775, FAX (212)233-6233.

LC HE
DD 384/.0971
ISSN 0836-0782
CN
CANADIAN TELECOM. [Can. telecom].
Added/Corp Canadian Business Telecommunications Alliance. Vol. 1, No 2 (Sept. 1987)-. Periodical. English. Six times a year. 45.00Can$. A B Y Group, 36 TorontoStreet, Suite 1160, Toronto, Ontario M5C 2C5 Canada. **Tel** (416)359-2911, FAX (416)359-9909. **ED** Arn Gable. **Circ:** 6,000. *Continues Canadian Telecom Directory and Buyer's Guide., 0843-1418.*

SZ
CCIR. (19??)-. English (French and Spanish). Irregular.
Price varies. International Telecommunication Union, place des Nations, CH-1211 Geneva 20 Switzerland. **Tel** 011 41 22 7305111, FAX 011 41 22 7337256.

UK
CEI. (19??)-. English. Twelve times a year. £33.00.
Quarto International Ltd., 4 Brandon Road, London N7 9TR United Kingdom. **Tel** 011 44 171 6092177, FAX 011 44 171 6094985. **Bk Rev. Ad Acc. Circ:** 24,029.
Continues Communications Engineering International, 0143-9561.

DD 384
ISSN 1054-7703
US
CELLULAR & MOBILE INTERNATIONAL. [Cell. mob. int.]. VFOAT
Cellular and Mobile International. (1991)-. Trade Publication. English. Six times a year. $29.41. Intertec Publishing Corporation, 9800 Metcalf, Overland Park KS 66212. **Tel** (913)341-1300. **(Subscription address:** Intertec Publishing Corporation, PO Box 2901, Overland Park KS 66212. **Tel** 800 441-0294.)

LC HD9696.R363 U617
DD 384.5/3
ISSN 0741-6520
US
CCC
CELLULAR BUSINESS. See
Communications-Radio.

DD 332
ISSN 0898-0403
US
TITLE CHANGE
CELLULAR INVESTOR. [Cell. investor].
Added/Corp Paul Kagan Associates. No. 1 (Mar 21 1988)-(199?). Newsletter. English. Paul Kagan Associates Inc., 126 Clock Tower Place, Carmel CA 93923-8734. **Tel** (408)624-1536, FAX (408)625-3225, telex ITT 4938124 PKA UI. *Continued by Wireless Telecom Investor, 1075-413X.*

DD 384
ISSN 1071-779X
US
CELLULAR MARKET FORECASTS. [Cell. mark. forecasts]. Added/Corp
Hershel Shosteck Associates. (1986)-. Periodical. English. Four times a year. $1295.00. Herchel Shosteck Association Ltd., 11160 Viers Mill Road, Suite 709, Wheaton MD 20902. **Tel** (301)589-2259, FAX (301)588-3311.
Desc: Measures, analyzes, and forecasts industry revenues, subscriber growth, and telephone sales.

US
TITLE CHANGE
CELLULAR / MOBILE COMMUNICATIONS DIRECTORY, THE.
Added/Corp Phillips Business Information, Inc. **VFOAT** Cellular Mobile Communications Directory. (199?)-(199?). English. Phillips Business Information Inc., 1201 Seven Locks Road, PO Box 61130, Potomac MD 20854. **Tel** (301)424-3338, (301)340-1520, (800)777-5005, FAX (301)424-4297, telex 358149. *Continues Mobile Communications Directory, 1055-1980.* Merged into *Wireless Industry Directory.*
Desc: Profiles suppliers of cellular/mobile products and services worldwide. Gives direct access to suppliers, colleagues, competitors and customers around the world.

DD 384
ISSN 1059-3888
US
CELLULAR PEOPLE. [Cell. people].
Added/Corp International Registry for Cellular Professionals. Vol. 1, Issue 1 (Dec. 1991)-. Periodical. English. Twelve times a year. $100.00 US; $130.00 other. Cellular People, c/o IRCP, PO Box 547756, Orlando FL 32854.

LC HE8801 .C44
DD 384.5/34
ISSN 1066-0518
US
CELLULAR RATES. [Cell. rates]. Added/Corp
Paul Kagan Associates. (Mar. 1992)-. English. Irregular. $695.00. Paul Kagan Associates Inc., 126 Clock Tower Place, Carmel CA 93923-8734. **Tel** (408)624-1536, FAX (408)625-3225, telex ITT 4938124 PKA UI. available on diskette (rates database).
Desc: Inventory of cellular rates - includes major rate differences by market and by company, activation fee and feature rates by company, MSA and RSA market pops, owner/operator directory, etc.

DD 338
ISSN 0892-2683
US
CELLULAR SALES & MARKETING. [Cell. sales mark.]. VFOAT
Cellular Sales and Marketing. Vol. 1, No. 1 (Feb. 1987)-. Periodical. English. Twelve times a year. $347.00. Creative Communications, PO Box

Communications —Telecommunication

1519-EBS, Herndon VA 22070. **Tel** (710)742-9696. **ED** Stuart Crump Jr. **Bk Rev**, (Qty: 1-2). available on an online database from NEWSNET.
  Desc: News and information on the sales and marketing of cellular and other personal communications technologies.

LC HE8811 .C445   ISSN 1052-7451
DD 384   US
CELLULAR TELEPHONE ATLAS, THE.
[Cell. teleph. atlas]. **Added/Corp** Paul Kagan Associates. (19??)-. English. One time a year. $395.00. Paul Kagan Associates Inc., 126 Clock Tower Place, Carmel CA 93923-8734. **Tel** (408)624-1536, FAX (408)625-3225, telex ITT 4938124 PKA UI.

LC HE8811 .C45   US
DD 384.5/3
         TITLE CHANGE
CELLULAR TELEPHONE DIRECTORY, THE.
Added/Corp Communications Publishing Service. 1st Edition (1987)-(19??). Directory. English. Communications Publishing Service, PO Box 500, Mercer Island WA 98040-0500. **Tel** (206)232-3464. *Continued by Cellular Travel Guide.*
  Desc: Complete fact book about the cellular telephone industry. Includes maps and instructions for using a car telephone in the US and Canada.

    US
CELLULAR TRAVEL GUIDE.
Added/Corp Communications Publishing Service. (19??)-. Directory. English. One time a year. $19.95. Communications Publishing Service, PO Box 500, Mercer Island WA 98040-0500. **Tel** (206)232-3464. *Continues The Cellular Telephone Directory.*

LC HE7791.F6 M5   ISSN 1073-9645
DD 338/.0029/47281   US
●CENTRAL AMERICA BUSINESS DIRECTORY, THE.
[Cent. Am. bus. dir.]. **VFOAT** InterCom Projects, Limited Business Directory; IPL Business Directory. (1994)-. English (Spanish). Irregular. $80.00. Intercom Projects Ltd., 118 South Miami Avenue, Suite 105, Miami FL 33130. *Continues Fax & Business Directory, 1052-2190.*

    HK
●CHINA FAX AND TELEX DIRECTORY.
See Business and Economics-Commerce.

LC HF5260.A3 C498
DD 650   HK
NLM TK 6011; C536
CHINA PHONE BOOK & BUSINESS DIRECTORY, THE.
See Business and Economics.

LC TK5102.3.C6 C49   ISSN 1078-2214
    US
●CHINA TELECOM NEWSLETTER.
Added/Corp Information Gatekeepers, Inc. **VFOAT** China Telecom. Vol. 1, No. 1 (Sept. 1994)-. Periodical. English. Twelve times a year. $575.00 US and Canada; $625.00 other. Information Gatekeepers Inc., 214 Harvard Avenue, Boston MA 02134. **Tel** (617)232-3111, (617)738-8088, (800)323-1088, FAX (617)734-8562.

    ISSN 1081-4094
DD 384   US
●CHINA TELECOM REPORT.
[China telecom rep.]. **Added/Corp** International Technology Consultants, Inc. (1994)-. Newsletter. English. Twelve times a year. $679.00. International Technology Consultants, 1724 Kalorama Road, Suite 210, Washington DC 20009. **Tel** (202)234-2138, FAX (202)483-7922. **ED** S. Blake Swensrud.

    ISSN 1017-5199
    HK
CHINA TELECOMMUNICATIONS CONSTRUCTION.
Trade Publication. Chinese. Six times a year (Feb, Apr, Jun, Aug, Oct, Dec). $98.00. Metropolitan Museum of Art, 1000 5th Avenue & 82nd Street, New York NY 10028. **Tel** (212)879-5500 ext. 2937, telex 4676. **ED** Rebecca Li. **Ad Acc, Adv Mgr:** Alan Law. **Circ:** 8,300 (ctrl).

    ISSN 1017-5199
UDC 384   HK
CHINA TELECOMMUNICATIONS CONSTRUCTION.
[China telecommun. constr.]. **VFOAT** Zhongguo Dianxin Jianshe. (1988)-. Trade Publication. Chinese. Six times a year. $80.00. China Telecommunications Construction Publishers, 3A Sing ku Commerical Building, 27 des Voeux Road West, Hong Kong Hong Kong. **Tel** 011 852 25172093, 011 852 25172095, FAX 011 852 25172101, telex 2359. **ED** Rebecca Li. **Ad Acc, Adv Mgr:** K.M. Han. **Circ:** 20,000 (ctrl).

    HK
    TITLE CHANGE
CHINA TELEX & FAX DIRECTORY.
Added/Corp Chung-kuo Tien Hua Pu Kung Ssu. **VFOAT** China Telex and FAX Directory. (1988/89)-(19??). Directory. English. China Phone Book Company Ltd,

GPO Box 11581, Hong Kong Hong Kong. **Tel** 011 852 25084448, FAX 011 852 25031526, telex 84958. *Continues China Telex Book. Continued by China Fax and Telex Directory.*

LC TK5101.A1 C583
    KO
CHONGI TONGSIN.
VFOAT KETRI Journal; The K.E.T.R.I. Journal; K.E.T.R.I. Journal. Periodical. Korean (Korean). Four times a year.

LC TK7800 .C44a
    CU
    SUSPENDED
CIC INFORMACION TECNICA. Main/Corp
Centro de Informacion de Comunicaciones. (19??)-(1990). Spanish. Four times a year. Ediciones Cubanas, Obispo 527 Altos ESQ Bernaza, CP 10100 Havana Cuba.

LC HE7771 .C65   ISSN 1043-545X
DD 384.1/4   US
COLUMBINE FAX DIRECTORY.
[Columbine FAX dir.]. 1989-. Directory. English. One time a year. $12.95 (copy), $10.36 (libraries) US; (add $2.50 for shipping, unless libraries prepay). Columbine Inc, PO Box 974, Blue Hill ME 04614-0974. **Tel** (207)326-4717, FAX (207)326-8639. **ED** Sally Beach and Bill Allen. **Circ:** 10,000.
  Desc: A portable directory of 63,000+ business and government facsimile phone numbers in USA, Canada, Mexico, and Caribbean.

    US
COMMON CARRIER SERVICES INFORMATION. Main/Corp
United States. Federal Communications Commission. (19??)-. Periodical. English. FCC / Federal Communications Commission, 1919 M Street Northwest, Room 538, Washington DC 20554. **Tel** (202)632-6302.

LC HE7761 .C66   ISSN 0743-4812
DD 384/.0973   US
    CCC
COMMON CARRIER WEEK.
(COMMON CARRIER WEEK : A SERVICE OF TELEVISION DIGEST, INC.). [Common carrier week]. (1984)-. Newsletter. English. One time a week. $724.00. Warren Publishing, Inc., 2115 Ward Court Northwest, Washington DC 20037. **Tel** (202)872-9200, FAX (202)293-3435. **ED** Arthur Brodsky. available on an online database from NEWSNET; and (files 16,636,648/Full-Text) DIALOG.
  Desc: Covering telecommunications industry-regulation changes, business strategies, new equipment, services, personnel, etc.
  Ind/Abst PROMT [Full Txt.]; PTS Newsl. Database [Full Txt.].

    ISSN 0264-4509
    UK
    CODEN CTUSD8
COMMUNICATE (HIGH WYCOMBE).
(COMMUNICATE.). [Communicate]. (19??)-. Periodical. English. Twelve times a year. $42.78. Link House Magazines Ltd., Link House, Dingwall Avenue, Croydon Surrey CR9 2TA United Kingdom. **Tel** 011 44 181 6862599, FAX 011 44 181 7600973, telex 947709. **ED** Annie Turner. **Ad Acc, Adv Mgr:** Stuart Giddings, **Tel** 071 403 8989. **Circ:** 17,118 (ctrl). Documents available from Ask*IEEE. *Continues Communicate for the Telecommunication User.*
  Desc: Coverage of all areas pertinent to those within large organizations who are responsible for the specification and management of data and telecommunication infrastructures.
  Ind/Abst Curr. Cit.; HILITES; Infomat Int. Bus.; INSPEC (Sep. 1987-).

    US
COMMUNICATIONS BUSINESS AND FINANCE.
(19??)-. English. Twenty-five times a year. $547.00 US; $673.00 other. Telecommunications Reports, 1333 H Street Northwest, 2nd Floor West Wester, Washington DC 20005. **Tel** (202)842-0520, (800)822-6338, FAX (202)842-3047. **(Subscription address:** Telecommunications Reports, PO Box 675, Cooper Station, New York NY 10276.)
  Desc: Covers mergers, acquisitions and other strategic alliances, new business plans and emerging industry trends.

    ISSN 0277-0679
    US
    CCC
COMMUNICATIONS DAILY.
(COMMUNICATIONS DAILY / TELEVISION DIGEST.). [Commun. dly.]. **Added/Corp** Television Digest, inc. (198?)-. Periodical. English. Seven times a week. $2593.00. Warren Publishing, Inc., 2115 Ward Court Northwest, Washington DC 20037. **Tel** (202)872-9200, FAX (202)293-3435. **ED** Mary Crowley. available on an online database from NEWSNET; Lexis-Nexis; (files 16,80,636/Full-Text) DIALOG; and DATA-STAR.
  Desc: Newsletter covering the entire telecommunications industry. Follows FCC, Congress, White House and all related news worldwide.

Ind/Abst PROMT [Full Txt.]; PTS Newsl. Database [Full Txt.]; Trade Ind. ASAP [Full Txt.]; Trade Ind. Index [Full Txt.].

LC TK5101.A1 C629   ISSN 0010-356X
DD 384/.05   US
    CCC
    CODEN CMUTAR
    TITLE CHANGE
COMMUNICATIONS (ENGLEWOOD. 1964).
(COMMUNICATIONS.). [Communications]. (1964)-(19??). Trade Publication. English. Argus Business, 6151 Powers Ferry Road Northwest, Atlanta GA 30339. **Tel** (404)995-2500, FAX (404)995-0400. **(Subscription address:** Sunbelt Fulfillment Services / Nashville, PO Box 41369, Nashville TN 37204. **Tel** (615)377-3322, (800)888-5139.) **ED** George Dennis. **Circ:** 20,000. available on microfilm and microfiche from University Microfilms International (UMI). Documents available from UMI Article Clearinghouse, Ask*IEEE. *Continued by Communications for the Wireless Communications Professional.*
  Ind/Abst ABI/INFORM Glob. Ed.; ABI/INFORM [Computer File] (Dec. 1978-Dec. 1980); Curr. Cit.; INSPEC (Jan. 1968-); PsycINFO (1990-); PsycLit; UMI ABI/Inform--Bus. Period. Ondisc [Full Txt.].

    US
COMMUNICATIONS FOR THE WIRELESS COMMUNICATIONS PROFESSIONAL.
(19??)-. Periodical. English. Twelve times a year. $39.00 US; $59.00 (surface mail), $99.00 (airmail) other. Argus Business, 6151 Powers Ferry Road Northwest, Atlanta GA 30339. **Tel** (404)995-2500, FAX (404)995-0400. **(Subscription address:** Sunbelt Fulfillment Services, PO Box 5039, Brentwood TN 37024. **Tel** (800)685-3435.) *Continues Communications.*

LC TK5101.A1 C638   ISSN 0305-2109
DD 621.38/05   US
    CODEN CINTDZ
COMMUNICATIONS INTERNATIONAL.
[Commun. int.]. (1974)-. Trade Publication. English. Twelve times a year. $135.00. EMAP Readerlink, Audit House, 260 Field End Road, Ruislip Middlesex HA4 9LT United Kingdom. **Tel** 011 44 1773 63100, FAX 011 44 1733 87367. available on an online database from Lexis-Nexis; and (file 648/Full-Text) DIALOG. Documents available from Ask*IEEE, BLDSC, FAXON Xpress, SWETS, UMI Article Clearinghouse.
  Ind/Abst Curr. Cit.; F&S Index Plus Text, Int. [Select. Cov.]; Infomat Int. Bus.; INSPEC (March 1975-); PROMT; Trade Ind. ASAP [Full Txt.]; Trade Ind. Index [Full Txt.].

LC HE8861 .A265   ISSN 0380-0334
DD 384/.0971   CN
COMMUNICATIONS (OTTAWA).
(COMMUNICATIONS.). [Communications]. **Main/Corp** Statistics Canada. Transportation and Communications Division. **Added/Corp** Statistics Canada. Public Utilities Section. Statistics Canada. Statistics Canada. Transportation and Communications Division. Statistics Canada. Services Division. **VFOAT** Communications. **VAT** Service Bulletin. Communications. Vol. 1, No. 4 (Aug. 1971)-. Periodical. English (French). Irregular. 53.00Can$ Canada; $64.00 US; $75.00 other. Statistics Canada Publications Sales and Services, R.H. Coats Building 6th Floor, Ottawa Ontario K1A 0T6 Canada. **Tel** (613)951-5078, (800)267-6677, FAX (613)951-1584, telex 053-3585. *Continues Communications (Canada. Dominion Bureau of Statistics)., 0380-0334.*
  Desc: Provides early release of summary information on telecommunications, including the telephone industry and other telecommunications carriers; radio and television broadcasting, cable television and miscellaneous data of general interest.

LC TK5101.A1 C642   ISSN 1053-9433
DD 621/.382   US
COMMUNICATIONS QUARTERLY.
(COMMUNICATIONS QUARTERLY : THE JOURNAL OF COMMUNICATIONS TECHNOLOGY.). [Commun. q.]. (Fall 1990)-. Periodical. English. Four times a year. $29.95. CQ Communications Inc, 76 North Broadway, Hicksville NY 11801. **Tel** (516)681-2922, FAX (516)681-2926.

    US
COMMUNICATIONS REGULATION.
(19??)-. English. Irregular (includes monthly updates). $995.00. Pike & Fischer Inc., 4600 East-West Highway, Suite 200, Bethesda MD 20814-1438. **Tel** (301)654-6262, FAX (301)654-6297.

    US
COMMUNICATIONS SERIES. COMMUNICATIONS NETWORKING SERVICES.
Added/Corp Datapro Information Services Group. **VFOAT** Communications Networking Services; Information Technology Solutions, Communications Series. Communications Networking Services. (Jan. 1992)-. Periodical. English. Twelve times a year. $485.00. Datapro Information Services Group, 600 Delran Parkway, Delran NJ 08075. **Tel**

Communications —Telecommunication

(609)764-0100, (800)328-2776, FAX (609)764-8953. **Continues in part** Datapro Reports on Telecommunications, 0735-8458.

US
COMMUNICATIONS SERIES. VOICE NETWORKING SYSTEMS. Added/Corp
Datapro Information Services Group. **VFOAT** Voice Networking Systems; Information Technology Solutions, Communications Series. Voice Networking Systems. (Jan. 1992)-. Periodical. English. Twelve times a year. $857.00. Datapro Information Services Group, 600 Delran Parkway, Delran NJ 08075. **Tel** (609)764-0100, (800)328-2776, FAX (609)764-8953. **Continues in part** Datapro Reports on Telecommunications, 0735-8458.

ISSN 1081-4655
US
●COMMUNICATIONS STANDARDS REVIEW--TELECOMMUNICATIONS.
VFOAT CSR-T. (1995)-. Periodical. English. Irregular (6 to 8 issues per year). $595.00. Communications Standards Review, 757 Greer Road, Palo Alto CA 94303. **Tel** (415)856-9018, FAX (415)856-6591. **ED** Elaine Baskin. **Circ:** 200 (ctrl). available on an online database. **Continues** Communications Standards Review, 1064-3907.
 Desc: Provides timely, detailed coverage of the lower layer (OSI layers 1-3) wide area networking wirelines technical standards committee work in TIA and ITU-T.

LC HE7601 .T442 ISSN 0746-8121
DD 384 US
CCC
COMMUNICATIONSWEEK (MANHASSET, N.Y.).
(COMMUNICATIONSWEEK.). [CommunicationsWeek]. **VFOAT** Communications Week. (1984)-. Periodical. English. One time a week (51 issues). $143.00. CMP Publications Inc., One Jericho Plaza, Wing A, 2nd Floor, Jericho NY 11753. **Tel** (516)733-6700. **(Subscription address:** CMP Publications, Inc. / Illinois, PO Box 5920, Department 100, Carol Stream IL 60197-5920.) available on an online database from NEWSNET; and (file 16/Full-Text) DIALOG. Documents available from BLDSC.
 Desc: Provides late breaking news for the US communications industry with particular emphasis on internetworking and intercommunications.
 Ind/Abst Bus. Source Plus; Bus. Source; Comput. Database; EP Collect.; F&S Index Plus Text, Int. [Full Txt.] [Select. Cov.]; Homework Help.; Lotus Notes; MasterFile FullTEXT 1000; MasterFile FullTEXT 350; MasterFile FullTEXT 650; MasterFile FullTEXT; OCLC; Telebase.

LC TK5102.3.F8 C65 ISSN 0242-1283
DD 621.38/05 FR
CODEN COTNDL
CEASED
COMMUTATION & TRANSMISSION.
[Commut. transm.]. **Added/Corp** SOTELEC. Vol. 1, No. 1 (Sept. 1979)-(1995). Periodical. English (French). Sotelec, 28 rue du Docteur Finlay, 75015 Paris France. **Tel** 011 33 1 40590505, FAX 011 33 1 40590707. **ED** Jean Duquesne. **Ad Acc, Adv Mgr:** Jean Duquesne. **Circ:** 7500 (ctrl). Documents available from Article Express International, Ask*IEEE.
 Ind/Abst Bioeng. Abstr.; Curr. Cit.; Ei Page One; Energy Res. Abstr. (April 1982-); Eng. Index Annu.; INSPEC (Sep. 1979-); SCISEARCH.

LC TK7800 .C65 ISSN 0898-3577
DD 621.381/0218 US
CCC
CODEN CENGE3
COMPLIANCE ENGINEERING. [Compliance eng.].
VFOAT CE. (198?)-. Periodical. English. Seven times a year (irregular; includes Compliance Engineering Handbook). $100.00. Compliance Engineering, 629 Massachusetts Avenue, Boxborough MA 01719. **Tel** (508)264-4208, FAX (508)635-9407. **(Subscription address:** Compliance Engineering European Edition. **Tel** 011 44 1483 271288.) **ED** Daniel Griffin, Glen Dash and Isidor Straus (Managing Editors). **Ad Acc, Adv Mgr:** Michael Costa and Michael Mintzer. available on an online database.
 Desc: The magazine for international regulatory compliance.

LC TK5105.5 .C647 ISSN 0169-7552
DD 621.382 NE
CCC
CODEN CNISE9CNETDP
Pr Rev.
COMPUTER NETWORKS AND ISDN SYSTEMS. See Computers-Computer Networks.

LC HD9696.C63 G733 ISSN 0964-4520
DD 338.47621381 UK
COMPUTING & COMMUNICATIONS DECISIONS. See Computers-Computer Industry and Industry Directories.

LC TK5104 .C64 ISSN 0095-9669
DD 621.38/0422 US
CODEN CSTRCQ
COMSAT TECHNICAL REVIEW. [COMSAT tech. rev.].
Main/Corp Communications Satellite Corporation. **Added/Corp** Communications Satellite Corporation. Technical Review. **VAT** Communications Satellite Technical Review. Vol. 1 (Fall 1971)-. Periodical. English (summaries and/or abstracts in French and Spanish). One time a year. $25.00. Communications Satellite Corporation, 22300 Comsat Drive, Clarksburg MD 20871. **Tel** (301)428-4512. Documents available from Article Express International, Ask*IEEE, CASDDS.
 Desc: Devoted exclusively to the advancement of satellite communications technology.
 Ind/Abst Bioeng. Abstr.; Chem. Abstr.; Ei Page One; Eng. Index Annu.; INSPEC (Fall 1971-); Int. Aerosp. Abstr.; Leadscan; SCISEARCH.

CU
COMUNICACIONES. Added/Corp Centro de Informacion de Comunicaciones.
(19??)-. Periodical. Spanish. Two times a year. Ediciones Cubanas, Obispo 527 Altos ESQ Bernaza, CP 10100 Havana Cuba. Index available. **Bk Rev. Circ:** 10,000 (ctrl).
 Desc: Investigates transmission systems worldwide, with economic and technical analysis allowing convenient selection for data transmission systems by means of communications channels.

HO
COMUNICADOR, EL. Added/Corp Empresa Hondurena de Telecomunicaciones.
Vol. 1, No. 1 (January/March 1981)-. Periodical. Spanish. Six times a year. Empresa Hondurena de Telecomunicaciones, Apartado Postal 1794, Tegucigalpa DC Honduras.

LC TK7885.A1 P47a ISSN 0896-582X
DD 004 US
CONFERENCE PROCEEDINGS / ANNUAL INTERNATIONAL PHOENIX CONFERENCE ON COMPUTERS AND COMMUNICATIONS. See Computers.

LC TK5101.A1 I3544a ISSN 0893-4266
DD 621.382 US
TITLE CHANGE
CONFERENCE PROCEEDINGS - IEEE PACIFIC RIM CONFERENCE ON COMMUNICATIONS, COMPUTERS AND SIGNAL PROCESSING.
(CONFERENCE PROCEEDINGS / IEEE PACIFIC RIM CONFERENCE ON COMMUNICATIONS, COMPUTERS AND SIGNAL PROCESSING.). [Conf. proc. - IEEE Pac. Rim Conf. Commun. Comput. Signal Process.]. **Added/Corp** Institute of Electrical and Electronics Engineers. Victoria Section ... [ET AL.]. (June 4-5, 1987)-(May 9th-10th, 1991). English. IEEE / Institute of Electrical and Electronics Engineers Inc., 345 East 47th Street, New York NY 10017-2394. **Tel** (908)981-1393, FAX (908)981-9667. **Continued by** IEEE Pacific Rim Conference on Communication, Computers and Signal Processing. Proceedings.
 Desc: Covers telecommunication, computers, electric filters (digital) and signal processing.

LC TK5101.A1 I145a ISSN 1054-5921
DD 621.382 US
CONFERENCE RECORD / IEEE GLOBAL TELECOMMUNICATIONS CONFERENCE & EXHIBITION. [Conf. rec.- IEEE Global Telecommun. Conf. Exhib.].
Added/Corp IEEE Communications Society. Institute of Electrical and Electronics Engineers. **VFOAT** IEEE GLOBECOM. (1988)-. English. Irregular. IEEE / Institute of Electrical and Electronics Engineers Inc., 345 East 47th Street, New York NY 10017-2394. **Tel** (908)981-1393, FAX (908)981-9667. **Continues** IEEE/IEICE Global Telecommunications Conference. Conference Record.
 Ind/Abst Comput. Inf. Syst. Abstr. J. [Full Cov.]; Elect. Comm. Abstr.; Environ. Eng. Abstr.; Manuf. Process Eng. Abstr.; Mech. Eng. Abstr.; Solid State Supercond. Abstr.

LC TK5101.A1 I16a ISSN 1044-4556
DD 621.382 US
CCC
CONFERENCE RECORD - IEEE INTERNATIONAL CONFERENCE ON COMMUNICATIONS.
(CONFERENCE RECORD.). [Conf. rec. - IEEE Intl. Conf. Commun.]. **Added/Corp** Institute of Electrical and Electronics Engineers. **VFOAT** Proceedings; IEEE ... International Communications Conference. ICC (1982)-. English. One time a year. IEEE / Institute of Electrical and Electronics Engineers Inc., 345 East 47th Street, New York NY 10017-2394. **Tel** (908)981-1393, FAX (908)981-9667. **Continues** International Conference on Communications. Conference Record, 0536-1486.

ISSN 0266-3279
UK
CONNECTIONS (LONDON).
(CONNECTIONS.). [Connections]. (Feb. 1984)-. Periodical. English. Twenty-four times a year. Television Digest Inc, 1836 Jefferson Place NW, Washington DC 20036.

US
CONVERGENCE NEWSLETTER. (19??)-.
Newsletter. English. Eleven times a year. $265.00. Information Gatekeepers Inc., 214 Harvard Avenue, Boston MA 02134. **Tel** (617)232-3111, (617)738-8088, (800)323-1088, FAX (617)734-8562.

US
TITLE CHANGE
CORPORATE SECURITY'S TECHNOLOGY ALERT. (19??)-(1995).
English. Telecommunications Reports, 1333 H Street Northwest, 2nd Floor West Tower, Washington DC 20005. **Tel** (202)842-0520, (800)822-6338, FAX (202)842-3047. **(Subscription address:** Telecommunications Reports, PO Box 675, Cooper Station, New York NY 10276.) **Merged into** Corporate Securitys with Technology Alert.

ISSN 8750-5568
US
CPC EAST COAST REPORT, THE. See Petroleum and Natural Gas.

ISSN 0747-9050
DD 384 US
TITLE CHANGE
CPE STRATEGIES. [CPE strategies].
Added/Corp Marketing Program and Services Group. **VFOAT** C.P.E. Strategies. Vol. 1, No. 1 (Jan. 1984)-(19??). Periodical. English. The ARIES Group MPSG, 1350 Piccard Drive, Suite 300, Rockville MD 20850. **Tel** (301)840-0800. **Merged into** Telecommunications Product Review, 0736-4156.

ISSN 0884-7983
DD 738 US
CROWN JEWELS OF THE WIRE. [Crown jewels wire].
VFOAT Crown Jewels. (1984)-. Periodical. English. Twelve times a year. $20.00. Crown Jewels of the Wire, PO Box 10003, St. Charles IL 60174. **Tel** (708)513-1544, FAX (708)513-8278. **ED** Carol M. MacDougald. Index available. cum. index. **Bk Rev. Ad Acc. Circ:** 1,700. **Continues** Insulators, 0738-3452.
 Desc: Devoted exclusively to insulator collecting, telephone/telegraph history and related collectibles.

LC WMLC 93/3957 ISSN 1194-9457
DD 343.7109/94/0264605 CN
●CRTC TELECOM DECISIONS, LETTER DECISIONS, AND PUBLIC NOTICES.
(CRTC TELECOM DECISIONS, LETTER DECISIONS, AND PUBLIC NOTICES = DECISIONS, LETTRES-DECISIONS ET AVIS PUBLICS DU CRTC EN MATIERE DE TELECOMMUNICATIONS.). [CRTC telecom decis. lett. decis. public not.]. **Main/Corp** Canadian Radio-Television and Telecommunications Commission. **VFOAT** Decisions, Lettres-Decisions et avis Publics du CRTC en Matiere de Telecommunications. **VAT** Canadian Radio-Television and Telecommunications Commission Telecom Decisions, Letter Decisions, and Public Notices. (1993)-. Periodical. English (French). One time a year. Receiver General for Canada / Ottawa, Canada Comm Group Publishing, Ottawa Ontario K1A 0S9 Canada. **Tel** (819)956-4802, (800)661-2868.

LC TK5101.A1 C75 ISSN 0393-2648
DD 621.38 IT
CSELT TECHNICAL REPORTS.
Added/Corp CSELT. Vol. 12, No. 3 (June 1984)-. Periodical. English (Italian). Six times a year. Free on request. Centro Studi e Laboratori Telecomunicazione Spa, Via Guglielmo Reiss Romoli 274, 10148 Turin Italy. **Tel** 39 11 21691, FAX 39 11 2169520, telex 220539. Index available. **Ad Acc. Circ:** 1,200 (ctrl). Documents available from Article Express International, Ask*IEEE. **Continues** CSELT Rapporti Tecnici.
 Desc: Reports documents presented by congress or published by CSELT.
 Ind/Abst Curr. Cit.; Eng. Index Annu.; INSPEC (Dec. 1984-); Int. Aerosp. Abstr.

ISSN 0894-6418
US
Pr Rev.
CSR HOTLINE. VAT Customer Service Research Hotline.
Vol. 1, No. 1 (1987)-. Periodical. English. Irregular. Freehold Galleries Inc., 80 Scenic Drive, Suite 8, Freehold NJ 07728. **Tel** (201)780-7020. **ED** Lee R. Van Vechten.
 Desc: Customer service reps skills training on telemarketing continuity program.

LC TK5101 ISSN 1024-5847
DD 621.382 HK
●CTC NEWS. VFOAT China Telecommunications Construction News.
(1995)-. Newsletter. English (Chinese). Twenty-two times a year. $395.00. China Telecommunications Construction Publishers, 3A Sing ku Commerical Building, 27 des Voeux Road West, Hong

Communications — Telecommunication

Kong Hong Kong. **Tel** 011 852 25172093, 011 852 25172095, FAX 011 852 25172101, telex 2359. **ED** T.P. Yuen.
Desc: Covers the events, developments and other news affecting telecommunication in China. Each issue covers a variety of topics such as plans of communications, administration, new products and services, major deals, ventures and contracts, and more. Includes regulations and standards.

ISSN 0745-3302
US

CUTW VOICE. See Business and Economics-Labor.

ISSN 0007-9227
US

CWA NEWS. See Business and Economics-Labor.

ISSN 1071-3212
DD 384 US

DAILY DIGEST (UNITED STATES. FEDERAL COMMUNICATIONS COMMISSION). (DAILY DIGEST.). [Dly. dig.]. **Added/Corp** United States. Federal Communications Commission. (198?)-. Periodical. English. Seven times a week. $300.00. International Transcriptions Services, 2100 M Street Northwest, Suite 140, Washington DC 20037. **Tel** (202)857-3813, FAX (202)857-3814, (202)296-0019. *Continues Daily Digest (United States. Federal Communications Commission), 1071-3212.*
Ind/Abst PTS Newsl. Database [Full Txt.].

ISSN 0712-3302
DD 621.38/0971 CN

DATACOMMUNICATOR. [Datacommun.]. **Added/Corp** Computer Communications Group (Canada). Trans Canada Telephone System. Vol. 1, No. 1 (4th Quarter 1979)-. Periodical. English. Six times a year. Free on request. Datacommunicator, 410 Laurier Avenue West, Room 970, Ottawa Ontario K1P 6H5 Canada. **Tel** (613)560-3021.

UK

DATAPRO MANAGEMENT OF INTERNATIONAL TELECOMMUNICATIONS. (19??)-. English. Twelve times a year. $626.00. Datapro International, McGraw Hill House, Shoppenhangers Road, Maidenhead Berkshire SL6 2QL United Kingdom. **Tel** 011 44 1628 773277, FAX 011 44 1628 773628.

ISSN 0710-1856
DD 384/.05 CN

DELTA REPORT, THE. [Delta rep.]. May 25, 1981-. Periodical. English. Twenty-four times a year. $250.00. Ted Bates Electronic Publications International, 790 Bay Street, Toronto Ontario M5G 1N9 Canada. *Continues Report (Ted Bates Electronic Publishing International), 0710-1848.*

LC TK5101.A1 D469
ISSN 0913-5693
JA
CCC
CODEN DJTGEB

DENSHI JOHO TSUSHIN GAKKAI SHI = THE JOURNAL OF THE INSTITUTE OF ELECTRONICS, INFORMATION, AND COMMUNICATION ENGINEERS. See Electronics.

LC TK5101.A1 D47
JA

DENSHI TSUSHIN NO GENJO TO TEMBO. Added/Corp Denki Tsushin Kyokai. Japan. Kagaku Gijutsucho. (1973)-. Japanese. ¥950. Okurasho Insatukyoku, (Printing Bureau Ministry of Finance), 2-4 Toranomon 2 chome, Minatoku Tokyo 105 Japan.

LC HE7771 .O75
ISSN 1046-7262
DD 384.1/4 US

DIAL-A-FAX DIRECTORY. [Dial-a-fax dir.]. **VFOAT** Dial a FAX Directory. 3rd Edition (1989)-. Directory. English. One time a year. $193.50. Dial A Fax Directories Corporation, 930 Fox Pavilion, Jenkintown PA 19046. **Tel** (215)887-5700, FAX (215)881-2239. *Continues Original FAX Phone Book, 0896-9434.*

ISSN 0710-2313
DD 354.71270087/4/05 CN

DIALOGUE - MANITOBA TELEPHONE SYSTEM. (DIALOGUE : AN EXCHANGE OF IDEAS AND OPINIONS ON NEW TELECOMMUNICATIONS SERVICES.). [Dialogue - Manit. Teleph. Syst.]. **VFOAT** Dialogue : Un Echange des Idees et Avis sur les Services Mouveaux de Telecomunications. Vol. 1, No. 1 (Mar. 1980)-. Periodical. English (French). Twelve times a year. Manitoba Telephone System, Box 6666, Winnipeg Manitoba R3C 3V6 Canada.

ISSN 1165-788X
FR

● **DIALOGUES (PARIS. 1993).** (1993)-. Periodical. French. Four times a year (Mar., June, Sept., Dec.). $32.81. Dawson France SA, BP 40, 91121 Palaiseau Cedex France. **Tel** 011 33 1 69104700, FAX 011 33 1 64548326, telex 220064F. *Continues France Telecom (Ed. Nationale), 0984-8916.*
Ind/Abst F&S Index Plus Text, Int. [Select. Cov.]; Infomat Int. Bus.; PROMT.

ISSN 0882-1143
DD 621 US

DIGEST OF TECHNICAL INFORMATION. [Dig. tech. inf.]. **Added/Corp** Bell Communications Research, Inc. **VFOAT** Bellcore Digest of Technical Information; Bell Communications Research Digest of Technical Information. Vol. 1, Issue 1 (Apr. 1984)-. Periodical. English. Twelve times a year. $110.00. Bell Communications Research, 60 New England Avenue, Piscataway NJ 08854. **Tel** (908)699-5800, FAX (908)699-0936.

ISSN 1185-0213
DD 384/.097124/05 CN

DIRECT LINE (SASKATOON). (DIRECT LINE.). [Direct line]. **Added/Corp** Sask Tel. Vol. 1, No. 1 (Summer 1990)-. Periodical. English. Four times a year. Free. H & W Publishing Company Ltd, 218-103rd Street East, Saskatoon Saskatchewan S7N 1Y7 Canada. **Tel** (306)373-0404, FAX (306)373-5553.

LC HE7893 .D57
DD 384.1/4 ES

DIRECTORIO TELEX (SAN SALVADOR, EL SALVADOR). (DIRECTORIO TELEX.). **Added/Corp** El Salvador. Administracion Nacional de Telecomunicaciones. (19??)-. Spanish. Antel Edif T Roble, Metrocentre Nte, San Salvador El Salvador.

ISSN 1322-350X
AT

DIRECTORY OF ELECTRONIC SERVICES AND COMMUNICATION NETWORKS. (19??)-. English. One time a year (March with updates in June, Sept., and Dec.). 217.87Aus$. Paul Budde Communication Pty Ltd, 2643 George Downes Drive, Bucketty NSW 2250 Australia. **Tel** 61 (0)49 988 144, FAX 61 (0)49 988 247.
Desc: Lists over 450 telecommunications and broadband services and networks. Each service/network is described in 300-500 words and includes address details and, if applicable, user charges.

LC TS2301.A7 D57
DD 688 US
CEASED

DIRECTORY OF MULTIMEDIA EQUIPMENT, SOFTWARE, AND SERVICES. Added/Corp International Communications Industries Association. **VFOAT** Multimedia Equipment, Software, and Service. 1st Ed. (1992)-3rd Ed. (1995). Directory. English. International Communications Industries, 3150 Spring Street, Fairfax VA 22031-2399. **Tel** (703)273-7200, FAX (703)278-8082. **ED** Diane V. Smith. **Bk Rev**. **Ad Acc**, **Adv Mgr:** Kim Williams, **Tel** (703)273-7200.

LC AS8 .D53
ISSN 1067-4217
DD 361.9/0973 US
NLM AG 521; D598

DIRECTORY OF NATIONAL HELPLINES. (DIRECTORY OF NATIONAL HELPLINES : A GUIDE TO TOLL-FREE PUBLIC SERVICE NUMBERS.). [Dir. natl. helplines]. (19??)-. Directory. English. One time a year. $9.00. Pierian Press, PO Box 1808, Ann Arbor MI 48106. **Tel** (313)434-5530, (800)678-2435, FAX (313)434-6409.

LC L
DD 370 US

DIRECTORY OF TELECOMMUNICATIONS SCHOOLS AND INSTITUTIONS. See Education.

ISSN 1068-2023
DD 363 US
TITLE CHANGE

DISPATCH CENTER MANAGEMENT. (1992)-(199?). Periodical. English. Fulcrum Group, PO Box 335, Schwenksville PA 19473. *Continues Telecommunicators Dispatch, 0887-1647. Merged with Fulcrum Report, 1068-0977 to form Public Safety On-Line, 1072-9321.*

LC HE8689 .I5713
DD 384.54/05 SZ

DOC. - C.C.I.R. See Communications-Radio.

LC HE8341 .D67
US

DOSSIER. ASIAN TELECOM SERVICE MARKETS. Added/Corp Northern Business Information. **VFOAT** Asian Telecom Service Markets. (19??)-. English. Irregular. $22500.00. Datapro

Information Services Group, 600 Delran Parkway, Delran NJ 08075. **Tel** (609)764-0100, (800)328-2776, FAX (609)764-8953.

LC HE8090.7 .A2
ISSN 1082-3379
DD 384/.0947/05 US

DOSSIER. EUROPEAN TELECOM SERVICE MARKETS. EASTERN EUROPEAN TELECOM OPERATORS. (DOSSIER, EUROPEAN TELECOM SERVICE MARKETS.). [Doss., Eur. telecom serv. mark., East. Eur. telecom oper.]. **Added/Corp** Northern Business Information. **VFOAT** European Telecom Service Markets. Eastern European Telecom Operators; Eastern European Telecom Operators. (1991)-. English. Northern Business Information, 157 Chambers Street, 7th Floor, New York NY 10007-1015. **Tel** (212)732-0775, FAX (212)233-6233. *Continues Eastern Europe and Soviet Union Telecom Markets, 1058-2037.*

ISSN 0991-2738
FR

DROIT DE L'INFORMATIQUE ET DES TELECOMS. VFOAT Computer & Telecoms Law Review Computer and Telecoms Law Review; Revue du Droit de l'Informatique et des Telecommunications; Droit de l'Informatique et des Telecommunications; Computer & Telecommunications Law Review; Computer and Telecommunications Law Review. (1988)-. French. Four times a year. $148.73. Editions des Parques, 119 rue de Flandre 75019 Paris France. **Tel** 011 33 1 40350303. *Continues Droit et Informatique, 0772-3660.*

US

● **EAST EUROPEAN AND FORMER SOVIET TELECOM REPORT.** (1995)-. English. Twelve times a year. $749.00. International Technology Consultants, 1724 Kalorama Road, Suite 210, Washington DC 20009. **Tel** (202)234-2138, FAX (202)483-7922. *Continues Eastern European and Former Soviet Telecom Report.*
Desc: Reporting on the political, legislative, financial and regulatory developments affecting the telecommunications, information technology, and broadcasting industries in Eastern Europe and the former Soviet Union.

US
TITLE CHANGE

EASTERN EUROPEAN AND FORMER SOVIET TELECOM REPORT. (19??)-(1995). Newsletter. English. International Technology Consultants, 1724 Kalorama Road, Suite 210, Washington DC 20009. **Tel** (202)234-2138, FAX (202)483-7922. *Continued by East European and Former Soviet Telecom Report.*

LC TK5101.A1 317
ISSN 1054-6499
DD 384/.0947 US
TITLE CHANGE

EASTERN EUROPEAN & SOVIET TELECOM REPORT. [East. Eur. Sov. telecom rep.]. **VFOAT** Eastern European and Soviet Telecom Report; EESTR. (1990)-(19??). Newsletter. English. International Technology Consultants, 1724 Kalorama Road, Suite 210, Washington DC 20009. **Tel** (202)234-2138, FAX (202)483-7922. **ED** Blake Swersmed. **Ad Acc**. **Circ:** 3000. available on an online database (text 16,636/Full-Text) from DIALOG; NEWSNET; and Predicasts, Inc. *Continued by Eastern European and Former Soviet Telecom Report.*
Desc: Washington based newsletter reporting on the political, legislative, financial and regulatory developments affecting the telecommunications, information technology, and broadcasting industries in Eastern Europe and the former Soviet Union.
Ind/Abst PROMT [Full Txt.]; PTS Newsl. Database [Full Txt.].

LC TK5101.A1 E33
ISSN 0012-9283
DD 621.38/05 FR

ECHO DES RECHERCHES, L'. [Echo rech.]. French (English). Four times a year. $82.03. Centre National d'Etudes des Telecommunications, 38-40 rue du General LeClerc, 92131 Issy les Moulineaux France. **Tel** 011 33 1 45294312 or, 45295108. Index available. **Bk Rev**. **Circ:** 10,000 (ctrl). Documents available from Ask*IEEE.
Desc: Telecom networks and services, switching and transmission systems, circuits, semiconductors, videocoms, image and speech processing, CAO, economic studies, management and reliability.
Ind/Abst Acoust. Abstr.; Energy Res. Abstr. (Dec. 1982-); INSPEC (1971-); World Publ. Monit.

LC LC5805 .E3
DD 371.3/078 US

ED. (ED : THE OFFICIAL PUBLICATION OF USDLA.). **Added/Corp** Applied Business Telecommunications. USDLA. (1988)-. Periodical. English. Twelve times a year. Included with USDLA membership. $100.00 (membership). Applied Business Telecommunications, Box 5106, San Ramon CA 94583. **Tel** (510)820-5563, FAX (510)820-5894.
Desc: Covers telecommunications in education.

Communications —Telecommunication

DD 384
ISSN 0890-9563
US
CEASED

EDGE (MORRISTOWN, N.J.). (EDGE.).
(1986)-(July 1994). Periodical. English. Vintage Systems Corporation, 103 Washington Street/Suite 378, Morristown NJ 07960. available on an online database (through Dialog).
Desc: Covers AT&T and the telecommunication industry; specializes in information on product offerings, organizational developments and internal/external influences on AT&T. Includes commentary and analysis.
Ind/Abst Comput. ASAP [Full Txt.]; Comput. Database [Full Txt.]; Trade Ind. Index [Full Txt.].

LC AN
DD 070
UDC 070:621.38
ISSN 1023-7135
UK

EEMA BRIEFING. [EEMA brief.]. VFOAT
European Electronic Messaging Association Briefing. (1987)-. Periodical. English. Six times a year (Feb., Apr., Jun., Aug., Oct., Dec.). 350.00F. EEMA Briefing, Alexander House, High Street, Inkberrow, Worcester, WR7 4DT United Kingdom. **Tel** 011 44 1386 793028, FAX 011 44 1386 793268. **ED** Freddie Dawkins (Editor's address: Media Training, Premier House, Room 521, 77 Oxford Street, London W1R 1RB United Kingdom; telephone: 011 44 181 500814). **Bk Rev. Ad Acc, Adv Mgr Tel** 011 44 1386 793028. **Circ:** 3,000 (ctrl).

ISSN 0731-0633
US
CODEN PREFDI

EFOC, FIBER OPTICS & COMMUNICATIONS PROCEEDINGS.
(EFOC ... FIBER OPTICS & COMMUNICATIONS PROCEEDINGS : PAPERS PRESENTED AT THE ... EUROPEAN FIBER OPTICS & COMMUNICATIONS EXPOSITION.). [EFOC, fiber optics commun. proc.].
Main/Conf European Fiber Optics & Communications Exposition. **VFOAT** EFOC; EFOC ... Fiber Optics & Communications; E.F.O.C. ... Fiber Optics and Communications Proceedings; European Fiber Optics & Communications; Fiber Optics and Communications; Papers Presented at the ... European Fiber Optics and Communications Exposition. (19??)-. Proceedings. English. One time a year. Information Gatekeepers Inc., 214 Harvard Avenue, Boston MA 02134. **Tel** (617)232-3111, (617)738-8088, (800)323-1088, FAX (617)734-8562. **ED** Polishuk, Kennelly and Fasano. Documents available from CASDDS.
Desc: Papers presented at the European fiber optics and local area networks trade shows and conferences.
Ind/Abst Chem. Abstr.; Curr. Cit.

LC TK5101.A1 E43
ISSN 1242-0565
FR
TITLE CHANGE

ELECTRICAL COMMUNICATION.
Added/Corp Alcatel N.V. 4th Quarter (1992)-(1995). Periodical. English (German, Spanish, Italian and French). Electrical Communication / Alcatel, 54 rue la Boetie, 75008 Paris Cedex 08 France. **Tel** 011 33 1 40761347, 011 33 1 40761349, FAX 011 33 1 40761426. **ED** Rod Hazell. available with illustrations; available with charts. **Continues** Electrical communication, 0013-4252. **Continued by** Alcatel Telecommunications Review.
Desc: Technical journal of Alcatel. Reports the research, development and production achievements of its affiliates worldwide.
Ind/Abst Soc. Sci. Cit. Index [Select. Cov.].

CL

ELECTRICIDAD & TELECOMUNICACIONES. See
Energy-Electric Power.

LC TK5105 .E42
DD 651.5/0285
ISSN 0965-2035
UK
CODEN ELDOEE

ELECTRONIC DOCUMENTS. [Electron. doc.].
Vol. 1, No. 1 (Jan. 1992)-. Periodical. English. Twelve times a year. $179.00. Learned Information Ltd., Woodside Hinksey Hill, Oxford OX1 5AU United Kingdom. **Tel** 011 44 1865 730275, FAX 011 44 1865 736354, telex 23667. **(Subscription address:** Information Today, 143 Old Marlton Pike, Medford NJ 08055-8750. **Tel** (609)654-6266, FAX (609)654-4309.) Documents available from Ask*IEEE.
Desc: Publication about storing and exchanging information without paper. Reviews a particular technology used to store and disseminate information electronically - from image filing, to hypertext, to fax on demand.
Ind/Abst INSPEC (1992-).

US

●ELECTRONIC INFORMATION REPORT.
English. Forty-six times a year. $449.00. SIMBA Information Inc., 213 Danbury Road, PO Box 7430, Wilton CT 06897-7430. **Tel** (203)834-0033 ext. 173, FAX (203)834-1771. **(Subscription address:** Simba Information Inc., PO Box 7430, Wilton CT 06897. **Tel** (203)834-0033 ext. 160, FAX (203)834-1771.)

LC HF
DD 651
US

●ELECTRONIC MAIL & MESSAGING SYSTEMS : EMMS. Added/Corp Business
Research Publications, Inc. **VFOAT** Electronic Mail and Messaging Systems; EMMS. (Feb. 1994)-. English. Twenty-five times a year. $595.00. Telecommunications Reports, 1333 H Street Northwest, 2nd Floor West Tower, Washington DC 20005. **Tel** (202)842-0520, (800)822-6338, FAX (202)842-3047. **(Subscription address:** Telecommunications Reports, PO Box 675, Cooper Station, New York NY 10276.) **Continues** Electronic Mail & Micro Systems, 8756-2537; **Absorbed** Telecom/Eye Bee Em, 0888-7292; Netline, 0892-9467 and Advanced Office Technologies Report, 1054-1462.

LC HF
DD 651
ISSN 8756-2537
US
CODEN EMSYEO
TITLE CHANGE

ELECTRONIC MAIL & MICRO SYSTEMS.
[Electron. mail micro syst.]. **Added/Corp** International Resource Development, Inc. **VFOAT** Electronic Mail and Micro Systems; EMMS; E.M.M.S. (19??)-(199?). Newsletter. English. Telecommunications Reports, 1333 H Street Northwest, 2nd Floor West Tower, Washington DC 20005. **Tel** (202)842-0520, (800)822-6338, FAX (202)842-3047. **(Subscription address:** Telecommunications Reports, PO Box 675, Cooper Station, New York NY 10276.) **ED** Eric Arnum. **Bk Rev. Continues** EMMS. Electronic Mail Messaging Systems, 0163-9811. **Continued by** Electronic Mail & Messaging Systems.
Desc: Information on the electronic mail market including CBMS, facsimile, telex, networking, modems, and EDI. Covers technology, user, product and legislative trends in graphic and record communications.
Ind/Abst Infomat Int. Bus.

LC HD9696.A3 U539
DD 381/.45/62130973
ISSN 0270-0093
US

ELECTRONIC MARKET DATA BOOK.
See Electronics.

LC TK5101.A1 E48
ISSN 0013-5119
UK
CCC
CODEN ECOAAS
CEASED

ELECTRONICS & COMMUNICATIONS ABSTRACTS. See Electronics.

LC TK7800 .E43859
DD 621.381/08
ISSN 1069-5303
US

●ELECTRONICS AND COMMUNICATIONS ABSTRACTS. See
Electronics-Abstracting, Bibliographies and Statistics.

ISSN 0231-066X
HU
UDC 016

ELEKTRONIKAI ES HRADASTECHNIKAI SZAKIRODALMI TAJEKOZTATO. See
Engineering-Electrical Engineering.

ISSN 0013-5771
RU
CODEN EKVZAO

ELEKTROSVIAZ (MOSKVA. 1934).
(ELEKTROSVIAZ; NAUCHNO-TEKHNICHESKII ZHURNAL.). [Elektrosviaz]. **Added/Corp** Soviet Union. Narodnyi Komissariat Sviazi. Soviet Union. Narodnyi Komissariat Sviazi. Soviet Union. Ministerstvo Sviazi. (1934)-. Periodical. Russian. Twelve times a year. $129.95. **(Subscription address:** East View Publications Inc., 3020 Harbor Lane North, Suite 110, Minneapolis MN 55447. **Tel** (800)477-1005, (612)550-0961, FAX (612)559-2931.) Documents available from Article Express International, Ask*IEEE.
Ind/Abst Ei Page One; Energy Res. Abstr.; Eng. Index Annu.; INSPEC (1968-); Int. Aerosp. Abstr.

LC TK7800 .E47
ISSN 0013-6123
IT
CODEN ETTCB9

ELETTRONICA E TELECOMUNICAZIONI. See Electronics.

LC HE7761
DD 384
UDC 38
US

ELLIOT GOLD'S TELESPAN. VFOAT
TeleSpan. (1991)-. Bulletin. English. Irregular (40 issues). $357.00. TeleSpan Publishing Corporation, 50 West Palm Street, Altadena CA 91001. **Tel** (818)797-5482, FAX (818)797-2035. **Bk Rev. Continues** TeleSpan, 0743-2283.

DD 006
ISSN 1078-9790
US
TITLE CHANGE

ENTERPRISE COMMUNICATIONS.
[Enterp. commun.]. Vol. 6, No. 9 (Sept. 1994)-(Sept. 1995). Periodical. English. Advanstar Communications Inc., 131 West First Street, Duluth MN 55802. **Tel** (218)723-9477, (800)346-0085, FAX (218)723-9437. **Continues** Voice Processing Magazine, 1042-0460.

Merged into America's Network.
Desc: Covers developments in computer-technology integration. Features new technology in networking, inbound/outbound call processing, updates on phone system and service suppliers.

US

EQUIPMENT RULES. (19??)-. English. Irregular
(Master Volume with bimonthly looseleaf reports). $355.00. Pike & Fischer Inc., 4600 East-West Highway, Suite 200, Bethesda MD 20814-1438. **Tel** (301)654-6262, FAX (301)654-6297. available on diskette.

ISSN 0014-0171
SW
CODEN ERREAO

ERICSSON REVIEW (ENGLISH EDITION). (ERICSSON REVIEW.). [Ericsson rev.].
Added/Corp Telefonaktiebolaget L. M. Ericsson. Vol. 12 (1935)-. Trade Publication. English (Swedish, French and Spanish). Four times a year. $35.00. Telefonaktiebolaget L M Ericsson, Telefonplan Hagersten, S-126 25 Stockholm Sweden. **Tel** 011 46 8 7190000, 7190069, FAX 011 46 8 184085, 6812710, telex 14910 ERIC S. **ED** Per Olof Thyselius. **Circ:** 16,000 (ctrl). Documents available from Article Express International, Ask*IEEE.
Continues L. M. Ericsson Review.
Desc: Market growth, updates, etc.
Ind/Abst Alum. Ind. Abstr.; Bioeng. Abstr.; Curr. Cit.; Ei Page One; Energy Res. Abstr. (June 1978-); Eng. Mater. Abstr.; Eng. Index Annu. [Select. Cov.]; INSPEC (1968-); Met. Abstr.; SCISEARCH; World Alum. Abstr.

LC HE7811 .C36a
DD 354.710087/4/05
CN

ESTIMATES. PART III, DEPARTMENT OF COMMUNICATIONS. Main/Corp Canada.
VFOAT Budget des Depenses. Partie III, Ministere des Communications. (198?)-. English (French). $9.00 Canada; $10.80 other. Canada Communication Group Publishers, Order Processing, Ottawa Ontario K1A 0S9 Canada. **Tel** (819)956-4800, (819)956-4802. **Continues** Canada. Estimates. Part III, Department of Communications, Communications Program, Arts and Culture Program.

ISSN 0999-582X
FR
UDC 654

ETUDES TELECOM PARIS. (ETUDES
TELECOM.). (1989)-. Periodical. French. Ten times a year (monthly except Aug. and Dec.). $964.00. Etudes Telecom Sarl, BP 61, 34131 Mauguio France. **Tel** 011 33 1 1667292585, FAX 011 33 1 1667294777. **ED** Roland DuBois.

US
TITLE CHANGE

EURO-EAST TELECOMMUNICATIONS.
(July 1991)-(Apr. 20, 1994). English. Probe Research Inc., Three Wing Drive, Suite 240, Cedar Knolls NJ 07927-1000. **Tel** (201)285-1500, FAX (201)285-1519. **Merged into** European Telecommunications.

LC HE8081 .E9
DD 384.6/094
UK
TITLE CHANGE

EURODATA FOUNDATION VOICEBOOK. Added/Corp Eurodata Foundation.
VFOAT Voicebook. (19??)-(19??). English. Eurodata Foundation, 175 Piccadilly, Empire House, London W1V 9DB United Kingdom. **Tel** 011 44 171 6291143, FAX 011 44 171 5830516. **Merged into** T Guide.

DD 384
ISSN 1056-2281
UK
CEASED

EUROPEAN CELLULAR. [Eur. cell.]. No. 1
(March 28, 1991)-(199?). Periodical. English. Kagan World Media Inc., 126 Clock Tower Place, Carmel CA 93923-8734. **Tel** (408)624-1536, FAX (408)625-3225. **(Subscription address:** Kagan World Media Ltd., 524 Fulham Road, London SW6 5NR United Kingdom. **Tel** 011 44 171 3718880, FAX 011 44 171 3718715.)
Desc: The facts and figures you need to understand and participate in cellular's rapid growth. The economics that come into play, the technologies, the marketing challenges, and the countries and companies that lead the way.

US

EUROPEAN CELLULAR/MOBILE COMMUNICATIONS DIRECTORY. (19??)-.
Directory. English. $159.00. Phillips Business Information Inc., 1201 Seven Locks Road, PO Box 61130, Potomac MD 20854. **Tel** (301)424-3338, (301)340-1520, (800)777-5005, FAX (301)424-4297, telex 358149.
Desc: European Market data, multinational associations serving Europe, mobile communications regulations and standards, cellular license of European countries, etc.

LC TK6570.M6 E93
DD 384.5/3
ISSN 1080-4625
US

●EUROPEAN CELLULAR/MOBILE COMMUNICATIONS DIRECTORY. [Eur.
cell./mob. commun. dir.]. **Added/Corp** Phillips Business Information, Inc. **VFOAT** European Cellular Mobile

1495

Communications —Telecommunication

Communications Directory. (1994)-. Directory. English. Irregular. Phillips Business Information Inc., 1201 Seven Locks Road, PO Box 61130, Potomac MD 20854. **Tel** (301)424-3338, (301)340-1520, (800)777-5005, FAX (301)424-4297, telex 358149.

US

EUROPEAN SATELLITE DIRECTORY.
(19??)-. Directory. English. $159.00. Phillips Business Information Inc., 1201 Seven Locks Road, PO Box 61130, Potomac MD 20854. **Tel** (301)424-3338, (301)340-1520, (800)777-5005, FAX (301)424-4297, telex 358149.
Desc: Includes European market research, satellite coverage maps, country profiles, etc.

LC HE   ISSN 8756-4459
DD 384

EUROPEAN TELECOMMUNICATIONS.
[Eur. telecommun.]. **Added/Corp** Probe Research Incorporated. (1983)-. Periodical. English. Twenty-four times a year (published the 1st and 15th of each month). $497.00. Probe Research Inc., Three Wing Drive, Suite 240, Cedar Knolls NJ 07927-1000. **Tel** (201)285-1500, FAX (201)285-1519. **ED** Paul Broadhead, Karl Kozarsky, Victor Schnee, Frank Barbetta. **Circ:** 300 (ctrl). Documents available from UMI Article Clearinghouse. **Absorbed** Euro-East Telecommunications.
Desc: Comprehensive coverage and analysis of the manufacturers, markets, and marketers in the telecommunications industry throughout Europe.
Ind/Abst ABI/INFORM Glob. Ed.; Trade Ind. Index.

LC TK5101.A1 E975   ISSN 1120-3862
DD 621.382/05
IT
CCC
CODEN ETTTET

EUROPEAN TRANSACTIONS ON TELECOMMUNICATIONS AND RELATED TECHNOLOGIES.
[Eur. trans. telecommun. relat. technol.]. **Added/Corp** Associazione Elettrotecnica ed Elettronica Italiana. Asociacion Electrotecnica y Electronica Espanola. **VFOAT** ETT. Vol. 1, No. 1 (Jan./Feb. 1990)-. Academic Scholarly Publication. English. Six times a year. L440000. Associazione Elettrotecnica Ed Elettronica, Italiana Viale Monza 259, 20126 Milan Italy. **Tel** 011 39 2 25779223. Documents available from Article Express International, The Genuine Article, Ask*IEEE, CASDDS. **Formed by the union of** Alta Frequenza, 0002-6557 **and** NTZ Archiv, 0170-172X.
Ind/Abst Chem. Abstr. (Jan./Feb. 1990-); Comput. Inf. Syst. Abstr. J. [Full Cov.]; Curr. Cit.; Curr. Contents Eng. Comput. Technol.; Ei Page One (Jan./Feb. 1990-); Elect. Comm. Abstr.; Electron. Commun. Abstr. J. (Jan./Feb. 1990-); EMBASE (Jan./Feb. 1990-); Energy Res. Abstr. (Jan./Feb. 1990-); Eng. Index Annu.; INSPEC (Jan./Feb. 1990-); Int. Aerosp. Abstr. (Jan./Feb. 1990-); ISMEC Bull. (Jan./Feb. 1990-); Manuf. Process Eng. Abstr.; Math. Rev. (Jan./Feb. 1990-); Nucl. Sci. Abstr. (Jan./Feb. 1990-); Res. Alert [Select. Cov.]; Saf. Sci. Abstr. J. (Jan./Feb. 1990-); SCISEARCH.

ISSN 1062-3787
US

EWP UPDATE, THE.
VAT Electronic White Pages Update. (1992)-. Periodical. English. Twelve times a year. Directorynet Inc., 600 Morgan Falls Road, Suite 100, Atlanta GA 30350.

LC HE8803 .G45a   ISSN 0096-9893
DD 353.007/232
US

EXAMINATION OF THE RURAL TELEPHONE BANK'S FINANCIAL STATEMENTS.
See Business and Economics-Accounting.

EXECUTIVE TELECOMMUNICATION PLANNING GUIDE.
Main/Corp Center for Communications Management, Ramsey, N.J. (1972)-. English. Twelve times a year. $572.40. CCMI, 11300 Rockville Pike 11th Floor, Rockville MD 20852-3003. cum. index.

ISSN 1054-9196
DD 658   US
CCC
CEASED

FACILITY STRATEGIES.
[Facil. strateg.]. (Jan. 1988)-(July 1994). Periodical. English. Facility Issues, PO Box 477, Tempe AZ 85280. **Tel** (602)941-5898, FAX (602) 423-9808.

US

FACSIMILE & VOICE SERVICES.
(Jan. 1991)-. English. Twelve times a year. $347.00 US and Canada; $367.00 other. Probe Research Inc., Three Wing Drive, Suite 240, Cedar Knolls NJ 07927-1000. **Tel** (201)285-1500, FAX (201)285-1519. **ED** Michael LaColla

and Adam Greenberg. **Circ:** 125 (ctrl).
Desc: Information on the emerging interactive communications market.

US

FAULKNER TELECOMMUNICATIONS STRATEGIES.
(19??)-. Periodical. English. Irregular. $1635.00. Faulkner Technical Reports, 7905 Browning Road, Suite 114, Pennsauken NJ 08109. **Tel** (800)843-0460.

US

FAULKNER TELECOMMUNICATIONS WORLD.
(19??)-. Periodical. English. Irregular. $1320.00 US; $1506.00 Canada; $1615.00 other. Faulkner Technical Reports, 7905 Browning Road, Suite 114, Pennsauken NJ 08109. **Tel** (800)843-0460.

LC TK6710 .F39   ISSN 0749-2715
DD 384.1/4
US

FAX/NET, PUBLIC ACCESS FACSIMILE STATION DIRECTORY.
VFOAT F.A.X./N.E.T., Public Access Facsimile Station Directory; Public Access Facsimile Station Directory. (19??)-. Directory. English. Perimeter Inc, PO Box 2401, Minneapolis MN 55402-0401.

GW

FAXES OF THE WORLD.
English (German). Two times a year. DM94.48 Germany; DM109.00 other. Interdata Verlag GmbH, Lahnstraße 27, W-5429 Katzenelnbogen Germany. **Tel** 49 6486 8085, FAX 49 6486 8000. **ED** Peter Wurr. Index available. **Circ:** 4,000 (ctrl).
Desc: A standard directory for the complete offerings of the facsimile world market. It includes directly comparable in-depth information about technical features, manufacturers, vendors, and prices.

ISSN 1053-234X
DD 621   US

FAXREPORTER (HACKENSACK, N.J.).
(FAXREPORTER.). [FAXreporter]. **Added/Corp** Buyers Laboratory. **VFOAT** FAX Reporter. (19?)-. Periodical. English. Twelve times a year. $395.00. Buyers Laboratory Inc., 20 Railroad Avenue, Hackensack NJ 07601. **Tel** (201)488-0404.

LC KF2763.3.A2 U535   ISSN 1057-5766
DD 353.0087/4
US

FCC RECORD.
(FCC RECORD : A COMPREHENSIVE COMPILATION OF DECISIONS, REPORTS, PUBLIC NOTICES AND OTHER DOCUMENTS OF THE FEDERAL COMMUNICATIONS COMMISSION OF THE UNITED STATES.). [FCC rec.].
Main/Corp United States. Federal Communications Commission. **VFOAT** Federal Communications Commission Record. **VAT** Federal Communications Commission Record. Vol. 1, No. 1 (Oct. 1-Oct. 10, 1986)-. Government Publication. English. Twenty-six times a year. $197.00. FCC / Federal Communications Commission, 1919 M Street Northwest, Room 538, Washington DC 20554. **Tel** (202)632-6302.
(Subscription address: Superintendent of Documents, US Government Printing Office, Washington DC 20402.)
Absorbed Federal Communications Commission Reports. United States. Federal Communications Commission.
Desc: An inclusive compilation of decisions, reports, public notices and other documents of the Federal Communications Commission of the United States.

US

FCC RULES.
(19??)-. English. Irregular (nine volumes with weekly looseleaf reports). $1040.00. Pike & Fischer Inc., 4600 East-West Highway, Suite 200, Bethesda MD 20814-1438. **Tel** (301)654-6262, FAX (301)654-6297.

ISSN 1051-1903
DD 384   US
CCC

FDDI NEWS.
[FDDI news]. **VFOAT** FDDI Newsletter. **VAT** Fiber Distributed Data Interface News. (1990)-. Newsletter. English. Twelve times a year. $575.00. Information Gatekeepers Inc., 214 Harvard Avenue, Boston MA 02134. **Tel** (617)232-3111, (617)738-8088, (800)323-1088, FAX (617)734-8562.
Desc: Covers the developing market and technology opportunities in the FDDI field.

ISSN 1051-1954
DD 384   US

FIBER DATACOM.
(FIBER DATACOM : MONTHLY NEWSLETTER ON WORLDWIDE APPLICATIONS OF FIBER OPTICS TO DATA COMMUNICATIONS). [Fiber datacom]. **VFOAT** Fiber Datacom Newsletter; Fiber Data Communication Newsletter. (1988)-. Newsletter. English. Twelve times a year. $575.00. Information Gatekeepers Inc., 214 Harvard Avenue, Boston MA 02134. **Tel** (617)232-3111, (617)738-8088, (800)323-1088, FAX (617)734-8562.

ISSN 1082-2119
DD 384   US

●**FIBER IN THE LOOP.** [Fiber loop]. **Added/Corp** Information Gatekeepers, Inc. Vol. 7, No. 7 (Apr. 1995)-. Newsletter. English. Twenty-four times a year. $575.00.

Information Gatekeepers Inc., 214 Harvard Avenue, Boston MA 02134. **Tel** (617)232-3111, (617)738-8088, (800)323-1088, FAX (617)734-8562. **Continues** Fiber to the Home, 1051-192X.

ISSN 1051-1946
DD 621   US
CCC

FIBER OPTIC SENSORS AND SYSTEMS.
(FIBER OPTIC SENSORS AND SYSTEMS : FOS2.). [Fiber opt. sens. syst.]. **VFOAT** FOS2; FOS2 Newsletter. (1987)-. Newsletter. English. Twelve times a year. $575.00. Information Gatekeepers Inc., 214 Harvard Avenue, Boston MA 02134. **Tel** (617)232-3111, (617)738-8088, (800)323-1088, FAX (617)734-8562.

ISSN 0275-0457
US
CCC

FIBER OPTICS AND COMMUNICATIONS.
[Fiber optics commun.]. **VFOAT** Fiber Optics and Communications Newsletter. (19??)-. Newsletter. English. Twelve times a year. $575.00. Information Gatekeepers Inc., 214 Harvard Avenue, Boston MA 02134. **Tel** (617)232-3111, (617)738-8088, (800)323-1088, FAX (617)734-8562. **Continues** Fiber Optics and Communications Newsletter, 0274-6271.

ISSN 1057-5375
DD 623   US

FIBER OPTICS BUSINESS NEWSLETTER.
[Fiber optics bus. newsl.]. **Added/Corp** Information Gatekeepers Inc. **VFOAT** Fiber Optics Business; FOB Newsletter. (199?)-. Newsletter. English. Twenty-four times a year. $575.00. Information Gatekeepers Inc., 214 Harvard Avenue, Boston MA 02134. **Tel** (617)232-3111, (617)738-8088, (800)323-1088, FAX (617)734-8562. **Continues** MFOC Newsletter, 1051-1911.

ISSN 0270-3068
US

FIBER OPTICS DIRECTORY UPDATE SERVICE.
[Fiber optics dir. update serv.]. (1980)-. Directory. English. Six times a year. $43.50. Patent Data Publications, 901 North President Street, Wheaton IL 60187. **Tel** (312)462-0818.

ISSN 1045-6422
DD 621   US
CCC
CODEN FOPMEW
CEASED

FIBER OPTICS MAGAZINE.
[Fiber opt. mag.]. (198?)-(March 1993). Periodical. English. Information Gatekeepers Inc., 214 Harvard Avenue, Boston MA 02134. **Tel** (617)232-3111, (617)738-8088, (800)323-1088, FAX (617)734-8562. **Formed by the union of** International Fiber Optics and Communications, 0199-5820 **and** Fiber Optics. Handbook & Buyers Guide.

ISSN 1051-189X
DD 384   US

FIBER OPTICS WEEKLY UPDATE.
[Fiber optics wkly. update]. (19??)-. Periodical. English. One time a week. $575.00. Information Gatekeepers Inc., 214 Harvard Avenue, Boston MA 02134. **Tel** (617)232-3111, (617)738-8088, (800)323-1088, FAX (617)734-8562. **Continues** Fiber Optics & Communications Weekly News Service, 0732-9407.

ISSN 1075-5268
DD 621   US

●**FIBER OPTICS YELLOW PAGES.** [Fiber opt. yellow pages]. **VFOAT** International Fiber Optics Yellow Pages. Vol. 14 (1993)-. Directory. English. One time a year. $69.95. Information Gatekeepers Inc., 214 Harvard Avenue, Boston MA 02134. **Tel** (617)232-3111, (617)738-8088, (800)323-1088, FAX (617)734-8562. **Continues** Fiber Optics Handbook & Buyers Guide, 1075-525X.

ISSN 1051-192X
DD 384   US
TITLE CHANGE

FIBER TO THE HOME.
[Fiber home]. (1989)-(1995). Periodical. English. Information Gatekeepers Inc., 214 Harvard Avenue, Boston MA 02134. **Tel** (617)232-3111, (617)738-8088, (800)323-1088, FAX (617)734-8562. **ED** Paul Polishuk. **Circ:** 1,000. **Continued by** Fiber in the Loop, 1082-2119.
Desc: Covers the range of technologies, disciplines, politics, regulation, and economics involved in bringing fiber optics to the home.

LC TA1800 .F536   ISSN 0890-653X
DD 621.36/92
US
CCC

FIBEROPTIC PRODUCT NEWS.
(FIBEROPTIC PRODUCT NEWS : FPN.). [Fiberopt. prod. news]. **VFOAT** FPN. Vol. 1, No. 1 (Jan./Feb. 1986)-. Periodical. English. Thirteen times a year. $115.00. Cahners Publishing Company, 249 West 17th Street, New York NY 10011. **Tel** (212)645-0067, FAX (212)242-6987. **(Subscription address:** Gordon Publications, Inc., Paid Circulation Department, 301

Communications — Telecommunication

Gibralter Drive, Box 650, Morris Plains NJ 07950-0650. **Tel** (201)292-5100 ext. 351, FAX (201)898-9281.) **ED** Holly Bigelow. Index available. **Bk Rev**. **Ad Acc**. **Circ:** 26,000 (ctrl). available on microfilm from University Microfilms International (UMI).
Desc: Provides the most complete coverage available of the design, application and technology of fiberoptic and related products. Includes product reviews, industry news and emerging technology.
Ind/Abst Infomat Int. Bus.

LC HE8531 .A94A
DD 354.940087/4/06   AT

FIGURES FOR THE YEAR ENDED MARCH 31 ... / THE OVERSEAS TELECOMMUNICATIONS COMMISSION (AUSTRALIA). **Main/Corp** Australia. Overseas Telecommunications Commission. English. One time a year.

ISSN 0267-1484
DD 384.041   UK

FIN TECH. 1, TELECOM MARKETS. [Fin Tech., 1, Telecom mark.]. (1984)-. Periodical. English. Twenty-four times a year. $1137.95. Financial Times / UK, Maple House, 149 Tottenham Court Road, London W1P 9LL United Kingdom. **Tel** 011 44 171 8962276, FAX 011 44 171 8962275, 011 44 171 8962399. **ED** Neil McCartney. Index available. available on microfiche; available on an online database from Lexis-Nexis; and DATA-STAR. Documents available from SWETS, UMI Article Clearinghouse.
Desc: International telecom finance, markets, and legislation.
Ind/Abst Infomat Int. Bus.; PROMT [Full Txt.]; PTS Newsl. Database [Full Txt.].

UK
FINTECH. MOBILE COMMUNICATIONS. (19??)-. English. Twenty-four times a year. £495.00. Financial Times Magazines, Greystoke Place, Fetter Lane, London EC4A 1ND United Kingdom. **Tel** 011 44 171 8316577. **ED** Neil McCartney. Index available. cum. index. available on microfiche.
Desc: International mobile communications, radiopaging, and cellular use.
Ind/Abst Infomat Int. Bus.; PROMT [Full Txt.]; PTS Newsl. Database [Full Txt.].

ISSN 0959-0188
DD 621.3692   UK

FOCUS, FIBRE OPTIC COMMUNICATION & USER SYSTEMS. [FOCUS, Fibre opt. commun. user syst.]. (1990)-. Trade Publication. English. Irregular (4-6 per year). $45.00. Focus Limited, Cotswold Kingston Ringwood, Hampshire BH24 3BQ United Kingdom. **Tel** 011 44 1425 473535, FAX 011 44 1425 480900. **ED** Bob Yates. Index available. cum. index. **Bk Rev**, (Qty: 6). **Ad Acc**, **Adv Mgr:** Alex Henner (UK)/ Willy R. Mattes (CN). **Circ:** 8,500 (ctrl).
Desc: Technical magazine covering optical communications.
Ind/Abst Curr. Cit.

ISSN 1181-8654
DD 384   CN

FORUM - CANADIAN TELEMATICS FORUM. (THE FORUM : THE OFFICIAL BULLETIN OF THE CANADIAN TELEMATICS FORUM.). [Forum -Can. Telemat. Forum]. **Added/Corp** Canadian Telematics Forum. **VFOAT** Forum. **VAT** Forum - Forum Telematique Canedien. Vol. 1, No. 1 (Fall 1990)-. Bulletin. English (French). Four times a year. Limited free distribution. Canadian Telematics Forum, 1 Desjardins Complex, South Tower, 36th Floor, Montreal Quebec H5B 1B2 Canada.

ISSN 0984-8916
FR
UDC 654 (44)
TITLE CHANGE
FRANCE TELECOM ED. NATIONALE. (FRANCE TELECOM.). [France Telecom Ed. nationale]. (1986)-(Dec. 1993). Periodical. French. France Telecom, 6 Place d'Alleray, 75740 Paris Cedex 15 France. **Tel** 011 33 1 44448360. **Continues** T (Paris. 1971), 0183-8636. **Continued by** Dialogues, 1165-788X.
Ind/Abst F&S Index Plus Text, Int. [Select. Cov.]; Infomat Int. Bus.; PROMT.

ISSN 0898-1027
DD 384   US
FRANCE TELECOM NEWS. [Fr. Telecom news]. **Added/Corp** France Telecom, Inc. **VFOAT** France Telecom. (19??)-. Periodical. English. France Telecom Inc, 1270 Avenue of the Americas/Room 2703, New York NY 10020.

FR
FRANCE TELECOM QUARTERLY. (19??)-. Periodical. French. Four times a year. 100.00F France; 150.00F other. Dawson France SA, BP 40, 91121 Palaiseau Cedex France. **Tel** 011 33 1 69104700, FAX 011 33 1 64548326, telex 220064F. **Continues** Telecommunications.

LC TK5101 .F8   **ISSN** 0342-0426
GW
CODEN FUTEDZ
FUNK-TECHNIK. AUSGABE ZV (MUNCHEN). (FUNK-TECHNIK.). [Funk-Tech., Ausg. ZV]. Vol. 1 (Dec. 13, 1946)-. Trade Publication. German. Twelve times a year. $50.00, $5.00 single issue, add $11.00 for postage. Verlag CF Mueller, Verlags GS, D-69018 Heidelberg Germany. **Tel** 011 49 6221 4890. **ED** Lothar Starke. **Bk Rev**. **Ad Acc**. Documents available from Ask*IEEE, CASDDS.
Desc: Technical journal for the radio and television industry and manufacturers.
Ind/Abst Chem. Abstr.; Energy Res. Abstr. (Sept. 1975-); INSPEC (1968-).

ISSN 1300-2732
DD 605   TU
●FUTURE'S TECHNOLOGIES. See Engineering-Electrical Engineering.

LC HF   **ISSN** 1120-219X
DD 380   IT
UDC 654.15
Pr Rev.   TITLE CHANGE
GIORNALE DELL'INSTALLATORE TELEFONICO, IL. [G. install. telef.]. (1983)-(1993). Periodical. Italian. Six times a year. Stammer Spa, Via della Liberazione 1, 20068 Peschiera Borromeo Italy. **Tel** 011 39 2 55302606, FAX 011 39 2 55302700, telex 321083. **ED** Girolamo Bellina. **Bk Rev**. **Ad Acc**. **Circ:** 4,500 (ctrl). **Continued by** Telephone Trade, 1122-424X.
Desc: Electricity and telephone engineering and installation.

LC HG1501   **ISSN** 1069-9899
DD 332.1   US
●GLOBAL FINANCIAL REPORT ON TELECOMMUNICATIONS AND COMPUTER COMPANIES. See Business and Economics-Banks and Banking.

ISSN 1065-8424
DD 384   US
SUSPENDED
GLOBAL TELECOM. [Global telecom]. Vol. 1, No. 1 (Sept. 1992)-(19??). Periodical. English. Ten times a year. $24.00. DB Publishing, 8547 East Araphoe Road, Suite J414, Greenwood Villagee CO 80112-9602. **Tel** (303)689-9126, FAX (303)689-9163.

ISSN 1059-4485
US
CCC
TITLE CHANGE
GLOBAL TELECOM REPORT. (1991)-(19??). Periodical. English. Phillips Business Information Inc., 1201 Seven Locks Road, PO Box 61130, Potomac MD 20854. **Tel** (301)424-3338, (301)340-1520, (800)777-5005, FAX (301)424-4297, telex 358149. available on an online database (file 636/Full-Text) from DIALOG. **Continued by** Wireless Business & Finance.
Ind/Abst PTS Newsl. Database [Full Txt.].

UK
GLOBAL TELECOMMS BUSINESS. (199?)-. English. Six times a year. £60.00 UK; $90.00 other. Euromoney Publications PLC, Nestor House, Playhouse Yard, London EC4Z 5EX United Kingdom. **Tel** 011 44 171 7798888, FAX 011 44 171 7798630, telex 290700 EUROMON G.
Desc: Magazine for the telecommunications industry. Reports on company management, marketing sales, mergers acquisitions, alliances, market performance, fund raising and regulatory issues.

LC HE7601 .G55
DD 384/.05   UK
GLOBAL TELECOMS BUSINESS. (19??)-. Periodical. English. Six times a year. $135.00. Euromoney Publications PLC, Nestor House, Playhouse Yard, London EC4Z 5EX United Kingdom. **Tel** 011 44 171 7798888, FAX 011 44 171 7798630, telex 290700 EUROMON G. **(Subscription address:** Euromoney Publications PLC, Perrymount Road Haywards Heath, West Sussex RH16 3DH United Kingdom. **Tel** 011 44 1444 440421.)

UK
●GLOBAL TELECOMS OPERATORS. (1995)-. English. FT Telecoms and Media Publishing, Maple House, 149 Tottenham Court Road, London W1P 9LL United Kingdom. **Tel** 011 44 171 8962234.

ISSN 1067-6317
DD 621   US
GLOBAL TELEPHONY. [Glob. teleph.]. Vol. 1, No. 1 (Feb. 1993)-. Periodical. English. Twelve times a year. $49.41 US; $29.41 Canada; $35.29 other. Intertec Publishing Corporation, 9800 Metcalf, Overland Park KS 66212. **Tel** (913)341-1300. **(Subscription address:** Intertec Publishing Corporation, PO Box 2901, Overland Park KS 66282. **Tel** 800 441-0294.)

LC TK5101   **ISSN** 1188-6307
DD 621.382   US
GLOSAS NEWS. [Glosas news]. **Added/Corp** Global Systems Analysis and Simulation Association in the United States of America. Vol. 1, No. 1 (Nov. 1991)-. Periodical. English. Six times a year. Free. Global Systems Analysis and Simulation Association, 43-23 Colden Street, Flushing NY 11355-3998. **Tel** (718)939-0928. available via Internet (message listserv@vm1.mcgill.ca, SUBSCRIBE GLOSAS).

US
GMRMLN FAX DIRECTORY. **Added/Corp** Greater Midwest Regional Medical Library Network. **VFOAT** FAX Directory. (19??)-. Directory. English. Management Office, Library of the Health Sciences, University of Illinois at Chicago, PO Box 7509, Chicago IL 60680.

LC JL267 .G68   **ISSN** 0701-9599
DD 354.713/00025   CN
GOVERNMENT OF ONTARIO TELEPHONE DIRECTORY. **VFOAT** Telephone Directory. **VAT** Telephone Directory - Government of Ontario; Government Telephone Directory (Toronto). Vol. 1973-. Directory. English. Two times a year. 6.73Can$. Ministry of Government Services / Treasurer of Ontario, 50 Grosvenor, Toronto Ontario M7A 1N8 Canada. **Tel** (416)326-5300. Index available. **Continues** Ontario Government Telephone Directory.

RU
GOVORIT I POKAZYVAET MOSKVA. **Added/Corp** Russia (1923-U.S.S.R.) Gosudarstvennyi Komitet po Televideniiu i Radioveshchaniiu. (19??)-. Periodical. Russian. One time a week. $199.95. **(Subscription address:** East View Publications Inc., 3020 Harbor Lane North, Suite 110, Minneapolis MN 55447. **Tel** (800)477-1005, (612)550-0961, FAX (612)559-2931.)

LC TK7800 .G17   **ISSN** 0097-7721
DD 621.3/05   US
GTE JOURNAL OF RESEARCH AND DEVELOPMENT. See Engineering-Electrical Engineering.

LC TK1 .S852   **ISSN** 0742-6151
DD 384   US
CODEN GAEJDG
GTE NETWORK SYSTEMS WORLD-WIDE COMMUNICATIONS JOURNAL. [GTE netw. syst. world-wide commun. j.]. **Added/Corp** GTE Network Systems. GTE Network Systems. Graphics and Composition Dept. **VFOAT** G.T.E. Network Systems World-Wide Communications Journal; G.T.E. Network Systems Journal; World-Wide Communications Journal; GTE Network Systems Journal. Vol. 21, No. 3 (3rd Quarter 1983)-. Periodical. English. Irregular. Automatic Electric Company, Northlake IL 60164. available on microfilm and microfiche from University Microfilms International (UMI). Documents available from UMI Article Clearinghouse, Ask*IEEE. **Continues** GTE Automatic Electric World-Wide Communications Journal, 0273-141X.
Ind/Abst ABI/INFORM Glob. Ed.; ABI/INFORM [Computer File] (1983-); INSPEC (1983-).

AG
GUIA TELEFONICA : SAN SALVADOR DE JUJUY. **Main/Corp** Empresa Nacional de Telecomunicaciones. **VFOAT** Guia Telefonica : Jujuy. (19??)-. Spanish. Empresa Nacional de Telecomunicaciones, Rivadavia 758, Catamarca Argentina.

LC TK5102.5 .H319 1988 Suppl.   **ISSN** 1051-7839
DD 384   US
HANDBOOK OF COMMUNICATIONS SYSTEMS MANAGEMENT. YEARBOOK. [Handb. commun. syst. manage., Yearb.] **VFOAT** Yearbook; Year Book. (1989)-. English. Irregular. $170.95. Auerbach Publishers Inc., Park Square Building, 31 St. James Avenue, Boston MA 02116. **Tel** (800)950-1207.

LC WMLC 93/3204   **ISSN** 1073-547X
DD 384   US
●HEALTHCARE TELECOM REPORT. See Medical Sciences.

ISSN 0892-5143
DD 384   US
HOME SATELLITE NEWSLETTER, THE. [Home satell. newsl.]. (1985)-. Newsletter. English. Twelve times a year. $275.00. Commtek Publishing Company, 8330 Boone Boulevard, Suite 600, Vienna VA 22182. **Tel** (703)827-0511.

LC TK5101.A1 H77
CC
HSIEN TAI TUNG HSIN. **VFOAT** Communications Today. (19??)-. Periodical. Chinese (English). Twelve times a year. Science Press, 16 Donghuangchenggen North Street, Beijing 100707, People's Republic of China. **Tel** 011 86 1 4019821, 011

86 1 4010642, FAX 011 86 1 4012180, 011 86 1 4019810, telex 210147. **Ad Acc. Circ:** 150,000.
Desc: Reports on the latest developments in communications, radio, TV and is distributed to executives and technical staff of communications services, manufacturers, government, departments and universities.

BE
CODEN ITMZEM

●**I & T MAGAZINE. Added/Corp** Commission of the European Communities. Directorate General for Industrial and Technological Affairs. Commission of the European Communities. Directorate-General for Telecommunications, Information Industries, and Innovation. **VFOAT** I and T Magazine. (Winter 1993)-. Periodical. English. Four times a year. Free. Commission of the European Communities, Directorate of General Information, Avenue D Auderghem, 45 Breydel boulevard, B 1049 Brussels Belgium. **Tel** 011 32 2 2357639, telex 21877 COMEU B. ***Continues*** *XIII Magazine.*

ISSN 1350-2425
UK
CCC

●**IEE PROCEEDINGS. COMMUNICATIONS. Added/Corp** Institution of Electrical Engineers. **VFOAT** Communications; IEE Proc.-Commun. Vol. 141, No. 1 (Feb. 1994)-. Periodical. English. Six times a year. $633.15. Institution of Electrical Engineers / IEE, Michael Faraday House, Six Hills Way, Stevenage Hertfordshire SG1 2AY United Kingdom. **Tel** 011 44 1438 313311, FAX 011 44 1438 742840, telex 825578 IEESTV G. **(Subscription address:** IEE / Peter Peregrinus Ltd., PO Box 96, Stevenage Herts SG1 2SD United Kingdom. **Tel** 011 44 1438 313311, FAX 011 44 438 742792, telex 825578 IEESTV G.**)** available on CD-ROM from University Microfilms International (UMI). Documents available from BLDSC, FAXON Xpress, The UnCover Company, SWETS, UMI Article Clearinghouse. ***Continues*** *IEE Proceedings. I, Communications, Speech and Vision, 0956-3776.*
Ind/Abst Curr. Cit.

LC TK1 .I1376 **ISSN** 0956-375X
DD 621.3848 UK
CODEN IPFPEV

Pr Rev. **TITLE CHANGE**

IEE PROCEEDINGS. F, RADAR AND SIGNAL PROCESSING. [IEE proc., F. Radar signal process.]. **Added/Corp** Institution of Electrical Engineers. **VFOAT** Radar and Signal Processing; IEE Proceedings. Part F, Radar and Signal Processing. **VAT** Institution of Electrical Engineers. F, Radar and Signal Processing. Vol. 136, Pt. F, No. 1 (Feb. 1989)-(1993). Academic Scholarly Publication. English. Institution of Electrical Engineers / IEE, Michael Faraday House, Six Hills Way, Stevenage Hertfordshire SG1 2AY United Kingdom. **Tel** 011 44 1438 313311, FAX 011 44 1438 742840, telex 825578 IEESTV G. **(Subscription address:** IEE / Peter Peregrinus Ltd., PO Box 96, Stevenage Herts SG1 2SD United Kingdom. **Tel** 011 44 1438 313311, FAX 011 44 438 742792, telex 825578 IEESTV G.**)** available on microfilm from University Microfilms International (UMI). Documents available from Article Express International, The Genuine Article, Ask*IEEE. ***Continues in part*** *IEE Proceedings. F, Communications, Radar, and Signal Processing, 0143-7070.* ***Continued by*** *IEE Proceedings. Radar, Sonar, and Navigation, 1350-2395.*
Ind/Abst Appl. Sci. Technol. Index; Bioeng. Abstr.; Curr. Cit.; Ei Page One; EMBASE; Energy Res. Abstr.; Eng. Index Annu.; INSPEC (April 1989-); Int. Aerosp. Abstr.; Math. Rev.; Res. Alert [Full Cov.]; Sci. Cit. Index; SCISEARCH.

LC TK1 .I13817 **ISSN** 0956-3776
DD 621.382 UK
CCC
CODEN IPIVEU
TITLE CHANGE

IEE PROCEEDINGS. I, COMMUNICATIONS, SPEECH, AND VISION. [IEE proc., I. Commun. speech vis.]. **Added/Corp** Institution of Electrical Engineers. **VFOAT** Communications, Speech, and Vision. **VAT** Institution of Electrical Engineers. I, Communications, Speech, and Vision. Vol. 136, Pt. 1, No. 1 (Feb. 1989)-(1993). Periodical. English. Institution of Electrical Engineers / IEE, Michael Faraday House, Six Hills Way, Stevenage Hertfordshire SG1 2AY United Kingdom. **Tel** 011 44 1438 313311, FAX 011 44 1438 742840, telex 825578 IEESTV G. **(Subscription address:** IEE / Peter Peregrinus Ltd., PO Box 96, Stevenage Herts SG1 2SD United Kingdom. **Tel** 011 44 1438 313311, FAX 011 44 438 742792, telex 825578 IEESTV G.**)** available on microfilm from University Microfilms International (UMI). Documents available from Article Express International, The Genuine Article. ***Continues in part*** *IEE Proceedings. F, Communications, Radar, and Signal Processing, 0143-7070.* ***Continued by*** *IEE Proceedings. Communications, 1350-2425.*
Ind/Abst Appl. Sci. Technol. Index (19??-19??); Curr. Cit.; Ei Page One (19??-19??); Eng. Index Annu. (19??-19??); Ergon. Abstr. (19??-19??); Int. Aerosp. Abstr. (19??-19??); Leadscan (19??-19??); Res. Alert (19??-19??) [Full Cov.]; Sci. Cit. Index (19??-19??); SCISEARCH (19??-19??).

LC TK1 .I1376 **ISSN** 1350-2395
DD 621.3848 UK
CODEN IRSNE2

●**IEE PROCEEDINGS. RADAR, SONAR, AND NAVIGATION. Added/Corp** Institution of Electrical Engineers. **VFOAT** Radar, Sonar, and Navigation. Vol. 141, No. 1 (Feb. 1994)-. Periodical. English. Six times a year. $633.15. Institution of Electrical Engineers / IEE, Michael Faraday House, Six Hills Way, Stevenage Hertfordshire SG1 2AY United Kingdom. **Tel** 011 44 1438 313311, FAX 011 44 1438 742840, telex 825578 IEESTV G. **(Subscription address:** IEE / Peter Peregrinus Ltd., PO Box 96, Stevenage Herts SG1 2SD United Kingdom. **Tel** 011 44 1438 313311, FAX 011 44 438 742792, telex 825578 IEESTV G.**)** available on CD-ROM from University Microfilms International (UMI). Documents available from BLDSC, FAXON Xpress, The UnCover Company, SWETS, UMI Article Clearinghouse. ***Continues*** *IEE Proceedings. Part F, Radar and Signal Processing, 0956-375X.*
Ind/Abst Curr. Cit.

ISSN 0263-5852
UK
CODEN ITESDS

IEE TELECOMMUNICATIONS SERIES. [IEE telecommun. ser.]. **Main/Corp** Institution of Electrical Engineers. **Added/Corp** Institution of Electrical Engineers. Telecommunications Series. **VFOAT** Telecommunications Series. **VAT** Institution of Electrical Engineers Telecommunications Series. (1975)-. Monographic series. English. Irregular. Price varies per volume. Institution of Electrical Engineers / IEE, Michael Faraday House, Six Hills Way, Stevenage Hertfordshire SG1 2AY United Kingdom. **Tel** 011 44 1438 313311, FAX 011 44 1438 742840, telex 825578 IEESTV G. **(Subscription address:** IEE / Peter Peregrinus Ltd., PO Box 96, Stevenage Herts SG1 2SD United Kingdom. **Tel** 011 44 1438 313311, FAX 011 44 438 742792, telex 825578 IEESTV G.**)**
Ind/Abst Curr. Cit.

LC TK5101.A1 I13a **ISSN** 0163-6804
DD 621/.38/05 US
CCC
CODEN ICOMD9

Pr Rev.

IEEE COMMUNICATIONS MAGAZINE. [IEEE commun. mag.]. **Main/Corp** IEEE Communications Society. **VAT** Institute of Electrical and Electronics Engineers Communications. Vol. 17 (Jan. 1979)-. Periodical. English. Twelve times a year. $145.00. IEEE / Institute of Electrical and Electronics Engineers Inc., 345 East 47th Street, New York NY 10017-2394. **Tel** (908)981-1393, FAX (908)981-9667. **(Subscription address:** IEEE / Institute of Electrical and Electronics Engineers, 445 Hoes Lane, PO Box 1331, Piscataway NJ 08855-1331. **Tel** (800)701-IEEE, (908)981-0060, FAX (908)981-9667, telex 833233.**)** **Bk Rev**. available on microfiche. Documents available from Article Express International, The Genuine Article, Ask*IEEE. ***Continues*** *IEEE Communications Society Magazine, 0148-9615.*
Desc: Covers all areas of communications: conferences, short courses, standards, governmental regulations and legislation, special feature technical articles; society news including administration and elections.
Ind/Abst Appl. Sci. Technol. Index; Bioeng. Abstr.; Comput. Inf. Syst. Abstr. J. [Full Cov.]; Comput. Bus.; Curr. Cit.; Curr. Contents Eng. Comput. Technol.; Ei Page One; Elect. Comm. Abstr.; Eng. Index Annu.; Expand. Acad. Index (1992-); Index IEEE Publ.; Inf. Sci. Abstr.; INIS Atomindex [Micro.]; INSPEC (Jan. 1979-); Int. Aerosp. Abstr.; Mech. Eng. Abstr.; Res. Alert [Full Cov.]; Sci. Cit. Index; SCISEARCH; Soc. Sci. Cit. Index [Select. Cov.]; World Publ. Monit.

LC TK5101.A1 I35 **ISSN** 0733-8716
DD 621.38/05 US
CCC
CODEN ISACEM

Pr Rev.

IEEE JOURNAL ON SELECTED AREAS IN COMMUNICATIONS. (IEEE JOURNAL ON SELECTED AREAS IN COMMUNICATIONS : A PUBLICATION OF THE IEEE COMMUNICATIONS SOCIETY.). [IEEE j. sel. areas commun.]. **Added/Corp** Institute of Electrical and Electronics Engineers. IEEE Comunications Society. **VFOAT** I.E.E.E. Journal on Selected Areas in Communications; Selected Areas in Communications. **VAT** Institute of Electrical and Electronics Engineers Journal on Selected Areas in Communications. Vol. SAC- 1, No. 1 (Jan. 1983)-. Periodical. English. Nine times a year. $295.00. IEEE / Institute of Electrical and Electronics Engineers Inc., 345 East 47th Street, New York NY 10017-2394. **Tel** (908)981-1393, FAX (908)981-9667. **(Subscription address:** IEEE / Institute of Electrical and Electronics Engineers, 445 Hoes Lane, PO Box 1331, Piscataway NJ 08855-1331. **Tel** (800)701-IEEE, (908)981-0060, FAX (908)981-9667, telex 833233.**)** Documents available from Article Express International, The Genuine Article, Ask*IEEE.
Desc: Covers all telecommunications, including telephone, telegraphy, facsimile, and point-to-point television by electromagnetic propagation, radio, wire, aerial, underground, coaxial, and submarine cables.
Ind/Abst Comput. Inf. Syst. Abstr. J. [Full Cov.]; Curr. Cit.; Curr. Contents Eng. Comput. Technol.; Ei Page One; Elect. Comm. Abstr.; Eng. Index Annu.; Index IEEE Publ.; Inf. Sci. Abstr.; INSPEC (Jan. 1983-); Int. Aerosp. Abstr.; Pollut. Abstr. Indexes; Res. Alert [Full Cov.]; Sci. Cit. Index; SCISEARCH; Soc. Sci. Cit. Index [Select. Cov.]; Solid State Supercond. Abstr.

LC TK5101.A1 I2 **ISSN** 0090-6778
DD 621.38/05 US
CCC
CODEN IECMBT

IEEE TRANSACTIONS ON COMMUNICATIONS. [IEEE trans. commun.]. **Main/Corp** IEEE Communications Society. **Added/Corp** Institute of Electrical and Electronics Engineers. **VFOAT** Transactions on Communications. Vol. 20 (Feb. 1972)-. Periodical. English. Thirteen times a year. $330.00. IEEE / Institute of Electrical and Electronics Engineers Inc., 345 East 47th Street, New York NY 10017-2394. **Tel** (908)981-1393, FAX (908)981-9667. **(Subscription address:** IEEE / Institute of Electrical and Electronics Engineers, 445 Hoes Lane, PO Box 1331, Piscataway NJ 08855-1331. **Tel** (800)701-IEEE, (908)981-0060, FAX (908)981-9667, telex 833233.**)** available on microfiche. Documents available from Article Express International, The Genuine Article, Ask*IEEE, CASDDS. ***Continues*** *IEEE Transactions on Communication Technology, 0018-9332.*
Desc: Covers all telecommunications including telephone, telegraphy, facsimile, and point-to-point television, and electromagnetic propagation including radio.
Ind/Abst Acoust. Abstr.; Appl. Sci. Technol. Index; Bioeng. Abstr.; Chem. Abstr.; Comput. Abstr.; Comput. Inf. Syst. Abstr. J. [Full Cov.]; Curr. Cit.; Curr. Contents Eng. Comput. Technol.; Ei Page One; Elect. Comm. Abstr.; Eng. Index Annu.; Expand. Acad. Index (1992-); Index IEEE Publ.; Inf. Sci. Abstr.; INSPEC (Feb. 1972-); Int. Aerosp. Abstr.; Math. Rev. (?-199?); Mech. Eng. Abstr.; Pollut. Abstr. Indexes; Res. Alert [Full Cov.]; Sci. Cit. Index; SCISEARCH; Solid State Supercond. Abstr.; Zentralbl. Math. Ihre Grenzgeb.

ISSN 0018-9375
US
CCC
CODEN IEMCAE

Pr Rev.

IEEE TRANSACTIONS ON ELECTROMAGNETIC COMPATIBILITY. [IEEE trans. electromagn. compat.]. **Added/Corp** IEEE Electromagnetic Compatibility Society. Institute of Electrical and Electronics Engineers. Electromagnetic Compatibility Group. **VFOAT** Transactions on Electromagnetic Compatibility; Electromagnetic Compatibility. Vol. EMC-6 (Jan. 1964)-. Periodical. English. Four times a year. $93.00. IEEE / Institute of Electrical and Electronics Engineers Inc., 345 East 47th Street, New York NY 10017-2394. **Tel** (908)981-1393, FAX (908)981-9667. **(Subscription address:** IEEE / Institute of Electrical and Electronics Engineers, 445 Hoes Lane, PO Box 1331, Piscataway NJ 08855-1331. **Tel** (800)701-IEEE, (908)981-0060, FAX (908)981-9667, telex 833233.**)** available on microfiche. Documents available from Article Express International, The Genuine Article, Ask*IEEE, CASDDS. ***Continues*** *IEEE Transactions on Radio Frequency Interference.*
Desc: Covers all areas of electromagnetic compatibility.
Ind/Abst Acoust. Abstr.; Bioeng. Abstr.; Chem. Abstr.; Curr. Cit.; Curr. Contents Eng. Comput. Technol.; Ei Page One; Elect. Comm. Abstr.; Eng. Index Annu.; Expand. Acad. Index (1992-); Index IEEE Publ.; INSPEC (1968-); Int. Aerosp. Abstr.; Res. Alert [Full Cov.]; Sci. Cit. Index; SCISEARCH; Solid State Supercond. Abstr.

LC Q350 .I2 **ISSN** 0018-9448
DD 001.53/9 US
CCC
CODEN IETTAW

IEEE TRANSACTIONS ON INFORMATION THEORY. (IEEE TRANSACTIONS ON INFORMATION THEORY / PROFESSIONAL TECHNICAL GROUP ON INFORMATION THEORY.). [IEEE trans. inf. theory]. **Added/Corp** Institute of Electrical and Electronics Engineers. Professional Technical Group on Information Theory. Institute of Electrical and Electronics Engineers. Information Theory Group. IEEE Information Theory Group. IEEE Information Theory Society. **VFOAT** Transactions on Information Theory; Information Theory. **VAT** Institute of Electrical and Electronics Engineers Transactions on Information Theory. Vol. IT-9, No. 1 (Jan. 1963)-. Academic Scholarly Publication. English. Seven times a year. $350.00. IEEE / Institute of Electrical and Electronics Engineers Inc., 345 East 47th Street, New York NY 10017-2394. **Tel** (908)981-1393, FAX (908)981-9667. **(Subscription address:** IEEE / Institute of Electrical and Electronics Engineers, 445 Hoes Lane, PO Box 1331, Piscataway NJ 08855-1331. **Tel** (800)701-IEEE, (908)981-0060, FAX (908)981-9667, telex 833233.**)** Documents available from Article Express International, The Genuine Article, Ask*IEEE, CASDDS. ***Continues*** *IRE Transactions on Information Theory, 0096-1000.*
Desc: Covers the theoretical and experimental aspects of information transmission, processing, and utilization.

Ind/Abst Acoust. Abstr.; Appl. Sci. Technol. Index (1991-); Bioeng. Abstr.; Chem. Abstr.; CompuMath Cit. Index [Full Cov.]; Comput. Abstr.; Comput. Database; Comput. Rev.; Curr. Cit.; Curr. Contents Eng. Comput. Technol.; Ei Page One; EMBASE; Eng. Index Annu.; Expand. Acad. Index (1992-); Index IEEE Publ.; Inf. Sci. Abstr. [Full Cov.]; INSPEC (1968-); Int. Aerosp. Abstr.; Math. Rev.; Oper. Res./Manage. Sci.; Pollut. Abstr. Indexes; Res. Alert [Full Cov.]; Sci. Cit. Index; SCISEARCH; Stat. Theory Method Abstr. (1968-1981, 1983-1984); Zentralbl. Math. Ihre Grenzgeb.

LC TK5101.A1 I37 **ISSN** 0916-8516 JA **CCC** **CODEN** ITCMEZ

IEICE TRANSACTIONS ON COMMUNICATIONS. **Added/Corp** Denshi Joho Tsushin Gakkai (Japan). **VFOAT** IEICE Transactions; Institute of Electronics, Information and Communication Engineers Transactions on communications; Transactions on Communications. Vol. E74, No. 1 (Jan. 1991)-. Periodical. English. Twelve times a year. $100.00. Denshi Joho Tsushin Gakkai / Institute of Electronics, Information and Communication Engineers, Kikai Shinko Kaikan, 5-8 Shiba Koen, 3-chome, Minatoku Tokyo 105 Japan. **(Subscription address:** Maruzen Company Ltd., PO Box 5050, Import & Export Department, Tokyo 100 31 Japan. **Tel** 011 81 3 32789224.**)** Documents available from The Genuine Article, Ask*IEEE. ***Continues in part*** *IEICE Transactions on Communications, Electronics, Information, and Systems, 0917-1673.*
Ind/Abst Curr. Cit.; Curr. Contents Eng. Comput. Technol.; INSPEC (Jan. 1992-); Res. Alert [Select. Cov.]; SCISEARCH; Soc. Sci. Cit. Index [Select. Cov.].

LC TK7800 .I2343 **ISSN** 0916-8508
DD 621.381/05 JA **CCC**

IEICE TRANSACTIONS ON FUNDAMENTALS OF ELECTRONICS, COMMUNICATIONS AND COMPUTER SCIENCES. **Added/Corp** Denshi Joho Tsushin Gakkai (Japan). **VFOAT** IEICE Transactions; Institute of Electronics, Information and Communication Engineers Transactions on Fundamentals of Electronics, Communications and Computer Sciences. Vol. E75-A, No. 1 (Jan. 1992)-. Periodical. English. Twelve times a year. $170.00. Denshi Joho Tsushin Gakkai / Institute of Electronics, Information and Communication Engineers, Kikai Shinko Kaikan, 5-8 Shiba Koen, 3-chome, Minatoku Tokyo 105 Japan. **(Subscription address:** Maruzen Company Ltd., PO Box 5050, Import & Export Department, Tokyo 100 31 Japan. **Tel** 011 81 3 32789224.**)** Documents available from The Genuine Article, Ask*IEEE. ***Continues in part*** *IEICE Transactions on Communications, Electronics, Information, and Systems, 0917-1673.*
Ind/Abst Curr. Cit.; Curr. Contents Eng. Comput. Technol.; INSPEC (Jan. 1991-); Res. Alert [Select. Cov.]; SCISEARCH; Soc. Sci. Cit. Index [Select. Cov.].

LC HE8805.M8 I5 **ISSN** 0361-3437
DD 384.6/3/09773 US

INCLUSIVE DIRECTORY OF INDEPENDENT OPERATING TELEPHONES. **Added/Corp** Missouri Public Service Commission. Office of Economic Research. (19??)-. Directory. English. One time a year. Missouri Public Service Commission / Office of Economic Research, PO Box 360, Jefferson City MO 65101.

US

●**INDIA TELECOM.** (1995)-. Newsletter. English. Twenty-four times a year. $795.00. Information Gatekeepers Inc., 214 Harvard Avenue, Boston MA 02134. **Tel** (617)232-3111, (617)738-8088, (800)323-1088, FAX (617)734-8562.

ISSN 0241-0362 FR
UDC 654 **TITLE CHANGE**

INF TELECOM ET TELEMATIQUE PARIS. [Inf telecom telemat. Paris]. (19??)-(19??). Periodical. French. Inf Telecom et Telematique, 5 rue du Helder, 75009 Paris France. **Tel** 42 47 13 42. ***Continues*** *Inf Telecom, 0338-8166.* ***Continued by*** *Le Quotidien des Telecoms.*
Ind/Abst Infomat Int. Bus.

ISSN 0931-3540 GW
UDC 681.3

INFO-MARKT. RATGEBER TELEKOMMUNIKATION. [Info-Markt, Ratg. Telekommun.]. (198?)-. German. Two times a year. $127.43. Infomarkt GmbH, Grafenberger Allee 368, D-40235 Duesseldorf Germany. **Tel** 011 49 211 669070.

ISSN 0742-633X US

INFOPRENEUR. Vol. 1, No. 1 (Jan. 31, 1984)-. Periodical. English. Twelve times a year. $39.00. Infopreneur, PO Box 4302, Annapolis MD 21403.

LC QA76 .I427
DD 004 IT

INFORMATICA 70 [I.E. SETTANTA]. **See** Computers-Electronic Data Processing.

LC HE7761 .I57 **ISSN** 1059-731X
DD 384 US

INFORMATION & INTERACTIVE SERVICES REPORT. [Inf. interact. serv. rep.]. **VFOAT** Information and Interactive Services Report. Vol. 12, No. 1 (Mar. 15, 1991)-. Periodical. English. Twenty-five times a year. $495.00. Telecommunications Reports, 1333 H Street Northwest, 2nd Floor West Tower, Washington DC 20005. **Tel** (202)842-0520, (800)822-6338, FAX (202)842-3047. **(Subscription address:** Telecommunications Reports, PO Box 675, Cooper Station, New York NY 10276. **)** Index available (free). ***Continues*** *Interactivity Report.*

LC HE7781 .I587 **ISSN** 1073-6921
DD 004.6/0973/05 US

●**INFORMATION INFRASTRUCTURE SOURCEBOOK.** [Inf. infrastruct. sourceb.]. **Added/Corp** John F. Kennedy School of Government. Science, Technology and Public Policy Program. John F. Kennedy School of Government. Information Infrastructure Project. (June 15, 1993)-. English. $85.00 per issue. Harvard University Center for Science & International Affairs, 79 JFK Street, School of Government, Cambridge MA 02138. **Tel** (617)495-1400. **(Subscription address:** Document Imaging Services, 1730 Cambridge Street, Room 202, Cambridge MA 02138. **Tel** (617)496-4077.**)**

ISSN 0961-7612 UK **CCC** **CODEN** IMRPE2
Pr Rev.

INFORMATION MANAGEMENT REPORT. (April 1991)-. Periodical. English. Twelve times a year. $384.00. Elsevier Advanced Technology, An Imprint of Elsevier Science Ltd., The Boulevard, Langford Lane, Kidlington, Oxford OX5 1GB United Kingdom. **Tel** 011 44 1865 843000, 011 44 1865 843699, FAX 011 44 1865 843010. **(Subscription address:** Elsevier Science Ltd. / Oxford Fulfillment Centre, PO Box 800, Kidlington OX5 1DX United Kingdom. **Tel** 011 44 865 843355.**)** available on an online database from Elsevier Electronic Subscriptions (EES); (File no. 636) DIALOG; and DATA-STAR. Documents available from Ask*IEEE, BLDSC, SWETS, CASDDS. ***Formed by the union of*** *Advanced Information Report* ***and*** *Outlook on Research Libraries.*
Ind/Abst Comput. Lit. Index; Inf. Manage. Technol.; INSPEC (April. 1991-).

ISSN 1078-6589
DD 384 US

●**INFORMATION SUPERHIGHWAYS.** **See** Computers-Computer Networks.

LC TK7800 .C53 CU

INGENIERIA ELECTRONICA, AUTOMATICA Y COMUNICACIONES. **See** Engineering-Electrical Engineering.

ISSN 1061-2629
DD 384 US

INSIDE BT. (INSIDE BT: A MANAGEMENT REPORT ON A LEADING WORLD PLAYER IN TELECOMMUNICATIONS AND INFORMATION TECHNOLOGY.). [Inside BT]. **VAT** Inside British Telecom. 3rd Ed. (1992)-. English. $399.00. Telecom Publishing Group, 1101 King Street, Suite 444, Alexandria VA 22314. **Tel** (703)683-4100, (800)327-7205, FAX (703)739-6490. ***Continues*** *Inside British Telecom, 1055-5234.*

ISSN 1061-2637
DD 384 US

INSIDE GTE. (INSIDE GTE: A PROFILE OF A LEADING MULTINATIONAL TELECOMMUNICATIONS COMPANY.). [Inside GTE]. **Added/Corp** Telecom Publishing Group. (1992)-. English. One time a year. $1195.00. Telecom Publishing Group, 1101 King Street, Suite 444, Alexandria VA 22314. **Tel** (703)683-4100, (800)327-7205, FAX (703)739-6490.

ISSN 1055-0283
DD 384 US

INSIDE MCI. (INSIDE MCI : A PROFILE : A MANAGEMENT REPORT ON MCI'S ORGANIZATIONAL STRUCTURE, MARKET POSITION, SERVICE OFFERINGS, AND STRATEGIC OUTLOOK.). [Inside MCI]. **Added/Corp** Telecom Publishing Group. (1991)-. English. $650.00. Telecom Publishing Group, 1101 King Street, Suite 444, Alexandria VA 22314. **Tel** (703)683-4100, (800)327-7205, FAX (703)739-6490.

ISSN 1065-6898 US

INSIDE MOTOROLA. (INSIDE MOTOROLA : A MANAGEMENT REPORT ON MOTOROLA'S ORGANIZATIONAL STRUCTURE, MARKET POSTITION AND STRATEGIC OUTLOOK.). **Added/Corp** Telecom Publishing Group. (1992)-. English. $995.00. Telecom Publishing Group, 1101 King Street, Suite 444, Alexandria VA 22314. **Tel** (703)683-4100, (800)327-7205, FAX (703)739-6490.

LC HD9696.T444 N675 **ISSN** 1071-8761
DD 384/.06/57 US

●**INSIDE NORTHERN TELECOM.** (INSIDE NORTHERN TELECOM : A PROFILE OF A LEADING TELECOMMUNICATIONS EQUIPMENT MANUFACTURER.). [Inside North. Telecom]. **Added/Corp** Telecom Publishing Group. (1993)-. Trade Publication. English. One time a year. $895.00. Telecom Publishing Group, 1101 King Street, Suite 444, Alexandria VA 22314. **Tel** (703)683-4100, (800)327-7205, FAX (703)739-6490.

ISSN 1065-8505 US

●**INSIDE SPRINT CORP.** **Added/Corp** Telecom Publishing Group. **VAT** Inside Sprint Corporation. (1993)-. Periodical. English. $995.00. Telecom Publishing Group, 1101 King Street, Suite 444, Alexandria VA 22314. **Tel** (703)683-4100, (800)327-7205, FAX (703)739-6490. ***Continues*** *Inside Sprint, 1058-9872.*

LC HE8846 .A535 **ISSN** 1055-9027
DD 384.6/3 US

INSIDE THE RHCS. (INSIDE THE RHCS : A MANAGEMENT REPORT ON THE SEVEN REGIONAL HOLDING COMPANIES.). [Inside RHCs]. **Added/Corp** Telecom Publishing Group. **VAT** Inside the Regional Holding Companies. (1987)-. English. Telecom Publishing Group, 1101 King Street, Suite 444, Alexandria VA 22314. **Tel** (703)683-4100, (800)327-7205, FAX (703)739-6490. **(Subscription address:** Telecom Publishing Group, PO Box 1455, Alexandria VA 22313. **Tel** 800 327-7205, (703)683-4100.**)**

ISSN 1073-7707
DD 338 US

●**INSIDE WIRELESS .** [Inside wirel.]. **Added/Corp** Four Pines Publishing. (1993)-. Periodical. English. Twenty-four times a year. $499.00. Four Pines Publishing, PO Box 3209, Boulder CO 80307. **Tel** (303)494-6522.

ISSN 1056-1412
DD 004 US

INTEGRATED MESSAGING NEWS. [Integr. messag. news]. **VFOAT** Integrated Messaging. Vol. 1, No. 1, (Mar. 1991)-. Periodical. English. Twelve times a year. $240.00. Stoneridge Technical Services, PO Box 1891, Rockville MD 20849. **Tel** (301)424-0114, FAX (301)424-8971. **ED** Bill Creitz. Index available. cum. index.

LC TK6271 .I57a **ISSN** 0275-0473
DD 621.38 US **CCC** **CODEN** IITPDH

INTELEC. **Main/Conf** International Telecommunications Energy Conference. **Added/Corp** IEEE Communications Society. Institution of Electrical Engineers. Electronics Division. Institution of Electrical Engineers. Power Division. Chartered Institution of Building Services. Nachrichtentechnische Gesellschaft. Svenska Elektroingenjorers Riksforening. **VFOAT** IEEE Intelec. **VAT** International Telecommunications Energy Conference. (1979)-. English. One time a year. must order direct. IEEE / Institute of Electrical and Electronics Engineers Inc., 345 East 47th Street, New York NY 10017-2394. **Tel** (908)981-1393, FAX (908)981-9667. **(Subscription address:** IEEE / Institute of Electrical and Electronics Engineers, 445 Hoes Lane, PO Box 1331, Piscataway NJ 08855-1331. **Tel** (800)701-IEEE, (908)981-0060, FAX (908)981-9667, telex 833233.**)** Documents available from Article Express International. ***Continues*** *International Telephone Energy Conference (Intelec).*
Ind/Abst Bioeng. Abstr.; Curr. Cit.; Ei Page One; Eng. Index Annu.; Index IEEE Publ.

LC HE8689 .I55 **ISSN** 0309-118X
DD 384.54/05 UK

INTERMEDIA (LONDON). (INTERMEDIA.). [InterMedia]. **Added/Corp** International Institute of Communications. International Broadcast Institute. Vol. 1 (March/April 1973)-. Trade Publication. English. Six times a year. $119.79. International Institute of Communications, Tavistock House South, Tavistock Square, London WC1H 9LF United Kingdom. **Tel** 44 71 3880671, FAX 44 71 3800623, telex 24578 IIC LDN G. **ED** Rex Malik. **Bk Rev. Circ:** 2,200. available on microfilm and microfiche from University Microfilms International (UMI). Documents available from UMI Article Clearinghouse. ***Supersedes*** *IBI Newsletter.*
Desc: Raises and discusses all the issues with an impact on policymaking in the fields of broadcasting, telecommunications and new technologies.
Ind/Abst ABI/INFORM Glob. Ed.; ABI/INFORM [Computer File] (Dec. 1977-Sept. 1981); Electron. Pub. Abstr.; Libr. Inf. Sci. Abstr.; World Publ. Monit.

ISSN 1069-7136
DD 384 UK

INTERNATIONAL CELLULAR. [Int. cell.]. (199?)-. Newsletter. English. Twelve times a year. $595.00. Kagan World Media Inc., 126 Clock Tower

Communications —Telecommunication

Place, Carmel CA 93923-8734. **Tel** (408)624-1536, FAX (408)625-3225. **(Subscription address:** Kagan World Media Ltd., 524 Fulham Road, London SW6 5NR United Kingdom. **Tel** 011 44 171 3718880, FAX 011 44 171 3718715.) available via fax. **Continues** European Cellular, 1056-2281.
Desc: Economics, technologies, and marketing challenges of the countries and companies foremost in the cellular field.

UK
TITLE CHANGE
INTERNATIONAL COMMUNICATIONS REPORT. (19??)-(1993). English. Wharton Publishing Limited, First Floor Regal House, Twickenham Middlesex, TW1 3QS United Kingdom. **Tel** 011 44 181 8916197. **ED** A Wharton. **Bk Rev. Merged with** Wharton Report; Computers and Communications.
Desc: Telecomms and data communications news.

US
NLM WV 22.1; I61
INTERNATIONAL DIRECTORY FOR TEXT TELEPHONE USERS. Added/Corp Telecommunications for the Deaf, Inc. **VFOAT** International Directory for TT Users; TDI Text Telephone Directory. (1992)-. English. One time a year. Telecommunication for the Deaf, 8719 Colesville Road, Suite 300, Silver Spring MD 20910. **Tel** (301)589-3786. **Continues** International Telephone Directory of TDD Users, 0898-3267.

UK
INTERNATIONAL DIRECTORY OF TELECOMMUNICATIONS. 1st Ed. (1984)-. Directory. English. Irregular. Longman Group Ltd., Fourth Avenue, Longman House, Harlow Essex CM19 5SR United Kingdom. **Tel** 011 44 1279 429655, FAX 011 44 1279 431067, telex 81259.

ISSN 1075-5276
DD 338 US
INTERNATIONAL ISDN YELLOW PAGES. See Computers-Computer Networks.

LC QC221 ISSN 0969-9112
DD 534 UK
Pr Rev.
●**INTERNATIONAL JOURNAL OF ACTIVE CONTROL. See** Electronics.

ISSN 1074-5351
DD 621 UK
●**INTERNATIONAL JOURNAL OF COMMUNICATION SYSTEMS.** [Int. j. commun. syst.]. Vol. 7, No. 1 (Jan.-Mar. 1994)-. Periodical. English. Four times a year. $625.00. John Wiley & Sons Ltd., Baffins Lane, Chichester, West Sussex PO19 1UD United Kingdom. **Tel** 011 44 1243 779777, FAX 011 44 1243 776128 BTG:JWP001, telex 86290 WIBOOKG. **(Subscription address:** John Wiley & Sons, Inc. / Philadelphia, PO Box 7247, Philadelphia PA 19170. **Tel** (212)850-6645, (800)225-5945.) **ED** J. Fox (managing editor), M. Vecchi (North American editor). Documents available from Article Express International, Ask*IEEE. **Continues** International Journal of Digital and Analog Communication Systems, 1047-9627.
Desc: Establishes a forum for research and development in the fast growing area of communication networks. Provides a single source of information on systems linked together by the common theme of using cable as their primary transmission means (over conventional copper or fiber).
Ind/Abst Curr. Cit.; Ei Page One; Eng. Index Annu.; INSPEC.

ISSN 1077-9124
US
●**INTERNATIONAL JOURNAL OF EDUCATIONAL TELECOMMUNICATIONS. Added/Corp** Association for the Advancement of Computing in Education. (1995)-. Periodical. English. Four times a year. $93.00. Association for the Advancement of Computing in Education, PO Box 2966, Charlottesville VA 22902. **Tel** (804)973-3987, FAX (804)978-7449.

LC TK5104 .I577 ISSN 0737-2884
DD 621.382/5/05 UK
CCC
CODEN IJSCEF
Pr Rev.
INTERNATIONAL JOURNAL OF SATELLITE COMMUNICATIONS. [Int. j. satell. commun.]. **VFOAT** Satellite Communications. Vol. 1, No. 1 (July-Sept. 1983)-. Trade Publication. English. Six times a year. $795.00. John Wiley & Sons Ltd., Baffins Lane, Chichester, West Sussex PO19 1UD United Kingdom. **Tel** 011 44 1243 779777, FAX 011 44 1243 776128 BTG:JWP001, telex 86290 WIBOOKG. **ED** B. G. Evans (chief editor), A. Stimson (editor, North America). **Bk Rev. Ad Acc. Circ:** 1,000. available on microfilm and microfiche from University Microfilms International (UMI). Documents available from Article Express International, The Genuine Article, Ask*IEEE.
Desc: Provides communication of the latest results and trends in this expanding field. Covering all aspects of the theory and practice of satellite systems and networks.
Ind/Abst Curr. Cit.; Curr. Contents Eng. Comput. Technol.; Ei Page One; Eng. Index Annu.; INSPEC (Oct./Dec. 1983-); Int. Aerosp. Abstr. (1984-); Res. Alert [Select. Cov.]; SCISEARCH.

ISSN 1068-9605
US
CCC
●**INTERNATIONAL JOURNAL OF WIRELESS INFORMATION NETWORKS.** (1994)-. Periodical. English. Four times a year. $165.00. Plenum Press, 233 Spring Street, New York NY 10013-1578. **Tel** (212)620-8000, (800)221-9369, FAX (212)463-0742, (212)807-1047, telex 23/421139.

LC TL512 .I68 ISSN 1041-4541
DD 629.1/025 US
INTERNATIONAL SATELLITE DIRECTORY. [Int. satell. dir.]. (1986)-. English. One time a year (Feb.). $268.50. Design Publishers, 800 Siesta Way, Sonoma CA 95476. **Tel** (707)939-9306, FAX (707)939-9235. **ED** Silvano Payne. Index available (Bound in next issue). **Ad Acc. Circ:** 3,500. available on diskette.
Desc: Contains complete information on the satellite communications industry.

ISSN 0227-1176
DD 384.1/4 CN
INTERNATIONAL TELEX. [Int. telex]. **VFOAT** Telex International. (1978)-. English (French). One time a year. Teleglobe Canada, 1000 de la Gauchetiere Street West, Montreal Quebec H3B 4X5 Canada. **Tel** (514)868-7465.

LC HE7621 .I58 ISSN 0099-2461
DD 384.1/4 US
INTERNATIONAL TELEX BOOK. AFRICAN-ASIAN-AUSTRALASIAN EDITION, THE. (THE INTERNATIONAL TELEX BOOK.). (19??)-. English. International Telex Corporation, 1313 Fulton National Bank Building, Atlanta GA 30303.

LC HE7621 .I59 ISSN 0094-6923
DD 384.1/4 US
INTERNATIONAL TELEX BOOK. AMERICAS EDITION. (THE INTERNATIONAL TELEX BOOK.). Vol. 1 (1974)-. English. International Telex Corporation, 1313 Fulton National Bank Building, Atlanta GA 30303.

LC HE7742 .I48 ISSN 0097-2525
DD 384/.025/4 US
INTERNATIONAL TELEX BOOK. EUROPEAN EDITION. (THE INTERNATIONAL TELEX BOOK.). (19??)-. English. International Telex Corporation, 1313 Fulton National Bank Building, Atlanta GA 30303.

LC HE7742 .I5
DD 384.1/4 GW
INTERNATIONAL TELEX (DARMSTADT, GERMANY). (INTERNATIONAL TELEX / J+W.). **VFOAT** Telex International; J+W International Telex. **VAT** Jaeger and Waldmann International Telex. 38th ed. (1990/91)-. English (French, German and Spanish). One time a year. $305.00. Telex-Verlag Jaeger+Waldmann GmbH, PO Box 111454, D-64229 Darmstadt Germany. **Tel** 011 49 6151 33020, FAX 011 49 6151 330250, telex 419389 TLX D. **Continues** Jaeger + Waldmann Telex + Teletex International.

LC HE7742 .I495
DD 384.1/4 GW
INTERNATIONAL TELEX-DIRECTORY ITD. VFOAT International Telex Directory ITD; ITD International Telex-Directory; ITD. (1986)-. Directory. English (French, German and Spanish). One time a year. $815.00, $1,290 (world edition). Telcom, Postfach 40 06 39, W-5000 Cologne 40 Germany. **Tel** 011 49 2234 40040, FAX 011 49 2234 400438, telex 8881686 DAMED. Index available. cum. index. **Ad Acc. Circ:** 20,000 (ctrl). available on CD-ROM. **Continues** ITV, Internationales Telex-Verzeichnis.

BE
INTERNATIONAL TELEX FAX DIRECTORY. Directory. English. One time a year. Interfax International Inc Ltd, rue Kindermans 18, B 1050 Brussels Belgium. **Tel** 011 32 2 640 54 30.

US
CEASED
INTERNATIONAL VOICE SYSTEMS REVIEW. (19??)-Vol. 1, No. 4 (1993). English. Media Dimensions Inc., 42 East 23rd Street, New York NY 10010-4410. **Tel** (212)717-1318. **Continues** International Voice Processing Review.
Ind/Abst Abstr. Hum. Comput. Interact.; HILITES.

LC HE7601 .I48a ISSN 1012-8719
DD 384/.05 UK
IPTC NEWS. [IPTC news]. **Main/Corp** International Press Telecommunications Council. **Added/Corp** International Press Telecommunications Council. News. **VAT** International Press Telecommunications Council News. (1991)-. Newsletter. English. Free to members. IPTC, 8 Sheet Street, Windsor, Barks SL4 1BG United Kingdom. **Tel** 011 44 1753 833728, FAX 011 44 1753 833750. **Bk Rev. Ad Acc. Circ:** 150 (ctrl). **Continues** International Press Telecommunications Council. I.P.T.C. Newsletter.
Desc: Concerned with the activities of the International Press Telecommunications Council and current press telecommunications developments.
Ind/Abst Print. Abstr.

LC QA75 ISSN 0735-1844
DD 004 US
CCC
ISDN (BROOKLINE, MASS.). See Computers-Computer Networks.

ISSN 1080-2991
DD 004 US
●**ISDN FOR SMALL BUSINESS. See** Computers-Computer Networks.

US
ISDN INFORMATION SOURCEBOOK. See Computers-Computer Networks.

ISSN 0899-9554
DD 384 UK
CCC
ISDN NEWS. See Computers-Computer Networks.

ISSN 1058-7470
DD 004 US
TITLE CHANGE
ISDN USER MAGAZINE. See Computers-Computer Networks.

ISSN 1078-1005
DD 004 US
ISDN USER NEWSLETTER. See Computers-Computer Networks.

LC HF3101 .I85
DD 338/.0029/445 IT
ITALIAN YELLOW PAGES FOR THE U.S.A. Added/Corp American Telephone and Telegraph Company. ItalCable (Firm) SEAT (Firm). (1987/1988)-. English.

ISSN 0932-6022
GW
CODEN ITGFEY
ITG-FACHBERICHTE. [ITG-Fachber.]. **Added/Corp** Informationstechnische Gesellschaft im VDE. **VFOAT** ITG Fachberichte. (1987)-. Monographic series. German. Irregular. Price varies per volume. VDE Verlag GmbH, Postfach 122305, D-10591 Berlin Germany. **Tel** 011 49 30 3480010, FAX 011 49 30 3417093. **Continues** NTG-Fachberichte, 0341-0196.
Ind/Abst Chem. Abstr. (19??-1988); Curr. Cit.; INSPEC (1988-).

ISSN 0268-9960
DD 338.4 UK
CCC
Pr Rev.
ITI. INTERNATIONAL TELECOMMUNICATIONS INTELLIGENCE. [ITI. Int. telecommun. intell.]. **VFOAT** International Telecommunications Intelligence. (1985)-. Trade Publication. English. One time a week (46 issues per year). $1018.17. MDIS Publications Limited, MDIS House, City Fields Business Park, City Fields Way, Chichester, West Sussex PO20 6FS United Kingdom. **Tel** 011 44 1243 533322, FAX 011 44 1243 533418. **ED** Neil Parker. **Bk Rev. Ad Acc. Circ:** 600.
Desc: Newsletter monitoring worldwide telecommmunications markets.

LC TK5101.A1 I87 ISSN 0235-2265
RU
ITOGI NAUKI I TEKHNIKI. SERIIA SVIAZ. **Added/Corp** Vsesoiuznyi Institut Nauchnoi i Tekhnicheskoi Informatsii (Soviet Union). **VFOAT** Sviaz; Seriia Sviaz; Itogi Nauki i Tekhniki. Sviaz. (1988)-. Periodical. Russian. Irregular. VINITI - Vsesoyuznyi Institut Nauchno-Tekhnicheskoi Informatsii, All-Union Scientific and Technical Information Institute, Baltiiskaia ulitsa 14, 125219 Moscow Russia. **Tel** 011 7 95 2384600, FAX 011 7 95 9430060, telex 411160. **Continues** Itogi Nauki i Tekhniki. Seriia Elektrosviaz, 0130-6804.

LC TK5101.A1 I472a
DD 621.38/05 US
TITLE CHANGE
ITS ... TECHNICAL PROGRESS REPORT FOR THE PERIOD ... . Main/Corp Institute for Telecommunication Sciences. **Added/Corp** United States. Dept. of Commerce. **VFOAT** Technical Progress Report. (19??)-(199?). English. Publications NTIA/ITS, 325 Broadway, Boulder CO 80303. **Tel** (303)497-3572.

Communications — Telecommunication

Continues Institute for Telecommunication Sciences., 0196-4410; ITS Annual Technical Progress Report. *Continued by* Institute for Telecommunication Sciences. Technical Progress Report.

SZ

●**ITU NEWSLETTER.** (1994)-. Newsletter. English. Ten times a year. Free on request. International Telecommunication Union, place des Nations, CH-1211 Geneva 20 Switzerland. **Tel** 011 41 22 7305111, FAX 011 41 22 7337256. **ED** Dominique Bourne. Index available. cum. index. **Bk Rev**. **Ad Acc**. **Circ**: 12,000 (ctrl). *Continues* Telecommunication Journal, 0497-137X.

LC HE8701
DD 384.6

GW

●**J & W BUSINESS INTERNATIONAL. INTERNATIONAL BUSINESS COMMUNICATIONS.** (1995)-. Directory. English. One time a year. $240.00. Verlag Jaeger & Waldmann GmbH, Birkenweg 8-10, 64295 Darmstadt Germany. **Tel** 011 49 6151 33020, FAX 011 49 6151 330250. **(Subscription address:** Universal Media Division / US Subscriptions, Division of Shamgar Inc., 212 Broadway, PO Box 45, Bethpage NY 11714. **Tel** (516)433-6767.**) ED** W. Lucius.

GW

J + W TELEFAX INTERNATIONAL. (19??)-. English. One time a year (Dec.). $330.00 (postage included). Telex-Verlag Jaeger+Waldmann GmbH, PO Box 111454, D-64229 Darmstadt Germany. **Tel** 011 49 6151 33020, FAX 011 49 6151 330250, telex 419389 TLX D. available on CD-ROM. *Continues* Telefax International.

LC UG590 .J35   **ISSN** 0144-0004
DD 355.8/5

UK
CCC

JANE'S MILITARY COMMUNICATIONS. See Military and Defense.

SP

JAPAN REPORT SERIES TELECOMMUNICATIONS. (19??)-. English. Twelve times a year. Newmedia International Japan, AV Infanta Carlota 123 5 A, 08029 Barcelona Spain. **Tel** 011 34 3 4195690, FAX 011 34 3 4144213.
Ind/Abst PROMT [Full Txt.]; PTS Newsl. Database [Full Txt.].

ISSN 1081-9983
DD 384

US

●**JAPAN TELECOM NEWSLETTER.** [Jap. telecom newsl.]. Vol. 1, No. 1 (Mar. 1995)-. Newsletter. English. Twenty-four times a year. $795.00 US and Canada; $845.00 other. Information Gatekeepers Inc., 214 Harvard Avenue, Boston MA 02134. **Tel** (617)232-3111, (617)738-8088, (800)323-1088, FAX (617)734-8562.

JA

JAPAN TELECOM REPORT. English. Twenty-four times a year. ¥200000.00 Japan; ¥220000.00 other. Egis KK, 22-1 Ichibancho Chiyoda-ku, Tokyo 102 Japan. **Tel** 011 81 3 3264 1060.
Desc: Provides in-depth analysis and market insight.

SP

JAPANESE REPORT SERIES : TELECOMMUNICATIONS. (19??)-. English. Twelve times a year. $370.00 US; £215.00 UK. Newmedia International Japan, AV Infanta Carlota 123 5 A, 08029 Barcelona Spain. **Tel** 011 34 3 4195690, FAX 011 34 3 4144213. **(Subscription address:** Newmedia International Japan Midland, Bank 196 Oxford Street, London W1A 1 EZ United Kingdom. **) *Continues*** Japan Report : Telecommunication.

US
TITLE CHANGE

JAPANESE TELECOMMUNICATIONS. (Jan. 1990)-(Apr. 15, 1994). English. Probe Research Inc., Three Wing Drive, Suite 240, Cedar Knolls NJ 07927-1000. **Tel** (201)285-1500, FAX (201)285-1519. **ED** Michael Galbraith, Karl Kozarsky, Victor Schnee, and Frank Barbetta. **Circ**: 100 (ctrl). ***Merged into*** Pacific Rim Telecommunications.

LC Z7165.J6 J63 HC465.A9

JA

JOHO SANGYO KIJI SAKUINSHU. SHINBUNHEN. **Added/Corp** Joho Kagaku Kenkyujo (Tokyo, Japan). (19??)-. Japanese. Two times a year. ¥38000. Joho Kagaku Kenkyujo, (Institute for Information Science), 5-36 Akasaka 6 chome, Minatoku Tokyo 107 Japan.

LC TK5101.A1 J68   **ISSN** 1047-0492
DD 621.382

US
CCC

JOURNAL OF COMMUNICATIONS TECHNOLOGY. [J. commun. technol.].
Added/Corp International Centers for Telecommunication Technology. **VFOAT** Communications Technology. Vol. 1, No. 1 (Feb. 1990)-.

Periodical. English. One time a year. Free on request. International Center for Telecommunication Technology, PO Box 3405, Terrehaute IN 47803. **Tel** (812)232-2208.

LC QC973 .D43   **ISSN** 0914-9260
DD 621.382

JA
CODEN JCRLEX

JOURNAL OF THE COMMUNICATIONS RESEARCH LABORATORY. [J. Commun. Res. Lab.]. **Added/Corp** Tsushin Sogo Kenkyujo (Japan). Vol. 35 No. 145 (July 1988)-. Periodical. English. Three times a year. Free. Communications Research Laboratory, 2 1 4 chome Nukuikitamachi, Koganei-shi, Tokyo Japan. Index available. cum. index. **Circ**: 1,000 (ctrl). Documents available from Article Express International, Ask*IEEE. ***Continues*** Journal of the Radio Research Laboratories, 0033-8001.
Desc: Concerned with communication and radio science.
Ind/Abst Ei Page One; Eng. Index Annu. [Select. Cov.]; INSPEC (1988-); Int. Aerosp. Abstr.

LC TK5101 .I55   **ISSN** 0377-2063
DD 621.38/05

II
CODEN JIETAU

JOURNAL OF THE INSTITUTION OF ELECTRONICS AND TELECOMMUNICATION ENGINEERS. [J. Inst. Electron. Telecommun. Eng.]. **Main/Corp** Institution of Electronics and Telecommunication Engineers (India). Vol. 19, No. 7 (July 1973)-. Periodical. English. Six times a year. $75.00. Institution of Electronics and Telecommunication Engineers, 2 Institutional Area, Lodi Road, New Delhi 110003 India. **Tel** 011 91 11 4631830, 011 91 11 4610324. **(Subscription address:** Prints India, 11 Darya Ganj, New Delhi 110002 India. **Tel** 011 91 11 3268645, FAX 011 91 11 3275542, telex 31-61087 PRIN-IN.**) ED** S C Bajpai. Index available. cum. index. **Circ**: 6,000 (ctrl). Documents available from Article Express International, Ask*IEEE, CASDDS. ***Continues*** Journal of the Institution of Telecommunication Engineers, 0020-353X. *Continued in part by* IETE Technical Review, 0255-9609.
Desc: Disseminates research and development work in electronics, communications, computer devices and instruments.
Ind/Abst Bioeng. Abstr.; Chem. Abstr.; Curr. Cit.; Ei Page One; Energy Res. Abstr. (March 1977-); Eng. Index Annu.; INSPEC (July 1973-); Int. Aerosp. Abstr.; Stat. Theory Method Abstr. (1978).

LC TK7800 .J7   **ISSN** 0251-1096
DD 621.381/05

II

JOURNAL OF THE INSTITUTION OF ENGINEERS (INDIA). ELECTRONICS & TELECOMMUNICATION ENGINEERING DIVISION. See Electronics.

US

JPRS REPORT. TELECOMMUNICATIONS. MICROFORM. **VFOAT** Telecommunications. **VAT** Joint Publications Research Service Report Telecommunications. (June 1987)-. English (Multiple languages). Irregular. Joint Publications Research Services, PO Box 12507, Arlington VA 22209. available on microfiche (Vols. for June 26, 1987- distributed to depository libraries). ***Continues*** Worldwide Report. Telecoomunications Policy, Research, and Development.

LC HE7601 .K33

JA

KAIGAI DENKI TSUSHIN. **VFOAT** Overseas Telecommunications Journal. Periodical. Japanese. Denki Tsushin Seisaku Sogo Kenkyujo, (Reseach Inst. of Telecom-Policies & Economics), 1-8 Motoakasaka 1 Chome, Minatoku Tokyo 107 Japan.

NP

KATHMANDU VALLEY TELEPHONE DIRECTORY. (Oct. 1991)-. Directory. English. Rs.125.00 (single issue). Kathmandu Valley Telephone Directory, PO Box 956, Kathmandu Nepal.

KE

KENYA FAX DIRECTORY, THE. (1991)-. Directory. English. Irregular. Target Mail & Services Ltd., PO Box 30759, Nairobi Kenya.

ISSN 1055-5544
DD 331

US

KERN REPORT, THE. See Business and Economics.

LC TK5101.A1 K43   **ISSN** 0950-4877
DD 621.382/05

UK

KEY ABSTRACTS. TELECOMMUNICATIONS. See Communications-Abstracting, Bibliographies and Statistics.

LC HE7601 .K65
DD 384/.05

SZ

KOMMUNIKATION. (19??)-. Periodical. German. Ten times a year (Jan/Feb & July/Aug issues are combined). $131.07. B & L Verlags AG, Steinwiesenstrasse 3, CH-8952 Schlieren Switzerland. **Tel** 011 41 1 7304066, FAX 011 41 1 7305841. **ED** Peter Boll. **Bk Rev**. **Ad Acc**.

LC HD9986.A1 K6

LU

KOMMUNIKATIONSDIENSTE, JAHRLICHE STATISTIKEN = COMMUNICATION SERVICES, ANNUAL STATISTICS. **Added/Corp** Statistical Office of the European Communities. **VFOAT** Kommunikationsdienste; Communications Services; Communication Services, Annual Statistics. (1991)-. Statistical Publication. English (German and French). Office for Official Publications of the European Communities, 2 rue Mercier, 2985 Luxembourg Luxembourg. **Tel** 011 352 499281, FAX 011 352 292942763. **(Subscription address:** SDU Staatsdrukkerij En, Uitgeverijbedrijf, PO Box 20014, 2500 EA Gravenhage Netherlands. **)**

LC HE8390.6 .A27b
DD 354.5950087/4/06

MY

LAPURAN TAHUNAN. **Main/Corp** Malaysia. Jabatan Telekom. **VFOAT** Annual Report. (19??)-?. English (Malay). One time a year. *Continued in part by* Annual Report.

LC HE9719
DD 384.51

US

LATIN AMERICAN SATELLITE DIRECTORY. (19??)-. Directory. English. One time a year. $177.00. Phillips Business Information, Inc., 1201 Seven Locks Road, PO Box 61130, Potomac MD 20854. **Tel** (301)424-3338, (301)340-1520, (800)777-5005, FAX (301)424-4297, telex 358149. **(Subscription address:** Phillips Publishing Inc., 7811 Montrose Road, Potomac MD 20854. **Tel** (800)777-5005 ext. 5450.**)**
Desc: Information on personnel shifts, system additions and satellite deployment; also Latin American market data, associations serving Latin American countries, etc.

ISSN 1062-3884
DD 384

US

LATIN AMERICAN TELECOM REPORT. [Lat. Am. telecom rep.]. **VFOAT** LATR. Vol. 1, No. 1 (Mar. 15, 1992)-. Trade Publication. English. Twelve times a year. $679.00. International Technology Consultants, 1724 Kalorama Road, Suite 210, Washington DC 20009. **Tel** (202)234-2138, FAX (202)483-7922. available on an online database (file 636/Full-Text) from DIALOG.

LC TA1800 .L55   **ISSN** 0741-5834
DD 621.36/92/05

US
CCC

LIGHTWAVE. [Lightwave]. **VFOAT** Light Wave. (Jan. 1984)-. Trade Publication. English. Thirteen times a year (annual with annual product listing). $75.00. PennWell Publishing Company, 1421 South Sheridan, PO Box 1260, Tulsa OK 74101. **Tel** (918)835-3161, (800)331-4463, FAX (918)831-9497. **(Subscription address:** Lightwave Magazine, PO Box 2139, Tulsa OK 74101. **Tel** (800)331-4463.**) ED** Sharon Scully. Index available. **Bk Rev**. **Ad Acc**. **Circ**: 15,000 (ctrl). available on microfilm and microfiche from University Microfilms International (UMI).
Desc: Serves a concentrated audience of fiber optics market including telecommunications, data communications, lightwave systems and components, sensing, process control, and military applications on all levels and job functions. Provides comprehensive coverage of fiber optics technology in all its applications including telecommunications, data communications, local area networks, and cable television distribution.
Ind/Abst Bus. Source Plus; Energy Inf. Abstr.; EP Collect.; Homework Help.; Infomat Int. Bus.; MasterFile FullTEXT 1000; MasterFile FullTEXT 350; MasterFile FullTEXT 650; MasterFile FullTEXT (Jan. 1995-); OCLC; Telebase.

UK
CODEN LICOEV

LINES OF COMMUNICATION : THE INDEPENDENT VOICE FOR THE TELECOMS TRADE AND INDUSTRY. (1987)-. Periodical. English. Twelve times a year. £28.50. Lines of Communication, Cheltonian House, Portsmouth Road, Esher Surrey KT10 9AA United Kingdom. Documents available from Ask*IEEE.
Ind/Abst HILITES; Infomat Int. Bus.; INSPEC (1989-1991).

US

LIST OF MATERIALS ACCEPTABLE FOR USE ON TELEPHONE SYSTEMS OF REA BORROWERS . **Added/Corp** United States. Rural Electrification Administration. (19??)-. Government Publication. English. One time a year (supplementary material). $63.00 US; $78.75 other. US Department of Agriculture, 14th Street and Independence Avenue SW, Washington DC 20250. **Tel** (202)720-5457. **(Subscription address:** Superintendent of Documents, US Government Printing Office, Washington DC 20402. **)** available on microfiche (Vols. for (1986-) distributed to depository libraries).

Desc: Gives names of manufacturers and catalog numbers for materials acceptable for use on telephone systems of REA borrowers.

LC Z5834.T4 I532a TK5101
DD 016.384 SZ
LIST OF PUBLICATIONS / INTERNATIONAL TELECOMMUNICATION UNION. See Communications-Abstracting, Bibliographies and Statistics.

ISSN 1067-6333
US
CCC
•**LOCAL TELECOM COMPETITION NEWS.** (1993)-. Periodical. English. Twenty-five times a year. $597.00. Phillips Business Information Inc., 1201 Seven Locks Road, PO Box 61130, Potomac MD 20854. **Tel** (301)424-3338, (301)340-1520, (800)777-5005, FAX (301)424-4297, telex 358149.

US
MANAGING VOICE NETWORKS. **Added/Corp** Datapro Research Corporation. **VFOAT** Datapro Managing Voice Networks. Vol. 1, No. 1 (Feb. 1992)-. Periodical. English. Two times a year. $926.00. Datapro Information Services Group, 600 Delran Parkway, Delran NJ 08075. **Tel** (609)764-0100, (800)328-2776, FAX (609)764-8953. ***Continues*** *Datapro Management of Telecommunications.*

ISSN 0849-0619
DD 971.27/43004951 CN
MANITOBA, WINNIPEG AND VICINITY CHINESE TELEPHONE DIRECTORIES. [Manit. Winn. vicin. Chin. teleph. dir.]. **VFOAT** Manitoba Chinese Telephone Directory; Chinese Telephone Directory, Manitoba. Vol. 35 (1987)-. English (summaries and/or abstracts in Chinese). Chinese Publicity Bureau Ltd., 459 East Hastings Street, Vancouver British Columbia V6A 1P5 Canada. **Tel** (604)254-2533. ***Continues*** *Chinese Directory & Telephone Book, Manitoba, Winnipeg and Vicinity., 0316-716X.*

ISSN 0076-4418
US
MARCONI'S INTERNATIONAL REGISTER. [Marconi's int. regist.]. **VFOAT** International Register. (1945)-. Directory. English. One time a year. $155.00 US; $161.00 other. Telegraphic Cable and Radio Register, 19 Dogwood Lane, Larchmont NY 10538. **Tel** (914)632-8171, FAX (914)698-1804. **ED** Joanne Clark. Index available (Pubd in Nov. issue). **Ad Acc, Adv Mgr:** L.G.Smith. **Circ:** 5,000 (ctrl). ***Continues*** *Marconi's International Register of Telegraphic and Trade Addresses.*
Desc: Business directory used by businesses, libraries, and government agencies. Includes communications and trade data for firms doing business internationally, providing contacts and sources.

LC HD9993.B63 M37
DD 338.7/6238/02573 US
MARINE INDUSTRY FAX DIRECTORY. **Added/Corp** National Marine Representatives' Association. 1st Ed. (1988)-. Directory. English. One time a year. $5.00 US; $7.00 Canada; $10.00 other. National Marine Representatives Association, PO Box 957075, Hoffman Estates IL 60195. **Tel** (312)213-0606, FAX (312)213-0705. **ED** Teddee Grace. **Ad Acc. Circ:** 2,000.
Desc: Names, addresses, phone/FAX numbers for almost 2,000 marine industry businesses.

ISSN 0748-9358
DD 535 US
MARKETING INTELLIGENCE. FIBEROPTIC. **Added/Corp** Kessler Marketing Intelligence. **VFOAT** Fiberoptic; F.M.I.; Fiberoptic Marketing Intelligence; FMI. (198?)-. Periodical. English. Twenty-six times a year. $375.00. Kessler Marketing Intelligence, 31 Bridge Street & Americas Cup Avenue, Newport RI 02840. **Tel** (401)849-6771, FAX (401)847-5866, telex 6502592954. **ED** Richard Mack. Index available ((available for $20.00 within US; $25.00 outside US. Please specify year.)). cum. index. **Circ:** 300.
Desc: International newsletter that analyzes developments and trends related to markets in the fiberoptics industry. It provides the market intelligence needed to make important long-term (and day-to-day) business decisions. Its purpose is to inform decision-makers involved in fiberoptics markets of emerging markets, competition, prices and technology affecting fiberoptics markets. Each issue contains a two-page report on Europe. Stockwatch, which tracks publicly-traded companies involved in fiberoptics, is included quarterly.

US
UDC 62
MCCARTHY TETRAULT REGULATORY REPORTER. (19??)-. English. Twenty-four times a year. 295.00Can$ (telecommunications); 550.00Can$ (telecommunications and broadcasting). McCarthy Tetrault, 275 Sparks Street, Suite 1000, Ottawa Ontario K1R 7X9 Canada. **Tel** (613)238-2000, FAX (613)563-9386, (613)563-7813. ***Continues*** *Clarkson Tetrault Regulatory Reporter.*
Desc: Provides a summary and analysis of all federal and provincial regulatory notices and decisions in Canadian telecommunications, broadcasting and transportation and summaries of judicial and executive appeals.

LC HE6005 .P67
DD 380.3/0944 FR
MESSAGES DES POSTES ET TELECOMMUNICATIONS. See Communications-Postal Communications.

US
MIC-TECH-TELECOMMUNICATIONS. (19??)-. English. Twelve times a year. $970.00. Management Information Corporation, 1111 Marlkress Road, Cherry Hill NJ 08003. **Tel** (609)424-1100. **ED** Donald Stuart. Index available. cum. index. ctrl circ. available on diskette.
Desc: Reference service on key systems, PBXs, ACDs, call accounting and voice mail.

US
MICROCELL NEWS. (Dec. 1989)-. English. Twenty-four times a year (published the 10th and 25th of each month). $497.00 US and Canada; $527.00 other. Probe Research Inc., Three Wing Drive, Suite 240, Cedar Knolls NJ 07927-1000. **Tel** (201)285-1500, FAX (201)285-1519. **ED** Frank Barbetta and Paul Broadhead. **Circ:** 400 (ctrl).
Desc: International source on cordless telephones, personal communications networks, micro cellular technology and the wireless office.

ISSN 1048-6976
DD 384 US
MICROCELL REPORT. (MICROCELL REPORT : THE JOURNAL OF MICROCELL TELECOMMUNICATIONS.). [Microcell rep.]. (Feb. 1990)-. Periodical. English. Twelve times a year. $397.00 North America; $417.00 other. Microcell Report, 150 West 22nd Street, Suite 1000, New York NY 10011. **Tel** (800)883-8989 or (212)366-9788, FAX (212)366-9798. **ED** Roger P Newell. Index available (Bound in issue, January). **Circ:** 300. available on an online database (files 16,636/Full-Text) from DIALOG.
Desc: Covers personal communications, services and personal communications networks (PCNS), telepoints and wireless PBXS.
Ind/Abst PROMT [Full Txt.]; PTS Newsl. Database [Full Txt.].

LC TK5101 **ISSN** 1358-040X
DD 621.3825 UK
•**MIDDLE EAST SATELLITE TODAY.** [Middle East satell. today]. (1995)-. Trade Publication. English. Six times a year. ICOM Publications Ltd., Chancery House, St. Nicholas Way, Sutton Surrey SM1 1JB United Kingdom. **Tel** 011 44 181 6421117, FAX 011 44 181 6421941. **Ad Acc. Circ:** 6,500.
Desc: Covers the satellite distribution market in the Middle East.

ISSN 0747-9565
US
MIDWEST MESSENGER. (19??)-. Periodical. English. Twenty-six times a year. $11.00. Plaindealer Publishing, Box 239, Tekamah NE 68061.

NE
MOBIELE TELECOMMUNICATIE. Dutch. Four times a year. Pietersen, Postbus 1029, 2430 AA Noorden The Netherlands. **Tel** 011 31 01724 9741.

GW
MOBILCOM FUNKSCHAU. (19??)-. German. Twelve times a year. DM240.00. Franzis Verlag GmbH, Gruberstrasse 46 A, D-85586 Poing Germany. **Tel** 011 49 8121 769433.

UK
MOBILE & CELLULAR. **VFOAT** Mobile and Cellular; Mobile & Cellular Magazine; Mobile and Cellular Magazine. (19??)-. Periodical. English. Twelve times a year. $88.99. Courtesy Publishing Ltd, 127 Oatlands Drive, Weybridge Surrey KT13 9LB United Kingdom. **Tel** 011 44 1932 820100. **ED** Richard Lambley. **Ad Acc. Circ:** 9,000 (ctrl). Documents available from Ask*IEEE.
Desc: Topical management issues and technical information on products and services in application news, market information, user abuse, company profiles, and updates of radio.
Ind/Abst HILITES; Infomat Int. Bus.; INSPEC (April 1991-).

UK
MOBILE & SATELLITE. English. Four times a year. Tempest Public Relations, PO Box 601, London SW12 9BU United Kingdom. **Tel** 011 44 181 6737744.

ISSN 1352-9226
DD 621.38 UK
•**MOBILE COMMUNICATIONS INTERNATIONAL.** [Mob. Commun. Int.]. (1993)-. Periodical. English. Ten times a year. $171.12. Cheerman Limited, Halpern House 301, 305 Euston Road, London NW1 3SS United Kingdom. **Tel** 011 44 171 3835757, FAX 011 44 171 3833181. **ED** Stuart Sharrock. **Ad Acc, Adv Mgr:** Roger Hinkson and Marc Florczak. ***Continues*** *Pan-European Mobile Communications, 0958-157X.*

ISSN 1350-7362
DD 338.47621382 UK
MOBILE EUROPE. [Mob. Eur.]. (1990)-. Periodical. English. Ten times a year. $128.34. Nexus Business Communications, Warwick House Azalea Drive, Kent BR8 8HY United Kingdom. **Tel** 011 44 1322 660070, FAX 011 44 1322 667633. **ED** David Bobbett. **Ad Acc. Circ:** 15,000 (ctrl).
Desc: News, views, product information, technology, developments, technical standards, policy updates and in depth market reports for CT2/Telepant, PMR and Satellite.

LC TK5700 **ISSN** 1359-4028
DD 621.38456 UK
•**MOBILE MIDDLE EAST, AFRICA.** [Mob. Middle East Afr.]. (1994)-. Trade Publication. English. Five times a year. Nexus Media Ltd., Nexus House, Azalea Drive, Swanley Kent BR8 8HY United Kingdom. **Tel** 011 1322 660070, FAX 011 1322 667633.

LC WMLC 93/1409 **ISSN** 1047-1952
DD 384 US
MOBILE OFFICE. [Mob. office]. (1990)-. Periodical. English. Twelve times a year. $23.90. Cowles Business Media Inc. / Connecticut, 6 River Bend Center, 911 Hope Street, Stamford CT 06907. **Tel** (203)358-9900, (800)775-3777, FAX (203)357-9014. **(Subscription address:** Neodata / Colorado, PO Box 2606, Boulder CO 80322. **) ED** Michael Meresman. **Ad Acc. Circ:** 150,000 (ctrl). ***Absorbed*** *Portable Office (Peterborough, N.H.), 1054-2736.*
Desc: Devoted to coverage of innovations in cellular communications and mobile technology along with practical applications. Product reviews, comparison reports, buyer's guides and a forum for ideas exchange.
Ind/Abst Microcomput. Abstr. (April 1992-).

ISSN 1062-6638
DD 384 US
MOBILE OFFICE MAGAZINE'S CELLULAR BUYERS' GUIDE. [Mob. off. mag. cell. buy. guide]. **VFOAT** Cellular Buyers' Guide. Vol. 1, No. 1 (Spring 1991)-. Consumer Publication. English. Four times a year. Curtco's Mobile Office Magazine Inc., Warner Plaza, 21800 Oxnard Street, Suite 250, Woodland Hills CA 91367.

ISSN 0737-5077
US
CCC
MOBILE PHONE NEWS. [Mob. phone news]. Vol. 1, No. 1 (June 10, 1983)-. Periodical. English. Fifty times a year. $697.00. Phillips Business Information Inc., 1201 Seven Locks Road, PO Box 61130, Potomac MD 20854. **Tel** (301)424-3338, (301)340-1520, (800)777-5005, FAX (301)424-4297, telex 358149. **ED** Kevin Dennehy and Paul Shultz. available on an online database from NEWSNET; Predicasts, Inc.; and (files 636,648/Full-Text) DIALOG.
Desc: Coverage of worldwide cellular marketing and business strategies.
Ind/Abst PTS Newsl. Database [Full Txt.]; Trade Ind. ASAP [Full Txt.]; Trade Ind. Index [Full Txt.].

ISSN 1044-1190
DD 384 US
CCC
MOBILE PRODUCT NEWS. [Mob. prod. news]. Vol. 1, No. 1 (June/July 1989)-. Trade Publication. English. Twelve times a year. $69.00. Phillips Business Information Inc., 1201 Seven Locks Road, PO Box 61130, Potomac MD 20854. **Tel** (301)424-3338, (301)340-1520, (800)777-5005, FAX (301)424-4297, telex 358149. **ED** David J. Durham, Barbara Bink, and Lanie Efron. Index available. **Ad Acc. Circ:** 17,746 (ctrl). ***Continues*** *Mobile Communications Business, 0897-4802.*
Desc: Introduces new products to large volume buyers in the mobile communications marketplace, including cellular, 2-way radio, paging, specialized mobile radio and improved mobile telephone services.

ISSN 1046-5286
DD 384 US
CCC
MOBILE SATELLITE NEWS (POTOMAC, MD.). (MOBILE SATELLITE NEWS.). [Mob. satell. news]. Vol. 1, No. 1 (Nov. 1989)-. Periodical. English. Twenty-five times a year. $597.00. Phillips Business Information Inc., 1201 Seven Locks Road, PO Box 61130, Potomac MD 20854. **Tel** (301)424-3338, (301)340-1520, (800)777-5005, FAX (301)424-4297, telex 358149. available on an online database (file 636/Full-Text) from DIALOG.
Ind/Abst PTS Newsl. Database [Full Txt.].

ISSN 1046-6061
DD 384 US
MOBILE SATELLITE REPORTS. [Mob. satell. rep.]. **VFOAT** MSR. (198?)-. Periodical. English. Twenty-six times a year. $526.18 Washington DC; $493.00 other US, Canada and Mexico; $514.00 other. Warren Publishing, Inc., 2115 Ward Court Northwest,

Communications — Telecommunication

Washington DC 20037. **Tel** (202)872-9200, FAX (202)293-3435. **ED** David Hartshorn. available on an online database (files 16,636/Full-Text) from DIALOG. **Continues** Mobile Satellite News, 0894-8690.
Desc: Report on aeronautical, maritime, and land mobile satellites, and radiodetermination.
Ind/Abst PROMT [Full Txt.]; PTS Newsl. Database [Full Txt.].

DD 621.384165 **ISSN** 0267-1255
UK
SUSPENDED

MOBILE TELECOMMUNICATIONS NEWS. [Mob. telecommun. news]. (1983)-Suspended (July 1995). Trade Publication. English. Ten times a year. £29.00 UK; £50.00 US £40.00 other. Wordcount Ltd, PO Box 48, Wormley, Godalming Surrey GU8 5TX United Kingdom. **Tel** 011 44 1428 684955, FAX 011 44 1428 684251. **ED** Kendrick Struthers Watson. **Bk Rev**. **Ad Acc**. **Circ:** 9,500 (ctrl).
Desc: Contains information on mobile communications including cellular, land-mobile radio, radiopaging, telepoint, and emerging technologies.
Ind/Abst Infomat Int. Bus.

AT

MOBILES. Vol. 1, No. 2 (July 1990)-. English. Twelve times a year. 375.00Aus$ Australia; 425.00Aus$ other. Teleresources Pty Ltd, PO Box 693, Brookvale NSW 2100 Australia. **Tel** 011 61 2 9752230, FAX 011 61 2 97522407.

IT

MODEM & TELECOMUNICAZIONI. Italian. Ten times a year (monthly except Jan. and Aug.). L100000 Italy; L200000 other. Edicomp Srl, Via Sannio 79, 00183 Rome Italy. **Tel** 011 39 6 7092444, FAX 011 39 6 77205150. **Ad Acc**.

DD 380 **ISSN** 0899-8108
US

MORNING FAX, THE. [Morning fax]. (1988)-. Periodical. English. One time a week. $179.00. The Morning Fax, 560 Hollywood, Detroit MI 48236-1319.

LC TK5981 .N3 **ISSN** 0323-4657
GW
CCC
CODEN NTELAP

NACHRICHTENTECHNIK - ELEKTRONIK. [Nachrichtentech., Elektron.]. **Added/Corp** Kammer der Technik. (1951)-. Trade Publication. German. Six times a year. $105.94. Verlag Technik GmbH Berlin, AM Friedrichshain 22, D-10407 Berlin Germany. **Tel** 011 49 30 428700. Documents available from Article Express International, Ask*IEEE, CASDDS. **Continues** Nachrichtentechnik.
Ind/Abst Bioeng. Abstr.; Chem. Abstr.; Curr. Cit.; Ei Page One; Eng. Index Annu.; INSPEC (1973-); Math. Rev.

LC TK6011 .N37 **ISSN** 0743-7072
DD 621.386/025/73 US

NATIONAL DIRECTORY OF COMMUNICATION CUSTOMER PREMISE EQUIPMENT WIRING & EQUIPMENT INSTALLERS, WITH RATE INFORMATION BY CITY, STATE & REGION, THE. (19??)-. Directory. English. One time a year. Carl D Southard Associates Inc, PO Box 30033, Raleigh NC 27622.

LC TK6710 .N37 **ISSN** 1045-9499
DD 384.1/4 US
TITLE CHANGE

NATIONAL FAX DIRECTORY. [Nat. fax dir.]. **Added/Corp** General Information, Inc. (1989)-(199?). Directory. English. One time a year. Gale Research Inc., 835 Penobscot Building, 645 Griswold Street, Detroit MI 48226. **Tel** (800)877-GALE, (313)961-2242, FAX (313)961-6083, (800)414-5043, telex TWX 810-221-7086. **ED** Karin E. Koek. available on magnetic tape; available on diskette. **Continued by** U.S. Fax Directory, 1084-4465.
Desc: Gives access to over 160,000 FAX numbers, verified for accuracy, for U.S. companies, organizations, government agencies, and libraries.

DD 610 **ISSN** 1073-595X
US

NATIONAL HEALTHLINES DIRECTORY. See Medical Sciences.

LC TK7800 .E445 **ISSN** 0177-5499
DD 621.38/05 GW
CCC
CODEN NETTEN

NET. NACHRICHTEN ELEKTRONIK + TELEMATIK (1984). (NET : NACHRICHTEN ELEKTRONIK + TELEMATIK.). [NET, Nachr. Elektron. + Telemat.]. **VFOAT** Nachrichten Elektronik + Telematik. (Jan. 1984)-. Trade Publication. German. Ten times a year. $108.00. R V Decker's Verlag, G Schenck, Huethig im Weiher 10, D-69121 Heidelberg Germany. **(Subscription address:** WEPF Publishing Services GmbH, Auf dem Wolf 4, CH-4018 Basel Switzerland. **Tel** 011 41 61 3115125.) Documents available from Ask*IEEE. **Continues** Nachrichten Elektronik + Telematik, 0723-8703.
Ind/Abst Energy Res. Abstr. (Oct. 1982-); F&S Index Plus Text, Int. [Select. Cov.]; INSPEC (June 1989-); PROMT.

US

●**NETWORK BRIEFING.** (1995)-. English. One time a week. $495.00. APT Data Services, 12 Sutton Row, 4th Floor, London W1V 5FH United Kingdom. **Tel** 011 44 171 2084200, FAX 011 44 171 4391105. **Continues** Network Week.

LC HD9696.T44 N47 **ISSN** 8755-2124
DD 384 US

NETWORK RESOURCE REPORT, THE. [Netw. resour. rep.]. **Added/Corp** Yankee Group. Vol. 1 (January 1984)-. Trade Publication. English. Irregular. The Yankee Group, 89 Broad Street, 14th Floor, Boston MA 02110. **Continues** Report on Electronic Mail, 0163-9846.

DD 384.05 **ISSN** 0965-3031
UK
TITLE CHANGE

NETWORK WEEK. [Netw. week]. **Added/Corp** APT Data Services. (1991)-(1995). Newsletter. English. APT Data Services, 12 Sutton Row, 4th Floor, London W1V 5FH United Kingdom. **Tel** 011 44 171 2084200, FAX 011 44 171 4391105. **ED** Chris Rose. **Circ:** 1,000 (ctrl). **Continues** Telegram (London. 1986), 0953-5284. **Continued by** Network Briefing.
Desc: Newsletter on telecommunications, containing news and analysis on the industry, plus marketing information.

LC QA76 .C5816 **ISSN** 0887-7661
DD 004.6/05 CCC

NETWORK WORLD. See Computers-Computer Networks.

DD 384 **ISSN** 0895-5077
US
CEASED

NETWORKS IN-DEPTH. (NETWORKS IN-DEPTH : MONTHLY REPORT BY RESTON CONSULTING GROUP, INC.). [Netw. in-depth]. **Added/Corp** Reston Consulting Group (Reston, Va.). **VFOAT** Networks In Depth. (April 1987)-Vol. 8 (1995). Periodical. English. Reston Consulting Group Inc, 462 Herndon Parkway, Suite 203, Herndon VA 22070. **Tel** (703)834-1155. **ED** Brij Bhushan. Index available. cum. index. **Circ:** 1,000.
Desc: Research on telecommunications products and services. Provides department reading in all areas of telecommunications.

DD 621.38 **ISSN** 0912-0076
JA
CEASED

NEW ERA OF TELECOMMUNICATIONS IN JAPAN. [New era telecommun. Jpn.]. (1985)-(June 1995). Periodical. English. Telecommunications Association, 1-chome Shin Yurakucho, Bld 12, Chiyoda-ku Tokyo 100 Japan. **Tel** 011 81 3 32155725, FAX 011 81 3 32016015, telex 27161.

LC HE7601 .N49 **ISSN** 1070-3683
DD 384/.05 US
CCC
CODEN NTQUFF

●**NEW TELECOM QUARTERLY.** [New telecom q.]. **Added/Corp** Technology Futures, Inc. **VFOAT** A.NTQ. Vol. 1 (1993)-. Trade Publication. English. Four times a year (Feb., May, Aug., Nov.). $120.00. Technology Futures Inc., 11709 Boulder Lasne, Austin TX 78726. **Tel** (512)258-8898, (800)835-3887, FAX (512)258-0087. **ED** Julia A. Marsh. **Ad Acc**. **Circ:** 1,000 (ctrl).
Desc: For those with a need to better understand changes occurring in the telecommunications industry.

ISSN 0380-478X
CN

NEWS LETTER - MCGILL UNIVERSITY COMPUTING CENTRE. See Computers.

US

NEXTNET. (19??)-. English. Twenty-five times a year. $498.00 North America; $533.00 other. Telecommunications Reports, 1333 H Street Northwest, 2nd Floor West Tower, Washington DC 20005. **Tel** (202)842-0520, (800)822-6338, FAX (202)842-3047. **Continues** Telecom Data Report.

LC HE7621 .N65 SZ
DD 384.1/025

NOMENCLATURE DES BUREAUX TELEGRAPHIQUES OUVERTS AU SERVICE INTERNATIONAL. **Added/Corp** International Telecommunication Union. **VFOAT** List of Telegraph Offices Open for International Service; Nomenclature des Bureaux Telegraphiques. (1971)-. English (French and Spanish). International Telecommunication Union, place des Nations, CH-1211 Geneva 20 Switzerland. **Tel** 011 41 22 7305111, FAX 011 41 22 7337256. **Continues** Nomenclature Officielle des Bureaux Telegraphiques Ouverts au Service International.

LC HE7601 .I532a **ISSN** 0252-1792
SZ

NOMENCLATURE DES VOIES DE TELECOMMUNICATION UTILISEES POUR LA TRANSMISSION DES TELEGRAMMES = LIST OF TELECOMMUNICATION CHANNELS USED FOR THE TRANSMISSION OF TELEGRAMS = NOMENCLATOR DE LA VIAS DE TELECOMUNICACION EMPLEADAS PARA LA TRANSMISION DEL TELEGRAMAS. **Main/Corp** International Telecommunication Union General Secretariat. **Added/Corp** International Telecommunications Union. General Secretariat. List of Telecommunication Channels Used for the Transmission of Telegrams. International Telecommunications Union. General Secretariat. Nomenclator de las Vias de Telecomunicacion Empleadas para la Transmision de Telegramas. **VFOAT** List of Telecommunication Channels Used for the Transmission of Telegrams; Nomenclator de las Vias de Telecomunicacion Empleadas para la Transmision de Telegramas. 1st Ed. (1977)-. Monographic series. Multiple languages (English, French and Spanish). Irregular. 50.00F. International Telecommunication Union, place des Nations, CH-1211 Geneva 20 Switzerland. **Tel** 011 41 22 7305111, FAX 011 41 22 7337256. **ED** Board. **Supersedes** International Telecommunication Union. General Secretariat. Nomenclature des Voies de Communication Radiotelegraphiques Entre Points Fixes.

DD 381 **ISSN** 1078-523X
US

●**NORTHERN BUSINESS INFORMATION'S TELECOM PERSPECTIVES.** [North. Bus. Inf. telecom perspect.]. **Added/Corp** Northern Business Information. McGraw-Hill, Inc. **VFOAT** Telecom Perspectives. (July 1994)-. Periodical. English. Twelve times a year. $995.00. Northern Business Information, 157 Chambers Street, 7th Floor, New York NY 10007-1015. **Tel** (212)732-0775, FAX (212)233-6233. **Formed by the union of** Telecom Market Letter, 0712-3663 and Telecom Strategy Letter, 0739-683X.

IT

NOTIZIARIO TELECOMUNICAZIONI INTERNAZIONALI. Italian. Irregular. L450000. Ediemme, Via Maroncelli 13, 20154 Milan Italy. **Tel** 2/6570270, 2/6570250, FAX 2/6552402.

FR

NOUVEL OBSERVATEUR ENTERPRISES ET TELECOMMUNICATIONS. (19??)-. French. Four times a year. 300.00F France; 380.00F other. 36 rue de Pispus 99, 75012 Paris France. **Tel** 011 33 1 43425800. **Continues** Telematique Magazine.

LC TK5101.A1 U55A **ISSN** 0271-9703
DD 621.38/05 US

NTIA REPORT. [NTIA rep.]. **VAT** National Telecommunications and Information Administration Report. Monographic series. English. Price varies per volume. US Department of Commerce / National Telecommunications & Information Administration, 14th Street & Constitution Avenue NW, Hoover Building, Room 4898, Washington DC 20230. **Tel** (202)482-1551, FAX (202)482-1635.

US

NTT NEWSLETTER. (19??)-. Newsletter. English. NTT Information Desk, 301 East 57th Street, New York NY 10022. **Tel** (212)593-6317. **Continues** NTT Topics, 0895-089X.

LC TK5101.A1 K37 **ISSN** 0915-2326
JA
CODEN NTTDEC

NTT R & D. [NTT R & D]. **Added/Corp** Denki Tsushin Kyokai (Japan) Nihon Denshin Denwa Kabushika Kaisha. Nihon Denshin Denwa Kabushika Kaisha. Gijutsu Joho Senta. **VFOAT** NTT R and D. (1989)-. Periodical. Japanese (English). Twelve times a year. $297.00. **(Subscription address:** Japan Publications Trading Company Ltd., PO Box 5030, Tokyo International, Tokyo 100-31 Japan. **Tel** 011 81 3 3292 3753.) Documents available from Article Express International, Ask*IEEE, CASDDS. **Continues** Kenkyu Jitsuyoka Hokoku, 0415-3200.
Desc: A specialty magazine providing in-depth introductions to NTT's latest research and development efforts.
Ind/Abst Chem. Abstr.; Ei Page One; Eng. Index Annu.; INSPEC (1989-).

Communications —Telecommunication

LC TK5101.A1 N83
DD 384/.0952/05
ISSN 0915-2334
JA
CODEN NTTREK
Pr Rev.
NTT REVIEW. [NTT rev.]. **Added/Corp** Nihon Denshin Denwa Kabushiki Kaisha. **VAT** Nippon Telegraph and Telephone Review. Vol. 1, No. 1 (May 1989)-. Academic Scholarly Publication. English. Six times a year. $200.00. (**Subscription address:** Maruzen Company Ltd., PO Box 5050, Import & Export Department, Tokyo 100 31 Japan. **Tel** 011 81 3 32789224.) Documents available from Article Express International, The Genuine Article, Ask*IEEE, CASDDS. **Formed by the union of** Japan Telecommunications Review, 0029-067X **and** Review of the Electrical Communication Laboratories, 0021-4744.
Desc: An English-language publication specially planned and edited to provide overseas readers with comprehensive information about NTT, including its business activities, technological trends, services and systems, and R&D and international activities.
Ind/Abst Chem. Abstr.; Curr. Cit.; Curr. Contents Eng. Comput. Technol.; Ei Page One; Eng. Index Annu.; INSPEC (May 1989-); Int. Aerosp. Abstr.; Res. Alert [Select. Cov.]; SCISEARCH.

JA
NTT SHISETSU. VFOAT Equipment on Telecommunication. Japanese. Twelve times a year. $88.00. Nippon Denshin Denwa K.K. Nettowaku Jigyo Honbu, (Telecommunications Network Sector Nippon Telegraph & Telephone Corp.), 12-1 Yurakucho 1 Chome, Chiyodaku Tokyo 100 Japan.

ISSN 0027-707X
GW
CCC
CODEN NAZEAA
NTZ : NACHRICHTENTECHNISCHE ZEITSCHRIFT. [NTZ Nachrichtentech. Z.]. **Added/Corp** Nachrichtentechnische Gesellschaft. **VFOAT** NTZ-Communications Journal. (Oct. 1955)-. Trade Publication. German (English). Twelve times a year. $284.64. VDE Verlag GmbH, Postfach 122305, D-10591 Berlin Germany. **Tel** 011 49 30 3480010, FAX 011 49 30 3417093. **ED** Jurgen Gabel. cum. index. **Bk Rev. Ad Acc. Circ:** 7,109 (ctrl). Documents available from Article Express International, Ask*IEEE. **Continues FS :** Fernmeldetechnische Zeitschrift, 0367-2166; **Absorbed** NTZ-Communications Journal.
Desc: Software in communication engineering and optical communication engineering.
Ind/Abst Curr. Cit.; Ei Page One; Eng. Index Annu.; F&S Index Plus Text, Int. [Select. Cov.]; INSPEC (March 1987-); PROMT.

LC Z7165.J3 O25 HC465.A9
JA
OA KANREN SHINBUN KIJI SORAN. **Added/Corp** Joho Kagaku Kenkyujo (Tokyo, Japan). (1984)-. Japanese. Two times a year. ¥48000. Joho Kagaku Kenkyujo, (Institute for Information Science), 5-36 Akasaka 6 chome, Minatoku Tokyo 107 Japan.

ISSN 0838-6811
DD 384.1/4
CN
CEASED
OFFICIAL FAX DIRECTORY (CANADIAN ED.). (THE OFFICIAL FAX DIRECTORY.). [Off. Fax dir.]. (1986/87)-(19??). Periodical. English. Telinfomatic Inc., 800 56 Aberfoyle Cres. 7th Floor, Toronto Ontario M8X 2W4 Canada. **Tel** (416)236-2001. **Continues** FAX Directory, 0834-1079.

LC TK5103.59 .O673
DD 621.36/92/05
JA
CODEN JAOFDJ
OPTICAL DEVICES & FIBERS. VFOAT Optical Devices and Fibers. (1982)-. Academic Scholarly Publication. English. One time a year. Elsevier Science Publishers / Tokyo, 20-12, Yushima 3-chome, Bunkyo-ku, Tokyo 113 Japan. **ED** Y Suematsu. Documents available from CASDDS.
Ind/Abst Chem. Abstr.

US
OVERSEAS COMMON CARRIER SECTION 214 APPLICATIONS ACCEPTED FOR FILING. Main/Corp United States. Federal Communications Commission. (19??)-. Periodical. English. FCC / Federal Communications Commission, 1919 M Street Northwest, Room 538, Washington DC 20554. **Tel** (202)632-6302.

LC TK6195 .P18
DD 621.385
ISSN 0092-8828
US
P.B.X. SYSTEMS GUIDE. (PBX SYSTEMS GUIDE.). [P.B.X. syst. guide]. **Added/Corp** Marketing Programs and Services Group. (March 1972)-. English. Irregular. $595.00. The AFIES Group MPSG, 1350 Piccard Drive, Suite 300, Rockville MD 20850. **Tel** (301)840-0800.

US
●**PACIFIC RIM TELECOMMUNICATIONS.** (May 1993)-. English. Twelve times a year. $389.00 US and Canada; $409.00 other. Probe Research Inc., Three Wing Drive, Suite 240, Cedar Knolls NJ 07927-1000. **Tel** (201)285-1500, FAX (201)285-1519. **Absorbed** Japanese Telecommunications.
Desc: Written by telecommunications experts in Japan, Hong Kong and Australia. Covers public network services, private networks, cellular, ISDN, CATV, plus information on current profit potential in the region.

LC TK6570.M6 T45
DD 384.5/3/05
ISSN 1075-7821
US
CEASED
PCIA JOURNAL. (PCIA JOURNAL : THE MAGAZINE FOR THE PERSONAL COMMUNICATIONS INDUSTRY.). [PCIA j.]. **Added/Corp** Personal Communications Industry Association. **VFOAT** Personal Communications Industry Association Journal. Vol. 18, No. 2 (Feb. 1994)-(May 1995). Periodical. English. Business Word Inc., 5350 South Roslyn Street, Suite 400, Englewood CO 80111-2125. **Tel** (303)290-8500, FAX (303)290-9025. Index available (published in Dec. issue). **Continues** Telocator, 0193-1458.

LC HE9715.U6 P37
DD 384
ISSN 1077-9035
US
●**... PCS ATLAS & DATABOOK, THE.** [PCS atlas datab.]. **Added/Corp** Paul Kagan Associates. **VFOAT** PCS Atlas and Databook. (1994)-. English. One time a year. $895.00. Paul Kagan Associates Inc., 126 Clock Tower Place, Carmel CA 93923-8734. **Tel** (408)624-1536, FAX (408)625-3225, telex ITT 4938124 PKA UI.
Desc: Comprehensive research and data on personal communications services (PCS). Maps of 51 major trading areas and the 492 basic trading areas within them as well as the cellular service areas that overlap. Also demographic and economic data about each PCS market.

US
TITLE CHANGE
PERSONAL DEVICES REPORT. (July 1994)-(1995). English. Phillips Business Information Inc., 1201 Seven Locks Road, PO Box 61130, Potomac MD 20854. **Tel** (301)424-3338, (301)340-1520, (800)777-5005, FAX (301)424-4297, telex 358149. **Merged into** Wireless Data News.
Desc: Provides current information on the personal devices market, including hardware, software, services, applications and wireless solutions.

LC HE9443 .P47a
DD 384.6/025/598
IO
PERTAMINA, PETUNJUK TELEPON. **Main/Corp** Pertamina (Organization). **Added/Corp** Pertamina (Organization). Dinas Humas. Pertamina (Organization). Divisi Telekomunikasi. Pertamina (Organization). Pertamina Telephone Directory. **VFOAT** Pertamina Telephone Directory. (1974/75)-. Multiple languages (English and Indonesian). Usaha Advertising Company, Jalan Kemiri No 22, Jakarta Indonesia.

LC HE7677.B2 P45
DD 332.1/025
ISSN 0882-8296
US
PETERSON DIRECTORY. [Peterson dir.]. **Added/Corp** Peterson Cipher Code Company. (19??)-. Directory. English. Every 2 years. $50.00. Peterson Cipher Code Company, 37 West Fort Lee Road, Bogota NJ 07603. **Continues** Peterson Cable Address Directory.

ISSN 1078-9782
DD 384
US
●**PHILLIPS BUSINESS INFORMATION'S WIRELESS PRODUCT NEWS.** [Phillips Bus. Info. wirel. prod. news]. **Added/Corp** Phillips Business Information, Inc. **VFOAT** Wireless Product News. Vol. 10, No. 10 (Oct. 1994)-. Periodical. English. Twelve times a year. Phillips Business Information Inc., 1201 Seven Locks Road, PO Box 61130, Potomac MD 20854. **Tel** (301)424-3338, (301)340-1520, (800)777-5005, FAX (301)424-4297, telex 358149. **Continues** Mobile Product News, 1044-1190.

ISSN 1046-2007
DD 384
US
PHONE+ (SCOTTSDALE, ARIZ.). (PHONE+ : THE MONTHLY JOURNAL FOR THE PUBLIC COMMUNICATIONS INDUSTRY.). [Phone+]. **VFOAT** Phone Plus. (198?)-. Periodical. English. Twelve times a year. $55.00. Taurus Publishing Inc., 4141 North Scottsdale Road, Suite 316, Scottsdale AZ 85251. **Tel** (602)483-0014 ext. 172. **Continues** Telecommunications Equipment Retailer, 1045-0106.

US
PHONEDISC USA RESIDENTIAL (EASTERN & WESTERN EDITIONS). (PHONEDISC USA RESIDENTIAL CD-ROM.). (19??)-. English. Four times a year. $203.00 (single user), $302.50 (networking 2-10), $402.00 (networking 11-20). Digital Directory Assistance, 6931 Arlington Road, Suite 405, Bethesda MD 20814. **Tel** (800)284-8353, (301)657-8548. Index available. **Circ:** 1,000. **Continues** PhoneDisc Eastern Edition. CD-ROM; PhoneDisc Western Edition. CD-ROM.
Desc: Telephone directory on CD-ROM.

ISSN 1064-1068
DD 621
US
POF NEWSLETTER. [POF newsl.]. **Added/Corp** Information Gatekeepers, Inc. **VAT** Plastic Optical Fibers Newsletter. Vol. 1, No. 1 (July 1992)-. Newsletter. English. Six times a year. $275.00. Information Gatekeepers, Inc., 214 Harvard Avenue, Boston MA 02134. **Tel** (617)232-3111, (617)738-8088, (800)323-1088, FAX (617)734-8562.

LC TK5103 .P56
RU
POLUPROVODNIKOVAIA ELEKTRONIKA V TEKHNIKE SVIAZI. (19??)-. Periodical. Russian. 0.90rub. Izdatelstvo Sviaz, Christoprudnyi Bulvar D 2, 101000 Moscow Russia.

ISSN 0891-5628
DD 384
US
POST (CARLE PLACE, N.Y.). (POST.). [Post] (1986)-. Trade Publication. English. Twelve times a year. $40.00. Testa Communications, 25 Willowdale Avenue, Port Washington NY 11050. **Tel** (516)767-2500, FAX (516)767-9335. **ED** Ken McGorry. **Ad Acc.** ctrl circ.
Desc: An audio, video, television, and film professional journal. Targets creative, management, and other professionals who work in or use the services of post facilities / production houses.

ISSN 0390-5942
IT
UDC 621.39
POSTE E TELECOMUNICAZIONI NELLO SVILUPPO DELLA SOCIETA. See Communications-Postal Communications.

LC HE7601
DD 384
ISSN 1081-4329
US
Pr Rev.
●**PREMIER TELECARD MAGAZINE.** [Prem. telecard mag.]. (1993)-. Periodical. English. Six times a year. $30.00 US; $60.00 other. BJE Graphics & Publishing Inc., 935 Riverside Avenue, Suite 18, Paso Robles CA 93446. **Tel** (805)547-8500, FAX (805)237-2530. (**Subscription address:** BJE Graphics & Publishing Inc., PO Box 2297, Paso Robles CA 93447. **Tel** (805)547-8500.) **ED** Sean McElhiney. **Ad Acc, Adv Mgr:** Joe Smith, **Tel** (805)547-8500 ext. 2. **Circ:** 5,000.
Desc: Contains articles which appeal to a wide range of interests, from basic collecting tips to technical explanations about this new collectible.

ISSN 0266-0288
UK
PRESTEL DIRECTORY, THE. [Prestel dir.]. Directory. English. Four times a year. $30.65. Directel Ltd, 54 Hagley Road/12th Floor Edgbaston, Birmingham B16 8PE United Kingdom. **Tel** 011 44 121 4556585. **ED** Dawn Howell. **Bk Rev. Ad Acc. Circ:** 65,000 (ctrl). **Absorbed** Prestel Magazine; **Continues** Viewdata and TV User.
Desc: News and views on the world of viewdata. Directory of information and advertisements about products, and services on prestel. In a classified subject index format.

LC TK6675 .P28
DD 384.55/5/097305
ISSN 1080-9570
US
●**PRIVATE CABLE & WIRELESS CABLE.** [Priv. cable wirel. cable]. **VFOAT** Wireless Cable; PCWC; Private Cable and Wireless Cable. (1994)-. Periodical. English. Twelve times a year. National Satellite Publishing Inc, 1909 Avenue G, PO Box 1489, Rosenberg TX 77471. **Tel** (713)342-9826, FAX (713)342-2488. **Continues** Private Cable, 0745-8711.

LC HE7601
DD 384
ISSN 1077-3487
US
●**PRIVATE LINE : A JOURNAL OF INQUIRY INTO THE TELEPHONE SYSTEM.** [Priv. line]. Vol. 1, No. 1 (June 1994)-. Consumer Publication. English. Six times a year. $27.00. Private Line, 5150 Fair Oaks Boulevard, No. 101-348, Carmichael CA 95608. **Tel** (916)488-4231, FAX (916)978-0810. (**Subscription address:** Private Line, 2605 Del Monte Street, West Sacramento CA 95691. **Tel** FAX (916)373-3089.) Index available. **Ad Acc, Adv Mgr:** Tom Farley, **Tel** (916)488-4231. **Circ:** 850. available with illustrations; available from an online database.
Desc: Focuses on the technological side of the telephone system.

LC HE7601 .P76
DD 384/.05
ISSN 0195-9174
US
CEASED
PROBE TELECOMMUNICATIONS JOURNAL. (May/July 1977)-(19??). Periodical. English. Probe Research Inc., Three Wing Drive, Suite 240, Cedar Knolls NJ 07927-1000. **Tel** (201)285-1500, FAX (201)285-1519.

Communications —Telecommunication

LC TK5101.A1 I3544a
DD 621.382
US
●**PROCEEDINGS / IEEE PACIFIC RIM CONFERENCE ON COMMUNICATIONS, COMPUTERS AND SIGNAL PROCESSING.** **Added/Corp** Institute of Electrical and Electronics Engineers. Victoria Section. Institute of Electrical and Electronics Engineers. Canadian Region. University of Victoria (B.C.). Faculty of Engineering. (May 19th-21st, 1993)-. English. Every 2 years. IEEE / Institute of Electrical and Electronics Engineers Inc., 345 East 47th Street, New York NY 10017-2394. **Tel** (908)981-1393, FAX (908)981-9667. *Continues IEEE Pacific Rim Conference on Communications, Computers and Signal Processing. Conference Proceedings, 0893-4266.*

ISSN 0896-7229
DD 384
CEASED
PROCOMM ENTERPRISES MAGAZINE. [Procomm Enterp. mag.]. **VFOAT** Procomm; Procomm Magazine. (May 1987)-(Dec. 1993). Trade Publication. English. Procomm Enterprises, PO Box 886, San Anselmo CA 94960. **Tel** (415)459-4669. **ED** Jason Bray. Index available. cum. index. **Bk Rev. Ad Acc. Circ:** 30,000; (ctrl).
Desc: A monthly journal for the professional telecommunications/MIS manager.

LC TK5101.A1 P7
PL
CODEN PZTKAP
PRZEGLAD TELEKOMUNIKACYJNY. **Added/Corp** Stowarzyszenie Elektryków Polskich. Sekcja Telekomunikacyjna. (1928)-. Periodical. Polish. Twelve times a year. $99.00. **(Subscription address:** Ars Polona-Ruch, PO Box 1001, Krakowskie Przedmiescie 7, 00-068 Warsaw Poland. **Tel** 011 48 22 261201.) Documents available from Ask*IEEE.
Ind/Abst Ceram. Abstr.; Energy Res. Abstr.; INSPEC (1968-).

LC HD9697.T453 U555
ISSN 1041-6943
DD 384.6/0973/05
US
PUBLIC COMMUNICATIONS MAGAZINE. [Public commun. mag.]. **VFOAT** Information Publishing Corporation's Public Communications Magazine. Vol. 5, No. 1 (Jan. 1989)-. Trade Publication. English. Twelve times a year. $39.00. Multi-Media Publishing Corporation, PO Box 42190, Houston TX 77242. **Tel** (800)825-0061, (713)783-8999, FAX (713)783-9567. **ED** Eric Stebel and Larry Terry (phone: (713)974-5252). **Ad Acc, Adv Mgr:** Denise Fisher, **Tel** (804)320-4675. **Circ:** 10,000; (ctrl).
Continues Payphone Magazine, 0890-6742.
Desc: Provides information on the public communications industry, including payphones, private and public payphone operators, operator services providers as well as equipment manufacturers.

LC HE7771 .P85
ISSN 1042-9336
DD 384.1/4
US
PUBLIC FAX DIRECTORY, THE. [Public FAX dir.]. **Added/Corp** Public FAX, Inc. (198?)-. Directory. English. Four times a year. $40.00. Public FAX Inc, 9 Executive Circle/#230, Irving CA 92714.

US
PUBLIC NOTICE - FEDERAL COMMUNICATIONS COMMISSION. CABLE TELEVISION AUTHORIZATION ACTIONS. See Communications-Television and Cable.

US
PUBLIC NOTICE - FEDERAL COMMUNICATIONS COMMISSION. DOMESTIC PUBLIC LAND MOBILE RADIO SERVICE. See Communications-Radio.

US
PUBLIC NOTICE - FEDERAL COMMUNICATIONS COMMISSION. EXPERIMENTAL ACTIONS. **Main/Corp** United States. Federal Communications Commission. **VFOAT** Experimental Actions. (19??)-. Periodical. English. FCC / Federal Communications Commission, 1919 M Street Northwest, Room 538, Washington DC 20554. **Tel** (202)632-6302.

US
PUBLIC NOTICE - FEDERAL COMMUNICATIONS COMMISSION. SAFETY AND SPECIAL ACTIONS. **Main/Corp** United States. Federal Communications Commission. (19??)-. Periodical. English. FCC / Federal Communications Commission, 1919 M Street Northwest, Room 538, Washington DC 20554. **Tel** (202)632-6302.

ISSN 1072-9321
US
●**PUBLIC SAFETY ON-LINE.** **VFOAT** Public Safety On Line. (1993)-. English. Fulcrum Group, PO Box 335, Schwenksville PA 19473. *Formed by the union of Fulcrum Report, 1068-0977 and Dispatch Center Mangement, 1068-2023.*

ISSN 0409-0179
DD 621.3
YU
PUBLIKACIJE. SERIJA : ELEKTRONIKA, TELEKOMUNIKACIJE, AUTOMATIKA. See Electronics.

LC HE255.3.A15 P85
ISSN 0788-3080
FI
PUHELINYRITYSTEN TILINPAATOSTILASTO. **Added/Corp** Finland. Tilastokeskus. **VFOAT** Telefonforetagens Bokslutsstatistik; Financial Statements Statistics of Telephone Companies. (1989)-. Finnish (English and Swedish). Tilastokeskus, PL 504, Annankatu 44, 00101 Helsinki Finland. **Tel** 011 358 0 17341, FAX 011 358 0 17342474, telex 1002111 TILASTO SF. *Separated from Liikenteen Tilinpaatostilasto, 0784-8463.*

LC HE8090.7 .A35
ISSN 1070-9339
DD 384/.0947/05
US
●**PYRAMID RESEARCH EASTERN EUROPE.** [Pyramid Res. East. Eur.]. **Added/Corp** Pyramid Research (Firm). **VFOAT** Eastern Europe. Vol. 1, No. 1 (Jan. 1993)-. Periodical. English. Twelve times a year. $595.00. Pyramid Research Inc., 14 Arrow Street, Cambridge MA 02138. **Tel** (617)868-4725.

FR
QUOTIDIEN DES TELECOMS, LE. (19??)-. French. Seven times a week. 7051.91F France; 7500.00F other. Edicom, 21 rue Tournefort, F 75005 Paris France. **Tel** 011 33 1 47072929, FAX 011 33 1 47073066, 011 33 1 4703129. *Continues INF Telecom & Telematique.*

LC TK7800 .R37
ISSN 0033-7900
GW
RADIO, FERNSEHEN, ELEKTRONIK. (Jan. 1968)-. Trade Publication. German. Twelve times a year. $78.30. Verlag Technik GmbH Berlin, AM Friedrichshain 22, D-10407 Berlin Germany. **Tel** 011 49 30 428700. Documents available from Ask*IEEE. *Continues Radio und Fernsehen.*
Ind/Abst INSPEC (Sept. 1968-).

ISSN 0986-2900
UDC 654.165
FR
RADIOCOMMUNICATIONS MAGAZINE. (1987)-. Periodical. French. Six times a year. $104.98. Radiocommunications, 41 Bd Anatole France, F-93285 St. Denis Cedex France. **Tel** 011 33 1 48206372.
Ind/Abst Infomat Int. Bus.

LC TK7800 .R383
ISSN 0321-222X
RU
CODEN RAELE8
RADIOELEKTRONIKA I ELEKTROSVIAZ. [Radioelektron. elektrosvaz]. **Added/Corp** Rigas Politehniskais Instituts. (1973)-. Academic Scholarly Publication. Russian. 1.27rub. Documents available from CASDDS.
Ind/Abst Chem. Abstr. (1984-).

ISSN 1079-7874
DD 384
US
RAIL PRICE ADVISOR. [Rail price advis.]. **Added/Corp** Escalation Consultants, Inc. **VFOAT** RPA. (19??)-. Periodical. English. Four times a year. $220.00. Escalation Consultants Inc., PO Box 3566, Gaitherburg MD 20885. **Tel** (301)977-7459.

LC HE8141 .D57c
DD 384/.0944
FR
RAPPORT D'ACTIVITE. **Main/Corp** France. Direction Generale des Telecommunications. (19??)-. French. One time a year.

LC TK6555 .R35
ISSN 1062-3779
DD 384.5/34
US
RCR'S PAGING HANDBOOK. [RCR's paging handb.]. **VFOAT** Paging Handbook. 1st Ed. (1992)-. English. Every 2 years. $69.00. RCR Publications Inc., 777 East Spear Boulevard, Denver CO 80203-4214. **Tel** (303)733-2500, FAX (303)733-9941.

LC TK5101.A1 R39
RU
REFERATIVNYI ZHURNAL. 29, SVIAZ. **Added/Corp** Vsesoiuznyi Institut Nauchnoi i Tekhnicheskoi Informatsii (Soviet Union). **VFOAT** Sviaz. (1987)-. Abstracting/Indexing Service. Russian. Twelve times a year. $499.95. VINITI - Vsesoyuznyi Institut Nauchno-Tekhnicheskoi Informatsii, All-Union Scientific and Technical Information Institute, Baltiiskaia ulitsa 14, 125219 Moscow Russia. **Tel** 011 7 95 2384600, FAX 011 7 95 9430060, telex 411160. **(Subscription address:** East View Publications Inc., 3020 Harbor Lane North, Suite 110, Minneapolis MN 55447. **Tel** (800)477-1005, (612)550-0961, FAX (612)559-2931.)

LC TK6552 .F4
ISSN 1066-2731
DD 621.38
US
REFERENCE DATA FOR ENGINEERS : RADIO, ELECTRONICS, COMPUTER, AND COMMUNICATIONS. See Communications-Radio.

LC HE9046 .T44a
DD 384.6/3/0981
BL
RELATORIO DA ADMINISTRACAO - TELEBRAS. **Main/Corp** Telebras. (19??)-. Portuguese. Telebras / Ambaixador, SCS 4-BL No 49 Edifico Ambaixador, CP 1218 AG No 4, Brasilia Brazil.

LC HE8523 .A28a
DD 658.1/594
SL
REPORT AND ACCOUNTS - SIERRA LEONE EXTERNAL COMMUNICATIONS LIMITED. **Main/Corp** Sierra Leone External Telecommunications Limited. (19??)-. English. One time a year. External Telecommunications Ltd, 7 Lightfoot Boston Street, Freetown Sierra Leone.

LC HE7601 .I5
DD 384.5/1/05
SZ
REPORT BY THE INTERNATIONAL TELECOMMUNICATION UNION ON TELECOMMUNICATION AND THE PEACEFUL USES OF OUTER SPACE. **Main/Corp** International Telecommunication Union. **VFOAT** Report ITU Space; Report ITU/Space. English. International Telecommunication Union, place des Nations, CH-1211 Geneva 20 Switzerland. **Tel** 011 41 22 7305111, FAX 011 41 22 7337256. *Continues Report on Telecommunication and the Peaceful Uses of Outer Space.*

LC HE9719 .I59a
ISSN 1082-4901
DD 341.7/577
US
TITLE CHANGE
REPORT - INTERNATIONAL TELECOMMUNICATIONS SATELLITE ORGANIZATION. See Law.

LC HE7351 .A22a
DD 354.680072/32
SA
REPORT OF THE AUDITOR-GENERAL ON THE ACCOUNTS OF THE DEPARTMENT OF POSTS AND TELECOMMUNICATIONS. See Communications-Postal Communications.

ISSN 0741-8361
US
CCC
REPORT ON AT & T, THE. [Rep. AT&T]. **Added/Corp** Capitol Publications, Inc. **VFOAT** Report on A.T. & T.; Report on A.T. and T. (198?)-. Periodical. English. Twenty-four times a year. $697.00. Telecom Publishing Group, 1101 King Street, Suite 444, Alexandria VA 22314. **Tel** (703)683-4100, (800)327-7205, FAX (703)739-6490.
Ind/Abst PTS Newsl. Database [Full Txt.]; Trade Ind. Index.

US
REPORT ON ELECTRIC COMMERCE. English. Twenty-six times a year. $554.00 US; $589.00 other. Telecommunications Reports, 1333 H Street Northwest, 2nd Floor West Tower, Washington DC 20005. **Tel** (202)842-0520, (800)822-6338, FAX (202)842-3047. **(Subscription address:** Telecommunications Reports, PO Box 675, Cooper Station, New York NY 10276.)

ISSN 8755-3511
DD 384
US
REPORT ON TELCO MARKETING, THE. [Rep. telco mark.]. **VFOAT** Telco Marketing. Vol. 1, No. 1 (May 31, 1984)-. Periodical. English. Twenty-six times a year. $237.00. Telecom Publishing Group, 1101 King Street, Suite 444, Alexandria VA 22314. **Tel** (703)683-4100, (800)327-7205, FAX (703)739-6490.

ISSN 1071-4197
DD 384
US
CCC
TITLE CHANGE
REPORT ON TELECOM ADVERTISING & PUBLISHING, TA. [TA rep. telecom advert. publ.]. **VFOAT** TA Report. (1985)-(199?). Periodical. English. SIMBA Information Inc., 213 Danbury Road, PO Box 7430, Wilton CT 06897-7430. **Tel** (203)834-0033 ext. 173, FAX (203)884-1771. **(Subscription address:** Simba Information Inc., PO Box 7430, Wilton CT 06897. **Tel** (203)834-0033 ext. 160, FAX (203)834-1771.) *Continued by Telecom Advertising Report, 1082-5908.*

LC HE7700 .I474
SZ
REPORT ON THE ACTIVITIES OF THE INTERNATIONAL TELECOMMUNICATION UNION. **Main/Corp** International Telecommunication Union. **Added/Corp**

Communications — Telecommunication

International Telecommunication Union. General Secretariat. International Telecommunication Union. Report by the Secretary General of the International Telecommunication Union. (19??)-. English (French and Spanish). One time a year. International Telecommunication Union, place des Nations, CH-1211 Geneva 20 Switzerland. **Tel** 011 41 22 7305111, FAX 011 41 22 7337256. **Circ:** 3,000.

LC HD
DD 338
UDC 654
ISSN 1251-8964
FR

●**RESEAUX & TELECOMS (PARIS-LA-DEFENSE).** (RESEAUX & TELECOMS.). **VFOAT** Reseaux et Telecoms (Paris-La-Defense). (1993)-. Periodical. French. Twelve times a year. 770.81F France; 800.00F other. IDG Communications / France, Immeuble La Fayette Cedex 65, F-92051 Paris la Defense 5 France. **Tel** 011 33 1 49047900, FAX 011 33 1 49047870, telex 613234. **Continues** Telecoms Reseaux International, 1163-9180.

LC HE8141 .F737a
DD 384/0944/05
FR

RESULTATS FINANCIERS. Main/Corp France. Direction Generale des Telecommunications. (19??)-. French. Ministere des Postes et Telecommunications, Direction Generale des Telecommunications, 20 Avenue de Segur, 75700 Paris France.

LC TK5101.A1 R46
DD 384/.05
BL

REVISTA NACIONAL DE TELECOMUNICACOES (INTERNATIONAL EDITION). (REVISTA NACIONAL DE TELECOMUNICACOES : RNT.). **VFOAT** RNT; R.N.T. (1979)-. Periodical. Portuguese (English; translations available in Portuguese). Twelve times a year. Grafica e Editora, Ave Paulista 1159, CJ 1204, CEP 01311, Sao Paulo Brazil.

LC TK5101.A1 T316
BL

REVISTA TELEBRAS. Main/Corp Telebras. Vol. 1 (Oct. 1976)-. Periodical. Portuguese. Three times a year. Free on request. Telecomunicacoes Brasileiras SA, SAS Quadro 6 / Bloco H, Lotes 5 a 8, Caixa Postal 11 1218, CEP 70 313 Brasilia DF Brazil. **ED** Francisco Solano Borges Filho. **Circ:** 12,000.

ISSN 0035-0516
AG
CODEN RTELB2

Pr Rev.
REVISTA TELEGRAFICA ELECTRONICA. See Electronics.

LC TA1001 .R42
ISSN 0379-2390
RM

REVISTA TRANSPORTURILOR SI TELECOMUNICATIILOR. See Transportation.

ISSN 1180-4831
DD 343.7109/9/05
CN

REVUE DE DROIT MEDIA & COMMUNICATIONS. [Rev. droit media commun.]. **VFOAT** Revue de Droit Media et Communications; Media & Communications Law Review; Media and Communications Law Review. Vol. 1, No. 1 (Aug. 1990)-. Periodical. English (French). Irregular. $115.00 (bound v. and parts service), $90.00 (members of Canadian Bar Association). Carswell / Canada, 2075 Kennedy Road, Scarborough Ontario M1T 3V4 Canada. **Tel** (416)298-5092, (800)387-5164, FAX (416)298-5094. **Ind/Abst** Index Can. Leg. Period. Lit. (1992-).

ISSN 1243-7492
FR

UDC 654
●**REVUE DES TELECOMMUNICATIONS (PARIS. 1992).** (1992)-. Periodical. French (English, German, Spanish and Italian). Four times a year. Free on request. Electrical Communication / Alcatel, 54 rue la Boetie, 75008 Paris Cedex 08 France. **Tel** 011 33 1 40761347, 011 33 1 40761349, FAX 011 33 1 40761426.

FR

REVUE FRANCE TELECOM. French. Four times a year. 100.00F France; 150.00F other. 6 Place d'Alleray, 75740 Paris Cedex 15 France. **Tel** 011 33 1 44442330. **Continues** Revue Francaise des Telecommunications.

ISSN 0035-3248
BE
CEASED

LC TK5101.A1 R44
DD 384/.0981
BL

RNT. VFOAT R.N.T.; Revista Nacional de Telecomunicacoes. Periodical. Portuguese (English). Twelve times a year. $50.00. Telepress Editora Ltda, Av Paulista N 1159 10 Andar, 01311 Sao Paulo SP Brazil. **Tel** 55 11 2841599. **ED** Ethevaldo Siqueira. **Ad Acc.** **Circ:** 16,500 (ctrl). **Continues** Revista Nacional de Telecomunicacoes (Brazilian Edition).
Desc: News reports on telecommunications, Brazilian electronics industry and computer industry, data transmission. Also covers satellite communications and audio and video technologies.

ISSN 1046-6045
DD 384
US
TITLE CHANGE

RSA NEWSLETTER, THE. [RSA newsl.]. **Added/Corp** Paul Kagan Associates. **VAT** Rural Service Areas Newsletter. No. 1 (Sept. 20, 1989)-(1994). Newsletter. English. Paul Kagan Associates Inc., 126 Clock Tower Place, Carmel CA 93923-8734. **Tel** (408)624-1536, FAX (408)625-3225, telex ITT 4938124 PKA UI. **Continued by** Wireless Market Stats.

US

RULES AND REGULATIONS - FEDERAL COMMUNICATIONS COMMISSION.
VOLUME 1. Main/Corp United States. Federal Communications Commission. **VFOAT** Federal Communications Commission Rules and Regulations, Volume 1. (1??)-. Periodical. English. FCC / Federal Communications Commission, 1919 M Street Northwest, Room 538, Washington DC 20554. **Tel** (202)632-6302.

US

RULES AND REGULATIONS - FEDERAL COMMUNICATIONS COMMISSION.
VOLUME 2. Main/Corp United States. Federal Communications Commission. **VFOAT** Federal Communications Commission Rules and Regulations, Volume 2. (19??)-. Periodical. English. FCC / Federal Communications Commission, 1919 M Street Northwest, Room 538, Washington DC 20554. **Tel** (202)632-6302.

US

RULES AND REGULATIONS - FEDERAL COMMUNICATIONS COMMISSION.
VOLUME 3. Main/Corp United States. Federal Communications Commission. **VFOAT** Federal Communications Commission Rules and Regulations, Volume 3. (19??)-. Periodical. English. FCC / Federal Communications Commission, 1919 M Street Northwest, Room 538, Washington DC 20554. **Tel** (202)632-6302.

US

RULES AND REGULATIONS - FEDERAL COMMUNICATIONS COMMISSION.
VOLUME 4. Main/Corp United States. Federal Communications Commission. **VFOAT** Federal Communications Commission Rules and Regulations, Volume 4. (19??)-. Periodical. English. FCC / Federal Communications Commission, 1919 M Street Northwest, Room 538, Washington DC 20554. **Tel** (202)632-6302.

US

RULES AND REGULATIONS - FEDERAL COMMUNICATIONS COMMISSION.
VOLUME 5. Main/Corp United States. Federal Communications Commission. **VFOAT** Federal Communications Commission Rules and Regulations, Volume 5. (1??)-. Periodical. English. $18.20 US; $22.75 other. FCC / Federal Communications Commission, 1919 M Street Northwest, Room 538, Washington DC 20554. **Tel** (202)632-6302.

US

RULES AND REGULATIONS - FEDERAL COMMUNICATIONS COMMISSION.
VOLUME 7. Main/Corp United States. Federal Communications Commission. **VFOAT** Federal Communications Commission Rules and Regulations, Volume 7. (1??)-. Periodical. English. $7.70 US; $9.65 other. FCC / Federal Communications Commission, 1919 M Street Northwest, Room 538, Washington DC 20554. **Tel** (202)632-6302.

US

RULES AND REGULATIONS - FEDERAL COMMUNICATIONS COMMISSION.
VOLUME 8. Main/Corp United States. Federal Communications Commission. **VFOAT** Federal Communications Commission Rules and Regulations, Volume 8. (19??)-. English. FCC / Federal Communications Commission, 1919 M Street Northwest, Room 538, Washington DC 20554. **Tel** (202)632-6302.

US

RULES AND REGULATIONS - FEDERAL COMMUNICATIONS COMMISSION.
VOLUME 9. Main/Corp United States. Federal Communications Commission. **VFOAT** Federal Communications Commission Rules and Regulations, Volume 9. (19??)-. English. FCC / Federal Communications Commission, 1919 M Street Northwest, Room 538, Washington DC 20554. **Tel** (202)632-6302.

US

RULES AND REGULATIONS - FEDERAL COMMUNICATIONS COMMISSION.
VOLUME 10. Main/Corp United States. Federal Communications Commission. **VFOAT** Federal Communications Commission Rules and Regulations, Volume 10. (19??)-. English. FCC / Federal Communications Commission, 1919 M Street Northwest, Room 538, Washington DC 20554. **Tel** (202)632-6302.

US

RULES AND REGULATIONS - FEDERAL COMMUNICATIONS COMMISSION.
VOLUME 11. (RULES AND REGULATIONS - FEDERAL COMMUNICATIONS COMMISSION. VOLUME 11.). **Main/Corp** United States. Federal Communications Commission. **VFOAT** Federal Communications Commission Rules and Regulations, Volume 11. (19??)-. English. Irregular. FCC / Federal Communications Commission, 1919 M Street Northwest, Room 538, Washington DC 20554. **Tel** (202)632-6302.

ISSN 0737-7649
US

RULES AND REGULATIONS. PART 99, DISASTER COMMUNICATIONS SERVICE. (RULES AND REGULATIONS - FEDERAL COMMUNICATIONS COMMISSION. PART 99. DISASTER COMMUNICATIONS SERVICE.). **Main/Corp** United States. Federal Communications Commission. **VFOAT** Disaster Communications Service. (19??)-. English. FCC / Federal Communications Commission, 1919 M Street Northwest, Room 538, Washington DC 20554. **Tel** (202)632-6302.

LC HE8801 .R86
DD 384.6/0973
ISSN 0744-2548
US

RURAL TELECOMMUNICATIONS. (RURAL TELECOMMUNICATIONS : JOURNAL OF THE NATIONAL TELEPHONE COOPERATIVE ASSOCIATION.). [Rural telecommun.]. **Added/Corp** National Telephone Cooperative Association. Vol. 1, No. 1 (Winter 1982)-. Trade Publication. English. Six times a year (Jan., Mar., May, July, Sept., Nov.). $30.00. Cooperative Association, 2626 Pennsylvania Avenue Northwest, Washington DC 20037-1695. **Tel** (202)298-2300, FAX (202)298-2320. **ED** Lisa Westbrook, (phone: (202)298-2374). Index available (Bound in the 6th issue, Nov/Dec). **Bk Rev. Ad Acc. Adv Mgr:** Dave Bolton, **Tel** (202)298-2331. **Circ:** 5,000. available on microfilm and microfiche from University Microfilms International (UMI); available on an online database (file 15/Full-Text) from DIALOG. Documents available from UMI Article Clearinghouse. **Continues** Phone Call.
Desc: Covers legislative, regulatory, marketing, and management issues affecting small and rural telephone companies.
Ind/Abst ABI/INFORM Glob. Ed.; ABI/INFORM [Computer File] (Winter 1986-); UMI ABI/Inform--Bus. Period. Ondisc (Spring 1987-) [Full Txt.].

ISSN 1066-9612
DD 384
US

RUSSIAN FIBER OPTICS AND TELECOMMUNICATIONS BUSINESS. [Russ. fiber opt. telecommun. bus.]. **Added/Corp** Sankt-Peterburgskii Elektrotekhnicheskii Institut Sviazi im. prof. M.A. Bonch-Bruevicha. Information Gatekeepers, Inc. **VFOAT** Russian Fiber Optics Business Magazine; Russian Fiber Optics. Vol. 1, No. 1 (Summer 1992)-. Periodical. Four times a year. $250.00. Information Gatekeepers Inc., 214 Harvard Avenue, Boston MA 02134. **Tel** (617)232-3111, (617)738-8088, (800)323-1088, FAX (617)734-8562.

ISSN 1080-2169
DD 384
US

●**RUSSIAN TELECOM.** [Russ. telecom]. Vol. 1, No. 1 (Dec. 1994)-. Periodical. English. Twelve times a year. $575.00. Information Gatekeepers Inc., 214 Harvard Avenue, Boston MA 02134. **Tel** (617)232-3111, (617)738-8088, (800)323-1088, FAX (617)734-8562.

LC KES393.A329 S27
DD 343.7124/09943
ISSN 0844-7020
CN

SASKATCHEWAN TELECOMMUNICATIONS / SASKATCHEWAN PUBLIC UTILITIES REVIEW COMMISSION. [Sask. Telecommun.]. **Main/Corp** Saskatchewan Public Utilities Review Commission. English. Sturdy-Stone Centre, 122 3rd Avenue North, Saskatoon Saskatchewan S7K 2H6 Canada.

US

SATCOM QUARTERLY. Added/Corp Jet Propulsion Laboratory (U.S.). **VAT** Satellite Communications Quarterly. No. 1 (1991)-. Periodical. English. Four times a year. Jet Propulsion Laboratory, 4800 Oak Grove Drive / MS264-786, Pasadena CA 91103. **Tel** (818)354-5090.

ISSN 1043-0865
DD 384
US

SATELLITE BUSINESS NEWS. [Satell. bus. news]. Vol. 1, No. 1 (Dec. 28, 1988)-. Periodical. English. Twenty-six times a year. $44.75. Satellite Business News, 1050 17th Street Northwest, Suite 400, Washington DC 20036. **Tel** (202)785-0505. **ED** Bob Scherman. **Ad Acc, Adv Mgr:** Collette Loescher, **Tel** same as publisher. **Circ:** 9,000 (ctrl).

Communications —Telecommunication

Desc: A satellite, television and business publication.
Ind/Abst F&S Index Plus Text, Int. [Select. Cov.]; Mark. Advert. Ref. Serv.; PROMT.

LC TK5104 .S3636   ISSN 0147-7439
DD 621.38/0422   US
    CCC
    CODEN SACODH

SATELLITE COMMUNICATIONS. [Satell. commun.]. Vol. 1 No. 1 (Oct. 1977)-.
Trade Publication. English. Twelve times a year. $42.00. Argus Business, 6151 Powers Ferry Road Northwest, Atlanta GA 30339. **Tel** (404)995-2500, FAX (404)995-0400. **(Subscription address:** Sunbelt Fulfillment Services / Nashville, PO Box 41369, Nashville TN 37204. **Tel** (615)377-3322, (800)888-5139.) **Bk Rev. Ad Acc. Circ:** 11,166. available on microfilm and microfiche from University Microfilms International (UMI); available on an online database (files 15,648/Full-Text) from DIALOG. Documents available from UMI Article Clearinghouse, Ask*IEEE.
Desc: Magazine about commercial satellite communications covering regulatory government issues, finance, military technology, education, space commercialization and international issues.
Ind/Abst ABI/INFORM Glob. Ed.; ABI/INFORM [Computer File] (Jan. 1979-); Curr. Cit.; Ei Page One; F&S Index Plus Text, Int. [Select. Cov.]; INSPEC (Jan. 1979-); Int. Aerosp. Abstr.; PROMT; Trade Ind. ASAP [Full Txt.]; Trade Ind. Index [Full Txt.]; UMI ABI/Inform--Bus. Period. Ondisc (Jan. 1988-) [Full Txt.].

    ISSN 1195-9304
DD 384.5/1/0971   CN

SATELLITE COMMUNICATIONS IN CANADA . [Satell. commun. Can.]. Added/Corp Kirk Satellite Communications. Telesat Canada. (1989)-.
English. Irregular. 145.00Can$ per volume. Satellite Information Service, 1601 Telesat Court, Gloucester Ontario K1B 5P4 Canada. **Tel** (613)748-8785.

    ISSN 0742-7077
DD 338   US

SATELLITE DIRECTORY AND BUYERS GUIDE. [Satell. dir. buy. guide]. VFOAT Satellite Directory & Buyers Guide. (1984)-.
Directory. English. One time a year. Steve Tolin, PO Box 2772, Palm Springs CA 92263. **Tel** (310)874-4331. **Continues in part** Video Product News, 0271-5953.

    ISSN 0161-3448
    US
    CCC

SATELLITE NEWS. Vol. 1 (May 1978)-.
Periodical. English. Fifty times a year (weekly). $897.00. Phillips Business Information Inc., 1201 Seven Locks Road, PO Box 61130, Potomac MD 20854. **Tel** (301)424-3338, (301)340-1520, (800)777-5005, FAX (301)424-4297, telex 358149. **ED** Diane Dowling. available on an online database from DIALOG. **Absorbed** World Satellite Update.
Desc: Briefings on the hard news, marketing strategies, new laws and technology in the satellite industry.
Ind/Abst PROMT; PTS Newsl. Database [Full Txt.]; Trade Ind. ASAP [Full Txt.]; Trade Ind. Index [Full Txt.].

LC HE9719 .S28   ISSN 0737-9250
DD 384.5/1/025   US

SATELLITE SERVICES SOURCEBOOK, THE. [Satell. serv. sourceb.]. Added/Corp Technical Marketing Services, Ltd. 1st Ed. (1982)-.
English. One time a year. Satellite Services Sourcebook, PO Box 2010, Orlando FL 32802. **Tel** (407)422-6095.

    US

SATELLITE SITUATION REPORT.
Added/Corp Goddard Space Flight Center. Office of Public Affairs. Goddard Space Flight Center. Mission Operations Division. Operations Center Branch. Goddard Space Flight Center. Mission Operations Division. Control Center Support Section. Goddard Space Flight Center. Mission Operations Division. Project Operations Branch. (19??)-. English. Two times a year. Goddard Space Flight Center NASA, Code 513, Greenbelt MD 20771. **Tel** (301)286-8956. available on microfiche (Vols. for (1987) distributed to depository libraries). Documents available from Documents on Demand.
Ind/Abst Am. Stat. Index.

LC TK5104 .S372   ISSN 1078-8298
DD 384.5/1   US
    TITLE CHANGE

SATELLITE SYSTEMS HANDBOOK.
(19??)-(1994). Directory. English. Phillips Business Information Inc., 1201 Seven Locks Road, PO Box 61130, Potomac MD 20854. **Tel** (301)424-3338, (301)340-1520, (800)777-5005, FAX (301)424-4297, telex 358149. **Merged into** World Satellite Almanac.
Desc: Provides technical details of all commercial satellite systems and operators. Included are EIRP footprint maps for satellites showing area coverage and signal strength, booking contacts and PTT decision makers.

    ISSN 1079-820X
DD 384   US

●**SATELLITE TECH JOURNAL.** [Satell. tech j.]. (1993)-. Periodical. English. Six times a year. $29.00. Morgan Communication Co., PO Box 475, Rose City MI 48654. **Tel** (517)685-3970.

    ISSN 0193-2861
    US
    CCC

SATELLITE WEEK. Vol. 1 (July 30, 1979)-.
Trade Publication. English. One time a week. $903.00. Warren Publishing, Inc., 2115 Ward Court Northwest, Washington DC 20037. **Tel** (202)872-9200, FAX (202)293-3435. **ED** Daniel Warren. available on an online database (files 16,80,636/Full-Text) from DIALOG.
Desc: Covering space technology and communications, including personnel, regulatory matters, features, current developments, key issues, etc.
Ind/Abst PROMT [Full Txt.]; PTS Newsl. Database [Full Txt.].

    ISSN 1059-8413
DD 384   US

SBN UPDATE. (SBN UPDATE : A NEWSLETTER OF THE SATELLITE BAR NETWORK.). [SBN update].
Added/Corp Satellite Bar Network.a. **VAT** Satellite Bar Network Update. Vol. 1, No. 1 (Sept. 1991)-. Newsletter. English. Satellite Bar Network, 8094 Rolling Road, Suite 900, Springfield VA 22153.

●**SHOSTECK'S CELLULAR STRATEGIES.** (1995)-. Newsletter. English. Six times a year. $347.00. Herchel Shosteck Association Ltd., 11160 Viers Mill Road, Suite 709, Wheaton MD 20902. **Tel** (301)589-2259, FAX (301)588-3311.
Desc: Industry information about cellular telephones for business executives.

    IT

SISTEMI DI TELECOMUNICAZIONI.
(19??)-. Italian. Eleven times a year. L80000 Italy; L150000 other. Edizioni Iens, Via Taramelli 19, 20124 Milan Italy. **Tel** 011 39 2 6881371.

LC TK5104 .S62   ISSN 0924-8625
DD 621.382/38   NE
    CCC
    CODEN SPCCEJ

SPACE COMMUNICATIONS. [Space commun.]. Vol. 7, No. 1 (Dec. 1989)-.
Periodical. English. Four times a year. $280.92. IOS Press, Van Diemenstraat 94, 1013 CN Amsterdam Netherlands. **Tel** 011 31 20 6382189, FAX 011 31 20 6203419. available in microform from University Microfilms International (UMI). Documents available from Article Express International, The Genuine Article, Ask*IEEE. **Continues** Space Communication and Broadcasting, 0167-9368.
Ind/Abst Curr. Cit.; Curr. Contents Eng. Comput. Technol.; Ei Page One; Eng. Index Annu.; INSPEC (1989-); Int. Aerosp. Abstr.; Res. Alert [Select. Cov.].

LC TL796.6.E2 S67
DD 384.5/1   US

SPACE SATELLITE HANDBOOK. See
Aeronautics, Astronautics.

    US

●**STATE AND LOCAL COMMUNICATIONS REPORT.** (1995)-. English. Twenty-five times a year. $499.00. Telecommunications Reports, 1333 H Street Northwest, 2nd Floor West Tower, Washington DC 20005. **Tel** (202)842-0520, (800)822-6338, FAX (202)842-3047. **(Subscription address:** Telecommunications Reports, PO Box 675, Cooper Station, New York NY 10276.) **Continues** Telecommunications Week.

    US

STATE DIRECTORY OF O.G.S. INTEGRATED TELECOMMUNICATIONS SYSTEMS. Added/Corp New York (State). Office of General Services. Division of Telecommunications. VAT
State directory of Office of General Services Integrated Telecommunications Systems. (1988)-. Directory. English. One time a year. $4.50. Office of General Services, 27 FL Corning Tower EMP ST PL, Albany NY 12242. **Tel** (518)474-5575, (518)474-7947. **Continues** Statewide Telephone Directory.

    US

STATE OF CALIFORNIA TELEPHONE DIRECTORY. Main/Corp California. Dept. of
General Services. **VFOAT** State Offices Telephone Directory. (April 1969)-. Directory. English. One time a year. $13.40. California General Services, Publication Section, PO Box 1015, North Highlands CA 95660. **Tel** (916)445-1020. **Continues** State Offices Telephone Directory.

LC JK7830 .S73   ISSN 1052-5114
DD 353.9788001/0025   US

STATE OF COLORADO TELEPHONE DIRECTORY. Added/Corp Colorado. Division of
Central Services. Colorado. Division of Communications.

(19??)-. Directory. English. One time a year. $10.00. Craftsman Publication, PO Box 12476, El Paso TX 79912. **Tel** (915)584-7791. available on microfiche (by National Directory Services, Spring, Tex.).

    ISSN 0741-8388
    US
    CCC

STATE TELEPHONE REGULATION REPORT. [State teleph. regul. rep.]. Added/Corp
Capitol Publications, Inc. Telecom Publishing Group. Vol. 1, No. 1 (Nov. 24, 1983)-. Periodical. English. Twenty-six times a year. $535.00. Telecom Publishing Group, 1101 King Street, Suite 444, Alexandria VA 22314. **Tel** (703)683-4100, (800)327-7205, FAX (703)739-6490. **(Subscription address:** Telecom Publishing Group, PO Box 1455, Alexandria VA 22313. **Tel** 800 327-7205, (703)683-4100.) available on an online database (file 636/Full-Text) from DIALOG.
Ind/Abst PTS Newsl. Database [Full Txt.].

LC HE8801 .S7   ISSN 0731-8251
DD 384.6/3   US
    TITLE CHANGE

STATISTICAL REPORT. RURAL TELEPHONE BORROWERS. See
Communications-Abstracting, Bibliographies and Statistics.

    ISSN 0161-5173
DD 384   US

STATISTICS OF COMMUNICATIONS COMMON CARRIERS. See
Communications-Abstracting, Bibliographies and Statistics.

LC HE8801 .S73   ISSN 1054-7886
DD 384.6/0973/021   US

STATISTICS OF THE LOCAL EXCHANGE CARRIERS. See
Communications-Abstracting, Bibliographies and Statistics.

    ISSN 1190-9978
DD 382   CN

●**STRATEGIE D'EXPORTATION DU CANADA, PLAN DE PROMOTION DU COMMERCE EXTERIEUR. 15, TECHNOLOGIES DE L'INFORMATION ET TELECOMMUNICATIONS.** [Strateg. export. Can. plan promot. commer. exter., 15 Technol. inf. telecommun.]. **Added/Corp** Canada. **VFOAT** Technologies de l'Information et Telecommunications. (1996)-. Government Publication. French. Irregular. **Continues** Plan de Promotion du Commerce Exterieur du Canada. 16, Technologie de l'Information, 1200-1376.

    ISSN 0970-1664
    II
UDC 621.39

STUDENTS' JOURNAL OF THE INSTITUTION OF ELECTRONICS AND TELECOMMUNICATION ENGINEERS.
See Engineering-Electrical Engineering.

    ISSN 1070-096X
DD 384   US

●**SUBMARINE FIBER OPTIC COMMUNICATIONS SYSTEMS.** (SUBMARINE FIBER OPTIC COMMUNICATIONS SYSTEMS : SFOCS.). [Submar. fiber optic commun. syst.]. **VFOAT** SFOCS; Submarine Fiber Optic Systems Newsletter. Vol. 1, No. 1 (June 1993)-. Newsletter. English. Twelve times a year. $575.00. Information Gatekeepers Inc., 214 Harvard Avenue, Boston MA 02134. **Tel** (617)232-3111, (617)738-8088, (800)323-1088, FAX (617)734-8562.

    ISSN 1048-8359
DD 371   US

T.I.E. NEWS. [T.I.E. news]. Added/Corp
International Society for Technology in Education. Special Interest Group for Telecommunications. **VFOAT** TIE News; Iste Sigtel Newsletter. **VAT** Telecommunications in Education News. Vol. 1, No. 1 (Winter 1990)-. Periodical. English. Four times a year. $29.00. International Society for Technology in Education ISTE, University of Oregon, 1787 Agate Street, Eugene OR 97403-1923. **Tel** (503)346-4414, FAX (503)346-5890.
Desc: Supports and promotes telecommunications as a tool for the enhancement of learning and the delivery of instruction.

    HK

TE & MS TELECOM ASIA. English (Chinese).
Four times a year. $25.00. Edgell Communications, Two Illinois Center, 24th Floor, 233 North Michigan Avenue, Chicago IL 60601. **Tel** (312)938-2381, FAX (312)938-4854. **ED** Bob Stoffels. **Bk Rev. Ad Acc. Circ:** 12,000 (ctrl).

Communications — Telecommunication

Desc: Circulated to government owned and operated telecommunications administration and to the communications departments of businesses, industry and others who use and operate commercial and private networks. It is edited for planning, engineering and operational managers responsible for the design, installation, marketing and maintenance of public or private telecom systems.

LC HE7601
DD 384.1
BE

TECH-EUROPE. **Added/Corp** Europe Information Service. **VAT** Tech Europe. (19??)-. Government Publication. English (French). Twelve times a year. $763.07. Europe Information Service, rue de Geneve 6, 1140 Brussels Belgium. **Tel** 011 32 2 242 6020, FAX 011 32 2 242 9549. **ED** Eve Damiens. **Ad Acc, Adv Mgr:** Lucyna Grauer. **Circ:** 500. available on an online database (file 636/Full-Text) from DIALOG.

LC TK5101.A1 I472a
DD 621.38/05
US

TECHNICAL PROGRESS REPORT FOR THE PERIOD ... / INSTITUTE FOR TELECOMMUNICATION SCIENCES OF THE NATIONAL TELECOMMUNICATIONS AND INFORMATION ADMINISTRATION. **Main/Corp** Institute for Telecommunication Sciences. **Added/Corp** United States. Dept. of Commerce. (199?)-. English. Publications NTIA/ITS, 325 Broadway, Boulder CO 80303. **Tel** (303)497-3572. **Continues** Institute for Telecommunication Sciences. ITS ... Technical Progress Report.

LC TK5101.A1 I355
DD 621.38/05
ISSN 0255-9609
II

TECHNICAL REVIEW - IETE. (IETE TECHNICAL REVIEW.). [Tech. rev. - IETE]. **Added/Corp** Institution of Electronics and Telecommunication Engineers (India). **VFOAT** I.E.T.E. Technical Review. Vol. 1, No. 1 (Jan. 1984)-. Periodical. English. Six times a year. Institution of Electronics and Telecommunication Engineers, 2 Institutional Area, Lodi Road, New Delhi 110003 India. **Tel** 011 91 11 4631830, 011 91 11 4610324. **(Subscription address:** Prints India, 11 Darya Ganj, New Delhi 110002 India. **Tel** 011 91 11 3268645, FAX 011 91 11 3275542, telex 31-61087 PRIN-IN.**) Bk Rev. Ad Acc.** Documents available from Ask*IEEE. **Separated from** Journal of the Institution of Electronics and Telecommunication Engineers. **Ind/Abst** Curr. Cit.; INSPEC (Jan. 1984-).

DD 338.4/762139/0971
ISSN 1180-3703
CN
CEASED

TECHNOLOGY WATCH (WILLOWDALE). See Computers-Computer Industry and Industry Directories.

DD 384
ISSN 1073-8134
US
CCC

●**TELCO BUSINESS REPORT.** [Telco bus. rep.]. **VFOAT** Telco Business. (1993)-. Periodical. English. Twenty-four times a year. Telecom Publishing Group, 1101 King Street, Suite 444, Alexandria VA 22314. **Tel** (703)683-4100, (800)327-7205, FAX (703)739-6490. **Continues** Telephone Week, 1062-4724.

US

TELCO COMPETITION REPORT. English. Twenty-six times a year. $499.00 US; $535.00 other. Telecommunications Reports, 1333 H Street Northwest, 2nd Floor West Tower, Washington DC 20005. **Tel** (202)842-0520, (800)822-6338, FAX (202)842-3047. **(Subscription address:** Telecommunications Reports, PO Box 675, Cooper Station, New York NY 10276. **)**

US

TELCOM DATA REPORT. (19??)-. English. Twenty-six times a year. $498.00 US; $533.00 other. Telecommunications Reports, 1333 H Street Northwest, 2nd Floor West Tower, Washington DC 20005. **Tel** (202)842-0520, (800)822-6338, FAX (202)842-3047. **(Subscription address:** Telecommunications Reports, PO Box 675, Cooper Station, New York NY 10276. **)**

LC HD
DD 338
ISSN 0890-1198
US
Pr Rev.

TELCOM HIGHLIGHTS. [Telcom highlights]. (19??)-. Periodical. English. One time a week. $425.00. Telcom Highlights, PO Box 1609, Paramus NJ 07653. **Tel** (201)265-7236, FAX (201)265-7236. **ED** George Chevalier. **Circ:** 450 (ctrl).

UDC 621.395
ISSN 0344-4724
GW
CCC

TELCOM REPORT DEUTSCHE AUSGABE. [Telcom rep. Dtsch. Ausg.]. (1978)-. Trade Publication. German. Six times a year. $87.51. Siemens AG ZWD V Verlag, Naegelsbachstrasse 26, D-91052 Erlangen Germany. **Tel** 011 49 9131 723004, FAX 011 49 9131 725022. **(Subscription address:** VCH Publishers Inc., 303 Northwest 12th Avenue, Journals Department, Deerfield FL 33442. **Tel** (800)367-8249, (305)428-5566.**) Continues** Telefon-Report, 0340-7535.

LC TK5101.A1 T29
DD 621.38/05
ISSN 0344-4880
GW
CCC

TELCOM REPORT (ENGLISH EDITION). (TELCOM REPORT.). [Telcom report]. **Added/Corp** Siemens Aktiengesellschaft. (Feb. 1978)-. Trade Publication. English. Six times a year. $86.00. Siemens AG ZWD V Verlag, Naegelsbachstrasse 26, D-91052 Erlangen Germany. **Tel** 011 49 9131 723004, FAX 011 49 9131 725022. **(Subscription address:** VCH Publishers Inc., 303 Northwest 12th Avenue, Journals Department, Deerfield FL 33442. **Tel** (800)367-8249, (305)428-5566.**)** Documents available from Article Express International, Ask*IEEE. **Continues** Telefon Report, 0341-6488. **Ind/Abst** Curr. Cit.; Ei Page One; Eng. Index Annu. [Select. Cov.]; Ergon. Abstr.; INSPEC (Jan./Feb. 1990-); World Publ. Monit.

LC HE8261 .T44
ISSN 0040-2427
SZ
CODEN TELEBZ

TELE. [Tele]. Periodical. German. One time a week. $84.70 Austria, Cyprus, Finland, France, Germany, Greece, Iceland, Italy, Malta, Netherlands, Norway, Portugal, Spain, Sweden, Turkey, Yugoslavia, Denmark, Luxembourg; $115.30 other. Ringier & Co. AG, Florastrasse, CH-4800 Zofingen Switzerland. **Tel** 011 41 62 503110. Documents available from Ask*IEEE. **Continues** Tekniska Meddelanden Fran K. Telegrafstyrelsen. **Ind/Abst** INSPEC (1971-); World Publ. Monit.

ISSN 0153-0747
FR

UDC 791

TELE 7 JOURS. VFOAT Tele Sept Jours. (1960)-. Periodical. French. One time a week. $104.98. Tele 7 Jours, 6 rue Ancelle, 9220 Neuilly SUR Seine France. **Tel** 011 33 1 408860000.

ISSN 0739-7208
US

TELE CONFERENCE. Added/Corp Applied Business Communications. Applied Business Telecommunications. **VFOAT** Teleconference. (198?)-. Periodical. English. Six times a year. $60.00. Applied Business Telecommunications, Box 5106, San Ramon CA 94583. **Tel** (510)820-5563, FAX (510)820-5894.

ISSN 0495-0127
SW

UDC 654

TELE ENGLISH EDITION. (TELE.). (1950)-. Periodical. English. Two times a year. Kr100.00. Swedish Telecommunication Administration, Marbackagatan 11, S-12386 Farsta Sweden. **Tel** 011 46 8 7131000, 7135862. Documents available from Ask*IEEE. **Ind/Abst** Ei Page One; INSPEC (1971-).

US

TELE-TIPS LONG DISTANCE RATE COMPARISON CHART. English. Every 2 years. $25.00. Telecommunications Research & Action Center, PO Box 12038, Washington DC 20005. **Tel** (202)466-8407. **ED** Jacci Gruninger. **Circ:** 5,000. **Continues** Citizens Media Directory. **Desc:** Newsletter that compares long distance rates.

LC WMLC 93/4942
US

●**TELECARD WORLD. VFOAT** Tele Card World; Multimedia Publishing's Telecard World. Vol. 1, No. 1 (1994)-. English. Twelve times a year. $36.00. Telecard World, PO Box 6246, Syracuse NY 13217. **Tel** (800)825-0061.

FR

TELECOM. French. Four times a year. 250.00F. AAIENST, 46 rue Barrault, 75634 Paris Cedex France. **Tel** 011 33 1 45509984, FAX 011 33 1 45896950. **ED** Jean-Philippe Henry. **Bk Rev. Ad Acc, Adv Mgr:** S. Mariani, **Tel** 011 33 1 45818048. **Circ:** 4,000. **Desc:** Information on communications technology.

LC HE
DD 384
ISSN 1082-5908
US

●**TELECOM ADVERTISING REPORT.** [Telecom advert. rep.]. **Added/Corp** SIMBA Information Inc. Vol. 11, No. 4 (Feb. 27, 1995)-. Periodical. English. Twenty-four times a year. $498.00. SIMBA Information Inc., 213 Danbury Road, PO Box 7430, Wilton CT 06897-7430. **Tel** (203)834-0033 ext. 173, FAX (203)884-1771. **Continues** TA Report on Telecom Advertising & Publishing, 1071-4197.

DD 384/.0971
ISSN 1195-5759
CN

TELECOM ADVISOR. (THE TELECOM ADVISOR.). [Telecom advis.]. **Added/Corp** Telecommunications Management Consultants. (Oct. 1988)-. English. Four times a year. 80.04Can$. TMC/Telecommunications Management Consultants Inc., 1500 West Georgia Street, Suite 1400, Vancouver BC V6G 2Z6 Canada. **Tel** (604)683-1103, (800)663-4TMC, FAX (604)685-1520. **ED** E. V. (Ted) Hird and Jeannie Coleman. **Ad Acc. Circ:** 2,200. **Desc:** Gives information on data and voice communications, as well as advice and projects management for clients.

LC TK5101.A1 T266
DD 384/.095
US

TELECOM ASIA : TECHNOLOGY FOR THE ASIAN/PACIFIC TELECOM NETWORK = YA-CHOU TIEN HSIN. Added/Corp Advanstar Communications. **VFOAT** Ya-Chou Tien Hsin. (199?)-. Periodical. English (Chinese). Six times a year. $120.00. CCI Asia Pacific Ltd, Unit 101, 1 F Pacific Plaza, 410 D Voeux Road, Hong Kong, Honk Kong. **Tel** 011 852 28580789, 011 852 29641330. **Continues** TE & M's Ttelecom Asia, 1055-4432. **Ind/Abst** MasterFile FullTEXT (Jan. 1995-).

ISSN 0339-9486
FR

UDC 65

TELECOM INFO. (TELECOM INFO. FRENCH EDITION.). (1975)-. Periodical. French. One time a week (except Aug. and certain holidays). 7300.00F France. Telecom Info, 3 rue Tronchet, F-75008 Paris France. **Tel** 011 33 1 42651152. **Desc:** Telecommunications business information in France and internationally.

ISSN 0712-3663
US

DD 381/.4562138/0971
TITLE CHANGE

TELECOM MARKET LETTER, THE. [Telecom mark. lett.]. **Added/Corp** Northern Business Intelligence. Northern Business Information. Vol. 1, No. 1 (April 15, 1980)-(199?). Periodical. English. Northern Business Information, 157 Chambers Street, 7th Floor, New York NY 10007-1015. **Tel** (212)732-0775, FAX (212)233-6233. **ED** Michael Miller. Index available. cum. index. **Circ:** 300 (ctrl). **Merged with** Telecom Strategy Letter, 0739-683X **to form** Northern Business Information's Telecom Perspectives, 1078-523X. **Desc:** Covers telecommunications news, interviews and analysis. **Ind/Abst** Predicasts.

US

TELECOM REPORTS WIRELESS NEWS. English. Twenty-six times a year. $497.00 US; $533.00 other. Telecommunications Reports, 1333 H Street Northwest, 2nd Floor West Tower, Washington DC 20005. **Tel** (202)842-0520, (800)822-6338, FAX (202)842-3047. **(Subscription address:** Telecommunications Reports, PO Box 675, Cooper Station, New York NY 10276. **)**

DD 621
ISSN 0898-9087
US

TELECOM RESOURCES. (TELECOM RESOURCES : A MONTHLY LISTING OF PUBLICATIONS BY TELECOM PUBLISHING GROUP.). [Telecom resour.]. **Added/Corp** Telecom Publishing Group. (1985)-. Periodical. English. Twelve times a year. Free on request. Telecom Publishing Group, 1101 King Street, Suite 444, Alexandria VA 22314. **Tel** (703)683-4100, (800)327-7205, FAX (703)739-6490.

DD 384/.09714
ISSN 0820-8018
CN

TELECOM (SAINTE-FOY). (TELECOM.). [Telecom]. Vol. 1, No. 1 (April 1978)-. Periodical. French. Free. Mediatheque Universite du Quebec, 2875 boulevard Laurier, Sainte-Foy Quebec G1V 2M3 Canada.

DD 384
ISSN 1064-1076
US

TELECOM STANDARDS NEWSLETTER. [Telecom stand. newsl.]. **Added/Corp** Information Gatekeepers, Inc. (1992)-. Newsletter. English. Twelve times a year. $195.00. Information Gatekeepers Inc., 214 Harvard Avenue, Boston MA 02134. **Tel** (617)232-3111, (617)738-8088, (800)323-1088, FAX (617)734-8562. **ED** R.T. Bobilin. **Desc:** A newsletter describing telecommunications standards activities.

DD 384
ISSN 1057-6002
US

TELECOM TEN YEAR CALENDAR. [Telecom ten year cal.]. **VFOAT** Telecom Calendar Newsletter. (199?)-. Newsletter. English. Four times a year. $275.00 US and Canada; $315.00 other. Information Gatekeepers Inc., 214 Harvard Avenue, Boston MA 02134. **Tel** (617)232-3111, (617)738-8088, (800)323-1088, FAX (617)734-8562.

JA

TELECOM TRIBUNE. Trade Publication. English. Twelve times a year. $50.00. **(Subscription address:** Japan Publications Trading Company Ltd., PO Box 5030, Tokyo International, Tokyo 100-31 Japan. **Tel** 011 81 3 3292 3753.**) Desc:** Trade journal specialized in telecommunications and high technology.

Communications — Telecommunication

LC HE8091 .B73   **ISSN** 0963-0597
UK
CODEN TEWOEL
TELECOM WORLD. [Telecom world].
Added/Corp British Telecom. **VFOAT** Telecom. (June 1991)-. Periodical. English. Four times a year. £14.00 UK; £18.50 Europe; £24.00 other. Just Write Publishing Ltd., PO Box 664 9, Andrewes House, London EC2Y 8EH United Kingdom. **Tel** 011 44 171 9200022, FAX 011 44 171 9200041. **ED** Justin Quillinan. **Bk Rev. Ad Acc. Circ:** 18,000 (ctrl). available on an online database (file 648/Full-Text) from DIALOG. Documents available from Ask*IEEE. **Continues** British Telecom World, 0953-8429. **Ind/Abst** INSPEC (1991-); Trade Ind. ASAP [Full Txt.]; Trade Ind. Index [Full Txt.].

NE
TELECOMBRIEF. English. Twenty-four times a year. EDP Publications BV, Postbus 9525, 4801 LM Breda The Netherlands. **Tel** 011 31 76 220059.

LC TF5101   **ISSN** 1355-3429
DD 621.3845   UK
●**TELECOMEUROPA'S ADVANCED CORDLESS COMMUNICATIONS.**
[Telecomeuropa's adv. cordless commun.]. **VFOAT** Advanced Cordless Communications. (1994)-. Newsletter. English. Twelve times a year. £595.00. Telecomeuropa, 3 Princes Building, George Street, Bath BA1 2ED United Kingdom. **Tel** 011 44 1225 445282, FAX 011 44 1225 445283. **ED** Ian Channing.

LC TF5101   **ISSN** 1357-3446
DD 384.3   UK
●**TELECOMEUROPA'S COMPUTER TELEPHONY WORLD REPORT.**
[Telecomeuropa's comput. teleph. world rep.]. **VFOAT** Computer Telephony World Report. (1995)-. Newsletter. English. Twelve times a year. £595.00. Telecomeuropa, 3 Princes Building, George Street, Bath BA1 2ED United Kingdom. **Tel** 011 44 1225 445282, FAX 011 44 1225 445283. **ED** Bob Whitehouse.

LC TF5101   **ISSN** 1354-1331
DD 621.382   UK
●**TELECOMEUROPA'S CUSTOMER CARE AND BILLING.** [Telecomeuropa's custom. care billing]. (1994)-. Newsletter. English. Twelve times a year. £595.00. Telecomeuropa, 3 Princes Building, George Street, Bath BA1 2ED United Kingdom. **Tel** 011 44 1225 445282, FAX 011 44 1225 445283. **ED** Cris Thomas.
Desc: Customer care billing for mobile and fixed network operators.

ISSN 0962-3825
DD 384.0947   UK
TELECOMEUROPA'S EASTERN EUROPE NEWSLETTER. [Telecomeur. East. Eur. newsl.]. (1991)-. Newsletter. English. Twelve times a year. £745.00. Telecomeuropa, 3 Princes Building, George Street, Bath BA1 2ED United Kingdom. **Tel** 011 44 1225 445282, FAX 011 44 1225 445283. **ED** Peter Purton.

ISSN 0958-8515
DD 621.382   UK
TELECOMEUROPA'S ISDN NEWSLETTER. [Telecomeur. ISDN newsl.]. **VFOAT** Telecomeuropa's Integrated Services Digital Networks Newsletter. (1989)-. Periodical. English. Twelve times a year. $847.05. Telecomeuropa, 3 Princes Building, George Street, Bath BA1 2ED United Kingdom. **Tel** 011 44 1225 445282, FAX 011 44 1225 445283.
Desc: Latest news and analysis on all aspects of telecommunications across Europe.

LC TF5101   **ISSN** 1357-2865
DD 621.382   UK
●**TELECOMEUROPA'S MARKETING TELECOMS.** [Telecomeur. mark. telecoms]. (1994)-. Newsletter. English. Twelve times a year. £595.00. Telecomeuropa, 3 Princes Building, George Street, Bath BA1 2ED United Kingdom. **Tel** 011 44 1225 445282, FAX 011 44 1225 445283. **ED** Lance Hiley.
Desc: Covers marketing and advertising for telecom equipment marketers and servicers.

ISSN 0958-8523
DD 621.3845   UK
●**TELECOMEUROPA'S PERSONAL COMMUNICATIONS NEWSLETTER.**
[Telecomeur. pers. commun. newsl.]. (1990)-. English. Twelve times a year. £325.00 UK; $500.00 US; DM970.00 Germany; 858.00F Switzerland; Kr3,380 Sweden; Fl1096 Netherlands; ¥74990 Japan; L709,560 Italy; 3,290F France; 660.00Aus$ Australia. Telecomeuropa, 3 Princes Building, George Street, Bath BA1 2ED United Kingdom. **Tel** 011 44 1225 445282, FAX 011 44 1225 445283.
Desc: Helps identify business opportunities, growth markets, potential partners and new product ideas in the world of cordless communications.

NE
TELECOMMAGAZINE. Dutch. Twelve times a year. VNU Business Publications BV, Postbus 9194, 1006 AC Amsterdam Netherlands. **Tel** 011 31 20 4875879.

ISSN 0957-4611
DD 016.62138   UK
TELECOMMS ABSTRACTS. [Telecomms abstr.]. (1989)-. Periodical. English. Six times a year. $121.50. Techgnosis Ltd., Blade House, Battersea Road, Cheshire SK4 3EA United Kingdom. **Tel** 011 44 161 4422639, FAX 011 44 161 4431162. **Continues** Telecomms Profile, 0265-170X.

ISSN 0951-4686
DD 384.6   UK
TELECOMMS REGULATION REVIEW.
[Telecomms regul. rev.]. **VFOAT** TRR. (1987)-. Periodical. English. Ten times a year (monthly except Dec. and one summer month). $727.26. Corby Communications, PO Box 139, Horley Surrey RH6 8YS United Kingdom. **Tel** 011 44 171 7370522, FAX 011 44 171 7375672.

LC HE7601 .J63   **ISSN** 0497-137X
DD 384/.05   SZ
CODEN TCJOA6
Pr Rev.   TITLE CHANGE
TELECOMMUNICATION JOURNAL (ENGLISH EDITION). (TELECOMMUNICATION JOURNAL.). [Telecommun. j.]. **Added/Corp** International Telecommunication Union. Vol. 29 (Jan. 1962)-Jan. (1994). Periodical. English (French and Spanish). International Telecommunication Union, place des Nations, CH-1211 Geneva 20 Switzerland. **Tel** 011 41 22 7305111, FAX 011 41 22 7337256. **ED** Rene Fontaine and Michael Woolley. Index Available, published separately, free-automatically sent. **Bk Rev. Ad Acc. Circ:** 7,000 (ctrl). Documents available from Article Express International, The Genuine Article, Ask*IEEE. **Supersedes in part** Journal UIT. **Continued by** ITU Newsletter.
Desc: Official journal of the International Telecommunication Union.
Ind/Abst Acoust. Abstr.; Appl. Sci. Technol. Index; Bioeng. Abstr.; Comput. Inf. Syst. Abstr. J. [Full Cov.]; Curr. Cit.; Curr. Contents Eng. Comput. Technol.; Ei Page One; Elect. Commun. Abstr.; Eng. Index Annu.; Inf. Sci. Abstr. (?-?); INSPEC (1968-); Int. Aerosp. Abstr.; Res. Alert [Select. Cov.]; Soc. Sci. Cit. Index [Select. Cov.].

LC TK5101.A1 T36   **ISSN** 0040-2486
AT
CODEN TCJAAW
TELECOMMUNICATION JOURNAL OF AUSTRALIA, THE. [Telecommun. j. Aust.]. **Added/Corp** Telecommunication Society of Australia. (1935)-. Periodical. English. Three times a year. 56.73Aus$. Telecomm Society of Australia, GPO Box 4050, Melbourne Victoria 3001 Australia. **Tel** 011 61 3 6390906, FAX 011 61 3 6391515. **ED** Fred Cox. **Ad Acc. Circ:** 7,000 (ctrl). Documents available from Article Express International, Ask*IEEE.
Ind/Abst Bioeng. Abstr.; Curr. Cit.; Ei Page One; Eng. Index Annu.; INSPEC (Feb. 1969-); Int. Aerosp. Abstr.

ISSN 1018-4864
NE
UDC 384   CCC
TELECOMMUNICATION SYSTEMS.
[Telecommun. syst.]. (1992)-. Periodical. English. Four times a year. 343.50F (includes distribution costs). Baltzer Science Publishers BV, Asterweg 1A, 1031 HL Amsterdam Netherlands. **Tel** 011 31 20 6370061, FAX 011 31 20 6323651.

LC TK5101.A1 T35
II
TELECOMMUNICATIONS. **Added/Corp** India. Posts and Telegraphs Dept. Technical & Development Circle. (1951)-. Periodical. English. Four times a year. $7.00. Posts and Telegraphs Department, Technical and Development Circle, Jabalpur India. **ED** B.C. Soni.
Desc: Provides information of use to those in the telecommunications field.
Ind/Abst Curr. Cit.

ISSN 0742-5384
DD 384   US
CCC
TELECOMMUNICATIONS ALERT.
[Telecommun. alert]. Vol. 1, No. 1 (Oct. 1983)-. Periodical. English. Twelve times a year. $274.00. United Communications Group, 11300 Rockville Pike, Suite 1100, Rockville MD 20852. **Tel** (301)816-8950 ext. 313, FAX (301)816-8945. available on an online database (file 636/Full-Text) from DIALOG.
Ind/Abst PTS Newsl. Database [Full Txt.].

LC HE7761 .T46
DD 384/.0973   US
TELECOMMUNICATIONS ANALYSIS & RESEARCH. **Added/Corp** Yankee Group. **VFOAT** Telecommunications Analysis and Research. (19??)-. Trade Publication. English. Four times a year. The Yankee Group, 89 Broad Street, 14th Floor, Boston MA 02110.

ISSN 0040-2508
DD 621   US
CCC
CODEN TCREAG
Pr Rev.
TELECOMMUNICATIONS AND RADIO ENGINEERING. [Telecommun. radio eng.]. **Added/Corp** Scripta Technica, Inc. **VFOAT** Telecommunications & Radio Engineering. (1964)-. Periodical. English (translations available in Russian). Twelve times a year. $1488.00. Scripta Technica, A Subsidiary of John Wiley & Sons Inc., 7961 Eastern Avenue, Silver Spring MD 20910. **Tel** (301)588-0484, FAX (301)588-5278. **(Subscription address:** John Wiley & Sons, Inc. / Philadelphia, PO Box 7247, Philadelphia PA 19170. **Tel** (212)850-6645, (800)225-5945.) **ED** Reuben Glass, City University, London. **Ad Acc. Circ:** 500. available on microfilm and microfiche from University Microfilms International (UMI). Documents available from Article Express International, The Genuine Article, Ask*IEEE, CASDDS. **Formed by the union of** Telecommunications and Radio Engineering. Part 1. Telecommunications, 0497-1396 **and** Telecommunications and Radio Engineering. Part 2. Radio Engineering, 0497-140X.
Desc: Deals with digital and analog wire, radio, video, satellite, and optical communications, facsimile, micro- and millimeter waves, switching, coding, signal processing, voice and pattern recognition, filters, antennas and waveguides.
Ind/Abst Curr. Cit.; Eng. Index Annu.; INSPEC (1968-); Res. Alert [Full Cov.]; SCISEARCH.

US
CEASED
TELECOMMUNICATIONS COST AND CALL MANAGEMENT. **Added/Corp** Faulkner Technical Reports, Inc. **VFOAT** Faulkner Report on Telecommunications Cost and Call Management. Vol. 5, No. 2 Sept. (1987)-(June 1993). Periodical. English. Faulkner Technical Reports, 7905 Browning Road, Suite 114, Pennsauken NJ 08109. **Tel** (800)843-0460. **Continues** Telephone Cost & Call Management.

ISSN 0735-388X
US
TELECOMMUNICATIONS COUNSELOR.
[Telecommun. couns.]. **Added/Corp** Voice & Data Resources, Inc. (Aug. 10, 1982)-. Periodical. English. Twelve times a year. $265.00. Voice and Data Resources Inc, 601 Bangs Avenue, Suite 903, Asbury Park NJ 07712. **Tel** (201)773-5566. **ED** Robert W. Ryley. **Bk Rev. Circ:** 500.
Desc: Executive report about business telephone equipment and services. Insider tips and money saving techniques.

ISSN 0889-907X
DD 384   US
TELECOMMUNICATIONS DEVELOPMENT REPORT. [Telecommun. dev. report]. Periodical. English. Twelve times a year. $795.00. Pyramid Research Inc., 14 Arrow Street, Cambridge MA 02138. **Tel** (617)868-4725.

LC TK5102.5 .T3965   **ISSN** 1055-8454
DD 384/.025   US
CODEN TDIREL
●**TELECOMMUNICATIONS DIRECTORY (DETROIT, MICH.).** (TELECOMMUNICATIONS DIRECTORY.). [Telecommun. dir.]. **Added/Corp** Gale Research Inc. **VFOAT** TD. 5th Ed. (1992/1993)-. Directory. English. $340.00. Gale Research Inc., 835 Penobscot Building, 645 Griswold Street, Detroit MI 48226. **Tel** (800)877-GALE, (313)961-2242, FAX (313)961-6083, (800)414-5043, telex TWX 810-221-7086. **ED** John Krol. available on magnetic tape; available on diskette. **Continues** Telecommunications Systems and Services Directory, 0738-3045.
Desc: Provides detailed descriptions and full contact information on more than 2,300 national and international communications systems and services, voice and data communication services, local area networks and more.

US
TELECOMMUNICATIONS - EXPORT LICENSING CONTROLS. See Business and Economics-Commerce.

ISSN 1356-6423
UK
●**TELECOMMUNICATIONS GUIDE TO THE FORMER SOVIET UNION, THE.**
(19??)-. English. Two times a year. £470.00. The CIS Technical Publishing Institute, 11-13 Charterhouse Buildings, London EC1M 7AN United Kingdom. **Tel** 011 44 171 4903774, FAX 011 44 171 4905371.
Desc: Covers all sectors of the telecommunications industry, including fixed, mobile and satellite networks and electronic and voice communication services.

SA
●**TELECOMMUNICATIONS IN AFRICA.**
(1995)-. English. Ten times a year. $20.93. AITEC, PO Box 2422, Pinegowrie 2123 South Africa.

Communications —Telecommunication

LC TK5101.A1 T32
DD 384
ISSN 0040-2494
US
CODEN TLCOAY

TELECOMMUNICATIONS (INTERNATIONAL ED.).
(TELECOMMUNICATIONS.). [Telecommunications]. Vol. 1, No. 1 (June 1967)-. Periodical. English. Twelve times a year. $75.00. Horizon House, 685 Canton Street, Norwood MA 02062. **Tel** (617)365-4595. **(Subscription address:** Telecommunications, PO Box 850949, Braintree MA 02185. **Tel** (617)356-6935.) Documents available from UMI Article Clearinghouse. *Continued in part by* Telecommunications. Euro-Global Ed.
 Ind/Abst ABI/INFORM [Computer File] (Jan. 1979-Aug. 1981); Bus. Period. Index; Curr. Cit.; Int. Aerosp. Abstr.

DD 343.94099405
ISSN 1038-1481
AT

TELECOMMUNICATIONS LAW AND POLICY REVIEW. See Law.

DD 384.30994
ISSN 1034-7496
AT
TITLE CHANGE

TELECOMMUNICATIONS MANAGEMENT AND MARKETING NEWSLETTER. [Telecommun. manage. mark. newsl.]. (1989)-(1995). Periodical. English. Twelve times a year. Paul Budde Communication Pty Ltd, 2643 George Downes Drive, Bucketty NSW 2250 Australia. **Tel** 61 (0)49 988 144, FAX 61 (0)49 988 247. *Continues* New Media Marketing Newsletter, 0816-6269. *Continued by* Australasian Telecommunications Marketing and Management Newsletter.
 Desc: Newsletter on national and international management and marketing applications in voice, data and video communication. Trends and development in telecommunications.

DD 384.05
ISSN 0264-4568
UK

TELECOMMUNICATIONS NEWS.
[Telecommun. news]. (1983)-. Periodical. English. Twenty-six times a year (Published on the 1st and 15th of each month). $539.03. Communications Team Ltd., 5 Riverside Woodburn Moor Near, Wycombe Buckinghamshire HP10 0NU United Kingdom. **Tel** 011 44 16285 23458. **ED** Alan Forberg. **Bk Rev. Circ:** 1,000.

LC TK5101.A1 T26
ISSN 0278-4831
US
CCC

TELECOMMUNICATIONS (NORTH AMERICAN EDITION).
(TELECOMMUNICATIONS.). [Telecommunications]. Vol. 15, No. 9 (Sept. 1981)-. Periodical. English. Twelve times a year. $75.00 US; $135.00 other. Horizon House, 685 Canton Street, Norwood MA 02062. **Tel** (617)365-4595. **ED** Anthony Rutkowski. **Bk Rev. Ad Acc. Circ:** 85,000 (ctrl). available on microfilm and microfiche from University Microfilms International (UMI). Documents available from UMI Article Clearinghouse.
 Desc: Management oriented publication aimed at providing technical, application, marketing and financial insight for those who acquire and make use of telecommunication technology through articles.
 Ind/Abst ABI/INFORM Glob. Ed.; ABI/INFORM [Computer File] (1981-); Acad. Search; Bus. ASAP (1990-) [Full Txt.]; Bus. Index (1985-); Bus. Period. Index; Bus. Source Plus; Bus. Source; Comput. ASAP [Full Txt.]; Comput. Bus.; Comput. Database [Full Txt.]; Comput. Lit. Index; Comput. Rev.; EP Collect.; F&S Index Plus Text, Int. [Select. Cov.]; Gen. BusinessFile (1985-); Gen. Period. Index (1988-); Homework Help.; INFO-SOUTH Abstr.; Infomat Int. Bus.; Inf. Sci. Abstr. (?-?); Mag. Search; MasterFile FullTEXT 1000; MasterFile FullTEXT 350; MasterFile FullTEXT 650; MasterFile FullTEXT (Jan. 1994-); OCLC; PROMT; Telebase; Trade Ind. ASAP [Full Txt.]; Trade Ind. Index [Full Txt.]; UMI ABI/Inform--Bus. Period. Ondisc (Mar. 1987-) [Full Txt.]; Vocat. Search; Wilson Bus. Abstr.

LC HE7601 .T44
DD 384/.05
ISSN 0308-5961
UK
CCC
CODEN TEPODJ
Pr Rev.

TELECOMMUNICATIONS POLICY.
[Telecomm. policy]. Vol. 1 (Dec. 1976)-. Periodical. English. Ten times a year. $597.00. Butterworth Heinemann Publishers, Linacre House Jordan Hill, Oxford OX2 8DP United Kingdom. **Tel** 011 44 1865 310366, FAX 011 44 1865 310898. **(Subscription address:** Elsevier Science Ltd. / Oxford Fulfillment Centre, PO Box 800, Kidlington OX5 1DX United Kingdom. **Tel** 011 44 865 843355.) **ED** Colin Blackman. Index available. **Bk Rev. Ad Acc.** available on microfilm and microfiche from University Microfilms International (UMI); available on an online database from Elsevier Electronic Subscriptions (EES). Documents available from Article Express International, The Genuine Article, UMI Article Clearinghouse, Ask*IEEE.
 Desc: An international and interdisciplinary journal concerned with the social, economic, political and regulatory aspects of telecommunications and information systems.

Ind/Abst ABI/INFORM Glob. Ed.; ABI/INFORM [Computer File] (March 1983-); Bioeng. Abstr.; Commun. Abstr.; Curr. Cit.; Curr. Contents Eng. Comput. Technol.; Curr. Contents Soc. Behav. Sci.; Ei Page One; Eng. Index Annu.; Expand. Acad. Index (1992-); INSPEC (Dec. 1977-); Int. Aerosp. Abstr.; J. Plan. Lit.; Newsp. Period. Abstr. (1992-); PAIS Int. Print; Res. Alert [Full Cov.]; Sci. Cit. Index; SCISEARCH; Soc. Sci. Cit. Index [Full Cov.].

ISSN 0736-4156
US

TELECOMMUNICATIONS PRODUCT REVIEW. [Telecommun. prod. news]. **Added/Corp** Marketing Programs and Services Group. (19??)-. Periodical. English. Twelve times a year. $199.00. The ARIES Group MPSG, 1350 Piccard Drive, Suite 300, Rockville MD 20850. **Tel** (301)840-0800. *Absorbed* CPE Strategies, 0747-9050.

LC HE7775 .T36
DD 384
ISSN 0163-9854
US

TELECOMMUNICATIONS REPORTS.
[Telecommun. rep.]. (Aug. 9, 1934)-. Periodical. English. One time a week (51 issues, published weekly on Monday). $695.00. Telecommunications Reports, 1333 H Street Northwest, 2nd Floor West Tower, Washington DC 20005. **Tel** (202)842-0520, (800)822-6338, FAX (202)842-3047. **(Subscription address:** Telecommunications Reports, PO Box 675, Cooper Station, New York NY 10276.) **ED** Victoria A. Mason. Index available (included in subscription). cum. index.
 Desc: Covers federal and state regulatory, legislative, technological, legal, and corporate news. International telecommunications events are also covered.
 Ind/Abst Trade Ind. Index.

DD 384
ISSN 1054-1942
US

TELECOMMUNICATIONS REPORTS INTERNATIONAL. [Telecommun. rep. int.]. **VFOAT** TR International. (1990)-. Periodical. English. Twenty-five times a year. $997.00. Telecommunications Reports, 1333 H Street Northwest, 2nd Floor West Tower, Washington DC 20005. **Tel** (202)842-0520, (800)822-6338, FAX (202)842-3047. **(Subscription address:** Telecommunications Reports, PO Box 675, Cooper Station, New York NY 10276.)

DD 384
ISSN 1080-0085
US

TELECOMMUNICATIONS REPORTS, WIRELESS NEWS. [Telecommun. rep. wirel. news]. **VFOAT** Wireless News; TR Wireless News. (199?)-. Periodical. English. Twenty-five times a year. $547.00 North America; $673.00 other. Telecommunications Reports, 1333 H Street Northwest, 2nd Floor West Tower, Washington DC 20005. **Tel** (202)842-0520, (800)822-6338, FAX (202)842-3047.

US

TELECOMMUNICATIONS RETAILER : TCR. VFOAT TCR; T.C.R. (June 1983)-. Periodical. English. Four times a year. Gordon Publications Inc., A Subsidiary of Cahners Publishing Company, 301 Gibraltar Drive, Box 650, Morris Plains NJ 07950. **Tel** (201)292-5100, (800)637-6081.

LC TK6011 .T23
DD 621.385/025/73
ISSN 0730-9872
US

TELECOMMUNICATIONS SOURCEBOOK. [Telecommun. sourceb.]. **Added/Corp** North American Telephone Association. **VFOAT** Telecommunications Source Book; NATA Telecommunications Sourcebook. (1982)-. English. One time a year (Nov.). $53.00. North American Telephone Association, 2000 M Street Northwest, Suite 550, Washington DC 20036. **Tel** (800)538-6282, (202)296-9800. *Continues* Interconnect Industry Directory.
 Ind/Abst Stat. Ref. Index.

LC HE7811 .A382
DD 384/.0971
ISSN 0703-7252
CN
CEASED

TELECOMMUNICATIONS STATISTICS. See Communications-Abstracting, Bibliographies and Statistics.

ISSN 1322-3518
AT
Pr Rev.

TELECOMMUNICATIONS STRATEGIES REPORT. English. One time a year. $185.91. Paul Budde Communications Pty Ltd, 2643 George Downes Drive, Bucketty NSW 2250 Australia. **Tel** 61 (0)49 988 144, FAX 61 (0)49 988 247. Index available. **Ad Acc. Circ:** 200 (ctrl). *Continues* Strategic VAS - Vans Report.
 Desc: Provides statistical information on the Australian telecommunication market and describes markets, trends, and developments around the world. The report highlights the latest in key markets such as networks, value added services, video based services, and mobile communications.

US
CEASED

TELECOMMUNICATIONS SYSTEMS GUIDE. English. Faulkner Technical Reports, 7905 Browning Road, Suite 114, Pennsauken NJ 08109. **Tel** (800)843-0460.

DD 384
ISSN 1040-418X
US
TITLE CHANGE

TELECOMMUNICATIONS WEEK (NEW YORK, N.Y.). (TELECOMMUNICATIONS WEEK.). [Telecommun. week]. (198?)-(1995). Trade Publication. English. Telecommunications Reports, 1333 H Street Northwest, 2nd Floor West Tower, Washington DC 20005. **Tel** (202)842-0520, (800)822-6338, FAX (202)842-3047. **(Subscription address:** Telecommunications Reports, PO Box 675, Cooper Station, New York NY 10276.) **ED** Karen Kinard. *Continued by* State and Local Communications Report.
 Desc: A newsletter covering the latest happenings in all aspects of the domestic telecommunications industry.

DD 363
ISSN 0887-1647
US
TITLE CHANGE

TELECOMMUNICATORS DISPATCH, THE. [Telecommun. dispatch]. (1985)-(199?). Periodical. English. J.D. Hamilton Associates, PO Box 95, Audubon PA 19407. **Tel** (610)666-7400. **ED** Pat Van Glesen. **Bk Rev.** *Continued by* Dispatch Center Management, 1068-2023.
 Desc: Publication of interest to public safety dispatch personnel and 1st line supervisors. Articles deal with training, stress, humorous happenings and interviews.

DD 384
ISSN 8756-7431
US
CCC

TELECOMMUTING REVIEW.
(TELECOMMUTING REVIEW : THE GORDON REPORT.). [Telecommut. rev.]. **Added/Corp** Gil Gordon Associates. **VFOAT** Gordon Report. Vol. 1, No. 1 (1984)-. Periodical. English. Twelve times a year. $157.00. Gil Gordon Associates, 10 Donner Court, Monmouth Junction NJ 08852. **Tel** (908)329-2266, FAX (908)329-2703. **ED** Gil Gordon. Index available. cum. index. **Bk Rev,** (Qty: 4). **Circ:** 250. available on an online database (file 675/Full-Text) from DIALOG.
 Ind/Abst Comput. ASAP [Full Txt.]; Comput. Database [Full Txt.].

FR
CEASED

TELECOMS MAGAZINE. (1990)-(1994). Periodical. French. Groupe Tests, 26 rue d'Oradour sur Glane, 75504 Paris Cedex 15 France. **Tel** 011 33 1 44253001, FAX 011 33 1 45573506. *Absorbed* Ressources Informatiques.

FR

TELECOMS MAGAZINE = ENTREPRISE COMMUNICATION RESEAUX. French. Telecoms Magazine, 5 place du Colonel Fabien, 75491 Paris Cedex 10 France.
 Ind/Abst Infomat Int. Bus.

LC HD
DD 338
UDC 654
ISSN 1163-9180
FR
TITLE CHANGE

TELECOMS RESEAUX INTERNATIONAL. VFOAT Telecoms Reseaux; Telecoms et Reseaux International. (1991)-(Summer 1993). Periodical. French. IDG Communications / France, Immeuble La Fayette Cedex 65, F-92051 Paris la Defense 5 France. **Tel** 011 33 1 49047900, FAX 011 33 1 49047870, telex 613234. *Continues* Telecoms International, 0987-4119. *Continued by* Reseaux & Telecoms (Paris-La-Defense), 1251-8964.

LC TK5101.A1 T363
ISSN 0495-0186
IT
CODEN TLCZAX

TELECOMUNICAZIONI. [Telecomunicazioni]. Periodical. Italian (summaries and/or abstracts in English). L2,000. Societa Telecomunicazioni Siemens, Piazzale Zavattari 12, Milan Italy. Documents available from Ask*IEEE.
 Ind/Abst INSPEC (June 1971-).

LC TK5102.5 .T4245
DD 384
US

TELECONFERENCING DIRECTORY. (CIP TELECONFERENCING DIRECTORY : WITH MARKET REPORTS.). **Added/Corp** University of Wisconsin--Extension. Center for Interactive Programs. **VFOAT** Teleconferencing Directory. 9th Ed. (1986)-. English. One time a year. University of Wisconsin-Extension / Center for Interactive Programs, Madison WI 53706. *Continues* Teleconferencing Directory, 0889-5147.

ISSN 1065-3007
DD 384 US
TELECONFERENCING NEWS. [Teleconf. news]. Vol. 1, No. 1 (June/July 1991)-. Periodical. English. Six times a year. $95.00. Knowledge Industry Publications Inc, 701 Westchester Avenue, White Plains NY 10604. **Tel** (914)328-9157, (800)800-5474, FAX (914)328-9093.

LC TK6001 .T43 **ISSN** 0740-9354
US
TELECONNECT. (TELECONNECT : THE VOICE OF THE TELEPHONE INTERCONNECT INDUSTRY.). [Teleconnect]. **Added/Corp** Telecom Library. (March 1983)-. Periodical. English. Twelve times a year. $15.00. Telecom Library Inc., 12 West 21st Street, New York NY 10010. **Tel** (212)691-8215, (800)542-7279. **ED** Rick Lunmann. **Bk Rev. Ad Acc, Adv Mgr:** Gerry Friesen, **Tel** (215)355-2886. **Circ:** 25,000. available on an online database (file 675/Full-Text) from DIALOG.
Ind/Abst Comput. ASAP [Full Txt.]; Comput. Database [Full Txt.].

US
TELECONS. (19??)-. English. Six times a year. $30.00 US; $70.00 other. Applied Business Telecommunications, Box 5106, San Ramon CA 94583. **Tel** (510)820-5563, FAX (510)820-5894.

UK
TELEFACTS. (19??)-. Periodical. English. Twelve times a year. £275.00 Europe, Middle East and Asia. ICW Publications Ltd., Chapter House, Hinderton Hall Estate, Neston S Wiral L64 7TS United Kingdom. **Tel** 011 44 151 3531234, FAX 011 44 151 3531011. **(Subscription address:** Datapro International, McGraw Hill House Shoppenhangers, Maidenhead Berkley SL6 2QL United Kingdom. **Tel** 011 44 628 773277.**)**

LC TK6710 .T43
DD 384.1/4 GW
TELEFAX INTERNATIONAL. Added/Corp Telex-Verlag Jaeger + Waldmann. **VFOAT** Telefax Facsimile Bureaufax. (198?)-. English. One time a year. Telex-Verlag Jaeger+Waldmann GmbH, PO Box 111454, D-64229 Darmstadt Germany. **Tel** 011 49 6151 33020, FAX 011 49 6151 330250, telex 419389 TLX D.
Desc: Contains all the necessary data required for the smooth handling of the telefax traffic, clearly arranged for effortless and quick use.

ISSN 0743-541X
DD 384 US
TELEFOCUS. [TeleFocus]. **Added/Corp** Touche Ross & Co. North American Telecommunications Organization. Touche Ross & Co. Washington Service Center. **VFOAT** Tele Focus. Vol. 1, No. 1 (June 1984)-. Periodical. English. Touche Ross, 1900 M Street Northwest, Washington DC 20036. **Tel** (202)955-4238.

ISSN 0940-7715
GW
UDC 33
TELEFONMARKETING-PRAXIS. [Telef.mark.-Prax.]. **VFOAT** TM. Telefonmarketing-Praxis; Telefonmarketing. (19??)-. Newsletter. German (English). Twelve times a year. DM20.00. Verlag Norbert Mueller AG & Co. KG, Postfach 450632, Munich 80906 Germany. **Tel** 011 44 89 35093-02, FAX 011 44 89 35093-218. **ED** Gerlinde Felix. Index available. **Circ:** 700 (ctrl).
Desc: Newsletter for successful telecommunication practices.

LC TK3 .F43 **ISSN** 0015-0118
GW
CCC
CODEN TPRAEV
TELEKOM PRAXIS . Added/Corp Germany (West). Fernmeldetechnisches Zentralamt. Deutsche Bundespost Telekom. Fernmeldetechnisches Zentralamt. **VFOAT** Telekom-Praxis. (Jan. 1990)-. Trade Publication. German. Twelve times a year. $227.07. Fachverlag Schiele und Schoen, Markgafenstrasse 11, D-10969 Berlin Germany. **Tel** 011 49 30 2516029. Documents available from Ask*IEEE. ***Continues*** *Fermelde Praxis.*
Ind/Abst INSPEC (Jan. 1990-).

XR
TELEKOMUNIKACE. Added/Corp Czechoslovakia. Federalni Ministerstvo Spoju. (1964)-. Periodical. Czech. Twelve times a year. $39.70. Nakladatelstvi Dopravy a Spoju, Transport and Communications, Hybernska 5, 11578 Prague 1 Czech Republic. **Tel** 011 42 2 2365774, FAX 011 42 2 2356772. **(Subscription address:** Artia Pegas Press Ltd., Palac Metro Narodni Trida 25, 11210 Prague 1 Czech Republic. **Tel** 011 42 2 24196265, 011 42 2 24196266.**)**

ISSN 0840-5476
DD 384/.05 CN
CCC
TELEMANAGEMENT (PICKERING). (TELEMANAGEMENT : THE ANGUS REPORT ON COMMUNICATIONS, SYSTEMS, SERVICES AND STRATEGIES.). [Telemanagement]. **Added/Corp** Angus Telemanagement Group. (Sept. 1988)-. Periodical. English. Ten times a year. 260.00Can$. Angus Telemanagement Group Inc., 8 Old Kingston Road, Ajax Ontario L1T 2Z7 Canada. **Tel** (905)686-5050, FAX (905)686-2655. **ED** Ian Angus and Liz Angus. Index available. cum. index. **Bk Rev. Circ:** 1,500 (ctrl). ***Formed by the union of*** *Telemanagement Report, 0824-2410* ***and*** *Telecom Systems and Strategies, 0832-9877.*
Desc: This magazine covers the latest news in telecommunication fields.

LC HF5415.1265 .T43 **ISSN** 0730-6156
DD 658.8/5 US
TELEMARKETING. See Business and Economics-Marketing and Purchasing.

LC TK5101.A1 T43 **ISSN** 0736-5853
DD 384 US
CCC
CODEN TEINEG
TELEMATICS AND INFORMATICS. [Telemat. inform.]. Vol. 1, No. 1 (1984)-. Periodical. English. Four times a year. $490.00. Pergamon Press, An Imprint of Elsevier Science Ltd., The Boulevard, Langford Lane, Kidlington, Oxford OX5 1GB United Kingdom. **Tel** 011 44 1865 843000, 011 44 1865 843699, FAX 011 44 1865 843010. **(Subscription address:** Elsevier Science Ltd. / Oxford Fulfillment Centre, PO Box 800, Kidlington OX5 1DX United Kingdom. **Tel** 011 44 865 843355.**) ED** Indu B. Singh. available on microfilm and microfiche from University Microfilms International (UMI); available on an online database from Elsevier Electronic Subscriptions (EES). Documents available from Ask*IEEE.
Desc: Publishes research and review articles in applied telecommunications and information sciences in business, industry, government and educational establishments.
Ind/Abst Abstr. Hum. Comput. Interact.; ACM Guide Comput. Lit.; Commun. Abstr.; Comput. Rev.; Curr. Cit.; Ei Page One; HILITES; Inf. Sci. Abstr. [Full Cov.]; INSPEC (1985-); Int. Aerosp. Abstr. (1984-).

LC TK5101.A1 T44 **ISSN** 0970-3934
DD 621.382/0954 II
CODEN TELIEG
TELEMATICS INDIA. [Telemat. India]. Vol. 1, No. 1 (Oct. 1987)-. Trade Publication. English. Twelve times a year. $25.00. **(Subscription address:** Prints India, 11 Darya Ganj, New Delhi 110002 India. **Tel** 011 91 11 3268645, FAX 011 91 11 3275542, telex 31-61087 PRIN-IN.**)**
Ind/Abst Curr. Cit.

ISSN 1071-135X
DD 338 US
●**TELEMEDIA NEWS AND VIEWS.** [Telemedia news views]. **VFOAT** TNV. (1993)-. Periodical. English. Twelve times a year. $295.00. Opus Research Incorporated, 345 Chenery Street, San Francisco CA 94131. **Tel** (800)428-6787, (415)239-0244, FAX (415)239-6932. **ED** Daniel N. Miller (editor's phone number: (415)239-6932). available on an online database from Information Access Company. ***Absorbed*** *800 900 Review; Audiotex Now.*
Desc: Provides market data and trend analysis for inactive services offered over the telephone lines worldwide.

LC HE **ISSN** 1320-2669
DD 384.09505 AT
●**TELENEWS ASIA.** [Telenews Asia]. (1993)-. Periodical. English. Twenty-five times a year. $801.62. Stuart Corner Information Services, Locked Bag 13, Rozelle NSW 2039 Australia. **Tel** 011 61 2 5557377, FAX 011 61 2 8182294. ***Continues*** *Asia Business Report, 1038-9717.*

US
TELEPHONE CONTACTS FOR DATA USERS. Main/Corp United States. Bureau of the Census. (19??)-. Government Publication. English. Irregular. Free on request. US Department of Commerce / Bureau of the Census, Data User Services Division, Customer Services, Washington DC 20233-0800. **Tel** (301)763-4100. **(Subscription address:** Superintendent of Documents, US Government Printing Office, Washington DC 20402. **)**
Desc: Lists names and telephone numbers of Census Bureau specialists in demographic and economic statistics, geography, statistical research and user services.

LC TK1 .T33 **ISSN** 0040-263X
DD 621.30 US
CCC
CODEN TPEMAW
TITLE CHANGE
TELEPHONE ENGINEER & MANAGEMENT. [Teleph. eng. manage.]. **VFOAT** TE&M; TE & M; TE and M. **VAT** Telephone Engineer and Management. Vol. 45, No. 10 (Oct. 1941)-Vol. 98, No. 3 (Feb. 1, 1994). Trade Publication. English. Advanstar Communications Inc., 131 West First Street, Duluth MN 55802. **Tel** (218)723-9477, (800)346-0085, FAX (218)723-9437. available on microfilm. Documents available from Ask*IEEE, UMI Article Clearinghouse. ***Continues*** *Telephone Engineer.* ***Continued by*** *America's Network, 1075-5292.*
Ind/Abst ABI/INFORM [Computer File] (Sept. 1978-); Acad. Search; EP Collect.; Homework Help.; INSPEC (Oct. 1968-); MasterFile FullTEXT 1000; MasterFile FullTEXT 350; MasterFile FullTEXT 650; MasterFile FullTEXT; OCLC; Predicasts; Telebase; Trade Ind. Index (1981-); Vocat. Search.

LC TK6195 .T45
US
TITLE CHANGE
TELEPHONE ENGINEER & MANAGEMENT DIRECTORY. VFOAT Telephone Engineer's Composite Catalog & Buyers' Directory. (1936)-(19??). Directory. English. Advanstar Communications Inc., 131 West First Street, Duluth MN 55802. **Tel** (218)723-9477, (800)346-0085, FAX (218)723-9437. **ED** Robert Stoffels and Cathy Zikur. **Ad Acc. Circ:** 8,000 (ctrl). ***Continued by*** *America's Network Directory.*
Desc: Directory serving executives in every segment of telecommunications. Includes extensive marketing data, complete directory of all U.S. telephone companies, foreign PTTs, interconnects, telecommunications and data communications equipment and service vendors, distribution of telecom equipment, etc.

LC HE8811 .P47
DD 384.60973 US
●**... TELEPHONE INDUSTRY DIRECTORY, THE. Added/Corp** Phillips Business Information, Inc. 7th Annual Ed. (1993)-. Directory. English. One time a year. $229.00. Phillips Business Information Inc., 1201 Seven Locks Road, PO Box 61130, Potomac MD 20854. **Tel** (301)424-3338, (301)340-1520, (800)777-5005, FAX (301)424-4297, telex 358149. ***Continues*** *Phillips Publishing's ... Telephone Industry Directory.*
Desc: Information on business contacts in more than 5,000 companies and 170 countries, including information on CPE and central office products as well as transmission equipment, access lines and rankings.

ISSN 0888-353X
DD 658 US
TELEPHONE MARKETING COUNCIL NEWSLETTER. See Business and Economics-Marketing and Purchasing.

ISSN 0271-5430
US
CCC
TITLE CHANGE
TELEPHONE NEWS. [Teleph. news]. Vol. 1 (Oct. 6, 1980)-(June 1993). Periodical. English. Phillips Business Information Inc., 1201 Seven Locks Road, PO Box 61130, Potomac MD 20854. **Tel** (301)424-3338, (301)340-1520, (800)777-5005, FAX (301)424-4297, telex 358149. **ED** Deborah Eby. available on an online database (files 16,636,638/Full-Text) from DIALOG. ***Absorbed*** *Telephone Bypass News; The Long Distance Letter; Telecom Insider.* ***Merged with*** *The Spectrum Report* ***and*** *Telecommunications Regulatory Monitor* ***to form*** *Washington Telecom News.*
Desc: A comprehensive source for telephone industry executives covering marketing, new products and services, regulation and competition in the newly deregulated environment.
Ind/Abst PROMT [Full Txt.]; PTS Newsl. Database [Full Txt.]; Trade Ind. ASAP [Full Txt.]; Trade Ind. Index [Full Txt.].

ISSN 0882-1461
US
CODEN TSERE4
TELEPHONE SELLING REPORT. See Business and Economics-Marketing and Purchasing.

LC HE8861 .S7b **ISSN** 0380-7843
DD 384.6/0971/021 CN
TELEPHONE STATISTICS. See Communications-Abstracting, Bibliographies and Statistics.

ISSN 0707-9753
DD 384.6/0971 CN
TELEPHONE STATISTICS (MONTHLY ED.). See Communications-Abstracting, Bibliographies and Statistics.

LC HE8805.W6 P8a **ISSN** 0097-9198
DD 385.6/3/09775 US
TELEPHONE STATISTICS : SELECTED FINANCIAL DATA FOR WISCONSIN TELEPHONE COMPANIES. See Communications-Abstracting, Bibliographies and Statistics.

LC HF **ISSN** 1122-424X
DD 380 IT
UDC 654.15
●**TELEPHONE TRADE.** [Telephone trade]. (1994)-. Periodical. Italian. Six times a year (Feb., Apr., June, Aug., Oct., Dec.). L50000 Italy; L100000 other. Stammer Spa, Via della Liberazione 1, 20068 Peschiera Borromeo Italy. **Tel** 011 39 2 55302606, FAX 011 39 2 55302700, telex 321083. **Bk Rev. Ad Acc. Circ:** 4,500 (ctrl). ***Continues*** *Il Giornale dell'Installatore Telefonico, 1120-219X.*

Communications —Telecommunication

DD 384
ISSN 1062-4724
US
CCC
TITLE CHANGE

TELEPHONE WEEK. [Teleph. week]. (Feb. 1992)-(19??). Periodical. English. Telecom Publishing Group, 1101 King Street, Suite 444, Alexandria VA 22314. **Tel** (703)683-4100, (800)327-7205, FAX (703)739-6490. available on an online database (file 636/Full-Text) from DIALOG. *Formed by the union of BOC Week and Independent Telco News, 1051-3124. Continued by Telco Business Report.*
Ind/Abst PTS Newsl. Database [Full Txt.].

LC TK1 .T36
DD 621
ISSN 0040-2656
US
CCC
CODEN TLPNAS

TELEPHONY. [Telephony]. **VFOAT** Global Telephony. Vol. 1 (Jan. 1901)-. Periodical. English. One time a week. $78.82. Intertec Publishing Corporation, 9800 Metcalf, Overland Park KS 66212. **Tel** (913)341-1300. **(Subscription address:** Intertec Publishing Corporation, PO Box 2901, Overland Park KS 66282. **Tel** 800 441-0294.) **ED** H.B. McMeal. **Circ:** 45,000. available on microform and microfiche from University Microfilms International (UMI); available on an online database (files 15,648,675/Full-Text) from DIALOG. Documents available from UMI Article Clearinghouse, Ask*IEEE. *Absorbed Telephone Magazine; American Telephone Journal.*
Desc: For executives and managers of companies that provide telecommunications services. Covers aspects of the daily business activities of local exchange and interexchange carriers as well as those of companies that supply customer premise equipment and attendant planning, installation and maintenance.
Ind/Abst ABI/INFORM Glob. Ed.; ABI/INFORM [Computer File] (Nov. 1978-); Acad. Search; Bus. ASAP (1990-) [Full Txt.]; Bus. Index (1985-); Bus. Period. Index; Bus. Source Plus; Bus. Source; Comput. ASAP [Full Txt.]; Comput. Bus. (19??-19??); Comput. Database [Full Txt.]; Curr. Cit.; EP Collect.; F&S Index Plus Text, Int. [Select. Cov.]; Gen. BusinessFile (1985-); Gen. Periodical. Index (1985-); Homework Help.; INFO-SOUTH Abstr.; Infomat Int. Bus.; INSPEC (May 1977-); Mag. Search; MasterFile FullTEXT 1000; MasterFile FullTEXT 350; MasterFile FullTEXT 650; MasterFile FullTEXT (July 1993-); OCLC; Predicasts; PROMT; Stat. Ref. Index; Telebase; Trade Ind. ASAP [Full Txt.]; Trade Ind. Index [Full Txt.]; UMI ABI/Inform--Bus. Period. Ondisc (Nov. 1987-) [Full Txt.]; Vocat. Search; Wilson Bus. Abstr.

LC HD9696.T44 T45
US
CEASED

TELEPHONY'S PUBLIC NETWORK TECHNOLOGY SOURCE. **VFOAT** Public Network Technology Source. (Sept. 14, 1992)-(19??). English. Intertec Publishing Corporation, 9800 Metcalf, Overland Park KS 66212. **Tel** (913)341-1300. *Continues Telephony's Buyers' Information.*

LC HF5415.1265 .T47
DD 658.8/5
ISSN 0886-9642
US

TELEPROFESSIONAL. See Business and Economics-Marketing and Purchasing.

LC TK5101.A1 T46
DD 621.38
ISSN 0040-2710
CN
CODEN TLSSAO

TELESIS (OTTAWA, ONT.). (TELESIS.). [Telesis]. **Added/Corp** Northern Electric Company. Bell-Northern Research. (Nov. 1967)-. Periodical. English. Three times a year. Free on request. Bell-Northern Research, Box 3511 Station C, Ottawa Ontario Canada. **Tel** (613)727-2211. **ED** John Lawlor. Index Available, published separately, free-automatically sent. **Circ:** 25,000 (ctrl). available on microfilm and microfiche from University Microfilms International (UMI). Documents available from Article Express International, UMI Article Clearinghouse, Ask*IEEE.
Desc: Describes BNR's efforts in the design of advanced telecommunications and integrated office systems for Northern Telecom.
Ind/Abst ABI/INFORM Glob. Ed.; ABI/INFORM [Computer File] (1986-); Bioeng. Abstr.; Curr. Cit.; Ei Page One; Eng. Index Annu.; INSPEC (Oct. 1970-); World Publ. Monit.

LC TK5101.A1 T4713
ISSN 0492-6110
DK
CODEN TLKKAS

TELETEKNIK (ENGLISH EDITION). (TELETEKNIK.). [Teletek.]. **Added/Corp** Denmark. Generaldirektoratet for Post- og Telegrafvaesenet. (1957)-. Periodical. English. Two times a year. Free on request. Teleteknik, Telegade 2, DK-2630 Taastrup Denmark. **Tel** 011 45 2 528022, FAX 011 45 2 527080, telex 22383. Documents available from Article Express International, Ask*IEEE.
Ind/Abst Ei Page One; Eng. Index Annu. [Select. Cov.]; INSPEC (1968-).

DD 384
ISSN 1074-5823
US

TELETIMES (WASHINGTON, D.C.). (TELETIMES.). [Teletimes]. **Added/Corp** United States Telephone Association. (1990)-. Periodical. English. Four times a year. United States Telephone Association, 1401 H Street NW Suite 600, Washington DC 20005. **Tel** (202)326-7270, FAX (202)326-7333. **ED** Ellen B. Mullally. **Ad Acc. Circ:** 3,500.
Desc: Highlights news and information from the telephone and telecommunications industries.

ISSN 1358-1465
UK

●**TELEWORKER.** (1993)-. Periodical. English. Six times a year. £24.50. Telecottage Association, The Other Cottage, Shortwood Nailsworth, Gloucestershire GL6 OSH United Kingdom. **Tel** 011 44 1453 834874, FAX 011 44 1453 836174. **ED** Alan Denbigh. **Bk Rev**, (Qty: 12). **Ad Acc, Adv Mgr:** Alan Denbigh, **Tel** 011 44 1453 834874. **Circ:** 5,000.
Desc: Aimed at teleworkers and telecentre managers.

LC HE7621 .T45
DD 384.1/025/73
ISSN 0091-3170
US

TELEX DIRECTORY. **VFOAT** RCA Telex Directory. Directory. Multiple languages (English, French, German and Spanish). RCA Global Communications, 60 Broad Street, New York NY 10004.

DD 354.710085
ISSN 1187-4848
CN

TETE-A-TETE (OTTAWA. 1991). See Communications-Radio.

LC TK5101.A1 T52
DD 621.38
CH

TIEN HSIN CHI SHU (JEN MIN YU TIEN CHU PAN SHE). (TIEN HSIN CHI SHU.). **VFOAT** Dianxin Jishu. Periodical. Chinese. NT$0.22. Pei-Ching Pao Kan Fa Hsing Chu; Beijing, People's Republic of China. **Tel** 011 86 1 483531.

LC TK5101.A1 T53
DD 621.38/05
CH

TIEN HSIN CHI SHU = TELECOMS TECHNICAL QUARTERLY. **Added/Corp** China (Republic : 1949-). Tien Hsin Tsung Chu. **VFOAT** Telecoms Technical Quarterly. (1981)-. Periodical. Chinese (summaries and/or abstracts in English). Four times a year. Directorate General of Telecommunications, 31 Aikuo East Road, Taipei 106 Taiwan.

ISSN 0374-3853
NE
CODEN NERTA9

TIJDSCHRIFT VAN HET NEDERLANDS ELEKTRONICA- EN RADIOGENOOTSCHAP (1973). See Electronics.

LC HE8221 .F56a
FI

TOIMINTAKERTOMUS. **Main/Corp** Telekehityskeskus (Finland). **VFOAT** Telekehityskeskuksen Toimintakertomus. (1990)-. Finnish. Telehityskeskus, Kiviaidankatu 2F, PL 64, 00211 Helsinki Finland. *Continues Teletutkimuskeskus (Finland). Toimintakertomus.*

LC HE8811 .T63
DD 384.6/025/73
ISSN 0146-6801
US

TOLL FREE BUSINESS. (19??)-. English. One time a year. $11.95. Toll Free Planning Services, Box 102, Minneapolis MN 55440. **Tel** (612)333-5511.

LC HE8811 .T64
DD 384.6/42
ISSN 0363-2962
US
SUSPENDED

TOLL FREE DIGEST. **VFOAT** Toll-Free Digest. Suspended (Jan. 1991). English. One time a year. $19.95. Toll-Free Digest Company Inc, PO Box 800, Claverack NY 12513. **Tel** (518)828-6400. **ED** Paul R Montana and Gary Montana. Index available. **Bk Rev.** ctrl circ.
Desc: Contains over 43,000 current toll-free listings.

ISSN 1143-3760
FR

UDC 330

TRANSFIL EUROPE PARIS. (TRANSFIL EUROPE.). (1987)-. Periodical. English (French, German, Spanish and Italian). Four times a year (with one supplement). 220.00F France; 260.00F other. St Diffusion, 29-31 Ave des Champs Elysees, 75008 Paris France. **Tel** 011 33 1 45638594, FAX 011 33 1 42893277. **ED** Pascal Caudebec. Index available. cum. index. **Ad Acc.** Acid Free. **Circ:** 9,000. available on diskette.
Desc: Information on telecommunications, non-ferrous and ferrous metals, optic fibers, and energy.

LC QA76.9.A25 T73
DD 384/.05
ISSN 0892-399X
US
CODEN TDCREP
TITLE CHANGE

TRANSNATIONAL DATA AND COMMUNICATIONS REPORT. (TRANSNATIONAL DATA AND COMMUNICATIONS REPORT : TDR.). [Transnatl. data commun. rep.]. **Added/Corp** Transnational Data Reporting Service. **VFOAT** Transnational Data Report; TDR. Vol. 9, No. 1 (Jan. 1986)-(1994). Periodical. English. Transnational Data Reporting Service Inc, PO Box 10528, Burke VA 22009. **Tel** (703)323-9116, FAX (703)250-4705. **ED** Timothy G. Donovan. Index available. **Bk Rev. Ad Acc. Circ:** 3,000. Documents available from Ask*IEEE. *Formed by the union of Transnational Data Report, 0167-6962 and Chronicle of International Communication, 0278-0011. Continued by I-Ways.*
Desc: A review of the international information policy, telecommunication policy and regulation, and related legal matters.
Ind/Abst Comput. Lit. Index; INSPEC (1986-); Libr. Inf. Sci. Abstr.; PAIS Int. Print; Pollut. Abstr. Indexes.

IT

TRASMISSIONI DATI E TELECOMUNICAZIONI. Italian. Gruppo Editoriale Jackson Spa, Via Gorki 69, 20092 Cinisello Balsamo Italy. **Tel** 011 39 2 66034401.

LC HE
DD 384
ISSN 0920-2706
NE
CODEN TRTLEK
CEASED

TRENDS IN TELECOMMUNICATIONS. [Trends telecommun.]. **Added/Corp** American Telephone and Telegraph Company. Philips Telecommunications, B.V. (Winter 1985)-(1995). Periodical. English. AT&T NSI, Postbus 1168, 1200 BD Hilversum Netherlands. **Tel** 011 31 35 871571. Documents available from Ask*IEEE.
Ind/Abst Curr. Cit.; INSPEC (1985).

ISSN 0390-5187
IT

UDC 656

TRIBUNA POSTALE E DELLE TELECOMUNICAZIONI. See Communications-Postal Communications.

LC HE7661
DD 384/.07/20713
ISSN 0842-0548
CN

TRIO NETWORK. (THE TRIO NETWORK / THE TELECOMMUNICATIONS RESEARCH INSTITUTE OF ONTARIO.). [TRIO netw.]. **Added/Corp** TRIO. **VAT** Telecommunications Research Institute of Ontario Network. Vol. 1, No. 1 (Oct. 1987)-. Periodical. English. Four times a year. Telecommunications Research Institute of Ontario Network, Suite 302, 1150 Morrison Drive, Ottawa, Ontario K2H 8S9.

LC QC676 .D46
ISSN 0914-9279
JA
CODEN TSKKED

TSUSHIN SOGO KENKYUJO KIHO. [Tsushin Sogo Kenkyujo kiho]. **Added/Corp** Yuseisho Tsushin Sogo Kenkyujo. **VFOAT** Review of the Communications Research Laboratory. (1988)-. Periodical. Japanese (summaries and/or abstracts in English). Four times a year. Denki Tsushin Shinkokai, Showa 63, Tokyo Japan. Documents available from Ask*IEEE. *Continues Denpa Kenkyujo Kiho, 0033-801X.*
Ind/Abst INSPEC (1988-); Int. Aerosp. Abstr.

DD 384
ISSN 0887-1701
US

TV TECHNOLOGY. [TV technol.]. **Added/Corp** Industrial Marketing Advisory Services. **VFOAT** TVT. **VAT** Television Technology. (19??)-. Trade Publication. English. Twelve times a year. Industrial Marketing Advisory, PO Box 1214, Falls Church VA 22041. **Tel** (703)998-7600, FAX (703)998-2966. **ED** Marlene Lane. **Ad Acc. Circ:** 20,000 (ctrl).

US

U.S. TELECOMMUNICATIONS. (Feb. 1990)-. English. Twenty-four times a year. $497.00 US and Canada; $527.00 other. Probe Research Inc., Three Wing Drive, Suite 240, Cedar Knolls NJ 07927-1000. **Tel** (201)285-1500, FAX (201)285-1519. **ED** Frank Barbetta, Peter Bernstein, and Jeffrey B. Berger. **Circ:** 200 (ctrl). *Absorbed Metropolitan Network News.*
Desc: An interpretive publication on competition and strategy in the U.S. telecom markets.

US
FI

UNITED NATIONS TELEPHONE DIRECTORY. FIJI, FEDERATED STATES OF MICRONESIA, KIRIBATI, MARSHALL ISLANDS, NAURU, SOLOMON ISLANDS, TONGA, TUVALU, VANUATU AND PACIFIC REGIONAL PROGRAMMES. **Main/Corp** United Nations Development Programme. Directory. English. United Nations Development Programme / Fiji, National Bank of

Fiji Building/2nd Floor, Cnr Victoria Parade & Gordon Street, Private Mail Bag, Suva Fiji. **Continues** Directory of United Nations personnel in Fiji, Kiribati, Nauru, Solomon Islands, Tonga, Tuvalu, Vanuatu, Federated States of Micronesia, Marshall Islands, Palau.

LC TK6710 .N37   **ISSN** 1084-4465
DD 384   US

●**UNITED STATES FAX DIRECTORY.** (U.S. FAX DIRECTORY.). [U.S. fax directory]. **VFOAT** United States Fax Directory. (1994)-. Directory. English. One time a year. Gale Research Inc., 835 Penobscot Building, 645 Griswold Street, Detroit MI 48226. **Tel** (800)877-GALE, (313)961-2242, **FAX** (313)961-6083, (800)414-5043, telex TWX 810-221-7086. **Continues** National Fax Directory, 1045-9499.
  Desc: Gives access to over 160,000 FAX numbers, verified for accuracy, for U.S. companies, organizations, government agencies, and libraries.

LC HE8701   **ISSN** 1358-8923
DD 384.6   UK

●**UP 2 DATE (LONDON).** [Up 2 date Lond.]. **VFOAT** Up Two Date. (1994)-. Consumer Publication. English. Four times a year. Mediamark Publishing International Ltd., 35 Gresse Street, Rathbone Place, London W1P 1PN United Kingdom. **Tel** 011 44 171 5803105, **FAX** 011 44 171 5801695. **ED** Lisa Phillips. **Circ:** 240,000.

LC HE7771 .U53
DD 384.5/1/02573   US

UPLINK DIRECTORY. Added/Corp Virginia A. Ostendorf, Inc. (1986)-. English. One time a year. $150.00. Virginia A. Ostendorf Inc, PO Box 2896, Littleton CO 80161-2896. **Tel** (307)797-3131.

    ISSN 1079-2937
DD 384   US

●**UTILITIES COMMUNICATIONS NEWS.** [Util. commun. news]. **VFOAT** UTN. Vol. 1, No. 1 (Sept. 1994)-. Newsletter. English. Twelve times a year. $575.00 US and Canada; $625.00 other. Information Gatekeepers Inc., 214 Harvard Avenue, Boston MA 02134. **Tel** (617)232-3111, (617)738-8088, (800)323-1088, **FAX** (617)734-8562.

    ISSN 0882-0295
DD 384   US
     CEASED

VAR (CAMDEN, ME.). (VAR.). [VAR]. **VAT** Value-Added Resellers. Vol. 1, No. 1 (July 1985)-(19??). Periodical. English. Camden Communications Inc, Highland Mill, PO Box 250, Camden ME 04843. **Tel** (800)253-5473.

    ISSN 0922-6540
UDC 614.842/614.847   NE
Pr Rev.

VERBINDING ROTTERDAM. (VERBINDING.). [Verbinding Rotterdam]. (1980)-. Periodical. Dutch. Ten times a year (monthly with June-July and Aug.-Sept. issues combined). $59.95. Verbinding Uitgeverij, Ab de Molenaarpad 4, 3069 ZC Rotterdam Netherlands. **Tel** 011 31 10 4553258, **FAX** 31-10-4374089. **ED** R. R. Van der Beek. cum. index. **Bk Rev**. **Ad Acc**. **Circ:** 5,000 (ctrl).
  Desc: Information and news about telecommunications for mobile telecommunications users, producers, control centers and alarm rooms.

LC HE7343 .A386a
DD 383.49   SA

VERSLAG VAN DIE GEKOSE KOMITEE OOR POS- EN TELEKOMMUNIKASIEWESE. REPORT OF THE SELECT COMMITTEE ON POSTS AND TELECOMMUNICATIONS. **See** Communications-Postal Communications.

    ISSN 1057-140X
DD 384   US

VIDEO CONFERENCING : ANALYSIS OF AN EMERGING TECHNOLOGY. [Video confer.]. 1st Ed. (1991)-. Periodical. English. $255.00 (single issue). Telecom Publishing Group, 1101 King Street, Suite 444, Alexandria VA 22314. **Tel** (703)683-4100, (800)327-7205, **FAX** (703)739-6490.

    ISSN 0967-2052
     UK

VOICE INTERNATIONAL. [Voice int.]. (1991)-. Trade Publication. English. Six times a year. $116.36. Europe Media Ltd., 14-47 Kings Terrace, London NW1 0JR United Kingdom. **Tel** 011 44 171 9116002, **FAX** 011 44 171 9116020. **Absorbed** World Telemedia.

    ISSN 0884-6685
DD 384   US

VOICE PROCESSING. See Computers-Artificial Intelligence.

DD 338.4/7621399   **ISSN** 1181-8204
     CN

VOICEPOWER REVIEW, THE. [VoicePower rev.]. **VFOAT** Voice Power Review. Vol. 1, No. 1 (Sept./Oct. 1990)-. Periodical. English. Irregular. Voicepower, Inc., PO Box 313, Don Mills Ontario M3C 2S7 Canada.

    ISSN 1069-7500
     US
     CCC

●**WASHINGTON TELECOM NEWS.** (June 1993)-. Periodical. English. One time a week (50 issues). $597.00. Phillips Business Information Inc., 1201 Seven Locks Road, PO Box 61130, Potomac MD 20854. **Tel** (301)424-3338, (301)340-1520, (800)777-5005, **FAX** (301)424-4297, telex 358149. **Formed by the union of** The Spectrum Report **and** Telephone News Telecommunications Regulatory Monitor.

     US

WASHINGTON TELECOMMUNICATIONS DIRECTORY. (198?)-. Directory. English. $35.00. Capitol Publications, 1101 King Street, Suite 444, Alexandria VA 22314. **Tel** (703)683-4100, (800)655-5597, **FAX** (703)739-6517, (800)645-4104. **(Subscription address:** Capitol Publications, PO Box 1455, Alexandria VA 22313. **Tel** (800)655-5597, **FAX** (703)739-6517.**)** **Continues** Washington Telecom Directory, 8755-2876.

     UK

●**WHAT CELLPHONE AND PERSONAL OFFICE.** (1995)-. English. Six times a year. $94.11. WV Publications, 57-59 Rochester Place, London NW1 9JU United Kingdom. **Tel** 011 44 171 4850011. **Continues** What Cellphone and Mobile Office.

LC HE8701   **ISSN** 1023-179X
DD 384.6   SA

●**WHAT MOBILE AND CELLPHONE MAGAZINE.** (1994)-. English. Twelve times a year. Blah Publishing, PO Box 9573, Hennopsmeer 0046 South Africa. **Ad Acc**.

    ISSN 1067-0793
DD 384   US

WHAT'S ON SATELLITE. [What's satell.]. (199?)-. English. Three times a year (Jan., May, Sept.). $133.50. Design Publishers, 800 Siesta Way, Sonoma CA 95476. **Tel** (707)939-9306, **FAX** (707)939-9235. **Continues** Business Telecommunications Directory, 1041-6137.

LC TK5101.A1 W48   **ISSN** 0730-3033
DD 621.38   US

WHO, WHAT, & WHERE IN COMMUNICATIONS SECURITY. [Who, what, where commun. secur.]. **Added/Corp** Marketing Consultants International. **VFOAT** Who, What, and Where in Communications Security. (1981)-. English. One time a year. Marketing Consultants International Inc, 645 East 1st Street, Hagerstown MD 21740.

LC TK5105.5 .W57   **ISSN** 1059-1028
DD 306   US
     CODEN WREDEM

●**WIRED (SAN FRANCISCO, CALIF.). See** Computers-Computer Networks.

     US

WIRELESS BUSINESS & FINANCE. (199?)-. Periodical. English. Twenty-five times a year. $597.00 US; $630.00 other. Phillips Business Information Inc., 1201 Seven Locks Road, PO Box 61130, Potomac MD 20854. **Tel** (301)424-3338, (301)340-1520, (800)777-5005, **FAX** (301)424-4297, telex 358149.

    ISSN 1058-6717
DD 384   US

WIRELESS CELLULAR. [Wirel. cell.]. **Added/Corp** Information Gatekeepers, Inc. **VFOAT** Wireless Cellular Newsletter. Vol. 1, No. 1 (Aug. 1991)-. Periodical. English. Twelve times a year. $575.00. Information Gatekeepers Inc., 214 Harvard Avenue, Boston MA 02134. **Tel** (617)232-3111, (617)738-8088, (800)323-1088, **FAX** (617)734-8562.

    ISSN 1067-9723
DD 338   US

WIRELESS DATA NETWORKS. (WIRELESS DATA NETWORKS : EMERGING TECHNOLOGIES AND MARKET OPPORTUNITIES.). [Wirel. data netw.]. (1991)-. Periodical. English. Every 2 years. $1,995.00. Telecom Publishing Group, 1101 King Street, Suite 444, Alexandria VA 22314. **Tel** (703)683-4100, (800)327-7205, **FAX** (703)739-6490.

    ISSN 1069-3416
     US
     CCC

●**WIRELESS DATA NEWS. Added/Corp** Phillips Business Information, Inc. (1993)-. Periodical. English. Twenty-five times a year. $597.00. Phillips Business

Communications —Telecommunication

Information Inc., 1201 Seven Locks Road, PO Box 61130, Potomac MD 20854. **Tel** (301)424-3338, (301)340-1520, (800)777-5005, **FAX** (301)424-4297, telex 358149.

    ISSN 1076-4240
DD 621   US

WIRELESS DESIGN & DEVELOPMENT. [Wirel. design dev.]. (199?)-. Periodical. English. Twelve times a year. $75.00. Cahners Publishing Company, 249 West 17th Street, New York NY 10011. **Tel** (212)645-0067, **FAX** (212)242-6987. **(Subscription address:** Gordon Publications, Inc., Paid Circulation Department, 301 Gibralter Drive, Box 650, Morris Plains NJ 07950-0650. **Tel** (201)292-5100 ext. 351, **FAX** (201)898-9281.**)**
  Desc: Provides information on commercial wireless technology.

    ISSN 1080-5249
DD 621   US

WIRELESS FOR THE CORPORATE USER. [Wirel. corp. user]. **VFOAT** Wireless. (1992)-. Periodical. English. Six times a year. $30.00 Canada and Mexico; $66.00 other. Probe Research Inc., Three Wing Drive, Suite 240, Cedar Knolls NJ 07927-1000. **Tel** (201)285-1500, **FAX** (201)285-1519. **ED** Peter Bernstein. **Ad Acc**. **Circ:** 85,000.
  Desc: Covers wireless communications of all types - voice, data, and cellular.

     US

WIRELESS INDUSTRY DIRECTORY. (199?)-. Directory. English. One time a year. $229.00. Phillips Business Information Inc., 1201 Seven Locks Road, PO Box 61130, Potomac MD 20854. **Tel** (301)424-3338, (301)340-1520, (800)777-5005, **FAX** (301)424-4297, telex 358149. **Absorbed** Cellular Mobile Communications Directory; Mobile Communications Directory.
  Desc: Profiles executive decision makers in 84 countries. The publication also provides information allowing access to the suppliers of cellular/mobile products and services worldwide.

    ISSN 1077-3991
DD 384   US

●**WIRELESS MARKET STATS.** [Wirel. mark. stats]. **Added/Corp** Paul Kagan Associates. No. 58 (June 30, 1994)-. Newsletter. English. Twelve times a year. $695.00. Paul Kagan Associates Inc., 126 Clock Tower Place, Carmel CA 93923-8734. **Tel** (408) 624-1536, **FAX** (408)625-3225, telex ITT 4938124 PKA UI. available via fax. **Continues** RSA Newsletter, 1046-6045.
  Desc: Guide to wireless telecom competition - analysis on metropolitan and rural cellular market efficiency, operating statistics, private deal market data, economic and demographic data for narrowband and broadband PCS, ESMR, paging, etc.

     US

WIRELESS MESSAGING REPORT. English. Twenty-six times a year. $449.00 US; $484.00 other. Telecommunications Reports, 1333 H Street Northwest, 2nd Floor West Tower, Washington DC 20005. **Tel** (202)842-0520, (800)822-6338, **FAX** (202)842-3047. **(Subscription address:** Telecommunications Reports, PO Box 675, Cooper Station, New York NY 10276.**)**

    ISSN 1058-6725
DD 384   US
     TITLE CHANGE

WIRELESS PCN TELECOMMUNICATIONS. [Wirel. PCN telecommun.]. **Added/Corp** Information Gatekeepers, Inc. **VFOAT** Wireless PCN; Wireless PCN Newsletter. **VAT** Wireless Personal Communications Network Telecommunications. Vol. 1, No. 1 (Aug. 1991)-(1995). Newsletter. English. Information Gatekeepers Inc., 214 Harvard Avenue, Boston MA 02134. **Tel** (617)232-3111, (617)738-8088, (800)323-1088, **FAX** (617)734-8562. **Continued by** Wireless PCS Telecommunications, 1082-2100.

    ISSN 1082-2100
DD 384   US

●**WIRELESS PCS TELECOMMUNICATIONS.** [Wirel. PCS telecommun.]. **Added/Corp** Information Gatekeepers, Inc. **VFOAT** Wireless PCS; Wireless PCS Newsletter. Vol. 5, No. 3 (Mar. 1995)-. Newsletter. English. Twelve times a year. $575.00. Information Gatekeepers Inc., 214 Harvard Avenue, Boston MA 02134. **Tel** (617)232-3111, (617)738-8088, (800)323-1088, **FAX** (617)734-8562. **Continues** Wireless PCN Newsletter, 1058-6725.

    ISSN 0929-6212
     NE
     CCC
     CODEN WPCOFW

●**WIRELESS PERSONAL COMMUNICATIONS.** (1994)-. Academic Scholarly Publication. English. Four times a year.

Communications —Telecommunication

$328.00. Kluwer Academic Publishers, Postbus 322, 3300 AH Dordrecht The Netherlands. **Tel** 011 31 78 524400, FAX 011 31 78 183273, telex 20083.

ISSN 1058-6695
DD 384 US

WIRELESS SATELLITE & BROADCASTING. [Wirel. satell. broadcast.]. **Added/Corp** Information Gatekeepers, Inc. **VFOAT** Wireless Satellite and Broadcasting Newsletter; Wireless Satellite and Broadcasting Newsletter; Wireless Satellite & Broadcasting Newsletter; Wireless Satellite Newsletter. Vol. 1, No. 1 (Aug. 1991)-. Periodical. English. Twelve times a year. $575.00 US and Canada; $625.00 other. Information Gatekeepers Inc., 214 Harvard Avenue, Boston MA 02134. **Tel** (617)232-3111, (617)738-8088, (800)323-1088, FAX (617)734-8562.

ISSN 1058-6709
DD 384 US

WIRELESS SPECTRUM MANAGEMENT. [Wirel. spectr. manage.]. **Added/Corp** Information Gatekeepers, Inc. **VFOAT** Wireless Spectrum Management Newsletter; Wireless Spectrum Newsletter. Vol. 1, No. 1 (Aug. 1991)-. Periodical. English. Twelve times a year. $575.00 US and Canada; $625.00 other. Information Gatekeepers Inc., 214 Harvard Avenue, Boston MA 02134. **Tel** (617)232-3111, (617)738-8088, (800)323-1088, FAX (617)734-8562.

ISSN 1075-413X
DD 332 US

●**WIRELESS TELECOM INVESTOR.** [Wirel. telecom invest.]. **Added/Corp** Paul Kagan Associates. No. 72 (Feb. 23, 1994)-. Newsletter. English. Twelve times a year. $695.00. Paul Kagan Associates Inc., 126 Clock Tower Place, Carmel CA 93923-8734. **Tel** (408)624-1536, FAX (408)625-3225, telex ITT 4938124 PKA UI. available via fax. **Continues** Cellular Investor, 0898-0403.
Desc: Analysis of private and public values of wireless telecommunications companies, including cellular telephone, ESMR and PCS.

ISSN 1057-5391
DD 384 US

WIRELESS TELECOMMUNICATIONS. [Wirel. telecommun.]. **Added/Corp** Information Gatekeepers, Inc. **VFOAT** Wireless Telecommunications Newsletter. Vol. 1, No. 1 (May 1991)-. Newsletter. English. Twelve times a year. $575.00 US and Canada; $625.00 other. Information Gatekeepers Inc., 214 Harvard Avenue, Boston MA 02134. **Tel** (617)232-3111, (617)738-8088, (800)323-1088, FAX (617)734-8562.

ISSN 1075-4385
DD 338 US

●**WIRELESS WORLD.** [Wirel. world]. **VFOAT** Wirelessworld. (1994)-. Periodical. English. Twelve times a year. Intertec Publishing Corporation, 9800 Metcalf, Overland Park KS 66212. **Tel** (913)341-1300. **ED** Rhonda L. Wickham. **Ad Acc.**
Desc: Contents include business news, new product information and in-depth reports on the wireless communication industry.

LC GV1201.5 ISSN 1081-7646
DD 790 US

●**WORLD OF PHONECARDS, THE.** See Hobbies.

LC TK5104 .W58 ISSN 0885-1611
DD 384.5/1 US

WORLD SATELLITE ALMANAC. [World satell. alm.]. **VFOAT** World Satellite. Vol. 1 (1985)-. English. $111.95 North America; $129.95 Europe, South America; $134.95 other. Phillips Business Information Inc., 1201 Seven Locks Road, PO Box 61130, Potomac MD 20854. **Tel** (301)424-3338, (301)340-1520, (800)777-5005, FAX (301)424-4297, telex 358149. **Absorbed** Satellite Systems Handbook.

LC TK5104 .W583 ISSN 1052-7842
DD 384.5/1/05 US

WORLD SATELLITE ANNUAL, THE. (THE ... WORLD SATELLITE ANNUAL.). [World satell. annu.]. (198?)-. English. $66.95. MLE Inc, PO Box 159, Winter Beach FL 32971. **Tel** (305)767-4687, FAX (305)767-6067.

LC TK5104 .S366 ISSN 1046-0950
DD 384.5/1/025 US
TITLE CHANGE

WORLD SATELLITE DIRECTORY (POTOMAC, MD.), THE. (THE ... WORLD SATELLITE DIRECTORY.). [World satell. dir.]. (1989)-(Jan. 1996). Directory. English. Phillips Business Information Inc., 1201 Seven Locks Road, PO Box 61130, Potomac MD 20854. **Tel** (301)424-3338, (301)340-1520, (800)777-5005, FAX (301)424-4297, telex 358149. **Continues** Satellite Directory, 0731-0293; **Absorbed** World Satellite Transponder Report. **Continued by** Satellite Industry Directory.
Desc: Business reference for the satellite industry with information on customers, colleagues, suppliers, and market data.

LC HE7621 .W67 ISSN 0364-3360
DD 384/.025 US

WORLD TELECOMMUNICATIONS DIRECTORY. (19??)-. Directory. English. Telecom Systems Group Inc, 579 Pompton Avenue, Cedar Grove NJ 07009.

UK

Pr Rev.
WORLD TELECOMMUNICATIONS MARKETFILE SERVICES. (19??)-. Trade Publication. English. Irregular. £1,750.00. Telecom Information Services Ltd, Argyle Circus #3, Bognor Regis, West Sussex PO21 1DS United Kingdom. **Tel** 011 44 1243 842082, FAX 011 44 1243 842083. Index available. cum. index. available on CD-ROM.
Desc: More than 750 of detailed analysis and statistics on 70 world telecommunications markets.

UK

WORLD TELECOMS DAILY. English. Seven times a week. £525.00 UK and Europe; $1050.00 other. Telecom Information Services Ltd, Argyle Circus #3, Bognor Regis, West Sussex PO21 1DS United Kingdom. **Tel** 011 44 1243 842082, FAX 011 44 1243 842083. **ED** Frazer Nicholson. ctrl circ.

ISSN 1017-6950
BE
CODEN XIMAEZ
TITLE CHANGE

XIII MAGAZINE (BRUXELLES). (XIII MAGAZINE.). [XIII mag.]. **Added/Corp** Commission of the European Communities. Directorate-General for Telecommunications, Information Industries, and Innovation. **VFOAT** 13 Magazine; Thirteen Magazine. No. 1 (Apr. 1991)-(1993). Periodical. English (French, Spanish, Italian and German). Commission of the European Communities, Directorate of General Information, Avenue D Auderghem, 45 Breydel boulevard, B 1049 Brussels Belgium. **Tel** 011 32 2 2357639, telex 21877 COMEU B. **ED** Michel Carpentier. Documents available from UMI Article Clearinghouse. **Continues** I'm. **Continued by** I & T Magazine.
Desc: Covers telecommunications and information technology programs and policy in Europe.
Ind/Abst ABI/INFORM Glob. Ed.; HILITES.

LC TK5101.A1 T45

BE
CODEN XMNREH
TITLE CHANGE

XIII MAGAZINE NEWS REVIEW. **Added/Corp** Commission of the European Communities. Directorate-General for Telecommunications, Information Industries and Innovation. **VFOAT** 13 Magazine News Review; Thirteen Magazine News Review. No. 1 (1991)-(1993). Periodical. English. Commission of the European Communities, Directorate of General Information, Avenue D Auderghem, 45 Breydel boulevard, B 1049 Brussels Belgium. **Tel** 011 32 2 2357639, telex 21877 COMEU B. **ED** Jean Siotis. **Continued by** I & T Magazine News Review.
Desc: Covers telecommunication and information technology programs in Europe. Details succinct operational information on results.

TELEVISION AND CABLE

LC PN4888.T4 A34 ISSN 0891-8775
DD 070.1/9 US

ABC NEWS INDEX. See Communications-Abstracting, Bibliographies and Statistics.

US

ABC NEWS TRANSCRIPTS [MICROFORM]. **Added/Corp** ABC News. (Jan. 1970)-. Periodical. English. Four times a year. $922.20. Primary Source Media, 12 Lunar Drive, Woodbridge CT 06525. **Tel** (800)444-0799, FAX (203)397-3893. Index available ($205.00).

ISSN 0810-6118
DD 354.940087454 AT

ABTEE. [Abtee]. (1982)-. Periodical. English. Twenty-six times a year. 75.00Aus$. Australian Broadcasting Tribunal, PO Box 1308, North Sydney 2059 Australia. **Tel** 02 959-7811.
Ind/Abst Aust. Educ. Index (199?)-.

ISSN 0821-0209
DD 269/.2 CN
UDC 269; 286.3

ACCENT ON ARTS. See Religions and Theology-Protestantism.

AT

ACTAC. (19??)-. English. Four times a year. 20.00Aus$. Australian Children's Television Action Committee, 4 Neath Street, Surrey Hill Victoria 3127 Australia. **Tel** 011 61 3 3870177, FAX 011 61 3 3878653. **ED** Mrs. Jo James (editor's address: 23 Maling Road, Canterbury 3126 Australia; telephone: 011 61 3 8366786,

or 8369445). **Bk Rev. Ad Acc. Circ:** 400.
Desc: Contains articles relating to the quality of children's television.

ISSN 0889-8170
US

ADVANCE (DES MOINES, IOWA). (ADVANCE.). **Added/Corp** Friends of Iowa Public Television. Vol. 1 (1971)-. Periodical. English. Twelve times a year. $30.00. Friends of Iowa Public TV, PO Box 6400, Johnston IA 50131-6450. **Tel** (515)253-9225, FAX (515)253-9791. **ED** Melanie Campbell (editor's address: PO Box 6400, Johnston, IA 50134; phone:(515)242-3148. **Circ:** 70,000.
Desc: Program listing for Iowa public television.

LC PN1993.5.A35 A47

RH

AFRICA FILM & TV. VFOAT Africa Film and TV; African Film and Television. (199?)-. English. Six times a year. $50.65. AFL / Zimbabwe, PO Box 6109, Harare Zimbabwe.

ISSN 0164-6508

AFTERNOON TV. VAT Afternoon Television. (19??)-. Periodical. English. Twelve times a year. $24.00. Dynasty Media Publishing Corporation, PO Box 1629, Englewood Cliff NJ 07632. **Tel** (212)371-4932.

ISSN 0278-9639

AIRWAVES. Added/Corp Friends of Channel 21 (Madison, Wis.) Wisconsin Public Radio Association. **VAT** Air Waves. Vol. 1, No. 1 (Dec. 1981)-. Periodical. English. Twelve times a year. $35.00. Friends of WHA-TV, 821 University Avenue, Madison WI 53706. **Tel** (608)262-5255. **ED** Pat Brown. **Circ:** 53,000.
Desc: Program guide for WHA-TV.

LC HF6146.T42 A45 ISSN 0889-2717
DD 659.14/3/02573 US

ALL TV PUBLICITY OUTLETS, NATIONWIDE. [All TV public. outlets nationwide]. **Added/Corp** Public Relations Plus, Inc. **VAT** All Television Publicity Outlets, Nationwide. No. 45 (1986)-. Periodical. English. Two times a year. Public Relations Plus Inc., PO Drawer 1197, New Milford CT 06776. **Tel** (800)-999-8448, FAX (203)355-8048. **Formed by the union of** TV Publicity Outlets, Nationwide **and** Cable TV Publicity Outlets, Nationwide.
Desc: Includes all stations and cable outlets displayed by market, key news, production and on-air contacts. Also covers stations that use interviews in news broadcasts, programs that use guests, and stations that send out news crews. Includes types of publicity materials used, programs that use VNRs, slides, film and tape, separate indexes for network shows, details on network and syndicated programs, at-a-glance market demographics, etc.

ISSN 1200-4170
DD 791.45/01/3 CN

ALLIANCE INFO. [Alliance info]. **Added/Corp** Alliance for Children and Television. (199?)-. Periodical. English (French). Twelve times a year. Free on request. Alliance for Children and Television, 344 Dupont Street, Suite 205, Toronto Ontario M5R 1V9 Canada. **Tel** (416)515-0466. **Continues** Children's Broadcast Institute (Newsletter), 0824-7005.

ISSN 1042-198X
DD 384 US

AMATEUR TELEVISION QUARTERLY. (AMATEUR TELEVISION QUARTERLY : ATVQ MAGAZINE.). [Amat. telev. q.]. **VFOAT** ATVQ Magazine; ATVQ. **VAT** Amateur Quarterly Magazine. Vol. 1, No. 1 (Aug. 1988)-. Periodical. English. Four times a year (Jan., Apr., July, Oct.). $18.00. Amateur Television Quarterly, 1545 Lee Street, Suite 73, Des Plaines IL 60018. **Tel** (708)298-2369, (708)298-2269, FAX (708)803-8994. **ED** Henry Rvh. Index available ($5.00). cum. index. **Bk Rev**, (Qty: 4-10). **Ad Acc, Adv Mgr:** Henry Rvh. **Circ:** 3,000.
Desc: News and information on interactive personal television via ham radio.

ISSN 0271-7263
US

AMERICAN BROADCASTING COMPANIES ANNUAL REPORT.
Main/Corp American Broadcasting Companies. **Added/Corp** American Broadcasting Companies. Annual Report. **VAT** American Broadcasting Companies, Incorporated, Annual Report. (1965)-. English. One time a year. ABC Schwann Publications, PO Box 41094, Nashville TN 37204. **Tel** (615)377-3322, (800)937-3513. **Continues** Annual Report - American Broadcasting-Paramount Theatres, Inc., 0401-7072.

II

ANANDALOKA. VFOAT Anandalok. (19??)-. Periodical. Bengali. Twenty-four times a year. Anandbazar Patrika Ltd, 689 Prafulla Sarkar Street, Calcutta 700 001 India.

Communications — Television and Cable

LC TK6675 .C66a **ISSN** 0198-0270
DD 621.388/5
CODEN ACRPDD
US

ANNUAL CONFERENCE ON CATV RELIABILITY.
(ANNUAL CONFERENCE ON CATV RELIABILITY : PAPERS.). [Annu. Conf. CATV Reliab.]. **Main/Conf** Conference on CATV Reliability. **Added/Corp** Society of Cable Television Engineers. Institute of Electrical and Electronics Engineers. IEEE Broadcast, Cable and Consumer Electronics Society. **VFOAT** CATV Reliability. 1st (1976)-. English. Irregular. Institution of Electrical Engineers / IEE, Michael Faraday House, Six Hills Way, Stevenage Hertfordshire SG1 2AY United Kingdom. **Tel** 011 44 1438 313311, FAX 011 44 1438 742840, telex 825578 IEESTV G. **(Subscription address:** IEE / Peter Peregrinus Ltd., PO Box 96, Stevenage Herts SG1 2SD United Kingdom. **Tel** 011 44 1438 313311, FAX 011 44 438 742792, telex 825578 IEESTV G.) Index Available published separately, bound from publisher, free-automatically sent.

LC HE8700.9
DD 384.55
UK

ANNUAL REPORT & ACCOUNTS / ITC.
Main/Corp Independent Television Commission. **VFOAT** Annual Report and Accounts. (19??)-. Corporate Report. English. Independent Television Commission, 33 Foley Street, London W1P 7LB United Kingdom. **Tel** 011 44 171 2553000, FAX 011 44 171 3067800. *Continues Independent Broadcasting Authority. Annual Report.*
Desc: Annual report from the Independent Television Commission.

LC HE8689.9.C3 C38a **ISSN** 0708-9392
DD 384.54/06/571
CN

ANNUAL REPORT - CANADIAN BROADCASTING CORPORATION.
(ANNUAL REPORT - CANADIAN BROADCASTING CORPORATION. RAPPORT ANNUEL - SOCIETE RADIO-CANADA.). **Main/Corp** Canadian Broadcasting Corporation. **Added/Corp** Canadian Broadcasting Corporation. Rapport Annuel de la Societe Radio-Canada. **VFOAT** Rapport Annuel - Societe Radio-Canada. (1938)-. English (French). One time a year. Free on request. Canadian Broadcasting Corp, PO Box 8478, 1500 Bronson Avenue, Ottawa Ontario K1G 3J5 Canada. **Tel** (613)724-1200. *Continues Canadian Broadcasting Corporation. Report of the Canadian Broadcasting Corporation., 0708-9392.*

LC HE8700.8 .N42a **ISSN** 0737-0733
DD 384.55/4/060.749
US

ANNUAL REPORT - NEW JERSEY NETWORK (FIRM).
(ANNUAL REPORT / NEW JERSEY NETWORK.). **Main/Corp** New Jersey Network (Firm). (19??)-. English. One time a year. New Jersey Network, 1573 Parkside Avenue, CN 777, Trenton NJ 08625. **Tel** (609)530-5031.

LC LB1044.7 .S59a
DD 371.33/58/09757
US

ANNUAL REPORT OF THE SOUTH CAROLINA EDUCATIONAL TELEVISION COMMISSION.
Main/Corp South Carolina. Educational Television Commission. (19??)-. English. One time a year. Educational Television Commission, 1101 George Rogers Boulevard, PO Box 11000, Columbia SC 29211. **Tel** (803)737-3527.

LC LB1044.7 .O537a **ISSN** 0198-988X
DD 371.3/358/09766
US

ANNUAL REPORT - OKLAHOMA EDUCATIONAL TELEVISION AUTHORITY. See Education-Teaching and Curriculum.

LC PN1993.5.U778 T46a
DD 353.97680085/4
US

ANNUAL REPORT / TENNESSEE FILM, TAPE, AND MUSIC COMMISSION. See Motion Picture.

ISSN 0748-6014
DD 338
US

ASIA CABLE.
[Asia cable]. (1984)-. Periodical. English. Twenty-six times a year. $259.00. Asia Cable, PO Box 307, Lake Oswego OR 97034. **Tel** (503)636-7058.

ISSN 1074-1127
DD 384
UK

●ASIA PACIFIC MEDIA INVESTOR.
[Asia Pac. media invest.]. No. 1 (Nov. 5, 1993)-. Newsletter. English. Twelve times a year. $695.00. Kagan World Media Inc., 126 Clock Tower Place, Carmel CA 93923-8734. **Tel** (408)624-1536, FAX (408)625-3225. **(Subscription address:** Kagan World Media Ltd., 524 Fulham Road, London SW6 5NR United Kingdom. **Tel** 011 44 171 3718880, FAX 011 44 171 3718715.) available via fax.
Desc: Analyses of strategic alliances, media convergence, cable/pay TV penetration, satellite growth, mergers and acquisitions, broadcast operations and regulatory developments of countries of the Asia Pacific region.

LC HE8700
DD 384.55
UK

●ASIA - PACIFIC SATELLITE.
(1995)-. Trade Publication. English. Four times a year. £30.00. ICOM Publications Ltd., Chancery House, St. Nicholas Way, Sutton Surrey SM1 1JB United Kingdom. **Tel** 011 44 181 6421117, FAX 011 44 181 6421941. **ED** R. Hawkes. **Ad Acc, Adv Mgr:** A. Wand. Full Page (B&W) $3,265.00. Full Page (Color) $4,675.00. Circ: 7,177 (ctrl).
Desc: Focuses on the satellite market in the Asia-Pacific region.

LC HE8700 **ISSN** 1355-0071
DD 384.55
UK

●ASIA - PACIFIC TELECOMS ANALYST.
(1994)-. Newsletter. English. Twenty-four times a year. £495.00. Financial Times Telecoms & Media Publishing, Maple House, 149 Tottenham Court Road, London W1P 9LL United Kingdom. **Tel** 011 44 171 8962234, FAX 011 44 171 8962256. **ED** Jenny Walker. available with charts.
Desc: Focuses on telecommunication developments in the Asia-Pacific region. Includes reports on business, legislation, technology, and market analyses.

UK

ASIA PACIFIC TV DATABOOK.
(19??)-. English. One time a year. $445.00. Kagan World Media Inc., 126 Clock Tower Place, Carmel CA 93923-8734. **Tel** (408)624-1536, FAX (408)625-3225. **(Subscription address:** Kagan World Media Ltd., 524 Fulham Road, London SW6 5NR United Kingdom. **Tel** 011 44 171 3718880, FAX 011 44 171 3718715.)
Desc: Analyses on each major television market of Asia and the Pacific Rim, with profiles of 13 Asia Pacific countries, advertising revenue and TV household projections, developments for cable and satellite expansion along with regulatory, advertising and industry names, addresses, phone and fax numbers.

LC HE8689.9.B7 A93
BL

AUDIENCIA.
(1976)-. Portuguese. Abert, Av Angelica No 421, Sao Paulo Brazil.

ISSN 0169-0256
NE

UDC 621.39

AV. AUDIOVISUEEL MAGAZINE.
(AV.). [AV. Audiov. mag.]. **VFOAT** Audiovisueel Magazine. (1982)-. Periodical. Dutch. Twelve times a year. $96.96. AV Press BV, Postbus 155, 6500 AD Nijmegen Netherlands. **Tel** 011 31 80 787444. *Absorbed Film en TV Maker, 0166-171X.*

LC PN1560 **ISSN** 1055-9825
DD 792
US
TITLE CHANGE

BACK STAGE SHOOT. See Business and Economics-Advertising and Public Relations.

LC HE8689.8 .B33 **ISSN** 0891-0103
DD 384.54/02573
US
TITLE CHANGE

BACON'S RADIO/TV DIRECTORY.
[Bacon's radio/TV dir.]. **Added/Corp** Bacon's PR and Media Information Systems. Bacon's Publishing Company. **VFOAT** Bacon's Radio TV Directory; Radio TV Directory; Radio/TV Directory. 1st Ed. (1987)-(19??). Directory. English. Bacon's Publishing Co., 332 South Michigan Avenue, Chicago IL 60604. **Tel** (312)922-2400, (800)621-0561, FAX (312)922-3127. *Continued by Bacon's Radio TV Cable Directory.*
Desc: Lists all U.S. radio, TV, and cable stations, including address, phone/fax, key station personnel. Target audience, station format, call letter, network affiliation provided. News/talk/interview shows and their editorial contracts, show profiles included. Network and syndicated programming provided. Free phone updating and midyear revisions provided.

LC TK6645 .E8
DD 384.55/53/0254
SZ

BANDES METRIQUE ET DECIMETRIQUE, LISTE DES STATIONS DE TELEVISION, ZONE EUROPEENNE DE RADIODIFFUSION.
Added/Corp European Broadcasting Union. Technical Centre. **VFOAT** Liste des Stations de Television; List of VHF/UHF Television Stations, European Broadcasting Area. No 30 (Sept. 1985)-. English (French). Six times a year. 70F. European Broadcasting Union, Case Postale 67, CH-1218 Geneva Switzerland. **Tel** 011 41 22 7172111, FAX 011 41 22 7985897, telex 41 57 00 EBU CH. *Continues Liste des Stations de Television, Zone Europeenne de Radiodiffusion.*

AT

B&T WEEKLY.
(19??)-. English. One time a week. 162.00Aus$ Australia; 260.00Aus$ New Zealand, Papua New Guinea; 280.00Aus$ Malaysia, Indonesia, Fiji; 282.00Aus$ Japan, India, Hong Kong; 330.00Aus$ US, Canada, Lebanon; 366.00Can$ Europe, Africa, former USSR. Thomson Publications / Australia, 47 Chippen Street, Chippendale New South Wales 2008 Australia. **Tel** 011 61 2 6992411, FAX 011 61 2 6991184, telex 122226. **(Subscription address:** Thomson Publications Australia, PO Box 815, Strawberry Hills, New South Wales, 2012 Australia. **Tel** 011 61 2 6992411.)

LC HE8699.A8 B7
DD 384.54/0994
AT

B&T YEAR BOOK.
VFOAT B & T Year Book; B and T Year Book. 17th Ed. (1974)-. English. One time a year. 120.86Aus$. Thomson Publications / Australia, 47 Chippen Street, Chippendale New South Wales 2008 Australia. **Tel** 011 61 2 6992411, FAX 011 61 2 6991184, telex 122226. **(Subscription address:** Thomson Publications Australia, PO Box 815, Strawberry Hills, New South Wales, 2012 Australia. **Tel** 011 61 2 6992411.) *Continues Broadcasting and Television Year Book.*

LC HE8689.9.G7 B75a
UK
TITLE CHANGE

BBC ANNUAL REVIEW. Main/Corp
British Broadcasting Corporation. **VFOAT** Annual Review. (1993)-(1993). English. BBC Publications, 35 Marylebone High Street, London W1 United Kingdom. **Tel** 011 44 71 580 5577. **(Subscription address:** Exel Logistics, Sir Thomas Longley Road, Rochester Kent ME2 4DU United Kingdom. **Tel** 011 44 1634 297123.) *Continues British Broadcasting Corporation. Annual Report & Accounts. Continued by British Broadcasting Corporation. BBC Report and Accounts.*

LC HE8689.9.G7 .B75a
DD 621
UK

●BBC REPORT AND ACCOUNTS. Main/Corp
British Broadcasting Corporation. **VFOAT** Report and Accounts; Annual Report and Accounts of the British Broadcasting Corporation for the Year .... (1994)-. English. One time a year. $15.38. BBC Publications, 35 Marylebone High Street, London W1 United Kingdom. **Tel** 011 44 71 580 5577. **(Subscription address:** Exel Logistics, Sir Thomas Longley Road, Rochester Kent ME2 4DU United Kingdom. **Tel** 011 44 1634 297123.) *Continues British Broadcasting Corporation. BBC Annual Review.*

UK

BBC RESEARCH AND DEVELOPMENT REPORT : BBC RD.
(19??)-. Periodical. English. £60.00 UK; £80.00 Europe; £85.00 other. British Broadcasting Corporation / Tadworth Surrey, Kingswood Warren, Tadworth Surrey KT20 6NP United Kingdom. **Tel** 011 44 1737 832361, FAX 011 44 1737 832336. *Continues BBC Research Department Report.* **Ind/Abst** Curr. Cit.

UK
TITLE CHANGE

BBC RESEARCH DEPARTMENT REPORTS.
(19??)-(19??). English. British Broadcasting Corporation / Tadworth Surrey, Kingswood Warren, Tadworth Surrey KT20 6NP United Kingdom. **Tel** 011 44 1737 832361, FAX 011 44 1737 832336. *Continued by BBC Research and Development Report : BBC RD.*

ISSN 0967-5442
DD 791.44
UK

BBC WORLDWIDE.
[BBC worldwide]. (1992)-. Periodical. English. Twelve times a year. $48.00. BBC World Service, PO Box 76, Bush House Strand, London WC2B 4PH United Kingdom. **Tel** 011 44 171 2572906, FAX 011 44 171 3790519. available in braille. *Continues London Calling (London, England: 1939), 0024-600X.*

LC PN1991 .L84
DD 384.545
UK

BBC WORLDWIDE : THE BBC WORLD SERVICE MAGAZINE. See Communications-Radio.

LC PN1993 .F665
DD 791.43/05
GW

BEITRAEGE ZUR FILM- UND FERNSEHWISSENSCHAFT : SCHRIFTENREIHE DER HOCHSCHULE FUR FILM UND FERNSEHEN DER DDR.
See Motion Picture.

LC PN1993.3 .F418
DD 384/.8/02541
UK

●BFI FILM AND TELEVISION HANDBOOK.
See Motion Picture.

ISSN 1056-6104
US

BIB TELEVISION PROGRAMMING SOURCE BOOKS.
Added/Corp Broadcast Information Bureau. **VAT** Broadcast Information Bureau Television Programming Source Books. (1991)-. English. One time a year. $860.00 US; $875.00 Canada; $915.00 other. North American Publishing Company, 401 North Broad Street, Philadelphia PA 19108. **Tel** (215)238-5300, (800)777-8074, FAX (215)238-5283. available on CD-ROM. *Continues Television Programming Source Books.*
Desc: Annual programming directory for the television

Communications —Television and Cable

industry and other organizations that show films or film clips. Provides data and rights information on every film, film package and series available in syndication.

UK

BLUE BOOK OF BRITISH BROADCASTING, THE. See Communications-Radio.

LC HE8689.9.U8 B64
DD 384.54/09895

UY

BOLETIN DE ANDEBU. Added/Corp Asociacion Nacional de Broadcasters Uruguayos. **VFOAT** Boletin de A.N.D.E.B.U. (19??)-. Spanish. Six times a year. Calle YI 1264, Montevideo Uruguay.

UK

BRAILLE TELEVISION TIMES. (19??)-. English. One time a week (every Friday). £88.40. Royal National Institute for the Blind, PO Box 173, Peterborough PE2 6WS United Kingdom. **Tel** 011 44 1733 3730777, FAX 011 44 1733 371555.
 Desc: Contains details of BBC1, BBC2, Thames Television and Channel 4. Around fifty percent of the programs shown on Thames Television are available in other ITV areas at the same time. However, some voluntary associations produce braille versions of regional ITV programs.

ISSN 0040-2788
UK

BROADCAST (BORDON). (BROADCAST.). [Broadcast]. **VFOAT** Broad Cast; Broadcast Incorporating Television Weekly. (1973)-. Trade Publication. English. One time a week. $256.68. Jeska & Harrington, 33 39 Bowling Green Lane, London EC1 R08A United Kingdom. **Tel** 011 44 171 8371212, FAX 011 44 171 83344518.
 Continues Television Mail; **Absorbed** Television Weekly, 0264-2905.
 Ind/Abst F&S Index Plus Text, Int. [Select. Cov.].

LC HE8689 .B743
DD 384.54/3/097305

US

BROADCAST CABLE FINANCIAL JOURNAL & CREDITOPICS. Added/Corp Broadcast Cable Financial Management Association. Broadcast Cable Credit Association. **VFOAT** Broadcast Cable Financial Journal and Creditopics. (May 1992)-. Periodical. English. Six times a year. Broadcast Cable Financial Management, 701 Lee Street, Suite 1010, Des Plaines IL 60016. **Tel** (708)296-0200. **Formed by the union of** Broadcast Cable Financial Journal **and** Creditopics.

ISSN 0155-3720
DD 384.0994
AT

BROADCAST ENGINEERING NEWS. [Broadcast eng. new]. **VFOAT** Broadcast Engineering News for Engineering Management in Radio and Television. (1974)-. Trade Publication. English. Twelve times a year. 54.27Aus$. Reed Business Publishing Pty Ltd. / Australia, PO Box 5487, W Chatswood New South Wales 2057, Australia. **Tel** 011 61 2 3725222, FAX 011 61 2 4197533. **ED** Bill Oawes. **Ad Acc, Adv Mgr:** Dion Stead. **Circ:** 3850 (ctrl).
 Desc: A consistent technical trade magazine for the industry in Australia and the region. Its main goal is to provide accurate and independent news and product information for the technical side of operations in the professional broadcast, video and audio industries.

LC TK6540 .B8433
 ISSN 0007-1994
US
CCC

BROADCAST ENGINEERING (OVERLAND PARK). (BROADCAST ENGINEERING.). Vol. 1 (May 1959)-. Trade Publication. English. Thirteen times a year. $55.29. Intertec Publishing Corporation, 9800 Metcalf, Overland Park KS 66212. **Tel** (913)341-1300. **(Subscription address:** Intertec Publishing Corporation, PO Box 2901, Overland Park KS 66282. **Tel** 800 441-0294.) **ED** Jerry Whitaker. **Ad Acc. Circ:** 35,000 (ctrl). available on microfilm and microfiche from University Microfilms International (UMI).
 Desc: Targets the key buyers of broadcast equipment, broadcast engineers and technical managers. Articles are written for and by engineers. Focuses on technological applications and developments with a how-to approach.
 Ind/Abst Ei Page One.

LC HE8689.8 .B74
DD 384.54/3/0973021
US

... BROADCAST FINANCIAL RECORD, THE. Added/Corp Paul Kagan Associates. (19??)-. English. One time a year. $345.00. Paul Kagan Associates, 126 Clock Tower Place, Carmel CA 93923-8734. **Tel** (408)624-1536, FAX (408)625-3225, telex ITT 4938124 PKA UI. **Continues** Broadcast Databook, 0276-4245.

ISSN 0269-493X
UK

BROADCAST HARDWARE INTERNATIONAL. [Broadcast hardw. int.]. **VFOAT** Hardware. (198?)-. Trade Publication. English. Six times a year. $102.67. Hardware Magazine Company Ltd, 48 The Broadway, Maidenhead Berkshire SL6 1PW United Kingdom. **Tel** 011 44 1628 773935, FAX 011 44 1628 773537, telex 265451. **ED** Dania Spaeks. **Ad Acc.** ctrl circ.

UK

BROADCAST (INTERNATIONAL). (19??)-. Periodical. English. One time a week. £85.00 UK; £95.00 Europe; £125.00 other. EMAP Media, 33 39 Bowling Green Lane, London EC1R 0DA United Kingdom. **Tel** 011 44 171 8371212, FAX 011 44 171 8334519.

LC HG450
DD 332.6
ISSN 0146-0110
US

BROADCAST INVESTOR. Added/Corp Paul Kagan Associates. (1975)-. Newsletter. English. Twelve times a year. $750.00. Paul Kagan Associates Inc., 126 Clock Tower Place, Carmel CA 93923-8734. **Tel** (408)624-1536, FAX (408)625-3225, telex ITT 4938124 PKA UI. Index available. available via fax.
 Desc: Newsletter on investments in private radio and television stations, and public broadcast companies; includes analysis of cash flow multiples and valuations of stations and companies.

LC HG450
DD 332.6
ISSN 0736-9069
US

BROADCAST INVESTOR CHARTS. [Broadcast investor charts]. **Added/Corp** Paul Kagan Associates. Issue #1 (Jan. 21, 1983)-. Newsletter. English. Twelve times a year. $450.00. Paul Kagan Associates Inc., 126 Clock Tower Place, Carmel CA 93923-8734. **Tel** (408)624-1536, FAX (408)625-3225, telex ITT 4938124 PKA UI. **ED** Dwight Beach. Index available. available via fax.
 Desc: Chart service showing stock price movements of 41 publicly-held broadcast companies for the past two years.

NE

BROADCAST MAGAZINE. (19??)-. Periodical. Dutch. Ten times a year. Fl150.00 Netherlands; Fl200.00 Europe; Fl250.00 other. Broadcast Press Hilversum BV, Postbus 576, 1200 And Hilversum Netherlands. **Tel** 011 31 35 258698.

US

BROADCAST RULES. (19??)-. English. Irregular (Master Volume with bimonthly looseleaf reports). $340.00. Pike & Fischer Inc., 4600 East-West Highway, Suite 200, Bethesda MD 20814-1438. **Tel** (301)654-6262, FAX (301)654-6297. available on diskette.

LC HE8689.8 .B75
US

... BROADCAST SERVICES GUIDE, THE. (19??)-. English. Broadcast Investment Analysts Inc, PO Box 17307, Washington DC 20041. **Continues** Broadcast Financial & Legal Services Guide.

ISSN 0749-2936
US

BROADCAST STATS. See Communications-Abstracting, Bibliographies and Statistics.

LC TK6540 .B846
DD 621.384
ISSN 0899-6725
US

BROADCAST TECHNICAL DATA AND APPLICATION INFORMATION MANUAL. [Broadcast tech. data appl. inf. man.]. **Added/Corp** Bill Daniels Co. **VFOAT** Technical Data and Application Information; Technical Data & Application Information; Broadcast Technical Data & Application Information. (1989). English. One time a year. $80.00. Bill Daniels Company, PO Box 2056, Shawnee Mission KS 66201. **Tel** (913)492-9900, (800)255-6038, FAX (913)492-2085.

CN

BROADCASTER DIRECTORY. (19??)-. Directory. English. One time a year. 39.95Can$. Southham Information & Technical Group Inc, 1450 Don Mills Road, Don Mills Ontario M3B 2X7 Canada. **Tel** (416)445-6641, (800)668-2374, FAX (416)442-2261.

ISSN 0008-3038
CN

BROADCASTER (TORONTO). (BROADCASTER.). Vol. 28, No. 10, (Oct. 1969)-. Periodical. English. Ten times a year. 35.00Can$. Southham Information & Technical Group Inc, 1450 Don Mills Road, Don Mills Ontario M3B 2X7 Canada. **Tel** (416)445-6641, (800)668-2374, FAX (416)442-2261. **ED** Ted Davis. **Bk Rev. Ad Acc. Circ:** 9,000 (ctrl). **Continues** Canadian Broadcaster, 0319-1389.
 Desc: Serving the broadcasting and related industries.

LC S
DD 630
US

●**BROADCASTERS LETTER.** See Agriculture.

DD 384
ISSN 1064-6124
US
TITLE CHANGE

BROADCASTING ABROAD. [Broadcast. abroad]. Vol. 1 (1989)-(19??). Periodical. English. Broadcasting & Cable International, 245 West 17th Street, New York NY 10011. **Tel** (212)337-6944, FAX (212)337-6948. **Continued by** Broadcasting & Cable International.

LC HE8689.8 .B77
DD 621
ISSN 1068-6827
US
CCC

●**BROADCASTING & CABLE.** [Broadcast. cable]. **VFOAT** Broadcasting and Cable. Vol. 123, No. 7 (Mar. 1, 1993)-. Trade Publication. English. One time a week (Monday). $117.00. Cahners Publishing Company, 249 West 17th Street, New York NY 10011. **Tel** (212)645-0067, FAX (212)242-6987. **(Subscription address:** Broadcasting & Cable, PO Box 6399, Torrance CA 90504-0399. **Tel** (800)554-5729.) available on an online database from Lexis-Nexis; and DIALOG. Documents available from UMI Article Clearinghouse.
 Continues Broadcasting (Washington, D.C. : 1957), 0007-2028.
 Desc: The weekly newsmagazine of tv, radio, cable and satellite.
 Ind/Abst ABI/INFORM [Computer File] (Feb. 1976-Jan. 1978); Biogr. Index; Bus. Period. Index; Mag. Search; MasterFile FullTEXT (Mar. 1993-); Trade Ind. Index (1981-?).

US

BROADCASTING & CABLE INTERNATIONAL. (19??)-. Trade Publication. English. Four times a year (Feb., Apr., Oct. Dec.). Free. Broadcasting & Cable International, 245 West 17th Street, New York NY 10011. **Tel** (212)337-6944, FAX (212)337-6948. **ED** Meredith Amdur, (editor's address: 54 Great Maribough, St. London W1V 1DD England, (phone: 011 44 71437 0493). **Ad Acc, Adv Mgr:** Randi Schatz, **Tel** (212)337-6944. **Circ:** 8,500 (ctrl). **Continues** Broadcasting Aboard, 1064-6124.
 Desc: Goes behind the headlines to bring analyses, special reports, and features.

ISSN 1071-9261
US

●**BROADCASTING & CABLE'S TV INTERNATIONAL. VFOAT** Broadcasting and Cable's TV International. (1993)-. Periodical. English. Twenty-six times a year. $566.00. Baskerville Communications, PO Box 5084, Thousand Oaks CA 91359. **Tel** (805)499-0721 ext. 289. **(Subscription address:** Nextech Customer Service, PO Box 303, Shrub Oak NY 10588-9904. **Tel** (914)962-6297, FAX (914)962-1338.) **ED** Tim Baskerville.

LC TK6675 .B76
DD 384.55/5/05
US

BROADCASTING. CABLE. VFOAT Cable. (1989)-. Periodical. English. Twenty-four times a year. Broadcasting Publications Inc, 1735 DeSales Street Northwest, Washington DC 20036. **Tel** (202)638-1022, ORDERS: (800)638-7827, FAX (202)331-1732.

LC HE8689.9.C3 B76
DD 384.54/53/0971
ISSN 0527-7418
CN

BROADCASTING STATIONS IN CANADA. Added/Corp Canadian Radio-Television Commission. **VFOAT** Stations de Radiodiffusion au Canada. (19??)-. Multiple languages (English and French). Information Canada, 171 Slater Street, Ottawa Ontario K1A 0S9 Canada. **Tel** (819)997-1095.

LC TK6540 .B85
DD 621
ISSN 0007-2028
US
CCC
TITLE CHANGE

BROADCASTING (WASHINGTON, D.C. 1957). (BROADCASTING.). [Broadcasting]. (Oct. 14, 1957)-. Periodical. English. Cahners Publishing Company, 249 West 17th Street, New York NY 10011. **Tel** (212)645-0067, FAX (212)242-6987. **ED** Donald V West. Index Available Received separately--bound from publisher. **Ad Acc. Circ:** 39,000 (ctrl). available on microfilm and microfiche from University Microfilms International (UMI); available on an online database. Documents available from UMI Article Clearinghouse.
 Continues Broadcasting, Telecasting; **Absorbed** Television (Television Magazine Corporation).
 Continued by Broadcasting & Cable, 1068-6827.
 Desc: Offers readers coverage of the entire broadcast and cable industry--all areas, all aspects. Programs, ratings, sales and marketing strategies, programming, new technology and more are all covered each week.
 Ind/Abst ABI/INFORM Glob. Ed.; ABI/INFORM [Computer File] (January 1992); Acad. Abstr. Full Text Elite; Acad. Abstr.; Acad. Ind. [Computer File] (1984-); Acad. Search; Biogr. Index; Bus. Period. Index (1985-); Bus. Period. Index (1981-); EP Collect.; Expand. Acad. Index (1984-); F&S Index Plus Text, Int. [Select. Cov.]; Gen. BusinessFile (1985-); Gen. Period. Index (1985-); Homework Help.; Index Period. Artic. Relat. Law; INFO-SOUTH Abstr.; Infobank (1979-); Mag. Search; Mark. Advert. Ref. Serv.; MasterFile FullTEXT 1000; MasterFile FullTEXT 350; MasterFile FullTEXT 650;

Communications — Television and Cable

MasterFile FullTEXT (July 1990-Feb. 1993); Newsp. Period. Abstr. (1988-); OCLC; PROMT; Pub. Lib. FullTEXT; Telebase; Topicator; Trade Ind. ASAP [Full Txt.]; Trade Ind. Index (Feb. 1976-Jan. 1978) [Full Txt.]; Urban Aff. Abstr.; Wilson Bus. Abstr.

CN

BT : BROADCAST TECHNOLOGY. (1992)-. Trade Publication. English. Twelve times a year. 24.01Can$. Diversified Publications Ltd, Box 420, Bolton Ontario L7E 5T3 Canada. **Tel** (416)857-6076, FAX (416)857-6045. *Continues Broadcast + Technology.*

ISSN 0709-0676
DD 384.54/0971 CN

BULLETIN - ASSOCIATION FOR THE STUDY OF CANADIAN RADIO AND TELEVISION. See Communications-Radio.

LC PN1993.5.I84 B84 ISSN 0216-3411
IO

BULLETIN KFT : MEDIA KARYAWAN FILM DAN TELEVISI INDONESIA. See Motion Picture.

LC HD30.34 .B87 ISSN 1052-3138
DD 384.55/6/02573 US

BUSINESS TELEVISION DIRECTORY, THE. [Bus. telev. dir.]. **Added/Corp** Irwin Communications. Telehealth Associates. (1988)-. Directory. English. Irregular. $295.00. Telehealth Asscioates, 11 Willow Street, Needham MA 02192.

LC HG450
DD 332.6 US

BUYING A BROADCAST STATION : A GUIDE TO DUE DILIGENCE. (19??)-. English. One time a year. $195.00. Paul Kagan Associates Inc., 126 Clock Tower Place, Carmel CA 93923-8734. **Tel** (408)624-1536, FAX (408)625-3225, telex ITT 4938124 PKA UI.
Desc: Business, legal and accounting issues raised by the acquisition of broadcast stations.

ISSN 0068-8401
CN
CODEN CENRE2
CEASED

C B C ENGINEERING REVIEW. **Main/Corp** Canadian Broadcasting Corporation. **VFOAT** Revue Technique de Radio-Canada. **VAT** Canadian Broadcasting Corporation Engineering Review. Vol. 1 (May 1967)-(April 1995). Periodical. English (French). Canadian Broadcasting Corporation, CP 6000, Montreal Quebec H3C 3A8 Canada. **Tel** (514)597-7666.

ISSN 1322-3534
AT

CABLE AND PAY TV NEWSLETTER. (19??)-. Newsletter. English. Twelve times a year. 295 Aus$ Australia; 328 Aus$ New Zealand; 335 Aus$ Asia; 345 Aus$ US and Europe. Paul Budde Communication Pty Ltd, 2643 George Downes Drive, Bucketty NSW 2250 Australia. **Tel** 61 (0)49 988 144, FAX 61 (0)49 988 247.
Desc: Discusses developments in the market for cable and pay television in Australia. Topics include: superhighways and superskyways, video-on-demand, interactive TV, multimedia, teleconferencing, homeshopping, etc.

UK

●**CABLE AND SATELLITE ASIA.** (Nov. 1994)-. English. Four times a year. $162.57. 21st Century Publishing, 531-583 Kings Road, London SW10 0TZ United Kingdom. **Tel** 011 44 71 3513612.

UK

CABLE & SATELLITE EUROPE. **VFOAT** Cable and Satellite Europe. (19??)-. Periodical. English. Twelve times a year. Cable & Satellite Magazine Ltd., 531-533 Kings Road, London SW10 0TZ United Kingdom. **Tel** 011 44 71 3513612. (**Subscription address:** Select Subscriptions Ltd., Northbridge Road, Berkhamsted HP4 1ST United Kingdom. **Tel** 011 44 1442 876661.)
Desc: Information on cable television and artificial satellites in telecommunication.
Ind/Abst Infomat Int. Bus.

ISSN 0268-215X
UK

CABLE & SATELLITE EXPRESS. [Cable satell. express]. **VFOAT** Cable and Satellite Express. (1986)-. Periodical. English. Twenty-five times a year. $663.10. Cable & Satellite Magazine Ltd., 531-533 Kings Road, London SW10 0TZ United Kingdom. **Tel** 011 44 171 3513612. (**Subscription address:** Select Subscriptions Ltd., Northbridge Road, Berkhamsted HP4 1ST United Kingdom. **Tel** 011 44 1442 876661.) *Continues Cable & Satellite News, 0267-4912.*

UK

CABLE & SATELLITE YEARBOOK. **VFOAT** Cable and Satellite Yearbook. (19??)-. English. One time a year. 21st Century Publishing, 531-583 Kings Road, London SW10 0TZ United Kingdom. **Tel** 011 44 71 3513612.

ISSN 1057-7378
DD 659 US

CABLE AVAILS. [Cable avails]. **VFOAT** Cable Avails. Vol. 1, No. 1 (Sept./Oct. 1991)-. Trade Publication. English. Twelve times a year. $35.00. Cable World Associates, 1905 Sherman Street, Suite 1000, Denver CO 80203. **Tel** (303)837-0900, FAX (303)837-0915.

DD 384.6/5/025 CN

CABLE COMMUNICATIONS. ANNUAL DIRECTORY AND BUYERS' GUIDE. (1974)-. Consumer Publication. English. *Supersedes Canadian Telephone and Cable Television Journal. Annual Directory and Buyers' Guide.*

LC HE8700.7.C6 C316 ISSN 0733-8600
DD 384.55/56/09776 US

CABLE COMMUNICATIONS IN MINNESOTA. [Cable commun. Minn.]. **Added/Corp** Minnesota Cable Communications Board. (19??)-. English. One time a year. Cable Communications in Minnesota, 500 Rice Street, St Paul MN 55103.

LC HE8700.7.C6 C36 ISSN 0318-0069
DD 384.55/56/0971 CN
SUSPENDED

CABLE COMMUNICATIONS MAGAZINE. [Cable commun. mag.]. **VFOAT** Cable Communications. Vol. 45, No. 5 (May 1979)-Suspended (Jan. 1995). Trade Publication. English. Six times a year. 22.41Can$. Premier Canada Cable TV Publishers, 57 Peachwood Court, Kitchener Ontario N2B 1S7 Canada. **Tel** (519)744-4111, FAX (519)744-1261. **ED** Udo Salewsky. Index available. cum. index. **Bk Rev. Ad Acc. Circ:** 6,300. *Continues Cable Communications, 0824-8435.*
Desc: Cable television publication providing news, views and analytical coverage of major issues, events and developments relative to the industry worldwide.
Ind/Abst Can. Bus. Index.

LC HE8700.72.U6 C24 ISSN 1053-9026
DD 384.55/52/02573 US
CEASED

CABLE CONTACTS. [Cable contacts]. **Added/Corp** BPi Media Services. **VFOAT** Cable Contacts Cable. (1990)-(19??). English. BPi Media Services, 1515 Broadway, New York NY 10036. **Tel** (800)753-6675, (518)753-6675, FAX (518)374-7889. **ED** Mitch Tebo.
Desc: Designed to help publicists target cable media. Focuses on the top 50 markets and contains information regarding over 700 local cable systems, over 220 satellite networks, pay services, superstations, associations, text services, independent producers, multiple system operators, and over 1200 programs. Provides comprehensive details on organization, staff, and programming.

LC HE8700.72.U6 C25 ISSN 1048-3764
DD 384.55/5/02573 US

CABLE CONTACTS YEARBOOK. [Cable contacts yearb.]. **VFOAT** Cable Contacts. (1983)-. English. One time a year. Larimi Communications Associates, 151 East 50th Street, New York NY 10022. **Tel** (212)819-9310.

LC HE7601 ISSN 0889-1885
DD 384 US

CABLE FRANCHISE ACTIVITY REPORTER, THE. [Cable franch. act. report.]. **Added/Corp** Cable Television Information Center (U.S.). **VFOAT** Cable Franchising Activity Reporter. (198?)-. Periodical. English. Six times a year. $250.00. Cable Television Information Center, 1500 North Beauregard Street, Suite 205, Alexanria VA 22311. *Continues Cable Franchise Activity Lists.*

ISSN 0191-4871
US

CABLE GUIDE. (19??)-. Periodical. English. Twenty-six times a year. $15.95. Cable Guide, PO Box 604, 5720 North US 1, Vero Beach FL 32960. **Tel** (407)567-9494. **ED** Paul E Ford. **Bk Rev. Ad Acc. Circ:** 15,000,000.
Desc: Cable and local television listings for Florida cablevision and Jones intercable subscribers in the county area.

US

CABLE GUIDE (WYOMING, MI). (CABLE GUIDE). (19??)-. English. One time a week. $29.00. Cable Guide Publications, PO Box 9114, Wyoming MI 49509. **Tel** (616)531-8711. **ED** David Kamps. **Ad Acc. Circ:** 30,000.

LC HE8700.7.C6 P8a ISSN 0364-8761
DD 384.55/47 US

CABLE HANDBOOK. **Main/Corp** Publi-Cable, Inc. (1976)-. English. GK Hall & Co., 100 Front Street, Riverside NJ 08075. **Tel** (800)257-5755 ext. 2223.

LC LB1044.7 .C116 ISSN 1054-5409
DD 371.3/358/05 US

CABLE IN THE CLASSROOM. [Cable classr.]. (1991)-. Periodical. English. Eleven times a year. $18.00. IDG Communications / New Hampshire, 86 Elm Street, Peterborough NH 03458. **Tel** (800)349-7327, FAX (603)924-6972. *Continues Connect (Boston, Mass.), 1047-7268.*

LC HE8700.7 .C32
DD 384.55/5025/73 US

●**CABLE INDUSTRY DIRECTORY.** **Added/Corp** Phillips Business Information, Inc. (1994)-. Directory. English. Irregular. $229.00. Phillips Business Information Inc., 1201 Seven Locks Road, PO Box 61130, Potomac MD 20854. **Tel** (301)424-3338, (301)340-1520, (800)777-5005, FAX (301)424-4297, telex 358149.
Desc: Provides market data, multimedia technological product developments, product and service information, and cable company business profiles.

ISSN 0214-1868
UDC 37.02 :806.0 SP

CABLE MADRID. (1988)-. Periodical. Spanish. Two times a year. $44.41. Revista Cable, C/Leiva 54-58 At.4, 08014 Barcelona Spain.

LC HG ISSN 1062-3515
DD 332 US

CABLE NETWORK INVESTOR. [Cable netw. invest.]. **Added/Corp** Paul Kagan Associates. No. 1 (Mar. 23, 1992)-. Newsletter. English. Twelve times a year. $695.00. Paul Kagan Associates Inc., 126 Clock Tower Place, Carmel CA 93923-8734. **Tel** (408)624-1536, FAX (408)625-3225, telex ITT 4938124 PKA UI. available via fax.
Desc: Private market values of public cable networks, recent data on public stock offerings, projections for growth of networks and programs, analyses of balance sheet leverage and equity, comparisons of companies, rankings of competitors and insights into corporate financings.

ISSN 0733-5504

CABLE PRODUCT NEWS. [Cable prod. news]. (1982)-. Periodical. English. Six times a year. Cable Product News, PO Box 2772, Palm Springs CA 92263. **Tel** (619)323-2000.

US

CABLE REPORT. 1- Mar. 1972-. Periodical. English. PO Box 6119, 541 North Fairbank Court, Chicago IL 60611.

US

CABLE SERVICES REPORT. **Main/Corp** National Cable Television Association. (19??)-. English. One time a year. National Cable Television Association, Research and Policy Analysis Department, 1724 Massachusetts Avenue Northwest, Washington DC 20036-1969. **Tel** (202)775-3350. *Continues NCTA Cable Services Directory.*

LC HE8700.72.U6 C28 ISSN 1076-6499
DD 384.55/5/0973021 US

●**CABLE STATISTICS BOOK, THE.** (THE CABLE STATISTICS BOOK : A FACTBOOK SUPPLEMENT FROM WARREN PUBLISHING, INC.). [Cable stat. book]. (1993)-. Statistical Publication. English. Irregular. Warren Publishing, Inc., 2115 Ward Court Northwest, Washington DC 20037. **Tel** (202)872-9200, FAX (202)293-3435.

ISSN 1059-681X
DD 384 US

CABLE SYSTEM MANAGER. [Cable syst. manager]. **VFOAT** Manager. (1991)-. Periodical. English. Twelve times a year. $225.00. Cowles Business Media Inc. / Connecticut, 6 River Bend Center, 911 Hope Street, Stamford CT 06907. **Tel** (203)358-9900, (800)775-3777, FAX (203)357-9014. (**Subscription address:** Cable World Associates, 1905 Sherman Street, Suite 800, Denver CO 80203. **Tel** (303)837-0900.)

ISSN 1082-4081
DD 384 US

CABLE TELCO CONVERGENCE GUIDEBOOK. [Cable telco converg. guideb.]. **Added/Corp** Paul Kagan Associates. **VFOAT** Telco Convergence Guidebook; Kagan Cable Telco Convergence Guidebook; Kagan Cable/Telco Convergence Guidebook; Cable/Telco Convergence Guidebook; Cable Telco Convergence. (19??)-. English. Irregular. $995.00. Paul Kagan Associates Inc., 126 Clock Tower Place, Carmel CA 93923-8734. **Tel** (408)624-1536, FAX (408)625-3225, telex ITT 4938124 PKA UI.

ISSN 1050-0553
DD 384 US

CABLE-TELCO REPORT, THE. See Communications-Telecommunication.

Communications —Television and Cable

LC HE8700.7.C6 C35 ISSN 0703-7244
DD 384.55/47 CN
CABLE TELEVISION. [Cable telev.]. **Main/Corp** Statistics Canada. Communications Section. **Added/Corp** Statistics Canada. Public Utilities Section. Statistics Canada. Communications Section. Statistics Canada. Communications and Information Section. Statistics Canada. Telecommunications Section. **VFOAT** Teledistribution. (1971)-. Periodical. English (French). One time a year. 40.00Can$. Statistics Canada Publications Sales and Services, R.H. Coats Building 6th Floor, Ottawa Ontario K1A 0T6 Canada. **Tel** (613)951-5078, (800)267-6677, **FAX** (613)951-1584, telex 053-3585. **Continues** Community Antenna Television, 0575-8238.
Desc: Covers wireline facilities, subscribers and contracts by area; operating revenue and expenses by area and by revenue group; employee statistics by area; income and surplus accounts; and assets, liabilities and net worth data.

LC HE8700.72.U6 C32
US
CABLE TELEVISION DEVELOPMENTS : DIRECTORY OF TOP 50 MSOS, DIRECTORY OF CABLE NETWORKS. **Added/Corp** National Cable Television Association. Research & Policy Analysis Dept. **VFOAT** Directory of Cable Networks; Directory of Top 50 MSOs. (19??)-. Corporate Report. English. Irregular. National Cable Television Association, Research and Policy Analysis Department, 1724 Massachusetts Avenue Northwest, Washington DC 20036-1969. **Tel** (202)775-3350.

US
CABLE TELEVISION INFORMATION. **Added/Corp** New York (State). Bureau of Mass Communications. (19??)-. English.

LC HE8700.7 .C34 ISSN 1044-9434
DD 384.55/5/02573 US
CABLE TELEVISION MARKETING HANDBOOK. [Cable telev. mark. handb.]. **Added/Corp** Associated Cable Enterprises Inc. **VFOAT** Cable Television Marketing Handbook. (1989)-. Trade Publication. English. Irregular. $59.95. Associated Cable Enterprises, 352 Park Avenue South, New York NY 10010.

US
CABLE TELEVISION SERVICE REGISTRATIONS. **Main/Corp** United States. Federal Communications Commission. (19??)-. English. FCC / Federal Communications Commission, 1919 M Street Northwest, Room 538, Washington DC 20554. **Tel** (202)632-6302. **Continues** United States. Federal Communications Commission. Cable Television Service Applications.

ISSN 0270-885X
DD 659 US
CABLE TV ADVERTISING. See Business and Economics-Advertising and Public Relations.

US
CABLE TV ADVERTISING REPORT. See Business and Economics-Advertising and Public Relations.

ISSN 1061-5652
DD 338 US
CABLE TV FINANCE (1992). (CABLE TV FINANCE.). [Cable TV Finance]. **Added/Corp** Paul Kagan Associates. **VFOAT** Cable Television Finance. No. 138 (Jan. 31, 1992)-. Newsletter. English. Twelve times a year. $695.00. Paul Kagan Associates Inc., 126 Clock Tower Place, Carmel CA 93923-8734. **Tel** (408)624-1536, **FAX** (408)625-3225, telex ITT 4938124 PKA UI. available via fax. **Continues** Cable TV Banker/Broker, 0893-2131.
Desc: Analyzes sources of funding for cable TV, selling and buying of cable systems, financing strategies and trends, and surveys of capital sources.

LC HE8700.7.C6 C3335
DD 384.55/47 US
CABLE TV FINANCIAL DATABOOK, THE. See Communications-Abstracting, Bibliographies and Statistics.

LC HG450 ISSN 0731-0250
DD 332.6 US
CABLE TV INVESTOR. [Cable TV investor]. **Added/Corp** Paul Kagan Associates. **VFOAT** Cable T.V. Investor; Cablecast. **VAT** Cable Television Investor. No. 290 (Dec. 17, 1981)-. Newsletter. English. Twelve times a year. $875.00. Paul Kagan Associates Inc., 126 Clock Tower Place, Carmel CA 93923-8734. **Tel** (408)624-1536, **FAX** (408)625-3225, telex ITT 4938124 PKA UI. **ED** Dwight Beach. **Ad Acc.** available via fax. **Continues** Cablecast, 0146-0380.
Desc: Newsletter on investments in private cable television systems and public cable television stocks. Includes analysis of cash flow multiple and value per subscriber.

LC HG450 ISSN 0732-7757
DD 332.6 US
CABLE TV INVESTOR CHARTS. (CABLE TV INVESTOR CHARTS / PK.). [Cable TV investor charts]. **Added/Corp** Paul Kagan Associates. **VFOAT** Cable T.V. Investor Charts; Cable Television Investor Charts. No. 1 (Mar. 1982)-. Newsletter. English. Twelve times a year. $450.00. Paul Kagan Associates Inc., 126 Clock Tower Place, Carmel CA 93923-8734. **Tel** (408)624-1536, **FAX** (408)625-3225, telex ITT 4938124 PKA UI. **ED** Dwight Beach. Index available. available via fax.
Desc: Chart service showing stock price movements of 37 publicly-held cable television companies. Each chart presents two years of stock price activity.

LC PN1992.3.U5 C27 ISSN 0277-1462
DD 791.45/75 US
CABLE TV MAGAZINE. **VAT** Cable Television Magazine. Vol. 1, No. 1 (Jan. 1981)-. Periodical. English. Irregular. Cable TV Magazine, 24 West 40th Street, New York NY 10018. **Tel** (212)719-4500.

ISSN 0278-503X
DD 384 US
CABLE TV PROGRAMMING. (CABLE TV PROGRAMMING.). [Cable TV program.]. **Added/Corp** Paul Kagan Associates. **VFOAT** Cable T.V. Programming. **VAT** Cable Television Programming. No. 1 (Sept. 25, 1981)-. Newsletter. English. Twelve times a year. $695.00. Paul Kagan Associates Inc., 126 Clock Tower Place, Carmel CA 93923-8734. **Tel** (408)624-1536, **FAX** (408)625-3225, telex ITT 4938124 PKA UI. **ED** Dwight Beach. Index available. available via fax.
Desc: Newsletter on the economics of basic and pay TV program networks. Case studies of cable system program line-ups.
Ind/Abst Predicasts.

ISSN 1068-9826
DD 343 US
●**CABLE TV REGULATION (1993).** (CABLE TV REGULATION.). [Cable TV regul.]. **Added/Corp** Paul Kagan Associates. No. 326 (Feb. 28, 1993)-. Newsletter. English. Twelve times a year. $625.00. Paul Kagan Associates Inc., 126 Clock Tower Place, Carmel CA 93923-8734. **Tel** (408)624-1536, **FAX** (408)625-3225, telex ITT 4938124 PKA UI. available via fax. **Continues** Cable TV Franchising, 0731-0269.
Desc: Tracks cable franchise awards and renewals. Analyzes developments in federal, state and local regulation of cable TV, including competitive overbuilds and rate changes.

CABLE TV RULES. (19??)-. English. Irregular (Master Volume with bimonthly looseleaf reports). $245.00. Pike & Fischer Inc., 4600 East-West Highway, Suite 200, Bethesda MD 20814-1438. **Tel** (301)654-6262, **FAX** (301)654-6297. available on diskette.

ISSN 0276-5713
DD 384 US
CABLE TV TECHNOLOGY. [Cable telev. technol.]. **Added/Corp** Paul Kagan Associates. **VFOAT** Cable T.V. Technology. **VAT** Cable Television Technology. No. 1 (Apr. 23, 1981)-. Newsletter. English. Twelve times a year. $650.00. Paul Kagan Associates Inc., 126 Clock Tower Place, Carmel CA 93923-8734. **Tel** (408)624-1536, **FAX** (408)625-3225, telex ITT 4938124 PKA UI. **ED** Dwight Beach. **Ad Acc.** available via fax.
Desc: Newsletter on technical advances, the construction of new systems and the rebuilding of existing systems. Analyzes growth in addressable converters, high definition TV, fiber optics, etc.

US
CABLE-VIDEO INDEX, THE. **VFOAT** Cable Video Index. Vol. 1, No. 1 (March 1983)-. English. Irregular. Cable-Video Index, PO Box 537, Muncie IN 47305.

ISSN 0745-6891
US
CABLE VIEWER MAGAZINE. (198?)-. Periodical. English. Twelve times a year. Cable Viewer Magazine, 3417 Plumtree Drive, Ellicott City MD 21043.

LC HE8700.7.C6 C334 ISSN 0361-8374
DD 384.55/47 US
CABLE VISION. [Cable vis.]. **VFOAT** CableVision. **VAT** Cablevision. (19??)-. Periodical. English. Twenty-four times a year. $59.00. Chilton, 825 7th Avenue, New York NY 10019. **Tel** (212)887-8560. (**Subscription address:** Cablevision, PO Box 7698, Riverton NJ 08077. **Tel** (609)786-0501.) **Circ:** 787,588. available on microfilm and microfiche from University Microfilms International (UMI).
Desc: Directed toward the management staff of cable operations. The publication tracks current trends and issues involving the cable television industry.
Ind/Abst Mark. Advert. Ref. Serv.; Stat. Ref. Index; Urban Aff. Abstr.

ISSN 0744-2327
US
CABLE WEEK. ORANGE-SEMINOLE-OSEOLA ED. (CABLE WEEK.). (198?)-. Periodical. English. One time a week. $20.00. Cable Week, 2120 1 2 South Orange Avenue, Orlando FL 32806. **Tel** (407)849-9927. **ED** Donna Yates. **Bk Rev.** **Ad Acc.** **Circ:** 12,000 (ctrl). **Continues** Cableweek TV News, 0191-9865.
Desc: Listings of cable channels. Also offers many special features.

LC WMLC 93/2312 HE8700.7 .C35 ISSN 1042-7228
DD 384 US
CABLE WORLD. [Cable world]. (1989)-. Trade Publication. English. One time a week. $60.00. Cable World Associates, 1905 Sherman Street, Suite 1000, Denver CO 80203. **Tel** (303)837-0900, **FAX** (303)837-0915. **Bk Rev.** **Ad Acc.** **Circ:** 14,000 (ctrl). **Continues** Marketing New Media, 0743-2178.
Ind/Abst F&S Index Plus Text, Int. [Select. Cov.]; Mark. Advert. Ref. Serv.; PROMT.

CN
CABLECASTER DIRECTORY. (19??)-. Directory. English. One time a year. 15.00Can$. Southam Information & Technical Group, 1450 Don Mills Road, Don Mills Ontario M3B 2X7 Canada. **Tel** (416)445-6641, (800)668-2374, **FAX** (416)442-2261.

LC HE8700 ISSN 0840-9153
DD 384.55/56/0971 CN
CABLECASTER (TORONTO). (CABLECASTER.). [Cablecaster]. Vol. 1, No. 1 (Feb. 1989)-. Periodical. English. Eight times a year. 30.00Can$. Southam Information & Technical Group Inc, 1450 Don Mills Road, Don Mills Ontario M3B 2X7 Canada. **Tel** (416)445-6641, (800)668-2374, **FAX** (416)442-2261.

ISSN 1069-6644
DD 384 US
CABLEFAX (DENVER, COLO.). (CABLEFAX.). [Cablefax]. (1990)-. Trade Publication. English. Five times a week (260 per year). $495.00. Phillips Business Information Inc., 1201 Seven Locks Road, PO Box 61130, Potomac MD 20854. **Tel** (301)424-3338, (301)340-1520, (800)777-5005, **FAX** (301)424-4297, telex 358149.

LC HE8700 ISSN 1084-9157
DD 384.55 US
UDC 38
CABLEGUIDE (NASHVILLE ED.). (CABLEGUIDE.). (19??)-. Periodical. English. Twenty-four times a year. Viacom Cablevision, 660 Mainstream Drive, Nashville TN 37208. **Continues** Nashville Cableguide, 1058-1782.

ISSN 0884-8025
US
CABLEPLUS MAGAZINE. **VFOAT** Cable Plus; Cable Plus Magazine; CablePlus. (1985)-. Periodical. English. Twelve times a year. Comcast of Maryland, 1830 York Road, Timonium MD 21093. **Tel** (301)252-1012. **Continues** Caltec Cabletelevision, 8750-7102.

US
TITLE CHANGE
CABLESPORTS NEWSLETTER. (19??)-(July 1994). Newsletter. English. QV Publishing Inc., 647 US Route One, PO Box 3000, York ME 03909. **Tel** (207)363-6222, **FAX** (207)363-6182. **ED** Dantina Gould. **Ad Acc, Adv Mgr:** Barry Gould, **Tel** (207)363-6222. **Circ:** 150 (ctrl). **Merged into** Phillips Business Information's Interactive Video News.
Desc: Covers updates all news and information regarding the cablesports business industry.

ISSN 0745-2969
US
CABLETIME. (CABLETIME.). (1982)-. Periodical. English. One time a week. Nor Cal Cablevision, 311 B Street, Yuba City CA 95991.

ISSN 0740-0527
US
TITLE CHANGE
CALIFORNIA CABLETTER. **VFOAT** California Cable Letter. Vol. 1, No. 1 (Jan. 1984)-(19??). Periodical. English. California Cable Letter, PO Box 7600, Santa Cruz CA 95061. **Tel** (408)426-5981. **ED** Thomas J. Karwin. **Bk Rev. Circ:** 200. **Continued by** Community Cable Letter, 1074-3936.
Desc: Reports and analyses on cable television services from consumer and community perspectives.

ISSN 0316-3083
DD 384/.0971 CN
CANADIAN COMMUNICATIONS REPORTS. **Added/Corp** Tele-Connect Publications. Vol. 1 (Sept. 1984)-Suspended (Oct. 1990)-Resumed publication (March 1, 1993)-. NewsletterNewsletter. English. Twenty times a year. 316.13Can$. Evert Communications Ltd, 1296 Carling Avenue, Ottawa Ontario, K1Z 7K8 Canada. **Tel** (613)728-4621, **FAX** (613)728-0385. **ED** Bryan Barney.

Communications —Television and Cable

Desc: Newsletter providing exclusive in-depth coverage of television, radio, cable TV, pay-TV, videotex, satellite technology, cellular radio and telecommunications.

ISSN 0193-5801
US

CATALOG OF TELEVISION AND AUDIOVISUAL MATERIALS. Main/Corp Agency for Instructional Television. **VFOAT** Television and Audiovisual Materials. (1978)-. Catalog. English. One time a year. Free. Agency for Instructional Television, PO Box A, Bloomington IN 47401.

LC TK6675 .C16
DD 384.55
ISSN 0091-1984
US

CATV SYSTEMS DIRECTORY, MAP SERVICE & HANDBOOK. Directory. English. $8.95. Communications Publishing Corporation, 1900 West Yale, Englewood CO 80110.

ISSN 0361-3135
US

CBS NEWS SPECIAL REPORT. Main/Corp CBS News. (1975)-. English. Microfilming Corporation of America, 21 Harristown Road, Glen Rock NJ 07452.

ISSN 0361-3097
US

CBS REPORTS. Main/Corp CBS News. (1975)-. English. Microfilming Corporation of America, 21 Harristown Road, Glen Rock NJ 07452.

LC TK6675 .C65
DD 621.388/57
ISSN 1044-2871
US

CED (DENVER, COLO.). (CED.). [CED]. **VFOAT** Communications Engineering and Design. Vol. 14, No. 9 (Sept. 1988)-. Periodical. English. Thirteen times a year. $54.00. Chilton, 825 7th Avenue, New York NY 10019. **Tel** (212)887-8560. **(Subscription address:** Cable Engineering Design, PO Box 7698, Riverton NJ 08077. **) Continues** Communications Engineering & Design, 0191-5428.

DD 384.5
ISSN 1195-3233
CN

CELLULAR NETWORKING PERSPECTIVES. [Cell. netw. perspect.]. No. 1 (July 1992)-. Periodical. English. Twelve times a year. 250.00Can$. Cellular Network Perspectives, 2636 Toronto Crescent NW, Calgary Alberta T2N 3W1 Canada. **Tel** (800)633-5514, (403)289-6609.

LC HE8700.72.U6 C43
DD 384.55/532
US

CHANNEL CAPACITY REPORT, THE. Added/Corp Paul Kagan Associates. (19??)-. Periodical. Irregular. $995.00. Paul Kagan Associates Inc., 126 Clock Tower Place, Carmel CA 93923-8734. **Tel** (408)624-1536, FAX (408)625-3225, telex ITT 4938124 PKA UI.

US

CHANNEL COMPRESSION : A STRATEGIC ANALYSIS. (19??)-. English. One time a year. $395.00. Paul Kagan Associates Inc., 126 Clock Tower Place, Carmel CA 93923-8734. **Tel** (408)624-1536, FAX (408)625-3225, telex ITT 4938124 PKA UI. available with charts.
Desc: Information on channel compression and how it will affect cable, DBS, wireless cable, telcos and broadcasters.

ISSN 1042-1238
US

CHANNEL GUIDE (MILWAUKEE, WIS.). (CHANNEL GUIDE.). **VFOAT** Channel Guide Magazine. (198?)-. English. Twenty-four times a year. $30.00. Verlag Technik GmbH Berlin, AM Friedrichshain 22, D-10407 Berlin Germany. **Tel** 011 49 30 428700.

LC PN1993.5.U74 C48
DD 384.55/025/7311
ISSN 0193-7596
US

CHICAGO CREATIVE DIRECTORY, THE. See Motion Picture.

LC PN1992.3.C6 C48
DD 791.45/0951
CC

CHUNG-KUO KUANG PO TIEN SHIH. VFOAT Zhongguo Guangbo Dianshi. (19??)-. Periodical. Chinese. Science Press, 16 Donghuangchenggen North Street, Beijing 100707, People's Republic of China. **Tel** 011 86 1 4019821, 011 86 1 4010642, FAX 011 86 1 4012180, 011 86 1 4019810, telex 210147.

IT

CIAK SI GIRA. See Motion Picture.

FR

CINEMACTION TV. VAT CinemAction Television. (1992)-. Periodical. French. Four times a year. Editions Corlet, Z1 route de Vire, 14110 Conde-sur-Noireau France.

US
CEASED

CLANDESTINE CONFIDENTIAL. (19??)-(1993). English. Gerry Dexter, RR #4 PO Box 110, Lake Geneva WI 53147. **Tel** (414) 248-4845.

DD 384
ISSN 1055-0461
US

COLLEGE BROADCASTER. See Communications-Radio.

LC HD9696.T463 U6345
DD 338.4/762138804/0973
US

COLOR TELEVISION RECEIVERS : QUARTERLY PROFITS AND CAPACITY AND CERTAIN ANNUAL EXPENDITURES OF U.S. PRODUCERS, QUARTERLY PRICES, ORDERS, AND INVENTORIES OF IMPORTERS. Added/Corp United States International Trade Commission. **VFOAT** Quarterly Profits and Capacity and Certain Annual Expenditures of U.S. Producers, Quarterly Prices, Orders, and Inventories of Importers. (1977)-. English. One time a year. United States International Trade Commission, 701 East Street Northwest, Washington DC 20436. **Tel** (202)482-5487.

LC HE8689 .C6613
DD 384.55/4/09171241
ISSN 0951-0826
UK

COMBROAD. (COMBROAD.). [COMBROAD]. **Added/Corp** Commonwealth Broadcasting Association. (19??)-. Periodical. English. Four times a year. $35.00. Commonwealth Broadcasting Association, Broadcasting House, London W1A 1AA United Kingdom. **Tel** 011 44 181 7655144, FAX 011 44 181 7655152. **ED** Stuart Revill. **Bk Rev. Ad Acc.**

LC HE8700.9.G7 C6
DD 384.55/4/02541
ISSN 0306-7718
UK

COMMERCIAL TELEVISION AND RADIO YEAR BOOK. VFOAT TV & Radio Year Book. (1974)-. English. One time a year. Mercury House Business Publications, Waterloo Road, London SE1 8W United Kingdom. **Continues** Commercial Television Yearbook, 0069-6668.

US

COMMON CARRIER RULES. (19??)-. English. Irregular (Master Volume with bimonthly looseleaf reports). $545.00. Pike & Fischer Inc., 4600 East-West Highway, Suite 200, Bethesda MD 20814-1438. **Tel** (301)654-6262, FAX (301)654-6297.

LC TK6675 .C656
DD 621.388/57
ISSN 0884-2272
US
CCC

COMMUNICATIONS TECHNOLOGY. (COMMUNICATIONS TECHNOLOGY : OFFICIAL TRADE JOURNAL OF THE SOCIETY OF CABLE TELEVISION ENGINEERS.). [Commun. technol.]. **Added/Corp** Society of Cable Television Engineers. Vol. 1, No. 1 (Mar. 1984)-. Trade Publication. English. Twelve times a year. $69.00. Phillips Business Information Inc., 1201 Seven Locks Road, PO Box 61130, Potomac MD 20854. **Tel** (301)424-3338, (301)340-1520, (800)777-5005, FAX (301)424-4297, telex 358149. ctrl circ. **Absorbed** Installer Technician.

DD 384.55/5/097105
ISSN 1192-5035
CN

COMMUNIQUE - ASSOCIATION CANADIENNE DE TELEVISION PAR CABLE (1992). (COMMUNIQUE.). [Commun. - Assoc. can. telev. cable]. **Added/Corp** Association Canadienne de Television par Cable. (1992)-. Periodical. French. Twelve times a year. Association Canadienne de Television par Cable, 1010 360 rue Albert, Ottawa Ontario, K1R 7X7 Canada. **Continues** Cable Communique (Bi-Hebdomadaire). Francais., 0710-2259.

DD 384.555097105
ISSN 1193-5898
CN

COMMUNIQUE - CANADIAN CABLE TELEVISION ASSOCIATION (1992). (COMMUNIQUE.). [Commun. - Can. Cable Telev. Assoc. 1992]. (1992)-. Trade Publication. English. Canadian Cable Television Association, 1010 360 Albert Street, Ottawa Ontario K1R 7X7 Canada. **Tel** (613)232-2631. **ED** Sylvie Powell. **Circ:** 2,500. **Continues** Cable Communique (Biweekly. English Ed.), 0710-2240.

DD 384
ISSN 1074-3936
US
SUSPENDED

COMMUNITY CABLE LETTER. [Community cable lett.]. Vol. 8, No. 1 (Jan. 1994)-Suspended (199?). Periodical. English. Twelve times a year. California Cable Letter, PO Box 7600, Santa Cruz CA 95061. **Tel** (408)426-5981. **Bk Rev. Circ:** 200. **Continues** California Cabletter, 0740-0527.
Desc: Reports and analyses on cable television services from consumer and community perspectives.

US
TITLE CHANGE

COMMUNITY TELEVISION REVIEW : CTR. Added/Corp National Federation of Local Cable Programmers (U.S.). **VFOAT** CTR. (19??)-(1993). Periodical. English. Alliance for Community Media, 666 11th Street Northwest, Suite 806, Washington DC 20001. **Tel** (202)393-2650, FAX (202)393-2653. **Continued by** Community Media Review.

LC HE8700.8 .C653
DD 384
ISSN 1076-237X
US

COMPETING VIDEO MEDIA. (COMPETING VIDEO MEDIA : A MARKET-BY-MARKET GUIDE : A FACTBOOK SUPPLEMENT FROM ...). [Compet. video media]. (19??)-. Trade Publication. English. Irregular. Warren Publishing, Inc., 2115 Ward Court Northwest, Washington DC 20037. **Tel** (202)872-9200, FAX (202)293-3435.

LC GV885.515.N37 C66
DD 796.323/64/0973
US

COMPLETE ... NATIONAL BASKETBALL ASSOCIATION TELEVISION SCHEDULE, THE. See Sports and Games.

LC HE8700
DD 384.55
ISSN 1358-112
UK

●COMPRESSION EXPRESS. (1995)-. Newsletter. English. Two times a month. £310.00. Route 104 Publishing, 104 City View, 463 Bethnal Green Road, London E2 9QY United Kingdom. **Tel** 011 44 171 6135553, FAX 011 44 171 7297723. **ED** Alan Burkett-Gray.
Desc: News on consumer equipment, industry deals and standards and digital broadcasting.

ISSN 0744-3269
US

COMTEC CABLE TELEVISION VIEWERS GUIDE. Added/Corp Comtec, Inc. **VFOAT** Comtec Viewers Guide. (19??)-. Periodical. English. Twelve times a year. Comtec Viewers Guide, 512 Kinoole Street, Hilo HI 96720. **Continues** Focus Hawaii, 0192-0014.

LC HE8700
DD 384.55
ISSN 1354-8565
UK

●CONVERGENCE: THE JOURNAL OF RESEARCH INTO NEW MEDIA TECHNOLOGIES. (1995)-. Academic Scholarly Publication. English. Two times a year. £40.00 (institutions), £18.00 (individuals). John Libbey & Company Ltd., 13 Smiths Yard, Summerley Street, London SW18 4HR United Kingdom. **Tel** 011 44 171 9472777, FAX 011 44 171 9472664, telex 94013503 JOHN G.
Desc: Discusses the creative, social, political and pedagogical issues in regard to new media technologies.

LC TK6630.A1 C67
DD 384.55/05
ISSN 0889-4523
US

CORPORATE TELEVISION. (CORPORATE TELEVISION : THE OFFICIAL MAGAZINE OF THE INTERNATIONAL TELEVISION ASSOCIATION.). [Corp. telev.]. **Added/Corp** International Television Association. Vol. 1, No. 1 (Sept. 1986)-. Periodical. English. Six times a year. $25.00. Media Horizons Inc, PO Box 150, Midland Park NJ 07432-0150. **Tel** (212)779-1919.

ISSN 0271-3438
US

COTA NEWSLETTER. [COTA Newsl.]. **Main/Corp** Consortium of Television Archivists. **VAT** Consortium of Television Archivists Newsletter. (1978)-. Newsletter. English. Six times a year. $10.00. Cota Newsletter, 2306 College Station, Pullman WA 99163.

US
CEASED

CPB REPORT. Added/Corp Corporation for Public Broadcasting. (1968)-(July 1995). Newsletter. English. Corporation for Public Broadcasting, 901 E Street Northwest, Washington DC 20001. **Tel** (202)879-9600. **ED** Jennifer Grossman. **Circ:** 2,165. **Continues** Memo - Corporation for Public Broadcasting; CPB Today.
Desc: Newsletter on CPB activities and other information pertaining to the public broadcasting industry.

LC HD9696.T464 C653a
DD 621.388/029/473
ISSN 1059-227X
US

CTL TOTAL VIDEO. (CTL TOTAL VIDEO : PRODUCT CATALOG / CTL.). [CTL total video]. **Main/Corp** Communications Televideo Ltd. **VFOAT** Total Video; Product Catalog. (19??)-. Catalog. English. Irregular. CTL Communications Televideo Ltd, 9301 Georgia Avenue, Silver Spring MD 20910.

LC P87 .C25
DD 791.43/7
ISSN 0007-9219
US

CTVD, CINEMA, TV DIGEST. VFOAT Cinema, TV Digest. **VAT** Cinema Television Digest : Cinema, Television Digest. Vol. 1 (Winter 1961/1962)-. Periodical. English. Irregular. $3.00 (per volume) North America; $4.00 (per volume) other. Hampton Books, Route 1 Box 202, Newberry SC 29108. **Tel** (803)276-6870. **ED** Ben Hamilton and Muriel Price Hamilton. **Ad Acc.**

DD 791
ISSN 1064-2579
US

CUE MAGAZINE. See Communications-Video.

Communications —Television and Cable

LC HD9696.R363 U67
DD 338.4/76213841/0973
US
CURRENT INDUSTRIAL REPORTS. MA-36M, RADIO AND TELEVISION RECEIVERS, PHONOGRAPHS, AND RELATED EQUIPMENT. See Communications-Radio.

ISSN 1072-8104
DD 791
US
DARK SHADOWS ANNOUNCEMENT, THE. [Dark shad. announc.]. **Added/Corp** Dark Shadows Fan Club. (1988)-. Newsletter. English. Four times a year. $20.00. Fan Club Publishing, PO Box 69A04, West Hollywood CA 90069. **Tel** (213)650-5112. **ED** Louis Wendruck. **Bk Rev. Ad Acc. Circ:** 1,000.
Desc: Publication of the Dark Shadows Fan Club. Newsletter for fans of the 1960s gothic soap opera. Offers photos, postcards, t-shirts, videos, articles about the stars of the show, episode guides and meetings.

ISSN 0164-8306
US
DAYTIME SERIAL NEWSLETTER. Vol. 1 (1972)-. Newsletter. English. Twelve times a year. $11.00 US; $12.00 Canada and Mexico. DSN Publications, PO Box 6, Mountain View CA 95014.

LC PN1992.8.S4 D39 **ISSN** 0011-7129
DD 051
US
DAYTIME TV. Vol. 1 (Winter 1970)-. Periodical. English. Six times a year. $14.95. Sterling Macfadden, 233 Park Avenue South, New York NY 10003. **Tel** (212)979-4800.

ISSN 1054-0814
DD 384
US
DBS REPORT, THE. [DBS rep.]. **Added/Corp** Paul Kagan Associates. (June 1990)-. Periodical. English. Twelve times a year. $595.00. Paul Kagan Associates Inc., 126 Clock Tower Place, Carmel CA 93923-8734. **Tel** (408)624-1536, FAX (408)625-3225, telex ITT 4938124 PKA UI. available via fax.
Desc: Analyzes direct-to-home satellite ventures on the television frontier. Projects future scenarios, costs, values.

LC PN1992.3.U5 D47 **ISSN** 1065-1535
DD 791.45/0973/05
US
TITLE CHANGE
DESTINATION DISCOVERY. [Destin. discov.]. Vol. 8, No. 6 (Sept. 1992)-(1995). Periodical. English. Discovery Channel, 7700 Wisconsin Avenue, Bethesda MD 20814. **Tel** (301)986-0444 ext. 5826. **(Subscription address:** Kable Publishers Aide / Illinois, 308 East Hitt Street, Subscription Department, Mt. Morris IL 61054-1473. **Tel** (815)734-1261.**) Continues** Discovery Channel, 0890-8540. **Merged into** Discovery Channel Monthly.

ISSN 1181-7917
DD 621.388/33/05
CN
TITLE CHANGE
DIGITAL EVOLUTION MAGAZINE. [Digit. evol. mag.]. **VFOAT** Digital Evolution. No. 16 (Aug./Sept. 1990)-No. 39 (Dec. 1992/Jan. 1993). Trade Publication. English. Castlestone Publishing Ltd., 3214 Wharton Way, Mississauga Ontario L4X 2C1 Canada. **Continues** Video News and Used., 0847-4990. **Continued by** VPM Magazine, 1193-994X.

LC TK6678 .D54 **ISSN** 0730-5613
DD 621.388
US
DIGITAL VIDEO. [Digit. video]. **Added/Corp** Society of Motion Picture and Television Engineers. (1977)-. Trade Publication. English. Irregular. $24.97. Tech Media Publishing, Inc, 80 Elm Street, Peterborough NH 03458. **Tel** (603)924-0100, FAX (603)924-0379. **(Subscription address:** Desktop Publishing, PO Box 594, Mt. Morris IL 61054. **Tel** (800)998-0806.**)**

LC HE8689.9.C3 D57 **ISSN** 0419-2273
DD 384.54/025/71
CN
DIRECTORY OF BROADCAST EXECUTIVES (TORONTO). (DIRECTORY OF BROADCAST EXECUTIVES.). 1963/64-. Directory. English. R.C. Ellis, 17 Dundonald Street, Toronto Canada.

UK
DIRECTORY OF EUROPEAN MEDIA REGULATION. (19??)-. English. One time a year. $395.00. Kagan World Media Inc., 126 Clock Tower Place, Carmel CA 93923-8734. **Tel** (408)624-1536, FAX (408)625-3225. **(Subscription address:** Kagan World Media Ltd., 524 Fulham Road, London SW6 5NR United Kingdom. **Tel** 011 44 171 3718880, FAX 011 44 171 3718715.**)**
Desc: Compiles data on ownership and advertising restrictions, license fees, TV and movie release windows, etc., for TV, cable TV, cinema, radio, video and telephony.

US
DIRECTORY OF MONTANA BROADCASTERS. Added/Corp Montana. University, Missoula. Bureau of Press and Broadcasting Research. (19??)-. Directory. English. One time a year. $18.00. Montana Broadcasters Association, PO Box 503, Helena MT 59624. **Tel** (406)442-3961, FAX (406)442-3987.

LC BV655.2.U5 D57
DD 384.54/53/02573
US
●**DIRECTORY OF RELIGIOUS MEDIA.** See Religions and Theology.

LC HE8700
DD 384.55
US
●**DISCOVERY CHANNEL MONTHLY.** (Jan. 1996)-. Periodical. English. Twelve times a year. $11.97. Discovery Channel, 7700 Wisconsin Avenue, Bethesda MD 20814. **Tel** (301)986-0444 ext. 5826. **Absorbed** Destination Discovery **and** TLC Monthly.

ISSN 0747-4644
DD 051
US
DISNEY CHANNEL MAGAZINE, THE. [Disney channel mag.]. **VFOAT** Disney Channel. (198?)-. Periodical. English. Six times a year. $12.00 (one-year), $22.00 (two-year) non-subscribers to Disney Channel; $6.00 (one-year), $12.00 (two-year) subscribers to Disney Channel. The Disney Channel, 3800 West Alameda Avenue, Burbank CA 91505. **Tel** (818)569-7768, FAX (818)569-7395. **ED** Mark Shuper. **Bk Rev. Ad Acc. Adv Mgr:** Myles Grossman, **Tel** (212)687-4442. **Circ:** 4,250,000 (ctrl).
Desc: Contains articles about Disney programs and movies, celebrity interviews, articles about families and parenting, and a pull-out section for kids. Includes programming highlights and listings section.

US
●**DOUBLETAKE.** (May 1995)-. English. Four times a year. $24.00. Circulation Specialists, 19 Brook Road, Needham MA 02194. **Tel** (617)455-0740, FAX (617)455-0743.

ISSN 0960-3352
UK
DOWNLINK : SATELLITE & CABLE INDUSTRY NEWS. (19??)-. English. Twelve times a year. $171.12. Nettlefold Weavers & Assn Ltd, 33 Alderney Street, Pimlico, London SW1V 4ES United Kingdom. **Tel** 011 44 171 8349970, FAX 011 44 171 8349928. **Continues** Satellite Industry Update, 0957-1671.

ISSN 0737-1659
US
DX NEWS. See Communications-Radio.

LC TK6540 .E22 **ISSN** 1019-6587
DD 621.3841/05
SZ
CODEN ETEREG
EBU TECHNICAL REVIEW. See Communications-Radio.

US
ECONOMICS OF BASIC CABLE NETWORKS, THE. Added/Corp Paul Kagan Associates. (19??)-. English. Irregular. $495.00. Paul Kagan Associates Inc., 126 Clock Tower Place, Carmel CA 93923-8734. **Tel** (408)624-1536, FAX (408)625-3225, telex ITT 4938124 PKA UI.
Desc: Analysis and financial profile of the largest ad-supported cable TV program networks. Includes financial and viewership data, advertising information, spending-to-income ratios compared to industry-wide benchmarks, etc.

US
ECONOMICS OF TV PROGRAMMING & SYNDICATION. (19??)-. English. One time a year. $495.00. Paul Kagan Associates, 126 Clock Tower Place, Carmel CA 93923-8734. **Tel** (408)624-1536, FAX (408)625-3225, telex ITT 4938124 PKA UI.

LC PN1991.3 .R8S6 **ISSN** 0131-694X
RU
EFIR. Added/Corp Gosudarstvennyi Komitet SSSR po Televideniiu i Radioveshchaniiu. Vsesoiuznaia Gosudarstvennaia Teleradioveshchatelnaia Kompaniia (Soviet Union). **VFOAT** Teleradio. (1991)-. Periodical. Russian. One time a week. $149.95. **(Subscription address:** East View Publications Inc., 3020 Harbor Lane North, Suite 110, Minneapolis MN 55447. **Tel** (800)477-1005, (612)550-0961, FAX (612)559-2931.**) Continues** Televidenie, Radioveshchanie.

LC TK7800 .E47 **ISSN** 0013-6123
IT
CODEN ETTCB9
ELETTRONICA E TELECOMUNICAZIONI. See Electronics.

ISSN 0896-2502
US
ELEVEN (CHICAGO, ILL.). (ELEVEN : 11.). **Added/Corp** WTTW (Television Station : Chicago, Ill.). **VFOAT** 11. Vol. 1, No. 1 (May 1987)-. Periodical. English. Twelve times a year. $40.00 (with annual subscription to WTTW/Chicago). WTTW Channel 11, PO Box 59111, Chicago IL 60659-0111. **Tel** (312)509-1111. **Continues** Dial Eleven.

LC PN1992.3.U5 E45 **ISSN** 0164-3495
DD 791.45/05
US
EMMY. [Emmy]. **Added/Corp** National Academy of Television Arts and Sciences (U.S.). **VFOAT** Emmy Magazine. Vol. 1 (Winter 1979)-. Trade Publication. English. Six times a year (Jan., Mar., May, July, Sept., Nov.). $28.00. Emmy Magazine, 5220 Lankershim Blvd, North Hollywood CA 91601. **Tel** (818)754-2800, FAX (818)761-2827. **ED** Hank Rieger. **Bk Rev. Ad Acc. Adv Mgr:** John Mccarthy. **Circ:** 15,000. available on an online database, CD-ROM, magnetic tape, and microfilm.
Desc: Explores issues, trends, and behind the scenes VIPs in broadcast and cable TV. Covers programming, new technology, and international developments.
Ind/Abst Access (1979-); Pop. Period. Index.

ISSN 0316-0076
DD 791.45/09714
CN
ENCYCLOPEDIE ARTISTIQUE. Vol. 1 (1973)-. Periodical. French. One time a year. Publications Eclair, 9393 Aveneu Edison, Montreal Quebec H1J 1T5 Canada.

ISSN 1058-109X
DD 791
US
EPI-LOG (DUNLAP, TENN.). (EPI-LOG : THE TELEVISION MAGAZINE OF SCIENCE FICTION, FANTASY, AND ADVENTURE.). [Epi-log]. **VFOAT** Epi Log. (1990)-. Periodical. English. Six times a year. $25.00 US; $30.00 Canada. Epi-Log, POO Box 1322, Dunlap TN 37327.

BE
SUSPENDED
ETUDES DE RADIO TELEVISION. See Communications-Radio.

LC PN1991.3.B4 E89 **ISSN** 0770-9994
BE
CEASED
ETUDES DE RADIO-TELEVISION - RTBF. (ETUDES DE RADIO-TELEVISION.). [Etud. radio-telev. - RTBF]. **Added/Corp** Radiodiffusion Television Belge. Bureau d'Etudes. Radio-Television Belge de la Communaute Culturelle Francaise. No. 1 (1963)-(19??). Periodical. French. RTBF Bureau d Estudes, Local 10M2, Bd Aug Reyers 52, 1040 Brussels Belgium. **Tel** 011 32 2 7372534, FAX 011 32 2 7334020.
Ind/Abst Sociol. Abstr.

ISSN 0012-8023
US
ETV NEWSLETTER. VFOAT The Biweekly News Report of Educational and Instructional Television. No. 1 (Dec. 1966)-. Newsletter. English. Twenty-six times a year. $200.00. Tepfer Publishing Company Inc., PO Box 597, Ridgefield CT 06877. **Tel** (203)454-2618, FAX (203)454-2618. **ED** Charles Tepfer. **Ad Acc.**
Desc: A news report of educational and public television and instructional technologies.

ISSN 1053-8313
DD 384
US
EURO CABLE TV PROGRAMMING. [Euro cable TV programm.]. No. 1 (Oct. 25, 1990)-. Newsletter. English. Twelve times a year. $595.00. Kagan World Media Inc., 126 Clock Tower Place, Carmel CA 93923-8734. **Tel** (408)624-1536, FAX (408)625-3225. **(Subscription address:** Kagan World Media Ltd., 524 Fulham Road, London SW6 5NR United Kingdom. **Tel** 011 44 171 3718880, FAX 011 44 171 3718715.**) ED** Paul Kagan. available via fax.
Desc: Analyses of programming economics, network values, carriage fees, viewer shares and the financial impact of changes in Europe's cable/DBS industries.

FR
EURODIENCE. (1987)-. French (English). Twelve times a year. 4500F. Institut National de L'Audiovisuel / INA, Direction de la Recherche, 4 Avenue de L'Europe No. 6, 94366 Bry Sur Marne Cedex France. **Tel** 011 33 1 49832140, FAX 011 33 1 49832582. Index available. cum. index. **Ad Acc, Adv Mgr:** Joelle Chausiemier, **Tel** 011 33 1 49 83 24 87. **Circ:** 1,000.
Desc: Provides the latest audience shares and detailed top 20 programmes from the largest European markets. Articles on programming and scheduling issues facing European today.

ISSN 1050-3579
DD 384
US
EUROPEAN CABLE/PAY TV. [Eur. cable/pay TV]. **VFOAT** European Cable Pay TV. No. 1 (Apr. 19, 1990)-. Newsletter. English. Twelve times a year. $695.00. Kagan World Media Inc., 126 Clock Tower Place, Carmel CA 93923-8734. **Tel** (408)624-1536, (408)625-3225. **(Subscription address:** Kagan World Media Ltd., 524 Fulham Road, London SW6 5NR United

Communications —Television and Cable

Kingdom. **Tel** 011 44 171 3718880, FAX 011 44 171 3718715.) available via fax. **Continues** Euromedia Investor.
Desc: Companies making pioneering moves in cable, cable funding, penetration, and new sources of programming.

US
EUROPEAN CABLE PAY TV DATABOOK. (19??)-. English (French). One time a year. $495.00. Kagan World Media Inc., 126 Clock Tower Place, Carmel CA 93923-8734. **Tel** (408)624-1536, FAX (408)625-3225. **(Subscription address:** Kagan World Media Ltd., 524 Fulham Road, London SW6 5NR United Kingdom. **Tel** 011 44 171 3718880, FAX 011 44 171 3718715.)
Desc: Data on current industry developments, projections of future events, complete history of each European country's growth of subscribers, homes passed and penetration rates. Also presents statistics on DTH/DBS markets, information on cable/pay TV in Eastern Europe and the addresses, phone numbers and key executive names for major operating companies in every European country.

UK
EUROPEAN CABLE PROGRAMME NETWORKS DATABOOK. (19??)-. English. One time a year. $395.00. Kagan World Media Inc., 126 Clock Tower Place, Carmel CA 93923-8734. **Tel** (408)624-1536, FAX (408)625-3225. **(Subscription address:** Kagan World Media Ltd., 524 Fulham Road, London SW6 5NR United Kingdom. **Tel** 011 44 171 3718880, FAX 011 44 171 3718715.)
Desc: Data on current industry developments, projections, history of each European country's growth of subscribers, homes passed and penetration rates. Also statistics on DTH markets, pay TV release windows and the addresses, phone numbers and executive names for major operating companies in every European country.

UK
EUROPEAN HOME VIDEO DATABOOK. See Communications-Video.

ISSN 0962-8312
UK
TITLE CHANGE
EUROPEAN MEDIA BULLETIN. [Eur. multimedia bull.]. (1991)-(199?). Bulletin. English. Digitalvision International Limited, 17 Totenham Court Road, 2nd Floor, London W1P 9DP United Kingdom. **Tel** 011 44 171 9163577, FAX 011 44 171 7217054. **ED** Isobel Pring and Claire Bayard-White. **Bk Rev. Circ:** 250.
Merged into Inside Multimedia.

ISSN 1052-5068
DD 384 US
EUROPEAN TELEVISION. [Eur. telev.]. **Added/Corp** Paul Kagan Associates. (Apr. 1989)-. Newsletter. English. Twelve times a year. $625.00. Kagan World Media Inc., 126 Clock Tower Place, Carmel CA 93923-8734. **Tel** (408)624-1536, FAX (408)625-3225. **(Subscription address:** Kagan World Media Ltd., 524 Fulham Road, London SW6 5NR United Kingdom. **Tel** 011 44 171 3718880, FAX 011 44 171 3718715.) available via fax. **Continues** Euro TV Investor, 1043-9420.
Desc: The valuation of private and public networks, stations, programme producers and distributors. Includes prices of the programmes, costs of spots, names of the buyers and owners and values of the markets.

UK
EUROPEAN TELEVISION DATABOOK. CHANNELS. (19??)-. English. One time a year. $395.00 ($595.00 for complete two-volume set). Kagan World Media Inc., 126 Clock Tower Place, Carmel CA 93923-8734. **Tel** (408)624-1536, FAX (408)625-3225. **(Subscription address:** Kagan World Media Ltd., 524 Fulham Road, London SW6 5NR United Kingdom. **Tel** 011 44 171 3718880, FAX 011 44 171 3718715.)
Desc: A guide to 23 countries and 52 channels; includes contact lists, advertising and license fee revenues, financial analysis of investment returns and cash flow margins.

UK
EUROPEAN TELEVISION DATABOOK. COUNTRIES. (19??)-. English. One time a year. $395.00 ($595.00 for complete two-volume set). Kagan World Media Inc., 126 Clock Tower Place, Carmel CA 93923-8734. **Tel** (408)624-1536, FAX (408)625-3225. **(Subscription address:** Kagan World Media Ltd., 524 Fulham Road, London SW6 5NR United Kingdom. **Tel** 011 44 171 3718880, FAX 011 44 171 3718715.)
Desc: A guide to 23 countries and 52 channels; includes contact lists, advertising and license fee revenues, financial analysis of investment returns and cash flow margins.

ISSN 1050-298X
DD 384 US
EUROPEAN TV SPORTS. [Eur. TV sports]. **Added/Corp** Kagan World Media, Inc. **VFOAT** TV Sports. No. 1 (Apr. 12, 1990)-. Newsletter. English. Twelve times a year. $595.00. Kagan World Media Inc., 126 Clock Tower Place, Carmel CA 93923-8734. **Tel** (408)624-1536, FAX (408)625-3225. **(Subscription address:** Kagan World Media Ltd., 524 Fulham Road, London SW6 5NR United Kingdom. **Tel** 011 44 171 3718880, FAX 011 44 171 3718715.) available via fax.
Desc: Current data on the business aspects of TV sports broadcasting. Includes rights fees, rights ownership, sponsorship, ad spending, team revenues/profits and regulatory changes.

UK
EUROPEAN TV SPORTS DATABOOK, THE. (19??)-. English. Irregular. $495.00. Kagan World Media Inc., 126 Clock Tower Place, Carmel CA 93923-8734. **Tel** (408)624-1536, FAX (408)625-3225. **(Subscription address:** Kagan World Media Ltd., 524 Fulham Road, London SW6 5NR United Kingdom. **Tel** 011 44 171 3718880, FAX 011 44 171 3718715.)
Desc: A source book on every major European sports network. Includes a channel-by-channel guide of who's buying what events in which markets, statistics on major sports rights transactions, portfolios of major sports distributors and contact lists of industry personnel.

LC PN1993.5.U8 E83 ISSN 0737-0113
DD 384/.8/025797 US
EVERGREEN STATE FILM & VIDEO INDEX, THE. See Communications-Abstracting, Bibliographies and Statistics.

US
FACTS AT A GLANCE, INTERNATIONAL CABLE. Added/Corp National Cable Television Association. National Cable Television Association. Research & Policy Analysis Dept. **VFOAT** International Cable. Vol. 1, No. 1 (Mar. 1991)-. Trade Publication. English. Irregular. National Cable Television Association, Research and Policy Analysis Department, 1724 Massachusetts Avenue Northwest, Washington DC 20036-1969. **Tel** (202)775-3350.

ISSN 1180-4785
DD 791.45/75/09713 CN
FEATURE (MONTREAL). (FEATURE.). [Feature]. (1990)-. Periodical. English. Twelve times a year. 12.00Can$. Feature Publishing Ltd, 2100 St. Catherine Street West, 9th Floor, Montreal, Quebec H3H 2T3 Canada. **Tel** (514)939-5024, FAX (514)939-1515. **ED** David Sherman. **Ad Acc. Circ:** 410,000.
Desc: Stories and descriptions of movies on Canadian English speaking pay television.

LC PN1990.83 .F38 ISSN 0147-4871
DD 384.54/05 US
FEEDBACK (WASHINGTON). (FEEDBACK.). **Added/Corp** Broadcast Education Association (U.S.). (19??)-. Trade Publication. English. Four times a year. Broadcast Education Association, 1771 North Street Northwest, Washington DC 20036-2891. **Tel** (202)429-5355, FAX (202)429-5406. **ED** Philip S. Kipper. **Circ:** 950 (ctrl).
Ind/Abst Curr. Index J. Educ.

ISSN 0345-3057
SW
FILMHAFTET : TIDSKRIFT OM FILM OCH TV. See Motion Picture.

ISSN 0821-6681
DD 384.54/025/713541 CN
FRAME BY FRAME (TORONTO, ONT.). (FRAME BY FRAME.). (1981)-. English. One time a year. Frame By Frame, 131 Hazelton Avenue, Toronto Ontario M5R 2E4 Canada.

LC TK7800 .F86 ISSN 0016-2841
GW
CCC
CODEN FUSHA2
FUNKSCHAU. See Electronics.

LC TK7800 .F862 ISSN 0172-2778
DD 621.38/05 GW
FUNKSCHAU. SONDERHEFT. See Electronics.

ISSN 1197-4788
DD 791.4/079/714 CN
GALA DES PRIX GEMEAUX. [Gala prix Gemeaux]. **Added/Corp** Academie Canadienne du Cinema & de la Television. (1992)-. French. Irregular. free on request. Academie Canadienne du Cinema et de la Television, Bureau 709, 3575 Boul. St-Laurent, Montreal, Quebec H2X 2T7 Canada. **Continues** Prix Gemeaux., 1182-2457.

LC PN1991.3.G5 G48A GH
DD 384.54/09667 SUSPENDED
GBC RADIO AND TV TIMES. See Communications-Radio.

ISSN 1066-8586
US
'GBH (BOSTON, MASS.). ('GBH.). **Added/Corp** WGBH Educational Foundation. (1991)-. Periodical. English. Twelve times a year. $40.00 membership. WGBH, 125 Western Avenue, Boston MA 02134. **Tel** (617)492-2777. **ED** Diane Carasik Dion.
Desc: Publication of the WGBH Educational Foundation. Contains highlights and TV listings.

LC TK6630 .G44
DD 621.388 JA
CODEN NHKGDR
GIKEN GEPPO. VFOAT NHK Technical Report; N.H.K. Giken Geppo; N.H.K. Technical report; NHK Giken Geppo. (19??)-. Academic Scholarly Publication. Japanese. Twelve times a year. ¥535 single issue. Nihon Hoso Shuppan Kyokai, 41-1 Udagawa-cho Shibuya-ku, Tokyo-to 150 Japan. Documents available from CASDDS.
Ind/Abst Chem. Abstr.

ISSN 0738-7555
US
CEASED
GPN NEWSLETTER. Added/Corp Great Plains National Instructional Television Library. **VFOAT** GP Newsletter. **VAT** Great Plains National Newsletter. (1974)-(Spring 1994). Newsletter. English. Great Plains National Instr TV Lib, 1800 North 33, Box 80669, Lincoln NE 68501. **Tel** (800)228-4630 (402)472-2007, FAX (402)472-1785, telex 484340. **Continues** GPN Newsletter, 0738-7555.

LC HE8700
DD 384.55 BL
●**GUIA DE PROGRAMACAO NET.** (1994)-. Consumer Publication. Portuguese. Twelve times a year. Editora Globo SA, Rua do Curtume 665, 05065-001 Sao Paulo SP Brazil. **Tel** 011 55 11 8746000, FAX 011 55 11 8612042.
Desc: Covers programming of Globo System cable network.

ISSN 1055-6141
PR
GUIA DE TELEVISION Y ENTRETENIMEINTO. (May 1991)-. Periodical. English (Spanish). Twelve times a year. $15.00. Casiano Communications, PO Box 12130, Loiza St. Station, San Juan Puerto Rico 00914. **Tel** (809)728-3000, (800)462-2185, FAX (809)268-1001, (809)728-7325.

LC HE8689 .C6614
DD 384.54/06/01 UK
HANDBOOK - COMMONWEALTH BROADCASTING ASSOCIATION.
Main/Corp Commonwealth Broadcasting Association. (19??)-. Trade Publication. English. Every 2 years. Commonwealth Broadcasting Association, Broadcasting House, London W1A 1AA United Kingdom. **Tel** 011 44 181 7655144, FAX 011 44 181 7655152. **ED** Stuart Revill. **Ad Acc, Adv Mgr:** Derek Inall, **Tel** 011 44 462 684231. **Circ:** 10,000.

US
HANDY POCKET DIRECTORY OF TELEVISION STATIONS IN OPERATION. (19??)-. Directory. English. Irregular. Free. Warren Publishing, Inc., 2115 Ward Court Northwest, Washington DC 20037. **Tel** (202)872-9200, FAX (202)293-3435. **ED** Michael Taliaferro.
Desc: Simplified instructional manual to the Television and Cable Factbook.

US
HARD REPORT. (19??)-. English. One time a week (50 issues). $250.00 radio station; $300.00 other. Hard Report Inc., 4 Trading Post Way, Medford Lakes NJ 08055. **Tel** (609)654-7272.

ISSN 0745-6565
US
HAWAII TV DIGEST. Vol. 1, No. 1 (Jan. 1983)-. Periodical. English. Twelve times a year. Free to subscribers of Oceanic Cablevision. Hawaii TV Digest, 2669 Kilihau Street, Honolulu HI 96819. **Ad Acc.** ctrl circ.

ISSN 1050-8996
DD 791 US
HBO'S GUIDE TO MOVIES ON VIDEOCASSETTE AND CABLE TV. [HBO's guide movies videocass. cable TV]. **Added/Corp** Home Box Office (Firm). **VFOAT** Guide to Movies on Videocassette and Cable TV; Movies on Videocassette and Cable TV. **VAT** Home Box Office's Guide to Movies on Videocassette and Cable Television. 1st Ed. (1990)-. English. One time a year. $12.95. Harper Collins Publishers, Keystone Industrial Park, Scranton PA 18512. **Tel** (800)242-7737, (800)233-4727, FAX (800)822-4090.
Desc: Lists more than 7,000 movies.

ISSN 0892-5771
DD 384 US
HDTV NEWSLETTER. [HDTV newsl.]. **VFOAT** HD TV Newsletter. **VAT** High Definition Television Newsletter. (1986)-. Newsletter. English. Ten times a year. $695.00. Advanced Television Publishing, 753 East Fall Creek Road, Alsea OR 97324. **Tel** (503)487-4186, FAX (503)222-2341. **ED** Dale Cripps and Sam Bush. Index available. available on an online database from NEWSNET.
Desc: Advanced television systems offering vastly

Communications —Television and Cable

improved image and sound quality; medium is being revolutionized by technology; new applications abound. Read by communications planners worldwide.

ISSN 1055-9280
US
CCC
TITLE CHANGE

HDTV REPORT. **VAT** High Definition Television Report. (1991)-(1995). Periodical. English. Phillips Business Information Inc., 1201 Seven Locks Road, PO Box 61130, Potomac MD 20854. **Tel** (301)340-3338, (301)340-1520, (800)777-5005, FAX (301)424-4297, telex 358149. available on an online database (file 636/Full-Text) from DIALOG. *Merged into Video Technology News.*
Ind/Abst PTS Newsl. Database [Full Txt.].

UK

HEADLINE NEWS CURRENT AWARENESS SERVICE. BATTERIES / NEW DEVELOPMENTS. (19??)-. English. Twelve times a year. £200.00. Evison Enterprises, 65 Ashey Road Ryde, Isle of Wight United Kingdom. **Tel** 011 44 1983 566541.

ISSN 0343-4206
GW
UDC 339.166 :[621.396.97 + 621.397.6]   CCC

HIFI & TV. **VFOAT** HiFi und TV. (1977)-. Periodical. German. Twenty-six times a year. $58.03. Josef Keller GmbH & Co. Verlags KG, Postfach 1455, D-82317 Starnberg Germany. **Tel** 011 49 (08151)771-0, FAX 011 49 (08151)771-152, telex 566438.

US

HIGH DEFINITION PRODUCTION. **Added/Corp** HDTV 1125/60 Group. **VFOAT** HD Production; High Definition. (19??)-. Periodical. English. Four times a year. CRN Inc, 8 Bond Street, Great Neck NY 11021.

LC PN1993.5.A1 H54   ISSN 0143-9685
DD 791.4/05   UK
CCC

HISTORICAL JOURNAL OF FILM, RADIO, AND TELEVISION. See Motion Picture.

ISSN 0287-3540
JA
DD 371.3
HOSO KYOIKU. See Education.

LC PN1992 .H67
JA

HOSOGAKU KENKYU. **Added/Corp** NHK Hoso Yoron Chosajo. NHK Hoso Bunka Kenkyujo. Hosogaku Kenkyushitsu. NHK Sogo Hoso Bunka Kenkyujo. Hosogaku Kenkyushitsu. NHK Sogo Hoso Bunka Kenkyujo. Hsogaku Kenkyubu. **VFOAT** Studies of Broadcasting. (1961)-. Periodical. Japanese (summaries and/or abstracts in English). ¥1500. Japan Broadcasting Corporation, 211 Atago Minato Ku, Tokyo 105 Japan.
Ind/Abst PAIS Int. Print.

LC PN1991.3.R8 H68
UN

HOVORYT I POKOZUIE UKRAINA. **Added/Corp** Ukraine. Derzhavnyi Komitet po Telebachenniu i Radiomovlenniu. **VFOAT** Govorit i Pokazyvaet Ukraina. (Feb. 1957)-. Ukrainian. One time a week. $119.95. **(Subscription address:** East View Publications Inc., 3020 Harbor Lane North, Suite 110, Minneapolis MN 55447. **Tel** (800)477-1005, (612)550-0961, FAX (612)559-2931.**)**

LC PN1991.3.U6 I3   ISSN 0748-0237
DD 384.54/025/796   US

IDAHO BROADCASTING GUIDE. See Communications-Radio.

ISSN 0018-9316
DD 384   US
CCC
CODEN IETBAC

Pr Rev.

IEEE TRANSACTIONS ON BROADCASTING. [IEEE trans. broadcast.]. **Added/Corp** IEEE Broadcasting Group. IEEE Professional Technical Group on Broadcasting. IEEE Broadcast, Cable and Consumer Electronics Society. **VFOAT** IEEE Transactions on Broadcasting; Broadcasting. Vol. BC-9 (Feb. 1963)-. Periodical. English. Four times a year. $50.00. IEEE / Institute of Electrical and Electronics Engineers Inc., 345 East 47th Street, New York NY 10017-2394. **Tel** (908)981-1393, FAX (908)981-9667. **(Subscription address:** IEEE / Institute of Electrical and Electronics Engineers Inc., 445 Hoes Lane, PO Box 1331, Piscataway NJ 08855-1331. **Tel** (800)701-IEEE, (908)981-0060, FAX (908)981-9667, telex 833233.**)** available on microfiche. Documents available from Article Express International, The Genuine Article, Ask*IEEE, CASDDS. *Continues* IRE Professional Group on Broadcasting. IRE Transactions on Broadcasting, 0096-1663.
Desc: Covers the field of broadcast technology, including the production, distribution, transmission, and propagation aspects of broadcasting.

Ind/Abst Acoust. Abstr.; Appl. Sci. Technol. Index (1991-); Bioeng. Abstr.; Chem. Abstr.; Curr. Cit.; Curr. Contents Eng. Comput. Technol.; Ei Page One; Eng. Index Annu.; Expand. Acad. Index (1992-); Index IEEE Publ.; INSPEC (1968-); Int. Aerosp. Abstr.; Res. Alert [Full Cov.]; Sci. Cit. Index; SCISEARCH.

ISSN 1051-8215
DD 621   US
CCC
CODEN ITCTEM

IEEE TRANSACTIONS ON CIRCUITS AND SYSTEMS FOR VIDEO TECHNOLOGY. (IEEE TRANSACTIONS ON CIRCUITS AND SYSTEMS FOR VIDEO TECHNOLOGY : A PUBLICATION OF THE CIRCUITS AND SYSTEMS SOCIETY.). [IEEE trans. circuits syst. video technol.]. **Added/Corp** IEEE Circuits and Systems Society. **VFOAT** Circuits and Systems for Video Technology. **VAT** Institute of Electrical and Electronics Engineers Transactions on Circuits and Systems for Video Technology. Vol. 1, No. 1 (March 1991)-. Periodical. English. Six times a year. $163.00. IEEE / Institute of Electrical and Electronics Engineers Inc., 345 East 47th Street, New York NY 10017-2394. **Tel** (908)981-1393, FAX (908)981-9667. **(Subscription address:** IEEE / Institute of Electrical and Electronics Engineers, 445 Hoes Lane, PO Box 1331, Piscataway NJ 08855-1331. **Tel** (800)701-IEEE, (908)981-0060, FAX (908)981-9667, telex 833233.**)** available on microfiche. Documents available from Article Express International, Ask*IEEE.
Desc: Emphasizes video processing algorithms, real-time implementation, VLSI architecture and technology, and related topics.
Ind/Abst Curr. Cit.; Ei Page One; Eng. Index Annu.; Expand. Acad. Index (1992-); Index IEEE Publ.; INSPEC (March 1991-).

ISSN 1064-6833
DD 384   US

INDEPENDENT TELEVISION. (INDEPENDENT TELEVISION : FROM THE ASSOCIATION OF INDEPENDENT TELEVISION STATIONS.). [Indep. telev.]. **Added/Corp** Association of Independent Television Stations. Vol. 1, No. 1 (Oct. 1990)-. Periodical. English. Four times a year. Crain Communications, Independent Television, 740 N. Rush Street, Chicago IL 60611. **Tel** (312)649-5200. *Continues* INTV Journal, 0899-787X.

ISSN 0822-9236
DD 384.55/56/072071   CN

INFO SID TELIDON II. (INFO SID TELIDON II : BULLETIN D'INFORMATION PUBLIE PAR LE GROUPE VIDEOTRON.). [Info SID TELIDON II]. **Added/Corp** Groupe Videotron. Groupe Videotron. Centre de Recherche. **VAT** Info Systeme d'Information A Domicile Telidon II. Vol. 1, No. 1 (Dec. 1980)-. Bulletin. French. Free. Groupe Videotron, 3700 boulevard Losch, St. Hubert Quebec J3Y 5T6 Canada.

ISSN 0258-9494
UDC 061 (100) :621.39   BE

INFORMATIONS MONDIALES - UNDA. **VFOAT** Informations Mondiales - Association Catholique Internationale pour la Radio et la t~el~evision; UNDA Informations Mondiales. (1977)-. Periodical. French. Eight times a year. $12.00 (one-year), $36.00 (three-year) Europe; $15.00 (one-year), $45.00 (three-year) other. UNDA Intl Cath Assn Radio & TV, 12 rue de l'Orme, B-1040 Brussels Belgium. **Tel** 011 32 2 7349708. **Bk Rev. Ad Acc. Circ:** 2,000. *Continues* Wide World of UNDA Newsletter.

ISSN 1064-7457
DD 384   US

INTERACTIVE TELEVISION REPORT. [Interact. telev. rep.]. (Sept. 1992)-. Periodical. English. Twelve times a year. $495.00. Intercor Inc, 575 Anton Boulevard, Suite 450, Costa Masa CA 92625. **Tel** (714)557-8800, FAX (714)557-5445.

ISSN 0020-6229
UK

INTERNATIONAL BROADCAST ENGINEER : IBE. [Int. broadcast eng.]. **VFOAT** IBE; IBE International Broadcast Engineer. (1964)-. Trade Publication. English. Seven times a year. $162.00. Argus Press Group, Queensway House, 2 Queensway Redhill, Surrey RH1 1QS United Kingdom. **Tel** 011 44 1737 768611, 011 44 1737 761685, FAX 011 44 1737 760510, telex 948669 TOPJNL G. **ED** David Sparks. **Ad Acc. Circ:** 8,500. Documents available from Ask*IEEE. *Formed by the union of* International Sound Engineer *and* International TV Technical Review.
Desc: Devoted to design and operation of professional TV broadcast equipment.
Ind/Abst Curr. Cit.; Curr. Technol. Index (1971-); INSPEC (1971-).

LC TK6540 .I562   ISSN 0957-4425
DD 621.3841/05   UK
CODEN IBSODS

INTERNATIONAL BROADCASTING. [Int. broadcast.]. (19??)-. Trade Publication. English. Ten times a year. $150.00. International Thomson Business Publications, 42 Bedford Square, London WC1B 3SC

United Kingdom. **Tel** 011 44 171 3236986. **(Subscription address:** EMAP Business Publishing, 4 Admiral House Cardinal Way, Middlesex HA3 5SQ United Kingdom. **Tel** 011 44 181 8684499.**) ED** Fergal Ringrose. **Ad Acc. Circ:** 10,000 (ctrl). Documents available from Ask*IEEE. *Continues* Broadcasting Systems & Operations, 0141-1748.
Desc: News and features covering broadcast technology throughout the world and of interest to broadcasters and equipment manufacturers.
Ind/Abst INSPEC (1980-); World Publ. Monit.

LC HE8700 .I56   ISSN 1069-5494
DD 384.55/5/068   US
CCC
CODEN ICABE9

INTERNATIONAL CABLE. [Int. cable]. (1990)-. Trade Publication. English. Twelve times a year. free to qualified personnel. Phillips Business Information Inc., 1201 Seven Locks Road, PO Box 61130, Potomac MD 20854. **Tel** (301)424-3338, (301)340-1520, (800)777-5005, FAX (301)424-4297, telex 358149. **ED** Shelly Ollig. **Bk Rev. Ad Acc.** ctrl circ. available with illustrations.
Ind/Abst INSPEC.

LC HE8700 .I57   ISSN 0895-2213
DD 384.55/05   US

INTERNATIONAL TELEVISION & VIDEO ALMANAC. [Int. telev. video alm.]. **VFOAT** International Television and Video Almanac; Television & Video Almanac. 32nd Ed. (1987)-. Trade Publication. English. One time a year. $88.50. Quigley Publications, 159 West 53rd Street, New York NY 10019. **Tel** (212)247-3100. **Bk Rev. Ad Acc.** *Continues* International Television Almanac, 0539-0761.

LC PN1992 .I57   UK
DD 384.55/4/05   SUSPENDED

INTERNATIONAL TV & VIDEO GUIDE. **VFOAT** International TV and Video Guide; TV and Video Guide; TV & Video Guide; International T.V. & Video Guide. **VAT** International Television and Video Guide. (1983)-Suspended with 1987 edition. Periodical. English. One time a year. $12.95. New York Zoetrope, 838 Broadway, New York NY 10003. **Tel** (212)420-0590. **ED** Richard Paterson. **Bk Rev. Ad Acc.**
Desc: Worldwide reports covering cable, TV movies, rock video, festivals, animation, schools, books, magazines and distribution. Also special features, directories, and photos. This is the complete source.

ISSN 0899-787X
DD 384   US
TITLE CHANGE

INTV JOURNAL. [INTV j.]. **VAT** Independent Television Journal. (198?)-(19??). Periodical. English. INTV Journal, 80 Fifth Avenue, New York NY 10011. *Continues* INTV Quarterly, 0882-2271. *Continued by* Independent Television, 1064-6833.

LC HE8700.8 .I58
DD 384.55/43   US

INVESTING IN TELEVISION. **Added/Corp** Broadcast Investment Analysts (Washington, D.C.). (19??)-. English. One time a year. $745.00. Broadcast Investment Analysts, PO Box 17307, Washington DC 20041. **Tel** (703)818-2425.

US

ITV RESOURCES IN THE DEFINED MINIMUM PROGRAM. **Added/Corp** South Carolina. Office of Instructional Technology. South Carolina Educational Television Network. English. *Continues* ITV and Radio Resources in the Defined Minimum Program.

LC TK6642 .D322   ISSN 0360-2419
DD 621.388/8/705   US

JACK DARR'S SERVICE CLINIC. See Electronics.

ISSN 1056-3342
DD 791   US

JEWISH TELEVIMAGE REPORT. [Jew. televimage rep.]. **Added/Corp** Jewish Televimages Resource Center. **VFOAT** JTVR. Premiere Issue (May 1991)-. Periodical. English. Nine times a year. $45.00. The Jewish Televimage Report, 78-46 265th Street, Floral Park NY 11004. **Tel** (718)962-1730. **ED** Jonathon Pearl. **Bk Rev.**
Desc: Guide to television's Jewish themes and characters. Provides news, analysis, commentary, advance notice, interviews, and behind-the-scenes information about TV's Jewish images.

LC PN1991 .J6   ISSN 0883-8151
DD 384.54/05   US

JOURNAL OF BROADCASTING & ELECTRONIC MEDIA. [J. broadcast. electron. media]. **Added/Corp** Broadcast Education Association (U.S.). **VFOAT** Journal of Broadcasting and Electronic Media; JOBEM. Vol. 29, No. 1 (Winter 1985)-. Academic Scholarly Publication. English. Four times a year (Feb., May, Aug., Oct.). $75.00. Broadcast Education Association, 1771 North Street Northwest, Washington DC 20036-2891. **Tel** (202)429-5355, FAX (202)429-5406.

ED A. Alexander. **Bk Rev**. available on microfilm and microfiche from University Microfilms International (UMI). Documents available from The Genuine Article, UMI Article Clearinghouse. ***Continues*** *Journal of Broadcasting, 0021-938X.*
Desc: Contains scholarly articles about developments, trends and research as well as reviews and criticism, written by academicians, researchers and other professionals in the field today.
Ind/Abst Acad. Abstr.; Acad. Ind. [Computer File] (1984, 1985, 1987-); Acad. Search; Arts Humanit. Citation Index [Full Cov.]; Commun. Abstr.; Curr. Cit.; Curr. Contents Arts Humanit.; Curr. Contents Soc. Behav. Sci.; Curr. Index J. Educ.; Curr. Law Index (1985-); EP Collect.; Expand. Acad. Index (1984-); Gen. Period. Index (1985-); Homework Help.; Humanit. Index; INFO-SOUTH Abstr.; Leg. Resour. Index (1985-); LegalTrac (1980-); Mag. Search; MasterFile FullTEXT 1000; MasterFile FullTEXT 350; MasterFile FullTEXT 650; MasterFile FullTEXT (July 1990-); Newsp. Period. Abstr. (1986-); OCLC; PAIS Int. Print (1991-); Psychol. Abstr. (1986-); PsycINFO (1990-); PsycLit; Pub. Lib. FullTEXT; Res. Alert [Full Cov.]; Sage Fam. Stud. Abstr.; Soc. Plann. Policy Dev. Abstr.; Soc. Sci. Cit. Index [Full Cov.]; Sociol. Abstr.; Telebase; Topicator.

LC PN1992 .J68 **ISSN** 0308-6801
DD 384.55/4/05 UK
JOURNAL OF CENTRE FOR ADVANCED TV STUDIES : JCATS. [JCATS. J. cent. adv. telev. stud.]. **Added/Corp** Centre for Advanced TV Studies (Great Britain). Vol. 6, No. 2 (Apr./Sept. 1978)-. Periodical. English. Two times a year. £23.00 UK; £28.00 other. Centre For Advanced TV Studies, 27 Theobald's Road, London WC1 8NW United Kingdom. ***Continues*** *Journal of the Centre for Advanced TV Studies.*

LC LB1044.7 .J68 **ISSN** 0260-7417
DD 371.3/358 UK
CCC
Pr Rev. TITLE CHANGE
JOURNAL OF EDUCATIONAL TELEVISION. (JOURNAL OF EDUCATIONAL TELEVISION : JOURNAL OF THE EDUCATIONAL TELEVISION ASSOCIATION.). [J. educ. telev.]. **Added/Corp** Educational Television Association (Great Britain). (1982)-(1995). Periodical. English. Carfax Publishing Company, PO Box 25, Abingdon, Oxfordshire OX14 3UE United Kingdom. **Tel** 011 44 1235 555335, FAX 011 44 1235 553559, telex 817484. **ED** Maire Messenger Davies. **Bk Rev**. **Ad Acc**. available on microfiche. Documents available from The Genuine Article. ***Continued by*** *Journal of Educational Media, 1358-1651.*
Ind/Abst Br. Educ. Index (?-?); Child. Lit. Abstr. (19??-?); Commun. Abstr. (?-?); Curr. Cit.; Curr. Contents Soc. Behav. Sci. (?-?); Curr. Index J. Educ. (?-?); Educ. Adm. Abstr. (?-?); Educ. Technol. Abstr. (?-?); EP Collect.; Homework Help.; Humanit. Source; Inf. Sci. Abstr. (?-?); MasterFile FullTEXT 1000; MasterFile FullTEXT 350; MasterFile FullTEXT 650; MasterFile FullTEXT (July 1994-); Multicult. Educ. Abstr. (?-?); Res. Alert (?-?) [Full Cov.]; Res. High. Educ. Abstr. (?-?); School Organ. Manage. Abstr. (?-?); Soc. Sci. Source; Soc. Sci. Cit. Index (?-?) [Full Cov.]; Sociol. Educ. Abstr. (?-?); Stud. Women Abstr. (?-?); Tech. Educ. Train. Abstr. (?-?); Telebase; World Mag. Bank.

ISSN 1045-5744
US
KAET MAGAZINE. Added/Corp KAET-TV (Television Station : Tempe, Ariz.). Vol. 14, Issue 7 (July 1989)-. English. Twelve times a year. Friends of Channel Eight, Arizona State University / KAET, Tempe AZ 85287-1405. **Tel** (602)965-3506, FAX (602)965-1000. **ED** Dorothy Mayer. ***Continues*** *Under Cover.*
Desc: Contains information on television programs, with emphasis on public television.

UK
KEMPS FILM, TV & VIDEO YEARBOOK. **VFOAT** Kemps Film, TV, and Video Yearbook. (19??)-. English. Reed Information Services Ltd., Windsor Court, East Grinstead House, East Grinstead RH19 1BR United Kingdom. **Tel** 011 44 1342 326972, FAX 011 44 1342 335977, telex 95127 INFSER G. ***Continues*** *Kemps International Film & Television Year Book.*

UK
●**KEY NOTE REPORT : TV AND VIDEO RENTAL.** (1994)-. Trade Publication. English. Irregular. Key Note Publications Ltd., Field House, 72 Oldfield Road, Hampton Middlesex TW12 2HQ United Kingdom. **Tel** 011 0181 7830755, FAX 011 0181 7831940.

LC HE **ISSN** 1064-1114
DD 384 US
KIDSNET (WASHINGTON, D.C.). (KIDSNET : FUTURE BULLETIN & CALENDAR.). [Kidsnet]. **Added/Corp** KIDSNET (Organization). **VFOAT** Future Bulletin & Calendar; Kidsnet Bulletin and Future Programming. (19??)-. Bulletin. English. Twelve times a year. $155.00. Kidsnet Clearinghouse, 6856 Eastern Avenue Northwest, Suite 208, Washington DC 20012. **Tel** (202)291-1400, FAX (202)882-7315. **ED** laura McGough. available on an online database.
Desc: Lists children's television, radio and home video. Quarterly calendar includes relevant legislation, conferences, grants, and services related to children and the media.

ISSN 1074-1135
DD 384 UK
●**LATIN AMERICAN CABLE & PAY TV.** [Lat. Am. cable pay TV]. **VFOAT** Latin American Cable and Pay TV. No. 1 (Sept. 22, 1993)-. Newsletter. English. Twelve times a year. $695.00. Kagan World Media Inc., 126 Clock Tower Place, Carmel CA 93923-8734. **Tel** (408)624-1536, FAX (408)625-3225. **(Subscription address:** Kagan World Media Ltd., 524 Fulham Road, London SW6 5NR United Kingdom. **Tel** 011 44 171 3718880, FAX 011 44 171 3718715.**)** available via fax.
Desc: Multichannel trends and market development in South America, Mexico, Central America and the Caribbean. Insights into financing, foreign investment deals, values, growth potential, programming regulation, operations and marketing in Latin America.

UK
LATIN AMERICAN CABLE PROGRAM NETWORKS DATABOOK. (19??)-. English. One time a year. $495.00. Kagan World Media Inc., 126 Clock Tower Place, Carmel CA 93923-8734. **Tel** (408)624-1536, FAX (408)625-3225. **(Subscription address:** Kagan World Media Ltd., 524 Fulham Road, London SW6 5NR United Kingdom. **Tel** 011 44 171 3718880, FAX 011 44 171 3718715.**)**
Desc: Research report on the programming, penetration and potential of Latin American cable and satellite program networks, including summaries of multichannel markets and contact lists of channel executives and organizations. Information on network development, program genre, lineups, advertising spot rates, financing and revenue streams, regulation, etc.

US
LATIN AMERICAN TELEVSION. (19??)-. English. Irregular. Baskerville Communications, PO Box 5084, Thousand Oaks CA 91359. **Tel** (805)499-0721 ext. 289. **(Subscription address:** Bakersville Communications, PO Box 303, Shrub Oak NY 10588. **Tel** (914)962-6297.**)**

ISSN 0226-7764
DD 371.3/358/09714 CN
LEGENDE. [Legende]. No. 1- 5 Oct. 1978-. Periodical. French. Twenty-six times a year. Free. Tele-Universite / Canada, 214 Av Saint-Sacrement, Quebec Quebec G1N 4M6 Canada.

ISSN 0996-7826
FR
UDC 7.096/.097
LETTRE. FRENCH TV MARKET NEWSLETTER, LA. (LA LETTRE. THE FRENCH TV MARKET NEWSLETTER.). **VFOAT** French TV Market Newsletter; Lettre (International Ed.). (1989)-. Newsletter. English. Ten times a year. $214.35. SIMAPRESS, 18 rue Seguier, 75006 Paris France. **Tel** 011 33 1 40 46 01 22, FAX 011 33 43 26 74 98. **ED** Maurice Chapot. **Ad Acc. Circ:** 1,000 (ctrl).
Desc: A professional letter of information on audiovisual media and communication.

ISSN 0108-5697
DK
LEVENDE BILLEDER. See Motion Picture.

BE
LIST OF EUROPEAN VHF SOUND BROADCASTING STATIONS. (19??)-. English (French). Six times a year. 70.00F. European Broadcasting Union, Case Postale 67, CH-1218 Geneva Switzerland. **Tel** 011 41 22 7172111, FAX 011 41 22 7985897, telex 41 57 00 EBU CH.

LC TK6645 .E8
DD 621.388 BE
LISTE DES STATIONS DE TELEVISION. ZONE EUROPEENNE. Main/Corp European Broadcasting Union. **VFOAT** Zone Europeenne; List of Television Stations. European Area. (195?)-. French (English). Six times a year. 70.00F Comes with Situation Edition and supplements. European Broadcasting Union, Case Postale 67, CH-1218 Geneva Switzerland. **Tel** 011 41 22 7172111, FAX 011 41 22 7985897, telex 41 57 00 EBU CH. ***Continues*** *Liste de Stations Europeennes de Television et de Radio-Difusion Sonore en Ondes Metriques.*

ISSN 0279-4152
US
LO-POWER COMMUNITY TV. [Lo-power community TV]. **VAT** Low Power Community Television. (19??)-. Periodical. English. Twelve times a year. Lo-Power Community TV, 7432 East Diamond, Scottsdale AZ 85257.

LC LB1044.8 .M37a **ISSN** 0732-8125
DD 371.3/358/09752 US
MARYLAND PUBLIC TV. Added/Corp Maryland Center for Public Broadcasting. **VFOAT** Maryland Public T.V.; Maryland Public Television. (19??)-. Periodical. English. Twelve times a year. Maryland Center for Public Broadcasting, Bonita Avenue, Owings Mills MD 21117. **Tel** (301)337-4081. ***Continues*** *Program Guide (Maryland Center for Public Broadcasting), 0363-9606.*

CN
MATTHEWS' CATV DIRECTORY. Directory. English. Two times a year. 115.00Can$; 275.00Can$ (combined with Matthews' Media Directory). Canadian Corporate News, 25 Adelaide Street East, Suite 500, Toronto Ontario M5C 3A1 Canada. **Tel** (416)362-5739, (800)363-9296, FAX (416)362-9693. ***Continues*** *Matthews' CATV.*

ISSN 1043-2639
DD 791 US
MAYBERRY GAZETTE, THE. [Mayberry gaz.]. **Added/Corp** Andy Griffith Show Appreciation Society. (1986)-. Periodical. English. Six times a year. $17.00 North America; $25.00 other. Mayberry Gazette, PO Box 330, Clemmons NC 27012. **Tel** (919)998-2860. **ED** John Meroney. **Bk Rev**. **Ad Acc**. **Circ:** 7,000.
Desc: A publication of the "Andy Griffith Show Appreciation Society."

LC HM **ISSN** 1038-6750
DD 302.230994 AT
MEDIA AUSTRALIA (RICHMOND NORTH). (MEDIA AUSTRALIA.). [Media Aust (Richmond North)]. (1992)-. Periodical. English. One time a week. 395.00Aus$ Australia; 465.00Aus$ other. Gold Group Asia Pacific Pty. Ltd., 394A Victoria Street, Richmond North 3121 Australia. **Tel** 011 61 3 4295599. ***Absorbed*** *Media Letter* ***and*** *Video Music Business.*

ISSN 0889-0951
DD 384 US
MEDIA SPORTS BUSINESS. [Media sports bus.]. (198?)-. Newsletter. English. Twelve times a year. $595.00. Paul Kagan Associates Inc., 126 Clock Tower Place, Carmel CA 93923-8734. **Tel** (408)624-1536, FAX (408)625-3225, telex ITT 4938124 PKA UI. **ED** Dwight Beach. available via fax. ***Continues*** *Pay TV Sports, 0734-8533.*
Desc: Newsletter on the economic power struggle among sports teams and the electronic media, with analysis of the value of sports media rights.

LC E743 **ISSN** 0543-3754
US
MEET THE PRESS : AMERICA'S PRESS CONFERENCE OF THE AIR. See History-History of North and South America.

ISSN 1191-7962
DD 791.450971622505 CN
METRO WEEKLY TELECASTER. [Metro wkly. telecaster]. **VFOAT** Telecaster. (1992)-. Periodical. English. One time a week. Fundy Group Publications, PO Box 128, 2 Second Street, Yarmouth Nova Scotia B5A 4B1 Canada. **Tel** (902)453-2330, (902)742-7111, FAX (902)455-7162. ***Continues*** *Metro Telecaster (1977), 0708-2568.*

ISSN 0913-0101
DD 621.319 JA
MITSUBISHI DENSEN KOGYO JIHO. [Mitsubishi Densen Kogyo jiho]. **VFOAT** Mitsubishi Cable Industries Review. (1986)-. Periodical. Multiple languages. Two times a year. Mitsubishi Cable Industries Ltd., Patent & Technology Administration Department, 15-26 Fukushima 7-chome, Fukushima-ku, Osaka-shi Osaka 553 Japan. ***Continues*** *Dainichi-Nippon Densen Jiho, 0011-5541.*
Ind/Abst Curr. Cit.

UK
MODERN REVIEW, THE. See Motion Picture.

LC PN1993.5.U755 M66
DD 384/.8/025776 US
MONTANA PRODUCTION GUIDE : A DIRECTORY OF PRODUCTION SERVICES, PERSONNEL, AND LOCATIONS IN MONTANA. See Motion Picture.

LC PN1992.8.F5 M68 **ISSN** 1053-5314
DD 016.79143/75 US
MOVIES ON TV AND VIDEOCASSETTE. [Movies TV videocass.]. **VAT** Movies on Television and Videocassette. (1989/1990)-. English. $8.99. Bantam Books Doubleday, 1540 Broadway, New York NY 10036. **Tel** (212)354-6500, (800)223-6834, FAX (212)492-9700. ***Continues*** *Movies on TV, 0160-4791.*

LC HE8700.7.C6 M84 **ISSN** 0276-8593
US
CCC
MULTICHANNEL NEWS. VFOAT Multi Channel News. (1980)-. Periodical. English. One time a week. $96.00. Chilton, 825 7th Avenue, New York NY 10019. **Tel** (212)887-8560. **(Subscription address:** Multichannel News, PO Box 7700, Riverton NJ 08077. **Tel** (800)360-7600.**) ED** Tom Southwick. **Bk Rev**. **Ad Acc. Circ:** 13,000 (ctrl). available on an online database (file 16,570,648/Full-Text) from DIALOG.
Desc: Covers news pertaining to the cable TV, pay TV

and MDS industries. Content is limited to news about events, finance, breakthroughs and related matters. **Ind/Abst** F&S Index Plus Text, Int. [Full Txt.] [Select. Cov.]; Mark. Advert. Ref. Serv. [Full Txt.]; PROMT [Full Txt.]; Trade Ind. ASAP [Full Txt.]; Trade Ind. Index [Full Txt.].

US

MUNSTERS & THE ADDAMS FAMILY REUNION, THE. English. Four times a year. $20.00. Fan Club Publishing, PO Box 69A04, West Hollywood CA 90069. **Tel** (213)650-5112. **ED** Louis Wendruck. **Bk Rev. Ad Acc. Circ:** 1,000.
Desc: Publication of the Munsters & The Addams Family fan club. Newsletter for fans of the 1960s television shows. Offers photos, postcards, t-shirts, videos, records, articles about stars of the show, and episode guides - all for sale.

ISSN 1065-0229
US

●**MUSIC VIDEO MAGAZINE.** **See** Music.

ISSN 1081-1893
DD 331 US

●**NABET-CWA NEWS.** [NABET-CWA news]. **Main/Corp** NABET-CWA. **VFOAT** NABET CWA News. (1994)-. Periodical. English. Six times a year. Corporation for Public Broadcasting, 901 E Street Northwest, Washington DC 20001. **Tel** (202)879-9600. ***Continues*** *National Association of Broadcast Employees and Technicians NABET News, 0027-5697.*

LC HD6350.B86 N18 **ISSN** 0027-5697
US
TITLE CHANGE

NABET NEWS. INTERNATIONAL EDITION. (NABET NEWS.). **Main/Corp** National Association of Broadcast Employees and Technicians. **Added/Corp** National Association of Broadcast Employees and Technicians. News. **VAT** National Association of Broadcast Employees and Technicians News International Edition. (19??)-(199?). Periodical. English. NABET News, 80 East Jackson Boulevard, Room 711, Chicago IL 60604. ***Continued by*** *NABET-CWA News, 1081-1893.*

LC HE8700 **ISSN** 1358-8931
DD 384.55 UK

●**NETWORK LONDON. 1995.** [Network Lond., 1995]. **VFOAT** CNN Network. (1995)-. Consumer Publication. English. Four times a year. Mediamark Publishing International Ltd., 35 Gresse Street, Rathbone Place, London W1P 1PN United Kingdom. **Tel** 011 44 171 5803105, FAX 011 44 171 5801695. **Circ:** 20,000.

LC PN1990.9.T34 N48 **ISSN** 0741-7225
DD 791.44/75/02574 US

NEW ENGLAND TALK SHOW DIRECTORY. (NEW ENGLAND TALK SHOW DIRECTORY : RADIO STATIONS, TELEVISION STATIONS.). **Added/Corp** New England Newsclip Agency, inc. (1983)-. Directory. English. One time a year. New England Newsclip Agency Inc, 5 Auburn Street, Framingham MA 01701. **Tel** (617)879-4460. **ED** Thomas M Georgon.

ISSN 0227-1532
DD 791.45/09718 CN

NEWFOUNDLAND TV TOPICS. **VFOAT** T V Topics. Vol. 1 (March 17-23, 1979)-. Periodical. English. One time a week. Robinson-Blackmore Publishing Ltd, PO Box 129, Grand Falls Newfoundland A2A 2J4 Canada. **Tel** (709)489-2162, FAX (709)489-4817.

ISSN 0468-1835
US

NIELSEN NEWSCAST, THE. **Added/Corp** A.C. Nielsen Company. (1951). Periodical. English. Irregular. AC Nielsen Company, Media Research Division, Neilsen Plaza, Northbrook IL 60062. **Tel** (312)498-6300.

US

NIELSEN REPORT ON TELEVISION . **Main/Corp** A.C. Nielsen Company. **Added/Corp** A.C. Nielsen Company. (1979)-. Periodical. English. One time a year. Free on request. AC Nielsen Company, Media Research Division, Neilsen Plaza, Northbrook IL 60062. **Tel** (312)498-6300. **ED** Larray Frerk. **Circ:** 28,000 (ctrl). ***Continues*** *Nielsen Television (Northbrook, Ill. : 1977).*
Desc: Contains highlights of trends in television, including facility growth, VCR, cable, and the audiences for electronic media.

LC PN1993.5.N55 N55 **ISSN** 1115-6848
DD 791.43/09669/05 NR

NIGERIAN FILM/TV INDEX, THE. **VFOAT** Nigerian Film, TV Index. (1992)-. English. Irregular. A-Productions Nigeria Ltd, PO Box 7340, Ikeja, Lagos State, Nigeria.

CN

NIGHTINGALE REPORT. **See** Motion Picture.

LC PN1992 .K16 **ISSN** 1050-513X
US

NINE (SEATTLE, WASH.). (NINE / KCTS.). **Added/Corp** KCTS (Television Station : Seattle, Wash.). **VFOAT** 9; KCTS Magazine; Nine Magazine. Vol. 4, No. 4 (Apr. 1990)-. Periodical. English. Twelve times a year. comes with membership. KCTS Seattle Channel 9, 401 Mercer Street, Seattle WA 98109. **Tel** (800)937-5287, FAX (206)443-6783. ***Continues*** *KCTS Magazine.*

LC TK6555 .J6 **ISSN** 0078-1347
DD 621.38416 US

NORTH AMERICAN RADIO-TV STATION GUIDE. **See** Communications-Radio.

ISSN 0713-648X
DD 372.13/358/09716 CN

NOVA SCOTIA SCHOOL TELEVISION. ELEMENTARY. **See** Education-Elementary Education.

US

NSI VIEWERS IN PROFILE REFERENCE VOLUMES : AVERAGE WEEKLY TELEVISION AUDIENCE ESTIMATES. **Added/Corp** A.C. Nielsen Company. **VFOAT** Viewers in Profile Reference Volumes; VIP Reference Volumes. **VAT** Nielsen Station Index Viewers in Profile Reference Volumes. (1983)-. Periodical. English. Six times a year. AC Nielsen Company, Media Research Division, Neilsen Plaza, Northbrook IL 60062. **Tel** (312)498-6300. ***Continues*** *NSI VIP Reference Volumes. Average Weekly Television Audience Estimates.*

UK

●**OFFICIAL MAGAZINE OF CORONATION STREET, THE.** (1994)-. Newsletter. English. Twelve times a year. $4.99 (per issues). Newsstand Publishing Services, Office Block One, Southlink Business Line, Southlink Oldham OL4 1DE United Kingdom. **Tel** 011 44 161 6240414, FAX 011 44 161 6284655. **ED** Brian Clark. **Ad Acc, Adv Mgr:** Alan Young, **Tel** 011 44 161 6240414. **Circ:** 6,000 (ctrl).
Desc: Dedicated to the long-running British television drama of "Coronation Street." It features star interviews, behind-the-scenes articles, memory-lane stories from the past episodes, profiles of actors and actresses and story-line updates.

LC PN1995.9.C54 O36 **ISSN** 0748-7606
DD 791.4/075/0973 US

OFFICIAL PRICE GUIDE TO RADIO, TV & MOVIE MEMORABILIA, THE. **Added/Corp** House of Collectibles. **VFOAT** Movie, T.V.; Movie, TV. 1st Ed. (1985)-. English. Irregular. $11.95. Random House Inc., 400 Hahn Road, Westminster MD 21157. **Tel** (800)726-0600, (800)733-3000, FAX (800)659-2436, (410)386-7013. **ED** T.E. Hudgeons III.

LC HE8700.7 .O5 **ISSN** 1076-0334
DD 384.55/5/05 US

●**ON DEMAND.** [On demand]. Vol. 1, No. 1 (June/July 1994)-. Periodical. English. Twelve times a year. $35.00. Cowles Business Media / Colorado, 1905 Sherman Street, Denver CO 80203. **Tel** (303)837-0900.

IT

ONDA TV. (19??)-. Italian. One time a week. L49900 Italy; L105000 other. Rusconi Editore Spa, Servicio Abbonements, Viale Le Sarca 235, 20126 Milan Italy. **Tel** 011 39 2 66192634, FAX 011 39 2 66192206.

ISSN 0747-4059
US

ONSAT. **VFOAT** On Sat. (19??)-. Periodical. English. One time a week. $59.95. Triple D Publishing Inc., PO Box 2384, Shelby NC 28151-2384. **Tel** (800)234-0021, FAX (704)484-8558.

ISSN 0896-6672
US

OREGON FOCUS (PORTLAND, OR.). (OREGON FOCUS.). [Or. focus]. **Added/Corp** Oregon Public Broadcasting. **VFOAT** Focus. Vol. 1, No. 1 (Oct. 1987)-. Periodical. English. Twelve times a year. $35.00 Comes with KOPB Portland Channel 10 membership. Oregon Public Broadcasting, PO Box 69485, Portland OR 97228. **Tel** (503)293-1908. ***Continues*** *Dial (Oregon Public Broadcasting).*

LC PN1990 .P35
KO

PANGSONG YONGU. **Added/Corp** Pangsong Wiwonhoe (Korea). **VFOAT** Broadcasting Quarterly. (1982)-. Periodical. Korean. Four times a year. Not for sale. Pangsong Wiwonhoe, 16F Boyung Building, 108 Phung-dong, Chongro-ku 110, Seoul South Korea.

LC HE8700.8 .P38 **ISSN** 1055-3789
DD 384.55/06/573 US
TITLE CHANGE

PAUL KAGAN'S RECORD OF TV STATION DEALS. [Paul Kagan's rec. TV stn. deals]. **Added/Corp** Paul Kagan Associates. **VFOAT** Record of TV Station Deals; Record of Television Station Deals. **VAT** Paul Kagan's Record of Television Station Deals. (1987)-(199?). English. Paul Kagan Associates Inc., 126 Clock Tower Place, Carmel CA 93923-8734. **Tel** (408)624-1536, FAX (408)625-3225, telex ITT 4938124 PKA UI. ***Continued by*** *TV Deal Record, 1070-2601.*

LC HE8700.72.U6 P39 **ISSN** 1058-9422
DD 384.55/54 US

... PAY-PER-VIEW REPORT, THE. [Pay-per-view rep.]. **Added/Corp** Paul Kagan Associates. **VAT** Pay Per View Report. (19??)-. English. One time a year. $345.00. Paul Kagan Associates Inc., 126 Clock Tower Place, Carmel CA 93923-8734. **Tel** (408)624-1536, FAX (408)625-3225, telex ITT 4938124 PKA UI.
Desc: Examines pay-per-view marketing expenditures, buy rates, revenues, penetrations and 10-year industry forecasts.

ISSN 0146-0072
DD 384 US

PAY TV NEWSLETTER, THE. [Pay TV newsl.]. **Added/Corp** Paul Kagan Associates. **VFOAT** Pay Television Newsletter. (19??)-. Newsletter. English. Twelve times a year. $695.00. Paul Kagan Associates Inc., 126 Clock Tower Place, Carmel CA 93923-8734. **Tel** (408)624-1536, FAX (408)625-3225, telex ITT 4938124 PKA UI. **ED** Dwight Beach. **Ad Acc.** available via fax.
Desc: Newsletter on pay television, premiere services and pay-per-view offered over cable, direct satellite and other over-the-air current. Includes ten-year projected analysis of subscribers, subscriptions and revenues.

ISSN 0896-1840
DD 384 US
TITLE CHANGE

PAYPERVIEWS (HARTSDALE, N.Y.). (PAYPERVIEWS.). [PayPerViews]. **VFOAT** Pay Per Views; PayPerViews Magazine. Vol. 1, No. 1 (Dec. 1, 1987)-(July 1994). Periodical. English. QV Publishing Inc., 647 US Route One, PO Box 3000, York ME 03909. **Tel** (207)363-6222, FAX (207)363-6182. ***Merged into*** *Phillips Business Information's Interactive Video News.*
Desc: Pay-per-view update reports and the latest news involving the pay-per-view industry.

LC HE **ISSN** 0895-4143
DD 384 US

PERFECT VISION, THE. [Perfect vis.]. (1986)-. Periodical. English. Four times a year. $39.95. Pearson Publishing Empire, PO Box 360, Sea Cliff NY 11579. **Tel** (516)676-2830, FAX (516)676-5469. **ED** Roy Frumkes (editor's address: 58 School Street, Glen Cove, NY 11542). Index available. **Ad Acc, Adv Mgr:** Rose Gunter. **Circ:** 20,000.
Desc: Includes critiques and reports on stereo broadcast systems, hi-fi video tapes, as well as laser disc technology and performance. The magazine's objective is to critically assess the medium. Film reviews are also included.

ISSN 0836-2114
DD 338.4/77914/0971 CN

PLAYBACK (TORONTO). (PLAYBACK : CANADA'S BROADCAST AND PRODUCTION JOURNAL.). [Playback]. **VFOAT** Video Innovations. (Sept. 29, 1986)-. Periodical. English. Twenty-five times a year. 93.50Can$. Brunico Communications Inc., 366 Adelaide Street West, Suite 500, Toronto Ontario M5V 1R9 Canada. **Tel** (416)408-2300, FAX (416)408-0807. **ED** Mark Smyka. **Ad Acc. Circ:** 10,000.
Desc: Covers the television and film industry in Canada.

BO

PORTAVOZ. **Added/Corp** Centro Impulsor del Video. No. 1 (Sept./Oct. 1991)-. Periodical. Spanish. Six times a year. Centro Impulsor del Video, Casilla #2104, Santa Cruz Bolivia.

LC PN1993 .P725
DD 791.43/05 IT

●**PREMIERE TV & CINEMA.** **See** Motion Picture.

ISSN 0745-8711
DD 621 US

PRIVATE CABLE. [Priv. cable]. **VFOAT** Private Cable Magazine. Periodical. English. Twelve times a year. $10.95. Wiesner Publishing Company, 1909 Avenue G, PO Box 1460, Rosenberg TX 77471. ***Continues*** *Satellite TV, 0744-9739;* ***Absorbed*** *TVRO Technology, 0885-7598.*

LC HE **ISSN** 1068-4514
DD 384 US

●**PRIVATE CABLE INVESTOR.** [Priv. cable invest.]. **Added/Corp** Paul Kagan Associates. No. 153 (Feb. 22, 1993)-. Newsletter. English. Twelve times a year. $595.00. Paul Kagan Associates Inc., 126 Clock Tower Place, Carmel CA 93923-8734. **Tel** (408)624-1536, FAX (408)625-3225, telex ITT 4938124 PKA UI. available via fax. ***Continues*** *SMATV News, 0734-5399.*
Desc: Across-the-board coverage of private cable (satellite master antenna) TV. Finance, investment, marketing, legal issues.

Communications —Television and Cable

LC TK6630.A1 P76   **ISSN** 0249-3756
DD 384/.05   FR
PROBLEMES AUDIOVISUELS. Added/Corp
Institut National de L'audiovisuel (France) Institut National de la Communication Audiovisuelle (France). (1981)-. French. Six times a year. Documentation Francaise, 29 quai Voltaire, 75344 Paris Cedex 7 France. **Tel** 011 33 1 40157000, FAX 011 33 1 40157230, telex 204 826 DOCFRAN.

ISSN 1067-439X
DD 791   US
PRODUCER (PORT WASHINGTON, N.Y.). (PRODUCER.). [Producer]. (199?)-. Trade
Publication. English. Six times a year. $15.00. Testa Communications, 25 Willowdale Avenue, Port Washington NY 11050. **Tel** (516)767-2500, FAX (516)767-9335. **ED** Ken McGorry. **Ad Acc.** ctrl circ. **Continues** Producers Quarterly, 1053-6450.
Desc: Covers audio, video, and film production with stories from the motion picture television, commercial, corporate, non-broadcast, and documentary realms.

LC PN1993.5.U77 B46a   **ISSN** 0732-6653
DD 384.55/025/7   US
PRODUCER'S MASTERGUIDE, THE. (THE
PRODUCER'S MASTERGUIDE / COMPILED, WRITTEN, AND EDITED BY SHMUEL BENSION.). [Prod. masterguide]. (1983)-. English. One time a year. $125.00. The Producers Masterguide, 60 East 8th Street, 31st Floor, New York NY 10003. **Tel** (800)622-6112, (212)777-4002, FAX (212)777-4101, (800)622-6116. **ED** Shmuel Bension. Index available. cum. index. **Ad Acc.** Circ: 18,000. **Continues** Bension, Shmuel. New York Production Manual, 0163-1276.
Desc: International production manual for motion picture, broadcast-television, commercials, cable and videotape industries in the United States, Canada, the United Kingdom, the Caribbean Islands, Australia, and New Zealand.

ISSN 1053-6450
DD 791   US
   TITLE CHANGE
PRODUCERS QUARTERLY. [Prod. q.].
(1990)-(199?). Periodical. English. Testa Communications, 25 Willowdale Avenue, Port Washington NY 11050. **Tel** (516)767-2500, FAX (516)767-9335. **Continued by** Producer (Port Washington, N.Y.), 1067-439X.

LC PN1993.5.F7 P75
DD 791.43/0232/05   FR
PROFESSIONNEL DU CINEMA, VIDEO, TELEVISION & CABLE, LE. (19??)-. English
(French). Four times a year. L'Europeenne de Productions, 12 rue Berteaux Dumas, 92200 Neuilly-sur-Seine, France.

ISSN 0161-9845
   US
PROGRAM GUIDE - SOUTH DAKOTA PUBLIC TELEVISION. Main/Corp South Dakota
Public Television. (19??)-. Periodical. English. Twelve times a year. $5.00. South Dakota Public Broadcast, Box 2218 B Pugsley Center, Brookings SD 57007. **Tel** (800)992-2077.

   US
PROJECT LOOK-LISTEN-THINK-RESPOND ANNUAL REPORT. (19??)- .Periodical. English.
$10.00. National Telemedia Council Inc, 120 East Wilson Street, Madison WI 53703. **Tel** (608)257-7712. **ED** Marieli Rowe, Mary Wyman, and Joan Maynard. **Circ:** 50 (ctrl).
Desc: Reports on the annual NTC Media Literacy Project Look, Listen, Think, Respond through which children in grades 1 through 12 (and some college classes) learn to evaluate and think about the television programming they consume.

LC PN1990.9.P82 P82   **ISSN** 0193-3663
DD 384.54/43   US
   CCC
PUBLIC BROADCASTING REPORT, THE. See Communications-Radio.

   US
PUBLIC NOTICE - FEDERAL COMMUNICATIONS COMMISSION. CABLE TELEVISION AUTHORIZATION ACTIONS. Main/Corp United States. Federal
Communications Commission. **VFOAT** Cable Television Authorization Actions. (19??)-. Periodical. English. FCC / Federal Communications Commission, 1919 M Street Northwest, Room 538, Washington DC 20554. **Tel** (202)632-6302.

   US
PUBLIC NOTICE - FEDERAL COMMUNICATIONS COMMISSION. CABLE TELEVISION CERTIFICATE OF COMPLIANCE ACTIONS. Main/Corp United
States. Federal Communications Commission. **VFOAT** Cable Television Certificate of Compliance Actions.

(19??)-. Periodical. English. FCC / Federal Communications Commission, 1919 M Street Northwest, Room 538, Washington DC 20554. **Tel** (202)632-6302.

LC PN1990.6.G7 P82   **ISSN** 0960-3999
   UK
PUBLIC OPINION AND BROADCASTING STANDARDS. Added/Corp Broadcasting
Standards Council (Great Britain). **VFOAT** Annual Review. (1990)-. Monographic series. English. Irregular. Price varies per volume. John Libbey Company Ltd, 13 Smith Yard, Summerley Street, London SW18 4HR United Kingdom. **Tel** 011 44 81 9472777. **(Subscription address:** Faber & Faber, Burnt Mill Elizabeth Way, Harlas Essex United Kingdom. **Tel** 011 44 1279 421352.**)**

LC HF5905 .S74   **ISSN** 1071-4707
DD 659.1/42/02573   US
●RADIO ADVERTISING SOURCE. See Communications-Radio.

ISSN 0575-9560
DD 384.54/0971/021   CN
RADIO AND TELEVISION BROADCASTING. See Communications-Radio.

LC TK6555 .R19   **ISSN** 0812-2016
DD 384.54/53/02594   AT
RADIO AND TELEVISION BROADCASTING STATIONS. See Communications-Radio.

LC PN1990.55 .R33   **ISSN** 1062-0737
DD 384.54/02573   US
RADIO & TELEVISION CAREER DIRECTORY. [Radio telev. career dir.]. Added/Corp
Career Press Inc. Visible Ink Press. **VFOAT** Radio and Television Career Directory. 1st Ed. (1991)-. Directory. English. $34.00 (hardcover); $17.95 (softcover). Gale Research Inc., 835 Penobscot Building, 645 Griswold Street, Detroit MI 48226. **Tel** (800)877-GALE, (313)961-2242, FAX (313)961-6083, (800)414-5043, telex TWX 810-221-7086.
Desc: Covers opportunities in radio and TV news, broadcast meteorology, radio programming, radio marketing, writing for TV, cable TV and other specialties.

LC TK6553.A1 R25   **ISSN** 0307-3165
DD 621.38   UK
RADIO AND TELEVISION SERVICING. See Communications-Radio.

LC TK6540 .R464
   GW
RADIO-, FERNSEH-, PHONO-PRAXIS. See Communications-Radio.

   PL
RADIO I TELEWIZJA. Periodical. Polish
(English). One time a week. **(Subscription address:** Ars Polona-Ruch, PO Box 1001, Krakowskie Przedmiescie 7, 00-068 Warsaw Poland. **Tel** 011 48 22 261201.**)**
Desc: Weekly television guide.

ISSN 0883-640X
DD 384   US
RADIO/TV HIGHLIGHTS. (RADIO/TV
HIGHLIGHTS : A WEEKLY REPORT FROM THE NATIONAL ASSOCIATION OF BROADCASTERS.). [Radio/TV highl.]. **Added/Corp** National Association of Broadcasters. **VFOAT** Radio TV Highlights; Highlights. **VAT** Radio/Television Highlights. (19??)-. Periodical. English. One time a week. National Association of Broadcasters, 1771 N Street NW/Suite 600, Washington DC 20036.

ISSN 1073-4562
DD 384   US
   CEASED
RAP (THOUSAND OAKS, CALIF.). (RAP :
RATINGS, ADVERTISING, PROGRAMMING.). [RAP]. **VFOAT** Ratings, Advertising, Programming. (1994)-(Oct. 1995). Periodical. English. Baskerville Communications, PO Box 5084, Thousand Oaks CA 91359. **Tel** (805)499-0721 ext. 289. **(Subscription address:** Nextech Customer Service, PO Box 303, Shrub Oak NY 10588-9904. **Tel** (914)962-6297, FAX (914)962-1338.**)**

LC HE8700.72.U6 R44
DD 384.55/47/0973021   US
   CEASED
REGIONAL CABLE REPORT, THE.
Added/Corp Paul Kagan Associates. Census Research Staff. (19??)-(19??). English. Paul Kagan Associates Inc., 126 Clock Tower Place, Carmel CA 93923-8734. **Tel** (408)624-1536, FAX (408)625-3225, telex ITT 4938124 PKA UI.

LC BV655 .R45   **ISSN** 0034-4079
DD 260   US
RELIGIOUS BROADCASTING. See Religions and Theology.

   UK
REPORT / BRITISH BROADCASTING CORPORATION RESEARCH DEPARTMENT ENGINEERING DIVISION.
(19??)-. English. British Broadcasting Corporation, Caversham Park, Reading RG4 8TZ United Kingdom. **Tel** 011 44 1734 472742, FAX 011 44 1734 463823, telex 848318.
Ind/Abst Curr. Cit.

   HK
... REPORT OF THE BROADCASTING AUTHORITY ON THE PROGRESS OF TELEVISION BROADCASTING IN HONG KONG, THE. Main/Corp Hong Kong. Broadcasting
Dept. (1987/1988)-. English. Irregular. Price varies per volume. Hong Kong Government Information Service, Beaconsfield House, 4 Queens Road, Hong Kong Hong Kong. **Tel** 011 852 284288014, 011 852 259881947, FAX 011 852 28459078, 011 852 25987482, telex 61190 HKGIS.

LC HE8689.9.N45 B76a
DD 384.54/060931   NZ
REPORT OF THE BROADCASTING CORPORATION OF NEW ZEALAND.
Main/Corp Broadcasting Corporation of New Zealand. (19??)-. English. One time a year. Price varies. Government Printing Office / New Zealand, 10 Mulgrave Street, Wellington New Zealand. **Tel** 011 64 4 4737211, FAX 011 64 4 734943, telex GOVPRINT NZ 31320.

LC PN1992.3.U5 R47   **ISSN** 0278-6397
   US
   SUSPENDED
RERUNS. [Reruns]. Vol. 1, No. 1 (Apr.
1980)-Suspended Vol. 7. English. Three times a year. $10.50 US; $11.00 Canada; $12.00 other. Reruns/The Magazine of Television History, PO Box 1057, Safford AZ 85548-1057. **Tel** (602)428-0307. **ED** Richard K Tharp. **Bk Rev. Circ:** 500.
Desc: Features detailed descriptions of U.S. television series including individual episode synopses. Feature articles on U.S. television including commercials.

LC LB1044.7 .R48
   BL
REVISTA BRASILEIRA DE TELEDUCACAO. Added/Corp Associacao
Brasileira de Teleducacao. (19??)-. Portuguese. Associacao Brasileira de Teleducacao, Caixa Postal No 56008, Rio de Janeiro Brazil.

LC PN1992.3.U5 R67   **ISSN** 0035-8355
DD 384.55/025/73   US
ROSS REPORTS TELEVISION. VFOAT Ross
Talent Report. (19??)-. Trade Publication. English. Twelve times a year. $42.75. Television Index Inc, 40/29 27th Street/2nd Floor, Long Island City NY 11101. **Tel** (718)937-3990. **ED** Timothy Hunter, Ron Brown and Jonathan Miller.
Desc: Television casting, scripts and production information; emphasizes New York contacts, as well as Los Angeles primetime and soap opera production and casting information.

LC PN1991.3.C9 N3
   XR
ROZHLAS. Added/Corp Ceskoslovensky Rozhlas.
Vol. 40 I./7. (Jan. 1973)-. Periodical. Czech. One time a week. kcs82.90. **(Subscription address:** Artia Pegas Press Ltd., Palac Metro Narodni Trida 25, 11210 Prague 1 Czech Republic. **Tel** 011 42 2 24196265, 011 42 2 24196266.**) Continues** Ceskoslovensky Rozhlas.

LC HE8690 .R8   **ISSN** 0035-9874
   GW
   CCC
RUNDFUNK UND FERNSEHEN.
Added/Corp Universitat Hamburg. Hans-Bredow-Institut Fur Rundfunk und Fernsehen. Vol. 1 (1953)-. Trade Publication. German. Four times a year (Mar., June, Oct., Dec.). $81.53. Verlag Hans Bredow Institut, Heimhuderstrasse 21, D-20148 Hamburg Germany. **Tel** 011 040 447034, FAX 011 040 447870. **Bk Rev. Ad Acc. Circ:** 1,200.
Desc: Radio and television sciences.
Ind/Abst Commun. Abstr. (?-?).

ISSN 0035-9890
   GW
   CODEN RUMIA5
RUNDFUNKTECHNISCHE MITTEILUNGEN. [Rundfunktech. Mitt.].
Added/Corp Institut fuer Rundfunktechnik G.m.b.H. (Feb. 1957)-. Trade Publication. German (summaries and/or abstracts in English and French). Four times a year. $79.84. Mensing & Company, Postfach 1769, D-22807 Norderstedt Germany. **Tel** 011 49 40 5252011, FAX 011 49 40 5251088, telex 211173 HORST D. **ED** R. Hengstler and H. Mucke. Index available. cum. index. **Bk Rev. Ad**

Communications —Television and Cable

Acc. Circ: 2,300. Documents available from Article Express International, Ask*IEEE. **Supersedes** *Nordwestdeutscher Rundfunk. Technische Hausmitteilungen* and *Rundfunktechnisches Institut, Nurnberg. Mitteilungen.*
Desc: Covers radio and television, scientific research and technical development in broadcasting.
Ind/Abst Acoust. Abstr.; Bioeng. Abstr.; Ei Page One; Energy Res. Abstr. (March 1982-); Eng. Index Annu.; INSPEC (1968-); Int. Aerosp. Abstr.
US

RUNDOWN. (19??)-. English. Fifty times a year (Weekly except first week in Aug. and last week in Dec.). $325.00. Rundown/Standish Publishing Company, PO Box 335, Ardmore PA 19003. **Tel** (610)519-9220, FAX (610)519-9221. **ED** Kim Standish.
US

S.E.T. FREE. Added/Corp Society for the Eradication of Television. **VFOAT** SET Free. (1990)-. Periodical. English. Four times a year. Society for the Eradication of Television, PO Box 10491, Oakland CA 94610-0491. **Tel** (510)763-8712. **Continues** *News and Notes From all Over.*
SA

SAFTTA NEWSLETTER. See Motion Picture.
IT

SATELLITE. (19??)-. Periodical. Italian. Eleven times a year. L64.000 Italy; L95.000 Europe; L125.000 other. Today, LGO Antonelli 27, 00145 Rome Italy. **Tel** 011 39 6 5417059, FAX 011 39 6 5940921.

ISSN 1043-0865
DD 384
US
SATELLITE BUSINESS NEWS. See Communications-Telecommunication.

LC PN1992.3.U5 S27 **ISSN** 1075-1823
DD 791.45/75/05
US
●**SATELLITE CHOICE.** [Satell. choice]. (June 1994)-. Periodical. English. Twelve times a year. $52.00. Fortuna Communications Corporation, 140 South Fortuna Boulevard, PO Box 308, Fortuna CA 95540. **Tel** (707)725-6951, FAX (707)725-4311.

ISSN 0843-8617
CN
SATELLITE ENTERTAINMENT GUIDE. (19??)-. Periodical. English. Twelve times a year. 52.00Can$. Satellite TV Guide Inc., 1109 Toronto Dominion Tower, Edmonton Alberta T5J 2Z1 Canada. **Tel** (403)424-6222.

LC PN1992 .S28 **ISSN** 0732-7668
DD 791.45/75/05
US
SATELLITE ORBIT. [Satell. orbit]. (1982)-. Periodical. English. Twelve times a year. $52.00. Commtek Publishing Company, 8330 Boone Boulevard, Suite 600, Vienna VA 22182. **Tel** (703)827-0511.

UK
SATELLITE TIMES. English. Satellite House, 85 Church Road, Crystal Palace, London SE19 2TA United Kingdom.

UK
SATELLITE TV FINANCE. (19??)-. English. Twenty-three times a year. £499.00. Financial Times Magazines, Greystoke Place, Fetter Lane, London EC4A 1ND United Kingdom. **Tel** 011 44 171 8316577. **ED** Peter Elman. **Circ:** 300. available on an online database (files 16,636/Full-Text) from DIALOG.
Desc: Covers developments of the satellite channels, the direct-to-home markets and ancillary businesses. Funding, policies against cable television, video and terrestrial television.
Ind/Abst PROMT [Full Txt.]; PTS Newsl. Database [Full Txt.].

ISSN 0896-3673
DD 384
US
CEASED
SATELLITE TV PRE-VUE. [Satell. TV pre-vue]. **VFOAT** Satellite TV Preview; TV Pre-Vue; T.V. Pre-Vue. **VAT** Satellite Television Pre-Vue. (19??)-(Dec. 1993). Trade Publication. English. Western Publications / New York, PO Box 460, Salamanca NY 14779. **Tel** (716)945-3488, FAX (716)945-3238. **ED** Sandra Jackson. **Circ:** 20,000.

ISSN 0744-7841
US
SATELLITE TV WEEK. NORTH AMERICAN EDITION. (SATELLITE TV WEEK.). (19??)-. Periodical. English. One time a week. $59.95. Satellite TV Week, PO Box 308, Fortuna CA 95540. **Tel** (707)725-1185, (800)345-8876, FAX (707)725-4311. **Ad Acc, Adv Mgr:** Dan Eliason, **Tel** (207)725-6951. **Circ:** 450,000.
Desc: Reports television program listings for over 115 satellite channels. Editoral sections contain relevant issues affecting the satellite industry as well as entertainment, sports, consumer electronics and personality interviews.

LC PN6120 **ISSN** 1075-8860
DD 808.838
●**SCI-FI ENTERTAINMENT.** [Sci Fi entertain.]. Vol. 1, No. 1 (June 1994)-. Consumer Publication. English. Six times a year. $14.95. Sovereign Media, PO Box 749, 487 Carlisle Drive, Herndon VA 22070. **Tel** (703)471-1556, FAX (703)471-1556. **(Subscription address:** Sci-Fi Entertainment, Box 709, Mt. Morris IL 61054-0709. **Tel** (800)933-6407.) **ED** Edward Flixman. **Circ:** 75,000.
Desc: Includes information on actors, writers, filmmakers, and films of the science fiction genre.

LC PN6120
DD 808.838
US
●**SCIENCE FICTION ENTERTAINMENT. See** Literature-Science Fiction, Fantasy and Horror.

UK
SCREEN. See Motion Picture.

LC PN1995.9.P7 R88 **ISSN** 1070-7573
DD 791.43/023/0977311
US
●**SCREEN (CHICAGO, ILL.). See** Motion Picture.

LC HE8700 .S37
UK
SCREEN DIGEST. VFOAT Screendigest. (1971)-. Periodical. English. Twelve times a year. $469.00. Screen Digest, 37 Gower Street, London WC1E 6HH United Kingdom. **Tel** 011 44 171 5802842, FAX 011 44 171 5800060. **ED** David Fisher. Index available. **Bk Rev.** available on an online database (files 16,636/Full-Text) from DIALOG.
Desc: Covers news, intelligence, business summaries, statistics and research on television, film, video and related industries, with a substantial annual index. Organized for use as permanent reference sources.
Ind/Abst Infomat Int. Bus.; Print. Abstr.; PROMT [Full Txt.]; PTS Newsl. Database [Full Txt.]; World Publ. Monit.

LC PN1993.5.G7 C5 **ISSN** 0307-4617
DD 338.4/7/791430941
UK
CCC
SCREEN INTERNATIONAL. See Motion Picture.

LC Z1223.Z7 S45 **ISSN** 0748-4836
DD 015.73/053
US
SELECTED AUDIOVISUAL MATERIALS PRODUCED BY THE UNITED STATES GOVERNMENT. See Communications-Abstracting, Bibliographies and Statistics.

ISSN 0319-5570
CN
SHELBURNE COUNTY TELECASTER. (1974)-. English. One time a week. Fundy Group Publications, PO Box 128, 2 Second Street, Yarmouth Nova Scotia B5A 4B1 Canada. **Tel** (902)453-2330, (902)742-7111, FAX (902)455-7162.

LC PN1560 **ISSN** 1074-5297
DD 792
US
●**SHOOT (NEW YORK, N.Y.). See** Business and Economics-Advertising and Public Relations.

LC HF6146.T42 S572
DD 384.55/51
US
SIMMONS STUDY OF MEDIA AND MARKETS. C-2, CABLE TELEVISION REPORT. NORTHEAST REGION.
Added/Corp Simmons Market Research Bureau. **VFOAT** Study of Media and Markets. C-2, Northeast Region; Cable Television Report; Study of Media and Markets; Cable Television Report. Northeast Region. (19??)-. Trade Publication. English. Irregular. Simmons Market Research Bureau, 420 Lexington Avenue, 8th Floor, New York NY 10017. **Tel** (212)916-8900.

LC HF6146.T42 S573
DD 384.55/51
US
SIMMONS STUDY OF MEDIA AND MARKETS. C-3, CABLE TELEVISION REPORT. EAST CENTRAL REGION.
Added/Corp Simmons Market Research Bureau. **VFOAT** Study of Media and Markets. C-3, East Central Region; Cable Television Report; Study of Media and Markets; Cable Television Report. East Central Region. (19??)-. Trade Publication. English. Irregular. Simmons Market Research Bureau, 420 Lexington Avenue, 8th Floor, New York NY 10017. **Tel** (212)916-8900.

LC HF6146.T42 S574
DD 384.55/51
US
SIMMONS STUDY OF MEDIA AND MARKETS. C-4, CABLE TELEVISION REPORT. WEST CENTRAL REGION.
Added/Corp Simmons Market Research Bureau. **VFOAT** Study of Media and Markets. C-4, West Central Region; Cable Television Report; Study of Media and Markets; Cable Television Report. West Central Region. (19??)-. Trade Publication. English. Irregular. Simmons Market Research Bureau, 420 Lexington Avenue, 8th Floor, New York NY 10017. **Tel** (212)916-8900.

LC HF6146.T42 S576
DD 384.55/51
US
SIMMONS STUDY OF MEDIA AND MARKETS. C-6, CABLE TELEVISION REPORT. PACIFIC REGION. Added/Corp Simmons Market Research Bureau. **VFOAT** Study of Media and Markets. C-6, Pacific Region; Cable Television Report; Study of Media and Markets; Cable Television Report. Pacific Region. (19??)-. English. Irregular. Simmons Market Research Bureau, 420 Lexington Avenue, 8th Floor, New York NY 10017. **Tel** (212)916-8900.

ISSN 0734-5399
DD 384
US
TITLE CHANGE
SMATV NEWS. [SMATV news]. **Added/Corp** Paul Kagan Associates, Inc. **VFOAT** S.M.A.T.V. News. No. 1 (Aug. 1982)-(19??). Periodical. English. Paul Kagan Associates Inc., 126 Clock Tower Place, Carmel CA 93923-8734. **Tel** (408)624-1536, FAX (408)625-3225, telex ITT 4938124 PKA UI. **ED** Dwight Beach. **Continued by** *Private Cable Investor*, 1068-4514.
Desc: Newsletter on the economic, technical, marketing and legal issues that impact SMATV (Satellite Master Antenna Television).

ISSN 0199-3003
US
SOAP OPERA STARS. (19??)-. Periodical. English. Four times a year. $8.00 (one-year), $15.00 (two-year). Sterling Macfadden, 233 Park Avenue South, New York NY 10003. **Tel** (212)979-4800.

US
SOLOMON INTERNATIONAL TELEVISION NEWSLETTER, THE. (19??)-. Newsletter. English. One time a week. $800.00 (one-year), $1400.00 (two-year), $1800.00 (three-year). Solomon Newsletter / Department of Circulation, 4000 Warner Boulevard, Burbank CA 91522. **Tel** (818)954-4049, FAX (213)654-6236. **ED** Kenneth J. Morris (editor's address: 3900 West Aiameda Avenue, Suite 1411, Burbank, CA 91505, phone: (818)954-4049). ctrl circ.

BE
SOMMET DE LA TVHD, LE. (19??)-. French. 3000F Belgium and Luxembourg; 510F France; 3100F other. Edimedia ASBL, rue de la Constitution 22, 1030 Brussels Belgium. **Tel** 011 32 2 2180031. **Bk Rev. Ad Acc.**

ISSN 0038-156X
IT
UDC 791
SORRISI E CANZONI TV. [Sorrisi canzoni TV]. **VFOAT** TV Sorrisi e Canzoni. (1972)-. Periodical. Italian. One time a week. L93600 Italy; L205400 other. Arnoldo Mondadori Editore, UFF Cont Abbonamenti, 20090 Segrate MI Italy. **Tel** 011 39 2 75422015, telex 320457 MONDMI I. **Continues** *Sorrisi e Canzoni d' Italia*, 1121-7502.

US
SOUTH CAROLINA SCENE: ETV/RADIO GUIDE. See Communications-Radio.

ISSN 1080-8809
US
SPANISH TV MAGAZINE. VIDEO TEACHING GUIDE. (1991)-. English. $440.00. Heinle & Heinle, UMBC 5401 Wilkens Avenue, Baltimore MD 21264. **Tel** (410)455-2156. **(Subscription address:** Pacific MT Network, 1550 Park Avenue, Denver CO 80218. **Tel** (303)837-8000.)

ISSN 0883-2560
DD 384
US
SPEC-COM. [Spec-com]. **VFOAT** Spec Com. Vol. 15, No. 3 (March/April 1985)-. Periodical. English. Six times a year. SPEC-COM Communications Inc, P O H, Lowden IA 52255-0408. **Tel** (319)944-7705. **ED** Mike Stone. Index available. cum. index. **Bk Rev. Ad Acc. Circ:** 2,000 (ctrl). **Continues** *A 5 Amateur Television Magazine*, 0279-4772.
Desc: Specialized communication journal of USATVS. Heavy in amateur "ham" television (FSTV-SSTV). Other modes include RTTY, packet radio, facsimile, TVRO, computers, satellites, lasers.

LC PN1993 .S677 **ISSN** 1051-0230
DD 791.43/05
US
SPECTATOR (LOS ANGELES, CALIF.).
See Motion Picture.

LC HE8689.9.G7 I528 **ISSN** 0962-1830
DD 384.55/4/0941
UK
SPECTRUM : THE QUARTERLY MAGAZINE OF THE INDEPENDENT TELEVISION COMMISSION. Added/Corp Independent Television Commission. No. 1 (Spring 1991)-. Periodical. English. Four times a year. Free on request. ITC, PO Box 777, Colchester CO1 1SE United Kingdom. **Tel** 011 44 1206 765601. **Continues** *Airwaves (London, England)*, 0267-3789.

Communications —Television and Cable

ISSN 1067-408X
DD 791
US
SPORTS CASTER. (SPORTS CASTER : THE COMPLETE GUIDE TO TELEVISED SPORTS.). [Sports caster]. **Added/Corp** Satellite Sports Networks. **VFOAT** Sportscaster. (1992)-. Periodical. English. Twelve times a year. Liberty Sports, 2080 N. Highway 360 #200, Grand Prarie TX 75050. **Tel** (214) 988-1088, FAX (214) 606-8651. **ED** Richard M. Hill. **Ad Acc. Circ:** 35,000.

LC HF5905 .S745
DD 384.55/43
ISSN 0038-9552
US
TITLE CHANGE
SPOT TELEVISION RATES AND DATA.
See Business and Economics-Advertising and Public Relations.

LC HF5905 .S745
DD 384.55/43
ISSN 1071-4596
US
TITLE CHANGE
SPOT TV & CABLE SOURCE. [Spot tv cable source]. **Added/Corp** Standard Rate & Data Service. **VFOAT** Spot TV and Cable Source; Spot Television and Cable Source; Spot Television and Cable Source. Vol. 75, No. 9 (Sept. 1993)-Vol. 75, No. 10 (Dec. 1993). Trade Publication. English. SRDS / Standard Rate & Data Service, 3004 Glenview Road, Wilmette IL 60091. **Tel** (708)375-5049, (800)851-7737, FAX (708)375-5003. **(Subscription address:** Neodata / Colorado, PO Box 2606, Boulder CO 80322. **) Continues** Spot Television Rates and Data, 0038-9552. **Continued by** TV & Cable Source, 1076-3988.

LC PN1993 .S68
DK
SPOTLIGHT. See Motion Picture.

US
STATE OF DBS, THE. (19??)-. English. One time a year. $495.00. Paul Kagan Associates Inc., 126 Clock Tower Place, Carmel CA 93923-8734. **Tel** (408)624-1536, FAX (408)625-3225, telex ITT 4938124 PKA UI.

US
STATUS REPORT OF PUBLIC BROADCASTING. Added/Corp Corporation for Public Broadcasting. National Center for Education Statistics. (1973)-. English. Corporation for Public Broadcasting, 901 E Street Northwest, Washington DC 20001. **Tel** (202)879-9600.

LC PN1992 .S85
DD 301.16/1
JA
STUDIES OF BROADCASTING.
Added/Corp NHK Hoso Bunka Kenkyujo. Hosogaku Kenkyushitsu. NHK Sogo Hoso Bunka Kenkyujo. Hosogaku Kenkyushitsu. No. 1 (1963)-. Periodical. English. One time a year. Japan Broadcasting Corporation, 211 Atago Minato Ku, Tokyo 105 Japan. **Circ:** 1,000 (ctrl).
Ind/Abst Int. Bibliogr. Sociol.

LC HF6146.T42 S867
DD 659.14/3/0973021
ISSN 1070-4507
US
STUDY OF MEDIA & MARKETS. CABLE TELEVISION VOLUME. ADDENDUM, CNN/HEADLINE NEWS (NET). [Study media mark., Cable telev. vol., Add. CNN/headl. news (NET)]. **Added/Corp** Simmons Market Research Bureau. **VFOAT** Study of Media and Markets. Cable Television Volume; Cable Television Volume; Addendum, CNN/Headline News (NET); SMM ... Cable Television Volume; Addendum, CNN/Headline News (NET). (19??)-. English. Irregular. Simmons Market Research Bureau, 420 Lexington Avenue, 8th Floor, New York NY 10017. **Tel** (212)916-8900.

DD 384
ISSN 1052-4290
US
SYNDICATION NEWS. [Synd. news]. (1990)-. Periodical. English. Twenty-six times a year. $195.00. Copley Entertainment Inc, 3006 Fairfield Avenue, Bridgeport CT 06605. **Tel** (203)333-6633, FAX (203)333-8844. **ED** Paul R. Krumins. ctrl circ. available via fax.

LC PN1992.8.F5 T54
DD 791.45/7
ISSN 0092-9263
US
T.L.F. QUARTERLY. (TLF QUARTERLY.). **Main/Corp** Time-Life Films. (1973)-. English. Four times a year. Time-Life Films, Room 33/43 Time-Life Building, New York NY 10020.

DD 791.45/09714
ISSN 0039-8551
CN
T V HEBDO (MONTREAL). (T V HEBDO.). [TV hebdo]. Vol. 15, No. 40 (May 3, 1975)-. Periodical. French. One time a week. 41.53Can$. TV Hebdo, 2001 University/5th Floor, Montreal Quebec H3A 2AG Canada. **Tel** (514)499-0561, FAX (514)843-3529. **ED** Louise Marie Cote. available on microfilm from Bibliotheque National du Quebec.
Desc: Provides television programming information and background articles on TV stars and programs. It recommends TV specials, sports and movie programs and discusses video releases and trends. Three regional editions published for Canada.

DD 791.45/09711
ISSN 0319-342X
CN
T V THIS WEEK. VFOAT This Week. (1975)-. English. One time a week. Davidson Advertising Ltd, 208-1062 Austin Road, Port Coquitlam British Columbia Canada. **Continues** This Week., 0319-3411.

LC PN1990.9.T34 T34
DD 791.44/5
ISSN 0731-9134
US
TALK SHOW DIRECTORY. Added/Corp National Research Bureau, inc. **VFOAT** Talk Show Directory for Radio and Television. (19??)-. Directory. English. National Research Bureau Inc. / Illinois, 150 North Wacker Drive, Suite 2222, Chicago IL 60606. **Tel** (312)541-0100.

LC PN1991.8.T35 T35
DD 791.44/6
ISSN 1045-9553
US
TALK SHOW "SELECTS". [Talk show sel.]. **Added/Corp** Broadcast Interview Source (Firm). (198?)-. English. One time a year. $185.00. Broadcast Interview Source, 2233 Wisconsin Avenue Northwest, Suite 540, Washington DC 20007-4104. **Tel** (800)955-0311, (202)333-4904, FAX (202)342-5411.

IT
TASCABILE TV. Italian. One time a week. L47000. Moreno Polidori Editore, Via di Novoli 75/U, 50127 Firenze Italy. **Tel** 011 39 55 431496.

DD 621.388/005
ISSN 0710-2267
CN
TECHNICAL COMMUNIQUE (CANADIAN CABLE TELEVISION ASSOCIATION). (TECHNICAL COMMUNIQUE.). [Tech. commun. - Can. Cable Telev. Assoc.]. **Added/Corp** Canadian Cable Television Association. **VFOAT** Communique Technique. **VAT** Communique Technique - Association Canadienne de Television Par Cable. (1976)-. Periodical. English. Twelve times a year. Free. Technical Communique, c/o CCTA Ottawa Ontario K1P 6A4 Canada. **Continues** Of Interest to Engineers and Technicians.

BL
TELA VIVA. (1992)-. Periodical. Portuguese. Twelve times a year. Glasberg Assessoria Consultoria e Representacoes Ltd, rue Sergipe 401, CEP 01243-906 Sao Paulo, Brazil.

DD 791.45/75
ISSN 0820-3334
CN
TELE DES ENFANTS, LA. [Tele enfants]. (1987)-. French. One time a year. 3.00Can$. Association Nationale des Telespectateurs, 4005 rue Bellechasse, Montreal Quebec H1X 1J6 Canada. **Continues** La Television des Enfants, 0820-3326.

UDC 791
ISSN 0757-0112
FR
TITLE CHANGE
TELE K7. VFOAT Tele K Sept. (1983)-(1993). Periodical. French. Societe Francaise d'Edition Presse, 48 50 boulevard Senard, 92210 Saint Cloud France. **Tel** 011 33 1 47112000. **Merged with** Tele 7 Video (Paris), 0996-5491 **to form** Tele K7, Tele 7 Video, 1248-9948.

UDC 7.096/.097(44)
ISSN 1248-9948
FR
●**TELE K7, TELE 7 VIDEO.** (1993)-. Periodical. French. Societe Francaise d'Edition Presse, 48 50 boulevard Senard, 92210 Saint Cloud France. **Tel** 011 33 1 47112000. **Formed by the union of** Tele K7, 0757-0112 **and** Tele 7 Video (Paris), 0996-5491.

SP
TELECAST AND BROADCAST. (19??)-. Spanish. Twelve times a year. Free on request. Stereofonia SA, C Card H Oria 171, Ciud Period, 28034 Madrid Spain. **Tel** 011 34 1 7307177, FAX 011 34 1 7308092.

ISSN 0315-8985
CN
TELENATION. Added/Corp Canadian Broadcasting League. (1972)-. Periodical. English. Twelve times a year. Canadian Broadcasting League, Box 1504, Ottawa Ontario K1P 5R5 Canada.

UDC 654.1
ISSN 1121-1814
IT
TELEPIU MILANO. (1987)-. Periodical. Italian. One time a week. L60800 Italy; L123200 other. Arnoldo Mondadori Editore, UFF Cont Abbonamenti, 20090 Segrate MI Italy. **Tel** 011 39 2 75422015, telex 320457 MONDMI I.

DD 791.45/09714
ISSN 0380-6073
CN
TELESEMAINE. Vol. 1 (Sept. 13-19, 1975)-. Periodical. French. One time a week. 0.35Can$ each number. Les Editions Tele Semaine Inc., CP 908 Succursale H, Montreal Quebec H3G 2L6 Canada.

DD 302.2/345/09714
ISSN 0712-6891
CN
SUSPENDED
TELESPECTATEUR, LE. [Telespectateur]. Vol. 1, No. 1 (Oct. 1979)-(19??). Periodical. French. Four times a year. 25.00Can$ Canada; 30.00Can$ other. Le Telespectateur, 4005 Bellechasse, Montreal Quebec H1X 1J6 Canada. **Tel** 729-6393. **Bk Rev. Ad Acc. Circ:** 2,000.
Desc: General information about broadcasting actuality.

LC PN1991.3.R8 S6
ISSN 0131-694X
RU
TELEVIDENIE, RADIOVESHCHANIE.
Added/Corp Russia (1923-U.S.S.R.) Gosudarstvennyi Komitet po Radioveshchaniiu Televideniiu. Vol. 19, No. 11 (Nov. 1970)-. Periodical. Russian. Twelve times a year. $129.95. **(Subscription address:** East View Publications Inc., 3020 Harbor Lane North, Suite 110, Minneapolis MN 55447. **Tel** (800)477-1005, (612)550-0961, FAX (612)559-2931.**) Continues** Sovetskoe Radio I Televidenie.

US
TELEVISION AND CABLE ACTION UPDATE. (19??)-. Periodical. English. One time a week. included in Television Digest Service. Warren Publishing, Inc., 2115 Ward Court Northwest, Washington DC 20037. **Tel** (202)872-9200, FAX (202)293-3435.

LC TK6540 .T453
DD 384.55/025/73
ISSN 0732-8648
CCC
TELEVISION & CABLE FACTBOOK.
VFOAT Television and Cable Factbook; T.V. and Cable Factbook; T.V. & Cable Factbook; TV & Cable Factbook. No. 51 (1982-83)-. Trade Publication. English. One time a year. $455.00. Warren Publishing, Inc., 2115 Ward Court Northwest, Washington DC 20037. **Tel** (202)872-9200, FAX (202)293-3435. **ED** Michael Taliaferro, Richard Koch and Daniel Kohlmeier. **Ad Acc. Continues** Television Factbook, 0082-268X.
Desc: Reference for television, cable systems, and cable and related stations. Edited for industry consultants, suppliers, manufacturers, specialists, personnel, etc.

LC PN1992 .T433
US
TELEVISION ANNUAL. Added/Corp Television Index, Inc. Vol. 1 (1989/1990)-. English. Television Index Inc, 40/29 27th Street/2nd Floor, Long Island City NY 11101. **Tel** (718)937-3990.

LC TK6540 .B8432
DD 621
ISSN 0898-767X
US
TELEVISION BROADCAST. (198?)-. Trade Publication. English. Twelve times a year. $38.00. Miller Freeman PSN Inc., 2 Park Avenue, Suite 1820, New York NY 10016. **Tel** (212)213-3444, FAX (212)213-3484. **ED** Ron Merrell. **Bk Rev. Ad Acc. Circ:** 25,000 (ctrl). **Continues** Television/Broadcast Communications, 0746-5777.
Desc: Production and engineering techniques, applications of new technology for television broadcast stations and teleproduction facilities.

LC HE8700 .T45
ISSN 0953-6841
UK
TELEVISION BUSINESS INTERNATIONAL : TBI. [TBI. Telev. bus. int.]. **VFOAT** TBI. (Feb. 1988)-. Periodical. English. Ten times a year. $102.67. 21st Century Publishing, 531-583 Kings Road, London SW10 0TZ United Kingdom. **Tel** 011 44 71 3513612. **(Subscription address:** Select Subscriptions Ltd., Northbridge Road, Berkhamsted HP4 1ST United Kingdom. **Tel** 011 44 1442 876661.**)**

LC HE8700.8 .T37
ISSN 0147-3352
US
CEASED
TELEVISION CONTACTS. Added/Corp Larimi Communications Associates. (19??)-(1993). English. Larimi Communications Associates, 151 East 50th Street, New York NY 10022. **Tel** (212)819-9310. **ED** Bob Del Pazzo.
Desc: Directory on television programming, listing national, syndicated and local program's guest, product and information requirements. Local listings include affiliation, personnel, etc.

LC HE8700.8 .T915
DD 384.55/025/73
ISSN 1056-0963
US
TELEVISION DATATRAK. (TV DATATRAK.). [Telev. datatrak]. **VAT** Television Datatrak. 1st Quarter (1991)-. English. Four times a year. $350.00. Bethlehem Publishing Inc, Box 119, Bethlehem NH 03574. **Tel** (212)832-7170.

LC HD9696.T463 U663
DD 381/.45621388/002573
US
TELEVISION DEALERS DIRECTORY.
Added/Corp American Business Directories, Inc. (19??)-. Directory. English. Irregular. $275.00. American Business Directories, Box 27347, 5711 South 86th Street, Omaha NE 68127. **Tel** (402)593-4600, FAX (402)331-1505.

Communications —Television and Cable

DD 384
ISSN 0497-1515
US
CCC

TELEVISION DIGEST WITH CONSUMER ELECTRONICS (1984). (TELEVISION DIGEST, WITH CONSUMER ELECTRONICS.). [Telev. dig. consum. electroni.]. **VFOAT** Weekly Television Digest, with Consumer Electronics. Vol. 24, No. 22 (May 28, 1984)-. Trade Publication. English. One time a week. $885.00. Warren Publishing, Inc., 2115 Ward Court Northwest, Washington DC 20037. **Tel** (202)872-9200, FAX (202)293-3435. *Continues* Weekly Television Digest with Consumer Electronics, 0897-5620.

LC PN1992 .T42
DD 791.45/0233/02573
ISSN 1055-0828
US

TELEVISION DIRECTORS GUIDE. [Telev. dir. guide]. **VFOAT** TV Directors Guide. 1st Ed. (1990)-. English. One time a year. $46.00. Lone Eagle Publishing Inc., 2337 Roscomare Road, Suite 9, Los Angeles CA 90077. **Tel** (310)471-8066, FAX (310)471-4969.

ISSN 0735-567X
US

TELEVISION EQUIPMENT SPECIFICATION SERVICE. (TESS : TELEVISION EQUIPMENT SPECIFICATION SERVICE.). [Telev. equip. specif. serv.]. **VFOAT** T.E.S.S. English. Irregular. Knowledge Industry Publications Inc, 701 Westchester Avenue, White Plains NY 10604. **Tel** (914)328-9157, (800)800-5474, FAX (914)328-9093.

LC PN1992.3.U5 T39
DD 016.79145/0973
ISSN 0149-7375
US

TELEVISION INDEX: NETWORK FUTURES, PROGRAM DEBUTS, RETURNS, SPECIALS AND CHANGES.
VFOAT Network Futures, Program Debuts, Returns, Specials and Changes. (19??)-. Periodical. English. One time a week. $250.00. Television Index Inc, 40/29 27th Street/2nd Floor, Long Island City NY 11101. **Tel** (718)937-3990. **ED** Jonathan Miller. Index available.
Desc: Report of series, specials and other production information on the three commercial networks covering production personnel and performers. Includes "TV pro-log", network futures and TV network movies.

LC PN1992.7 .T455
US

TELEVISION INDEX. WRITERS DIRECTORY. **Added/Corp** Television Index, Inc. **VFOAT** Writers Directory. (19??)-. Directory. English. Irregular. Television Index Inc, 40/29 27th Street/2nd Floor, Long Island City NY 11101. **Tel** (718)937-3990.

ISSN 1058-1030
US

TELEVISION LISTING CO. **Added/Corp** Television Listing Co. **VFOAT** T.L.C. (1991)-. Periodical. English. One time a week. Free. Television Listing Co., 1500 Adams Avenue, Suite 206, Costa Mesa CA 92626.

LC TK6630.A1 T425
DD 621.388/005
ISSN 0308-454X
UK
CODEN TELED3

TELEVISION (LONDON). (TELEVISION.). [Television]. **Added/Corp** Royal Television Society (Great Britain). (1976)-. Trade Publication. English. Eight times a year. $123.21. Royal Television Society, 100 Grays Inn Road, Holborn Hall, London WC1X 8AL United Kingdom. **Tel** 011 44 171 4301000, FAX 011 44 171 4300924. **ED** Harvey Lee. Index available. **Bk Rev. Ad Acc. Circ:** 4,000 (ctrl). Documents available from Article Express International, Ask*IEEE, CASDDS. *Continues* Royal Television Society (Great Britain). Journal.
Desc: Publishes articles on matters of concern to those who work in television program making management and engineering.
Ind/Abst Bioeng. Abstr.; Chem. Abstr.; Educ. Technol. Abstr.; Ei Page One; Eng. Index Annu.; INSPEC (March-April 1976-).

ISSN 0032-647X
UK
CCC
CODEN TVSCAC

TELEVISION (LONDON. 1970). [Telev. Lond. 1970]. (1970)-. Trade Publication. English. Twelve times a year. $54.60. Reed Business Publishing / West Sussex, England, Perrymount Road, Haywards Heath, West Sussex RH16 3DH United Kingdom. **Tel** 011 44 1444 441212, FAX 011 44 1444 445447. *Continues* Practical Television.
Ind/Abst Curr. Cit.

DD 384
ISSN 0894-5225
US

TELEVISION MARKET INSIGHT. [Telev. mark. insight]. **VFOAT** TMI. (June 15, 1987)-. Periodical. English. Twelve times a year. $300.00. Hawthorne Communications Inc, PO Box 1238, Canal Street Station, New York NY 10013. **Tel** (212)475-3227.

LC AI3 .T44
DD 011
ISSN 0085-7157
US

TELEVISION NEWS INDEX AND ABSTRACTS. See Communications-Abstracting, Bibliographies and Statistics.

ISSN 0085-7157
US

TELEVISION NEWS INDEX AND ABSTRACTS : ANNUAL INDEX. See Communications-Abstracting, Bibliographies and Statistics.

LC PN1992 .T45
ISSN 0040-2796
US

TELEVISION QUARTERLY (BEVERLY HILL). (TELEVISION QUARTERLY.). [Televis. q.]. **Added/Corp** National Academy of Television Arts and Sciences (U.S.) Syracuse University. Television and Radio Center. Vol. 1 (Feb. 1962)-. Periodical. English. Four times a year. $30.00. National Academy of TV Arts and Sciences, 111 West 57th Street/#1020, New York NY 10019. **Tel** (212)586-8424, FAX (212)246-8129. **ED** Richard Pack. **Bk Rev. Ad Acc. Circ:** 14,000 (ctrl). available on microfilm and microfiche from University Microfilms International (UMI). Documents available from The Genuine Article, UMI Article Clearinghouse.
Desc: The official journal of the national academy of Television Arts and Sciences. Discusses the social, political, economic, and technological issues caused and solved by television. Writers and subjects include industry professionals and personalities.
Ind/Abst Arts Humanit. Citation Index [Full Cov.]; Curr. Contents Arts and Humanities; Expand. Acad. Index (1988-); Film Lit. Index (19??-); Newsp. Period. Abstr. (1989-); PAIS Int. Print; Read. Guide Abstr. Select Ed.; Read. Guide Period. Lit. (1991-); Res. Alert [Full Cov.].

LC HE8689 .R62
DD 384.54/05
ISSN 0271-4809
US

TELEVISION/RADIO AGE COMMUNICATIONS COURSEBOOK.
VAT Television Radio Age Communications Coursebook. (1977/78)-. English. One time a year. $22.00. Communications Research Institute, 515 Madison Avenue 2100, New York NY 10022. **Tel** (212)752-9635.

UK

TELEVISION; SERVICING, CONSTRUCTION, COLOUR, DEVELOPMENTS. Vol. 21, No. 241 (Oct. 1970)-. English. $49.80 US and Canada; $39.14 UK and Eire; $46.21 other. IPC Magazines Ltd., Perrymount Road, Haywards Heath, West Sussex RH16 3DH United Kingdom. **Tel** 011 44 1444 440421, FAX 011 44 1444 445599. Documents available from Ask*IEEE.
Ind/Abst INSPEC (Aug. 1971-).

ISSN 0887-1000
US

TELEVISION TRENDS. (1990)-. Periodical. English. Twenty-six times a year. $96.00. Rundown/Standish Publishing Company, PO Box 335, Ardmore PA 19003. **Tel** (610)519-9220, FAX (610)519-9221.

DD 384.55/0971/021
ISSN 1181-6643
CN
CEASED

TELEVISION VIEWING. (TELEVISION VIEWING.). [Telev. viewing]. **Added/Corp** Statistics Canada. Education, Culture and Tourism Division. **VFOAT** Ecoute de la Television. (1989)-(1993). English (French). Statistics Canada Publications Sales and Services, R.H. Coats Building 6th Floor, Ottawa Ontario K1A 0T6 Canada. **Tel** (613)951-5078, (800)267-6677, FAX (613)951-1584, telex 053-3585. *Continues* Television Viewing in Canada, 1180-3304.
Desc: An annual analysis of the television viewing patterns of Canadians, including charts and tables, beginning with survey data from the fall of 1985.

LC PN1992.7 .T46
DD 791
ISSN 0894-8658
US

TELEVISION WRITERS GUIDE. [Telev. writ. guide]. **Added/Corp** Lone Eagle Publishing Co. **VFOAT** Television Writers. 1st Ed. (1989)-. English. One time a year. $51.00. Lone Eagle Publishing Inc., 2337 Roscomare Road, Suite 9, Los Angeles CA 90077. **Tel** (310)471-8066, FAX (310)471-4969.

LC PN1992.3.U5 T45
DD 791.45/75/097305
ISSN 1063-7087
US

TELEVISION YEARBOOK, THE. (THE TELEVISION YEARBOOK : COMPLETE DETAILED LISTINGS FOR THE ... SEASON.). [Telev. yearb.]. (1991)-. English. One time a year. The Putnam Publishing Group, 390 Murray Hill Parkway East, Rutherford NJ 07073. **Tel** (800)631-8571.

LC PN1992 .T47
DD 384.55/4/05
UK

TELEVISUAL. **VFOAT** Televisual Magazine. Periodical. English. Twelve times a year. Centaur Communications Ltd., St. Giles House, 50 Poland Street, London W1V 4AX United Kingdom. **Tel** 011 44 171 4394222, FAX 011 44 171 7346748, telex 261352. available on an online database (files 771,772/Full-Text) from DIALOG. *Continues* Corporate Video.

ISSN 0049-3325
NE

UDC 654.195+ 654.197

TELEVIZIER LEIDEN. (TELEVIZIER.). [Televizier Leiden]. **Added/Corp** Gemene Vereniging Radio-Omroep RO. **VFOAT** Televizier(Amsterdam); Televizier (Hilversum). (1960)-. Periodical. Dutch. One time a week. $45.38. Avro Ledenservice, Postbus 5000, 1200 EW Hilversum Netherlands. **Tel** 011 31 35 717911. *Absorbed* TV Film, 0929-1628.

LC PN1992.3.B8 T18
BU

TELEVIZIIA, RADIO. See Communications-Radio.

ISSN 0386-6831
JA

TEREBIJON GAKKAISHI. See Engineering.

DD 354.710085
ISSN 1187-4848
CN

TETE-A-TETE (OTTAWA. 1991).
(TETE-A-TETE : CRTC, OBSERVATIONS, RENSEIGNEMENTS ET PLAINTES.). [Tete-a-tete]. **Main/Corp** Conseil de la Radiodiffusion et des Telecommunications Canadiennes. **VFOAT** Tete-a-Tete. (1991)-. French (English).

LC HE8700.9.A67 T55
SU

TILIFIZYUN AL-KHALIJ. **Added/Corp** Jihaz Tilifizyun Al-Khalij. **VFOAT** Gulf TV.; Majallat Tilifizyun Al-Khalij. (19??)-. Periodical. Arabic. Four times a year. Jihaj Tilifizyun Al-Khalij, PO Box 6802, Al-Riyad 11452 Saudi Arabia.

LC PN1993 .T55
DD 791.43/05
ISSN 0040-7836
II

TIME & TIDE. See Motion Picture.

DD 384
ISSN 1050-1398
US

TOPICS CATALOG. [Top. cat.]. (Spring 1990)-. Catalog. English. Four times a year. $5.40 (single issue). Journal Graphics Inc, 267 Broadway, New York NY 10007. **ED** Gary Tilzer. available on diskette (in a variety of sizes and formats).

ISSN 0040-2672
SP

UDC 654.19

TP. TELEPROGRAMA. [TP. Teleprogr.]. **VFOAT** Teleprograma. (1966)-. Periodical. Spanish. One time a week. $43.88. Cempro, Plaza Conde Valle Suchil 20, 28015 Madrid Spain. **Tel** 011 34 1 4462050, 011 34 1 4472700.

ISSN 1059-9657
US

TV 2 (SAINT PAUL, MINN.). (TV 2.). **Added/Corp** Twin Cities Public Television (Saint Paul, Minn.). (19??)-. Periodical. English. Twelve times a year. $35.00 (individuals), $25.00 (senior citizens), $40.00 (family), $66.00 (supporting), $120.00 (sponsor club) Comes with Twin Cities Public Television Inc. membership. Twin Cities Public Television, 172 East 4th Street, St. Paul MN 55101. **Tel** (612)222-1717. *Continues* Scene, 0744-5741.

DD 384
ISSN 1054-4259
US

TV & CABLE PUBLICITY OUTLETS. [TV cable public. outlets]. **VFOAT** TV and Cable Publicity Outlets; Television and Cable Publicity Outlets. (19??)-. Trade Publication. English. Four times a year. $239.00. Morgan-Rand Publications Inc., 1800 Byberry Road 800, Huntington Valley PA 19006. **Tel** (215)938-5511, FAX (215)988-0402. *Continues* All TV & Cable Publicity Outlets.

LC TK6540 .T9
DD 384.55/025/73
ISSN 1076-6626
US

●TV & CABLE SALES REPS & INTERCONNECTS. [TV & Cable Sales Reps & Interconnects]. **VFOAT** TV and Cable Sales Reps and Interconnects; Television and Cable Sales Representatives and Cable Interconnects. (1993)-. Trade Publication. English. Irregular. Warren Publishing, Inc., 2115 Ward Court Northwest, Washington DC 20037. **Tel** (202)872-9200, FAX (202)293-3435.

LC HF5905 .S745
DD 384.55/43
ISSN 1076-3988
US

●TV & CABLE SOURCE. [TV cable source]. **Added/Corp** Standard Rate & Data Service. **VFOAT** TV and Cable Source; Television & Cable Source; Television and Cable Source; SRDS TV and Cable Source; SRDS Television and Cable Source; SRDS Television & Cable Source; SRDS TV & Cable Source. Vol. 76, No. 1 (Mar. 1994)-. Periodical. English. Four times a year. $369.00. SRDS, Standard Rate & Data Service, 3004 Glenview Road, Wilmette IL 60091. **Tel** (708)375-5049, (800)851-7737, FAX (708)375-5003. **(Subscription**

Communications —Television and Cable

address: Real Time Publications Service, PO Box 1962, Danbury CT 06813.) *Continues Spot TV & Cable Source, 1071-4596.*

ISSN 1064-9433
US

TV BLUEPRINT. VAT Television Blueprint. Vol. 13, No. 9 (Sept. 1992)-. Periodical. English. Twelve times a year. TV Blueprint, 135 Oval Drive, Islandia NY 11722. *Continues Premium Channels TV Blueprint, 1040-5534.*

TV BROADCAST FINANCIAL DATA. Main/Corp United States. Federal Communications Commission. **Added/Corp** United States. Federal Communications Commission. Final TV broadcast financial data. (19??)-. English. One time a year. FCC, 1919 M Street NW, Washington DC 20554. **Tel** (202)632-6302.

ISSN 0887-5847
DD 791 US

TV COLLECTOR, THE. [TV collect.]. **VAT** Television Collector. (19??)-. Periodical. English. Six times a year (Jan., Mar., May, July, Sept., Nov.) $20.00. The TV Collector, PO Box 1088, Easton MA 02334. **Tel** (508)238-1179. **ED** Diane L. Albert. Index available. cum. index. **Bk Rev**, (Qty: 10). **Ad Acc, Adv Mgr:** D. Albert. **Circ:** 2,000 (ctrl).
Desc: In-depth background articles about television shows and stars of the past and interviews with actors and actresses. Lists the classified ads forum to buy-sell-trade videotapes, memorabilia, upcoming TV highlights, and information on where old television shows are currently being aired.

ISSN 1070-2601
DD 380 US

TV DEAL RECORD, THE. [TV deal rec.]. **Added/Corp** Paul Kagan Associates. (199?)-. English. One time a year. $195.00. Paul Kagan Associates Inc., 126 Clock Tower Place, Carmel CA 93923-8734. **Tel** (408)624-1536, **FAX** (408)625-3225, telex ITT 4938124 PKA UI. *Continues Paul Kagan's Record of TV Station Deals, 1055-3789.*
Desc: Record of all TV station deals proposed and filed with the FCC in the last decade. Includes cash flow multiples, prior sale prices, terms of deals, seller financing values, etc.

LC HE8700.8 .T917 ISSN 0884-1098
DD 384.54/43 US

TV DIMENSIONS. [TV Dimens.]. **Added/Corp** Media Dynamics, Inc. **VFOAT** T.V. Dimensions. **VAT** Television Dimensions. (19??)-. English. One time a year. $117.50. Media Dynamics Inc., 18 East 41st Street, Suite 1806, New York NY 10017. **Tel** (212)683-7895.

ISSN 1049-1163
US

TV ENTERTAINMENT. VAT Television Entertainment. Periodical. English (Spanish). Twelve times a year. $24.00. TV Entertainment, 309 Lakeside Drive, Horsham PA 19044-2313. **ED** Cable Neulaus. **Ad Acc.** ctrl circ. *Continues TV Entertainment Monthly, 1044-0682.*
Desc: Consumer magazine about TV programming and the entertainment industry.

ISSN 1054-2329
DD 384 US

TV ETC. [TV etc.]. **Added/Corp** Media Research Center. **VAT** Television Etcetera. (19??)-. Trade Publication. English. Twelve times a year. $35.00. Media Research Center, 113 Southwest Street, 2nd Floor, Alexandria VA 22314. **Tel** (703)683-9733, **FAX** (703)683-9736. **ED** Sandy Crawford, (phone: (703)683-9733). **Ad Acc.** ctrl circ.

LC HE8700.8 .T92 ISSN 0736-2986
DD 384.55/4/068 US

TV EXECUTIVE, THE. [TV exec.]. **VFOAT** Television Executive; Executive. (1983)-. Trade Publication. English. Two times a year. TV Trade Media Inc., 216 E 75th Street No. PW, New York NY 10021. **Tel** (212)288-1549, **FAX** (212)734-9033, telex 428669. **ED** Dom Serafini. **Bk Rev. Ad Acc. Circ:** 10,000 (ctrl).
Desc: A business journal for top level TV management.

ISSN 0039-8543
US

TV GUIDE. [TV guide]. **VAT** Television Guide. Vol. 1 (April 3-9, 1953)-. Periodical. English. One time a week. $45.24. News America Publishing Inc., PO Box 500, Radnor PA 19088. **Tel** (610)293-8500. **Ad Acc.** Documents available from UMI Article Clearinghouse.
Desc: Contains news and features on television stars and programs. Also contains a listing of channels and broadcast times for current television programs.
Ind/Abst Acad. Index. Full Text Elite; Acad. Abstr.; Access (1975-1988); EP Collect.; Gen. Period. Index (1985-); Homework Help.; Mag. Artic. Summar. Elite; Mag. Artic. Summar. Select; Mag. Artic. Summar. CD-ROM; Mag. Index Plus (1989-); Mag. Index. Sel. (1986-); Mag. Search; MasterFile FullTEXT 1000; MasterFile FullTEXT 350; MasterFile FullTEXT 650; MasterFile FullTEXT (Apr. 1984-); Newsp. Period. Abstr.

(1988-); OCLC; Pub. Lib. FullTEXT; Read. Guide Abstr. Select Ed.; Read. Guide Period. Lit.; Telebase; Mag. Index (1977-).

UK

TV GUIDE MONTHLY. English. Twelve times a year. £12.00 UK; £12.50 EIRE; £25.00 Europe; £50.00 other. Murdoch Magazines (England), Finum House, 48 Leicester Square, London WC2H 7FB United Kingdom. **Tel** 011 44 71 930-9300.

LC PN1992.3.G43 T2

GW

TV HOEREN UND SEHEN. (19??)-. Periodical. German. One time a week. Heinrich Bauer Verlag, Burchardstr 11, D-20095 Hamburg Germany. **Tel** 011 49 40 30190. **(Subscription address:** Deutscher Pressevertrieb Buch, POB 101602 Hansa GMBH, D-20010 Hamburg Germany. **Tel** 011 49 40 23711249.)

ISSN 0744-5504
US

TV LINK. (198?)-. Periodical. English. Twelve times a year. $24.00. TV Link, PO Box 65, Dahlonega GA 30533.

LC PN4784.T4 T8 ISSN 1051-3590
DD 070.1/95 US
CEASED

TV NEWS CONTACTS. [TV news contacts]. **Added/Corp** BPi Media Services. **VFOAT** Television News Contacts. (1990)-(199?). English. BPi Media Services, 1515 Broadway, New York NY 10036. **Tel** (800)753-6675, (518)753-6675, **FAX** (518)374-7889. *Continues TV News (New York, N.Y.), 1048-2210.*

US

TV PRO-LOG. VFOAT TV Pro Log. (19??)-. Periodical. English. One time a week. $100.00. Television Index Inc, 40/29 27th Street/2nd Floor, Long Island City NY 11101. **Tel** (718)937-3990. **ED** Timothy Hunter.
Desc: Newsletter on present and future television programming, basically on the three commercial networks.

LC HG ISSN 0885-2340
DD 332 US

TV PROGRAM INVESTOR. [TV program investor]. **VAT** Television Program Investor. No. 1 (Sept. 13, 1985)-. Newsletter. English. Twelve times a year. $595.00. Paul Kagan Associates Inc., 126 Clock Tower Place, Carmel CA 93923-8734. **Tel** (408)624-1536, **FAX** (408)625-3225, telex ITT 4938124 PKA UI. **ED** Dwight Beach. available via fax.
Desc: Newsletter on trends in television program syndication, the value of television programs and networks, the value of public and private companies engaged in the TV program business, plus analysis of mergers and acquisitions.

ISSN 1040-6123
DD 384 US

TV PROGRAM STATS. See Communications-Abstracting, Bibliographies and Statistics.

US

●**TV SPORTS FILE. See** Sports and Games.

LC PN1992 .T2 ISSN 0041-4530
US

TV STAR PARADE. VAT Television Star Parade. (1951)-. Periodical. English. Six times a year. Ideal Publ Co, 2 Park Avenue, 16th Place, New York NY 10016.

LC HE8700.8 .T924 ISSN 1050-3633
DD 384.55// US

TV STATION & CABLE OWNERSHIP DIRECTORY. [TV stn. cable ownersh. dir.]. **Added/Corp** Warren Publishing. **VFOAT** Ownership Directory; TV Station and Cable Ownership Directory. **VAT** Television Station and Cable Ownership Directory; Television Station and Cable Ownership Directory. (Spring 1990)-. Directory. English. Two times a year. $195.00. Warren Publishing, Inc., 2115 Ward Court Northwest, Washington DC 20037. **Tel** (202)872-9200, **FAX** (202)293-3435.

ISSN 1061-8317
US

TV STATION LOG. VFOAT TV Log. **VAT** Television Station Log. (1992)-. English. $9.95. Dajja Enterprises, PO Box 24, Cambridge WI 53523-0024.

ISSN 1382-2713
NE

●**TV STUDIO.** (1993)-. Dutch. One time a week. $42.64. Katholieke Radio OMROEP, Postbus 10050, 1201 DB Hilversum Netherlands. **Tel** 011 31 35 714714. *Continues Studio, 1382-2721.*

LC PN1992.3.U5 T23
DD 791.U5/0973 US

TV. THE TELEVISION ANNUAL. VFOAT TV; Television Annual. (1979)-. English. One time a year. Macmillan Publishing Company / New York, 866 3rd Avenue, New York NY 10022. **Tel** (212)702-2000, (800)257-5755. available in paper back.

ISSN 0039-8624
UK
SUSPENDED

TV TIMES. (19??)-(19??). English. One time a week. £160.00. IPC Television Publishing Group, 11th Floor, Kings Reach Tower, Stamford Street, London SE1 9LS United Kingdom. **Tel** 011 44 171 2615000.

LC HE8700
DD 384.55 GW

●**TV TODAY.** (1994)-. Consumer Publication. English. Twenty-four times a year. DM58.50. Magazin Verlag am Fleetrand, Brieffach 01, 20444 Hamburg Germany. **Tel FAX** 011 49 40 37037988. **ED** Andreas Schmidt.

ISSN 1064-2676
US

TV VIDEO. (TV VIDEO [VIDEORECORDING].). **VAT** Television Video. (1992)-. English. Twelve times a year. TV Video, 15900 South Crenshaw Boulevard, #G-403, Gardena CA 90249.

ISSN 0810-249X
AT

TV WEEK MELBOURNE. (1957)-. Periodical. English. One time a week. 94.06Aus$. Pacific Publications Pty Ltd, 32 Walsh Street, Melbourne Victoria 3000 Australia. **Tel** 011 61 3 3207000.

LC HE8700 .T18 ISSN 0142-7466
DD 384.55/05 UK

TV WORLD. [TV World]. **VAT** Television World. (1977)-. Trade Publication. English. Ten times a year. $145.00. Jeska & Harrington, 33 39 Bowling Green Lane, London EC1 R08A United Kingdom. **Tel** 011 44 171 8371212, **FAX** 011 44 171 83344518. **(Subscription address:** EMAP Business Publishing, 4 Admiral House Cardinal Way, Middlesex HA3 5SQ United Kingdom. **Tel** 011 44 181 8684499.) **ED** Alison Homewood. **Ad Acc. Circ:** 9,529.

ISSN 0199-4484
US

TV WORLD. VAT Television World. Vol. 4 (Jan. 14/20, 1978)-. Periodical. English. Twenty-six times a year. TV World, 505 Eighth Avenue, Suite 1804, New York NY 10018. *Continues Cable TV World.*
Desc: Includes all cable and regular TV program listings in New York City.

ISSN 0957-3844
UK

TV ZONE. (1989)-. Periodical. English. Twelve times a year. $66.74. Visual Imagination, 1 Blades Court Deodar Road, London SW15 2NU United Kingdom. **Tel** 011 44 181 8751520, **FAX** 011 44 181 8751588. **ED** S. Payne. **Ad Acc.**
Desc: Contains information on cult television programs.

UK

UK TELEVISION DATABOOK. (19??)-. English. One time a year. $445.00. Kagan World Media Inc., 126 Clock Tower Place, Carmel CA 93923-8734. **Tel** (408)624-1536, **FAX** (408)625-3225. **(Subscription address:** Kagan World Media Ltd., 524 Fulham Road, London SW6 5NR United Kingdom. **Tel** 011 44 171 3718880, **FAX** 011 44 171 3718715.)
Desc: Reference guide to the television industry in the U.K. Information on regulation, advertising, independent production companies, cable/satellite services, etc.

LC HE8700.66.U6 U558
DD 384.55 US

UNIVERSE ESTIMATES SUMMARY. Added/Corp Arbitron Company. Arbitron Ratings/Television. (1981/82)-. English. Arbitron Ratings, 142 West 57th Street, 14th Floor, New York NY 10019-3301. *Formed by the union of ADI Book; Population Book and Television Households Book.*

ISSN 0922-2642
NE

UDC 654.19

VARA TV MAGAZINE. [VARA tv mag.]. **VFOAT** Vereniging Arbeiders Radio Amateurs TV Magazine. (1988)-. Periodical. Dutch. One time a week. $42.33. Veren Arbeiders Radio Amateurs, Postbus 333, 1200 AH Hilversum Netherlands. **Tel** 011 31 35 711911. *Continues VARA Gids, 0922-2634.*

LC PN1992.3.U5 V37 ISSN 1064-9557
DD 791 US

VARIETY AND DAILY VARIETY TELEVISION REVIEWS. [Var. Dly. var. telev. rev.]. **VFOAT** Television Reviews; Variety Television Reviews. Vol. 16 (1989/1990)-. English. Every 2 years. $165.00. Garland Publishing, 1000A Sherman Avenue, Hamden CT 06514. **Tel** (800)627-6273, (203)281-4487, **FAX** (203)230-1186. *Continues Variety Television Reviews, 1064-9565.*

ISSN 1078-1544
US

●**VARIETY DEAL MEMO. VFOAT** Deal Memo. (1994)-. Periodical. English. Twenty-four times a year. $497.00. Baskerville Communications, PO Box 5084, Thousand Oaks CA 91359. **Tel** (805)499-0721 ext. 289.

UK

VETERANS NEWSLETTER (CINEMA & TELEVISION VETERANS). See Motion Picture.

Communications —Television and Cable

DD 384   **ISSN** 1041-0643   US   CCC

VIA SATELLITE. [Via satell.]. (1986)-. Trade Publication. English. Twelve times a year. $49.00. Phillips Business Information Inc., 1201 Seven Locks Road, PO Box 61130, Potomac MD 20854. **Tel** (301)424-3338, (301)340-1520, (800)777-5005, FAX (301)424-4297, telex 358149.
  Ind/Abst F&S Index Plus Text, Int. [Select. Cov.]; PROMT.

ISSN 1064-4520   US

VIEWFINDER (LEWISTON, MAINE). (VIEWFINDER.). **Added/Corp** WCBB (Television station : Lewiston, Me.) Colby College. Bates College. Bowdoin College. (July 1992)-. Periodical. English. Twelve times a year. Viewfinder, 1450 Lisbon Road, Lewiston ME 04240. *Continues* WCBB 10 Pulse.

ISSN 0142-8543   UK   CCC

VISION. **Added/Corp** British Academy of Film and Television Arts. No. 1 (March 1976)-. Periodical. English. Twenty-four times a year. $196.79. SUBIS, Mansion House 19 Kingfield Road, Sheffield S11 9AS United Kingdom. **Tel** 011 44 114 2554433, FAX 011 44 114 255 4626. **Bk Rev.** *Supersedes* Society of Film and Television Arts. Journal.

DD 791   **ISSN** 1064-8658   US

VISIONS MAGAZINE (BOSTON, MASS.). See Communications-Video.

LC HE8700.7.C6 C13   **ISSN** 1047-9902
DD 912/.13845547/05   US

WARREN PUBLISHING'S CABLE & STATION COVERAGE ATLAS. [Warren Publ. cable stn. cover. atlas]. **Added/Corp** Warren Publishing. **VFOAT** Warren Publishing's Cable and Station Coverage Atlas; Cable and Station Coverage Atlas; Cable & Station Coverage Atlas. (1989)-. Trade Publication. English. One time a year. $401.50 Washington DC; $379.00 other US; $405.00 other. Warren Publishing, Inc., 2115 Ward Court Northwest, Washington DC 20037. **Tel** (202)872-9200, FAX (202)293-3435. *Continues* Television Digest's Cable & Station Coverage Atlas, 0895-2035.

ISSN 1067-6252   US   CCC

●**WARREN'S CABLE REGULATION MONITOR.** **VFOAT** Monitor. (1993)-. Periodical. English. One time a week. $557.00. Warren Publishing, Inc., 2115 Ward Court Northwest, Washington DC 20037. **Tel** (202)872-9200, FAX (202)293-3435.

LC PN1993
DD 808.823   US

●**WESTERN CLIPPINGS.** See Motion Picture.

LC PN1992.3.U5 W45   **ISSN** 1041-2700
DD 791.45/09753   US

WETA (WASHINGTON, D.C.). (WETA.). **Added/Corp** Greater Washington Educational Telecommunications Association. **VFOAT** WETA Magazine. **VAT** Washington Educational Telecommunications Association. (1988)-. Periodical. English. Twelve times a year. Greater WETA, Box 2626, Washington DC 20013. *Continues* Dial WETAS, 0898-1779.
  Ind/Abst Index Vet.; Rev. Agric. Entomol.; Rev. Med. Vet. Entomol.; Small Anim. Abstr. Bibliogr.

LC PN1990 .C617
DD 384.54/06/01   UK

WHO'S WHO - COMMONWEALTH BROADCASTING ASSOCIATION. **Main/Corp** Commonwealth Broadcasting Association. (1980)-. Directory. English. One time a year. Commonwealth Broadcasting Association, Broadcasting House, London W1A 1AA United Kingdom. **Tel** 011 44 181 7655144, FAX 011 44 181 7655152. **ED** Stuart Revill. **Ad Acc, Adv Mgr:** Derek Inall, **Tel** 011 44 462 684231. **Circ:** 10,000. *Continues* Who's Who in Commonwealth Broadcasting.
  Desc: Journal specializing in all fields of broadcasting, providing information on the progress of broadcast technology.

DD 384   **ISSN** 1058-9384   US

WHRO MAGAZINE. [WHRO mag.]. **Added/Corp** WHRO (Television Station : Norfolk, Va.) WHRO (Radio Station : Norfolk, Va.) Hampton Roads Educational Telecommunications Association. Vol. 1, No. 1 (Sept. & Oct. 1991)-. Periodical. English. Six times a year. $35.00 (includes membership). Hampton Roads Educational Telecommunications Association, 5200 Hampton Boulevard, Norfolk VA 23508. *Continues* Dimensions (Norfolk, Va.), 1047-5532.

LC HE8700.72.U6 W57   **ISSN** 1068-4360
DD 384.55/5/097305   US

●**... WIRELESS CABLE DATABOOK, THE.** [Wirel. cable datab.]. **Added/Corp** Paul Kagan Associates. (1993)-. English. One time a year. $215.00. Paul Kagan Associates Inc., 126 Clock Tower Place, Carmel CA 93923-8734. **Tel** (408)624-1536, FAX (408)625-3225, telex ITT 4938124 PKA UI. available with charts.
  Desc: Information on the wireless cable industry - charts and tables with industry frequencies, sub counts, revenue projections, pay network subscriber shares, license fees, etc.

ISSN 1075-1483
DD 384   US

●**WIRELESS CABLE INVESTOR.** [Wirel. cable invest.]. **Added/Corp** Paul Kagan Associates. No. 409 (Jan. 31, 1994)-. Newsletter. English. Twelve times a year. $550.00. Paul Kagan Associates Inc., 126 Clock Tower Place, Carmel CA 93923-8734. **Tel** (408)624-1536, FAX (408)625-3225, telex ITT 4938124 PKA UI. **ED** Dwight Beach. available via fax. *Continues* Wireless Investor, 1054-6960.
  Desc: Newsletter on the wireless cable, multipoint distribution pay TV industry.

LC PN1990.6.K6 W64   KO

WOLGAN PANGSONG. **Added/Corp** Hanguk Pangsong Saoptan. **VFOAT** Pangsong. 1st Vol. (August 1982)-. Periodical. Korean. Twelve times a year. Hanguk Pangsons Saoptan, 1 Youido-dong, Yongdungpo-ku, Seoul South Korea.

LC PN1995.9.W6 W678   **ISSN** 1030-8644
DD 384/.8/02594   AT

WOMEN WORKING IN FILM, TELEVISION & VIDEO. **Added/Corp** WIFT (Organization). **VFOAT** National Register of Women Working in Film, Television & Video; National Directory of Women Working in Film, Television & Video. (1988)-. Trade Publication. English. Irregular. Women in Film and Television Inc, PO Box 648, Broadway NSW 2007 Australia.

WORLD BROADCASTING INFORMATION. (19??)-. English. One time a week. £365.00 UK; £390.00 (airmail) Europe; £405.00 (airmail) other. British Broadcasting Corporation, Caversham Park, Reading RG4 8TZ United Kingdom. **Tel** 011 44 1734 472742, FAX 011 44 1734 463823, telex 848318.
  Ind/Abst PTS Newsl. Database [Full Txt.].

ISSN 1072-6144
DD 384   US

●**WORLD GUIDE TO TELEVISION & FILM.** [World guide telev. film]. **VFOAT** World Guide to Television and Film; BIB World Guide to Television & Film. (1994)-. English. One time a year. $455.00. North American Publishing Company, 401 North Broad Street, Philadelphia PA 19108. **Tel** (215)238-5300, (800)777-8074, FAX (215)238-5283. *Continues* World Guide to Television & Programming, 1058-1944.

LC PN1992.1 .T37   **ISSN** 1058-1944
DD 384.55/4/025   US

TITLE CHANGE

WORLD GUIDE TO TELEVISION & PROGRAMMING. [World guide telev. program.]. **VFOAT** World Guide; World Guide to Television and Programming; BIB World Guide to Television & Programming. (1992)-(1994). English. North American Publishing Company, 401 North Broad Street, Philadelphia PA 19108. **Tel** (215)238-5300, (800)777-8074, FAX (215)238-5283. *Continues* TBI's World Guide, 1052-7192. *Continued by* World Guide to Television & Film, 1072-6144.
  Desc: Covers market opportunities and key personnel at every broadcast, cable, pay-TV, and satellite network and station in the world. Includes regulatory agencies, trade associations, trade events, equipment suppliers and distributors listed with their top programs available for export. Also includes 10,477 contact names, addresses, phone and FAX numbers.

WORLD SATELLITE TRANSPONDER LOADING REPORT. (19??)-. English. Four times a year. $150.00 North America; $175.00 other. MLE Inc, PO Box 159, Winter Beach FL 32971. **Tel** (305)767-4687, FAX (305)767-6067.

US

●**WORLDNET AT A GLANCE.** **Added/Corp** United States Information Agency. (Oct. 1993)-. English. Irregular. Worldnet Television and Film Service / US Information Agency, 601 D Street Northwest, Washington DC 20547.

LC E839.5 .N38a   **ISSN** 0197-7474
DD 973.92/05   US

WPIX EDITORIALS. **Main/Corp** New York. Television Station WPIX. (19??)-. English. One time a year. WPIX, 11 WPIX Plaza, New York NY 10017. **Tel** (212)949-1100, FAX (212)210-2805, telex 710-581-27698.

ISSN 1055-2960   US

Pr Rev.
WXXI (ROCHESTER, N.Y.). See Communications-Radio.

ISSN 0748-9560
DD 384   US

ZA NETWORK NEWS REPORTS. [ZA netw. news rep.]. **Added/Corp** Zatyko Associates. **VFOAT** Z.A. Network News Reports; Network News Reports. **VAT** Zatyko Associates Network News Reports. (19??)-. Periodical. English. Twelve times a year. $295.00. Zatyko Associates, 202 Fashion Lane #115, Tustin CA 92680.

LC HE8700
DD 384.55   GW

●**ZAP! FERNSEHEN UND BUECHER.** (1995)-. Consumer Publication. English. Twelve times a year. DM2.00. Stiftung Lesen, Fischtorplatz 23, 55116 Mainz Germany. **Tel** 011 49 6131 288900, FAX 011 49 6131 230333. **Circ:** 10,000.

ISSN 0261-1686
DD 778.5905   UK

ZERB. [Zerb]. (1978)-. Periodical. English. Two times a year (March, Sept.). $20.53. Vernon Dyer, 43 Mote Park Saltash, Cornwall PL12 4JY United Kingdom. **Tel** 011 44 1752 845434, FAX 011 44 1822 614405. **Ad Acc, Adv Mgr:** Ian Lewis. *Continues* Journal - Guild of Television Cameramen.

VIDEO

ISSN 0834-0730
DD 017/.537   CN

4-H AUDIO VISUAL CATALOGUE. [4-H audio vis. cat.]. **Main/Corp** Saskatchewan 4-H Program. **VFOAT** Saskatchewan 4-H Audio Visual Catalogue. **VAT** Four-H Audio Visual Catalogue. (1986)-. English. Irregular. Saskatchewan 4-H Office, University of Saskatchewan, Saskatoon, Saskatchewan S7N 0W0 Canada. *Continues* University of Saskatchewan. 4-H Audio Visual Catalogue., 0834-0730.

US

A/V ACCESS. See Library and Information Sciences.

ISSN 0883-7090
DD 791   US

ADULT VIDEO NEWS. [Adult video news]. (198?)-. Periodical. English. Twelve times a year. $44.95. Adult Video News Publications, 8600 West Chester Park/Suite 300, Upper Darby PA 19082. **Tel** (610)789-2085, FAX (215)446-0237. **ED** Paul Fishbein. **Bk Rev. Ad Acc. Circ:** 27,000 (ctrl).
  Desc: Complete coverage of the field of adult video. Features reviews of every video release, interviews, feature stories, profiles and industry news.

LC PN1992.95 .V56   UK

AL-VIDYU AL-ARABI. **VFOAT** Videoarab; Video Arab; Majallat Al-Vidyu Al-Arabi. (1983)-. Periodical. Arabic. Twelve times a year. Trytel International Publications Ltd, 26/28 Agnes Road, London W3 7YF United Kingdom.

ISSN 1130-4855
UDC 681.84   SP

ALTA FIDELIDAD EN AUDIO Y EN VIDEO. [Alta fidel. audio video]. **VFOAT** Alta Fidelidad. (1990)-. Periodical. Spanish. Twelve times a year. $75.50. MC Ediciones, C Monasterio 23, 08034 Barcelona Spain. **Tel** 011 34 93 280 43 44.

US

AMERICAN CINEMATOGRAPHER VIDEO MANUAL. (19??)-. English. American Society of Cinematographers, Box 2230, Hollywood CA 90028. **Tel** (213)969-4333.

US

AMERICAN FILM AND VIDEO FESTIVAL. **Main/Conf** American Film and Video Festival (New York, N.Y.). **Added/Corp** Educational Film Library Association. **VFOAT** Film and Video Festival. (1986)-. English. One time a year. American Film and Video Association, 85 Van Reypen Street, Jersey City NJ 07306. **ED** Ray Rolff. *Continues* American Film Festival.

Communications —Video

LC PN1993.3 .A476
DD 384/.8/02544
FR
ANNUAIRE DU CINEMA, TELEVISION, VIDEO. (1986)-. French. Irregular. Editions Bellefaye, 38 rue Etienne-Marcel, 75002 Paris France. **Continues** Annuaire du Cinema et Television.

LC PN1993.5.U778 T46a
DD 353.97680085/4
US
ANNUAL REPORT / TENNESSEE FILM, TAPE, AND MUSIC COMMISSION. See Motion Picture.

US
CEASED
ATS VIDEO MAGAZINE. (19??)-(19??). English. ATS Video Magazine, PO Box 1007, 127 Main Street North, Woodbury CT 06798. **Tel** (203)263-0006.

LC TS2301.A7 A78
DD 384
ISSN 0305-2249
UK
CCC
TITLE CHANGE
AUDIO VISUAL. [Audio vis.]. Vol. 1 (Jan. 1972)-(19??). Periodical. English. Emap Vision, 19 Scarbrook Road, Croydon CR9 1QH United Kingdom. **Tel** 01-760 9690, FAX 01-681 1672, telex 946665. **ED** Peter Lloyd. **Bk Rev. Ad Acc. Circ:** 20,000 (ctrl) available on microfilm and microfiche from University Microfilms International (UMI). Documents available from Ask*IEEE. **Supersedes** Film User, 0015-1459; Absorbed Computer Images International **and** Multi Media. **Continued by** AV Magazine.
Desc: Promotes the effective use of audio-visual techniques, and advises users on the equipment, materials and services available to them.
Ind/Abst Anbar Account. Finan. Abstr. (19??-) [Full Txt.]; Anbar Mark. Distr. Abstr. (19??-) [Full Txt.]; Anbar Top Manage. Abstr. (19??-) [Full Txt.]; Curr. Cit.; Fluid Abstr., Civil Eng. (19??-); Fluid Abstr. Proc. Eng. (19??-); FLUIDEX (1973-1990); INSPEC (Sept. 1983-); Manage. Bibliogr. Rev. (19??-); Med. Rev. Dig. (19??-); Oper. Prod. Manage. Abstr. (19??-) [Full Txt.]; Person. Train. Abstr. (19??-) [Full Txt.]; Women Manage. Rev. (19??-) [Full Txt.]; World Publ. Monit. (19??-).

ISSN 0822-823X
DD 017/.537
CN
AUDIO VISUAL CATALOGUE - PACIFIC VOCATIONAL INSTITUTE. (AUDIO VISUAL CATALOGUE.). [Audio vis. cat. - Pac. Vocat. Inst.]. **Main/Corp** Pacific Vocational Institute. **VAT** Audio-Visual Resource Catalogue. **VAT** Audio-Visual Resource Catalogue - Pacific Vocational Institute. 1983-. English. One time a year. Free to Colleges in British Columbia. Pacific Vocational Institute, 3650 Willingdon Avenue, Burnaby British Columbia V5G 3H1 Canada.

UK
AUDIO VISUAL MAGAZINE. (19??)-. English. Twelve times a year. £33.00 UK; £50.00 other. EMAP Readerlink, Audit House, 260 Field End Road, Ruislip Middlesex HA4 9LT United Kingdom. **Tel** 011 44 1773 63100, FAX 011 44 1733 87367. **Continues** Computer Images.

NE
TITLE CHANGE
AUDIO VISUEEL MAGAZINE. (19??)-(19??). Dutch. AV Press BV, Postbus 155, 6500 AD Nijmegen Netherlands. **Tel** 011 31 80 787444. **Continued by** AV, 0169-0256.

LC TR
DD 770
ISSN 1320-6672
AT
TITLE CHANGE
AUSTRALIAN CAMERA AND SHOOTING VIDEO. See Photography.

LC TR
DD 770.994
ISSN 1039-7949
AT
●**AUSTRALIAN CAMERA, PHOTO, VIDEO, DIGITAL. See** Photography.

ISSN 1031-5462
AT
AUSTRALIAN FILM DATA. See Motion Picture.

UK
●**AV MAGAZINE.** (1995)-. English. Twelve times a year. £45.00. EMAP Business Publishing Ltd., 260 Field End Road, Audit House, Ruislip Middlesex HA4 9LT United Kingdom. **Tel** 011 44 181 9563000, FAX 011 44 181 4293117. **Continues** Audio Visual.
Desc: Promotes the effective use of audio-visual techniques, and advises users on the equipment, materials and services available to them.

LC TK7881.4 .A97
DD 621.388/33/05
ISSN 0747-1335
US
CCC
AVIDEO. (AV VIDEO.). [AV video]. **VFOAT** A.V. Video. **VAT** Audiovideo Video. Vol. 6, No. 2 (Feb. 1984)-. Periodical. English. Twelve times a year. $53.00. Knowledge Industry Publications Inc, 701 Westchester Avenue, White Plains NY 10604. **Tel** (914)328-9157, (800)800-5474, FAX (914)328-9093. **ED** Phil Kurz. Index available. **Ad Acc. Circ:** 60,000 (ctrl) available on microfilm and microfiche from University Microfilms International (UMI). **Continues** Audio Visual Directions, 0746-8989.
Desc: For readers who create or present video, audiovisuals and computer graphics in their professional capacities in business, industry, government, health care and financial and educational institutions.
Ind/Abst Pollut. Abstr. Indexes.

US
BASIC 2 REPORT. (19??)-. English. Six times a year. $24.00. VCR Inc, PO Box 90967, Austin TX 78709. **Tel** (512)892-6115.

LC PN1998 .B46
DD 016.79143/75
ISSN 1076-3783
US
●**BEST FAMILY VIDEOS FOR THE DISCRIMINATING VIEWER, THE.** [Best fam. videos discrim. viewer]. **VFOAT** Family Videos for the Discriminating Viewer; Best Family Videos. (1994)-. English. Every 2 years. Northfield Press, 215 West Locust, Chicago IL 60610.

LC PN1995.9.N4 B52
DD 016.79143/09/093520396073 791
ISSN 0882-7532
US
BLACK VIDEO GUIDE, THE. See Motion Picture.

LC HD9697.V543 U517
ISSN 1068-6363
US
BLUE BOOK (WHITE PLAINS, N.Y.). (THE BLUE BOOK.). [Blue book]. (19??)-. English. Irregular. Knowlege Industry Publications, 701 Westchester Avenue, White Plains NY 10604.

ISSN 0841-2545
DD 384/.029/471
CN
BROADCAST PRODUCT NEWS. See Communications-Telecommunication.

ISSN 0842-0165
DD 791.43
CN
BULLETIN DE L'ALLIANCE DE LA VIDEO ET DU CINEMA INDEPENDANT. See Motion Picture.

LC TR845
DD 778.5990285416
ISSN 1357-0633
UK
●**BUSINESS VIDEO. See** Computers-Computer Graphics and Design.

LC TK9960 .B89
DD 621.388
US
BUYERS GUIDE & TEST ANNUAL. VFOAT Buyers Guide and Test Annual. **VAT** Buyers Guide and Test Annual. (1987)-. English. Irregular. $3.95. Video Magazine, 460 West 34th Street, New York NY 10001. **Continues** Video Magazine ... Buyer's Guide & Test annual.

UK
CAMCORDER USER. (1988)-. English. Twelve times a year. $94.11. WV Publications, 57-59 Rochester Place, London NW1 9JU United Kingdom. **Tel** 011 44 171 4850101.

LC TR882 .C36
DD 778.59/9
ISSN 1048-8804
US
CAMCORDER (VENTURA, CALIF.). (CAMCORDER.). [Camcorder]. (Dec. 1989)-. Periodical. English. Six times a year. $23.00. Miller Magazines Inc, 4880 Market Street, Ventura CA 93003. **Tel** (805)664-3824, FAX (805)664-3875. **Continues** Camcorder Report, 1047-8787.

US
●**CATALOG OF CAPTIONED EDUCATIONAL VIDEOS AND FILMS. See** Education-Special Education and Rehabilitation.

ISSN 0895-2094
DD 791
US
CHILDREN'S VIDEO REVIEW NEWSLETTER. [Child. video rev. newsl.]. **VFOAT** Children's Video Review; CVR. Vol. 1, No. 1 (Apr./May 1987)-. Newsletter. English. Six times a year. $36.00. Children's Video Review Newsletter, 16765 Lena Court, Grass Valley CA 95949. **Tel** (916)273-7471, FAX (916)273-6542. **ED** Eveline Carsman. cum. index. ctrl circ.
Desc: Reviews of 15-20 newly released videocassettes for pre-school to middle-school children. Videos are selected for educational, literary and recreational use. Videos comply with public and school library standards.

LC LB1043.2.C2 Z92
DD 017/.5/09714
ISSN 0706-2257
CN
CHOIX: DOCUMENTATION AUDIOVISUELLE. Added/Corp Quebec (Province). Centrale des Bibliotheques. (1978)-. French. One time a year. 32.01Can$. Services Documentaires Multimedia Inc, 75 rue de Port-Royal, Suite 300, Montreal Quebec H3L 3T1 Canada. **Tel** (514)382-0895, FAX (514)384-9139. Index available. cum. index. **Bk Rev.**
Circ: 400 (ctrl). available on microfiche.
Desc: Lists and analyzes audiovisual materials, mostly of a documentary nature for all ages and types of audiences.

ISSN 0895-805X
DD 791
US
CINEVUE. (CINEVUE : A PUBLICATION OF ASIAN CINEVISION.). [CineVue]. **Added/Corp** Asian CineVision (Organization). **VFOAT** Cine Vue. Vol. 1, No. 1 (April 1986)-. Periodical. English. Four times a year. $20.00. Asian Cinevision Inc, 32 East Broadway, New York NY 10002. **Tel** (212)925-8685. **ED** Bill J. Gee. **Bk Rev. Ad Acc. Circ:** 16,000.
Desc: Focuses on Asian American media arts. Contains news reports, features on filmmakers and video artists, and reviews of new and important works.

ISSN 1061-4850
DD 011
US
COMPLETE GUIDE TO SPECIAL INTEREST VIDEOS, THE. [Complete guide spec. interest videos]. (1991)-. English. James-Robert Publishing, Ontario Commerce Center, 3535 East Inland Empire Boulevard, Ontario CA 91764.

ISSN 1076-7959
DD 004
US
●**COMPUTER VIDEO (FALLS CHURCH, VA.).** (COMPUTER VIDEO.). [Comput. video]. Vol. 1, No. 1 (July/Aug. 1994)-. Periodical. English. Six times a year. J R S Publishing, Inc, 5827 Columiba Pike, 3rd Floor, Falls Church VA 22041. **Tel** (703) 998-7600, FAX (703) 998-2966. **ED** John Spofford. **Ad Acc, Adv Mgr:** Mike Dahle. **Circ:** 50,000.
Desc: Designed to bridge the gap between the converging worlds on professional video and computer systems. Topics covered include computer import/video export, studio production, editing, automation and design.

LC HD9696.T464 C653a
DD 621.388/029/473
ISSN 1059-227X
US
CTL TOTAL VIDEO. See Communications-Television and Cable.

ISSN 1064-2579
DD 791
US
CUE MAGAZINE. (CUE MAGAZINE : NORTHERN CALIFORNIA FILM, VIDEO, TELEVISION PRODUCTION.). [Cue.mag.]. (19??)-. Periodical. English. Twelve times a year. $24.00. Cue Magazine, 1430 Benito Avenue, Burlingame CA 94010. **Tel** (415)348-8004, FAX (415)348-7781. **ED** Pat Henry and Karen Pathmell (editor's address: PO Box 2027 Burlingame CA 94011-2027). **Ad Acc.** ctrl circ.

ISSN 0743-2402
US
CVC VIDEO REPORT. VFOAT C.V.C. Video Report. (1983)-. Periodical. English. Twenty-two times a year (twice a month except Jan. and Aug.). $195.00. Creative Video Consulting, 648 Broadway, New York NY 10012. **Tel** (212)533-9870.

ISSN 0710-1562
DD 018/.137
CN
CVPOP. CENTRE VIDEO POPULAIRE DE LA RIVE-SUD. (CVPOP : REPERTOIRE DES VIDEOGRAMMES / CENTRE VIDEO POPULAIRE DE LA RIVE-SUD.). [CVPOP. Cent. video pop. Rive-Sud]. **Main/Corp** Centre Video Populaire de la Rive-Sud. No. 1-. Periodical. French. Free.

BE
DIFFUSION DES PROGRAMMES AUDIOVISUELS, LA. (19??)-. French. 1100F Belgium and Luxembourg; 320F France; 2200F other. Edimedia ASBL, rue de la Constitution 22, 1030 Brussels Belgium. **Tel** 011 32 2 2180031. **Bk Rev. Ad Acc.**

ISSN 1181-7917
DD 621.388/33/05
CN
TITLE CHANGE
DIGITAL EVOLUTION MAGAZINE. See Communications-Television and Cable.

LC TR899 .D4
DD 778.59
ISSN 1075-251X
US
●**DIGITAL VIDEO MAGAZINE.** [Digit. video mag.]. **VFOAT** Digital Video. (1994)-. Periodical. English. Twelve times a year. $24.97. Tech Media Publishing, Inc, 80 Elm Street, Peterborough NH 03458. **Tel** (603)924-0100, FAX (603)924-0379. **Ad Acc, Adv Mgr:** Michael McGoldrick. **Circ:** 60,000. **Continues** Desktop Video World, 1067-7720.
Desc: Aimed at the merging computer and video markets and is designed for computer users, multimedia producers and videographers. Contains articles on video and computer technology, as well new products available.

UK
DIRECTORY OF EUROPEAN MEDIA REGULATION. See Communications-Television and Cable.

Communications —Video

LC TS2301.A7 A8
DD 621.38/044/0294 2 19
US
●**DIRECTORY OF VIDEO, COMPUTER, AND AUDIO-VISUAL PRODUCTS, THE.** **Added/Corp** International Communications Industries Association. **VFOAT** Directory of Video, Computer, & Audio-Visual Products. 38th Ed. (1993)-. Directory. English. One time a year. $77.50. International Communications Industries, 3150 Spring Street, Fairfax VA 22031-2399. **Tel** (703)273-7200, FAX (703)278-8082. **Continues** Equipment Directory of Video, Computer, and Audio-Visual Products.

LC HD9697.V543 U5244
DD 381/.45621388332/02573
ISSN 1053-9069
US
DIRECTORY OF VIDEO RETAILERS. [Dir. video retail.]. (1991)-. Directory. English. One time a year (June). $180.00. Palm Springs Media Inc, PO Box 2740, Palm Springs CA 92262. **Tel** (619)322-3050.

LC HD9697.P563 U533
DD 381/.4578149/02573
ISSN 1045-523X
US
... DIRECTORY. RECORDING SERVICE-SOUND AND VIDEO, THE. [Dir., Rec. serv.-sound video]. **Added/Corp** American Business Directories, Inc. **VFOAT** Recording Service-Sound and Video; Recording Service-Sound and Video; Directory of Recording Service-Sound and Video. (19??)-. English. Irregular. American Business Directories, Box 27347, 5711 South 86th Street, Omaha NE 68127. **Tel** (402)593-4600, FAX (402)331-1505.

LC LB1044.Z9 E37
DD 011/.37
ISSN 0000-135X
US
EDUCATIONAL FILM & VIDEO LOCATOR OF THE CONSORTIUM OF COLLEGE AND UNIVERSITY MEDIA CENTERS AND R. R. BOWKER. [Educ. film video locator Consort. Coll. Univ. Media Cent. R. R. Bowker]. **Added/Corp** Consortium of College and University Media Centers. R.R. Bowker Company. **VFOAT** Educational Film and Video Locator of the Consortium of College and University Media Centers and R.R. Bowker; Educational Film & Video Locator. 4th Ed. (1991)-. English. Irregular. $175.00. R.R. Bowker, A Reed Reference Publishing Company, Part of Reed International PLC, PO Box 31, 121 Chanlon Drive, New Providence NJ 07974. **Tel** (908)464-6800, (800)521-8110, FAX (908)665-6688, telex 138-755. **Continues** Educational Film/Video Locator of the Consortium of University Film Centers and R.R. Bowker, 0000-0973.
Desc: Union listing of videos and films. Indexes some 52,000 videos and films available for rental from the 46 Consortium media centers.

LC LB1043.Z9 E34 LB1044.75.Z9 E34
DD 371.3/07/8
ISSN 1068-9206
US
EDUCATORS GUIDE TO FREE VIDEOTAPES. [Educ. guide free videotapes]. **Added/Corp** Educators Progress Service. **VFOAT** Guide to Free Videotapes; Educators Guide to Free Audio and Video Materials. 39th Ed. (1992)-. English. One time a year. $32.95. Educators Progress Service Inc., 214 Center Street, Randolph WI 53956. **Tel** (414)326-3126. **Continues in part** Educators Guide to Free Audio and Video Materials, 0160-1296.

ISSN 1191-2286
DD J054/.1
CN
EN PRIMEUR JEUNE S. [En primeur jeune S]. **VFOAT** En Primeur Jeunesse. Vol. 1, No. 1 (1991)-. Periodical. French. Four times a year (Jan., Apr., July, Oct.). 12.00Can$ Canada; 18.00Can$ others. Tribute Publishers Inc., 900A Don Mills Road, Suite 1000, Don Mills Ontario M3C 1V6 Canada. **Tel** (816)445-0544, FAX (816)445-2894. **ED** Sandra Stewart. **Ad Acc. Circ:** 50,000 (ctrl).
Desc: Movies and video stories for kids aged 8 to 12 years old.

ISSN 1055-2839
DD 384
US
EUROPEAN HOME VIDEO. [Eur. home video]. No. 1 (Jan. 22, 1991)-. Newsletter. English. Twelve times a year. $595.00. Kagan World Media Inc., 126 Clock Tower Place, Carmel CA 93923-8734. **Tel** (408)624-1536, FAX (408)625-3225. **(Subscription address:** Kagan World Media Ltd., 524 Fulham Road, London SW6 5NR United Kingdom. **Tel** 011 44 171 3718880, FAX 011 44 171 3718715.) available via fax.
Desc: Analysis of the economics of the business, the revenues of the industry, the hardware growth and software distribution, retail updates, rentals and sales.

UK
EUROPEAN HOME VIDEO DATABOOK. (19??)-. English. One time a year. $445.00. Kagan World Media Inc., 126 Clock Tower Place, Carmel CA 93923-8734. **Tel** (408)624-1536, FAX (408)625-3225. **(Subscription address:** Kagan World Media Ltd., 524 Fulham Road, London SW6 5NR United Kingdom. **Tel** 011 44 171 3718880, FAX 011 44 171 3718715.)
Desc: Contains market analysis in European countries - includes industry projections for retail revenue, supplier revenue, VCR and TV households and VCR penetration as well as insights on window release times, censorship, and the development of pay TV.

ISSN 0950-737X
DD 778.53
UK
Pr Rev.
EYEPIECE. (EYEPIECE : JOURNAL OF THE GUILD OF BRITISH CAMERA TECHNICIANS.). [Eyepiece]. (1978)-. Trade Publication. English. Six times a year. $59.89. Guild of British Camera Technicians, 5-11 Taunton Road/Metro Centre, Greenford Middlesex UB6 8UQ United Kingdom. **Tel** 011 44 181 5789243, FAX 011 44 181 5755972. **ED** Charles Hewitt and Kerry Anne Burrows. Index available. cum. index. **Ad Acc, Adv Mgr:** Ron Bowyer, **Tel** 081 464 6738. **Acid Free. Circ:** 3,500-5,000 (ctrl). **Continues** Eyepiece/GBCT News.
Desc: Movies and cinefilm and video making films, commercials, pop promotions, etc.
Ind/Abst Film Lit. Index (19??-).

LC N6512.5 V53 .F45
US
Pr Rev.
FELIX. See The Arts.

LC LB1044.Z9 F58
DD 011
ISSN 0898-1582
US
NLM LB 1044; F487
FILM & VIDEO FINDER. [Film video finder]. **Added/Corp** National Information Center for Educational Media. **VFOAT** Film Video Finder; NICEM Film and Video Finder; NICEM Film & Video Finder. 1st Ed. (1987)-. English. One time a year. Price varies per volume. Plexus Publishing Inc., 143 Old Marlton Pike, Medford NJ 08055. **Tel** (609)654-6500, FAX (609)654-4309. **ED** J. C. Johnstone, Patricia Smith and Camille Fullington. **Bk Rev. Circ:** 2,000 (ctrl). available on CD-ROM from SilverPlatter (US). **Formed by the union of** Index to Educational Videotapes, 0734-6921 **and** Index to 16mm Educational Films, 0734-5488.
Desc: Indexes 16mm films and video cassettes of an educational, informational or documentary nature. Gives current information on name and address of producer and distributor. Lists 90,000 films or videotapes.

LC PN1993.5.C2 F55
DD 015.71037
ISSN 0836-1002
CN
FILM/VIDEO CANADIANA. See Motion Picture.

ISSN 0257-7852
SZ
UDC 791.4
FILMBULLETIN ZURICH. [Filmbulletin Zur.]. (1959)-. Bulletin. German. Six times a year. $62.23. Film Bulletin, Postfach 6887, Ch 8023 Zurich Switzerland. **Tel** 011 41 52 256444.

ISSN 0882-8490
DD 791
US
FILMS/VIDEO. See Motion Picture.

LC TR845
DD 778.5
ISSN 1070-7999
US
FOOTAGE (NEW YORK, N.Y.). See Motion Picture.

ISSN 0214-2244
SP
UDC 77
FV. FOTO-VIDEO ACTUALIDAD. See Photography.

ISSN 0161-9055
US
HOME VIDEO REPORT, THE. (1978)-. Periodical. English. Twenty-four times a year. $95.00. Knowledge Industry Publications Inc, 701 Westchester Avenue, White Plains NY 10604. **Tel** (914)328-9157, (800)800-5474, FAX (914)328-9093. **Continues** Video Publisher, 0300-7057.

ISSN 1191-9795
DD 709.1
CN
IMAGES DU FUTUR. See The Arts-Computer Applications.

LC WMLC 93/5017 HD9697.M68 I5
DD 778
ISSN 0889-6208
US
CCC
TITLE CHANGE
IN MOTION FILM & VIDEO PRODUCTION MAGAZINE. [In motion film video prod. mag.]. **VFOAT** In Motion Film and Video Production Magazine; Film and Video Product in Magazine; In Motion. (198?)-(1995). Trade Publication. English. Phillips Business Information Inc., 1201 Seven Locks Road, PO Box 61130, Potomac MD 20854. **Tel** (301)424-3338, (301)340-1520, (800)777-5005, FAX (301)424-4297, telex 358149. ctrl circ. **Continues** Maryland In Motion Film & Video Production Directory. **Merged into** Film & Video.
Desc: Covers film and video production techniques.

ISSN 1077-8918
DD 791
US
INDEPENDENT FILM & VIDEO, THE. See Motion Picture.

LC LB1043.Z9 I54
DD 011/.37/025
ISSN 1044-3967
US
INDEX TO AV PRODUCERS & DISTRIBUTORS. **Added/Corp** National Information Center for Educational Media. **VFOAT** Index to AV Producers and Distributors. **VAT** Index to Audio Visual Products and Distributors. 7th Ed. (1989)-. English. Every 2 years. $94.00. Plexus Publishing Inc., 143 Old Marlton Pike, Medford NJ 08055. **Tel** (609)654-6500, FAX (609)654-4309. **Continues** Index to Producers & Distributors, 1045-392X.
Desc: Contains over 22,000 producers and distributors of AV materials of all kinds, current and archival. It lists all companies and institutions involved in the production and dissemination of non-print media.

LC HE8700 .I57
DD 384.55/05
ISSN 0895-2213
US
INTERNATIONAL TELEVISION & VIDEO ALMANAC. See Communications-Television and Cable.

LC PN1992 .I57
DD 384.55/4/05
UK
SUSPENDED
INTERNATIONAL TV & VIDEO GUIDE. See Communications-Television and Cable.

US
KAGAN'S THE STATE OF HOME VIDEO. **Added/Corp** Paul Kagan Associates. **VFOAT** State of Home Video. (19??)-. English. Irregular. $495.00. Paul Kagan Associates Inc., 126 Clock Tower Place, Carmel CA 93923-8734. **Tel** (408)624-1536, FAX (408)625-3225, telex ITT 4938124 PKA UI.

UK
KEMPS FILM, TV & VIDEO YEARBOOK. See Communications-Television and Cable.

ISSN 0847-3935
DD 791.43/05
CN
KIDS TRIBUTE. See Children and Youth Interests.

BE
MARCHE MONDIAL DE L'AUDIOVISUEL, LE. (19??)-. French. 60000F Belgium and Luxembourg; 9500F France; 62000F other. Edimedia ASBL, rue de la Constitution 22, 1030 Brussels Belgium. **Tel** 011 32 2 2180031. **Bk Rev. Ad Acc.**

ISSN 1073-8924
US
MARKEE (SANFORD, FLA.). See Motion Picture.

US
MICROCOMPUTER AND VIDEO PURCHASING AND USAGE PLANS ... SCHOOL YEAR : .... ANNUAL TECHNOLOGY SURVEY OF SELECTED U.S. SCHOOL DISTRICTS. See Computers.

LC TK6655.V5 M63
DD 621.388/332
US
MODERN PHOTOGRAPHY'S ... VIDEO GUIDE. **VFOAT** Video Guide. (1987)-. English. Irregular. $3.95. ABC Consumer Magazine, 825 7th Avenue, New York NY 10019. **Tel** (212)887-8469.

LC PN1998 .M65
DD 011/.37/05
US
MOTION PICTURE ANNUAL, THE. See Motion Picture.

LC PN1992.95 .V4945
DD 016.79143/75
ISSN 1051-5488
US
CEASED
MOVIE MARKETPLACE. [Movie marketpl.]. **VFOAT** Movie Market Place; Video Marketplace. Vol. 3, No. 6 (Aug. 1990)-(Jan./Feb. 1995). Periodical. English. Century Publishing Company, 990 Grove Street, Evanston IL 60201-4370. **Tel** (708)491-6440, (800)321-3333, FAX (708)491-0459. **(Subscription address:** Kable Publishers Aide / Illinois, 308 East Hitt Street, Subscription Department, Mt. Morris IL 61054-1473. **Tel** (815)734-1261.) **Continues** Video Marketplace, 0895-2892.
Desc: Features articles, plus 5,000 videos for sale.

LC PN1992.8.F5 M68
DD 016.79143/75
ISSN 1053-5314
US
MOVIES ON TV AND VIDEOCASSETTE. See Communications-Television and Cable.

ISSN 1081-1893
DD 331
US
●**NABET-CWA NEWS.** See Communications-Television and Cable.

ISSN 0846-4065
DD 384.3/54/0601
CN
NEWSLETTER / INTERNATIONAL INTERACTIVE COMMUNICATIONS SOCIETY, TORONTO. [Newsl. - Int. Interact.

Communications — Video

Commun. Soc. Tor.]. **Added/Corp** International Interactive Communications Society. Toronto Chapter. **VFOAT** IICS Toronto Chapter Newsletter. **VAT** International Interactive Communications Society Toronto Chapter Newsletter. (Nov. 1987)-. Newsletter. English. Twelve times a year. fre to members of the International Interactive Communications Society. International Interactive Communications Society / Toronto, c/o C.A.V. Productions Inc, 189 Church Street, Toronto, Ontario M5B 1Y7 Canada.

ISSN 0829-4968
DD 363.1/89 CN

NEWSLETTER - LABOUR COUNCIL OF METROPOLITAN TORONTO. AD HOC COMMITTEE ON VDTS. (NEWSLETTER.). [Newsl. - Labour Counc. Metrop. Tor., Ad Hoc Comm. VDTs]. **Added/Corp** Labour Council of Metropolitan Toronto. Ad hoc Committee on VDTs. **VAT** VDT newsletter; Video display terminals newsletter. (1982)-. Newsletter. English. Four times a year. 5.00Can$. Labour Council of Metropolitan Toronto, Ad hoc Committee on VDT's, Room 407, 15 Gervais Drive, Don Mills, Ontario M3C 1Y8 Canada. **Continues** Health Alert., 0712-3795.

ISSN 0840-3910
DD 791.43/05 CN

NOUVELLES DU VIDEO. See Motion Picture.

ISSN 1056-103X
DD 791 US

OUT IN VIDEO. See The Arts-Performing Arts.

LC PN1993 .P315
DD 791.43/05 IT

PATALOGO. CINEMA + TELEVISIONE + VIDEO, IL. See Motion Picture.

ISSN 1076-4526
DD 384 US
CCC

•**PHILLIPS BUSINESS INFORMATION'S INTERACTIVE VIDEO NEWS.** [Phillips Bus. Inf. interact. video news]. **Added/Corp** Phillips Business Information, Inc. **VFOAT** Interactive Video News. Vol. 2, No. 11 (May 31, 1994)-. Periodical. English. Twenty-five times a year. $597.00. Phillips Business Information Inc., 1201 Seven Locks Road, PO Box 61130, Potomac MD 20854. **Tel** (301)424-3338, (301)340-1520, (800)777-5005, **FAX** (301)424-4297, telex 358149. **Formed by the union of** Video Services News, 1067-3849 and Video Marketing News, 0196-4429; **Absorbed** PayPerViews; On-Demand Video; CableSports.

ISSN 1036-384X
DD 380.1457710994 AT

PHOTO & VIDEO RETAILER. See Photography.

LC HF
DD 381 US

PHOTO TRADE NEWS. See Photography.

ISSN 0227-115X
DD 778.5/349/060714 CN

PLEIN CADRE. [Plein cadre]. **Added/Corp** Association Pour le Jeune Cinema Quebecois. (1979)-. Periodical. French. Twelve times a year. $7.74. Association Pour le Jeune Cinema Quebecois, 1415 Est rue Jarry, Montreal Quebec M2E 2Z7 Canada. **Tel** (514)374-4700. **Supersedes** Debobinons, 0319-5899.

US

PROCEEDINGS. See Computers-Computer Systems.

ISSN 1067-439X
DD 791 US

PRODUCER (PORT WASHINGTON, N.Y.). See Communications-Television and Cable.

ISSN 0261-1910
UK

PROFESSIONAL VIDEO INTERNATIONAL YEARBOOK. 1984/85-. English. One time a year. Link House Publications, 15400 Knoll Trail, Suite 450, Dallas TX 75248. **Tel** (214)233-5156. **Continues** International Video Yearbook.

LC HF **ISSN** 1053-8968
DD 381 US
TITLE CHANGE

PTN (MELVILLE, N.Y.). See Photography.

ISSN 1061-0499
US

RECOMMENDED VIDEOS FOR SCHOOLS. [Recomm. videos sch.]. (1991)-. Periodical. English. $50.00. ABC Clio Inc, PO Box 1911, 130 Cremona, Santa Barbara CA 93116. **Tel** (805)968-1911, (800)422-2546, **FAX** (805)685-9685.

LC PN1995 .E318
DD 791.43/75/05 US
TITLE CHANGE

ROGER EBERT'S MOVIE HOME COMPANION. See Motion Picture.

LC PN1992 .S28 **ISSN** 0732-7668
DD 791.45/75/05 US

SATELLITE ORBIT. See Communications-Television and Cable.

ISSN 0279-201X
US

SMART. **Added/Corp** Society of Audio/Video Consultants. (1987?)-. Periodical. English. Six times a year. SAC Joseph Jerry, PO Box 9197, Palm Springs CA 92263.

LC TK6655.V5 S67 **ISSN** 1148-4322
DD 621.389/3 FR

SON, MUSIQUE, VIDEO MAG. **VFOAT** Son Mag; Son, Musique, Video. (19??)-. Periodical. French. Twelve times a year. EMMPS, 1 boulevard Ney, 75018 Paris France. **Tel** 011 33 1 40360197, **FAX** 011 33 1 40361196. **Continues** Son, Video Magazine, 0765-3530.

LC TK7881.6 .S73
US

STEREO REVIEWS TAPE RECORDING BUYERS' GUIDE. See Sound Recordings and Systems.

LC TK7881.6 .B53 TK7881.6 .B532
DD 621.389/32/0294 US
TITLE CHANGE

TAPE/DISC DIRECTORY / BILLBOARD. See Sound Recordings and Systems.

LC AI3 .T44 **ISSN** 0085-7157
DD 011 US

TELEVISION NEWS INDEX AND ABSTRACTS. See Communications-Abstracting, Bibliographies and Statistics.

LC PN1992 .T47
DD 384.55/4/05 UK

TELEVISUAL. See Communications-Television and Cable.

ISSN 1064-2676
US

TV VIDEO. See Communications-Television and Cable.

LC TR593 .H534 **ISSN** 1018-7928
DD 621.36/7 US

ULTRAHIGH- AND HIGH-SPEED PHOTOGRAPHY, VIDEOGRAPHY, AND PHOTONICS. See Photography.

LC PN1992.95 **ISSN** 1066-8810
DD 384 US

VARIETY'S VIDEO DIRECTORY PLUS. (VARIETY'S VIDEO DIRECTORY PLUS [COMPUTER FILE].). [Var. video dir. plus]. **Added/Corp** R.R. Bowker Company. **VFOAT** Video Directory Plus; Video Directory. (1986)-. Directory. English. Four times a year. $395.00. R.R. Bowker Electronic Publishing, A Reed Reference Publishing Company, Part of Reed International PLC, 121 Chanlon Drive, New Providence NJ 07974. **Tel** (800)323-3288.
Desc: Includes over 88,000 citations with complete, current and reliable video information.

NE

VIDEO & AUDIO REPORT. Dutch. Eleven times a year. Fl81.95. Kern Advertising, Postbus 92, 2040 AB Zandvoort Netherlands. **Tel** 0 2507 19092, **FAX** 0 2507 16002. **Bk Rev**. **Ad Acc**. **Circ**: 5,000 (ctrl).
Desc: Information for the professional and semi-professional video and audio branch.

CN

VIDEO AND FILM CATALOGUE. See Motion Picture.

LC TK6650 .V5 **ISSN** 1046-3860
DD 621.388/332 US

VIDEO & TELEVISION. (VIDEO & TELEVISION BLUEBOOK). [Video televi.]. **Added/Corp** Orion Research Corporation. **VFOAT** Video and Television. (198?)-. English. One time a year (Dec). $129.00. Orion Research Corporation, 14555 North Scottsdale Road, Suite 330, Scottsdale AZ 85260. **Tel** (800)844-0759, (602)951-1114, **FAX** (602)951-1117. **ED** Roger Rohrs. **Continues** Video (San Luis Obispo, Calif.), 0883-5888.
Desc: Hardbound, 320-page book lists and 13,000 video products, with a chart of equivalent models.

LC PN1992 .V53 **ISSN** 0278-5013
DD 384.55/4/05 US

VIDEO AGE INTERNATIONAL. [Video age int.]. **VAT** Videoage International. (19??)-. Trade Publication. English (Spanish, French and Italian). Six times a year. $30.00. TV Trade Media Inc., 216 E 75th Street No. PW, New York NY 10021. **Tel** (212)288-1549, **FAX** (212)734-9033, telex 428669. **ED** DoM Serafini. **Bk Rev**, (Qty: 20-25/yr). **Ad Acc**. **Circ**: 12,000. available on an online database (file 648/Full-Text) from DIALOG.
Desc: Business journal on international TV, broadcasting and production.
Ind/Abst Trade Ind. ASAP [Full Txt.]; Trade Ind. Index [Full Txt.].

LC PN1992.93 .V5 Z692.V52 V45 **ISSN** 1055-0267
DD 384.55/8/05 US
CEASED

VIDEO ANNUAL, THE. [Video annu.]. (1991)-(1994). English. ABC Clio Inc, PO Box 1911, 130 Cremona, Santa Barbara CA 93116. **Tel** (805)968-1911, (800)422-2546, **FAX** (805)685-9685.

FR

VIDEO BROADCAST. (19??)-. French. Eleven times a year. 440.74F France; 570.00F other. Photovision Svc Abonnement, 90 rue de Flandre, 75947 Paris Cedex 19 France. **Tel** 011 33 1 43296370.

LC HD9697.V543 U546 **ISSN** 0279-571X
DD 621.388/33 US

VIDEO BUSINESS. [Video bus.]. Vol. 1, No. 1 (Jan. 1981)-. Periodical. English. One time a week. $70.00. Chilton, 825 7th Avenue, New York NY 10019. **Tel** (212)887-8560.
Ind/Abst Trade Ind. ASAP [Full Txt.]; Trade Ind. Index [Full Txt.].

UK

VIDEO CAMERA. (19??)-. English. Twelve times a year. $40.00 US and Canada. IPC Magazines Ltd., Perrymount Road, Haywards Heath, West Sussex RH16 3DH United Kingdom. **Tel** 011 44 1444 440421, **FAX** 011 44 1444 445599.

ISSN 0896-2871
DD 384 US

VIDEO CHOICE. [Video choice]. Vol. 1, No. 1 (March 1988)-. Periodical. English. Twelve times a year. $24.95 US; $31.75 other. Video Choice, 331 Jaffrey Road, Peterborough NH 03458. **Tel** (603)924-7271. **ED** Deborah Navas. **Ad Acc**.
Desc: A family-oriented home video magazine, reviews and rates at least 80 new videos each month and provides updates on new video equipment.

ISSN 8756-5250
DD 001 SUSPENDED

VIDEO COMPUTING. See Computers-Optical Storage, CD-ROM Applications.

LC N6494.V53 V53
US

VIDEO EIGHTIES MAGAZINE. **VFOAT** Video 80s Magazine; Video Eighties. (198?)-. Periodical. English. Four times a year. San Francisco Video Festival, PO Box 11320, San Francisco CA 94101-7320. **Continues** Video (San Francisco, Calif.).

ISSN 0888-0492
DD 384 US

VIDEO EXTRA. [Video extra]. (April 1986)-. Periodical. English. Twelve times a year. $18.00. Home Viewer Publishers, 121 South 13th Street/2nd Floor, Philadelphia PA 19107. **Continues in part** Home Viewer.

ISSN 0228-6726
DD 384.55/05 CN
CEASED

VIDEO GUIDE (VANCOUVER). (VIDEO GUIDE.). [Video guide]. Vol. 1, No. 1 (Feb./Mar. 1978)-(19??). Periodical. English. Video Guide, 1102 Homer Street V6B 2X6 Canada. **Tel** (604)688-4336. **ED** Shawn Preus. Index available. cum. index. **Bk Rev**. **Ad Acc**. **Circ**: 200 (ctrl).
Desc: Devoted to continued awareness, appreciation, and development of video and videoarts. International, national, and local issues and events.

LC HD9696.T463 U693 **ISSN** 0730-6180
DD 338.7/621388/02573 US

VIDEO INDUSTRY DIRECTORY. [Video ind. dir.]. (1981)-. Directory. English. One time a year. Reese Publishing Company Inc, 460 West 34th Street, New York NY 10001. **Tel** (212)947-6500.

LC PN1992.95 .V492 **ISSN** 1059-2245
DD 016.79145/75 US

VIDEO INK. [Video Ink]. (Jan/Feb 1991)-. Periodical. English. Irregular. $30.00. Dunton Campbell Press, PO Box 990, Kenosha WI 53141. **Tel** (414)654-7727.

ISSN 1046-0837
US

VIDEO INSIDER. [Video insider]. (1983)-. Periodical. English. One time a week. Video Insider, 223 Conestoga Road, Wayne PA 19087. **Tel** (610)688-7030, **FAX** (215)687-5543.

ISSN 1042-7694
DD 384 US

VIDEO INVESTOR. [Video investor]. **Added/Corp** Paul Kagan Associates. No. 54 (Jan. 31, 1989)-. Newsletter. English. Twelve times a year. $625.00. Paul Kagan Associates Inc., 126 Clock Tower Place, Carmel CA 93923-8734. **Tel** (408)624-1536, **FAX** (408)625-3225,

telex ITT 4938124 PKA UI. available via fax. ***Continues*** *VCR Letter, 8755-9927.*
Desc: Looks inside the business of renting and selling video cassettes. Estimates of retail and wholesale transactions and inventories.

LC Z692.V52 V52 **ISSN** 0887-6851
DD 025 US
VIDEO LIBRARIAN, THE. [Video libr.]. Vol. 1, No. 1 (March 1, 1986)-. Newsletter. English. Six times a year. $47.00. Video Librarian, PO Box 2725, Bremerton WA 98310. **Tel** (360)377-2231, FAX (360)692-7608. **ED** Randy Pitman. Index available (Nov.). **Bk Rev**, (Qty: 10 or less). **Circ:** 750.
Desc: Articles and news on the subject of video in public schools and libraries. Reviews approximately 100 videos per issue.

LC TK6630.A1 V49 **ISSN** 1044-7288
DD 778.59/9/05 US
CCC
VIDEO MAGAZINE. [Video mag.]. **VFOAT** Video. Vol. 11, No. 6 (Sept. 1987)-. Periodical. English. Ten times a year. $18.00. Hachette Magazines Inc., 1633 Broadway, New York NY 10019. **Tel** (212)767-6000. **(Subscription address:** Kable Publishers Aide / Illinois, 308 East Hitt Street, Subscription Department, Mt. Morris IL 61054-1473. **Tel** (815)734-1261.**)** available on microfilm and microfiche from University Microfilms International (UMI). Documents available from UMI Article Clearinghouse. ***Continues*** *Video, 0147-8907.*
Ind/Abst Abr. Read. Guide Period. Lit.; Acad. Abstr. Full Text Elite; Acad. Abstr.; Acad. Search; EP Collect.; Gen. Period. Index (1989-); Homework Help.; Mag. Artic. Summar. Elite; Mag. Artic. Summar. Select; Mag. Artic. Summar. CD-ROM; Mag. Index Plus (1989-); Mag. Index. Sel. (1989-); MasterFile FullTEXT 1000; MasterFile FullTEXT 350; MasterFile FullTEXT 650; MasterFile FullTEXT (July 1989-); Newsp. Period. Abstr. (1986-); OCLC; Pub. Lib. FullTEXT; Read. Guide Abstr. Select Ed.; Read. Guide Period. Lit.; Telebase; Mag. Index (1989-); Vocat. Search.

LC TK9960 .V536
DD 621.388/332/05 IT
VIDEO MAGAZINE. Vol. 1, No. 1 (Sept. 1981)-. Periodical. Italian (Italian). Twelve times a year. 27.000.

LC TK9961 .V54 **ISSN** 1070-2709
DD 621.388/33/05 US
VIDEO MAGAZINE SPECIAL BUYER'S GUIDE & TEST ANNUAL. [Video mag. spec. buy. guide test annu.]. **VFOAT** Buyer's Guide & Test Annual; Buyer's Guide and Test Annual; Video Magazine Buyer's Guide & Test Annual; Video Special. (19??)-. English. Irregular. Video Magazine, 460 West 34th Street, New York NY 10001. ***Separated from*** *Video Magazine Special, 0887-557X.*

ISSN 0836-6055
DD 381/.4579143/05 CN
VIDEO MARKETING. [Video mark.]. (1986)-. Trade Publication. English. Eight times a year. Video Marketing / US, 1680 Vine Street/Suite 820, Hollywood CA 90028. **Tel** (310)462-6350. **ED** Larry Anklewicz.

LC TK6655.V5 V53
US
TITLE CHANGE
VIDEO MARKETING NEWS. Vol. 11, No. 19 (Oct. 15, 1990)-(1994). Periodical. English. Phillips Business Information Inc., 1201 Seven Locks Road, PO Box 61130, Potomac MD 20854. **Tel** (301)424-3338, (301)340-1520, (800)777-5005, FAX (301)424-4297, telex 358149. available on an online database (files 570,636,648/Full-Text) from DIALOG. ***Continues*** *Video Marketing Newsletter, 0196-4429;* ***Absorbed*** *VideoNews International; Home Video Publisher.* ***Merged with*** *Video Services News, 1067-3849* ***to form*** *Phillips Business Information's Interactive Video News, 1076-4526.*
Ind/Abst Mark. Advert. Ref. Serv. [Full Txt.]; PTS Newsl. Database [Full Txt.]; Trade Ind. ASAP [Full Txt.]; Trade Ind. Index [Full Txt.].

LC HD9696.T463 U695 **ISSN** 0740-4247
DD 381/.45621388332 US
VIDEO MARKETING SURVEYS AND FORECASTS. [Video mark. surv. forecasts]. Vol. 1, No. 1 (Sept. 1983)-. Periodical. English. Twelve times a year. $4,500.00. Video Marketing / US, 1680 Vine Street/Suite 820, Hollywood CA 90028. **Tel** (310)462-6350. **ED** Steve Rosen. cum. index.
Desc: Provides between 300 and 400 capsule market surveys and forecasts in the form of charts, graphs, tables, lists and diagrams. Areas of coverage include home video, cable TV, computers, computer software, video games, satellites, broadcasting, motion pictures and consumer electronics.

ISSN 0888-9538
DD 384 US
CCC
VIDEO MONITOR (SILVER SPRING, MD.). (VIDEO MONITOR.). [Video monit.]. Vol. 4 No. 6 (June 1986)-. Periodical. English. Twelve times a year. $98.00 individuals, $108.00 institutions. Communication Research Associates Inc., 10606 Mantz Road, Silver Spring MD 20903-1228. **Tel** (301)445-3230, FAX (301)314-9981.

ISSN 1063-5106
DD 791 US
CEASED
VIDEO MOVIES (BREMERTON, WASH.). (VIDEO MOVIES.). [Video movies]. Vol. 1, No. 1 (July 1992)-(Oct. 1993). Periodical. English. Video Librarian, PO Box 2725, Bremerton WA 98310. **Tel** (360)377-2231, FAX (360)692-7608. **ED** Randy Pisman. Index available (Jan./Feb. iss.). **Circ:** 215.
Desc: Critical reviews of forthcoming video movie releases for libraries and collectors, with information on stars, original production date for theaters or TV, price, distributor, and potential audience.

ISSN 0738-7563
US
VIDEO NETWORKS. [Video netw.]. **Added/Corp** Bay Area Video Coalition (San Francisco, Calif.). (19??)-. Periodical. English. Six times a year. $20.00. Bay Area Video Coalition, 1111 17th Street, San Francisco CA 94107. **Tel** (415)861-3282, FAX (415)861-4316. **ED** Sally Jo Fifer. **Bk Rev**. **Ad Acc. Circ:** 8,000 (ctrl).
Desc: Covers funding, festival, distribution and exhibition opportunities for independent video artists and producers. It also funds reviews, artist profiles and articles on production.

ISSN 8755-7290
DD 384 US
VIDEO NOW. [Video now]. Vol. 1, No. 1 (Nov. 1984)-. Periodical. English. Twelve times a year. $12.00 US; $15.00 Canada. Video Now, PO Box 1470 Murray Hill Station, New York NY 10016.

LC PN1992.95 .V5 **ISSN** 0272-1236
DD 381/.4579143/029573 US
VIDEO PROGRAMS INDEX, THE. [Video programs index]. 1st- Ed.; 1976-. English. One time a year. Video Programs Index, 15 Madison Avenue, Summit NJ 07901.

LC TK6655.V5 V5374 **ISSN** 0887-3836
DD 338.4/7/77859 US
CEASED
VIDEO REGISTER AND TELECONFERENCING RESOURCES DIRECTORY, THE. 9th Ed. (1987)-12th Ed. Directory. English. Knowledge Industry Publications Inc, 701 Westchester Avenue, White Plains NY 10604. **Tel** (914)328-9157, (800)800-5474, FAX (914)328-9093. ***Formed by the union of*** *Teleconferencing Resources Directory, 0739-2966* ***and*** *Video Register, 0190-3705.*

UK
VIDEO RETAILER. (19??)-. Periodical. English. Twelve times a year. £24.00 UK; £31.00 other. Link House Magazines Ltd., Link House, Dingwall Avenue, Croydon, Surrey CR9 2TA United Kingdom. **Tel** 011 44 181 6862599, FAX 011 44 181 7600973, telex 947709. **(Subscription address:** Link House Magazines Ltd., 120-126 Lavendar Avenue, Mitcham Surrey CR4 3HP United Kingdom. **Tel** 011 44 181 6466672.**)**

ISSN 0196-8793
US
VIDEO REVIEW (NEW YORK, N.Y.). (VIDEO REVIEW.). [Video rev.]. Vol. 1 (April 1980)-. Periodical. English. Eight times a year. $15.97 US; $27.80 Canada; $37.80 other. Media Works Group, 271 North Avenue, Suite 318, New Rochelle NY 10801. **Tel** (914)576-8800, (914)576-8815. **(Subscription address:** Neodata / Colorado, PO Box 2606, Boulder CO 80322. **)** available on microfilm and microfiche from University Microfilms International (UMI). Documents available from UMI Article Clearinghouse.
Ind/Abst Acad. Abstr. Full Text Elite; Acad. Abstr.; Acad. Search; EP Collect.; Gen. Period. Index (1989-); Homework Help.; INFO-SOUTH Abstr.; Mag. Artic. Summar. Elite; Mag. Artic. Summar. Select; Mag. Artic. Summar. CD-ROM; Mag. Index Plus (1989-); Mag. Index. Sel. (1989-); Mag. Search; MasterFile FullTEXT 1000; MasterFile FullTEXT 350; MasterFile FullTEXT 650; MasterFile FullTEXT (Jan. 1993-); Newsp. Period. Abstr. (1988-); OCLC; Pop. Period. Index; Pub. Lib. FullTEXT; Read. Guide Period. Lit.; Resource/One Ondisc (1988-); Telebase; Mag. Index (1989-).

ISSN 0838-9586
DD 778.59/9/05 CN
VIDEO SCENE (1987). (VIDEO SCENE.). [Video scene (1987)]. Vol. 7, No. 3 (Dec. 1987)-. Periodical. English. Six times a year. $10.00. Video Science, 5th Floor/6 Adelaide Street East, Toronto Ontario M5C 1H6 Canada. ***Continues*** *Video Scene & Electronics, 0834-373X.*

ISSN 1067-3849
DD 384 US
CCC
TITLE CHANGE
VIDEO SERVICES NEWS / PHILLIPS BUSINESS INFORMATION, INC. [Video serv. news]. **Added/Corp** Phillips Business Information, Inc. (1993)-(June 1994). Periodical. English. Phillips Business Information Inc., 1201 Seven Locks Road, PO Box 61130, Potomac MD 20854. **Tel** (301)424-3338, (301)340-1520, (800)777-5005, FAX (301)424-4297, telex 358149. ***Merged with*** *Video Marketing News, 0196-4429* ***to form*** *Phillips Business Information's Interactive Video News, 1076-4526.*

ISSN 1057-8250
DD 384 US
TITLE CHANGE
VIDEO SHOPPER. [Video shopp.]. (1991)-(199?). Periodical. English. Reese Communications Inc., 460 West 34th Street, New York NY 10001. **Tel** (212)947-6500. ***Merged into*** *Movie Collectors World.*

ISSN 1046-607X
DD 791 US
VIDEO SOFTWARE MAGAZINE. [Video softw. mag.]. **VFOAT** VSM. (198?)-. Periodical. English. Twelve times a year. $60.00. Chilton, 825 7th Avenue, New York NY 10019. **Tel** (212)887-8560. ***Continues*** *Video Software Dealer, 0894-3001.*

LC PN1992.95 .V52 **ISSN** 0748-0881
DD 011/.37 US
NLM LB 1044.7; V652
VIDEO SOURCE BOOK, THE. [Video source book]. **Added/Corp** National Video Clearinghouse. 1st. Ed. (1979)-. Directory. English. $260.00. Gale Research Inc., 835 Penobscot Building, 645 Griswold Street, Detroit MI 48226. **Tel** (800)877-GALE, (313)961-2242, FAX (313)961-6083, (800)414-5043, telex TWX 810-221-7086. **ED** Julia C. Furtaw. **Ad Acc.** available on magnetic tape; available on diskette.
Desc: Over 91,000 entries describe 130,000 currently available video programs in all areas of entertainment, education, culture, medicine, and business. Up to twenty points of information given for each video in an easy-to-read entry and page format. Listings indicate how the title may be acquired and the name, address, and phone number of the distributor is given for each video. A separate section of the directory provides a complete listing of the name, address, and telephone numbers for 2,500 distributors.

LC HD9697.V543 U55 **ISSN** 0195-1750
DD 381/.4562138833 US
VIDEO STORE. [Video store]. (1979)-. Trade Publication. English. One time a week. $62.00. Advanstar Communications Inc., 131 West First Street, Duluth MN 55802. **Tel** (218)723-9477, (800)346-0085, FAX (218)723-9437. **(Subscription address:** Advanstar / Minnesota, 131 West First Street, Duluth MN 55802. **) ED** Frank Moldstad, Charles Orton, Van Wallach and Kathleen Wakeman. Index available. **Ad Acc. Circ:** 40,000 (ctrl). available on an online database (files 16,570/Full-Text) from DIALOG.
Desc: For retailers of prerecorded videotapes, videodiscs, blank tapes and accessories. An aid in solving retail business problems such as inventory management, product buying and competitive stances.
Ind/Abst Bus. Source Plus; Bus. Source; EP Collect.; F&S Index Plus Text, Int. [Full Txt.] [Select. Cov.]; Homework Help.; Mark. Advert. Ref. Serv. [Full Txt.]; MasterFile FullTEXT 1000; MasterFile FullTEXT 350; MasterFile FullTEXT 650; MasterFile FullTEXT (Jan. 1995-); OCLC; PROMT [Full Txt.]; Telebase.

LC PN1992.95 .V48
DD 791.43/75/0953 GW
VIDEO (STUTTGART, GERMANY). (VIDEO.). (19??)-. Periodical. German. Twelve times a year. $90.00. Vereinigte Motor Verlag GmbH, Motor Presse, POB 106036, D-70049 Stuttgart Germany. **Tel** 011 49 711 1821506, 011 49 711 1821545. **(Subscription address:** German Language Publications Inc., 153 South Dean Street, Englewood NJ 07631. **Tel** (201)871-1010, (800)457-4443.**)**

LC TK6680 .V53 **ISSN** 0361-0942
DD 384.55/5/05 US
CCC
VIDEO SYSTEMS. [Video syst.]. **Added/Corp** Intertec Publishing Corporation. Vol. 1 (Nov./Dec. 1975)-. Trade Publication. English. Twelve times a year. $49.41. Intertec Publishing Corporation, 9800 Metcalf, Overland Park KS 66212. **Tel** (913)341-1300. **(Subscription address:** Intertec Publishing Corporation, PO Box 2901, Overland Park KS 66282. **Tel** 800 441-0294.**) ED** David Hodes. **Ad Acc. Circ:** 21,000 (ctrl).
Desc: Covers the corporate video production with a how-to editorial approach; discusses production techniques, new technologies and industry developments. Targets video professionals at production and post-production facilities, and at in-house corporate video production departments.
Ind/Abst Educ. Technol. Abstr.

ISSN 1040-2772
DD 384 US
CCC
VIDEO TECHNOLOGY NEWSLETTER. [Video technol. newsl.]. Vol. 1, No. 1 (Sept. 26, 1988)-. Newsletter. English. Twenty-five times a year. $595.00 US; $630.00 other. Phillips Business Information Inc., 1201 Seven Locks Road, PO Box 61130, Potomac MD 20854. **Tel** (301)424-3338, (301)340-1520, (800)777-5005, FAX (301)424-4297, telex 358149. available on an online database (file 636/Full-Text) from

DIALOG. **Absorbed in part** Home Media Technology News; **Absorbed** Advanced Technology Newsletter **and** HDTV Report.

LC TK6650 .V49   **ISSN** 0736-2587
DD 621.388/3/0294   US
VIDEO TEST ANNUAL AND BUYER'S GUIDE. Periodical. English. One time a year. $3.95. Video Magazine, 460 West 34th Street, New York NY 10001. **Continues** Video. Buyer's Guide, 0731-0846.

ISSN 1075-8704
DD 791   US
VIDEO TOASTER USER. [Video Toaster user]. **VFOAT** VTU. (1992)-. Periodical. English. Twelve times a year. $36.00. AVID Publications, 273 North Mathilda Avenue, Sunnyvale CA 94086. **Tel** (408)774-6770, FAX (408)774-6783. **ED** Jim Plant. **Ad Acc. Adv Mgr.** Mark Holland. **Circ:** 30,000 **Continues** Bread Box.
Desc: Magazine providing coverage of the video production industry, with particular emphasis on the Video Toaster desktop video system.

ISSN 1070-9991
DD 791.43   US
VIDEO WATCHDOG. See Motion Picture.

ISSN 0196-5905
US
CCC
VIDEO WEEK. [Video week]. Vol. 1 (Feb. 4, 1980)-. Trade Publication. English. One time a week. $850.00. Warren Publishing, Inc., 2115 Ward Court Northwest, Washington DC 20037. **Tel** (202)872-9200, FAX (202)293-3435. **ED** David Lachenbruch. available on an online database (files 16,636/Full-Text) from DIALOG.
Desc: Covers cable TV, subscription TV, satellite-to-home broadcasting, videocassettes, videodiscs, videogames and home computer entertainment.
Ind/Abst PROMT [Full Txt.]; PTS Newsl. Database [Full Txt.].

ISSN 0277-3481
US
VIDEO X. (19??)-. Periodical. English. Twelve times a year. Video X, 300 West 43rd Street/Suite 601, New York NY 10036.

ISSN 1035-9508
DD 778.59905   AT
VIDEOCAMERA AND ELECTRONIC IMAGING. [Videocamera and electron. imaging]. (1991)-. Periodical. English. Twelve times a year. 48.51Aus$. Video Camera, PO Box 874, Mona Vale NSW 2103 Australia. **Tel** 011 61 2 9795977, FAX 011 61 2 992016.

LC PN1993.5.L3 V53   MX
VIDEOGRAFIA LATINOAMERICANA.
Added/Corp Universidad de Guadalajara. Departamento Television y Video. (19??)-. Spanish. Irregular. VideoFilVideo, Apartado Postal 39-130, Guadalajara, Jal. 44130, Mexico.

LC TK6630.A1 V53   **ISSN** 0363-1001
DD 621.388/005   US
VIDEOGRAPHY. [Videography]. Vol. 1 (Apr. 1976)-. Trade Publication. English. Twelve times a year. $30.00 (one-year); $50.00 (two-year); $70.00 (three-year) US and Canada. Miller Freeman PSN Inc., 2 Park Avenue, Suite 1820, New York NY 10016. **Tel** (212)213-3444, FAX (212)213-3484. **ED** Brian McKernan. **Bk Rev. Ad Acc. Circ:** 28,000 (ctrl). available on microfilm and microfiche from University Microfilms International (UMI). **Absorbed** Corporate Video Decisions.
Desc: For the video professional. News, analysis, equipment, services, production, technology, interviews and expert commentary.
Ind/Abst EP Collect.; Film Lit. Index; Homework Help.; Index Period. Artic. Relat. Law; MasterFile FullTEXT 1000; MasterFile FullTEXT 350; MasterFile FullTEXT 650; MasterFile FullTEXT; OCLC; Telebase.

LC PN1998 .V45   **ISSN** 0193-9602
DD 016.79145   US
VIDEOLOG : PROGRAMS FOR GENERAL INTEREST AND ENTERTAINMENT, THE. 1979-. English. One time a year. $20.00. Esselte Video, Inc., Order Center, Department 100, PO Box 978, Edison NJ 08817.
Supersedes in part Video Bluebook, 0146-860X.

ISSN 0889-4973
DD 384   US
VIDEOMAKER. [Videomaker]. **VFOAT** Video Maker. Vol. 1, No. 1 (June/July 1986)-. Periodical. English. Twelve times a year. $22.50. Videomaker, PO Box 4591, Chico CA 95927. **Tel** (916)891-8410, FAX (916)891-8443. **ED** Stephen Muratore. **Bk Rev,** (Qty: 12 per month). **Ad Acc. Circ:** 75,000.
Desc: Provides comprehensive coverage of videomaking tools, tips, and techniques for consumers involved with videomaking as a hobby, in business or in education. Complementing its role as a how-to source for video camera enthusiasts, Videomaker addresses the various aspects of the personal-video phenomenon: products, services, trends, and potentials.

ISSN 0164-5862
US
VIDEOPHILE, THE. (197?)-. Periodical. English. Six times a year. $10.00. Videophile, 2003 Apalachees Parkway 312, Tallahassee FL 32301. **Tel** (904)878-5346.

IT
VIDEOTEL INTERNATIONAL REVIEW. (19??)-. Italian. Ten times a year. L30000.00. Edicomp Srl, Via Sannio 79, 00183 Rome Italy. **Tel** 011 39 6 7092444, FAX 011 39 6 77205150. **Ad Acc.**

NE
VIDEOVISIE. Trade Publication. Dutch. Fl100.00 Netherlands; Fl125.00 other. Kabelvisie BV, PB 70486, 1007 KL Amsterdam, The Netherlands. **ED** Jan Boers. Index available. **Bk Rev. Ad Acc. Circ:** 5,000.
Desc: Trade magazine on professional video and and broadcasting technology and trade information.

ISSN 1064-8658
DD 791   US
VISIONS MAGAZINE (BOSTON, MASS.). (VISIONS MAGAZINE : FILM/TELEVISION ARTS.). [Vis. mag.]. (1991)-. Periodical. English. Four times a year (Spring, Summer, Fall, Winter). $45.00 (institutions); $20.00 (individuals). Boston Center for the Arts, 551 Tremont Street, Studio 212, Boston MA 02116. **Tel** (617)695-1360, FAX (617)695-1277. **ED** Marie-France Alderman. **Bk Rev,** (Qty: 4). **Ad Acc. Circ:** 25,000.

LC HD9697.V543 U5493   **ISSN** 1062-8894
DD 381/.45621388332/029473   US
VSDA MEMBERSHIP DIRECTORY. [VSDA membsh. dir.]. **Main/Corp** Video Software Dealers Association. (1991)-. Directory. English. Video Software Dealers Association, PO Box 8500, Philadelphia PA 19178.

LC PN1992.95 .A9
DD 791.43/05   AT
SUSPENDED
WHAT'S ON VIDEO AND CINEMA. Vol. 5, No. 51 (March 1986)-?. Periodical. English. Twelve times a year. $20.00. Video & Cinema Subscriptions, PO Box 1024, Richmond North 3121 Australia. **Tel** (03)429-5599. **Bk Rev. Ad Acc. Circ:** 135,000. **Continues** Australian Video and Cinema.

COMPUTERS

ISSN 0299-5948
FR
01 INFORMATIQUE. ANNUAIRE. See Computers-Computer Industry and Industry Directories.

ISSN 1070-6097
DD 004   US
3X/400 SYSTEMS MANAGEMENT. [3X/400 syst. manag.]. **VFOAT** 3X 400 Systems Management; Systems Management 3X 400; Systems Management 3X/400. (199?)-. Periodical. English. Twelve times a year. $42.00. Hunter Publishing Company Inc., 25 Northwest Point Boulevard, Suite 800, Elk Grove Village IL 60007-1036. **Tel** (708)427-9512, FAX (708)427-2097. **Continues** Systems 3X/400, 1055-7768.

ISSN 0176-8824
GW
64'ER. [64'er]. **VFOAT** Vierundsechziger. (1984)-. Periodical. German. Twelve times a year. $99.03. Verlag Markt & Technik, Hans Pinsel Str 2, W-8013 Haar B Munich Germany. **Tel** 011 49 89 461300, FAX 11 49 89 4613774.

ISSN 1056-2222
DD 651   US
501 (C)OMPUTING NEWS : AN INFORMATION NEWSLETTER SERVING THE 501(C) NON-PROFIT COMMUNITY. [501 (C)omput. news]. **VFOAT** 501 Computing News; 501(C) Computing News; Five O One C Computing News. Vol. 1, No. 1 (1991)-. Newsletter. English. Four times a year. $150.00. Communal Computing, PO Box 6599, Silver Springs MD 20916-6599.

ISSN 0885-4017
US
CCC
A2-CENTRAL. Vol.5, No.1 (Feb. 1989)-. Periodical. English. Twelve times a year. $59.95. Resource Central, Box 11250, Overland Pard KS 66207. **Tel** (913)469-6502. Bound Index published separately, free upon request. **Continues** Open-Apple.
Desc: Information about the Apple II computer.

LC QA76.88   **ISSN** 1064-9409
DD 004   US
ACCESS / NATIONAL CENTER FOR SUPERCOMPUTING APPLICATIONS.
[Access - Natl. Cent. Supercomput. Appl.]. **Added/Corp** National Center for Supercomputing Applications. **VFOAT** National Center for Supercomputing Applications Access. Vol. 1, No. 1 (May/June 1987)-. Periodical. English. Two times a year. Free on request. National Center for Supercomputing Applications, 605 East Springfield Avenue, Champaign IL 61820. **Tel** (217)244-4130. available via Internet (http://www.ncsa.uiuc.edu/Pubs/access/accessDir.html).
Formed by the union of News (National Center for Supercomputing Applications) **and** User Bulletin (National Center for Supercomputing Applications).

ISSN 0254-3133
SZ
CEASED
ACCIS NEWSLETTER. [ACCIS newsl.].
Added/Corp United Nations. Advisory Committee for the Co-ordination of Information Systems. Vol. 1, No. 1 (May 1983)-(Fall 1994). Newsletter. English. ACCIS Newsletter, ACCIS Secretary Palais Nations, 1211 Geneva 10 Switzerland. **Tel** 011 41-22-7988591, FAX 011 41-22-7401269, telex 412962. **Circ:** 1,200. **Continues** IOB Newsletter, 0379-1947.

LC QA76.5 .C617   **ISSN** 0360-0300
DD 651.8   US
CCC
Pr Rev.
ACM COMPUTING SURVEYS. [ACM comput. surv.]. **Main/Corp** Association for Computing Machinery. **Added/Corp** Association for Computing Machinery. **VFOAT** Computing Surveys. **VAT** Association for Computing Machinery Computing Surveys. Vol. 3, No. 2 (June 1971)-. Periodical. English. Four times a year (Mar., June, Sept., Dec.). $115.00. ACM / Association for Computing Machinery, 1515 Broadway, 17th Floor, New York NY 10036. **Tel** (212)869-7440, FAX (212)869-0481. **(Subscription address:** Association for Computing Machinery, PO Box 12114, Church Street Station, New York NY 10249. **Tel** (212)626-0500.) Index available (bound in last issue). available on microfilm and microfiche from University Microfilms International (UMI). Documents available from Article Express International, The Genuine Article, UMI Article Clearinghouse, Ask*IEEE. **Continues** Computing Surveys, 0010-4892.
Ind/Abst ABI/INFORM Glob. Ed.; ABI/INFORM [Computer File] (Dec. 1990-); Abstr. Hum. Comput. Interact. (June 1971-); ACM Guide Comput. Lit.; Appl. Sci. Technol. Index (June 1971-); CompuMath Cit. Index [Full Cov.]; Comput. Abstr. (June 1971-); Comput. Database; Comput. Lit. Index; Comput. Rev. (June 1971-); Curr. Cit.; Curr. Contents Eng. Comput. Technol.; Ei Page One; Eng. Index Annu.; Ergon. Abstr. (June 1971-); Inf. Sci. Abstr. (1987-?); INSPEC (June 1971-); Int. Aerosp. Abstr. (June 1971-); Math. Rev. (June 1971-199?); Res. Alert [Full Cov.]; Sci. Cit. Index; SCISEARCH; Soc. Sci. Cit. Index [Select. Cov.]; Trade Ind. Index (1981-?); UMI ABI/Inform--Bus. Period. Ondisc (Dec. 1990-) [Full Txt.]; Zentralbl. Math. Ihre Grenzgeb. (June 1971-).

US
ACM NO-NONSENSE GUIDE TO COMPUTING CAREERS. See Occupations and Careers.

ISSN 0163-6774
US
Pr Rev.
ACRONYMS. Added/Corp Michigan State University. Computer Laboratory. User Information Center. (19??)-. Newsletter. English. Eight times a year. Free. Michigan State University / Computer Lab User, Information Center, East Lansing MI 48824. **Tel** (517)355-0335. **ED** Marilyn Everingham Stone and Linda Dunn. Index available. cum. index. **Circ:** 3,000.
Desc: Contains site-specific information and general-interest computer articles and lists educational resources.

LC QA75 .A18   **ISSN** 0355-2713
DD 510   FI
CODEN ASMSD7
TITLE CHANGE
ACTA POLYTECHNICA SCANDINAVICA. MATHEMATICS AND COMPUTER SCIENCE SERIES. MA. See Mathematics.

AT
Pr Rev.
AD CYCLE NEWSLETTER. Vol. 1, No. 1 (April 1990)-. Newsletter. English. Twelve times a year. 157.86Aus$. **(Subscription address:** DP Professional Book Service, PO Box 1, Teven New South Wales 2478 Australia. **Tel** 011 61 066 878076.) **ED** Eric Garrigue Vesely. Index available. cum. index. **Bk Rev. Circ:** 20.
Desc: Complete information on AD/Cycle.

US
ADA BUFFET. CD-ROM. (19??)-. English. Irregular. $247.05 US; $250.65 Canada; $300.50 other. Alde Publishing, PO Box 39326, Minneapolis MN 55396.

Computers

Tel (612)474-3755. **(Subscription address:** Islo Tech Inc., PO Box 39326, Edina MN 55439. **Tel** (612)474-3755.**)**

US

ADA JOURNEYMAN. (19??)-. English. $1295.00. Alde Publishing, PO Box 39326, Minneapolis MN 55396. **Tel** (612)474-3755.

US

ADA WHITESANDS. CD-ROM. (19??)-. English. Irregular. $106.55. Alde Publishing, PO Box 39326, Minneapolis MN 55396. **Tel** (612)474-3755. **(Subscription address:** Islo Tech Inc., PO Box 39326, Edina MN 55439. **Tel** (612)474-3755.**)**

ISSN 1073-1016
DD 371 US

●**ADMINISTRATIVE COMPUTING. See** Education-School Management and Organization.

LC QA76 .A3 ISSN 0065-2458
DD 510.78 US
CCC
CODEN ADCOA7
Pr Rev.

ADVANCES IN COMPUTERS. [Adv. comput.]. Vol. 1 (1960)-. Monographic series. English. Irregular. Price varies per volume. Academic Press Inc., 6277 Sea Harbor Drive, Orlando FL 32887. **Tel** (800)543-9534, (407)345-4100, FAX (407)352-3445. **ED** Franz L. Alt. Documents available from Article Express International, The Genuine Article, Ask*IEEE.
Ind/Abst Bioeng. Abstr.; CompuMath Cit. Index [Full Cov.]; Ei Page One; Eng. Index Annu.; INSPEC; Math. Rev.; Res. Alert [Full Cov.]; SCISEARCH; Zentralbl. Math. Ihre Grenzgeb.

LC QA76.27 .A35 ISSN 0741-9341
DD 001.64/05 US
SUSPENDED

ADVANCES IN COMPUTING RESEARCH. [Adv. comput. res.]. Vol. 1 (1983)-(199?). Periodical. English. One time a year. $90.25. JAI Press Inc., 55 Old Post Road, Suite 2, PO Box 1678, Greenwich CT 06836-1678. **Tel** (203)661-7602, FAX (203)661-0792. **ED** Franco Preparata. Documents available from BLDSC.

ISSN 1053-184X
DD 621 US
CCC

ADVANCES IN INFORMATION STORAGE SYSTEMS. [Adv. inf. storage syst.]. Vol. 1 (1991)-. Periodical. English. Irregular. Price varies. American Society of Mechanical Engineers, 22 Law Drive, Fairfield NJ 07007. **Tel** (201)882-1167, (212)705-7722 (editorial).

LC QA76.58 .A39 ISSN 1057-3461
DD 004/.35 US
CEASED

ADVANCES IN PARALLEL COMPUTING (GREENWICH, CONN.). (ADVANCES IN PARALLEL COMPUTING.). [Adv. parallel comput.]. Vol. 1 (1990)-(19??). Periodical. English. JAI Press Inc., 55 Old Post Road, Suite 2, PO Box 1678, Greenwich CT 06836-1678. **Tel** (203)661-7602, FAX (203)661-0792. **ED** David Evans.
Desc: Survey articles of current interest in parallelism and research topics in parallelism, which are constantly appearing and progressing in new directions. Includes and explores topics that have been identified as future research areas.
Ind/Abst Math. Rev.

LC TK5102.5 .A335 ISSN 1058-8957
DD 621.38/043 US

ADVANCES IN STATISTICAL SIGNAL PROCESSING. [Adv. stat. signal process.]. **VFOAT** Estimation. Vol. 1 (1987)-. Statistical Publication. English. $78.75. JAI Press Inc., 55 Old Post Road, Suite 2, PO Box 1678, Greenwich CT 06836-1678. **Tel** (203)661-7602, FAX (203)661-0792. **ED** Vincent Poor.

LC QA75 ISSN 1083-1339
DD 005.43 US

●**AGILITY AND VIRTUAL ORGANIZATION.** (1996)-. Periodical. English. Four times a year. $150.00 US; $174.00 other. John Wiley & Sons, Inc., 605 Third Avenue, New York NY 10158-0012. **Tel** (212)850-6000, (212)850-6645, FAX (212)850-6088, telex 12-7063. **(Subscription address:** John Wiley & Sons, Inc., 605 Third Avenue, New York NY 10158-0012. **Tel** (212)850-6645, FAX (212)850-6021.**)**

ISSN 0738-5978
US
CODEN AGRCE3

AGRICOMP. See Agriculture-Computer Applications.

LC HD9999.M47 A392
US

●**AIIM BUYING GUIDE. Added/Corp** Association for Information and Image Management (U.S.). (1995)-. English. One time a year. $70.75 (nonmembers), $54.00 (members). Association for Information & Image Management, Business Office, 1100 Wayne Avenue/Suite 1100, Silver Spring MD 20910. **Tel** (301)587-8202, FAX (301)587-2711. **Continues in part** AIIM Buying Guide and Membership Directory.

LC HD9999.M47 A39
US
TITLE CHANGE

AIIM BUYING GUIDE AND MEMBERSHIP DIRECTORY : THE INFORMATION MANAGEMENT SOURCEBOOK. Added/Corp Association for Information and Image Management (U.S.). **VFOAT** Information Management Sourcebook. (1994)-(1994). English. Association for Information & Image Management, Business Office, 1100 Wayne Avenue/Suite 1100, Silver Spring MD 20910. **Tel** (301)587-8202, FAX (301)587-2711. **Continues** Information Management Sourcebook, 0897-3199. **Split into** AIIM Buying Guide **and** AIIM Membership Directory.

US

●**AIIM MEMBERSHIP DIRECTORY [COMPUTER FILE]. Added/Corp** Association for Information and Image Management (U.S.). (1995)-. English. Association for Information & Image Management, Business Office, 1100 Wayne Avenue/Suite 1100, Silver Spring MD 20910. **Tel** (301)587-8202, FAX (301)587-2711. **Continues in part** AIIM Buying Guide and Membership Directory.

ISSN 0961-7302
DD 004.165 UK

AMIGA SHOPPER. [Amiga shopp.]. (1991)-. Periodical. English. Twelve times a year. Future Publishing Ltd., Cary Court, Somerton, Somerset TA11 6TB United Kingdom. **Tel** 011 44 1225 442244, FAX 011 44 1225 45827378.

LC QA1 .B7658a ISSN 1010-5433
DD 510 RM
CODEN AUBMDG

ANALELE UNIVERSITATII BUCURESTI. MATEMATICA. See Mathematics-Computer Applications.

RM

ANALELE UNIVERSITATII DIN GALATI. FASCICULA III. See Engineering-Electrical Engineering.

ISSN 1066-8845
DD 004 US
TITLE CHANGE

ANDREW SEYBOLD'S OUTLOOK ON MOBILE COMPUTING. [Andrew Seybold's outlook mob. comput.]. **VFOAT** Outlook on Mobile Computing. (1993)-(1995). Periodical. English. Pinecrest Press, PO Box 917, Brookdale CA 95007. **Tel** (408)338-7701, FAX (408)338-7806. **Merged with** Andrew Seybold's Outlook on Professional Computing, 0895-3821 **to form** Andrew Seybold's Outlook on Communications and Computing, 1080-4056.

ISSN 0738-419X
US

ANNEX COMPUTER REPORT. [Annex comput. rep.]. **Added/Corp** Annex Holdings, Inc. **VFOAT** Computer Report. (19??)-. Periodical. English. Twelve times a year. $775.00. Annex Research, 5110 North 40th Street, Phoenix AZ 85018. **Tel** (602)956-8586, FAX (602)956-8594, telex 156309. **ED** Bob Djurdjevic.
Desc: News & analysis of market trends in the computer industry.

LC KF390.5.C6 C645 ISSN 1052-8350
DD 346 US

ANNUAL COMPUTER LAW INSTITUTE. See Law-Computer Applications.

LC QA76 .I489A ISSN 0098-2431
DD 331.1/142 US

ANNUAL REPORT - THE INSTITUTE FOR CERTIFICATION OF COMPUTER PROFESSIONALS. Main/Corp Institute for the Certification of Computer Professionals. English. One time a year. Institute for the Certification of Computer Professionals, PO Box 1442, Chicago IL 60690.

LC HD9696.C63 B72 ISSN 0101-8477
BL

ANUARIO DE INFORMATICA CWB. **VFOAT** Anuario CWB de Informatica. **VAT** Anuario de Informatica Computerworld do Brasil; Anuario Computerworld do Brasil de Informatica. Portuguese. One time a year. Computerworld do Brasil Servicos e Publicacoes Ltda, rua Alcindo Guanabara, 25/100. Andar 20.031 Rio de Janeiro RJ Brazil. **Tel** (202)452-4200. **Continues** Anuario de Informatica DN.

ISSN 0953-4474
DD 658.054165 UK
TITLE CHANGE

APPLE BUSINESS. [Apple bus.]. (1988)-(19??). Periodical. English. EMAP Readerlink, Audit House, 260 Field End Road, Ruislip Middlesex HA4 9LT United Kingdom. **Tel** 011 44 1773 63100, FAX 011 44 1733 87367. **Absorbed by** Macworld, 0957-2341.
Ind/Abst HILITES.

ISSN 1122-9268
IT

APPLICANDO (CINISELLO BALSAMO). (APPLICANDO.). (1983)-. Periodical. Italian. Eleven times a year. L65400. Gruppo Editoriale JCE SRL, Via Ferri 6, 20092 Cinisello B Milan Italy. **Tel** 011 39 2 660251, FAX 011 39 2 66025343. **ED** Renato Gelforte.
Bk Rev. Ad Acc. Circ: 10,000.
Desc: Magazine devoted to Macintosh environments.

ISSN 0741-0603
DD 622 US

APPLICATION OF COMPUTERS AND OPERATIONS RESEARCH IN THE MINERAL INDUSTRY. See Earth Sciences-Computer Applications.

ISSN 0888-2231
DD 610 US

APPLICATIONS OF COMPUTER SCIENCE SERIES. [Appl. comput. sci. ser.]. (19??)-. Monographic series. English. Price varies per volume. Computer Science Press Inc, 9125 Fall River Lane, Potomac MD 20854. **Tel** (301)251-9050. **ED** Arthur D Friedmann. Index available. ctrl circ.
Desc: This series of text and reference works examines a broad range of applications of computers and computer science from business to architecture.

LC QA1 .A6473 ISSN 0096-3003
DD 519.4/05 US
CCC
NLM W1 AP526 CODEN AMHCBQ
Pr Rev.

APPLIED MATHEMATICS AND COMPUTATION. See Mathematics-Computer Applications.

LC QA76.9.M35 A66 ISSN 0867-857X
DD 004 PL

APPLIED MATHEMATICS AND COMPUTER SCIENCE. Added/Corp Wyzsza Szkola Inzynierska w Zielonej Gorze. Lubuskie Towarzystwo Naukowe. Technical University of Zielona Gora. (199?)-. Periodical. English. Four times a year. $120.00. **(Subscription address:** Ars Polona-Ruch, PO Box 1001, Krakowskie Przedmiescie 7, 00-068 Warsaw Poland. **Tel** 011 48 22 261201.**)**

ISSN 0954-8912
DD 004.09536
UK

ARABIAN BUSINESS COMPUTING. [Arab. bus. comput.]. (1988)-. English. One time a year. $25.67. Information Technology Publishing Company, Angus House, 13 Tilehouse Street HITC, Hertfordshire SG5 2DU United Kingdom. **Tel** 011 44 1462 420785, FAX 011 44 1462 420786.

UK

ARABIAN SYSTEMS GUIDE. (1988)-. Trade Publication. English. One time a year. $15.00. Information Technology Publishing Company, Angus House, 13 Tilehouse Street HITC, Hertfordshire SG5 2DU United Kingdom. **Tel** 011 44 1462 420785, FAX 011 44 1462 420786. **ED** Rob Corder. **Ad Acc, Adv Mgr:** Damon Thomson, **Tel** 44 462 420 205. **Circ:** 12,000 (ctrl).
Desc: Information on computing systems for the Middle East.

ISSN 0961-8414
DD 004 UK

ARCHIMEDES WORLD. [Arch. world]. (1991)-. Periodical. English. Twelve times a year. $99.25. Argus Specialist Publications, Argus House, Boundary Way / Hemel, Hempstead Herts HP27ST United Kingdom. **Tel** 011 44 181 6671033, FAX 011 44 181 6889573, telex 948669 TOPJNL G. **Continues** A & B Computing, 0264-4584.
Desc: Devoted entirely to the Acorn Risc OS Computers. Offers existing and prospective owners new developments on software, plus features, reviews and technical information.

ISSN 1121-2462
IT

UDC 651

ARCHIVI & COMPUTER. [Arch. comput.]. (1991)-. Periodical. Multiple languages. Four times a year. L42580. Archivi Computer, Arc Storico Via Ser Ridolfo 4, 56027 San Miniato PI Italy. **Tel** 011 39 571

400151, FAX 011 39 571 400262. **ED** Roberto Cerri. Index available. **Bk Rev**, (Qty: varies). **Ad Acc**, **Adv Mgr:** Cerri Roberto. **Circ:** 1,300 (ctrl).

GW

•ASPEKTE KOMPLEXER SYSTEME. (1994)-. Monographic series. German. Irregular. DM58.00. F.A. Brockhaus AG, Postfach 100311, 68033 Mannheim Germany. **Tel** 011 0621 390101, FAX 011 0621 3901389.

LC HD9696.S64 A87 **ISSN** 1051-4163
DD 006.5/05 US

ASR NEWS : AUTOMATIC SPEECH RECOGNITON NEWS. See Communications-Computer Applications.

LC TK1 .B425 **ISSN** 8756-2324
DD 621.38/05 US
CCC
NLM W1; AT205D

AT&T TECHNICAL JOURNAL. See Communications-Telecommunication.

LC QA **ISSN** 1040-6034
DD 004 US

ATLANTA COMPUTER CURRENTS. [Atlanta comput. curr.]. **VFOAT** Computer Currents. (1988)-. Periodical. English. Twelve times a year. $15.00. Jaye Communications, 550 Interstate North Parkway, Suite 150, Atlanta GA 30339. **Tel** (404)984-9444, FAX (404)612-0780. **ED** Mike Adkinson. **Ad Acc.**

FR

AU SERVICE DE L' ENSEIGNMENT INFORMATIQUE. (19??)-. French. Editions Creatives, 4 rue des Marguerites, 67850 Herrlisheim France. **Tel** 011 33 88 967731.

LC HE **ISSN** 1039-3994
DD 384.3099405 AT

AUSTRALASIAN EDI REPORT. [Australas. EDI rep]. (1993)-. Periodical. English. Ten times a year. 295.00Aus$. Technosocial Research Services, GPO Box 1240L, Melbourne Victoria 3001 Australia. **Tel** 011 61 3 96021544, FAX 011 61 3 96023216. ***Continues*** *EDI Research Australia, 1034-8360.*

ISSN 1034-4942
AT
Pr Rev.

AUSTRALASIAN JOURNAL OF COMBINATORICS, THE. See Mathematics.

AT

AUSTRALASIAN WHEELS FOR THE MIND. [Australas. wheel. mind]. **Added/Corp** Australasian Apple University Consortium ple Computer Australia Pty. Ltd. (1990)-. English. Two times a year (June, Dec.). 15.00Aus$ Australia and New Zealand; 25.00Aus$ other. Anutech Pty. Limited, GPO Box 4, Canberra ACT 2601 Australia. **Tel** 011 61 6 2492479, FAX 011 61 6 2575088. ***Continues*** *Wings for the Mind, 1032-3805.*

LC QA76 .A86 **ISSN** 0004-8917
DD 651.8/05 AT
CCC
CODEN ACMJB2
Pr Rev.

AUSTRALIAN COMPUTER JOURNAL, THE. [Aust. comput. j.]. **Added/Corp** Australian Computer Society. Vol. 1, No. 1 (Nov. 1967)-. Periodical. English. Four times a year (Feb., May, Aug., Nov.). 41.11Aus$. Australian Computer Society South Australian Branch, GPO Box 2423, Adelaide South Australia, 5001 Australia. **Tel** 011 61 8 2315088. **ED** D. N. Wilson. Index available. **Bk Rev. Ad Acc. Circ:** 12,500 (ctrl). available on microfilm and microfiche from University Microfilms International (UMI). Documents available from Article Express International, The Genuine Article, Ask*IEEE.
Desc: Research articles regarding computing and advanced technology.
Ind/Abst ACM Guide Comput. Lit.; Bioeng. Abstr.; CompuMath Cit. Index [Full Cov.]; Comput. Abstr.; Comput. Lit. Index; Comput. Rev.; Curr. Cit.; Ei Page One (May 1970-); Energy Res. Abstr.; Eng. Index Annu.; INSPEC (May 1970-); Int. Civil Eng. Abstr.; Math. Rev.; Pollut. Abstr. Indexes (May 1970-); Res. Alert [Full Cov.]; SCISEARCH; Soft. Abstr. Eng.; Zentralbl. Math. Ihre Grenzgeb.

US
Pr Rev.

AUTHORWARE MAGAZINE. (19??)-. English. Four times a year. $20.00 North America, $30.00 other. Authorware Inc, 275 Shoreline Drive, Suite 535, Redwood City CA 94065. **Tel** (612)921-8555, FAX (612)921-8556. **ED** Kathy Nordgaard. Index available. **Circ:** 5,000 (ctrl). available on diskette.
Desc: Focuses on issues and trends in interactive multimedia computing and instructional design.

CN

•AUTOCAD USER. See Computers-Computer Assisted Instruction.

ISSN 1060-1317
DD 005 US

AUTOCAD WORLD. [AutoCAD world]. **VFOAT** Auto CAD World. Vol. 1, No. 1 (Feb. 28, 1992)-. Trade Publication. English. Thirteen times a year. $38.00. Publications & Communications, 12416 Hymeadow Drive, Austin TX 78750. **Tel** (512)250-9023, (800)678-9724, FAX (512)331-3900, telex 384303. **(Subscription address:** Publications & Communications, PO Box 399, Cedar Park TX 78630. **) Circ:** 30,000.
Desc: Focuses on news and new product information in the AutoCAD industry. Delivers fast breaking news, as well as current product releases, application and site profiles, and industry updates.

ISSN 1352-8971
UK

•AXIS : THE UCISA JOURNAL OF ACADEMIC COMPUTING AND INFORMATION SYSTEMS. Added/Corp UCISA (Association). Vol. 1, No. 1 (1994)-. Periodical. English. Four times a year. $128.34. Whurr Publishers Ltd., 19B Compton Terrace, London N1 2UN United Kingdom. **Tel** 011 44 171 3595979, FAX 011 44 171 2265290. **(Subscription address:** Whurr Publications Ltd., Distribution Centre, Blackhorse Road, Letchworth SG6 1HN United Kingdom. **Tel** 011 44 1462 672555.) ***Continues*** *University Computing, 0265-4385.*
Ind/Abst Curr. Cit.

ISSN 0860-1674
PL
UDC 681.3

BAJTEK. [Bajtek]. (1985)-. Periodical. Polish. Twelve times a year. zl.5.00. **(Subscription address:** Ars Polona-Ruch, PO Box 1001, Krakowskie Przedmiescie 7, 00-068 Warsaw Poland. **Tel** 011 48 22 261201.)

ISSN 0892-6778
DD 332 US
CCC
CODEN BASREM
CEASED

BANKING SOFTWARE REVIEW. See Business and Economics-Computer Applications.

LC HG1501
DD 332.1 FR

BANQUE ET INFORMATIQUE. See Business and Economics-Banks and Banking.

ISSN 8756-0046
DD 004 US

BAY AREA COMPUTER CURRENTS. See Computers-Computer Industry and Industry Directories.

ISSN 1041-4770
DD 001 US

BCS UPDATE. [BCS update]. **Added/Corp** Boston Computer Society. **VAT** Boston Computer Society Update. (Nov. 1988)-. Periodical. English. Twelve times a year. $39.00 (regular); $35.00 (associate membership); $100.00 (institutional membership and non-profit only); $150.00 (sustaining membership); $400.00 (corporate membership) Only available with Boston Computer Society Membership. Boston Computer Society, One Kendall Square, Cambridge MA 02139. **Tel** (617)367-8080, 252-0600, FAX (617)577-9365. **ED** Mary McCann. **Bk Rev. Ad Acc. Circ:** 33,000. available on microfilm and microfiche from University Microfilms International (UMI). ***Continues*** *Computer Update, 0748-6588.*
Desc: Featuring provocative reporting and commentary on the latest developments in personal computers and the BCS.

ISSN 0263-7561
DD 001.6404 UK
CEASED

BEEBUG. [BEEBUG]. **VFOAT** BEEBUG Newsletter. (1982)-(April 1994). Periodical. English. Beebug Ltd., 117 Hatfield Road, St. Albans Hertfordshire, AL1 4JS United Kingdom. **Tel** 011 44 1727 40303, FAX 011 44 1727 860263. available in microform. Documents available from Ask*IEEE.
Desc: Matter related to Acorn computers, BBC Micro and Master computers, or the Archimedes and A3000 computers.
Ind/Abst INSPEC (1984-1988).

LC BF180 .B4 **ISSN** 0743-3808
DD 150/.72 US
CCC
NLM W1 BE126H **CODEN** BRMCEW

BEHAVIOR RESEARCH METHODS, INSTRUMENTS, & COMPUTERS : A JOURNAL OF THE PSYCHONOMIC SOCIETY, INC. See Psychology.

US

BENCHMARK REPORT. Added/Corp Association of Computer Users. Vol. 1, No. 1 (Nov. 1978)-. Periodical. English. Association of Small Computer Users, PO Box 9003, Boulder CO 80301.

ISSN 1066-0380
DD 004 US

BENCHMARKS (DENTON, TEX.). (BENCHMARKS.). [Benchmarks Dent. Tex.]. (1980)-. Periodical. English. Irregular (9 issues). Computing Center, Box 13495, University of North Texas, Denton TX 76203. **Tel** (817)656-2324, FAX (817)565-4060. **ED** Claudia Lynch, (817)565-4068. Index available (bound in Jan. issue). **Bk Rev. Circ:** 1,000.
Desc: Provides timely information about topics of interest to the academic computing community.

LC HC79.I55 B46 **ISSN** 1061-9216
DD 650 US

BEYOND COMPUTING. [Beyond comput.]. **Added/Corp** International Business Machines Corporation. Vol. 1, No. 1 (1992)-. Periodical. English. Nine times a year. $29.50. IBM Magazines, 590 Madison Avenue, 32nd Floor, New York NY 10022. **Tel** (212)745-6429, FAX (212)745-7984. **(Subscription address:** Omeda Communications, 3005 Macarthur Boulevard, Northbrook IL 60062. **Tel** (708)564-1385.) **ED** Eileen Feretic (editor's phone: (212)745-6336). **Ad Acc. Circ:** 200,000 (ctrl).
Desc: Strives to inform and educate information technology executives about how companies integrate business strategy and the use of information technology.

IT

BIT. No. 1- Mar./Apr. 1967-. Periodical. Italian. Eleven times a year. L49680. Gruppo Editoriale Jackson Spa, Via Gorki 69, 20092 Cinisello Balsamo Italy. **Tel** 011 39 2 66034401. Index available. **Bk Rev. Ad Acc. Circ:** 45,000 (ctrl).
Desc: Covers news, hardware tests, software tests, personal and home computers, and programs.

ISSN 0896-2774
US

BIT DROPPER, THE. (THE BIT DROPPER : OFFICIAL PUBLICATION OF THE SAN FRANCISCO BAY AREA CHAPTERS, ASSOCIATION FOR COMPUTING MACHINERY.). **Added/Corp** Association for Computing Machinery. Peninsula Chapter. Association for Computing Machinery. Golden Gate Chapter. (19??)-. Periodical. English. Twelve times a year. The Bit Dropper, 1082 East El Camino Real, Sunnyvale CA 94087.

LC QA76 .N62 **ISSN** 0006-3835
DD 001.64/05 DK
CODEN NBITAB
Pr Rev. **TITLE CHANGE**

BIT (NORDISK TIDSKRIFT FOR INFORMATIONSBEHANDLING). (BIT.). [BIT (Nord. Tidskr. Inf.-behandl.)]. **VFOAT** B.I.T.; BIT. Computer Science, Numerical Mathematics. (1967)-(1994). Periodical. English. Four times a year. BIT Scandinavian Computer Soc, PO Box 113, DK-1004 Copenhagen K Denmark. **Tel** 011-45-1-125033, FAX 011-45-33122342, telex 41325. **(Subscription address:** Allen Press, PO Box 1897, Lawrence KS 66044. **Tel** (800)627-0629.) **ED** Carl-Erik Froberg. Index available. cum. index. **Bk Rev. Circ:** 1,000. Documents available from Article Express International, The Genuine Article, Ask*IEEE. ***Continues*** *Nordisk Tidskrift for Informationsbehandling.* ***Continued in part by*** *Nordic Journal of Computing. BIT. Numerical Mathematics;* ***Continued by*** *BIT. Numerical Mathematics.*
Desc: Publishes original research papers in the rapidly expanding field of numerical analysis. The essential areas covered are development and analysis of numerical methods as well as the design and use of algorithms for scientific computing. Topics emphasized are stability theory, numerical linear algebra, and approximation.
Ind/Abst ACM Guide Comput. Lit.; Bioeng. Abstr.; CompuMath Cit. Index [Full Cov.]; Comput. Abstr.; Comput. Rev.; Curr. Cit.; Ei Page One; Eng. Index Annu.; INSPEC (1968-); Math. Rev.; Res. Alert [Full Cov.].

LC QA76 .N62
DD 004 DK

•BIT. NUMERICAL MATHEMATICS. VFOAT Numerical Mathematics; BIT. Vol. 35, No. 1 (Mar. 1995)-. English. Four times a year (Mar., June, Sept., Dec.). $160.00. BIT Scandinavian Computer Soc, PO Box 113, DK-1004 Copenhagen K Denmark. **Tel** 011-45-1-125033, FAX 011-45-33122342, telex 41325. **(Subscription address:** Allen Press, PO Box 1897, Lawrence KS 66044. **Tel** (800)627-0629.) ***Continues*** *BIT, 0006-3835.*
Desc: Publishes original research papers in the rapidly expanding field of numerical analysis.

ISSN 0891-2955
DD 001 US

BITS & BYTES REVIEW. (BITS & BYTES REVIEW : B & B REVIEW.). [Bits bytes rev.]. **VFOAT** Bits and Bytes Review; B & B Review; B and B Review. Vol. 1, No. 1 (Oct. 1986)-. Academic Scholarly Publication. English. Four times a year. $70.00. Bits & Bytes Computer Resources, 623 North Iowa Avenue, Whitefish MT 59937. **Tel** (406)862-7280, FAX (408)862-1124. **ED** John J. Hughes. Index available. cum. index. ctrl circ. Documents available from Ask*IEEE.
Desc: An academic computer journal distinguished by its detailed and thorough reviews of innovative products and resources. Each review clearly explains a product's

Computers

features and evaluates its suitability for a range of selected tasks.
Ind/Abst INSPEC (1986-).

LC QA76.8.A662 A66   ISSN 0739-2095
DD 001.64/029/473   US
BLUE BOOK FOR THE APPLE COMPUTER, THE. [Blue book Apple comput.]. **VFOAT** Apple 2 Blue Book; Apple Two Blue Book. 2nd Ed.-. English. $24.95. Widl Video Publications, 5245 West Diversey, Chicago IL 60639. **Continues** Apple II Blue Book, 0731-2873.

ISSN 1047-496X
DD 004   US
BOCOEX INDEX, THE. (THE BOCOEX INDEX [COMPUTER FILE] : CLOSING PRICES ON THE BOSTON COMPUTER EXCHANGE FOR THE WEEK ENDING ...). [BoCoEx index]. **Added/Corp** Boston Computer Exchange. **VAT** Boston Computer Exchange Index. (1986-). Periodical. English. One time a week. $250.00. The Boston Computer Exchange, Box 1177, Boston MA 02103. **Tel** (617)542-4414.
Desc: Online access via: CompuServe, American CitiNet, Delphi and other networks.

ISSN 0210-9743
UDC 681.3   SP
BOLETIN DEL CENTRO DE CALCULO DE LA UNIVERSIDAD COMPLUTENSE. [Bol. Cent. Calc. Univ. Complut.]. **VFOAT** Boletin - Centro de Calculo de la Universidad de Madrid. (1968)-. Periodical. Spanish. Three times a year. Free to Universities on request; $6.00 other. Editorial Complutense, Donoso Cortes 65, Primera Planta, 28015 Madrid Spain. **Tel** 011 34 1 3946372, 011 34 1 3946373, 011 34 1 3946374.

ISSN 0939-3498
UDC 651.74   GW
TITLE CHANGE
BRIEF-BERATER, DER. [Brief-Berat.]. (1991)-(199?). German. Verlag Norman Rentrop, Theodor Heuss Strasse 4, D-53177 Bonn Germany. **Tel** 011 49 228 82050, FAX 011 49 228 364411, telex 17228309 TTX D. **Merged into** Texten und Schreiben der Brief Berater.

ISSN 0265-5217
NLM W1; BR535E   UK
Pr Rev.   **TITLE CHANGE**
BRITISH JOURNAL OF HEALTHCARE COMPUTING, THE. See Medical Sciences-Computer Applications.

LC QA   ISSN 0252-9742
DD 510   NE
BULLETIN OF THE EUROPEAN ASSOCIATION FOR THEORETICAL COMPUTER SCIENCE. **Added/Corp** European Association for Theoretical Computer Science. **VFOAT** EATCS Bulletin. (19??)-. Bulletin. English. Three times a year. DM42.00 US, Canada, and Israel; DM46.00 Japan; DM50.00 other. European Association for Theoretical Computer Science (EATCS), Fachbereich 17 U-GH Paderborn, W-4790 Paderborn Germany. **ED** G Rozenberg, President EATCS. Documents available from Ask*IEEE.
Desc: Publishes papers in the fast evolving field of theoretical computer science. The publication deals with the classical theories of automata and formal languages as well as newer areas, such as the formal semantics of programming languages and the study of algorithms and their complexity.
Ind/Abst Curr. Cit.; INSPEC (June 1981-).

US
BUS DATABASE. (1994)-. English. Three times a year. $65.00 (regular), $199.00 (professional). Octoplus Corporation, 1275 North University Avenue, Unit 7, Provo UT 84604. **Tel** (801)373-0696, FAX (801)373-0695. **ED** Jay Vilhena. **Ad Acc. Formed by the union of** Supermicro **and** Futurebus + Design.

LC Z7146.C81 B963 HF5548.125   ISSN 0741-2363
DD 016.65/002854   US
BUSINESS COMPUTER INDEX, THE. See Business and Economics-Computer Applications.

ISSN 0265-1564
DD 658.054   UK
TITLE CHANGE
BUSINESS COMPUTING & COMMUNICATIONS. [Bus. comput. commun.]. **VFOAT** Business Computing and Communications. (1983)-19??). Periodical. English. Morgan Grampian, 40 Beresford Street Woolwich, London SE18 6BQ United Kingdom. **Tel** 011 44 181 8557777, FAX 011 44 181 8555548, telex 896238. **Merged into** What's New in Computing.
Ind/Abst Infomat Int. Bus.

ISSN 0957-4085
UK
CODEN CLAPEE   **TITLE CHANGE**
C & L APPLICATIONS. See Library and Information Sciences.

LC QA76.73.C15 C193   ISSN 1075-2838
DD 005.13/3   US
CODEN CCUJEX
●**C/C++ USERS JOURNAL.** [C/C++ users j.]. **VFOAT** C/C Plus Plus Users Journal. Vol. 12, No. 7 (July 1994)-. Periodical. English. Twelve times a year (source code disk available). $34.95. R & D Publications, 1601 West 23rd Street, Suite 200, Lawrence KS 66046. **Tel** (913)841-1631, FAX (913)841-2624. **Continues** C Users Journal, 0898-9788.
Desc: Directed towards the professional C and C++ programmer. Includes tutorials, product user reports, case studies, and code listings to explain how developers can efficiently build C programs.

ISSN 1049-1244
DD 004   US
C2C CURRENTS JAPAN. COMPUTERS. [C2C curr. Jpn., Comput.]. **VFOAT** Computers. English. Twelve times a year. $200.00. SCAN C2C Inc., 500 E Street Southwest, Suite 800 8th Floor, Washington DC 20024. **Tel** (202)863-3850, (800)525-3865, FAX (202)863-3855. Index available. cum. index. available on an online database from DATA-STAR; and DIALOG; available on CD-ROM from DIALOG.
Desc: Listings of Japanese science, technical and business journals in the field of computers.

ISSN 0160-9025
US
CODEN CCOCDF
CA SELECTS: COMPUTERS IN CHEMISTRY. See Chemistry and Chemicals-Computer Applications.

ISSN 0890-1821
DD 621   US
CODEN CSMMEC
CA SELECTS: MEMORY & RECORDING DEVICES & MATERIALS. See Chemistry and Chemicals-Abstracting, Bibliographies and Statistics.

ISSN 0925-7977
NE
UDC 681.51
CA TECHNIEK. [CA tech.]. **VFOAT** Computer Aided Techniek. (1991)-. Trade Publication. Dutch. Ten times a year. $99.35. Array Publications, Antwoordnummer 10235, 2400 Alphen Rijn Netherlands. **Tel** 011 31 1720 24177. **Continues** CA Techniek in Bedrijf, 0924-9605.

ISSN 8755-3732
DD 336   US
CAAS NEWS. See Real Estate.

ISSN 1043-6448
DD 621   US
CAD/CAM, CAE, SURVEY, REVIEW, AND BUYERS' GUIDE. [CAD/CAM CAE surv. rev. buy. guide]. **Added/Corp** Daratech (U.S.). **VFOAT** Survey, Review, and Buyers' Guide; Daratech CAD/CAM, CAE Industry Update. (19??)-. Consumer Publication. English. Twelve times a year. $972.00. Daratech Inc., PO Box 410, 140 6th Street, Cambrridge MA 02238. **Tel** (617)354-2339, FAX (617)354-7822. **ED** Bruce Jenkins. Index available. **Continues** U.S. Directory of Vendors, 0735-861X.
Desc: Source of CAD/CAM, CAE industry, company and product data that profiles systems and vendors, provides forecasts for revenue growth, market share and other industry statistics.

ISSN 1052-0856
DD 670   US
CAD/CAM WATCH. [CAD/CAM watch]. **Added/Corp** TechniCom, Inc. **VFOAT** CAD, CAM Watch. **VAT** Computer Aided Design/Computer Aided Manufacturing Watch; Computer Aided Design, Computer Aided Manufacturing Watch. Vol. 1, Issue 1 (Dec. 1989)-. Periodical. English. Eight times a year (published every 6 weeks). $149.00. TechniCom Inc., PO Box 4195, Clifton NJ 07012. **Tel** (201)470-9110, FAX (201)778-6465. **ED** Raymond Kurland. Index available. cum. index.
Desc: Newsletter focusing on the mechanical CAD/CAM industry and its supporting technologies.

ISSN 1037-8529
AT
CAD USER AUSTRALIA NEW ZEALAND. (1991)-. English. Seven times a year. 45.22Aus$. CAD User Pty Ltd., First Floor 1342 Toorak Road, Burwood VICT 3125 Australia. **Tel** 011 61 3 889 3161, FAX 011 61 3 889 1290.

LC T57.6 .C64   ISSN 0008-9737
BE
CODEN CCROAT
CAHIERS - CENTRE D'ETUDES DE RECHERCHE OPERATIONNELLE. [Cah. Cent. etud. rech. oper.]. **Main/Corp** Centre d'Etudes de Recherche Operationnelle, Brussels. **Added/Corp** Universite Libre de Bruxelles. Centre d'Etudes de Recherche Operationnelle. Vol. 1, (1958)-. Periodical. French (French). Four times a year. $55.97. Centre d'Etudes de Recherche Operationnelle, ULB Campus Place CP 210, Triomphe B 1050, Brussels Belgium. **Tel** 011 32 2 6502111. Documents available from Ask*IEEE.
Ind/Abst Comput. Rev.; INSPEC (1978-); Int. Abstr. Oper. Res. [Full Cov.]; Math. Rev.; Stat. Theory Method Abstr. (1969-1975, 1977-1984, 1987).

LC QA75 .C33   ISSN 0363-0102
DD 510/.28   US
CALCULATOR LIB. Vol. 1 (May 1976)-. Periodical. English. Six times a year. $8.00. Technological Developments, PO Box 2151, Oxnard CA 93034.

LC U168 .C34   US
DD 355.4/11/0285   CEASED
CALS/ENTERPRISE INTEGRATION JOURNAL. **VFOAT** CALS Enterprise Integration Journal; Computer-Aided Acquisitions and Logistics Support Enterprise Integration Journal. Vol. 3, No. 3 (Summer 1994)-(Mar. 1995). Periodical. English. CALS Journal, 14407 Big Basin Way, Saratoga CA 95070. **Tel** (408)867-8601, FAX (408)867-9800. **ED** Jeff Hill. Index available. **Ad Acc, Adv Mgr:** Bill Sleight. **Circ:** 10,000. **Continues** CALS Journal, 1061-2572.

LC U168 .C34   ISSN 1061-2572
DD 355.4/11/0285   US
TITLE CHANGE
CALS JOURNAL. [CALS j.]. **VAT** Computer-Aided Acquisition and Logistics Support Journal. Vol. 1, No. 1 (Spring 1992)-(1994). Periodical. English. CALS Journal, 14407 Big Basin Way, Saratoga CA 95070. **Tel** (408)867-8601, FAX (408)867-9800. **ED** Jeff Hill. Index available. **Ad Acc, Adv Mgr:** Bill Sleight. **Circ:** 10,000. **Continued by** CALS/Enterprise Intergration Journal.
Desc: A new publication for the international CALS community, is a forum for detailed information, insights and perspectives on the CALS initiative. Articles offer practical guidelines, business insights, strategic direction and case studies on CALS planning and implementation.

UK
CAMBRIDGE COMPUTER SCIENCE TEXTS. (1972)-. Monographic series. English. Price varies per volume. Cambridge University Press, The Edinburgh Building, Shaftesbury Road, Cambridge CB2 2RU United Kingdom. **Tel** 011 44 1223 312393, FAX 011 44 1223 315052, telex 851-817256.
Ind/Abst Math. Rev. (1988-); Zentralbl. Math. Ihre Grenzgeb.

UK
CAMBRIDGE TRACTS IN THEORETICAL COMPUTER SCIENCE. (1987)-. Monographic series. English. Irregular. Price varies per volume. Cambridge University Press, The Edinburgh Building, Shaftesbury Road, Cambridge CB2 2RU United Kingdom. **Tel** 011 44 1223 312393, FAX 011 44 1223 315052, telex 851-817256. **Subscription address:** Cambridge University Press / North America, 110 Midland Avenue, Port Chester NY 10573. **Tel** (800)431-1580, (914)937-9600.)
Desc: Series of tracts devoted to theoretical computer science. Topics include extensions of first-order logic and Godel's proof.
Ind/Abst Curr. Cit.; Math. Rev. (1988-); Zentralbl. Math. Ihre Grenzgeb.

ISSN 1071-2976
DD 004   US
Pr Rev.
CANDLE COMPUTER REPORT. [Candle comput. rep.]. **Added/Corp** Candle Corp. (1978)-. Periodical. English. Twelve times a year. Free on request. Candle Corporation, 2425 Olympic Boulevard, Santa Monica CA 90404. **Tel** (310)829-5800, FAX (310)582-4233. **ED** Denise Hamilton. Index available. **Circ:** 10,000 (ctrl). available on an online database.

LC QA76 .E215   ISSN 1049-2194
DD 004.5/05   US
CODEN CAMRE3
CAPACITY MANAGEMENT REVIEW. (CAPACITY MANAGEMENT REVIEW : CMR : A MONTHLY REPORT ON MANAGING COMPUTER PERFORMANCE.). [Capacity manage. rev.]. **Added/Corp** Applied Computer Research (Firm). **VFOAT** CMR. Vol. 18, No. 1 (Jan. 1990)-. Academic Scholarly Publication. English. Twelve times a year. $250.00. Institute for Computer Capacity Management, 1020 8th Avenue South, Suite 6, Naples FL 33940. **Tel** (813)261-6945, FAX (813)261-5456. **Bk Rev. Circ:** 1,000. available on microfilm and microfiche from University Microfilms International (UMI); available on an online database (file 15/Full-Text) from DIALOG. Documents available from UMI Article Clearinghouse, Ask*IEEE, CASDDS. **Continues** EDP Performance Review, 0091-7206.
Ind/Abst ABI/INFORM [Computer File] (1990-); ACM Guide Comput. Lit. (19??-1989); Chem. Abstr. (1990-); Comput. Lit. Index; Curr. Cit.; INSPEC (Jan. 1990-); UMI ABI/Inform--Bus. Period. Ondisc [Full Txt.].

Computers

DD 004   ISSN 0893-3049   US

CAPITAL COMPUTER DIGEST. [Cap. comput. dig.]. **VFOAT** Computer Digest. (1986)-. Periodical. English. Twelve times a year. $5.00. Clark Publishing Company, 1313 Dolly Madison Boulevard, Suite 303, McClean VA 22181. **Tel** (703)525-7900.

US

CAPSTONE LETTER. English. Six times a year. $75.00. Capstone Group Inc., 164 Old Elm Street, Mansfield MA 02048. **Tel** (617)523-1959. **ED** Clifford Jones, (phone: (508)261-9658). **Circ:** 100. **Desc:** In-depth information on building practice systems with CAPS.

ISSN 1017-6764   BB

CARIBBEAN JOURNAL OF MATHEMATICAL AND COMPUTING SCIENCES. See Mathematics-Computer Applications.

LC QC801
DD 551   US

CAS NEWSLETTER. See Earth Sciences-Geophysics.

ISSN 0277-0407   US   CEASED

CCAN. See Building and Construction.

ISSN 0160-8711   US

CCIS NEWSLETTER. Main/Corp Rutgers University, New Brunswick, N.J. Center for Computer and Information Services. **VAT** Center for Computer and Information Services Newsletter. Newsletter. English. Four times a year. $1.00. Center for Computer and Information Services, Rutgers University, PO Box 879, Piscataway NJ 08854.

US   CEASED

CD-I NEWS. VFOAT CDI News. (19??)-(1994). English. Link Resources Corporation, 79 Fifth Avenue, New York NY 10003. **Tel** (212)473-5600.

UK   CEASED

CDS INFO PLUS. (19??)-Vol. 8 (19??). Periodical. English. Coveford Data Systems Limited, 52 Park Street, Camberley Surrey GU15 3PT United Kingdom. **Tel** 011 44 1276 681261, FAX 011 44 1276 25845, telex 858062. **ED** Jane Anderson. Index available. cum. index. **Circ:** 550.
Desc: Designed for technical managers and senior technical personnel responsible for technical planning and support in the IBM and IBM compatible mainframe arena.

DD 540   ISSN 0886-6716   US   CCC   CODEN CDANEK

CHEMICAL DESIGN AUTOMATION NEWS. See Chemistry and Chemicals-Computer Applications.

LC QD39.3.E46 C43
DD 540   US

CHEMPUTER BUYERS' GUIDE. See Chemistry and Chemicals-Computer Applications.

DD 004   ISSN 1079-6606   US
Pr Rev.

CHERYL WATSON'S TUNING LETTER. [Cheryl Watson's tuning lett.]. **VFOAT** Tuning Letter. (1991)-. Periodical. English. Six times a year. $445.00. Watson and Walker Inc., 1605 Main Street, Suite 900, Sarasota FL 34236. **Tel** (800)553-4562, (813)366-7708, FAX (813)366-6479. Index available. cum. index. **Circ:** 1,300.
Desc: Practical journal of MVS tuning and measurement advice.

LC QA
DD 004   ISSN 1085-0767   US
UDC 68
●**CHICAGO COMPUTER GUIDE.** [Chic. comput. guide]. (1995)-. Periodical. English. Twelve times a year. $19.95. Chicago Computer Guide, 29 South La Salle Street, Suite 1218, Chicago IL 60603. **Tel** (312)332-0419, FAX (312)332-6113. **ED** McKinley Blumenberg. **Circ:** 70,000. **Continues** Computer Guide (Chicago, Ill.), 1071-7749.

ISSN 1073-0486   US   CCC
Pr Rev.

●**CHICAGO JOURNAL OF THEORETICAL COMPUTER SCIENCE.** See Mathematics-Computer Applications.

LC HD30.2 .C4744
DD 658.4/038/05   ISSN 0899-0182   US   CODEN CIOJEB   CEASED

CHIEF INFORMATION OFFICER JOURNAL. See Business and Economics-Computer Applications.

IT

CHIP. Italian. Gruppo Editoriale JCE SRL, Via Ferri 6, 20092 Cinisello B Milan Italy. **Tel** 011 39 2 660251, FAX 011 39 2 66025343.

UDC 621.391   ISSN 0211-2841   SP   CEASED

CHIP MADRID. [ChipMadr.]. (1981)-(Jan. 1994). Periodical. Spanish. VNU Business Publications / Spain, Cinca 13, 28002 Madrid Spain. **Tel** 011 34 1 563-8100, FAX 011 34 1 563-7572. **Ad Acc. Circ:** 10,000.

DD 205   ISSN 0882-0961   US

CHRISTIAN COMPUTER NEWS. [Christ. comput. news]. Periodical. English. Six times a year. $15.00. Christian Computer News, 5795 Lawndale, Hudsonville MI 49426. **Continues** CCUA News.

DD 004   ISSN 1063-7672   US

CHRISTIAN COMPUTING MAGAZINE. See Religions and Theology.

LC QA75
DD 004   ISSN 1053-7473   US

CHURCH COMPUTING NEWS. [Church comput. news]. (1990)-. Periodical. English. Four times a year. Communal Computing, PO Box 6599, Silver Springs MD 20916-6599.

CU

CID : ELECTRONICA Y PROCESO DE DATOS EN CUBA. VFOAT Electronica y Proceso de Datos en Cuba; Revista Cid. Periodical. Spanish. Four times a year. $16.00. Ediciones Cubanas, Obispo 527 Altos ESQ Bernaza, CP 10100 Havana Cuba. **Circ:** 6,000 (ctrl).
Desc: Articles on electronic computation in general, peripheral equipment and electronic and digital systems, written by outstanding Cuban specialists.

UDC 338.3   ISSN 0179-2679   GW

CIM-MANAGEMENT. [CIM-Manage.]. **VFOAT** Computer Integrated Manufacturing-Management. (1985)-. Periodical. German. Six times a year. $191.76. R Oldenbourg Verlag, Postfach 801360, D-81613 Munich Germany. **Tel** 011 49 89 450190, FAX 011 49 89 45019305. Index available. **Bk Rev. Ad Acc. Circ:** 5,600.

ISSN 1032-3007   AT

CIT TASK FORCE REPORT. [CIT task force rep.]. **VAT** Computing and Information Technology Task Force Report. No. 1; 1988-. Monographic series. English. Irregular. Price varies per volume. Bond University, Gold Coast Law School, Queensland 4229 Australia. **Tel** 011 61 75 925011, FAX 011 61 75 952246.

FR

CLASSIFICATION AUTOMATIQUE ET PERCEPTION PAR ORDINATEUR. (19??)-. Monographic series. French. Irregular. Price varies per volume. Institut National de Recherche et Informatique en Automatique, SEDIS Diffusion, Domaine de Voluceau-Rocquencourt, BP 105, 78153 Le Chesnay Cedex France. **Tel** 011 33 1 39635627, FAX 011 33 1 39635228, telex 697033 F.

DD 027   ISSN 0738-8845   US

CMC NEWS. [CMC news]. **VAT** Computers and the Media Center News. (197?)-. Periodical. English. Three times a year. 14.00. CMC News, 515 Oak Street North, Cannon Falls MN 55009. **Tel** (507)263-3711. **ED** Jim Deacon. **Circ:** 1400. Documents available from Ask*IEEE.
Desc: Provides information on the application of microcomputers in library/media centers.
Ind/Abst INSPEC (Spring 1984-).

US

CMG PROCEEDINGS. (19??)-. Proceedings. English. One time a year. $125.00 (US), $175.00 (Canada), $200.00 (other) includes CMG membership and Proceedings. Computer Measurement Group, Inc., 414 Plaza Drive / Suite 209, Westmont IL 60559. **Tel** (708)655-1812. **(Subscription address:** Commputer Measurement Group Inc. / CMG, Department 77-6023, Chicago IL 60678-6023. **Tel** (312)527-6652.) **Circ:** 3,500.
Desc: Proceedings for the international conference for the management and performance evaluation of enterprise computing systems.
Ind/Abst Curr. Cit.

US

CMG TRANSACTIONS. (19??)-. English. Four times a year. $125.00 (US), $175.00 (Canada), $200.00 (other) includes CMG membership and Proceedings. Computer Measurement Group, Inc., 414 Plaza Drive / Suite 209, Westmont IL 60559. **Tel** (708)655-1812. **(Subscription address:** Commputer Measurement Group Inc. / CMG, Department 77-6023, Chicago IL 60678-6023. **Tel** (312)527-6652.) **ED** Dale Doolittle and Phil Clark (Doolittle's address: Storage Technology Corporation, 500 North Westshore Boulevard, Suite 830, Tampa, Florida 33609; telephone: (813)287-8036; FAX: (813)287-2212). **Circ:** 3,500.
Desc: Directed toward CPE (Computer Performance Evaluation) analysts and professionals interested in the development of the CPE technology.

UDC 681.3.02   ISSN 0178-8728   GW

COGITO DARMSTADT. [Cogito Darmst.]. (1985)-. Trade Publication. German. Six times a year. $110.54. Verlag Hoppenstedt & Company, Postfach 100139, D-64201 Darmstadt Germany. **Tel** 011 49 6151 380436, 011 49 6151 380361.

DD 006   ISSN 1057-8374   US

COGNIZER REPORT. (1991)-. Periodical. English. Twelve times a year. $125.00 North America; $165.00 other. Frontline Strategies, 516 Southeast, Chkalov Drive, Suite 164, Vancouver WA 98684. **Tel** (201)892-5880. **ED** Martin Middlewood. Index available (Dec. iss. each year). **Bk Rev. Circ:** 100. **Continues** Neural Networks Today, 1054-8556.

US

COLLECTED ALGORITHMS FROM ACM. Added/Corp Association for Computing Machinery. **VAT** Collected Algorithms from Association for Computing Machinery. Vol. 1 (1980)-. English. Four times a year. $430.00. ACM / Association for Computing Machinery, 1515 Broadway, 17th Floor, New York NY 10036. **Tel** (212)869-7440, FAX (212)869-0481. **(Subscription address:** Association for Computing Machinery, PO Box 12114, Church Street Station, New York NY 10249. **Tel** (212)626-0500.)

ISSN 0149-1989   US   CCC

●**COLLECTED ALGORITHMS FROM ACM. SUPPLEMENT.** [Collect. algorithms ACM, Suppl.]. **Main/Corp** Association for Computing Machinery. **Added/Corp** Association for Computing Machinery. Collected Algorithms From ACM. **VAT** Collected Algorithms from Association for Computing Machinery. (Supplement). (19??)-. Periodical. English. Four times a year (Jan., Apr., July, Oct.). $448.00. ACM / Association for Computing Machinery, 1515 Broadway, 17th Floor, New York NY 10036. **Tel** (212)869-7440, FAX (212)869-0481.
Desc: Offers code listings for all algorithms printed in ACM journals - in machine readable and microfiche form. Remarks and certifications are also given, often with driver code.

FR

COLLECTION DE L'OPI. (19??)-. Monographic series. French. Irregular. Price varies per volume. Institut National de Recherche et Informatique en Automatique, SEDIS Diffusion, Domaine de Voluceau-Rocquencourt, BP 105, 78153 Le Chesnay Cedex France. **Tel** 011 33 1 39635627, FAX 011 33 1 39635228, telex 697033 F.

ISSN 1062-4791   US

COLORADO COMPUTER RESOURCES. Added/Corp Addams-Pike Associates. (1992)-. Periodical. English. Two times a year. $40.00. Addams-Pike Associates, 3973 Promontory Court, Boulder CO 80304.

ISSN 0742-3519   US

COLUMBUS COMPUTER XCHANGE. VFOAT Columbus Computer Exchange. (198?)-. Periodical. English. Eleven times a year. $10.00. Columbus Computer Exchange, PO Box 755, 58 Larrimer, Worthington OH 43085. **Tel** (614)846-5644.

LC QA164 .C665
DD 511/.6/05   ISSN 0963-5483   UK   CCC

COMBINATORICS, PROBABILITY & COMPUTING : CPC. See Mathematics-Computer Applications.

ISSN 0746-3197   US

COMMANDER (TACOMA, WASH.). (COMMANDER.). [Commander]. Periodical. English. Twelve times a year. $22.00 US; $26.00 Canada and

Computers

Mexico; $37.00 (surface mail), $54.00 (airmail) other. Micro Systems Specialties, PO Box 98827, Tacoma WA 98498.

ISSN 1157-8637
FR

UDC 681.3
COMMUNICATIONS & STRATEGIES MONTPELLIER. (COMMUNICATIONS & STRATEGIES.). [Commun. strategies Montpellier]. **VFOAT** Communications et Strategies (Montpellier). (1991)-. Periodical. Multiple languages. Four times a year. $185.91. IDATE, BP 4167, 34092 Montpellier CED 5 France. **Tel** 011 33 67 144444, **FAX** 011 33 67 144400. **ED** Jacques Alaudis. Index available. cum. index. **Bk Rev. Circ:** 1,000 (ctrl). **Continues** Bulletin de l'IDATE, 0249-2571.

LC QA76 .A772
DD 001.64/05
ISSN 0001-0782
CCC
NLM Z 699.A1 C734
CODEN CACMA2
Pr Rev.

COMMUNICATIONS OF THE ACM.
[Commun. ACM]. **Added/Corp** Association for Computing Machinery. **VFOAT** Communications of the A.C.M. **VAT** Communications of the Association for Computing Machinery. Vol. 2, No. 11 (Nov. 1959)-. Periodical. English. Twelve times a year. $129.00. ACM / Association for Computing Machinery, 1515 Broadway, 17th Floor, New York NY 10036. **Tel** (212)869-7440, **FAX** (212)869-0481. **(Subscription address:** Association for Computing Machinery, PO Box 12114, Church Street Station, New York NY 10249. **Tel** (212)626-0500.) **ED** Peter J. Denning. **Ad Acc. Circ:** 77,000. available on microfilm and microfiche from University Microfilms International (UMI); available on an online database (files 15,675/Full-Text) from DIALOG. Documents available from Article Express International, The Genuine Article, UMI Article Clearinghouse, Ask*IEEE. **Continues** Communications of the Association for Computing Machinery, 0001-0782.
Desc: Provides a comprehensive overview of computing.
Ind/Abst ABI/INFORM Glob. Ed. (March 1972-March 1973); ABI/INFORM [Computer File] (March 1972-March 1973); Abstr. Hum. Comput. Interact.; Acad. Abstr.; Acad. Ind. [Computer File] (1989-); Acad. Search; Appl. Sci. Technol. Index; Bioeng. Abstr.; CompuMath Cit. Index [Full Cov.]; Comput. Abstr.; Comput. ASAP [Full Txt.]; Comput. Database [Full Txt.]; Comput. Lit. Index; Comput. Rev.; Curr. Cit.; Curr. Contents Eng. Comput. Technol.; Data Process. Dig.; Ei Page One; Eng. Index Annu.; EP Collect.; Ergon. Abstr.; Expand. Acad. Index (1989-); Geol. Abstr.; GeoRef; HILITES; Homework Help.; Index Period. Artic. Relat. Law; INFO-SOUTH Abstr.; Inf. Sci. Abstr.; INIS Atominex [Micro.]; INSPEC (1968-); Int. Abstr. Oper. Res. [Select. Cov.]; Int. Aerosp. Abstr.; MasterFile FullTEXT 1000; MasterFile FullTEXT 350; MasterFile FullTEXT 650; MasterFile FullTEXT (Jan. 1991-); Math. Rev. (?-199?); MLA Int. Bibl. Books Artic. Mod. Lang. Lit.; Newsp. Period. Abstr. (1990-); OCLC; Oper. Res./Manage. Sci. (1968-); Pollut. Abstr. Indexes; Qual. Control Appl. Stat. (1968-); Res. Alert [Full Cov.]; Robotics Abstr.; Sci. Cit. Index.; SCISEARCH; Soc. Sci. Cit. Index [Select. Cov.]; Telebase; UMI ABI/Inform--Bus. Period. Ondisc [Full Txt.]; Zentralbl. Math. Ihre Grenzgeb.

US

COMPCON : PROCEEDINGS. Added/Corp
Institute of Electrical and Electronics Engineers. Computer Society. (1967)-. Proceedings. English. One time a year. $80.00. IEEE Computer Society, 10662 Los Vaqueros Circle, PO Box 3014, Los Alamitos CA 90720-1264. **Tel** (714)821-8380, (800)272-6657, **FAX** (714)821-4641. Documents available from Article Express International. **Continues** COMPCON. Digest of Papers.
Desc: General proceedings of the Institute of Electrical and Electronics Engineers.
Ind/Abst Bioeng. Abstr.; Comput. Lit. Index; Curr. Cit.; Ei Page One; Eng. Index Annu.

US

COMPILER (NORRIS, TENN.), THE. (THE COMPILER.). [Compiler]. Added/Corp Forest Resources Systems Institute (U.S.). Vol. 1, Issue 1 (Nov. 1983)-. Periodical. English. Four times a year (Mar., June, Sept., Dec.,). $80.00. Forest Resources Systems Institute, 122 Helton Court, Florence AL 35630-1433. **Tel** (205)767-0250, **FAX** (205)767-3768. **ED** David Gilluly. **Ad Acc, Adv Mgr:** V. Stacey, **Tel** (205)767-0250. **Circ:** 600.
Desc: Use and applications of computers in forestry and related fields.

US

COMPLETE LIBRARIES GROUP USER MANUAL. English. Irregular. Visual Numerics, PO Box 4605, Houston TX 77210. **Tel** (800)222-4675.
ISSN 0195-8526
US

●**COMPU-FAX.** (197?)-. Periodical. English. Six times a year. $18.00. Data Processing Management Association, 505 Busse Highway, Park Ridge IL 60068-3191. **Tel** (708)825-8124 ext.252. Fax (708)825-1693.

US

●**COMPU-MGR TELE-MGR. See** Communications-Computer Applications.

JM

COMPUTA. (June 1990)-. English. Twelve times a year. Personal Computer Users of Jamaica (PCJAM), 56 Dumbarton Avenue, Kingston 10 Jamaica. **ED** Sandi Bell.
Desc: Geared toward the PC users of Jamaica.

LC QA267 .C732
ISSN 1016-3328
SZ
CODEN CPTCEU

COMPUTATIONAL COMPLEXITY. See
Mathematics.

LC HB143.5 .C66 HB143.5 .C65
DD 658/.05
ISSN 0927-7099
NE
CCC
CODEN CNOMEL

Pr Rev.
●**COMPUTATIONAL ECONOMICS. See** Business and Economics-Computer Applications.

ISSN 1055-677X
US

COMPUTATIONAL FLUID DYNAMICS (NEW YORK, N.Y.). See Engineering-Computer Applications.

LC Z6654.C17 C64 QA75.5
DD 016.00164
NLM Z 699.A1 C736
ISSN 0010-4469
UK

COMPUTER ABSTRACTS. See
Computers-Abstracting, Bibliographies and Statistics.

US
TITLE CHANGE
COMPUTER ABSTRACTS ON DISKETTE. See Computers-Abstracting, Bibliographies and Statistics.

DD 658
ISSN 8756-8780
US

COMPUTER AIDED SELLING. See Business and Economics-Computer Applications.

LC QA76 .C548
DD 016.0016/4
ISSN 0036-8113
UK
CCC
CODEN CCABB8

COMPUTER & CONTROL ABSTRACTS.
See Computers-Abstracting, Bibliographies and Statistics.

ISSN 0308-4221
UK
CODEN CPUABQ
COMPUTER APPLICATIONS. See Science and Technology-Computer Applications.

LC T61 .C575
DD 620/.0071/1
ISSN 1061-3773
US
CODEN CAPEED

COMPUTER APPLICATIONS IN ENGINEERING EDUCATION. See Engineering-Computer Applications.

DD 005
ISSN 1062-9734
CEASED

COMPUTER ASSISTED REHABILITATION THERAPY. (COMPUTER ASSISTED REHABILITATION THERAPY: UTILIZING THE BRACY PROCESS APPROACH AND SOFTWARE.). [Compu. assist. rehabil. ther.]. **Added/Corp** Psychological Software Services. **VFOAT** CART. Vol. 1, No. 1 (Jan./Feb. 1992)-(1993). Periodical. English. Psychological Software Services, Inc., 6555 Carrollton Avenue, Indianapolis IN 46220. **Tel** (317)257-9672.

LC QA75.5 .C589
DD 001.64
ISSN 0737-0334
US

COMPUTER BOOK REVIEW. [Comput. book rev.]. (1983)-. Periodical. English. Six times a year. $30.00. Computer Book Review, 735 Ekekela Place, Honolulu HI 96817. **ED** Carlene Char. Index available. cum. index. **Bk Rev.** available on an online database from DIALOG. Documents available from BLDSC.
Desc: Critically reviews new, computer-related titles. All subjects and publishers. Focuses on books of interest to users, professionals and students.
Ind/Abst Book Rev. Index (1984-); Microcomput. Abstr. (Nov. 1987-).

UK
COMPUTER BUSINESS REVIEW. English.
Twelve times a year. $195.00. APT Data Services, 12 Sutton Row, 4th Floor, London W1V 5FH United Kingdom. **Tel** 011 44 171 2084200, **FAX** 011 44 171 4391105.

AT
COMPUTER COMMENTARY. (19??)-.
English. Eleven times a year. 283.65Aus$. Hicorp Marketing, PO Box N542 Grosvenor Place, Sydney NSW 2000 Australia. **Tel** 011 61 2 2412933. **Continues** Australian Computer Commentary.

LC TK7885 .D55
DD 621.39/029/4
ISSN 1058-2606
US
COMPUTER COMPENDIUM. [Comput. compend.]. (June 1991/1992)-. Periodical. English. Twenty-four times a year. Computer Publishers Inc., 2604 East Dempster Street, PO Box 5045, Des Plains IL 60017-5045. **Continues** Digital Digest, 1048-4442.

DD 001
US
COMPUTER CRAFTSMAN JOURNAL.
[Comput. craftsm. j.]. Vol. 1, No. 1, (1984)-. Periodical. English. Twelve times a year. $36.00 US; $48.00 other. Support Group Inc, PO Box 130, McHenry MD 21541.

LC TK7888.3 .C65
DD 621.3819/582
ISSN 0010-4566
US
CCC
CODEN CMPDAM
Pr Rev.
COMPUTER DESIGN (WINCHESTER).
(COMPUTER DESIGN.). [Comput. des.]. Vol. 1 (Jan. 1962)-. Trade Publication. English. Twelve times a year. $99.00. PennWell Publishing Company, 1421 South Sheridan, PO Box 1260, Tulsa OK 74101. **Tel** (918)835-3161, (800)331-4463, **FAX** (918)831-9497. **(Subscription address:** Computer Design, Publishing Services, PO Box 3466, Tulsa OK 74101. **Tel** (918)832-9263, **FAX** (918)832-9295.) available on microfilm and microfiche from University Microfilms International (UMI); available on an online database (file 675/Full-Text) from DIALOG. Documents available from Article Express International, The Genuine Article, Ask*IEEE, BLDSC, FAXON Xpress, The UnCover Company, SWETS, UMI Article Clearinghouse.
Desc: Positioned to serve system design managers and senior engineers who design and/or integrate hardware and software into computers, computer peripherals and other electronic products that incorporate microprocessors, board-level computers and computers.
Ind/Abst ACM Guide Comput. Lit.; Acoust. Abstr.; Appl. Sci. Technol. Index; Bioeng. Abstr.; Bus. Source Plus; Bus. Source; CompuMath Cit. Index [Full Cov.]; Comput. ASAP [Full Txt.]; Comput. Database [Full Txt.]; Comput. Lit. Index; Comput. Rev.; Curr. Cit.; Ei Page One; Eng. Index Annu. [Select. Cov.]; EP Collect.; Homework Help.; Inf. Sci. Abstr. (?-?); INSPEC (Sept. 1968-); MasterFile FullTEXT 1000; MasterFile FullTEXT 350; MasterFile FullTEXT 650; MasterFile FullTEXT (Jan. 1995-); OCLC; Res. Alert [Full Cov.]; SCISEARCH; Telebase.

ISSN 0739-0874
DD 338
US
CODEN CERTDR
COMPUTER ECONOMIC$ REPORT.
(COMPUTER ECONOMIC$ REPORT : THE FINANCIAL ADVISOR OF DATA PROCESSING USERS.). [Comput. econ. rep.]. **VFOAT** Computer Economics Report. (1979)-. Periodical. English. Twelve times a year. $595.00. Computer Economics Inc., 5841 Edison Place, Carlsbad CA 92008. **Tel** (800)326-8100, (619)438-8100, **FAX** (619)431-1126. **ED** Lee Kroon. Index available (bound in Jan. issue). Documents available from Ask*IEEE.
Desc: The newsletter covers new Data Processing (DP) equipment trends and forecasts, evaluation of DP acquisition methods, cost control techniques, financial management of DP operations, analyses of new product announcements, evaluation of price versus performance, residual value forecasts and used computer market.
Ind/Abst Comput. Lit. Index; INSPEC (March 1984-).

ISSN 0890-4308
US
COMPUTER ECONOMICS SOURCEBOOK. (1986)-. Periodical. English. Twelve times a year. $1495.00. Computer Economics Inc., 5841 Edison Place, Carlsbad CA 92008. **Tel** (800)326-8100, (619)438-8100, **FAX** (619)431-1126.
Desc: A financial guide to DP equipment acquisition and control of DP expenses. Covers list and used equipment prices, residual value forecasts, leasing rates, operating costs, acquisition and disposition strategies, and required support resources.

SZ
COMPUTER FORUM. German. Twelve times a year. 68.00F Switzerland; 88.00F Europe; 102.00F other. Diagonal Verlags Ag, Taefernstrasse 2, CH-5405 Baden Switzerland. **Tel** 011 41 56 834550.

Computers

COMPUTER FREEBIE$. VFOAT Computer Freebies. (1992)-. Periodical. English. Six times a year. $12.00. Old Town Graphics & Publishing, PO Box 47, Howard Beach NY 11414.

ISSN 0192-6349
US

COMPUTER HOT LINE. (19??)-. Periodical. English. One time a week. $84.00. United Advertising Periodicals, 15400 Knoll Trail Suite 400, Dallas TX 75248. Tel (214)233-5131. Index available. Ad Acc. ctrl circ.

ISSN 0889-082X

DD 338

COMPUTER INDUSTRY REPORT. See Computers-Electronic Data Processing.

NE

COMPUTER INFO. (19??)-. Periodical. English. Eleven times a year. Fl50.00. Sala Communications, Postbus 43048, 1009 ZA Amsterdam Netherlands. Tel 011 31 20 6273198.

ISSN 1061-6403
US

DD 004

COMPUTER INFO. [Comput. Inf.] (1992)-. Periodical. English. Twelve times a year. $1.00 (single issue). Computer Info, 9514 Mcneil Road, Suite 207, Austin TX 78758.

LC QA76 .C57
DD 510.78

ISSN 0010-4620
UK
CCC
CODEN CMPJA6

Pr Rev.

COMPUTER JOURNAL. (THE COMPUTER JOURNAL.). [Comput. j.]. **Added/Corp** British Computer Society. Vol. 1 (April 1958)-. Periodical. English. Ten times a year. $560.00. Oxford University Press / UK, Walton Street, Oxford OX6 6DP United Kingdom. Tel 011 44 1865 56767, FAX 011 44 1865 267773, telex 851/837330 OXPRES G. **(Subscription address:** Oxford University Press / USA, Journals Marketing Department, Oxford University Press, 2001 Evans Road, Cary NC 27513. Tel (800)451-7556, (919)677-0977, FAX (919)677-1714.**)** ED P. Hammersley. Index available (free). **Bk Rev** available on microfilm and microfiche from University Microfilms International (UMI). Documents available from Article Express International, The Genuine Article, Ask*IEEE, CASDDS.
Desc: Technical, commercial and academic papers deal with all areas including advanced programming, computer science theory, hardware and logic design, and business applications.
Ind/Abst Abstr. Hum. Comput. Interact.; ACM Guide Comput. Lit.; Appl. Sci. Technol. Index; Bioeng. Abstr.; BMT Abstr.; Chem. Abstr.; CompuMath Cit. Index [Full Cov.]; Comput. Abstr.; Comput. Lit. Index; Comput. Rev.; Contents Pages Manage.; Curr. Cit.; Curr. Contents Eng. Comput. Technol.; Educ. Technol. Abstr.; Ei Page One; Eng. Index Annu.; Ergon. Abstr.; HILITES; INSPEC (1968-); Int. Aerosp. Abstr.; J. Ferrocement; Libr. Inf. Sci. Abstr.; Manage. Market. Abstr.; Math. Rev.; MLA Int. Bibl. Books Artic. Mod. Lang. Lit.; Res. Alert [Full Cov.]; SCISEARCH; Soc. Sci. Cit. Index [Select. Cov.]; Stat. Theory Method Abstr. (1967-1977); World Publ. Monit.; Zentralbl. Math. Ihre Grenzgeb.

ISSN 0748-9331
US

DD 621

COMPUTER JOURNAL (KALISPELL, MONT.). (THE COMPUTER JOURNAL.). [Comput. j.]. (198?)-. Periodical. English. Six times a year (Jan., Mar., May, July, Sept., Nov.). $22.00. The Computer Journal, PO Box 535, Lincoln CA 95648. Tel (908)645-1670, (800)424-8825. ED Bill Kibler. Bk Rev. Ad Acc. Circ: 1,500. **Continues** Computer Hacker.
Desc: Details of computers; primary, classical and older systems.

LC KF905.C6 C638
DD 343 73/078004/0269 347.303780040269

ISSN 0894-1858
US

COMPUTER LAW FORMS HANDBOOK. See Law.

LC KFM2484.5.C65.C65 A133
DD 343.744/07800164 44037800164
US
CEASED

COMPUTER LAW NEWSLETTER. See Law-Computer Applications.

ISSN 0824-4790
CN

DD 346.71/07

COMPUTER LAW (TORONTO). See Law-Computer Applications.

ISSN 1076-9862
US

●**COMPUTER LIFE.** (1994)-. Periodical. English. Twelve times a year. $25.00. Ziff-Davis, One Park Avenue, 5th Floor, New York NY 10016. Tel (212)503-3500. **(Subscription address:** Neodata / Colorado, PO Box 2606, Boulder CO 80322.**)** available via Internet (http://www.ziff.com/).
Desc: Contains practical, how-to guidance, in-depth articles, and special features.
Ind/Abst Acad. Abstr.; Acad. Search; Bus. Source Plus; Bus. Source; EP Collect.; Homework Help.; Mag. Artic. Summar. Elite; Mag. Artic. Summar. Select; Mag. Artic. Summar. CD-ROM; MasterFile FullTEXT 1000; MasterFile FullTEXT 350; MasterFile FullTEXT 650; MasterFile FullTEXT (Jan. 1995-); OCLC; Pub. Lib. FullTEXT; Telebase; Vocat. Search; World Mag. Bank.

US

COMPUTER LITERACY NEWSLETTER. (19??)-. Newsletter. English. Twelve times a year. $19.00. Computer Literacy Workshop, 4500 Bissonnet, Suite 330, Bellaire TX 77401. Tel (713)667-7121, FAX (713)667-3962. ED Margaret Luellen Briggs. Bk Rev, (Qty: 12). Circ: 2,500 (ctrl).
Desc: User's journal for personal computers and Macintoshes. Includes tips, tricks, and more.

LC TK7885.A1 I5
DD 001.6/4/05

ISSN 0018-9162
US
CCC
CODEN CPTRB4

Pr Rev.

COMPUTER (LONG BEACH, CALIF.). (COMPUTER.). [Computer]. **Added/Corp** IEEE Computer Society. Vol. 3, No. 5 (Sept./Oct. 1970)-. Periodical. English. Twelve times a year. $455.00. IEEE / Institute of Electrical and Engineers Inc., 345 East 47th Street, New York NY 10017-2394. Tel (908)981-1393, FAX (908)981-9667. **(Subscription address:** IEEE / Institute of Electrical and Electronics Engineers, 445 Hoes Lane, PO Box 1331, Piscataway NJ 08855-1331. Tel (800)701-IEEE, (908)981-0060, FAX (908)981-9667, telex 833233.**)** ED Marilyn Potes. Index available. Bk Rev. Ad Acc. Circ: 92,774. available on microfiche. Documents available from Article Express International, The Genuine Article, Ask*IEEE. **Continues** Institute of Electrical and Electronics Engineers. Computer Group. Computer Group News, 0537-9229.
Desc: Provides tutorial, survey, and applications-oriented articles on hardware, software, and systems for practicing engineers and scientists. Includes product reviews, new products, conference news, and more.
Ind/Abst Abstr. Hum. Comput. Interact.; ACM Guide Comput. Lit.; Appl. Sci. Technol. Index; Bioeng. Abstr.; CompuMath Cit. Index [Full Cov.]; Comput. Bus. (19??-19??); Comput. Database; Comput. Rev. (19??-19??); Curr. Cit.; Curr. Contents Eng. Comput. Technol.; Data Process. Dig.; Ei Page One; Eng. Index Annu.; Ergon. Abstr.; HILITES; HTFS Dig.; Index IEEE Publ.; Inf. Sci. Abstr.; INSPEC (Nov./Dec. 1971-); Int. Aerosp. Abstr. (1984-); J. Ferrocement; Res. Alert [Full Cov.]; Sci. Cit. Index; SCISEARCH; Soc. Sci. Cit. Index [Select. Cov.].

ISSN 0747-749X
US

COMPUTER MEDIA DIRECTORY. (198?)-. Directory. English. Four times a year. $407.00. Morrissey Standard, 742 Gilman Street, Berkeley CA 94710. Tel (713)524-6565. ED Lola Wilkerson. Index available. available on diskette.

LC QA76.5 .C61263
DD 004/.05

ISSN 1050-396X
US

COMPUTER NEWS INTERNATIONAL. [Comput. news int.]. VFOAT CNI. Vol. 2, No. 2 (May 1990)-. Periodical. English (Spanish). Six times a year. $25.00 US; $43.00 Canada. SFS Corporation, 1 Northwest 40th Street, Suite 205, Miami FL 33137. Tel (305)576-6999. **Continues** Florida Computer News.

ISSN 0840-3929
CN

DD 004/.05

Pr Rev.

COMPUTER PAPER (BRITISH COLUMBIA ED.). (THE COMPUTER PAPER.). [Comput. pap.]. (Feb. 1988)-. Periodical. English. Twelve times a year. 19.96Can$. Canada Computer Paper, Inc, 3661 West 4th Avenue, Suite 8, Vancouver BC V6R 1P2 Canada. Tel (604)733-5596, FAX (604)732-4380. ED Douglas Alder. Index available (1.95Can$). cum. index. Bk Rev. Ad Acc. Adv Mgr: Hari Singh. Circ: 350,000 (ctrl). available via Internet.
Desc: Provides a Canadian focus on current computing products and issues.

ISSN 1064-7007
US

DD 004

COMPUTER PARTNER LEADS. [Comput. partn. leads]. (1992)-. Periodical. English. One time a week. $375.00. RM Publishing Corporation, 29327 Stonecrest Road, Rolling Hills Estates CA 90274.

ISSN 0722-0987
GW

UDC 681.31

CEASED

COMPUTER PERSONLICH. [Comput. pers.]. (1982)-(Jan. 1995). Periodical. German. Verlag Markt & Technik, Hans Pinsel Str 2, W-8013 Haar B Munich Germany. Tel 011 49 89 461300, FAX 11 49 89 4613774. **(Subscription address:** DSB ABO Betreuung GmbH, Heiner Fleischmann Strasse 2, D-74168 Neckarsulm Germany. Tel 011 49 71329590.**) Absorbed** PC Plus Technik (1990), 0940-9238.

ISSN 1194-305X
CN

DD 004

COMPUTER POST. [Comput. post]. Vol. 1, No. 1 (July 1991)-. Periodical. English. Twelve times a year. 29.46Can$. Business and Technology Publications Co., #301 - 68 Higgins Avenue, Winnipeg Manitoba R3B 0A5 Canada. Tel (204)947-9766, FAX (204)947-9767. ED Sylvia Douglas and Robert Li. Bk Rev, (Qty: 5). Ad Acc, Adv Mgr: Brent Aubertin, Tel (204)947-9766. Circ: 11,000 (ctrl).
Desc: Designed for people who use computers in their day to day work routine. Helps businesses and organizations make informed buying decisions.

LC PL1074.5 .C66
DD 495.1/0285

ISSN 0715-9048
US
CODEN CPCLE6

COMPUTER PROCESSING OF CHINESE & ORIENTAL LANGUAGES. See Linguistics.

ISSN 0899-126X
US

DD 004

Pr Rev.

COMPUTER PROTOCOLS. [Comput. protoc.]. (1988)-. Periodical. English. Twelve times a year. $150.00 North America; $165.00 other. W V Publishing Company, PO Box 138, Babson Park, Boston MA 02157. ED Mark Wright. available on an online database from NEWSNET; (file 636/Full-Text) DIALOG; and DATA-STAR.
Desc: Covers news and developments of computer communication protocols and their related products. Information is presented on LANs, gateways, and bridges.
Ind/Abst PTS Newsl. Database [Full Txt.].

ISSN 0276-9972
US
CEASED

COMPUTER PUBLICITY NEWS. See Business and Economics-Advertising and Public Relations.

JA

COMPUTER REPORT. (19??)-. Japanese. Twelve times a year. ¥18000.00. Japan Management Science Institute, 4-18-3-309 Minami Aoyama, Minato-ku Tokyo Japan. Tel 011 81 3 3401 3110.

LC QA76.5 .C6132
DD 001.64/05

ISSN 0254-7813
II
CODEN CSINET

COMPUTER SCIENCE AND INFORMATICS. [Comput. sci. inform.]. **Added/Corp** Computer Society of India. Vol. 12, No. 1 (1982)-. Academic Scholarly Publication. English. Two times a year. $20.00. Computer Society of India, 15 Haji Ali Park, Bombay 400 034 India. ED S.V. Rangaswamy Documents available from Ask*IEEE. **Continues** Computer Society of India. Journal, 0379-5152.
Ind/Abst Curr. Cit.; INSPEC (1982-).

LC QA
DD 001.6

US

COMPUTER SCIENCE AND SCIENTIFIC COMPUTING. (19??)-. Monographic series. English. Irregular. Price varies per volume. Academic Press Inc., 6277 Sea Harbor Drive, Orlando FL 32887. Tel (800)543-9534, (407)345-4100, FAX (407)352-3445. **Continues** Computer Science and Applied Mathematics.

ISSN 0899-3408
US
CCC

DD 004

COMPUTER SCIENCE EDUCATION. See Education-Higher Education.

LC QA
DD 621.381
US

COMPUTER SCIENCE LIBRARY. OPERATING AND PROGRAMMING SYSTEMS SERIES, THE. VFOAT Operating and Programming Systems Series. (1977)-. Monographic series. English. Irregular. Price varies per volume. Elsevier Science Publishing Company Inc, Madison Square Station, PO Box 882, New York NY 10159-0882. Tel (212)633-3950, FAX (212)633-3990. ED P. J. Denning. Documents available from Ask*IEEE. **Continues** Elsevier Computer Science Library. Operating and Programming Systems Series.
Ind/Abst INSPEC.

Computers

ISSN 1065-2078
DD 371
US
COMPUTER SCIENCE SYLLABUS.
[Comput. sci. syllabus]. **Added/Corp** Apple Computer, Inc. (1992)-. Periodical. English. Four times a year. $24.00 (individuals), $48.00 (institutions) US; $60.00 other. Syllabus Press, 1307 South Mary Avenue, Suite 218, Sunnydale CA 94087-0716. **Tel** (408)773-0670, FAX (408)746-2711. **ED** John P. Noon. **Ad Acc. Circ**: 60,000. available on an online database.
Desc: Dedicated to computer science education. Each issue covers new technology trends, languages, campus profiles, industry news, products, resources for columns, and opinions from well-known computer science faculty and industry figures.

ISSN 1053-9808
DD 621
US
COMPUTER SCIENCE. VERY LARGE SCALE INTEGRATION.
[Comput. sci., Very large scale integr.]. **VFOAT** Very Large Scale Integration. (1986)-. Monographic series. English. Irregular. Price varies per volume. University Microfilms International, 300 North Zeeb Road, Ann Arbor MI 48106-1346. **Tel** (313)761-4700, (800)521-0600 Exts. 2490, 2491, FAX (313)973-1540.

US
COMPUTER-SPECS.
(19??)-. English. Irregular. Silverplatter Information Inc., 100 River Ridge Drive, Norwood MA 02062. **Tel** (800)343-0064, (617)769-2599, FAX (617)769-8763. **Continues** Compu-Info.

ISSN 0885-2308
DD 006
UK
CCC
NLM W1; CO457KE
CODEN CSPLEO
COMPUTER SPEECH & LANGUAGE. See
Linguistics-Computer Applications.

LC QA76.9.S8 C64
ISSN 0920-5489
DD 004/.0218
SZ
CCC
CODEN CSTIEZ
Pr Rev.
COMPUTER STANDARDS & INTERFACES.
[Comput. stand. interfaces]. **VFOAT** Computer Standards and Interfaces. Vol. 5, No. 1 (1986)-. Academic Scholarly Publication. English. Seven times a year. $592.00. Elsevier Science Publishers BV, PO Box 211, 1000 AE Amsterdam Netherlands. **Tel** 011 31 20 4853641, 011 31 20 4853642, FAX 011 31 20 4853598. **ED** J L Berg, H Schumny, and R A Rosner. available on microfilm and microfiche from University Microfilms International (UMI); available on an online database from Elsevier Electronic Subscriptions (EES). Documents available from Article Express International, The Genuine Article, Ask*IEEE. **Formed by the union of** Computers & Standards, 0167-8051 **and** Interfaces in Computing, 0252-7308.
Desc: Intended to inform the international EDP community about computer standards work at the international and national levels and to provide an international forum for discussion of computer interfaces and standards.
Ind/Abst ACM Guide Comput. Lit.; CompuMath Cit. Index [Full Cov.]; Comput. Abstr.; Comput. Lit. Index; Comput. Rev.; Curr. Cit.; Ei Page One; Eng. Index Annu.; Inf. Sci. Abstr. (?-?); INSPEC (1986-); Res. Alert [Full Cov.]; SCISEARCH; Zentralbl. Math. Ihre Grenzgeb.

ISSN 0280-9982
SW
UDC 681.3
COMPUTER SWEDEN.
[Comput. Swed.]. (1983)-. Periodical. Swedish. Forty-eight times a year. $119.41. CW Communications AB, Sturegatan 11, S 10678 Stockholm Sweden. **Tel** 011 46 8 453-6000. **ED** Lars Dahmen. **Bk Rev. Ad Acc. Circ**: 21000 (ctrl). available on microfilm from University Microfilms International (UMI).

ISSN 0887-5553
US
COMPUTER SYSTEMS JOURNAL.
(1991)-. Periodical. English. Twelve times a year. $36.00. Feedbak Publications, PO Box 201404, Austin TX 78720.

UK
CEASED
COMPUTER TALK.
(1978)-(199?). Periodical. English. Reed Business Publishing / West Sussex, England, Perrymount Road, Haywards Heath, West Sussex RH16 3DH United Kingdom. **Tel** 011 44 1444 441212, FAX 011 44 1444 445447. available on an online database (file 648/Full-Text) from DIALOG. Documents available from Ask*IEEE.
Ind/Abst INSPEC (1980-1984).

US
CEASED
COMPUTER TRADE SHOW WORLD.
(Aug. 1992)-(April 1995). Periodical. English. Publications & Communications, 12416 Hymeadow Drive, Austin TX 78750. **Tel** (512)250-9023, (800)678-9724, FAX (512)331-3900, telex 384303.
Desc: Official publication of the Computer Exhibit Managers Association.

UK
COMPUTER TRADE WEEKLY. (19??)-.
Periodical. English. One time a week. £80.00 Europe; £150.00 other Europe; £250.00 other. CTW / Computer Trade Weekly Circulation Department, Troopers Yard, 23 Bancroft, Hitchin Hertfordshire SG5 1JW United Kingdom. **Tel** 011 44 1462 442486. **ED** Stuart Dinsey. **Ad Acc, Adv Mgr**: Russell Beadle, **Tel** 011 44 462 4424741. ctrl circ.

LC KK164.C66 C66
ISSN 0179-1990
DD 343.43/07800164 344.3037800164
GW
CCC
CODEN CRECE3
COMPUTER UND RECHT (KOLN). See
Law.

LC KF390.5.C6 A134
ISSN 8756-2642
DD 343.73/07800164 347.3037800164
US
SUSPENDED
COMPUTER USER'S LEGAL REPORTER, THE. See Law.

ISSN 1053-3834
US
COMPUTER USER'S SURVIVAL MAGAZINE, THE.
(THE COMPUTER USER'S SURVIVAL MAGAZINE [COMPUTER FILE].). [Comput. user's surv. mag.]. Vol. 1, Issue 1- (1990)-. Periodical. English. Twelve times a year. $35.00. J P Walman, Box 31, F.D.R. Station, New York NY 10150.
Desc: System requirements: IBM compatible computer.

ISSN 1076-7959
DD 004
US
●COMPUTER VIDEO (FALLS CHURCH, VA.). See Communications-Video.

ISSN 1065-8246
DD 005
US
CEASED
COMPUTER VIRUS DEVELOPMENTS QUARTERLY.
(Fall 1992)-(March 1995). Periodical. English. **VFOAT** CVDQ. American Eagle Publications Inc., PO Box 41401, Tucson AZ 85717. **Tel** (502)888-4957.

AT
COMPUTER WEEK.
(19??)-. English. Forty-Five times a year. 69.89Aus$. Peter Isaacson Publications, 46-50 Porter Street, Prahran Victoria, 3181 Australia. **Tel** 011 61 3 2457777, FAX 011 61 3 2457606. **Continues** Pacific Computer Weekly.

ISSN 0254-2188
SA
UDC 681.3
COMPUTER WEEK.
[Comput. week]. (1978)-. Periodical. English. One time a week (50 issues per year). $59.79. Systems Publishers Pty Ltd, PO Box 41345, Craighall 2024 South Africa. **Tel** 011 27 11 7891808, 7891809, FAX 011 27 11 7894725.

ISSN 0010-4787
UK
CCC
CODEN COMWAA
COMPUTER WEEKLY.
[Comput. wkly.]. (1966)-. Trade Publication. English. One time a week. $213.00. Reed Business Publishing / West Sussex, England, Perrymount Road, Haywards Heath, West Sussex RH16 3DH United Kingdom. **Tel** 011 44 1444 441212, FAX 011 44 1444 445447. available on microfilm from University Microfilms International (UMI); available on an online database (files 648,675/Full-Text) from DIALOG. Documents available from Ask*IEEE.
Ind/Abst Anbar Account. Finan. Abstr. [Full Txt.]; Anbar Mark. Distr. Abstr. [Full Txt.]; Anbar Top Manage. Abstr. [Full Txt.]; Comput. ASAP [Full Txt.]; Comput. Database [Full Txt.]; Educ. Technol. Abstr.; F&S Index Plus Text, Int. [Select. Cov.]; HILITES; Infomat Int. Bus.; Inf. Manage. Technol.; INSPEC (March 1972-); Manage. Bibliogr. Rev.; Oper. Prod. Manage. Abstr. [Full Txt.]; Person. Train. Abstr. [Full Txt.]; PROMT; Trade Ind. ASAP [Full Txt.]; Trade Ind. Index [Full Txt.]; Women Manage. Rev. [Full Txt.]; World Publ. Monit.

ISSN 0268-716X
DD 338.47004
UK
COMPUTERGRAM INTERNATIONAL.
[Computergram int.]. (1984)-. Trade Publication. English. Irregular (250 issues). $995.00. APT Data Services, 12 Sutton Row, 4th Floor, London W1V 5FH United Kingdom. **Tel** 011 44 171 2084200, FAX 011 44 171 4391105. **Circ**: 3,000. available on an online database from NEWSNET. Documents available from BLDSC. **Absorbed** Technology Research.
Ind/Abst Comput. ASAP [Full Txt.]; Comput. Database [Full Txt.]; Infomat Int. Bus.; PROMT [Full Txt.]; PTS Newsl. Database [Full Txt.]; Trade Ind. ASAP [Full Txt.]; Trade Ind. Index [Full Txt.].

ISSN 0969-2053
UK
●COMPUTERGRAM WEEKLY. (1993)-. English.
One time a week. $540.74. APT Data Services, 12 Sutton Row, 4th Floor, London W1V 5FH United Kingdom. **Tel** 011 44 171 2084200, FAX 011 44 171 4391105.

LC HG450
ISSN 0734-4597
DD 332.6
US
COMPUTERIZED INVESTING. See Business and Economics-Investments.

LC CS42 .C58
ISSN 0743-7919
DD 929/.373
US
UDC 929.52
COMPUTERIZED SURNAME MAGAZINE. See Genealogy and Heraldry-Computer Applications.

ISSN 0771-7784
BE
UDC 681.3
COMPUTERRECHT. (1984)-. Periodical. Dutch.
Six times a year. $126.76. Kluwer BV, Postbus 23, 7400 GA Deventer Netherlands. **Tel** 011 31 5700 33155, 011 31 5700 47421, FAX 011 31 5700 11504, telex 42829.
(Subscription address: Libresso BV, Postbus 23, 7400 GA Deventer Netherlands. **Tel** 011 30 5700 47333, 011 31 5700 33155.)

ISSN 0010-4809
DD 574
US
CCC
NLM W1 CO457R
CODEN CBMRB7
Pr Rev.
COMPUTERS AND BIOMEDICAL RESEARCH. See Medical Sciences-Computer Applications.

US
COMPUTERS AND BUSINESS EQUIPMENT. See Business and Economics-Office Equipment and Services.

LC QD39.3.E46 C647
ISSN 0097-8485
DD 542/.8
UK
CCC
NLM W1 CO457RI
CODEN COCHDK
Pr Rev.
COMPUTERS & CHEMISTRY. See Chemistry and Chemicals-Computer Applications.

UK
COMPUTERS & COMMUNICATIONS.
(19??)-. Newsletter. English. Twelve times a year. £210.00 UK; £230.00 US, Canada and Mexico. Wharton Publishing Limited, First Floor Regal House, Twickenham Middlesex, TW1 3QS United Kingdom. **Tel** 011 44 181 8916197.
Desc: Written by the expert researchers and consultants of WIS. The target audience is the MIS and administrative manager who has so many decisions to make. This report provides a second and informed input into the potential of all the new systems.
Ind/Abst Curr. Lit. Sci. Sci.

LC QE48.8 .C62
ISSN 0098-3004
DD 550/.28/54
UK
CCC
CODEN CGEODTCGOSDN
Pr Rev.
COMPUTERS & GEOSCIENCES. See Earth Sciences-Computer Applications.

ISSN 0140-3249
UK
CODEN CLAWDY
COMPUTERS AND LAW. See Law-Computer Applications.

ISSN 0888-2193
DD 510
US
COMPUTERS AND MATH SERIES. See Mathematics-Computer Applications.

LC T57.6.A1 C65
ISSN 0305-0548
DD 001.4/24/05
US
CCC
CODEN CMORAP
Pr Rev.
COMPUTERS & OPERATIONS RESEARCH. VFOAT Comput. oper. res.].
Computers & Operations Research and their Application to Problems of World Concern. **VAT** Computers and Operations Research. Vol. 1 (March 1974)-. Periodical. English. Twelve times a year. $1128.00. Pergamon Press, An Imprint of Elsevier Science Ltd., The Boulevard, Langford Lane, Kidlington, Oxford OX5 1GB United Kingdom. **Tel** 011 44 1865 843000, 011 44 1865 843699, FAX 011 44 1865 843010. (**Subscription address**: Elsevier Science Ltd. / Oxford Fulfillment Centre, PO Box 800, Kidlington OX5 1DX United Kingdom. **Tel** 011 44 865 843355.) **ED** Samuel Raff. available on microfilm and microfiche from University Microfilms International (UMI); available on an online database from Elsevier Electronic Subscriptions (EES). Documents available from Article Express International,

Computers

The Genuine Article, UMI Article Clearinghouse, Ask*IEEE.
Desc: Provides an international forum for the application of computers and operations research techniques to problems in these and related fields.
Ind/Abst ABI/INFORM Glob. Ed.; ABI/INFORM [Computer File] (Spring 1978-)(spring 1978-); Acad. Search; ACM Guide Comput. Lit.; Bioeng. Abstr.; Bus. Index (1985-); Bus. Source Plus; Bus. Source; CompuMath Cit. Index [Full Cov.]; Comput. Inf. Syst. Abstr. J. [Full Cov.]; Comput. Database; Comput. Rev.; Curr. Cit.; Curr. Contents Eng. Comput. Technol.; Ei Page One; EMBASE; Eng. Index Annu.; EP Collect.; Gen. BusinessFile (1985-); Gen. Period. Index (1985-); GeoRef; Homework Help.; Inf. Sci. Abstr.; INSPEC (March 1974-); Int. Abstr. Oper. Res. [Full Cov.]; Mag. Search; Manuf. Process Eng. Abstr.; MasterFile FullTEXT 1000; MasterFile FullTEXT 350; MasterFile FullTEXT 650; MasterFile FullTEXT (July 1993-); Math. Rev.; Mech. Eng. Abstr.; OCLC; Oper. Res./Manage. Sci.; Pollut. Abstr. Indexes; Qual. Control Appl. Stat.; Res. Alert [Full Cov.]; SCISEARCH; Soc. Sci. Cit. Index [Select. Cov.]; Solid State Supercond. Abstr.; Telebase; Trade Ind. Index; Zentralbl. Math. Ihre Grenzgeb.

LC QA76 .C5812
DD 301.24/3
ISSN 0095-2737
US
CODEN CMSCD3

COMPUTERS & SOCIETY. See Social Sciences.

US

COMPUTERS & SOFTWARE - EXPORT LICENSING CONTROLS. See Business and Economics-Commerce.

LC N380 .C663
DD 702/.85
ISSN 1048-6798
SZ
CCC
CODEN CHIAEF

COMPUTERS AND THE HISTORY OF ART. See The Arts-Computer Applications.

LC HF5679 .C587
DD 657/.028/5
ISSN 0883-1866
US
CCC
CODEN CACCEA
TITLE CHANGE

COMPUTERS IN ACCOUNTING. See Business and Economics-Computer Applications.

ISSN 0953-3257
UK
TITLE CHANGE

COMPUTERS IN AFRICA. (19??)-(19??).
English. Africa File Ltd., 37 Fairhazel Gardens, London NW6 3QN United Kingdom. **Tel** 011 44 148 0830724, FAX 011 44 148 0831131, telex 932524. **Continued by** Computers & Communications in Africa.

UK
CEASED

COMPUTERS IN DEFENSE. (19??)-(19??).
English. Eaglehead Publishing Ltd, 98 Maybury Woking, Woking Surrey GU21 5JL United Kingdom. **Tel** 011 44 1483 740271.

LC TA345 .I5485a
DD 620
ISSN 1065-3201
US
CCC

COMPUTERS IN ENGINEERING. See Engineering-Computer Applications.

LC TK7885.A1 C613
DD 338.4/7/001640254
UK

COMPUTERS IN EUROPE. 1st- Ed.; 1971-.
English. One time a year. Richard Williams and Partners, GPO Box 8, Llandudno Wales United Kingdom. **Formed by the union of** British Commercial Computer Digest; European Computer Users Handbook **and** European Computer Survey.

DD 616
ISSN 0745-1075
US
CCC

NLM W1; CO457Y

TITLE CHANGE

COMPUTERS IN HEALTHCARE. See Medical Sciences-Computer Applications.

LC BF39.5 .C663
DD 150/.28/5
ISSN 0747-5632
US
CCC

NLM W1; CO457YB
CODEN CHBEEQ

COMPUTERS IN HUMAN BEHAVIOR. See Psychology.

ISSN 0736-8593
US
CCC

NLM W1; CO4572BC
Pr Rev.

COMPUTERS IN NURSING. See Medical Sciences-Computer Applications.

ISSN 0738-3614
US

NLM W1; CO4572H
CODEN CPSHD5

COMPUTERS IN PSYCHIATRY/PSYCHOLOGY. See Medical Sciences-Psychiatry.

ISSN 0741-5893
US

COMPUTERS-R-DIGITAL. [Comput.-r-digit.].
VFOAT Computers R Digital; Computers R Digital Monthly; Computers-R-Digital Monthly. Periodical. English. Twelve times a year. Free to qualified professionals. Directory Database, Box 8669, Red Bank NJ 07701.

ISSN 0970-0129
II

UDC 681.3

COMPUTERS TODAY. [Comput. today]. (1985-).
English. Twelve times a year. $60.00. Computers Today, Faribadad 121 007, Haryana India. (**Subscription address:** Prints India, 11 Darya Ganj, New Delhi 110002 India. **Tel** 011 91 11 3268645, FAX 011 91 11 3275542, telex 31-61087 PRIN-IN.)

ISSN 0736-3893
US

Pr Rev.

COMPUTERTALK FOR THE PHARMACIST. See Pharmacy and Pharmacology-Computer Applications.

ISSN 0886-4225
US

COMPUTERWHAT?. **VFOAT** Computer What?. (1987-). Periodical. English. Twelve times a year. $12.00. Seidman & Seidman, 1200 Smith Street, Suite 500, Houston TX 77002. **Tel** (713)659-6551.

ISSN 0170-5121
GW

COMPUTERWOCHE. [Computerwoche]. **VFOAT** CW. (1974-). Trade Publication. German. One time a week. DM245.00 Germany; DM265.70 Switzerland; DM360.00 other. IDG Communications Verlag AG / Germany, Rheinstrasse 26 28, D-80803 Munich Germany. **Tel** 011 49 89 360860. available on microfilm from University Microfilms International (UMI).
Ind/Abst F&S Index Plus Text, Int. [Select. Cov.]; Infomat Int. Bus.; PROMT.

DD 004/.0971/05
ISSN 1195-6100
CN

●**COMPUTERWORLD CANADA (DOWNSVIEW).** (COMPUTERWORLD CANADA.). [ComputerWorld Can.]. **VFOAT** Computer World Canada; LTI's Focus Issue. Vol. 9, No. 14 (July 16, 1993)-. Periodical. English. Twenty-six times a year. 55.00Can$. Laurentian Technomedia, 501 Oakdale Road, Downsview Ontario M3N 1W7 Canada. **Tel** (416)746-7360, (613)475-3217. **Continues** Direct Access (Toronto, Ont.)., 0827-5033.

SP

COMPUTERWORLD ESPANA. Trade Publication. Spanish. Irregular. $200.00. IDG Communications / Spain, Rafael Calvo 18, 28010 Madrid Spain. **Tel** 011 34 1 3194014, 3087233. available on microfilm from University Microfilms International (UMI).

LC QA76 .C5816
DD 004
ISSN 0010-4841
US
CCC
CODEN CMPWAB

COMPUTERWORLD (FRAMINGHAM, MASS.). See Computers-Computer Industry and Industry Directories.

ISSN 0392-8845
IT

UDC 681.3

COMPUTERWORLD ITALIA. [Computerworld Ital.]. (1982-). Periodical. Italian. Forty-Five times a year. L64040. IDG Communications Italia SRL, Via Mecenate 30 14, 20138 Milan Italy. **Tel** 011 39 2 58011660, FAX 011 39 2 58011670. **Ad Acc. Circ:** 25,000 (ctrl).
Desc: Covers computers, telecommunications, hardware and software.

DD 001.64095
ISSN 0217-8362
SI
CEASED

COMPUTERWORLD SINGAPORE.
(COMPUTERWORLD : THE NEWSPAPER FOR THE COMPUTER COMMUNITY.). [Computerworld Singap.]. (1985)-(Sept. 1994). Trade Publication. English. Asia Computerworld Commun Ltd, 701-4 Kam Chung Blg, 54 Jaffe R, Wanchai Hong Kong. **Tel** 011 852 28613238, FAX 011 852 28610953. **ED** Donald Tennant. **Ad Acc,**
Adv Mgr: Vera Chan. **Circ:** 3500. available on microfilm from University Microfilms International (UMI). **Continues** Asian Computer World, 0217-5665.

UK

COMPUTING & COMMUNICATIONS DECISIONS. See Communications-Computer Applications.

DD 004.6
ISSN 1188-3383
CN

COMPUTING & COMMUNICATIONS NEWSLETTER. See Communications-Computer Applications.

DD 004
ISSN 1184-7557
CN

COMPUTING & COMMUNICATIONS NEWSLETTER. See Communications-Computer Applications.

DD 004
ISSN 1053-7856
US

COMPUTING ARCHIVE. (COMPUTING ARCHIVE [COMPUTER FILE]. BIBLIOGRAPHY AND REVIEWS FROM ACM.). [Comput. arch.]. **Added/Corp** Association for Computing Machinery. **VFOAT** CA. Vol. 1, Issue 1 (1991)-. Bibliography. English. One time a year. $1299.00 nonmember. ACM / Association for Computing Machinery, 1515 Broadway, 17th Floor, New York NY 10036. **Tel** (212)869-7440, FAX (212)869-0481.
Desc: Contains citations of journal articles and conference papers, and citations from scholarly and industrial periodicals.

DD 004
ISSN 0954-7479
UK

COMPUTING, COMMUNICATIONS & MEDIA TREND MONITOR. [Comput. commun. media trend monit.]. **Added/Corp** lib. **VFOAT** Trend Monitor. (1988-). Periodical. English. Four times a year. £450.00. Trend Monitor International, 3 Tower Street, Portsmouth PO1 2JR United Kingdom. **Tel** 011 44 1705 864714, FAX 011 44 1705 828009. **ED** J. Wyllie. Index available. **Circ:** 400.
Desc: Supplies intelligence relating to technologies and markets in computing, communications, media, and socio-technologies.

ISSN 0266-4283
UK
CEASED

COMPUTING EQUIPMENT. [Comput. equip.]. (1984)-(1994). Periodical. English. IML Group, Blair House, 184-186 High Street, Tonbridge Kent, TN9 1BQ United Kingdom. **Tel** 011 44 1732 359990, FAX 011 44 1732 770049.
Ind/Abst HILITES.

LC Z5640 .H54 QA76
DD 004
ISSN 0887-1175
US

COMPUTING INFORMATION DIRECTORY. [Comput. inf. dir.]. **VFOAT** CID. (1985)-. Directory. English. One time a year. $229.95. Hildebrandt Inc, PO Box 576, Pullman WA 99163. **Tel** (509)332-5340. **ED** Darlene M. Hildebrant. **Continues** Computer Science Resources.
Desc: Covers computer science and computer science literature.

ISSN 1340-7228
JA

●**COMPUTING JAPAN.** [Comput. Jpn.]. **VFOAT** Magazine of Computing Trends, Technology and Resources in Japan. (1994-). Periodical. English. Twelve times a year. $95.00. Kimihira & Taylor Associates Inc, 2463 Torrance Boulevard, Torrance CA 90501. **Tel** (310)320-2445, FAX (310)320-3228.

ISSN 0226-9201
CN

DD 001.64/07/11713541

COMPUTING NEWS. [Comput. news - York Univ.]. **Added/Corp** York University (Toronto, Ont.) Dept. of Academic Computing. **VFOAT** Computing Newsletter. **VAT** York University Computing News; Computing Newsletter - York University. Vol. 13, No. 1 (Jan./Feb. 1981)-. Periodical. English. Twelve times a year. Free. Newsletter Editor, Computing Services, T103 Steacie York University, 4700 Keele Street, Downsview Ontario M3J 1P3 Canada. **Tel** 736-5257, FAX 736-5700. **ED** Cecil O. Humphrey. Index available. **Bk Rev. Circ:** 1200 (ctrl). **Continues** York University (Toronto, Ont.). Dept. of Computer Services. DCS Newsletter, 0228-0434.

ISSN 0737-8556
US

NLM W1; CO4575

COMPUTING PHYSICIAN. See Medical Sciences-Computer Applications.

LC QA76.5 .C616
DD 004
ISSN 1069-384X
US

COMPUTING RESEARCH NEWS.
(COMPUTING RESEARCH NEWS : THE NEWS JOURNAL OF THE COMPUTING RESEARCH ASSOCIATION.). [Comput. res. news]. **Added/Corp** The Computing Research Association. Vol. 1, No. 1 (Summer

Computers

1989)-. Periodical. English. Five times a year (Jan., Mar., May, Sept., Nov.) $25.00. Computing Research Association, 1875 Connecticut Avenue Northwest, Suite 718, Washington DC 20009. **Tel** (202)234-2111, FAX (202)667-1066. **ED** John Bass. **Ad Acc, Adv Mgr:** Joan Bass, **Tel** (202)234-2111. **Circ:** 5,000 (ctrl).
 Desc: This covers information of interest to computing research community.

LC QA75 **ISSN** 1084-015X
DD 005 US
COMPUTISTS' COMMUNIQUE, THE. (THE COMPUTISTS' COMMUNIQUE [COMPUTER FILE].). [Comput. commun.]. **Added/Corp** Computists International. (1991)-. Periodical. English. Forty-Four times a year. Comes with Computists International membership. Computists International, 4064 Sutherland Drive, Palo Alto CA 94303. **Tel** (415)493-7390. **ED** Kenneth I. Laws. **Circ:** 1,000. available via Internet (laws@ai.sri.com).

US
COMPUTOREDGE. (19??)-. English. Fifty times a year (publishes weekly except Christmas and New Years). $35.00. Computoredge, PO Box 83086, San Diego CA 92138. **Tel** (619)573-0315. **ED** Pam Lance. Index available. **Ad Acc. Circ:** 50,000 (ctrl). available on an online database. **Continues** Byte Buyer, 0889-8200.
 Desc: A computer related magazine.

 ISSN 0748-3104
DD 384 US
COMUNICACIONES (CORAL GABLES, FLA.). See Communications-Computer Applications.

LC QA76.58 .C66 **ISSN** 1040-3108
DD 004/.35 UK
 CCC
 CODEN CPEXEI
CONCURRENCY (CHICHESTER, ENGLAND). (CONCURRENCY PRACTICE AND EXPERIENCE.). [Concurrency]. **VFOAT** Concurrency. (1989)-. Periodical. English. Eight times a year. $550.00. John Wiley & Sons Ltd., Baffins Lane, Chichester, West Sussex PO19 1UD United Kingdom. **Tel** 011 44 1243 779777, FAX 011 44 1243 776128 BTG:JWP001, telex 86290 WIBOOKG. **(Subscription address:** John Wiley & Sons, Inc. / Philadelphia, PO Box 7247, Philadelphia PA 19170. **Tel** (212)850-6645, (800)225-5945.) **ED** G. C. Fox, A. J. G. Hey, and P. Messina. available on microfilm and microfiche from University Microfilms International (UMI). Documents available from The Genuine Article, Ask*IEEE.
 Desc: Journal relays practical experience of concurrent machines and focuses especially upon concurrent solutions to specific problems, concurrent algorithms and computational methods, programming environments, operating systems and tools, new languages, performance design, analysis, models and results.
 Ind/Abst ACM Guide Comput. Lit.; CompuMath Cit. Index [Full Cov.]; Comput. Abstr.; Comput. Rev.; Curr. Cit.; Data Process. Dig.; INSPEC (Sep. 1989-); Res. Alert [Full Cov.]; SCISEARCH.

LC TK7885.A1 P47a **ISSN** 0896-582X
DD 004 US
CONFERENCE PROCEEDINGS / ANNUAL INTERNATIONAL PHOENIX CONFERENCE ON COMPUTERS AND COMMUNICATIONS. [Conf. proc. - Annu. Int. Phoenix Conf. on Comput. Commun.]. **Added/Corp** Institute of Electrical and Electronics Engineers. IEEE Computer Society. IEEE Communications Society. 3rd (1984)-. English. IEEE Computer Society, 10662 Los Vaqueros Circle, PO Box 3014, Los Alamitos CA 90720-1264. **Tel** (714)821-8380, (800)272-6657, FAX (714)821-4641. **Continues** Phoenix Conference on Computers and Communications. Conference Proceedings.
 Ind/Abst Curr. Cit.

US
●**CONFERENCE PROCEEDINGS / ELECTRO ... INTERNATIONAL.** See Engineering-Electrical Engineering.

LC TK5101.A1 I3544a **ISSN** 0893-4266
DD 621.382 US
 TITLE CHANGE
CONFERENCE PROCEEDINGS - IEEE PACIFIC RIM CONFERENCE ON COMMUNICATIONS, COMPUTERS AND SIGNAL PROCESSING. See Communications-Telecommunication.

 ISSN 1070-0994
DD 004 US
●**CONNECT (ANN ARBOR, MICH.).** (CONNECT : THE MODEM USER'S RESOURCE.). [Connect]. Vol. 1, No. 1 (May/June 1993)-. Periodical. English. Six times a year (Jan., Mar., May, July, Sept., Nov.) $18.00. Pegasus Press, 3487 Braeburn Circle, Ann Arbor MI 48108. **Tel** (313)973-9825, FAX (313)973-0411. **ED** William Rall. **Bk Rev. Ad Acc. Adv Mgr Tel:** (310)572-7272. **Circ:** 65,000.

LC TK3521 .I57 **ISSN** 1078-1528
DD 621.319/3 US
 CODEN CNNSEY
●**CONNECTOR SPECIFIER.** [Connect. specif.]. (June 1994)-. Periodical. English. Twelve times a year. $55.00. IHS Publishing Group, 17730 West Peterson Road, Libertyville IL 60048. **Tel** (708)362-8711, FAX (708)362-3484. **Ad Acc.** ctrl circ. **Continues** InterConnection Technology, 1065-0415.
 Ind/Abst INSPEC.

 ISSN 0264-6854
 UK
 CODEN CNSCEB
CONSTRUCTION COMPUTING. [Constr. comput.]. **Added/Corp** Chartered Institute of Building (Great Britain). (198?)-. Trade Publication. English. Four times a year. $51.33. Chartered Institute of Building, Englemere Kings Ride, Ascot Berkshire SL5 8BJ United Kingdom. **Tel** 011 44 1344 23355, FAX 011 44 1344 23467. **ED** Paul Barton, Pauline Sargent. **Bk Rev. Ad Acc. Circ:** 30,000 (ctrl). Documents available from Ask*IEEE.
 Desc: The application of computing to construction.
 Ind/Abst Curr. Cit.; INSPEC (1985-).

 NE
 CODEN CTITEK
Pr Rev.
CONTEMPORARY TOPICS IN INFORMATION TRANSFER. Vol. 1 (1982)-. Monographic series. English. Irregular. Price varies per volume. Elsevier Science Publishers BV, PO Box 211, 1000 AE Amsterdam Netherlands. **Tel** 011 31 20 4853641, 011 31 20 4853642, FAX 011 31 20 4853598. Documents available from Ask*IEEE.
 Ind/Abst INSPEC.

 ISSN 0734-757X
 US
CONTRIBUTIONS TO THE STUDY OF COMPUTER SCIENCE. [Contrib. study comput. sci.]. (1983)-. Monographic series. English. Greenwood Press Inc., PO Box 5007, Westport CT 06881-5007. **Tel** (203)226-3571, FAX (203)222-1502.

 ISSN 0266-2493
DD 629.8 UK
CONTROL SYSTEMS TONBRIDGE. (CONTROL SYSTEMS.). [Control syst. Tonbridge]. (1983)-. Trade Publication. English. Ten times a year. $188.23. IML Group, Blair House, 184-186 High Street, Tonbridge Kent, TN9 1BQ United Kingdom. **Tel** 011 44 1732 359990, FAX 011 44 1732 770049. **ED** Paul Hanifan. **Ad Acc, Adv Mgr:** Paul Johnson. **Continues** Transducer Technology.
 Ind/Abst Infomat Int. Bus.

LC QA402.3 .C639 **ISSN** 0911-0704
DD 629.9/312/05 JA
Pr Rev. CEASED
CONTROL THEORY AND ADVANCED TECHNOLOGY. **VFOAT** Control-Theory and Advanced Technology; C-TAT; C.T.A.T. Vol. 1 No. 1 (Apr. 1985)-Vol. 10 (1995). Periodical. English. MITA Press, 2-12 Hongo 3, Bunkyo-ku, Tokyo 113 Japan. **Tel** 011 81 3 3818 1011, FAX 011 81 3 3818 1016, telex 2722813. **(Subscription address:** Japan Publications Trading Company Ltd., PO Box 5030, Tokyo International, Tokyo 100-31 Japan. **Tel** 011 81 3 3292 3753.) **ED** Y. Sunahara and D.P. Atherton. Index available (December). **Bk Rev,** (Qty: 1-2). **Circ:** 400 (ctrl). Documents available from Article Express International, The Genuine Article.
 Desc: Dealing with control system and information sciences and related areas. Publishes original scientific and technical papers, short papers, correspondence, or technical notes.
 Ind/Abst CompuMath Cit. Index [Full Cov.]; Curr. Contents Eng. Comput. Technol.; Eng. Index Annu.; Math. Rev. (1988-); Res. Alert [Full Cov.]; SCISEARCH.

 ISSN 0935-0381
 GW
UDC 33
CONTROLLING. [Controlling]. (1989)-. Trade Publication. German. Six times a year. DM178.00. CH Beck Verlagsbuchhandlung, D-80791 Munich Germany. **Tel** 011 49 89 381891.

 ISSN 1067-3121
DD 621
 TITLE CHANGE
CONTROLS DIGEST. [Controls dig.]. (Mar. 1993)-(199?). Periodical. English. Controls Digest, Box 5268, Carefree AZ 85377. **Continues** PLC Insider's Newsletter, 1040-9718. **Continued by** Industrial Controls Intelligence & The PLC Insider's Newsletter.

 ISSN 0745-1342
 US
CPA COMPUTER REPORT. See Business and Economics-Computer Applications.

LC QA75.5 .C67
DD 004 US
CPSR NEWSLETTER, THE. **Added/Corp** Computer Professionals for Social Responsibility. **VAT** Computer Professionals for Social Responsibility Newsletter. (1983)-. Newsletter. English. Four times a year. $40.00 Basic membership; $50.00 library membership; $75.00 regular membership. Computer Professional Social Responsibility, PO Box 717, Palo Alto CA 94302. **Tel** (415)322-3778, FAX (415)322-3798.

LC QA76.8.C7 C73a
DD 004.1/1 US
 CODEN CRCHE8
CRAY CHANNELS. **Main/Corp** Cray Research, Inc. (19??)-. Periodical. English. Four times a year. Cray Research Inc., 608 2nd Avenue South, Suite 1200, Minneapolis MN 55402. **Tel** (612)334-6450.
 Desc: Contains information on supercomputers and Cray computers.
 Ind/Abst Curr. Cit.

 ISSN 0899-8159
DD 005 US
CRYPTOSYSTEMS JOURNAL. Vol. 1, No. 1 (May 1988)-. Periodical. English. Irregular. $70.00. Cryptosystems Journal, 485 Middle Holland Road, Holland PA 18966. **Tel** (215)579-9888. **ED** Tony S. Patti. **Bk Rev.**
 Desc: A unique international journal devoted to the implementation of cryptographic systems on IBM personal computers. Includes complete programs with source code on diskette.

 ISSN 1172-2002
DD 378.00285 004.05 NZ
●**CSC NEWSLETTER CHRISTCHURCH.** [CSC newsl. Christch.]. **VFOAT** Computer Services Centre Newsletter (Christchurch). (1993)-. Periodical. English. Eleven times a year (monthly except Jan.). Free on request. University of Canterbury / Computer Centre, Private Bag, Christchurch New Zealand. **Tel** 011 64 3 667001. **Bk Rev. Circ:** 350-500. **Continues** Newsletter - Computer Services Centre, University of Canterbury, 1170-9251.
 Desc: News, views, and the future directions of the University of Canterbury's Computer Services Center.

 ISSN 0724-8679
 GW
UDC 681.322-181.48
C'T. [C't]. (1983)-. Periodical. German. Twelve times a year. $81.98. Verlag Heinz Heise GmbH und Co, Postfach 610407, D-30604 Hannover Germany. **Tel** 011 49 511 53520, FAX 011 49 511 5352129.

 UK
CU AMIGA. (19??)-. English. Twelve times a year. £29.00. EMAP Images, Priory Court, 30-32 Farringdon Lane, London EC1R 3AU United Kingdom. **Tel** 011 44 171 9726700, FAX 011 44 171 9726710. **Continues** Commodore User.

 ISSN 0748-898X
DD 001 US
CURRENT INDEX OF COMPUTER LITERATURE. [Curr. index comput. lit.]. **Added/Corp** Information Research Institute. **VFOAT** Computer Literature; CICL. Vol. 1, No. 1 (Apr. 1984)-. Periodical. English. Twelve times a year. $180.00. CICL, PO Box 676, Bala-Cynwyd PA 19004.

 US
CURRENT INDUSTRIAL REPORTS. ELECTRONIC BULLETIN BOARD. Bulletin. English. Irregular. US Department of Commerce / Bureau of the Census, Data User Services Division, Customer Services, Washington DC 20233-0800. **Tel** (301)763-4100. **(Subscription address:** Superintendent of Documents, US Government Printing Office, Washington DC 20402.)

LC QA75.5 .C87 **ISSN** 0011-3794
DD 016.00164 US
CURRENT PAPERS ON COMPUTERS & CONTROL. See Computers-Abstracting, Bibliographies and Statistics.

LC QA75-76.95 **ISSN** 1186-8783
DD 004.071/1712338 CN
 CEASED
CURRENTS (CALGARY). (CURRENTS.). [Currents]. **Added/Corp** University of Calgary. Dept. of Academic Computing Services. Vol. 1, No. 1 (Spring 1991)-Vol. 4, No. 2 (Summer 1994). Periodical. English. Academic Computing Services, University of Calgary, Publications Coordinator, 2500 University Drive NW, Calgary Alberta T2N 1N4 Canada.

 NE
CWI TRACT / CENTRUM VOOR WISKUNDE EN INFORMATICA. See Mathematics-Computer Applications.

ISSN 1079-2112
DD 004 US
•CYBERNAUTICS DIGEST. [Cybernaut. dig.]. Vol. 1, No. 1 (Nov. 1994)-. Periodical. English. Twelve times a year. $24.00. KFH Publications Inc., 3530 Bagley Avenue North, Seattle WA 98103. **Tel** (206)547-4950, FAX (206)547-5355.

LC QA75 **ISSN** 0093-7290
DD 004.05 US
CCC
NLM Z 699.A1 D223
DATA CHANNELS. [Data channels]. Vol. 1 (Feb. 1974)-. Trade Publication. English. Twenty-five times a year. $697.00. Phillips Business Information Inc., 1201 Seven Locks Road, PO Box 61130, Potomac MD 20854. **Tel** (301)424-3338, (301)340-1520, (800)777-5005, FAX (301)424-4297, telex 358149. **ED** Anita Taff-Rice. available on an online database (files 636,648/Full-Text) from DIALOG. ***Absorbed*** *Computer Digest, 0163-4194; Data Processing in Education, 0162-5268; Applied Networks Report; Telemedia Monitor.*
Desc: Inside briefings on the entire data computer industry, local area networking, integrated offices, new technologies, regulations, the competition, etc. Also provides contacts for information, hardware and software, etc.
Ind/Abst Comput. Lit. Index; Predicasts; PTS Newsl. Database [Full Txt.].

BE
DATA NEWS. (19??)-. French (Dutch). Forty-three times a year. 2000F Belgium; 2500F Luxembourg and Netherlands; 3500F Europe; 4500F other. IUM Diligentia NV, Hulstlaan 42, 1170 Brussels Belgium. **Tel** 011 32 2 6738170, FAX 011 32 2 6603600.

US
DATAEASE DIALOGUE. (19??)-. English. Ten times a year. $149.00. DataEase International, 7 Cambridge Drive, Trumbull CT 06611. **Tel** (203)374-8000, (800)243-5123. ***Absorbed*** *Expertease.*

LC T175 .M26 **ISSN** 0011-6963
DD 607/.2 US
CCC
CODEN DTMNAT
Pr Rev.
DATAMATION. [Datamation]. Vol. 5, No. 3 (May/June 1959)-. Trade Publication. English. Twenty-four times a year. $75.00 US; $110.00 Canada and Mexico; $195.00 Japan, Australia and New Zealand; $165.00 other. Cahners Publishing Company, 249 West 17th Street, New York NY 10011. **Tel** (212)645-0067, FAX (212)242-6987. **(Subscription address:** Cahners Publishing Company / Colorado, Paid Subscription Service Center, PO Box 7610, Highlands Ranch CO 80126-7610. **Tel** (303)470-4466, FAX (303)470-4691.) **ED** David R. Brousell. Index available. **Bk Rev. Ad Acc. Circ:** 200,000. available on microfilm and microfiche from University Microfilms International (UMI); available in reprints from University Microfilms International (UMI); available on an online database (files 647,648,675/Full-Text) from DIALOG; available in microform. Documents available from Article Express International, The Genuine Article, UMI Article Clearinghouse, Ask*IEEE, Magazine Collection. ***Continues*** *Magazine of Datamation.*
Desc: Journal for the enterprising professional. Interprets the technologies, products and events of significance in the rapidly evolving world of information systems. Analyzes the latest advancements in PC/workstations, networks, software and midrange/mainframe computers. Every issue provides commentary on new product introductions, forecasts of economic trends, and personal interviews with industry leaders.
Ind/Abst ABI/INFORM Glob. Ed.; ABI/INFORM [Computer File] (Oct. 1971-); Acad. Abstr. Full Text Elite; Acad. Abstr.; Acad. Ind. [Computer File] (1984-); Acad. Search; Account. Art.; Anbar Account. Finan. Abstr. [Full Txt.]; Anbar Mark. Distr. Abstr. [Full Txt.]; Anbar Top Manage. Abstr. [Full Txt.]; Appl. Sci. Technol. Index; Art Archaeol. Tech. Abstr.; Bus. Index (1985-); Bus. Period. Index; Bus. Source Plus; Bus. Source; CompuMath Cit. Index [Full Cov.]; Comput. ASAP [Full Txt.]; Comput. Bus.; Comput. Database [Full Txt.]; Comput. Ind. Update; Comput. Lit. Index; Comput. Rev.; Consum. Index Prod. Eval. Inf. Source; Curr. Cit.; Curr. Contents Eng. Comput. Technol.; Data Process. Dig.; Eng. Index Annu. [Select. Cov.]; EP Collect.; Ergon. Abstr.; Expand. Acad. Index (1984-); F&S Index Plus Text, Int. [Select. Cov.]; GATFWORLD (1984); Gen. BusinessFile (1985-); Gen. Period. Index (1985-); HILITES; Homework Help.; Index Period. Artic. Relat. Law (19??-19??); INFO-SOUTH Abstr.; Infomat Int. Bus.; Inf. Instruc. Technol.; Inf. Sci. Abstr.; INIS Atomindex [Micro.]; INSPEC (1968-); Int. Labour Doc.; Mag. Artic. Summar. Elite; Mag. Artic. Summar. Select; Mag. Artic. Summar. CD-ROM; Mag. Index Plus (1989-); Mag. Search; Manage. Market. Abstr.; Manage. Bibliogr. Rev.; MasterFile FullTEXT 1000; MasterFile FullTEXT 350; MasterFile FullTEXT 650; MasterFile FullTEXT (Jan. 1984-); Math. Rev.; Microcomput. Abstr. (Jan. 1985-); Newsp. Period. Abstr. (1988-); OCLC; Oper. Prod. Manage. Abstr. [Full Txt.]; Oper. Res./Manage. Sci.; Person. Train. Abstr. [Full Txt.]; PROMT; Pub. Lib. FullTEXT; Qual. Control Appl. Stat.; Res. Alert [Full Cov.]; Resource/One Ondisc (1988-); Risk Abstr. (19??-19??); Robotics Abstr.; Selec. Coop. Index Manage. Period.; SCISEARCH; Soc. Sci. Cit. Index [Select. Cov.]; Stat. Ref. Index; Telebase; Mag. Index (1977-); Trade Ind. ASAP [Full Txt.]; Trade Ind. Index (1981-) [Full Txt.]; Urban Aff. Abstr.; Vocat. Search; Wilson Bus. Abstr.; Women Manage. Rev. [Full Txt.]; World Ceram. Abstr.; World Publ. Monit.

US
DATAPRO INFORMATION MANAGEMENT & WORKFLOW. (19??)-. English. $1,720.00. Datapro Information Services Group, 600 Delran Parkway, Delran NJ 08075. **Tel** (609)764-0100, (800)328-2776, FAX (609)764-8953.

US
DATAPRO MASTER INDEX [COMPUTER FILE]. **Added/Corp** Datapro Research Corporation. (19??)-. English. Four times a year. $49.95. Datapro Information Services Group, 600 Delran Parkway, Delran NJ 08075. **Tel** (609)764-0100, (800)328-2776, FAX (609)764-8953.

LC T58.6 **ISSN** 1081-874X
DD 658 US
DATAPRO ON CD-ROM. INFORMATION MANAGEMENT & WORKFLOW ANALYST [COMPUTER FILE]. [Datapro CD-ROM, inf. manag. workflow anal.]. **Added/Corp** Datapro Information Services Group. **VFOAT** Information Management & Workflow Analyst; Information Management and Workflow Analyst. (199?)-. English. Twelve times a year. Datapro Information Services Group, 600 Delran Parkway, Delran NJ 08075. **Tel** (609)764-0100, (800)328-2776, FAX (609)764-8953.

US
CODEN DRIBEV
TITLE CHANGE
DATATRENDS REPORT ON DEC AND IBM, THE. Vol. 10, No. 7 (July 1990)-(19??). Periodical. English. DataTrends Publications, 895 Harrison Street SE, Suite B, Leesburg VA 22075. **Tel** (703)779-0574, (800)766-8130, FAX (703)779-2267. available on an online database (file 636/Full-Text) from DIALOG. ***Continues*** *Monosson Report on DEC and IBM, 1040-0966.* ***Continued by*** *DataTends Report on DEC, 1064-377X.*
Ind/Abst PTS Newsl. Database [Full Txt.].

US
DATATRENDS REPORT ON DEC AND IBM. (19??)-. Academic Scholarly Publication. English. Twelve times a year. $625.00. DataTrends Publications, 895 Harrison Street SE, Suite B, Leesburg VA 22075. **Tel** (703)779-0574, (800)766-8130, FAX (703)779-2267. Documents available from CASDDS. ***Continues*** *Terry Shannon on DEC, 1068-8412.*
Ind/Abst Chem. Abstr.

ISSN 0280-6622
SW
DATAVARLDEN. [Datavarlden]. (1983)-. Periodical. Swedish. Thirty-six times a year. $187.38. Fackpressforlaget, Box 3188, S 103 63 Stockholm Sweden. **Tel** 011 46 8 7365600. ***Absorbed*** *Datavarlden och Datafolket, 0284-6691.*
Ind/Abst Infomat Int. Bus.

ISSN 0950-5482
UK
DEC COMPUTING. [DEC comput.]. **VAT** Digital Equipment Corporation Computing. (198?)-. Trade Publication. English. Twenty-six times a year. $136.89. VNU Business Publications BV, 32-34 Broadwick Street, London W1A 2HG United Kingdom. **Tel** 011 44 171 4394242 ext. 2222, FAX 011 44 171 4379638, telex 23918 VNU G, 8952440. Documents available from Ask*IEEE.
Ind/Abst INSPEC (Oct. 1986-).

ISSN 0263-6530
DD 001.64 UK
CCC
DEC USER. [DEC user]. **VFOAT** Digital Equipment Corporation User. (1982)-. Periodical. English. Twelve times a year. $116.36. EMAP Readerlink, Audit House, 260 Field End Road, Ruislip Middlesex HA4 9LT United Kingdom. **Tel** 011 44 1773 63100, FAX 011 44 1733 87367. available on an online database from DIALOG. Documents available from Ask*IEEE. ***Continues*** *Network(Richmond), 0263-3280.*
Ind/Abst Comput. ASAP [Full Txt.]; Comput. Database [Full Txt.]; Curr. Cit.; INSPEC (April 1983-).

FR
DECISION INFORMATIQUE. (19??)-. French. Soc Presse Publs Specialisees, 5 Place du Colonel Fabien, 75491 Paris Cedex 10 France. **Tel** 011 33 1 42402201.

US
•DELPHI DEVELOPERS EXCHANGE. (1995)-. English. Twelve times a year. $99.00. IDG Newsletter Corporation, 77 Franklin Street, Suite 310, Boston MA 02110. **Tel** (617)482-8470, (800)807-0771, FAX (617)338-0164. **(Subscription address:** IDG Newsletters, PO Box 145, Oxon Hill MD 20750. **Tel** (800)549-9494.)

ISSN 1082-3948
US
•DELPHI DEVELOPER'S JOURNAL. **Added/Corp** Cobb Group. (1995)-. Periodical. English. Twelve times a year. $59.00. Cobb Group, 9420 Bunsen Parkway #300, Louisville KY 40220. **Tel** (502)491-1900, (800)223-8720, FAX (502)491-4200.

ISSN 1080-0662
DD 005 US
•DELPHI INFORMANT MAGAZINE. [Delphi inf. mag.]. **VFOAT** Delphi Informant. Vol. 1, No. 1 (1995)-. Periodical. English. Twelve times a year. $49.95. Informant Communications Group Inc, 10519 East Stockton Boulevard, Suite 142, Elk Grove CA 95624-9743. **Tel** (916)686-6610, FAX (916)686-8497.

ISSN 0710-1856
DD 384/.05 CN
DELTA REPORT, THE. See Communications-Telecommunication.

ISSN 1076-3481
DD 004 US
CODEN DTREEV
•DEMAND-SIDE TECHNOLOGY REPORT. [Demand-side technol. rep.]. **Added/Corp** Cutter Information Corp. **VFOAT** Demand Side Technology Report. (1993)-. Periodical. English. Twelve times a year. $457.00. Cutter Information Corporation, 37 Broadway, Arlington MA 02174-5539. **Tel** (617)648-8700, (800)964-5118, FAX (617)648-8707, (617)648-1950, telex 650 100 9891.

US
DENTAL COMPUTERTALK. See Medical Sciences-Computer Applications.

LC QA76.5 .I58 **ISSN** 0731-3071
DD 004.2 US
CCC
CODEN DPFTDL
DIGEST OF PAPERS - INTERNATIONAL SYMPOSIUM ON FAULT-TOLERANT COMPUTING (1979). (DIGEST OF PAPERS / THE ... ANNUAL INTERNATIONAL CONFERENCE ON FAULT-TOLERANT COMPUTING.). [Dig. pap. - Int. Symp. Fault-Toler. Comput.]. **Main/Conf** International Symposium on Fault-Tolerant Computing. **Main/Corp** International Symposium on Fault-Tolerant Computing. **Added/Corp** IEEE Computer Society. IEEE Computer Society. Fault-Tolerant Computing Technical Committee. Denshi Tsushin Gakkai. Denshi Joho Tsushin Gakkai (Japan) IFIP WG 10.4 on Reliable Computing and Fault Tolerance. **VAT** Digest of Papers - International Symposium on Fault Tolerant Computing. 8th (June 21-23, 1978)-. Proceedings. English. One time a year. $100.00. IEEE Computer Society, 10662 Los Vaqueros Circle, PO Box 3014, Los Alamitos CA 90720-1264. **Tel** (714)821-8380, (800)272-6657, FAX (714)821-4641. Documents available from Article Express International. ***Continues*** *International Symposium on Fault-Tolerant Computing. Proceedings.*
Ind/Abst Bioeng. Abstr.; Curr. Cit.; Ei Page One; Eng. Index Annu.; Index IEEE Publ.

LC QA75.5 .D55 **ISSN** 1048-4639
DD 004.16 US
DIGITAL DESKTOP REVIEW. [Digit. deskt.]. Periodical. English. Twelve times a year. $42.00. Publications & Communications, 12416 Hymeadow Drive, Austin TX 78750. **Tel** (512)250-9023, (800)678-9724, FAX (512)331-3900, telex 384303. **ED** Aubrey McAuley.
Desc: Targets users of DEC workstations and UNIX systems; coverage includes networking of DEC and non-DEC systems.

US
DIGITAL IMAGING REPORT. See Publishing.

US
•DIGITAL KIDS. See Children and Youth Interests.

LC TK5102.5 .D4463 **ISSN** 1051-2004
DD 621.382/2 US
CCC
CODEN DSPREJ
Pr Rev.
DIGITAL SIGNAL PROCESSING. [Digit. signal process.]. Vol. 1, No. 1 (Jan. 1991)-. Academic Scholarly Publication. English. Four times a year. $179.00. Academic Press Inc., 6277 Sea Harbor Drive, Orlando FL 32887. **Tel** (800)543-9534, (407)345-4100, FAX (407)352-3445. **ED** John Hershey and Rao Yarlagadda. Documents available from Ask*IEEE.
Desc: Illuminates and explores the path of creativity in the field of signal processing. The content is diverse, covering new technologies, new significant programs, and breakthroughs in the field. A central theme is chosen for each issue to cover important topics in breadth. Publishes advice from the experts. Publishes unique articles describing how readers devised a trick or reached an important conclusion in signal processing.
Ind/Abst Curr. Cit.; INSPEC (Jan. 1991-).

Computers

DD 004
ISSN 1067-7224
US
CODEN DSJOEE
Pr Rev.
DIGITAL SYSTEMS JOURNAL. [Digit. syst. j.]. Vol. 14, No. 6 (Nov./Dec. 1992)-. Trade Publication. English. Six times a year. $60.00. Professional Press Inc, 101 Witmer Road, Horsham PA 19044. **Tel** (215)957-1500, FAX (215)957-1050. **(Subscription address:** Professional Press, PO Box 218, Horsham PA 19044. **) Continues** VAX Professional, 8750-9628. **Ind/Abst** Curr. Cit.

DD 004
ISSN 1059-9991
US
CEASED
DIGITAL'S RDB WORLD. [Digital's Rdb world]. **VFOAT** Rdb World. (1992)-(199?). Periodical. English. Publications & Communications, 12416 Hymeadow Drive, Austin TX 78750. **Tel** (512)250-9023, (800)678-9724, FAX (512)331-3900, telex 384303.

DD 004
ISSN 1070-3950
US
DIRECTORY OF COMPUTER AND HIGH TECHNOLOGY GRANTS. [Dir. comput. high technol. grants]. (1991)-. English. Every 2 years. $52.50. Research Grant Guides, PO Box 1214, Loxahatchee FL 33470. **Tel** (407)795-6129, FAX (407)795-7794.

US
DIRECTORY OF COMPUTER EDUCATION AND RESEARCH. 1st Ed. (1973)-. Directory. English. Six times a year. Scinece and Technology Press, PO Box 614, Latham NY 12110. **ED** T C Hsiao.

US
NLM W 22; AA1 D599
Pr Rev.
DIRECTORY OF MEDICAL COMPUTER SYSTEMS. See Medical Sciences-Computer Applications.

LC TS2301.A7 A8
DD 621.38/044/0294 2 19
US
●**DIRECTORY OF VIDEO, COMPUTER, AND AUDIO-VISUAL PRODUCTS, THE. See** Communications-Video.

ISSN 0234-0860
RU
CCC
CODEN DIMAEJ
DISKRETNAIA MATEMATIKA. Added/Corp Akademiia Nauk SSSR. Otdelenie Matematiki. (1989)-. Academic Scholarly Publication. Russian. Four times a year. $106.00. Izdatelstvo Nauka / Akademiia Nauk, (Publishing House of the Russian Academy of Sciences), Leninskii Porspekt 14, 117901 Moscow Russia. **Tel** 011 95 9542153, FAX 011 95 9382144, telex 411964. **(Subscription address:** East View Publications Inc., 3020 Harbor Lane North, Suite 110, Minneapolis MN 55447. **Tel** (800)477-1005, (612)550-0961, FAX (612)559-2931.**)**

DD 636.089/0285
ISSN 1180-338X
CN
●**DISKUSSIONS (GUELPH).** (DISKUSSIONS.). [Diskussions]. **Added/Corp** Ontario Veterinary College. Computer Group. Vol. 1, Issue 1 (Fall 1990)-. Periodical. English. Three times a year. COUGH Computer Group, Ontario Veterinary College, University of Guelph, Guelph Ontario N1G 2W1 Canada. **Continues** COUGH., 0823-7654.

DD 004/.06/071233
ISSN 0840-6235
CN
DISPATCH / UNIVERSITY OF ALBERTA, UNIVERSITY COMPUTING SYSTEMS. [Dispatch - Univ. Alta., Univ. Comput. Syst.]. **Added/Corp** University of Alberta. University Computing Systems. **VAT** University Computing Systems Dispatch. Vol. 1, No. 1 (Sept. 1988)-. Periodical. English. Ten times a year (publishes monthly except July and Aug.). Free on request. University of Alberta / University Computing Services, 352 General Services Building, Edmonton Alberta T6G 2H1 Canada. **Tel** (403)432-2462. **Continues** Computing Services Bulletin (1985), 0829-3635.

LC TK7872.I6 D57
DD 621.381/542
JA
CODEN DDEVE7
DISPLAY DEVICE : ELECTRONIC DISPLAY DEVICE AND APPLICATION TECHNOLOGY. VFOAT Display Devices. (1990)-. Trade Publication. English. Two times a year (Spring and Fall). $38.00. Dempa Publications Inc., 1 11 15 Higashi Gotanda, Shinagawa ku Tokyo 141 Japan. **Tel** 011 81 3 34456111. Documents available from Ask*IEEE. **Desc:** Monitors the world of electronics displays. Twice a year, it outlines the fast-growing trends in CRTs, VFDs, LCDs, PDPs, LEDs and EL devices and related technologies in up-to-the-minute detail. **Ind/Abst** F&S Index Plus Text, Int. [Select. Cov.]; INSPEC (Spring 1991-); PROMT.

DD 004
ISSN 0888-4129
US
DISTRIBUTED PROCESSING PRODUCT REPORTS. [Distrib. process. prod. rep.]. Periodical. English. Twelve times a year. $721.00. Management Information Corporation, 1111 Marlkress Road, Cherry Hill NJ 08003. **Tel** (609)424-1100. **ED** David Axner. Index available. **Continues** Datacomm & Distributed Processing Report, 0161-7508. **Desc:** Subscription service offering evaluations of mini, medium, and large scale computers.

UDC 658.8
ISSN 0757-309X
FR
DISTRIBUTIQUE. (1983)-. Periodical. French. Ten times a year (monthly except Jan. and Aug.). $137.80. IDG Communications / France, Immeuble La Fayette Cedex 65, F-92051 Paris la Defense 5 France. **Tel** 011 33 1 49047900, FAX 011 33 1 49047870, telex 613234. available on microfilm from University Microfilms International (UMI).

NE
DM-M DATABASE MAGAZINE. English. Database Magazine, Antwoordnummer 10235, 2400 Alphen Rijn Netherlands.

US
●**DOCUMENT IMAGING REPORT.** (1993)-. English. Twenty-five times a year. $597.00. Phillips Business Information Inc., 1201 Seven Locks Road, PO Box 61130, Potomac MD 20854. **Tel** (301)424-3338, (301)340-1520, (800)777-5005, FAX (301)424-4297, telex 358149. **Continues** Electronic Imaging Report; **Absorbed** Imaging Business Report.

UDC 681.3
ISSN 0934-2842
GW
DOS EXTRA. [DOS extra]. **VFOAT** Disk Operating System Extra. (1987)-. Periodical. German. Four times a year. DM70.00. DMV Daten Medien Verlagsgesellschaft, Gruber Strasse 46A, Postfach 1236, D-85586 Poing Germany. **Tel** 011 49 8121 769335.

UDC 681.3
ISSN 0933-1557
GW
DOS INTERNATIONAL. VFOAT Disk Operating System International. (1987)-. Periodical. German. Twelve times a year. DM90.00. DMV Daten Medien Verlagsgesellschaft, Gruber Strasse 46A, Postfach 1236, D-85586 Poing Germany. **Tel** 011 49 8121 769335. **ED** DMV Verlag Eschwege, Telephone: 0565/8090. Index available. cum. index. **Bk Rev. Ad Acc. Circ:** 230,000 (ctrl).

NE
TITLE CHANGE
DOS SPECIAL. VFOAT Disk Operating System Special. (1988)-(1993). Dutch. Sala Communications, Postbus 43048, 1009 ZA Amsterdam Netherlands. **Tel** 011 31 20 6273198. **Continues in part** PC Business Info, 0920-3311. **Continued by** DOS-WIN Special, 0929-5011.

ISSN 0929-5011
NE
●**DOS-WIN SPECIAL. VFOAT** Disk Operating System-Windows Special. (1993)-. Dutch. Four times a year. Sala Communications, Postbus 43048, 1009 ZA Amsterdam Netherlands. **Tel** 011 31 20 6273198. **Continues** DOS Special, 0929-4929.

ISSN 0991-2738
FR
DROIT DE L'INFORMATIQUE ET DES TELECOMS. See Communications-Telecommunication.

LC QA
DD 004
US
●**DV FULL MOTION.** (1996)-. English. Six times a year (Jan., Mar., May, July, Sept., Nov.) $49.95. ActiveMedia inc, 120 Bedford Center, Suite 4, Bedford NH 03110. **Tel** (603)472-2421, FAX (603)472-2419.

US
EASY ACT!. (19??)-. Newsletter. English. Twelve times a year. $79.00 US; $94.00 Canada; $99.00 other. Pinnacle Publishing Inc, PO Box 888, Kent WA 98035. **Tel** (206)251-1900, (800)231-1293, FAX (206)251-5057. **Desc:** Offers tips and solutions for ACT! users. Contains easy-to-use tips, shortcuts, and time saving ACT! techniques.

DD 005
ISSN 1076-0814
US
CEASED
EASY APPROACH. [Easy approach]. Vol. 1, Issue 1 (1994)-(June 1995). Newsletter. English. Pinnacle Publishing Inc, PO Box 888, Kent WA 98035. **Tel** (206)251-1900, (800)231-1293, FAX (206)251-5057. **Desc:** Newsletter on Lotus Approach for Windows. Offers time saving tips for Approach users who want to get more from their databases. Gives you practical advice on setting up databases, generating reports and mail merges, speeding up searches, writing macros and formulas, using Approach with other software, accessing existing data with Approach, and much more.

DD 004
ISSN 0954-870X
UK
EDI INTERFACE. [EDI interface]. **VFOAT** EDInterface (London). (1988)-. Periodical. English. Six times a year. $76.75. Mundy Perry Limited, 102 108 Clerkenwell Road, London EC1M 5SA United Kingdom. **Tel** 011 44 171 4170073, FAX 011 44 171 4170075, telex 922015.

LC QA76.9.T48 E34
DD 651.5/0285
ISSN 1058-0379
US
TITLE CHANGE
EDMS JOURNAL. [EDMS j.]. **Added/Corp** Delphi Consulting Group. **VFOAT** Electronic Document Management Systems Journal. Vol. 2, Issue 1 (Sept. 1991)-(199?). Periodical. English. Delphi Consulting Group Inc, 266 Beacon Street, Boston MA 02114-1224. **Tel** (617)247-1511, FAX (617)247-4957. **ED** Thomas M Kaulopoulos. Index available ((bound in each issue)). cum. index. **Ad Acc, Adv Mgr:** Debra Fitzgibbons, **Tel** 617-247-1511. **Circ:** 2500 (ctrl). **Continues** Text Management Journal, 1051-2454. **Continued by** Electronic Document Management Systems Journal, 1067-7003. **Desc:** Devoted to providing users and evaluators of text retrieval, imaging and multimedia with current industry information.

UK
ELECTRICAL REVIEW. See Engineering-Computer Applications.

DD 006
ISSN 1053-0924
US
ELECTRONIC ATLAS NEWSLETTER, THE. See Geography.

UK
CEASED
ELECTRONIC DOCUMENTS NEWS BULLETIN. VFOAT News Bulletin. (Jan. 1992)-(19??). Bulletin. English. Learned Information Ltd., Woodside Hinksey Hill, Oxford OX1 5AU United Kingdom. **Tel** 011 44 1865 730275, FAX 011 44 1865 736354, telex 23667. **Desc:** Covers both the creation and distribution of electronic documents. Each edition investigates key issues, both practical and technological, such as replacing your filing cabinets with discs; exchanging documents without using paper; sending sound, text and images together by phone or replacing printed books with electronic books. **Ind/Abst** Inf. Manage. Technol. (19??-19??); Int. Aerosp. Abstr. (19??-19??).

DD 338
ISSN 1057-0942
US
TITLE CHANGE
ELECTRONIC IMAGING REPORT. See Engineering-Computer Applications.

LC HE6239.E54 E57
DD 384.1/4
ISSN 0735-2379
US
ELECTRONIC MAIL EXECUTIVES DIRECTORY. [Electron. mail exec. dir.]. **Added/Corp** International Resource Development, inc. (1980)-. Directory. English. One time a year. $595.00. International Resource Development Inc, PO Box 1716, New Canaan CT 06840-1716. **Tel** (203)966-2525, telex 64 3452. **ED** Diam Tomck. **Desc:** Results of primary survey of approximately 1,000 major US corporations. (All raw survey data provided). Plans for procurement of microcomputers and software. Centralized/decentralized procurement policies, etc.

US
ELECTRONIC MAP CABINET. See Geography.

ISSN 1072-1959
US
●**ELECTRONIC MESSAGING UPDATE. See** Communications-Computer Applications.

DD 004
ISSN 1069-4021
US
●**EMBEDDED COMPUTER TRENDS.** No. 53 (Feb. 1993)-. Periodical. English. Twelve times a year. $295.00. InfoBUS Publishing, PO Box 15, Needham MA 02194. **Tel** (617)449-2033, FAX (617)449-1193. **ED** Warren Andrews (editors address: 261 Concord Street, West Glouster, MA 01930 (508)843-2511). **Continues** InfoBUS Report.

DD 005
ISSN 1040-3272
US
CCC
CODEN EYPRE4
EMBEDDED SYSTEMS PROGRAMMING. [Embedded syst. program.]. Vol. 1, No. 1 (1988)-. English. Twelve times a year. $50.00. Miller Freeman Inc, 600 Harrison Street, San Francisco CA 94107. **Tel** (415)905-2337, (415)905-2200, FAX

Computers

(415)905-2240, telex 278273. **(Subscription address:** Palm Coast Data, PO Box 420163, Agency Department, Palm Coast FL 32142. **Tel** (904)445-4662 ext. 669, (800)829-5475.**) ED** Tyler Sperry. **Ad Acc. Circ:** 26,000 (ctrl). available on microfilm and microfiche from University Microfilms International (UMI). Documents available from Ask*IEEE.
Desc: Edited for design engineers, engineering managers, software developers and programmers who use embedded systems development. Editorial includes coverage of microprocessors and microcontrollers, high-level languages and real-time operating systems.
Ind/Abst ACM Guide Comput. Lit. (19??-); Comput. Rev. (19??-); INSPEC (1992-).

US
EMPLOYMENT MARKETPLACE. See Occupations and Careers.

LC TK7885 **ISSN** 1077-2642
DD 621.39 US
●**ENGINEERING DESIGN AND AUTOMATION. See** Engineering.

PL
ENTER WARSZAWA. (ENTER.). (1990)-. Polish. Twelve times a year. $45.00. **(Subscription address:** Ars Polona-Ruch, PO Box 1001, Krakowskie Przedmiescie 7, 00-068 Warsaw Poland. **Tel** 011 48 22 261201.**)**

ISSN 1078-9790
DD 006 US
TITLE CHANGE
ENTERPRISE COMMUNICATIONS. See Communications-Telecommunication.

US
ENTERPRISE DSI INFODISK. (19??)-. Periodical. English. Six times a year. $6975.00 US; $7673.00 Canada; $8370.00 other. Faulkner Technical Reports, 7905 Browning Road, Suite 114, Pennsauken NJ 08109. **Tel** (800)843-0460.

ISSN 1076-1462
DD 004 US
●**ENTERPRISE NETWORKING.** (ENTERPRISE NETWORKING : THE JOURNAL OF THE ASSOCIATION OF BANYAN USERS INTERNATIONAL.). [Enterp. netw.]. **Added/Corp** Association of Banyan Users International (U.S.). Vol. 7, No. 2 (Mar./Apr. 1994)-. Periodical. English. Six times a year. $30.00. Association of Banyan Users International, 401 North Michigan Avenue, Chicago IL 60611. **Tel** (312)644-6610. **Continues** ABUI Network News, 1061-5547.

LC WMLC 93/1282 QA76.8.I1015 E5 **ISSN** 1053-6566
DD 004 US
Pr Rev.
ENTERPRISE SYSTEMS JOURNAL. [Enterp. syst. j.]. **VFOAT** Enterprise Systems. Vol. 5, No. 10 (Oct. 1990)-. Trade Publication. English. Twelve times a year. $60.00. Cardinal Business Media / Texas, 12225 Greenville Avenue, Suite 700, Dallas TX 75243. **Tel** (214)669-9000, **FAX** (214)669-9909. **(Subscription address:** Enterprise Systems Journal, PO Box 740908 Circulations Department, Dallas TX 75243. **) Ad Acc. Circ:** 90,000 (ctrl). **Continues** Mainframe Journal, 0895-5751.
Desc: Edited for those MIS/DP professionals and corporate managers who are primarily involved in the use of IBM and/or compatible mainframe computer systems.

ISSN 8755-1047
DD 001 US
EPSON WORLD. [Epson world]. Vol. 1, No. 1 (Fall 1984)-. Periodical. English. Four times a year. $17.97. Camden Communications Inc, Highland Mill, PO Box 250, Camden ME 04843. **Tel** (800)253-5473. Documents available from Ask*IEEE.
Ind/Abst INSPEC (1985-).

ISSN 8750-622X
DD 001 US
EPSONCONNECTION. [EpsonConnection]. **VFOAT** Epson Connection; EC. Periodical. English. Twelve times a year. $24.00 US; $30.00 Canada. Epsonconnection, PO Box 14027, Detroit MI 48214.

ISSN 0960-085X
UK
CCC
Pr Rev.
EUROPEAN JOURNAL OF INFORMATION SYSTEMS. (EUROPEAN JOURNAL OF INFORMATION SYSTEMS : AN OFFICIAL JOURNAL OF THE OPERATIONAL RESEARCH SOCIETY.). [Eur. J. Inf. Syst.]. **Added/Corp** Operational Research Society (Great Britain). Vol. 1, No. 1 (Jan. 1991)-. Trade Publication. English. Four times a year. $265.23. Macmillan Magazines Ltd., Brunel Road, Basingstoke, Hampshire RG21 6XS United Kingdom. **Tel** 011 44 1256 29242, **FAX** 011 44 1256 812358, telex 858493. **ED** J. Liebenau and S. Smithson. Index available. cum. index. **Bk Rev. Ad Acc. Circ:** 4,000. available on microfilm and microfiche from University Microfilms International (UMI). Documents available from

UMI Article Clearinghouse, Ask*IEEE. **Absorbed** Journal of Applied Systems Analysis, 0308-9541.
Desc: A mixture of research articles and case studies of interest to professionals in academia industry, commerce, and government.
Ind/Abst ABI/INFORM Glob. Ed.; ACM Guide Comput. Lit.; Comput. Rev.; Curr. Cit.; INSPEC (Jan. 1991-); Int. Abstr. Oper. Res. [Full Cov.].

UK
EXPERT SYSTEMS APPLICATIONS. English. Twelve times a year. £300.00 UK; £450.00 other. IML Group, Blair House, 184-186 High Street, Tonbridge Kent, TN9 1BQ United Kingdom. **Tel** 011 44 1732 359990, **FAX** 011 44 1732 770049. **ED** Andrew Bond. **Continues** Expert Systems User.

ISSN 1047-7705
DD 005 US
TITLE CHANGE
EXPERTEASE (FEDERAL WAY, WASH.). (EXPERTEASE : MAKING DATAEASE EASIER.). [ExpertEase]. **VFOAT** Expert Ease. Vol. 1, Issue 1 (Nov. l989)-(19??). Periodical. English. DataEase International, 7 Cambridge Drive, Trumbull CT 06611. **Tel** (203)374-8000, (800)243-5123. **Merged into** Dataease Dialogue.

US
EXPORTING COMPUTERS WITHOUT A VALIDATED LICENSE. See Business and Economics-Commerce.

AT
FARM COMPUTING. See Agriculture-Computer Applications.

US
FAULKNER CLIENT SERVER INFODISK. (19??)-. Periodical. English. Four times a year. $1413.00. Faulkner Technical Reports, 7905 Browning Road, Suite 114, Pennsauken NJ 08109. **Tel** (800)843-0460.

US
FAULKNER COMPUTER AND COMMUNICATIONS LIBRARY. See Communications-Computer Applications.

US
FAULKNER DATAWORLD. (19??)-. Periodical. English. Twelve times a year. $1460.00 US; $1678.00 Canada; $2080.00 other. Faulkner Technical Reports, 7905 Browning Road, Suite 114, Pennsauken NJ 08109. **Tel** (800)843-0460.

US
FAULKNER DATAWORLD INFODISC. (19??)-. Periodical. English. Four times a year. $1707.00 US; $1957.00 Canada; $2077.00 other. Faulkner Technical Reports, 7905 Browning Road, Suite 114, Pennsauken NJ 08109. **Tel** (800)843-0460.

US
FAULKNER EDP LIBRARY. (19??)-. Periodical. English. Twelve times a year. $6305.00 US; $7152.00 Canada; $7780.00 other (renewals only). Faulkner Technical Reports, 7905 Browning Road, Suite 114, Pennsauken NJ 08109. **Tel** (800)843-0460.

US
FAULKNER ELECTRONIC OFFICE AUTOMATION. See Business and Economics-Office Equipment and Services.

US
FAULKNER IMAGING SYSTEMS. (19??)-. Periodical. English. Twelve times a year. $645.00 US; $728.00 Canada; $920.00 other. Faulkner Technical Reports, 7905 Browning Road, Suite 114, Pennsauken NJ 08109. **Tel** (800)843-0460.

US
FAULKNER MICRODATA INFODISK. (19??)-. Periodical. English. Six times a year. $1313.00 US; $1533.00 Canada; $1698.00 other. Faulkner Technical Reports, 7905 Browning Road, Suite 114, Pennsauken NJ 08109. **Tel** (800)843-0460.

US
FAULKNER STANDARD EDP REPORTS. (19??)-. Periodical. English. Irregular. $3880.00 US; $4358.00 Canada; $4965.00 other. Faulkner Technical Reports, 7905 Browning Road, Suite 114, Pennsauken NJ 08109. **Tel** (800)843-0460.

LC AS4 .W6514 **ISSN** 0015-0770
US
FIELDS WITHIN FIELDS WITHIN FIELDS. **Added/Corp** World Institute. **VFOAT** Fields within Fields. No. 1 (Spring 1968)-. Periodical. English. Four times a year. World Institute Council, 171 West Street, Brooklyn NY 11222. Index available. cum. index. ctrl circ. available on microfilm from University Microfilms International

(UMI).
Desc: Solutions to mankind's problems using systems thinking.

LC HG1709 .F53 **ISSN** 0743-0159
DD 332/.028/5 US
FINANCIAL COMPUTING. See Business and Economics-Computer Applications.

US
FLEXLINES. Trade Publication. English. Six times a year. $24.00 US and Puerto Rico; $75.00 other. Data Access Corporation, 5753 Miami Drive East, Miami Lakes FL 33014. **Tel** (305)825-7070, **FAX** (305)825-2450.

ISSN 1067-6244
DD 004 US
●**FM TECHNOLOGY REPORT.** [FM technol. rep.]. Vol. 2, No. 9 (Feb. 1993)-. Periodical. English. Twelve times a year. $115.00. Graphic Systems, 1815 Massachussetts Avenue, Suite 308, Cambridge MA 02140. **Tel** (617)492-1148. **Continues** GSI Report on Real Estate and Facility Management Automation, 1056-5604.

ISSN 1023-0114
SZ
UDC 681.3
FORUM LOGICIEL. [Forum logiciel]. (1991)-. Periodical. French. Six times a year. 240.00F. Martinig & Associes, Avenue Nestle 28, CH 1800 Vevey Switzerland. **Tel** 011 41 219221300, **FAX** 011 41 219221300.

PL
FOUNDATIONS OF COMPUTING AND DECISION SCIENCE. English. Four times a year. Price on request. **(Subscription address:** Ars Polona-Ruch, PO Box 1001, Krakowskie Przedmiescie 7, 00-068 Warsaw Poland. **Tel** 011 48 22 261201.**)**
Continues Foundations of Control Engineering.

US
FRAMERS FORUM. English. Four times a year. $29.95 US; $42.95 other. Framers Forum Magazine, 37213 Wildcat Mountain Drive, Eagle Creek OR 97022. **Tel** (503)637-3275, **FAX** (503)637-6876. **ED** Patrick Walsh. **Bk Rev. Ad Acc.** ctrl circ.

US
Pr Rev.
FUNDAMENTAL STUDIES IN COMPUTER SCIENCE. Vol. 1 (1973)-. English. Irregular. Elsevier Science Publishing Company Inc, Madison Square Station, PO Box 882, New York NY 10159-0882. **Tel** (212)633-3950, **FAX** (212)633-3990. Documents available from Ask*IEEE.
Ind/Abst INSPEC.

LC CS14 .G46 **ISSN** 0735-0287
DD 929/.1/02854 US
GENEALOGICAL COMPUTER PIONEER. See Genealogy and Heraldry-Computer Applications.

LC CS14 .G465 **ISSN** 0277-5913
DD 929/.1/028542 US
Pr Rev.
GENEALOGICAL COMPUTING. See Genealogy and Heraldry-Computer Applications.

ISSN 1067-8719
DD 025 US
●**GILBANE REPORT ON OPEN INFORMATION & DOCUMENT SYSTEMS, THE.** [Gilbane rep. open inf. doc. syst.]. **VFOAT** Gilbane Report. Vol. 1, No. 1 (Mar. 1993)-. Periodical. English. Six times a year. $225.00. Cap Ventures, One Snow Road, Marshfield MA 02050. **Tel** (617)837-7200, , **FAX** (617)837-8856. **ED** Frank Silbane. **Circ:** 2,000.
Desc: Analysis of technology and trends in information and document management, electronic delivery, text retrieval, publishing, reengineering, and standards.

UK
GOVERNMENT COMPUTING. (19??)-. English. Government Computing / England, Southbank House, Black Prince Road, London FE1 7SJ United Kingdom. **Tel** 011 44 171 5829191, **FAX** 011 44 171 5871810.

US
●**GOVERNMENT IMAGING.** (May 1992)-. English. Ten times a year. Free. Government Imaging, 1734 Elkton Road, Suit 200, Silver Spring MD 20903. **Tel** (301)445-4405, **FAX** (301)445-5722. **ED** Robert V. Head. Index Available Published separately--free--upon request. **Ad Acc. Circ:** 35,000 (ctrl).
Desc: Information on document imaging.

LC QA76.27 .G69
DD 004 US
●**GRADUATE ASSISTANTSHIP DIRECTORY IN COMPUTING. Added/Corp** Association for Computing Machinery. **VFOAT** GAD; Graduate Assistantship Directory. (1994)-. Directory.

English. One time a year (Apr.). $22.00. ACM / Association for Computing Machinery, 1515 Broadway, 17th Floor, New York NY 10036. **Tel** (212)869-7440, FAX (212)869-0481. **(Subscription address:** Association for Computing Machinery, PO Box 12114, Church Street Station, New York NY 10249. **Tel** (212)626-0500.) ***Continues*** *Graduate Assistantship Directory in the Computer Sciences, 0072-5234.*

LC WMLC L 83/8317 QA76.27 .G73 **ISSN** 0072-5234
DD 004 US
TITLE CHANGE

GRADUATE ASSISTANTSHIP DIRECTORY IN THE COMPUTER SCIENCES. **Added/Corp** Association for Computing Machinery. **VFOAT** Graduate Assistantship Directory; GAD; ACM Graduate Assistantship Directory. (19??)-(1993). Directory. English. ACM / Association for Computing Machinery, 1515 Broadway, 17th Floor, New York NY 10036. **Tel** (212)869-7440, FAX (212)869-0481. ***Continued by*** *Graduate Assistantship Directory in Computing.*
Desc: Contains information about assistantships and fellowships available in university computing science departments and university computing centers for graduate study.

LC QA
DD 004 GW

●**GRADUATE TEXTS IN COMPUTER SCIENCE.** (1994)-. Monographic series. English. Irregular. DM56.00. Springer-Verlag GmbH & Company KG, Heidelberger Platz 3, D-14197 Berlin Germany. **Tel** 011 49 30 8207223, FAX 011 49 30 8214091, telex 183 319 SPBLN D. **(Subscription address:** Springer-Verlag New York Inc. / North America, PO Box 2485, Journal Fulfillment, Secaucus NJ 07096. **Tel** (201)348-4033, (800)777-4643, FAX (201)348-4505.) **ED** D. Gries, F. Schneider.
Desc: Contains information on graduate level computer science.

LC QA76.16 .G84 **ISSN** 0748-6235
DD 001.64/029/4 US

GUIDE TO FREE COMPUTER MATERIALS. **See** Education-Teaching and Curriculum.

LC QA76.8.T18 T77 **ISSN** 0734-3159
DD 001.64 US

H & E COMPUTRONICS INC. [H & E Comput. Inc.]. **VFOAT** H and E Computronics Inc; H & E Computronics Monthly News Magazine; Computronics; H&E Computronics Inc. Monthly News Magazine; H&E Computronics Monthly News Magazine. Issue No. 18 (Jan. 1980)-. Periodical. English. Twelve times a year. $24.00 US; $36.00 other. H & E Computronics Inc, 50 North Pascack Road, Spring Valley NY 10977. ***Continues*** *TRS-80 Monthly News Magazine, 0734-3175.*

ISSN 0936-1375
GW
UDC 061.68 :5
CODEN 061.68 :608.3

HANDBUCH DER DATENBANKEN FUER NATURWISSENSCHAFT, TECHNIK, PATENTE. (1988)-. German. One time a year. DM295.00. Verlag Hoppenstedt und Co, Havelstr 9, Postfach 4006, D-6100 Darmstadt Germany. **Tel** 6151-380-1, FAX 6151/380-360, telex 419258 HOPP D. **ED** Dr Schulte-Hillen BDU. **Bk Rev. Ad Acc. Circ:** 600.
Desc: Gives information on 930 databases worldwide. Descriptions of the databases inform about technical literature, research projects, and patent documents. Each entry gives information on producer, provider, type of database, subjects covered, sources, data compiled, how-to get access to the database and languages used.

ISSN 0255-030X
DD 001.64/05 CN

HANDI-COMMUNICATIONS. **See** Communications-Computer Applications.

ISSN 0842-5353
DD 362.1/1/0684 CN

HEALTHCARE COMPUTING & COMMUNICATIONS CANADA. **See** Medical Sciences-Computer Applications.

LC QA76.8.H16 H48 **ISSN** 0018-1153
DD 004 US
CODEN HPJOAX

HEWLETT-PACKARD JOURNAL. (HEWLETT-PACKARD JOURNAL : TECHNICAL INFORMATION FROM THE LABORATORIES OF HEWLETT-PACKARD COMPANY.). [Hewlett-Packard j.]. **Added/Corp** Hewlett-Packard Company. **VAT** Hewlett Packard Journal. Vol. 1, No. 8 (1950)-. Periodical. English. Irregular. Free on request. Hewlett Packard, 1000 Northeast Circle Boulevard, Corvallis OR 97330. **Tel** (503)757-2000. available on CD-ROM; available on microfilm and microfiche from University Microfilms International (UMI); available on an online database (file 675/Full-Text) from DIALOG. Documents available from Article Express International, The Genuine Article, Ask*IEEE. ***Continues*** *HP Journal.*
Ind/Abst AESIS Q.; Bus. Source Plus; Bus. Source; Comput. ASAP [Full Txt.]; Comput. Database [Full Txt.]; Curr. Cit.; Curr. Contents Eng. Comput. Technol.; Ei Page One; Eng. Index Annu. [Select. Cov.]; EP Collect.; Homework Help.; INSPEC (1968-); Int. Civil Eng. Abstr.; MasterFile FullTEXT 1000; MasterFile FullTEXT 350; MasterFile FullTEXT 650; MasterFile FullTEXT (Jan. 1995-); OCLC; Res. Alert [Select. Cov.]; SCISEARCH; Telebase.

LC QA76.88 .H544 **ISSN** 1068-0365
DD 004 US
CODEN HPCREB
CEASED

HIGH-PERFORMANCE COMPUTING REVIEW. [High-perform. comput. rev.]. **VFOAT** High Performance Computing Review. Vol. 1, No. 1 (Winter 1992)-Vol. 1, No. 6 (Aug. 1993). Periodical. English. Publications & Communications, 12416 Hymeadow Drive, Austin TX 78750. **Tel** (512)250-9023, (800)678-9724, FAX (512)331-3900, telex 384303. ***Continues*** *Supercomputing Review, 1048-6836.*

US

HIGH TECH PROCUREMENT. (19??)-. English. Twelve times a year. $495.00. International Computer Negotiations Inc., PO Drawer 2970, Winter Park FL 32790. **Tel** (407)740-0700.

ISSN 0193-466X
US

HIRSCH REPORT, THE. [Hirsch rep.]. **Main/Corp** Hirsch, Phil. (197?)-. Periodical. English. Six times a year. $96.00. Hirsch Report, PO Box 34616, Bethesda MD 20034. **Tel** (301)340-6773. **ED** Phil Hirsch.
Desc: Covers data communications.

LC D16.12 .H56 **ISSN** 0957-0144
DD 901 UK
CCC
NLM W1; HI82L

HISTORY & COMPUTING. **See** History-Computer Applications.

ISSN 0939-2602
GW
UDC 33

HMD. THEORIE UND PRAXIS DER WIRTSCHAFTSINFORMATIK. **VFOAT** Theorie und Praxis der Wirtschaftsinformatik. (1989)-. Trade Publication. German. Six times a year. $165.81. Forkel Verlag GmbH, Postfach 2120, D-65011 Wiesbaden Germany. **Tel** 011 49 611 278030. **(Subscription address:** WEPF Publishing Services GmbH, Auf dem Wolf 4, CH-4018 Basel Switzerland. **Tel** 011 41 61 3115125.) ***Continues*** *Handbuch der Modernen Datenverarbeitung HMD, 0723-5208.*

ISSN 1044-4319
DD 005 US
CCC
CEASED

HOTLINE ON OBJECT-ORIENTED TECHNOLOGY. [Hotline object-oriented technol.]. **VFOAT** Hotline on Object Oriented Technology; Hot Line on Object-Oriented Technology; HOOT. Vol. 1, No. 1 (Nov. 1989)-Vol. 4, No. 4 (Feb. 1993). Periodical. English. SIGS Publications Inc. / New York, 71 West 23rd Street, 3rd Floor, New York NY 10010-4102. **Tel** (212)242-7447.
Ind/Abst Abstr. Hum. Comput. Interact. (?-?).

LC QA76.8.H48 H63 **ISSN** 1075-0703
DD 005.4/469 US

●**HP-UX/USR (SUNNYVALE, CALIF.).** (HP-UX/USR : HANDS-ON SOLUTIONS FOR HP-UX USERS.). [HP-UX/usr]. **Added/Corp** Interex (Organization). Vol. 1, No. 1 (Mar. 1993)-. Newsletter. English. Twelve times a year. Interex, PO Box 3439, Sunnyvale CA 94088. **Tel** (408)747-0227, FAX (408)736-2156, telex 4971527. **ED** Richard Kranz. **Circ:** 8,000.
Desc: Newsletter for Hewlett-Packard computer users.

ISSN 1060-5916
US

HR COMPUTING. (1992)-. Directory. English. One time a year. $79.95. DGM Associates, PO Box 10639, Marina del Rey CA 90292. **Tel** (310)578-1428.
Desc: Directory of software products and services for human resources.

LC QA76.9.S88 H84 **ISSN** 0737-0024
DD 004/.01/9 US
CODEN HCINE6

HUMAN-COMPUTER INTERACTION. [Hum.-comput. interact.]. **VFOAT** Human Computer Interaction. Vol. 1, No. 1 (1985)-. Periodical. English. Four times a year. $215.00. Lawrence Erlbaum Associates, Inc., 10 Industrial Avenue, Mahwah NJ 07430. **Tel** (201)236-9500, (800)926-6579, FAX (201)666-2394. **ED** Thomas P. Moran. **Ad Acc.** Full Page (B&W) $375.00. Half Page (B&W) $275.00. Documents available from Article Express International, Ask*IEEE.
Desc: Journal of theoretical, empirical and methodological issues of user psychology and of system design.
Ind/Abst Abstr. Hum. Comput. Interact.; Comput. Abstr.; Comput. Inf. Syst. Abstr. J. [Full Cov.]; Curr. Cit.; Ei Page One; Eng. Index Annu.; Ergon. Abstr.; HILITES; INSPEC (1987-1988); Psychol. Abstr. (1985-); PsycINFO (1990-); PsycLit.

ISSN 0825-5784
DD 001.64/04 CN

HYPERION PC. [Hyperion PC]. **VAT** Hyperion Personal Computer. Vol. 1, No. 1 (1984)-. Periodical. English. Six times a year. $27.00 (12 issues). Hyperion PC, Suite 400/22 Metcalfe Street, Ottawa Ontario K1P 5L1 Canada.

ISSN 0954-917X
UK

I T L G. [I T L G]. **VFOAT** Information Technology for Local Government. (1988)-. Government Publication. English. Ten times a year. $119.79. Government Computing / England, Southbank House, Black Prince Road, London FE1 7SJ United Kingdom. **Tel** 011 44 171 5829191, FAX 011 44 171 5871810. **(Subscription address:** Pillar Publications, 45 Woodland Grove, Waybridge Surrey KT13 9EQ, United Kingdom. **Tel** 011 44 932 820282, FAX 011 44 932 858035.)

US

I WAY. (19??)-. English. Business Computer Publishing Inc., 80 Elm Street, Peterborough NH 03458. **Tel** (800)349-7327. **(Subscription address:** Kable Publishers Aide / Illinois, 308 East Hitt Street, Subscription Department, Mt. Morris IL 61054-1473. **Tel** (815)734-1261.)

UK

IBEX BULLETIN. (19??)-. Bulletin. English. Twelve times a year. $460.00. Xephon, 27-35 London Road, Newbury Berkshire RG13 1JL United Kingdom. **Tel** 011 44 1635 33823, FAX 011 44 1635 38345. **(Subscription address:** Xephon, 1301 West Highway, Suite 201 450, Lewisville TX 75067.) **ED** Harold Lewis and Chris Bunyan. Index available. cum. index. **Circ:** 1,000.
Desc: Statistical review of the IBM mainframe marketplace based on monthly surveys of 1000 mainframe sites.

ISSN 0018-8662
GW
CODEN IBMNAQ

IBM NACHRICHTEN. [IBM Nachr.]. **Added/Corp** IBM Deutschland. **VAT** International Business Machines Nachrichten. No. 104 (Oct. 1951)-. Periodical. German. Four times a year. IBM Deutschland GmbH, Postfach 80 0880, 7000 Stuttgart 80 Germany. cum. index. ***Supersedes*** *Hollerith-Nachrichten.*
Ind/Abst Bioeng. Abstr.; Energy Res. Abstr. (Dec. 1976-); Libr. Inf. Sci. Abstr.; Soc. Plann. Policy Dev. Abstr.; Sociol. Abstr.

US
TITLE CHANGE

IBM OS/2 DEVELOPER. **VFOAT** IBM OS 2 Developer. (19??)- Vol. 5, No. 3 (July/Aug. 1993). Periodical. English. Miller Freeman Inc., 600 Harrison Street, San Francisco CA 94107. **Tel** (415)905-2337, (415)905-2200, FAX (415)905-2240, telex 278273. ***Continued by*** *OS/2 Developer, 1073-0729.*

LC Z5642.6.I25 I25 QA76.8.I2594 **ISSN** 0741-2355
DD 016.00164 US

IBM PC INDEX, THE. [IBM PC index]. **VFOAT** I.B.M. P.C. INDEX. Vol. 1, No. 1 (July/Aug. 1983)-. English. Six times a year (with annual cumulations). $24.00. BP Publications, 465 Chestnut Tree Hill Road, Southbury CT 06488-1955. **Tel** (203)264-2143. **ED** Beverly A Pajer.

ISSN 0950-303X
DD 004.165 UK

IBM SYSTEM USER. [IBM syst. user]. (1983)-. Periodical. English. Twelve times a year. $145.45. APT Data Services, 12 Sutton Row, 4th Floor, London W1V 5FH United Kingdom. **Tel** 011 44 171 2084200, FAX 011 44 171 4391105. **(Subscription address:** Computer Action Ltd. / UK, Central House, 27 Park Street, Croyden Surrey CRO 1YD, United Kingdom.) ***Continues*** *IBM User, 0261-3654.*
Ind/Abst Comput. ASAP [Full Txt.]; Comput. Database [Full Txt.].

ISSN 0018-8689
US
CODEN IBMTAA

IBM TECHNICAL DISCLOSURE BULLETIN. [IBM tech. dis. bull.]. **Added/Corp** International Business Machines Corporation. **VAT** International Business Machines Technical Disclosure Bulletin. Vol. 1 (June 1958)-. Bulletin. English. Twelve times a year. Free. IBM Corporation, Corporate Technical Publications, Armonk NY 10504. **Tel** (914)765-1900. Documents available from Article Express International, Ask*IEEE.
Ind/Abst Ei Page One; Eng. Index Annu.; INIS Atomindex [Micro.]; INSPEC (1968-1986).

LC TK7895.S62 M45 **ISSN** 1074-6269
DD 621.39/8 US
CCC

●**IC CARD SYSTEMS & DESIGN.** [IC card syst. des.]. **VFOAT** IC Card Systems and Design; IC Card. Vol. 3, No. 1 (Jan./Feb. 1993)-. Trade Publication. English. Six times a year. $36.00. Argus Business, 6151 Powers Ferry Road Northwest, Atlanta GA 30339. **Tel** (404)995-2500, FAX (404)995-0400. ***Continues*** *Memory Card Systems & Design, 1055-5188.*

ISSN 0801-5775
NO

ICAME JOURNAL / INTERNATIONAL COMPUTER ARCHIVE OF MODERN ENGLISH. **See** Linguistics-Computer Applications.

LC QA75.5 .I567a **ISSN** 0142-1557
DD 001.64/05 UK
CCC
CODEN ITJOD7
TITLE CHANGE

ICL TECHNICAL JOURNAL. [ICL tech. j.]. **Main/Corp** International Computers, Ltd. **Added/Corp** International Computers, Ltd. Technical Journal. **VFOAT** I.C.L. Technical Journal. **VAT** International Computers, Limited Technical Journal. Vol. 1 (Nov. 1978)-(1993). Periodical. English. Oxford University Press / UK, Walton Street, Oxford OX2 6DP United Kingdom. **Tel** 011 44 1865 56767, FAX 011 44 1865 267773, telex 851/837330 OXPRES G. **(Subscription address:** Oxford University Press / USA, Journals Marketing Department, Oxford University Press, 2001 Evans Road, Cary NC 27513. **Tel** (800)451-7556, (919)677-0977, FAX (919)677-1714.**) ED** J.M.M. Pinkerton. Index available. **Ad Acc. Circ:** 7,000. available on microfilm and microfiche from University Microfilms International (UMI). Documents available from Article Express International, Ask*IEEE. ***Continued by*** *Ingenuity, 1354-9952.*
Desc: Up-to-date practical applications and developments in the fields of computers and information science and technology.
Ind/Abst Abstr. Hum. Comput. Interact. (?-?); Bioeng. Abstr. (?-?); Curr. Cit.; Curr. Technol. Index (?-?); Ei Page One (?-?); Eng. Index Annu. (?-?); Ergon. Abstr. (?-?); INSPEC (Nov. 1978-); World Publ. Monit. (?-?).

FR

ICONES / LE JOURNAL DU MACINTOSH. (19??)-. French. Six times a year. 176.30F France; 230.00F Europe; 290.00F other. Icones, 15 Ave Delroy, 59100 Roubaix France. **Tel** 011 33 20 705490.

JA

ICOT JOURNAL. **Added/Corp** Institute for New Generation Computer Technology. **VFOAT** ICOT Journal Digest. No. 1 (June 1983)-. Periodical. English. Shinsedai Konpyuta Gijutsu Kaihatsu Kiko, (Inst. for New Generation Computer Technology), 4-28 Mita 1 Chome, Minatoku Tokyo 108 Japan.
Ind/Abst Abstr. Hum. Comput. Interact.

LC HF5416 .B363 **ISSN** 0892-676X
DD 006.4/2 US
CCC

ID SYSTEMS. [ID syst.]. **Added/Corp** North American Technology (Firm). Vol. 7, No. 1 (Jan./Feb. 1987)-. Periodical. English. Ten times a year. $55.00. Helmers Publishing Inc., 174 Concord Street, PO Box 874, Peterborough NH 03458-0874. **Tel** (603)924-9631, FAX (603)924-7408. **ED** Deborah Navas. Index available. **Bk Rev. Ad Acc. Circ:** 50,000 (ctrl). ***Continues*** *Bar Code News, 8750-8702.*
Desc: Journal of automated data collection, provides information to users of bar code equipment and other types of automatic identification equipment, such as optical character recognition, voice recognition and radio frequency identification.
Ind/Abst Abstr. Bull. Inst. Pap. Sci. Tech.; Ei Page One; Graph. Arts Bull. Inst. Pap. Sci. Technol. (April, July, Nov. 1989); Int. Packag. Abstr.

UK

IEE DIGITAL ELECTRONICS AND COMPUTING SERIES. **See** Electronics.

LC TK1 .I1373 **ISSN** 1350-2387
DD 621.305/6 UK
CCC
CODEN ICDTEA
Pr Rev.

•IEE PROCEEDINGS. COMPUTERS AND DIGITAL TECHNIQUES. **Added/Corp** Institution of Electrical Engineers. **VFOAT** Computers and Digital Techniques; IEE Proc.-Comput. Digit. Tech. Vol. 141, No. 1 (Jan. 1994)-. Periodical. English. Six times a year. $633.15. Institution of Electrical Engineers / IEE, Michael Faraday House, Six Hills Way, Stevenage Hertfordshire SG1 2AY United Kingdom. **Tel** 011 44 1438 313311, FAX 011 44 1438 742840, telex 825578 IEESTV G. **(Subscription address:** IEE / Peter Peregrinus Ltd., PO Box 96, Stevenage Herts SG1 2SD United Kingdom. **Tel** 011 44 1438 313311, FAX 011 44 438 742792, telex 825578 IEESTV G.**)** available on CD-ROM from University Microfilms International (UMI). Documents available from BLDSC, FAXON Xpress, The UnCover Company, SWETS, UMI Article Clearinghouse. ***Continues*** *IEE Proceedings. E, Computers and Digital Techniques, 0143-7062.*
Ind/Abst Curr. Cit.

ISSN 1070-9924
DD 004 US
CCC
CODEN ISCEE4

•IEEE COMPUTATIONAL SCIENCE AND ENGINEERING. **See** Engineering-Computer Applications.

LC QA76.76.E95 I35 **ISSN** 0885-9000
DD 006.3/3/05 US
CCC
CODEN IEEXE7
Pr Rev.

IEEE EXPERT. [IEEE expert]. **Added/Corp** Institute of Electrical and Electronics Engineers. IEEE Computer Society. **VFOAT** Expert. **VAT** Institute of Electrical and Electronics Engineers Expert. Vol. 1, No. 1 (Spring 1986)-. Periodical. English. Six times a year. $270.00. IEEE / Institute of Electrical and Electronics Engineers Inc., 345 East 47th Street, New York NY 10017-2394. **Tel** (908)981-1393, FAX (908)981-9667. **(Subscription address:** IEEE / Institute of Electrical and Electronics Engineers, 445 Hoes Lane, PO Box 1331, Piscataway NJ 08855-1331. **Tel** (800)701-IEEE, (908)981-0060, FAX (908)981-9667, telex 833233.**) ED** True Seaborn. Index available. **Bk Rev. Ad Acc. Circ:** 15,940. available on microfiche. Documents available from Article Express International, The Genuine Article, Ask*IEEE.
Desc: Development and application of expert systems and artificial intelligence, including knowledge engineering, database and data engineering, planning and problem solving, natural language processing, and medical and industrial applications.
Ind/Abst Abstr. Hum. Comput. Interact.; CompuMath Cit. Index [Full Cov.]; Comput. Inf. Syst. Abstr. J. [Full Cov.]; Comput. Database; Curr. Cit.; Curr. Contents Eng. Comput. Technol.; Ei Page One; Elect. Comm. Abstr.; Eng. Index Annu.; Ergon. Abstr.; Expand. Acad. Index (1992-); Index IEEE Publ. (Spring 1986-); Inf. Sci. Abstr.; INSPEC (1986-); Int. Aerosp. Abstr.; Oper. Res./Manage. Sci.; Res. Alert [Full Cov.]; SCISEARCH; Soc. Sci. Cit. Index [Select. Cov.].

ISSN 1070-986X
DD 006 US

•IEEE MULTIMEDIA. [IEEE multimed.]. **Added/Corp** Institute of Electrical and Electronics Engineers. **VFOAT** Multimedia. (1994)-. Periodical. English. Four times a year. $210.00. IEEE / Institute of Electrical and Electronics Engineers Inc., 345 East 47th Street, New York NY 10017-2394. **Tel** (908)981-1393, FAX (908)981-9667. **(Subscription address:** IEEE / Institute of Electrical and Electronics Engineers, 445 Hoes Lane, PO Box 1331, Piscataway NJ 08855-1331. **Tel** (800)701-IEEE, (908)981-0060, FAX (908)981-9667, telex 833233.**)**
Desc: Focuses on multimedia computing and communications systems. Covers hardware and software for media compression, media storage and transport, workstation support, data modeling, and abstractions to embed multimedia in applications programs.

ISSN 1063-6706
DD 006 US
CCC
CODEN IEFSEV

•IEEE TRANSACTIONS ON FUZZY SYSTEMS. (IEEE TRANSACTIONS ON FUZZY SYSTEMS : A PUBLICATION OF THE IEEE NEURAL NETWORKS COUNCIL.). [IEEE trans. fuzzy syst.]. **Added/Corp** IEEE Neural Networks Council. Institute of Electrical and Electronics Engineers. **VAT** Institute of Electrical and Electronics Engineers Transactions on Fuzzy Systems. Vol. 1, No. 1 (Feb. 1993)-. Periodical. English. Four times a year. $200.00. IEEE / Institute of Electrical and Electronics Engineers Inc., 345 East 47th Street, New York NY 10017-2394. **Tel** (908)981-1393, FAX (908)981-9667. **(Subscription address:** IEEE / Institute of Electrical and Electronics Engineers, 445 Hoes Lane, PO Box 1331, Piscataway NJ 08855-1331. **Tel** (800)701-IEEE, (908)981-0060, FAX (908)981-9667, telex 833233.**) ED** James Bezdek.
Desc: Provides the latest developments in the theory, design, and application of fuzzy systems. Major topics include fuzzy estimation, prediction, and control; approximate reasoning; intelligent systems design; fuzzy neuro-computing; and propagation and optimization.

LC TK7874 .I3273 **ISSN** 1063-8210
DD 621.39/5 US
CCC
CODEN IEVSE9

•IEEE TRANSACTIONS ON VERY LARGE SCALE INTEGRATION (VLSI) SYSTEMS. [IEEE trans. very large scale integr. (VLSI) syst.]. **Added/Corp** Institute of Electrical and Electronics Engineers. IEEE Circuits and Systems Society. IEEE Computer Society. IEEE Solid-State Circuits Council. **VFOAT** Very Large Scale Integration (VLSI) Systems. **VAT** Institute of Electrical and Electronics Engineers Transactions on Very Large Scale Integration (VLSI) Systems. Vol. 1, No. 1 (Mar. 1993)-. Periodical. English. Four times a year. $240.00. IEEE / Institute of Electrical and Electronics Engineers Inc., 345 East 47th Street, New York NY 10017-2394. **Tel** (908)981-1393, FAX (908)981-9667. **(Subscription address:** IEEE / Institute of Electrical and Electronics Engineers, 445 Hoes Lane, PO Box 1331, Piscataway NJ 08855-1331. **Tel** (800)701-IEEE, (908)981-0060, FAX (908)981-9667, telex 833233.**)**
Desc: Includes major aspects of the design and implementation of VLSI/VLSI and microelectronic systems. Topics of special interest include: systems specifications, design and partitioning, high performance computing and communication systmes, systems networks, wafer-scale integration and multichip module systems and their applications.

ISSN 0916-8532
JA
CCC

IEICE TRANSACTIONS ON INFORMATION AND SYSTEMS. **Added/Corp** Denshi Joho Tsushin Gakkai (Japan). **VFOAT** IEICE Transactions; Institute of Electronics, Information and Communication Engineers Transactions on Information and systems; Transactions on Information and Systems. (1992)-. Periodical. English. Twelve times a year. $170.00. Denshi Joho Tsushin Gakkai / Institute of Electronics, Information and Communication Engineers, Kikai Shinko Kaikan, 5-8 Shiba Koen, 3-chome, Minatoku Tokyo 105 Japan. **(Subscription address:** Maruzen Company Ltd., PO Box 5050, Import & Export Department, Tokyo 100 31 Japan. **Tel** 011 81 3 32789224.**)** Documents available from The Genuine Article, Ask*IEEE. ***Continues in part*** *IEICE Transactions on Communications, Electronics, Information, and Systems, 0917-1673.*
Ind/Abst Curr. Cit.; Curr. Contents Eng. Comput. Technol. (19??-); INSPEC (Jan. 1992-); Res. Alert (19??-) [Select. Cov.]; SCISEARCH (19??-).

LC TS500 **ISSN** 0924-5812
DD 681 NE
UDC 681

IFIP CONGRESS SERIES. [IFIP congr. ser.]. **VFOAT** International Federation for Information Processing Congress Series. (1957)-. Monographic series. English. Elsevier Science Publishers BV, PO Box 211, 1000 AE Amsterdam Netherlands. **Tel** 011 31 20 4853641, 011 31 20 4853642, FAX 011 31 20 4853598.
Ind/Abst Zentralbl. Math. Ihre Grenzgeb.

ISSN 1024-8102
AU
UDC 659.2

IFIP NEWSLETTER. [IFIP newsl.]. **VFOAT** International Federation for Information Processing Newsletter; Newsletter - IFIP. (1984)-. Periodical. English. Four times a year. International Federation for Information Processing / IFIP, Hofstrasse 3A-2361, Laxenburg Austria. **Circ:** 4,000. available via Internet (http://www.dit.upm.es/~cdk/ifip.html).

ISSN 0889-9134
DD 004 US

II COMPUTING. [II comput.]. **VFOAT** 2 Computing; II Computing--For Apple II Users; II Computing, for Apple II Users. Vol. 1, No. 1 (Oct./Nov. 1985)-. Periodical. English. Six times a year. $11.97 (regular edition), $59.95 (action edition). II Computing, PO Box 1922, Marion OH 43306. **Tel** (415)957-0886. **ED** Anita Malnig. **Circ:** 50,000.

ISSN 1012-909X
AU
CODEN ICOSDR

IIASA COLLABORATIVE PROCEEDINGS SERIES. [IIASA collab. proc. ser.]. **Added/Corp** International Institute for Applied Systems Analysis. **VAT** International Institute for Applied Systems Analysis Collaborative Proceedings Series. (1981)-. Academic Scholarly Publication. English. International Institute for Applied Systems Analysis, Publications Department, A-2361 Laxenburg Austria. **Tel** 2236-71521 302, FAX 2236-71313, telex 079137 IIASAA. Documents available from BIOSIS Document Express, CASDDS.
Ind/Abst Biol. Abstr. (?-1983); Chem. Abstr. (1981-1982); Math. Rev.; Zentralbl. Math. Ihre Grenzgeb.

AU

IIASA PUBLICATIONS. **Main/Corp** International Institute for Applied Systems Analysis. (1974)-. Periodical. English. Irregular. S150.00. International Institute for Applied Systems Analysis, Publications Department, A-2361 Laxenburg Austria. **Tel** 2236-71521 302, FAX 2236-71313, telex 079137 IIASAA. cum. index. **Circ:** 5,000.
Desc: Publishes publications dealing with all aspects of systems analysis and cooperates with other publishers on specific ventures.

ISSN 0969-6008
UK
CODEN IMAPEJ

IMAGE PROCESSING. **VFOAT** Image Processing Magazine. (Summer 1989)-. Periodical. English. Six times a year (Jan., Mar., May, Jul., Sept., Nov.). $85.56. European Technology Publishing, Ltd., Preston Barn Preston Lane, Marlborough Wilshire SN8 2HF United Kingdom. **Tel** 011 44 1672 21096. Documents available from Ask*IEEE.
Ind/Abst Curr. Cit.; Inf. Manage. Technol.; INSPEC (Summer 1989-).

Computers

DD 621
ISSN 1083-2912
US
IMAGING MAGAZINE. [Imaging mag.]. (199?)-. Periodical. English. Twelve times a year. $17.95. Telecom Library Inc., 12 West 21st Street, New York NY 10010. **Tel** (212)691-8215, (800)542-7279. *Continues Imaging (New York, N.Y.), 1063-4320.*

LC TK8315 .I453
DD 621.36/7
ISSN 1063-4320
US
TITLE CHANGE
IMAGING (NEW YORK, N.Y.). (IMAGING : THE IMAGING INDUSTRY MAGAZINE.). [Imaging]. **VFOAT** Imaging Magazine. (1992)-(199?). Trade Publication. English. Telecom Library Inc., 12 West 21st Street, New York NY 10010. **Tel** (212)691-8215, (800)542-7279. **(Subscription address:** Imaging Magazine, 1265 Industrial Highway, Southampton PA 18966. **Tel** 800 677-3435, (215)355-2886, FAX (215)355-1068.) *Continued by Imaging Magazine, 1083-2912.*
Desc: Critical reviews of imaging products and services.

US
IMAGING SOLUTIONS INFODISK. (19??)-. Periodical. English. Four times a year. $1007.00 US; $1167.00 Canada; $1267.00 other. Faulkner Technical Reports, 7905 Browning Road, Suite 114, Pennsauken NJ 08109. **Tel** (800)843-0460.

LC TS176 .I5437
DD 670
ISSN 1074-228X
US
●**INDUSTRIAL COMPUTING (1993). See** Engineering-Computer Applications.

DD 621
ISSN 1074-0511
US
●**INDUSTRIAL CONTROLS INTELLIGENCE & THE PLC INSIDER'S NEWSLETTER.** [Ind. controls intell. PLC insid. newsl.]. **VFOAT** Industrial Controls Intelligence and the PLC Insider's Newsletter. (Jan. 1994)-. Newsletter. English. Twelve times a year. $195.00. Carefree Communications, PO Box 5268, Carefree AZ 85377. **Tel** (602)488-1462, FAX (602)488-5376. **ED** Jack Grenard. **Bk Rev**, (Qty: 2-3). *Continues Controls Digest, 1067-3121.*
Desc: Informs the vendors and their executives of news, trends, opinions, new products, technology in the industrial controls arena.

DD 004
ISSN 1187-7081
CN
CODEN IFCAE3
INFO CANADA (DOWNSVIEW). (INFO CANADA.). [Info Can.]. Vol. 16, No. 9 (Sept. 1991)-. Trade Publication. English. Twelve times a year. 90.00Can$. Laurentian Media Inc, 501 Oakdale Road, Downsview Ontario M3N 1W7 Canada. **Tel** (416)746-7360, (800)565-4007, FAX (416)746-1421. *Continues Computer Data, 0383-7319; Absorbed I.T. Magazine (Toronto, Ont.). Continued in part by Network World Canada, 1187-2985.*
Ind/Abst Comput. Lit. Index; Curr. Cit.; PROMT.

DD 004/.05
ISSN 1189-6515
CN
●**INFO-TECH MAGAZINE.** [Info-tech mag.]. **VFOAT** Informatique & Technologie Magazine; Informatique et Technologie Magazine. (1993)-. Periodical. French. Twelve times a year. 23.28Can$. Publications Transcontinental Inc, 1100 Rene-Levesque, 24FI boulevard West, Montreal Quebec H3B 4X9 Canada. **Tel** (514)392-9000, FAX (514)392-4724. *Formed by the union of Informatique & Bureautique., 0227-8332 and Info-Log Magazine., 0847-4915.*

DD 004
ISSN 1074-522X
US
●**INFO TO GO! (GARDEN GROVE, CALIF.).** (INFO TO GO!). [Info go!]. Vol. 1, Issue 1 (Jan. 1994)-. Periodical. English. Twelve times a year. $48.00. Info to Go! Publications, PO Box 272, Garden Grove CA 92642. available via Internet.

DD 004
ISSN 0889-6836
US
INFOCUS (PHILADELPHIA, PA.). (INFOCUS.). [Infocus]. **VFOAT** In Focus. (198?)-. Periodical. English. Six times a year (Jan., Mar., May, July, Sept., Nov.). $52.00. Infocus Inc., 37 South Main Street, Yardley PA 19067. **Tel** (215)321-2200. *Continues Sselect.*

LC TR835 .J67
DD 686
ISSN 0892-3876
US
CODEN INFREN
INFORM (SILVER SPRING, MD.). See Photography.

DD 354.71270071/4/0285
ISSN 0848-757X
CN
INFORM (WINNIPEG). (INFORM : TOTAL SOLUTIONS FOR YOUR INFORMATION MANAGEMENT : A QUARTERLY PUBLICATION OF MANITOBA DATA SERVICES.). [Inform]. **Main/Corp** Manitoba Data Services. Vol. 10, No. 3 (Summer 1990)-. Periodical. English. Four times a year. Manitoba Data Services, 215 Garry Street/10th Floor, Winnipeg Manitoba R3C 3P3 Canada. *Continues Manitoba Data Services. Manitoba Data Services Computing Report., 0826-3620.*

BE
INFORMATIC USERS. Dutch (French). Ten times a year (no issue in July and Aug.). 928F Belgium; 1734F North America; 1203F other. Ecopress SA, Revenue Van Volxem 281, 1190 Brussels Belgium. **ED** Jean-Claude Verset and Renee Baguette. **Ad Acc. Circ:** 14,000 (ctrl). *Continues Paninformatic.*

ISSN 0392-8888
IT
UDC 681.3
TITLE CHANGE
INFORMATICA OGGI. [Inform. oggi]. (1980)-(19??). Periodical. Italian. Gruppo Editoriale Jackson Spa, Via Gorki 69, 20092 Cinisello Balsamo Italy. **Tel** 011 39 2 66034401. *Continued by Informatica Oggi e Unix.*

IT
INFORMATICA OGGI E UNIX. (19??)-. Italian. Eleven times a year. L70400 Italy; L140800 other. Gruppo Editoriale Jackson Spa, Via Gorki 69, 20092 Cinisello Balsamo Italy. **Tel** 011 39 2 66034401. *Continues Informatica Oggi.*

IT
INFORMATICA OGGI MENSILE. Italian. Gruppo Editoriale Jackson Spa, Via Gorki 69, 20092 Cinisello Balsamo Italy. **Tel** 011 39 2 66034401.

IT
INFORMATICA OGGI SETTIMANALE. Italian. Gruppo Editoriale Jackson Spa, Via Gorki 69, 20092 Cinisello Balsamo Italy. **Tel** 011 39 2 66034401.

ISSN 0178-3564
GW
CCC
Pr Rev.
INFORMATIK - FORSCHUNG UND ENTWICKLUNG. (1986)-. German. Four times a year. DM368.00. Springer-Verlag GmbH & Company KG, Heidelberger Platz 3, D-14197 Berlin Germany. **Tel** 011 49 30 8207223, FAX 011 49 30 8214091, telex 183 319 SPBLN D. **(Subscription address:** Springer-Verlag New York Inc. / North America, PO Box 2485, Journal Fulfillment, Secaucus NJ 07096. **Tel** (201)348-4033, (800)777-4643, FAX (201)348-4505.) **ED** A. Endres. Index available. **Ad Acc. Circ:** 700. available on microfilm and microfiche from University Microfilms International (UMI). Documents available from Ask*IEEE.
Ind/Abst INSPEC (March 1986-).

LC Q350 .I5
DD 001.53/9
ISSN 0890-5401
US
CCC
CODEN INFCEC
Pr Rev.
INFORMATION AND COMPUTATION. [Inf. comput.]. Vol. 72, No. 1 (Jan. 1987)-. Academic Scholarly Publication. English. Sixteen times a year. $1215.00. Academic Press Inc., 6277 Sea Harbor Drive, Orlando FL 32887. **Tel** (800)543-9534, (407)345-4100, FAX (407)352-3445. **ED** Albert R. Meyer. **Bk Rev** Documents available from Article Express International, The Genuine Article, Ask*IEEE. *Continues Information and Control, 0019-9958.*
Desc: Publishes original papers in all areas of theoretical computer science and computational aspects of information theory. Survey articles of exceptional quality are published occasionally. Emphasizes papers contributing new results in active theoretical areas.
Ind/Abst ACM Guide Comput. Lit.; Bioeng. Abstr.; CompuMath Cit. Index [Full Cov.]; Comput. Rev.; Curr. Cit.; Curr. Contents Eng. Comput. Technol.; Ei Page One; Eng. Index Annu.; Inf. Sci. Abstr.; INIS Atomindex [Micro.]; INSPEC (1987-); Int. Aerosp. Abstr.; Math. Rev. (1987-); MLA Int. Bibl. Books Artic. Mod. Lang. Lit.; Res. Alert [Full Cov.]; Sci. Cit. Index; SCISEARCH; Soc. Sci. Cit. Index [Select. Cov.]; Zentralbl. Math. Ihre Grenzgeb.

LC TK7885
DD 621.39
ISSN 0929-9610
NE
●**INFORMATION AND SYSTEMS ENGINEERING. See** Library and Information Sciences.

ISSN 0924-3461
FR
INFORMATION, COMPUTER, COMMUNICATIONS POLICY. [Inf. comput. commun. policy]. **Added/Corp** Organisation for Economic Co-Operation and Development. Organisation for Economic Co-Operation and Development. Working Party on Information, Computer and Communications Policy. **VFOAT** ICCP. (1979)-. Monographic series. English (French). Irregular. Price varies per volume. OECD Publications and Information Center, 2 rue Andre-Pascal, 75775 Paris Cedex 16 France. **Tel** 011 33 1 49104262, US:(202)785-6323, FAX 011 33 1 45248500, 011 33 1 45248176, telex 620 160 OCDE. **(Subscription address:** OECD Publications Center, 2001 L Street, Suite 700, Washington DC 20036. **Tel** (202)822-3873, (202)785-6323.) Documents available from Ask*IEEE.
Ind/Abst INSPEC.

LC HD9980
DD 338.4/7005740971
ISSN 1195-3616
CN
CODEN INHIE6
●**INFORMATION HIGHWAYS. See** Industry and Production.

ISSN 1053-0428
US
INFORMATION INDUSTRY SCAN. VFOAT Scan. (1991)-. Periodical. English. Twenty-four times a year. $345.00. Current Awareness, 177 Main Street, Suite 235, Fort Lee NJ 07024. **Tel** (201)461-5136.

DD 025
ISSN 1046-9303
US
TITLE CHANGE
INFORMATION MANAGEMENT BULLETIN. (INFORMATION MANAGEMENT BULLETIN : AN OFFICIAL PUBLICATION OF THE INFORMATION RESOURCES MANAGEMENT ASSOCIATION.). [Inf. manage. bull.]. **Added/Corp** Information Resources Management Association. (1988)-(1995). Bulletin. English. (Feb., Aug.). Idea Group Publishing, 4811 Jonestown Road, Suite 230, Harrisburg PA 17109. **Tel** (800)345-4332, (717)541-9150, FAX (717)541-9159. **ED** Mehdi Khosrowpour. **Bk Rev**, (Qty: 2-3). **Ad Acc. Circ:** 1,000 (ctrl). *Continued by Information Management, 1080-286X.*
Desc: Covers current and future issues and trends in the field of information technology.

LC HD9999.M47 A39
DD 338.7/68643
ISSN 0897-3199
US
TITLE CHANGE
INFORMATION MANAGEMENT SOURCEBOOK. (INFORMATION MANAGEMENT SOURCEBOOK : THE AIIM BUYING GUIDE AND MEMBERSHIP DIRECTORY.). [Inf. manage. sourceb.]. **Added/Corp** Association for Information and Image Management (U.S.). **VFOAT** AIIM Buying Guide and Membership Directory. (1987)-(19??). Directory. English. Association for Information & Image Management, Business Office, 1100 Wayne Avenue/Suite 1100, Silver Spring MD 20910. **Tel** (301)587-8202, FAX (301)587-2711. **ED** Meg Buckley. Index available. **Ad Acc. Circ:** 8,000. *Continues AIIM Buying Guide. Continued by AIIM Buying Guide.*
Desc: Identifies the manufacturers of the products and services of the information and image management industry. Includes company listings, company profiles, products and services, and membership directory of the Association for Information and Image Management.

US
INFORMATION SYSTEMS SPENDING: AN ANALYSIS OF TRENDS AND STRATEGIES. (1990)-. Periodical. English. One time a year. $895.00. Computer Economics Inc, 5841 Edison Place, Carlsbad CA 92008. **Tel** (800)326-8100, (619)438-8100, FAX (619)431-1126. **ED** Michael C. Erbschloe.

ISSN 0266-8513
UK
INFORMATION TECHNOLOGY & PUBLIC POLICY. [Inf. technol. public policy]. **VFOAT** Information Technology and Public Policy. (1985)-. Periodical. English. Three times a year (Feb., July, Nov.). $77.01. Pitcom Secretariat, West Heaton, Old Hillside Road, Winchester 5022 5LN United Kingdom. **Tel** telex 817484. **ED** Kate Norman. **Ad Acc, Adv Mgr:** MJ Hughes. **Circ:** 500 (ctrl). Documents available from Ask*IEEE. *Continues PITCOM, 0263-614X.*
Ind/Abst Abstr. Hum. Comput. Interact.; Curr. Cit.; HILITES; INSPEC (Feb. 1985-).

DD 004.02594
ISSN 1036-0352
AT
INFORMATION TECHNOLOGY INDEX. [Inf. technol. index]. (1991)-. English. One time a year. 69.89Aus$. Peter Isaacson Publications, 46-50 Porter Street, Prahran Victoria, 3181 Australia. **Tel** 011 61 3 2457777, FAX 011 61 3 2457606. *Continues DP Index and Software Register, 0813-4758.*

ISSN 0249-3381
FR
UDC 02
INFORMATIQUE DOCUMENTAIRE PARIS, L'. (L'INFORMATIQUE DOCUMENTAIRE.). [Inform. doc. Paris]. **VFOAT** Bulletin du Centre des Hautes Etudes Internationales d'Informatique Documentaire. (1981)-. Bulletin. French. Four times a year. $98.43. CID / Informatique Documentaire, 36 Bis rue Ballu, 75009 Paris France. **Tel** 011 33 1 42850475.

FR
INFORMATIQUE. E33. French. Irregular. 791.28F France; 825.00F other. Institut de l'Information Scientifique et Technique (INIST), 2 Allee du Parc de

Computers

Brabois, 54514 Vandoeuvre Nancy Cedex France. **Tel** 011 33 83 504600, FAX 011 33 83 504650. **Continues** Pascal Explore. E33: Informatique.

US

INFOTECH NEWS. (19??)-. English. Six times a year. $100.00 (subscribers to ICMA Management Information Service or McGraw Hill Product Info Network; $130.00 other. International City Management Association, 777 North Capitol Street NE, Suite 500, Washington DC 20002. **Tel** (202)289-4262, (800)745-8780, FAX (202)962-3500. **Continues** Microsoftware News.

LC TK7800 .C53

CU

INGENIERIA ELECTRONICA, AUTOMATICA Y COMUNICACIONES. **See** Engineering-Electrical Engineering.

LC QA75.5 .I567a ISSN 1354-9952

UK

●**INGENUITY.** **Added/Corp** International Computers, Ltd. (May 1994)-. Periodical. English. Two times a year. $120.00. Oxford University Press / UK, Walton Street, Oxford OX2 6DP United Kingdom. **Tel** 011 44 1865 56767, FAX 011 44 1865 267773, telex 851/837330 OXPRES G. **(Subscription address:** Oxford University Press / USA, Journals Marketing Department, Oxford University Press, 2001 Evans Road, Cary NC 27513. **Tel** (800)451-7556, (919)677-0977, FAX (919)677-1714.) **ED** J.M.M. Pinkerton. Index available. **Ad Acc.** **Circ:** 7,000. available on microfilm and microfiche from University Microfilms International (UMI). **Continues** International Computers, Ltd. ICL Technical Journal, 0142-1557.
Desc: Up-to-date practical applications and developments in the fields of computers and information science and technology.
Ind/Abst Curr. Cit.

AU

INIS, CHARACTER SET REPRESENTATION AND CODING RULES. **Added/Corp** International Atomic Energy Agency. 2nd Ed. (1982)-. English. Irregular. International Atomic Energy Agency IAEA, Wagramerstrasse 5, PO Box 100, A-1400 Vienna Austria. **Continues** INIS Magnetic and Punched Paper Tape Codes and Character Sets.

ISSN 1060-0922
DD 004 *US*

INITIATIVE (AUSTIN, TEX.), THE. (THE INITIATIVE : THE OFFICIAL NEWSLETTER OF THE CAD FRAMEWORK INITIATIVE, INC.). [Initiative]. **Added/Corp** CAD Framework Initiative, Inc. Fall (1991)-. Newsletter. English. Four times a year. Free on request. CAD Framework Initiative, 4030 Braker Laneste 550, Austin TX 78759. **Tel** (512)338-3739.

ISSN 0756-7677
FR

INRIATHEQUE ROCQUENCOURT, L'. [Inriatheque Rocquencourt]. (1981)-. Periodical. French. Forty-Five times a year. Institut National de Recherche et Informatique en Automatique, SEDIS Diffusion, Domaine de Voluceau-Rocquencourt, BP 105, 78153 Le Chesnay Cedex France. **Tel** 011 33 1 39635627, FAX 011 33 1 39635228, telex 697033 F. available on microfiche. **Continues** L'Iriatheque (Rocquencourt), 0181-6276.

ISSN 1056-8964
US

INSIDE ASHLAR VELLUM. (1991)-. Periodical. English. Twelve times a year. $49.00. Calispill Computer Consultants, PO Box 234, Cusick WA 99119.

ISSN 0953-2625
DD 338.4700405 *UK*

INSIDE IT. [Inside IT]. **VFOAT** Inside Information Technology. (1987)-. Periodical. English. Twelve times a year. $342.24. Tossa House, Main Road, Smalley, Derby DE7 6EF United Kingdom. **Tel** 011 44 1332 881779, FAX 011 44 1332 780008. **ED** John Barker. **Continues** Ed-IT World.

ISSN 1065-8475
US
CEASED

INSIDE OBJECTVISION. **Added/Corp** Cobb Group. **VFOAT** Inside Object Vision. (1992)-Vol. 1 No. 10 (Aug. 1993). Periodical. English. Cobb Group, 9420 Bunsen Parkway #300, Louisville KY 40220. **Tel** (502)491-1900, (800)223-8720, FAX (502)491-4200.

ISSN 1071-2968
DD 004 *US*

INSIDE OPERATIONS. (INSIDE OPERATIONS : THE CANDLE VIEW.). [Inside opera.]. **Added/Corp** Candle Corp. (1988)-. Periodical. English. Twelve times a year. Free on request. Candle Corporation, 2425 Olympic Boulevard, Santa Monica CA 90404. **Tel** (310)829-5800, FAX (310)582-4233. **Circ:** 30,000 (ctrl).

ISSN 1081-3314
US

●**INSIDE SOLARIS.** **Added/Corp** Cobb Group. (1995)-. Periodical. English. Twelve times a year. $99.00. Cobb Group, 9420 Bunsen Parkway #300, Louisville KY 40220. **Tel** (502)491-1900, (800)223-8720, FAX (502)491-4200.

ISSN 1079-4573
US

●**INSIDE THE NEW COMPUTER INDUSTRY.** (1994)-. Trade Publication. English. Eleven times a year. $675.00. Andrew Allison, 25420 Via Cicindela, Carmel CA 93923. **Tel** (408)626-4361. **Continues** RISC Management : Analysis & Comment on the Impact of RISC Technology, 1051-1393; **Absorbed** Benchpress Quarterly.

ISSN 1059-387X
US

INSIDE TRAC, THE. **See** Business and Economics-Marketing and Purchasing.

LC LB1028.3 .I52 ISSN 0892-4872
DD 005 *US*
CCC

INSTRUCTION DELIVERY SYSTEMS. [Instr. deliv. syst.]. Vol. 1, No. 1 (Jan./Feb. 1987)-. Periodical. English. Six times a year. $40.00 (North America), $55.00 (other) including postage (members of Society for Applied Learning Technology); $60.00 (North America), $75.00 (other) including postage (nonmembers). Society for Applied Learning Technology, 50 Culpeper Street, Warrenton VA 22186. **Tel** (703)347-0055, FAX (703)349-3169. **Ad Acc.** **Circ:** 18,000 (ctrl).
Ind/Abst ACM Guide Comput. Lit.; Comput. Rev.; Curr. Index J. Educ.

ISSN 0263-6522
UK
CCC
CODEN ICIIDZ

INTEGRATED CIRCUITS INTERNATIONAL. **See** Electronics.

ISSN 1046-932X
DD 004 *US*

INTEGRATED IMAGE. [Integr. image]. Vol. 1, Issue 1 (Winter 1990)-. Periodical. English. Four times a year. Free. International Society of WANG Users, One Industrial Avenue, Lowell MA 01851. **Tel** (508)967-4322.
Desc: In-house WANG publication of business solutions.

ISSN 1080-2797
US

●**INTEGRATED SYSTEM DESIGN.** **Added/Corp** Verecom Group. (1995)-. Trade Publication. English. Twelve times a year. $48.00. ASIC Technology & News, 5150 El Camino Real, Suite A 31, Los Altos CA 94022. **Tel** (415)903-0140. **Continues** ASIC & EDA, 1067-9804.

UK

INTEGRATION. Periodical. English. Twelve times a year. £50.00 UK; £80.00 (airmail) Europe; £70.00 other. VNU Business Publications BV, 32-34 Broadwick Street, London W1A 2HG United Kingdom. **Tel** 011 44 171 4394242 ext. 2222, FAX 011 44 171 4379638, telex 23918 VNU G, 8952440.

ISSN 1042-4296
DD 004 *US*

INTELLIGENCE (NEW YORK, N.Y. 1984). (INTELLIGENCE.). [Intelligence]. (May 1984)-. Periodical. English. Sixteen times a year (Monthly with four seasonal special issues). $395.00. Intelligence, PO Box 20008, New York NY 10025. **Tel** (212)222-1123, FAX (212)222-1123. **ED** Edward Rosenfeld. **Bk Rev**, (Qty: 12). **Ad Acc.**
Desc: News and developments affecting the future of computing.
Ind/Abst Abstr. Hum. Comput. Interact.

LC QA76.9.H85 I59 ISSN 0953-5438
DD 004/.01/9 *UK*
CCC
CODEN INTCEE

INTERACTING WITH COMPUTERS. [Interact. comput.]. **Added/Corp** British Computer Society. Human Computer Interaction Specialist Group. Vol. 1, No. 1 (April 1989)-. Periodical. English. Four times a year. $366.00. Butterworth Heinemann Publishers, Linacre House Jordan Hill, Oxford OX2 8DP United Kingdom. **Tel** 011 44 1865 310366, FAX 011 44 1865 310898. **(Subscription address:** Elsevier Science Ltd. / Oxford Fulfillment Centre, PO Box 800, Kidlington OX5 1DX United Kingdom. **Tel** 011 44 865 843355.) **ED** Dan Diaper. Index available. cum. index. **Bk Rev.** **Ad Acc.** **Circ:** 1,200 (ctrl). available on microfilm and microfiche from University Microfilms International (UMI); available on an online database from Elsevier Electronic Subscriptions (EES). Documents available from The Genuine Article, Ask*IEEE.
Desc: Aims to act as an international forum for the discussion of HCI issues, to foster communication between academic researchers and industry practitioners, to encourage the flow of information across the boundaries of the contributing disciplines, and to stimulate ideas and provoke widespread discussion with a forward-looking perspective.
Ind/Abst Abstr. Hum. Comput. Interact.; ACM Guide Comput. Lit.; CompuMath Cit. Index [Full Cov.]; Comput. Abstr.; Comput. Rev.; Curr. Cit.; Curr. Cont. Eng. Comput. Technol.; Ergon. Abstr.; HILITES; INSPEC (April 1989-); Res. Alert [Full Cov.]; Soc. Sci. Cit. Index [Select. Cov.].

ISSN 1072-5520
DD 005 *US*

●**INTERACTIONS (NEW YORK, N.Y.).** (INTERACTIONS.). [Interactions]. **Added/Corp** Association for Computing Machinery. Vol. 1, No. 1 (Jan. 1994)-. Periodical. English. Four times a year. $135.00. ACM / Association for Computing Machinery, 1515 Broadway, 17th Floor, New York NY 10036. **Tel** (212)869-7440, FAX (212)869-0481. **(Subscription address:** Association for Computing Machinery, PO Box 12114, Church Street Station, New York NY 10249. **Tel** (212)626-0500.)

ISSN 0953-8771
DD 621.388332 *UK*

INTERACTIVE UPDATE. [Interact. update]. (1987)-. Periodical. English. Six times a year.
Ind/Abst Abstr. Hum. Comput. Interact.

ISSN 1077-8047
US

●**INTERACTIVITY (SAN FRANCISCO, CALIF.).** (INTERACTIVITY.). (1994)-. English. Six times a year. $19.97. Miller Freeman Inc., 600 Harrison Street, San Francisco CA 94107. **Tel** (415)905-2337, (415)905-2200, FAX (415)905-2240, telex 278273. **ED** Dominic Milano. **Ad Acc, Adv Mgr:** Carol Robinson, **Tel** (415)655-4281. **Circ:** 40,000.
Desc: A journal about multimedia for multimedia professionals.

LC TK3521 .I57 ISSN 1065-0415
DD 621.381 *US*
CODEN IECHEH
TITLE CHANGE

INTERCONNECTION TECHNOLOGY. [InterConnect. technol.]. **Added/Corp** International Institute of Connector and Interconnection Technology. **VFOAT** Connection Technology. Vol. 8, No. 8 (Aug. 1992)-(199?). Periodical. English. IHS Publishing Group, 17730 West Peterson Road, Libertyville IL 60048. **Tel** (708)362-8711, FAX (708)362-3484. Documents available from Ask*IEEE. **Continues** Connection Technology, 8756-4076. **Continued by** Connector Specifier, 1078-1528.
Ind/Abst INSPEC (1992-?).

ISSN 1078-7259
DD 004 *US*

●**INTER@CTIVE WEEK (PRINT).** (INTER@CTIVE WEEK.). [Inter@ct. week]. **VFOAT** Interactive Week; Inter@ctive; A.Interactive. Vol. 1, No. 1 (Oct. 10, 1994)-. Periodical. English. Twenty-six times a year. Free (qualified subscribers), $60.00 (other). Interactive Enterprises, 100 Q Roosevelt, Suite 508, Garden City NY 11530. **Tel** (516)229-3700. available via Internet (http://www.ziff.com/).

ISSN 1049-8982
DD 004 *US*

INTEREXPRESS (SUNNYVALE, CALIF.). (INTEREXPRESS : THE NEWS PUBLICATION FOR HEWLETT-PACKARD USERS WORLDWIDE.). [INTEREXpress]. **Added/Corp** Interex (organization). **VFOAT** INTEREX Press; HP Users Interexpress. Vol. 8, No. 3/4 (Mar./Apr. 1990)-. Periodical. English. Twelve times a year. $30.50 (included in membership). Interex, PO Box 3439, Sunnyvale CA 94088. **Tel** (408)747-0227, FAX (408)736-2156, telex 4971527. **Continues** Interrupt, 0739-6465.

IT

INTERFACCIA. Italian. Etas Periodici Spa, Via Mecenate 91, 20138 Milan Italy.

JA

INTERFACE. Japanese. Twelve times a year. $136.00. C Q Shuppan K.K. (C Q Publishing Company), 14-4 Sugamo 1-chome, Toshimo-ku, Tokyo 170 Japan.

ISSN 0020-5419
US

INTERFACE (BETHESDA). (INTERFACE.). **Added/Corp** National Institutes of Health. Computer Center. Division of Computer Research and Technology. (1968)-. Periodical. English. Irregular. Free. US Department of Health and Human Services National Institutes of Health, 9000 Rockville Pike, Bethesda MD 20892. **Tel** (301)496-9291, FAX (301)496-2443. Index available (Bound in last issue).

ISSN 1071-295X
DD 004 *US*

INTERFACE (SANTA MONICA, CALIF.). (INTERFACE : CANDLE'S VIEW ON IBM'S DATABASE WORLD.). [Interface]. **Added/Corp** Candle Corp. (1991)-.

Computers

Periodical. English. Free on request. Candle Corporation, 2425 Olympic Boulevard, Santa Monica CA 90404. **Tel** (310)829-5800, FAX (310)582-4233.

US

INTERNAL CONTROLS. (19??)-. English.
Irregular. FTP Technical Library, 3230 Commander Drive, Carrollton TX 75006.

ISSN 1076-8696
DD 004 US

INTERNATIONAL BUSINESS SCHOOLS COMPUTING QUARTERLY. See Business and Economics-Computer Applications.

LC K564.C6 A1555   ISSN 1067-6171
DD 343.099/9 342.3999   US
  CODEN ICOLE7
  CEASED

INTERNATIONAL COMPUTER LAWYER, THE. See Law-Computer Applications.

LC HD9696.C6 I55   ISSN 0897-411X
DD 338.4/7004/05   US
  CEASED

INTERNATIONAL COMPUTER UPDATE.
[Int. comput. update]. Jan. (1988)-(199?). Periodical. English. IDG International News Group, 41 West Street 8th Floor, Boston MA 02111. **Tel** (617)423-9030.
Desc: A briefing on the important international news from the IDG News Service. Provides market information in a concise, easy-to-read format.

US

INTERNATIONAL CONFERENCE ON RAPID PROTOTYPING. (19??)-. English. One time a year. $135.00. University of Dayton, 300 College Park Avenue, Dayton OH 45469. **Tel** (513)229-4214.

LC TR835 .I53   ISSN 1053-8291
DD 338.4/768643/025   US
NLM TR 835; I614

INTERNATIONAL IMAGING SOURCE BOOK. (INTERNATIONAL IMAGING SOURCE BOOK: INCLUDING MICROGRAPHICS AND OPTICAL IMAGING.). [Int. imaging source book]. (1992)-. English. One time a year (Dec.). $207.00. Phillips Business Information Inc., 1201 Seven Locks Road, PO Box 61130, Potomac MD 20854. **Tel** (301)424-3338, (301)340-1520, (800)777-5005, FAX (301)424-4297, telex 358149.
Continues International Micrographics Source Book, 0272-0310.

ISSN 0167-9945
NE
CCC
NLM W1; IN766DJ   CODEN IJMCEJ
Pr Rev.

INTERNATIONAL JOURNAL OF CLINICAL MONITORING AND COMPUTING. [Int. j. clin. monit. comput.]. Vol. 1, No. 1 (1984)-. Periodical. English. Four times a year. $264.00. Kluwer Academic Publishers, Postbus 322, 3300 AH Dordrecht The Netherlands. **Tel** 011 31 78 524400, FAX 011 31 78 183273, telex 20083. **ED** Omar Prakash and Iikka Kalli. Bk Rev. Ad Acc. Acid Free. Circ: 1,000. available on microfilm and microfiche from University Microfilms International (UMI). Documents available from The Genuine Article, BIOSIS Document Express, Ask*IEEE.
Desc: Original articles, clinical communications and review articles on all aspects of patient monitoring and the use of computers.
Ind/Abst Biol. Abstr. (1984-); Curr. Aware. Biol. Sci.; CABS; Curr. Cit.; Curr. Contents Clin. Med.; EMBASE; Index Med. (Vol. 1, No. 1, 1984-); INSPEC (1987-); Int. Nurs. Index; Ref. Upd. Deluxe Ed.; Res. Alert [Select. Cov.]; SCISEARCH.

LC QA76 .I59   ISSN 0020-7160
  UK
  CCC
  CODEN IJCMAT
Pr Rev.

INTERNATIONAL JOURNAL OF COMPUTER MATHEMATICS. See Mathematics.

US

•INTERNATIONAL JOURNAL OF COMPUTER RESEARCH. (1994)-. Periodical. English. Four times a year. $225.00. Nova Science Publishers Inc., 6080 Jericho Turnpike, Suite 207, Commack NY 11725-2808. **Tel** (516)499-3103, (516)499-3106, FAX (516)499-3146. *Continues* Journal of Computer Abstracts and Research, 1077-6265.

LC TA1632 .I56   ISSN 0920-5691
DD 006.3/7/05   US
  CCC
  CODEN IJCVEQ
Pr Rev.

INTERNATIONAL JOURNAL OF COMPUTER VISION. [Int. j. comput vis.]. VFOAT Computer Vision. Vol. 1, No. 1 (1987)-. Periodical. English. Twelve times a year. $838.00. Kluwer Academic Publishers / Massachusetts, PO Box 358, Accord Station, Hingham MA 02018. **Tel** (617)871-6600. **ED** Takeo Kanade, Robert Bolles, Olivier Fougeras. Ad Acc. Acid Free. Circ: 360. available on microfilm and microfiche from University Microfilms International (UMI). Documents available from Article Express International, The Genuine Article, Ask*IEEE.
Desc: Provides a forum for the dissemination of new research results in the rapidly growing field of computer vision. Publishes high quality and original papers on the computational aspects of vision, including vision algorithms, systems, artificial intelligence approaches and computer architectures for vision, as well as the applications of computer vision with special emphasis on robotics and photo interpretation.
Ind/Abst Abstr. Hum. Comput. Interact. (1991-); ACM Guide Comput. Lit.; Appl. Sci. Technol. Index (1991-); CompuMath Cit. Index [Full Cov.]; Comput. Rev.; Curr. Cit.; Curr. Contents Eng. Comput. Technol.; Ei Page One; Eng. Index Annu.; INSPEC (1987-); Refer. Z.; Res. Alert [Full Cov.]; SCISEARCH.

NE

INTERNATIONAL JOURNAL OF COMPUTERS FOR MATHEMATICAL LEARNING. (19??)-. English. Three times a year. $200.07. Kluwer Academic Publishers, Postbus 322, 3300 AH Dordrecht The Netherlands. **Tel** 011 31 78 524400, FAX 011 31 78 183273, telex 20083.

LC QA75.5 .I624   ISSN 0129-0541
DD 004/.05   SI
  CCC
  CODEN IFCSEN
Pr Rev.

INTERNATIONAL JOURNAL OF FOUNDATIONS OF COMPUTER SCIENCE. VFOAT Foundations of Computer Science. Vol. 1, No. 1 (March 1990)-. Periodical. English. Four times a year. $286.00. World Scientific Publishing Company, PO Box 128, Farrer Road, Singapore 9128 Singapore. **Tel** 011 65 3825663, FAX 011 65 3825919, telex RS 28561 WSPC. **(Subscription address:** World Scientific Publishing Company, Inc., 1060 Main Street, Suite 1 B, River Edge NJ 07661. **Tel** (800)227-7562, (201)487-9655.) **ED** E. Engeler, T. Ito, D.T. Lee, R. Parikh and J. Tucker. Circ: 200. Documents available from Ask*IEEE.
Desc: Contributes new theoretical results in all areas of the foundations of computer science.
Ind/Abst Curr. Cit.; INSPEC (Sep. 1990-); Math. Rev.; Zentralbl. Math. Ihre Grenzgeb.

ISSN 1071-5819
UK
CCC

•INTERNATIONAL JOURNAL OF HUMAN-COMPUTER STUDIES. (1994)-. Academic Scholarly Publication. English. Twelve times a year. $1155.06. Academic Press Ltd., A Division of Harcourt Brace & Company Ltd., 24-28 Oval Road, London NW1 7DX United Kingdom. **Tel** 011 44 171 2674466, FAX 011 44 171 4822293, 011 44 171 4854752, telex 25775 ACPRES G. **(Subscription address:** Harcourt Brace & Company, Ltd., Foots Cray High Street, Sidcup Kent DA14 5HP United Kingdom. **Tel** 011 44 181 3003322, FAX 011 44 181 3090807, telex 896 377 ACADEM.) *Continues* International Journal of Man-Machine Studies, 0020-7373; *Absorbed* Knowledge Acquisition, 1042-8143.
Ind/Abst Curr. Cit.

LC QA76.5 .I567   ISSN 0890-2720
DD 004.1/1   US
  CCC
  CODEN IJSAE9
Pr Rev.   TITLE CHANGE

INTERNATIONAL JOURNAL OF SUPERCOMPUTER APPLICATIONS, THE. [Int. j. supercomput. appl.]. Added/Corp M.I.T. Press. VFOAT Supercomputer Applications. Vol. 1, No. 1 (Spring 1987)-Vol. 7, No. 4 (Winter 1993). Periodical. English. Massachusetts Institute of Technology (MIT) Press, 55 Hayward Street, Cambridge MA 02142. **Tel** (617)253-2889, (617)625-8481, FAX (617)258-6779. **ED** Joanne L. Martin and Jack Dongarra. Bk Rev. Ad Acc. Circ: 900. available on microfilm from University Microfilms International (UMI). Documents available from The Genuine Article, Ask*IEEE. *Continued by* International Journal of Supercomputing Applications and High Performance Computing, 1078-3482.
Desc: Forum for the exchange of experiences in supercomputing, with an emphasis on techniques that apply to classes of problems across disciplines. Contains methods for analyzing, measuring and applying algorithms and solution schemes related to particular application areas. Issues contain essays, product reviews, news from international supercomputer centers and editorials.
Ind/Abst ACM Guide Comput. Lit.; Appl. Mech. Rev.; CompuMath Cit. Index [Full Cov.]; Comput. Rev.; Curr. Cit.; Curr. Contents Eng. Comput. Technol.; Inf. Sci. Abstr.; INIS Atomindex [Micro.]; INSPEC (1988-?); Int. Aerosp. Abstr.; Res. Alert [Full Cov.]; Sci. Cit. Index; SCISEARCH; Soc. Sci. Cit. Index [Select. Cov.].

LC QA76.5 .I567   ISSN 1078-3482
DD 004   US
  CCC

•INTERNATIONAL JOURNAL OF SUPERCOMPUTER APPLICATIONS AND HIGH PERFORMANCE COMPUTING, THE. [Int. j. supercomput. appl. high perform. comput.]. Added/Corp M.I.T. Press. VFOAT Supercomputer Applications and High Performance Computing; Supercomputer Applications. Vol. 8, No. 1 (Spring 1994)-. Periodical. English. Four times a year. $222.00. Massachusetts Institute of Technology (MIT) Press, 55 Hayward Street, Cambridge MA 02142. **Tel** (617)253-2889, (617)625-8481, FAX (617)258-6779. **ED** Joanne L. Martin and Jack Dongarra. *Continues* International Journal of Supercomputer Applications, 0890-2720.
Desc: For researchers of supercomputing and high-performance computing applications in disciplines such as computer science, biology, artificial intelligence, meteorology, aerodynamics, economics, and graphics.
Ind/Abst Curr. Cit.; INSPEC.

LC Q375 .I59   ISSN 0218-4885
DD 006.3/3/05   SI

•INTERNATIONAL JOURNAL OF UNCERTAINTY, FUZZINESS AND KNOWLEDGE BASED SYSTEMS. VFOAT Uncertainty, Fuzziness, and Knowledge-based Systems; IJUFKS. Vol. 1, No. 1 (Sept. 1993)-. Periodical. English. Four times a year. $180.00. World Scientific Publishing Company, PO Box 128, Farrer Road, Singapore 9128 Singapore. **Tel** 011 65 3825663, FAX 011 65 3825919, telex RS 28561 WSPC. **(Subscription address:** World Scientific Publishing Company, Inc., 1060 Main Street, Suite 1 B, River Edge NJ 07661. **Tel** (800)227-7562, (201)487-9655.) **ED** B. Bouchon-Meunier.
Desc: Forum for research on various methodologies for the management of imprecise, vague, uncertain or incomplete information. Deals with methods to represent and manipulate imperfectly described pieces of knowledge.

US

INTERNATIONAL PAF USERS GROUP SOFTWARE. (19??)-. English. Four times a year (March, June, Sept., Dec.). $15.00. International PAF Users Group, 2463 Ledgewood Drive, West Jordan UT 84084. **Tel** (801)967-8400. **ED** Vance Parker. Index available. Bk Rev. (Qty: 2). Ad Acc. Circ: 2,500 (ctrl).
Ind/Abst Genealogical Period. Annu. Index.

UK

•INTERNATIONAL REVIEW OF LAW, COMPUTERS, AND TECHNOLOGY. See Law-Computer Applications.

ISSN 0733-1932
UK

INTERNATIONAL SERIES IN MODERN APPLIED MATHEMATICS AND COMPUTER SCIENCE. See Mathematics-Computer Applications.

UK

INTERNATIONAL SERIES OF MONOGRAPHS ON COMPUTER SCIENCE, THE. (19??)-. Monographic series. English. Irregular. Price varies per volume. Oxford University Press / UK, Walton Street, Oxford OX2 6DP United Kingdom. **Tel** 011 44 1865 56767, FAX 011 44 1865 267773, telex 851/837330 OXPRES G. **(Subscription address:** Oxford University Press / USA, Journals Marketing Department, Oxford University Press, 2001 Evans Road, Cary NC 27513. **Tel** (800)451-7556, (919)677-0977, FAX (919)677-1714.) **ED** D Gabbay, Z. Galil, J.E. Hopcroft, G.D. Plotkin, J.T. Schwartz, D.S. Scott, J. Vuillemin and A. Yonesawa.
Ind/Abst Math. Rev.; Zentralbl. Math. Ihre Grenzgeb.

ISSN 0271-7379
UK

INTERNATIONAL SERIES ON APPLIED SYSTEMS ANALYSIS. [Int. ser. appl. syst. anal.]. Added/Corp International Institute for Applied Systems Analysis. VFOAT Wiley IIASA International Series on Applied Systems Analysis. Vol. 1 (1977)-. English. John Wiley & Sons, Inc., 605 Third Avenue, New York NY 10158-0012. **Tel** (212)850-6000, (212)850-6645, FAX (212)850-6088, telex 12-7063. **(Subscription address:** John Wiley & Sons / UK, Baffins Lane, Chichester, West Sussex PO19 1UD United Kingdom. **Tel** 011 44 1243 779777, FAX 011 44 243 776128, telex 86290 WIBOOKG.)
Ind/Abst Zentralbl. Math. Ihre Grenzgeb.

ISSN 1050-9070
DD 005   US
  CODEN ISPEEZ

INTERNATIONAL SPECTRUM. [Int. spectr.]. Added/Corp International Database Management Association. (198?)-. Trade Publication. English. Six times a year. $40.00. IDBMA Spectrum Magazine, 10675 Treena Street, Suite 103, San Diego CA 92131. **Tel** (619)578-3152, FAX (619)271-1032. **ED** Nichelle

Computers

Johnson. **Ad Acc, Adv Mgr:** Jill Dennis. **Circ:** 50,000 (ctrl). Documents available from Ask*IEEE.
Desc: Covers computers, new products (both hardware and software), business solutions, and industry news. Provides product reviews.
Ind/Abst INSPEC (1988-1990).

ISSN 0969-6016
UK
CCC

●**INTERNATIONAL TRANSACTIONS IN OPERATIONAL RESEARCH : A JOURNAL OF THE INTERNATIONAL FEDERATION OF OPERATIONAL RESEARCH SOCIETIES. Added/Corp** International Federation of Operational Research Societies. **VFOAT** ITOR; Int. Trans. Opl. Res. Vol. 1, No. 1 (Jan. 1994)-. Periodical. English. Four times a year. $276.00. Pergamon Press, An Imprint of Elsevier Science Ltd., The Boulevard, Langford Lane, Kidlington, Oxford OX5 1GB United Kingdom. **Tel** 011 44 1865 843000, 011 44 1865 843699, **FAX** 011 44 1865 843010.
(Subscription address: Elsevier Science Ltd. / Oxford Fulfillment Centre, PO Box 800, Kidlington OX5 1DX United Kingdom. **Tel** 011 44 865 843355.**) ED** Peter C. Bell. available on an online database from Elsevier Electronic Subscriptions (EES).
Desc: Strives to advance the understanding and practice of operational research.

ISSN 0965-528X
UK
CCC
TITLE CHANGE
INTERNATIONAL YEARBOOK OF LAW, COMPUTERS, AND TECHNOLOGY. See Law-Computer Applications.

US
INTERNET BUSINESS REPORT. (19??)-. English. Twelve times a year. $395.00 US and Canada. CMP Publications Inc., One Jericho Plaza, Wing A, 2nd Floor, Jericho NY 11753. **Tel** (516)733-6700.
(Subscription address: CMP Publications, Inc. / New York, PO Box 4037, Church Street Station, New York NY 10261-4037. **Tel** (516)733-6800.**) ED** Robert Hertzberg.
Desc: Provides independent information on the Internet. Includes facts about Internet investment, research outlays, sales and marketing costs.

LC L
DD 371
ISSN 1064-4326
US
●**INTERPERSONAL COMPUTING AND TECHNOLOGY.** (INTERPERSONAL COMPUTING AND TECHNOLOGY [COMPUTER FILE] : IPCT.). [Interpers. comput. technol.]. **Added/Corp** Georgetown University. Center for Teaching & Technology. **VFOAT** IPCT-J; IPCT Electronic Journal; IPCT. Vol. 1, No. 1 (Jan. 1993)-. Periodical. English. Four times a year. Georgetown University Center for Teaching and Technology, 238 Reiss Science, Washington DC 20057-1001. available via Internet (gopher: guvm.ccf.georgetown.edu 70).

LC QA75.5 .C588
DD 004/.05
ISSN 1051-9246
US
INTRODUCING COMPUTERS. [Introd. comput.]. (1989)-. English. One time a year. $25.95. John Wiley & Sons Inc / New Jersey, 1 Wiley Drive, Somerset NJ 08875. **Tel** (800)225-5945, (908)469-4400.
(Subscription address: John Wiley & Sons / UK, Baffins Lane, Chichester, West Sussex PO19 1UD United Kingdom. **Tel** 011 44 1243 779777, FAX 011 44 243 776128, telex 86290 WIBOOKG.**) Continues** Computer Annual, 0749-9221.

US
IS CAPACITY MANAGEMENT HANDBOOK SERIES. English. Two times a year. $750.00 US; $825.00 other. Institute for Computer Capacity Management, 1020 8th Avenue South, Suite 6, Naples FL 33940. **Tel** (813)261-8945, FAX (813)261-5456.

ISSN 0931-0827
GW
UDC 621.39.037.37
ISDN-REPORT. [ISDN-Rep.]. **VFOAT** Integrated Services Digital Network-Report. (1986)-. Trade Publication. German. Twelve times a year. $191.91. Neue Mediengesellschaft Ulm, Konrad Celtis Strasse 77, D-81369 Muendhen Germany. **Tel** 011 49 89 74117190, FAX 011 49 731 152077. **ED** G. Heutscher.

DD 001
ISSN 0893-7109
US
ITC NEWS - UNITED STATES. DEPT. OF AGRICULTURE. INFORMATION TECHNOLOGY CENTER. See Library and Information Sciences.

UK
●**ITEXT.** (1995)-. English. Six times a year. £80.00 UK and Europe; US$ 140.00 other. Oxford University Press / UK, Walton Street, Oxford OX2 6DP United Kingdom. **Tel** 011 44 1865 56767, FAX 011 44 1865 267773, telex 851/837330 OXPRES G. **(Subscription address:** Oxford University Press / USA, Journals Marketing Department, Oxford University Press, 2001 Evans Road, Cary NC 27513. **Tel** (800)451-7556, (919)677-0977, FAX (919)677-1714.**)**

DD 025.040941
ISSN 0265-5551
UK
IT'S NEWS (LONDON. 1983). (INFORMATION TECHNOLOGY'S NEWS (LONDON. 1983).). [IT's news Lond. 1983]. (1983)-. Periodical. English. Twelve times a year. $325.00. Fadum Enterprises Inc, PO Box 3436, Boulder CO 80307. **Tel** (303)447-1711, FAX (303)447-8373.
Ind/Abst Curr. Cit.

UDC 50/59
ISSN 0935-9680
GW
IX-MULTIUSER-MULTITASKING-MAGAZIN. [IX-Multiuser-Multitask.-Mag.]. Trade Publication. German. Twelve times a year. $68.17. Verlag Heinz Heise GmbH und Co, Postfach 610407, D-30604 Hannover Germany. **Tel** 011 49 511 53520, FAX 011 49 511 5352129.

SP
JAPAN REPORT SERIES INFORMATION TECHNOLOGY. (19??)-. English. Twelve times a year. $430.00. Newmedia International Japan, AV Infanta Carlota 123 5 A, 08029 Barcelona Spain. **Tel** 011 34 3 4195690, FAX 011 34 3 4144213. **(Subscription address:** Newmedia International Japan Midland, Bank 196 Oxford Street, London W1A 1 EZ United Kingdom. **)**
Ind/Abst PROMT [Full Txt.]; PTS Newsl. Database [Full Txt.].

LC QA75
DD 004
ISSN 1058-7306
SZ
CCC
JAPANESE TECHNOLOGY REVIEWS. SECTION B, COMPUTERS AND COMMUNICATION. See Communications-Computer Applications.

DD 005
ISSN 1057-9303
US
JEWISH COMPUTING CATALOG, THE. [Jew. comput. cat.]. **VFOAT** Springwells Jewish Computing Catalog. (1992)-. Catalog. English. Two times a year. $15.00. Springwells Company, PO Box 12346, Boulder CO 80303.

ISSN 1058-1812
US
JEWISH COMPUTING JOURNAL. (1992)-. Periodical. English. Two times a year. $25.00. Springwells Company, PO Box 12346, Boulder CO 80303.

ISSN 1058-1790
US
JEWISH COMPUTING NEWS. (1992)-. Periodical. English. Twelve times a year. $35.00. Springwells Company, PO Box 12346, Boulder CO 80303.

LC QA75.5 .C528
DD 004/.05
ISSN 0254-4164
CH
CODEN JIXUDT
JISUANJI XUEBAO. [Jisuanji xuebao]. **VFOAT** Chinese Journal of Computers. (1978)-. Periodical. Chinese. Six times a year. $84.60. Science Press, 16 Donghuangchenggen North Street, Beijing 100707, People's Republic of China. **Tel** 011 86 1 4019821, 011 86 1 4010642, FAX 011 86 1 4012180, 011 86 1 4019810, telex 210147. **(Subscription address:** China International Book Trading Corporation, PO Box 399, Library Service Department, Beijing 100044 People's Republic of China. **Tel** 011 86 1 8414284, FAX 011 86 1 8412023, telex 22496 CIBTC CN.**)** Documents available from Ask*IEEE.
Ind/Abst INSPEC (1981-); Math. Rev.

LC QA75.5 .C543
DD 004/.05
ISSN 1001-4160
CC
CODEN JYYHE6
Pr Rev.
JISUANJI YU YINGYONG HUAXUE. See Chemistry and Chemicals-Computer Applications.

BE
JOURNAL DE REFLEXION SUR L'INFORMATIQUE. (19??)-. French. Three times a year. 800.00F Belgium; 1000.00F other. Institut de l'Informatique, 21 rue de Grandgagnage, 5000 Namur Belgium. **Tel** 011 32 81 724964, FAX 011 32 81 724967. **ED** Jacques Berleur. Index available.
Desc: A journal based on a sociological analysis of computer development in our society.

LC QA76.6 .J69
DD 511/.8
ISSN 0196-6774
US
CCC
CODEN JOALDV
Pr Rev.
JOURNAL OF ALGORITHMS. See Mathematics.

ISSN 1074-3111
US
●**JOURNAL OF AMERICAN UNDERGROUND COMPUTING, THE.** (THE JOURNAL OF AMERICAN UNDERGROUND COMPUTING [COMPUTER FILE].). **VFOAT** TJOAUC. (1994)-. English. Four times a year. Scott Davis, 10111 North Lamar, Suite 25, Austin TX 78753-3601. **Tel** (512)339-0602. available via Internet (sub@fennec.com).
Desc: Covers all aspects of "underground" computing.

LC QD1 .A495
DD 029/.9/54
ISSN 0095-2338
US
CCC
NLM Z 1007 J85
CODEN JCISD8
JOURNAL OF CHEMICAL INFORMATION AND COMPUTER SCIENCES. See Chemistry and Chemicals-Computer Applications.

ISSN 0090-1091
US
NLM W1 JO587K
CODEN JCLCB
JOURNAL OF CLINICAL COMPUTING. See Medical Sciences-Computer Applications.

ISSN 1077-6265
US
TITLE CHANGE
JOURNAL OF COMPUTER ABSTRACTS AND RESEARCH. See Computers-Abstracting, Bibliographies and Statistics.

LC QA75.5 .I97
DD 004/.05
ISSN 1064-2307
US
CCC
CODEN JSSIE5
JOURNAL OF COMPUTER AND SYSTEMS SCIENCES INTERNATIONAL. [J. comput. syst. sci. int.]. Vol. 30, No. 5 (Sept.-Oct. 1992)-. Academic Scholarly Publication. English (translations available in Russian). Six times a year. $1632.00. Scripta Technica, A Subsidiary of John Wiley & Sons Inc., 7961 Eastern Avenue, Silver Spring MD 20910. **Tel** (301)588-0484, FAX (301)588-5278.
(Subscription address: John Wiley & Sons, Inc. / Philadelphia, PO Box 7247, Philadelphia PA 19170. **Tel** (212)850-6645, (800)225-5945.**) ED** Robert N. McDonough and Reed K. Even. Documents available from Article Express International, Ask*IEEE, CASDDS. **Continues** Izvestiia Akademii Nauk SSSR. Tekhnicheskaia Kibernetika. English. Soviet Journal of Computer and Systems Sciences, 0882-4002.
Desc: Emphasizes practical applications of computer, cognitive and system sciences and at the same time reflects the traditional excellence of Russian mathematics.
Ind/Abst Bioeng. Abstr.; Chem. Abstr.; CompuMath Cit. Index [Full Cov.]; Curr. Cit.; Ei Page One; Electron. Commun. Abstr. J.; Eng. Index Annu.; INIS Atomindex [Micro.]; INSPEC (Oct. 1968-); ISMEC Bull.; Math. Rev.; Nucl. Sci. Abstr.; Pollut. Abstr. Indexes; Saf. Sci. Abstr. J.; Sci. Cit. Index; SCISEARCH; Soc. Sci. Index [Select. Cov.].

ISSN 1000-9000
CC
CCC
CODEN JCTEEM
JOURNAL OF COMPUTER SCIENCE AND TECHNOLOGY. [J. comput. sci. technol.]. (198?)-. Periodical. English. Four times a year. $410.00. Allerton Press Inc., 150 Fifth Avenue, New York NY 10011. **Tel** (212)924-3950, FAX (212)463-9684, telex 427441 ALPRES. **ED** Xia Peisu, Wang Xuan and Zhou Chaochen. Documents available from Article Express International, Ask*IEEE.
Desc: Covers aspects of computer science and technology. Accepts papers of original research and innovatory applications from all parts of the world. Provides not only a window for the other part of the world to have a better understanding of developments of computer science and technology in China, but also a chance for international communication in the computer field.
Ind/Abst Abstr. Hum. Comput. Interact.; Comput. Abstr.; Comput. Rev.; Curr. Cit.; Ei Page One; Eng. Index Annu. [Select. Cov.]; HILITES; INSPEC (Jan. 1988-); Math. Rev.; Zentralbl. Math. Ihre Grenzgeb.

ISSN 0887-3801
DD 624
US
CCC
CODEN JCCEE5
JOURNAL OF COMPUTING IN CIVIL ENGINEERING. See Engineering-Computer Applications.

LC QA76.9.T48 J68
DD 506
ISSN 0969-9325
UK
Pr Rev.
TITLE CHANGE
JOURNAL OF DOCUMENT AND TEXT MANAGEMENT. Added/Corp Institute of Information Scientists. (1993)-(1995). Periodical. English. Taylor Graham Publishing, 500 Chesham House, 150 Regent Street, London W1R 5FA United Kingdom. **Bk Rev. Ad Acc. Continued by** New Review of Document and Text Management.

DD 658 ISSN 0891-5865 US CEASED

JOURNAL OF DOCUMENTATION PROJECT MANAGEMENT. [J. doc. proj. manage.]. **Added/Corp** Sandra Pakin and Associates. **VFOAT** JDPM. (Winter 1987)-(1994). Periodical. English. Sandra Pakin & Associates, 6007 North Sheridan Road, Chicago IL 60660. **Tel** (312)271-2848. **ED** Deanna Bethke, Sandra Pakin. Index available. cum. index. ***Continues** Sandra Pakin & Associates Folio, 0731-7212.*
Desc: Planning, developing, and managing computer end-user documentation projects. Articles are written by documentation consultants, based on their field experiences over the past two decades.

LC T58.64 .J68 **ISSN** 1062-7375
DD 658 US
CODEN JGLMEY
Pr Rev.

●**JOURNAL OF GLOBAL INFORMATION MANAGEMENT.** [J. glob. inf. manag.]. **Added/Corp** Information Resources Management Association. **VFOAT** Global Information Management. Vol. 1, No. 1 (Winter 1993)-. Periodical. English. Four times a year. $125.00. Idea Group Publishing, 4811 Jonestown Road, Suite 230, Harrisburg PA 17109. **Tel** (800)345-4332, (717)541-9150, FAX (717)541-9159. **ED** Prashant Palvia. Index available (bound in 2nd issue). **Bk Rev.** (Qty: 4). **Ad Acc. Circ:** 300 (ctrl).
Desc: Focuses on providing coverage of research findings and expert advice on the development, utilization and management of global information technology.
Ind/Abst Inf. Sci. Abstr. [Full Cov.].

LC WMLC 93/1308 **ISSN** 0888-7985
DD 025 US
CODEN JINFE3

JOURNAL OF INFORMATION SYSTEMS, THE. **See** Business and Economics-Computer Applications.

LC QA76.27 .J68 **ISSN** 1055-3096
DD 004/.071 US

JOURNAL OF INFORMATION SYSTEMS EDUCATION. (JOURNAL OF INFORMATION SYSTEMS EDUCATION / THE DATA PROCESSING MANAGEMENT ASSOCIATION'S SPECIAL INTEREST GROUP FOR EDUCATION (EDSIG).). [J. inf. syst. educ.]. **Added/Corp** Data Processing Management Association. Special Interest Group for Education. Vol. 3, No. 1 (Spring 1991)-. Periodical. English. Four times a year. $35.00. Journal of Information Systems Education, Computer Technology Department, Knoy Hall, Purdue University, West Lafayette IN 47907. ***Continues** CIS Educator Forum, 1055-310X.*

DD 006 **ISSN** 1040-0370 US **CCC**

JOURNAL OF INTERACTIVE INSTRUCTION DEVELOPMENT. [J. interact. instr. dev.]. **Added/Corp** Communicative Technology Corporation. Vol. 1, No. 1 (Summer 1988)-. Trade Publication. English. Four times a year. $60.00. Society for Applied Learning Technology, 50 Culpeper Street, Warrenton VA 22186. **Tel** (703)347-0055, FAX (703)349-3169. **ED** Dr. Ann Barron (Editor's telephone: (813)974-1631). **Circ:** 700 (paid).

LC QA76 .J678 **ISSN** 0863-0445
DD 004/.05 GW
CODEN JGCSE7

JOURNAL OF NEW GENERATION COMPUTER SYSTEMS. [J. new gener. comput. syst.]. **VFOAT** Zhurnal Novykh Pokolenii Vychislitelnykh Sistem. Vol. 1, No. 1 (1988)-. Periodical. English (Russian). Two times a year. $88.00 (academic institutions), $138.00 (corporate institutions). Gordon & Breach Science Publishers, PO Box 90, Reading, Berkshire RG1 8JL United Kingdom. **Tel** 011 44 1734 560080, FAX 011 44 1734 568211. Index available. **Bk Rev. Ad Acc. Circ:** 1,780. Documents available from Ask*IEEE.
Ind/Abst INSPEC (1989-); Math. Rev. (1988-); Zentralbl. Math. Ihre Grenzgeb.

LC HV7936.A8 J68 **ISSN** 1058-8663
DD 363.2/0285 US
CEASED

JOURNAL OF PUBLIC SAFETY COMPUTING, THE. **See** Law-Computer Applications.

LC QA76.88 .J68 **ISSN** 0920-8542
DD 004.1/1/05 US
CCC
CODEN JOSUED
Pr Rev.

JOURNAL OF SUPERCOMPUTING, THE. [J. supercomput.]. **Added/Corp** Supercomputing Research Center (Lanham, Md.). Vol. 1, No. 1 (1987)-. Periodical. English. Four times a year. $364.00. Kluwer Academic Publishers / Massachusetts, PO Box 358, Accord Station, Hingham MA 02018. **Tel** (617)871-6600. **ED** Richard Draper and J. Riganati. **Acid Free.** available on microfilm and microfiche from University Microfilms International (UMI). Documents available from Article Express International, The Genuine Article, Ask*IEEE.
Desc: A technical journal publishing theoretical, practical, tutorial and survey papers on all aspects of supercomputing. The papers published generally fall into areas such as technology, architecture and systems, algorithms, languages and programs, performance measures and methods, and applications.
Ind/Abst ACM Guide Comput. Lit.; CompuMath Cit. Index [Full Cov.]; Comput. Abstr. (1987-); Comput. Rev.; Curr. Cit.; Curr. Contents Eng. Comput. Technol.; Ei Page One; Eng. Index Annu.; INSPEC (1987-); Res. Alert [Full Cov.]; Sci. Cit. Index; SCISEARCH; Zentralbl. Math. Ihre Grenzgeb.

LC QA76.95 .J68 **ISSN** 0747-7171
DD 510/.285 UK
CCC
CODEN JSYCEH
Pr Rev.

JOURNAL OF SYMBOLIC COMPUTATION. **See** Mathematics-Computer Applications.

ISSN 0925-4676
US
CCC
CODEN JSINE4
Pr Rev.

JOURNAL OF SYSTEMS INTEGRATION. [J. syst. integr.]. (1991)-. Periodical. English. Four times a year. $338.00. Kluwer Academic Publishers / Massachusetts, PO Box 358, Accord Station, Hingham MA 02018. **Tel** (617)871-6600. **ED** Peter Ng, Raymond Yeh, and C.V. Ramamoorthy. **Acid Free.** available on microfilm and microfiche from University Microfilms International (UMI). Documents available from Ask*IEEE.
Desc: The scope of this journal generally parallels the definition of the integration of computer systems. However, it deals with the general integration of processes and systems, and the development of mechanisms and tools enabling solutions to multidisciplinary problems found in the computer services and manufacturing industries. This journal focuses on process characterization, to understand current process capabilities, behaviors and interfaces, re-engineering and simplification of processes from a system perspective, convergence on a common system architecture with a unified language for data management, and automation of the processes and systems. The aim is to provide an international and interdisciplinary forum for the dissemination of new theoretical and applied research results, application information and the developments concerning management of systems integration.
Ind/Abst INSPEC (Aug. 1991-).

LC QA76 .A77 **ISSN** 0004-5411
DD 001.6/4/05 US
CCC
NLM Z 699.A1 A849J **CODEN** JACOAH
Pr Rev.

JOURNAL OF THE ASSOCIATION FOR COMPUTING MACHINERY. [J. Assoc. Comput. Mach.]. **Main/Corp** Association for Computing Machinery. Vol. 1 (Jan. 1954)-. Periodical. English. Six times a year. $175.00. ACM / Association for Computing Machinery, 1515 Broadway, 17th Floor, New York NY 10036. **Tel** (212)869-7440, FAX (212)869-0481. **(Subscription address:** Association for Computing Machinery, PO Box 12114, Church Street Station, New York NY 10249. **Tel** (212)626-0500.**)** **ED** F. Thomson Leighton. cum. index. **Circ:** 15,900. available on microfilm and microfiche from University Microfilms International (UMI). Documents available from Article Express International, The Genuine Article, Ask*IEEE, CASDDS.
Desc: Offers a broad range of scientific material that keeps computer scientists aware of the latest issues and advances.
Ind/Abst Appl. Sci. Technol. Index; Bioeng. Abstr.; Chem. Abstr.; CompuMath Cit. Index [Full Cov.]; Comput. Abstr.; Comput. Database; Comput. Rev.; Curr. Cit.; Curr. Contents Eng. Comput. Technol.; Ei Page One; Eng. Index Annu.; Expand. Acad. Index (1992-); Inf. Sci. Abstr. [Full Cov.]; INIS Atomindex [Micro.]; INSPEC (Jan. 1968-); Int. Abstr. Oper. Res. [Select. Cov.]; Int. Aerosp. Abstr.; Math. Rev. [Full Cov.]; Pollut. Abstr. Indexes; Res. Alert [Full Cov.]; Sci. Cit. Index; SCISEARCH; Soc. Sci. Cit. Index [Select. Cov.]; Stat. Theory Method Abstr. (1969); UMI ABI/Inform--Bus. Period. Ondisc (Jan. 1991-) [Full Txt.]; Zentralbl. Math. Ihre Grenzgeb.

DD 005 **ISSN** 1045-926X UK
CODEN JVLCE7

JOURNAL OF VISUAL LANGUAGES AND COMPUTING. [J. vis. lang. comput.]. Vol. 1, No. 1 (Mar. 1990)-. Academic Scholarly Publication. English. Four times a year. $213.90. Academic Press Ltd., A Division of Harcourt Brace & Company Ltd., 24-28 Oval Road, London NW1 7DX United Kingdom. **Tel** 011 44 171 2674466, FAX 011 44 171 4822293, 011 44 171 4854752, telex 25775 ACPRES G. **(Subscription address:** Harcourt Brace & Company, Ltd., Foots Cray High Street, Sidcup Kent DA14 5HP United Kingdom. **Tel** 011 44 181 3003322, FAX 011 44 181 3090807, telex 896 377 ACADEM.**)** **ED** S. K. Chang and S. Levialdi. Documents available from Ask*IEEE.
Desc: A forum for researchers, practitioners, and developers to exchange ideas and results for the advancement of visual languages and its implication to the art of computing. Publishes research papers, state-of-the-art surveys, and review articles in all aspects of visual languages.
Ind/Abst Curr. Cit.; INSPEC (March 1990-).

ISSN 0950-4788
UK

KEY ABSTRACTS. COMPUTER COMMUNICATIONS & STORAGE. **See** Engineering-Abstracting, Bibliographies and Statistics.

UK

KEY ABSTRACTS. HUMAN-COMPUTER INTERACTION. **See** Computers-Abstracting, Bibliographies and Statistics.

UK

KEY ABSTRACTS. NEURAL NETWORKS. **See** Computers-Abstracting, Bibliographies and Statistics.

LC TK1005 .K49 **ISSN** 0950-4834
DD 621.319/1/05 UK

KEY ABSTRACTS. POWER SYSTEMS AND APPLICATIONS. **See** Computers-Abstracting, Bibliographies and Statistics.

LC HD9680 **ISSN** 1357-1370
DD 338.4762138 UK

●**KEY NOTE MARKET REVIEW. MULTIMEDIA IN THE UK.** **See** Business and Economics-Advertising and Public Relations.

LC T58.6 .K575
DD 003/.05 RU

KLASSIFIKATORY I DOKUMENTY V ASU. **Added/Corp** Vsesoiuznyi Nauchno-Issledovatelskii Institut Tekhnicheskoi Informatsii, Klassifikatsii i Kodirovaniia (Soviet Union). **VFOAT** Klassifikatory I Dokumenty v A.S.U. Vol. 1 (1981)-. Periodical. Russian. Irregular. $219.95. VINITI - Vsesoyuznyi Institut Nauchno-Tekhnicheskoi Informatsii, All-Union Scientific and Technical Information Institute, Baltiiskaia ulitsa 14, 125219 Moscow Russia. **Tel** 011 7 95 2384600, FAX 011 7 95 9430060, telex 411160. **(Subscription address:** East View Publications Inc., 3020 Harbor Lane North, Suite 110, Minneapolis MN 55447. **Tel** (800)477-1005, (612)550-0961, FAX (612)559-2931.**)**
Desc: Covers materials on these subjects: information supply of automated control systems; systems of classification and coding of technical and economic information, unification of documents; development and application of of all-union classification schemes and unified document system, etc.

US

KLUWER INTERNATIONAL SERIES IN ENGINEERING AND COMPUTER SCIENCE, THE. **See** Engineering-Computer Applications.

US

KNOW NEWS ... IS GOOD NEWS. **VFOAT** Know News. Vol. 12, No. 2 (Summer 1990)-. English. Information on Demand Inc, 8000 Westpark Drive, McLean VA 22102. **Tel** (800)999-4463, (703)442-0303, FAX (703)442-0907.
Desc: This publication promotes the services offered by "Information On Demand".

LC QA76.76.E95 K575 **ISSN** 0950-7051
DD 006.3/3 UK
CCC
CODEN KNSYET
Pr Rev.

KNOWLEDGE-BASED SYSTEMS (GUILDFORD, SURREY). (KNOWLEDGE-BASED SYSTEMS.). [Knowl.-based syst.]. **VFOAT** Knowledge Based Systems. Vol. 1, No. 1 (Dec. 1987)-. Periodical. English. Eight times a year. $552.00. Butterworth Heinemann Publishers, Linacre House Jordan Hill, Oxford OX2 8DP United Kingdom. **Tel** 011 44 1865 310366, FAX 011 44 1865 310898. **(Subscription address:** Elsevier Science Ltd. / Oxford Fulfillment Centre, PO Box 800, Kidlington OX5 1DX United Kingdom. **Tel** 011 44 865 843355.**)** **ED** E. A. Edmonds. Index available. cum. index. **Bk Rev. Ad Acc. Circ:** 800 (ctrl). available on microfilm and microfiche from University Microfilms International (UMI); available on an online database from Elsevier Electronic Subscriptions (EES). Documents available from The Genuine Article, Ask*IEEE.
Desc: An international, interdisciplinary and applications-oriented journal on knowledge-based systems.
Ind/Abst Abstr. Hum. Comput. Interact.; CompuMath Cit. Index [Full Cov.]; Comput. Lit. Index; Curr. Cit.; INSPEC (Dec. 1987-); Res. Alert [Full Cov.]; Sci. Cit. Index; SCISEARCH; Soc. Sci. Cit. Index [Select. Cov.].

Computers

LC QA75.5 .K76
KO
KOMPYUTO PIJON. VFOAT The Computer Vision; Computer Vision. First issue 1983. Periodical. Korean (Korean). Twelve times a year. W2.000. Chongbo Sidae, 36-4 Yourdo Dong, Yongdungpo-Ku Seoul Korea.

LC HD9696.C63 J323
DD 338.47621381
JA
KOMPYUTOPIA = COMPUTOPIA. VFOAT Computopia. (1967)-. Periodical. Japanese. Twelve times a year. $138.00. Kompyuta Eji Sha, Kasumigaseki Building, 30-kai, 2-5, Kasumigaseki 3-chome, Chiyoda-ku, Tokyo 100 Japan. **ED** Teijiro Kubo. **Circ:** 61,500.
Desc: An all-around journal of computers.

LC HF5548.2 .K9
DD 651
KO
KYONGYONG KWA KOMPYUTO. See Business and Economics-Computer Applications.

ISSN 0921-5034
NE
LANGUAGE AND COMPUTERS. See Linguistics.

ISSN 0962-9580
DD 344.103999
UK
LAW, COMPUTERS & ARTIFICIAL INTELLIGENCE. See Law-Computer Applications.

LC K12 .A93649
DD 340/.068
ISSN 1055-128X
US
CCC
LAW OFFICE COMPUTING. See Law-Computer Applications.

LC KF320.A9 L396
DD 340
ISSN 1047-6482
US
LAW OFFICE TECHNOLOGY REVIEW. See Law-Computer Applications.

ISSN 1044-4785
US
LAX (GLENDALE, CALIF.). (LAX.). [LAX]. VFOAT L A X Magazine; LAX Magazine; L.A.X.; L A X. **VAT** Language Art Expression. Vol. 1, No. 1 (1989)-. Periodical. English. Three times a year. $18.00. L.A.X. Axis, 103 W California Street, Glendale CA 91203.

ISSN 0302-9743
GW
CCC
CODEN LNCSD9
LECTURE NOTES IN COMPUTER SCIENCE. [Lect. notes comput. sci.]. (1973)-. Monographic series. Multiple languages. Irregular. Price varies per volume. Springer-Verlag GmbH & Company KG, Heidelberger Platz 3, D-14197 Berlin Germany. **Tel** 011 49 30 8207223, FAX 011 49 30 8214091, telex 183 319 SPBLN D. **(Subscription address:** Springer-Verlag New York Inc. / North America, PO Box 2485, Journal Fulfillment, Secaucus NJ 07096. **Tel** (201)348-4033, (800)777-4643, FAX (201)348-4505.) Documents available from The Genuine Article, BIOSIS Document Express, Ask*IEEE.
Desc: Contains information on storage units, system analysis, software, hardware, languages, and data structures.
Ind/Abst Biol. Abstr. (?-1985); CompuMath Cit. Index [Full Cov.]; Curr. Cit.; Ei Page One; GeoRef; INSPEC; Math. Rev.; Res. Alert [Full Cov.]; SCISEARCH; Soc. Sci. Cit. Index [Select. Cov.]; Zentralbl. Math. Ihre Grenzgeb.

ISSN 0177-1205
GW
UDC 621.382
LEITERPLATTEN. [Leiterplatten]. VFOAT ZEV-Leiterplatten. (198?)-. Periodical. German. Ten times a year. $91.24. Roman Th Stadtmueller, Birkenstrasse 12, 8609 Bischberg Germany.

ISSN 1165-6816
FR
UDC 681.3
●**LETTRE DES SSII PARIS, LA.** (LA LETTRE DES SSII.). (1993)-. Periodical. French. One time a week. $656.17. Publications GRD, 85 rue du Dessous des Berges, 75013 Paris France. **Tel** 011 33 1 53828253. **Continues** Logiciels & Services Herdo, 0986-2986.

US
CEASED
LIE GROUPS. SERIES B, SYSTEMS INFORMATION AND CONTROL. VFOAT Systems Information and Control. Vol. 1 (1983)-Series Completed (19??). Monographic series. English. Math Science Press, 53 Jordan Road, Brookline MA 02146. **Tel** (617)738-0307. **Separated from** Lie Groups. History, Frontiers, and Applications, 1045-6368.
Ind/Abst Zentralbl. Math. Ihre Grenzgeb.

IT
LINEA EDP. Italian. One time a week. L135000.00. Alfa Linea Srl, Viale Sondrio 5, 20124 Milan Italy. **Tel** 011 39 2 66987575. **ED** Alfa Linea. Index available. **Bk Rev.**

Ad Acc, Adv Mgr: Giacomo Bernini. ctrl circ.
Desc: Weekly magazine about news on information technology.

ISSN 1049-4928
DD 025
US
LINK (CHAMPAIGN, ILL.), THE. (THE LINK : THE NEWSLETTER OF THE ILLINOIS LIBRARY COMPUTER SYSTEMS ORGANIZATION.). [Link]. **Added/Corp** Illinois Library Computer Systems Organization. Vol. 1, No. 1 (April 1990)-. Newsletter. English. Six times a year. Free on request. Illinois Library Computer Systems Office, 205 Johnstowne Centre, 502 East John Street, Champaign IL 61820.

ISSN 0296-8754
FR
UDC 681.3
LOGICIELS ET SERVICES. [Logiciels serv.]. (1984)-. Periodical. French. Twelve times a year. 391.77F France; 630.00F other. Publications GRD, 85 rue du Dessous des Berges, 75013 Paris France. **Tel** 011 33 1 53828253. **Continues** Logiciels & Services Informatiques, 0754-1503.

ISSN 0897-9308
DD 004
US
LOS ANGELES COMPUTER CURRENTS. See Computers-Computer Industry and Industry Directories.

ISSN 1074-0392
DD 004
US
●**MAC HOME JOURNAL.** [Mac home j.]. VFOAT MacHome Journal. (1993)-. Periodical. English. Twelve times a year. $19.95. Antic Publishing, 544 2nd Street, San Francisco CA 94170. **Tel** (415)957-1911. **(Subscription address:** Kable Publishers Aide / Illinois, 308 East Hitt Street, Subscription Department, Mt. Morris IL 61054-1473. **Tel** (815)734-1261.)

ISSN 1195-8367
DD 005.4
CN
●**MACBIZ CANADA.** [MacBiz Can.]. Vol. 1, No. 1 (March 1994)-. Periodical. English. Six times a year. $24.00 US; $25.00 Canada. Macbiz Publishing, 30 Wertheim Court, Suite 24, Richmond Hill ONT, L4B 1B9 Canada. **Tel** (905)764-6420.

ISSN 1058-6601
DD 006
US
●**MACPREPRESS.** [MacPrePress]. VFOAT Mac Prepress. (1989)-. Periodical. English. Forty-Five times a year. $295.00. Prepress Information Service, 12 Burr Road, Westport CT 06880. **Tel** (203)227-2357, FAX (203)454-4962. **ED** Kathleen Turkel. cum. index. **Circ:** 400.
Desc: Prepress information and news.

ISSN 1072-5466
DD 005
US
●**MACROCOSM (OVERLAND PARK, KAN.).** (MACROCOSM [COMPUTER FILE].). [Macrocosm]. (Sept. 1993)-. Periodical. English. Twelve times a year. $59.95. Resource Central, Box 11250, Overland Pard KS 66207. **Tel** (913)469-6502.

ISSN 1065-3929
DD 005
US
MACROMEDIA USER JOURNAL. (MACROMEDIA USER JOURNAL : FOR MULTIMEDIA DEVELOPERS AND USERS OF MACROMEDIA PROGRAMS.). [Macromedia user j.]. No. 9 (July/Aug. 1992)-. Periodical. English. Twelve times a year. $128.00. HyperMedia Communications, 901 Mariner's Island Boulevard, Suite 365, San Mateo CA 94404. **Tel** (415)573-5170. **(Subscription address:** Macromedia User Journal, PO Box 10285, Des Moines IA 50381.) **Continues** MacroMind Developer Letter.

ISSN 1074-679X
DD 006
US
●**MAGAZINE OF ARTIFICIAL INTELLIGENCE IN FINANCE, THE.** See Business and Economics-Computer Applications.

US
MAINFRAME COMPUTERS. **Added/Corp** Auerbach Publishers. (1982)-. English. Auerbach Publishers Inc., Park Square Building, 31 St. James Avenue, Boston MA 02116. **Tel** (800)950-1207. **Supersedes** Computer Systems.

US
MAINFRAME REPORT. (19??)-. Periodical. English. Thirteen times a year. $1045.00. Faulkner Technical Reports, 7905 Browning Road, Suite 114, Pennsauken NJ 08109. **Tel** (800)843-0460.

GW
MANAGEMENT & COMPUTER. See Business and Economics-Computer Applications.

IT
CEASED
MANAGEMENT E INFORMATICA. (19??)-(Dec. 1993). Italian. Franco Angeli Riviste SRL, Viale Monza 106, 20127 Milan Italy. **Tel** 011 39 2 2827651, 011 39 2 289562, FAX 011 39 2 258004, telex 051-511650. Documents available from Ask*IEEE.
Ind/Abst INSPEC (Jan. 1980-).

LC T58.6 .M55
DD 658.4/038
ISSN 0276-7783
US
CCC
CODEN MISQDP
Pr Rev.
MANAGEMENT INFORMATION SYSTEMS QUARTERLY. See Business and Economics-Computer Applications.

DD 004
US
MANAGING INFORMATION TECHNOLOGY. **Added/Corp** Datapro Information Services Group. VFOAT Datapro Managing Information Technology. Vol. 1, No. 1 (Aug. 1991)-. English. Twelve times a year. Datapro Information Services Group, 600 Delran Parkway, Delran NJ 08075. **Tel** (609)764-0100, (800)328-2776, FAX (609)764-8953. **Continues** Datapro Management of EDP Systems.

ISSN 1358-1066
UK
●**MANUFACTURING COMPUTER SOLUTIONS.** (19??)-. English. Twelve times a year. $154.01. Findlay Publications Ltd., Franks Hall, Horton Kirby, Dartford Kent DA4 9LL United Kingdom. **Tel** 011 44 1322 614060, FAX 011 44 1322 613943.
Ind/Abst Curr. Cit.

ISSN 0888-6989
DD 670
US
CEASED
MAPNETTER NEWSLETTER, THE. [MAPNetter newsl.]. VFOAT MAP Netter Newsletter; MAPnetter. Vol. 1, No. 1 (July 1986)-Vol. 7, No. 12 (Jan. 1993). Newsletter. English. Architecture Technology Corporation, PO Box 24344, Minneapolis MN 55424. **Tel** (612)935-2035.

ISSN 0954-7126
UK
MAPPING AWARENESS. [Mapp. aware.]. VFOAT Mapping Awareness and Integrated Spatial Information Systems. (1987)-. Periodical. English. Ten times a year. £65.00 UK; £75.00 other Europe; £85.00 other. Miles Arnold, High Winds Cassington, Oxford OX8 1DL United Kingdom. **Tel** 011 44 1865 880236, FAX 011 44 1865 883301. **ED** Peter Shand. **Bk Rev. Ad Acc. Circ:** 8,000 (ctrl).

LC G70.2 .M37
DD 910
ISSN 0954-7126
UK
Pr Rev.
●**MAPPING AWARENESS.** See Geography-Cartography.

LC QA
DD 004
NE
MARKETONS BV. (19??)-. Newsletter. Dutch. Twenty times a year. Fl275.00. Intl Info Research, Postbus 1310, Nijmegen 6501 BH Netherlands. **Tel** 31-80-224200, FAX 31-80-603176. **ED** W. Y. M. Veldkamp. **Circ:** 1,500.
Desc: Newsletter for the information technology world.

ISSN 1067-0688
DD 511
US
●**MATHEMATICAL MODELLING AND SCIENTIFIC COMPUTING.** See Mathematics-Computer Applications.

NE
MB PRODUCTIETECHNIEK. Dutch. Tech Uitgeverij Vey Mestdagh, Markt 51, 4331 LK Middelburg Netherlands.

ISSN 0882-3979
DD 001
US
MCGRAW-HILL'S COMPUTER CAREERS. See Occupations and Careers.

ISSN 0393-0599
IT
UDC 681.3
MEDIA DUEMILA. [Media duemila]. (1983)-. Periodical. Italian. Eleven times a year. L40880. Gutenberg 2000 s.r.l., C S Massimo D Azeglio 60, 10126 Turin Italy. **Tel** 011 39 11 6504430.

ISSN 0162-2382
US
NLM W1 ME265
MEDICAL COMPUTING SERIES. See Medical Sciences-Computer Applications.

ISSN 0307-7640
UK
CCC
NLM W1; ME342C
CODEN MINFDZ
Pr Rev.
MEDICAL INFORMATICS. See Medical Sciences-Computer Applications.

Computers

ISSN 1075-0924
US
CEASED

METHODS OF LOGIC IN COMPUTER SCIENCE. (1994)-Vol. 2 (1995). Periodical. English. Ablex Publishing Corporation, 355 Chestnut Street, Norwood NJ 07648. **Tel** (201)767-8450, (201)767-8455 (Customer Service), FAX (201)767-6717.

US

Pr Rev.
MIC-TECH-UNIX. English. Twelve times a year. $891.00 US; $986.00 other postage) other. Management Information Corporation, 1111 Marlkress Road, Cherry Hill NJ 08003. **Tel** (609)424-1100. Index available. cum. index. ctrl circ. available on diskette.
Desc: Reference service on UNIX operating systems and UNIX standards.

ISSN 1122-0368
IT
UDC 681.3
MICRO & SOFT. [Micro Soft]. **VFOAT** Micro and Soft. (1992)-. Periodical. Italian. Four times a year. L15000 Italy; L30000 Europe; L50000 other. Gruppo Editoriale Jackson Spa, Via Gorki 69, 20092 Cinisello Balsamo Italy. **Tel** 011 39 2 66034401.

ISSN 0883-4296
US
DD 338
MICRO ECONOMICS. See Business and Economics.

US

MICROCOMPUTER AND VIDEO PURCHASING AND USAGE PLANS ... SCHOOL YEAR : .... ANNUAL TECHNOLOGY SURVEY OF SELECTED U.S. SCHOOL DISTRICTS. Added/Corp Quality Education Data, Inc. **VFOAT** Annual Technology Survey of Selected U.S. School Districts. (19??)-. Periodical. English. Irregular. Quality Education Data, 1600 Broadway, Suite 1200, Denver CO 80202. **Tel** (303)860-1832.

ISSN 0726-352X
AT
DD 001.6404
MICROCOMPUTER NEWS. [Microcomput. news]. (1981)-. Periodical. English. Irregular.
Ind/Abst Aust. Educ. Index.

ISSN 0883-9808
US
DD 686
MICROGRAPHICS NEWSLETTER. [Microgr. newsl.]. Vol. 7, No. 1 (Jan. 1975)-. Newsletter. English. Twelve times a year. $178.00. Microfilm Publishing Inc., PO Box 950, Larchmont NY 10538-0950. **Tel** (914)834-3044. **ED** Mitchell M. Badler and Dorothy Miceli. **Bk Rev. Ad Acc.** available on microfilm and microfiche from University Microfilms International (UMI). **Continues** Microfilm Newsletter, 0026-2749.
Desc: News of the micrographics and related industries for users, vendors and other interested parties.
Ind/Abst Inf. Manage. Technol. (19??-).

ISSN 0889-9533
US
DD 070
TITLE CHANGE
MICROPUBLISHING REPORT. See Publishing-Computer Applications.

ISSN 1065-9900
US
DD 004
MICROQUEST REPORT. [Microquest rep.]. (1989)-. Periodical. English. Twelve times a year. $495.00 US; $550.00 other. Microquest, 454 Las Gallinas Avenue, Suite 250, San Rafael CA 94903. **Tel** (415)479-4723, FAX (415)479-8636. **ED** Mark Ross.

ISSN 1081-3497
US
●**MICROSOFT CERTIFIED PROFESSIONAL MAGAZINE.** (1995)-. Periodical. English. Six times a year. $19.95. Quickstart Technologies, 1500 Quail Street, 6th Floor, Newport Beach CA 92660. **Tel** (714)476-7575, (714)476-1015.

US
●**MICROSOFT MAGAZINE.** (Fall 1994)-. Periodical. English. Four times a year. Microsoft, One Microsoft Way, Redmond WA 98052-6399. **Tel** (206)882-8080, (800)MSPRESS, FAX (615)793-3915. **ED** Sharon McKenna.
Desc: Ideas relevant to Microsoft customers.

ISSN 0933-9434
GW
UDC 681.3
MICROSOFT-SYSTEM-JOURNAL. (1988)-. Periodical. German. Six times a year. $114.22. Vogel Verlag, Postfach 6740, D-97064 Wuerzburg Germany. **Tel** 011 49 931 4182145, 011 49 931 4182483, FAX 011 49 931 4182670, telex 841 680131.

ISSN 1052-3561
US
DD 004
MIDRANGE COMPUTING. [Midrange comput.]. **VFOAT** Computing. (Jan. 1990)-. Trade Publication. English. Twelve times a year. $99.00. Midrange Computing, 5650 El Camino Real, Suite 225, Carlsbad CA 92008. **Tel** (619)931-8615, (800)477-5665, FAX (619)931-9935. **Continues** DataNetwork, 1052-3553.

ISSN 1120-5164
IT
UDC 681.3
CEASED
MINISISTEMI. [Minisistemi]. (1989)-(19??). Periodical. Italian. Arnoldo Mondadori Editore, UFF Cont Abbonamenti, 20090 Segrate MI Italy. **Tel** 011 39 2 75422015, telex 320457 MONDMI I.

ISSN 1060-3565
US
●**MIS MANAGEMENT REVIEW. VFOAT** Management Information Systems Management Review; MIS Professional. (1992)-. Periodical. English. Twelve times a year. $30.00. Computech, Larry M Singer, 2187 Tuliptree Avenue, Columbus OH 43229.

US
MISINFORMATION. English. Irregular (six-eight issues per year). $20.00. Chris Miksanek, Box 305, Burbank CA 91503. **ED** Chris Miksanek. **Ad Acc. Circ:** 1,500.
Desc: Computer humor newsletter.

ISSN 0891-4702
US
DD 004
MIT PRESS SERIES IN INFORMATION SYSTEMS. [MIT Press ser. inf. syst.]. **VFOAT** Information Systems Series. (1985)-. Monographic series. English. Irregular. Price varies per volume. Massachusetts Institute of Technology (MIT) Press, 55 Hayward Street, Cambridge MA 02142. **Tel** (617)253-2889, (617)625-8481, FAX (617)258-6779. (**Subscription address:** MIT Press Books, 55 Hayward Street, Cambridge MA 02142.) **ED** Michael Lesk. Documents available from Ask*IEEE.
Ind/Abst INSPEC (1985-).

US
●**MOBILE LETTER.** (1995)-. English. Twelve times a year. $495.00. IDG Newsletter Corporation, 77 Franklin Street, Suite 310, Boston MA 02110. **Tel** (617)482-8470, (800)807-7100, FAX (617)338-0164.

ISSN 0242-5769
FR
UDC 681.3
CCC
MONDE INFORMATIQUE, LE. [Monde inform]. (1981)-. Periodical. French. One time a week (except July 15 to Sept. 1). $227.91. IDG Communications / France, Immeuble La Fayette Cedex 65, F-92051 Paris la Defense 5 France. **Tel** 011 33 1 49047900, FAX 011 33 1 49047870, telex 613234. **Ad Acc. Circ:** 35,000 (ctrl). available on microfilm from University Microfilms International (UMI).
Ind/Abst Infomat Int. Bus.

IT
MONDO AUTOCAD. Italian. Irregular. L50000 Italy; L100000 other. Franco Ziviani Editore, Via Aldrovandi 3, 20129 Milan Italy. **Tel** 011 39 2 29404781.

ISSN 0892-5445
US
DD 004
MONEY MACHINE. [Money mach.]. **VFOAT** Commodore Money Machine; Money Machine Magazine. Issue 1 (Nov./Dec. 1986)-. Periodical. English. Six times a year. $16.00. Money Machine, PO Box 2618, 2142 East Silver Springs Boulevard, Ocala FL 32678.

ISSN 1074-6501
US
DD 005
●**MORPH'S OUTPOST ON THE DIGITAL FRONTIER.** [Morph's Outpost digit. front.]. (1993)-. Periodical. English. Twelve times a year. $34.95. Morphs Outpost Inc., PO Box 469054, Escondido CA 92046. **Tel** (510)210-8170.

ISSN 0741-8035
US
MSC/NASTRAN APPLICATION MANUAL. IBM EDITION. (MSC/NASTRAN APPLICATION MANUAL.). **Added/Corp** MacNeal-Schwendler Corporation. **VFOAT** M.S.C./N.A.S.T.R.A.N. Application Manual; Application Manual. (19??)-. English. Irregular (Must specify type of computer and operating system). $100.00 US; $50.00 other. MacNeil Schwendler, 815 Colorado Boulevard, Los Angeles CA 90041. **Tel** (213)259-3888, FAX (213)259-3800, telex 4720462.

ISSN 0960-1295
UK
LC QA76.9.M35 M3874
DD 004/.01/51
CCC
MSCS (CAMBRIDGE). (MATHEMATICAL STRUCTURES IN COMPUTER SCIENCE : MSCS). [MSCS]. **Added/Corp** University of Cambridge. **VFOAT** MSCS. Vol. 1, No. 1 (March 1991)-. Academic Scholarly Publication. English. Six times a year. $248.00. Cambridge University Press, The Edinburgh Building, Shaftesbury Road, Cambridge CB2 2RU United Kingdom. **Tel** 011 44 1223 312393, FAX 011 44 1223 315052, telex 851-817256. (**Subscription address:** Cambridge University Press / North America, 110 Midland Avenue, Port Chester NY 10573. **Tel** (800)431-1580, (914)937-9600.) **ED** G. Longo.
Desc: Journal of theoretical computer science which focuses on the application of ideas from the structural side of mathematics and mathematical logic to computer science.
Ind/Abst Math. Rev.; Zentralbl. Math. Ihre Grenzgeb.

ISSN 0923-8182
NE
UDC 681.31 :658.012.4
Pr Rev.
MULTI-MEDIA COMPUTING. [Multi-media comput.]. (1989)-. Periodical. Dutch. Eleven times a year (with July and Aug. combined). Fl125.00. Nanton Press Uitgeverij BV, Postbus 93, 3720 AB Bilthoven Netherlands. **Tel** 011 31 30 290644. Index available. **Bk Rev. Ad Acc.** ctrl circ. **Continues** Mini/Micro Computer, 0167-6547.

ISSN 0923-6082
US
LC TK5102.5 .M84
DD 621.382/2
CCC
CODEN MUSPE5
Pr Rev.
MULTIDIMENSIONAL SYSTEMS AND SIGNAL PROCESSING. [Multidimens. syst. signal process.]. Vol. 1, No. 1 (March 1990)-. Periodical. English. Four times a year. $338.00. Kluwer Academic Publishers / Massachusetts, PO Box 358, Accord Station, Hingham MA 02018. **Tel** (617)871-6600. **ED** Nirmal K. Bose, Marwan Simaan, and Jan Biemond. **Acid Free.** available on microfilm and microfiche from University Microfilms International (UMI). Documents available from Article Express International, The Genuine Article, Ask*IEEE.
Desc: An archival, peer-reviewed, technical journal publishing survey and original papers, spanning fundamentals as well as applicable research contributions. While the subject of multidimensional systems is concerned with mathematical issues designed to tackle a broad range of models, its applications in signal processing have been known to cover spatial and temporal signals of diverse physical origin.
Ind/Abst ACM Guide Comput. Lit.; CompuMath Cit. Index [Full Cov.]; Comput. Rev.; Curr. Contents Eng. Comput. Technol.; Ei Page One; Eng. Index Annu.; Inf. Sci. Abstr. (Mar. 1990-); INSPEC (March 1990-); Math. Rev.; Res. Alert [Full Cov.]; Sci. Cit. Index; SCISEARCH; Zentralbl. Math. Ihre Grenzgeb.

ISSN 1065-7657
US
DD 005
TITLE CHANGE
MULTILINGUAL COMPUTING. (MULTILINGUAL COMPUTING : MAGAZINE AND BUYER'S GUIDE.). [Multiling. comput.]. **VFOAT** Multilingual Computing Magazine. (1992)-(19??). Periodical. English. Multilingual Computing Inc., 111 Cedar Street, Suite 5, Sandpoint ID 83864. **Tel** (208)263-8178, FAX (208)263-6310. **Formed by the union of** Worldwide Product Directory **and** SESAME Bulletin, 0950-2025. **Split into** Multilingual Computing Magazine **and** Multilingual Computing Buyer's Guide.

US
●**MULTILINGUAL COMPUTING MAGAZINE.** (199?)-. Periodical. English. Six times a year. $35.00. Multilingual Computing Inc., 111 Cedar Street, Suite 5, Sandpoint ID 83864. **Tel** (208)263-8178, FAX (208)263-6310. **ED** Seth Thomas Schneider. **Ad Acc.** Separated from Multilingual Computing : Magazine and Buyer's Guide, 1065-7657.
Desc: A journal of language technology for computers.

ISSN 1051-953X
US
DD 004
MULTIMEDIA COMPUTING & PRESENTATIONS. VFOAT Multimedia Computing and Presentations. (1988)-. Periodical. English. Twelve times a year. $449.00 North America; $499.00 other. Multimedia Computing Corporations, 3501 Ryder Street, Santa Clara CA 95051. **ED** Nick Arnett. available on an online database (file 675/Full-Text) from DIALOG.
Desc: Written for industry professionals and investors on multimedia market and product strategies. Also includes new products and general news in the industry.
Ind/Abst Comput. ASAP [Full Txt.]; Comput. Database [Full Txt.].

UK
MULTIMEDIA INTERNATIONAL. (19??)-. English. Twelve times a year. £254.00 UK; $445.00 US. World Business Publications Ltd., 960 High Road, Britannia 4th Floor, London N12 9RY United Kingdom. **Tel** 011 44 181 4465141, FAX 011 44 181 4463659, telex 9419208.

Computers

LC QA76.575 .M84   ISSN 1046-3550
DD 006.6   US
    CCC
CODEN MULREA
CEASED

MULTIMEDIA REVIEW. (MULTIMEDIA REVIEW : THE JOURNAL OF MULTIMEDIA COMPUTING.). [Multimed. rev.]. Vol. 1, No. 1 (Spring 1990)-Vol. 4 No. 2 (1993). Periodical. English. Mecklermedia Corporation, 11 Ferry Lane West, Westport CT 06880. **Tel** (203)226-6967, (800)632-5537, FAX (203)454-5840. **ED** Sandra Kay Helsel and Judith Paris Roth. Documents available from Ask*IEEE.
Desc: Devoted to analysis of trends, paradigms, and strategies affecting the creation and production, design and development, and implementation and use of multimedia programs and configurations.
Ind/Abst Curr. Cit.; HILITES; INSPEC (Winter 1990-).

    ISSN 1060-7684
DD 005   US
CODEN MUCOEO
TITLE CHANGE

MUMPS COMPUTING. [MUMPS comput.]. **Added/Corp** MUMPS Users' Group. (1992)-(19??). Periodical. English. M Technology Association, 1738 Elton Road, Suite 205, Silver Springs MD 20903. **Tel** (301)431-4070, FAX (301)431-0017. Documents available from Ask*IEEE. **Continues** Quarterly MUG, 0193-0885. **Continued by** M Computing, 1072-3226.
Ind/Abst INSPEC (1992-); Microcomput. Abstr.

    ISSN 0258-1248
    GW
    CCC
CODEN NASFEG

NATO ASI SERIES. SERIES F, COMPUTER AND SYSTEM SCIENCES. [NATO ASI ser., Ser. F : Comput. syst. sci.]. **Added/Corp** North Atlantic Treaty Organization. Scientific Affairs Division. **VFOAT** Computer and System Sciences. **VAT** North Atlantic Treaty Organization Advanced Science Institutes Series. Series F, Computer and System Sciences. No. 1 (1983)-. Monographic series. English. Irregular. Price Varies per volume. Springer-Verlag GmbH & Company KG, Heidelberger Platz 3, D-14197 Berlin Germany. **Tel** 011 49 30 8207223, FAX 011 49 30 8214091, telex 183 319 SPBLN D. **(Subscription address:** Springer-Verlag New York Inc. / North America, PO Box 19386 Books, Newark NJ 07195. **Tel** (201)348-4033.)
Ind/Abst Curr. Cit.

    ISSN 0890-5673
DD 333   US

NATURAL RESOURCES COMPUTER NEWSLETTER. See Environmental Issues-Computer Applications.

LC Z699.A1 N354   ISSN 0548-0027
DD 025.04   RU
CODEN NIPSBP

NAUCHNO-TEKHNICHESKAIA INFORMATSIIA. SERIIA 2. INFORMATSIONNYE PROTSESSY I SISTEMY. [Naucno-teh. inf. - Vses. inst. naucn. teh. inf., Ser. 2]. **Added/Corp** Vsesoiuznyi Institut Nauchnoi i Tekhnicheskoi Informatsii (Soviet Union). **VFOAT** Informatsionnye Protsessy i Sistemy. (1967)-. Academic Scholarly Publication. Russian. Twelve times a year. $79.95. VINITI - Vsesoyuznyi Institut Nauchno-Tekhnicheskoi Informatsii, All-Union Scientific and Technical Information Institute, Baltiiskaia ulitsa 14, 125219 Moscow Russia. **Tel** 011 7 95 2384600, FAX 011 7 95 9430060, telex 411160. **(Subscription address:** East View Publications Inc., 3020 Harbor Lane North, Suite 110, Minneapolis MN 55447. **Tel** (612)477-1005, (612)550-0961, FAX (612)559-2931.) Documents available from The Genuine Article, Ask*IEEE, CASDDS. **Supersedes in part** Nauchno-Tekhnicheskaia Informatsiia.
Ind/Abst Chem. Abstr.; CompuMath Cit. Index [Full Cov.]; INSPEC (1969-); Res. Alert [Full Cov.]; Soc. Plann. Policy Dev. Abstr.; Soc. Sci. Cit. Index [Full Cov.].

    US

NCAIR NEWS. Added/Corp National Center for Automated Information Retrieval. **VAT** National Center for Automated Information Retrieval News. Vol. 1 (Nov. 1977)-. Periodical. English. Four times a year. Free on request. National Center Automated Information Retrieval, 330 Madison Avenue, New York NY 10017. **Tel** (212)661-1260.

    ISSN 1069-126X
DD 621   US
    CCC

●**NETWORK ECONOMICS LETTER.** [Netw. econ. lett.]. Vol. 1 No. 1 (June 1993)-. Periodical. English. Twelve times a year. $395.00. Computer Economics Inc., 5841 Edison Place, Carlsbad CA 92008. **Tel** (800)326-8100, (619)438-8100, FAX (619)431-1126.

    ISSN 0269-3089
    UK
CODEN NWRKEA

NETWORK (LONDON. 1985). (NETWORK.). [Network]. (1985)-. Trade Publication. English. Twelve times a year. $136.89. VNU Business Publications BV, 32-34 Broadwick Street, London W1A 2HG United Kingdom. **Tel** 011 44 171 4394242 ext. 2222, FAX 011 44 171 4379638, telex 23918 VNU G, 8952440. Documents available from Ask*IEEE.
Ind/Abst Curr. Cit.; INSPEC (1985-).

LC HE   ISSN 0953-8402
DD 384   UK
UDC 38   CCC
CEASED

NETWORK MONITOR. [Netw. monit.]. (1988)-(1993). Academic Scholarly Publication. English. Elsevier Science Publishers Ltd., Crown House, Linton Road, Barking Essex IG11 8JU United Kingdom. **Tel** 011 44 181 5947272, FAX 011 44 181 5945942, telex 896950. available on microfilm from University Microfilms International (UMI); available on an online database (file 636/Full-Text) from DIALOG. **Continues** Open Systems and Software, 0956-4063.
Ind/Abst PTS Newsl. Database [Full Txt.].

LC QA76.5 .N447   ISSN 0288-3635
DD 004/.05   JA
    CCC
Pr Rev.

NEW GENERATION COMPUTING. Vol. 1, No. 1 (1983)-. Periodical. English. Four times a year. $322.00. Springer-Verlag Tokyo, 37-3 Hongo 3-Chrome, Bunkyo-ku, Tokyo 113 Japan. **Tel** 011 81 3 38120331, FAX 011 81 3 38120719, telex 26536 SREBS J. **(Subscription address:** Springer-Verlag New York Inc. / North America, PO Box 2485, Journal Fulfillment, Secaucus NJ 07096. **Tel** (201)348-4033, (800)777-4643, FAX (201)348-4505.) **ED** K. Fuchi. available on microfilm and microfiche from University Microfilms International (UMI). Documents available from The Genuine Article, Ask*IEEE.
Desc: Presents critical perspectives of Fifth Generation research.
Ind/Abst Abstr. Hum. Comput. Interact.; ACM Guide Comput. Lit.; CompuMath Cit. Index [Full Cov.]; Comput. Abstr.; Comput. Rev.; Curr. Cit.; Curr. Contents Eng. Comput. Technol.; INSPEC (1983-); Res. Alert [Full Cov.]; SCISEARCH; Soc. Sci. Cit. Index [Select. Cov.]; Zentralbl. Math. Ihre Grenzgeb.

    US

NEW GENERATION COMPUTING SERIES. Monographic series. English. Irregular. Price varies per volume. Marcel Dekker Inc., 270 Madison Avenue, New York NY 10016. **Tel** (212)696-9000, (800)228-1160, FAX (212)685-4540, telex 421419. **(Subscription address:** Marcel Dekker Inc., PO Box 5017, Monticello NY 12701. **Tel** (800)228-1160.)
Desc: Topics covered have included supercomputing in engineering analysis and parallel processing in computational mechanics.

    UK

●**NEW REVIEW OF DOCUMENT AND TEXT MANAGEMENT.** (1995)-. English. One time a year. $125.00. Taylor Graham Publishing, 500 Chesham House, 150 Regent Street, London W1R 5FA United Kingdom. **Continues** Journal of Document and Text Management.

    ISSN 0114-4596
    NZ

NEW ZEALAND JOURNAL OF COMPUTING. (1989)-. English.
Ind/Abst ACM Guide Comput. Lit.; Comput. Rev.

    ISSN 0380-478X
    CN

NEWS LETTER - MCGILL UNIVERSITY COMPUTING CENTRE. Main/Corp McGill University. Computing Centre. (1969)-. Periodical. English. Six times a year. McGill University / Computing Centre, 853 Sherbrooke Street West, Montreal Quebec H3A 2K6 Canada. **Tel** (514)398-4850. **ED** Barbara Fox. Index available. **Circ:** 3,100 (ctrl).
Desc: Computing and telecommunication news for the McGill University user community.

    UK
CODEN NRSEEU

NEWS / RADIOSUISSE SERVICES. Added/Corp RadioSuisse Services. **VFOAT** RadioSuisse Services News. Vol. 11, No. 3 (Mar. 1992)-. Academic Scholarly Publication. English. Twelve times a year. Documents available from CASDDS. **Continues** Data-Star News.
Ind/Abst Chem. Abstr.

    ISSN 0743-5894
    US

NEWSBIT (LINDEN, N.J.). (NEWSBIT.). **VFOAT** News Bit. Vol. 1, No. 1 (Aug. 1984)-. Periodical. English. Twelve times a year. Newsbit Inc, 18 East Price Street, Linden NJ 07036.

    ISSN 0714-6647
DD 025/.063/00971326   CN

NEWSLETTER - SOCIAL SCIENCE COMPUTING LABORATORY. See Social Sciences.

    US

NEWSLETTER - THE UNIVERSITY OF TENNESSEE COMPUTING CENTER. Main/Corp University of Tennessee, Knoxville. Computing Center. **VFOAT** UTCC Newsletter. Newsletter. English. 200 Stokely Management Center, University of Tennessee, Knoxville TN 37916.

    ISSN 0744-8821
DD 004   US
CEASED

NEWSLETTER-UNIVERSITY OF WASHINGTON. (NEWSLETTER / UNIVERSITY OF WASHINGTON, ACADEMIC COMPUTER CENTER.). [Newsl. - Univ. Wash., Acad. Comput. Cent.]. **Main/Corp** University of Washington. Academic Computer Center. **Added/Corp** University of Washington. Academic Computer Center. (1964)-(19??). Newsletter. English. University of Washington Academic Computer Center, 3737 Brooklyn Avenue NE, Seattle WA 98105. **Tel** (206)543-5818.

    ISSN 0891-1037
DD 338   US
Pr Rev.

NEWTON-EVANS RESEARCH COMPANY'S MARKET TRENDS DIGEST FOR THE COMPUTER, COMMUNICATIONS, AND CONTROLS INDUSTRIES. [Newton-Evans Res. Co. mark. trends dig. comput. commun. controls ind.]. **Added/Corp** Newton-Evans Research Company. **VFOAT** Market Trends Digest. (1985)-. Periodical. English. Eight times a year (Jan., Mar., May, July, Aug., Sept., Nov., Dec.). $295.00. Newton-Evans Research Company, 10176 Baltimore National Pike/Suite 204, Ellicott City MD 21042. **Tel** (410)465-7316, (800)222-2856, FAX (410)750-7429. **ED** Loretta Smolenski. **Circ:** 1,250 (ctrl).
Desc: Survey findings including summaries of multi-client studies of the markets for microcomputers, datacomm and computer-based control systems. Exclusive excerpts from certain proprietary studies.

    ISSN 1061-6616
DD 004   US
CEASED

NEXTWORLD (SAN FRANCISCO, CALIF.). (NEXTWORLD.). [Nextworld]. **VFOAT** Next World. (1991)-(April 1994). Periodical. English. Integrated Media Inc., 501 2nd Street, San Francisco CA 94107. **Tel** (415)978-3306, (415)243-4188.

LC QA76.5 .N543
DD 004   JA

NIHON NO DENSHI KEISANKI. Added/Corp Nihon Denshi Kogyo Shinko Kyokai. Nihon Denshi Keisanki Kabushiki Kaisha. (19??)-. Japanese. One time a year. Nihon Denshi Kogyo Shinko Kyokai, (Japan Electric Industry Development Corporation), 5-8 Shiba Koen 3-chome, Minatoku Tokyo 105 Japan.

    ISSN 0934-8778
    GW

NJW-COR COMPUTERREPORT : DER NEUEN JURISTISCHEN WOCHENSCHRIFT : INFORMATIONSMANAGEMENT AND BUROORGANISATION IN DER JUSTISCHEN PRAXIS. See Law-Computer Applications.

    ISSN 1064-0444
    US

NORTH JERSEY COMPUTERUSER. VFOAT North Jersey Computer User; North Jersey Computeruser Magazine. (1992)-. Periodical. English. Twelve times a year. Free (North Jersey area), $12.00 (elsewhere). North Jersey ComputerUser, Box 1057, Hightstown NJ 08520.

    ISSN 1076-2515
DD 005   US

●**NOTES REPORT, THE.** [Notes rep.]. (1993)-. Periodical. English. Twelve times a year. $295.00. IDG Newsletter Corporation, 77 Franklin Street, Suite 310, Boston MA 02110. **Tel** (617)482-8470, (800)807-0771, FAX (617)338-0164. **(Subscription address:** Lotus Publishing, PO Box 120102, Boston MA 02112.) **ED** Jim O'Donnell. **Ad Acc, Adv Mgr:** Scott Tharler. **Circ:** 2,000.
Desc: Guide for getting the most from Notes software. Includes tips, techniques, and step-by-step guides.

Computers

UDC 681.3

ISSN 1251-8905
FR

●**NOUVEL ESPACE : PARIS.** (NOUVEL ESPACE.). (1994)-. Periodical. French. Six times a year. $148.73. Groupe Creations, 40 rue de Chabrol, 75010 Paris France. **Tel** 011 33 1 42464473, **FAX** 011 33 1 42461438.

ISSN 0262-5369
UK

NPL REPORT DITC. [NPL rep. DITC]. **VFOAT** National Physical Laboratory Report Division of Information Technology and Computing. (1982)-. Monographic series. English. Irregular. Price varies per volume. National Physical Laboratory, Teddington Middlesex TW11 0LW United Kingdom. **Continues** NPL Report DNACS, 0143-7348.
Ind/Abst Curr. Cit.

LC QA
DD 004
US

NTIS ALERT. COMPUTERS, CONTROL & INFORMATION THEORY. Added/Corp United States. National Technical Information Service. (19??)-. Periodical. English. Twenty-four times a year. $165.00 US; $235.00 other. National Technical Information Service - NTIS, Room 2027S, 5285 Port Royal Road, Springfield VA 22161. **Tel** (703)487-4630, (703)487-4660, (703)487-4650, **FAX** (703)321-8547, telex 89-9405. Index available. **Continues** Computers, Control & Information Theory / NTIS, 0364-796X.

ISSN 0969-9767
UK
CCC

●**OBJECT ORIENTED SYSTEMS.** (1994)-. Periodical. English. Four times a year. $246.00. Chapman & Hall, 2-6 Boundary Row, London SE1 8HN United Kingdom. **Tel** 011 44 171 8650066, **FAX** 011 44 171 5229623, telex 290164 CHAPMA G. **(Subscription address:** International Thomson Publishing Services Ltd., North Way Andover, Hampshire SP10 5BE United Kingdom. **Tel** 011 44 1264 332424.)

ISSN 0941-1968
GW
CCC

OFFENE SYSTEME. (1992)-. German. Four times a year. $206.00. Springer-Verlag GmbH & Company KG, Heidelberger Platz 3, D-14197 Berlin Germany. **Tel** 011 49 30 8207223, **FAX** 011 49 30 8214091, telex 183 319 SPBLN D. **(Subscription address:** Springer-Verlag New York Inc. / North America, PO Box 2485, Journal Fulfillment, Secaucus NJ 07096. **Tel** (201)348-4033, (800)777-4643, **FAX** (201)348-4505.)

ISSN 1065-9560
US

●**OFFICIAL COMPUTER USER'S TRAVEL COMPANION (ASIAN ED.).** (OFFICIAL COMPUTER USER'S TRAVEL COMPANION.). (1993)-. Periodical. English. Four times a year. $39.00. Design Network International, Ltd., 417 Central Avenue, Highland Park IL 60035. **Tel** (708)831-0300.

ISSN 1065-9579
US

●**OFFICIAL COMPUTER USER'S TRAVEL COMPANION (EUROPEAN ED.).** (OFFICIAL COMPUTER USER'S TRAVEL COMPANION.). (1993)-. Periodical. English. Four times a year. $39.00. Design Network International, Ltd., 417 Central Avenue, Highland Park IL 60035. **Tel** (708)831-0300.

ISSN 1065-9536
US

●**OFFICIAL COMPUTER USER'S TRAVEL COMPANION (NORTH AMERICAN ED.).** (OFFICIAL COMPUTER USER'S TRAVEL COMPANION.). (1993)-. Periodical. English. Four times a year. $39.00. Design Network International, Ltd., 417 Central Avenue, Highland Park IL 60035. **Tel** (708)831-0300.

GW
CODEN OCOLD4

ONLINE (COLOGNE, GERMANY : 1982). (ONLINE.). **Added/Corp** Anwenderverband Deutscher Informationsverarbeiter. (198?)-. Periodical. German. Twelve times a year. $143.55. Datacom Zeitschriften Verlag, Postfach 1502, D-50105 Bergheim Germany. **Tel** 011 49 2271 6080, **FAX** 011 49 2271 608290. **ED** Berthold Wesseler. Index available. cum. index. **Bk Rev. Ad Acc.** Circ: 16,000 (ctrl). Documents available from Article Express International, Ask*IEEE. **Continues** Anwenderverband Deutscher Informationsverarbeiter. ADI-Nachrichten/Online.
Desc: Hardware, software, micros, telecommunications, applications, and surveys.
Ind/Abst Bioeng. Abstr.; Ei Page One; Eng. Index Annu.; INSPEC (1981-).

US

OPEN CHANNEL. (1983)-. English. Ten times a year. Free. The Open Channel Newsletter, Information Technology Information Services, University of Houston, Houston TX 77204-1961. **Tel** (713)743-1500. **ED** James N. Bradley. Index available. **Circ:** 2,600 (ctrl).
Desc: The computing and communications newsletter for the University of Houston.

ISSN 1079-753X
US

●**OPENVIEW ADVISOR. VFOAT** Open View Advisor. (1995)-. Periodical. English. Twelve times a year. $595.00. McGraw Hill Publishing Company, Inc., 1221 Avenue of the Americas, New York NY 10020. **Tel** (212)512-6410, (800)525-5003, **FAX** (212)512-6111. **(Subscription address:** Openview Advisor, PO Box 5048, Brentwood TN 37024. **Tel** (800)598-0474.)
Desc: News and analysis strictly devoted to openview-related topics.

LC QA76.6 .O625
DD 621.3819/52

ISSN 0163-5980
US
CCC
CODEN OSRED8

OPERATING SYSTEMS REVIEW. See Computers-Software.

ISSN 0030-3658
DD 001
US
Pr Rev.

OPERATIONS RESEARCH/MANAGEMENT SCIENCE. See Computers-Abstracting, Bibliographies and Statistics.

ISSN 1055-6788
DD 004
UK
CCC

OPTIMIZATION METHODS AND SOFTWARE. See Mathematics-Computer Applications.

ISSN 1066-9493
DD 658
US
CEASED

OPTIV (MCLEAN, VA.). (OPTIV.). [Optiv]. **Added/Corp** Corporation for Open Systems International. Vol. 1, No. 1 (Fall 1991)-(1993). Periodical. English. Corporation for Open Systems International, 8260 Willow Oaks Corporation Drive, Suite 700, Fairfax VA 22031. **Tel** (703)205-2700.

ISSN 1065-3171
DD 005
US

ORACLE MAGAZINE. [Oracle mag.]. (1987)-. Trade Publication. English. Four times a year (Seasonally). Free on request. Oracle Magazine, 500 Oracle Parkway, MS 659510, Redwood Shores CA 94065. **Tel** (415)506-4763, **FAX** (415)506-7122. **ED** Julie Gibbs (phone: (415)506-3052). **Bk Rev. Ad Acc. Adv Mgr:** Kevin Canady, **Tel** (415)506-3430. **Circ:** 74,000 (ctrl).
Desc: Provides coverage of the information management market. Features products news, commentary by industry experts, articles on tools, productivity, and coverage on every major computing environment from mainframes to PC's.

ISSN 1052-3367
DD 004
US
CEASED

ORACLE NEWS. [Oracle news]. (Sept. 24, 1990)-(Aug. 1993). Periodical. English. Publications & Communications, 12416 Hymeadow Drive, Austin TX 78750. **Tel** (512)250-9023, (800)678-9724, **FAX** (512)331-3900, telex 384303.

FR

ORDINATEUR INDIVIDUEL, L'. French. Eleven times a year. 300.00F France; 83.50Can$ Canada; 420.00F other. Soc Presse Publs Specialisees, 5 Place du Colonel Fabien, 75491 Paris Cedex 10 France. **Tel** 011 33 1 42402201.

LC WMLC 93/1125
DD 005
ISSN 0899-1499
US
CCC
CODEN OJCOE3
Pr Rev.

ORSA JOURNAL ON COMPUTING. [ORSA j. comput.]. **Added/Corp** Operations Research Society of America. **VFOAT** ORSA Journal on Computing. **VAT** Operations Research Society of America Journal on Computing. Vol. 1, No. 1 (Winter 1989)-. Periodical. English. Four times a year. $120.00. Operations Research Society of America, 1314 Guilford Avenue, Baltimore MD 21202. **Tel** (410)850-0300, (800)850-0300. **ED** Harvey J. Greenberg. Index available. cum. index. **Bk Rev. Circ:** 1,500 (ctrl). Documents available from Article Express International, Ask*IEEE.
Desc: Explores the interface between operations research and computer science.
Ind/Abst Comput. Inf. Syst. Abstr. J. [Full Cov.]; Curr. Cit.; Eng. Index Annu.; INSPEC (1989-); Int. Abstr. Oper. Res. [Select. Cov.]; Math. Rev.

ISSN 1073-1547
DD 004
US

●**OS/2 MAGAZINE.** [OS/2 mag.]. Vol. 1, No. 1 (Dec. 1993)-. Periodical. English. Twelve times a year. $39.95. Miller Freeman Inc., 600 Harrison Street, San Francisco CA 94107. **Tel** (415)905-2337, (415)905-2200, **FAX** (415)905-2240, telex 278273. **(Subscription address:** Neodata / Colorado, PO Box 2606, Boulder CO 80322.)

ISSN 0898-0489
DD 004
US

OSI PRODUCT & EQUIPMENT NEWS. (OSI PRODUCT & EQUIPMENT NEWS : OPEN.). [OSI prod. equip. news.]. **VFOAT** OSI Product and Equipment News; OPEN; OPEN, OSI Product & Equipment News. **VAT** Open Systems Interconnect Product & Equipment News. Vol. 1, No. 1 (May 12, 1988)-. Periodical. English. Twelve times a year. $550.00 US, Canada and Mexico; $598.00 other. DataTrends Publications, 895 Harrison Street SE, Suite B, Leesburg VA 22075. **Tel** (703)779-5774, (800)766-8130, **FAX** (703)779-2267. available on an online database (file 636/Full-Text) from DIALOG.
Ind/Abst PTS Newsl. Database [Full Txt.].

ISSN 0888-6997
DD 004
US

OSINETTER NEWSLETTER, THE. [OSINetter newsl.]. **VFOAT** OSI Netter Newsletter; OSINetter. **VAT** Open Systems Interconnection Netter Newsletter. Vol. 1, No. 1 (Aug. 1986)-. Newsletter. English. Twelve times a year. $372.00. Architecture Technology Corporation, PO Box 24344, Minneapolis MN 55424. **Tel** (612)935-2035.
Desc: Covers product and company activity in the rapidly evolving area of open systems interconnection.

ISSN 1080-5079
DD 368
US

●**P/C BEST'S LOSS RESERVES [COMPUTER FILE].** [P/C Best's loss reserv.]. **Added/Corp** A.M. Best Company. **VFOAT** Best's Loss Reserves. (1993)-. English. Irregular. $8500.00. AM Best Company, Ambest Road, Oldwick NJ 08858. **Tel** (908)439-2200 ext. 5653, **FAX** (908)439-3296, telex 837744.

ISSN 0817-6213
DD 004.05
AT
TITLE CHANGE

PACIFIC COMPUTER WEEKLY. [Pac. comput. wkly.]. (1974)-(19??). Periodical. English. Peter Isaacson Publications, 46-50 Porter Street, Prahran Victoria, 3181 Australia. **Tel** 011 61 3 2457777, **FAX** 011 61 3 2457606. **Continues** Australian Computer Weekly, 0310-5865. **Continued by** Computer Week.

ISSN 1054-3929
DD 004
US
CEASED

PARADIGM SHIFT : PATRICIA SEYBOLD'S GUIDE TO THE INFORMATION REVOLUTION. [Paradig. shift]. **Added/Corp** Patricia Seybold's Office Computing Group. **VFOAT** PS; P.S. (1990)-(April 1994). Periodical. English. Patricia Seybolds Office Computing Group, 148 State Street, Suite 700, Boston MA 02109. **Tel** (617)742-5200, (800)826-2424, **FAX** (617)742-1028. **Continues** P.S. Postscript on Information Technology, 1041-4630.
Desc: Captures the actual experiences of users shifting to the new paradigm of distributed computing as they tall their stories in interviews with Patricia Seybold.

ISSN 0953-7252
UK
CODEN PINTE9

PARALLELOGRAM INTERNATIONAL. **VFOAT** Parallelogram. (1988)-. Trade Publication. English. Ten times a year (Monthly with July/Aug. and Dec./Jan. combined). $99.00. Fitzroy Publishing, 46 Old Compton Street, London W1V 5PB United Kingdom. **Tel** 011 44 171 4377005, **FAX** 011 44 171 4342225. Documents available from Ask*IEEE. **Continues** Parallelogram, 0953-7252.
Desc: The magazine of super performance computing.
Ind/Abst INSPEC (June/July 1991-Oct./Nov. 1991).

ISSN 1130-9954
SP

PC ACTUAL. [Pc acutal]. **VFOAT** Personal Computer Actual. (1991)-. Trade Publication. Spanish. Twelve times a year. $52.31. VNU Business Publications / Spain, Cinca 13, 28002 Madrid Spain. **Tel** 011 34 1 563-8100, **FAX** 011 34 1 563-7572. **Continues** PC Magazine Actual, 0214-9931.

US
Pr Rev.

PC GUIDE USA. CD-ROM. English. $199.95 US; $249.00 other. Macguide Magazine Inc, 444 17th Street, Suite 200, Denver CO 80217. **Ad Acc. Circ:** 1,000. available on diskette; available in print.

ISSN 0177-0977
GW

UDC 681.322-181.48
PC-MAGAZIN. [PC-Mag.]. **VFOAT** Personal-Computer-Magazin. (1984)-. Periodical. German. One time a week. $245.50. Verlag Markt & Technik, Hans Pinsel Str 2, W-8013 Haar B Munich Germany. **Tel** 011 49 89 461300, **FAX** 11 49 89 4613774.

Computers

ISSN 0936-4315
UDC 519 GW

PC-NETZE. [PC-Netze]. **VFOAT** Personal-Computer-Netze. (1989)-. Periodical. German. Twelve times a year. $92.12. Datacom Zeitschriften Verlag, Postfach 1502, D-50105 Bergheim Germany. **Tel** 011 49 2271 6080, FAX 011 49 2271 608290.

ISSN 0940-6743
UDC 519 GW

PC-PRAXIS (1989). [PC-Prax. 1989]. **VFOAT** Personalcomputer-Praxis (1989). (1989)-. Periodical. German. Twelve times a year. $57.58. Data Becker GmbH & Company KG, PC Praxis, Merowingerstr 30, W-4000 Dusseldorf 1 Germany. **Tel** 011 49 211 3100159, FAX 011 49 211 3190877. **ED** Achim Becker (phone: (0049) 211 31081 0). Index available. **Bk Rev. Ad Acc, Adv Mgr:** Peter Staesche, **Tel** 211 31081 50. **Circ:** 227,000 (ctrl). **Continues** Data-Welt (1985), 0930-4975. **Desc:** User magazine.

ISSN 1121-3337
UDC 681.3 IT

PC PROFESSIONALE. [PC Prof.]. **VFOAT** Personal Computer Professionale. (1991)-. Periodical. Italian. Eleven times a year. L36680. Arnoldo Mondadori Editore, UFF Cont Abbonamenti, 20090 Segrate MI Italy. **Tel** 011 39 2 75422015, telex 320457 MONDMI I.

IT

PC WEEK. (19??)-. Italian. Forty-Five times a year. L75250 Italy; L128850 other. Arnoldo Mondadori Editore, UFF Cont Abbonamenti, 20090 Segrate MI Italy. **Tel** 011 39 2 75422015, telex 320457 MONDMI I.

ISSN 0175-0496
UDC 681.322-181.48 GW

PC-WELT. [PC-Welt]. **VFOAT** Personal-Computer-Welt. (1984)-. Trade Publication. German. Twelve times a year. DM54.00 Germnay; DM72.00 other. IDG Communications Verlag AG / Germany, Rheinstrasse 26 28, D-80803 Munich Germany. **Tel** 011 49 89 360860. **(Subscription address:** DSB ABO Betreuung GmbH, Heiner Fleischmann Strasse 2, D-74168 Neckarsulm Germany. **Tel** 011 49 71329590.) available on microfilm from University Microfilms International (UMI). **Absorbed** Micro-Computerwelt, 0721-6432.

FR

PCTE NEWSLETTER. Newsletter. English. Four times a year. free trial subscription. Jeane Claude Rault, EC2 2169 rue de la Garenne, 92200 Nanterre Cedex France. **Tel** 33 1 67 80 70 00, FAX 33 1 47806629. **ED** Ian Campbell. Index available. **Bk Rev. Ad Acc.** ctrl circ.

ISSN 0739-0653
US

PEEK (65). **VFOAT** Peek Sixty-Five. (19??)-. Periodical. English. Twelve times a year. $22.00 US; $30.00 Canada and Mexico; $40.00 other. Peek (65), PO Box 586, Pacifica CA 94044. **Tel** (415)359-5708. **ED** Richard L. Trethewey. **Bk Rev. Ad Acc. Circ:** 800. **Desc:** Articles, reviews (software and hardware), models, fixes, etc., for Ohio scientific and compatible computers, (personal and business).

ISSN 1054-4011
DD 006 US

PEN-BASED COMPUTING. (PEN-BASED COMPUTING : THE JOURNAL OF STYLUS SYSTEMS.). [Pen-based comput.]. **VFOAT** Pen Based Computing. Vol. 1, No. 1 (Jan. 22, 1991)-. Periodical. English. Twelve times a year. 200.00Can$. Volksware Inc, 301 349 Wesr Georgia Street, Vancouver British Columbia, V6B 3W5 Canada. **Tel** (604)472-1315. **ED** Nicholas Baran, Jon Erickson. **Bk Rev.** **Desc:** Newsletter covering product and technology relating to pen-based computing.

ISSN 1062-6344
US

PEN COMPUTER REPORT. (1992)-. Periodical. English. Twelve times a year. $195.00. Business Computer Publishing Inc., 80 Elm Street, Peterborough NH 03458. **Tel** (800)349-7327.

LC QA76.9.H85 B75a
DD 004/.01/9 UK

PEOPLE AND COMPUTERS. **Added/Corp** British Computer Society. Human Computer Interaction Specialist Group. (1991)-. English. One time a year. Cambridge University Press, The Edinburgh Building, Shaftesbury Road, Cambridge CB2 2RU United Kingdom. **Tel** 011 44 1223 312393, FAX 011 44 1223 315052, telex 851-817256. **Continues** British Computer Society. Human Computer Interaction Specialist Group. Conference. People and Computers. **Ind/Abst** Curr. Cit.

ISSN 0882-3480
DD 621 US

PERFORMANCE REVIEW (RESTON, VA.), THE. (THE PERFORMANCE REVIEW.). [Perform. rev.]. Vol. 1, No. 1 (Jan. 1985)-. Periodical. English. Twelve times a year. $195.00. Systems Performance Group Inc, PO Box 1053, Bethesda MD 20827. **Tel** (301)762-9108. **Circ:** 1,000. **Desc:** A newsletter presenting case studies from actual consulting experiences.

US

PERSPECTIVES IN COMPUTING (BOSTON, MASS.). (PERSPECTIVES IN COMPUTING.). (198?)-. Monographic series. English. Irregular. Price varies per volume. Academic Press Inc., 6277 Sea Harbor Drive, Orlando FL 32887. **Tel** (800)543-9534, (407)345-4100, FAX (407)352-3445. **Continues** Notes and Reports in Computer Science and Applied Mathematics, 1053-1262. **Ind/Abst** Math. Rev.; Zentralbl. Math. Ihre Grenzgeb.

ISSN 0931-1084
UDC 519.68 GW

PETRI NET NEWSLETTER. [Petri net newsl.]. (1986)-. Periodical. English. Three times a year. $19.20. Gesellschaft fur Informatik, Godesberger Allee 99, W-5300 Bonn 2 F R Germany. **Continues** Newsletter - Special Interest Group Petri Nets and Related System Models, Gesellschaft feur Informatik, 0173-7473. **Desc:** Topics include: technical information, information on software packages, correspondence, problems and puzzles, conference announcements, conference reports, and abstracts of available publications.

ISSN 1080-7187
DD 384 US

●**PHILLIPS BUSINESS INFORMATION'S PCS WEEK.** **See** Communications.

US
CEASED

PHILOSOPHY AND COMPUTING. **See** Philosophy.

US

PI QUALITY. English. Four times a year. $74.00. Hitchcock Publishing Company, 191 South Gary Avenue, Carol Stream IL 60188. **Tel** (708)665-1000. **Bk Rev. Ad Acc. Circ:** 40,000 (ctrl). **Desc:** Targeting processing industries with an editorial focusing on analytical instruments in quality assurance. Quality control applications from laboratories to on-line processing.

ISSN 1066-2154
DD 005 US

PICKWORLD IRVINE, CALIF. (PICKWORLD.). [Pickworld Irvine Calif.]. **VFOAT** Pick World. (1984)-. Trade Publication. English. Six times a year. Free on request. Pick Systems, 1691 Browning, Irvine CA 92714. **Tel** (714)261-7425, FAX (714)250-8187. **ED** Erin Jones. **Ad Acc.**

ISSN 0930-5157
UDC 681.3 GW CCC

PIK. PRAXIS DER INFORMATIONSVERARBEITUNG UND KOMMUNIKATION. [PIK, Prax. Inf.verarb. Kommun.]. **VFOAT** Praxis der Informationsverarbeitung und Kommunikation. (1986)-. Periodical. German. Four times a year. DM228.00. K.G. Saur Verlag KG, A Reed Reference Publishing Company, Part of Reed International PLC, Ortlerstrasse 8, D-81373 Munich Germany. **Tel** 011 49 89 769020, FAX 011 49 89 76902150, telex 5212067-SAUR-D. **Bk Rev. Ad Acc, Adv Mgr:** Elisabeth Grubev, **Tel** 089-76902235. ctrl circ. available on CD-ROM from K G Saur; available on microfiche from K G Saur. **Continues** Das Rechenzentrum, 0343-317X.

ISSN 1058-8787
DD 658 US
CODEN PIQUER

Pr Rev.

PIQUALITY. [PIQuality]. **VFOAT** PI Quality. **VAT** Process Industries Quality. (1991)-. Periodical. English. Six times a year. $35.00 (U.S.), $45.00 (Can.). PI Quality, 191 South Gary, Carol Stream IL 60188. **ED** Dan Byrnes and David Toy. **Ad Acc, Adv Mgr:** Jim Losm, **Tel** (708)462-2316. **Acid Free. Circ:** 42,000 (ctrl). available on microfilm and microfiche from University Microfilms International (UMI). **Desc:** Serves the quality function in the process industries and independent laboratories responsible for test, inspection, measurement evaluation and control of process and product quality as obtained through analytical instruments, sensors, SPC/SQC systems, computer software and hardware taking place in laboratories or online.

FR

PIXEL : LE MAGAZINE DES NOUVELLES IMAGES. (19??)-. Trade Publication. French. Six times a year. 190.00F France; 224.00F other. Pixel, 71 rue Maubeuge, 75010 Paris France. **Tel** 011 33 1 48786090.

US

PLANET STUDIO. (19??)-. English. Six times a year. $59.95. IDG Communications / New Hampshire, 86 Elm Street, Peterborough NH 03458. **Tel** (800)349-7327, FAX (603)924-6972.

ISSN 1061-3838
DD 620 US

POINT LINE POLY. PC. (POINT LINE POLY. PC : A TECHNICAL FRIEND FOR PC ARC/INFO USERS.). [Point line poly, PC]. **VFOAT** Point Line Poly; PLP; PC. Vol. 1, No. 1 (1992)-. Periodical. English. Six times a year. $35.00. Stover Publishing Company Inc., 19 South Street, Proctor VT 05765. **Tel** (802)459-6358. **ED** Dan Stover. Index available (bound in Nov. issue). **Circ:** 100 (ctrl).

ISSN 0888-0131
DD 004 US
CODEN POOHEK

PORTABLE 100 (1986). (PORTABLE 100.). [Portable 100]. **VFOAT** Portable One Hundred. Vol. 3, No. 12 (Aug. 1986)-. Periodical. English. Eleven times a year (monthly with combined July/Aug.). $19.95 (one-year), $34.95 (two-year), $49.95 (three-year) US; $24.95 (one-year) $44.95 (two-year) Canada and Mexico; $39.95 (one-year), $74.95 (two-year) other. Portable Computing Intl Corp, PO Box 428, Peterborough NH 03458. **Tel** (603)-924-9455. **ED** Terry Kepher. (index published separately). cum. index. **Bk Rev,** (Qty: 4-6). **Ad Acc, Adv Mgr:** Bob Liddil. Documents available from Ask*IEEE. **Continues** Portable 100/200/600, 0888-0131. **Ind/Abst** INSPEC (1986-); Microcomput. Abstr. (Feb. 1985-).

ISSN 1064-8801
US
CEASED

POWER USER. (1991)-Vol. 3. English. Falsoft Inc., PO Box 385, Prospect KY 40059. **Tel** (502)228-4492, FAX (502)228-5121. **ED** Lawrence C Falk. **Desc:** Newsletter with information and programs to enhance your computer's operation. Also, comes with a quarterly disk.

LC QA297 .P64
DD 515 PL
CODEN PIPPE7

PRACE IPI PAN = ICS PAS REPORTS. **See** Mathematics-Computer Applications.

ISSN 0965-6219
DD 004.16 UK

PRACTICAL PC. [Pract. PC]. (1992)-. Periodical. English. Twelve times a year. $173.00. AIM Nexus, HHL Subs, PO Box 10, Pallion Indt Estate, Sunderland SR4 6SN United Kingdom. **Tel** 011 44 191 510 2290, FAX 011 44 191 567 1176.

ISSN 0888-2096
DD 004 US

PRINCIPLES OF COMPUTER SCIENCE SERIES. [Princ. comput. sci. ser.]. (19??)-. Monographic series. English. Irregular. Price varies per volume. Computer Science Press Inc, 9125 Fall River Lane, Potomac MD 20854. **Tel** (301)251-9050. **ED** Alfred V. Aho and Jeffrey D. Ullman. Index available. ctrl circ. **Desc:** Books for the foundations of computer science at the college and professional level, as well as outstanding research works at the forefront of computer research. **Ind/Abst** Math. Rev.

ISSN 0738-6613
US

PRINTOUT (NEWTONVILLE, MASS.). **See** Printing Industry.

LC Q350 .P7213
ISSN 0032-9460
US
CCC
CODEN PRITA9

PROBLEMS OF INFORMATION TRANSMISSION. [Probl. inf. transm.]. **Added/Corp** Consultants Bureau. Vol. 1 (Jan./Mar. 1965)-. Academic Scholarly Publication. English (Russian). Four times a year. $945.00. Consultants Bureau, A Division of Plenum Publishing Corporation, 233 Spring Street, New York NY 10013. **Tel** (212)620-8000, (212)620-8466, FAX (212)463-0742, telex 23/421139. **ED** V. I. Siforov. Index available. available on microfilm and microfiche from University Microfilms International (UMI). Documents available from Article Express International, Ask*IEEE, CASDDS. **Desc:** Covers topics such as statistical information, theory coding, theories and techniques, noisy channels, theory of random process and bionics. **Ind/Abst** Bioeng. Abstr.; Chem. Abstr.; Comput. Rev.; Ei Page One; Eng. Index Annu.; Inf. Sci. Abstr.; INSPEC

Computers

(1968-); Math. Rev.; Pollut. Abstr. Indexes; Stat. Theory Method Abstr. (1986-1987); Zentralbl. Math. Ihre Grenzgeb.

LC QA76.9.A73 S9a **ISSN 1063-6897**
DD 004.2/2 US
PROCEEDINGS. [Proc. - Int. Symp. Comput. Archit.]. **Added/Corp** Sigarch. IEEE Computer Society. Technical Committee on Computer Architecture. **VFOAT** Computer Architecture; IEEE ... Annual International Symposium on Computer Architecture; Conference Proceedings. (May 28 - June 1, 1989)-. English. One time a year. ACM / Association for Computing Machinery, 1515 Broadway, 17th Floor, New York NY 10036. **Tel** (212)869-7440, FAX (212)869-0481. *Continues International Symposium on Computer Architecture. Conference Proceedings, 0884-7495.*
Ind/Abst Curr. Cit.

US
PROCEEDINGS ACM SIGUCCS USER SERVICES CONFERENCE. Proceedings. English. One time a year. ACM / Association for Computing Machinery, 1515 Broadway, 17th Floor, New York NY 10036. **Tel** (212)869-7440, FAX (212)869-0481.
Ind/Abst Curr. Cit.

LC TA1650 .I349 **ISSN 1063-6919**
DD 006.4/2 US
CCC
PROCEEDINGS / CVPR, IEEE COMPUTER SOCIETY CONFERENCE ON COMPUTER VISION AND PATTERN RECOGNITION. [Proc. - IEEE Comput. Soc. Conf. Comput. Vis. Pattern Recognit.]. **Added/Corp** IEEE Computer Society. Technical Committee on Pattern Analysis and Machine Intelligence. June 19-23, (1983)-. Proceedings. English. IEEE Computer Society, 10662 Los Vaqueros Circle, PO Box 3014, Los Alamitos CA 90720-1264. **Tel** (714)821-8380, (800)272-6657, FAX (714)821-4641. *Continues IEEE Computer Society Conference on Pattern Recognition and Image Processing. Proceedings.*
Ind/Abst Curr. Cit.; Index IEEE Publ.

US
CEASED
PROCEEDINGS / FALL JOINT COMPUTER CONFERENCE ; SPONSORED BY ACM AND COMPUTER SOCIETY OF THE IEEE. **Added/Corp** IEEE Computer Society. Association for Computing Machinery. (1986)-(19??). Proceedings. English. ACM / Association for Computing Machinery, 1515 Broadway, 17th Floor, New York NY 10036. **Tel** (212)869-7440, FAX (212)869-0481. *Formed by the union of Compcon. Proceedings - Compcon and ACM Conference. Proceedings.*

LC TK5105.5 .I32a **ISSN 0743-166X**
DD 621 US
CCC
PROCEEDINGS / IEEE INFOCOM. See Library and Information Sciences-Computer Applications.

LC TK7888.4 .I35a
DD 621.395/05 US
PROCEEDINGS / IEEE INTERNATIONAL CONFERENCE ON COMPUTER DESIGN : VLSI IN COMPUTERS SPONSORED BY IEEE COMPUTER SOCIETY AND IEEE CIRCUITS AND SYSTEMS SOCIETY TECHNICAL COMMITTEES. **Main/Conf** IEEE International Conference on Computer Design : VLSI in Computers. **Added/Corp** IEEE Computer Society. IEEE Circuits and Systems Society. Institute of Electrical and Electronics Engineers. IEEE Electron Devices Society. **VFOAT** Computer Design : VLSI in Computers; VLSI Computers. (198?)-. Periodical. English. One time a year. $100.00 (latest edition). IEEE / Institute of Electrical and Electronics Engineers Inc., 345 East 47th Street, New York NY 10017-2394. **Tel** (908)981-1393, FAX (908)981-9667. **(Subscription address:** IEEE / Institute of Electrical and Electronics Engineers, 445 Hoes Lane, PO Box 1331, Piscataway NJ 08855-1331. **Tel** (800)701-IEEE, (908)981-0060, FAX (908)981-9667, telex 833233.**)**
Ind/Abst Index IEEE Publ.

LC TK5101.A1 I3544a
DD 621.382 US
●**PROCEEDINGS / IEEE PACIFIC RIM CONFERENCE ON COMMUNICATIONS, COMPUTERS AND SIGNAL PROCESSING.** See Communications-Telecommunication.

US
PROCEEDINGS / INTERNATIONAL CONFERENCE ON COMPUTERS AND APPLICATIONS. **Main/Conf** International Conference on Computers and Applications. **VFOAT** IEEE ... International Conference on Computers & Applications. Computers and Applications. 1st (1984)-. Proceedings. English.
Ind/Abst Index IEEE Publ.

LC TK5103.7 .I57a **ISSN 1015-8057**
DD 621.382 SZ
PROCEEDINGS / INTERNATIONAL ZURICH SEMINAR ON DIGITAL COMMUNICATIONS. See Communications-Computer Applications.

LC QA76.9.A43 A34a **ISSN 1071-9040**
DD 005.1 US
PROCEEDINGS OF THE ANNUAL ACM-SIAM SYMPOSIUM ON DISCRETE ALGORITHMS. See Mathematics.

LC QA267 .A27a **ISSN 0737-8017**
DD 511 US
PROCEEDINGS OF THE ... ANNUAL ACM SYMPOSIUM ON THEORY OF COMPUTING. [Proc. annu. ACM Symp. Theory Comput.]. **Main/Conf** ACM Symposium on Theory of Computing. **Added/Corp** ACM Special Interest Group for Automata and Computability Theory. 14th (1982)-. Proceedings. English. One time a year. $114.00. ACM / Association for Computing Machinery, 1515 Broadway, 17th Floor, New York NY 10036. **Tel** (212)869-7440, FAX (212)869-0481. *Continues ACM Symposium on Theory of Computing. Conference Proceedings of the ... Annual ACM Symposium on Theory of Computing, 0734-9025.*
Ind/Abst Curr. Cit.

LC T58.6 .I57
US
PROCEEDINGS OF THE ... INTERNATIONAL CONFERENCE ON INFORMATION SYSTEMS. **Added/Corp** Society for Management Information Systems (U.S.). Research and Education in Information Systems. Association for Computing Machinery. Special Interest Group on Business Data Processing. Institute of Management Sciences. College on Information Systems. (Dec. 8-10, 1980)-. Proceedings. English. One time a year. $68.00. ACM / Association for Computing Machinery, 1515 Broadway, 17th Floor, New York NY 10036. **Tel** (212)869-7440, FAX (212)869-0481.
Ind/Abst Curr. Cit.

ISSN 0276-699X
US
PROCEEDINGS OF THE MUMPS USERS' GROUP MEETING. [Proc. MUMPS Users' Group Meet.]. **Main/Conf** Mumps Users' Group. Meeting. **VFOAT** MUGM. **VAT** Proceedings of the Massachusetts General Hospital Utility Multiprograming System User's Group Meeting. (19??)-. Proceedings. English. M Technology Association, 1738 Elton Road, Suite 205, Silver Springs MD 20903. **Tel** (301)431-4070, FAX (301)431-0017.

LC QA76.88 .S856 **ISSN 1063-9535**
DD 004.1/1 US
CCC
PROCEEDINGS - SUPERCOMPUTING. (SUPERCOMPUTING PROCEEDINGS.). [Proc. - Supercomput.]. **Added/Corp** IEEE Computer Society. Technical Committee on Supercomputing Applications. IEEE Computer Society. Technical Committee on Computer Architecture. IEEE Computer Society. Sigarch. (1988)-. Proceedings. English. One time a year. IEEE Computer Society, 10662 Los Vaqueros Circle, PO Box 3014, Los Alamitos CA 90720-1264. **Tel** (714)821-8380, (800)272-6657, FAX (714)821-4641. available on microfiche.

LC QA76.9.C62 S95a **ISSN 1063-6889**
DD 004/.01/51 US
PROCEEDINGS / SYMPOSIUM ON COMPUTER ARITHMETIC. See Mathematics-Computer Applications.

US
Pr Rev.
PROCEEDINGS / THE ANNUAL SYMPOSIUM ON COMPUTER APPLICATIONS IN MEDICAL CARE. See Medical Sciences-Computer Applications.

NE
PROCESS TECHNOLOGY PROCEEDINGS. (1984)-. Academic Scholarly Publication. English. Price varies per volume. Elsevier Science Publishers BV, PO Box 211, 1000 AE Amsterdam Netherlands. **Tel** 011 31 20 4853641, 011 31 20 4853642, FAX 011 31 20 4853598. Documents available from CASDDS.
Ind/Abst Chem. Abstr.; Curr. Cit.

ISSN 1050-7043
DD 004 US
PRODUCT DATA INTERNATIONAL. [Prod. data int.]. **VFOAT** PDI. (Sept. 1990)-. Periodical. English. Six times a year (Jan., Mar., May, July, Sept., Nov.). $395.00. Warthen Technical Information Services, N5303 Broughton Road, Albany WI 53502-9725. **Tel** (608)862-1702, FAX (608)862-1702. **ED** Barbara D. Warthen. Index available (published separately). **Bk Rev,** (Qty: varies). **Ad Acc.** available on an online database.
Desc: Report on 16ES, PDES, STEP (data exchange/integration standards) and related activities for computer integrated manufacturing and construction.

ISSN 0889-3438
DD 005 US
PROFESSIONAL REPORT (BOSTON, MASS.). See Computers-Word Processing.

LC Z678.9.A1 P76 **ISSN 0033-0337**
DD 025.3/028/5 UK
CCC
CODEN PRGRDU
Pr Rev.
PROGRAM (ASLIB). See Library and Information Sciences.

ISSN 0743-1597
DD 621 US
PROGRESS IN COMPUTER SCIENCE. [Prog. comput. sci.]. Vol. 1 (1981)-. Monographic series. English. Irregular. Price varies per volume. Birkhauser Boston, Inc., c/o Springer Publishers New York Inc., Customer Service Department, 333 Meadowlands Parkway, Secaucus NJ 07096-2491. **Tel** (201)348-4033, (800)777-4643, FAX (201)348-4505. **(Subscription address:** Birkhauser Boston Books, c/o Springer Verlag, PO Box 19386, Newark NJ 07195. **Tel** (201)348-4033.**)**
Ind/Abst Math. Rev.; Zentralbl. Math. Ihre Grenzgeb.

PROGRESSIONS : A TECHNICAL JOURNAL FOR DEVELOPERS IN PROGRESS. (19??)-. Newsletter. English. Six times a year. $58.00 US; $69.00 Canada; $76.00 other. Progressions, PO Box 51623, Palo Alto CA 94303. **Tel** (415)857-0686, FAX (415)857-0779. **ED** John and Constance Campbell. **Ad Acc.** Circ: 3,000.
Desc: Technical newsletter on the Progress computer language.

ISSN 0556-2678
DD 006 US
PUBLICATIONS IN CONDUCT AND COMMUNICATION. **Main/Corp** University of Pennsylvania. **Added/Corp** University of Pennsylvania Series in Conduct and Communication. **VFOAT** Conduct and Communication. 1 (1969)-. English. Irregular. The University of Pennsylvania Press, 418 Service Drive, 1300 Blockley Hall, Philadelphia PA 19104. **Tel** (215)898-6264. Index available. **Bk Rev**

ISSN 0885-7881
DD 658 US
PUBLICATIONS IN OPERATIONS RESEARCH SERIES. [Publ. oper. res. ser.]. Vol. 1, (1977)-. Monographic series. English. Price varies per volume. Elsevier Science Publishing Company Inc, Madison Square Station, PO Box 882, New York NY 10159-0882. **Tel** (212)633-3950, FAX (212)633-3990.
Ind/Abst Math. Rev.; Zentralbl. Math. Ihre Grenzgeb.

ISSN 0886-8174
PUGET SOUND COMPUTER USER. **VFOAT** Computer User. Vol. 1, No. 1 (March 1986)-. Periodical. English. Twelve times a year. $12.00. KFH Publications Inc., 3530 Bagley Avenue North, Seattle WA 98103. **Tel** (206)547-4950, FAX (206)547-5355. **ED** Terry Hansen. **Ad Acc, Adv Mgr:** Ray Kehl, **Tel** (206)547-4950. Circ: 85,000 (ctrl). available on an online database.
Desc: Covers business technology, office automation, and computers.

IT
CEASED
QUADERNI DI INFORMATICA. (19??)-(June 1993). Italian. Quaderni Informatica Bulletin, Italia via Vida 11, 20127 Milan Italy. **Tel** 011 39 2 67793223.

UK
QUALITY INTELLIGENCE INTERNATIONAL. (19??)-. English. Twelve times a year. £249.00 UK; $435.00 US. World Business Publications Ltd., 960 High Road, Britannia 4th Floor, London N12 9RY United Kingdom. **Tel** 011 44 181 4465141, FAX 011 44 181 4463659, telex 9419208.

ISSN 1076-7452
DD 338 US
●**QUICK-SOLUTIONS (FORT WASHINGTON, MD.).** See Business and Economics-Small Business.

UK
RACF UPDATE. (19??)-. English. Twelve times a year. $266.95. Xephon, 27-35 London Road, Newbury Berkshire RG13 1JL United Kingdom. **Tel** 011 44 1635 33823, FAX 011 44 1635 38345. **(Subscription address:** Xephon, 1301 West Highway, Suite 201 450, Lewisville TX 75067. **)**

Computers

DD 005
ISSN 0890-0019
US
CEASED
RAISED DOT COMPUTING NEWSLETTER. [Rais. dot comput. newsl.]. (Feb. 1983)-(Jan. 1994). Newsletter. English. Raised Dot Computing, 408 South Baldwin Street, Madison WI 53703. **Tel** (608)257-9595, FAX (608)241-2498. **ED** Caryn Navy. **Circ:** 265. available on audiocassette.
Desc: This newsletter provides information in software, and articles of interest to the blind community and reviews new technology for the blind..

DD 621
ISSN 1059-6399
US
RAPID PROTOTYPING REPORT. (RAPID PROTOTYPING REPORT : THE NEWSLETTER OF THE DESKTOP MANUFACTURING INDUSTRY.). (1991)-. Newsletter. English. Twelve times a year. $295.00. CAD CAM Publishing, 1010 Turquoise Street, Suites 320, San Diego CA 92109. **Tel** (619)488-0533. **ED** Geoff Smith-Moritz.
Desc: Reports on current developments in the use of new technology to produce prototype parts from computer models.
LC QA76.27 .F69a

DD 004.06
FR
RAPPORT NATIONAL DE CONJONCTURE SCIENTIFIQUE: INFORMATIQUE ET MOYENS DE CALCUL POLYVALENTS. Main/Corp France. Centre National de la Recherche Scientifique. Comite National de la Recherche Scientifique. (19??)-. French. CNRS / Institut d'Information Scientifique et Technique, (Centre National de la Recherche Scientifique), 15 Quai Anatole France, 75700 Paris France. **Tel** 011 33 1 47531515, FAX 011 33 1 45517307, telex 260034.

ISSN 0742-5600
US
REAL ESTATE COMPUTER REVIEW. See Business and Economics-Computer Applications.

ISSN 1077-2014
UK
●**REAL-TIME IMAGING.** (1995)-. Academic Scholarly Publication. English. Six times a year. $171.12. Academic Press Ltd., A Division of Harcourt Brace & Company Ltd., 24-28 Oval Road, London NW1 7DX United Kingdom. **Tel** 011 44 171 2674466, FAX 011 44 171 4822293, 011 44 171 4854752, telex 25775 ACPRES G. (**Subscription address:** Harcourt Brace & Company, Ltd., Foots Cray High Street, Sidcup Kent DA14 5HP United Kingdom. **Tel** 011 44 181 3003322, FAX 011 44 181 3090807, telex 896 377 ACADEM.)

DD 004
ISSN 1059-552X
TITLE CHANGE
REAL-TIME INTERFACE. [Real-time interface]. **Added/Corp** Interex (Organization). **VFOAT** Real Time Interface. Vol. 1, No. 1 (Aug. 1991)-(199?). Periodical. English. Interex, PO Box 3439, Sunnyvale CA 94088. **Tel** (408)747-0227, FAX (408)736-2156, telex 4971527. **Continues** TC Interface, 0888-3033. **Merged into** HPUX User.

LC QA76.54 .R429
DD 004/.33/05
ISSN 0922-6443
US
CCC
CODEN RESYE9
Pr Rev.
REAL-TIME SYSTEMS. [Real-time syst.]. **VFOAT** Real Time Systems. Vol. 1, No. 1 (June 1989)-. Periodical. English. Six times a year. $499.00. Kluwer Academic Publishers / Massachusetts, PO Box 358, Accord Station, Hingham MA 02018. **Tel** (617)871-6600. **ED** John A Stankovic, Wolfgang A Halang and Mario Tokoro. **Acid Free.** available on microfilm and microfiche from University Microfilms International (UMI). Documents available from Article Express International, The Genuine Article, Ask*IEEE.
Desc: Publishes papers that concentrate on real-time computing principles and applications, research papers, invited papers, project reports and case studies, standards and corresponding proposals for general discussion, and a partitioned tutorial on real-time systems as a continuing series. It provides a single-source coverage of the state of the art in this exciting and expanding field. It covers the following topics: requirements engineering, specification and verification techniques, design methods and tools, programming languages, operating systems, scheduling algorithms, architecture and hardware (especially interfacing), fault tolerance, distributed and other novel architectures, communications, distributed databases.
Ind/Abst ACM Guide Comput. Lit.; CompuMath Cit. Index [Full Cov.]; Comput. Inf. Syst. Abstr. J. [Full Cov.]; Comput. Rev.; Curr. Cit.; Curr. Contents Eng. Comput. Technol.; Elect. Comm. Abstr.; Eng. Index Annu.; Inf. Sci. Abstr. (June 1989-); INSPEC (June 1989-) [Full Cov.]; Res. Alert [Full Cov.]; Zentralbl. Math. Ihre Grenzgeb.

DD 005
ISSN 0894-3117
US
CEASED
REFERENCECLIPPER. (REFERENCE(CLIPPER).). [Ref.Clipp.]. **VFOAT** Reference Clipper. Vol. 1, No. 1 (June 1987)-(Jan. 1995). Periodical. English. Pinnacle Publishing Inc., PO Box 888, Kent WA 98035. **Tel** (206)251-1900, (800)231-1293, FAX (206)251-5057.

UDC 519
ISSN 0941-9780
GW
REIHE INFORMATIK. [Reihe Inform.]. **VFOAT** Skripten zur Informatik. (1969)-. Monographic series. Multiple languages. Irregular. Price varies per volume.
Ind/Abst Zentralbl. Math. Ihre Grenzgeb.

UDC 007
ISSN 0168-6542
NE
REPEAT. [Repeat]. (1983)-. Periodical. Dutch. Ten times a year. $236.39. G I G A, Postbus 91, 1700 Heerhugowaard Netherlands. **Tel** 011 31 2207 45620, FAX 011 31 2207 40765. **Continues** Reproduktie, 0166-4905.

ISSN 0742-5341
US
CCC
REPORT ON IBM, THE. [Rep. IBM]. **VFOAT** Report on I.B.M. Vol. 1, No. 1 (Feb. 15, 1984)-. Periodical. English. One time a week (Fifty times a year). $775.00. DataTrends Publications, 895 Harrison Street SE, Suite B, Leesburg VA 22075. **Tel** (703)779-0574, (800)766-8130, FAX (703)779-2267.
Ind/Abst Comput. Lit. Index; PTS Newsl. Database [Full Txt.].

LC QA75
DD 005
ISSN 1072-9453
US
●**REPORT ON MICROSOFT, THE.** [Rep. Microsoft]. Vol. 1, No. 1 (Oct. 25, 1993)-. Periodical. English. Twenty-six times a year. $395.00. DataTrends Publications, 895 Harrison Street SE, Suite B, Leesburg VA 22075. **Tel** (703)779-0574, (800)766-8130, FAX (703)779-2267.

LC AZ105 .R47
DD 001.3/0285
UK
RESEARCH IN HUMANITIES COMPUTING : SELECTED PAPERS FROM THE AALC / ACH CONFERENCE. See Humanities.

ISSN 0953-7767
UK
RESEARCH MONOGRAPHS IN PARALLEL AND DISTRIBUTED COMPUTING. [Res. monogr. parallel distrib. comput.]. (1989)-. Monographic series. English. Irregular. Price varies per volume. Pitman Publishing Ltd, 12 14 Slaidburn Cres, Southport Merseyside, PR9 9YF United Kingdom. **Tel** 011 44 1704 26881, FAX 011 44 1704 231970, telex 261367.

UK
RESEARCH REPORT / UNIVERSITY OF WARWICK, DEPARTMENT OF COMPUTER SCIENCE. Added/Corp University of Warwick. Dept. of Computer Science. (19??)-. Monographic series. English. Irregular. Price varies per volume.

DD 006
ISSN 1050-3978
US
Pr Rev.
RESOLUTION. (RESOLUTION : PROFESSIONAL APPLICATIONS OF TRUEVISION-BASED IMAGING SYSTEMS.). [Resolution]. Vol. 1, No. 1 (Summer 1990)-. Periodical. English. Four times a year. Free to US; $24.00 (one-year), $40.00 (two-year) Europe, Canada, Mexico; $34.00 (one-year), $58.00 (two-year) other. Camden News Media, 21 Elm Street, PO Box 1328, Camden ME 04348. **Tel** (800)344-3115, FAX (207)236-6018. **ED** Tom McMillan. Index available. cum. index. **Bk Rev**. **Ad Acc**. **Circ:** 50,000 (ctrl).

DD 005.1
ISSN 0955-8500
UK
REVMEDIA LONDON. (REVMEDIA.). [REVMEDIALond.]. (1989)-. Periodical. English. Ten times a year. £95.00 (UK); $199.00 (US); 240.00Can$ (Canada and Mexico). Sprezzatura Ltd, Po Box 266, London SW11 2JH United Kingdom. **Tel** 011 44 171 2287566, FAX 011 44 171 2285982. **ED** A P McAuley (editor's phone: 44 71 9246793). Index Available Received separately--bound from publisher (May). cum. index. **Bk Rev** (Qty: Occasionally). **Ad Acc, Adv Mgr:** C A McKenney. **Circ:** 400 (ctrl).
Desc: Covers in depth technical info on a PC database package called Advanced Revelation

US
REVTECH. (19??)-. English. Twelve times a year. $55.00 US; $65.00 Canada and Mexico; $75.00 other. Revtech, PO Box 1237, Longview WA 98632. **Tel** (800)422-2511, (206)577-8989. **ED** Betty Erickson. **Bk Rev**, (Qty: 6). **Ad Acc, Adv Mgr:** Betty. **Circ:** 2,000 (ctrl).
Desc: News and information on computers.

FR
REVUE FRANCAISE D'AUTOMATIQUE, INFORMATIQUE, RECHERCHE OPERATIONNELLE. Added/Corp Association Francais Pour la Cybernetique Economique et Technique. (1972)-. Periodical. Multiple languages (English and French). Seventeen times a year. 2987.27F France; 4110.00F other. Dunod Gauthier Villars, 15 rue Gossin, 92543 Montrouge Cedex France. **Tel** 011 33 1 46565266, 011 33 1 40926527, FAX 011 33 1 40926597. (**Subscription address:** Centrale des Revues, 11 rue Gossin, 92543 Montrouge Cedex France. **Tel** 011 33 1 46565266.) **Continues** Revue Francaise d'Informatique et de Recherche Operationnelle.
Ind/Abst Stat. Theory Method Abstr. (1969, 1976-1978).

DD 004
ISSN 1051-1393
US
TITLE CHANGE
RISC MANAGEMENT. (RISC MANAGEMENT : ANALYSIS & COMMENTARY ON THE IMPACT OF RISC TECHNOLOGY.). [RISC manage.]. **VAT** Reduced Instruction Set Computer Management. (Aug. 1988)-(1994). Periodical. English. WaterTechnics, PO Box 2307, Santa Cruz CA 95063-2307. **Tel** (408)761-3987, FAX (408)761-5468. available on an online database (files 16,636/Full-Text) from DIALOG. **Continued by** Inside the New Computer Industry, 1079-4573.
Ind/Abst PROMT (19??-19??) [Full Txt.]; PTS Newsl. Database (19??-19??) [Full Txt.].

ISSN 0966-1913
UK
RISC USER. [RISC user]. (1987)-. Periodical. English. Ten times a year. £78.72. Beebug Ltd., 117 Hatfield Road, St. Albans Hertfordshire, AL1 4JS United Kingdom. **Tel** 011 44 1727 840303, FAX 011 44 1727 860263. **ED** Alan Wrigley. Index available. cum. index. **Bk Rev**. **Ad Acc**. **Circ:** 10,000 (ctrl). available in microform; available on diskette.
Desc: Matter related to Acorn computers, BBC Micro and Master computers or the Archimedes and A3000 computers.

LC NC
DD 746
UDC 681.3
ISSN 0390-668X
IT
CODEN RIINDL
RIVISTA DI INFORMATICA. [Riv. Inform.]. (1970)-. Periodical. Multiple languages. Four times a year. L177000. Masson SPA, via Statuto 2/4, 20121 Milan Italy. **Tel** 011 39 2 63671, FAX 011 39 2 6367211. **ED** Arrigo L. Frisiani. **Bk Rev**. **Ad Acc**. **Circ:** 2,100 (ctrl). Documents available from Ask*IEEE.
Desc: Includes all the aspects of the theory and practice of computers and computing.
Ind/Abst Curr. Cit.; Inf. Sci. Abstr.; INSPEC (June 1974-).

LC QA76 .A775
DD 510/78
US
ROSTER OF MEMBERS. See Computers-Abstracting, Bibliographies and Statistics.

LC TK7874 .M478
DD 621.381/7/05
ISSN 1063-7397
US
CCC
CODEN RUICE5
RUSSIAN MICROELECTRONICS. [Russ. microelectron.]. **Added/Corp** Consultants Bureau. (1992)-. Periodical. English (translations available in Russian). Six times a year. $885.00. MAIK Nauka / Interperiodica, Ulitsa Profsoyuznaia 90, Moscow 117864 Russia. Documents available from Article Express International, Ask*IEEE. **Continues** Soviet Microelectronics, 0363-8529.
Ind/Abst Bioeng. Abstr.; Curr. Cit.; Ei Page One; Eng. Index Annu.; INSPEC; Pollut. Abstr. Indexes.

LC K22 .U83
DD 340/.028/5
ISSN 0735-8938
US
CODEN RCTJDM
RUTGERS COMPUTER & TECHNOLOGY LAW JOURNAL. [Rutgers comput. technol. law j.]. **Added/Corp** Rutgers Law School (Newark, N.J.). **VFOAT** Rutgers Computer and Technology Law Journal. Vol. 8, No. 2 (1981)-. Periodical. English. Two times a year (Apr., June). $34.00. Rutgers Law School, 15 Washington Street, 14th Floor, Newark NJ 07102. **Tel** (201)648-5549. **ED** Adam M. Stengel (Managing Business Editor). cum. index. **Bk Rev**. **Ad Acc**. **Circ:** 1,500. available on microfilm and microfiche from University Microfilms International (UMI). Documents available from Ask*IEEE. **Continues** Rutgers Journal--Computers, Technology and the Law, 0278-5633.
Desc: Explores the legal technology as it progresses. Includes articles in biotechnology, intellectual property and telecommunications.
Ind/Abst Bowne Dig. Corp. Sec. Lawyers; Comput. Lit. Index; Crim. Justice Abstr.; Curr. Law Index (1980-); Index Leg. Period.; INSPEC (1981-); Leg. Resour. Index (1981-); LegalTrac (1981-).

Computers

SACRA BLUE. [Sacra blue]. **Added/Corp** Sacramento PC Users Group (California). (198?)-. Periodical. English. Twelve times a year. comes with Sacramento PC Users Group Inc membership. Sacramento PC Users Group Inc, PO Box 162227, Sacramento CA 95816. **Tel** (916)386-9856.

ISSN 0891-6799
US
DD 004

LC K23 .A55
DD 343.73/07800164 347.3037800164 #2 19
ISSN 0882-3383
US

SANTA CLARA COMPUTER AND HIGH-TECHNOLOGY LAW JOURNAL. See Law-Computer Applications.

US

SCANNING SOURCEBOOK, THE. English. $895.00 US; $995.00 other. Association for Information & Image Management, Business Office, 1100 Wayne Avenue/Suite 1100, Silver Spring MD 20910. **Tel** (301)587-8202, FAX (301)587-2711.
Desc: Directed towards present and prospective users of electronic systems for correspondence management, audit trails, technical publications, electronic publishing, office automation, processing, drawing reproduction digital archival systems, mechanical, facility and electrical CAD engineering, etc.

LC QA
DD 001.6/4/071171332
ISSN 0316-8573
CN

SCHOOL OF COMPUTER SCIENCE. UNIVERSITY OF WINDSOR. (THE SCHOOL OF COMPUTER SCIENCE : CALENDAR.). **Main/Corp** University of Windsor. School of Computer Science. (1974)-. Periodical. English. University of Windsor School of Computer Science, Windsor Ontario N9B 3P4 Canada.

DD 006
ISSN 0891-9003
US
CCC
CODEN SCOAEG

SCIENTIFIC COMPUTING & AUTOMATION. See Science and Technology-Computer Applications.

DD 004
ISSN 0887-9338
US

SCOPE/36. [Scope 36]. **VFOAT** Scope 36; Scope Thirty Six. (19??)-. Periodical. English. Twelve times a year. Scope Publications Inc, PO Box 437, Lake Mary FL 32746.

UK

SCREEN AND DISPLAY. (19??)-. English. Twelve times a year. £30.00. A E Morgan Publications Ltd, Stanley House, 9 West Street, Epsom Surrey KT18 7RL United Kingdom. **Tel** 011 44 1372 741411, FAX 011 44 1372 744493, telex 291561 VIA SOS G.

LC TK7882.I6 S38
DD 621.38
ISSN 0887-915X
US
CCC

SEMINAR LECTURE NOTES / SID, SOCIETY FOR INFORMATION DISPLAY. [Semin. lect. notes - Soc. Inf. Displ.]. **Added/Corp** Society for Information Display. (197?)-. Periodical. English. $80.00. Society for Information Display, 1526 Brookhollow Drive, Suite 82, Santa Ana CA 92705. **Tel** (714)545-1526, FAX (714)545-1547.
Ind/Abst Curr. Cit.

LC QA76.58 .S46
DD 004/.35/05
ISSN 0894-2226
US

SERLIN REPORT ON PARALLEL PROCESSING, THE. [Serlin rep. on parallel process.]. **Added/Corp** ITOM International Co. **VFOAT** Report on Parallel Processing; Parallel Processing; PP. Issue No. 1 (June 3, 1987)-. Trade Publication. English. Twelve times a year. $695.00. ITOM International Company, Box 1450, Los Altos CA 94023. **Tel** (415)948-4516, FAX (415)948-9153. **ED** Omri Serlin. Index available (bound in Dec. issue). **Bk Rev**.
Desc: Reports and analyzes business and technical developments in massively-parallel systems, supercomputers, and workstation clusters, used mainly in technical applications.

UK
CODEN STHDA3

SHD. **VFOAT** SHD Storage/Handling/Distribution. **VAT** Storage Handling Distribution. Vol. 20, No. 1 (Apr. 1976)-. Periodical. English. Twelve times a year. £85.00 other. Turret Group, 177 Hagden Lane, Watford Hertfordshire WD1 8LN United Kingdom. **Tel** 011 44 1923 228577, FAX 011 44 1923 221346. Documents available from Ask*IEEE. **Continues** SHD Storage Handling Distribution.
Ind/Abst INSPEC (March 1981)-; Int. Packag. Abstr.; Manage. Market. Abstr.

LC QA1 .S145
DD 505
US

SIAM NEWS : A PUBLICATION OF SOCIETY FOR INDUSTRIAL AND APPLIED MATHEMATICS. See Mathematics-Computer Applications.

DD 004
ISSN 1062-8053
US
TITLE CHANGE

SIBERIAN JOURNAL OF COMPUTER MATHEMATICS. See Mathematics-Computer Applications.

LC QA76.9.A25 S53
DD 005.8/05
ISSN 0277-920X
US
CODEN SSARE7

SIG SECURITY, AUDIT & CONTROL REVIEW. [SIG secur., audit, control rev.]. **Added/Corp** Association for Computing Machinery. Special Interest Group on Security, Audit, and Control. **VFOAT** S.I.G. Security, Audit, and Control Review; Security, Audit & Control Review; Security, Audit, and Control Review; S.I.G.S.A.C. Review; SIGSAC Review. **VAT** Special Interest Group Security, Audit, and Control Review. Vol. 1, No. 1 (Winter 1981)-. Periodical. English. Four times a year. $31.00. ACM / Association for Computing Machinery, 1515 Broadway, 17th Floor, New York NY 10036. **Tel** (212)869-7440, FAX (212)869-0481. **(Subscription address:** Association for Computing Machinery, PO Box 12114, Church Street Station, New York NY 10249. **Tel** (212)626-0500.)
Ind/Abst Comput. Rev. (Winter 1989)-; Curr. Cit.

LC QA267 .S53
DD 511.3
ISSN 0163-5700
US
CODEN SIGNDM

SIGACT NEWS. [SIGACT news]. **Main/Corp** ACM Special Interest Group for Automata and Computability Theory. **Added/Corp** ACM Special Interest Group for Automata and Computability Theory. **VAT** Special Interest Group on Automata and Computability Theory. (196?)-. Periodical. English. Four times a year. $39.00. ACM / Association for Computing Machinery, 1515 Broadway, 17th Floor, New York NY 10036. **Tel** (212)869-7440, FAX (212)869-0481. **(Subscription address:** Association for Computing Machinery, PO Box 12114, Church Street Station, New York NY 10249. **Tel** (212)626-0500.) Documents available from Ask*IEEE.
Ind/Abst Abstr. Hum. Comput. Interact. (July 1974-); ACM Guide Comput. Lit.; Comput. Rev. (July 1974-); INSPEC (July 1974-); Zentralbl. Math. Ihre Grenzgeb. (July 1974-).

LC R858.A1 S54
DD 610/.285
ISSN 0163-5697
US
CODEN SINWDG

SIGBIO NEWSLETTER. See Medical Sciences-Computer Applications.

LC QA297 .A76a
DD 519.4
ISSN 0163-5778
US
CODEN SNEWD6

SIGNUM NEWSLETTER. See Mathematics-Computer Applications.

LC QA155.7.E4 A68a
DD 512/.0285
ISSN 0163-5824
US
CODEN SIGSBZ

SIGSAM BULLETIN. See Mathematics-Computer Applications.

DD 338
ISSN 0896-4068
US

SILVERPLATTER EXCHANGE, THE. [SilverPlatter exch.]. **VFOAT** Silver Platter Exchange. Vol. 1, No. 1 (Jan. 1988)-. Periodical. English. Two times a year (July & Dec.). Free on request. Silverplatter Information Inc., 100 River Ridge Drive, Norwood MA 02062. **Tel** (800)343-0064, (617)769-2599, FAX (617)769-8763. **ED** Elizabeth Morley.
Desc: News for and about CD-ROM users.
Ind/Abst Libr. Inf. Sci. Abstr.

DD 004
ISSN 1060-6068
US

SIMPLE TIMES, THE. (THE SIMPLE TIMES : THE BIMONTHLY NEWSLETTER OF SNMP TECHNOLOGY, COMMENT, AND EVENTS.). [Simple times]. **Added/Corp** Dover Beach Consulting, Inc. Vol. 1, No. 1 (Mar./Apr. 1992)-. Newsletter. English. Six times a year. Free on request. SNMP Research Inc., 3001 Kimberling Heights Road, Knoxville TN 37920. **Tel** (615)573-1434.

DD 004
ISSN 1079-5677
US

●**SIMPLY SECURE.** [Simply secure]. **Added/Corp** Cobb Group. Vol. 1, No. 1 (Dec. 1994/Jan. 1995)-. Periodical. English. Six times a year. $49.00. Cobb Group, 9420 Bunsen Parkway #300, Louisville KY 40220. **Tel** (502)491-1900, (800)223-8720, FAX (502)491-4200.

US

SIXTH GENERATION SYSTEMS. (July 1990)-. English. Twelve times a year. $79.00. Sixth Generation Systems, PO Box 155, Vicksburg MI 49097. **Tel** (616)649-3772. **Continues** Neurocomputers, 0897-1585.

DD 702
ISSN 0748-2043
US

SMALL COMPUTERS IN THE ARTS NEWS. See The Arts-Computer Applications.

DD 658
ISSN 1080-1545
US
TITLE CHANGE

SMART COMPUTER & SOFTWARE RETAILING. [Smart comput. softw. retail.]. **VFOAT** Smart Computer and Software Retailing; Smart. (Jan. 1995)-(1995). Periodical. English. Cahners Publishing Company, 249 West 17th Street, New York NY 10011. **Tel** (212)645-0067, FAX (212)242-6987. **(Subscription address:** Cahners Publishing Company / Colorado, Paid Subscription Service Center, PO Box 7610, Highlands Ranch CO 80126-7610. **Tel** (303)470-4466, FAX (303)470-4691.) **Merged into** Twice.

DD 004
ISSN 0893-0406
US

SNA MONTHLY REVIEW. [SNA mon. rev.]. **VFOAT** Monthly Review. (198?)-. Periodical. English. Twelve times a year. $497.00. Network Technology Group, PO Box 630, Belmont MA 02178. **Tel** (617)236-8741.

UK

SOFTSEL RESELLER. (19??)-. English. Softsel Computer Products, 546 North Oak Street, Inglewood CA 90312.

ISSN 0268-6708
UK

SOFTWARE USER'S YEAR BOOK, THE. (1985/86)-. English. One time a year. VNU Business Publications BV, 32-34 Broadwick Street, London W1A 2HG United Kingdom. **Tel** 011 44 171 4394242 ext. 2222, FAX 011 44 171 4379638, telex 23918 VNU G, 8952440. **Formed by the union of** International Directory of Software and Microcomputer Software Directory.

US
CEASED

SOURCE DATA : THE DATAPOINT CUSTOMER MAGAZINE. (19??)-(19??). English. Datapoint Corporation, M O Beyland, 9725 Datapoint Drive, Box MS-T-94, San Antonio TX 78284. **Tel** (512)699-7414.

DD 381
ISSN 0897-4128
US
SUSPENDED

SOURCE FILE. [Source file]. **Added/Corp** Applied Computer Research (Firm). **VFOAT** Sourcefile. Vol. 7, No. 4 (Nov. 1987)-?. Periodical. English. Six times a year. $85.00. Applied Computer Research Inc., 11242 North 19th Avenue, Phoenix AZ 85029. **Tel** (602)995-5929, FAX (602)995-0905. **Continues** Sources (Phoenix, Ariz.), 0743-4367.

LC QA76 .S647
DD 004/.05
ISSN 1015-7999
SA
CODEN SACJE3

SOUTH AFRICAN COMPUTER JOURNAL = SUID-AFRIKAANSE REKENAARTYDSKRIF. **Added/Corp** Computer Society of South Africa. South African Institute of Computer Scientists. **VFOAT** SACJ; SART; Suid-Afrikaanse Rekenaartydskrif; Computer Science and Information Systems; Rekenaarwetenskap en Inligtingstelsels; SACJ/SART. No. 1 (Jan. 1990)-. Periodical. English (Afrikaans). Irregular (2 or 3 issues per year). South Africa Computer Society, PO Box 1714, Halfway House, 1685 South Africa. **Tel** 011 27 11 3151319.
Desc: Covers computer science and information technology.
Ind/Abst Curr. Cit.

ISSN 1068-557X
US
CODEN SPEWEL

SPEC NEWSLETTER. [SPEC newsl.]. **Added/Corp** Standard Performance Evaluation Corporation. **VFOAT** Standard Performance Evaluation Corporation Newsletter. (198?)-. Newsletter. English. Four times a year (Mar., June, Sept., Dec.). $550.00. SPEC / NCGA, 2722 Merrilee Drive, Suite 200, Fairfax VA 22031. **Tel** (703)698-9600, FAX (703)560-2752. **Circ:** 300.

NE

SPECIAL TOPICS IN SUPERCOMPUTING. Vol. 1 (1987)-. Monographic series. English.
Ind/Abst Math. Rev. (1988-); Zentralbl. Math. Ihre Grenzgeb.

LC QA75
DD 004
GW

●**SPRINGER SERIES IN OPERATIONS RESEARCH.** (1994)-. Monographic series. English. Irregular. DM88.00. Springer-Verlag GmbH & Company KG, Heidelberger Platz 3, D-14197 Berlin Germany. **Tel** 011 49 30 8207223, FAX 011 49 30 8214091, telex 183

Computers

319 SPBLN D. **ED** P. Glynn.
  Desc: Aimed at management scientists and operations researchers.

GW
ST COMPUTER. (19??)-. German. Eleven times a year. DM80.00. PSH Medienvertriebs GmbH, Georgenstrasse 38 b, D-64297 Darmstadt Germany. **Tel** 011 49 61 51 947723, FAX 011 49 61 51 947725, 947718. (**Subscription address:** MAXON Computer GmbH, Postfach 59 69, D 65734 Eschborn Germany. **Tel** 011 49 61 96 481814, FAX 011 49 61 96 41137.) **ED** Harald Egel. **Ad Acc.**

NE
ST NEWS. (1986)-. English. Four times a year (irregular). Free. Richard Karsmakers, Looplantsoen 50, NL-3523 GV Utrecht Netherlands. **Tel** 011 31 0 30 887482. **ED** Richard Karsmakers. **Bk Rev**, (Qty: 5-20).
  Desc: Disk magazine for users of Atari ST/TT/Falcon computers. Available on 3.5" DD disk.

US
STANDARD VIEW / STANVIEW. (19??)-. English. Four times a year. $100.00 nonmembers, $25.00 members. ACM / Association for Computing Machinery, 1515 Broadway, 17th Floor, New York NY 10036. **Tel** (212)869-7440, FAX (212)869-0481.

ISSN 0889-6216
DD 004 US
CEASED
START (SAN FRANCISCO, CALIF.). (START.). [STart]. Vol. 1, No. 1 (Summer 1986)-(19??). Periodical. English. Antic Publishing, 544 2nd Street, San Francisco CA 94170. **Tel** (415)957-1911. **Bk Rev**. **Ad Acc. Circ:** 50,000.
  Desc: Articles, programs, tutorials and software reviews for Atari ST users of all levels.
  Ind/Abst Comput. Rev. Index (Fall 1987-).

LC QA76.9.D32 S73   ISSN 1050-2378
DD 005.74/025/73 US
STATE DATA AND DATABASE FINDER. [State data database finder]. **Added/Corp** Information USA, Inc. Ed. 1 (1989)-. English. One time a year. $145.00. Information USA, PO Box E, Kensington MD 20895. **Tel** (301)924-0556, (800)955-7693, FAX (301)946-3004. **ED** Andrew Naprawa. available on diskette.
  Desc: State level information "on everthing from legislation, insurance, taxes and education, to agriculture, food and drugs, and overseas markets."

LC QA274.A1 S78   ISSN 1045-1129
DD 519.2/05 US
CCC
CODEN SSTREY
STOCHASTICS AND STOCHASTICS REPORT. See Mathematics.

ISSN 0141-1004
UK
STUDIES IN OPERATIONS RESEARCH. [Stud. oper. res.]. (1972)-. Monographic series. English. Irregular. Price varies per volume. Gordon & Breach Science Publishers, PO Box 90, Reading, Berkshire RG1 8JL United Kingdom. **Tel** 011 44 1734 560080, FAX 011 44 1734 568211.

ISSN 1054-5417
DD 005 US
SUBSCRIBER NEWS : PRACTICAL INFORMATION FOR USERS OF FATE, FET, FIT, AND FGT. [Subscr. news]. **Added/Corp** Shepard's/McGraw-Hill. (Mar. 1991)-. Periodical. English. Four times a year. Free with software subscription. Shepards McGraw-Hill Inc, 555 Middle Creek Parkway, PO Box 35300, Colorado Springs CO 80935-3530. **Tel** (719)488-3000, (800)458-8811, FAX (800)525-0053.

LC WMLC 93/5125 QA75.5 .S86   ISSN 1053-9239
DD 004 US
SUNEXPERT (BROOKLINE, MASS.). (SUNEXPERT.). [SunExpert]. **VFOAT** SunExpert Magazine; Sun Expert; Sun Expert Magazine. Vol. 1, No. 1 (Nov. 1989)-. Periodical. English. Twelve times a year. $60.00. Computer Publishing Group, 1330 Beacon Street, Brookline MA 02146. **Tel** (617)739-7001, FAX (617)739-7003. **Bk Rev**, (Qty: 20+). **Ad Acc. Circ:** 73,000 (ctrl).
  Desc: Supported by in-house test lab in the Sun market. Tests and evaluates products in an environment that mirrors the readers' workplace.

ISSN 1043-2418
DD 004 US
SUPER GROUP MAGAZINE. [Super Group mag.]. **VFOAT** SuperGroup Magazine. (198?)-. Periodical. English (German and French). Six times a year. $60.00 (one-year), $110.00 (two-year), $150.00 (three-year). Vertitech Publications, 1787 East Fort Union Boulevard, Suite 107, Salt Lake City UT 84121. **Tel** (801)942-6655, (801)356-3434, FAX (801)942-8675. **ED** Kathy Anderson. Index available. cum. index. **Ad Acc. Circ:** 6,000 (ctrl). **Continues** SuperGroup Association Magazine, 0738-4572.
  Ind/Abst Comput. ASAP [Full Txt.]; Comput. Database [Full Txt.].

ISSN 0168-7875
NE
CODEN SPCOEL
Pr Rev.
SUPERCOMPUTER. [Supercomputer]. **VFOAT** Super Computer. (May 1984)-. Periodical. English. Six times a year. $225.00. ASFRA BV, Voorhaven 33, 1135 BL Edam The Netherlands. **Tel** 011 31 02993 72751, FAX 011 31 02993 72877. **Bk Rev**. **Ad Acc. Circ:** 450. Documents available from The Genuine Article, Ask*IEEE.
  Ind/Abst CompuMath Cit. Index [Full Cov.]; Curr. Cit.; Curr. Contents Eng. Comput. Technol.; INSPEC (Jan. 1988-); Res. Alert [Full Cov.].

ISSN 1064-1750
DD 005 US
SUPPORT@FTP.COM (WAKEFIELD, MASS.). (SUPPORT@FTP.COM.). [Support@ftp.com]. **VFOAT** Supportftp.com Newsletter. Vol. 1, No. 1 (Mar. 1992)-. Newsletter. English. Four times a year. Free. FTP Software, 26 Princess Street, Wakefield MA 01880-3004.

ISSN 0281-9015
SW
UDC 681.3
SVENSKA PC-WORLD. [Sven. PC-world]. (1984)-. Periodical. Swedish. Six times a year. $76.14. IDG, Sturegatan 11, S-10678 Stockholm Sweden. **Tel** 011 46 8 4536000.
  Ind/Abst Infomat Int. Bus.

LC QA76.9.C55 S93   ISSN 1072-2483
DD 005.75/05 US
●**SYBASE (EMERYVILLE, CALIF.).** (SYBASE.). [Sybase]. **VFOAT** Sybase Magazine. (1993)-. Periodical. English. Four times a year. Free. Sybase, 6475 Christie Avenue, Emeryville CA 94608. **Tel** (510) 596-3500, FAX (510) 658-9441. **ED** John A. Barry. **Ad Acc.**

LC QA76.8.T145 S92   ISSN 0734-0133
DD 001.64 US
SYNTAX QUARTERLY. (SYNTAX QUARTERLY : SQ : A PUBLICATION OF THE HARVARD GROUP.). **VFOAT** SQ; S.Q. Vol. 1, No. 1 (Winter 1982)-. Periodical. English. Four times a year. The Harvard Group Inc, PO Box 667, Harvard MA 01451-0667.

ISSN 0714-7864
DD 001.64/05 CN
SYSTEMLETTER. (SYSTEMLETTER : A DIGEST OF CURRENT INFORMATION FOR DATACROWN USERS.). [Systemletter]. **VAT** Datacrown Systemletter. Vol. 1, No. 1 (Sept./Oct. 1979)-. Periodical. English. Datacrown, 650 McNicoll Avenue Canada. **Continues** Shared Processing, 0703-8658.

ISSN 0893-9586
DD 004 US
SYSTEMTALK. [Systemtalk]. **VFOAT** System Talk. (198?)-. Periodical. English. Eight times a year (Jan,. Feb., Apr., May, July, Sept., Oct., Nov.). $30.00 (one-year), $50.00 (two-year) US; $35.00 (one-year), $60.00 (two-year) Canada; $40.00 (one-year), $70.00 (two-year) other. MSGI Publications, 8A Catherineberg Charlo Amalie, St. Thomas 00802, U. S. Virgin Islands. **Tel** 800-322-6744.
  Desc: Targeted toward Prime computer users.

ISSN 0891-303X
DD 338 US
TECHNICAL COMPUTING. [Tech. comput.]. (Nov. 1986)-. Periodical. English. Twelve times a year. $175.00. Technical Computing, 9714 South Rice Avenue, Houston TX 77096. **Tel** (713)774-3942. **Bk Rev**. available on an online database (files 16,636/Full-Text) from DIALOG.
  Ind/Abst PROMT; PTS Newsl. Database [Full Txt.].

ISSN 1038-5231
DD 620.00420285 AT
TECHNICAL COMPUTING (ALEXANDRIA). [Tec. comput. Alex.]. **Added/Corp** Association for Computer Aided Design (Australia). (1992)-. Trade Publication. English. Four times a year. 28.78Aus$. Association for Computer Aided Design, 16 High Street, Glen Iris Victoria 3146 Australia. **Tel** 11 61 03 8856586, FAX 11 61 03 8855974. **Continues** ACADS Quarterly, 0817-072X.

FR
TECHTRADE. English. Irregular. $130.00. Innovation 128, 24 rue du Quatre Septembre, 75002 Paris France. **Tel** 011 33 1 42680971.

FR
TECTONIQUE, GEOPHYSIQUE INTERNE F45. French. Irregular. 1056.74F France; 1095.00F other. CNRS / Institut d'Information Scientifique et Technique, (Centre National de la Recherche Scientifique), 15 Quai Anatole France, 75700 Paris France. **Tel** 011 33 1 47531515, FAX 011 33 1 45517307, telex 260034. **Continues** Pascal Folio, F45. Tectonique, Geophysique Interne.

LC T58.6 .R53a
DD 338 LV
TEORETICHESKIE VOPROSY AVTOMATIZIROVANNYKH SISTEM UPRAVLENIIA. Main/Corp Petera Stuckas Latvijas Valsts Universitate. Ekonomiskas Kibernetikas Katedra. Vol. 1 (1973)-. Russian. 0.70rub each issue. Redktsionno-Izdatelskii Otdel LGU, 50 Bulv Rainisa 19 50, Riga Latvia.

FR
TERMINAL / INFORMATIQUE CULTURE SOCIETE. French. Six times a year. 290.00F (individuals), 600.00F (individuals) France; 360.00F (individuals), 670.00F (institutions) Europe; 400.00F (individuals), 710.00F (institutions) other. C3I, Ctr Info Initv Infrmsatn, 18 rue de Chatillon, F-75014 Paris France. **Tel** 011 33 1 45395008.

ISSN 1068-8412
DD 004 US
CCC
CODEN TSHDEB
TITLE CHANGE
TERRY SHANNON ON DEC. [Terry Shannon DEC]. Vol. 12, No. 9 (Sept. 1992)-(19??). Academic Scholarly Publication. English. DataTrends Publications, 895 Harrison Street SE, Suite B, Leesburg VA 22075. **Tel** (703)779-0574, (800)766-8130, FAX (703)779-2267. Documents available from CASDDS. **Continues** DataTrends Report on DEC, 1064-377X. **Continued by** Datatrends Report on DEC and IBM.
  Ind/Abst Chem. Abstr.

UK
TEST CADMAT : INTERFACING DESIGN AND TEST. (19??)-. English. Nine times a year. $174.00. Angel Publishing Ltd., 361 373 City Road, 5th Floor, London EC1V 1LR United Kingdom. **Tel** 011 44 71 417 7400, FAX 011 44 71 417 7500. **Continues** Test.

ISSN 0172-8288
GW
UDC 651.7
TITLE CHANGE
TEXTEN + SCHREIBEN. **VFOAT** Texten und Schreiben. (1979)-(Jan. 1995). Periodical. German. Verlag Norman Rentrop, Theodor Heuss Strasse 4, D-53177 Bonn Germany. **Tel** 011 49 228 82050, FAX 011 49 228 364411, telex 17228309 TTX D. **Merged into** Texten und Schreiben der Brief Berater.

GW
●**TEXTEN UND SCHREIBEN BRIEF BERATER.** **VFOAT** Texten und Schreiben. (1995)-. English. Twelve times a year. $152.00. Verlag Norman Rentrop, Theodor Heuss Strasse 4, D-53177 Bonn Germany. **Tel** 011 49 228 82050, FAX 011 49 228 364411, telex 17228309 TTX D. **Absorbed** Texten und Schreiben, 0172-8288 **and** Der Brief Berater, 0939-3498.

ISSN 0172-603X
TEXTS AND MONOGRAPHS IN COMPUTER SCIENCE. [Texts monogr. comput. sci.]. (1975)-. Monographic series. English. Irregular. Price varies per volume. Springer-Verlag New York Inc., 175 Fifth Avenue, New York NY 10010. **Tel** (212)460-1500 ext 256, FAX (212)533-3503, telex 232 235 SPB UR. (**Subscription address:** Springer-Verlag New York Inc. / North America, PO Box 19386 Books, Newark NJ 07195. **Tel** (201)348-4033.) Documents available from Ask*IEEE.
  Desc: Contains articles on programming (modula-2) and compiler construction.
  Ind/Abst INSPEC; Math. Rev.

LC QA267 .T46   ISSN 0304-3975
DD 001.6/4/05 NE
CCC
CODEN TCSCDI
Pr Rev.
THEORETICAL COMPUTER SCIENCE. [Theor. comput. sci.]. **Added/Corp** European Association for Theoretical Computer Science. Vol. 1 (June 1975)-. Academic Scholarly Publication. English. Thirty-four times a year (17 vols.). $3425.00. Elsevier Science Publishers BV, PO Box 211, 1000 AE Amsterdam Netherlands. **Tel** 011 31 20 4853641, 011 31 20 4853642, FAX 011 31 20 4853598. **ED** M Nivat and M Paterson. **Ad Acc. Circ:** 500 (ctrl). available on microfilm and microfiche from University Microfilms International (UMI); available on an online database from Elsevier Electronic Subscriptions (EES). Documents available from The Genuine Article, Ask*IEEE.
  Desc: Derives its motivation from the problems of practical computation.
  Ind/Abst ACM Guide Comput. Lit.; CompuMath Cit. Index [Full Cov.]; Comput. Abstr.; Comput. Inf. Syst. Abstr. J. (1975-) [Full Cov.]; Comput. Rev. (1975-); Curr. Cit.; Curr. Contents Eng. Comput. Technol.; Elect. Comm. Abstr.; Inf. Sci. Abstr. (?-?); INSPEC (1975-); Math. Rev.;

Computers

Res. Alert [Full Cov.]; Sci. Cit. Index; SCISEARCH; Soc. Sci. Cit. Index [Select. Cov.]; Solid State Supercond. Abstr.; Zentralbl. Math. Ihre Grenzgeb. (1975-).

ISSN 0954-7096
DD 005.43   UK
THREADS LONDON. (THREADS.). [Threads Lond.]. (1988)-. Periodical. English. Four times a year. Free. Instruction Set City House, 190 City Road, London EC1V 2QH United Kingdom. **Tel** 011 44 171 2512128, FAX 011 44 171 2512853.

UK
TIP APPLICATIONS. See Library and Information Sciences.

ISSN 1063-973X
DD 651   US
TOWARD AN ELECTRONIC PATIENT RECORD. See Medical Sciences-Computer Applications.

ISSN 0827-2131
DD 001.64/05   CN
TRACE NEWSLETTER - TORONTO REGION AGGREGATION OF COMPUTER ENTHUSIASTS. (TRACE NEWSLETTER.). **VAT** Toronto Region Aggregation of Computer Enthusiasts Newsletter. No. 65 (Oct. 1983)-. Newsletter. English. Six times a year. $1.00 each number. Trace Newsletter, PO Box 6922 Station A, Toronto Ontario M5W 1X6 Canada. **Continues** TRACE Newsletter (Toronto Region Association of Computer Enthusiasts), 0827-2069.

CH
TRADE WINNERS COMPUTERS. English. One time a week. $120.00. Trade Winners, 11 Floor 3 190 Section 2 Keelung Road, Taipei Taiwan. **Tel** 011 886 2 7333988.

ISSN 0887-1450
DD 004   US
TRAINING SOLUTIONS / DIGITAL CONTROLS. [Train. solut.]. **Added/Corp** Digital Controls, Inc. (19??)-. Periodical. English. Six times a year. Free to retail computer stores, corporate training departments, and other concerned with computer applications training. Training Solutions, 5555 Oakbrook Parkway/Suite 200, Norcross GA 30093. **Tel** (404)441-3332.

UK
TRAINING TECHNOLOGY. English. Twelve times a year. £30.00 UK; £38.00 other. Fitzalan Publications Ltd, 100 Great Portland Street, London W1N 5PD United Kingdom. **Tel** 011 44 171 0480861266, FAX 011 44 171 480861212.

FR
TRAITEMENT DE TEXTE. French. Irregular. 350.00F. Traitement de Texte, 11 rue de Provence, 75009 Paris France.

ISSN 0898-2333
DD 004   US
TRANSFER (SANTA BARBARA, CALIF.). (TRANSFER.). [Transfer]. **Added/Corp** Protocol Engines Incorporated. (Jan. & Feb. 1988)-. Periodical. English. Six times a year (Feb., Apr., June, Aug., Oct., Dec.). $150.00. Protocol Engines Inc., 1900 State Street, Santa Barbara CA 93101. **Tel** (805)965-0825, FAX (805)687-2984. **ED** Megan Mori. Index available (Bound in 6th issues in December). cum. index. **Circ:** 1,000.

LC QA76.5 .T673   **ISSN 1070-454X**
DD 004/.35   UK
CODEN TCOMET
Pr Rev.
●**TRANSPUTER COMMUNICATIONS.** [Transput. commun.]. (1993)-. Periodical. English. Four times a year. $250.00. John Wiley & Sons Ltd., Baffins Lane, Chichester, West Sussex PO19 1UD United Kingdom. **Tel** 011 44 1243 779777, FAX 011 44 1243 776128 BTG:JWP001, telex 86290 WIBOOKG. (**Subscription address:** John Wiley & Sons, Inc. / Philadelphia, PO Box 7247, Philadelphia PA 19170. **Tel** (212)850-6645, (800)225-5945.) **ED** P. H. Welch.
Desc: Publishes papers on theory, technology and applications of transputer and associated hardware and software. Transputers are designed for a whole range of high performance applications, many of which have strong safety or finance critical requirements combined with highly complex and ever changing specifications that include real-time constraints.

US
TRENDS AND APPLICATIONS. Added/Corp IEEE Computer Society. United States. National Bureau of Standards. (1976)-. English. One time a year. $40.00. IEEE Computer Society, 10662 Los Vaqueros Circle, PO Box 3014, Los Alamitos CA 90720-1264. **Tel** (714)821-8380, (800)272-6657, FAX (714)821-4641. **Bk Rev.** ctrl circ. **Continues** Computer Networks: Trends and Applications, Proceedings of the Symposium.
Desc: Focuses on the latest developments in the computer science field by changing its theme and emphasis.
Ind/Abst Index IEEE Publ.

LC QA75   **ISSN 1081-1109**
DD 004   US
●**TRI-CITY COMPUTING MAGAZINE.** [Tri-City Comput. Mag.]. **VFOAT** TCCM. (Oct. 1994)-. Consumer Publication. English. Twelve times a year. $14.00. AJA Consulting, 141 South Lake Avenue, Albany NY 12208. **Tel** (518)446-1944. **ED** Anthony J. Ardito. Index available. cum. index. **Bk Rev.**, (Qty: 12). **Ad Acc.**, **Adv Mgr:** Josie Soto. **Circ:** 20,000 (ctrl).
Desc: Covering the national and capital region of New York State computer information. Columns on the Internet, computer education, OS/2, MAC, C programming, Autocad, entertainment and educational software, BBS information, and Windows. Includes profiles of New York based computer firms.

ISSN 0892-2845
DD 004   US
UNISYS WORLD. [Unisys world]. (1986)-. Trade Publication. English. Twelve times a year. $92.00. Publications & Communications, 12416 Hymeadow Drive, Austin TX 78750. **Tel** (512)250-9023, (800)678-9724, FAX (512)331-3900, telex 384303. (**Subscription address:** Publications & Communications, PO Box 399, Cedar Park TX 78630.) **Circ:** 15,000. available on microfilm from University Microfilms International (UMI). **Continues** Burroughs World, 0743-9474; **Absorbed** The Bulletin, 0895-0326.
Desc: Keeps readers abreast of the latest happenings of interest to the Unisys user. A source of news, product information, user profiles, technical articles, user group information and special features.
Ind/Abst INSPEC (1986-1989).

ISSN 0913-0748
DD 001.642   JA
UNIX MAGAZINE. [UNIX mag.]. **VFOAT** Yunikkusu Magajin. (1986)-. Periodical. Japanese. Twelve times a year. $172.00. Asuki K.K., (Ascii Co. Ltd.), 11-1 Minamiaoyama 6 Chome, Minatoku Tokyo 107 Japan. (**Subscription address:** Maruzen Company Ltd., PO Box 5050, Import & Export Department, Tokyo 100 31 Japan. **Tel** 011 81 3 32789224.)

ISSN 0176-8654
UDC 681.3.066   GW
    CCC
UNIX/MAIL. [Unix/mail]. (1983)-. Trade Publication. German. Six times a year. $157.98. Carl Hanser Verlag, Postfach 860420, D-81631 Munich Germany. **Tel** 011 49 89 998300, FAX 011 49 89 981264.

FR
CEASED
UNIXSYSTEM. (19??)-(19??). French. Societe Parisienne d'Edition, 9 Passage des Marais 9, 75010 Paris France. **Tel** 011 33 1 42089582.

LC QA76.9.H85 U73   **ISSN 0924-1868**
DD 004/.01/9   NE
    CCC
    CODEN UMUIEQ
Pr Rev.
USER MODELING AND USER-ADAPTED INTERACTION. [User model. user-adapt. interact.]. **VFOAT** User Modeling and User Adapted Interaction; UMUAI. Vol. 1, No. 1 (1991)-. Periodical. English. Four times a year. $280.00. Kluwer Academic Publishers, Postbus 322, 3300 AH Dordrecht The Netherlands. **Tel** 011 31 78 524400, FAX 011 31 78 183273, telex 20083. **ED** Alfred Kobsa. **Acid Free.** available on microfilm and microfiche from University Microfilms International (UMI). Documents available from Ask*IEEE.
Desc: Provides an interdisciplinary forum for the dissemination of new research results on all aspects of user modeling and user-adapted interaction. Publishes original papers contributing to these fields, including the following areas: acquisition of user and student models; conceptual models, mental models; dialog planning and response tailoring; levels of user expertise; explanation strategies; intelligent information retrieval; plan recognition and generation; presentation planning; recognition and correction of misconceptions; user stereotypes; formal representation of ur
Ind/Abst INSPEC (1991-).

US
USER'S GUIDE TO COMPUTER CONTRACTING. (19??)-. English. One time a year. $75.00. Prentice-Hall Law and Business, 270 Sylvan Avenue, Englewood Cliffs NJ 07632. **Tel** (800)223-0231, (201)894-8538, FAX (201)894-8666.

US
UTAH DATA GUIDE : A NEWSLETTER FOR DATA USERS. Added/Corp Utah State Data Center. Utah. Office of the Utah State Planning Coordinator. Utah. Office of Planning and Budget. Vol. 1, No. 1 (Summer 1982)-. Newsletter. English. Four times a year. Free on request. State Planning & Budget Office / Utah, 116 State Capitol, Salt Lake City UT 84114. **Tel** (801)538-1027, 538-1036.

LC QA   **ISSN 0315-3681**
DD 004   CN
    CCC
    CODEN UTMADA
Pr Rev.
UTILITAS MATHEMATICA. See Mathematics-Computer Applications.

LC QA75   **ISSN 1080-8434**
DD 004   US
●**VB TECH JOURNAL : YOUR VISUAL BASIC RESOURCE.** [VB tech j.]. **VFOAT** Visual Basic Tech Journal. Vol. 1, No. 1 (1995)-. Trade Publication. English. Twelve times a year. $19.95. Oakley Publishing Company, PO Box 70087, Eugene OR 97401-9943. **Tel** (800)234-0386, (503)747-0800. **ED** J.D. Hildenbrand. **Ad Acc.**

ISSN 0955-1433
DD 005.133   UK
VECTOR LONDON. (VECTOR.). [VectorLond.]. (1984)-. Periodical. English. Four times a year. $265.23. British Computer Society / Swindon, PO Box 1454 Station Road, Swindon SN1 1TG United Kingdom. **Tel** 011 44 1793 480269. **Ad Acc. Circ:** 900.

LC HG1501
DD 332.1   US
VENTURE FINANCE. See Finance.

US
VIRGINIA DISC [COMPUTER FILE].
Added/Corp Virginia Polytechnic Institute and State University. Nimbus Records (Firm) Virginia Center for Innovative Technology. State Council of Higher Education for Virginia. (1988)-. Periodical. English. Virginia Polytechnic Institute and State University, 617 North Main Street, Blacksburg VA 24060. **Tel** (313)764-4392.

LC QA76.76.C68 V58   **ISSN 1061-8384**
DD 005.8   US
VIRUS NEWS AND REVIEWS. (VIRUS NEWS AND REVIEWS : VNR.). [Virus news rev.]. **Added/Corp** International Computer Security Association. Virus Research Center. **VFOAT** VNR. (Jan. 1992)-. Periodical. English. Twelve times a year. $395.00 (nonmembers); $365.00 (members). Virus Research Center of the ICSA, 5435 Connecticut Avenue NW, Suite 33, Washington DC 20015. **Tel** (202)364-8252.

ISSN 1065-514X
    US
●**VLSI DESIGN (PHILADELPHIA, PA.).** (VLSI DESIGN: AN INTERNATIONAL JOURNAL OF CUSTOM-CHIP DESIGN, SIMULATION, AND TESTING.). (1993)-. Periodical. English. Four times a year. $192.00 (academic institutions), $299.00 (corporate institutions). Gordon & Breach Science Publishers, Inc., PO Box 786, Cooper Station, New York NY 10276. **Tel** (212)206-8900, FAX (212)645-2459.
Desc: Presents papers on state-of-the-art research and development and tutorials in VLSI design, testing, implementation, systems, simulation and analysis.

LC QA75.5 .V95
DD 001.64/05   RU
VYCHISLITELNYE SISTEMY (MOSCOW, R.S.F.S.R.). (VYCHISLITELNYE SISTEMY.). Vol. 1 (1980)-. Periodical. Russian (summaries and/or abstracts in English). Izdatelstvo Statistika, Ulitsa Kirova 39, Moscow Russia.
Ind/Abst Zentralbl. Math. Ihre Grenzgeb.

ISSN 0897-9316
DD 004   US
WASHINGTON, D.C. COMPUTER CURRENTS. See Computers-Computer Industry and Industry Directories.

ISSN 0950-1800
DD 651   UK
WHARTON REPORT. [Whart. rep.]. (1984)-. Newsletter. English. Twelve times a year. $316.58. Wharton Publishing Limited, First Floor Regal House, Twickenham Middlesex, TW1 3QS United Kingdom. **Tel** 011 44 181 8916197. **ED** Andrea Wharton. **Continues** Wharton Market Report.
Desc: Devotes its entire pages to a single topic, and employs the technical knowledge and skills of the Wharton Information Systems researchers and consultants to evaluate the topic indepth. The topics include company, market, application and hardware profiles.

ISSN 0262-2734
DD 001.6405   UK
    CEASED
WHAT'S NEW IN COMPUTING. [What's new comput.]. (1981)-(July 1994). Trade Publication. English. Morgan Grampian, 40 Beresford Street Woolwich, London SE18 6BQ United Kingdom. **Tel** 011 44 181 8557777, FAX 011 44 181 8555548, telex 896413.
Ind/Abst EP Collect.; Homework Help.; MasterFile FullTEXT 1000; MasterFile FullTEXT 350; MasterFile FullTEXT 650; MasterFile FullTEXT; OCLC; Telebase; World Mag. Bank.

Computers —Abstracting, Bibliographies and Statistics

AT
CEASED
WHAT'S NEW IN COMPUTING. (19??)-(Nov. 1995). English. Westwick Farrow, PO Box 289, Wahroonga New South Wales, 2076 Australia. **Tel** 011 61 02 4872700. **Continues** Business & Computing Communications.

ISSN 0140-3435
UK
CCC
CODEN WHCOD8
CEASED
WHICH COMPUTER?. [Which comput.?]. (1977)-(Oct. 1994). Periodical. English. EMAP Readerlink, Audit House, 260 Field End Road, Ruislip Middlesex HA4 9LT United Kingdom. **Tel** 011 44 1773 63100, FAX 011 44 1733 87367. **ED** Jim Wright. **Bk Rev. Ad Acc. Circ:** 31,438 (ctrl). Documents available from Ask*IEEE.
Desc: Covering all aspects of personal computing within the business environment in a non-technical way.
Ind/Abst Comput. ASAP [Full Txt.]; Comput. Database [Full Txt.]; HILITES; Infomat Int. Bus.; INSPEC (Oct. 1978-); Int. Civil Eng. Abstr.; Microcomput. Abstr. (1985-?); Women Manage. Rev. [Full Txt.]; World Ceram. Abstr.; World Publ. Monit.; World Text. Abstr.

US
WHO'S WHO IN ELECTRONIC COMMERCE. (19??)-. Directory. English. One time a year. $199.00; includes a copy of the EDI Yellow Pages. Phillips Business Information Inc., 1201 Seven Locks Road, PO Box 61130, Potomac MD 20854. **Tel** (301)424-3338, (301)340-1520, (800)777-5005, FAX (301)424-4297, telex 358149. **Continues** EDI Directory.
Desc: Information on electronic data interchange (EDI) networks, services, translation software, consulting and related services. Includes market research data on the status, growth, and standards of the electronic commerce marketplace.

ISSN 0277-2647
UK
WILEY SERIES IN COMPUTING. [Wiley ser. comput.]. (19??)-. Monographic series. English. Irregular. Price varies per volume. John Wiley & Sons Ltd., Baffins Lane, Chichester, West Sussex PO19 1UD United Kingdom. **Tel** 011 44 1243 779777, FAX 011 44 1243 776128 BTG:JWP001, telex 86290 WIBOOKG.
(Subscription address: John Wiley & Sons Inc / New Jersey, PO Box 2575, Secaucus NJ 07096-2575. **)** Documents available from Ask*IEEE.
Ind/Abst INSPEC.

ISSN 0940-8029
GW
UDC 519
TITLE CHANGE
WINDOS. [WinDos]. (1991)-(Sept. 1993). Periodical. German. DMV Daten Medien Verlagsgesellschaft, Gruber Strasse 46A, Postfach 1236, D-85586 Poing Germany. **Tel** 011 49 8121 769335. **Continued by** Windows Konkret.

GW
●**WINDOWS KONKRET.** (Sept. 1993)-. German. Twelve times a year. DM82.50 Germany; DM110.00 other Europe; DM150.00 other. DMV Daten Medien Verlagsgesellschaft, Gruber Strasse 46A, Postfach 1236, D-85586 Poing Germany. **Tel** 011 49 8121 769335. **ED** Wilfried F. Platten. **Ad Acc. Continues** Windos, 0940-8029.

UK
WINDOWS MAGAZINE. English. Twelve times a year. £27.00 (one-year), £47.25 (two-year) UK; £51.25 (one-year), £89.75 (two-year) other Europe; £81.00 (one-year), £141.75 (two-year) other. Dennis Publishing Ltd, 19 Bolsover Street, London W1P 7HJ United Kingdom. **Tel** 011 44 181 6311433, FAX 011 44 181 6365668, telex 8954139.

US
●**WIRELESS MEDIA & MESSAGING. See** Communications-Computer Applications.

LC QA76.5 .E54
DD 004
ISSN 0937-6429
GW
CCC
CODEN WIINE9
WIRTSCHAFTSINFORMATIK. [Wirtschaftsinformatik]. **Added/Corp** Hochschullehrer fuer Betriebswirtschaft. Wissenschaftliche Kommission Wirtschaftsinformatik. **VFOAT** Wirtschafts Informatik. Vol. 32, No. 1 (Feb. 1990)-. Periodical. German (summaries and/or abstracts in English; table of contents in English). Six times a year. $288.49. Vieweg Publishing, PO Box 5829, D-65049 Wiesbaden Germany. **Tel** 011 49 611 160230, FAX 011 49 611 534430. **ED** Paul Schmitz. Index available. **Bk Rev. Ad Acc. Circ:** 2,100. Documents available from Article Express International, The Genuine Article, Ask*IEEE. **Continues** Angewandte Informatik, 0013-5704.
Desc: Scientific papers and other information on applications of computers in business, administration, science and other areas.
Ind/Abst ACM Guide Comput. Lit.; CompuMath Cit.

Index [Full Cov.]; Comput. Rev.; Curr. Cit.; Curr. Contents Eng. Comput. Technol.; Ei Page One; Eng. Index Annu.; INSPEC (Feb. 1990-); Res. Alert [Full Cov.]; Soc. Sci. Cit. Index [Select. Cov.].

LC TK7885.A1 W57
DD 621.39
KO
WOLGAN KOMPYUTO HAKSUP. VFOAT Kompyuto Haksup. Vol. 1 (1983)-. Periodical. Korean. Twelve times a year. W15,000. Chusik Hoesa Minkom, 44-31 Youido-dong Yongdunpo-ku, Seoul Korea.

DD 621
ISSN 1073-2233
US
CODEN WPITE8
WORK PROCESS IMPROVEMENT TODAY. [Work process improv. today]. **Added/Corp** Association for Work Process Improvement. **VFOAT** Today. (19??)-. Periodical. English. Six times a year. $195.00 US; $205.00 Canada and Mexico; $215.00 others Comes with membership. Association for Work Process Improvement, 185 Devonshire Street, Suite 770, Boston MA 02110. **Tel** (617)426-1167, FAX (617)426-8911. **ED** Franklin Cooper. **Ad Acc. Circ:** 10,000. **Continues** Remittance and Document Processing Today, 1050-9186.
Desc: Written for application specialists focusing on technology and systems. Covers topics including client server, image and data compression, electronic image management, CAR, OCR, MICR, and many others.
Ind/Abst INSPEC.

US
WORKSTATION ADVISORY SERVICE. (19??)-. English. Six times a year. $895.00. Computer Economics Inc., 5841 Edison Place, Carlsbad CA 92008. **Tel** (800)326-8100, (619)438-8100, FAX (619)431-1126.

LC QA76.76.W56 X22
DD 005.4/3
ISSN 1058-5591
CODEN XRESEA
X RESOURCE, THE. (THE X RESOURCE: A PRACTICAL JOURNAL OF THE X WINDOW SYSTEM.). [X resour.]. **VFOAT** Practical Journal of the X Window System. Issue 1 (Winter 1992)-. Periodical. English. Four times a year (Jan., Apr., July, Oct.). $90.00 US; $100.00 Canada and Mexico; $140.00 Central and South America, Europe and Africa; $150.00 other. O'Reilly & Associates, 103 Morris Street, Sebastapol CA 95472. **Tel** (707)829-0515, (800)338-6887, FAX (707)829-0104.
Ind/Abst Comput. Rev.

LC Q
DD 500
NLM W1 YA459
ISSN 0091-0287
US
YALE SCIENTIFIC. See Science and Technology.

LC A
DD 001.640405
ISSN 0725-3931
AT
YOUR COMPUTER MOSMAN. [Your comput. Mosman]. (1981)-. Periodical. English. Twelve times a year. 45.22Aus$. Federal Publishing Co Pty Ltd., PO Box 199, 180 Bourke Road, Alexandria New South Wales 2015 Australia. **Tel** 011 61 2 3539992, FAX 011 61 2 66923059935. **(Subscription address:** Federal Publishing Co. Pty Ltd., PO Box 199, Alexandria NSW 2015 Australia. **Tel** 011 61 2 3530666.**)**

IT
ZEROUNO. (19??)-. Italian. L61600 Italy; L85200 other. Arnoldo Mondadori Editore, UFF Cont Abbonamenti, 20090 Segrate MI Italy. **Tel** 011 39 2 75422015, telex 320457 MONDMI I.

ABSTRACTING, BIBLIOGRAPHIES AND STATISTICS

ISSN 0269-8862
UK
CCC
CEASED
ABSTRACTS IN ARTIFICIAL INTELLIGENCE / THE TURING INSTITUTE. Added/Corp Turing Institute (Glasgow, Scotland). **VFOAT** Turing Institute Abstracts in Artificial Intelligence; Turing Institute Abstracts. Vol. 1, No. 1 (July 1986)-(1995). Periodical. English. Springer-Verlag London Ltd., Springer House, 8 Alexandra Road Wimbledon, London SW19 7JZ United Kingdom. **Tel** 011 44 181 9471280, 011 44 181 9475885, FAX 011 44 181 9474651, telex 21531 SPRGB G. **(Subscription address:** Springer-Verlag New York Inc. / North America, PO Box 2485, Journal Fulfillment, Secaucus NJ 07096. **Tel** (201)348-4033, (800)777-4643, FAX (201)348-4505.**) ED** Jon S. Ritchie.
Desc: Providing access to English language artificial intelligence abstracts from around the world. Provides an environment for research, training, and development in applied artificial intelligence.

LC QA76.9.H85 A27
DD 004/.01/9
ISSN 1042-0193
US
CCC
SUSPENDED
ABSTRACTS IN HUMAN-COMPUTER INTERACTION. [Abstr. hum.-comput. interact.]. **Added/Corp** Ergosyst Associates. **VAT** Abstracts in Human Computer Interaction. Vol. 1, Issue 1 (Mar. 1990)-Suspended with Vol. 1, No. 2 (199?). Abstracting/Indexing Service. English. Four times a year. Ergosyst Associates Inc, 123 West Eighth Street, Suite 1012, Lawrence KS 66044-2605. **Tel** (913)842-7334, FAX (913)842-7348. Index available. cum. index. **Bk Rev. Ad Acc. Acid Free.** available on CD-ROM.
Desc: International abstracting journal monitoring scientific, technical, and other professional and trade literature relevant to computer usability and covering innovative techniques, systems, and products involving computer-based interaction with users and operators.

LC QA75.5 .A75a
DD 016.00164
ISSN 0149-1199
US
ACM GUIDE TO COMPUTING LITERATURE. [ACM guide comput. lit.]. **Main/Corp** Association for Computing Machinery. **Added/Corp** Association for Computing Machinery. Guide to Computing Literature. **VAT** Association for Computing Machinery Guide to Computing Literature. (1977)-. Abstracting/Indexing Service. English. One time a year (July). $200.00. ACM / Association for Computing Machinery, 1515 Broadway, 17th Floor, New York NY 10036. **Tel** (212)869-7440, FAX (212)869-0481. **(Subscription address:** Association for Computing Machinery, PO Box 12114, Church Street Station, New York NY 10249. **Tel** (212)626-0500.**) Circ:** 2,000. available on an online database from DIALOG.
Continues Computing Reviews. Bibliography and Subject Index of Current Computing Literature.
Desc: Covers books, reports, theses, articles and papers from journals and proceedings from both ACM and other sources.

LC Z
DD 004
ISSN 0770-0512
BE
CODEN BORSEG
BELGIAN JOURNAL OF OPERATIONS RESEARCH, STATISTICS AND COMPUTER SCIENCE. [Belg. j. oper. res. stat. comput. sci.]. **VFOAT** Revue Belge de Recherche Operationelle, de Statistique et d'Informatique. Vol. 25, No. 1 (March 1985)-. Periodical. English. Four times a year. $44.77. Ecole Royale Militaire Mathematique Appliquee, AV de la Renaissance 30, B 1040 Brussels Belgium. Documents available from Ask*IEEE.
Continues Revue Belge de Statistique, d'Informatique et de Recherche Operationnelle, 0373-9597.
Ind/Abst INSPEC (March 1985-); Int. Abstr. Oper. Res. (1985-) [Full Cov.]; Math. Rev. (1985-); Zentralbl. Math. Ihre Grenzgeb. (1985-).

LC TS155.6 .C328
DD 670/.285
ISSN 0882-1437
US
CAD/CAM ABSTRACTS. [CAD CAM abstr.]. **Added/Corp** EIC Intelligence Inc. **VFOAT** CAD CAM Abstracts; CAD CAM. Vol. 1, No. 1 (1984)-. English. Six times a year. £60.00 UK. Techgnosis Ltd., Blade House, Battersea Road, Cheshire SK4 3EA United Kingdom. **Tel** 011 44 161 4422639, FAX 011 44 161 4431162. **ED** Barry Lenson. Index available. **Bk Rev.** ctrl circ. available on CD-ROM (SuperTech Abstracts Plus).
Desc: A journal covering all aspects of CAD/CAM. Includes abstracts of journal articles, reports, conference proceedings, monograph research studies, etc.

LC Z6654.C17 C64 QA75.5
DD 016.00164
NLM Z 699.A1 C736
ISSN 0010-4469
UK
COMPUTER ABSTRACTS. [Comput. abstr.]. **Added/Corp** Technical Information Company. Vol. 4 (Jan. 1960)-. Abstracting/Indexing Service. English. Twelve times a year. $1999.00. MCB University Press, 60 62 Toller Lane, Bradford, West Yorkshire BD8 9BY United Kingdom. **Tel** 011 44 1274 785280, FAX 011 44 1274 785220, telex 51317-MCBUNI-G. **(Subscription address:** MCB University Press / US and Canada Subscriptions, PO Box 10812, Birmingham AL 35201-0812. **Tel** (205)995-1567, (800)633-4931, FAX (205)995-1588.**) ED** Chris Matthews. **Circ:** 1,200.
Continues Computer Bibliography.
Desc: Information source with articles abstracted from journals published in the field of computer science. Listing includes computer theory, mathematics, programming, data transfer, hardware, and others.

US
TITLE CHANGE
COMPUTER ABSTRACTS ON DISKETTE. (19??)-(1993). English. Nova Science Publishers Inc., 6080 Jericho Turnpike, Suite 207, Commack NY 11725-2808. **Tel** (516)499-3103, (516)499-3106, FAX (516)499-3146. **Continued by** Journal of Computer Abstracts and Research, 1077-6265.

US
TITLE CHANGE

COMPUTER ABSTRACTS ON MICROFICHE. Vol. 4, No. 1 (Jan. 1989)-(1993). English. Nova Science Publishers Inc., 6080 Jericho Turnpike, Suite 207, Commack NY 11725-2808. **Tel** (516)499-3103, (516)499-3106, FAX (516)499-3146. ***Continues*** *Computer Information Review.* ***Continued by*** *Journal of Computer Abstracts and Research.*
Desc: Covers books, conference proceedings, technical reports, patents, government reports, dissertations and software.

LC QA76 .C548 **ISSN** 0036-8113
DD 016.0016/4 UK
CCC
CODEN CCABB8

COMPUTER & CONTROL ABSTRACTS. [Comput. control abstr.]. **Added/Corp** Institution of Electrical Engineers. Institute of Electrical and Electronics Engineers. **VFOAT** Computer and Control Abstracts. Vol. 4, No. 32 (Jan. 1969)-. Abstracting/Indexing Service. English. Twelve times a year. £930.00. Institution of Electrical Engineers / IEE, Michael Faraday House, Six Hills Way, Stevenage Hertfordshire SG1 2AY United Kingdom. **Tel** 011 44 1438 313311, FAX 011 44 1438 742840, telex 825578 IEESTV G. **(Subscription address:** IEE / Peter Peregrinus Ltd., PO Box 96, Stevenage Herts SG1 2SD United Kingdom. **Tel** 011 44 1438 313311, FAX 011 44 438 742792, telex 825578 IEESTV G.) **ED** Gill Wheeler. Index available (published separately). available on CD-ROM; available on microfilm (16MM open reel or cartridge - 35MM open reel only 1898-1990) from INSPEC/IEE; available on microfiche (1974 to present) from INSPEC/IEE; available on an online database from STN International; Orbit Search Service; Fiz-Technik; European Space Agency; DIALOG; DATA-STAR; CEDOCAR; and BRS. Documents available from BLDSC, CASDDS. ***Continues*** *Control Abstracts.*
Desc: Offers an information service on all aspects of computer installations, applications, hardware, peripherals, and software as well as control engineering, robotics, systems theory and artificial intelligence.
Ind/Abst Math. Rev.

LC QA76 .I46
DD 016.0016/4 US

•**COMPUTER AND INFORMATION SYSTEMS ABSTRACTS.** **Added/Corp** Cambridge Scientific Abstracts, Inc. Engineering Information, Inc. Vol. 41, No. 1 (1993)-. Periodical. English. Twelve times a year. $1,150.00 US; $1,345.00 other. Cambridge Scientific Abstracts, 7200 Wisconsin Avenue, #601, Bethesda MD 20814-4823. **Tel** (301)961-6750, (800)843-7751, FAX (301)961-6720. available via Internet (to the current year's abstracts and five-year backfiles) from Cambridge Scientific Abstracts. ***Continues*** *Computer and Information Systems Abstracts Journal, 0191-9776.*

US

COMPUTER ASAP [ONLINE DATABASE]. (19??)-. Abstracting/Indexing Service. English. Information Access Company, 362 Lakeside Drive, Foster City CA 94404. **Tel** (800)227-8431, (800)458-1565.
Desc: Covers aspects of the computer, telecommunications and electronics industries. Detailed product announcements, evaluations and comparisons, industry and market trends, best buys, company and biographical profiles, and financial information on computer, electronic and telecommunications firms are all included.

LC HD **ISSN** 0732-8346
DD 338 US
CCC
CEASED

COMPUTER BUSINESS (LOS ANGELES, CALIF.). (COMPUTER BUSINESS.). [Comput. bus.]. **Added/Corp** Contemporary Communications, Inc. Round Table Associates. (Jan. 1978)-(Dec. 1995). Abstracting/Indexing Service. English. Twelve times a year. $180.00. Round Table Associates / SAB Inc., PO Box 45923, Los Angeles CA 90045-0923. **Tel** (213)649-2846. **ED** Abe H. Hassan.
Desc: Brief abstracts of articles appearing in the trade and business press, in 20 categories.

US

COMPUTER DATABASE [ONLINE DATABASE]. (19??)-. Abstracting/Indexing Service. English. Information Access Company, 362 Lakeside Drive, Foster City CA 94404. **Tel** (800)227-8431, (800)458-1565.
Desc: Covers the computer, telecommunications and electronics industries. Provides answers to questions regarding hardware, software, peripherals, and high tech fields such as robotics, neural networks, satellite communications and videotex.

LC HD9696.C6 C63 **ISSN** 0744-0081
DD 338.7/6100164/05 US

COMPUTER INDUSTRY UPDATE. [Comput. ind. update]. **Added/Corp** IMR, Inc. (19??)-. Abstracting/Indexing Service. English. Twelve times a year. $395.00. Industry Market Reports Inc., PO Box 681, Los Altos CA 94023. **Tel** (415)941-6679. **ED** George Weiser. available on diskette (with search software).
Desc: A complete abstracting service reviewing major weekly computer trade publications. Vendor announcements and articles are summarized and organized by vendor within the following market segments: mainframes, minicomputers, terminals and workstations, peripherals, personal computers, and networking.

LC QA76 .Q3 **ISSN** 0270-4846
DD 016.00164 US
CCC

COMPUTER LITERATURE INDEX. [Comput. lit. index]. **Added/Corp** Applied Computer Research (Firm). Vol. 10, No. 1 (April 1980)-. Abstracting/Indexing Service. English. Four times a year (with annual cumulation). $198.50. Applied Computer Research Inc., 11242 North 19th Avenue, Phoenix AZ 85029. **Tel** (602)995-5929, FAX (602)995-0905. **(Subscription address:** Applied Computer Research, PO Box 82266, Phoenix AZ 85071. **Tel** (602)995-5929.) **ED** Janet Butler. cum. index. available on microfilm from University Microfilms International (UMI). ***Continues*** *Quarterly Bibliography of Computers and Data Processing, 0048-6132.*
Desc: The index organizes the DP literature for each quarter by subject matter, and briefly describes the purpose and content of each article, paper, or book.

ISSN 1040-5003
DD 004 US

COMPUTER REVIEW INDEX. [Comput. rev. index]. **Added/Corp** Schenectady County Public Library (Schenectady, N.Y.). Vol. 1, No. 1 (March 1986)-. Abstracting/Indexing Service. English. Twelve times a year. $40.00. Sullivan Computer Services, 1297 Keyes Avenue, Schenectady NY 12309. **ED** Robert G. Sullivan.
Desc: A guide to reviews of computer hardware, software, and online services in library and computer journals. Each issue includes more than 1400 citations of over 1000 products.

ISSN 0309-8885
UK

COMPUTING JOURNAL ABSTRACTS. Vol. 1 (1969)-. English. Twelve times a year. $287.48. Techgnosis Ltd., Blade House, Battersea Road, Cheshire SK4 3EA United Kingdom. **Tel** 011 44 161 4422639, FAX 011 44 161 4431162.

LC QA76 .C5854 **ISSN** 0010-4884
DD 001.6/05 US
CCC
NLM Z 699.A1 C76 **CODEN** CPGRA6

COMPUTING REVIEWS. [Comput. rev.]. **Added/Corp** Association for Computing Machinery. Vol. 1, No. 1 (Feb. 1960)-. Abstracting/Indexing Service. English. Twelve times a year. $145.00. ACM / Association for Computing Machinery, 1515 Broadway, 17th Floor, New York NY 10036. **Tel** (212)869-7440, FAX (212)869-0481. **(Subscription address:** Association for Computing Machinery, PO Box 12114, Church Street Station, New York NY 10249. **Tel** (212)626-0500.) **ED** Aaron Finerman and Carol A. Meyer. cum. index. **Circ:** 8,500. available on microfilm and microfiche from University Microfilms International (UMI); available on an online database from DIALOG. Documents available from BLDSC, UMI Article Clearinghouse, CASDDS.
Desc: Prints critiques of the current literature covering the topics of hardware, software, systems theory, systems applications and computing milieu.
Ind/Abst Abstr. Hum. Comput. Interact.; Ergon. Abstr.; Math. Rev.; Oper. Res./Manage. Sci.

LC QA75.5 .C87 **ISSN** 0011-3794
DD 016.00164 UK

CURRENT PAPERS ON COMPUTERS & CONTROL. [Curr. pap. comput. control]. **Added/Corp** Institution of Electrical Engineers. Institute of Electrical and Electronics Engineers. **VFOAT** C.P.C.; Current Papers in Computers & Control; Current Papers in Computers and Control; Currnet Papers in Computers & Control; CPC. No. 32 (Jan. 1969)-. Abstracting/Indexing Service. English. Twelve times a year. $395.00. Institution of Electrical Engineers / IEE, Michael Faraday House, Six Hills Way, Stevenage Hertfordshire SG1 2AY United Kingdom. **Tel** 011 44 1438 313311, FAX 011 44 1438 742840, telex 825578 IEESTV G. **(Subscription address:** IEE / Peter Peregrinus Ltd., PO Box 96, Stevenage Herts SG1 2SD United Kingdom. **Tel** 011 44 1438 313311, FAX 011 44 438 742792, telex 825578 IEESTV G.) ***Continues*** *Current Papers on Control.*
Desc: Gives the title and full details of the bibliographic reference of each article selected from the world's scientific and technical literature.

LC HF5548 .D3 **ISSN** 0011-6858
DD 651.2605 US
CCC
NLM Z 699.A1 D225

DATA PROCESSING DIGEST. Vol. 1 (April 1955)-. Abstracting/Indexing Service. English. Twelve times a year. $180.00. Data Processing Digest Inc, PO Box 1249, Los Angeles CA 90078-1249. **Tel** (213)851-3156, FAX (213)851-3156. **ED** M. Milligan. **Circ:** 4,500. available on microfilm and microfiche from University Microfilms International (UMI).
Desc: Contains information of interest to Data Processing and Information Systems professionals and executives in the fields of business, education, and computers and computer science.
Ind/Abst Comput. Rev.; Data Process. Dig.

ISSN 0886-2400
DD 004 US
CEASED

DATACOM READER SERVICE. [DataCom read. serv.]. **VFOAT** DataCom Reader. Vol., No. 1 (Oct. 1982)-(19??). Abstracting/Indexing Service. English. Architecture Technology Corporation, PO Box 24344, Minneapolis MN 55424. **Tel** (612)935-2035. ***Continues*** *Monthly Newsletter for the Datacomm's Industry.*
Desc: An abstracting service drawn from the previous month's new product announcements listed in several key trade publications, including Computerworld, Data Communications, and Telephone.

LC AI **ISSN** 1200-5290
DD 016.004 CN

FLASH INFORMATION ONLINE. (FLASH INFORMATION.). [Flash. inf. Online]. (1993)-. Bulletin. Multiple languages. One time a week. Free. Centre for Information Technology Innovation, 1575 Chomeday, Laval Quebec H7V 2X2 Canada. **Tel** (514)973-5740, FAX (514)973-5757. **Circ:** 3,000. available via Internet (gopher://gopher.nlc-bnc.ca/11gopher$root_pub%3a%5b flash%5d).
Desc: Provides bibliographic information for R&D and information technology professionals.

ISSN 1053-1742
DD 005 US

FORMAT (ANN ARBOR, MICH.). **See** Library and Information Sciences.

US

HILITES DATABASE [ONLINE DATABASE]. **VFOAT** HCI Information and LITerature Enquiry Service. (19??)-. Abstracting/Indexing Service. English. Ergosyst Associates Inc, 123 West Eighth Street, Suite 1012, Lawrence KS 66044-2605. **Tel** (913)842-7334, FAX (913)842-7348. available on CD-ROM.
Desc: Covers the scientific, technical, professional and commercial English-language literature relevant to the usability and human engineering of computer hardware and software and of systems and products involving computer-based interaction with users, programmers, and operators -- human-computer interaction (HCI).

UK
CODEN IMTHEM

INFORMATION MANAGEMENT & TECHNOLOGY. **See** Library and Information Sciences-Abstracting, Bibliographies and Statistics.

ISSN 1077-6265
US
TITLE CHANGE

JOURNAL OF COMPUTER ABSTRACTS AND RESEARCH. (1994)-(1994). English. Nova Science Publishers Inc., 6080 Jericho Turnpike, Suite 207, Commack NY 11725-2808. **Tel** (516)499-3103, (516)499-3106, FAX (516)499-3146. ***Continues*** *Computer Abstracts on Diskette; Computer Abstracts on Microfiche.* ***Continued by*** *International Journal of Computer Research.*

LC Q334 .K48 **ISSN** 0950-477X
DD 006.3 UK

KEY ABSTRACTS. ARTIFICIAL INTELLIGENCE. [Key abstr., Artif. intell.]. **Added/Corp** INSPEC (Information Service) Institute of Electrical and Electronics Engineers. **VFOAT** Artificial Intelligence. (Jan. 1987)-. Abstracting/Indexing Service. English. Twelve times a year. $185.00. Institution of Electrical Engineers / IEE, Michael Faraday House, Six Hills Way, Stevenage Hertfordshire SG1 2AY United Kingdom. **Tel** 011 44 1438 313311, FAX 011 44 1438 742840, telex 825578 IEESTV G. **(Subscription address:** IEEE / Institute of Electrical and Electronics Engineers, 445 Hoes Lane, PO Box 1331, Piscataway NJ 08855-1331. **Tel** (800)701-IEEE, (908)981-0060, FAX (908)981-9667, telex 833233.) ***Continues*** *Key Abstracts. Systems Theory, 0306-5553.*
Desc: Covers theory and applications of artificial intelligence, knowledge engineering and expert systems.
Ind/Abst HILITES.

LC Z5640 **ISSN** 0954-9153
DD 016.004 UK

KEY ABSTRACTS. BUSINESS AUTOMATION. **Added/Corp** INSPEC (Information Service) Institute of Electrical and Electronics Engineers. **VFOAT** Business Automation. (Jan. 1989)-. Abstracting/Indexing Service. English. Twelve times a year. $185.00. Institution of Electrical Engineers / IEE, Michael Faraday House, Six Hills Way, Stevenage Hertfordshire SG1 2AY United Kingdom. **Tel** 011 44 1438 313311, FAX 011 44 1438 742840, telex 825578 IEESTV G. **(Subscription address:** IEEE / Institute of Electrical and Electronics Engineers, 445 Hoes Lane, PO Box 1331, Piscataway NJ 08855-1331. **Tel** (800)701-IEEE, (908)981-0060, FAX (908)981-9667, telex 833233.)

available on an online database from STN International; Orbit Search Service; Fiz-Technik; European Space Agency; DIALOG; DATA-STAR; CEDOCAR; and BRS. ***Continues*** *IT Focus, 0264-9152.*
Desc: Covers communications, computers and office systems in business and commerce including banking, financial markets and retailing.
Ind/Abst HILITES.

UK

KEY ABSTRACTS. FACTORY AUTOMATION. Abstracting/Indexing Service. English. Twelve times a year. $178.00. Institution of Electrical Engineers / IEE, Michael Faraday House, Six Hills Way, Stevenage Hertfordshire SG1 2AY United Kingdom. **Tel** 011 44 1438 313311, FAX 011 44 1438 742840, telex 825578 IEESTV G. **(Subscription address:** IEEE / Institute of Electrical and Electronics Engineers, 445 Hoes Lane, PO Box 1331, Piscataway NJ 08855-1331. **Tel** (800)701-IEEE, (908)981-0060, FAX (908)981-9667, telex 833233.**)**
Ind/Abst HILITES.

UK

KEY ABSTRACTS. HUMAN-COMPUTER INTERACTION. Abstracting/Indexing Service. English. Twelve times a year. $178.00. Institution of Electrical Engineers / IEE, Michael Faraday House, Six Hills Way, Stevenage Hertfordshire SG1 2AY United Kingdom. **Tel** 011 44 1438 313311, FAX 011 44 1438 742840, telex 825578 IEESTV G. **(Subscription address:** IEEE / Institute of Electrical and Electronics Engineers, 445 Hoes Lane, PO Box 1331, Piscataway NJ 08855-1331. **Tel** (800)701-IEEE, (908)981-0060, FAX (908)981-9667, telex 833233.**)**
Ind/Abst HILITES.

ISSN 0952-7052
UK

KEY ABSTRACTS. MACHINE VISION. **Added/Corp** Institution of Electrical Engineers. Institute of Electrical and Electronics Engineers. **VFOAT** Machine Vision; Machine Vision, Key Abstracts. (19??)-. Abstracting/Indexing Service. English. Twelve times a year. $185.00. Institution of Electrical Engineers / IEE, Michael Faraday House, Six Hills Way, Stevenage Hertfordshire SG1 2AY United Kingdom. **Tel** 011 44 1438 313311, FAX 011 44 1438 742840, telex 825578 IEESTV G. **(Subscription address:** IEEE / Institute of Electrical and Electronics Engineers, 445 Hoes Lane, PO Box 1331, Piscataway NJ 08855-1331. **Tel** (800)701-IEEE, (908)981-0060, FAX (908)981-9667, telex 833233.**)** available on CD-ROM from University Microfilms International (UMI); available on an online database from STN International; Orbit Search Service; Fiz-Technik; European Space Agency; DIALOG; DATA-STAR; CEDOCAR; and Belindis.
Desc: Covers machine vision and pattern recognition, information theory, digital picture processing, image sensing devices, machine vision applications.

UK

KEY ABSTRACTS. NEURAL NETWORKS. Abstracting/Indexing Service. English. Twelve times a year. $178.00. Institution of Electrical Engineers / IEE, Michael Faraday House, Six Hills Way, Stevenage Hertfordshire SG1 2AY United Kingdom. **Tel** 011 44 1438 313311, FAX 011 44 1438 742840, telex 825578 IEESTV G. **(Subscription address:** IEEE / Institute of Electrical and Electronics Engineers, 445 Hoes Lane, PO Box 1331, Piscataway NJ 08855-1331. **Tel** (800)701-IEEE, (908)981-0060, FAX (908)981-9667, telex 833233.**)**

LC TK1005 .K49 **ISSN** 0950-4834
DD 621.319/1/05 UK

KEY ABSTRACTS. POWER SYSTEMS AND APPLICATIONS. [Key abstr., Power syst. appl.]. **Added/Corp** INSPEC (Information Service) Institute of Electrical and Electronics Engineers. **VFOAT** Power Systems and Applications; Key Abstracts. Power Systems & Applications; Power Systems & Applications. (Jan. 1987)-. Abstracting/Indexing Service. English. Twelve times a year. $225.00. Institution of Electrical Engineers / IEE, Michael Faraday House, Six Hills Way, Stevenage Hertfordshire SG1 2AY United Kingdom. **Tel** 011 44 1438 313311, FAX 011 44 1438 742840, telex 825578 IEESTV G. **(Subscription address:** IEEE / Institute of Electrical and Electronics Engineers, 445 Hoes Lane, PO Box 1331, Piscataway NJ 08855-1331. **Tel** (800)701-IEEE, (908)981-0060, FAX (908)981-9667, telex 833233.**)** ***Continues*** *Key Abstracts. Power Transmission and Distribution, 0306-5561.*
Desc: Covers articles on power networks and systems, power apparatus, electric machines power utilisation and industrial applications of power.

LC Z5853.A8 K49 TJ213 **ISSN** 0950-4842
DD 629.8 UK

KEY ABSTRACTS. ROBOTICS & CONTROL. [Key abstr. Robot. control]. **Added/Corp** INSPEC (Information Service) Institute of Electrical and Electronics Engineers. **VFOAT** Key Abstracts. Robotics and Control; Robotics & Control; Robotics and Control. (Jan. 1987)-. Abstracting/Indexing Service. English. Twelve times a year. $185.00. Institution of Electrical Engineers / IEE, Michael Faraday House, Six Hills Way, Stevenage Hertfordshire SG1 2AY United Kingdom. **Tel** 011 44 1438 313311, FAX 011 44 1438 742840, telex 825578 IEESTV G. **(Subscription address:** IEEE / Institute of Electrical and Electronics Engineers, 445 Hoes Lane, PO Box 1331, Piscataway NJ 08855-1331. **Tel** (800)701-IEEE, (908)981-0060, FAX (908)981-9667, telex 833233.**)** ***Continues*** *Key Abstracts. Industrial Power and Control Systems, 0306-5596.*
Desc: Covers articles on robots and their applications to materials handling, industrial production systems and transportation systems.

ISSN 0950-4869
UK

KEY ABSTRACTS. SOFTWARE ENGINEERING. [Key abstr. Softw. eng.]. **Added/Corp** Institution of Electrical Engineers. Institute of Electrical and Electronics Engineers. **VFOAT** Software Engineering. (19??)-. Abstracting/Indexing Service. English. Twelve times a year. $185.00. Institution of Electrical Engineers / IEE, Michael Faraday House, Six Hills Way, Stevenage Hertfordshire SG1 2AY United Kingdom. **Tel** 011 44 1438 313311, FAX 011 44 1438 742840, telex 825578 IEESTV G. **(Subscription address:** IEEE / Institute of Electrical and Electronics Engineers, 445 Hoes Lane, PO Box 1331, Piscataway NJ 08855-1331. **Tel** (800)701-IEEE, (908)981-0060, FAX (908)981-9667, telex 833233.**)** Index available.
Desc: Covers articles on program support, high-level programming languages, operating systems, database management systems and software development management.

LC QA75.5 .M5 **ISSN** 1074-3995
DD 016.00416 US

●**MICROCOMPUTER ABSTRACTS.** [Microcomput. abstr.]. **Added/Corp** Learned Information (Firm). **VFOAT** Micro Computer Abstracts. Vol. 15, No. 1 (Mar. 1994)-. Abstracting/Indexing Service. English. Four times a year. $195.00. Information Today Inc., 143 Old Marlton Pike, Medford NJ 08055-8750. **Tel** (609)654-6266, (609)654-4888 (editorial), FAX (609)654-4309. **ED** Judith W. Bouchard and Elisa K. Miller. Index available. cum. index. available on CD-ROM from SilverPlatter (US). ***Continues*** *Microcomputer Index, 8756-7040.*
Desc: Covers microcomputer publications.

LC QA75.5 .M5 **ISSN** 8756-7040
DD 016.00416 US
TITLE CHANGE

MICROCOMPUTER INDEX. [Microcomput. index]. **Added/Corp** Microcomputer Information Services. Database Services (Mountain View, Calif.) Learned Information (Firm). **VFOAT** Micro Computer Index. (1980)-(1993). Abstracting/Indexing Service. English. Information Today Inc., 143 Old Marlton Pike, Medford NJ 08055-8750. **Tel** (609)654-6266, (609)654-4888 (editorial), FAX (609)654-4309. **ED** Lisa R. Jasper and William Spence. Index available. cum. index. **Bk Rev.** available on an online database (File 233) from DIALOG; available on CD-ROM. ***Continued by*** *Microcomputer Abstracts, 1074-3995.*
Desc: Covers microcomputer publications. Topics include software and hardware, networks, communications, databases, books, industry events and corporate information.

LC HD9696.C6 M5 **ISSN** 0741-6016
DD 338.4/700164 US

MICROCOMPUTER INDUSTRY UPDATE. [Microcomput. ind. update]. (Sept. 1983)-. Abstracting/Indexing Service. English. Twelve times a year. $355.00. Industry Market Reports Inc., PO Box 681, Los Altos CA 94023. **Tel** (415)941-6679. **ED** George Weiser. available on diskette (with search software).
Desc: Summaries from the weekly computer trade press of product announcements and articles of interest organized by the market segments of personal computers, software, peripherals, local area networks and distribution.

US

NEWSBANK REFERENCE SERVICE COMPUTER FILE. **Added/Corp** NewsBank, Inc. **VFOAT** NewsBank Electronic Index. (1992)-. Periodical. English. Twelve times a year. Newsbank Inc., 58 Pine Street, New Canaan CT 06840. **Tel** (800)243-7694, (800)762-8182, FAX (203)966-6254. ***Continues*** *NewsBank Electronic Information System.*
Desc: Index to the Newsbank microfiche products: NewsBank, Review of the Arts, and Names in the News.

ISSN 0030-3658
DD 001 US
Pr Rev.

OPERATIONS RESEARCH/MANAGEMENT SCIENCE. [Oper. res./manage. sci.]. **Added/Corp** Executive Sciences Institute. **VAT** Operations Research, Management Science. Vol. 1 (1961)-. Abstracting/Indexing Service. English. Six times a year. $151.00. Executive Sciences Institute, 1005 Mississippi Avenue, PO Box 4318, Davenport IA 52808-4318. **Tel** (319)324-4463, FAX (319)322-3725. **(Subscription address:** Executive Sciences Institute, PO Box 4318, Davenport IA 52808. **Tel** (319)324-4463.**)** **ED** Bruce Brocka. Index available (annual). **Bk Rev. Circ:** 1,000.
Desc: Operations research, management science, management information systems, computers, simulation, mathematical programming, queueing, practical applications.

LC QA76 .A775
DD 510/78 US

ROSTER OF MEMBERS. **Main/Corp** Association for Computing Machinery. (Apr. 1, 1959)-. English. Every 2 years (every two years). $30.00. **ACM** / Association for Computing Machinery, 1515 Broadway, 17th Floor, New York NY 10036. **Tel** (212)869-7440, FAX (212)869-0481. **(Subscription address:** Association for Computing Machinery, PO Box 12114, Church Street Station, New York NY 10249. **Tel** (212)626-0500.**)**
Desc: An alphabetic and geographic cross-listing of the names and addresses of 60,000 regular, associate and student members of the ACM as of June 30, 1983.

ISSN 1064-8860
DD 005 US
CCC

SOFT WATCH. [Soft watch]. **Added/Corp** Applied Computer Research (Firm). **VFOAT** SoftWatch. Vol. 1, No. 1 (Jan./Mar. 1992)-. Abstracting/Indexing Service. English. Four times a year. $95.00. Applied Computer Research Inc., 11242 North 19th Avenue, Phoenix AZ 85029. **Tel** (602)995-5929, FAX (602)995-0905. **(Subscription address:** Applied Computer Research, PO Box 82266, Phoenix AZ 85071. **Tel** (602)995-5929.**)** **ED** Alan Howard.
Desc: Provides abstracts and summaries of articles dealing with computer application development and software from over two hundred periodicals.

ISSN 0790-150X
IE

SOFTWARE ABSTRACTS FOR ENGINEERS : SAFE. See Engineering-Computer Applications.

LC HD9696.C63 C334a **ISSN** 1181-9847
DD 338.4/7004/0971021 CN

SOFTWARE DEVELOPMENT AND COMPUTER SERVICE INDUSTRY. (SOFTWARE DEVELOPMENT AND COMPUTER SERVICE INDUSTRY = INDUSTRIE DE LA PRODUCTION DE LOGICIELS ET DES SERVICES INFORMATIQUES.). [Softw. dev. comput. serv. ind.]. **Added/Corp** Statistics Canada. Services, Science and Technology Division. **VFOAT** Industrie de la Production de Logiciels et des Services Informatiques. (1991)-. Trade Publication. English (French). One time a year. 28.00Can$ Canada; $34.00 US; $40.00 other. Statistics Canada Publications Sales and Services, R.H. Coats Building 6th Floor, Ottawa Ontario K1A 0T6 Canada. **Tel** (613)951-5078, (800)267-6677, FAX (613)951-1584, telex 053-3585. ***Continues*** *Computer Service Industry, 0318-4064.*

LC QA76.753 .S67 **ISSN** 0000-006X
DD 005.36/029/473 US
NLM QA 76.753; S681

SOFTWARE ENCYCLOPEDIA, THE. [Softw. encycl.]. **Added/Corp** R.R. Bowker Company. (1985/86)-. English. One time a year. $229.95. R.R. Bowker, A Reed Reference Publishing Company, Part of Reed International PLC, PO Box 31, 121 Chanlon Drive, New Providence NJ 07974. **Tel** (908)464-6800, (800)521-8110, FAX (908)665-6688, telex 138-755. available on magnetic tape and an online database.
Desc: Lists over 21,000 new and established software programs.

LC QA276.4 .S73 **ISSN** 0960-3174
DD 519.5 UK
CCC
Pr Rev.

STATISTICS AND COMPUTING. Vol. 1, No. 1 (Sept. 1991)-. Periodical. English. Four times a year. $290.00. Chapman & Hall, 2-6 Boundary Row, London SE1 8HN United Kingdom. **Tel** 011 44 171 8650066, FAX 011 44 171 5229623, telex 290164 CHAPMA G. **ED** David J. Hand. **Bk Rev. Ad Acc, Adv Mgr:** Rachel Kelly, **Tel** 44-71-865-0066.
Desc: Publishes articles which cover the entire range of interaction between statistics and computer science. Contains original research reports, review papers, discussion papers and occasional special issues.
Ind/Abst CompuMath Cit. Index [Full Cov.]; Curr. Index Stat.

ISSN 0095-4179
US

TRW SOFTWARE SERIES : INDEX TO PUBLICATIONS IN PRINT. [TRW soft. ser., Index publ. print]. **Added/Corp** TRW Systems Group. Systems Engineering and Integration Division. No. 1 (July 1974)-. Periodical. English. TRW Space & Technology Group, One Space Park, R11 1373, Redondo Beach CA 90278. ***Supersedes*** *TRW Software Bibliography.*

ARTIFICIAL INTELLIGENCE

ISSN 0269-8862
UK
CCC
CEASED

ABSTRACTS IN ARTIFICIAL INTELLIGENCE / THE TURING INSTITUTE. See Computers-Abstracting, Bibliographies and Statistics.

LC QL750 .A36 **ISSN** 1059-7123
DD 591.51/05 US
CCC
NLM W1; AD116 **CODEN** ADBEEA
Pr Rev.
ADAPTIVE BEHAVIOR. See Zoology.

ISSN 0169-1864
NE
CODEN ADROEI

ADVANCED ROBOTICS. (ADVANCED ROBOTICS : THE INTERNATIONAL JOURNAL OF THE ROBOTICS SOCIETY OF JAPAN.). [Adv. robot.]. **Added/Corp** Robotics Society of Japan. Vol. 1, No. 1 (1986)-. Periodical. English. Six times a year. DM500.00. VSP International Science Publishers, Godfried van Seystlaan 47, 3703 BR Zeist Netherlands. **Tel** 011 31 3404 25790, FAX 011 31 3404 32081, telex 40217 USP NL. **(Subscription address:** VSP International Science Publishers, PO Box 346, 3700 AH Zeist Netherlands. **Tel** 011 31 30 6925790, FAX 011 31 30 6932081.**) ED** T. Fukuda. Documents available from Article Express International, Ask*IEEE.
Desc: Interdisciplinary journal which integrates publication of all aspects of research on robotics science and engineering with special emphasis being placed on work done in Japan.
Ind/Abst Abstr. Hum. Comput. Interact.; Curr. Cit.; Ei Page One; Eng. Index Annu.; Inf. Sci. Abstr. (?-?); INSPEC (1987-).

LC QA76.87 .A375 **ISSN** 1060-2410
DD 006.3 US
ADVANCES IN CONNECTIONIST AND NEURAL COMPUTATION THEORY. [Adv. connect. neural comput. theory]. Vol. 1 (1991)-. Monographic series. English. Irregular. Price varies per volume. Ablex Publishing Corporation, 355 Chestnut Street, Norwood NJ 07648. **Tel** (201)767-8450, (201)767-8455 (Customer Service), FAX (201)767-6717.

LC QA76.76.E95 A4 **ISSN** 1074-7532
DD 004 US
•**ADVANCES IN EXPERT SYSTEMS FOR MANAGEMENT.** [Adv. expert syst. manag.]. Vol. 1 (1993)-. English. One time a year. $73.25. JAI Press Inc., 55 Old Post Road, Suite 2, PO Box 1678, Greenwich CT 06836-1678. **Tel** (203)661-7602, FAX (203)661-0792. **ED** William Wallace.

LC QA76.87 .A38 **ISSN** 1049-5258
DD 006.3 US
ADVANCES IN NEURAL INFORMATION PROCESSINGS SYSTEMS. [Adv. neural inf. process. syst.]. (1989)-. English. One time a year. $63.00. Morgan Kaufman Publishers, 2483 Old Middlefield, Suite 103, PO Box 50490, Palo Alto CA 94303. **Tel** (415)578-9911, (800)745-7323, FAX (415)578-0672. **ED** Douglas Sery.
Desc: Collected papers from the "Advances in Neural Information Processing Systems" conference.
Ind/Abst Curr. Cit.

ISSN 0749-1603
DD 629 US
ADVANCES IN ROBOTICS. [Adv. robot.]. (1985)-. Monographic series. English. Irregular. Price varies per volume. John Wiley & Sons, Inc., 605 Third Avenue, New York NY 10158-0012. **Tel** (212)850-6000, (212)850-6645, FAX (212)850-6088, telex 12-7063. **(Subscription address:** John Wiley & Sons / UK, Baffins Lane, Chichester, West Sussex PO19 1UD United Kingdom. **Tel** 011 44 1243 779777, FAX 011 44 243 776128, telex 86290 WIBOOKG.**)**
Ind/Abst Math. Rev. (1987-).

ISSN 0951-5666
GW
CCC
CODEN AISCEM
AI & SOCIETY. [AI & soc.]. **VFOAT** AI and Society. **VAT** Artificial Intelligence & Society; Artificial Intelligence and Society. Vol. 1, No. 1 (July/Sept. 1987)-. Periodical. English. Four times a year. $243.00. Springer-Verlag London Ltd., Springer House, 8 Alexandra Road Wimbledon, London SW19 7JZ United Kingdom. **Tel** 011 44 181 9471280, 011 44 181 9475885, FAX 011 44 181 9474651, telex 21531 SPRGB G. **(Subscription address:** Springer-Verlag New York Inc. / North America, PO Box 2485, Journal Fulfillment, Secaucus NJ 07096. **Tel** (201)348-4033, (800)777-4643, FAX (201)348-4505.**) ED** Karamjit S Gill, James Finkelstein, David Smith and Janet Vaux. available on microfilm and microfiche from University Microfilms International (UMI). Documents available from Ask*IEEE.
Desc: Covers problems of knowledge and skill transfer, AI and human decision making, ethical issues of AI, AI automation and control, management support systems, communication technologies and culture, expert systems in industry, commerce and medicine, human-centered manufacturing systems, relationship between civil and military research, AI and social action in education, training, health, welfare, law, the arts, etc.
Ind/Abst Abstr. Hum. Comput. Interact.; ACM Guide Comput. Lit.; Comput. Abstr.; Comput. Rev.; Curr. Cit.; INSPEC (Jan./March 1989-)(Jan.-Mar. 1989-).

LC HC10 .A635 **ISSN** 1051-8266
DD 333.7/0285/633 US
CODEN AIALER
AI APPLICATIONS. [AI appl.]. **VAT** Artificial Intelligence Applications. Vol. 5, No. 1 (1991)-. Periodical. English. Three times a year. $72.00. AI Applications, PO Box 3066, Moscow ID 83843. **Tel** (208)885-7033, FAX (208)885-6226, telex 5107760923. **ED** Molly Stock. Index available. cum. index. **Ad Acc.** ctrl circ. Documents available from The Genuine Article. ***Continues** AI Applications in Natural Resource Management, 0896-6664.*
Ind/Abst Curr. Aware. Biol. Sci., CABS; Curr. Contents Agric. Biol. Environ. Sci.; Res. Alert [Select. Cov.].

LC Q334 .A46 **ISSN** 0921-7126
DD 006.3/05 NE
CCC
CODEN ACMMEE
AI COMMUNICATIONS. (AI COMMUNICATIONS : THE EUROPEAN JOURNAL ON ARTIFICIAL INTELLIGENCE.). [Ai commun.]. **Added/Corp** European Coordinating Committee for Artificial Intelligence. **VFOAT** European Journal on Artificial Intelligence; Aicom. **VAT** Artificial Intelligence Communications. (19??)-. Periodical. English. Four times a year. $222.68. IOS Press, Van Diemenstraat 94, 1013 CN Amsterdam Netherlands. **Tel** 011 31 20 6382189, FAX 011 31 20 6203419. Documents available from Ask*IEEE.
Ind/Abst ACM Guide Comput. Lit.; Comput. Rev.; Curr. Cit.; Ei Page One; INSPEC (Jan. 1988-); Zentralbl. Math. Ihre Grenzgeb.

LC Q334 .A53a **ISSN** 1050-7965
DD 006.3/025 US
AI DIRECTORY. [AI dir.]. **Added/Corp** American Association for Artificial Intelligence. **VAT** Artificial Intelligence Directory. (1990)-. Directory. English. One time a year. American Association for Artificial Intelligence, 445 Burgess Drive, Menlo Park CA 94025-3496. **Tel** (415)328-3123, FAX (415)321-4457. **ED** David Hamilton. Index available. **Bk Rev**, (Qty: 8-15). **Ad Acc, Adv Mgr:** Mike Hamilton, **Tel** (415)853-0197. **Circ:** 12,000 (ctrl). ***Continues** Membership Directory (American Association for Artificial Intelligence).*
Desc: Strives to disseminate articles representing current artificial intelligence. Articles are selected for appeal to the broad spectrum of researchers in this field and related areas.

LC Q334 .A53 **ISSN** 0888-3785
DD 006 US
CCC
CEASED
AI EXPERT. [AI expert]. **VAT** Artificial Intelligence Expert. Vol. 1, No. 1 (1986)-(1994). Periodical. English. Miller Freeman Inc., 600 Harrison Street, San Francisco CA 94107. **Tel** (415)905-2337, (415)905-2200, FAX (415)905-2240, telex 278273. **(Subscription address:** Neodata / Colorado, PO Box 2606, Boulder CO 80322. **) ED** Craig LaGrow. **Circ:** 35,000. available on an online database from Mead Data Central; NEXIS; and (file 675/Full-Text) DIALOG; available on microfilm and microfiche from University Microfilms International (UMI); available on microfiche (from University Microfilms Intl.). Documents available from Ask*IEEE.
Desc: Focuses on practical implementations and techniques used in artificial intelligence today. Written for AI professionals such as software developers, technical managers, programmers, engineers and consultants; articles cover the latest technology and practical applications.
Ind/Abst Abstr. Hum. Comput. Interact. (19??-199?); ACM Guide Comput. Lit. (19??-199?); Comput. ASAP (19??-199?) [Full Txt.]; Comput. Database (19??-199?) [Full Txt.]; Comput. Lit. Index (19??-199?); Comput. Rev. (19??-199?); Curr. Cit.; F&S Index Plus Text, Int. (19??-199?) [Select. Cov.]; INSPEC (May 1990-199?); Oper. Res./Manage. Sci. (19??-199?); PROMT (19??-199?).

LC Q334 .A5 **ISSN** 0738-4602
DD 001.53/5/05 US
CCC
Pr Rev.
AI MAGAZINE. [AI mag.]. **Added/Corp** American Association for Artificial Intelligence. **VFOAT** A.I. Magazine. **VAT** Artificial Intelligence Magazine. Vol. 1, No. 1 (Spring 1980)-. Trade Publication. English. Four times a year (March, June, Sept., Dec.). Comes with American Association for Artificial Intelligence membership. American Association for Artificial Intelligence, 445 Burgess Drive, Menlo Park CA 94025-3496. **Tel** (415)328-3123, FAX (415)321-4457. **ED** Ramesh Patil. Index available. **Bk Rev**, (Qty: 8-15). **Ad Acc, Adv Mgr:** Mike Hamilton, **Tel** (415)853-0197. **Circ:** 12,000 (ctrl). available on microfilm and microfiche from University Microfilms International (UMI). Documents available from Article Express International, The Genuine Article, Ask*IEEE.
Desc: Disseminates articles representing the current trends in artificial intelligence. Articles selected for appeal to the broad spectrum of researchers in artificial intelligence and related areas.
Ind/Abst Abstr. Hum. Comput. Interact.; ACM Guide Comput. Lit.; Appl. Sci. Technol. Index; CompuMath Cit. Index [Full Cov.]; Comput. Lit. Index; Comput. Rev.; Curr. Cit.; Curr. Contents Eng. Comput. Technol.; Eng. Index Annu.; Expand. Acad. Index (1992-); Fluid Abstr., Civil Eng.; Fluid Abstr. Proc. Eng.; FLUIDEX; INSPEC (May 1990-); PsycINFO; Res. Alert [Full Cov.]; Sci. Cit. Index; SCISEARCH; Soc. Sci. Cit. Index [Select. Cov.].

LC Q334 .A517 **ISSN** 1054-8645
DD 006.3/05 US
AI REVIEW OF PRODUCTS, SERVICES, AND RESEARCH. [AI rev. prod. serv. res.]. **Added/Corp** American Association for Artificial Intelligence. **VFOAT** Review of Products, Services, and Research; AI Review. **VAT** Artificial Intelligence Review of Products, Services, and Research. (19??)-. English. American Association for Artificial Intelligence, 445 Burgess Drive, Menlo Park CA 94025-3496. **Tel** (415)328-3123, FAX (415)321-4457. Documents available from Article Express International.
Ind/Abst Ei Page One; Eng. Index Annu. [Select. Cov.].

US
AI SOURCEBOOK: THE AI TRENDS ANNUAL REPORT. (19??)-. English. One time a year. $600.00. Relayer Group, 8232 East Buckskin Road/2nd Floor, Scottsdale AZ 85255. **Tel** (602)585-8587, FAX (602)585-3067. **ED** H Dewquist. Index available.
Desc: Contains discussion of all AI technologies, products, companies, as well as markets and analysis of trends and future projections.

ISSN 0893-6552
DD 658 US
AI TODAY. [AI today.]. **VAT** Artificial Intelligence Today. (1986)-. Periodical. English. Six times a year. $49.95. Yellowstone Information Services, 7 View Road, Elkview WV 25071. **Tel** (304)965-5548. **ED** Roger C. Thibault, Ron Phillips, Jim Golden and Marilyn Windecker. Index available. cum. index. **Bk Rev. Ad Acc. Circ:** 10,000 (ctrl). available on diskette (certain sections on 5 1/4 inch disk).
Desc: The magazine of applied artificial intelligence. Primary topics include expert systems, natural language systems, intelligent databases, robotics, computervision, knowledge acquisition, and speech processing. Hardware coverage includes personal computers, work stations, mini-computers, mainframes, and super computers. Focus is applications of products.

ISSN 8756-7687
DD 338 US
AI TRENDS (MONTHLY). (AI TRENDS.). [AI trends]. **VFOAT** AI Trends Newsletter. **VAT** Artificial Intelligence Trends. Vol. 1, No. 1 (Oct. 1984)-. Periodical. English. Twelve times a year. $295.00 US; $345.00 other. Relayer Group, 8232 East Buckskin Road/2nd Floor, Scottsdale AZ 85255. **Tel** (602)585-8587, FAX (602)585-3067. **ED** H P Newquist. cum. index. **Bk Rev.** ***Continues** Technology Trends Newsletter, 0736-5071.*
Desc: Covers expert systems, natural language software, computer aided instruction, visual recognition, voice recognition, AI computers, fifth generation programs, semiconductor technology, mornmachine interfaces, artificial vision, government activities, corporate profiles, and research and investment activities.
Ind/Abst Abstr. Hum. Comput. Interact.; Comput. Lit. Index.

ISSN 1354-2001
DD 006.3 UK
•**AI WATCH.** [AI Watch]. **VFOAT** Artificial Intelligence Watch. (1994)-. English. Twelve times a year. $675.93. AI Intelligence, PO Box 95, Oxford OX2 7XL United Kingdom. **Tel** 011 44 1865 59872, FAX 011 44 1865 59872. **ED** Alex Goodall. ***Continues** Machine Intelligence News, 0267-0429.*

ISSN 0953-6000
DD 006.3 UK
AIRING EDINBURGH. (AIRING.). [Airing Edinb.]. (1987)-. Periodical. English. Three times a year.
Ind/Abst Abstr. Hum. Comput. Interact.

ISSN 0268-4179
UK
CODEN AISBEJ
AISB QUARTERLY. (AISB QUARTERLY : NEWSLETTER OF THE SOCIETY FOR THE STUDY OF ARTIFICIAL INTELLIGENCE & SIMULATION OF BEHAVIOUR.). [AISB q.]. **Added/Corp** Society for the Study of Artificial Intelligence and Simulation of Behaviour. **VFOAT** A.I.S.B. Quarterly; AISB. **VAT** Artificial Intelligence and Simulation of Behaviour Quarterly; Artificial Intelligence & Simulation of Behaviour Quarterly. (19??)-. Newsletter. English. Four times a year

(Mar., May, Sept., Dec.). $94.11. AISB Administration / Society for the Study of Artificial Intelligence and Simulation of Behaviour, University of Sussex, Falmer, Brighton BN1 9QH United Kingdom. **Tel** 011 44 1273 678448, FAX 011 44 1273 671320. Documents available from Ask*IEEE.
Ind/Abst Curr. Cit.; Ei Page One; INSPEC (Spring 1988-).

ISSN 1012-2443
NE
CCC
CODEN AMAIEC
Pr Rev.

ANNALS OF MATHEMATICS AND OF ARTIFICIAL INTELLIGENCE. Vol. 1, No. 1/4 (Sept. 1990)-. Periodical. English. Two times a year. $582.51. Baltzer Science Publishers BV, Asterweg 1A, 1031 HL Amsterdam Netherlands. **Tel** 011 31 20 6370061, FAX 011 31 20 6323651. Documents available from Ask*IEEE.
Ind/Abst Curr. Cit.; Ei Page One; INSPEC (Jan. 1991-); Math. Rev.

LC TL797 .W67a
DD 629.47/4 US

ANNUAL WORKSHOP ON SPACE OPERATIONS APPLICATIONS AND RESEARCH (SOAR ...). **See** Aeronautics, Astronautics.

ISSN 1019-0716
US

APPLICATIONS OF ARTIFICIAL INTELLIGENCE: KNOWLEDGE-BASED SYSTEMS. **Added/Corp** Society of Photo-Optical Instrumentation Engineers. (1992)-. English. $57.00 (members), $76.00 other. International Society for Optical Engineering, PO Box 10, Bellingham WA 98227-0010. **Tel** (360)676-3290, FAX (360)647-1445, telex 46-7053. **ED** U.M. Fayyad and R. Uthurusamy. ***Continues in part*** *Applications of Artificial Intelligence, 0893-9810.*

LC Q334 .A677 **ISSN** 0883-9514
DD 006 US
CCC
CODEN AAINEH

APPLIED ARTIFICIAL INTELLIGENCE. [Appl. artif. intell.]. Vol. 1, No. 1 (1987)-. Periodical. English. Six times a year. $325.00. Taylor & Francis Ltd. / UK, Rankine Road, Basingstoke, Hampshire RG24 8PR United Kingdom. **Tel** 011 44 1256 840366, FAX 011 44 1256 479438, telex 858540. **(Subscription address:** Taylor & Francis Inc., 1900 Frost Road, Suite 101, Bristol PA 19007-1598. **Tel** (215)785-5800, (800)821-8312, FAX (215)785-5515.**)** **ED** Robert Trappl (editor's address: Austrian Research Institute for Artificial Intelligence, Schottengasse 3, 1010 Vienna Austria). Index available. **Bk Rev. Ad Acc. Circ:** 1,000. available on microfilm and microfiche from University Microfilms International (UMI). Documents available from Article Express International, The Genuine Article, Ask*IEEE.
Desc: This current, solidly researched material spans the uses of expert systems, evaluations of existing AI systems and tools, theoretical research relevant to potential applications, and coverage of economic, social, and cultural impacts of AI.
Ind/Abst Abstr. Hum. Comput. Interact.; ACM Guide Comput. Lit.; CompuMath Cit. Index [Full Cov.]; Comput. Abstr.; Comput. Rev.; Curr. Cit.; Eng. Index Annu.; Ergon. Abstr.; INSPEC (1987-); Res. Alert [Full Cov.]; Soc. Sci. Cit. Index [Select. Cov.].

ISSN 0924-669X
NE
CCC
CODEN APITE4
Pr Rev.

APPLIED INTELLIGENCE. (1991)-. Periodical. English. Four times a year. $312.00. Kluwer Academic Publishers, Postbus 322, 3300 AH Dordrecht The Netherlands. **Tel** 011 31 78 524400, FAX 011 31 78 183273, telex 20083. **ED** Moonis Ali. **Acid Free.** available on microfilm and microfiche from University Microfilms International (UMI). Documents available from Ask*IEEE.
Desc: Focus is on research in artificial intelligence and neural networks. The journal adresses issues involving solutions of real-life manufacturing, defense, management, government and industrial problems which are too complex to be solved through conventional approaches and which require the simulation of intelligent thought processes, heuristics, applications of knowledge, and distributed and parallel processing.
Ind/Abst INSPEC (1991-); Zentralbl. Math. Ihre Grenzgeb.

DD 629.8/05 PL

ARCHIVES OF CONTROL SCIENCES. **See** Computers-Automation.

LC Q335 .A785 **ISSN** 0004-3702
DD 001.5/35/05 NE
CCC
NLM W1 AR955K **CODEN** AINTBB
Pr Rev.

ARTIFICIAL INTELLIGENCE. [Artif. intell.]. Vol. 1 (Spring 1970)-. Academic Scholarly Publication. English. Sixteen times a year (8 volumes). $1976.00. Elsevier Science Publishers BV, PO Box 211, 1000 AE Amsterdam Netherlands. **Tel** 011 31 20 4853641, 011 31 20 4853642, FAX 011 31 20 4853598. **ED** Daniel G Bobrow and M Brady. available on microfilm and microfiche from University Microfilms International (UMI); available on an online database from Elsevier Electronic Subscriptions (EES). Documents available from Article Express International, The Genuine Article, Ask*IEEE.
Desc: Studies and reports on the learning of heuristics, scene analysis, induction, heuristic search, theorem-proving, artificial paranoia, reasoning by analogy protocol analysis, sentence comprehension, robot planning, question answering, interpretation of imperfect line data, chess programs, etc.
Ind/Abst Abstr. Hum. Comput. Interact.; ACM Guide Comput. Lit.; Appl. Sci. Technol. Index; Bioeng. Abstr.; CompuMath Cit. Index [Full Cov.]; Comput. Abstr.; Comput. Inf. Syst. Abstr. J. [Full Cov.]; Comput. Rev.; Curr. Cit.; Curr. Contents Eng. Comput. Technol.; Curr. Contents Soc. Behav. Sci.; Ei Page One; Elect. Comm. Abstr.; Eng. Index Annu.; GeoRef; Inf. Sci. Abstr. [Full Cov.]; INSPEC (Spring 1971-); Linguist. Lang. Behav. Abstr.; Manuf. Process Eng. Abstr.; Math. Rev.; Oper. Res./Manage. Sci.; Res. Alert [Full Cov.]; Sci. Cit. Index; SCISEARCH; Soc. Plann. Policy Dev. Abstr.; Soc. Sci. Cit. Index [Full Cov.]; Sociol. Abstr.; Zentralbl. Math. Ihre Grenzgeb.

UK

ARTIFICIAL INTELLIGENCE. (19??)-. English. Four times a year. $175.00. Pineridge Press Limited, 54 Newton Road, Mumbles Swansea SA3 4BQ United Kingdom.
Desc: Directed at reporting recent developments in artificial intelligence, including theoretical models and industrial applications, CAD/CAM, expert systems, modelling programming, interfacing, etc.

ISSN 0924-8463
NE
CCC
CODEN AINLEO
Pr Rev.

ARTIFICIAL INTELLIGENCE AND LAW. **VFOAT** AI and Law; AI & Law. Vol. 1, No. 1 (1992)-. Periodical. English. Four times a year. $258.00. Kluwer Academic Publishers, Postbus 322, 3300 AH Dordrecht The Netherlands. **Tel** 011 31 78 524400, FAX 011 31 78 183273, telex 20083. **ED** Donald H. Berman and Carole Hafner. **Bk Rev. Acid Free.** available on microfilm and microfiche from University Microfilms International (UMI).
Desc: The scope of the journal is as follows: theoretical or empirical studies in artificial intelligence, cognitive psychology, jurisprudence, linguistics, or philosophy which addresses the development of formal or computational models of legal knowledge, reasoning, and decision making; in-depth studies of innovative artificial intelligence systems that are being used in the legal domain; and studies which address the ethical and social implications of the field.

LC TA174 .A78 **ISSN** 0890-0604
DD 620/.00425/028563 UK
CCC
CODEN AIEMEG

ARTIFICIAL INTELLIGENCE FOR ENGINEERING DESIGN, ANALYSIS AND MANUFACTURING. (ARTIFICIAL INTELLIGENCE FOR ENGINEERING DESIGN, ANALYSIS AND MANUFACTURING : AIEDAM.). [Artif. intell. eng. des. anal. manuf.]. **VFOAT** AI EDAM; AIEDAM. Vol. 1, No. 1 (1987)-. Academic Scholarly Publication. English. Five times a year. $210.00. Cambridge University Press, The Edinburgh Building, Shaftesbury Road, Cambridge CB2 2RU United Kingdom. **Tel** 011 44 1223 312393, FAX 011 44 1223 315052, telex 851-817256. **(Subscription address:** Cambridge University Press / North America, 110 Midland Avenue, Port Chester NY 10573. **Tel** (800)431-1580, (914)937-9600.**)** **ED** Clive L. Dym. Documents available from Ask*IEEE.
Desc: A forum that is set for engineers and designers who see the leverage that artificial intelligence (AI) technologies can bring to bear on difficult engineering problems; and for researchers in artificial intelligence and computer science who are interested in applications.
Ind/Abst CompuMath Cit. Index [Full Cov.]; Curr. Cit.; INSPEC (1989-); Soc. Sci. Cit. Index [Select. Cov.].

LC TA345 .I569 **ISSN** 0954-1810
DD 620/.00285/63 UK
CCC
CODEN AIENEJ
Pr Rev.

ARTIFICIAL INTELLIGENCE IN ENGINEERING. [Artif. intell. eng.]. Vol. 4, No. 1 (Jan. 1989)-. Academic Scholarly Publication. English. Four times a year. $374.00. Elsevier Applied Science, An Imprint of Elsevier Science Ltd., The Boulevard, Langford Lane, Kidlington, Oxford OX5 1GB United Kingdom. **Tel** 011 44 1865 843000, 011 44 1865 843699, FAX 011 44 1865 843010. **(Subscription address:** Elsevier Science Ltd. / Oxford Fulfillment Centre, PO Box 800, Kidlington OX5 1DX United Kingdom. **Tel** 011 44 865 843355.**)** available on an online database from Elsevier Electronic Subscriptions (EES). Documents available from Article Express International, Ask*IEEE. ***Continues*** *International Journal for Artificial Intelligence in Engineering, 0267-9264.*
Ind/Abst Curr. Cit.; Eng. Index Annu.; Fluid Abstr., Civil Eng.; Fluid Abstr. Proc. Eng.; FLUIDEX; INSPEC (Jan. 1989-); Int. Civil Eng. Abstr.; Soft. Abstr. Eng.

ISSN 0933-3657
NE
CCC
NLM W1; AR955S **CODEN** AIMEEW
Pr Rev.

ARTIFICIAL INTELLIGENCE IN MEDICINE. [Artif. intell. med.]. **VFOAT** AIM. Vol. 1 No. 1 (1989)-. Academic Scholarly Publication. English. Six times a year (1 volume). $293.00. Elsevier Science Publishers BV, PO Box 211, 1000 AE Amsterdam Netherlands. **Tel** 011 31 20 4853641, 011 31 20 4853642, FAX 011 31 20 4853598. **ED** K S Zadeh. **Bk Rev. Ad Acc.** available on an online database from Elsevier Electronic Subscriptions (EES). Documents available from Article Express International, The Genuine Article, Ask*IEEE.
Desc: Publishes original articles from a variety of interdisciplinary perspectives, particularly concerning intelligent databases, medical knowledge engineering, AI-based clinical decision-making, books and libraries, intelligent devices and instruments, and medical artificial intelligence tools.
Ind/Abst Comput. Inf. Syst. Abstr. J. [Full Cov.]; Curr. Cit.; EMBASE; Eng. Index Annu.; Index Med.; INSPEC (1989-); Res. Alert [Full Cov.]; Soc. Sci. Cit. Index [Select. Cov.].

LC Q334 .A8 **ISSN** 0269-2821
DD 006.3 UK
CCC
CODEN AIRVE6
Pr Rev.

ARTIFICIAL INTELLIGENCE REVIEW, THE. [Artif. intell. rev.]. Vol. 1, No. 1 (July 1986)-. Periodical. English. Six times a year. $338.00. Kluwer Academic Publishers, Postbus 322, 3300 AH Dordrecht The Netherlands. **Tel** 011 31 78 524400, FAX 011 31 78 183273, telex 20083. **ED** Masoud Yazdani. **Acid Free.** available on microfilm and microfiche from University Microfilms International (UMI). Documents available from Article Express International, The Genuine Article, Ask*IEEE.
Desc: This scholarly publication offers multiple perspectives on significant developments in artificial intelligence, cognitive science and related disciplines. It illustrates the variety of styles and points of view which characterizes research in this important field of scientific discovery.
Ind/Abst Abstr. Hum. Comput. Interact. (1987-); CompuMath Cit. Index [Full Cov.]; Comput. Abstr.; Curr. Cit.; Curr. Contents Eng. Comput. Technol.; Educ. Technol. Abstr. (1987-); Eng. Index Annu. [Select. Cov.]; INSPEC (1987-); Res. Alert [Full Cov.]; SCISEARCH; Soc. Sci. Cit. Index [Select. Cov.]; Zentralbl. Math. Ihre Grenzgeb.

ISSN 0272-1686
US

ARTIFICIAL INTELLIGENCE SERIES, THE. [Artif. intell. ser.]. Monographic series. English. Price varies per volume. John Wiley & Sons, Inc., 605 Third Avenue, New York NY 10158-0012. **Tel** (212)850-6000, (212)850-6645, FAX (212)850-6088, telex 12-7063. **(Subscription address:** John Wiley & Sons / UK, Baffins Lane, Chichester, West Sussex PO19 1UD United Kingdom. **Tel** 011 44 1243 779777, FAX 011 44 243 776128, telex 86290 WIBOOKG.**)**

LC QH324.2 .A74 **ISSN** 1064-5462
DD 574/.01/13 US
CCC
NLM W1; AR955TM **CODEN** ARLIEY

●**ARTIFICIAL LIFE.** **See** Biology.

LC Q300 **ISSN** 0929-5593
DD 003 NE
Pr Rev. **CCC**

●**AUTONOMOUS ROBOTS.** Vol. 1, No. 1 (1994)-. Academic Scholarly Publication. English. Four times a year. Kluwer Academic Publishers, Postbus 322, 3300 AH Dordrecht The Netherlands. **Tel** 011 31 78 524400, FAX 011 31 78 183273, telex 20083.

LC HD9744.E433 U62 **ISSN** 1071-1317
DD 355 US
CCC

●**C4I NEWS.** [Cp4sl news]. **VFOAT** C 4 I News; C Four I News. **VAT** Command, Control, Communications, Computers, and Intelligence News. (1993)-. Periodical. English. Twenty-five times a year. $595.00. Phillips Business Information Inc., 1201 Seven Locks Road, PO

Box 61130, Potomac MD 20854. **Tel** (301)424-3338, (301)340-1520, (800)777-5005, FAX (301)424-4297, telex 358149.

ISSN 0823-9339
DD 001.53/5/05 CN

CANADIAN ARTIFICIAL INTELLIGENCE NEWSLETTER. [Can. artif. intell.]. **VFOAT** Intelligence Artificielle au Canada; Intelligence Artificial Intelligence Newsletter; Newsletter. No. 1 (Sept. 1984)-. Newsletter. English (French). Four times a year. Free to members. CSCSI/SCEIO, c/o Canadian Information Processing Society Canada. Documents available from Ask*IEEE. ***Continues*** *Newsletter (Canadian Society for Computational Studies of Intelligence), 0828-685X.*
Ind/Abst Abstr. Hum. Comput. Interact.; INSPEC (July 1989-).

ISSN 0773-4182
BE

CC AI. VFOAT CC-AI; CCAI; Communication and Cognition, Artificial Intelligence. (1985)- Periodical. English (French and German). Four times a year (Mar., July, Aug., Dec.). $145.52. Communication & Cognition, Blandijnberg 2, Dr Vandamme, B-9000 Ghent Belgium. **Tel** 11 32 91 643952, FAX (32) 91 24 16 21. **ED** F. Vandamme. Index available (Last iss.). **Bk Rev. Ad Acc, Adv Mgr:** Yves Devlieher, **Tel** 32 9 264 39 52. **Circ:** 300 (ctrl). available on diskette.
Desc: For the integrated study of artificial intelligence, cognitive science, and applied epistemology. Covers techniques of AI as enriched by research in such fields as mathematics, linguistics, logic, epistemology and the cognitive sciences and biology.
Ind/Abst Abstr. Hum. Comput. Interact.

LC BF311 .C552 **ISSN** 0364-0213
DD 155.4/05 US
CCC
NLM W1 CO107T **CODEN** COGSD5
Pr Rev.

COGNITIVE SCIENCE. [Cogn. sci.]. Vol. 1 (Jan. 1977)-. Periodical. English. Four times a year. $165.00. Ablex Publishing Corporation, 355 Chestnut Street, Norwood NJ 07648. **Tel** (201)767-8450, (201)767-8455 (Customer Service), FAX (201)767-6717. **ED** Martin Ringle. Index available. cum. index. **Bk Rev. Ad Acc. Circ:** 2,000. Documents available from The Genuine Article, BIOSIS Document Express, Ask*IEEE, UMI Article Clearinghouse. ***Absorbed*** *Cognition and Brain Theory, 0193-5488.*
Desc: This journal provides a timely flow of information in the field of cognitive science.
Ind/Abst Abstr. Anthropol. (19??-); Abstr. Hum. Comput. Interact.; Biol. Abstr.; Curr. Cit.; Curr. Contents Soc. Behav. Sci.; EMBASE; Ergon. Abstr.; Expand. Acad. Index (1992-); INSPEC (1987-); Int. Bibliogr. Sociol.; Linguist. Lang. Behav. Abstr.; Math. Rev.; MLA Int. Bibl. Books Artic. Mod. Lang. Lit.; Newsp. Period. Abstr. (1992-); Psychol. Abstr. (1977-); PsycINFO; PsycLit; Res. Alert [Full Cov.]; Soc. Plann. Policy Dev. Abstr.; Soc. Sci. Cit. Index [Full Cov.]; Sociol. Abstr.

US

COGNIZER REPORT. English. $125.00 North America; $165.00 other. Frontline Strategies, 516 Southeast, Chkalov Drive, Suite 164, Vancouver WA 98684. **Tel** (201)892-5880. **ED** Martin Middlewood. Index available. **Bk Rev. Circ:** 100. ***Continues*** *Neural Networks Today.*
Desc: Devoted to covering advanced computing topics, including neural networks, fuzzy logic, genetic algorithms, artificial life, etc. Also provides timely network application coverage in plain English.

UK

COMLINE INDUSTRIAL REPORT SERIES. ROBOTICS. English. Twelve times a year. £410.00. MicroInfo Ltd., PO Box 3, Omega Park, Alton Hampshire GU34 2PG United Kingdom. **Tel** 011 44 1420 86848, FAX 011 44 1420 89889, telex 858431 MINFO G.

LC Q334 .C65 **ISSN** 0824-7935
DD 006.3/05 CN
CCC
CODEN COMIE6
Pr Rev.

COMPUTATIONAL INTELLIGENCE. [Comput. intell.]. **Added/Corp** National Research Council Canada. **VFOAT** Comput. Intell. Vol. 1, No. 1 (Feb. 1985)-. Periodical. English (French). Four times a year. $259.00. Blackwell Publishers, 238 Main Street, Cambridge MA 02142. **Tel** (617)547-7110, (800)835-6770, FAX (617)547-0789. **ED** N Cercone and G McCalla. Index available. **Ad Acc. Circ:** 800. available on microfilm from University Microfilms International (UMI). Documents available from Ask*IEEE.
Desc: Publishes high-quality theoretical and experimental research papers in computational intelligence.
Ind/Abst Abstr. Hum. Comput. Interact. ACM Guide Comput. Lit.; Comput. Abstr.; Comput. Rev.; Curr. Cit.; INSPEC (1987-).

ISSN 0232-0274
XO

COMPUTERS AND ARTIFICIAL INTELLIGENCE. Added/Corp Ustav Technickej Kibernetiky SAV. **VFOAT** Vychislitelnye Mashiny i Iskusstvennyi Intellekt. (1982)-. Periodical. English (Russian). Six times a year. DM490.00. Slovenska Akademia Vied / Slovak Academy of Sciences, PO Box 57, 81005 Bratislava Slovakia. **Tel** 011 42 7 3782715, 011 42 7 3782925, FAX 011 42 7 496849, telex 93261. **(Subscription address:** Kubon & Sagner, ABT Zeitschriftenimport, D 80328 Munich Germany. **Tel** 011 49 89 54218130.) Documents available from The Genuine Article, Ask*IEEE.
Ind/Abst Abstr. Hum. Comput. Interact.; ACM Guide Comput. Lit.; CompuMath Cit. Index [Full Cov.]; Comput. Abstr.; Comput. Rev.; Curr. Cit.; Curr. Contents Eng. Comput. Technol.; Ei Page One; INSPEC (1984-); Math. Rev.; Res. Alert [Full Cov.]; SCISEARCH; Zentralbl. Math. Ihre Grenzgeb.

LC QA76.87 .C66 **ISSN** 0954-0091
DD 004 UK
CCC
NLM W1; CO727J **CODEN** CNTSEU

CONNECTION SCIENCE. [Connect. sci.]. Vol. 1, No. 1 (1989)-. Periodical. English. Four times a year (Mar., June, Sept., Dec.). $442.00. Carfax Publishing Company, PO Box 25, Abingdon, Oxfordshire OX14 3UE United Kingdom. **Tel** 011 44 1235 555335, FAX 011 44 1235 553559, telex 817484. **ED** Noel. E. Sharkey. Index available. cum. index. available on microfiche. Documents available from Ask*IEEE.
Desc: Covers current connectionist issues in human and artificial intelligence, cognitive science, computational neuroscience and advanced computer science.
Ind/Abst Acad. Search; Bus. Source Plus; Bus. Source; Curr. Cit.; EP Collect.; Ergon. Abstr.; Homework Help.; INSPEC (1989-); Linguist. Lang. Behav. Abstr.; MasterFile FullTEXT 1000; MasterFile FullTEXT 350; MasterFile FullTEXT 650; MasterFile FullTEXT (July 1994-); Soc. Plann. Policy Dev. Abstr.; Sociol. Abstr.; Telebase.

ISSN 1061-3099
DD 003 US
CCC

CYBEREDGE JOURNAL. [Cyberedge j.]. (1991)-. Periodical. English. Six times a year. $249.00. CyberEdge Journal, #1 Gate Six Road, Suite G, Sausalito CA 94965. **Tel** (415)331-3343, FAX (415)331-3643. **ED** Ben Delaney. **Bk Rev**, (Qty: 10-15). **Ad Acc. Circ:** 3,000.

ISSN 1079-2694
DD 006 US

•**CYBEREDGE JOURNAL'S VIRTUAL REALITY PRODUCTS.** [CyberEdge j. virtual real. prod.]. Vol. 1, No. 1 (Nov./Dec. 1994)-. English. Six times a year. $14.95. Delaney Companies / Cyberedge Journal, 1 Gate Six Road, Suite G, Sausalito CA 94965. **Tel** (415)331-3343.

US

ELECTRONIC HOUSE : INTELLIGENCE REPORT. (19??)-. English. Twelve times a year. $249.00. Electronic House, Inc., PO Box 339, Stillwater OK 74076. **Tel** (405)624-8015, FAX (405)743-3374. **ED** Lisa Montgomery. **Ad Acc, Adv Mgr:** Steve Gragert. ctrl circ.

LC QA76.9.H85 **ISSN** 1081-3055
DD 302 US

•**ELECTRONIC JOURNAL ON VIRTUAL CULTURE.** (ELECTRONIC JOURNAL ON VIRTUAL CULTURE [COMPUTER FILE].). [Electron. j. virtual cult.]. **VFOAT** EJVC. Vol. 3, No. 1 (Feb. 5, 1995)-. Periodical. English. Twelve times a year. Free. EJVC, 961 South Lincoln Street, Kent OH 44240. **ED** E Stepp (editor's address: Marshall University, Huntington, WV 25755-2440). available via Internet (message listserv@kentvm.kent.edu, SUBSCRIBE EJVC-L). ***Continues*** *Arachnet Electronic Journal on Virtual Culture, 1068-5723.*
Desc: Provides news and information on virtual culture. Encourages scholarly thought and research.

LC TA345 .E5346 **ISSN** 0952-1976
DD 620/.00285/63 UK
CCC
CODEN EAAIE6

ENGINEERING APPLICATIONS OF ARTIFICIAL INTELLIGENCE. **See** Engineering-Computer Applications.

LC QA76.76.E95 E973 **ISSN** 0266-4720
DD 006.3/3 UK
CCC
CODEN EXSYEX

EXPERT SYSTEMS. [Expert syst.]. Vol. 1, No. 1 (July 1984)-. Periodical. English. Four times a year. $132.00. Learned Information Ltd., Woodside Hinksey Hill, Oxford OX1 5AU United Kingdom. **Tel** 011 44 1865 730275, FAX 011 44 1865 736354, telex 23667. **(Subscription address:** Information Today, 143 Old Marlton Pike, Medford NJ 08055-8750. **Tel** (609)654-6266, FAX (609)654-4309.) **ED** Ian F. Croall, Geneva L. Henry, Mitsori Ishizuka. available on microfilm and microfiche from University Microfilms International (UMI). Documents available from Article Express International, Ask*IEEE.
Desc: Contains articles about the basic principles of expert systems and related areas. Features the latest developments in connected fields such as fifth generation computing and knowledge engineering - developing working systems from the knowledge of human instructors. Provides news about products and services, developments in the technical and applied aspects of expert systems, etc.
Ind/Abst Abstr. Hum. Comput. Interact.; Comput. Abstr.; Contents Pages Manage.; Curr. Cit.; Ei Page One; Eng. Index Annu.; HILITES; Inf. Sci. Abstr.; INSPEC (July 1984-); Microcomput. Abstr. (Feb. 1989-).

UK
CODEN ESBUE3
CEASED

EXPERT SYSTEMS AI IN BUSINESS. VFOAT Expert Systems/AI; Expert Systems AI in Business. **VAT** Expert Systems Artificial Intelligence in Business. Vol. 1, No. 1 (June 1987)-(19??). Periodical. English. Learned Information Ltd., Woodside Hinksey Hill, Oxford OX1 5AU United Kingdom. **Tel** 011 44 1865 730275, FAX 011 44 1865 736354, telex 23667.
Ind/Abst Abstr. Hum. Comput. Interact. (19??-19??).

LC QA76.76.E95 E9767 **ISSN** 0953-5551
DD 658.4/038/0285633 UK
CODEN ESIMEE
TITLE CHANGE

EXPERT SYSTEMS FOR INFORMATION MANAGEMENT. [Expert syst. inf. manag.]. Vol. 1, No. 1 (Spring 1988)-(19??). Periodical. English. Taylor Graham Publishing, 500 Chesham House, 150 Regent Street, London W1R 5FA United Kingdom. **Bk Rev. Ad Acc.** Documents available from Ask*IEEE. ***Continued by*** *International Journal of Applied Expert Systems.*
Ind/Abst Abstr. Hum. Comput. Interact.; ACM Guide Comput. Lit.; Comput. Rev.; Curr. Cit.; INSPEC (1988-).

UK
TITLE CHANGE

EXPERT SYSTEMS USER. Vol. 2, No. 10 (1987)-(1994). English. IML Group, Blair House, 184-186 High Street, Tonbridge Kent, TN9 1BQ United Kingdom. **Tel** 011 44 1732 359990, FAX 011 44 1732 770049. Documents available from Ask*IEEE. ***Continued by*** *Expert Systems Applications.*
Ind/Abst Abstr. Hum. Comput. Interact.; INSPEC (Nov. 1985-).

LC QA76.76.E95 E986 **ISSN** 0957-4174
DD 006.3/3 US
CCC
CODEN ESAPEH

EXPERT SYSTEMS WITH APPLICATIONS. [Expert syst. appl.]. Vol. 1, No. 1 (1990)-. Periodical. English. Eight times a year. $1164.00. Pergamon Press, An Imprint of Elsevier Science Ltd., The Boulevard, Langford Lane, Kidlington, Oxford OX5 1GB United Kingdom. **Tel** 011 44 1865 843000, 011 44 1865 843699, FAX 011 44 1865 843010. **(Subscription address:** Elsevier Science Ltd. / Oxford Fulfillment Centre, PO Box 800, Kidlington OX5 1DX United Kingdom. **Tel** 011 44 865 843355.) **ED** Jay Liebowitz. available on microfilm and microfiche from University Microfilms International (UMI); available on an online database from Elsevier Electronic Subscriptions (EES). Documents available from Article Express International, The Genuine Article, Ask*IEEE.
Ind/Abst ACM Guide Comput. Lit.; Civ. Struct. Eng. Abstr.; CompuMath Cit. Index [Full Cov.]; Comput. Inf. Syst. Abstr. J. [Full Cov.]; Comput. Rev.; Curr. Cit.; Curr. Contents Eng. Comput. Technol.; Ei Page One; Elect. Comm. Abstr.; Eng. Index Annu.; Environ. Eng. Abstr.; HILITES; INSPEC (1990-); Int. Aerosp. Abstr. (1991-); Manuf. Process Eng. Abstr.; Mech. Eng. Abstr.; Res. Alert [Full Cov.]; Risk Abstr.; SCISEARCH; Soc. Sci. Cit. Index [Select. Cov.]; Solid State Supercond. Abstr.

LC Q334 **ISSN** 1059-6119
DD 006 US
CEASED

FREELANCE GRAPHICS REPORT, THE. (1992)-(Sept. 1993). Periodical. English. Lotus Publishing, 77 Franklin Street 320, Boston MA 02110. **Tel** (617)482-8470, (800)234-1089.

ISSN 1189-6078
DD 006.3 CN
SUSPENDED

ICO. INTELLIGENCE ARTIFICIELLE ET SCIENCES COGNITIVES AU QUEBEC. (ICO.). [ICO, Intell. artif. sci. cogn. Que.]. **VFOAT** Intelligence Artificielle et Sciences Cognitives au Quebec; ICO Quebec. (19??)-Suspended (19??). Periodical. French. Three times a year (Feb., May, Oct.). 116.00 Can$ Canada; 126.00Can$ US; 140.00Can$ other (libraries); 100.00Can$ Canada; 110.00Can$ US; 140.00Can$ other. GIRICO, 276 rue St Jacques, Bureau 912, Montreal Quebec, H3B 3G1 Canada. **Tel** (514)985-5459, FAX (514)985-2720. **ED** Ghislain Levesque. **Bk Rev**, (Qty: 3). **Ad Acc. Circ:** 1,000.
Desc: Research and development review in the domain of cognitive and computer science.
Ind/Abst Repere (1991-).

DD 629 ISSN 1070-9932 US

•IEEE ROBOTICS AND AUTOMATION MAGAZINE. [IEEE robot. autom. mag.]. **Added/Corp** Institute of Electrical and Electronics Engineers. **VFOAT** Robotics & Automation; Robotics and Automation. **VAT** Institute of Electrical and Electronics Engineers Robotics & Automation. (1994)-. Periodical. English. Four times a year. $75.00. IEEE / Institute of Electrical and Electronics Engineers Inc., 345 East 47th Street, New York NY 10017-2394. **Tel** (908)981-1393, FAX (908)981-9667. **(Subscription address:** IEEE / Institute of Electrical and Electronics Engineers, 445 Hoes Lane, PO Box 1331, Piscataway NJ 08855-1331. **Tel** (800)701-IEEE, (908)981-0060, FAX (908)981-9667, telex 833233.**) ED** Michael Leahy.
Desc: Deals with prototyping, demonstration and evaluation, and commercialization of robotic and automation technology and systems. Serves as a forum for the application of theory to real-world systems, with an emphasis on implementation.

DD 006 ISSN 1045-9227 US CCC CODEN ITNNEP

IEEE TRANSACTIONS ON NEURAL NETWORKS. (IEEE TRANSACTIONS ON NEURAL NETWORKS.). [IEEE trans. neural netw.]. **Added/Corp** IEEE Neural Networks Council. **VFOAT** Transactions on Neural Networks. **VAT** Institute of Electrical and Electronics Engineers Transactions on Neural Networks. Vol. 1 No. 1 (Mar. 1990)-. Periodical. English. Six times a year. $360.00. IEEE / Institute of Electrical and Electronics Engineers Inc., 345 East 47th Street, New York NY 10017-2394. **Tel** (908)981-1393, FAX (908)981-9667. **(Subscription address:** IEEE / Institute of Electrical and Electronics Engineers, 445 Hoes Lane, PO Box 1331, Piscataway NJ 08855-1331. **Tel** (800)701-IEEE, (908)981-0060, FAX (908)981-9667, telex 833233.**)** Documents available from Article Express International, The Genuine Article, Ask*IEEE.
Desc: Devoted to the science and technology of neural networks, which disclose significant technical knowledge, exploratory developments, and applications of neural networks from biology to software to hardware. Emphasis is on artificial neural networks.
Ind/Abst Appl. Sci. Technol. Index (1991-); CompuMath Cit. Index [Full Cov.]; Comput. Abstr.; Comput. Inf. Syst. Abstr. J. [Full Cov.]; Curr. Cit.; Curr. Contents Eng. Comput. Technol.; Ei Page One; Elect. Comm. Abstr.; Eng. Index Annu.; Expand. Acad. Index (1992-); Index IEEE Publ.; INSPEC (March 1990-); Int. Aerosp. Abstr.; Res. Alert [Full Cov.]; Sci. Cit. Index; SCISEARCH; Soc. Sci. Cit. Index [Select. Cov.].

LC Q327 .I19 ISSN 0162-8828
DD 006.42 US CCC CODEN ITPIDJ
Pr Rev.

IEEE TRANSACTIONS ON PATTERN ANALYSIS AND MACHINE INTELLIGENCE. [IEEE trans. pattern anal. mach. intell.]. **Added/Corp** IEEE Computer Society. Institute of Electrical and Electronics Engineers. **VAT** Institute of Electrical and Electronics Engineers Transactions on Pattern Analysis and Machine Intelligence. Vol. PAMI-1 (Jan. 1979)-. Periodical. English. Twelve times a year. $475.00. IEEE / Institute of Electrical and Electronics Engineers Inc., 345 East 47th Street, New York NY 10017-2394. **Tel** (908)981-1393, FAX (908)981-9667. **(Subscription address:** IEEE / Institute of Electrical and Electronics Engineers, 445 Hoes Lane, PO Box 1331, Piscataway NJ 08855-1331. **Tel** (800)701-IEEE, (908)981-0060, FAX (908)981-9667, telex 833233.**) ED** Theo Pavlidis. Index available. available on microfiche. Documents available from Article Express International, The Genuine Article, Ask*IEEE.
Desc: Contains technical research papers on image processing, computer vision, robotics, speech recognition, natural language understanding, expert systems, knowledge representation, inference, and search strategies.
Ind/Abst Abstr. Hum. Comput. Interact.; ACM Guide Comput. Lit.; Appl. Sci. Technol. Index (1991-); Bioeng. Abstr.; CompuMath Cit. Index [Full Cov.]; Comput. Abstr.; Comput. Inf. Syst. Abstr. J. [Full Cov.]; Comput. Rev.; Curr. Cit.; Curr. Contents Eng. Comput. Technol.; Ei Page One; Elect. Comm. Abstr.; Eng. Index Annu.; Expand. Acad. Index (1992-); GeoRef; Index IEEE Publ.; Inf. Sci. Abstr.; INSPEC (Jan. 1979-); Int. Aerosp. Abstr.; Mech. Eng. Abstr.; Pollut. Abstr. Indexes; Res. Alert [Full Cov.]; Robotics Abstr.; Sci. Cit. Index; SCISEARCH; Soc. Sci. Cit. Index [Select. Cov.]; Zentralbl. Math. Ihre Grenzgeb.

LC TJ210.2 .I33 ISSN 1042-296X
DD 628.8/92/05 US CCC CODEN IRAUEZ
Pr Rev.

IEEE TRANSACTIONS ON ROBOTICS AND AUTOMATION. (IEEE TRANSACTIONS ON ROBOTICS AND AUTOMATION : A PUBLICATION OF THE IEEE ROBOTICS AND AUTOMATION SOCIETY.). [IEEE trans. robot. autom.]. **Added/Corp** Institute of Electrical and Electronics Engineers. IEEE Robotics and Automation Society. **VAT** Institute of Electrical and Electronics Engineers Transactions on Robotics and Automation. Vol. 5, No. 1 (Feb. 1989)-. Periodical. English. Six times a year. $195.00. IEEE / Institute of Electrical and Electronics Engineers Inc., 345 East 47th Street, New York NY 10017-2394. **Tel** (908)981-1393, FAX (908)981-9667. **(Subscription address:** IEEE / Institute of Electrical and Electronics Engineers, 445 Hoes Lane, PO Box 1331, Piscataway NJ 08855-1331. **Tel** (800)701-IEEE, (908)981-0060, FAX (908)981-9667, telex 833233.**)** available on microfilm from the publisher. Documents available from Article Express International, The Genuine Article, Ask*IEEE. ***Continues*** *IEEE Journal of Robotics and Automation, 0882-4967.*
Desc: Covers theory and applications in robot dynamics and control.
Ind/Abst CompuMath Cit. Index [Full Cov.]; Comput. Abstr.; Comput. Inf. Syst. Abstr. J. [Full Cov.]; Curr. Cit.; Curr. Contents Eng. Comput. Technol.; Ei Page One; Elect. Comm. Abstr.; Eng. Index Annu.; Index IEEE Publ. (1989-); Inf. Sci. Abstr.; INSPEC (1989-); Int. Aerosp. Abstr.; Manuf. Process Eng. Abstr.; Mech. Eng. Abstr.; Res. Alert [Full Cov.]; Soc. Sci. Cit. Index [Select. Cov.]; Solid State Supercond. Abstr.

LC Q334 .I568a ISSN 1045-0823
DD 006.3 US CCC

IJCAI (UNITED STATES). (IJCAI : PROCEEDINGS OF THE CONFERENCE / SPONSORED BY THE INTERNATIONAL JOINT CONFERENCES ON ARTIFICIAL INTELLIGENCE.). [IJCAI]. **Added/Corp** International Joint Conferences on Artificial Intelligence. **VFOAT** Proceedings of the International Joint Conference on Artificial Intelligence. 5th (1977)-. Proceedings. English. Every 2 years. $75.00. Morgan Kaufmann Publishers, 340 Pine Street, 6th Floor, San Francisco CA 94014. **Tel** (415)578-9911, (800)745-7323. ***Continues*** *International Joint Conference on Artificial Intelligence. Advance Papers of the ... International Joint Conference on Artificial Intelligence.*

DD 006 ISSN 0886-8042 US

IMAGE PROCESSING TECHNOLOGY. [Image process. technol.]. (Jan. 1986)-. Periodical. English. Twelve times a year. $125.00 US; $175.00 other. Robert Griffiths Associates, 110 Brainerd Road/Suite A, Allston MA 02134.

ISSN 0143-991X UK CCC CODEN IDRBAT
Pr Rev.

INDUSTRIAL ROBOT, THE. [Ind. rob.]. Vol. 1 (Sept. 1973)-. Trade Publication. English. Six times a year. $1159.00. MCB University Press, 60 62 Toller Lane, Bradford, West Yorkshire BD8 9BY United Kingdom. **Tel** 011 44 1274 785280, FAX 011 44 1274 785200, telex 51317-MCBUNI-G. **(Subscription address:** MCB University Press / US and Canada Subscriptions, PO Box 10812, Birmingham AL 35201-0812. **Tel** (205)995-1567, (800)633-4931, FAX (205)995-1588.**) ED** Clive Loughlin. **Bk Rev**. Documents available from Article Express International, Ask*IEEE.
Desc: Aimed primarily to keep engineers and directors all over the world fully informed on the latest developments in robotics technology and the increasing contribution robots are making to the growing levels of automation in industry.
Ind/Abst Appl. Sci. Technol. Index; Bioeng. Abstr.; BMT Abstr. (?-199?); Curr. Cit.; Curr. Technol. Index; Ei Page One; Eng. Index Annu.; Expand. Acad. Index (1992-); F&S Index Plus Text, Int. [Select. Cov.]; Fluid Abstr., Civil Eng.; Fluid Abstr. Proc. Eng.; FLUIDEX (1973-); INSPEC (Sept. 1979-); Pollut. Abstr. Indexes; PROMT; Robotics Abstr.; Trade Ind. Index.

UK

•INFORMATION AND COMMUNICATIONS TECHNOLOGY LAW. (1995)-. English. Three times a year. $232.00. Carfax Publishing Company, PO Box 25, Abingdon, Oxfordshire OX14 3UE United Kingdom. **Tel** 011 44 1235 555335, FAX 011 44 1235 553559, telex 817484. ***Continues*** *Law Computers and Artificial Intelligence.*

DD 006 ISSN 1054-8696 US CCC

INTELLIGENT SYSTEMS REPORT. (INTELLIGENT SYSTEMS REPORT : ISR.). [Intell. syst. rep.]. **VFOAT** ISR. Vol. 7, No. 21 (Nov. 1990)-. Periodical. English. Twelve times a year. $299.00. ISR: Intelligent Systems Report, 2555 Cumberland Parkway/Suite 299, Atlanta GA 30339-3908. **Tel** (404)434-2187, FAX (404)432-6969. **ED** David Blanchard. Index Bound in First Issue. **Bk Rev**, (Qty: 12). **Circ:** 500. available on an online database (file 648/Full-Text) from DIALOG. ***Formed by the union of*** *Alweek, 0897-3466* ***and*** *Neural network news, 1051-5410.*
Desc: Provides information on the integration and application of advanced decision - support technologies in a variety of industries.
Ind/Abst Comput. Lit. Index; Trade Ind. ASAP [Full Txt.]; Trade Ind. Index [Full Txt.].

DD 371.334 ISSN 0957-9133 UK CCC CEASED

INTELLIGENT TUTORING MEDIA. [Intell. tutor. media]. **VFOAT** ITM. Intelligent Tutoring Media. (1990)-(1994). Periodical. English. Learned Information Ltd., Woodside Hinksey Hill, Oxford OX1 5AU United Kingdom. **Tel** 011 44 1865 730275, FAX 011 44 1865 736354, telex 23667. Documents available from Ask*IEEE.
Desc: Aims to provide a forum for the communication and packaging of knowledge using advanced information technologies.
Ind/Abst Curr. Cit.; Ergon. Abstr. (19??-19??); HILITES (19??-19??); INSPEC (1990-19??); Microcomput. Abstr. (Feb. 1989-19??).

UK

INTERNATIONAL JOURNAL OF APPLIED EXPERT SYSTEMS. (1993)-. English. Three times a year. $111.00 US; £57.00 other. Taylor Graham Publishing, 500 Chesham House, 150 Regent Street, London W1R 5FA United Kingdom. ***Continues*** *Expert Systems for Information Management.*

LC QA76.76.E95 I577 ISSN 0888-613X
DD 006.3/01/511322 US CCC CODEN IJARE4
Pr Rev.

INTERNATIONAL JOURNAL OF APPROXIMATE REASONING. (INTERNATIONAL JOURNAL OF APPROXIMATE REASONING : OFFICIAL PUBLICATION OF THE NORTH AMERICAN FUZZY INFORMATION PROCESSING SOCIETY.). [Int. j. approx. reason.]. **Added/Corp** North American Fuzzy Information Processing Society. Vol. 1, No. 1 (Jan. 1987)-. Academic Scholarly Publication. English. Eight times a year (2 volumes). $474.00. Elsevier Science Publishing Company Inc, Madison Square Station, PO Box 882, New York NY 10159-0882. **Tel** (212)633-3950, FAX (212)633-3990. **ED** James C Bezdek. **Ad Acc.** available on microfilm and microfiche from University Microfilms International (UMI); available on an online database from Elsevier Electronic Subscriptions (EES). Documents available from Article Express International, Ask*IEEE.
Desc: Represents all theoretical and applied approaches toward approximate reasoning in the design of (artificially) intelligent computer systems.
Ind/Abst ACM Guide Comput. Lit.; Comput. Rev.; Curr. Cit.; Ei Page One; Eng. Index Annu.; INSPEC (1987-); Math. Rev. (1987-); Soc. Plann. Policy Dev. Abstr.; Zentralbl. Math. Ihre Grenzgeb.

SI

•INTERNATIONAL JOURNAL OF COOPERATIVE INFORMATION SYSTEMS. (1995)-. English. Four times a year. $250.00. World Scientific Publishing Company, PO Box 128, Farrer Road, Singapore 9128 Singapore. **Tel** 011 65 3825663, FAX 011 65 3825919, telex RS 28561 WSPC. ***Continues*** *International Journal of Intelligent and Cooperative Information Systems.*
Desc: Provides a forum for presentation and discussion of the potential roles and nature of the emerging notion of Intelligent and Cooperative Information Systems (ICIS).

DD 006 ISSN 0894-9077 US CCC CODEN IJSYED

INTERNATIONAL JOURNAL OF EXPERT SYSTEMS. [Int. j. expert syst.]. Vol. 1, No. 1 (Sept. 1987)-. Periodical. English. Four times a year. $225.00. JAI Press Inc., 55 Old Post Road, Suite 2, PO Box 1678, Greenwich CT 06836-1678. **Tel** (203)661-7602, FAX (203)661-0792. **ED** Mehdi T. Harandi. Index available. cum. index. **Ad Acc. Circ:** 500. available on microfiche. Documents available from Article Express International, Ask*IEEE.
Desc: Seeks original research and survey papers on all aspects of expert systems and related subjects.
Ind/Abst Abstr. Hum. Comput. Interact.; ACM Guide Comput. Lit.; Comput. Rev.; Curr. Cit.; Ei Page One; Eng. Index Annu. [Select. Cov.]; Fluid Abstr., Civil Eng.; Fluid Abstr. Proc. Eng.; FLUIDEX; INSPEC (1987/1988-); Soc. Plann. Policy Dev. Abstr.

LC QA76.9.D3 I565 ISSN 0218-2157
DD 006.3 SI CODEN IICSEA TITLE CHANGE

INTERNATIONAL JOURNAL OF INTELLIGENT & COOPERATIVE INFORMATION SYSTEMS : IJICIS. **VFOAT** IJICIS; International Journal of Intelligent and Cooperative Information Systems. Vol. 1, No. 1 (Mar. 1992)-(1995). Periodical. English. World Scientific Publishing Company, PO Box 128, Farrer Road, Singapore 9128 Singapore. **Tel** 011 65 3825663, FAX 011 65 3825919, telex RS 28561 WSPC. **(Subscription address:** World Scientific Publishing Company, Inc., 1060 Main Street, Suite 1 B, River Edge NJ 07661. **Tel** (800)227-7562, (201)487-9655.**) ED** Mike P. Papazoglou. ***Continued by*** *International Journal of Cooperative Information Systems.*

Desc: Provides a forum for presentation and discussion of the potential roles and nature of the emerging notion of Intelligent and Cooperative Information Systems (ICIS).

LC Q334 .I573 **ISSN** 0884-8173
DD 006.3/05 US
CCC
CODEN IJISED
Pr Rev.

INTERNATIONAL JOURNAL OF INTELLIGENT SYSTEMS. [Int. j. intell. syst.]. Vol. 1, No. 1 Spring (1986)-. Periodical. English. Twelve times a year. $900.00. John Wiley & Sons, Inc., 605 Third Avenue, New York NY 10158-0012. **Tel** (212)850-6000, (212)850-6645, FAX (212)850-6088, telex 12-7063. **(Subscription address:** John Wiley & Sons / UK, Baffins Lane, Chichester, West Sussex PO19 1UD United Kingdom. **Tel** 011 44 1243 779777, FAX 011 44 243 776128, telex 86290 WIBOOKG.**)** **ED** Ronald R. Yager. **Ad Acc.** available on microfilm and microfiche from University Microfilms International (UMI). Documents available from Article Express International, The Genuine Article, Ask*IEEE.
Desc: Devoted to the systematic development of the theory necessary for the construction of intelligent systems. Editorial matters include research papers, tutorial reviews, short communications on theoretical as well as developmental issues.
Ind/Abst Abstr. Hum. Comput. Interact.; CompuMath Cit. Index [Full Cov.]; Comput. Rev.; Curr. Cit.; Curr. Contents Eng. Comput. Technol.; Ei Page One; Eng. Index Annu.; INSPEC (Winter 1988-); Res. Alert [Full Cov.]; SCISEARCH; Soc. Sci. Cit. Index [Select. Cov.]; Zentralbl. Math. Ihre Grenzgeb.

ISSN 0954-9889
UK
NLM W1; IN76957 **CODEN** IJNNEN
Pr Rev. **CEASED**

INTERNATIONAL JOURNAL OF NEURAL NETWORKS. (THE INTERNATIONAL JOURNAL OF NEURAL NETWORKS.). [Int. j. neural netw.]. **VFOAT** Neural Networks. Vol. 1 No. 1 (Jan. 1989)-(19??). Periodical. English. Learned Information Ltd., Woodside Hinksey Hill, Oxford OX1 5AU United Kingdom. **Tel** 011 44 1865 730275, FAX 011 44 1865 736354, telex 23667. **ED** Kamal N Karna and Ian F Croall. Documents available from Ask*IEEE.
Desc: Approaches the problem of getting computers to perform intelligently by the simulation of the neural networks of the brain. Dedicated to technology transfer and should become an essential tool for the developer, researcher, and user of neural networks. Includes substantial refereed papers that survey critical research areas of application domains, or summarize neural network state-of-the-art.
Ind/Abst INSPEC (1989-19??); Zentralbl. Math. Ihre Grenzgeb. (19??-19??).

LC QA76.87 .I58 **ISSN** 0129-0657
DD 006.3 SI
CCC
NLM W1; IN7698 **CODEN** IJSZEG
Pr Rev.

INTERNATIONAL JOURNAL OF NEURAL SYSTEMS. Vol. 1, No. 1 (1989)-. Periodical. English. Six times a year. $275.00. World Scientific Publishing Company, PO Box 128, Farrer Road, Singapore 9128 Singapore. **Tel** 011 65 3825663, FAX 011 65 3825919, telex RS 28561 WSPC. **(Subscription address:** World Scientific Publishing Company, Inc., 1060 Main Street, Suite 1 B, River Edge NJ 07661. **Tel** (800)227-7562, (201)487-9655.**)** **ED** B. Lautrup and S. Brunak. cum. index. **Circ:** 200. Documents available from The Genuine Article, Ask*IEEE.
Desc: Information on neural networks, neural circuitry and computer simulation. Involves physics, biology, psychology, computer science and engineering.
Ind/Abst ACM Guide Comput. Lit.; Comput. Rev.; Curr. Cit.; Index Med.; INSPEC (1989-); Res. Alert [Full Cov.]; Soc. Sci. Cit. Index [Select. Cov.].

LC Q327 .I63 **ISSN** 0218-0014
DD 006.4 SI
CCC
CODEN IPJIEI
Pr Rev.

INTERNATIONAL JOURNAL OF PATTERN RECOGNITION AND ARTIFICIAL INTELLIGENCE. [Int. j. pattern recogn. artif. intell.]. Vol. 1, No. 1 (April 1987)-. Periodical. English. Eight times a year. $426.00. World Scientific Publishing Company, PO Box 128, Farrer Road, Singapore 9128 Singapore. **Tel** 011 65 3825663, FAX 011 65 3825919, telex RS 28561 WSPC. **(Subscription address:** World Scientific Publishing Company, Inc., 1060 Main Street, Suite 1 B, River Edge NJ 07661. **Tel** (800)227-7562, (201)487-9655.**)** **ED** H. Bunke and P.S.P. Wang. Index available. **Ad Acc, Adv Mgr:** Gilbert Low. **Circ:** 250. Documents available from Ask*IEEE.
Desc: Publishes papers on pattern recognition and artificial intelligence, with particular emphasis on papers in the intersection of both fields.
Ind/Abst Comput. Rev.; Curr. Cit.; INSPEC (June 1988-).

LC TJ210.2 .I6 **ISSN** 0826-8185
DD 629.8/92/05 US
CODEN IJAUED

INTERNATIONAL JOURNAL OF ROBOTICS & AUTOMATION. [Int. j. robot. autom.]. **Added/Corp** International Association of Science and Technology for Development. **VFOAT** International Journal of Robotics and Automation; Robotics and Automation; Robotics & Automation. Vol. 1, No. 1 (1986)-. Periodical. English. Four times a year. $255.00. IASTED- International Association of Science and Technology for Development, PO Box 2481, Anaheim CA 92814. **Tel** (714)778-3230, (800)995-2161, FAX (714)535-2662. **ED** Professor T C Hsia. **Bk Rev. Ad Acc.** Documents available from Ask*IEEE.
Ind/Abst Curr. Cit.; INSPEC (1986-); Int. Labour Doc.; Oper. Res./Manage. Sci.; Qual. Control Appl. Stat.; Robotics Abstr.

LC TJ211 .I485 **ISSN** 0278-3649
DD 629.8/92/05 US
CCC
Pr Rev.

INTERNATIONAL JOURNAL OF ROBOTICS RESEARCH, THE. [Int. j. rob. res.]. **VFOAT** Robotics Research. Vol. 1, No. 1 (Spring 1982)-. Academic Scholarly Publication. English. Six times a year. $215.00. Massachusetts Institute of Technology (MIT) Press, 55 Hayward Street, Cambridge MA 02142. **Tel** (617)253-2889, (617)625-8481, FAX (617)258-6779. **ED** J. Michael Brady. **Ad Acc.** available on microfilm and microfiche from University Microfilms International (UMI). Documents available from Article Express International, The Genuine Article, Ask*IEEE.
Desc: Information on the advances in robotics science from relevant areas such as computer science, mechanical and electrical engineering, and artificial intelligence.
Ind/Abst ACM Guide Comput. Lit.; Appl. Sci. Technol. Index (1991-); CompuMath Cit. Index [Full Cov.]; Comput. Inf. Syst. Abstr. J. [Full Cov.]; Comput. Rev. (1983-); Curr. Cit.; Curr. Contents Eng. Comput. Technol.; Ei Page One; Elect. Comm. Abstr.; Eng. Index Annu.; Ergon. Abstr.; Inf. Sci. Abstr.; INSPEC (Fall 1983-); Int. Aerosp. Abstr. (1983-); Manuf. Process Eng. Abstr.; Math. Rev. (1991-); Res. Alert [Full Cov.]; Robotics Abstr.; Sci. Cit. Index; SCISEARCH.

LC QA76.758 .I5745 **ISSN** 0218-1940
DD 005.1/05 SI
CCC
CODEN ISEKEW

INTERNATIONAL JOURNAL OF SOFTWARE ENGINEERING AND KNOWLEDGE ENGINEERING. [Int. j. softw. eng. knowl. eng.]. **VFOAT** Journal of Software Engineering and Knowledge Engineering. Vol. 1, No. 1 (Mar. 1991)-. Periodical. English. Four times a year. $218.00. World Scientific Publishing Company, PO Box 128, Farrer Road, Singapore 9128 Singapore. **Tel** 011 65 3825663, FAX 011 65 3825919, telex RS 28561 WSPC. **(Subscription address:** World Scientific Publishing Company, Inc., 1060 Main Street, Suite 1 B, River Edge NJ 07661. **Tel** (800)227-7562, (201)487-9655.**)** **ED** S.K. Chang. Documents available from The Genuine Article, Ask*IEEE.
Desc: Concentrates on the interplay between software engineering and knowledge engineering: how their methods can be applied to each other. Includes papers on object-oriented systems, rapid prototyping, software reuse, logic programming, deductive database systems, and other related topics.
Ind/Abst CompuMath Cit. Index [Full Cov.]; Curr. Cit.; INSPEC (1991-); Res. Alert [Full Cov.]; SCISEARCH; Soc. Sci. Cit. Index [Select. Cov.].

ISSN 1081-1451
US

●**INTERNATIONAL JOURNAL OF VIRTUAL REALITY : A MULTIMEDIA PUBLICATION, THE.** **VFOAT** Virtual Reality. (1995)-. Periodical. English. Four times a year. $225.00. IPI Press, 2608 North Cascade Avenue, Colorado Springs CO 80907. **Tel** (800)474-4587.

ISSN 0218-2130
DD 006.305 SI

INTERNATIONAL JOURNAL ON ARTIFICIAL INTELLIGENCE TOOLS. [Int. j. artif. intell. tools]. (1992)-. Periodical. English. Four times a year. $221.00. World Scientific Publishing Company, PO Box 128, Farrer Road, Singapore 9128 Singapore. **Tel** 011 65 3825663, FAX 011 65 3825919, telex RS 28561 WSPC. **(Subscription address:** World Scientific Publishing Company, Inc., 1060 Main Street, Suite 1 B, River Edge NJ 07661. **Tel** (800)227-7562, (201)487-9655.**)** **ED** NG Bourbakis.
Desc: Promotes general and/or special purpose artificial intelligence tools. Covers topics such as expert systems, knowledge bases and environments, artificial intelligence for software engineering, and machine learning tools.

LC TJ210.5 .I58 **ISSN** 0739-1595
DD 629.8/92/05 US

INTERNATIONAL ROBOTICS YEARBOOK, THE. [Int. rob. yearb.]. 1st Ed.-. English. One time a year. $50.00. Ballinger Publishing Company, 10 East 53rd Street, New York NY 10022-5244. **ED** I Aleksander.
Desc: A comprehensive guide to contemporary industrial and academic activity in the field of robotics. Detailed specifications are included on all the robot models available at present, and information given on the manufacturers, suppliers and distributors of these systems.

ISSN 1061-6608
DD 006 US

IRIS UNIVERSE. (IRIS UNIVERSE : THE MAGAZINE OF VISUAL COMPUTING.). [IRIS universe]. (1987)-. Periodical. English. Four times a year. $14.00. Silicon Graphics, Inc, 2011 North Shoreline Blvd, Mountain View CA 94043-1389. **Tel** (415) 390-1278, FAX (415) 390-1737. **ED** Anne-Marie Gambelin. **Ad Acc. Circ:** 40,000.
Desc: Written to appeal to users of computer visualization, from the most technically oriented to the novice. Presents new products available along with the latest in techniques and technology.

ISSN 0912-8085
JA

JINKO CHINO GAKKAISHI = JOURNAL OF JAPANESE SOCIETY FOR ARTIFICIAL INTELLIGENCE. **Added/Corp** Jinko Chino Gakkai. **VFOAT** Journal of Japanese Society for Artificial Intelligence. (1986)-. Periodical. Japanese (summaries and/or abstracts in English). Four times a year. Do Gakkai, Keto Tsushin 19-ban 30-go Mita, 2-chome Minato-ku, Tokyo 108 Japan.
Ind/Abst Curr. Cit.

LC Q334 .J68 **ISSN** 1076-9757
DD 006 US

●**JOURNAL OF ARTIFICIAL INTELLIGENCE RESEARCH (PRINT), THE.** (THE JOURNAL OF ARTIFICIAL INTELLIGENCE RESEARCH.). [J. artif. intell. res.]. **VFOAT** JAIR. Vol. 1 (Aug. 1993/June 1994)-. Periodical. English. One time a year. $75.00. Morgan Kaufmann Publishers, 340 Pine Street, 6th Floor, San Francisco CA 94014. **Tel** (415)578-9911, (800)745-7323. available via Internet (http://www.cs.washington.edu/research/jair/home.html).
Desc: Covers all areas of artificial intelligence.

LC QA76.87 .J67 **ISSN** 1073-5828
DD 006.3 US
CODEN JANNE5
CEASED

JOURNAL OF ARTIFICIAL NEURAL NETWORKS. [J. artif. neural netw.]. (1994)-(1995). Periodical. English. Ablex Publishing Corporation, 355 Chestnut Street, Norwood NJ 07648. **Tel** (201)767-8450, (201)767-8455 (Customer Service), FAX (201)767-6717.

LC WMLC 93/1866 **ISSN** 0168-7433
NE
CCC
CODEN JAREEW
Pr Rev.

JOURNAL OF AUTOMATED REASONING. **See** Computers-Automation.

LC Q334 .J68 **ISSN** 0952-813X
DD 006.3/05 UK
CCC
CODEN JEAIEL

JOURNAL OF EXPERIMENTAL & THEORETICAL ARTIFICIAL INTELLIGENCE. [J. exp. theor. artif. intell.]. **VFOAT** Journal of Experimental and Theoretical Artificial Intelligence; JETAI. Vol. 1, No. 1 (Jan.-Mar. 1989)-. Periodical. English. Four times a year. $255.00. Taylor & Francis Ltd. / UK, Rankine Road, Basingstoke, Hampshire RG24 8PR United Kingdom. **Tel** 011 44 1256 840366, FAX 011 44 1256 479438, telex 858540. **(Subscription address:** Taylor & Francis Inc., 1900 Frost Road, Suite 101, Bristol PA 19007-1598. **Tel** (215)785-5800, (800)821-8312, FAX (215)785-5515.**)** **ED** Eric Dietrich (editor's address: Department of Philosophy, Program in Philosophy and Computer and Systems Science, State University of New York, Binghamton, NY 13901). Index available. **Ad Acc.** available on microfilm and microfiche from University Microfilms International (UMI). Documents available from Ask*IEEE.
Desc: Aims to advance scientific research in artificial intelligence by providing a public forum for the presentation, evaluation and criticism of research results, the discussion of methodological issues, and the communication of positions, preliminary findings and research directions. The journal features work in all subfields of AI research that adopts a scientific rather than engineering methodology, including work on problem-solving, perception, learning, knowledge representation, memory and neural system modelling.

Ind/Abst ACM Guide Comput. Lit.; Comput. Rev.; Curr. Cit.; INSPEC (1989-); Soc. Sci. Cit. Index [Select. Cov.]; Zentralbl. Math. Ihre Grenzgeb.

LC TJ210.2 .J68 **ISSN** 0921-0296
DD 629.8/92 NE
CCC
CODEN JIRSES

Pr Rev.
JOURNAL OF INTELLIGENT & ROBOTIC SYSTEMS. See Computers-Automation.

US
•**JOURNAL OF INTELLIGENT CONTROL, NEUROCOMPUTING AND FUZZY LOGIC.** (1994)-. Periodical. English. Four times a year. $285.00. Nova Science Publishers Inc., 6080 Jericho Turnpike, Suite 207, Commack NY 11725-2808. **Tel** (516)499-3103, (516)499-3106, FAX (516)499-3146.

LC QA76.9.D3 J683 **ISSN** 0925-9902
DD 006.3 US
CCC
CODEN JIISEH

Pr Rev.
JOURNAL OF INTELLIGENT INFORMATION SYSTEMS. VFOAT Intelligent Information systems. Vol. 1, No. 1 (Aug. 1992)-. Periodical. English. Six times a year. $453.00. Kluwer Academic Publishers / Massachusetts, PO Box 358, Accord Station, Hingham MA 02018. **Tel** (617)871-6600. **ED** Larry Kerschberg, Zbigniew Ras and Maria Zemankova. **Acid Free.** available on microfilm and microfiche from University Microfilms International (UMI).
Desc: The mission is to present research and development focused on the integration of artificial intelligence and database management technologies to provide models, architectures, tools and techniques for the next generation of systems. Focuses on the creation of information systems that exhibit intelligent behavior and embody intelligence in their reasoning and management processes.

ISSN 0956-5515
UK
CCC
CODEN JIMNEM

Pr Rev.
JOURNAL OF INTELLIGENT MANUFACTURING. [J. intell. manuf.]. Vol. 1, No. 1 (March 1990)-. Periodical. English. Six times a year. $455.00. Chapman & Hall, 2-6 Boundary Row, London SE1 8HN United Kingdom. **Tel** 011 44 171 8650066, FAX 011 44 171 5229623, telex 290164 CHAPMA G. **ED** Andrew Kusiak, U. Rembold, H. Yamashina. Documents available from The Genuine Article, Ask*IEEE.
Desc: Publishes quality papers on applications of artificial intelligence in manufacturing. Informs readers on the effective design, development and use of intelligent systems.
Ind/Abst CompuMath Cit. Index [Full Cov.]; Curr. Cit.; INSPEC (March 1990-); Res. Alert [Full Cov.]; SCISEARCH; Soc. Sci. Cit. Index [Select. Cov.].

LC TA418.9.S62 J68 **ISSN** 1045-389X
DD 620.1/1 US
CCC
CODEN JMSSER

JOURNAL OF INTELLIGENT MATERIAL SYSTEMS AND STRUCTURES. See Engineering-Mechanical Engineering and Machinery.

ISSN 0334-1860
UK
NLM W1; JO716CM **CODEN** JISYEH

Pr Rev.
JOURNAL OF INTELLIGENT SYSTEMS. [J. intell. syst.]. **VFOAT** Intelligent Systems. Vol. 1, No. 1 (Aug.-Dec. 1987)-. Periodical. English. Four times a year. $250.00. Freund Publishing House Ltd., PO Box 35010, 61 Nachmani Street, Tel Aviv 61350 Israel. **Tel** 011 972 3 5628540, FAX 011 972 3 5628538. **(Subscription address:** Freund Publishing House Ltd., Suite 500, Chesham House 150 Regent Street, London W1R 5FA United Kingdom. **Tel** 011 44 178 172811, FAX 011 972 3 615335.) **ED** M. Wright, R. Holte, L. Kohout and P. Thomas. **Ad Acc.** Documents available from Ask*IEEE.
Desc: Publishes original research papers, review articles and brief notes on an interdisciplinary level whose focal point is the field of intelligent systems. This field includes artificial intelligence techniques and theories, models and computational theories of human cognition, perception and motivation, brain models, artificial neural nets and neural computing.
Ind/Abst INSPEC (1987-); Zentralbl. Math. Ihre Grenzgeb.

LC QA76.63 .J68 **ISSN** 0955-792X
DD 004/.01/5113 UK
CCC
CODEN JLCOEU

JOURNAL OF LOGIC AND COMPUTATION. [J. log. comput.]. Vol. 1, No. 1 (July 1990)-. Periodical. English. Six times a year. $295.00. Oxford University Press / UK, Walton Street, Oxford OX2 6DP United Kingdom. **Tel** 011 44 1865 56767, FAX 011 44 1865 267773, telex 851/837330 OXPRES G. **(Subscription address:** Oxford University Press / USA, Journals Marketing Department, Oxford University Press, 2001 Evans Road, Cary NC 27513. **Tel** (800)451-7556, (919)677-0977, FAX (919)677-1714.) available on microfilm and microfiche from University Microfilms International (UMI). Documents available from Ask*IEEE.
Ind/Abst INSPEC (July 1990-); Math. Rev.; Zentralbl. Math. Ihre Grenzgeb.

LC TJ210.3 .J68 **ISSN** 0741-2223
DD 629.8/92 US
CCC

Pr Rev.
JOURNAL OF ROBOTIC SYSTEMS. [J. robot. syst.]. Vol. 1, No. 1 (Spring 1984)-. Academic Scholarly Publication. English. Twelve times a year. $888.00. John Wiley & Sons, Inc., 605 Third Avenue, New York NY 10158-0012. **Tel** (212)850-6000, (212)850-6645, FAX (212)850-6088, telex 12-7063. **(Subscription address:** John Wiley & Sons / UK, Baffins Lane, Chichester, West Sussex PO19 1UD United Kingdom. **Tel** 011 44 1243 779777, FAX 011 44 243 776128, telex 86290 WIBOOKG.) **ED** Gerardo Beni and Susan Hackwood. **Ad Acc. Circ:** 700. available on microfilm and microfiche from University Microfilms International (UMI). Documents available from Article Express International, The Genuine Article, UMI Article Clearinghouse, Ask*IEEE.
Desc: Serves the robotics community by presenting scholarly theoretical and applied contributions on the design and implementation of robotic systems, including robotic task ware. Other areas explored are control, automation and mechatronics.
Ind/Abst ABI/INFORM Glob. Ed.; Appl. Sci. Technol. Index; Civ. Struct. Eng. Abstr.; CompuMath Cit. Index [Full Cov.]; Comput. Inf. Syst. Abstr. J. [Full Cov.]; Curr. Cit.; Curr. Contents Eng. Comput. Technol.; Ei Page One; Elect. Comm. Abstr.; Eng. Index Annu.; Inf. Sci. Abstr.; INSPEC (Spring 1985-); Int. Aerosp. Abstr.; Manuf. Process Eng. Abstr.; Mech. Eng. Abstr.; Res. Alert [Full Cov.]; Risk Abstr.; Robotics Abstr.; Sci. Cit. Index; SCISEARCH; Zentralbl. Math. Ihre Grenzgeb.

ISSN 0915-3942
DD 629.8 JA

JOURNAL OF ROBOTICS AND MECHATRONICS. [J. robot. mechatronics]. (1989)-. Periodical. English. Six times a year. $778.28. **(Subscription address:** Maruzen Company Ltd., PO Box 5050, Import & Export Department, Tokyo 100 31 Japan. **Tel** 011 81 3 32789224.)

LC Q334 .K48 **ISSN** 0950-477X
DD 006.3 UK

KEY ABSTRACTS. ARTIFICIAL INTELLIGENCE. See Computers-Abstracting, Bibliographies and Statistics.

ISSN 0952-7052
UK

KEY ABSTRACTS. MACHINE VISION. See Computers-Abstracting, Bibliographies and Statistics.

LC Z5853.A8 K49 TJ213 **ISSN** 0950-4842
DD 629.8 UK

KEY ABSTRACTS. ROBOTICS & CONTROL. See Computers-Abstracting, Bibliographies and Statistics.

LC QA76.76.E95 K578 **ISSN** 0269-8889
DD 006.3/3 UK
CCC
CODEN KEREE3

KNOWLEDGE ENGINEERING REVIEW, THE. [Knowl. eng. rev.]. **Added/Corp** Cambridge University Press. British Computer Society. Specialist Group on Expert Systems. (1984)-. Academic Scholarly Publication. English. Four times a year. $180.00. Cambridge University Press, The Edinburgh Building, Shaftesbury Road, Cambridge CB2 2RU United Kingdom. **Tel** 011 44 1223 312393, FAX 011 44 1223 315052, telex 851-817256. **(Subscription address:** Cambridge University Press / North America, 110 Midland Avenue, Port Chester NY 10573. **Tel** (800)431-1580, (914)937-9600.) **ED** John Fox and P. Jackson. **Bk Rev.** available on microfilm from University Microfilms International (UMI). Documents available from Ask*IEEE.
Desc: This publication is committed to the critical development of this field, the clarification of its methods and concepts, and the dissemination of knowledge and results.
Ind/Abst Comput. Lit. Index; Curr. Cit.; Fluid Abstr., Civil Eng.; Fluid Abstr. Proc. Eng.; FLUIDEX (1987-1989); HILITES; INSPEC (1987-).

ISSN 0895-7533
DD 629 US
CCC
NLM W1; LA149 **CODEN** LRAUEY

LABORATORY ROBOTICS AND AUTOMATION. [Lab. robot. autom.]. Vol. 1, No. 1 (Jan. 1989)-. Academic Scholarly Publication. English. Six times a year. $294.00. VCH Publishers Inc, 220 East 23rd Street, New York NY 10010. **Tel** (212)683-8333, FAX (212)481-0897. **(Subscription address:** VCH Publishers Inc., 303 Northwest 12th Avenue, Journals Department, Deerfield FL 33442. **Tel** (800)367-8249, (305)428-5566.) **ED** Jeffrey W Hurst. Index available. **Bk Rev. Ad Acc.** Documents available from Ask*IEEE, CASDDS.
Ind/Abst Chem. Abstr. (1989-); Curr. Cit.; INSPEC (Jan. 1989-).

UK
Pr Rev. **TITLE CHANGE**
LAW COMPUTERS & ARTIFICIAL INTELLIGENCE. VFOAT Law Computers and Artificial Intelligence. Vol. 1, No. 1 (1992)-(1995). Periodical. English. Triangle Journals Ltd., PO Box 65, Wallingford Oxfordshire OX10 0YG United Kingdom. **Tel** 011 44 1491 838013, FAX 011 44 1491 834968. **ED** A. Adam, D. Bainbridge, C. Beardon. **Bk Rev. Circ:** 500. available in microform from University Microfilms International (UMI). ***Continued by** Information and Communications Technology Law.*

LC Q334 .L4
GW

LECTURE NOTES IN ARTIFICIAL INTELLIGENCE. (1988)-. Periodical. English. Irregular. Price varies. Springer-Verlag GmbH & Company KG, Heidelberger Platz 3, D-14197 Berlin Germany. **Tel** 011 49 30 8207223, FAX 011 49 30 8214091, telex 183 319 SPBLN D. **(Subscription address:** Springer-Verlag New York Inc. / North America, PO Box 2485, Journal Fulfillment, Secaucus NJ 07096. **Tel** (201)348-4033, (800)777-4643, FAX (201)348-4505.) Documents available from Ask*IEEE.
Ind/Abst CompuMath Cit. Index [Full Cov.]; INSPEC; Math. Rev.; Soc. Sci. Cit. Index [Select. Cov.].

ISSN 0923-0459
NE
NLM W1; MA16G

MACHINE INTELLIGENCE AND PATTERN RECOGNITION. [Mach. intell. pattern recognit.]. Vol. 1 (1985)-. Monographic series. English. Irregular. Price varies per volume. Elsevier Science Publishers BV, PO Box 211, 1000 AE Amsterdam Netherlands. **Tel** 011 31 20 4853641, 011 31 20 4853642, FAX 011 31 20 4853598. ***Absorbed** Progress in Pattern Recognition.*
Ind/Abst Curr. Cit.; Math. Rev.; Zentralbl. Math. Ihre Grenzgeb.

ISSN 0267-0429
UK
TITLE CHANGE

MACHINE INTELLIGENCE NEWS. Vol. 1, No. 1 (Oct. 1984)-(19??). Periodical. English. AI Intelligence, PO Box 95, Oxford OX2 7XL United Kingdom. **Tel** 011 44 1865 59872, FAX 011 44 1865 59872. **ED** Janet Vaux. **Bk Rev.** ***Merged into** AI Watch, 1354-2001.*
Desc: Monthly newsletter covering artificial intelligence and advanced information technology, primarily from an industrial perspective.
Ind/Abst Abstr. Hum. Comput. Interact.; Fluid Abstr., Civil Eng.; Fluid Abstr. Proc. Eng.; FLUIDEX; HILITES.

LC Q325.5 .M32 **ISSN** 0885-6125
DD 006.3/1 US
CCC
CODEN MALEEZ

Pr Rev.
MACHINE LEARNING. [Mach. learn.]. Vol. 1, No. 1 (1986)-. Periodical. English. Twelve times a year. $814.00. Kluwer Academic Publishers / Massachusetts, PO Box 358, Accord Station, Hingham MA 02018. **Tel** (617)871-6600. **ED** Thomas G. Dietterich. **Acid Free.** available on microfilm and microfiche from University Microfilms International (UMI). Documents available from Article Express International, The Genuine Article, Ask*IEEE.
Desc: An international forum for research on computational approaches to learning. Publishes articles reporting substantive research results on a wide range of learning methods applied to a variety of task domains.
Ind/Abst Abstr. Hum. Comput. Interact.; ACM Guide Comput. Lit.; Appl. Sci. Technol. Index (1991-); Appl. Soc. Sci. Index Abstr. (1991-); CompuMath Cit. Index [Full Cov.]; Comput. Rev.; Curr. Cit.; Curr. Contents Eng. Comput. Technol.; Ei Page One; Eng. Index Annu. [Select. Cov.]; INSPEC (1986-); Res. Alert [Full Cov.]; Sci. Cit. Index; SCISEARCH; Soc. Sci. Cit. Index [Select. Cov.]; Zentralbl. Math. Ihre Grenzgeb.

ISSN 0896-0348
DD 629 US

MILITARY ROBOTICS. [Mil. robot.]. Vol. 1, No. 1 (Oct. 9, 1987)-. Periodical. English. Twenty-four times a year. $295.00. L & B Ltd., 19 Rock Creek Church Road NW, Washington DC 20011. **Tel** (202)723-1600, FAX (202)726-2979. **ED** Joseph A Lovece, Steven M Shaker, Robert Finkelstein, and Gwen E Benson-Walker. **Bk Rev.** ctrl circ. available on an online database (file 636/Full-Text) from DIALOG; and NEWSNET.
Desc: Covers government and military applications of robotics including remotely piloted aircraft, unmanned submarines, teleoperated combat vehicles, cruise

missiles, unmanned spacecraft, automation technology, and teleoperated and autonomous weapons.
Ind/Abst PTS Newsl. Database [Full Txt.].

LC Q334 .M56 **ISSN** 0924-6495
DD 006.3 NE
CCC
CODEN MMACEO
Pr Rev.

MINDS AND MACHINES (DORDRECHT). (MINDS AND MACHINES.). [Minds mach.]. Vol. 1, No. 1 (Feb. 1991)-. Periodical. English. Four times a year. $351.00. Kluwer Academic Publishers, Postbus 322, 3300 AH Dordrecht The Netherlands. **Tel** 011 31 78 524400, FAX 011 31 78 183273, telex 20083. **ED** James Fetzer. available on microfilm and microfiche from University Microfilms International (UMI). Documents available from The Genuine Article, Ask*IEEE.
Desc: Features that make this journal distinctive within the field are strong stands on controversial issues, important articles exceeding normal journal length, special issues devoted to specific topics, critical responses to previously published pieces, and review essays discussing current situations.
Ind/Abst ACM Guide Comput. Lit.; Comput. Rev.; INSPEC (1991-); Res. Alert [Full Cov.]; Soc. Sci. Cit. Index [Select. Cov.].

LC QA76.87 .N46 **ISSN** 0954-898X
DD 006.3 UK
CCC
NLM W1; NE235S **CODEN** NEWKEB

NETWORK (BRISTOL). (NETWORK : COMPUTATION IN NEURAL SYSTEMS.). [Network]. **Added/Corp** Institute of Physics (Great Britain) American Institute of Physics. Vol. 1, No. 1 (Jan. 1990)-. Periodical. English. Four times a year (February, May, August and November). $420.00. Institute of Physics, Techno House, Redcliffe Way, Bristol BS1 6NX United Kingdom. **Tel** 011 44 117 9297481, FAX 011 44 117 9294318, telex 449149 INSTP G. **(Subscription address:** American Institute of Physics, Publishing Sales, 500 Sunnyside Blvd., Woodbury NY 11797. **Tel** (516)576-2200.**)** **ED** Daniel J Amit. Index available in last issue of volume--attached. available on microfiche. Documents available from The Genuine Article, Ask*IEEE.
Desc: Provides a forum for integrating theoretical and experimental findings across relevant interdisciplinary boundaries. Publishes review articles and has sections on rapid communications, comments and discussion, and suggested cross-disciplinary reading.
Ind/Abst CompuMath Cit. Index [Full Cov.]; Curr. Cit.; INSPEC (Jan. 1990-); Res. Alert [Full Cov.]; SCISEARCH.

LC QA76.5 .N4255 **ISSN** 0899-7667
DD 006.3 US
CCC
CODEN NEUCEB
Pr Rev.

NEURAL COMPUTATION. [Neural comput.]. Vol. 1, No. 1 (Spring 1989)-. Periodical. English. Six times a year. $220.00. Massachusetts Institute of Technology (MIT) Press, 55 Hayward Street, Cambridge MA 02142. **Tel** (617)253-2889, (617)625-8481, FAX (617)258-6779. **ED** Terrence Sejnowski. **Bk Rev. Ad Acc. Circ:** 1,100. available on microfilm and microfiche from University Microfilms International (UMI). Documents available from The Genuine Article, Ask*IEEE.
Desc: Provides a forum for the dissemination of research results and for reviews of research areas in neural computation.
Ind/Abst ACM Guide Comput. Lit.; CompuMath Cit. Index [Full Cov.]; Comput. Rev.; Curr. Cit.; Curr. Contents Eng. Comput. Technol.; Ei Page One; INSPEC (Spring 1989-); Psychol. Abstr. (1989-); PsycINFO; PsycLit; Res. Alert [Full Cov.]; Sci. Cit. Index; Soc. Plann. Policy Dev. Abstr.

ISSN 0941-0643
UK
CCC
NLM W1; NE32T

•**NEURAL COMPUTING & APPLICATIONS.** **VFOAT** Neural Computing and Applications. Vol. 1, No. 1 (1993)-. Trade Publication. English. Four times a year. $250.00. Springer-Verlag London Ltd., Springer House, 8 Alexandra Road Wimbledon, London SW19 7JZ United Kingdom. **Tel** 011 44 181 9471280, 011 44 181 9475885, FAX 011 44 181 9474651, telex 21531 SPRGB G.
Ind/Abst CSA Neuro. Abstr.

ISSN 1210-0552
XR
UDC 612.8 :681.324
Pr Rev.

NEURAL NETWORK WORLD. [Neural Netw. World]. (1991)-. Periodical. English. Six times a year. DM540.00. VSP International Science Publishers, Godfried van Seystlaan 47, 3703 BR Zeist Netherlands. **Tel** 011 31 3404 25790, FAX 011 31 3404 32081, telex 40217 USP NL. **(Subscription address:** VSP International Science Publishers, PO Box 346, 3700 AH Zeist Netherlands. **Tel** 011 31 30 6925790, FAX 011 31 30 6932081.**)** **ED** Mirko Novak.
Desc: Provides the latest developments in the field of information technology, with attention being focused on neurocomputing based on the application of artificial neural networks.

LC QA76.5 .N434 **ISSN** 0893-6080
DD 006.3 US
CCC
NLM W1; NE321 **CODEN** NNETEB
Pr Rev.

NEURAL NETWORKS. (NEURAL NETWORKS : THE OFFICIAL JOURNAL OF THE INTERNATIONAL NEURAL NETWORK SOCIETY.). [Neural netw.]. **Added/Corp** International Neural Network Society. Vol. 1, No. 1 (1988)-. Periodical. English. Nine times a year. $735.00. Pergamon Press, An Imprint of Elsevier Science Ltd., The Boulevard, Langford Lane, Kidlington, Oxford OX5 1GB United Kingdom. **Tel** 011 44 1865 843000, 011 44 1865 843699, FAX 011 44 1865 843010. **(Subscription address:** Elsevier Science Ltd. / Oxford Fulfillment Centre, PO Box 800, Kidlington OX5 1DX United Kingdom. **Tel** 011 44 865 843355.**)** **ED** Shun-Ichi Armari, Stephen Grossberg and John Taylor. available on microfilm and microfiche from University Microfilms International (UMI); available on an online database from Elsevier Electronic Subscriptions (EES). Documents available from Article Express International, The Genuine Article, BIOSIS Document Express, Ask*IEEE.
Desc: Publishes research concerned with the modelling of brain and behavioral processes and the application of these models to computer and related technologies.
Ind/Abst Abstr. Hum. Comput. Interact.; ACM Guide Comput. Lit.; Appl. Sci. Technol. Index (1991-); Biol. Abstr.; Biostatistica; Chemorecept. Abstr.; CompuMath Cit. Index [Full Cov.]; Comput. Inf. Syst. Abstr. J. [Full Cov.]; Comput. Rev.; CSA Neuro. Abstr. (?-?); Curr. Aware. Biol. Sci., CABS; Curr. Cit.; Curr. Contents Eng. Comput. Technol.; Ei Page One; Elect. Comm. Abstr.; Eng. Index Annu.; Inf. Sci. Abstr.; INSPEC (1988-); Microcomput. Abstr. (Jan. 1989-); Oper. Res./Manage. Sci.; Psychol. Abstr. (1989-); PsycINFO; PsycLit; Res. Alert [Full Cov.]; Sci. Cit. Index; SCISEARCH; Soc. Sci. Cit. Index [Select. Cov.]; Zentralbl. Math. Ihre Grenzgeb.

UK

NEURAL TECHNOLOGY UPDATE. (19??)-. English. Twelve times a year. $295.00. Graeme Publishing Corporation, 10 Northern Boulevard, Amhurst NH 03031. **Tel** (603)672-3652. ***Continues** Synapse Connection.*

LC QA76.87 .N487 **ISSN** 0925-2312
NE
CCC
CODEN NRCGEO
Pr Rev.

NEUROCOMPUTING (AMSTERDAM). (NEUROCOMPUTING.). [Neurocomputing]. (1989)-. Academic Scholarly Publication. English. Sixteen times a year. $924.00. Elsevier Science Publishers BV, PO Box 211, 1000 AE Amsterdam Netherlands. **Tel** 011 31 20 4853641, 011 31 20 4853642, FAX 011 31 20 4853598. **ED** David Sanchez. **Bk Rev. Ad Acc. Circ:** 200. available on microfilm and microfiche from University Microfilms International (UMI); available on an online database from Elsevier Electronic Subscriptions (EES). Documents available from Article Express International, The Genuine Article, Ask*IEEE.
Desc: Covers recent fundamental contributions in the field of neurocomputing. Also covers advances in hardware and software development for neurocomputing in different fields.
Ind/Abst CompuMath Cit. Index [Full Cov.]; Comput. Inf. Syst. Abstr. J. [Full Cov.]; Curr. Cit.; Ei Page One; EMBASE; Eng. Index Annu.; INSPEC (June 1990-); Int. Aerosp. Abstr.; Res. Alert [Full Cov.]; Soc. Sci. Cit. Index [Select. Cov.]; Zentralbl. Math. Ihre Grenzgeb.

ISSN 0918-2187
JA

NIKKEI INTERIJENTO SHISUTEMU. **VFOAT** Nikkei Intelligent Systems. (1992)-. Periodical. Japanese. Twenty-four times a year. ¥136000. Nihon Keizai Shimbun Inc., 9-5 Otemachi 1 Chome, Chiyoda-ku Tokyo 100 Japan. **Tel** 011 81 3 32700251, 011 81 3 52108502 (Nikkei Business Publications Inc.), FAX 011 81 3 52552661, 011 81 3 52108119 (Nikkei Business Publications Inc.). ***Continues** Nikkei AI, 0911-5560.*
Desc: Latest in artificial intelligence.

LC TK7895.M4 O6847 **ISSN** 1060-992X
DD 006.3 US
CCC
CODEN OMNNE8

OPTICAL MEMORY & NEURAL NETWORKS. [Opt. mem. neural netw.]. **VFOAT** Optical Memory and Neural Networks. Vol. 1, No. 1 (1992)-. Periodical. English. Four times a year. $280.00. Allerton Press Inc., 150 Fifth Avenue, New York NY 10011. **Tel** (212)924-3950, FAX (212)463-9684, telex 427441 ALPRES.
Ind/Abst INSPEC (1992-).

LC Z5853 .R58 TJ211 **ISSN** 1146-5425
DD 016.67042/72 FR

PASCAL. E34, ROBOTICS, CONTROL THEORY AND INDUSTRIAL PROCESSES AUTOMATION. **Added/Corp** Institut de l'information Scientifique et Technique (France). **VFOAT** Robotique, Automatique et Automatisation des Processus Industriels; Robotics, Control Theory and Industrial Processes Automation; PASCAL. N.E34, P.Robotics, Control Theory and Industrial Processes automation. (1990)-. Periodical. French. Twelve times a year. 720F (surface mail), 780F (airmail). Centre de Documentation Scientifique et Technique, Centre National de la Recherche Scientifique, 26 rue Boyer, 75971 Paris Cedex 20 France. **Tel** (1) 43 58 35 59, telex CNRSDOC 220880F. ***Continues** PASCAL Explore. E34, Robotique, Automatique et Automatisation des Processus Industriels.*

LC Q327 .P36 **ISSN** 0031-3203
DD 006.4 UK
CCC
NLM Z 699.A1 P316 **CODEN** PTNRA8
Pr Rev.

PATTERN RECOGNITION. [Pattern recogn.]. **Added/Corp** Pattern Recognition Society. Vol. 1 (July 1968)-. Academic Scholarly Publication. English. Twelve times a year. $1292.00. Pergamon Press, An Imprint of Elsevier Science Ltd., The Boulevard, Langford Lane, Kidlington, Oxford OX5 1GB United Kingdom. **Tel** 011 44 1865 843000, 011 44 1865 843699, FAX 011 44 1865 843010. **(Subscription address:** Elsevier Science Ltd. / Oxford Fulfillment Centre, PO Box 800, Kidlington OX5 1DX United Kingdom. **Tel** 011 44 865 843355.**)** **ED** Robert Ledley. available on microfilm and microfiche from Microfilms International Marketing Corp.; available on an online database from Elsevier Electronic Subscriptions (EES). Documents available from Article Express International, The Genuine Article, BIOSIS Document Express, Ask*IEEE.
Ind/Abst Abstr. Hum. Comput. Interact.; ACM Guide Comput. Lit.; Bioeng. Abstr.; Biol. Abstr.; CompuMath Cit. Index [Full Cov.]; Comput. Inf. Syst. Abstr. J. [Full Cov.]; Comput. Rev.; Curr. Aware. Biol. Sci., CABS; Curr. Cit.; Curr. Contents Eng. Comput. Technol.; Curr. Contents Soc. Behav. Sci.; Ecol. Abstr.; Ei Page One; EMBASE; Eng. Index Annu.; Geogr. Abstr. Phys. Geogr.; Inf. Sci. Abstr.; INSPEC (Nov. 1968-); Int. Aerosp. Abstr.; Math. Rev.; Life Sci. Collect.; Pollut. Abstr. Indexes; Res. Alert [Full Cov.]; Sci. Cit. Index; SCISEARCH; Soc. Sci. Cit. Index [Select. Cov.]; World Publ. Monit.; Zentralbl. Math. Ihre Grenzgeb.

LC TK7882.P3 P396 **ISSN** 0167-8655
DD 006.4 NE
CCC
CODEN PRLEDG
Pr Rev.

PATTERN RECOGNITION LETTERS. [Pattern recogn. lett.]. **Added/Corp** International Association for Pattern Recognition. Vol. 1, No. 1 (Oct. 1982)-. Academic Scholarly Publication. English. Fourteen times a year. $1122.00. Elsevier Science Publishers BV, PO Box 211, 1000 AE Amsterdam Netherlands. **Tel** 011 31 20 4853641, 011 31 20 4853642, FAX 011 31 20 4853598. **ED** E Backer and E S Gelsema. available on microfilm and microfiche from University Microfilms International (UMI); available on an online database from Elsevier Electronic Subscriptions (EES). Documents available from The Genuine Article, Ask*IEEE.
Desc: Takes a novel approach to the publication of research work in the field of pattern recognition.
Ind/Abst Abstr. Hum. Comput. Interact.; ACM Guide Comput. Lit.; CompuMath Cit. Index [Full Cov.]; Comput. Rev. (Oct. 1982-); Curr. Cit.; Curr. Contents Eng. Comput. Technol.; Geogr. Abstr. Phys. Geogr. (Oct. 1982-); INSPEC (Oct. 1982-); Math. Rev.; Res. Alert [Full Cov.]; Robotics Abstr.; SCISEARCH; Soc. Sci. Cit. Index [Select. Cov.]; Stat. Theory Method Abstr. (1983, 1986); Zentralbl. Math. Ihre Grenzgeb.

ISSN 0894-0711
DD 006 US
CCC
CODEN PCAIE5

PC AI. [PC AI]. Vol. 1, No. 1 (Spring 1987)-. Trade Publication. English. Six times a year (Jan., Mar., May, July, Sept., Nov.). $32.00. PC AI Magazine, 3310 West Bell Road, Suite 119, Phoenix AZ 85023. **Tel** (602)971-1869, FAX (602)971-2321. **ED** Joseph Schmuller. Index Available Published separately--free--upon request. cum. index. **Bk Rev**, (Qty: 3-6). **Ad Acc, Adv Mgr:** Robin Okun, **Tel** (602)971-1869. **Circ:** 20,000.
Desc: This publication is geared toward practical applications of today's computers. Covers the development in expert system, networks, languages and others areas of artificial intelligence.
Ind/Abst Curr. Cit.; Microcomput. Abstr. (May 1992-).

ISSN 0748-9315
DD 629 US

PERSONAL ROBOTICS MAGAZINE. **VFOAT** P.R.M.; PRM. (Mar. 1984)-. Periodical. English. Six times a year. $21.00 US; $25.00 other. KLH Publishing, PO Box 421, Rheem Valley CA 94570.

ISSN 0737-8505
US

PERSONAL ROBOTICS NEWS. [Pers. robot. news]. Vol. 1, No. 1 (Aug. 1983)-. Periodical. English. Twelve times a year. $125.00. PRN Corporation, PO Box

Computers — Artificial Intelligence

10058, Berkeley CA 94709. Documents available from Ask*IEEE.
Ind/Abst INSPEC (1985).

US

Pr Rev.
PERSPECTIVES IN ARTIFICIAL INTELLIGENCE.
(19??)-. English. Irregular. Academic Press Ltd., A Division of Harcourt Brace & Company Ltd., 24-28 Oval Road, London NW1 7DX United Kingdom. **Tel** 011 44 171 2674466, FAX 011 44 171 4822293, 011 44 171 4854752, telex 25775 ACPRES G.
Ind/Abst Curr. Cit.

LC TA167 .P69   ISSN 1054-7460
DD 006   US
    CCC

PRESENCE (CAMBRIDGE, MASS.).
(PRESENCE: TELEOPERATORS AND VIRTUAL ENVIRONMENTS.). [Presence]. **VFOAT** Teleoperators and Virtual Environments. Vol. 1, No. 1 (Winter 1992)-. Periodical. English. Four times a year. $165.00. Massachusetts Institute of Technology (MIT) Press, 55 Hayward Street, Cambridge MA 02142. **Tel** (617)253-2889, (617)625-8481, FAX (617)258-6779. **ED** Thomas B. Sheridan, Thomas A. Furness III and Nathaniel I. Durlach. available on microfilm and microfiche from University Microfilms International (UMI).
Desc: Filled with research and designs applicable to these advanced eletromechanical and computer devices. Devoted to teleoperators and virtual environments. Also includes information on man-machine systems, human-computer interaction, and robotics.
Ind/Abst Comput. Rev.; Ergon. Abstr.; Inf. Sci. Abstr.; Int. Aerosp. Abstr.

US

PROCEEDINGS / AAAI- ... NATIONAL CONFERENCE ON ARTIFICIAL INTELLIGENCE. Added/Corp American Association for Artificial Intelligence. **VFOAT** AAAI-. 5th (Aug. 11-15, 1986)-. Proceedings. English. American Association for Artificial Intelligence, 445 Burgess Drive, Menlo Park CA 94025-3496. **Tel** (415)328-3123, FAX (415)321-4457. **Continues** National Conference on Artificial Intelligence. Proceedings of the [sic] National Conference on Artificial Intelligence.
Ind/Abst Curr. Cit.

LC Q334 .C66a   ISSN 1043-0989
DD 006.3   US

PROCEEDINGS / CONFERENCE ON ARTIFICIAL INTELLIGENCE APPLICATIONS.
[Proceedings - Conf. Artif. Intell. Appl.]. **Added/Corp** IEEE Computer Society. American Association of Artificial Intelligence. **VFOAT** IEEE Conference on Artificial Intelligence Applications. 3rd (1987)-. Proceedings. English. IEEE / Institute of Electrical and Electronics Engineers Inc., 345 East 47th Street, New York NY 10017-2394. **Tel** (908)981-1393, FAX (908)981-9667. **Continues** Conference on Artificial Intelligence Applications. Conference on Artificial Intelligence Applications, 1043-0970.
Ind/Abst Civ. Struct. Eng. Abstr.; Comput. Inf. Syst. Abstr. J. [Full Cov.]; Elect. Comm. Abstr.; Environ. Eng. Abstr.; Manuf. Process Eng. Abstr.; Mech. Eng. Abstr.; Solid State Supercond. Abstr.

UK

PROCEEDINGS OF THE ... ANNUAL BRITISH ROBOT ASSOCIATION CONFERENCE. **Main/Corp** British Robot Association. Conference. 8th (May 14-17, 1985)-. English. One time a year. British Robot Association, Aston Science Park, Love Lane, Birmingham B7 4BJ United Kingdom. **Tel** 011 44 121 3590981, FAX 011 44 121 3590433. **Continues** Proceedings of the ... British Robot Association Annual Conference.

ISSN 0710-0825
DD 006.3   CN
    TITLE CHANGE

PROCEEDINGS OF THE ... BIENNIAL CONFERENCE OF THE CANADIAN SOCIETY FOR COMPUTATIONAL STUDIES OF INTELLIGENCE. [Proc. bienn. conf. Can. Soc. Comput. Stud. Intell.]. **Main/Corp** Canadian Society for Computational Studies of Intelligence. Conference. **VFOAT** Proceedings, CSCSI/SCEIO Conference; Compte-Rendu de la ... Conference Biennale de la Societe Canadienne des Etudes d'Intelligence par Ordinateur. Proceedings. English (French). Conference Proceedings, Canadian Society for Computational Studies of Intelligence, c/o CIPS National Office, 5th Floor 243 College Street, Toronto Ontario M5T 2Y1 Canada. **Continues** Proceedings of ... CSCSI/SCEIO National Conference, 0710-0833. **Continued by** Canadian Conference on Artificial Intelligence. Proceedings, 0834-6267.
Ind/Abst Curr. Cit.

ISSN 1240-3946
    FR
UDC 658.8
PRODUCTIQUE AFFAIRES PARIS.
(PRODUCTIQUE AFFAIRES.). (1992)-. Periodical. French. Eighteen times a year. $546.80. A Jour, 11 rue du Marche St. Honore, 75001 Paris France. **Tel** 011 33 1 44553849. **Continues** Robots (Cergy), 0752-4978.

LC QA76.87 .P76   ISSN 1055-713X
DD 006.3   US
    CODEN PNNEEX
PROGRESS IN NEURAL NETWORKS.
[Prog. neural netw.]. Vol. 1 (1991)-. Periodical. English. Irregular. $45.00. Ablex Publishing Corporation, 355 Chestnut Street, Norwood NJ 07648. **Tel** (201)767-8450, (201)767-8455 (Customer Service), FAX (201)767-6717. **ED** Omid Omiduar.
Desc: Series including research on various topics pertaining to neural networks.

ISSN 0939-4818
    US
NLM W1; RE232KJ
RESEARCH NOTES IN NEURAL COMPUTING. [Res. notes neural comput.]. Vol. 1 (1989)-. Monographic series. English. Irregular. Price varies per volume. Springer-Verlag New York Inc., 175 Fifth Avenue, New York NY 10010. **Tel** (212)460-1500 ext 256, FAX (212)533-3503, telex 232 235 SPB UR. **(Subscription address:** Springer-Verlag New York Inc. / North America, PO Box 2485, Journal Fulfillment, Secaucus NJ 07096. **Tel** (201)348-4033, (800)777-4643, FAX (201)348-4505.)
Ind/Abst Zentralbl. Math. Ihre Grenzgeb.

ISSN 0212-3754
    SP
UDC 621-52
    TITLE CHANGE
REVISTA DE ROBOTICA. [Rev. rob.]. (1982)-(1993). Periodical. Spanish. Pulsar SA, Gran Via Corts Catalanes 322 324, 08004 Barcelona Spain. **Tel** 011 34 3 4254544. **Continued by** Automatizacion Integrada y Revista de Robotica.

FR
REVUE D'INTELLIGENCE ARTIFICIELLE ET SYSTEMS EXPERTS. French. 2800.00F France; 3320.80F other. Agence de l'Intelligence Artificielle, 221 rue St. Honore, 75001 Paris France. **Tel** 011 33 1 42615171.

LC TJ210.4 .R53   ISSN 0741-9473
DD 629.8/92   US
RIA ROBOTICS GLOSSARY. [RIA rob. gloss.]. **VFOAT** Robotics Glossary; R.I.A. Robotics Glossary. **VAT** Robotics Institute of America Robotics Glossary. No. 1-. English.

ISSN 1040-2012
DD 621   US
    CODEN RLECEO
RLE CURRENTS. [RLE curr.]. **Added/Corp** Massachusetts Institute of Technology. Research Laboratory of Electronics. **VFOAT** RLE Currents. **VAT** Research Laboratory of Electronics Currents. Vol. 1, No. 1 (Dec. 1987)-. English. Every 2 years. free. RLE Currents, 36-412, Research Laboratory of Electronics, Massachusetts Institute of Technology, 77 Massachusetts Avenue, Cambridge MA 02139. **ED** Jonathan Allen Ticchi, and Dorothy A Fleischer. Documents available from Ask*IEEE.
Desc: Contains articles on recent research and developments within the electronics field.
Ind/Abst INSPEC (June 1989-).

LC QA   ISSN 1060-4375
DD 006.3   US
ROBOT EXPLORER. [Robot explor.]. (1992)-. Newsletter. English. Six times a year. $14.95 North America; $29.95 other. Appropriate Solutions Inc, PO Box 458, Peterborough NH 03458-0458. **Tel** (603)924-6079, FAX (603)924-9441. **ED** Ray Cote. **Bk Rev**. **Circ:** 500.
Desc: Presents topics devoted to the non-industrial usages of robotics.

ISSN 0387-1940
    JA
    CODEN ROBBDQ
ROBOT (TOKYO, 1971). (ROBOT.). [Robot]. (1971)-. Periodical. Japanese. Six times a year. $110.00. Japan Industrial Robot Association, 3 5 8 Shibakoen Minato-ku, Tokyo 105 Japan. **(Subscription address:** Maruzen Company Ltd., PO Box 5050, Import & Export Department, Tokyo 100 31 Japan. **Tel** 011 81 3 32789224.) **ED** Kanji Yonemoto. **Ad Acc, Adv Mgr:** Keiichi Takai. **Circ:** 3,500. Documents available from Ask*IEEE.
Desc: Contains a foreword, commentary, special issues, information on technology and application, research and development, new products, and interviews.
Ind/Abst Curr. Cit.; INSPEC (Feb. 1984-).

ISSN 0724-1712
    GW
UDC 658.52.011.56
ROBOTER. (1983)-. Trade Publication. German. Six times a year. $132.04. Verlag Moderne Industrie, Justus von Liebigstrasse 1, D-86899 Landsberg Lech Germany. **Tel** 011 49 8191 125453.

ISSN 0178-0026
    GW
    CCC
    CODEN RBTSE9
Pr Rev.
ROBOTERSYSTEME. [Robotersysteme]. Vol. 1, No. 1 (1985)-. Periodical. German (English). Four times a year. DM358.00. Springer-Verlag GmbH & Company KG, Heidelberger Platz 3, D-14197 Berlin Germany. **Tel** 011 49 30 8207223, FAX 011 49 30 8214091, telex 183 319 SPBLN D. **(Subscription address:** Springer-Verlag New York Inc. / North America, PO Box 2485, Journal Fulfillment, Secaucus NJ 07096. **Tel** (201)348-4033, (800)777-4643, FAX (201)348-4505.) **ED** U Rembold and H J Warnecke. available on microfilm and microfiche from University Microfilms International (UMI). Documents available from Article Express International, The Genuine Article, Ask*IEEE.
Ind/Abst Coal Abstr.; CompuMath Cit. Index [Full Cov.]; Curr. Contents Eng. Comput. Technol.; Eng. Index Annu.; INSPEC (1988-); Res. Alert [Full Cov.]; Robotics Abstr.

LC TJ210.2 .R6   ISSN 0263-5747
DD 629.8/92/05   UK
    CCC
Pr Rev.
ROBOTICA. [Robotica]. Vol. 1, Pt. 1 (Jan. 1983)-. Academic Scholarly Publication. English. Six times a year. $315.00. Cambridge University Press, The Edinburgh Building, Shaftesbury Road, Cambridge CB2 2RU United Kingdom. **Tel** 011 44 1223 312393, FAX 011 44 1223 315052, telex 851-817256. **(Subscription address:** Cambridge University Press / North America, 110 Midland Avenue, Port Chester NY 10573. **Tel** (800)431-1580, (914)937-9600.) **ED** J. Rose. **Bk Rev**. **Ad Acc. Circ:** 400. available on microfilm from University Microfilms International (UMI). Documents available from Article Express International, The Genuine Article, Ask*IEEE.
Desc: Provides an international forum for the multi-disciplinary subject of robotics and encourages developments in this field of automation with regard to industry, education and research. Covers the many aspects of robotics, including sensory perception, software, kinematics and dynamics involved in robot design, world model representation, artificial intelligence, development of relevant educational courses, training methods, analysis of managerial and social policy, economic and cost problems, and items of theoretical and practical interest. Particular stress is placed on practical applications of theoretical concepts in the industrial field and also on many aspects of artificial intelligence and its impact on automation.
Ind/Abst Abstr. Hum. Comput. Interact.; Agric. Eng. Abstr. (1991-); Comput. Rev.; Curr. Cit.; Curr. Contents Eng. Comput. Technol.; Eng. Index Annu.; Ergon. Abstr.; Inf. Sci. Abstr.; INSPEC (Jan. 1984-); Pollut. Abstr.; Indexes; Postharvest News Inf.; Res. Alert [Select. Cov.]; Robotics Abstr.

LC TJ210.2 .R62   ISSN 0921-8890
DD 629.8/92/05   NE
    CCC
    CODEN RASOEJ
Pr Rev.
ROBOTICS AND AUTONOMOUS SYSTEMS. [Robot. auton. syst.]. **VFOAT** Robotics. Vol. 4, No. 1, March (1988)-. Academic Scholarly Publication. English. Eight times a year (2 volumes). $549.00. Elsevier Science Publishers BV, PO Box 211, 1000 AE Amsterdam Netherlands. **Tel** 011 31 20 4853641, 011 31 20 4853642, FAX 011 31 20 4853598. available in microform from University Microfilms International (UMI); available on an online database from Elsevier Electronic Subscriptions (EES). Documents available from Article Express International, Ask*IEEE.
Continues Robotics, 0167-8493.
Ind/Abst Comput. Inf. Syst. Abstr. J. [Full Cov.]; Curr. Cit.; Elect. Comm. Abstr.; Eng. Index Annu.; Expand. Acad. Index (1992-); INSPEC (Nov. 1988-); Mech. Eng. Abstr.; Solid State Supercond. Abstr.

LC TS191.8 .R5593   ISSN 0736-5845
DD 670/.285   US
    CCC
Pr Rev.
ROBOTICS AND COMPUTER-INTEGRATED MANUFACTURING. See Industry and Production-Computer Applications.

LC TJ210.3 .W66A   ISSN 0891-4621
DD 629.8/92   US
    CCC
    SUSPENDED
ROBOTICS AND EXPERT SYSTEMS.
(ROBOTICS AND EXPERT SYSTEMS : PROCEEDINGS OF ROBEXS.). [Robot. expert syst.]. **Main/Corp** Workshop on Robotics and Expert Systems. **VFOAT** Proceedings of ROBEXS. 1st (1985)-Suspended (1989).

Proceedings. English. One time a year. Instrument Society of America, 67 Alexander Drive, Research Triangle NC 27709. **Tel** (919)549-8411, FAX (919)549-8288, telex 802 540.

US

ROBOTICS TODAY. Added/Corp Robotics International of SME. Vol. 1, No. 1 (Spring 1988)-. Periodical. English. Four times a year (Mar., June, Sept., Dec.). $70.00. Society of Manufacturing Engineers, One SME Drive, PO Box 930, Member's Records Dept., Dearborn MI 48121-0930. **Tel** (313)271-1500, FAX (313)271-2861, telex 297742 SME UR (VIA RCA). ***Continues*** *Robotics Today, 0193-6913.*
Ind/Abst ABI/INFORM Glob. Ed.; ABI/INFORM [Computer File]; Alum. Ind. Abstr.; Comput. ASAP [Full Txt.]; Comput. Database [Full Txt.]; INSPEC; Met. Abstr.; Robotics Abstr.; Trade Ind. ASAP [Full Txt.]; Trade Ind. Index [Full Txt.].

LC TS191.8 .R63 **ISSN** 0734-287X
DD 629.8/92/05 US
ROBOTICS TODAY (ANNUAL ED.). (ROBOTICS TODAY.). [Robot. today]. **Added/Corp** Robotics International of SME. (1982)-. English. One time a year. Society of Manufacturing Engineers, One SME Drive, PO Box 930, Member's Records Dept., Dearborn MI 48121-0930. **Tel** (313)271-1500, FAX (313)271-2861, telex 297742 SME UR (VIA RCA).

LC TJ210.2 .R63 **ISSN** 0737-5700
DD 629.8/92/05 US
ROBOTICS UPDATE. Vol. 1, No. 1 (Apr. 1983)-. Periodical. English. Twelve times a year. $67.00. Robotics Update Circulation Department, 10076 Boca Entrada Boulevard, Boca Raton FL 33433.

LC TS191.8 .R635 **ISSN** 0737-7908
DD 629.8/92/05 US
CCC
CEASED
ROBOTICS WORLD. [Rob. world]. Vol. 1, No. 1 (Jan. 1983)-(1995). Periodical. English. Argus Business, 6151 Powers Ferry Road Northwest, Atlanta GA 30339. **Tel** (404)995-2500, FAX (404)995-0400. **ED** Andrea Ashmore. **Circ:** 23,051. available on microfilm and microfiche from University Microfilms International (UMI); available on an online database (file 15/Full-Text) from DIALOG. Documents available from Article Express International.
Ind/Abst Appl. Sci. Technol. Index; Curr. Cit.; Eng. Index Annu.; Robotics Abstr.

US

ROBOTICS WORLD DIRECTORY. (1986)-. Directory. English. One time a year. $45.95. Communications Channels Inc, 6255 Barfield Road, Atlanta GA 30328-4369. **Tel** (404)256-9800, FAX (404)256-3116. **ED** Barbara Katinsky Also available in microform. **Ad Acc.** ***Continues*** *Robotics World. Directory Issue.*

LC Q334 .S54 **ISSN** 1053-4830
DD 006.3 US
SIGART BULLETIN. [SIGART bull.]. **Added/Corp** SIGART. Vol. 1, No. 1 (Jan./April 1990)-. Bulletin. English. Four times a year (Jan., Apr., July, Oct.). $25.00. ACM / Association for Computing Machinery, 1515 Broadway, 17th Floor, New York NY 10036. **Tel** (212)869-7440, FAX (212)869-0481. **(Subscription address:** Association for Computing Machinery, PO Box 12114, Church Street Station, New York NY 10249. **Tel** (212)626-0500.) ***Continues*** *SIGART Newsletter, 0163-5719.*
Ind/Abst Ergon. Abstr.

IT

SISTEMI INTELLIGENTI. Vol. 1, No. 1 (April 1989)-. Periodical. Italian. Three times a year. L62000.00 Italy; L120000.00 (surface mail), L140000.00 (airmail) other. Societa Editrice il Mulino, Strada Maggiore 37, 40125 Bologna Italy. **Tel** 011 39 51 256011, FAX 011 39 51 256034. **ED** Domenico Parisi. **Bk Rev. Ad Acc. Circ:** 2,000.
Ind/Abst Neuropsych. Abstr.; Psychoanal. Abstr.; PsycINFO (1989-); PsycScan: Appl. Exp. Eng. Psych.; PsycScan: LD/MR.

LC TK7882.S65 S677 **ISSN** 1070-857X
DD 006.4/54/05 US
•**SPEECH RECOGNITION UPDATE.** [Speech recognit. update]. **Added/Corp** TMA Associates. No. 1 (Jan. 1993)-. Periodical. English. Six times a year. $395.00. TMA Associates, PO Box 17568, Encino CA 91416. **Tel** (818) 708-0962, FAX (8181) 345-2980. **ED** William S. Meisel.

ISSN 0924-3542
NE
STUDIES IN COMPUTER SCIENCE AND ARTIFICIAL INTELLIGENCE. [Stud. comput. sci. artif. intell.]. (1986)-. Monographic series. English. Irregular. Elsevier Science Publishers BV, PO Box 211, 1000 AE Amsterdam Netherlands. **Tel** 011 31 20 4853641, 011 31 20 4853642, FAX 011 31 20 4853598. **(Subscription address:** Elsevier Science Inc. / New York Books, 655 Avenue of the Americas, New York NY 10010. **Tel** (212)633-3650.)
Ind/Abst Math. Rev.; Zentralbl. Math. Ihre Grenzgeb.

LC HD9696.R62 T43 **ISSN** 0741-367X
DD 338.4/7629892 US
TECHNICAL INSIGHTS ANNUAL REPORT ON INDUSTRIAL ROBOTS. [Tech. insights annu. rep. ind. robots]. **VFOAT** Annual Report on Industrial Robots. 1983/1984-. English. One time a year. $175.00. Technical Insights Inc., PO Box 1304, Fort Lee NJ 07024-9967. **Tel** (201)568-4744, FAX (201)568-8247, telex 425900 SWIFT UI.

ISSN 0040-1927
IT
TECNICHE DELL AUTOMAZIONE & ROBOTICA. (19??)-. Italian. Twelve times a year. L64720. Etas SRL, Via Mecenate 89, 20138 Milan Italy. **Tel** 011 39 2 580841.

UK
TRANSLATING AND THE COMPUTER : PROCEEDINGS OF A CONFERENCE JOINTLY SPONSORED BY ASLIB, THE ASSOCIATION FOR INFORMATION MANAGEMENT; THE ASLIB TECHNICAL TRANSLATION GROUP; THE TRANSLATORS' GUILD. Proceedings. English. One time a year. ASLIB, Information House, 20-24 Old Street, London EC1V 9AP United Kingdom. **Tel** 011 44 171 2534488, FAX 011 44 171 4300514, telex 23667 AJLIB G.
Ind/Abst Curr. Cit.

LC HD9696.C63 U59348 **ISSN** 1065-271X
DD 004 US
TITLE CHANGE
VIRTUAL REALITY MARKET PLACE. [Virtual real. mark. place]. **VFOAT** Virtual Reality; Virtual Reality Market Place Company Directory. (1993)-(1993). Trade Publication. English. Mecklermedia Corporation, 11 Ferry Lane West, Westport CT 06880. **Tel** (203)226-6967, (800)632-5537, FAX (203)454-5840. ***Continued by*** *Virtual Reality World's Virtual Reality Market Place.*
Desc: Profiles of companies offering VR products and services.

LC QA76.9.C65 V5 **ISSN** 1052-6242
DD 003 US
CEASED
VIRTUAL REALITY REPORT. [Virtual real. rep.]. Vol. 1, No. 1 (Jan./Feb. 1991)-(1994). Periodical. English. Mecklermedia Corporation, 11 Ferry Lane West, Westport CT 06880. **Tel** (203)226-6967, (800)632-5537, FAX (203)454-5840. **(Subscription address:** Fulco, 30 Broad Street, Denville NJ 07834. **Tel** (800)783-4903, (201)627-2427.) **ED** Sandra Helsel. Index available. cum. index. **Bk Rev. Ad Acc. Circ:** 900.
Desc: Reports on the organizing consciousness of an emerging new discipline and its requisite concepts and technologies. Each issue brings news, reviews, analysis and interviews from the professionals who are pioneering in artificial reality, cyberspace, and virtual reality.

ISSN 1074-1038
DD 006 US
VIRTUAL REALITY SPECIAL REPORT. [Virtual real. spec. rep.]. **VFOAT** Virtual Reality. (1994)-. Periodical. English. Four times a year. $32.00. Miller Freeman Inc., 600 Harrison Street, San Francisco CA 94107. **Tel** (415)905-2337, (415)905-2200, FAX (415)905-2240, telex 278273.

LC QA76.575 .V55 **ISSN** 1060-9547
DD 006 US
CCC
TITLE CHANGE
VIRTUAL REALITY WORLD. [Virtual real. world]. Vol. 1, No. 1 (Spring 1993)-Vol. 2, No. 6 (Nov./Dec. 1994). Periodical. English. Six times a year. Mecklermedia Corporation, 11 Ferry Lane West, Westport CT 06880. **Tel** (203)226-6967, (800)632-5537, FAX (203)454-5840. **(Subscription address:** Fulco, 30 Broad Street, Denville NJ 07834. **Tel** (800)783-4903, (201)627-2427.) ***Continued by*** *VR World.*

LC HD9696.C63 U59348 **ISSN** 1081-7824
DD 006 US
CEASED
VIRTUAL REALITY WORLD'S VIRTUAL REALITY MARKET PLACE. See Computers-Computer Industry and Industry Directories.

ISSN 0884-6685
DD 384 US
VOICE PROCESSING. (VOICE PROCESSING : THE NEWSLETTER OF VOICE STORE & FORWARD, RECOGNITION, RESPONSE.). [Voice process.]. (19??)-. Newsletter. English. Twenty-four times a year. $497.00 US and Canada; $527.00 other. Probe Research Inc., Three Wing Drive, Suite 240, Cedar Knolls NJ 07927-1000. **Tel** (201)285-1500, FAX (201)285-1519. **ED** Frank Barbetta, Adam Greenberg, Chris Seelbach, Karl Kozarsky, and Victor Schnee. Index available. **Circ:** 400 (ctrl).
Desc: A publication of the voice (messaging, response, synthesis, recognition) industries.

LC QA76.575 .V55 **ISSN** 1060-9547
US
CCC
CEASED
VR WORLD. VFOAT Virtual Reality World. Vol. 3, No. 1 (Jan./Feb. 1995)-(July 1995). Periodical. English. Mecklermedia Corporation, 11 Ferry Lane West, Westport CT 06880. **Tel** (203)226-6967, (800)632-5537, FAX (203)454-5840. **(Subscription address:** Meckler Media Ltd., Artillery House Artillery Row, London SW1P 1RT United Kingdom. **Tel** 011 44 171 9760405, FAX 011 44 171 9760506.) ***Continues*** *Virtual Reality World.*

AUTOMATION

ISSN 0885-5684
DD 670 US
CCC
ADVANCED MANUFACTURING TECHNOLOGY. [Adv. manuf. technol.]. **Added/Corp** Technical Insights, Inc. Vol. 6, No. 1 (Jan. 14, 1985)-. Periodical. English. Twelve times a year. $630.00. Technical Insights Inc., PO Box 1304, Fort Lee NJ 07024-9967. **Tel** (201)568-4744, FAX (201)568-8247, telex 425900 SWIFT UI. **ED** Ed Flinn. available on an online database from NEXIS; and (file 636/Full-Text) DIALOG. Documents available from Ask*IEEE. ***Continues*** *Industrial Robots International, 0197-9280.*
Desc: Focuses on technological advances leading to the factory of the future.
Ind/Abst Curr. Cit.; INSPEC (Feb. 1987-); PTS Newsl. Database [Full Txt.].

LC QA76.9.I58 A38 **ISSN** 0748-8602
DD 004/.01/905 US
ADVANCES IN HUMAN-COMPUTER INTERACTION. [Adv. hum.-comput. interact.]. **VFOAT** Advances in Human Computer Interaction. Vol. 1 (1985)-. English. One time a year. Price varies per volume. Ablex Publishing Corporation, 355 Chestnut Street, Norwood NJ 07648. **Tel** (201)767-8450, (201)767-8455 (Customer Service), FAX (201)767-6717. **ED** Rex Hartson and Deborah Hix.
Desc: Annual book series consisting of state-of-the-art articles on all facets of human-computer interaction.

RU
AKTIVNYE SISTEMY. (1973)-. Russian. Irregular.

US
ANNUAL RESEARCH REVIEW / THE ROBOTICS INSTITUTE. Main/Corp Carnegie-Mellon University. Robotics Institute. (1983)-. Academic Scholarly Publication. English. One time a year. Free on request. Carnegie Mellon University Robotics Institute, 5000 Forbes Avenue, Pittsburgh PA 15213-3891. **Tel** (412)268-3818. **ED** Sean Brady.

LC CD973.D3 A7 **ISSN** 1042-1467
DD 025.3/16 US
CODEN AMUIEA
ARCHIVES & MUSEUM INFORMATICS. [Arch. mus. inform.]. **Added/Corp** Archives & Museum Informatics (Firm). **VFOAT** Archives and Museum Informatics; Archival Informatics Newsletter. Vol. 3, No. 1 Spring (1989)-. Periodical. English. Four times a year. $90.00. Archives & Museum Informatics, 5501 Walnut Street, Suite 203, Pittsburgh PA 15232-2311. **Tel** (412)683-9775, FAX (412)683-7366. **ED** David Bearman. Index available (published in August). **Circ:** 500. Documents available from Ask*IEEE. ***Continues*** *Archival Informatics Newsletter & Technical Reports. Part 1, Archival Informatics Newsletter, 0892-2179.*
Desc: Reports on developments in uses of automated techniques in archival repositories and museums. Features critical reviews of software, essays on issues in archiving automated records and managing collections, and reports and evaluations of on-going projects.
Ind/Abst Ei Page One; INSPEC (Spring 1990-).

LC TJ212 .A7 **ISSN** 1230-2384
DD 629.8/05 PL
ARCHIVES OF CONTROL SCIENCES. [Arch. control sci.]. **Added/Corp** Polska Akademia Nauk. Komitet Automatyki i Robotyki (Polish Academy of Sciences. Committee of Automated Control and Robotics). Vol. 1, No. 1/2 (1992)-. Periodical. English. Four times a year. $50.00. Panstwowe Wydawnictwo Naukowe / PWN, (Polish Scientific Publishers PWN Ltd.), Ul. Miodowa 10, PO Box 391, 00-251 Warsaw Poland. **Tel** 011 48 22 312738, FAX 011 48 22 267163. **(Subscription address:** Ars Polona-Ruch, PO Box 1001, Krakowskie Przedmiescie 7, 00-068 Warsaw Poland. **Tel** 011 48 22 261201.) ***Continues*** *Archiwum Automatyki i Robotyki.*
Ind/Abst INSPEC (1992-).

LC TS178.4 .A84 **ISSN** 0144-5154
DD 671.42/7 UK
CCC
CODEN ASAUDL
ASSEMBLY AUTOMATION. [Assem. autom.]. Vol. 1, No. 1 (Nov. 1980)-. Trade Publication. English. Four times a year. $869.00. MCB University Press, 60 62 Toller Lane, Bradford, West Yorkshire BD8 9BY United Kingdom. **Tel** 011 44 1274 785280, FAX 011 44 1274 785200, telex 51317-MCBUNI-G. **(Subscription address:** MCB University Press / US and Canada Subscriptions, PO Box 10812, Birmingham AL 35201-0812. **Tel** (205)995-1567, (800)633-4931, FAX (205)995-1588.**) ED** Clive Loughlin. **Bk Rev**. Documents available from Article Express International, UMI Article Clearinghouse, Ask*IEEE.
Desc: Emphasizes trends towards flexible manufacture. Of interest to engineers, managers and researchers with responsibilities in small scale as well as large volume manufacture.
Ind/Abst ABI/INFORM Glob. Ed.; Bioeng. Abstr.; Curr. Cit.; Ei Page One; Eng. Index Annu.; Fluid Abstr., Civil Eng.; Fluid Abstr. Proc. Eng.; FLUIDEX; INSPEC (May 1981-); Pollut. Abstr. Indexes; Robotics Abstr.

ISSN 1051-3396
DD 004 US
AUTOMATED AGENCY REPORT, THE. [Autom. agency rep.]. Vol. 6, No. 6 (June 1990)-. Periodical. English. Twelve times a year. $175.00. Automation Management Group, PO Box 7024, Boulder CO 80306. **Tel** (303)449-9898. ***Continues*** *Agency Automation Report, 0888-8205.*

LC TJ212 .A7375 **ISSN** 0146-4116
DD 629.8/028/54 US
CCC
CODEN ACCSCE
AUTOMATIC CONTROL AND COMPUTER SCIENCES. [Autom. control comput. sci.]. Vol. 6 (1972)-. Academic Scholarly Publication. English (Russian). Six times a year. $985.00. Allerton Press Inc., 150 Fifth Avenue, New York NY 10011. **Tel** (212)924-3950, FAX (212)463-9684, telex 427441 ALPRES. Index available. **Bk Rev**. Documents available from Article Express International, Ask*IEEE, CASDDS. ***Continues*** *Automatic Control, 0005-1047.*
Desc: Provides information on automatic control, electronic data processing and software.
Ind/Abst ACM Guide Comput. Lit.; Bioeng. Abstr.; Chem. Abstr.; Comput. Rev.; Curr. Cit.; Ei Page One; Eng. Index Annu.; INSPEC (1976-); Math. Rev.; Pollut. Abstr. Indexes; Zentralbl. Math. Ihre Grenzgeb.

ISSN 0890-9768
DD 658 US
CCC
CODEN AIDNEE
AUTOMATIC I.D. NEWS. [Autom. I.D. news]. **VFOAT** Automatic ID News. **VAT** Automatic Identification News. (19??)-. Trade Publication. English. Thirteen times a year. $41.00. Advanstar Communications Inc., 131 West First Street, Duluth MN 55802. **Tel** (218)723-9477, (800)346-0085, FAX (218)723-9437. **Circ:** 12,000.
Ind/Abst Bus. Source Plus; EP Collect.; Homework Help.; MasterFile FullTEXT 1000; MasterFile FullTEXT 350; MasterFile FullTEXT 650; MasterFile FullTEXT (Jan. 1995-); OCLC; Telebase.

US
AUTOMATIC I.D. NEWS EUROPE. (19??)-. Trade Publication. English. Thirteen times a year. £72.00 Western Europe; £102.00 other. Advanstar Communications Inc., 131 West First Street, Duluth MN 55802. **Tel** (218)723-9477, (800)346-0085, FAX (218)723-9437. **(Subscription address:** Advanstar Communications / UK Subscriptions, Park West Sealand Road, Chester CH1 4RN United Kingdom. **Tel** 011 44 1244 378888.**)**
Ind/Abst MasterFile FullTEXT (Jan. 1995-).

ISSN 0213-3113
SP
UDC 62-52
Pr Rev.
AUTOMATICA E INSTRUMENTACION. [Autom. instrum.]. (1985)-. Periodical. Spanish. Ten times a year. $220.27. CETISA Boixareu Editores SA, C Concepcion Arenal 5 7, 08027 Barcelona Spain. **Tel** 011 34 3 3527061. Index available. cum. index. **Bk Rev**. **Ad Acc.** ctrl circ. Documents available from Ask*IEEE. ***Continues*** *Tecnica de la Regulacion y Mando Automatico, 0040-1722.*
Desc: Industrial automation, control engineering and machine design.
Ind/Abst Curr. Cit.; Fluid Abstr., Civil Eng.; Fluid Abstr. Proc. Eng.; FLUIDEX (199?-); INSPEC (Sep. 1985-).

LC TJ212 .A74 **ISSN** 0005-1098
DD 629.8/05 UK
CCC
CODEN ATCAA9
Pr Rev.
AUTOMATICA (OXFORD). (AUTOMATICA : THE JOURNAL OF IFAC, THE INTERNATIONAL FEDERATION OF AUTOMATIC CONTROL.). [Automatica]. **Added/Corp** International Federation of Automatic Control. Vol. 1 (Jan./March 1963)-. Periodical. English (French and German; summaries and/or abstracts in Russian). Twelve times a year. $1284.00. Pergamon Press, An Imprint of Elsevier Science Ltd., The Boulevard, Langford Lane, Kidlington, Oxford OX5 1GB United Kingdom. **Tel** 011 44 1865 843000, 011 44 1865 843699, FAX 011 44 1865 843010. **(Subscription address:** Elsevier Science Ltd. / Oxford Fulfillment Centre, PO Box 800, Kidlington OX5 1DX United Kingdom. **Tel** 011 44 865 843355.**) ED** Hulbert Kwakernaak. available on microfilm and microfiche from University Microfilms International (UMI); available on an online database from Elsevier Electronic Subscriptions (EES). Documents available from Article Express International, The Genuine Article, Ask*IEEE, Documents on Demand.
Desc: Publishes papers on theoretical and experimental research and its practical application to all types of control systems.
Ind/Abst Abstr. Bull. Inst. Pap. Sci. Tech.; Abstr. Hum. Comput. Interact.; ACM Guide Comput. Lit.; Appl. Mech. Rev.; Aqualine Abstr.; Bioeng. Abstr.; CompuMath Cit. Index [Full Cov.]; Comput. Abstr.; Comput. Rev.; Curr. Cit.; Curr. Contents Eng. Comput. Technol.; Ei Page One; EMBASE; Energy Inf. Abstr.; Eng. Index Annu.; Environ. Abstr.; Ergon. Abstr.; HILITES; Inf. Sci. Abstr.; INSPEC (1968-); Int. Aerosp. Abstr. (1991-); Math. Rev.; Res. Alert [Full Cov.]; Sci. Cit. Index; SCISEARCH; Zentralbl. Math. Ihre Grenzgeb.

ISSN 0005-1128
NE
CODEN AUTOA7
AUTOMATIE. [Automatie]. Vol. 1 (1957)-. Academic Scholarly Publication. English. Twelve times a year. $75.37. Uitgeverij Adex, Postbus 328, 3760 AH Soest Netherlands. **Tel** 011 31 2155 10034. Documents available from Ask*IEEE.
Ind/Abst Curr. Cit.; EMBASE; F&S Index Plus Text, Int. [Select. Cov.]; INSPEC (1968-).

JA
AUTOMATION. (19??)-. Japanese. Twelve times a year. $236.00. Nikkan Kogyo Shinbun Ltd. (Industrial Daily News Ltd.), 1-8-10 Kudan Kita Chiyoda-ku, Tokyo 102 Japan.

ISSN 0110-6295
NZ
CODEN AUCODR
AUTOMATION AND CONTROL. [Autom. control]. **Added/Corp** Automatic Control and Instrumentation Society (NZ). (1971)-. Trade Publication. English. Eleven times a year. $50.92. Matrix Publishing, PO Box 99 731 Newmarket, Auckland New Zealand. **Tel** 011 64 9 3795393. **ED** Ross MacKay. Index available. **Bk Rev**. **Ad Acc. Circ:** 7,000 (ctrl). Documents available from Article Express International, Ask*IEEE. ***Absorbed*** *Electronics and Communications.*
Desc: Practical information on control of industrial processes, electricity, instrumentation, computers, communications, pneumatics and hydraulics, with emphasis on New Zealand industry applications.
Ind/Abst Eng. Index Annu. [Select. Cov.]; INSPEC (1976-).

LC TJ212 .A9135 **ISSN** 0005-1179
DD 629.8/05 US
CCC
CODEN AURCAT
Pr Rev.
AUTOMATION AND REMOTE CONTROL. [Autom. remote control]. **Added/Corp** Consultants Bureau. Consultants Bureau Enterprises. Massachusetts Institute of Technology. Instrument Society of America. Vol. 17 (Jan. 1956)-. Academic Scholarly Publication. English (Russian). Twenty-four times a year. $1565.00. Consultants Bureau, A Division of Plenum Publishing Corporation, 233 Spring Street, New York NY 10013. **Tel** (212)620-8000, (212)620-8466, FAX (212)463-0742, telex 23/421139. **ED** N. A. Kuznetsov. available on microfilm and microfiche from University Microfilms International (UMI). Documents available from Article Express International, The Genuine Article, Ask*IEEE, CASDDS.
Desc: Coverage of research conducted in active areas of automation and remote control technology. Publishes research dealing in all phases of automatic control theory.
Ind/Abst Appl. Mech. Rev.; Bioeng. Abstr.; Chem. Abstr. (?-1982); CompuMath Cit. Index [Full Cov.]; Comput. Abstr.; Comput. Rev.; Curr. Cit.; Curr. Contents Eng. Comput. Technol.; Ei Page One; Eng. Index Annu.; Inf. Sci. Abstr.; INIS Atomindex [Micro.]; INSPEC (Sept. 1969-); Int. Aerosp. Abstr.; Math. Rev.; Pollut. Abstr. Indexes; Res. Alert [Full Cov.]; Sci. Cit. Index; SCISEARCH; Soc. Sci. Cit. Index [Select. Cov.]; Zentralbl. Math. Ihre Grenzgeb.

ISSN 0005-1152
UK
CODEN ATMNBV
TITLE CHANGE
AUTOMATION (LONDON). (AUTOMATION.). [Automation]. (1966)-(19??). Periodical. English. United Trade Press Ltd, 33/35 Bowling Green Lane, London EC1R 0DA United Kingdom. **Tel** 011 44 171 8371212. available on microfilm and microfiche from University Microfilms International (UMI). Documents available from Ask*IEEE. ***Merged into*** *Production & Industrial Equipment Digest.*
Ind/Abst BMT Abstr. (-19??); Bus. Index (1987-1991); Data Process. Dig.; Ergon. Abstr. (1973-?); Fluid Abstr., Civil Eng.; Fluid Abstr. Proc. Eng.; FLUIDEX (1973-); Gen. BusinessFile (1987-1991); INSPEC (Nov. 1968-); Pap. Board Abstr.; Print. Abstr.; UMI ABI/Inform--Bus. Period. Ondisc [Full Txt.].

ISSN 0005-125X
XR
CODEN AUTMAZ
AUTOMATIZACE. [Automatizace]. **Added/Corp** Statni Nakladatelstvi Technicke Literatury. (1958)-. Academic Scholarly Publication. Czech. Twelve times a year. $106.30. **(Subscription address:** Artia Pegas Press Ltd., Palac Metro Narodni Trida 25, 11210 Prague 1 Czech Republic. **Tel** 011 42 2 24196265, 011 42 2 24196266.**)** Documents available from Article Express International, Ask*IEEE.
Ind/Abst Alum. Ind. Abstr.; Bioeng. Abstr.; Ei Page One; EMBASE; Eng. Index Annu.; INSPEC (1968-); Int. Aerosp. Abstr.; Met. Abstr.; Saf. Health Work.

LC TJ212 .A865 **ISSN** 0133-1620
HU
AUTOMATIZALAS. [Automatizalas]. **Added/Corp** KGM Muszaki Tudomanyos Tajekoztato Intezet. Muszaki Informacios Osztaly. (1967)-. Periodical. Hungarian (summaries and/or abstracts in English, German and Russian). Twelve times a year. Prodinform Muszaki Tanacsodo Vallalat, (Prodinform Technical Consulting Company), Munkacsy Mihaly u. 16, PO Box 453, H-1372 Budapest Hungary. **Tel** 361-317-569. **(Subscription address:** Kultura, PO Box 143, H-1300 Budapest 3 Hungary. **Tel** 011 36 1 2500194.**) Bk Rev**. **Ad Acc. Circ:** 1550.
Desc: Co-sponsored by the Hungarian Foreign Trade Office.
Ind/Abst Energy Res. Abstr. (Aug. 1982-).

ISSN 0865-7580
HU
UDC 681.3
AUTOMATIZALAS ES ROBOTTECHNIKA. [Autom. robottech.]. (1990)-. Periodical. Multiple languages. Twelve times a year. ***Continues*** *Automatizalas, 0133-1620.*
Ind/Abst Fluid Abstr., Civil Eng.; Fluid Abstr. Proc. Eng.; FLUIDEX (19??-).

ISSN 0231-0643
HU
UDC 016
CODEN 681.5
AUTOMATIZALASI, SZAMTASTECHNIKAI ES MERESTECHNIKAI SZAKIRODALMI TAJEKOZTATO. (1983)-. Periodical. Hungarian. Twelve times a year. Orszagos Muszaki Informacios Kozpont es Konyvtar (O.M.I.K.K.), National Technical Information Centre and Library Museum, Muzeum u. 17, PO Box 12, 1428 Budapest Hungary. **Tel** 011 36 1 1181994, FAX 011 36 1 1382414, telex 22-4944 OMIKK H. **ED** Pal Konyves Toth. **Circ:** 185.
Desc: Information on computers, computer science, robots, and control.

IT
AUTOMAZIONE E STRUMENTAZIONE. **Added/Corp** Associazione Nazionale italiana per L'Automazione. Vol. 1 (1953)-. Periodical. Italian. Twelve times a year. L80000 Italy; L100000 other. Editrice Bias, Viale Premuda 2, 20129 Milan Italy. **Tel** 011 39 2 55181842. Index available. Documents available from Ask*IEEE. ***Absorbed*** *Automazione.*
Ind/Abst INSPEC (1968-).

LC TS500 **ISSN** 0392-8829
DD 681 IT
UDC 681.326
AUTOMAZIONE OGGI. [Autom. oggi]. (1983)-. Periodical. Italian. Eleven times a year. L49000. Gruppo Editoriale Jackson Spa, Via Gorki 69, 20092 Cinisello Balsamo Italy. **Tel** 011 39 2 66034401.

LC TJ212 .A97 **ISSN** 0132-4160
LV
CCC
CODEN AVYTAK
AVTOMATIKA I VYCISLITEL'NAYA TEHNIKA (RIGA). (AVTOMATIKA I VYCHISLITEL'NAIA TEKHNIKA.). [Avtom. vycisl. teh.]. **Added/Corp** Latvijas PSR Zinatnu Akademija. Elektronikas un Skaitlosanas Tehnikas Instituts (Latvijas PSR Zinatnu Akademija). **VFOAT** Trudy Instituta; AVT. Vol. 1 (1967)-. Periodical. Russian. Six times a year. Latvian Academy of Sciences, Institute of Electronic and Computer Science, Dzerbenes iela, 14 Riga LV-1006 Latvia. **Tel** 371 2 554500. **(Subscription address:** Victor Kamkin, 4956 Boiling Brook Parkway, Rockville MD 20852. **Tel** (301)881-5973.**) ED** J. Bilinskis. Index available. **Bk Rev**. **Circ:** 70,000. Documents available from Article Express International, The Genuine Article, Ask*IEEE.
Desc: Provides information on automatic control, electronic data processing and software.

Computers —Automation

LC TJ212 .A93   **ISSN** 0572-2691
DD 621.317   UN
    CCC
Pr Rev.   **TITLE CHANGE**

Ind/Abst Eng. Index Annu.; INSPEC (1968-); Math. Rev.; Res. Alert [Select. Cov.]; SCISEARCH; Zentralbl. Math. Ihre Grenzgeb.

AVTOMATIKA (KIEV). (AVTOMATIKA.).
[Avtomatika]. **Added/Corp** Institut Kibernetiki im. V.M. Glushkova. Instytut Kibernetyky (Akademiia Nauk Ukrainskoi RSR). No. 1 (1978)-(1993). Academic Scholarly Publication. Russian (summaries and/or abstracts in English and Ukrainian; table of contents in English). Izdatelstvo Naukova Dumka / Ukrainian Academy of Sciences, Yu. A. Khramov, Dir., Ul. Repina 3, 252 601 Kiev Ukraine. **Tel** 011 7 44 4303441, 011 7 44 2254182, telex 131376. **(Subscription address:** East View Publications Inc., 3020 Harbor Lane North, Suite 110, Minneapolis MN 55447. **Tel** (800)477-1005, (612)550-0961, FAX (612)559-2931.) **ED** AG Ivakhnenko, VV Pavlov. Index available. cum. index. **Bk Rev. Ad Acc. Circ:** 2,290 (ctrl). Documents available from The Genuine Article, Ask*IEEE, CASDDS. **Continues** Avtomatika. **Continued by** Problemy Upravleniia i Avtomatiki.
Ind/Abst Alum. Ind. Abstr.; Chem. Abstr.; Curr. Contents Eng. Comput. Technol.; Eng. Mater. Abstr.; INSPEC (1978-); Int. Aerosp. Abstr.; Math. Rev.; Met. Abstr.; Pollut. Abstr. Indexes; Res. Alert [Select. Cov.]; SCISEARCH; Zentralbl. Math. Ihre Grenzgeb.

    ISSN 0320-7102
    RU
    CCC
    CODEN AVMEBI

AVTOMETRIJA (NOVOSIBIRSK).
(AVTOMETRIIA.). [Avtometrija]. **Added/Corp** Akademiia Nauk SSSR. Sibirskoe Otdelenie. No. 1 (1965)-. Periodical. Russian. Six times a year. $129.95. **(Subscription address:** East View Publications Inc., 3020 Harbor Lane North, Suite 110, Minneapolis MN 55447. **Tel** (800)477-1005, (612)550-0961, FAX (612)559-2931.) Documents available from Article Express International, Ask*IEEE, CASDDS.
Ind/Abst Chem. Abstr.; Ei Page One; Eng. Index Annu.; INSPEC (1968-); Math. Rev.

    BE

BELEIDSINFORMATICA. (19??)-. Periodical.
Dutch. Four times a year. 500F. Contactgroep Beleidsinformatica, Dekenstraat 2, 3000 Louvain Belgium. **ED** F. Put. Index available. **Circ:** 600 (ctrl).
Desc: Discusses an issue of computer automation that is presently of interest.

    ISSN 0303-1276
    FR

BULLETIN DE LIAISON DE LA RECHERCHE EN INFORMATIQUE ET AUTOMATIQUE. [Bull. liaison rech. inform. autom.]. **Added/Corp** Institut de Recherche d'Informatique et d'Automatique. (19??)-. Bulletin. French. Irregular (5 to 6 per year). Free on request. Institut National de Recherche et Informatique en Automatique, SEDIS Diffusion, Domaine de Voluceau-Rocquencourt, BP 105, 78153 Le Chesnay Cedex France. **Tel** 011 33 1 39635627, FAX 011 33 1 39635228, telex 697033 F. **ED** Nicole Ray. Documents available from Ask*IEEE.
Desc: Information on the various aspects of automation, including algorithms, transport vehicles, and the integration of automation.
Ind/Abst INSPEC (1987-); Math. Rev.

    FR

BULLETIN L'AFRI. (19??)-. Bulletin. French.
Irregular. Association Francaise de Robotique Industrielle, 4 place Jussieu Tour 66, F 75252 Paris Cedex 5 France. **Tel** 011 33 1 43547170, FAX 011 33 1 43547170.

LC TJ212 .B87   **ISSN** 0296-8517
DD 629.8/05   FR
    CODEN BEAUE3
    TITLE CHANGE

BUREAU D'ETUDES AUTOMATISMES.
[Bur. etudes autom.]. No. 19 (Sept. 1985)-(19??). Periodical. French. CEP Information Technologie, Immeuble Europais, 26 rue d'Oradour sur Glane, 75504 Paris Cedex 15 France. **Tel** 011 33 1 44253131, FAX 011 31 1 45573506, telex 270589F. Documents available from Ask*IEEE. **Formed by the union of** Bureaux d'Etudes **and** Nouvel Automatisme, 0220-8482. **Continued by** Bureaux d'Etudes, 1148-7305.
Ind/Abst INSPEC (1985-?).

LC Z678.93.L63 C33   **ISSN** 1065-0741
DD 004   US
    CCC

●CAMPUS-WIDE INFORMATION SYSTEMS. (CAMPUS-WIDE INFORMATION SYSTEMS : CWIS.). [Campus-wide inf. syst.]. **VFOAT** Campus-Wide Information Systems; Campus Wide Information Systems; CWIS. Vol. 10, No. 1 (Jan./Feb. 1993)-. Periodical. English. Four times a year. $179.00. MCB University Press, 60 62 Toller Lane, Bradford, West Yorkshire BD8 9BY United Kingdom. **Tel** 011 44 1274 785280, FAX 011 44 1274 785200, telex 51317-MCBUNI-G. **ED** Les Lloyd. **Continues** Academic and Library Computing, 1055-4769.
Desc: Covers the use and development of campus-wide information systems, networks and on-line interfaces. Devoted to discussing and providing examples of implementation of networking students, libraries and university/college administration.
Ind/Abst Comput. Database; Inf. Sci. Abstr.; Microcomput. Abstr.

LC GA101 .C33   **ISSN** 0008-7041
    UK
    CCC
    CODEN CGJLA8
Pr Rev.

CARTOGRAPHIC JOURNAL, THE. See
Geography-Cartography.

LC TJ212 .T9844   **ISSN** 1044-064X
DD 629.8   US
    CCC
    CODEN CJAUEF

CHINESE JOURNAL OF AUTOMATION.
[Chin. j. autom.]. **Added/Corp** Chinese Association of Automation. Vol. 1, No. 1 (1989)-. Periodical. English (translations available in Chinese). Four times a year. $455.00. Allerton Press Inc., 150 Fifth Avenue, New York NY 10011. **Tel** (212)924-3950, FAX (212)463-9684, telex 427441 ALPRES.
Ind/Abst INSPEC (1991-).

    ISSN 0931-3125
    GW
UDC 681.323 :658.5

CIM-PRAXIS. See Industry and Production-Computer Applications.

LC TJ212   **ISSN** 0361-1442
DD 001.6/4/05   US
    CODEN CPLEAQ

COMPUTERS AND PEOPLE. [Comput. people]. Vol. 23 (Jan. 1974)-. Academic Scholarly Publication. English. Irregular. Price varies per volume. Academic Press Inc., 6277 Sea Harbor Drive, Orlando FL 32887. **Tel** (800)543-9534, (407)345-4100, FAX (407)352-3445. Index available. cum. index. **Bk Rev. Circ:** 2,600. available on microfilm from University Microfilms International (UMI). Documents available from Ask*IEEE, UMI Article Clearinghouse. **Continues** Computers and Automation (Newtonville, Mass. : 1973), 0887-4549.
Desc: Series that provides significant and clear information to the intelligent reader to understand and apply to computers. Covers applications and implications of information.
Ind/Abst ABI/INFORM Glob. Ed.; ABI/INFORM [Computer File] (Jan. 1974-Sept. 1981); Account. Art.; Bus. Index (1988-); Bus. Period. Index; Comput. Rev.; EMBASE; Gen. BusinessFile (1988-); Gen. Period. Index (1985-); GeoRef; INIS Atomindex [Micro.]; INSPEC (Jan. 1974-); Trade Ind. Index [Full Txt.].

    ISSN 0956-3385
    UK
    CCC
    CODEN CCEJEL

COMPUTING & CONTROL ENGINEERING JOURNAL. [Comput. control eng. j.]. **Added/Corp** Institution of Electrical Engineers. **VFOAT** Computing and Control Engineering Journal. Vol. 1, No. 1 (Jan. 1990)-. Periodical. English. Six times a year. $217.33. Institution of Electrical Engineers / IEE, Michael Faraday House, Six Hills Way, Stevenage Hertfordshire SG1 2AY United Kingdom. **Tel** 011 44 1438 313311, FAX 011 44 1438 742840, telex 825578 IEESTV G. **(Subscription address:** IEE / Peter Peregrinus Ltd., PO Box 96, Stevenage Herts SG1 2SD United Kingdom. **Tel** 011 44 1438 313311, FAX 011 44 438 742792, telex 825578 IEESTV G.) Documents available from Article Express International, Ask*IEEE. **Absorbed** Computer-Aided Engineering Journal, 0263-9327.
Ind/Abst Curr. Cit.; Ei Page One; Eng. Index Annu.; INSPEC (1990-).

LC TJ212 .A738   **ISSN** 0730-9538
DD 629.8/05   US
    CODEN CONCER

CONTROL AND COMPUTERS. [Control comput.]. **Added/Corp** International Association of Science and Technology for Development. Vol. 9, No. 1 (1981)-. Periodical. English (French). Three times a year. $187.00. IASTED- International Association of Science and Technology for Development, PO Box 2481, Anaheim CA 92814. **Tel** (714)778-3230, (800)995-2161, FAX (714)535-2662. **ED** Prof M H Hamza. Index available. **Bk Rev. Ad Acc. Circ:** 500. Documents available from Ask*IEEE. **Continues** Automatic Control Theory & Applications, 0315-8934.
Desc: Covers all aspects of automatic control theory and its applications with special emphasis on computers in control. Includes book reviews, conferences, call for papers, new publications, and advertisements.
Ind/Abst Curr. Cit.; INSPEC (1981-); Int. Aerosp. Abstr. (1983-); Math. Rev.

LC QA402.3 .C62   **ISSN** 0324-8569
DD 629.8/312/05   PL
    CODEN CCYBAP

CONTROL AND CYBERNETICS. See
Computers-Cybernetics.

LC TJ212 .C593   **ISSN** 0010-8022
DD 629.8/05 629.8   UK
    CCC
    CODEN CTLIAW

CONTROL & INSTRUMENTATION. [Control & instrum.]. **VAT** Control and instrumentation. Vol. 1 (May 1969)-. Trade Publication. English. Twelve times a year. $180.00. Morgan Grampian, 40 Beresford Street Woolwich, London SE18 6BQ United Kingdom. **Tel** 011 44 181 8557777, FAX 011 44 181 8555548, telex 896238. **ED** B Tinham. **Bk Rev. Ad Acc. Circ:** 18,000 (ctrl). available on microfilm and microfiche from University Microfilms International (UMI); available on an online database (files 16,648/Full-Text) from DIALOG. Documents available from Article Express International, The Genuine Article, Ask*IEEE. **Formed by the union of** Control (London) **and** M & I, Measurement and Instrument Review.
Desc: Leading specialist British journal for control engineering, instrumentation technology and systems design in process, manufacturing and service sectors.
Ind/Abst Agric. Eng. Abstr.; Coal Abstr.; Curr. Cit.; Curr. Contents Eng. Comput. Technol.; Curr. Technol. Index; Eng. Index Annu. [Select. Cov.]; Ergon. Abstr.; F&S Index Plus Text, Int. [Select. Cov.]; Fluid Abstr., Civil Eng.; Fluid Abstr. Proc. Eng.; FLUIDEX (1973-); HTFS Dig.; Infomat Int. Bus.; INSPEC (May 1969-); Int. Aerosp. Abstr.; Int. Build. Serv. Abstr.; Proc. Chem. Eng.; PROMT [Full Txt.]; Res. Alert [Select. Cov.]; SCISEARCH; Theor. Chem. Eng.; Trade Ind. ASAP [Full Txt.]; Trade Ind. Index [Full Txt.]; World Ceram. Abstr.; World Surf. Coat. Abstr.; World Text. Abstr.

LC TS156.8 .C675   **ISSN** 1013-2287
    CU
    CODEN CCAZAB

CONTROL CIBERNETICA Y AUTOMATIZACION. See
Computers-Cybernetics.

LC TJ212 .C6   **ISSN** 0010-8049
DD 621.8 620   US
    CCC
    CODEN CENGAX
Pr Rev.

CONTROL ENGINEERING. See
Engineering-Computer Applications.

    ISSN 1083-9240
DD 005   US

CONTROL INDUSTRY INSIDE REPORT.
[Control ind. inside rep.]. (19??)-. Periodical. English. Twenty-six times a year. $100.00. FTT Associates, 827 Fairlawn Avenue, Libertyville IL 60048. **Tel** (708)362-0283, FAX (708)362-0289. **ED** Felix Tancula.
Desc: A summary of information interested in the field of automation.

    ISSN 0730-8809
    US
    CCC

DATAPRO REPORTS ON BANKING AUTOMATION. See Business and Economics-Computer Applications.

    US
    CEASED

DATAPRO REPORTS ON OFFICE AUTOMATION. See Business and Economics-Computer Applications.

    ISSN 0730-8817
    US
    CCC
Pr Rev.

DATAPRO REPORTS ON RETAIL AUTOMATION. See Business and Economics-Computer Applications.

    ISSN 0929-5585
    NE
    CCC

DESIGN AUTOMATION FOR EMBEDDED SYSTEMS. (19??)-. English. Four times a year. $295.00. Kluwer Academic Publishers, Postbus 322, 3300 AH Dordrecht The Netherlands. **Tel** 011 31 78 524400, FAX 011 31 78 183273, telex 20083.

    GW
    CODEN EKANAJ

ELEKTRO AUTOMATION. See
Engineering-Electrical Engineering.

LC TK7874.6 .E88a
DD 621.39/5   US
    TITLE CHANGE

EUROPEAN TEST CONFERENCE. PROCEEDINGS OF THE... EUROPEAN TEST CONFERENCE. (19??)-(19??).
Proceedings. English. IEEE / Institute of Electrical and

Electronics Engineers Inc., 345 East 47th Street, New York NY 10017-2394. **Tel** (908)981-1393, FAX (908)981-9667. **Merged with** Proceedings / The European Conference on Design Automation, 1066-1409 to form European Design and Test Conference. Proceedings.

ISSN 0169-5509
NE

UDC 681.3.01
EXCERPTA INFORMATICA. [Excerpta inform.]. (1985)-. Periodical. English. Eleven times a year. Fl240.00. Tilburg University Library, PO Box 90153, 5000 LE Tilburg Netherlands. **Tel** 011 31 13 662510, 354066, FAX 011 31 13 662996. **ED** J G B Prinsen and H Roes. Index available. cum. index. **Bk Rev. Ad Acc. Circ:** 1,500. **Continues** New Literature on Automation, 0028-6095.
 Desc: Contains books an articles in the field of applied computer science and automation. Special attention is paid to European publications.

ISSN 1070-9932
DD 629 US
●**IEEE ROBOTICS AND AUTOMATION MAGAZINE.** See Computers-Artificial Intelligence.

LC TJ212 .I48 **ISSN** 0018-9286
US
CCC
CODEN IETAA9
Pr Rev.
IEEE TRANSACTIONS ON AUTOMATIC CONTROL. [IEEE trans. automat. contr.]. **Added/Corp** IEEE Control Systems Society. IEEE Automatic Control Group. Institute of Electrical and Electronics Engineers. Automatic Control Group. **VFOAT** Transactions on Automatic Control; Automatic Control. Vol. AC-8 (Jan. 1963)-. Periodical. English. Twelve times a year. $420.00. IEEE / Institute of Electrical and Electronics Engineers Inc., 345 East 47th Street, New York NY 10017-2394. **Tel** (908)981-1393, FAX (908)981-9667. **(Subscription address:** IEEE / Institute of Electrical and Electronics Engineers, 445 Hoes Lane, PO Box 1331, Piscataway NJ 08855-1331. **Tel** (800)701-IEEE, (908)981-0060, FAX (908)981-9667, telex 833233.) available on microfiche. Documents available from Article Express International, The Genuine Article, Ask*IEEE, CASDDS. **Continues** Institute of Radio Engineers. Professional Group on Automatic Control. IRE Transactions on Automatic Control, 0096-199X.
 Desc: Covers the theory, design and application of control systems.
 Ind/Abst Abstr. Bull. Inst. Pap. Sci. Tech.; Acoust. Abstr.; Appl. Sci. Technol. Index (1991-); Bioeng. Abstr.; Chem. Abstr.; CompuMath Cit. Index [Full Cov.]; Comput. Abstr.; Curr. Cit.; Curr. Contents Eng. Comput. Technol.; Ei Page One; Eng. Index Annu.; Expand. Acad. Index (1992-); Index IEEE Publ.; INSPEC (1968-); Int. Abstr. Oper. Res. [Select. Cov.]; Int. Aerosp. Abstr.; Math. Rev.; Res. Alert [Full Cov.]; Sci. Cit. Index; SCISEARCH; Stat. Theory Method Abstr. (1986); Zentralbl. Math. Ihre Grenzgeb.

LC TJ210.2 .I33 **ISSN** 1042-296X
DD 628.8/92/05 US
CCC
CODEN IRAUEZ
Pr Rev.
IEEE TRANSACTIONS ON ROBOTICS AND AUTOMATION. See Computers-Artificial Intelligence.

ISSN 0962-9505
UK
CCC
CODEN ISYSEK
CEASED
IFAC SYMPOSIA SERIES. [IFAC symp. ser.]. **Added/Corp** International Federation of Automatic Control. **VAT** International Federation of Automatic Control Symposia Series. (19??)-(1993). Monographic series. English. Pergamon Press, An Imprint of Elsevier Science Ltd., The Boulevard, Langford Lane, Kidlington, Oxford OX5 1GB United Kingdom. **Tel** 011 44 1865 843000, 011 44 1865 843699, FAX 011 44 1865 843010. **ED** Janos Gertler. Documents available from Article Express International, Ask*IEEE, CASDDS. **Continues** IFAC Proceedings Series, 0742-5953.
 Ind/Abst Chem. Abstr.; Curr. Cit.; Ei Page One; Eng. Index Annu.; INSPEC.

LC TA1632 .I487 **ISSN** 0748-0059
DD 621.36/7 US
NLM W1; IM457J
IMAGE UNDERSTANDING. [Image underst.]. (1984)-. Monographic series. English. Irregular. Price varies per volume. Ablex Publishing Corporation, 355 Chestnut Street, Norwood NJ 07648. **Tel** (201)767-8450, (201)767-8455 (Customer Service), FAX (201)767-6717. **ED** Shimon Ullman and Whitman Richards.
 Desc: Book series reporting recent studies in computational vision.

LC T59.5 .I45
SZ
CODEN IHPREV
INDUSTRIAL HANDLING REVUE. **Added/Corp** International Fachmesse fuer Automatisierung und Rationalisierung des Industriellen Arbeitsplatzes. (19??)-. Periodical. German (German). Three times a year. 30.00F Switzerland; 40.00F other. AGIFA Verlag AG, Bruggacherstrasse 26, CH-8117 Faellanden Switzerland. **Tel** 011 41 1 8256464.

LC Q184 .I25
DD 681/.029/4 US
●**INSTRUMENTATION & AUTOMATION NEWS : IAN.** See Engineering.

ISSN 1079-8587
US
●**INTELLIGENT AUTOMATION AND SOFT COMPUTING / WORLD AUTOMATION CONGRESS.** **Added/Corp** World Automation Congress. (1995)-. Periodical. English. Four times a year. $195.00. Autosoft Press, PO Box 14155, Albuquerque NM 87191.

LC QC53 .I58 **ISSN** 0889-8308
DD 530/.7 US
CCC
NLM W1; IN652F **CODEN** IICOEW
Pr Rev. TITLE CHANGE
INTELLIGENT INSTRUMENTS & COMPUTERS. [Intell. instrum. comput.]. **VFOAT** Intelligent Instruments and Computers; Instruments and Computers; Instruments & Computers. Vol. 3, No. 1 (Jan. 1985)-(19??). Academic Scholarly Publication. English. Elsevier Science Publishing Company Inc, Madison Square Station, PO Box 882, New York NY 10159-0882. **Tel** (212)633-3950, FAX (212)633-3990. **ED** Richard C Graham. Index available. Ad Acc. Circ: 1,000. Documents available from Article Express International, Ask*IEEE, CASDDS. **Continues** Computer Applications in the Laboratory, 0724-0031. **Merged into** Chemometrics and Intelligent Laboratory Systems.
 Desc: International journal for scientists and engineers who use computers in their laboratory and field work.
 Ind/Abst Abstr. Bull. Inst. Pap. Sci. Tech.; Chem. Abstr. (1985-); Chem. Hazards Ind.; Ei Page One; Eng. Index Annu.; Gas Abstr.; INSPEC (1985-); Lab. Hazards Bull.; Mass Spect. Bull.

LC QA76.9.H85 I62 **ISSN** 1044-7318
DD 004/.01/9 US
CODEN IJHIEC
Pr Rev.
INTERNATIONAL JOURNAL OF HUMAN-COMPUTER INTERACTION. [Int. j. hum.-comput. interact.]. **VFOAT** Human-Computer Interaction. **VAT** International Journal of Human Computer Interaction. Vol. 1, No. 1 (1989)-. Academic Scholarly Publication. English. Four times a year. $145.00. Ablex Publishing Corporation, 355 Chestnut Street, Norwood NJ 07648. **Tel** (201)767-8450, (201)767-8455 (Customer Service), FAX (201)767-6717. **ED** Garriel Salvendy and Michael Smith. Index available. cum. index. **Bk Rev. Ad Acc. Circ:** 500. Documents available from Ask*IEEE.
 Desc: This scholarly publication provides a scientific forum for the integration of ergonomic, health, cognitive, and social aspects of how computers in all areas of life from leisure, to education, to work.
 Ind/Abst Abstr. Hum. Comput. Interact.; Curr. Cit.; Ergon. Abstr.; HILITES; Inf. Sci. Abstr.; INSPEC (1990-); Psychol. Abstr. (1989-); PsycINFO; PsycLit.

LC TS155.6 .I5935 **ISSN** 1045-2699
DD 670/.285 US
CCC
CODEN IHFMEY
INTERNATIONAL JOURNAL OF HUMAN FACTORS IN MANUFACTURING, THE. **VFOAT** Human Factors in Manufacturing. Vol. 1, No. 1 Jan. (1991)-. Periodical. English. Four times a year. $256.00. John Wiley & Sons Inc., 605 Third Avenue, New York NY 10158-0012. **Tel** (212)850-6000, (212)850-6645, FAX (212)850-6088, telex 12-7063. **(Subscription address:** John Wiley & Sons / UK, Baffins Lane, Chichester, West Sussex PO19 1UD United Kingdom. **Tel** 011 44 1243 779777, FAX 011 44 243 776128, telex 86290 WIBOOKG.) **ED** Waldemar Karwowski and Gavriel Salvendy. available on microfilm and microfiche from University Microfilms International (UMI). Documents available from Article Express International, Ask*IEEE.
 Desc: An international journal providing a forum for the dissemination of scientific results on the human aspects of advanced manufacturing technologies.
 Ind/Abst Comput. Inf. Syst. Abstr. J. [Full Cov.]; Curr. Cit.; Ei Page One; Eng. Index Annu.; Ergon. Abstr.; INSPEC (Jan. 1991-); Int. Labour Doc.; Manuf. Process Eng. Abstr.

Computers —Automation

LC TJ210.2 .I6 **ISSN** 0826-8185
DD 629.8/92/05 US
CODEN IJAUED
INTERNATIONAL JOURNAL OF ROBOTICS & AUTOMATION. See Computers-Artificial Intelligence.

JA
JAPANESE JOURNAL OF ADVANCED AUTOMATION TECHNOLOGY. (19??)-. Periodical. English. Six times a year. ¥72000. **(Subscription address:** Maruzen Company Ltd., PO Box 5050, Import & Export Department, Tokyo 100 31 Japan. **Tel** 011 81 3 32789224.)

ISSN 0287-8461
DD 629.8 JA
JIDOKA GIJUTSU. [Jidoka gijutsu]. **VFOAT** Mechanical Automation. (1969)-. Periodical. Japanese. Twelve times a year. $230.00. Kogyo Chsakai, (Kogyo Chosakai Publishing Co. Ltd.), 14-7 Hongo 2 Chome, Bunkyoku Tokyo 113 Japan.

LC Z7165.J6 J63 HC465.A9
JA
JOHO SANGYO KIJI SAKUINSHU. SHINBUNHEN. See Communications-Telecommunication.

LC WMLC 93/1866 **ISSN** 0168-7433
NE
CCC
CODEN JAREEW
Pr Rev.
JOURNAL OF AUTOMATED REASONING. [J. autom. reason.]. Vol. 1, No. 1 (1985)-. Periodical. English. Six times a year. $461.00. Kluwer Academic Publishers, Postbus 322, 3300 AH Dordrecht The Netherlands. **Tel** 011 31 78 524400, FAX 011 31 78 183273, telex 20083. **ED** Deepak Kapur. Index available. **Bk Rev. Ad Acc. Acid Free. Circ:** 750. available on microfilm and microfiche from University Microfilms International (UMI). Documents available from Article Express International, Ask*IEEE.
 Desc: The main fields covered are automated theorem proving, logic programming, expert systems, program synthesis and validation, artificial intelligence, computational logic, robotics, and various industrial applications. The papers share the common feature of focusing on some aspect of automated reasoning, a field whose objective is the design and implementation of a computer program that serves as an assistant in solving problems and in answering questions that require reasoning.
 Ind/Abst ACM Guide Comput. Lit.; Comput. Abstr. (1987-); Comput. Rev. (1985-); Curr. Cit.; Ei Page One; Eng. Index Annu. [Select. Cov.]; INSPEC (1985-); Math. Rev.; Zentralbl. Math. Ihre Grenzgeb. (1985-).

LC TJ212 .A918 **ISSN** 1064-2315
DD 629.8 US
CCC
JOURNAL OF AUTOMATION AND INFORMATION SCIENCES. [J. autom. inf. sci.]. Vol. 25, No. 1 (Jan.-Feb. 1992)-. Academic Scholarly Publication. English (translations available in Russian). Six times a year. $954.00. Scripta Technica, A Subsidiary of John Wiley & Sons Inc., 7961 Eastern Avenue, Silver Spring MD 20910. **Tel** (301)588-0484, FAX (301)588-5278. **(Subscription address:** John Wiley & Sons, Inc. / Philadelphia, PO Box 7247, Philadelphia PA 19170. **Tel** (212)850-6645, (800)225-5945.) **ED** Robert N. McDonough, Johns Hopkins University, MD. Documents available from Article Express International, Ask*IEEE, CASDDS. **Continues** Soviet Journal of Automation and Information Sciences, 0882-570X.
 Desc: A source of information for computer-oriented scientists and engineers concerned with pragmatic solutions to control problems in a wide variety of areas. Topics covered includes dynamics of control systems, identification theory, adaptive and optimal control, fuzzy system estimation and control, as well as information processing.
 Ind/Abst Bioeng. Abstr.; Chem. Abstr.; Ei Page One; Electron. Commun. Abstr. J.; EMBASE; Eng. Index Annu.; Eng. Index Energy Abstr.; INSPEC; Int. Aerosp. Abstr.; ISMEC Bull.; Math. Rev.; Nucl. Sci. Abstr.; Pollut. Abstr. Indexes; Saf. Sci. Abstr. J.

LC TJ210.2 .J68 **ISSN** 0921-0296
DD 629.8/92 NE
CCC
CODEN JIRSES
Pr Rev.
JOURNAL OF INTELLIGENT & ROBOTIC SYSTEMS. [J. intell. & robotic syst.]. **VFOAT** Journal of Intelligent and Robotic Systems. Vol. 1, No. 1 (1988)-. Periodical. English. Twelve times a year. $712.00. Kluwer

Computers —Automation

Academic Publishers, Postbus 322, 3300 AH Dordrecht The Netherlands. **Tel** 011 31 78 524400, FAX 011 31 78 183273, telex 20083. **ED** Spyros G. Tzafestas. **Acid Free.** available on microfilm and microfiche from University Microfilms International (UMI). Documents available from The Genuine Article, Ask*IEEE. *Absorbed Mechatronic Systems Engineering, 0924-3992.*
Desc: Provides a source linking all fields where system intelligence plays a dominant role in the theory and practice of intelligent robotic systems. Topics of particular relevance are: computer integrated manufacturing systems, computer vision, diagnostic systems, expert systems, intelligent systems, learning theory, robot languages, and robotic systems.
Ind/Abst CompuMath Cit. Index [Full Cov.]; Curr. Cit.; Curr. Contents Eng. Comput. Technol.; INSPEC (1988-); Psychol. Abstr. (1988-); PsycINFO; PsycLit; Res. Alert [Full Cov.]; SCISEARCH; Soc. Sci. Cit. Index [Select. Cov.]; Zentralbl. Math. Ihre Grenzgeb.

LC TJ1 .M328
DD 621
ISSN 1052-6188
US
CCC

JOURNAL OF MACHINERY MANUFACTURE AND RELIABILITY. See Engineering-Mechanical Engineering and Machinery.

DD 629.8
ISSN 0915-3942
JA

JOURNAL OF ROBOTICS AND MECHATRONICS. See Computers-Artificial Intelligence.

ISSN 1167-8127
FR

UDC 681.5

JOURNAL ROBOTIQUE INFORMATIQUE INDUSTRIELLE, LE.
(1991)-. Periodical. French. Eleven times a year. $141.07. Saincy Communication, 15 rue d'Hauteville, 75010 Paris France. **Tel** 011 33 1 482240240. *Continues Le Journal de la Robotique (Paris), 0764-5171.*

UK

KEY ABSTRACTS. FACTORY AUTOMATION. See Computers-Abstracting, Bibliographies and Statistics.

ISSN 0952-7052
UK

KEY ABSTRACTS. MACHINE VISION.
See Computers-Abstracting, Bibliographies and Statistics.

LC T57.5 .A86
YU

KIBERNETIKA, AUTOMATIZACIJA POSLOVANJA : MESECNI CASOPIS ZAVODA ZA EKONOMSKI EKSPERTIZE.
See Computers-Cybernetics.

LC Q300 .K53
DD 001.53/05
ISSN 0739-8417
US
CCC

KIBERNETIKA I VYCHISLITELNAIA TEKHNIKA. ENGLISH. See Computers-Cybernetics.

LC Q300 .K5289
ISSN 0454-9910
UN
CODEN KVYTAS

KIBERNETIKA I VYCISLITELNAJA TEHNIKA (KIEV). See Computers-Cybernetics.

DD 629
ISSN 0895-7533
US
CCC
NLM W1; LA149
CODEN LRAUEY

LABORATORY ROBOTICS AND AUTOMATION. See Computers-Artificial Intelligence.

DD 380.1/45670427/029471
ISSN 1192-5973
CN

●MANUFACTURING & PROCESS AUTOMATION. [Manuf. process autom.]. VFOAT
Manufacturing and Process Automation; Automation; Manufacturing & Process Automation, Products, Systems, Techology. Vol. 7, No. 6 (Jan./Feb. 1993)-. Trade Publication. English. Six times a year (Jan., Mar., May, July, Sept., Nov.). 61.00Can$. Kerrwil Publications Ltd., 395 Matheson Boulevard E, Mississauga Ontario L4Z 2H2 Canada. **Tel** (905)890-1846. *Continues Automation Systems (Mississauga, Ont)., 1181-7003.*

LC TS155.A1 M39
DD 670/.285
ISSN 0748-948X
US
CCC
CODEN MASYES

MANUFACTURING SYSTEMS. See Industry and Production-Computer Applications.

DD 338
ISSN 1064-1343
US
CEASED

MATRIX (WASHINGTON, D.C. 1992).
(MATRIX : THE TWICE MONTHLY INDUSTRY NEWS REPORT FOR THE INTEGRATED BUILDING SYSTEM CONTROL AND AUTOMATION PROFESSION.).
[Matrix]. (1992)-(199?). Trade Publication. English. Matrix, 1223 Potomac Street NW, Washington DC 20007-3212.

ISSN 0924-3992
NE
CCC
CODEN MSYEEM
TITLE CHANGE

MECHATRONIC SYSTEMS ENGINEERING. [Mechatron. syst. eng.]. Vol. 1 No. 1 (1990)-(199?). Periodical. English. Kluwer Academic Publishers, Postbus 322, 3300 AH Dordrecht The Netherlands. **Tel** 011 31 78 524400, FAX 011 31 78 183273, telex 20083. available on microfilm and microfiche from University Microfilms International (UMI). Documents available from Article Express International, Ask*IEEE. *Absorbed by Journal of Intelligent and Robotic Systems, 0921-0296.*
Ind/Abst Ei Page One; Eng. Index Annu.; INSPEC (1990-).

ISSN 0931-3907
GW
UDC 681.5(058)

MESSEN, REGELN, AUTOMATISIEREN.
[Mess. Regeln Autom.]. (1986)-. German. One time a year. $26.87. Verlag Hoppenstedt & Company, Postfach 100139, D-64201 Darmstadt Germany. **Tel** 011 49 6151 380436, 011 49 6151 380361. *Continues Messtechnik + Regelungstechnik + Automatik, 0174-3651.*

US

MIC/SUB-IMAGING AND OFFICE SYSTEMS. [DISKETTE]. (19??)-. English.
Twelve times a year. $930.00. Management Information Corporation, 1111 Marlkress Road, Cherry Hill NJ 08003. **Tel** (609)424-1100. Index available. cum. index. ctrl circ.
Desc: Description, analysis, and pricing of imaging and office automation systems.

LC HG1709 .N37a
DD 332.1/028/54
ISSN 0095-5396
US

NATIONAL OPERATIONS AND AUTOMATION CONFERENCE PROCEEDINGS, THE. See Business and Economics-Banks and Banking.

DD 629.8929994
ISSN 0726-3716
AT

NEWSLETTER OF THE AUSTRALIAN ROBOT ASSOCIATION. [Newsl. Aust. Robot Assoc.]. (1982)-. Trade Publication. English. Four times a year (Jan., Apr., July, Oct). 41.11Aus$. Australian Robot Association, GPO Box 1527, Sydney NSW 2001, Australia. **Tel** 11 61 27959 3239, FAX 11 61 2 9594632. **ED** Michael Kassler. **Bk Rev**, (Qty: 10). **Ad Acc. Circ:** 500.

LC Z7165.J3 O25 HC465.A9
JA

OA KANREN SHINBUN KIJI SORAN. See Communications-Telecommunication.

ISSN 0737-8122
US

OFFICE MANAGEMENT. See Business and Economics.

LC QA402.3 .O66
DD 629.8/312
ISSN 0143-2087
UK
CCC
CODEN OCAMD5
Pr Rev.

OPTIMAL CONTROL APPLICATIONS & METHODS. [Optim. control appl. methods]. VFOAT
Optimal Control Applications and Methods. (Jan./Mar. 1980)-. Periodical. English. Five times a year (quarterly plus special issue). $875.00. John Wiley & Sons Ltd., Baffins Lane, Chichester, West Sussex PO19 1UD United Kingdom. **Tel** 011 44 1243 779777, FAX 011 44 1243 776128 BTG:JWP001, telex 86290 WIBOOKG.
(**Subscription address:** John Wiley & Sons, Inc. / Philadelphia, PO Box 7247, Philadelphia PA 19170. **Tel** (212)850-6645, (800)225-5945.) **ED** Bion L. Pierson.
Circ: 600. available on microfilm and microfiche from University Microfilms International (UMI). Documents available from Article Express International, The Genuine Article, Ask*IEEE.
Desc: The journal presents an interdisciplinary forum for the reporting of interesting optimal control applications emphasizing both the commonality of the underlying theory and the diversity of its applications.
Ind/Abst CompuMath Cit. Index [Full Cov.]; Curr. Cit.; Curr. Contents Eng. Comput. Technol.; Eng. Index Annu.; INSPEC (March 1980-); Int. Abstr. Oper. Res. [Select. Cov.]; Res. Alert [Full Cov.]; SCISEARCH; Zentralbl. Math. Ihre Grenzgeb.

LC TJ1313 .P6
ISSN 0032-4140
PL
CODEN PAUKAP

POMIARY, AUTOMATYKA, KONTROLA.
[Pomiary autom. kontr.]. **Added/Corp** Naczelna Organizacja Techniczna (Poland). (July 1955)-. Academic Scholarly Publication. Polish (table of contents in Multiple languages). Twelve times a year. Price on request.
(**Subscription address:** Ars Polona-Ruch, PO Box 1001, Krakowskie Przedmiescie 7, 00-068 Warsaw Poland. **Tel** 011 48 22 261201.) Documents available from Ask*IEEE, CASDDS.
Ind/Abst Ceram. Abstr.; Chem. Abstr.; Energy Res. Abstr. (Oct. 1982-); INSPEC (1968-); Int. Aerosp. Abstr.; Saf. Health Work.

LC TJ212 .P633
ISSN 0137-3595
PL

POSTEPY CYBERNETYKI. [Post. cybern.].
Added/Corp Polskie Towarzystwo Cybernetyczne. (1978)-. Periodical. Polish (summaries and/or abstracts in English and Russian). Four times a year. $40.00.
(**Subscription address:** Ars Polona-Ruch, PO Box 1001, Krakowskie Przedmiescie 7, 00-068 Warsaw Poland. **Tel** 011 48 22 261201.)
Ind/Abst Math. Rev.; Zentralbl. Math. Ihre Grenzgeb.

LC TA167 .P69
DD 006
ISSN 1054-7460
US
CCC

PRESENCE (CAMBRIDGE, MASS.). See Computers-Artificial Intelligence.

LC TK7874.6 .E88a
DD 621.39/5
ISSN 1066-1409
US
TITLE CHANGE

PROCEEDINGS - EUROPEAN CONFERENCE ON DESIGN AUTOMATION. (PROCEEDINGS / EUROPEAN CONFERENCE ON DESIGN AUTOMATION AND THE EUROPEAN EVENT IN ASIC DESIGN.). [Proc. - Eur. Conf. Des. Autom.]. **Added/Corp** EDAC Association. EDA Association. (1990)-(Feb. 22-25, 1993). Proceedings. English. IEEE / Institute of Electrical and Electronics Engineers Inc., 345 East 47th Street, New York NY 10017-2394. **Tel** (908)981-1393, FAX (908)981-9667. *Formed by the union of Euro ASIC, 1064-5322 and Proceedings, the European Conference on Design Automation. Merged with European Test Conference. Proceedings of the ... European Test Conference to form European Design and Test Conference. Proceedings.*

LC TJ210.3 .I58a
DD 629.8/92/05
ISSN 1050-4729
US
CCC

PROCEEDINGS / IEEE INTERNATIONAL CONFERENCE ON ROBOTICS AND AUTOMATION. [Proc. - IEEE Int. Conf. Robot. Autom.]. **Added/Corp** IEEE Robotics and Automation Council. IEEE Computer Society. IEEE Robotics and Automation Society. **VFOAT** Proceedings ... IEEE International Conference on Robotics and Automation; Robotics and Automation. (1986)-. Proceedings. English. One time a year. $300.00. IEEE Computer Society, 10662 Los Vaqueros Circle, PO Box 3014, Los Alamitos CA 90720-1264. **Tel** (714)821-8380, (800)272-6657, FAX (714)821-4641. *Continues IEEE International Conference on Robotics and Automation. IEEE International Conference on Robotics and Automation : [Proceedings], 1049-3492.*
Ind/Abst Curr. Cit.

LC TK7874.6 .E89a
DD 621.3815
US

●PROCEEDINGS / THE EUROPEAN DESIGN AND TEST CONFERENCE.
(1994)-. English. IEEE / Institute of Electrical and Electronics Engineers Inc., 345 East 47th Street, New York NY 10017-2394. **Tel** (908)981-1393, FAX (908)981-9667. *Formed by the union of European Conference on Design Automation. Proceedings and European Test Conference. Proceedings of the ... European Test Conference.*

ISSN 1240-3946
FR
UDC 658.8

PRODUCTIQUE AFFAIRES PARIS. See Computers-Artificial Intelligence.

ISSN 1018-0303
BE

REAL TIME MAGAZINE. [Real time mag.].
(1991)-. Periodical. English. Four times a year (Jan., Apr., July, Oct.). 2400F Belgium; 8000F other. RT Consult, rue de la Justice 23, 1070 Brussels Belgium. **Tel** 011 32 2 5205577, FAX 011 32 2 5208309. **ED** Professor M. Timmerman. **Bk Rev. Ad Acc. Adv Mgr:** Rene Giden.

Computers —Computer Assisted Instruction

Circ: 3,000. **Continues** VME Bus (Brussel), 1013-364X.
Desc: Focused on the field of real-time and embedded systems design.

GW

REGELUNGS TECHNIK. Vol. 26, (1978)-. Periodical. English. Twelve times a year. Documents available from Ask*IEEE.
Ind/Abst INSPEC (1968-).

ISSN 0387-1940
JA
CODEN ROBBDQ

ROBOT (TOKYO, 1971). See Computers-Artificial Intelligence.

ISSN 0724-1712
GW

UDC 658.52.011.56
ROBOTER. (19??)-. Periodical. German. Twenty-four times a year. $132.04. Verlag Moderne Industrie, Justus von Liebigstrasse 1, D-86899 Landsberg Lech Germany. **Tel** 011 49 8191 125453.

ISSN 0178-0026
GW
CCC
CODEN RBTSE9
Pr Rev.
ROBOTERSYSTEME. See Computers-Artificial Intelligence.

US
ROBOTICS TODAY. See Computers-Artificial Intelligence.

ISSN 0233-6944
RU
SBORNIK TRUDOV (VSESOIUZNYI NAUCHNO-ISSLEDOVATELSKII INSTITUT PRIKLADNYKH AVTOMATIZIROVANNYKH SISTEM (SOVIET UNION). (SBORNIK TRUDOV.).
Added/Corp Vsesoiuznyi Nauchno-Issledovatelskii Institut Prikladnykh Avtomatizirovannykh Sistem (Soviet Union) Nauchnyi Sovet po Kompleksnoi Probleme "Kibernetika" (Akademiia Nauk SSSR). (1984)-. Monographic series. Russian. Price varies per volume.

ISSN 0273-3080
US
SCAN NEWSLETTER. VFOAT Scanning, Coding & Automation Newsletter. **VAT** Scanning, Coding and Automation Newsletter. (19??)-. Newsletter. English. Twelve times a year. $195.00. Scan Newsletter, Ltd., 11 Middle Neck Road, Great Neck NY 11021. **Tel** (516)487-6370, FAX (516)487-6449. **ED** George Goldberg. Index available ((published separately)). **Bk Rev.**
Desc: Management newsletter for all industries involved with bar code scanning and other automatic identification technologies.

JA
SENSOR GIJUTSU: SENSOR TECHNOLOGY. See Computers-Cybernetics.

ISSN 1356-3378
DD 670.42
UK
●**SERVICE ROBOT. See** Engineering-Industrial Engineering.

ISSN 0163-5743
US
CODEN SIGDDQ
SIGDA NEWSLETTER. [SIGDA newsl.].
Main/Corp Association for Computing Machinery. Special Interest Group on Design Automation. **Added/Corp** ACM Special Interest Group on Design Automation. **VAT** Special Interest Group on Design Automation Newsletter. (19??)-. Newsletter. English. Two times a year. $18.00. ACM / Association for Computing Machinery, 1515 Broadway, 17th Floor, New York NY 10036. **Tel** (212)869-7440, FAX (212)869-0481. available via Internet (http://kona.ee.pitt.edu/newsletter/). Documents available from Ask*IEEE.
Ind/Abst Abstr. Hum. Comput. Interact.; ACM Guide Comput. Lit.; Comput. Rev.; INSPEC (Aug. 1980-).

LC Z5853.A8 S57 TJ213
DD 016.6298/05
RU
SISTEMY AVTOMATICHESKOGO UPRAVLENIIA / INSTITUT PROBLEM UPRAVLENIIA, NAUCHNO-TEKHNICHESKAIA BIBLIOTEKA. Added/Corp Institut Problem Upravleniia (Akademiia Nauk SSSR). Nauchno-Tekhnicheskaia Biblioteka. (19??)-. Russian. One time a week (48 issues per year). $180.00. Gosudarstvennaia Biblioteka, Informatsionnyi Tsentr, Imeni V. I. Lenina, Prospekt Kalinina 3, 121019 Moscow Russia. **(Subscription address:** Victor Kamkin, 4556 Boiling Brook Parkway, Rockville MD 20852. **Tel** (301)881-5973.)
Desc: Information on automation control.

NE
STUDIES IN AUTOMATION AND CONTROL. (1978)-. Monographic series. English.
Ind/Abst Zentralbl. Math. Ihre Grenzgeb.

ISSN 1073-0516
US
CCC
●**TRANSACTIONS ON COMPUTER-HUMAN INTERACTION.**
Added/Corp Association for Computing Machinery. **VFOAT** Transactions on Computer Human Interaction. (1994)-. Periodical. English. Four times a year. $95.00. ACM / Association for Computing Machinery, 1515 Broadway, 17th Floor, New York NY 10036. **Tel** (212)869-7440, FAX (212)869-0481.

LC TJ212 .T984
DD 629.8/05
ISSN 0254-4156
CC
CODEN ZIXUDZ
Pr Rev.
TZU TUNG HUA HSUEH PAO. Added/Corp Chung-kuo Tzu Tung Hua Hsueh Hui. **VFOAT** Acta Automatica Sinica. (1963)-. Academic Scholarly Publication. Chinese (summaries and/or abstracts in English). Six times a year. $83.50. Science Press, 16 Donghuangchenggen North Street, Beijing 100707, People's Republic of China. **Tel** 011 86 1 4019821, 011 86 1 4010642, FAX 011 86 1 4012180, 011 86 1 4019810, telex 210147. **Circ:** 11,100. Documents available from BLDSC, Ask*IEEE.
Desc: Contains information from automation research in China.
Ind/Abst Ei Page One; INSPEC (Jan. 1981-); Int. Aerosp. Abstr. (1984-); Math. Rev.

LC QA
DD 004
US
USSR AND EASTERN EUROPE SCIENTIFIC ABSTRACTS. CYBERNETICS, COMPUTERS, AND AUTOMATION TECHNOLOGY. See Computers-Cybernetics.

ISSN 0926-3241
NE
UDC 681.31
VIP. VAKBLAD VOOR IMAGE PROCESSING. (VIP.). [VIP, Vakbl. image process.].
VFOAT Vakblad Voor Image Processing. (1989)-. Periodical. Dutch. Ten times a year. G I G A, Postbus 91, 1700 Heerhugowaard Netherlands. **Tel** 011 31 2207 45620, FAX 011 31 2207 40765. **ED** Roelof P. Koedijker. **Bk Rev. Ad Acc, Adv Mgr:** Dennis Landman.
Desc: This magazine contains editorial news of microfilm and electronic document management systems, image automation and application.

LC QA76.575 .V55
DD 006
ISSN 1060-9547
US
CCC
TITLE CHANGE
VIRTUAL REALITY WORLD. See Computers-Artificial Intelligence.

UK
WHAT'S NEW IN INSTRUMENTATION. English. Four times a year. £30.00 UK and Northern Ireland; $80.00 other. Morgan Grampian, 40 Beresford Street Woolwich, London SE18 6BQ United Kingdom. **Tel** 011 44 181 8557777, FAX 011 44 181 8555548, telex 896238.

COMPUTER ASSISTED INSTRUCTION

LC QA76.27 .T474
DD 004
ISSN 1078-2192
US
●**3C ON-LINE.** (3C ON-LINE : A QUARTERLY PUBLICATION OF THE ASSOCIATION FOR COMPUTING MACHINERY SPECIAL INTEREST GROUP FOR COMPUTING AT COMMUNITY COLLEGES.). [3C on-line]. **Added/Corp** Association for Computing Machinery. Special Interest Group for Computing at Community Colleges. **VFOAT** Three C On Line; 3C On Line; 3C Online; SIG3C. Vol. 1, No. 1 (Oct. 1994)-. Periodical. English. Four times a year. $30.00. ACM / Association for Computing Machinery, 1515 Broadway, 17th Floor, New York NY 10036. **Tel** (212)869-7440, FAX (212)869-0481. **(Subscription address:** Association for Computing Machinery, PO Box 12114, Church Street Station, New York NY 10249. **Tel** (212)626-0500.)

ISSN 0828-6949
DD 371.3/9445/05
CN
ATACC NEWSLETTER. [ATACC newsl.]. **VAT** Alberta Teachers' Association Computer Council Newsletter. Vol. 2, No. 2 (July 1983)-. Newsletter. English. Four times a year. 30.00Can$ includes ATACC Journal subscription. Alberta Teachers Association, 11010 142 Street, Barnett House, Edmonton Alberta T5N 2R1 Canada. **Tel** (403)453-2411. ctrl circ. **Continues** ATACC (Alberta Teachers' Association. Computer Council), 0824-2208.

ISSN 0816-9020
AT
AUSTRALIAN EDUCATIONAL COMPUTING. See Education-Computer Applications.

ISSN 1039-7841
AT
Pr Rev.
AUSTRALIAN JOURNAL OF INFORMATION SYSTEMS, THE. (19??)-. Academic Scholarly Publication. English. Two times a year. 32.88Aus$. AJET Publications Ltd., PO Box 772, Belconnen ACT 2616 Australia. **Tel** 011 61 6 735405, 011 61 6 2591980, FAX 011 61 6 735403. **ED** John Hedberg. **Bk Rev**, (Qty: 3). **Circ:** 800.

CN
●**AUTOCAD USER. VFOAT** Auto Computer Assisted Design User. (1993)-. English. Four times a year (Feb., May, Aug., Nov.). 14.40Can$. Autocad User, 1011 Upper Middle Road East, PO Box 1235, Oakville Ontario L6H 5Z9 Canada. **Tel** (905)845-1347, FAX (905)845-5521. **ED** R. Erickson. **Ad Acc, Adv Mgr:** M. Sean, **Tel** (905)475-4231. **Circ:** 17,000 (ctrl).

ISSN 0835-0280
DD 371.3/9445/05
CN
BUS (ST-LAURENT). (LE BUS.). [Bus].
Added/Corp Association Quebecoise des Utilisateurs de l'Ordinateur au Primaire et au Secondaire. Vol. 1, No 1 (Jan./Feb. 1984)-. Periodical. French. Six times a year. Free for members. Association Quebecoise des Utilisateurs de l'Ordinateur au Primaire-Secondaire, Bureau 530, 7400 boulevard St. Laurent, 5e Etage, Montreal Quebec H2R 2Y1 Canada. **Tel** (514)873-3827.
Ind/Abst Repere (1991-).

ISSN 0959-6259
DD 005.369
UK
Pr Rev.
CAD USER. [CAD user]. (198?)-. Periodical. English (French, Swedish and German). Ten times a year. $92.40. Compudraft Ltd., 24 High Street, Beckenham Kent, BR3 1AY United Kingdom. **Tel** 011 44 181 6633818, FAX 011 44 181 6633822. **ED** Brian Wall. Index available. **Bk Rev. Ad Acc, Adv Mgr:** Adam Ramzi, **Tel** 081 663 3818. **Circ:** 21,407 (ctrl).
Desc: Focuses on AutoCAD and its related hardware and software. All publications feature the latest information on AutoCAD, including product reviews and launches, industry news and regular user profiles showing the application of AutoCAD across a wide variety of industries.

LC P53.28 .C34
DD 418/.00285
ISSN 0742-7778
US
Pr Rev.
CALICO JOURNAL. [CALICO j.]. **Added/Corp** CALICO (Organization). **VAT** Computer Aided Language Learning & Instruction Consortium Journal. Vol. 1, No. 1, June (1983)-. Periodical. English. Four times a year. $65.00. Duke University / CALICO, 014 Language Center, Box 90267, Durham NC 27708-0267. **Tel** (919)660-3180, FAX (919)660-3183. **ED** Eleanor Johnson. **Ad Acc. Circ:** 6,000 (ctrl). Documents available from Ask*IEEE.
Desc: Devoted to the application of high technology to the teaching and learning of languages.
Ind/Abst Curr. Cit.; Curr. Index J. Educ.; INSPEC (Sep. 1984-).

LC LB2395.7 .C37
DD 378/.00285
ISSN 1065-9447
US
TITLE CHANGE
CAMPUS TECH. See Education-Computer Applications.

ISSN 0727-1255
DD 371.0205
AT
CCC
CLASSROOM. See Education-Teaching and Curriculum.

ISSN 0726-2132
DD 001.64071
AT
TITLE CHANGE
CLASSROOM COMPUTING. See Education-Computer Applications.

ISSN 1049-9059
DD 407
US
CCC
CODEN CLJOEM
CLL JOURNAL : COMPUTER-ASSISTED ENGLISH LANGUAGE LEARNING JOURNAL. See Linguistics.

US
COGNITION AND COMPUTING. (1987)-. English. Irregular. Price varies. Ablex Publishing Corporation, 355 Chestnut Street, Norwood NJ 07648. **Tel** (201)767-8450, (201)767-8455 (Customer Service),

Computers — Computer Assisted Instruction

FAX (201)767-6717. **ED** John B. Black and Elliot Soloway.
Desc: Series of monographs, edited volumes and texts.

LC LB1028.43 .C63 ISSN 0731-4213
DD 378/.179445/05 US
  CCC
  CEASED

COLLEGIATE MICROCOMPUTER. See Education-Computer Applications.

AT

COM 3. (19??)-. English. Four times a year. Comes with Computer Education Group of Victoria membership. Computer Education Group of Victoria, 217 Church Street, Room 42, Richmond No VIC 3121 Australia. **Tel** 011 61 3 4279189.
Ind/Abst Aust. Educ. Index (199?-).

ISSN 0818-1748
AT

COMPUTER DOWNLOAD. (1982)-. English. Irregular. Department of Education / Queensland, PO Box 33, North Quay Queensland 4000 Australia.
Ind/Abst Aust. Educ. Index.

LC QA76.27 .C65 ISSN 0010-4590
DD 001.64/071 UK
  CODEN CPECBK

COMPUTER EDUCATION. See Education-Computer Applications.

DD 001 ISSN 8755-5816
  US

COMPUTER INSTRUCTOR, THE. [Comput. instr.]. Vol. 1, No. 1 (Nov. 1984)-. Periodical. English. Four times a year. $6.00. The Computer Instructor, 614 Santa Barbara Street, Santa Barbara CA 93101. **Tel** (805)963-0439. **ED** Lisa Timmon. **Circ:** 30,100.

LC LB1576.7 .C6 ISSN 8755-4615
DD 428 US
  CODEN CHCMEM
Pr Rev.

COMPUTERS AND COMPOSITION. [Comput. compos.]. Vol. 1, No. 1 (Nov. 1983)-. Periodical. English. Three times a year. $79.50. Ablex Publishing Corporation, 355 Chestnut Street, Norwood NJ 07648. **Tel** (201)767-8450, (201)767-8455 (Customer Service), FAX (201)767-6717. **ED** Cynthia L. Selfe and Gail E. Hawisher. **Bk Rev.** (Qty: 3). **Circ:** 700. Documents available from Ask*IEEE.
Desc: A journal devoted to exploring the use of computers in writing classes, writing programs, and writing research. Provides a forum for discussing issues connected with writing and computer use. Also information about integrating computers into writing programs on the basis of theoretical and pedagogical decisions along with empirical evidence.
Ind/Abst Curr. Cit.; Curr. Index J. Educ. (March 1990); Educ. Index (1992-); INSPEC (Aug. 1987-).

LC Z699.5.H8 C65 ISSN 0010-4817
DD 025.04 NE
  CCC
NLM Z 699.A1 C7363 CODEN COHUAD
Pr Rev.

COMPUTERS AND THE HUMANITIES. [Comput. humanit.]. Vol. 1 (Sept. 1966)-. Academic Scholarly Periodical. English. Six times a year. $326.00. Kluwer Academic Publishers, Postbus 322, 3300 AH Dordrecht The Netherlands. **Tel** 011 31 78 524400, FAX 011 31 78 183273, telex 20083. **ED** Glyn Holmes, Terrence Erdt, Joel Goldfield, and Christian Delcourt (European editor). **Acid Free.** available on microfilm and microfiche from University Microfilms International (UMI). Documents available from The Genuine Article, UMI Article Clearinghouse, Ask*IEEE.
Desc: Publishes work on computer applications in the humanities, including work on literature of all periods and genres, languages and linguistics, musicology, history, art history, and humanistically oriented social science. Publishes reports on the latest research in these areas, as well as pedagogical applications.
Ind/Abst Abstr. Engl. Stud.; Acad. Search; Am. Hist. Life (1967-); Am. Humanit. Index; Annu. Bibliogr. Engl. Lang. Lit.; ARTbibliogr. Mod.; ARTbibliogr. Curr. Titles; Arts Humanit. Citation Index [Full Cov.]; BHA : Biblio. Hist. Art; Book Rev. Index (1984-); CompuMath Cit. Index [Full Cov.]; Comput. Lit. Index; Comput. Rev.; Curr. Cit.; Curr. Contents Arts Humanit.; Curr. Index J. Educ. (March 1990); Data Process. Dig.; Educ. Technol. Abstr.; EP Collect.; Expand. Acad. Index (1989-); Homework Help.; Humanit. Index; Humanit. Source; INFO-SOUTH Abstr.; Inf. Instruc. Technol. (1984-); INSPEC (May 1969-); Linguist. Lang. Behav. Abstr.; Mag. Search; MasterFile FullTEXT 1000; MasterFile FullTEXT 350; MasterFile FullTEXT 650; MasterFile FullTEXT (Jan. 1994-); MLA Int. Bibl. Books Artic. Mod. Lang. Lit.; Music Index (?-19??); Newsp. Period. Abstr. (1991-); OCLC; Res. Alert [Full Cov.]; RILM Abstr.; Romant. Move.; SCISEARCH; Soc. Plann. Policy Dev. Abstr.; Soc. Sci. Cit. Index [Select. Cov.]; Sociol. Abstr.; Telebase.

LC LB1028.43 .C6455
DD 371.3/34/097305 US

COMPUTERS IN EDUCATION (GUILFORD, CONN.). See Education-Computer Applications.

DD 371 ISSN 0888-2177
  US

COMPUTERS IN EDUCATION SERIES. See Education-Computer Applications.

DD 001.64/05 ISSN 0823-9940
  CN
  CEASED

COMPUTERS IN EDUCATION (TORONTO, ONT.). See Education-Computer Applications.

LC LB1028.43 .C6475 ISSN 0738-0569
DD 370/.285 US
Pr Rev.

COMPUTERS IN THE SCHOOLS. See Education-Computer Applications.

DD 001 ISSN 8756-596X
  US

COMPUTING AND THE CLASSICS. Vol. 2, No. 1 (Nov. 1984)-. Periodical. English. Four times a year. Free. Joseph Tebben Classics Department, The Ohio State University, Newark OH 43055. **Tel** (614)366-9338. **ED** Joseph R Tebben (Editor's Address: 1179 University Drive, Newark, OH 43055). **Circ:** 500 (ctrl).
Desc: Reports on the use of computers for instruction and research in the field of classics.

LC LB1028.5 .C575 ISSN 0278-9175
DD 371.3/9445 US
  CCC
  TITLE CHANGE

COMPUTING TEACHER, THE. See Education-Computer Applications.

ISSN 0959-3004
UK

CTISS FILE. (THE CTISS FILE.). [CTISS file]. **Added/Corp** CTISS. **VFOAT** Computers in Teaching Initiative Support Service File. (1986)-. Periodical. English. Two times a year. Free on request. University of Oxford / CTISS, 13 Banbury Road, Oxford OX2 6NN United Kingdom. **Tel** 011 44 1865 273273, FAX 011 44 1865 273275. **Ad Acc. Circ:** 5,000.
Ind/Abst Abstr. Hum. Comput. Interact.; HILITES.

ISSN 0712-2519
DD 371.3/9445/060711 CN

CUE (VANCOUVER). (CUE : THE NEWSLETTER OF CUBEC / COMPUTER-USING EDUCATORS OF BRITISH COLUMBIA.). [CUE]. **Added/Corp** Computer-Using Educators of British Columbia. **VFOAT** Newsletter of CUEBC; Journal of CUBEC; Journal of the Computer Using Educators of British Columbia; C.U.E. Journal. Vol. 1, No. 1 (Oct. 1981)-. Newsletter. English. Irregular. British Columbia Teachers Federation, 100-550 West 6th Avenue, Vancouver British Columbia V5Z 4P2 Canada. **Tel** (604)871-2283, (800)663-9163, FAX (604)871-2294, (604)871-2290.
Ind/Abst Can. Educ. Index.

DD 001 ISSN 0749-9302
  US

DIGEST OF SOFTWARE REVIEWS : EDUCATION, THE. See Education-Computer Applications.

LC LB1028.3 .E316 ISSN 1065-6901
DD 371.3/078 US
  TITLE CHANGE

ED-TECH REVIEW. [Ed-tech rev.]. **Added/Corp** Association for the Advancement of Computing in Education. **VFOAT** Ed Tech Review. (Spring/Summer 1993)-(1993). Periodical. English. Association for the Advancement of Computing in Education, PO Box 2966, Charlottesville VA 22902. **Tel** (804)973-3987, FAX (804)978-7449. **Continued by** Educational Technology Review.

LC LB1028.43 .E47 ISSN 1061-5008
DD 370/.285/4 US
  CCC

EDUCATION TECHNOLOGY NEWS. See Education-Computer Applications.

LC LB1028.5 .E38
DD 370 UK
  CODEN ECTEEZ

EDUCATIONAL COMPUTING AND TECHNOLOGY. See Education-Computer Applications.

LC LB1028.5 .E333 ISSN 1055-8683
DD 371.3/078 US
  CCC
  TITLE CHANGE

EDUCATIONAL IRM QUARTERLY. [Educ. IRM q.]. **Added/Corp** International Society for Technology in Education. Vol. 1, No. 1 (Fall 1991)-(1994). Periodical. English. International Society for Technology in Education ISTE, University of Oregon, 1787 Agate Street, Eugene OR 97403-1923. **Tel** (503)346-4414, FAX (503)346-5890. **Absorbed by** Computing Teacher.

ISSN 0424-5997
US
TITLE CHANGE

Pr Rev.
EDUCATIONAL RESOURCES & TECHNIQUES. Added/Corp Texas Association for Educational Technology. Texas Audio Visual Education Association. **VAT** Educational Resources and Techniques. Vol. 1 (1964)-(1995). Periodical. English. Education Resources Techniques, PO Box 5155, Denton TX 76203. **Tel** (917)565-3790. **ED** Ron Johnson. **Bk Rev. Ad Acc. Circ:** 300 (ctrl). available on microfilm and microfiche from University Microfilms International (UMI). **Continued by** Texas Technology Connection.
Desc: Articles, editorials on the use of technology and related software in instructional settings.

LC LB1028.3 .E316 ISSN 1081-8677
DD 371 US

●**EDUCATIONAL TECHNOLOGY REVIEW.** [Educ. technol. rev.]. **Added/Corp** Association for the Advancement of Computing in Education. **VFOAT** Edutional Tech. No. 3 (Autumn/Winter 1994)-. Periodical. English. Two times a year. $43.00. Association for the Advancement of Computing in Education, PO Box 2966, Charlottesville VA 22902. **Tel** (804)973-3987, FAX (804)978-7449. **Continues** Ed-Tech Review, 1065-6901.

LC QA76 .B725
DD 001.6/4/071041 UK

EDUCATIONAL YEARBOOK. English. One time a year. **Continues** BCS Educational Yearbook.

ISSN 1065-9447
US

●**EDUCATORS' TECH EXCHANGE : AN EDUTECH PUBLICATION FOR THE ACADEMIC COMPUTING COMMUNITY.** Vol. 1, No. 2 (Summer 1993)-. Periodical. English. Four times a year. Free to members of the education community. Edutech, PO Box 52180, Pacific Grove CA 93950-9935. **Tel** (408)375-3700. **Continues** Campus Tech.

LC LB1028.5 .E43 ISSN 0278-3258
DD 371.3/9445/05 US
  CODEN ELEADA

ELECTRONIC LEARNING. [Electron. learn.]. Vol. 1, No. 1 (Sept./Oct. 1981)-. Trade Publication. English. Six times a year. $23.95. Scholastic Inc, 730 Broadway, New York NY 10003. **Tel** (416)883-5300, FAX (212)505-3653. **(Subscription address:** Neodata / Colorado, PO Box 2606, Boulder CO 80322.) available on microfilm and microfiche from University Microfilms International (UMI); available on an online database (files 647,675/Full-Text) from DIALOG. Documents available from Ask*IEEE, UMI Article Clearinghouse, Magazine Collection.
Desc: Helps teachers and others who work with children keep up with their professions.
Ind/Abst Acad. Abstr. Full Text Elite; Acad. Abstr.; Acad. Search; ACM Guide Comput. Lit.; Comput. ASAP [Full Txt.]; Comput. Database [Full Txt.]; Comput. Rev.; Contents Pages Educ.; Curr. Cit.; Curr. Index J. Educ.; Educ. Index; EP Collect.; Gen. Period. Index (1992-); Homework Help.; INFO-SOUTH Abstr.; Inf. Sci. Abstr. (?-?); INSPEC (Sept./Oct. 1981-); Mag. Artic. Summar. Elite; Mag. Artic. Summar. Select.; Mag. Artic. Summar. CD-ROM; Mag. ASAP Plus [Full Txt.]; Mag. ASAP Sel. [Full Txt.]; Mag. Express (1988-) [Full Txt.]; Mag. Index Plus (1989-); Mag. Index Sel. Microfiche (1990-) [Full Txt.]; Mag. Index. Sel. (1986-); Mag. Search; MasterFile FullTEXT 1000; MasterFile FullTEXT 350; MasterFile FullTEXT 650; MasterFile FullTEXT (July 1989-); Microcomput. Abstr. (Sept. 1981-); Mid. Search; Newsp. Period. Abstr. (1988-); OCLC; Prim. Search; Pub. Lib. FullTEXT; Resource/One Ondisc; Telebase; Mag. Index (1977-); TOM Gen. Index (1987-) [Full Txt.]; Vocat. Search.

US

FLORIDA TECHNOLOGY IN EDUCATION QUARTERLY : A PUBLICATION OF FLORIDA A&M UNIVERSITY IN CONJUNCTION WITH THE STATE OF FLORIDA, DEPARTMENT OF EDUCATION.
Added/Corp Florida Agricultural and Mechanical University. Florida. Dept. of Education. **VFOAT** FTEQ. Vol. 3, No. 2 (Winter 1991)-. Periodical. English. Four times a year. $20.00. Florida A&M University College of Education, GEC-C Room 201-B, Tallahassee FL 32307. **Tel** (904)599-3289. **Continues** Florida Educational Computing Quarterly.

LC LB1028.7 .S87 ISSN 1060-9504
DD 371.3/9445 US

HIGH/SCOPE BUYER'S GUIDE TO CHILDREN'S SOFTWARE. See Education-Computer Applications.

LC LB1028.7 .S87
DD 370 US

HIGH/SCOPE SURVEY OF EARLY CHILDHOOD SOFTWARE. See Education-Computer Applications.

LC QA76.76.H92 H97 **ISSN** 0955-8543
DD 025.04 UK
TITLE CHANGE

HYPERMEDIA. [Hypermedia]. (Spring 1989)-(1995). Periodical. English. Taylor Graham Publishing, 500 Chesham House, 150 Regent Street, London W1R 5FA United Kingdom. Documents available from Ask*IEEE. ***Continued by** New Review of Hypermedia and Multimedia Applications and Research.*
Ind/Abst Abstr. Hum. Comput. Interact.; ACM Guide Comput. Lit.; Comput. Rev.; Curr. Cit.; HILITES; INSPEC (Spring 1989-); Libr. Inf. Sci. Abstr.

US

HYPERNEXUS. English. Four times a year. $29.00 (one-year), $55.00 (two-year) US; $39.00 (one-year), $75.00 (two-year) other. International Society for Technology in Education ISTE, University of Oregon, 1787 Agate Street, Eugene OR 97403-1923. **Tel** (503)346-4414, FAX (503)346-5890.
Desc: Journal of hypermedia and multimedia. Contains articles on projects, lesson plans, and theoretical issues.

ISSN 0831-540X
DD 370/.28/5 CN

INFO CDAME. (INFO CDAME : INFORMATION BULLETIN OF CDAME, A CENTRE FOR THE DEVELOPMENT OF MICROCOMPUTER APPLICATIONS IN EDUCATION.). [Info CDAME.]. **Added/Corp** Centre de Developpement des Applications de la Micro-Informatique a des Fins Educatives. Conseil Scolaire de L'ile de Montreal. **VFOAT** Info CDAME. **VAT** Info Centre de Developpement des Applications de la Micro--Informatique a des Fins Educatives. Vol. 1, No. 1 (Oct. 1985)-. Bulletin. English (French). Six times a year. Free. Centre de Developpement des Applications de la Micro-Informatique a des Fins Educatives, Conseil Scolaire de l'Ile de Montreal, 500 boulevard Cremazie East, Montreal Quebec H2P 1E7 Canada.

LC Z699.A1 I536 **ISSN** 1055-3916
DD 371 US

INFORMATION SEARCHER. **See** Education-Computer Applications.

ISSN 0954-7940
DD 004.07 UK

IT TRAINING. [IT train.]. (?989)-. Trade Publication. English. Six times a year. $85.56. Training Information Network, Jubilee House, The Oaks Ruislip, Middlesex HA4 7LF United Kingdom. **Tel** 011 44 1895 622112, FAX 011 44 1895 621582. **ED** Colin Steed. **Bk Rev. Ad Acc, Adv Mgr:** Sam Stevens. ctrl circ.

LC RC429 .J68 **ISSN** 8756-7342
DD 616.85/506 US
NLM W1; JO379L
CEASED

JOURNAL FOR COMPUTER USERS IN SPEECH AND HEARING. **See** Physically Impaired.

LC LB1028.43 .J68 **ISSN** 1043-1020
DD 371.3/34/05 US
CCC
CODEN JAIEEL

JOURNAL OF ARTIFICIAL INTELLIGENCE IN EDUCATION. [J. artif. intell. educ.]. **Added/Corp** Association for the Advancement of Computing in Education. Vol. 1, No. 1 (Fall 1989)-. Periodical. English. Four times a year. $103.00. Association for the Advancement of Computing in Education, PO Box 2966, Charlottesville VA 22902. **Tel** (804)973-3987, FAX (804)978-7449. **ED** Dr. Gary H. Marks. Index available. cum. index. **Bk Rev. Circ:** 3,000. available on microfilm and microfiche from University Microfilms International (UMI). Documents available from Ask*IEEE.
Desc: Publishes articles that advance knowledge and theory on how intelligent computer technologies can enhance learning and teaching.
Ind/Abst ACM Guide Comput. Lit.; Comput. Rev.; Curr. Cit.; Educ. Adm. Abstr.; INSPEC (Fall 1989-); Microcomput. Abstr. (Fall 1989-).

LC LB1028.5 .J68 **ISSN** 0266-4909
DD 370 UK
CCC
CODEN JCALEG

JOURNAL OF COMPUTER ASSISTED LEARNING. [J. comput. assist. learn.]. **VFOAT** JCAL. Vol. 1, No. 1 (Mar./Apr. 1985)-. Academic Scholarly Publication. English. Four times a year. $225.00. Blackwell Scientific Publications Ltd, Marston Book Services, PO Box 88, Oxford OX2 ONE United Kingdom. **Tel** 011 44 1865 206206, FAX 011 44 1865 206219, telex 837 515 MARDIS G. **ED** Robert Lewis. Index available. **Circ:** 900. available on microfilm and microfiche from University Microfilms International (UMI). Documents available from Ask*IEEE.
Ind/Abst Br. Educ. Index; Comput. Abstr.; Curr. Cit.; Curr. Index J. Educ.; Curr. Titles Dent.; Educ. Technol. Abstr.; Inf. Sci. Abstr. (?-?); INSPEC (March 1989-); Psychol. Abstr. (1985-); PsycINFO (1990-); PsycLit; Res. High. Educ. Abstr.; Soc. Plann. Policy Dev. Abstr.; Tech. Educ. Train. Abstr.

LC LB1028.5 .J613 **ISSN** 0098-597X
DD 371.39/445/05 US
CCC
CODEN JCOID8
Pr Rev. **CEASED**

JOURNAL OF COMPUTER-BASED INSTRUCTION. [J. comput.-based instr.]. **Added/Corp** Association for the Development of Computer-Based Instructional Systems. Vol. 1, (Aug. 1974)-(19??). English. ADCIS International Headquarters, 30600 Telegraph Road, Suite 1305, Bingham Farms MI 40825. **ED** Kristine Mraz. cum. index. **Bk Rev.** available on microfilm and microfiche from University Microfilms International (UMI). Documents available from The Genuine Article, Ask*IEEE.
Desc: Contains original research, critical analyses, case study and applications reports related to design, development, evaluation and implementation of computer-based learning systems.
Ind/Abst Abstr. Hum. Comput. Interact.; ACM Guide Comput. Lit.; Comput. Rev.; Contents Pages Educ.; Curr. Cit.; Curr. Index J. Educ.; Educ. Index; Educ. Technol. Abstr.; Eng. Mater. Abstr.; HILITES; Inf. Sci. Abstr. (?-?); INSPEC (Feb. 1977-); Psychol. Abstr. (1974-); PsycINFO; PsycLit; Res. Alert [Full Cov.]; Soc. Sci. Cit. Index [Full Cov.]; Tech. Educ. Train. Abstr.

US

JOURNAL OF COMPUTER SCIENCE EDUCATION. **See** Education-Computer Applications.

LC QA20.C65 J68 **ISSN** 0731-9258
DD 507/.8 US
CCC
CODEN JCMTDV
Pr Rev.

JOURNAL OF COMPUTERS IN MATHEMATICS AND SCIENCE TEACHING, THE. **See** Education-Computer Applications.

ISSN 0735-6331
DD 371 US
CODEN JERSEY
Pr Rev.

JOURNAL OF EDUCATIONAL COMPUTING RESEARCH. [J. educ. comput. res.]. Vol. 1, No. 1 (1985)-. Periodical. English. Eight times a year. $193.00. Baywood Publishing Company Inc., 26 Austin Avenue, PO Box 337, Amityville NY 11701. **Tel** (516)691-1270, (800)638-7819, FAX (516)691-1770. **ED** Robert H. Seidman. Index available. cum. index. **Bk Rev.** Documents available from Article Express International, The Genuine Article, Ask*IEEE.
Desc: Brings together original articles on important empirical research, conceptual and theoretical analyses, design and development studies, and critical reviews in this important field.
Ind/Abst Comput. Abstr.; Comput. Lit. Index; Contents Pages Educ.; Curr. Cit.; Curr. Contents Soc. Behav. Sci.; Curr. Index J. Educ.; Educ. Index; Educ. Technol. Abstr.; Ei Page One; Eng. Index Annu.; HILITES; Inf. Sci. Abstr. (?-?); INSPEC (1985-); Linguist. Lang. Behav. Abstr.; Psychol. Abstr. (1986-); PsycINFO; PsycLit; Res. Alert [Full Cov.]; Soc. Plann. Policy Dev. Abstr.; Soc. Sci. Cit. Index [Full Cov.]; Sociol. Abstr.; Stud. Women Abstr.; Tech. Educ. Train. Abstr.

LC LB2846 .A78 **ISSN** 0888-6504
DD 371.2/00285 US
CCC
CODEN JRCEE8

JOURNAL OF RESEARCH ON COMPUTING IN EDUCATION. [J. res. comput. educ.]. **Added/Corp** International Association for Computing in Education. Vol. 20, No. 2 (Winter 1987)-. Periodical. English. Four times a year. $74.00. International Society for Technology in Education ISTE, University of Oregon, 1787 Agate Street, Eugene OR 97403-1923. **Tel** (503)346-4414, FAX (503)346-5890. **Bk Rev. Ad Acc. Circ:** 2,000. available on microfilm and microfiche from University Microfilms International (UMI). Documents available from Ask*IEEE. ***Continues** AEDS Journal, 0001-1037.*
Desc: Articles on research, system or project descriptions and evaluations, assessments of the state of the art, and theoretical or conceptual positions that relate to the field of educational computing.
Ind/Abst Acad. Search; Comput. Rev.; Curr. Cit.; Curr. Index J. Educ. (Winter 1987-);; Educ. Index (Winter 1987-);; Educ. Technol. Abstr.; Electron. Commun. Abstr. J. (winter 1987-); EP Collect.; Homework Help.; INFO-SOUTH Abstr.; Inf. Sci. Abstr. (?-?); INSPEC (Winter 1987-); ISMEC Bull. (winter 1987-); Mag. Search; MasterFile FullTEXT 1000; MasterFile FullTEXT 350; MasterFile FullTEXT 650; MasterFile FullTEXT (July 1993-); Microcomput. Abstr. (Spring 1990-); OCLC; Pollut. Abstr. Indexes (Winter 1987-);; Saf. Sci. Abstr. J. (winter 1987-); Tech. Educ. Train. Abstr.; Telebase.

US

KIDTECH NEWS. (19??)-. Newsletter. English. KidTECH, PO Box 200, New York NY 10044.
Desc: Newsletter for consumers and is dedicated to providing information about the home and school electronic learning environments.

ISSN 0866-9619
PL
UDC 681.322

KOMPUTER W SZKOLE. (1990)-. Periodical. Polish. Twelve times a year. Price on request. **(Subscription address:** Ars Polona-Ruch, PO Box 1001, Krakowskie Przedmiescie 7, 00-068 Warsaw Poland. **Tel** 011 48 22 261201.)

LC LB1028.5 .C575 **ISSN** 1082-5754
DD 371.3/9445 US

•**LEARNING AND LEADING WITH TECHNOLOGY.** (LEARNING AND LEADING WITH TECHNOLOGY : THE ISTE JOURNAL OF EDUCATIONAL TECHNOLOGY PRACTICE AND POLICY.). [Learn. lead. technol.]. **Added/Corp** International Society for Technology in Education. Vol. 22, No. 8 (May 1995)-. Periodical. English. Eight times a year. $61.00. International Society for Technology in Education ISTE, University of Oregon, 1787 Agate Street, Eugene OR 97403-1923. **Tel** (503)346-4414, FAX (503)346-5890. **ED** Anita Best and David Moursund. Index available. cum. index. **Bk Rev. Ad Acc. Circ:** 14,000 (ctrl). available on microfilm and microfiche from University Microfilms International (UMI). Documents available from Ask*IEEE. ***Continues** Computing Teacher, 0278-9175.*
Desc: For persons interested in the instructional use of computers. Emphasis is on teaching about computers, teaching using computers, teacher education and impact on curriculum.
Ind/Abst Contents Pages Educ.; Curr. Cit.; Curr. Index J. Educ.; Educ. Index (1992-); Educ. Technol. Abstr.; Inf. Sci. Abstr.; INSPEC (Oct. 1983-);; Microcomput. Abstr. (Feb. 1981-);.

ISSN 0821-3623
DD 371.3/9445/0971 CN

LEARNING WITH COMPUTERS. [Learn. comput.]. **VFOAT** Apprendre Avec l'Ordinateur. (1983)-. Periodical. English (French; summaries and/or abstracts in French). Irregular. $18.00. Learning With Computers, PO Box 185, West Hill, Ontario M1E 4R4 Canada.

ISSN 0993-2801
FR
UDC 681.3:37 (443.822)

LETTRE DE CLEO, LA. **VFOAT** La Lettre de Centre Lorrain d'Enseignement Assiste par Ordinateur. (1987)-. Periodical. French. Ten times a year. $42.85. CLEO, Ban la Dame, 54390 Frouard France. **Tel** 011 33 83 243783.

US

MACADEMIC. CD-ROM. English. Irregular. $149.00. Quantum Leap Technologies, 1399 Southeast 9th Avenue, Suite 4, Hialeah FL 33010-5999. **Tel** (305)885-9985, (800)762-2877, FAX (305)762-9986. Index available.
Desc: Features a wide range of educational software from art and music to math and science, plus study programs in foreign languages, religion, health and computer programing. Also included in the library of over 7,500 programs and files, is a large fun and games section featuring hundreds of educational games and quizzes with an element of entertainment. This disc also contains a number of resources for the education professional, including grading and quiz making programs.

LC LB1028.5 .M128 **ISSN** 0732-6718
DD 371.3/9445 US
CCC
CODEN MMLEDG
SUSPENDED

MACHINE-MEDIATED LEARNING. [Mach.-mediat. learn.]. **VFOAT** Machine Mediated Learning. Vol. 1, No. 1 (1983)-Suspended (1995). Periodical. English. Four times a year. $125.00. Lawrence Erlbaum Associates, Inc., 10 Industrial Avenue, Mahwah NJ 07430. **Tel** (201)236-9500, (800)926-6579, FAX (201)666-2394. **ED** Edward A. Friedman and Alan Lesgold. **Bk Rev. Ad Acc.** Full Page (B&W) $300.00. Half Page (B&W) $200.00. **Circ:** 400 (ctrl). Documents available from Ask*IEEE.
Desc: Focuses on the scientific, technological and managerial aspects of the application of machines to instruction and training.
Ind/Abst Abstr. Hum. Comput. Interact.; ACM Guide Comput. Lit.; Comput. Rev.; Contents Pages Educ.; Curr. Index J. Educ. (March 1990); Educ. Technol. Abstr.; Ergon. Abstr.; Inf. Sci. Abstr.; INSPEC (1989-).

LC QA13 .M16 **ISSN** 0730-8639
DD 510/.711 US
CODEN MCEDDA
Pr Rev.

MATHEMATICS AND COMPUTER EDUCATION. **See** Mathematics.

LC LB1028.5 .N29A **ISSN** 0730-7675
DD 371.3/9445/02573 US

MEMBERSHIP DIRECTORY - NATIONAL SOCIETY FOR PERFORMANCE AND INSTRUCTION. (MEMBERSHIP DIRECTORY / NSPI.). **Main/Corp** National Society for Performance and Instruction. **VFOAT** N.S.P.I. Membership Directory; NSPI Membership

Computers —Computer Assisted Instruction

Directory. Directory. English. Ten times a year. $A125.00 US; $175.00 other. National Society for Performance & Instruction, 1300 L Street Northwest, Suite 1250, Washington DC 20005. **Tel** (202)408-7969, FAX (202)408-7972. **ED** Sivasailam Thiagarajan. **Bk Rev. Ad Acc. Circ:** 3,000.
Desc: Publishes practical articles, theoretical and conceptual discussions, procedural models and their applications, research reports, case histories, research reviews, and short essays on topics related to improving human performance through a wide range of strategies.

ISSN 1046-1981
DD 372   US
CCC
CODEN MWEDEF

MICROSOFT WORKS IN EDUCATION.
See Education-Computer Applications.

UK

●NEW REVIEW OF HYPERMEDIA AND MULTIMEDIA APPLICATIONS AND RESEARCH.
(1995)-. English. One time a year. $130.00. Taylor Graham Publishing, 500 Chesham House, 150 Regent Street, London W1R 5FA United Kingdom. **Continues** Hypermedia.

ISSN 0821-3674
DD 371.3/9445/097127   CN

NEWSLETTER - MANITOBA ASSOCIATION FOR EDUCATIONAL DATA SYSTEMS.
(NEWSLETTER / MAN-AEDS.). [Newsl. - Manit. Assoc. Educ. Data Syst.]. **VAT** Newsletter - MAN-AEDS. (1975)-. Newsletter. English. Six times a year. Free to members. Manitoba Association for Educational Data Systems, 1577 Wall Street East, Winnipeg Manitoba R3E 2S5 Canada.

LC L   ISSN 1081-2687
DD 371.334   US

●ONLINE EDUCATOR, THE.
[Online educ.]. Vol. 1.1 (Nov. 1994)-. Periodical. English. Ten times a year. $29.00 US; $35.00 Canada and Mexico; $45.00 other. Hass Associates, Box 151141, West Bloomfield MI 48324. **Tel** (810)932-3993. **Circ:** 200. available via Internet (http://www.cris.com/~felixg/OE/OEWELCOME.html).
Desc: Provides information on how to make the Internet a valuable classroom tool. Gives teachers, and other readers, the "Online Basics" and more.

LC LB1028.7 .O54   ISSN 1053-4326
DD 373.13/9445/0973   US

ONLY THE BEST.
See Education-Computer Applications.

ISSN 1184-9770
DD 371.3   CN
Pr Rev.

OUTPUT (RICHMOND HILL).
(OUTPUT.). [Output]. **Added/Corp** Educational Computing Organization of Ontario. **VFOAT** ECOO Output. Vol. 12, No. 1 (Apr. 1991)-. Periodical. English. Four times a year (Jan., Apr., July, Sept.). 32.01Can$. Educational Computing Organization of Ontario, PO Box 2699, Station B, Richmond Hill Ontario L4E 1A7 Canada. **Tel** (416)773-3981, FAX (416)773-6963. **ED** Brenda Kosky (editor's address: 500 Glencairn Avenue, Suite 301, Toronto, Ontario M6B 1Z1 Canada. **Bk Rev**, (Qty: 1-5). **Ad Acc. Circ:** 1,600 (ctrl). **Continues** ECOO Output, 0829-3864.

LC LB1028.5 .N3a   ISSN 0884-1985
DD 371.3/9445   US

PERFORMANCE & INSTRUCTION
(1985). (PERFORMANCE + INSTRUCTION.). [Perform. instr.]. **Added/Corp** National Society for Performance and Instruction. **VFOAT** Performance and Instruction. Vol. 24, No.1 (Feb. 1985)-. Periodical. English. Ten times a year (May/June & Nov/Dec. issues combined). $50.00. National Society for Performance & Instruction, 1300 L Street Northwest, Suite 1250, Washington DC 20005. **Tel** (202)408-7969, FAX (202)408-7972. **Ad Acc.** available on microfilm and microfiche from University Microfilms International (UMI). **Continues** Performance & Instruction Journal, 8750-0191.
Desc: This journal is dedicated to the advancement of performance science and technology. Practical articles on topics related to improving human performance.
Ind/Abst AGRICOLA [Select. Cov.]; Contents Pages Educ.; Curr. Cit.]; Curr. Index J. Educ.; Psychol. Abstr. (1985)-.

ISSN 0732-0175
US

PROCEEDINGS OF THE INTERNATIONAL SYMPOSIUM ON COMPUTER AIDED SEISMIC ANALYSIS AND DISCRIMINATION.
See Science and Technology.

ISSN 0958-8671
UK
NLM W1; PS746VP

PSYCHOLOGY SOFTWARE NEWS : NEWSLETTER OF THE COMPUTERS IN TEACHING INITIATIVE CENTRE FOR PSYCHOLOGY.
Added/Corp Computers in Teaching Initiative Centre for Psychology. (19??)-. Newsletter. English. Four times a year. £34.00 (institutions), £16.00 (individuals) UK; £38.00 (institutions), £18.00 (individuals) other. University of York / CTI Centre for Psychology, Heslington, York Y01 2DD United Kingdom. **Tel** 011 44 1904 433154, FAX 011 44 1904 433181.

AT

QUICK.
(19??)-. English. Comes with Computer Group of Queensland membership. Computer Education Group of Queensland, GPO 1669, Brisbane Queensland 4001 Australia. **Tel** 011 61 7 3528515, FAX 011 61 7 3566178. **Ind/Abst** Aust. Educ. Index.

BE
CEASED

SCHOOL EN COMPUTER.
(19??)-(19??). French. School en Computer, Bloesemlaan 17, 3360 Korbeek Lo Belgium. **ED** H. Christiaen. **Bk Rev. Ad Acc. Circ:** 450.
Desc: Background articles, reviews of programs for use of computers in education.

LC HV1569.5 .S53   ISSN 0163-5727
DD 362   US
CODEN SGNWD2

SIGCAPH NEWSLETTER.
(SIGCAPH NEWSLETTER : A QUARTERLY PUBLICATION OF THE ACM SPECIAL INTEREST GROUP ON COMPUTERS AND THE PHYSICALLY HANDICAPPED.). [SIGCAPH newsl.]. **Added/Corp** ACM--SIGCAPH. **VFOAT** S.I.G.C.A.P.H. Newsletter. **VAT** Special Interest Group on Computers and the Physically Handicapped Newsletter. (1973)-. Newsletter. English. Three times a year. $30.00. ACM / Association for Computing Machinery, 1515 Broadway, 17th Floor, New York NY 10036. **Tel** (212)869-7440, FAX (212)869-0481. **(Subscription address:** Association for Computing Machinery, PO Box 12114, Church Street Station, New York NY 10249. **Tel** (212)626-0500.) Documents available from Ask*IEEE. **Continues** SICCAPH Newsletter.
Ind/Abst ACM Guide Comput. Lit.; Comput. Rev. (Spring 1980-); Ergon. Abstr. (Spring 1980-); INSPEC (Spring 1980-).

LC LB1028.43 .S52   ISSN 0893-2999
DD 370   US

SIGCUE OUTLOOK.
[SIGCUE outlook]. **Added/Corp** Association for Computing Machinery. Special Interest Group on Computer Uses in Education. **VFOAT** Outlook. **VAT** Special Interest Group on Computer Uses in Education Outlook. Vol. 19, Nos. 1/2 (Spring/Summer 1986)-. Periodical. English. Three times a year. $36.00. ACM / Association for Computing Machinery, 1515 Broadway, 17th Floor, New York NY 10036. **Tel** (212)869-7440, FAX (212)869-0481. **(Subscription address:** Association for Computing Machinery, PO Box 12114, Church Street Station, New York NY 10249. **Tel** (212)626-0500.) Documents available from Ask*IEEE. **Continues** SIGCUE Bulletin, 0163-5735.
Ind/Abst Abstr. Hum. Comput. Interact.; ACM Guide Comput. Lit.; Comput. Rev. (1986-); Ergon. Abstr.; INSPEC (1986-).

ISSN 1048-8340
DD 371   US

SIGTC CONNECTIONS.
(SIGTC CONNECTIONS / INTERNATIONAL SOCIETY FOR TECHNOLOGY IN EDUCATION, ISTE, SPECIAL INTEREST GROUP FOR TECHNOLOGY COORDINATORS.). [SIGTC connect.]. **Added/Corp** International Society for Technology in Education. International Society for Technology in Education. Special Interest Group for Technology Coordinators. **VAT** Special Interest Group for Technology Coordinators Connections. (19?)-. Periodical. English. Four times a year. $29.00. International Society for Technology in Education ISTE, University of Oregon, 1787 Agate Street, Eugene OR 97403-1923. **Tel** (503)346-4414, FAX (503)346-5890. **Continues** SIGCC Bulletin, 1040-4465.
Desc: Provides a way to identify problems and solutions, share information, and develop policy papers on issues facing technology coordinators.

LC LB1043 .E654
DD 370   US

●SOFTWARE AND NETWORKS FOR LEARNING.
Vol. 20, No. 5 (Sept. 1994)-. Periodical. English. Nine times a year. $65.00. Sterling Harbor Press Inc., PO Box 3894, Santa Barbara CA 93130. **Tel** (805)687-0904, FAX (805)687-0904. **Continues** EPIEgram (Water Mill, N.Y. : 1988), 1046-1493.

LC LB1028.3 .T28   ISSN 0898-3348
DD 372   US

T.H.E. JOURNAL. SOURCE GUIDE OF HIGH-TECHNOLOGY PRODUCTS FOR EDUCATION.
See Education-Computer Applications.

ISSN 0742-4930

TEACHING, LEARNING, COMPUTING :
TLC. See Education-Computer Applications.

LC LB1028.43 .C53   ISSN 1053-6728
DD 371.3/9445   US

TECHNOLOGY & LEARNING.
See Education-Computer Applications.

LC LB1043 .A815   ISSN 8756-3894
DD 371.3/07/8   US
CODEN TETREF
Pr Rev.

TECHTRENDS.
See Education-Computer Applications.

LC LB1028.3 .J69   ISSN 0192-592X
DD 371.3/07/8   US
CODEN THEJD4

THE JOURNAL.
(THE JOURNAL : TECHNOLOGICAL HORIZONS IN EDUCATION.). [THE journal]. **VFOAT** Technological Horizons in Education; T.H.E. Journal. **VAT** Technological Horizons in Education Journal. (May 1974)-. Periodical. English. Eleven times a year. Free on request. Information Synergy Inc, 150 El Camnio Real, Suite 112, Tustin CA 92680. **Tel** (714)730-4011. available on microfilm and microfiche from University Microfilms International (UMI). Documents available from Ask*IEEE.
Ind/Abst Acad. Search; ACM Guide Comput. Lit.; Comput. ASAP [Full Txt.]; Comput. Database [Full Txt.]; Comput. Lit. Index; Comput. Rev.; Educ. Index (Jan. 1982-); EP Collect.; Homework Help.; Inf. Instruc. Technol.; INSPEC (1982-1984); MasterFile FullTEXT 1000; MasterFile FullTEXT 350; MasterFile FullTEXT 650; MasterFile FullTEXT (July 1993-); Microcomput. Abstr. (Jan. 1982-?); OCLC; Telebase.

ISSN 1040-4694
DD 371   US
CCC

UPDATE - INTERNATIONAL COUNCIL FOR COMPUTERS IN EDUCATION
(U.S.). See Education.

AT

VICTORIAN BULLETIN.
See Education-Computer Applications.

COMPUTER CRIMES AND SECURITY

LC QA76.9.A25 A15   ISSN 0749-3851
DD 621.382   US

2600.
[2600]. (19??)-. **VFOAT** Twenty-Six Hundred; Twenty Hundred; Twenty-Six Hundred Magazine; 2600 Magazine. (Jan. 1984)-. Periodical. English. Four times a year (Mar., June, Sept., Dec.). $50.00. 2600 Enterprises, Box 752, Middle Island NY 11953-0752. **Tel** (516)751-2600, FAX (516)751-2608. **ED** Emmanuel Goldstein. **Circ:** 6,000.
Desc: Information about the world of telephones and computers written from the perspective of 'computer hackers' and 'phone phreaks'. With emphasis on privacy and security issues.

LC QA76.9.A25 A36   ISSN 0197-1514
DD 658.4/78   US
CEASED

ADVANCES IN COMPUTER SECURITY MANAGEMENT.
[Adv. comput. secur. manage.]. Vol. 1 (1980)-Completed Series (1993). Periodical. English. John Wiley & Sons Ltd., Baffins Lane, Chichester, West Sussex PO19 1UD United Kingdom. **Tel** 011 44 1243 779777, FAX 011 44 1243 776128 BTG:JWP001, telex 86290 WIBOOKG.

LC KF390.5.C6 A492   ISSN 8755-1675
DD 343.73/078004/02648 347.3037800402648   US

AMERICAN COMPUTER LAW DIGEST.
See Law-Computer Applications.

US

ASSETS PROTECTION.
(19??)-. English. Six times a year. $56.00 US; $68.00 Canada and Mexico; $88.00 other. Assets Protection, PO Box 5323, Madison WI 53705. **Tel** (608)833-8099, FAX (608)271-4520. **Absorbed** Corporate Compliance Report.
Desc: Focus is on how to establish, monitor, assess and maintain internal controls that detect and prevent loss of assets. Reviews focus on uncovering duplicate payments, overpayments, excessive charges, and false claims. Techniques and aids for valuations or loss estimations are presented. Legal aspects emphasizes statutes and cases relevant to prosecution, restitution or recovery.

ISSN 0746-7281
DD 658 US
CCC

AUERBACH DATA SECURITY MANAGEMENT. [Auerbach data secur. manage.]. **Added/Corp** Auerbach Publishers. **VFOAT** Data Security Management. (1983)-. English. Six times a year. $395.65. Auerbach Publishers Inc., Park Square Building, 31 St. James Avenue, Boston MA 02116. **Tel** (800)950-1207. **ED** Alan Berman and Rich Mansfield. ***Continues*** *Data Security Management, 0736-363X.*
Desc: A reference service dealing with all aspects of the discipline in 80+ articles. Each article is about 20 pages. The book is chock full of figures, charts, and checklists.

ISSN 0822-6709
DD 346.71/07 CN
CEASED

CANADIAN COMPUTER LAW REPORTER. See Law.

LC QA75 **ISSN** 1244-4901
DD 005.8 FR
UDC 061.22:681.3(44)

CHAOS DIGEST SAINT-OUEN. (CHAOS DIGEST.). (1993)-. Periodical. English. One time a week. Free. Chaos Computer Club, BP155, 93404 St Ouen Cedex France. **Tel** 011 33 1 47874083, FAX 011 33 1 47877070. available via Internet (message linux-activists-request@niksula.hut.fi,X-Mn.Admin: join CHAOS_DIGEST).
Desc: Covers computer fraud, hacking and other computer security issues.

ISSN 0265-1866
DD 368.400941 UK

CLAIMANTS UNDER THREAT. [Claimants under threat]. **VFOAT** CUT (London). (1983)-. Periodical. English. Six times a year. £60.00 UK; £64.00 other Europe; £66.00 other. Techgnosis Ltd., Blade House, Battersea Road, Cheshire SK4 3EA United Kingdom. **Tel** 011 44 161 4422639, FAX 011 44 161 4431162.

ISSN 1352-6278
DD 005.8 UK

COMPUTER & COMMUNICATIONS SECURITY REVIEWS. [Comput. commun. secur. rev.]. **VFOAT** Computer and Communications Security Reviews. (1992)-. Periodical. English. Four times a year (Mar., June, Sept., Dec.). £60.00 individuals, £95.00 institutions. Northgate Consultants Ltd, Ivy Dene Lode Farm Lode, Cambridgeshire CB5 9HF United Kingdom. **Tel** 011 44 223 334678. **ED** Ross Anderson. **Bk Rev**, (Qty: 20). available via electronic mail.
Desc: Published research in cryptology, computer security, and related topics.

ISSN 0142-0496
DD 364 NE
CCC
CODEN CFSBEK

COMPUTER FRAUD & SECURITY BULLETIN. [Comput. fraud secur. bull.]. **VAT** Computer Fraud and Security Bulletin. (1978)-. Bulletin. English. Twelve times a year. $417.00. Elsevier Advanced Technology, An Imprint of Elsevier Science Ltd., The Boulevard, Langford Lane, Kidlington, Oxford OX5 1GB United Kingdom. **Tel** 011 44 1865 843000, 011 44 1865 843699, FAX 011 44 1865 843010. **(Subscription address:** Elsevier Science Ltd. / Oxford Fulfillment Centre, PO Box 800, Kidlington OX5 1DX United Kingdom. **Tel** 011 44 865 843355.) **ED** Robin Arnfield and Fred Lafferty. available on microfilm from University Microfilms International (UMI); available on an online database from Elsevier Electronic Subscriptions (EES); DIALOG; and DATA-STAR. Documents available from Ask*IEEE, BLDSC, SWETS.
Desc: Contains information on computer crime.
Ind/Abst Comput. Lit. Index; Comput. Rev.; Curr. Cit.; Data Process. Dig.; INSPEC (May 1982-); PTS Newsl. Database [Full Txt.].

UK
CODEN CLSRE8
Pr Rev.

COMPUTER LAW AND SECURITY REPORT, THE. Vol. 1, Issue 1 (May/June 1985)-. Periodical. English. Eight times a year. $415.00. Elsevier Advanced Technology, An Imprint of Elsevier Science Ltd., The Boulevard, Langford Lane, Kidlington, Oxford OX5 1GB United Kingdom. **Tel** 011 44 1865 843000, 011 44 1865 843699, FAX 011 44 1865 843010. **(Subscription address:** Elsevier Science Ltd. / Oxford Fulfillment Centre, PO Box 800, Kidlington OX5 1DX United Kingdom. **Tel** 011 44 865 843355.) **ED** Stephen Saxby, David Davies. Index available. **Bk Rev. Circ:** 500. available in microform from University Microfilms International (UMI); available on an online database from Elsevier Electronic Subscriptions (EES). Documents available from Ask*IEEE.
Desc: Reports on computer security, risk management, and the law governing information technology and computer use. Read by senior level corporate managers responsible for computer security and lawyers.
Ind/Abst Curr. Cit.; INSPEC (May/June 1985-)(1985-).

LC KF390.5.C6 A493 **ISSN** 0741-8809
DD 343.73/078004 347.30478004 US

COMPUTER LAW MONITOR, THE. See Law.

LC KF390.5.C6 C649 **ISSN** 0739-7771
DD 343.73/07800164 347.3037800164 US

COMPUTER LAW REPORTER. See Law.

NE

COMPUTER LAW SERIES. See Law.

LC KF390.5.C6 C653 **ISSN** 0747-8933
DD 343.73/07800164 347.3037800164 US

COMPUTER LAW STRATEGIST. See Law.

LC QA
DD 004 US

COMPUTER SECURITY. **Added/Corp** Computer Security Institute (Hudson, Mass.). (197?)-. Periodical. English. Six times a year. Computer Security Institute / San Francisco, 600 Harrison Street, San Francisco CA 94107. **Tel** (415)905-2200, (415)905-2263.
Ind/Abst Risk Abstr.

LC QA76.9.A25 C637 **ISSN** 0742-0633
DD 005.8/05 US
SUSPENDED

COMPUTER SECURITY ALERT. [Comput. secur. alert]. **VFOAT** Alert. Vol. 1, No. 1 (July 1983)-(Sept. 1984). Periodical. English. Twelve times a year. Advent Group, 500 Northeast Spanish River, Boulevard 8, Boca Raton FL 33431. **Tel** (305)392-5411.

ISSN 0738-4262
DD 658 US

COMPUTER SECURITY, AUDITING AND CONTROLS. [Comput. secur. audit. controls]. **VFOAT** COM-S.A.C. Vol. 1, No. 1 (Jan. 1974)-. Trade Publication. English. Four times a year. $75.00. Management Advisory Publications, 57 Greylock Road, PO Box 81151, Wellesley Hills MA 02181-0001. **Tel** (617)235-2895, FAX (617)235-5446. **ED** Javier F. Kuong. Index available. **Bk Rev. Ad Acc.** ctrl circ. Documents available from Ask*IEEE.
Desc: Articles, tutorials and in-depth coverage of topics on computer security, auditing and internal controls, and the most comprehensive digest of all literature on computer security, and other courses.
Ind/Abst Data Process. Dig.; INSPEC.

ISSN 0882-1453
DD 364 US

COMPUTER SECURITY DIGEST. [Comput. secur. dig.]. **Added/Corp** Computer Protection Systems, Inc. (198?)-. Periodical. English. Twelve times a year. $125.00. Computer Protection System Inc., 150 North Main Street, Plymouth MI 48170. **Tel** (313)459-8787, FAX (313)459-2720. **ED** Jack Bologna. **Bk Rev. Circ:** 150.
Desc: Provides subscribers with digests of current incidents involving computer security breaches and computer-related crime.

US

COMPUTER SECURITY INSTITUTE. English. Computer Security Institute, 360 Church Street/Suite 110, Northborough MA 01532. **Tel** (508)393-2600, FAX (508)393-3888.

LC QA76.9.A25 C65 **ISSN** 0277-0865
DD 658.4/78 US

COMPUTER SECURITY JOURNAL. [Comput. secur. j.]. **Added/Corp** Computer Security Institute (San Francisco, Calif.). Vol. 1, No. 1 (Spring 1981)-. Periodical. English. Two times a year. $85.00. Miller Freeman Inc., 600 Harrison Street, San Francisco CA 94107. **Tel** (415)905-2337, (415)905-2200, FAX (415)905-2240, telex 278273. **ED** Russell Kay. Index available. **Circ:** 30,000 (ctrl). available on an online database (file 485/Full-Text) from DIALOG. Documents available from Ask*IEEE.
Desc: Comprehensive, regular forum for new ideas and useful information about current security products and practices designed for corporate managers, DP personnel, security officers, and EDP auditors.
Ind/Abst Account. Tax Datab. (1981-) [Full Txt.]; Comput. Database (19??-); Curr. Cit.; INSPEC (Summer 1984-).

LC QA76.9.A25 B89
DD 005.8/029/40973 US

COMPUTER SECURITY PRODUCTS BUYERS GUIDE. **Added/Corp** Computer Security Institute (San Francisco, Calif.). (1992)-. English. Computer Security Institute / San Francisco, 600 Harrison Street, San Francisco CA 94107. **Tel** (415)905-2200, (415)905-2263. ***Continues*** *Buyers Guide (Computer Security Institute (San Francisco, Calif.)), 1059-5317.*

LC KF3024.C6 C656 **ISSN** 1041-7133
DD 346.7304/82 US

COMPUTER SOFTWARE. (COMPUTER SOFTWARE : PROTECTION AND MARKETING.). [Comput. softw.]. English. Irregular. Practising Law Institute, 810 Seventh Avenue, New York NY 10019-5818. **Tel** (212)765-5700, FAX (212)581-4670 general correspondence, (212)265-4742 orders and billing inquiries.

LC KF3024.C6 C657
DD 346.7304/82 US

COMPUTER SOFTWARE AND CHIPS : PROTECTION AND MARKETING. (1985)-. English. Irregular. Practising Law Institute, 810 Seventh Avenue, New York NY 10019-5818. **Tel** (212)765-5700, FAX (212)581-4670 general correspondence, (212)265-4742 orders and billing inquiries. **ED** Morton David Goldberg.

LC QA76.9.A25 C664 **ISSN** 0167-4048
DD 005.8/05 UK
CCC
Pr Rev.

COMPUTERS & SECURITY. [Comput. secur.]. **VFOAT** Computers and Security. Vol. 1, No. 1 (Jan. 1982)-. Periodical. English. Eight times a year. $339.00 The Americas; £227.00 other. Elsevier Advanced Technology, An Imprint of Elsevier Science Ltd., The Boulevard, Langford Lane, Kidlington, Oxford OX5 1GB United Kingdom. **Tel** 011 44 1865 843000, 011 44 1865 843699, FAX 011 44 1865 843010. **(Subscription address:** Elsevier Science Ltd. / Oxford Fulfillment Centre, PO Box 800, Kidlington OX5 1DX United Kingdom. **Tel** 011 44 865 843355.) **ED** Harold Joseph Highland. **Bk Rev. Ad Acc. Circ:** 750. available on microfilm and microfiche from University Microfilms International (UMI); available on an online database from Elsevier Electronic Subscriptions (EES). Documents available from Article Express International, UMI Article Clearinghouse, Ask*IEEE.
Desc: Provides the international community with information about all phases of computer security in depth and in sufficient detail to be readily understood by its varied professional readers.
Ind/Abst ABI/INFORM Glob. Ed.; ABI/INFORM [Computer File] (Jan. 1983-); ACM Guide Comput. Lit.; Anbar Account. Finan. Abstr. [Full Txt.]; Anbar Mark. Distr. Abstr. [Full Txt.]; Anbar Top Manage. Abstr. [Full Txt.]; Comput. Abstr.; Comput. Lit. Index; Comput. Rev.; Curr. Cit.; Data Process. Dig.; Ei Page One; Eng. Index Annu.; Gen. BusinessFile (1992-); INSPEC (Jan. 1982-); Manage. Bibliogr. Rev.; Oper. Prod. Manage. Abstr. [Full Txt.]; Person. Train. Abstr. [Full Txt.]; Pollut. Abstr. Indexes; Women Manage. Rev. [Full Txt.]; World Publ. Monit.

US

COMPUTING AND COMMUNICATIONS LAW AND PROTECTION REPORT. (19??)-. English. Twelve times a year. $84.00 US; $96.00 Canada and Mexico; $116.00 other. Assets Protection, PO Box 5323, Madison WI 53705. **Tel** (608)833-8099, FAX (608)271-4520. ***Continues*** *Computing and Communications Protection.*
Desc: Reports on the spectrum of legal liability risks arising from an absence of or inadequate data processing information systems protection, including the lack of confidentiality and privacy safeguards for information, electronic commerce and data communication networks, and records retention and storage.

LC HV8290 .A8
DD 658.47 US
TITLE CHANGE

COMPUTING AND COMMUNICATIONS PROTECTION. **VFOAT** Computing and Communications Protection. Vol. 16, No. 1 (Jan. 1992)-(1994). Periodical. English. Assets Protection, PO Box 5323, Madison WI 53705. **Tel** (608)833-8099, FAX (608)271-4520. ***Continues*** *Data Processing and Communications Security, 0749-1484.* ***Continued by*** *Computing and Communications Law and Protection Report.*

ISSN 0899-4595
DD 658 US
Pr Rev.

CONTINGENCY PLANNING & RECOVERY JOURNAL : CPR-J. [Cont. plan. recovery j.]. **Added/Corp** Contingency Planning & Recovery Institute. **VFOAT** CPR-J; Contingency Planning and Recovery Journal. Vol. 2, No. 1 (1988)-. Trade Publication. English. Four times a year. $65.00. Management Advisory Publications, 57 Greylock Road, PO Box 81151, Wellesley Hills MA 02181-0001. **Tel** (617)235-2895, FAX (617)235-5446. **ED** Javier F. Kuong. cum. index. **Bk Rev. Ad Acc.** ***Continues*** *Contingency Planning & Recovery Report, 0899-4994.*
Desc: A journal for business continuity professionals. Devoted to computer contingency planning, disaster recovery and business continuity. Current trends and developments included.

LC Z102.5 .C79 **ISSN** 0161-1194
DD 001.34/36/05 US
CCC
CODEN CRYPE6

CRYPTOLOGIA. [Cryptologia]. **Added/Corp** Albion College. Dept. of Mathematics. Rose-Hulman Institute of Technology. Vol. 1 (Jan. 1977)-. Periodical. English. Four times a year (Jan., Apr., Jul., Oct.). $40.00. Rose Hulman Institute of Technology, 5500 Wabash Avenue, Terre Haute IN 47803. **Tel** (812)877-8412, FAX (812)877-3198. **ED** Brian J Winkel. Index available. cum. index. **Bk Rev. Ad Acc. Circ:** 1,000 (ctrl). available on microfilm and microfiche from University Microfilms International (UMI).

Documents available from Ask*IEEE.
Desc: Devoted to all aspects of cryptology including computer security, mathematics, codes and ciphers, cryptanalysis, assessment of cryptosystems, history, military science, literature, ancient languages, cipher devices.
Ind/Abst ACM Guide Comput. Lit.; Comput. Rev.; Curr. Cit.; INSPEC (July 1990-); Math. Rev.; Zentralbl. Math. Ihre Grenzgeb.

LC KF3024.C6 C656
DD 346.7304/82 347.306482 US
CURRENT DEVELOPMENTS IN COMPUTER SOFTWARE PROTECTION. **Added/Corp** Practising Law Institute. (1991)-. English. Practising Law Institute, 810 Seventh Avenue, New York NY 10019-5818. **Tel** (212)765-5700, FAX (212)581-4670 general correspondence, (212)265-4742 orders and billing inquiries. ***Continues*** *Computer Software (New York, N.Y.), 1041-7133.*

LC HV8290 .A8 **ISSN** 0749-1484
DD 658.4/78 US
TITLE CHANGE
DATA PROCESSING & COMMUNICATIONS SECURITY. **See** Computers-Electronic Data Processing.

ISSN 1065-9986
DD 005 US
Pr Rev.
DATA SECURITY LETTER. [Data secur. lett.]. **Added/Corp** Trusted Information Systems, Inc. (1988)-. Periodical. English. Nine times a year. $345.00. Data Security Letter, 3060 Washington Road, Route 97, Glenwood MD 21738. **Tel** (301)854-5338, FAX (301)854-5363. **ED** Sharon Osuna. Index available. **Bk Rev**, (Qty: 3-4). **Circ:** 500 (ctrl).
Desc: Covers pertinent legislation, conferences and workshops, security standards and guidelines, interviews, and research results.

US
DATAPRO REPORTS ON INFORMATION SECURITY. **See** Computers-Computer Systems.

ISSN 0170-7256
GW
UDC 342.7 **CCC**
DATENSCHUTZ-BERATER. [Datenschutz-Berat.]. **VFOAT** DSB. Datenschutz-Berater. (197?)-. Trade Publication. German. Twelve times a year. $225.69. Handelsblatt GmbH, Postfach 102716, D-40018 Duesseldorf Germany. **Tel** 011 49 211 8871730, FAX 011 49 211 133523, telex 172114489.

ISSN 0736-6981
US
CCC
CODEN EDPCDF
EDPACS. (EDPACS : THE EDP AUDIT, CONTROL AND SECURITY NEWSLETTER.). [EDPACS]. **VFOAT** E.D.P.A.C.S.; EDP Audit, Control and Security Newsletter; E.D.P. Audit, Control and Security Newsletter. Vol. 1 (April 1973)-. Newsletter. English. Twelve times a year. $177.25. Auerbach Publishers Inc., Park Square Building, 31 St. James Avenue, Boston MA 02116. **Tel** (800)950-1207. **ED** Rich Mansfield. Index available. cum. index. **Bk Rev. Circ:** 6,000. Documents available from UMI Article Clearinghouse, Ask*IEEE.
Desc: Articles, news items, new product information, book reviews, and abstracts of worldwide publications in computer audit and security. Adopted by two professional societies.
Ind/Abst ABI/INFORM Glob. Ed.; ABI/INFORM [Computer File] (June 1975-April 1979); Account. Tax Datab. (1974-); Comput. Lit. Index; INSPEC (Jan. 1980-).

ISSN 1066-7822
DD 005 US
CODEN ISUNEJ
INFO SECURITY NEWS. [Info secur. news]. (199?)-. Periodical. English. Six times a year. $50.00. MIS Training Institute Press Inc., 498 Concord Street, Framingham MA 01701. **Tel** (508)879-9792. **ED** David Bernstein. **Ad Acc. Circ:** 28,000 (ctrl). ***Continues*** *ISPNews, 1051-2500.*

ISSN 0968-5227
UK
CODEN IMCSE4
INFORMATION MANAGEMENT & COMPUTER SECURITY. **VFOAT** Information Management and Computer Security; IMCS. (199?)-. Periodical. English. Five times a year. $1189.00. MCB University Press, 60 62 Toller Lane, Bradford, West Yorkshire BD8 9BY United Kingdom. **Tel** 011 44 1274 785280, FAX 011 44 1274 785200, telex 51317-MCBUNI-G. **(Subscription address:** MCB University Press / US and Canada Subscriptions, PO Box 10812, Birmingham AL 35201-0812. **Tel** (205)995-1567, (800)633-4931, FAX (205)995-1588.) **ED** Kevin Fitzgerald & John Beaumont. Index available. ***Absorbed*** *Computer Control Quarterly, 0813-7099; International Journal of Information Resource Management.*
Ind/Abst Curr. Cit.

UK
INFORMATION SECURITY SERVICE. (19??)-. English. Twelve times a year. $1,168.00. Datapro International, McGraw Hill House, Shoppenhangers Road, Maidenhead Berkshire SL6 2QL United Kingdom. **Tel** 011 44 1628 773277, FAX 011 44 1628 773628.

ISSN 1065-898X
DD 004 US
INFORMATION SYSTEMS SECURITY. [Inf. syst. secur.]. **Added/Corp** Information Systems Security Association. Vol. 1, No. 1, (Spring 1992)-. Trade Publication. English. Four times a year. $165.75. Auerbach Publishers Inc., Park Square Building, 31 St. James Avenue, Boston MA 02116. **Tel** (800)950-1207. **ED** Robert M Elliot. **Bk Rev**, (Qty: 12). **Ad Acc.**
Ind/Abst EP Collect.; Homework Help.; MasterFile FullTEXT 1000; MasterFile FullTEXT 350; MasterFile FullTEXT 650; MasterFile FullTEXT (Jan. 1995-); OCLC; Telebase.

LC K87 .I53
DD 343/.0999 342.3999 FR
INFORMATIQUE ET SCIENCES JURIDIQUES. **Added/Corp** Centre National de la Recherche Scientifique. Centre de Documentation Sciences Humaines. (19??)-. French (English and German). Two times a year. 165.00F. CNRS / Institut d'Information Scientifique et Technique, (Centre National de la Recherche Scientifique), 15 Quai Anatole France, 75700 Paris France. **Tel** 011 33 1 47531515, FAX 011 33 1 45517307, telex 260034. **Bk Rev. Circ:** 250 (ctrl).
Desc: Covers computer law, computer criminality, computer contracts, data security, data protection, legal data bank, computer in a law practice, society and technology, intellectual property and computers.

ISSN 1079-5669
US
•**INTERNET SECURITY MONTHLY.** **See** Computers-Computer Networks.

ISSN 0950-7388
DD 658.478 UK
ISM. INFORMATION SECURITY MONITOR. [ISM, Inf. secur. monit.]. **VFOAT** Information Security Monitor. (1985)-. Periodical. English. Twelve times a year. $426.09. Legal Studies & Services Publ Ltd., 9-13 St. Andrew Street, London EC4A 3AE United Kingdom. **Tel** 011 44 171 9362016. **(Subscription address:** IBC Subscription Services, IBC House, Vickers Drive, Weybridge, Surrey KT13 OXS United Kingdom. **Tel** 011 44 1932 354020.) **ED** Vincent Jones. **Bk Rev**, (Qty: 5).

ISSN 0926-227X
NE
UDC 681.3 **CCC**
JOURNAL OF COMPUTER SECURITY. [J. comput. secur.]. (1992)-. Periodical. English. Four times a year. $232.96. IOS Press, Van Diemenstraat 94, 1013 CN Amsterdam Netherlands. **Tel** 011 31 20 6382189, FAX 011 31 20 6203419.

LC K10 .O8733 **ISSN** 0729-1485
DD 343.94/0999 349.403999 AT
JOURNAL OF LAW AND INFORMATION SCIENCE. **See** Law.

ISSN 1353-4858
UK
NETWORK SECURITY. **See** Computers-Computer Networks.

ISSN 1353-4858
UK
NETWORK SECURITY NEWSLETTER. (199?)-. Newsletter. English. Twelve times a year. $454.00. Elsevier Advanced Technology, An Imprint of Elsevier Science Ltd., The Boulevard, Langford Lane, Kidlington, Oxford OX5 1GB United Kingdom. **Tel** 011 44 1865 843000, 011 44 1865 843699, FAX 011 44 1865 843010. **(Subscription address:** Elsevier Science Ltd. / Oxford Fulfillment Centre, PO Box 800, Kidlington OX5 1DX United Kingdom. **Tel** 011 44 865 843355.) **ED** John Meyer.
Desc: Concentrates on the technical and management solutions to international network security problems.

ISSN 1079-1302
US
•**NETWORK SECURITY OBSERVATIONS.** (1994)-. English. Irregular (5 or 6 per year). $225.00. Network Security Observations, Suite 400, 1825 I Street Northwest, Washington DC 20006. **Tel** (202)775-4947, FAX (202)429-9574, telex 440557 hqwdc. **ED** Dr. F. Bertil Fortrie. **Circ:** 2,200.

ISSN 0883-5608
DD 651 US
PERSONAL IDENTIFICATION NEWS. (PERSONAL IDENTIFICATION NEWS : PIN.). [Pers. identif. news]. **Added/Corp** Warfel & Miller. **VFOAT** PIN. (Apr. 1985)-. Periodical. English. Eleven times a year (also free directory). $345.00. Warfel & Miller Inc., 11619 Danville Drive, Rockville MD 20852. **Tel** (301)881-6668. **ED** Benjamin Miller and George Warfel Sr. Index available. **Bk Rev.**
Desc: Covers state-of-the art methods of identifying people (i.e. plastic cards, smart cards, biometrics) for industrial and government applications. Computer security, electronic funds transfer, and access control.

ISSN 0736-6817
US
POLICIES AND METHODOLOGIES. DATA PROCESSING SECURITY AND CONTROL. [Policies methodol., Data process. secur. control]. **VFOAT** Data Processing Security and Control. (1983)-. Periodical. English. Four times a year. Auerbach Publishers Inc., Park Square Building, 31 St. James Avenue, Boston MA 02116. **Tel** (800)950-1207.

LC KF1262.A15 P68 **ISSN** 0145-7659
DD 342.73/0858/05 347.30285805 US
Pr Rev.
PRIVACY JOURNAL. [Priv. j.]. Vol. 1, No. 1 (Nov. 1974)-. Periodical. English. Twelve times a year. $118.00. Privacy Journal, PO Box 28577, Providence RI 02908. **Tel** (401)274-7861. **ED** Robert Ellis Smith. Index available. cum. index. **Circ:** 5,000 (ctrl). available on CD-ROM; available on microfilm and microfiche from University Microfilms International (UMI).
Desc: Newsletter on new technology, legislation and court cases affecting personal privacy, including medical, credit, government and financial records, plus wiretaps and lie detectors.

LC QA76.9.A25 S94a **ISSN** 1063-7109
DD 004 US
CCC
TITLE CHANGE
PROCEEDINGS - IEEE COMPUTER SOCIETY SYMPOSIUM ON RESEARCH IN SECURITY AND PRIVACY. (PROCEEDINGS / IEEE COMPUTER SOCIETY SYMPOSIUM ON RESEARCH IN SECURITY AND PRIVACY ; SPONSORED BY THE IEEE COMPUTER SOCIETY, TECHNICAL COMMITTEE ON SECURITY AND PRIVACY IN COOPERATION WITH THE INTERNATIONAL ASSOCIATION FOR CRYPTOLOGIC RESEARCH (IACR).). [Proc. - IEEE Comput. Soc. Symp. Res. Secur. Priv.]. **Added/Corp** IEEE Computer Society. Technical Committee on Security and Privacy. International Association for Cryptologic Research. **VFOAT** IEEE Symposium on Security and Privacy. (1990)-(May 16-18, 1994). Proceedings. English. IEEE Computer Society, 10662 Los Vaqueros Circle, PO Box 3014, Los Alamitos CA 90720-1264. **Tel** (714)821-8380, (800)272-6657, FAX (714)821-4641. Documents available from Article Express International. ***Continues*** *IEEE Symposium on Security and Privacy. Proceedings of the ... IEEE Symposium on Security and Privacy, 1063-9578.* ***Continued by*** *IEEE Symposium on Security and Privacy. Proceedings, 1081-6011.*
Ind/Abst Curr. Cit. (?-?); Eng. Index Annu. (?-?).

LC QA76.9.A25 S94a **ISSN** 1081-6011
DD 621 US
•**PROCEEDINGS - IEEE SYMPOSIUM ON SECURITY AND PRIVACY.** (PROCEEDINGS.). [Proc. - IEEE Symp. Secur. Priv.]. **Added/Corp** IEEE Computer Society. IEEE Computer Society Technical Committee on Security and Privacy. International Association for Cryptologic Research. (May 8-10, 1995)-. English. IEEE Computer Society, 10662 Los Vaqueros Circle, PO Box 3014, Los Alamitos CA 90720-1264. **Tel** (714)821-8380, (800)272-6657, FAX (714)821-4641. Documents available from Article Express International. ***Continues*** *IEEE Computer Society Symposium on Research in Security and Privacy. Proceedings, 1063-7109.*
Ind/Abst Curr. Cit.; Eng. Index Annu.

LC KK6071.5.A13 R43 **ISSN** 0178-8930
DD 340 GW
RECHT DER DATENVERARBEITUNG : RDV. **Added/Corp** Gesellschaft fuer Datenschutz und Datensicherung. **VFOAT** RDV. Vol. 1 (Nov. 1985)-. Trade Publication. German (English). Five times a year. $158.44. Datakongext-Verlag GmbH, AAchener Strasse 1052/PF 400253, W-5000 Cologne 40 F R Germany. **Tel** 011-49-221-486503, FAX 011-49-221-484391. **ED** George Wrouka, Rudolf Schomerus, and Peter Gola. Index available. cum. index. **Bk Rev. Ad Acc.** ctrl circ.
Desc: Serves as a comprehensive source of information for all legal aspects of data processing. Publishes articles, legal decisions and current findings which will be of interest to the manager, lawyer, judge and to data security personnel.

LC QA75 **ISSN** 1352-4097
DD 005.8 UK
•**SECURE COMPUTING.** [Secur. comput.]. (1994)-. Trade Publication. English. Twelve times a year. £225.00. West Coast Publishing Ltd., William Knox House, Britannic Way, Llandarcy, Swansea SA10 6EL United Kingdom. **Tel** 011 44 1792 324000, FAX 011 44 1792 324001. **ED** Paul Robinson. **Bk Rev**, (Qty: Ray Pooley). **Circ:** 5,000. Documents available from BLDSC.

Computers —Computer Engineering

Continues *Virus News International, 0960-3921.*
Desc: Topics include hacking, viruses, and illegal software use.

ISSN 1068-8374
US
CCC

●**SECURITY TECHNOLOGY NEWS.** (1993)-. Newsletter. English. Twenty-five times a year. $495.00. Phillips Business Information Inc., 1201 Seven Locks Road, PO Box 61130, Potomac MD 20854. **Tel** (301)424-3338, (301)340-1520, (800)777-5005, FAX (301)424-4297, telex 358149.
Desc: Business opportunities and applications in the emerging security markets.

ISSN 0882-665X
DD 621 US
SMART CARDS AND COMMENTS. [Smart cards comments]. Vol. 1, No. 1 (Mar. 1985)-. Periodical. English. Ten times a year. $300.00. Smart Cards and Comments, 221 Yarborough Lane, Redwood City CA 94061. **Tel** (415)365-3211, FAX (415)363-2198. **ED** Jerome Svigals. Index available. **Bk Rev**, (Qty: 6). **Circ:** 300.
Desc: Provides a constant stream of market place reports, results and concrete specifics derived from new product application results. Your source of information, examples and guidance.

LC KD667.C65 C66
DD 343.41/0999/05 344.10399905 UK
CODEN TCLPEN
TOLLEY'S COMPUTER LAW AND PRACTICE. See Law.

LC QA76.76.C68 V57 ISSN 0956-9979
DD 005.8/05 UK
CCC
CODEN VBULE3
VIRUS BULLETIN. (VIRUS BULLETIN : THE AUTHORITATIVE INTERNATIONAL PUBLICATION ON COMPUTER VIRUS PREVENTION, RECOGNITION, AND REMOVAL.). [Virus bull.]. (1989)-. Bulletin. English. Twelve times a year. $29.50. Virus Bulletin Ltd., Abingdon Science Park, Abingdon, Oxfordshire OX14 3YS United Kingdom. **Tel** 011 44 1235 555139, FAX 011 44 1235 559935. **ED** Richard Ford. Index available. cum. index. **Ad Acc.** Documents available from Ask*IEEE.
Desc: Computer virus prevention, recognition and removal.
Ind/Abst INSPEC (July 1989-).

COMPUTER ENGINEERING

LC QA76.9.H85 A27 ISSN 1042-0193
DD 004/.01/9 US
CCC
SUSPENDED
ABSTRACTS IN HUMAN-COMPUTER INTERACTION. See Computers-Abstracting, Bibliographies and Statistics.

LC TK7885 ISSN 1084-4309
DD 621.39 US
●**ACM TRANSACTIONS ON DESIGN AUTOMATION OF ELECTRONIC SYSTEMS. Added/Corp** Association for Computing Machinery. (1996)-. Periodical. English. Four times a year. $35.00 (members), $150.00 (nonmembers). ACM / Association for Computing Machinery, 1515 Broadway, 17th Floor, New York NY 10036. **Tel** (212)869-7440, FAX (212)869-0481. **(Subscription address:** Association for Computing Machinery, PO Box 12114, Church Street Station, New York NY 10249. **Tel** (212)626-0500.)

LC QA76.758 .A35 ISSN 1049-331X
DD 005.1/05 US
CCC
CODEN ATSMER
ACM TRANSACTIONS ON SOFTWARE ENGINEERING AND METHODOLOGY. See Computers-Software.

LC QA75 .A18 ISSN 1237-2404
DD 51.28 FI
CODEN APOSEV
●**ACTA POLYTECHNICA SCANDINAVICA. MATHEMATICS AND COMPUTING IN ENGINEERING SERIES.** See Mathematics.

ISSN 0169-1864
NE
CODEN ADROEI
ADVANCED ROBOTICS. See Computers-Artificial Intelligence.

US
CEASED
APPLICATION DEVELOPMENT TOOLS. (19??)-(1994). English. Sentry Publishing Co., 1900 West Park Drive, Westborough MA 01581. **Tel** (508)366-2031, FAX (508)836-4732. **Continues** *Case Product Guide.*
Desc: Features descriptions and comparisons of more than 500 software development tools offered by more than 300 vendors.

US
●**APPLICATION DEVELOPMENT TRENDS.** (Jan. 1994)-. Trade Publication. English. Nine times a year. $49.00. Software Productivity Group, 386 West Main Street, Suite 2, Northboro MA 01532. **Tel** (508)393-7100, FAX (508)393-3388. **Continues** *CASE Trends, 1046-5944.*
Desc: Focuses on the experiences of serious practitioners in the pursuit of state-of-the-art software development options. Coverage features implementation experiences, interviews, graphic presentation of information, technical product summaries and analyses, and updates on key industry trends.

ISSN 0895-2108
DD 005 US
CCC
TITLE CHANGE
C/A/S/E OUTLOOK. [C/A/S/E outlook]. **Added/Corp** CASE Consulting Group. **VFOAT** C A S E Outlook; Computer Aided Software Engineering Outlook; CASE Outlook. **VAT** Computer-Aided Software Engineering Outlook. Vol. 1, No. 1 (July 1987)-(19??). Periodical. English. CASE Consulting Group Inc, 11830 Southwest Kerr Parkway, Suite 315, Lake Oswego OR 97035. **Tel** (503)245-6880, FAX 503 245-6935. **ED** Gene Forte. Index available. **Bk Rev**, (Qty: 6-10 / year). **Circ:** 1000 (ctrl). **Merged into** *Application Development Strategies.*
Desc: Covers developments in the field of computer-aided software engineering (CASE).

LC TK1 .C34 ISSN 0840-8688
DD 621.3 CN
CODEN CJEEEL
Pr Rev.
CANADIAN JOURNAL OF ELECTRICAL AND COMPUTER ENGINEERING. [Can. j. electr. comput. eng.]. **Added/Corp** Canadian Society for Electrical Engineering. **VFOAT** Revue Canadienne de Genie Electrique et Informatique. Vol. 13 No. 2 (1988)-. Periodical. English (French). Four times a year (Jan., Apr., July, Oct.). 90.00Can$. Canadian Journal Electrical and Computer Engineering, University of Laval, Department of Electrical Engineering, Quebec Quebec G1K 7P4 Canada. **Tel** (604)721-8617, FAX (604)721-8676, telex (049) 7222. **ED** Michael Lecours (phone: (418)656-2966). Index available. **Ad Acc, Adv Mgr Tel** (604)721-8617. **Circ:** 1,066. Documents available from Article Express International, Ask*IEEE. **Continues** *Canadian Electrical Engineering Journal, 0700-9216.*
Desc: Covers electrical energy, communications, networks, circuit theory, power engineering, power electronics, electrical machines, transmission, generation, distribution, and utility.
Ind/Abst Curr. Cit.; Eng. Index Annu.; INIS Atomindex [Micro.]; INSPEC (1988-).

LC QA76.758 .C38 ISSN 1046-5944
DD 005.1 US
CCC
TITLE CHANGE
CASE TRENDS. [CASE trends]. **Added/Corp** Software Productivity Group, Inc. **VAT** Computer-Aided Software Engineering Trends. (1989)-(1994). Periodical. English. Software Productivity Group, 386 West Main Street, Suite 2, Northboro MA 01532. **Tel** (508)393-7100, FAX (508)393-3388. **ED** Eliot Weinman. Index available. **Bk Rev. Ad Acc. Circ:** 10,400. **Continued by** *Application Development Trends.*
Desc: This guide helps steer readers through the maze of conflict and confusion arising from the use of CASE technology.

LC QA76.9.A73 C64 ISSN 0163-5964
DD 001.64 US
CODEN CANED2
COMPUTER ARCHITECTURE NEWS. [Comput. archit. news]. **Added/Corp** Association for Computing Machinery. Special Interest Committee on Computer Architecture. Sigarch. **VFOAT** S.I.G.A.R.C.H. Computer Architecture News; SIGARCH Computer Architecture News. (1972)-. Periodical. English. Five times a year. $55.00. ACM / Association for Computing Machinery, 1515 Broadway, 17th Floor, New York NY 10036. **Tel** (212)869-7440, FAX (212)869-0481. **(Subscription address:** Association for Computing Machinery, PO Box 12114, Church Street Station, New York NY 10249. **Tel** (212)626-0500.) Documents available from Ask*IEEE.
Ind/Abst Abstr. Hum. Comput. Interact. (Aug. 1981-); ACM Guide Comput. Lit.; Comput. Rev. (Aug. 1981-); Curr. Cit.; INSPEC (Aug. 1981-).

US
COMPUTER SCIENCE AND COMPUTER ENGINEERING. (19??)-. English. Irregular. Price varies. Ablex Publishing Corporation, 355 Chestnut Street, Norwood NJ 07648. **Tel** (201)767-8450, (201)767-8455 (Customer Service), FAX (201)767-6717. **ED** George W. Zobrist.

ISSN 0888-2088
DD 005 US
COMPUTER SOFTWARE ENGINEERING SERIES. [Comput. softw. eng. ser.]. (19??)-. Monographic series. English. Irregular. Price varies per volume. Computer Science Press Inc, 9125 Fall River Lane, Potomac MD 20854. **Tel** (301)251-9050. **ED** Arthur D Friedman. Index available. ctrl circ. Documents available from Ask*IEEE.
Desc: Explores the frontiers of software engineering and the foundations of computer science.
Ind/Abst INSPEC; Math. Rev.

LC QA75.5 .C5965 ISSN 0267-6192
DD 004/.05 UK
CCC
CODEN CSSEEI
Pr Rev.
COMPUTER SYSTEMS SCIENCE AND ENGINEERING. [Comput. syst. sci. eng.]. Vol. 1, No. 1 (Oct. 1985)-. Periodical. English. Six times a year. £199.00 Europe; £210.00 other. CRL Publishing Ltd., PO Box 31, Market Harborough, Leicestershire LE16 9RQ United Kingdom. **Tel** 011 44 1 85886382, FAX 011 44 1 85886635. **ED** Jeremy Thompson. Index available. cum. index. **Bk Rev. Ad Acc.** available on microfilm and microfiche from University Microfilms International (UMI). Documents available from Article Express International, The Genuine Article, Ask*IEEE.
Desc: A international journal covering theoretical developments in computer systems science and their applications in computer systems engineering.
Ind/Abst ACM Guide Comput. Lit.; CompuMath Cit. Index [Full Cov.]; Comput. Inf. Syst. Abstr. J. [Full Cov.]; Comput. Lit. Index; Comput. Rev.; Curr. Cit.; Ei Page One; Elect. Comm. Abstr.; Eng. Index Annu.; INSPEC (1985-); Res. Alert [Full Cov.]; SCISEARCH; Soc. Sci. Cit. Index [Select. Cov.]; Solid State Supercond. Abstr.; Zentralbl. Math. Ihre Grenzgeb.

LC TK7885.A1 C612 ISSN 0045-7906
DD 621.3819/5/05 US
CCC
CODEN CPEEBQ
COMPUTERS & ELECTRICAL ENGINEERING. [Comput. electr. eng.]. **VFOAT** Computers and Electrical Engineering. Vol. 1 (June 1973)-. Periodical. English. Six times a year. $730.00. Pergamon Press, An Imprint of Elsevier Science Ltd., The Boulevard, Langford Lane, Kidlington, Oxford OX5 1GB United Kingdom. **Tel** 011 44 1865 843000, 011 44 1865 843699, FAX 011 44 1865 843010. **(Subscription address:** Elsevier Science Ltd. / Oxford Fulfillment Centre, PO Box 800, Kidlington OX5 1DX United Kingdom. **Tel** 011 44 865 843355.) Index available. available on microfilm and microfiche from University Microfilms International (UMI); available on an online database from Elsevier Electronic Subscriptions (EES). Documents available from Ask*IEEE.
Ind/Abst Curr. Cit.; Energy Res. Abstr. (Mar. 1978-); INSPEC (June 1973-); Int. Aerosp. Abstr.; Math. Rev.; Pollut. Abstr. Indexes; Soc. Sci. Cit. Index [Select. Cov.].

LC TK7801 .A8a ISSN 1058-6393
DD 621.38 US
CCC
CONFERENCE RECORD / ASILOMAR CONFERENCE ON SIGNALS, SYSTEMS & COMPUTERS. [Conf. rec. - Asilomar Conf. Signals, Syst. Comput.]. **Main/Conf** Asilomar Conference on Signals, Systems & Computers. **Added/Corp** Naval Postgraduate School (U.S.) IEEE Acoustics, Speech, and Signal Processing Society. 20th (1986)-. Periodical. English. Irregular. $140.00 (new 26th edition). IEEE Computer Society, 10662 Los Vaqueros Circle, PO Box 3014, Los Alamitos CA 90720-1264. **Tel** (714)821-8380, (800)272-6657, FAX (714)821-4641. **Continues** *Asilomar Conference on Circuits, Systems, and Computers. Conference Record.*
Ind/Abst Curr. Cit.

US
DATA ENGINEERING. Main/Conf International Conference on Data Engineering. **Added/Corp** IEEE Computer Society. **VFOAT** COMPDEC. 1st (1984)-. Proceedings. English. One time a year. $120.00. IEEE Computer Society, 10662 Los Vaqueros Circle, PO Box 3014, Los Alamitos CA 90720-1264. **Tel** (714)821-8380, (800)272-6657, FAX (714)821-4641.

ISSN 0888-2118
DD 621 US
DIGITAL SYSTEM DESIGN SERIES. [Digit. syst. des. ser.]. (19??)-. Monographic series. English. Irregular. Price varies per volume. Computer Science Press Inc, 9125 Fall River Lane, Potomac MD 20854. **Tel** (301)251-9050. **ED** Arthur D Friedman. Index available. ctrl circ. Documents available from Ask*IEEE.
Desc: The text and reference works in this series offer a comprehensive examination of issues relevant to the design of computer systems.
Ind/Abst INSPEC.

LC TK7882.I6 D58 **ISSN** 0141-9382
DD 621 UK
CCC
CODEN DISPDP
Pr Rev.
DISPLAYS. [Displays]. Vol. 1, No. 1 (April 1979)-. Academic Scholarly Publication. English. Four times a year. $366.00. Butterworth Heinemann Publishers, Linacre House Jordan Hill, Oxford OX2 8DP United Kingdom. **Tel** 011 44 1865 310366, FAX 011 44 1865 310898. **(Subscription address:** Elsevier Science Ltd. / Oxford Fulfillment Centre, PO Box 800, Kidlington OX5 1DX United Kingdom. **Tel** 011 44 865 843355.) **ED** Angela Jamesoi. Index available. cum. index. **Bk Rev. Ad Acc.** available on microfilm and microfiche from University Microfilms International (UMI); available on an online database from Elsevier Electronic Subscriptions (EES). Documents available from Article Express International, The Genuine Article, Ask*IEEE, CASDDS.
Desc: Covers both the research and commercial development stages of display technology. It caters for the scientist developing new display technologies and the engineer wishing to apply them. Contributions published include review articles, original research papers, and technical notes of applications, techniques and systems.
Ind/Abst Abstr. Hum. Comput. Interact.; Bioeng. Abstr.; Chem. Abstr.; CompuMath Cit. Index [Full Cov.]; Curr. Cit.; Ei Page One; Eng. Index Annu.; INSPEC (1979-); Res. Alert [Full Cov.]; SCISEARCH; Soc. Sci. Cit. Index [Select. Cov.].

UK
DISTRIBUTED SYSTEMS ENGINEERING JOURNAL. (July 1993)-. English. Four times a year. $134.00. Institute of Physics, Techno House, Redcliffe Way, Bristol BS1 6NX United Kingdom. **Tel** 011 44 117 9297481, FAX 011 44 117 9294318, telex 449149 INSTP G. **(Subscription address:** American Institute of Physics, Publishing Sales, 500 Sunnyside Blvd., Woodbury NY 11797. **Tel** (516)576-2200.) available on microfiche.
Desc: The area of interest of this journal centers on the integration of processing, storage and communication subsystems within an overall parallel processing and on practical engineering papers rather than theoretical approaches.

LC TK7885
DD 621.39 GW
•**EUROPEAN JOURNAL OF CONTROL.** (1996)-. English. Four times a year. $224.00. Springer-Verlag GmbH & Company KG, Heidelberger Platz 3, D-14197 Berlin Germany. **Tel** 011 49 30 8207223, FAX 011 49 30 8214091, telex 183 319 SPBLN D. **(Subscription address:** Springer-Verlag New York Inc. / North America, PO Box 2485, Journal Fulfillment, Secaucus NJ 07096. **Tel** (201)348-4033, (800)777-4643, FAX (201)348-4505.) **ED** I.D. Landau.

ISSN 0268-6872
UK
CODEN EXEEE5
Pr Rev.
EXE. (EXE : THE SOFTWARE DEVELOPER'S MAGAZINE.). [EXE]. **VFOAT** EXE Magazine. Vol. 4, Issue 8 (Feb. 198?)-. Trade Publication. English (German). Twelve times a year. $119.79. Process Communications Ltd, 50 Poland Street, St. Giles House, London W1V 4AX United Kingdom. **Tel** 011 44 171 2875000. **ED** Will Watts. Index available (published separately). cum. index. **Bk Rev**, (Qty: 22). **Ad Acc, Adv Mgr:** Sandra Inniss-Palmer, **Tel** 81-994-6477. **Circ:** 17,000. available on an online database (file 675/Full-Text) from DIALOG. Documents available from Ask*IEEE.
Ind/Abst Abstr. Hum. Comput. Interact.; Comput. ASAP [Full Txt.]; Comput. Database [Full Txt.]; Curr. Cit.; INSPEC (Oct. 1987-).

LC Z **ISSN** 1350-4967
DD 011 UK
•**FOCUS ON BRITISH ENGINEERING AND COMPUTER SCIENCES RESEARCH.** (1994)-. Bibliography. English. Twelve times a year. £26.00. British Library / Document Supply Centre, Boston Spa, Wetherby West Yorkshire LS23 7BQ United Kingdom. **Tel** 011 44 1937 546060, FAX 011 44 1937 546333, telex 557381. **(Subscription address:** Turpin Distribution Services Limited, Blackhorse Road, Letchworth, Hertfordshire SH6 1HN United Kingdom. **Tel** 011 44 1462 672555, FAX 011 44 1462 480947.) Index available. **Ad Acc.** Documents available from BLDSC.

ISSN 1073-922X
US
•**GAME DEVELOPER.** See Computers-Computer Games.

ISSN 1166-4738
FR
CODEN GLSEED
Pr Rev.
GENIE LOGICIEL & SYSTEMES EXPERTS. See Computers-Software.

ISSN 1040-6433
DD 001 US
Pr Rev.
HEURISTICS (ROCKVILLE, MD.). (HEURISTICS : QUARTERLY JOURNAL OF THE INTERNATIONAL ASSOCIATION OF KNOWLEDGE ENGINEERS.). [Heuristics]. **Added/Corp** International Association of Knowledge Engineers. Vol. 1, No. 1 (Sept. 1988)-. Periodical. English. Four times a year. $150.00. Systemsware Corporation, 973-C Russell Avenue, Gaithersburg MD 20879. **Tel** (301)948-3515, FAX (301)926-4243. **ED** Dr. John Coyne (editor's address; 1923 Rhode Island Avenue, McLean, VA 22101, (phone: (202)994-5819). **Bk Rev**, (Qty: 4). **Ad Acc, Adv Mgr:** V. Sullivan, **Tel** (301)948-4890. **Circ:** 2,000.
Ind/Abst HILITES.

LC TK1 .I1373 **ISSN** 0143-7062
DD 621.39/05 UK
CCC
CODEN IPETD3
Pr Rev. **TITLE CHANGE**
IEE PROCEEDINGS. PART E. COMPUTERS AND DIGITAL TECHNIQUES. (IEE PROCEEDINGS. E, COMPUTERS AND DIGITAL TECHNIQUES.). [IEE proc. E]. **Added/Corp** Institution of Electrical Engineers. **VFOAT** I.E.E. Proceedings. E, Computers and Digital Techniques; Computers and Digital Techniques; I.E.E. Proceedings. Part E, Computers and Digital Techniques; IEE Proceedings, Part E, Computers and Digital Techniques. **VAT** Institute of Electrical Engineers. Part E, Computers and Digital Techniques. Vol. 127, No. 1 (Jan. 1980)-Vol. 140, No. 6 (Nov. 1993). Academic Scholarly Publication. English. Institution of Electrical Engineers / IEE, Michael Faraday House, Six Hills Way, Stevenage Hertfordshire SG1 2AY United Kingdom. **Tel** 011 44 1438 313311, FAX 011 44 1438 742840, telex 825578 IEESTV G. **(Subscription address:** IEE / Peter Peregrinus Ltd., PO Box 96, Stevenage Herts SG1 2SD United Kingdom. **Tel** 011 44 1438 313311, FAX 011 44 438 742792, telex 825578 IEESTV G.) available on microfilm from University Microfilms International (UMI). Documents available from Article Express International, The Genuine Article, Ask*IEEE. ***Continues in part*** *Proceedings of the Institution of Electrical Engineers, 0020-3270;* ***Absorbed*** *IEE Journal on Computers and Digital Techniques.* ***Continued by*** *IEE Proceedings. Computers and Digital Techniques.*
Ind/Abst Acoust. Abstr.; Appl. Sci. Technol. Index; Bioeng. Abstr.; CompuMath Cit. Index [Full Cov.]; Comput. Database; Curr. Contents Eng. Comput. Technol.; Ei Page One; EMBASE; Energy Res. Abstr. (July 1980-); Eng. Index Annu.; INSPEC (Jan. 1980-); Int. Aerosp. Abstr.; Math. Rev.; Res. Alert [Full Cov.]; Sci. Cit. Index (19??-19??); SCISEARCH.

ISSN 0740-7475
DD 621 US
CCC
Pr Rev.
IEEE DESIGN & TEST OF COMPUTERS. (IEEE DESIGN & TEST OF COMPUTERS / IEEE COMPUTER SOCIETY [AND] THE INSTITUTE OF ELECTRICAL AND ELECTRONICS ENGINEERS, INC.). [IEEE des. test comput.]. **Added/Corp** IEEE Computer Society. Institute of Electrical and Electronics Engineers. **VFOAT** IEEE Design and Test of Computers; Design & Test of Computers; Design and Test of Computers; IEEE Design & Test. **VAT** Institute of Electrical and Electronics Engineers design & test of computers. Vol. 1, No. 1 (Feb. 1984)-. Periodical. English. Four times a year. $230.00. IEEE / Institute of Electrical and Electronics Engineers Inc., 345 East 47th Street, New York NY 10017-2394. **Tel** (908)981-1393, FAX (908)981-9667. **(Subscription address:** IEEE / Institute of Electrical and Electronics Engineers, 445 Hoes Lane, PO Box 1331, Piscataway NJ 08855-1331. **Tel** (800)701-IEEE, (908)981-0060, FAX (908)981-9667, telex 833233.) **ED** Vishwani Agrawal. Index available. **Ad Acc. Circ:** 6,800. available on microfiche. Documents available from Article Express International, The Genuine Article, Ask*IEEE.
Desc: Addresses the concurrent engineering of chips, assemblies, and systems for computer design and for all types of computer applications, including avionics and fail-safe systems.
Ind/Abst Abstr. Hum. Comput. Interact.; CompuMath Cit. Index [Full Cov.]; Comput. Inf. Syst. Abstr. J. [Full Cov.]; Comput. Database; Curr. Cit.; Curr. Contents Eng. Comput. Technol.; Ei Page One; Elect. Comm. Abstr.; Eng. Index Annu.; Index IEEE Publ.; Inf. Sci. Abstr.; INSPEC (Feb. 1984-); Int. Aerosp. Abstr. (1984-); Mech. Eng. Abstr.; Oper. Res./Manage. Sci.; Pollut. Abstr. Indexes; Res. Alert [Full Cov.]; SCISEARCH; Solid State Supercond. Abstr.

LC QA76.76.E95 I36 **ISSN** 1041-4347
DD 006/3/3/05 US
CCC
CODEN ITKEEH
IEEE TRANSACTIONS ON KNOWLEDGE AND DATA ENGINEERING. [IEEE trans. knowl. data eng.]. **Added/Corp** Institute of Electrical and Electronics Engineers. IEEE Computer Society. **VFOAT** Institute of Electrical and Electronics Engineers Transactions on Knowledge and Data Engineering; Transactions on Knowledge and Data Engineering; Knowledge and Data Engineering. **VAT** Institute of Electrical and Electronics Engineers Transactions on Knowledge and Data Engineering. Vol. 1, No. 1 (Mar. 1989)-. Periodical. English. Six times a year. $375.00. IEEE / Institute of Electrical and Electronics Engineers Inc., 345 East 47th Street, New York NY 10017-2394. **Tel** (908)981-1393, FAX (908)981-9667. **(Subscription address:** IEEE / Institute of Electrical and Electronics Engineers, 445 Hoes Lane, PO Box 1331, Piscataway NJ 08855-1331. **Tel** (800)701-IEEE, (908)981-0060, FAX (908)981-9667, telex 833233.) **ED** Gail S. Ferenc. Index available. **Circ:** 6,000. available on microfiche. Documents available from Article Express International, The Genuine Article, Ask*IEEE.
Desc: Designed to provide an international and interdisciplinary forum to publish results on the research, design and development of data engineering methodologies, strategies and systems.
Ind/Abst CompuMath Cit. Index [Full Cov.]; Comput. Abstr.; Curr. Cit.; Curr. Contents Eng. Comput. Technol.; Ei Page One; Eng. Index Annu.; Index IEEE Publ.; INSPEC (March 1989-); Int. Aerosp. Abstr.; Res. Alert [Full Cov.]; Soc. Sci. Cit. Index [Select. Cov.]; Zentralbl. Math. Ihre Grenzgeb.

ISSN 1045-9227
DD 006 US
CCC
CODEN ITNNEP
IEEE TRANSACTIONS ON NEURAL NETWORKS. See Computers-Artificial Intelligence.

LC QA76.6 .I17 **ISSN** 0098-5589
DD 001.6/425/05 US
CCC
CODEN IESEDJ
Pr Rev.
IEEE TRANSACTIONS ON SOFTWARE ENGINEERING. [IEEE trans. softw. eng.]. **Added/Corp** IEEE Computer Society. **VFOAT** Transactions on Software Engineering; Software Engineering. **VAT** Institute of Electrical and Electronics Engineers Transactions on Software Engineering. Vol. SE-1 (March 1975)-. Periodical. English. Twelve times a year. $485.00. IEEE / Institute of Electrical and Electronics Engineers Inc., 345 East 47th Street, New York NY 10017-2394. **Tel** (908)981-1393, FAX (908)981-9667. **(Subscription address:** IEEE / Institute of Electrical and Electronics Engineers, 445 Hoes Lane, PO Box 1331, Piscataway NJ 08855-1331. **Tel** (800)701-IEEE, (908)981-0060, FAX (908)981-9667, telex 833233.) **ED** Gail S. Ferenc. Index available. available on microfiche. Documents available from Article Express International, The Genuine Article, UMI Article Clearinghouse, Ask*IEEE.
Desc: Concentrates on research on software and systems requirements specification, design, development, testing, management, and documentation. Includes development and maintenance methods and models, assessment methods, project management, tools, and environments.
Ind/Abst ABI/INFORM Glob. Ed.; ABI/INFORM [Computer File] (May 1978-); ACM Guide Comput. Lit.; Acoust. Abstr.; Appl. Sci. Technol. Index (1991-); Bioeng. Abstr.; CompuMath Cit. Index [Full Cov.]; Comput. Abstr.; Comput. Database; Comput. Lit. Index; Comput. Rev.; Curr. Cit.; Curr. Contents Eng. Comput. Technol.; Ei Page One; Eng. Index Annu.; Expand. Acad. Index (1992-); Gen. BusinessFile (1992-); HILITES; Index IEEE Publ.; Inf. Sci. Abstr.; INSPEC (March 1975-); Int. Aerosp. Abstr.; Oper. Res./Manage. Sci.; Pollut. Abstr. Indexes; Res. Alert [Full Cov.]; Sci. Cit. Index; SCISEARCH; Soc. Sci. Cit. Index [Select. Cov.]; Zentralbl. Math. Ihre Grenzgeb.

ISSN 0963-9640
DD 620.0028563 UK
CCC
CEASED
INTELLIGENT SYSTEMS ENGINEERING. [Intell. syst. eng.]. (1992)-Vol. 3 (1994). Periodical. English. Institution of Electrical Engineers / IEE, Michael Faraday House, Six Hills Way, Stevenage Hertfordshire SG1 2AY United Kingdom. **Tel** 011 44 1438 313311, FAX 011 44 1438 742840, telex 825578 IEESTV G. **(Subscription address:** IEE / Peter Peregrinus Ltd., PO Box 96, Stevenage Herts SG1 2SD United Kingdom. **Tel** 011 44 1438 313311, FAX 011 44 438 742792, telex 825578 IEESTV G.)

ISSN 0952-8091
SZ
CODEN IJCTEK
INTERNATIONAL JOURNAL OF COMPUTER APPLICATIONS IN TECHNOLOGY. See Science and Technology-Computer Applications.

LC TK7885 **ISSN** 0969-1170
DD 621.39 UK
INTERNATIONAL JOURNAL OF ENGINEERING INTELLIGENT SYSTEMS FOR ELECTRICAL ENGINEERING AND COMMUNICATIONS. **VFOAT** Engineering Intelligent Systems for Electrical Engineering and communications; Engineering Intelligent Systems.

Computers — Computer Engineering

(19??)-. Periodical. English. Four times a year. $222.45. CRL Publishing Ltd., PO Box 31, Market Harborough, Leicestershire LE16 9RQ United Kingdom. **Tel** 011 44 1 85886382, FAX 011 44 1 85886635. **ED** Jeremy Thompson.

LC TK7885   **ISSN** 1381-2416
DD 621.39   NE
    CCC
Pr Rev.
●**INTERNATIONAL JOURNAL OF SPEECH TECHNOLOGY. See** Linguistics-Computer Applications.

    ISSN 0980-1529
    FR
UDC 681.3
    TITLE CHANGE
IX-MAGAZINE PARIS. (IX MAGAZINE.). (1986)-(19??). Periodical. French. Publications GRD, 85 rue du Dessous des Berges, 75013 Paris France. **Tel** 011 33 1 53828253. *Merged into Logiciels and Systemes.*

LC QA75.5 .J627   **ISSN** 1069-5451
DD 004/.05   US
    CEASED
JOURNAL OF COMPUTER AND SOFTWARE ENGINEERING. [J. comput. softw. engin.]. Vol. 1, No. 1 (1993)-Vol. 3 (1995). Periodical. English. Ablex Publishing Corporation, 355 Chestnut Street, Norwood NJ 07648. **Tel** (201)767-8450, (201)767-8455 (Customer Service), FAX (201)767-6717.

LC TK7885.A1 J68
DD 621.39/.05   II
JOURNAL OF THE INSTITUTION OF ENGINEERS (INDIA). COMPUTER ENGINEERING DIVISION. Added/Corp Institution of Engineers (India). Computer Engineering Division. **VFOAT** Computer Engineering Division; IE (I) Journal-CO. (19??)-. Periodical. English. Two times a year. $5.00. Institution of Engineers India, 8 Gokhale Road, Calcutta 700020 India. **Tel** 011 91 33 288311, 011 91 33 288334, FAX 011 91 33 288345, telex 21 7885 IEIC IN. *Continues Journal of the Institution of Engineers (India), 0368-2498.*
Ind/Abst Int. Aerosp. Abstr. (1983-).

    FR
●**LOGICIELS AND SYSTEMES.** (1995)-. French. Ten times a year. 630.00F. Publications GRD, 85 rue du Dessous des Berges, 75013 Paris France. **Tel** 011 33 1 53828253. *Absorbed IX Magazine.*

LC TK7874.5 .M45
DD 621.397/3   US
MEMORY DISCONTINUED DEVICES. Ed. 1- (1987). English. One time a year. $65.00. D A T A Inc, 9889 Willow Creed Road, PO Box 26875, San Diego CA 92126. **Tel** (619)578-7600, telex 910 530606. **ED** Steven D'Adolf.
Desc: Contains specifications on 10,000 devices from 119 manufacturers.

LC TK7885   **ISSN** 0946-7076
DD 621.39   GW
UDC 62
Pr Rev.
●**MICROSYSTEM TECHNOLOGIES.** [Microsyst. technol.]. (1994)-. Academic Scholarly Publication. English (German). Four times a year. DM400.00. Springer-Verlag GmbH & Company KG, Heidelberger Platz 3, D-14197 Berlin Germany. **Tel** 011 49 30 8207223, FAX 011 49 30 8214091, telex 183 319 SPBLN D. **(Subscription address:** Springer-Verlag New York Inc. / North America, PO Box 2485, Journal Fulfillment, Secaucus NJ 07096. **Tel** (201)348-4033, (800)777-4643, FAX (201)348-4505.) **ED** H. Reichl. available in microform from University Microfilms International (UMI). Documents available from BLDSC.
Desc: Covers information on miniaturized systems in telecommunications and technology.

    ISSN 1351-3249
    UK
    CCC
●**NATURAL LANGUAGE ENGINEERING.** Vol. 1 (1995)-. English. Four times a year. $118.00 US, Canada and Mexico; £79.00 other. Cambridge University Press, The Edinburgh Building, Shaftesbury Road, Cambridge CB2 2RU United Kingdom. **Tel** 011 44 1 223 312393, FAX 011 44 1 223 315052, telex 851-817256. **(Subscription address:** Cambridge University Press / North America, 110 Midland Avenue, Port Chester NY 10573. **Tel** (800)431-1580, (914)937-9600.) **ED** Branimir Boguraev, Roberto Garigliano and John I. Tait.
Desc: Designed for professionals and researchers in all areas of computerized language processing. Covers machine translation, information retrieval, speech recognition and generation, dialogue systems, knowledge bases for natural language processing, text analysis and integrated systems.

    ISSN 1055-6923
    US
NETWARE PROGRAMMER'S JOURNAL. (1991)-. Periodical. English. Twelve times a year. Roseware, 8515 Cyrus Place, Alexandria VA 22308.

LC TK7885.A1 O36   **ISSN** 1048-8928
DD 621.395   US
OEM INTEGRATOR, THE. (OEM INTEGRATOR : FOR DESIGNERS OF OPEN SYSTEMS.). **VAT** Original Equipment Manufactures Integrator. Vol. 1, No. 1 (Spring 1990)-. Trade Publication. English. Six times a year (Feb., Apr., June, Aug., Oct., Dec.). $60.00. Transatlantic Publishing, 18 Main Street, Concord MA 01742. **Tel** (617)259-9207.

LC QA75.5 .O33   **ISSN** 1071-8990
DD 338.4/762139/05   US
●**OEM MAGAZINE.** (OEM MAGAZINE : FOR SYSTEMS AND SOFTWARE BUILDERS.). [OEM mag.]. **VAT** Original Equipment Manufacturer Magazine. Vol. 1, No. 1 (July 1993)-. Periodical. English. Nine times a year. $79.00. CMP Publications Inc., One Jericho Plaza, Wing A, 2nd Floor, Jericho NY 11753. **Tel** (516)733-6700. **(Subscription address:** CMP Publications, Inc. / New York, PO Box 4037, Church Street Station, New York NY 10261-4037. **Tel** (516)733-6800.)
Ind/Abst Bus. Source Plus; EP Collect.; Homework Help.; Lotus Notes; MasterFile FullTEXT 1000; MasterFile FullTEXT 350; MasterFile FullTEXT 650; MasterFile FullTEXT; OCLC; Telebase.

LC QA76.76.O63 I23   **ISSN** 1073-0729
DD 005/.265   US
●**OS/2 DEVELOPER. See** Computers-Software.

    ISSN 1051-9696
DD 005   US
    TITLE CHANGE
PARADOX DEVELOPER'S JOURNAL. [Paradox dev. j.]. **Added/Corp** Cobb Group. Vol. 1, No. 1 (Sept. 1990)-(199?). Periodical. English. Cobb Group, 9420 Bunsen Parkway #300, Louisville KY 40220. **Tel** (502)491-1900, (800)223-8720, FAX (502)491-4200. *Continued by Paradox for Windows Developer's Journal, 1082-1678.*

    ISSN 1082-1678
DD 005   US
    CEASED
PARADOX FOR WINDOWS DEVELOPER'S JOURNAL. [Paradox Windows dev. j.]. Vol. 6, No. 2 (Feb. 1995)-(Nov. 1995). Periodical. English. Cobb Group, 9420 Bunsen Parkway #300, Louisville KY 40220. **Tel** (502)491-1900, (800)223-8720, FAX (502)491-4200. *Continues Paradox Developer's Journal, 1051-9696.*

    ISSN 0895-5069
DD 620   US
PC CAD DIGEST. (PC CAD DIGEST : THE JOURNAL OF THE PRODESIGN II USER GROUP.). [PC CAD dig.]. **Added/Corp** ProDesign User Group (Seattle, Wash.). **VAT** Personal Computer Computer-Aided Design Digest. Vol. 1, Issue 1 (July 1987)-. Periodical. English. Six times a year. $24.00 (membership). RCM Communications, PO Box 1188, Graham WA 98338.
Desc: User group publications for CAD software prodesign - fast/easy CAD.

    ISSN 1063-6382
DD 004   US
    CCC
PROCEEDINGS / INTERNATIONAL CONFERENCE ON DATA ENGINEERING. See Computers-Data Base Management.

LC QA402 .S7a   **ISSN** 0094-2898
DD 003   US
    CCC
    CODEN PASTDB
PROCEEDINGS OF THE ANNUAL SOUTHEASTERN SYMPOSIUM ON SYSTEM THEORY. (PROCEEDINGS.). [Proc. annu. Southeast. Symp. Syst. Theory]. **Added/Corp** North Carolina State University at Raleigh. Dept. of Computer Science. Duke University. Dept. of Electrical Engineering. University of North Carolina at Chapel Hill. Dept. of Statistics. (1969)-. Proceedings. English. One time a year. $100.00. IEEE Computer Society, 10662 Los Vaqueros Circle, PO Box 3014, Los Alamitos CA 90720-1264. **Tel** (714)821-8380, (800)272-6657, FAX (714)821-4641.
Ind/Abst Curr. Cit.

    ISSN 0989-7100
    FR
UDC 681.5
ROBOTS EXPERT PARIS. (1988)-. Periodical. French. Societe Parisienne d'Edition, 9 Passage des Marais 9, 75010 Paris France. **Tel** 011 33 1 42089582. *Continues Robots Ingenierie (Paris), 0767-4694.*

    US
SOFTWARE DEVELOPER'S MONTHLY. (19??)-. English. Twelve times a year. $295.00 US; $395.00 North America; other. Sourceview Press, PO Box 578, Concord CA 94522. **Tel** (510)827-0810. **ED** Michael Dean. Index available. **Bk Rev. Ad Acc.**

Desc: Articles relating to software development activities. Emphasis is on activities developers must do not related to programming.

    ISSN 1070-8588
DD 005   US
    CCC
●**SOFTWARE DEVELOPMENT. See** Computers-Software.

    ISSN 0964-6841
DD 005.1   UK
    CCC
SOFTWARE DEVELOPMENT MONITOR. [Softw. dev. monit.]. (1991)-. Periodical. English. Twelve times a year. $738.00 The Americas; £495.00 other. Elsevier Advanced Technology, An Imprint of Elsevier Science Ltd., The Boulevard, Langford Lane, Kidlington, Oxford OX5 1GB United Kingdom. **Tel** 011 44 1865 843000, 011 44 1865 843699, FAX 011 44 1865 843010. **(Subscription address:** Elsevier Science Ltd. / Oxford Fulfillment Centre, PO Box 800, Kidlington OX5 1DX United Kingdom. **Tel** 011 44 865 843355.) *Continues Monitor.*

LC QA76.758 .S656   **ISSN** 0268-6961
DD 005.1/05   UK
    CCC
    CODEN SEJOED
Pr Rev.
SOFTWARE ENGINEERING JOURNAL. [Softw. eng. j.]. **Added/Corp** British Computer Society. Institution of Electrical Engineers. Vol. 1, No. 1 (Jan. 1986)-. Periodical. English. Six times a year. $231.02. Institution of Electrical Engineers / IEE, Michael Faraday House, Six Hills Way, Stevenage Hertfordshire SG1 2AY United Kingdom. **Tel** 011 44 1438 313311, FAX 011 44 1438 742840, telex 825578 IEESTV G. **(Subscription address:** IEE / Peter Peregrinus Ltd., PO Box 96, Stevenage Herts SG1 2SD United Kingdom. **Tel** 011 44 1438 313311, FAX 011 44 1438 742792, telex 825578 IEESTV G.) Documents available from Article Express International, The Genuine Article, Ask*IEEE. *Continues Software & Microsystems, 0261-3182.*
Ind/Abst Abstr. Hum. Comput. Interact.; ACM Guide Comput. Lit.; CompuMath Cit. Index [Full Cov.]; Comput. Rev.; Curr. Cit.; Ei Page One; Eng. Index Annu.; HILITES; INSPEC (1986); Res. Alert [Full Cov.].

LC QA76.758 .S6467   **ISSN** 0163-5948
DD 005.1/05   US
    CODEN SFENDP
SOFTWARE ENGINEERING NOTES. (SOFTWARE ENGINEERING NOTES : AN INFORMAL NEWSLETTER OF THE SPECIAL INTEREST GROUP ON SOFTWARE ENGINEERING.). [Softw. eng. notes]. **Added/Corp** Sicsoft. ACM Sigsoft. Special Interest Group on Software Engineering. **VFOAT** SEN; ACM SIGSOFT Software Engineering Notes. Vol. 1 (1976)-. Newsletter. English. Five times a year. $33.00. ACM / Association for Computing Machinery, 1515 Broadway, 17th Floor, New York NY 10036. **Tel** (212)869-7440, FAX (212)869-0481. **(Subscription address:** Association for Computing Machinery, PO Box 12114, Church Street Station, New York NY 10249. **Tel** (212)626-0500.) Documents available from Ask*IEEE.
Ind/Abst Abstr. Hum. Comput. Interact. (July 1980-); ACM Guide Comput. Lit.; Comput. Lit. Index; Comput. Rev. (July 1980-); Curr. Cit.; Ergon. Abstr. (July 1980-); HILITES; INSPEC (1986-).

    ISSN 1067-1293
DD 005   US
    CEASED
SOFTWARE ENGINEERING STRATEGIES. [Softw. eng. strateg.]. (1993)-Vol. 2, No. 1. Trade Publication. English. Auerbach Publishers Inc., Park Square Building, 31 St. James Avenue, Boston MA 02116. **Tel** (800)950-1207.

    ISSN 1064-878X
DD 338   US
SOFTWARE MANUFACTURING NEWS. See Computers-Software.

LC TA345 .S598   **ISSN** 8756-1085
DD 620/.0028/553   US
SOFTWHERE. ENGINEERING. See Computers-Software.

    ISSN 0921-1373
    NE
UDC 621.39
TELESCOPE B'S-GRAVENHAGE. (TELESCOPE.). [Telescope B's-Gravenhage]. (1982)-. Periodical. Dutch. Four times a year. Free on request. PTT Telecom BV, Antwoordnummer 10011, 2500 VB Den Haag Netherlands. **Tel** 011 31 70 3434154.

LC TA1 .T493   **ISSN** 0893-7877
DD 620/.005   US
    CODEN TITJEJ
TEXAS INSTRUMENTS TECHNICAL JOURNAL. [Tex. instrum. tech. j.]. **Added/Corp** Texas Instruments Incorporated. **VFOAT** TI Technical Journal. Vol. 3, No. 3 (May/June 1986)-. Periodical. English. Six times a year. Free on request. Texas

Computers —Computer Engineering

Instruments, PO Box 405, MS 3455, Lewisville TX 75067. **Tel** (214)917-3906. **Continues** Texas Instruments Engineering Journal, 0882-2557.

ISSN 0886-2362
DD 621 US
TOKEN PERSPECTIVES NEWSLETTER. [Token perspect. newsl.]. **Added/Corp** Architecture Technology Corporation. Vol. 1, No. 1 (Dec. 1983)-. Newsletter. English. Twelve times a year. $312.00. Architecture Technology Corporation, PO Box 24344, Minneapolis MN 55424. **Tel** (612)935-2035.

ISSN 1063-2662
DD 004 US
TOOL WATCH. (TOOL WATCH : ENABLING OPEN APPLICATIONS DEVELOPMENT.). [Tool watch]. Vol. 1, No. 1 (1992)-. Monographic series. English. Twelve times a year. $295.00 (one-year), $499.00 (two-year). Hurwitz Consulting Group, 44 Pleasant Street, Suite 200, Watertown MA 02172. **Tel** (617)926-5500, FAX (617)926-5222. **ED** Chet Geschickter. Index available. cum. index.

COMPUTER GAMES

LC GV1449.3 .A38
DD 794.1/7 UK
ADVANCES IN COMPUTER CHESS. Vol. 1 (1977)-. English. Price varies per volume. Edinburgh University Press Ltd., 22 George Square, Edinburgh EH8 9LF United Kingdom. **Tel** 011 44 131 6506207, FAX 011 44 131 6620053. **ED** M. R. B. Clarke.

ISSN 0731-5686
US
ATARI AGE. **Added/Corp** Atari Club (Philadelphia, Pa.). Vol. 1, No. 1 (May/June 1982)-. Periodical. English. Six times a year. Atari Club, 1700 Walnut Street, Philadelphia PA 19103.

ISSN 0261-3697
DD 794.05 UK
CCC
COMPUTER & VIDEO GAMES. [Comput. video games]. **VFOAT** Computer and Video Games. (1981)-. Periodical. English. Twelve times a year. $56.47. EMAP Images, Priory Court, 30-32 Farringdon Lane, London EC1R 3AU United Kingdom. **Tel** 011 44 171 9726700, FAX 011 44 171 9726710. **(Subscription address:** EMAP Images, PO Box 500, Leicester LE99 0AA United Kingdom. **Tel** 011 44 116 2468811.**)**

LC WMLC 91/4736 **ISSN** 1062-113X
DD 794 US
COMPUTER GAME REVIEW AND CD-ROM ENTERTAINMENT. [Comput. game rev. CD-ROM entertain.]. **VFOAT** CGR; Computer Game Review and 16-bit Entertainment; A.Computer game review. Apr. 1992-. Periodical. English. Twelve times a year. $19.95 US, $29.95 other. Sendai Publications, 1920 Highland Avenue, Suite 222, Lombard IL 60148. **Tel** (708)916-7222. **ED** Steve Honeywell. **Continues** Computer Game Review and 16-bit Entertainment, 1060-4693.

LC GV1469.3 .V55 **ISSN** 0748-4461
DD 794.8/2/05 US
COMPUTER GAMES. [Comput. games]. Vol. 2, No. 3 (Dec./Jan. 1984)-. Periodical. English. Six times a year. $15.00. Carnegie Corporation of New York, 437 Madison Avenue, New York NY 10022. **Tel** (212)371-3200. **Continues** Video Games Player, 0748-4453.

US
COMPUTER GAMES STRATEGY PLUS. English. Twelve times a year. $32.00. Strategy Plus, PO Box 21, Hancock VT 05748. **Tel** (802)767-4622, FAX (802)767-4623. **ED** Steve Wartofsky. **Ad Acc. Circ:** 65,000.
Desc: Aimed at the adult computer game player. Includes reviews, previews, and news of games available today. Categories include: hints, simulations, strategy, sports, features and more to help both beginners and experts.

LC GV1469.15 .C65 **ISSN** 0744-6667
DD 794.8/2 US
COMPUTER GAMING WORLD. [Comput. gaming world]. (1981)-. Periodical. English. Twelve times a year. $28.00. Ziff-Davis, One Park Avenue, 5th Floor, New York NY 10016. **Tel** (212)503-3500. **(Subscription address:** Neodata / Colorado, PO Box 2606, Boulder CO 80322. **) ED** Russell Sipe and Johnny L. Wilson. Index available. **Ad Acc. Circ:** 25,000 (ctrl). available on an online database from Information Access Company; available via Internet (http://www.ziff.com/).
Desc: Reviews of computer games. Focuses on games of strategy and adventure.
Ind/Abst Abstr. Hum. Comput. Interact. (?-?).

LC WMLC 93/5026 **ISSN** 1077-3967
DD 794 US
●**COMPUTER PLAYER.** [Comput. play.]. (1994)-. Periodical. English. Twelve times a year. $21.95. LFP Inc., 8484 Wilshire Boulevard, Suite 900, Beverly Hills CA 90210. **Tel** (213)651-5400.

LC QA76.5 .C725 **ISSN** 0735-6668
DD 001.64 US
CREATIVE COMPUTING BUYER'S GUIDE TO PERSONAL COMPUTERS, PERIPHERALS, AND ELECTRONIC GAMES. **See** Computers-Microcomputers, Personal Computers.

ISSN 8750-1937
US
CURRENT NOTES. **Added/Corp** Washington Area Atari Computer Enthusiasts. (19??)-. Periodical. English. Six times a year. $24.00. Current Notes, 122 North Johnson Road, Sterling VA 22170. **Tel** (703)450-4761. **ED** Joseph Waters. Index available. **Bk Rev**, (Qty: 2). **Ad Acc. Circ:** 3,000 (ctrl).
Desc: Includes news, reviews, tutorials, and commentaries for the Atari home computer owner on computing, word processing, desktop publishing, MIDI, telecommunications, and new computing technology.

ISSN 1079-2120
US
●**CYBERSURFER.** **See** Computers-Computer Networks.

ISSN 1070-3020
DD 794 US
DIEHARD GAME FAN. [Diehard game fan]. **VFOAT** Die Hard Game Fan; Diehard Gamefan. (1992)-. Periodical. English. Twelve times a year. $47.40. Die Hard Game Fan, 5137 Clareton Drive #210, Agoura CA 91301. **Tel** (818) 706-3260, FAX (818) 706-1367.

ISSN 1059-5457
DD 794 US
DIGITAL GAMES REVIEW. **See** Sports and Games.

ISSN 0825-0049
DD 794.1/05 CN
ECHEC +. [Echec +]. **VAT** Echec Plus. No. 34 (March/April 1984)-. Periodical. French. Six times a year. 27.21 can$. Quebec Chess Federation, PO Box 640, Station C, Montreal Quebec H2L 4L5 Canada. **Tel** (514)252-3034, FAX (514)251-8038. Index available. **Bk Rev. Ad Acc, Adv Mgr:** Robert Finta, **Tel** same as publisher. **Circ:** 2,500. **Continues** Petit Roque, 0227-8340.
Desc: Contains international and national tournament news, games, analysis, problems, and contests. Authoritative articles and columns on middle end games and chess computers.

ISSN 0746-2999
US
TITLE CHANGE
ELECTRONIC ENTERTAINMENT. [Electron. entertain.]. (Sept. 1983)-(Jan. 1996). Periodical. English. Infotainment World Inc., 951 Mariners Island Boulevard #700, San Mateo CA 94404. **Tel** (415)349-4300. **(Subscription address:** Neodata / Colorado, PO Box 2606, Boulder CO 80322. **) Continues** Arcade (Long Beach, Calif.), 0736-0304. **Continued by** PC Entertainment.

ISSN 1073-4791
DD 629 US
●**FULL THROTTLE.** [Full throttle]. **Added/Corp** Cobb Group. Vol. 1, No. 1 (Dec./Jan. 1993-94)-. Periodical. English. Six times a year. $29.00. Cobb Group, 9420 Bunsen Parkway #300, Louisville KY 40220. **Tel** (502)491-1900, (800)223-8720, FAX (502)491-4200.

ISSN 1073-922X
US
●**GAME DEVELOPER.** (1994)-. Periodical. English. Four times a year. $39.95. Miller Freeman Inc., 600 Harrison Street, San Francisco CA 94107. **Tel** (415)905-2377, (415)905-2200, FAX (415)905-2240, telex 278273.

LC WMLC 93/4612 **ISSN** 1067-6392
DD 794 US
Pr Rev.
GAME INFORMER MAGAZINE. (GAME INFORMER MAGAZINE : FOR VIDEO GAME ENTHUSIASTS.). [Game inf. mag.]. **VFOAT** Game Informer. (199?)-. Periodical. English. Six times a year. $19.98. Sunrise Publications Inc., 10120 West 76th Street, Eden Prairie MN 55344. **Tel** (612)946-7274, FAX (612)946-8155. **ED** Andy McNamara. **Ad Acc, Adv Mgr:** Kimberley Benike, **Tel** (612)946-8159. **Circ:** 200,000 (ctrl). available on an online database from America Online; and Compuserve Inc.
Desc: Entertains and informs game players of all ages, with emphasis on the coverage of video games. Areas covered include new product and game reviews, industry news updates and an open forum for readers.

LC GV1469.15 .G35 **ISSN** 1068-1809
DD 794.8 US
TITLE CHANGE
GAME PLAYERS NINTENDO-SEGA. [Game play. Nintendo-Sega]. **VFOAT** Game Players Nintendo Sega; Game Players. (June 1993)-(1993). Periodical. English. GP Publications, 1350 Old Bayshore, Burlingame CA 94010. **Tel** (415)696-1688. **Formed by the union of** Game Players Nintendo Guide, 1059-2172 **and** Game Players Sega Guide, 1065-3376. **Continued by** Game Players Sega-Nintendo, 1074-2425.

LC WMLC L 83/9156 **ISSN** 1065-3376
DD 794 US
TITLE CHANGE
GAME PLAYERS SEGA GUIDE. [Game play. Sega guide]. Vol. 3, No. 4 (Aug./Sept. 1992)-(1993). Periodical. English. GP Publications, 1350 Old Bayshore, Burlingame CA 94010. **Tel** (415)696-1688. **Continues** Game Player's Sega Genesis Strategy Guide, 1052-763X. **Merged with** Game Players Nintendo Guide, 1059-2172 **to form** Game Players Nintendo-Sega, 1068-1809.

ISSN 1074-2425
US
●**GAME PLAYERS SEGA-NINTENDO.** (1994)-. English. Twelve times a year. $24.95. Imagine Publishing Inc., 1350 Old Bayshore Highway, Suite 210, Burlingame CA 94010. **Tel** (415)696-1688, FAX (415)696-1678. **Continues** Game Players Nintendo Sega.

LC GV1469.15 .G38 **ISSN** 1050-5601
DD 793.93/2 US
GAME PLAYERS STRATEGY GUIDE TO GAME BOY GAMES. [Game play. strategy guide Game Boy games]. **VFOAT** Players Strategy Guide to Game Boy Games. Vol. 1, No. 1 (Summer 1990)-. Periodical. English. Four times a year. Signal Research Inc / North Carolina, PO Box 29364, 300 Westgate Drive, Greensboro NC 27407. **Tel** (919)299-9902, (201)703-9500, FAX (919)854-0963.

LC GV1312
DD 794.8 SP
●**HI-TECH.** (1994)-. Consumer Publication. Spanish. Twelve times a year. 3800ptas. Hobby Press SA, Los Ciruelos 4, 28700 S. Sebastian Reyes, Madrid Spain. **Tel** 011 34 1 6548199. **Ad Acc.**

ISSN 0920-234X
CN
UDC 51
Pr Rev.
ICCA JOURNAL. **VFOAT** International Computer Chess Association Journal. (1983)-. Periodical. English. Four times a year. $80.00. Queen Mary and Westfield College, Mile End Road, London E1 4NS United Kingdom. **Tel** 011 44 171 9755200, FAX 011 44 171 9806533. Documents available from The Genuine Article. **Ind/Abst** CompuMath Cit. Index [Full Cov.]; Res. Alert [Full Cov.].

SZ
●**INTERNATIONAL SOCIETY OF DYNAMIC GAMES. ANNALS.** (1994)-. Monographic series. English. Irregular. Birkhauser Verlag Ag, Klosterberg 23, PO Box 133, CH-4010 Basel Switzerland. **Tel** 011 41 61 2717400, FAX 011 41 61 2717666, telex 963475 birk ch.

ISSN 1354-3350
UK
●**KEY NOTE REPORT. ELECTRONIC GAMES.** [Key Note rep., Electron. games]. **VFOAT** Electronic Games. (1994)-. English. Key Note Publications Ltd., Field House, 72 Oldfield Road, Hampton Middlesex TW12 2HQ United Kingdom. **Tel** 011 0181 7830755, FAX 011 0181 7831940.

ISSN 1058-9171
US
MEGA PLAY. [Mega play]. (1990)-. Periodical. English. Six times a year. $14.95 US, $24.95 Canada. Sendai Publications, 1920 Highland Avenue, Suite 222, Lombard IL 60148. **Tel** (708)916-7222.
Desc: Written for computer game enthusiasts with concentration on Sega Genesis, Sega CDs, and the new game gear for the Sega system.

US
●**PC ENTERTAINMENT.** (1995)-. English. Twelve times a year. $24.00. Infotainment World Inc., 951 Mariners Island Boulevard #700, San Mateo CA 94404. **Tel** (415)349-4300. **(Subscription address:** Neodata / Colorado, PO Box 2606, Boulder CO 80322. **) Continues** Electronic Entertainment.

ISSN 1080-4471
DD 794 US
PC GAMER. [PC gamer]. **VAT** Personal Computer Gamer. (199?)-. Periodical. English. Twelve times a year. $47.95. Imagine Publishing Inc., 1350 Old Bayshore Highway, Suite 210, Burlingame CA 94010. **Tel** (415)696-1688, FAX (415)696-1678. **ED** Selby Bateman. **Circ:** 75,000. **Continues** Game Players PC

Entertainment, 1059-2180.
Desc: Covers computer games for IBM PC's and compatible computers.

ISSN 1351-3540
US

●**PC GAMER.** (1993)-. English. Twelve times a year. $47.95. Imagine Publishing Inc., 1350 Old Bayshore Highway, Suite 210, Burlingame CA 94010. **Tel** (415)696-1688, FAX (415)696-1678. **(Subscription address:** Neodata / Colorado, PO Box 2606, Boulder CO 80322.) *Continues Game Players.*

LC GV1312 ISSN 1351-0290
DD 794.8 UK

●**PC GAMES LONDON.** [PC games Lond.]. **VFOAT** Personal Computer Games. (1994)-. Consumer Publication. English. Twelve times a year. £55.00. EMAP Images, Priory Court, 30-32 Farringdon Lane, London EC1R 3AU United Kingdom. **Tel** 011 44 171 9726700, FAX 011 44 171 9726710. **Ad Acc.** available on CD-ROM; available on diskette.

ISSN 1042-2943
DD 794 US
CCC
TITLE CHANGE

PC GAMES (PETERBOROUGH, N.H.). (PC GAMES.). [PC games]. **VFOAT** PCGames; PCGames Magazine. **VAT** Personal Computer Games. (1989)-(19??). Periodical. English. IDG Communications / New Hampshire, 86 Elm Street, Peterborough NH 03458. **Tel** (800)349-7327, FAX (603)924-6972. *Continues PC Resource's PC Games, 1042-1351. Continued by Electronic Entertainment, 0746-2999.*

ISSN 0897-893X
DD 794 US
SUSPENDED

PCGAMES. (PCGAMES [COMPUTER FILE].). [PC games]. **VAT** Personal Computer Games. No. 1, (1988)-(19??). Periodical. English. Four times a year. $29.00. PCGames, 80 Elm Street, Peterborough NH 03458. **Tel** (603)924-0100, FAX (603)924-6838. **ED** Chuck Weston. **Ad Acc. Circ:** 160,000.
Desc: Reflects the growth in the exploding computer and video entertainment industry. Features computer game software, as well as the latest technology. Also offers hints and tips about games, and strategies to play those games. System requirements: IBM-PC, Tandy-1000 series and compatibles, 256K, MS-DOS.

LC GV1199 ISSN 1352-4267
DD 793 UK

●**SEGA MAGAZINE.** [Sega mag.]. (1994)-. Consumer Publication. English. Twelve times a year. £34.00. EMAP Images, Priory Court, 30-32 Farringdon Lane, London EC1R 3AU United Kingdom. **Tel** 011 44 171 9726700, FAX 011 44 171 9726710. **(Subscription address:** Tower Publishing, Tower House, Sovereign Park, Market Harborough, Leicester LE16 9EF United Kingdom. **Tel** 011 44 1858 468811, FAX 011 44 1858 432164.) **Ad Acc.**

US
CEASED

SEGAVISIONS. (19??)-(Sept. 1995). English. Infotainment World Inc., 951 Mariners Island Boulevard #700, San Mateo CA 94404. **Tel** (415)349-4300. **(Subscription address:** Neodata / Colorado, PO Box 2606, Boulder CO 80322.) **ED** N. Lavoroff. **Circ:** 1,000,000 (ctrl).

ISSN 1070-5090
DD 741 US

●**SONIC THE HEDGEHOG.** No. 1 (Mar. 1993)-. Periodical. English. Twelve times a year. Archie Comic Publications, 325 Fayette Avenue, Mamaroneck NY 10543. **Tel** (914)381-5155.

LC QA76.5 .S6517 ISSN 0882-6862
DD 004.16 US

ST. GAME. [St.Game]. **VFOAT** Saint Game. Vol. 4 (March/April 1984)-. Periodical. English. Six times a year. $12.00. Softalk, 11021 Magnolia Boulevard North, Hollywood CA 91601. *Continues Softline, 0745-4988.*
Ind/Abst Microcomput. Abstr. (1984-?).

ISSN 0934-3237
UDC 681.3 GW
CEASED

ST-MAGAZIN 68000ER. [ST-Mag. 68000er].
VFOAT ST-Magazin Achtundsechzigtausender. (1988)-(Aug. 1993). Periodical. Multiple languages. PSH Medienvertriebs GmbH, Georgenstadt Strasse 38 b, D-64297 Darmstadt Germany. **Tel** 011 49 61 51 947723, FAX 011 49 61 51 947725, 947718. *Continues 68000er, 0933-2308.*

LC WMLC 93/4525 ISSN 1078-5132
DD 794 US

STRATEGY PLUS. [Strategy plus]. **VFOAT** Computer Games. (19??)-. Periodical. English. Twelve times a year. $36.00. Strategy Plus Inc., PO Box 21, Hancock VA 05748. **Tel** (802)767-4622.

LC GV1469.3 .V522 ISSN 1071-5290
DD 794.8/05 US

VIDEO GAME BUYER'S GUIDE. (THE ... VIDEO GAME BUYER'S GUIDE.). [Video game buy. guide]. **VFOAT** Electronic Gaming Monthly Presents The ... Video Game Buyer's guide; Electronic Gaming Monthly's ... Video Game Buyer's Guide; EGM Buyer's Guide. (1990)-. English. Irregular. Electronic Gaming Monthly, 1920 Highland Avenue, Suite 100, Lombard IL 60148. *Continues Buyer's Guide (Lisle, Ill.).*

ISSN 1059-2938
DD 794 US
TITLE CHANGE

VIDEO GAMES & COMPUTER ENTERTAINMENT. [Video games comput. entertain.]. **VFOAT** Video Games and Computer Entertainment; Videogames & Computer Entertainment; VG&CE. (1988)-(19??). Periodical. English. LFP Inc., 8484 Wilshire Boulevard, Suite 900, Beverly Hills CA 90210. **Tel** (213)651-5400. *Continued by Video Games The Ultimate Gaming Magazine.*

LC GV1469.3 .V56 ISSN 1074-3774
DD 794.8/05 US

●**VIDEOGAMES (BEVERLY HILLS, CALIF.).** (VIDEOGAMES.). [VideoGames]. **VFOAT** Video Games. Vol. 5, No. 9 (Sept. 1993)-. Periodical. English. Twelve times a year. L. F. P. Inc., 9171 Wilshire Boulevard, Suite 300, Beverly Hills CA 90210. **Circ:** 300,000. *Continues VideoGames & Computer Entertainment, 1059-2938.*
Desc: Features information on Nintendo, Atari, Sega, 3DO, CD-I and Arcade Gaming.

ISSN 0954-867X
DD 794.802855365 UK
TITLE CHANGE

ZZAP! 64. [Zzap! 64]. **VFOAT** Zzap! Sixty Four. (1985)-(1993). Periodical. English. Euro Press Sales and Distribution Ltd., Case Mill Temeside, Ludlow, Shropshire SY8 1JW United Kingdom. **Tel** 011 44 151 3571275, FAX 011 44 151 3572813. **ED** Stuart Wynne. **Bk Rev. Ad Acc. Circ:** 55,900. *Continued by Commodore Force.*
Desc: Reviews, previews, and features on all aspects of computer game playing on The Commodore C-64, C-128 and Amiga computer.

COMPUTER GRAPHICS AND DESIGN

ISSN 1058-9503
DD 760 US

3D ARTIST. See The Arts-Graphic Arts.

LC NC ISSN 0953-2331
DD 745.40285 UK

3D (LONDON). (3D.). [3D Lond.]. **VFOAT** Three D (London). (1988)-. Periodical. English. Twelve times a year. EMAP Business Publishing Ltd., 260 Field End Road, Audit House, Ruislip Middlesex HA4 9LT United Kingdom. **Tel** 011 44 181 9563000, FAX 011 44 181 4293117. available on an online database from DIALOG. *Continues in part CadCam International, 0261-6920.*
Ind/Abst Comput. ASAP [Full Txt.]; Comput. Database [Full Txt.].

LC QA76.9.S88 A27 ISSN 0734-2071
DD 001.64/05 US
CCC
Pr Rev.

ACM TRANSACTIONS ON COMPUTER SYSTEMS. See Computers-Computer Systems.

LC T385 .A28 ISSN 0730-0301
DD 006.6 US
CCC
CODEN ATGRDF
Pr Rev.

ACM TRANSACTIONS ON GRAPHICS. [ACM trans. graph.]. **Added/Corp** Association for Computing Machinery. **VFOAT** Transactions on Graphics; A.C.M. Transactions on Graphics. **VAT** Association for Computing Machinery Transactions on Graphics. Vol. 1, No. 1 (Jan. 1982)-. Periodical. English. Four times a year. $125.00. ACM / Association for Computing Machinery, 1515 Broadway, 17th Floor, New York NY 10036. **Tel** (212)869-7440, FAX (212)869-0481. **ED** Jim Foley. Index available (bound in Oct. issue). **Circ:** 9,000. available on microfilm and microfiche from University Microfilms International (UMI); available on an online database (indexing and abstracting) from Knowledge Index; DIALOG; DATA-STAR; Compuserve Inc.; BRS/Colleague; BRS After Dark; and BRS. Documents available from Article Express International, The Genuine Article, Ask*IEEE.
Desc: Covers every aspect of the use and development of computer graphics.
Ind/Abst Abstr. Hum. Comput. Interact.; ACM Guide Comput. Lit.; Appl. Sci. Technol. Index (1991-); CompuMath Cit. Index [Full Cov.]; Comput. Abstr.; Comput. Database; Comput. Index; Comput. Rev.; Curr. Cit.; Ei Page One; Eng. Index Annu.; Ergon. Abstr.;

GeoRef; HILITES; INSPEC (Oct. 1982-); Int. Aerosp. Abstr. (1983-); Res. Alert [Full Cov.]; SCISEARCH; Zentralbl. Math. Ihre Grenzgeb.

LC T385 .A365 ISSN 0197-7040
DD 621.39/9 US
GW

ADVANCES IN COMPUTER GRAPHICS HARDWARE. (1987)-. Trade Publication. English. One time a year.

ISSN 0197-7040
US
TITLE CHANGE

ANDERSON REPORT, THE. [Anderson rep.]. (197?)-(1994). Periodical. English. Altus Inc., 1901 East Fourth Street, Suite 310, Santa Ana CA 92705. **Tel** (714)542-0700, FAX (714)542-0783. **ED** B. J. Anderson. Index available. **Bk Rev.** ctrl circ. **Merged into** *Engineering Automation Report, 1065-6952.*
Desc: Features late-breaking news, industry happenings, trends, new products, software news and services, plus an inside report on computer graphics, CAD/CAM, and CAE.

LC NX180.T4 D57
DD 700/.1/0502573 US

ARTISTS USING SCIENCE AND TECHNOLOGY DIRECTORY. See The Arts-Art.

LC TH437 .A95 ISSN 0926-5805
DD 624/.0285 NE
CCC
CODEN AUCOES
Pr Rev.

AUTOMATION IN CONSTRUCTION. See Building and Construction.

LC TK7881.4 .A97 ISSN 0747-1335
DD 621.388/33/05 US
CCC

AVIDEO. See Communications-Video.

LC WMLC 91/1059
DD 004 CI

BIT. See Computers-Electronic Data Processing.

LC TR845 ISSN 1357-0633
DD 778.5990285416 UK

●**BUSINESS VIDEO.** [Bus. video]. (1994)-. Trade Publication. English. Six times a year. £30.00. EMAP Media, 33 39 Bowling Green Lane, London EC1R 0DA United Kingdom. **Tel** 011 44 171 8371212, FAX 011 44 171 8334519. **(Subscription address:** Readerlink, Audit House, 260 Field End Lane, Eastcote Ruislip, Middlesex HA4 9LT United Kingdom. **Tel** 011 44 181 8684499, FAX 011 44 181 4293117.) **ED** Chris Histed. **Ad Acc, Adv Mgr:** Chris Histed. **Circ:** 8,499.
Desc: Includes information on desktop video editing, graphics, and audio for those creating corporate videos.

ISSN 0263-6190
UK
CODEN CCDGD6

CAD/CAM DIGEST. See Engineering-Computer Applications.

ISSN 8755-8637
DD 670 US

CAD EDUCATOR, THE. [CAD educ.]. **VAT** Computer Aided Design Educator. Vol. 1, No. 1 (Nov./Dec. 1984)-. Periodical. English. Five times a year. $21.00 US; $27.00 Canada. The CAD Educator Inc, 717 West Wood Drive, PO Box 47150, Phoenix AZ 85029. **Tel** (602)256-1355.

ISSN 0896-3266
DD 620 US

CAD EVOLUTION. [CAD evol.]. **Added/Corp** Evolution Computing User Group. **VAT** Computer Aided Design Evolution. Vol. 1, No. 1 (Nov./Dec. 1987)-. Periodical. English. Six times a year. $24.00. Martin Publishing, 21300 68 W/Suite 203, Lynnwood WA 98036.
Desc: User group publications for computer-aided-design software.

LC TA174 .C255 ISSN 1055-8926
DD 620/.0042/0285662 US

CAD INDUSTRY DIRECTORY (HARDWARE ED.). (CAD INDUSTRY DIRECTORY / COMPILED BY ARIEL COMMUNICATIONS, INC.). [CAD ind. dir.]. **Added/Corp** Ariel Communications, Inc. **VAT** Computer Aided Design Industry Directory. (1991)-. Directory. English. One time a year. $19.95. OmRay Inc., PO Box 203550, Austin TX 78720-3550. **Tel** (512)250-1700, FAX (512)250-1016. *Continues Resources Directory (Austin, Tex.), 1044-2847.*

NE

CAD MAGAZINE. English. Eight times a year. Fl137.00. CAD Magazine BV, Postbus 397, 3300 AJ Dordrecht Netherlands. **Tel** 011 31 78 314565.

ISSN 1183-9414
DD 620/.0042/0285 CN
CAD SYSTEMS. [CAD syst.]. **VFOAT** Computer Aided Design Systems. Vol. 9, No. 4 (Sept. 1991)-. Trade Publication. English. Six times a year. 61.00Can$. Kerrwil Publications Ltd., 395 Matheson Boulevard E, Mississauga Ontario L4Z 2H2 Canada. **Tel** (905)890-1846. ***Formed by the union of*** *Architectural Engineering Construction Magazine, 1187-0524* ***and*** *CAD/CAM Systems, 0847-5547.*

LC T385 .C338 **ISSN** 0820-5450
DD 006.6/05 US
CCC
CADALYST. (CADALYST : THE NEWSLETTER OF THE AUTOCAD USERS' GROUP.). [CADalyst]. **Added/Corp** AutoCAD Users' Group. **VFOAT** Journal of the AutoCAD Users' Group; Journal for AutoCAD Users. (1984)-. Trade Publication. English. Twelve times a year. $39.00. Advanstar Communications Inc., 131 West First Street, Duluth MN 55802. **Tel** (218)723-9477, (800)346-0085, FAX (218)723-9437.
Desc: Provides practical information to users and managers of CAD systems based on AutoCAD, Generic CADD, and the spectrum of application software built around these products.

ISSN 0963-5750
UK
CADCAM LONDON. (CADCAM.). [Cadcam Lond.]. (1990)-. Periodical. English. Twelve times a year. $135.18. EMAP Readerlink, Audit House, 260 Field End Road, Ruislip Middlesex HA4 9LT United Kingdom. **Tel** 011 44 1773 63100, FAX 011 44 1733 87367. **ED** David Allen. **Bk Rev. Ad Acc. Circ:** 20,000 (ctrl). available on an online database from DIALOG. ***Continues*** *CadCam International, 0261-6920.*
Desc: Technical reviews of computer aided design hardware and software.
Ind/Abst BMT Abstr. (?-199?); Comput. ASAP [Full Txt.]; Comput. Database [Full Txt.]; Fluid Abstr., Civil Eng.; Fluid Abstr. Proc. Eng.; FLUIDEX; Trade Ind. ASAP [Full Txt.]; Trade Ind. Index [Full Txt.].

LC T385 .C32 **ISSN** 0887-9141
DD 620 US
CCC
CODEN CADEEL
CADENCE (AUSTIN, TEX.). (CADENCE.). [Cadence]. Vol. 1, No. 1 (1986)-. Periodical. English. Twelve times a year. $39.95. Miller Freeman Inc., 600 Harrison Street, San Francisco CA 94107. **Tel** (415)905-2337, (415)905-2200, FAX (415)905-2240, telex 278273. **(Subscription address:** Neodata / Colorado, PO Box 2606, Boulder CO 80322. **) ED** Kelly Johnson and David Baceskl. Index available. **Bk Rev. Ad Acc. Circ:** 50,000. available on diskette. Documents available from Ask*IEEE.
Desc: Using Auto CAD computer aided design (CAD) software in professional applications such as architecture, engineering, manufacturing or drafting.
Ind/Abst Acad. Abstr. Full Text Elite; Acad. Abstr.; Acad. Search; EP Collect.; Homework Help.; INFO-SOUTH Abstr. (19??-); INSPEC (Apr. 1989-1991); Mag. Artic. Summar. Elite; Mag. Artic. Summar. Select; Mag. Artic. Summar. CD-ROM; Mag. Search (19??-); MasterFile FullTEXT 1000; MasterFile FullTEXT 350; MasterFile FullTEXT 650; MasterFile FullTEXT (July 1990-); Microcomput. Abstr. (Feb. 1989-); OCLC; Pub. Lib. FullTEXT; Telebase; Vocat. Search.

LC TA174 .C58 **ISSN** 0010-4485
DD 620/.00425/02854 UK
CCC
CODEN CAIDA5
Pr Rev.
COMPUTER AIDED DESIGN. [Comput. aided des.]. **VFOAT** Computer-Aided Design ; CAD . Vol. 1 (Autumn 1968)-. Periodical. English. Twelve times a year. $764.00. Butterworth Heinemann Publishers, Linacre House Jordan Hill, Oxford OX2 8DP United Kingdom. **Tel** 011 44 1865 310366, FAX 011 44 1865 310898. **(Subscription address:** Elsevier Science Ltd. / Oxford Fulfillment Centre, PO Box 800, Kidlington OX5 1DX United Kingdom. **Tel** 011 44 865 843355.**) ED** Jennifer Smith. Index available. **Bk Rev. Ad Acc. Circ:** 2,500. available on microfilm and microfiche from University Microfilms International (UMI); available on an online database from Elsevier Electronic Subscriptions (EES). Documents available from Article Express International, The Genuine Article, Ask*IEEE.
Desc: Covers the latest developments and applications of CAD in every field. Areas covered are mechanical engineering and manufacture, civil and structural engineering, architecture and building design, electronic engineering, chemical engineering, expert systems, the user interface, databases, simulation, geometric modelling, numerical control and social implications of CAD and more.
Ind/Abst ACM Guide Comput. Lit.; Archit. Period. Index (1978-); Bioeng. Abstr.; BMT Abstr. (?-199?); CompuMath Cit. Index [Full Cov.]; Comput. Abstr.; Comput. Database; Comput. Rev.; Curr. Cit.; Curr. Contents Eng. Comput. Technol.; Curr. Technol. Index; Ei Page One; Eng. Index Annu.; Fluid Abstr., Civil Eng.; Fluid Abstr. Proc. Eng.; FLUIDEX (1973-); Geogr. Abstr. Human Geogr. (?-?); Inf. Sci. Abstr. (?-?); INSPEC (Winter 1969-); Int. Civil Eng. Abstr.; Life Sci. Collect.; Res. Alert [Full Cov.]; Robotics Abstr.; SCISEARCH; World Publ. Monit.; Zentralbl. Math. Ihre Grenzgeb.

ISSN 0991-1960
FR
COMPUTER AIDED DESIGN. FRENCH EDITION. (19??)-. Periodical. French. Twelve times a year. $433.07. SGAO, 8 rue Henri Becquerel, 92508 Rueil Malmaison France. **Tel** 011 33 1 47104900, FAX 011 33 1 47104949. **ED** Patrice Elu.
Desc: Computer aided design newsletter. Hardware and software evolutions in the field of CAD/CAM.

LC Z5838.D5 V35 TK7868.D5 **ISSN** 0191-2305
DD 016.6213815/02854 US
COMPUTER AIDED DESIGN OF DIGITAL SYSTEMS. Vol. 1 (1974)-. English. One time a year. $7.50. Computer Science Press Inc, 9125 Fall River Lane, Potomac MD 20854. **Tel** (301)251-9050.

ISSN 0276-749X
US
COMPUTER AIDED DESIGN REPORT. [Comput. aided des. rep.]. **VFOAT** Computer Aided Design. Vol. 1, No. 1 (April 1981)-. Periodical. English. Twelve times a year. $189.00. CAD CAM Publishing, 1010 Turquoise Street, Suites 320, San Diego CA 92109. **Tel** (619)488-0533. **ED** Steve Wolfe. Index available (free). cum. index. **Bk Rev. Circ:** 2,600 (ctrl). available on microfiche. ***Absorbed*** *CAD/CIM Alert, 8756-842X.*
Desc: Reports on current developments in the use of computers by engineers designing manufactured products. Topics include computer graphics, CAD/CAM/CAE, engineering analysis, and design automation techniques.
Ind/Abst Text. Technol. Dig.

ISSN 1063-312X
DD 702 US
COMPUTER ARTIST. [Comput. artist]. Vol. 1, No. 1 (Spring 1992)-. Trade Publication. English. Six times a year. $29.70. PennWell Publishing Company, 1421 South Sheridan, PO Box 1260, Tulsa OK 74101. **Tel** (918)835-3161, (800)331-4463, FAX (918)831-9497. **(Subscription address:** Computer Artist, Publishing Services, PO Box 3188, Tulsa OK 74101. **Tel** (918)831-9405, FAX (918)831-9295.**)**
Desc: Designed to meet the needs of a wide range of non-technical creative professionals who use computer workstations. Directed at art and creative directors, graphic designers, illustrators and other professionals.
Ind/Abst Bus. Source Plus; Bus. Source; EP Collect.; Homework Help.; MasterFile FullTEXT 1000; MasterFile FullTEXT 350; MasterFile FullTEXT 650; MasterFile FullTEXT (Jan. 1995-); OCLC; Telebase.

LC T385 .C56 **ISSN** 0097-8930
DD 001.55 US
CODEN CGRADI
COMPUTER GRAPHICS. [Comput. graph.]. **Added/Corp** SIGGRAPH. SIGGRAPH. SIGGRAPH ... Conference Proceedings. (19??)-. Trade Publication. English. Four times a year (Jan., Apr., July, Oct.). $85.00. ACM / Association for Computing Machinery, 1515 Broadway, 17th Floor, New York NY 10036. **Tel** (212)869-7440, FAX (212)869-0481. **(Subscription address:** Association for Computing Machinery, PO Box 12114, Church Street Station, New York NY 10249. **Tel** (212)626-0500.**)** Documents available from Article Express International, Ask*IEEE. ***Continued in part by*** *Computer Graphics Proceedings, Annual Conference Series, 1069-529X.*
Ind/Abst Abstr. Hum. Comput. Interact.; ACM Guide Comput. Lit.; Bioeng. Abstr.; Comput. Lit. Index; Comput. Rev.; Curr. Cit.; Ei Page One; Eng. Index Annu.; Ergon. Abstr.; GeoRef; HILITES; INSPEC (July 1980-); World Publ. Monit.

LC T385 .C5746 **ISSN** 0167-7055
DD 006.6 NE
CCC
CODEN CGFODY
Pr Rev.
COMPUTER GRAPHICS FORUM : A JOURNAL OF THE EUROPEAN ASSOCIATION FOR COMPUTER GRAPHICS. Vol. 1, No. 1 (Mar. 1982)-. Academic Scholarly Publication. English. Five times a year. $340.00. Basil Blackwell Publishers Ltd., 108 Cowley Road, Oxford 0X4 1JF United Kingdom. **Tel** 011 44 1235 465500, FAX 011 44 1235 465556, telex 837022 OXBOOK G. **(Subscription address:** Blackwell Publishers / UK, 108 Cowley Road, Oxford OX4 1JF United Kingdom. **Tel** 011 44 1865 791100, FAX 011 44 1865 791347.**) ED** Hans Peter Feidel and Philip Willis. **Bk Rev. Ad Acc, Adv Mgr:** Paula Stewart, **Tel** 0865 791100. **Circ:** 1430 (ctrl). available on microfilm from University Microfilms International (UMI). Documents available from Article Express International, Ask*IEEE.
Desc: Features refereed articles on the theory and practice of computer graphics. A unique forum for computer graphics developments internationally, transcending the limitations which are typical of national publications.
Ind/Abst ACM Guide Comput. Lit.; Comput. Abstr.; Comput. Lit. Index; Comput. Rev.; Curr. Cit.; Ei Page One; Eng. Index Annu.; Ergon. Abstr.; Geogr. Abstr. Phys. Geogr.; HILITES; INSPEC (March 1982-).

ISSN 0276-2811
US
COMPUTER GRAPHICS NEWS (WASHINGTON, D.C.). (COMPUTER GRAPHICS NEWS.). [Comput. graph. news]. April 1980-. Periodical. English. Irregular. Free to clients. Aui Data Graphics, 600 Maryland Avenue SW, Washington DC 20024.

LC T385 .C584 **ISSN** 1069-529X
DD 006 US
•**COMPUTER GRAPHICS PROCEEDINGS, ANNUAL CONFERENCE SERIES.** (COMPUTER GRAPHICS PROCEEDINGS, ANNUAL CONFERENCE SERIES / SPONSORED BY THE ASSOCIATION FOR COMPUTING MACHINERY'S SPECIAL INTEREST GROUP ON COMPUTER GRAPHICS.). [Comput. graph. proc. annu. conf. ser.]. **Added/Corp** SIGGRAPH. **VFOAT** Annual Conference Series. (1993)-. Proceedings. English. ACM / Association for Computing Machinery, 1515 Broadway, 17th Floor, New York NY 10036. **Tel** (212)869-7440, FAX (212)869-0481. **(Subscription address:** Association for Computing Machinery, PO Box 12114, Church Street Station, New York NY 10249. **Tel** (212)626-0500.**)** ***Continues in part*** *Computer Graphics, 0097-8930.*

LC T385 .C558 **ISSN** 0271-4159
DD 001.55/3 US
CCC
CODEN CGWODH
COMPUTER GRAPHICS WORLD. [Comput. graph. world]. Vol. 3, No. 2 (March/April 1980)-. Trade Publication. English. Twelve times a year. $50.00. PennWell Publishing Company, 1421 South Sheridan, PO Box 1260, Tulsa OK 74101. **Tel** (918)835-3161, (800)331-4463, FAX (918)831-9497. **(Subscription address:** Computer Graphics World, Publishing Services, PO Box 122, Tulsa OK 74101. **Tel** (918)831-9400, FAX (918)832-9295.**)** Index available. **Bk Rev. Ad Acc. Circ:** 50,000 (ctrl). available on microfilm and microfiche from University Microfilms International (UMI); available on an online database (files 648,675/Full-Text) from DIALOG. Documents available from Ask*IEEE, BLDSC, FAXON Xpress, The UnCover Company, SWETS, UMI Article Clearinghouse. ***Continues*** *Computer Graphics, 0162-3273.*
Desc: Purpose is to communicate business and technology developments in an array of commercial applications, and to provide analysis of their impact on product strategies and market trends.
Ind/Abst Abstr. Hum. Comput. Interact.; Bus. Source Plus; Bus. Source; Comput. ASAP [Full Txt.]; Comput. Database [Full Txt.]; Comput. Lit. Index; Curr. Cit.; EP Collect.; F&S Index Plus Text, Int. [Select. Cov.]; HILITES; Homework Help.; INSPEC (Feb. 1983-); MasterFile FullTEXT 1000; MasterFile FullTEXT 350; MasterFile FullTEXT 650; MasterFile FullTEXT (Jan. 1995-); Microcomput. Abstr. (Jan. 1985-); OCLC; Print. Abstr.; PROMT; Telebase; Trade Ind. ASAP [Full Txt.]; Trade Ind. Index [Full Txt.]; World Publ. Monit.

LC T385 .C59315 **ISSN** 0895-2760
DD 006.6/025 US
SUSPENDED
COMPUTER GRAPHICS WORLD BUYERS GUIDE. [Comput. graph. world buy. guide]. **VFOAT** CGW Buyers Guide. (19??)-Suspended (1993). Trade Publication. English. One time a year. PennWell Publishing Company, 1421 South Sheridan, PO Box 1260, Tulsa OK 74101. **Tel** (918)835-3161, (800)331-4463, FAX (918)831-9497. **ED** Thomas McMillan and Janice Bremer. **Ad Acc. Circ:** 16,000. ***Continues*** *Computer Graphics Directory.*
Desc: A current reference for graphics products and services; serves OEMs, VARs, product developers, manufacturers and decision makers in business and industry.

UK
TITLE CHANGE
COMPUTER IMAGES. (19??)-(19??). English. EMAP Readerlink, Audit House, 260 Field End Road, Ruislip Middlesex HA4 9LT United Kingdom. **Tel** 011 44 1773 63100, FAX 011 44 1733 87367. ***Merged with*** *Multi Media* ***to form*** *Audio Visual, 0305-2249.*

ISSN 1042-1130
DD 006 US
COMPUTER IMAGES. [Comput. images]. (1988)-. English. One time a year. $19.95. Camelot Publishing Company, PO Box 1357, Ormond Beach FL 32175. **Tel** (904)672-5672. **ED** Donald D Spencer.
Desc: Covers diverse examples of computer-generated images. The work is representative of art produced by secondary school students, college students, art teachers, computer graphics professionals, artists, and others. The images are created by people of all ages, using computer systems such as microcomputers.

LC TR894 .B88 **ISSN** 0883-5683
DD 778.5 US
CCC
CEASED

COMPUTER PICTURES. [Comput. pict.]. **VFOAT** Business Screen's Computer Pictures; Computer Pictures Magazine. Vol. 1, No. 1 (Jan./Feb. 1983)-(Jan./Feb. 1995). Periodical. English. Montage Publishing Inc., 701 Westchester Avenue, White Plains NY 10604. **Tel** (800)800-5474, (914)329-9157, FAX (914)328-9093. available on an online database (file 648/Full-Text) from DIALOG. ***Continues** Business Screen (New York, N.Y.), 0734-1911.*
Desc: Written for producers of graphic and multimedia presentations. It covers corporate graphics applications, software, input and output devices, multimedia, prepress imaging, new products and industry news developments.
Ind/Abst Acad. Search; Bus. ASAP (1990-) [Full Txt.]; Bus. Index (1985-); EP Collect.; Gen. BusinessFile (1985-); Gen. Period. Index (1985-); Homework Help.; INFO-SOUTH Abstr.; Mag. Search; MasterFile FullTEXT 1000; MasterFile FullTEXT 350; MasterFile FullTEXT 650; MasterFile FullTEXT (Jan. 1994-); OCLC; Telebase; Trade Ind. ASAP [Full Txt.]; Trade Ind. Index [Full Txt.].

US

●**COMPUTER VISION AND IMAGE UNDERSTANDING.** (1993)-. Academic Scholarly Publication. English. Six times a year. $385.00 US and Canada; $441.00 other. Academic Press Inc., 6277 Sea Harbor Drive, Orlando FL 32887. **Tel** (800)543-9534, (407)345-4100, FAX (407)352-3445. ***Continues** CVGIP: Image Understanding, 1049-9660.*

ISSN 0232-0274
XO

COMPUTERS AND ARTIFICIAL INTELLIGENCE. **See** Computers-Artificial Intelligence.

LC T385 .C595 **ISSN** 0097-8493
DD 001.55 US
CCC
CODEN COGRD2
Pr Rev.

COMPUTERS & GRAPHICS. [Comput. graph.]. **VAT** Computers and Graphics. Vol. 1 (May 1975)-. Periodical. English. Six times a year. $972.00. Pergamon Press, An Imprint of Elsevier Science Ltd., The Boulevard, Langford Lane, Kidlington, Oxford OX5 1GB United Kingdom. **Tel** 011 44 1865 843000, 011 44 1865 843699, FAX 011 44 1865 843010. **(Subscription address:** Elsevier Science Ltd. / Oxford Fulfillment Centre, PO Box 800, Kidlington OX5 1DX United Kingdom. **Tel** 011 44 865 843355.**) ED** Jose Encarnacao. available on microfilm and microfiche from University Microfilms International (UMI); available on an online database from Elsevier Electronic Subscriptions (EES). Documents available from Article Express International, The Genuine Article, Ask*IEEE.
Desc: Dedicated to the dissemination of information on the application and use of computer graphics techniques. Encourages articles on: (1) research and applications of computer graphics. Emphasis is placed on graphical man/machine interaction and the application of graphics to problem solving, (2) tutorial papers on computer graphics, (3) information on innovative uses of various graphics devices and systems.
Ind/Abst Abstr. Hum. Comput. Interact.; Bioeng. Abstr.; BMT Abstr.; CompuMath Cit. Index [Full Cov.]; Comput. Abstr.; Comput. Rev.; Curr. Cit.; Curr. Contents Eng. Comput. Technol.; Ei Page One; Eng. Index Annu.; Ergon. Abstr.; Fluid Abstr., Civil Eng.; Fluid Abstr. Proc. Eng.; FLUIDEX (1975-); GeoRef; HILITES; Inf. Sci. Abstr.; INSPEC (May 1975-); Int. Aerosp. Abstr.; Pollut. Abstr. Indexes; Res. Alert [Full Cov.]; SCISEARCH; Soc. Sci. Cit. Index [Select. Cov.]; World Publ. Monit.

US

COMPUTERS & GRAPHICS. MICROFORM. **VAT** Computers and Graphics. Vol. 1, No. 1 (May 1975)-. Periodical. English. Six times a year. University Microfilms International, 300 North Zeeb Road, Ann Arbor MI 48106-1346. **Tel** (313)761-4700, (800)521-0600 Exts. 2490, 2491, FAX (313)973-1540.

LC T385 .C665 **ISSN** 1063-7591
DD 006.6/869 US

COREL MAGAZINE. [Corel mag.]. Vol. 1, No. 1 (Apr. 1992)-. Trade Publication. English. Twelve times a year. $39.95. Ariel Communications Inc., PO Box 203550, Austin TX 78720. **Tel** (512)250-1700 (800)486-4995, FAX (512)250-1016.

LC NC998.6.G7 X993
DD 741.6 UK

●**CREATIVE TECHNOLOGY.** **See** The Arts-Graphic Arts.

LC T385 .C89 **ISSN** 1049-9652
DD 621.39/9 US
CCC
CODEN CGMPE5
TITLE CHANGE

CVGIP. GRAPHICAL MODELS AND IMAGE PROCESSING. (COMPUTER VISION, GRAPHICS, AND IMAGE PROCESSING. GRAPHICAL MODELS AND IMAGE PROCESSING.). [CVGIP, Graph. models image process.]. **VFOAT** Graphical Models and Image Processing; CVGIP. **VAT** Computer Vision, Graphics, and Image Processing. Graphical Models and Image Processing. Vol. 53, No. 1 (Jan. 1991)-(1993). Academic Scholarly Publication. English. Academic Press Inc., 6277 Sea Harbor Drive, Orlando FL 32887. **Tel** (800)543-9534, (407)345-4100, FAX (407)352-3445. **ED** Norman Badler and Rama Chellappa. Documents available from Article Express International, Ask*IEEE. ***Continues in part** Computer Vision, Graphics, and Image Processing, 0734-189X. **Continued by** Graphical Models and Image Processing.*
Desc: Focuses on the synthesis methods and computational models underlying computer-generated or processed imagery. Features original research papers, expository and review papers, and papers that embody novel concepts in applications and techniques.
Ind/Abst ACM Guide Comput. Lit. (19??-19??); Appl. Sci. Technol. Index (1991-199?); CompuMath Cit. Index (19??-19??) [Full Cov.]; Comput. Database (19??-19??); Curr. Cit.; Curr. Contents Eng. Comput. Technol. (19??-19??); Eng. Index Annu. (19??-19??); Geogr. Abstr. Phys. Geogr. (19??-19??); INSPEC (Jan. 1991-199?); Sci. Cit. Index (19??-19??); SCISEARCH (19??-19??).

LC TA1632 .C88 **ISSN** 1049-9660
DD 621.39/9 US
CCC
CODEN CIUNEJ
TITLE CHANGE

CVGIP. IMAGE UNDERSTANDING. [CVGIP, Image underst.]. **VFOAT** Computer Vision, Graphics, and Image Processing. Image Understanding; Image Understanding. Vol. 53, No. 1 (Jan. 1991)-(1993). Academic Scholarly Publication. English. Academic Press Inc., 6277 Sea Harbor Drive, Orlando FL 32887. **Tel** (800)543-9534, (407)345-4100, FAX (407)352-3445. Documents available from Article Express International, The Genuine Article, Ask*IEEE. ***Continues in part** Computer Vision, Graphics, and Image Processing, 0734-189X. **Continued by** Computer Vision and Image Understanding.*
Desc: Focus of this journal is the computer analysis of pictorial information. Publishes papers covering all aspects of image analysis from the low-level, iconic processes of early vision to the high-level, symbolic processes of recognition and interpretation. A wide range of topics in the image understanding area is covered, including papers offering insights that differ from predominant views.
Ind/Abst ACM Guide Comput. Lit.; Appl. Sci. Technol. Index (1991-); CompuMath Cit. Index [Full Cov.]; Comput. Database; Comput. Rev.; Curr. Cit.; Curr. Contents Eng. Comput. Technol.; Eng. Index Annu.; Geogr. Abstr. Phys. Geogr.; INSPEC (Jan. 1991-); Res. Alert [Full Cov.]; Sci. Cit. Index; SCISEARCH; Soc. Sci. Cit. Index [Select. Cov.].

ISSN 1053-7848
US

DALIBRARY. **Added/Corp** Association for Computing Machinery. **VFOAT** DAL; DA Library. **VAT** Design Automation Library. (1991)-. English. One time a year. $1499.00 nonmembers; $999.00 members. ACM / Association for Computing Machinery, 1515 Broadway, 17th Floor, New York NY 10036. **Tel** (212)869-7440, FAX (212)869-0481.

LC NE **ISSN** 1320-3088
DD 760 AT

●**DESIGN GRAPHICS.** **See** The Arts-Graphic Arts.

LC NK1170 .S7
DD 745.4/071/173 US

DESIGN STATEMENTS / AMERICAN CENTER FOR DESIGN. **Added/Corp** American Center for Design. (199?)-. Periodical. English. Three times a year. $25.00. American Center for Design, 233 East Ontario St. 500, Chicago IL 60611. **Tel** (312)787-2018. ***Continues** Statements (Chicago, Ill. : 1985), 1054-7746.*

LC TA **ISSN** 1066-7504
DD 620 US
CCC
CEASED

DESIGN TECHNOLOGIES. **See** Engineering-Industrial Engineering.

LC Z278 **ISSN** 1037-7603
DD 070.505 AT

DESKTOP MAGAZINE. [Deskt. mag.]. **VFOAT** Desktop. (1991)-. Periodical. English. Eleven times a year. 47.00Aus$ Australia; 85.00Aus$ New Zealand; 95.00Aus$ Papua New Guinea; 105.00Aus$ Fiji and Singapore; 120.00Aus$ other. Niche Publishing Pty Ltd., 165 Fitzroy Street, St. Kilda West 3182 Australia. **Tel** 011 61 3 5255566, FAX 011 61 3 5255627. **ED** Amanda Wise (phone: (02)310 1142). **Bk Rev. Ad Acc, Adv Mgr Tel** 03 525 5566. **Circ:** 7,500. ***Continues** Desktop Electronic Publishing and Graphics, 1036-2207.*
Desc: Magazine is geared toward the desktop publisher, graphic designer or anyone interested in producing media via desktop computer. Covers all aspects of design, pre-press, and production.

LC TK7874 .I3235a **ISSN** 1063-6757
DD 621.395 US

DIGEST OF TECHNICAL PAPERS - IEEE INTERNATIONAL CONFERENCE ON COMPUTER-AIDED DESIGN. (DIGEST OF TECHNICAL PAPERS.). [Dig. tech. papers - IEEE Int. Conf. Computer-Aided Des.]. **Added/Corp** IEEE Computer Society. IEEE Circuits and Systems Society. IEEE Electron Devices Society. Institute of Electrical and Electronics Engineers. ACM Special Interest Group on Design Automation. **VFOAT** Computer-Aided Design; ICCAD. (19??)-. English. IEEE, Institute of Electrical and Electronics Engineers Inc., 445 Hoes Lane, Piscataway NJ 08855. **Tel** (908)981-0060.
Ind/Abst Curr. Cit.

ISSN 0943-6987
GW
UDC 772 :519

DIGITAL IMAGING. [Digit. imaging]. **VFOAT** Imaging (Munchen). (1992)-. Periodical. German. Four times a year (Mar., June, Sept., Dec.). $45.45. Ringier Verlag GmbH, Gustav Heinemann Ring 212, D-81739 Munich Germany. **Tel** 011 49 89 638180. **(Subscription address:** DSB ABO Betreuung GmbH, Heiner Fleischmann Strasse 2, D-74168 Neckarsulm Germany. **Tel** 011 49 71329590.**)**

US

DIGITAL MEDIA. (19??)-. Periodical. English. Six times a year. $140.00. Euromoney Publications PLC, Nestor House, Playhouse Yard, London EC4Z 5EX United Kingdom. **Tel** 011 44 171 7798888, FAX 011 44 171 7798630, telex 290700 EUROMON G.

ISSN 1067-8506
DD 702 US
TITLE CHANGE

DIRECTORY OF ARTISTS USING SCIENCE AND TECHNOLOGY. **See** The Arts-Art.

ISSN 0840-5905
DD 338.4/0066/025 CN

DIRECTORY OF COMPUTER ANIMATION PRODUCERS. [Dir. comput. animat. prod.]. (199?)-. Directory. English. Computer Animation News People Inc, 109 Vanderhoof Avenue, Suite Two, Toronto Ontario M4G 2H7 Canada. **Tel** (416)424-4657, FAX (416)424-4617. ***Continues** International Directory of Computer Animation Producers, 0840-5905.*
Desc: A directory of computer animation and graphics production companies with listing of names and addresses. Includes a complete profile and full course data for listed schools.

IT
SUSPENDED

DISEGNO MAGAZINE. (19??)-Suspended (19??). Italian. Twelve times a year. Esse s.r.l., via Renato Serra 14, 20148 Milan Italy. **Tel** 011 39 2 39210300. **ED** Roberto Salardi. **Bk Rev. Ad Acc. Circ:** 30,000 (ctrl).
Desc: Draws in a broad sense from graphics to engineering, architecture to packaging, computer graphics and computer science.

LC HD9680 **ISSN** 1195-7778
DD 338.4/7004/0971305 CN

●**ELECTRONIC LINK MAGAZINE.** [Electron. link mag.]. **VFOAT** Link. Vol. 1, No. 1 (Apr./May 1994)-. Periodical. English. Four times a year. 27.00Can$. Applied Arts, 885 Don Mills Road Suite 324, Don Mills Ontario M3C 1V9 Canada. **Tel** (905)510-0909.

LC TA174 .E56 **ISSN** 0177-0667
DD 624 US
CCC
CODEN ENGCE7
Pr Rev.

ENGINEERING WITH COMPUTERS. **See** Engineering-Computer Applications.

ISSN 1077-0291
DD 005 US
CEASED

FBC (MADISON, ALA.). (FBC : THE VISUALIZATION NEWSLETTER.). [FbC]. (1993)-(Nov./Dec. 1995). Newsletter. English. ModelVision, 8006 Old Madison Pike, Suite 11, Madison AL 35758. **Tel** (205)461-0878, FAX (204)461-0879. **ED** Janet Hanson. **Circ:** 150. ***Continues** Flashy But Cheap, 1064-6027.*
Desc: Dedicated to Intergraph Corporation's ModelView 3D image rendering and animation software. Provides articles and tips on how to use ModelView.

ISSN 0168-874X
NE
CCC
Pr Rev.

FINITE ELEMENTS IN ANALYSIS AND DESIGN. **See** Engineering-Computer Applications.

ISSN 1064-6027
DD 005
US
TITLE CHANGE

FLASHY BUT CHEAP. [Flashy cheap]. (19??)-(199?). Periodical. English. ModelVision, 8006 Old Madison Pike, Suite 11, Madison AL 35758. **Tel** (205)461-0878, FAX (204)461-0879. **ED** Janet Hanson. **Circ:** 150. ***Continued by*** *FbC, 1077-0291.*
Desc: Dedicated to Intergraph Corporation's ModelView 3D image rendering and animation software. Provides articles and tips on how to use ModelView.

US

FULL SPECTRUM. CD-ROM. (19??)-. English. Irregular. $306.55. Alde Publishing, PO Box 39326, Minneapolis MN 55396. **Tel** (612)474-3755. **(Subscription address:** Islo Tech Inc., PO Box 39326, Edina MN 55439. **Tel** (612)474-3755.) ctrl circ.
Desc: Extensive collection of copyright-free decorative type clipart. This library of ready-to-use clip-art and quick copy-art is aimed at people interested in an addition to their CD-ROM library or desktop publishing system.

ISSN 1077-3169
US
CCC

•GRAPHICAL MODELS AND IMAGE PROCESSING. (1995)-. Academic Scholarly Publication. English. Six times a year. $288.00 US and Canada; $339.00 other. Academic Press Inc., 6277 Sea Harbor Drive, Orlando FL 32887. **Tel** (800)543-9534, (407)345-4100, FAX (407)352-3445. **(Subscription address:** Academic Press Inc., PO Box 620000, Orlando FL 32891-8340. **Tel** (800)543-9534.) ***Continues*** *GVGIP. Graphical Models and Image Processing, 1049-9652.*
Ind/Abst Curr. Cit.; Soc. Sci. Cit. Index [Select. Cov.].

ISSN 1060-5282
DD 006
US
TITLE CHANGE

HIGH COLOR. (HIGH COLOR : THE MAGAZINE OF PC GRAPHICS.). [High color]. (1992)-(1993). Periodical. English. Image Tech, 21 Elm Street 3rd Floor, Box 1347, Camden ME 04843. **Tel** (207)236-6267, FAX (207)236-6018. **ED** Lafe Lou. **Bk Rev**, (Qty: 120). **Ad Acc. Circ:** 75,000 (ctrl). ***Continued by*** *PC Graphics & Video.*

LC NC1000 .H68 ISSN 0886-0483
DD 741.6
US
CODEN HOWWEH

HOW (BETHESDA, MD.). (HOW.). [How]. Vol. 1, No. 1 (Nov./Dec. 1985)-. Periodical. English. Six times a year. $47.00. F&W Publications, 1507 Dana Avenue, Cincinnati OH 45207. **Tel** (513)531-2222, FAX (513)531-1843. **(Subscription address:** CDS Agency Hard Copy, PO Box 4966, Des Moines A 50340. **Tel** (515)247-7569.) available on microfilm from University Microfilms International (UMI).
Desc: Contains ideas and techniques in graphic design that explore the studios of art directors, production designers and computer graphics professionals. Explores the world of graphic design, including the latest in publication design. Feature articles include: production, marketplace, software review, and specifications - news of people, places and things from the world of design.
Ind/Abst Abstr. Bull. Inst. Pap. Sci. Tech.

LC T385 .I18 ISSN 0272-1716
DD 001.64/43
US
CCC
CODEN ICGADZ

Pr Rev.

IEEE COMPUTER GRAPHICS AND APPLICATIONS. [IEEE comput. graph. appl.]. **Added/Corp** IEEE Computer Society. National Computer Graphics Association (U.S.). **VFOAT** Computer Graphics and Applications. **VAT** Institute of Electrical and Electronics Engineers Computer Graphics and Applications. Vol. 1, No. 1 (Jan. 1981)-. Periodical. English. Six times a year. $265.00. IEEE / Institute of Electrical and Electronics Engineers Inc., 345 East 47th Street, New York NY 10017-2394. **Tel** (908)981-1393, FAX (908)981-9667. **(Subscription address:** IEEE / Institute of Electrical and Electronics Engineers, 445 Hoes Lane, PO Box 1331, Piscataway NJ 08855-1331. **Tel** (800)701-IEEE, (908)981-0060, FAX (908)981-9667, telex 833233.) **ED** John Staudhammer. Index available. **Bk Rev. Ad Acc. Circ:** 12,234. available on microfiche. Documents available from Article Express International, The Genuine Article, Ask*IEEE.
Desc: Provides technology transfer in business graphics, human factors in graphics system design, CAD/CAM/CAE workstations, display technology, and distributed graphics techniques.
Ind/Abst Abstr. Hum. Comput. Interact.; Appl. Sci. Technol. Index; CompuMath Cit. Index [Full Cov.]; Comput. Database; Comput. Lit. Index; Comput. Rev.; Curr. Cit.; Curr. Contents Eng. Comput. Technol.; Ei Page One; Eng. Index Annu.; Ergon. Abstr.; Expand. Acad. Index (1992-); HILITES; Index IEEE Publ.; Inf. Sci. Abstr.; INSPEC (Jan. 1981-); Int. Aerosp. Abstr.; Pollut. Abstr. Indexes; Res. Alert [Full Cov.]; Sci. Cit. Index; SCISEARCH; Soc. Sci. Cit. Index [Select. Cov.]; World Publ. Monit.

LC Q334
DD 006.6
US

•IEEE JOURNAL OF TECHNOLOGY COMPUTER AIDED DESIGN. (1996)-. English. Irregular. Free. IEEE / Institute of Electrical and Electronics Engineers Inc., 345 East 47th Street, New York NY 10017-2394. **Tel** (908)981-1393, FAX (908)981-9667. **(Subscription address:** IEEE / Institute of Electrical and Electronics Engineers, 445 Hoes Lane, PO Box 1331, Piscataway NJ 08855-1331. **Tel** (800)701-IEEE, (908)981-0060, FAX (908)981-9667, telex 833233.)
Ind/Abst INSPEC.

US

IEEE VISUALIZATION AND COMPUTER GRAPHICS. Periodical. English. Four times a year. $225.00. IEEE / Institute of Electrical and Electronics Engineers Inc., 345 East 47th Street, New York NY 10017-2394. **Tel** (908)981-1393, FAX (908)981-9667. **(Subscription address:** IEEE / Institute of Electrical and Electronics Engineers, 445 Hoes Lane, PO Box 1331, Piscataway NJ 08855-1331. **Tel** (800)701-IEEE, (908)981-0060, FAX (908)981-9667, telex 833233.) **ED** Ane E. Kaufman.
Desc: Combines the field of scientific visualization with the technologies of computer graphics, image and signal processing, computer vision, CAD and user interfaces.

LC TA1632 .I45 ISSN 0262-8856
DD 621.36/7
UK
CCC

Pr Rev.

IMAGE AND VISION COMPUTING. [Image vis. comput.]. Vol. 1, No. 1 (Feb. 1983)-. Periodical. English. Ten times a year. $637.00. Butterworth Heinemann Publishers, Linacre House Jordan Hill, Oxford OX2 8DP United Kingdom. **Tel** 011 44 1865 310366, FAX 011 44 1865 310898. **(Subscription address:** Elsevier Science Ltd. / Oxford Fulfillment Centre, PO Box 800, Kidlington OX5 1DX United Kingdom. **Tel** 011 44 865 843355.) **ED** Steve Hitchcock. Index available. **Bk Rev. Ad Acc. Circ:** 400. available on microfilm and microfiche from University Microfilms International (UMI); available on an online database from Elsevier Electronic Subscriptions (EES). Documents available from Article Express International, The Genuine Article, Ask*IEEE.
Desc: Provides communication between workers from different backgrounds involved in clarifying, analysing and processing pictures generated electronically by TV cameras, X-ray apparatus, electron microscopes, ultrasonic, sensors and thermographic equipment.
Ind/Abst Abstr. Hum. Comput. Interact.; ACM Guide Comput. Lit.; CompuMath Cit. Index [Full Cov.]; Comput. Rev.; Curr. Cit.; Curr. Contents Eng. Comput. Technol.; Ei Page One; Eng. Index Annu.; Inf. Sci. Abstr. (?-?); INSPEC (Feb. 1984-); Res. Alert [Full Cov.]; Robotics Abstr.; Sci. Cit. Index; SCISEARCH; Soc. Sci. Cit. Index [Select. Cov.]; World Publ. Monit.

ISSN 1071-0728
US

•INSIDE AUTOCAD. **Added/Corp** Cobb Group. (1993)-. Periodical. English. Twelve times a year. $99.00. Cobb Group, 9420 Bunsen Parkway #300, Louisville KY 40220. **Tel** (502)491-1900, (800)223-8720, FAX (502)491-4200.

LC QA75.5 .J6 ISSN 0387-5806
DD 004
JA
CCC

JOHO SHORI GAKKAI RONBUN SHI = TRANSACTIONS OF INFORMATION PROCESSING SOCIETY OF JAPAN. See Computers-Electronic Data Processing.

ISSN 1040-7847
DD 006
US
SUSPENDED

JOURNAL OF THEORETICAL GRAPHICS AND COMPUTING. [J. theor. graph. comput.]. (1988)-(19??). Periodical. English. Twelve times a year. $48.00 US (individuals), $96.00 US (institutions); $56.00 other (individuals), $104.00 other (institutions). Society for Theoretical and Computational Graphics, PO Box 77353, Atlanta GA 30357-7353.

LC P93.5 .J68 ISSN 1047-3203
DD 302.23
US
CCC
CODEN JVCRE7

JOURNAL OF VISUAL COMMUNICATION AND IMAGE REPRESENTATION. [J. vis. commun. image represent.]. **VFOAT** Visual Communication and Image Representation. Vol. 1, No. 1 (Sept. 1990)-. Academic Scholarly Publication. English. Four times a year. $210.00. Academic Press Inc., 6277 Sea Harbor Drive, Orlando FL 32887. **Tel** (800)543-9534, (407)345-4100, FAX (407)352-3445. **ED** Yehoshua Y. Zeevi and T. Russell Hsing. Documents available from Ask*IEEE.
Desc: Publishes papers on the state-of-the-art of visual communication and image representation with emphasis on novel technologies and theoretical work. The field of visual communication and image representation is considered in its broadest sense and covers both digital and analog aspects as well as processing and communication in biological visual systems.
Ind/Abst Curr. Cit.; Ei Page One; INSPEC (Sept. 1990-).

LC TR897.5 .J68 ISSN 1049-8907
DD 006.6
UK
CCC
CODEN JVCAEO

JOURNAL OF VISUALIZATION AND COMPUTER ANIMATION, THE. [J. vis. comput. animat.]. Vol. 1, Issue 1 (Aug. 1990)-. Periodical. English. Four times a year (Jan., Apr., July, Oct.). $425.00. John Wiley & Sons Ltd., Baffins Lane, Chichester, West Sussex PO19 1UD United Kingdom. **Tel** 011 44 1243 779777, FAX 011 44 1243 776128 BTG:JWP001, telex 86290 WIBOOKG. **(Subscription address:** John Wiley & Sons, Inc. / Philadelphia, PO Box 7247, Philadelphia PA 19170. **Tel** (212)850-6645, (800)225-5945.) **ED** N. M. Thalmann and D. Thalmann. available on microfilm and microfiche from University Microfilms International (UMI). Documents available from Ask*IEEE.
Desc: Publishes research papers on the technological developments, both hardware and software, that will make animation tools more accessible to end-users.
Ind/Abst Curr. Cit.; HILITES; INSPEC (Aug. 1990-).

LC TS155.6 .K49 ISSN 1064-2145
DD 670/.285
US
CODEN KESOE4

KEY SOLUTIONS. [Key solut.]. **Added/Corp** Valve Engineering Associates. Vol. 1, No. 1 (Sept./Oct. 1992)-. Periodical. English. Ten times a year. $29.95. Value Engineering Assoicates, PO Box 11978, Spokane WA 99211. **Tel** (509)928-5169.

ISSN 1076-7819
DD 004
US

LIGHTWAVEPRO (SUNNYVALE, CALIF.). (LIGHTWAVEPRO.). [Lightwavepro]. (199?)-. Periodical. English. Twelve times a year. $72.00. AVID Publications, 273 North Mathilda Avenue, Sunnyvale CA 94086. **Tel** (408)774-6770, FAX (408)774-6783.

IT
SUSPENDED

LIST : PROGRAMMI PER IL TUO HOME COMPUTER. See Computers-Programs and Programming.

ISSN 1059-4132
DD 004
US

MACARTIST (SANTA ANA, CALIF.). (MACARTIST : THE NEWSLETTER FOR MACINTOSH ARTISTS.). [MacArtist]. (199?)-. Newsletter. English. Twelve times a year. $47.97. MacArtist, 8146 SW Hall Boulevard R16, Beaverton OR 97008.

LC T385 .M3647 ISSN 8756-0690
DD 006.6/025
US

MARQUIS WHO'S WHO DIRECTORY OF COMPUTER GRAPHICS. [Marquis who's who dir. comput. graph.]. **VFOAT** Who's Who Directory of Computer Graphics. 1st Ed. (1984)-. Directory. English. Marquis Who's Who, A Reed Reference Publishing Company, Part of Reed International PLC, 121 Chanlon Road, New Providence NJ 07974. **Tel** (908)464-6800, (800)521-8110, FAX (908)665-6688, telex 138 755.

US
CODEN MCNREU

MCN. **VFOAT** MicroCAD News. Vol. 6, No. 1 (Jan. 1991)-. Periodical. English. Twelve times a year. OmRay Inc., PO Box 203550, Austin TX 78720-3550. **Tel** (512)250-1700, FAX (512)250-1016. Documents available from Ask*IEEE. ***Continues*** *MicroCAD News, 0895-4151.*
Ind/Abst INSPEC (Jan. 1991-).

ISSN 0883-9808
DD 686
US

MICROGRAPHICS NEWSLETTER. See Computers.

LC P93.5 .N49 ISSN 1063-6471
DD 700/.28
US

NEW MEDIA SHOWCASE. (NEW MEDIA SHOWCASE : THE DIGITAL SOURCEBOOK.). [New media showc.]. **Added/Corp** American Showcase, Inc. (1991)-. English. One time a year. $35.00. American Showcase, 915 Broadway, 14th Floor, New York NY 10010. **Tel** (212)673-6600, FAX (212)673-9795, telex 880356 AMSHOW P.
Desc: Includes articles on digital technology and its related fields. Also lists names, addresses and telephone numbers of professionals working in these fields.

ISSN 0912-1609
DD 001.64
JA

NIKKEI CG. [Nikkei CG]. **VFOAT** Nikkei Computer Graphics. (1986)-. Trade Publication. Japanese. Twelve times a year. ¥12600. Nihon Keizai Shimbun Inc., 9-5 Otemachi 1 Chome, Chiyoda-ku Tokyo 100 Japan. **Tel** 011 81 3 32700251, 011 81 3 52108502 (Nikkei Business Publications Inc.), FAX 011 81 3 52552661, 011 81 3 52108119 (Nikkei Business Publications Inc.). **ED** Shigeru Ishii. **Circ:** 20,000.

ISSN 1056-6023
DD 686 US
Pr Rev.
PAGE (CHICAGO, ILL.), THE. See Computers-Desktop Publishing.

LC T385 .P383 **ISSN** 1077-5862
DD 006.6/05 US
•PC GRAPHICS & VIDEO. [PC graph. video]. **VFOAT** PC Graphics and Video. Vol. 3, No. 1 (Jan./Feb. 1994)-. Periodical. English. Twelve times a year. $29.95. Advanstar Communications Inc., 131 West First Street, Duluth MN 55802. **Tel** (218)723-9477, (800)346-0085, FAX (218)723-9437. **(Subscription address:** Advanstar Communications / New Jersey, PO Box 7683, Riverton NJ 08077. **Tel** (800)9496525, (503)343-1200.) **ED** Lafe Lou. **Bk Rev**, (Qty: 120). **Ad Acc**. **Circ:** 75,000 (ctrl). ***Continues*** *High Color, 1060-5282.*
Desc: Features applications for electronic business presentations, color desktop publishing, multimedia, animation, and computer graphic arts.

ISSN 1065-156X
DD 006 US
PC GRAPHICS REPORT, THE. (THE PC GRAPHICS REPORT : THE JPA NEWSLETTER ON DESKTOP GRAPHICS.). [PC graph. rep.]. **Added/Corp** Jon Peddie Associates. **VFOAT** JPA Graphics Report; JPA PC Graphics Report. **VAT** Jon Peddie Associates Graphics Report; Jon Peddie Associates PC Graphics Report. (19??)-. Periodical. English. Fifty times a year. $2300.00. Jon Peddie Associates, 6201 Ascot Drive, Oakland CA 94920. **Tel** (415)435-1775.

ISSN 0392-8217
IT
UDC 681.3
PIXEL. [Pixel]. (1980)-. Periodical. Italian. Ten times a year. L81750. Editrice Il Rostro Sas, 6A Via Monte Generoso, 20155 Milan Italy. **Tel** 011 39 2 39217306, 39262186.
Ind/Abst Curr. Cit.

ISSN 0835-8095
DD 778.5/2345/0285 CN
CEASED
PIXEL (TORONTO). (PIXEL : THE COMPUTER ANIMATION NEWSLETTER.). [Pixel]. **VFOAT** Computer Animation Newsletter. Vol. 1, No. 1 (Apr. 6, 1984)-(199?). Newsletter. English. Computer Animation News People Inc, 109 Vanderhoof Avenue, Suite Two, Toronto Ontario M4G 2H7 Canada. **Tel** (416)424-4657, FAX (416)424-4617. **ED** Robi Roncarelli. Index available (bound in last issue). cum. index. **Bk Rev**.
Desc: A monthly consultation with a computer animation expert filled with market information, and knowledge of the industry.

LC T385 .P528
DD 006.6/05 FR
PIXEL VISION. No. 1 (1990)-. Trade Publication. English. Five times a year. $35.00. Pixel, 71 rue Maubeuge, 75010 Paris France. **Tel** 011 33 1 48786090. **(Subscription address:** Zoom Pixel / US Subscriptions, PO Box 1138, Madison Square Station, New York NY 10159. **Tel** (212)481-3398, (212)431-6054.)

LC T385 .P58 **ISSN** 1049-8052
DD 001 US
CODEN PIXLEZ
SUSPENDED
PIXEL (WATSONVILLE, CALIF.). (PIXEL : THE MAGAZINE OF SCIENTIFIC VISUALIZATION.). [Pixel]. Vol. 1, No. 1 (Jan./Feb. 1990)-Suspended (19??). Trade Publication. English. Six times a year. $42.00. Pixel Communications Inc., Box 12715, Research Triangle Park NC 27709-2715. **Tel** (718)624-3386.
Ind/Abst ACM Guide Comput. Lit.; Comput. Rev.

US
PROCEEDINGS / ... ANNUAL WORKSHOP ON INTERACTIVE COMPUTING, CAD/CAM, ELECTRICAL ENGINEERING EDUCATION. See Engineering-Electrical Engineering.

LC TA174 .D46a
DD 624 US
•PROCEEDINGS / DESIGN AUTOMATION CONFERENCE. See Engineering-Computer Applications.

LC QA76.9.I58 C35a **ISSN** 0713-5424
DD 006.6 CN
CCC
PROCEEDINGS - GRAPHICS INTERFACE. (PROCEEDINGS / GRAPHICS INTERFACE / COMPTES RENDUS / INTERFACE GRAPHIQUE.). [Proc. - Graph. Interface]. **Added/Corp** National Research Council Canada. Canadian Information Processing Society. Canadian Man-Computer Communications Society. National Computer Graphics Association of Canada. Computer Graphics Society. Ecole des Hautes etudes Commerciales (Montreal, Quebec) Canadian Image Processing and Pattern Recognition Society. Canadian Society for Computational Studies of Intelligence. SIGGRAPH. **VFOAT** Comptes Rendus Interface Graphique; Graphics Interface. **VAT** Comptes Rendus - Interface Graphique. (1982)-. Proceedings. English (French). One time a year. 40.01Can$. Canadian Information Processing Society, 430 King Street West, Suite 106, Toronto Ontario M5V 1L5 Canada. **Tel** (416)593-4040, FAX (416)593-5184. Documents available from Article Express International. ***Continues*** *Canadian Man-Computer Communications Conference. Proceedings of the ... Canadian Man-Computer Communications Conference, 0228-4022.*
Ind/Abst ACM Guide Comput. Lit.; Curr. Cit.; Eng. Index Annu.

LC T385 .N372A **ISSN** 0732-8028
DD 006.6 US
PROCEEDINGS OF THE ... ANNUAL CONFERENCE AND EXPOSITION OF THE NATIONAL COMPUTER GRAPHICS ASSOCIATION, INC. [Proc. annu. conf. expos. Natl. Comput. Graph. Assoc.]. **Main/Conf** National Computer Graphics Association (U.S.). **Main/Corp** National Computer Graphics Association (US). Conference and Exposition. **VFOAT** N.C.G.A. Conference Proceedings; NCGA ... Conference Proceedings; Conference Proceedings. (1981)-. Proceedings. English. One time a year. $55.00 (per vol.), $150.00 (full set). National Computer Graphics Association, 2722 Merrilee Drive/#200, Fairfax VA 22031. **Tel** (703)698-9600, telex 510 601 1247 NCGA UQ. ctrl circ. ***Continues*** *Proceedings of the ... Conference of the National Computer Graphics Association, 0278-0615.*
Desc: Published tutorials and technical sessions from national conference.

ISSN 1171-8897
DD 745.4099305 NZ
PRODESIGN AUCKLAND. (PRODESIGN.). [Prodesign Auckl.]. **VFOAT** Design; Pro Design. (1992)-. Periodical. English. Six times a year. $34.38. Associated Group Media Ltd, Private Bag 99915, Newmarket, Auckland 1031 New Zealand. **Tel** 11 64 9 3795393, FAX 11 64 9 3089523, telex 79121057.

ISSN 1048-8863
DD 006 US
CEASED
QUARKXPRESS IN-DEPTH. [QuarkXPress in-depth]. **VFOAT** Quark XPress In-Depth; In-Depth. (1990)-(Aug. 1993). Periodical. English. Mindcraft Publishing Corp, 52 Domino Drive, Concord MA 01742. **Tel** (508)371-1660. **ED** Matt Laurence.

LC Q334 **ISSN** 1064-5004
DD 006 US
REAL TIME GRAPHICS. [Real time graph.]. Vol. 1, No. 1 (July 1992)-. Periodical. English. Ten times a year. $185.00. Computer Graphics Systems Development, 2483 Old Middlefield Way #140, Mountain View CA 94043. **Tel** (415)903-4920, FAX (415)967-5252. **ED** Roy W. Latham (Editor's telephone: (415)903-4922). Index available. cum. index (Once a year). **Bk Rev**, (Qty: 2-3). **Ad Acc**, **Adv Mgr:** L. Adams, **Tel** (415)903-4924. **Circ:** 500.

LC T385 .S53 **ISSN** 1057-7041
DD 004.165 US
SILICON GRAPHICS WORLD. [Silicon graph.]. Vol. 1, No. 1 (July/Aug. 1991)-. Periodical. English. Twelve times a year. $45.00. Publications & Communications, 12416 Hymeadow Drive, Austin TX 78750. **Tel** (512)250-9023, (800)678-9724, FAX (512)331-3900, telex 384303.
Desc: Providing news covering the Silicon Graphics computer system line. Includes user profiles and technical articles.

ISSN 1055-2774
DD 621 US
STEP-BY-STEP ELECTRONIC DESIGN. [Step step electron. des.]. **VFOAT** Step by Step Electronic Design; Electronic Design. (1989)-. Periodical. English. Twelve times a year. $48.00. Dynamic Graphics Inc., 6000 North Forest Park Drive, Peoria IL 61614. **Tel** (800)255-8800, FAX (309)688-5873. **(Subscription address:** Dynamic Graphics Inc., PO Box 1901, Peoria IL 61656. **Tel** (309)688-8800, 800-255-8800.)
Ind/Abst Abstr. Bull. Inst. Pap. Sci. Tech.

ISSN 0886-7682
DD 760 US
CODEN SSGRE3
STEP-BY-STEP GRAPHICS. See The Arts-Graphic Arts.

LC NC997 **ISSN** 1202-0249
DD 741.6 CN
STUDIO (REXDALE). See The Arts-Graphic Arts.

LC NE
DD 760 IT
SUSPENDED
UOVO DI COLOMBO. See The Arts-Graphic Arts.

ISSN 1075-8704
DD 791 US
VIDEO TOASTER USER. See Communications-Video.

ISSN 0247-4352
FR
UDC 621.39 **CCC**
VIDEOTEX PARIS. [Videotex Paris]. (1980)-. Periodical. French. Thirty times a year. $721.78. A Jour, 11 rue du Marche St. Honore, 75001 Paris France. **Tel** 011 33 1 44553849.

LC T385 .V57 **ISSN** 0178-2789
DD 006.6/05 GW
CCC
CODEN VICOE5
VISUAL COMPUTER, THE. [Vis. comput.]. **Added/Corp** Computer Graphics Society. Vol. 1, No. 1 (July 1985)-. Periodical. English. Ten times a year. $767.00. Springer-Verlag GmbH & Company KG, Heidelberger Platz 3, D-14197 Berlin Germany. **Tel** 011 49 30 8207223, FAX 011 49 30 8214091, telex 183 319 SPBLN D. **(Subscription address:** Springer-Verlag New York Inc. / North America, PO Box 2485, Journal Fulfillment, Secaucus NJ 07096. **Tel** (201)348-4033, (800)777-4643, FAX (201)348-4505.) **ED** T L Kunii. available on microfilm and microfiche from University Microfilms International (UMI). Documents available from Article Express International, Ask*IEEE.
Desc: Dedicated to reporting on state-of-the-art technology in the fields of computer vision, graphics, and imaging with specific focus on applications.
Ind/Abst ACM Guide Comput. Lit.; Comput. Rev.; Curr. Cit.; Ei Page One; Eng. Index Annu.; Inf. Sci. Abstr.; INSPEC (1986-); Zentralbl. Math. Ihre Grenzgeb.

LC NC998.6.G7 X993
DD 741.6 UK
TITLE CHANGE
XYZ DESIGN & DIRECTION. See The Arts-Graphic Arts.

COMPUTER INDUSTRY AND INDUSTRY DIRECTORIES

ISSN 0299-5948
FR
01 INFORMATIQUE. ANNUAIRE. VFOAT Zero un Informatique. 1987-. French. One time a year. 01 Informatique, 5 place du Colonel-Fabien, F-75491 Paris Cedex 10 France. ***Continues*** *01 Digest (Edition France), 0246-697X.*

LC HD9696.C63 F715 **ISSN** 0997-654X
DD 338.4/7004/096605 FR
01 REFERENCES (PARIS). (01 REFERENCES.). **VFOAT** Zero un References. No. 1 (Feb 1989)-. Periodical. French. 01 Informatique, 5 place du Colonel-Fabien, F-75491 Paris Cedex 10 France. ***Continues*** *01 Informatique Magazine, 0985-2999.*
Ind/Abst Repere (1989-).

LC HE8461 .A37 **ISSN** 1053-2897
DD 302.2/096/05 US
AFRICA COMMUNICATIONS. See Communications.

LC HF5415.5 .F53 **ISSN** 1049-2135
DD 658.8/12 US
AFSM INTERNATIONAL. (AFSM INTERNATIONAL : JOURNAL.). [AFSM Int.]. **Added/Corp** AFSM International (Organization). **VFOAT** AFSMI Journal; Field Service Manager. (198?)-. Periodical. English. Twelve times a year. $65.00. AFSM International, 1342 Colonial Boulevard, Suite 25, Fort Myers FL 33907. **Tel** (813)275-7887. **ED** Leonard Mafrica. **Bk Rev**. **Ad Acc**. **Circ:** 6,000 (ctrl). available on microfilm from University Microfilms International (UMI). ***Continues*** *Field Service Manager, 0199-8889.*
Desc: Professional journal for the executives and managers of the high technology service industry.

LC HD9696.C6 A45 **ISSN** 1050-0367
DD 338 US
ALLIANCE ALERT. ELECTRONICS/COMPUTER HARDWARE / INDUSTRIAL AUTOMATION. [Alliance alert, Electron./comput. hardw./ind. autom.]. **VFOAT** Electronics/Computer Hardware/Industrial Automation; Electronics, Computer Hardware, Industrial Automation. Vol. 1, Issue 1 (Apr. 1990)-. Periodical. English. Four times a year. $395.00 (1 industry), $635.00 (2 industries), $855.00 (3 industries), $975.00 (4 industries), $1095.00 (5 industries). Securities Data Company, 40 West 57th Street, 11th Floor, New York NY 10019. **Tel** (212)765-5311. available on an online database (files 16,636/Full-Text) from DIALOG.
Ind/Abst PROMT [Full Txt.]; PTS Newsl. Database [Full Txt.].

LC HD9696.C6 A455 **ISSN** 1053-0665
DD 338.7/61004/02573 US
ALLIANCE ALERT. SOFTWARE / INFORMATION SERVICES. [Alliance alert, Softw./inf. serv.]. **VFOAT** Software/Information Services.; Software, Information Services. Vol. 1, Issue 1 (Apr. 1990)-. Periodical. English. Four times a year. $395.00 (1

industry), $635.00 (2 industries), $855.00 (3 industries), $975.00 (4 industries), $1095.00 (5 industries). Securities Data Company, 40 West 57th Street, 11th Floor, New York NY 10019. **Tel** (212)765-5311. available on an online database (files 16,636/Full-Text) from DIALOG. **Ind/Abst** PROMT [Full Txt.]; PTS Newsl. Database [Full Txt.].

LC HD9696.C6 A85A **ISSN** 0098-8324
DD 338.4/7/621381950973 US

ANNUAL ADAPSO INDUSTRY REPORT. **Main/Corp** Association of Data Processing Service Organizations. **VFOAT** Computer Services Industry. **VAT** Annual Association of Data Processing Service Organizations Industry Report. English. One time a year. Quantum Science Corporation, 245 Park Avenue, New York NY 10017.

LC HD9696.C64 M365A **ISSN** 0715-6758
DD 354.71270071 CN

ANNUAL REPORT / MANITOBA DATA SERVICES. [Annu. rep. - Manit. Data Serv.]. **Main/Corp** Manitoba Data Services. 1976/77-. English. One time a year. Free. Manitoba Data Services, 215 Garry Street/10th Floor, Winnipeg Manitoba R3C 3P3 Canada.

LC HD9696.C64 S27A **ISSN** 0703-4849
DD 338.7/61/0016 CN

ANNUAL REPORT OF THE SASKATCHEWAN COMPUTER UTILITY CORPORATION OF THE PROVINCE OF SASKATCHEWAN. **Main/Corp** Saskatchewan Computer Utility Corporation. 1973-. Periodical. English. One time a year. Saskatchewan Computer Utility Corporation, 400 Campion College Building, Regina Campus, Regina Saskatchewan S4S 0A2 Canada.

LC QA75 **ISSN** 0950-5075
DD 004.09536 UK

ARABIAN COMPUTER NEWS. [Arab. comput. news]. (1986)-. Periodical. English. Ten times a year. $102.67. Information Technology Publishing Company, Angus House, 13 Tilehouse Street HITC, Hertfordshire SG5 2DU United Kingdom. **Tel** 011 44 1462 420785, FAX 011 44 1462 420786. **ED** M. Bayman. **Bk Rev.** **Ad Acc.** ctrl circ. available via Internet (acn@rhillc.demon.co.uk).
Desc: Covers business and technology involved in the computer industry of the Middle East.

ISSN 0129-5896
DD 338.4762138195 SI

ASIA COMPUTER WEEKLY. [Asia comput. wkly.]. (1979)-. Newspaper. English. One time a week. $199.00. Asian Business Press Pte Ltd, PO Box 219, 9118 Singapore Singapore. **Tel** 011 65 2943366. **ED** Eileen Lian, Singapore 294-3366. **Bk Rev.** **Ad Acc, Adv Mgr:** Jeff Chua, **Tel** 294-3366. **Circ:** 20 000 (ctrl).
Desc: Computer industry newspaper serving Hong Kong, Singapore, Taiwan, Korea, Thailand, Philippines, Indonesia, Malaysia, Vietnam and China.
Ind/Abst J. Ferrocement.

LC QA75.5 .A73
DD 004 HK

ASIAN COMPUTER DIRECTORY. **See** Computers-Electronic Data Processing.

LC HD9696.C63 A823 **ISSN** 0254-5586
DD 338.4/700164/095 HK

ASIAN SOURCES COMPUTER PRODUCTS. [Asian sources comput. prod.]. **VFOAT** Computer Products. (1983)-. Periodical. English. Twelve times a year. $85.00. Trade Media Ltd / Hong Kong, GPO Box 11411, Hong Kong Hong Kong. **Tel** 011 852 25554777, FAX 011 852 28700637. **Ad Acc.** ctrl circ. Documents available from Ask*IEEE.
Desc: Provides coverage of the Asian computer scene. Editorial reports on emerging technologies, plus over 350 product advertisements each month from manufacturers dealing with the computer industry.
Ind/Abst INSPEC (June 1983-Dec. 1986).

LC HD9696.C63 **ISSN** 0731-9304
DD 338.4/700164/0973 US

AUERBACH REPORTER. [Auerbach report.]. **VFOAT** Reporter. (19??)-. Periodical. English. Twelve times a year. Auerbach Publishers Inc., Park Square Building, 31 St. James Avenue, Boston MA 02116. **Tel** (800)950-1207.

ISSN 8756-0046
DD 004 US

BAY AREA COMPUTER CURRENTS. [Bay area comput. curr.]. **VFOAT** Computer Currents. (198?)-. Periodical. English. Twenty-five times a year. $29.95. Computer Currents, 5720 Hollis Street, Emeryville CA 94608. **Tel** (415)547-6800, (800)365-7773, FAX (415)547-4613. **ED** Miriam Liekin. Index available ($2.00). ***Continues** Bay Area Computer Classifieds.*
Desc: Industry news local features, informative reviews, helpful tips and up-to-date computer prices.

ISSN 0897-9324
DD 004 US

BOSTON COMPUTER CURRENTS. [Boston comput. curr.]. **VFOAT** Computer Currents. Vol. 2, No. 8 (Aug. 1987)-. Periodical. English. Twelve times a year. $19.95. Computer Currents, 5720 Hollis Street, Emeryville CA 94608. **Tel** (415)547-6800, (800)365-7773, FAX (415)547-4613. ***Absorbed** Boston Computer News.*
Desc: Industry news, local features, informative reviews, helpful tips and up-to-date computer prices.

LC HD9696.C63 F725
DD 338.47621381 FR

BOTTIN INFORMATIQUE. **Added/Corp** Didot-Bottin (Firm). 1987-. French. One time a year. Societe Didot-Bottin, 28 rue du Docteur-Finlay, 75738 Paris Cedex 15 France.

UK

BRITAIN'S COMPUTER INDUSTRY. Trade Publication. English. One time a year. Jordan Publishing Ltd., 21 St. Thomas Street, Bristol BS1 6JS United Kingdom. **Tel** 011 44 117 9230600, FAX 011 44 117 230063, telex 499119. **Ad Acc.** available on diskette.
Desc: Overview of industry, financial and marketing information of top UK companies.

ISSN 0847-4362
DD 338.4/700416/0971 CN
CEASED

BUSINESS COMPUTER RESELLER NEWS. [Bus. comput. resell. news]. **VFOAT** Business Computer News. Vol. 1, No. 1 (Dec. 11, 1989)-(19??). Periodical. English. Moorshead Magazines Ltd., 10 Gateway Boulevard, Suite 490, North York Ontario M3C 3T4 Canada. **Tel** (416)696-5488, FAX (416)696-7395.

LC HF5001 .B837 **ISSN** 8756-9639
DD 001.55/05 US

BUSINESS MEDIA WEEK. **See** Business and Economics.

ISSN 0315-1417
DD 001.4/24/06271 CN

C O R S BULLETIN. **Main/Corp** Canadian Operational Research Society. **VFOAT** Bulletin S C R O. **VAT** SCRO. Bulletin. (July 1971)-. Bulletin. English (French). Four times a year. 45.00Can$ membership rate (available to members only). Canadian Operational Research Society, PO Box 2225 Postal Station D, Ottawa Ontario K1P 5W4 Canada. **Tel** (613)992-4079. **ED** Karen Elliot. **Ad Acc. Circ:** 600 (ctrl). ***Supersedes** Canadian Operational Research Society. Bulletin, 0319-6178.*
Desc: General descriptive articles or announcements on competitions for awards and prizes, announcements of annual conference or news items, and list of meetings of various societies.

ISSN 0731-079X
US

CACHE REGISTER, THE. (THE CACHE REGISTER / CHICAGO AREA COMPUTER HOBBYIST EXCHANGE.). **VAT** Chicago Area Computer Hobbyist Exchange Register. Periodical. English. Twelve times a year. $20.00 (membership). CACHE Register, 1744 W Devon, Chicago IL 60660. **Tel** (708)470-1664. **(Subscription address:** Chicago Area Computer Hobbyist Exchange, 117 West Harrison Street, Suite 640-C176, Chicago IL 60605. **)** **ED** Kevin Bryson. **Bk Rev.** **Ad Acc. Circ:** 250 (ctrl).
Desc: Newsletter for members of CACHE (Chicago Area Computer Hobbyists' Exchange). Reviews, articles, meeting notices, humor, tutorials, editorials, software previews and reviews.

DD 001.6/4/05 CN

CANADIAN DATASYSTEMS. REFERENCE MANUAL. 5th- 1975-. English. One time a year. $30.00. Maclean Hunter Canada / Montreal, 1001 bvd. de Maisonneuve W., Montreal Quebec H3A 3E1 Canada. **Tel** (514)845-5141, FAX (514)845-4302, telex 055-60604. ***Continues** Canadian Computer Reference Manual.*
Desc: A buyers' guide featuring key information on Canadian EDP organizations, trade names of products, services offered by suppliers, and range of EDP products available.

US
CEASED

CASE BUYERS GUIDE. (19??)-(19??). English. CASE Consulting Group Inc, 11830 Southwest Kerr Parkway, Suite 315, Lake Oswego OR 97035. **Tel** (503)245-6880, FAX 503 245-6935. ***Continues** CASE Industry Directory.*

ISSN 0893-4843
DD 338 US
CCC

CD COMPUTING NEWS. **See** Computers-Optical Storage, CD-ROM Applications.

LC HD9696.O67 C377 **ISSN** 1047-966X
DD 338.4/76213976 US
CEASED

CD-ROM MARKET PLACE. [CD-ROM mark. place]. **VFOAT** CD ROM Market Place. (1991)-(1994). Directory. English. Mecklermedia Corporation, 11 Ferry Lane West, Westport CT 06880. **Tel** (203)226-6967, (800)632-5537, FAX (203)454-5840. Index available. **Ad Acc. Circ:** 2,000.
Desc: A directory of all CD-ROM publishers, international in scope.

LC HD9696.O67 C38 **ISSN** 1048-406X
DD 621.39/76 US
SUSPENDED

CD-ROM SHOPPERS GUIDE. **See** Computers-Optical Storage, CD-ROM Applications.

LC HD9696.C6 C46
DD 338.47621381 KO

CHONGBO SANOP. **VFOAT** Information Industry. Periodical. Korean (Korean). Six times a year. Chonguk Kyongjein Yonhaphoe, 1-124 Youido-dong, Yongdungpo-ku, Seoul South Korea.

LC HD9811.A1 I57a **ISSN** 1051-2721
DD 621.388/332/025 US

COMPLETE MEMBERSHIP DIRECTORY OF THE INTERACTIVE MULTIMEDIA ASSOCIATION, THE. [Complete membersh. dir. Interact. Multimed. Assoc.]. **Main/Corp** Interactive Multimedia Association. **VFOAT** IMA Membership Directory. (1992)-. Directory. English. One time a year. Interactive Multimedia Association, 48 Maryland Avenue, Suite 202, Annapolis MD 21401. **Tel** (410)626-1380, FAX (410)263-0590. ***Continues** Interactive Video Industry Association. Interactive Video Industry Directory, 1046-2767.*

LC QA **ISSN** 1072-3544
DD 004 US

COMPU-MART (RICHARDSON, TEX.). (COMPU-MART.). **VFOAT** Compu Mart. (1991)-. Periodical. English. One time a week. $80.00. James Publishing & Associates, 899 Presidential Drive, Suite 110, Richardson TX 75081. **Tel** (800)864-1155, FAX (214)238-1132. **ED** Sarah Klein. Index available (bound in every issue). **Ad Acc, Adv Mgr:** Jennifer Hopper, **Tel** (800)864-1155. **Circ:** 140,000 (ctrl).
Desc: Computer equipment and service for the secondary market.

LC QA76.6 .C634
DD 001.64/25/029459 HK

COMPUTER-ASIA SOFTWARE GUIDE. **See** Computers-Software.

LC HD **ISSN** 0732-8346
DD 338 US
CCC

COMPUTER BUSINESS (LOS ANGELES, CALIF.). **See** Computers-Abstracting, Bibliographies and Statistics.

LC QA76.5 .C612562 **ISSN** 0882-7818
DD 001.64 US

COMPUTER BUYING GUIDE. **See** Computers-Microcomputers, Personal Computers.

ISSN 1071-2216
DD 004 US

COMPUTER CONFERENCE ANALYSIS NEWSLETTER, THE. [Comput. conf. anal. newsl.]. **Added/Corp** Guidelines (Firm). **VFOAT** Conference Analysis Newsletter. (1989)-. Newsletter. English. Irregular. $495.00. Guidelines / Pennsylvania, 2512 Deep Creek Road, Perkiomenville PA 18074. **Tel** (215)234-4449. available on an online database (file 675/Full-Text) from DIALOG.
Desc: Covers the most important conferences, shows, meetings and symposiums in the computer industry.
Ind/Abst Bus. Source Plus; Bus. Source; Comput. ASAP [Full Txt.]; Comput. Database [Full Txt.]; EP Collect.; Homework Help.; MasterFile FullTEXT 1000; MasterFile FullTEXT 350; MasterFile FullTEXT 650; MasterFile FullTEXT; OCLC; Telebase.

UK

COMPUTER CONTRACTOR. Trade Publication. English. Twenty-six times a year. £60.00 UK; £90.00 (airmail) Europe; £70.00 (surface mail) other. VNU Business Publications BV, 32-34 Broadwick Street, London W1A 2HG United Kingdom. **Tel** 011 44 171 4394242 ext. 2222, FAX 011 44 171 4379638, telex 23918 VNU G, 8952440.

ISSN 1184-2369
DD 381.45004/0971/05 CN

COMPUTER DEALER NEWS (1990). (COMPUTER DEALER NEWS.). [Comput. deal. news]. Vol. 6, No. 21 (Oct. 1990)-. Periodical. English. Twenty-six times a year. 120.05Can$. Plesman Publications Ltd., 2005 Sheppard Avenue East, 4th Floor, Willowdale Ontario M2J 5B1 Canada. **Tel** (416)497-9562, FAX (416)497-9427. available on an online database (file 648/Full-Text) from DIALOG. ***Continues** Canadian Computer Dealer News., 0834-4612 **and** SI Business, 0849-1801.*
Ind/Abst Trade Ind. ASAP [Full Txt.]; Trade Ind. Index [Full Txt.].

ISSN 1193-1272
DD 381 CN
COMPUTER DEALER NEWS SOURCE GUIDE. [Comput. deal. news source guide]. **VFOAT** Source Guide; CDN Source Guide. (1992)-. Trade Publication. English. $30.00. Plesman Publications Ltd., 2005 Sheppard Avenue East, 4th Floor, Willowdale Ontario M2J 5B1 Canada. **Tel** (416)497-9562, FAX (416)497-9427. ***Continues*** *Canadian Computer Dealer News Source Guide., 0842-5531.*

LC HD9696.C63 U51496 **ISSN** 0883-4881
DD 004/.029/473 US
COMPUTER (DURANGO, COLO.). (COMPUTER.). **VFOAT** Orion Computer Blue Book. English. One time a year. (call for price and availability). Orion Research Corporation, 14555 North Scottsdale Road, Suite 330, Scottsdale AZ 85260. **Tel** (800)844-0759, (602)951-1114, FAX (602)951-1117. **ED** Roger Rohrs.
Desc: Hardbound, 450-page book lists 12,250 hardware products, including systems, modems, monitors, plotters, printers, disk drives, terminals and expansion cards.

ISSN 0966-7849
DD 338.47004 UK
COMPUTER FINANCE. [Comput. financ.]. (1992)-. Periodical. English. Twelve times a year. $495.00. APT Data Services, 12 Sutton Row, 4th Floor, London W1V 5FH United Kingdom. **Tel** 011 44 171 2084200, FAX 011 44 171 4391105. ***Continues*** *IBM Futures, 0958-4579.*

LC HD9696.A1 C65 **ISSN** 0893-0791
DD 338.7/61004/02573 US
COMPUTER INDUSTRY ALMANAC. [Comput. ind. alm.]. (1987)-. Trade Publication. English. One time a year. $60.00. Computer Industry Almanac Inc., 225 Allen Way, Incline Village, Lake Tahoe NV 89451. **Tel** (702)831-2288. **ED** Egil Juliussen, Portia Isaacson and Luanne Kruse.
Desc: Insider's guide to people, companies, products and trends in the fascinating, fast-paced computer industry; lists award winners, publications, associations, users, groups, etc.

LC HD9696.C6 C6 **ISSN** 0894-6213
DD 380.1/45004021 US
CCC
COMPUTER INDUSTRY FORECASTS (1987). (COMPUTER INDUSTRY FORECASTS.). [Comput. ind. forecasts]. **Added/Corp** Data Analysis Group. 4th Quarter (1987)-. Trade Publication. English. Four times a year (Jan., April, July, Oct.). $325.00. Data Analysis Group, 3201 Hanson H Road, Box 4210, Georgetown CA 95634. **Tel** (916)333-4001, FAX (916)333-1247. **ED** Keith Parker. Index available. cum. index. available on magnetic tape (Lotus 1-2-3 Formated Disk); available on an online database from Lexis-Nexis. ***Continues*** *Computer Industry Abstracts, 0883-931X.*
Desc: Reference tool providing complete coverage of business information on computers, peripherals and software. Market data is needed for forecasting and planning the following sales and shipment forecasts, market share and installed base.
Ind/Abst Comput. Database.

ISSN 0955-2111
DD 004.0941 UK
COMPUTER INDUSTRY GUIDE. (THE COMPUTER INDUSTRY GUIDE.). [Comput. ind. guide]. (1989)-. Trade Publication. English. Two times a year (Mar. & Sept.). $77.01. KIS Publications, PO Box 1500, Bournemouth, Dorset BH3 7YB United Kingdom. **Tel** 011 44 1202 761928, FAX 011 44 1202 535278. **ED** Peter Kammerling (editors telephone: 202 529028). **Circ:** 2,000.
Desc: Provides an overview of the 17 main computer companies, including company background, financial position, marketing strategy, products & strengths/weaknesses. It also has sections on networking, open systems, UNIX companies, software houses, & abbreviations/acronyms.

LC KF390.5.C6 C63 **ISSN** 0740-1469
DD 346.7304/82 347.306482 US
COMPUTER INDUSTRY LITIGATION REPORTER. **See** Copyright, Intellectual Property.

LC HD9696.C6 C63 **ISSN** 0744-0081
DD 338.7/6100164/05 US
COMPUTER INDUSTRY UPDATE. **See** Computers-Abstracting, Bibliographies and Statistics.

LC Z286.C65 C66 **ISSN** 0740-4085
DD 381.45002 US
COMPUTER PUBLISHERS & PUBLICATIONS. [Comput. publ. publ.]. **Added/Corp** Communications Trends, Inc. **VFOAT** Computer Publishers and Publications. (1984)-. Directory. English. Irregular. $205.00. SIMBA Information Inc., 213 Danbury Road, PO Box 7430, Wilton CT 06897-7430. **Tel** (203)834-0033 ext. 173, FAX (203)884-1771. **(Subscription address:** Simba Information Inc., PO Box 7430, Wilton CT 06897. **Tel** (203)834-0033 ext. 160, FAX (203)834-1771.) **ED** Efrem Sigel and Frederica Evan.
Desc: Contains entries for more than 1,200 computer periodicals. Entries for publishers provide full name, address and phone number, contact person and key personnel, year founded, brief description, details concerning periodicals and books published, and more. Coverage includes the U.S., U.K., Canada, Australia, and other English-speaking countries.

US
CEASED
COMPUTER SOFTWARE & SERVICES REPORT. (19??)-(19??). English. Deboever and Associates, 1740 Massachusetts Avenue, Boxborough MA 01719. **Tel** (508)264-0155. ***Continues*** *Computer Services Report.*

ISSN 0010-4760
UK
CODEN COSVA3
COMPUTER SURVEY. [Comput. surv.]. Vol. 1, No. 1 (June 1962)-. Periodical. English. Six times a year. $248.13. Inn Data Ltd, PO Box 372, Wimbledon Lnd SW19 6LH United Kingdom. **Tel** 011 44 81 7802095. **ED** Georgina Dodd. **Circ:** 2,500. Documents available from Ask*IEEE.
Desc: For UK, Ireland, France, Belgium, and the Netherlands. Provides a list of computer installations, their applications, the peripheral and terminals they support, and the networks they form.
Ind/Abst Comput. Lit. Index; INSPEC (May/June 1969-).

LC HD9696.C6 C634 **ISSN** 1059-7018
DD 380.1/456213776 US
COMPUTER TAPE OUTLOOK. HALF-INCH PRODUCTS. [Comput. tape outlook, Half-inch prod.]. **Added/Corp** Freeman Associates. **VFOAT** Half-Inch Products; Computer Tape Outlook. Half Inch Products. (1991)-. English. Freeman Associates, 311 East Carrillo Street, Santa Barbara CA 93101.

LC HD9696.A963 U634 **ISSN** 0746-3405
DD 670.42/7/097305 US
COMPUTERIZED MANUFACTURING. [Comput. manuf.]. **Added/Corp** Technical Database Corp. Vol. 1, No. 1 (May/June 1983)-. Periodical. English. Ten times a year. TECSPEC, PO Box 617024, Orlando FL 32861. **Tel** (407)295-1094, FAX (407)293-4948. **ED** Philip C. Flora. **Circ:** 4,000.
Desc: Covers new products in the following areas: robotics, CAD, CAM, programmable controllers, engineering/manufacturing software, computer vision systems, industrial sensors.

LC QA75.5 .C61137
DD 338.4/7004/096 UK
•**COMPUTERS & COMMUNICATIONS IN AFRICA.** **See** Computers-Electronic Data Processing.

LC Z5640 .C648 QA76 **ISSN** 0894-8941
DD 016.004 19 004 US
COMPUTERS AND COMPUTING INFORMATION RESOURCES DIRECTORY. [Comp. comp. inf. resour. dir.]. **Added/Corp** Gale Research Company. **VFOAT** CCIRD. 1st Ed. (1987)-. Directory. English. One time a year (May). $205.00. Gale Research Inc., 835 Penobscot Building, 645 Griswold Street, Detroit MI 48226. **Tel** (800)877-GALE, (313)961-2242, FAX (313)961-6083, (800)414-5043, telex TWX 810-221-7086. **ED** Martin Connors.
Desc: Gives current data and services from over 4,000 live sources ranging from worldwide associations and user groups to consultants and research organizations.

LC HD9696.C63 G734 **ISSN** 0588-9448
DD 338.4/7/621381950941 UK
COMPUTERS (CROYDON). (COMPUTERS; AN ANNUAL SURVEY OF THE COMPUTER INDUSTRY IN BRITAIN.). Trade Publication. English. One time a year. £30.00. Digest Data Books, Park House, Park Street, Croydon Surrey United Kingdom.

LC QA76 .C5816 **ISSN** 0010-4841
DD 004 US
CCC
CODEN CMPWAB
COMPUTERWORLD (FRAMINGHAM, MASS.). (COMPUTERWORLD.). **VAT** Computer World. (1967)-. Trade Publication. English. One time a week. $48.00. CW Communications, 375 Cochituate Road, Box 9171, Framingham MA 01701. **Tel** (508)879-0700. **ED** Bill Laberis. Index available. **Ad Acc, Adv Mgr:** Kevin McPherson. **Circ:** 137,000. available in microform from University Microfilms International (UMI); available on an online database from Lexis-Nexis; and (files 15,674/Full-Text) DIALOG. Documents available from Ask*IEEE, UMI Article Clearinghouse, BLDSC, FAXON Xpress, The UnCover Company, SWETS, CASDDS.
Desc: Paid newspaper for MIS/DP and other information systems professionals who plan, evaluate, specify, acquire, implement and manage information and data/telecomm systems in business, government, education and vendor organizations. Content includes news, executive reports, editorials, commentaries, columnists, viewpoints, product spotlights and announcements and in-depth reports.
Ind/Abst ABI/INFORM Glob. Ed.; ABI/INFORM [Computer File] (May 1976-); Acad. Ind. [Computer File] (1992-); Acad. Search; Bus. Index (1985-); Comput. Bus. (19??-19??); Comput. Database; Comput. Ind. Update; Comput. Lit. Index; Data Process. Dig.; EP Collect.; Expand. Acad. Index (1992-); F&S Index Plus Text, Int. [Select. Cov.]; GATFWORLD (1984); Gen. BusinessFile (1985-); Gen. Period. Index (1985-); Homework Help.; INFO-SOUTH Abstr.; INSPEC (June 1981-); Law Office Inf. Serv.; Mag. Index Plus (1992-); Mag. Search; MasterFile FullTEXT 1000; MasterFile FullTEXT 350; MasterFile FullTEXT 650; MasterFile FullTEXT (July 1993-); Microcomput. Abstr. (Jan. 1985-); Microcomput. Ind. Update; Newsp. Period. Abstr. (1992-); OCLC; PROMT; Telebase; Trade Ind. Index (1981-); UMI ABI/Inform--Bus. Period. Ondisc [Full Txt.].

LC HD9696.C63 G733 **ISSN** 0964-4520
DD 338.47621381 UK
COMPUTING & COMMUNICATIONS DECISIONS. **Added/Corp** TechGnosis Ltd. National Computing Centre Limited. **VFOAT** Computing and Communications Decisions. (19??)-. English. One time a year. $119.79. Techgnosis Ltd., Blade House, Battersea Road, Cheshire SK4 3EA United Kingdom. **Tel** 011 44 161 4422639, FAX 011 44 161 4431162.

LC QA76.25 .C56 **ISSN** 1070-728X
DD 004/.023/73 US
•**COMPUTING AND SOFTWARE DESIGN CAREER DIRECTORY.** [Comput. softw. des. career dir.]. 1st Ed. (1993)-. Directory. English. $34.00 (hardcover), $17.95 (softcover). Gale Research Inc., 835 Penobscot Building, 645 Griswold Street, Detroit MI 48226. **Tel** (800)877-GALE, (313)961-2242, FAX (313)961-6083, (800)414-5043, telex TWX 810-221-7086.
Desc: Discusses such jobs as a Windows programmer, systems analyst, technical writer, local area network administrator and many other related specialties.

LC HD9696.C6 C64 **ISSN** 0144-3097
DD 338.4/700164/094 UK
CODEN CPTGB5
COMPUTING (LONDON. 1980). (COMPUTING.). [Computing]. **Added/Corp** British Computer Society. Vol. 8, No. 1 (Jan. 3, 1980)-. Periodical. English. One time a week. $205.35. VNU Business Publications BV, 32-34 Broadwick Street, London W1A 2HG United Kingdom. **Tel** 011 44 171 4394242 ext. 2222, FAX 011 44 171 4379638, telex 23918 VNU G, 8952440. Documents available from Ask*IEEE. ***Continues*** *Computing Europe, 0307-8965.*
Ind/Abst Abstr. Hum. Comput. Interact.; CompuMath Cit. Index [Full Cov.]; Curr. Cit.; Curr. Technol. Index; F&S Index Plus Text, Int. [Select. Cov.]; HILITES; Infomat Int. Bus.; Inf. Manage. Technol. (19??-); INSPEC (Aug. 1980-); Libr. Inf. Sci. Abstr.; PROMT; World Publ. Monit.; Zentralbl. Math. Ihre Grenzgeb.

UK
CONNECT. Issue 1 (1990)-. Periodical. English. Reed Business Publishing / West Sussex, England, Perrymount Road, Haywards Heath, West Sussex RH16 3DH United Kingdom. **Tel** 011 44 1444 441212, FAX 011 44 1444 445447.

LC QA76.6 .C72 **ISSN** 0734-3361
DD 001.64/2 US
CREATIVE COMPUTING SOFTWARE BUYER'S GUIDE. **VFOAT** Creative Computing Buyer's Guide; Software Buyer's Guide. English. One time a year. $3.95 each. AHL Computing Inc, 39 East Hanover Avenue, Morris Plains NJ 07950.

LC HD9696.C63 B73
DD 338.47621381 BL
CEASED
DADOS E IDEIAS. Vol. 1 (August/Sept. 1975)-(19??). Periodical. Portuguese. Servico Federal de Processamento de Dados, Administracao Central DSS, rua da Lapa 236 - 100, 2000 Rio de Janeiro Brazil.

LC QA76.9.D3 D26 **ISSN** 0737-951X
DD 001.64/42 US
CCC
DATA BASE ALERT. **See** Computers-Data Base Management.

LC HD9696.C63 U51592 **ISSN** 0744-1673
DD 001.64/029/473 US
DATA SOURCES. (DATA SOURCES : THE COMPREHENSIVE GUIDE TO THE INFORMATION PROCESSING INDUSTRY : EQUIPMENT, SOFTWARE, SERVICES, COMPANIES, AND PEOPLE.). [Data sources]. **Added/Corp** Ziff-Davis Publishing Company. Vol. 1, No. 1 (Autumn 1981)-. Directory. English. Two times a year (Jan. and June). $495.00. Ziff-Davis, One Park Avenue, 5th Floor, New York NY 10016. **Tel** (212)503-3500.
Desc: A directory of all software and hardware products, from micros to mainframes. For all DP buying decisions and analysis, provides information on 30,000 systems and applications software packages, 19,000 hardware and communications products, and 10,000 company profiles.

Computers —Computer Industry and Industry Directories

DD 004
ISSN 0886-2400
US CEASED
DATACOM READER SERVICE. See Computers-Abstracting, Bibliographies and Statistics.

LC TK7885.A4 D37
DD 621.3819/5/0294
ISSN 0270-9872
US
DATAGUIDE. [Dataguide]. **VAT** Data Guide. Vol. 1 (Spring 1980)-. English. Two times a year. $50.00 US; $75.00 other. Technical Publishing Company / New York, 875 3rd Avenue, New York NY 10022. **Tel** (312)635-9920.

LC HD9696.C63 S84
DD 338
SW
DATAMARKNADEN. Added/Corp Svenska Dataforeningen. (197?)-. Swedish. Svenska Dataforeningen, Ravinvagen 32 183 40 Taby, Stockholm Sweden. **Continues** Svenska Foreningens Matrikel.

ISSN 0730-8795
US CCC
DATAPRO DIRECTORY OF MICROCOMPUTER SOFTWARE. [Datapro dir. microcomput. softw.]. **Added/Corp** Datapro Research Corporation. **VFOAT** Directory of Microcomputer Software. (1981)-. Directory. English. Twelve times a year. $1008.00. Datapro Information Services Group, 600 Delran Parkway, Delran NJ 08075. **Tel** (609)764-0100, (800)328-2776, FAX (609)764-8953.

DD 004
ISSN 1055-8497
US
DATATRENDS NEWS DIGEST. [DataTrends news dig.]. **VFOAT** Data Trends News Digest. (Feb. 1991)-. Periodical. English. Twelve times a year. DataTrends Publications, 895 Harrison Street SE, Suite B, Leesburg VA 22075. **Tel** (703)779-0574, (800)766-8130, FAX (703)779-2267.

US
DECISIONS IN COMPUTER MANAGEMENT. Trade Publication. English. Twelve times a year.

DD 338.4/7004/0971
ISSN 0842-1951
CN
DIRECTION INFORMATIQUE. [Dir. inform.]. Vol. 1, No. 1 (June 1988)-. Periodical. French. Twelve times a year. 60.82Can$. Plesman Publications Ltd., 2005 Sheppard Avenue East, 4th Floor, Willowdale Ontario M2J 5B1 Canada. **Tel** (416)497-9562, FAX (416)497-9427.
Ind/Abst Can. Period. Index (Jan. 1990-); Repere (1988-1991).

LC HD9696.C63 U515948
DD 381/.45004/02573
ISSN 1066-9698
US
DIRECTORY OF COMPUTER & SOFTWARE RETAILERS (TAMPA, FLA.). (DIRECTORY OF COMPUTER & SOFTWARE RETAILERS.). [Dir. comput. softw. retail.]. **Added/Corp** Business Guides, Inc. **VFOAT** Directory of Computer and Software Retailers. (199?)-. Periodical. English. One time a year. $280.00 continental US; $290.00 other US; $305.00 other. Lebhar Friedman Inc., PO Box 31203, Tampa FL 33633. **Tel** (800)944-4676, (813)664-6707. **Continues** Directory of Computer & Software Storefront Dealers, 1067-1072.
Desc: Directory of computer and software retailers.

LC HD9696.C6 D57
DD 621.3819/58/0294
ISSN 0277-3694
US
DIRECTORY OF COMPUTER DEALERS. INTERNATIONAL EDITION. (DIRECTORY OF COMPUTER DEALERS.). [Dir. compuut. deal.]. **VFOAT** CEIB Directory of Computer Dealers. Directory. English. $12.00.

ISSN 0735-617X
US
DIRECTORY OF INDEPENDENT IBM PERSONAL COMPUTER HARDWARE AND SOFTWARE, THE. VFOAT Directory of Independent I.B.M. Personal Computer Hardware and Software. (1984)-. Directory. English. One time a year. $31.95. Infopro Inc, 6048 Edge Avenue, Be Salem PA 19020. **Tel** (215)750-1023.

LC Z5641 .D57 QA76
DD 016.00164/05
ISSN 0742-6755
US
DIRECTORY OF INFORMATION AGE NEWSLETTERS. [Dir. inf. age newsl.]. 1st Ed.-. Newsletter. English. Irregular. $95.00. Frank Communications Group, PO Box 144, Mcnt Vernon NH 03057.

LU
DIRECTORY OF PUBLIC DATABASES PRODUCED BY THE INSTITUTIONS OF THE EUROPEAN COMMUNITIES / OFFICE FOR OFFICIAL PUBLICATIONS OF THE EUROPEAN COMMUNITIES. Added/Corp Office for Official Publications of the European Communities. **VFOAT** Directory of Public Databases. (198?)-. Directory. English. Irregular. Free on request. Office for Official Publications of the European Communities, 2 rue Mercier, 2985 Luxembourg Luxembourg. **Tel** 011 352 499281, FAX 011 352 292942763.

LC TA1635 .D57
DD 004.5/6
ISSN 1052-4053
US SUSPENDED
DISC. (DISC MAGAZINE.). [DISC mag.]. (1990)-Suspended (199?). Periodical. English. Twelve times a year. Helgerson Associates, 7 Cottonwood Lane, Hilton Head Island SC 29926. **ED** Linda W. Helgerson. **Bk Rev. Ad Acc. Circ:** 5,000 (ctrl). available on CD-ROM.
Desc: A technical publication for producers and suppliers of CD-ROM products and services.

DD 384
ISSN 0894-9212
US CCC
EDI NEWS. [EDI news]. **Added/Corp** Phillips Publishing. **VAT** Electronic Data Interchange News. Vol. 1, No. 1 (Sept. 1987)-. Periodical. English. Twenty-five times a year. $597.00. Phillips Business Information Inc., 1201 Seven Locks Road, PO Box 61130, Potomac MD 20854. **Tel** (301)424-3338, (301)340-1520, (800)777-5005, FAX (301)424-4297, telex 358149. **ED** Lane Cooper and Susan Aluise. **Bk Rev.** available on an online database from NEXIS; and (file 636/Full-Text) DIALOG. **Absorbed** Electronic Trade and Transport News; Just in Time / Quick Response News; EDI Executive.
Desc: Reports on developments in the electronic data interchange (EDI) arena. Covers user, vendor, and standard issues both nationally and internationally. Uses surveys of market developments, user case studies, product profiles, and reports on standard updates and related issues.
Ind/Abst PTS Newsl. Database [Full Txt.].

UDC 05
US
EDI YELLOW PAGES INTERNATIONAL. (19??)-. Directory. English. One time a year. Phillips Business Information Inc., 1201 Seven Locks Road, PO Box 61130, Potomac MD 20854. **Tel** (301)424-3338, (301)340-1520, (800)777-5005, FAX (301)424-4297, telex 358149. **ED** Anna Lee Payne. **Ad Acc. Circ:** 33,000 (ctrl). available on diskette. **Absorbed in part by** EDI Directory.
Desc: Directory listing users and service providers in the field of electronic data interchange, worldwide. Also a source on E01, a calendar of events and tips on implementation.

US
EDP WEEKLY. VFOAT Computer Age--EDP Weekly. Vol. 28, No. 1 (Jan. 5, 1987)-. Periodical. English. One time a week. $495.00. Millin Publishing Group Inc., 714 Church Street, Alexandria VA 22314. **Tel** (703)739-8500. **ED** Charles Bailey, Mike Cotter and Terry Miller. **Bk Rev,** (Qty: 10). **Circ:** 1,000. available on an online database, CD-ROM, magnetic tape, and microfilm from University Microfilms International (UMI); available on an online database from Information Access Company. **Continues** Computer Age. EDP Weekly; **Absorbed** Data/Comm Industry Report, 0149-9556; The Robotics Report, 0889-5759.
Desc: The nation's oldest independent computer publication, reports industry-wide corporate and governmental announcements, developments and strategies, with special features on mini and micro computers, data/comm, robotics, electronic funds transfer, and world trade.
Ind/Abst Comput. Lit. Index; Comput. Rev.

LC TD173.5 .E59
DD 628/.0285/536
ISSN 1043-9056
US
ENVIRONMENTAL SOFTWARE DIRECTORY. See Environmental Issues-Computer Applications.

SP
Pr Rev. SUSPENDED
EUROPEAN MAC PROFESSIONAL. (Feb. 1990)-(199?). Spanish (French). Twelve times a year. 7200ptas. European Macintosh, Jose Ortega u Gasset 21-30, 28006 Madrid Spain. **Tel** (34) 1 4350010, telex 4316312. Index available. cum. index. **Bk Rev. Ad Acc. Desc:** Information on the Macintosh market internationally and for Spain.

US
EUROPEAN MONITOR NEWSLETTER. (19??)-. Newsletter. English. Twelve times a year. $550.00. K-III Press Inc., 424 West 33rd Street, New York NY 10001. **Tel** (212)714-3100, (800)221-5488.
Desc: Provides monthly news and views on the personal computer markets of Europe.

ISSN 0741-0050
US CCC
EXECUTIVE COMPUTING. Added/Corp Association of Computer Users (U.S.). Vol. 10, No. 7 (July 1984)-. Periodical. English. Twelve times a year. $99.00. Intercom Group, 1250 45th Street, Suite 200, Emeryville CA 94608. **Tel** (800)959-1059, (510)596-9337, FAX (510)596-9331. **Continues** Hillel Segal's Executive Computing Newsletter, 0741-0050.

LC HD9696.C63 U51643
DD 338.4/762138195/0973
ISSN 0191-2135
US
EXECUTIVE PERSPECTIVE. Vol. 1 (Feb. 1979)-. Periodical. English. Four times a year. $380.00 US and Canada, $415.00 other, $795.00 general, $825.00 US federal, state, and local government and academic libraries. Computer and Communications Industry Association, 666 11th Street NW/#600, Washington DC 20001-4542.

LC HD9696.C6 F73
DD 338
ISSN 1058-8299
US
FREEMAN REPORTS. MASS STORAGE OUTLOOK. [Freeman rep., Mass storage outlook]. **Added/Corp** Freeman Associates. **VFOAT** Mass Storage Outlook. (1991)-. English. Freeman Associates, 311 East Carrillo Street, Santa Barbara CA 93101.

ISSN 1069-5656
US
●**FRINGE WARE REVIEW.** [Fringe ware rev.]. (1993)-. Periodical. English. Four times a year. $25.00. FringeWare Inc., PO Box 49921, Austin TX 78765-9921. **Tel** (512)477-1366. **ED** Paco Xander Nathan, Jon Lebkowsky.
Desc: Provides information on gizmos, non-mainstream software and subversive media through essays, fiction, interviews, tutorials, comics and reviews.

LC QA76.9.D32 G36
DD 025.04/029/6
ISSN 1066-8934
US CODEN GDDAE6
●**GALE DIRECTORY OF DATABASES.** [Gale dir. databases]. **Added/Corp** Gale Research Inc. **VFOAT** Directory of Databases. (Jan. 1993)-. Directory. English. Two times a year. $300.00. Gale Research Inc., 835 Penobscot Building, 645 Griswold Street, Detroit MI 48226. **Tel** (800)877-GALE, (313)961-2242, FAX (313)961-6083, (800)414-5043, telex TWX 810-221-7086. **ED** Kathleen Young Maraccio. available on magnetic tape; available on diskette; available on CD-ROM from SilverPlatter (US); available on an online database (File Name: CUADRA) from Questel; DATA-STAR; and (File Name: CUAD) ORBIT. **Formed by the union of** Computer-Readable Data Bases, 0271-4477; Directory of Online Databases, 0193-6840 **and** Directory of Portable Databases, 1045-8352.
Desc: Profiles more than 8,400 databases available in a variety of computer-readable formats. Provides descriptions and contact information for nearly 5,200 online databases made publicly available from the producer or an online service.

LC HD9696.C6 G43
DD 338.47621381
JA
GEKKAN KOMPYUTA DAIJESUTO. VFOAT Kompyuta Daijesuto; Computer Digest. (Dec. 1975)-. Periodical. Japanese. ¥8160. Tie Shi Kikaku Shuppanbu, c/o Dai 2 Bunsei Building, 11-7 Toranomon 1, Minato-ku 105, Tokyo-to Japan.

NE
GEOSCIENCE SOFTWARE DIRECTORY FOR THE IBM PC & COMPATIBLES. See Earth Sciences-Computer Applications.

DD 001
ISSN 0738-4300
US CCC
GOVERNMENT COMPUTER NEWS. See Public Administration.

ISSN 1080-1618
US
●**GOVERNMENT COMPUTER NEWS, STATE AND LOCAL.** See Public Administration.

DD 354.41000285
ISSN 0951-7537
UK
GOVERNMENT COMPUTING. See Public Administration.

DD 004/.023/71
ISSN 1186-1460
CN
GRADUATE COMPUTERWORLD. [Grad. computerworld]. **VFOAT** Graduate Computer World. Vol. 1, No. 1 (Sept. 1990)-. Trade Publication. English. Four times a year. Limited free distribution. Graduate Computerworld, 501 Oakville Road, Downsview Ontario M3N 1W7 Canada.

LC QA76.6 .G825
DD 001.64/2/029473
ISSN 0740-8374
US CCC
TITLE CHANGE
GUIDE TO SOFTWARE PRODUCTIVITY AIDS. [Guide softw. prod. aids]. **Added/Corp** Applied Computer Research (Firm). (Summer 1983)-(19??). Periodical. English. Applied Computer Research Inc., 11242 North 19th Avenue, Phoenix AZ 85029. **Tel** (602)995-5929, FAX (602)995-0905. **(Subscription address:** Applied Computer Research, PO Box 82266, Phoenix AZ 85071. **Tel** (602)995-5929. **ED** Janet M. Fraser. **Continued by** Library of Programmer's and

Computers —Computer Industry and Industry Directories

Developer's Tools.
Desc: A directory of commercial software tools to improve the productivity of conventional system development and equip the information center with user friendly packages.

ISSN 0897-0289
DD 658 US
IBM DIRECTIONS. [IBM dir.]. **Added/Corp** International Business Machines Corporation. Information Systems Group. **VFOAT** Directions. **VAT** International Business Machines Directions. (April 1987)-. Periodical. English. Four times a year. International Business Machines Corp, Information Systems Group, Dept DCX, 4111 Northside Parkway, Atlanta GA 30327.

LC QA76.6 .I16
DD 001.64/25/05
ISSN 0734-466X
US
CODEN ISJODY
ICP SOFTWARE JOURNAL. See Computers-Software.

ISSN 1041-4320
DD 621 US
IMAGING TECHNOLOGY REPORT. See Computers-Optical Storage, CD-ROM Applications.

LC TS176 .I5437
DD 670/.285/05
ISSN 1045-0203
US
CCC
CODEN ICPCEJ
TITLE CHANGE
INDUSTRIAL COMPUTING PLUS PROGRAMMABLE CONTROLS. [Ind. comput. plus program. controls]. **Added/Corp** Instrument Society of America. **VFOAT** Industrial Computing; Industrial Computing/Programmable Controls. Vol. 8, No. 7 (Sept./Oct. l989)-(19??). Trade Publication. English. Instrument Society of America, 67 Alexander Drive, Research Triangle NC 27709. **Tel** (919)549-8411, **FAX** (919)549-8288, telex 802 540. **Ad Acc. Circ:** 40,000. available on microfilm from University Microfilms International (UMI). Documents available from Article Express International. **Continues** Programmable Controls, 0747-4458; Industrial Computing. **Continued by** Industrial Computing, 1074-228X.
Desc: Targets decision makers who purchase products in the computer industry.
Ind/Abst Ei Page One (?-?); Eng. Index Annu. (?-?); Microcomput. Abstr. (Sept. 1989-).

ISSN 0733-9305
US
INFOPERSPECTIVES. [Infoperspectives]. **Added/Corp** Computer Intelligence Corp. Technology News of America. **VFOAT** Info Perspectives. (Sept. 1982)-. Periodical. English. Twelve times a year. $485.00. Technology News of America, 110 Greene Street, Room 1101, New York NY 10012. **Tel** (212)334-9750, **FAX** (212)334-9491, telex 668758. **ED** Sharon Brady. ctrl circ. available on microfilm from University Microfilms International (UMI). **Continues** Mainstream, 0272-4545; **Absorbed** Computer and Communications Buyer.
Desc: Trends in computing are presented using statistical data. These trends are interpreted and analysed for the computer user.
Ind/Abst Comput. Lit. Index; Trade Ind. Index.

ISSN 1044-8764
DD 338 UK
INFOPERSPECTIVES INTERNATIONAL. [Infoperspectives int.]. (1989)-. Periodical. English. Twelve times a year. $641.70. Technology News Limited, 110 Cloucester Avenue, London NW1 8JA United Kingdom. **Tel** 011 44 171 4832681, **FAX** 011 44 171 4834541.

ISSN 0950-9879
UK
CCC
INFORMATION WORLD REVIEW. See Computers-Optical Storage, CD-ROM Applications.

LC HD9696.C63 J313
DD 338.4/7004/0952
JA
INFORMATIZATION WHITE PAPER. **Added/Corp** Nihon Joho Shori Kaihatsu Kyokai. (1987)-. English. One time a year. $43.23. Japan Information Processing Development Center, 3 5 8 Shibakoen, Minato-ku Tokyo 105 Japan. **Tel** 011 81 3 3432 9384, **FAX** 011 81 3 3432 9389. **Continues** Computer White Paper.
Desc: A review on the state of computer utilization and trends in the information and telecommunications industries in Japan.

LC QA75.5 .I56
DD 004
ISSN 0199-6649
US
CCC
CODEN INWODU
INFOWORLD. [InfoWorld]. **VFOAT** Info World. Vol. 2 (Feb. 18, 1980)-. Trade Publication. English. One time a week (51 issues). $145.00. InfoWorld, 155 Bovet Road, Suite 800, San Mateo CA 94402. **Tel** (800)227-8365, (415)572-7341, (415)312-0691, **FAX** (415)328-1049, (415)312-0547, telex MNPK 176072. **(Subscription address:** Infoworld, PO Box 1172, Skokie IL 60076. **) ED** Jonathan Sacks. Index available. **Ad Acc. Circ:** 160,000 (ctrl). available on microfilm and microfiche from University Microfilms International (UMI); available on an online database from NEXIS; and (files 15,648,675/Full-Text) DIALOG. Documents available from UMI Article Clearinghouse, Ask*IEEE. **Continues** *Intelligent Machines Journal, 0164-3878*.
Desc: Delivers industry news, analysis and product reviews to more than 140,000 qualified volume buyers of PC systems, software and related products.
Ind/Abst ABI/INFORM Glob. Ed.; ABI/INFORM [Computer File] (March 1986-); Acad. Ind. [Computer File] (1992-); Acad. Search; Bus. Source Plus; Bus. Source; Can. Index (?-?); Comput. Bus.; Comput. Database; Comput. Rev. Index (1986-); EP Collect.; Expand. Acad. Index (1992-); F&S Index Plus Text, Int. [Select. Cov.]; Gen. Period. Index (1992-); Homework Help.; INFO-SOUTH Abstr.; INSPEC (July 1981-); Mag. Index Plus (1992-); Mag. Search; MasterFile FullTEXT 1000; MasterFile FullTEXT 350; MasterFile FullTEXT 650; MasterFile FullTEXT (July 1993-); Microcomput. Abstr. (Jan. 1981-);(1981-); Microcomput. Ind. Update; Newsp. Period. Abstr. (1991-); OCLC; Predicasts; PROMT; Telebase; Trade Ind. Index; UMI ABI/Inform--Bus. Period. Ondisc (Nov. 1987-) [Full Txt.].

ISSN 1077-548X
DD 004 US
● **INSIDE SCO UNIX SYSTEMS.** [Inside SCO UNIX syst.]. **Added/Corp** Cobb Group. Vol. 1, No 1 (Sept. 1994)-. Periodical. English. Twelve times a year. $119.00 US; $139.00 other. Cobb Group, 9420 Bunsen Parkway #300, Louisville KY 40220. **Tel** (502)491-1900, (800)223-8720, **FAX** (502)491-4200.

UK
CEASED
INSIGHT IBM. **Added/Corp** International Business Machines Corporation. (19??)-(19??). Periodical. English. Xephon, 27-35 London Road, Newbury Berkshire RG13 1JL United Kingdom. **Tel** 011 44 1635 33823, **FAX** 011 44 1635 38345. **ED** Mark Lillycrop. **Circ:** 2,500.
Desc: Monthly journal analyzing strategic developments in the IBM mainframe marketplace.

UK
INSIGHT IS. (19??)-. English. Twelve times a year. $355.00. Xephon, 27-35 London Road, Newbury Berkshire RG13 1JL United Kingdom. **Tel** 011 44 1635 33823, **FAX** 011 44 1635 38345. **(Subscription address:** Xephon, 1301 West Highway, Suite 201 450, Lewisville TX 75067. **) Continues** Insight IBM.

LC QA76.6 .I554
DD 001.64/25/0294
ISSN 0260-3438
UK
INTERNATIONAL DIRECTORY OF SOFTWARE. See Computers-Software.

LC HD9696.C6 I57
DD 382/.450053/025
ISSN 0887-4921
US
INTERNATIONAL DIRECTORY OF SYSTEMS HOUSES AND COMPUTER OEM'S. [Int. dir. syst. houses comput. OEM's]. (1986)-. English. One time a year (March). $345.00. Technical Publishing, 199 Wells Avenue, Newton Centre MA 02159. **Tel** (617)964-8890. available on magnetic tape (9-track); available on diskette (5-1/4"). **Continues** International Directory of Computer & Software Sales Agents & Distributors, 0882-3324.
Desc: Source for ISO's, VAR's, OEM's of computers, peripherals and software worldwide (excluding USA).

LC HD9696.C63 J3214
DD 338.47621381
JA
JOHOKA HAKUSHO = INFORMATIZATION WHITE PAPER. **VFOAT** Informatization White Paper. (1987)-. Japanese. One time a year. ¥4200. Konpyuta Eijisha, Kasumigaseki Building, 2-5 Kasumigaseki 3, Chiyoda-ku, Tokyo-to 100 Japan. **Continues** Konpyuta Hakusho.

ISSN 0897-9308
DD 004 US
LOS ANGELES COMPUTER CURRENTS. [Los Angel. comput. curr.]. **VFOAT** Computer Currents. (198?)-. Periodical. English. Twelve times a year. $19.95. Computer Currents, 5720 Hollis Street, Emeryville CA 94608. **Tel** (415)547-6800, (800)365-7773, **FAX** (415)547-4613. **Continues** Computer Currents (Greater Los Angeles Computer Magazine).
Desc: Industry news, local features, informative reviews, helpful tips and up-to-date computer prices.

ISSN 0899-1642
DD 004 US
MAC SUBJECTS. [Mac subj.]. **VAT** Macintosh Subjects. Vol. 1, No. 1 (Jan. 1988)-. Periodical. English. Six times a year. $30.00. Pointer Publications, Box 70065, Marietta GA 30007. available on diskette.
Desc: Provides product name and subject. Also indexes hardware.

LC QA76.8.M3 M29
DD 004.165
ISSN 0892-8118
US
CODEN MWEEEI
MACWEEK. [MacWeek]. **VFOAT** Mac Week. Vol. 1, No. 1 (March 9, 1987)-. Periodical. English. Forty-eight times a year. $125.00. Ziff-Davis, One Park Avenue, 5th Floor, New York NY 10016. **Tel** (212)503-3500. **(Subscription address:** JCI, PO Box 1766, Riverton NJ 08077. **) ED** Dan Farber. **Bk Rev. Ad Acc, Adv Mgr:** Peter J Longo. ctrl circ. available on an online database (file 675/Full-Text) from DIALOG; available via Internet (http://www.ziff.com/).
Desc: Covers the Macintosh industry. Provides news on products, companies and technology trends as they apply to the Macintosh platform.
Ind/Abst Comput. ASAP [Full Txt.]; Comput. Database [Full Txt.]; Comput. Rev. Index (Dec. 8, 1987-); Expand. Acad. Index (1992-); Microcomput. Abstr. (June 1989-).

LC HD9696.A1 M34
DD 338.47621381
KO
MAIKURO SOPUTUWEO. **Added/Corp** Chongbo Sidae (Firm). Vol. 1 (1983)-. Periodical. Korean. Chusik Hoesa Chongbo Sidae, 36-4 Youido-dong Yongdungpo-ku, Seoul Korea.

LC QA76.55 .M37
DD 004/.33/0257
NLM QA 76.215; M357
ISSN 0884-044X
US
MARQUIS WHO'S WHO DIRECTORY OF ONLINE PROFESSIONALS. [Marquis who's who dir. online prof.]. **Added/Corp** Marquis Who's Who, Inc. **VFOAT** Directory of Online Professionals; Who's Who Directory of Online Professionals. (1984)-. English. Marquis Who's Who, A Reed Reference Publishing Company, Part of Reed International PLC, 121 Chanlon Road, New Providence NJ 07974. **Tel** (908)464-6800, (800)521-8110, **FAX** (908)665-6688, telex 138 755.

LC TK7874.5 .M45
DD 621.397/3
US
MEMORY DISCONTINUED DEVICES. See Computers-Computer Engineering.

LC HD9696.C63 U52555
DD 001.64
ISSN 0747-511X
US
MICROCOMPUTER VENDOR DIRECTORY. Directory. English. $9.95. Auerbach Publishers Inc., Park Square Building, 31 St. James Avenue, Boston MA 02116. **Tel** (800)950-1207.

ISSN 1065-0148
DD 004 US
MICROTIMES (PLEASANT HILL, CALIF.). See Computers-Microcomputers, Personal Computers.

ISSN 0743-037X
DD 001 US
NEW IN COMPUTING MAGAZINE AND BUYER'S GUIDE. [New comput. mag. buy. guide]. Vol. 1, No. 11-. Periodical. English. Four times a year. $12.97 US, $15.00 Canada. Computer Education Services of America, 1020 North Broadway/Suite 111, Milwaukee WI 53202. **Tel** (414)272-9977.

ISSN 0917-9364
JA
NIKKEI INFOBESU UNIX. See Computers-Software.

LC HD9696.C63 J347
DD 338.47621381
ISSN 0285-4619
JA
NIKKEI KONPYUTA. **VFOAT** Nikkei Computer. (1981)-. Trade Publication. Japanese. Twenty-four times a year. $482.00. Nihon Keizai Shimbun Inc., 9-5 Otemachi 1 Chome, Chiyoda-ku Tokyo 100 Japan. **Tel** 011 81 3 32700251, 011 81 3 52108502 (Nikkei Business Publications Inc.), **FAX** 011 81 3 52552661, 011 81 3 52108119 (Nikkei Business Publications Inc.). **(Subscription address:** Maruzen Company Ltd., PO Box 5050, Import & Export Department, Tokyo 100 31 Japan. **Tel** 011 81 3 32789224.)

LC HD9696.C63 J35
DD 338.47621381
JA
NIKKEI PASOKON. See Computers-Microcomputers, Personal Computers.

ISSN 0914-0379
DD 651 JA
NIKKEI UOTCHA. IBM-BAN. [Nikkei uotcha. IBM-ban]. **VFOAT** Nikkei Watcher on IBM. (1987)-. Periodical. Japanese. Twenty-six times a year. Nihon Keizai Shimbun Inc., 9-5 Otemachi 1 Chome, Chiyoda-ku Tokyo 100 Japan. **Tel** 011 81 3 32700251, 011 81 3 52108502 (Nikkei Business Publications Inc.), **FAX** 011 81 3 52552661, 011 81 3 52108119 (Nikkei Business Publications Inc.). **ED** Katsumi Tanaka.
Desc: Newsletter on IBM's strategies and approaches to the industry.

ISSN 1043-9854
DD 004 US
CEASED
NINA LYTTON'S OPEN SYSTEMS ADVISOR. [Nina Lytton's open syst. advis.]. **VFOAT** Open Systems Advisor. (April 1989)-Vol. 4 No. 10 (19??). Periodical. English. Open Systems Advisor, 268 Newbury Street, Boston MA 02116. **Tel** (617)859-0859. **ED** Nina Lytton. Index available. ctrl circ.
Desc: In-depth analysis of strategic issues and changing industry structure in the movement toward open systems.

Computers —Computer Industry and Industry Directories

LC HD62.6 .N655
DD 004/.029/473
ISSN 1049-9210
US
NONPROFIT COMPUTER SOURCEBOOK. [Nonprofit comput. sourceb.]. **VFOAT** Nonprofit Computer Source Book. (1990)-. English. One time a year. $75.00. Taft Group, 835 Penobscott Building, Customer Service, Detroit MI 48226. **Tel** (800)877-8238, FAX (313)961-6083.

LC QA76.215 .O34
DD 001.64/025/74
ISSN 0276-6442
US
OFFICIAL DIRECTORY OF DATA PROCESSING, COMPUTER USERS EASTERN USA. **VFOAT** Official Directory of Data Processing, Eastern Computer Users. Directory. English. One time a year. $120.00. Official Directories and Services, Inc., Box 488, Gresham OR 97030.

LC QA76.215 .O343
DD 001.64/25/75
ISSN 0276-6434
US
OFFICIAL DIRECTORY OF DATA PROCESSING, COMPUTER USERS SOUTHERN USA. **VFOAT** Official Directory of Data Processing, Southern Computer Users. Directory. English. One time a year. $120.00. Official Directories and Services, Inc., Box 488, Gresham OR 97030.

ISSN 0278-5889
US
OFFICIAL DIRECTORY OF DATA PROCESSING, COMPUTER USERS WESTERN USA. [Off. dir. data process. Comput. users West USA]. **VFOAT** Computer Users Western USA; Western U.S.A. Computer Users; Western Directory of U.S.A. System Users. (1981)-. Directory. English. Irregular. $175.00. Official Directory of Data Processing, Box 488, Gresham OR 97030. **Tel** (503)667-4669. **ED** R. F. Knudson. **Circ**: 5,000. **Continues** Official Directory of Data Processing, EDP Systems Users Western U.S.A., 0278-6109.
Desc: USA end-user computer sites with in-depth information on computer installations including computer manufacturer and model number, computer, executives' names and titles plus programming languages.

LC QA76.215 .O345
DD 001.64/25/77
ISSN 0276-6450
US
OFFICIAL DIRECTORY OF DATA PROCESSING, EDP SYSTEM USERS MIDWESTERN USA. **VFOAT** Official Directory of Data Processing, Midwestern System Users. Directory. English. One time a year. $90.00. Official Directories and Services, Inc., Box 488, Gresham OR 97030.

LC HD9999.I493 U668
DD 338.4/702504/097305
ISSN 1057-3666
US
ONLINE SERVICES : REVIEW, TRENDS & FORECAST. [Online serv.]. **Added/Corp** Simba Information Inc. (1990)-. English. One time a year. $701.00. SIMBA Information Inc., 213 Danbury Road, PO Box 7430, Wilton CT 06897-7430. **Tel** (203)834-0033 ext. 173, FAX (203)884-1771.
Desc: Includes over four hundred pages of statistics, trend analysis and forecasts. Covers profiles of key industry players as well as emerging online companies.

DD 004
ISSN 1069-0409
US
●**OPEN SYSTEMS PRODUCTS DIRECTORY.** [Open syst. prod. dir.]. **Added/Corp** UniForum. (1993)-. English. Irregular. $155.00. UniForum, 2901 Tasman Dr., Suite 201, Santa Clara CA 95054. **Tel** (408)986-8840, FAX (408)986-1645. **Continues** UniForum Products Directory, 0886-2575.

DD 004.16
ISSN 0950-5474
UK
PC DEALER. [PC deal.]. **VFOAT** Personal Computer Dealer. (1986)-. Trade Publication. English. One time a week. Free on request. VNU Business Publications BV, 32-34 Broadwick Street, London W1A 2HG United Kingdom. **Tel** 011 44 171 4394242 ext. 2222, FAX 011 44 171 4379638, telex 23918 VNU G, 8952440.

LC HD9696.C63 U515946
DD 001.64
ISSN 0746-6773
US
PC RETAILING. See Business and Economics-Computer Applications.

US
PC TELEMART SOFTWARE DIRECTORY. **Added/Corp** PC Telemart, Inc./Vanloves. **VFOAT** P.C. Telemart Software Directory; Software Directory; Yellow Pages to the World of Microcomputers. 8th ed. (1984)-. Directory. English. **Continues** PC Clearinghouse Directory.

DD 004
ISSN 0893-8075
US
PCNETTER NEWSLETTER, THE. [PCNetter newsl.]. **VFOAT** PC Netter Newsletter; PCNetter; PC Netter. (Oct. 1986)-. Newsletter. English. Twelve times a year. $275.00. Architecture Technology Corporation, PO Box 24344, Minneapolis MN 55424. **Tel** (612)935-2035.
Desc: Provides a monthly overview of important industry news as well as new product introductions in the key areas of communications, hardware, software, and workstations/servers.

ISSN 0273-8201
US
PRINTOUT (SAINT CLOUD, MINN.). (PRINTOUT.). Vol. 1, No. 1 (Nov. 1980)-. Periodical. English. Six times a year.
Ind/Abst Print. Abstr.

LC HD9696.C63 U5156a
DD 338.4/7/001642
ISSN 0069-8148
US
CODEN CPRPBM
PROCEEDINGS OF THE ANNUAL COMPUTER PERSONNEL RESEARCH CONFERENCE. [Proc. annu. Comput. Pers. Res. Conf.]. **Main/Conf** Computer Personnel Research Conference. **Added/Corp** Association for Computing Machinery. Special Interest Group on Computer Personnel Research. (19??)-. Proceedings. English. One time a year. $56.00. ACM / Association for Computing Machinery, 1515 Broadway, 17th Floor, New York NY 10036. **Tel** (212)869-7440, FAX (212)869-0481. Documents available from Article Express International.
Ind/Abst Bioeng. Abstr.; Comput. Lit. Index; Ei Page One; Eng. Index Annu.

DD 338
ISSN 1064-1394
US
PROGRAMMABLE LOGIC, NEWS & VIEWS. [Program. log. news views]. **VFOAT** Programmable Logic, News and Views; News and Views. Vol. 1, No. 1 (Apr. 1992)-. Periodical. English. Twelve times a year. $395.00. Information Associates, 1259 El Camino Real, Suite 231, Menlo Park CA 94025. **Tel** (415)322-0247, FAX (415)322-0469.

LC HD9696.C6 P84
DD 001.64
ISSN 0749-4920
US
PULSE (YANKEE GROUP). (PULSE.). [Pulse]. English. The Yankee Group, 89 Broad Street, 14th Floor, Boston MA 02110.

LC QA
DD 004
ISSN 1080-076X
US
RED HERRING (REDWOOD CITY, CALIF.), THE. (THE RED HERRING.). [Red herring]. (199?)-. Periodical. English. Twelve times a year. $89.00. Red Herring, PO Box 620453, Woodside CA 94062. **Tel** (415)865-2277.

LC HD9696.C63 U582
DD 338.4/7004/097305
ISSN 1047-935X
US
RELEASE 1.0. [RELease 1.0.]. **VFOAT** RELease One Point Zero. (198?)-. Periodical. English. Fifteen times a year. $595.00. EDventure Holdings Inc., 104 5th Avenue, 20th Floor, New York NY 10011-6987. **Tel** (212)924-8800. available on an online database (file 675/Full-Text) from DIALOG. **Continues** Rosen Electronics Letter, 0737-6677.
Ind/Abst Comput. ASAP [Full Txt.]; Comput. Database [Full Txt.]; Comput. Lit. Index.

LC HD9696.C63 U568
DD 004/.068/8
ISSN 1042-7325
US
CCC
RESELLER MANAGEMENT. [Resell. manage.]. Vol. 12, No. 1 (Jan. 1989)-. Trade Publication. English. Twelve times a year. $69.90. Cahners Publishing Company, 249 West 17th Street, New York NY 10011. **Tel** (212)645-0067, FAX (212)242-6987. **(Subscription address:** Cahners Publishing Company / Colorado, Post Subscription Service Center, PO Box 7610, Highlands Ranch CO 80126-7610. **Tel** (303)470-4466, FAX (303)470-4691.) **Formed by the union of** Computer Dealer, 0160-8916 **and** Computer Reseller Monthly, 0890-3980.
Desc: Focus is on resellers of personal computers and related peripherals. This includes VARs, system integrators, software developers, systems houses and consultants.
Ind/Abst ACM Guide Comput. Lit.

LC QA76.8.A66 R48
DD 001.64
ISSN 0740-7866
US
RESOURCE DIRECTORY FOR THE APPLE COMPUTER, THE. [Resour. dir. Apple comput.]. Directory. English. $9.95. Scribner Book Companies, 5245 West Diversey Avenue, Chicago IL 60639. **Tel** (201)256-0700.

ISSN 1130-622X
SP
UDC 681.3
CEASED
REVISTA MICROSOFT PARA PROGRAMADORES. [Rev. microsoft program.]. **VFOAT** RMP. (1991)-(Sept. 1995). Periodical. Spanish. Anaya Multimedia, Juan Ignacio Luca de Tena, 15, 28027 Madrid Spain. **Tel** 011 34 1 917429479, FAX 011 34 1 912304419.

LC HD9696.C6 R54
DD 380.1/456213976
US
RIGID DISK DRIVE MAGNETIC HEAD/MEDIA MARKET, AND TECHNOLOGY UPDATE. See Computers-Optical Storage, CD-ROM Applications.

LC HD9696
DD 338.47621381
US
SALES SOFTWARE SUPPLIERS DIRECTORY. See Computers-Computer Sales, Service and Supply.

LC QA76.753 .S38
DD 005.3/029/473
ISSN 1047-1812
US
TITLE CHANGE
SCOUT MID-RANGE SOFTWARE DIRECTORY. See Computers-Software.

LC HD9696.C6 S44
DD 338.47621381
JA
SEKAI KONPYUTA NENKAN. **VFOAT** Computer Yearbook. Japanese. One time a year. ¥6800. Konpyuta Eijisha, Kasumigaseki Building, 2-5 Kasumigaseki 3, Chiyoda-ku, Tokyo-to 100 Japan.

US
SELECTWARE SYSTEM. CD-ROM. English. Four times a year. $99.00 US; $114.00 Canada; $139.00 other. Selectware Technologies Inc., 29200 Vassar, Suite 200, Livonia MI 48152. **ED** Joseph Dandy (contact person). Index available. cum. index. **Ad Acc**.
Desc: Covers over 300 software demonstration systems.

LC HD9696.C63 U58337
DD 338.4/762139/097305
ISSN 1046-1965
US
SERVICE NEWS (YARMOUTH, ME.). (SERVICE NEWS : FOR COMPUTER/ELECTRONIC SERVICE AND SUPPORT PROFESSIONALS.). Vol. 8, No. 10 (Oct. 1988)-. Periodical. English. Twelve times a year. $45.00. United Publications Inc., PO Box 995, 38 Lafayette Street, Yarmouth ME 04096. **Tel** (207)846-0600, FAX (207)846-0657. **Continues** Computer/Electronic Service News, 0744-1584.
Ind/Abst F&S Index Plus Text, Int. [Select. Cov.]; PROMT.

DD 381.45004/0971/05
ISSN 0849-1801
CN
TITLE CHANGE
SI BUSINESS. (SI BUSINESS : THE MAGAZINE FOR CANADIAN SYSTEMS INTEGRATORS & VARS.). [SI bus.]. **VFOAT** Systems Integrators Business. Vol. 1, No. 1 (Jan./Feb. 1990)-(1993). Periodical. English. Plesman Publications Ltd., 2005 Sheppard Avenue East, 4th Floor, Willowdale Ontario M2J 5B1 Canada. **Tel** (416)497-9562, FAX (416)497-9427. **Continues** Systems Integrator., 0846-5258. **Merged into** Computer Dealer News, 0834-4612.

DD 384
ISSN 1042-7252
US
SOFTWARE INDUSTRY REPORT. See Computers-Software.

LC HF5439.C67 S66
DD 338.7/610016425/02573
ISSN 8756-9833
US
SOFTWARE WRITERS MARKET (POMONA, N.Y.). (SOFTWARE WRITERS MARKET.). [Softw. writ. mark.]. (1982)-. English. One time a year. $19.95. IPF Publications, PO Box 3600 146 Country Club Lane, Pomona NY 10970.

LC KF6768.C66 S73
DD 343
ISSN 1063-2522
US
STATE-BY-STATE SUMMARY OF SOFTWARE SALES & USE TAX. **VFOAT** State by State Summary of Software Sales & Use Tax; Software sales and Use Tax. 1st ed. (1992)-. English. One time a year. $450.00. Kutish Publications, PO Box 181916, Coronado CA 92178-1916. **Tel** (619)552-0523, FAX (619)522-0525.
Desc: A sourcebook dedicated to software taxation issues. It includes documents from the states with an interpretation as to what each document means, where it is applicable and how to use it to your advantage.

DD 338
ISSN 8756-7822
US
STEWART ALSOP'S P.C. LETTER. [Stewart Alsop's P.C. lett.]. **VFOAT** P.C. Letter. **VAT** Stewart Alsop's Personal Computer Letter. Issue 1.1 (Jan. 15, 1985)-. Periodical. English. Twenty-two times a year. $495.00. PC Letter, 155 Bovet Road, Suite 800, San Mateo CA 94402. **Tel** (415)312-0691, FAX (415)312-0547. **ED** David Coursey. Index available (free). **Circ**: 600. available on an online database from America Online.
Desc: Analysis and evaluation of recent events and emerging trends in the personal computer industry.
Ind/Abst Trade Ind. Index [Full Txt.].

LC HD9696.C63 U585 ISSN 0192-9690
DD 338.4/7/62138195 US
SURVEY OF THE MINI/MICROCOMPUTER MARKET. 1977-. English. One time a year. G S Grumman/Cowen & Company, 28 State Street, Boston MA 02109.

LC HD9696.C63 U5855
DD 381/.45621381958/0973 US
SYSTEM TREND SERVICE. Added/Corp Computer Intelligence Corporation (U.S.). (19??)-. English. Four times a year. $15.00. Computer Intelligence Corporation, 3344 North Torrey Pines Court, La Jolla CA 92037. **Tel** (619)450-1667. **ED** Paul Hairopoulos. ctrl circ.
 Desc: A analytical overview of the computer market place. It covers IBM, PCMS, DEC, HP, and others. All major hardware and mainframe software is included.

ISSN 1180-3703
DD 338.4/762139/0971 CN
CEASED
TECHNOLOGY WATCH (WILLOWDALE). (TECHNOLOGY WATCH.). [Technol. watch]. **Added/Corp** Evans Research Corporation. **VFOAT** Watch. Vol. 3, No. 9 (Oct. 1989)-(May 1995). Newsletter. English. Evans Research Corporation, 2005 Sheppard Avenue East, 4th Floor, Willowdale Ontario M2J 5B1 Canada. **Tel** (416)498-6664, (416)497-9562, FAX (416)498-7275. **ED** Charles Whaley. **Continues** ERC Update., 0843-0845.
 Desc: Contains a compilation of Evans Research Corporation findings and announcements.

NE
TELINDUS NEWS. See Communications-Computer Applications.

ISSN 1044-3312
US
ULTIMATE NETWORKING DIRECTORY, THE. See Computers-Computer Networks.

ISSN 0895-0334
DD 004 US
CEASED
UNISYS WORLD. EUROPE. [Unisys world, Eur.]. Vol. 1, No. 1 (June 1987)-(April 1994). Trade Publication. English. Publications & Communications, 12416 Hymeadow Drive, Austin TX 78750. **Tel** (512)250-9023, (800)678-9724, FAX (512)331-3900, telex 384303.

ISSN 0958-6253
DD 005.43 UK
CEASED
UNIX/BUSINESS. (UNIX BUSINESS MAGAZINE.). [UNIX/bus.]. (1989)-(1993). Periodical. English. 4GL Publications Co Ltd, 4 Carlton Court, Fifth Avenue, Team Valley Gateshead, Tyne and Wear NE11 0A2 United Kingdom. **Tel** 011 44 191 4820220, FAX 011 44 191 4825668. **ED** David Errington. Bk Rev. **Ad Acc.** Circ: 11,000 (ctrl). **Absorbed** Access Magazine, 0958-6253.
 Desc: Offers topical news, reviews and feature articles to individuals involved in the UNIX, Pick and Open systems marketplace.

LC HD9696.C6 U54 ISSN 0886-2575
DD 004.165/05 US
TITLE CHANGE
UNIX PRODUCTS DIRECTORY. [UNIX prod. dir.]. **Added/Corp** Usr Group. **VFOAT** USR/Group Directory. 5th Ed. (Winter 1986)-(199?). English. USR Group, 4655 Old Ironsides Drive/Suite 200, Santa Clara CA 95054. **Tel** (408)986-8840, FAX (408)986-1645. **Ad Acc.** Circ: 6,000-10,000. **Continues** UNIX Products Catalog, 0886-2583. **Continued by** Open Systems Products Directory, 1069-0409.

LC QA76.76.O63 U55 ISSN 0742-3136
DD 001.64 US
CCC
CODEN UNRED5
UNIX REVIEW. [UNIX rev.]. **VFOAT** U.N.I.X. Review. Vol. 1, No. 1 (June/July 1983)-. Periodical. English. Twelve times a year. $55.00. Miller Freeman Inc., 600 Harrison Street, San Francisco CA 94107. **Tel** (415)905-2231, (415)905-2200, FAX (415)905-2204, telex 278273. **(Subscription address:** Palm Coast Data, PO Box 420163, Agency Department, Palm Coast FL 32142. **Tel** (904)445-4662 ext. 669, (800)829-5475.) **ED** J. D. Hildebrand. available on microfilm and microfiche from University Microfilms International (UMI); available on an online database (files 15,675/Full-Text) from DIALOG. Documents available from Ask*IEEE, UMI Article Clearinghouse.
 Desc: Devoted to the computer industry and other business professionals involved in the design, development, implementation, purchase, use or assessment of UNIX and UNIX-like systems. Feature articles focus on analysis of technologies while the magazine's departments section covers industry news, corporate developments and products.
 Ind/Abst ABI/INFORM Glob. Ed. (19??-); ABI/INFORM [Computer File] (Nov. 1987-); Comput. ASAP (19??-) [Full Txt.]; Comput. Database (19??-) [Full Txt.]; Curr. Cit.; Data Process. Dig. (19??-); INSPEC (Sept. 1987-); Microcomput. Abstr. (May 1988-); UMI ABI/Inform--Bus. Period. Ondisc (Nov. 1987-) [Full Txt.].

LC HC110.H53 U67 ISSN 1052-0341
DD 338.4/762/00097305 US
UPSIDE (U.S. ED.). (UPSIDE.). [Upside]. **VFOAT** Upside Magazine. (1989)-. Trade Publication. English. Twelve times a year. $48.00. Upside Magazine, 1159 Triton Drive, Foster City CA 94404. **Tel** (415)377-0950, FAX (415)377-1961. **ED** Eric Nee. **Ad Acc. Circ:** 50,000 (ctrl).
 Desc: Delivers perspective on the people and companies creating the digital revolution.

ISSN 0742-6089
US
USED COMPUTER GUIDE. [Used comput. guide]. (1984)-. Periodical. English. Four times a year. $37.50. Hansen Publishing Company, PO Box 1194, Mercer Island WA 98040.

LC HD9696.C63 U59344 ISSN 0894-5802
DD 381/.45004/097305 US
CCC
VARBUSINESS. [VARbusiness]. **VFOAT** VAR Business; Computer Systems News; Value Added Resellers Business. **VAT** Value Added Resellers Business. (1985)-. Periodical. English. Eighteen times a year. $89.00. CMP Publications Inc., One Jericho Plaza, Wing A, 2nd Floor, Jericho NY 11753. **Tel** (516)733-6700. **(Subscription address:** CMP Publications, Inc. / New York, PO Box 4037, Church Street Station, New York NY 10261-4037. **Tel** (516)733-6800.) **ED** Ellen Pearlman. Index available. cum. index. **Ad Acc. Circ:** 50,226 (ctrl). available on an online database. **Separated from** Systems and Network Integration.
 Desc: Emphasis geared toward the value added resellers and dealers.
 Ind/Abst Bus. Source Plus; EP Collect.; F&S Index Plus Text, Int. [Full Txt.] [Select. Cov.]; Homework Help.; Lotus Notes; MasterFile FullTEXT 1000; MasterFile FullTEXT 350; MasterFile FullTEXT 650; MasterFile FullTEXT; Microcomput. Abstr. (Jan. 1989-); OCLC; PROMT [Full Txt.]; Telebase.

LC HD9696.C63 U59348 ISSN 1065-271X
DD 004 US
TITLE CHANGE
VIRTUAL REALITY MARKET PLACE. See Computers-Artificial Intelligence.

LC HD9696.C63 U59348 ISSN 1081-7824
DD 006 US
CEASED
VIRTUAL REALITY WORLD'S VIRTUAL REALITY MARKET PLACE. [Virtual real. world's virtual real. mark. place]. **VFOAT** Virtual Reality Market Place. (1994)-(1994). Periodical. English. Mecklermedia Corporation, 11 Ferry Lane West, Westport CT 06880. **Tel** (203)226-6967, (800)632-5537, FAX (203)454-5840. **Continues** Virtual Reality Market Place, 1065-271X.

ISSN 0270-8507
US
VLSI UPDATE. Added/Corp Advanced Associates. **VAT** Very Large Scale Integration Update. (1978)-. Periodical. English. Twelve times a year. $147.00 US. Advanced Associates, PO Box 830766, Richardson TX 75083-0766. **Tel** (214)341-0370.
 Desc: Evaluates and forecasts trends and developments in the microchip industry from the perspective of an engineering group tracking the technology since RCTL days.

ISSN 0896-2111
DD 004 US
WANG IN THE NEWS. [Wang news]. Vol. 1, No. 4 (Nov. 1987)-. Trade Publication. English. Twelve times a year. $45.00. Publications & Communications, 12416 Hymeadow Drive, Austin TX 78750. **Tel** (512)250-9023, (800)678-9724, FAX (512)331-3900, telex 384303. **Continues** News (Marlin, Tex.), 0895-0318.
 Desc: Dedicated to the Wang computer user. Includes news, new products, features, technical columns, and software reviews.

LC QA76.5 .W352 ISSN 0882-8962
DD 004.16/025/753 US
WASHINGTON-AREA MICROCOMPUTER DIRECTORY, THE. (THE WASHINGTON-AREA MICROCOMPUTER DIRECTORY : A BUYERS/USERS GUIDE TO MICROCOMPUTER-RELATED GOODS AND SERVICES IN THE WASHINGTON METROPOLITAN AREA.). [Wash.-area microcomput. dir.]. **Added/Corp** New Local Resources, Inc. **VFOAT** Washington Area Microcomputer Directory; Microcomputer Directory. (19??)-. Directory. English. Irregular. $8.95. New Local Resources Inc, PO Box 2133, Silver Spring MD 20902.

ISSN 0897-9316
DD 004 US
WASHINGTON, D.C. COMPUTER CURRENTS. [Wash. D. C. comput. curr.]. **VFOAT** Computer Currents; Washington Computer Currents. Vol. 1, No. 1 (Jan. 1988)-. Periodical. English. Irregular. Computer Currents, 5720 Hollis Street, Emeryville CA 94608. **Tel** (415)547-6800, (800)365-7773, FAX (415)547-4613.

ISSN 1193-073X
DD 004.025713 CN
WHO'S WHO (ONTARIO ED.). (WHO'S WHO.). [Who's Who Ont. ed.]. (1992)-. Directory. English. One time a year. Who's Who Publications, 268 Lakeshore East/Suite 510, Port Credit Ontario L5G 1H1 Canada. **Tel** (416)271-1601, FAX (416)271-4522. **Continues** Who's Who in Systems (Ontario Ed.), 1187-0990.
 Desc: Provides alphabetical listings of 10,500 MIS centres across Canada, describes systems, technology activity and the executives in charge at end-user sites.

ISSN 1193-3593
DD 004/.025/714 CN
WHO'S WHO (PQ/ATLANTIC ED.). (WHO'S WHO.). [Who's who]. (1992)-. English. One time a year. Who's Who Publications, 268 Lakeshore East/Suite 510, Port Credit Ontario L5G 1H1 Canada. **Tel** (416)271-1601, FAX (416)271-4522. **ED** Roy Whitseed. **Continues** Who's Who in Computing (Eastern Edition)., 0845-2784.
 Desc: Provides alphabetical listings of 10,500 MIS centres across Canada, describes systems, technology advances and the executives in charge at end-user sites.

ISSN 1193-3607
DD 004/.025/712 CN
WHO'S WHO (WESTERN CANADA ED.). (WHO'S WHO.). [Who's who]. (1992)-. Directory. English. $595.00. Who's Who Publications, 268 Lakeshore East/Suite 510, Port Credit Ontario L5G 1H1 Canada. **Tel** (416)271-1601, FAX (416)271-4522. **Continues** Who's Who in Computing (Western Edition)., 0845-2792.
 Desc: Provides alphabetical listings of 10,500 MIS centres across Canada, describes systems, technology activity and the executives in charge at end-user sites.

LC QA76.76.W56 W56 ISSN 1049-071X
DD 005.4/3 US
CODEN WSGUEM
CEASED
WINDOWS SHOPPER'S GUIDE, THE. See Computers-Programs and Programming.

LC HD9696.C6 W67 ISSN 1074-3308
DD 621.39/16/029473 US
WORKGROUP COMPUTING SERIES. DIRECTORY OF MICROCOMPUTER HARDWARE. See Computers-Hardware.

COMPUTER MUSIC

US
COMPUTER MUSIC AND DIGITAL AUDIO SERIES, THE. (1985)-. Monographic series. English. Irregular. Price varies per volume. A-R Editions Inc., 801 Deming Way, Madison WI 53717. **Tel** (800)736-0700, (608)836-9000.

LC ML1 .C857 ISSN 0148-9267
DD 789.9 US
CCC
CODEN CMUJDY
Pr Rev.
COMPUTER MUSIC JOURNAL. [Comput. music j.]. **VFOAT** Computer Music. Vol. 1, No. 1 (Feb. 1977)-. Periodical. English. Four times a year. $115.00. Massachusetts Institute of Technology (MIT) Press, 55 Hayward Street, Cambridge MA 02142. **Tel** (617)253-2889, (617)625-8481, FAX (617)258-6779. **ED** Stephen Travis Pope. cum. index. Bk Rev. Ad Acc. Circ: 3,700 (ctrl). available on microfilm and microfiche from University Microfilms International (UMI). Documents available from Article Express International, The Genuine Article, Ask*IEEE.
 Desc: Concentrates on skills, technologies, and promises of digital sound and musical applications of computers.
 Ind/Abst Acoust. Abstr.; Arts Humanit. Citation Index [Full Cov.]; CompuMath Cit. Index [Full Cov.]; Comput. Rev.; Curr. Cit.; Curr. Contents Arts Humanit.; Curr. Contents Eng. Comput. Technol.; Ei Page One; Eng. Index Annu. [Select. Cov.]; Inf. Sci. Abstr. (?-?); INSPEC (Dec. 1978-); Music Artic. Guide; Music Index; Pollut. Abstr. Indexes; Res. Alert [Full Cov.]; RILM Abstr.; Sci. Cit. Index; SCISEARCH.

LC ML73 .D57 ISSN 1057-9478
DD 780/.01/02584 US
Pr Rev.
COMPUTING IN MUSICOLOGY. (COMPUTING IN MUSICOLOGY : A DIRECTORY OF RESEARCH.). [Comput. musicol.]. **Added/Corp** Center for Computer Assisted Research in the Humanities. (Oct. 1989)-. Directory. English. One time a year. $29.00. Center for Computer Assisted Research, 525 Middlefield Road, Suite 120, Menlo Park CA 94025. **Tel** (415)322-7050, FAX (415)329-8365. **ED** Walter B. Hewlett and Eleanor Selfridge-Field. cum. index. Circ: 3500 (ctrl). **Continues** Directory of Computer Assisted Research in Musicology.

Computers —Computer Music

LC ML197 .F44 1979
DD 780/.904
GW
FEEDBACK PAPERS. (March 1971)-. Periodical. German (English). Irregular. Feedback Studio Koln Johannes Fritsch, Genter Strasse 23, 5000 Cologne 1 Germany. **Bk Rev. Circ:** 200.
 Desc: Special new-music (electronic and computer music) papers since 1977.

US
INTERNATIONAL COMPUTER MUSIC CONFERENCE PROCEEDINGS. (19??)-. Proceedings. English. $75.00. Computer Music Association, 2040 Polk Street, Suite 330, San Francisco CA 94101. **Tel** (817)566-2235.
 Ind/Abst Curr. Cit.

ISSN 1080-2770
DD 005
US
●**MUSIC & COMPUTERS.** See Music-Computer Applications.

LC ML73 .K49
DD 789.9/9/05
ISSN 0896-4750
US
MUSIC, COMPUTERS & SOFTWARE. (MUSIC, COMPUTERS & SOFTWARE : MCS.). [Music comput. softw.]. **VFOAT** MCS; Music, Computers, and Software. Vol. 2, No. 2 May (1987)-. Periodical. English. Twelve times a year. Keyboards Computers and Software, 190 East Main Street, Huntington NY 11743. **Continues** Keyboards, Computers & Software, 0886-6228.

LC ML1 .P109
DD 780/.5
ISSN 0031-6016
US
PERSPECTIVES OF NEW MUSIC. [Perspect. new music]. **Added/Corp** Fromm Music Foundation. Vol. 1 (Fall 1962)-. Academic Scholarly Publication. English. Two times a year (winter and summer). $75.00. Perspectives of New Music Inc., University of Washington, School Music DN-10, Seattle WA 98195. **Tel** (206)543-0196. **ED** Benjamin Boretz (address: Music Program Zero, Box 175 Bard College, Annandale on Hudson, NY 12504). **Tel**: (914)758-5785). Index available. cum. index (three year cum.). **Bk Rev. Ad Acc. Circ:** 2,000. available on microfilm and microfiche from University Microfilms International (UMI). Documents available from The Genuine Article, UMI Article Clearinghouse.
 Desc: Scholarly journal concentrating on atonal, serial, electronic, and computer music by living composers, and abstract or speculative matters relevant thereto.
 Ind/Abst Acad. Search; Am. Bibliogr. Slavic East Europ. Stud.; Arts Humanit. Citation Index [Full Cov.]; Curr. Contents Arts Humanit.; EP Collect.; Expand. Acad. Index (1989-); Homework Help.; Humanit. Index; Humanit. Source; INFO-SOUTH Abstr.; Mag. Search; MasterFile FullTEXT 1000; MasterFile FullTEXT 350; MasterFile FullTEXT 650; MasterFile FullTEXT (Jan. 1993-); Music Artic. Guide; Music Index; Newsp. Period. Abstr. (1991-); OCLC; Pub. Lib. FullTEXT; Res. Alert [Full Cov.]; RILM Abstr.; Telebase; Vocat. Search.

COMPUTER NETWORKS

LC TK5105.5 .A13
DD 004.6/05
ISSN 1051-9637
US
3TECH (SANTA CLARA, CALIF.). (3TECH : THE 3COM TECHNICAL JOURNAL.). [3TECH]. **Added/Corp** 3Com Corporation. **VFOAT** ThreeTECH; Three Tech; ThreeTECH ThreeCom's Technical Journal; 3TECH 3Com's Technical Journal. (Summer 1990)-. Periodical. Four times a year. Free on request. 3 Com/CSI, PO Box 58145, 5400 Bayfront Plaza, Santa Clara CA 95052. **Tel** (408)764-5000, (800)638-3266, FAX (408)764-5001.

UK
●**3W : GLOBAL NETWORKING NEWSLETTER.** **VFOAT** 3W Magazine; Three W. Issue 3 (Jan./Feb. 1994)-. Newsletter. English. Six times a year. $51.33. 3W, 461 West 49th Street, Suite 338, New York NY 10010. **Continues** World Wide Web Global Network Newsletter, 1350-2263.

ISSN 1072-0030
DD 004
US
CCC
●**ADVANCED INTELLIGENT NETWORK NEWS.** [Adv. intell. netw. news]. (1993)-. Periodical. English. Twenty-five times a year. $597.00. Phillips Business Information Inc., 1201 Seven Locks Road, PO Box 61130, Potomac MD 20854. **Tel** (301)424-3338, (301)340-1520, (800)777-5005, FAX (301)424-4297, telex 358149. available on an online database from NEWSNET. **Continues** AIN Report.

ISSN 1056-7119
US
TITLE CHANGE
ADVANCED INTELLIGENT NETWORKS REPORT. (1991)-(1993). Periodical. English. Phillips Business Information Inc., 1201 Seven Locks Road, PO Box 61130, Potomac MD 20854. **Tel** (301)424-3338, (301)340-1520, (800)777-5005, FAX (301)424-4297, telex 358149. **Continued by** Advanced Intelligent Network News, 1072-0030.
 Ind/Abst PTS Newsl. Database [Full Txt.].

ISSN 1038-359X
AT
AUSTRALIAN NEW ZEALAND LAN MAGAZINE. (19??)-. Periodical. English. Eleven times a year. 37.00Aus$. Australian Consolidated Press Ltd., Private Bag 92615 Symonds St, Auckland New Zealand. **Tel** 011 64 9 3735408, FAX 011 64 9 3022889.

LC QA
DD 004
US
BANYAN TECHNICAL JOURNAL. (19??)-. Periodical. English. Six times a year (Jan., Mar., May, Jul., Sept., Nov.). $299.00. Wellesley Information Services, 108 Arnold Road, Newton MA 02159. **Tel** (617)969-6666, FAX (617)969-9998. **Continues** Vines Observer, 1070-5082.

ISSN 0045-1991
CN
CEASED
BIG BYTE, THE. See Computers-Computer Systems.

ISSN 1059-0544
DD 384
US
CCC
BROADBAND NETWORKING NEWS. See Communications-Telecommunication.

US
BURTON GROUP NEWS ANALYSIS. English. Seventeen times a year. $795.00. Burton Group, 2649 East Union Boulevard, Salt Lake City UT 84121. **Tel** (801)943-1966, (800)824-9924.

ISSN 0384-5702
CN
DD 001.6/44/04
C C N G REPORT. **Main/Corp** University of Waterloo. Computer Communications Network Group. EL- 1973-. Periodical. English. Computer Communications Network Group E-4, 2369 University of Waterloo, Waterloo Ontario N2L 3G1 Canada.

LC Z678.93.L63 C33
DD 004
ISSN 1065-0741
US
CCC
●**CAMPUS-WIDE INFORMATION SYSTEMS.** See Computers-Automation.

ISSN 1189-461X
CN
CIMI NEWS. See Museums and Galleries.

ISSN 1081-3187
US
●**CISCO WORLD.** (1995)-. Periodical. English. Twelve times a year. $39.00. Publications & Communications, 12416 Hymeadow Drive, Austin TX 78750. **Tel** (512)250-9023, (800)678-9724, FAX (512)331-3900, telex 384303. **ED** Robert Martin. **Ad Acc, Adv Mgr:** Tricia Winton. **Circ:** 20,000 (ctrl).
 Desc: About networking and connectivity.

ISSN 0964-8844
UK
CLIENT SERVER. (CLIENT SERVER NEWS.). [Client serv.]. (1991)-. English. Twelve times a year. £395.00 UK and Europe; $595.00 US and Canada; £405.00 other. APT Data Services, 12 Sutton Row, 4th Floor, London W1V 5FH United Kingdom. **Tel** 011 44 171 2084200, FAX 011 44 171 4391105.

ISSN 1059-3470
DD 005
US
CCC
CLIENT/SERVER COMPUTING. [Client/server comput.]. **VFOAT** Client Server Computing; Client/Server Computing Supplement. (Sept. 1991)-. Trade Publication. English. Four times a year. $65.00. Sentry Publishing Co., 1900 West Park Drive, Westborough MA 01581. **Tel** (508)366-2031, FAX (508)836-4732.
 Desc: Focuses on the management of client/server technology - the platforms, the networks, and the software products that are the building blocks of next generation information systems.

LC TK7885
DD 621.39
US
●**CLIENT/SERVER TODAY.** (1994)-. English. Twelve times a year. $65.00 US; $96.00 (GST included) Canada; $90.00 Mexico; $120.00 (surface mail) other. Cahners Publishing Company, 249 West 17th Street, New York NY 10011. **Tel** (212)645-0067, FAX (212)242-6987. **(Subscription address:** Cahners Publishing Company / Colorado, Paid Subscription Service Center, PO Box 7610, Highlands Ranch CO 80126-7610. **Tel** (303)470-4466, FAX (303)470-4691.)
 Desc: Fulfills the information needs of computer professionals who are implementing or managing client/server strategies.

LC HD66 .C545
DD 658.3128
ISSN 0968-2082
UK
CCC
Pr Rev.
●**COLLABORATIVE COMPUTING.** (March 1994)-. Academic Scholarly Publication. English. Four times a year. $248.13. Chapman & Hall, 2-6 Boundary Row, London SE1 8HN United Kingdom. **Tel** 011 44 171 8650066, FAX 011 44 171 5229623, telex 290164 CHAPMA G. **(Subscription address:** International Thomson Publishing Services Ltd., North Way Andover, Hampshire SP10 5BE United Kingdom. **Tel** 011 44 1264 332424.) **ED** Board. available with charts; available with illustrations; available on an online database. Documents available from BLDSC.
 Desc: Emphasizes computer-supported cooperative work and computer-mediated communications.

US
COMMUNICATIONS SERIES. COMMUNICATIONS NETWORKING SERVICES. See Communications-Telecommunication.

ISSN 1058-8965
DD 004
US
CODEN CSMGES
COMPUSERVE MAGAZINE. [CompuServe mag.]. **Added/Corp** CompuServe Incorporated. (19??)-. Periodical. English. Twelve times a year. $30.00. CompuServe Inc, PO Box 20212, 5000 Arlington Centre Boulevard, Columbus OH 43220. **Tel** (614)457-8600, FAX (614)457-0348. available on an online database from Compuserve Inc. **Continues** Online Today, 0891-4672.
 Desc: Illustrates how CompuServe helps manage resources, communicates, informs, and entertains.
 Ind/Abst Trade Ind. Index.

LC TK5105.5 .C6377
DD 004
ISSN 0146-4833
US
CODEN CCRED2
COMPUTER COMMUNICATION REVIEW. [Comput. commun. rev.]. **Added/Corp** Association for Computing Machinery. Special Interest Group on Data Communications. Vol. 1, No. 2 (Mar. 1971)-. Periodical. English. Four times a year (quarterly with one Proceedings issue). $37.00. ACM / Association for Computing Machinery, 1515 Broadway, 17th Floor, New York NY 10036. **Tel** (212)869-7440, FAX (212)869-0481. **(Subscription address:** Association for Computing Machinery, PO Box 12114, Church Street Station, New York NY 10249. **Tel** (212)626-0500.) Documents available from Ask*IEEE. **Continues** ACM SIGCOMM Newsletter.
 Ind/Abst ACM Guide Comput. Lit.; Comput. Rev. (July 1981-); Curr. Cit.; Ei Page One; INSPEC (July 1981-).

LC TK5105.5 .C6373
DD 384
ISSN 0140-3664
UK
CCC
CODEN COCOD7
Pr Rev.
COMPUTER COMMUNICATIONS. [Comput. commun.]. Vol. 1, No. 1 (Feb. 1978)-. Periodical. English. Fourteen times a year. $835.00. Butterworth Heinemann Publishers, Linacre House Jordan Hill, Oxford OX2 8DP United Kingdom. **Tel** 011 44 1865 310366, FAX 011 44 1865 310898. **(Subscription address:** Elsevier Science Ltd. / Oxford Fulfillment Centre, PO Box 800, Kidlington OX5 1DX United Kingdom. **Tel** 011 44 865 843355.) **ED** Helen Sawyer. Index available. cum. index. **Bk Rev. Ad Acc. Circ:** 1,000. available on microfilm and microfiche from University Microfilms International (UMI); available on an online database from Elsevier Electronic Subscriptions (EES). Documents available from Article Express International, The Genuine Article, Ask*IEEE.
 Desc: Focuses on developments in networking and distributed computing techniques, communications hardware and software, and standardization. Applications, such as videotex, electronic mail, distributed database systems, EFTS and POS networks, are covered in detail.
 Ind/Abst ACM Guide Comput. Lit.; Bioeng. Abstr.; CompuMath Cit. Index [Full Cov.]; Comput. Database; Comput. Lit. Index; Comput. Rev.; Curr. Cit.; Curr. Contents Eng. Comput. Technol.; Ei Page One; Eng. Index Annu.; Inf. Sci. Abstr. (?-?); INSPEC (1978-); Manage. Market. Abstr.; Pollut. Abstr. Indexes; Res. Alert [Full Cov.]; SCISEARCH; Soc. Sci. Cit. Index [Select. Cov.]; World Publ. Monit.

LC TK5105.5 .C647
DD 621.382
ISSN 0169-7552
NE
CCC
CODEN CNISE9CNETDP
Pr Rev.
COMPUTER NETWORKS AND ISDN SYSTEMS. [Comput. netw. ISDN syst.]. **Added/Corp** International Council for Computer Communication. Vol. 9, No. 1 (Jan. 1985)-. Academic Scholarly Publication. English. Fourteen times a year. $881.00. Elsevier Science Publishers BV, PO Box 211, 1000 AE Amsterdam Netherlands. **Tel** 011 31 20 4853641, 011 31 20 4853642, FAX 011 31 20 4853598. **ED** P H Enslow (Editor's Address: College of Computing, Georgia Institute of Technology, Atlanta, GA 30332). Index

available. cum. index. **Ad Acc**, **Adv Mgr:** W Van Cattenburch. available on microfilm and microfiche from University Microfilms International (UMI); available on an online database from Elsevier Electronic Subscriptions (EES). Documents available from Article Express International, The Genuine Article, UMI Article Clearinghouse, Ask*IEEE. ***Continues*** *Computer Networks, 0376-5075.*
Desc: Provides a publication vehicle for complete coverage of all topics of interest to those involved in the area. Material on all aspects of the design, implementation, use and management of computer and telecommunication networks, communication sub-systems, and integrated services digital networks is included.
Ind/Abst ABI/INFORM Glob. Ed.; ABI/INFORM [Computer File] (February 1981-); Commun. Abstr.; CompuMath Cit. Index [Full Cov.]; Comput. Abstr.; Comput. Lit. Index; Comput. Rev.; Curr. Cit.; Ei Page One; Eng. Index Annu.; Gen. BusinessFile (1992-); Inf. Sci. Abstr.; INSPEC (Feb. 1985-); Linguist. Lang. Behav. Abstr.; Res. Alert [Full Cov.]; SCISEARCH; Soc. Plann. Policy Dev. Abstr.; Soc. Sci. Cit. Index [Select. Cov.]; Sociol. Abstr.; Zentralbl. Math. Ihre Grenzgeb.

LC TK5105.5 .C6472
DD 004.6 NE
•COMPUTER NETWORKS FOR RESEARCH IN EUROPE. Added/Corp International Council for Computer Communication. Reseaux Associes pour la Recherche Europeenne. European Academic and Research Network. **VFOAT** CNRE. (1993)-. Academic Scholarly Publication. English. Four times a year (1 volume). Fl220.00; Fl1300.00 combination subscription with Computer Networks and ISDN Systems. Elsevier Science Publishers BV, PO Box 211, 1000 AE Amsterdam Netherlands. **Tel** 011 31 20 4853641, 011 31 20 4853642, FAX 011 31 20 4853598. available on an online database from Elsevier Electronic Subscriptions (EES).

ISSN 0925-9724
NE
CCC
CODEN CSCWEQ
Pr Rev.
COMPUTER SUPPORTED COOPERATIVE WORK : CSCW : AN INTERNATIONAL JOURNAL. VFOAT CSCW. Vol. 1, No. 1-2 (1992)-. Periodical. English. Four times a year. $280.00. Kluwer Academic Publishers, Postbus 322, 3300 AH Dordrecht The Netherlands. **Tel** 011 31 78 524400, FAX 011 31 78 183273, telex 20083. **ED** Kjeld Schmidt. **Acid Free.** available on microfilm and microfiche from University Microfilms International (UMI). Documents available from Ask*IEEE.
Desc: Provides an interdisciplinary forum for the debate and exchange of ideas concerning theoretical, practical, technical and social issues in CSCW. The journal facilitates the discussion of all issues that arise in connection with the computerized support of cooperative work.
Ind/Abst INSPEC (1992-).

ISSN 0899-9783
DD 004 US
COMPUTER WORKSTATIONS. [Comput. workstn.]. (July 1988)-. Periodical. English. Twelve times a year. $150.00. WV Publishing Company, PO Box 138, Babson Park, Boston MA 02157. available on an online database (file 636/Full-Text) from DIALOG.
Ind/Abst PTS Newsl. Database [Full Txt.].

ISSN 1077-5803
DD 004 US
CODEN CLSJEI
•COMPUTERWORLD CLIENT/SERVER JOURNAL. [Comput.world client/serv. j.]. **VFOAT** Client/Server Journal. Vol. 1, No. 1 (Nov. 1993)-. Periodical. English. Four times a year. Comes with Computerworld - $48.00 US; $110.00 Canada; $150.00 Mexico, Central and South America. CW Communications, 375 Cochituate Road, Box 9171, Framingham MA 01701. **Tel** (508)879-0700.

US
COMPUTING STRATEGY SERVICE. English. Irregular. $5,000.00. Forrester Research Inc., 1 Brattle Square, Cambridge MA 02138. **Tel** (617)497-7090.

LC QA **ISSN** 0894-5926
DD 004 US
CONNEXIONS (CUPERTINO, CALIF.). (CONNEXIONS.). **VFOAT** Connections; ConneXions, The Interoperability Report; Interoperability Report. (Spring 1987)-. Trade Publication. English. Twelve times a year. $150.00. Interop Company, 303 Vintage Park Drive, Suite 201, Foster City CA 94404-1138. **Tel** (415)578-6900, FAX (415)525-0194. **ED** Ole Jacobsen. Index available (free). **Bk Rev**.
Desc: Covers interoperability issues, in particular the Internet suite of protocols (TCP/IP), OSI and related LAN/WAN protocols.

ISSN 1058-6806
DD 338 US
CONNEXIONS (MANASSAS, VA.). (CONNEXIONS : NETWORKING FOR HOMEBASED MOTHERS & PROFESSIONALS.). (1990)-. Periodical. English. Four times a year. $14.95. Connexions / Manassas, PO Box 1461, Manassas VA 22110.

ISSN 1071-6327
DD 004 US
COOK REPORT ON INTERNET, NREN, THE. [Cook rep. Internet NREN]. **Added/Corp** Cook Network Consultants. (199?)-. Periodical. English. Twelve times a year. $175.00. Cook Network Consultants, 431 Greenway Avenue, Ewing NJ 08618. **Tel** (609)882-2572.

ISSN 1065-8610
DD 004 US
CEASED
CORPORATE COMPUTING. [Corp. comput.]. Vol. 1, No. 1 (June/July 1992)-(Aug. 1993). Periodical. English. Corporate Computing, PO Box 7644, Riverton NJ 08077-7644. **Tel** (609)461-2100.

ISSN 1059-4590
DD 657 US
Pr Rev.
CPA'S PC NETWORK ADVISOR. See Business and Economics-Computer Applications.

ISSN 1079-2120
US
•CYBERSURFER. (CYBERSURFER : THE MAGAZINE OF ENTERTAINMENT TECHNOLOGY.). **Added/Corp** Starlog Group. (1995)-. Periodical. English. Four times a year. $16.97. Starlog Press Inc., 475 Park Avenue South, New York NY 10016. **Tel** (212)689-2830, FAX (212)889-7933.

LC QA75.5 .D35 **ISSN** 0363-6399
DD 001.6/4/05 US
CCC
CODEN DACODM
DATA COMMUNICATIONS. [Data commun.]. Vol. 3, No. 1 (May/June 1974)-. Periodical. English. Seventeen times a year (monthly with additional issues March, June, Sept., Oct., Nov.). $125.00. McGraw Hill Publishing Company, Inc., 1221 Avenue of the Americas, New York NY 10020. **Tel** (212)512-6410, (800)525-5003, FAX (212)512-6111. **(Subscription address:** Data Communications, PO Box 477, Hightstown NJ 08520. **)** Index available. ctrl circ. available on microfilm and microfiche from University Microfilms International (UMI); available on an online database from Dow Jones News/Retrieval; NEWSNET; NEXIS; and (file 624/Full-Text) DIALOG. Documents available from UMI Article Clearinghouse, Ask*IEEE. ***Continues*** *Data Communications Systems.*
Desc: Worldwide technical magazine edited for the user and purchaser of computer and communication systems, including local and wide area networks and voice/data informations networks.
Ind/Abst ABI/INFORM Glob. Ed.; ABI/INFORM [Computer File] (March 1975-); Acad. Search; Bus. Index (1985-); Bus. Period. Index; Bus. Source Plus; Bus. Source; Comput. Bus. (19??-19??); Comput. Database; Comput. Lit. Index; Comput. Rev.; Ei Page One; EP Collect.; F&S Index Plus Text, Int. [Select. Cov.]; Gen. BusinessFile (1985-); Gen. Period. Index (1985-); Homework Help.; INFO-SOUTH Abstr.; Infomat Int. Bus.; Inf. Instruc. Technol.; Inf. Sci. Abstr.; INSPEC (Nov. 1981-); Mag. Search; Manage. Market. Abstr.; MasterFile FullTEXT 1000; MasterFile FullTEXT 350; MasterFile FullTEXT 650; MasterFile FullTEXT (July 1993-); Microcomput. Abstr. (Jan. 1985-); OCLC; PROMT; Telebase; Trade Ind. Index (1981-); UMI ABI/Inform--Bus. Period. Ondisc [Full Txt.]; Wilson Bus. Abstr.; World Publ. Monit.

US
DATA COMMUNICATIONS INTERNATIONAL. (19??)-. English. Twelve times a year. $150.00 (one-year), $225.00 (two-year). McGraw Hill Publishing Company, Inc., 1221 Avenue of the Americas, New York NY 10020. **Tel** (212)512-6410, (800)525-5003, FAX (212)512-6111. **(Subscription address:** Data Communications International, Box 477, Hightstown NJ 08520. **)** Index available. **Ad Acc. Circ:** 18,669.
Desc: Networking magazine for the user and purchaser of computer and communication systems.

US
Pr Rev.
DATA NETWORKING / DATAPRO. Added/Corp Datapro Information Services Group. Vol. 1, No. 1 (Aug. 1991)-. Periodical. English. Twelve times a year. $1723.00. Datapro Information Services Group, 600 Delran Parkway, Delran NJ 08075. **Tel** (609)764-0100, (800)328-2776, FAX (609)764-8953. Index available. cum. index. available on microfilm; available on microfiche. ***Continues*** *Datapro Reports on Data Communications, 0730-8787.*
Desc: Information on data communication equipment, standards networking services, internetworking and interoperability issues make up the focus of this comprehensive publication.

ISSN 0265-4490
UK
DATABASE AND NETWORK JOURNAL. See Computers-Data Base Management.

UK
CEASED
DATACOM : THE JOURNAL OF INTERCONNECTION AND NETWORKING. (19??)-(June 1995). English. Datacom, 2nd Floor/155 Farringdon Road, London EC1R 3AD United Kingdom. **Tel** 011 44 171 2516222.

UK
DATAPRO INTERNATIONAL NETWORK SERIES. (19??)-. English. Irregular. $1,963.00. Datapro International, McGraw Hill House, Shoppenhangers Road, Maidenhead Berkshire SL6 2QL United Kingdom. **Tel** 011 44 1628 773277, FAX 011 44 1628 773628.

US
DATAPRO MANAGING DATA NETWORKS. Added/Corp Datapro Research Corporation. **VFOAT** Managing Data Networks. (Aug. 1991)-. Periodical. English. Twelve times a year. $1031.00. Datapro Information Services Group, 600 Delran Parkway, Delran NJ 08075. **Tel** (609)764-0100, (800)328-2776, FAX (609)764-8953. ***Continues*** *Datapro Management of Data Communications.*

ISSN 0107-7481
DD 025.04 DK
DISPLAY. [Display Kbh.]. (1982)-. Periodical. Danish. Ten times a year. $62.22. Dansk Diane Center, Sigurdsgade 41, DK 2200 Copenhagen N Denmark. **Tel** 011 45 31 816666. **ED** Karen Bonnis. **Bk Rev. Circ:** 7,000.

LC QA76.9.D5 D493 **ISSN** 0178-2770
DD 004/.36/05 GW
CCC
CODEN DICOEB
Pr Rev.
DISTRIBUTED COMPUTING. See Computers-Electronic Data Processing.

ISSN 1359-4699
DD 004.6 UK
•DISTRIBUTED COMPUTING DIRECTIONS. [Distrib. comput. dir.]. **VFOAT** DC Directions. (1995)-. Periodical. English. Six times a year. $1069.50. Technology Appraisals Ltd., 82 Hampton Road, Twickenham TW2 5QS United Kingdom. **Tel** 011 44 181 8933986. ***Separated from*** *OSN Open Systems Network and Computing, 1359-4702.*

ISSN 1068-6266
DD 004 US
DISTRIBUTED COMPUTING MONITOR. [Distrib. comput. monit.]. Vol. 7, No. 6 (June 1992)-. Periodical. English. Twelve times a year. $550.00. Patricia Seybolds Office Computing Group, 148 State Street, Suite 700, Boston MA 02109. **Tel** (617)742-5200, (800)826-2424, FAX (617)742-1028. ***Continues*** *Network Monitor, 1058-4153.*

ISSN 1079-4727
DD 004 US
CCC
•DISTRIBUTED SYSTEMS MANAGEMENT REPORT. [Distrib. syst. manag. rep.]. **Added/Corp** Leesburg, VA : Datatrends Publications. Vol. 7, No. 10 (Oct. 1994)-. Periodical. English. Twelve times a year. $550.00. DataTrends Publications, 895 Harrison Street SE, Suite B, Leesburg VA 22075. **Tel** (703)779-0574, (800)766-8130, FAX (703)779-2267. ***Continues*** *OPEN (Vienna, Va.), 1072-7760.*

LU
ECHO NEWS. Main/Corp European Commission Host Organisation. English. Six times a year. European Commission Host Organisation, POB 2373, L-1023 Luxembourg Luxembourg. **Tel** 011 352 48 8041, 011 352 48 8040, telex 2181. **ED** Bernice Sweeney.

ISSN 1063-8431
DD 004 US
EDGE (HACKETTSTOWN, N.J.). (EDGE : WORK-GROUP COMPUTING REPORT.). [Edge]. (1990)-. Periodical. English. Twenty-six times a year. $7000.00. Edge Publishing, PO Box 471, Hackettstown NJ 07840. **Tel** (908)852-7217, FAX (908)850-8304. available on an online database (files 636,648,675/Full-Text) from DIALOG.
Ind/Abst Comput. ASAP [Full Txt.]; Comput. Database [Full Txt.]; PTS Newsl. Database [Full Txt.]; Trade Ind. Index [Full Txt.].

LC QA75 **ISSN** 1082-8761
DD 004 US
•EI JOURNAL. (EI JOURNAL : ENTERPRISE INTERNETWORKING.). [EI j.]. **VFOAT** Enterprise Internetworking Journal. Vol. 3, No. 5 (May 1995)-. Periodical. English. Twelve times a year. Cardinal Business Media / Texas, 12225 Greenville Avenue, Suite

Computers —Computer Networks

700, Dallas TX 75243. **Tel** (214)669-9000, FAX (214)669-9909. **Continues** IBM Internet Journal, 1068-1396.

LC QA75   ISSN 1054-1055
DD 004   US
EJOURNAL (ALBANY, N.Y.). (EJOURNAL [COMPUTER FILE] : AN ELECTRONIC JOURNAL CONCERNED WITH THE IMPLICATIONS OF ELECTRONIC NETWORKS AND TEXTS.). **Added/Corp** State University of New York at Albany. **VFOAT** E Journal. **VAT** Electronic Journal. Vol. 1, Issue 1 (Mar. 1991)-. Periodical. English. Irregular. Free. The University of New York at Albany, Department of English, Albany NY 12222. **Tel** (518)442-4091. available via Internet (message to Listserv@albany.edu, SUBSCRIBE EJRNL).
Desc: Covers electronic networks and "texts." Discusses all aspects of computer-mediated networks.

    ISSN 1044-9892
DD 384   UK
    CCC
ELECTRONIC MESSAGING NEWS. See Communications.

    UK
ENTERPRISE CLIENT/SERVER. (19??)-. English. Twelve times a year. $300.00. Xephon, 27-35 London Road, Newbury Berkshire RG13 1JL United Kingdom. **Tel** 011 44 1635 33823, FAX 011 44 1635 38345. **(Subscription address:** Xephon, 1301 West Highway, Suite 201 450, Lewisville TX 75067.)

    ISSN 0741-0050
    US
    CCC
EXECUTIVE COMPUTING. See Computers-Computer Industry and Industry Directories.

    US
FAULKNER ENTERPRISE NETWORKING. (19??)-. Periodical. English. Twelve times a year. $1395.00 US; $1589.00 Canada; $1820.00 other. Faulkner Technical Reports, 7905 Browning Road, Suite 114, Pennsauken NJ 08109. **Tel** (800)843-0460.

    US
FAULKNER LOCAL AREA NETWORKING. (19??)-. Periodical. English. Twelve times a year. $835.00 US; $937.00 Canada; $1119.00 other. Faulkner Technical Reports, 7905 Browning Road, Suite 114, Pennsauken NJ 08109. **Tel** (800)843-0460.

LC JK468.A8 F42   ISSN 1057-5804
DD 353.04/0285   US
FEDERAL ADP AND TELECOMMUNICATIONS STANDARDS INDEX. See Communications-Computer Applications.

LC TK5105.5 .F89   ISSN 1059-0846
DD 004.6/2   US
FUTUREBUS+ DESIGN. [Futurebus+ des.]. **VFOAT** Futurebus Plus Design. Issue No. 1 (Jan./Feb. 1991)-. Periodical. English. Six times a year. Supermicro, 1275 North University/Unit 7, Provo UT 84604.

    ISSN 1057-1620
DD 004   US
GLOBAL NETWORKS. [Glob. netw.]. Vol. 1, No. 1 (Spring 1991)-. Periodical. English. Four times a year. $75.00. Network World Inc., 161 Worcester Road, Framingham MA 01701-9172.

LC QA76.9.A25 T73   ISSN 0892-399X
DD 004   US
●**I-WAYS : DIGEST OF THE GLOBAL INFORMATION INFRASTRUCTURE COMMISSION. Added/Corp** Transnational Data Reporting Service. Center for Strategic and International Studies (Washington, D.C.) International Communications Studies Program. Global Information Infrastructure Commission. **VFOAT** I Ways; Digest of the Global Information Infrastructure Commission. Vol. 18, No. 1 (Jan./Feb. 1995)-. Periodical. English. Six times a year. $310.00. Transnational Data Reporting Service Inc, PO Box 10528, Burke VA 22009. **Tel** (703)323-9116, FAX (703)250-4705. **Continues** Transnational Data and Communications Report.
Desc: A review of the international information policy, telecommunication policy and regulation, and related legal matters.

LC TK5105.875.I57 I26   ISSN 1068-1396
DD 004.6   US
Pr Rev.   TITLE CHANGE
IBM INTERNET JOURNAL. [IBM internet j.]. **VFOAT** Internet Journal. **VAT** International Business Machines Internet Journal. (1993)-(199?). Periodical. English. Cardinal Business Media / Texas, 12225 Greenville Avenue, Suite 700, Dallas TX 75243. **Tel** (214)669-9000, FAX (214)669-9909. **Continued by** El Journal, 1082-8761.

LC TK5105.5 .I3   ISSN 1063-6692
DD 004.6/05   US
    CODEN IEANEP
●**IEEE / ACM TRANSACTIONS ON NETWORKING.** (IEEE/ACM TRANSACTIONS ON NETWORKING : A JOINT PUBLICATION OF THE IEEE COMMUNICATIONS SOCIETY, THE IEEE COMPUTER SOCIETY, AND THE ACM WITH ITS SPECIAL INTEREST GROUP ON DATA COMMUNICATION.). [IEEE/ACM trans. netw.]. **Added/Corp** Institute of Electrical and Electronics Engineers. IEEE Communications Society. IEEE Computer Society. Association for Computing Machinery. Special Interest Group on Data Communications. **VFOAT** Transactions on Networking; Networking. **VAT** Institute of Electrical and Electronics Engineers, Association for Computing Machinery Transactions on Networking. Vol. 1, No. 1 (Feb. 1993)-. Periodical. English. Six times a year. $265.00. ACM / Association for Computing Machinery, 1515 Broadway, 17th Floor, New York NY 10036. **Tel** (212)869-7440, FAX (212)869-0481. **(Subscription address:** Institute of Electrical and Electronics Engineers, 445 Hoes Lane, PO Box 1331, Piscataway NJ 08855-1331. **Tel** (800)701-IEEE, (908)981-0060, FAX (908)981-9667, telex 833233.)
Desc: Covers research in the networking aspects of communications. Major topics include protocols, internetworking, network management, and applications for computer communications, multimedia, and multiple-service capabilities.

LC TK5105.5 .I324   ISSN 0890-8044
DD 004.6   US
    CCC
IEEE NETWORK. [IEEE netw.]. **Added/Corp** IEEE Communications Society. Institute of Electrical and Electronics Engineers. **VFOAT** Network; IEEE Network Magazine. **VAT** Institute of Electrical and Electronics Engineers Network. Vol. 1, No. 1 (Jan. 1987)-. Periodical. English. Six times a year. $130.00. IEEE / Institute of Electrical and Electronics Engineers Inc., 345 East 47th Street, New York NY 10017-2394. **Tel** (908)981-1393, FAX (908)981-9667. **(Subscription address:** IEEE / Institute of Electrical and Electronics Engineers, 445 Hoes Lane, PO Box 1331, Piscataway NJ 08855-1331. **Tel** (800)701-IEEE, (908)981-0060, FAX (908)981-9667, telex 833233.) Documents available from Article Express International, Ask*IEEE.
Desc: Covers network protocols and architectures, protocol design and validation, communication software and its development and test, network control and signaling, network management, and practical network implementations.
Ind/Abst Comput. Database; Curr. Cit.; Ei Page One; Eng. Index Annu.; Expand. Acad. Index (1992-); Index IEEE Publ. (Jan. 1987-); Inf. Sci. Abstr.; INSPEC (Jan. 1987-); Int. Aerosp. Abstr.

    ISSN 0926-549X
    NE
    CCC
    CODEN ITCCE5
IFIP TRANSACTIONS. C, COMMUNICATION SYSTEMS. (IFIP TRANSACTIONS. C, COMMUNICATION SYSTEMS / INTERNATIONAL FEDERATION FOR INFORMATION PROCESSING, TECHNICAL COMMITTEE 6.). [IFIP trans. C, Commun. syst.]. **Added/Corp** International Federation for Information Processing. Technical Committee 6. (1992)-. Academic Scholarly Publication. English. Irregular. Price varies per volume. Elsevier Science Publishers BV, PO Box 211, 1000 AE Amsterdam Netherlands. **Tel** 011 31 20 4853641, 011 31 20 4853642, FAX 011 31 20 4853598.
Ind/Abst CompuMath Cit. Index [Full Cov.]; Curr. Cit.; Soc. Sci. Cit. Index [Select. Cov.].

    ISSN 1079-4069
    US
●**INFOBAHN (FOSTER CITY, CALIF.).** (INFOBAHN : THE MAGAZINE OF INTERNET CULTURE.). (1995)-. Periodical. English. Six times a year. $24.95. Postmodern Communications Inc., Post Office Box 4216, Foster City CA 94404.

    ISSN 1065-0660
    US
INFORMATION FOR NETWORK USERS. (INFORMATION FOR NETWORK USERS [COMPUTER FILE].). (1992)-. Periodical. English. Free.

LC HE7781 .I587   ISSN 1073-6921
DD 004.6/0973/05   US
●**INFORMATION INFRASTRUCTURE SOURCEBOOK. See** Communications-Telecommunication.

    ISSN 1078-6589
DD 384   US
●**INFORMATION SUPERHIGHWAYS.** [Inf. superhighw.]. **VFOAT** Information Superhighways Newsletter. Vol. 1, No. 1 (Sept. 1994)-. Newsletter. English. Twelve times a year. $575.00. Information Gatekeepers Inc., 214 Harvard Avenue, Boston MA 02134. **Tel** (617)232-3111, (617)738-8088, (800)323-1088, FAX (617)734-8562.

    US
INFORMATION TECHNOLOGY DIGEST. See Computers-Microcomputers, Personal Computers.

    NZ
●**INFOSYS.** (1994)-. Newsletter. English. One time a week. Massey University Information Systems Department, Palmerston North New Zealand. **Tel** 011 64 9 4439612, FAX 011 64 9 4439640.

    ISSN 1077-0259
DD 005   US
●**INSIDE LANTASTIC.** [Inside LANtastic]. **Added/Corp** Cobb Group. Vol. 1, No. 1 (Aug. 1994)-. Periodical. English. Twelve times a year. $99.00. Cobb Group, 9420 Bunsen Parkway #300, Louisville KY 40220. **Tel** (502)491-1900, (800)223-8720, FAX (502)491-4200.

LC TK5105.875.I57 I53   ISSN 1075-7902
DD 004.6/7   US
●**INSIDE THE INTERNET.** [Inside Internet]. **Added/Corp** Cobb Group. (1994)-. Periodical. English. Twelve times a year. $49.00. Cobb Group, 9420 Bunsen Parkway #300, Louisville KY 40220. **Tel** (502)491-1900, (800)223-8720, FAX (502)491-4200.

    ISSN 1080-4927
DD 004   US
●**INTERACTIVE AGE.** [Interact. age]. (Sept. 26, 1994)-. Periodical. English. Twenty-six times a year. $79.00 US; $94.00 Canada; $179.00 Mexico, Central & South America, Europe; $200.00 other. CMP Publications Inc., One Jericho Plaza, Wing A, 2nd Floor, Jericho NY 11753. **Tel** (516)733-6700. **(Subscription address:** CMP Publications, Inc. / Illinois, PO Box 5920, Department 100, Carol Stream IL 60197-5920.) **ED** David Klein.
Ind/Abst Bus. Source Plus; EP Collect.; Homework Help.; MasterFile FullTEXT 1000; MasterFile FullTEXT 350; MasterFile FullTEXT 650; MasterFile FullTEXT; OCLC; Telebase.

    ISSN 1075-5276
DD 338   US
INTERNATIONAL ISDN YELLOW PAGES. [Int. ISDN yellow pages]. **VFOAT** ISDN Yellow Pages. (199?)-. Directory. English. One time a year. $49.95. Information Gatekeepers Inc., 214 Harvard Avenue, Boston MA 02134. **Tel** (617)232-3111, (617)738-8088, (800)323-1088, FAX (617)734-8562. **Continues** ISDN Handbook & Buyers Guide.
Desc: Business directory for the integrated services digital network industry.

LC QA76.87 .I58   ISSN 0129-0657
DD 006.3   SI
    CCC
NLM W1; IN7698   CODEN IJSZEG
Pr Rev.
INTERNATIONAL JOURNAL OF NEURAL SYSTEMS. See Computers-Artificial Intelligence.

    ISSN 1082-393X
    US
●**INTERNET BUSINESS ADVANTAGE (LOUISVILLE, KY.).** (INTERNET BUSINESS ADVANTAGE.). **Added/Corp** Cobb Group. (1995)-. Periodical. English. Twelve times a year. $59.00. Cobb Group, 9420 Bunsen Parkway #300, Louisville KY 40220. **Tel** (502)491-1900, (800)223-8720, FAX (502)491-4200.

    ISSN 1078-6422
DD 658   US
●**INTERNET BUSINESS ADVANTAGE : ONLINE SOLUTIONS FOR BUSINESS SUCCESS.** [Internet bus. advant.]. Vol. 1, No. 1 (1994)-. Periodical. English. Twelve times a year. $59.00. Wentworth Publishing Company, 1866 Colonial Village Lane, Lancaster PA 17605. **Tel** (800)331-5196, (717)393-1000, FAX (717)393-5752.

LC TK5105.875.I57 I5   ISSN 1192-8646
DD 384.3   CN
    CCC
    CODEN IBUJEO
●**INTERNET BUSINESS JOURNAL, THE.** [Internet bus. j.]. Vol. 1, No. 1 (June/July 1993)-. Periodical. English. Twelve times a year. 75.00Can$. Strangelove Press, 208 Somerset Street East, Suite A, Ottawa Ontario K1N 6V2 Canada. **Tel** (613)565-0982. available via Internet (email mstrange@fonorola.net).

    ISSN 1082-1880
    US
●**INTERNET (CARLSBAD, CALIF.).** (INTERNET : WHAT'S WORKING FOR BUSINESS.). (1995)-. Periodical. English. Twelve times a year. $250.00. Computer Economics Inc., 5841 Edison Place, Carlsbad CA 92008. **Tel** (800)326-8100, (619)438-8100, FAX (619)431-1126.

    US
●**INTERNET CONNECTION, THE. See** Communications-Computer Applications.

LC HE7601 ISSN 1076-4143
DD 384 US
●INTERNET HOMESTEADER. SERIES A, LIBRARY AND INFORMATION SCIENCE, THE. [Internet homestd., Ser. A Libr. inf. sci.]. **Added/Corp** SUNY/OCLC Network. State University of New York. Office of Library Services. Vol. 1, no. 1 (Apr. 1994)-. Periodical. English. Twelve times a year. $29.00. Homesteader Editor SUNY, Office Library Services, SUNY Plaza, Albany NY 12246. **Tel** (518)443-5444.

LC K
DD 340 US
●INTERNET LAWYER. See Law-Computer Applications.

ISSN 1070-9851
DD 004 US
TITLE CHANGE
INTERNET LETTER, THE. (Oct. 1993)-(1995). Periodical. English. Net Week Inc., 220 National Press Building, Washington DC 20045. **Tel** (202)638-6020, (800)638-9335. ***Merged into*** *Internet Week.*

LC TK5105.5 .E42 ISSN 1066-2243
DD 004.6/7 US
CCC
CODEN IRESEF
●INTERNET RESEARCH. [Internet res.]. Vol. 3, No. 1 (Spring 1993)-. Periodical. English. Four times a year. $239.00. Mecklermedia Corporation, 11 Ferry Lane West, Westport CT 06880. **Tel** (203)226-6967, (800)632-5537, FAX (203)454-5840. **(Subscription address:** Fulco, 30 Broad Street, Denville NJ 07834. **Tel** (800)783-4903, (201)627-2427.**)** Documents available from Ask*IEEE. ***Continues*** *Electronic Networking, 1051-4805.*
Ind/Abst INSPEC; Soc. Sci. Cit. Index [Select. Cov.].

ISSN 1079-5669
US
●INTERNET SECURITY MONTHLY. (1994)-. English. Twelve times a year. $75.00. Network Security Observations, Suite 400, 1825 I Street Northwest, Washington DC 20006. **Tel** (202)775-4947, FAX (202)429-9574, telex 440557 hqwdc. **ED** Dr. F. Bertil Fortrie. **Circ:** 7,500.

ISSN 1078-540X
DD 384 US
●INTERNET VOYAGER. [Internet voyag.]. Vol. 1, No. 1 (1994)-. Periodical. English. Twelve times a year. $78.00. Blue Dolphin Communications, PO Box 216, Wayland MA 01778. **Tel** (508)443-8214.

LC TK5105.5 .R448
DD 384.3 US
CODEN IERNE8
INTERNET WORLD. [Internet world]. Vol. 3, No. 7 (Sept. 1992)-. English. Eleven times a year. $29.00. Mecklermedia Corporation, 11 Ferry Lane West, Westport CT 06880. **Tel** (203)226-6967, (800)632-5537, FAX (203)454-5840. **(Subscription address:** Kable Publishers Aide / Illinois, 308 East Hitt Street, Subscription Department, Mt. Morris IL 61054-1473. **Tel** (815)734-1261.**)** ***Continues*** *Research & Education Networking, 1051-4791.*
Desc: For Internet users; contains information on computer systems, online systems, and computer networks.

LC TK5105.875.I57 I585 ISSN 1066-9973
DD 025 US
TITLE CHANGE
INTERNET WORLD'S ON INTERNET. [Internet world's internet]. **VFOAT** On Internet. (1994)-(1995). English. Mecklermedia Corporation, 11 Ferry Lane West, Westport CT 06880. **Tel** (203)226-6967, (800)632-5537, FAX (203)454-5840. ***Continued by*** *Official Internet World Internet Yellow Pages.*

LC TK5105.875.I57 H34
DD 621.382 US
●INTERNET YELLOW PAGES, THE. See Communications-Computer Applications.

LC TK5105.7 .I568 ISSN 1079-0373
DD 004.6/05 US
●INTERNETWORK (FORT WASHINGTON, PA.). (INTERNETWORK.). [Internetwork]. **VFOAT** Inter Network. Vol. 5, No. 9 (Sept. 1994)-. Periodical. English. Twelve times a year. $75.00. Cardinal Business Media / Pennsylvania, 1300 Virginia Drive, Suite 400, Fort Washington PA 19034. **Tel** (215)643-8112. ***Continues*** *LAN Computing, 1055-1808.*

LC TK5105.5 .I63 ISSN 1049-8915
DD 004.6 UK
CCC
CODEN IREEE7
INTERNETWORKING (CHICHESTER, ENGLAND). (INTERNETWORKING : RESEARCH AND EXPERIENCE.). [Internetworking]. **VFOAT** Journal of Internetworking Practice and Experience; Internetworking, Research and Experience. (1990)-. Trade Publication. English. Four times a year. $315.00. John Wiley & Sons Ltd., Baffins Lane, Chichester, West Sussex PO19 1UD United Kingdom. **Tel** 011 44 1243 779777, FAX 011 44 1243 776128 BTG:JWP001, telex 86290 WIBOOKG. **(Subscription address:** John Wiley & Sons, Inc. / Philadelphia, PO Box 7247, Philadelphia PA 19170. **Tel** (212)850-6645, (800)225-5945.**)** **ED** D. E. Comer, R. E. Droms, D. L. Estrin, and L. Svobodova. available on microfilm and microfiche from University Microfilms International (UMI). Documents available from Ask*IEEE.
Desc: Provides a focus for original results of research in interconnection and interoperability of computer networks and systems, a mechanism for quality control and verification through the refereeing process, and opportunities for comment and debate in a public and easily accessible forum.
Ind/Abst Data Process. Dig.; INSPEC (Sep. 1990-).

LC TK5105.5 .I64
DD 004.6/05 US
INTEROPERABILITY. Vol. 2, No. 1 (Fall 1991)-. English. Miller Freeman Inc., 600 Harrison Street, San Francisco CA 94107. **Tel** (415)905-2337, (415)905-2200, FAX (415)905-2240, telex 278273.

LC QA ISSN 1082-9849
DD 004.6 US
●IOMA'S REPORT ON MANAGING LAN COSTS. **Added/Corp** Institute of Management & Administration. **VFOAT** Institute of Management & Administration Report on Managing LAN Costs. (1995)-. Periodical. English. Twelve times a year. $245.00. Institute of Management and Administration, 29 West 35th Street, 5th Floor, New York NY 10001-2299. **Tel** (212)244-0360, FAX (212)564-0465.

LC QA75 ISSN 0735-1844
DD 004 US
CCC
ISDN (BROOKLINE, MASS.). (ISDN.). [ISDN]. **Added/Corp** Information Gatekeepers, Inc. **VFOAT** I.S.D.N.; I.S.D.N. News; ISDN News. **VAT** Integrated Services Digital Network. Vol. 5, No. 8 (Aug. 1982)-. Newsletter. English. Twelve times a year. $575.00. Information Gatekeepers Inc., 214 Harvard Avenue, Boston MA 02134. **Tel** (617)232-3111, (617)738-8088, (800)323-1088, FAX (617)734-8562. ***Continues*** *International Data Networks, 0270-2738.*

ISSN 1080-2991
DD 004 US
●ISDN FOR SMALL BUSINESS. [ISDN small bus.]. **Added/Corp** Information Gatekeepers, Inc. **VAT** Integrated Services Digital Network for Small Business. (1994)-. Newsletter. English. Twelve times a year. $29.95 US and Canada; $39.95 other. Information Gatekeepers Inc., 214 Harvard Avenue, Boston MA 02134. **Tel** (617)232-3111, (617)738-8088, (800)323-1088, FAX (617)734-8562.

US
ISDN INFORMATION SOURCEBOOK. (19??)-. Periodical. English. Irregular. $295.00. Information Gatekeepers Inc., 214 Harvard Avenue, Boston MA 02134. **Tel** (617)232-3111, (617)738-8088, (800)323-1088, FAX (617)734-8562.

ISSN 0899-9554
DD 384 UK
CCC
ISDN NEWS. [ISDN news]. **VAT** Integrated Services Digital Network News. (Aug. 1988)-. Periodical. English. Twenty-five times a year (biweekly). $597.00. Omnicom PPI Limited, (A Phillips Business Information company), Forum Chambers, The Forum Stevenage Hertfordshire SG1 1EL United Kingdom. **Tel** 011 44 1438 742424, FAX 011 44 1438 740154. **ED** John Lilley, Jennifer Whalen (US editor). available on an online database (file 636/Full-Text) from DIALOG.
Ind/Abst PTS Newsl. Database [Full Txt.].

ISSN 1058-7470
DD 004 US
TITLE CHANGE
ISDN USER MAGAZINE. [ISDN user mag.]. **VFOAT** I.S.D.N. User Magazine; ISDN User. **VAT** Integrated Services Digital Network User Magazine. (198?)-(199?). Periodical. English. Information Gatekeepers Inc., 214 Harvard Avenue, Boston MA 02134. **Tel** (617)232-3111, (617)738-8088, (800)323-1088, FAX (617)734-8562. ***Continues*** *ISDN User.* ***Continued by*** *ISDN User Newsletter, 1078-1005.*

ISSN 1078-1005
DD 004 US
ISDN USER NEWSLETTER. [ISDN user newsl.]. **VAT** Integrated Services Digital Network User Newsletter. (199?)-. Newsletter. English. Six times a year. $80.00. Information Gatekeepers Inc., 214 Harvard Avenue, Boston MA 02134. **Tel** (617)232-3111, (617)738-8088, (800)323-1088, FAX (617)734-8562. ***Continues*** *ISDN User Magazine, 1058-7470.*

LC HD9696.C63 J3214
DD 338.47621381 JA
JOHOKA HAKUSHO = INFORMATIZATION WHITE PAPER. See Computers-Computer Industry and Industry Directories.

LC QA76.87 .J67 ISSN 1073-5828
DD 006.3 US
CODEN JANNE5
CEASED
JOURNAL OF ARTIFICIAL NEURAL NETWORKS. See Computers-Artificial Intelligence.

ISSN 0926-6801
NE
CCC
JOURNAL OF HIGH SPEED NETWORKS. (19??)-. Periodical. English. Four times a year. $274.07. IOS Press, Van Diemenstraat 94, 1013 CN Amsterdam Netherlands. **Tel** 011 31 20 6382189, FAX 011 31 20 6203419.

LC TK5105.5 .J68 ISSN 0966-9248
DD 621.382 UK
CODEN JIFNEL
Pr Rev. TITLE CHANGE
JOURNAL OF INFORMATION NETWORKING. (1993)-(1995). Periodical. English. Taylor Graham Publishing, 500 Chesham House, 150 Regent Street, London W1R 5FA United Kingdom. **Bk Rev. Ad Acc.** ***Continued by*** *New Review of Information Networking.*

ISSN 1064-7570
DD 004 US
CCC
CODEN JNSMEG
●JOURNAL OF NETWORK AND SYSTEMS MANAGEMENT. [J. netw. syst. manag.]. Vol. 1, No. 1 (Mar. 1993)-. Periodical. English. Four times a year. $195.00. Plenum Press, 233 Spring Street, New York NY 10013-1578. **Tel** (212)620-8000, (800)221-9369, FAX (212)463-0742, (212)807-1047, telex 23/421139.

ISSN 0899-9309
DD 005 US
KERMIT NEWS. [Kermit news]. **Added/Corp** Columbia University. Center for Computing Activities. Vol. 1, No. 1 (July 1986)-. Periodical. English. Irregular (usually once every two years). Free. Kermit Distribution and Development, Columbia University, Academic Information Systems, 612 West 115th Street, New York NY 10025. **Tel** (212)854-3703, FAX (212)663-8202.

LC TK5105.7 .L35 ISSN 1055-1808
DD 004.6/8/05 US
LAN COMPUTING. [LAN comput.]. **VAT** Local Area Network Computing. (Sept. 1990)-. Periodical. English. Twelve times a year. free (to qualified professionals). Professional Press Inc, 101 Witmer Road, Horsham PA 19044. **Tel** (215)957-1500, FAX (215)957-1050. available on an online database (file 675/Full-Text) from DIALOG.
Desc: A new tabloid written for managers of multivendor networks. Editorial reports on developments in open systems, interoperability and industry standards to help managers understand issues and trends in networking.
Ind/Abst Comput. ASAP [Full Txt.]; Comput. Database [Full Txt.].

NE
Pr Rev.
LAN MAGAZINE. Dutch. Fl175.00. LAN Magazine BV, Spaarne 55, 2011 CE Haarlem Netherlands. **Tel** 023-366814, FAX 023-360724. **ED** Frank Keiren. Index available. cum. index. **Bk Rev. Ad Acc. Circ:** 12,000. available on an online database (file 675/Full-Text) from DIALOG.
Desc: A magazine for professionals in networking.
Ind/Abst Comput. ASAP [Full Txt.]; Comput. Database [Full Txt.].

LC TK5105.7 .L363 ISSN 1051-4066
DD 004.6/8 US
CEASED
LAN REPORTER. [LAN report.]. **Added/Corp** National Software Testing Laboratories. **VAT** Local Area Network Reporter. Vol. 1, No. 1 (May 1990)-(Jan. 1994). Periodical. English. National Software Testing Laboratories, PO Box 1000, Plymouth Meeting Corporate Center, Plymouth Meeting PA 19462. **Tel** (610)941-9600, (800)328-2776, FAX (215)941-9952. Index available (free).
Desc: Tests standalone and networked software applications, environments and hardware. The service compares networked and workgroup products head-to-head.

LC TK5105.7 .L585 ISSN 1069-5621
DD 004.6/05 US
CCC
●LAN (SAN FRANCISCO, CALIF.). (LAN : THE NETWORK SOLUTIONS MAGAZINE.). [LAN]. **VFOAT** LAN Magazine. Vol. 8, No. 3 (Mar. 1993)-. Periodical. English. Twelve times a year. $29.97. Miller Freeman Inc., 600 Harrison Street, San Francisco CA 94107. **Tel** (415)905-2337, (415)905-2200, FAX (415)905-2240, telex 278273. **(Subscription address:** Neodata / Colorado, PO Box 2606, Boulder CO 80322.**)** ***Continues*** *Local Area Network Magazine, 0898-0012;* ***Absorbed*** *Network Administrator.*

LC TK5105.7 .L36 ISSN 1042-4695
DD 004 US
CCC
CODEN LTECEE
CEASED

LAN TECHNOLOGY. [LAN technol.]. **VAT** Local Area Network Technology. Vol. 5, No. 1 (Jan. 1989)-(1993). Periodical. English. M & T Publishing Inc., 411 Borel Avenue, Suite 100, San Mateo CA 94402. **Tel** (415)358-9500, FAX (415)358-9732. available on microfilm and microfiche from University Microfilms International (UMI); available on an online database (file 675/Full-Text) from DIALOG. ***Continues** Micro/Systems Journal, 8750-9482.*
Desc: Written for network programmers and systems integrators, LAN Technology, supports its readers with the latest information on computer integration, multitasking, languages, and operating systems.
Ind/Abst Comput. ASAP [Full Txt.]; Comput. Database [Full Txt.]; Microcomput. Abstr. (Jan. 1989-).

LC WMLC 93/1068 TK5105.7 .N67 ISSN 1040-5917
DD 004 US

LAN TIMES. [LAN times]. **Added/Corp** Novell, Inc. **VFOAT** Local Area Network Times. **VAT** Local Area Network Times. (198?)-. Periodical. English. Twenty-six times a year. Free on request. McGraw Hill Publishing Company, Inc., 1221 Avenue of the Americas, New York NY 10020. **Tel** (212)512-6410, (800)525-5003, FAX (212)512-6111. **(Subscription address:** LAN Times, PO Box 652, Hightstown NJ 08520. **)** available on microfilm and microfiche from University Microfilms International (UMI); available on an online database from Dow Jones News/Retrieval; NEWSNET; Lexis-Nexis; and (file 624/Full-Text) DIALOG.
Desc: Serves the network computing industry. Qualified subscribers include network manager, MIS/DP managers, system integrators, resellers, engineers, and system supervisors.
Ind/Abst Comput. Bus. (19??-); Comput. Database; Microcomput. Abstr. (Sept. 1989-).

US

LANBOOK. **Added/Corp** Architecture Technology Corporation. **VAT** Local Area Network Book. 6th Ed. (1988)-. English. Irregular. Architecture Technology Corporation, PO Box 24344, Minneapolis MN 55424. **Tel** (612)935-2035. ***Continues** Localnetter Designer's Handbook, 0740-6932.*

GW

LANLINE. English. Twelve times a year. DM90.00 Germany; DM97.50 other. Vogel Verlag, Postfach 6740, D-97064 Wuerzburg Germany. **Tel** 011 49 931 4182145, 011 49 931 4182483, FAX 011 49 931 4182670, telex 841 680131.

LC TK5105 .L57 ISSN 0739-988X
DD 004.6/16/05 US
CCC
CODEN LIUPDL

LINK-UP (MINNEAPOLIS, MINN. 1983). (LINK-UP.). [Link-up]. **Added/Corp** On-Line Communications, Inc. Learned Information (Firm). **VFOAT** Link Up; Linkup. Vol. 1, No. 1 (Sept. 1983)-. Periodical. English. Six times a year. $28.95. Information Today Inc., 143 Old Marlton Pike, Medford NJ 08055-8750. **Tel** (609)654-6266, (609)654-4888 (editorial), FAX (609)654-4309. **ED** Loraine Page. **Bk Rev. Photos. Ad Acc, Adv Mgr:** Michael V. Zarrello. Full Page (B&W) $1,765.00. Half Page (B&W) $1,225.00. Full Page (Color) $900.00 for four-color. Half Page (Color) $900.00 for four-color. **Pub. Size:** Tabloid. **Circ:** 10,000 (ctrl). available on microfilm and microfiche from University Microfilms International (UMI); available on an online database (file 648/Full-Text) from DIALOG. Documents available from UMI Article Clearinghouse, Ask*IEEE. ***Absorbed** Modem Notes.*
Desc: Provides coverage of online services, business databases, and hardware and software, and details on bulletin board systems. Report news of the online services industry, features how-to articles on an online communications topic and spotlights online services.
Ind/Abst ABI/INFORM Glob. Ed.; ABI/INFORM [Computer File] (Sept. 1987-); Aust. Libr. Inf. Sci. Abstr. (1981-); Curr. Cit.; Foods Adlibra; INSPEC (1985-1986); Microcomput. Abstr. (July 1988-); Trade Ind. ASAP [Full Txt.]; Trade Ind. Index [Full Txt.]; UMI ABI/Inform--Bus. Period. Ondisc (Sept. 1987-) [Full Txt.].

LC TK5105.7 .L585 ISSN 0898-0012
DD 004.6/05 US
CCC
CODEN LANNER
TITLE CHANGE

LOCAL AREA NETWORK MAGAZINE : LAN, THE. [Local area netw. mag.]. **VFOAT** LAN; LAN Magazine. (198?)-(1993). Periodical. English. Miller Freeman Inc., 600 Harrison Street, San Francisco CA 94107. **Tel** (415)905-2337, (415)905-2200, FAX (415)905-2240, telex 278273. **ED** Patricia Schnaidt. available on microfilm and microfiche from University Microfilms International (UMI). ***Continued by** LAN.*
Desc: Product oriented magazine designed to assist users with the purchasing, installation and management of Lan Systems. Includes a tutorial series offering practical advice for everyday network problems.

ISSN 1051-1962
DD 004 US

LOCAL AREA NETWORKS. (LOCAL AREA NETWORKS : LAN.). [Local area netw.]. **VFOAT** LAN; LAN Newsletter; Local Area Network Newsletter. (19??)-. Newsletter. English. Twelve times a year. $575.00. Information Gatekeepers Inc., 214 Harvard Avenue, Boston MA 02134. **Tel** (617)232-3111, (617)738-8088, (800)323-1088, FAX (617)734-8562. ***Continues** Local Area Networks Newsletter, 0897-3210.*

ISSN 0886-2397
DD 004 US

LOCALNETTER NEWSLETTER, THE. [Localnetter newsl.]. **Added/Corp** Architecture Technology Corporation. Vol. 1, No. 1 (Apr. 1981)-. Newsletter. English. Twelve times a year. $300.00. Architecture Technology Corporation, PO Box 24344, Minneapolis MN 55424. **Tel** (612)935-2035.

UK
TITLE CHANGE

MAINFRAME CLIENT/SERVER. (19??)-(19??). English. Xephon, 27-35 London Road, Newbury Berkshire RG13 1JL United Kingdom. **Tel** 011 44 1635 33823, FAX 011 44 1635 38345. ***Continued by** Enterprise Client/Server.*

ISSN 1057-5383
DD 004 US

MAN (BOSTON, MASS.). (MAN : A MONTHLY NEWSLETTER COVERING WORLDWIDE DEVELOPMENTS IN THE "METROPOLITAN AREA NETWORKS" MARKETS, APPLICATIONS, TECHNOLOGY.). [MAN]. **Added/Corp** Information Gatekeepers, Inc. **VFOAT** MAN Newsletter; Metropolitan Area Networks. (199?)-. Newsletter. English. Twelve times a year. $575.00. Information Gatekeepers Inc., 214 Harvard Avenue, Boston MA 02134. **Tel** (617)232-3111, (617)738-8088, (800)323-1088, FAX (617)734-8562.

ISSN 0954-712636
UK
Pr Rev. TITLE CHANGE

MAPPING AWARENESS & GIS EUROPE. (19??)-(19??). English (Dutch and French). Longman Geoinformation, 307 Cambridge Science Park, Milton Road Cambridge CB4 4ZD, United Kingdom. **Tel** 011 44 1223 423020, FAX 011 44 1223 425787. Index available. **Bk Rev. Ad Acc. Circ:** 8,000 (ctrl). ***Continued by** Mapping Awareness, 0954-7126.*
Desc: Covers all aspects of integrated spatial information (GIS/LIS) with articles on strategy, networking. Pilot studies and case histories are included.

ISSN 1073-0958
US

●MATRIX MAPS QUARTERLY. 3rd Quarter, (1993)-. Periodical. English. Four times a year. $400.00. Matrix Information and Directory Services, 1106 Clayton Lane, Suite 500W, Austin TX 78723. **Tel** (512)451-7602, FAX (512)450-1436. available via Internet (http://www.mids.org).
Desc: Publication of maps for computer networks.

ISSN 1059-0749
DD 004 US

MATRIX NEWS. [Matrix news]. **Added/Corp** Matrix Information and Directory Services. Vol. 1, No. 1 (Apr. 1991)-. Newsletter. English. Twelve times a year. $30.00. Matrix Information and Directory Services, 1106 Clayton Lane, Suite 500W, Austin TX 78723. **Tel** (512)451-7602, FAX (512)450-1436. **ED** John Quarterman. cum. index. **Bk Rev**, (Qty: 8-10). **Circ:** 1,000. available on an online database (mids @ tic.com) from the publisher.
Desc: Information about cross-network topics. It is not internet-specific but a great deal of the articles are about the internet.

LC HE ISSN 1040-7022
DD 384 US
CCC

MOBILE DATA REPORT. [Mob. data rep.]. **Added/Corp** Waters Information Services. Vol. 1, No. 1 (Sept. 15, 1988)-. Periodical. English. Twenty-four times a year. $547.00. Telecom Publishing Group, 1101 King Street, Suite 444, Alexandria VA 22314. **Tel** (703)683-4100, (800)327-7205, FAX (703)739-6490. **(Subscription address:** Telecom Publishing Group, PO Box 1455, Alexandria VA 22313. **Tel** 800 327-7205, (703)683-4100.**)** **ED** Alan Reiter. available on an online database (files 16,636/Full-Text) from DIALOG. ***Absorbed** En Route Technology, 1057-5618.*
Desc: Covers radio-based information network industry.
Ind/Abst PROMT [Full Txt.]; PTS Newsl. Database [Full Txt.].

ISSN 1070-2792
DD 004 US

MONITOR (ROCKVILLE, MD.). See Computers-Microcomputers, Personal Computers.

ISSN 0954-6561
UK
SUSPENDED

MULTI-USER COMPUTING. (19??)-(Dec. 1990). English. Eleven times a year (publishes monthly with July/Aug. issues combined). Storyplace Limited, 42 Colebrooke Row, London N1 8AF United Kingdom. **Tel** 011 44 171 3593003, FAX 011 44 171 2268113. ***Absorbed** IX Magazine, 0267-5692.*

ISSN 1077-4440
US

●MULTIMEDIA NETWORK TECHNOLOGY REPORT. (1994)-. English. Twenty-six times a year. $395.00. DataTrends Publications, 895 Harrison Street SE, Suite B, Leesburg VA 22075. **Tel** (703)779-0574, (800)766-8130, FAX (703)779-2267.

ISSN 1079-4689
US
CCC

●MULTIMEDIA PRODUCER. (1995)-. Periodical. English. Twelve times a year. $40.00. Knowledge Industry Publications Inc, 701 Westchester Avenue, White Plains NY 10604. **Tel** (914)328-9157, (800)800-5474, FAX (914)328-9093.

ISSN 1080-2681
US

●NET (GREENSBORO, N.C.), THE. See Communications-Computer Applications.

LC QA75 ISSN 1081-5066
DD 004 US

●NET.TECH (LOVELAND, COLO.). (NET.TECH.). [Net.tech]. **VFOAT** Net Tech. Vol. 1, No. 1 (Jan. 1995)-. Periodical. English. Twelve times a year. $119.00. Duke Communications International, 221 East 29th Street, Loveland CO 80539. **Tel** (303)663-4700, (800)373-3853, FAX (303)667-2321, telex 6502618199. available via Internet (http://duke.com/dukesubs.html).
Desc: Newsletter covering Internet connection technology, including network productivity, security, software selection, and more.

LC QA75 ISSN 1078-7593
DD 004 US

●NETCETERA (BELLEVUE, WASH.). (NETCETERA [COMPUTER FILE].). [NetCetera]. **Added/Corp** NorthWestNet. Northwest Academic Computing Consortium. Vol. 1, Issue 1 (Feb. 8, 1994)-. Periodical. English. One time a week. Free. NorthWestNet, 15400 Southeast 30th Place, Suite 202, Bellevue WA 98007. **Tel** (205)562-3000, FAX (206)562-4822. available via Internet (gopher://gopher.nwnet.net:70/11/nwnet-info/netcetera).
Desc: Provides information on new Internet tools and resources.

ISSN 1078-4632
US

●NETGUIDE (MANHASSET, N.Y.). (NETGUIDE.). (1994)-. Periodical. English. Twelve times a year. $22.97. CMP Publications Inc., One Jericho Plaza, Wing A, 2nd Floor, Jericho NY 11753. **Tel** (516)733-6700. **(Subscription address:** Palm Coast Data, PO Box 420163, Agency Department, Palm Coast FL 32142. **Tel** (904)445-4662 ext. 669, (800)829-5475.**)**
Ind/Abst Bus. Source Plus; EP Collect.; Homework Help.; Lotus Notes; MasterFile FullTEXT 1000; MasterFile FullTEXT 350; MasterFile FullTEXT 650; MasterFile FullTEXT; OCLC; Telebase.

ISSN 0892-9467
DD 004 US
TITLE CHANGE

NETLINE. [Netline]. **Added/Corp** Hyatt Research Corporation. Vol. 4 (Jan. 1987)-(19??). Periodical. English. Telecommunications Reports, 1333 H Street Northwest, 2nd Floor West Tower, Washington DC 20005. **Tel** (202)842-0520, (800)822-6338, FAX (202)842-3047. **(Subscription address:** Telecommunications Reports, PO Box 675, Cooper Station, New York NY 10276. **)** **ED** Dennis M. Kouba. available on an online database (file 636/Full-Text) from DIALOG. ***Continues** PC Netline, 0749-8578. **Merged into** Electronic Mail & Micro Systems.*
Desc: Analysis and reports on computer network products, companies, trends and user concerns.
Ind/Abst PTS Newsl. Database [Full Txt.].

UK

NETUSER. (19??)-. English. Six times a year. $115.34. Paragon Publishing Ltd., Paragon House St. Peters Road, Bournemouth Dorset BH12JS United Kingdom. **Tel** 011 44 1202 299900.

ISSN 1076-3422
DD 004 US

NETWARE CONNECTION. [NetWare connect.]. **Added/Corp** Netware Users International. (May/June 1990)-. Periodical. English. Six times a year (Jan., Mar., May, July, Sept., Nov.). Free on request. Netware Users International, 122 East 1700 South, Provo UT 84606. **Tel** (801)429-7000. **ED** Debi Pearson, (editor's address: PO Box 19007, Provo, UT 84605, phone: (801)429-5861). **Ad Acc. Circ:** 140,000 (ctrl).

ISSN 1080-3971
US

●NETWARE/INTERNET EXCHANGE. See Communications-Computer Applications.

Computers —Computer Networks

ISSN 1055-6923
US
NETWARE PROGRAMMER'S JOURNAL. See Computers-Computer Engineering.

DD 004   **ISSN** 1058-2800
US
NETWARE SOLUTIONS. [NetWare solut.]. **VFOAT** Net Ware Solutions. (1991)-. Trade Publication. English. Twelve times a year. $35.40. New Media Publications, Inc., 10711 Burnet Road, Suite 305, Austin TX 78758-4459. **Tel** (512)873-7761, FAX (512)873-7782. **ED** Deni Connor.

DD 004   **ISSN** 1040-4503
US
CEASED
NETWARE TECHNICAL JOURNAL. See Computers-Software.

DD 004   **ISSN** 1073-1164
US
TITLE CHANGE
NETWORK ADMINISTRATOR. [Netw. adm.]. (1994)-(1995). Trade Publication. English. R & D Publications, 1601 West 23rd Street, Suite 200, Lawrence KS 66046. **Tel** (913)841-1631, FAX (913)841-2624. **ED** Robert Ward. **Bk Rev**, (Qty: 2-4). **Ad Acc**, **Adv Mgr:** Donna Ward, **Tel** (913)841-0239. **Circ:** 10,000. **Merged into LAN.**
Desc: Provides technical information for PC network administrators; focuses on solutions for optimizing, tuning, and troubleshooting PC networks.

LC QA76.87 .N46   **ISSN** 0954-898X
DD 006.3   UK
CCC
NLM W1; NE235S   **CODEN** NEWKEB
NETWORK (BRISTOL). See Computers-Artificial Intelligence.

LC TK5105.5 .N4653   **ISSN** 1046-4468
DD 004.6/05   US
CCC
NETWORK COMPUTING. [Netw. comput.]. Vol. 1, Issue 1 (Oct. 1990)-. Periodical. English. Irregular (15 issues). $60.00. CMP Publications Inc., One Jericho Plaza, Wing A, 2nd Floor, Jericho NY 11753. **Tel** (516)733-6700. (**Subscription address:** CMP Publications, Inc. / Illinois, PO Box 5920, Department 100, Carol Stream IL 60197-5920.) **ED** Gary A. Bolles (editor's E-mail: gbolles@nwc.com.). **Ad Acc**. ctrl circ.
Desc: Focuses on the network as the basic business environment for computing. Covers connecting computers, networking opportunities and technical solutions for networking problems.
Ind/Abst Bus. Source Plus; EP Collect.; F&S Index Plus Text, Int. [Full Txt.] [Select. Cov.]; Homework Help.; Lotus Notes; MasterFile FullTEXT 1000; MasterFile FullTEXT 350; MasterFile FullTEXT 650; MasterFile FullTEXT; OCLC; PROMT [Full Txt.]; Telebase.

ISSN 0966-7873
UK
NETWORK COMPUTING. (19??)-. English. Eight times a year. £39.00 (one-year), £69.00 (two-year) UK; £69.00 (one-year), £99.00 (two-year) other. Compudraft Ltd., 24 High Street, Beckenham Kent, BR3 1AY United Kingdom. **Tel** 011 44 181 6633818, FAX 011 44 181 6633822. **ED** Brian Wall. **Bk Rev**. **Ad Acc**, **Adv Mgr:** Stuart Leigh. **Circ:** 20,000 (ctrl).
Desc: A new independent magazine dedicated to NetWare and the associated products and services that contribute to Novell's position as the leader in the evolving technology of networking computers. Each issue of Network Computing covers: Novell and Industry news and analysis, case studies, in-depth product/service reviews, personality profiles, training and development features on Novell NetWare, and technical tips and much more.

DD 004   **ISSN** 1043-1217
US
CCC
NETWORK MANAGEMENT SYSTEMS & STRATEGIES. [Netw. manage. sys. strategies]. **VFOAT** NMS&S; Network Management Systems and Strategies. Vol. 1, No. 1 (Jan. 30, 1989)-. Periodical. English. Twenty-six times a year. $465.00. DataTrends Publications, 895 Harrison Street SE, Suite B, Leesburg VA 22075. **Tel** (703)779-0574, (800)766-8130, FAX (703)779-2267. available on an online database (file 636/Full-Text) from DIALOG.
Ind/Abst PTS Newsl. Database [Full Txt.].

UK
●**NETWORK POLICY BRIEFING.** (1995)-. English. Six times a year. $367.91. Technology Appraisals Ltd., 82 Hampton Road, Twickenham TW2 5QS United Kingdom. **Tel** 011 44 181 8933986. **Separated from** OSN Open Systems and Computing.

US
●**NETWORK PROFESSIONAL JOURNAL.** (1995)-. Trade Publication. English. Twelve times a year. $48.00. Network Professional Association, 151 East 1700 South, Provo UT 84606. **Tel** (801)379-0330. **ED** Scott Hatch. **Continues** Network News.

ISSN 1353-4858
UK
NETWORK SECURITY. (19??)-. Periodical. English. Twelve times a year. $454.00. Elsevier Science Publishers Ltd., Crown House, Linton Road, Barking Essex IG11 8JU United Kingdom. **Tel** 011 44 181 5947272, FAX 011 44 181 5945942, telex 896950.

ISSN 1353-4858
UK
NETWORK SECURITY NEWSLETTER. See Computers-Computer Crimes and Security.

US
NETWORK STRATEGY SERVICE. (19??)-. English. Irregular. $5,000.00. Forrester Research Inc., 1 Brattle Square, Cambridge MA 02138. **Tel** (617)497-7090.

US
●**NETWORK VAR.** (1995)-. English. Twelve times a year. $39.00. Miller Freeman Inc., 600 Harrison Street, San Francisco CA 94107. **Tel** (415)905-2337, (415)905-2200, FAX (415)905-2240, telex 278273. (**Subscription address:** Stacks, PO Box 469050, Escondido CA 92046.) **Continues** Stacks.

LC QA76 .C5816   **ISSN** 0887-7661
DD 004.6/05   US
CCC
NETWORK WORLD. [Netw. world]. Vol. 3, No. 3 (March 1986)-. Trade Publication. English. One time a week. $95.00. Network World, Box 9172, Framingham MA 01701. **Tel** (800)622-1108. available on microfilm and microfiche from University Microfilms International (UMI); available on an online database (files 15,674/Full-Text) from DIALOG. Documents available from UMI Article Clearinghouse. **Continues** On Communications, 8750-7854.
Desc: Communications publication dedicated to networking.
Ind/Abst ABI/INFORM Glob. Ed.; ABI/INFORM [Computer File] (March 1986-); Comput. Database; Comput. Ind. Update (19??-); Comput. Lit. Index; F&S Index Plus Text, Int. [Select. Cov.]; PROMT; Trade Ind. Index; UMI ABI/Inform--Bus. Period. Ondisc (Nov. 1987-) [Full Txt.].

DD 004.6   **ISSN** 1187-2985
CN
NETWORK WORLD CANADA. [Netw. world Can.]. **VFOAT** Directory of Suppliers. Vol. 1, No. 1 (Apr. 1991)-. Trade Publication. English. Twelve times a year. 45.00Can$. Laurentian Technomedia, 501 Oakdale Road, Downsview Ontario M3N 1W7 Canada. **Tel** (416)746-7360, (613)475-3217. **Separated from** Info Canada (Downsview, Ont.), 1187-7081.

LC TK5101.A1 T3   **ISSN** 1052-049X
DD 621   US
CCC
CEASED
NETWORKING MANAGEMENT. [Netw. manage.]. Vol. 7, No. 5 (May 1989)-(June 1993). Periodical. English. PennWell Publishing Company, 1421 South Sheridan, PO Box 1260, Tulsa OK 74101. **Tel** (918)835-3161, (800)331-4463, FAX (918)831-9497. **ED** John M Lusa. Index available. cum. index. **Ad Acc**. **Circ:** 63,000 (ctrl). available on microfilm and microfiche from University Microfilms International (UMI); available on an online database (files 15,675/Full-Text) from DIALOG. Documents available from UMI Article Clearinghouse, Ask*IEEE. **Continues** TPT.
Desc: Magazine of solutions and applications for MIS, voice and data professionals who plan, implement, support and manage their organizations' networks. The target audience are individuals in large, information-intensive organizations who plan, develop and operate private voice and data communications networks.
Ind/Abst ABI/INFORM Glob. Ed.; ABI/INFORM [Computer File] (Nov. 1988-); Comput. ASAP [Full Txt.]; Comput. Database [Full Txt.]; Comput. Lit. Index; F&S Index Plus Text, Int. [Select. Cov.]; INSPEC (1988-); PROMT; UMI ABI/Inform--Bus. Period. Ondisc (Dec. 1987-) [Full Txt.].

DD 003/.05   **ISSN** 0028-3045
US
CODEN NTWKAA
Pr Rev.
NETWORKS (NEW YORK). (NETWORKS.). [Networks]. Vol. 1 (1971)-. Periodical. English. Eight times a year. $696.00. John Wiley & Sons, Inc., 605 Third Avenue, New York NY 10158-0012. **Tel** (212)850-6000, (212)850-6645, FAX (212)850-6088, telex 12-7063. (**Subscription address:** John Wiley & Sons / UK, Baffins Lane, Chichester, West Sussex PO19 1UD United Kingdom. **Tel** 011 44 1243 779777, FAX 011 44 243 776128, telex 86290 WIBOOKG.) **ED** Frank T. Boesch, I. T. Frisch, and D. J. Kleitman. available on microfilm and microfiche from University Microfilms International (UMI). Documents available from Article Express International, The Genuine Article, Ask*IEEE.
Desc: Focuses on both applications and theory for innovations in design and use of computer networks, telecommunications, transportation systems, power grids, distribution systems and other networks.

Ind/Abst CompuMath Cit. Index [Full Cov.]; Comput. Control Abstr.; Comput. Rev.; Curr. Cit.; Curr. Contents Eng. Comput. Technol.; Math. Rev.; Res. Alert [Full Cov.]; Sci. Cit. Index; SCISEARCH.

ISSN 1210-0552
XR
UDC 612.8 :681.324
Pr Rev.
NEURAL NETWORK WORLD. See Computers-Artificial Intelligence.

LC QA76.87 .N492   **ISSN** 1061-5369
DD 004/.3   US
CCC
Pr Rev.
●**NEURAL, PARALLEL & SCIENTIFIC COMPUTATIONS.** [Neural parallel sci. comput.]. **VFOAT** Neural, Parallel, and Scientific Computations. Vol. 1, No. 1 (Mar. 1993)-. Periodical. English. Four times a year. $250.00. Dynamic Publishers Inc., PO Box 48654, Atlanta GA 30362. **Tel** (404)451-3616, FAX (404)451-3616. **ED** Dr. M. Sambandham (editor's address: Morehouse College, Department of Math, Atlanta, GA 30314; phone: (404)681-2800 ext. 2455). Index available in last issue of volume--attached. cum. index. **Bk Rev**, (Qty: 15). **Ad Acc**, **Adv Mgr:** S. Revathi, **Tel** (404)458-7932. **Circ:** 150.
Desc: Covers all branches of mathematics and computer science which use all or any one of neural computing, parallel computing, and scientific computing. Also publishes research papers.

UK
NEURAL TECHNOLOGY UPDATE. See Computers-Artificial Intelligence.

UK
●**NEW REVIEW OF INFORMATION NETWORKING.** (1995)-. English. One time a year. $125.00. Taylor Graham Publishing, 6th Floor, 150 Regent Street, London W1R 5FA United Kingdom. **Continues** Journal of Information Networking.

ISSN 1065-0652
US
NEWS FOR NETWORK USERS. (NEWS FOR NETWORK USERS [COMPUTER FILE].). (1992)-. Periodical. English. Free.

DD 004   **ISSN** 1060-7803
US
TITLE CHANGE
NEWS- INTERNET SOCIETY (PRINT ED.). (NEWS- INTERNET SOCIETY.). [News- Internet Soc.]. **Added/Corp** Internet Society. **VFOAT** Internet Society News. (1992)-(199?). Periodical. English. Internet Society, 1895 Preston White Drive, Suite 100, Reston VA 22091. **Tel** (703)620-8990. **Continued by** Onthe Internet.

US
CEASED
NEWSBYTES : NEWS NETWORK. (19??)-(19??). English. Metatec Discovery Systems, 7001 Discovery Boulevard, Dublin OH 43017. **Tel** (614)766-3101, (800)637-3472. available on an online database (files 16,636,649,675/Full-Text) from DIALOG.
Desc: A news network on CD-ROM.
Ind/Abst Comput. ASAP [Full Txt.]; Comput. Database [Full Txt.]; PROMT [Full Txt.]; PTS Newsl. Database [Full Txt.].

LC QA75   **ISSN** 1070-1737
DD 004   US
NORTHWESTNET NODE NEWS (ONLINE). (NORTHWESTNET NODE NEWS [COMPUTER FILE].). [NorthWestNet node news]. **Added/Corp** Northwest Academic Computing Consortium. (Feb. 1992)-. Periodical. English. Four times a year. Free. NorthWestNet, 15400 Southeast 30th Place, Suite 202, Bellevue WA 98007. **Tel** (205)562-3000, FAX (206)562-4822. available via Internet (ftp://ftp.nwnet.net/nodenews).

LC TK5105.5 .N68   **ISSN** 1077-0321
DD 004.6/05   US
●**NOVELL APPLICATION NOTES.** [Novell appl. notes]. **Added/Corp** Novell, Inc. **VFOAT** Application Notes. (1994)-. Periodical. English. Twelve times a year. $95.00. Novell Incorporated, PO Box 5205, Denver CO 80217. **Tel** (801)429-5900, FAX (303)294-0930. **Continues** NetWare Application Notes.

LC QA75   **ISSN** 1072-5172
DD 004   US
NSF NETWORK NEWS (PRINT). (NSF NETWORK NEWS.). [NSF netw. news]. **Added/Corp** NSF Network Service Center. InterNIC Information Services. (1987)-. Periodical. English. Four times a year. Free on request. General Atomics, PO Box 85608, San Diego CA 92186-9784. **Tel** (619)455-4600, FAX (619)455-4640. available via Internet (http://www.internic.net/newsletter).
Desc: Provides information on the NSFNET and the Internet.

Computers —Computer Networks

LC TK7885.A1 O36   **ISSN** 1048-8928
DD 621.395   US
OEM INTEGRATOR, THE. See
Computers-Computer Engineering.

   US
●**OFFICIAL INTERNET WORLD INTERNET YELLOW PAGES.** See
Communications-Computer Applications.

   US
ONTHE INTERNET. (199?)-. Periodical. English. Six times a year (Bimonthly). $22.00. Internet Society, 1895 Preston White Drive, Suite 100, Reston VA 22091. **Tel** (703)620-8990. **Continues** News: Internet Society.

ISSN 1072-7760
   US
TITLE CHANGE
OPEN (VIENNA, VA). (OPEN : THE INTERNATIONAL NEWSLETTER OF MULTIVENDOR NETWORKING TECHNOLOGIES, TRENDS, AND PRODUCTS.). **Added/Corp** Vienna, VA : Datatrends Publications. **VFOAT** OSI Product and Equipment News. (1992)-(1994). Newsletter. English. DataTrends Publications, 895 Harrison Street SE, Suite B, Leesburg VA 22075. **Tel** (703)779-0574, (800)766-8130, FAX (703)779-2267. **Continues** OSI Product & Equipment News, 0898-0489. **Continued by** Distributed Systems Management Report, 1079-4727.

   UK
P.C. NETWORK ADVISOR. (July 1990)-. English. £225.00. International Technology Publishing, PO Box 2JD/Suite 4 2JD United Kingdom. **Tel** 011 44 171 7249306, FAX 011 44 171 7063296.

ISSN 1076-917X
DD 005   US
●**PATHWORKS MANAGER.** [Pathworks manager]. Vol. 1, No. 1 (Oct. 1994)-. Periodical. English. Twelve times a year. $199.00. Pathworks Manager, 1300 Virginia Drive, Suite 400, Fort Washington PA 19034. **Tel** (800)769-7993, (215)643-8112, FAX (215)643-8099.

   UK
PC LAN. See Computers-Microcomputers, Personal Computers.

ISSN 1077-4696
DD 384   UK
   CCC
●**PHILLIPS BUSINESS INFORMATION'S COMMUNICATIONS STANDARDS NEWS.** See Communications-Computer Applications.

LC TK5105.5 .C66a
DD 621.382   US
PROCEEDINGS / CONFERENCE ON LOCAL COMPUTER NETWORKS.
Main/Conf Conference on Local Computer Networks. **Added/Corp** IEEE Computer Society. Technical Committee on Computer Communications. Institute of Electrical and Electronics Engineers. **VFOAT** IEEE ... Local Computer Networks; Local Computer Networks; IEEE Conference on Local Computer Networks. 11th (1986)-. Proceedings. English. One time a year. $90.00. IEEE Computer Society, 10662 Los Vaqueros Circle, PO Box 3014, Los Alamitos CA 90720-1264. **Tel** (714)821-8380, (800)272-6657, FAX (714)821-4641. **Continues** Conference on Local Computer Networks, 0742-1303.
Ind/Abst Index IEEE Publ.

LC QA76.9.D5 I568a   **ISSN** 1063-6927
DD 004/.36/05   US
PROCEEDINGS OF THE INTERNATIONAL CONFERENCE ON DISTRIBUTED COMPUTING SYSTEMS.
(PROCEEDINGS / THE ... INTERNATIONAL CONFERENCE ON DISTRIBUTED COMPUTING SYSTEMS.). [Proc. Int. Conf. Distributed Comput. Syst.]. **Added/Corp** IEEE Computer Society. IEEE Computer Society. TC on Distributed Processing. Joho Shori Gakkai (Japan). **VFOAT** Proceedings of the ... International Conference on Distributed Computing Systems. 10th (May 28-June 1, 1990)-. Proceedings. English. One time a year. $120.00. IEEE Computer Society, 10662 Los Vaqueros Circle, PO Box 3014, Los Alamitos CA 90720-1264. **Tel** (714)821-8380, (800)272-6657, FAX (714)821-4641. **Continues** International Conference on Distributed Computing Systems. International Conference on Distributed Computing Systems : [Proceedings].
Ind/Abst Curr. Cit.

LC QA76.87 .P76   **ISSN** 1055-713X
DD 006.3   US
   CODEN PNNEEX
PROGRESS IN NEURAL NETWORKS.
See Computers-Artificial Intelligence.

   US
QUERY. (1992)-. English. Four times a year. $24.00 (individuals), $48.00 (institutions) US; $55.00 other. Syllabus Press, 1307 South Mary Avenue, Suite 218, Sunnydale CA 94087-0716. **Tel** (408)773-0670, FAX (408)746-2711. **ED** John P. Noon. **Ad Acc.** **Circ:** 30,000.

available on an online database.
Desc: Covers the integration of computer technology into administrative environments. Topics include enterprise computing, client/server architecture, and networking/connectivity. Each issue has feature articles, news, resources, and in-depth looks at how campuses can better accommodate their computing needs.

ISSN 0926-6364
   NE
Pr Rev.
●**RANDOM OPERATORS AND STOCHASTIC EQUATIONS.** Vol. 1, No. 1 (1993)-. Periodical. English. Four times a year. DM650.00. VSP International Science Publishers, Godfried van Seystlaan 47, 3703 BR Zeist Netherlands. **Tel** 011 31 3404 25790, FAX 011 31 3404 32081, telex 40217 USP NL. (**Subscription address:** VSP International Science Publishers, PO Box 346, 3700 AH Zeist Netherlands. **Tel** 011 31 30 6925790, FAX 011 31 30 6932081.) **ED** V. Girko.
Desc: Publishes original and translated articles on the theory of random operators and stochastic analysis. In addition to articles, issues contain reviews, short communications, tutorial articles, notices and announcements.

LC QA75   **ISSN** 1076-4429
DD 004   US
●**REAL-TIME ENGINEERING : COMPUTING WITH A DEADLINE.**
[Real-time eng.]. **VFOAT** Real Time Engineering. Vol. 1, No. 1 (Spring 1994)-. Trade Publication. English. Four times a year. Free US and Canada; $50.00 other. Real-Time Engineering, 11051 Pinto Drive, Fountain Hills AZ 85268. **Tel** (602)837-3756. (**Subscription address:** Micrology Pbt. Inc., 2618 South Shannon Drive, Tempe AZ 85282. **Tel** (602)968-9265.) **ED** John Black. available with illustrations.
Desc: Covers the real-time computing industry and includes information on software, hardware, developments and applications.

LC TK7885
DD 621.39   NE
Pr Rev.
●**REAL-TIME SAFETY CRITICAL SYSTEMS.** See Computers-Computer Systems.

LC HD9696.O67 S45
DD 338.74621381   JA
SEKAI CD-ROM SORAN = CD-ROM DIRECTORY OF THE WORLD. See
Computers-Data Base Management.

LC QA75.5 .S53   **ISSN** 0736-6892
DD 004.05/6   US
   CODEN SSNRD3
SIGUCCS NEWSLETTER. See
Computers-Electronic Data Processing.

ISSN 0928-4869
   NE
UDC 681.31   CCC
Pr Rev.
SIMULATION PRACTICE AND THEORY.
[Simul. pract. theory]. (1993)-. Academic Scholarly Publication. English. Six times a year (1 volume). $250.00. Elsevier Science Publishers BV, PO Box 211, 1000 AE Amsterdam Netherlands. **Tel** 011 31 20 4853641, 011 31 20 4853642, FAX 011 31 20 4853598. **ED** L. Dekker. **Bk Rev.** **Ad Acc.** **Adv Mgr:** W Van Cattenburch. available on an online database from Elsevier Electronic Subscriptions (EES).
Desc: Provides a forum for high-quality original research and tutorial papers in the field of simulation.

LC TK5105.5 .S723   **ISSN** 1070-8596
DD 004.6/05   US
   CCC
   TITLE CHANGE
STACKS (SAN FRANCISCO, CALIF.).
(STACKS : THE NETWORK JOURNAL.). [Stacks]. **VFOAT** Network Journal; Stacks, The Network Journal. (May 1993)-(1995). Periodical. English. Miller Freeman Inc., 600 Harrison Street, San Francisco CA 94107. **Tel** (415)905-2337, (415)905-2200, FAX (415)905-2240, telex 278273. (**Subscription address:** Sunbelt Fulfillment Services, PO Box 5039, Brentwood TN 37024. **Tel** (800)685-3435.) **Continued by** Network VAR.

   US
STACKS: THE NETWORK JOURNAL.
(19??)-. English. Irregular. $39.00 US; $45.00 Canada and Mexico; $54.00 (surface mail), $79.00 (airmail) other. Miller Freeman Inc., 600 Harrison Street, San Francisco CA 94107. **Tel** (415)905-2337, (415)905-2200, FAX (415)905-2240, telex 278273. (**Subscription address:** Sunbelt Fulfillment Services, PO Box 5039, Brentwood TN 37024. **Tel** (800)685-3435.)

   US
●**SUPPORT ON SITE FOR NETWORKS.**
(1995)-. English. Twelve times a year. $1495.00. Computer Library, One Park Avenue, Fifth Floor, New York NY 10016. **Tel** (212)503-4409, FAX (212)503-4414.

LC HE7601
DD 384.1   US
●**TECHNOLOGY FOR COMMUNICATIONS.**
(1995)-. Newsletter. English. Twelve times a year. $149.00. Ragan Communications Inc., 212 West Superior Street, Suite 200, Chicago IL 60610. **Tel** (312)335-0037, (800)878-5331, FAX (312)335-9583. **ED** Steve Crescenzo.
Desc: Information on using cyberspace technology.

ISSN 1058-6733
   US
   CEASED
TECHNOLOGY TUTORIALS ENTERPRISE NETWORKING.
(TECHNOLOGY TUTORIALS ENTERPRISE NETWORKING / JOSEPH NETWORKS GROUP.). [Technol. tutor. enterp. netw.]. **Added/Corp** Joseph Networks Group. Information Gatekeepers, Inc. **VFOAT** Enterprise Networking Newsletter; Wireless PCN Newsletter. Vol. 1, Issue 1 (July 1990)-(Dec. 1994). Trade Publication. English. Information Gatekeepers Inc., 214 Harvard Avenue, Boston MA 02134. **Tel** (617)232-3111, (617)738-8088, (800)323-1088, FAX (617)734-8562.

LC TK5101.A1 T43   **ISSN** 0736-5853
DD 384   US
   CCC
   CODEN TEINEG
TELEMATICS AND INFORMATICS. See
Communications-Telecommunication.

   NE
Pr Rev.
●**TELETRAFFIC SCIENCE AND ENGINEERING.** (1994)-. Proceedings. English. Irregular. Elsevier Science Publishers BV, PO Box 211, 1000 AE Amsterdam Netherlands. **Tel** 011 31 20 4853641, 011 31 20 4853642, FAX 011 31 20 4853598. available on an online database from Elsevier Electronic Subscriptions (EES).

LC QA76.9.A25 T73   **ISSN** 0892-399X
DD 384/.05   US
   CODEN TDCREP
   TITLE CHANGE
TRANSNATIONAL DATA AND COMMUNICATIONS REPORT. See
Communications-Telecommunication.

ISSN 1044-3312
   US
ULTIMATE NETWORKING DIRECTORY, THE. (1990)-. Directory. English. One time a year. $10.00. Jag Publishers Ltd., PO Box 271, Greenvale NY 11548. **Tel** (516)625-3033, FAX (516)625-3411.

ISSN 0736-4083
   US
Pr Rev.   CEASED
UNIQUE (EAST HANOVER, N.J.).
(UNIQUE.). [Unique]. **Added/Corp** InfoPro Systems. Vol. 2, No. 4 (Dec. 1982)-(19??). Periodical. English. TPCI, 13 Moresby Drive, Xanata Ontario K2M 2A2 Can. **Tel** (613)592-6625, FAX (613)592-8125. **ED** Tim Parker. **Bk Rev.** (Qty: 5). **Circ:** 2000 (ctrl). available on CD-ROM from Information Access Company. **Continues** UNIX Software List, 0731-1028.

LC QA   **ISSN** 1070-5082
DD 004   US
   TITLE CHANGE
VINES OBSERVER. [VINES obs.]. **Added/Corp** Wellesley Information Services. (19??)-(May 1995). Periodical. English. Wellesley Information Services, 108 Arnold Road, Newton MA 02159. **Tel** (617)969-6666, FAX (617)969-9998. **ED** Bonnie Penzias. Index available. cum. index. **Circ:** 700-1,200. **Continued by** Banyan Technical Journal.

LC QA75
DD 004   US
●**VIRTUAL CITY.** (1995)-. Consumer Publication. English. Four times a year. Newsweek, 251 West 57th Street, New York NY 10019. **Tel** (201)445-4000. **Ad Acc.**
Desc: User-friendly lifestyle magazine for the interactive world.

ISSN 1063-3839
DD 332   US
   CEASED
WALL STREET NETWORK NEWS. [Wall Str. netw. news]. **Added/Corp** Waters Information Services. Vol. 1, No. 1 (June 19, 1992)-(June 17, 1994). Periodical. English. Waters Information Services, PO Box 2248, Binghamton NY 13902-2248. **Tel** (607)770-8535, FAX (607)798-1692. available on an online database (files 16,636/Full-Text) from DIALOG.

ISSN 0734-6182
   US
WILEY SEARCH UPDATE USER NETWORK. [Wiley search update user netw.]. **VFOAT** Wiley Search Update. Vol. 1, No. 1 (Oct. 1982)-. Periodical. English. Four times a year. John Wiley & Sons, Inc., 605 Third Avenue, New York NY 10158-0012. **Tel** (212)850-6000, (212)850-6645, FAX (212)850-6088,

telex 12-7063. **(Subscription address:** John Wiley & Sons / UK, Baffins Lane, Chichester, West Sussex PO19 1UD United Kingdom. **Tel** 011 44 1243 779777, FAX 011 44 243 776128, telex 86290 WIBOOKG.**)**

LC TK5105.5 .W57 **ISSN** 1059-1028
DD 306 US
CODEN WREDEM

•WIRED (SAN FRANCISCO, CALIF.). (WIRED.). [Wired]. **VFOAT** Chuan Lien hao. (1993)-. Consumer Publication. English. Twelve times a year. $80.00 (institutions), $39.95 (individuals) US; $103.00 (institutions), $64.00 (individuals) Canada and Mexico; $110.00 (institutions), $79.00 (individuals) other. Wired Ventures Ltd., 544 2nd Street, 3rd Floor, San Francisco CA 94107. **Tel** (415)904-0660, FAX (415)904-0669. **(Subscription address:** Wired Ventures Ltd., PO Box 191826, San Francisco CA 94119. **Tel** (800)677-3361.**)** **ED** Louis Rossetto. Index available. cum. index (online). **Bk Rev**, (Qty: 40). **Ad Acc**, **Adv Mgr:** Kathleen Lyman. **Circ:** 200,000. available on an online database from AOL.
Desc: Consumer magazine for the digital generation, tracking technology's impact on business, culture, and society at large. Examines the people, companies, and ideas that are merging computers, consumer electronics, communications, and entertainment.
Ind/Abst Access (1993-).

LC TK5103.2 .W5 **ISSN** 1022-0038
DD 621.382 NE

•WIRELESS NETWORKS. **Added/Corp** Association for Computing Machinery. **VFOAT** WN. Vol. 1, No. 1 (Feb. 1995)-. Periodical. English. Four times a year. 176.50F (includes distribution costs). Baltzer Science Publishers BV, Asterweg 1A, 1031 HL Amsterdam Netherlands. **Tel** 011 31 20 6370061, FAX 011 31 20 6323651.

LC QA75
DD 004 US

•WORLD WIDE WEB. (1995)-. English. Twelve times a year. $24.00. Scream Press, 509 Enterprise Drive, Rohnert Park CA 94928.

COMPUTER SALES, SERVICE AND SUPPLY

UK

BLACKWELL PERSONAL COMPUTER MARKETS. **See** Computers-Microcomputers, Personal Computers.

ISSN 0840-7312
DD 338.4/7004/05 CN

CANADIAN COMPUTER RESELLER. [Can. comput. reseller]. (Oct./Nov. 1987)-. Periodical. English. Irregular. 48.02Can$. MacLean Hunter Ltd. Business Publishers / Canada, Box 9100, Station A, Toronto Ontario M5W 1A5 Canada. **Tel** (416)596-5000, , FAX (416)596-5552. **(Subscription address:** Indas Customer Service, 35 Riviera Drive, Building 17, Markham Ontario L3R 8N4 Canada. **Tel** (905)946-0406.**)**

US

CAO/CAM/CAE PRODUCTS DATABASE. English. One time a year. $49.00 (per database), $124.00 (for all five databases). TECSPEC, PO Box 617024, Orlando FL 32861. **Tel** (407)295-1094, FAX (407)293-4948. Index available. cum. index. available on diskette.
Desc: Directory of products (hardware/software) in the CAD/CAM/CAE areas, with company contacts, specifications, etc.

ISSN 1058-8329
DD 004 US

CCRA NEWSLETTER : THE OFFICIAL MONTHLY NEWSLETTER OF THE CAMPUS COMPUTER RESELLERS ALLIANCE, THE. [CCRA newsl.]. **Added/Corp** National Association of College Stores (U.S.). Campus Computer Resellers Alliance. **VAT** Campus Computer Resellers Alliance Newsletter. No. 1 (Sept. 1991)-. Newsletter. English. Twelve times a year. Campus Computer Resellers Alliance, 500 East Lorain Street, Oberlin OH 44074-1294.

UK
CEASED

COMMODORE FORCE. (19??)-(19??). English. Euro Press Sales and Distribution Ltd., Case Mill Temeside, Ludlow, Shropshire SY8 1JW United Kingdom. **Tel** 011 44 151 3571275, FAX 011 44 151 3572813. ***Continues*** *Zzap! 64, 0954-867X.*

ISSN 0272-4553
US
TITLE CHANGE

COMPUTER AND COMMUNICATIONS BUYER. [Comput. commun. buy.]. **Added/Corp** Technology News of America. (1979)-(Jan. 1995). Periodical. English. Technology News of America, 110 Greene Street, Room 1101, New York NY 10012. **Tel** (212)334-9750, FAX (212)334-9491, telex 668758. **ED** Hesh Wiener. ctrl circ. available on microfilm from University Microfilms International (UMI). ***Merged into*** *Infoperspectives.*
Desc: Reporting on costs of computer purchase, sale or lease aimed at large mainframe users. Data and analysis of equipment markets.

LC HF5410
DD 658.8 GW

•COMPUTER BUSINESS. (1995)-. Trade Publication. German. One time a week. Computerwoche Verlag GmbH, Rheinstrasse 28, 80803 Munich Germany. **Tel** 011 49 89 36086299, FAX 011 49 89 36086325, telex 5215250-COMW-D.

LC QA76.5 .C6125617 **ISSN** 0738-9213
DD 004/.029 004 US

COMPUTER BUYER'S GUIDE AND HANDBOOK. **See** Computers-Microcomputers, Personal Computers.

ISSN 0734-0583
US

COMPUTER DIRECTORY AND BUYERS' GUIDE, THE. [Comput. dir. buy. guide]. (19??)-. Consumer Publication. English. One time a year. $35.00. Berkeley Enterprises Inc, 815 Washington Street, Newtonville MA 02160. **Tel** (617)332-5453. **ED** Judith P. Callahan. **Ad Acc. Circ:** 1,800.
Desc: A basic buyers' guide to the organizations available for supplying, designing, and using data processing and computing systems.

LC HD9696.C6 C6 **ISSN** 0894-6213
DD 380.1/45004021 US
CCC

COMPUTER INDUSTRY FORECASTS (1987). **See** Computers-Computer Industry and Industry Directories.

ISSN 0886-7194
DD 005 US
CEASED

COMPUTER MARKETING NEWSLETTER, THE. [Comput. mark. newsl.]. (19??)-Vol. 17 (May 1994). Newsletter. English. M. V. Publishing Company, PO Box 3649, Newport Beach CA 92659. **Tel** (714)548-9151, FAX (714)548-6727. **ED** Gerard Guyod. Index available. cum. index. **Bk Rev**, (Qty: varies). **Circ:** 3,000. available on microfilm from University Microfilms International (UMI).
Desc: Insiders news and information for computer communications industry, sales and marketing executives.

ISSN 0045-7841
DD 004 US

COMPUTER PRICE GUIDE. [Comput. price guide]. **Added/Corp** Computer Merchants, inc. **VFOAT** Computer Price Guide. The Blue Book of Used IBM Computer Prices. (197?)-. Periodical. English. Four times a year. $125.00. Computer Merchants Inc, PO Box 1006, 22 Saw Mill River Road, Hawthorne NY 10532. **Tel** (914)592-1060, FAX (914)592-3625. **ED** Svend E. Hartmann. ctrl circ.
Desc: Contains prices, market information, and editorial comment about the market for used IBM computers from mainframes to PCs.

ISSN 1052-3502
DD 004 US

COMPUTER PRICE WATCH. [Comput. price watch]. (19??)-. Periodical. English. Twelve times a year. $110.00. Computer Information Resources, PO Box 13176, Arlington TX 76094. **Tel** (817)654-0346. **ED** Dale Taylor. ctrl circ.

BE
UDC 62

COMPUTER PRODUCT NEWS. English. Ten times a year. $111.94. Pan European Publishing Company, rue Verte 216, 1210 Brussels 21 Belgium. **Tel** 011 32 2 2420611. **(Subscription address:** Elsevier Librico NV, Div Pepco Groenstraat 216, 1210 Brussels 21 Belgium. **Tel** 011 32 2 2422992.**)** **ED** Nadia Liefsoens. **Bk Rev**. **Ad Acc**, **Adv Mgr:** Leo Por, **Tel** 011 32 2 2422992. **Circ:** 50,000 (ctrl).

ISSN 0893-8377
DD 381 US
CCC

COMPUTER RESELLER NEWS. No. 166 (Aug. 18, 1986)-. Periodical. English. One time a week (51 issues). $189.00. CMP Publications Inc., One Jericho Plaza, Wing A, 2nd Floor, Jericho NY 11753. **Tel** (516)733-6700. **(Subscription address:** CMP Publications, Inc. / New York, PO Box 4037, Church Street Station, New York NY 10261-4037. **Tel** (516)733-6800.**)** **ED** John Russell. Index available. cum. index. **Ad Acc. Circ:** 64,000 (ctrl). available on an online database from NEWSNET; and (file 16/Full-Text) DIALOG. Documents available from BLDSC, UMI Article Clearinghouse. ***Continues*** *Computer Retail News, 0744-673X;* ***Separated from*** *Systems and Network Integration.*
Desc: Provides timely analysis and market research statistics pertaining to the microcomputer reseller industry.
Ind/Abst Comput. Database; EP Collect.; F&S Index Plus Text, Int. [Full Txt.] [Select. Cov.]; Homework Help.; MasterFile FullTEXT 1000; MasterFile FullTEXT 350; MasterFile FullTEXT 650; MasterFile FullTEXT; Microcomput. Abstr. (Sept. 1985-); Microcomput. Ind. Update; OCLC; PROMT [Full Txt.]; Telebase; Trade Ind. Index.

LC CURRENT ISSUES ONLY **ISSN** 1066-7598
DD 338 US

COMPUTER RETAIL WEEK. [Comput. retail week]. (1990)-. Periodical. English. Thirty-nine times a year. $179.95. CMP Publications Inc., One Jericho Plaza, Wing A, 2nd Floor, Jericho NY 11753. **Tel** (516)733-6700. **(Subscription address:** CMP Publications, Inc. / New York, PO Box 4037, Church Street Station, New York NY 10261-4037. **Tel** (516)733-6800.**)** available on an online database (file 16/Full-Text) from DIALOG.
Desc: Targeted specifically to computer superstores, mass merchants and retailers. Serves the information needs of executives, merchandise and sales managers, buyers, salespeople and all other key personnel within the computer retail industry.
Ind/Abst EP Collect.; F&S Index Plus Text, Int. [Full Txt.] [Select. Cov.]; Homework Help.; MasterFile FullTEXT 1000; MasterFile FullTEXT 350; MasterFile FullTEXT 650; MasterFile FullTEXT; OCLC; PROMT; Telebase.

LC TK7887 .C67 **ISSN** 1073-2861
DD 621.39/16 US

•COMPUTER SERVICE & REPAIR MAGAZINE. **See** Computers-Microcomputers, Personal Computers.

ISSN 0886-0556
US

COMPUTER SHOPPER. [Comput. shopp.]. Vol. 1, No. 1 (198?)-. Periodical. English. Twelve times a year. $40.00. Ziff-Davis, One Park Avenue, 5th Floor, New York NY 10016. **Tel** (212)503-3500. **(Subscription address:** Neodata / Colorado, PO Box 2606, Boulder CO 80322. **)** available on an online database (file 675/Full-Text) from DIALOG; available via Internet (http://www.ziff.com/).
Desc: Shop-direct guide to computer deals. Features over 1,000 mail-order ads for hardware, software, peripherals and accessories for IBM, Macintosh and Unix Systems, plus a quick-reference product index. Includes a hardware buyer's guide with comparison charts and purchasing tips, inside programming techniques, a section on how to buy direct, and more.
Ind/Abst Comput. ASAP [Full Txt.]; Comput. Database [Full Txt.]; Comput. Rev. Index (1986-).

ISSN 0268-6821
DD 651.8 UK

COMPUTER USERS' YEAR BOOK. [Comput. users' year book]. (1969)-. English. One time a year (Dec.). $256.68. VNU Business Publications BV, 32-34 Broadwick Street, London W1A 2HG United Kingdom. **Tel** 011 44 171 4394242 ext. 2222, FAX 011 44 171 4379638, telex 23918 VNU G, 8952440. **ED** Alan Reid. Index available. cum. index. **Bk Rev**. **Ad Acc.** ctrl circ. available on diskette.
Desc: Directory of computer equipment, services, end users and suppliers. UK's top reference source for DP managers.

US

CTOSIAN. English. Twelve times a year. $75.00 (one-year), $120.00 (two-year). Executive Productivity System, PO Box 15539, Chesapeake VA 23328. **Tel** (804) 547-0209, FAX (804) 547-5518. **ED** Carla Whitmore. Index available. cum. index. **Bk Rev**. **Ad Acc**, **Adv Mgr:** Teresa Davis, **Tel** (804) 547-8382. **Circ:** 1,300.
Desc: The magazine for BTOS/CTOS resellers and users.

ISSN 8750-3697
DD 001 US
CCC

CULPEPPER LETTER, THE. **See** Computers-Software.

ISSN 0842-1951
DD 338.4/7004/0971 CN

DIRECTION INFORMATIQUE. **See** Computers-Computer Industry and Industry Directories.

LC HD9696.C63 U516314 **ISSN** 0884-8300
DD 381/.45004/02573 US

DIRECTORY OF VARS, THE. (THE ... DIRECTORY OF VARS.). [Dir. VARS]. **VFOAT** Directory of Value Added Resellers. (1985)-. Periodical. English. One time a year. $290.00. Lebhar Friedman Inc., PO Box 31203, Tampa FL 33633. **Tel** (800)944-4676, (813)664-6707. **ED** Carl Skeps. Index available. available on diskette (and telemarketing cards); available on magnetic tape; available on labels.
Desc: Provides complete company profiles on 4,000 VARs, including value added dealers, systems houses, systems integrators, and system specialists serving a wide variety of end users.

Computers —Computer Sales, Service and Supply

DD 025
ISSN 1079-8668
US
●**GEAC SERVICEPLUS CUSTOMER UPDATE.** [Geac serv.plus cust. update]. **Added/Corp** Geac Computers, Inc. **VFOAT** Serviceplus Customer Update. (1994)-. Periodical. English. Twelve times a year. Free on request. GEAC Computers Inc, 320 Nevada Street, Newtonville MA 02160. **Tel** (617)965-6310.

LC TK7887.7 .H35
DD 681/.62/029473
ISSN 1058-2444
US
HARD COPY OBSERVER, THE. See Business and Economics-Office Equipment and Services.

US
HOW TO BUY & PRICE A USED COMPUTER. English. One time a year. $39.00. Orion Research Corporation, 14555 North Scottsdale Road, Suite 330, Scottsdale AZ 85260. **Tel** (800)844-0759, (602)951-1114, FAX (602)951-1117.

DD 338.4/7004/09714/05
ISSN 0847-4915
CN
CODEN ILMAER
CEASED
INFO-LOG MAGAZINE. (INFO-LOG MAGAZINE.). [Info-log mag.]. (1990)-(1993). Periodical. French. Information Logiciel, 3480 rue Saint Denis, Montreal Quebec H2X 3L3 Canada. **Tel** (514)288-8875. Documents available from Ask*IEEE. **Continues** Informateur-Logiciel., 0832-638X.
Ind/Abst INSPEC (Jan. 1990-); Repere (19??-19??).

LC HD9801.U544 I274
DD 001.64
ISSN 0743-9695
US
INTERNATIONAL REGISTER OF MARKETERS AND SUPPORTERS OF IBM PRODUCTS. **VFOAT** International Register. (Fall 1984)-. English. Two times a year. $17.50 US; $27.50 other. Basic Society Inc, PO Box 226049, Dallas TX 75222.

US
LESSOR'S GUIDE TO RESIDUAL VALUES - COMPUTER. English. One time a year. Orion Research Corporation, 14555 North Scottsdale Road, Suite 330, Scottsdale AZ 85260. **Tel** (800)844-0759, (602)951-1114, FAX (602)951-1117.

US
TITLE CHANGE
MAINFRAME MARKET MONTHLY. (19??)-(19??). English. Xephon, 27-35 London Road, Newbury Berkshire RG13 1JL United Kingdom. **Tel** 011 44 1635 33823, FAX 011 44 1635 38345. **Merged into** Insight IBM.
Desc: Up-to-the-minute market intelligence and reliable figures on prices, discounts and residual values- IBM compatible mainframe market.

US
MIC/INFO. English. One time a week. $2,095 US; $2320.00 other. Management Information Corporation, 1111 Marlkress Road, Cherry Hill NJ 08003. **Tel** (609)424-1100. Index available. cum. index. ctrl circ. available on diskette.
Desc: Vendor news releases on new products, company organization and finances.

US
MIC/TECH-DATA COMMUNICATIONS. English. Twelve times a year. $966.00 US; $1051.00 other. Management Information Corporation, 1111 Marlkress Road, Cherry Hill NJ 08003. **Tel** (609)424-1100. Index available. cum. index. ctrl circ.
Desc: Descriptions and pricing of data communication products.

US
MIC/TECH-MAINFRAME AND MINICOMPUTER. English. Twelve times a year. $1,145 US; $1230.00 other. Management Information Corporation, 1111 Marlkress Road, Cherry Hill NJ 08003. **Tel** (609)424-1100. Index available. cum. index. ctrl circ. available on diskette.
Desc: Descriptions and pricing of minicomputers, super minis, mainframes, and super computers.

US
MIC/TECH-MICROCOMPUTER AND WORKSTATION. English. Twelve times a year. $845.00 US; $930.00 other. Management Information Corporation, 1111 Marlkress Road, Cherry Hill NJ 08003. **Tel** (609)424-1100. Index available. cum. index. ctrl circ. available on diskette.
Desc: Descriptions and pricing of personal computers, laptops, portables, and workstations.

ISSN 0277-0059
US
MICRO MOONLIGHTER. [Micro moonlighter]. No. 1 (May 1981)-. Periodical. English. Twelve times a year. $25.00 US; $29.00 other. Association of Electronic Cottagers, 4121 Buckhorn Court, Lewisville TX 75028.

US
MICROLEADS U.S. & CANADIAN DEALER DIRECTORY. Directory. English. One time a year. $995.00. Chromatic Communications, PO Box 30127, Walnut Creek CA 94598. **Tel** (510)945-1602, (800)782-DISK, FAX (707)746-0542. **ED** Michael Shipp.
Desc: List over 6,000 microcomputer retailers in the U.S. Listings include company name, address, phone, key contacts and their appropriate titles as well as the brands of computers they sell. Each listing is either confirmed via written survey or through a telephone conservation with the store owner or manager.

LC HD9696.C63 U5278
DD 004/.029/473
ISSN 1056-0386
US
MICROLEADS VENDOR DIRECTORY. [MicroLeads vend. dir.]. **VFOAT** Vendor Directory; Microcomputer Vendor Directory. (1988)-. Directory. English. One time a year. $495.00. Chromatic Communications, PO Box 30127, Walnut Creek CA 94598. **Tel** (510)945-1602, (800)782-DISK, FAX (707)746-0542. Index available. cum. index. available on diskette. **Continues** Personal Computer, an Industry Source Book, 0739-3687.
Desc: Includes company profiles and industry members directly involved in the microcomputer Industry. Each listing contains market research information such as sales volume, year started, number of employees, type of entity, key contacts, machine specialization, industry specialization, application specialization, as well as detailed product line descriptions.

US
CEASED
MULTILINGUAL COMPUTING BUYER'S GUIDE. (199?)-(1994). Consumer Publication. English. Multilingual Computing Inc., 111 Cedar Street, Suite 5, Sandpoint ID 83864. **Tel** (208)263-8178, FAX (208)263-6310. **Separated from** Multilingual Computing : Magazine and Buyer's Guide, 1065-7657.

LC HD9696.C6 O75
DD 004.16/029/473
ISSN 1056-8573
US
ORION COMPUTER PRICE WATCH. [Orion comput. price watch]. **Added/Corp** Orion Research Corporation. **VFOAT** Computer Price Watch. (Winter 1991)-. English. Four times a year. $39.95 (single issue). Orion Research Group, 1315 Main Avenue, #230, Durango CO 81301.

DD 001.6404
ISSN 0266-8483
UK
CEASED
PC BUSINESS WORLD. [PC bus. world]. **VFOAT** Personal Computer Business World. (1984)-(19??). Periodical. English. IDG Communications Ltd. / London, 99 Grays Inn Road, London WC1X 8UT United Kingdom. **Tel** 011 44 181 6860371, FAX 011 44 181 4052347. **(Subscription address:** Tower Publishing, Tower House, Sovereign Park, Market Harborough, Leicester LE16 9EF United Kingdom. **Tel** 011 44 1858 468811, FAX 011 44 1858 432164.)
Ind/Abst HILITES.

DD 004
ISSN 1075-6159
US
●**PC TROUBLESHOOTER, THE.** **VFOAT** Personal Computer Troubleshooter. (1993)-. Periodical. English. Six times a year. $97.50. Landmark Research, 703 Grand Central Street, Clearwater FL 34616. **Tel** (800)683-6696 ext. 505.

LC QA76.8.I2594 P3
DD 001.64
ISSN 0737-8939
US
CCC
CODEN PCWDDV
PC WORLD. See Computers-Microcomputers, Personal Computers.

ISSN 0954-6286
UK
CEASED
PC YEAR BOOK. [PC year b.]. (1987)-(1993). English. VNU Business Publications BV, 32-34 Broadwick Street, London W1A 2HG United Kingdom. **Tel** 011 44 171 4394242 ext. 2222, FAX 011 44 171 4379638, telex 23918 VNU G, 8952440. **Continues** Microcomputer Users' Year Book, 0269-3232.
Desc: Contains information on equipment, software, services and suppliers.

LC HD9696
DD 338.47621381
US
SALES SOFTWARE SUPPLIERS DIRECTORY. **Added/Corp** Sales Automation Association. **VFOAT** SAA Sales Software Suppliers Directory. (1991)-. Directory. English. Sales Automation Association, 1105 Washington, Dearborn MI 48124.

LC HD9696.C63 C334a
DD 338.4/0971021
ISSN 1181-9847
CN
SOFTWARE DEVELOPMENT AND COMPUTER SERVICE INDUSTRY. See Computers-Abstracting, Bibliographies and Statistics.

US
TIMIX BUYERS' GUIDE. (19??)-. Consumer Publication. English. One time a year. $5.00. TIMIX, Box 201897, Austin TX 78720. **Tel** (512)250-7151. **ED** Bethany Powell. **Ad Acc. Circ:** 10,000 (ctrl).
Desc: Index of hardware, software, services, and supplies for users to Texas Instruments computers.

US
CEASED
VERTICAL APPLICATION RESELLER. (19??-Dec. 1994).Trade Publication. English. Six times a year. $30.00 US, Canada and Mexico; $35.00 (surface mail); $69.00 (airmail) other. Gordon Publications Inc., A Subsidiary of Cahners Publishing Company, 301 Gibraltar Drive, Box 650, Morris Plains NJ 07950. **Tel** (201)292-5100, (800)637-6081.
Desc: Provides information to high-end vertical resellers in manufacturing/process, retail, professional/service, wholesale distribution/government/institution, and healthcare industries.

SI
WHAT'S NEW IN COMPUTING. (19??)-. English. Twelve times a year. $50.00 (airmail) Asia; $60.00 (airmail) other. Asian Business Press Pte Limited / Singapore, 100 Beach Road, 26-00 Shaw Towers, Singapore 0718 Singapore. **Tel** 65-2943366, FAX 65-2985534, telex RS 25280 ABPSIN. **ED** T C Seow. **Ad Acc. Circ:** 18,000 (ctrl). **Continues** Business Computing & Communications.
Desc: Asian buyers guide to software and systems.
Ind/Abst Infomat Int. Bus.

US
WORKGROUP COMPUTING SERIES. PERIPHERALS. See Computers-Microcomputers, Personal Computers.

COMPUTER SYSTEMS

ISSN 0298-2285
FR
01 INFORMATIQUE (HEBDOMADAIRE). (01 INFORMATIQUE.). **VFOAT** Zero un Informatique. (1986)-. Periodical. French. Fifty times a year. 954.95F France; 1535.00F other. Groupe Tests, 26 rue d'Oradour sur Glane, 75504 Paris Cedex 15 France. **Tel** 011 33 1 44253001, FAX 011 33 1 45573506. Documents available from Ask*IEEE. **Continues** 01 Hebdo, 0398-1169.
Ind/Abst INSPEC (June/July 1988-); Repere.

DD 004
ISSN 1061-7663
US
A/E/C SYSTEMS COMPUTER SOLUTIONS. [A/E/C syst. comput. solut.]. **VFOAT** A E C Systems Computer Solutions. Premiere Issue (Autumn 1991)-. Periodical. English. Four times a year. $56.00. A/E/C Systems Computer Solutions, PO Box 310318, Newington CT 06131-0318. **Tel** (203)666-1326, FAX (203)666-4782.
Desc: Each issue contains a practical blend of "how to" features and case studies of real value to the practicing professional. It is written by users for users and do not allow vendor sales pitches disguised as articles.

LC QA76.9.S88 A27
DD 001.64/05
ISSN 0734-2071
US
CCC
Pr Rev.
ACM TRANSACTIONS ON COMPUTER SYSTEMS. [ACM trans. comput. syst.]. **Added/Corp** Association for Computing Machinery. **VFOAT** A.C.M. Transactions on Computer Systems; Transactions on Computer Systems. **VAT** Association for Computing Machinery Transactions on Computer Systems. Vol. 1, No. 1 (Feb. 1983)-. Periodical. English. Four times a year (Feb., May., Aug., Nov.). $125.00. ACM / Association for Computing Machinery, 1515 Broadway, 17th Floor, New York NY 10036. **Tel** (212)869-7440, FAX (212)869-0481. **(Subscription address:** Association for Computing Machinery, PO Box 12114, Church Street Station, New York NY 10249. **Tel** (212)626-0500.) **ED** Anita K. Jones. available on microfilm and microfiche from University Microfilms International (UMI). Documents available from Article Express International, The Genuine Article, Ask*IEEE.
Desc: Reports valuable and original work in the design, implementation and use of computer systems.
Ind/Abst Abstr. Hum. Comput. Interact.; ACM Guide Comput. Lit.; Appl. Sci. Technol. Index (1991-); CompuMath Cit. Index [Full Cov.]; Comput. Database; Comput. Lit. Index; Comput. Rev.; Curr. Cit. Curr. Contents Eng. Comput. Technol.; Ei Page One; Eng. Index Annu.; Inf. Access [Annex] (1992-); Inf. Sci. Abstr.; INSPEC (Jan. 1983-); Res. Alert [Full Cov.]; Sci. Cit. Index; SCISEARCH.

Computers — Computer Systems

LC QA75.5 .A3395 ISSN 1061-8929
DD 004/.05 US
CEASED

ADVANCES IN THE IMPLEMENTATION AND IMPACT OF COMPUTER SYSTEMS. [Adv. implement. impact comput. syst.]. Vol. 1 (1991)-(19??). English. JAI Press Inc., 55 Old Post Road, Suite 2, PO Box 1678, Greenwich CT 06836-1678. **Tel** (203)661-7602, FAX (203)661-0792.

ISSN 0129-5896
DD 338.4762138195 SI

ASIA COMPUTER WEEKLY. See Computers-Computer Industry and Industry Directories.

ISSN 0735-9985
DD 658 US
CCC

AUERBACH SYSTEMS DEVELOPMENT MANAGEMENT. [Auerbach syst. dev. manage.]. **Added/Corp** Auerbach Publishers. **VFOAT** Systems Development Management. (1976)-. Periodical. English. Six times a year. $498.95 US. Auerbach Publishers Inc., Park Square Building, 31 St. James Avenue, Boston MA 02116. **Tel** (800)950-1207. **ED** Ian A. Gilhooley and Ruth Mills.
 Desc: The one information service designed for the manager of the systems development function, providing the information needed to effectively manage projects-from user needs identification through planning, design, implementation to evaluation and improvement. Describes techniques, methods, and tools for the efficient use of current technology.

LC QA76.758 .A98 ISSN 0928-8910
DD 004 US
CCC
CODEN ASOEEA

●**AUTOMATED SOFTWARE ENGINEERING. See** Computers-Software.

ISSN 0045-1991
CN
CEASED

BIG BYTE, THE. Added/Corp University of Calgary. Data Centre. University of Calgary. Dept. of Computer Services. Vol. 1 (June 1968)-(June 1994). Periodical. English. University Calgary Computing Services, 2920 24th Avenue Northwest, Calgary Alberta Canada. **Tel** (403)220-6616, FAX (403)282-9199. **ED** Jackie Bell. **Circ:** 1,800 (ctrl).

LC KF3024.C6 C657
DD 346.7304/82 US

COMPUTER SOFTWARE AND CHIPS : PROTECTION AND MARKETING. See Computers-Computer Crimes and Security.

ISSN 0957-2945
DD 005 UK

COMPUTER SYSTEMS EUROPE. [Comp. syst. Eur.]. **VFOAT** Computer Systems. (19??)-. Periodical. English. Twelve times a year. VNU Business Publications BV, 32-34 Broadwick Street, London W1A 2HG United Kingdom. **Tel** 011 44 171 4394242 ext. 2222, FAX 011 44 171 4379638, telex 23918 VNU G, 8952440.
 Ind/Abst Informat Int. Bus.

LC TK7885.A1 C6114 ISSN 0278-9647
DD 621.3819/58/05 US
CCC

COMPUTER TECHNOLOGY REVIEW. [Comput. tech. rev.]. Vol. 1, No. 1 (Spring/Summer 1981)-. Periodical. English. Sixteen times a year. $84.00. West World Productions, 924 Westwood Boulevard, Suite 650, Los Angeles CA 90024. **Tel** (310)208-1335, FAX (310)208-1054. **ED** George McNamara. **Ad Acc, Adv Mgr:** Carol Stagg, **Tel** (310)208-1335. **Circ:** 67,000 (ctrl). Documents available from UMI Article Clearinghouse.
 Desc: Explores technological innovations on computers, peripherals and systems. Provides articles across the spectrum of computer systems technology.
 Ind/Abst ABI/INFORM Glob. Ed.; ABI/INFORM [Computer File] (December 1985-); Comput. Lit. Index; Ei Page One; Graph. Arts Bull. Inst. Pap. Sci. Technol. (Jan. 1989-Feb. 1989, April 1989, June 1989-July 1989, Sept. 1989-Nov. 1989).

LC TK7885 ISSN 1352-9404
DD 621.39 UK

●**COMPUTING AND INFORMATION SYSTEMS.** (1994)-. Academic Scholarly Publication. English. Three times a year. £50.00. University of Paisley, Department of Computing and Information Systems, High Street, Paisley PA1 2BE United Kingdom. **Tel** 011 44 141 8483301, FAX 011 44 141 8483542. **ED** M.K. Crowe. Documents available from BLDSC.

US

DATAPRO COMPUTER SYSTEMS SERIES / OVERVIEWS. (19??)-. English. $485.00. Datapro Information Services Group, 600 Delran Parkway, Delran NJ 08075. **Tel** (609)764-0100, (800)328-2776, FAX (609)764-8953.

US

DATAPRO COMPUTER SYSTEMS SERIES / PERIPHERALS. (19??)-. English. $485.00. Datapro Information Services Group, 600 Delran Parkway, Delran NJ 08075. **Tel** (609)764-0100, (800)328-2776, FAX (609)764-8953.

US

DATAPRO COMPUTER SYSTEMS SERIES / SOFTWARE. (19??)-. English. $485.00. Datapro Information Services Group, 600 Delran Parkway, Delran NJ 08075. **Tel** (609)764-0100, (800)328-2776, FAX (609)764-8953.

US

DATAPRO COMPUTER SYSTEMS SERIES / SYSTEMS. (19??)-. English. $485.00. Datapro Information Services Group, 600 Delran Parkway, Delran NJ 08075. **Tel** (609)764-0100, (800)328-2776, FAX (609)764-8953.

UK

DATAPRO ENTERPRISE SYSTEMS / INTERNATIONAL EDITION. (19??)-. English. Irregular. $584.00. Datapro Information Services Group, 600 Delran Parkway, Delran NJ 08075. **Tel** (609)764-0100, (800)328-2776, FAX (609)764-8953.

UK

DATAPRO MIDRANGE SYSTEMS / INTERNATIONAL EDITION. (19??)-. English. Twelve times a year. $1,031.00. Datapro International, McGraw Hill House, Shoppenhangers Road, Maidenhead Berkshire SL6 2QL United Kingdom. **Tel** 011 44 1628 773277, FAX 011 44 1628 773628.

US

DATAPRO REPORTS ON INFORMATION SECURITY. (19??)-. English. Twelve times a year. $1,116.00. Datapro Information Services Group, 600 Delran Parkway, Delran NJ 08075. **Tel** (609)764-0100, (800)328-2776, FAX (609)764-8953.

US

DATAPRO REPORTS ON UNIX SYSTEMS & SOFTWARE. (19??)-. English. Twelve times a year. $866.00. Datapro Information Services Group, 600 Delran Parkway, Delran NJ 08075. **Tel** (609)764-0100, (800)328-2776, FAX (609)764-8953.

US

DATAPRO WORKSTATIONS & SERVERS / ISSUES. (19??)-. English. $433.00. Datapro Information Services Group, 600 Delran Parkway, Delran NJ 08075. **Tel** (609)764-0100, (800)328-2776, FAX (609)764-8953.

US

DATAPRO WORKSTATIONS & SERVERS / SYSTEMS. (19??)-. English. $433.00. Datapro Information Services Group, 600 Delran Parkway, Delran NJ 08075. **Tel** (609)764-0100, (800)328-2776, FAX (609)764-8953.

LC QA76.8.D43 D433 ISSN 0744-9216
DD 001.64 US
TITLE CHANGE

DEC PROFESSIONAL, THE. [DEC prof.]. **VFOAT** DEC Professional Magazine. **VAT** Digital Equipment Corporation Professional. Vol. 1, No. 1 (July 1982)-(1995). Trade Publication. English. Professional Press Inc, 101 Witmer Road, Horsham PA 19044. **Tel** (215)957-1500, FAX (215)957-1050. (**Subscription address:** Professional Press, PO Box 218, Horsham PA 19044.) **ED** Linda D Biasio and Lou Pilla. Index available. cum. index. **Bk Rev. Ad Acc. Circ:** 95,510 (ctrl). available on microfilm and microfiche from University Microfilms International (UMI); available on an online database (file 675/Full-Text) from DIALOG. Documents available from Ask*IEEE, Documents on Demand. **Absorbed** Personal and Professional, 0746-3960. **Continued by** Digital Age.
 Desc: Serves the total DEC community with articles that span developments in networking, programming languages, database management systems, hardware and peripherals.
 Ind/Abst Comput. ASAP [Full Txt.]; Comput. Database [Full Txt.]; Comput. Rev. index (April 1987-); Curr. Cit.; Environ. Abstr.; INSPEC (June 1983-); Microcomput. Abstr. (Jan. 1986-).

LC TK7885 ISSN 0929-5585
DD 621.39 NE
CCC

●**DESIGN AUTOMATION FOR EMBEDDED SYSTEMS.** (1995)-. Academic Scholarly Publication. English. Four times a year. Kluwer Academic Publishers, Postbus 322, 3300 AH Dordrecht The Netherlands. **Tel** 011 31 78 524400, FAX 011 31 78 183273, telex 20083.

US

●**DIGITAL AGE.** (1995)-. English. Twelve times a year. $30.00. Professional Press Inc, 101 Witmer Road, Horsham PA 19044. **Tel** (215)957-1500, FAX (215)957-1050. **Continues** DEC Professional.

ISSN 1047-1693
DD 338 US
CCC
CODEN DDREEL

DIGITAL DIRECTIONS REPORT. See Computers-Electronic Data Processing.

LC QA76.8.D43 D545 ISSN 1065-7452
DD 004.1/4 US

DIGITAL NEWS & REVIEW. [Digit. news rev.]. **VFOAT** Digital News and Review. Vol. 9, No. 16 (Aug. 24, 1992)-. Trade Publication. English. Twenty-four times a year. $95.90. Cahners Publishing Company, 249 West 17th Street, New York NY 10011. **Tel** (212)645-0067, FAX (212)242-6987. (**Subscription address:** Cahners Publishing Company / Colorado, Paid Subscription Service Center, PO Box 7610, Highlands Ranch CO 80126-7610. **Tel** (303)470-4466, FAX (303)470-4691.) available on an online database (files 648,675/Full-Text) from DIALOG. **Formed by the union of** Digital News (Boston, Mass.), 0891-9860 **and** Digital Review (New York, N.Y.), 0739-4314.
 Desc: The independent news, labs and technology source for the digital world.

ISSN 1079-4727
DD 004 US
CCC

●**DISTRIBUTED SYSTEMS MANAGEMENT REPORT. See** Computers-Computer Networks.

ISSN 1081-7905
US

●**DO IT WITH MACINTOSH SYSTEM 7.5.** **VFOAT** Do it with MacOS. (1995)-. Periodical. English. Twelve times a year. $59.00. IDG Newsletter Corporation, 77 Franklin Street, Suite 310, Boston MA 02110. **Tel** (617)482-8470, (800)807-0771, FAX (617)338-0164.

LC QA871 .D96 ISSN 0268-1110
DD 003/.05 UK
CCC

DYNAMICS AND STABILITY OF SYSTEMS. Vol. 1, No. 1 (1986)-. Periodical. English. Four times a year. $342.00. Oxford University Press / UK, Walton Street, Oxford OX2 6DP United Kingdom. **Tel** 011 44 1865 56767, FAX 011 44 1865 267773, telex 851/837330 OXPRES G. (**Subscription address:** Oxford University Press / USA, Journals Marketing Department, Oxford University Press, 2001 Evans Road, Cary NC 27513. **Tel** (800)451-7556, (919)677-0977, FAX (919)677-1714.) **ED** Koncay Huseyin. Index available. **Ad Acc.** available on microfilm and microfiche from University Microfilms International (UMI). Documents available from Article Express International.
 Desc: International journal designed to serve as an outlet for original research work concerning the stability, instability, bifurcation and oscillatory behaviour of natural and man-made systems.
 Ind/Abst Eng. Index Annu.; Math. Rev. (1986-); Zentralbl. Math. Ihre Grenzgeb.

LC QA75 ISSN 0969-7977
DD 004 UK

●**ELECTRONIC JOURNAL OF STRATEGIC INFORMATION SYSTEMS.** **VAT** SISE - Journal. (1994)-. Academic Scholarly Publication. English. One time a year. University of Sheffield / Information Studies Department, 211 Portobello Street, Regents Court, Room 315, Sheffield S10 2UH United Kingdom. **Tel** 011 44 742 768555, FAX 011 44 742 780300. **ED** Luis Zeredo.

US

FAULKNER MANAGING DISTRIBUTED SYSTEMS. (19??)-. Periodical. English. Twelve times a year. $495.00 US; $545.00 Canada; $595.00 other. Faulkner Technical Reports, 7905 Browning Road, Suite 114, Pennsauken NJ 08109. **Tel** (800)843-0460.

US

FAULKNER MANAGING OPEN SYSTEMS. (19??)-. Periodical. English. Irregular (2 volumes and monthly supplements). $1035.00 US;

Computers — Computer Systems

$1175.00 Canada; $1326.00 other. Faulkner Technical Reports, 7905 Browning Road, Suite 114, Pennsauken NJ 08109. **Tel** (800)843-0460.
US

FAULKNER SYSTEMS SOFTWARE REPORTS. (19??)-. Periodical. English. Irregular. $670.00 US; $755.00 Canada; $790.00 other. Faulkner Technical Reports, 7905 Browning Road, Suite 114, Pennsauken NJ 08109. **Tel** (800)843-0460.

DD 353 **ISSN** 0893-052X
US

FEDERAL COMPUTER WEEK. [Fed. comput. week]. (1987)-. Periodical. English. Thirty-six times a year. $95.00. Federal Computer Week, 3110 Fairview Park Drive, Suite 1040, Falls Church VA 22042. **Tel** (703)876-5100. **ED** Anne A. Armstrong. Index available. **Ad Acc, Adv Mgr:** Julie Savage. **Circ:** 61,500 (ctrl).
Desc: Data for the federal government buyers of computer and communications systems and for the companies that sell them hardware, software and services.
Ind/Abst Comput. Database.

DD 001 **ISSN** 0883-8194
US

FOCUS (AUSTIN, TEX. 1985). (FOCUS : THE MAGAZINE OF THE NORTH AMERICAN DATA GENERAL USERS GROUP.). [Focus]. **Added/Corp** North American Data General Users Group. (Sept. 1985)-. Periodical. English. Twelve times a year. $48.00. Turnkey Publishing, PO Box 200549, Austin TX 78731. **Tel** (512)335-2286. **ED** Greg Farman. **Bk Rev. Ad Acc. Circ:** 8,000 (ctrl).
Desc: Technical and management information to help users of Data General computer systems get better use from their investments.

LC QA75.5 .F66 **ISSN** 0934-5043
DD 004/.05 UK
CCC
CODEN FACME5

FORMAL ASPECTS OF COMPUTING. [Form. asp. comput.]. **Added/Corp** British Computer Society. Specialist Group in Formal Aspects of Computing Science. Vol. 1, No. 1 (Jan./March 1989)-. Trade Publication. English. Six times a year. $334.00. Springer-Verlag London Ltd., Springer House, 8 Alexandra Road Wimbledon, London SW19 7JZ United Kingdom. **Tel** 011 44 181 9471280, 011 44 181 9475885, FAX 011 44 181 9474651, telex 21531 SPRGB G. **(Subscription address:** Springer-Verlag New York Inc. / North America, PO Box 2485, Journal Fulfillment, Secaucus NJ 07096. **Tel** (201)348-4033, (800)777-4643, FAX (201)348-4505.**)** **ED** C B Jones, D J Cooke, D Gries, and R C Shaw. Documents available from Ask*IEEE.
Desc: Provides a basis on which complex systems can be designed and analysed.
Ind/Abst Comput. Abstr.; Comput. Rev.; INSPEC (Jan./March 1990-)(Jan./Mar. 1990-); Zentralbl. Math. Ihre Grenzgeb.

LC QA76.9.S88 F675 **ISSN** 0925-9856
DD 004.2/1 US
CCC
CODEN FMSDE6
Pr Rev.
FORMAL METHODS IN SYSTEM DESIGN. Vol. 1, No. 1 (July 1992)-. Periodical. English. Six times a year. $493.00. Kluwer Academic Publishers / Massachusetts, PO Box 358, Accord Station, Hingham MA 02018. **Tel** (617)871-6600. **ED** R.K. Brayton, E.M. Clarke and P.A. Subrahmanyam. **Acid Free.** available on microfilm and microfiche from University Microfilms International (UMI). Documents available from Article Express International.
Desc: The focus of this journal is on formal methods for designing, implementing, and validating the correctness of hardware (VLS) and software systems.
Ind/Abst Comput. Rev.; Eng. Index Annu.; Inf. Sci. Abstr.; Zentralbl. Math. Ihre Grenzgeb.

LC QA75.5 .F87 **ISSN** 0167-739X
DD 004/.05 NE
CCC
Pr Rev.
FUTURE GENERATIONS COMPUTER SYSTEMS : FGCS. [FGCS, Future gener. comput. syst.]. **VFOAT** Future Generation Computer Systems; FGCS. Vol. 1, No. 1 (July 1984)-. English. Six times a year (1 volume). $555.00. Elsevier Science Publishers BV, PO Box 211, 1000 AE Amsterdam Netherlands. **Tel** 011 31 20 4853641, 011 31 20 4853642, FAX 011 31 20 4853598. **ED** H Aiso, F Kuo and R van de Riet. available on microfilm and microfiche from University Microfilms International (UMI); available on an online database from Elsevier Electronic Subscriptions (EES). Documents available from Article Express International, Ask*IEEE.
Desc: Devoted to all major developments in the field of new computer systems.
Ind/Abst ACM Guide Comput. Lit.; Civ. Struct. Eng. Abstr.; Comput. Inf. Syst. Abstr. J. [Full Cov.]; Comput. Lit. Index; Comput. Rev.; Curr. Cit.; Ei Page One; Elect. Comm. Abstr.; Eng. Index Annu.; INSPEC (March 1986-); Manuf. Process Eng. Abstr.

LC SD144.A15 G57 **ISSN** 1054-0563
DD 634.9/0975 US
GIS APPLICATION NOTE. See Forests and Forestry.
UK

HANDBOOK OF IBM TERMINOLOGY, THE. (19??)-. English. Two times a year. $111.23. Xephon, 27-35 London Road, Newbury Berkshire RG13 1JL United Kingdom. **Tel** 011 44 1635 33823, FAX 011 44 1635 38345.
NE

NLM W1; HU447L
HUMAN FACTORS IN INFORMATION TECHNOLOGY. (1989)-. Monographic series. English. Price varies per volume. Elsevier Science Publishers BV, PO Box 211, 1000 AE Amsterdam Netherlands. **Tel** 011 31 20 4853641, 011 31 20 4853642, FAX 011 31 20 4853598. **ED** H.-J. Bullinger, P.G. Polson.
Desc: Covers a wide range of topics dealing with all aspects of human factors in the applications of information technology.
Ind/Abst Curr. Cit.

LC TA168 .I5 **ISSN** 0018-8670
DD 620.7/05 US
CCC
CODEN IBMSA7
Pr Rev.
IBM SYSTEMS JOURNAL. See Computers-Electronic Data Processing.

ISSN 1063-6552
US
CCC
●**IEEE PARALLEL & DISTRIBUTED TECHNOLOGY : SYSTEMS & APPLICATIONS.** **Added/Corp** IEEE Computer Society. Institute of Electrical and Electronics Engineers. **VFOAT** Parallel & Distributed Technology; Systems & Applications; IEEE Parallel and Distributed Technology; Systems and Applications; IEEE P&DT; P&DT. **VAT** Institute of Electrical and Electronics Engineers Parallel and Distributed Technology. Vol. 1, No. 1 (Feb. 1993)-. Periodical. English. Six times a year. $20.00 members; $36.00 (nonmembers). IEEE Computer Society, 10662 Los Vaqueros Circle, PO Box 3014, Los Alamitos CA 90720-1264. **Tel** (714)821-8380, (800)272-6657, FAX (714)821-4641. **ED** Michael J. Quinn, Oregon State University.
Desc: Emphasizes practical experience and new ideas; provides information on advances in parallel and distributed computing technology, specifics on unique features and applications, and an awareness of the trends in this rapidly evolving area. Covers topics such as computational models, distributed databases, high speed networks, numerical algorithms, parallel and distributed computer architectures, and supercomputing; also includes coverage of current developments in the field.

LC TK7885.A1 I2 **ISSN** 0018-9340
DD 621.3819/5/05 US
CCC
CODEN ITCOB4
Pr Rev.
IEEE TRANSACTIONS ON COMPUTERS. [IEEE trans. comput.]. **Main/Corp** Institute of Electrical and Electronics Engineers. **Added/Corp** Institute of Electrical and Electronics Engineers. Transactions on Computers. Vol. C-17 (Jan. 1968)-. Academic Scholarly Publication. English. Twelve times a year. $540.00. IEEE / Institute of Electrical and Electronics Engineers Inc., 345 East 47th Street, New York NY 10017-2394. **Tel** (908)981-1393, FAX (908)981-9667. **(Subscription address:** IEEE / Institute of Electrical and Electronics Engineers, 445 Hoes Lane, PO Box 1331, Piscataway NJ 08855-1331. **Tel** (800)701-IEEE, (908)981-0060, FAX (908)981-9667, telex 833233.**)** **ED** Tse-Yun Feng. Index available. available on microfiche. Documents available from Article Express International, The Genuine Article, Ask*IEEE, CASDDS. **Continues** IEEE Transactions on Electronic Computers, 0367-7508.
Desc: Contains technical research papers on the theory, design, and application of computer systems. Regularly features a range of topics such as computer systems and subsystems, interconnection networks, VLSI and digital devices, computational methods, parallel processing, and others.
Ind/Abst Abstr. Hum. Comput. Interact.; ACM Guide Comput. Lit.; Acoust. Abstr.; Appl. Sci. Technol. Index (1991-); Bioeng. Abstr.; Chem. Abstr.; CompuMath Cit. Index [Full Cov.]; Comput. Abstr.; Comput. Inf. Syst. Abstr. J. [Full Cov.]; Comput. Database; Comput. Lit. Index; Comput. Rev.; Curr. Cit.; Curr. Contents Eng. Comput. Technol.; Ei Page One; Elect. Comm. Abstr.; Eng. Index Annu.; Expand. Acad. Index (1992-); Index IEEE Publ.; Inf. Sci. Abstr.; INIS Atomindex [Micro.]; INSPEC (1968-); Int. Abstr. Oper. Res. [Select. Cov.]; Int. Aerosp. Abstr.; Math. Rev.; Pollut. Abstr. Indexes; Res. Alert [Full Cov.]; Sci. Cit. Index [Select. Cov.]; Solid State Supercond. Abstr.; Zentralbl. Math. Ihre Grenzgeb.

LC Q300 .I43 **ISSN** 0018-9472
DD 001.53/05 US
CCC
NLM W1 I224E CODEN ISYMAW
Pr Rev. TITLE CHANGE
IEEE TRANSACTIONS ON SYSTEMS, MAN, AND CYBERNETICS. See Computers-Cybernetics.
US

●**IEEE TRANSACTIONS ON SYSTEMS, MAN, AND CYBERNETICS. PART A.** See Computers-Cybernetics.
US

●**IEEE TRANSACTIONS ON SYSTEMS, MAN, AND CYBERNETICS. PART B.** See Computers-Cybernetics.
US

IMA BULLETIN : THE NEWSLETTER OF THE INTERNATIONAL MIDI ASSOCIATION, THE. **Added/Corp** International MIDI Association. (19??)-. Bulletin. English. Four times a year. $125.00. International MIDI Association, 5316 West 57th Street, Los Angeles CA 90056-1339. **Tel** (310)649-6434. **ED** Stephanie Westfall. **Bk Rev. Circ:** 1,500 (ctrl).

ISSN 0716-0658
CL
UDC 681.3
Pr Rev.
INFORMATICA. REVISTA DE COMPUTACION Y SISTEMAS. [Inform., Rev. comput. sist.]. (1979)-. Periodical. Spanish. Eleven times a year (monthly except Feb.). $100.00. Publicaciones Computacion Ltd., Casilla 13220 Javier Valencia, 21 Santiago Chile. **Tel** 011 56 2 2232616. **ED** Jorge Gatica. **Bk Rev,** (Qty: 6). **Ad Acc, Adv Mgr:** Javier Valencia Jara, **Tel** 011 56 2 2042828. Full Page (B&W) $1,540.00. Half Page (B&W) $720.00. Full Page (Color) $2,050.00. Half Page (Color) $1,285.00. **Circ:** 15,000 (ctrl).
Desc: Covers hardware technology, software and data processing at a nationwide/worldwide level, management and communications.

LC QA402 .L357 **ISSN** 0923-0408
DD 003/.71/05 NE
CCC
CEASED

INFORMATION AND DECISION TECHNOLOGIES (AMSTERDAM). (INFORMATION AND DECISION TECHNOLOGIES.). [Inf. decis. technol.]. Vol. 14 No. 1 (1988)-Vol. 19. Academic Scholarly Publication. English. Elsevier Science Publishers BV, PO Box 211, 1000 AE Amsterdam Netherlands. **Tel** 011 31 20 4853641, 011 31 20 4853642, FAX 011 31 20 4853598. available on microfilm and microfiche from University Microfilms International (UMI). Documents available from Article Express International, The Genuine Article, Ask*IEEE. **Continues** Large Scale Systems in Information and Decision Technologies, 0167-420X.
Ind/Abst CompuMath Cit. Index [Full Cov.]; Comput. Inf. Syst. Abstr. J. [Full Cov.]; Curr. Cit.; Curr. Contents Eng. Comput. Technol.; Ei Page One; Eng. Index Annu.; Hum. Resour. Abstr.; INSPEC (1988-); Int. Abstr. Oper. Res. [Select. Cov.]; Manuf. Process Eng. Abstr.; Math. Rev./ Mech. Eng. Abstr.; Res. Alert [Full Cov.]; Sci. Cit. Index; SCISEARCH; Soc. Sci. Cit. Index [Select. Cov.].

UK
CODEN ISYJER
●**INFORMATION SYSTEMS JOURNAL.** Vol. 4, No. 1 (Jan. 1994)-. Academic Scholarly Publication. English. Four times a year. $222.00. Blackwell Scientific Publications Ltd, Marston Book Services, PO Box 88, Oxford OX2 ONE United Kingdom. **Tel** 011 44 1865 206206, FAX 011 44 1865 206219, telex 837 515 MARDIS G. **Continues** Journal of Information Systems (Oxford, England), 0959-2954.

LC T58.6 .J65 **ISSN** 1058-0530
DD 658/.054 658 US
CCC
CODEN ISYME2
Pr Rev.
INFORMATION SYSTEMS MANAGEMENT. See Business and Economics-Computer Applications.

LC QC53 .I58 **ISSN** 0889-8308
DD 530/.7 US
CCC
NLM W1; IN652F CODEN IICOEW
Pr Rev. TITLE CHANGE
INTELLIGENT INSTRUMENTS & COMPUTERS. See Computers-Automation.

ISSN 1080-4927
DD 004 US
●**INTERACTIVE AGE.** See Computers-Computer Networks.

LC QA76.76.E95 E9767 **ISSN** 0969-9317
DD 006.3/3/05 UK
CODEN IAESEW
TITLE CHANGE

INTERNATIONAL JOURNAL OF APPLIED EXPERT SYSTEMS. (1993)-(1995). Periodical. English. Taylor Graham Publishing, 500 Chesham House, 150 Regent Street, London W1R 5FA United Kingdom. ***Continues** Expert Systems for Information Management, 0953-5551.* ***Continued by** International Journal of Applied Expert Systems.*

LC Q295 .I58 **ISSN** 0308-1079
DD 003/.05 US
CCC
CODEN IJGSAX

Pr Rev.
INTERNATIONAL JOURNAL OF GENERAL SYSTEMS. [Int. j. gen. syst.]. (197?)-. Periodical. English. Four times a year (1 volume). $1017.00 (academic institutions), $1586.00 (corporate institutions). Gordon & Breach Science Publishers, Inc., PO Box 786, Cooper Station, New York NY 10276. **Tel** (212)206-8900, FAX (212)645-2459. **ED** George J. Klir. **Bk Rev. Ad Acc.** Documents available from Article Express International, The Genuine Article, BIOSIS Document Express, Ask*IEEE.
Ind/Abst Bioeng. Abstr.; Biol. Abstr. (-1984); CompuMath Cit. Index [Full Cov.]; Comput. Rev.; Curr. Cit.; Curr. Contents Eng. Comput. Technol.; Curr. Contents Phys. Chem. Earth Sci.; Curr. Contents Soc. Behav. Sci.; Ei Page One; Eng. Index Annu.; INSPEC (1974-); Math. Rev.; Res. Alert [Full Cov.]; Sci. Cit. Index; SCISEARCH; Soc. Sci. Cit. Index [Full Cov.]; Zentralbl. Math. Ihre Grenzgeb.

LC TK7874.7 .I54
DD 621.381/05 SI
CODEN IHSSEF

●INTERNATIONAL JOURNAL OF HIGH SPEED ELECTRONICS AND SYSTEMS. Vol. 4, No. 1 (Mar. 1993)-. Periodical. English. Four times a year. $319.00. World Scientific Publishing Company, PO Box 128, Farrer Road, Singapore 9128 Singapore. **Tel** 011 65 3825663, FAX 011 65 3825919, telex RS 28561 WSPC. ***Continues** International Journal of High Speed Electronics, 0129-1564.*
Ind/Abst Curr. Cit.

LC QA76.5 .J7 **ISSN** 0022-0000
DD 651.8/05 US
CCC
CODEN JCSSBM

Pr Rev.
JOURNAL OF COMPUTER AND SYSTEM SCIENCES. [J. comput. syst. sci.]. Vol. 1 (Apr. 1967)-. Academic Scholarly Publication. English. Six times a year. $748.00. Academic Press Inc., 6277 Sea Harbor Drive, Orlando FL 32887. **Tel** (800)543-9534, (407)345-4100, FAX (407)352-3445. **ED** E. K. Blum. Documents available from Article Express International, The Genuine Article, BIOSIS Document Express, Ask*IEEE.
Desc: Original research in computer science and in system science, with particular attention given to the pertinent mathematical theory and its application.
Ind/Abst ACM Guide Comput. Lit.; Bioeng. Abstr.; Biol. Abstr.; CompuMath Cit. Index [Full Cov.]; Comput. Rev.; Curr. Cit.; Curr. Contents Eng. Comput. Technol.; Ei Page One; Eng. Index Annu.; Inf. Sci. Abstr.; INSPEC (Oct. 1968-); Int. Abstr. Oper. Res. [Select. Cov.]; Int. Aerosp. Abstr.; Math. Rev.; Pollut. Abstr. Indexes; Res. Alert [Full Cov.]; Soc. Sci. Cit. Index [Select. Cov.]; Zentralbl. Math. Ihre Grenzgeb.

ISSN 0959-2954
UK
CCC
TITLE CHANGE

JOURNAL OF INFORMATION SYSTEMS. Vol. 1, No. 1 (Jan. 1991)-(199?). Academic Scholarly Publication. English. Blackwell Scientific Publications Ltd, Marston Book Services, PO Box 88, Oxford OX2 ONE United Kingdom. **Tel** 011 44 1865 206206, FAX 011 44 1865 206219, telex 837 515 MARDIS G. **ED** David Avison and Guy Fitzgerald. available on microfilm and microfiche from University Microfilms International (UMI). ***Continued by** Information Systems Journal.*
Desc: Seeks to provide a natural home for articles on research, practice, experience, current issues and debates concerning information systems.
Ind/Abst Bus. Source Plus; Bus. Source; EP Collect.; Homework Help.; MasterFile FullTEXT 1000; MasterFile FullTEXT 350; MasterFile FullTEXT 650; MasterFile FullTEXT; OCLC; Telebase.

ISSN 1070-0056
DD 621 US
CODEN JMSIEV

●JOURNAL OF MICROELECTRONIC SYSTEMS INTEGRATION. [J. microelectron. syst. integr.]. Vol. 1, No. 1 (Mar. 1993)-. Periodical. English. Four times a year. $175.00. Plenum Press, 233 Spring Street, New York NY 10013-1578. **Tel** (212)620-8000, (800)221-9369, FAX (212)463-0742, (212)807-1047, telex 23/421139.

LC QC20.7.N6 J68 **ISSN** 0938-8974
DD 003/.75 US
CCC
CODEN JNSCEK

JOURNAL OF NONLINEAR SCIENCE. [J. nonlinear sci.]. Vol. 1, No. 1 (1991)-. Periodical. English. Six times a year. $349.00. Springer-Verlag New York Inc., 175 Fifth Avenue, New York NY 10010. **Tel** (212)460-1500 ext 256, FAX (212)533-3503, telex 232 235 SPB UR. **(Subscription address:** Springer-Verlag New York Inc. / North America, PO Box 2485, Journal Fulfillment, Secaucus NJ 07096. **Tel** (201)348-4033, (800)777-4643, FAX (201)348-4505.) **ED** E A Kuznetsov and S R Wiggins. available on microfilm and microfiche from University Microfilms International (UMI). Documents available from The Genuine Article.
Desc: Publishes innovative, high-quality research papers that augment the fundamental ways we analyze, describe and predict aspects of our nonlinear world.
Ind/Abst CompuMath Cit. Index [Full Cov.]; Curr. Contents Phys. Chem. Earth Sci.; Math. Rev.; Res. Alert [Full Cov.]; Sci. Cit. Index.

LC HD30.213 .J68 **ISSN** 0963-8687
DD 658.4/038/05 UK
CCC
CODEN JSIYE3

JOURNAL OF STRATEGIC INFORMATION SYSTEMS, THE. **VFOAT** Strategic Information Systems. Vol. 1, No. 1 (Dec. 1991)-. Periodical. English. Four times a year. $274.00. Butterworth Heinemann Publishers, Linacre House Jordan Hill, Oxford OX2 8DP United Kingdom. **Tel** 011 44 1865 310366, FAX 011 44 1865 310898. **(Subscription address:** Elsevier Science Ltd. / Oxford Fulfillment Centre, PO Box 800, Kidlington OX5 1DX United Kingdom. **Tel** 011 44 865 843355.) available on microfilm and microfiche from University Microfilms International (UMI); available on an online database from Elsevier Electronic Subscriptions (EES). Documents available from Ask*IEEE. ***Continues** Information Age, 0261-4103.*
Ind/Abst Curr. Cit.; INSPEC (Dec. 1991-).

ISSN 0923-0459
NE

NLM W1; MA16G
MACHINE INTELLIGENCE AND PATTERN RECOGNITION. **See** Computers-Artificial Intelligence.

ISSN 0895-5697
DD 658 US

MARKETING COMPUTERS. [Mark. comput.]. Vol. 7, No. 9 Sept. (1987)-. Periodical. English. Twelve times a year. $36.00. Billboard Publications Inc., 1515 Broadway Billboard, New York NY 10036. **Tel** (212)764-7300, FAX (305)755-7048, telex WU TWX 710-581-6279. available on an online database (files 16,570,648/Full-Text) from DIALOG. ***Continues** Adweek's Computer & Electronics Marketing, 0884-5549.*
Desc: Focuses on micro, mini, mainframe, communications, peripherals and business computer systems.
Ind/Abst F&S Index Plus Text, Int. [Full Txt.] [Select. Cov.]; Mark. Advert. Ref. Serv.; PROMT [Full Txt.]; Trade Ind. ASAP [Full Txt.]; Trade Ind. Index [Full Txt.].

US

Pr Rev.
MIC / TECH-COMPUTERS. (19??)-. English. Twelve times a year. $1470.00. Management Information Corporation, 1111 Marlkress Road, Cherry Hill NJ 08003. **Tel** (609)424-1100. Index available. cum. index. ctrl circ. available on diskette.
Desc: Reference service on micros, workstations, minis, mainframes, and supercomputers.

LC HG1501
DD 332.1 US

MIC/TECH-RETAIL AND BANKING. English. Twelve times a year. $891.00 US; $976.00 other. Management Information Corporation, 1111 Marlkress Road, Cherry Hill NJ 08003. **Tel** (609)424-1100. Index available. cum. index.
Desc: Descriptions and pricing of POS terminals, systems, ATM's and bank processing systems.

ISSN 1081-9355
DD 004 US

●MICROSOFT SQL SERVER PROFESSIONAL. [Microsoft SQL Server prof.]. **VFOAT** SQL Server. Vol. 1, No. 1 (1995)-. Newsletter. English. Twelve times a year. $199.00. Pinnacle Publishing Inc., PO Box 888, Kent WA 98035. **Tel** (206)251-1900, (800)231-1293, FAX (206)251-5057.
Desc: This newsletter cuts through Microsoft SQL Server's complexity and gives you the no-nonsense information you need to run a leaner, tighter client/server system.

LC HD9696.M844 U5
DD 338.47621381 US
TITLE CHANGE

... MULTIMEDIA DIRECTORY, THE. **Added/Corp** Phillips Publishing, Inc. 1st Ed. (1991/1992)-(1993). English. Phillips Business Information Inc., 1201 Seven Locks Road, PO Box 61130, Potomac MD 20854. **Tel** (301)424-3338, (301)340-1520, (800)777-5005, FAX (301)424-4297, telex 358149. ***Continued by** The Multimedia & CD Directory.*

LC QA75
DD 004 US

●NETNEWS. (1994)-. Trade Publication. English. Four times a year. Free on request. TDA Group, PO Box 1360, Los Altos CA 94023. **Tel** (800)551-2832. **ED** Lorrie Nelson. **Bk Rev. Photos. Ad Acc, Adv Mgr:** Mary Lachapelle, **Tel** (415)948-3140 ext. 105. Half Page (B&W) $5,150.00. Full Page (Color) $8,000,00. **Acid Free. Circ:** 180,000 (ctrl). available via Internet.
Desc: Covers computer systems networking, including hardware, software and management.

UK

●NEW REVIEW OF APPLIED EXPERT SYSTEMS. (1995)-. English. One time a year. $125.00. Taylor Graham Publishing, 500 Chesham House, 150 Regent Street, London W1R 5FA United Kingdom. ***Continues** International Journal of Applied Expert Systems.*

LC QA75 **ISSN** 1040-6093
DD 004 US
TITLE CHANGE

NEWS 3X/400. [News 3X/400]. **VFOAT** News 3X 400; News Three X Four Hundred. (1988)-(199?). Trade Publication. English (Italian). Sixteen times a year. Duke Communications International, 221 East 29th Street, Loveland CO 80539. **Tel** (303)663-4700, (800)373-3853, FAX (303)667-2321, telex 6502618199. **(Subscription address:** Intelligent Technologies Publications Pty Ltd, Parramatta NSW 2150, PO Box 800, Parramatta NSW 2124 Australia. **Tel** 011 61 02 891 9136, FAX 011 61 02 891 9137.) **ED** Trish Faubion. **Ad Acc. Circ:** 31,000. available on microfiche. ***Continues** News/34-38, 8750-1678.* ***Continued by** News/400, 1084-7626.*
Desc: A technical computer magazine for users of the IBM System/34, System/36, System/38 and AS/400. It has information and solutions to questions pertaining to these four specific computers.

ISSN 0917-5342
JA

NIKKEI JOHO SUTORATEJI. **VFOAT** Nikkei Information Strategy. (1992)-. Periodical. Japanese. Twelve times a year. Nihon Keizai Shimbun Inc., 9-5 Otemachi 1 Chome, Chiyoda-ku Tokyo 100 Japan. **Tel** 011 81 3 32700251, 011 81 3 52108502 (Nikkei Business Publications Inc.), FAX 011 81 3 52552661, 011 81 3 52108119 (Nikkei Business Publications Inc.). **ED** Takaki Kamimura.
Desc: Information for proper use and construction of information systems.

LC QA75.5 .O33 **ISSN** 1071-8990
DD 338.4/762139/05 US

●OEM MAGAZINE. **See** Computers-Computer Engineering.

LC HF5548.125 .O45 **ISSN** 0898-2015
DD 650/.0285 US

ONLINE ACCESS. **See** Computers-Online Computing and Information.

ISSN 1068-5553
DD 004 US
CODEN OINSET

OPEN INFORMATION SYSTEMS. (OPEN INFORMATION SYSTEMS : GUIDE TO UNIX AND OTHER OPEN SYSTEMS.). [Open inf. syst.]. **Added/Corp** Patricia Seybold Group. Vol. 7, No. 6 (June 1992)-. Academic Scholarly Publication. English. Twelve times a year. $550.00. Patricia Seybolds Office Computing Group, 148 State Street, Suite 700, Boston MA 02109. **Tel** (617)742-5200, (800)826-2424, FAX (617)742-1028. Documents available from CASDDS. ***Continues** UNIX in the Office, 1058-4161.*
Ind/Abst Chem. Abstr.

ISSN 0741-2851
US
CCC
CODEN OSCOEW
TITLE CHANGE

OPEN SYSTEMS COMMUNICATION. [Open syst. commun.]. **Added/Corp** Omnicom, Inc. (Jan. 1984)-(1994). Periodical. English. Phillips Business Information Inc., 1201 Seven Locks Road, PO Box 61130, Potomac MD 20854. **Tel** (301)424-3338, (301)340-1520, (800)777-5005, FAX (301)424-4297, telex 358149. available on an online database (file 636/Full-Text) from DIALOG. ***Continues** OSI Communication, 0740-4433;* ***Absorbed** Open Systems Report.* ***Merged into** Phillip's Business Communication's Communications Standards News, 1077-4696.*

LC HD9696.C6 U55 **ISSN** 1061-0839
DD 005.4/3 US
CCC
CEASED

OPEN SYSTEMS TODAY. [Open syst. today]. (1992)-(19??). Trade Publication. English. CMP Publications Inc., One Jericho Plaza, Wing A, 2nd Floor, Jericho NY 11753. **Tel** (516)733-6700. **(Subscription address:** CMP Publications, Inc. / Illinois, PO Box 5920, Department 100, Carol Stream IL 60197-5920. **)** available

Computers —Computer Systems

on an online database (file 16/Full-Text) from DIALOG. **Continues** UNIX Today!, 1040-5038.
 Desc: Newspaper of UNIX and Interoperable Computing, covers technology issues including migrating UNIX in all its varieties, interoperability, portability, cross platform applications development, building/deploying graphical applications, and downsizing.
 Ind/Abst Comput. Ind. Update (19??-); PROMT [Full Txt.].

LC QA
DD 004   AU
OPTIONS. **Added/Corp** International Institute for Applied Systems Analysis. (19??)-. Periodical. English. Four times a year. International Institute for Applied Systems Analysis, Publications Department, A-2361 Laxenburg Austria. **Tel** 2236-71521 302, FAX 2236-71313, telex 079137 IIASAA.
 Ind/Abst For. Abstr.

ISSN 1063-7192
US
CCC
CODEN PAAPEC

●**PARALLEL ALGORITHMS AND APPLICATIONS.** (1993)-. Periodical. English. Four times a year. $288.00 (academic institutions), $448.00 (corporate institutions). Gordon & Breach Science Publishers, Inc., PO Box 786, Cooper Station, New York NY 10276. **Tel** (212)206-8900, FAX (212)645-2459.
 Desc: Publishes papers relating to parallel and multiprocessor computer systems covering the areas of parallel algorithms and parallel applications.

ISSN 0167-8191
NE
CCC
CODEN PACOEJ
Pr Rev.
PARALLEL COMPUTING. [Parallel comput.]. Vol. 1, No. 1 (Aug. 1984)-. Academic Scholarly Publication. English. Fourteen times a year. $1131.00. Elsevier Science Publishers BV, PO Box 211, 1000 AE Amsterdam Netherlands. **Tel** 011 31 20 4853641, 011 31 20 4853642, FAX 011 31 20 4853598. **ED** M Feilmeier, G R Joubert, U Schendel, B L Buzbee, D J Evans and H Kashiwagi. available on microfilm and microfiche from University Microfilms International (UMI); available on an online database from Elsevier Electronic Subscriptions (EES). Documents available from The Genuine Article, Ask*IEEE.
 Desc: Features original research work, tutorial and review articles as well as accounts of practical experience with, and techniques for, the use of parallel computers.
 Ind/Abst CompuMath Cit. Index [Full Cov.]; Comput. Abstr.; Comput. Inf. Syst. Abstr. J. [Full Cov.]; Comput. Rev. (1985-); Curr. Cit.; Curr. Contents Eng. Comput. Technol.; Elect. Comm. Abstr.; Environ. Eng. Abstr.; INSPEC (Aug. 1984-); Math. Rev. (1985-); Mech. Eng. Abstr.; Res. Alert [Full Cov.]; SCISEARCH; Soc. Sci. Cit. Index [Select. Cov.]; Solid State Supercond. Abstr.; Zentralbl. Math. Ihre Grenzgeb.

ISSN 1071-2259
US
DD 004
PC STREET PRICE INDEX, THE. [PC str. price index]. (19??)-. Periodical. English. Twelve times a year. $245.00. Metro Computing, PO Box 1430, Cherry Hill NJ 08034. **Tel** (609)784-8866, FAX (609)784-9814. **ED** John R. Murphy. Index available. **Ad Acc, Adv Mgr:** John R. Murphy. Full Page (B&W) $595.00. **Circ:** 500. available on diskette. **Continues in part** Computer Report & The PC Street Price Index, 1063-8369.
 Desc: Features technical information and actual retail prices for over 2,000 IBM, IBM-Compatible and Macintosh personal computers, computer peripherals and software.

US
PERSONAL AND DEPARTMENTAL COMPUTING CORPORATE PLANNER. (1990)-. Periodical. English. Twelve times a year. $595.00. Computer Economics Inc., 5841 Edison Place, Carlsbad CA 92008. **Tel** (800)326-8100, (619)438-8100, FAX (619)431-1126. **ED** Michael C. Erbschloe.
 Desc: Up-to-date guide to the acquisition, management and cost control of desktop and network systems.

ISSN 1077-4696
DD 384   UK
CCC

●**PHILLIPS BUSINESS INFORMATION'S COMMUNICATIONS STANDARDS NEWS.** See Communications-Computer Applications.

ISSN 0032-8154
RU
CODEN PRSUBT
PRIBORY I SISTEMY UPRAVLENIJA. (PRIBORY I SISTEMY UPRAVLENIIA). [Prib. sist. upr.]. Vol. 1, (1967)-. Academic Scholarly Publication. Russian. Twelve times a year. $218.01. **(Subscription address:** East View Publications Inc., 3020 Harbor Lane North, Suite 110, Minneapolis MN 55447. **Tel** (800)477-1005, (612)550-0961, FAX (612)559-2931.**)** Index available in last issue of volume--attached. Documents available from Ask*IEEE, CASDDS. **Continues** Pribcrostroenie, 0100-6614.

Ind/Abst Alum. Ind. Abstr.; Chem. Abstr.; Dairy Sci. Abstr.; Energy Res. Abstr. (Oct. 1982-); Eng. Mater. Abstr.; INSPEC (1968-); Math. Rev.; Met. Abstr.; Pollut. Abstr. Indexes.

US
PROCEEDINGS. Main/Corp Interactive Multimedia Association Compatibility Project. **Added/Corp** Interactive Multimedia Association. **VFOAT** IMA Compatibility Project Proceedings. Vol. 1, No. 1 (Sept. 1991)-. Proceedings. English. Six times a year. IMA Compatibility Project Headquarters, 9 Randall Court, Annapolis MD 21401.

LC QA76.9.I58 C35a   ISSN 0713-5424
DD 006.6   CN
CCC
PROCEEDINGS - GRAPHICS INTERFACE. See Computers-Computer Graphics and Design.

LC QA402 .S7a   ISSN 0094-2898
DD 003   US
CCC
CODEN PASTDB
PROCEEDINGS OF THE ANNUAL SOUTHEASTERN SYMPOSIUM ON SYSTEM THEORY. See Computers-Computer Engineering.

LC TA168 .H37a
DD 624   US
PROCEEDINGS OF THE ... HAWAII INTERNATIONAL CONFERENCE ON SYSTEM SCIENCES. Added/Corp University of Hawaii (System) Association for Computing Machinery. IEEE Computer Society. Pacific Research Institute for Information Systems and Management. **VFOAT** HICSS. 25th (1992)-. English. IEEE Computer Society, 10662 Los Vaqueros Circle, PO Box 3014, Los Alamitos CA 90720-1264. **Tel** (714)821-8380, (800)272-6657, FAX (714)821-4641. **Continues** Hawaii International Conference on System Sciences. Proceedings of the ... Annual Hawaii International Conference on System Sciences, 1060-3425.
 Ind/Abst Curr. Cit.; Eng. Index Annu.

LC Z   ISSN 1048-6542
DD 025   US
CODEN PACRES
PUBLIC-ACCESS COMPUTER SYSTEMS REVIEW (ELECTRONIC ED.), THE. (THE PUBLIC-ACCESS COMPUTER SYSTEMS REVIEW [COMPUTER FILE]). [Public-access computer syst. rev.]. **Added/Corp** University of Houston. Libraries. **VFOAT** Public Access Computer Systems Review; PACS Review. Vol. 1, No. 1, (1990)-. Periodical. English. Three times a year. University of Houston Library, 4800 Calhoun Road, Houston TX 77004. **Tel** (713)749-4710. available via Internet (gopher info.lib.uh.edu).
 Desc: Covers information storage and retrieval systems.

LC QA75   ISSN 1076-4429
DD 004   US
●**REAL-TIME ENGINEERING : COMPUTING WITH A DEADLINE.** See Computers-Computer Networks.

LC TK7885
DD 621.39   NE
Pr Rev.
●**REAL-TIME SAFETY CRITICAL SYSTEMS.** (1994)-. Monographic series. English. Irregular. Elsevier Science Publishers BV, PO Box 211, 1000 AE Amsterdam Netherlands. **Tel** 011 31 20 4853641, 011 31 20 4853642, FAX 011 31 20 4853598.

ISSN 1073-5402
DD 004   US
RELIABILITY RATINGS VAX/ALPHA ADVISOR. [Reliab. rat. VAX/Alpha advis.]. **VFOAT** Reliability Ratings VAX Alpha Advisor; VAX Alpha Advisor; VAX/Alpha Advisor. (199?)-. Periodical. English. Twelve times a year. $512.00. United Communications Group, 11300 Rockville Pike, Suite 1100, Rockville MD 20852. **Tel** (301)816-8950 ext. 313, FAX (301)816-8945. **Continues** Reliability Ratings. Field Research Report for the VAX and Alpha Environments.

LC QA76.53 .R45   ISSN 0098-0722
DD 001.6/44/04   US
REMOTE COMPUTING DIRECTORY. Directory. English. Quantum Science Corporation, 245 Park Avenue, New York NY 10017.

ISSN 0905-0167
DK
SCANDINAVIAN JOURNAL OF INFORMATION SYSTEMS. [Scand. j. inf. syst.]. **Added/Corp** Aalborg Universitetscenter. Institute of Electronic Systems. Department of Mathematics and Computer Science. Information Systems Group. (1989)-. Periodical. English. Two times a year. kr2200.00. Information System Group, Aalborg Univ. F Bajersvej 7 E, DK 9220 Aalborg Denmark. **Tel** 011 45 98158522.

Documents available from Ask*IEEE.
 Ind/Abst ACM Guide Comput. Lit.; Comput. Rev.; Curr. Cit.; INSPEC (Aug. 1990-).

LC QA76.75 .S35   ISSN 1060-1074
DD 005.4/469   US
CEASED
SCO MAGAZINE. [SCO mag.]. (Nov. 1991)-(Apr. 1993). Periodical. English. CMP Publications Inc., One Jericho Plaza, Wing A, 2nd Floor, Jericho NY 11753. **Tel** (516)733-6700.
 Desc: For builders and buyers of SCO Open Systems. Independent publication exclusively for the SCO community.

LC QA75   ISSN 1075-3265
DD 004   US
●**SCO WORLD.** **VAT** Santa Cruz Operations World. (1994)-. Trade Publication. English. Twelve times a year. $15.00. SCO World Magazine, PO Box 59662, Boulder CO 80323. **(Subscription address:** Neodata / Colorado, PO Box 2606, Boulder CO 80322. **) ED** Michael Burgard. **Ad Acc.** Full Page (B&W) $5,595.00. **Circ:** 42,000.

LC T57.6 .S513   ISSN 0374-4507
DD 600   JA
SHISUTEMU, SEIGYO, JOHO. **Added/Corp** Shisutemu Seigyo Joho Gakkai. **VFOAT** Systems, Control, and Information. (1989-). Periodical. Japanese. Twelve times a year. Yamabana Itchodencho, Sakyo-ku (606), Kyoto Japan. Documents available from Ask*IEEE.
 Continues Shisutemu to Seigyo.
 Ind/Abst Curr. Cit.; INSPEC (Jan. 1989-).

LC H61.3 .S57   ISSN 0736-6906
DD 300/.285   US
CODEN SGBUD4
SIGCHI BULLETIN. (SIGCHI BULLETIN : A QUARTERLY PUBLICATION OF THE SPECIAL INTEREST GROUP ON COMPUTER & HUMAN INTERACTION). [SIGCHI bull.]. **Added/Corp** SIGCHI (Group : U.S.). **VFOAT** S.I.G.C.H.I. Bulletin. **VAT** Special Interest Group on Computer & Human Interaction Bulletin. Vol. 14 (July 1982)-. Bulletin. English. Four times a year. $57.00. ACM / Association for Computing Machinery, 1515 Broadway, 17th Floor, New York NY 10036. **Tel** (212)869-7440, FAX (212)869-0481. **(Subscription address:** Association for Computing Machinery, PO Box 12114, Church Street Station, New York NY 10249. **Tel** (212)626-0500.**)** Documents available from Ask*IEEE. **Continues** SIGSOC Bulletin, 0163-5794.
 Ind/Abst Abstr. Hum. Comput. Interact. (July 1982-); Comput. Rev. (July 1982-); Curr. Cit.; Ergon. Abstr. (July 1982-); HILITES; INSPEC (July 1982-).

LC QA76.76.H94 S53
DD 005.75   US
SIGLINK NEWSLETTER: QUARTERLY NEWSLETTER OF THE SPECIAL INTEREST GROUP ON HYPERTEXT, ASSOCIATION FOR COMPUTING MACHINERY. **Added/Corp** Association for Computing Machinery. Special Interest Group on Hypertext. Vol. 1, No. 1 (Mar. 1992)-. Newsletter. English. Three times a year. $56.00. ACM / Association for Computing Machinery, 1515 Broadway, 17th Floor, New York NY 10036. **Tel** (212)869-7440, FAX (212)869-0481.
 Ind/Abst ACM Guide Comput. Lit.; Comput. Rev.

LC HF5547.5.A1 S53   ISSN 0894-0819
DD 651.8/05   US
CODEN SIGBEL
SIGOIS BULLETIN. [SIGOIS bull.]. **Added/Corp** SIGOIS (Group). **VAT** Special Interest Group on Office Information Systems Bulletin. Vol. 7, Nos. 2-3 (Summer/Fall 1986)-. Bulletin. English. Three times a year. $46.00. ACM / Association for Computing Machinery, 1515 Broadway, 17th Floor, New York NY 10036. **Tel** (212)869-7440, FAX (212)869-0481. **(Subscription address:** Association for Computing Machinery, PO Box 12114, Church Street Station, New York NY 10249. **Tel** (212)626-0500.**)** Documents available from Ask*IEEE. **Continues** SIGOA Bulletin, 0893-2867.
 Ind/Abst ACM Guide Comput. Lit.; Comput. Rev. (1986-); Curr. Cit.; Ergon. Abstr.; HILITES; INSPEC (1986-).

ISSN 0270-7284
US
SNA PERSPECTIVE. [SNA perspect.]. **Added/Corp** Communications Solutions. **VAT** Systems Network Architecture Perspective. Vol. 1 (June 1980)-. Periodical. English. Twelve times a year. $395.00 US; $445.00 other (all postage included). Saratoga Group, 12930 Saratoga Avenue, Suite A-1, Saratoga CA 95070. **Tel** (408)446-9115, FAX (408)446-9134. **ED** Donald Czubek. Index available (subject and title index included in Jan. issue). cum. index. **Circ:** 5,000 (ctrl).
 Desc: IBM System Network Architecture (SNA) products, operations, and analysis including third party vendors with perspective on what these network tools mean for users and manufacturers.

DD 004 ISSN 1060-3751 US CCC

STRATEGIC SYSTEMS. [Strateg. syst.]. **Added/Corp** Nims Associates. Applied Computer Research (Firm). Vol. 4, No. 6 (Jan. 1992)-. Periodical. English. Four times a year (supplements). Comes with Managing System Development. Applied Computer Research Inc., 11242 North 19th Avenue, Phoenix AZ 85029. **Tel** (602)995-5929, FAX (602)995-0905. **(Subscription address:** Applied Computer Research, PO Box 82266, Phoenix AZ 85071. **Tel** (602)995-5929.) ***Continues** SAA Age, 0899-5664.*

DD 004 ISSN 1058-5400 US

SUN OBSERVER (U.S. ED.), THE. (THE SUN OBSERVER.). [Sun obs.]. Vol. 1, No. 5 (Dec. 1988)-. Trade Publication. English. Twelve times a year. $45.00. Publications & Communications, 12416 Hymeadow Drive, Austin TX 78750. **Tel** (512)250-9023, (800)678-9724, FAX (512)331-3900, telex 384303. **Circ:** 30,000. ***Continues** SunTimes, 0899-448X.*
Desc: News tabloid that features the latest products and innovations for the Sun Microsystems market. Profiles people using Sun Systems, focuses on companies that have created a vast array of peripheral hardware and software for Sun Systems, and highlights Sun's direction by providing in-depth interviews with executives at the company.

LC QA76.76.O63 S944 ISSN 1061-2688
DD 005.4/3 US
CODEN SYADE7

SYS ADMIN (LAWRENCE, KAN.). (SYS ADMIN : THE JOURNAL FOR UNIX SYSTEM ADMINISTRATORS.). [Sys admin]. **VFOAT** Sysadmin. Vol. 1, No. 1 (1992)-. Trade Publication. English. Six times a year. $39.00. R & D Publications, 1601 West 23rd Street, Suite 200, Lawrence KS 66046. **Tel** (913)841-1631, FAX (913)841-2624. Documents available from CASDDS.
Desc: Offers technical information for UNIX system administrators who seek to improve the performance or extend the capabilities of their system. Coverage spans a variety of hardware platforms, and popular UNIX versions.
Ind/Abst Chem. Abstr.

SZ

SYSDATA. **See** Computers-Electronic Data Processing.

LC QA75.5 .S6 ISSN 1055-7768
DD 004.1/45 US
CCC
TITLE CHANGE

SYSTEMS 3X/400. [Systems 3X/400]. **VFOAT** Systems 3X 400; Systems Three X Four Hundred. Vol. 19, No. 3 (Mar. 1991)-(199?). Periodical. English. Hunter Publishing Company Inc., 25 Northwest Point Boulevard, Suite 800, Elk Grove Village IL 60007-1036. **Tel** (708)427-9512, FAX (708)427-2097. Documents available from Ask*IEEE. ***Continues** Systems 3X & AS World, 1044-1239.* ***Continued by** 3X/400 Systems Management, 1070-6097.*
Ind/Abst Comput. Lit. Index; Gen. BusinessFile (1992-); INSPEC.

LC QA75.5 .S982 ISSN 0882-1666
DD 004/.05 US
CCC
CODEN SCJAEP

SYSTEMS AND COMPUTERS IN JAPAN. [Syst. comput. Jpn.]. **Added/Corp** Denshi Tsushin Gakkai. Denshi Joho Tsushin Gakkai (Japan). Vol. 16, No. 1 (Jan./Feb. 1985)-. Periodical. English (translations available in Japanese). Fourteen times a year. $1638.00. Scripta Technica, A Subsidiary of John Wiley & Sons Inc., 7961 Eastern Avenue, Silver Spring MD 20910. **Tel** (301)588-0484, FAX (301)588-5278. **(Subscription address:** John Wiley & Sons, Inc. / Philadelphia, PO Box 7247, Philadelphia PA 19170. **Tel** (212)850-6645, (800)225-5945.) **ED** Shunichi Toida, Dept. of Computer Scienec, Old Dominion University, Norfolk, VA. available on microfilm and microfiche from University Microfilms International (UMI). Documents available from Article Express International, Ask*IEEE. ***Continues** Systems, Computers, Controls, 0096-8765.*
Desc: Communicate information from the research centers of Japan to broader audience of specialists. Such issues as computer architecture, large system design, advanced digital circuitry, data transmissions, interface devices, data processing programming techniques, automata, formal language and biomedical applications of computers are covered.
Ind/Abst Bioeng. Abstr.; Comput. Rev.; Curr. Cit.; Ei Page One; Eng. Index Annu.; INSPEC (1985-); Int. Aerosp. Abstr.; ISMEC Bull.; Math. Rev. (1985-1986); Pollut. Abstr. Indexes; Robotics Abstr.; Saf. Sci. Abstr. J.; Zentralbl. Math. Ihre Grenzgeb.

LC Q295 .S9565 ISSN 0894-9859
DD 003 US
CCC
CODEN SYPREM

SYSTEMS PRACTICE. [Syst. pract.]. Vol. 1, No. 1 (March 1988)-. Periodical. English. Six times a year. $265.00. Plenum Press, 233 Spring Street, New York NY 10013-1578. **Tel** (212)620-8000, (800)221-9369, FAX (212)463-0742, (212)807-1047, telex 23/421139. **ED** Robert L. Flood. available on microfilm and microfiche from University Microfilms International (UMI). Documents available from The Genuine Article.
Desc: This interdisciplinary journal is concerned with work that aims to find utility in applying the concepts of systems science.
Ind/Abst Abstr. Anthropol.; Curr. Cit.; Curr. Contents Soc. Behav. Sci.; Res. Alert [Full Cov.]; Soc. Sci. Cit. Index [Full Cov.].

DD 338 ISSN 1074-732X US CCC

•SYSTEMS REENGINEERING ECONOMICS. [Syst. reengineering econ.]. **Added/Corp** Computer Economics, Inc. Vol. 1, No. 1 (May 1994)-. Newsletter. English. Twelve times a year. $395.00. Computer Economics Inc., 5841 Edison Place, Carlsbad CA 92008. **Tel** (800)326-8100, (619)438-8100, FAX (619)431-1126. **ED** Teresa Elms. Index available. available with charts.
Desc: Gives various details on information systems and business process reengineering.

LC Q295 .S96 ISSN 0137-1223
DD 003/.05 PL
CODEN SYSCDP

SYSTEMS SCIENCE. [Syst. sci.]. Vol. 1 (1975)-. English (summaries and/or abstracts in Russian and Polish). Four times a year. $68.00. Wrocaw Technical University, Ul Janiszewskiego 11/17, 50-372 Wroclaw Poland. **Tel** 011 48 71 203328. **(Subscription address:** Ars Polona-Ruch, PO Box 1001, Krakowskie Przedmiescie 7, 00-068 Warsaw Poland. **Tel** 011 48 22 261201.) **ED** Zdziskaw Bubnicki. **Bk Rev. Ad Acc. Circ:** 600 (ctrl). Documents available from Article Express International, Ask*IEEE.
Desc: General systems and control theory, system identification, modelling and simulation, system optimization, large scale systems, computer networks, and applications of systems theory.
Ind/Abst Bioeng. Abstr.; Ei Page One; Eng. Index Annu.; GeoRef; INSPEC (1975-); Math. Rev.; Pollut. Abstr. Indexes; Zentralbl. Math. Ihre Grenzgeb.

DD 005 ISSN 1052-2581 US
CODEN TESUEJ
TITLE CHANGE

TECHNICAL SUPPORT. [Tech. support]. **Added/Corp** National Systems Programmers Association. Vol. 1, No. 1 ([Jan./Feb. 1987])-(1993). Periodical. English. National Systems Programmers Association, 4811 South 76th Street, Suite 210, Milwaukee WI 53220. **Tel** (414)423-2420, FAX (414)423-2433. ***Continued by** Information Technologies, 1069-8140.*

LC QA76.64 ISSN 1074-3227
DD 006.3 US
Pr Rev.

•THEORY AND PRACTICE OF OBJECT SYSTEMS. [Theory pract. object syst.]. **Added/Corp** John Wiley & Sons. **VFOAT** TAPOS. (1995)-. Academic Scholarly Publication. English. Four times a year. $170.00. John Wiley & Sons, Inc., 605 Third Avenue, New York NY 10158-0012. **Tel** (212)850-6000, (212)850-6645, FAX (212)850-6088, telex 12-7063. **(Subscription address:** John Wiley & Sons / UK, Baffins Lane, Chichester, West Sussex PO19 1UD United Kingdom. **Tel** 011 44 1243 779777, FAX 011 44 243 776128, telex 86290 WIBOOKG.)

ISSN 0940-9262 GW
UDC 519

TOOLBOX. [DOS toolbox]. **VFOAT** Disk Operating Systems Toolbox. (1991)-. Periodical. German. Four times a year. $115.15. DMV Daten Medien Verlagsgesellschaft, Gruber Strasse 46A, Postfach 1236, D-85586 Poing Germany. **Tel** 011 49 8121 769335.

DD 332 ISSN 0892-5542 US

TRADING SYSTEMS TECHNOLOGY. [Trading syst. technol.]. (1987)-. Periodical. English. Twenty-four times a year. $895.00. Waters Information Services, PO Box 2248, Binghamton NY 13902-2248. **Tel** (607)770-8535, FAX (607)798-1692. **ED** Corey Bock, Ann Goodman and Dennis P. Waters. Index available (free). available on an online database (files 16,636/Full-Text) from DIALOG.
Desc: Covers information systems used in investment community.
Ind/Abst PROMT [Full Txt.]; PTS Newsl. Database [Full Txt.].

ISSN 0925-4986 NE
UDC 681.324

TRANSPUTER AND OCCAM ENGINEERING SERIES. [Transput. OCCAM eng. ser.]. (1990)-. Monographic series. English. Irregular. Price varies per volume. IOS Press, Van Diemenstraat 94, 1013 CN Amsterdam Netherlands. **Tel** 011 31 20 6382189, FAX 011 31 20 6203419.
Desc: Titles in this series deal with progress reports on transputer-based parallel computer developments.

LC Z253.4.T47 T83 ISSN 0896-3207
DD 686 US

TUGBOAT (PROVIDENCE, R.I.). (TUGBOAT.). [TUGboat]. **Added/Corp** TEX Users Group. **VFOAT** Tug Boat. **VAT** TEX Users Group Boat. Vol. 1, No. 1 (Oct. 1980)-. Periodical. English. Three times a year. $60.00. TEX Users Group, 1850 Union Street 1637, San Francisco CA 94123. **Tel** (415)982-8449. Index available (bound in all issues).

DD 005.43 ISSN 0952-3359 UK

UNIGRAM. X. [Unigram. X]. **VFOAT** Unigram/X. (1984)-. Periodical. English. One time a week. $595.00. APT Data Services, 12 Sutton Row, 4th Floor, London W1V 5FH United Kingdom. **Tel** 011 44 171 2084200, FAX 011 44 171 4391105. **(Subscription address:** Unigram.X, 3 Maple Place, Glen Head NY 11545. **Tel** (516)759-7028, FAX (516)759-2025.) **ED** William Fellows. **Ad Acc, Adv Mgr:** S Thompson. **Circ:** 2,000. available on diskette; available via electronic mail.
Desc: Weekly Unix information newsletter.

LC QA76.8.U55 U55 ISSN 0279-1579
DD 004 US
Pr Rev.

UNISPHERE. (1981)-. Trade Publication. English. Twelve times a year. $40.00. Cardinal Business Media / Texas, 12225 Greenville Avenue, Suite 700, Dallas TX 75243. **Tel** (214)669-9000, FAX (214)669-9909. **ED** Martha Humphries. **Ad Acc. Circ:** 22,000 (ctrl). Documents available from Ask*IEEE.
Desc: Unisys computer users exchange of ideas and information, including new releases from Unisys, technical evaluations, user forum, and account spotlights.
Ind/Abst Curr. Cit.; INSPEC.

DD 004 ISSN 1059-9967 US
TITLE CHANGE

UNISYS WORLD OPEN SYSTEMS NEWS. [Unisys world open syst. news]. **VFOAT** Open Systems News; Unisys World/Open Systems News. (19??)-(19??). Trade Publication. English. Publications & Communications, 12416 Hymeadow Drive, Austin TX 78750. **Tel** (512)250-9023, (800)678-9724, FAX (512)331-3900, telex 384303. ***Formed by the union of** Network Computing News **and** Convergent World, 0892-2802.* ***Merged into** Unisys World, 0892-2845.*

UK

UNIX & OPEN SYSTEMS SERVICE. (19??)-. English. Twelve times a year. $1,036.00. Datapro International, McGraw Hill House, Shoppenhangers Road, Maidenhead Berkshire SL6 2QL United Kingdom. **Tel** 011 44 1628 773277, FAX 011 44 1628 773628.

LC QA ISSN 0956-2753
DD 005.43 UK
UDC 68
Pr Rev.

UNIX NEWS (LONDON). (UNIX NEWS.). [UNIX news Lond.]. (1989)-. Trade Publication. English. Twelve times a year. $188.23. APT Data Group PLC, 12 Sutton Row, 4th Floor, London W1V 5FH United Kingdom. **Tel** 011 44 171 2084200. **(Subscription address:** Computer Action, Garrard House 2 6 Homesdale Road, Bromley Kent BR3 9TW United Kingdom. **Tel** 011 44 181 4028181, FAX 011 44 181 4028383.) **ED** John Abbott and Andrea Lord. Index available. cum. index. **Bk Rev**, (Qty: 60). **Ad Acc, Adv Mgr:** Oren Wolfe, **Tel** 011 44 171 5287083. **Circ:** 10,500 (ctrl). available on an online database (file 16/Full-Text) from DIALOG. Documents available from FAXON Xpress.
Desc: For managers of computer departments using UNIX and open systems. Articles on news in the UNIX arena, hardware and software reviews, industry focus, and features.
Ind/Abst F&S Index Plus Text, Int. [Full Txt.] [Select. Cov.]; HILITES; PROMT [Full Txt.].

LC QA76.76.O63 U552189 ISSN 1059-4159
DD 004.1 US

UNIX SYSTEM PRICE PERFORMANCE GUIDE. [UNIX syst. price perform. guide]. **Added/Corp** AIM Technology (Organization). **VFOAT** UNIX Price Performance Guide. (Spring 1991)-. English. Four times a year (Seasonally). $39.95. Aim Technology, 4699 Old Ironsides Drive, Suite 150, Santa Clara CA 95054. **Tel** (408)748-8649, FAX (408)748-0161. **Circ:** 20,000.

US

VME, VXI, FUTUREBUS+ COMPATIBLE PRODUCTS DIRECTORY / VITA. **Added/Corp** VFEA International Trade Association. **VFOAT** VERSAmodule Europe, VMEbus Extensions for Instrumentation, Futurebus+ Compatible Products Directory; VME, VXI, Futurebus+ Products Directory. 1st Ed. (1990)-. Directory. English. VFEA International Trade Association, 10229 North Scottsdale Road, Suite B, Scottsdale AZ 85253.

LC TK7885.A1 V87 ISSN 1072-9933
DD 006 US

VXI JOURNAL. (VXI JOURNAL : THE MAGAZINE OF HIGH PERFORMANCE INSTRUMENTATION.). [VXI j.]. **VAT** Sixteen Journal. (19??)-. Periodical. English. Four times a year (Jan., Apr., July, Oct.). $24.00. Technical Communications / Michigan, 25875 Jefferson, St Clair Shores MI 48081. **Tel** (810)774-8180, FAX (810)774-8182. **ED** Wayne Kristoff (editor's address: 11051 Pinto Drive, Fountain Hills, AZ 85268 (phone: (602)837-3756). **Ad Acc, Adv Mgr:** Todd Bowman, **Tel** (810)774-8180. **Circ:** 7,000 (ctrl).

US

WORKGROUP COMPUTING SERIES. SYSTEMS. See Computers-Microcomputers, Personal Computers.

CYBERNETICS

LC Q300 .A27 ISSN 0324-721X
DD 001.53/05 HU
CODEN ACCYDX
Pr Rev.

ACTA CYBERNETICA (SZEGED). (ACTA CYBERNETICA.). [Acta cybern.]. (19??)-. Periodical. English. Two times a year. Attila Jozsef University, Exchange Librarian, Dugonics ter 13, PO Box 393, Szeged H 6701 Hungary. **(Subscription address:** Kultura, PO Box 143, H-1300 Budapest 3 Hungary. **Tel** 011 36 1 2500194.) **ED** Ferenc Gecseg, Janos Csirik. Index available. **Bk Rev. Circ:** 400. Documents available from Article Express International, Ask*IEEE.
Ind/Abst ACM Guide Comput. Lit.; Comput. Rev.; Ei Page One; Eng. Index Annu.; INSPEC (Vol. 8, No. 1 1987-); Math. Rev.; Zentralbl. Math. Ihre Grenzgeb.

ISSN 0320-720X
UN
CODEN ASAUAI

ADAPTIVNYE SISTEMY AVTOMATICESKOGO UPRAVLENIA. (ADAPTIVNYE SISTEMY AVTOMATICHESKOGO UPRAVLENIIA; TRUDY SEMINARA.). [Adapt. sist. avtom. upr.]. **Added/Corp** Instytut Kibernetyky (Akademiia Nauk Ukrainskoi RSR). **VFOAT** Trudy Seminara Adaptivnye Sistemy Avtomaticheskogo Upravleniia. No. 1 (1968)-. Academic Scholarly Publication. Russian. Izdatelstvo Naukova Dumka / Ukrainian Academy of Sciences, Yu. A. Khramov, Dir., Ul. Repina 3, 252 601 Kiev Ukraine. **Tel** 011 7 44 4303441, 011 7 44 2254182, telex 131376. **(Subscription address:** Scripta Technica, Subsidiary of: John Wiley & Sons, Inc, 7961 Eastern Avenue, Silver Springs MD 20910. **Tel** (301) 588-0484, FAX (301) 588-5278.) Documents available from CASDDS.
Ind/Abst Chem. Abstr. (-1981); Math. Rev.

LC TA167 .A37 ISSN 0882-6137
DD 620.8/05 US
CCC
CEASED

ADVANCES IN MAN-MACHINE SYSTEMS RESEARCH. [Adv. man-mach. syst. res.]. **VFOAT** Advances in Man Machine Systems Research. Vol. 1 (1984)-(19??). English. JAI Press Inc., 55 Old Post Road, Suite 2, PO Box 1678, Greenwich CT 06836-1678. **Tel** (203)661-7602, FAX (203)661-0792.

LC QA268.5 .S9a
US

ANNUAL SYMPOSIUM ON FOUNDATIONS OF COMPUTER SCIENCE. (PROCEEDINGS ... ANNUAL SYMPOSIUM ON FOUNDATIONS OF COMPUTER SCIENCE.). [Annu. Symp. Found. Comput. Sci.]. **Main/Conf** Symposium on Foundations of Computer Science. **Added/Corp** IEEE Computer Society. Technical Committee on Mathematical Foundations of Computing. ACM Special Interest Group for Automata and Computability Theory. University of California, Berkeley. Dept. of Electrical Engineering and Computer Sciences. **VFOAT** IEEE ... Annual Symposium on Foundations of Computer Science; Foundations of Computer Science; Annual Symposium on Foundations of Computer Science. 31st (Oct. 22-24, 1990)-. Proceedings. English. One time a year. $110.00. IEEE Computer Society, 10662 Los Vaqueros Circle, PO Box 3014, Los Alamitos CA 90720-1264. **Tel** (714)821-8380, (800)272-6657, FAX (714)821-4641. **Bk Rev.** ctrl circ. ***Continues** Annual Symposium on Foundations of Computer Science, 0272-5428.*
Desc: Topics include analysis of algorithms, computational complexity, formal languages, switching and automata theory of computation, theory of programming and formal semantics.
Ind/Abst Eng. Index Annu.; Index IEEE Publ.; INSPEC.

US

ASC CYBERNETICS FORUM. Vol. 7 (Spring 1975)-. English. Four times a year. American Society for Cybernetics, Dept Management Science, George Washington University, Washington DC 20052. **Tel** (202)676-7530. ***Continues** ASC Forum.*
Ind/Abst Comput. Rev.

LC Q350 .K92 ISSN 0340-1200
DD 574 GW
CCC
NLM W1 BI742 CODEN BICYAF
Pr Rev.

BIOLOGICAL CYBERNETICS. See Biology-Computer Applications.

ISSN 0374-6569
UN
CODEN BNKABJ

BIONIKA (KIEV). (BIONIKA.). [Bionika]. **Added/Corp** Akademiia Nauk Ukrainskoi RSR. Instytut Hidromekhaniky (Akademiia Nauk Ukrainskoi RSR). (1969)-. Monographic series. Russian. Irregular. $179.95. Izdatelstvo Naukova Dumka / Ukrainian Academy of Sciences, Yu. A. Khramov, Dir., Ul. Repina 3, 252 601 Kiev Ukraine. **Tel** 011 7 44 4303441, 011 7 44 2254182, telex 131376. **(Subscription address:** East View Publications Inc., 3020 Harbor Lane North, Suite 110, Minneapolis MN 55447. **Tel** (800)477-1005, (612)550-0961, FAX (612)559-2931.) Documents available from Ask*IEEE, CASDDS.
Desc: Information on bionics.
Ind/Abst Chem. Abstr. (?-1977); INSPEC (1972-); Int. Aerosp. Abstr.

LC QA276 .B85 ISSN 0286-522X
DD 519.5/05 JA

BULLETIN OF INFORMATICS AND CYBERNETICS. (BULLETIN OF INFORMATICS AND CYBERNETICS / RESEARCH ASSOCIATION OF STATISTICAL SCIENCES.). [Bull. inform. cybern.]. **Added/Corp** Tokei Kagaku Kenkyukai (Japan). Vol. 20, No. 1/2 (March 1982)-. Bulletin. English. Two times a year. $94.00. Tosio Kitagawa, Research Association of Statistical Sciences, Kyushu University 33, Fukuoka 812 Japan. **Tel** 011 81 92 6411101, FAX 011 81 92 6112668. **(Subscription address:** Maruzen Company Ltd., PO Box 5050, Import & Export Department, Tokyo 100 31 Japan. **Tel** 011 81 3 32789224.) **ED** T Kitagawa, H Akaike, S Arikawa, Ch Asano, H Enomoto, N Furukawa, C Hayashi, S Kano, S Moriguti, J Nagumo, M Okamoto, S Ohsuga, Y Shimazu, Y Sunahara, K Takeuchi, and S Yamamoto. **Circ:** 600. Documents available from Ask*IEEE. ***Continues** Bulletin of Mathematical Statistics, 0007-4993.*
Desc: Covers information science, computer science, mathematical statistics, mathematical programming, cybernetics, data analysis, computation theory, information theory, knowledge science, and control theory.
Ind/Abst Inf. Sci. Abstr.; INSPEC (March 1984-); Math. Rev.; Stat. Theory Method Abstr. (1983-1984, 1986-1987); Zentralbl. Math. Ihre Grenzgeb.

LC TJ212 .B87 ISSN 0296-8517
DD 629.8/05 FR
CODEN BEAUE3
TITLE CHANGE

BUREAU D'ETUDES AUTOMATISMES. See Computers-Automation.

US

COGNIZER REPORT. See Computers-Artificial Intelligence.

US

•**CONFERENCE PROCEEDINGS / INTERNATIONAL CONFERENCE ON SYSTEMS, MAN, AND CYBERNETICS.** **Added/Corp** Institute of Electrical and Electronics Engineers. (1993)-. Proceedings. English. IEEE / Institute of Electrical and Electronics Engineers Inc., 345 East 47th Street, New York NY 10017-2394. **Tel** (908)981-1393, FAX (908)981-9667. ***Continues** IEEE International Conference on Systems, Man, and Cybernetics. International Conference on Systems, Man, and Cybernetics : Proceedings.*

LC QA402.3 .C62 ISSN 0324-8569
DD 629.8/312/05 PL
CODEN CCYBAP

CONTROL AND CYBERNETICS. [Control cybern.]. **Added/Corp** Instytut Cybernetyki Stosowanej (Polska Akademia Nauk) Instytut Badan Systemowych (Polska Akademia Nauk). Vol. 1 (1972)-. Periodical. English (summaries and/or abstracts in Polish and Russian). Four times a year. $80.00. **(Subscription address:** Ars Polona-Ruch, PO Box 1001, Krakowskie Przedmiescie 7, 00-068 Warsaw Poland. **Tel** 011 48 22 261201.) Documents available from Ask*IEEE.
Ind/Abst INSPEC (1972-); Math. Rev.; Zentralbl. Math. Ihre Grenzgeb.

LC TS156.8 .C675 ISSN 1013-2287
CU
CODEN CCAZAB

CONTROL CIBERNETICA Y AUTOMATIZACION. [Control cibern. autom.]. Periodical. Spanish. Four times a year. $12.00. Ediciones Cubanas, Obispo 527 Altos ESQ Bernaza, CP 10100 Havana Cuba. **Circ:** 10,000 (ctrl). Documents available from Ask*IEEE.
Desc: Contains information on the application of cybernetics to industrial processes. Previously unpublished papers on these branches by outstanding Cuban researchers with broad experience and scientific precision in these fields.
Ind/Abst INSPEC (Jan.-March 1969-).

LC Q350 .C9 ISSN 0011-4227
DD 621.34 510.78 BE
NLM W1 CY348 CODEN CYBEA5
Pr Rev.

CYBERNETICA. (CYBERNETICA : REVUE DE L'ASSOCIATION INTERNATIONALE DE CYBERNETIQUE.). [Cybernetica]. **Added/Corp** International Association for Cybernetics. (1958)-. Periodical. English (French). Four times a year. $120.00. Association Internationale de Cybernetique, place Andre Rijckmans Palais, 5000 Namur Belgium. **Tel** 011 32 81 735209, FAX 011 32 81 742945, telex 59 101. **Bk Rev. Circ:** 1,000 (ctrl). Documents available from Article Express International, The Genuine Article, BIOSIS Document Express, Ask*IEEE.
Desc: Covers cybernetics, general systems, artificial intelligence, computers, automation, technology and information.
Ind/Abst ACM Guide Comput. Lit.; Bioeng. Abstr.; Biol. Abstr.; CompuMath Cit. Index [Full Cov.]; Comput. Rev.; Curr. Cit.; Curr. Contents Eng. Comput. Technol.; Curr. Contents Soc. Behav. Sci.; Ei Page One; EMBASE; Eng. Index Annu.; INSPEC (1970-); Math. Rev.; Life Sci. Collect.; Res. Alert [Full Cov.]; SCISEARCH; Soc. Sci. Cit. Index [Full Cov.]; Zentralbl. Math. Ihre Grenzgeb.

LC Q300 .J68 ISSN 0196-9722
DD 001.5/05 US
CCC
CODEN CYSYDH
Pr Rev.

CYBERNETICS AND SYSTEMS. [Cybern. syst.]. **Added/Corp** Osterreichische Studiengellschaft fuer Kybernetik. Vol. 11 (June/Aug. 1980)-. Periodical. English. Six times a year. $560.00. Taylor & Francis Ltd. / UK, Rankine Road, Basingstoke, Hampshire RG24 8PR United Kingdom. **Tel** 011 44 1256 840366, FAX 011 44 1256 479438, telex 858540. **(Subscription address:** Taylor & Francis Inc., 1900 Frost Road, Suite 101, Bristol PA 19007-1598. **Tel** (215)785-5800, (800)821-8312, FAX (215)785-5515.) **ED** Robert Trappl (editor's address: University of Vienna, Department of Medical Cybernetics and Artificial Intelligence, Freyung 6, 1010 Vienna Austria). **Bk Rev. Ad Acc. Circ:** 600. available on microfilm and microfiche from University Microfilms International (UMI). Documents available from Article Express International, The Genuine Article, BIOSIS Document Express, Ask*IEEE. ***Continues** Journal of Cybernetics, 0022-0280.*
Desc: Offers a worldwide alert system for all the latest developments in cybernetics, enhancing communication among researchers in the field. Refereed articles provide original research based on fundamental insight, mathematical explication, and empirical verification, ranging from artificial intelligence to economics. Journal includes the International Cybernetics Newsletter.
Ind/Abst Abstr. Hum. Comput. Interact.; ACM Guide Comput. Lit.; Bioeng. Abstr.; Biol. Abstr.; Comput. Abstr.; Comput. Rev.; Curr. Cit.; Curr. Contents Eng. Comput. Technol.; Ei Page One; Eng. Index Annu.; INSPEC (June/Aug. 1980-); Math. Rev.; Pollut. Abstr. Indexes; Res. Alert [Select. Cov.]; Sci. Cit. Index; SCISEARCH; Zentralbl. Math. Ihre Grenzgeb.

ISSN 1060-0396
DD 003 US
CCC
CODEN CYASEC

CYBERNETICS AND SYSTEMS ANALYSIS. [Cybern. syst. anal.]. **Added/Corp** Consultants Bureau. Vol. 27, No. 4 (July/Aug. 1991)-. Academic Scholarly Publication. English (Russian). Six times a year. $1145.00. Consultants Bureau, A Division of Plenum Publishing Corporation, 233 Spring Street, New York NY 10013. **Tel** (212)620-8000, (212)620-8466, FAX (212)463-0742, telex 23/421139. Documents available from Article Express International, The Genuine Article, Ask*IEEE, CASDDS. ***Continues** Cybernetics, 0011-4235.*
Ind/Abst Appl. Mech. Rev.; Bioeng. Abstr.; Chem. Abstr.; Coal Abstr.; CompuMath Cit. Index [Full Cov.]; Curr. Contents Eng. Comput. Technol.; Ei Page One; Eng. Index Annu.; Inf. Sci. Abstr.; INIS Atomindex [Micro.]; INSPEC; Int. Aerosp. Abstr.; Math. Rev.; Pollut. Abstr. Indexes; Res. Alert [Full Cov.]; Soc. Plann. Policy Dev. Abstr.; Sociol. Abstr.

ISSN 0424-267X
RM
CODEN ECECAI

ECONOMIC COMPUTATION AND ECONOMIC CYBERNETICS STUDIES AND RESEARCH. [Econ. comput. econ. cybern. stud. res.]. **Added/Corp** Academia de Studii Economice (Romania). (1966)-. Periodical. English (summaries and/or abstracts in French and Russian). Four times a year. $185.00. **(Subscription address:** Orion Press SRL, SPL Independentei 202-A, Bucharest 6 Romania. **Tel** 011 401 3122425.) Documents available from Article Express International, Ask*IEEE.
Ind/Abst Bioeng. Abstr.; Comput. Abstr.; Comput. Rev.;

Econ. Lit. Index; Ei Page One; Eng. Index Annu.; INSPEC (1968-); Int. Abstr. Oper. Res. [Select. Cov.]; J. Econ. Lit.; Math. Rev.; Stat. Theory Method Abstr. (1984, 1986-1987); Zentralbl. Math. Ihre Grenzgeb.

AU

ERGOTHERAPIE. German. Four times a year. Verband der Diplom Ergotherapie, Sperrgasse 8, A 1150 Vienna Austria. **Tel** 011 43 1 8929380.

LC H9 .G4 **ISSN** 0072-0798
DD 006 US

GENERAL SYSTEMS. (GENERAL SYSTEMS : YEARBOOK OF THE SOCIETY FOR THE ADVANCEMENT OF GENERAL SYSTEMS THEORY.). [Gen. syst.]. **Added/Corp** Society for the Advancement of General Systems Theory. Society for General Systems Research. International Society for the Systems Sciences. Vol. 1 (1956)-. English. One time a year. $35.00. International Society Systems Sciences, PO Box 6808, Louisville KY 40206. **Tel** (502)899-3332. **ED** William J. Reckmeyer.
Ind/Abst Int. Polit. Sci. Abstr.

LC QA76.38 .G53 **ISSN** 0207-0111
UN
CODEN GVMKD2

GIBRIDNYE VYCHISLITELNYE MASHINY I KOMPLEKSY. [Gibrid. vycisl. mas. kompleksy]. **Added/Corp** Instytut Elektrodynamiky (Akademiia nauk Ukrainskoi RSR). Sektor Elektroniki i Modelirovaniia. Institut Problem Modelirovaniia v Energetike (Akademiia Nauk Ukrainskoi RSR). (1979)-. Academic Scholarly Publication. Russian. Documents available from CASDDS.
Ind/Abst Chem. Abstr.; Int. Aerosp. Abstr.; Math. Rev.

ISSN 0017-4939
GW

GRUNDLAGENSTUDIEN AUS KYBERNETIK UND GEISTESWISSENSCHAFT. [Grundlagenstud. Kybern. Geisteswiss.]. (1960)-. Periodical. German (French and English). Four times a year. DM94.00 Germany; DM102.00 other. Institut fuer Kybernetik, Kleinenberger WEG 16B, D-33100 Paderborn Germany. **Tel** 011 49 5152 64200. **ED** Helmar Frank. Index available. **Circ:** 130.
Ind/Abst Energy Res. Abstr. (March 1982-); Soc. Plann. Policy Dev. Abstr.; Sociol. Abstr.

LC Q300 .I43 **ISSN** 0018-9472
DD 001.53/05 US
CCC
NLM W1 I224E **CODEN** ISYMAW
Pr Rev. **TITLE CHANGE**

IEEE TRANSACTIONS ON SYSTEMS, MAN, AND CYBERNETICS. [IEEE trans. syst. man cybern.]. **Added/Corp** Institute of Electrical and Electronics Engineers. Systems, Man, and Cybernetics Group. IEEE Systems, Man, and Cybernetics Society. **VFOAT** Transactions on Systems, Man, and Cybernetics. Vol. SMC-1, No. 1 (Jan. 1971)-(1995). Periodical. English. IEEE / Institute of Electrical and Electronics Engineers Inc., 345 East 47th Street, New York NY 10017-2394. **Tel** (908)981-1393, FAX (908)981-9667. **(Subscription address:** IEEE / Institute of Electrical and Electronics Engineers, 445 Hoes Lane, PO Box 1331, Piscataway NJ 08855-1331. **Tel** (800)701-IEEE, (908)981-0060, FAX (908)981-9667, telex 833233.**)** Documents available from Article Express International, The Genuine Article, Ask*IEEE, Documents on Demand. ***Formed by the union of*** *IEEE Transactions on Systems Science and Cybernetics, 0536-1567* ***and*** *IEEE Transactions on Man-Machine Systems.* ***Split into*** *IEEE Transactions on Systems, Man, and Cybernetics Part A* ***and*** *IEEE Transactions on Systems, Man, and Cybernetics Part B. Cybernetics.*
Desc: Covers the fields of man-machine systems, systems science, systems and engineering, and cybernetics.
Ind/Abst Abstr. Hum. Comput. Interact.; Bioeng. Abstr.; Biostatistica; Coal Abstr.; CompuMath Cit. Index [Full Cov.]; Comput. Abstr.; Comput. Database; Comput. Rev.; Curr. Cit.; Curr. Contents Eng. Comput. Technol.; Ei Page One; Energy Inf. Abstr.; Eng. Index Annu.; Environ. Abstr.; Ergon. Abstr.; Expand. Acad. Index (1992-); Health Plan. Adminis.; Highw. Res. Abstr.; HILITES; Index IEEE Publ. (Jan. 1971-); Inf. Sci. Abstr. [Full Cov.]; INIS Atomindex [Micro.]; INSPEC (Jan. 1972-); Int. Abstr. Oper. Res. [Select. Cov.]; Int. Aerosp. Abstr.; Math. Rev.; Oper. Res./Manage. Sci.; Psychol. Abstr. (1971-); PsycINFO; PsycLit; PsycScan: Appl. Psych.; Res. Alert [Full Cov.]; Robotics Abstr.; Sci. Cit. Index; SCISEARCH; Soc. Sci. Cit. Index [Select. Cov.]; Zentralbl. Math. Ihre Grenzgeb.

US

•IEEE TRANSACTIONS ON SYSTEMS, MAN, AND CYBERNETICS. PART A. (1995)-. English. Twelve times a year. $175.00 US, Canada, and Mexico; $190.00 other. IEEE / Institute of Electrical and Electronics Engineers Inc., 345 East 47th Street, New York NY 10017-2394. **Tel** (908)981-1393, FAX (908)981-9667. ***Separated from*** *IEEE Transactions on Systems, Man, and Cybernetics.*

LC Q300 **ISSN** 1083-4419
DD 003.5 US

•IEEE TRANSACTIONS ON SYSTEMS, MAN AND CYBERNETICS. PART B. CYBERNETICS. **Added/Corp** Institute of Electrical and Electronics Engineers. **VFOAT** Cybernetics. (1996)-. Periodical. English. Six times a year. $175.00. IEEE / Institute of Electrical and Electronics Engineers Inc., 345 East 47th Street, New York NY 10017-2394. **Tel** (908)981-1393, FAX (908)981-9667. ***Separated from*** *IEEE Transactions on Systems, Man and Cybernetics, 0018-9472.*

LC Q300 .A38a
RU

INFORMATSIONNYE MATERIALY; KIBERNETIKA. **Main/Corp** Akademiia Nauk SSSR. Nauchnyi Sovet po Kompleksnoi Proplema Kibernetika. (1967)-. Russian. Izdatelstvo Nauka / Akademiia Nauk, (Publishing House of the Russian Academy of Sciences), Leninskii Porspekt 14, 117901 Moscow Russia. **Tel** 011 95 9542153, FAX 011 95 9382144, telex 411964.

LC TA167 .I5 **ISSN** 0020-7373
DD 620.8/05 UK
CCC
NLM W1 IN769R **CODEN** IJMMBC
Pr Rev. **TITLE CHANGE**

INTERNATIONAL JOURNAL OF MAN-MACHINE STUDIES. [Int. j. man-mach. stud.]. **VFOAT** International Journal of Man Machine Studies. Vol. 1-39 (Jan. 1969)-(Dec. 1993). Academic Scholarly Publication. English. Harcourt Brace & Company Ltd., Foots Cray High Street, Sidcup Kent DA14 5HP United Kingdom. **Tel** 011 44 181 3003322, FAX 011 44 181 3090807. **ED** B R Gaines and D R Hill. cum. index. Documents available from Article Express International, The Genuine Article, BIOSIS Document Express, Ask*IEEE, CASDDS. ***Continued by*** *International Journal of Hhuman-Computer Studies, 1071-5819.*
Desc: Publishes original research over the whole spectrum of studies on both the theory and practice of humans and computers acting together in various ways and for various purposes, the journal covers the boundaries between: computing and artificial intelligence; psychology; linguistics; mathematics; engineering and social organisation.
Ind/Abst Abstr. Hum. Comput. Interact.; ACM Guide Comput. Lit.; Appl. Sci. Technol. Index; Bioeng. Abstr.; Biol. Abstr.; Chem. Abstr.; CompuMath Cit. Index [Full Cov.]; Comput. Abstr.; Comput. Rev.; Curr. Cit.; Curr. Contents Eng. Comput. Technol.; Curr. Contents Soc. Behav. Sci.; Educ. Technol. Abstr.; Ei Page One; EMBASE; Eng. Index Annu.; Ergon. Abstr.; HILITES; Inf. Sci. Abstr.; INSPEC (April 1970-); Int. Aerosp. Abstr.; Math. Rev.; Pollut. Abstr. Indexes; Psychol. Abstr. (1971-); PsycINFO; PsycLit; PsycScan: Appl. Psych.; Res. Alert [Full Cov.]; SCISEARCH; Soc. Sci. Cit. Index [Full Cov.]; Tech. Educ. Train. Abstr.; Zentralbl. Math. Ihre Grenzgeb.

LC TJ212 .I8 **ISSN** 0130-6774
RU

ITOGI NAUKI I TEKHNIKI. SERIIA TEKHNICHESKAIA KIBERNETIKA. **Added/Corp** Vsesoiuznyi Institut Nauchnoi i Tekhnicheskoi Informatsii (Soviet Union). **VFOAT** Seriia Tekhnicheskaia Kibernetika; Tekhnicheskaia Kibernetika Itogi Nauki i Tekhniki. (1979)-. Periodical. Russian. Irregular. VINITI - Vsesoyuznyi Institut Nauchno-Tekhnicheskoi Informatsii, All-Union Scientific and Technical Information Institute, Baltiiskaia ulitsa 14, 125219 Moscow Russia. **Tel** 011 7 95 2384600, FAX 011 7 95 9430060, telex 411160. **(Subscription address:** Mezhdunarodnaya Kniga, Dimitrova ulitsa 39, 113095 Moscow Russia. **)** ***Continues*** *Itogi Nauki i Tekhniki. Tekhnicheskaia Kibernetika.*

LC QA76 .E525 **ISSN** 0863-0593
DD 004/.05 GW
CODEN JICYE5
SUSPENDED

JOURNAL OF INFORMATION PROCESSING AND CYBERNETICS : EIK. [J. Inf. Process. Cybern.]. **Added/Corp** Mathematische Gesellschaft der DDR. Deutsche Akademie der Wissenschaften zu Berlin. Zentralinsitut fuer Kybernetik und Informationsprozesse. **VFOAT** EIK. Vol. 23, No. 1 (1987)-Suspended with Vol. 30 (1995). Periodical. English (French, German and Russian). Six times a year. $275.00. Akademie-Verlag GmbH, Postfach, D-13162 Berlin Germany. **Tel** 011 49 30 47889300, FAX 011 49 30 47889357. **(Subscription address:** VCH Publishers Inc., 303 Northwest 12th Avenue, Journals Department, Deerfield FL 33442. **Tel** (800)367-8249, (305)428-5566.**)** Documents available from Ask*IEEE. ***Continues*** *Elektronische Informationsverarbeitung und Kybernetik, 0013-5712.*
Ind/Abst ACM Guide Comput. Lit.; Comput. Rev.; Ei Page One; Inf. Sci. Abstr. [Full Cov.]; INSPEC (1987-); Math. Rev. (1987-); World Ceram. Abstr.; Zentralbl. Math. Ihre Grenzgeb.

LC T57.5 .A86
YU

KIBERNETIKA, AUTOMATIZACIJA POSLOVANJA : MESECNI CASOPIS ZAVODA ZA EKONOMSKI EKSPERTIZE. **Added/Corp** Zavod za Ekonomske Ekspertize. **VFOAT** Automatizacija Poslovanja. Vol. 21, No. 10 (Oct. 1980)-. Periodical. Serbo-Croatian (Roman). Twelve times a year. Zavod za Ekonomske Ekspertize, 11071 Novi Belgrad Palmira, Toljatija 3, Postanski Fah 104, Belgrad Yugoslavia. ***Continues*** *Automatizacija Poslovanja.*

LC TJ212 .K48
UN

KIBERNETIKA I SISTEMNYI ANALIZ : KSA. **Added/Corp** Institut Kibernetiki im. V.M. Glushkova. **VFOAT** KSA. (July- Aug. 1991)-. Periodical. Russian (summaries and/or abstracts in English and Ukrainian). Six times a year. $99.95. Izdatelstvo Naukova Dumka / Ukrainian Academy of Sciences, Yu. A. Khramov, Dir., Ul. Repina 3, 252 601 Kiev Ukraine. **Tel** 011 7 44 4303441, 011 7 44 2254182, telex 131376. **(Subscription address:** East View Publications Inc., 3020 Harbor Lane North, Suite 110, Minneapolis MN 55447. **Tel** (800)477-1005, (612)550-0961, FAX (612)559-2931.**)** ***Continues*** *Kibernetika (Kiev, Ukraine), 0023-1274.*
Ind/Abst Math. Rev.

LC Q300 .K53 **ISSN** 0739-8417
DD 001.53/05 US
CCC

KIBERNETIKA I VYCHISLITELNAIA TEKHNIKA. ENGLISH. (CYBERNETICS AND COMPUTING TECHNOLOGY.). [Cybern. comput. technol.]. **VFOAT** Kibernetika i Vychislitelnaya Tekhnika. No. 1 (1982)-. Periodical. English (Russian; translations available in Russian). Four times a year. $820.00. Allerton Press Inc., 150 Fifth Avenue, New York NY 10011. **Tel** (212)924-3950, FAX (212)463-9684, telex 427441 ALPRES. Documents available from Article Express International, Ask*IEEE.
Desc: Papers on the application of control systems, computer science, CAD and AI to areas such as human factors, engineering, medical diagnosis test procedures, and transportation systems.
Ind/Abst Ei Page One; Eng. Index Annu.; INSPEC (1984-); Math. Rev.

LC Q300 .K5289 **ISSN** 0454-9910
UN
CODEN KVYTAS

KIBERNETIKA I VYCISLITELNAJA TEHNIKA (KIEV). (KIBERNETIKA I VYCHISLITELNAIA TEKHNIKA.). [Kibern. vycisl. teh.]. **Added/Corp** Instytut Kibernetiki (Akademiia Nauk Ukrainskoi RSR) Institut Kibernetiki im. V.M. Glushkova. (1969)-. Academic Scholarly Publication. Russian. Four times a year. $750.00. Izdatelstvo Naukova Dumka / Ukrainian Academy of Sciences, Yu. A. Khramov, Dir., Ul. Repina 3, 252 601 Kiev Ukraine. **Tel** 011 7 44 4303441, 011 7 44 2254182, telex 131376. Documents available from Ask*IEEE, CASDDS.
Ind/Abst Chem. Abstr. (1969-1982); INSPEC (1972-); Int. Aerosp. Abstr.; Math. Rev.

LC Q300 .K98 **ISSN** 0368-492X
DD 001.53/05 UK
CCC
CODEN KBNTA3
Pr Rev.

KYBERNETES. [Kybernetes]. **VFOAT** Kybernetes. Vol. 1, No. 1 (Jan. 1972)-. Periodical. English. Nine times a year. $2329.00. MCB University Press, 60 62 Toller Lane, Bradford, West Yorkshire BD8 9BY United Kingdom. **Tel** 011 44 1274 785280, FAX 011 44 1274 785200, telex 51317-MCBUNI-G. **(Subscription address:** MCB University Press / US and Canada Subscriptions, PO Box 10812, Birmingham AL 35201-0812. **Tel** (205)995-1567, (800)633-4931, FAX (205)995-1588.**) ED** Brina Rudall. Index available. **Bk Rev. Circ:** 500 (ctrl). Documents available from Article Express International, The Genuine Article, BIOSIS Document Express, Ask*IEEE, Documents on Demand.
Desc: Seeks to provide an interdisciplinary and international platform for everyone involved in the field.
Ind/Abst Abstr. Hum. Comput. Interact.; Bioeng. Abstr.; Biol. Abstr.; CompuMath Cit. Index [Full Cov.]; Comput. Rev.; Curr. Cit.; Curr. Contents Eng. Comput. Technol.; Ei Page One; Energy Inf. Abstr.; Eng. Index Annu.; Environ. Abstr.; Inf. Sci. Abstr.; INSPEC (Jan. 1972-); Res. Alert [Full Cov.]; SCISEARCH; Soc. Sci. Cit. Index [Select. Cov.]; Zentralbl. Math. Ihre Grenzgeb. (Jan. 1972-).

LC Q300 .K92 **ISSN** 0023-5954
XR
CODEN KYBNAI
Pr Rev.

KYBERNETIKA. [Kybernetika]. **Added/Corp** Ceskoslovenska Akademie ved. Kyberneticka Komise. Ceskoslovenska Kyberneticka Spolecnost. Ceskoslovenska Akademie ved. Ustav Teorie Informace a Automatizace. Vol. 1 (1965)-. Periodical. Multiple languages (Czech; summaries and/or abstracts in English and German). Six times a year. $219.55. **(Subscription address:** Kubon & Sagner, ABT Zeitschriftenimport, D 80328 Munich Germany. **Tel** 011 49 89 54218130.**) ED**

Stanislav Kubik, Karel Sladky. Index available. **Bk Rev. Circ:** 1,150 (ctrl). Documents available from Article Express International, The Genuine Article, Ask*IEEE.
Desc: An international journal publishing original research and review papers devoted to system and control theory, computer science, information theory, operations research and related branches of mathematics.
Ind/Abst Bioeng. Abstr.; CompuMath Cit. Index [Full Cov.]; Curr. Contents Eng. Comput. Technol.; Ei Page One; Eng. Index Annu.; INSPEC (1968-); Int. Aerosp. Abstr. (1984-); Math. Rev.; Res. Alert [Full Cov.]; SCISEARCH; Soc. Plann. Policy Dev. Abstr.; Soc. Sci. Cit. Index [Select. Cov.]; Sociol. Abstr.; Stat. Theory Method Abstr. (1972, 1977-1981, 1986-1987); Zentralbl. Math. Ihre Grenzgeb.

LC TA1632 .M3355 **ISSN** 0932-8092
DD 006.4/2 US
CCC
CODEN MVAPEO

MACHINE VISION AND APPLICATIONS. [Mach. vis. appl.]. Vol. 1, No. 1 (1988)-. Periodical. English. Six times a year. $332.00. Springer-Verlag New York Inc., 175 Fifth Avenue, New York NY 10010. **Tel** (212)460-1500 ext 256, FAX (212)533-3503, telex 232 235 SPB UR. **(Subscription address:** Springer-Verlag New York Inc. / North America, PO Box 2485, Journal Fulfillment, Secaucus NJ 07096. **Tel** (201)348-4033, (800)777-4643, FAX (201)348-4505.) **ED** Ramesh Jain, Andre Oosterlinck, Jorge Sanz, Jack Sklansky, and Masahiko Yachida. Index available. cum. index. **Bk Rev. Ad Acc. Circ:** 400. available on microfilm and microfiche from University Microfilms International (UMI). Documents available from Article Express International, BIOSIS Document Express, Ask*IEEE.
Desc: Publishes high-quality technical contributions in machine vision research and development.
Ind/Abst Abstr. Hum. Comput. Interact.; ACM Guide Comput. Lit.; Biol. Abstr.; Comput. Rev.; Curr. Cit.; Ei Page One; Eng. Index Annu.; Inf. Sci. Abstr. (?-?); INSPEC (1988-).

LC Q300 .M33
RU

MATHEMATICHESKIE VOPROSY KIBERNETIKI. Added/Corp Akademiia Nauk SSSR. Otdelenie Matematiki. Vol. 1 (1988)-. Academic Scholarly Publication. Russian. One time a year. Izdatelstvo Nauka / Akademiia Nauk, (Publishing House of the Russian Academy of Sciences), Leninskii Porspekt 14, 117901 Moscow Russia. **Tel** 011 95 9542153, FAX 011 95 9382144, telex 411964. ***Continues in part*** *Kibernetika i Vychislitelnaia Tekhnika (Moscow, R.S.F.S.R.), 0555-277X.*
Ind/Abst Zentralbl. Math. Ihre Grenzgeb.

LC TA1650 .R382 **ISSN** 1054-6618
DD 006.4/2 US
Pr Rev.

PATTERN RECOGNITION AND IMAGE ANALYSIS. **See** Mathematics.

LC TJ212 .P68 **ISSN** 0204-9848
DD 621.317 BU
CODEN PTKRDU

PROBLEMI NA TEKHNICHESKATA KIBERNETIKA I ROBOTIKATA. Added/Corp Bulgarska Akademiia na Naukite. **VFOAT** Problems of Engineering Cybernetics and Robotics. (19??)-. Academic Scholarly Publication. Bulgarian (summaries and/or abstracts in English and Russian). Irregular. .89lv per issue. Bulgarska Akademiia na Naukite, 7 Noemvri 1, Sofia Bulgaria. **Circ:** 470. Documents available from Ask*IEEE. ***Continues*** *Problemi na Tekhnicheskata Kibernetika.*
Desc: Covers automatic control, cybernetics and robotics.
Ind/Abst INSPEC (1981-); Int. Aerosp. Abstr.; Math. Rev.; Zentralbl. Math. Ihre Grenzgeb.

LC Q300 .P73 **ISSN** 0555-2656
UN
NLM W1 PR577K **CODEN** PBNKAV

PROBLEMY BIONIKI. [Probl. bioniki]. **Added/Corp** Kharkovskii Institut Radicelektroniki. (1968)-. Academic Scholarly Publication. Russian. Documents available from CASDDS.
Ind/Abst Chem. Abstr. (1968-1983); Int. Aerosp. Abstr.; Zentralbl. Math. Ihre Grenzgeb.

LC Q295 .R49 **ISSN** 0980-1472
DD 003 FR
CCC
CODEN RISYE3

REVUE INTERNATIONALE DE SYSTEMIQUE. [Rev. int. syst.]. **Added/Corp** Association Francaise Pour la Cybernetique Economique et Technique. **VFOAT** Systemique. Vol. 1, No. 1 (1987)-. Periodical. French (English). Five times a year. $273.40. Dunod Gauthier Villars, 15 rue Gossin, 92543 Montrouge Cedex France. **Tel** 011 33 1 46565266, 011 33 1 40926527, FAX 011 33 1 40926597. **(Subscription address:** Centrale des Revues, 11 rue Gossin, 92543 Montrouge Cedex France. **Tel** 011 33 1 46565266.)
Ind/Abst Zentralbl. Math. Ihre Grenzgeb.

LC HD28 .S36
DD 658.4/005 II
Pr Rev.

SCIMA. Added/Corp Society of Management Science and Applied Cybernetics. Vol. 1 (1972)-. Periodical. English. Three times a year. $60.00. Society of Management Science & Applied Cybernetics, Room #306, CSIR Complex, NPL Campus, New Delhi 110012 India. **Tel** 011 91 11 5732193, FAX 011 91 11 343703, telex 3161635. **(Subscription address:** Prints India, 11 Darya Ganj, New Delhi 110002 India. **Tel** 011 91 11 3268645, FAX 011 91 11 3275542, telex 31-61087 PRIN-IN.) **ED** A Ghosal. Index available. **Bk Rev. Ad Acc. Circ:** 250.
Desc: Management science or cybernetics with emphasis on applications in economics, social science and industry; system studies for developing countries; new developments in cybernetics.
Ind/Abst Zentralbl. Math. Ihre Grenzgeb.

JA

SENSOR GIJUTSU: SENSOR TECHNOLOGY. Japanese. Thirteen times a year. $248.00. Joho Chosakai, (Information Research Center Co. Ltd.), 8-1 Kudan Kita 1 Chome, Chiyodaku Tokyo 102 Japan.

LC TJ212 .B74
PL

SERIA MONOGRAFIE - POLITECHNIKA WROCLAWSKA, INSTYTUT CYBERNETYKI TECHNICZNEJ. Main/Corp Politechnika Wroclawska. Instytut Cybernetyki Technicznej. **VFOAT** Monografie - Politechnika Wroclawska, Instytut Cybernetyki Technicznej. (1974)-. Monographic series. Polish (summaries and/or abstracts in English and Russian). Price varies per volume. **(Subscription address:** Ars Polona-Ruch, PO Box 1001, Krakowskie Przedmiescie 7, 00-068 Warsaw Poland. **Tel** 011 48 22 261201.)

ISSN 0275-5807
DD 001 US

STUDIES IN CYBERNETICS. [Stud. cybern.]. Vol. 1 (1981)-. Monographic series. English. Irregular. Price varies per volume. Gordon & Breach Science Publishers, Inc., PO Box 786, Cooper Station, New York NY 10276. **Tel** (212)206-8900, FAX (212)645-2459. Documents available from Ask*IEEE.
Ind/Abst INSPEC; Zentralbl. Math. Ihre Grenzgeb.

ISSN 0160-6409
US

SYSTEMS, MAN, AND CYBERNETICS REVIEW. Added/Corp IEEE Systems, Man, and Cybernetics Society. (19??)-. Periodical. English. Four times a year. Institution of Electrical Engineers / IEE, Michael Faraday House, Six Hills Way, Stevenage Hertfordshire SG1 2AY United Kingdom. **Tel** 011 44 1438 313311, FAX 011 44 1438 742840, telex 825578 IEESTV G. **(Subscription address:** IEE / Peter Peregrinus Ltd., PO Box 96, Stevenage Herts SG1 2SD United Kingdom. **Tel** 011 44 1438 313311, FAX 011 44 438 742792, telex 825578 IEESTV G.)

LC QA
DD 004 US

USSR AND EASTERN EUROPE SCIENTIFIC ABSTRACTS. CYBERNETICS, COMPUTERS, AND AUTOMATION TECHNOLOGY. VFOAT Cybernetics, Computers, and Automation Technology. No. 1- Mar. 1973-. English. National Technical Information Service - NTIS, Room 2027S, 5285 Port Royal Road, Springfield VA 22161. **Tel** (703)487-4630, (703)487-4660, (703)487-4650, FAX (703)321-8547, telex 89-9405. ***Formed by the union of*** *East European Scientific Abstracts. Cybernetics, Computers, and Automation Technology* ***and*** *USSR Scientific Abstracts. Cybernetics, Computers and Automation Technology.*

LC QA1 .V43a **ISSN** 0278-6419
DD 510/.5 US
CCC
CODEN MUCTD4

VESTNIK MOSKOVSKOGO UNIVERSITETA. SERIIA XV, VYCHISLITELNAIA MATEMATIKA I KIBERNETIKA. ENGLISH. (MOSCOW UNIVERSITY COMPUTATIONAL MATHEMATICS AND CYBERNETICS.). [Moscow. Univ. comput. math. cybern.]. **Added/Corp** Moskovskii Gosudarstvennyi Universitet Im. M.V. Lomonosova. **VFOAT** Computational Mathematics and Cybernetics. (1979)-. Periodical. English (Russian). Four times a year. $855.00. Allerton Press Inc., 150 Fifth Avenue, New York NY 10011. **Tel** (212)924-3950, FAX (212)463-9684, telex 427441 ALPRES. Documents available from Article Express International, Ask*IEEE.
Ind/Abst Bioeng. Abstr.; Ei Page One; Eng. Index Annu.; INSPEC (1978-); Zentralbl. Math. Ihre Grenzgeb.

LC Q300 .V66 **ISSN** 0321-2769
DD 003.5 UZ
CODEN VPKBAH

VOPROSY KIBERNETIKI (TASKENT). (VOPROSY KIBERNETIKI.). [Vopr. kibern.]. **Added/Corp** Institut Kibernetiki s V TS (Uzbekiston SSR Fanlar Akademiiasi). No. 38 (1970)-. Academic Scholarly Publication. Russian. Irregular. Documents available from CASDDS. ***Supersedes in part*** *Voprosy Kibernetiki i Vychislitelnoi Matematiki.*
Ind/Abst Chem. Abstr. (19??-1973); Math. Rev.; Zentralbl. Math. Ihre Grenzgeb.

DATA BASE MANAGEMENT

LC QA76.9.D3 A88a **ISSN** 0362-5915
DD 001.6/442 US
CCC
CODEN ATDSD3
Pr Rev.

ACM TRANSACTIONS ON DATABASE SYSTEMS. [ACM trans. database syst.]. **Main/Corp** Association for Computing Machinery. **Added/Corp** Association for Computing Machinery. Transactions on Database Systems. **VAT** Association for Computing Machinery Transactions on Database Systems. Vol. 1 (Mar. 1976)-. Periodical. English. Four times a year (Mar., June, Sept., Dec.). $124.00. ACM / Association for Computing Machinery, 1515 Broadway, 17th Floor, New York NY 10036. **Tel** (212)869-7440, FAX (212)869-0481. **(Subscription address:** Association for Computing Machinery, PO Box 12114, Church Street Station, New York NY 10249. **Tel** (212)626-0500.) **ED** Gio Wiederhold. available on microfilm and microfiche from University Microfilms International (UMI). Documents available from Article Express International, The Genuine Article, Ask*IEEE.
Desc: Reports on work done in database management and design. Covers the development and validation of abstractions and models to describe database applications, formalization and design methods which exploit the knowledge for effective processing of data.
Ind/Abst ACM Guide Comput. Lit.; Appl. Sci. Technol. Index; Bioeng. Abstr.; CompuMath Cit. Index [Full Cov.]; Comput. Abstr.; Comput. Database; Comput. Lit. Index; Comput. Rev.; Curr. Cit.; Curr. Contents Eng. Comput. Technol.; Ei Page One; Eng. Index Annu.; Ergon. Abstr.; Expand. Acad. Index (1992-); HILITES; Index Sci. Rev.; Inf. Sci. Abstr.; INSPEC (March 1976-); Math. Rev.; Pollut. Abstr. Indexes; Res. Alert [Full Cov.]; Sci. Cit. Index; SCISEARCH; Soc. Sci. Cit. Index [Select. Cov.]; Zentralbl. Math. Ihre Grenzgeb.

LC QA76.9.D3 A345 **ISSN** 0196-8718
DD 658/.054 US
CEASED

ADVANCES IN DATA BASE MANAGEMENT. [Adv. data base manage.]. Vol. 1 (1980)-Completed Series Vol. 2 (19??). Periodical. English. John Wiley & Sons Inc / New Jersey, 1 Wiley Drive, Somerset NJ 08875. **Tel** (800)225-5945, (908)469-4400.

US

ADVANCES IN DATA BASE THEORY. Vol. 1 (1981)-. Monographic series. English. Irregular. Prices varies per volume. Plenum Press, 233 Spring Street, New York NY 10013-1578. **Tel** (212)620-8000, (800)221-9369, FAX (212)463-0742, (212)807-1047, telex 23/421139. Documents available from Ask*IEEE.
Ind/Abst INSPEC.

ISSN 0735-9977
DD 658 US
CCC

AUERBACH DATA BASE MANAGEMENT. [Auerbach data base manage.]. **Added/Corp** Auerbach Publishers. **VFOAT** Auerbach Database Management; Data Base Management. (1976)-. Trade Publication. English. Six times a year. $490.65 US and Canada. Auerbach Publishers Inc., Park Square Building, 31 St. James Avenue, Boston MA 02116. **Tel** (800)950-1207. **ED** Susan M. McDermott. Index available. **Ad Acc, Adv Mgr:** Phil Brady, **Tel** (212)971-5120. **Circ:** 600.
Desc: Information service for the manager of the data resource function. Provides the information needed to effectively evaluate, plan, develop, implement, and maintain an efficient data base management system. Includes current techniques, terminology, technology, and issues directed at DP management, data administrators, and user departments.

ISSN 0811-4927
AT

AUSTRALIAN DATABASE DEVELOPMENT ASSOCIATION NEWSLETTER. (1983)-. Newsletter. English. (comes with Australian Database Development Association membership). Australian Database Development Association, PO Box 53, Hawthorn VIC 3122 Australia. **Tel** 61 3 8181760, or 8503361.
Ind/Abst Aust. Educ. Index (19??-); Aust. Libr. Inf. Sci. Abstr. (1983-).

ISSN 0765-1325
FR
UDC 002 : 681.3
Pr Rev.
BASES PARIS. See Computers-Online Computing and Information.

ISSN 0742-4574
DD 005
US
CCC
CEASED
BOXES AND ARROWS. [Boxes arrows]. (198?)-(Dec. 1994). Periodical. English. Boxes and Arrows Inc, 5111-6 Baymeadows Road, Suite 255, Jacksonville FL 32217. **Tel** (904)446-4908.

ISSN 0951-6050
UK
CAB INTERNATIONAL DATABASE NEWS. [CAB Int. database news]. **VFOAT** Database News; Commonwealth Agricultural Bureaux International Database News. (1987)-. Periodical. English. Four times a year. Free on request. CAB International Centre, Wallingford, Oxfordshire OX10 8DE United Kingdom. **Tel** 011 44 1491 832111, FAX 011 44 1491 833508, telex 847964 COMAGG G. ***Continues** CAB Abstracts Online Newsletter.*
Desc: Focusing on the development, coverage and applications of the CAB ABSTRACTS database.

LC QA76.9.D32 D36 ISSN 0903-1871
DK
DANSKE INFORMATIONSBASER. Vol. 1 (1987)-. Danish. One time a year.

LC QA76.9.D26 D38 ISSN 0169-023X
DD 005.74/05
NE
CCC
CODEN DKENEW
Pr Rev.
DATA & KNOWLEDGE ENGINEERING. [Data know. eng.]. **VFOAT** Data and Knowledge Engineering; DKE. Vol. 1, No. 1 (June 1985)-. Academic Scholarly Publication. English. Nine times a year (3 volumes). $768.00. Elsevier Science Publishers BV, PO Box 211, 1000 AE Amsterdam Netherlands. **Tel** 011 31 20 4853641, 011 31 20 4853642, FAX 011 31 20 4853598. **ED** Peter Chen and R van de Riet. available on microfilm and microfiche from University Microfilms International (UMI); available on an online database from Elsevier Electronic Subscriptions (EES). Documents available from Article Express International, Ask*IEEE.
Desc: Serves designers, managers and users of database systems, expert systems, and knowledge-based systems. Identifies, investigates, and analyzes the underlying principles in the design and effective use of these systems.
Ind/Abst ACM Guide Comput. Lit.; Comput. Abstr.; Comput. Lit. Index; Comput. Rev.; Curr. Cit.; Ei Page One; Eng. Index Annu.; Inf. Sci. Abstr. (?-?); INSPEC (June 1985-); Zentralbl. Math. Ihre Grenzgeb.

LC QA76.9.D3 D26 ISSN 0737-951X
DD 001.64/42
US
CCC
DATA BASE ALERT. [Data base alert]. **VFOAT** Database Alert. Vol. 1, No. 1 (May 1983)-. English. Twelve times a year. Comes with Database Directory Service. Knowledge Industry Publications Inc, 701 Westchester Avenue, White Plains NY 10604. **Tel** (914)328-9157, (800)800-5474, FAX (914)328-9093.

LC QA76.9.D3 D295 ISSN 0749-6680
DD 011/.3
US
NLM Z 699.22; C738
DATA BASE DIRECTORY. [Data base dir.]. **Added/Corp** American Society for Information Science. Knowledge Industry Publications, Inc. **VFOAT** Database Directory. (1984-85)-. Directory. English. Irregular. $195.00. Knowledge Industry Publications Inc, 701 Westchester Avenue, White Plains NY 10604. **Tel** (914)328-9157, (800)800-5474, FAX (914)328-9093. ***Continues** Computer-Readable Data Bases.*

ISSN 0735-3677
DD 005
US
CODEN DBNEDK
DATA BASE NEWSLETTER (PRINCETON, N.J.). (DATA BASE NEWSLETTER.). [Data base newsl.]. **Added/Corp** Database Research Group. Performance Development Corporation. **VFOAT** Database Newsletter. (1972)-. Newsletter. English. Six times a year. $129.00. Database Research Group Inc., 1 State Street, Suite 1150, Boston MA 02109. **Tel** (617)227-2583, FAX (617)227-2396. **ED** Ron Ross. **Bk Rev**. Documents available from Ask*IEEE.
Ind/Abst Comput. Lit. Index; INSPEC (July/Aug. 1991-).

LC QA76.9.D3 D34 ISSN 0740-6800
DD 005.74/05
US
CODEN RMNTDO
DATA BASE PRODUCT REPORTS / MIC. [Data base prod. rep.]. **Added/Corp** Management Information Corporation. **VFOAT** Database Product Reports. (198?)-. Periodical. English. Twelve times a year. $721.00. Management Information Corporation, 1111 Marlkress Road, Cherry Hill NJ 08003. **Tel** (609)424-1100.

LC QA76.9.D3 D3575 ISSN 0740-5200
DD 001.64/2
US
TITLE CHANGE
DATA BASED ADVISOR. [Data based advis.]. **VFOAT** Databased Advisor. (1983)-(1995). Periodical. English. Data Based Solutions Inc, 4010 Morena Boulevard, Suite 200, San Diego CA 92117. **Tel** (619)483-6400, (800)336-6060, FAX (619)483-9851. **(Subscription address:** Data Based Solutions Inc., PO Box 469013, Escondido CA 92046. **) ED** John L. Hawkins. Index available. **Bk Rev**. **Ad Acc**. **Circ:** 40,000. available on an online database (file 675/Full-Text) from DIALOG; and NEXIS. ***Continued by** Data Based Application Development Advisor, 1082-1252.*
Desc: For users of microcomputer database management systems to maximize system performance. Articles provide techniques for improving productivity and efficiency, programming tips, software reviews, tutorials, database application design, and programs in source code, ready to input and use.
Ind/Abst ACM Guide Comput. Lit.; Comput. ASAP [Full Txt.]; Comput. Bus. (19??-); Comput. Database [Full Txt.]; Comput. Rev. (1985-1989); Curr. Cit.; Data Process. Dig. (1985-1989); Microcomput. Abstr. (Dec. 1991-); Text. Technol. Dig. (1985-1989).

ISSN 1082-1252
DD 004
US
●**DATA BASED APPLICATION DEVELOPMENT ADVISOR.** [Data based appl. dev. advis.]. **VFOAT** Application Development; DBA; Data Based Advisor. Vol. 13, No. 6 (July 1995)-. Periodical. English. Twelve times a year. $39.00. Advisor Publications Group, 4010 Morena Boulevard, Suite 200, San Diego CA 92117. **Tel** (800)336-6060, (619)483-6400, FAX (619)483-9851. ***Continues** Data Based Advisor, 0740-5200.*
Desc: For users of microcomputer database management systems to maximize system performance. Articles provide techniques for improving productivity and efficiency, programming tips, software reviews, tutorials, database application design, and programs in source code, ready to input and use.

ISSN 1043-0571
DD 004
US
DATA MANAGEMENT JOURNAL, THE. [Data manage. j.]. Vol. 4 No. 1 (1989)-. Periodical. English. Four times a year. $275.00. Number Company, 12007 Bobwhite Drive, Suite 101, Catharpin VA 22018. **Tel** (800)431-3282, (703)497-1400. ***Continues** VSAM Performance Notebook, 0893-8709.*

LC QA76.9.D3 A19 ISSN 1067-3717
DD 005.74/05
US
●**DATA MANAGEMENT REVIEW.** [Data manage. rev.]. Vol. 3, No. 1 (Jan. 1993)-. Periodical. English. Twelve times a year. Free on request. Powell Publishing Inc., 19380 Emerald Drive, Waukesha WI 53186. **Tel** (414)792-9696, FAX (414)792-9777. **ED** Ronal Powell (editor's phone number: (414)792-9668). **Ad Acc. Circ:** 55,000 (ctrl). ***Continues** Data Base Management (Milwaukee, Wis.), 1066-5498.*

ISSN 0265-4490
UK
DATABASE AND NETWORK JOURNAL. [Datab. netw. j.]. Vol. 13, No. 2 (1983)-. Periodical. English. Four times a year (Mar., June, Sept., Dec.). $221.00. A. P. Publications Ltd, 377 Saint Johns Street, London EC1V 4LD United Kingdom. **Tel** 011 44 171 8375921, FAX 011 44 171 8371197, telex 8955107. **ED** E. Patterson. Index available. **Bk Rev. Circ:** 1,000. Documents available from Article Express International, Ask*IEEE. ***Continues** Database Journal, 0141-0849; **Absorbed** PC Business Software.*
Desc: Provides an update on new software and software technology in the fields of database and networks computing.
Ind/Abst BMT Abstr. (-199?); Comput. Lit. Index; Comput. Rev.; Curr. Cit.; Eng. Index Annu.; INSPEC (1983-); Pollut. Abstr. Indexes.

ISSN 0840-7797
DD 338.4/7005740971
CN
TITLE CHANGE
DATABASE CANADA. [Database Can.]. **Added/Corp** Database Canada Inc. Vol. 1, Issue 1, (1988)-. Periodical. English. Information Highways, 162 Joicey Boulevard, Toronto Ontario M5M 2V2 Canada. **Tel** (416)488-7372, FAX (416)488-7078. **ED** Jacqueline Halupka and Beverly Watters. Index available. **Bk Rev**. **Ad Acc. Circ:** 500. ***Continued by** Information Highways.*
Desc: A forum for exchange of news, views and products for Canadian information industry.

LC QA76.9.D3 D3588 ISSN 0895-4518
DD 005.74/05
US
CCC
CODEN DPDEEZ
Pr Rev.
DATABASE PROGRAMMING & DESIGN. [Database program. des.]. **VFOAT** Database Programming and Design. Vol. 1, No. 1 (1987)-. Periodical. English. Twelve times a year. $47.00. Miller Freeman Inc., 600 Harrison Street, San Francisco CA 94107. **Tel** (415)905-2337, (415)905-2200, FAX (415)905-2240, telex 278273. **(Subscription address:** Neodata / Colorado, PO Box 2606, Boulder CO 80322. **) ED** David Stoddor and Linda Comer. Index available. **Bk Rev**. **Ad Acc. Circ:** 25,000. available on microfilm and microfiche from University Microfilms International (UMI). Documents available from Ask*IEEE.
Desc: Contains practical and everyday solutions for selecting and using database management systems.
Ind/Abst Comput. Database (19??-); Comput. Lit. Index (19??-); Curr. Cit.; Data Process. Dig. (19??-); INSPEC (Jan. 1990-).

ISSN 1042-2595
DD 005
US
CODEN DARVEH
DATABASE REVIEW. [Database rev.]. **Added/Corp** Colin J. White Consulting (Firm). **VFOAT** Data Base Review. Vol. 1, No. 1 (Feb. 1989)-(1994). Periodical. English. Six times a year. $96.00 school, $120.00 regular, US and Canada; $108.00 school, $135.00 regular, other. Database Associates, PO Box 215, Morgan Hill CA 95038. **Tel** (408)779-0436, FAX (408)779-3274. Documents available from Ask*IEEE. ***Absorbed by** InfoDB, 0891-6004.*
Desc: Review of key developments in the database marketplace.
Ind/Abst INSPEC (April 1990-).

US
CEASED
DATABASE SEARCH AIDS. (19??)-(19??). Monographic series. English. Online Inc., 462 Danbury Road, Wilton CT 06897. **Tel** (203)761-1466, (800)248-8466, FAX (203)761-1444.

LC Z699.A1 D375 ISSN 0891-6713
DD 025.5/24
US
CCC
CODEN DASEE5
TITLE CHANGE
DATABASE SEARCHER. [Database search.]. Vol. 3, No. 1 (Jan. 1987)-(1993). Periodical. English. Mecklermedia Corporation, 11 Ferry Lane West, Westport CT 06880. **Tel** (203)226-6967, (800)632-5537, FAX (203)454-5840. **ED** Barbara Quint. **Bk Rev**. **Ad Acc. Circ:** 2,500. available on microfilm and microfiche from University Microfilms International (UMI); available on an online database (file 648/Full-Text) from DIALOG. Documents available from Ask*IEEE. ***Continues** Database End User, 0882-326X. **Continued by** Document Delivery World, 1067-0815.*
Desc: A journal for professional online searcher and librarians with online/database news.
Ind/Abst Cumul. Index Nurs. Allied Health Lit.; Inf. Sci. Abstr.; INSPEC (1987-); Int. Aerosp. Abstr.; Libr. Inf. Sci. Abstr.; Libr. Lit.; Microcomput. Abstr. (June 1987-); Trade Ind. ASAP [Full Txt.]; Trade Ind. Index [Full Txt.].

LC Z699.A1 D37 ISSN 0162-4105
DD 029.7/05
US
CCC
CODEN DTBSDQ
DATABASE (WESTON). (DATABASE.). [Database]. **VFOAT** Database Magazine. Vol. 1 (Sept. 1978)-. Periodical. English. Six times a year. $110.00. Online Inc., 462 Danbury Road, Wilton CT 06897. **Tel** (203)761-1466, (800)248-8466, FAX (203)761-1444. **(Subscription address:** Kinokuniya Company Ltd., 38-1 Sakuragaoka 5, chome Setagaya-ku, Tokyo 156 Japan. **Tel** FAX 011 03 3439 0136.**) ED** Paula Hane. Index Available in first issue of next volume--attached. **Bk Rev**, (Qty: (3/4 per issue)). **Ad Acc, Adv Mgr:** Corky Murray, **Tel** (203)761-1466. **Circ:** 3,550 (ctrl). available on an online database (in full text) from DIALOG; available on microfilm and microfiche from University Microfilms International (UMI). Documents available from The Genuine Article, Ask*IEEE, UMI Article Clearinghouse.
Desc: Presents lengthy, in-depth articles on database usage, with comparisons and evaluations. Each issue contains how-to-articles that provide comparative analysis and tips and techniques for online searching.
Ind/Abst Acad. Abstr.; Acad. Search; ACM Guide Comput. Lit.; AESIS Q.; Appl. Sci. Technol. Index; Bus. Period. Index; Bus. Source Plus; Bus. Source; CompuMath Cit. Index [Full Cov.]; Comput. Rev. Index (1988-); Comput. Rev.; Cumul. Index Nurs. Allied Health Lit.; Curr. Cit.; Curr. Index J. Educ.; Ei Page One; EP Collect.; Expand. Acad. Index (1992-); Homework Help.; Index Period. Artic. Relat. Law (19??-19??); INFO-SOUTH Abstr.; Inf. Instruc. Technol.; Inf. Sci. Abstr. [Full Cov.]; INSPEC (Sept. 1978-); Int. Aerosp. Abstr.; Int. Civil Eng. Abstr.; Leg. Inf. Manage. Index (19??-); Libr. Inf. Sci. Abstr.; Libr. Lit.; Mag. Artic. Summar. Elite; Mag. Artic. Summar. Select; Mag. Artic. Summar. CD-ROM; Mag. Search; MasterFile FullTEXT 1000; MasterFile FullTEXT 350; MasterFile FullTEXT 650; MasterFile FullTEXT (July 1993-) [Full Txt.]; Microcomput. Abstr. (Jan. 1985-); Newsp. Period. Abstr. (1992-); OCLC; Pub. Lib. FullTEXT; Res. Alert [Full Cov.]; Soc. Sci. Cit. Index [Select. Cov.]; Soft. Abstr. Eng.; Telebase; Trade Ind. ASAP [Full Txt.]; Trade Ind. Index [Full Txt.]; UMI ABI/Inform--Bus. Period. Ondisc [Full Txt.]; Vocat. Search; Wilson Bus. Abstr.; World Mag. Bank.

LC Z699.A1 D38 ISSN 0275-9152
DD 025.3/028/54
US
DATABASES ONLINE. (DATABASES ONLINE IN ....). [Databases online]. (1981)-. English. One time a year. $15.00 members, $18.00 nonmembers. American

Society of Information Science, 8720 George Avenue, Suite 501, Silver Spring MD 20910. **Tel** (301)495-0900, FAX (301)495-0810.

US

DATAPRO WORKGROUP COMPUTING SERIES / DISTRIBUTED DATABASES. (19??)-. English. Irregular. $443.00. Datapro Information Services Group, 600 Delran Parkway, Delran NJ 08075. **Tel** (609)764-0100, (800)328-2776, FAX (609)764-8953.

UK

DB2 UPDATE. (19??)-. Trade Publication. English. Twelve times a year. $320.00. Xephon, 27-35 London Road, Newbury Berkshire RG13 1JL United Kingdom. **Tel** 011 44 1635 33823, FAX 011 44 1635 38345. **(Subscription address:** Xephon, 1301 West Highway, Suite 201 450, Lewisville TX 75067. **) ED** Steve Piggit, 011 44 635 38323. Index available ((bound in Nov. issue)). cum. index. **Circ:** 1000. available on an online database from Bulletin Board.
Desc: Technical journal with annotated listings, and hints on getting the best out of IBM's software. Over half the articles in each issue are specifications of user-written utilities, exits, macros, and other extensions and modifications, usually with full source listings.

LC QA76.9.D3 D389 **ISSN** 1041-5173
DD 005.74/05 US
CCC
CODEN DBMSEO

DBMS (REDWOOD CITY, CALIF.). (DBMS.). [DBMS]. **VAT** Database management systems. Vol. 1, No. 1 (Sept. 1988)-. Periodical. English. Twelve times a year. $24.95. Miller Freeman Inc., 600 Harrison Street, San Francisco CA 94107. **Tel** (415)905-2337, (415)905-2200, FAX (415)905-2240, telex 278273. **(Subscription address:** Hutchins & Associates Inc, 1865 East Valley Parkway, Suite 206, Escondido CA 92072. **Tel** (619)745-0685.**) ED** James E. Fawcette. **Ad Acc. Circ:** 50,000. available on microfilm and microfiche from University Microfilms International (UMI); available on an online database (file 675/Full-Text) from DIALOG. Documents available from Ask*IEEE. ***Continues in part*** *Business Software.*
Desc: Practical and technical publication that describes how to use and develop databases. Targeting those who create software applications for database management systems. Provides technical information on the future core technology for PC's.
Ind/Abst Comput. ASAP (19??-) [Full Txt.]; Comput. Bus. (19??-); Comput. Database (19??-) [Full Txt.]; Curr. Cit.; INSPEC (Sep. 1988-); Microcomput. Abstr. (Sept. 1988-).

ISSN 1164-0642
FR
UDC 681.3:654(44)

DIRECTORY OF FRENCH VIDEOTEX DATABASES FOR COMPANIES. (1991)-. English. Irregular. 170.00F. Editions FLA Consultants, 27 rue de la Vistule, 75013 Paris France. **Tel** 011 33 1 45827575, FAX 33 1 45824604. **ED** Beatrice Riou.

LC QA76.9.D5 D4855 **ISSN** 0926-8782
DD 005.75/8 US
CCC
CODEN DAATES

Pr Rev.
●**DISTRIBUTED AND PARALLEL DATABASES.** (1993)-. Periodical. English. Four times a year. $303.00. Kluwer Academic Publishers / Massachusetts, PO Box 358, Accord Station, Hingham MA 02018. **Tel** (617)871-6600. **ED** Ahmed K. Elmagarmid. **Acid Free.** available on microfilm and microfiche from University Microfilms International (UMI). Documents available from Article Express International.
Desc: Publishes papers in all the traditional areas of database research, including transaction models, processing and management, query processing, data fragmentation, placement and allocation, replication protocols, and reliability and fault tolerance.
Ind/Abst Comput. Lit. Index; Comput. Rev.; Eng. Index Annu.; Inf. Sci. Abstr.; Math. Rev.

LC QA76.9.D32 F4 **ISSN** 0897-4810
DD 005.74/025/73 US
SUSPENDED

FEDERAL DATA BASE FINDER, THE. [Fed. data base finder]. **Added/Corp** Information USA, Inc. **VFOAT** Federal Database Finder; Federal Databases Finder. 1st Ed. (1985)-(19??). English. Irregular. $125.00. Information USA, PO Box E, Kensington MD 20895. **Tel** (301)924-0556, (800)955-7693, FAX (301)946-3004.

LC QA76.9.D3 F54 **ISSN** 0896-0313
DD 005 US

FILEMAKER REPORT, THE. See Computers-Software.

LC QA **ISSN** 0740-4980
DD 004.2 US
CCC

FT SYSTEMS. VFOAT F.T. Systems. (1982)-. Trade Publication. English. Twelve times a year. $695.00. ITOM International Company, Box 1450, Los Altos CA 94023. **Tel** (415)948-4516, FAX (415)948-9153. **ED** Omri Serlin. Index available (published in Jan., free upon request). **Bk Rev**.
Desc: Reports and analyzes business and technical developments in online transaction processing (OLTP), fault-tolerant systems, and parallel commercial systems.

ISSN 0197-0178
US
CCC

IDP REPORT. [IDP rep.]. **VFOAT** I.D.P. Report. **VAT** Information and Data Base Publishing Report. Vol. 1 (Feb. 10, 1980)-. Periodical. English. Forty-six times a year. $399.00. SIMBA Information Inc., 213 Danbury Road, PO Box 7430, Wilton CT 06897-7430. **Tel** (203)834-0033 ext. 173, FAX (203)884-1771. **(Subscription address:** Simba Information Inc., PO Box 7430, Wilton CT 06897. **Tel** (203)834-0033 ext. 160, FAX (203)834-1771.**)** available on an online database (files 16,636/Full-Text) from DIALOG.
Desc: Information on electronic information services for various markets, including business, consumer and professional markets.
Ind/Abst Comput. Lit. Index; PROMT [Full Txt.]; PTS Newsl. Database [Full Txt.]; Trade Ind. Index.

ISSN 0926-549X
NE
CCC
CODEN ITCCE5

IFIP TRANSACTIONS. C, COMMUNICATION SYSTEMS. See Computers-Computer Networks.

LC QA76.9.D3 I517 **ISSN** 0891-6004
DD 005.74 #2 19 US
CODEN IFDBEB

INFODB. [InfoDB]. **Added/Corp** Colin J. White Consulting (Firm). **VFOAT** Info DB. (1986)-. Periodical. English. Four times a year. $475.00. Database Associates, PO Box 215, Morgan Hill CA 95038. **Tel** (408)779-0436, FAX (408)779-3274. Documents available from Ask*IEEE. ***Absorbed*** *Database Review, 1042-2595.*
Desc: Technical journal for database users. Produces articles relevant to the design and development of DBMS applications.
Ind/Abst Curr. Cit.; INSPEC (Summer 1988-).

LC HD28 .I447 **ISSN** 0378-7206
DD 658/.05/405 NE
CCC
CODEN IMANDC

Pr Rev.
INFORMATION & MANAGEMENT. [Inf. manage.]. **VAT** Information and Management. Vol. 1 (Nov. 1977)-. Academic Scholarly Publication. English. Twelve times a year (2 vols.). $645.00. Elsevier Science Publishers BV, PO Box 211, 1000 AE Amsterdam Netherlands. **Tel** 011 31 20 4853641, 011 31 20 4853642, FAX 011 31 20 4853598. **ED** E H Sibley and Henry C Lucas Jr. **Bk Rev. Ad Acc.** available on microfilm and microfiche from University Microfilms International (UMI); available on an online database from Elsevier Electronic Subscriptions (EES). Documents available from Article Express International, The Genuine Article, UMI Article Clearinghouse, Ask*IEEE. ***Supersedes*** *Management Datamatics;* ***Absorbed*** *Systems, Objectives, Solutions, 0165-7747.*
Desc: Resulted from a reassessment of the impact and role of advanced information and data handling technology in today's complex economic and social environment.
Ind/Abst ABI/INFORM Glob. Ed.; ABI/INFORM Ondisc: Expr. Ed.; ABI/INFORM [Computer File] (March 1981-); ACM Guide Comput. Lit.; Anbar Account. Finan. Abstr. [Full Txt.]; Anbar Mark. Distr. Abstr. [Full Txt.]; Anbar Top Manage. Abstr. [Full Txt.]; Appl. Sci. Technol. Index; Arts Humanit. Citation Index [Select. Cov.]; Bioeng. Abstr.; CompuMath Cit. Index [Full Cov.]; Comput. Abstr.; Comput. Lit. Index; Comput. Rev.; Contents Pages Manage.; Curr. Cit.; Ei Page One; Eng. Index Annu.; Gen. BusinessFile (1992-); HILITES; Inf. Sci. Abstr. [Full Cov.]; INSPEC (Nov. 1977-); Int. Abstr. Oper. Res. [Select. Cov.]; Libr. Inf. Sci. Abstr.; Manage. Bibliogr. Rev.; Oper. Prod. Manage. Abstr. [Full Txt.]; Person. Train. Abstr. [Full Txt.]; Res. Alert [Full Cov.]; SCISEARCH; Soc. Sci. Cit. Index [Select. Cov.]; Women Manage. Rev. [Full Txt.].

LC QA76.9.D3 I53 **ISSN** 0306-4379
DD 029.7/05 UK
CCC
CODEN INSYD6

Pr Rev.
INFORMATION SYSTEMS (OXFORD). (INFORMATION SYSTEMS.). [Inf. syst.]. Vol. 1 (Jan. 1975)-. Periodical. English. Eight times a year. $840.00. Pergamon Press, An Imprint of Elsevier Science Ltd., The Boulevard, Langford Lane, Kidlington, Oxford OX5 1GB United Kingdom. **Tel** 011 44 1865 843000, 011 44 1865 843699, FAX 011 44 1865 843010. **(Subscription address:** Elsevier Science Ltd. / Oxford Fulfillment Centre, PO Box 800, Kidlington OX5 1DX United Kingdom. **Tel** 011 44 865 843355.**) ED** Hans-Jochen Schneider. available on microfilm and microfiche from University Microfilms International (UMI); available on an online database from Elsevier Electronic Subscriptions (EES). Documents available from Article Express International, The Genuine Article, BIOSIS Document Express, Ask*IEEE. ***Continues*** *Database Technology.*
Ind/Abst ACM Guide Comput. Lit.; Bioeng. Abstr.; Biol. Abstr.; CompuMath Cit. Index [Full Cov.]; Comput. Lit. Index; Comput. Rev.; Curr. Cit.; Curr. Contents Eng. Comput. Technol.; Ei Page One; EMBASE; Eng. Index Annu.; Inf. Sci. Abstr. [Full Cov.]; INSPEC (Nov. 1985-)(Jan. 1975-); Libr. Inf. Sci. Abstr.; Math. Rev.; Pollut. Abstr. Indexes; Res. Alert [Full Cov.]; SCISEARCH; World Publ. Monit.; Zentralbl. Math. Ihre Grenzgeb.

LC QA76.9.D3 I5457 **ISSN** 1061-3293
DD 005.75/65 US
CEASED

INSIDE DBASE. [Inside dBase]. **Added/Corp** Cobb Group. (Mar. 1992)-(Oct. 1995). Periodical. English. Cobb Group, 9420 Bunsen Parkway #300, Louisville KY 40220. **Tel** (502)491-1900, (800)223-8720, FAX (502)491-4200.

LC HF5548.2 .J6 **ISSN** 0898-171X
DD 658/.05/05 US
CCC

INSIDE DPMA. See Business and Economics-Computer Applications.

SI

●**INTERNATIONAL JOURNAL OF COOPERATIVE INFORMATION SYSTEMS. See** Computers-Artificial Intelligence.

LC QA76.9.D3 I565 **ISSN** 0218-2157
DD 006.3 SI
CODEN IICSEA
TITLE CHANGE

INTERNATIONAL JOURNAL OF INTELLIGENT & COOPERATIVE INFORMATION SYSTEMS : IJICIS. See Computers-Artificial Intelligence.

LC QA76.9.D3 J68 **ISSN** 1063-8016
DD 005 US
CODEN JDAMEQ

Pr Rev.
JOURNAL OF DATABASE MANAGEMENT. (JOURNAL OF DATABASE MANAGEMENT : AN OFFICIAL PUBLICATION OF THE INTERNATIONAL DATA MANAGEMENT INSTITUTE OF THE INFORMATION RESOURCES MANAGEMENT ASSOCIATION.). [J. database manage.]. **Added/Corp** International Data Management Institute. **VFOAT** Database Management. Vol. 4, No. 1 (Winter 1993)-. Periodical. English. Four times a year (Jan., Apr., July, Oct.). $110.00. Idea Group Publishing, 4811 Jonestown Road, Suite 230, Harrisburg PA 17109. **Tel** (800)345-4332, (717)541-9150, FAX (717)541-9159. **ED** Mehdi Khosrowpour. Index available (Bound in Mar. iss.). cum. index. **Bk Rev**, (Qty: 4). **Ad Acc. Circ:** 400 (ctrl). ***Continues*** *Journal of Database Administration, 1047-9430.*
Desc: Aimed at designers, developers, educators, researchers, consultants, and administrators of database management systems. The major emphasis of topics is on a variety of database issues ranging from strategic planning to performance tuning, optimization, and issues concerning the greater utilization and management of database technology.
Ind/Abst Inf. Sci. Abstr. [Full Cov.].

LC QA76.9.D3 J683 **ISSN** 0925-9902
DD 006.3 US
CCC
CODEN JIISEH

Pr Rev.
JOURNAL OF INTELLIGENT INFORMATION SYSTEMS. See Computers-Artificial Intelligence.

LC QA76.73.M15 M15 **ISSN** 1072-3226
DD 005.13/3 US
CODEN MCPUEF

Pr Rev.
●**M COMPUTING.** [M comput.]. **Added/Corp** M Technology Association. (1993)-. Periodical. English. Five times a year. comes with membership. M Technology Association, 1738 Elton Road, Suite 205, Silver Springs MD 20903. **Tel** (301)431-4070, FAX (301)431-0017. ***Continues*** *MUMPS Computing, 1060-7684.*
Desc: Dealing with all aspects of M technology.

LC HF5548.125 .O45 **ISSN** 0898-2015
DD 650/.0285 US

ONLINE ACCESS. See Computers-Online Computing and Information.

ISSN 1063-6382
DD 004 US
CCC

PROCEEDINGS / INTERNATIONAL CONFERENCE ON DATA ENGINEERING. [Proc. - Int. Conf. Data Eng.]. **Added/Corp** IEEE Computer Society. **VFOAT** Data Engineering. 3rd (1987)-. Proceedings. English. One time a year. $120.00. IEEE Computer Society, 10662 Los Vaqueros Circle, PO Box 3014, Los Alamitos CA 90720-1264. **Tel** (714)821-8380, (800)272-6657, FAX (714)821-4641. ***Continues*** *International Conference on Data Engineering. International Conference on Data Engineering : [Proceedings].*
Ind/Abst Curr. Cit.

Computers —Desktop Publishing

LC QA76.9.D3 A294a   **ISSN** 1055-6338
DD 005.74/05   US

PROCEEDINGS OF THE ... ACM SIGACT-SIGMOD-SIGART SYMPOSIUM ON PRINCIPLES OF DATABASE SYSTEMS. [Proc. ACM SIGACT-SIGMOD-SIGART Symp. Princ. Database syst.]. **Main/Conf** ACM SIGACT-SIGMOD-SIGART Symposium on Principles of Database Systems. **Added/Corp** ACM Special Interest Group for Automata and Computability Theory. Association for Computing Machinery. Special Interest Group on Management of Data. SIGART. 6th (Mar. 1987)-. Proceedings. English. $23.00 (members), $31.00 (nonmembers). ACM / Association for Computing Machinery, 1515 Broadway, 17th Floor, New York NY 10036. **Tel** (212)869-7440, FAX (212)869-0481. *Continues ACM SIGACT-SIGMOD Symposium on Principles of Database Systems. Proceedings of the ... ACM SIGACT-SIGMOD Symposium on Principles of Database Systems.*
Ind/Abst Curr. Cit.

   ISSN 1053-1238
DD 005   US

QUARTERLY BULLETIN OF THE COMPUTER SOCIETY OF THE IEEE TECHNICAL COMMITTEE ON DATA ENGINEERING. [Q. bull. Comput. Soc. IEEE Tech. Comm. Data Eng.]. **VFOAT** Data Engineering; Database Engineering; Database Engineering Bulletin; DE; Quarterly Bulletin of the Computer Society Technical Committee Database Engineering; Quarterly Bulletin of the Computer Society Technical Committee Data Engineering. Vol. 10, No. 3 (Sept. 1987)-. Bulletin. English. Four times a year. IEEE Computer Society, 10662 Los Vaqueros Circle, PO Box 3014, Los Alamitos CA 90720-1264. **Tel** (714)821-8380, (800)272-6657, FAX (714)821-4641. *Continues Quarterly Bulletin of the IEEE Computer Society Technical Committee on Database Engineering.*
Ind/Abst Comput. Rev.

   ISSN 1052-3820
DD 005   US

QUICK ANSWER, THE. (THE QUICK ANSWER : THE INDEPENDENT MONTHLY GUIDE TO Q&A EXPERTISE.). [Quick answ.]. Vol. 1, Issue 1 (June 1990)-. Periodical. English. Twelve times a year. $85.48. Marble Publications, PO Box 9034, Gaithersburg MD 20898. **Tel** (800)780-5474.

LC QA76.9.D3 R437   **ISSN** 1074-6404
DD 005.75/6/05   US
Pr Rev.

●**RELATIONAL DATABASE JOURNAL.** [Relat. database j.]. **Added/Corp** Cardinal Business Media, Inc. Vol. 2, No. 2 (May-July 1993)-. Periodical. English. Six times a year. 30.00Aus$. Cardinal Business Media / Texas, 12225 Greenville Avenue, Suite 700, Dallas TX 75243. **Tel** (214)669-9000, FAX (214)669-9909. **ED** Carol McGowan. **Ad Acc. Circ:** 35,000 (ctrl). *Continues DB2 Journal, 1069-2134.*

LC HD9696.O67 S45
DD 338.74621381   JA

SEKAI CD-ROM SORAN = CD-ROM DIRECTORY OF THE WORLD. **Added/Corp** Kyodo Keikaku Kabushiki Kaisha. Shuppan Jigyobu. Kyodo Keikaku Kabushiki Kaisha. Data Net Henshubu. **VFOAT** CD-ROM Directory of the World. (198?)-. Periodical. Japanese. One time a year. ¥20000. Kyodo Keikaku Co., Ltd., Publishing Department, Futaba Bldg. 3-4-18, Mita Minato-ku, Tokyo 108 Japan.

LC QA76.9.D3 F43   **ISSN** 0163-5808
   US
   CODEN SRECD8

SIGMOD RECORD. [SIGMOD rec.]. **Main/Corp** Association for Computing Machinery. Special Interest Group on Management of Data. **Added/Corp** Association for Computing Machinery. Special Interest Group on Management of Data. Association for Computing Machinery. Special Interest Group on Management of Data Records. **VFOAT** SIGMOD. **VAT** Special Interest Group on Management of Data Record. Vol. 8, No. 3 (Sept. 1976)-. Periodical. English. Four times a year. $27.00. ACM / Association for Computing Machinery, 1515 Broadway, 17th Floor, New York NY 10036. **Tel** (212)869-7440, FAX (212)869-0481. Documents available from Article Express International, Ask*IEEE. *Continues FDT Bulletin.*
Ind/Abst ACM Guide Comput. Lit.; Comput. Rev. (Jan. 1981-); Curr. Cit.; Eng. Index Annu.; INSPEC (Jan. 1981-).

LC QA76.9.D3 S6   **ISSN** 1066-7911
DD 005.75/65   US

●**SMART ACCESS.** [Smart Access]. **VFOAT** Smart Microsoft Access. Vol. 1, No. 1 (Feb. 1993)-. Newsletter. English. Twelve times a year. $139.00 US; $154.00 Canada; $159.00 other (includes companion disks). Pinnacle Publishing Inc., PO Box 888, Kent WA 98035. **Tel** (206)251-1900, (800)231-1293, FAX (206)251-5057. available on CD-ROM from the publisher.
Desc: Newsletter for developers and power users working with Microsoft Access. Packed with information for the Microsoft Access professional; time saving tips on database design, queries and dynasets, form controls, Access Wizards and more.

   UK

UNIFACTS. (19??)-. English. Four times a year. $77.01. Database Solutions, Kinetic Court Theobard Street, Hertfordshire Barehamwood WD6 4PJ United Kingdom. **Tel** 011 44 181 9532519, FAX 011 44 181 2076717. **ED** Hitesh Patel.

   ISSN 1066-8888
DD 004   US

VLDB JOURNAL, THE. (THE VLDB JOURNAL : VERY LARGE DATA BASES : A PUBLICATION OF THE VLDB ENDOWMENT.). [VLDB j.]. **Added/Corp** VLDB Endowment. **VFOAT** Very Large Data Bases. **VAT** Very Large Data Bases Journal. Vol. 1, No. 1 (July 1992)-. Periodical. English. Four times a year (Jan., Apr., July, Oct.). $192.00. Boxwood Press, 183 Ocean View Boulevard, Pacific Grove CA 93950. **Tel** (408)375-9110, FAX (408)375-0430. **ED** Hans J. Schek, (editor's address: Department of Informatik, Swiss Federal Institute of Technology, Ch 8092 Zurich Switzerland, phone: (41 1 262 3973). Index available. cum. index. **Circ:** 650.

   ISSN 0206-4715
   RU

VOPROSY SISTEMOTEKHNIKI. **Added/Corp** Russian S.F.S.R. Ministerstvo Vysshego i Srednego Spetsialnogo Obrazovaniia. Vol. 5 (1980)-. Monographic series. Russian. Price varies per volume. St. Petersburg State University / Izdatelstvo Leningradskogo Universiteta, Universitetskaia Nab 7/9, 199034 St. Petersburg Russia. **Tel** 011 7 812 2189788, FAX 011 7 812 2185152, telex 121481. *Continues Avtomatizirovannye Sistemy Upravleniia.*

   ISSN 0960-5061
DD 658.4038   UK

WHICH EUROPEAN DATABASE?. [Which Eur. database?]. (1990)-. English. One time a year. $324.00. Headland Business Information, 1 Henry Smiths Terrace, Headland Cleveland, TS24 0PD United Kingdom. **Tel** 011 44 429 231902, FAX 011 44 429 861403.

DESKTOP PUBLISHING

LC Z286.D47 .A43   **ISSN** 1081-4477
DD 070   US

●**ADOBE MAGAZINE.** [Adobe mag.]. **Added/Corp** Adobe Systems. **VFOAT** Adobe. Vol. 6, No. 3 (Jan./Feb. 1995)-. Periodical. English. Seven times a year. Adobe Systems Inc, 411 1st Avenue South, Suite 200, Seattle WA 98104. **Tel** (206)622-5500. *Continues Aldus Magazine, 1046-0616.*

   ISSN 1043-6065
DD 070   US
   TITLE CHANGE

BOVE & RHODES INSIDE REPORT ON DESKTOP PUBLISHING AND MULTIMEDIA. [Bove Rhodes inside rep. deskt. publ. multimed.]. **VFOAT** Bove and Rhodes Inside Report on Desktop Publishing and Multimedia; Bove and Rhodes Inside Report; Bove & Rhodes Inside Report. (Nov. 1988)-(19??). Trade Publication. English. HyperMedia Communications, 901 Mariner's Island Boulevard, Suite 365, San Mateo CA 94404. **Tel** (415)573-5170. Index available. **Circ:** 1,000. *Continues Desktop Publishing, Bove and Rhodes' Inside Report. Continued by Inside Report on New Media.*
Desc: Covers desktop publishing and media.

LC Z286.D47 P47   **ISSN** 1060-2208
DD 070   US
   CCC
   TITLE CHANGE

BUSINESS PUBLISHING (CAROL STREAM, ILL.). See Publishing.

   ISSN 0896-3541
DD 070   US

CASH ON YOUR DESKTOP PUBLISHING REPORT. [Cash your deskt. publ. rep.]. **VFOAT** Cash on Your Desktop; Publishing Report. (1988)-. Periodical. English. Twenty-four times a year. $49.00. Arcsoft Publishers, PO Box 132, Woodsboro MD 21798. **Tel** (301)845-8856.

   ISSN 1058-3580
   US

COLOR DESKTOP PUBLISHING PRODUCTS MONTHLY. (1991)-. Periodical. English. Twelve times a year. $195.00. The Color Resource, 708 Montgomery Street, San Francisco CA 94111. **Tel** (415)398-5337, (800)827-3311.

LC Z48 .C65   **ISSN** 1055-9701
DD 686.2/3042   US
   CCC
Pr Rev.

COLOR PUBLISHING. See Publishing.

   IT

COMPUTER GRAFICA E DESKTOP PUBLISHING. Italian. Gruppo Editoriale Jackson Spa, Via Gorki 69, 20092 Cinisello Balsamo Italy. **Tel** 011 39 2 66034401.

LC Z286.D47 D445   **ISSN** 1050-1800
DD 686.2/2544   US
   CEASED

DESKTOP COMMUNICATIONS. [Deskt. commun.]. **VFOAT** Desk Top Communications; Desk Top; Desktop. (1990)-(Feb. 1993). Periodical. English. International Desktop Communications Ltd, 530 5th Avenue, 84th Floor, New York NY 10036-5101. **Tel** (212)867-9650, FAX (212)867-9657. **Ad Acc. Circ:** 80,000 (ctrl). *Continues ITC Desktop, 1042-3923.*
Ind/Abst Abstr. Bull. Inst. Pap. Sci. Tech.; ACM Guide Comput. Lit.; Comput. Database; Comput. Rev.

   ISSN 1062-5437
   US

DESKTOP IMPRESSIONS. (1992)-. Periodical. English. Twelve times a year. Free with membership. Windows Publishing Group, PO Box 3488, Chatsworth CA 91313-3488.

   US
   SUSPENDED

DESKTOP PUBLISHER. (19??)-Suspended (1994). English. Six times a year. $49.95 North America; $89.95 other. Yellowstone Information Services, 7 View Road, Elkview VW 25071. **Tel** (304)965-5548. **ED** Roger C. Thibault, Mark G. Thibault. Index available. **Bk Rev.** **Ad Acc. Circ:** 2,000 (ctrl). available on diskette.
Desc: The publication of applied desktop publishing. Coverage includes software, hardware, and application articles.

LC HF5548.125 .D47   **ISSN** 0890-7226
DD 004/.029   US

DESKTOP PUBLISHING AND OFFICE AUTOMATION BUYER'S GUIDE AND HANDBOOK. Periodical. English. Two times a year. $32.00 (subscription as part of Computer Buyer's Guide and Handbook). Computer's Buyer's Guide and Handbook, PO Box 318, Mt Morris IL 61054-9942.

   SA

●**DIGITAL IMAGING AND PUBLISHING.** (1995)-. English. Nine times a year (7 issues yearly and 2 special issues). $62.63. Graphix, PO Box 751119, Grandview 2047 South Africa. **Tel** 011 27 11 6224800. *Continues DTP Today.*

   ISSN 1016-1287
   SA
   TITLE CHANGE

DTP TODAY. [DTP today]. **VFOAT** Desktop Publishing Today. (1988)-(July 1995). Periodical. English. Graphix, PO Box 751119, Grandview 2047 South Africa. **Tel** 011 27 11 6224800. *Continued by Digital Imaging Publishing.*

LC Z253.53 .E44   **ISSN** 0838-9535
DD 686.2/2544536   CN

ELECTRONIC COMPOSITION & IMAGING. [Electron. compos. imaging]. **VFOAT** Electronic Composition and Imaging; Graphic Perspective; EC&I. (May/June 1987)-. Periodical. English. Six times a year. 24.01Can$. Youngblood Communications, 2240 Midland Avenue, Suite 201, Scarborough Ontario M1P 4R8 Canada. **Tel** (416)299-6007, FAX (416)299-6674. *Absorbed Graphic Perspective, 0835-0914.*
Ind/Abst Can. Period. Index (1991-).

   US

ELECTRONIC PUBLISHING. (19??)-. Periodical. Eighteen times a year. $30.00 North America; $165.00 other. PennWell Publishing Company, 1421 South Sheridan, PO Box 1260, Tulsa OK 74101. **Tel** (918)835-3161, (800)331-4463, FAX (918)831-9497. (**Subscription address:** Electronic Publishing, PO Box 2709, Tulsa OK 74101. **Tel** (918)831-9537.)
Desc: Focuses on typesetting and electronic publishing systems for both commercial and corporate markets - a news-oriented tabloid, covering printers, newspaper and commercial publishers, typesetting and art service markets.
Ind/Abst MasterFile FullTEXT (Jan. 1995-).

DD 071
UDC 07   US

ELECTRONIC PUBLISHING DIGEST. English. Twelve times a year. $195.00 (one-year), $345.00 (two-year) US; $230.00 (one-year), $415.00 (two-year) Canada; $250.00 (one-year), $455.00 (two-year) other. Vista Information Systems, PO Drawer 4430, Boulder CO 80306-4430.

Desc: Review of electronic publishing industry, including word processing, authoring, graphics, image, page layout, fonts and laser printers.

ISSN 0954-3244
UK

EPJOURNAL. **VFOAT** EP Journal. (Feb. 1984)-. English. Twelve times a year. £260.00 £200.00 (libraries). Electronic Publ Services Ltd, 104A St. John Street, London EC1M 4EH United Kingdom. **Tel** 011 44 171 4901185, FAX 011 44 171 4904706.

ISSN 1042-3737
DD 070 US
CODEN EPNWEE

EPSIG NEWS. [EPSIG news]. **Added/Corp** Association of American Publishers. Electronic Publishing Special Interest Group. **VAT** Electronic Publishing Special Interest Group News. Vol. 1 No. 1 (Sept. 1987)-. Periodical. English. Four times a year. comes with membership. OCLC Asia Pacific Services, 6565 Frantz Road, Dublin OH 43017. **Tel** (800)848-5878, (614)764-6394 or 6000, FAX (614)764-6096.

US

FRAMER'S FORUM MAGAZINE : THE MAGAZINE FOR DOCUMENT PUBLISHERS. English. Four times a year. $24.95 USI; $29.95 other. Framer's Forum Magazine, 37213 SE WildCat Mountain Drive, Eagle Creek OR 97022. **Tel** (503)637-3275, FAX (503)637-6876.
Desc: In each issue there will be special topics that include template design, multiple platform networking, add-on utilities (grammar checkers, fax and imposition software, fonts), and much more. Also there will be how-to topics like autonumbering, anchored frames, indexing, conditional text, kerning, book building as just a few of the many nuts and bolts articles. In addition, there will be regular features and third party solutions like database publishing, document management, filters, and printers.

US

FULL SPECTRUM. CD-ROM. **See** Computers-Computer Graphics and Design.

LC Z252.5.O5 R39 **ISSN** 1043-1942
DD 686.2/315/05 US
CCC

IN-PLANT REPRODUCTIONS (1988). **See** Printing Industry.

LC Z286.D47 J69

US
TITLE CHANGE

JOURNAL. **Added/Corp** National Association of Desktop Publishers (U.S.). **VFOAT** Desktop Publishers Journal; National Association of Desktop Publishers Journal; NADTP Journal. **VAT** NADTP Journal Jan. 1992. (1990)-(1995). Periodical. English. National Association of Desktop Publishers, 462 Old Boston Street, Topsfield MA 01983. **Tel** (800)874-4113, (508)887-7900, FAX (508)887-6117. ***Continues*** *Journal (National Association of Desktop Publishers (U.S.)), 0897-6503.* ***Continued by*** *National Association of Desktop Publishers Journal.*

US

•JOURNAL OF NATIONAL ASSOCIATION OF DESKTOP PUBLISHERS. (1995)-. English. Twelve times a year. $48.00. National Association of Desktop Publishers, 462 Old Boston Street, Topsfield MA 01983. **Tel** (800)874-4113, (508)887-7900, FAX (508)887-6117. ***Continues*** *Journal.*

ISSN 0260-6666
DD 025.0405 UK

MONITOR ABINGDON. **See** Computers-Online Computing and Information.

ISSN 0897-4764
DD 070 US

NATIONAL ASSOCIATION OF DESKTOP PUBLISHERS FORUM, THE. **See** Publishing-Computer Applications.

ISSN 1056-6023
DD 686 US
Pr Rev.

PAGE (CHICAGO, ILL.), THE. (THE PAGE.). [Page]. (198?)-. Periodical. English. Twelve times a year. $69.00. Cobb Group, 9420 Bunsen Parkway #300, Louisville KY 40220. **Tel** (502)491-1900, (800)223-8720, FAX (502)491-4200. **ED** David Doty. Index available. cum. index. **Bk Rev**, (Qty: 10 per year). **Circ:** 3,000.
Desc: A visual guide to desktop publishing on the MacIntosh computer.

ISSN 1056-540X
DD 004 US
CEASED

PC PUBLISHING AND PRESENTATIONS. [PC publ. present.]. **VFOAT** PC Publishing & Presentations. **VAT** Personal Computer Publishing and Presentations. (1991)-(1993). Periodical. English. PC Publishing, 950 Lee Street, Des Plaines IL 60016. **Tel** (312)296-0770. ***Continues*** *PC Publishing, 0896-8209.*
Ind/Abst Abstr. Bull. Inst. Pap. Sci. Tech.

US

PERSONAL COMPOSITION REPORT, THE. **VFOAT** PCR. Vol. 7, No. 6 (Sept. 1985)-. Periodical. English. Ten times a year. $100.00. Graphic Dimensions, 134 Caversham Woods, Pittsford NY 14534-2834. **Tel** (716)381-3428. **ED** Michael L Kleper. **Bk Rev**. ***Continues*** *Digest of Information on Phototypesetting.*
Desc: Covers the desktop publishing and personal typesetting field for word processing, personal computer and typesetting users worldwide.
Ind/Abst Graph. Arts Bull. Inst. Pap. Sci. Technol. (March 1989, July 1989, Sept. 1989, Dec. 1989).

UK

•PREPRESS COMMENTARY. (1995)-. English. Ten times a year. $342.24. Pira International, Randalls Road Leatherhead, Surrey KT22 7RU United Kingdom. **Tel** 011 44 1372 802050, FAX 011 44 1372 802239, telex 929810. ***Continues*** *Desktop Publishing Commentary.*

ISSN 0928-6500
NE

PREPRESS COMPUTING MAGAZINE. (1991)-. English. Irregular. $174.53. Uitgeverij Nanton Press BV, Postbus 93, Leijenseweg 115C, 3720 AB Bilthoven Netherlands. **Tel** 011 31 30 290644, FAX 011 31 30 286224. ***Continues*** *Prepress Magazine, 0925-0999.*

NE

PROOF : MAANBLAD VOOR DESKTOP PUBLISHING EN GRAFISCHE TOEPASSINGEN. (19??)-. Periodical. English. Ten times a year. Fl85.00. Multiple Informatica Publ BV, Postbus 177, 1000 AD Amsterdam Netherlands. **Tel** 011 31 20 6385509.

LC Z286.D47 P83 **ISSN** 0897-6007
DD 070.5/028/5 US

PUBLISH! (SAN FRANCISCO, CALIF.). (PUBLISH! : THE HOW-TO MAGAZINE OF DESKTOP PUBLISHING.). [Publish!]. **VFOAT** Desktop Publishing. Vol. 1, No. 1 (Sept./Oct. 1986)-. Periodical. English. Twelve times a year. $39.90. PCW Communications Inc., 501 Second Street, San Francisco CA 94107. **Tel** (415)243-0500, (415)978-3146. **(Subscription address:** Sunbelt Fulfillment Services, PO Box 5039, Brentwood TN 37024. **Tel** (800)685-3435.**)** **ED** Susan Gubernat. **Ad Acc.** Documents available from UMI Article Clearinghouse.
Desc: Contains facts on establishing your own publishing system. Includes reviews of hardware and software, new product listings, tips and shortcuts.
Ind/Abst Abstr. Bull. Inst. Pap. Sci. Tech.; Comput. Database; Comput. Rev. Index (Oct. 1987-); Gen. Period. Index (1992-); Graph. Arts Bull. Inst. Pap. Sci. Technol. (Feb. 1989-March 1989, May 1989, July 1989, Sept. 1989-Oct. 1989); Mag. Index Plus (1992-); Microcomput. Abstr. (July 1986-); Newsp. Period. Abstr. (1992-).

LC Z284. .P86 **ISSN** 1048-3055
DD 380 US
CCC

PUBLISHING & PRODUCTION EXECUTIVE. **See** Publishing.

LC Z286.D47 S53 **ISSN** 0889-9762
DD 686 US
CCC

SEYBOLD REPORT ON DESKTOP PUBLISHING, THE. Vol. 1, No. 1 (Sept. 8, 1986)-. Trade Publication. English. Twelve times a year. $365.00. Seybold Publications Inc., 428 West Baltimore Pike, PO Box 644, Media PA 19063. **Tel** (610)565-2480, (800)325-3830, FAX (610)565-4659, or 3261, telex 4991494. Index available. **Bk Rev**. available on an online database (file 675/Full-Text) from DIALOG. Documents available from Ask*IEEE. ***Separated from*** *Seybold Report on Publishing Systems, 0736-7260.*
Ind/Abst Abstr. Bull. Inst. Pap. Sci. Tech.; Bus. Source Plus; Comput. ASAP [Full Txt.]; Comput. Database [Full Txt.]; Curr. Cit.; EP Collect.; Graph. Arts Bull. Inst. Pap. Sci. Technol. (Jan. 1989, March 1989-April 1989, June 1989-July 1989, Sept. 1989-Oct. 1989); Homework Help.; INSPEC (1986-); MasterFile FullTEXT 1000; MasterFile FullTEXT 350; MasterFile FullTEXT 650; MasterFile FullTEXT; OCLC; Telebase.

UK

TEXT & IMAGE NEWS. **See** Computers-Word Processing.

ISSN 0194-4851
DD 070 US
TITLE CHANGE

TYPEWORLD. **See** Printing Industry.

US

WORKGROUP COMPUTING SERIES. INFORMATION DELIVERY. **Added/Corp** Datapro Information Services Group. **VFOAT** Information Delivery. (June 1992)-. Periodical. English. Irregular. $551.00. Datapro Information Services Group, 600 Delran Parkway, Delran NJ 08075. **Tel** (609)764-0100, (800)328-2776, FAX (609)764-8953. ***Continues in part*** *Datapro Reports on Electronic Publishing.*

US

WORKGROUP COMPUTING SERIES. MULTIMEDIA SOLUTIONS / DATAPRO. **Added/Corp** Datapro Information Services Group. **VFOAT** Multimedia Solutions. (June 1992)-. Periodical. English. Irregular. $344.00. Datapro Information Services Group, 600 Delran Parkway, Delran NJ 08075. **Tel** (609)764-0100, (800)328-2776, FAX (609)764-8953. ***Continues in part*** *Datapro Reports on Electronic Publishing.*

ELECTRONIC DATA PROCESSING

LC QA75.5 .A75a **ISSN** 0149-1199
DD 016.00164 US

ACM GUIDE TO COMPUTING LITERATURE. **See** Computers-Abstracting, Bibliographies and Statistics.

LC HF5548.2 .A335 **ISSN** 1046-8188
DD 651.8 US
CCC
CODEN ATISET

ACM TRANSACTIONS ON INFORMATION SYSTEMS : PUBLICATION OF THE ASSOCIATION FOR COMPUTING MACHINERY. [ACM trans. inf. sys.]. **Added/Corp** Association for Computing Machinery. **VFOAT** Transactions on Information Systems. **VAT** Association for Computing Machinery Transactions on Information Systems. Vol. 7, No. 1 (Jan. 1989)-. Academic Scholarly Publication. English. Four times a year. $125.00. ACM / Association for Computing Machinery, 1515 Broadway, 17th Floor, New York NY 10036. **Tel** (212)869-7440, FAX (212)869-0481. **(Subscription address:** Association for Computing Machinery, PO Box 12114, Church Street Station, New York NY 10249. **Tel** (212)626-0500.**)** **ED** Robert B. Allen. Documents available from Article Express International, The Genuine Article, Ask*IEEE, CASDDS. ***Continues*** *ACM Transactions on Office Information Systems, 0734-2047.*
Ind/Abst Abstr. Hum. Comput. Interact.; ACM Guide Comput. Lit.; Chem. Abstr. (1989); CompuMath Cit. Index [Full Cov.]; Comput. Database; Comput. Lit. Index; Comput. Rev.; Curr. Cit.; Curr. Contents Eng. Comput. Technol.; Ei Page One; Eng. Index Annu.; Ergon. Abstr.; Expand. Acad. Index (1992-); HILITES; Inf. Sci. Abstr.; INSPEC (Jan. 1989-); Res. Alert [Full Cov.]; Sci. Cit. Index; SCISEARCH; Soc. Sci. Cit. Index [Select. Cov.].

LC QA76 .A265 **ISSN** 0001-5903
DD 001.6/4/05 GW
CCC
CODEN AINFA2
Pr Rev.

ACTA INFORMATICA. [Acta inf.]. Vol. 1 (1971)-. Periodical. Multiple languages (English, French and German). Eight times a year. $852.00. Springer-Verlag GmbH & Company KG, Heidelberger Platz 3, D-14197 Berlin Germany. **Tel** 011 49 30 8207223, FAX 011 49 30 8214091, telex 183 319 SPBLN D. **(Subscription address:** Springer-Verlag New York Inc. / North America, PO Box 2485, Journal Fulfillment, Secaucus NJ 07096. **Tel** (201)348-4033, (800)777-4643, FAX (201)348-4505.**)** **ED** F L Bauer, M Broy, E W Dijkstra, D Gries, A J Perlis, and W M Turski. available on microfilm and microfiche from University Microfilms International (UMI). Documents available from Article Express International, The Genuine Article, Ask*IEEE, CASDDS.
Desc: Provides international dissemination of contributions on the art, discipline and science of informatics.
Ind/Abst ACM Guide Comput. Lit.; Bioeng. Abstr.; Chem. Abstr.; CompuMath Cit. Index [Full Cov.]; Comput. Abstr.; Comput. Rev.; Curr. Cit.; Curr. Contents Eng. Comput. Technol.; Ei Page One; Eng. Index Annu.; Inf. Sci. Abstr.; INSPEC (1972-); Int. Abstr. Oper. Res. [Select. Cov.]; Math. Rev.; Res. Alert [Full Cov.]; Sci. Cit. Index; SCISEARCH; Zentralbl. Math. Ihre Grenzgeb.

ISSN 0893-0570
DD 005 US

ADA STRATEGIES. [Ada strateg.]. (March 1987)-. Trade Publication. English. Twelve times a year. $337.00. Software Strategies and Tactics, Route 2 Box 713, Harpers Ferry WV 25425. **Tel** (304)725-6542, FAX (304)725-6543. **ED** Ralph E. Crafts. **Ad Acc. Circ:** 200 (ctrl).
Desc: Focuses on competitive issues, including: Congressional awareness and actions; DoD policies and regulations; applicable standards and technologies; case histories of Ada projects; international Ada efforts; and commercial usage of Ada technology.

US

ADVANCES IN DATA BASE THEORY. **See** Computers-Data Base Management.

Computers — Electronic Data Processing

LC TK5105 .A3
DD 621.38/05
ISSN 0197-1476
US

ADVANCES IN DATA COMMUNICATIONS MANAGEMENT.
[Adv. data commun. manage.]. Vol. 1 (1980)-. Monographic series. English. Irregular. Price varies per volume. Vieweg Publishing, PO Box 5829, D-65048 Wiesbaden Germany. **Tel** 011 49 611 160230, FAX 011 49 611 534430.

LC HF5548.125 .A38
DD 658/.054/05
ISSN 0196-8696
US

ADVANCES IN DATA PROCESSING MANAGEMENT.
[Adv. data process. manage.]. Vol. 1 (1980)-. Periodical. English. Irregular. Price varies. John Wiley & Sons Inc / New Jersey, 1 Wiley Drive, Somerset NJ 08875. **Tel** (800)225-5945, (908)469-4400. **(Subscription address:** John Wiley & Sons / UK, Baffins Lane, Chichester, West Sussex PO19 1UD United Kingdom. **Tel** 011 44 1243 779777, FAX 011 44 243 776128, telex 86290 WIBOOKG.) Documents available from Ask*IEEE.
Ind/Abst INSPEC.

LC QA76.9.D5 A36
DD 001.64
ISSN 0197-1433
US

ADVANCES IN DISTRIBUTED PROCESSING MANAGEMENT.
[Adv. distrib. process. manage.]. Vol. 1 (1980)-. Monographic series. English. Irregular. Price varies per volume. Vieweg Publishing, PO Box 5829, D-65048 Wiesbaden Germany. **Tel** 011 49 611 160230, FAX 011 49 611 534430.

LC HD30.213 .A38
US

●ADVANCES IN MANAGERIAL COGNITION AND ORGANIZATIONAL INFORMATION PROCESSING. See Industry and Production.

LC QA75.5 .A414
ISSN 0178-4617
US
CCC
CODEN ALGOEJ
Pr Rev.

ALGORITHMICA.
[Algorithmica]. Vol. 1, No. 1 (1986)-. Academic Scholarly Publication. English. Twelve times a year. $299.00. Springer-Verlag New York Inc., 175 Fifth Avenue, New York NY 10010. **Tel** (212)460-1500 ext 256, FAX (212)533-3503, telex 232 235 SPB UR. **(Subscription address:** Springer-Verlag New York Inc. / North America, PO Box 2485, Journal Fulfillment, Secaucus NJ 07096. **Tel** (201)348-4033, (800)777-4643, FAX (201)348-4505.) **ED** C K Wong. available in microform from University Microfilms International (UMI). Documents available from Article Express International, The Genuine Article, Ask*IEEE.
Desc: Publishes papers on algorithms with a strong emphasis on practical application. Keeps the reader at the forefront of new technologies, methodologies, applications by publishing research results of the application of algorithms to areas such as VLSI, distributed computing, parallel processing, automated design, robotics, graphics, database design, and software tools.
Ind/Abst CompuMath Cit. Index [Full Cov.]; Comput. Rev.; Curr. Cit.; Curr. Contents Eng. Comput. Technol.; Ei Page One; Eng. Index Annu.; INSPEC (1986-); Int. Abstr. Oper. Res. [Select. Cov.]; Math. Rev. (1986-); Res. Alert [Full Cov.]; Sci. Cit. Index; SCISEARCH; Zentralbl. Math. Ihre Grenzgeb.

AT

ANNUAL REPORT / CSIRONET. Main/Corp
CSIRONET (Organization : Australia). (1985)-. English. One time a year. CSIRO Publications, PO Box 89, 314 Albert Street, East Melborne Victoria 3002 Australia. **Tel** 011 61 3 4187333, 4187217, FAX 011 61 3 4190459, telex AA 30236.

LC TK7885
DD 621.39
ISSN 0941-0635

APPLIED SIGNAL PROCESSING.
(1992)-. Academic Scholarly Publication. English. Four times a year. $243.00. Springer-Verlag London Ltd., Springer House, 8 Alexandra Road Wimbledon, London SW19 7JZ United Kingdom. **Tel** 011 44 181 9471280, 011 44 181 9475885, FAX 011 44 181 9474651, telex 21531 SPRGB G. **(Subscription address:** Springer-Verlag New York Inc. / North America, PO Box 2485, Journal Fulfillment, Secaucus NJ 07096. **Tel** (201)348-4033, (800)777-4643, FAX (201)348-4505.) **ED** M. Sandler and A.C. Davies. Documents available from BLDSC.

LC QA75.5 .A73
DD 004
HK

ASIAN COMPUTER DIRECTORY. (1985)-.
Directory. English. One time a year. $103.00. Computer Publications Ltd, Washington Place 1st Floor, 230 Wanchai Road, Wanchai Hong Kong. **Tel** 011 852 5 28327123, FAX 011 852 5 28329208. **Continues** Asian Computer Yearbook.

LC QA76.9.D6 S96
DD 004
ISSN 0731-1001
US

ASTERISK (NEW YORK, N.Y.).
(ASTERISK : THE JOURNAL OF COMPUTER DOCUMENTATION.). [Asterisk]. **Added/Corp** Association for Computing Machinery. Special Interest Group on Systems Documentation. **VFOAT** Journal of Computer Documentation; Asterisk Journal. Vol. 1, No. 1 (Mar. 1991)-. Periodical. English. Four times a year. $25.00. ACM / Association for Computing Machinery, 1515 Broadway, 17th Floor, New York NY 10036. **Tel** (212)869-7440, FAX (212)869-0481. **(Subscription address:** Association for Computing Machinery, PO Box 12114, Church Street Station, New York NY 10249. **Tel** (212)626-0500.) Documents available from Ask*IEEE. **Continues** ACM SIGDOC Asterisk, 0731-1001.
Ind/Abst INSPEC.

ISSN 1067-5221
US

ATM NEWSLETTER. (ATM NEWSLETTER : ASYNCHRONOUS TRANSFER MODE.).
[ATM newsl.]. **Added/Corp** Information Gatekeepers, Inc. **VFOAT** Asynchronous Transfer Mode. **VAT** Asynchronous Transfer Mode Newsletter. Vol. 1, No. 1 (Nov. 1992)-. Newsletter. English. Twelve times a year. $575.00. Information Gatekeepers Inc., 214 Harvard avenue, Boston MA 02134. **Tel** (617)232-3111, (617)738-8088, (800)323-1088, FAX (617)734-8562.

DD 658
ISSN 0736-3648
US
CCC

AUERBACH DATA CENTER OPERATIONS MANAGEMENT.
[Auerbach data cent. oper. manage.]. **VFOAT** Data Center Operations Management. (1977)-. Trade Publication. English. Six times a year. Auerbach Publishers Inc., Park Square Building, 31 St. James Avenue, Boston MA 02116. **Tel** (800)950-1207. **ED** Layne Bradley and Kim Kelly.
Desc: Up-to-date articles on all aspects of data center management, including planning, budgeting, workflow management, maintenance and security of DP facilities, disaster recovery planning, equipment selection and acquisition, data center personnel management, computer performance evaluation, capacity planning, and magnetic media management.

DD 658
ISSN 0736-0002
US
CCC

AUERBACH DATA COMMUNICATIONS MANAGEMENT.
[Auerbach data commun. manage.]. **VFOAT** Data Communications Management. (1975)-. Trade Publication. English. Six times a year. $395.00. Auerbach Publishers Inc., Park Square Building, 31 St. James Avenue, Boston MA 02116. **Tel** (800)950-1207. **ED** Paul Berk. Index available. **Circ:** 400.
Desc: Provides data and data/voice communications managers, DP departments, consultants with information on management, planning, control, technologies, networks, hardware, software, standards, and applications.

LC HF5601
DD 657
ISSN 0746-7265
US
CCC

AUERBACH EDP AUDITING. See Business and Economics-Accounting.

LC QA76.5 .A78
DD 338.4/7/62138195025
ISSN 0361-2783
US

AUERBACH GUIDE TO COMPUTING EQUIPMENT SPECIFICATIONS. English.
Two times a year. Auerbach Publishers Inc., Park Square Building, 31 St. James Avenue, Boston MA 02116. **Tel** (800)950-1207. **Continues** Auerbach Computer Characteristics Digest, 0004-7708.

DD 658
ISSN 1045-7879
US
Pr Rev.

AUERBACH INFORMATION MANAGEMENT. (AUERBACH INFORMATION MANAGEMENT : STRATEGY, SYSTEMS, AND TECHNOLOGIES.).
[Auerbach inf. manage.]. **Added/Corp** Auerbach Publishers. **VFOAT** Information Management. Vol. 1, (1989)-. Trade Publication. English. Six times a year. $495.00. Auerbach Publishers Inc., Park Square Building, 31 St. James Avenue, Boston MA 02116. **Tel** (800)950-1207. **ED** Karen Brogno. Index available. **Circ:** 1000. **Continues** Auerbach Data Processing Management, 0735-9993.
Desc: Publishes articles for all levels of managers in the IS department to help them work effectively. Covers general and strategic management and staffing issues, directions in technology, systems development and resource and communications network management.

US

BBP MANAGER'S LETTER. See Business and Economics-Management.

LC QA75.5
DD 004/.05
ISSN 0144-929X
UK
CCC
CODEN BEITD5
Pr Rev.

BEHAVIOUR & INFORMATION TECHNOLOGY.
[Behav. inf. technol.]. **VFOAT** Behaviour and Information Technology. Vol. 1, No. 1 (Jan.-Mar. 1982)-. Periodical. English. Six times a year. $310.00. Taylor & Francis Ltd. / UK, Rankine Road, Basingstoke, Hampshire RG24 8PR United Kingdom. **Tel** 011 44 1256 840366, FAX 011 44 1256 479438, telex 858540. **(Subscription address:** Taylor & Francis Inc., 1900 Frost Road, Suite 101, Bristol PA 19007-1598. **Tel** (215)785-5800, (800)821-8312, FAX (215)785-5515.) **ED** T. F. M. Stewart, S. J. Payne and Ahmet Cakir. available on microfilm from University Microfilms International (UMI). Documents available from The Genuine Article, Ask*IEEE.
Desc: Deals with the human aspects of information technology in three broad areas: computing, telecommunications and office automation. Covers research and development related to the design, use and impact of information technology.
Ind/Abst Abstr. Hum. Comput. Interact.; Anbar Account. Finan. Abstr. [Full Txt.]; Anbar Mark. Distr. Abstr. [Full Txt.]; Anbar Top Manage. Abstr. [Full Txt.]; CompuMath Cit. Index [Full Cov.]; Comput. Abstr.; Comput. Rev.; Curr. Cit.; Curr. Contents Soc. Behav. Sci.; Ei Page One; Ergon. Abstr.; HILITES; Inf. Sci. Abstr.; INSPEC (Jan.-March 1982); Manage. Market. Abstr.; Manage. Bibliogr. Rev.; Oper. Prod. Manage. Abstr. [Full Txt.]; Person. Train. Abstr. [Full Txt.]; Pollut. Abstr. Indexes; Psychol. Abstr. (1982-); PsycINFO (1990-); PsycLit; Res. Alert [Full Cov.]; Soc. Sci. Cit. Index [Full Cov.]; Women Manage. Rev. [Full Txt.]; World Publ. Monit.

LC WMLC 91/1059
DD 004
CI

BIT. Added/Corp Galerije Grada Zagreba. VFOAT Bit
International. No. 1 (1968)-. Periodical. Serbo-Croatian (Roman). **Ad Acc. Circ:** 45,287.
Desc: Information on electronic data processing, computer graphics and information theory.
Ind/Abst SCISEARCH.

LC QA75.5 B72A
BL

BOLETIM TECNICO - CAPRE. Main/Corp
Brazil. Comissao de Coordenacao das Atividades de Processamento Electronico. Vol. 1 (Jan./March 1979)-. Bulletin. Portuguese.

ISSN 0193-9734
US

BUSINESS DATA PROCESSING: A WILEY SERIES. See Business and Economics-Computer Applications.

ISSN 0339-3097
FR
CCC
CODEN CADODG

CAHIERS DE L'ANALYSE DES DONNEES, LES. [Cah. anal. donnees]. VFOAT
Analyse des Donnees. Vol. 1 (1976)-. Periodical. French (summaries and/or abstracts in English). Four times a year. $166.22. Dunod Gauthier Villars, 15 rue Gossin, 92543 Montrouge Cedex France. **Tel** 011 33 1 46565266, 011 33 1 40926527, FAX 011 33 1 40926597. **(Subscription address:** Centrale des Revues, 11 rue Gossin, 92543 Montrouge Cedex France. **Tel** 011 33 1 46565266.) **ED** J. Benzecri. Index available. **Bk Rev**. **Ad Acc. Circ:** 900.
Desc: Publishes results of specific studies, statistics and programs designed for data analysis.
Ind/Abst Br. Archaeol. Bibliogr. (?-?); Energy Res. Abstr. (April 1982-); GeoRef; Stat. Theory Method Abstr. (1978-1983, 1986-1987); Zentralbl. Math. Ihre Grenzgeb.

FR
CEASED

CAHIERS MANAGEMENT INFORMATIQUE. (19??)-(1993). French (English).
Technology Transfer Yphise, 53 BD Sebastopol, F 75001 Paris France. **Tel** 011 33 1 45088670.
Desc: Data processing management.

LC TK7870 .C24
DD 621.381
IT

CAMAC BULLETIN. See Electronics.

DD 380.1/45/621381950971
ISSN 0704-7932
CN

CANADA'S DATA PROCESSING MARKET.
(1978)-. English. One time a year. $50.00 per vol. Maclean Hunter Canada / Montreal, 1001 bvd. de Maisonneuve W., Montreal Quebec H3A 3E1 Canada. **Tel** (514)845-5141, FAX (514)845-4302, telex 055-60604. **Continues** Canada's Data Processing Industry, 0317-0411.

DD 004/.06/071 ISSN 1182-3097
CN
CCC
CEASED

CANADIAN INFORMATION PROCESSING. [Can. inf. process.]. **Added/Corp** Canadian Information Processing Society. **VFOAT** Informatique Canadienne. (April/May 1990)-(Oct./Dec. 1993). Periodical. English (French). Canadian Information Processing Society, 430 King Street West, Suite 106, Toronto Ontario M5V 1L5 Canada. **Tel** (416)593-4040, FAX (416)593-5184. **ED** Patrick McAuley. **Ad Acc.** ***Continues*** *C I P S Review, 0701-8681.*
Desc: Examines trends and issues in the information technology profession and industry.
Ind/Abst Can. Period. Index (19??-); Comput. Lit. Index.

LC QA75.5 .C53
DD 001.64/05 CH
CHI SUAN CHI KO HSUEH. VFOAT Jisuanjikexue. Periodical. Chinese. Six times a year. NT$0.40. Post Office Chung-Ching Shih, Chung-Ching Shih, People's Republic of China. **Tel** 3578.

LC Microfilm 05496 QA QA75.5
NE
COMPUTABLE. (19??)-. Periodical. Dutch (Dutch). One time a week. $116.35. VNU Business Publications BV, Postbus 9194, 1006 AC Amsterdam Netherlands. **Tel** 011 31 20 4875879.

LC QA75.5 .C587 **ISSN** 0194-357X
DD 001 US
CODEN COMPER
CEASED
COMPUTE (GREENSBORO). (COMPUTE.). [Compute]. Iss. 1 (Fall 1979)-(Sept. 1994). Periodical. English. General Media Publishing Company, 1965 Broadway, New York NY 10023. **Tel** (212)496-6100. **ED** Peter Scisco, Keith Ferrell, Denny Atkin, Heidi E H Aycock, and Richard C Leinecker (editors address: 324 W Wendover Avenue/Suite 200, Greensboro, NC 27408; editor's telephone number: (919)275-9809). Index available. **Bk Rev. Ad Acc. Circ:** 275,000. available on microfilm and microfiche from University Microfilms International (UMI); available on an online database (files 647,648/Full-Text) from DIALOG. Documents available from Ask*IEEE, UMI Article Clearinghouse. ***Continues*** *PET Gazette;* ***Absorbed*** *Recreational Computing, 0164-5846; Home and Educational Computing, 0743-9679;* ***Continues*** *Compute's Gazette.*
Desc: Offers in-depth feature articles, industry news, interviews with leaders in the personal computer field, product information, reviews of hardware and software, plus regular columns for Amiga, Apple, Atari ST, Commodore, IBM PC, Tandy, and compatible machines. The general focus is on using the personal computer at home, work, and in the school.
Ind/Abst Abr. Read. Guide Period. Lit.; Acad. Abstr. Full Text Elite; Acad. Abstr.; Acad. Ind. [Computer File] (1989-); Acad. Search; Bus. Source Plus; Bus. Source; EP Collect.; Expand. Acad. Index (1989-); Gen. Period. Index (1985-); Homework Help.; INFO-SOUTH Abstr.; INSPEC (May 1982-); Int. Civil Eng. Abstr.; Mag. Artic. Summar. Elite; Mag. Artic. Summar. Select; Mag. Artic. Summar. CD-ROM; Mag. ASAP Plus [Full Txt.]; Mag. ASAP Sel. [Full Txt.]; Mag. Index Plus (1989-); Mag. Index. Sel. (1989-); Mag. Search; MasterFile FullTEXT 1000; MasterFile FullTEXT 350; MasterFile FullTEXT 650; MasterFile FullTEXT (Mar. 1984-Sept. 1994); Microcomput. Abstr. (Jan. 1985-); Newsp. Period. Abstr. (1988-); OCLC; Pub. Lib. FullTEXT; Read. Guide Abstr. Select Ed.; Read. Guide Period. Lit.; Resource/One Ondisc (1988-); Soft. Abstr. Eng.; Telebase; Mag. Index; TOM Gen. Index (1989-) [Full Txt.]; Trade Ind. ASAP [Full Txt.]; Trade Ind. Index [Full Txt.]; Vocat. Search; World Mag. Bank.

LC QA76 .I46
DD 016.0016/4 US
•**COMPUTER AND INFORMATION SYSTEMS ABSTRACTS. See** Computers-Abstracting, Bibliographies and Statistics.

ISSN 0960-2593
DD 005.8 UK
CCC
Pr Rev.
COMPUTER AUDIT UPDATE. [Comput. audit update]. (1991)-. Periodical. English. Twelve times a year (plus 2 supplements). $396.00. Elsevier Advanced Technology, An Imprint of Elsevier Science Ltd., The Boulevard, Langford Lane, Kidlington, Oxford OX5 1GB United Kingdom. **Tel** 011 44 1865 843000, 011 44 1865 843699, FAX 011 44 1865 843010. **(Subscription address:** Elsevier Science Ltd. / Oxford Fulfillment Centre, PO Box 800, Kidlington OX5 1DX United Kingdom. **Tel** 011 44 865 843355.) available on an online database from Elsevier Electronic Subscriptions (EES); and DIALOG. ***Continues*** *Update on Computer Audit, Control and Security, 0953-5217.*
Desc: Encompasses both managerial and technical aspects of auditing electronic data processing systems.
Ind/Abst Curr. Cit.; PTS Newsl. Database [Full Txt.].

LC QA76 .C56 **ISSN** 0010-4531
DD 510.78 UK
CCC
CODEN COBUAH
COMPUTER BULLETIN. (THE COMPUTER BULLETIN / THE BRITISH COMPUTER SOCIETY.). [Comput. bull.]. **Added/Corp** British Computer Society. Vol. 1, No. 2 (Aug. 1957)-. Bulletin. English. Six times a year. $80.00. Oxford University Press / UK, Walton Street, Oxford OX2 6DP United Kingdom. **Tel** 011 44 1865 56767, FAX 011 44 1865 267773, telex 851/837330 OXPRES G. **(Subscription address:** Oxford University Press / USA, Journals Marketing Department, Oxford University Press, 2001 Evans Road, Cary NC 27513. **Tel** (800)451-7556, (919)677-0977, FAX (919)677-1714.) available on microfilm and microfiche from University Microfilms International (UMI). Documents available from Article Express International, Ask*IEEE. ***Continues*** *London Computer Group Bulletin.*
Desc: Fills the gap between academic computing journals and user magazines. It contains articles covering developments and application in practice, case studies and state-of-the-art reviews, industry profiles, regular news from Europe, USA, Japan, and Australia, as well as education and regular input from British Computer Society specialist groups.
Ind/Abst Abstr. Hum. Comput. Interact.; ACM Guide Comput. Lit.; BMT Abstr. (?-199?); Comput. Lit. Index; Comput. Rev. (Dec. 1974-); Curr. Cit.; Educ. Technol. Abstr. (Dec. 1974-); Ei Page One; Eng. Index Annu.; HILITES; INSPEC (Dec. 1974-); Stat. Theory Method Abstr. (1968-1969, 1971-1972); Stud. Women Abstr.; Tech. Educ. Train. Abstr. (Dec. 1974-); World Publ. Monit.

ISSN 1054-5026
DD 338 US
CODEN CEIEE6
Pr Rev.
COMPUTER ECONOMIC$ REPORT (INTERNATIONAL ED.). (COMPUTER ECONOMIC$ REPORT.). [Comput. econ. rep.]. **VFOAT** Computer Economics Report. (1979)-. Periodical. English. Twelve times a year. $595.00. Computer Economics Inc., 5841 Edison Place, Carlsbad CA 92008. **Tel** (800)326-8100, (619)438-8100, FAX (619)431-1126. **ED** Lee Kroon and Michael Erbschloe. Index available. cum. index. Documents available from Ask*IEEE.
Desc: A financial advisor for data processor users. Provides cost comparisons, price performance analyses and new product forecasts.
Ind/Abst Curr. Cit.; INSPEC (July 1990-).

ISSN 0889-082X
DD 338 US
COMPUTER INDUSTRY REPORT. [Comput. ind. rep.]. **Added/Corp** International Data Corporation. **VFOAT** Gray Sheet Computer Industry Report. Vol. 22, No. 1 (April 30, 1986)-. Trade Publication. English. Twenty-four times a year. $495.00. International Data Corporation, 5 Speen Street, PO Box 9015, Framingham MA 01701. **Tel** (508)872-8200, (508)935-4443. **(Subscription address:** IDG Newsletters, PO Box 145, Oxon Hill MD 20750. **Tel** (800)549-9494.) **ED** Peter Burris. ctrl circ. ***Continues*** *EDP Industry Report, 0742-647X;* ***Absorbed*** *IBM Watch.*
Desc: Provides original research that identifies and explains trends in the worldwide IT industry. Applies methodology to analyzing, segmenting and sizing worldwide computer markets to deliver market data.
Ind/Abst Acad. Search; Bus. ASAP (1992-) [Full Txt.]; Bus. Index (1986-); Bus. Source Plus; Bus. Source; Comput. Lit. Index; EP Collect.; Gen. BusinessFile (1986-); Gen. Period. Index (1986-); Homework Help.; INFO-SOUTH Abstr.; Mag. Search; MasterFile FullTEXT 1000; MasterFile FullTEXT 350; MasterFile FullTEXT 650; MasterFile FullTEXT (July 1993-); OCLC; Predicasts; Telebase; Trade Ind. ASAP [Full Txt.]; Trade Ind. Index (1986-) [Full Txt.].

LC QA76 .Q3 **ISSN** 0270-4846
DD 016.00164 US
CCC
COMPUTER LITERATURE INDEX. See Computers-Abstracting, Bibliographies and Statistics.

ISSN 0319-6216
DD 370/.28/5 CN
COMPUTER STUDIES NEWSLETTER. Issue 1- Sept. 1971-. Newsletter. English. J Dale Burnett, Faculty of Education, Queen's University, Kingston Ontario K7L 2N6 Canada.

LC QA76 .C576 **ISSN** 0163-4003
DD 004/.05 US
NLM Z 699.A1 C743
COMPUTER YEARBOOK (DETROIT). (COMPUTER YEARBOOK.). [Comput. yearb.]. 1972-. English. One time a year. International Electronics Information Service, 200 Park Avenue/Suite 303 East, New York NY 10017. ***Supersedes*** *Computer Yearbook and Directory.*

LC QA75.5 .C61137
DD 338.4/7004/096 UK
•**COMPUTERS & COMMUNICATIONS IN AFRICA. VFOAT** Computers and Communications in Africa; Computers in Africa. Vol. 7, No. 2 (Mar./Apr. 1993)-. Trade Publication. English. Ten times a year. $51.33. Africa File Ltd., 37 Fairhazel Gardens, London NW6 3QN United Kingdom. **Tel** 011 44 148 0830724, FAX 011 44 148 0831131, telex 932524. ***Continues*** *Computers in Africa & Telecoms Update.*

ISSN 0898-1221
DD 004 UK
CCC
COMPUTERS & MATHEMATICS WITH APPLICATIONS (1987). See Mathematics-Computer Applications.

ISSN 1077-5803
DD 004 US
CODEN CLSJEI
•**COMPUTERWORLD CLIENT/SERVER JOURNAL. See** Computers-Computer Networks.

LC QA76 .C777 **ISSN** 0010-485X
AU
CCC
CODEN CMPTA2
Pr Rev.
COMPUTING. [Computing]. **VFOAT** Archives for Informatics and Numerical Computation; Archiv fur Informatik und Numerik. Vol. 1 (1966)-. Periodical. English (German; summaries and/or abstracts in German and English). Eight times a year. $745.00. Springer-Verlag Vienna, Sachsenplatz 4 6, PO Box 89, A-1201 Vienna Austria. **Tel** 011 43 1 33024150, FAX 011 43 1 330242665. **(Subscription address:** Springer-Verlag New York Inc. / North America, PO Box 2485, Journal Fulfillment, Secaucus NJ 07096. **Tel** (201)348-4033, (800)777-4643, FAX (201)348-4505.) **ED** R Albrecht, W Haendler, W W Knoedel, W L Miranker, H J Stetter, and Hj. Wacker. available on microfilm and microfiche from University Microfilms International (UMI). Documents available from Article Express International, The Genuine Article, Ask*IEEE. ***Continues*** *Mathematik-Technik-Wirtschaft.*
Desc: Presents the latest research results from computer science and numerical computation. The journal is international and is intended for professionals and students in all fields of scientific computing, for computer center staff, and software and hardware manufacturers.
Ind/Abst ACM Guide Comput. Lit.; Appl. Mech. Rev.; Bioeng. Abstr.; Comput. Rev.; Curr. Cit.; Ei Page One; Eng. Index Annu.; INIS Atomindex [Micro.]; INSPEC (1968-); Int. Abstr. Oper. Res. [Select. Cov.]; Int. Aerosp. Abstr.; Math. Rev.; Res. Alert [Full Cov.]; Sci. Cit. Index; SCISEARCH; Stat. Theory Method Abstr. (1969-1977, 1979-1984); Women Manage. Rev. [Full Txt.].

ISSN 0319-0161
DD 001.6/4/05 CN
COMPUTING CANADA. [Comput. Can.]. Vol. 1 (May 1975)-. English. Twenty-six times a year. 64.02Can$. Plesman Publications Ltd., 2005 Sheppard Avenue East, 4th Floor, Willowdale Ontario M2J 5B1 Canada. **Tel** (416)497-9562, FAX (416)497-9427. **ED** Martin Slofstra. **Bk Rev. Ad Acc, Adv Mgr:** Carmen Girard, **Tel** (416)497-9562. **Circ:** 32,000 (ctrl). available on an online database (files 648,675/Full-Text) from DIALOG. Documents available from UMI Article Clearinghouse.
Desc: Coverage of news, issues, and trends of interest to computer users and data processing (DP/MIS) professionals in Canada.
Ind/Abst ABI/INFORM Glob. Ed.; ABI/INFORM [Computer File] (July 1980-); Can. Period. Index (19??-); Comput. ASAP [Full Txt.]; Comput. Database [Full Txt.]; F&S Index Plus Text, Int. [Select. Cov.]; PROMT; Trade Ind. ASAP [Full Txt.]; Trade Ind. Index [Full Txt.].

LC TA345 **ISSN** 0010-4876
DD 502/.8/54 US
COMPUTING REPORT IN SCIENCE AND ENGINEERING. See Science and Technology-Computer Applications.

LC QA76 .C5854 **ISSN** 0010-4884
DD 001.6/05 US
CCC
NLM Z 699.A1 C76 **CODEN** CPGRA6
COMPUTING REVIEWS. See Computers-Abstracting, Bibliographies and Statistics.

ISSN 0380-9501
DD 001.6/4 CN
COMPUTING STUDIES. 1- 1975-. Monographic series. English. Price varies per volume. Computing Centre University of New Brunswick, PO Box 4400, Fredericton New Brunswick E3B 5G4 Canada.

LC QA75.5 .C6114
DD 001.64/05 MX
COMUNIDAD INFORMATICA. No. 1 (May/June 1978)-. Periodical. Spanish. Four times a year.

UK
CONNECT. See Computers-Computer Industry and Industry Directories.

MX
CURSOR. Added/Corp Instituto Tecnologico y de Estudios Superiores de Monterrey. Campus Monterrey. Direccion de Informatica. (198?)-. Periodical. Spanish.

Twelve times a year. Instituto Tecnologico y de Estudios Superiores de Monterrey, Centro de Desarrollo Industrial CETEC, Torre Norte Nivel VI, Ave. Eugenio Garza Sada 2501 Sur, 64849 Monterrey NL Mexico.

LC HD9696.C63 B73
DD 338.47621381
BL
CEASED

DADOS E IDEIAS. See Computers-Computer Industry and Industry Directories.

LC QA76.9.D26 D38   ISSN 0169-023X
DD 005.74/05
NE
CCC
CODEN DKENEW
Pr Rev.

DATA & KNOWLEDGE ENGINEERING. See Computers-Data Base Management.

LC QA75 .D3155   ISSN 0095-0033
DD 658/.05/405
US
CODEN DTBSAN
Pr Rev.   **TITLE CHANGE**

DATA BASE. [Data base]. **Added/Corp** Association for Computing Machinery. Special Interest Group on Business Data Processing. Association for Computing Machinery. Special Interest Group on Business Information Technology. Vol. 1 (Spring 1969)-Vol. 24 (1994). English. Four times a year (Feb., May, Aug., Dec.). ACM / Association for Computing Machinery, 1515 Broadway, 17th Floor, New York NY 10036. **Tel** (212)869-7440, FAX (212)869-0481. **(Subscription address:** Association for Computing Machinery, PO Box 12114, Church Street Station, New York NY 10249. **Tel** (212)626-0500.**) ED** James C. Wetherbe. Index available (free). cum. index. **Bk Rev.** ctrl circ. Documents available from The Genuine Article, Ask*IEEE. **Continues** SIGBDP Newsletter. **Continued by** Data Base for Advances in Information Systems.
Desc: A communication of the Association of Computing Machinery special interest group on business data processing providing a vehicle for research of practical significance to practitioners in the field of information systems.
Ind/Abst ACM Guide Comput. Lit.; Bus. Educ. Index; CompuMath Cit. Index [Full Cov.]; Comput. Lit. Index; Comput. Rev.; Curr. Cit.; Ergon. Abstr.; INSPEC (Spring 1969-1997); J. Plan. Lit.; Res. Alert [Full Cov.]; SCISEARCH.

LC QA76 .D3155
DD 658/.05/405
US
CODEN DTBSAN

●**DATA BASE FOR ADVANCES IN INFORMATION SYSTEMS : A QUARTERLY PUBLICATION OF SIGBIT, THE.** **Added/Corp** Association for Computing Machinery. Special Interest Group on Business Information Technology. **VFOAT** Database for Advances in Information Systems; Advances in Information Systems; Db Advances in Information Systems. Vol. 26, No. 1 (Feb. 1995)-. Periodical. English. Four times a year (Feb., May, Aug., Dec.). $38.00. ACM / Association for Computing Machinery, 1515 Broadway, 17th Floor, New York NY 10036. **Tel** (212)869-7440, FAX (212)869-0481. **(Subscription address:** Association for Computing Machinery, PO Box 12114, Church Street Station, New York NY 10249. **Tel** (212)626-0500.**) ED** James C. Wetherbe. Index available (free). cum. index. **Bk Rev.** ctrl circ. **Continues** Data Base, 0095-0033.
Ind/Abst ACM Guide Comput. Lit.; Bus. Educ. Index; CompuMath Cit. Index; Comput. Lit. Index; Comput. Rev.; Curr. Cit.; Ergon. Abstr.; INSPEC; J. Plan. Lit.; Res. Alert; SCISEARCH.

LC QA75   ISSN 0093-7290
DD 004.05
US
CCC

NLM Z 699.A1 D223
DATA CHANNELS. See Computers.

LC QA76 .D315   ISSN 0105-9912
DK

DATA (KBENHAVN. 1971). (DATA.). [Data]. Periodical. Multiple languages (Danish, English and Swedish). Irregular. kr100.00. Box 113, DK 1004 Copenhagen K Denmark. Documents available from Ask*IEEE.
Ind/Abst Comput. Rev.; INSPEC (1979-).

LC QA75.5 .D36
DD 001.6/4
AU
DATA PRESS. 1976- 1. German. Billrothstrasse 14, 1190 Vienna Austria.

LC HV8290 .A8   ISSN 0749-1484
DD 658.4/78
US
TITLE CHANGE

DATA PROCESSING & COMMUNICATIONS SECURITY. [Data process. commun. secur.]. **VFOAT** Data Processing and Communications Security. Vol. 8, No. 1 (Sept./Oct. 1983)-(1993). Periodical. English. Assets Protection, PO Box 5323, Madison WI 53705. **Tel** (608)833-8099, FAX (608)271-4520. **ED** Paul Shaw. **Bk Rev. Ad Acc. Circ:** 5,000. available on microfilm and microfiche from University Microfilms International (UMI). **Continues** Assets Protection, 0098-9169. **Continued by** Computing and Communications Protection.
Desc: A resource of facts and ideas for solving computer security problems, with practical advice and guidance from professionals in security, data processing, communications, law and auditing.
Ind/Abst Comput. Lit. Index; Crim. Justice Period. Index.

LC HF5548 .D3   ISSN 0011-6858
DD 651.2605
CCC

NLM Z 699.A1 D225
DATA PROCESSING DIGEST. See Computers-Abstracting, Bibliographies and Statistics.

LC QA75.5 .A4a   ISSN 0192-3986
DD 353.9/798/0081
US

DATA PROCESSING IN ALASKA. **Main/Corp** Alaska. Dept. of Administration. Division of Data Processing. **Added/Corp** Alaska. Dept. of Administration. Division of Data Processing. Annual Report of Data Processing in the State of Alaska. Alaska. Dept. of Administration. Division of Data Processing. Consulting Services Section. **VFOAT** Annual Report of Data Processing in the State of Alaska. (1977)-. English. One time a year. Department of Administration / Juneau, Alaska, Pouch C, Juneau AK 99811.

    ISSN 1065-7177
DD 658
US
TITLE CHANGE
DATA PROCESSING MANAGER'S BULLETIN. See Business and Economics-Management.

LC QA75.5 .D365   ISSN 0374-289X
DD 001.64/04
GW
CODEN DARPAT
DATA REPORT. [Data rep.]. Vol. 1 (March 1966)-. Periodical. German (summaries and/or abstracts in English). Irregular. DM12.00 single issue. Siemens Aktiengesellschaft / Hellabrunner, Hellabrunner Strasse 1, W-8000 Munich 90 Germany. Documents available from Ask*IEEE.
Ind/Abst Energy Res. Abstr. (Aug. 1976-); INSPEC (Sept. 1968-).

DD 025.5205   ISSN 0959-6429
UK
DATACOMMS BOOK, THE. [DataComms book]. (1986)-. Trade Publication. English. One time a year. $116.36. VNU Business Publications BV, 32-34 Broadwick Street, London W1A 2HG United Kingdom. **Tel** 011 44 171 4394242 ext. 2222, FAX 011 44 171 4379638, telex 23918 VNU G, 8952440.

    ISSN 0045-9704
US
CEASED
DATAPRO 70. (DATAPRO 70; THE EDP BUYER'S BIBLE.). [Datapro 70]. Periodical. Datapro Research Corporation. **VAT** Datapro Seventy. (1975)-(19??). Periodical. English. Datapro Information Services Group, 600 Delran Parkway, Delran NJ 08075. **Tel** (609)764-0100, (800)328-2776, FAX (609)764-8953. **ED** Mary Heminway.
Desc: Compiles and digests information on mainframes, plug compatibles, mega-mainframes, peripherals, systems software, communications links, CAD/CAM systems and graphic systems.

    ISSN 0730-7497
US
CEASED
DATAPRO BANKNEWS. See Business and Economics-Computer Applications.

DD 001   ISSN 8756-6516
US
DATAPRO MANAGEMENT OF APPLICATIONS SOFTWARE. See Computers-Programs and Programming.

US
DATAPRO MANAGING INFORMATION TECHNOLOGY. **Added/Corp** Managing Information Technology. (1991)-. Periodical. English. Twelve times a year. $937.00. Datapro Information Services Group, 600 Delran Parkway, Delran NJ 08075. **Tel** (609)764-0100, (800)328-2776, FAX (609)764-8953.

    ISSN 0730-7500
US
DATAPRO MININEWS. INTERNATIONAL EDITION. (DATAPRO MININEWS.). [Datapro mininews, Int. ed.]. **Added/Corp** Datapro Research Corporation. **VFOAT** Mininews. (19??)-. Periodical. English (French and German). Twelve times a year. $130.00. Datapro Information Services Group, 600 Delran Parkway, Delran NJ 08075. **Tel** (609)764-0100, (800)328-2776, FAX (609)764-8953.

    ISSN 0730-7519
US
CEASED
DATAPRO NEWSCOM. INTERNATIONAL EDITION. (DATAPRO NEWSCOM.). [Datapro newscom, Int. ed.]. **Added/Corp** Datapro Research Corporation. (1972)-(19??). Periodical. English (French and German). Datapro Information Services Group, 600 Delran Parkway, Delran NJ 08075. **Tel** (609)764-0100, (800)328-2776, FAX (609)764-8953.

DD 004/.07/1171344   ISSN 0225-4034
CN
DCS NEWSLETTER. [DCS newsl. - Dep. Comput. Serv., Univ. Waterloo]. **Added/Corp** University of Waterloo. Dept. of Computing Services. (1981-1982)-. Newsletter. English. Twelve times a year. Users Services, Department of Computing Services, University of Waterloo, Waterloo Ontario N2L 3G1 Canada. **Tel** (519)885-1211. **Continues** University of Waterloo. Dept. of Computing Services. Newsletter - Department of Computing Services, University of Waterloo., 0841-7644.

    ISSN 0285-9394
DD 001.6
JA
CEASED
DETA TSUSHIN. [Deta Tsushin]. **VFOAT** Data Communication and Processing; Gekkan Deta Tsushin (Tokyo. 1969). (1969)-(19??). Periodical. Japanese. Joho Kenkyu Shuppan Kai Publ, Akasaka 9 1 7 Minato-ku, Tokyo 107 Japan. **Tel** 011 81 3 34983171. Documents available from Ask*IEEE.
Ind/Abst INSPEC (1986-).

    ISSN 1047-1693
DD 338
US
CCC
CODEN DDREEL
DIGITAL DIRECTIONS REPORT. (DIGITAL DIRECTIONS REPORT : THE FINANCIAL ADVISOR TO DEC USERS.). [Digit. dir. rep.]. (Oct. 1989)-. Academic Scholarly Publication. English. Twelve times a year. $525.00. Computer Economics Inc., 5841 Edison Place, Carlsbad CA 92008. **Tel** (800)326-8100, (619)438-8100, FAX (619)431-1126. **ED** Michael Erbschloe. Documents available from CASDDS.
Desc: Publication providing details on the financial ramifications of future DEC products. Delivered in a concisely written 8-page format, the Report gives you the critical information you need to control costs, develop cost-effective strategies and understand the impact of rapidly changing DEC technologies.
Ind/Abst Chem. Abstr. (1990).

LC HD9696.C63 U516313
DD 338.4./7004/02574
US
DIRECTORY OF TOP COMPUTER EXECUTIVES. **Added/Corp** Applied Computer Research (Firm). (Spring 1985)-. Directory. English. Two times a year. $285.00. Applied Computer Research Inc., 11242 North 19th Avenue, Phoenix AZ 85029. **Tel** (602)995-5929, FAX (602)995-0905. **(Subscription address:** Applied Computer Research, PO Box 82266, Phoenix AZ 85071. **Tel** (602)995-5929.**) Continues in part** Directory of Top Computer Executives.

LC HD9696.C63 U5163133
DD 338.4/7004/02578
US
DIRECTORY OF TOP COMPUTER EXECUTIVES. **Added/Corp** Applied Computer Research (Firm). (Spring 1985)-. Directory. English. Two times a year. $285.00. Applied Computer Research Inc., 11242 North 19th Avenue, Phoenix AZ 85029. **Tel** (602)995-5929, FAX (602)995-0905. **(Subscription address:** Applied Computer Research, PO Box 82266, Phoenix AZ 85071. **Tel** (602)995-5929.**) Continues in part** Directory of Top Computer Executives.

LC QA76.9.D5 D493   ISSN 0178-2770
DD 004/.36/05
GW
CCC
CODEN DICOEB
Pr Rev.
DISTRIBUTED COMPUTING. [Distrib. comput.]. Vol. 1, No. 1 (Jan. 1986)-. Periodical. English. Four times a year. $250.00. Springer-Verlag GmbH & Company KG, Heidelberger Platz 3, D-14197 Berlin Germany. **Tel** 011 49 30 8207223, FAX 011 49 30 8214091, telex 183 319 SPBLN D. **(Subscription address:** Springer-Verlag New York Inc. / North America, PO Box 2485, Journal Fulfillment, Secaucus NJ 07096. **Tel** (201)348-4033, (800)777-4643, FAX (201)348-4505.**) ED** F B Schneider. available on microfilm and microfiche from University Microfilms International (UMI). Documents available from Article Express International, The Genuine Article, Ask*IEEE.
Desc: Provides a forum for original and significant contributions in the field of distributed computing.
Ind/Abst CompuMath Cit. Index [Full Cov.]; Comput. Abstr.; Comput. Rev.; Curr. Cit.; Curr. Contents Eng. Comput. Technol.; Eng. Index Annu.; Inf. Sci. Abstr.; INSPEC (Jan. 1986-); Math. Rev.; Res. Alert [Full Cov.]; SCISEARCH; Zentralbl. Math. Ihre Grenzgeb.

LC QA76.9.D5 D62   ISSN 0967-1846
DD 004/.36/05
UK
CODEN DSENEK
●**DISTRIBUTED SYSTEMS ENGINEERING : A JOINT PUBLICATION OF THE BRITISH COMPUTER SOCIETY, THE INSTITUTION OF ELECTRICAL ENGINEERS, AND INSTITUTE OF PHYSICS PUBLISHING.** **Added/Corp** British Computer Society. Institution of Electrical Engineers

Institute of Physics Publishing. Vol. 1, No. 1 (Sept. 1993)-. Periodical. English. Four times a year. $204.00. Institute of Physics, Techno House, Redcliffe Way, Bristol BS1 6NX United Kingdom. **Tel** 011 44 117 9297481, FAX 011 44 117 9294318, telex 449149 INSTP G. **(Subscription address:** American Institute of Physics, 500 Sunnyside Boulevard, Publishing Sales, Woodbury NY 11797. **Tel** (516)576-2200.)

LC HF5738 .D638 **ISSN** 1079-5928
DD 651.5/8/05 US

●**DOCUMENT MANAGEMENT (1994).** (DOCUMENT MANAGEMENT.). [Doc. manag.]. Vol. 4, Issue 3 (May/June 1994)-. Periodical. English. Six times a year. $30.00. Pinnacle Peak Publishing Ltd., 8711 East Pinnacle Peak Road #249, Scottsdale AZ 85255-9978. **Tel** (602)224-9777, FAX (602)585-7417. ***Continues*** *Document Management & Windows Imaging, 1071-8567.*

LC HF5738 .D63 **ISSN** 1071-8567
DD 651.5/8/05 US
TITLE CHANGE

DOCUMENT MANAGEMENT & WINDOWS IMAGING. [Doc. manag. windows imaging]. **VFOAT** Document Management and Windows Imaging; Document Management. Vol. 2, Issue 5 (Sept./Oct. 1992)-(199?). Periodical. English. Pinnacle Peak Publishing Ltd., 8711 East Pinnacle Peak Road #249, Scottsdale AZ 85255-9978. **Tel** (602)224-9777, FAX (602)585-7417. ***Continues*** *Document Management, 1057-0365.* ***Continued by*** *Document Management.*

ISSN 0890-4316
DD 658 US
TITLE CHANGE

DP BUDGET. (DP BUDGET : THE PLANNING ASSISTANT FOR MIS DIRECTORS.). [DP budg.]. **Added/Corp** Computer Economics, Inc. Vol. 5, No. 2 (Feb. 1986)-Vol. 13, No. 4 (Apr. 1994). Periodical. English. Computer Economics Inc., 5841 Edison Place, Carlsbad CA 92008. **Tel** (800)326-8100, (619)438-8100, FAX (619)431-1126. **ED** Eva Young. ***Continues*** *Computer Executive Letter, 0739-2265.* ***Continued by*** *IS Budget, 1076-2620.*
Desc: Provides analyses of DP expenses, salaries of DP personnel, software, equipment and communications cost comparisons and focuses of increasing productivity and improving the return of your DP investment.

LC Discard **ISSN** 0730-6806
US

DP DIRECTORY. [DP dir.]. **VFOAT** D.P. Directory. **VAT** Data Processing Directory. (19??)-. Directory. English. Twelve times a year. $48.00. DP Directory, PO Box 38, Glastonbury CT 06025.
Desc: Publishing of tables of contents of dozens of other data processing magazines.

ISSN 0711-7884
DD 001.64/05 CN
CEASED

DP MARKET FACTS. [DP mark. facts]. **VFOAT** Market Facts. **VAT** Data Processing Market Facts. Vol. 1, No. 1 (Mar. 25, 1982)-(1993). Periodical. English. DP Market Facts, Suite 105/208 Evans Avenue, Toronto Ontario M8Z 1J7 Canada. **Tel** (416)622-5452. **ED** Brett Graham. **Circ:** 150 (ctrl).
Desc: Data processing, industry news, products, people, corporate profiles, emphasis on Canadian companies, current information and exclusivity are key features.

LC Z7164.C81 E34 H5548.33 **ISSN** 1045-5698
DD 016.004 US
SUSPENDED

EDI (DALLAS, TEX.). (EDI.). [EDI]. **VFOAT** Electrical Design and Installation. **VAT** Electronic Data Interchange. (1986)- Suspended Dec. 1991. English. Twelve times a year. $48.00 US; $58.00 Canada and Mexico; $60.00 other. EDI, PO Box 1506, 452 Hudson Terrace, Englewood Cliffs NJ 07632. **Tel** (201)568-2930, FAX (201)568-2988. **Ad Acc.** ctrl circ.

LC HF5548.33 .E35 **ISSN** 1055-0399
DD 658/.05 US
Pr Rev.

EDI WORLD. [EDI world]. **VAT** Electronic Data Interchange World. Vol. 1, No. 1 (Jan. 1991)-. Periodical. English. Twelve times a year. $29.95. EDI World Inc, 2021 Coolidge Street, Hollywood FL 33020-2400. **Tel** (305)925-5900, FAX (305)925-7533. **ED** Michael S. McGarr. **Bk Rev. Ad Acc, Adv Mgr:** R. Sessa. **Circ:** 42,000 (ctrl).
Desc: Written for corporate decision makers, covering evolving information technologies with comprehensive feature articles, tutorials, and case studies written by leading industry experts. Cross industry editorial content covers topics ranging from Electronic Data Interchange implementation to workflow automation and automatic data collection. Other topics include Business Process Re-engineering, Financial EDI and the development of ANSI X12 and EDIFACT standards.

LC HF5548.35 .E36 **ISSN** 0885-0445
DD 657 US
CCC
CODEN EAJOEZ
TITLE CHANGE

EDP AUDITOR JOURNAL, THE. [EDP audit. j.]. **Added/Corp** EDP Auditors Foundation. **VFOAT** EDP Auditor; EDP Journal. **VAT** Electronic Data Processing Auditor Journal. Vol. 4 (1989)-(1993). Periodical. English. EDP Auditors Association Inc, PO Box 74171, Chicago IL 60690. **Tel** (708)253-1545, FAX (708)253-1443. **ED** Michael Cangemi. **Bk Rev. Ad Acc, Adv Mgr:** M. Faddock. **Circ:** 12,000 (ctrl). Documents available from Ask*IEEE. ***Continues*** *EDP Auditor.* ***Continued by*** *IS Audit & Control Journal, 1076-4100.*
Desc: Addresses the entire control community, including computer security and quality assurance. Five technical articles and papers, editorials, book reviews and a 'current events' column that addresses information control issues and related fields are included in each issue.
Ind/Abst Account. Index Suppl. (1983-); Account. Tax Datab. (1974-); Curr. Cit.; Data Process. Dig. (?-?); INSPEC (1983-).

LC QA76 .E355 **ISSN** 0377-7154
DD 001.6/4/05 UA
CODEN ECJODE

EGYPTIAN COMPUTER JOURNAL, THE. [Egypt. comput. j.]. **Added/Corp** Jamiat al-Qahirah. Mahad al-Dirasat wa-al-Buhuth al-Ihsaiyah. Vol. 1 (June 1973)-. English. Two times a year. $15.00. Institute of Statistical Study Research, PO Box 1017, 5 Tharwat Street, Giza, Cairo Egypt. **Tel** 011 20 2 718355, 011 20 2 718496. Documents available from Ask*IEEE.
Ind/Abst INSPEC (June-Dec. 1979-); Math. Rev.

LC HF5601
DD 657 LV

EKONOMISKAS INFORMACIJAS APSTRADES MEHANIZACIJA. Main/Corp Petera Stuckas Latvijas Valsts Universitate. Ekonomiskas Informacijas Mehanizetas Apstrades Organizacijas Katedra. (19??)-. Latvian.
Desc: Information on electronic data processing, accounting, and punched card systems.

LC HD4966.D372 U633 **ISSN** 0193-7979
DD 331.2/81/001640973 US

ELECTRONIC DATA PROCESSING SALARY SURVEY. **See** Business and Economics-Labor.

LC QA75.5 .E55 **ISSN** 0204-3572
DD 001.64/05 UN
CCC
CODEN ELMODO

ELEKTRONNOE MODELIROVANIE. [Elektron. model.]. **Added/Corp** Akademiia Nauk SSSR. Otdelenie Fiziko-Tekhnicheskikh Problem Energetiki. Akademiia Nauk Ukrainskoi RSR. Viddilennia Fizyko-Tekhnichnykh Problem Energetyky. (Sept./Oct. 1979)-. Academic Scholarly Publication. Russian (summaries and/or abstracts in English). Six times a year. $109.95. Izdatelstvo Naukova Dumka / Ukrainian Academy of Sciences, Yu. A. Khramov, Dir., Ul. Repina 3, 252 601 Kiev Ukraine. **Tel** 011 7 44 4303441, 011 7 44 2254182, telex 131376. **(Subscription address:** East View Publications Inc., 3020 Harbor Lane North, Suite 110, Minneapolis MN 55447. **Tel** (800)477-1005, (612)550-0961, FAX (612)559-2931.) Documents available from Ask*IEEE, CASDDS.
Ind/Abst Chem. Abstr.; INSPEC (Jan./Feb. 1980-); Int. Aerosp. Abstr.; Math. Rev.

LC TK3 .E6 **ISSN** 0932-383X
DD 621 AU
CCC
CODEN EIEIEE

ELEKTROTECHNIK UND INFORMATIONSTECHNIK : E&I. **See** Engineering-Electrical Engineering.

LC Z699.5.C27 E86 **ISSN** 0834-3888
CN
Pr Rev.

ESPIAL CANADIAN DATA BASE DIRECTORY, THE. [Espial Can. data base dir.]. (1987)-. Directory. English (French). One time a year. 36.02Can$. Espial Productions Ltd., 85 Roe Avenue, Toronto Ontario M5M 2H6 Canada. **Tel** (416)485-8063. **ED** H Campbell. Index available. cum. index. **Ad Acc, Adv Mgr:** H. Cambell, **Tel** (416)485-8063. **Circ:** 1,500. available on an online database from SDM. ***Continues*** *Espial Data Base Directory, 0706-1781.*
Desc: A comprehensive listing of national and international databases containing references to Canadian topics; 356 databases analysed and ranked in terms of Canadian content.

ISSN 0251-4230
PO

ESTUDOS MATEMATICA E INFORMATICA, INSTITUTO GULBENKIAN DE CIENCIA. (ESTUDOS. MATEMATICA E INFORMATICA.). [Estud. mat. inform., Inst. Gulbenkian Cienc.]. **VFOAT** Matematica e Informatica. (1979)-. Monographic series. English (Portuguese). Price varies per volume.
Ind/Abst Math. Rev.; Zentralbl. Math. Ihre Grenzgeb.

ISSN 1180-3711
DD 338.4/7004/0971 CN

EVANS REPORT, THE. [Evans rep.]. **Added/Corp** Evans Research Corporation. Vol. 19 No. 1 (1990)-. Periodical. English. Irregular. 556.22Can$. Evans Research Corporation, 2005 Sheppard Avenue East, 4th Floor, Willowdale Ontario M2J 5B1 Canada. **Tel** (416)498-6664, (416)497-9562, FAX (416)498-7275. **ED** Charles Whaley. Documents available from Ask*IEEE. ***Continues*** *EDP In-Depth Reports, 0315-3819.*
Ind/Abst INSPEC (1990-).

ISSN 0892-4856
DD 005 US

GREGORY'S A-SERIES TECHNICAL JOURNAL. [Gregory's A-ser. tech. j.]. **VFOAT** A-Series Technical Journal; Gregory's A Series Technical Journal; A.A series technical journal. Vol. 0, No. 1 (Nov./Dec. 1986)-. Periodical. English. Ten times a year. $225.00. Gregory Publishing Company, 333 Cobalt Drive/Suite 107, Sunnyvale CA 94086. **Tel** (408)727-4660, FAX (408)720-1949. **ED** Donald Gregory. Index available (published separately). cum. index. **Circ:** 1,000.
Desc: Covers technical topics on A-series system software and related topics.

LC QA76 .H627 **ISSN** 0046-7847
DD 001.6/4/05 US
CODEN HNCJA3

HONEYWELL COMPUTER JOURNAL, THE. [Honeywell comput. j.]. Academic Scholarly Publication. English (summaries and/or abstracts in French, German, Italian and Spanish). Four times a year. $10.00. Honeywell Information Systems Inc, PO Box 6000, Phoenix AZ 85005. Documents available from Article Express International, CASDDS.
Ind/Abst Chem. Abstr.; Ei Page One; Eng. Index Annu.

LC QA75 **ISSN** 1188-522X
DD 004.16/09713/83 CN

HUM (OTTAWA). (HUM.). [Hum]. **VFOAT** Hum Magazine; Government Computer Magazine. (1991)-. Trade Publication. English. Eleven times a year. 34.95Can$ Canada; 89.95Can$ US and Mexico; 120.00 other. Hum Magazine, 557 Cambridge Street, Suite 202, Ottawa Ont K1S 4J4 Canada. **Tel** (613)237-4862, FAX (613)237-4232. **ED** Tim Lougheed (editor's phone: (613)746-7227). **Bk Rev**, (Qty: 4). **Ad Acc, Adv Mgr:** Lori Cunningham, **Tel** (613)237-4862. Full Page (B&W) 1590.00Can$. Full Page (Color) 2400.00Can$. **Circ:** 13,000 (ctrl).
Desc: Canada's national magazine for information technology in the public sector.

LC HF5548.2 .E15 **ISSN** 0896-3231
DD 651 US
TITLE CHANGE

I/S ANALYZER. [I/S anal.]. **Added/Corp** United Communications Group. **VFOAT** IS Analyzer. **VAT** Information Systems Analyzer. Vol. 25, No. 9 (Sept. 1987)-(1994). Periodical. English. United Communications Group, 11300 Rockville Pike, Suite 1100, Rockville MD 20852. **Tel** (301)816-8950 ext. 313, FAX (301)816-8945. Index available (bound in all issues). available on microfilm and microfiche from University Microfilms International (UMI). Documents available from UMI Article Clearinghouse, Ask*IEEE. ***Continues*** *EDP Analyzer, 0012-7523.* ***Continued by*** *I/S Analyzer Case Studies, 1080-1146.*
Desc: Offers advice and analysis on how to manage an information systems organization.
Ind/Abst ABI/INFORM Glob. Ed.; ABI/INFORM [Computer File] (Sept. 1987-); Acad. Search; Appl. Sci. Technol. Index (Sept. 1987-); Bus. Index (1988-); Bus. Period. Index (Sept. 1987-); Comput. Lit. Index; Curr. Cit.; Data Process. Dig.; Energy Res. Abstr. (Sept. 1987-); EP Collect.; Gen. BusinessFile (1988-); Gen. Period. Index (1988-); Homework Help.; INSPEC (Sept. 1987-); MasterFile FullTEXT 1000; MasterFile FullTEXT 350; MasterFile FullTEXT 650; MasterFile FullTEXT (July 1993-); OCLC; SCISEARCH; Telebase; Trade Ind. Index; World Publ. Monit. (Sept. 1987-).

LC HF5548.2 .E15 **ISSN** 1080-1146
DD 651 US

●**I/S ANALYZER CASE STUDIES.** [I/S anal. case stud.]. **Added/Corp** United Communications Group. **VFOAT** IS Analyzer Case Studies. Vol. 33, No. 3 (March 1994)-. Periodical. English. Twelve times a year. $325.00. United Communications Group, 11300 Rockville Pike, Suite 1100, Rockville MD 20852. **Tel** (301)816-8950 ext. 313, FAX (301)816-8945. ***Continues*** *I/S Analyzer, 0896-3231.*
Desc: Offers advice and analysis on how to manage an information systems organization.
Ind/Abst ABI/INFORM Glob. Ed.; ABI/INFORM [Computer File] (Sept. 1987-); Appl. Sci. Technol. Index (Sept. 1987-); Bus. Index (1988-); Bus. Period. Index (Sept. 1987-); Comput. Lit. Index; Data Process. Dig.; Energy Res. Abstr. (Sept. 1987-); Gen. BusinessFile (1988-); Gen. Period. Index (1988-); INSPEC (Sept. 1987-); SCISEARCH; Trade Ind. Index; World Publ. Monit. (Sept. 1987-).

LC HF5548.125 .C3 **ISSN** 1196-4715
DD 004/.05 CN
CODEN ITMGEX
TITLE CHANGE

I.T. MAGAZINE (TORONTO). (I.T. MAGAZINE.). **VFOAT** Information Technology Magazine; IT Magazine; I.T. Mag. (Tor.). Vol. 25, No. 1 (Jan. 1993)-Vol. 26, No. 2 (Feb. 1994). Periodical. English. Laurentian Media Inc, 501 Oakdale Road, Downsview Ontario M3N 1W7 Canada. **Tel** (416)746-7360, (800)565-4007, FAX (416)746-1421. ***Continues*** *Canadian Datasystems, 0008-3364.* ***Absorbed by*** *Info Canada (Downsview, Ont.), 1187-7081.*

LC QA76.9.A25 T73 **ISSN** 0892-399X
DD 004 US

●**I-WAYS : DIGEST OF THE GLOBAL INFORMATION INFRASTRUCTURE COMMISSION.** **See** Computers-Computer Networks.

LC TK7800 .I14 **ISSN** 0018-8646
DD 621.3072 US
CCC
CODEN IBMJAE

Pr Rev.
IBM JOURNAL OF RESEARCH AND DEVELOPMENT. **See** Engineering-Computer Applications.

LC TA168 .I5 **ISSN** 0018-8670
DD 620.7/05 US
CCC
CODEN IBMSA7

Pr Rev.
IBM SYSTEMS JOURNAL. [IBM syst. j.]. **Added/Corp** International Business Machines Corporation. **VFOAT** I.B.M. Systems Journal. **VAT** International Business Machines Systems Journal. Vol. 1 (Sept. 1962)-. Periodical. English. Four times a year (Feb., May, Aug., Nov.). $55.00. IBM Corporate Technical Publications, Thomas J. Watson Research Center, PO Box 218, Yorktown Heights NY 10598. **Tel** (914)945-3000, (914)241-4184, (914)742-5928. **ED** Gene F. Hoffnagle. cum. index. **Bk Rev. Circ:** 100,000. available on microfilm and microfiche from University Microfilms International (UMI); available on an online database (file 15/Full-Text) from DIALOG. Documents available from Article Express International, The Genuine Article, UMI Article Clearinghouse, Ask*IEEE, CASDDS.
Desc: Published for the software and systems professional community worldwide.
Ind/Abst ABI/INFORM Glob. Ed.; ABI/INFORM [Computer File] (May 1979-); ACM Guide Comput. Lit.; Acoust. Abstr.; Appl. Sci. Technol. Index; Bioeng. Abstr.; BMT Abstr. (?-199?); Chem. Abstr.; CompuMath Cit. Index [Full Cov.]; Comput. Abstr.; Comput. Database; Comput. Lit. Index; Comput. Rev.; Curr. Cit.; Curr. Contents Eng. Comput. Technol.; Ei Page One; Electron. Pub. Abstr.; Electron. Commun. Abstr. J.; EMBASE; Energy Res. Abstr.; Eng. Index Annu.; EP Collect.; Ergon. Abstr.; Gen. BusinessFile (1992-); Homework Help.; Inf. Sci. Abstr. (?-?); INIS Atomindex [Micro.]; INSPEC (1968-); Int. Aerosp. Abstr.; MasterFile FullTEXT 1000; MasterFile FullTEXT 350; MasterFile FullTEXT 650; MasterFile FullTEXT (Jan. 1995-); Math. Rev.; Nucl. Sci. Abstr.; OCLC; Oper. Res./Manage. Sci.; Qual. Control Appl. Stat.; Res. Alert [Full Cov.]; Sci. Cit. Index; SCISEARCH; Ship Abstr.; Soc. Plann. Policy Dev. Abstr.; Soc. Sci. Cit. Index [Select. Cov.]; Telebase; UMI ABI/Inform--Bus. Period. Ondisc (1987-) [Full Txt.]; World Publ. Monit.; Zentralbl. Math. Ihre Grenzgeb.

ISSN 0334-6056
IS
UDC 681.3
ICA INFORMATION. **See** Public Administration-Computer Applications.

ISSN 0969-823X
DD 658.05 UK
IDPM JOURNAL. [IDPM j.]. **VFOAT** Institute of Data Processing Management Journal. (1992)-. Periodical. English. Four times a year (Feb., Apr., Aug., Nov.). £76.00. IDPM Publications Ltd., IDPM House, Edington Way, Ruxley, Sidcup Kent DA14 5HR United Kingdom. **Tel** 011 44 181 3080747. ***Continues*** *Information Management Journal, 0265-5306.*
Ind/Abst Curr. Cit.

LC QA76.17 .A56 **ISSN** 1058-6180
DD 001.6/09 US
CCC
CODEN IAHCEX

IEEE ANNALS OF THE HISTORY OF COMPUTING. [IEEE ann. hist. comput.]. **Added/Corp** IEEE Computer Society. Institute of Electrical and Electronics Engineers. **VFOAT** Annals of the History of Computing. **VAT** Institute of Electrical and Electronics Engineers Annals of the History of Computing. Vol. 14, No. 1 (1992)-. Periodical. English. Four times a year. $160.00. IEEE / Institute of Electrical and Electronics Engineers Inc., 345 East 47th Street, New York NY 10017-2394. **Tel** (908)981-1393, FAX (908)981-9667. **(Subscription address:** IEEE / Institute of Electrical and Electronics Engineers, 445 Hoes Lane, PO Box 1331, Piscataway NJ 08855-1331. **Tel** (800)701-IEEE, (908)981-0060, FAX (908)981-9667, telex 833233.**)** available on microfiche. Documents available from Article Express International, The Genuine Article. ***Continues*** *Annals of the History of Computing, 0164-1239.*
Desc: Serves as a of computing and the impact of computing on society.
Ind/Abst Acad. Search; Am. Hist. Life (1979-); CompuMath Cit. Index [Full Cov.]; Comput. Lit. Index; Curr. Cit.; Curr. Contents Eng. Comput. Technol.; Ei Page One; Eng. Index Annu.; EP Collect.; Homework Help.; INFO-SOUTH Abstr.; Mag. Search; MasterFile FullTEXT 1000; MasterFile FullTEXT 350; MasterFile FullTEXT 650; MasterFile FullTEXT (July 1993-); Math. Rev.; OCLC; Res. Alert [Full Cov.]; SCISEARCH; Soc. Sci. Cit. Index [Select. Cov.]; Telebase.

ISSN 1063-6552
US
CCC

●**IEEE PARALLEL & DISTRIBUTED TECHNOLOGY : SYSTEMS & APPLICATIONS.** **See** Computers-Computer Systems.

LC QA76.58 .I44 **ISSN** 1045-9219
DD 004/.35/05 US
CCC
CODEN ITDSEO

IEEE TRANSACTIONS ON PARALLEL AND DISTRIBUTED SYSTEMS. (IEEE TRANSACTIONS ON PARALLEL AND DISTRIBUTED SYSTEMS : A PUBLICATION OF THE IEEE COMPUTER SOCIETY.). [IEEE trans. parallel distrib. syst.]. **Added/Corp** Institute of Electrical and Electronics Engineers. IEEE Computer Society. **VFOAT** Parallel and Distributed Systems. **VAT** Institute of Electrical and Electronics Engineering Transactions on Parallel and Distributed Systems. Vol. 1, No. 1 (Jan. 1990)-. Periodical. English. Twelve times a year. $480.00. IEEE / Institute of Electrical and Electronics Engineers Inc., 345 East 47th Street, New York NY 10017-2394. **Tel** (908)981-1393, FAX (908)981-9667. **(Subscription address:** IEEE / Institute of Electrical and Electronics Engineers, 445 Hoes Lane, PO Box 1331, Piscataway NJ 08855-1331. **Tel** (800)701-IEEE, (908)981-0060, FAX (908)981-9667, telex 833233.**) ED** Gail S. Ferenc. Index available. available on microfiche. Documents available from Article Express International, The Genuine Article, Ask*IEEE.
Desc: Devoted to hardware/software issues and applications studies specifically for parallel and/or distributed computing systems. Covers architecture, software, algorithms and applications for parallel and distributed systems. Typical subjects include design, analysis, and implementation of multiple-processor systems, VLSI, languages and compilers, operating systems, databases, parallel models of computation, performance measurement, reliability and fault-tolerance issues.
Ind/Abst Appl. Sci. Technol. Index (1991-); CompuMath Cit. Index [Full Cov.]; Comput. Abstr.; Curr. Contents Eng. Comput. Technol.; Ei Page One; Eng. Index Annu.; Expand. Acad. Index (1992-); Index IEEE Publ.; INSPEC (Jan. 1990-); Int. Aerosp. Abstr.; Math. Rev.; Res. Alert [Full Cov.]; Sci. Cit. Index; SCISEARCH; Soc. Sci. Cit. Index [Select. Cov.]; Zentralbl. Math. Ihre Grenzgeb.

LC HF5736 .I453 **ISSN** 1060-894X
DD 651.5/3 US
IMAGINGWORLD (CAMDEN, ME.). (IMAGING WORLD.). [ImagingWorld]. **VFOAT** Imaging World. Vol. 1, Issue 1 (Jan. 1992)-. Periodical. English. Twelve times a year. $48.00. IW Publishing, 49 Bayview, Suite 200, Camden ME 04843. **Tel** (207)236-8524, FAX (207)236-8524. **ED** Bruce Taylor. Index Bound in First Issue. **Ad Acc, Adv Mgr Tel** (207)236-8524. **Circ:** 60,000 (ctrl).
Desc: A trade that features important news and information to the electronic imaging industry. Focus is on trends and analysis, new products, and case studies.

LC TR835 .I46a **ISSN** 0019-0012
DD 001.55/23/05 US
CODEN IMGCB7

IMC JOURNAL. [IMC j.]. **Added/Corp** International Micrographic Congress. International Information Management Congress. **VFOAT** I.M.C. Journal. **VAT** International Micrographic Congress Journal. (Fall 1967)-. Periodical. English. Six times a year (Jan., Mar., May, July, Sept., Nov.). $38.00. International Information Management Congress, 1650 38th Street, Suite 205W, Boulder CO 80301. **Tel** (303)440-7085, FAX (303)440-7234. **ED** Bill MacArthur. **Ad Acc, Adv Mgr:** Chris Lacy. **Circ:** 30,000. available on microfilm and microfiche from University Microfilms International (UMI). Documents available from Ask*IEEE, UMI Article Clearinghouse.
Desc: Application and technical articles on document-based information systems.
Ind/Abst ABI/INFORM Glob. Ed.; ABI/INFORM [Computer File] (Fall 1976-); ACM Guide Comput. Lit.; Anbar Account. Finan. Abstr. [Full Txt.]; Anbar Mark. Distr. Abstr. [Full Txt.]; Anbar Top Manage. Abstr. [Full Txt.]; Bus. Educ. Index; Comput. Lit. Index; Comput. Rev. (1979-); Curr. Cit.; Data Process. Dig.; Ei Page One; Inf. Instruc. Technol.; INSPEC (1979-); Int. Aerosp. Abstr.; Libr. Inf. Sci. Abstr.; Manage. Bibliogr. Rev.; Oper. Prod. Manage. Abstr. (Fall 1976-) [Full Txt.]; Person. Train. Abstr. (1979-) [Full Txt.]; Women Manage. Rev. (1979-) [Full Txt.].

LC Q183.9 .I49 **ISSN** 0899-8248
DD 500/.28/5 US
CCC
CODEN ICOEEK
CEASED

IMPACT OF COMPUTING IN SCIENCE AND ENGINEERING. **See** Science and Technology-Computer Applications.

LC HD28 .I4424 **ISSN** 0263-5577
DD 650/.05 UK
CCC
CODEN IMDSD8

INDUSTRIAL MANAGEMENT & DATA SYSTEMS. **See** Business and Economics-Management.

ISSN 0226-6598
DD 001.64/06/0714 CN
INFO-QUEBEC. (L'INFO-QUEBEC.). [Info-Que.]. **Added/Corp** Association Canadienne des Cadres en Informatique. Section de Quebec. Association Canadienne de l'Informatique. Section de Qu,ebec. F,ed,eration de l'informatique du Qu,ebec. (1976)-. Periodical. French. Nine times a year. 40.01Can$. Federation de l'Informatique, 1155 boulevard Rene-Levesque Ouest, 21e Etage, Montreal Quebec H3B 2J9 Canada. **Tel** (514)395-8689, FAX (514)395-9007. **Ad Acc**. ctrl circ.

ISSN 0260-7247
DD 338.470016405 UK
CEASED

INFOMATICS. [Infomatics]. (1980)-(19??). Periodical. English. VNU Business Publications BV, 32-34 Broadwick Street, London W1A 2HG United Kingdom. **Tel** 011 44 171 4394242 ext. 2222, FAX 011 44 171 4379638, telex 23918 VNU G, 8952440.
Ind/Abst Curr. Cit.

ISSN 0315-5986
CN
CCC
CODEN INFRCL

Pr Rev.
INFOR. INFORMATION SYSTEMS AND OPERATIONAL RESEARCH. (INFOR.). [INFOR, Inf. syst. oper. res.]. **Added/Corp** Canadian Information Processing Society. Canadian Operational Research Society. **VFOAT** Canadian Journal of Operational Research and Information Processing; Journal Canadien de Recherche Operationnelle et d'Informatique. **VAT** Information Systems and Operational Research; Systemes d'Information et Recherche Operationnelle. Vol. 9, (March 1971)-. Periodical. English (French; summaries and/or abstracts in French and English). Four times a year (Mar., June, Sep., Dec.). 80.00Can$. University of Toronto Press, 5201 Dufferin Street, Downsview Ontario M3H 5T8 Canada. **Tel** (416)667-7781, (416)667-7810, FAX (416)667-7881. **ED** Dr. David Wright. **Circ:** 540 (ctrl). available on microfilm and microfiche from University Microfilms International (UMI). Documents available from Article Express International, The Genuine Article, UMI Article Clearinghouse, Ask*IEEE. ***Continues*** *Canadian Operational Research Society. C O R S Journal.*
Desc: Publishes theoretical and applied papers in operations research (management science) and in information systems. Papers are selected from submissions from authors around the world on the basis of the contribution to knowledge and the anticipated interest in our readership.
Ind/Abst ABI/INFORM Glob. Ed.; ABI/INFORM [Computer File] (Feb. 1988-); Bioeng. Abstr.; Comput. Lit. Index; Curr. Cit.; Curr. Contents Eng. Comput. Technol.; Ei Page One; Eng. Index Annu.; Inf. Sci. Abstr. (?-?); INSPEC (March 1971-); Int. Abstr. Oper. Res. [Full Cov.]; Int. Aerosp. Abstr.; Math. Rev.; Oper. Res./Manage. Sci.; Qual. Control Appl. Stat.; Res. Alert [Select. Cov.]; SCISEARCH.

LC QA76 .I427
DD 004 IT
INFORMATICA 70 [I.E. SETTANTA]. (Oct.1972)-. Italian. Six times a year. L54500. Editrice IL Crogiolo SRL, Via Valdolenga 117, 15046 South Salvator Monf AL Italy. **Tel** 011 39 131 239450.

LC QA75.5 .I53 **ISSN** 0390-2439
DD 029.7/05 IT
INFORMATICA & [I.E. E] DOCUMENTAZIONE. [Inform. doc.]. **Added/Corp** Inforav (Organization). Vol. 1 (March 1974)-. Periodical. Italian (summaries and/or abstracts in English and French). Four times a year. L102190. Infor Av, Ple Clodio 14, 00195 Rome Italy. **Tel** 011 39 6 39725631, FAX 011 39 6 39725633. Index available. **Bk Rev. Ad Acc. Circ:** 2,000 (ctrl).
Desc: Presents new applications of computer science.
Ind/Abst Comput. Rev.; Libr. Inf. Sci. Abstr.; Libr. Lit.

ISSN 0716-0658
CL

UDC 681.3
Pr Rev.
INFORMATICA. REVISTA DE COMPUTACION Y SISTEMAS. See Computers-Computer Systems.

LC QA75.5 .I5 **ISSN** 0170-6012
DD 001.64/05 GW
CCC

INFORMATIK-SPEKTRUM. (INFORMATIK-SPEKTRUM : ORGAN DER GESELLSCHAFT FUER INFORMATIK E.V.). [Inform.-Spektrum]. **Added/Corp** Gesellschaft fuer Informatik. (Aug. 1978)-. Periodical. German (summaries and/or abstracts in English). Six times a year. DM348.00. Springer-Verlag GmbH & Company KG, Heidelberger Platz 3, D-14197 Berlin Germany. **Tel** 011 49 30 8207223, FAX 011 49 30 8214091, telex 183 319 SPBLN D. **(Subscription address:** Springer-Verlag New York Inc. / North America, PO Box 2485, Journal Fulfillment, Secaucus NJ 07096. **Tel** (201)348-4033, (800)777-4643, FAX (201)348-4505.) **ED** W Brauer. **Bk Rev.** available on microfilm from University Microfilms International (UMI). Documents available from Ask*IEEE.
Desc: Offers current, practical and applicable information on technological and scientific advances from all fields of information science through survey articles, new project reports and future trends. Of interest to the informed user as well as the computer specialist.
Ind/Abst Comput. Rev.; Curr. Cit.; Energy Res. Abstr. (Dec. 1979-); INSPEC (1986-); Zentralbl. Math. Ihre Grenzgeb.

LC HD28 .I447 **ISSN** 0378-7206
DD 658/.05/405 NE
CCC
CODEN IMANDC

Pr Rev.
INFORMATION & MANAGEMENT. See Computers-Data Base Management.

LC HF5548.2 .D3 **ISSN** 0950-5849
DD 004/.05 UK
CCC
CODEN ISOTE7

Pr Rev.
INFORMATION AND SOFTWARE TECHNOLOGY. [Inf. softw. technol.]. Vol. 29, No. 1 (Jan./Feb. 1987)-. Periodical. English. Twelve times a year. $500.00. Butterworth Heinemann Publishers, Linacre House Jordan Hill, Oxford OX2 8DP United Kingdom. **Tel** 011 44 1865 310366, FAX 011 44 1865 310898. **(Subscription address:** Elsevier Science Ltd. / Oxford Fulfillment Centre, PO Box 800, Kidlington OX5 1DX United Kingdom. **Tel** 011 44 865 843355.) **ED** Judith Murray. Index available. **Bk Rev. Ad Acc.** available on microfilm and microfiche from University Microfilms International (UMI); available on an online database from Elsevier Electronic Subscriptions (EES). Documents available from Article Express International, The Genuine Article, UMI Article Clearinghouse, Ask*IEEE. ***Continues** Data Processing (London, England), 0011-684X.*
Desc: Closes the gap between the theories of software engineering and the application of information technology within organizations. Covers the entire area of information processing, from state-of-the-art research, through software developments and implementation, to information systems management.
Ind/Abst ABI/INFORM Glob. Ed.; ABI/INFORM [Computer File] (June 1984-); Abstr. Hum. Comput. Interact.; ACM Guide Comput. Lit.; Anbar Account. Finan. Abstr. [Full Txt.]; Anbar Mark. Distr. Abstr. [Full Txt.]; Anbar Top Manage. Abstr. [Full Txt.]; Appl. Sci. Technol. Index (1987-); CompuMath Cit. Index [Full Cov.]; Comput. Lit. Index; Comput. Rev.; Curr. Cit.; Curr. Contents Eng. Comput. Technol.; Data Process. Dig.; Ei Page One; Eng. Index Annu.; Ergon. Abstr.; HILITES; Inf. Sci. Abstr. (?-?); INSPEC (1987-); Manage. Market. Abstr.; Manage. Bibliogr. Rev.; Oper. Prod. Manage. Abstr. [Full Txt.]; Person. Train. Abstr. [Full Txt.]; Res. Alert [Full Cov.]; SCISEARCH; Soc. Sci. Cit. Index [Select. Cov.]; Women Manage. Rev. [Full Txt.].

LC QA76 .I47 **ISSN** 0020-0190
DD 004 NE
CCC
CODEN IFPLAT

Pr Rev.
INFORMATION PROCESSING LETTERS. [Inf. process. lett.]. Vol. 1 (1971)-. Academic Scholarly Publication. English. Twenty-four times a year (4 vols.). $1146.00. Elsevier Science Publishers BV, PO Box 211, 1000 AE Amsterdam Netherlands. **Tel** 011 31 20 4853641, 011 31 20 4853642, FAX 011 31 20 4853598. available on microfilm and microfiche from University Microfilms International (UMI); available on an online database from Elsevier Electronic Subscriptions (EES). Documents available from Article Express International, The Genuine Article, UMI Article Clearinghouse, Ask*IEEE.
Desc: The aim of the journal is to allow rapid dissemination of interesting results in the field of information processing in the form of short concise papers.
Ind/Abst ABI/INFORM Glob. Ed.; ABI/INFORM [Computer File] (Feb. 1981-); ACM Guide Comput. Lit.; Bioeng. Abstr.; CompuMath Cit. Index [Full Cov.]; Comput. Abstr.; Comput. Rev.; Curr. Cit.; Curr. Contents Eng. Comput. Technol.; Ei Page One; Eng. Index Annu.; INSPEC (Feb. 1972-); Int. Abstr. Oper. Res. [Select. Cov.]; Math. Rev.; Pollut. Abstr. Indexes; Res. Alert [Full Cov.]; SCISEARCH; Soc. Sci. Cit. Index [Select. Cov.]; Zentralbl. Math. Ihre Grenzgeb.

LC QA76.27 .I534 **ISSN** 1047-7047
DD 658.4/038/011 US
Pr Rev.
INFORMATION SYSTEMS RESEARCH. [Inf. syst. res.]. **Added/Corp** Institute of Management Sciences. **VFOAT** ISR. Vol. 1, No. 1 (March 1990)-. Trade Publication. English. Four times a year. $105.00. Institute of Management Sciences, 290 Westminster Street, Providence RI 02903. **Tel** (401)274-2525, FAX (401)274-3189. **ED** John L. King. **Ad Acc, Adv Mgr:** Pamela Battis. **Circ:** 1800 (ctrl).
Desc: For advancing the understanding and practice of information systems in organizations through theoretical and empirical research.

LC QA76 .E53 **ISSN** 0944-2774
DD 004/.05 GW
CODEN ITINEY

●**INFORMATIONSTECHNIK UND TECHNISCHE INFORMATIK : IT + TI.** **Added/Corp** Gesellschaft fuer Informatik. Fachbereich 3--"Technische Informatik und Architektur von Rechensystemen." Gesellschaft fuer Informatik. Fachbereich 4--"Informationstechnik und Technische Nutzung der Informatik.". **VFOAT** IT + TI; IT und TI. Vol. 35, No. 1 (Feb. 1993)-. Periodical. German. Six times a year. $234.75. R Oldenbourg Verlag, Postfach 801360, D-81613 Munich Germany. **Tel** 011 49 89 450190, FAX 011 49 89 45019305. ***Continues** IT (Munich, Germany), 0179-9738.*
Ind/Abst Curr. Cit.

LC QA75.5 .I5344 **ISSN** 8750-6874
DD 004/.05 US
CCC
CODEN INFWE4

INFORMATIONWEEK (MANHASSET, N.Y.). (INFORMATIONWEEK.). **VFOAT** Information Week. Issue 001 (Jan. 14, 1985)-. Periodical. English. Fifty-two times a year. $63.95. CMP Publications Inc., One Jericho Plaza, Wing A, 2nd Floor, Jericho NY 11753. **Tel** (516)733-6700. **(Subscription address:** CMP Publications, Inc. / Illinois, PO Box 5920, Department 100, Carol Stream IL 60197-5920. **) ED** Dennis Eskow. **Bk Rev. Ad Acc. Circ:** 141,385 (ctrl). Documents available from Ask*IEEE. ***Continues** Information Systems News, 0199-0691.*
Desc: Written exclusively for information managers who are increasingly involved in computer, communications and corporate planning.
Ind/Abst Bus. Source Plus; Comput. Bus. (19??-); Comput. Database; Comput. Ind. Update (1986-); Comput. Lit. Index; EP Collect.; F&S Index Plus Text, Int. [Full Txt.] [Select. Cov.]; Graph. Arts Bull. Inst. Pap. Sci. Technol. (Jan. 1989); Homework Help.; INSPEC (July 1986-); MasterFile FullTEXT 1000; MasterFile FullTEXT 350; MasterFile FullTEXT 650; MasterFile FullTEXT; Microcomput. Abstr. (Jan. 1985-); OCLC; PROMT [Full Txt.]; Telebase; Trade Ind. Index.

LC QA75.5 .I537 **ISSN** 0750-1080
DD 001.64/05 FR
INFORMATIQUE PROFESSIONNELLE, L'. [Inform. prof.]. No. 1 (Mar. 1982)-. French. Ten times a year. $546.80. Bouhot & Le Gendre Publishers, 75 Bis rue de Bellevue, F 92100 Boulogne France. **Tel** 011 33 1 46040708. **(Subscription address:** Centrale des Revues, 11 rue Gossin, 92543 Montrouge Cedex France. **Tel** 011 33 1 46565266.) cum. index. **Bk Rev. Circ:** 2,500.
Ind/Abst Repere (1983-).

ISSN 0706-1773
DD 001.64/05 CN
INFORMATIQUE QUEBEC. [Inform. Que.]. Vol. 1 (Oct. 1979)-. Periodical. French. Twelve times a year. 11.61Can$. Les Publications Informatique, Quebec Ltee 254 Av, Bloomfield Outremont, Quebec H2V 3R4. **Tel** (514)270-5481. **Ad Acc. Circ:** 37,000.
Desc: Data and word processing new products/communications.

LC QC53 .I58 **ISSN** 0889-8308
DD 530/.7 US
CCC
NLM W1; IN652F **CODEN** IICOEW
Pr Rev. **TITLE CHANGE**
INTELLIGENT INSTRUMENTS & COMPUTERS. See Computers-Automation.

ISSN 0279-2664
DD 004 US
INTERACT (LOS ALTOS, CALIF.). (INTERACT.). [Interact]. **Added/Corp** HP 3000 International User's Group (U.S.) Interex (Organization). **VFOAT** Interact Magazine. Vol. 1, Issue 1 (June/July 1981)-. Periodical. English. Twelve times a year. $49.50. Interex, PO Box 3439, Sunnyvale CA 94088. **Tel** (408)747-0227, FAX (408)736-2156, telex 4971527.
Ind/Abst Abstr. Hum. Comput. Interact.

LC QA76.27 .I56 **ISSN** 0163-6626
DD 001.64/07/1 US
CODEN INFCDB
CEASED

INTERFACE. [Interface]. Vol. 1 (Winter 1979)-(1994). Periodical. English. Mitchell Publishing, 55 Francisco Street, Suite 200, San Francisco CA 94133. **Tel** (415)433-2821. **ED** Erika Berg and John Ambrose (phone: (408)724-0195). **Bk Rev. Ad Acc, Adv Mgr:** Judith Hug, **Tel** (408)724-0915. **Circ:** 2,000. Documents available from Ask*IEEE.
Ind/Abst Abstr. Hum. Comput. Interact.; Comput. Lit. Index; Contents Pages Educ.; HILITES; INSPEC (Winter 1979-).

LC QA76.5 .I563 **ISSN** 0129-0533
DD 004.1/1/05 SI
CCC
CODEN IHSCEZ

INTERNATIONAL JOURNAL OF HIGH SPEED COMPUTING. VFOAT Journal of High Speed Computing. Vol. 1, No. 1 (May 1989)-. Periodical. English. Four times a year. $319.00. World Scientific Publishing Company, PO Box 128, Farrer Road, Singapore 9128 Singapore. **Tel** 011 65 3825663, FAX 011 65 3825919, telex RS 28561 WSPC. **(Subscription address:** World Scientific Publishing Company, Inc., 1060 Main Street, Suite 1 B, River Edge NJ 07661. **Tel** (800)227-7562, (201)487-9655.) **ED** W. Jalby, Y. Muraoka and H. Simon. Documents available from Ask*IEEE.
Desc: Information on supercomputers and electronic data processing.
Ind/Abst Comput. Abstr.; Curr. Cit.; INSPEC (1989-); Zentralbl. Math. Ihre Grenzgeb.

LC TA1630 .I55 **ISSN** 1047-8507
DD 621.36/7 UK
CODEN IJOCET
CEASED

INTERNATIONAL JOURNAL OF OPTICAL COMPUTING. [Int. j. opt. comput.]. **VFOAT** Optical Computing. Vol. 1, No. 1 (Oct. 1990)-(199?). Periodical. English. John Wiley & Sons Ltd., Baffins Lane, Chichester, West Sussex PO19 1UD United Kingdom. **Tel** 011 44 1243 779777, FAX 011 44 1243 776128 BTG:JWP001, telex 86290 WIBOOKG. **ED** J A Neff, G Lebreton, V Morozov, and Y Ichioka. available in microform. Documents available from Ask*IEEE.
Desc: Promotes an exchange of new ideas and results between scientists in academic, government and industrial research centers worldwide who are involved in optics for information processing / computing.
Ind/Abst ACM Guide Comput. Lit.; Comput. Rev.; INSPEC (Oct. 1990-?).

LC Q101 .I694a **ISSN** 0374-3365
DD 505 GW
CODEN IWKLAL

INTERNATIONALES WISSENSCHAFTLICHES KOLLOQUIUM : VORTRAEGE. See Science and Technology.

LC HF5548.35 .E36 **ISSN** 1076-4100
DD 657 US
●**IS AUDIT & CONTROL JOURNAL.** [IS audit control j.]. **Added/Corp** Information Systems Audit and Control Association. **VFOAT** IS Audit and Control Journal; Information Systems Audit and Control Journal. (1994)-. Periodical. English. Six times a year. $50.00. EDP Auditors Association Inc, PO Box 74171, Chicago IL 60690. **Tel** (708)253-1545, FAX (708)253-1443. **ED** Michael Cangemi. **Bk Rev. Ad Acc, Adv Mgr:** M. Faddock. **Circ:** 12,000 (ctrl). Documents available from Ask*IEEE. ***Continues** EDP Auditor Journal, 0885-0445.*
Desc: Addresses the entire control community, including computer security and quality assurance. Includes technical articles and papers, editorials, book reviews addressing information control issues and related fields.
Ind/Abst Account. Index Suppl.; Curr. Cit.; INSPEC.

ISSN 1076-2620
DD 658 US
CCC
●**IS BUDGET.** (IS BUDGET : THE PLANNING ASSISTANT FOR MIS EXECUTIVES.). [IS budg.]. **Added/Corp** Computer Economics, Inc. Vol. 13, No. 5 (May 1994)-. Periodical. English. Twelve times a year. $495.00. Computer Economics Inc., 5841 Edison Place, Carlsbad CA 92008. **Tel** (800)326-8100, (619)438-8100, FAX (619)431-1126. **ED** Eva Young. ***Continues** DP Budget, 0890-4316.*
Desc: Provides analyses of IS expenses, salaries of IS personnel, software, equipment and communications cost comparisons and focuses of increasing productivity and improving the return of your IS investment.

LC QA76 .G44A **ISSN** 0343-3110
DD 001.6/4 GW
JAHRESTAGUNG - GESELLSCHAFT FUER INFORMATIK E.V. (JAHRESTAGUNG.). **Main/Corp** Gesellschaft fur Informatik. **VFOAT** Proceedings. Multiple languages (English and German). One time a year. Springer-Verlag GmbH & Company KG, Heidelberger Platz 3, D-14197 Berlin Germany. **Tel** 011 49 30 8207223, FAX 011 49 30 8214091, telex 183 319 SPBLN D. **(Subscription address:** Springer-Verlag New

York Inc. / North America, PO Box 2485, Journal Fulfillment, Secaucus NJ 07096. **Tel** (201)348-4033, (800)777-4643, FAX (201)348-4505.)

LC HF5548.2 .N48758a **ISSN** 0910-6707
DD 338.4/7004/095205 JA
CODEN JCQUEL
Pr Rev. **TITLE CHANGE**

JAPAN COMPUTER QUARTERLY. [Jpn. comput. q.]. **Added/Corp** Nihon Joho Shori Kaihatsu Kyokai. No. 59 (1984)-(1993). Periodical. English. Japan Information Processing Development Center, 3 5 8 Shibakoen, Minato-ku Tokyo 105 Japan. **Tel** 011 81 3 3432 9384, FAX 011 81 3 3432 9389. **ED** Yuji Yamadori. **Circ:** 500. Documents available from Ask*IEEE. ***Continues*** *JIPDEC Report.* ***Continued by*** *JIPDEC Informatization Quarterly, 1340-3346.*
Ind/Abst INSPEC (1988-199?).

ISSN 1340-3346
JA
Pr Rev.

•JIPDEC INFORMATIZATION QUARTERLY. [JIPDEC informatization q.]. (1993)-. Periodical. English. Four times a year (Jan., Apr., Jul., Oct.). ¥13000. Japan Information Processing Development Center, 3 5 8 Shibakoen, Minato-ku Tokyo 105 Japan. **Tel** 011 81 3 3432 9384, FAX 011 81 3 3432 9389. **ED** Yuji Yamadori. **Circ:** 500. Documents available from Ask*IEEE. ***Continues*** *Japan Computer Quarterly, 0910-6707.*
Desc: A form of a magazine containing a number of articles dealing with specific trends and developments in the field of information processing in Japan.
Ind/Abst Curr. Cit.

LC QA75.5 .J6 **ISSN** 0387-5806
DD 004 JA
CCC

JOHO SHORI GAKKAI RONBUN SHI = TRANSACTIONS OF INFORMATION PROCESSING SOCIETY OF JAPAN. **Added/Corp** Joho Shori Gakkai (Japan). **VFOAT** Transactions of Information Processing Society of Japan. (19??)-. Periodical. Japanese (English). Twelve times a year. $176.00. Joho Shori Gakkai, (Information Processing Soc. of Japan), 4-2 Azabudai 2 Chome, Minatoku Tokyo 106 Japan. **(Subscription address:** Maruzen Company Ltd., PO Box 5050, Import & Export Department, Tokyo 100 31 Japan. **Tel** 011 81 3 32789224.) Documents available from Ask*IEEE.
Ind/Abst INSPEC (1979-).

LC QA76 .J627 **ISSN** 0388-5038
DD 004 JA

JOHO SHORI KENKYU. (19??)-. Japanese. One time a year. Central Research Institute of Electric, Information System Department, c/o Otemachi Building, 6-1 Otemachi 1-chome, Chiyoda-ku 100 Tokyo Japan. **Tel** +81-3-201-6601, FAX +81-3-287-2880, telex CRIEPI 528517. **ED** Information Division, CRIEPI. Index available. **Bk Rev. Circ:** 800 (ctrl). Documents available from Ask*IEEE.
Desc: Research reports in information and distributes to electric power companies.
Ind/Abst INSPEC (1985-).

ISSN 0887-4417
DD 004 US
CODEN JCISE9

JOURNAL OF COMPUTER INFORMATION SYSTEMS, THE. [J. comput. inf. syst.]. Vol. 26, No. 1 (Fall 1985)-. Periodical. English. Four times a year. $45.00. International Association Computer Information System, Oklahoma State University, 220 CBA GD Nord, Stillwater OK 74078. **Tel** (405)744-8632. **ED** J. Cretta Horn Nord (editor's address: Oklahoma State University, College of Business Administration, Stillwater, OK 74078). **Bk Rev. Ad Acc. Circ:** 1,100 (ctrl). available on microfilm from University Microfilms International (UMI). Documents available from Ask*IEEE. ***Continues*** *Journal of Data Education, 0022-0310.*
Ind/Abst Bus. Educ. Index; Curr. Cit.; INSPEC (1985-).

LC QA **ISSN** 1063-2239
DD 004 US
CODEN JEUCEZ
Pr Rev.

JOURNAL OF END USER COMPUTING. [J. end user comput.]. Vol. 4 No. 3 (Summer 1992)-. Periodical. English. Four times a year. $110.00. Idea Group Publishing, 4811 Jonestown Road, Suite 230, Harrisburg PA 17109. **Tel** (800)345-4332, (717)541-9150, FAX (717)541-9159. **ED** Mehdi Khosrowpour. Index available. cum. index. **Bk Rev**, (Qty: 4). **Ad Acc. Circ:** 500 (ctrl). Documents available from Ask*IEEE. ***Continues*** *Journal of Microcomputer Systems Management, 1043-6464.*
Desc: Focuses on providing coverage of research findings and expert advice on the development, utilization and management of end user computing in organizations.
Ind/Abst Curr. Cit.; INSPEC (1992-).

ISSN 0268-3962
UK
CCC
CODEN JINTEB

JOURNAL OF INFORMATION TECHNOLOGY : JIT. [JIT, J. inf. technol.]. **Added/Corp** Association for Information Technology (Great Britain). **VFOAT** JIT. Vol. 1, No. 1 (Feb. 1986)-. Periodical. English. Four times a year. $295.00. Chapman & Hall, 2-6 Boundary Row, London SE1 8HN United Kingdom. **Tel** 011 44 171 8650066, FAX 011 44 171 5229623, telex 290164 CHAPMA G. **ED** Anne Leeming, Leslie Willcocks. Documents available from Ask*IEEE.
Desc: Bridges the gap between those who research and develop new techniques and applications in the field of information technology, and those who apply this technology in an industrial or business environment.
Ind/Abst Abstr. Hum. Comput. Interact.; Contents Pages Manage.; Curr. Cit.; Educ. Technol. Abstr.; Ergon. Abstr.; HILITES; INSPEC (1987-); Libr. Inf. Sci. Abstr.; Soc. Sci. Cit. Index [Select. Cov.].

ISSN 0742-1222
DD 658 US
CCC
CODEN JMISEB

JOURNAL OF MANAGEMENT INFORMATION SYSTEMS. **See** Library and Information Sciences.

LC QA76.5 .J73 **ISSN** 0743-7315
DD 004/.35 US
CCC
CODEN JPDCER
Pr Rev.

JOURNAL OF PARALLEL AND DISTRIBUTED COMPUTING. [J. parallel distrib. comput.]. Vol. 1, No. 1 (Aug. 1984)-. Academic Scholarly Publication. English. Sixteen times a year. $548.00. Academic Press Inc., 6277 Sea Harbor Drive, Orlando FL 32887. **Tel** (800)543-9534, (407)345-4100, FAX (407)352-3445. **ED** Kai Hwang and Howard Jay Siegel. Documents available from Article Express International, The Genuine Article, Ask*IEEE.
Desc: Directed to researchers, engineers, educators, managers, programmers, and users of computers who have particular interests in parallel processing and/or distributed computing.
Ind/Abst ACM Guide Comput. Lit.; CompuMath Cit. Index [Full Cov.]; Comput. Rev.; Curr. Cit.; Curr. Contents Eng. Comput. Technol.; Ei Page One; Eng. Index Annu.; Inf. Sci. Abstr.; INSPEC (1985-); Int. Aerosp. Abstr.; Math. Rev.; Res. Alert [Full Cov.]; Sci. Cit. Index; SCISEARCH; Zentralbl. Math. Ihre Grenzgeb.

LC QA76 .S524
DD 001.6/4/05 SI

JOURNAL - SINGAPORE COMPUTER SOCIETY. **Main/Corp** Singapore Computer Society. Vol. 1 (Dec. 1971)-. English. Three times a year. Free to members. Singapore Computer Society, PO Box 2570, Singapore Singapore. **ED** Juzar Motiwalla. **Bk Rev. Ad Acc. Circ:** 2,000 (ctrl).
Desc: Articles on computer application and research.

LC QA74 .K4B
JA

KOHO - KEIO GIJUKU DAIGAKU JOHO KAGAKU KENKYUJO. **Main/Corp** Keio Gijuku Daigaku, Tokyo Joho Kagaku Kenkyujo. Japanese. One time a year. Free. Keio Gijuku Daigaku Joho Kagaku Kenkyuho, 1-1 Hiyoshi 4 Kohoku-ku 223, Yokohama Japan. **Tel** 44-61-2739. **Circ:** 200 (ctrl).
Desc: Report on the staff's activity and introduction to the institute.

LC QA75.5 .K67A
KO

KOMPYUTO CHONGNAM. **Main/Corp** Korea (Republic). Kwahak Kisulcho. Korean.

UK

MAINFRAME MARKET MONITOR. (19??)-. English. Four times a year. $1530.00. Xephon, 27-35 London Road, Newbury Berkshire RG13 1JL United Kingdom. **Tel** 011 44 1635 33823, FAX 011 44 1635 38345. **(Subscription address:** Xephon, 1301 West Highway, Suite 201 450, Lewisville TX 75067.)

LC QA76.9.P75 M36
FI

MAN-COMPUTER INTERFACE. **Added/Corp** Tampereen Yliopisto. Matemaattisten Tieteiden Laitos. **VFOAT** Man Computer Interface. (19??)-. Finnish (English; summaries and/or abstracts in English). One time a year. University of Tampere, PO Box 617, SF Sales Office, 33101 Tampere Finland. **ED** Prof Pertti Jarvinen (phone: 358 31 156777). Index available. **Circ:** 50 (ctrl).
Desc: Essays written by computer science students.

LC QA76.9.S88 S97
US

•MANAGING SYSTEM DEVELOPMENT. **Added/Corp** Applied Computer Research (Firm). Vol. 13, No. 1 (Jan. 1993)-. Newsletter. English. Twelve times a year. $198.50. Applied Computer Research Inc., 11242 North 19th Avenue, Phoenix AZ 85029. **Tel** (602)995-5929, FAX (602)995-0905. **(Subscription address:** Applied Computer Research, PO Box 82266, Phoenix AZ 85071. **Tel** (602)995-5929.) ***Continues*** *System Development, 0275-6617.*
Desc: For data processing professionals who need to know the latest findings in system development productivity.
Ind/Abst Curr. Cit.

LC QA76.5 .M522 **ISSN** 0141-9331
DD 004.2 UK
CCC
CODEN MIMID5
Pr Rev.

MICROPROCESSORS AND MICROSYSTEMS. [Microprocess. microsyst.]. Vol. 2, No. 4 (Aug. 1978)-. Periodical. English. Ten times a year. $479.00. Butterworth Heinemann Publishers, Linacre House Jordan Hill, Oxford OX2 8DP United Kingdom. **Tel** 011 44 1865 310366, FAX 011 44 1865 310898. **(Subscription address:** Elsevier Science Ltd. / Oxford Fulfillment Centre, PO Box 800, Kidlington OX5 1DX United Kingdom. **Tel** 011 44 865 843355.) **ED** Steve Hitchcock. Index available. cum. index. **Bk Rev. Ad Acc. Circ:** 2,000 (ctrl). available on microfilm and microfiche from University Microfilms International (UMI); available on an online database from Elsevier Electronic Subscriptions (EES). Documents available from Article Express International, The Genuine Article, Ask*IEEE. ***Continues*** *Microprocessors.*
Desc: Serves the professional computing and engineering community with practical papers on the design and implementation of microprocessor-based computer and control systems. Chip-level to systems-level architecture designs are covered; together with the application of associated software tools.
Ind/Abst ACM Guide Comput. Lit.; Bioeng. Abstr.; CompuMath Cit. Index [Full Cov.]; Comput. Abstr.; Comput. Database; Comput. Rev.; Curr. Cit.; Curr. Contents Eng. Comput. Technol.; Curr. Technol. Index; Ei Page One; Eng. Index Annu.; Inf. Sci. Abstr. (?-?); INSPEC (1979-); Pollut. Abstr. Indexes; Res. Alert [Full Cov.]; SCISEARCH; World Ceram. Abstr.

LC QA75.5 .N3a
JA

NAGOYA DAIGAKU OGATA KEISANKI SENTA NYUSU. COMPUTATION CENTER NEWS. **Main/Corp** Nagoya Daigaku. Ogata keisanki Senta. **Added/Corp** Nagoya Daigaku. Ogata Keisanki Senta. Computation Center News. **VFOAT** Computation Center News. (19??)-. Japanese. Nagoya Daigaku Ogata Keisanki, Senta Furocho Cigusa-ku, Nagoya 464 Japan.

LC QA75.5 .T63A **ISSN** 0385-2814
JA

NEMPO - TOKYO DAIGAKU OGATA KEISANKI SENTA. **Main/Corp** Tokyo Daigaku. Ogata Keisanki Senta. **VFOAT** Annual Report. (19??)-. Japanese. One time a year (published in Aug.). University of Tokyo Computer Centre, 11-16 Yayoi 2-chome Bunkyo-ku, Tokyo 113 Japan. **Tel** 011 3 812 2111, FAX 011 3 814 7279. **ED** Haruhisa Ishida (editor's phone: 011 81 3 3818 0287). **Circ:** 450 (ctrl).
Desc: Reports on the various activities and usage statistics of the Computer Centre during each academic year.

ISSN 0914-9317
DD 001.64 JA

NIKKEI DETAPURO EDP. **VFOAT** Nikkei Datapro EDP. (1981)-. Japanese. Irregular. Nihon Keizai Shimbun Inc., 9-5 Otemachi 1 Chome, Chiyoda-ku Tokyo 100 Japan. **Tel** 011 81 3 32700251, 011 81 3 52108502 (Nikkei Business Publications Inc.), FAX 011 81 3 52552661, 011 81 3 52108119 (Nikkei Business Publications Inc.). **ED** Hisashi Okamura.
Desc: Journal for electronic data processing.

LC P98 .N63 **ISSN** 1049-9865
DD 410/.28/5 US

NOTES ON COMPUTING (1987). **See** Linguistics-Computer Applications.

LC QA76 .O86 **ISSN** 0303-8351
DD 004 SZ
CODEN OUTPDV

OUTPUT. [Output]. **Added/Corp** Universite de Fribourg. Institut pour l'Automation et la Recherche Operationnelle. Schweizerische Vereinigung fuer Datenverarbeitung. (19??)-. Periodical. German (summaries and/or abstracts in French). Twelve times a year. $144.27. Fachpresse Goldach Hudson & Co, Abteilung Vertrieb 272, CH-9403 Goldach Switzerland. **Tel** 011 41 71 416611. **ED** Hans Wittwer, Hans Ulrich Beglinger, Peter Heuberger, Louis A. Venetz. Index available. **Bk Rev. Ad Acc. Circ:** 12,000 (ctrl). available on videocassette. Documents available from Ask*IEEE.
Desc: The Swiss magazine for information management and data processing.
Ind/Abst Curr. Cit.; Energy Res. Abstr. (March 1982-); INSPEC (Dec. 1978-).

Computers —Electronic Data Processing

DD 001.64   ISSN 0824-5894   CN
OVERVIEW - COMPUTING SERVICES. UNIVERSITY OF ALBERTA. (OVERVIEW.). (1983)-. Monographic series. English. Price varies per volume. Overview Computing Services, University of Alberta, Edmonton Alberta T6G 2H1 Canada.

DD 658   ISSN 1069-9228   US   TITLE CHANGE
PC MANAGER'S LETTER. See Business and Economics-Computer Applications.

LC QA76.9.E95 P47   ISSN 0166-5316
DD 001.64/028/7   NE   CCC   CODEN PEEVD9
Pr Rev.
PERFORMANCE EVALUATION. [Perform. eval.]. Vol. 1, No. 1 (Jan. 1981)-. Academic Scholarly Publication. English. Twelve times a year. $810.00. Elsevier Science Publishers BV, PO Box 211, 1000 AE Amsterdam Netherlands. **Tel** 011 31 20 4853641, 011 31 20 4853642, FAX 011 31 20 4853598. **ED** Martin Reiser and Werner Bux. Index available. **Ad Acc**, **Adv Mgr:** W Van Cattenburch, **Tel** 31 20 515 3220. available on microfilm and microfiche from University Microfilms International (UMI); available on an onl ne database from Elsevier Electronic Subscriptions (EES). Documents available from Article Express International, The Genuine Article, Ask*IEEE.
Desc: Serves system theorists, designers, implementors and analysts who are concerned with performance aspects of computer systems, compute· communications, and distributed systems.
Ind/Abst ACM Guide Comput. Lit.; Biceng. Abstr.; CompuMath Cit. Index [Full Cov.]; Comput. Abstr.; Comput. Lit. Index; Comput. Rev.; Curr. Cit.; Ei Page One; Eng. Index Annu. [Select. Cov.]; INSPEC (Jan. 1981-); Math. Rev.; Pollut. Abstr. Indexes; Res. Alert [Full Cov.]; SCISEARCH; Soc. Sci. Index [Select. Cov.]; Zentralbl. Math. Ihre Grenzgeb.

LC QA75.5 .P45   ISSN 0147-3077
DD 016.0016/4   US   SUSPENDED
PERIODICAL GUIDE FOR COMPUTERISTS. 1976-?. English. One time a year. $2.50 single issue. Applegate Computer Enterprises, 470 Slagel Creek Road, Grant Pass OR 97526.

DD 610   ISSN 0891-8163   US
NLM W1; PH761T
PHYSICIANS & COMPUTERS. See Medical Sciences-Computer Applications.

ISSN 0736-6817   US
POLICIES AND METHODOLOGIES. DATA PROCESSING SECURITY AND CONTROL. See Computers-Computer Crimes and Security.

LC QA75.5 .P715   RU
PRIKLADNAIA INFORMATIKA. Vol. 1 (1981)-. Russian. Izdatelstvo Finansy I Statistika, Ulitsa Chernyshvskogo 7 K-142, 101000 Moscow Russia.

UN   CODEN PUINFH
●**PROBLEMY UPRAVLENIIA I INFORMATIKI.** **Added/Corp** Instytut Kibernetyky Imeni V.M. Hlushkova AN Ukrainy. (1994)-. Periodical. Russian (summaries and/or abstracts in English and Ukrainian). Six times a year. Izdatelstvo Naukova Dumka / Ukrainian Academy of Sciences, Yu. A. Khramov, Dir., Ul. Repina 3, 252 601 Kiev Ukraine. **Tel** 011 7 44 4303441, 011 7 44 2254182, telex 131376. *Continues Avtomatika, 0572-2691.*

LC QA76.6 .C6296a   ISSN 0730-3157
DD 004.1   US   CCC
PROCEEDINGS - INTERNATIONAL COMPUTER SOFTWARE & APPLICATIONS CONFERENCE. (PROCEEDINGS, COMPSAC : THE IEEE COMPUTER SOCIETY'S ... INTERNATIONAL COMPUTER SOFTWARE & APPLICATIONS CONFERENCE.). [Proc. - Int. Comput. Softw. Appl. Conf.]. **Main/Conf** COMPSAC. **Added/Corp** IEEE Computer Society. **VFOAT** Computer Software and Applications; I.E.E.E. COMPSAC; Computer Software & Applications; IEEE COMPSAC. 1 (Nov. 8-11, 1977)-. Proceedings. English. One time a year. $80.00. IEEE Computer Society, 10662 Los Vaqueros Circle, PO Box 3014, Los Alamitos CA 90720-1264. **Tel** (714)821-8380, (800)272-6657, FAX (714)821-4641. **Bk Rev**. **Ad Acc**. ctrl circ.
Desc: Focuses on software techniques, methodologies and applications.
Ind/Abst Comput. Lit. Index; Curr. Cit.; Index IEEE Publ.

LC QA76.6 .N373a   ISSN 0270-5257
DD 004.16   US   CCC   CODEN PCSEDE
PROCEEDINGS - INTERNATIONAL CONFERENCE ON SOFTWARE ENGINEERING. [Proc. - Int. Conf. Softw. Eng.]. **Main/Conf** International Conference on Software Engineering. **Added/Corp** IEEE Computer Society. Association for Computing Machinery. United States. National Bureau of Standards. ACM Sigsoft. **VFOAT** Software Engineering. 2nd (1976)-. Proceedings. English. One time a year. $90.00. IEEE Computer Society, 10662 Los Vaqueros Circle, PO Box 3014, Los Alamitos CA 90720-1264. **Tel** (714)821-8380, (800)272-6657, FAX (714)821-4641. Documents available from Article Express International. *Continues Proceedings of the National Conference on Software Engineering.*
Ind/Abst Bioeng. Abstr.; Curr. Cit.; Ei Page One; Eng. Index Annu.; Index IEEE Publ.

LC QA76.9.D5 A34a   US
DD 004/.36
PROCEEDINGS OF THE ... ANNUAL ACM SYMPOSIUM ON PRINCIPLES OF DISTRIBUTED COMPUTING. **Main/Conf** ACM Symposium on Principles of Distributed Computing. **Added/Corp** ACM Special Interest Group for Automata and Computability Theory. ACM Special Interest Group in Operating Systems. 2nd (Aug. 17-19, 1983)-. English. One time a year. ACM / Association for Computing Machinery, 1515 Broadway, 17th Floor, New York NY 10036. **Tel** (212)869-7440, FAX (212)869-0481. *Continues ACM SIGACT-SIGOPS Symposium on Principles of Distributed Computing. ACM SIGACT-SIGOPS Symposium on Principles of Distributed Computing : [Papers].*
Ind/Abst Curr. Cit.

LC TA168 .H37a   US
DD 624
PROCEEDINGS OF THE ... HAWAII INTERNATIONAL CONFERENCE ON SYSTEM SCIENCES. See Computers-Computer Systems.

LC TS156.8 .I53   ISSN 1058-8655
DD 004   US   CODEN PINDET
PROCEEDINGS OF THE INDUSTRIAL COMPUTING CONFERENCE. See Industry and Production-Computer Applications.

LC QA76.6 .I548a   ISSN 0190-3918
DD 001/.6/4   US   CCC
PROCEEDINGS OF THE INTERNATIONAL CONFERENCE ON PARALLEL PROCESSING. [Proc. Int. Conf. Parallel Process.]. **Main/Conf** International Conference on Parallel Processing. **Added/Corp** Institute of Electrical and Electronics Engineers. Wayne State University. Dept. of Electrical and Computer Engineering. IEEE Computer Society. Association for Computing Machinery. Pennsylvania State University. **VFOAT** Parallel Processing. (1976)-. Proceedings. English. One time a year. $150.00. IEEE Computer Society, 10662 Los Vaqueros Circle, PO Box 3014, Los Alamitos CA 90720-1264. **Tel** (714)821-8380, (800)272-6657, FAX (714)821-4641. Documents available from Article Express International, Ask*IEEE. *Continues Sagamore Computer Conference. Proceedings of the ... Sagamore Computer Conference on Parallel Processing (1975).*
Ind/Abst Curr. Cit.; Ei Page One; Eng. Index Annu.; Index IEEE Publ.; INSPEC.

LC QA75.5 .S9574a   ISSN 1043-6871
DD 004/.01/5113   US
PROCEEDINGS / SYMPOSIUM ON LOGIC IN COMPUTER SCIENCE. [Proc. - Symp. Logic Comput. Sci.]. **Main/Conf** Symposium on Logic in Computer Science. **Added/Corp** IEEE Computer Society. Technical Committee on Mathematical Foundations of Computing. Association for Symbolic Logic. ACM Special Interest Group for Automata and Computability Theory. European Association for Theoretical Computer Science. **VFOAT** Logic in Computer Science. (June 16-18, 1986)-. Proceedings. English. One time a year. $90.00. IEEE Computer Society, 10662 Los Vaqueros Circle, PO Box 3014, Los Alamitos CA 90720-1264. **Tel** (714)821-8380, (800)272-6657, FAX (714)821-4641.
Ind/Abst Comput. Inf. Syst. Abstr. J. [Full Cov.]; Elect. Comm. Abstr.

US   CODEN SPADDB
PROCEEDINGS - SYMPOSIUM ON MACHINE PROCESSING OF REMOTELY SENSED DATA. **Main/Conf** Symposium on Machine Processing of Remotely Sensed Data. **VFOAT** Machine Processing of Remotely Sensed Data. 1- 1973-. Proceedings. English. One time a year. Lars, 345 East 47th Street, New York NY 10017. Documents available from Article Express International.
Ind/Abst Bioeng. Abstr.; Ei Page One; Eng. Index Annu.; GeoRef.

ISSN 0210-122X   SP
UDC 681
PROCESO DE DATOS. [Proceso datos]. (1967)-. Periodical. Spanish. Eleven times a year (monthly except Aug.). $25.00 (one-year), $44.00 (two-year) Spain; $38.00 (one-year), $70.00 (two-year) other. Prodace SA, Ferraz 11, Madrid 8 Spain.

LC QA1 .R455   ISSN 0988-3754
DD 511   CCC   CODEN RITAE4
Pr Rev.
RAIRO. INFORMATIQUE THEORIQUE ET APPLICATIONS. [Inform. theor. appl.]. **Added/Corp** Association Francaise Pour la Cybernetique Economique et Technique. Centre National de la Recherche Scientifique (France). **VFOAT** Informatique Theorique et Applications; Theoretical Informatics and Applications. (1986)-. Periodical. English (French and German; summaries and/or abstracts in English, German and French). Six times a year. $344.48. Dunod Gauthier Villars, 15 rue Gossin, 92543 Montrouge Cedex France. **Tel** 011 33 1 46565266, 011 33 1 40926527, FAX 011 33 1 40926597. **(Subscription address:** Centrale des Revues, 11 rue Gossin, 92543 Montrouge Cedex France. **Tel** 011 33 1 46565266.) Documents available from The Genuine Article, Ask*IEEE. *Continues RAIRO: Informatique Theorique, 0399-0540.*
Ind/Abst CompuMath Cit. Index; INSPEC (1986-); Math. Rev. (1986); Res. Alert; Soc. Sci. Cit. Index [Select. Cov.].

DD 000   CN
RAPPORT DE RECHERCHE (UNIVERSITE LAVAL. DEPARTEMENT D'INFORMATIQUE). (RAPPORT DE RECHERCHE.). **Added/Corp** Universite Laval. Departement d'Informatique. (1975)-. Monographic series. French. Price varies per volume. Dep d'Informatique Faculte des Sciences et de Genie, Universite Laval, Quebec Quebec G1K 7P4 Canada.

DD 000   CN
RAPPORT TECHNIQUE (UNIVERSITE LAVAL. DEPARTEMENT D'INFORMATIQUE). (RAPPORT TECHNIQUE / DEPARTEMENT D'INFORMATIQUE, FACULTE DES SCIENCES ET DE GENIE, UNIVERSITE LAVAL.). RT/7501-. Monographic series. English (French). Price varies per volume. Dep d'Informatique Faculte des Sciences et de Genie, Universite Laval, Quebec Quebec G1K 7P4 Canada.

FR
RAPPORTS DE RECHERCHE / INRIA. **Added/Corp** Institut National de Recherche en Informatique et en Automatique (France). No. 1 (1980)-. Monographic series. English. Price varies per volume. Institut National de Recherche en Informatique et en Automatique, SEDIS Diffusion, Domaine de Voluceau-Rocquencourt, BP 105, 78153 Le Chesnay Cedex France. **Tel** 011 33 1 39635627, FAX 011 33 1 39635228, telex 697033 F.
Ind/Abst Curr. Cit.

ISSN 0300-3450   GW   CODEN RTDVAQ   CEASED
RECHENTECHNIK DATENVERARBEITUNG. [Rechentech. Datenverarb.]. (1966)-(19??). German. Computerwoche Verlag GmbH, Rheinstrasse 28, 80803 Munich Germany. **Tel** 011 49 89 36086299, FAX 011 49 89 36086325, telex 5215250-COMW-D. Documents available from Ask*IEEE.
Desc: Intended for information experts in science and industry, and for all those benefitting from or using electronic data processing equipment, personal and workstation computers. Features modern examples of EDP problems and daily assignments.
Ind/Abst INSPEC (Jan. 1973-).

DD 001.64   ISSN 0822-997X   CN
REFERENCE - COMPUTING SERVICES. UNIVERSITY OF ALBERTA. (REFERENCE / COMPUTING SERVICES, THE UNIVERSITY OF ALBERTA.). [Ref. - Comput. Serv., Univ. Alta.]. Monographic series. English. Price varies per volume. Computing Services, 352 General Services Building, University of Alberta, Edmonton Alberta T6G 2H1 Canada. *Continues Reference Manual (University of Alberta. Computing Services), 0318-2142.*

LC HF5548.125 .R46   ISSN 1050-9186
DD 651.8/05   US   TITLE CHANGE
REMITTANCE AND DOCUMENT PROCESSING TODAY. [Remit. doc. process. today]. **Added/Corp** Recognition Technologies Users

Association. **VFOAT** Today. (198?)-(1993). Periodical. English. Association for Work Improvement, 185 Devonshire Street, Suite 770, Boston MA 02110. **Tel** (617)426-1167, FAX (617)426-8911. **ED** Franklin Cooper. Index available. cum. index. **Ad Acc.** ctrl circ. Documents available from Ask*IEEE. **Continues** *Recognition Technologies Today, 0883-5594.* **Continued by** *Work Process Improvement Today, 1073-2233.*
Desc: For data processing managers and professionals concerned with management and productivity of the automated information processing environment, specifically OCR image, and MICR technology applications in remittance and document processing.
Ind/Abst INSPEC (1987-).

LC QA76 .T54   ISSN 0564-8742
DD 651.8   JA
    CODEN TUCRA4

REPORT OF THE COMPUTER CENTRE, UNIVERSITY OF TOKYO.
[Rep. Comput. Cent. Univ. Tokyo]. Vol. 1, No. 1 (April/Sept. 1968)-. Japanese. Free (academic institutions). University of Tokyo Computer Centre, 11-16 Yayoi 2-chome Bunkyo-ku, Tokyo 113 Japan. **Tel** 011 3 812 2111, FAX 011 3 814 7279. **ED** Haruhisa Ishida. Index available. **Circ:** 500 (ctrl).
Desc: Reports on the R&D activities at the computer center. Detailed statistics of computer usage and some technical reports are included.
Ind/Abst Math. Rev.

LC QA76.5 .S398   ISSN 0743-6599
DD 004   US

SELECTED COMPUTER ARTICLES.
[Sel. comput. artic.]. (19??)-. English. US Department of the Defense National Defense University, 4th & P Streets SW, Fort McNair Building 62, Washington DC 20319. **Tel** (202)475-1966, FAX (202)287-9388.

LC QA76 .S555   ISSN 0097-5397
DD 001.6/4/05   US
    CCC
    CODEN SMJCAT
Pr Rev.
SIAM JOURNAL ON COMPUTING. See
Mathematics-Computer Applications.

LC QA76.27 .A79a   ISSN 0097-8418
DD 001.6/4/0711   US
    CODEN SIGSD3

SIGCSE BULLETIN.
[SIGCSE bull.]. **Added/Corp** Association for Computing Machinery. Special Interest Group on Computer Science Education. **VAT** Special Interest Group on Computer Science Education Bulletin. (1969)-. Bulletin. English. Four times a year. $30.00. ACM / Association for Computing Machinery, 1515 Broadway, 17th Floor, New York NY 10036. **Tel** (212)869-7440, FAX (212)869-0481. **(Subscription address:** Association for Computing Machinery, PO Box 12114, Church Street Station, New York NY 10249. **Tel** (212)626-0500.) Documents available from Article Express International, Ask*IEEE.
Ind/Abst ACM Guide Comput. Lit.; Bioeng. Abstr.; Comput. Rev.; Curr. Cit.; Ei Page One; Eng. Index Annu.; Ergon. Abstr.; INSPEC (Feb. 1980-).

LC QA75.5 .S53   ISSN 0736-6892
DD 004.05/6   US
    CODEN SSNRD3

SIGUCCS NEWSLETTER.
[SIGUCCS newsl.]. **Added/Corp** Association for Computing Machinery. Special Interest Group on University and College Computing Services. **VFOAT** S.I.G.U.C.C.S. Newsletter. **VAT** Special Interest Group on University and College Computing Services Newsletter. Vol. 11, No. 4 (Winter 1981)-. Newsletter. English. Four times a year (Mar., June, Sept., Dec.). $53.00. ACM / Association for Computing Machinery, 1515 Broadway, 17th Floor, New York NY 10036. **Tel** (212)869-7440, FAX (212)869-0481. **(Subscription address:** Association for Computing Machinery, PO Box 12114, Church Street Station, New York NY 10249. **Tel** (212)626-0500.) **ED** Alicia Towster. **Bk Rev.** ctrl circ. Documents available from Ask*IEEE. **Continues** *SIGUCC Newsletter, 0163-5832.*
Ind/Abst ACM Guide Comput. Lit.; Comput. Rev. (Winter 1981-); INSPEC (Winter 1981-).

LC QA75.5 .S56
DD 001.6/4/05   BL

SISTEMAS.
Added/Corp Sao Paulo, Brazil (City). Universidade. Centro de Procesamento de Dados. Vol. 1 (July/August 1976)-. Periodical. Portuguese. Six times a year. Universidade de Sao Paulo / Botelho, Av Dr Carlos Botelho 1465 - Caixa Postal 378, Sao Carlos 13.560 Brazil.
Desc: Information on electronic data processing.

LC QA75.5 .S585
    RU
SISTEMY I SREDSTVA INFORMATIKI.
Added/Corp Institut Problem Informatiki (Akademiia Nauk SSSR). (1989)-. Russian. One time a year. Izdatelstvo Nauka / Akademiia Nauk, (Publishing House of the Russian Academy of Sciences), Leninskii Porspekt 14, 117901 Moscow Russia. **Tel** 011 95 9542153, FAX 011 95 9382144, telex 411964.

    ISSN 0179-3632
    GW
SPRINGER SERIES IN COMPUTATIONAL MATHEMATICS.
[Springer ser. comput. math.]. (1983)-. Monographic series. English. Irregular. Price varies per volume. Springer-Verlag GmbH & Company KG, Heidelberger Platz 3, D-14197 Berlin Germany. **Tel** 011 49 30 8207223, FAX 011 49 30 8214091, telex 183 319 SPBLN D. **(Subscription address:** Springer-Verlag New York Inc. / North America, PO Box 2485, Journal Fulfillment, Secaucus NJ 07096. **Tel** (201)348-4033, (800)777-4643, FAX (201)348-4505.)
Ind/Abst Math. Rev. (1988-); Zentralbl. Math. Ihre Grenzgeb.

    SZ
SYSDATA.
(19??)-. Trade Publication. German. Twelve times a year. 50.00F Switzerland; 100.00F other. Verlag Binkert AG, Baslerstrasse 15, CH-4335 Laufenburg Switzerland. **Tel** 011 41 64 697272, FAX 011 41 64 697333. **ED** R Bachmann. **Bk Rev. Ad Acc, Adv Mgr:** B U Schonenberger. **Circ:** 27000. Documents available from Ask*IEEE. **Continues** *Sysdata & Burotechnik.*
Desc: Trade journal for commercial EDP, office automation, management, communication and office equipment.
Ind/Abst INSPEC (Sept. 1981-).

DD 001.6/4   ISSN 0042-0204
    CN
TECHNICAL REPORT (UNIVERSITY OF TORONTO. DEPT. OF COMPUTER SCIENCE).
(TECHNICAL REPORT - UNIVERSITY OF TORONTO, DEPARTMENT OF COMPUTER SCIENCE). [Tech rep. - Dep. Univ. Toronto, Dep. Comput. Sci.]. (1968)-. Monographic series. English. Price varies per volume. Department of Computer Science, Toronto Ontario M5S 1A7 Canada.

LC QA75.5 .T43   ISSN 0752-4072
DD 001.64/05   FR
    CCC
    CODEN TTSIDJ

TECHNIQUE ET SCIENCE INFORMATIQUES : TSI.
[TSI. Tech. sci. inform.]. **VFOAT** TSI; T.S.I. Vol. 1, No. 1 (Jan./Feb. 1982)-. Periodical. English (French). Six times a year. $514.00. Editions Hermes, 14 rue Lantiez, 75017 Paris France. **Tel** 11 33 1 42294466. Documents available from The Genuine Article, Ask*IEEE.
Ind/Abst CompuMath Cit. Index [Full Cov.]; Comput. Rev.; INSPEC (1982); Res. Alert [Full Cov.]; Zentralbl. Math. Ihre Grenzgeb.

LC QA76.9.A25 T73   ISSN 0892-399X
DD 384/.05   US
    CODEN TDCREP
    TITLE CHANGE
TRANSNATIONAL DATA AND COMMUNICATIONS REPORT. See
Communications-Telecommunication.

    ISSN 0821-1043
DD 001.64   CN
TUTORIAL (UNIVERSITY OF ALBERTA. COMPUTING SERVICES).
(TUTORIAL / COMPUTING SERVICES, UNIVERSITY OF ALBERTA.). [Tutor. - Comput. Serv. Univ. Alta.]. Periodical. English. University of Alberta / University Computing Services, 352 General Services Building, Edmonton Alberta T6G 2H1 Canada. **Tel** (403)432-2462.

LC QA76.8.U55 U55   ISSN 0279-1579
DD 004   US
Pr Rev.
UNISPHERE. See Computers-Computer Systems.

LC T58.6 .U66   ISSN 0130-5395
    UN
UDC 62.52
    CODEN UPSMBC
UPRAVLJAJUSCIE SISTEMY I MASINY (KIEV, 1972).
(UPRAVLIAIUSHCHIE SISTEMY I MASHINY.). [Upr. sist. mas.]. **VFOAT** USI M. (1972)-. Periodical. Russian (summaries and/or abstracts in English). Six times a year. $129.00 domestic airmail; $134.00 international airmail. **(Subscription address:** Victor Kamkin, 4956 Boiling Brook Parkway, Rockville MD 20852. **Tel** (301)881-5973.) Documents available from CASDDS.
Ind/Abst Chem. Abstr.; Int. Aerosp. Abstr.; Math. Rev.; Pollut. Abstr. Indexes.

LC QA75.5 .M67a   ISSN 0137-0782
    RU
    CODEN VMUKD8
VESTNIK MOSKOVSKOGO UNIVERSITETA. SERIIA XV. VYCHISLITELNAIA MATEMATIKA I KIBERNETIKA.
[Vestn. Moskovskogo univ. Ser. 15. Vycisl. mat. kibern.]. **Main/Corp** Moskovskii Gosudarstvennyi Universitet. (1977)-. Periodical. Russian (summaries and/or abstracts in English). Four times a year. $49.95. Izdatelstvo Moskovskogo Universiteta, K-9 Ulitsa Gertsena 5/7, 103009 Moscow Russia. **Tel** (301)881-5973. **(Subscription address:** East View Publications Inc., 3020 Harbor Lane North, Suite 110, Minneapolis MN 55447. **Tel** (800)477-1005, (612)550-0961, FAX (612)559-2931.) Documents available from Ask*IEEE.
Ind/Abst INSPEC (1978-); Math. Rev.; Stat. Theory Method Abstr. (1987).

LC TK7885.A1 V89
DD 621.39   RU
VYCHISLITELNAIA TEKHNIKA.
Added/Corp Kuibyshevskii Politekhnicheskii Institut Imeni V. Kuibysheva. Vol. 1 (1973)-. Russian. Forty-eight times a year. $180.00. Redaktsionno-Izdatelskii Otdel Kpti, 445010 Ulitsa Calaktionovskaia 141, Kuibyshev Russia.

LC QA75.5 .V934
    RU
    CODEN VTSSD3
VYCHISLITELNAIA TEKHNIKA SOTSIALISTICHESKIKH STRAN.
Added/Corp Mezhpravitelstvennaia Komissiia po Sotrudnichestvu Sotsialisticheskikh Stran v Oblasti Vychislitelnoi Tekhniki. Vol. 1 (1977)-. Academic Scholarly Publication. Russian. Statistika, Ulitsa Kirova 39, Moscow Russia. Documents available from CASDDS.
Ind/Abst Chem. Abstr. (1977-1980).

LC QA75.5 .V945
    RU
VYCHISLITELNYE PROTSESSY I SISTEMY.
Added/Corp Akademiia Nauk SSSR. Otdel Vychislitelnoi Matematiki. (1983)-. Academic Scholarly Publication. Russian. Izdatelstvo Nauka / Akademiia Nauk, (Publishing House of the Russian Academy of Sciences), Leninskii Porspekt 14, 117901 Moscow Russia. **Tel** 011 95 9542153, FAX 011 95 9382144, telex 411964. **ED** G.I. Marchuk.
Ind/Abst Zentralbl. Math. Ihre Grenzgeb.

    ISSN 0268-523X
DD 670   UK
WHAT'S NEW IN PROCESSING.
[What's new process.]. (1985)-. Periodical. English. Twelve times a year. £60.00 UK and Northern Ireland; $145.00 other. Morgan Grampian, 40 Beresford Street Woolwich, London SE18 6BQ United Kingdom. **Tel** 011 44 181 8557777, FAX 011 44 181 8555548, telex 896238.

LC QA75   ISSN 0945-9448
DD 004   GW
● **X-CHANGE.** (1994)-. Trade Publication. English. Four times a year. DM78.00. Beuth Verlag GmbH, Burggrafenstrasse 6, D-10787 Berlin Germany. **Tel** 011 49 30 260112573, FAX 011 49 30 24399926. **ED** Christian-Hinrich Dorner.

LC QA76 .Y43   ISSN 0303-1381
    IS
YEDION LE-TEKNOLOGYAH SEL MEDA U-MAHSEVIM.
(YEDION LE-TEKHNOLOGYAH SHEL MEDA U-MAHSHEVIM.). Periodical. Hebrew. Iltam, Rehov Keren Hayesod 18, POB 7170, Jerusalem Israel.

    ISSN 0860-0295
    PL
ZESZYTY NAUKOWE UNIWERSYTETU JAGIELLONSKIEGO. PRACE INFORMATYCZNE.
VFOAT Prace Informatyczne; Acta Litterarumque. Schedae Informaticae; Schedae Informaticae. (1985)-. Polish (English; summaries and/or abstracts in English). Irregular. **(Subscription address:** Ars Polona-Ruch, PO Box 1001, Krakowskie Przedmiescie 7, 00-068 Warsaw Poland. **Tel** 011 48 22 261201.)

HARDWARE

LC WMLC 93/1471   ISSN 1052-6366
DD 004   US
ACCESS TO WANG.
[Access Wang]. **VFOAT** Access. Vol. 5, No. 9 (May 1988)-. Trade Publication. English. Twelve times a year. $30.00. New Media Publications, Inc., 10711 Burnet Road, Suite 305, Austin TX 78758-4459. **Tel** (512)873-7761, FAX (512)873-7782. Documents available from Ask*IEEE. **Continues** *Access (Austin, Tex. : 1985), 0890-2321.*
Ind/Abst INSPEC (1988-1989).

    ISSN 1074-9306
DD 004   US
    SUSPENDED
● **ADVANCED SYSTEMS. See**
Computers-Software.

LC QA76.8.T18 A44   ISSN 0277-2418
DD 001.64   US
ALTERNATE SOURCE, THE.
(198?)-. Periodical. English. $18.00. The Alternate Source, 704 North Pennsylvania, Lansing MI 48906.

Computers —Hardware

AMAZING COMPUTING FOR THE COMMODORE AMIGA. [Amaz. comput. Commodore Amiga]. **VFOAT** Amazing Computing; Amazing Computing. (19??)-. Periodical. English. Twelve times a year. $27.00 (surface mail); $99.00 (airmail). Poetry in Motion Publications Inc., PO Box 2140, Fall River MA 02722. **Tel** (508)678-4200, (800)345-3360, FAX (508)675-6002. **Continues** Amazing Computing, 0886-9480.
ISSN 1053-4547
DD 004
US

AMIGA USER, THE. Periodical. English. Six times a year. $20.00. Amiga Atlanta, 4280 Village Square Lane, Stone Mountain GA 30083.
ISSN 0889-5783
US

AMIGA USER INTERNATIONAL. [Amiga user int.]. (1988)-. Periodical. English. Twelve times a year. $164.61. HYA Limited, PO Box 10, Lazahold Limited, Sunderland SR4 6SN United Kingdom. **Tel** 011 44 191 5102290, FAX 011 44 191 5100155. **Continues** Commodore Business and Amiga User.
ISSN 0955-1077
DD 004.165
UK

AMIGA WORLD. [Amiga world]. **VFOAT** AmigaWorld. Vol. 1, No. 1 (Premiere Issue 1985)-(Apr. 1995). Periodical. English. IDG Communications / New Hampshire, 86 Elm Street, Peterborough NH 03458. **Tel** (800)349-7327, FAX (603)924-6972. (Subscription address: Kable Publishers Aide / Illincis, 308 East Hitt Street, Subscription Department, Mt. Morris IL 61054-1473. **Tel** (815)734-1261.)
Ind/Abst Comput. Rev. Index (Nov. 1987-); Microcomput. Abstr. (Sept. 1990).
ISSN 0883-2390
DD 004
US CEASED

APPLE ACCESS. Vol. 1 (Jan. - June 1984)-. English. Two times a year. Stony Point Publications, Box 4467, Petaluma CA 94953.
LC Z5642.6.A66 A65 QA76.8.A66
DD 016.004165
ISSN 0749-5277
US

APPLE INDEX, THE. [Apple index]. Vol. 1, No. 1 (July/Aug. 1983)-. English. Six times a year. $22.00. BP Publications, 465 Chestnut Tree Hill Road, Southbury CT 06488-1955. **Tel** (203)264-2143. **ED** Beverly A Pajer.
LC Z5642.6.A66 A66 QA76.8.A66
DD 016.00164
ISSN 0741-2347
US

ATARI EXPLORER. [Atari explor.]. Feb. 1985-. Periodical. English. Six times a year. $14.95 (one-year), $39.95 (three-year), $2.95 (single issue). Atari (US) Corporation, PO Box 3427, Sunnyvale CA 94088-3427. **Continues** Atari Connection, 0739-2516.
Ind/Abst Comput. Rev. Index (Nov.-Dec. 1987-).
LC QA76.8.A82 A85
DD 004.165
ISSN 0882-3340
US

ATARI MAGAZINE. Added/Corp Atari France. (1987)-. Periodical. French. Eleven times a year. $76.56. Artipresse, 79 Avenue Louis Roche, 92238 Gennev Cedex France. **Tel** 011 33 1 40853190. **ED** Sergo Fenez. Index available. **Bk Rev. Ad Acc. Circ:** 30,000.
Desc: Dedicated to the Atari computer user.
UDC 681.3
ISSN 0992-2016
FR

ATARI USER. [Atari user]. (1985)-. Periodical. English. Twelve times a year. £15.00 UK; £18.00 Europe and Eire; £33.00 other. Database Publ, Europa House, Adlington House, Adlington Macclesfield, SK10 5NP United Kingdom. Index available. **Ad Acc. Circ:** 20,000.
Desc: Periodical dedicated to the Atari Computer.
DD 004.16
ISSN 0266-545X
UK
Pr Rev.

CAO/CAM/CAE PRODUCTS DATABASE. See Computers-Computer Sales, Service and Supply.

CD-ROM INFORMATION PRODUCTS. (19??)-(Dec. 1993). Trade Publication. English. Ashgate Publishing Company, Old Post Road, Brookfield VT 05036. **Tel** (800)535-9544, (802)276-3837, FAX (802)276-3837. **ED** Chris Armstrong and Andy Large.
Desc: Contains evaluations of international CD-ROM products. Written to assist with the assessment of new products in this dynamic field.
ISSN 0967-8123
UK CEASED

COMPUTE IT. (19??)-. English. Twelve times a year. £20.40. Royal National Institute for the Blind, PO Box 173, Peterborough PE2 6WS United Kingdom. **Tel** 011 44 1733 3730777, FAX 011 44 1733 371555.
Desc: Designed for the computer enthusiast or amateur; provides information on the latest hardware and software developments.
UK

COMPUTER DATA STORAGE NEWSLETTER. See Computers-Optical Storage, CD-ROM Applications.
UDC 681.3
ISSN 0988-3452
FR

COMPUTER PRICE GUIDE. See Computers-Computer Sales, Service and Supply.
DD 004
ISSN 0045-7841
US

COMPUTER REVIEW. [Comput. rev.]. (1974)-. English. Two times a year (Jan. and Jul.). $385.00. Computer Review, 19 Pleasant Street, Gloucester MA 01930. **Tel** (508)283-2100. Index available (free). **Bk Rev. Ad Acc. Circ:** 1,000 (ctrl). available on CD-ROM. Documents available from Ask*IEEE. **Continues** Computer Characteristics Review, 0010-454X.
Desc: Covers over 850 mainframe and minicomputer systems, including applications, specifications, software, prices, features, peripherals and languages. Directory of manufacturers listing is also included.
Ind/Abst Comput. Rev.; INSPEC (1978-1987).
LC TK7885.A1 C56
DD 338.4/7/621381958
ISSN 0093-416X
US CODEN CMRVCK

COMPUTER SOFTWARE/HARDWARE INDEX. See Computers-Software.
LC QA76.75 .C65
DD 016.00164/25
ISSN 0882-5629
UK

DATAPRO PERIPHERALS / INTERNATIONAL EDITION. (19??)-. English. Irregular. $584.00. Datapro International, McGraw Hill House, Shoppenhangers Road, Maidenhead Berkshire SL6 2QL United Kingdom. **Tel** 011 44 1628 773277, FAX 011 44 1628 773628.
UK

DIRECTORY OF SPARC-BASED HARDWARE PRODUCTS & COMPANINES. [Dir. SPARC-based hardw. prod. co.]. (1991)-. Directory. English. Four times a year. $695.00. Desktop Strategies, 23190 Ravensbury Avenue, Los Altos CA 94022. **Tel** (415)948-3927, FAX (011)948-3590. **ED** Susan Mason.
Desc: Stay current with new products, competitor products, and market directions.
LC QA76.9.S88 F675
DD 004.2/1
ISSN 1065-187X
DD 004
ISSN 0925-9856
US CCC CODEN FMSDE6
Pr Rev.

FORMAL METHODS IN SYSTEM DESIGN. See Computers-Computer Systems.
LC QA76.5 .F87
DD 004/.05
ISSN 0167-739X
NE CCC
Pr Rev.

FUTURE GENERATIONS COMPUTER SYSTEMS : FGCS. See Computers-Computer Systems.
LC QA
DD 005.3
ISSN 0958-1790
UK

INSIDE INFORMATION (WHITCHURCH). See Computers-Software.
LC QA76.5 .I563
DD 004.1/1/05
ISSN 0129-0533
SI CCC CODEN IHSCEZ

INTERNATIONAL JOURNAL OF HIGH SPEED COMPUTING. See Computers-Electronic Data Processing.
ISSN 1120-8465
IT

M. MACINTOSH MAGAZINE. [M. Macintosh mag.]. **VFOAT** Macintosh Magazine. (1989)-. Periodical. Italian. Eleven times a year. L68130. MGE Communications, Via Cola Di Rienzo 163, 00192 Rome Italy. **Tel** 011 39 6 3243289, FAX 011 39 6 3293088. **ED** Santo Strati. Index available. cum. index. **Bk Rev. Ad Acc. Circ:** 25,000. available on diskette.
Desc: General information about software, hardware, and literature of the Macintosh Computer International Guide to Products.
UDC 681.3
ISSN 1040-0966
DD 004
US TITLE CHANGE

MONOSSON REPORT ON DEC AND IBM, THE. [Monosson rep. DEC IBM]. **VAT** Monosson Report on Digital Equipment Corporation and International Business Machines. (June 1988)-(19??). Periodical. English. DataTrends Publications, 895 Harrison Street SE, Suite B, Leesburg VA 22075. **Tel** (703)779-0574, (800)766-8130, FAX (703)779-2267. available on an online database (file 636/Full-Text) from DIALOG. **Continues** Monosson on DEC, 0884-4097. **Continued by** Datatrends Report on DEC and IBM.
LC QA75
DD 004
ISSN 1040-6093
US TITLE CHANGE

NEWS 3X/400. See Computers-Computer Systems.
US
Pr Rev.

●**NPI TECHNO VIEW TIMES.** (1995)-. Newsletter. English. Six times a year. Free. Nosh Productions, Inc., 220 Clara Street, San Francisco CA 94107. **Tel** (415)896-6674, FAX (415)896-6675. **ED** Marla Rabin. **Bk Rev. Circ:** 4,500. available via Internet.
Desc: General computer information on hardware and software aimed at everyone from the novice to the experienced user.
IT

PERSONAL COMPUTER. See Computers-Software.
ISSN 1073-6425
US CCC

●**PETROSYSTEMS WORLD.** See Petroleum and Natural Gas-Computer Applications.
ISSN 1040-9718
DD 621
US TITLE CHANGE

PLC INSIDER'S NEWSLETTER, THE. [PLC insid. newsl.]. **VAT** Programmable Logic Controller Insider's Newsletter. (198?)-(199?). Newsletter. English. Carefree Communications, PO Box 5268, Carefree AZ 85377. **Tel** (602)488-1462, FAX (602) 488-5376. **ED** Jack Grenard. **Bk Rev.** (Qty: 3 /yr). **Ad Acc.** ctrl circ. available on diskette. **Continues** PC Insider. **Continued by** Controls Digest, 1067-3121.
Desc: Carries news and features of interest to executives of companies that make and sell programmable logic controllers. Such news includes people and jobs, a calendar of events, new products (both hardware and software), distribution, legislation, industry trends, and signed opinion pieces. Uses no pictures.
ISSN 1061-1509
DD 363
US
Pr Rev. SUSPENDED

POLICE COMPUTER REVIEW. See Law-Computer Applications.
LC TK7887.7 .P73
DD 621.398/7
ISSN 0890-7234
US

PRINTERS BUYER'S GUIDE AND HANDBOOK. [Print. buy. guide handb.]. Guide #1 (1985)-. English. Two times a year. $4.95 (single copy). Printers Buyer's Guide and Handbook, PO Box 318, Mt Morris IL 61054-9942. **Tel** (212)807-8220, FAX (212)807-8737. **ED** Ephraim Schwartz, editor's address: 150 5th Avenue, Suite 714, New York City, NY 10011. **Ad Acc, Adv Mgr:** Mary Wohlberg. **Circ:** 50,000.
Desc: This publication reviews and features articles on computer printers.
US

RESIDUAL VALUE FORECASTS FOR DEC SYSTEMS AND PERIPHERALS. (19??)-. English. Four times a year. $1495.00. Computer Economics Inc., 5841 Edison Place, Carlsbad CA 92008. **Tel** (800)326-8100, (619)438-8100, FAX (619)431-1126. **ED** Michael E Erbschloe.
Desc: Provides accurate residual value forecasts for over 140 DEC machines, from the largest data center processor to the smallest desktop peripheral.

RESIDUAL VALUE FORECASTS FOR IBM SYSTEMS AND PERIPHERALS. (1989)-. English. Four times a year. $2495.00. Computer Economics Inc., 5841 Edison Place, Carlsbad CA 92008. **Tel** (800)326-8100, (619)438-8100, FAX (619)431-1126.
ISSN 1059-9975
DD 004
US CEASED

RISC WORLD. [Risc world]. (1991)-(1995). Trade Publication. English. Publications & Communications, 12416 Hymeadow Drive, Austin TX 78750. **Tel** (512)250-9023, (800)678-9724, FAX (512)331-3900, telex 384303. **Circ:** 10,000. **Continues** Risc 6000 World, 1068-4778.
Desc: Dedicated to users of IBM's AIX operating system products. AIX represents IBM's UNIX offering. The publication features product and news developments from IBM's workstation family of systems. It also reports on third parties active in the AIX client/server reseller market.
BE

SAMSON PERSONAL COMPUTER. Dutch (French). Twenty-four times a year. 4452.00F. Wolters Kluwer Samson Personal Computer, Koutrveldstraat 14, 1831 Diegem Belgium. **Tel** 723 11 11. **ED** Marilyn

Computers —Microcomputers, Personal Computers

Kindermans, phone:723-10-81, Kouterveld 14- B 1831 Diegem, Belgium. Index available. **Bk Rev**.
Desc: A newsletter about PC hardware and software.

DD 004   **ISSN** 0888-1057 US
ST WORLD. [ST world]. Periodical. English. Twelve times a year. $18.00 US; $22.00 Canada. Atari ST Council, 2463 Latona Court Northeast, Salem OR 97303.

LC WMLC 93/4036   **ISSN** 0742-938X
DD 363   US
    CCC
    CEASED
VDT NEWS. See Public Health and Safety.

    ISSN 0270-8507 US
VLSI UPDATE. See Computers-Computer Industry and Industry Directories.

LC HD9696.C6 W67   **ISSN** 1074-3308
DD 621.39/16/029473   US
WORKGROUP COMPUTING SERIES. DIRECTORY OF MICROCOMPUTER HARDWARE. [Workgr. comput. ser., Dir. microcomput. hardw.]. **Added/Corp** Datapro Information Services Group. **VFOAT** Directory of Microcomputer Hardware. Vol. 1, No. 2 (Sept. 1992)- . Directory. English. Four times a year. $791.00. Datapro Information Services Group, 600 Delran Parkway, Delran NJ 08075. **Tel** (609)764-0100, (800)328-2776, FAX (609)764-8953.
Formed by the union of Workgroup Computing Series. Hardware Product Directory **and** Workgroup Computing Series. Hardware Vendor Directory.

MICROCOMPUTERS, PERSONAL COMPUTERS

LC QA76.8.A177 A255   **ISSN** 1053-7929
DD 004.165   US
    CEASED
AC'S TECH FOR THE COMMODORE AMIGA. [AC's tech Commodore Amiga]. **VFOAT** Tech for the Commodore Amiga; AC's Tech. **VAT** Amazing Computing's Tech for the Commodore Amiga. Vol. 1, No. 1 (1991)-(1995). Periodical. English. Poetry in Motion Publications Inc., PO Box 2140, Fall River MA 02722. **Tel** (508)678-4200, (800)345-3360, FAX (508)675-6002. **ED** Don Hicks. Index available. cum. index. **Ad Acc, Adv Mgr:** Donna Viveiros. ctrl circ.
Desc: A technical magazine for the Amiga computers.

LC QA76.5 .A3375   **ISSN** 0883-1262
DD 621.391/6/05   US
ADVANCED MICRO DEVICES ... ANNUAL PROCEEDINGS. [Adv. Micro Devices annu. proc.]. **VFOAT** AMD Annual Proceedings. 1985-. Proceedings. English (French, German, Italian and Japanese). One time a year. Product Public Relations, 901 Thompson Place, Sunnyvale CA 94088.

LC H61.3 .A38   **ISSN** 1047-2010
DD 300/.285   US
ADVANCES IN SOCIAL SCIENCE AND COMPUTERS. See Social Sciences.

    ISSN 0843-9753
DD 005.26   CN
    CEASED
ALGORITHM, THE PERSONAL PROGRAMMING NEWSLETTER. (ALGORITHM.). [Algorithm pers. program. newsl.]. **VFOAT** Algo-Rithm. (Nov./Dec. 1989)-(19??). Periodical. English. Algorithm Publications, PO Box 29237, Westmount Post Street, London Ontario N6K 1M6 Canada. **Tel** (519)432-8042.

LC QA76.5 .S442   **ISSN** 0895-3821
DD 004.16/05   US
    CODEN ASOCE4SOPCE9
    TITLE CHANGE
ANDREW SEYBOLD'S OUTLOOK ON PROFESSIONAL COMPUTING. [Andrew Seybold's outlook prof. comput.]. **VFOAT** Outlook on Professional Computing. Vol. 5, No. 12 (Aug. 31, 1987)-(19??). Periodical. English. Pinecrest Press, PO Box 917, Brookdale CA 95007. **Tel** (408)338-7701, FAX (408)338-7806. **ED** Andrew M. Seybold. Index available. cum. index. **Bk Rev**. available on CD-ROM and diskette from Ziff Communications. Documents available from Ask*IEEE. **Continues** Seybold Outlook on Professional Computing, 0887-5758. **Merged with** Andrew Seybold's Outlook on Mobile Computing, 1066-8845 **to form** Andrew Seybold's Outlook on Communications and Computing, 1080-4056.
Desc: Volume buyer, end user, assistance in analysis on hardware and software.
Ind/Abst Comput. Bus. (19??-199?); INSPEC (Aug. 31, 1987-); SCISEARCH; World Publ. Monit. (Aug. 31, 1987-).

    ISSN 0882-0406
DD 001   US
APPLE BITS. [Apple bits]. (19??)-. Periodical. English. Twelve times a year. comes with Apple Bits Users Group membership. Apple Bits Users Group Inc, Box 368, Mission KS 66201-0368. **Tel** (816)523-1007.

LC Z678.93.A65 A67   **ISSN** 1057-1159
DD 025/.00285/5369   US
APPLE LIBRARY USERS GROUP NEWSLETTER. See Library and Information Sciences-Computer Applications.

    ISSN 0992-3012
UDC 681.3   FR
    CEASED
APPLE MAGAZINE LES ULIS. (APPLE MAGAZINE.). **Added/Corp** Apple Computer France. (1988)-(Sept. 1993). Periodical. French. Apple Magazine, 12 Avenue de l'Oceanie, 91956 Lis Ullis Cedex France. **Tel** 011 33 1 69863400.

    NE
APPLE WORLD MAGAZINE. (19??)-. Periodical. English. Eleven times a year. Fl70.75. Nanton Press Uitgeverij BV, Postbus 93, 3720 AB Bilthoven Netherlands. **Tel** 011 31 30 290644. **Continues** Appleblad.

    ISSN 0847-5644
DD 005.265   CN
ATARISTE. (L'ATARISTE.). **VFOAT** Atari-ST-e. Vol. 4, No. 1 (Sept. 1989)-. Periodical. French. Irregular. $27.00 North America; $44.00 other. L'AtariSTe, 955 rue Poirier, McMasterville Quebec J3G 1K6 Canada. **Tel** (514)467-1019, FAX (514)464-4999. **ED** Paul Potters. Index available. **Bk Rev**. **Ad Acc**. **Circ:** 1,400.
Continues ST-tique, 0841-6974.
Desc: For use with Atari ST computers.

    ISSN 1071-3093
DD 004   US
AUDIO MICROCOMPUTER REPORT [SOUND RECORDING]. [Audio microcomput. rep.]. **Added/Corp** Totaltape, Inc. (19??)-. English. Twelve times a year. $240.00. Totaltape Publishing Company, 9417 Princess Palm Avenue, Tampa FL 33619. **Tel** (800)874-7877, (813)621-6200. Index available.

    AT
AUSTRALIAN AND NEW ZEALAND PC USER. (19??)-. Periodical. English. Twelve times a year. 55.00Aus$ Australia; 147.00NZ$ New Zealand; 125.00Aus$ other. Australian Consolidated Press Ltd., Private Bag 92615 Symonds St, Auckland New Zealand. **Tel** 011 64 9 3735408, FAX 011 64 9 3022889.
Continues Australian PC User.

    AT
AUSTRALIAN MACUSER. (19??)-. Periodical. English. Eleven times a year. 50.00Aus$ Australia; 80.00Aus$ New Zealand; 109.30Aus$ other. Australian Consolidated Press Ltd., Private Bag 92615 Symonds St, Auckland New Zealand. **Tel** 011 64 9 3735408, FAX 011 64 9 3022889.

    ISSN 0813-1384
DD 001.6405   AT
AUSTRALIAN PC WORLD. [Aust. PC World]. **VFOAT** Australian Personal Computer World. (1984)-. Periodical. English. Twelve times a year. 53.44Aus$. IDG Communications Pty Ltd. / Australia, 88 Christie Street, PO Box 295, St. Leonards 2065 Australia. **Tel** 011 61 2 4395133.

    ISSN 0725-4415
DD 001.640405   AT
AUSTRALIAN PERSONAL COMPUTER. [Aust. pers. comput.]. **VFOAT** APC. (1980)-. Periodical. English. Twelve times a year. 57.55Aus$. Australian Consolidated Press Ltd., Private Bag 92615 Symonds St, Auckland New Zealand. **Tel** 011 64 9 3735408, FAX 011 64 9 3022889.
Ind/Abst EP Collect.; Homework Help.; MasterFile FullTEXT 1000; MasterFile FullTEXT 350; MasterFile FullTEXT 650; MasterFile FullTEXT (Sept. 1994-); Telebase; World Mag. Bank.

    ISSN 1063-8296
DD 005   US
    TITLE CHANGE
AVID (CUPERTINO, CALIF.). (AVID : THE AMIGA-VIDEO JOURNAL.). [Avid]. **VFOAT** Amiga-Video Journal; Amiga Video Journal. (199?)-(1993). Periodical. English. AVID Publications, 273 North Mathilda Avenue, Sunnyvale CA 94086. **Tel** (408)774-6770, FAX (408)774-6783. **Continued by** Amiga Video Graphics Magazine.

LC QA   **ISSN** 0746-598X
DD 510   US
BARON'S MICROCOMPUTING REPORTS. [Baron's MicroComput. rep.]. **Added/Corp** Computer Information Resources (Firm). **VFOAT** Microcomputing Reports; Microcomputing;

Baron's Micro Computing Reports. Vol. 1, No. 1 (July 1983)-. Periodical. English. Twelve times a year. Baron's Micro Computing, PO Box 695, New York NY 10956. **Tel** (212)832-1171.

    ISSN 0962-9475
    UK
    CODEN BACREA
BBC ACORN USER. [BBC Acorn user]. (198?)-. Periodical. English. Twelve times a year. £22.95 UK; £49.00 Europe; £69.00 other. Redwood Publishing, Fulham House Goldsworth Road, Woking Surrey GU21 1LZ United Kingdom. **Tel** 011 44 1483 747008, FAX 011 44 1483 776573. Documents available from Ask*IEEE.
Continues Acorn User, 0263-7456.
Ind/Abst INSPEC (Jan. 1989-).

LC QA76.5 .B474   **ISSN** 0275-455X
DD 658/.054   US
BEST OF PERSONAL COMPUTING, THE. See Computers-Minicomputers.

    UK
BLACKWELL PERSONAL COMPUTER MARKETS. (19??)-. English. Twenty-four times a year. £877.00. Highdon Publishing Ltd., PO Box 1626, London N5 1JF United Kingdom. **Tel** 011 44 171 2268155. **Continues** Fintech 3 Personal Computer Markets.

LC QA76.8.M3 B58   **ISSN** 0899-1014
DD 004   US
... BMUG NEWSLETTER, THE. Added/Corp BMUG, Inc. (Spring 1986)-. Newsletter. English. Two times a year (Jan., and July). $45.00 US, $57.00 Canada, $77.00 other (individuals); $120.00 US, $132.00 Canada, $152.00 other (corporate) Comes with Berkeley Macintosh Users Group membership. Berkeley Macintosh Users Group - BMUG, 1442A Walnut Street, Suite 62, Berkeley CA 94709. **Tel** (800)776-2684, (510)549-2684, FAX (510)849-9026. **ED** Hars Hansen. **Bk Rev**. **Circ:** 12,000 (ctrl). **Continues** Newsletter (Berkeley Macintosh Users Group), 0899-0980.

LC QA76.8.A66 B66   **ISSN** 0736-2692
DD 001.64/25/0294   US
    CEASED
BOOK OF APPLE SOFTWARE, THE. See Computers-Software.

LC QA76.8.A82 B65   **ISSN** 0736-2706
DD 001.64/2   US
BOOK OF ATARI SOFTWARE, THE. See Computers-Software.

    ISSN 0882-0651
DD 004   US
BROWN BOOK (OAKLAND, CALIF.), THE. (THE BROWN BOOK.). [Brown book]. (1985)-. Periodical. English. Four times a year. $250.00. Brown Book Corporation, 10 State Street/#A, Sanata Barbara CA 93101-3528. **Tel** (805)965-7544. **ED** Sherolyn Smith and Fred Brown.
Desc: The industry guide for microcomputer pricing similar in concept to the Kelly Blue Book for automobiles.

    ISSN 0838-438X
DD 004.16/029/4   CN
    CEASED
BUSINESS COMPUTER NEWS. See Business and Economics-Computer Applications.

    ISSN 0847-4362
DD 338.4/700416/0971   CN
    CEASED
BUSINESS COMPUTER RESELLER NEWS. See Computers-Computer Industry and Industry Directories.

    GR
●**BUSINESS INTERNET NEWSLETTER.** (1995)-. Newsletter. Greek, Modern. Twelve times a year. Compupress S.A., 44 Syngrou, 117 42 Athens Greece. **Tel** 011 30 1 9238672, FAX 011 30 1 9216847.

    ISSN 1188-2697
DD 004.16   CN
CENTRAL ALBERTA BITS & BYTES. (THE CENTRAL ALBERTA BITS & BYTES : NEWSLETTER OF THE KNEEHILL COMPUTER CLUB & THE PARKLAND PC USERS CLUB.). [Centr. Alta. bits bytes]. **Added/Corp** Kneehill Computer Club. Parkland PC Users Club. **VFOAT** Bits & Bytes. Fall (1991)-. Newsletter. English. Four times a year. $15.00 per year. Guidepost Publications, PO Box 1233, Three Hills Alberta T0M 2A0 Canada.

    ISSN 0170-6632
    GW
    CCC
    CODEN CHIPDP
CHIP. [Chip]. (Sept./Oct. 1978)-. Trade Publication. German. Twelve times a year. $96.54. Vogel Verlag, Postfach 6740, D-97064 Wuerzburg Germany. **Tel** 011 49 931 4182145, 011 49 931 4182483, FAX 011 49 931 4182670, telex 841 680131. Documents available from Ask*IEEE.
Ind/Abst INSPEC (May 1979-).

Computers —Microcomputers, Personal Computers

DD 004
Pr Rev.
ISSN 0896-8985
US
CIRCUIT CELLAR INK. See
Engineering-Computer Applications.

UK
COMMODORE COMPUTING. English. Twelve times a year. £15.00 UK; £20.00 Europe; £28.00 other. Croftward Ltd, 40 Bowling Green Lane, London EC1R 0NE United Kingdom. **Tel** 01 278 0333.

FR
COMPATIBLES PC MAGAZINE. French. Laser Presse SA, 175 Jean Jaures, 75019 Paris France.

DD 001.64/04
ISSN 0827-262X
CN
COMPUTEK. [Computek]. Vol. 1, No. 1 (Sept./Oct. 1984)-. Periodical. English. Twelve times a year. $19.50. IBIS Publishing Inc, 844 West 15th Street, N Vancouver British Columbia V7P 1M6 Canada. **Tel** (604)986-9501. **Continues** Compuwest.

LC QA76.5 .C6125617
DD 004/.029 004
ISSN 0738-9213
US
COMPUTER BUYER'S GUIDE AND HANDBOOK. [Comput. buy. guide handb.]. **VFOAT** Computer. (198?)-. Periodical. English. Six times a year. $28.95. Bedford Comm, 150 Fifth Avenue, Suite 714, New York NY 10011. **Tel** (212)807-8220, FAX (212)807-8737. **(Subscription address:** Kable Publishers Aide / Illinois, 308 East Hitt Street, Subscription Department, Mt. Morris IL 61054-1473. **Tel** (815)734-1261.) **ED** Ephraim Schwartz. **Bk Rev. Ad Acc, Adv Mgr:** Mary Wohlberg. **Circ:** 50,000.
Desc: This publication reviews and features personal computers.
Ind/Abst Comput. Rev. Index (July-August 1987-).

LC QA76.5 .C612562
DD 001.64
ISSN 0882-7818
US
COMPUTER BUYING GUIDE. (COMPUTER BUYING GUIDE : RATING THE BEST COMPUTERS, PERIPHERALS & SOFTWARE / BY THE EDITORS OF CONSUMER GUIDE.). [Comput. buy. guide]. **VFOAT** Rating the Best Computers, Peripherals & Software. (1984-)-. Consumer Publication. English. One time a year. $99.00 (Consumer Guide subscription package). Publications International Ltd, 7373 North Cicero Avenue, Lincolnwood IL 60646. **Tel** (708)676-3470.

LC QA76.5 .C61262
DD 001.64/029/4
ISSN 0743-457X
US
COMPUTER GUIDE. See
Computers-Minicomputers.

DD 005
ISSN 8750-4375
US
COMPUTER LIVING, NEW YORK. [Comput. living N.Y.]. **VFOAT** Computer Living/New York; Computer Living/NY. (198?)-. Periodical. English. Twelve times a year. $25.00. Wolf Communications, 5793 Tyndell Avenue, Riverdale NY 10471. **Bk Rev. Ad Acc.**

DD 004
ISSN 0888-1987
US
COMPUTER PERIODICALS INDEX. [Comput. per. index]. Vol. 1, No. 1 (Jan. 1986)-. Periodical. English. Twelve times a year. CPI Publications Inc, PO Box 353, One Prestwick Circle, Palm Beach Garden FL 33410.

DD 004
ISSN 0899-3025
US
COMPUTER RAMBLINGS. See
Agriculture-Computer Applications.

LC QA76.5 .C61264
DD 004.16/05
ISSN 0748-8610
US
COMPUTER RETAILERS' GUIDE. [Comput. retail. guide]. Vol. 1, No. 001 (Winter 1985)-. Periodical. English. Four times a year. Free to qualified subscribers, $130.00 US; $160.00 other. Circulation Department of the Computer Retailers' Guide, Box 2110, Manhasset NY 11030. **Continues** Computer Retail News. Retailers' Guide, 0884-7444.

DD 004
ISSN 1040-5003
US
COMPUTER REVIEW INDEX. See
Computers-Abstracting, Bibliographies and Statistics.

LC TK7887 .C67
DD 621.39/16
ISSN 1073-2861
US
●**COMPUTER SERVICE & REPAIR MAGAZINE.** [Comput. serv. repair mag.]. **VFOAT** Computer Service and Repair Magazine. Vol. 1, Issue 1 (Jan./Feb. 1994)-. Periodical. English. Six times a year. Quantum Publishing Company, 8281 S. Yukon Way, Littleton CO 80123. **Tel** (303) 933-3033, FAX (303) 727-6765. **ED** Frank G. Gallo. **Ad Acc. Circ:** 14,000.

LC QA76.5 .C6129
DD 004.165
ISSN 0895-7398
US
COMPUTER SHOPPER'S PC CLONES. [Comput. shopp. PC clones]. **VFOAT** PC Clones. **VAT** Computer Shopper's Personal Computer Clones. Vol. 1, No. 1 (1987)-. Periodical. English. Irregular. $3.95 US single issue; $4.95 Canada single issue. Patch Publishing, 5211 South Washington Avenue, Titusville FL 32780. **Tel** (407)268-5010, FAX (407)267-7216.

LC TK7800 .C66
DD 621.39/16
ISSN 1055-5072
US
TITLE CHANGE
COMPUTERCRAFT (HICKSVILLE, N.Y.). (COMPUTERCRAFT.). [ComputerCraft]. **VFOAT** Computer Craft. Vol. 1, No. 1 (Apr. 1991)-Vol. 3, No. 12 (Dec. 1993). Periodical. English. CQ Communications Inc, 76 North Broadway, Hicksville NY 11801. **Tel** (516)681-2922, FAX (516)681-2926. **Continues** Modern Electronics (Hicksville, N.Y.), 0748-9889. **Continued by** MicroComputer Journal.
Ind/Abst Acad. Search; EP Collect.; Homework Help.; MasterFile FullTEXT 1000; MasterFile FullTEXT 350; MasterFile FullTEXT 650; MasterFile FullTEXT (July 1993-Dec. 1993); OCLC; Telebase.

DD 004
ISSN 8756-7911
US
COMPUTERITER. [Computeriter]. **Added/Corp** Creative Business Communications. (1985)-. Periodical. English. Twelve times a year. $40.00. Computeriter Microcomputer, PO Box 476, Columbia MD 21045. **Tel** (301)596-5591. **ED** Linda J. Elengold and Mark A. Elengold. **Bk Rev. Circ:** 4,000.
Desc: Contains microcomputer news and views for the writer/editor.

LC QA76.5 .C6145
DD 001.64/05
ISSN 0737-4313
US
COMPUTERS (GREENWICH, CONN.). See
Computers-Minicomputers.

LC CS14 .C65
DD 929/.1/02854
ISSN 0263-3248
UK
CODEN CGENER
COMPUTERS IN GENEALOGY. See
Genealogy and Heraldry-Computer Applications.

DD 001.64/04
ISSN 0823-6437
CN
CEASED
COMPUTING NOW!. See
Computers-Minicomputers.

COMPUTING TODAY (LONDON).
ISSN 0142-7210
UK
CODEN COMTD4
CEASED
(COMPUTING TODAY.). [Comput. today]. (1978)-(19??). Periodical. English. Infonet Ltd, 5 Riverpark Industrial Area, Billets Lane, Berkhamsted HP4 1HL United Kingdom. **ED** Henry Budgett. **Bk Rev. Ad Acc. Circ:** 35,000. Documents available from Ask*IEEE. **Formed by the union of** Microcomputer Printout **and** Business Micro.
Desc: General information for home computer enthusiasts, professional users, scientific, technical and education.
Ind/Abst INSPEC (April 1980-); World Ceram. Abstr.

LC QA76.753 .C638
DD 005.36/029//673
ISSN 1045-7445
US
TITLE CHANGE
CONNECTION, THE. (THE CONNECTION : PROGRAMMER'S CONNECTION BUYER'S GUIDE.). [Connection]. **Added/Corp** Programmer's Connection (Firm). **VFOAT** Programmer's Connection Buyer's Guide. (19??)-(199?). English. Programmers Connection, 7249 Whipple Avenue NW, North Canton OH 44720. **Tel** (216)494-3781, FAX (216)494-5260. **ED** Scott DiBattista. **Ad Acc, Adv Mgr:** Gina Cope, **Tel** (216)494-1996. **Circ:** 195,000 (ctrl). **Continued by** Programmer's PROVANTAGE Computer Products Buyer's Guide, 1076-9714.
Desc: Resource for information and pricing of microcomputer hardware and software products. Also included are feature editorials on current issues in the computer industry and a technical question and answer section.
Ind/Abst ACM Guide Comput. Lit. (?-?); Comput. Rev. (?-?).

DD 004.165
ISSN 0953-1378
UK
CONNECTIVITY LONDON. [Connectivity Lond.]. (1988)-. Periodical. English. Twelve times a year. Comes with Personal Computer Users Group membership. Personal Computer Users Group, PO Box 360, Harrow HA1 4LQ England. **Tel** 011 44 181 8631191, FAX 011 44 181 8636095. **ED** Alan Jay. **Bk Rev,** (Qty: 12). **Ad Acc.** ctrl circ. **Continues** IBM PC User Group Newsletter, 0952-0449.

LC QA75.5 .M49
DD 004.16/05
UK
CONSERVATION MICRO NEWS. VFOAT Micro News. Periodical. English. Four times a year. Micro News Publications Circulation Department, c/o Nicholson Harris Associates, 25 Queen Anne's Gate, London SW1H 9BU United Kingdom. **Continues** Micro News (Haywards Heath, England), 0267-6265.

LC QA76.5 .C725
DD 001.64
ISSN 0735-6668
US
CREATIVE COMPUTING BUYER'S GUIDE TO PERSONAL COMPUTERS, PERIPHERALS, AND ELECTRONIC GAMES. [Creat. comput. buy. guide pers. comput. peripher. electron. games]. **VFOAT** Buyer's Guide to Personal Computers, Peripherals, and Electronic Game; Creative Computing Buyer's Guide. (1987?)-. English. One time a year. $3.95. AHL Computing Inc, 39 East Hanover Avenue, Morris Plains NJ 07950.

DD 005
ISSN 1052-1941
US
DATAPRO SOFTWARE FINDER (MICROCOMPUTER ED.). See
Computers-Software.

US
DATAPRO WORKGROUP COMPUTING SERIES / DEVELOPMENT TOOLS. See
Computers-Software.

US
DATAPRO WORKGROUP COMPUTING SERIES / DISTRIBUTED DATABASES. See Computers-Data Base Management.

US
DATAPRO WORKGROUP COMPUTING SERIES / STRATEGIES & LAN SERVICES. See Computers-Software.

UK
DATAPRO WORKSTATIONS / INTERNATIONAL EDITION. (19??)-. English. Twelve times a year. $584.00. Datapro International, McGraw Hill House, Shoppenhangers Road, Maidenhead Berkshire SL6 2QL United Kingdom. **Tel** 011 44 1628 773277, FAX 011 44 1628 773628.

II
DATAQUEST : DQ. VFOAT DQ. (19??)-. Periodical. English. Twelve times a year. $120.00. Cyber Media, New Delhi India. **(Subscription address:** Prints India, 11 Darya Ganj, New Delhi 110002 India. **Tel** 011 91 11 3268645, FAX 011 91 11 3275542, telex 31-61087 PRIN-IN.)

NLM W1; DE184K
Pr Rev.
ISSN 0738-9744
US
DENTAL COMPUTER NEWSLETTER. See
Medical Sciences-Computer Applications.

DD 004.165/05
ISSN 1191-0755
CN
DEPECHE MAC. [Depeche Mac]. **VFOAT** Depeche Macintosh. No. 1 (Feb. 1992)-. Periodical. French. Twelve times a year. Limited free distribution. F. Cordeau, 8-625 Outremont, Outremont (Quebec) H2V 3M8.

LC QA76.8.A66 D47
DD 004.16
Pr Rev.
ISSN 1047-0735
US
DEVELOP (CUPERTINO, CALIF.). (DEVELOP : THE APPLE TECHNICAL JOURNAL.). [Develop]. **Added/Corp** Apple Computer, Inc. Developer Technical Communications Group. (Jan. 1990)-. Periodical. English. Four times a year. $30.00. Apple Computer Inc., 20525 Mariani Avenue, Cupertino CA 95014. **Tel** (408)996-1010, (619)558-7150. **(Subscription address:** Kable Publishers Aide / Illinois, 308 East Hitt Street, Subscription Department, Mt. Morris IL 61054-1473. **Tel** (815)734-1261.)

LC QA76.8.D43 D545
DD 004.1/4
ISSN 1065-7452
CCC
DIGITAL NEWS & REVIEW. See
Computers-Computer Systems.

LC QA76.8.M3 D56
DD 005.75/65
ISSN 1057-4506
US
DIMENSIONS (WINONA, MINN.). (DIMENSIONS : THE JOURNAL OF THE 4TH DIMENSION ENVIRONMENT.). [Dimensions]. Vol. 1, No. 1 (Sept./Oct. 1991)-. Periodical. English. Six times a year (Jan., Mar., May, July, Sept., Nov.). $69.00. Blackledge Publishing Company, PO Box 1262, 1126 East Broadway, Winona MN 55987. **Tel** (800)424-4855, (507)452-0023, FAX (507)452-0037. **ED** David Graves. **Ad Acc, Adv Mgr:** Gloria, **Tel** (507)452-0023.

ISSN 0735-617X
US
DIRECTORY OF INDEPENDENT IBM PERSONAL COMPUTER HARDWARE AND SOFTWARE, THE. See
Computers-Computer Industry and Industry Directories.

Computers —Microcomputers, Personal Computers

LC QA276.4 .D57
DD 519.5/028/55369 US
DIRECTORY OF STATISTICAL MICROCOMPUTER SOFTWARE. See Mathematics-Computer Applications.

LC QA76.6 .D574 ISSN 1063-9748
DD 001.64/25/029473 US
DIRECTORY OF U.S. GOVERNMENT SOFTWARE FOR MAINFRAMES AND MICROCOMPUTERS. See Computers-Software.

LC QA76.5 .D723 ISSN 1079-8595
DD 005 US
CEASED
DR. DOBB'S DEVELOPER UPDATE. [Dr. Dobb's dev. update]. (Mar. 1994)-(Jan. 1996). Periodical. English. Miller Freeman Inc., 600 Harrison Street, San Francisco CA 94107. **Tel** (415)905-2337, (415)905-2200, FAX (415)905-2240, telex 278273.

LC QA76.5 .D617 ISSN 1044-789X
DD 005 US
CCC
CODEN DDJOEB
Pr Rev.
DR. DOBB'S JOURNAL (1989). See Computers-Programs and Programming.

ISSN 0747-3931 US
EASY HOME COMPUTER. [Easy home comput.]. Periodical. English. Six times a year. $22.00 US, $43.00 Canada. Pumpkin Press Inc, Empire State Building, 350 Fifth Avenue, New York NY 10118. **Tel** (212)947-4322, FAX (212)563-4774.

US
EDP WEEKLY. See Computers-Computer Industry and Industry Directories.

ISSN 0886-6643
DD 644 US
ELECTRONIC HOUSE. [Electron. house]. **VFOAT** Electronic House Buying Guide. Vol. 1, No. 1 (Jan./Feb. 1986)-. Periodical. English. Six times a year. $19.95. Electronic House, Inc., PO Box 339, Stillwater OK 74076. **Tel** (405)624-8015, FAX (405)743-3374. **ED** Lisa Montgomery (phone: (219)291-5115).
Desc: Designed for anyone interested in the future of homes and home electronics.
Ind/Abst Index Inf. (1990-).

US
END-USER COMPUTING MANAGEMENT. English. Six times a year. $395.00. Auerbach Publishers Inc., Park Square Building, 31 St. James Avenue, Boston MA 02116. **Tel** (800)950-1207. **ED** Nancy Tyson. Index available. **Circ:** 500.
Desc: Practical advice for those in charge of managing and supporting end-user computing or of the information center in their organizations. Topic categories include the user interface, training, staffing, data base, data communications and systems design and development.

US
END-USER COMPUTING MANAGEMENT.
EUROPEAN MONITOR NEWSLETTER. See Computers-Computer Industry and Industry Directories.

ISSN 0896-7725
DD 005 US
CEASED
EXPERT (LOUISVILLE, KY.). (THE EXPERT.). [Expert]. **Added/Corp** Cobb Group. Vol. 1, No. 1 (Aug. 1988)-(Jan. 1996). Periodical. English. Cobb Group, 9420 Bunsen Parkway #300, Louisville KY 40220. **Tel** (502)491-1900, (800)223-8720, FAX (502)491-4200.
Desc: Microsoft Excel and DOS (windows).

ISSN 1076-7754 US
●**FAMILY PC.** [Family personal computer]. (1994)-. Periodical. English. Ten times a year. $12.95. FamilyFun, 114 5th Avenue, 15th Floor, New York NY 10011. **Tel** (212) 633-3628, (800)413-9749. **(Subscription address:** CDS Agency Hard Copy, PO Box 4966, Des Moines IA 50340. **Tel** (515)247-7569.)
Ind/Abst Acad. Abstr.; Acad. Search; Bus. Source Plus; Bus. Source; EP Collect.; Homework Help.; Mag. Artic. Summar. Elite; Mag. Artic. Summar. Select; Mag. Artic. Summar. CD-ROM; MasterFile FullTEXT 1000;

MasterFile FullTEXT 350; MasterFile FullTEXT 650; MasterFile FullTEXT (Oct. 1994-); Pub. Lib. FullTEXT; Telebase; Vocat. Search; World Mag. Bank.

US
FAULKNER MICROCOMPUTER AND SOFTWARE. (19??)-. Periodical. English. Twelve times a year. $970.00 US; $1103.00 Canada; $1270.00 other. Faulkner Technical Reports, 7905 Browning Road, Suite 114, Pennsauken NJ 08109. **Tel** (800)843-0460.

US
FLOPPYLAND. COMPUTER DISK. English. $5.00 to start and $3.00 per month thereafter. Stone Mountain Software, PO Box 870183, Stone Mountain GA 30087. **Tel** (404)979-4729. **ED** James W Mangham (Editor's Address: 4586 Ashington Drive, Lithonia, GA 30058). **Circ:** 100. **Continues** Marriage Connection. [Computer File].
Desc: A general exchange of views between subscribers.

ISSN 1049-7757
DD 004 US
FOUR HUNDRED (NEW YORK, N.Y.), THE. (THE FOUR HUNDRED : THE MIDRANGE SYSTEMS STRATEGY JOURNAL.). [Four hundred]. Vol. 1, No. 1 (1990)-. Periodical. English. Twelve times a year. $249.00. Technology News of America, 110 Greene Street, Room 1101, New York NY 10012. **Tel** (212)334-9750, FAX (212)334-9491, telex 668758.

LC QA76.5.G368 JA
GEKKAN RAMU. See Computers-Minicomputers.

LC QA76.5 .G654 ISSN 1040-1636
DD 004.16 US
GOVERNMENT MICRO USER'S GUIDE, THE. [Gov. micro user's guide]. **VFOAT** Micro User's Guide. Vol. 1, No. 1 (Winter 1987)-. Periodical. English. Four times a year. Free (US government installations worldwide). Government Technology Services Inc, 14130-B Sullyfield Circle, Chantilly VA 22021. **Continues** Government Micro User's Catalog.

ISSN 0882-6587
DD 320 US
GOVERNMENT MICROCOMPUTER LETTER. See Public Administration-Computer Applications.

NE
HANDBOEK MACINTOSH & NIEUWSBRIEF. (19??)-. Dutch. Uitgeverij Tutein Nolthenius, Postbus 51344, 1007 EH Amsterdam Netherlands. **Tel** 020-6613999. **Circ:** 1500.
Desc: Contains software reviews, product descriptions and varied Macintosh news.

ISSN 0737-6219 US
HEALTHCARE MICROCOMPUTING NETWORK. See Medical Sciences-Computer Applications.

ISSN 8750-4928
DD 658 US
HOME COMPUTER & SOFTWARE MERCHANDISING. See Business and Economics-Computer Applications.

ISSN 0747-055X
DD 001 US
HOME COMPUTER MAGAZINE. [Home comput. mag.]. Periodical. English. Ten times a year. $25.00 US; $32.00 Canada. Emerald Valley Publishing Company, PO Box 21910, Eugene OR 97402. **Continues** 99'er Home Computer Magazine, 0745-6913.
Ind/Abst Microcomput. Abstr. (Jan. 1985-Dec. 1986).

LC QA76.5 .F328 ISSN 0899-7373
DD 004.16/05 US
HOME OFFICE COMPUTING. [Home off. comput.]. **VFOAT** Home-Office Computing. **VAT** Home-office computing. Vol. 6, No. 9 (Sept. 1988)-. Trade Publication. English. Twelve times a year. $19.97. Scholastic Inc, 2931 East McCarty Street, PO Box 3710, Jefferson City MO 65102-9957. **Tel** (314)636-5271, (800)631-1586. **(Subscription address:** Home Office Computing, PO Box 53561, Boulder CO 80322-3561. **)** available on microfilm and microfiche from University Microfilms International (UMI); available on an online database (files 647,675/Full-Text) from DIALOG. Documents available from UMI Article Clearinghouse. **Continues** Family & Home Office Computing, 0896-6028.
Desc: Published for the home office "techno-preneur." Covers every aspect of working from home, from designing the perfect workspace to interviewing an accountant, and from finding the prices on computers and software to checking out the phone system. Also gives tax tips, legal advice, sales and marketing help, desktop publishing, and more.
Ind/Abst Abr. Read. Guide Period. Lit.; Acad. Abstr. Full Text Elite; Acad. Abstr.; Acad. Search; Comput. ASAP [Full Txt.]; Comput. Bus. (19??-); Comput. Database [Full Txt.]; EP Collect.; Gen. Period. Index (1989-); Homework

Help.; Mag. Artic. Summar. Elite; Mag. Artic. Summar. Select; Mag. Artic. Summar. CD-ROM; Mag. ASAP Plus [Full Txt.]; Mag. ASAP Sel. [Full Txt.]; Mag. Express (1988-) [Full Txt.]; Mag. Index Plus (1989-); Mag. Index. Sel. (1989-); Mag. Search; MasterFile FullTEXT 1000; MasterFile FullTEXT 350; MasterFile FullTEXT 650; MasterFile FullTEXT (Sept. 1988-); Microcomput. Abstr. (Sept. 1988-); Newsp. Period. Abstr. (1988-); OCLC; Pub. Lib. FullTEXT; Read. Guide Abstr. Select Ed.; Read. Guide Period. Lit.; Resource/One Ondisc; Telebase; Mag. Index (1989-); TOM Gen. Index (1993-) [Full Txt.]; Vocat. Search.

ISSN 1073-1784
DD 005 US
●**HOME PC.** [Home PC]. **VAT** Home Personal Computer. Vol. 1, No. 1 (June 1994)-. Periodical. English. Twelve times a year. $21.97. CMP Publications Inc., One Jericho Plaza, Wing A, 2nd Floor, Jericho NY 11753. **Tel** (516)733-6700. **(Subscription address:** Home PC, PO Box 420285, Palm Coast FL 32142-0285. **Tel** (904)445-4662, ext. 420, FAX (904)445-2728 attn: agency order.)
Ind/Abst EP Collect.; Homework Help.; Lotus Notes; MasterFile FullTEXT 1000; MasterFile FullTEXT 350; MasterFile FullTEXT 650; MasterFile FullTEXT; OCLC; Telebase.

ISSN 1260-6421
FR
●**HOME PC PARIS.** (HOME PC). (1994)-. French. $153.10. Edicorp Publications, 73 boulevard de Clichy, F-75009 Paris France. **Tel** 011 33 1 44539191. **(Subscription address:** Home PC, Service Abonnement, 36 rue de Picpus, 75012 Paris France. **Tel** 011 33 1 43420060.**)**

ISSN 0740-3186
DD 001 US
HOT COCO. [Hot CoCo]. **VFOAT** Hot Co Co. Vol. 1, No. 1 (June 1983)-. Periodical. English. Twelve times a year. $27.97. Hot Coco, PO Box 975, Farmingdale NY 11737. available on microfilm and microfiche from University Microfilms International (UMI).
Ind/Abst Microcomput. Abstr. (June 1983-Feb. 1986).

ISSN 0737-8076
US
CEASED
HOT OFF THE COMPUTER. See Library and Information Sciences-Computer Applications.

LC QA76.8.H48 C46 ISSN 0892-2829
DD 004 US
HP CHRONICLE, THE. [HP chron.]. **VFOAT** Chronicle. **VAT** Hewlett-Packard Chronicle; Hewlett Packard Chronicle. (1986)-. Periodical. English. Twelve times a year. $45.00. Publications & Communications, 12416 Hymeadow Drive, Austin TX 78750. **Tel** (512)250-9023, (800)678-9724, FAX (512)331-3900, telex 384303. **(Subscription address:** Publications & Communications, PO Box 399, Cedar Park TX 78630. **)** **ED** Ron Seybold. **Circ:** 16,500. **Continues** Chronicle (Austin, Tex.), 0741-0522; **Absorbed** Workstation, 1059-9959.
Desc: Devoted exclusively to Hewlett-Packard 3000 computer users. Features the latest news, productivity tips, new products, classifieds.

ISSN 0895-0342
DD 004 US
CEASED
HP CHRONICLE. EUROPE, THE. [HP chron., Eur.]. **VAT** Hewlett Packard Chronicle. Europe. Vol. 1, No. 1 (Aug. 1987)-(1993). Periodical. English. Publications & Communications, 12416 Hymeadow Drive, Austin TX 78750. **Tel** (512)250-9023, (800)678-9724, FAX (512)331-3900, telex 384303. **ED** Melba Ferguson.
Desc: A trade publication for European Hewlett-Packard computer users, focused on news and information specifically related to the European Hewlett-Packard market.

ISSN 1065-6189
DD 004 US
HP PALMTOP PAPER, THE. [HP palmtop paper]. **VFOAT** Hewlitt-Packard Palmtop Paper. (199?)-. Periodical. English. Six times a year. $39.00. Thaddeus Computing Incorporated, PO Box 869, Fairfield IA 52556. **Tel** (800)373-6114, (515)472-6330, FAX (515)472-1879. **ED** Rich Hall. **Ad Acc. Circ:** 12,000. available on diskette.
Desc: For users of Hewlett-Packard 200LX, 100LX, and 95LX Palmtop computers.

LC QA76.8.H48 H62 ISSN 0896-145X
DD 004 US
HP PROFESSIONAL. [HP prof.]. **Added/Corp** Hewlett-Packard Company. **VAT** Hewlett Packard Professional. Vol. 1, No. 1 (May 1987)-. Trade Publication. English. Twelve times a year. $30.00. Professional Press Inc, 101 Witmer Road, Horsham PA 19044. **Tel** (215)957-1500, FAX (215)957-1050. **(Subscription address:** Professional Press, PO Box 218, Horsham PA 19044. **)** **ED** Thomas M Halligan, Andrea J Zavod, David B Miller, Linda DiBiasio. **Ad Acc. Circ:** 35,000 (ctrl). available on microfilm and microfiche from University Microfilms International (UMI); available on an online database (file 675/Full-Text) from DIALOG.

Computers —Microcomputers, Personal Computers

Desc: Contributed articles describing helpful techniques, solutions to general problems, challenges, and opportunities and methods to extract performance from a Hewlett-Packard 9000, 3000, or 1000 personal computer or work station. These articles supplement staff-written sections on new products, industry news and product reviews.
Ind/Abst Comput. ASAP [Full Txt.]; Comput. Database [Full Txt.]; Microcomput. Abstr. (May 1987-).

ISSN 0953-4091
UK
CODEN HPWOEY
CEASED

HP WORLD. (HP WORLD : THE INDEPENDENT EUROPEAN MAGAZINE FOR HEWLETT PACKARD COMPUTER USERS.). [HP world]. **VAT** Hewlett Packard World. Vol. 1, No. 1 (Jan. 1988)-(Aug. 1993). Periodical. English. INFAR Ltd, 20 Marine Road, Eastbourne BN22 7AU United Kingdom. **Tel** 011 44 1323 412252, FAX 011 44 1323 412272. Documents available from Ask*IEEE.
Ind/Abst INSPEC (Spring 1991-).

US

HPUX USER. (199?)-. Periodical. English. Six times a year. $49.50. Interex, PO Box 3439, Sunnyvale CA 94088. **Tel** (408)747-0227, FAX (408)736-2156, telex 4971527. **Absorbed** Real-Time Interface, 1059-552X.

LC QA76.5 H74
DD 001.6404
CC
HSIAO HSING WEI HSING CHI SUAN CHI HSI TUNG. See Computers-Minicomputers.

US
ICP SOFTWARE DIRECTORY. MICROCOMPUTER SERIES. See Computers-Programs and Programming.

LC QA76.5 .I276
DD 001.64
ISSN 0272-1732
US
CCC
CODEN IEMIDZ
Pr Rev.
IEEE MICRO. [IEEE MICRO]. Added/Corp IEEE Computer Society. **VFOAT** Micro. **VAT** Institute of Electrical and Electronics Engineers Micro. Vol. 1, No. 1 (Feb. 1981)-. Periodical. English. Six times a year. $270.00. IEEE / Institute of Electrical and Electronics Engineers Inc., 345 East 47th Street, New York NY 10017-2394. **Tel** (908)981-1393, FAX (908)981-9667. **(Subscription address:** IEEE / Institute of Electrical and Electronics Engineers, 445 Hoes Lane, PO Box 1331, Piscataway NJ 08855-1331. **Tel** (800)701-IEEE, (908)981-0060, FAX (908)981-9667, telex 833233.) **ED** James J. Farrell III. Index available. **Bk Rev. Ad Acc. Circ:** 18,520. available on microfiche. Documents available from Article Express International, The Genuine Article, Ask*IEEE.
Desc: Microprocessor and microcomputer design and use; departments cover news, new products, software reviews, standards, legal issues and interviews.
Ind/Abst Acoust. Abstr.; Appl. Sci. Technol. Index; Bioeng. Abstr.; CompuMath Cit. Index [Full Cov.]; Comput. Inf. Syst. Abstr. J. [Full Cov.]; Comput. Bus.; Comput. Database; Comput. Rev.; Curr. Cit.; Curr. Contents Eng. Comput. Technol.; Ei Page One; Elect. Comm. Abstr.; Eng. Index Annu.; Ergon. Abstr.; Expand. Acad. Index (1992-); Index IEEE Publ.; Inf. Sci. Abstr.; INSPEC (Feb. 1981-); Pollut. Abstr. Indexes; Res. Alert [Full Cov.]; Sci. Cit. Index; SCISEARCH; Soc. Sci. Cit. Index [Select. Cov.]; Solid State Supercond. Abstr.

LC QA76.8.A66 T96
US
CEASED
II ALIVE. VFOAT Two Alive; 2 Alive. (1993)-Vol. 3 (1995). Periodical. English. Quality Computers, PO Box 349, St. Clair Shores MI 48080. **Tel** (800) 777-3642, FAX (810) 774-2698. **ED** Jerry Kindall. **Ad Acc. Circ:** 20,000.
Desc: Written for Apple II personal computer users both in the home and the office.

LC QA76.8.A66 I5
DD 004
ISSN 1054-6456
US
CEASED
INCIDER A+. [InCider A+]. **VFOAT** InCider A Plus; InCider A+; InCider A plus; InCider. Vol. 7, No. 11 (November 1989)-(July 1993). Periodical. English. IDG Communications / New Hampshire, 86 Elm Street, Peterborough NH 03458. **Tel** (800)349-7327, FAX (603)924-6972. available on microfilm and microfiche from University Microfilms International (UMI). Documents available from Ask*IEEE, UMI Article Clearinghouse. **Continues** InCider, 0740-0101.
Ind/Abst Acad. Search; EP Collect.; Homework Help.; INFO-SOUTH Abstr.; INSPEC; Mag. Search; MasterFile FullTEXT 1000; MasterFile FullTEXT 350; MasterFile FullTEXT 650; MasterFile FullTEXT (July 1993-July 1993); Microcomput. Abstr. (1989-); Newsp. Period. Abstr. (1988-); OCLC; Telebase.

ISSN 0981-6402
FR
UDC 681.3
INFO PC (NEUILLY-SUR-SEINE). (INFO PC.). **VFOAT** InfoPC (Neuilly-sur-Seine); Info Personal Computer (Neuilly-sur-Seine). (1986)-. Periodical.

French. Eleven times a year. $103.90. IDG Communications / France, Immeuble La Fayette Cedex 65, F-92051 Paris la Defense 5 France. **Tel** 011 33 1 49047900, FAX 011 33 1 49047870, telex 613234. **Continues** O.P.C., 0762-9249.

LC QA76.5 .I442
DD 004.16/029
ISSN 1067-1595
CEASED
INFO WORLD DIRECT. [Info world dir.]. **VFOAT** InfoWorld Direct. Vol. 2, No. 10 (Nov. 1992)-(19??). Trade Publication. English. InfoWorld, 155 Bovet Road, Suite 800, San Mateo CA 94402. **Tel** (800)227-8365, (415)572-7341, (415)312-0691, FAX (415)328-1049, (415)312-0547, telex MNPK 176072. **Continues** Computer Buying World, 1057-9982.

ISSN 0941-6048
GW
INFODOC. (19??)-. German. Six times a year. $133.57. FBO Fachverlag GmbH, Postfach 316, D-76482 Baden-Baden Germany. **Tel** 011 49 7221 271066, 011 49 7221 271067, 011 49 7221 271068, FAX 011 49 7221 33228. **Continues** Mikrodok.

LC Z678.9.A1 I544
DD 025.3/0285
ISSN 0737-7770
CCC
CODEN IIOMEI
INFORMATION INTELLIGENCE, ONLINE LIBRARIES, AND MICROCOMPUTERS. See Library and Information Sciences-Computer Applications.

US
INFORMATION TECHNOLOGY DIGEST. Vol. 1, No.1 Jan. (1992)-. Periodical. English. Fourteen times a year. Free on request. Document Support Staff, 611 Church, 2nd Floor, Ann Arbor MI 48104. **Tel** (313)998-7624. **Formed by the union of** U-M Computing News; UIS Newsletter **and** Communication Lines.

ISSN 8755-6286
DD 001
US
CCC
INFORMATION TODAY. See Library and Information Sciences-Computer Applications.

LC QA75.5 .I56
DD 004
ISSN 0199-6649
US
CCC
CODEN INWODU
INFOWORLD. See Computers-Computer Industry and Industry Directories.

ISSN 1049-5320
DD 005
US
INSIDE DOS. See Computers-Software.

ISSN 1047-6067
DD 005
US
CEASED
INSIDE MICROSOFT BASIC. See Computers-Software.

ISSN 1046-9648
DD 005
US
INSIDE MICROSOFT WORKS. See Computers-Software.

LC QA
DD 005.3
ISSN 1083-1754
US
•**INSIDE PAGEMAKER.** See Computers-Software.

ISSN 1045-6775
DD 005
US
CEASED
INSIDE TURBO PASCAL. See Computers-Software.

LC QA76.5 .I5635
DD 004.1/4
ISSN 0702-0481
CODEN IJMMDE
INTERNATIONAL JOURNAL OF MINI & MICROCOMPUTERS. See Computers-Minicomputers.

LC QA76.5 .J72
DD 004.16/05
ISSN 0745-7138
UK
CCC
CODEN JMIADO
Pr Rev.
TITLE CHANGE
JOURNAL OF MICROCOMPUTER APPLICATIONS. [J. microcomput. appl.]. (Jan. 1982)-(1995). Academic Scholarly Publication. English. Academic Press Ltd., A Division of Harcourt Brace & Company Ltd., 24-28 Oval Road, London NW1 7DX United Kingdom. **Tel** 011 44 171 2674466, FAX 011 44 171 4822293, 011 44 171 4854752, telex 25775 ACPRES G. **(Subscription address:** Harcourt Brace & Company, Ltd., Foots Cray High Street, Sidcup Kent DA14 5HP United Kingdom. **Tel** 011 44 181 3003322, FAX 011 44 181 3090807, telex 896 377 ACADEM.) **ED** J. R. Muhlbacher and M. J. Taylor. Documents available from Article Express International, The Genuine Article, Ask*IEEE. **Continues** Microcomputer Applications (Liverpool Lancashire), 0143-3792. **Continued by**

Journal of Network and Computer Applications.
Desc: Provides an interdisciplinary forum for the presentation of full-length papers and shorter communications on software and hardware design techniques of interesting or novel applications of microcomputers.
Ind/Abst Abstr. Hum. Comput. Interact.; ACM Guide Comput. Lit.; CompuMath Cit. Index [Full Cov.]; Comput. Rev.; Curr. Cit.; Ei Page One; Eng. Index Annu.; Inf. Sci. Abstr. (?-?); INSPEC (Jan. 1982-); Res. Alert [Full Cov.]; SCISEARCH; Soc. Sci. Cit. Index [Select. Cov.]; World Ceram. Abstr.; World Publ. Monit.

UK
•**JOURNAL OF NETWORK AND COMPUTER APPLICATIONS.** (1995)-.
English. Academic Press Ltd., A Division of Harcourt Brace & Company Ltd., 24-28 Oval Road, London NW1 7DX United Kingdom. **Tel** 011 44 171 2674466, FAX 011 44 171 4822293, 011 44 171 4854752, telex 25775 ACPRES G. **Continues** Journal of Microcomputer Applications.

NE
Pr Rev.
•**JOURNAL OF SYSTEMS ARCHITECTURE.** (1995)-. Academic Scholarly Publication. English. Ten times a year. $616.00. Elsevier Science Publishers BV, PO Box 211, 1000 AE Amsterdam Netherlands. **Tel** 011 31 20 4853641, 011 31 20 4853642, FAX 011 31 20 4853598. **(Subscription address:** Elsevier Science BV / Maryland, PO Box 64698, Baltimore MD 21264.) available on an online database from Elsevier Electronic Subscriptions (EES). **Continues** Microprocessing and Microprogramming.

LC QA76.8.I2593 J7
DD 004.165
ISSN 0742-6607
US
JR. (PETERBOROUGH, N.H.). (JR.). [Jr]. **VFOAT** Junior. Vol. 1, No. 1 (May 1984)-. Periodical. English. Twelve times a year. $19.97 US: $22.97 Canada and Mexico. Wayne Green Inc, PO Box 903, Farmingdale NY 11737.
Ind/Abst Microcomput. Abstr. (Jan. 1984-August 1984-).

ISSN 0262-2955
UK
CCC
NLM W1; LA219U
CODEN LMICDI
LABORATORY MICROCOMPUTER. See Science and Technology-Computer Applications.

LC TJ223.M53 L32
DD 621.815
ISSN 0897-0130
US
SUSPENDED
LABORATORY PC USER. See Science and Technology-Computer Applications.

LC TK5105.7 .L36
DD 004
ISSN 1042-4695
US
CCC
CODEN LTECEE
CEASED
LAN TECHNOLOGY. See Computers-Computer Networks.

LC WMLC 93/1068 TK5105.7 .N67
DD 004
ISSN 1040-5917
US
LAN TIMES. See Computers-Computer Networks.

LC KF320.A9 L42
DD 340/.028/5416
ISSN 0740-0942
US
LAWYER'S PC, THE. See Law-Computer Applications.

LC TK5105 .L57
DD 004.6/16/05
ISSN 0739-988X
US
CCC
CODEN LIUPDL
LINK-UP (MINNEAPOLIS, MINN. 1983). See Computers-Computer Networks.

IT
SUSPENDED
LIST : PROGRAMMI PER IL TUO HOME COMPUTER. See Computers-Programs and Programming.

LC QA76.6 .L363
DD 001.64/25
ISSN 0741-7667
US
LSI JOURNAL. See Computers-Programs and Programming.

LC R858.A1 M18
DD 610/.28/5
ISSN 0724-6811
US
CCC
NLM W1; MD9994
Pr Rev.
M.D. COMPUTING. See Medical Sciences-Computer Applications.

ISSN 1045-5825
DD 005
US
Pr Rev.
MAC/CHICAGO (CHICAGO, ILL.). (MAC/CHICAGO). [Mac/CHICAGO]. **VFOAT** Mac Chicago; Resource for Chicagoland Macintosh Users. (1989)-. Trade Publication. English. Six times a year.

Computers —Microcomputers, Personal Computers

$12.00. Mac/CHICAGO, 515 East Golf Road, Suite 201, Arlington Heights IL 60005. **Tel** (708)439-6575. **ED** Jennifer Dees. Index available. cum. index. **Bk Rev**. **Ad Acc**, **Adv Mgr**: Jennifer Dees. **Circ**: 11,000 (ctrl).
 Desc: For MacIntosh computer users in the Chicago metropolitan area. Covers local users, product and service resources, tips and techniques, and software reviews. Provides local area trade directory for Mac related products and services. Local and national columnists cover the latest Mac news.

US
MAC HOME JOURNAL. (19??)-. English. Six times a year. $11.95 (one-year), $19.95 (two-year) US; $16.95 (one-year), $31.95 (two-year) other. Antic Publishing Company, 544 Second Street, San Francisco CA 94107. **Tel** (415)957-1911, FAX (415)882-9502. **(Subscription address**: Kable Publishers Aide / Illinois, 308 East Hitt Street, Subscription Department, Mt. Morris IL 61054-1473. **Tel** (815)734-1261.**) ED** Sandra Anderson. **Bk Rev**. **Ad Acc**. **Circ**: 125,000.

FR
MAC INFORMATIQUE. French. Exa Publications, 10 rue Fresnel, 75116 Paris France. **Tel** 011 33 1 47235570.

AT
MAC-LINK. (19??)-. English. Two times a year. 16.44Aus$. Microcomputer Applications Centre, PO Box 88, South Melbourne 3205 Australia. **Tel** 011 61 3 2545454, FAX 011 61 3 6961956. **ED** Kaitlin Swindon. **Bk Rev**. **Ad Acc**.
 Desc: Gives updated and new ideas on electronic equipment for people with disabilities.

US
MAC REPORT, THE. (19??)-. English. One time a week. $220.00. The Mac Report, 101 Church Street #410, Nashville TN 37201. **Tel** (615)256-5044, FAX (615)256-7124. **ED** Patrick McCoy. **Ad Acc**.

ISSN 0899-1642
DD 004 US
MAC SUBJECTS. See Computers-Computer Industry and Industry Directories.

ISSN 0891-0243
DD 004 US
MAC TITLES IN PRINT. [MAC titles print].
VFOAT MAC TIP. **VAT** MacIntosh Titles in Print. Vol. 1, Issue 1 (Nov. 1986)-. Periodical. English. Twelve times a year. $48.00. Mac Titles in Print, PO Box 748, El Toro CA 92630. **Tel** (714)472-4790.

US
CEASED
MACACADEMY MENTOR. (19??)-(Dec. 1993). English. Florida Marketing International Inc, 477 South Nova Road, Ormond Beach FL 32174. **Tel** (904) 677-1918, FAX (904) 677-6717. **ED** LaDell Crookston (editors telephone: (904) 673-6229. ctrl circ.
 Desc: Covers Macintosh computers & software.

ISSN 1047-8221
DD 005 US
MACBARGAIN CONNECTION NEWSLETTER : MONEY-SAVING NEWS AND INFO ABOUT APPLE MACINTOSH PRODUCTS AND SERVICES. [MacBargain connect. newsl.]. Vol. 1, No. 1 (Nov./Dec. 1989)-. Newsletter. English. Twelve times a year. Century Micropublishing, 146 Main Street, Suite 101, Salem NH 03079. **Tel** (603)898-2854.

US
MACHACKER. (19??)-. English. Six times a year. Dail's Software Co., PO Box 2861, Newport News VA 23602. **Continues** Macazine, 8756-6117.
 Desc: Available for use on a Macintosh.

ISSN 0894-9603
DD 330 US
MACINTOSH BUSINESS LETTER, THE.
[Macintosh bus. lett.]. Vol. 1, No. 1 (Oct. 30, 1987)-. Periodical. English. Twelve times a year. $295.00 US; $370.00 other. MBL Publications Inc, 153 California Avenue, Suite F213, Palo Alto CA 94306.

ISSN 1055-7350
DD 004 US
MACINTOSH CONSTRUCTION FORUM.
[Macintosh constr. forum]. (1987)-. Periodical. English. Six times a year. $75.00. Macintosh Construction Forum, PO Box 1272, Sandpoint ID 83864. **Tel** (208)263-3078.

ISSN 1048-3535
DD 004 US
MACINTOSH DISCOUNT REPORTER NEWSLETTER, THE. [Macintosh discount report. newsl.]. **VFOAT** Macintosh Discount Reporter. Vol. 1, No. 1 (Jan. 1990). Newsletter. English. Ten times a year. $49.00 (new), $99.00 (renewal) US; $79.00 other. Century Micropublishing, 146 Main Street, Suite 101, Salem NH 03079. **Tel** (603)898-2854. **ED** Russell Marano. **Bk Rev**. **Circ**: 400. **Continues** Macintosh Connection, 0748-8807.
 Desc: Includes news, trends on Mac pricing and contacts.

NE
MACINTOSH MAGAZINE. (19??)-. English. Six times a year. IDG Communications / Netherlands, Postbus 5446, 2000 GK Haarlem Netherlands. **Tel** 011 31 23 366814.

ISSN 1070-6720
DD 005 US
MACINTOSH TIPS & TRICKS (PRINT).
(MACINTOSH TIPS & TRICKS.). [Macintosh tips tricks]. **VFOAT** Macintosh Tips and Tricks. Vol. 1, Issue 1 (Sept. 1992)-. Newsletter. English. Twelve times a year. $19.95. Giles Road Press, PO Box 212, Harrington Park NJ 07640-0212. **Tel** (201)767-7001, FAX (201)767-7457. **ED** Maria L. Langer. **Circ**: 15,000. available on an online database from GEnie; America Online; and Compuserve Inc.
 Desc: A news and productivity newsletter for Macintosh computer users. Each issue features product news, illustrated how-to articles, and shortcuts for "Quick Tips" that help readers work better or faster. An editor's column offers insights on Macintosh computing. Letters to the Editor give readers a chance to share what's on their mind.

ISSN 0887-9648
DD 004 US
MACINTOUCH. [MacInTouch]. **VFOAT** Mac In Touch. (1985)-. Periodical. English. Twelve times a year. $24.00. Sdmug, PO Box 12568, La Jolla CA 92039. **ED** Paul Taylor. **Bk Rev**. **Ad Acc**.
 Desc: Information and articles on the Macintosh user's groups.

IT
CEASED
MACNEWS. (19??)-(19??). Italian. Soft Publishing, Cas Post 628, 35129 Padua Italy. **Tel** 011 39 49 772290.

ISSN 0891-365X
DD 004 US
MACTIMES. [MacTimes]. **VFOAT** Mac Times. **VAT** Macintosh Times. (198?)-. Periodical. English. Six times a year. MacTimes Inc, PO Box 40, 1174 Barnes Street, Franklin Square NY 11010.

ISSN 0269-3275
UK
MACUSER LONDON. (MACUSER.). [MacUser Lond.]. (1985)-. Periodical. English. Twenty-four times a year. $208.77. Dennis Publishing Ltd, 19 Bolsover Street, London W1P 7HJ United Kingdom. **Tel** 011 44 181 6311433, FAX 011 44 181 6365668, telex 8954139. **ED** Caroline Bassett. **Bk Rev**. **Ad Acc**, **Adv Mgr**: Caroline Evans. **Circ**: 30,000.
 Desc: News, reviews, features, advice and analysis of Apple-Macintosh products and technology. Aimed at users of Apple-Macintosh.

LC QA76.8.M3 M36
DD 004.165 **ISSN** 0884-0997 US
CODEN MCUSEY
MACUSER (NEW YORK, N.Y.). (MACUSER.). [MacUser]. **VFOAT** Mac User. **VAT** Macintosh User. Vol. 1, No. 1 (Oct. 1985)-. Periodical. English. Twelve times a year. $27.00. Ziff-Davis, One Park Avenue, 5th Floor, New York NY 10016. **Tel** (212)503-3500. **(Subscription address**: Neodata / Colorado, PO Box 2606, Boulder CO 80322.) available on an online database (files 647,675/Full-Text) from DIALOG; available via Internet (http://www.ziff.com/). Documents available from UMI Article Clearinghouse.
 Desc: Delivers over 250 product reviews, coverage of important Macintosh applications including graphics, telecommunications, networking, games and education. Special power user hints and techniques written to help users expand the performance of their system.
 Ind/Abst Acad. Ind. [Computer File] (1987-); Acad. Search; Comput. ASAP [Full Txt.]; Comput. Bus. (19??-); Comput. Database [Full Txt.]; Comput. Rev. Index (Oct. 1986-); EP Collect.; Expand. Acad. Index (1987-); Gen. Period. Index (1987-); HILITES; Homework Help.; INFO-SOUTH Abstr.; Mag. ASAP Plus [Full Txt.]; Mag. ASAP Sel. [Full Txt.]; Mag. Index Plus (1989-); Mag. Index. Sel. (1987-); Mag. Search; MasterFile FullTEXT 1000; MasterFile FullTEXT 350; MasterFile FullTEXT 650; MasterFile FullTEXT (July 1993-); Microcomput. Abstr. (Sept. 1987-); Newsp. Period. Abstr. (1988-); OCLC; Telebase; Mag. Index. (1977-); TOM Gen. Index (1993-) [Full Txt.].

ISSN 0957-2341
UK
MACWORLD (LONDON). (MACWORLD : THE MACINTOSH MAGAZINE.). [MacWorld]. **VAT** Macintosh World. (1989). Vol. 5 (1993)-. Periodical. English. Twelve times a year. $94.11. IDG Communications Ltd. / London, 99 Grays Inn Road, London WC1X 8UT United Kingdom. **Tel** 011 44 181 6860371, FAX 011 44 181 4052347. **ED** Peter Wonlock. **Bk Rev**. **Ad Acc**. **Circ**: 26,898 (ctrl). **Absorbed** Apple Business, 0953-4474.

LC QA76.8.M3 M3
DD 004.165 **ISSN** 0741-8647 US
CODEN MACWEA
MACWORLD (SAN FRANCISCO, CALIF.). (MACWORLD : THE MACINTOSH MAGAZINE.). [Macworld]. **VAT** Macintosh World. Vol. 1, No. 1 (Feb. 1984)-. Periodical. English. Twelve times a year. $18.00. PCW Communications Inc., 501 Second Street, San Francisco CA 94107. **Tel** (415)243-0500, (415)978-3146. **(Subscription address**: MacWorld, Subscription Department, PO Box 54529, Boulder CO 80322-4529. **Tel** (800)288-6848, (303)447-9330 (outside continental US).) available on magnetic tape, an online database, and CD-ROM; available on microfilm and microfiche from University Microfilms International (UMI); available on an online database (file 15/Full-Text) from DIALOG. Documents available from UMI Article Clearinghouse.
 Desc: Designed especially for users of the MacIntosh. Includes hardware and software reviews, hands-on instruction, etc.
 Ind/Abst Acad. Abstr.; Acad. Ind. [Computer File] (1992-); Acad. Search; Comput. Bus. (19??-); Comput. Database; Comput. Rev. Index (1986-); Curr. Cit.; EP Collect.; Expand. Acad. Index (1992-); Gen. Period. Index (1992-); HILITES; Homework Help.; INFO-SOUTH Abstr.; Mag. Artic. Summar. Elite; Mag. Artic. Summar. Select; Mag. Artic. Summar. CD-ROM; Mag. Index Plus (1989-); Mag. Search; MasterFile FullTEXT 1000; MasterFile FullTEXT 350; MasterFile FullTEXT 650; MasterFile FullTEXT (Jan. 1992-); Microcomput. Abstr. (Feb. 1984-); Newsp. Period. Abstr. (1988-); OCLC; Pop. Period. Index; Pub. Lib. FullTEXT; Read. Guide Period. Lit.; Telebase; Mag. Index (1977-); TOM Gen. Index (1987-); Vocat. Search.

LC HD9696.A1 M34
DD 338.47621381 KO
MAIKURO SOPUTUWEO. See Computers-Computer Industry and Industry Directories.

ISSN 1048-6933
DD 658 US
CODEN MEUCEY
CEASED
MANAGING END-USER COMPUTING.
[Manag. end-user comput.]. **VFOAT** Managing End User Computing. Vol. 1, No. 1 (Aug. 1987)-(April 1993). Periodical. English. Auerbach Publishers Inc., Park Square Building, 31 St. James Avenue, Boston MA 02116. **Tel** (800)950-1207. **ED** Nancy Tyson, (212)971-5275. **Bk Rev**, (Qty: up to 12)). **Circ**: 1,000.
 Desc: Practical advice about how to manage end-user computing in your organization, including suggestions and guidelines for supporting and training end-users.

GW
MC COMPUTERPRAXIS FUER TECHNISCHE ANWENDER. (19??)-. German. Twelve times a year. DM84.00 Germany; DM96.00 other. Franzis Verlag GmbH, Gruberstrasse 46 A, D-85586 Poing Germany. **Tel** 011 49 8121 769433. **Continues** MC Die Mikrocomputerzeitschrift.

ISSN 0720-4442
GW
CCC
CODEN MDMZDL
TITLE CHANGE
MC : DIE MIKROCOMPUTER-ZEITSCHRIFT.
VFOAT Mikrocomputer-Zeitschrift; Mikrocomputer Zeitschrift. (19??)-(19??). Trade Publication. German. Franzis Verlag GmbH, Gruberstrasse 46 A, D-85586 Poing Germany. **Tel** 011 49 8121 769433. **Circ**: 62,643. Documents available from Ask*IEEE. **Continued by** MC Computerpraxis fuer Technische Anwender.
 Ind/Abst Infomat Int. Bus.; INSPEC (Sept. 1990-).

IT
MC : MICROCOMPUTER. (19??)-. Italian. Eleven times a year. L230000 America and Asia; L64000 Italy; L165000 Europe; L285000 other. Technimedia Srl, Via Carlo Perrier 9, 00157 Rome Italy. **Tel** 011 39 6 418921.

US
MCPS OVERSEAS AND STATESIDE UPDATES/MICRO COMPUTERS PROCESSING SYSTEM. English. $150.00. Williams Consulting Service, 2626 Burton Road, Utica KY 42376. **Tel** (502)729-4273.

ISSN 0733-2394
US
MEMORY AND MICROCOMPUTERS.
Periodical. English. Irregular. $292.00 (corporations), $178.00 (academic libraries). Gordon & Breach Science Publishers, Inc., PO Box 786, Cooper Station, New York NY 10276. **Tel** (212)206-8900, FAX (212)645-2459.

Computers —Microcomputers, Personal Computers

ISSN 0958-4668
UK
MICRO ABSTRACTS. (19??)-. English. Six times a year. £60.00 UK; £64.00 Europe; £66.00 other. Techgnosis Ltd., Blade House, Battersea Road, Cheshire SK4 3EA United Kingdom. **Tel** 011 44 161 4422639, FAX 011 44 161 4431162.

LC HF5469.55.U6 M53   ISSN 8755-2132
DD 381/.1   US
MICRO AND PERSONAL COMPUTERS USED IN THE CONVENIENCE STORE INDUSTRY. Added/Corp National Association of Convenience Stores (U.S.). **VFOAT** Directory of Micro and Personal Computers Used in the Convenience Store Industry. (19??)-. Trade Publication. English. One time a year. $50.00. National Association of Convenience Stores, 1605 King Street, Alexandria VA 22314. **Tel** (703)684-3600.

ISSN 0177-5235
GW
CODEN MCCOEY
MICRO COMPUTER COLLEG. [Micro-Comput.-Coll.]. **VFOAT** Microcomputer Colleg. (19??)-. Periodical. German. Six times a year. Bertelsmann Fachzeitschriften GmbH, Carl Bertelsmann Strasse 270, D-33311 Frankfurt Germrany. **Tel** 011 49 5241 802199. Documents available from Ask*IEEE.
Ind/Abst INSPEC (1985-).

ISSN 0732-9512
US
MICRO DISCOVERY. [Micro discov.]. (1983)-. Periodical. English. Twelve times a year. $15.00 (schools and libraries) US; $25.00 (schools and libraries) other.

ISSN 0836-3587
CN
DD 658/.024/0285416
MICRO-GAZETTE. See Business and Economics-Small Business.

ISSN 0748-8483
DD 004   US
MICRO MAINFRAME CONNECTION. Vol. 1, No. 1 (Oct. 1984)-. Periodical. English. Twelve times a year. $165.00 US; $195.00 other. Daymaker Publishing Company, 13324 Hawthorne Blvd. Suite 133, Hawthorne CA 90250.

ISSN 0742-9398
US
MICRO MONEY. [Micro money]. Periodical. English. Twelve times a year. $55.00. How Publishing Company, PO Box 218, Washington IL 61571. **ED** Harry Wahl. **Bk Rev**. **Ad Acc**.
Desc: How to make money with microcomputers and related products. Gives markets, product sources, opportunities and how-to information.

ISSN 0277-0059
US
MICRO MOONLIGHTER. See Computers-Computer Sales, Service and Supply.

FR
MICRO ORDINATEUR. French. Societe de Presse et Services, 49 rue de L'Universite, 75007 Paris France.

LC QA76.5 .M5216
DD 001.64/04/02947   US
MICRO SHOPPER. (19??)-. English. $3.95 each issue. Microage Wholesale, 1425 W 12th Place, Tempe AZ 85281.

ISSN 0183-5084
FR
UDC 681.3
CEASED
MICRO SYSTEMES (PARIS. 1978). [Micro syst. Paris, 1978]. (1978)-(1993). Periodical. French. Micro-Systemes, 2/12 rue Bellevue, F-75940 Paris Cedex 19 France. **Tel** 011 33 1 42003305.
Ind/Abst Repere (1985-).

UK
MICRO USER. (19??)-. English. £24.95 UK; £49.00 Europe; £69.00 other. Database Publ, Europa House, Adlington House, Adlington Macclesfield, SK10 5NP United Kingdom. **Continues** BBC Micro User.
Ind/Abst Int. Civil Eng. Abstr.

LC QA75.5 .M5   ISSN 1074-3995
DD 016.00416   US
●**MICROCOMPUTER ABSTRACTS. See** Computers-Abstracting, Bibliographies and Statistics.

LC QA76.5 .M52167   ISSN 0820-0750
DD 001.64   US
MICROCOMPUTER APPLICATIONS (ANAHEIM). (MICROCOMPUTER APPLICATIONS : AN OFFICIAL JOURNAL OF THE INTERNATIONAL SOCIETY FOR MINI AND MICROCOMPUTERS.). [Microcomput. appl.]. **Added/Corp** International Society for Mini-Microcomputers. Vol. 1, No. 1 (1982)-. Periodical. English. Three times a year (Jan., May, Sep.). $172.00. ISMM- International Society of Mini and Microcomputers,

PO Box 2481, Anaheim CA 92814. **Tel** FAX (714)535-2662. **ED** Prof L Miller. Index available. **Bk Rev**. **Ad Acc**. **Circ:** 200. Documents available from Ask*IEEE.
Desc: Covers mini and microcomputers including technology, hardware, software, systems, networks, education and applications. It includes book reviews, conferences, call for papers, new publications, and ads.
Ind/Abst Comput. Abstr.; Curr. Cit.; INSPEC (1984-); Int. Civil Eng. Abstr.; Soft. Abstr. Eng.

LC QA75.5 .M5   ISSN 8756-7040
DD 016.00416   US
TITLE CHANGE
MICROCOMPUTER INDEX. See Computers-Abstracting, Bibliographies and Statistics.

LC HD9696.C6 M5   ISSN 0741-6016
DD 338.4/700164   US
MICROCOMPUTER INDUSTRY UPDATE. See Computers-Abstracting, Bibliographies and Statistics.

LC TK7800 .M43   US
DD 621.39/16
●**MICROCOMPUTER JOURNAL. VFOAT** Micro Computer Journal. Vol. 1, No. 1 (Jan./Feb. 1994)-. Periodical. English. Six times a year. $14.95. CQ Communications Inc, 76 North Broadway, Hicksville NY 11801. **Tel** (516)681-2922, FAX (516)681-2926.
Continues ComputerCraft, 1055-5072.
Ind/Abst MasterFile FullTEXT (Jan. 1994-).

DD 004   ISSN 1041-8563
US
MICROCOMPUTER SOLUTIONS (U.S. ED.). (MICROCOMPUTER SOLUTIONS.). [Microcomput. solut.]. **Added/Corp** Intel Corporation. **VFOAT** Solutions. (Nov./Dec. 1987-)-. Periodical. English. Six times a year. **Continues** Solutions (U.S. ed. : Santa Clara, Calif.), 1041-8547.
Ind/Abst ACM Guide Comput. Lit.; Comput. Rev.

DD 005   ISSN 1055-3258
US
MICROCOMPUTER TRAINER, THE. [Microcomput. train.]. (Apr. 1991)-. Periodical. English. Eleven times a year (monthly with July/Aug. issue combined). $195.00 US; $210.00 Canada and Mexico; $220.00 other. Systems Literary Inc., PO Box 2487, Seacaucus NJ 07096-2487. **Tel** (201)330-8923, FAX (201)330-0163. **ED** Loretta Weiss Morris.

LC HD9696.C63 U52555   ISSN 0747-511X
DD 001.64   US
MICROCOMPUTER VENDOR DIRECTORY. See Computers-Computer Industry and Industry Directories.

LC Z678.93.M53 M54   ISSN 0742-2342
DD 025.6/2   US
CCC
MICROCOMPUTERS FOR INFORMATION MANAGEMENT. See Library and Information Sciences.

ISSN 0743-0302
US
MICROCOMPUTERS FOR LIBRARIES. See Library and Information Sciences-Computer Applications.

LC TA345 .M487   ISSN 0885-9507
DD 624/.028/5416   UK
CCC
CODEN MCENE7
MICROCOMPUTERS IN CIVIL ENGINEERING. See Engineering-Computer Applications.

LC HE147.6 .M53   ISSN 0741-5451
DD 388.4/028/5425   US
MICROCOMPUTERS IN TRANSPORTATION. SOFTWARE AND SOURCE BOOK. See Transportation-Computer Applications.

ISSN 0823-0234
DD 001.64/04   CN
MICROMONTH. [Micromonth]. Periodical. English. Twelve times a year. $95.00. DP Market Facts, Suite 105/208 Evans Avenue, Toronto Ontario M8Z 1J7 Canada. **Tel** (416)622-5452.

ISSN 1065-6111
US
MICROPRENEUR (NORTHWOOD, N.H.). (MICROPRENEUR.). **Added/Corp** Micropreneur Assistance Center. (1992)-. Periodical. English. Twelve times a year. Micropreneur Assistance Center, Upper Deerfield Road, Northwood NH 03261.

ISSN 0740-3526
US
MICROPRO USERS' MONTHLY. (MICROPRO USERS' MONTHLY : MUM.). [Micropro users' mon.]. **VFOAT** M.U.M.; MUM. Vol. 1, No (Nov.

1983)-. Periodical. English. Twelve times a year. $36.00. MUM, 700 Larkspur Landing/Suite 120, Larkspur CA 94939.

LC QA76.5 .E89a   ISSN 0165-6074
DD 004.16   NE
CCC
CODEN MMICDT
TITLE CHANGE
Pr Rev.
MICROPROCESSING AND MICROPROGRAMMING. [Microprocess. microprogram.]. **Added/Corp** Euromicro. Vol. 7, No. 1 (Jan. 1981)-(1995). Academic Scholarly Publication. English. Elsevier Science Publishers BV, PO Box 211, 1000 AE Amsterdam Netherlands. **Tel** 011 31 20 4853641, 011 31 20 4853642, FAX 011 31 20 4853598. **ED** M Sami and L Richter. Index available. **Bk Rev**, (Qty: 10). **Ad Acc, Adv Mgr:** W Van Cattenburch. available on microfilm and microfiche from University Microfilms International (UMI). Documents available from Article Express International, The Genuine Article, BIOSIS Document Express, UMI Article Clearinghouse, Ask*IEEE. **Continues** Euromicro Journal, 0167-3858. **Continued by** Journal of Systems Architecture.
Desc: Facilitates the international flow of information in the field of microprocessing and microprogramming.
Ind/Abst ABI/INFORM Glob. Ed.; ABI/INFORM [Computer File] (Jan. 1981-); Abstr. Hum. Comput. Interact.; ACM Guide Comput. Lit.; Bioeng. Abstr.; Biol. Abstr. (-1987); CompuMath Cit. Index [Full Cov.]; Comput. Abstr.; Comput. Inf. Syst. Abstr. J. [Full Cov.]; Comput. Lit. Index; Comput. Rev.; Curr. Cit.; Ei Page One; Elect. Comm. Abstr.; Eng. Index Annu.; Gen. BusinessFile (1992-); Inf. Sci. Abstr. (?-); INSPEC (Jan. 1981-); Res. Alert [Full Cov.]; SCISEARCH.

DD 004   ISSN 0899-9341
US
MICROPROCESSOR REPORT.
[Microprocess. rep.]. (Sept. 1987)-. Periodical. English. Seventeen times a year. $495.00. MicroDesign Resources Inc., 874 Gravenstein Highway South, Suite 14, Sebastopol CA 95472. **Tel** (707)823-4004, (800)527-0288, FAX (707)823-0504. available on an online database (files 648,675/Full-Text) from DIALOG.
Ind/Abst Comput. Database ASAP [Full Txt.]; Comput. Database [Full Txt.]; Trade Ind. ASAP [Full Txt.]; Trade Ind. Index [Full Txt.].

LC QA76.5 .M5227   ISSN 0889-9932
DD 005.36/05   US
CCC
CODEN MSJOED
MICROSOFT SYSTEMS JOURNAL. See Computers-Software.

ISSN 0968-4743
DD 005.369   UK
MICROSOFT SYSTEMS JOURNAL LONDON. See Computers-Software.

FR
MICROSYSTEMES. French. Les Publ Georges Ventillard, 2 A 12 rue de Bellevue, 75019 Paris Cedex 19 France. **Tel** 011 33 1 44848484.

LC HD9696.C6 M53   ISSN 0743-6343
DD 001.64   US
MICROSYSTEMS COMPETITIVE REVIEW. Added/Corp Systems Marketing Associates. **VFOAT** M.C.R.; MCR. (19??)-. English. Two times a year. $450.00. Systems Marketing Associates, 3328 E Cherokee Street, Phoenix AZ 85044-3512.

ISSN 1063-1488
DD 004   US
MICROSYSTEMS HANDBOOK. [Microsyst. handb.]. **Added/Corp** National Software Testing Laboratories. **VFOAT** NSTL Microsystems Handbook. (1992)-. English. NSTL, Inc., Plymouth Corporate Center, Plymouth Meeting PA 19462.

ISSN 1065-0148
DD 004   US
MICROTIMES (PLEASANT HILL, CALIF.). (MICROTIMES.). **VFOAT** Micro Times. (19??)-. Periodical. English. Fourteen times a year. $35.00. BAM Publications Inc., 3470 Buskirk Avenue, Pleasant Hill CA 94523. **Tel** (510)934-3700, FAX (510)934-3958. **ED** Mary Eisenhart. **Ad Acc**. **Circ:** 235,000 (ctrl).

ISSN 0836-5482
DD 650/.028/5416   CN
MICROVIEW (TORONTO). See Business and Economics-Computer Applications.

ISSN 0163-6294
US
MICRU REALITY. Added/Corp Microdata Reality Users Group, Chicago. (Jan. 1978)-. Periodical. English. Four times a year. Cerebratonia Renaissance Press, 70 East Main Street, PO Box 259, Lake Zurich IL 60047.

LC QA76.76.D47 M53   ISSN 1050-0324
DD 005.1   US
MIDNIGHT ENGINEERING. See Engineering.

Computers —Microcomputers, Personal Computers

ISSN 0344-8010
GW
TITLE CHANGE
MIKRODOK (BADEN-BADEN, GERMANY). (MIKRODOK.). (198?)-(1993). Periodical. German. FBO Fachverlag GmbH, Postfach 316, D-76482 Baden-Baden Germany. **Tel** 011 49 7221 271066, 011 49 7221 271067, 011 49 7221 271068, FAX 011 49 7221 33228. *Continues* Mikrodok, 0343-0286. *Continued by* Infodoc.

US
MIMI, PROCEEDINGS OF THE INTERNATIONAL SYMPOSIUM ON MINI AND MICRO COMPUTERS. See Computers-Minicomputers.

ISSN 0179-0382
GW
CODEN MMMAEA
MINI-MICRO-MAGAZIN. See Computers-Minicomputers.

LC WMLC 93/1409 **ISSN 1047-1952**
DD 384 US
MOBILE OFFICE. See Communications-Telecommunication.

ISSN 1070-2792
DD 004 US
MONITOR (ROCKVILLE, MD.). (MONITOR.). [Monitor]. **Added/Corp** Capital PC User Group. **VFOAT** Capital PC Monitor Magazine; Capital PC Monitor. (19??)-. Periodical. English. Twelve times a year. $35.00. Capital PC User Group Inc, 51 Monroe Street, Plaza East Two, Rockville MD 20850. **Tel** (301)762-9372. *Continues Capital PC Monitor, 0884-0830.*

GR
●**MULTIMEDIA AND CD-ROM.** (1995)-. Greek, Modern. Twelve times a year. Dr28000.00. Compupress S.A., 44 Syngrou, 117 42 Athens Greece. **Tel** 011 30 1 9238672, FAX 011 30 1 9216847.

ISSN 1073-4759
DD 006 US
CCC
●**MULTIMEDIA WORLD.** [Multimed. world]. **VFOAT** Multimedia World Magazine. Vol. 1, No. 1 (Dec. 1993)-. Trade Publication. English. Twelve times a year. $17.97. PCW Communications Inc., 501 Second Street, San Francisco CA 94107. **Tel** (415)243-0500, (415)978-3146. **(Subscription address:** Neodata / Colorado, PO Box 2606, Boulder CO 80322.) *Separated from* PC World, 0737-8939; *Absorbed* CD-ROM World.

US
Pr Rev.
NERVLINE. A MICROCOMPUTER INFORMATION RETRIEVAL SYSTEM IN THE CLINICAL NEUROSCIENCES. See Medical Sciences-Computer Applications.

LC PN4784.E5 N49 **ISSN 0888-1596**
DD 070/.028/541605 US
NEWS COMPUTING JOURNAL. See Journalism.

ISSN 0289-6508
DD 621.38195 JA
NIKKEI BAITO. [Nikkei baito]. **VFOAT** Nikkei Byte. (1984)-. Periodical. Japanese. One time a week. $276.00. Nihon Keizai Shimbun Inc., 9-5 Otemachi 1 Chome, Chiyoda-ku Tokyo 100 Japan. **Tel** 011 81 3 32700251, 011 81 3 52108502 (Nikkei Business Publications Inc.), FAX 011 81 3 52552661, 011 81 3 52108119 (Nikkei Business Publications Inc.). **(Subscription address:** Maruzen Company Ltd., PO Box 5050, Import & Export Department, Tokyo 100 31 Japan. **Tel** 011 81 3 32789224.) **Desc:** Information on advances in personal computer technology for professionals and amateurs.

ISSN 0915-2490
DD 001.64 621.38195 JA
NIKKEI DETAPURO MAIKURO PUROSESA. **VFOAT** Nikkei Datapro Maikuro Purosesa. (1989)-. Japanese. Irregular. Nihon Keizai Shimbun Inc., 9-5 Otemachi 1 Chome, Chiyoda-ku Tokyo 100 Japan. **Tel** 011 81 3 32700251, 011 81 3 52108502 (Nikkei Business Publications Inc.), FAX 011 81 3 52552661, 011 81 3 52108119 (Nikkei Business Publications Inc.). **ED** Hisashi Okamura.

ISSN 0914-9368
DD 001.64 621.38195 JA
NIKKEI DETAPURO PASOKON. VFOAT Nikkei Datapro Pasokon. (1985)-. Japanese. Irregular. Nihon Keizai Shimbun Inc., 9-5 Otemachi 1 Chome, Chiyoda-ku Tokyo 100 Japan. **Tel** 011 81 3 32700251, 011 81 3 52108502 (Nikkei Business Publications Inc.), FAX 011 81 3 52552661, 011 81 3 52108119 (Nikkei Business Publications Inc.). **ED** Hisashi Okamura.

ISSN 0914-0212
DD 001.64 JA
NIKKEI DETAPURO WAKU SUTESHON. See Business and Economics-Office Equipment and Services.

LC HD9696.C63 J35 **ISSN 0287-9506**
DD 338.47621381 JA
NIKKEI PASOKON. **VFOAT** Nikkei Personal Computing. (1983)-. Periodical. Japanese. Twenty-four times a year. $490.00. Nikkei Magurohirusha, 1 Kanda Ogawa-machi 1 Chiyoda-ku, Tokyo-to 101 Japan. **Tel** 03-233-8171. **(Subscription address:** Maruzen Company Ltd., PO Box 5050, Import & Export Department, Tokyo 100 31 Japan. **Tel** 011 81 3 32789224.) **ED** Kouichi Shiraishi. Index available. cum. index. **Bk Rev. Ad Acc. Circ:** 138,725. **Desc:** Articles include information on how to utilize personal computers, evaluation on the software presently in the market, and case studies on the use of personal computers.

ISSN 0731-8367
US
●**ON-LINE (DURHAM, N.H.).** (ON-LINE : NEWSLETTER OF UNH COMPUTER SERVICES.). **Main/Corp** University of New Hampshire. Computer Service. **VFOAT** Online. Newsletter. English. Six times a year. $10.00. Newsletter Computer Services, Kingsbury Hall, University of New Hampshire, Durham NH 03824. **Tel** (603)862-2323. **ED** James W Cerny. **Circ:** 1,650 (ctrl).
Desc: Newsletter for computer services to communicate with user community.

LC TS540 **ISSN 1381-2882**
DD 681 NE
UDC 681.31+621.39
●**ORGANIZE AMSTERDAM. See** Business and Economics-Management.

SP
P C DISC. (19??)-. Spanish. Eleven times a year. P C Disc SA, Ferraz 11, 28008 Madrid Spain. **Tel** (91)247 30 00, 541 34 00, FAX (91)248 1123. **ED** Javier San Roman. **Bk Rev. Ad Acc. Circ:** 18,990. available on diskette.

ISSN 0747-9573
DD 001 US
CEASED
PACKAGED SOFTWARE REPORTS / MIC. See Business and Economics-Computer Applications.

ISSN 1074-7257
DD 005 US
●**PAGE PC, THE.** [Page PC]. **Added/Corp** Cobb Group. **VAT** Page Personal Computer. Vol. 1, No. 1 (Feb. 1994)-. Periodical. English. Twelve times a year. $69.00. Cobb Group, 9420 Bunsen Parkway #300, Louisville KY 40220. **Tel** (502)491-1900, (800)223-8720, FAX (502)491-4200.

LC QA76.8.I2594 P285 **ISSN 0743-2534**
DD 016.004165 US
PC ABSTRACTS. [PC abstr.]. **VFOAT** P.C. Abstracts. **VAT** Personal Computer Abstracts. (1983)-. English. Two times a year. $15.95. Walter Gaber, 9754 South Houston, Jenks OK 74037-3409.

ISSN 0925-5745
NE
UDC 681.31
PC ACTIVE. [PC Act.]. **VFOAT** Personal Computer Active. (1989)-. Periodical. Dutch. Eleven times a year. F79.00 (latest volume). M Stok, Postbus 2545, 1000 CM Amsterdam Netherlands. **Tel** 011 31 20 6242636. **ED** A. Withop. **Bk Rev. Ad Acc. Adv Mgr:** R Lie, **Tel** 020-6249969. **Circ:** 30,000 (ctrl). *Continues* PC Amstrad, 0925-5737; MSX-MX DOC Computer Magazine.

ISSN 0894-0711
DD 006 US
CCC
CODEN PCAIE5
PC AI. See Computers-Artificial Intelligence.

LC TK7887 .P4 **ISSN 1045-5701**
DD 621.39/16/0288 US
PC COMPUTER MAINTENANCE ANNUAL. (PC COMPUTER ... MAINTENANCE ANNUAL.). [PC comput. maint. annu.]. (1988/89)-. English. Irregular (4 updates set per year). $294.95. Champions Management Support Services, 128-B Meadowlake Drive, Downingtown PA 19335. **Tel** (908)276-3477, FAX (301)604-9248. **ED** Ken Lachnicht. available on CD-ROM.

ISSN 0899-1847
DD 004 US
PC/COMPUTING (NEW YORK, N.Y.). (PC/COMPUTING.). [PC/Computing]. **VFOAT** PC Computing. Vol. 1, No. 1 (Aug. 1988)-. Periodical. English. Twelve times a year. $25.00. Ziff-Davis, One Park Avenue, 5th Floor, New York NY 10016. **Tel** (212)503-3500. **(Subscription address:** Neodata / Colorado, PO Box 2606, Boulder CO 80322.) available on an online database from NEXIS; available via Internet (http://www.ziff.com/). Documents available from UMI Article Clearinghouse. *Absorbed* Personal Computing, 0192-5490.
Desc: Designed to help executives find PC solutions to everyday business problems and to get the most out of their PC's. Offers problem-solving product reviews, reports on new and future technologies, a help section to speed up day-to-day operations.
Ind/Abst Abr. Read. Guide Period. Lit. (1991-); Acad. Abstr. Full Text Elite; Acad. Abstr.; Acad. Search; ACM Guide Comput. Lit.; Comput. ASAP [Full Txt.]; Comput. Bus. (19??-); Comput. Database [Full Txt.]; Comput. Rev.; EP Collect.; Homework Help.; INFO-SOUTH Abstr.; Mag. Artic. Summar. Elite; Mag. Artic. Summar. Select; Mag. Artic. Summar. CD-ROM; Mag. ASAP Plus [Full Txt.]; Mag. ASAP Sel. [Full Txt.]; Mag. Index Plus (1989-); Mag. Index Sel. Microfiche (1988-) [Full Txt.]; Mag. Index. Sel. (1988-); Mag. Search; MasterFile FullTEXT 1000; MasterFile FullTEXT 350; MasterFile FullTEXT 650; MasterFile FullTEXT (Jan. 1991-); Microcomput. Abstr. (Aug. 1988-); Newsp. Period. Abstr. (1990-); OCLC; Pub. Lib. FullTEXT; Read. Guide Abstr. Select Ed.; Read. Guide Period. Lit. (1991-); Telebase; Mag. Index (1988-); TOM Gen. Index (1988-) [Full Txt.]; Vocat. Search.

LC QA76.9.E94 P38 **ISSN 1042-3575**
DD 004/.029/673 US
CCC
PC DIGEST RATINGS REPORT. [PC dig. rat. rep.]. **Added/Corp** National Software Testing Laboratories. **VFOAT** PC Digest Microsystems Reporter; PC Digest Ratings Report, Microsystems Reporter; PC Digest Ratings Report, Peripherals Reporter; PC Digest Microsystems Handbook; PC Digest. **VAT** Personal Computer Digest Ratings Report. Vol. 3, No. 1 (1989-)-. Periodical. English. Fifteen times a year. $450.00. National Software Testing Laboratories, PO Box 1000, Plymouth Meeting Corporate Center, Plymouth Meeting PA 19462. **Tel** (610)941-9600, (800)328-2776, FAX (215)941-9952. **(Subscription address:** McGraw Hill / PC Digest, PO Box 551, Hightstown NJ 08520.) Index available (free). cum. index. ctrl price. *Continues* PC Digest (Philadelphia, PA.), 0891-575X.
Desc: Tests standalone and networked microcomputers and peripherals. Provides head-to-head comparisons between hardware products.

ISSN 0964-1661
DD 004.16 UK
PC DIRECT. [PC direct]. (1991)-. Periodical. English. Twelve times a year. $107.76. Ziff Davis Ltd., Cottons Centre Hay's Lane, London SE1 2QT United Kingdom. **Tel** 011 44 171 3786800, FAX 011 44 171 3786702. **ED** Karen Packham. **Ad Acc, Adv Mgr:** Emma Roffey.

ISSN 1045-7240
DD 004 US
PC FAST FACTS. (PC FAST FACTS : THE EXECUTIVE'S GUIDE TO PC PRODUCT RATINGS.). [PC fast facts]. **VAT** Personal Computer Fast Facts. (1989)-. Periodical. English. Twelve times a year. $89.00. Whitney-Stearns Corporation, 130 Oxford Street, Irvine CA 92715. **Tel** (714)253-5797.

US
CEASED
PC HOME JOURNAL. (19??)-(Feb./March 1993). English. Antic Publishing Company, 544 Second Street, San Francisco CA 94107. **Tel** (415)957-1911, FAX (415)882-9502. **ED** Sandra Anderson. **Bk Rev. Circ:** 75,000.

UK
PC LAN. Periodical. English. Twelve times a year. £50.00 UK; £80.00 (airmail) Europe; £70.00 (surface mail) other. VNU Business Publications BV, 32-34 Broadwick Street, London W1A 2HG United Kingdom. **Tel** 011 44 171 4394242 ext. 2222, FAX 011 44 171 4379638, telex 23918 VNU G, 8952440.

ISSN 1043-1314
DD 004 US
PC LAPTOP COMPUTERS MAGAZINE. **VFOAT** PC Lap Top Computers Magazine; PC Laptop; Laptop Computers Magazine; PClaptop. **VAT** Personal Computer Laptop Computers Magazine. (Apr. 1989)-. Periodical. English. Twelve times a year. $24.95. LFP Inc., 8484 Wilshire Boulevard, Suite 900, Beverly Hills CA 90210. **Tel** (213)651-5400. **(Subscription address:** Kable Publishers Aide / Illinois, 308 East Hitt Street, Subscription Department, Mt. Morris IL 61054-1473. **Tel** (815)734-1261.)
Ind/Abst Microcomput. Abstr. (Feb. 1992-).

ISSN 0953-7708
UK
PC MAGAZINE. **VAT** Personal Computer Magazine. Vol. 1, Issue 1 (May 1988)-. Periodical. English. Twelve times a year. $111.17. Ziff Davis UK Ltd., Cottons Centre Hay's Lane, London SE1 2QT United Kingdom. **Tel** 011 44 171 3786800, FAX 011 44 171 3786702. **ED** Tony Westbrook and Steve Malone. **Ad Acc, Adv Mgr:** Tim Munson.

IT
PC MAGAZINE. Italian. Eleven times a year. L61600 Italy; L123200 other. Gruppo Editoriale Jackson Spa, Via Gorki 69, 20092 Cinisello Balsamo Italy. **Tel** 011

39 2 66034401.
Ind/Abst Graph. Arts Bull. Inst. Pap. Sci. Technol. (Feb. 1989-March 1989, May 1989, July 1989, Oct. 1989-); HILITES; Microcomput. Ind. Update.

LC QA76.8.I1015 **ISSN** 1078-8085
DD 004 US

•PC MAGAZINE CD. (PC MAGAZINE CD [COMPUTER FILE].). [PC mag. CD]. (1993)-. English. Four times a year. $50.00. Ziff-Davis, One Park Avenue, 5th Floor, New York NY 10016. **Tel** (212)503-3500. **(Subscription address:** Neodata / Colorado, PO Box 2606, Boulder CO 80322. **)**

LC QA
DD 004 CH

PC MAGAZINE. CHINESE EDITION. (19??)-. Chinese. Twelve times a year. $150.00 Hong Kong; $186.00 Asia; $239.00 US and Europe. Transdata Research Company, Nan Ching East Road, 4th Floor 51 Section 4, Taipei Taiwan. **Tel** 011 8862 7153000.

ISSN 1069-9953
DD 004 US

PC MAGAZINE EN ESPANOL. [PC mag. esp.]. (19??)-. Periodical. Spanish. Twelve times a year. $29.75. Editorial America SA, 6355 Northwest 36th Street, Miami FL 33166. **Tel** (305)871-6400. **(Subscription address:** CDS / SIFD Agency Control, 1901 Bell Avenue, Des Moines IA 50315. **Tel** (515)246-6812.**)**

LC QA76.8.I1015 P38 **ISSN** 0888-8507
DD 004.165 US

PC MAGAZINE (NEW YORK, N.Y.). (PC MAGAZINE : THE INDEPENDENT GUIDE TO IBM-STANDARD PERSONAL COMPUTERS.). [PC mag.]. **VFOAT** PC. **VAT** Personal Computer Magazine. Vol. 5, No. 2 (Jan. 28, 1986)-. Periodical. English. Twenty-two times a year (publishes twice a month and one issue in July and Aug.). $50.00. Ziff-Davis, One Park Avenue, 5th Floor, New York NY 10016. **Tel** (212)503-3500. **(Subscription address:** Neodata / Colorado, PO Box 2606, Boulder CO 80322. **)** available on an online database from DIALOG; available on CD-ROM; available on microfilm and microfiche from Ziff Communications; available via Internet (http://www.ziff.com/). Documents available from UMI Article Clearinghouse. ***Continues** PC (San Francisco, Calif.), 0745-2500.*
Desc: Provides business users and corporate buyers with information and evaluations of software, hardware and peripherals, exclusive comparative product reviews and test reports from PC labs.
Ind/Abst Acad. Abstr.; Acad. Ind. [Computer File] (1984-); Acad. Search; Bus. ASAP (1990-) [Full Txt.]; Bus. Index (1985-); Comput. ASAP [Full Txt.]; Comput. Bus.; Comput. Database [Full Txt.]; Comput. Rev. Index (1986-); Curr. Cit.; Curr. Lit. Fam. Plan. (19??-199?); EP Collect.; Expand. Acad. Index (1984-); Gen. BusinessFile (1985-); Gen. Period. Index (1985-); Homework Help.; Index Period. Artic. Relat. Law; INFO-SOUTH Abstr.; Inf. Manage. Technol. (19??-); Mag. Artic. Summar. Elite; Mag. Artic. Summar. Select; Mag. Artic. Summar. CD-ROM; Mag. ASAP Plus [Full Txt.]; Mag. ASAP Sel. [Full Txt.]; Mag. Index Plus (1989-); Mag. Index Sel. Microfiche (1986-) [Full Txt.]; Mag. Index. Sel. (1986-); Mag. Search; MasterFile FullTEXT 1000; MasterFile FullTEXT 350; MasterFile FullTEXT 650; MasterFile FullTEXT (Jan. 1992-); Microcomput. Abstr. (Jan. 1982-); Newsp. Period. Abstr. (1988-); OCLC; Pub. Lib. FullTEXT; Telebase; TOM Gen. Index (1988-) [Full Txt.]; Trade Ind. ASAP [Full Txt.]; Trade Ind. Index [Full Txt.]; Vocat. Search.

LC QA
DD 005 PO
UDC 68

PC MAGAZINE. PORTUGUESE EDITION. (19??)-. Periodical. Portuguese. Twelve times a year. 44$30 Portugal; 74$30 other. PC Magazine, Rua D Estefania 32 1, 1000 Lisbon Portugal.

BE
CEASED

PC MICRO MAGAZINE. (19??)-(19??). Multiple languages (French and Dutch). Ecopress S A, rue de la Petite ILE 1, 1070 Brussels Belgium. **Tel** 011 32 2 5251411. ***Continues** Micro Magazine.*

LC QA76.5.P364 **ISSN** 1052-1186
DD 004.16.05 US
CCC

PC NOVICE. [PC novice]. **VAT** Personal Computer Novice. Vol. 1, Issue 1 (May 1990)-. Periodical. English. Twelve times a year. $24.00. Peed Corporation, 120 West Harvest Drive, PO Box 85380, Lincoln NE 68501. **Tel** (800)424-7900, (402)477-8900. **Ad Acc.**
Desc: The magazine for computer newcomers. Designed to help beginners learn about the basics of personal computing. Articles are written in a readable, plain-English style, and topics include hardware, software and DOS.
Ind/Abst Abr. Read. Guide Period. Lit.; Comput. Bus. (19??-); Read. Guide Period. Lit.

NE

PC PLUS. (19??)-. English. VNU Business Publications BV, Postbus 9194, 1006 AC Amsterdam Netherlands. **Tel** 011 31 20 4875879.

UK

PC PLUS. No. 1 (Oct. 1986)-. English. Twelve times a year. Future Publishing Ltd., Cary Court, Somerton, Somerset TA11 6TB United Kingdom. **Tel** 011 44 1225 442244, FAX 011 44 1225 45827378.

ISSN 1065-9099
US

•PC PRESENTATIONS, PRODUCTIONS. **VFOAT** PC Presentations/Productions. **VAT** Personal Computer Presentations, Productions. (1993)-. Periodical. English. Six times a year. $28.00. Pisces Publishing Group, 417 Bridgeport Avenue, Devon CT 06460. **Tel** (203)877-4427, FAX (203)877-1927.

US

PC QUOTES. (1985)-. Periodical. English. Twelve times a year. David S Cook Publishing Company, PO Box 229, Keystone Heights FL 32656.

US

PC REPORT. English. Twelve times a year. $40.00 US; $75.00 other (members only). The Boston Computer Society, One Kendall Square, Cambridge MA 02139-1562. **Tel** (617)367-8080. **ED** Art Bevilacqua. **Bk Rev. Ad Acc. Circ:** 15,000 (ctrl).

LC QA76.75 .P36 **ISSN** 1042-0681
DD 005.3/25 US
Pr Rev.

PC-SIG MAGAZINE. **See** Computers-Software.

LC QA76.5 .P3654 **ISSN** 1052-6579
DD 004.16 US
CEASED

PC SOURCES. [PC sources]. **VAT** Personal Computer Sources. Vol. 1, No. 10 (Oct. 1990)-(1993). Periodical. English. Ziff-Davis, One Park Avenue, 5th Floor, New York NY 10016. **Tel** (212)503-3500. **ED** Peter McKie.
Desc: Specs and upgrading information. A forward look at PC product classes coming to the mail-order front. Includes product reviews to help professionals make the most of the computer market.
Ind/Abst Comput. ASAP [Full Txt.]; Comput. Database [Full Txt.].

ISSN 1031-3966
DD 004.1605 AT

PC SUPPORT ADVISOR (SYDNEY). [PC support advis. Syd.]. **VFOAT** Personal Computer Support Advisor. (1988)-. Periodical. English. Twelve times a year. $641.70. International Technology Publishing Inc., GPO Box 4730, Sydney NSW 2001 Australia. **Tel** 011 61 2 2614683.

LC QA76.76.D47 P38 **ISSN** 1053-6205
DD 005.265 US
TITLE CHANGE

PC TECHNIQUES. **See** Computers-Software.

LC QA76.5 .P743 **ISSN** 1040-6484
DD 004.16/05 US
CCC

PC TODAY. [PC today]. **VFOAT** Processor PC Today. **VAT** Personal Computer Today. Vol. 2, No. 9 (Oct. 1988)-. Periodical. English. Twelve times a year. $24.00. Peed Corporation, 120 West Harvest Drive, PO Box 85380, Lincoln NE 68501. **Tel** (800)424-7900, (402)477-8900. **ED** Steven Mann. Index available. **Ad Acc. Circ:** 200,000 (ctrl). ***Continues** Processor (Lincoln, Neb.).*
Desc: Designed to help the small business person get the most out of personal computers. Helps the reader find out about hardware and software and strives to give a growing business a competitive edge.
Ind/Abst Comput. Bus. (19??-).

ISSN 0960-0124
UK
TITLE CHANGE

PC TODAY MACCLESFIELD. (PC TODAY.). [PC today Macclesfield]. **VFOAT** Personal Computing Today (Macclesfield). (1990)-(19??). Periodical. English. Europress Direct, PO Box 2, Ellesmere Port Wirral, Cheshire L65 3EA United Kingdom. **Tel** 011 44 171 0513571275, FAX 011 44 171 0513572813. ***Continues** PC. Personal Computing with the Amstrad, 0952-3014. **Merged into** PC Works.*

ISSN 1075-6159
DD 004 US

•PC TROUBLESHOOTER, THE. **See** Computers-Computer Sales, Service and Supply.

ISSN 0263-5720
UK
CCC

PC USER (LONDON, ENGLAND). (PC USER.). **VFOAT** PC User Magazine. **VAT** Personal Computer User. (198?)-. Periodical. English. Twenty-four times a year. $205.35. EMAP Business & Computer Publishing Ltd., 1 Lincoln Court 1 Lincoln Road, Peterborough PE1 2RP United Kingdom. **Tel** 011 44 1733 68900, FAX 011 44 1733 349290. **ED** Chris Long. **Bk Rev. Ad Acc. Circ:** 39,213 (ctrl). available on CD-ROM; available on an online database (files 648,675/Full-Text) from DIALOG.
Desc: The UK's top PC magazine for users of IBM and compatible personal computers. Includes exclusive reviews, up to date news and buyer's guide on all PC hardware and software.
Ind/Abst Comput. ASAP [Full Txt.]; Comput. Database [Full Txt.]; Inf. Manage. Technol.; Int. Civil Eng. Abstr.; Soft. Abstr. Eng.; Trade Ind. ASAP [Full Txt.]; Trade Ind. Index [Full Txt.].

ISSN 1065-8645
DD 005 US

PC VISION. [PC vis.]. **VAT** Personal Computer Vision. Vol. 1, Issue 1 (Sept. 1992)-. Periodical. English. Twelve times a year. $30.00. PC Vision, PO Box 744, Clovis CA 93613-0744.

ISSN 1030-6137
AT

PC WEEK (AUSTRALIAN EDITION). (PC WEEK.). (1987)-. Periodical. English. One time a week. 81.40Aus$. Australian Consolidated Press Ltd., Private Bag 92615 Symonds St, Auckland New Zealand. **Tel** 011 64 9 3735408, FAX 011 64 9 3022889.

LC QA75.5 .P37 **ISSN** 0740-1604
DD 001.64 US

PC WEEK (U.S. ED.). (PC WEEK.). [PC week]. **VFOAT** Week. **VAT** Personal Computer Week. Vol. 1, No. 1 (July 18, 1983)-. Periodical. English. One time a week. $195.00. Ziff-Davis, One Park Avenue, 5th Floor, New York NY 10016. **Tel** (212)503-3500. **Ad Acc. Circ:** 175,000 (ctrl). available on an online database (files 647,648,675/Full-Text) from DIALOG; available via Internet (http://www.ziff.com/). Documents available from UMI Article Clearinghouse.
Desc: Each issue provides news and industry updates, expert opinions, and buying guidance.
Ind/Abst Acad. Search; Bus. ASAP (1990-) [Full Txt.]; Bus. Index (1985-); Bus. Source Plus; Bus. Source; Comput. ASAP [Full Txt.]; Comput. Bus. (19??-); Comput. Database [Full Txt.]; Comput. Rev. Index (April 1986-); Curr. Lit. Fam. Plan. (19??-199?); EP Collect.; F&S Index Plus Text, Int. [Select. Cov.]; Gen. BusinessFile (1985-); Gen. Period. Index (1985-); Homework Help.; INFO-SOUTH Abstr.; Mag. ASAP Plus [Full Txt.]; Mag. Index Plus (1989-); Mag. Search; MasterFile FullTEXT 1000; MasterFile FullTEXT 350; MasterFile FullTEXT 650; MasterFile FullTEXT (Jan. 1993-); Microcomput. Abstr. (Jan. 1985-); Microcomput. Ind. Update; Newsp. Period. Abstr. (1989-); OCLC; PROMT; Pub. Lib. FullTEXT; Telebase; Mag. Index (1983-); Trade Ind. ASAP [Full Txt.]; Trade Ind. Index [Full Txt.]; Vocat. Search.

ISSN 0269-3011
UK
CODEN PCWKEJ

PC WEEK (UK ED.). (PC WEEK.). [PC week]. **VFOAT** Week. **VAT** Personal Computer Week. (Wednesday, September 4, 1985)-. Trade Publication. English. One time a week. $171.12. VNU Business Publications BV, 32-34 Broadwick Street, London W1A 2HG United Kingdom. **Tel** 011 44 171 4394242 ext. 2222, FAX 011 44 171 4379638, telex 23918 VNU G, 8952440. Documents available from Ask*IEEE.
Ind/Abst INSPEC (1985-).

UK

PC WORKS. **VFOAT** Personal Computing Today (Macclesfield). (19??)-. Periodical. English. Twelve times a year. £65.50 Europe; £78.50 others. IDG Media, Media House, Adlington Park, Macclesfield SK10 4NP United Kingdom. **Tel** 011 44 1625 878888. ***Absorbed** PC Today, 0960-0124.*

LC QA76.8.I2594 P3 **ISSN** 0737-8939
DD 001.64 US
CCC
CODEN PCWDDV

PC WORLD. [PC world]. **VFOAT** P.C. World. Vol. 1, No. 1 (1983)-. Periodical. English. Twelve times a year. $29.90. PCW Communications Inc., 501 Second Street, San Francisco CA 94107. **Tel** (415)243-0500, (415)978-3146. **(Subscription address:** Neodata / Colorado, PO Box 2606, Boulder CO 80322. **) ED** David Bunnell. available on microfilm and microfiche from University Microfilms International (UMI). Documents available from Ask*IEEE, UMI Article Clearinghouse. ***Absorbed** PC Resource, 0892-0575. **Continued in part by** Multimedia World, 1073-4759.*
Desc: Covers the IBM PC and compatibles market; aims to give business decision makers solutions to their business problems, and help them buy personal computers and related products.
Ind/Abst Abstr. Bull. Inst. Pap. Sci. Tech.; Acad. Abstr. Full Text Elite; Acad. Abstr.; Acad. Ind. [Computer File]

Computers —Microcomputers, Personal Computers

(1992-); Acad. Search; Comput. Bus. (1983-); Comput. Database; Comput. Rev. Index (1986-); Curr. Cit.; Data Process. Dig.; Ei Page One; EP Collect.; Expand. Acad. Index (1992-); Gen. Period. Index (1992-); Graph. Arts Bull. Inst. Pap. Sci. Technol. (Jan. 1989); Homework Help.; INFO-SOUTH Abstr.; INSPEC (Feb. 1985-); J. Ferrocement; Mag. Artic. Summar. Elite; Mag. Artic. Summar. Select; Mag. Artic. Summar. CD-ROM; Mag. Index Plus (1992-); Mag. Search; MasterFile FullTEXT 1000; MasterFile FullTEXT 350; MasterFile FullTEXT 650; MasterFile FullTEXT (June 1986-); Microcomput. Abstr. (March 1983-); Microcomput. Ind. Update; Newsp. Period. Abstr. (1988-); OCLC; Pop. Period. Index; Pub. Lib. FullTEXT; Read. Guide Period. Lit.; Resource/One Ondisc (1988-); Telebase; Vocat. Search.

SP

PC WORLD. (19??)-. Spanish. Eleven times a year. $180.00. IDG Communications / Spain, Rafael Calvo 18, 28010 Madrid Spain. **Tel** 011 34 1 3194014, 3087233. available on microfilm from University Microfilms International (UMI).

ISSN 1120-8066
IT

UDC 681.3
PC WORLD ITALIA. **VFOAT** Personal Computer World Italia. (1990)-. Periodical. Italian. Eleven times a year. L88.000 Italy; L138.000 Europe; L204.000 other. IDG Communications Italia SRL, Via Mecenate 30 14, 20138 Milan Italy. **Tel** 011 39 2 58011660, FAX 011 39 2 58011670.

US
CEASED
PC WORLD. LOTUS EDITION. (PC WORLD.). Vol. 10, No. 12 (Dec. 1992)-Vol. 17, No. 7 (199?). Periodical. English. PCW Communications Inc., 501 Second Street, San Francisco CA 94107. **Tel** (415)243-0500, (415)978-3146. **(Subscription address:** Neodata / Colorado, PO Box 2606, Boulder CO 80322.) **Continues** Lotus (Cambridge, Mass.), 8756-7334.

ISSN 0213-1307
SP

UDC 681.3
PC WORLD MADRID. **VFOAT** Personal Computer World (Madrid); PC World Espa*f*na. (1985)-. Periodical. Spanish. Eleven times a year. 7920ptas Spain; 8910ptas other; $180.00 other. IDG Communications / Spain, Rafael Calvo 18, 28010 Madrid Spain. **Tel** 011 34 1 3194014, 3087233.

ISSN 0801-5236
DD 001.64 NO
PC WORLD NORGE (1987). (PC WORLD NORGE.). [PC World Nor. 1987]. (1987)-. Periodical. Norwegian. Eleven times a year. Kr440.00. Oslo IDG Communications Norge, Hovinveien 43, 0576 Oslo 5 Norway. **Tel** 011 47 22 688090. **Continues** PC Mikrodata, 0800-9465.

LC QA76.5 .P366 ISSN 0747-0460
DD 004.16 US
PCM. [PCM]. **VAT** Portable Computing Magazine. (July 1983)-. Periodical. English. Twelve times a year. $34.00 US; $46.00 Canada; $78.00 (surface mail); $126.00 (airmail) other. Falsoft Inc., PO Box 385, Prospect KY 40059. **Tel** (502)228-4492, FAX (502)228-5121. **ED** Lawrence C. Falk. Index available. **Ad Acc, Adv Mgr:** Carol Fenwick, **Tel** (502)228-4492. **Circ:** 50,000. available on diskette.
Desc: Personal computer magazine for Tandy computer users.
Ind/Abst Microcomput. Abstr. (Jan. 1985-).

HK
PCWORLD. (19??)-. English (Chinese). Twelve times a year. HK$380.00 (one-year), HK$720.00 (two-year) Hong Kong; 81.00Sing$ (one-year), 150.00Sing$ (two-year) Singapore; 130.00Mal$ (one-year), 240.00Mal$ (two-year) Malaysia; $90.00 (one-year), $180.00 (two-year) countries within Asia; $135.00 (one-year), $270.00 (two-year) countries outside Asia. Asia Computerworld Communication, 701-4 Kam Chung Blg, 54 Jaffe R, Wanchai Hong Kong. **Tel** 011 852 28613238, FAX 011 852 28610953. **ED** Laura Janney. **Ad Acc, Adv Mgr:** Vera Chan. **Circ:** 3500.

ISSN 0744-2475
US
PEELINGS II : THE MAGAZINE OF APPLE SOFTWARE EVALUATION. See Computers-Software.

LC QA75 ISSN 1235-1199
DD 004 FI
UDC 681.3
PELIT (1992). (PELIT.). (1992)-. Periodical. Finnish. Eight times a year. Erikoislehdet Oy, Tecnopress, PO Box 16, SF 00381 Helsinki Finland. **Tel** 358-0-120-5911, FAX 358-0-120-5999. **ED** Eskoensio Pipatti. **Circ:** 15,000.

ISSN 1063-1496
DD 004 US
PERIPHERALS HANDBOOK. [Peripher. handb.]. **Added/Corp** National Software Testing Laboratories. **VFOAT** NSTL Peripherals Handbook. (1992)-. English. NSTL, Inc., Plymouth Corporate Center, Plymouth Meeting PA 19462.

LC QA76.8.I2594 P47 ISSN 0737-2906
DD 001.64 US
PERSONAL COMPUTER AGE. [Pers. comput. age]. Vol. 1/1 (Jan. 1982)-. Periodical. English. Twelve times a year. $24.00 US; $29.00 Canada. CRC Publishing, 8138 Foothill Boulevard, Sunland CA 91040. **Tel** (310)352-7811.
Ind/Abst Microcomput. Abstr. (Nov. 1982-May 1984).

ISSN 0957-2279
UK
PERSONAL COMPUTER MAGAZINE (LONDON). (PERSONAL COMPUTER MAGAZINE.). [Pers. comput. mag.]. **VFOAT** Personal Computer. (1988)-. Trade Publication. English. Twelve times a year. $85.56. VNU Business Publications BV, 32-34 Broadwick Street, London W1A 2HG United Kingdom. **Tel** 011 44 171 4394242 ext. 2222, FAX 011 44 171 4379638, telex 23918 VNU G, 8952440. **Continues** PC (U.K. Ed.), 0267-4815.
Ind/Abst HILITES.

US
PERSONAL COMPUTER OUTLOOK. English. One time a year. $595.00. Technologic Partners, 419 Park Avenue South, Suite 500, New York NY 10016. **Tel** (212)696-7910.

ISSN 0894-3532
DD 004 US
PERSONAL COMPUTER REPORT (MINEOLA, N.Y.). (THE PERSONAL COMPUTER REPORT.). [Pers. comput. rep.]. **Added/Corp** Micro Business Systems (Mineola, N.Y.). Vol. 1, No. 1 (Nov. 1984)-. Periodical. English. Twelve times a year. $495.00. Advanced Microcomputers Inc, Box 645, Mineola NY 11501. **Tel** (718)341-3724. **(Subscription address:** Personal Computer Report, 144-21 167th Street, Springfield Gardens NY 11434.) **ED** Julian Benfield. **Bk Rev.** ctrl circ.
Desc: Timely evaluation and forecast of friends and products in the personal computer industry.

ISSN 0142-0232
UK
CODEN PCWODU
PERSONAL COMPUTER WORLD. See Business and Economics-Computer Applications.

NE
PERSONAL COMPUTERS MAGAZINE. (19??)-. English. VNU Business Publications BV, Postbus 9194, 1006 AC Amsterdam Netherlands. **Tel** 011 31 20 4875879.

ISSN 0275-6900
US
PERSONAL COMPUTING INDUSTRY REPORT. [Pers. comput. ind. Rep.]. Periodical. English. Twelve times a year. $255.00. Vantage Research Inc., 2680 Bayshore Road, Mountail View CA 94043.

LC TA345 .P46 ISSN 0748-0016
DD 620/.0028/5416 US
CCC
CODEN PEGNEU
PERSONAL ENGINEERING & INSTRUMENTATION NEWS. See Engineering-Computer Applications.

ISSN 0732-7501
US
PORTABLE COMPANION, THE. [Portable companion]. (1982)-. Periodical. English. Six times a year. $25.00. Osborne Computer, 125 Fremont Avenue, Los Altos CA 94022. **Tel** (415)887-8080. **ED** Tony Bove and Cheryl Rhodes. **Bk Rev. Ad Acc.**
Desc: The magazine for Osborne computer users.

LC QA76.5 .P6345 ISSN 0738-1220
DD 001.64/05 US
PORTABLE COMPUTER. [Portable comput.]. Vol. 1, No. 1 (Feb./Mar. 1983)-. Periodical. English. Six times a year. $22.00. Portable Computer, 500 Howard Street, San Francisco CA 94105. **Tel** (415)397-1881. **ED** Stephen J Schneiderman. available on microfilm and microfiche from University Microfilms International (UMI).
Ind/Abst Microcomput. Abstr. (Feb. 1983-Dec. 1984).

LC QA76.8.C63 C65 ISSN 0739-8018
DD 004 US
POWER PLAY. [Power play]. **Added/Corp** Commodore Business Machines. Computer Systems Division. **VFOAT** Commodore Power Play. (1982)-. Periodical. Four times a year. $10.00 US; $15.00 other. Commodore Business Machines, 1200 Wilson Drive, West Chester PA 19380.

LC QA76.5 .R498A ISSN 0278-291X
DD 001.64/04 US
PROCEEDINGS - ROCKY MOUNTAIN SYMPOSIUM ON MICROCOMPUTERS: SYSTEMS, SOFTWARE, ARCHITECTURE. (PROCEEDINGS ... ANNUAL ROCKY MOUNTAIN SYMPOSIUM ON MICROCOMPUTERS, SYSTEMS, SOFTWARE, ARCHITECTURE.). **Main/Conf** Rocky Mountain Symposium on Microcomputers: Systems, Software, Architecture. 1st (Aug. 31-Sept. 2, 1977)-. Proceedings. English. One time a year. IEEE Computer Society, 10662 Los Vaqueros Circle, PO Box 3014, Los Alamitos CA 90720-1264. **Tel** (714)821-8380, (800)272-6657, FAX (714)821-4641.

ISSN 1076-9714
DD 005 US
●**PROGRAMMER'S PROVANTAGE COMPUTER PRODUCTS BUYER'S GUIDE.** See Computers-Programs and Programming.

US
PROGRAMMERS ROM. CD-ROM. See Computers-Programs and Programming.

LC QA76.8.T183 R34 ISSN 0746-4797
DD 001.64 US
RAINBOW (PROSPECT, KY.). (THE RAINBOW.). [Rainbow]. Vol. 1, No. 1-. Periodical. English. Twelve times a year. $31.00 US; $38.00 Canada; $85.00 (surface mail), $103.00 (airmail) other. Falsoft Inc., PO Box 385, Prospect KY 40059. **Tel** (502)228-4492, FAX (502)228-5121. **ED** Cray Augsburg. **Bk Rev. Ad Acc. Circ:** 50,000. available on diskette; available on an online database (file 675/Full-Text) from DIALOG.
Desc: Articles, tutorials, program listings for the Tandy Color Computer.
Ind/Abst Comput. Rev.

LC Z52.5.I27 R37 ISSN 0742-0684
DD 652/.5 US
RATINGS BOOK, THE. See Computers-Word Processing.

US
RBBS-PC IN A BOX. CD-ROM. See Computers-Software.

LC HF5548.4.I25 R78 ISSN 1061-0030
DD 004.165 US
CEASED
RS/MAGAZINE (BROOKLINE, MASS.). (RS/MAGAZINE : THE JOURNAL FOR IBM WORKSTATION USERS.). [RS/mag.]. **VFOAT** RS Magazine. Vol. 1, No. 1 (Jan. 1992)-(1995). Periodical. English. Computer Publishing Group, 1330 Beacon Street, Brookline MA 02146. **Tel** (617)739-7001, FAX (617)739-7003. **ED** Ann Knowles. **Circ:** 40,000 (ctrl). **Continued by** RS/The PowerPC Magazine, 1082-2313.

ISSN 1082-2313
DD 004 US
●**RS / THE POWERPC MAGAZINE.** [RS PowerPC mag.]. Vol. 4, No. 3 (Mar. 1995)-. Periodical. English. Twelve times a year. Computer Publishing Group, 1330 Beacon Street, Brookline MA 02146. **Tel** (617)739-7001, FAX (617)739-7003. **Continues** RS/Magazine, 1061-0030.

LC QA76.8.M3 S44 ISSN 1072-0995
DD 502/.85/4165 US
CODEN SITJE8
●**SCITECH JOURNAL.** (SCITECH JOURNAL : OFFICIAL JOURNAL OF THE MACINTOSH SCIENTIFIC AND TECHNICAL USERS ASSOCIATION.). [SciTech j.]. **Added/Corp** Macintosh Scientific and Technical Users Association. **VFOAT** Sci Tech Journal. Vol. 3, No. 1 (Jan. 1993)-. Periodical. English. Six times a year. MacSciTech, 49 Midgley Lane, Worcester MA 01604. **Tel** (508)755-5242, FAX (508)795-1636. **ED** Shari L.S. Worthington. **Ad Acc, Adv Mgr:** Jerry Caswell. **Continues** SciTech Quarterly.

LC TK7800
DD 621.381 US
●**SELLING NETWORKS.** (1994)-. Trade Publication. English. Six times a year. McGraw Hill Information Systems Company, 1221 Avenue of the Americas, New York NY 10020. **Tel** (212)512-2000, (800)525-5003, FAX (212)512-6111.

LC QA76.753 .S52 ISSN 1042-0681
DD 005.365 US
CEASED
SHAREWARE MAGAZINE. See Computers-Software.

LC QA76.5 .S54 ISSN 1078-134X
DD 004 US
CODEN SGBLEC
●**SIGICE BULLETIN.** (SIGICE BULLETIN : A MONTHLY PUBLICATION OF THE ACM SPECIAL INTEREST GROUP ON INDIVIDUAL COMPUTING ENVIRONMENTS.). [SIGICE bull.]. **Added/Corp** Association for Computing Machinery. Special Interest

Computers — Microcomputers, Personal Computers

Group on Individual Computing Environments. **VFOAT** Special Interest Group on Individual Computing Environments bulletin; ACM SIGICE Bulletin; Association for Computing Machinery Special Interest Group on Individual Computing Environments Bulletin. Vol. 19, No. 3 (Feb. 1994)-. Periodical. English. Four times a year. $38.00. ACM / Association for Computing Machinery, 1515 Broadway, 17th Floor, New York NY 10036. **Tel** (212)869-7440, FAX (212)869-0481. **(Subscription address:** Association for Computing Machinery, PO Box 12114, Church Street Station, New York NY 10249. **Tel** (212)626-0500.) **Continues** SIGSMALL/PC Notes, 0893-2875.

ISSN 0743-8656
US

SMALL COMPUTERS IN BIOMEDICAL RESEARCH. See Medical Sciences-Computer Applications.

LC H61.3 .S616   **ISSN 0894-4393**
DD 300/.28/5   US
   CCC

SOCIAL SCIENCE COMPUTER REVIEW. [Soc. sci. comput. rev.]. **Added/Corp** North Carolina State University. Social Science Research and Instructional Computing Laboratory. **VFOAT** SSCORE. Vol. 6, No. 1 (Spring 1988)-. Periodical. English. Four times a year. $105.00. Duke University Press, PO Box 90660, Durham NC 27708-0660. **Tel** (919)687-3600, (919)688-5134 (orders), FAX (919)688-4574, telex 802829. **ED** G. David Garson. **Bk Rev. Ad Acc. Circ:** 1,000. available on microfilm and microfiche from University Microfilms International (UMI). Documents available from Ask*IEEE. **Continues** Social Science Microcomputer Review, 0885-0011.
   Desc: Each issue includes comprehensive reports on new microcomputing products related to the social sciences, a tutorials section for beginning users and more.
   Ind/Abst Comput. Lit. Index; Comput. Rev.; Curr. Cit.; Curr. Index J. Educ. (March 1990-199?) INSPEC (Spring 1988-); J. Plan. Lit.; Psychol. Abstr. (1988-); PsycINFO; PsycLit; Soc. Plann. Policy Dev. Abstr.; Soc. Res. Methodol. Abstr. (1988-).

ISSN 0755-3579
FR
UDC 681.3
   TITLE CHANGE

SOFT & MICRO. (SOFT & MICRO : LE PREMIER MAGAZINE DES APPLICATIONS ET DU LOGICIEL.). [Soft micro]. **VFOAT** Soft et Micro. (1984-)-(19??). Periodical. French. Excelsior Publications, 1 rue du Colonel Pierre Avia, 75503 Paris Cedex 15 France. **Tel** 011 33 1 46484848, FAX 011 33 1 46484758. **Merged into** Science et Vie Micro, 0760-6516.
   Ind/Abst Repere (1989-).

LC QA76.5 .S652   **ISSN 0742-5058**
DD 001.64/.029/473   US

SOFTWARE EXPRESS. See Computers-Software.

ISSN 1070-101X
DD 005   US
   SUSPENDED

SOFWIN REPORTS. [Sofwin rep.]. (1992)-Suspended (19??). Periodical. English. Twelve times a year. $99.00. Sofwin Publishing Company, 613 Old Farm Road, Columbus OH 43213. **Tel** (614)866-9966, FAX (614)866-9960. **ED** Michael Blaisdell (editor's address: 3016 Fairview, Alamiena, CA phone: (510)865-1323). **Circ:** 1,000. available on an online database from Compuserve Inc.
   Desc: PC system performance measurement & analysis and productivity.

LC Z5642.3 .S17 QA76.6   **ISSN 0160-0400**
DD 016.0016/425   US

SSI. (SSI.). **VFOAT** Index to Published Microcomputer Software; Shreier Index to Published Microcomputer Software. Vol. 1 (Jan./July 1978)-. Periodical. English. Two times a year. SSI, 4327 East Grove Street, Phoenix AZ 85040.

LC QA76.5 .S6517   **ISSN 0882-6862**
DD 004.16   US

ST. GAME. See Computers-Computer Games.

LC QA76.5 .S89436   **ISSN 1054-5980**
DD 004.16/05   US
   TITLE CHANGE

SUNWORLD. (PETERBOROUGH, N.H.). [SunWorld]. **VFOAT** Sun World. (1991)-(199?). Periodical. English. Integrated Media Inc., 501 2nd Street, San Francisco CA 94107. **Tel** (415)978-3306, (415)243-4188. **Continues** SunTech Journal, 1046-5456. **Continued by** Advanced Systems, 1074-9306.

LC HD9697.C63 U585   **ISSN 0192-9690**
DD 338.4/7/62138195   US

SURVEY OF THE MINI/MICROCOMPUTER MARKET. See Computers-Computer Industry and Industry Directories.

ISSN 1166-4770
FR
UDC 681.3

SVM MAC PARIS. (SVM MAC.). **VFOAT** Science et Vie Micro (Paris). (1991)-. Periodical. French. Eleven times a year. $87.71. Excelsior Publications, 1 rue du Colonel Pierre Avia, 75503 Paris Cedex 15 France. **Tel** 011 33 1 46484848, FAX 011 33 1 46484758. **Continues** SVM Macintosh, 0992-5120.

LC QA76.8.T145 S9   **ISSN 0279-5701**
DD 001.64   US

SYNC. [Sync]. **VFOAT** S.Y.N.C. Magazine; SYNC Magazine. Vol. 1, No. 1 (Jan./Feb. 1981)-. Periodical. English. Six times a year. Creative Computing, 39 East Hanover Avenue, Morris Plains NJ 07950.
   Ind/Abst Microcomput. Abstr. (Jan. 1981-April 1982).

ISSN 1047-1367
DD 005   US
   CEASED

TECHNOTES DBASE IV. [TechNotes dBase IV]. **Added/Corp** Ashton-Tate. **VFOAT** TechNotes/DBase IV; Tech Notes DBase IV; TechNotes DBase 4; Tech Notes DBase Four; Tech Notes DBase 4; Tech Notes DBase Four. (1988)-(1993). Periodical. English. Borland International, PO Box 660001, 1800 Green Hills, Scotts Valley CA 95067. **Tel** (408)438-8400, FAX (408)438-8696. **Continues** TechNotes (Culver City, Calif.), 0883-6493.

ISSN 0743-5878
DD 004   US

TIME-LIFE ACCESS. APPLE. VFOAT Time Life Access. Apple; Apple. Vol. 1, No. 1 (May 1984)-(?). Periodical. English. Boston Publishing Company, A subsidiary of Time Life Books, 306 Dartmouth Street, Boston MA 02116.

ISSN 0743-5886
DD 004   US

TIME-LIFE ACCESS. IBM. VFOAT Time Life Access. IBM; IBM. Vol. 1, No. 1 (May 1984)-. Periodical. English. Twelve times a year. $48.00. Boston Publishing Company, A subsidiary of Time Life Books, 306 Dartmouth Street, Boston MA 02116.

ISSN 0825-0367
DD 001.64/04   CN

TPUG MAGAZINE. [TPUG mag.]. **VAT** Toronto Pet Users Group Magazine. Feb. 1984-. Periodical. English. Irregular. 25.00Can$ Canada; 45.00Can$ other. TPUG Inc., Suite 1 1912A Avenue Road, Toronto Ontario M5M 4A1. **Tel** (416)253-9637. **ED** Nick Sullivan. **Bk Rev. Ad Acc. Circ:** 27,000.
   Desc: Reviews, programs and a wide range of articles relating to all Commodore computers and their varied uses. Includes recreational, educational, small business and computer science applications.

ISSN 0827-2530
DD 001.64/04   CN

TRANSACTOR, THE. [Transactor]. **Added/Corp** Commodore Business Machines. (March 1978)-. Periodical. English. Six times a year. 21.00Can$, 40.00Can$ (airmail). Transactor Publishing, 85 West Wilmot Unit 10, Richmond Hill L4B 1K7 Canada. **Tel** (416)764-5273. **ED** Karl Hilden. **Bk Rev. Ad Acc. Circ:** 72,000 (ctrl).
   Desc: Covers advanced technical information for Commodore computers.

ISSN 1193-1477
DD 381/.456123916/0971   CN

TRENDS IN THE CANADIAN PC MARKET. [Trends Can. PC Mark.]. **Added/Corp** Evans Research Corporation. **VFOAT** Trends in the Canadian Personal Computer Market. (Jan. 1992)-. English. $1,975.00 per volume. Evans Research Corporation, 2005 Sheppard Avenue East, 4th Floor, Willowdale Ontario M2J 5B1 Canada. **Tel** (416)498-6664, (416)497-9562, FAX (416)498-7275. **Continues** The Canadian PC Market., 1193-1469.

ISSN 0749-5897
DD 001   US

TRULY PORTABLE. [Truly portable]. Vol. 1, No. 1 (Dec. 1984)-. Periodical. English. Six times a year. Truly Portable, 6540 Dana Street, PO Box 2916, Oakland CA 94609-1108. **Tel** (415)658-1889. **ED** Rachel Holmen. **Bk Rev. Circ:** 1,000.

ISSN 0739-6473
US

TS USER. VFOAT T.S. User. **VAT** Timex Sinclair User. (19??)-. Periodical. English. Twelve times a year. $16.95. YAGSEE, PO Box 155, Vicksburg MI 49097.

ISSN 0892-4961
DD 004   US
Pr Rev.   **CEASED**

TUG LINES. See Computers-Programs and Programming.

ISSN 0736-4083
US
Pr Rev.   **CEASED**

UNIQUE (EAST HANOVER, N.J.). See Computers-Computer Networks.

ISSN 1161-3157
FR
UDC 681.3

UNIVERS MAC PARIS. (UNIVERS MAC.). (1991)-. Periodical. French. Twelve times a year. $96.68. Pressimage, 19 rue Hegesippe Moreau, 75018 Paris France. **Tel** 011 33 1 45223860, 011 33 1 43870139. **(Subscription address:** Pressimage Svc Abonnement, 36 rue de Picpus, 75012 Paris France. **Tel** 011 33 1 43420060.)

ISSN 0895-8688
DD 005   US

UPTIME (COMMODORE C64 AND 128). See Computers-Software.

LC QA76.76.D47 P38
DD 005.265   US

●**VISUAL DEVELOPER.** See Computers-Software.

LC TK7895.B87 V597   **ISSN 0884-1357**
DD 621.39/16   US

VMEBUS SYSTEMS. (VMEBUS SYSTEMS : OFFICIAL QUARTERLY JOURNAL OF THE VMEBUS INTERNATIONAL TRADE ASSOCIATION.). [VMEbus syst.]. **Added/Corp** VMEbus International Trade Association. **VFOAT** VME Bus Systems. **VAT** Versa Module Europe Bus Systems. Vol. 1, No. 1 (Summer 1985)-. Periodical. English. Six times a year (Feb., Apr., June, Aug., Oct., Dec.). $24.00. Technical Communications / Michigan, 2875 Jefferson, St Clair Shores MI 48081. **Tel** (810)774-8180, FAX (810)774-8182. **ED** John Black (editor's address: 2618 South Shannon, Tempe, AZ 85282, phone: (602)963-5581). **Ad Acc, Adv Mgr:** Todd Bowman, **Tel** (810)7748180. **Circ:** 24,000 (ctrl).

ISSN 0748-7886
DD 001   US
   CEASED

VS NEWS. [VS news]. **VFOAT** V.S. News. (198?)-(1993). Periodical. English. Information Exchange Corporation, 786 Rockrimmon Road, Stamford CT 06903. **Tel** (203)329-1132, FAX (203)322-0419. **ED** Harry Berkley. **Ad Acc, Adv Mgr:** Joan Berkley. **Circ:** 1,200 (ctrl). **Continues** VS News & World Report.
   Desc: Independent newsletter for Wang computer users. Only source of accurate third party technical information on wang with help and advice for all classes of users.

ISSN 0740-8919
US
   CEASED

WALL STREET MICRO INVESTOR. See Business and Economics-Computer Applications.

LC QA76.8.A66 W36   **ISSN 1056-7682**
DD 004.165   US
Pr Rev.

WASHINGTON APPLE PI. (WASHINGTON APPLE PI : THE JOURNAL OF WASHINGTON APPLE PI, LTD.). [Wash. apple pi]. **Added/Corp** Washington Apple PI (Group). (19??)-. Periodical. English. Twelve times a year. $39.00. Washington Apple PI, 7910 Woodmont Avenue, Suite 910, Bethesda MD 20814. **Tel** (301)654-8060. **ED** Kathryn Murray. Index available. **Bk Rev. Ad Acc, Adv Mgr:** Beth Medlin, **Tel** (301)654-8060. **Circ:** 4,000 (ctrl).
   Desc: How-to articles, question and answer columns, and reports of meetings. Information on developments in microcomputers and WAP activities.

LC QA76.5 .W352   **ISSN 0882-8962**
DD 004.16/025/753   US

WASHINGTON-AREA MICROCOMPUTER DIRECTORY, THE. See Computers-Computer Industry and Industry Directories.

LC TK7885.A1 W39
DD 001.6404/05   CH

WEI HSING CHI SUAN CHI. VFOAT Weixing Jisuanji. (19??)-. Periodical. Chinese. Six times a year. NT$0.75. Post Office Chung-Ching Shih, Chung-Ching Shih, People's Republic of China. **Tel** 3578.

ISSN 0264-441X
UK
   TITLE CHANGE

WHAT MICRO?. [What micro?]. (1982)-(19??). Periodical. English. VNU Business Publications BV, 32-34 Broadwick Street, London W1A 2HG United Kingdom. **Tel** 011 44 171 4394242 ext. 2222, FAX 011 44 171 4379638, telex 23918 VNU G, 8952440. Documents available from Ask*IEEE. **Continued by** What PC?.
   Ind/Abst INSPEC (April 1985-).

LC QA75
DD 004   UK

WHAT PC?. (19??)-. Periodical. English. Twelve times a year. £21.00 UK; £36.00 (airmail) Europe. VNU Business Publications BV, 32-34 Broadwick Street,

London W1A 2HG United Kingdom. **Tel** 011 44 171 4394242 ext. 2222, FAX 011 44 171 4379638, telex 23918 VNU G, 8952440.

LC QA76.5 .T415
DD 004.16/05 US

•WINDOWS DEVELOPERS JOURNAL. (1995)-. Trade Publication. English. Twelve times a year. $34.99. Miller Freeman Inc., 600 Harrison Street, San Francisco CA 94107. **Tel** (415)905-2337, (415)905-2200, FAX (415)905-2240, telex 278273. **(Subscription address:** Neodata / Boulder, CO, Agency Processing, PO Box 8034, Boulder CO 80306. **Tel** (800)264-9717.) ***Continues*** *Windows/DOS Developers Journal.*

LC QA76.5 .T415 **ISSN** 1059-2407
DD 004.16/05 US
TITLE CHANGE

WINDOWS/DOS DEVELOPER'S JOURNAL. [Windows/DOS dev. j.]. **VFOAT** Windows DOS Developer's Journal; Windows/DOS; Windows DOS. (Dec. 1991)-(Oct. 1995). Trade Publication. English. R & D Publications, 1601 West 23rd Street, Suite 200, Lawrence KS 66046. **Tel** (913)841-1631, FAX (913)841-2624. ***Continues*** *Tech Specialist, 1049-913X.* ***Continued by*** *Windows Developers Journal.*
Ind/Abst Comput. ASAP [Full Txt.]; Comput. Database [Full Txt.].

ISSN 0896-7717
DD 005 US
CEASED

WORD FOR WORD. See Computers-Software.

US

WORKGROUP COMPUTING SERIES. DESKTOP APPLICATIONS. See Computers-Software.

LC HD9696.C6 W67 **ISSN** 1074-3308
DD 621.39/16/029473 US

WORKGROUP COMPUTING SERIES. DIRECTORY OF MICROCOMPUTER HARDWARE. See Computers-Hardware.

US

WORKGROUP COMPUTING SERIES. INFORMATION DELIVERY. See Computers-Desktop Publishing.

US

WORKGROUP COMPUTING SERIES. MULTIMEDIA SOLUTIONS / DATAPRO. See Computers-Desktop Publishing.

US

WORKGROUP COMPUTING SERIES. PERIPHERALS. **Added/Corp** Datapro Information Services Group. **VFOAT** Peripherals; Information Technology Solutions, Workgroup Computing Series. Peripherals. (June 1992)-. Periodical. English. Twelve times a year. $428.00. Datapro Information Services Group, 600 Delran Parkway, Delran NJ 08075. **Tel** (609)764-0100, (800)328-2776, FAX (609)764-8953. ***Continues in part*** *Datapro Reports on Microcomputers, 0741-2541.*

US

WORKGROUP COMPUTING SERIES. SYSTEMS. **Added/Corp** Datapro Information Services Group. **VFOAT** Systems; Information Technology Solutions, Workgroup Computing Series. Systems. (June 1992)-. Periodical. English. Twelve times a year. $551.00. Datapro Information Services Group, 600 Delran Parkway, Delran NJ 08075. **Tel** (609)764-0100, (800)328-2776, FAX (609)764-8953. ***Continues in part*** *Datapro Reports on Microcomputers.*

ISSN 1059-9959
DD 004 US
TITLE CHANGE

WORKSTATION (AUSTIN, TEX.). (WORKSTATION.). [Workstation]. (19??)-(19??). Periodical. English. Publications & Communications, 12416 Hymeadow Drive, Austin TX 78750. **Tel** (512)250-9023, (800)678-9724, FAX (512)331-3900, telex 384303. ***Continues*** *HP Design & Automation, 0896-212X.* ***Merged into*** *HP Chronicle, 0892-2829.*

ISSN 1049-491X
DD 338 US
CEASED

WORKSTATION NEWS. [Workstn. news]. (1990)-(Sept. 1993). Trade Publication. English. Data Base Publications, 9390 Research Blvd, Ste 11 300, Austin TX 78759. **Tel** (512)343-9066, FAX (512)345-1935. **ED** Carl Furry.
Desc: Tabloid aimed at 35,000 workstation users and volume buyers; editorial covers company, product, financial, market and application news.

ISSN 0263-0885
DD 001.6404 AT

YOUR COMPUTER. [Your comput.]. (1981)-. Periodical. English. Twelve times a year. 112.00Aus$. Federal Publishing Co Pty Ltd., PO Box 199, 180 Bourke Road, Alexandria New South Wales 2015 Australia. **Tel** 011 61 2 3539992, FAX 011 61 2 66923059935.
Ind/Abst AESIS Q.; EP Collect.; Homework Help.; MasterFile FullTEXT 1000; MasterFile FullTEXT 350; MasterFile FullTEXT 650; MasterFile FullTEXT (Sept. 1994-); Telebase; World Mag. Bank.

MINICOMPUTERS

LC QA76.5 .B474 **ISSN** 0275-455X
DD 658/.054 US

BEST OF PERSONAL COMPUTING, THE. [Best. Pers. comput.]. Vol. 1 (1979)-. Periodical. English. $7.50. Editor Personal Computing, 1050 Commonwealth Avenue, Boston MA 02215.

LC QA76.5 .B9 **ISSN** 0360-5280
DD 001.6/4/05 US
CCC
CODEN BYTEDJ
Pr Rev.

BYTE. [Byte]. (Sept. 1975)-. Periodical. English. Twelve times a year. $29.95. McGraw Hill Publishing Company, Inc., 1221 Avenue of the Americas, New York NY 10020. **Tel** (212)512-6410, (800)525-5003, FAX (212)512-6111. **(Subscription address:** BYTE, PO Box 555, Hightstown NJ 08520. **) ED** Philip Lemmons. **Bk Rev. Ad Acc. Circ:** 416,219. available on microfilm and microfiche from University Microfilms International (UMI); available on an online database from NEWSNET; Lexis-Nexis; Dow Jones News/Retrieval; and (file 624/Full-Text) DIALOG. Documents available from Article Express International, The Genuine Article, UMI Article Clearinghouse, Ask*IEEE.
Desc: Gives technical information on all aspects of microcomputing hardware, software, peripherals, languages, programming, communications, applications, graphics and artificial intelligence.
Ind/Abst ABI/INFORM Glob. Ed.; ABI/INFORM [Computer File] (Dec. 1977-Nov. 1980); Abstr. Hum. Comput. Interact.; Acad. Abstr. Full Text Elite; Acad. Abstr.; Acad. Ind. [Computer File] (1984-); Acad. Search; ACM Guide Comput. Lit.; Appl. Sci. Technol. Index; Bioeng. Abstr.; Book Rev. Index (1984-); Bus. Index (1985-); Bus. Period. Index; Bus. Source Plus; Bus. Source; Can. Index (?-?); Can. Period. Index; CompuMath Cit. Index [Full Cov.]; Comput. Bus.; Comput. Database; Comput. Rev. Index (1986-); Comput. Rev.; Curr. Cit.; Curr. Contents Eng. Comput. Technol.; Curr. Lit. Fam. Plan. (19??-199?); Ei Page One; Eng. Index Annu. [Select. Cov.]; EP Collect.; Ergon. Abstr.; Expand. Acad. Index (1984-); Fluid Abstr., Civil Eng.; Fluid Abstr. Proc. Eng.; FLUIDEX (?-19??); Gen. BusinessFile (1985-); Gen. Period. Index (1985-); GeoRef; Graph. Arts Bull. Inst. Pap. Sci. Technol. (Jan. 1989-March 1989, July 1989, Nov. 1989); HILITES; Homework Help.; Index Inf. (1977-1984); INFO-SOUTH Abstr.; Infomat Int. Bus.; Inf. Manage. Technol.; Inf. Sci. Abstr. (?-?); INSPEC (July 1977-); J. Ferrocement; Mag. Artic. Summar. Elite; Mag. Artic. Summar. Select; Mag. Artic. Summar. CD-ROM; Mag. Express (1988-) [Full Txt.]; Mag. Index Plus (1989-); Mag. Index. Sel. (1986-); Mag. Search; MasterFile FullTEXT 1000; MasterFile FullTEXT 350; MasterFile FullTEXT 650; MasterFile FullTEXT (Jan. 1984-); Math. Rev.; Microcomput. Abstr. (Jan. 1981-); Microcomput. Ind. Update; Newsp. Period. Abstr. (1988-); OCLC; Oper. Res./Manage. Sci.; Pub. Lib. FullTEXT; Read. Guide Abstr. Select Ed.; Read. Guide Period. Lit.; Res. Alert [Full Cov.]; Resource/One Ondisc; Robotics Abstr.; Sci. Cit. Index; SCISEARCH; Soc. Sci. Cit. Index [Select. Cov.]; Telebase; Mag. Index (1977-); Trade Ind. Index (1981-); Vocat. Search; Wilson Bus. Abstr.; World Publ. Monit.

LC QA76.5 .C61262 **ISSN** 0743-457X
DD 001.64/029/4 US

COMPUTER GUIDE. [Comput. guide]. **VFOAT** CESS Computer Guide; C.E.S.S. Computer Guide. 1983-. English. One time a year. $34.25. Computer & Electronic Supply Services (CESS), PO Box 345, MIT Branch PO, Cambridge MA 02139.

LC HD **ISSN** 1081-7549
DD 001.64/029/4 US

COMPUTER SYSTEMS SERIES. OVERVIEWS. (COMPUTER SYSTEMS SERIES. OVERVIEWS : CONCEPTS, MARKETS, TECHNOLOGIES, SPECIFICATIONS, RATINGS.). [Comput. syst. ser., Overviews]. **Added/Corp** Datapro Information Services Group. **VFOAT** Overviews. Vol. 1, No. 1 (Oct. 1991)-. Periodical. English. Twelve times a year. DataPro Research Corporation, 600 Delran Parkway, Customer Service, Delran NJ 08075. **Tel** (609)764-0100, telex 4761231. ***Continues in part*** *Datapro 70, 0045-9704* ***and*** *Datapro Research Corporation. Datapro Reports on Minicomputers, 0275-0813.*

ISSN 1081-7557
DD 621.3819/532/0212 US

COMPUTER SYSTEMS SERIES. PERIPHERALS. [Comput. syst. ser., Peripher.]. **Added/Corp** Datapro Information Services Group. **VFOAT** Peripherals. Vol. 1, No. 1 (Oct. 1991)-. Periodical. English. Twelve times a year. DataPro Research Corporation, 600 Delran Parkway, Customer Service, Delran NJ 08075. **Tel** (609)764-0100, telex 4761231. ***Continues in part*** *Datapro 70, 0045-9704* ***and*** *Datapro Research Corporation. Datapro Reports on Minicomputers, 0275-0813.*

LC HD **ISSN** 1081-7573
DD 005.3/05 US

COMPUTER SYSTEMS SERIES. SOFTWARE. [Comput. syst. ser., Softw.]. **Added/Corp** Datapro Information Services Group. **VFOAT** Software. Vol. 1, No. 1 (Oct. 1991)-. Periodical. English. Twelve times a year. DataPro Research Corporation, 600 Delran Parkway, Customer Service, Delran NJ 08075. **Tel** (609)764-0100, telex 4761231. ***Continues in part*** *Datapro 70, 0045-9704* ***and*** *Datapro Research Corporation. Datapro Reports on Minicomputers, 0275-0813.*

LC HD **ISSN** 1081-7565
DD 001.64/029/4 US

COMPUTER SYSTEMS SERIES. SYSTEMS. [Comput. syst. ser., Syst.]. **Added/Corp** Datapro Information Services Group. **VFOAT** Systems. Vol. 1, No. 1 (Oct. 1991)-. Periodical. English. Twelve times a year. DataPro Research Corporation, 600 Delran Parkway, Customer Service, Delran NJ 08075. **Tel** (609)764-0100, telex 4761231. ***Continues in part*** *Datapro 70, 0045-9704* ***and*** *Datapro Research Corporation. Datapro Reports on Minicomputers, 0275-0813.*

ISSN 0742-5902
US

COMPUTER USER (MINNEAPOLIS, MINN.). (COMPUTER USER.). [Comput. user]. **Added/Corp** Computer User Publications, Inc. (Minneapolis, Minn.). MSP Publications, Inc. (Minneapolis, Minn.). (198?)-. Periodical. English. Twelve times a year. $12.00. M.S.P. Communications, 220 south Sixth Street, Suite 500, Minneapolis MN 55402. **Tel** (612) 339-7571, FAX (612) 339-5806. **Circ:** 60,000. ***Continues*** *Twin Cities Computer User.*
Desc: Features a mix of hardware and software product reviews, along with technical features and business articles addressing the information needs of corporate and small-business computer professionals and owners.

LC QA76.5 .C6145 **ISSN** 0737-4313
DD 001.64/05 US

COMPUTERS (GREENWICH, CONN.). (COMPUTERS.). [Computers]. **VFOAT** Mechanix Illustrated Computers. (198?)-. Periodical. English. Four times a year. CBS Publications, 1515 Broadway, New York NY 10036. **Tel** (212)767-6000.

LC Z678.9.A1 S6 **ISSN** 1041-7915
DD 025.30285/416 US
CCC
CODEN CPLIE8

COMPUTERS IN LIBRARIES. See Library and Information Sciences-Computer Applications.

ISSN 0823-6437
DD 001.64/04 CN
CEASED

COMPUTING NOW!. [Comput. now!]. (April 1983)-(July 1995). Periodical. English. Moorshead Magazines Ltd., 10 Gateway Boulevard, Suite 490, North York Ontario M3C 3T4 Canada. **Tel** (416)696-5488, FAX (416)696-7395. **ED** Frank Lenk (Editor's Phone: (416)696-5488). Index available. cum. index. **Bk Rev. Ad Acc, Adv Mgr:** David Stone, **Tel** (416)696-5488. **Circ:** 15,000. available on microfiche from University Microfilms International (UMI); and Micromedia Limited.
Desc: Allows users of personal and small business micro-computers to understand these powerful tools. Contains articles to help the beginner choose his or her system as well as material on using it at virtually every level of application. Includes market surveys, industry news and product reviews, and programs readers can use on their own systems.
Ind/Abst Can. Index; Can. Period. Index (19??-).

LC HD **ISSN** 0275-0813
DD 338 US
CCC
TITLE CHANGE

DATAPRO REPORTS ON MINICOMPUTERS. **Main/Corp** Datapro Research Corporation. **Added/Corp** Datapro Research Corporation. Datapro Mininews. **VFOAT** Minicomputers. (1973)-(199?). Periodical. English. DataPro Research Corporation, 600 Delran Parkway, Customer Service, Delran NJ 08075. **Tel** (609)764-0100, telex 4761231. **ED** Alan T. Hirsch. Each issue contains an index to its own contents (no volume index)--loose. cum. index. **Bk Rev.** ***Continues*** *Datapro Mininews, 0730-7500.* ***Split into*** *Computer Systems Series. Peripherals, 1081-7557; Computer Systems Series. Software, 1081-7573; Computer Systems Series. Systems, 1081-7565* ***and*** *Computer Systems Series. Overviews, 1081-7549.*
Desc: Provides analysis of trends and events in the medium-scale computer market place (including supermicros, minicomputers, and superminis) technologies.

Computers —Minicomputers

DATAPRO REPORTS ON MINICOMPUTERS. INTERNATIONAL EDITION. (DATAPRO REPORTS ON MINICOMPUTERS.). Added/Corp Datapro Research Corporation. (197?)-. Periodical. English. Twelve times a year. $1283.00. Datapro International, McGraw Hill House, Shoppenhangers Road, Maidenhead Berkshire SL6 2QL United Kingdom. **Tel** 011 44 1628 773277, FAX 011 44 1628 773628.

LC Z678.9 .I57   ISSN 0264-0473
DD 025/.02/02854   UK
    CCC
Pr Rev.

ELECTRONIC LIBRARY. See Library and Information Sciences-Computer Applications.

    US

FAULKNER MINICOMPUTER REPORTS. (19??)-. Periodical. Eng ish. Twelve times a year. $1065.00 US; $1310.00 other. Faulkner Technical Reports, 7905 Browning Road, Suite 114, Pennsauken NJ 08109. **Tel** (800)843-0460.

LC QA76.5.G368
    JA
GEKKAN RAMU. VFOAT Ramu; RAM : Random Access Magazine; R.A.M.; RAM. Period.cal. Japanese. Twelve times a year. ¥560 single issue. Kosaido Shuppan, 23-13 Shiba 3 Minato-ku, Tokyo-to 105 Japan.

LC QA76.5 H74
DD 001.6404   CC
HSIAO HSING WEI HSING CHI SUAN CHI HSI TUNG. VFOAT Mini-Micro Systems. (19??)-. Periodical. Chinese. Twelve times a year. Chung-Kuo Kuo Chi Tu Shu Mao I Tsung Kung SSU, PO Box 2820, Beijing, People's Republic of China.

    ISSN 8755-6286
DD 001   US
    CCC

INFORMATION TODAY. See Library and Information Sciences-Computer Applications.

LC QA75.5 .I56   ISSN 0199-6649
DD 004   US
    CCC
    CODEN INWODU
INFOWORLD. See Computers-Computer Industry and Industry Directories.

LC QA76.5 .I5635   ISSN 0702-0481
DD 004.1/4   US
    CODEN IJMMDE
INTERNATIONAL JOURNAL OF MINI & MICROCOMPUTERS. [Int. j. mini microcomput.]. Added/Corp International Society for Mini-Micro Computers. VFOAT International Journal of Mini and Microcomputers. VAT International Journal of Mini and Microcomputers. Vol. 1, No. 1 (1978)-. Periodical. English. Three times a year (Jan., May, Sep.). $197.00. ISMM- International Society of Mini and Microcomputers, PO Box 2481, Anaheim CA 92814. **Tel** FAX (714)535-2662. **ED** Dr B Furht. Index available. **Bk Rev. Ad Acc. Circ:** 300 (ctrl). Documents available from Ask*IEEE.
Desc: All aspects of mini and microcomputers including technology, hardware, software, systems, education, networks, distributed processing and applications.
Ind/Abst Comput. Abstr.; Curr. Cit.; Ei Page One; INSPEC (1980-); Int. Aerosp. Abstr.

LC TK7888.3 .K67   ISSN 0192-5334
DD 001.64/044   US
KIPS BOOK, THE. 1st- Ed.; 1978-. English. One time a year. SBS Publishers, PO Box 9747, San Jose CA 95157.

    ISSN 1041-8237
DD 005   US
    CODEN MISYEG
MIDRANGE SYSTEMS. Vol. 1, No. 1 (Sept. 1988)-. Trade Publication. English. Twenty-six times a year. $75.00. Professional Press Inc, 101 Witmer Road, Horsham PA 19044. **Tel** (215)957-1500, FAX (215)957-1050. **(Subscription address:** Professional Press, PO Box 218, Horsham PA 19044.) available on an online database (file 675/Full-Text) from DIALOG.
Ind/Abst Comput. ASAP [Full Txt.]; Comput. Database [Full Txt.]; F&S Index Plus Text, Int. [Select. Cov.]; PROMT.

    US
MIMI, PROCEEDINGS OF THE INTERNATIONAL SYMPOSIUM ON MINI AND MICRO COMPUTERS. Added/Corp IEEE Computer Society. Institute of Electrical and Electronics Engineers. Canadian Region. VFOAT Proceedings of the International Symposium on Mini and Micro Computers. (1976)-. Proceedings. English. Irregular. Price varies per volume. Acta Press, PO Box 3243 Station B, Calgary Alberta T2M 4L8 Canada. **Tel** (403)288-1195, FAX (403)247-6851. **(Subscription address:** IASTED, PO Box 24281, Anaheim CA 92814. **Tel** (800)995-2161.)
Ind/Abst Curr. Cit.

    ISSN 0179-0382
    GW
    CODEN MMMAEA
MINI-MICRO-MAGAZIN. (MINIMICRO MAGAZIN.). [Mini-Micro-Mag.]. VFOAT Mini Micro Magazin. (1985)-. Periodical. German. Ten times a year. $139.71. PR & Marketing Verlag, Birkenweg 8, D 83129 Hoeslwang Germany. **Tel** 011 49 8055 1584, FAX 011 49 8055 8051.
Ind/Abst Curr. Cit.; INSPEC (1987-).

LC QA76.5 .S658   ISSN 0194-018X
DD 382/.450016/404   US
SOURCE BOOK OF MINICOMPUTERS. (19??)-. English. One time a year. GML Corporation, 594 Marrett Road, Lexington MA 02173. **Tel** (617)861-0515.

    ISSN 1000-1220
DD 621.38195   CC
XIAOXING WEIXING JISUANJI XITONG. VFOAT Mini-Micro Systems. (1982)-. Periodical. Chinese. Twelve times a year. Zhongguo Kexueyuan / Shenyang Jisuan Jishu Yanjiusuo, Chinese Academy of Sciences, Shenyang Institute of Computing Technology, 100 Sanhao Jie, Shenyang, Liaoning 110003 People's Republic of China. **ED** Luan Guixing.

ONLINE COMPUTING AND INFORMATION

    ISSN 0894-9948
    US
ARIZONA ONLINE USER GROUP. VFOAT Arizona On Line User Group Newsletter; AOLUG Newsletter. No. 3, (Oct./Nov. 1978)-. Periodical. English. Five times a year. $13.00. Arizona Online Users Group, Science-Engineering Library, University Arizona, Tucson AZ 85721. **Tel** (602)621-6375, FAX (602)621-9733. **ED** B. Brin. **Circ:** 90 (ctrl). **Continues** Arizona Libraries Online News.
Desc: Newsletter for members in Arizona Online Users Group. This group promotes the uses of electronic information retrieval systems in Arizona libraries and information centers.

    ISSN 0765-1325
    FR
UDC 002 : 681.3
Pr Rev.
BASES PARIS. (1985)-. Periodical. French. Eleven times a year. $369.63. Editions FLA Consultants, 27 rue de la Vistule, 75013 Paris France. **Tel** 011 33 1 45827575, FAX 33 1 45824604. **ED** M. Francois Libmann. Index available. **Bk Rev**, (Qty: 20). **Ad Acc. Circ:** 800.
Desc: Covers current events in electronic information; birth and death of databases, meeting agenda, accounts of conferences and thematic surveys. Information is checked and presented from a user point of view.

    ISSN 1055-2812
DD 004   US
BBS CALLERS DIGEST. [BBS callers dig.]. (1990)-. Periodical. English. Twelve times a year. $25.00. Callers Digest, PO Box 416, Mt Laurel NJ 08054. **Bk Rev. Ad Acc, Adv Mgr:** Richard Paquette. **Circ:** 12,000. available on an online database.
Desc: Used to call local bulletin board systems.

    ISSN 0747-5438
    US
    CCC
BNA ONLINE. VFOAT B.N.A. Online. VAT Bureau of National Affairs Online. Vol. 1, No. 1 (Apr. 1984)-. Periodical. English. Six times a year. Free on request. Bureau of National Affairs Inc., 9435 Key West Avenue, Rockville MD 20850. **Tel** (800)372-1033, (301)258-1033, FAX (301)948-5823. **ED** Rhonda Oziel.

LC QA76.9.B84 B6   ISSN 1054-2760
DD 004.693/05   US
BOARDWATCH MAGAZINE. [Boardwatch mag.]. VFOAT Board Watch Magazine. (1989)-. Periodical. English. Twelve times a year. $36.00. Denver PC Boardwatch, 5970 South Vivian Street, Littleton CO 80127. **Tel** (303)973-6038. **Continues** Denver PC Boardwatch, 0894-5209.

    UK
CAB ABSTRACTS ONLINE MANUAL. Added/Corp C.A.B. International. VAT Commonwealth Agricultural Bureaus abstracts Online Manual. (19??)-. English.

    ISSN 0967-8123
    UK
Pr Rev.   CEASED
CD-ROM INFORMATION PRODUCTS. See Computers-Hardware.

    ISSN 1081-3187
    US
●**CISCO WORLD.** See Computers-Computer Networks.

    US
●**CYBERMARKETING LETTER.** (1995)-. English. Twelve times a year. $299.00. Cybermarketing Letter, 184 Palisade Avenue, Dobbs Ferry NY 10522. **Tel** (914)693-5950.

LC QA75   ISSN 1085-2417
DD 004.6   US
●**CYBERSKEPTIC'S GUIDE TO INTERNET RESEARCH, THE.** (1996)-. Periodical. English. Ten times a year. $149.00. Bibliodata, PO Box 61, Needham Heights MA 02194. **Tel** (617)444-1154, FAX (617)449-4584.

LC Z699.A1 D375   ISSN 0891-6713
DD 025.5/24   US
    CCC
    CODEN DASEE5
    TITLE CHANGE
DATABASE SEARCHER. See Computers-Data Base Management.

LC Z699.A1 D38   ISSN 0275-9152
DD 025.3/028/54   US
DATABASES ONLINE. See Computers-Data Base Management.

LC Z699.4.D18 D54a
DD 025.04   US
DIALOG DATABASE CATALOG. Main/Corp DIALOG Information Services. VFOAT Database Catalog; DIALOG. (19??)-. Catalog. English. One time a year. $3.00. Knight Ridder Information Inc., 2440 El Camino Real, Mountain View CA 94040. **Tel** (415)254-7000. **Continues** DIALOG Information Retrieval Service. Database Catalog.

    ISSN 1067-0815
    US
    CCC
    CEASED
DOCUMENT DELIVERY WORLD. (1993)-(Dec. 1993). Trade Publication. English. Mecklermedia Corporation, 11 Ferry Lane West, Westport CT 06880. **Tel** (203)226-6967, (800)632-5537, FAX (203)454-5840.

    ISSN 1071-247X
    US
    CCC
●**ELECTRONIC MARKETPLACE REPORT.** See Business and Economics-Commerce.

LC Z699.5.C27 E86   ISSN 0834-3888
    CN
Pr Rev.
ESPIAL CANADIAN DATA BASE DIRECTORY, THE. See Computers-Electronic Data Processing.

LC QA   ISSN 0740-4980
DD 004.2   US
    CCC
FT SYSTEMS. See Computers-Data Base Management.

    ISSN 1081-2385
    US
●**GALE GUIDE TO INTERNET DATABASES.** Added/Corp Gale Research Inc. (1995)-. English. $95.00. Gale Research Inc., 835 Penobscot Building, 645 Griswold Street, Detroit MI 48226. **Tel** (800)877-GALE, (313)961-2242, FAX (313)961-6083, (800)414-5043, telex TWX 810-221-7086.

    ISSN 1072-0413
    US
●**GNN MAGAZINE.** (GNN MAGAZINE [COMPUTER FILE].). Added/Corp O'Reilly & Associates. VAT Global Network Navigator Magazine. (1993)-. Periodical. English. One time a week. Free. Global Network Navigator, 103 Morris Street, Sebastopol CA 95472. **Tel** (707)829-0515, FAX (707)829-0104. **ED** Joan Callahan. **Circ:** 85,000. available via Internet (URL http://gnn.com/).
Desc: Interactive guide to the Internet. Provides direct links to more than 1,300 information resources.

    ISSN 1078-4942
DD 384   US
●**INFORMATION FREEWAY REPORT, THE.** [Inf. freeway rep.]. Added/Corp Washington Researchers (Firm). Vol. 1, No. 1 (June 1994)-. Periodical. English. Twelve times a year. $160.00. Washington Researchers, PO Box 19005, 20th Street Station, Washington DC 20036. **Tel** (202)333-3533, (202)333-3499, FAX (202)625-0656.

Computers —Online Computing and Information

LC Z678.9.A1 I544
DD 025.3/0285
ISSN 0737-7770
US
CCC
CODEN IIOMEI
INFORMATION INTELLIGENCE, ONLINE LIBRARIES, AND MICROCOMPUTERS. See Library and Information Sciences-Computer Applications.

ISSN 0194-0694
US
CCC
CODEN IIONDK
INFORMATION INTELLIGENCE ONLINE NEWSLETTER. [Inf. intell. online newsl.]. **Main/Corp** Information Intelligence, Inc. **VFOAT** Online Newsletter. Vol. 1 (Jan. 1980)-. Newsletter. English. Ten times a year. $62.50. Information Intelligence Inc., PO Box 31098, Phoenix AZ 85046. **Tel** (602)996-2283, (800)228-9982, telex 703787. **ED** Richard S. Huleatt and George S. Machovec. Index available. cum. index. **Bk Rev. Ad Acc.** available on CD-ROM from NEWSNET; DATA-STAR; CARL; and DIALOG; available on an online database. Documents available from Ask*IEEE.
Desc: International in scope covering all aspects of online and CD-ROM developments throughout the world. Regular feature sections include new online/CD-ROM developments and events, mergers and acquisitions, editorials which reflect events or product developments that impact on online users, people in the news, telecommunications and networks, new equipment and developments, microcomputer hardware and software, etc.
Ind/Abst INSPEC (Jan. 1982-); Int. Aerosp. Abstr.; Libr. Inf. Sci. Abstr.

ISSN 0020-0220
US
INFORMATION RETRIEVAL & LIBRARY AUTOMATION. [Inf. retr. libr. autom.]. **VFOAT** Information Retrieval & Library Automation Newsletter. **VAT** Information Retrieval and Library Automation. Vol. 9, No. 2 (July 1973)-. Periodical. English. Twelve times a year. $66.00. Lomond Publications, PO Box 88, Mt Airy MD 21771. **Tel** (301)829-1496, (800)443-6299. **ED** Maxine Mattery Johnson. Index available. cum. index. **Bk Rev.** ctrl circ. available on microfilm and microfiche from University Microfilms International (UMI). Documents available from Ask*IEEE. **Continues** Information Retrieval & Library Automation Letter.
Desc: A summary of research, events and literature of scientific and technical information systems.
Ind/Abst Book Rev. Index; Comput. Lit. Index; Data Process. Dig.; Inf. Sci. Abstr.; INSPEC (Aug. 1983-Dec. 1986); Leg. Inf. Manage. Index (19??-); Libr. Inf. Sci. Abstr.; Pollut. Abstr. Indexes.

ISSN 0950-9879
UK
CCC
INFORMATION WORLD REVIEW. See Computers-Optical Storage, CD-ROM Applications.

ISSN 0241-2640
FR
CCC
CODEN NFTCDC
INFOTECTURE. (1979)-. French. Twenty-two times a year. 2938.30F France; 3100.00F other. A Jour, 11 rue du Marche St. Honore, 75001 Paris France. **Tel** 011 33 1 44553849.
Desc: Journal of online databases and optical memory products. Covers the activities of the main producers and service companies, and the development of products and markets.

ISSN 1081-0625
US
●**INTERJOURNAL (BOSTON, MASS.).** (INTERJOURNAL.). **Added/Corp** Boston University. Center for Computational Science. (1995)-. English. InterJournal, ECS Department, Boston University, 44 Cummungton Street, Boston MA 02215. **Tel** (617)353-2843, FAX (617)353-6440. **ED** Yaneer Bar-Yam. available via Internet (http://dynamics.bu.edu:80/InterJournal/).
Desc: Central database consists of comments, abstracts, and relevant manuscript information. Source of information for users of the Internet.

ISSN 1082-1945
US
●**INTERNET MARKETING AND TECHNOLOGY REPORT.** (1995)-. Periodical. English. Twelve times a year. $247.00. Computer Economics Inc., 5841 Edison Place, Carlsbad CA 92008. **Tel** (800)326-8100, (619)438-8100, FAX (619)431-1126.

ISSN 1081-2482
US
●**INTERNET (POTOMAC, MD.).** (INTERNET [COMPUTER FILE].). (1995)-. Periodical. English. One time a week. $397.00. Phillips Business Information Inc., 1201 Seven Locks Road, PO Box 61130, Potomac MD 20854. **Tel** (301)424-3338, (301)340-1520, (800)777-5005, FAX (301)424-4297, telex 358149.

ISSN 1081-2474
US
●**INTERNET WEEK.** (1995)-. Periodical. English. Fifty times a year. $497.00. Phillips Business Information Inc., 1201 Seven Locks Road, PO Box 61130, Potomac MD 20854. **Tel** (301)424-3338, (301)340-1520, (800)777-5005, FAX (301)424-4297, telex 358149. available via Internet. **Absorbed** Internet Letter.

NE
Pr Rev.
●**JOURNAL OF SYSTEMS ARCHITECTURE.** See Computers-Microcomputers, Personal Computers.

ISSN 8756-4149
DD 001
US
LOG/ON (LOUISVILLE, KY.). (LOG/ON.). **Added/Corp** Data Courier, inc. **VFOAT** Log On; Logon. (Jan./Feb. 1983)-. Periodical. English. Twelve times a year. Free on request. UMI/Data Courier, 620 South 3rd Street, Louisville KY 40202. **Tel** (800)626-2823, (502)583-4111, FAX (502)589-5572, telex 204235. **ED** Rae Helton. **Circ:** 8,000 (ctrl). **Continues** Database news, 0743-0035.
Desc: Online database news from UMI.

LC QA76.5 .E89a
DD 004.16
ISSN 0165-6074
NE
CCC
CODEN MMICDT
TITLE CHANGE
Pr Rev.
MICROPROCESSING AND MICROPROGRAMMING. See Computers-Microcomputers, Personal Computers.

UK
MONITOR. Added/Corp Learned Information (Firm). No. 1 (March 1981)-. Periodical. English. Twelve times a year. £175.00. Learned Information Ltd., Woodside Hinksey Hill, Oxford OX1 5AU United Kingdom. **Tel** 011 44 1865 730275, FAX 011 44 1865 736354, telex 23667. Documents available from Ask*IEEE.
Desc: Provides informed description and analysis of events in the sphere of information transfer via electronic media. Offers a comprehensive record of what is happening in the international information industry as well as interpretation of the month's news. Includes timely reports on online and optical media, videotex, telecommunications policy and micros, with updates and analyses of events as they occur in the field.
Ind/Abst INSPEC (Feb. 1982-); Int. Aerosp. Abstr.

ISSN 0260-6666
DD 025.0405
UK
MONITOR ABINGDON. [Monitor Abingdon]. (1981)-. Newsletter. English. Twelve times a year. $290.00. Learned Information Ltd., Woodside Hinksey Hill, Oxford OX1 5AU United Kingdom. **Tel** 011 44 1865 730275, FAX 011 44 1865 736354, telex 23667. **(Subscription address:** Information Today, 143 Old Marlton Pike, Medford NJ 08055-8750. **Tel** (609)654-6266, FAX (609)654-4309.)

ISSN 1077-4173
US
●**NET GUIDE.** (Dec. 1994)-. English. Twelve times a year. $22.97 US. CMP Publications Inc., One Jericho Plaza, Wing A, 2nd Floor, Jericho NY 11753. **Tel** (516)733-6700. **(Subscription address:** Net Guide, PO Box 420285, Palm Coast FL 32142-0285. **Tel** (904)445-4662, ext. 420, FAX (904)445-2728 attn: agency order.**)**
Desc: For the explorers of cyberspace. As a guide to the online world, it provides hundreds of new online listings each month, as well as articles explaining the various aspects of the information superhighway.

ISSN 1355-7602
DD 004.6
UK
●**NET: THE INTERNET MAGAZINE.** [.net, internet mag.]. **VFOAT** Internet Magazine; Net. (1994)-. Periodical. English. Twelve times a year. £17.40 UK; £38.95 Europe; £67.95 others. Future Publishing Ltd., Cary Court, Somerton, Somerset TA11 6TB United Kingdom. **Tel** 011 44 1225 442244, FAX 011 44 1225 45827378. **Continues** Net Magazine - Internet Magazine.

ISSN 0749-338X
DD 025
US
SUSPENDED
NEWSLETTER / MAP ONLINE USERS GROUP. See Library and Information Sciences.

ISSN 0957-8544
DD 025.524
UK
NEWSLETTER - UK ONLINE USER GROUP. (NEWSLETTER.). [Newsl. - UK Online User Group]. **VFOAT** Newsletter - United Kingdom Online User Group. (197?)-. Newsletter. English. Six times a year. £35.00. Learned Information Ltd., Woodside Hinksey Hill, Oxford OX1 5AU United Kingdom. **Tel** 011 44 1865 730275, FAX 011 44 1865 736354, telex 23667.
Desc: Acts as a forum for information about online developments and training, and a consumer group acting as an intermediary between individual users and service suppliers.

ISSN 0895-187X
DD 005
US
OMNI ONLINE DATABASE DIRECTORY. See Library and Information Sciences-Computer Applications.

ISSN 0827-4932
DD 025/.04/06071133
CN
ON LINE/ON WARD. (VOLUG.). **Added/Corp** Vancouver Online Users' Group. **VFOAT** Online/Onward. No. 27 (Sept. 1981)-. Periodical. English. Irregular. 16.01Can$. Vancouver Online Users Group, 623 West 14th Avenue 402, Vancouver British Columbia V5Z 1P7 Canada. **Tel** (604)822-9392. **Continues** On Line/On Ward, 0827-4932.

LC HF5548.125 .O45
DD 650/.0285
ISSN 0898-2015
US
ONLINE ACCESS. [Online access]. Vol. 2, No. 3 (May/June 1987)-. Periodical. English. Twelve times a year. $29.70. Chicago Fine Print, 900 North Franklin, Suite 310, Chicago IL 60610. **Tel** (312)573-1700, FAX (312)573-0520. **ED** Tracy Weisman. **Ad Acc, Adv Mgr:** Robert Jordan, **Tel** (312)573-1700. **Circ:** 65,000. available on microfiche from University Microfilms International (UMI). **Continues** Online Access Guide.
Desc: International magazine for people interested in learning about online services, gateways, transactional, interactive and electronic mail services, and commercial databases.
Ind/Abst Comput. Rev.

LC Z699.A1 O5
DD 025.04
ISSN 1353-2642
UK
CCC
CODEN ONCDEW
Pr Rev.
●**ONLINE & CDROM REVIEW : THE INTERNATIONAL JOURNAL OF ONLINE & OPTICAL INFORMATION SYSTEMS. VFOAT** Online & CD ROM Review; Online and CDROM Review; Online and CD ROM Review; Online & CDROM; Online and CDROM; Online & CD ROM; Online and CD ROM. Vol. 17, No. 1 (Feb. 1993)-. Academic Scholarly Publication. English. Six times a year (Feb., Apr., Jun., Aug., Oct., Dec.). $115.00. Learned Information Ltd., Woodside Hinksey Hill, Oxford OX1 5AU United Kingdom. **Tel** 011 44 1865 730275, FAX 011 44 1865 736354, telex 23667. **(Subscription address:** Information Today, 143 Old Marlton Pike, Medford NJ 08055-8750. **Tel** (609)654-6266, FAX (609)654-4309.) **ED** Martha E. Williams (editor's address: University of Illinois, Urbana, IL 61801 USA; E-mail: mewillia@ux1.cso.uiuc.edu) and Forbes Gibb (editor's address: University of Strathclyde, Glasgow G1 1XH Scotland; E-mail: forbes@dis.strath.ac.uk). Index available (bound in Apr. issue). **Bk Rev. Ad Acc, Adv Mgr:** Michael Hislop (Europe) and Michael V. Zarrello (US), **Tel** 011 44 1865 730275 ext. 226 (Europe) or (609)654-4888 (US). Documents available from CASDDS. **Continues** On-Line Review, 0309-314X.
Desc: Concentrates on online information sources, systems and services. Concerned with the analysis, storage and retrieval of information held on both magnetic and optical media.
Ind/Abst Chem. Abstr.; Curr. Cit.

LC HF54.5 .O54
DD 380.1025
ISSN 0953-5055
UK
TITLE CHANGE
ONLINE BUSINESS SOURCEBOOK. See Business and Economics-Computer Applications.

UK
ONLINE/CD-ROM BUSINESS SOURCEBOOK. See Business and Economics-Computer Applications.

LC QA76.9.D3 O54a
DD 004.09
US
CEASED
ONLINE/CD-ROM ... CONFERENCE PROCEEDINGS. Added/Corp Online Inc. **VFOAT** ONLINE/CD-ROM. (1990)-(19??). English. Online Inc., 462 Danbury Road, Wilton CT 06897. **Tel** (203)761-1466, (800)248-8466, FAX (203)761-1444. **Continues** ONLINE ... Conference Proceedings, 1051-9890.

ISSN 0887-6215
US
ONLINE COMMUNICATIONS. (1986)-. Periodical. English. Twelve times a year. $40.00. Online Information Consultants Inc, PO Box 1431, Springfield OR 97477.

ISSN 0816-956X
DD 025.040994
AT
ONLINE CURRENTS. [Online curr.]. (1986)-. Periodical. English. Ten times a year (monthly with Jan./Feb. and July/Aug. issues combined). 127.44Aus$. Enterprise Information Management Pty., Ltd., 6/217 Eastern Valley Way, Willoughby 2068, New South Wales Australia. **Tel** 011 61 2 9587099, FAX 011 61 2 99580699. **ED** Julia Bale. **Bk Rev,** (Qty: 2). **Ad Acc, Adv Mgr:** P. Johnstone.
Desc: A newsletter covering the online and CD-ROM

industry.
Ind/Abst AESIS Q.; Aust. Educ. Index; Aust. Libr. Inf. Sci. Abstr. (1986-).

LC L **ISSN** 1081-2687
DD 371.334 US

•**ONLINE EDUCATOR, THE.** See Computers-Computer Assisted Instruction.

ISSN 0967-6090 UK

ONLINE FILES. [Online files]. (1992)-. English. Four times a year. $128.34. Effective Technical Marketing Ltd., Enterprise House / Wilton Road, Humberston Grimsby DN36 4AS United Kingdom. **Tel** 011 44 1472 210707, FAX 011 44 1472 699027. **ED** Alan Baldwin. **Circ:** 300. available on diskette. ***Continues** Clover Comparative Cost Chart for Online Files, 0959-5619.*
Desc: A guide to searching the online databases on the world's major host systems.

ISSN 1040-6646
DD 025 US
Pr Rev.

ONLINE HOTLINE NEWS SERVICE. See Library and Information Sciences.

US
TITLE CHANGE

ONLINE REVIEW: THE INTERNATIONAL JOURNAL OF ONLINE INFORMATION SYSTEMS. Vol. 1, No. 1 (March 1977)-(197?). Periodical. English. Learned Information Ltd., Woodside Hinksey Hill, Oxford OX1 5AU United Kingdom. **Tel** 011 44 1865 730275, FAX 011 44 1865 736354, telex 23667. ***Continued by** Online & CD ROM Review, 0309-314X.*
Ind/Abst Abstr. Hum. Comput. Interact.; Int. Packag. Abstr.

LC Z699 **ISSN** 1085-5068
DD 025.04 US

•**ONLINE TACTICS.** (Oct. 1995)-. English. Twelve times a year. $345.00. SIMBA Information Inc., 213 Danbury Road, PO Box 7430, Wilton CT 06897-7430. **Tel** (203)834-0033 ext. 173, FAX (203)884-1771.

LC Z699.A1 O54 **ISSN** 0146-5422
DD 001.6/4404 US
CCC
CODEN ONLIDN
Pr Rev.

ONLINE (WESTON, CONN.). (ONLINE.). [Online]. Vol. 1 (Jan. 1977)-. Academic Scholarly Publication. English. Six times a year. $110.00. Online Inc., 462 Danbury Road, Wilton CT 06897. **Tel** (203)761-1466, (800)248-8466, FAX (203)761-1444. **(Subscription address:** Kinokuniya Company Ltd., 38-1 Sakuragaoka 5, chome Setagaya-ku, Tokyo 156 Japan. **Tel** FAX 011 03 3439 0136.**) ED** Nancy Garman. Index Available in first issue of next volume--attached. **Bk Rev**, (Qty: (3/4 per issue)). **Ad Acc, Adv Mgr:** Corky Murray, **Tel** (203)761-1466. **Circ:** 5,100 (ctrl). available on an online database (in full text) from DIALOG; available on microfilm and microfiche from University Microfilms International (UMI). Documents available from Article Express International, The Genuine Article, Ask*IEEE, UMI Article Clearinghouse, CASDDS.
Desc: Edited for professional users of online database services. Feature articles, columns and new reports cover the entire spectrum of the field: new databases, searching tips, management information centers, training, terminals, printers, microcomputers and other equipment.
Ind/Abst Acad. Ind. [Computer File] (1992-); Acad. Search; ACM Guide Comput. Lit.; Bioeng. Abstr.; Bus. Index (1985-); Bus. Period. Index; Bus. Source Plus; Chem. Abstr. (1977-1985); CompuMath Cit. Index [Full Cov.]; Comput. Rev.; Cumul. Index Nurs. Allied Health Lit.; Curr. Cit.; Curr. Contents Eng. Comput. Technol.; Curr. Contents Soc. Behav. Sci.; Curr. Index J. Educ.; Ei Page One; Eng. Index Annu.; EP Collect.; Expand. Acad. Index (1992-); F&S Index Plus Text, Int. [Select. Cov.]; Gen. BusinessFile (1985-); Gen. Period. Index (1985-); Health Devices Alerts; Homework Help.; Index Period. Artic. Relat. Law; INFO-SOUTH Abstr.; Inf. Instruc. Technol.; Inf. Sci. Abstr. [Full Cov.]; INSPEC (Jan. 1977-); Int. Aerosp. Abstr.; Leg. Inf. Manage. Index (19??-); Libr. Inf. Sci. Abstr.; Libr. Lit.; Mag. ASAP Plus; Mag. Index Plus (1989-); Mag. Search; MasterFile FullTEXT 1000; MasterFile FullTEXT 350; MasterFile FullTEXT 650; MasterFile FullTEXT (July 1993-); Microcomput. Abstr. (Jan. 1985-); Newsp. Period. Abstr. (1988-); OCLC; Res. Alert [Full Cov.]; SCISEARCH; Soc. Sci. Cit. Index [Full Cov.]; Telebase; Mag. Index (1977-); Trade Ind. ASAP [Full Txt.]; Trade Ind. Index (1981-) [Full Txt.]; UMI ABI/Inform--Bus. Period. Ondisc (Jan. 1988-) [Full Txt.]; Wilson Bus. Abstr.

LC QA76.55 .N372a **ISSN** 0739-1471
DD 001.64/404 US
CCC
CODEN PNOMDR

PROCEEDINGS - NATIONAL ONLINE MEETING. (PROCEEDINGS / NATIONAL ONLINE MEETING; COMPILED BY MARTHA E. WILLIAMS, THOMAS H. HOGAN.). [Proc. - Natl. Online Meet.]. **VFOAT** Proceedings of the ... National Online Meeting. 2nd (1981)-. Proceedings. English. One time a year. £55.00. Learned Information Ltd., Woodside Hinksey Hill, Oxford OX1 5AU United Kingdom. **Tel** 011 44 1865 730275, FAX 011 44 1865 736354, telex 23667. **(Subscription address:** Information Today, 143 Old Marlton Pike, Medford NJ 08055-8750. **Tel** (609)654-6266, FAX (609)654-4309.**) ED** Martha E. Williams. Documents available from Article Express International.
Desc: Collection of papers on new online tools and resources.
Ind/Abst Bioeng. Abstr.; Curr. Cit.; Ei Page One; Eng. Index Annu.

LC Z699.A1 S4 **ISSN** 1070-4795
DD 025.3/132 US
CCC
CODEN SMDPE8

•**SEARCHER (MEDFORD, N.J.).** (SEARCHER : THE MAGAZINE FOR DATABASE PROFESSIONALS.). [Searcher]. Vol. 1, No. 1 (May 1993)-. Periodical. English. Ten times a year. $55.95. Information Today Inc., 143 Old Marlton Pike, Medford NJ 08055-8750. **Tel** (609)654-6266, (609)654-4888 (editorial), FAX (609)654-4309. **(Subscription address:** Learned Information Ltd., Woodside, Hinksey Hill, Oxford OX 15 AU United Kingdom. **) ED** Barbara Quint. **Photos**. **Ad Acc, Adv Mgr:** Michael V. Zarrello. Full Page (B&W) $780.00. Half Page (B&W) $520.00. Full Page (Color) $900.00 for four-color. Half Page (Color) $900.00 for four-color. **Pub. Size:** Standard. **Circ:** 3,500.
Desc: Explores and deliberates on a range of issues important to the professional database searcher. Centers on the needs of the experienced, knowledgeable searcher and combines evaluations of data content with discussions of delivery media.

LC Z699.5.E6 S54 **ISSN** 0163-5840
DD 025/.04 US
CODEN FASRDV

SIGIR FORUM. [SIGIR forum]. **Added/Corp** Association for Computing Machinery. Special Interest Group on Information Retrieval. **VFOAT** S.I.G.I.R. Forum. **VAT** Special Interest Group on Information Retrieval Forum. (196?)-. Monographic series. English. Three times a year. $32.00. ACM / Association for Computing Machinery, 1515 Broadway, 17th Floor, New York NY 10036. **Tel** (212)869-7440, FAX (212)869-0481. **(Subscription address:** Association for Computing Machinery, PO Box 12114, Church Street Station, New York NY 10249. **Tel** (212)626-0500.**)** Documents available from Article Express International, Ask*IEEE.
Ind/Abst ACM Guide Comput. Lit.; Comput. Rev. (Summer 1980-); Curr. Cit.; Eng. Index Annu.; INSPEC (Summer 1980-); Libr. Inf. Sci. Abstr.

LC QA76.55 .S68 **ISSN** 0270-496X
DD 025/.04/05 US

SOURCEWORLD. [Sourceworld]. **VAT** Source World. Vol. 1 (Mar. 1980)-. Periodical. English. Six times a year. Free to members. Source Telecomputing Corporation, 1616 Anderson Road, McLean VA 22102. **Tel** (703)734-7500, telex 440486 SOURC UI. **ED** Laura Penny. **Ad Acc.** ctrl circ.
Desc: Magazine sent to members of the source.

ISSN 1084-2063 US

•**WEBSIGHT (BEVERLY HILLS, CALIF.).** (WEBSIGHT : THE WORLD WIDE WEB MAGAZINE.). (1995)-. Periodical. English. Six times a year. $14.95. Navigate Media, 9520 Jefferson Boulevard, Culver City CA 90232. **Tel** (310)838-6200.

GR

•**WORLD OF INTERNET.** (1995)-. Consumer Publication. Greek, Modern. Twelve times a year. Dr17000. Compupress S.A., 44 Syngrou, 117 42 Athens Greece. **Tel** 011 30 1 9238672, FAX 011 30 1 9216847.

OPTICAL STORAGE, CD-ROM APPLICATIONS

LC TK8315 .A37 **ISSN** 1042-0711
DD 770 US
CODEN ADIMEZ

ADVANCED IMAGING (WOODBURY, N.Y.). (ADVANCED IMAGING.). [Adv. imaging]. (Oct. 1988)-. Trade Publication. English. Twelve times a year. $60.00. PTN Publishing Company, 445 Broad Hollow Road, Melville NY 11747. **Tel** (516)845-2700, FAX (516)845-7109. **ED** Barry Mazor. **Ad Acc. Circ:** 35,000 (ctrl). available on microfilm and microfiche from University Microfilms International (UMI). Documents available from Article Express International. ***Continues** Tech Photo Pro Imaging Systems, 1040-0141; **Absorbed** AVC Presentation for the Visual Communicator.*
Desc: Application and technology features covering all forms and markets of electronic imaging.
Ind/Abst Acad. Search; Ei Page One; Eng. Index Annu. [Select. Cov.]; EP Collect.; Graph. Arts Bull. Inst. Pap. Sci. Technol. (May 1989-June 1989, Aug. 1989-Nov. 1989); Homework Help.; Index Inf. (1990-); MasterFile FullTEXT 1000; MasterFile FullTEXT 350; MasterFile FullTEXT 650; MasterFile FullTEXT (Jan. 1994-); OCLC; Telebase.

LC HD9697.V543 U517 **ISSN** 1068-6363 US

BLUE BOOK (WHITE PLAINS, N.Y.). See Communications-Video.

US

C LIBRARY. CD-ROM. English. $99.00. Alde Publishing, PO Box 39326, Minneapolis MN 55396. **Tel** (612)474-3755.
Desc: This CD-ROM contains a huge selection of C programs, source code and public domain utilities.

ISSN 0848-8649
DD 025.3/0285/574 CN
CEASED

CANADIAN CD-ROM NEWS. [Can. CD-ROM news]. **Added/Corp** CD ROM Interest Group. Canadian Library Association : CD ROM Interest Group. **VFOAT** Canadian CD ROM News. **VAT** Canadian Compact Disc Read Only Memory News. Vol. 4 No. 1 (Sept./Oct. 1989)-Vol. 8 No. 4 (1994). Periodical. English. Pelican Island Information, PO Box 24004, London Ontario N6H 5C4 Canada. **Tel** (519)679-9107, FAX (519)661-3866. **ED** Paul Nicholls. Index available. **Bk Rev. Ad Acc. Circ:** 500. ***Continues** Canadian CD ROM Newsletter, 0832-5979.*

ISSN 0893-4843
DD 338 US
CCC

CD COMPUTING NEWS. [CD comput. news]. **VAT** Compact Disc Computing News. Vol. 1, No. 1 (April 1987)-. Periodical. English. Twelve times a year. $150.00. Worldwide Videotex, PO Box 3273, Boynton Beach FL 33424-3273. **Tel** (407)738-2276, FAX (407)738-2275. **ED** Mark Wright. **Bk Rev**, (Qty: 12). available on an online database (file 636/Full-Text) from DIALOG; and NEWSNET.
Desc: News and information on CD-ROM products, developments, companies and marketing strategies. Written for industry professionals and librarians.
Ind/Abst PTS Newsl. Database [Full Txt.].

ISSN 1122-6455 IT
UDC 681.3

•**CD-ROM & MULTIMEDIA.** [CD-ROM Multimed.]. **VFOAT** Compact Disc-Reed Only Memory e Multimedia. (1994)-. Periodical. Italian. Six times a year. L81750. Tecniche Nuove SPA, Via Ciro Menotti 14, 20129 Milan Italy. **Tel** 011 39 2 75701, FAX 011 39 2 7570205, telex 334647 TECHS I. ***Continues** High Tech, 1120-2548.*

ISSN 0892-0176
DD 621 US

CD-ROM APPLICATIONS FORUM. [CD-ROM appl. forum]. **Added/Corp** Special Interest Group on CD-ROM Applications & Technology. **VFOAT** CD ROM Applications Forum. **VAT** Compact Disc, Read-Only Memory Applications Forum. Vol. 1, No. 1 (May 1987)-. Periodical. English. Twelve times a year. $297.00 individuals, $118.00 libraries. AllTech Communications Inc, PO Box 8285, Cincinnati OH 45208-0285.

US

CD-ROM DATABASES. English. Twelve times a year. $150.00. Worldwide Videotex, PO Box 3273, Boynton Beach FL 33424-3273. **Tel** (407)738-2276, FAX (407)738-2275. **ED** Mark Wright. **Bk Rev**, (Qty: 12). available on an online database (file 636/Full-Text) from DIALOG; and NEWSNET.
Desc: CD-ROM directory, includes titles, prices, and categories, and a separate directory of CD-ROM vendors.
Ind/Abst PTS Newsl. Database [Full Txt.].

US

CD-ROM DEVELOPERS LAB. CD-ROM. (19??)-. English. Two times a year. $400.00 US; $432.00 other. Software Mart Incorporated, 3933 Steck Street, Suite B115, Austin TX 78759. **Tel** (512)346-7887.

LC Z699.22 **ISSN** 1062-6891
DD 070 US
CODEN CDRDE7
TITLE CHANGE

CD-ROM DIRECTORY ON DISC, THE. (THE CD-ROM DIRECTORY ON DISC [COMPUTER FILE].). [CD-ROM dir. disc]. (19??)-(199?). Directory. English. Task Force Pro Libra Ltd., 17-18 Britton Street, London EC1M 5NQ United Kingdom. **Tel** 011 44 171 2515522, FAX 011 44 171 2518318. **(Subscription address:** TFPL Inc. / North America Subscriptions, 1301 20th Street Northwest #702, Washington DC 20036. **Tel** (202)296-6009.**)** available in print. ***Continued by** CD-ROM Directory.*

LC HD9696.O67 C37
UK

•**CD-ROM DIRECTORY ... WITH MULTIMEDIA CD'S, THE.** **VFOAT** CD ROM Directory with Multimedia CD's; CD-ROM Directory. 9th Ed. (1993)-. Periodical. English. One time a year (Dec.). Task Force Pro Libra Ltd., 17-18 Britton Street, London EC1M 5NQ United Kingdom. **Tel** 011 44 171 2515522, FAX 011 44 171 2518318. **(Subscription address:** TPFL

Computers —Optical Storage, CD-ROM Applications

Inc., 1301 20th Street Northwest #702, Washington DC 20036. **Tel** (202)296-6009.) **Continues** CD-ROM Directory.

LC HD9696.O67 C375
UK

CD-ROM DIRECTORY [COMPUTER FILE], THE. (199?)-. Directory. English. Two times a year. Task Force Pro Libra Ltd., 17-18 Britton Street, London EC1M 5NQ United Kingdom. **Tel** 011 44 171 2515522, FAX 011 44 171 2518318. **Continues** CD-ROM Directory On Disc.

LC TA1635 .C38   ISSN 1042-8623
DD 004.5/6   US

CD-ROM ENDUSER. [CD-ROM endUser]. **VFOAT** CD-ROM End User. **VAT** Compact Disk-Read-Only Memory Enduser. Vol. 1, No. 1 (May 1989)-. Periodical. English. Twelve times a year. Free (qualified end users), $19.95 US; $29.95 other. Helgerson Associates, 7 Cottonwood Lane, Hilton Head Island SC 29926. **ED** Linda W Helgerson, Martin G Ennis, and Jeff A Blakeman. Index available. **Bk Rev. Ad Acc. Circ:** 18,000 (ctrl). available on CD-ROM.
Desc: Features in-depth coverage of a major CD-ROM application area, military, business, education, etc. Regular columnists with reviews of books and CD-ROM titles, user interfaces, games and future entertainment.

LC Z5771
DD 011.7   UK

●**CD-ROM FINDER : THE WORLD OF CD-ROM PRODUCTS FOR INFORMATION SEEKERS.** See Library and Information Sciences-Abstracting, Bibliographies and Statistics.

ISSN 0967-8123
UK
Pr Rev.   **CEASED**

CD-ROM INFORMATION PRODUCTS. See Computers-Hardware.

ISSN 0987-8238
FR
UDC 778

CD ROM INTERNATIONAL. **VFOAT** Compact Disc Read Only Memory International. (1987)-. Periodical. English. Eighteen times a year. $546.80. A Jour, 11 rue du Marche St. Honore, 75001 Paris France. **Tel** 011 33 1 44553849. **ED** Sotives Eleftheriou. **Bk Rev. Ad Acc. Circ:** 500.
Desc: News of the CD-ROM industry.

LC HD9696.O67 C377   ISSN 1047-966X
DD 338.4/76213976   US
   CEASED

CD-ROM MARKET PLACE. See Computers-Computer Industry and Industry Directories.

LC TA1635 .C337   ISSN 1075-1106
DD 004   US
   CODEN CNEEEF
   CEASED

CD-ROM NEWS EXTRA. (CD-ROM NEWS EXTRA : THE BIMONTHLY NEWS SUPPLEMENT TO CD-ROM PROFESSIONAL MAGAZINE.). [CD-ROM **VFOAT** Compact Disc Read Only Memory News Extra. Vol. 1, No. 1 (Feb. 1993)-(Oct. 1994). Periodical. English. Online Inc., 462 Danbury Road, Wilton CT 06897. **Tel** (203)761-1466, (800)248-8466, FAX (203)761-1444.

ISSN 0954-3600
DD 004.56   UK

CD-ROM NEWSLETTER ALTON. (CD-ROM NEWSLETTER.). [CD-ROM newsl. Alton]. **VFOAT** Compact Disc-Read Only Memory Newsletter (Alton). (1987)-. Newsletter. English. Six times a year (Jan., Mar., May, July, Sept., Nov.). $162.57. MicroInfo Ltd., PO Box 3, Omega Park, Alton Hampshire GU34 2PG United Kingdom. **Tel** 011 44 1420 86848, FAX 011 44 1420 89889, telex 858431 MINFO G. **ED** Roy B. Selwyn. **Bk Rev.**
Desc: Covers all aspects of CD-ROM and related CD technologies. Reports on software, hardware introductions and database products.

ISSN 1076-0415
US
   SUSPENDED

CD-ROM POCKET GUIDE. (1994)- Suspended (1995). English. Four times a year. Online Inc., 462 Danbury Road, Wilton CT 06897. **Tel** (203)761-1466, (800)248-8466, FAX (203)761-1444.

ISSN 1079-6800
DD 004   US
   CEASED

CD-ROM POWER. [CD-ROM power]. (Feb. 1995)-(Oct. 1995). Periodical. English. LFP Inc., 8484 Wilshire Boulevard, Suite 900, Beverly Hills CA 90210. **Tel** (213)651-5400.
US

CD-ROM ... PRODUCT GUIDE. Added/Corp Bureau of Electronic Publishing. **VFOAT** CD-ROM Product Guide. (19??)-. English. Bureau of Electronic Publishing Inc., 141 New Road, Parsippany NJ 07054. **Tel** (201)808-2700, FAX (201)808-2676.

LC TA1635 .L37   ISSN 1049-0833
DD 004.5/6   US
   CODEN CRPFEX

CD-ROM PROFESSIONAL. [CD-ROM prof.]. **VAT** Compact Disc Read Only Memory Professional; CD ROM Professional. Vol. 3, No. 3 (May 1990)-. Periodical. English. Twelve times a year (subscription includes demofloppy). $98.00. Online Inc., 462 Danbury Road, Wilton CT 06897. **Tel** (203)761-1466, (800)248-8466, FAX (203)761-1444. **ED** Nancy K. Herther (editor's telephone: (612)771-9939). Index available. **Bk Rev,** (Qty: 36). **Ad Acc; Adv Mgr:** John Bryans. **Circ:** 6000. available on microfilm and microfiche from University Microfilms International (UMI); available on an online database (file 648/Full-Text) from DIALOG. Documents available from Ask*IEEE, BLDSC, CASDDS, FAXON Xpress, SWETS, UMI Article Clearinghouse. **Continues** Laserdisk Professional, 0896-4149.
Desc: Edited to provide practical information on all aspects of CD-ROM use, including evaluation, purchase and operation of equipment and publishing activities. Each issue contains approximately 150 pages of feature articles; news pages; columns on hardware development; product reviews; practical instruction on CD-ROM publishing; user evaluations of commercially available discs; product comparisons; answers to reader's questions; book and magazine reviews; and interviews with industry executives.
Ind/Abst Acad. Abstr.; ACM Guide Comput. Lit.; Comput. Rev.; Cumul. Index Nurs. Allied Health Lit.; Curr. Cit.; Curr. Index J. Educ.; EP Collect.; Expand. Acad. Index (1992-); Homework Help.; Inf. Instruc. Technol. (May 1990-); Inf. Manage. Technol.; Inf. Sci. Abstr. (May 1990-) [Full Cov.]; INSPEC (May 1990-); Int. Aerosp. Abstr.; Libr. Inf. Sci. Abstr.; Mag. Artic. Summar. Elite; Mag. Artic. Summar. Select; Mag. Artic. Summar. CD-ROM; MasterFile FullTEXT 1000; MasterFile FullTEXT 350; MasterFile FullTEXT 650; MasterFile FullTEXT; Microcomput. Abstr. (Jan. 1992-); Mid. Search; Newsp. Period. Abstr. (1992-); OCLC; Telebase; Trade Ind. ASAP [Full Txt.]; Trade Ind. Index [Full Txt.]; UMI ABI/Inform--Bus. Period. Ondisc [Full Txt.].

ISSN 1075-7694
DD 004   US
   CEASED

CD-ROM REPORTER. [CD ROM report.]. **VFOAT** CD ROM Reporter. (1993)-(1995). Periodical. English. Centos, 5024 Katella Avenue, Suite 161, Los Alamitos CA 90720.

LC HD9696.O67 C38   ISSN 1048-406X
DD 621.39/76   US
   SUSPENDED

CD-ROM SHOPPERS GUIDE. [CD-ROM shoppers guide]. **VFOAT** CD ROM Shoppers Guide. Vol. 1, No. 1 (Spring 1990)-. Periodical. English. Four times a year. $12.95 US; $19.95 other. DDRI Inc, 510 North Washington Street/Suite 401, Falls Church VA 22046-3537. **Tel** (703)237-0682, FAX (703)532-5447.
Desc: Consumers buying guide for CD-ROM titles and drives, including worldwide distributors of these products.
US

CD-ROM SOURCEDISC [COMPUTER FILE], THE. Added/Corp Helgerson Associates, Inc. **VFOAT** CD-ROM Sourcedisc. Titles; Titles. **VAT** Compact Disc Read-Only Memory Sourcedisc. (Nov. 1990)-. Periodical. English. Twenty-four times a year. Helgerson Associates, 7 Cottonwood Lane, Hilton Head Island SC 29926. Index available. cum. index. **Circ:** 5,000.
Desc: Descriptions of all commercially available CD-ROM titles with demonstrations.

LC TA1635 .C43   ISSN 1069-4099
DD 006.6   US

●**CD-ROM TODAY.** [CD-ROM today]. **VFOAT** CD ROM Today. (July 1993)-. Periodical. English. Six times a year. $49.95. Imagine Publishing Inc, 1350 Old Bayshore Highway, Suite 210, Burlingame CA 94010. **Tel** (415)696-1688, FAX (415)696-1678. **ED** Daniel Tynan. **Photos. Ad Acc. Adv Mgr:** Patricia Neuray.
Desc: A journal of personal multimedia covering the latest in CD-ROM technology.

LC Z681.3.O67 C3   ISSN 1066-274X
DD 025   US
   CCC
   CODEN CDWOEV
   TITLE CHANGE

CD-ROM WORLD. [CD-ROM world]. **VFOAT** CD ROM World. **VAT** Compact Disc Read Only Memory World. Vol. 8, No. 1 (Jan. 1993)-(Feb. 1995). Periodical. English. PCW Communications Inc., 501 Second Street, San Francisco CA 94107. **Tel** (415)243-0500, (415)978-3146. **(Subscription address:** Kable Publishers Aide / Illinois, 308 East Hitt Street, Subscription Department, Mt. Morris IL 61054-1473. **Tel** (815)734-1261.) Documents available from Ask*IEEE. **Continues** CD-ROM Librarian, 0893-9934. **Merged into** Multimedia World, 1073-4759.
Desc: A magazine for the CD-ROM user. Contains articles, interviews, CD-ROM reviews, equipment reviews, round-ups and much more.
Ind/Abst Curr. Cit.; INSPEC.

LC TK7882.C56 C34   ISSN 0891-8198
DD 025.3/44/025   US
   CCC

CD-ROMS IN PRINT. [CD-ROMs print]. **VFOAT** CD ROMS in Print. **VAT** Compact Disc-Read Only Memories in Print; CD ROMs in Print. (1987)-. Directory. English. One time a year (annually in print, semi-annually on CD-ROM). $99.95, £65.00. Gale Research Inc., 835 Penobscot Building, 645 Griswold Street, Detroit MI 48226. **Tel** (800)877-GALE, (313)961-2242, FAX (313)961-6083, (800)414-5043, telex TWX 810-221-7086. **ED** Norman Desmarals. Index available. cum. index. **Ad Acc. Circ:** 2,900.
Desc: The most comprehensive listing of CD-ROM products, providers, and distributors available, including annotated descriptions, subject classification for each CD-ROM title, an index of data providers, and distributors, title index, CD-ROM player index, subject index and glossary of terms.

ISSN 1052-2638
DD 025   US
   CODEN CRPREZ

●**CD-ROMS IN PRINT (CD-ROM).** (CD-ROMS IN PRINT. [COMPUTER FILE].). [CD-ROMs print]. **VFOAT** CD Roms in Print. **VAT** Compact Disc-Read Only Memories in Print. 1st (1995)-. Periodical. English. Two times a year. $99.95. Mecklermedia Corporation, 11 Ferry Lane West, Westport CT 06880. **Tel** (203)226-6967, (800)632-5537, FAX (203)454-5840. **(Subscription address:** Meckler Media Ltd., Artillery House Artillery Row, London SW1P 1RT United Kingdom. **Tel** 011 44 171 9760405, FAX 011 44 171 9760506.) available in print.

ISSN 0897-3296
DD 005   US
   CCC

CDROM DATABASES. [CDROM databases]. **VFOAT** CD ROM Databases. Vol. 1, No. 1 (Jan. 1988)-. Periodical. English. Twelve times a year. $150.00. Worldwide Videotex, PO Box 3273, Boynton Beach FL 33424-3273. **Tel** (407)738-2276, FAX (407)738-2275. **ED** Mark Wright. ctrl circ. available on an online database from NEWSNET; and DIALOG.
Desc: Provides titles, prices and subject categories of CD-ROM databases currently being marketed. Lists the names, addresses, and telephone numbers of all vendors who supply these CD-ROM databases. Listed first by title order and then by vendor name and category.

ISSN 0895-3902
DD 621   US

COMPACT DISC NEWS. [Compact disc news]. **VFOAT** CD News. Vol. 1, No. 1 (Aug. 1987)-. Periodical. English. Twelve times a year. $32.00. Atlantic Book Company, 4201 University Drive No 102, Durham NC 27707.

ISSN 0988-3452
FR
UDC 681.3

COMPUTER DATA STORAGE NEWSLETTER. (1988)-. Periodical. English. Twelve times a year. $396.98. Micro-Journal SARL, 11 rue de Provence, 75009 Paris France. **Tel** 011 33 1 42463056, FAX 011 33 1 48242276. **ED** Jean-Jacques Maleval. Index available. cum. index. **Bk Rev,** (Qty: 12).
Desc: News report on the magnetic optical disk and tape industry.

ISSN 1051-6700
US

CONNECTIONS (PROVIDENCE, R.I.). (CONNECTIONS [COMPUTER FILE] : THE COSA JOURNAL.). **Added/Corp** Company of Science & Art. **VFOAT** Connections, The CoSA Journal. (1991)-. Periodical. English. Twelve times a year. $100.00. The Company of Science & Art Inc., 14 Imperial Place, Suite 203, Providence RI 02903.

LC TK7895.M4 D39   ISSN 1078-0920
DD 621.39/7/05   US

●**DATA STORAGE.** [Data storage]. Vol. 1, No. 1 (Sept. 1994)-. Trade Publication. English. Six times a year. $33.00 US and Canada; $89.00 other. PennWell Publishing Company, 1421 South Sheridan, PO Box

1260, Tulsa OK 74101. **Tel** (918)835-3161, (800)331-4463, FAX (918)831-9497. **(Subscription address:** Data Storage Magazine, Publishing Services, PO Box 1260, Tulsa OK 74101. **Tel** (918)831-9812, FAX (918)831-9497.)
Desc: Contains data storage device technology and manufacturing with technical features related to the data storage industry.

ISSN 0267-5447
NE
CCC

DATA STORAGE REPORT. Vol. 1 No. 1 (Mar. 1985)-. Trade Publication. English. Twelve times a year. $385.00 US; $424.00 other. Jonas Press Publishing Company, 53 Park Belmont Place, San Jose CA 95136-2506. **Tel** (408)629-8249, FAX (408)629-8249. available on microfilm from University Microfilms International (UMI); available on an online database (file 636/Full-Text) from DIALOG.
Desc: Covers all aspects of the mass storage industry including technology, legislation and litigation, finance and marketing. Reviews the entire field from floppy disks to Winchesters, and from videodiscs through optical data disks to CD-ROM.
Ind/Abst PTS Newsl. Database [Full Txt.].

LC Z699.A1 D375 **ISSN** 0891-6713
DD 025.5/24 US
CCC
CODEN DASEE5
TITLE CHANGE

DATABASE SEARCHER. See Computers-Data Base Management.

US

DATAPRO REPORTS ON DOCUMENT IMAGING SYSTEMS. **Added/Corp** Datapro Research Corporations. **VFOAT** Document Imaging Systems; Reports on Document Imaging Systems. (Feb. 1990)-. Periodical. English. Twelve times a year. $1008.00. Datapro Information Services Group, 600 Delran Parkway, Delran NJ 08075. **Tel** (609)764-0100, (800)328-2776, FAX (609)764-8953. Each issue contains an index to its own contents (no volume index)--loose.

LC TK5105 .V52 **ISSN** 1054-9692
DD 004 US
CCC
CODEN DIATEG
TITLE CHANGE

DOCUMENT IMAGE AUTOMATION. [Doc. image autom.]. Vol. 11, No. 2 (March/April 1991)-(19??). Periodical. English. Phillips Business Information Inc., 1201 Seven Locks Road, PO Box 61130, Potomac MD 20854. **Tel** (301)424-3338, (301)340-1520, (800)777-5005, FAX (301)424-4297, telex 358149. available on microfilm and microfiche from University Microfilms International (UMI). Documents available from Article Express International, The Genuine Article, UMI Article Clearinghouse, Ask*IEEE. ***Continues*** *Optical Information Systems, 0886-5809.* ***Absorbed by*** *Document Imaging Report.*
Ind/Abst ABI/INFORM Glob. Ed.; ABI/INFORM [Computer File] (Winter 1981-); CompuMath Cit. Index [Full Cov.]; Curr. Cit.; Curr. Index J. Educ.; Eng. Index Annu.; Inf. Sci. Abstr. [Full Cov.]; INSPEC (March/April 1991-); Leg. Inf. Manage. Index (19??-199?); Libr. Inf. Sci. Abstr.; Libr. Lit.; Microcomput. Abstr. (July 1991-); Res. Alert [Full Cov.]; SCISEARCH; Trade Ind. ASAP [Full Txt.]; Trade Ind. Index [Full Txt.]; UMI ABI/Inform--Bus. Period. Ondisc [Full Txt.].

ISSN 1054-9706
DD 004 US
CCC
CODEN DIAUEJ
TITLE CHANGE

DOCUMENT IMAGE AUTOMATION UPDATE. [Doc. image autom. update]. (1991)-(19??). Periodical. English. Mecklermedia Corporation, 11 Ferry Lane West, Westport CT 06880. **Tel** (203)226-6967, (800)632-5537, FAX (203)454-5840. available on an online database (files 16,636,648/Full-Text) from DIALOG. ***Continues*** *Optical Information Systems Update, 0887-5162.* ***Absorbed by*** *Document Imaging Report.*
Ind/Abst Comput. Lit. Index; PROMT; PTS Newsl. Database [Full Txt.].

LC Z699.5.C27 E86 **ISSN** 0834-3888
CN
Pr Rev.

ESPIAL CANADIAN DATA BASE DIRECTORY, THE. See Computers-Electronic Data Processing.

LC Z681.3.O67 A27 **ISSN** 1053-6396
DD 001/.3 US
CODEN FACDEC

FAXON GUIDE TO CD-ROM. [Faxon guide CD ROM]. **Added/Corp** Faxon Company. **VFOAT** Guide to CD-ROM; Faxon Guide to Compact Disc-Read Only Memory. **VAT** Faxon Guide to CD ROM. (1991)-. English. One time a year. $12.00. FW Faxon Company Inc., Faxon Building, 15 Southwest Drive, Westwood MA 02090. **Tel** (617)329-3350. ***Continues*** *Access Faxon, 0897-6139.*

ISSN 1054-9315
DD 342 US

GRID NEWS (LANSING, MICH.). (GRID NEWS [COMPUTER FILE].). [GRID news]. **Added/Corp** World GRID Association. **VAT** General Resources for Information Distribution News. Vol. 2, No. 1 (Jan. 22, 1991)-. Periodical. English. World GRID Association, PO Box 15061, Lansing MI 48911.
Desc: Available on BITNET, FidoNet, and Point-to-Point.
Ind/Abst Energy Inf. Abstr.

US

HANDBOOK OF OPTICAL MEMORY SYSTEMS & UPDATES. (19??)-. English. Seven times a year (Handbook is published in Sept. & updates are in Jan., Mar., May, July, Sept., Nov.). $199.50. Optical Disk Institute, 567 Walnut Street, PO Box 289, Newtonville MA 02160. **Tel** (617)964-3925. **ED** C. Peter Waegemann. Index Bound in First Issue. cum. index. **Bk Rev.**
Desc: This handbook is of interest to any person who works in a supervisory position or information systems position.

ISSN 1041-4320
DD 621 US

IMAGING TECHNOLOGY REPORT. [Imaging technol. rep.]. (198?)-. Periodical. English. Twenty-five times a year. $489.00. Business Research Publications, 1333 H Street Northwest, 2nd Floor West, Washington DC 20005. **Tel** (202)842-3022, (800)822-6338, FAX (202)842-3023. available in microform from University Microfilms International (UMI).
Desc: The monthly review of business imaging that reports on technology, application, vendors, markets, problems, research, innovations, products and trends. It covers optical disk, electronic imaging, CD-Rom, interactive videodisk and other growing imaging technologies. In non-technical language, this journal keeps readers up to date on a rapidly changing field that impacts present information management systems as well as future ones.

ISSN 0194-0694
US
CCC
CODEN IIONDK

INFORMATION INTELLIGENCE ONLINE NEWSLETTER. See Computers-Online Computing and Information.

ISSN 0950-9879
UK
CCC

INFORMATION WORLD REVIEW. [Inf. world rev.]. No. 197 (197?)-. Trade Publication. English. Eleven times a year. $62.95. Learned Information Ltd., Woodside Hinksey Hill, Oxford OX1 5AU United Kingdom. **Tel** 011 44 1865 730275, FAX 011 44 1865 736354, telex 23667. **(Subscription address:** Information Today, 143 Old Marlton Pike, Medford NJ 08055-8750. **Tel** (609)654-6266, FAX (609)654-4309.) available on microfilm and microfiche from University Microfilms International (UMI).
Desc: Source for both users and producers of electronic information services. Keeps readers informed about the launch of new products and services, industry and market news, user experiences, trends and company profiles. Articles are written by experts from throughout Europe and the United States.
Ind/Abst Abstr. Hum. Comput. Interact.; Curr. Cit.; Fluid Abstr., Civil Eng.; Fluid Abstr. Proc. Eng.; FLUIDEX (1973-); HILITES; Infomat Int. Bus.; Inf. Manage. Technol. (19??-); Libr. Inf. Sci. Abstr. (1973-).

ISSN 0847-0456
DD 004.5 CN
CEASED

INTERNATIONAL CD-ROM REPORT, THE. [Int. CD-ROM rep.]. **Added/Corp** Innotech Inc. **VFOAT** International Compact Disk Readable-Only-Memory-Report. Vol. 1, No. 1 (Sept. 1989)-(199?). Periodical. English. Innotech Inc., 2001 Sheppard Avenue East 118, North York Ontario M2J 4Z7 Canada. **Tel** (416)492-3838. **ED** Reuben Lando. Index available. **Bk Rev. Ad Acc. Circ:** 30,000.
Desc: Contains information for the general reader interested in the developments taking place in the optical publishing world of CD-ROM.

LC Z265 .I565 **ISSN** 0958-9961
UK
CCC
CODEN IMOTEX

INTERNATIONAL JOURNAL OF MICROGRAPHICS & OPTICAL TECHNOLOGY. [Int. j. microgr. opt. technol.]. **VFOAT** International Journal of Micrographics and Optical Technology; Micrographics & Optical Technology; Micrographics and Optical Technology. Vol. 7, No. 1 (1989)-. Periodical. English. Four times a year. $224.00. Pergamon Press, An Imprint of Elsevier Science Ltd., The Boulevard, Langford Lane, Kidlington, Oxford OX5 1GB United Kingdom. **Tel** 011 44 1865 843000, 011 44 1865 843699, FAX 011 44 1865 843010. **(Subscription address:** Elsevier Science Ltd. / Oxford Fulfillment Centre, PO Box 800, Kidlington OX5 1DX United Kingdom. **Tel** 011 44 865 843355.) **ED** Don Avedon. available on microfilm and microfiche from University Microfilms International (UMI); available on an online database from Elsevier Electronic Subscriptions (EES). Documents available from Ask*IEEE. ***Continues*** *International Journal of Micrographics & Video Technology, 0743-9636.*
Ind/Abst Curr. Cit.; Inf. Sci. Abstr.; INSPEC (1989-).

US

LEGALITY OF MICROFILM. English. Irregular (2-4 issues per year). $210.00 (new subscription), $85.00 renewal. Cohasset Associates, 505 North Lake Shore Drive, Suite 3806, Chicago IL 60611. **Tel** (312)527-1550.

ISSN 1120-8465
IT
UDC 681.3

M. MACINTOSH MAGAZINE. See Computers-Hardware.

LC TK7895.M3 I57 **ISSN** 0738-923X
DD 621.397 US

MAGNETIC MEDIA INTERNATIONAL NEWSLETTER. **Added/Corp** Magnetic Media Information Services (Firm). (198?)-. Newsletter. English. Six times a year (Every 10 weeks). $1,500. Magnetic Media Information Services, 841 Ikena Circle, Honolulu HI 96821. **Tel** (808)373-5330, FAX (808)377-5668. **ED** Laurence B. Lueck. ***Continues*** *International Newsletter (Magnetic Media Information Services (Firm)), 0738-923X.*
Desc: Concerned with technology, marketing and trends in all forms of recordable and recorded media, whether magnetic, optical or solid state.

ISSN 0990-7939
FR
UDC 681.3

MEMOIRES OPTIQUES & SYSTEMES. **VFOAT** Memoires Optiques et Systemes. (1988)-. Periodical. French. Twelve times a year (10 regular issues, 2 double issues). $262.47. Arca Editions, BP 303, 56008 Vannes Cedex France. **Tel** 011 33 97 478306, FAX 011 33 97 474946. ***Continues*** *Memoires Optiques, 0755-432X.*

LC TR835 .M497a **ISSN** 0882-3294
DD 686.4/3/028 US
CCC
CEASED

MICROGRAPHICS AND OPTICAL STORAGE EQUIPMENT REVIEW. [Microgr. opt. storage equip. rev.]. Vol. 10 (1985)-Vol. 18 (1993). English. Mecklermedia Corporation, 11 Ferry Lane West, Westport CT 06880. **Tel** (203)226-6967, (800)632-5537, FAX (203)454-5840. **ED** William Saffady. Index available. **Bk Rev.** ***Continues*** *Micrographics Equipment Review, 0362-1006.*
Desc: In-depth reviews and tutorials on new equipment for library applications.

LC TA1635 .M53 **ISSN** 1042-0908
DD 004.5/6 US

MICROSOFT CD-ROM YEARBOOK, THE. [Microsoft CD-ROM yearb.]. **Added/Corp** Microsoft Press. **VFOAT** CD-ROM Yearbook; Microsoft CD ROM Yearbook; CD ROM Yearbook. **VAT** Microsoft CD ROM yearbook; CD ROM yearbook. (1989/90)-. English. One time a year. $79.95. Microsoft, One Microsoft Way, Redmond WA 98052-6399. **Tel** (206)882-8080, (800)MSPRESS, FAX (615)793-3915. **(Subscription address:** Publishers Resources Inc., 1224 Heil Quaker Boulevard, PO Box 7017, La Vergne TN 37086.)

LC HD9696.M84 M84
US

... MULTIMEDIA & CD DIRECTORY, THE. **Added/Corp** Phillips Business Information, Inc. **VFOAT** Multimedia and CD Directory; Multimedia and Compact Disc Directory. (19??)-. Directory. English. $199.00. Phillips Business Information Inc., 1201 Seven Locks Road, PO Box 61130, Potomac MD 20854. **Tel** (301)424-3338, (301)340-1520, (800)777-5005, FAX (301)424-4297, telex 358149.
Desc: Information on new sources of multimedia and optical storage products, applications, and services.

ISSN 1046-8684
DD 004 US

NEW MEDIA NEWS (BOSTON, MASS.). (NEW MEDIA NEWS / THE BOSTON COMPUTER SOCIETY.). [New media news]. **Added/Corp** Boston Computer Society. BCS Hypermedia/Optical Disc Publishing Special Interest Group. Vol. 3, No. 1 (Winter 1989)-. Trade Publication. English. Four times a year. The Boston Computer Society, One Kendall Square, Cambridge MA 02139-1562. **Tel** (617)367-8080. ***Continues*** *Optical Insights, 0897-0874.*

UK

OMNI : OPTICAL MEDIA NEWS AND INFORMATION. **VFOAT** OMNI. Vol. 1, Issue No. 1 (Apr. 1991)-. Periodical. English. Twelve times a year. $299.46. MicroInfo Ltd., PO Box 3, Omega Park, Alton Hampshire GU34 2PG United Kingdom. **Tel** 011 44 1420 86848, FAX 011 44 1420 89889, telex 858431 MINFO G.

Computers —Programs and Programming

ED Roy Selwyn. **Bk Rev.** *Formed by the union of Document Image Processing and Optical Data Systems.*
Desc: Important news source concerned with the application of optical technologies to the solution of information storage and retrieval problems. It features all known formats of optical disks, microfilm and related developments. There are regular items on applications, equipment, supplies and services as they concern DIP, business systems, data processing, engineering maintenance support services, libraries and other associated fields.

LC Z699.A1 O5   ISSN 1353-2642
DD 025.04   UK
     CCC
     CODEN ONCDEW
Pr Rev.

●**ONLINE & CDROM REVIEW : THE INTERNATIONAL JOURNAL OF ONLINE & OPTICAL INFORMATION SYSTEMS.** See Computers-Online Computing and Information.

     ISSN 0816-956X
DD 025.040994   AT

ONLINE CURRENTS. See Computers-Online Computing and Information.

LC TA1630 .O625   ISSN 0954-2264
DD 621.36/7/05   UK
     CCC
     CODEN OCOPEH
Pr Rev.   TITLE CHANGE

OPTICAL COMPUTING & PROCESSING. [Opt. comput. process.]. **VFOAT** Optical Computing and Processing. Vol. 1, No. 1 (Jan./Mar. 1991)-(1993). Periodical. English. Taylor & Francis Ltd. / UK, Rankine Road, Basingstoke, Hampshire RG24 8PR United Kingdom. **Tel** 011 44 1256 840366, FAX 011 44 1256 479438, telex 858540. (**Subscription address:** Taylor & Francis Inc., 1900 Frost Road, Suite 101, Bristol PA 19007-1598. **Tel** (215)785-5800, (800)821-8312, FAX (215)785-5515.) **ED** T. J. Hall (editor's address: Physics Department, King's College, Strand, London WC2R 2LS UK). Index available. **Bk Rev**. **Ad Acc**. **Circ**: 400. Documents available from Ask*IEEE. *Absorbed by International Journal of Optoelectronics, 0952-5432.*
Desc: Optical telecommunication and optical information processing have many areas in common. Ideas originating in one field are beginning to be considered in the other, and so each area is able to provide the other with new concepts, applications and technologies. Aims to create a major forum to unite and stimulate work and to facilitate a freer exchange of information between the various groups involved in the study of transmission, processing and storage of data by optical or optoelectronic processes. Besides including optical and optoelectronic systems, the journal will also cover the way the subject impinges on electronics and on computing science.
Ind/Abst ACM Guide Comput. Lit.; Comput. Rev.; Ei Page One; INSPEC (Jan.-March 1991-).

     ISSN 0741-5869
DD 338   CCC

OPTICAL MEMORY NEWS. [Opt. mem. news]. Issue No. 12 (Nov.-Dec. 1983)-. Periodical. English. Twenty-five times a year. $547.00. Phillips Business Information Inc., 1201 Seven Locks Road, PO Box 61120, Potomac MD 20854. **Tel** (301)424-3338, (301)340-1520, (800)777-5005, FAX (301)424-4297, telex 358149. **ED** David Herzberg. available from an online database (file 636/Full-Text) from DIALOG. *Continues Optical Memory Newsletter Including Interactive Videodisks, 0731-9452; Absorbed Optical & Magnetic Report, 1047-5117.*
Desc: Covers worldwide business development in the optical memory field, new products, standard activities, applications and industry trends.
Ind/Abst Inf. Instruc. Technol.; Inf. Manage. Technol. (19??-); PTS Newsl. Database [Full Txt.].

LC TK7895.M4 O686   ISSN 8755-1195
DD 621.397/67/0294   US
     CCC

OPTICAL MEMORY REPORT, THE. [Optic. mem. rep.]. **Added/Corp** Rothchild Consultants. (1984)-. English. One time a year. $1,995.00. Rothchild Consultants, 256 Laguna Honda Boulevard, San Francisco CA 94116-1496. **Tel** (415)681-3700, FAX (415)681-3732, telex 910-350-6063. **ED** Edward S. Rothchild.
Desc: Comprehensive reference guide to and for the optical memory industry. Technology explanation, product specifications, company profiles, market projections and glossary of terms.

     ISSN 0167-8949
     NE

PROFILE (AMSTERDAM). (PROFILE : EXCERPTA MEDICA NEWSLETTER.). [Profile]. **Added/Corp** Excerpta Medica (Firm). Vol. 1, No. 1 (1982)-. Newsletter. English. Four times a year. Elsevier Science Publishers BV, PO Box 211, 1000 AE Amsterdam Netherlands. **Tel** 011 31 20 4853641, 011 31 20 4853642, FAX 011 31 20 4853598.

LC TK5102.5 .R372   ISSN 8755-3619
DD 621.38/043

REAL-TIME SIGNAL PROCESSING. See Electronics.

LC HD9696.C6 R54
DD 380.1/456213976   US

RIGID DISK DRIVE MAGNETIC HEAD/MEDIA MARKET, AND TECHNOLOGY UPDATE. **Added/Corp** Peripheral Research Corporation. (19??)-. English. One time a year (November). $945.00. Peripheral Research Corporation, 351 South Hitchcock Way #B-200, Santa Barbara CA 93105. **Tel** (805)963-8081, FAX (805)569-2512.

     ISSN 1062-8568
     US

ROM (CEDAR FALLS, IOWA). (ROM.). (1992)-. Periodical. English. Six times a year. $35.00. Freiberg Publishing Company, PO Box 7, Cedar Falls IA 50613. **Tel** (319)277-3599, FAX (319)277-3783.

     ISSN 0893-9462
DD 621   US

SMART CARD MONTHLY. [Smart card mon.]. (May 1987)-. Periodical. English. Twelve times a year. $595.00. Smart Card Concepts, 1168 Date Street, PO Box 370968, Montara CA 94037. **Tel** (415)728-3920, FAX (415)728-8675. **ED** Stephan Seidman. **Bk Rev**.
Desc: Technology, market and applications for Integrated Circuit Cards, Smart Cards and related storage methods.

     US

●**SUPPORT ON SITE FOR APPLICATIONS.** (1995)-. English. Twelve times a year. $1295.00. Computer Library, One Park Avenue, Fifth Floor, New York NY 10016. **Tel** (212)503-4409, FAX (212)503-4414.

     UK

TEXT & IMAGE NEWS. See Computers-Word Processing.

     ISSN 8756-5250
DD 001   SUSPENDED

VIDEO COMPUTING. [Video comput.]. Suspended (Feb 1989). Periodical. English. Twelve times a year. $130.00 (one-year), $230.00 (two-year) US; $150.00 (one-year) other. Video Computing, PO Box 372401, Satellite Beach FL 32937. **Tel** (305)768-2778, (205)991-6925, FAX (205)991-1479, telex 78-2661. (**Subscription address:** Video Computing, PO Box 11127, Birmingham AL 35202.) **ED** Gwendolyn De Cort. **Bk Rev**. **Ad Acc**. **Circ**: 40,000.
Desc: The journal of interactive video and optical storage technology.

PROGRAMS AND PROGRAMMING

     US

ACCESS PROGRAMMING FOR DUMMIES. (19??)-. English. $23.90. Cary Prague Books and Software, 60 Krawski Drive, South Windsor CT 06074. **Tel** (800)277-3117.

LC QA76.73.A35 A3   US

●**ACM ADA LETTERS : A BIMONTHLY PUBLICATION OF SIGADA, THE ACM SPECIAL INTEREST GROUP ON ADA.** **Added/Corp** SIGAda. **VFOAT** Ada Letters; Association for Computing Machinery Ada Letters. Vol. 13, No. 4 (July/Aug. 1993)-. Periodical. English. Six times a year. $58.00. ACM / Association for Computing Machinery, 1515 Broadway, 17th Floor, New York NY 10036. **Tel** (212)869-7440, FAX (212)869-0481. *Continues Ada Letters, 0736-721X.*
Ind/Abst Curr. Cit.

LC QA76.7 .A24   ISSN 1057-4514
DD 005.1/05   CCC
     CODEN ALPSE8
     TITLE CHANGE

ACM LETTERS ON PROGRAMMING LANGUAGES AND SYSTEMS. [ACM lett. program. lang. syst.]. **Added/Corp** Association for Computing Machinery. **VFOAT** LOPLAS; Letters on Programming Languages and Systems. **VAT** Association for Computing Machinery Letters on Programming Languages and Systems. (1992)-(1993). Periodical. English. ACM / Association for Computing Machinery, 1515 Broadway, 17th Floor, New York NY 10036. **Tel** (212)869-7440, FAX (212)869-0481. **ED** Charles N. Fisher. Documents available from Article Express International. *Absorbed by Association for Computing Machinery. ACM Transactions on Programming Languages and Systems, 0164-0925.*
Desc: Features publication of short papers describing research and development efforts in programming languages and related systems.
Ind/Abst Comput. Rev.; Ei Page One; Eng. Index Annu.

LC QA76.7 .S54
DD 001.64/24/05   US

ACM SIGPLAN NOTICES : A MONTHLY PUBLICATION OF THE SPECIAL INTEREST GROUP ON PROGRAMMING LANGUAGES. **Added/Corp** ACM Special Interest Group in Programming Languages. **VFOAT** Notices; SIGPLAN Notices. **VAT** Association for Computing Machinery Special Interest Group on Programming Languages notices; Special Interest Group on Programming Languages Notices. Vol. 26, No. 10 (Oct. 1991)-. Periodical. English. Twelve times a year. $57.00. ACM / Association for Computing Machinery, 1515 Broadway, 17th Floor, New York NY 10036. **Tel** (212)869-7440, FAX (212)869-0481. (**Subscription address:** Association for Computing Machinery, PO Box 12114, Church Street Station, New York NY 10249. **Tel** (212)626-0500.) *Continues SIGPLAN Notices, 0352-1340.*

LC QA76.6 .A8a   ISSN 0098-3500
DD 510/.28/542505   CCC
     CODEN ACMSCU
Pr Rev.

ACM TRANSACTIONS ON MATHEMATICAL SOFTWARE. See Mathematics-Computer Applications.

LC QA76.7 .A77a   ISSN 0164-0925
DD 001.64/2   US
     CCC
     CODEN ATPSDT
Pr Rev.

ACM TRANSACTIONS ON PROGRAMMING LANGUAGES AND SYSTEMS. [ACM trans. program. lang. syst.]. **Main/Corp** Association for Computing Machinery. **Added/Corp** Association for Computing Machinery. Transactions on Programming Languages and Systems. **VAT** Association for Computing Machinery Transactions on Programming Languages and Systems. Vol. 1 (July 1979)-. Periodical. English. Six times a year (bimonthly). $180.00. ACM / Association for Computing Machinery, 1515 Broadway, 17th Floor, New York NY 10036. **Tel** (212)869-7440, FAX (212)869-0481. (**Subscription address:** Association for Computing Machinery, PO Box 12114, Church Street Station, New York NY 10249. **Tel** (212)626-0500.) available on microfilm and microfiche from University Microfilms International (UMI). Documents available from Article Express International, The Genuine Article, Ask*IEEE. *Absorbed ACM Letters on Programming Languages and Systems, 1057-4514.*
Ind/Abst ACM Guide Comput. Lit.; Appl. Sci. Technol. Index (1991-); CompuMath Cit. Index [Full Cov.]; Comput. Abstr.; Comput. Database; Comput. Lit. Index; Comput. Rev.; Curr. Cit.; Curr. Contents Eng. Comput. Technol.; Educ. Technol. Abstr.; Ei Page One; Eng. Index Annu.; Ergon. Abstr. (?-?); Expand. Acad. Index (1992-); Index Sci. Rev.; Inf. Sci. Abstr.; INIS Atomindex [Micro.]; INSPEC (1979-); Int. Aerosp. Abstr.; Res. Alert [Full Cov.]; Sci. Cit. Index; SCISEARCH; Zentralbl. Math. Ihre Grenzgeb.

     ISSN 1064-1505
DD 005   US

ADA IC NEWSLETTER. (ADA IC NEWSLETTER.). [Ada IC newsl.]. **Added/Corp** Ada Information Clearinghouse. **VFOAT** AdaIC Newsletter. **VAT** Ada Information Clearinghouse Newsletter. (19??)-. Newsletter. English. Four times a year (Mar., June, Sept., Dec.). Free on request. Ada Information Clearinghouse, c/o IIT Research Institute, PO Box 46593, Washington DC 20050-6593. **Tel** (703)635-1477, (800)232-4211, FAX (703)685-7019. **ED** Susan Carlson, John Walker. **Bk Rev**, (Qty: 1-2). **Circ**: 16,000. available on CD-ROM; available from an online database from Internet; Compuserve Inc.; and Bulletin Board.
Desc: Provides information on the Ada community, and on Ada - an internationally standardized, general-purpose computer programming language used in a wide variety of applications and designed to provide inherent support to sound software engineering.

LC QA76.73.A35 A3   ISSN 0736-721X
DD 001.64/24   US
     CODEN AALEE5
     TITLE CHANGE

ADA LETTERS. (ADA LETTERS : A BIMONTHLY PUBLICATION OF ADATEC.). [Ada lett.]. **Added/Corp** AdaTEC. Association for Computing Machinery. Vol. 1, No. 1 (July/Aug. 1981)-(1993). Periodical. English. ACM / Association for Computing Machinery, 1515 Broadway, 17th Floor, New York NY 10036. **Tel** (212)869-7440, FAX (212)869-0481. Documents available from Article Express International, Ask*IEEE. *Continued by ACM Ada Letters.*
Ind/Abst ACM Guide Comput. Lit.; Comput. Rev. (May-June 1988-); Ei Page One; Eng. Index Annu.; INSPEC (Vol. 8, May-June 1988-).

LC WMLC 93/1357 ISSN 0268-652X
NE
CCC
CODEN ADUSEB
TITLE CHANGE

ADA USER. [Ada user]. (198?)-(1994). Periodical. English. IOS Press, Van Diemenstraat 94, 1013 CN Amsterdam Netherlands. **Tel** 011 31 20 6382189, FAX 011 31 20 6203419. **ED** D. Simpson. Documents available from Ask*IEEE. ***Continues*** *Ada UK News, 0264-2085.* ***Continued by*** *Ada User Journal, 1381-6551.*
Ind/Abst INSPEC (1987-?).

LC WMLC 93/1357 ISSN 1381-6551
NE
UDC 800.92
CODEN ADUSEB

●**ADA USER JOURNAL.** [Ada user j.]. **Added/Corp** a Language UK. (1994)-. Periodical. English. Four times a year. Fl300.00. IOS Press, Van Diemenstraat 94, 1013 CN Amsterdam Netherlands. **Tel** 011 31 20 6382189, FAX 011 31 20 6203419. **ED** D. Simpson. Documents available from Ask*IEEE. ***Continues*** *Ada User, 0268-652X.*
Desc: Publishes material which promotes the effective development and use of the Ada language. Promotes the communication of ideas and information about the technology of software engineering and the commercial implications of policy decisions and attitudes to embedded computer systems.
Ind/Abst Curr. Cit.; INSPEC (1987-).

LC Z5642.3 .A57 QA76.6
RU

ALGORITMY I PROGRAMMY. **Added/Corp** Gosudarstvennaia Publichnaia Nauchno-Tekhnicheskaia Biblioteka SSSR. Russia (U.S.S.R.). Gosudarstvennyi Komitet po Nauke i Tekhnike. No. 1 (1968)-. Multiple languages (Russian and Multiple languages). Four times a year. $150.00. GPNTB SSR, 103031 Kuznetskii Most 12, Moscow Russia. **(Subscription address:** Victor Kamkin, 4956 Boiling Brook Parkway, Rockville MD 20852. **Tel** (301)881-5973.**)**

ISSN 1057-2325
DD 004 US

AMI PRO REPORT, THE. [Ami pro rep.]. **VFOAT** Lotus Newsletters. Vol. 1, No. 1 (1991)-. Periodical. English. Twelve times a year. $59.00. IDG Newsletter Corporation, 77 Franklin Street, Suite 310, Boston MA 02110. **Tel** (617)482-8470, (800)807-0771, FAX (617)338-0164. **(Subscription address:** Neodata / Colorado, PO Box 2606, Boulder CO 80322. **)**

LC QA76 .A63 ISSN 0066-4138
DD 510.78 UK
CCC
NLM Z 699.A1 A615 CODEN ARVAAM

ANNUAL REVIEW IN AUTOMATIC PROGRAMMING. [Annu. rev. autom. program.]. Vol. 1 (1960)-. English. Two times a year. $226.00. Pergamon Press, An Imprint of Elsevier Science Ltd., The Boulevard, Langford Lane, Kidlington, Oxford OX5 1GB United Kingdom. **Tel** 011 44 1865 843000, 011 44 1865 843699, FAX 011 44 1865 843010. **(Subscription address:** Elsevier Science Ltd. / Oxford Fulfillment Centre, PO Box 800, Kidlington OX5 1DX United Kingdom. **Tel** 011 44 865 843355.**)** available on microfilm and microfiche from University Microfilms International (UMI); available on an online database from Elsevier Electronic Subscriptions (EES). Documents available from Ask*IEEE.
Desc: Provides review articles on topics of interest to professionals in the field of computer software. Each year, the editors identify areas in which there has been sufficient progress to justify an article that provides a comprehensive review.
Ind/Abst Comput. Rev.; Ei Page One; INSPEC (1969-); Zentralbl. Math. Ihre Grenzgeb.

LC QA76.73.A27 A195 ISSN 0163-6006
DD 001.64/24 US
CODEN APLQD9

APL QUOTE QUAD. [APL quote quad]. **Added/Corp** ACM Special Interest Group in Programming Languages. Technical Committee on APL. SIGAPL. **VFOAT** APL Quote-Quad. Vol. 1, No. 4 (Jan. 1970)-. Periodical. English. Four times a year (Mar., May, Sept., Dec.). $40.00. ACM / Association for Computing Machinery, 1515 Broadway, 17th Floor, New York NY 10036. **Tel** (212)869-7440, FAX (212)869-0481. **(Subscription address:** Association for Computing Machinery, PO Box 12114, Church Street Station, New York NY 10249. **Tel** (212)626-0500.**)** Documents available from Article Express International, Ask*IEEE. ***Continues*** *Share APL360 Newsletter.*
Ind/Abst ACM Guide Comput. Lit.; Comput. Rev.; Curr. Cit.; Eng. Index Annu.; INSPEC (Dec. 1980-).

LC HF5548.4.A68 A67 ISSN 0898-1183
DD 005.369 US

APPLEWORKS JOURNAL. (APPLEWORKS JOURNAL : INFORMATION & NEWS FOR APPLEWORKS USERS.). [AppleWorks j.]. **VFOAT** Apple Works Journal. Vol. 1, No. 1 (1987)-. Periodical. English. Twelve times a year. IDG International News Group, 41 West Street 8th Floor, Boston MA 02111. **Tel** (617)423-9030. ***Formed by the union of*** *Main Menu, 0890-2585* ***and*** *AppleWorks Exclusive Reference, 0891-8236.*

US

APPLICATION DEVELOPMENT STRATEGIES. (19??)-. English. Twelve times a year. $387.00 US, Canada and Mexico; $455.00 other. Cutter Information Corporation, 37 Broadway, Arlington MA 02174-5539. **Tel** (617)648-8700, (800)964-5118, FAX (617)648-8707, (617)648-1950, telex 650 100 9891. ***Continues*** *CASE Outlook; CASE Strategies, 1045-1986.*

LC QA76.6 .V56A ISSN 0145-9880
DD 001.6/425 US

APPLICATIONS PROGRAMS. **Main/Corp** The Viola Grange (Firm). Vol. 1-. English. Viola Grange, Box 965, Estacada OR 97023.

US

●**APPLIED COMPUTING REVIEW : A PUBLICATION OF THE SPECIAL INTEREST GROUP ON APPLIED COMPUTING.** **See** Computers-Software.

LC QA
DD 005 US

BASICALY SPEAKING. (1990)-. Newsletter. English. Twelve times a year. $24.00. Information Management Systems, 1165 North Industrial Park Drive, Orem UT 80457-2807. **Tel** (800)750-6390, (801)226-6390, FAX (801)226-6291. **ED** Alan C. Earnshaw. **Bk Rev**, (Qty: 1-2). **Ad Acc. Circ:** 365.
Desc: Monthly newsletter devoted to programming in PowerBASIC. Contains feature articles on programming topics, helpful hints, and overviews of add-on products for PowerBASIC.

ISSN 1071-7463
US

●**BTRIEVE DEVELOPER'S JOURNAL.** (1993)-. Periodical. English. Four times a year. $49.00. Btrieve Developer's Journal, 2416 Hillsboro Road, Suite 201, Nashville TN 37212. **Tel** (615)386-3100.

LC HD9696.C63 ISSN 0885-8055
DD 658/.0553/05 US
CODEN BSREE2

BUSINESS SOFTWARE REVIEW. **See** Business and Economics-Computer Applications.

ISSN 1040-6042
DD 005 US
CCC
CODEN CRPTE7

C++ REPORT, THE. (THE C++ REPORT : THE INTERNATIONAL NEWSLETTER FOR C++ PROGRAMMERS.). [C++ rep.]. **VFOAT** C plus plus report. **VAT** C Plus Plus Report. Vol. 1, No. 1 (Jan. 1989)-. Newsletter. English. Nine times a year. $139.00. SIGS Publications Inc. / New York, 71 West 23rd Street, 3rd Floor, New York NY 10010-4102. **Tel** (212)242-7447. Documents available from Ask*IEEE.
Desc: Newsletter with latest trends in research applications, language developments in C++. Programming tips, inside news and reviews, tutorials, literature summaries and the C++ puzzle.
Ind/Abst INSPEC (June 1991-).

US
CEASED

C USER'S GROUP LIBRARY DIRECTORY, THE. (19??)-(1995). Directory. English. R & D Publications, 1601 West 23rd Street, Suite 200, Lawrence KS 66046. **Tel** (913)841-1631, FAX (913)841-2624. **ED** Bernard Williams. Index available. cum. index. **Circ:** 6,000. available on CD-ROM from Walnut Creek.
Desc: Catalog and index of C Users Group Library of C language source code. Each volume in the library is summarized and each file in the volume is explained in a capsule description. The key word and title combined index accesses all files.

LC QA76.73.C15 C193 ISSN 0898-9788
DD 005.13/3 US
TITLE CHANGE

C USERS JOURNAL, THE. [C users j.]. Vol. 6, No. 1 (Dec./Jan. 1988)-(1994). Periodical. English. R & D Publications, 1601 West 23rd Street, Suite 200, Lawrence KS 66046. **Tel** (913)841-1631, FAX (913)841-2624. **ED** Diane Thomas, P.J. Plauger. Index available. **Bk Rev**, (Qty: 12-24). **Ad Acc, Adv Mgr:** Jeff Dickey-Chasins. **Circ:** 40,000. available on CD-ROM; available on an online database (file 675/Full-Text) from DIALOG. ***Formed by the union of*** *C Journal, 8756-9736* ***and*** *C Users' Group Newsletter.* ***Continued by*** *C/C++ Users Journal, 1075-2838.*
Desc: Technical journal for C programmers. Provides advanced solutions to real-world programming problems.
Ind/Abst Comput. ASAP [Full Txt.]; Comput. Database [Full Txt.].

UK
Pr Rev.

CICS UPDATE. (19??)-. English. Twelve times a year. $225.00. Xephon, 27-35 London Road, Newbury Berkshire RG13 1JL United Kingdom. **Tel** 011 44 1635 33823, FAX 011 44 1635 38345. **(Subscription address:** Xephon, 1301 West Highway, Suite 201 450, Lewisville TX 75067. **) ED** Steve Piggott. Index available. cum. index. **Circ:** 4,000.
Desc: Technical hints and tips for CICS systems programmers.

ISSN 1044-4750
DD 005 US
CEASED

CLARION TECH JOURNAL, THE. [Clar. tech j.]. (July/Aug. 1989)-(1995). Periodical. English. PC Information Group Inc, PO Box 1301, 1126 East Broadway, Winona MN 55987. **Tel** (800)321-8285, (507)452-2824, FAX (507)452-0037. **ED** Randy Goodhew. **Ad Acc, Adv Mgr Tel** (507)452-2824.

US

COBOL INFORMATION BULLETIN. (19??)-. Bulletin. English. Irregular. COBOL Information Bulletin, 311 First Street Northwest, Suite 500, Washington DC 20001. **Tel** (202)737-8888.

LC QC100 .U565 HF5548 ISSN 0591-0218
US
CEASED

CODASYL COBOL JOURNAL OF DEVELOPMENT. [CODASYL COBOL j. dev.]. **Main/Corp** Conference on Data Systems Languages. Programming Language Committee. **Added/Corp** United States. National Bureau of Standards. **VFOAT** COBOL Journal of Development. **VAT** Conference on Data Systems Languages Cobol Journal of Development. (1968)-(1993). English. Journal of Development, 845 La Para Avenue, Palo Alto CA 94306. **Tel** (408)285-0892. ***Continues*** *COBOL, 0574-962X.*

LC QA76.7 .C646 ISSN 0749-2839
DD 005.13/3 US
CCC
CODEN COMLEF
TITLE CHANGE

COMPUTER LANGUAGE. [Comput. lang.]. Vol. 1, No. 1 (Sept. 1984)-(19??). Periodical. English. Miller Freeman Inc., 600 Harrison Street, San Francisco CA 94107. **Tel** (415)905-2337, (415)905-2200, FAX (415)905-2240, telex 278273. **ED** Craig LaGrow. **Ad Acc. Circ:** 45,000. available on microfilm and microfiche from University Microfilms International (UMI); available on an online database (file 675/Full-Text) from DIALOG; and NEXIS. Documents available from Ask*IEEE. ***Continued by*** *Software Development.*
Desc: Dedicated to the professional engineer and programmer who writes software. Editorial includes in-depth coverage of the entire spectrum of languages, programming tools and techniques, as well as practical and theoretical developments in the software design field.
Ind/Abst Abstr. Bull. Inst. Pap. Sci. Tech.; Comput. Inf. Syst. Abstr. J. [Full Cov.]; Comput. ASAP [Full Txt.]; Comput. Database [Full Txt.]; Comput. Lit. Index; Comput. Rev. Index (Oct. 1987-); Curr. Cit.; INSPEC (1986-); Microcomput. Abstr. (Dec. 1985-); Robotics Abstr.

LC QA76.7 .C647 ISSN 0096-0551
DD 001.6/424/05 US
CCC
CODEN COLADA
Pr Rev.

COMPUTER LANGUAGES. [Comput. lang.]. Vol. 1 (Jan. 1975)-. Periodical. English. Four times a year. $552.00. Pergamon Press, An Imprint of Elsevier Science Ltd., The Boulevard, Langford Lane, Kidlington, Oxford OX5 1GB United Kingdom. **Tel** 011 44 1865 843000, 011 44 1865 843699, FAX 011 44 1865 843010. **(Subscription address:** Elsevier Science Ltd. / Oxford Fulfillment Centre, PO Box 800, Kidlington OX5 1DX United Kingdom. **Tel** 011 44 865 843355.**) ED** Robert S. Ledley. Index available. available on microfilm and microfiche from University Microfilms International (UMI); available on an online database from Elsevier Electronic Subscriptions (EES). Documents available from Article Express International, The Genuine Article, Ask*IEEE.
Desc: Publishes articles presenting original work and review articles on programming systems, structures and theories. The objective is to concentrate on programming languages and the theory of such languages. Topics to be included are syntax, parsing, compilers, programming (theories, documentation) and the theory of algorithms, but no actual algorithms.
Ind/Abst Abstr. Hum. Comput. Interact.; ACM Guide Comput. Lit.; Bioeng. Abstr.; CompuMath Cit. Index [Full Cov.]; Comput. Abstr.; Comput. Rev.; Curr. Cit.; Curr. Contents Eng. Comput. Technol.; Ei Page One; Eng. Index Annu.; Ergon. Abstr.; Expand. Acad. Index (1992-); Inf. Sci. Abstr.; INSPEC (Jan. 1975-); Int. Aerosp. Abstr.; Math. Rev.; Pollut. Abstr. Indexes; Res. Alert [Full Cov.]; SCISEARCH; Zentralbl. Math. Ihre Grenzgeb.

Computers —Programs and Programming

NLM W1; CO457I
Pr Rev.
ISSN 0169-2607
NE
CCC
CODEN CMPBEK
COMPUTER METHODS AND PROGRAMS IN BIOMEDICINE. See Biology-Computer Applications.

LC HD8039.D37 C73
ISSN 0160-2497
US
CODEN CPPNB6
COMPUTER PERSONNEL. [Comput. pers.]. **Added/Corp** Association for Computing Machinery. Special Interest Group on Computer Personnel Research. Vol. 1, No. 1 (Apr. 1969)-. Periodical. English. Four times a year. $26.00 nonmembers; $18.00 members. ACM / Association for Computing Machinery, 1515 Broadway, 17th Floor, New York NY 10036. **Tel** (212)869-7440, FAX (212)869-0481. Documents available from Ask*IEEE. **Ind/Abst** ACM Guide Comput. Lit.; Comput. Rev. (1974-); Ergon. Abstr.; INSPEC (1974-).

LC QC52 .C65
DD 530/.028/5
Pr Rev.
ISSN 0010-4655
NE
CCC
CODEN CPHCBZ
COMPUTER PHYSICS COMMUNICATIONS. See Physics-Computer Applications.

DD 004
ISSN 1040-5003
US
COMPUTER REVIEW INDEX. See Computers-Abstracting, Bibliographies and Statistics.

LC QA76.73.O63 C66
DD 005.4/3
Pr Rev.
ISSN 0895-6340
US
CCC
CODEN CMSYE2
COMPUTING SYSTEMS. (COMPUTING SYSTEMS : THE JOURNAL OF THE USENIX ASSOCIATION.). [Comput. syst.]. **Added/Corp** USENIX Association. EUUG (Society). Vol. 1, No. 1 (Winter 1988)-. Periodical. English. Four times a year. $82.00. Massachusetts Institute of Technology (MIT) Press, 55 Hayward Street, Cambridge MA 02142. **Tel** (617)253-2889, (617)625-8481, FAX (617)258-6779. **ED** David S. Presotto. **Circ:** 5,400. Documents available from Article Express International, Ask*IEEE. **Desc:** Dedicated to the analysis and understanding of the theory, design, art, engineering, and implementation of advanced computing systems, with an emphasis on systems inspired or influenced by the UNIX tradition. **Ind/Abst** Comput. Abstr.; Comput. Inf. Syst. Abstr. J. [Full Cov.]; Curr. Cit.; Ei Page One; Eng. Index Annu.; Inf. Sci. Abstr. (?-?); INSPEC (Winter 1988-).

LC QA76.7 .A25a
DD 001.64/24/05
ISSN 0730-8566
US
CCC
CODEN CRLADV
CONFERENCE RECORD OF THE ... ANNUAL ACM SYMPOSIUM ON PRINCIPLES OF PROGRAMMING LANGUAGES. [Conf. rec. annu. ACM Symp. Princ. Program. Lang.]. **Main/Conf** ACM Symposium on Principles of Programming Languages. **Added/Corp** ACM Special Interest Group for Automata and Computability Theory. ACM Special Interest Group in Programming Languages. **VFOAT** Conference Record of the ... Annual ACM SIGPLAN-SIGACT Symposium on Principles of Programming Languages. 5th (Jan. 23-25, 1978)-. English. One time a year. $70.00. ACM / Association for Computing Machinery, 1515 Broadway, 17th Floor, New York NY 10036. **Tel** (212)869-7440, FAX (212)869-0481. **Ad Acc.** ctrl circ. Documents available from Article Express International, Ask*IEEE. **Continues** Conference Record of the ... ACM Symposium on Principles of Programming Languages, 0743-9016. **Ind/Abst** Bioeng. Abstr.; Curr. Cit.; Ei Page One; Eng. Index Annu.

LC QA76.753 .C638
DD 005.36/029//673
ISSN 1045-7445
US
TITLE CHANGE
CONNECTION, THE. See Computers-Microcomputers, Personal Computers.

DD 006
Pr Rev.
ISSN 1072-9224
US
CEASED
CONVERGE (SUNNYVALE, CALIF.). (CONVERGE : THE MULTIMEDIA DEVELOPER'S RESOURCE.). [Converg.]. Vol. 4, No. 1 (1994)-No. 5 (1994). Periodical. English. Multi Facet Communications, 499 South Sunnyvale Avenue, Sunnyvale CA 94086. **Tel** (408)749-0549. **Continues** QuickTime Forum, 1062-9009.

LC QA76.6 .D57
DD 005.3/029/473
ISSN 1043-9935
US
COSMIC SOFTWARE CATALOG. See Aeronautics, Astronautics-Computer Applications.

LC QA76.9.D3 D3588
DD 005.74/05
Pr Rev.
ISSN 0895-4518
CCC
CODEN DPDEEZ
DATABASE PROGRAMMING & DESIGN. See Computers-Data Base Management.

DD 001
ISSN 8756-6516
US
DATAPRO MANAGEMENT OF APPLICATIONS SOFTWARE. [Datapro manage. appl. softw.]. **Added/Corp** Datapro Research Corporation. Vol. 7, No. 1 (Jan. 1985)-. Periodical. English. Twelve times a year. $937.00. Datapro Information Services Group, 600 Delran Parkway, Delran NJ 08075. **Tel** (609)764-0100, (800)328-2776, FAX (609)764-8953. **ED** James H. Shelton. **Circ:** 2,000. **Continues** Datapro Applications Software Solutions, 0730-8760. **Desc:** Contains reports related to the development and acquisition of computer applications software.

US
DB2 FOR THE COBOL PROGRAMMER. Monographic series. English. Irregular. $32.50. Mike Murach & Associates, 4697 West Jacqelyn Avenue, Fresno CA 93722. **Tel** (209)275-3335, (800)221-5528, FAX (209)275-9035. **Desc:** An introductory course to master the essentials of DB2 programming.

ISSN 1082-4375
US
●**DELPHI DEVELOPER.** (1995)-. Newspaper. English. Twelve times a year. $149.00 US; $164.00 Canada; $169.00 other. Pinnacle Publishing Inc., PO Box 888, Kent WA 98035. **Tel** (206)251-1900, (800)231-1293, FAX (206)251-5057.

LC QA76.8.A66 D47
DD 004.16
Pr Rev.
ISSN 1047-0735
US
DEVELOP (CUPERTINO, CALIF.). See Computers-Microcomputers, Personal Computers.

DD 004
Pr Rev.
ISSN 1067-7224
US
CODEN DSJOEE
DIGITAL SYSTEMS JOURNAL. See Computers.

LC WMLC 93/4657
US
●**DIRECTIONS ON MICROSOFT : THE INDEPENDENT VIEW OF MICROSOFT TECHNOLOGY & STRATEGY.** (Oct. 1994)-. Periodical. English. Twelve times a year. $595.00. Redmond Communications Inc, 15127 Northeast 24th, Suite 293, Redmond WA 98052. **Tel** (206)882-3396, FAX (206)885-0848. **Continues** Microsoft Directions.

DD 005
ISSN 1078-795X
US
●**DO IT WITH LOTUS SMARTSUITE.** [Do Lotus SmartSuite Windows]. **VFOAT** Do it with Lotus SmartSuite. (1994)-. Periodical. English. Twelve times a year. $49.00. IDG Newsletter Corporation, 77 Franklin Street, Suite 310, Boston MA 02110. **Tel** (617)482-8470, (800)807-0771, FAX (617)338-0164. **ED** Jim Welp. **Desc:** Tips and techniques for Lotus Smartsuite users.

LC QA76.5 .D723
DD 005
ISSN 1079-8595
US
CEASED
DR. DOBB'S DEVELOPER UPDATE. See Computers-Microcomputers, Personal Computers.

LC QA76.5 .D617
DD 005
Pr Rev.
ISSN 1044-789X
US
CCC
CODEN DDJOEB
DR. DOBB'S JOURNAL (1989). (DR. DOBB'S JOURNAL : SOFTWARE TOOLS FOR THE PROFESSIONAL PROGRAMMER.). [Dr. Dobb's j.]. **VFOAT** Dr. Dobb's Journal of Software Tools. (Feb. 1989)-. Trade Publication. English. Twelve times a year. $29.97. Miller Freeman Inc., 600 Harrison Street, San Francisco CA 94107. **Tel** (415)905-2337, (415)905-2200, FAX (415)905-2240, telex 278273. (**Subscription address:** Neodata / Colorado, PO Box 2606, Boulder CO 80322.) available on microfilm and microfiche from University Microfilms International (UMI); available on an online database. Documents available from The UnCover Company, ADONIS, BLDSC, Ask*IEEE, UMI Article Clearinghouse. **Continues** Dr. Dobb's Journal of Software Tools for the Professional Programmer, 0888-3076. **Desc:** Loaded with the latest on popular programming languages, practical code examples, algorithms, program listings, technical coverage of different computing architectures, and operating systems. **Ind/Abst** Acad. Search; ACM Guide Comput. Lit. (19??-); Bus. Source Plus; Bus. Source; Comput. ASAP (19??-) [Full Txt.]; Comput. Database (19??-) [Full Txt.]; Comput. Rev. (19??-); Curr. Cit.; Ei Page One (19??-); EP Collect.; Homework Help.; INFO-SOUTH Abstr. (19??-); INSPEC (1989-); Mag. Artic. Summar. Elite; Mag. Artic. Summar. Select; Mag. Artic. Summar. CD-ROM; Mag. Search (19??-); MasterFile FullTEXT 1000; MasterFile FullTEXT 350; MasterFile FullTEXT 650; MasterFile FullTEXT (Mar. 1984-June 1989); Newsp. Period. Abstr. (1992-); OCLC; Telebase.

DD 005
ISSN 1076-3473
US
CEASED
ED YOURDON'S GUERRILLA PROGRAMMER. [Ed Yourdon's guerrilla program.]. **Added/Corp** Cutter Information Corp. **VFOAT** Guerrilla Programmer. (Jan. 1994)-(Aug. 1995). Periodical. English. Cutter Information Corporation, 37 Broadway, Arlington MA 02174-5539. **Tel** (617)648-8700, (800)964-5118, FAX (617)648-8707, (617)648-1950, telex 650 100 9891.

DD 005
ISSN 0896-7725
US
CEASED
EXPERT (LOUISVILLE, KY.). See Computers-Microcomputers, Personal Computers.

US
FACHTAGUNG UEBER PROGRAMMIERSPRACHEN. **Main/Corp** Gesellschaft fur Informatik. Multiple languages (English and German). Springer-Verlag New York Inc., 175 Fifth Avenue, New York NY 10010. **Tel** (212)460-1500 ext 256, FAX (212)533-3503, telex 232 235 SPB UR. (**Subscription address:** Springer-Verlag New York Inc. / North America, PO Box 2485, Journal Fulfillment, Secaucus NJ 07096. **Tel** (201)348-4033, (800)777-4643, FAX (201)348-4505.)

LC QA76.73.F23 F64
DD 005.74
ISSN 1074-4037
US
CEASED
FOCUS SYSTEMS JOURNAL ENCYCLOPEDIA. [FOCUS syst. j. encycl.]. **VFOAT** Systems Journal Encyclopedia. (1989)-Vol. 7, No. 2 (1994). Periodical. English. Information Builders, 1250 Broadway, New York NY 10001. **Tel** (212)736-4433, FAX (212)594-1450, telex 661558. **Desc:** Magazine for the FOCUS, Level5, EDA/SQI user. Consists of tips and techniques.

LC QA76.73.F25 F67
DD 005
ISSN 1061-7264
US
FORTRAN FORUM. [Fortran forum]. **Added/Corp** ACM Special Interest Group in Programming Languages. Vol. 3, No. 3 (Dec. 1984)-. Periodical. English. Three times a year. $20.00. ACM / Association for Computing Machinery, 1515 Broadway, 17th Floor, New York NY 10036. **Tel** (212)869-7440, FAX (212)869-0481. (**Subscription address:** Association for Computing Machinery, PO Box 12114, Church Street Station, New York NY 10249. **Tel** (212)626-0500.) **Continues** Fortec Forum, 0735-3731. **Ind/Abst** ACM Guide Comput. Lit.; Comput. Rev.

DD 005
Pr Rev.
ISSN 1060-0221
US
FORTRAN JOURNAL. [Fortran j.]. **Added/Corp** Fortran Users Group (U.S.) (1989)-. Periodical. English. Six times a year (Jan., Mar., May, July, Sept., Nov.). $100.00. Fortran Users Group, PO Box 4201, Fullerton CA 92634. **Tel** (714)441-2022. **ED** Charles Ritz. **Bk Rev.** (Qty: 6). **Ad Acc. Circ:** 1,200.

DD 005
ISSN 1042-6302
US
FOXTALK (FEDERAL WAY, WASH.). (FOXTALK.). [Foxtalk]. **VFOAT** Fox Talk. Vol. 1, Issue 1 (Feb. 1989)-. Newsletter. English. Twelve times a year. $149.00 US; $164.00 Canada; $469.00 other. Pinnacle Publishing Inc., PO Box 888, Kent WA 98035. **Tel** (206)251-1900, (800)231-1293, FAX (206)251-5057. **Desc:** Newsletter for developers using FoxPro and Visual FoxPro 3.0.

LC QA75.5 .F87
DD 004/.05
Pr Rev.
ISSN 0167-739X
NE
CCC
FUTURE GENERATIONS COMPUTER SYSTEMS : FGCS. See Computers-Computer Systems.

LC QA76.76.T49 G58
DD 005.1/05
ISSN 1075-7813
US
GNU'S BULLETIN. (GNU'S BULLETIN : NEWSLETTER OF THE FREE SOFTWARE FOUNDATION.). [GNU's bull.]. **Added/Corp** Free Software Foundation. (June 1987)-. Newsletter. English. Four times a year. Free. Free Software Foundation Inc., 675 Massachusetts Avenue, Cambridge MA 02139-3309. available via Internet (gnu@prep.ai.mit.edu).

ISSN 0892-4856
DD 005 US
GREGORY'S A-SERIES TECHNICAL JOURNAL.
See Computers-Electronic Data Processing.

US
ICP SOFTWARE DIRECTORY. MICROCOMPUTER SERIES.
VFOAT Microcomputer Series. **VAT** International Computer Programs Software Directory. Microcomputer Series. 56th Ed. (Autumn 1986)-. Directory. English. Two times a year. International Computer Programs Inc / Barbara Lahiff, 823 East Westfield Boulevard, Indianapolis IN 46220. **Tel** (800)428-6179, (317)251-7727. ***Continues in part*** *ICP Software Directory.*

LC QA76.6 .I17 **ISSN** 0098-5589
DD 001.6/425/05 US
CCC
CODEN IESEDJ
Pr Rev.
IEEE TRANSACTIONS ON SOFTWARE ENGINEERING.
See Computers-Computer Engineering.

US
INFORMATION TECHNOLOGY DIGEST.
See Computers-Microcomputers, Personal Computers.

ISSN 1078-8786
US
•INSIDE DBASE FOR WINDOWS.
Added/Corp Cobb Group. (1994)-. Periodical. English. Twelve times a year. $69.00. Cobb Group, 9420 Bunsen Parkway #300, Louisville KY 40220. **Tel** (502)491-1900, (800)223-8720, FAX (502)491-4200.

ISSN 1076-8106
DD 005 US
•INSIDE MICROSOFT POWERPOINT.
[Inside Microsoft PowerPoint]. **Added/Corp** Cobb Group. Vol. 1, No. 1 (May. 1994)-. Periodical. English. Twelve times a year. $49.00. Cobb Group, 9420 Bunsen Parkway #300, Louisville KY 40220. **Tel** (502)491-1900, (800)223-8720, FAX (502)491-4200.

ISSN 1071-8168
DD 005 US
INSIDE NATURAL.
[Inside Nat.]. (199?)-. Periodical. English. Four times a year (Feb., May, Aug., Nov.). $95.00. S. L. Robinson & Associates Inc., PO Box L1235, 28 Teal Drive, Langhorne PA 19047. **Tel** (215)741-0820.

NE
INTEL 16 BIT ASSEMBLER HANDBOEK.
(19??)-. Dutch. Twenty-four times a year. Fl55.00. Weka Uitgeverij BV, Postbus 61196, 1005 HD Amsterdam Netherlands. **Tel** 011 31 20 6867131. **ED** F Spiekerman.
Desc: Programing in 16/32 bit on the PC.

LC QA76.5 .I564 **ISSN** 0885-7458
DD 004/.35 US
CCC
CODEN IJPPE5
Pr Rev.
INTERNATIONAL JOURNAL OF PARALLEL PROGRAMMING.
[Int. j. parallel program.]. **VFOAT** Parallel Programming. Vol. 15 No. 1 (Feb. 1986)-. Periodical. English. Six times a year. $475.00. Plenum Press, 233 Spring Street, New York NY 10013-1578. **Tel** (212)620-8000, (800)221-9369, FAX (212)463-0742, (212)807-1047, telex 23/421139. **ED** Julius T. Tou. Index available. available on microfilm and microfiche from University Microfilms International (UMI). Documents available from Article Express International, The Genuine Article, UMI Article Clearinghouse, Ask*IEEE. ***Continues*** *International Journal of Computer & Information Sciences, 0091-7036.*
Ind/Abst ABI/INFORM Glob. Ed.; ABI/INFORM [Computer File] (1986-); ACM Guide Comput. Lit.; Bioeng. Abstr. (1986-); CompuMath Cit. Index [Full Cov.]; Comput. Abstr.; Comput. Rev.; Curr. Cit.; Ei Page One (1986-); Eng. Index Annu.; Gen. BusinessFile (1992-); Inf. Sci. Abstr.; INSPEC (1986-); Math. Rev.; MLA Int. Bibl. Books Artic. Mod. Lang. Lit.; Refer. Z. (1986-); Res. Alert [Full Cov.]; SCISEARCH; Soc. Plann. Policy Dev. Abstr.; Sociol. Abstr. (1986-); Zentralbl. Math. Ihre Grenzgeb.

ISSN 1042-5721
DD 005 US
Pr Rev.
JOURNAL OF C LANGUAGE TRANSLATION, THE.
[J. C lang. transl.]. Vol. 1, No. 1 (June 1989)-. Periodical. English. Four times a year. $235.00. Journal of C Language Translation, PO Box 349, Cambridge MA 02238. **Tel** (617)492-3869, FAX (617)492-4407. **ED** John R. Levine. Index available (published separately). cum. index. **Bk Rev**, (Qty: 1).

LC QA76.73.F24 J68 **ISSN** 0738-2022
DD 001.64/24 US
CCC
CODEN JFAREL
Pr Rev.
JOURNAL OF FORTH APPLICATION AND RESEARCH, THE.
[J. Forth appl. res.]. Vol. 1, Issue 1 (Sept. 1983)-. Periodical. English. Four times a year. $145.00 (institutions), $60.00 (individuals) US; $65.00 (individuals) Canada and Mexico; $75.00 (individuals) Europe and Asia; $160.00 (institutions) other. Institute for Applied FORTH Research Inc, 70 Elmwood Avenue, Rochester NY 14611. **Tel** (716)235-0168, FAX (716)328-6426. **ED** Steve Lewis, c/o FORTH Institute. **Bk Rev. Circ:** 400 (ctrl). Documents available from Article Express International, Ask*IEEE.
Desc: Current applications and development in the use of the computer language forth. Also reviews, conference abstracts, and technical notes.
Ind/Abst ACM Guide Comput. Lit.; Comput. Lit. Index; Comput. Rev.; Ei Page One; Eng. Index Annu.; INSPEC (Sept. 1983-).

ISSN 1080-5230
US
•JOURNAL OF FUNCTIONAL AND LOGIC PROGRAMMING [COMPUTER FILE].
(1995)-. Periodical. English. Four times a year. $125.00. Massachusetts Institute of Technology (MIT) Press, 55 Hayward Street, Cambridge MA 02142. **Tel** (617)253-2889, (617)625-8481, FAX (617)258-6779.

LC QA76.62 .J68 **ISSN** 0956-7968
DD 005.1/1 UK
CCC
CODEN JFPRES
JOURNAL OF FUNCTIONAL PROGRAMMING.
[J. funct. program.]. Vol. 1, Pt. 1 (Jan. 1991)-. Academic Scholarly Publication. English. Six times a year. $182.00. Cambridge University Press, The Edinburgh Building, Shaftesbury Road, Cambridge CB2 2RU United Kingdom. **Tel** 011 44 1223 312393, FAX 011 44 1223 315052, telex 851-817256. **(Subscription address:** Cambridge University Press / North America, 110 Midland Avenue, Port Chester NY 10573. **Tel** (800)431-1580, (914)937-9600.**)** **ED** RJM Hughes, PL Wadler, P Hudak, H Barendregt. **Bk Rev. Ad Acc.** available on microfilm and microfiche from University Microfilms International (UMI). Documents available from Ask*IEEE.
Desc: Devoted to this important area of computer science. Covers new languages and extensions, reasoning, proof and program transformation, program synthesis, implementation techniques, type theory, parallelism, and applications. Of interest to computer scientists, engineers working in parallelism, and mathematicians working in theoretical computer science.
Ind/Abst INSPEC (1991-); Math. Rev.

ISSN 0743-1066
DD 511 US
CCC
CODEN JLPRE2
Pr Rev.
JOURNAL OF LOGIC PROGRAMMING, THE.
[J. log. program.]. **Added/Corp** Syracuse University. Logic Programming Research Center. Vol. 1, No. 1 (June 1984)-. Academic Scholarly Publication. English. Twelve times a year (4 volumes). $735.00. Elsevier Science Publishing Company Inc, Madison Square Station, PO Box 882, New York NY 10159-0882. **Tel** (212)633-3950, FAX (212)633-3990. **ED** J A Robinson and Jean-Louis Lassez. **Ad Acc.** available on microfilm and microfiche from University Microfilms International (UMI); available on an online database from Elsevier Electronic Subscriptions (EES). Documents available from Article Express International, The Genuine Article, Ask*IEEE.
Desc: Publishes original research papers, survey and review articles, tutorial expositions, and historical studies in logic programming.
Ind/Abst ACM Guide Comput. Lit.; CompuMath Cit. Index [Full Cov.]; Comput. Abstr.; Comput. Rev.; Curr. Cit.; Ei Page One; Eng. Index Annu.; INSPEC (June 1984-); Math. Rev.; Res. Alert [Full Cov.]; SCISEARCH; Soc. Sci. Cit. Index [Select. Cov.]; Zentralbl. Math. Ihre Grenzgeb.

LC QA76.6 .J72 **ISSN** 0896-8438
DD 005 US
CCC
CODEN JOOPEC
Pr Rev.
JOURNAL OF OBJECT-ORIENTED PROGRAMMING.
[J. object-oriented program.]. **VFOAT** Journal of Object Oriented Programming; JOOP. Vol. 1, No. 1 (April/May 1988)-. Periodical. English. Nine times a year. $199.00. SIGS Publications Inc. / New York, 71 West 23rd Street, 3rd Floor, New York NY 10010-4102. **Tel** (212)242-7447. **ED** Richard S. Wiener. Documents available from The Genuine Article, Ask*IEEE.
Desc: Features research articles and tutorial papers dealing with problem-solving techniques, reusable components, applications in artificial intelligence, software maintenance and language development.
Ind/Abst ACM Guide Comput. Lit.; CompuMath Cit. Index [Full Cov.]; Comput. Database; Comput. Rev.; Curr. Cit.; Fluid Abstr., Civil Eng.; Fluid Abstr. Proc. Eng.; FLUIDEX; INSPEC (Feb. 1990-); Res. Alert [Full Cov.]; SCISEARCH; Soc. Sci. Cit. Index [Select. Cov.].

LC QA76.7 .I69 **ISSN** 0963-9306
DD 005.13/05 UK
CCC
CODEN JPLAER
•JOURNAL OF PROGRAMMING LANGUAGES.
[J. program. lang.]. (1993)-. Periodical. English. Four times a year. $246.00. Chapman & Hall, 2-6 Boundary Row, London SE1 8HN United Kingdom. **Tel** 011 44 171 8650066, FAX 011 44 171 5229623, telex 290164 CHAPMA G. **(Subscription address:** International Thomson Publishing Services Ltd., North Way Andover, Hampshire SP10 5BE United Kingdom. **Tel** 011 44 1264 332424.**)** **ED** D. Watson.
Desc: Covers the broad range of topics relevant to the design and implementation of programming languages. Seeks to present work of practical relevance, to disseminate knowledge obtained from experiment and observation, supported by discussion of theory where it is appropriate. Also seeks to present material of a tutorial nature, reviewing recent research work in specific fields relevant to the scope of the journal and incorporating significant bibliographies.

LC QA76.5 .J74 **ISSN** 0164-1212
DD 001.64/05 US
CCC
CODEN JSSODM
Pr Rev.
JOURNAL OF SYSTEMS AND SOFTWARE, THE.
[J. syst. softw.]. **VFOAT** JSS. Vol. 1 (1979)-. Academic Scholarly Publication. English. Twelve times a year (4 volumes). $725.00. Elsevier Science Publishing Company Inc, Madison Square Station, PO Box 882, New York NY 10159-0882. **Tel** (212)633-3950, FAX (212)633-3990. **ED** Robert Glass. available on microfilm and microfiche from University Microfilms International (UMI); available on an online database from Elsevier Electronic Subscriptions (EES). Documents available from Article Express International, The Genuine Article, UMI Article Clearinghouse, Ask*IEEE.
Desc: Publishes papers covering all aspects of programming methodology, software engineering and related hardware-software systems.
Ind/Abst ABI/INFORM Glob. Ed.; ABI/INFORM [Computer File] (Winter 1979-); ACM Guide Comput. Lit.; Bioeng. Abstr.; CompuMath Cit. Index [Full Cov.]; Comput. Abstr.; Comput. Database; Comput. Lit. Index; Comput. Rev.; Curr. Cit.; Ei Page One; Eng. Index Annu.; Gen. BusinessFile (1992-); INSPEC (1979-); Int. Aerosp. Abstr.; Math. Rev.; Res. Alert [Full Cov.]; SCISEARCH.

FR
Pr Rev.
LETTRE ADA, LA.
(1987)-. French. Ten times a year. $317.14. EC2 / Editions Colloques et Conseil, 269 rue de la Garenne, 92024 Nanterre Cedex France. **Tel** 011 33 1 47807000, FAX 011 33 1 47806629. **ED** Jean Claude Rault. Index available. cum. index. **Bk Rev. Ad Acc. Circ:** 300.
Desc: Information newsletter with technical and commercial content dedicated to the Ada programming language.

US
LIBRARY OF PROGRAMMER'S AND DEVELOPER'S TOOLS.
(19??)-. Monographic series. English. $275.00 (full set), $65.00 (single book) US; $290.00 (full set), $80.00 (single book) other. Applied Computer Research Inc., 11242 North 19th Avenue, Phoenix AZ 85029. **Tel** (602)995-5929, FAX (602)995-0905. **(Subscription address:** Applied Computer Research, PO Box 82266, Phoenix AZ 85071. **Tel** (602)995-5929.**)** ***Continues*** *Guide to Software Productivity Aids.*

LC QA76.76.O63 L546 **ISSN** 1075-3583
DD 005.4/3 US
•LINUX JOURNAL.
[Linux j.]. **VFOAT** LJ. (1994)-. Periodical. English. Twelve times a year. $19.00. Linux Journal, PO Box 85867, Seattle WA 98145-1867. **Tel** (206) 352-3622, FAX (206) 352-1047. **ED** Michael K. Johnson.
Desc: Devoted to information on Linux technologies. Features tutorials, reviews or related products, and columns on GNU, Debian, and programming.

LC QA76.73.L23 L57 **ISSN** 0892-4635
DD 005.13/3 US
CCC
CODEN LSCOEX
Pr Rev.
LISP AND SYMBOLIC COMPUTATION.
[LISP symb. comput.]. Vol. 1, No. 1 (June 1988)-. Periodical. English. Four times a year. $319.00. Kluwer Academic Publishers / Massachusetts, PO Box 358, Accord Station, Hingham MA 02018. **Tel** (617)871-6600. **ED** Robert R. Kessler, Carolyn Talcott, and Jan Zubkoff. **Acid Free.** available on microfilm and microfiche from University Microfilms International (UMI). Documents available from Ask*IEEE.
Desc: An international journal that presents a forum for current and evolving symbolic computing, focusing on

LISP and object-oriented programming.
Ind/Abst ACM Guide Comput. Lit.; Comput. Rev.; Curr. Cit.; Ei Page One; INSPEC (June 1988-).

LC QA76.73.L23 L58 **ISSN** 1045-3563
DD 005.13/3 US
LISP POINTERS. [LISP pointers]. **Added/Corp** ACM Special Interest Group in Programming Languages. Vol. 1, No. 1 (Apr./May 1987)-. Periodical. English. Four times a year. $30.00. ACM / Association for Computing Machinery, 1515 Broadway, 17th Floor, New York NY 10036. **Tel** (212)869-7440, FAX (212)869-0481. **(Subscription address:** Association for Computing Machinery, PO Box 12114, Church Street Station, New York NY 10249. **Tel** (212)626-0500.**)**

IT
SUSPENDED
LIST : PROGRAMMI PER IL TUO HOME COMPUTER. (19??)-(Dec. 1991). Italian. Twelve times a year. L30'000 Italy; L72'000 US. Edicomp Srl, Via Sannio 79, 00183 Rome Italy. **Tel** 011 39 6 7092444, FAX 011 39 6 77205150. **ED** Renzo Rubeo. **Circ:** 110,000.

LC QA76.73.L63 L6 **ISSN** 0888-6970
DD 005.13/3 US
CCC
LOGO EXCHANGE. [Logo exch.]. **Added/Corp** ISTE Special Interest Group for Logo-Using Educators. Vol. 5, No. 1 (Sept. 1986)-. Periodical. English. Four times a year. $34.00. International Society for Technology in Education ISTE, University of Oregon, 1787 Agate Street, Eugene OR 97403-1923. **Tel** (503)346-4414, FAX (503)346-5890. ***Formed by the union of*** *National Logo Exchange, 0734-1717* ***and*** *International Logo Exchange, 0883-1505.*
Desc: Ideas from top Logo educators, with current information on Logo research, resources, and methods.

LC QA76.6 .L363 **ISSN** 0741-7667
DD 001.64/25 US
LSI JOURNAL. [LSI j.]. **VFOAT** L.S.I. Journal. Vol. 2 No. 4 (Oct.1 1983)-. English. Four times a year. $12.95. Logical Systems, Inc., 8970 North 55th Street, PO Box 23956, Milwaukee WI 53223. ***Continues*** *LDOS Quarterly, 0737-9161.*

LC QA76.8.M3 M32 **ISSN** 1067-8360
DD 005 US
•**MACTECH MAGAZINE.** [MacTech mag.]. **VFOAT** Mac Tech Magazine. Vol. 9, No. 1 (Jan. 1993)-. Trade Publication. English. Twelve times a year. $47.00. Xplain Corporation, PO Box 250055, Los Angeles CA 90025. **Tel** (310)575-4343, FAX (310)575-0925. ***Continues*** *MacTutor, 8756-8810.*

US
MACTUTOR COMPANION SOURCE CODE DISKS. (19??)-. English. Twelve times a year. $47.00 US; $77.00 Canada and Mexico; $97.00 other. Xplain Corporation, PO Box 250055, Los Angeles CA 90025. **Tel** (310)575-4343, FAX (310)575-0925. **ED** Neil Ticktin and Don Bresee. Index available. **Bk Rev. Ad Acc, Adv Mgr:** Barbara McRice. **Circ:** 13,000. available on CD-ROM.
Desc: Information, newsbits and dialogue regarding macintosh computer programming and development.

ISSN 1061-5733
DD 004 US
MAPLE TECHNICAL NEWSLETTER, THE. [Maple tech. newsl.]. **Added/Corp** Waterloo Maple Software. **VFOAT** Maple Tech. (1991)-. Newsletter. English. Two times a year. $52.00. Birkhauser Boston, Inc., c/o Springer Publishers New York Inc., Customer Service Department, 333 Meadowlands Parkway, Secaucus NJ 07096-2491. **Tel** (201)348-4033, (800)777-4643, FAX (201)348-4505. **ED** Dr. Tony Scott. ***Continues*** *Maple Newsletter, 1074-3790.*
Desc: A forum for users of applications written in the Maple language, a means of introducing new and extended capabilities of Maple, and examples of problems solved using the Maple computer algebra system. Presents applications not only in mathematics and physics, in which the power of symbolic computation has been amply demonstrated, but other scientific, technical or industrial endeavors as well.
Ind/Abst Math. Rev.; Zentralbl. Math. Ihre Grenzgeb.

UK
Pr Rev.
MVS UPDATE. (19??)-. English. Twelve times a year. $430.00. Xephon, 27-35 London Road, Newbury Berkshire RG13 1JL United Kingdom. **Tel** 011 44 1635 33823, FAX 011 44 1635 38345. **(Subscription address:** Xephon, 1301 West Highway, Suite 201 450, Lewisville TX 75067. **) ED** Steve Piggot. **Bk Rev. Circ:** 2,500. available via electronic mail.
Desc: Technical hints and tips for MVS systems programmers.

LC QA76.64 .O57 **ISSN** 1055-6400
DD 005.1/1 US
CODEN OOMEEO
OOPS MESSENGER. (OOPS MESSENGER : A QUARTERLY PUBLICATION OF THE SPECIAL INTEREST GROUP ON PROGAMMING LANGUAGES.). [OOPS messenger]. **Added/Corp** ACM Special Interest Group in Programming Languages. **VFOAT** ACM SIGPLAN Messenger; Messenger. **VAT** Object Oriented Programming Systems Messenger; Association for Computing Machinery Special Interest Group in Programming Languages Messenger. Vol. 1, No. 1 (Aug. 1990)-. Periodical. English. Four times a year. $25.00. ACM / Association for Computing Machinery, 1515 Broadway, 17th Floor, New York NY 10036. **Tel** (212)869-7440, FAX (212)869-0481. **(Subscription address:** Association for Computing Machinery, PO Box 12114, Church Street Station, New York NY 10249. **Tel** (212)626-0500.**)** Documents available from Ask*IEEE.
Ind/Abst Curr. Cit.; HILITES; INSPEC (Aug. 1990-).

ISSN 0953-5349
UK
OOPS REPORT, THE. [OOPS rep.]. **VFOAT** Object-Oriented Programming Systems Report. (1988)-. Periodical. English. Four times a year.
Ind/Abst Abstr. Hum. Comput. Interact.

ISSN 1078-7518
DD 005 US
•**ORACLE DEVELOPER.** [Oracle dev.]. **VFOAT** Oracle. Vol. 1, No. 1 (1994)-. Newsletter. English. Twelve times a year. $199.00. Pinnacle Publishing Inc., PO Box 888, Kent WA 98035. **Tel** (206)251-1900, (800)231-1293, FAX (206)251-5057.
Desc: Newsletter for developers using Oracle's tools and DMBS's. Provides techniques for optimizing the power of Oracle servers and for creating applications in the Oracle Cooperative Development Environment.

LC QA75 **ISSN** 1068-6835
DD 005 US
SUSPENDED
OS/2 MONTHLY. [OS/2 mon.]. **VFOAT** OS 2 Monthly. (1992)-Suspended (199?). Periodical. English. Twelve times a year. $80.00 US; $90.00 Canada and Mexico; $120.00 other. JDS Publishing, PO Box 4351, Highland Park NJ 08904. **Tel** (908)247-0952.

ISSN 1064-6736
DD 005 US
PAGEMAKER IN-DEPTH (1992). (PAGEMAKER IN-DEPTH : THE JOURNAL FOR INVOLVED USERS OF PAGEMAKER.). [PageMaker in-depth]. **VFOAT** Page Maker In-Depth; PageMaker In Depth; In-Depth; In Depth. No. 7 (1992)-. Periodical. English. Twelve times a year. $69.00. MindCraft Publishing Corporation, PO Box 256, Lincoln MA 01773-0256. ***Formed by the union of*** *PageMaker In-Depth (Macintosh Ed.), 1052-6560* ***and*** *PageMaker In-Depth (Windows Ed.), 1054-8173.*

ISSN 1058-7071
DD 005 US
Pr Rev.
PARADOX INFORMANT. Vol. 1, No. 1 (Aug. 1990)-. Periodical. English. Twelve times a year. $49.95. Informant Communications Group Inc, 10519 East Stockton Boulevard, Suite 142, Elk Grove CA 95624-9743. **Tel** (916)686-6610, FAX (916)686-8497. **ED** Mitchell Koulouris, Jerry Coffey. Index Available Published separately--free--upon request. cum. index. **Bk Rev**, (Qty: 48). **Ad Acc, Adv Mgr:** Mitchell Koulouris. **Circ:** 12,000.
Desc: An independently published magazine covering Borland International's Relational Database Software, Paradox, both DOS and Windows versions. Contains useful tips and techniques for users of all levels.

LC QA76.58 .P3779 **ISSN** 0129-6264
DD 004/.35 SI
CODEN PPLTEE
PARALLEL PROCESSING LETTERS. [Parallel process. lett.]. Vol. 1, No. 1 (Sept. 1991)-. Periodical. English. Four times a year. $215.00. World Scientific Publishing Company, PO Box 128, Farrer Road, Singapore 9128 Singapore. **Tel** 011 65 3825663, FAX 011 65 3825919, telex RS 28561 WSPC. **(Subscription address:** World Scientific Publishing Company, Inc., 1060 Main Street, Suite 1 B, River Edge NJ 07661. **Tel** (800)227-7562, (201)487-9655.**) ED** Michel Cosnard.
Desc: Covers topics such as the design and analysis of parallel and distributed algorithms, the theory of parallel computation, parallel programming languages, parallel programming environments, parallel architectures and VLSI circuits.

LC QA76.73.P2 P39 **ISSN** 0748-4127
DD 001.64/24 US
PASCAL & MODULA2. [Pascal Modula2]. **VFOAT** Pascal and Modula2; Pascal and Modula 2; Pascal & Modula Two; Pascal & Modula 2; Pascal and Modula Two. No. 27 (Nov. 83)-. Periodical. English. Four times a year. $25.00 members. Pascal & Modula2, 2903 Huntington Road, Cleveland OH 44210. ***Continues*** *Pascal News, 0739-1900.*

US
PC TELEMART SOFTWARE DIRECTORY. **See** Computers-Computer Industry and Industry Directories.

ISSN 0744-2475
US
PEELINGS II : THE MAGAZINE OF APPLE SOFTWARE EVALUATION. **See** Computers-Software.

US
SUSPENDED
POSTSCRIPT REVIEW. (19??)-(1990). English. Four times a year. Postscript Language, 2 Haven Avenue, Port Washington NY 11050. **Tel** (516)767-2233. ***Continues*** *Postscript Language Journal.*

ISSN 1078-1889
US
•**POWERBUILDER DEVELOPER'S JOURNAL.** **VFOAT** Power Builder Developer's Journal. (1994)-. Periodical. English. Twelve times a year. $119.00. Powerbuilder Developers Journal, 46 Holly Street, Jersey City NJ 07305. **Tel** (201) 332-1515.

ISSN 1077-6117
DD 005 US
•**POWERSOURCE (KENT, WASH.).** (POWERSOURCE.). [Powersource]. **VFOAT** Power Source. Vol. 1, No. 1 (1994)-. Newsletter. English. Twelve times a year. $249.00. Pinnacle Publishing Inc., PO Box 888, Kent WA 98035. **Tel** (206)251-1900, (800)231-1293, FAX (206)251-5057.
Desc: Newsletter for developers using PowerBuilder. Packed with time saving tips and shortcuts, in-depth articles on current development topics, and tools and solutions from PowerBuilder experts.

ISSN 1074-8970
DD 005 US
PROCEEDINGS - INTERNATIONAL CONFERENCE ON COMPUTER LANGUAGES. (PROCEEDINGS.). [Proceedings - Int. Conf. Comput. Lang.]. **Added/Corp** IEEE Computer Society. Technical Committee on Computer Languages. **VFOAT** Proceedings of the ... International Conference on Computer Languages. (1988)-. Proceedings. English. Every 2 years. $60.00. IEEE Computer Society, 10662 Los Vaqueros Circle, PO Box 3014, Los Alamitos CA 90720-1264. **Tel** (714)821-8380, (800)272-6657, FAX (714)821-4641. ***Continues*** *IEEE Computer Society International Conference on Computer Languages. Proceedings.*

LC HD9696.C63 U5156a **ISSN** 0069-8148
DD 338.4/7/001642 US
CODEN CPRPBM
PROCEEDINGS OF THE ANNUAL COMPUTER PERSONNEL RESEARCH CONFERENCE. **See** Computers-Computer Industry and Industry Directories.

LC QA75.5 .S9574a **ISSN** 1043-6871
DD 004/.01/5113 US
PROCEEDINGS / SYMPOSIUM ON LOGIC IN COMPUTER SCIENCE. **See** Computers-Electronic Data Processing.

ISSN 0953-9344
DD 005.105 UK
PROGRAM NOW. [Program now]. (1987)-. Trade Publication. English. Six times a year. Intra Press, Intra House, 193 Uxbridge Road, London W12 9RA United Kingdom. **Tel** 011 44 181 7438888, FAX 011 44 181 7433062. ***Continues*** *Program (London. 1987), 0952-8865.*
Ind/Abst Abstr. Hum. Comput. Interact.

ISSN 1076-9714
DD 005 US
•**PROGRAMMER'S PROVANTAGE COMPUTER PRODUCTS BUYER'S GUIDE.** [Program. PROVANTAGE comput. products buyer's guide]. **Added/Corp** PROVANTAGE Corp. **VFOAT** PROVANTAGE Computer Products Buyer's Guide. (1994)-. Periodical. English. Four times a year. Programmers Connection, 7249 Whipple Avenue NW, North Canton OH 44720. **Tel** (216)494-3781, FAX (216)494-5260. **ED** Scott DiBattista. **Ad Acc, Adv Mgr:** Gina Cope, **Tel** (216)494-1996. **Circ:** 195,000 (ctrl). ***Continues*** *Connection (North Canton, Ohio), 1045-7445.*
Desc: Resource for information and pricing of microcomputer hardware and software products. Also included are feature editorials on current issues in the computer industry and a technical question and answer section.
Ind/Abst ACM Guide Comput. Lit. (?-?); Comput. Rev. (?-?).

US
PROGRAMMERS ROM. CD-ROM. English. Irregular. $74.95. Quanta Press, Inc., 1313 Fifth Street Southeast, Suite 208C, Minneapolis MN 55414. **Tel** (612)379-3956, FAX (612)623-4570.
Desc: Gives the expert and amateur programmer hundreds of megabytes of DOS based public domain source codes, libraries and applications.

Computers —Programs and Programming

LC QA76 .P695
DD 001.6/42/05
ISSN 0361-7688
US
CCC
CODEN PCSODA
PROGRAMMING AND COMPUTER SOFTWARE. [Program. comput. softw.]. **VFOAT** Programmirovanie. Vol. 1 (Jan./Feb. 1975)-. Periodical. English (Russian). Six times a year. $695.00. MAIK Nauka / Interperiodica, Ulitsa Profsoyuznaia 90, Moscow 117864 Russia. **ED** V.P. Ivannikov. available on microfilm and microfiche from University Microfilms International (UMI). Documents available from Article Express International, The Genuine Article, Ask*IEEE.
Desc: Provides automative reports on current progress in programming and the use of computers.
Ind/Abst Bioeng. Abstr.; CompuMath Cit. Index [Full Cov.]; Comput. Abstr.; Comput. Rev.; Curr. Cit.; Ei Page One; Eng. Index Annu.; Inf. Sci. Abstr.; INSPEC (July/Aug. 1975-); Math. Rev.; Pollut. Abstr. Indexes; Res. Alert [Full Cov.]; Zentralbl. Math. Ihre Grenzgeb.

LC QA76 .P697
ISSN 0132-3474
RU
CODEN PROGD3
PROGRAMMIROVANIE. [Programmirovanie]. **Added/Corp** Akademiia Nauk SSSR. (Jan./Feb. 1975)-. Academic Scholarly Publication. Russian. Six times a year. $142.00. Izdatelstvo Nauka / Akademiia Nauk, (Publishing House of the Russian Academy of Sciences), Leninskii Porspekt 14, 117901 Moscow Russia. **Tel** 011 95 9542153, FAX 011 95 9382141, telex 411964. **(Subscription address:** East View Publications Inc., 3020 Harbor Lane North, Suite 110, Minneapolis MN 55447. **Tel** (800)477-1005, (612)550-0961, FAX (612)559-2931.) Documents available from Article Express International, Ask*IEEE.
Ind/Abst Energy Res. Abstr. (Mar. 1982-); Eng. Index Annu.; INSPEC (March/April 1975-); Math. Rev.; Zentralbl. Math. Ihre Grenzgeb.

LC QA76.5 .I22a
DD 001.6/425
ISSN 0091-469X
US
RECORD - I.E.E.E. SYMPOSIUM ON COMPUTER SOFTWARE RELIABILITY. (RECORD.). **Main/Conf** IEEE Symposium on Computer Software Reliability. **Added/Corp** Institute of Electrical and Electronics Engineers. Institute of Electrical and Electronics Engineers. Long Island Section. **VAT** Record - Institute of Electrical and Electronics Engineers Symposium on Computer Software Reliability. (1973)-. English. Irregular. $12.00. Institution of Electrical Engineers / IEE, Michael Faraday House, Six Hills Way, Stevenage Hertfordshire SG1 2AY United Kingdom. **Tel** 011 44 1438 313311, FAX 011 44 1438 742840, telex 825578 IEESTV G. **(Subscription address:** IEE / Peter Peregrinus Ltd., PO Box 96, Stevenage Herts SG1 2SD United Kingdom. **Tel** 011 44 1438 313311, FAX 011 44 438 742792, telex 825578 IEESTV G.)

ISSN 0822-997X
CN
DD 001.64
REFERENCE - COMPUTING SERVICES. UNIVERSITY OF ALBERTA. See Computers-Electronic Data Processing.

DD 004
ISSN 1073-5410
US
RELIABILITY RATINGS WORKSTATION ADVISOR. [Reliab. rat. workstn. advis.]. **VFOAT** Workstation Advisor. (199?)-. Periodical. English. Twelve times a year. $525.00. United Communications Group, 11300 Rockville Pike, Suite 1100, Rockville MD 20852. **Tel** (301)816-8950 ext. 313, FAX (301)816-8945.
Continues Reliability Ratings. Industry Report on Unix Workstations and Peripherals.

LC QA75
DD 004
ISSN 1075-2528
US
Pr Rev.
●**REPORT ON OBJECT ANALYSIS AND DESIGN.** (1994)-. Academic Scholarly Publication. English. Six times a year. $199.00. SIGS Publications Inc. / New York, 71 West 23rd Street, 3rd Floor, New York NY 10010-4102. **Tel** (212)242-7447. **ED** Richard Wiener. **Bk Rev. Ad Acc.** Documents available from BLDSC.
Desc: Covers analysis and design that is language-independent and object-oriented.

LC QA75.5
DD 005
ISSN 1083-155X
US
REVTECH MAGAZINE. See Computers-Software.

LC WMLC L 90/0008
DD 005
ISSN 1051-8118
US
TITLE CHANGE
REVUSER (PHILADELPHIA, PA.). See Computers-Software.

LC QA76.6 .S427
DD 001.64/2/05
ISSN 0167-6423
NE
CCC
CODEN SCPGD4
Pr Rev.
SCIENCE OF COMPUTER PROGRAMMING. [Sci. comput. program.]. Vol. 1, No. 1,2 (Oct. 1981)-. Academic Scholarly Publication. English. Six times a year (2 vols.). $518.00. Elsevier Science Publishers BV, PO Box 211, 1000 AE Amsterdam Netherlands. **Tel** 011 31 20 4853641, 011 31 20 4853642, FAX 011 31 20 4853598. **ED** M Sintzoff. **Bk Rev. Ad Acc.** ctrl circ. available on microfilm and microfiche from University Microfilms International (UMI); available on an online database from Elsevier Electronic Subscriptions (EES). Documents available from Article Express International, The Genuine Article, Ask*IEEE.
Desc: Contains research papers, short notices, occasional survey articles, and possibly book announcements and book reviews.
Ind/Abst ACM Guide Comput. Lit.; CompuMath Cit. Index [Full Cov.]; Comput. Abstr. (Oct. 1981-); Comput. Database; Comput. Lit. Index; Comput. Rev. (Oct. 1981-); Curr. Cit.; Eng. Index Annu.; INSPEC (Oct. 1981-); Int. Abstr. Oper. Res. [Select. Cov.]; Math. Rev.; Pollut. Abstr. Indexes; Res. Alert [Full Cov.]; Zentralbl. Math. Ihre Grenzgeb.

LC QA76.6 .S428
DD 502/.8551
ISSN 1058-9244
US
CCC
CODEN SCIPEV
SCIENTIFIC PROGRAMMING. See Science and Technology.

ISSN 0229-1231
CN
DD 001.64/25
SCRIPT USER'S GUIDE. [SCRIPT user's guide]. **Added/Corp** University of Waterloo. Dept. of Computing Services. (197?)-. English. One time a year. $2.00 per no. Computer Reference Room, University of Waterloo, Waterloo Ontario N2L 3G1 Canada.

DD 005
ISSN 1047-4544
US
CODEN SIFOEL
SIG FORTH. (SIG FORTH : NEWSLETTER OF THE ASSOCIATION FOR COMPUTING MACHINERY'S SPECIAL INTEREST GROUP ON FORTH.). [SIG Forth]. **Added/Corp** Association for Computing Machinery. Special Interest Group on Forth. **VFOAT** SIGForth; ACM SIGForth Newsletter; SIG Forth Newsletter. **VAT** Special Interest Group on Forth. Vol. 1, No. 1 (Spring 1989)-. Newsletter. English. Four times a year. $33.00. ACM / Association for Computing Machinery, 1515 Broadway, 17th Floor, New York NY 10036. **Tel** (212)869-7440, FAX (212)869-0481. **(Subscription address:** Association for Computing Machinery, PO Box 12114, Church Street Station, New York NY 10249. **Tel** (212)626-0500.) Documents available from Ask*IEEE.
Ind/Abst ACM Guide Comput. Lit.; Comput. Rev.; INSPEC (Spring 1989-).

US
SIGMICRO CONFERENCE PROCEEDINGS. (19??)-. Proceedings. English. Four times a year. $35.00. ACM / Association for Computing Machinery, 1515 Broadway, 17th Floor, New York NY 10036. **Tel** (212)869-7440, FAX (212)869-0481.
Continues SIGMICRO Newsletter, 1050-916X.

DD 005
ISSN 1071-1910
US
SINGER REPORT ON MANAGED CARE SYSTEMS AND TECHNOLOGY, THE. [Singer rep. manag. care syst. technol.]. **Added/Corp** Charles J. Singer & Co. (19??)-. Periodical. English. Nine times a year (every 6 weeks). $395.00. Charles J. Singer & Co, 401 Edgewater Place, Suite 580, Building 1 Unit 18, Wakefield MA 01880. **Tel** (617)246-7585 ext.228, FAX (617)246-7737. **ED** Rich Luhr. Index available. ctrl circ.

LC QA76.73.S59 S63
DD 005.13/3
ISSN 1056-7976
US
CCC
SMALLTALK REPORT, THE. [Smalltalk rep.]. **VFOAT** Small Talk Report. (1991)-. Periodical. English. Nine times a year. $199.00. SIGS Publications Inc. / New York, 71 West 23rd Street, 3rd Floor, New York NY 10010-4102. **Tel** (212)242-7447.

UK
SNA UPDATE. (19??)-. English. Four times a year. $165.00. Xephon, 27-35 London Road, Newbury Berkshire RG13 1JL United Kingdom. **Tel** 011 44 1635 33823, FAX 011 44 1635 38345. **(Subscription address:** Xephon, 1301 West Highway, Suite 201 450, Lewisville TX 75067.)
Desc: Provides systems programmers with the practical techniques, the proven tools, and most important of all - the enhanced professional expertise needed to improve the performance, integrity, usability, and reliability of their systems.

LC QA76.5 .S653
DD 001.6/425/05
ISSN 0038-0644
UK
CCC
CODEN SPEXBL
Pr Rev.
SOFTWARE : PRACTICE & EXPERIENCE. See Computers-Software.

LC QA76.75 .S64
DD 005.3
ISSN 8755-7169
US
SOFTWARE REVIEWS ON FILE. See Computers-Software.

LC QA76 .S563
DD 001.6/42
ISSN 0038-0652
UK
CODEN SOFWBG
SOFTWARE WORLD. See Computers-Software.

LC HF5439.C67 S66
DD 338.7/610016425/02573
ISSN 8756-9833
US
SOFTWARE WRITERS MARKET (POMONA, N.Y.). See Computers-Computer Industry and Industry Directories.

ISSN 1068-0950
US
DD 005
SQL FORUM. (SQL FORUM : THE JOURNAL FOR THE INTERNATIONAL SQL SERVER COMMUNITY.). [SQL forum]. Vol. 1, No. 1 (1991)-. Periodical. English. Six times a year. $84.00. SQL Forum, PO Box 240, Lynnwood WA 98046. **Tel** (206)382-6607, FAX (206)771-4783. **ED** Karl V Fischer (editor's address: 1510 10th Place North, Edmonds WA 98020; editor's phone: (206)771-3896). Index available. **Bk Rev. Ad Acc, Adv Mgr:** Marya C Fischer. **Circ:** 2,500 (ctrl).
Desc: An independent computer journal devoted exclusively to the SQL Server Product.

LC Z5642.3 .S17 QA76.6
DD 016.0016/425
ISSN 0160-0400
US
SSI. See Computers-Microcomputers, Personal Computers.

ISSN 1074-7249
US
DD 005
●**STUFF YOU GOTTA KNOW ABOUT MICROSOFT WINDOWS.** [Stuff You Gotta Know About Microsoft Wind.]. **Added/Corp** Cobb Group. Vol. 1, No. 1 (Feb. 1994)-. Periodical. English. Twelve times a year. $39.00. Cobb Group, 9420 Bunsen Parkway #300, Louisville KY 40220. **Tel** (502)491-1900, (800)223-8720, FAX (502)491-4200.

DD 005
ISSN 1067-9197
US
CODEN TAGGEP
TAG (STERLING, VA.). (TAG : THE SGML NEWSLETTER.). []. **Added/Corp** SGML Associates. BDS, Inc. Graphic Communications Association (U.S.). **VFOAT** SGML Newsletter. Vol. 1, Issue 1 (May/June 1987)-. Newsletter. English. Twelve times a year. $180.00. SGML Associates, 6360 South Gibraltar Circle, Aurora CO 80016. **Tel** (303)680-0875, FAX (303)680-4906. **ED** Brian Travis. **Bk Rev,** (Qty: 3). **Circ:** 300 (ctrl).
Desc: Includes articles, reviews, product news, tutorials, standards updates, user group information, case studies, technical tips and techniques for the new or experienced SGML user.

DD 005
ISSN 1065-2590
US
CEASED
TECHJOURNAL (SANTA CLARA, CALIF.). (TECHJOURNAL.). [TechJournal]. **Added/Corp** Software Publishing Corporation. **VFOAT** Tech Journal. (1991)-Vol. 4 No. 4 (1994). Periodical. English. Software Publishing Corporation, PO Box 54983, Santa Clara CA 95056. **Tel** (408)988-7518, (800)234-2500, FAX (408)980-0729.

LC QA75.5 .T43
DD 001.64/05
ISSN 0752-4072
FR
CCC
CODEN TTSIDJ
TECHNIQUE ET SCIENCE INFORMATIQUES : TSI. See Computers-Electronic Data Processing.

DD 005
ISSN 1076-5506
US
TICK, TICK, TICK. [Tick tick tick]. (199?)-. Periodical. English. Four times a year. $75.00. 2000 AD Inc., PO Box 020538, Brooklyn NY 11202. **Tel** (718)643-8425.

AJ
TRUDY VYCHISLITELNOGO TSENTRA. **Added/Corp** Vychislitelnyi Tsentr (Azerbaijan SSR Ermlar Akademiiasy). **VFOAT** Hesablama Markazinin Asarlari. (1962)-. Russian. Izdatelstvo Elm, Ul. Narimonova 37, 370073 Baku Azerbaijan.
Ind/Abst Zentralbl. Math. Ihre Grenzgeb.

ISSN 0892-4961
US
DD 004
Pr Rev.
CEASED
TUG LINES. [TUG lines]. **VAT** Turbo User Group Lines. Vol. 1, Issue 1 (June/July 1984)-No. 57 (Dec. 1993). Periodical. English. TUG/PRO, PO Box 1510, Poulsbo WA 98370. **Tel** (206)779-9508, FAX (206)779-8311. **ED** Don Taylor. **Bk Rev. Ad Acc, Adv Mgr:** C D Taylor. **Circ:** 3,000. available on diskette.
Desc: Coverage of language products published by Borland International.

ISSN 1069-0417
DD 004 US
UNIFORUM MONTHLY. [UniForum mon.]. **Added/Corp** UniForum. (1991)-. Periodical. English. Twelve times a year. $100.00. UniForum, 2901 Tasman Dr., Suite 201, Santa Clara CA 95054. **Tel** (408)986-8840, FAX (408)986-1645. **Ad Acc, Adv Mgr:** Dick Shippee. **Circ:** 7,200. ***Continues*** *CommUNIXations.*
Desc: Designed to meet the information needs of the computing industry and specifically the UNIX systems market.

ISSN 1069-0395
DD 004 US
UNINEWS (SANTA CLARA, CALIF.). (UNINEWS.). [UniNews]. **Added/Corp** UniForum. (1990)-. Periodical. English. Twenty-four times a year. UniForum, 2901 Tasman Dr., Suite 201, Santa Clara CA 95054. **Tel** (408)986-8840, FAX (408)986-1645. **Circ:** 6,000. ***Continues*** */usr/digest.*

ISSN 1077-6087
DD 004 US
●**VISUAL BASIC DEVELOPER.** [Vis. basic dev.]. Vol. 1, No. 1 (1994)-. Newsletter. English. Twelve times a year. $179.00. Pinnacle Publishing Inc., PO Box 888, Kent WA 98035. **Tel** (206)251-1900, (800)231-1293, FAX (206)251-5057.
Desc: Newsletter for developers using Visual Basic. Provides in-depth technical articles, tips, and shortcuts that help you get the most out of Visual Basic and add-in tools.

LC QA76.73.B3 B3963 ISSN 1075-1955
DD 005.26/ US
●**VISUAL BASIC PROGRAMMER'S JOURNAL.** [Vis. Basic program. j.]. **VFOAT** Visual Basic. (Aug./Sept. 1993)-. Periodical. English. Six times a year. $34.97. Fawcette Technical Publications, 209 Hamilton Avenue, Palo Alto CA 94301. **Tel** (800)848-5523, (415)833-7100. **(Subscription address:** Neodata / Colorado, PO Box 2606, Boulder CO 80322. **)** ***Continues*** *BasicPro, 1066-5978.*

ISSN 1079-0608
DD 005 US
CODEN VCDEF7
●**VISUAL C++ DEVELOPER.** [Vis. C++ dev.]. **VFOAT** Visual C Plus Plus Developer. Vol. 1, No. 1 (Fall 1994)-. Newsletter. English. Twelve times a year. $149.00. Pinnacle Publishing Inc., PO Box 888, Kent WA 98035. **Tel** (206)251-1900, (800)231-1293, FAX (206)251-5057.
Desc: Technical newsletter for developers using Visual C++ and related add-in products. Contains in-depth technical articles and time saving tips needed to build state-of-the art programs in less time.

ISSN 1080-2908
US
CEASED
VISUAL OBJECTS DEVELOPER. (1995)-(July 1995). Newsletter. English. Pinnacle Publishing Inc., PO Box 888, Kent WA 98035. **Tel** (206)251-1900, (800)231-1293, FAX (206)251-5057.
Desc: Technical newsletter for developers using CA-Visual Objects. Provides practical techniques for optimizing the power of Visual Objects, tips to increase productivity, and news and reviews to keep you up-to-date on Computer Associates and third-party vendors.

ISSN 0229-124X
DD 001.64/24 CN
VM/370 CMS EXEC USER'S GUIDE. [VM/370 CMS EXEC user's guide]. **VFOAT** VM/370 Exec User's Guide. Aug. 14, 1980-. Periodical. English. $1.00 each number. Computer Reference Room, University of Waterloo, Waterloo Ontario N2L 3G1 Canada.

UK
VM UPDATE. (19??)-. English. Twelve times a year. $235.00. Xephon, 27-35 London Road, Newbury Berkshire RG13 1JL United Kingdom. **Tel** 011 44 1635 33823, FAX 011 44 1635 38345. **(Subscription address:** Xephon, 1301 West Highway, Suite 201 450, Lewisville TX 75067. **) ED** Trevor Eddolls. Index available. cum. index. **Bk Rev. Circ:** 1,800.
Desc: Programs, hints and tips from users of VM/CMS operating systems.

UK
VSAM UPDATE. (19??)-. English. Four times a year. £100.00. Xephon, 27-35 London Road, Newbury Berkshire RG13 1JL United Kingdom. **Tel** 011 44 1635 33823, FAX 011 44 1635 38345. **(Subscription address:** Xephon, 1301 West Highway, Suite 201 450, Lewisville TX 75067. **) ED** Trevor Eddolls. Index available. cum. index. **Bk Rev. Circ:** 400.
Desc: Programs, hints and tips for people working with VSAM files.

UK
Pr Rev.
VSE UPDATE. (19??)-. English. Four times a year. $135.00. Xephon, 27-35 London Road, Newbury Berkshire RG13 1JL United Kingdom. **Tel** 011 44 1635 33823, FAX 011 44 1635 38345. **(Subscription address:** Xephon, 1301 West Highway, Suite 201 450, Lewisville TX 75067. **) ED** Trevor Eddolls. Index available. cum. index. **Bk Rev**, (Qty: 2). **Circ:** 400 (ctrl). available on an online database from Bulletin Board.
Desc: Aimed mainly at VSE systems programmers and other VSE technical staff. It contains program codes to enhance the performance and ease of use of VSE.

LC QA76 .M617 ISSN 0507-5386
RU
VYCHISLITELNYE METODY I PROGRAMMIROVANIE. [Vycisl. metody programm.]. **Added/Corp** Moskovskii Gosudarstvennyi Universitet Im. M.V. Lomonosova. Vychislitelnyi Tsentr. **VFOAT** Chislennye Metody v Gazovoi Dinamike. (1962)-. Academic Scholarly Publication. Russian. Two times a year. Price varies per volume. Izdatelstvo Moskovskogo Universiteta, K-9 Ulitsa Gertsena 5/7, 103009 Moscow Russia. **Tel** (301)881-5973. Documents available from CASDDS.
Ind/Abst Chem. Abstr.; Int. Aerosp. Abstr. (1984-); Math. Rev.; Zentralbl. Math. Ihre Grenzgeb.

ISSN 0828-5624
DD 001.64/25 CN
WATCOM NEWS. [WATCOM news]. **Added/Corp** Waterloo Computing Systems. University of Waterloo. Computer Systems Group. **VAT** Waterloo Computer Systems Group News. (May 1984)-. Periodical. English. Irregular. Free on request. Watcom Products Inc, 415 Philip Street, Waterloo Ontario N2L 3X2 Canada. **Tel** (519)886-3700, telex 06-955458. **ED** Janet E. Cater. Index available. **Circ:** 7,000 (ctrl). ***Formed by the union of*** *Infowat, 0822-8159* ***and*** *Watnews.*
Desc: Announces new products and describes product applications from its users.

ISSN 1060-1066
US
CCC
WINDOWS MAGAZINE. **VFOAT** Windows. (1991)-. English. Fourteen times a year (monthly with two special issues). $24.94. CMP Publications Inc., One Jericho Plaza, Wing A, 2nd Floor, Jericho NY 11753. **Tel** (516)733-6700. **(Subscription address:** Windows Magazine, PO Box 420285, Palm Coast FL 32142-0285. **Tel** (904)445-4662, ext. 420, FAX (904)445-2728 attn: agency order.**)**
Desc: Dedicated to the latest in Windows innovation. You'll get hard-hitting software reviews; insightful coverage of the full range of Window-related products; comprehensive explorations of the newest advances in desktop publishing, multimedia and networking; and tips to help you supercharge your Windows system.
Ind/Abst Bus. Source Plus; EP Collect.; Homework Help.; Lotus Notes; MasterFile FullTEXT 1000; MasterFile FullTEXT 350; MasterFile FullTEXT 650; MasterFile FullTEXT; OCLC; Telebase.

LC QA76.76.W56 W56 ISSN 1049-071X
DD 005.4/3 US
CODEN WSGUEM
CEASED
WINDOWS SHOPPER'S GUIDE, THE. (THE WINDOWS SHOPPER'S GUIDE : THE SOURCEBOOK FOR MICROSOFT WINDOWS APPLICATIONS & SERVICES.). [Windows shopp. guide]. Vol. 1, No. 1 (1989)-Vol. 5 (1993). Periodical. English. Whitefox Communications Inc, 1800 NW 169th Place, Suite 700 B, Beaverton OR 97006. **Tel** (503)629-5612, FAX (503)645-8642. **ED** Mike Jones. **Ad Acc, Adv Mgr:** Jolene Andoniodis, **Tel** (503)629-5612. **Circ:** 25,000.
Desc: Buyers reference for Microsoft Windows applications and services. It features vendor, product, consulting and pricing information for over 1,400 products form over 800 vendors, makes finding Windows application fun and easy for users at every level.

LC QA76.76.W56 W564 ISSN 1065-9641
DD 005.4/3 US
●**WINDOWS SOURCES.** [Windows sources]. (1993)-. Periodical. English. Twelve times a year. $28.00. Ziff-Davis, One Park Avenue, 5th Floor, New York NY 10016. **Tel** (212)503-3500. **(Subscription address:** Neodata / Colorado, PO Box 2606, Boulder CO 80322. **) ED** Jim Louderback. **Ad Acc.** available on an online database (file 675/Full-Text) from DIALOG; available via Internet (http://www.ziff.com/).
Desc: Contains undocumented user secrets, time-saving tips, labs-based reviews, benchmark test result, and advice on how to choose and use the best Windows products.

ISSN 1061-3501
DD 005 US
WINDOWS TECH JOURNAL. [Windows tech j.]. **VFOAT** Windows Tech. Vol. 1, No. 1 (Jan. 1992)-. Trade Publication. English. Twelve times a year. $29.95. Oakley Publishing Company, PO Box 70087, Eugene OR 97401-9943. **Tel** (800)234-0386, (503)747-0800.

ISSN 1065-3481
DD 005 US
CCC
CEASED
WINDOWS USER. [Windows user]. Vol. 1, No. 1 (1992)-(Aug. 1993). Periodical. English. Wandsworth Publishing, PO Box 304, Brookfield CT 06804. **Tel** (203)775-0190. **ED** Steven Bobker. **Ad Acc. Circ:** 150,000.
Desc: Covers the hardware, software and peripheral products for Windows, providing users with evaluation, advice and recommendations. The title is solutions oriented, dedicated to increasing the productivity of users.

LC QA76.76.W56 X2 ISSN 1056-7003
DD 005.4/3 US
CCC
CODEN XJOUEA
X JOURNAL, THE. [X j.]. (1991)-. Periodical. English. Six times a year. $99.00. SIGS Publications Inc. / New York, 71 West 23rd Street, 3rd Floor, New York NY 10010-4102. **Tel** (212)242-7447.

LC QA
DD 005.1 US
●**X-RAY MAGAZINE.** (1995)-. English. Six times a year (Feb., Apr., June, Aug., Oct., Dec.). Free. X-Ray Magazine, PO Box 200068, Denver CO 80220. **Tel** (303)394-3423.

SIMULATION

LC QA76.9.C65 A3 ISSN 1049-3301
DD 003/.3/05 US
CCC
CODEN ATMCEZ
ACM TRANSACTIONS ON MODELING AND COMPUTER SIMULATION : A PUBLICATION OF THE ASSOCIATION FOR COMPUTING MACHINERY. [ACM trans. model. comput. simul.]. **Added/Corp** Association for Computing Machinery. **VFOAT** Transactions on Modeling and Computer Simulation. **VAT** Association for Computing Machinery Transactions on Modeling and Computer Simulation. Vol. 1, No. 1 (Jan. 1991)-. Trade Publication. English. Four times a year (Jan., Apr., July, Oct.). $115.00. ACM / Association for Computing Machinery, 1515 Broadway, 17th Floor, New York NY 10036. **Tel** (212)869-7440, FAX (212)869-0481. **(Subscription address:** Association for Computing Machinery, PO Box 12114, Church Street Station, New York NY 10249. **Tel** (212)626-0500.**) ED** Richard E. Nance. Documents available from Article Express International, Ask*IEEE.
Desc: Primary resource for technical research material on all aspects of computer simulation and the modeling of complex systems studied through simulation techniques.
Ind/Abst ACM Guide Comput. Lit.; Comput. Rev.; Ei Page One; Eng. Index Annu.; INSPEC (Vol. 1, No. 1 Jan. 1991-).

ISSN 0761-2494
FR
UDC 658.5:681.3 CCC
ADVANCES IN MODELLING & SIMULATION. **VFOAT** Advances in Modelling and Simulation. (1984)-. Periodical. English. One time a year. $78.50. JAI Press Inc., 55 Old Post Road, Suite 2, PO Box 1678, Greenwich CT 06836-1678. **Tel** (203)661-7602, FAX (203)661-0792.
Ind/Abst Curr. Cit.

ISSN 1045-5795
DD 384 US
Pr Rev.
AUDIOTEX UPDATE. [Audiotex update]. (1989)-. Periodical. English. Twelve times a year. $150.00 North America; $165.00 other. Worldwide Videotex, PO Box 3273, Boynton Beach FL 33424-3273. **Tel** (407)738-2276, FAX (407)738-2275. **ED** Mark Wright. **Bk Rev.** available on an online database from NEWSNET; DATA-STAR; and (file 636/Full-Text) DIALOG.
Desc: Provides news and information about audiotex and voice processing industry and products. This includes voice processing, voice information products, services, companies, and marketing strategies.
Ind/Abst PTS Newsl. Database [Full Txt.].

LC QA276.A1 C655 ISSN 0361-0918
DD 591.5/05 US
CCC
CODEN CSSCDB
COMMUNICATIONS IN STATISTICS : SIMULATION AND COMPUTATION. [Commun. stat., Simul. comput.]. **VFOAT** Simulation and Computation. Vol. B5 (1976)-. Periodical. English. Four times a year. $625.00. Marcel Dekker Inc., 270 Madison Avenue, New York NY 10016. **Tel** (212)696-9000, (800)228-1160, FAX (212)685-4540, telex 421419. **(Subscription address:** Marcel Dekker Inc., PO Box 5017, Monticello NY 12701. **Tel** (800)228-1160.**) ED** William B. Smith, W. R. Schucany and A. M. Kshirsagar. **Bk Rev. Ad Acc.** available on microfiche. Documents available from The Genuine Article, Ask*IEEE. ***Supersedes in part*** *Communications in Statistics, 0090-3272.*
Desc: Deals with problems at the interface of statistics and computer science - including tables of, and algorithms for, statistical functions and numerical solutions to outstanding problems, whether by simulation or the use of special functions.
Ind/Abst Biostatistica; CompuMath Cit. Index [Full Cov.];

Computers —Simulation

Curr. Cit.; Curr. Contents Phys. Chem. Earth Sci.; Curr. Index Stat.; INSPEC (1976-); Int. Aerosp. Abstr.; Math. Rev. (1987-); Oper. Res./Manage. Sci.; Phys. Briefs; Qual. Control Appl. Stat.; Res. Alert [Full Cov.]; Sci. Cit. Index (19??-19??); SCISEARCH; Soc. Sci. Cit. Index [Select. Cov.]; Stat. Theory Method Abstr. (1977-1984, 1986-1987); Zentralbl. Math. Ihre Grenzgeb.

LC TA1632 .C65925   ISSN 1077-3142
DD 006.4/2/05   US
   CCC

●**COMPUTER VISION AND IMAGE UNDERSTANDING.** (COMPUTER VISION AND IMAGE UNDERSTANDING : CVIU.). [Comput. vis. image underst.]. **VFOAT** CVIU. Vol. 61, No. 1 (Jan. 1995)-. Periodical. English. Six times a year. $427.00. Academic Press Inc., 6277 Sea Harbor Drive, Orlando FL 32887. **Tel** (800)543-9534, (407)345-4100, **FAX** (407)352-3445. (**Subscription address:** Academic Press Inc., PO Box 620000, Orlando FL 32891-8340. **Tel** (800)543-9534.) **Continues** CVGIP. Image Understanding, 1049-9660.
Ind/Abst Curr. Cit.

   ISSN 0924-6703
   US
   CCC
   CODEN DEDAEE

Pr Rev.
DISCRETE EVENT DYNAMIC SYSTEMS. (DISCRETE EVENT DYNAMIC SYSTEMS: THEORY & APPLICATIONS.). [Discret. event dyn. syst.]. Vol. 1, No. 1 (May 1991)-. Periodical. English. Four times a year. $370.00. Kluwer Academic Publishers / Massachusetts, PO Box 358, Accord Station, Hingham MA 02018. **Tel** (617)871-6600. **ED** Yu-Chi Ho. **Acid Free.** available on microfilm and microfiche from University Microfilms International (UMI). Documents available from Article Express International, Ask*IEEE.
Desc: Covers three broad areas: theory and formal models, performance and control, and applications. Within those broad areas, papers are published specifically devoted to the dynamics of discrete event systems, control and optimization, and the interface with operations research and computer science. The scope of the journal is defined by its emphasis on the modeling of discrete events by dynamic systems, and on problems of their control and optimization.
Ind/Abst Eng. Index Annu.; INSPEC (May 1991-); Zentralbl. Math. Ihre Grenzgeb.

   ISSN 1063-1100
   US
   CCC
   CODEN ENSIEH

ELECTRONIC SIMULATION. See Electronics.

LC TD169 .E647   ISSN 0266-9838
DD 363.7/0028/5   UK
   CCC
   CODEN ENSOEZ

Pr Rev.
ENVIRONMENTAL SOFTWARE. See Environmental Issues-Computer Applications.

   ISSN 0177-6843
   GW

UDC 519.872.8
FACHBERICHTE SIMULATION. (1984)-. Monographic series. German. Irregular. Price varies per volume. Springer-Verlag GmbH & Company KG, Heidelberger Platz 3, D-14197 Berlin Germany. **Tel** 011 49 30 8207223, **FAX** 011 49 30 8214091, telex 183 319 SPBLN D. (**Subscription address:** Springer-Verlag New York Inc. / North America, PO Box 2485, Journal Fulfillment, Secaucus NJ 07096. **Tel** (201)348-4033, (800)777-4643, **FAX** (201)348-4505.)
Ind/Abst Zentralbl. Math. Ihre Grenzgeb.

LC QA75.5 .F67   ISSN 0889-4833
DD 620

FOREFRONTS. [Forefronts]. **Added/Corp** Cornell Theory Center. Vol. 1, No. 1 (May 1985)-. Periodical. English. Four times a year. Free. Cornell Theory Center, Engineering and Theory Center Building, Cornell University, Ithaca NY 14853-3801. available via Internet (gopher.tc.cornell.edu).

LC LT
DD 371.397   US

GUIDE TO SIMULATIONS/GAMES FOR EDUCATION AND TRAINING, THE. 2nd Edition (1973)-. English. Irregular. $49.95 (latest edition). SAGE Periodical Press, 2455 Teller Road, Thousand Oaks CA 91320. **Tel** (805)499-0721, **FAX** (805)499-0871, telex 100799. **Acid Free.**

LC QA76.9.C65 I56   ISSN 1055-8470
DD 003/.3/05   US

INTERNATIONAL JOURNAL IN COMPUTER SIMULATION. [Inter. j. comput. simul.]. **VFOAT** Computer Simulation. Vol. 1, No. 1 (1991)-. Periodical. English. Four times a year. $130.00. Ablex Publishing Corporation, 355 Chestnut Street, Norwood NJ 07648. **Tel** (201)767-8450, (201)767-8455 (Customer Service), **FAX** (201)767-6717. **ED** George Zobrist.
Desc: Focuses on computer simulation of special interest to computer scientists, engineers, and research and development simulationists in academic and industry.
Ind/Abst Inf. Sci. Abstr.

LC TA342 .I57   ISSN 0228-6203
DD 001.4/34   US
   CODEN IMSIEK

INTERNATIONAL JOURNAL OF MODELLING & SIMULATION. (INTERNATIONAL JOURNAL OF MODELLING & SIMULATION : A JOURNAL OF THE INTERNATIONAL ASSOCIATION OF SCIENCE AND TECHNOLOGY FOR DEVELOPMENT, IASTED.). [Int. j. model. simul.]. **Added/Corp** International Association of Science and Technology for Development. **VFOAT** International Journal of Modelling and Simulation. Vol. 1, No. 1 (1981)-. Periodical. English (French and German). Four times a year. $239.00. IASTED- International Association of Science and Technology for Development, PO Box 2481, Anaheim CA 92814. **Tel** (714)778-3230, (800)995-2161, **FAX** (714)535-2662. **ED** Dr S Sengupta. Index available.
Bk Rev. Ad Acc. Circ: 300. Documents available from Ask*IEEE.
Desc: Covers modelling, simulation, languages, software, hardware, methodology, statistical techniques, numerical and graphical methods, tutorials, surveys and applications.
Ind/Abst Curr. Cit.; INSPEC (1986-); Int. Aerosp. Abstr. (1984-).

   UK
TITLE CHANGE
JANE'S MILITARY TRAINING AND SIMULATION SYSTEMS. See Military and Defense.

   UK
●**JANE'S SIMULATION AND TRAINING SYSTEMS.** See Military and Defense.

LC QA   ISSN 1048-9533
DD 510   US

JOURNAL OF APPLIED MATHEMATICS AND STOCHASTIC ANALYSIS. [J. appl. math. stoch. anal.]. **Added/Corp** Society of Applied Mathematics, Modeling, and Simulation. **VFOAT** J.A.M.S.A.; JAMSA. Vol. 3, No. 1 (Spring 1990)-. Periodical. English. Four times a year (Apr., July, Oct., Dec./Jan.). $135.00. North Atlantic Science Publishing Company, PO Box 1017, Melbourne FL 32902-1017. **Tel** (407)951-8306, **FAX** (407)726-8200. **ED** Jewgeni Dshalalow (address: Department of Applied Mathematics, Florida Institute of Technology, Melbourne, Fl 32901) (phone: (407)768-8000 ext. 8091). **Ad Acc. Circ:** 200 (ctrl). **Continues** Journal of Applied Mathematics and Simulation, 0893-5688.
Ind/Abst Math. Rev.; Zentralbl. Math. Ihre Grenzgeb.

LC RC512
DD 616.89   US
NLM W1; JO595KL
●**JOURNAL OF COMPUTATIONAL NEUROSCIENCE.** See Medical Sciences-Neurology.

   ISSN 0924-0136
   NE
   CCC
   CODEN JMPTEF

Pr Rev.
JOURNAL OF MATERIALS PROCESSING TECHNOLOGY. See Engineering-Materials Science.

LC QA276.A1 J58   ISSN 0094-9655
DD 519.5/028/54   US
   CCC
   CODEN JSCSAJ

JOURNAL OF STATISTICAL COMPUTATION AND SIMULATION. [J. stat. comput. simul.]. **VFOAT** JSCS. Vol. 1 (Jan. 1972)-. Statistical Publication. English. Four times a year. $764.00 (academic institutions), $1191.00 (corporate institutions). Gordon & Breach Science Publishers, Inc., PO Box 786, Cooper Station, New York NY 10276. **Tel** (212)206-8900, **FAX** (212)645-2459. **ED** R. Krutchkoff. Index available. **Bk Rev. Ad Acc.** Documents available from Ask*IEEE.
Desc: Publishes significant and original work in areas of statistics which are related to or dependent on the computer.
Ind/Abst Comput. Rev.; Curr. Cit.; Curr. Index Stat.; EMBASE; INSPEC (July 1972-); Math. Rev.; Stat. Theory Method Abstr. (1974-1975, 1977-1984, 1986-1987); Zentralbl. Math. Ihre Grenzgeb.

   US

JOURNAL OF THE SOCIETY FOR COMPUTER SIMULATIONS. (19??)-. English. Twelve times a year. comes with membership. The Society for Computer Simulation, PO Box 17900, San Diego CA 92117-7900. **Tel** (619)277-3888, **FAX** (619)277-3930.

LC QA76.4 .I63   ISSN 0378-4754
DD 001.4/24   NE
   CCC
   CODEN MCSIDR

Pr Rev.
MATHEMATICS AND COMPUTERS IN SIMULATION. [Math. comput. simul.]. **Added/Corp** International Association for Mathematics and Computers in Simulation. Vol. 19 (Mar. 1977)-. Academic Scholarly Publication. English (French). Twelve times a year (2 volumes). $872.00. Elsevier Science Publishers BV, PO Box 211, 1000 AE Amsterdam Netherlands. **Tel** 011 31 20 4853641, 011 31 20 4853642, **FAX** 011 31 20 4853598. **ED** R. Vichnevetsky. **Bk Rev. Ad Acc. Circ:** 600. available on microfilm and microfiche from University Microfilms International (UMI); available from an online database from Elsevier Electronic Subscriptions (EES). Documents available from Article Express International, The Genuine Article, Ask*IEEE. **Continues** Transactions of the International Association for Mathematics and Computers in Simulation.
Desc: Provides forum for the dissemination of information in the field of computer simulation of systems.
Ind/Abst ACM Guide Comput. Lit.; Bioeng. Abstr.; Biostatistica; Coal Abstr.; CompuMath Cit. Index [Full Cov.]; Comput. Abstr.; Comput. Rev.; Curr. Cit.; Ei Page One; Energy Res. Abstr. (Feb. 1979-); Eng. Index Annu. [Select. Cov.]; GeoRef; INSPEC (March 1977-); Int. Abstr. Oper. Res. [Select. Cov.]; Math. Rev.; Oper. Res./Manage. Sci.; Pollut. Abstr. Indexes; Qual. Control Appl. Stat.; Res. Alert [Full Cov.]; SCISEARCH; Soc. Sci. Cit. Index [Select. Cov.]; Zentralbl. Math. Ihre Grenzgeb.

LC TA407 .M565   ISSN 0965-0393
DD 620.1/1/015118   UK
   CCC
   CODEN MSMEEU

MODELLING AND SIMULATION IN MATERIALS SCIENCE AND ENGINEERING. See Engineering-Materials Science.

   UK
PERSPECTIVES ON ACADEMIC GAMING & SIMULATION. See Education-Computer Applications.

LC T57.62 .S57   US

PROCEEDINGS / ANNUAL SIMULATION SYMPOSIUM. Added/Corp Society for Computer Simulation. IEEE Computer Society. Association for Computing Machinery. (Apr. 6-9, 1992)-. Proceedings. English. One time a year. $80.00. IEEE Computer Society, 10662 Los Vaqueros Circle, PO Box 3014, Los Alamitos CA 90720-1264. **Tel** (714)821-8380, (800)272-6657, **FAX** (714)821-4641. **Continues** Record of Proceedings, 0272-4715.

LC QA76 .S863a   ISSN 0094-7474
DD 001.6/424   US
   CCC
   CODEN PSCCD6

PROCEEDINGS OF THE SUMMER COMPUTER SIMULATION CONFERENCE. [Proc. Summer Comput. Simul. Conf.]. **Added/Corp** Association for Computing Machinery. American Institute of Aeronautics and Astronautics. American Institute of Chemical Engineers. American Geophysical Union. Society for Computer Simulation. (19??)-. Proceedings. English. One time a year (published in July). $180.00. The Society for Computer Simulation, PO Box 17900, San Diego CA 92117-7900. **Tel** (619)277-3888, **FAX** (619)277-3930. **ED** David Braxton. Index available (bound in issue). **Circ:** 1,200. Documents available from Article Express International, Ask*IEEE, CASDDS.
Desc: Contains papers on computer simulation presented at the summer conference in a wide variety of areas.
Ind/Abst Bioeng. Abstr.; Chem. Abstr.; Curr. Cit.; Ei Page One; Eng. Index Annu.; INSPEC (1985-).

LC T57.62 .C64a   ISSN 0891-7736
DD 001.4/34   US
   CCC

PROCEEDINGS - WINTER SIMULATION CONFERENCE. (PROCEEDINGS OF THE ... WINTER SIMULATION CONFERENCE.). [Proc. - Winter Simul. Conf.]. **Added/Corp** Institute of Electrical and Electronics Engineers. **VFOAT** Proceedings; Winter Simulation Conference Proceedings. (1980)-. Proceedings. English. One time a year (published in Dec.). $180.00. The Society for Computer Simulation, PO Box 17900, San Diego CA 92117-7900. **Tel** (619)277-3888, **FAX** (619)277-3930. Index available (bound in issue). **Continues** Winter Simulation Conference. Winter Simulation Conference, 0743-1902.
Ind/Abst Curr. Cit.; Index IEEE Publ.

LC QA76.9.C65 S644   US

SCS MEMBERSHIP DIRECTORY.
Main/Corp Society for Computer Simulation. **VFOAT** Society for Computer Simulation Membership Directory.

(19??)-. Directory. English. The Society for Computer Simulation, PO Box 17900, San Diego CA 92117-7900. **Tel** (619)277-3888, FAX (619)277-3930.

LC H62 .S477 **ISSN** 1046-8781
DD 003/.3 US
CCC
CODEN SIGAEI
Pr Rev.

SIMULATION & GAMING. [Simul. gaming]. **Added/Corp** Association for Business Simulation and Experiential Learning. North American Simulation and Gaming Association. International Simulation and Gaming Association. **VFOAT** Simulation and Gaming. Vol. 21, No. 1 (Mar. 1990)-. Periodical. English. Four times a year (Mar., June, Sept., Dec.). $200.00. SAGE Periodical Press, 2455 Teller Road, Thousand Oaks CA 91320. **Tel** (805)499-0721, FAX (805)499-0871, telex 100799. **ED** David Crookall. **Bk Rev. Ad Acc. Acid Free.** available on microfilm and microfiche from University Microfilms International (UMI). Documents available from The Genuine Article, Ask*IEEE, UMI Article Clearinghouse. ***Continues** Simulation & Games, 0037-5500.*
Desc: Publishes theoretical and empirical papers related to man, man-machine, and machine simulations of social processes.
Ind/Abst ABC POL SCI; Acad. Search; ACM Guide Comput. Lit.; Commun. Abstr.; Comput. Rev.; Curr. Cit.; Curr. Index J. Educ.; EP Collect.; Expand. Acad. Index (1989-); Homework Help.; Hum. Resour. Abstr.; INFO-SOUTH Abstr.; INSPEC (March 1970-); J. Plan. Lit.; Mag. Search; MasterFile FullTEXT 1000; MasterFile FullTEXT 350; MasterFile FullTEXT 650; MasterFile FullTEXT (Jan. 1994-); Med. Rev. Dig.; Newsp. Period. Abstr. (1991-); OCLC; Pollut. Abstr. Indexes; Psychol. Abstr. (1972-); PsycINFO; Res. Alert [Full Cov.]; Sage Public Adm. Abstr.; Soc. Plann. Policy Dev. Abstr.; Soc. Sci. Source; Soc. Sci. Cit. Index [Full Cov.]; Soc. Sci. Index; Soc. Sci. Index Fulltext (March 1990-) [Full Txt.]; Sociol. Abstr.; Telebase.

LC LB1029.S53 S52 **ISSN** 1351-4644
DD 370 UK

•SIMULATION AND GAMING YEARBOOK. **See** Education-Computer Applications.

LC QA76.9.C65 S62 **ISSN** 1060-3689
DD 004 US
CODEN SIDIER

SIMULATION DIGEST. (SIMULATION DIGEST : A JOINT PUBLICATION OF SIGSIM, THE SPECIAL INTEREST GROUP ON SIMULATION, ACM PRESS [AND] TCSIM, THE SIMULATION TECHNICAL COMMITTEE, IEEE COMPUTER SOCIETY.). [Simul. dig.]. **Added/Corp** ACM Special Interest Group on Simulation. IEEE Computer Society. Technical Committee on Simulation. Vol. 19, No. 3 (Sept. 1988)-. Periodical. English. Three times a year. $25.00. ACM / Association for Computing Machinery, 1515 Broadway, 17th Floor, New York NY 10036. **Tel** (212)869-7440, FAX (212)869-0481. **(Subscription address:** Association for Computing Machinery, PO Box 12114, Church Street Station, New York NY 10249. **Tel** (212)626-0500.) Documents available from Ask*IEEE. ***Formed by the union of** Simuletter, 0163-6103 **and** Modeling.*
Ind/Abst Abstr. Hum. Comput. Interact.; INSPEC (1988-1989).

LC TA343 .S52 **ISSN** 0037-5497
DD 001.4/24 US
CCC
CODEN SIMUA2
Pr Rev.

SIMULATION (SAN DIEGO, CALIF.). (SIMULATION.). [Simulation]. **VFOAT** SCI Simulation; SCS Simulation. Vol. 1 (Fall 1963)-. Trade Publication. English. Twelve times a year. $149.00. The Society for Computer Simulation, PO Box 17900, San Diego CA 92117-7900. **Tel** (619)277-3888, FAX (619)277-3930. **ED** Ron Belpedio, M. Zhody, Charles Shub and C. G. Stockton. Index available (bound in Dec. issue). cum. index. **Bk Rev. Ad Acc. Acid Free. Circ:** 4,100. available on microfilm and microfiche from University Microfilms International (UMI). Documents available from Article Express International, The Genuine Article, Ask*IEEE, CASDDS, Documents on Demand.
Desc: Contains technical articles on all aspects of computer simulation with features, calendar of events, meetings and conferences, and industry news.
Ind/Abst Abstr. Hum. Comput. Interact.; ACM Guide Comput. Lit.; Appl. Sci. Technol. Index; Bioeng. Abstr.; Biostatistica; BMT Abstr. (-199?); Book Rev. Index (?-Jan. 1989); Chem. Abstr. (1963-1983); Coal Abstr.; CompuMath Cit. Index [Full Cov.]; Comput. Abstr.; Comput. Database; Comput. Rev.; Curr. Cit.; Curr. Contents Eng. Comput. Technol.; Ei Page One; Electron. Commun. Abstr. J.; EMBASE; Energy Inf. Abstr.; Energy Res. Abstr. (Oct. 1976-); Eng. Index Annu.; Environ. Abstr.; Inf. Sci. Abstr. (?-?); INSPEC (1968-); Int. Abstr. Oper. Res. [Select. Cov.]; Int. Aerosp. Abstr.; Oper. Res./Manage. Sci.; Life Sci. Collect.; Qual. Control Appl. Stat.; Res. Alert [Full Cov.]; Soc. Plann. Policy Dev. Abstr.; Soc. Sci. Cit. Index [Select. Cov.]; Sociol. Abstr.; Zentralbl. Math. Ihre Grenzgeb.

ISSN 0735-9276
US
CCC
CODEN SMCPAX

SIMULATION SERIES. [Simul. ser.]. **Added/Corp** Society for Computer Simulation. Vol. 10, No. 1 (1981)-. Proceedings. English. Four times a year. $250.00. The Society for Computer Simulation, PO Box 17900, San Diego CA 92117-7900. **Tel** (619)277-3888, FAX (619)277-3930. Documents available from Ask*IEEE. ***Continues** Simulation Proceedings Series, 0886-1889.*
Ind/Abst Curr. Cit.; Ei Page One; INSPEC.

UK

SIMULATIONS AND GAMING YEARBOOK. (19??)-. Periodical. English. One time a year. £18.00 (individuals), £28.00 (institutions) UK; £20.00 (individuals), £28.00 (institutions) other Comes with Society for Advancement of Games and Simulations in Education and Training membership. SAGSET / Society for Advancement of Games and Simulations in Education and Training, Gala House, 3 Raglan Road, Edgbaston Birmingham B5 7RA United Kingdom. **Tel** 011 44 121 4466166.

LC WMLC 93/3892 **ISSN** 0883-7066
DD 003 US
CCC
CODEN SDREEG

SYSTEM DYNAMICS REVIEW. **See** Mathematics-Computer Applications.

LC QA402 .S969 **ISSN** 0232-9298
DD 003 GW
CCC
CODEN SAMSEC
Pr Rev.

SYSTEMS ANALYSIS, MODELLING, SIMULATION. **See** Mathematics-Computer Applications.

ISSN 0740-6797
DD 001 US
CCC
Pr Rev.

TRANSACTIONS OF THE SOCIETY FOR COMPUTER SIMULATION. [Trans. Soc. Comput. Simul.]. **Added/Corp** Society for Computer Simulation. **VFOAT** Transactions of SCS. Vol. 1, No. 1 (May 1984)-. Trade Publication. English. Four times a year (Jan., Apr., July, Oct.). $145.00. The Society for Computer Simulation, PO Box 17900, San Diego CA 92117-7900. **Tel** (619)277-3888, FAX (619)277-3930. **ED** Paul A. Luker and Ron Belpedio. **Acid Free. Circ:** 800. available on microfiche. Documents available from Article Express International, Ask*IEEE.
Desc: Presents papers dealing with theoretical and practical applications in all areas of simulation. Each issue features articles on the most innovative developments in computer modeling.
Ind/Abst ACM Guide Comput. Lit.; Biostatistica; Comput. Rev.; Curr. Cit.; Ei Page One; Eng. Index Annu.; INSPEC (Dec. 1984-); Int. Abstr. Oper. Res. [Select. Cov.]; Int. Aerosp. Abstr. (1984-).

UK

VIRTUAL REALITY SOCIETY JOURNAL. (19??)-. English. Every 2 years. $160.00. Virtual Reality Society, PO Box 316 Heywards Heath, West Sussex RH 17 5YA United Kingdom. **Tel** 011 44 1444 414792.

SOFTWARE

ISSN 1058-6954
DD 004 US

1-2-3 FOR MACINTOSH REPORT, THE. [1-2-3 Macintosh rep.]. **VFOAT** 1 2 3 for Macintosh Report; One Two Three for Macintosh Report. Vol. 1 No. 1 (1992)-. Periodical. English. Twelve times a year. $36.00. Lotus Publishing, 77 Franklin Street 320, Boston MA 02110. **Tel** (617)482-8470, (800)234-1089. **Circ:** 10,000.

ISSN 1057-2333
DD 005 US

1-2-3 FOR WINDOWS REPORT, THE. [1 2 3 Windows rep.]. **VFOAT** 1 2 3 for Windows Report; One Two Three for Windows Report. Vol. 1, No. 1 (1991)-. Periodical. English. Twelve times a year. $69.00. IDG Newsletter Corporation, 77 Franklin Street, Suite 310, Boston MA 02110. **Tel** (617)482-8470, (800)807-0771, FAX (617)338-0164. **ED** Richard Cranford. **Ad Acc. Circ:** 9,000.

ISSN 1065-0768
DD 005 US
CEASED

1-2-3 SOFTWARE CONNECTION. (123 SOFTWARE CONNECTION [COMPUTER FILE].). [1-2-3 softw. connect.]. **Added/Corp** Cobb Group. **VFOAT** 1, 2, 3 Software Connection; One, Two, Three Software Connection. (Aug. 1992)-(Apr. 1995). English. Cobb Group, 9420 Bunsen Parkway #300, Louisville KY 40220. **Tel** (502)491-1900, (800)223-8720, FAX (502)491-4200.

ISSN 0896-033X
DD 005 US

1 SOFT DECISION NEWS. [1 Soft Decis. news]. **VFOAT** One Soft Decision News. Vol. 1, No. 1 (May 1987)-. Periodical. English. Eight times a year. $50.00 (10 issues). 1 Soft Decision Inc, PO Box 346, San Rafael CA 94915. **Tel** (415)491-1616.

ISSN 0891-5121
DD 004 US

123 USER'S JOURNAL. [123 user's j.]. **Added/Corp** Cobb Group. **VFOAT** One Two Three User's Journal; Cobb Group's 123 User's Journal; 1-2-3 User's Journal. (198?)-. English. Twelve times a year. $59.00. Cobb Group, 9420 Bunsen Parkway #300, Louisville KY 40220. **Tel** (502)491-1900, (800)223-8720, FAX (502)491-4200.
Desc: Focuses on 1-2-3 applications, macros, shortcuts and techniques that allow users to master this complex software.

LC KF320.A9 A23 **ISSN** 0883-4695
DD 340/.028/553 US

ABA SOFTWARE REVIEW. **See** Law-Computer Applications.

ISSN 0741-997X
US
CCC
SUSPENDED

ABSOLUTE REFERENCE. (198?)-Suspended (19??). Periodical. English. Twelve times a year. $60.00 US; $80.00 other. Micromedia Publishers Inc., 55 Park Place, Morristown NJ 07963. **Tel** (201)644-5554. **ED** Sharon L. Sears. Index available (included with subscription).
Desc: Includes 1-2-3 and Symphony applications, reviews, and articles to help users increase their productivity and discover new tips.

ISSN 1066-7253
DD 005 US
TITLE CHANGE

ACCESS ADVISOR. [Access advis.]. **Added/Corp** Advisor Communications International, Inc. Vol. 1, No. 1 (1993)-(199?). Periodical. English. Advisor Publications Group, 4010 Morena Boulevard, Suite 200, San Diego CA 92117. **Tel** (800)336-6060, (619)483-6400, FAX (619)483-9851. **(Subscription address:** Advisor Publications Group, PO Box 17902, San Diego CA 92117. **Tel** (619)483-6400.) available on diskette. ***Continued by** Access Visual Basic Advisor.*

US

ACCESS VISUAL BASIC ADVISOR. (199?)-. Periodical. English. Twelve times a year. $29.00 US; $49.00 Canada; $69.00 other. Advisor Publications Group, 4010 Morena Boulevard, Suite 200, San Diego CA 92117. **Tel** (800)336-6060, (619)483-6400, FAX (619)483-9851. **(Subscription address:** Advisor Publications Group, PO Box 17902, San Diego CA 92117. **Tel** (619)483-6400.) ***Continues** Access Advisor.*

ISSN 1043-0768
DD 005 US
TITLE CHANGE

ACKNOWLEDGE : THE WINDOW LETTER. Vol. 1, No. 1 (Jan. 1989)-(19??). Periodical. English. Mendham Technology Group, 144 Talmadge Road, Mendham NJ 07945. **Tel** (201)543-2273, FAX (201)543-6033. **ED** Carole Patton. Index available. **Bk Rev. Circ:** 2,600. available on an online database from Information Access Company. ***Continued by** The Window Letter.*

LC QA76.758 .A35 **ISSN** 1049-331X
DD 005.1/05 US
CCC
CODEN ATSMER

ACM TRANSACTIONS ON SOFTWARE ENGINEERING AND METHODOLOGY. [ACM trans. softw. eng. methodol.]. **Added/Corp** Association for Computing Machinery. **VFOAT** Transactions on Software Engineering and Methodology. **VAT** Association for Computing Machinery Transactions on Software Engineering and Methodology. Vol. 1, No. 1 (Jan. 1992)-. Periodical. English. Four times a year (Jan., Apr., July, Oct.). $105.00. ACM / Association for Computing Machinery, 1515 Broadway, 17th Floor, New York NY 10036. **Tel** (212)869-7440, FAX (212)869-0481. **(Subscription address:** Association for Computing Machinery, PO Box 12114, Church Street Station, New York NY 10249. **Tel** (212)626-0500.) **ED** W. Richards Adrion. Documents available from Article Express International.
Ind/Abst ACM Guide Comput. Lit.; Comput. Rev.; Ei Page One; Eng. Index Annu.

ISSN 1074-9306
DD 004 US
SUSPENDED

•ADVANCED SYSTEMS. [Adv. syst.]. Vol. 7, No. 2 (Feb. 1994)-Suspended with Vol. 8, No. 5 (1995). Periodical. English. Twelve times a year. Integrated

Computers —Software

Media Inc., 501 2nd Street, San Francisco CA 94107. **Tel** (415)978-3306, (415)243-4188. **(Subscription address:** Advanced Systems, PO Box 41534, Nashville TN 37204 **)** *Continues* SunWorld (Peterborough, N.H.), 1054-5980.

LC QA76.75 .A38   **ISSN** 1044-7997
DD 005.3/05   US
ADVANCES IN SOFTWARE SCIENCE AND TECHNOLOGY. [Adv. softw. sci. technol.]. (1989)-. Academic Scholarly Publication. English. One time a year. $64.95 (Vol. 4). Academic Press Inc., 6277 Sea Harbor Drive, Orlando FL 32887. **Tel** (800)543-9534, (407)345-4100, FAX (407)352-3445. **Circ:** 1,500.

LC Z286.D47 .A43   **ISSN** 1046-0616
DD 070   US
                 TITLE CHANGE
ALDUS MAGAZINE. [Aldus mag.]. **Added/Corp** Aldus Corporation. (1989)-(1994). Periodical. English. Aldus Corporation, 411 First Avenue South, Suite 200, Seattle WA 98104-2871. **Tel** (206)622-5500. **ED** Harry Edwards. **Ad Acc. Circ:** 230,000 (ctrl). *Continued by Adobe Magazine, 1081-4477.*
  Desc: Contains hands-on techniques that can be put to work immediately to enhance the reader's documents. Feature articles include step-by-step implementation stories.
  Ind/Abst ACM Guide Comput. Lit.; Comput. Database; Comput. Rev.; HILITES.

                 ISSN 1062-5895
DD 005   US
ALPHA FORUM. (ALPHA FORUM: THE INDEPENDENT GUIDE TO ALPHA FOUR EXPERTISE.). [Alpha forum]. Vol. 1, Issue 1 (May 1992)-. Newsletter. English. Twelve times a year. $79.00. Pinnacle Publishing Inc., PO Box 888, Kent WA 98035. **Tel** (206)251-1900, (800)231-1293, FAX (206)251-5057.
  Desc: Newsletter for users of Alpha Software's Alpha Four and Alpha Five. Each issue includes in-depth application advice from expert authors, step-by-step design procedures, time saving shortcuts, Q&A and tips columns, and much more.

                 ISSN 1048-5600
DD 004   US
                 CCC
AMERICAN PROGRAMMER. [Am. Program.]. (1988)-. Periodical. English. Twelve times a year. $415.00. Cutter Information Corporation, 37 Broadway, Arlington MA 02174-5539. **Tel** (617)648-8700, (800)964-5118, FAX (617)648-8707, (617)648-1950, telex 650 100 9891. **ED** Toni Nash. Index available. cum. index. **Bk Rev**.
  Desc: Covers the American software scene with emphasis on events that impact the US marketplace.
  Ind/Abst Curr. Cit.

LC QA   **ISSN** 1022-7091
DD 005.3   NE
                 CCC
Pr Rev.
●**ANNALS OF SOFTWARE ENGINEERING.** (1995)-. Academic Scholarly Publication. English. Four times a year. Fl255.79. Baltzer Science Publishers BV, Asterweg 1A, 1031 HL Amsterdam Netherlands. **Tel** 011 31 20 6370061, FAX 011 31 20 6323651.

                 US
APDA TOOLS CATALOG. UPDATE. **Added/Corp** Apple Programmer's and Developer's Association. **VFOAT** Apple Programmer's and Developer's Association Catalog. Update. (19??)-. Catalog. English. Three times a year (March, July, Nov.). Free on request. APDA Apple Computer Inc., PO Box 319, Buffalo NY 14207. **Tel** 800-282-2732.
  Desc: This publication contains information about software development tools for Macintosh and Windows.

                 US
APPLE SOFTWARE DIRECTORY. **VFOAT** P.C. Telemart/Vanloves Apple Software Directory; PC Telemart/Vanloves Apple Software Directory. 1984-. Directory. English. *Continues* Vanloves ... Apple II/III Software Directory, 0732-0612.

                 ISSN 0893-4118
DD 004   US
                 CEASED
APPLE-WORKS FORUM. [Apple-works forum]. **Added/Corp** National AppleWorks Users Group (U.S.). **VFOAT** Apple Works Forum; Appleworks Forum. (1987)-(1995). Newsletter. English. National Appleworks Users Group : NAUG, PO Box 87453, Canton MI 48187. **Tel** (313)454-1115, FAX (313)454-1965. **ED** Cathleen Merritt. cum. index. **Ad Acc. Circ:** 10,000. available on diskette. *Continues* Forum (Canton, Mich.), 0892-9734.
  Desc: Newsletter with articles that describe how to use Appleworks, answer frequently asked questions, review enhancement programs and accessories, and contain special offers for readers.

                 ISSN 0730-1391
                 US
APPLESOURCE. [Applesource]. **VFOAT** Apple Source. (June 1982)-. Periodical. English. Three times a year. $25.00. American Software Publishing Co., 1010 16th Street NW, Washington DC 20036.

                 US
                 CEASED
APPLICATION DEVELOPMENT TOOLS. See Computers-Computer Engineering.

                 US
●**APPLICATION DEVELOPMENT TRENDS.** See Computers-Computer Engineering.

                 US
●**APPLIED COMPUTING REVIEW : A PUBLICATION OF THE SPECIAL INTEREST GROUP ON APPLIED COMPUTING.** **Added/Corp** SIGAPP. ACM Press. **VFOAT** ACR. Vol. 1, No. 1 (Winter 1993)-. Periodical. English. Four times a year. $30.00. ACM / Association for Computing Machinery, 1515 Broadway, 17th Floor, New York NY 10036. **Tel** (212)869-7440, FAX (212)869-0481.

LC G70.2 .A73   **ISSN** 1064-6108
DD 363   US
ARC NEWS (REDLANDS, CALIF.). (ARC NEWS.). [ARC news]. **Added/Corp** Environmental Systems Research Institute (Redlands, Calif.). (19??)-. Periodical. English. Four times a year (Feb., May, Aug., Nov.). Free on request. Environmental Systems Research Institute (ESRI), 380 New York Street, Redlands CA 92373. **Tel** (909)793-2853, FAX (909)793-5953, telex 9103321317. **ED** Karen Hunter. **Bk Rev**, (Qty: 4). **Ad Acc, Adv Mgr:** Karen Hunter. **Circ:** 80,000.
  Desc: Written for the ESRI software user community, as well as others interested in mapping and geographic information systems (GIS).

                 ISSN 0740-6738
                 US
ASTRO-TALK. **Added/Corp** Matrix User's Group. Matrix Software, Inc. **VFOAT** Astro Talk. (1984)-. Periodical. English. Six times a year. $9.95. Matrix Software, 315 Marion Avenue, Big Rapid MI 49307. **Tel** (616)796-2483. **ED** Michael Erlewine, (616)796-6343. **Circ:** 2,000.
  Desc: A product release information source for matrix software. Includes interviews with Astrologists.

LC QA76.758 .A98   **ISSN** 0928-8910
DD 004   CCC
                 CODEN ASOEEA
●**AUTOMATED SOFTWARE ENGINEERING.** Vol. 1, No. 1 (Mar. 1994)-. Periodical. English. Four times a year. $377.00. Kluwer Academic Publishers, Postbus 322, 3300 AH Dordrecht The Netherlands. **Tel** 011 31 78 524400, FAX 011 31 78 183273, telex 20083.

                 UK
BLACKWELL SOFTWARE MARKETS. (19??)-. English. Twenty-four times a year. £380.00. Highdon Publishing Ltd., PO Box 1626, London N5 1JF United Kingdom. **Tel** 011 44 171 2268155. *Continues Fintech 5 Software Markets.*

LC QA76.8.M3 B58   **ISSN** 0899-1014
DD 004   US
... **BMUG NEWSLETTER, THE.** See Computers-Microcomputers, Personal Computers.

LC QA76.8.A66 B66   **ISSN** 0736-2692
DD 001.64/25/0294   US
                 CEASED
BOOK OF APPLE SOFTWARE, THE. [Book Apple softw.]. (1983)-(199?). English. Arrays Inc, 6611 Valjean Avenue/Suite 109, Van Nuys CA 91406. **Tel** (818)994-1899. *Continues* Book of Apple Computer Software, 0736-2692.

LC QA76.8.A82 B65   **ISSN** 0736-2706
DD 001.64/2   US
BOOK OF ATARI SOFTWARE, THE. [Book Atari softw.]. **VFOAT** Atari Software. 1983-. English. One time a year. $19.95. Book Company, 11223 South Hindry Avenue, Los Angeles CA 90045.

                 ISSN 1073-4805
DD 005   US
●**BORLAND C++ DEVELOPER'S JOURNAL.** [Borland C++ dev. j.]. **Added/Corp** Cobb Group. **VFOAT** Borland C Plus Plus Developer's Journal. Vol. 1, No. 1 (Jan. 1994)-. Periodical. English. Twelve times a year. $69.00 US; $89.00 other. Cobb Group, 9420 Bunsen Parkway #300, Louisville KY 40220. **Tel** (502)491-1900, (800)223-8720, FAX (502)491-4200. *Continues Inside Turbo C++, 1052-9489.*

LC HF5548.125 .B884   **ISSN** 0887-9478
DD 650/.028/5536   US
BUSINESS SOFTWARE DIRECTORY. See Business and Economics-Computer Applications.

                 US
CAO/CAM/CAE PRODUCTS DATABASE. See Computers-Computer Sales, Service and Supply.

                 US
                 CEASED
CASE BUYERS GUIDE. See Computers-Computer Industry and Industry Directories.

LC QA76.758 .C38   **ISSN** 1046-5944
DD 005.1   US
                 CCC
                 TITLE CHANGE
CASE TRENDS. See Computers-Computer Engineering.

                 IT
CATALOGO SOFTWARE. (19??)-. Periodical. Italian. Six times a year. IPSOA Editore SRL, Casella Postale 12055, Mastrangelo, 20120 Milan Italy. **Tel** 011 39 2 82476248. Index available (Included).

                 SP
●**CD-ROM MAGAZINE.** (1995)-. Spanish. Twelve times a year. 9750ptas. Hobby Press SA, Los Ciruelos 4, 28700 S. Sebastian Reyes, Madrid Spain. **Tel** 011 34 1 6548199.

                 ISSN 1074-7443
                 US
                 CCC
●**CHINESE JOURNAL OF ADVANCED SOFTWARE RESEARCH.** (1994)-. Periodical. English (translations available in Chinese). Four times a year. $260.00. Allerton Press Inc., 150 Fifth Avenue, New York NY 10011. **Tel** (212)924-3950, FAX (212)463-9684, telex 427441 ALPRES.

                 ISSN 1190-8874
DD 006.6/869   CN
●**CHRIS DICKMAN'S COREL DRAW JOURNAL.** [Chris Dickman's Corel Draw j.]. **Added/Corp** Corel Systems Corporation. **VFOAT** Corel Draw Journal. (1994)-. Periodical. English. Ten times a year. $47.00 (one-year); $87.00 (two-year). Kazak Communications, 16 Ottawa Street, Toronto Ontario M4T 2B6 Canada. **Tel** (416)924-0759. *Continues* Dickman, Chris. Chris Dickman's Mastering Corel Draw, 1192-9006.

                 ISSN 1059-6542
DD 005   US
CLARISWORKS JOURNAL. [ClarisWorks j.]. **Added/Corp** ClarisWorks Users Group. Vol. 1, No. 1 (Feb. 1992)-. Newsletter. English. Ten times a year (Published monthly with June/July, Aug/Sept combined.). $29.00 US; $39.00 Canada and Mexico; $43.00 other (comes with membership). Clarisworks Users Group, Box 701010, Plymouth MI 48170. **Tel** (313)454-1969, FAX (313)454-1965. Index available. cum. index. **Bk Rev**. **Ad Acc**.
  Desc: A newsletter filled with articles that help users get the most from CLARISWORKS. Includes tips, hints, suggestions and ideas that enhance users' personal and professional productivity.

                 ISSN 1068-0675
DD 005   US
●**CLIPPER ADVISOR.** [Clipp. advis.]. Vol. 1, No. 1 (May/June 1993)-. Periodical. English. Six times a year (Jan., Mar., May, July, Sept., Nov.). $39.00 US; $49.00 Canada; $59.00 other. Advisor Publications Group, 4010 Morena Boulevard, Suite 200, San Diego CA 92117. **Tel** (800)336-6060, (619)483-6400, FAX (619)483-9851. **(Subscription address:** Advisor Publications Group, PO Box 17902, San Diego CA 92117. **Tel** (619)483-6400.**)** available on diskette.

                 ISSN 0985-0791
                 FR
UDC 681.3
COLLECTION CXP CATALOGUES DE PROGICIELS. [Collect. CXP cat. progiciels]. **VFOAT** CXP Collection Software Product Catalogues; CXP Collection Software Packages Directories; CXP Catalogues de Progiciels; Collection CXP des Catalogues de Progiciels; Collection CXP-Catalogues de Prologiciels; CXP-Catalogues de Prologicies. (1987)-. Monographic series. Multiple languages. One time a year. $1321.36. CXP Centre d'Experimentation des Produits Logiciels, 19-21 rue de la Rochefoucauld, 75009 Paris France. **Tel** 011 33 1 43879028, FAX 011 33 1 44709110. *Formed by the union of Catalogue des Progiciels pour Micro-Ordinateurs, 0768-942X and Guide Europeen des Progiciels, 0294-0701.*

Computers —Software

LC TK5101.A1 C626
DD 621.382
ISSN 1057-0071
US
CEASED
COMMUNICATION & COMPUTER NEWS. See Communications-Computer Applications.

UK
COMPUTE IT. See Computers-Hardware.

US
TITLE CHANGE
COMPUTER ABSTRACTS ON MICROFICHE. See Computers-Abstracting, Bibliographies and Statistics.

LC QA76.6 .C634
DD 001.64/25/029459
HK
COMPUTER-ASIA SOFTWARE GUIDE. VFOAT C.A. Software Guide; CA Software Guide. (1983)-. English. One time a year. Syme Media Enterprises, 6-12 Wing Kut Street, Central Hong Kong.

LC QA76.7 .C646
DD 005.13/3
ISSN 0749-2839
US
CCC
CODEN COMLEF
TITLE CHANGE
COMPUTER LANGUAGE. See Computers-Programs and Programming.

LC QA76.5 .C61264
DD 004.16/05
ISSN 0748-8610
US
COMPUTER RETAILERS' GUIDE. See Computers-Microcomputers, Personal Computers.

LC QA75.5 QA75.5 .C616
DD 004
ISSN 1062-8509
CODEN COSLEB
COMPUTER SELECT. (COMPUTER SELECT [COMPUTER FILE].). [Comput. sel.]. (Feb. 1991)-. English. Twelve times a year. $1250.00. Computer Library, One Park Avenue, Fifth Floor, New York NY 10016. **Tel** (212)503-4409, FAX (212)503-4414.
Continues Computer Library (New York, N.Y.), 1062-8517 **and** Computer Library (Ziff CD Rom), 1049-7412.

LC QA76.75 .C65
DD 016.00164/25
ISSN 0882-5629
US
COMPUTER SOFTWARE/HARDWARE INDEX. [Comput. softw./hardw. index]. VFOAT Computer Software, Hardware Index. Vol. 1, No. 1 (Jan. 1984)-. Periodical. English. Six times a year. $60.00. Computer Software Hardware, PO Box 7991, Haledon NJ 07503.

LC QA76.753 .C635
DD 005.36/5
US
COMPUTE!'S PC SOFTWARE BUYER'S GUIDE. Added/Corp Compute! Publications, Inc. VFOAT Compute!'s PC Software Buyer's Guide; PC Software Buyer's Guide. (19??)-. English. $3.95. Compute! Publications Inc, PO Box 5406, Greensboro NC 27403. **Tel** (919)275-9809.

DD 005
ISSN 1054-0784
US
TITLE CHANGE
COMPUTHINK WINDOWS WATCHER, THE. [CompuThink windows watch.]. VFOAT Windows Watcher. (Sept. 1990)-(1995). Newsletter. English. Computhink Inc, 15127 Northeast 24th, Suite 344, Redmond WA 98052. **Tel** (206)881-7354, FAX (206)883-1452. **(Subscription address:** Cobb Group, 9420 Bunsen Parkway, Louisville KY 40220. **Tel** (502)491-1900, (800)223-8721.**) ED** Jesse Berst. **Ad Acc. ctrl circ. Continued by** Windows Watcher.
Desc: An independent newsletter that focuses exclusively on news and analysis of Windows markets, trends, and technologies. Our goal is to provide readers with new perspectives about the Windows industry-what's happening, why its happening and what's coming in the future.

DD 005
ISSN 8756-730X
US
CONSUMER SOFTWARE NEWS. [Consum. softw. news]. (1985)-. Periodical. English. Twelve times a year. Consumer Software News, 906 North 101st Street, Seattle WA 98133.

US
TITLE CHANGE
CORELATION MAGAZINE. (19??)-(1995). English. Association of Corel Artists & Designers, 1309 Riverside Drive, Burbank CA 91506. **Tel** (310)452-5637. **Continued by** Power Graphics Report.
Desc: Contains numerous articles and features about CorelDRAW! software. Created to assist all users better understand the product, its uses and techniques.

DD 005
ISSN 1068-8285
US
Pr Rev.
CPA SOFTWARE NEWS, THE. See Business and Economics-Computer Applications.

LC QA76.6 .C72
DD 001.64/2
ISSN 0734-3361
US
CREATIVE COMPUTING SOFTWARE BUYER'S GUIDE. See Computers-Computer Industry and Industry Directories.

DD 001
ISSN 8750-3697
US
CCC
CULPEPPER LETTER, THE. [Culpepper lett.]. **Added/Corp** Culpepper and Associates. No. 21 (Sept./Oct. 1984)-. Periodical. English. Twelve times a year. $295.00. Culpepper & Associates, Inc., 7000 Peachtree Dunwoody Road 10, Atlanta GA 30328. **Tel** (404)668-0616, FAX (404)668-1095. **ED** Mark Pryor. **Circ:** 1,000 (ctrl). **Continues** Salt 'N Pepper, 0738-5757.
Desc: The software executive's guide to sales productivity. Practical advice on software sales and marketing issues. Exclusive survey-based industry data. Software sales trends.

US
DATAPRO COMPUTER SYSTEMS SERIES / SOFTWARE. See Computers-Computer Systems.

UK
DATAPRO CORPORATE SOFTWARE & SOLUTIONS / INTERNATIONAL EDITION. See Business and Economics-Computer Applications.

UK
DATAPRO DESKTOP SOFTWARE & SOLUTIONS / INTERNATIONAL EDITION. (19??)-. English. Twelve times a year. $1,036.00. Datapro International, McGraw Hill House, Shoppenhangers Road, Maidenhead Berkshire SL6 2QL United Kingdom. **Tel** 011 44 1628 773277, FAX 011 44 1628 773628.

ISSN 0730-8779
US
CCC
CODEN DDSODL
DATAPRO DIRECTORY OF SOFTWARE. [Datapro dir. softw.]. **Added/Corp** Datapro Research Corporation. (1975)-. Academic Scholarly Publication. English. Twelve times a year. $949.00. Datapro Information Services Group, 600 Delran Parkway, Delran NJ 08075. **Tel** (609)764-0100, (800)328-2776, FAX (609)764-8953. Each issue contains an index to its own contents (no volume index). -loose. cum. index. Documents available from CASDDS.
Continues Software Catalog. Microcomputers.
Ind/Abst Chem. Abstr. (1989-).

DD 384
ISSN 1082-2828
US
TITLE CHANGE
DATAPRO REPORTS ON INTERNATIONAL COMMUNICATIONS EQUIPMENT. [Datapro rep. int. commun. equip.]. **Added/Corp** Datapro Research Group. Datapro Information Services Group. VFOAT International Communications Equipment. (1989)-(1995). Periodical. English. Datapro Information Services Group, 600 Delran Parkway, Delran NJ 08075. **Tel** (609)764-0100, (800)328-2776, FAX (609)764-8953. **Merged into** Datapro Voice Networking Systems.

UK
TITLE CHANGE
DATAPRO REPORTS ON INTERNATIONAL COMMUNICATIONS SOFTWARE. See Communications-Computer Applications.

US
DATAPRO REPORTS ON UNIX SYSTEMS & SOFTWARE. See Computers-Computer Systems.

LC QA76.75
DD 005
ISSN 1052-195X
US
DATAPRO SOFTWARE FINDER (COMPLETE ED.). (DATAPRO SOFTWARE FINDER [COMPUTER FILE].). [Datapro softw. finder]. **Added/Corp** Datapro Research Group. (Winter 1991)-. English. Four times a year. $1288.53. Datapro Information Services Group, 600 Delran Parkway, Delran NJ 08075. **Tel** (609)764-0100, (800)328-2776, FAX (609)764-8953.
Desc: Reference guide to business and professional software, including product profiles, vendor directory, and glossary of computer-related terms.

DD 005
ISSN 1052-1941
US
DATAPRO SOFTWARE FINDER (MICROCOMPUTER ED.). (DATAPRO SOFTWARE FINDER [COMPUTER FILE].). [Datapro softw. finder]. **Added/Corp** Datapro Research Group. (Winter 1991)-. Periodical. English. Four times a year. $760.31. Datapro Information Services Group, 600 Delran Parkway, Delran NJ 08075. **Tel** (609)764-0100, (800)328-2776, FAX (609)764-8953.

DD 005
ISSN 1052-1968
US
DATAPRO SOFTWARE FINDER (MID-RANGE/MAINFRAME ED.). (DATAPRO SOFTWARE FINDER [COMPUTER FILE].). [Datapro softw. finder]. **Added/Corp** Datapro Research Group. (Winter 1991)-. Periodical. English. Four times a year. $760.31. Datapro Information Services Group, 600 Delran Parkway, Delran NJ 08075. **Tel** (609)764-0100, (800)328-2776, FAX (609)764-8953.
Desc: System requirements: IBM or compatible PC; 640K RAM; 2MB free on hard disk; MS-DOS or PC-DOS 3.1 or higher; monitor (color or monochrome); CD-ROM drive; printer (optional).

US
●**DATAPRO VOICE NETWORKING SYSTEMS.** (1995)-. English. Twelve times a year. $1066.00. Datapro Information Services Group, 600 Delran Parkway, Delran NJ 08075. **Tel** (609)764-0100, (800)328-2776, FAX (609)764-8953. **Absorbed** Datapro Reports on Communications Equipment.

US
DATAPRO WORKGROUP COMPUTING SERIES / DEVELOPMENT TOOLS. (19??)-. English. Irregular. $344.00. Datapro Information Services Group, 600 Delran Parkway, Delran NJ 08075. **Tel** (609)764-0100, (800)328-2776, FAX (609)764-8953.

US
DATAPRO WORKGROUP COMPUTING SERIES / STRATEGIES & LAN SERVICES. (19??)-. English. Twelve times a year. $443.00. Datapro Information Services Group, 600 Delran Parkway, Delran NJ 08075. **Tel** (609)764-0100, (800)328-2776, FAX (609)764-8953.

II
DATAQUEST : DQ. See Computers-Microcomputers, Personal Computers.

DD 005
ISSN 1072-6802
US
●**DBASE ADVISOR.** [dBASE adv.]. VFOAT dBASE Advisor Magazine. Vol. 1, No. 1 (Sept./Oct. 1994)-. Periodical. English. Six times a year. $60.00. Data Based Solutions Inc, 4010 Morena Boulevard, Suite 200, San Diego CA 92117. **Tel** (619)483-6400, (800)336-6060, FAX (619)483-9851. **(Subscription address:** Dbase Advisor, PO Box 469025, Escondido CA 92046. **)**

IT
DEC DIRECT SOFTWARE. Italian. Three times a year. Free. Digital Equipment, V Pacinotti 22, 16151 Geneva Italy. **Tel** 011 39 167802075.

ISSN 1074-8911
US
●**DIGITAL UNIX NEWS.** (1994)-. Periodical. English. Four times a year. Free. Publications & Communications, 12416 Hymeadow Drive, Austin TX 78750. **Tel** (512)250-9023, (800)678-9724, FAX (512)331-3900, telex 384303. available via Internet (email unix-news@pa.dec.com subject: help).
Desc: Targeted at users of UNIX products, services, and third party applications.

LC HD9696.C63 U515948
DD 381/.45004/02573
ISSN 1066-9698
US
DIRECTORY OF COMPUTER & SOFTWARE RETAILERS (TAMPA, FLA.). See Computers-Computer Industry and Industry Directories.

LC QA76.6
DD 001.642
US
DIRECTORY OF COMPUTER SOFTWARE APPLICATIONS. ATMOSPHERIC SCIENCES, A. See Science and Technology-Computer Applications.

LC HD9502
DD 333.79
US
DIRECTORY OF COMPUTER SOFTWARE APPLICATIONS. ENERGY, A. **Added/Corp** United States. National Technical Information Service. VFOAT Energy. (1977)-. Directory. English. National Technical Information Service - NTIS, Room 2027S, 5285 Port Royal Road, Springfield VA 22161. **Tel** (703)487-4630, (703)487-4660, (703)487-4650, FAX (703)321-8547, telex 89-9405.

LC Q
DD 500
US
DIRECTORY OF COMPUTER SOFTWARE APPLICATIONS. ENVIRONMENTAL POLLUTION & CONTROL, A. See Environmental Issues-Computer Applications.

Computers — Software

LC TA
DD 620 US
DIRECTORY OF COMPUTER SOFTWARE APPLICATIONS. MARINE ENGINEERING, A. See Engineering-Computer Applications.

LC HE9661
DD 387.7 US
DIRECTORY OF COMPUTER SOFTWARE APPLICATIONS. TRANSPORTATION, A. Added/Corp National Technical Information Service (U.S.). **VFOAT** Transportation. (197?)-. Directory. English. One time a year. $59.00 North America; $75.00 other. National Technical Information Service - NTIS, Room 2027S, 5285 Port Royal Road, Springfield VA 22161. **Tel** (703)487-4630, (703)487-4660, (703)487-4650, FAX (703)321-8547, telex 89-9405.

US
NLM WY 18; D598
DIRECTORY OF EDUCATIONAL SOFTWARE FOR NURSING. See Medical Sciences-Nursing.

LC SD381.5 .D57 **ISSN** 1053-8453
DD 634.9/0285/5369 US
DIRECTORY OF FORESTRY AND NATURAL RESOURCES COMPUTER SOFTWARE. See Forests and Forestry.

LC Z678.9.A3 D6 **ISSN** 1071-264X
DD 025.3/44/025 US
●**DIRECTORY OF LIBRARY AUTOMATION SOFTWARE, SYSTEMS, AND SERVICES.** See Library and Information Sciences-Computer Applications.

LC TS2301.A7 D57
DD 688 US
CEASED
DIRECTORY OF MULTIMEDIA EQUIPMENT, SOFTWARE, AND SERVICES. See Communications-Telecommunication.

LC QA76.6 .D574 **ISSN** 1063-9748
DD 001.64/25/029473 US
DIRECTORY OF U.S. GOVERNMENT SOFTWARE FOR MAINFRAMES AND MICROCOMPUTERS. [Dir. U.S. gov. softw. mainframes microcomput.]. **Added/Corp** Federal Computer Products Center (U.S.) United States. National Technical Information Service. **VFOAT** U.S. Government Software for Mainframes and Microcomputers; Directory of United States Government Software for Mainframes and Microcomputers; United States Government Software for Mainframes and Microcomputers; Directory of US Government Software for Mainframes and Microcomputers; US Government Software for Mainframes and Microcomputers; Directory of U.S. Government Software. (1992)-. Directory. English. One time a year. $75.00. National Technical Information Service - NTIS, Room 2027S, 5285 Port Royal Road, Springfield VA 22161. **Tel** (703)487-4630, (703)487-4660, (703)487-4650, FAX (703)321-8547, telex 89-9405. **Continues** Directory of Computer Software, 0748-1543.

ISSN 0899-4838
DD 005 US
DISKWORLD FOR THE MACINTOSH. (DISKWORLD FOR THE MACINTOSH [COMPUTER FILE].). [Diskworld Macintosh]. No. 1- (1988)-. Periodical. English. Twelve times a year. $89.95. Loadstar Inc., PO Box 30007, Shreveport LA 71130. **Tel** (318)221-8718.

ISSN 1080-398X
US
●**DO IT WITH MICROSOFT OFFICE FOR WINDOWS. VFOAT** Do it with Microsoft Office. (1995)-. Periodical. English. Twelve times a year. $59.00. IDG Newsletter Corporation, 77 Franklin Street, Suite 310, Boston MA 02110. **Tel** (617)482-8470, (800)807-0771, FAX (617)338-0164.

ISSN 1080-3998
US
CEASED
DO IT WITH VISIO FOR WINDOWS. VFOAT Do it with Visio. (1995)-(Apr. 1995). Periodical. English. IDG Newsletter Corporation, 77 Franklin Street, Suite 310, Boston MA 02110. **Tel** (617)482-8470, (800)807-0771, FAX (617)338-0164.

ISSN 1055-0569
DD 005 US
CEASED
DOS AUTHORITY, THE. (THE DOS AUTHORITY : TIPS & TECHNIQUES FOR MS-DOS & PC-DOS.). [DOS auth.]. Vol. 1, No. 1 (Mar. 1991)-(Dec. 1995). Periodical. English. Cobb Group, 9420 Bunsen Parkway #300, Louisville KY 40220. **Tel** (502)491-1900, (800)223-8720, FAX (502)491-4200. **Desc:** Covers information on PC DOS and MS-DOS.

ISSN 1056-7364
DD 005 US
TITLE CHANGE
DOS RESOURCE GUIDE. [DOS resour. guide]. No. 1 (1991)-(1994). Periodical. English. IDG Communications / New Hampshire, 86 Elm Street, Peterborough NH 03458. **Tel** (800)349-7327, FAX (603)924-6972. (**Subscription address:** Kable Publishers Aide / Illinois, 308 East Hitt Street, Subscription Department, Mt. Morris IL 61054-1473. **Tel** (815)734-1261.) **ED** Michael J. Comendul. **Continued by** DOS World, 1078-876X.
Desc: Devoted to MS-DOS; includes tricks, tips, hints, and useful programs.

ISSN 1065-0776
DD 005 US
DOS SOFTWARE CONNECTION. (DOS SOFTWARE CONNECTION [COMPUTER FILE].). [DOS softw. connect.]. **Added/Corp** Cobb Group. (Aug. 1992)-. English. Twelve times a year. $59.00. Cobb Group, 9420 Bunsen Parkway #300, Louisville KY 40220. **Tel** (502)491-1900, (800)223-8720, FAX (502)491-4200.

ISSN 1078-876X
US
●**DOS WORLD.** (1994)-. Periodical. English. Six times a year. $23.70. IDG Communications / New Hampshire, 86 Elm Street, Peterborough NH 03458. **Tel** (800)349-7327, FAX (603)924-6972. (**Subscription address:** Kable Publishers Aide / Ohio, PO Box 1958, Marion OH 43305.) **Continues** DOS Resource Guide, 1056-7364.

ISSN 0885-0305
DD 004 US
EASY COMPUTING. (EASY COMPUTING [COMPUTER FILE].). [Easy comput.]. (198?)-. Periodical. English. Six times a year. $39.95. D M Software Publishers, 1510 South 97th Street, Tacoma WA 98444.
Desc: System requirements: IBM PC and compatibles; 256K; color monitor.

ISSN 1082-4359
US
●**EASY ECCO.** (1995)-. Periodical. English. Twelve times a year. $49.95. Learning Associates Inc., PO Box 78, Dickeyville WI 53808. **Tel** (800)980-0052.

LC QA76.753 .E385 **ISSN** 0892-2527
DD 370/.285/536 US
EDUCATIONAL SOFTWARE PC COMPATIBILITY GUIDE, THE. See Education-Computer Applications.

LC HD9696.C6 E54 **ISSN** 1069-0557
DD 621.3/0285 US
●**EL&P U.S. ELECTRIC UTILITY INDUSTRY SOFTWARE DIRECTORY.** See Energy-Electric Power.

ISSN 1382-3256
DD 005.3 NE
●**EMPIRICAL SOFTWARE ENGINEERING.** (1996)-. Academic Scholarly Publication. English. Three times a year. $295.99. Kluwer Academic Publishers, Postbus 322, 3300 AH Dordrecht The Netherlands. **Tel** 011 31 78 524400, FAX 011 31 78 183273, telex 20083. (**Subscription address:** Kluwer Academic Publishers / Netherlands, PO Box 322, 3300 AH Dordrecht Netherlands. **Tel** 011 31 78 392392, FAX 011 31 78 546474.)

ISSN 0892-5496
DD 652 US
Pr Rev.
ENABLE EXCHANGE NEWSLETTER. (198?)-. Newsletter. English. Twelve times a year. $39.00 US and Canada; $44.00 (includes postage) other. Key Publications, 3221 Ruckriegel Parkway, Louisville KY 40299. **Tel** (502)267-9557, FAX (502)267-1722. **ED** Yvonne Johnson. **Circ:** 1,000.
Desc: Articles covering Enable (a PC program written by The Software Group).

US
●**ENABLE SUBSCRIPTION PLAN.** English. Four times a year. $95.00 (The customers must have Enable Software Package). Enable Software Inc., 313 Ushers Road, Northway Ten Executive Park, Ballston Lake NY 12019-1591. **Tel** (800)766-7079 or (518)877-8600.
Desc: Up-to-date on current inside information for various Enable products.

ISSN 1065-6952
DD 004 US
ENGINEERING AUTOMATION REPORT. See Engineering-Computer Applications.

LC TD169 .E647 **ISSN** 0266-9838
DD 363.7/0028/5 UK
CCC
CODEN ENSOEZ
Pr Rev.
ENVIRONMENTAL SOFTWARE. See Environmental Issues-Computer Applications.

LC TD173.5 .E59 **ISSN** 1043-9056
DD 628/.0285/536 US
ENVIRONMENTAL SOFTWARE DIRECTORY. See Environmental Issues-Computer Applications.

ISSN 1043-2884
DD 005 US
ENVIRONMENTAL SOFTWARE REPORT. See Environmental Issues-Computer Applications.

LC LB1043 .E654 **ISSN** 1046-1493
DD 371 US
TITLE CHANGE
EPIEGRAM (1988). See Education-Computer Applications.

ISSN 0886-9812
US
CEASED
EXCELLENCE (LOUISVILLE, KY.). (EXCELLENCE.). **Added/Corp** Cobb Group. Vol. 1, No. 1 (Jan. 1986)-(Dec. 1994). Periodical. English. Cobb Group, 9420 Bunsen Parkway #300, Louisville KY 40220. **Tel** (502)491-1900, (800)223-8720, FAX (502)491-4200. **Desc:** Independent journal exclusively for Microsoft Excel users. Timesaving tips, Excel applications, sample macros, feature articles, reviews of Excel-related products and much more.

ISSN 0268-6872
UK
CODEN EXEEE5
Pr Rev.
EXE. See Computers-Computer Engineering.

ISSN 1053-1599
DD 658 US
EXECUTIVE BRIEFING, CASE. [Exec. brief. CASE]. **VAT** Executive Briefing, Computer-Aided Software Engineering. (Jan./Feb. 1991)-. Periodical. English. Six times a year. $125.00. Executive Briefing, Case, 3150 SE 22nd Avenue, Portland OR 97202.

LC QA **ISSN** 1084-1962
DD 005.3 US
●**EXPLORING ORACLE DEVELOPER/2000, DESIGNER/2000. Added/Corp** Cobb Group. **VFOAT** Exploring Oracle Developer 2000, Designer 2000. (1995)-. Periodical. English. Twelve times a year. $129.00. Cobb Group, 9420 Bunsen Parkway #300, Louisville KY 40220. **Tel** (502)491-1900, (800)223-8720, FAX (502)491-4200.

ISSN 1070-8383
US
●**EXPLORING WINDOWS NT. Added/Corp** Cobb Group. (1993)-. Periodical. English. Twelve times a year. $119.00. Cobb Group, 9420 Bunsen Parkway #300, Louisville KY 40220. **Tel** (502)491-1900, (800)223-8720, FAX (502)491-4200.

US
FAULKNER APPLICATIONS SOFTWARE REPORTS. (19??)-. Periodical. English. Irregular. $670.00 US; $790.00 other. Faulkner Technical Reports, 7905 Browning Road, Suite 114, Pennsauken NJ 08109. **Tel** (800)843-0460.

US
FAULKNER MICROCOMPUTER AND SOFTWARE. See Computers-Microcomputers, Personal Computers.

US
FAULKNER SOFTWARE REPORTS. (19??)-. Periodical. English. Twelve times a year. $1035.00 US; $1175.00 Canada; $1275.00 other. Faulkner Technical Reports, 7905 Browning Road, Suite 114, Pennsauken NJ 08109. **Tel** (800)843-0460.

US
FAULKNER SYSTEMS SOFTWARE REPORTS. See Computers-Computer Systems.

ISSN 1077-0291
DD 005 US
CEASED
FBC (MADISON, ALA.). See Computers-Computer Graphics and Design.

LC K
DD 340 US
FEDERAL TAXATION OF COMPUTER SOFTWARE. (1993)-. Periodical. English. Irregular. $125.00. Kutish Publications, PO Box 181916, Coronado CA 92178-1916. **Tel** (619)552-0523, FAX (619)522-0525.

Computers —Software

Desc: A guide to structuring your software transactions. This publication deals with the confusing, detailed issues that surround federal software taxation: the buying and selling of software, employmnet software employment issues affecting the ownership of employee-generated material, and much more.

LC QA76.9.D3 F54   ISSN 0896-0313
DD 005   US
FILEMAKER REPORT, THE. [FileMak. rep.]. **VFOAT** Filemaker + Report; Filemaker Plus Report; +Filemaker+ Report. (Jan. 1987?)-. Periodical. English. Ten times a year. $49.00. WaterTechnics, PO Box 2307, Santa Cruz CA 95063-2307. **Tel** (408)761-3987, FAX (408)761-5468.

    ISSN 1064-6027
DD 005   US
    TITLE CHANGE
FLASHY BUT CHEAP. See Computers-Computer Graphics and Design.

LC QA76.9.S88 F675   ISSN 0925-9856
DD 004.2/1   US
    CCC
    CODEN FMSDE6
Pr Rev.
FORMAL METHODS IN SYSTEM DESIGN. See Computers-Computer Systems.

LC QA76.73.F24 F46   ISSN 0884-0822
DD 001   US
    CODEN FODMD5
FORTH DIMENSIONS. [Forth dimens.]. **Added/Corp** Forth Interest Group (Calif.). Vol. 1 (June/July 1978)-. Trade Publication. English. Six times a year. Free to members; $40.00 (membership). FORTH Interest Group, PO Box 2154, Oakland CA 94621. **Tel** (408)277-0668.
Ind/Abst Curr. Cit.

    ISSN 1066-7261
DD 005   US
●**FOXPRO ADVISOR.** [FoxPro advis.]. **Added/Corp** Advisor Communications International, Inc. Vol. 1, No. 1 (1993)-. Periodical. English. Twelve times a year. $49.00. Advisor Publications Group, 4010 Morena Boulevard, Suite 200, San Diego CA 92117. **Tel** (800)336-6060, (619)483-6400, FAX (619)483-9851. (**Subscription address:** Advisor Publications Group, PO Box 17902, San Diego CA 92117. **Tel** (619)483-6400.) available on diskette.

    ISSN 1070-0315
DD 005   US
    CEASED
FOXPRO DEVELOPER'S JOURNAL. [FoxPro dev. j.]. **Added/Corp** Cobb Group. Vol. 1, No. 1 (July 1993)-(Dec. 1995). Periodical. English. Cobb Group, 9420 Bunsen Parkway #300, Louisville KY 40220. **Tel** (502)491-1900, (800)223-8720, FAX (502)491-4200.

    US
FRAMEFOCUS. English. Four times a year. Frame Technology Corporation, Editor FrameFocus, 1010 Rincon Circle, San Jose CA 95131. **Tel** (408)433-3311.
Desc: Newsletter providing information on Frame products and services.

    US
FULL PAGES IMAGES. (19??)-. English. Irregular. $506.00 (one disc) US and Canada; $519.00 (one disc) other. Artbeats, PO Box 20083, San Bernardino CA 92404. **Tel** (714)881-1200. (**Subscription address:** Artbeats, 2611 South Myrtle Road, Myrtle Creek OR 97457. **Tel** (503)863-4429.) **Circ:** 1,000.
Desc: Includes Adobe illustrator files, a section of business card templates, and a large collection of examples showing how the images are used.

    ISSN 1166-4738
    FR
    CODEN GLSEED
Pr Rev.
GENIE LOGICIEL & SYSTEMES EXPERTS. [Genie logiciel syst. experts]. **VFOAT** Genie Logiciel et Systemes Experts; Genie Logiciel. (198?)-. Trade Publication. French. Four times a year. $244.92. EC2 / Editions Colloques et Conseil, 269 rue de la Garenne, 92024 Nanterre Cedex France. **Tel** 011 33 1 47807000, FAX 011 33 1 47806629. Index available. cum. index. **Bk Rev**. **Ad Acc. Circ:** 1,500. Documents available from Ask*IEEE. **Continues** Genie Logiciel, 0295-6322.
Desc: Entirely dedicated to software engineering.
Ind/Abst Curr. Cit.; INSPEC (March 1987-).

    NE
GEOSCIENCE SOFTWARE DIRECTORY FOR THE IBM PC & COMPATIBLES. See Earth Sciences-Computer Applications.

LC QA76.5 .G845   ISSN 0294-0701
DD 001.6/4/0294   FR
GUIDE EUROPEEN DES PROGICIELS. EDITION COMPLEMENTAIRE / CXP.
1983-. French. One time a year.

    US
GUIDE TO REAL ESTATE AND MORTGAGE BANKING SOFTWARE. See Business and Economics-Computer Applications.

LC QA76.6 .G825   ISSN 0740-8374
DD 001.64/2/029473   US
    CCC
    TITLE CHANGE
GUIDE TO SOFTWARE PRODUCTIVITY AIDS. See Computers-Computer Industry and Industry Directories.

LC QA76.76.A65 H36   ISSN 1056-0998
DD 005.1/068   US
HANDBOOK OF SYSTEMS MANAGEMENT, DEVELOPMENT AND SUPPORT. YEARBOOK. [Handb. syst. manage. dev. support, Yearb.]. **VFOAT** Systems Management Development and Support. (1991)-. Trade Publication. English. One time a year. $185.95. Auerbach Publishers Inc., Park Square Building, 31 St. James Avenue, Boston MA 02116. **Tel** (800)950-1207.

    NE
HARD EN SOFTWARETUNING VOOR IBM PCS EN COMPATIBLES. (19??)-. Periodical. Dutch. Irregular. Fl68.00 (includes binder). Weka Uitgeverij BV, Postbus 61196, 1005 HD Amsterdam Netherlands. **Tel** 011 31 20 6867131. **ED** F. Spiekerman.
Desc: Software for personal computers.

LC QA76.76.R44 H55   ISSN 0967-2648
DD 005.1   UK
    CCC
●**HIGH INTEGRITY SYSTEMS.** Vol. 1, No. 1 (1994)-. Periodical. English. Six times a year. $239.57. Oxford University Press / UK, Walton Street, Oxford OX2 6DP United Kingdom. **Tel** 011 44 1865 56767, FAX 011 44 1865 267773, telex 851/837330 OXPRES G.

    ISSN 8750-4928
DD 658   US
HOME COMPUTER & SOFTWARE MERCHANDISING. See Business and Economics-Computer Applications.

LC QA76.75 .H97   ISSN 1045-4624
DD 005.26/05   US
HYPERLINK MAGAZINE. [HyperLink mag.]. **VFOAT** HyperLink. Vol. 1, No. 1 (April/May 1988)-. Periodical. English. Six times a year. $25.00, $73.00 (includes diskette) US; $40.00, $94.00 (includes diskette) Canada and Mexico; $61.00, $127.00 (includes diskette) other. Publishers Guild Inc, Box 7723, Eugene OR 97401. **Tel** (503)484-5157. **ED** Roger Wood. Index available. **Bk Rev. Ad Acc. Circ:** 10,000. available on diskette.
Desc: A journal of graphical user interfaces on personal computers in particular: Hypercard, Supercard, Plus (trademark), Wingz (trademark), and Orache.

    UK
IASB : INTERNATIONAL ACCOUNTANCY SOFTWARE BULLETIN. See Business and Economics-Computer Applications.

    ISSN 0747-2102
    US
ICP ADMINISTRATIVE & ACCOUNTING SOFTWARE. See Business and Economics-Computer Applications.

    US
ICP REFERENCE SERIES SOFTWARE DIRECTORY. **Main/Corp** International Computer Programs, Inc. **VFOAT** ICP Software Directory. Directory. English. Two times a year. International Computer Programs Inc / Barbara Lahiff, 823 East Westfield Boulevard, Indianapolis IN 46220. **Tel** (800)428-6179, (317)251-7727.

LC HG1709 .I57A   ISSN 0094-8020
DD 332.1/028/54   US
ICP SOFTWARE GUIDE : BANKING. See Business and Economics-Computer Applications.

LC QA76.6 .I16   ISSN 0734-466X
DD 001.64/25/05   US
    CODEN ISJODY
ICP SOFTWARE JOURNAL. [ICP softw. j.]. **VFOAT** I.C.P. Software Journal; Software Journal; ICP Journal. **VAT** International Computer Programs Software Journal. Vol. 3, No. 1 (Spring 1982)-. Periodical. English. Four times a year. $10.00 for residents of the UK, or employees of this publication. International Computer Programs Inc / Barbara Lahiff, 823 East Westfield Boulevard, Indianapolis IN 46220. **Tel** (800)428-6179,
(317)251-7727. Documents available from Ask*IEEE. **Continues** ICP Journal of Software Products and Services, 0734-4678.
Ind/Abst INSPEC (Spring 1982-).

    ISSN 1081-7913
DD 005   US
●**IDG'S WINDOWS 95 JOURNAL.** [IDG's Windows 95 j.]. **VFOAT** Windows 95 Journal. Vol. 1, No. 1 (May 1995)-. Periodical. English. Twelve times a year. $79.00. IDG Newsletter Corporation, 77 Franklin Street, Suite 310, Boston MA 02110. **Tel** (617)482-8470, (800)807-0771, FAX (617)338-0164.

LC QA76.75 .I35   ISSN 0740-7459
DD 005.3/05   US
    CCC
Pr Rev.
IEEE SOFTWARE. [IEEE softw.]. **Added/Corp** IEEE Computer Society. **VFOAT** Software. Vol. 1, No. 1 (Jan. 1984)-. Periodical. English. Six times a year. $275.00. IEEE / Institute of Electrical and Electronics Engineers Inc., 345 East 47th Street, New York NY 10017-2394. **Tel** (908)981-1393, FAX (908)981-9667. (**Subscription address:** IEEE / Institute of Electrical and Electronics Engineers, 445 Hoes Lane, PO Box 1331, Piscataway NJ 08855-1331. **Tel** (800)701-IEEE, (908)981-0060, FAX (908)981-9667, telex 833233.) **ED** Bruce D. Shriver. Index available. **Bk Rev**. **Ad Acc.** available on microfiche. Documents available from Article Express International, The Genuine Article, Ask*IEEE.
Desc: Written for systems analysts, software architects, database designers and managers, programmers, data processing managers, and software engineers and scientists.
Ind/Abst Abstr. Hum. Comput. Interact.; Appl. Sci. Technol. Index (1991-); CompuMath Cit. Index [Full Cov.]; Comput. Inf. Syst. Abstr. J. [Full Cov.]; Comput. Bus.; Comput. Database; Comput. Lit. Index; Curr. Cit.; Curr. Contents Eng. Comput. Technol.; Data Process. Dig.; Ei Page One; Eng. Index Annu.; Expand. Acad. Index (1992-); HILITES; Index IEEE Publ.; Inf. Sci. Abstr.; INSPEC Jan. 1984-); Oper. Res./Manage. Sci.; Pollut. Abstr. Indexes; Res. Alert [Full Cov.]; SCISEARCH; Soc. Sci. Cit. Index [Select. Cov.].

LC QA76.6 .I17   ISSN 0098-5589
DD 001.6/425/05   US
    CCC
    CODEN IESEDJ
Pr Rev.
IEEE TRANSACTIONS ON SOFTWARE ENGINEERING. See Computers-Computer Engineering.

LC HF5548.2 .D3   ISSN 0950-5849
DD 004/.05   UK
    CCC
    CODEN ISOTE7
Pr Rev.
INFORMATION AND SOFTWARE TECHNOLOGY. See Computers-Electronic Data Processing.

    US
INFOROM. (19??)-. Directory. English. Four times a year. $296.00. International Computer Programs Inc / Barbara Lahiff, 823 East Westfield Boulevard, Indianapolis IN 46220. **Tel** (800)428-6179, (317)251-7727.

    ISSN 1052-2662
DD 005   US
    CEASED
INSIDE 1-2-3 RELEASE 3. [Inside 1-2-3 release 3]. **Added/Corp** Cobb Group. **VFOAT** Inside One-Two-Three Release Three; Inside 1 2 3 Release 3. Vol. 1, No. 1 (Oct. 1990)-Vol. 5, No. 3. Periodical. English. Cobb Group, 9420 Bunsen Parkway #300, Louisville KY 40220. **Tel** (502)491-1900, (800)223-8720, FAX (502)491-4200.

LC QA76.9.D3 I5457   ISSN 1061-3293
DD 005.75/65   US
    CEASED
INSIDE DBASE. See Computers-Data Base Management.

    ISSN 1049-5320
DD 005   US
INSIDE DOS. (INSIDE MS-DOS : TIPS & TECHNIQUES FOR MS-DOS AND PC-DOS.). [Inside DOS]. **Added/Corp** Cobb Group. Vol. 1, No. 1 (May 1990)-. Periodical. English. Twelve times a year. $49.00. Cobb Group, 9420 Bunsen Parkway #300, Louisville KY 40220. **Tel** (502)491-1900, (800)223-8720, FAX (502)491-4200.

    ISSN 1068-6908
DD 005   US
●**INSIDE FILEMAKER PRO.** [Inside FileMaker Pro]. **Added/Corp** Cobb Group. **VFOAT** Inside File Maker Pro. Vol. 1, No. 1 (May 1993)-. Periodical. English. Twelve times a year. $59.00. Cobb Group, 9420 Bunsen Parkway #300, Louisville KY 40220. **Tel** (502)491-1900, (800)223-8720, FAX (502)491-4200.

Computers —Software

INSIDE HYPERCARD. [Inside HyperCard]. **Added/Corp** Cobb Group. **VFOAT** Inside Hyper Card. Vol. 1, No. 1 (Mar. 1991)-(Apr. 1995). Periodical. English. Cobb Group, 9420 Bunsen Parkway #300, Louisville KY 40220. **Tel** (502)491-1900, (800)223-8720, FAX (502)491-4200.
Desc: Covers Claris Hypercard - Macintosh.
LC QA76.8.M3 I57 ISSN 1052-9470
DD 005 US
CEASED

INSIDE INFORMATION (WHITCHURCH). (INSIDE INFORMATION.). [Inside inf. Whitchurch]. (1989)-. Directory. English. Six times a year. $325.13. Codehigh Limited, Sedgewell House, Sedgewell Road, Reading Berkshire RG4 9TA United Kingdom. **Tel** 011 44 1734 724905, FAX 011 44 1734 723353. **ED** Michael S. Harper. Index available. cum. index. **Ad Acc.**
Desc: Product directory of all the PC software and hardware available in the United Kingdom.
LC QA ISSN 0958-1790
DD 005.3 UK

●**INSIDE MICROSOFT ACCESS.** [Inside Microsoft Access]. **Added/Corp** Cobb Group. Vol. 1, No. 1 (Feb./Mar. 1993)-. Periodical. English. Twelve times a year. $69.00. Cobb Group, 9420 Bunsen Parkway #300, Louisville KY 40220. **Tel** (502)491-1900, (800)223-8720, FAX (502)491-4200.
DD 005 ISSN 1067-8204
US

INSIDE MICROSOFT BASIC. [Inside microsoft BASIC]. **Added/Corp** Cobb Group. Vol. 1, No. 1 (Mar. 1990)-(April/May 1994). Periodical. English. Cobb Group, 9420 Bunsen Parkway #300, Louisville KY 40220. **Tel** (502)491-1900, (800)223-8720, FAX (502)491-4200. **Continues** Inside Quickbasic.
DD 005 ISSN 1047-6067
US
CEASED

INSIDE MICROSOFT C. [Inside microsoft C]. **Added/Corp** Cobb Group. Vol. 1, No. 1 (Mar. 1990)-(1993). Periodical. English. Cobb Group, 9420 Bunsen Parkway #300, Louisville KY 40220. **Tel** (502)491-1900, (800)223-8720, FAX (502)491-4200. **Continued by** Microsoft C/C++ Developer's Journal, 1068-5669.
DD 005 ISSN 1047-6075
US
CODEN IMICEK
TITLE CHANGE

●**INSIDE MICROSOFT EXCEL. Added/Corp** Cobb Group. (1994)-. Periodical. English. Twelve times a year. $59.00. Cobb Group, 9420 Bunsen Parkway #300, Louisville KY 40220. **Tel** (502)491-1900, (800)223-8720, FAX (502)491-4200.
DD 005 ISSN 1075-1580
US

●**INSIDE MICROSOFT OFFICE. Added/Corp** Cobb Group. (1995)-. Periodical. English. Twelve times a year. $69.00. Cobb Group, 9420 Bunsen Parkway #300, Louisville KY 40220. **Tel** (502)491-1900, (800)223-8720, FAX (502)491-4200.
DD 005 ISSN 1081-3667
US

●**INSIDE MICROSOFT PROJECT.** [Inside Microsoft proj.]. **Added/Corp** Cobb Group. Vol. 2, No. 1 (Sept./Oct. 1994)-. Periodical. English. Six times a year. $49.00. Cobb Group, 9420 Bunsen Parkway #300, Louisville KY 40220. **Tel** (502)491-1900, (800)223-8720, FAX (502)491-4200. **Continues** Project Views.
DD 658 ISSN 1077-8985
US

●**INSIDE MICROSOFT VISUAL C++. Added/Corp** Cobb Group. (1995)-. Periodical. English. Twelve times a year. $69.00. Cobb Group, 9420 Bunsen Parkway #300, Louisville KY 40220. **Tel** (502)491-1900, (800)223-8720, FAX (502)491-4200. **Continues** Inside Microsoft C/C++ Developer's Journal, 1068-5669.
DD 005 ISSN 1081-4450
US

INSIDE MICROSOFT WINDOWS. Added/Corp Cobb Group. Vol. 1, No. 1 (Sept. 1990)-. Periodical. English. Twelve times a year. $49.00. Cobb Group, 9420 Bunsen Parkway #300, Louisville KY 40220. **Tel** (502)491-1900, (800)223-8720, FAX (502)491-4200.
DD 005 ISSN 1051-9734
US

●**INSIDE MICROSOFT WINDOWS 95. Added/Corp** Cobb Group. (1995)-. Periodical. English. Twelve times a year. $49.00. Cobb Group, 9420 Bunsen Parkway #300, Louisville KY 40220. **Tel** (502)491-1900, (800)223-8720, FAX (502)491-4200.
ISSN 1082-1988
US

●**INSIDE MICROSOFT WINDOWS (NETWORKING ED.).** (INSIDE MICROSOFT WINDOWS.). **Added/Corp** Cobb Group. (1994)-. Periodical. English. Twelve times a year. Cobb Group, 9420 Bunsen Parkway #300, Louisville KY 40220. **Tel** (502)491-1900, (800)223-8720, FAX (502)491-4200.
ISSN 1074-7265
US

ISSN 1079-9451
CEASED

INSIDE MICROSOFT WORD 6/MAC. Added/Corp Cobb Group. **VFOAT** Inside Microsoft Word 6 MAC; Inside Microsoft Word Six MAC. (1995)-(Oct. 1995). Periodical. English. Cobb Group, 9420 Bunsen Parkway #300, Louisville KY 40220. **Tel** (502)491-1900, (800)223-8720, FAX (502)491-4200.
ISSN 1046-9648
US

INSIDE MICROSOFT WORKS. [Inside Microsoft Works]. **Added/Corp** Cobb Group. Vol. 1, No. 1 (Dec. 1989)-. Periodical. English. Twelve times a year. $49.00. Cobb Group, 9420 Bunsen Parkway #300, Louisville KY 40220. **Tel** (502)491-1900, (800)223-8720, FAX (502)491-4200.
DD 004 ISSN 1061-7647
US

INSIDE NETWARE. [Inside NetWare]. **Added/Corp** Cobb Group. Vol. 1, No. 1 (Apr. 1992)-. Periodical. English. Twelve times a year. $99.00. Cobb Group, 9420 Bunsen Parkway #300, Louisville KY 40220. **Tel** (502)491-1900, (800)223-8720, FAX (502)491-4200. Absorbed Netware Advisor.

INSIDE OS/2. [Inside OS/2]. **Added/Corp** Cobb Group. **VFOAT** Inside OS 2; Inside OS Two; Inside OS2. Vol. 1, No. 1 (July 1992)-. Periodical. English. Twelve times a year. $49.00. Cobb Group, 9420 Bunsen Parkway #300, Louisville KY 40220. **Tel** (502)491-1900, (800)223-8720, FAX (502)491-4200.
LC QA76.76.O63 I548 ISSN 1063-3146
DD 005.4/469 US

●**INSIDE PAGEMAKER. Added/Corp** Cobb Group. (1995)-. Periodical. English. Twelve times a year. $59.00 (US); $79.00 (other). Cobb Group, 9420 Bunsen Parkway #300, Louisville KY 40220. **Tel** (502)491-1900, (800)223-8720, FAX (502)491-4200.
LC QA ISSN 1083-1754
DD 005.3 US

INSIDE PARADOX FOR DOS. [Inside Paradox DOS]. (Feb. 1995)-(Oct. 1995). Periodical. English. Cobb Group, 9420 Bunsen Parkway #300, Louisville KY 40220. **Tel** (502)491-1900, (800)223-8720, FAX (502)491-4200. **Continues** Paradox User's Journal, 0889-2911.
ISSN 1082-166X
US
CEASED

●**INSIDE PARADOX FOR WINDOWS.** [Inside Paradox Windows]. **Added/Corp** Cobb Group. Vol. 1, No. 1 (May 1993)-. Periodical. English. Twelve times a year. $79.00. Cobb Group, 9420 Bunsen Parkway #300, Louisville KY 40220. **Tel** (502)491-1900, (800)223-8720, FAX (502)491-4200.
DD 005 ISSN 1069-0956
US

INSIDE PC TOOLS. [Inside PC tools]. **Added/Corp** Cobb Group. Vol. 1, No. 1 (Apr. 1992)-(Dec. 1993). Periodical. English. Cobb Group, 9420 Bunsen Parkway #300, Louisville KY 40220. **Tel** (502)491-1900, (800)223-8720, FAX (502)491-4200.
DD 004 ISSN 1061-5865
US
CEASED

INSIDE QUATTRO PRO. (INSIDE QUATTRO PRO / COBB.). [Inside Quattro Pro]. **Added/Corp** Cobb Group. (Jan. 1991)-(1995). Periodical. English. Cobb Group, 9420 Bunsen Parkway #300, Louisville KY 40220. **Tel** (502)491-1900, (800)223-8720, FAX (502)491-4200. **Continues** For Quattro, 0895-5603.
DD 005 ISSN 1053-1467
US
CEASED

●**INSIDE QUATTRO PRO FOR WINDOWS.** [Inside Quattro Pro Windows]. **Added/Corp** Cobb Group. Vol. 1, No. 1 (Jan. 1993)-. Periodical. English. Twelve times a year. $59.00. Cobb Group, 9420 Bunsen Parkway #300, Louisville KY 40220. **Tel** (502)491-1900, (800)223-8720, FAX (502)491-4200.
DD 004 ISSN 1066-5218
US

●**INSIDE SCO UNIX SYSTEMS. See** Computers-Computer Industry and Industry Directories.
ISSN 1077-548X
US

INSIDE TURBO C++. [Inside Turbo C++]. **Added/Corp** Cobb Group. **VFOAT** Inside Turbo C Plus Plus. Vol. 1, No. 1 (Mar. 1991)-(1993). Periodical. English. Cobb Group, 9420 Bunsen Parkway #300, Louisville KY 40220. **Tel** (502)491-1900, (800)223-8720, FAX (502)491-4200. **Continued by** Borland C++ Developer's Journal, 1073-4805.
Desc: Covers Borland Turbo C++ - DOS.
DD 005 ISSN 1052-9489
US
TITLE CHANGE

INSIDE TURBO PASCAL. [Inside Turbo Pascal]. Vol. 1, No. 1 (Sept. 1989)-(August 1993). Periodical. English. Cobb Group, 9420 Bunsen Parkway #300, Louisville KY 40220. **Tel** (502)491-1900, (800)223-8720, FAX (502)491-4200. **ED** Blake Ragsdale. Index available. ctrl circ.
DD 005 ISSN 1045-6775
US
CEASED

●**INSIDE VISUAL BASIC FOR WINDOWS.** [Inside Vis. Basic Windows]. **Added/Corp** Cobb Group. Vol. 3, No. 1 (Jan. 1993)-. Periodical. English. Twelve times a year. $59.00. Cobb Group, 9420 Bunsen Parkway #300, Louisville KY 40220. **Tel** (502)491-1900, (800)223-8720, FAX (502)491-4200. **Continues** Inside Visual Basic, 1059-1788.
ISSN 1066-7555
US

●**INSIDE VISUAL FOXPRO. Added/Corp** Cobb Group. (1995)-. Periodical. English. Twelve times a year. $69.00. Cobb Group, 9420 Bunsen Parkway #300, Louisville KY 40220. **Tel** (502)491-1900, (800)223-8720, FAX (502)491-4200.
ISSN 1082-2356
US

INSIDE WORD FOR WINDOWS. [Inside Word Windows]. **Added/Corp** Cobb Group. Vol. 1, No. 1 (June 1990)-(Dec. 1995). Periodical. English. Cobb Group, 9420 Bunsen Parkway #300, Louisville KY 40220. **Tel** (502)491-1900, (800)223-8720, FAX (502)491-4200.
DD 005 ISSN 1049-0795
US
CEASED

INSIDE WORD (MACINTOSH ED.). (INSIDE WORD : TIPS & TECHNIQUES FOR MICROSOFT WORD ON THE MACINTOSH.). [Inside Word]. **Added/Corp** Cobb Group. Vol. 1, No. 1 (Aug. 1987)-. Periodical. English. Twelve times a year. $49.00. Cobb Group, 9420 Bunsen Parkway #300, Louisville KY 40220. **Tel** (502)491-1900, (800)223-8720, FAX (502)491-4200.
Desc: A journal of information for Microsoft Word 3.0 users on creating polished, professional documents and overcoming problems.
DD 005 ISSN 0893-9349
US

INSIDE WORD (PC ED.). (INSIDE WORD : TIPS & TECHNIQUES FOR MICROSOFT WORD 5.5 [ON THE PC].). [Inside word]. **Added/Corp** Cobb Group. Vol. 1, No. 1 (Mar. 1991)-(March 1994). Periodical. English. Cobb Group, 9420 Bunsen Parkway #300, Louisville KY 40220. **Tel** (502)491-1900, (800)223-8720, FAX (502)491-4200.
DD 005 ISSN 1052-7605
US
CEASED

INSIDE WORDPERFECT. [Inside WordPerfect]. **Added/Corp** Cobb Group. **VFOAT** Inside Word Perfect. Vol. 1, No. 1 (March 1990)-. Periodical. English. Twelve times a year. $69.00. Cobb Group, 9420 Bunsen Parkway #300, Louisville KY 40220. **Tel** (502)491-1900, (800)223-8720, FAX (502)491-4200. Index available. cum. index. ctrl circ.
DD 652 ISSN 1046-9656
US
CODEN INWOEV

INSIDE WORDPERFECT WINDOWS. [Inside WordPerfect windows]. **Added/Corp** Cobb Group. **VFOAT** Inside Word Perfect for Windows. Vol. 1, No. 1 (July 1992)-. Periodical. English. Twelve times a year. $69.00. Cobb Group, 9420 Bunsen Parkway #300, Louisville KY 40220. **Tel** (502)491-1900, (800)223-8720, FAX (502)491-4200.
DD 005 ISSN 1063-2727
US

INSIDE WORKS FOR WINDOWS. [Inside works windows]. **Added/Corp** Cobb Group. Vol. 1, No. 1 (April 1992)-. Periodical. English. Twelve times a year. $49.00. Cobb Group, 9420 Bunsen Parkway #300, Louisville KY 40220. **Tel** (502)491-1900, (800)223-8720, FAX (502)491-4200.
LC HG8075 .I56 ISSN 1061-5873
DD 368/.00285/53 US
CCC

INSURANCE & TECHNOLOGY. See Insurance-Computer Applications.
ISSN 1054-0733
US

Computers —Software

●INTELLIGENT AUTOMATION AND SOFT COMPUTING See Computers-Automation.

ISSN 1052-7214
DD 006
US
CCC
CODEN INSSEN

INTELLIGENT SOFTWARE STRATEGIES. (INTELLIGENT SOFTWARE STRATEGIES / FROM CUTTER INFORMATION CORP.). [Intell. softw. strateg.]. **Added/Corp** Cutter Information Corp. (July 1990)-. Periodical. English. Twelve times a year. $447.00. Cutter Information Corporation, 37 Broadway, Arlington MA 02174-5539. **Tel** (617)648-8700, (800)964-5118, FAX (617)648-8707, (617)648-1950, telex 650 100 9891. available on an online database (file 636/Full-Text) from DIALOG. *Continues* Expert Systems Strategies, 0887-221X.
 Ind/Abst PTS Newsl. Database [Full Txt.].

ISSN 1048-0501
DD 610
US

INTERACTIVE HEALTHCARE NEWSLETTER. See Public Health and Safety.

ISSN 0791-4326
DD 620.0285
IE

INTERNATIONAL DIRECTORY OF CIVIL ENGINEERING/CONSTRUCTION SOFTWARE. See Engineering-Computer Applications.

LC QA76.6 .I554   ISSN 0260-3438
DD 001.64/25/0294
UK

INTERNATIONAL DIRECTORY OF SOFTWARE. [Int. dir. softw.]. 1980-81-. Directory. English. Every 2 years. Cuyb Publications Ltd., 1st Federal Building, Suite 401, Pottstown PA 19464.

LC QA76.758 .I5745   ISSN 0218-1940
DD 005.1/05
SI
CCC
CODEN ISEKEW

INTERNATIONAL JOURNAL OF SOFTWARE ENGINEERING AND KNOWLEDGE ENGINEERING. See Computers-Artificial Intelligence.

LC HD9696.C6 I59   ISSN 1050-4354
DD 005.1/029/4
US

INTERNATIONAL OOP DIRECTORY. VAT International Object-Oriented Programming Directory. (1990)-. Directory. English. One time a year. $54.00. SIGS Publications Inc. / New York, 71 West 23rd Street, 3rd Floor, New York NY 10010-4102. **Tel** (212)242-7447. **(Subscription address:** SIGS Publications Inc, PO Box 2029, Langhorne PA 19047. **Tel** (212)242-7447.)

ISSN 1065-1349
DD 005
US
Pr Rev.

●INTERNATIONAL PERSPECTIVES IN SOFTWARE ENGINEERING. [Int. perspect. softw. eng.]. **Added/Corp** Rocky Mountain Institute of Software Engineering. Vol. 1, Issue 1 (Mar. 1993)-. Periodical. English. Four times a year (Jan., Apr., July, Oct.). Free on request. Rocky Mountain Institute of Software Engineering, 1113 Spruce Street, Boulder CO 80302. **Tel** (303)449-9779, FAX (303)938-5005. **ED** William E. Riddle. **Circ:** 140.
 Desc: Includes articles on software process, education, and development.

LC TK7885
DD 621.39
UK

●INTERNATIONAL SMART CARD INDUSTRY GUIDE. (1995)-. Directory. English. Irregular. Smart Card News Ltd., 31 Ashdown Avenue, Saltdean Brighton, BN2 8AH United Kingdom. **Tel** 011 1273 302503, FAX 011 1273 300991.

US

●JOHN MARSHALL JOURNAL OF COMPUTER & INFORMATION LAW, THE. See Law-Computer Applications.

ISSN 1050-429X
DD 540
US

JOURNAL OF CHEMICAL EDUCATION. SOFTWARE, B. See Chemistry and Chemicals-Computer Applications.

LC QA75.5 .J627   ISSN 1069-5451
DD 004/.05
US
CEASED

JOURNAL OF COMPUTER AND SOFTWARE ENGINEERING. See Computers-Computer Engineering.

LC QA76.76.S64 J68   ISSN 1040-550X
DD 005.1/6/05
UK
CODEN JSMPEU

JOURNAL OF SOFTWARE MAINTENANCE. [J. softw. maint.]. **VFOAT** Software Maintenance. (1989)-. Periodical. English. Six times a year. $645.00. John Wiley & Sons Ltd., Baffins Lane, Chichester, West Sussex PO19 1UD United Kingdom. **Tel** 011 44 1243 779777, FAX 011 44 1243 776128 BTG:JWP001, telex 86290 WIBOOKG. **(Subscription address:** John Wiley & Sons, Inc. / Philadelphia, PO Box 7247, Philadelphia PA 19170. **Tel** (212)850-6645, (800)225-5945.) **ED** K. H. Bennett and N. Chapin. available on microfilm and microfiche from University Microfilms International (UMI). Documents available from Ask*IEEE.
 Desc: Conveys the results of academic research and practical experience into the computing community. Topics covered include: software evolution lifestyles, software maintenance management, tools, environments, metrics and productivity methods, quality assurance, theory of software maintenance, maintainability of new software, methods for software maintenance, and impact for maintenance of new software practices.
 Ind/Abst ACM Guide Comput. Lit.; Comput. Lit. Index; Comput. Rev.; Curr. Cit.; Data Process. Dig.; INSPEC (Sept. 1989-).

LC QA76.5 .J74   ISSN 0164-1212
DD 001.64/05
US
CCC
CODEN JSSODM
Pr Rev.

JOURNAL OF SYSTEMS AND SOFTWARE, THE. See Computers-Programs and Programming.

ISSN 0950-4869
UK

KEY ABSTRACTS. SOFTWARE ENGINEERING. See Computers-Abstracting, Bibliographies and Statistics.

LC HA32 .K49   ISSN 0197-7342
DD 001
US

KEYWORDS. [Keywords]. No. 21 (May/June 1980)-. Periodical. English. Four times a year. Free. SPSS Inc, 444 North Michigan Avenue/Suite 3300, Chicago IL 60611. **Tel** (312)329-2400, FAX (312)329-2431, telex 910/221-1 910/221-1396. **Circ:** 25,000. *Continues* SPSS Inc. Newsletter, 0160-7669.
 Desc: Newsletter for users of SPSS statistical and data analysis software.
 Ind/Abst Inf. Sci. Abstr.

ISSN 0895-0008
DD 330
US

KNOWLEDGE CENTER COURSEWARE LIBRARY. (KNOWLEDGE CENTER COURSEWARE LIBRARY [COMPUTER FILE].). [Knowl. cent. coursew. libr.]. **VFOAT** Knowledge Center Course Ware Library. (198?)-. Monographic series. English. Learncom, 215 First Street, Cambridge MA 02142.
 Desc: System requirements: IBM PC or compatible computer; 265K; DOS 2.0 or higher; two disk drives; color RGB monitor.

ISSN 1081-5872
US

●LAUNCH (SANTA MONICA, CALIF.). (LAUNCH). (1995)-. Periodical. English. Six times a year. $35.99. Launch Magazine, PO Box 4926, Manchester NH 03108. **Tel** (800)955-2862, FAX (310)576-6070.

LC QA76.6 .S637   ISSN 0742-5759
DD 001.64/25
CCC
CODEN LSREEA
Pr Rev.

LIBRARY SOFTWARE REVIEW. See Library and Information Sciences-Computer Applications.

ISSN 0886-4144
DD 004
US

LOADSTAR. (LOADSTAR [COMPUTER FILE].). [Loadstar]. **VFOAT** Load Star. (1984)-. Periodical. English. Twelve times a year. $69.95. Loadstar Inc., PO Box 30007, Shreveport LA 71130. **Tel** (318)221-8718. available on diskette.
 Desc: Available on 5 1/4" diskettes.

ISSN 1040-5542
DD 051
US

LOADSTAR 128 QUARTERLY. (LOADSTAR 128 QUARTERLY [COMPUTER FILE].). [Loadstar 128 q.]. **VFOAT** Loadstar One Twenty-Eight Quarterly; Loadstar 128; Loadstar. No. 1- (1988)-. Periodical. English. Four times a year. $39.95 US; $49.95 Canada and Mexico. Loadstar Inc., PO Box 30007, Shreveport LA 71130. **Tel** (318)221-8718.
 Desc: System requirements: Commodore 128.

ISSN 1079-235X
DD 005
US

●LOTUS NOTES ADVISOR. [Lotus notes advis.]. Vol. 1, No. 1 (1995)-. Periodical. English. Six times a year. $39.00. Advisor Publications Group, 4010 Morena Boulevard, Suite 200, San Diego CA 92117. **Tel** (800)336-6060, (619)483-6400, FAX (619)483-9851.

ISSN 1055-7504
US

LOTUS ON WINDOWS. (1991)-. Periodical. English. Twelve times a year. $49.00. Lotus Publishing Corporation, PO Box 54395, Boulder CO 80321-4395.

ISSN 1059-7344
US

●LOTUS WORKS REPORT, THE. (1993)-. Periodical. English. Six times a year. $18.00. The Lotus Works Report, PO Box 55087, Boulder CO 80322.

ISSN 1062-452X
DD 005
US

MACAUTHORITY (LOUISVILLE, KY.), THE. (THE MACAUTHORITY: TIPS & TECHNIQUES FOR APPLE MACINTOSH.). [MacAuthority]. **Added/Corp** Cobb Group. Vol. 1, No. 1 (June 1992)-. Periodical. English. Twelve times a year. $49.00. Cobb Group, 9420 Bunsen Parkway #300, Louisville KY 40220. **Tel** (502)491-1900, (800)223-8720, FAX (502)491-4200.

ISSN 1063-2700
DD 005
US

MACAUTHORITY SOFTWARE CONNECTION. (MACAUTHORITY SOFTWARE CONNECTION [COMPUTER FILE].). [MacAuthority softw. connect.]. **Added/Corp** Cobb Group. (June 1992)-. Periodical. English. Twelve times a year. $59.00. Cobb Group, 9420 Bunsen Parkway #300, Louisville KY 40220. **Tel** (502)491-1900, (800)223-8720, FAX (502)491-4200.

MATERIAL SAFETY DATA SHEETS. (19??)-. English. Four times a year. Silverplatter Information Inc., 100 River Ridge Drive, Norwood MA 02062. **Tel** (800)343-0064, (617)769-2599, FAX (617)769-8763.

ISSN 1080-9082
US

●MAXIMIZE (PETERBOROUGH, N.H.). (MAXIMIZE : THE PRACTICAL GUIDE TO WINDOWS.). (1995)-. English. Six times a year. $15.97. IDG Communications / New Hampshire, 86 Elm Street, Peterborough NH 03458. **Tel** (800)349-7327, FAX (603)924-6972. **(Subscription address:** Kable Publishers Aide / Ohio, PO Box 1958, Marion OH 43305.)

ISSN 0891-5318
DD 005
US

MERIDIAN SOFTWARE ANALYSIS BULLETIN. [Meridian softw. anal. bull.]. **Added/Corp** Meridian Software Analysis. **VFOAT** Software Analysis Bulletin. (1989)-. Bulletin. English. Twelve times a year. FAX Communications Inc, 665 Third Street/Suite 340, San Francisco CA 94107.

US

MIC/SUB-APPLICATION DEVELOPMENT. [DISKETTE]. (19??)-. English. Twelve times a year. $1,340.00. Management Information Corporation, 1111 Markkress Road, Cherry Hill NJ 08003. **Tel** (609)424-1100. Index available. cum. index. ctrl circ.
 Desc: Analysis service on database management systems and CASE software products.

ISSN 0738-6354
US

MICRO SOFTWARE MARKETING. [Micro softw. mark.]. (198?)-. Periodical. English. Twelve times a year. $87.00. Micro Software Marketing, PO Box 380, Congers NY 10920. **Tel** (914)268-5925. **ED** Scott Witt. **Bk Rev.**
 Desc: The industry newsletter for those who create, package, and market software for microcomputers.

ISSN 8755-5786
DD 001
US
SUSPENDED

MICRO SOFTWARE REPORT. See Library and Information Sciences-Computer Applications.

ISSN 1068-5669
DD 005
US
TITLE CHANGE

MICROSOFT C/C++ DEVELOPER'S JOURNAL. [Microsoft C/C++ dev. j.]. **Added/Corp** Cobb Group. Vol. 4, No. 4 (Apr. 1993)-(1994). Periodical. English. Cobb Group, 9420 Bunsen Parkway #300, Louisville KY 40220. **Tel** (502)491-1900, (800)223-8720, FAX (502)491-4200. *Continues* Inside Microsoft C, 1047-6075. *Continued by* Inside Microsoft Visual C++ Journal, 1081-1450.

Computers —Software

DD 005.369
ISSN 0964-0029
UK
MICROSOFT MAGAZINE. [Microsoft mag.]. **Added/Corp** Microsoft Corporation. (1990)-. Periodical. English. Four times a year.
Ind/Abst HILITES.

LC QA76.5 .M5227
DD 005.36/05
ISSN 0889-9932
US
CCC
CODEN MSJOED
MICROSOFT SYSTEMS JOURNAL. [Microsoft syst. j.]. **VFOAT** Systems Journal; MSJ. Vol. 1, No. 1 (Oct. 1986)-. Periodical. English (Japanese and German). Twelve times a year. $50.00. Miller Freeman Inc., 600 Harrison Street, San Francisco CA 94107. **Tel** (415)905-2337, (415)905-2200, FAX (415)905-2240, telex 278273. (**Subscription address:** Neodata / Colorado, PO Box 2606, Boulder CO 80322.) **ED** Jonathon Lazarus and Tony Rizzo. Index available. cum. index. available on microfilm and microfiche from University Microfilms International (UMI); available on an online database (file 675/Full-Text) from DIALOG. Documents available from Ask*IEEE.
Desc: Articles for programmers and systems designers on software subjects and new hardware related to software enhancement.
Ind/Abst Comput. ASAP (19??-) [Full Txt.]; Comput. Database (19??-) [Full Txt.]; Comput. Rev. Index (1987-); Curr. Cit.; INSPEC (Nov. 1988-).

DD 005.369
ISSN 0968-4743
UK
MICROSOFT SYSTEMS JOURNAL LONDON. [Microsoft syst. j. Lond.]. **VFOAT** MSJ (London). (1992)-. Periodical. English. Ten times a year. $82.13. TPD Publishing Ltd., 1 4 Warple Way Long Island House, London W3 0RG United Kingdom. **Tel** 011 44 181 7401740.
Ind/Abst Curr. Cit.

DD 005
ISSN 1079-5405
US
●**MICROSOFT WORD FOR WINDOWS SOFTWARE CONNECTION.** (MICROSOFT WORD FOR WINDOWS SOFTWARE CONNECTION [COMPUTER FILE].). [Microsoft word windows softw. connect.]. **Added/Corp** Cobb Group. (Sept. 1993)-. Periodical. English. Twelve times a year. $59.00. Cobb Group, 9420 Bunsen Parkway #300, Louisville KY 40220. **Tel** (502)491-1900, (800)223-8720, FAX (502)491-4200.

LC QA76.76.D47 M53
DD 005.1
ISSN 1050-0324
US
MIDNIGHT ENGINEERING. See Engineering.

DD 005
Pr Rev.
ISSN 1062-0451
US
MONASH SOFTWARE LETTER. [Monash softw. lett.]. (July 1991)-. Periodical. English. Twelve times a year. $347.00. Monash Software Letter, 888 Seventh Avenue, New York NY 10019. **Tel** (212)315-3120. **ED** Curt A. Monash. Index available. cum. index.

DD 005
ISSN 1051-8592
US
MS-DOS COLLECTION. (MS-DOS COLLECTION [COMPUTER FILE].). [MS-DOS collect.]. (1989)-. Periodical. English. Four times a year $99.00. Selectware Technologies Inc, 29200 Vassar, Suite 200, Livonia MI 48152.
Desc: System requirements: IBM AT, PS/2 or compatible; 640K RAM; 1MB of hard disk space; EGA or VGA; CD-ROM drive with Microsoft Extensions.

GR
●**MULTIMEDIA AND CD-ROM.** See Computers-Microcomputers, Personal Computers.

ISSN 1380-7501
NE
CCC
●**MULTIMEDIA TOOLS AND APPLICATIONS.** (1995)-. English. Six times a year. $537.00. Kluwer Academic Publishers, Postbus 322, 3300 AH Dordrecht The Netherlands. **Tel** 011 31 78 524400, FAX 011 31 78 183273, telex 20083. **ED** Borko Furht.
Desc: Publishes original research articles on multimedia development and performance measurement tools, user interfaces, and case studies of multimedia applications. Intended for both academic practitioners and industrial scientists and engineers.

LC QA76.76.O63 I53
DD 005
ISSN 1079-3135
US
●**NASPA TECHNICAL SUPPORT.** [NaSPA tech. support.]. **Added/Corp** NaSPA, Inc. **VFOAT** Technical Support. Vol. 2, No. 6 (Oct. 1994)-. Periodical. English. Twelve times a year. $45.00. National Systems Programmers Association, 4811 South 76th Street, Suite 210, Milwaukee WI 53220. **Tel** (414)423-2420, FAX (414)423-2433. **Continues** In-Depth Report. 370/390 Operating Systems, 1072-7647.

DD 005.1
ISSN 1183-3955
CN
NATIONAL DIRECTORY FOR SOFTWARE ADAPTATION. [Natl. dir. softw. adapt.]. **Added/Corp** Services Documentaires Multimedia. Canadian Association of Data, Professional Services and Software Organizations. Spring (1991)-. Directory. English. $10.00. Services Documentaires Multimedia Inc, 75 rue de Port-Royal, Suite 300, Montreal Quebec H3L 3T1 Canada. **Tel** (514)382-0895, FAX (514)384-9139.

ISSN 0739-697X
US
NEAS. NEWSLETTER OF ENGINEERING ANALYSIS SOFTWARE. See Engineering-Computer Applications.

DD 005
ISSN 1079-5421
US
●**NETWARE SOFTWARE CONNECTION.** (NETWARE SOFTWARE CONNECTION [COMPUTER FILE].). **Added/Corp** Cobb Group. (1993)-. Periodical. English. Twelve times a year. $59.00. Cobb Group, 9420 Bunsen Parkway #300, Louisville KY 40220. **Tel** (502)491-1900, (800)223-8720, FAX (502)491-4200.

DD 004
ISSN 1040-4503
US
CEASED
NETWARE TECHNICAL JOURNAL. [NetWare tech. j.]. **Added/Corp** Novell, Inc. **VFOAT** Netware. (Oct. 1988)-(June 1994). Periodical. English. McGraw Hill Publishing Company, Inc., 1221 Avenue of the Americas, New York NY 10020. **Tel** (212)512-6410, (800)525-5003, FAX (212)512-6111.
Desc: Targets network integrators, developers, programmers, systems analysts and other technical professionals who are responsible for optimizing and enhancing NetWare networking environments.

NEWS IBM. (19??)-. English. One time a week. $775.00. Xephon, 27-35 London Road, Newbury Berkshire RG13 1JL United Kingdom. **Tel** 011 44 1635 33823, FAX 011 44 1635 38345. (**Subscription address:** Xephon, 1301 West Highway, Suite 201 450, Lewisville TX 75067.) **ED** Trevor Eddolls. Index available ((sent with issue)). cum. index. **Bk Rev** (Qty: 6).
Desc: New products and new versions and releases of products are described for mainframes, communications, mid-range and PCs. All IBM related.

NEWSBANK REFERENCE SERVICE COMPUTER FILE. See Computers-Abstracting, Bibliographies and Statistics.

DD 001.64
ISSN 0911-5862
JA
NIKKEI DETAPURO SOFUTO. **VFOAT** Nikkei Datapro Sofuto. (1986)-. Japanese. Irregular. Nihon Keizai Shimbun Inc., 9-5 Otemachi 1 Chome, Chiyoda-ku Tokyo 100 Japan. **Tel** 011 81 3 32700251, 011 81 3 52108502 (Nikkei Business Publications Inc.), FAX 011 81 3 52552661, 011 81 3 52108119 (Nikkei Business Publications Inc.). **ED** Hisashi Okamura.

ISSN 0917-9364
JA
NIKKEI INFOBESU UNIX. **VFOAT** Nikkei Infobase UNIX. (1992)-. Periodical. Japanese. One time a year. Nihon Keizai Shimbun Inc., 9-5 Otemachi 1 Chome, Chiyoda-ku Tokyo 100 Japan. **Tel** 011 81 3 32700251, 011 81 3 52108502 (Nikkei Business Publications Inc.), FAX 011 81 3 52552661, 011 81 3 52108119 (Nikkei Business Publications Inc.).
Desc: UNIX system and product information.

US
Pr Rev.
●**NPI TECHNO VIEW TIMES.** See Computers-Hardware.

DD 005
ISSN 1055-3614
US
CCC
OBJECT MAGAZINE. [Object mag.]. **Added/Corp** COOT, Inc. **VFOAT** Object. (May/June 1991)-. Periodical. English. Six times a year. $119.00. SIGS Publications Inc. / New York, 71 West 23rd Street, 3rd Floor, New York NY 10010-4102. **Tel** (212)242-7447. (**Subscription address:** SIGS Publications Inc, PO Box 2029, Langhorne PA 19047. **Tel** (212)242-7447.)

LC QA276.4 .O27
DD 519.5/0285/5369
ISSN 1057-2902
US
OBSERVATIONS (CARY, N.C.). See Mathematics-Computer Applications.

LC QA75.5 .O33
DD 338.4/762139/05
ISSN 1071-8990
US
●**OEM MAGAZINE.** See Computers-Computer Engineering.

DD 004
ISSN 1081-9371
US
●**OFFICE DEVELOPER.** [Off. dev.]. (1995)-. Newsletter. English. Twelve times a year. $149.00. Pinnacle Publishing Inc., PO Box 888, Kent WA 98035. **Tel** (206)251-1900, (800)231-1293, FAX (206)251-5057.
Desc: Newsletter for Microsoft Office developers and power users.

LC QA76.76.O63 U57
DD 005.4/3
ISSN 1078-2370
US
●**OPEN COMPUTING.** [Open comput.]. Vol. 11, No. 8 (Aug. 1994)-. Periodical. English. Twelve times a year. $18.00. McGraw Hill Publishing Company, Inc., 1221 Avenue of the Americas, New York NY 10020. **Tel** (212)512-6410, (800)525-5003, FAX (212)512-6111. (**Subscription address:** McGraw Hill Book Company, Princeton Road, Hightstown NJ 08520. **Tel** (717)794-5461.) available on an online database from Dow Jones News/Retrieval; NEWSNET; DIALOG; and Lexis-Nexis. **Continues** UnixWorld's Open Computing, 1072-4044.
Ind/Abst Microcomput. Abstr.

DD 004
ISSN 1069-0409
US
●**OPEN SYSTEMS PRODUCTS DIRECTORY.** See Computers-Computer Industry and Industry Directories.

LC QA76.6 .O625
DD 621.3819/52
ISSN 0163-5980
US
CCC
CODEN OSRED8
OPERATING SYSTEMS REVIEW. [Oper. syst. rev.]. **Added/Corp** ACM Special Interest Group in Operating Systems. (19??)-. Periodical. English. Four times a year. $30.00. ACM / Association for Computing Machinery, 1515 Broadway, 17th Floor, New York NY 10036. **Tel** (212)869-7440, FAX (212)869-0481. (**Subscription address:** Association for Computing Machinery, PO Box 12114, Church Street Station, New York NY 10249. **Tel** (212)626-0500.) Documents available from Article Express International, Ask*IEEE. **Continues** SIGOPS Bulletin.
Ind/Abst Abstr. Hum. Comput. Interact.; ACM Guide Comput. Lit.; Bioeng. Abstr.; Comput. Rev.; Curr. Cit.; Ei Page One; Eng. Index Annu.; INSPEC (July 1974-).

LC QA76.76.O63 I23
DD 005/.265
ISSN 1073-0729
US
●**OS/2 DEVELOPER.** [OS/2 dev.]. **VFOAT** OS 2 developer. (1993)-. Periodical. English. Six times a year. $39.95. Miller Freeman Inc., 600 Harrison Street, San Francisco CA 94107. **Tel** (415)905-2337, (415)905-2200, FAX (415)905-2240, telex 278273. (**Subscription address:** Hallmark Data Systems, PO Box 1165, Skokie IL 60076.) **Continues** IBM OS/2 Developer.

DD 005
ISSN 1079-5413
CEASED
OS/2 SOFTWARE CONNECTION [COMPUTER FILE]. [OS/2 softw. connect.]. **Added/Corp** Cobb Group. (1993)-(Nov. 1995). Periodical. English. Cobb Group, 9420 Bunsen Parkway #300, Louisville KY 40220. **Tel** (502)491-1900, (800)223-8720, FAX (502)491-4200.

DD 005
ISSN 1069-6814
US
●**OS2 PROFESSIONAL.** [OS2 prof.]. **VFOAT** OS 2 Professional; OS/2 Professional. Vol. 1, No. 1 (Jan. 1993)-. Periodical. English. Ten times a year. $25.00. IF Computer Media, 172 Rollins Aveune, Rockville MD 20852. **Tel** (301)770-3333, FAX (301)770-7062. **ED** Edwin Brauk. Index available. cum. index. **Bk Rev**. **Ad Acc, Adv Mgr:** Richard Dubin, **Tel** (518)489-4034. **Circ:** 80,000.
Desc: Workstyle and lifestyle for the users of OS/2 software.

LC QA76.8.I2598 P33
DD 658/.0553
ISSN 0741-4978
US
Pr Rev.
PAC-FINDER SYSTEM 34/36 SOFTWARE DIRECTORY. [Pac-finder syst. 34/36 softw. dir.]. **Added/Corp** Mincron SBC Corporation. **VFOAT** Pac-Finder System Thirty-Four, Thirty-Six Software Directory; Pacfinder System System 34/36 Software Directory; Pac Finder System 34/36 Software Directory. (1984)-. Directory. English. One time a year. Elsevier Science Publishing Company Inc, Madison Square Station, PO Box 882, New York NY 10159-0882. **Tel** (212)633-3950, FAX (212)633-3990.

DD 001
ISSN 0747-9573
US
CEASED
PACKAGED SOFTWARE REPORTS / MIC. See Business and Economics-Computer Applications.

DD 005
ISSN 1051-9696
US
TITLE CHANGE
PARADOX DEVELOPER'S JOURNAL. See Computers-Computer Engineering.

Computers —Software

DD 005
ISSN 1082-1678
US
CEASED
PARADOX FOR WINDOWS DEVELOPER'S JOURNAL. See Computers-Computer Engineering.

ISSN 0889-2911
US
TITLE CHANGE
PARADOX USER'S JOURNAL. [Paradox user's j.]. Vol. 1, No. 1 (June 1986)-(19??). Periodical. English. Cobb Group, 9420 Bunsen Parkway #300, Louisville KY 40220. **Tel** (502)491-1900, (800)223-8720, FAX (502)491-4200. *Continued by Inside Paradox for DOS.*

LC QA76.6 .S615
DD 004
ISSN 0954-2833
UK
CODEN PBSOE4
TITLE CHANGE
PC BUSINESS SOFTWARE. See Business and Economics-Computer Applications.

DD 051
ISSN 0897-8913
US
SUSPENDED
PC DISK QUARTERLY. (PC DISK QUARTERLY [COMPUTER FILE].). [PC disk q.]. **VAT** Personal Computer Disk Quarterly. Vol. 1 (Winter 1987/1988)-(19??). Periodical. English. Four times a year. $59.00. PC Disk Quarterly, 425 Edwards, Suite 1306, Shreveport LA 71101-3125.

LC QA75
DD 005
ISSN 0890-4863
US
PC LIFE. (PC LIFE [COMPUTER FILE].). [PC life]. Vol. 1, No. 1 (July/Aug. 1986)-. Periodical. English. Six times a year. Microstar Graphics, 413 University Building, Syracuse NY 13202.

UK
PC PLUS. See Computers-Microcomputers, Personal Computers.

LC QA76.75 .P36
DD 005.3/25
ISSN 1042-0681
US
Pr Rev.
PC-SIG MAGAZINE. **VFOAT** PC SIG Magazine. **VAT** PC-Software Interest Group Magazine. (198?)-. Periodical. English. Six times a year. $14.95 US; $38.00 Canada and Mexico. PC-SIG Inc, 1030 East Duane Avenue, Sunnyvale CA 94086. **Tel** (408)730-9291, (800)245-6717, FAX (408)730-2107. **ED** Michael Callahan. Index available. **Bk Rev**, (Qty: (unlimited)). **Ad Acc**, **Adv Mgr:** Jerry Pearson, **Tel** (408)730-9291. **Circ:** 100,000. *Continues PC-SIG News.*
Desc: Shareware product reviews, hardware reviews, Shareware and commercial products compared, information for beginners and programmers, book reviews and industry related articles.

LC QA76.753 .P34
DD 005.365
ISSN 1069-0913
US
PC SOFTDIR. (PC SOFTDIR : PUBLICATION OF DOS AND WINDOWS SOFTWARE, INCLUDING NETWORK VERSIONS.). **VFOAT** PC SoftDIR. [PC SoftDIR]. (Summer 1992)-. Periodical. English. Four times a year. $24.00 (one-year), $44.00 (two-year). ElJen Inc., 2839 Timber Knoll, Valrico FL 33594. **Tel** (813)654-1168, FAX (813)654-6906. (**Subscription address:** Eljen Publishing, PO Box 3065, Brandon FL 33509. **Tel** (813)654-1168.) **ED** Richard J. Adams.
Desc: DOS and Windows software resource directory. Lists the various products from about 450 North American software publishers.

LC QA76.5 .P3654
DD 004.16
ISSN 1052-6579
US
CEASED
PC SOURCES. See Computers-Microcomputers, Personal Computers.

LC QA76.76.D47 P38
DD 005.265
ISSN 1053-6205
US
TITLE CHANGE
PC TECHNIQUES. [PC tech.]. **VAT** Personal Computer Techniques. (1990)-(1995). Trade Publication. English. Coriolis Group, 7339 East Acoma Drive, Suite 7, Scottsdale AZ 85260. **Tel** (602)483-0192, FAX (602)483-0193. **ED** Jeff Duntemann. **Bk Rev**, (Qty: 25). **Ad Acc**, **Adv Mgr:** T.Mayer. **Circ:** 27,000. *Continued by Visual Developer.*
Desc: Explains programming languages, operating systems and databases for PC software developers with plain-language discussion, graphic examples and reviews of PC programming products and technical books.

US
PEACHTREE QUARTERLY. (19??)-. Periodical. English. Four times a year. Peachtree Software Inc, 1505 Pavilion Place, Norcross GA 30093. **Tel** (404)564-5800.

ISSN 0744-2475
US
PEELINGS II : THE MAGAZINE OF APPLE SOFTWARE EVALUATION. [Peelings II]. **VFOAT** Peelings 2; Peelings Two. Periodical. English. Twelve times a year. Peelings II Inc, 945 Brook Circle, Las Cruces NM 88001.
Ind/Abst Microcomput. Abstr. (Jan. 1982-April 1984).

DD 338
ISSN 1055-2596
CEASED
PENVISION NEWS. [PenVision news]. **VFOAT** Pen Vision News. Vol. 1, No. 1 (Jan. 1991)-(Aug. 1994). Periodical. English. Lempesis Research, 4806 Smith Gate Court, Pleasanton CA 94566. **Tel** (510)484-0397, FAX (510)484-1427. **ED** William J. Lempesis. **Circ:** 500.
Desc: Focuses on Pen-Based computer hardware, software and user issues. Includes coverage of PDAS.

US
PERFECTOFFICE EXPERT. (19??)-. English. Twelve times a year. $69.00. WordPerfect Publishing Corporation, MS7100, 1555 North Technology Way, Orem UT 84057-2399. **Tel** (800)321-4566, (801)222-2685.

LC QA76.9.E94 P46
DD 001.64/028/7
ISSN 0163-5999
US
CODEN PEREDN
PERFORMANCE EVALUATION REVIEW. (PERFORMANCE EVALUATION REVIEW : A QUARTERLY PUBLICATION OF THE SPECIAL INTEREST COMMITTEE ON MEASUREMENT AND EVALUATION.). [Perform. eval. rev.]. **Added/Corp** Association for Computing Machinery. Special Interest Committee on Measurement and Evaluation. ACM-Sigmetrics. **VFOAT** PER Quarterly. Vol. 1, No. 1 (Mar. 1972)-. Periodical. English. Four times a year. $25.00. ACM / Association for Computing Machinery, 1515 Broadway, 17th Floor, New York NY 10036. **Tel** (212)869-7440, FAX (212)869-0481. (**Subscription address:** Association for Computing Machinery, PO Box 12114, Church Street Station, New York NY 10249. **Tel** (212)626-0500.) Documents available from Article Express International, Ask*IEEE.
Ind/Abst ACM Guide Comput. Lit.; Bioeng. Abstr.; Comput. Lit. Index; Comput. Rev. (Spring 1980-); Curr. Cit.; Ei Page One; Eng. Index Annu.; INSPEC (Spring 1980-).

IT
PERSONAL COMPUTER. (19??)-. Italian. Eleven times a year. Systems SRL, Via Olanda 6, 20083 Gaggiano Mi Italy. **Tel** 011 39 2 90841814. **ED** M. Di Pisa. **Circ:** 24,000 (ctrl).
Desc: Covers PC hardware and software.

LC K
DD 340
US
PERSONAL PROPERTY TAXATION OF COMPUTER SOFTWARE. (1992)-. English. Irregular. $125.00. Kutish Publications, PO Box 181916, Coronado CO 92178-1916. **Tel** (619)552-0523, FAX (619)522-0525.
Desc: Provides a brief overview of personal property taxation software: what it is, how it affects software, valuation of software for personal property taxes, and some standard exemptions to personal property tax.

LC TN860 .P54
DD 665.5/028/55369
US
PETROLEUM SOFTWARE DIRECTORY. See Petroleum and Natural Gas-Computer Applications.

LC TN860 .S668
DD 665.5/0285/55369
US
PETROLEUM SOFTWARE SOURCEBOOK FOR PERSONAL COMPUTERS. See Petroleum and Natural Gas-Computer Applications.

ISSN 1073-6425
US
CCC
●**PETROSYSTEMS WORLD.** See Petroleum and Natural Gas-Computer Applications.

UK
Pr Rev.
PHOENICS JOURNAL OF COMPUTATIONAL FLUID DYNAMICS & ITS APPLICATIONS, THE. (1988)-. English. Four times a year (Jan., May, Sept, Dec.). $213.90. Chamber Limited Bakery House, 40 High Street, Wimbledon London SW19 5AU United Kingdom. **Tel** 011 44 171 9477651, FAX 011 44 171 8793497. **ED** Professor D. Brian Spalding. **Ad Acc**, **Adv Mgr:** Miss S.J. Barnes. **Acid Free. Circ:** 250 (ctrl). Documents available from BLDSC.
Desc: A technical periodical to promote the exchange of knowledge and skills among PHOENICS Computational Fluid Dynamics (CFD) users around the world. Contains industrial applications of PHOENICS software, results from academic research and new PHOENICS features.

DD 621
ISSN 1040-9718
US
TITLE CHANGE
PLC INSIDER'S NEWSLETTER, THE. See Computers-Hardware.

US
●**POWER GRAPHICS REPORTS.** (1995)-. English. Four times a year. $24.00. Association of Corel Artists & Designers, 1309 Riverside Drive, Burbank CA 91506. **Tel** (310)452-5637. *Continues CORELation.*

ISSN 1078-1889
US
●**POWERBUILDER DEVELOPER'S JOURNAL.** See Computers-Programs and Programming.

LC QA76.6 .C6296a
DD 004.1
ISSN 0730-3157
US
CCC
PROCEEDINGS - INTERNATIONAL COMPUTER SOFTWARE & APPLICATIONS CONFERENCE. See Computers-Electronic Data Processing.

LC QA76.6 .N373a
DD 004.16
ISSN 0270-5257
US
CCC
CODEN PCSEDE
PROCEEDINGS - INTERNATIONAL CONFERENCE ON SOFTWARE ENGINEERING. See Computers-Electronic Data Processing.

ISSN 1083-4532
US
●**PROCESS INSIGHT REVIEW.** (1995)-. Periodical. English. Eleven times a year. $395.00. QSoft Solutions Corporation, 445 West Commercial Street, Box 556, East Rochester NY 14445. **Tel** (716)264-9700, FAX (716)264-9702. **ED** Paul Wetenhall. **Bk Rev**, (Qty: 30).
Desc: Summarizes worthwhile reading, highlights upcoming events of interest, provides user experiences, and offers our opinions about emerging trends.

DD 005
ISSN 1040-1482
US
PRODUCTIVITY SOFTWARE. [Prod. softw.]. Vol. 1, No. 1 (Jan. 1988)-. Periodical. English. Twelve times a year. $12.50 North America. Worldwide Videotex, PO Box 3273, Boynton Beach FL 33424-3273. **Tel** (407)738-2276, FAX (407)738-2275. available on an online database (file 636/Full-Text) from DIALOG.
Ind/Abst PTS Newsl. Database [Full Txt.].

LC QA76 .P695
DD 001.6/42/05
ISSN 0361-7688
US
CCC
CODEN PCSODA
PROGRAMMING AND COMPUTER SOFTWARE. See Computers-Programs and Programming.

LC QA76 .P697
ISSN 0132-3474
RU
CODEN PROGD3
PROGRAMMIROVANIE. See Computers-Programs and Programming.

DD 006
ISSN 1048-8863
US
CEASED
QUARKXPRESS IN-DEPTH. See Computers-Computer Graphics and Design.

CN
Pr Rev.
QUARTERLY REPORT ON ENERGY RELATED SOFTWARE IN CALGARY. See Energy-Computer Applications.

ISSN 1079-9923
US
●**QUICK$ENSE FOR WINDOWS.** **Added/Corp** Cobb Group. **VFOAT** Quick Sense for Windows; QuickSense for Windows. (1995)-. Periodical. English. Twelve times a year. $39.00. Cobb Group, 9420 Bunsen Parkway #300, Louisville KY 40220. **Tel** (502)491-1900, (800)223-8720, FAX (502)491-4200.

US
RBBS-PC IN A BOX. CD-ROM. English. Two times a year. $104.95 US; $749.00 (bundled with a CD-ROM drive). Quanta Press, Inc., 1313 Fifth Street Southeast, Suite 208C, Minneapolis MN 55414. **Tel** (612)379-3956, FAX (612)623-4570.
Desc: Over 15,000 DOS compatible shareware and freeware software programs on one CD-ROM disc. The end-user may run this as a bulletin board disc or as a software archive.

LC HD9696.C63 U582
DD 338.4/7004/097305
ISSN 1047-935X
US
RELEASE 1.0. See Computers-Computer Industry and Industry Directories.

Computers —Software

LC QA75.5
DD 005
ISSN 1083-155X
US
REVTECH MAGAZINE. [RevTech mag.]. (19??)-. Periodical. English. Twelve times a year. $49.00. Infocus Inc., 37 South Main Street, Yardley PA 19067. **Tel** (215)321-2200. **Continues** Revtech; **Absorbed** Revuser, 1051-8118.
 Desc: Deals with the Revelation software computer program.

LC WMLC L 90/0008
DD 005
ISSN 1051-8118
US
TITLE CHANGE
REVUSER (PHILADELPHIA, PA.). (REVUSER.). [Revuser]. **VFOAT** Rev User; Revuser Magazine. **VAT** Revelation User. Vol. 1, No. 2 (Jan./Feb. 1990)-(1994). Periodical. English. Infocus Inc., 37 South Main Street, Yardley PA 19067. **Tel** (215)321-2200. **Merged into** RevTech Magazine, 1083-155X.

US
RIGHT STUFFED. CD-ROM, THE. (19??)-. English. $99.00. Quantum Leap Technologies, 1399 Southeast 9th Avenue, Suite 4, Hialeah FL 33010-5999. **Tel** (305)885-9985, (800)762-2877, FAX (305)762-9986. Index available. cum. index.
 Desc: Covers software/shareware for Macintosh.

BE
SAMSON PERSONAL COMPUTER. See Computers-Hardware.

LC QA276.4 .S23a
DD 005.3
ISSN 0270-9422
US
SAS COMMUNICATIONS. [SAS commun.]. **Main/Corp** SAS Institute. (197?)-. Periodical. English (Japanese). Four times a year. SAS Institute Inc., Box 8000, SAS Circle, Cary NC 27512. **Tel** (919)677-8000, FAX (919)677-8123. **ED** Pamela Meek. Index available. cum. index. **Ad Acc. Circ:** 80,000 (ctrl).
 Desc: News and features related to SAS software; targeted for the SAS software user.

US
●**SCOUT BUSINESS SOFTWARE DIRECTORY.** (1995)-. Directory. English. Two times a year (March and Sept.). $65.00. Software Press, 2214 Eagleview Circle, Longmont CO 80501. **Tel** (303)772-0321, FAX (303)772-4069. **Ad Acc, Adv Mgr:** C. Minear. **Continues** Scout Mid-Range Software Directory.

LC QA76.753 .S38
DD 005.3/029/473
ISSN 1047-1812
US
TITLE CHANGE
SCOUT MID-RANGE SOFTWARE DIRECTORY. [Scout mid-range softw. dir.]. **VFOAT** Scout MidRange Software Directory. (19??)-(1995). Directory. English. Software Press, 2214 Eagleview Circle, Longmont CO 80501. **Tel** (303)772-0321, FAX (303)772-4069. **Ad Acc, Adv Mgr:** Dusty Johnson. **Circ:** 5,000. **Continued by** Scout Business Software Directory.
 Desc: Contains more than 400 pages of directory information on IBM System/36,/38 and AS/400 computers.

US
SELECTWARE SYSTEM. CD-ROM. See Computers-Computer Industry and Industry Directories.

LC QA76.75 .S52
US
SHAREWARE GRAB-BAG [COMPUTER FILE]. (198?)-. English. Irregular. $112.74 Minnesota residents; $106.80 other. Alde Publishing, PO Box 39326, Minneapolis MN 55396. **Tel** (612)474-3755.
 Desc: Contains over 6500 shareware programs for the IBM PC/XT/AT/PS2 and compatibles in high sierra format.

LC QA76.753 .S52
DD 005.365
ISSN 1042-0681
US
CEASED
SHAREWARE MAGAZINE. **Added/Corp** PC Software Interest Group (Sunnyvale, Calif.). **VFOAT** Shareware. Vol. 3, No. 1 (Jan./Feb. 1988)-(Sept./Oct. 1993). Periodical. English. PC-SIG Inc, 1030 East Duane Avenue, Sunnyvale CA 94086. **Tel** (408)730-9291, (800)245-6717, FAX (408)730-2107. **ED** Michelle Ramage. Index available. cum. index. **Bk Rev. Ad Acc. Circ:** 100,000 (ctrl).
 Desc: In-depth reviews of shareware. Light hearted, humorous, human interest pieces.

ISSN 1120-3595
IT
SUSPENDED
UDC 681.3
SISTEMI SOFTWARE. [Sist. softw.]. (1990)-Suspended (1994). Periodical. Italian. Twelve times a year. Edizioni Ritman, via Varesina 76, 20156 Milan Italy. **Tel** 011 39 2 38008859, FAX 011 39 2 66982686.

ISSN 0755-3579
FR
TITLE CHANGE
UDC 681.3
SOFT & MICRO. See Computers-Microcomputers, Personal Computers.

ISSN 0882-3499
DD 005
US
SOFT-LETTER. [Soft-lett.]. **VFOAT** Soft Letter. (198?)-. Periodical. English. Twenty-four times a year. $345.00. Soft-Letter, 17 Main Street, Watertown MA 02172. **Tel** (617)924-3944, FAX (617)924-7288. **ED** Jeffrey Tarter. **Circ:** 1,500 (ctrl). available on CD-ROM from Computer Library; available on an online database (file 675/Full-Text) from DIALOG; and Information Access Company. Documents available.
 Desc: Newsletter which focuses on trends and strategies in software publishing and development. Topics include market intelligence, product design, distribution, new technologies, company operating statistics and an annual ranking by revenues of the top 100 independent micro software companies in the U.S.
 Ind/Abst Comput. ASAP [Full Txt.]; Comput. Database [Full Txt.]; Comput. Lit. Index.

ISSN 1064-8860
DD 005
US
CCC
SOFT WATCH. See Computers-Abstracting, Bibliographies and Statistics.

ISSN 1065-7290
DD 005
US
SOFTAWARENESS (AUSTIN, TEX.). (SOFTAWARENESS : A CAD/CAM/CAE JOURNAL & GUIDE.). [Softawareness]. Vol. 1, No. 1 (Nov. 1992)-. Trade Publication. English. Twelve times a year. $24.95. OmRay Inc., PO Box 203550, Austin TX 78720-3550. **Tel** (512)250-1700, FAX (512)250-1016.

ISSN 0886-4152
DD 004
US
SOFTDISK. (SOFTDISK [COMPUTER FILE].). [Softdisk]. (Oct. 1981)-. Periodical. English. Twelve times a year. $69.95 US; $89.95 Canada and Mexico; $109.95 other. Loadstar Inc., PO Box 30007, Shreveport LA 71130. **Tel** (318)221-8718.
 Desc: Available on 5 1/4" diskettes. System requirements: Apple II+, IIe and IIc; 48K, DOS 3.3; some programs require additional peripherals.

GW
Pr Rev.
SOFTWARE ABC. German. DM100.00. Wirtschaft Recht und Steuern Verlag, Faunhofstr 5, Postfach 1363, D-8033 Planegg Germany. **Tel** 089/8577944-47, FAX 857 7990, telex 772442 HANFED. Index available. cum. index. **Circ:** 10,000.
 Desc: Provides information on software and how to improve your current software.

ISSN 1075-0932
US
●**SOFTWARE CEO.** [Softw. CEO]. **VFOAT** Software Chief Executive Officer; Software CEO Magazine. Vol. 1, No. 1 (Nov./Dec. 1994)-. Periodical. English. Twelve times a year. $25.00. Oaktree Publishing, 21041 Western Avenue, Suite 160, Torrance CA 90501. **Tel** (310)787-2193.

ISSN 0945-8115
GW
●**SOFTWARE CONCEPTS & TOOLS.** **Added/Corp** Association for Computing Machinery. **VFOAT** Software Concepts and Tools. Vol. 15, No. 1 (1994)-. Periodical. English. Four times a year. $184.00. Springer-Verlag GmbH & Company KG, Heidelberger Platz 3, D-14197 Berlin Germany. **Tel** 011 49 30 8207223, FAX 011 49 30 8214091, telex 183 319 SPBLN D. **(Subscription address:** Springer-Verlag New York Inc. / North America, PO Box 2485, Journal Fulfillment, Secaucus NJ 07096. **Tel** (201)348-4033, (800)777-4643, FAX (201)348-4505.) **Continues** Structured Programming, 0935-1183.
 Ind/Abst Curr. Cit.

US
SOFTWARE DEVELOPER'S MONTHLY. See Computers-Computer Engineering.

ISSN 1070-8588
DD 005
US
CCC
●**SOFTWARE DEVELOPMENT.** [Softw. dev.]. (July 1993)-. Trade Publication. English. Twelve times a year. $39.00. Miller Freeman Inc., 600 Harrison Street, San Francisco CA 94107. **Tel** (415)905-2337, (415)905-2200, FAX (415)905-2240, telex 278273. **(Subscription address:** Sunbelt Fulfillment Services, PO Box 5039, Brentwood TN 37024. **Tel** (800)685-3435.) **ED** Larry O'Brien. **Circ:** 70,000.
 Desc: Highlights products intended to aid quality control, increase productivity, and streamline the development process for the corporate developer.

ISSN 0964-6841
DD 005.1
UK
CCC
SOFTWARE DEVELOPMENT MONITOR. See Computers-Computer Engineering.

US
SOFTWARE DIGEST. (19??)-. Periodical. English. Twelve times a year. $470.00. National Software Testing Laboratories, PO Box 1000, Plymouth Meeting Corporate Center, Plymouth Meeting PA 19462. **Tel** (610)941-9600, (800)328-2776, FAX (215)941-9952. **(Subscription address:** McGraw Hill / PC Digest, PO Box 551, Hightstown NJ 08520. **)**
 Desc: Tests standalone and networked software applications and environments. Provides comparisons between software applications and environments.

LC QA76.76.E93 R37
DD 005.3
ISSN 0893-6455
US
CCC
SOFTWARE DIGEST RATINGS REPORT. [Softw. dig. rat. rep.]. **Added/Corp** National Software Testing Laboratories. **VFOAT** Ratings Report. Vol. 4, No. 1 (Jan. 1987)-. Periodical. English. Twelve times a year. $450.00. National Software Testing Laboratories, PO Box 1000, Plymouth Meeting Corporate Center, Plymouth Meeting PA 19462. **Tel** (610)941-9600, (800)328-2776, FAX (215)941-9952. **(Subscription address:** National Software Testing Lab, 625 Ridge Pike, Conshohocken PA 19428. **Tel** (610)941-9600.) Index available. cum. **Circ:** 8,000 (ctrl). **Continues** Ratings Newsletter, 0899-7365.
 Desc: Independent and comparative data on IBM PC Business Software, ratings given based on actual user and technical tests.
 Ind/Abst Comput. Rev. Index (Oct. 1987-).

UK
SOFTWARE DIRECTORY FOR THE OFFSHORE INDUSTRY. Directory. English. Every 2 years. £85.00. Marine Technology Directorate Limited, 19 Buckingham Street, London WC2N 6EF United Kingdom. **Tel** 011 44 171 3210674, FAX 011 44 171 9304323. **ED** Sharon Clark. available on microfiche.
 Desc: Identifies range of programs and location of software publishers; offers information on pipeline, drilling and production programs.

ISSN 1071-3441
DD 004
US
SOFTWARE DIRECTORY. SYSTEMS & UTILITIES. (SOFTWARE DIRECTORY. SYSTEMS & UTILITIES : MAINFRAME, MINICOMPUTER & MICROCOMPUTER BUSINESS SOFTWARE.). [Softw. dir., Syst. util.]. **Added/Corp** International Computer Programs, Inc. **VFOAT** Systems & Utilities; Systems and Utilities; Mainframe, Minicomputer & Microcomputer Business Software; ICP Software Directory. Systems & Utilities. **VAT** International Computer Programs Software Directory -- Systems & Utilities. 71st Ed. (Sept. 1992)-. English. Three times a year. International Computer Programs Inc / Barbara Lahiff, 823 East Westfield Boulevard, Indianapolis IN 46220. **Tel** (800)428-6179, (317)251-7727. **Formed by the union of** Software Directory. Datacenter Manager, 1049-0337 **and** Software Directory. System Builder, 1049-0345.

ISSN 1065-6146
DD 658
US
CCC
CODEN SECLE3
SOFTWARE ECONOMICS LETTER. (SOFTWARE ECONOMICS LETTER: MAXIMIZING OUR RETURN ON CORPORATE SOFTWARE.). [Softw. econ. lett.]. (1992)-. Periodical. English. Twelve times a year. $395.00. Computer Economics Inc., 5841 Edison Place, Carlsbad CA 92008. **Tel** (800)326-8100, (619)438-8100, FAX (619)431-1126.

LC QA76.758 .S656
DD 005.1/05
ISSN 0268-6961
UK
CCC
CODEN SEJOED
Pr Rev.
SOFTWARE ENGINEERING JOURNAL. See Computers-Computer Engineering.

LC QA76.758 .S6467
DD 005.1/05
ISSN 0163-5948
US
CODEN SFENDP
SOFTWARE ENGINEERING NOTES. See Computers-Computer Engineering.

ISSN 1067-1293
DD 005
US
CEASED
SOFTWARE ENGINEERING STRATEGIES. See Computers-Computer Engineering.

LC QA76.5 .S652
DD 001.64/.029/473
ISSN 0742-5058
US
SOFTWARE EXPRESS. [Softw. express]. (19??)-. Periodical. English. Irregular. $14.95. SKU, 2600 Tenth Street, Berkeley CA 94710.

ISSN 0965-6545
DD 005.3 UK
SOFTWARE FUTURES. [Softw. futures]. (1991)-. English. Twelve times a year. $495.00. APT Data Services, 12 Sutton Row, 4th Floor, London W1V 5FH United Kingdom. **Tel** 011 44 171 2084200, FAX 011 44 171 4391105.

ISSN 1063-147X
DD 005 US
SOFTWARE HANDBOOK (PLYMOUTH MEETING, PA.). (SOFTWARE HANDBOOK.). [Softw. handb.]. **Added/Corp** National Software Testing Laboratories. **VFOAT** NSTL Software Handbook. (1992)-. English. NSTL, Inc., Plymouth Corporate Center, Plymouth Meeting PA 19462.

ISSN 0883-5772
DD 338 US
SOFTWARE INDUSTRY BULLETIN. [Softw. indus. bull.]. **Added/Corp** Digital Information Group. (198?)-. Bulletin. English. Forty-eight times a year. $495.00. Digital Information Group, 51 Bank Street, Stamford CT 06901. **Tel** (800)255-0942, FAX (203)977-8310. **ED** Jeff Silverstein.

LC HD9696.C63 U58388
DD 338.4/70053/097305 US
SOFTWARE INDUSTRY FACTBOOK. **Added/Corp** Digital Information Group. **VFOAT** Software Industry Fact Book. (19??)-. Periodical. English. One time a year. $795.00. Digital Information Group, 51 Bank Street, Stamford CT 06901. **Tel** (800)255-0942, FAX (203)977-8310.

ISSN 1042-7252
DD 384 US
SOFTWARE INDUSTRY REPORT. [Softw. ind. rep.]. (1989)-. Periodical. English. Twenty-four times a year. $495.00. Millin Publishing Group Inc., 714 Church Street, Alexandria VA 22314. **Tel** (703)739-8500. **ED** Mike Cotter and Charles Bailey. Index available (bound in all issues). **Bk Rev. Circ:** 1000. available on an online database (file 648/Full-Text) from DIALOG; and Information Access Company. ***Continues*** *Computer Age. Software Industry Report.*
Desc: Tracks worldwide industry and government software activities and opportunities with an emphsis on innovative strategies for MIS executives, market research and new developments in systems technology. Topics covered include CASE, Ada, AI, Cals, ISDN, open systems, MAP/TOP, object-oriented design, EDI, expert systems and neural networks.
Ind/Abst Trade Ind. ASAP [Full Txt.]; Trade Ind. Index [Full Txt.].

LC QA76.6 .T4429a
DD 001.64/25/0216 US
SOFTWARE INVENTORY CATALOG. **Main/Corp** Texas. Office of the State Auditor. System/Administrative Services Division. (1978)-. Catalog. English. One time a year. Office of the State Auditor, Sam Houston State Office Building, PO Box 12067, Austin TX 78711.

ISSN 0747-6027
DD 001 US
SOFTWARE JOURNAL, THE. [Softw. j.]. Vol. 1, No. 1 (April 1984)-. Periodical. English. Irregular. Software Journal Inc., Pioneer Building, 600 First Avenue, Suite 427, Seattle WA 98104. available on microfilm from University Microfilms International (UMI).

LC KF390.5.C6 A497 ISSN 0897-2680
DD 342 US
SOFTWARE LAW BULLETIN, THE. See Law-Computer Applications.

LC K23 .O35 ISSN 0886-3628
DD 343.73/07800164 347.3037800164 US
CCC
TITLE CHANGE
SOFTWARE LAW JOURNAL. See Law.

LC QA76.75 .S63 ISSN 0897-8085
DD 005 US
CCC
CODEN SMWMEQ
SOFTWARE MAGAZINE (WESTBOROUGH, MASS.). (SOFTWARE MAGAZINE.). [Softw. mag.]. Vol. 8 No. 1 (Jan. 1988)-Vol.13 (Jan. 1993)-. Trade Publication. English. Twelve times a year. $65.00. Sentry Publishing Company, PO Box 542, Winchester MA 01890. **Tel** (508)366-2031. **ED** Michael Bucker. **Ad Acc. Circ:** 90,000 (ctrl). available on microfilm and microfiche from University Microfilms International (UMI); available on an online database (files 15,675/Full-Text) from DIALOG. Documents available from UMI Article Clearinghouse. ***Continues*** *Software News, 0279-9782.*
Desc: Aimed at managers of corporate software resources.
Ind/Abst ABI/INFORM Glob. Ed.; ABI/INFORM [Computer File] (Feb 1988-); Bus. Educ. Index; Comput. ASAP [Full Txt.]; Comput. Database [Full Txt.]; Comput. Ind. Update; Comput. Lit. Index; Curr. Cit.; Microcomput. Abstr. (Jan. 1988-); UMI ABI/Inform--Bus. Period. Ondisc (Feb. 1988-) [Full Txt.].

ISSN 0741-4501
US
CCC
CODEN SMNEEP
SOFTWARE MAINTENANCE NEWS. (SOFTWARE MAINTENANCE NEWS / SIGMA, SPECIAL INTEREST GROUP ON SOFTWARE MAINTENANCE.). [Softw. maint. news]. **Added/Corp** Data Processing Management Association. SIGMA. Vol. 1, No. 1 (Nov. 1983)-. Periodical. English. Six times a year. $60.00 US and Canada; $95.00 other. Software Maintenance News Inc, 141 Saint Marks Place, Suite 5F, Staten Island NY 10301. **Tel** (415)969-5522, FAX (415)969-5949. **ED** Nicholas Zvegintzov. **Bk Rev**, (Qty: 2). **Ad Acc, Adv Mgr:** Judith Marx Golub. **Circ:** 3,000. Documents available from Ask*IEEE.
Desc: Reports monthly on people and technology that enhance, adapt, or correct software, or that support non-technical users. We welcome readers' stories on people, practices, techniques, tools, systems, management, and all other topics relating to dealing with existing software.
Ind/Abst ACM Guide Comput. Lit.; Comput. Rev. (1986-); Data Process. Dig. (1986-); INSPEC (1986-).

ISSN 0960-0906
DD 005.1 UK
SOFTWARE MANAGEMENT. [Softw. manag.]. **VFOAT** Software Management Magazine. (1988)-. Periodical. English. Twelve times a year. $150.59. Process Communications Ltd, 50 Poland Street, St. Giles House, London W1V 4AX United Kingdom. **Tel** 011 44 171 2875000. ***Continues*** *EXE's Software Management, 0953-9735.*
Ind/Abst Curr. Cit.; HILITES.

ISSN 1064-878X
DD 338 US
SOFTWARE MANUFACTURING NEWS. [Softw. manuf. news]. Vol. 1, No. 1 (Aug. 1992)- Vol. 2 & 3 No.1 (Jan. 1993-94)- (Aug. Periodical. English. Twelve times a year. $347.00. Webster Communications, 4255 South Buckley Road, Suite 118, Aspen CO 80013. **Tel** (303)766-1687, FAX (303)766-3483. **Ad Acc.**
Desc: Worldwide coverage of the business and technology of software production, manufacturing and distribution.

ISSN 1060-3964
DD 658 US
SOFTWARE MARKETING JOURNAL. [Softw. mark. j.]. (Jan/Feb 1992)-. Periodical. English. Six times a year. $395.00. Kawalek & Associates, 455 Embaracadero, San Francisco CA 94111.

US
•**SOFTWARE PATENTS.** (1995)-. English. John Wiley & Sons, Inc., 605 Third Avenue, New York NY 10158-0012. **Tel** (212)850-6000, (212)850-6645, FAX (212)850-6088, telex 12-7063. **(Subscription address:** John Wiley & Sons, Inc. / Philadelphia, PO Box 7247, Philadelphia PA 19170. **Tel** (212)850-6645, (800)225-5945.**)**

LC QA76.5 .S653 ISSN 0038-0644
DD 001.6/425/05 UK
CCC
CODEN SPEXBL
Pr Rev.
SOFTWARE : PRACTICE & EXPERIENCE. [Softw. pract. exp.]. **VFOAT** Software, Practice and Experience; Software. **VAT** Software, Practice and Experience. Vol. 1 (Jan./March 1971)-. Periodical. English. Thirteen times a year (monthly with 1 Special Issue). $995.00. John Wiley & Sons Ltd., Baffins Lane, Chichester, West Sussex PO19 1UD United Kingdom. **Tel** 011 44 1243 779777, FAX 011 44 1243 776128 BTG:JWP001, telex 86290 WIBOOKG. **(Subscription address:** John Wiley & Sons, Inc. / Philadelphia, PO Box 7247, Philadelphia PA 19170. **Tel** (212)850-6645, (800)225-5945.**) ED** J. A. Campbell and D. E. Comer. **Bk Rev. Ad Acc. Circ:** 3,200. available on microfilm and microfiche from University Microfilms International (UMI). Documents available from Article Express International, The Genuine Article, Ask*IEEE.
Desc: An established forum for all who design, implement or maintain software. The journal is concerned with details and experience of the tools or methods used to achieve those results.
Ind/Abst Abstr. Hum. Comput. Interact.; ACM Guide Comput. Lit.; Appl. Sci. Technol. Index; Bioeng. Abstr.; CompuMath Cit. Index [Full Cov.]; Comput. Inf. Syst. Abstr. J. [Full Cov.]; Comput. Lit. Index; Comput. Rev.; Curr. Cit.; Curr. Contents Eng. Comput. Technol.; Data Process. Dig.; Educ. Technol. Abstr.; Ei Page One; Eng. Index Annu.; GeoRef; HILITES; Inf. Sci. Abstr.; INSPEC (Jan./March 1971-); J. Ferrocement; Math. Rev.; Pollut. Abstr. Indexes; Res. Alert [Full Cov.]; SCISEARCH; World Publ. Monit.; Zentralbl. Math. Ihre Grenzgeb.

LC QA76 ISSN 1077-4866
DD 005.3 UK
Pr Rev.
•**SOFTWARE PROCESS IMPROVEMENT AND PRACTICE.** (1995)-. Academic Scholarly Publication. English. Two times a year. $175.00. John Wiley & Sons Ltd., Baffins Lane, Chichester, West Sussex PO19 1UD United Kingdom. **Tel** 011 44 1243 779777, FAX 011 44 1243 776128 BTG:JWP001, telex 86290 WIBOOKG. **(Subscription address:** John Wiley & Sons, Inc. / Philadelphia, PO Box 7247, Philadelphia PA 19170. **Tel** (212)850-6645, (800)225-5945.**)** available in microform from University Microfilms International (UMI).

ISSN 1070-5457
US
•**SOFTWARE PROCESS, QUALITY & ISO 9000.** **VFOAT** Software Process, Quality and ISO 9000. (1993)-. Periodical. English. Twelve times a year. $150.00. Systems & Software / A Division of Intergratise Inc., PO Box 225, Holmdel NJ 07733. **Tel** (908)966-0005, FAX (908)946-4149. **ED** Gargi Adhikari. Index available. cum. index. **Bk Rev**, (Qty: 20). **Circ:** 2,000 (ctrl). ***Continues*** *Software Quality & ISO 9000, 1070-0145.*
Desc: News and information on software process, quality systems, process assessment and registrations.

ISSN 1032-1071
DD 005.3 AT
SOFTWARE PRODUCTIVITY REVIEW. [Softw. prod. rev.]. **Added/Corp** Australian Software Research Centre. (1988)-. Periodical. English. Six times a year. 325.00Aus$. Australian Software Centre, PO Box 214, Summer Hill New South Wales, 2130 Australia. **Tel** 02 9226767, FAX 02 7993665. **ED** D. Hiton. ***Continues*** *Australasian Software Report, 0314-9285.*

ISSN 1069-1278
DD 005 US
•**SOFTWARE PUBLISHER.** [Softw. publ.]. (1993)-. English. Twelve times a year. Webcom Communications Corporation, 10555 East Darthmouth Avenue, #330, Aurora CO 80014. **Tel** (303) 745-5711, FAX (303) 745-5712. **ED** Sheila Galatowitsch. **Ad Acc, Adv Mgr:** David Crosby. **Circ:** 20,000.
Desc: Written for executives and managers of software publishing companies. Includes features and news articles covering topics ranging from sales and marketing to financial and legal management.

ISSN 0963-9314
DD 005 UK
CCC
CODEN SQJOET
SOFTWARE QUALITY JOURNAL. Vol. 1, No. 1 (Mar. 1992)-. Periodical. English. Four times a year. $255.00. Chapman & Hall, 2-6 Boundary Row, London SE1 8HN United Kingdom. **Tel** 011 44 171 8650066, FAX 011 44 171 5229623, telex 290164 CHAPMA G. **ED** K. Croucher, W. Harrison. Documents available from The Genuine Article.
Desc: Deals with both technical and managerial aspects of software quality. Offers a balanced coverage of practical and research-based material, and relates software quality to wider quality issues.
Ind/Abst CompuMath Cit. Index [Full Cov.]; Res. Alert [Full Cov.].

ISSN 1042-9255
DD 005 US
SOFTWARE QUALITY WORLD. [Softw. qual. world]. (Nov. 1989)-. Periodical. English. Twelve times a year. $50.00 (individuals). ProQual Inc., PO Box 337, Medfield MA 02052. **Tel** (508)359-7273.

ISSN 1078-9847
DD 005 US
•**SOFTWARE QUARTERLY.** (SOFTWARE QUARTERLY : SQ : IBM'S MAGAZINE OF SOFTWARE TECHNOLOGIES.). [Softw. q.]. **Added/Corp** International Business Machines Corporation. Software Solutions Division. **VFOAT** SQ. Vol. 1, No. 1 (Fall/Winter 1994)-. Periodical. English. Four times a year. $19.00. IBM Magazines, 590 Madison Avenue, 32nd Floor, New York NY 10022. **Tel** (212)745-6429, FAX (212)745-7984.

US
SOFTWARE REFERENCE GUIDE. **Added/Corp** International City Management Association. International City/County Management Association. (1986/1987)-. English. One time a year. $45.00. International City Management Association, 777 North Capitol Street NE, Suite 500, Washington DC 20002. **Tel** (202)289-4262, (800)745-8780, FAX (202)962-3500. **(Subscription address:** International City Management Association, PO Box 2011, Annapolis Junction MD 20701. **)**

LC QA76.75 .S64 ISSN 8755-7169
DD 005.3 US
SOFTWARE REVIEWS ON FILE. [Softw. rev. file]. **Added/Corp** Facts on File, Inc. Vol. 1, Issue 1 (Jan. 1985)-. Periodical. English. Twelve times a year. $259.00. Facts on File Publications, 11 Penn Plaza, 15th Floor, New York NY 10001. **Tel** (212)967-8000, (800)322-8755. **ED** Scott F Night, Karen M Rufa. Index available. cum. index. **Circ:** 1,500.
Desc: Journal with 200 review condensations of more than 50 software programs, collected in a buchram binder with monthly cumulative index.

US
SOFTWARE STRATEGY SERVICE. English. Irregular. $5,000.00. Forrester Research Inc., 1 Brattle Square, Cambridge MA 02138. **Tel** (617)497-7090.

Computers —Software

SOFTWARE SYSTEMS AND TECHNIQUES ABSTRACTS. (19??)-. English. Six times a year. £60.00 UK; £64.00 Europe; £66.00 other. Techgnosis Ltd., Blade House, Battersea Road, Cheshire SK4 3EA United Kingdom. **Tel** 011 44 161 4422639, FAX 011 44 161 4431162.
ISSN 0958-465X
UK
LC QA76.76.T48 S65
DD 005.1/4/05
ISSN 0960-0833
UK
CODEN JTREET

Pr Rev.
SOFTWARE TESTING, VERIFICATION & RELIABILITY. (JOURNAL OF SOFTWARE TESTING VERIFICATION AND RELIABILITY.). [Softw. test. verif. reliab.]. **VFOAT** Software Testing, Verification and Reliability. Vol. 2, No. 1 (May 1992)-. Periodical. English. Four times a year. $255.00. John Wiley & Sons Ltd., Baffins Lane, Chichester, West Sussex PO19 1UD United Kingdom. **Tel** 011 44 1243 779777, FAX 011 44 1243 776128 BTG:JWP001, telex 86290 WIBOOKG. (**Subscription address:** John Wiley & Sons, Inc. / Philadelphia, PO Box 7247, Philadelphia PA 19170. **Tel** (212)850-6645, (800)225-5945.) **ED** Derek Yates and Lee White. **Bk Rev. Ad Acc. Circ:** 500. *Continues Journal of Software Testing, Verification, and Reliability.*
Desc: Provides primary information on solving problems in the fields of software testing and reliability. Promotes sound theoretical foundations for practical methods.
UK

SOFTWARE USERS YEAR BOOK CD-ROM. (19??)-. Periodical. English. One time a year. £344.00. VNU Business Publications BV, 32-34 Broadwick Street, London W1A 2HG United Kingdom. **Tel** 011 44 171 4394242 ext. 2222, FAX 011 44 171 4379638, telex 23918 VNU G, 8952440.
LC QA76 .S563
DD 001.6/42
ISSN 0038-0652
UK
CODEN SOFWBG

SOFTWARE WORLD. [Softw. world]. Vol. 1, Autumn (1969)-. Periodical. English. Four times a year (Jan., Apr., July, Oct.). $221.00. A. P. Publications Ltd, 377 Saint Johns Street, London EC1V 4LD United Kingdom. **Tel** 011 44 171 8375921, FAX 011 44 171 8371197, telex 8955107. **ED** E. Patterson. Index available. **Bk Rev. Circ:** 1,000. available on microfilm and microfiche from University Microfilms International (UMI). Documents available from Ask*IEEE.
Desc: International news and features of computer software products.
Ind/Abst Comput. Lit. Index; Comput. Rev./ INSPEC (Summer 1970-); Pollut. Abstr. Indexes (Summer 1970-).
LC QA76 .S563
DD 001.6/42
ISSN 1023-0661
SA

●**SOFTWARE WORLD.** (1994)-. Trade Publication. English. Thomson Publications Pty, PO Box 56182, Pinegowrie 2123 South Africa. **Tel** 011 27 11 7892144.
LC HF5439.C67 S66
DD 338.7/610016425/02573
ISSN 8756-9833
US

SOFTWARE WRITERS MARKET (POMONA, N.Y.). See Computers-Computer Industry and Industry Directories.
LC HD9000.1 .S64
DD 630/.68
ISSN 8756-1050
US

SOFTWHERE. AGRI-BUSINESS. See Agriculture-Computer Applications.
LC TA345 .S598
DD 620/.0028/553
ISSN 8756-1085
US

SOFTWHERE. ENGINEERING. [Softwhere, Eng.]. **VFOAT** Engineering Softwhere. Fall 1984-. English. Two times a year. Moore Data Management Services, Minneapolis MN 55416. **Tel** (612)588-7205.
LC R858.A1 S63
DD 001
NLM W 22; AA1 S65
ISSN 8756-1077
US

SOFTWHERE. HEALTH CARE. See Medical Sciences-Computer Applications.
ISSN 8756-1093
DD 001
US

SOFTWHERE. INSURANCE. See Insurance-Computer Applications.
LC KF242.A1 S64
DD 001
ISSN 8756-1107
US

SOFTWHERE. LEGAL. See Law-Computer Applications.
US

STORE CHECK REPORT. See Business and Economics-Computer Applications.
ISSN 1054-3902
DD 005
US

SYMANTEC. (CUPERTINO, CALIF.). (SYMANTEC.). **Added/Corp** Symantec Corp. **VFOAT** Symantec Magazine. Vol. 1, Issue 1 (Autumn 1990)-. Periodical. English. Four times a year. $16.00. Symantec Corporation, 10201-T Torre Avenue, Cupertino CA 95014. **Tel** (408)253-9600, (800)441-7234, FAX (408)253-3968. **Ad Acc. Circ:** 650,000.
ISSN 0968-0349
UK

TAGLINE (OLNEY). See Publishing.
ISSN 1076-5506
DD 005
US

TICK, TICK, TICK. See Computers-Programs and Programming.
ISSN 0095-4179
US

TRW SOFTWARE SERIES : INDEX TO PUBLICATIONS IN PRINT. See Computers-Abstracting, Bibliographies and Statistics.
NE

UNIX INFO. (19??)-. Dutch. Irregular (8 issues). Fl80.00. Sala Communications, Postbus 43048, 1009 ZA Amsterdam Netherlands. **Tel** 011 31 20 6273198.
LC HD9696.C6 U54
DD 004.165/05
ISSN 0886-2575
US
TITLE CHANGE

UNIX PRODUCTS DIRECTORY. See Computers-Computer Industry and Industry Directories.
ISSN 0730-255X
US

UNIX TOPICS FOR USERS. [UNIX top. users]. **Added/Corp** International Technical Seminars. **VFOAT** U.N.I.X. Topics for Users; UTC. Vol. 1, No. 1 (1981)-. Periodical. English. Six times a year. $95.00. International Technical Seminars, 47 Potomac Street, San Francisco CA 94117. **Tel** (415)621-6415.
ISSN 1062-5003
DD 004
US

UNIX USER. [Unix user]. Vol. 1, #1 (Nov. 1991)-. Periodical. English. Six times a year. $35.00. Hanson Computer Consulting, 1931 West Wilson Street, Suite 342, Batavia IL 60510.
LC QA76.76.O63 U57
DD 005.4/3
ISSN 0739-5922
US
TITLE CHANGE

UNIX/WORLD. [UNIX/world]. **VFOAT** UnixWorld Magazine; Unixworld. **VAT** UNIX World. (1984)-(1993). Periodical. English. McGraw Hill Publishing Company, Inc., 1221 Avenue of the Americas, New York NY 10020. **Tel** (212)512-6410, (800)525-5003, FAX (212)512-6111. (**Subscription address:** Open Computing, PO Box 570, Hightstown NJ 08520.) **ED** David Flack. Index available. cum. index. **Ad Acc. Circ:** 52,000. available on microfilm and microfiche from University Microfilms International (UMI). *Continued by UnixWorld's Open Computing, 1072-4044.*
Desc: Designed to educate and inform people interested in multiuser, multitasking, and open systems computing. For the beginner and expert system user. Features include looks at UNIX related marketing issues, profiles of domestic and international players and their strategies in the UNIX market, etc.
Ind/Abst Comput. Lit. Index; Microcomput. Abstr. (Dec. 1985-Nov. 1986)(1985-).
LC QA76.76.O63 U57
DD 005
ISSN 1072-4044
US
CODEN OPCOEB
TITLE CHANGE

UNIXWORLD'S OPEN COMPUTING. [UnixWorld's open comput.]. **VFOAT** Open Computing. Vol. 11, No. 1 (Jan. 1994)-Vol. 11, No. 7 (July 1994). Trade Publication. English. McGraw Hill Publishing Company, Inc., 1221 Avenue of the Americas, New York NY 10020. **Tel** (212)512-6410, (800)525-5003, FAX (212)512-6111. (**Subscription address:** McGraw Hill Book Company, Princeton Road, Hightstown NJ 08520. **Tel** (717)794-5461.) *Continues UNIX/World, 0739-5922. Continued by Open Computing, 1078-2370.*
Ind/Abst Microcomput. Abstr.
ISSN 0899-2010
DD 005
US

UPTIME (APPLE IIGS). (UPTIME [COMPUTER FILE].). [Uptime]. **VFOAT** Up Time; Uptime. GS. Vol. 1, No. 1 (1988)-. Periodical. English. Twelve times a year. Viking Technologies Inc, PO Box 299, Newport RI 02840.
Desc: System requirements: Apple IIGS.
ISSN 0895-8688
DD 005
US

UPTIME (COMMODORE C64 AND 128). (UPTIME [COMPUTER FILE].). [Uptime]. **VFOAT** Up Time. (198?)-. Periodical. English. Twelve times a year. $69.95. Viking Technologies Inc, PO Box 299, Newport RI 02840.
LC QA76.76.D47 P38
DD 005.265
US

●**VISUAL DEVELOPER.** (1995)-. English. Six times a year. $21.95. Coriolis Group, 7339 East Acoma Drive, Suite 7, Scottsdale AZ 85260. **Tel** (602)483-0192, FAX (602)483-0193. *Continues PC Techniques.*
IT

●**WIN.** (1994)-. Trade Publication. Italian. Eleven times a year. L45.000. Gruppo Editoriale JCE SRL, Via Ferri 6, 20092 Cinisello B Milan Italy. **Tel** 011 39 2 660251, FAX 011 39 2 66025343.
US

WINDOW LETTER, THE. (19??)-. English. Twelve times a year. $245.00. Mendham Technology Group, 144 Talmadge Road, Mendham NJ 07945. **Tel** (201)543-2273, FAX (201)543-6033. *Continues Acknowledge : The Window Letter.*
Desc: For windows and presentation manager developers and users.
LC QA75
DD 004
ISSN 1085-1291
US

●**WINDOWS 95 PROFESSIONAL.** **Added/Corp** Cobb Group. (1995)-. Periodical. English. Twelve times a year. $99.00. Cobb Group, 9420 Bunsen Parkway #300, Louisville KY 40220. **Tel** (502)491-1900, (800)223-8720, FAX (502)491-4200.
ISSN 1081-9363
DD 004
US
CEASED

WINDOWS '95 TRANSITION REPORT. [Windows '95 transit. rep.]. **VFOAT** Windows '95. (1995)-(Aug. 1995). Newsletter. English. Pinnacle Publishing Inc., PO Box 888, Kent WA 98035. **Tel** (206)251-1900, (800)231-1293, FAX (206)251-5057.
Desc: Newsletter for professionals who are moving their companies to Windows 95.
US

WINDOWS LETTER. (19??)-. English. Twelve times a year. $245.00. Mendham Technology Group, 144 Talmadge Road, Mendham NJ 07945. **Tel** (201)543-2273, FAX (201)543-6033. **ED** C. J. Patton. *Continues Acknowledge Windows Letter.*
NE

WINDOWS MAGAZINE. Dutch. Six times a year. Fl5950.00. Windows Magazine AB Service, Postbus 77, 5126 GZ Gilze Netherlands. **Tel** 011 31 1615 7450.
US

●**WINDOWS NT MAGAZINE.** (1995)-. English. Twelve times a year. $39.95. Duke Communications International, 221 East 29th Street, Loveland CO 80539. **Tel** (303)663-4700, (800)373-3853, FAX (303)667-2321, telex 6502618199.
ISSN 1065-3627
DD 005
US
TITLE CHANGE

WINDOWS REPORT, THE. [Windows rep.]. **Added/Corp** Cobb Group. (Sept. 7, 1992)-(1995). Periodical. English. Cobb Group, 9420 Bunsen Parkway #300, Louisville KY 40220. **Tel** (502)491-1900, (800)223-8720, FAX (502)491-4200. *Continued by Windows 95 Professional.*
ISSN 1065-0784
DD 005
US

WINDOWS SOFTWARE CONNECTION. (WINDOWS SOFTWARE CONNECTION [COMPUTER FILE].). [Windows softw. connect.]. **Added/Corp** Cobb Group. (Aug. 1992)-. English. Twelve times a year. $59.00. Cobb Group, 9420 Bunsen Parkway #300, Louisville KY 40220. **Tel** (502)491-1900, (800)223-8720, FAX (502)491-4200.
ISSN 1075-6167
DD 005
US

●**WINDOWS TROUBLESHOOTER, THE.** (1993)-. Periodical. English. Twelve times a year. $49.00. Landmark Research, 703 Grand Central Street, Clearwater FL 34616. **Tel** (800)683-6696 ext. 505.
UK

WINDOWS USER. (19??)-. English. Twelve times a year. $84.40. Reed Business Publishing Group / England, Quadrant House, Quadrant Sutton Surrey, SM2 5AS United Kingdom. **Tel** 011 44 1444 445599, FAX 011 44 1444 440421.
US

●**WINDOWS WATCHER.** (1995)-. Newsletter. English. Twelve times a year. $495.00. Computhink Inc, 15127 Northeast 24th, Suite 344, Redmond WA 98052. **Tel** (206)881-7354, FAX (206)883-1452. *Continues Computhink Windows Watcher.*
Desc: Focuses on news and analysis of Windows markets, trends, and technologies. Provides new perspectives about the Windows industry.

Computers —Word Processing

DD 005
ISSN 0896-7717
US
CEASED
WORD FOR WORD. [Word word]. **Added/Corp** Cobb Group. Vol. 1, No. 1 (May, 1988)-(Feb./March 1993). Periodical. English. Cobb Group, 9420 Bunsen Parkway #300, Louisville KY 40220. **Tel** (502)491-1900, (800)223-8720, FAX (502)491-4200.
Desc: Designed for those who use Microsoft Word 4.0 and those who train and support other Word 4.0 users. Includes news and answers about Microsoft Word 4.0.

UK
WORDPERFECT. (19??)-. English. Two times a year. $25.67. Wordperfect Publishing, Weybridge Business Park, Adlestone Road, Adlestone Surrey KT15 2UU United Kingdom. **Tel** 011 44 1345 125289.

DD 005
ISSN 1070-3896
US
●**WORDPERFECT FOR THE LAW OFFICE.**
See Law-Computer Applications.

LC Z52.5.W65 W6847
ISSN 1058-9783
DD 652.5/536
US
WORDPERFECT FOR WINDOWS MAGAZINE. [WordPerfect Windows mag.]. **VFOAT** Word Perfect for Windows Magazine. (Jan. 1992)-. Periodical. English. Twelve times a year. $24.00. Wordperfect Publishing Corporation, 270 West Center Street, Orem UT 84057. **Tel** (801)226-5555, (800)228-9626, FAX (801)227-3478. **ED** Clair F. Rees and Allen Biehl. Index available. cum. index (on disk).
Ad Acc, Adv Mgr: Maurice Beaujeu. **Circ:** 35,000 (ctrl).
Desc: How-to articles relating to WordPerfect 5.1 for Windows and other WPCorp software. Also includes reviews of compatible third party products.

DD 005
ISSN 1053-9638
US
CEASED
WORDPERFECT REPORT. [WordPerfect rep.]. **Added/Corp** WordPerfect Corporation. **VFOAT** Word Perfect Report. Vol. 4, No. 4 (Nov. 1990)-(Summer/Fall 1994). Periodical. English. WordPerfect Publishing Corporation, MS7100, 1555 North Technology Way, Orem UT 84057-2399. **Tel** (800)321-4566, (801)222-2685. **ED** Alex Caldiero. **Continues** WPCorp Report, 1040-1210.
Desc: An update of software and events.

DD 652
ISSN 1063-2719
US
CEASED
WORDPERFECT SOFTWARE CONNECTION. See Computers-Word Processing.

US
WORKGROUP COMPUTING SERIES. DESKTOP APPLICATIONS. Added/Corp Datapro Information Services Group. **VFOAT** Desktop Applications. (June 1992)-. Periodical. English. Twelve times a year. $428.00. Datapro Information Services Group, 600 Delran Parkway, Delran NJ 08075. **Tel** (609)764-0100, (800)328-2776, FAX (609)764-8953. **Continues in part** Datapro Reports on Microcomputers, 0741-2541.

US
WORKGROUP COMPUTING SERIES. SYSTEMS SOFTWARE (OS/NOS/GUI). Added/Corp Datapro Information Services Group. **VFOAT** Systems Software (OS/NOS/GUI); Systems Software; Information Technology Solutions, Workgroup Computing Series. Systems Software (OS/NOS/GUI); Workgroup Computing Series. Systems Software OS, Network OS, Graphical User Interfaces. (June 1992)-. Periodical. English. Twelve times a year. $428.00. Datapro Information Services Group, 600 Delran Parkway, Delran NJ 08075. **Tel** (609)764-0100, (800)328-2776, FAX (609)764-8953. **Continues in part** Datapro Reports on Microcomputers.

DD 005
ISSN 0895-4372
US
CEASED
WORKSHOP (LOUISVILLE, KY.). (THE WORKSHOP.). [Workshop]. **Added/Corp** Cobb Group. Vol. 1, No. 1 (Apr. 1988)-(Sept. 1994). Periodical. English. Cobb Group, 9420 Bunsen Parkway #300, Louisville KY 40220. **Tel** (502)491-1900, (800)223-8720, FAX (502)491-4200.
Desc: Newsletter for Microsoft and software for the PC user.

DD 006
ISSN 1062-6336
US
X-HEIGHT (WESTPORT, CONN.). (X-HEIGHT.). [X-height]. **VFOAT** X Height. (199?)-. Periodical. English. Two times a year. Free to Fonthaus customers. Fonthaus Inc., 1375 King's Highway, Fairfield CT 06430. **Tel** (203)367-1993. **Circ:** 20,000 (ctrl).

WORD PROCESSING

DD 378
ISSN 1047-2452
US
COMPUTER-ASSISTED COMPOSITION JOURNAL, THE. [Comput.-assist. compos. j.]. **Added/Corp** Methodist College (Fayetteville, N.C.). **VFOAT** CACJ. Vol. 1, No. 1 (Summer 1986)-. Periodical. English. Three times a year. $25.00. Human Technology Interface, 163 Wood Wedge Way, Sanford NC 27330. **Tel** (919)499-9216, FAX (919)499-9216.

LC HF5548.2 .D537
ISSN 0278-9663
DD 652
US
DIRECTORY OF WORD PROCESSING MANAGEMENT. [Dir. word process. manage.]. Premier Issue 1981-. Directory. English. Two times a year. $160.00 per copy. Word Systems Division, Applied Management Services, Box 73, Massapequa Park NY 11762.

DD 005
ISSN 1078-7968
US
●**DO IT WITH MICROSOFT PUBLISHER FOR WINDOWS.** [Do it Microsoft publ. Windows]. **VFOAT** Microsoft Publisher. Vol. 1, No. 1 (Nov. 1994)-. Periodical. English. Twelve times a year. $59.00. IDG Newsletter Corporation, 77 Franklin Street, Suite 310, Boston MA 02110. **Tel** (617)482-8470, (800)807-0771, FAX (617)338-0164. **ED** Scot Fields. **Circ:** 10,000.
Desc: Tips and Techniques for Microsoft Publisher users.

DD 001.64/05
ISSN 0706-1773
CN
INFORMATIQUE QUEBEC. See Computers-Electronic Data Processing.

DD 652
ISSN 1073-936X
US
●**INSIDE MICROSOFT WORD 6.** [Inside Miscosoft Word 6]. **Added/Corp** Cobb Group. **VFOAT** Inside Microsoft Word Six. Vol. 1, No. 1 (Jan. 1994)-. Periodical. English. Twelve times a year. $59.00. Cobb Group, 9420 Bunsen Parkway #300, Louisville KY 40220. **Tel** (502)491-1900, (800)223-8720, FAX (502)491-4200.

LC KF320.A9 P45
ISSN 1049-3964
DD 340/.068/2
US
PERFECT LAWYER, THE. See Law-Computer Applications.

DD 005
ISSN 0889-3438
US
PROFESSIONAL REPORT (BOSTON, MASS.). (THE PROFESSIONAL REPORT : THE INDEPENDENT REPORT FOR WANG PROFESSIONAL SYSTEM USERS.). [Prof. rep.]. (198?)-. Periodical. English. Twelve times a year. $75.00. Computer Group, Inc., PO Box 82, Cambridge MA 02238-0179. **ED** Jay Honeycutt. **Circ:** 1,300. **Continues** Wang Professional, 0740-0888.
Ind/Abst Bus. Index (1985-1986); Gen. BusinessFile (1985-1986); Gen. Period. Index (1985-1986); INFO-SOUTH Abstr.; Mag. Search.

LC Z52.5.I27 R37
ISSN 0742-0684
DD 652/.5
US
RATINGS BOOK, THE. (THE RATINGS BOOK / FROM THE SOFTWARE TESTING LABORATORIES OF SOFTWARE DIGEST.). [Rat. book]. Vol. 1 (1984/85) -. English. Twelve times a year. Software Digest Inc, 1 Wynnewood Road, Wynnewood PA 19096.

DD 652
ISSN 0890-524X
US
SCROLL (MALVERNE, N.Y.). (SCROLL : OFFICIAL NEWSLETTER OF THE WORD/PROCESSING USERS' GROUP.). **Added/Corp** Word/Processing Users' Group (Malverne, N.Y.). (1986)-. Newsletter. English. Six times a year. $25.00. Charles Babbage Memorial Fund, 7958 SW 105 Place, Miami FL 33173. **Tel** (305)274-0099. **ED** David Rafky. cum. index.
Bk Rev. Ad Acc. ctrl circ.
Desc: Newsletter for computer users of Wordstar word processing software.

UK
TEXT & IMAGE NEWS. Newsletter. English. Twelve times a year. £210.00 UK; £230.00 US, Canada and Mexico. Wharton Publishing Limited, First Floor Regal House, Twickenham Middlesex, TW1 3QS United Kingdom. **Tel** 011 44 181 8916197.
Desc: First concentrated on word processing systems. Now in addition to word processing, desktop publishing and more recently electronic document management is now focused on as well.

LC Z52.2 .T49
ISSN 1053-900X
DD 652.505
US
CODEN TTECEY
TEXT TECHNOLOGY. [TEXT technol.]. **Added/Corp** Wright State University. Vol. 1, No. 1 (Jan. 1991)-. Periodical. English. Four times a year. $72.00. TEXT Technology, 221 Beadle Hall, Dakota State University, Madison SD 57042. **Tel** (605)256-5270. **ED** Jim Schwartz and Arthur Molitierno. **Bk Rev. Ad Acc. Circ:** 1,000. Documents available from Ask*IEEE. **Continues** Research in Word Processing Newsletter, 0748-5484.
Desc: Brings to academic and corporate writers and teachers of writing analysis of microcomputer hardware and software, discussions of programming techniques, book reviews, updates of significant events in computing worldwide, an annotated bibliography, and much more.
Ind/Abst INSPEC (Jan. 1991-).

DD 362
ISSN 0890-2658
US
VIEWPOINT. See Education-Special Education and Rehabilitation.

ISSN 0277-268X
US
WILEY WORD PROCESSING SERIES. [Wiley word process. ser.]. Monographic series. English. Irregular. Price varies per volume. John Wiley & Sons, Inc., 605 Third Avenue, New York NY 10158-0012. **Tel** (212)850-6000, (212)850-6645, FAX (212)850-6088, telex 12-7063. **(Subscription address:** John Wiley & Sons / UK, Baffins Lane, Chichester, West Sussex PO19 1UD United Kingdom. **Tel** 011 44 1243 779777, FAX 011 44 243 776128, telex 86290 WIBOOKG.)

ISSN 0196-8114
US
WORD PROCESSING (FRANKLIN LAKES). (WORD PROCESSING.). [Word process.]. Periodical. English. Office Products Division, International Business Machines Corporation, 400 Parson's Pond Drive, Franklin Lakes NJ 07147.

ISSN 0895-0628
US
WORD PROCESSING, QUALITY CLINIC. [Word process. qual. clin.]. **Added/Corp** Bureau of Business Practice. **VFOAT** Word Processsing. (19??)-. Periodical. English. Twenty-four times a year. $59.76 US; $73.56 Canada. Bureau of Business Practice, 24 Rope Ferry Road, Waterford CT 06386. **Tel** (800)243-0876, (203)442-4365, (800)876-9105, FAX (203)443-1123.

US
WORD PROCESSING SKILLS PROGRAM. English. Twenty-four times a year. $87.96 US; $107.52 Canada (includes Word Processing Quality Clinic, Office Skills Workshop, and Office Guide). Bureau of Business Practice, 24 Rope Ferry Road, Waterford CT 06386. **Tel** (800)243-0876, (203)442-4365, (800)876-9105, FAX (203)443-1123.

LC Z52.5.W65 W75
ISSN 1042-5152
DD 686.2/254436
US
CODEN WORPEY
WORDPERFECT (OREM, UTAH). (WORDPERFECT : THE MAGAZINE.). [WordPerfect]. **VFOAT** WordPerfect, The Magazine; Word Perfect; WP Magazine; WordPerfect Magazine. (Jan. 1989)-. Periodical. English. Twelve times a year. $24.00. Wordperfect Publishing Corporation, 270 West Center Street, Orem UT 84057. **Tel** (801)226-5555, (800)228-9626, FAX (801)227-3478. **ED** Lisa Bearnson. Index available. **Ad Acc, Adv Mgr:** Mo Beaujeu. **Circ:** 240,000 (ctrl).
Desc: How-to articles for using WordPerfect. Applications including macros and forms. Basic articles also. Includes reviews of add-on products compatible with WordPerfect.

DD 652
ISSN 1063-2719
US
CEASED
WORDPERFECT SOFTWARE CONNECTION. (WORDPERFECT SOFTWARE CONNECTION [COMPUTER FILE].). [WordPerfect softw. connect.]. **Added/Corp** Cobb Group. (July 1992)-(Apr. 1995). Periodical. English. Cobb Group, 9420 Bunsen Parkway #300, Louisville KY 40220. **Tel** (502)491-1900, (800)223-8720, FAX (502)491-4200.

US
WORDPERFECTIONIST, THE. Added/Corp WordPerfect Support Group. (198?)-. Periodical. English. Twelve times a year. $69.00. Cobb Group, 9420 Bunsen Parkway #300, Louisville KY 40220. **Tel** (502)491-1900, (800)223-8720, FAX (502)491-4200. **ED** Richard P. Wilkes and Alessondra B. Wilkes. **Bk Rev. Circ:** 40,000.
Desc: Provides tips and tricks and informs members with Word Perfectionist Corporation products.

US
CEASED
WRITING NOTEBOOK. See Education-Computer Applications.

Consumer Education and Protection

CONSUMER EDUCATION AND PROTECTION

LC HC360.C63 D46b
DK

AARSBERETNING. Main/Corp Denmark. Forbrugerstyrelsen. (1988)-. Danish. J H Schultz Boghandel, 19 Montergade, DK-1057 K Copenhagen Denmark. **Continues in part** Denmark. Forbrugerklagenaevnet. Aarsberetning, 0106-4932; Denmark. Forbrugerombudsmanden. Beretning - Forbrugerombudsmanden, 0106-2328.

ISSN 0010-9975
US

ACCI NEWSLETTER. Added/Corp American Council on Consumer Interests. Vol. 37, No. 6 (September 1989)-. Newsletter. English. Six times a year. $125.00 US; $137.00 Canada and Mexico; $143.00 other Comes with American Council on Consumer Interests membership. American Council on Consumer Interest, 240 Stanley Hall, University of Missouri, Columbia MO 65211. **Tel** (314)882-3817, FAX (314)884-6571. **Continues** Newsletter (American Council on Consumer Interests), 0010-9975.

US

ACUPOLL REPORTS - FOODS & BEVERAGES. See Business and Economics-Marketing and Purchasing.

LC TT955
DD 646.7
US

ACUPOLL REPORTS - HEALTH & BEAUTY AIDS & HOUSEHOLD PRODUCTS. (19??)-. English. Twelve times a year. $1995.00. Marketing Intelligence Service Ltd., 6473D Route 64, Naples NY 14512. **Tel** (716)374-6326, (800)836-5710, FAX (714)374-5217, telex 469979. **Desc:** Published in conjunction with AcuPOLL RESEARCH, Inc. - contains quantitative data on the consumer appeal for the most significant, innovative and impactful grocery store products entering test market or national distribution.

LC HF5415.3 .A84b
DD 658.8/34
ISSN 0098-9258
US
Pr Rev.

ADVANCES IN CONSUMER RESEARCH. [Adv. consum. res.]. **Main/Corp** Association for Consumer Research (U.S.). Vol. 1 (1974)-. English. One time a year (May). $59.00. Association for Consumer Research, Brigham Young University, 632 TNRB, Provo UT 84602. **Tel** (801)378-2080, FAX (801)378-5984. **Circ:** 1,300. Documents available from The Genuine Article. **Supersedes** Association for Consumer Research (U.S.). Proceedings of the Annual Conference), 0084-6856. **Desc:** Current research on consumer behavior. **Ind/Abst** Acad. Abstr.; Acad. Search; Arts Humanit. Citation Index [Select. Cov.]; Curr. Cit.; EP Collect.; Homework Help.; INFO-SOUTH Abstr.; Mag. Search; Manage. Contents (1974-); MasterFile FullTEXT 1000; MasterFile FullTEXT 350; MasterFile FullTEXT 650; MasterFile FullTEXT (Jan. 1992-); OCLC; Pub. Lib. FullTEXT; Res. Alert [Full Cov.]; Soc. Sci. Cit. Index [Full Cov.]; Telebase.

LC HC110.C63 A63
DD 363
ISSN 1044-7385
US

ADVANCING THE CONSUMER INTEREST. (ADVANCING THE CONSUMER INTEREST : ACI.). [Adv. consum. interest]. **Added/Corp** American Council on Consumer Interests. **VFOAT** ACI. Vol. 1, No. 1 (1989)-. Trade Publication. English. Two times a year (Apr., Oct.). $125.00 US; $137.00 Canada and Mexico; $143.00 other Comes with American Council on Consumer Interests membership. American Council on Consumer Interest, 240 Stanley Hall, University of Missouri, Columbia MO 65211. **Tel** (314)882-3817, FAX (314)884-6571.

ISSN 0950-5458
DD 361.06
UK

ADVISER (WOLVERHAMPTON). [Adviser Wolverh.]. (1986)-. Periodical. English. Six times a year. $59.89. NACAB, 65 Waterloo Road, Wolverhampton WV1 4QU United Kingdom. **Tel** 011 44 1902 310568, FAX 011 44 1902 710068. **ED** Peter Madge and Jill Newton. Index available (published in Sept. issue). cum. index. **Bk Rev. Ad Acc, Adv Mgr:** H.A. Horton. **Circ:** 3,750. Formed by the union of Rights Workers' Bulletin, 0267-727X; Housing Aid **and** In the Black. **Desc:** Guide to housing, benefits, employment, consumer and money advice. Includes information on the law, procedure and practice. Also provides news, reviews, comments and case law, including abstracts. **Ind/Abst** Curr. Cit.

LC HC465.C6 A67
JA

AKUROSU. See Business and Economics-Economic History, Conditions.

LC TX335 .M246
LE

AL-MALAYIN = AL MALAYEEN. VFOAT Al Malayeen; Malayeen. Vol. 1, No. 1 (April 1983)-. Periodical. Arabic. Twelve times a year. 15.00 single issue. Al-Muassasah Al-Ammah Lil-Ilam, Beirut Lebanon.

LC TX335 .M87
JO

AL-MUSTAHLIK = AL MUSTAHLEK. **VFOAT** Mustahlek; Almustahlek. (19??)-. Periodical. Arabic (English). Twelve times a year. Majallat Al-Mustahlik, S B 9415, Amman Jordan. **Tel** 637912. **Bk Rev. Ad Acc. Circ:** 22,000. **Desc:** Aims at increasing the public awareness of their local industry; stresses quality rather than price or outlooks.

LC HC101 .A547
ISSN 0276-2900
US
CCC

AMERICAN MARKETPLACE. Vol. 7, No. 14 (July 10, 1986)-. Periodical. English. Twenty-six times a year (every other Thursday). $364.00. Business Publishers Inc., 951 Pershing Drive, Silver Spring MD 20910-4464. **Tel** (301)587-6300, (800)274-0122, FAX (301)585-9075. available for an online database from NEWSNET; and (files 16,636/Full-Text) DIALOG; available with charts. **Absorbed** U.S. Census Report. **Desc:** Provides news on marketing trends, census data, new non-governmental marketing studies, demographic shifts, the economy and experts in the field. Also provides insight and data on all the breaking news in the "numbers" field, and gives the information in a usable form. Each issue also contains US Census Report. **Ind/Abst** PROMT [Full Txt.]; PTS Newsl. Database [Full Txt.].

ISSN 1052-3065
DD 542
US
CCC

ANALYTICAL CONSUMER. [Anal. consum.]. No. 1 (Sept. 1990)-. Periodical. English. Eleven times a year. $260.00. Analytical Consumer Inc., 118 Pheasant Hill Lane, Carlisle MA 01741-1540. **Tel** (508)369-9079. **ED** Jo Rita Jordan, PhD. **Absorbed** Microscope Technology and News.

LC HC110.C63 C69a
DD 381/.06/273
ISSN 0094-8853
US

ANNUAL REPORT - COUNCIL OF BETTER BUSINESS BUREAUS. Main/Corp Council of Better Business Bureaus. (19??)-. English. One time a year. Free on request. Council of Better Business Bureaus, 4200 Wilson Boulevard, Suite 800, Arlington VA 22203. **Tel** (703)276-0100, FAX (703)525-8277. **Desc:** Information on better business bureaus and consumer protection.

LC KFN5375 .A243
US

ANNUAL REPORT / NEW YORK STATE ASSEMBLY, COMMITTEE ON CONSUMER AFFAIRS & PROTECTION. Main/Corp New York (State). Legislature. Assembly. Standing Committee on Consumer Affairs and Protection. **VFOAT** Annual Report of the New York State Assembly Standing Committee on Consumer Affairs and Protection. (1980)-. English. One time a year. Free on request. Consumer Affairs & Protection, Capitol Room 513, Albany NY 12248. **Tel** (518)455-4355. **Continues** New York (State). Legislature. Assembly. Standing Committee on Consumer Affairs and Protection. Report. **Desc:** Information on consumer protection.

LC HC117.N8 N62a
DD 354.7160082/042/06
ISSN 0713-715X
CN

ANNUAL REPORT - NOVA SCOTIA DEPARTMENT OF CONSUMER AFFAIRS. (ANNUAL REPORT FOR THE YEAR ENDED MARCH 31 ... / NOVA SCOTIA DEPARTMENT OF CONSUMER AFFAIRS.). [Annu. rep. - N.S. Dep. Consum. Aff.]. **Main/Corp** Nova Scotia. Dept. of Consumer Affairs. **VFOAT** Annual Report for the Fiscal Year Ending March 31 ... . (197?)-(199?). English. One time a year. Free on request. Nova Scotia Department of Consumer Affairs, PO Box 998, Halifax Nova Scotia B3J 2X3 Canada. **Tel** (902)424-4690.

LC HC607.W47 W45a
DD 354.9410082/042/06
AT

ANNUAL REPORT OF THE COMMISSIONER FOR CONSUMER AFFAIRS FOR THE YEAR ENDED JUNE 30 ... . Main/Corp Western Australia. Bureau of Consumer Affairs. (1982)-. English. One time a year. Free on request. Ministry of Consumer Affairs, Po Box 6355, East Perth, 6004 Australia. **Tel** 09 222-0666.

LC HC607.T37 T38a
DD 354.9460082/042/06
AT

ANNUAL REPORT OF THE CONSUMER AFFAIRS COUNCIL UPON THE ACTIVITIES OF THE COUNCIL. Main/Corp Tasmania. Consumer Affairs Council. (1976)-. English. One time a year. Free on request. OFC Consumer Affairs, GPO 1244J, Hobart Tasman 7001 Australia. **Tel** 011 61 2 302662. **Continues** Annual Report of the Consumers Protection Council Upon the Activities of the Council.

LC HC107.S73 C637a
DD 353.97570082/042/06
US

ANNUAL REPORT OF THE DEPARTMENT OF CONSUMER AFFAIRS OF THE STATE OF SOUTH CAROLINA. Main/Corp South Carolina. Dept. of Consumer Affairs. (19??)-. English. One time a year (Jan.). Free on request. South Carolina Department of Consumer Affairs, PO Box 5757, Columbia SC 29250. **Tel** (803)734-9458, FAX (803)734-9365.

US

ANNUAL REPORT OF THE FEDERAL TRADE COMMISSION. See Business and Economics-Commerce.

LC HB235.H75 A56
DD 338.5/28/095125
HK

ANNUAL REPORT ON THE CONSUMER PRICE INDEX. See Business and Economics.

LC HD2767.M62 M56a
DD 353.97760087
US

ANNUAL REPORT / RESIDENTIAL UTILITY CONSUMER UNIT, OFFICE OF CONSUMER SERVICES, MINNESOTA DEPARTMENT OF COMMERCE. See Public Administration-Public Utilities.

ISSN 0739-3857
US

ARIZONA CONSUMER, THE. Added/Corp Arizona Consumers' Council. (19??)-. Periodical. English. Four times a year (Mar., June, Sept., Dec.). $16.00. Arizona Consumers Council, PO Box 1288, Phoenix AZ 85001. **Tel** (602)265-9625. **ED** Phyllis Rowe.

LC TK7881.8 .A93
DD 747/.9
ISSN 1041-5378
US

AUDIO/VIDEO INTERIORS. See Sound Recordings and Systems.

ISSN 0922-2367
NE
UDC 681.846

AUDIO VIDEO TOTAAL. (1986)-. Periodical. Dutch. Eleven times a year. $92.16. Kombi Media Advertising BV, Postbus 4, 1730 AA Winkel, Netherlands. **Tel** 011 31 2262 2982.

ISSN 0897-9278
DD 362
US

AUGMENTATIVE COMMUNICATION NEWS. See Physically Impaired.

ISSN 0145-6776
US

AUTO INDEX, THE. See Transportation-Automobiles.

ISSN 1053-2021
DD 643
US

BARGAIN HUNTERS AND BUDGETEERS OPPORTUNITY NEWSLETTER. [Bargain hunt. budg. oppor. newsl.]. Vol. 1 (1990)-. Newsletter. English. Every 2 years. $5.00. Prosperity & Profits Unlimited, PO Box 416, Denver CO 80201-0416. **Tel** (303)575-5676. **ED** A.C. Doyle. **Circ:** 1,800. **Desc:** Bargain outlet possibilities.

ISSN 0730-9376
US

BAY AREA CONSUMERS' CHECKBOOK. Added/Corp Center for the Study of Services (San Francisco, Calif.). **VFOAT** Checkbook. Vol. 1, No. 1 (Spring 1982)-. Periodical. English. Irregular. Center for the Study of Services, 733 15th Street NW, Suite 820, Washington DC 20005. **Tel** (202)347-9612, 347-7283.

LC TX335.A1 C5754
DD 640.73/05
ISSN 0882-729X
US

BEST BUYS & DISCOUNT PRICES. **VFOAT** Best Buys and Discount Prices; Best Buys; Consumer Guide; Consumer Guide Best Buys & Discount Prices; Consumer Guide Best Buys and Discount Prices. (19??)-. English. One time a year. $99.00 (Consumer Guide subscription package). Publications International Ltd., 7373 North Cicero Avenue, Lincolnwood IL 60646. **Tel** (708)676-3470. **ED** Ann Taylor. **Circ:** 650,000. **Continues** Consumer Buying Guide : Best Buys &

Consumer Education and Protection

Discount Prices.
Desc: Consumer guide that aims to point out good buys in both products and prices.

ISSN 1071-9717
US
●**BORN TO SHOP. GREAT BRITAIN.** VFOAT Great Britain. (1994)-. English. Every 2 years. $12.00. Harper Collins Publishers, Keystone Industrial Park, Scranton PA 18512. **Tel** (800)242-7737, (800)233-4727, FAX (800)822-4090. **Continues** Born to Shop. England, Scotland, and Ireland, 1068-2287.

ISSN 1066-2782
US
●**BORN TO SHOP. NEW ENGLAND.** (1993)-. English. Every 2 years. $10.00. Harper Collins Publishers, Keystone Industrial Park, Scranton PA 18512. **Tel** (800)242-7737, (800)233-4727, FAX (800)822-4090.

ISSN 1066-2790
US
●**BORN TO SHOP. PARIS.** (1993)-. English. Every 2 years. $10.00. Harper Collins Publishers, Keystone Industrial Park, Scranton PA 18512. **Tel** (800)242-7737, (800)233-4727, FAX (800)822-4090. **Continues** Born to Shop. France.

ISSN 1064-5756
DD 659
US
BRANDADVANTAGE (WILMETTE, ILL.). (BRANDADVANTAGE : A PROFILE OF CONSUMER BRAND USAGE.). [BrandAdvantage]. **Added/Corp** Simmons Market Research Bureau. Standard Rate & Data Service. **VFOAT** Brand Advantage. (1992)-. English. $1,250.00. SRDS / Standard Rate & Data Service, 3004 Glenview Road, Wilmette IL 60091. **Tel** (708)375-5049, (800)851-7737, FAX (708)375-5003.

LC HC110.C63 U47b ISSN 0193-0362
DD 353.007/7 US
BUDGET REQUEST - U.S. CONSUMER PRODUCT SAFETY COMMISSION. See Public Health and Safety.

ISSN 0469-9076
US
BULLETIN. **Main/Corp** National Consumers League. (1961)-. Bulletin. English. Six times a year. $50.00 non-profit organizations; $125.00 profit making organizations; $25.00 individuals. National Consumers League, 1701 K Street Northwest, Suite 1200, Washington DC 20006. **Tel** (202)835-3323, FAX (202)835-0747. **ED** Cleo Manuel. **Bk Rev**. **Circ:** 3,000.
Desc: National consumer interest newsletter containing legislative update. Health care, food and drug safety and guest articles. Consumer power in marketplace and workplace.

LC HF5429.235.U5 B87 ISSN 1042-6175
DD 381./1/02573 US
Pr Rev.
BUSINESS OPPORTUNITIES HANDBOOK. See Business and Economics.

LC TX335 .B84 ISSN 0149-0338
DD 640.73/05 US
BUYER'S GUIDE REPORTS : SHOPPER'S GUIDE. [Buy. guide rep., Shopp. guide]. **VFOAT** Shopper's Guide. English. $3.00. DMR Publications Inc., 1410 East Capitol Drive, Milwaukee WI 53211. **Tel** (414)961-0120.

ISSN 0711-7256
DD 381./3/09711 CN
CAL NEWS. [CAL news]. Periodical. English. Consumer Action League, 353 East Avenue, Vancouver 10 BC V5T 2C4 Canada. **Continues** News (Consumer Action League), 0711-7248.

ISSN 1190-9846
DD 382 CN
●**CANADA'S EXPORT STRATEGY, THE INTERNATIONAL TRADE BUSINESS PLAN. 9, CONSUMER PRODUCTS.** See Business and Economics-Commerce.

ISSN 0008-3275
DD 640.73 CN
CCC
CEASED
CANADIAN CONSUMER (1963). (CANADIAN CONSUMER.). [Can. consum.]. **Added/Corp** Consumers' Association of Canada. **VFOAT** Consommateur; Canadian Consumer. Vol. 1-8, No. 3 (June 1963)-(Nov./Dec. 1970); Vol. 1 (Jan./Feb. 1971)-(Apr. 1993). Periodical. English (French). Consumers Association of Canada, PO Box 9300, Ottawa Ontario K1G 3T9 Canada. **Tel** (613)238-2533, FAX (613)723-9783. **ED** Paul Reynolds. Index available. cum. index. **Circ:** 150,000 (ctrl). available on microfiche from University Microfilms International (UMI). Documents available from UMI Article Clearinghouse. **Continues** CAC Bulletin, 0826-5402. **Continued in part by** Consommateur Canadien, 0315-1867.
Ind/Abst Acad. Abstr. Full Text Elite; Acad. Abstr.; Acad. Search; BioBusiness; Can. Index; Can. Period. Index; Consum. Index Prod. Eval. Inf. Source; Energy Res. Abstr. (Oct. 1981-); EP Collect.; Foods Adlibra; Gen. Period. Index (1985-); Homework Help.; INFO-SOUTH Abstr.; INIS Atomindex [Micro.]; Mag. Artic. Summar. Elite; Mag. Artic. Summar. Select; Mag. Artic. Summar. CD-ROM; Mag. Index Plus (1989-); Mag. Search; MasterFile FullTEXT 1000; MasterFile FullTEXT 350; MasterFile FullTEXT 650; MasterFile FullTEXT (Jan. 1990-Apr. 1993); Newsp. Period. Abstr. (1988-); OCLC; Pub. Lib. FullTEXT; Telebase; Mag. Index (1983-); TOM Gen. Index (1989-); Vocat. Search.

US
CAR AND DRIVER BUYERS GUIDE TO ... NEW CARS. See Transportation-Automobiles.

LC HC5428 .C3
US
●**CATALYST : THE NATIONAL CONSUMER GUIDE.** (1993)-. Consumer Publication. English. Two times a year. $21.00. Consumer Direct Access, Inc, 345 California Street, 21st Floor, San Francisco CA 94104. **Tel** (415) 693-5600, FAX (415) 693-5601. **ED** Carol Patterson. **Ad Acc**. **Circ:** 750,000.
Desc: Provides consumers with the phone numbers of consumer goods manufacturers, national service providers, and direct marketing companies.

LC TT950
DD 646.72 US
CATEGORY REPORT - HEALTH & BEAUTY AIDS. CRH. (19??)-. English. Twelve times a year. $1050.00 US; $1055.00 Canada; $1100.00 Europe and Pan America; $1135.00 other. Marketing Intelligence Service Ltd., 6473D Route 64, Naples NY 14512. **Tel** (716)974-6326, (800)836-5710, FAX (714)374-5217, telex 469979.
Desc: Combines domestic and foreign new product information for the health and beauty aids industry. Includes product and packaging descriptions with illustrations, manufacturing and marketing innovations, emerging trends, and other background information.

LC KFT1430.A59 C38 ISSN 0197-193X
DD 343/.73/071/05 US
CAVEAT VENDOR. **Added/Corp** State Bar of Texas. Consumer Law Section. (19??)-. Periodical. English. Caveat Vendor, PO Box 12487 Capitol Station, Austin TX 78711.

ISSN 0732-8281
US
CFANEWS (WASHINGTON, D.C.). (CFANEWS.). **Added/Corp** Consumer Federation of America. **VFOAT** CFA News; C.F.A. News. **VAT** Consumer Federation of America News. (19??)-. Consumer Publication. English. Eight times a year. $25.00. Consumer Federation of America, 1424 16th Street Northwest, Suite 604, Washington DC 20036. **Tel** (202)387-6121.

ISSN 0196-3813
US
CHAN. CONSUMER HEALTH ACTION NETWORK. **Added/Corp** Consumer Coalition for Health. Public Citizen Health Research Group. **VFOAT** CHAN. (197?)-. Periodical. English. Six times a year. Free to members. CHAN, 2000 P Street NW/Suite 708, Washington DC 20036.

ISSN 0895-9064
DD 640 US
CHICAGO CONSUMER (CHICAGO, ILL. : 1987). (CHICAGO CONSUMER.). [Chic. consum.]. (1987)-. Periodical. English. Six times a year. $20.00. Chicago Consumer, 1968 Somerset, Wheaton IL 60187. **Tel** (708)462-0090.

LC Discard
AT
CHOICE (CHIPPENDALE, N.S.W.). (CHOICE : THE JOURNAL OF THE AUSTRALIAN CONSUMERS' ASSOCIATION.). (1960)-. English. Twelve times a year. 64.13Aus$. Australian Consumers Association, 57 Carrington Road, Marrickville New South Wales 2204 Australia. **Tel** 11 61 02 558 0099, FAX 11 61 02 5589341. **ED** Cathy Gram. Index available. **Circ:** 200,000 (ctrl).
Desc: Reports on goods and services and research into consumer issues.
Ind/Abst MasterFile FullTEXT (Sept. 1994-).

LC GV1040 ISSN 0142-890X
DD 796.6 UK
Pr Rev.
CLASSIC BIKE. See Bicycles and Cycling.

ISSN 1183-7446
DD 339.4 CN
CLAYTON CONSUMER REPORT. [Clayton consum. rep.]. **Added/Corp** Clayton Research Associates. Vol. 1, No. 1 (June 1991)-. Newsletter. English. Twelve times a year. 272.11Can$. Clayton Research Associates Ltd, 1580 Kingston Road, Scarborough Ontario M1N 1S2 Canada. **Tel** (905)699-5645, FAX (416)699-6252. **ED** Mary Webb. ctrl circ. **Continues** Canadian Retailing, 0824-6890.
Desc: Detailed Canadian consumer newsletter which provides an ongoing forecast of Canadian consumer spending and discusses trends in retailing and commercial real estate.

LC KFC375.A15 C2
DD 343/.794/0705 US
CLM, CONSUMER LAW MONTHLY. See Law.

DK
CO-OP CONSUMERS. **Added/Corp** International Co-operative Alliance. Consumer Committee. (1980)-. Periodical. English. Four times a year. FDB, Co-Op Denmark, Roskildevej 65, DK-2620 Albertslund Denmark. **Continues** International Co-operative Alliance. Consumer Affairs Bulletin.

US
CONSU/STATS I. CD-ROM. English. Irregular. $65.00 US and Canada; $69.00 Minnesota residents; $150.00 Africa, Russia and Eastern Europe; $130.00 India; $115.00 other. Hopkins Technology, 421 Hazel Lane, Suite 120, Hopkins MN 55343. **Tel** (612)931-9376, FAX (612)931-9377.
Desc: Covers hundreds of characteristics of thousands of consumer units and family members in a hundred geographical areas, including income and expenditures by commodity.

ISSN 0165-6775
UDC 64-03 NE
CONSUMENTENGIDS. [Consumentengids]. (1953)-. Consumer Publication. Dutch (English). Twelve times a year. Fl56.90. Consumentenbond, Leeghwatersplein 26, 2521 CV Den Haag Netherlands. **Tel** 011 31 70 3847400.

DD 339.4 US
CONSUMER ACTION. **Main/Corp** New York (State). Bureau of Consumer Frauds and Protection. Vol. 1 (June 1969)-. Periodical. English. Two times a year. New York State Department of Law, Bureau of Consumer Frauds and Protection, Albany NY 12201.

ISSN 1036-1162
DD 381.330994 AT
CONSUMER ACTION CANBERRA. [Consum. action Canberra]. **Added/Corp** Australian Federation of Consumer Organizations. (1991)-. Periodical. English. Six times a year. 45.22Aus$. Australian Federation Consumer, Level 1, 40 Mort Street, Braddon 2601 Australia. **Tel** 011 61 6 2576469. **ED** Kylie Preece. **Circ:** 900. **Continues** Consumer Views, 0812-5074.
Desc: The voice for consumer groups in Australia.

ISSN 0270-0999
US
CONSUMER AFFAIRS LETTER, THE. Vol. 1, (May 1980)-. Newsletter. English. Twelve times a year. $125.00. The Consumer Affairs Letter, PO Box 65313, Washington DC 20035. **Tel** (202)362-4279. **ED** George Idelson. Index available (publish separately in January issue). cum. index. **Bk Rev**.
Desc: Report on the activities, issues and personalities of the consumer and public interest movement.
Ind/Abst Acad. Abstr.; Acad. Search; EP Collect.; Homework Help.; INFO-SOUTH Abstr.; Mag. Search; MasterFile FullTEXT 1000; MasterFile FullTEXT 350; MasterFile FullTEXT 650; MasterFile FullTEXT (Jan. 1992-); OCLC; Pub. Lib. FullTEXT; Telebase.

DD 339.4 US
CONSUMER ALERT. **Added/Corp** United States. Federal Trade Commission. Vol. 1, No. 1, (Feb. 1971)-. Periodical. English. Irregular. Federal Trade Commission, 6th Street & Pennsylvania Northwest, Washington DC 20590. **Tel** (202)326-2000. **ED** Barbara Keating. **Bk Rev**. ctrl circ. Documents available from UMI Article Clearinghouse.
Desc: Covers national issues affecting consumers. This includes news about legislation and regulations affecting the marketplace. Covers consumer products as well as services.
Ind/Abst Mag. Search; Newsp. Period. Abstr.

ISSN 0740-4964
US
CONSUMER ALERT COMMENTS. (CONSUMER ALERT COMMENTS : NEWSLETTER OF CONSUMER ALERT.). **Added/Corp** Consumer Alert (Organization). (197?)-. Newsletter. English. Six times a year. $75.00. Consumer Alert, 1024 J Street/Suite 425, Modesto CA 95354. **Tel** (209)524-1738, FAX (209)538-0609. **ED** Barbara Keating. **Bk Rev**. ctrl circ. **Continues** Consumer Alert.
Desc: Covers national issues affecting consumers. This includes news about legislation and regulations affecting the marketplace. Coverage includes consumer interest products as well as services.
Ind/Abst Acad. Abstr. Full Text Elite; Acad. Abstr.; Acad. Search; EP Collect.; Health Source Plus; Health Source; Homework Help.; Mag. Artic. Summar. Elite; Mag. Artic. Summar. Select; Mag. Artic. Summar. CD-ROM; MasterFile FullTEXT 1000; MasterFile FullTEXT 350; MasterFile FullTEXT 650; MasterFile FullTEXT; OCLC; Pub. Lib. FullTEXT; Telebase; Vocat. Search.

Consumer Education and Protection

LC TX335 .C6385
DD 640.73 US
CONSUMER BUYING GUIDE (SKOKIE, ILL.). (CONSUMER BUYING GUIDE.). VFOAT Consumer Guide. (19??)-. Consumer Publication. English. One time a year. $5.99. Publications International Ltd., 7373 North Cicero Avenue, Lincolnwood IL 60646. **Tel** (708)676-3470. **Bk Rev.** ctrl circ.

ISSN 0790-486X
IE
CONSUMER CHOICE. Vol. 1 (March 1985)-. English. Twelve times a year. £49.00. Consumers Association of Ireland, 45 Upper Mount Street, Dublin 2 Ireland. **Tel** 011 353 1 686 6836.

US
CONSUMER CLOSE-UPS. Added/Corp Cornell University. Dept. of Consumer Economics and Housing. (19??)-. Periodical. English. Six times a year. $12.00. Cornell University / Consumer Economics & Housing Department, Rensselaer Hall, Ithaca NY 14853. **Tel** (607)256-2261.

LC T12 .R66 ISSN 0160-2225
DD 381/.3 US
CONSUMER COMPLAINT GUIDE. (1971)-. English. One time a year. $4.95. Macmillan Publishing Company / New York, 866 3rd Avenue, New York NY 10022. **Tel** (212)702-2000, (800)257-5755. **(Subscription address:** Macmillan Publishing, Front and Brown Street, Riverside NJ 08075. **Tel** (800)257-5755.**)**

ISSN 1046-1876
DD 658 US
CONSUMER CONFIDENCE SURVEY. [Consum. confid. surv.]. **Added/Corp** Consumer Research Center. (Dec. 1987)-. Periodical. English. Twelve times a year. $195.00. Conference Board, 845 Third Avenue, New York NY 10022. **Tel** (212)759-0900 ext. 582, (800)872-6273, FAX (212)980-7014. *Continues Consumers Confidence, 1046-1884.*
Desc: Reflects prevailing business conditions and likely developments for the months ahead. Designated by the U.S. Department of Commerce as an economic indicator.

LC KF1040.Z9 C65
DD 346.73/073 347.30673 US
CONSUMER CREDIT AND OTHER RETAIL BANKING DEVELOPMENTS. See Law-Banking Law.

LC KF1039.A15 C6 ISSN 0300-6034
US
CCC
CONSUMER CREDIT AND TRUTH-IN-LENDING COMPLIANCE REPORT. See Law.

ISSN 0128-1143
DD 381.33 MY
CONSUMER CURRENTS. [Consum. Curr.]. (1978)-. Periodical. English. Twelve times a year. $50.00. Consumers International, Regional Office For Asia & Pacific, PO Box 1045, 10830 Penang Malaysia. **Tel** 011 604 2291396, FAX 011 604 2286506. **Bk Rev**, (Qty: 40). **Circ:** 350 (ctrl).
Desc: Brings together news items of relevance to groups and individuals who serve the consumer interest, particularly in the Third World.
Ind/Abst Hum. Rights Intern. Rep.

US
CONSUMER DIGEST. Added/Corp Cooperative Extension Association of Suffolk County. (19??)-. Periodical. English. Cooperative Extension Association of Suffolk County, 246 Griffing Avenue, Riverhead NY 11901.

ISSN 0276-1270
US
CONSUMER FEDERATION OF AMERICA. English. Consumer Federation of America, 1424 16th Street Northwest, Suite 604, Washington DC 20036. **Tel** (202)387-6121.

LC TL5 .C65 ISSN 0097-8337
DD 629.22/22/05 US
CONSUMER GUIDE : AUTO. See Transportation-Automobiles.

LC TL162 .C67 ISSN 0364-0809
DD 629.22/22 US
CONSUMER GUIDE: CARS. See Transportation-Automobiles.

LC TJ163.5.D86 C66 ISSN 1052-9179
DD 644 US
CONSUMER GUIDE TO HOME ENERGY SAVINGS. See Heating, Plumbing, and Refrigeration.

ISSN 0883-1149
DD 640 US
CONSUMER HOTLINE, THE. [Consum. hotline]. **Added/Corp** Comp-U-Card International. Vol. 1, No. 1 (June 1985)-. Newsletter. English. Twelve times a year. $20.00. The Consumer Hotline, 777 Summer Street, Stamford CT 06901. **Tel** (203)324-9261. **ED** Susan Crandell. **Circ:** 10,000 (ctrl).
Desc: A newsletter concerning consumer electronics, computers, photography, and home appliances.

ISSN 1054-4909
DD 384 US
CONSUMER INFORMATION APPLIANCE. [Consum. inf. appl.]. (1990)-. Periodical. English. Twelve times a year. $475.00. Jupiter Communications, 594 Broadway, Suite 1003, New York NY 10012. **Tel** (212)941-9252. available on an online database from NEWSNET.

US
CONSUMER INFORMATION CATALOG, THE. Added/Corp Consumer Information Center (U.S.). (Summer 1977)-. Catalog. English. Four times a year. Consumer Information Catalog, Public Documents Distribution Center, Pueblo CO 81009. **Tel** (202)501-1794. *Continues Consumer Information (Consumer Information Center (U.S.)).*

ISSN 0190-2938
US
CONSUMER INFORMATION SERIES (WASHINGTON. 1971). (CONSUMER INFORMATION SERIES.). **Added/Corp** United States. General Services Administration. (1971)-. Monographic series. English. Irregular. Price varies per volume. Consumer Information Center, Public Documents Distribution Center, Pueblo CO 81009. **Tel** (202)501-1794.

LC HC110.C63 A67a
DD 330 US
●**CONSUMER INTERESTS ANNUAL : ANNUAL CONFERENCE OF THE AMERICAN COUNCIL ON CONSUMER INTERESTS. Main/Corp** American Council on Consumer Interests. Conference. 40th (Mar. 23-26, 1994)-. English. American Council on Consumer Interest, 240 Stanley Hall, University of Missouri, Columbia MO 65211. **Tel** (314)882-3817, FAX (314)884-6571. *Continues American Council on Consumer Interests. Conference. Proceedings ... Annual Conference of the American Council on Consumer Interests, 0275-1356.*

US
●**CONSUMER MAGAZINE ADVERTISING SOURCE.** (1995)-. English. Twelve times a year. $550.99. SRDS / Standard Rate & Data Service, 3004 Glenview Road, Wilmette IL 60091. **Tel** (708)375-5049, (800)851-7737, FAX (708)375-5003. **(Subscription address:** Real Time Publications Service, PO Box 1962, Danbury CT 06813. **)** *Continues Consumer Magazine Agri Media Source.*

LC HF5905 .S725 ISSN 1071-4537
DD 659.1/025/73 US
TITLE CHANGE
CONSUMER MAGAZINE & AGRI-MEDIA SOURCE. See Business and Economics-Advertising and Public Relations.

US
CONSUMER MAGAZINE PROFILES. (19??)-. Periodical. English. Twelve times a year. $485.00. SRDS / Standard Rate & Data Service, 3004 Glenview Road, Wilmette IL 60091. **Tel** (708)375-5049, (800)851-7737, FAX (708)375-5003. **(Subscription address:** Neodata / Colorado, PO Box 2606, Boulder CO 80322. **)**

LC HC110.C6 C567 ISSN 0734-4341
DD 349.4/7/0973 US
CONSUMER MARKETS SERVICE. [Consum. mark. serv.]. **Added/Corp** Data Resources, Inc. Consumer Research Division. VFOAT C.M.S. Bulletin; CMS Bulletin. (19??)-. Bulletin. English. DRI McGraw Hill, 24 Hartwell Avenue, Lexington MA 02173. **Tel** (617)863-5100, FAX (617)860-6464, (617)860-6416.

ISSN 1055-0666
DD 384 US
CONSUMER MEDIA TECH. See Business and Economics-Marketing and Purchasing.

LC HC79.C63 O75a
DD 381/.3/05 FR
CONSUMER POLICY IN OECD COUNTRIES. Added/Corp Organisation for Economic Co-Operation and Development. VFOAT Consumer Policy. (1983)-. English. One time a year. OECD Publications and Information Center, 2 rue Andre-Pascal, 75775 Paris Cedex 16 France. **Tel** 011 33 1 49104262, US:(202)785-6323, FAX 011 33 1 45248500, 011 33 1 45248176, telex 620 160 OCDE. *Continues Organisation for Economic Co-Operation and Development. Annual Reports on Consumer Policy in OECD Member Countries, 0376-8058.*

UK
CONSUMER POLICY REVIEW. Added/Corp Consumers' Association. Vol. 1, No. 1 (Jan. 1991)-. English. Four times a year (Jan., Apr., July, Oct.). $154.01. Consumers Association, Castlemead, Gascoyne Way, Hertford SG14 1LH United Kingdom. **Tel** 011 44 1992 587773, FAX 011 44 1992 500369.
Ind/Abst Sage Public Adm. Abstr.; Sage Urban Stud. Abstr.

LC HB235.J25 J3a
DD 338.5/28/097292 JM
CONSUMER PRICE INDICES, ANNUAL REVIEW. Added/Corp Jamaica. Dept. of Statistics. Statistical Institute of Jamaica. (1972)-. English. One time a year. $31.50. Statistical Institute of Jamaica, 9 Swallowfield Road, PO Box 643, Kingston 5 Jamaica. **Tel** 011 809 92621756, FAX 011 809 9264859.

LC HV676.A1 U53a ISSN 0147-3360
DD 614.8/53/0973 US
CONSUMER PRODUCT HAZARD INDEX. See Public Health and Safety.

LC KF1296.A59 C66 ISSN 1052-9632
DD 346.7303/8/05 347.3063805 US
CONSUMER PRODUCT LITIGATION REPORTER. See Law.

LC KFW2630.A59 C66 ISSN 0362-157X
DD 353.9/787/0082 US
CONSUMER PROTECTION REPORT.
Main/Corp Wisconsin. Office of Consumer Protection. (19??)-. Consumer Publication. English. Twelve times a year. $145.00. National Association of Attorneys General, 444 North Capitol Street, Suite 339, Washington DC 20001. **Tel** (202)434-8000, FAX (202)434-8008. *Continues Wisconsin. Office of Consumer Protection. Annual Report, 0740-9931.*

LC KF1602 .C66
DD 343.73/071 347.30371 US
CONSUMER PROTECTION REPORT.
Added/Corp National Association of Attorneys General. (19??)-. Newsletter. English. Ten times a year. $145.00. National Association of Attorneys General, 444 North Capitol Street, Suite 339, Washington DC 20001. **Tel** (202)434-8000, FAX (202)434-8008. **ED** Emmit Carlton. *Continues Consumer Protection Newsletter, 0191-8567.*

ISSN 1053-1424
US
CONSUMER REFERENCE DISC.
Added/Corp National Information Services Corporation. (1990)-. Periodical. English. Two times a year. $711.00 US; $725.00 other. National Information Services Corporation, 3100 St. Paul Street, Wyman Towers, Suite 6, Baltimore MD 21218. **Tel** (410)243-0797, FAX (410)243-0982.
Desc: CD-ROM containing information from Consumers Index and Consumers Health & Nutrition Index. Abstracts and indexes over 25,000 product evaluations, recalls, alerts, and warnings as well as 8,000 articles on travel and transporation, finance, jobs, computers, food, health etc.

LC TX335.A1 C6 ISSN 0010-7174
DD 640.73/0973 US
NLM W1 CO755K
CONSUMER REPORTS. [Consum. rep.].
Added/Corp Consumers Union of United States. VFOAT CU. Vol. 7, No. 6 (June 1942)-. Consumer Publication. English. Thirteen times a year (monthly plus Buying Guide in Dec.). $24.00. Consumers Union, 101 Truman Avenue, Yonkers NY 10703. **Tel** (800)288-7898, (914)378-2000, FAX (914)378-2900. **(Subscription address:** Neodata / Colorado, PO Box 2606, Boulder CO 80322. **) ED** Eileen Denver (Executive Editor), David Heim (Managing Editor). Index available (free). cum. index. **Circ:** 4,500,000. available on CD-ROM; available on microfilm and microfiche from University Microfilms International (UMI); available on an online database from Lexis-Nexis; and (files 646,647,648/Full-Text) DIALOG. Documents available from UMI Article Clearinghouse, Documents on Demand, BLDSC, FAXON Xpress, The UnCover Company, SWETS, CASDDS. *Continues Consumers Union of United States. Consumers Union Reports; Absorbed Bread & Butter.*
Desc: A product-test and consumer advisory publication. Publishes results of tests on products ranging from major purchases such as automobiles and appliances to everyday items such as foods and cleaning products. Also examines money management, health, medical matters and nutrition.
Ind/Abst ABI/INFORM Glob. Ed. (1984-); ABI/INFORM [Computer File] (March 1975-); Abr. Read. Guide Period. Lit.; Acad. Abstr. Full Text Elite; Acad. Abstr.; Acad. Ind. [Computer File] (1984-); Acad. Search; AGRICOLA [Select. Cov.]; Art Index; Biol. Dig.; Can. Index (?-?); Can. Period. Index (19??-); Ceram. Abstr.; Comput. Rev. Index (1986-); Consum. Health Nutr. Index; Consum. Index Prod. Eval. Inf. Source; Cumul. Index Nurs. Allied Health Lit.; Curr. Lit. Fam. Plan.; Dent. Abstr. (1992-); Energy Inf.

Abstr.; Environ. Abstr.; EP Collect.; Expand. Acad. Index (1984-); F&S Index Plus Text, Int. [Select. Cov.]; Film Lit. Index; Foods Adlibra; Gen. Period. Index (1985-); Health Plan. Adminis.; Health Ref. Cent. (1987-) [Select. Cov.]; Homework Help.; Index Period. Artic. Relat. Law; INFO-SOUTH Abstr.; Infobank (Jan. 1969-); Int. Pharm. Abstr.; Mag. Artic. Summar. Elite; Mag. Artic. Summar. Select; Mag. Artic. Summar. CD-ROM; Mag. Index Plus (1989-); Mag. Index Sel. Microfiche (1986-) [Full Txt.]; Mag. Index. Sel. (1986-); Mag. Search; Mark. Advert. Ref. Serv.; MasterFile FullTEXT 1000; MasterFile FullTEXT 350; MasterFile FullTEXT 650; MasterFile FullTEXT (Jan. 1984-); Mid. Search; Newsp. Period. Abstr. (1986-); OCLC; Prim. Search; Pub. Lib. FullTEXT; Read. Guide Abstr. Select Ed.; Read. Guide Period. Lit.; Resource/One Ondisc (1986-); Telebase; Mag. Index (1977-); TOM Gen. Index (1985-) [Full Txt.]; Vocat. Search.

US

CONSUMER REPORTS. BUYING GUIDE ISSUE. **Added/Corp** Consumers Union of United States. **VFOAT** Buying Guide Issue. (194?)-. Consumer Publication. English. One time a year (Dec.). $11.86. Consumers Union, 101 Truman Avenue, Yonkers NY 10703. **Tel** (800)288-7898, (914)378-2000, FAX (914)378-2900. **(Subscription address:** St. Martin's Press, 175 5th Avenue, New York NY 10010. **Tel** (800)221-7945.**)** ***Continues*** *CU Buying Guide.*

LC TX335 **ISSN** 1053-1416
DD 640.73 US

CONSUMER REPORTS ON CD-ROM (ADVANCED USER'S ED.). **See** Business and Economics.

ISSN 1053-1408
US

CONSUMER REPORTS ON CD-ROM (BEGINNER'S ED.). **See** Business and Economics.

ISSN 1058-0832
DD 613 US
CODEN CREHEI

CONSUMER REPORTS ON HEALTH. [Consum. rep. health]. **Added/Corp** Consumer Union of United States. (199?)-. English. Twelve times a year. $24.00. Consumers Union, 101 Truman Avenue, Yonkers NY 10703. **Tel** (800)288-7898, (914)378-2000, FAX (914)378-2900. **(Subscription address:** Neodata / Colorado, PO Box 2606, Boulder CO 80322. **)** available on an online database (files 149,646/Full-Text) from DIALOG. ***Continues*** *Consumer Reports Health Letter, 1044-3193.*
Desc: Consumer-oriented reports on nutrition, medications, exercise, health fraud, new medical treatments, prevention, and more.
Ind/Abst Foods Adlibra; Health Index (1991-); Mag. Search.

LC G149 .C65 **ISSN** 1060-1511
DD 381 US

CONSUMER REPORTS TRAVEL BUYING GUIDE. **See** Travel and Tourism.

ISSN 0887-8439
DD 910 US
CODEN CRTLE3

CONSUMER REPORTS TRAVEL LETTER. [Consum. rep. travel lett.]. **Added/Corp** Consumers Union of United States. **VFOAT** Travel Letter. Vol. 1, No. 1 (1985)-. Periodical. English. Twelve times a year. $39.00. Consumers Union, 101 Truman Avenue, Yonkers NY 10703. **Tel** (800)288-7898, (914)378-2000, FAX (914)378-2900. **(Subscription address:** Neodata / Colorado, PO Box 2606, Boulder CO 80322. **)** available on an online database (files 646,647/Full-Text) from DIALOG. Documents available from UMI Article Clearinghouse, CASDDS.
Desc: Offers a complete independent source of unbiased, expert travel guidance. Provides inside information to make trips more enjoyable and travel dollars go farther.
Ind/Abst Gen. Period. Index (1992-); Mag. Index Plus (1992-); Newsp. Period. Abstr. (1989-); Mag. Index (Jan. 1990-).

LC HC110.C63 C638 **ISSN** 0738-0518
DD 381/.33/02573 US

CONSUMER SOURCEBOOK. [Consum. sourceb]. **Added/Corp** Gale Research Company. Gale Research Inc. 1st Ed. (1974)-. English. Irregular. $210.00. Gale Research Inc., 835 Penobscot Building, 645 Griswold Street, Detroit MI 48226. **Tel** (800)877-GALE, (313)961-2242, FAX (313)961-6083, (800)414-5043, telex TWX 810-221-7086. **ED** Shawn Brennan. available on magnetic tape; available on diskette.
Desc: Provides a comprehensive digest of accessible resources and advisory information for the American consumer. Identifies and describes more than 10,000 programs and services available to the general public at little or no cost. These services are provided by federal, state, county, and local governments and their agencies as well as by organizations and associations. FAX numbers are also provided.

ISSN 0313-7732
DD 330.994 AT

CONSUMER SURVEYS. INTERIM REPORT. [Consum. surv., Interim rep.]. (1976)-. Periodical. English. Twelve times a year. 184.99Aus$. Institute of Applied Economic and Social Research / Australia, University of Melbourne, Economics Building, Parkville Victoria 3052 Australia. **Tel** 011 61 3 3445330, FAX 011 61 3 3445630, telex 35185.

LC HC101 .C744 **ISSN** 0952-9543
DD 339.4/7/097305 UK

CONSUMER USA. **VFOAT** Consumer U.S.A. **VAT** Consumer United States of America. (1988)-. Trade Publication. English. Irregular. $550.00 US; £275.00 other. Euromonitor Publications Ltd., 60-61 Britton Street, London EC1M 5NA United Kingdom. **Tel** 011 44 171 2518024, FAX 011 44 171 6083149, telex 21120.
Desc: Contains profiles of major consumer goods manufacturers, a directory of major retailers in the United States, and a guide to official and nonofficial business information sources.

LC TX335 .C663 **ISSN** 0273-2475
DD 640/.73/05 US

CONSUMERISM (BOCA RATON). (CONSUMERISM.). Vol. 1, Article 1 (1979)-. English. One time a year. Social Issues Resources Series Inc, PO Box 2348, Boca Raton FL 33427. **Tel** (800)327-0513, (407)994-0079.
Desc: Interdisciplinary resource material consisting of reprinted articles from popular and professional journals, newspapers, magazines and government documents.

LC TX335.A1 C648 **ISSN** 0010-7182
DD 640 US

CONSUMERS DIGEST (CHICAGO, ILL.). (CONSUMERS DIGEST.). [Consum. dig.]. Vol. 6, No. 5 (Sept./Oct. 1967)-. Periodical. English. Six times a year. $15.97. Consumers Digest, 5705 North Lincoln Avenue, Chicago IL 60659. **Tel** (312)275-3590, FAX (312)275-7273. **(Subscription address:** CDS Agency Hard Copy, PO Box 4966, Des Moines IA 50340. **Tel** (515)247-7569.**)** **ED** John Manos. **Ad Acc. Circ:** 750,000. available on microfilm and microfiche from University Microfilms International (UMI); available on an online database (file 647/Full-Text) from DIALOG. Documents available from UMI Article Clearinghouse. ***Continues*** *Consumers Digest Magazine.*
Ind/Abst Abr. Read. Guide Period. Lit.; Acad. Abstr. Full Text Elite; Acad. Abstr.; Acad. Search; Consum. Index Prod. Eval. Inf. Source; EP Collect.; Foods Adlibra; Gen. Period. Index (1985-); Homework Help.; INFO-SOUTH Abstr.; Mag. Artic. Summar. Elite; Mag. Artic. Summar. Select; Mag. Artic. Summar. CD-ROM; Mag. Index Plus (1989-); Mag. Search; MasterFile FullTEXT 1000; MasterFile FullTEXT 350; MasterFile FullTEXT 650; MasterFile FullTEXT (Mar. 1984-) [Full Txt.]; Newsp. Period. Abstr. (1988-); OCLC; Pub. Lib. FullTEXT; Read. Guide Period. Lit.; Telebase; Mag. Index (1977-); Vocat. Search.

ISSN 0117-0171
PH

CONSUMERS' FORUM. [Consum. forum]. **Added/Corp** Citizens' Alliance for Consumer Protection (Philippines). (1982)-. Periodical. English. Six times a year. CACP / Citizens' Alliance for Consumer Protection, Manila Philippines.
Ind/Abst Hum. Rights Intern. Rep.

LC TX335 .C676 **ISSN** 0094-0534
DD 016.64073 US
NLM Z 5776.C65 C758

CONSUMERS INDEX TO PRODUCT EVALUATIONS AND INFORMATION SOURCES. **See** Consumer Education and Protection-Abstracting, Bibliographies and Statistics.

US

CONSUMERS INFORMATION GUIDE. (19??)-. Periodical. English. Twelve times a year. $57.90. National Research Bureau Inc. / Iowa, 200 North Fourth, PO Box 1, Burlington IA 52601. **Tel** (319)752-5415, FAX (319)752-3421.

LC TX335.A1 C68 **ISSN** 0095-2222
DD 640.73/05 US
CODEN CRMZA6

CONSUMERS' RESEARCH MAGAZINE. [Consum. res. mag.]. **Added/Corp** Consumers' Research, Inc. **VFOAT** Consumers' Research. Vol. 56, No. 6 (June 1973)-. Periodical. English. Twelve times a year. $24.00. Consumers Research Magazine, 800 Maryland Avenue Northeast, Washington DC 20002. **Tel** (202)546-1713. **(Subscription address:** Consumers Research, PO Box 5025, Brentwood TN 37024. **Tel** (615)377-3322.**)** **ED** John W. Merline. Index available. cum. index. **Bk Rev. Ad Acc. Circ:** 20,000. available in braille; available on microfilm and microfiche from University Microfilms International (UMI); available on an online database (file 647/Full-Text) from DIALOG; available on CD-ROM from University Microfilms International (UMI). Documents available from UMI Article Clearinghouse, Magazine Collection, FAXON Xpress, The UnCover Company, SWETS. ***Continues*** *Consumer Bulletin, 0010-7123.*
Desc: Dedicated to providing information on topics such as airline and highway safety, the hazards of radon gas, cable TV, health care, pesticides, picking good stocks and more. Covers all the issues that affect pocketbooks and choices in the marketplace.
Ind/Abst Acad. Abstr. Full Text Elite; Acad. Abstr.; Acad. Ind. [Computer File] (1984-); Acad. Search; BioBusiness (1973-); Consum. Index Prod. Eval. Inf. Source; EP Collect.; Expand. Acad. Index (1984-); Film Lit. Index; Foods Adlibra; Gen. Period. Index (1985-); Homework Help.; INFO-SOUTH Abstr.; Mag. Artic. Summar. Elite; Mag. Artic. Summar. Select; Mag. Artic. Summar. CD-ROM; Mag. Express (1986-) [Full Txt.]; Mag. Index Plus (1989-); Mag. Index Sel. Microfiche (1986-) [Full Txt.]; Mag. Index. Sel. (1986-); Mag. Search; MasterFile FullTEXT 1000; MasterFile FullTEXT 350; MasterFile FullTEXT 650; MasterFile FullTEXT (Jan. 1984-) [Full Txt.]; Newsp. Period. Abstr. (1986-); OCLC; Pub. Lib. FullTEXT; Read. Guide Abstr. Select Ed.; Read. Guide Period. Lit.; Resource/One Ondisc; Telebase; Text. Technol. Dig.; Mag. Index (1977-); TOM Gen. Index (1985-) [Full Txt.]; Vocat. Search; World Mag. Bank.

ISSN 0069-9241
US

CONSUMERS' RESEARCH MAGAZINE. HANDBOOK OF BUYING ISSUE. (1973/74)-. English. One time a year. Consumer Research Inc, 401 C Street/Suite 301, Washington DC 20002. available on microfilm from University Microfilms International (UMI). ***Continues*** *Consumer Bulletin Annual.*

ISSN 0728-3008
DD 381.30994 AT

CONSUMING INTEREST. CHIPPENDALE. [Consum. interest Chippendale]. (1979)-. Periodical. English. Irregular (4 issues). 28.78Aus$. Australian Consumers Association, 57 Carrington Road, Marrickville New South Wales 2204 Australia. **Tel** 11 61 02 558 0099, FAX 11 61 02 5589341.

ISSN 0822-6598
DD 640.73/05 CN

COOPRIX INFORMATION (1983). (COOPRIX INFORMATION.). [Cooprix inf.]. **Added/Corp** Cooperative des Consommateurs de Montreal. Vol. 6, No. 7 (March 1983)-. Periodical. French. Twelve times a year. Coop des Consommateurs de Montreal, 1601 boulevard Roland-Therrien, Longueuil Quebec J4J 5C5 Canada. ***Continues*** *Coop Information, 0820-9944.*

LC HG1501 **ISSN** 0738-6877
DD 332.1 US

CREDIT CODE LETTER, THE. **Added/Corp** Texas. Office of Consumer Credit Commissioner. Vol. 1, No. 1 (June 2, l981)-. Newsletter. English. Fifty-two times a year (Published on Tuesdays). $40.00. Office of Consumer Credit Commissioner, 2601 North Lamar, Austin TX 78705. **Tel** (512)479-1280. **ED** Leslie Pettijohn (editor's phone number: (512)479-1291). **Circ:** 900.
Desc: Established as a vehicle to notify creditors of usury rate ceilings in effect from time to time. Subsequently, information about official interpretations of the Texas Credit Code was added, and information on credit and credit related legislation appears when the State Legislature is active. Miscellaneous information thought to be of interest to subscribers may appear from time to time.

ISSN 1055-9981
US

CREDIT REPORT MAGAZINE : CR : A PUBLICATION OF THE NATIONAL CONSUMER ADVOCATE ASSOCIATION. **Added/Corp** National Consumer Advocate Association. **VFOAT** CR; Credit Report. (1991)-. Periodical. English. Four times a year. National Consumer Advocate Association, 5141-43 Chestnut Street, Philadelphia PA 19139.

ISSN 0176-3288
GW

UDC 621.39:681.32

DATACOM. [Datacom]. (1984)-. Periodical. German. Twelve times a year. $147.39. Datacom Zeitschriften Verlag, Postfach 1502, D-50105 Bergheim Germany. **Tel** 011 49 2271 6080, FAX 011 49 2271 608290. Index available. cum. index. **Bk Rev. Ad Acc. Circ:** 11,000 (ctrl). available on diskette.

ISSN 0225-2686
DD 381/.025/713541 CN

DIRECTORY & CONSUMER GUIDE - BETTER BUSINESS BUREAU GREATER TORONTO. [Dir. consum. guide - Better Bus. Bur., Greater Toronto]. **Main/Corp** Better Business Bureau Greater Toronto. 1980-. Directory. English. One time a year. Free. Better Business, Greater Toronto, Suite 901321 Bloor Street, Toronto Ontario M4W 3K6 Canada. ctrl circ. ***Continues*** *Better Business Bureau, Greater Toronto. Directory, 0708-9759.*

LC HD9696.A3 U5373 **ISSN** 0419-2508
US

DIRECTORY OF CONSUMER ELECTRONICS. **See** Home Economics-Household Appliances.

Consumer Education and Protection

LC HC110.C6 D5
DD 339.4/7/02573
NLM WA 22 AA1 D3
ISSN 0070-5586
US
DIRECTORY OF GOVERNMENT AGENCIES SAFEGUARDING CONSUMER AND ENVIRONMENT. 1st-Ed.; 1968-. Directory. English. One time a year. Serina Press, 70 Kennedy Street, Alexandria VA 22305.

LC AS8 .D53
DD 361.9/0973
NLM AG 521; D598
ISSN 1067-4217
US
DIRECTORY OF NATIONAL HELPLINES. See Communications-Telecommunication.

US
DO'S AND DON'TS IN ADVERTISING. See Business and Economics-Advertising and Public Relations.

ISSN 0744-690X
US
EASTERN ARKANSAS WEEKLY SHOPPING GUIDE. (19??)-. English. One time a week. $12.00 including subscription to Evening Times. Crittenden Publishing Company, PO Box 459, West Memphis AR 72303. **Tel** (501)735-1010, FAX (501)735-1020.

ISSN 8750-6009
US
EAU CLAIRE COUNTY BUYER'S GUIDE. (198?)-. Newspaper. English. One time a week. Eau Claire County Buyer's Guide, PO Box 209, Eau Claire WI 54702.

LC TL162 .E338
DD 629.2/222/029473
ISSN 0732-5835
US
TITLE CHANGE
EDMUND'S ... ECONOMY CAR BUYING GUIDE. See Transportation-Automobiles.

LC TL162 .V36
DD 629.223
ISSN 1079-1477
US
TITLE CHANGE
EDMUND'S NEW PICKUPS, VANS & SPORT UTILITIES BUYER'S GUIDE. See Transportation-Automobiles.

LC TL162 .V36
DD 629.223
ISSN 1081-6917
US
TITLE CHANGE
EDMUND'S NEW VANS, PICKUPS & SPORT UTILITIES BUYER'S GUIDE. See Transportation-Automobiles.

DD 629
ISSN 1055-2170
US
EDMUND'S PRESENTS ... ECONOMY CAR BUYING GUIDE. See Transportation-Automobiles.

DD 629
ISSN 1079-1515
US
●**EDMUND'S USED CARS PRICES & RATINGS.** See Transportation-Automobiles.

LC TL162 .V36
DD 629.223
ISSN 1077-2111
US
TITLE CHANGE
EDMUND'S VAN, PICKUP, SPORT UTILITY. See Transportation-Automobiles.

DD 640.73/097127
ISSN 0821-512X
CN
EDUCATED CONSUMER. [Educ. consum.]. (Feb. 2, 1981)-. Periodical. English. $0.50 per issue. Educated Consumer, 341 Wardlaw Avenue, Winnipeg Manitoba R3L 1P9 Canada.

LC TX1 .E662
US
EDUCATORS GUIDE TO FREE HOME ECONOMICS AND CONSUMER EDUCATION MATERIALS. See Home Economics.

ISSN 1060-4545
US
ELDER UPDATE. See Senior Citizens.

LC HC271 .A218 HC280.C6
DD 330.944 S 339.4/7/0944
FR
EQUIPEMENT DES MENAGES EN BIENS DURABLES AU DEBUT DE ..., L'. See Consumer Education and Protection-Abstracting, Bibliographies and Statistics.

LC HG1501
DD 332.1
ISSN 0423-8710
CCC
EVERYBODY'S MONEY. [Everybody's money]. (1961)-. Periodical. English. Four times a year. $4.00 US. Credit Union National Association, PO Box 431, Madison WI 53701. **Tel** (608)231-4088, (800)356-9655, FAX (608)231-4370. **ED** James Hanson. Index available. **Bk Rev. Circ:** 1,100,000. available on microfilm.
Desc: Money management guide for credit union members and potential members. Emphasis on wise borrowing and buying, and on regular saving habits.
Ind/Abst Consum. Index Prod. Eval. Inf. Source.

DD 640.73/0971
ISSN 0710-5878
CN
FACS SHEET. See Home Economics.

ISSN 0146-2857
FACTORY OUTLET NEWSLETTER, THE. (19??)-. Newsletter. English. Six times a year. $5.00. Factory Outlet Newsletter, PO Box 95L, Oradell NJ 07649.

LC HV
DD 363.0941
ISSN 0956-5590
FAILSAFE (LONDON). (FAILSAFE.). [FailSafe Lond.]. (1989)-. Periodical. English. Twelve times a year. $167.69. European Business Publishing, Sampford Lodge, Oxenden Square, Herne Bay Kent CT6 8TW United Kingdom. **Tel** 011 44 122 7362233, FAX 011 44 122 4940863. **ED** R. Mackmurdo (Editor's telephone: 011 44 122 7362233). **Circ:** 2,000.
Desc: For information of management or legal issues on claims, recalls, and developments in safety, law and practice.

DD 338.476151095
ISSN 1354-5299
UK
●**FAR EAST FOCUS.** See Public Health and Safety.

LC HD9000.9.U5 A1735
DD 640.73
NLM W1 F203E
ISSN 0362-1332
US
CODEN FDACBH
FDA CONSUMER. See Public Health and Safety.

LC KF1039.A15 F42
DD 346.73/073 347.30673
ISSN 0730-5028
FEDERAL FINANCIAL REGULATORY DIGEST. See Law.

LC KFN5630.A15 N48
DD 344.747/042/05 347.47044205
ISSN 1057-2759
US
FOOD, DRUG, COSMETIC, AND MEDICAL DEVICE LAW DIGEST. See Law.

ISSN 1057-7785
US
CODEN FNCNEV
CEASED
FOOD NEWS FOR CONSUMERS / UNITED STATES DEPT. OF AGRICULTURE, FOOD SAFETY AND QUALITY SERVICE. See Food and Food Industry.

LC HF5429.235.U5 F7
DD 658.8/708/05
ISSN 0882-5505
FRANCHISE HANDBOOK, THE. See Business and Economics-Retail.

ISSN 0148-2092
US
FREEBIES (SANTA MONICA). (FREEBIES.). Vol. 1 (Feb. 1978)-. Periodical. English. Five times a year. $12.50. Freebies Magazine, 1135 Eugenia Place, Carpinteria CA 93013. **Tel** (805)566-1225. **ED** Linda Cook. **Ad Acc. Circ:** 450,000 (ctrl).
Desc: A selection of free or almost free materials for teachers, children and adult consumers. Full-length articles, with consumer information.

LC HV
DD 362
ISSN 1066-2367
US
GETTING THE MOST FOR YOUR MEDICAL DOLLAR. [Get. most your med. dollar]. (1992)-. Periodical. English. Four times a year. $20.00. People's Medical Society, 462 Walnut Street, Allentown PA 18102. **Tel** (610)770-1670, FAX (610)770-0607.
Ind/Abst Acad. Abstr.; Acad. Search; EP Collect.; Health Source Plus; Health Source; Homework Help.; Mag. Artic. Summar. Elite; Mag. Artic. Summar. Select; Mag. Artic. Summar. CD-ROM; MasterFile FullTEXT 1000; MasterFile FullTEXT 350; MasterFile FullTEXT 650; MasterFile FullTEXT (Jan. 1994-) [Full Txt.]; OCLC; Pub. Lib. FullTEXT; Telebase.

ISSN 8750-8524
US
GOODS AND SERVICES BULLETIN, THE. Added/Corp Massachusetts. Office of the Secretary of State. **VFOAT** Goods & Services Bulletin. Vol. 1, No. 1 (Aug. 1984)-. Bulletin. English. One time a week. $45.00. Secretary of State Commonwealth of Massachusetts, State House, Boston MA 02133.

DD 640
ISSN 1049-2747
US
CODEN GCLEEH
CEASED
GREEN CONSUMER LETTER, THE. See Environmental Issues.

LC HF5429.215.U6 G84
US
GUIDE TO THE NATION'S BEST OUTLETS. Added/Corp Outletbound. **VFOAT** Outlet Bound. (1990/1991)-. English. Every 2 years. $6.95 US; $7.95 Canada. Outletbound, PO Box 1255-OB, Orange CT 06477.

DD 640.73/09713/533
ISSN 0707-3941
CN
HALTON CONSUMER. (Sept. 14, 1977)-. Periodical. English. One time a week. Free. Metrospan Community Newspapers, 44 Lesmill Road, Don Mills Ontario M3B 2T5. ctrl circ.

DD 381/.0971
ISSN 0225-4190
CN
CEASED
HANDBOOK OF CANADIAN CONSUMER MARKETS. [Handb. Can. consum. mark.]. **Added/Corp** Conference Board in Canada. (1979)-(19??)-. Periodical. English. Conference Board of Canada, 255 Smyth Road, Ottawa Ontario K1H 8M7 Canada. **Tel** (613)526-3280, FAX (613)526-4857, telex 053-3034.

ISSN 0738-811X
US
NLM W1; HE333
HEALTH FACTS. See Public Health and Safety.

LC TH
DD 693
GW
●**HEIMKINO.** See Electronics.

LC TX335 .H445
DD 640.73/05
ISSN 0363-9185
US
HELP (WASHINGTON). (HELP.). (1976/77)-. English. $4.95. Consumer News Inc., 813 National Press Building, Washington DC 20009.

NE
HI FI VIDEO TEST. See Sound Recordings and Systems.

ISSN 1145-0673
FR
UDC 339.379.8
Pr Rev.
INC HEBDO CONSOMMATEURS ACTUALITES. VFOAT Consommateurs Actualites (1986); Institut National de la Consommation Hebdo Consommateurs Actualites. (1986)-. Periodical. French. One time a week. $166.22. Institut National Consommation, 80 rue Lecourbe, 75732 Paris Cedex 15 France. **Tel** 011 33 1 45662146, 011 33 1 45662101. Index available. cum. index. **Bk Rev. Circ:** 60,000.
Continues CA. Consommateurs Actualite, 0339-154X.
Desc: Consumer affiliations, activities, economy, law, legislation, Europe, insurance, health, housing, environment, ecology and advertising.

FP
INDICE MENSUEL DES PRIX DE DETAIL A LA CONSOMMATION. Added/Corp Institut Territorial de la Statistique (French Polynesia). (Jan. 1990)-. Periodical. French. Twelve times a year. **Continues** Indice des Prix de Detail a la Consommation Familiale, 0761-2982.

ISSN 0019-9907
NE
INFORMATIE. [Informatie]. (1958)-. Academic Scholarly Publication. Dutch. Eleven times a year (July/Aug. issues combined). $133.61. Kluwer Berdijfswetenschappen, Postbus 4, 2400 Alphen Rijn Netherlands. **Tel** 011 31 01720 66855. **(Subscription address:** Intermedia BV, Postbus 4, 2400 MA Alphen AD Rijn Netherlands. **Tel** 011 31 1720 66481.) available on microfilm from University Microfilms International (UMI). Documents available from UMI Article Clearinghouse, Ask*IEEE.
Ind/Abst ABI/INFORM Glob. Ed.; ABI/INFORM [Computer File] (March 1981-); Curr. Cit.; EMBASE; INSPEC (1972-).

DD 363.7/009718
ISSN 0713-1682
CN
INFORMATION REPORT - DEPARTMENT OF CONSUMER AFFAIRS AND ENVIRONMENT, RESEARCH AND ASSESSMENT BRANCH. (INFORMATION REPORT.). [Inf. rep. - Dep. Consum. Aff. Environ., Res. Assess. Branch]. **Added/Corp** Newfoundland. Dept. of Consumer Affairs and Environment. Research and Assessment Branch. (197?)-. Monographic series. English. Price varies per volume. Department of Consumer Affairs and Environment, 95 Bonaventure Avenue, St. John's Newfoundland A1C 5T7 Canada.

ISSN 0199-5073
US
INLAND EMPIRE MAGAZINE. (1976)-. Periodical. English. Twelve times a year. $21.00. Don Lorenzi & Associates, 3769 Tibbetts Street, Suite A,

Consumer Education and Protection

Riverside CA 92506. **Tel** (909)682-3026, FAX (909)682-0246. **ED** Donald D. Lorenzi. **Bk Rev**, (Qty: 50). **Ad Acc, Adv Mgr:** Brenda Lorenzi. **Circ:** 54,000 (ctrl). **Continues** Inland Empire, 0193-1490.
Desc: Lifestyle, entertainment, leisure, business, and health for Southern California.

UK
INTERNATIONAL CONSUMER DIRECTORY. Added/Corp International Organization of Consumers' Unions. (1989)-. Directory. English. Every 2 years. Fl25.00. International Organization of Consumers Unions / Netherlands, 9 Emmastraat, NL 2500 The Hague, Netherlands. **Tel** 011 31 70 476331, FAX 011 31 70 476331. **Continues** Consumer Directory.
Desc: Reference source for detailed information on which consumer organization is doing what, where and how: addresses, principal officers, telex and telephone numbers, finances, regular publications and specific areas of work.

LC HC79.C63 I57   **ISSN** 0929-8347
DD 640.73   NE

●INTERNATIONAL JOURNAL FOR CONSUMER SAFETY. Added/Corp European Consumer Safety Association. (1994)-. Periodical. English. Four times a year. $311.06. Aeolus Press, PO Box 740, 4116 ZJ Buren The Netherlands. **Tel** 011 31 34472055, FAX 011 31 34472562.

ISSN 1055-3649
DD 381   US

INTERNATIONAL PARALLELS. See Business and Economics-Marketing and Purchasing.

US
INTERNATIONAL PRODUCT ALERT. See Business and Economics-Marketing and Purchasing.

ISSN 0730-2045
INVESTIGATOR (EL PASO, TEX.), THE. (THE INVESTIGATOR.). [Investigator]. Vol. 1, No. 1 (Sept. 1981)-. Periodical. English. $18.00. The Investigator, 930 Thunderbird, El Paso TX 79912.

ISSN 1081-163X
DD 629   US
●JAPANESE AUTO SHOPPER. See Transportation-Automobiles.

LC HC110.C6 J65   **ISSN** 0022-0078
US
CCC
Pr Rev.
JOURNAL OF CONSUMER AFFAIRS, THE. [J. consum. aff.]. Added/Corp American Council on Consumer Interests. Council on Consumer Information. Vol. 1 (Summer 1967)-. Periodical. English. Two times a year (June, Dec.). $125.00 US; $137.00 Canada and Mexico; $143.00 other Comes with American Council on Consumer Interests membership. American Council on Consumer Interest, 240 Stanley Hall, University of Missouri, Columbia MO 65211. **Tel** (314)882-3817, FAX (314)884-6571. **ED** Carole Makela. Index available. **Bk Rev**. **Ad Acc**. **Circ:** 1,750 (ctrl). available on microfilm and microfiche from University Microfilms International (UMI). Documents available from The Genuine Article, UMI Article Clearinghouse.
Desc: An interdisciplinary academic journal focusing on research, on consumer issues, consumer education, and public policy, with selected book reviews.
Ind/Abst ABI/INFORM Glob. Ed.; ABI/INFORM Ondisc: Expr. Ed.; ABI/INFORM [Computer File] (Winter 1972-); Acad. Abstr. Full Text Elite; Acad. Abstr.; Acad. Search; AGRICOLA [Select. Cov.]; Book Rev. Index (?-Dec. 1988); Bus. ASAP (1990-) [Full Txt.]; Bus. Educ. Index; Bus. Index (1985-); Bus. Period. Index; Bus. Source Plus; Commun. Abstr. (?-?); Consum. Index Prod. Eval. Inf. Source; Curr. Cit.; Curr. Contents Soc. Behav. Sci.; Curr. Index J. Educ. (March 1990); Econ. Lit. Index; EP Collect.; Gen. BusinessFile (1985-); Gen. Period. Index (1985-); Homework Help.; INFO-SOUTH Abstr.; J. Econ. Lit.; Mag. Artic. Summar. Elite; Mag. Artic. Summar. Select; Mag. Artic. Summar. CD-ROM; Mag. Search; Manage. Contents; MasterFile FullTEXT 1000; MasterFile FullTEXT 350; MasterFile FullTEXT 650; MasterFile FullTEXT (July 1990-); Newsp. Period. Abstr. (1992-); OCLC; PAIS Int. Print (1991-); Res. Alert [Full Cov.]; Soc. Sci. Cit. Index [Full Cov.]; Telebase; Trade Ind. ASAP [Full Txt.]; Trade Ind. Index [Full Txt.]; UMI ABI/Inform--Bus. Period. Ondisc (Winter 1987-) [Full Txt.]; Wilson Bus. Abstr.

LC HF5415.3 .Z44   **ISSN** 0168-7034
DD 381/.3/05   NE
CCC
Pr Rev.
JOURNAL OF CONSUMER POLICY. [J. consum. policy]. Vol. 6, No. 1 (1983)-. Academic Scholarly Publication. English (summaries and/or abstracts in German). Four times a year. $229.00. Kluwer Academic Publishers, Postbus 322, 3300 AH Dordrecht The Netherlands. **Tel** 011 31 78 524400, FAX 011 31 78 183273, telex 20083. **(Subscription address:** Kluwer Academic Publishers / US Subscriptions, PO Box 253, Accord Station, Hingham MA 02018. **Tel** (617)871-6600.)

ED F. Olander, N. Reich and G. Scherhorn. **Bk Rev**. **Ad Acc**. **Acid Free**. **Circ:** 700. available on microfilm and microfiche from University Microfilms International (UMI). Documents available from The Genuine Article, UMI Article Clearinghouse. **Continues** Zeitschrift fur Verbraucherpolitik, 0342-5843.
Desc: An international scholarly journal which encompasses a diverse range of issues involving consumer affairs, including empirical research on consumer and producer conduct.
Ind/Abst ABI/INFORM Glob. Ed.; ABI/INFORM Ondisc: Expr. Ed.; ABI/INFORM [Computer File] (March 1985-); AGRICOLA [Select. Cov.]; Bus. ASAP (1992-) [Full Txt.]; Bus. Index (1986-); Commun. Abstr. (?-?); Curr. Cit.; Curr. Contents Soc. Behav. Sci.; Econ. Lit. Index; Energy Res. Abstr. (1983-); Gen. BusinessFile (1986-); Gen. Period. Index (1986-); Mag. Search; MasterFile FullTEXT (Jan. 1991-); PAIS Int. Print; Res. Alert [Full Cov.]; Soc. Sci. Cit. Index [Full Cov.]; Trade Ind. ASAP [Full Txt.]; Trade Ind. Index [Full Txt.]; UMI ABI/Inform--Bus. Period. Ondisc (Dec. 1987-) [Full Txt.].

LC HF5415.32 .J677   **ISSN** 1057-7408
DD 658.8/342/05   US
JOURNAL OF CONSUMER PSYCHOLOGY: OFFICIAL JOURNAL OF THE SOCIETY FOR CONSUMER PSYCHOLOGY. See Business and Economics-Advertising and Public Relations.

LC HF5415.32 .J68   **ISSN** 0899-8620
DD 658.8/12/05   US
Pr Rev.
JOURNAL OF CONSUMER SATISFACTION, DISSATISFACTION, AND COMPLAINING BEHAVIOR. (JOURNAL OF CONSUMER SATISFACTION, DISSATISFACTION, AND COMPLAINING BEHAVIOR : CS/D&CB.). Added/Corp Consumer Satisfaction, Dissatisfaction, and Complaining Behavior, Inc. **VFOAT** CS/D&CB; JCS/D&CB. Vol. 1 (1988)-. English. $15.00. Association for Consumer Research, Brigham Young University, 632 TNRB, Provo UT 84602. **Tel** (801)378-2080, FAX (801)378-5984.

ISSN 0309-3891
UK
CCC
JOURNAL OF CONSUMER STUDIES AND HOME ECONOMICS. [J. consum. stud. home econ.]. **VAT** Journal of Consumer Studies & Home Economics. Vol. 1 (March 1977)-. Academic Scholarly Publication. English. Four times a year. $253.00. Blackwell Scientific Publications Ltd, Marston Book Services, PO Box 88, Oxford OX2 ONE United Kingdom. **Tel** 011 44 1865 206206, FAX 011 44 1865 206219, telex 837 515 MARDIS G. **ED** Ann Maree Rees. Index available. **Bk Rev**. **Ad Acc**. **Circ:** 550. available on microfilm and microfiche from University Microfilms International (UMI).
Desc: Aimed at people working in the field of consumer studies and home economics. Covers significant developments and ideas, including research papers, review articles, short communications, news, comments and correspondence.
Ind/Abst AGRICOLA [Full Cov.]; Art Archaeol. Tech. Abstr.; Educ. Technol. Abstr.; EMBASE; Energy Res. Abstr. (July 1981-); PAIS Int. Print (1991-); Stud. Women Abstr.; Tech. Educ. Train. Abstr.; World Text. Abstr.

LC HF5428 .J68   **ISSN** 0969-6989
DD 381/.1/094105   UK
Pr Rev.
●JOURNAL OF RETAILING AND CONSUMER SERVICES. See Business and Economics-Retail.

ISSN 0262-6624
DD 784.54005   UK
KERRANG!. See Music.

AU
KONSUMENT. (19??)-. German. Twelve times a year. S348.00 Austria; S432.00 other. Verein Konsumenteninformation, Postfach 440, 1061 Vienna Austria. Index available. **Circ:** 100,000 (ctrl).

ISSN 0929-0001
NE
●KRITISCH CONSUMEREN. (1993)-. Dutch. Irregular (8 issues). Fl44.00 (membership and subscription), Fl22.00 (membership). Alternatieve Konsumenten Bond, PB 61236, 1005 HE Amsterdam Netherlands. **Tel** 011 31 20 6863587, 011 31 20 6863338. **Continues** Voeding & Milieu, 0926-0447.

ISSN 0834-2423
DD 338.4/76292222/05   CN
LEMON-AID (1985). See Transportation-Automobiles.

LC HF5415.33.U6 L56   **ISSN** 1057-8080
DD 304.6/0973/021   US
CEASED
LIFESTYLE ZIP CODE ANALYST, THE. [Lifestyle zip code anal.]. Added/Corp Standard Rate & Data Service. National Demographics & Lifestyles.

(1991)-(19??). Trade Publication. English. SRDS / Standard Rate & Data Service, 3004 Glenview Road, Wilmette IL 60091. **Tel** (708)375-5049, (800)851-7737, FAX (708)375-5003. **(Subscription address:** Neodata / Colorado, PO Box 2606, Boulder CO 80322.)

ISSN 0047-486X
US
LIVING IN SOUTH CAROLINA. Added/Corp South Carolina Electric Cooperative Association. (19??)-. Periodical. English. Twelve times a year. $2.00. Living in South Carolina, 808 Knox Abbott Drive, Cayce SC 29033. **Tel** (803)796-6060, FAX (803)796-6064. **ED** Larry Cribb. **Bk Rev**, (Qty: 10-15). **Ad Acc**. **Circ:** 394,000 (ctrl).
Desc: Consumer news and ideas for improving the quality of life are featured. Also covers recreation and outdoor sports.

LC KF1602 .L69   **ISSN** 1041-5114
DD 343.73/071/05 347.3037105   US
LOYOLA CONSUMER LAW REPORTER. See Law.

LC TX336 .M33
US
MADE IN THE USA. Added/Corp Made in the USA Foundation. (1990)-. English. One time a year. $12.95 US; $18.95 other. National Press Books / Maryland, 7200 Wisconsin Avenue, Suite 212, Bethesda MD 20814. **Tel** (301)657-1616. Index available. cum. index. available on CD-ROM.
Desc: Information on consumer education and commercial products.

LC TX335 .M2215
IS
MAH KEDAI. No. 1- February 1975-. Periodical. Hebrew. Six times a year. 5.00 single issue. Ha-Moatsah Ha-Yisreelit Le-Tsarkhanut, Rehov Hauniversitah 42, Tel-Aviv Israel.

ISSN 0848-1989
DD 640./73/060718   CN
MANITOBA CONSUMER (1985). (MANITOBA CONSUMER.). [Manit. consum.]. Added/Corp Consumers' Association of Canada. Manitoba Branch. (Spring 1985)-. English. Free to members of CAC-Manitoba. Consumers' Association of Canada, Manitoba Branch, 21-1373 Portage Avenue, Winnipeg Manitoba R3G 0V8 Canada. **Continues** Update (Consumers' Association of Canada. Manitoba Branch)., 0826-2977.

ISSN 0262-5601
UK
MATCH WEEKLY. [Match wkly.]. (1979)-. Periodical. English. One time a week. £111.23. EMAP Pursuit Publishing, Apex House 7th Fl. Oundle Road, Peterborough PE2 9NP United Kingdom. **Tel** 011 44 1733 264666. **ED** Paul Stratton.

ISSN 0317-9303
DD 640.73   CN
MEMOIRE AUX GOUVERNEMENTS CANADIEN ET QUEBECOIS. Main/Corp Federation des Associations Cooperatives d'Economie Familiale du Quebec. (1968)-. Periodical. French. Free to minister and members of the Federation. Federation des Associations Cooperatives d'Economie Familiale du Quebec, 3510 Est boulevard St. Joseph, Montreal Quebec H1X 1W6 Canada.

ISSN 0734-3108
US
MOBIUS (ALEXANDRIA, VA.). See Business and Economics.

LC TX335 .M65   **ISSN** 0026-9646
DD 640.73/05   CCC
MONEYSWORTH (NEW YORK). (MONEYSWORTH.). Vol. 1, (Oct. 19, 1970)-. Periodical. English. Four times a year. Moneysworth, 251 West 57th Street, New York NY 10019. **Tel** (212)581-2000. available on microfilm and microfiche from University Microfilms International (UMI).
Ind/Abst Mag. Index (1977-Spring 1984).

ISSN 0027-2302
DD 388.3   UK
MOTORISTS GUIDE TO NEW & USED CAR PRICES. See Transportation-Automobiles.

US
NAD CASE REPORT. See Business and Economics-Advertising and Public Relations.

ISSN 0270-2835
US
NATIONAL ASSOCIATION OF CONSUMER AGENCY ADMINISTRATORS NEWS. Added/Corp National Association of Consumer Agency Administrators (U.S.). Vol. 2, No. 6 (March 1979)-. Periodical. English. Ten times a year. $75.00. The National Association of Consumer Agency Administrators, 1010 Vermont Avenue West, Suite 514, Washington DC 20005. **Tel** (202)347-7395. **ED** Pauline D. Flynn. Index available. **Bk**

Rev.
Desc: News from state, county and municipal consumer protection offices throughout the nation. Information on court decisions and federal agency actions which affect consumer protection.

LC HF5469.7 **ISSN** 1055-8268
DD 381.17 US

●NATIONAL AUCTIONS & SALES. **VFOAT** National Auctions and Sales. (1993)-. Periodical. English. Four times a year. $29.99. Publishing & Business Consultants, PO Box 75392, Los Angeles CA 90075. **Tel** (213)732-3477, FAX (213)732-9123. **ED** Andeson Napoleon Atia. **Ad Acc.** Full Page (B&W) $5750.00. Half Page (B&W) $3575.00. Full Page (Color) $8750.00 (two-color). Half Page (Color) $5500.00 (two-color). **Circ:** 166,000.
Desc: Features articles on taxes, financing and transportation. Of interest to those determined to get basic items at cost-effective prices.

ISSN 1068-0845
US

NATIONAL BOYCOTT NEWS. **Added/Corp** Institute for Consumer Responsibility. (19??)-. Periodical. English. Irregular. $20.00 (US and Canada); $30.00 (other) nonprofit organizations; $40.00 (US and Canada); $50.00 (other) corporations; $10.00 organizations and individuals. National Boycott News, 6506 28th Avenue Northeast, Seattle WA 98115. **Tel** (206)523-0421, (206) 524-7726. **ED** Todd Putnam.
Desc: Monitors and reports on organized consumer activity, boycotts in particular.
Ind/Abst Altern. Press Index (199?-); Hum. Rights Intern. Rep.

ISSN 0734-8274
US

NATIONAL STUDY OF SUPERMARKET SHOPPERS. CENSUS PROFILE, THE. [Natl. stud. supermark. shopp., Census profile]. **Added/Corp** Burgoyne, Inc. **VFOAT** Census Profile. (1977)-. English. Burgoyne Inc., Central Trust Building, Cincinnati OH 45202. ***Continues in part*** *Food Shopping Habits Study of Super Market Shoppers, their Buying Habits and Attitudes, 0160-9017.*

ISSN 0890-3417
DD 614 US

NCAHF NEWSLETTER. (NCAHF NEWSLETTER : QUALITY IN THE HEALTH MARKETPLACE.). **Added/Corp** National Council Against Health Fraud (U.S.). **VAT** National Council Against Health Fraud Newsletter. (1977)-. Newsletter. English. Six times a year. $15.00. National Council Against Health Fraud, PO Box 1276, Loma Linda CA 92354. **Tel** (909)824-4690, FAX (909)824-4838. **ED** William T. Jarvis. **Bk Rev. Circ:** 1,500. available on an online database (file 149/Full-Text) from DIALOG; available in microform.
Desc: Designed to analyze and expose fraudulent medical practices. Covers such topics as faith healing, nutritional fads, and questionable alternative health care.
Ind/Abst Acad. Search; Consum. Health Nutr. Index; EP Collect.; Health Index (1989-); Health Period. Database [Full Txt.]; Health Ref. Cent. (Jan. 1989-) [Full Txt.] [Full Cov.]; Health Source Plus; Health Source; Homework Help.; MasterFile FullTEXT 1000; MasterFile FullTEXT 350; MasterFile FullTEXT 650; MasterFile FullTEXT (July 1994-) [Full Txt.]; OCLC; Telebase.

ISSN 0958-7349
DD 306.3 UK
TITLE CHANGE

NEW CONSUMER. [New consum.]. (1989)-(1993). Periodical. English. New Consumer, 52 Elswick Road, Newcastle Upon Tyne NE4 6JH United Kingdom. **Tel** 011 44 191 2721148, FAX 011 44 191 2721615. **ED** Richard Adams. **Bk Rev**, (Qty: 12). **Circ:** 1,000 (ctrl). ***Continued by*** *New Consumer Briefing, 1357-017X.*
Desc: Provides people with information and practical strategies for integrating their economic choices with their values and lifestyle.

ISSN 1357-017X
DD 339.47 UK

●NEW CONSUMER BRIEFING. [New consum. brief.]. (1994)-. Periodical. English. Four times a year. $42.78. New Consumer, 52 Elswick Road, Newcastle Upon Tyne NE4 6JH United Kingdom. **Tel** 011 44 191 2721148, FAX 011 44 191 2721615. **ED** Richard Adams. **Bk Rev**, (Qty: 12). **Circ:** 1,000 (ctrl). ***Continues*** *New Consumer, 0958-7349.*
Desc: Provides people with information and practical strategies for integrating their economic choices with their values and lifestyle.

ISSN 0364-6777
US

NEW FOR CONSUMERS. (19??)-. English. Free. Consumer Information Center, Public Documents Distribution Center, Pueblo CO 81009. **Tel** (202)501-1794. **ED** Tim Burr. **Circ:** 6,000 (ctrl).
Desc: Informs citizens through the media about consumer topics and the availability of federal consumer booklets from Pueblo, Colorado.

LC TL162 .V36 **ISSN** 1081-0110
DD 629.223 US

●NEW PICKUP, VAN & SPORT UTILITY PRICES. See Transportation-Automobiles.

ISSN 0193-4635
US

NEWS - CONSUMER FEDERATION OF AMERICA. **Main/Corp** Consumer Federation of America. (19??)-. Periodical. English. Twelve times a year. $25.00. Consumer Federation of America, 1424 16th Street Northwest, Suite 604, Washington DC 20036. **Tel** (202)387-6121. **ED** Barbara Roper. **Bk Rev. Circ:** 1,500.
Desc: Consumer news on the legislative and regulatory areas of energy, utility, phone, and banking issues highlighted.

US

NORTH DAKOTA R E C MAGAZINE. See Business and Economics-Cooperatives.

ISSN 1044-3134
DD 328 US

NYPIRG AGENDA. See Environmental Issues.

GW

OEKO TEST. (19??)-. German. Twelve times a year. DM65.00 Germany; DM80.00 other. Oeko Test Verlag GmbH & Co., Postfach 900766 Betriebsgesellschaft, D-6000 Frankfurt 90 Germany. **Tel** 011 49 69 79209660.

LC AP66 .O65
AG

OPINION, LA. (July 1976)-. Periodical. Spanish. One time a week. Editorial Olta, LaFayette 1910, Buenos Aires, Argentina.

ISSN 1064-4628
DD 629 US
TITLE CHANGE

PACE BUYER'S GUIDES. DOMESTIC & FOREIGN TRUCK, VAN, 4X4 PRICES, NEW & USED. See Transportation-Automobiles.

ISSN 0279-4209
US

PENNYSAVER SHOPPING GUIDE. (19??)-. Periodical. English. One time a week. ***Continues*** *Halifax Shopping Guide, 0191-5169.*

LC HC110.C63 P44 **ISSN** 0148-0030
DD 381/.3 US

PEOPLE POWER. (1977)-. Consumer Publication. English. One time a year. $7.95 per issue. International Research & Evaluation, Research Publications Division, 7325 Humboldt Avenue South, Minneapolis MN 55423. **Tel** (612)888-9635, FAX (612)869-2675, telex 29-1008. **ED** Randall Voight and Rick Danford. Index available. cum. index. **Bk Rev. Circ:** 351,050. available on microfiche; available on diskette.
Desc: Reference source designed not only as a problem solving instrument, but also as a guide for people to voice their concerns.
Ind/Abst Acad. Abstr.; EP Collect.; Health Source Plus; Health Source; Homework Help.; Mag. Search; MasterFile FullTEXT 1000; MasterFile FullTEXT 350; MasterFile FullTEXT 650; MasterFile FullTEXT (Jan. 1993-); OCLC; Pub. Lib. FullTEXT; Telebase.

US

PICKUP, VAN & 4WD ROAD TEST ANNUAL AND BUYERS' GUIDE. See Transportation-Automobiles.

LC HD3514 .S65 **ISSN** 0234-8098
RU

POTREBITELSKAIA KOOPERATSIIA : PK. **VFOAT** PK. (1991)-. Periodical. Russian. Twelve times a year. ***Continues*** *Sovetskaia Potrebitelskaia Kooperatsiia.*

LC HG1501 **ISSN** 0198-9936
DD 332.1 US

POWELL ALERT, THE. (19??)-. Periodical. English. Twenty-six times a year. $36.00 (one-year), $55.00 (two-year). Reserve Research Ltd, C/O L.M. Powell, 622 Congress Street, PO Box 4135 Station A, Portland ME 04101. **Tel** (207)774-4971. **ED** Larson M. Powell.
Desc: Consumer-oriented financial planning report covering outlook for stock and bond markets interest rates, estate planning, taxes, insurance, health, travel, real estate and more.

ISSN 0738-5676
US
SUSPENDED

POWER LINE (WASHINGTON, D.C.), THE. See Energy-Electric Power.

LC HG **ISSN** 0888-2762
DD 332 US

PRIVILEGED INFORMATION. [Privil. inf.]. (1985)-. Consumer Publication. English. Twelve times a year. $48.00. Boardroom Reports Inc., 330 West 42nd Street, 14th Floor, New York NY 10036. **Tel** (212)239-9000. **ED** Martin Edelston, A.K. Brownfield, Devin-Adair Mahony. **Circ:** 100,001.
Desc: The report on America's consumer secrets.

LC HC110.C63 A67a **ISSN** 0275-1356
DD 381/.3/0973 US
Pr Rev. **TITLE CHANGE**

PROCEEDINGS ... ANNUAL CONFERENCE OF THE AMERICAN COUNCIL ON CONSUMER INTERESTS. [Proc. annu. conf. Am. Counc. Consum. Interests]. **Main/Corp** American Council on Consumer Interests. Conference. (1970)-39th (March 31/April 3, 1993). Proceedings. English. American Council on Consumer Interest, 240 Stanley Hall, University of Missouri, Columbia MO 65211. **Tel** (314)882-3817, FAX (314)884-6571. **ED** Virginia Haldeman. Index available. **Bk Rev. Ad Acc. Circ:** 1,100 (ctrl). available on microfilm from ERIC. ***Continues*** *Council on Consumer Information. Conference. Proceedings of Annual Conference.* ***Continued by*** *American Council on Consumer Interests. Conference. Consumer Interests Annual.*
Desc: A collection of the papers, panel discussions, and invited speakers' presentations at the annual convention.

ISSN 0098-7530
US
CCC

PRODUCT SAFETY LETTER. [Prod. saf. newsl.]. **VFOAT** PSL. (1972)-. Newsletter. English. One time a week (published Monday). $907.00. Washington Business Information Inc., 1117 North 19th Street, Suite 200, Arlington VA 22209. **Tel** (703)247-3434, (800)426-0416, FAX (703)247-3421. **ED** Todd Leeuwenburgh.
Desc: Monitors the CPS and other agencies. Offers advance notice of rules that hit production and sale of products ranging from TV's to toys, cleaners to clothing.

ISSN 0701-8517
CN

PROTEGEZ-VOUS. [Prot.-vous]. **Added/Corp** Quebec (Province). Office de la Protection du Consommateur. Vol. 1 (April 1973)-. Periodical. French. Twelve times a year. 18.64Can$ Canada; 30.00Can$ other. Protegez Vous, 25 boulevard Taschereau, Suite 201, Greenfield Quebec J4V 2G8 Canada. **Tel** (514)923-9381, FAX (514)923-0864.
Ind/Abst Can. Period. Index (19??-); Repere (1979-)(1983-).

ISSN 0738-5927
US

PUBLIC CITIZEN. (THE PUBLIC CITIZEN.). [Public citiz.]. **Added/Corp** Public Citizen, inc. (1976)-. Periodical. English. Six times a year. $25.00. Public Citizens Congress Watch, 2000 P Street NW Suite 600, Washington DC 20036. **Tel** (202)833-3000, FAX (202)296-1727. **ED** Peter Nye. **Bk Rev. Ad Acc. Circ:** 42,000.
Desc: Consumer safety and health issues, safe energy alternatives, government irresponsibility and corporate wrong-doing. Profiles individuals in the consumer movement. Oriented to politics and consumer affairs. Reporting, analytical features, and profiles on newsmakers.
Ind/Abst Acad. Abstr.; Acad. Search; Altern. Press Index; EP Collect.; Homework Help.; INFO-SOUTH Abstr.; Mag. Search; MasterFile FullTEXT 1000; MasterFile FullTEXT 350; MasterFile FullTEXT 650; MasterFile FullTEXT (Jan. 1992-); OCLC; Pub. Lib. FullTEXT; Telebase.

ISSN 0033-5932
FR
UDC 33

QUE CHOISIR ? PARIS. [Que choisir ? Paris]. (1961)-. Periodical. French. Eleven times a year (monthly with July/Aug. combined). 259.55F France; 331.05F other. Union Federale des Consummateurs, 11 rue Guenot, 75555 Paris Cedex 11 France. **Tel** 011 33 1 43485548.

LC HG **ISSN** 1053-9719
DD 332 US
Pr Rev.

RAM RESEARCH'S CARDTRAK. [RAM Res. cardtrak]. **Added/Corp** RAM Research/Publishing Co. **VFOAT** Cardtrak. No. 1 (Jan. 1991)-. Periodical. English. Twelve times a year. $60.00. RAM Research Corporation, PO Box 1700 (College Estates), Frederick MD 21701. **Tel** (301)695-4660, (301)662-6640, FAX (301)695-0160. **ED** Robert B. Mckinley (editor's address: Box 1916, College Estate, Frederick MD 21702). **Circ:** 100,000.
Desc: Covers all types of bank credit cards. Each issue surveys over 500 issuers offering low interest rate, no annual fee, gold cards and secured cards. A two-page commentary on the latest deals is also included in each issue.

LC HC117.Q4 Q29a **ISSN** 0319-8774
DD 354.7140082/042/06 CN

RAPPORT ANNUEL - CONSEIL DE LA PROTECTION DU CONSOMMATEUR. **Main/Corp** Quebec (Province). Conseil de la Protection

Consumer Education and Protection

du Consommateur. (1975)-. French. Editeur Officiel du Quebec, 1283 boulevard Charest Ouest, Quebec Quebec G1N 2C9 Canada. **Continues** *Quebec (Province). Consumer Protection Council. Rapport Annuel du Conseil de la Protection du Consommateur., 0319-8774.*

ISSN 1053-0525
DD 363 US
RECYCLING RELATED NEWSLETTERS, PUBLICATIONS, PERIODICALS, ETC. See Environmental Issues.

ISSN 0896-7350
US
REFUND EXPRESS. [Refund express]. (198?)-. Periodical. English. Twelve times a year. $3.00 (sample), $14.00 (6 months), $23.00 (one-year). Sandy Ennis, PO Box 10, Allen Park MI 48101. **Tel** (313)381-8686.

US
REFUNDING MAKES CENTS. (19??)-. English. Twelve times a year. $12.00. Refunding Makes Cents, PO Box R, Farmington UT 84025.

ISSN 0736-1688
US
REFUNDING UPDATE. VFOAT Refunds. (198?)-. English. Irregular. $6.95 US; $8.95 Canada; $10.95 other. Prosperity & Profits Unlimited, PO Box 416, Denver CO 80201-0416. **Tel** (303)575-5676. **ED** A. Doyle. **Circ:** 1500.
Desc: An introduction to refunding.

ISSN 0194-0139
US
REFUNDLE BUNDLE. (19??)-. Periodical. English. Six times a year (Jan., Mar., May, July, Sept., Nov.). $19.87. Refundle Bundle, PO Box 141 Centuck Station, Yonkers NY 10710. **Tel** (914)472-2227. **ED** Susan J. Samtur and Stephen M. Samtur. **Ad Acc. Circ:** 15,000 (ctrl).
Desc: A guide to couponing and refunding including good shopping techniques in the supermarket. Consumer features on couponing and refunding.

LC HC107.C23 C633b ISSN 0360-8050
DD 381/.3 US
REPORT TO THE GOVERNOR AND THE LEGISLATURE - STATE OF CALIFORNIA, DEPARTMENT OF CONSUMER AFFAIRS. (REPORT TO THE GOVERNOR AND THE LEGISLATURE.). **Main/Corp** California. Dept. of Consumer Affairs. (19??)-. English. California Department of Consumer Affairs, 1020 North Street, Room 510, Sacramento CA 95814. **Tel** (916)445-4465, FAX (916)443-1601.

US
RESEARCH ALERT. VFOAT RA. (198?)-. Periodical. English. Twenty-four times a year. $369.00. EPM Communications Inc., 488 East 18th Street, Brooklyn NY 11226. **Tel** (718)469-9330, FAX (718)469-7124. **Continues** *MIN/Research Alert, 0739-363X.*
Ind/Abst Mark. Advert. Ref. Serv. [Full Txt.]; PROMT [Full Txt.]; PTS Newsl. Database [Full Txt.].

ISSN 0227-1184
DD 334/.5/0971447 CN
RIPOSTE (1980). (LA RIPOSTE.). [Riposte]. **Added/Corp** Association Cooperative d'Economie Familiale de Quebec. Vol. 3 (Winter 1980)-. Periodical. French. Four times a year. Association Cooperative d'Economie Familiale de Quebec, 1215 rue de la Visitation, Montreal Quebec H2L 3B5 Canada. **Tel** (514)598-7288. **Continues** *Association Cooperative d'Economie Familiale de Quebec. Le Journal de l'A. C. E. F. de Quebec, 0705-7059.*

LC TX ISSN 0196-383X
DD 640 US
CEASED
ROADRUNNER REFUNDER. (197?)-(Aug. 1993). Periodical. English. Roadrunner Refunder, 5812 West Elm, Phoenix AZ 85031. **Tel** (602)846-5437. **ED** Jan Neuberger. **Ad Acc. Circ:** 8000.

ISSN 0899-9414
DD 977 US
ROCKFORD MAGAZINE. (June 1986)-. Periodical. English. Twelve times a year. $17.95. Rockford Magazine, PO Box 678, Rockford IL 61105. **Tel** (815)961-2400, (800)383-4567, FAX (815)961-2279. **ED** Craig Schmidt. **Ad Acc, Adv Mgr:** G. Kazuk. ctrl circ.

US
RUNZHEIMER MEAL LODGING COST INDEX. (19??)-. English. Irregular (also updates). Price varies. Runzheimer International / Wisconsin, Runzheimer Park, Rochester WI 53167. **Tel** (414)767-2200, FAX (414)767-2254, (800)558-1702. Index available (free). available on diskette.

ISSN 0379-8992
DD 640.7306268 SA
SA - VERBRUIKER, DIE. [SA - verbruiker]. **VFOAT** Suid-Afrika Verbruiker; South Africa Consumer; SA Consumer. (1978)-. Periodical. Multiple languages (Afrikaans and English). Four times a year (Mar., June, Sept., Nov.). Free on request. South Africa Consumer / SA Consumer, PO Box 56658, 0007 Arcadia South Africa. **Tel** 011 27 12 3202000, FAX 011 27 12 3201111. **ED** Thariza Steyo. Index available. cum. index. **Circ:** 50,000.

US
SALES PRO. See Business and Economics-Marketing and Purchasing.

LC Z6951 .S32 PN4877
DD 051 US
SAMIR HUSNI'S GUIDE TO THE NEW CONSUMER MAGAZINES PUBLISHED IN ... . VFOAT Samir Husni's Guide to New Consumer Magazines. Vol. 7 (1992)-. Periodical. English. One time a year. $63.95. Cowles Business Media Inc. / Connecticut, 6 River Bend Center, 911 Hope Street, Stamford CT 06907. **Tel** (203)358-9900, (800)775-3777, FAX (203)357-9014. **Continues** *Samir Husni's Guide to New Magazines, 0892-7170.*

ISSN 0276-4601
US
SAN DIEGO CONSUMER'S VOICE. VFOAT Consumer's Voice. Vol. 1, No. 1 (May 1981)-. Periodical. English. Twelve times a year. $9.00. San Diego Consumer's Voice, PO Box 1099, Eneinitas CA 92024.

ISSN 0193-4384
US
SEARS. (SEARS; CATALOG.). **Main/Corp** Sears, Roebuck and Company. **VFOAT** Catalog. (19??)-. Catalog. English. Two times a year. Sears Roebuck and Company, 7236 East Harry, Wichita KS 67207. **Continues** *Consumers Guide.*

US
●**SECONDARY MARKET ANNUAL GUIDE, THE.** (1994)-. Directory. English. One time a year. $100.00. Penton Publishing, 1100 Superior Avenue, Cleveland OH 44114-2543. **Tel** (216)696-7000, FAX (216)696-0836. **(Subscription address:** Penton Publishing, PO Box 96732, Chicago IL 60693. **)**
Desc: Directory of dealers covering used capital equipment markets, from airplanes to x-ray machines.

ISSN 1059-5384
US
SELF-STORAGE RENTAL GUIDE (SOUTHERN CALIFORNIA ED.). (SELF-STORAGE RENTAL GUIDE.). **VFOAT** Self Storage Rental Guide. (1992)-. English. Four times a year. $10.00. Self-Storage Rental Guide, PO Box 270212, San Diego CA 92198-2212.

UK
SERVICE STATION SHOPPER SURVEY. (19??)-. English. Irregular. £1500.00. Euromonitor Publications Ltd., 60-61 Britton Street, London EC1M 5NA United Kingdom. **Tel** 011 44 171 2518024, FAX 011 44 171 6083149, telex 21120.
Desc: A quantitative consumer survey that details habits and attitudes towards using on-site shops in service stations in the UK.

LC HC465.C63 S48
JA
SHIRYO SHOHISHA GYOSEI. Added/Corp Japan. Keizai Kikakucho. Shohisha Gyoseika. **VFOAT** Shohisha Gyosei. (19??)-. Periodical. Japanese. ¥780. Okurasho Insatuykyoku, (Printing Bureau Ministry of Finance), 2-4 Toranomon 2 chome, Minatoku Tokyo 105 Japan.

LC HC465.C63 T64a
JA
SHOHISHA SODAN JIREI SHU. Main/Corp Tokyo-to Shohisha Senta. (19??)-. Japanese. Tokyo-To Shohisha Senta, 10-1 Yurakucho 2-Chome, Chiyoda-ku 100, Tokyo Japan.

ISSN 1056-6473
US
SHOP 'TIL YA DROP. (1991)-. Periodical. English. Twelve times a year. Free. S3 Publishing, Inc., 353 Kellogg Boulevard, St. Paul MN 55101-1411.

UK
SHOP WINDOW. (19??)-. English. Twelve times a year. £10.20. Royal National Institute for the Blind, PO Box 173, Peterborough PE2 6WS United Kingdom. **Tel** 011 44 1733 3730777, FAX 011 44 1733 371555.
Desc: Contains product reviews, helpful tips, articles on food and drink, travel information and readers comments and suggestions.

LC Discard

US
SHOPPER & OBSERVER NEWS, THE. VFOAT Shopper and Observer News. (1958)-. Periodical. English. Fifty-two times a year (Wed.). $35.00. Ruskin Shopper & Observer News, PO Box 5, Ruskin FL 33570. **Tel** (813)645-3111. **ED** Sherrie Cole. Index available. cum. index. **Ad Acc. Circ:** 25,000 (ctrl).
Desc: Local community news and advertising.

ISSN 1055-2324
US
SHOPPER'S GUIDE (COLORADO SPRINGS, COLO.), THE. (THE SHOPPER'S GUIDE.). (1991)-. Periodical. English. Two times a year. $11.95. Marsham Corporation, PO Box 88005, Colorado Springs CO 80908.

LC HF5035 .D53 ISSN 1066-9701
DD 381/.025/73 US
●**SHOPPING CENTER DIRECTORY.** [Shopp. cent. dir.]. **Added/Corp** National Research Bureau, Inc. **VFOAT** NRB Shopping Center Directory. 33rd Ed. (1993)-. Directory. English. One time a year. $625.00 (complete 5-volume set). National Research Bureau Inc. / Virginia, 3975 Fair Ridge Drive Suite 200N, Fairfax VA 22033. **Tel** (800)456-4555, FAX (703)934-9607. **ED** Nancy D. Veatch. **Continues** *Directory of Shopping Centers in the United States.*

US
SHOPPING CENTERS ON DEMAND : CONTACT REPORT SERIES. (19??)-. English. National Research Bureau Inc. / Illinois, 150 North Wacker Drive, Suite 2222, Chicago IL 60606. **Tel** (312)541-0100.

US
SHOPPING CENTERS ON DEMAND : FACILITY REPORT SERIES. (19??)-. English. National Research Bureau Inc. / Illinois, 150 North Wacker Drive, Suite 2222, Chicago IL 60606. **Tel** (312)541-0100.

US
SHOPPING CENTERS ON DEMAND : LOCATION REPORT SERIES. (19??)-. English. National Research Bureau Inc. / Illinois, 150 North Wacker Drive, Suite 2222, Chicago IL 60606. **Tel** (312)541-0100. **(Subscription address:** National Research Bureau Inc., 3975 Fair Ridge Drive 200N, Fairfax VA 22033. **Tel** (800)456-4555, (703)934-2616.**)**

US
SHOPPING CENTERS ON DEMAND : RETAIL REPORT SERIES. (19??)-. English. National Research Bureau Inc. / Illinois, 150 North Wacker Drive, Suite 2222, Chicago IL 60606. **Tel** (312)541-0100. **(Subscription address:** National Research Bureau Inc., 3975 Fair Ridge Drive 200N, Fairfax VA 22033. **Tel** (800)456-4555, (703)934-2616.**)**

US
SHOPPING CENTERS ON DEMAND : TRANSACTIONS REPORT SERIES. (19??)-. English. National Research Bureau Inc. / Illinois, 150 North Wacker Drive, Suite 2222, Chicago IL 60606. **Tel** (312)541-0100. **(Subscription address:** National Research Bureau Inc., 3975 Fair Ridge Drive 200N, Fairfax VA 22033. **Tel** (800)456-4555, (703)934-2616.**)**

AT
SHOPPING CENTRE NEWS. (19??)-. English. Six times a year. 85.00Aus$ Australia; 98.00Aus$ New Zealand; 125.00Aus$ other. Rillage Publishing, PO Box 363, Rozelle NSW 2039 Australia. **Tel** 011 61 02 5557494, FAX 011 61 02 8104392. **ED** Sabina Rust. **Ad Acc.**

ISSN 0260-3004
DD 784.5 UK
SMASH HITS. See Music.

LC HC110.C63 A24 ISSN 0190-2210
DD 381/.3/0973 US
STATE CONSUMER ACTION. Main/Corp United States. Office of Consumer Affairs. (1971)-. Government Publication. English. One time a year. $1.05. Superintendent of Documents, US Government Printing Office, Washington DC 20402. **Tel** (202)275-3328, FAX (202)786-2377.

LC HF5415.126 .F33 ISSN 1049-6092
DD 381/.1 US
STATISTICAL FACT BOOK - DIRECT MARKETING ASSOCIATION (U.S.). (STATISTICAL FACTBOOK.). [Stat. fact book - Direct Mark. Assoc. (U. S.)]. **Added/Corp** Direct Marketing Association (U.S.). **VFOAT** DMA Statistical Fact Book. **VAT** Statistical Factbook. (1988)-. Statistical Publication. English. One time a year. $104.95. Direct Marketing Association Inc, 11 West 42nd Street, New York NY 10036. **Tel** (212)768-7277, FAX (212)599-1268. **Continues** *Fact Book (Direct Marketing Association (U.S.)), 0888-5362.*

Consumer Education and Protection

DD 382   **ISSN** 1190-9854   CN
● **STRATEGIE D'EXPORTATION DU CANADA, PLAN DE PROMOTION DU COMMERCE EXTERIEUR. 9, BIENS DE CONSOMMATION.** See Business and Economics-Commerce.

LC HC110.C6 T43
DD 658.8/348   **ISSN** 0741-7047   US
TEEN LEADER SYNDICATED STUDY. [Teen lead. synd. study]. No. 1 (Winter 1982-83)-. English. One time a year. Teen-Age Research Unlimited, 721 North McKinley Road, Lake Forest IL 60045. **Tel** (312)295-5580.

SZ
TEST. (19??)-. German (French). Six times a year. 40.00F other. FPC, Monbijoustrasse 61, 3007 Bern Switzerland. **Tel** 011 41 31 453444, 011 41 31 460027. **ED** Stiftung fur Konsumentenschutz. **Bk Rev**. **Circ**: 10,000.
Desc: Tests on commodities, reports about nutrition, and environmental safety.

UDC 351.82   **ISSN** 0772-9405   BE
TEST ACHATS MAGAZINE. [Test achats mag.]. **VFOAT** Test Aankoop Magazine. (1984)-. Periodical. Multiple languages (French and Dutch). Eleven times a year. $97.31. Association des Consommateurs, rue de Hollande 13, 1060 Brussels Belgium. **Tel** 011 32 2 5423211, **FAX** 011 32 2 5423250.
Continues Test Achats, 0772-974X.

UDC 658.62/.64.018   **ISSN** 0040-3946   GW
TEST BERLIN, WEST. ZEITSCHRIFT. [Test Berl. West, Z.]. (1966)-. Periodical. German. Twelve times a year. DM76.20. Stiftung Warentest, Postfach 304141, D-10724 Berlin Germany. **Tel** 011 49 30 2623014.

US
TEXAS CONSUMER LAW REPORTER. (19??)-. English. Twelve times a year. $195.00. Texas Consumer Law Reporter, Box 12841, Capitol Station, Austin TX 78711. **Tel** (512)473-8696.

ISSN 1060-961X   US
THRIFT SHOPPING IN YOUR NEIGHBORHOOD. (1992)-. English. $5.00 (single issue). CNC Productions, PO Box 60091, Palo Alto CA 94306.

ISSN 0169-1570   NE
TIJDSCHRIFT VOOR CONSUMENTENRECHT. [Tijdschr. consum. recht]. **VFOAT** Consumentenrecht. No. 1 (1985)-. Periodical. Dutch (English). Four times a year. Fl102.00. Kluwer BV, Postbus 23, 7400 GA Deventer Netherlands. **Tel** 011 31 5700 33155, 011 31 5700 47421, **FAX** 011 31 5700 11504, telex 42829.

LC HD2428.C3 T73   US
TRADE AND PROFESSIONAL ASSOCIATIONS IN CALIFORNIA : A DIRECTORY. **Added/Corp** Center for California Public Affairs. (1979)-. Directory. English. Irregular. California Institute of Public Affairs, PO Box 189040, Claremont College, Sacramento CA 95818. **Tel** (916)442-2472, **FAX** (916)442-2478. Each issue contains an index to its own contents (no volume index)--loose.
Desc: Lists over 1,800 associations with addresses and phone numbers. Indexed by subject and key word. A unique guide to sources of information and help in California on hundreds of topics ranging from accounting and baking to yachts and zoology.

ISSN 0399-1466   FR
TRAVAUX DE L'ASSOCIATION HENRI CAPITANT POUR LA CULTURE JURIDIQUE FRANCAISE. **Main/Corp** Association Henri Capitant des Amis de la Culture Juridique Francaise. Vol. 1 (1945)-. French. Dalloz, 35 rue Tournefort, 75204 Paris Cedex 05 France. **Tel** 011 33 1 40515434, 011 33 1 40515454, **FAX** 011 33 1 45873748, telex 206 446 F.
Desc: Reports on sessions where such topics as consumer protection, dangerous substances and the judge's role in economic problems were discussed.
Ind/Abst Index Foreign Leg. Per.

LC TL230.A1 T6885
DD 629.2/24/029473   **ISSN** 8756-5129   US   SUSPENDED
TRUCK & TRAILER BUYER'S GUIDE. See Transportation-Automobiles.

ISSN 0273-9402   US
TRUCK BLUE BOOK. See Transportation-Automobiles.

LC TX335 .T88
KO
TUSAN. **Added/Corp** Tongyang Maekchu Chusik Hoesa. (19??)-. Periodical. Korean. Six times a year. Not for sale. Tongyang Maekchu Chusik Hosea, 582 Yongdungpo-dong, Yongdungpo-ku Seoul Korea.

IT
UNC NOTIZIE. Italian. Seven times a week. L250.000. Unione Naz Consumatori, Via A Doria 48, 00192 Rome Italy. **Circ**: 3,000 (ctrl).
Desc: News on the consumption market.

LC TX335.A1 U8   **ISSN** 0126-950X   MY
UTUSAN KONSUMER. **Added/Corp** Persatuan Penggunap Pulau Pinang. (19??)-. Periodical. English (Chinese, Malay and Tamil). Twenty-four times a year. $22.00. Consumers Association of Penang, 87 Cantonment Road, 10250 Penang Malaysia. **Tel** 011 60 604 373 511. **Bk Rev**. available on microfiche.
Ind/Abst Hum. Rights Intern. Rep. (19??-).

LC HC380.C63 S933c
SW
VAD VI GOER. **Main/Corp** Sweden. Konsumentverket. (19??)-. Swedish. Konsumentverket, Box 503, 162 15 Vallingby Sweden.

ISSN 8750-1430   US
VALLEY MAGAZINE (GRANADA HILLS, CALIF.). (VALLEY MAGAZINE.). **VFOAT** Valley. (198?)-. Periodical. English. Twelve times a year. $10.00. World of Communications, 16800 Devonshire, Suite 275, Granada Hills CA 91344. **Tel** (818)368-3353. **ED** Barbara Wernik. **Ad Acc**, **Adv Mgr**: Fred Braden. **Circ**: 30,000. **Continues** Big Valley, 0164-8799.
Desc: A regional publication that concentrates on issues and concerns as they relate to the citizens of the San Fernando, Santa Clarity, San Gabriel, Lonejo and Simi Valleys in Southern California.

LC HF5429.215.U6 V34
US
VALUE RETAIL NEWS : THE JOURNAL OF VALUE-ORIENTED RETAILING & DEVELOPMENT. See Business and Economics-Retail.

LC TL162 .V36
DD 629.223   **ISSN** 1043-8270   US   TITLE CHANGE
VAN, PICKUP, SPORT UTILITY BUYER'S GUIDE. See Transportation-Automobiles.

LC HC290.5.C6 V47
DD 381/.3/0943   GW
VERBRAUCHERDIENST. **Added/Corp** Bundesausschuss fuer Volkswirtliche Aufklaerung. (19??)-. Periodical. German. Twelve times a year. AID, Postfach 200153, 5300 Bonn 2 Germany. Index available. **Bk Rev**. **Circ**: 17,000 (ctrl). **Continues** Verbraucherdienst. Ausgabe B.
Desc: Information for consultants on food and food products. Articles on nutrition, health, legal orders and new scientific findings.
Ind/Abst Food Sci. Technol. Abstr.

LC KF919.C6 A138
DD 343/.73/08   **ISSN** 0363-9517   US
WARRANTY WATCH. **Added/Corp** Federal State Reports, Inc. (19??)-. English. Federal State Reports Inc., PO Box 986 Courthouse Station, Arlington VA 22216.

LC TX335 .W28
DD 640.73   **ISSN** 0272-0469   US
WASHINGTON CONSUMER'S CHECKBOOK. **Added/Corp** Washington Center for the Study of Services. **VFOAT** Checkbook. Vol. 1, No. 1 (Winter 1976)-. Periodical. English. Two times a year. $25.00. Center for Study of Services, 733 15th Street Northwest, Suite 820, Washington DC 20005. **Tel** (202)347-9612, (202)347-7283. **ED** Robert Krughoff. Index available. cum. index. **Circ**: 35,000.
Desc: Evaluations of local consumer services like auto repair shops and retailers in the areas of price and quality.

LC TX335.A1 W5
DD 643   **ISSN** 0043-4841   UK
WHICH? (LONDON). (WHICH?). [Which?]. **Added/Corp** Consumers' Association. (Oct. 1957)-. Periodical. English. Twelve times a year. Consumers Association, Castlemead, Gascoyne Way, Hertford SG1 1LH United Kingdom. **Tel** 011 44 1992 587773, **FAX** 011 44 1992 500369. Index available (free).

Ind/Abst Archit. Period. Index (1959-); Consum. Index Prod. Eval. Inf. Source; Curr. Cit.; Infomat Int. Bus.; World Ceram. Abstr.; World Text. Abstr.

LC WMLC L 82/155
DD 332.1   **ISSN** 0512-5847   US
WHO'S WHO OF CONSUMER CREDIT MANAGEMENT, A. **Added/Corp** Society of Certified Consumer Credit Executives. (19??)-. English. One time a year. Society of Certified Consumer Credit Executives, 7405 University Drive, St. Louis MO 63130. **Tel** (314)991-3030.

ISSN 0195-4636   US
WORKBOOK, THE. See Environmental Issues-Conservation and Natural Resources.

LC TX335 .W675
DD 640.73   US
WORLD ALMANAC CONSUMER INFORMATION KIT, THE. **VFOAT** Consumer Information Kit. (198?)-. English. World Almanac Publications, 200 Park Avenue, New York NY 10166.

LC TX336 .P46
DD 640/.73/05   **ISSN** 1050-8163   US
ZILLIONS (MOUNT VERNON, N.Y.). See Children and Youth Interests.

ABSTRACTING, BIBLIOGRAPHIES AND STATISTICS

AT
AUSTRALIAN CONSUMER DIRECTORY. (19??)-. Directory. English. Six times a year. 330.47Aus$. International Public Relations Pty Ltd., 33 Walsh Street, West Melbourne Victoria 3003 Australia. **Tel** 011 61 3 3299333, **FAX** 011 61 3 92099320.

LC TX335 .C676
DD 016.64073   **ISSN** 0094-0534   US
NLM Z 5776.C65 C758
CONSUMERS INDEX TO PRODUCT EVALUATIONS AND INFORMATION SOURCES. [Consum. index prod. eval. inf. source]. **VFOAT** Consumers Index. (1973)-. Abstracting/Indexing Service. English. Five times a year (published quarterly with one annual). $231.00. Pierian Press, PO Box 1808, Ann Arbor MI 48106. **Tel** (313)434-5530, (800)678-2435, **FAX** (313)434-6409. **ED** C. Edward Wall, Mary K. Hashman (Managing Editor). **Bk Rev**. **Ad Acc**. **Circ**: 2,000 (ctrl). available on CD-ROM (and machine readable format) from National Information Service Corporation (NISC); available on an online database from OCLC EPIC. Documents available from The UnCover Company.
Desc: An index to evaluations, descriptions, and recalls of specific products and facilities, as well as more general information on consumerism appearing in over 90 magazines. Entries are arranged under 17 subject groupings. The products and subjects of greatest interest to education, libraries, business offices and general consumers are covered.

LC HC271 .A218 HC280.C6
DD 330.944 S 339.4/7/0944   FR
EQUIPEMENT DES MENAGES EN BIENS DURABLES AU DEBUT DE ..., L'. (1976)-. Statistical Publication. French. One time a year. CNGP INSEE - Institut National de la Statistique et des Estudes Economiques, BP 2718, 1 rue V Auriol, F 80027 Amiens Cedex 1 France. **Tel** 011 33 22 927322. **Continues** Equipement des Menages au Debut de ... .
Desc: Statistics on household goods in French homes, categorized by region, income, number of persons, and socio-professional level.

COPYRIGHT, INTELLECTUAL PROPERTY

LC K1 .I6
DD 346.5204/8 345.20648   JA
A.I.P.P.I. : JOURNAL OF THE JAPANESE GROUP OF AIPPI. **Added/Corp** Japanese Group of AIPPI. **VFOAT** AIPPI Journal. (19??)-. Periodical. English. Six times a year. $130.00. Kokusai Kogyo Shoyuken Hogo Kyokai Nihon Bukai, (Japanese Group of International Association for the Protection of Industrial Property), 8-1 Toranomon 2 Chome, Minatoku Tokyo 105 Japan. (**Subscription address**: Maruzen Company Ltd., PO Box 5050, Import & Export Department, Tokyo 100 31 Japan. **Tel** 011 81 3 32789224.) ctrl circ.
Desc: Journal published by the Japanese group of AIPPI; International Association for the Protection of the Industrial Property.

Copyright, Intellectual Property

ADAMS CHRONICLE, THE. [Adams chron.].
ISSN 1040-4449
DD 006
US
(1988)-. Periodical. English. Twelve times a year. $160.00. Adams Communications, 2101 Crystal Plaza, Suite 203, Alexnadria VA 22202. **Tel** (703)548-8261, FAX (703)548-0213. **ED** Russ Adams.
Desc: Newsletter gives last information about patents, financial information and industry news in the automatic indentification and bar code industry.

LC KF2972 .A47
DD 346.7304/8/05 347.3064805
US
AIPLA BULLETIN / AMERICAN INTELLECTUAL PROPERTY LAW ASSOCIATION, INC. Main/Corp American Intellectual Property Law Association. **VAT** American Intellectual Property Law Association Bulletin. (July/Aug. 1984)-. Bulletin. English. Six times a year. $40.00. American Intellectual Property Law Association, 2001 Jefferson Davis Highway/Suite 203, Arlington VA 22202. **Tel** (703)415-0780. **Circ:** 6,000. **Continues** *American Intellectual Property Law Association. AIPLA.*

LC K1 .M46
ISSN 0883-6078
DD 346.7304/86/05 347.30648605
US
AIPLA QUARTERLY JOURNAL. [AIPLA q. j.]. **Added/Corp** American Intellectual Property Law Association. **VAT** American Intellectual Property Law Association Quarterly Journal. Vol. 12, No. 1 (1984)-. Periodical. English. Four times a year. $45.00. American Intellectual Property Law Association, 2001 Jefferson Davis Highway/Suite 203, Arlington VA 22202. **Tel** (703)415-0780. Index available (free). **Continues** *American Patent Law Association. APLA Quarterly Journal, 0091-0538.*
Ind/Abst Curr. Law Index (1984-); Index Leg. Period.; Leg. Resour. Index (1984-); LegalTrac (1980-).

LC KF2995 .A14
ISSN 0191-3077
DD 346/.73/0482
US
ALI-ABA COURSE OF STUDY. THE COPYRIGHT ACT OF 1976 : MATERIALS. Main/Conf ALI-ABA Course of Study: The Copyright Act of 1976. **VAT** American Law Institute-American Bar Association Course of Study. The Copyright Act of 1976: Materials. English. American Law Institute, 4025 Chestnut Street, Philadelphia PA 19104-3099. **Tel** (215)243-1661, (800)253-6397, FAX (215)243-1664.

LC KF3178.36 .A37
ISSN 0899-191X
DD 346.7304/88/02648 347.3648802648
US
ALLEN'S TRADEMARK DIGEST. (ALLEN'S TRADEMARK DIGEST : ATD.). [Allen's trademark dig.]. **Added/Corp** United States. Patent and Trademark Office. **VFOAT** Trademark Digest; ATD. Vol. 1, No. 1 (July 10, 1987)-. English. Twelve times a year. $350.00. Allens Trademark Digest, 901 Main Street, Box 176, Osterville MA 02655. **Tel** (508)420-6051, FAX (508)428-1900.

LC T321.V1 A85a
ISSN 0312-3278
DD 602/.75
AT
ALPHABETICAL INDEX OF CONSTITUENT PARTICULARS OF TRADE MARKS. (ALPHABETICAL INDEX OF CONSTITUENT PARTICULARS OF TRADE MARKS, (TRADE MARKS ACT 1955-1966).). **Main/Corp** Australia. Trade Marks Office. (1947)-. English. Six times a year. 515.00Aus$. Commissioner of Patents, PO Box 200, Woden Australian Capital Territory 2606 Australia. **Tel** 011 61 6 2832211, FAX 011 61 6 811841, telex COMPAT 61517. **ED** V. Yourgand. cum. index. **Circ:** 60 (ctrl).

LC KF2972 D .A45
ISSN 0835-7560
DD 346.7304/8/05 347.3064805
CN
AMERICAN & WORLD INTELLECTUAL PROPERTY REPORT. [Am. world intellect. prop. rep.]. **VFOAT** American and World Intellectual Property Report. Vol. 1, No. 1; Nov. 1987-. Periodical. English. Twelve times a year. $150.00 US. American & World Intellectual Property Report, 2 Bloor Street, Toronto Ontario M4W 3E2 Canada.

US
AMERICA'S INVENTOR : OFFICIAL NEWSLETTER OF THE NATIONAL CONGRESS OF INVENTOR ORGANIZATIONS. Added/Corp National Congress of Inventor Organizations. Vol. 1, No. 1 (1991)-. Newsletter. English. Four times a year (Feb, May, Aug., Nov.). $50.00. National Congress of Inventor Organizations, NCIO, PO Box 268, Logan UT 84321. **Tel** (801)753-4700, FAX (801)753-7544.

ISSN 0170-9291
GW
UDC 347.77
CCC
AMTSBLATT DES EUROPAISCHEN PATENTAMTS. [Amtsbl. Eur. Pat.amts]. **VFOAT** Official mail of the European Patent Office; Journal Officiel de l'Office Europeen des Brevets; Amtsblatt - Europaisches Patentamt; Official Journal - European Patent Office; Journal Officiel - Office Europeen des Brevets. (1977)-. Periodical. Multiple languages. Twelve times a year. DM200.00 Europe; DM290.00 other. European Patent Office, Schottenfeldgasse 29, A 1060 Vienna Austria. **Tel** 011 43 1 52126543.

FR
ANNALES DE LA PROPRIETE INDUSTRIELLE, ARTISTIQUE ET LITTERAIRE. Added/Corp Association des Ingenieurs-Conseils en Matiere de Proprlete Industrielle (France) Compagnie des Ingenieurs-Conseils en Propriete Industrielle. Vol. 1 (1855)-. Periodical. French. Four times a year. $138.45. Annales de la Propriete, 10 Square Henri Pate, 75016 Paris France. **Tel** 011 33 1 42247300.

LC Z649.F35 A56
ISSN 1074-3316
DD 025.1/2
US
ANNUAL AUTHORIZATIONS SERVICE. TITLE AND FEES. [Annu. auth. serv., Title fees]. **Added/Corp** Copyright Clearance Center (Salem, Mass.). (19??)-. English. Two times a year. $100.00. Copyright Clearance Center, 222 Rosewood Drive, Danvers MA 01923. **Tel** (508)750-8400. **Formed by the union of** *Schedule A and Catalog of Publisher Information, 1065-7916.*

LC T321.V1 A84A
DD 929.9
AT
ANNUAL RECORD OF TRADE MARKS OFFICE PROCEEDINGS. Main/Corp Australia. Patent, Trade Marks, and Designs Office. (19??)-. Proceedings. English. One time a year. Commissioner of Patents / Australia, PO Box 200, Patent Office Woden, Australian Capital Territories, 2606 Australia. **Tel** 011 61 6 2832211.

LC T257.A2 C47A
DD 608.7/062/0421
UK
ANNUAL REPORT OF THE COUNCIL OF THE CHARTERED INSTITUTE OF PATENT AGENTS FOR THE YEAR ENDED ... - (LONDON, ENG.). Main/Corp Chartered Institute of Patent Agents (London, Eng.). Council. **VFOAT** Journal of the Chartered Institute of Patent Agents, Annual Report ... Annual Accounts ... List of Members. (19??)-. English. One time a year. Staple Inn Buildings, London WC1V 7PZ United Kingdom.
Continues *Chartered Institute of Patent Agents (London, Eng.). List of Members, Annual Report, and Annual Accounts.*

ISSN 0090-2845
US
ANNUAL REPORT OF THE REGISTER OF COPYRIGHTS. (ANNUAL REPORT OF THE REGISTER OF COPYRIGHTS FOR THE FISCAL YEAR ENDING ... - LIBRARY OF CONGRESS.). [Annu. rep. Regist. Copyr.]. **Main/Corp** Library of Congress. Copyright Office. 32nd (1969)-. English. One time a year. Library of Congress, 101 Independence Avenue SE, Washington DC 20540. **Tel** (202)287-5000. **Circ:** 250. available on microfiche (Vols. for (1985-) distributed to depository libraries). **Continues** *Report of the Register of Copyrights.*
Desc: Report to the Librarian of Congress by the Register of Copyrights.

ISSN 0814-9046
DD 346.9404802642
AT
AUSTRALIAN INTELLECTUAL PROPERTY CASES. See Law.

LC T321.A2 A87
DD 608.794
AT
AUSTRALIAN OFFICIAL JOURNAL OF PATENTS (CANBERRA, A.C.T. : 1987). (AUSTRALIAN OFFICIAL JOURNAL OF PATENTS.). **Added/Corp** Australia. Patent Office. Vol. 1, No. 1 (Jan. 23, 1987)-. English. One time a week. 304.20Aus$. Commissioner of Patents, Patent Office, PO Box 200, Woden Australian Capital Territory 2606 Australia. **Tel** 011 61 6 2832211, FAX 06 2811841, telex COMPATA 61517. **ED** S McKenzie. Index available. **Ad Acc. Circ:** 255 (ctrl). Documents available from Petroleum Abstracts Document Delivery Service. **Continues in part** *Australian Official Journal of Patents, Trade Marks, and Designs.*
Desc: Proceedings under the Patents Act; abridgments of accepted complete patent specifications.
Ind/Abst Pet. Abstr.

LC T321.V1 A88
DD 602/.75/0994
AT
AUSTRALIAN OFFICIAL JOURNAL OF TRADE MARKS. Added/Corp Australia. Patent Office. Vol. 1, No. 1 (22 Jan. 1987)-. English. One time a week. 337.10Aus$. Commissioner of Patents, Patent Office, PO Box 200, Woden Australian Capital Territory 2606 Australia. **Tel** 011 61 6 2832211, FAX 06 2811841, telex COMPATAA 61517. **Continues in part** *Australian Official Journal of Patents, Trade Marks, and Designs.*

ISSN 0941-0007
GW
UDC 62
CODEN 66/68
AUSZUGE AUS DEN EUROPAISCHEN PATENTSCHRIFTEN. TEIL I, GRUND- UND ROHSTOFFINDUSTRIE, CHEMIE UND HUTTENWESEN, BAUWESEN, BERGBAU. VFOAT WILA-EPS. Teil I. (1992)-. Multiple languages. One time a week. $1160.70. Wila Verlag/Wilhelm Lampl GMBH, Landsberger Str 191A, D-80687 Munich Germany. **Tel** 011 49 89 5795285. **Separated from** *Auszeuge Aus den Europaischen Patentschriften, 0720-9339.*

ISSN 0941-0015
GW
UDC 62
AUSZUGE AUS DEN EUROPAISCHEN PATENTSCHRIFTEN. TEIL II, ELEKTROTECHNIK, PHYSIK, FEINMECHANIK UND OPTIK, AKUSTIK. VFOAT WILA-EPS. Teil II. (1992)-. Multiple languages. One time a week. $1160.70. Wila Verlag/Wilhelm Lampl GMBH, Landsberger Str 191A, D-80687 Munich Germany. **Tel** 011 49 89 5795285. **Separated from** *Auszuege Aus den Europaischen Patentschriften, 0720-9339.*

ISSN 0941-0023
GW
UDC 62
AUSZUGE AUS DEN EUROPAISCHEN PATENTSCHRIFTEN. TEIL III, UBRIGE VERARBEITUNGSINDUSTRIE UND ARBEITSVERFAHREN, MASCHINEN- UND FAHRZEUGBAU, ERNAHRUNG, LANDWIRTSCHAFT. VFOAT WILA-EPS. Teil III. (1992)-. Multiple languages. One time a week. $1160.70. Wila Verlag/Wilhelm Lampl GMBH, Landsberger Str 191A, D-80687 Munich Germany. **Tel** 011 49 89 5795285. **Separated from** *Auszuege Aus den Europaischen Patentschriften, 0720-9339.*

ISSN 0005-0571
GW
UDC 62/69(088.8):347.773
AUSZUGE AUS DEN GEBRAUCHSMUSTERN. AUSGABE A. [Auszuge Gebrauchsmustern, Ausg. A]. (1964)-. German. One time a week. $1332.03. Wila Verlag/Wilhelm Lampl GMBH, Landsberger Str 191A, D-80687 Munich Germany. **Tel** 011 49 89 5795285.

LC T201 .P64a
PL
BIULETYN - POLAND. URZAD PATENTOWY. Main/Corp Poland. Urzad Patentowy. Vol. 1 (Feb. 26, 1973)-. Polish. Twenty-six times a year. Price varies. **(Subscription address:** Ars Polcna-Ruch, PO Box 1001, Krakowskie Przedmiescie 7, 00-068 Warsaw Poland. **Tel** 011 48 22 261201.)

ISSN 0148-7965
US
CCC
BNA'S PATENT, TRADEMARK & COPYRIGHT JOURNAL. Added/Corp Bureau of National Affairs (Washington, D.C.). **VFOAT** B.N.A.'s Patent, Trademark, and Copyright Journal. **VAT** Bureau of National Affairs' Patent, Trademark and Copyright Journal. No. 7 (Dec. 17, 1970)-. Periodical. English. One time a week. $1101.00. Bureau of National Affairs Inc., 9435 Key West Avenue, Rockville MD 20850. **Tel** (800)372-1033, (301)258-1033, FAX (301)948-5823. **ED** Jeffery M Samuels. **Circ:** 2,500 (ctrl). available on an online database from Lexis-Nexis; and West Services, Inc. **Continues** *Patent, Trademark & Copyright Journal.*
Desc: Provides an in-depth review of significant current developments in the intellectual property field. Covers congressional activity, court decisions, relevant conferences, professional associations, international developments, plus actions of the Patent and Trademark Office and the Copyright Office.

SP
BOLETIN DE RESUMENES DE PATENTES. (19??)-. Spanish. Twenty-six times a year. 8100.00ptas Spain; 11400.00ptas other. Registro Propiedad Industrial, Calle Panama 1 Info Tecnologia, 28071 Madrid Spain. **Tel** 011 34 1 3495331, 011 34 1 3495335. **Continues** *Informacion Tecnologica de Patentes.*

LC Z609 .B64
MX
BOLETIN DEL DERECHO DE AUTOR. Added/Corp Mexico. Direccion General del Derecho de Autor. No. 1 (1965)-. Spanish (English and French). Four times a year. $17.50. UNESCO / France, 31 rue Francois Bonvin, 75732 Paris Cedex 15 France. **Tel** 011 33 1 45684564, 011 33 1 45684565, FAX 011 33 1 45669270,

Copyright, Intellectual Property

telex 204461 Paris. (**Subscription address:** UNIPUB, 4611 F Assembly Drive, Lanham MD 20706. **Tel** (800)274-4888, (301)459-7666.)

US

BOOK OF AMERICAN TRADE MARKS, THE. VFOAT Trade Marks. (1977)-. Monographic series. English. One time a year. Price varies per volume. Art Direction Book Company, 10 East 39th Street, 6th Floor, New York NY 10016. **Tel** (212)889-6500. **ED** David E. Carter. *Continues Trademarks, 0145-5834.*
Desc: Over 1,000 internationally acclaimed trademarks, logos, and corporate symbols. An index of companies, designers and addresses complete this design idea resource for visual professionals and corporate executives.

LC T223.V4 A25   **ISSN** 1047-6407
DD 602/.75   US

BRANDS AND THEIR COMPANIES. [Brands co.]. 8th Ed. (1990)-. English. One time a year. $425.00. Gale Research Inc., 835 Penobscot Building, 645 Griswold Street, Detroit MI 48226. **Tel** (800)877-GALE, (313)961-2242, FAX (313)961-6083, (800)414-5043, telex TWX 810-221-7086. **ED** Meghan O'Meara. available on diskette; available on magnetic tape; available on an online database (File 116) from DIALOG. *Formed by the union of Trade Names Dictionary, 0272-8818 and New Trade Names, 0272-8826.*
Desc: Provides current information about consumer brands and their manufacturers.

LC KU1104.A13 B85   **ISSN** 0311-2934
DD 346.9404/82 349.406482   AT

BULLETIN. Added/Corp Australian Copyright Council. (19??)-. Bulletin. English. Four times a year (Feb., May, Aug., Nov.). 42.76Aus$. Australian Copyright Council, 245 Chalmers Street, Suite 3, Redfern NSW 2016 Australia. **Tel** 011 61 2 3181788, FAX 011 61 2 6983536.
Ind/Abst Aust. Educ. Index (199?-).

ISSN 1185-7250
DD 354.710082   CN

BULLETIN - COPYRIGHT BOARD CANADA. (BULLETIN.). [Bull. - Copyr. Board Can.]. **Main/Corp** Copyright Board Canada. **VFOAT** Bulletin. **VAT** Bulletin - Commission du Droit d'Auteur Canada. No. 1 (Oct. 1991)-. Bulletin. English (French). Four times a year.

LC T319.A4 V124A
DD 602/.75   AE

BULLETIN DE L'INSTITUT ALGERIEN DE NORMALISATION ET DE PROPRIETE INDUSTRIELLE. Main/Corp Mahad Al-Jazairi Lil-Tawhid Al-Sinai Wa-Al-Milkiyah Al-Sinaiyah. Bulletin. French. Institut Algerien de Normalisation et de Propriete Industrielle, 5 rue Abou Hamou Moussa, Alger Algeria.

LC TS171.A1 B85   **ISSN** 0250-7730
DD 745.2/027   SZ

BULLETIN DES DESSINS ET MODELES INTERNATIONAUX : PUBLICATION MENSUELLE DU BUREAU INTERNATIONAL DE L'ORGANISATION MONDIALE DE LA PROPRIETE INTELLECTUELLE. Added/Corp World Intellectual Property Organization. International Bureau. **VFOAT** International Designs Bulletin. (19??)-. Bulletin. English (French). Twelve times a year. 200.00F Switzerland; $135.00 US. Bureau International de l'Organisation Mondiale de la Propriete Intellectuelle, 34 Chemin des Colombettes Case Postale 1211 Geneva 20 Switzerland. **Tel** 011 41 22 999111, telex 22376 OMPI. **Ad Acc.**
Desc: Gives deposits under the Hague Agreement concerning the protection of industrial designs.

ISSN 0304-2928
UDC 347.78   FR
CODEN NU053

BULLETIN DU DROIT D'AUTEUR. [Bull. droit auteur]. (1967)-. Periodical. French. Four times a year. $17.50. UNESCO / France, 31 rue Francois Bonvin, 75732 Paris Cedex 15 France. **Tel** 011 33 1 45684564, 011 33 1 45684565, FAX 011 33 1 45669270, telex 204461 Paris. (**Subscription address:** UNIPUB, 4611 F Assembly Drive, Lanham MD 20706. **Tel** (800)274-4888, (301)459-7666.) *Continues in part Copyright Bulletin (Multilingual Ed.), 0010-8634.*

LC T271 .A233   **ISSN** 0750-7674
DD 608.744/05   FR
CODEN BOPBEN

BULLETIN OFFICIEL DE LA PROPRIETE INDUSTRIELLE BREVETS D'INVENTION ABREGES ET LISTES. See Copyright, Intellectual Property-Abstracting, Bibliographies and Statistics.

LC T271.V1 F7A
DD 602/.75   FR

BULLETIN OFFICIEL DE LA PROPRIETE INDUSTRIELLE (PARIS, FRANCE). (BULLETIN OFFICIEL DE LA PROPRIETE INDUSTRIELLE.). Bulletin. French. 50.00F. Departement de Diffusion de l'Imprimerie Nationale, BP 514, 59505 Douai Cedex France. **Tel** (1)42 94 52 52, telex 290 368 INPI PARIS. Documents available from Petroleum Abstracts Document Delivery Service.
Desc: Statistics, industrial property.
Ind/Abst Pet. Abstr.

ISSN 0849-3154
DD 608.771/05   CN

BULLETIN - PATENT AND TRADE INSTITUTE OF CANADA (1990). (BULLETIN.). [Bull. - Pat. Trademark Inst. Can.]. **Added/Corp** Patent and Trademark Institute of Canada. #139 (Sept. 1990)-. Bulletin. English. Six times a year. Free to members. Patent and Trademark Institute of Canada, PO Box 1298 Station B, Ottawa Ontario K1P 5R3 Canada. **Tel** (613)234-0516, FAX (613)234-0671. *Continues Newsletter - Patent and Trademark Institute of Canada., 0380-6375.*

ISSN 0840-7266
DD 346.7104/8/05   CN

CAHIERS DE PROPRIETE INTELLECTUELLE, LES. [Cah. prop. intellect.]. **VFOAT** Propriete Intellectuelle. Vol. 1, No. 1 (Oct. 1988)-. Periodical. French. Three times a year (Jan., May, Oct.). 79.95Can$. Editions Yvon Blais, Case Postale 180, Cowansville Quebec J2K 3H6 Canada. **Tel** (514)263-1086, (800)363-3047, FAX (514)263-9256.
Ind/Abst Can. Legal Lit.; Index Can. Leg. Period. Lit.

ISSN 0824-5452
DD 346.7104/82/05   CN

CANADIAN COPYRIGHT INSTITUTE. (CANADIAN COPYRIGHT INSTITUTE : [NEWSLETTER].). [Can. Copyr. Inst.]. **Added/Corp** Canadian Copyright Institute. (May 1980)-. Newsletter. English. 80.04Can$. Canadian Copyright Institute, 35 Spadina Road, Toronto Ontario M5R 2S9 Canada. **Tel** (416)975-1756.

LC KE2775.8 .C36   **ISSN** 0824-2623
DD 346.7104/8   CN

CANADIAN INTELLECTUAL PROPERTY REPORTS. [Can. intellect. prop. rep.]. Vol. 1, Pt. 1 (March 1984)-. Periodical. English. Twelve times a year. 130.00Can$ Canada, 113.25Can$ other. Carswell / Canada, 2075 Kennedy Road, Scarborough Ontario M1T 3V4 Canada. **Tel** (416)298-5092, (800)387-5164, FAX (416)298-5094. **ED** Lise Bertrand, Claude Brunet, Jean-Francois Buffoni, Stephane Gilker, Theresa Siok, Celine Tremblay, Raymond Trudeau, Jean-Pierre Blais, Wilbrod Claude Decarie. Index available. cum. index. **Ad Acc.**
Desc: Features all important decisions in intellectual property law selected by experts. Includes cases on copyright, industrial designs, patents of intervention, and trade marks.
Ind/Abst Can. Legal Lit.

ISSN 0825-7256
DD 608.7/71   CN

CANADIAN INTELLECTUAL PROPERTY REVIEW. (CANADIAN INTELLECTUAL PROPERTY REVIEW / PATENT AND TRADEMARK INSTITUTE OF CANADA.). [Can. intellect. prop. rev.]. **Added/Corp** Patent and Trademark Institute of Canada. **VFOAT** Revue Canadienne de Propriete Intellectuelle; **P.T.I.C.** Review; Revue I.C.B.M. **VAT** Patent and Trademark Institute of Canada Review; Revue Institut Canadien des Bbrevets et Marques. Vol. 1 No. 1 (June 1984)-. Periodical. English (French; summaries and/or abstracts in French). Three times a year. 55.00Can$ (per issue). Patent and Trademark Institute of Canada, PO Box 1298 Station B, Ottawa Ontario K1P 5R3 Canada. **Tel** (613)234-0516, FAX (613)234-0671. *Continues Patent and Trademark Institute of Canada. Bulletin - Patent and Trademark Institute of Canada., 0380-6367.*
Ind/Abst Index Can. Leg. Period. Lit.

LC T201-342   **ISSN** 1181-3369
DD 608.77105   CN

CANADIAN PATENT. VFOAT Brevet Canadien. (19??)-. English.
Ind/Abst Field Crop Abstr.; Potato Abstr.; Rice Abstr.; Soils Fert.; Soyabean Abstr.; Wheat Barley Trit. Abstr.

ISSN 0008-4689
CN

CANADIAN PATENT REPORTER. Vol. 1-65, Pt. 3, (July 1941)-. Periodical. English. 260.00Can$. Canada Law Book Inc., 240 Edward Street, Aurora Ontario L4G 3S9 Canada. **Tel** (800)263-3269, (905)841-6472, FAX (905)841-5085. **ED** W. Frank H. Mulock, Gary O'Neill. **Bk Rev**. **Ad Acc.** *Absorbed Patent, Trade Mark Design and Copyright Cases (Canada), 0700-8929.*
Desc: Reports all significant Canadian cases on patents, industrial design, copyright and trademark law.
Ind/Abst Can. Legal Lit.; Index Can. Leg. Period. Lit.

LC T223.A2 C38   **ISSN** 0748-8858
DD 608.773   US

CATALOG OF GOVERNMENT PATENTS. [Cat. gov. pat.]. 1966-76-. Catalog. English. One time a year. $29.00. National Technical Information Service - NTIS, Room 2027S, 5285 Port Royal Road, Springfield VA 22161. **Tel** (703)487-4630, (703)487-4660, (703)487-4650, FAX (703)321-8547, telex 89-9405.

UK

CHEMICAL PATENTS INDEX. See Chemistry and Chemicals-Abstracting, Bibliographies and Statistics.

ISSN 1062-8827
DD 608   US

CHEMICAL VAPOR DEPOSITION PATENTS. [Chem. vapor depos. pat.]. Vol. 1, No. 1 (Jan. 1992)-. Periodical. English. Twelve times a year. $1200.00. Roex Technologies, PO Box 12025, Santa Rosa CA 95406-2025. **Tel** (707)575-4681.
Desc: Unites the developments in chemical vapor deposition.

LC T305.A2 J36a   JA

CHUMOKU HATSUMEI NO SENTEI. **Main/Corp** Japan. Kagaku Gijutsucho. Shinkokyoku. (1977)-. Japanese. Kagaku Gijutsucho Kagaku Gijutsu Shinkokyoku, (Science & Technology Promotion Bureau Science & Technology Agency), 2-1 Kasumigaseki 2 Chome, Chiyodaku Tokyo 100 Japan.

HK
CODEN CCLPE6

CHUNG-KUO CHUAN LI YU SHANG PIAO. Added/Corp Hsiang-Kang Chuang-Kuo Chuan Li Yu Shang Piao Tsa Chih She. **VFOAT** China Patents and Trademarks; China Patents & Trademarks; Zhong Guo Zhuan Li Yu Shang Biao. (1985)-China. Periodical. Chinese (English). Four times a year (Jan., Apr., July, Oct.). $50.00. Peace Book Company Ltd, 903 Wing on House, 71 des Voeux Road C, Room 1502, Hong Kong Hong Kong. **Tel** 011 852 28046687, FAX 011 852 28046409, telex 76929.

UK

CIPA. English. £40.00 UK; £50.00 other. Chartered Institute of Patent Agents, Staple Inn Buildings, High Holborn, London WC1V 7P2 United Kingdom. **Tel** 01 405 9450.

UK

CIPA GUIDE TO THE PATENTS ACTS. English. One time a year. £48.00 (supplement). Sweet & Maxwell Ltd., South Quay Plaza, 183 Marsh Wall 7th Floor, London E14 9FT United Kingdom. **Tel** 011 44 171 5388686, FAX 011 44 171 5389508, telex 929089 ITPINF G.

ISSN 0082-9692
DD 655.673   US

CIRCULAR - COPYRIGHT OFFICE. (CIRCULAR.). **Added/Corp** Library of Congress. Copyright Office. (19??)-. Monographic series. English. Price varies per volume. Copyright Office, Library of Congress, Washington DC 20559.

US

CLIENT&TIMES. (19??)-. Newsletter. English. Thomson and Thomson Inc., 500 Victory Road, North Quincy MA 02171. **Tel** (617)479-1600, (800)692-8833, FAX (617)786-8273, telex 440388.
Desc: Newsletter that strives to educate professionals about intellectual property issues.

US

CODE OF FEDERAL REGULATIONS. 37, PATENTS, TRADEMARKS, AND COPYRIGHTS. Added/Corp United States. Office of the Federal Register. **VFOAT** Patents, Trademarks, and Copyrights; CFR. 37, Patents, Trademarks, and Copyrights. (19??)-. Government Publication. English. One time a year. $30.00. Superintendent of Documents, US Government Printing Office, Washington DC 20402. **Tel** (202)725-3328, FAX (202)786-2377. (**Subscription address:** US Government Bookstore, O'Neil Building, 2023 3rd Avenue North, Birmingham AL 35203.) available on microfiche (Vols. for (1984)- distributed to some depository libraries).
Desc: Special edition of the Federal Register, containing a codification of documents.

LC T223.V4 A253   **ISSN** 1047-6393
DD 602/.75   US

COMPANIES AND THEIR BRANDS. [Co. brands]. 8th Ed. (1990)-. English. One time a year. $410.00. Gale Research Inc., 835 Penobscot Building, 645 Griswold Street, Detroit MI 48226. **Tel** (800)877-GALE, (313)961-2242, FAX (313)961-6083, (800)414-5043, telex TWX 810-221-7086. **ED** Meghan O'Meara. available on diskette; available on magnetic tape; available on an online database (File 116) from DIALOG. *Continues Trade Names Dictionary. Company Index, 0277-0369.*

Copyright, Intellectual Property

Desc: Comprehensive list of manufacturers, distributors, marketers, and importers of consumer trade names, brands, and trademarks.

COMPENDIUM OF COPYRIGHT OFFICE PRACTICES. Main/Corp Library of Congress. Copyright Office. (1970)-. Government Publication. English. One time a year (2 semiannual supplements). $62.00 domestic; $77.50 other. Superintendent of Documents, US Government Printing Office, Washington DC 20402. **Tel** (202)275-3328, FAX (202)786-2377.
Desc: A general guide to the operating problems and practices for the staff of the Copyright Office with individual cases that represent common fact situations. Also known as Compendium II.

LC KF390.5.C6 C63   ISSN 0740-1469
DD 346.7304/82 347.306482   US

COMPUTER INDUSTRY LITIGATION REPORTER. [Comput. ind. litig. rep.]. (1983)-. Trade Publication. English. Twenty-four times a year. $850.00. Andrews Publications Inc., 1646 West Chester Pike, PO Box 1000, Westtown PA 19395. **Tel** (610)399-6600, (800)345-1101, FAX (610)399-6610. **ED** Leonard E. B. Andrews. cum. index. **Ad Acc.**
Desc: Reports on copyright, patent and trademark claims, theft of trade secrets cases, significant user/vendor contract-misrepresentation claims, consultant liability questions, and other evolving issues as they relate to the computer industry.

    ISSN 0010-8634
    FR
NLM Z 552 C785

COPYRIGHT BULLETIN : QUARTERLY REVIEW / UNESCO. Added/Corp Unesco. Vol. 1, No. 1 (1976)-. Bulletin. English (French, Spanish and Russian). Four times a year. $25.00. UNESCO / France, 31 rue Francois Bonvin, 75732 Paris Cedex 15 France. **Tel** 011 33 1 45684564, 011 33 1 45684565, FAX 011 33 1 45669270, telex 204461 Paris. **(Subscription address:** UNIPUB, 4611 F Assembly Drive, Lanham MD 20706. **Tel** (800)274-4888, (301)459-7666.) **Bk Rev**. **Circ:** 1,900. available on microfilm and microfiche from University Microfilms International (UMI). *Continues in part Copyright Bulletin.*
Desc: Covers international developments in copyright law. Significant documents are published with accounts of meetings and bibliographies on the subject. Keeps journalists, publishers, librarians, lawyers and other individuals up to date on interesting developments in the copyright field.
Ind/Abst Index Foreign Leg. Per.; Middle East Abstr. Index; PAIS Int. Print (1991-).

LC K   ISSN 0010-8626
DD 340   SZ
    TITLE CHANGE

COPYRIGHT (GENEVA). (COPYRIGHT.). Added/Corp World Intellectual Property Organization. United International Bureaux for the Protection of Intellectual Property. Vol. 1 (1965)-(19??). Periodical. English (French). World Intellectual Property Organization, WIPO OMPI 34 Chem Colombettes, 1211 Geneva 20 Switzerland. **Tel** 011 41 22 7309111. Index available. **Bk Rev**. **Ad Acc**. **Circ:** 1,000. *Merged with Industrial Property (World Intellectual Property Organization)* to form *Industrial Property and Copyright, 1020-2196.*
Desc: Review of the International (Berne) Union for the Protection of Literary and Artistic Works. Includes state of ratifications, texts of laws, court decisions, studies, and news items.
Ind/Abst BHA : Biblio. Hist. Art; Index Foreign Leg. Per.

LC KF2987 .C65   ISSN 0884-4437
DD 346.7304/82/05 347.30648205   US

COPYRIGHT LAW JOURNAL, THE. (THE COPYRIGHT LAW JOURNAL : AN ANALYSIS OF CURRENT CASES AND DEVELOPMENTS AFFECTING INTELLECTUAL PROPERTY RIGHTS.). [Copyr. law j.]. Vol. 1, No. 1 (July 1984)-. Periodical. English. Six times a year. $375.00. Copyright Law Journal, PO Box 3897, San Francisco CA 94119. **Tel** (510)685-5111. **ED** N. Boorstyn.

    US

COPYRIGHT LAW REPORTER. Main/Corp Commerce Clearing House. (1978)-. English. $340.00. Commerce Clearing House Inc., 4025 West Peterson Avenue, Chicago IL 60646-6085. **Tel** (312)583-8500, FAX (708)940-4600. **ED** A.E. Schechter.
Desc: Sets out and explains today's Copyright Revision Act rules. Reports new and proposed regulations, current case law, activities and views of the regulators and the regulated and other developments.

LC KF3035.A75 C6   ISSN 0069-9950
DD 346.7304/82 347.306482   US

COPYRIGHT LAW SYMPOSIUM. [Copyr. law sympo.]. Added/Corp Nathan Burkan Memorial Competition. American Society of Composers, Authors and Publishers. (1939)-. Monographic series. English. Irregular. Price varies per volume. Columbia University Press, 136 South Broadway, Irvington NY 10533. **Tel** (914)591-9111. **Circ:** 2,000.
Ind/Abst Curr. Law Index (1980-); Index Leg. Period.; Leg. Resour. Index (1980-); LegalTrac (1980-).

    ISSN 0069-9969
    US

COPYRIGHT LAWS AND TREATIES OF THE WORLD. Main/Corp Unesco. (19??)-. English. Irregular. $695.00 (complete set). Bureau of National Affairs Inc., 9435 Key West Avenue, Rockville MD 20850. **Tel** (800)372-1033, (301)258-1033, FAX (301)948-5823.

LC KF3045.3.A15 C67   ISSN 0884-1306
    US

COPYRIGHT MANAGEMENT CIRCLE. [Copyr. manage. circ.]. Periodical. English. Twelve times a year. $100.00. Copyright Management Circle, 127 Flora Vista, Camarillo CA 93010.

    ISSN 0725-0509
DD 346.0482   AT

COPYRIGHT REPORTER. [Copyr. rep.]. (1981)-. Periodical. English. Four times a year. 98.66Aus$. Australian Copyright Council, 245 Chalmers Street, Suite 3, Redfern NSW 2016 Australia. **Tel** 011 61 2 3181788, FAX 011 61 2 6983536.
Ind/Abst Aust. Leg. Mon. Dig.

    ISSN 0725-0509
    AT

COPYRIGHT REPORTER : JOURNAL OF THE COPYRIGHT SOCIETY OF AUSTRALIA. Added/Corp Copyright Society of Australia. Australian Copyright Council. (1981)-. English. Four times a year. 98.66Aus$. Australian Copyright Council, 245 Chalmers Street, Suite 3, Redfern NSW 2016 Australia. **Tel** 011 61 2 3181788, FAX 011 61 2 6983536.

LC K1411.2 .C66   ISSN 0950-2505
DD 346.04/82/05 342.648205   UK

COPYRIGHT WORLD. [Copyr. world]. Issue 1 (Nov. 1988)-. Periodical. English. Ten times a year. $450.00. Intellectual Property Publishing, 3rd Floor Brigade House, Parsons GRN, London SW6 7NE United Kingdom. **Tel** 011 44 171 7367111.
Ind/Abst Curr. Cit.; Index Leg. Period.

    ISSN 0590-711X
    US

CPDA NEWS. Main/Corp Council for Periodical Distributors Associations. **VAT** Council for Periodical Distributors Associations News. Periodical. English. Twelve times a year. CPDA News, 60 East 42nd Street, NY NY 10165.

    ISSN 1062-2535
DD 346   US

CPS EXPRESS. (CPS EXPRESS: A NEWS BULLETIN FROM THE NACS COPYRIGHT PERMISSIONS SERVICE.). [CPS express]. Added/Corp National Association of College Stores (U.S.) Copyright Permissions Service. **VAT** Copyright Permissions Service Express. (March 1992)-. Bulletin. English. Twelve times a year. Free on request. National Association of College Stores, 500 East Lorain Street, Oberlin OH 44074. **Tel** (216)775-7777.

LC KF2995 .C87   ISSN 0733-0243
DD 346.7304/82 347.306482   US

CURRENT DEVELOPMENTS IN COPYRIGHT LAW. [Curr. dev. copyr. law]. Added/Corp Practising Law Institute. (19??)-. English. Practising Law Institute, 810 Seventh Avenue, New York NY 10019-5818. **Tel** (212)765-5700, FAX (212)581-4670 general correspondence, (212)265-4742 orders and billing inquiries.

    UK
NLM QV 772; C9765
Pr Rev.   TITLE CHANGE

CURRENT OPINION IN THERAPEUTIC PATENTS. Vol. 1, No. 1 (Jan. 1991)-(19??). Periodical. English. Current Science / England, Middlesex House, 34-42 Cleveland Street, London W1P 6LB United Kingdom. **Tel** 011 44 171 5808393, 011 44 171 3230323, FAX 011 44 171 5805646. **(Subscription address:** Current Science, 20 North 3rd Street, Philadelphia PA 19106. **Tel** (800)552-5866.) **ED** Emma Weitkamp. **Bk Rev**. **Ad Acc**. **Circ:** 100. *Formed by the union of Current Cardiovascular Patents; Current Antimicrobial Patents and Current CNS Patents. Continued by Expert Opinion on Therapeutic Patents, 0962-2594.*
Desc: Summaries and critical appraisals of key patents and patent applications in all therapeutic areas.
Ind/Abst EMBASE.

    ISSN 0903-8825
DD 346.489 048 4   DK

DANSK MONSTERTIDENDE. [Dan. monstertid.]. (1988)-. Periodical. Danish. Twenty-four times a year. $159.30. Patentdirektoratet, Helgeshoj Alle 81, DK-2630 Taastrup Denmark. **Tel** 011 45 43 717171, FAX 011 45 43 717170, telex 16046 DPODK.
Continues Registreringstidende for Monstre, 0106-5246.

    ISSN 0011-6416
    DK
CODEN DAPAA8

DANSK PATENTTIDENDE. [Dan. patenttid.]. (1896)-. Academic Scholarly Publication. Danish. One time a week. kr1,000. Patentdirektoratet, Helgeshoj Alle 81, DK-2630 Taastrup Denmark. **Tel** 011 45 43 717171, FAX 011 45 43 717170, telex 16046 DPODK. Index available. **Circ:** 500. Documents available from CASDDS.
Ind/Abst Chem. Abstr.

LC KF2994.A1 C63   ISSN 0070-3176
DD 346/.73/04820264   US
NLM Z 644 D294

DECISIONS OF THE UNITED STATES COURTS INVOLVING COPYRIGHT. [Decis. U.S. courts involv. copyr.]. Added/Corp Library of Congress. Copyright Office. **VFOAT** Copyright Decisions. (1914)-. Government Publication. English. Irregular. $45.00. Superintendent of Documents, US Government Printing Office, Washington DC 20402. **Tel** (202)275-3328, FAX (202)786-2377. cum. index.
Desc: Information as decided by United States courts regarding copyright law.

    ISSN 1067-201X
DD 929   US

●**DIRECTORY OF CANADIAN TRADEMARKS, THE.** [Dir. Can. trademarks]. **VFOAT** Canadian Trademarks. (1993)-. English (French). One time a year. $225.00. Thomson and Thomson Inc., 500 Victory Road, North Quincy MA 02171. **Tel** (617)479-1600, (800)692-8833, FAX (617)786-8273, telex 440388.
Desc: Lists all active pending and registered trademarks filed with Consumer and Corporate Affairs Canada since 1867. Includes trademark, owner name, international classes (assigned by Thomson & Thomson), and registration/serial number.

LC KF3165.A3 D557   ISSN 1064-0355
DD 346.7304/8/025 347.30648025   US

●**DIRECTORY OF INTELLECTUAL PROPERTY ATTORNEYS.** See Law.

    US

DIRECTORY OF U.S. GOVERNMENT INVENTIONS, THE. **VFOAT** Directory of US Government Inventions; Directory of United States Government Inventions. (1991)-. English. One time a year. $225.00. Government Data Publications / New York, GDP Building, 1661 McDonald Avenue, Brooklyn NY 11230. **Tel** (718)627-0819.

LC T223.V4 A219   ISSN 1042-0665
DD 602/.75/0973   US

DIRECTORY OF U.S. TRADEMARKS, THE. Added/Corp Thomson & Thomson. **VFOAT** Directory of US Trademarks; Directory of United States Trademarks; U.S. Trademarks. (1992)-. Directory. English. One time a year. $1215.00. Thomson and Thomson Inc., 500 Victory Road, North Quincy MA 02171. **Tel** (617)479-1600, (800)692-8833, FAX (617)786-8273, telex 440388. **ED** Lisa M. DePasquale. *Continues Compu-mark Directory of U.S. Trademarks, 1042-0665.*
Desc: Includes pending and registered marks, and contains a total of over one million new and updated transactions.

    ISSN 0012-3420
    IT

DIRITTO DI AUTORE, IL. Added/Corp Societa Italiana degli Autori ed Editori. Vol. 1 (Jan./Mar 1930)-. Periodical. Italian. Four times a year. L71450. Giuffre Editore SPA, Via Busto Arsizio 40, 20151 Milan Italy. **Tel** 011 398 2 38089200. **ED** Mario Fabiani. **Bk Rev**. **Ad Acc**. **Circ:** 800.
Desc: Deals with doctrinal developments, new legislation and jurisprudential decisions in Italy and abroad on copyright.
Ind/Abst Index Foreign Leg. Per.

LC K   ISSN 0992-8421
DD 340   FR
UDC 347.77

DOSSIERS BREVETS... CENTRE DU DROIT DE L'ENTREPRISE. (DOSSIERS BREVETS.). [Doss. brev. - Cent. droit entrep.]. (19??)-. French. Eighteen times a year (6 regular issues and 12 monthly supplements). $218.73. Centre Droit de l'Entreprise, 39 rue de l'Universite, F-34060 Montpellier Cedex France. **Tel** 011 33 67615484.

    SZ

DROIT D'AUTEUR. French. Twelve times a year. 160.00F. World Intellectual Property Organization, WIPO OMPI 34 Chem Colombettes, 1211 Geneva 20 Switzerland. **Tel** 011 41 22 7309111.
Ind/Abst LABORDOC.

Copyright, Intellectual Property

LC WMLC 93/1743 — ISSN 1120-1819
DD 015.4 — IT
Pr Rev.
EDIZIONI PER LA CONSERVAZIONE. See Publishing-Books and Bookmaking.

BE
EURO TRADEMARK JOURNAL. (19??)-. English. One time a week. Compu Mark, St. Petersbliet 7, B-2000 Antwerp Belgium. **Tel** 011 32 3 2318850. **(Subscription address:** Thomson & Thomson, 500 Victory Road, North Quincy MA 02171. **Tel** (617)479-1600.)
Desc: Covers key countries and lists applications in the product and service class(es) selected. Allows tracking of competitor and industry new product introductions.

ISSN 0170-9305
GW
UDC (088.8) — CCC
EUROPAISCHES PATENTBLATT. [Eur. Patentbl.]. **VFOAT** European Patent Bulletin; Bulletin Europeen des Brevets. (1978)-. Bulletin. German (English and French). One time a week. $1266.63. European Patent Office, Schottenfeldgasse 29, A 1060 Vienna Austria. **Tel** 011 43 1 52126543.

LC K5 .U72 — ISSN 0142-0461
DD 346.404/8/05 — UK
CODEN EIPRES
EUROPEAN INTELLECTUAL PROPERTY REVIEW. **Added/Corp** World Intellectual Property Organization. (Oct. 1978)-. Periodical. English. Twelve times a year. $598.92. Sweet & Maxwell Ltd., South Quay Plaza, 183 Marsh Wall 7th Floor, London E14 9FT United Kingdom. **Tel** 011 44 171 5388686, FAX 011 44 171 5389508, telex 929089 ITPINF G. **ED** Hugh Brett. Index available. cum. index. **Bk Rev. Ad Acc. Circ:** 1,000.
Desc: The global movement by national governments to attempt to adjust their intellectual property laws to cope with the rapid developments of new technology makes this essential reading for all those advising on the commercial exploitation of intellectual property rights.
Ind/Abst Curr. Cit.; Index Leg. Period.; Leg. Resour. Index; LegalTrac (1990-); Plant Breed. Abstr.; World Agric. Econ. Rural Sociol. Abstr.

ISSN 0269-0802
DD 608.74 — UK
CCC
EUROPEAN PATENT OFFICE REPORTS. [Eur. pat. off. rep.]. **Added/Corp** European Patent Office. **VFOAT** EPOR. Vol. 1, Issue 1 (1986)-. Periodical. English. Eight times a year. $465.45. Sweet & Maxwell Ltd., South Quay Plaza, 183 Marsh Wall 7th Floor, London E14 9FT United Kingdom. **Tel** 011 44 171 5388686, FAX 011 44 171 5389508, telex 929089 ITPINF G. **ED** Brian Reid and Jonathan Turner. Index available. cum. index. **Ad Acc.**
Desc: Service for intellectual property lawyers and patent agents, presenting EPO decisions in an accessible form.

ISSN 0270-3076
US
FIBER OPTICS CROSS-REFERENCE PATENT ABSTRACTS SERVICE. [Fiber optics corss-ref. pat. abstr. serv.]. **VFOAT** Fiber Optics X-R Patent Abstracts. **VAT** Fiber Optics Cross Reference Patent Abstracts Service. (1980)-. Periodical. English. Twenty-four times a year. $130.00 US and Canada; $156.00 other. Patent Data Publications, 901 North President Street, Wheaton IL 60187. **Tel** (312)462-0818.

ISSN 0270-3084
US
FIBER OPTICS PATENT ABSTRACTS SERVICE. [Fiber optics pat. abstr. serv.]. **VFOAT** Fiber Optics Patent Abstracts. (1980)-. Periodical. English. Patent Data Publications, 901 North President Street, Wheaton IL 60187. **Tel** (312)462-0818.

ISSN 0968-0322
UK
FINANCIAL TIMES MUSIC & COPYRIGHT. **VFOAT** Financial Times Music and Copyright; Music & Copyright; Music and Copyright. (19??)-. Periodical. English. Twenty-four times a year. $992.50. Financial Times / UK, Maple House, 149 Tottenham Court Road, London W1P 9LL United Kingdom. **Tel** 011 44 171 8962276, FAX 011 44 171 8962275, 011 44 171 8962399.

LC KD1365.A2 F54 — ISSN 0141-9455
DD 346/.4204/86 — UK
CCC
FLEET STREET REPORTS. **Added/Corp** European Law Centre. (199?)-. Periodical. English. Twelve times a year. $581.81. Sweet & Maxwell Ltd., South Quay Plaza, 183 Marsh Wall 7th Floor, London E14 9FT United Kingdom. **Tel** 011 44 171 5388686, FAX 011 44 171 5389508, telex 929089 ITPINF G. **Continues** Fleet Street Reports of Industrial Property Cases from the Commonwealth and Europe, 0141-9455.
Ind/Abst Aust. Leg. Mon. Dig.

LC K6 .O725 — ISSN 1056-4128
DD 346.04/8 342.648 — US
TITLE CHANGE
FORDHAM ENTERTAINMENT, MEDIA & INTELLECTUAL PROPERTY LAW FORUM. See Law-Entertainment Law.

ISSN 1079-9699
DD 346 — US
•**FORDHAM INTELLECTUAL PROPERTY, MEDIA & ENTERTAINMENT LAW JOURNAL.** See Law-Entertainment Law.

ISSN 0952-2522
DD 608.741 — UK
FUTURE (LONDON. 1987). [Future Lond., 1987]. (1987)-. Periodical. English. Four times a year. $20.53. Institute of Patentees & Inventors, 189 Regent Street, Suite 505A, Triumph House, London W1R 7WF United Kingdom. **Tel** 011 44 171 2427812, FAX 011 44 171 2427812. **Bk Rev. Ad Acc. Circ:** 1,100. **Continues** Inventor, 0579-8388.

LC T228.A2 M48A
MX
GACETA DE INVENCIONES Y MARCAS. **Main/Corp** Mexico. Direccion General de Invenciones y Marcas. Spanish. Twelve times a year. Secertaria de Industria y Comercio-Direccion General, Mexico DF Mexico.

LC T223.J4 U54b — ISSN 0160-9491
DD 608/.7/73 — US
GENERAL INFORMATION CONCERNING PATENTS. **Added/Corp** United States. Patent Office. United States. Patent and Trademark Office. (1922)-. Government Publication. English. US Department of Commerce, 14th Street & Constitution Avenue NW, Washington DC 20230. **Tel** (202)482-2000, FAX (202)482-3772.

LC T273.A2 G468
DD 608/.7/43 — UK
GERMAN PATENTS GAZETTE : PARTS I-III COMPLETE. **VAT** German Patents Gazette: Parts One-Three Complete. Periodical. English. One time a week. Derwent Publications Ltd., Derwent House 14, Great Queen Street, London WC2B 5DF United Kingdom. **Tel** 011 44 171 3442800, FAX 011 44 171 3442899.

LC T273.A2 G47 — ISSN 0533-7542
DD 608/.7/43 — UK
GERMAN PATENTS GAZETTE : SECTION III, MECHANICAL & GENERAL. [Ger. pat. gaz., Sect. 3, mech. gen.]. **VAT** German Patents Gazette. Section Three, Mechanical and General. (1968)-. Periodical. English (German). Irregular. Derwent Publications Ltd., Derwent House 14, Great Queen Street, London WC2B 5DF United Kingdom. **Tel** 011 44 171 3442800, FAX 011 44 171 3442899. **(Subscription address:** Derwent Inc., 1420 Spring Hill Road, Suite 525, McLean VA 22102. **Tel** (703)790-0400.)

GW
GEWERBLICHER RECHTSSCHUTZ UND URHEBERRECHT. **Added/Corp** Deutsche Vereinigung fuer Gewerblichen Rechtsschutz und Urheberrecht. (1896)-. Periodical. German. Twelve times a year. $492.00. VCH Gesellschaft GmbH, Postfach 101161, D-69451 Weinheim Germany. **Tel** 011 49 6201 606459, FAX 011 49 6201 606184. **(Subscription address:** VCH Publishers Inc., 303 Northwest 12th Avenue, Journals Department, Deerfield FL 33442. **Tel** (800)367-8249, (305)428-5566.) **Supersedes** Zeitschrift fur Gewerblichen Rechtsschutz.
Ind/Abst Index Foreign Leg. Per.; World Agric. Econ. Rural Sociol. Abstr.

LC K9 .P18
DD 346.4704/8 344.70648 — UK
I. P. REPORTS FROM SOCIALIST COUNTRIES. Vol. 1 (June 1979)-. Periodical. English. Two times a year. $110.33. International Thomson Business Publications, 42 Bedford Square, London WC1B 3SC United Kingdom. **Tel** 011 44 171 3236986.

ISSN 0019-1272
DD 341 — US
IDEA (CONCORD, N.H.). (IDEA.). [Idea]. **Added/Corp** George Washington University. Patent, Trademark, and Copyright Research Institute. George Washington University. PTC Research Institute. Franklin Pierce Law Center. PTC Research Foundation. Vol. 8, No. 1 (Spring 1964)-. Periodical. English. Four times a year (Jan., Apr., May, July). $68.00. PTC Research Foundation, 2 White Street, Concord NH 03301. **Tel** (603)228-1541, FAX (603)224-3342. **ED** Dawn Noel Buonocore. Index available. cum. index. **Circ:** 800. available on microfiche (1984-); available with charts. **Continues** Patent, Trade-Mark, and Copyright Journal of Research and Education, 0893-1429.
Desc: Contains information about patent laws and legislation.
Ind/Abst Curr. Law Index (1980-); Gen. Period. Index (1985-); Index Leg. Period.; Leg. Contents, LC; Leg. Resour. Index (1980-); LegalTrac (1980-); Mag. Search; PAIS Int. Print.

LC K9 .I17 — ISSN 0018-9855
DD 341/.758/05 — GW
CCC
CODEN IICLDM
IIC; INTERNATIONAL REVIEW OF INDUSTRIAL AND COPYRIGHT LAW. [IIC. Int. rev. ind. prop. copyr. law]. **Added/Corp** Max-Planck-Institut fuer Auslandisches und Internationales Patent-, Urheber- und Wettbewerbsrecht. **VFOAT** International Review of Industrial Property and Copyright Law. (1970)-. Periodical. English. Six times a year. $364.00. VCH Gesellschaft GmbH, Postfach 101161, D-69451 Weinheim Germany. **Tel** 011 49 6201 606459, FAX 011 49 6201 606184. **(Subscription address:** VCH Publishers Inc., 303 Northwest 12th Avenue, Journals Department, Deerfield FL 33442. **Tel** (800)367-8249, (305)428-5566.) **ED** F K Beier and G Schricker. **Bk Rev. Ad Acc. Circ:** 1,360. available on microfilm. Documents available from The Genuine Article.
Desc: Articles, decisions and other materials of international importance in the fields of patents, copyrights, designs, trademarks, unfair competition, and related antitrust problems.
Ind/Abst Arts Humanit. Citation Index [Select. Cov.]; Curr. Cit.; Curr. Contents Soc. Behav. Sci.; Index Foreign Leg. Per.; Res. Alert [Select. Cov.]; Soc. Sci. Cit. Index [Select. Cov.].

ISSN 1056-1536
DD 621 — US
IMPACT PUMP NEWS & PATENTS. See Engineering-Mechanical Engineering and Machinery.

ISSN 1056-1544
DD 621 — US
IMPACT VALVE NEWS & PATENTS. See Engineering-Mechanical Engineering and Machinery.

LC T223.V4 A2 — ISSN 0099-0809
DD 602/.75 — US
INDEX OF TRADEMARKS ISSUED FROM THE UNITED STATES PATENT AND TRADEMARK OFFICE. **Added/Corp** United States. Patent and Trademark Office. **VFOAT** Index of Trademarks; Index of Trademarks Registered with the United States Patent and Trademark Office. (1974)-. Government Publication. English. Irregular. $20.00. Superintendent of Documents, US Government Printing Office, Washington DC 20402. **Tel** (202)275-3328, FAX (202)786-2377. available on microfiche (Vols. for (1980-1981) distributed to some depository libraries). **Continues** Index of Trademarks Issued from the United States Patent Office.

LC T223 .A25 — ISSN 0161-9470
DD 608/.7/012 — US
INDEX TO THE U.S. PATENT CLASSIFICATION. **Added/Corp** United States. Patent and Trademark Office. **VFOAT** Index to Classification. **VAT** Index to the United States Patent Classification. (Dec. 1977)-. Government Publication. English. One time a year. $37.00. Superintendent of Documents, US Government Printing Office, Washington DC 20402. **Tel** (202)275-3328, FAX (202)786-2377. **Continues** United States. Patent Office. Index to Classification.

ISSN 0019-8625
SZ
INDUSTRIAL PROPERTY. **Added/Corp** Bureaux Internationaux Reunis pour la Protection de la Propriete Industrielle. (1962)-. Periodical. English. Twelve times a year. 180.00F (surface mail), 200.00F (airmail), 18.00F Europe; 23.00F other (single copies). World Intellectual Property Organization, WIPO OMPI 34 Chem Colombettes, 1211 Geneva 20 Switzerland. **Tel** 011 41 22 7309111. Index available. **Bk Rev. Ad Acc. Circ:** 1,400 (ctrl). **Supersedes** Industrial Property Quarterly.
Desc: Review of the International (Paris) Union for the Protection of Industrial Property and the Special Unions and Agreements concerning industrial property. States ratifications, texts of laws, court decisions, studies, book reviews and news items.
Ind/Abst Index Foreign Leg. Per.

LC K1403 .I53 — ISSN 1020-2196
DD 341.7/58 — SZ
CODEN IPCOFE
•**INDUSTRIAL PROPERTY AND COPYRIGHT : MONTHLY REVIEW OF THE WORLD INTELLECTUAL PROPERTY ORGANIZATION.** **Added/Corp** World Intellectual Property Organization. (1995)-. Periodical. English. Twelve times a year. World Intellectual Property Organization, WIPO OMPI 34 Chem Colombettes, 1211 Geneva 20 Switzerland. **Tel** 011 41 22 7309111. **Formed by the union of** Industrial Property (World Intellectual Property Organization) **and** Copyright, 0010-8626.

Copyright, Intellectual Property

NE
TITLE CHANGE
INFORMATIERECHT. Added/Corp Vereniging voor Auteursrecht (Netherlands). Vol. 10, No. 1 (Feb. 1986)-(19??). Periodical. Dutch. Libresso BV, Postbus 878, 7400 GA Deventer Netherlands. **Tel** 011 31 5700 47421. **ED** H. Cohen Jehoram, A. W. Hins and J. H. Spoor. **Circ:** 800. **Continues** Auteursrecht. **Continued by** Informatierecht AMI.

LC T273 .A35 ISSN 0863-2790
DD 608 GW
INNOVATION & MANAGEMENT. VFOAT Innovation and Managment. (1990)-. German. Twelve times a year. $115.15. Verlag die Wirtschaft Berlin, Am Friedrichshain 22, D-10407 Berlin Germany. **Tel** 011 49 30 42151421. **(Subscription address:** Verlag Wirtschaft Huss GmbH, Am Friedrichshain 22, D 10407 Berlin Germany. **)** Index available. cum. index. **Circ:** 20,000. **Continues** Neuerer, 0028-3584.
Desc: Information on intellectual property, patents, trends, design management, law and enterprise proposal systems.

LC T ISSN 1081-8332
DD 602 US
 CODEN INPTFC
●**INSIDE THE PTO.** [Inside PTO]. **VFOAT** Inside the Patent and Trademark Office. Vol. 1, No. 1 (Feb. 27, 1995)-. Periodical. English. Twenty-four times a year. $475.00 US governments; $425.00 other governments; $550.00 other. Questel Publishing, 8000 Westpark Drive, McClean VA 22102. **Tel** (800)326-1710. available via Internet (http://www.questel.orbit.com/questelpub/).
Desc: Provides information from the US Patent and Trademark Office.

US
INTELLECTUAL FREEDOM ACTION NEWS. (19??)-. English. Twelve times a year. $20.00. American Library Association, 50 East Huron Street, Chicago IL 60611. **Tel** (312)944-6780, (800)545-2433, FAX (312)337-6787. **(Subscription address:** American Library Association, Subscription Department, 434 West Downer, Aurora IL 60506-9936. **Tel** (708)892-7465, FAX (708)892-7466.**) Continues** OIF Memorandum.

UK
INTELLECTUAL PROPERTY FRAUD REPORTER. Vol. 1, No. 2 (Jan. 11, 1990)-. English. Twelve times a year. $450.00. Intellectual Property Fraud Reporter, Leconfield House, Curson Street, London W1Y 8AS United Kingdom. **Tel** 011 44 171 4954655, FAX 011 44 171 4953101. **(Subscription address:** Intellectual Property Fraud, PO Box 27376, Washington DC 20038. **Tel** (202)662-5368.**)**

LC K9 .N7477 ISSN 0824-7064
DD 346.04/8/05 CN
 CCC
INTELLECTUAL PROPERTY JOURNAL. [Intellect. prop. j.]. Vol. 1, No. 1 (July 1984)-. Periodical. English (French). Three times a year. Price varies. Carswell / Canada, 2075 Kennedy Road, Scarborough Ontario M1T 3V4 Canada. **Tel** (416)298-5092, (800)387-5164, FAX (416)298-5094. **ED** David Vaver. **Bk Rev. Ad Acc.**
Desc: Covers matters of interest relating to patents, trademarks, copyright, designs, trade secrets, and competitive torts.
Ind/Abst Can. Legal Lit.; Curr. Law Index (1980-); Index Can. Leg. Period. Lit.; Leg. Resour. Index (1980-); LegalTrac (1984-).

LC K9 .N74774 ISSN 0892-2365
DD 346.04/8/05 342.64805 UK
 CCC
 CODEN IPLAEG
INTELLECTUAL PROPERTY LAW (CHUR, SWITZERLAND). (INTELLECTUAL PROPERTY LAW.). [Intellect. prop. law]. Vol. 1, No. 1 (Aug. 1987)-. Periodical. English. Irregular (1 volume). £102.00. Harwood Academic Publishers, PO Box 90, Reading RG1 8JL United Kingdom. **Tel** 011 44 1734 560080, FAX 011 44 1734 568211. **ED** Allen S. Melser. Index available. **Bk Rev. Ad Acc. Continues** A Practical Approach to Patents, Trademarks and Copyrights, 0142-5927.
Desc: The journal provides practical advice on matters relating to intellectual property law.
Ind/Abst Leg. Resour. Index; LegalTrac (1980-).

LC KF3114.A1 P3 ISSN 0193-4864
DD 346/.73/04805 US
INTELLECTUAL PROPERTY LAW REVIEW. [Intellect. prop. law rev.]. **Added/Corp** Clark Boardman Company. (1978)-. English. One time a year. $104.00. Clark Boardman Callaghan, 155 Pfingsten Road, Deerfield IL 60015. **Tel** (800)323-8067. **ED** Robert Bouchard. **Continues** Patent Law Review, 0079-0168.
Ind/Abst Leg. Resour. Index (1980-); LegalTrac (1983-).

LC KF2976.3 .I58 ISSN 1078-2796
DD 346.7304/8 347.30648 US
INTELLECTUAL PROPERTY LITIGATION REPORTER. [Intellect. prop. litig. report.]. **VFOAT** Andrews Intellectual Property Litigation Reporter. (19??)-. English. Twenty-four times a year. $550.00. Andrews Publications Inc., 1646 West Chester Pike, PO Box 1000, Westtown PA 19395. **Tel** (610)399-6600, (800)345-1101, FAX (610)399-6610.

LC K1401.A13 I58
DD 346.04/8/05 UK
INTELLECTUAL PROPERTY NEWSLETTER. Added/Corp Centre for Legal and Business Information. (197?)-. Newsletter. English. Twelve times a year. $342.24. Monitor Press, Rectory Road, Great Waldingfield, Sudbury Suffolk CO10 0TL United Kingdom. **Tel** 011 44 1787 378607, FAX 011 44 1787 880201. Index available. **Bk Rev.** ctrl circ.
Desc: Reports on patents, trademarks, commercial secrets and the increasing trend towards legislation about all forms of unfair competition.

 ISSN 0812-2024
 AT
INTELLECTUAL PROPERTY REPORTS. (19??)-. Periodical. English. Irregular. Butterworths Pty Ltd., 271-273 Lane Cove Road, PO Box 345, North Ryde, New South Wales 2113 Australia. **Tel** 011 61 2 3354444, FAX 011 61 2 3354655. **(Subscription address:** Butterworth Pty Ltd. / Australia, 35 Mitchell, North Sydney New South Wales 2060 Australia. **)** Index available.
Desc: Contains all major decisions from the High Court of Australia, the Federal Court of Australia and the Supreme Courts of all States of Australia as well as the Copyright Tribunal, the Patent Trade Marks and Designs Tribunal and other relevant bodies.
Ind/Abst Aust. Leg. Mon. Dig.

 ISSN 1079-2422
DD 346 US
●**INTELLECTUAL PROPERTY STRATEGIST.** [Intell. prop. strateg.]. (1994)-. Periodical. English. Twelve times a year. $95.00. Leader Publications, 345 Park Avenue South, New York NY 10010. **Tel** (800)888-8300 ext. 6170, (212)545-6170, FAX (212)696-1848.

 ISSN 0169-1074
 NE
INTELLECTUELE EIGENDOM & RECLAMERECHT. [Intellect. eigend. reclamer.]. **VFOAT** Intellectuele Eigendom en Reclamerecht. (1985)-. Periodical. Dutch. Six times a year. $158.36. W. E. J. Tjeenk Willink, Box 25, 8000 AA Zwolle Netherlands. **Tel** 011 31 38 228819, 011 31 38 211444.

 ISSN 0967-3466
DD 342.64800947 UK
●**INTELPROP NEWS.** [Intelprop news]. (1992)-. Periodical. English. Ten times a year. $444.92. Interforum Services Ltd., 565 Fulham Road, London SW6 1ES United Kingdom. **Tel** 011 41 171 3869322, FAX 011 41 171 3818914. **ED** David Jones-Robinson. **Circ:** 300 (ctrl).
Desc: Intellectual property and licensing in Russia, Ukraine, Eastern Europe and Central Asia.

 ISSN 8755-9609
DD 608 US
INTERNATIONAL INVENTION REGISTER. [Int. invent. regist.]. (19??)-. Periodical. English. Four times a year. $18.00 US; $27.40 other. Catalyst, PO Box 547, Fallbrook CA 92028. **ED** Dudley Rosborough. **Bk Rev. Ad Acc. Circ:** 27,500.
Desc: About 2,000 patents offered with free computer information to manufacturers.

LC CC135 .I594 ISSN 0940-7391
 GW
 CCC
INTERNATIONAL JOURNAL OF CULTURAL PROPERTY. Added/Corp International Cultural Property Society. **VFOAT** Cultural property; IJCP. Vol. 1, No. 1 (1992)-. Periodical. English. Two times a year. $180.40. Walter de Gruyter Inc., PO Box 303421, D-10728 Berlin Germany. **Tel** 011 49 30 260050, FAX 011 49 30 26005251, telex 184027.
Ind/Abst BHA : Biblio. Hist. Art.

UK
INTERNATIONAL LICENSING DIRECTORY, THE. (19??)-. Directory. English. One time a year (March). $190.00. A4 International, Hagley Chambers, 10-C Hagley Road, Stourbridge D78 1PS United Kingdom. **Tel** 011 44 1384 440591, FAX 011 44 1384 440582. **(Subscription address:** A4 Publications, PO Box 830410, Birmingham AL 35201. **Tel** (800)633-4931.**) ED** Francesca Ash and Adam Driscoll. **Bk Rev. Ad Acc. Adv Mgr:** Jerry Wooldridge. **Circ:** 3,000.
Desc: Complete licensing directory with 400 pages of more than 1800 licensors and agents in 63 countries.

 ISSN 0742-4825
 US
INTERNATIONAL TECHNOLOGY DISCLOSURES. (198?)-. English. Twelve times a year. $100.00 US, Canada and Mexico; $150.00 other. International Technology Disclosures Inc., PO Box 371, Tinley Park IL 60477. **Tel** (708)687-6070. **ED** Mary C. Sanders. ctrl circ.

LC T339 .I58 ISSN 1044-4742
DD 608 US
INVENTING AND PATENTING SOURCEBOOK. [Inventing pat. sourceb.]. **Added/Corp** Gale Research Inc. **VFOAT** Inventing & Patenting Sourcebook. 1st Ed. (1990)-. English. Every 2 years. $85.00. Gale Research Inc., 835 Penobscot Building, 645 Griswold Street, Detroit MI 48226. **Tel** (800)877-GALE, (313)961-2242, FAX (313)961-6083, (800)414-5043, telex TWX 810-221-7086. **ED** Richard C. Levy.
Desc: An all-around "how-to" guide for inventors, innovators, and marketers of new products and inventions. Takes users step by step from the patenting process to the trade show floor. Includes more than 35 usable forms, sample agreements, and declarations needed to file for patents and copyrights. Provides listings of information sources and contacts. Chapter introductions describe how to use each resource.

 ISSN 0706-6902
DD 608/.7/71 CN
INVENTORS DIGEST. VFOAT Canadian Inventors Digest. Vol. 1 (Jan./Feb. 1990)-. Periodical. English. Six times a year. United Inventors of Canada, PO Box 1328, Sudbury P3E 5K4 Canada. **Tel** (705)673-2444.

 ISSN 1011-3649
 HK
IP ASIA: INTELLECTUAL PROPERTY, MARKETING AND COMMUNICATIONS LAW. **VAT** Intellectual Property Asia. No. 1 (January 1988)-. Periodical. English. Ten times a year. $595.00. Asia Law & Practice Ltd, 2F 29 Hollywood Road, Central Hong Kong Hong Kong. **Tel** 011 852 25449918, FAX 011 852 25440040, 011 852 25437617.

LC KF2972 .P65
DD 346.7304/8/05 347.3064805 US
●**IPL NEWSLETTER : A PUBLICATION OF THE AMERICAN BAR ASSOCIATION SECTION OF INTELLECTUAL PROPERTY LAW. Added/Corp** American Bar Association. Section of Intellectual Property Law. **VFOAT** Newsletter. **VAT** Intellectual Property Law Newsletter. Vol. 12, No. 1 (Fall 1993)-. Periodical. English. Four times a year. American Bar Association, 750 North Lake Shore Drive, Chicago IL 60611. **Tel** (312)988-5500, (312)988-5241, FAX (312)988-6014, telex 270593. **Continues** PTC Newsletter, 0736-8232.

 ISSN 1080-8655
DD 608 US
 CEASED
IT'S NEW! : THE MAGAZINE ABOUT INVENTIONS, INNOVATIVE PRODUCTS, TRENDS. [It's new!]. **VFOAT** ItsNEW. (Apr. 1995)-(Sept/Oct. 1995). Periodical. English. Sunshine Publishing Co., 7060 Convoy Court, San Diego CA 92111. **Tel** (800)333-9345, (619)278-9080. **(Subscription address:** Kable News Co. Inc. / Illinois, 308 East Hitt Street, PO Box 564, Mt. Morris IL 61054-0564. **Tel** (800)967-6572.**)**

LC T285.A2 O8 ISSN 0208-287X
 RU
 CCC
IZOBRETENIIA : OFITSIALNYI PATENTNYI BIULLETEN. (19??)-. Periodical. Russian. One time a week. **(Subscription address:** East View Publications Inc., 3020 Harbor Lane North, Suite 110, Minneapolis MN 55447. **Tel** (800)477-1005, (612)550-0961, FAX (612)559-2931.**) Continues** Otkrytiia, Izobreteniia, 0208-287X.
Ind/Abst Abstr. Bull. Inst. Pap. Sci. Tech.

LC T273.H3 G47A
 GW
JAHRESBERICHT - DEUTSCHES PATENTAMT. Main/Corp Germany (Federal Republic, 1949-). Patentamt. German. Free. Deutsches Patentamt, Zweibruckenstrasse 12, 8000 Munich 2 Germany. **Tel** 089-21950, telex 523534 BPBM D.

LC T273.D7 J33
 GW
JAHRESVERZEICHNIS DER AUSLEGESCHRIFTEN UND ERTEILTEN PATENTE. Added/Corp Carl Heymanns Verlag. (19??)-. German. Irregular. DM220.00 Germany;

DM204.60 other. Carl Heymanns Verlag KG, Luxemburger Strasse 449, D-50939 Cologne Germany. **Tel** 011 49 221 460100, telex 8 881 888.

DD 346/.52/0486 JA
JAPAN PATENTS & TRADEMARKS. **Added/Corp** Suzuye (T) & Company. **VAT** Japan Patents and Trademarks. (1974)-. Periodical. English. Four times a year. $100.00. Suzuye Sogo Kenkyusho Inc., 3-7-2 Kasumigaseki, Chiyoda-ku Tokyo 100 Japan. **Tel** 011 81 3 3502 3181, telex 2224135 SUZUP J. **ED** H. Nakamori. **Circ:** 2,000.
Desc: Japanese industrial law reviews and court decisions.

LC T305 .A3 **ISSN** 0021-5333 UK
JAPANESE PATENTS ABSTRACTS. **Added/Corp** Derwent Information Service. Interpas. Vol. 1, No. 1 (July 21,1961)-. Periodical. English. One time a week. Derwent Publications Ltd., Derwent House 14, Great Queen Street, London WC2B 5DF United Kingdom. **Tel** 011 44 171 3442800, FAX 011 44 171 3442899.

US
•**JOURNAL OF COPYRIGHT INFORMATION.** **VFOAT** JOCI. Vol. 1, No. 1 (1994)-. Periodical. English. Twelve times a year. $300.00. Journal of Copyright Information, PO Box 421043, Plymouth MN 55442. **Tel** (612)593-4005, FAX (612)881-3684. **ED** Mr. Kim Brown. **Ad Acc.** ctrl circ.
Desc: A monthly guide to copyright information and developments.

LC K10 .O8683
DD 346.7304/8 347.30648 US
•**JOURNAL OF INTELLECTUAL PROPERTY LAW.** See Law.

LC KF2972 .J68 **ISSN** 1041-3952
DD 346.7304/8/05 347.3064805 US
JOURNAL OF PROPRIETARY RIGHTS, THE. See Law.

LC KF2987 .C66 **ISSN** 0886-3520
DD 346.7304/82/05 347.30648205 US
CODEN JCUSEZ
Pr Rev.
JOURNAL OF THE COPYRIGHT SOCIETY OF THE U.S.A. [J. Copyr. Soc. U. S. A.]. **Added/Corp** Copyright Society of the U.S.A. **VFOAT** Journal of the Copyright Society; Journal, Copyright Society of the U.S.A. Vol. 29, No. 2 (Dec. 1981)-. Periodical. English. Four times a year (Jan., Apr., Jul., Oct.). $125.00. Fred B. Rothman & Company, 10368 West Centennial Road, Littleton CO 80127. **Tel** (800)457-1986, (303)979-5657, FAX (303)978-1457, telex 87669. **ED** William Patry. cum. index. available on microfilm; available on an online database from DIALOG; WILSONLINE; Mead Data Central; (file 80) OCLC EPIC; and BRS. Documents available from The Genuine Article. ***Continues*** *Bulletin of the Copyright Society of the U.S.A., 0010-8642.*
Desc: This publication contains articles concerning copyright and copyright law.
Ind/Abst Curr. Contents Soc. Behav. Sci.; Curr. Law Index (1982-); Index Leg. Period.; Leg. Resour. Index (1982-)(1981-); LegalTrac (1982-); Res. Alert [Full Cov.]; Soc. Sci. Cit. Index [Full Cov.].

LC K16 .A73 **ISSN** 0882-9098
DD 346.7304/86/05 347.30648605 US
CCC
JOURNAL OF THE PATENT AND TRADEMARK OFFICE SOCIETY. [J. Pat. Trademark Off. Soc.]. **Added/Corp** Patent and Trademark Office Society (U.S.). Vol. 67, No. 1 (Jan. 1985)-. Periodical. English. Twelve times a year. $35.00. Patent and Trademark Office Society, PO Box 2600, Arlington VA 22202. **Tel** (703)308-4917. **ED** Louis S. Farfas. Index available ($40.00 extra). **Bk Rev. Ad Acc. Circ:** 4,300 (ctrl). ***Continues*** *Patent Office Society (U.S.) Journal of the Patent Office Society, 0096-3577.*
Desc: Articles on intellectual property law, including patent, trademark, copyright, trade secret law, approached from the legislative, executive and judicial perspectives and private viewpoint.
Ind/Abst Account. Art.; Curr. Law Index (1985-); Fed. Tax Artic.; Gen. BusinessFile (1992-); Index Leg. Period.; Leg. Resour. Index (1985-); LegalTrac (1985-).

LC T305.A2 K6 JA
KOGYO GIJUTSUIN TOKKYO SHOROKUSHU. **Added/Corp** Kogyo Gijutsuin (Japan) Nihon Sangyo Gijutsu Shinko Kyokai. **VFOAT** Kokuyu Tokkyo Shorokushu. (19??)-. Periodical. Japanese. One time a year. Nihon Sangyo Gijutsu Shinko Kyokai, (Japan Industrial Technology Association), 7-4 Nishishinbashi 2 chome, Minatoku Tokyo 105 Japan.

ISSN 0385-6909 JA
KOKUSAI KOGYO SHOYUKEN HOGO KYOKAI, NIHON BUKAI GEPPO. **VFOAT** A.I.P.P.I.; Journal of the Japanese Group of the International Association for the Protection of Industrial Property; AIPPI. (1956)-. Periodical. Japanese. Twelve times a year. ¥500 per issue. Kokusai Kogyo Shoyuken Hogo Kyokai Aippi Nihon Bukai, c/o Toranomon Denki Building, 8-ban 1-go Toranomon 2-chome Minato-ku, Tokyo-to Japan.

LC T306.5.A2 K65 KO
KONGGAE TUKHO KONGBO. **VFOAT** Official Gazette of the Unexamined Patent. Vol. 1 (1983)-. Korean (Korean). Hanguk Palmyong Tukho Hyophoe, 814-5 Yoksam-dong Kangnam-ku, Seoul 135 South Korea.

ISSN 1073-8983
DD 338 UK
LICENSING BUSINESS REVIEW. [Licens. bus. rev.]. (19??)-. Newsletter. English. Ten times a year (monthly with July/Aug. and Dec./Jan. issues combined). $250.00. A4 International, Hagley Chambers, 10-C Hagley Road, Stourbridge D78 1PS United Kingdom. **Tel** 011 44 1384 440591, FAX 011 44 1384 440582. **ED** Paul Wooding. **Ad Acc.** ***Continues*** *North American Licensing Tribune.*
Desc: Newsletter focusing on developments in the North American intellectual property/licensing market.

US
LICENSING REPORT. English. One time a week. $175.00 (one-year) US and Canada; $300.00 (one-year) other. Adventure Publishing Group Inc., 264 West 40th Street, New York NY 10018. **Tel** (212)575-4510, FAX (212)575-4521, telex 177368 IEBUT.

ISSN 0966-3568
DD 338 US
LICENSING REPORTER EUROPE. [Licens. report. Eur.]. (19??)-. Periodical. English. Twenty-two times a year. $250.00. A4 International, Hagley Chambers, 10-C Hagley Road, Stourbridge D78 1PS United Kingdom. **Tel** 011 44 1384 440591, FAX 011 44 1384 440582. **(Subscription address:** A4 Publications, PO Box 830430, Birmingham AL 35201. **Tel** (800)633-4931.**) ED** Francesca Ash. **Ad Acc, Adv Mgr:** Jerry Wooldridge, **Tel** 384-4400591. **Circ:** 2,000 (ctrl).
Desc: Newsletter concentrating on developments in the European intellectual property/licensing market.

UK
•**LICENSING TODAY INTERNATIONAL.** (1993)-. English. Four times a year (Jan., Mar., June, Sept.). $25.67. A4 International, Hagley Chambers, 10-C Hagley Road, Stourbridge D78 1PS United Kingdom. **Tel** 011 44 1384 440591, FAX 011 44 1384 440582.
Desc: A magazine for those involved in the licensing and merchandising industries, focusing on trends, developments, key players, news and information from people who do business in these areas.

US
LIGHTBULB / INVENT!, THE. **Added/Corp** Inventors Workshop International Education Foundation. **VFOAT** Lightbulb Invent!; Lightbulb and Invent! Magazine. No. 12 (Fall 1992)-. Trade Publication. English. Six times a year. $24.95. Inventors Workshop International, 7322 Mason Avenue, Canoga Park CA 91306. **Tel** (818)340-4268, FAX (818)884-8312. ***Continues*** *Invent!, 1040-3485.*

US
LIST OF RECENT ACCESSIONS AND FOREIGN PATENT TRANSLATIONS OF THE SCIENTIFIC LIBRARY. **Main/Corp** United States. Patent and Trademark Office. Periodical. English. US Department of Commerce / Patent and Trademark Office, 211 Crystal Drive, Suite 700, Arlington VA 20002. **Tel** (703)305-4537, FAX (703)305-6369.

SZ
LIST OF SELECTED WIPO MEETINGS. **Main/Corp** World Intellectual Property Organization. English. One time a year. World Intellectual Property Organization, WIPO OMPI 34 Chem Colombettes, 1211 Geneva 20 Switzerland. **Tel** 011 41 22 7309111.

LC KF3093.2 .L58 **ISSN** 8756-9647
DD 346.7304/86 347.306486 US
LITALERT (VIENNA, VA.). (LITALERT.). [Litalert]. **Added/Corp** INFAX Corporation. (Jan. 1985)-. Periodical. English. Twelve times a year. $345.00. Rapid Patent Service, PO Box 2527, Eads Station, Arlington VA 22202. **Tel** (800)336-5010. **ED** Gerry Jones. Index available. **Circ:** 200 (ctrl).
Desc: Listing of patent and trademark infringement law suits in US District Courts including docket numbers, plaintiffs and defendants. Approximately 200 cases per month.

ISSN 0960-5002
DD 658.575 UK
MANAGING INTELLECTUAL PROPERTY. [Manag. intellect. prop.]. (1990)-. Trade Publication. English. Twelve times a year. $440.00. Euromoney Publications PLC, Nestor House, Playhouse Yard, London EC4Z 5EX United Kingdom. **Tel** 011 44 171 7798888, FAX 011 44 171 7798630, telex 290700 EUROMON G. **(Subscription address:** Euromoney Publications PLC, Perrymount Road Haywards Heath, West Sussex RH16 3DH United Kingdom. **Tel** 011 44 1444 440421.**)**
Desc: For the corporation or financing institution, and advisers in private practice. Covers the protection of the assets of the corporation or financial institution--ideas, trade marks, licenses and patents--with advice and guidance on the developments.
Ind/Abst Curr. Cit.

LC T201-342
DD 608 US
MANUAL OF CLASSIFICATION. **Main/Corp** United States. Patent and Trademark Office. Office of Documentation Planning, Support, and Control. (Jan. 1979)-. Government Publication. English. Irregular. $82.00 US; $102.50 other. US Department of Commerce, 14th Street & Constitution Avenue NW, Washington DC 20230. **Tel** (202)482-2000, FAX (202)482-3772. **(Subscription address:** Superintendent of Documents, US Government Printing Office, Washington DC 20402. **)** ***Continues*** *United States. Patent and Trademark Office. Manual of Classification.*
Desc: Lists the numbers and descriptive titles of the Patent Office classes and subclasses, as well as the Design Classes.

ISSN 0364-2453 US
MANUAL OF PATENT EXAMINING PROCEDURE. **Main/Corp** United States. Patent and Trademark Office. (1975)-. Government Publication. English. Irregular. $78.00 domestic; $97.50 other. US Department of Commerce, 14th Street & Constitution Avenue NW, Washington DC 20230. **Tel** (202)482-2000, FAX (202)482-3772. **(Subscription address:** Superintendent of Documents, US Government Printing Office, Washington DC 20402. **)** ***Continues*** *Manual of Patent Examining Procedures.*
Desc: Provides information on the practices and procedures relative to the prosecution of patent applications before the Patent and Trademark Office.

LC T236.V1 A74A
DD 608.78 AG
MARCAS DE FABRICA, COMERCIO Y AGRICULTURA. **Main/Corp** Argentine Republic. Direccion Nacional de la Propiedad Industrial. (19??)-. Periodical. Spanish. Twelve times a year. 25.00Arg$ Argentina; 15.120Arg$ other. Direccion Nacional de la Propiedad Industrial, Avda Julio A Roca, 651 2do Subsuelo, Buenos Aires Argentina. **Tel** 30-2656. **ED** Miguel R Solanet. **Circ:** 300. available on diskette.
Desc: An official gazette that contains the bibliographic data, logos and isotopes of the industrial trademarks and designations approved by virtue of the Law 22.362. The description includes notations of the International Classification of Marks.

ISSN 0947-787X GW
MARKENBLATT. (19??)-. Periodical. German. Twenty-four times a year. $533.77. Wila Verlag/Wilhelm Lampl GMBH, Landsberger Str 191A, D-80687 Munich Germany. **Tel** 011 49 89 5795285. ***Absorbed*** *Warenzeichenblatt Teil I, 0043-0331* ***and*** *Warenzeichenblatt Teil II, 0043-034X.*

LC T325 .U5
DD 602/.75 SZ
MARQUES INTERNATIONALES : ORGANE OFFICIEL DU BUREAU INTERNATIONAL DE L'UNION POUR LA PROTECTION DE LA PROPRIETE INDUSTRIELLE, LES. **Added/Corp** International Bureau for the Protection of Industrial Property. World Intellectual Property Organization. United International Bureaux for the Protection of Intellectual Property. World Intellectual Property Organization. International Bureau. (189?)-. Periodical. English. Twelve times a year. 450.00F. World Intellectual Property Organization, WIPO OMPI 34 Chem Colombettes, 1211 Geneva 20 Switzerland. **Tel** 011 41 22 7309111.

LC KF2972 .M4 **ISSN** 1065-9390
DD 346.7304/8/05 347.3064805 US
CCC
MEALEY'S LITIGATION REPORTS. INTELLECTUAL PROPERTY. See Law.

LC KF3109 .M39 **ISSN** 1070-4043
DD 346.7304/86 347.306486 US
•**MEALEY'S LITIGATION REPORTS. PATENTS.** See Law.

ISSN 0734-3086 US
TITLE CHANGE
MEMORANDUM - AMERICAN LIBRARY ASSOCIATION. OFFICE FOR INTELLECTUAL FREEDOM. (MEMORANDUM.). [Memo. - Am. Libr. Assoc., Off. Intellect. Freedom]. **Main/Corp** American Library Association. Office for Intellectual Freedom. (19??)-(19??). Periodical. English. American Library Association, 50 East Huron Street, Chicago IL 60611. **Tel** (312)944-6780, (800)545-2433, FAX (312)337-6787.

Copyright, Intellectual Property

(Subscription address: American Library Association, Subscription Department, 434 West Downer, Aurora IL 60506-9936. **Tel** (708)892-7465, FAX (708)892-7466.) **ED** Judith F. Krug. **Circ:** 725 (ctrl). **Continued by** *Intellectual Freedom Action News*.
Desc: A brief information communication designed for members of American Library Association Chapters giving news about legislation and Supreme Court decisions affecting intellectual freedom.

LC T232.V1 N48a

NE
MERKENBLAD - BUREAU VOOR DE INDUSTRIELE EIGENDOM, NEDERLANDSE ANTILLEN. Main/Corp
Netherlands Antilles. Bureau voor de Industriele Eigendom. (19??)-. Periodical. Dutch. Twelve times a year. $240.00. Bureau voor de Industriele Eigendom AFD Admin., PO Box 3068, Curacao Netherlands Antilles. **Tel** 011 599 9 657800, FAX 011 599 9 657815.

ISSN 0026-6884
GW
UDC 347.77
MITTEILUNGEN DER DEUTSCHEN PATENTANWALTE. [Mitt. dtsch. Pat.anwalte].
(1934)-. Periodical. German. Twelve times a year. $141.24. Carl Heymanns Verlag KG, Luxemburger Strasse 449, D-50939 Cologne Germany. **Tel** 011 49 221 460100, telex 8 881 888.

LC T236.U3 A74A
DD 608.78
AG
MODELOS Y DISENOS INDUSTRIALES.
Main/Corp Argentine Republic. Direccion Nacional de la Propiedad Industrial. (19??)-. Periodical. Spanish. Twelve times a year. 25.00Arg$ Argentina; 15.120Arg$ other. Direccion Nacional de la Propiedad Industrial, Avda Julio A Roca, 651 2do Subsuelo, Buenos Aires Argentina. **Tel** 30-2656. **ED** Miguel Solanet. **Circ:** 300.
Desc: Contains the bibliographic data and drawings of the industrial models and designs

ISSN 1075-234X
US
CCC
●MULTIMEDIA AND TECHNOLOGY LICENSING LAW REPORT. See
Communications-Computer Applications.

LC T321.V1 N35
DD 016.9299
AT
NAME OF APPLICANTS FOR THE REGISTRATION OF TRADE MARKS.
Added/Corp Australia. Patent, Trade Marks, and Designs Office. Australia. Patent Office. **VFOAT** Name of Applicants for Registration of Trade Marks. (19??)-. English. Australia Patent Office, Canberra ACT Australia.

JA
NIHON RAISENSHINGU NENKAN.
Added/Corp Shohinkaken Shiryo Senta (Tokyo, Japan). (1984)-. Japanese. One time a year. ¥20000. Shohinkaken Shiryo Senta, c/o Shuwa Nagasaka, 102 13-9 Roppongi 5 Minato-ku, Tokyo-to 106 Japan.

US
NIMMER ON COPYRIGHT. (NIMMER ON COPYRIGHT; A TREATISE ON THE LAW OF LITERARY, MUSICAL AND ARTISTIC PROPERTY, AND THE PROTECTION OF IDEAS). Added/Corp
United States. Laws, Statutes, Etc. (1963)-. Periodical. English. One time a year. Matthew Bender & Company Inc., 1275 Broadway, Albany NY 12204. **Tel** (800)833-9844, (518)487-3000.

ISSN 0027-6723
SW
UDC 347.77
NIR. NORDISKT IMMATERIELLT RATTSSKYDD. [NIR, Nord. immater. rattsskydd].
VFOAT Nordiskt Immateriellt Rattsskydd. (1932)-. Periodical. Multiple languages (Norwegian, English, Swedish, Danish, French and German). Four times a year. Kr450.60. Institute for Intellectual Property, Skavlotsvagen 2 S 183 67 Taby, 10691 Stockholm Sweden. **Tel** 46 8 782 2950.
Ind/Abst Selec. Coop. Index Manage. Period.

ISSN 0029-2206
NO
CODEN NOTIAM
NORSK TIDENDE FOR DET INDUSTRIELLE RETTSVERN. DEL I : PATENTER. [Nor. tid. ind. rettsvern, Del I, Patenter].
Academic Scholarly Publication. Norwegian. One time a week. Kr300.00. Styret for det Industrielle Rettsvern, Boks 8160 Dep, N-0033 Oslo 1 Norway. **Tel** 011 47 2 461000, FAX 011 47 2 609843, telex 19152 NOPAT W. Index available. ctrl circ. Documents available from CASDDS.
Ind/Abst Chem. Abstr.

LC HF5429.255 .N67
UK
TITLE CHANGE
NORTH AMERICAN LICENSING INDUSTRY BUYERS GUIDE. Added/Corp
International Licensing Industry Merchandisers' Association. (1991/1992)-(199?). Consumer Publication. English. A4 International, Hagley Chambers, 10-C Hagley Road, Stourbridge D78 1PS United Kingdom. **Tel** 011 44 1384 440591, FAX 011 44 1384 440582. **Continues** U.S. Licensing Industry Buyers Guide. **Merged into** International Licensing Directory.

LC K12 .I25
DD 364.04/8 342.648
ISSN 0270-174X
US
NOUVELLES, LES. [LES nouv.]. Main/Corp
Licensing Executives Society (U.S.A.). **Added/Corp** Licensing Executives Society International. Licensing Executives Society (U.S.A.). Nouvelles. **VAT** Licensing Executives Society Nouvelles. (19??)-. Periodical. English. Four times a year (Mar., June, Sept., Dec.). $70.00. Licensing Executive Society / Jack Stuart Ott, 1444 West 10th Street, Suite 403, Cleveland OH 44113-1221. **Tel** (216)241-3940, FAX (216)771-8478. **ED** Jack Stuart Ott. Index available. **Bk Rev. Circ:** 5,400 (ctrl).
Desc: Articles relating to transfer of technology and industrial or intellectual property rights throughout the world.

LC K1411
DD 346.0482
NTIS ALERT. GOVERNMENT INVENTIONS FOR LICENSING. Added/Corp
United States. National Technical Information Service. (19??)-. Periodical. English. Twenty-four times a year. $265.00 US; $385.00 other. National Technical Information Service - NTIS, Room 2027S, 5285 Port Royal Road, Springfield VA 22161. **Tel** (703)487-4630, (703)487-4660, (703)487-4650, FAX (703)321-8547, telex 89-9405. **Continues** Government Inventions for Licensing / NTIS, 0364-6491.
Desc: Provides information on government R&D inventions available for licensing. Summarizes inventions from all government agencies.

US
NYPTC BULLETIN. See Law.

ISSN 0253-5327
AU
CODEN ORPBAD
OESTERREICHISCHES PATENBLATT.
[Oesterr. Patentbl.]. Academic Scholarly Publication. German. Twelve times a year. S1580 Austria; $90.04 US. Osterreichisches Patentamt, 1 Kohlmarkt 8-10, A-1014 Vienna Austria. **Tel** 011 43 222 53424, FAX 011 43 222 53424250, telex 136847. Index available. **Circ:** 500 (ctrl). Documents available from CASDDS.
Ind/Abst Chem. Abstr.

LC T223 .A23
DD 608/.7/73
ISSN 0098-1133
US
CODEN OGUPE7OGXXDB
OFFICIAL GAZETTE OF THE UNITED STATES PATENT AND TRADEMARK OFFICE. PATENTS. [Off. gaz. U.S. Pat. Trademark Off. Pat.]. Added/Corp
United States. Patent and Trademark Office. Vol. 931 (Feb. 4, 1975)-. Government Publication. English. Twelve times a year. $523.00 US; $653.75 other. US Department of Commerce, 14th Street & Constitution Avenue NW, Washington DC 20230. **Tel** (202)482-2000, FAX (202)482-3772. (**Subscription address:** Superintendent of Documents, US Government Printing Office, Washington DC 20402.) available on microfilm and microfiche from University Microfilms International (UMI). Documents available from BIOSIS Document Express, CASDDS. **Continues** Official Gazette of the United States Patent Office. Patents.
Desc: Contains the patents, patent office notices, and designs issued each week.
Ind/Abst Abstr. Bull. Inst. Pap. Sci. Tech.; BioBusiness (1985-); Biol. Abstr. (1985-); Chem. Abstr.

LC T223.V13 A34
DD 602/.75
ISSN 0360-5132
US
OFFICIAL GAZETTE OF THE UNITED STATES PATENT AND TRADEMARK OFFICE. TRADEMARKS. Added/Corp
United States. Patent and Trademark Office. **VFOAT** Official Gazette. Vol. 931, No. 2 (Feb. 11, 1975)-. Government Publication. English. One time a week. $470.00. US Department of Commerce, 14th Street & Constitution Avenue NW, Washington DC 20230. **Tel** (202)482-2000, FAX (202)482-3772. (**Subscription address:** Superintendent of Documents, US Government Printing Office, Washington DC 20402.) available on microfilm and microfiche from University Microfilms International (UMI). **Continues** Official Gazette. Trademarks.
Desc: Contains trademarks, trademark notices, marks published for opposition, trademark registrations issued, and an Index of Registrants.
Ind/Abst Alum. Ind. Abstr.; Met. Abstr.

LC T257 .A2
ISSN 0030-0330
UK
CCC
CODEN OFJBAZ
OFFICIAL JOURNAL (PATENTS). [Off. j., Pat.]. Main/Corp
Great Britain. Patent Office. No. 2196 (Feb. 18, 1931)-. English. One time a week. $1163.62. Patent Office / Wales, Room GY62 Concept House, Cardiff Road, Newport Gwent NP9 1RH United Kingdom. **Tel** 011 44 1633 814843. **Ad Acc**. Documents available from Petroleum Abstracts Document Delivery Service, CASDDS. **Continues** Great Britain. Patent Office. Illustrated Official Journal (Patents).
Ind/Abst Chem. Abstr.; Pet. Abstr.; World Ceram. Abstr.; World Text. Abstr.

AU
OSTERREICHISCHER MARKENANZEIGER. German. Twelve times a year. S600.00.
Osterreichisches Patentamt, 1 Kohlmarkt 8-10, A-1014 Vienna Austria. **Tel** 011 43 222 53424, FAX 011 43 222 53424250, telex 136847. Index available.

LC KF3124 .O9
DD 346/.73/04860269
ISSN 0160-5623
US
OUTLINE OF PTO PATENT INTERFERENCE PRACTICE. VAT
Outline of Patent and Trademark Office Patent Interference Practice. (19??)-. English. Outline of PTO Patent Interference Practice, 3449 North Western Avenue, Chicago IL 60618. **Continues** Outline of Patent Office Interference Practice.

LC T306.5.A2 P35
KO
PALMYONG TUKHO. VFOAT
Invention and Patent; Invention & Patent. Periodical. Korean (Korean). Twelve times a year. Hanguk Palmyong Tukho Hyophoe, 814-5 Yoksam-dong Kangnam-ku, Seoul 135 South Korea. ctrl circ.

LC T289.A2 S94a
SW
PATENT. Main/Corp
Sweden. Kungl. Patent- Och Registreringsverket. (19??)-. Swedish. Myron J Biggar Group Inc., PO Box 239, 692 Brandywine Road, Nazareth PA 18054. **Tel** (610)759-5367, FAX (610)759-0406.
Ind/Abst Maize Abstr.

LC TP
DD 665
ISSN 1065-0482
US
PATENT ABSTRACTS. AGRICULTURALS. (PATENT ABSTRACTS. AGRICULTURALS.). [Pat. abstr., Agric.]. Added/Corp
American Petroleum Institute. Central Abstracting & Information Services. **VFOAT** Agriculturals. (Jan. 6, 1992)-. English. One time a week. American Petroleum Institute, 275 Seventh Avenue, New York NY 10001. **Tel** (212)366-4040, FAX (212)366-4298.

ISSN 1066-2103
US
●PATENT ABSTRACTS. ENVIRONMENT, TRANSPORT & STORAGE. (PATENT ABSTRACTS. ENVIRONMENT, TRANSPORT & STORAGE.). [Pat. abstr., Environ. transp. storage]. Added/Corp
American Petroleum Institute. Central Abstracting and Indexing Service. **VFOAT** Environment, Transport & Storage. (1993)-. English. One time a week. American Petroleum Institute, 275 Seventh Avenue, New York NY 10001. **Tel** (212)366-4040, FAX (212)366-4298.

LC T215
DD 608.7
RU
●PATENT ABSTRACTS IN ENGLISH.
(1994)-. Bulletin. English. Twelve times a year. All-Russia Scientific and Research Institute of Patent Information, Raushskaya nab. 4, 113035 Moscow Russia. **Tel** 011 7 095 2393010, FAX 011 7 095 2311121, telex 411093 POISK SU.

DD 665
ISSN 1065-0466
US
PATENT ABSTRACTS. PETROLEUM & SPECIALTY PRODUCTS. [Pat. abstr., Pet. spec. prod.]. Added/Corp
American Petroleum Institute. Central Abstracting & Information Services. **VFOAT** Petroleum & Specialty Products. (Jan. 6, 1992)-. English. One time a week. American Petroleum Institute, 275 Seventh Avenue, New York NY 10001. **Tel** (212)366-4040, FAX (212)366-4298.

DD 665
ISSN 1065-0458
US
PATENT ABSTRACTS. PETROLEUM PROCESSES. (PATENT ABSTRACTS. PETROLEUM PROCESSES.). [Pat. abstr., Pet. processes]. Added/Corp
American Petroleum Institute. Central Abstracting & Information Services. **VFOAT** Petroleum Processes. (Jan. 6, 1992)-. English. One time a week. American Petroleum Institute, 275 Seventh Avenue, New York NY 10001. **Tel** (212)366-4040, FAX (212)366-4298.

Copyright, Intellectual Property

DD 665   **ISSN** 1065-044X   US
PATENT ABSTRACTS. PETROLEUM SUBSTITUTES. [Pat. abstr., Pet. substit.].
Added/Corp American Petroleum Institute. Central Abstracting & Information Services. **VFOAT** Petroleum Substitutes. (Jan. 6, 1992)-. Abstracting/Indexing Service. English. One time a week. American Petroleum Institute, 275 Seventh Avenue, New York NY 10001. **Tel** (212)366-4040, FAX (212)366-4298.

DD 665   **ISSN** 1065-2167
PATENT ABSTRACTS. POLYMERS. See
Chemistry and Chemicals-Abstracting, Bibliographies and Statistics.

US
PATENT AND TRADEMARK FORMS.
(19??)-. English. Irregular (supplements and revisions published annually). Clark Boardman Callaghan, 155 Pfingsten Road, Deerfield IL 60015. **Tel** (800)323-8067.

US
PATENT AND TRADEMARK OFFICE NOTICES. Main/Corp United States. Patent and Trademark Office. **VFOAT** U.S. Patent and Trademark Office Official Gazette. (19??)-. Government Publication. English. One time a week. $159.00. Superintendent of Documents, US Government Printing Office, Washington DC 20402. **Tel** (202)275-3328, FAX (202)786-2377.

LC KF3116 .P32   **ISSN** 0272-8621
DD 343.73/072 347.30372
PATENT ANTITRUST. Added/Corp Practising Law Institute. (19??)-. Monographic series. English. Every 2 years (every 2 years). $55.00. Practising Law Institute, 810 Seventh Avenue, New York NY 10019-5818. **Tel** (212)765-5700, FAX (212)581-4670 general correspondence, (212)265-4742 orders and billing inquiries.

LC KF3120.Z9 P28
DD 346.7304/86 347.306486   US
●PATENT APPLICATIONS HANDBOOK.
Added/Corp Clark Boardman Callaghan. (1993)-. English. One time a year. $105.00. Clark Boardman Callaghan, 155 Pfingsten Road, Deerfield IL 60015. **Tel** (800)323-8067.

US
PATENT DIGEST. English. Twelve times a year. $60.00. Gas Appliance Manufacturers Association, 1901 North Moore Street, Arlington VA 22209. **Tel** (703)525-9565, FAX (703)525-8159.

DD 608   **ISSN** 1065-0423   US
PATENT INDEX. (PATENT INDEX : INCLUDING BIBLIOGRAPHIC LIST, PATENT NUMBER LIST, ASSIGNEE INDEX / CENTRAL ABSTRACTING & INFORMATION SERVICES, AMERICAN PETROLEUM INSTITUTE.). [Pat. index]. **Added/Corp** American Petroleum Institute. Central Abstracting and Information Services. **VFOAT** American Petroleum Institute Patent Index. (Jan. 1992)-. English. Twelve times a year. American Petroleum Institute, 275 Seventh Avenue, New York NY 10001. **Tel** (212)366-4040, FAX (212)366-4298. **Continues** Patents Alphabetical Subject Index.

ISSN 1071-2631
DD 608   US
PATENT INTELLIGENCE AND TECHNOLOGY REPORT. [Pat. intell. technol. rep.]. **Added/Corp** IFI/Plenum Data Company. IFI/Plenum Data Corporation. (19??)-. English. One time a year. $395.00. IFI Plenum Data Corporation, 302 Swann Avenue, Alexandria VA 22301. **Tel** (703)683-1085, FAX (703)683-0246, telex 901-831.

US
PATENT LAW ANNUAL. See Law.

LC KF3114 .P36   **ISSN** 0192-8198
DD 346.7304/86 347.306486   US
PATENT LAW HANDBOOK. (1978)-. English. One time a year. Clark Boardman Callaghan, 155 Pfingsten Road, Deerfield IL 60015. **Tel** (800)323-8067.
ED Patricia Brantly. Index available.
Desc: Survey of law of patents.

LC T322.N7 A2
DD 608.79(3-4)   NZ
PATENT OFFICE JOURNAL. Main/Corp New Zealand. Patent Office. (19??)-. Periodical. English. Twelve times a year. $51.58. Government Printing Office / New Zealand, 10 Mulgrave Street, Wellington New Zealand. **Tel** 011 64 4 4737211, FAX 011 64 4 734943, telex GOVPRINT NZ 31320. (**Subscription address:** Government Printing Office / New Zealand, PO Box 12052, Wellington New Zealand. **Tel** 011 64 4 4737211.)
Desc: The official record of all patents and trademarks registered in New Zealand.

US
PATENT OFFICE RULES AND PRACTICES. (19??)-. English. Irregular. $299.00. Matthew Bender & Company Inc., 1275 Broadway, Albany NY 12204. **Tel** (800)833-9844, (518)487-3000.

LC KF3091.9 .P37   **ISSN** 0741-1219
DD 346.7304/8 347.30648   US
PATENT, TRADEMARK, AND COPYRIGHT LAWS. [Pat. trademark copyr. laws]. **Added/Corp** Bureau of National Affairs (Washington, D.C.). (1984 Ed.)-. English. Irregular. $60.00. Bureau of National Affairs Inc., 9435 Key West Avenue, Rockville MD 20850. **Tel** (800)372-1033, (301)258-1033, FAX (301)948-5823. **Continues** Patent and Trademark Laws, 0736-9670.

ISSN 0950-2513   UK
CODEN PAWOEH
PATENT WORLD. [Pat. world]. (Jan. 1987)-. Periodical. English. Ten times a year. $450.00. Intellectual Property Publishing, 3rd Floor Brigade House, Parsons GRN, London SW7 7NE United Kingdom. **Tel** 011 44 171 7367111.
Ind/Abst BioBusiness (1989-); Curr. Cit.; Index Leg. Period.

ISSN 0031-2894   GW
UDC 347.771/773:070.481
PATENTBLATT. [Patentblatt]. **VFOAT** Patenblatt. Vierteljahrliches Namensverzeichnis; Vierteljahrliches Namensverzeichnis zum Patentblatt. (1968)-. German. One time a week. $984.14. Carl Heymanns Verlag KG, Luxemburger Strasse 449, D-50939 Cologne Germany. **Tel** 011 49 221 460100, telex 8 881 888.
Ind/Abst Abstr. Bull. Inst. Pap. Sci. Tech.

ISSN 1064-2692
DD 608   US
CODEN USPAEJ
CEASED
PATENTIMAGES (NEW HAVEN, CONN.). (PATENTIMAGES [COMPUTER FILE].). [PatentImages]. **VFOAT** Patent Images. (Jan. 1, 1991)-(1993). English. MicroPatent, 250 Dodge Avenue, New Haven CT 06511. **Tel** (800)648-6787, (203)466-5055.

LC T319.S7 A3   **ISSN** 0031-286X
DD 608.768/05   SA
CODEN PASDEW
PATENTJOERNAAL INSLUITENDE HANDELSMERKE, MODELLE EN OUTEURSREG IN ROLPRENTE. (PATENT JOURNAL, INCLUDING TRADE MARKS DESIGNS AND COPYRIGHT IN CINEMATOGRAPH FILMS.). [Pat.j. insl. handelsmerke modelle out.reg rolpr.]. **Added/Corp** South Africa. Patent Designs, Trade Marks, and Copyright Office. **VFOAT** Patentjoernaal, Insluitende Handelsmerke Modele en Outeursreg in Rolprente. Vol. 13, No. 11 (Nov. 1980)-. Government Publication. Afrikaans (English). Twelve times a year. $4.47. Staatsdrukkery Government Printing Works, Bosmanstraat/Visagiestraat, Private Bag X85, Pretoria 0001 South Africa. **Tel** 011 27 12 3239731, FAX 011 27 12 3230009. Documents available from CASDDS. **Continues** Patentjoernaal, Insluitende Handelsmerke en Modelle, 0031-286X.
Ind/Abst Chem. Abstr. (1983-).

LC T201 .P43   **ISSN** 0031-2908
YU
PATENTNI GLASNIK. Periodical. Serbo-Croatian (Roman). Six times a year. 1,560.00 Din. Savezni Zavod za Patente, Uzun Mirkova 1, Belgrade Yugoslavia. **Tel** 011-636-466, telex 12761 SZPAT YU. Index available. cum. index. **Ad Acc. Circ:** 800.
Desc: Contains all information about patents, trademarks, designs, models and other official information.

ISSN 0388-7081   JA
PATENTS & LICENSING. **VFOAT** Patents and Licensing. (19??)-. Periodical. English. Six times a year. $130.00. (**Subscription address:** Maruzen Company Ltd., PO Box 5050, Import & Export Department, Tokyo 100 31 Japan. **Tel** 011 81 3 32789224.)

US
PATENTS THROUGHOUT THE WORLD. (19??)-. English. Irregular. Clark Boardman Callaghan, 155 Pfingsten Road, Deerfield IL 60015. **Tel** (800)323-8067.

LC K1503.3197.A6
SZ
PCT APPLICANT'S GUIDE. English. World Intellectual Property Organization, WIPO OMPI 34 Chem Colombettes, 1211 Geneva 20 Switzerland. **Tel** 011 41 22 7309111.

SZ
PCT GAZETTE. **Added/Corp** World Intellectual Property Organization. International Bureau. **VFOAT** Gazette of International Patent Applications. (May 11, 1978)-. Periodical. English. Twenty-six times a year. 480.00F. World Intellectual Property Organization, WIPO OMPI 34 Chem Colombettes, 1211 Geneva 20 Switzerland. **Tel** 011 41 22 7309111.
Desc: Provides summaries of international patent applications as they are published by the World Intellectual Property Organization in Geneva, Switzerland.
Ind/Abst Potato Abstr.

RU
●POLEZNYE MODELI, PROMYSHLENNYE OBRAZTSY : OFITSIALNYI BIULLETEN KOMITETA ROSSIISKOI FEDERATSII PO PATENTAM I TOVARNYM ZNAKAM.
Added/Corp Komitet Rossiiskoi Federatsii Po Patentam i Tovarnym Znakam. (1994)-. Periodical. Russian. Twelve times a year. **Continues** Promyshlennye Obraztsy, Tovarnye Znaki, 0208-2888.

US
POLP ASIST [COMPUTER FILE].
Added/Corp United States. Patent and Trademark Office. **VFOAT** ASIST. (Jan. 1991)-. Periodical. English. Four times a year. US Department of Commerce / Patent and Trademark Office, 211 Crystal Drive, Suite 700, Arlington VA 20002. **Tel** (703)305-4537, FAX (703)305-6369.
Desc: System requirements: AT class PC (or better) with DOS 3.1 or higher, MS-DOS CD-ROM extensions 2.x, 20MB hard disk 640K RAM, floppy disk drive, monitor (EGA recommended), CD-ROM drive, printer.

LC K16 .R216   **ISSN** 0142-5927
DD 346.7304/8 347.30648   SZ
CODEN PPTCD2
PRACTICAL APPROACH TO PATENTS, TRADEMARKS AND COPYRIGHTS, A.
[Pract. approach pat. trademarks copyr.]. Vol. 1, No. 1 (Oct. 1979)-. Periodical. English. Four times a year. $47.50. Harwood Academic Publishers, PO Box 90, Reading RG1 8JL United Kingdom. **Tel** 011 44 1734 560080, FAX 011 44 1734 568211.
Ind/Abst LegalTrac (1980-1982).

ISSN 0208-2888   RU
TITLE CHANGE
PROMYSHLENNYE OBRAZTSY, TOVARNYE ZNAKI : OFITSIALNYI BIULLETEN GOSUDARSTVENNOGO KOMITETA SSSR PO DELAM IZOBRETENII I OTKRYTII. Added/Corp
Gosudarstvennyi Komitet SSSR Po Delam Izobretenii i Otkrytii. Vsesoiuznyi Nauchno-Issledovatelskii Pnstitut Patentnoi Informatsii (Soviet Union). (1983-(1993). Periodical. Russian. **Continues in part** Otkrytiia, Izobreteniia, Promyshlennye Obraztsy, Tovarnye Znaki, 0021-3373. **Continued by** Poleznye Modeli, Promyshlennye Obraztsy.
Ind/Abst Abstr. Bull. Inst. Paper Chem.

LC T201 .P96
SZ
PROPRIETE INDUSTRIELLE, LE.
Periodical. French. Twelve times a year. World Intellectual Property Organization, WIPO OMPI 34 Chem Colombettes, 1211 Geneva 20 Switzerland. **Tel** 011 41 22 7309111.

LC T201 .P964   **ISSN** 0862-8726
XR
PRUMYSLOVE VLASTNICTVI. Added/Corp
Czechoslovakia. Federalni Urad Pro Vynalezy. (1991)-. Periodical. Czech (summaries and/or abstracts in English, French, German and Russian; table of contents in English, French, German and Russian). Twelve times a year. $93.20. (**Subscription address:** Kubon & Sagner, ABT Zeitschriftenimport, D 80328 Munich Germany. **Tel** 011 49 89 54218130.) **Continues** Vynalezy a Zlepsovaci Navrhy, 0139-701X.
Desc: Specifically looks at patents.

LC Z5073 .U27 S698   **ISSN** 0740-2848
DD 630   US
PUBLICATIONS AND PATENTS - UNITED STATES. AGRICULTURAL RESEARCH SERVICE. EASTERN REGIONAL RESEARCH CENTER (1981).
(PUBLICATIONS AND PATENTS.). [Publ. pat. - U.S., Agric. Res. Serv., East. Reg. Res. Cent. (1981)].
Main/Corp United States. Agricultural Research Service. Eastern Regional Research Center. Jan.-June 1981-. English. Two times a year. US Department of Agriculture / Philadelphia, Agricultural Research Service, Northeastern Region, Eastern Regional Research Center, 600 East Mermaid Lane, Philadelphia PA 19118. **Continues** United States. Science and Education Administration. Eastern Regional Research Center. Publications and Patents.

LC K1411 .N38   **ISSN** 0899-0859
DD 016.344/099 016.342499   US
RECENT TITLES IN LAW FOR THE SUBJECT SPECIALIST. COPYRIGHT AND ENTERTAINMENT LAW. See
Law-Entertainment Law.

Copyright, Intellectual Property

LC T267 .A23a   ISSN 0034-1851
DD 608/.7/493
BE
CODEN REBIA8

RECUEIL DES BREVETS D'INVENTION.
[Recl. brev. invent.]. **Main/Corp** Belgium. Service de la Propriete Industrielle et Commerciale. **Added/Corp** Belgium. Service de la Proprieté Industrielle et Commerciale. Belgium. Office de la Propriete Industrielle. **VFOAT** Verzameling der Uitvindingsoctrooien. No. 1 (1974)-. Academic Scholarly Publication. French (Dutch). Irregular (Thirteen times a year). $149.24. Office Proprieté Industrielle, 26 rue J A de Mot, B 1040 Brussels Belgium. **Tel** 011 32 2 233611, FAX 011 32 2 2308300, telex 20627. Index available. cum. index. **Bk Rev**. available on an online database from Belindis. Documents available from CASDDS.
Desc: Contains all patent applications made in Belgium during the month and the whole year as well as the European patents that have an effect in Belgium.
Ind/Abst Chem. Abstr.

BE
REPERTOIRE ALPHAPHONETIQUE DES MARQUES FRANCAISES : RAMF. (19??)-. French. Compu Mark, St. Petersbliet 7, B-2000 Antwerp Belgium. **Tel** 011 32 3 2318850.

LC PQ6001 .R39
DD 860/.9
SP
REPUBLICA DE LAS LETRAS : ORGANO DE LA ASOCIACION COLEGIAL DE ESCRITORES DE ESPANO. See Literature.

LC K19 .D87   ISSN 0326-0763
DD 346.04/8 342.648
AG
Pr Rev.
REVISTA DEL DERECHO INDUSTRIAL. See Law.

LC K19 .I44
DD 346.704/8 347.0648
BL
REVISTA INTERAMERICANA DE DIREITO INTELECTUAL : RIDI. VFOAT RIDI; Interamerican Review of Intellectual Property Law. Periodical. English (Portuguese and Spanish). $12.00. Editora Revista dos Tribunais, rua Conde do Pinhal 78, 01501 Sao Paulo SP Brazil. **Tel** 011 55 11 372433. **ED** Alvaro Malheiros. **Bk Rev. Circ:** 5,000.
Desc: Articles and commentaries of intellectual property law.

ISSN 0227-2180
DD 346.7104/82
CN
REVUE CANADIENNE DU DROIT D'AUTEUR. (LA REVUE CANADIENNE DU DROIT D'AUTEUR : LA PROPRIETE LITTERAIRE ET ARTISTIQUE.). [Rev. can. droit auteur]. **Added/Corp** Association Canadienne du Droit d'Auteur. Vol. 1, No. 1 (1980)-. Periodical. French. Four times a year. $9.00. Revue Canadienne du Droit, CP 907 Station H, Montreal Quebec H2G 2M9 Canada. **Tel** (514)842-9378.
Ind/Abst Index Can. Leg. Period. Lit.; Repere (1983-).

BE
REVUE DE DROIT INTELLECTUAL L'INGENIEUR-CONSEIL. (1911)-. French (Dutch). Six times a year. 3000F Belgium; 3900F other. Avenue de la Toison D or 63, B-1060 Brussels Belgium. **Tel** (02)537.13.08, FAX (02)537.56.09, telex 23.701. Index available. **Bk Rev. Circ:** 700.
Ind/Abst Music Artic. Guide (?-19??).

FR
REVUE DU DROIT DE LA PROPRIETE INTELLECTUELLE. VFOAT R.D.P.I. No. 37 (Oct. 1991)-. Periodical. French. Six times a year. Editions CEDAT, 21 rue Chevert, 75007 Paris France. **Tel** 011 33 1 45558573. **Formed by the union of** Revue du Droit de la Proprieté Industrielle **and** Cahiers du Droit d'Auteur.

LC T201 .R4   ISSN 0242-1623
DD 608/.05
FR
REVUE INTERNATIONALE DE LA PROPRIETE INDUSTRIELLE ET ARTISTIQUE : RIPIA. Added/Corp Union des Fabricants pour la Protection Internationale de la Propriete Industrielle et Artistique. **VFOAT** RIPIA. (19??)-. Periodical. French. 450.00F. Union des Fabricants, 16 rue de la Faisanderie, 75016 Paris France. **Tel** 011 33 1 45015111. **Continues** Revue Internationale de la Proprieté Industrielle.

ISSN 0035-3515
FR
REVUE INTERNATIONALE DU DROIT D'AUTEUR. [Rev. int. droit auteur]. (1953)-. French (English, Spanish and German). Four times a year (Jan., Apr., July, Oct.). $220.91. SACEM, 225 Charles de Gaulle, 92200 Neuilly/S-Seine France. **Tel** 011 33 1 47154715. Index Available in first issue of next volume--attached. cum. index.
Ind/Abst Index Foreign Leg. Per.

ISSN 0035-614X
IT
RIVISTA DI DIRITTO INDUSTRIALE.
(19??)-. English. Four times a year. L102080. Giuffre Editore SPA, Via Busto Arsizio 40, 20151 Milan Italy. **Tel** 011 398 2 38089200. **ED** Vincenzo Franceschelli. Index available. **Bk Rev. Ad Acc. Circ:** 1,200.
Desc: Two-part periodical featuring 1) studies and doctrine, 2) jurisprudence on copyright and intellectual property.

ISSN 0582-9917
DD 346
US
SHEPARD'S UNITED STATES PATENTS AND TRADEMARKS CITATIONS. See Law.

LC T241.V4 A26
BL
SINAL, REGISTRO DE MARCAS E SIMBOLOS. Portuguese. Editora de Guias, PO Box 4724, 01310 Sao Paulo Brazil. **Tel** 288-7667.

LC T285.A2 S68
DD 608/.7/47
UK
SOVIET INVENTIONS ILLUSTRATED : PARTS I-III COMPLETE. VAT Soviet Inventions Illustrated: Parts One-Three Complete. Periodical. English. One time a week. $580.00. Derwent Publications Ltd., Derwent House 14, Great Queen Street, London WC2B 5DF United Kingdom. **Tel** 011 44 171 3442800, FAX 011 44 171 3442899.

LC T201
DD 929
UK
SOVIET INVENTIONS ILLUSTRATED. SECTIONS P, Q: GENERAL/MECHANICAL. VFOAT General/Mechanical. (Jan. 12, 1977)-. Periodical. English. Irregular. Price varies per volume. Derwent Publications Ltd., Derwent House 14, Great Queen Street, London WC2B 5DF United Kingdom. **Tel** 011 44 171 3442800, FAX 011 44 171 3442899. **Continues** Soviet Inventions Illustrated. Part II: Mechanical & General.
Desc: Abstracts of Soviet patent and author's certificates.

LC T223.V4 P357   ISSN 0148-3498
DD 929
US
TM, TRADEMARK DIRECTORY. VFOAT Trademark Directory. Directory. English. National Paint and Coatings Association, Trademark Bureau, 1500 Rhode Island Avenue NW, Washington DC 20005.

LC K24 .R26   ISSN 0041-056X
DD 346.04/88/05 342.648805
US
TRADE-MARK REPORTER, THE.
[Trademark report.]. **Added/Corp** United States Trademark Association. **VFOAT** Trademark Reporter. **VAT** Trade Mark Reporter. Vol. 1, No. 1 (June 1911)-. Trade Publication. English. Six times a year. $50.00. International Trademark Association, 1133 Avenue of the Americas, New York NY 10036. **Tel** (212)768-9887. **ED** Jerre B. Swann and Charlotte Jones. Index available. cum. index. **Bk Rev. Circ:** 2,300 (ctrl). available on microfilm and microfiche from University Microfilms International (UMI). **Absorbed** Bulletin of the United States Trademark Association.
Ind/Abst Account. Art.; Fed. Tax Artic.; Index Leg. Period.; Law Office Inf. Serv.; Leg. Resour. Index; LegalTrac (1980-).

LC T257.V1 T7
UK
TRADE MARKS JOURNAL, THE.
Added/Corp Great Britain. Patent Office. (1876)-. Periodical. English. One time a week. $1060.95. Patent Office / Wales, Room GY62 Concept House, Cardiff Road, Newport Gwent NP9 1RH United Kingdom. **Tel** 011 44 1633 814843.

LC T226.V1 T7   ISSN 0041-0438
CN
TRADE MARKS JOURNAL (OTTAWA).
(TRADE MARKS JOURNAL. JOURNAL DES MARQUES DE COMMERCE.). **Added/Corp** Canada. Trade Marks Office. **VFOAT** Journal des Marques de Commerce. Vol. 1, (Sept. 29, 1954)-. Periodical. English (French). One time a week. 72.00Can$ Canada; 86.40Can$ other. Canada Communication Group Publishers, Order Processing, Ottawa Ontario K1A 0S9 Canada. **Tel** (819)956-4800, (819)956-4802.

ISSN 1070-6151
US
●**TRADEMARK ALERT - CANADA.** (1993)-. Periodical. English. One time a week. $925.00. Thomson and Thomson Inc., 500 Victory Road, North Quincy MA 02171. **Tel** (617)479-1600, (800)692-8833, FAX (617)786-8273, telex 440388.
Desc: Provides the first notification of new filing and reports trademarks prior to their publication in the Official Gazette. Lists all the owners who have filed that week, providing an overview of industry and competitor activity for market research purposes. Each record includes trademark, U.S. Class(es), first use date, applicant name, design indicator, serial number, filing date, and goods/services description.

LC T223.V3 T73   ISSN 1072-6233
DD 602/.75/0973
US
●**TRADEMARK INDEX OF US PATENT & TRADEMARK OFFICE FEDERAL RECORDS, THE.** [Trademark index US Pat. Trademark Off. fed. rec.]. **Added/Corp** Thomson & Thomson. **VFOAT** Trademark Index. **VAT** Trademark Index of United States Patent & Trademark Office Federal Records. (1994)-. English. One time a year. $245.00. Thomson and Thomson Inc., 500 Victory Road, North Quincy MA 02171. **Tel** (617)479-1600, (800)692-8833, FAX (617)786-8273, telex 440388.
Desc: Lists over 720,000 active trademarks registered at the U.S. Patent and Trademark Office from 1884 to the present. Includes trademark, owner name, registration date, registration number, and design indicator.

LC KF3176.A32 T7   ISSN 0731-5813
DD 346.7304/88 347.306488
TRADEMARK LAW HANDBOOK.
(TRADEMARK LAW HANDBOOK / THE UNITED STATES TRADEMARK ASSOCIATION.). [Trademark law handb.]. **Added/Corp** United States Trademark Association. (1981)-. English. One time a year. $75.00. Clark Boardman Callaghan, 155 Pfingsten Road, Deerfield IL 60015. **Tel** (800)323-8067.
Desc: A survey of year's past legal developments.

US
TRADEMARK MANUAL OF EXAMINING PROCEDURE (TMEP). Main/Corp United States Patent and Trademark Office. (1974)-. Government Publication. English. Irregular. $19.00 US; $23.75 other. Superintendent of Documents, US Government Printing Office, Washington DC 20402. **Tel** (202)275-3328, FAX (202)786-2377.
Desc: Provides trademark examiners in the Patent Office, trademark applicants, and attorneys for applicants with a reference work on the practices and procedures relative to prosecution of applications to register marks in the Patent Office.

LC T223.V4 A27   ISSN 0082-5786
DD 602/.75
US
TRADEMARK REGISTER OF THE UNITED STATES, THE. [Trademark regist. U.S.]. **Added/Corp** Patent Searching Service. (1968)-. English. One time a year. $355.00. Trademark Register, National Press Building 1297, Washington DC 20045. **Tel** (202)662-1233, FAX (202)347-4408. **ED** Diane Christen and Judy Semsak. Index available (bound in issue). available on an online database from Minitel Services Inc. **Continues** Trademark Renewal Register, 0564-0539.
Desc: All the currently registered trademarks in the US Patent and Trademark office since 1881.

LC KF3181.A329 P38   ISSN 0149-6387
DD 346/.73/0488
US
TRADEMARK RULES OF PRACTICE OF THE PATENT AND TRADEMARK OFFICE WITH FORMS AND STATUTES.
Main/Corp United States Patent and Trademark Office. (1976)-. Government Publication. English. US Department of Commerce, 14th Street & Constitution Avenue NW, Washington DC 20230. **Tel** (202)482-2000, FAX (202)482-3772. **Continues** Trademark Rules of Practice of the Patent Office, with Forms and Statutes.

ISSN 1062-7766
DD 741
US
TRADEMARK TRENDS. (TRADEMARK TRENDS : A MONTHLY REVIEW OF CREATIVE LOGOS & TRADEMARKS AS REGISTERED WEEKLY WITH U.S. TRADEMARK OFFICE.). [Trademark trends]. **Added/Corp** American Professional Graphic Artists. (19??)-. Periodical. English. Twelve times a year. $59.00. Board Report Publishing Company, PO Box 4416, Circulation Department, Denver CO 80204. **Tel** (303)839-9058, FAX (303)839-1272. **ED** Drew Miller. ctrl circ.
Desc: A compendium of new logo designs as being registered with the US Trademark office.

ISSN 0950-2564
UK
TRADEMARK WORLD. (TRADEMARK WORLD : THE INTERNATIONAL JOURNAL FOR TRADEMARK PROFESSIONALS.). [Trademark world]. Issue 1 (1986)-. Periodical. English. Ten times a year. $450.00. Intellectual Property Publishing, 3rd Floor Brigade House, Parsons GRN, London SW6 7NE United Kingdom. **Tel** 011 44 171 7367111. **Continues** Trademark America.
Ind/Abst Index Leg. Period. (1992-).

US
TRADEMARKS AND UNFAIR COMPETITION. (19??)-. English. Irregular (5 volume set). $495.00. Clark Boardman Callaghan, 155 Pfingsten Road, Deerfield IL 60015. **Tel** (800)323-8067.

TRADEMARKS, COPYRIGHTS, AND UNFAIR COMPETITION : ALI-ABA COURSE OF STUDY MATERIALS.
[Trademarks, copyr. unfair compet.]. **Added/Corp** American Law Institute-American Bar Association Committee on Continuing Professional Education. **VFOAT** ALI-ABA Course of Study Materials; Trademarks/Copyrights/Unfair Competition. (Nov. 17-18,

Copyright, Intellectual Property

1989)-. English. One time a year. $80.00. American Law Institute, 4025 Chestnut Street, Philadelphia PA 19104-3099. **Tel** (215)243-1661, (800)253-6397, FAX (215)243-1664. **Continues** ALI-ABA Course of Study. Unfair Competition, Trademarks, and Copyrights : Materials, 0191-1996.

GW

TRANSPATENT. (19??)-. German. Twelve times a year. DM18.00. Transpatent GmbH, Postfach 80 05, D-4000 Duesseldorf 1 Germany. **Tel** 011 49 211 312073.
Desc: Law and comments in the field of intellectual property all over the world.

LC T306.5.H3 T84

KO

TUKHOCHONG YONBO. VFOAT Annual Report of the Office of Patents Administration. Korean (Korean). One time a year. Tukhochong, 58-3 Socho-dong, Kangnam-ku, Seoul South Korea.

LC TP210 .U5   ISSN 0362-4358
DD 016.66/002/72   US

U.S. CHEMICAL PATENT INDEX. VAT United States Chemical Patent Index. English. Patent Publications, Inc., 20 nassau Street, Princeton NJ.

US

U.S. PATENT CLASSIFICATION - NUMERIC LISTING. Added/Corp United States. Patent and Trademark Office. **VFOAT** Patent Classification - Numeric Listing. (19??)-. Government Publication. English. Two times a year. $705.00. Superintendent of Documents, US Government Printing Office, Washington DC 20402. **Tel** (202)275-3328, FAX (202)786-2377.
Desc: Sequenced by patent numbers. Identifies the class and subclass to which a particular patent has been assigned as an original, a cross-reference, or an unofficial cross-reference.

ISSN 0041-803X
DD 346   US
CCC

UNITED STATES PATENTS QUARTERLY, THE. [U.S. pat. q.]. **Added/Corp** Bureau of National Affairs (Washington, D.C.). **VFOAT** USPQ. Vol. 1 (Mar. 4-June 1, 1929)-. Periodical. English. One time a week. $636.00. Bureau of National Affairs Inc., 9435 Key West Avenue, Rockville MD 20850. **Tel** (800)372-1033, (301)258-1033, FAX (301)948-5823. **ED** Cynthia J. Bolbach.
Desc: A weekly service reporting all important decisions dealing with patents, trademarks, copyrights, unfair competition, trade secrets, and computer chip protection.
Ind/Abst Nematol. Abstr.

US

UNITED STATES STATUTORY INVENTION REGISTRATION [MICROFORM]. Main/Corp United States. Patent and Trademark Office. **VFOAT** Statutory Invention Registration; U.S.S.I.Reg. (19??)-. Academic Scholarly Publication. English. US Department of Commerce / Patent and Trademark Office, 211 Crystal Drive, Suite 700, Arlington VA 20002. **Tel** (703)305-4537, FAX (703)305-6369. Documents available from CASDDS.
Ind/Abst Chem. Abstr.

LC HV7742 .A24A   ISSN 0343-690X
GW

VERFASSUNGSSCHUTZBERICHT. German. One time a year. Der Bundesminister des Innern, Graurheindorfer Strasse 198, W-5300 Bonn Germany. **Continues** Germany (West). Bundesministerium des Innern. Referat Offentlichkeitsarveit. Verfassungsschutz.

DD 346.6804/82

SA

VERSLAE VAN DIE GEKOSE KOMITEE OOR DIE WETSONTWERP OP OUTEURSREG. REPORTS OF THE SELECT COMMITTEE ON THE COPYRIGHT BILL. Main/Corp South Africa. Parliament. House of Assembly. Select Committee on the Copyright Bill. **Added/Corp** South Africa. Parliament. House of Assembly. Select Committee on the Copyright Bill. **VFOAT** Reports of the Select Committee on the Copyright Bill. (19??)-. Afrikaans (English). Government Printer / South Africa, Bosman Street, Private Bag X85, Pretoria 0001 South Africa. **Tel** 011 27 12 3239731 ext. 262.

LC T26.C9 V47   ISSN 0231-9942
XR
CODEN VFAVET

VESTNIK FEDERALNIHO URADU PRO VYNALEZY. CAST A, VYNALEZY. Added/Corp Czechoslovakia. Federalni Urad pro Vynalezy. **VFOAT** Vynalezy. (19??)-. Academic Scholarly Publication. Czech (table of contents in English, French, German and Russian). Twelve times a year. $117.00. Postovni Novinova Sluzba, Ustredni Expedice Tisku, Odd Vyvoz Tisku, Jindrisska 14, Prague 1 Czech Republic. **Circ:** 2,300. Documents available from CASDDS.
Ind/Abst Chem. Abstr.

LC T265.3.D7 V47   ISSN 0231-9985
XR

VESTNIK FEDERALNIHO URADU PRO VYNALEZY. CAST B, OCHRANNE ZNAMKY, PRUMYSLOVE UZORY. Added/Corp Czechoslovakia. Federalni Urad pro Vynalezy. **VFOAT** Ochranne Znamky, Prumyslove Vzory. (19??)-. Periodical. Czech (table of contents in English, French, German and Russian). Twelve times a year. $117.00. Federal Office for Inventions, Revolucni 7, Prague 1 Czech Republic. **Circ:** 2,300.

LC AP8 .V5   ISSN 0042-7195
II

VISVA-BHARATI QUARTERLY. [Visvabharati q.]. **Added/Corp** Visva-Bharati. **VFOAT** Visvabharati Quarterly. Vol. 1 (Apr. 14, 1923)-. Periodical. English. Four times a year (Feb., May, Aug., Nov.). $12.00. Visva-Bharati, 6 Acharya Jagadish Bose Road, Calcutta 700017 India. **Tel** 011 91 33 449868.
Ind/Abst MLA Int. Bibl. Books Artic. Mod. Lang. Lit.

LC T273.V1 A33

GW
CEASED

WARENZEICHEN- UND MUSTERBLATT. Added/Corp Germany (East). Amt fuer Erfindungs- und Patentwesen. (19??)-(1993). Periodical. German. Verlag die Wirtschaft Berlin, Am Friedrichshain 22, D-10407 Berlin Germany. **Tel** 011 49 30 42151421. **(Subscription address:** Verlag Wirtschaft Huss GmbH, Am Friedrichshain 22, D 10407 Berlin Germany. **) Continues** Warenzeichenblatt.
Desc: Publishes all merchandise marks, origin details and industrial designs registered with the GDR Inventions and Patent Office. Includes articles on content-related, creative and legal questions connected with designs and trademarks.

LC T223.D7 W48 T223 .A232   ISSN 1049-8168
DD 608.773   US

WHO'S INVENTING WHAT?. (WHO'S INVENTING WHAT? : PATENTS GRANTED IN THE UNITED STATES AS REPORTED IN THE OFFICIAL GAZETTE OF THE UNITED STATES PATENT AND TRADEMARK OFFICE). [Who's invent. what?]. Issue 1 (Jan. through Mar. 1990)-. Periodical. English. Four times a year. $195.00. Gale Research Inc., 835 Penobscot Building, 645 Griswold Street, Detroit MI 48226. **Tel** (800)877-GALE, (313)961-2242, FAX (313)961-6083, (800)414-5043, telex TWX 810-221-7086. **ED** Donna Wood.
Desc: Each issue presents information on 20-25,000 patents, including patent titles, U.S. patent numbers, name of inventor, and date issued.

LC K1544.A485 W47   ISSN 0899-1766
DD 346.04/8/025 342.648025   US

WHO'S WHO IN INTELLECTUAL PROPERTY. (WHO'S WHO IN INTELLECTUAL PROPERTY : WWIIP.). [Who's who intellect. prop.]. **VFOAT** WWIIP. 1st Ed. (1989-1990)-. Periodical. English. Every 2 years (published every other year in March). $254.00. Who's Who in Intellectual Property, PO Box 3856, North New Hyde Park NY 11040-9886. **Tel** (516)627-4468, FAX (516)742-5368. **ED** Eric D. Offner and Gary D. Offner. Index available. **Bk Rev. Circ:** 1,500.

LC K1401.A13 W67   ISSN 0952-7613
DD 346.04/8/05 342.64805   UK

WORLD INTELLECTUAL PROPERTY REPORT. Added/Corp BNA International Inc. (198?)-. Periodical. English. Twelve times a year. $695.00. BNA International Inc., Herron, HSE Dean 10 Farrar Street, 6th Floor, London SW1H 0DX United Kingdom. **Tel** 011 44 171 2228931, FAX 011 44 171 2220294, telex 262570 BNA LONG. **ED** Joel Kolko. Index available. cum. index. **Bk Rev. Circ:** 2,000 (ctrl).
Desc: Covers intellectual property questions and insights on preparing strategies and advice for clients on how business operations are affected by actions involving rules, regulations, treaties, proposals, court cases, conventions, enforcement and legislation.

LC T210 .W67   ISSN 0172-2190
DD 025/.06608   UK
CCC
CODEN WPAID2

WORLD PATENT INFORMATION. [World pat. inf.]. **Added/Corp** World Intellectual Property Organization. Commission of the European Communities. Vol. 1 (July 1979)-. Periodical. English (summaries and/or abstracts in French and German). Four times a year. $366.00. Pergamon Press, An Imprint of Elsevier Science Ltd., The Boulevard, Langford Lane, Kidlington, Oxford OX5 1GB United Kingdom. **Tel** 011 44 1865 843000, 011 44 1865 843699, FAX 011 44 1865 843010. **(Subscription address:** Elsevier Science Ltd. / Oxford Fulfillment Centre, PO Box 800, Kidlington OX5 1DX United Kingdom. **Tel** 011 44 865 843353.**) ED** Vincent Dodd. **Bk Rev. Ad Acc.** available on microfilm and microfiche from University Microfilms International (UMI); available on an online database from Elsevier Electronic Subscriptions (EES). Documents available from Ask*IEEE.
Ind/Abst Art Archaeol. Tech. Abstr.; Curr. Cit.; Inf. Sci. Abstr.; INSPEC (April 1981-); Libr. Inf. Sci. Abstr.; World Surf. Coat. Abstr.

US

WORLD PATENT LAW AND PRACTICE. Vol. 1 1968-. Periodical. English. Matthew Bender & Company Inc., 1275 Broadway, Albany NY 12204. **Tel** (800)833-9844, (518)487-3000.

US

WORLD PATENT LAW AND PRACTICE : PATENT STATUTES, REGULATION AND TREATIES. (1974)-. Newspaper. English. Irregular. $294.00. Matthew Bender & Company Inc., 1275 Broadway, Albany NY 12204. **Tel** (800)833-9844, (518)487-3000.

UK

WORLD PATENTS ABSTRACTS: EUROPEAN PATENTS REPORT. CHEMICAL. (19??)-. English. Irregular. $2400.00 North America. Derwent Publications Ltd., Derwent House 14, Great Queen Street, London WC2B 5DF United Kingdom. **Tel** 011 44 171 3442800, FAX 011 44 171 3442899. **(Subscription address:** Derwent Inc., 1420 Spring Hill Road, Suite 525, McLean VA 22102. **Tel** (703)790-0400.**)**

UK

WORLD PATENTS ABSTRACTS: UNITED STATES PATENTS ABSTRACTS. CHEMICAL. (19??)-. English. £1540.00. Derwent Publications Ltd., Derwent House 14, Great Queen Street, London WC2B 5DF United Kingdom. **Tel** 011 44 171 3442800, FAX 011 44 171 3442899.

LC T201 .P256   ISSN 0278-8047
DD 608.7/05   US

WORLD TECHNOLOGY PATENT LICENSING GAZETTE. [World technol. patent licens. gaz.]. **Added/Corp** Techni Research Associates. **VFOAT** WT-PLG. (Feb. 1975)-. Periodical. English. Six times a year. $163.00. Techni Research Associates Inc, PO Box T, Willow Grove PA 19090. **Tel** (215)657-1753, (215)657-1754, FAX (215)576-7924. **ED** Louis F. Schiffman, Ph.D. **Bk Rev.** available on microfilm from University Microfilms International (UMI). **Continues** Patent Licensing Gazette.
Desc: Describes new products and processes available for license or acquisition, business opportunities in technology, patent information and news items in technology transfer.

BE

WORLD TRADEMARK JOURNAL. (19??)-. English. One time a week. Compu Mark, St. Petersbliet 7, B-2000 Antwerp Belgium. **Tel** 011 32 3 2318850. **(Subscription address:** Thomson & Thomson, 500 Victory Road, North Quincy MA 02171. **Tel** (617)479-1600.**)**
Desc: Covers over two hundred countries and lists applications in the product and service class(es) selected. Allows tracking of competitor and industry new product introductions.

LC T295.P7 A118   ISSN 0477-1826
PL

WYKAZ PATENTOW NA WYNALAZKI UDZIELONYCH PRZEZ URZAD PATENTOWY PRL W ROKU ... . Main/Corp Urzad Patentowy Polskiej Rzeczypospolitej Ludowej. Polish. **Continues** Wykaz Patentow Udzielonych Przez Urzad Patentowy RZ.P. W Latach ... .

LC T212 .X47   ISSN 0361-4190
DD 681/.65   US

XEROX DISCLOSURE JOURNAL. Added/Corp Xerox Corporation. Vol. 1 (Jan. 1976)-. Periodical. English. Twelve times a year. Xerox Corporation, Xerox Square, Library 021, Rochester NY 14644. **Tel** 800 832-6979 ext. 501.
Ind/Abst Graph. Arts Bull. Inst. Pap. Sci. Technol. (March 1989, June 1989).

ISSN 0334-3332
IS
CODEN ISPDBT

YOMAN HA-PATENTIM VEHA-MIDGAMIN. [Pat. des. j.]. **Main/Corp** Israel. Lishkat Ha-Patentim. **VFOAT** Patents and Designs Journal. May 1968-. Academic Scholarly Publication. Multiple languages (English and Hebrew). 45.00. Documents available from CASDDS. **Supersedes in part** Yoman Ha-Patentim, Ha-Midgamim Ve-Simane Ha-Mishar; **Continues** Abridgments of Patent Specifications.
Ind/Abst Chem. Abstr.

LC K29 .U18
DD 346/.52/048605   JA
YUASA AND HARA PATENT NEWS.
Added/Corp Yuasa Hara Horitsu Tokkyo Jimusho. (July 1974)-. Periodical. English. Four times a year. Section 206, New Ohtemachi Building 2-1, Ohtemachi 2-chome, Chiyoda-ku 100 Japan.

RH
ZIMBABWE PATENT AND TRADE MARKS JOURNAL. (19??)-. English. One time a week. 54.00Zin$. Zimbabwe Government Printing, PO Box 8062, Causeway Harare Zimbabwe. **Tel** 011 263 4 706161.

LC KK6946.A13 Z86   ISSN 0177-6762
GW
CCC
ZUM : ZEITSCHRIFT FUER URHEBER- UND MEDIENRECHT/FILM UND RECHT.
See Motion Picture.

ABSTRACTING, BIBLIOGRAPHIES AND STATISTICS

LC T271 .A233   ISSN 0750-7674
DD 608.744/05   FR
CODEN BOPBEN
BULLETIN OFFICIEL DE LA PROPRIETE INDUSTRIELLE BREVETS D'INVENTION ABREGES ET LISTES. [Bull. off. propr. ind., Brev. invent. Abr. listes]. **Added/Corp** Institut National de la Propriete Industrielle (France). **VFOAT** Brevets d'Invention; Brevets d'Invention, Abreges et Listes; Brevets d'Invention, Abreges et Listes, Topographies de Produits Semi-Conducteurs; A.Brevets d'Invention, Topographies de Produits Semi-Conducateurs; Brevets d'Invention, Certificats Complementaires de Protection, Topographies de Produits semi-conducteurs; BOPI; B.O.P.I. Vol. 23 E No. 16 (April 23, 1982)-. Bulletin. French. Irregular. Price varies. Imprimerie Nationale / France, BP 514, 59505 Douai Cedex France. **Tel** 011 33 27 937090. cum. index. available in microform; available on an online database. Documents available from CASDDS. **Formed by the union of** Bulletin Officiel de la Propriete Industrielle. Abreges, 0151-0592 **and** Bulletin Officiel de la Propriete Industrielle. Listes.
Desc: Official Gazette of French Patents Bibliographical data and abstracts of published specifications arranged by publication number and IPC. Lists of published specifications arranged by name of applicant, IPX and priority data. Also contains a list of granted patents and other lists.
Ind/Abst Abstr. Bull. Inst. Pap. Sci. Tech.; Chem. Abstr. (1984-).

ISSN 1065-0474
DD 665   US
PATENT ABSTRACTS. CHEMICAL PRODUCTS. [Pat. abstr., Chem. prod.]. **Added/Corp** American Petroleum Institute. Central Abstracting & Information Services. **VFOAT** Chemical Products. (Jan. 6, 1992)-. English. One time a week. American Petroleum Institute, 275 Seventh Avenue, New York NY 10001. **Tel** (212)366-4040, FAX (212)366-4298.

DANCE

ISSN 0261-6939
UK
CEASED
2 D DRAMA, DANCE. See Theater.

LC GV1587 .A35   ISSN 1053-4261
DD 792.8/2/05   SZ
CCC
CODEN ADLAEE
ADVANCED LABANOTATION. [Adv. labanot.]. Vol. 1, Pt. 1 (1991)-. Periodical. English. £42.00. Harwood Academic Publishers, PO Box 90, Reading RG1 8JL United Kingdom. **Tel** 011 44 1734 560080, FAX 011 44 1734 568211. **ED** Ann Hutchinson Guest.
Desc: Explains step by step, and in depth, the symbols, rules and current usage of the movement notation system which originated in Germany in the 1920s and is now widely used all over the world in movement research and education with particular focus on dance.

ISSN 1063-8024
US
ALAMO AREA SQUARE AND ROUND DANCE ASSOCIATION NEWSLETTER.
Added/Corp Alamo Area Square and Round Dance Association. **VFOAT** AASRDA Newsletter. (1992)-. Newsletter. English. Twelve times a year. $7.00. Alamo Area Square and Round Dance Association, 9302 Lamerton, San Antonio TX 78250.

LC GV1587.5 .A53   ISSN 0197-6869
DD 793.3/2   US
AMERICAN DANCE DIRECTORY. [Amer. dance dir.]. **Added/Corp** Association of American Dance Companies. (1980)-. Directory. English. $10.00. Association of American Dance Companies, 162 West 56th Street, New York NY 10019-6021.

ISSN 0300-7448
US
AMERICAN DANCE GUILD NEWSLETTER. [Am. Dance Guild newsl.]. **Main/Corp** American Dance Guild. (1955)-. Newsletter. English. Four times a year (Jan., Apr., July, Sept.). Comes with American Dance Guild membership - $80.00 (institutions), $50.00 (individuals). American Dance Guild Inc., 31 West 21st Street, 3rd Floor, New York NY 10010. **Tel** (212)627-3790. **ED** Karen Deaver. **Bk Rev**, (Qty: 1). **Ad Acc. Circ:** 450.

LC RC489.D3 A42   ISSN 0146-3721
DD 615/.8515   US
CCC
NLM W1 AM45LT
AMERICAN JOURNAL OF DANCE THERAPY. See Psychology.

LC GV1763 .A58   ISSN 0091-3383
DD 793.3/4/05   US
AMERICAN SQUARE DANCE. [Am. sq. dance.]. **VFOAT** American Squaredance Magazine; American Squaredance. Vol. 27 (Jan. 1972)-. Periodical. English. Twelve times a year. $20.00. American Square Dance, 661 Middlefield Road, Salinas CA 93906. **Tel** (408)443-0761, (408)44-9724, FAX (408)443-6402. **ED** Stan Burdick and Cathie Burdick. Index available. cum. index. **Bk Rev. Ad Acc. Circ:** 24,000 (ctrl). available on microfilm and microfiche from University Microfilms International (UMI). **Continues** New Square Dance, 0091-3359.
Desc: Covers all phases of the square dance activity.

LC GV1796.F55 A56
DD 793.3/05   SP
ANUARIO FLAMENCO Y GUIA DE FESTIVALES. VFOAT Anuario Flamenco. (1988)-. Spanish. One time a year. **Continues** Guia de Festivales.

LC GV1703.N36 A7   ISSN 0148-5865
DD 792   US
ARABESQUE (NEW YORK, N.Y.). See Music.

ISSN 0882-3472
DD 792   US
ATTITUDE (BROOKLYN (NEW YORK, N.Y.)). (ATTITUDE : THE DANCERS' MONTHLY.). [Attitude]. Vol. 1, No. 1 (May 1982)-. Trade Publication. English. Four times a year. $20.00. Dance Giant Steps Inc., 1040 Park Place, Suite C-5, Brooklyn NY 11213. **Tel** (718)773-3046. **ED** Bernadine Jennings and Arthur T. Wilson; Telephone: (718)773-3046. **Bk Rev. Ad Acc. Circ:** 6,000.
Desc: Trade journal of dance news, features, and reviews of New York, written as a tool of audience development. Special emphasis on minority, ethnic and emerging dance artists.

ISSN 0889-8847
DD 792   US
ATTITUDES & ARABESQUES. [Attitudes arab.]. **Added/Corp** Mid-Peninsula Dance Guild (Calif.). **VFOAT** Attitudes and Arabesques. Vol. 1, No. 1 (May 1980)-. Periodical. English. Twelve times a year. $30.00. Mid-Peninsula Dance Guild, 1313 Newell Road, Palo Alto CA 94303. **Tel** (415)326-0775. **ED** Leslie Getz (editor's address: 1075 Marcussen Drive, Menlo Park, CA 94025, phone: (415)326-9775). **Bk Rev. Ad Acc:** 200.
Ind/Abst SPORT Discus; SportSearch (May 1987-).

LC GV1580 .A9   ISSN 0248-7845
DD 792   FR
AVANT-SCENE. BALLET/DANSE, L'.
VFOAT Avant-Scene. Ballet/Danse; Avant Scene Ballet Danse; Ballet Danse. (Jan./Mar. 1980)-. Periodical. French. Four times a year. 156F. L'Avant Scene, 6 rue Git le Couer, 75006 Paris France. **Tel** 011 33 1 46342820, FAX 011 33 1 43545014.

LC GV1787
DD 792.8084   US
BALLET. French. One time a year. Macmillan Publishing Company / New York, 866 3rd Avenue, New York NY 10022. **Tel** (212)702-2000, (800)257-5755. **(Subscription address:** Macmillan Publishing, Front and Brown Street, Riverside NJ 08075. **Tel** (800)257-5755.)

ISSN 0824-9970
DD 792.8/0971   CN
BALLET CANADA INTERNATIONAL.
[Ballet Can. int.]. Vol. 2, No. 3 (June 1982)-. Periodical. English. Four times a year. $1.50 per no. Ballet Canada International, 246 East Broadway/Suite 1, Vancouver British Columbia V5T 1W3 Canada. **Continues** Ballet Canada, 0824-9962.

US
BALLET DANCER. VFOAT Ballet Dancer Combined With Opera World. Vol. 1 (1980)-. Periodical. English. Ballet Dancer, 1170 Broadway, New York NY 10001. **Formed by the union of** Ballet Dancer **and** Opera World.

ISSN 0045-1347
CN
BALLET-HOO. Added/Corp Royal Winnipeg Ballet. Royal Winnipeg Ballet. Friends. No. 1 (Oct. 1969)-. Periodical. English. Four times a year (Mar., May, Oct., Dec.). 5.80Can$. Royal Winnipeg Ballet, 380 Graham Avenue, Winnipeg Manitoba R3C 4K2 Canada. **Tel** (204)956-0183, FAX (204)943-1994. **ED** Debbie Mennig. **Ad Acc. Circ:** 10,000 (ctrl).
Desc: A four-color glossy containing news about the artists and activities of the Royal Winnipeg Ballet, as well as dance features.

UK
BALLET IN LONDON YEARBOOK.
(1988/89)-. English. One time a year. Boland Publ, Bondway Business Centre, 71 Bondway, London SW8 1SQ United Kingdom.

LC GV1787 .B275   ISSN 0522-0653
US
CCC
BALLET REVIEW. [Ballet rev.]. **Added/Corp** Dance Research Foundation. **VFOAT** BR. Vol. 1 (1965)-. Periodical. English. Four times a year. $42.00. Dance Research Foundation Incorporated, 150 Claremont Avenue/Suite 2C, New York NY 10027. **Tel** (212)662-6515, (800)348-8001. **ED** Francis Mason. **Bk Rev. Ad Acc. Circ:** 4,000. Documents available from The Genuine Article.
Desc: Appears with historical and critical articles, interviews, catalogues of important exhibitions and photographic portfolios.
Ind/Abst Arts Humanit. Citation Index [Full Cov.]; Curr. Contents Arts Humanit.; Humanit. Index; Middle East Abstr. Index; Res. Alert [Full Cov.].

LC GV1787 .B2743   ISSN 0722-6268
DD 792.8/05   GW
TITLE CHANGE
BALLETT INTERNATIONAL. VFOAT Ballett und Tanz International; Tanz International; Ballett International Newsletter; Ballett + Tanz International. Vol. 5, No. 1 (Jan. 1982)-(1993). Trade Publication. English (German). Ballett International Verlags GmbH, PF 250126 Kartaeusergasse 36, W 5000 Cologne 1 F R Germany. **Tel** 011 49 221 316021. **ED** Rolf Garske. **Bk Rev. Ad Acc. Circ:** 12,000. Documents available from The Genuine Article. **Continues** Ballett Info. **Continued in part by** Tanz International (1993); **Merged with** Tanz Aktuell, 0933-0585 **to form** Ballett International, Tanz Aktuell, 0947-0484.
Desc: Covers all aspects of dance with an emphasis on avant-garde and ballet: historical essays, portraits, reviews, international reports, news articles and media.
Ind/Abst Arts Humanit. Citation Index (?-?) [Full Cov.]; Curr. Contents Arts Humanit. (?-?); Res. Alert (?-?) [Full Cov.]; Soc. Sci. Cit. Index (?-?) [Select. Cov.].

LC GV1787 .B2744   ISSN 0947-0484
GW
●**BALLETT INTERNATIONAL, TANZ AKTUELL. VFOAT** Ballet International/Tanz Aktuell. (1994)-. Periodical. German (English). Twelve times a year. $104.79. Erhard Friedrich Verlag, Postfach 100150, D-30917 Seelze Germany. **Tel** 011 49 511 4000452. **Formed by the union of** Ballett International. English **and** Tanz Aktuell, 0933-0585.
Desc: Covers all aspects of dance with an emphasis on avant-garde and ballet: historical essays, portraits, reviews, international reports, news articles and media.

LC GV1580 .B28   ISSN 0720-3896
DD 793.3/05   GW
BALLETT-JOURNAL/DAS TANZARCHIV. VFOAT Ballett Journal das Tanzarchiv. Vol. 1 (1981)-. Periodical. German. Four times a year. $55.27. Ulrich Steiner Verlag fur Tanzliteratur, Kielsberg 60, 5063 Overath-Immekeppel Germany. **Formed by the union of** Tanzarchiv **and** Ballett-Journal.

LC GV1787 .B278
DD 792.8/05   IT
BALLETTO OGGI. VFOAT Ballettoggi. No. 16 (Nov. 1983)-. Periodical. Italian. Six times a year. L49000. Balletto Oggi, Alzaia Naviglio, Grande 46, 20144 Milan Italy. **Tel** 011 39 2 58111192. **(Subscription address:** Italia Srl, C SO Brescia 75, 10152 Turin, Italy. **Tel** 011 39 11 2480870.) **Continues** Balletto.

UK
BALLROOM DANCING TIMES, THE. Vol. 1, No. 1 (Oct. 1956)-. Periodical. English. Twelve times a year. $31.00. Dancing Times Ltd, Clerkenwell House, 45-47 Clerkenwell Green, London EC1R 0BE United

Dance

Kingdom. **Tel** 011 44 171 2503006, FAX 011 44 171 2536679. **ED** Mary Clarke. **Bk Rev. Ad Acc. Circ:** 3,000.

ISSN 1072-5156
US

BALLROOM REVIEW, THE. (1991)-. English. Irregular (Published every 5-6 weeks). $25.00. TBR Communications Ltd., 60 Gramercy Park North, New York NY 10010. **Tel** (212)673-3442, FAX (212)673-3442. **ED** Nicholas M. Ullo. **Bk Rev. Ad Acc. Circ:** 3,000.
Desc: Feature articles cover the history of dance, dance music, and dancers. Also provides news of ballroom dance events.

LC GR142.R43 B47
DD 793.3/1942/06042293
UK

BERKSHIRE FOLK / ENGLISH FOLK DANCE AND SONG SOCIETY. See Music.

PE
BOLETIN DE MUSICA Y DANZA. See Music.

ISSN 0270-8981
US

BULLETIN - DANCE FILMS ASSOCIATION, INC. Main/Corp Dance Films Association. **VFOAT** DFA Bulletin. Jan. 1980-. Bulletin. English. Dance Films Association Inc, 1133 Broadway/Suite 507, New York NY 10010.

ISSN 0840-9633
CN
DD 793.3/09714
TITLE CHANGE

BULLETIN - REGROUPEMENT DES PROFESSIONNELS DE LA DANSE DU QUEBEC. (BULLETIN.). [Bull. - Regroup. prof. danse Qu,e]. **Added/Corp** Regroupement des Professionnels de la Danse du Quebec. **VFOAT** Bulletin du Regroupement des Professionnels de la Danse du Quebec inc; Bulletin du R.P.D.Q. (Sept. 1987)-Vol. 10, No. 1 (Feb. 1994). Bulletin. French. Regroup Professionnels Danse Quebec, 3575 boulevard St. Laurent, Bureau 818, Montreal Quebec H2X 2T7 Canada. **Tel** (514)849-4003, FAX (514)849-3288. **Continues** Regroupement des Professionnels de la Danse du Quebec (Bulletin d'information), 0845-2806. **Continued by** Bulletin (Regroupement Quebecois de la Danse), 1200-5096.

ISSN 1200-5096
CN
DD 792.8/09714/05

●**BULLETIN / REGROUPEMENT QUEBECOIS DE LA DANSE.** [Bull. - Regroup. qu,e. danse]. **Added/Corp** Regroupement Quebecois de la Danse. Vol. 10, No. 2 (July 1994)-. Periodical. French. (five or six issues per year). 25.00Can$. Regroup Professionnels Danse Quebec, 3575 boulevard St. Laurent, Bureau 818, Montreal Quebec H2X 2T7 Canada. **Tel** (514)849-4003, FAX (514)849-3288. **Continues** Bulletin (Regroupement des Professionnels de la Danse du Quebec), 0840-9633.

ISSN 0228-1767
CN
DD 793.3/0971

CANADIAN DANCE NEWS. [Can. dance news]. Vol. 1 (June 1980)-. Periodical. English. Twelve times a year. $9.95. Canadian Dance News, 155A George Street, Toronto Ontario M5A 2M8 Canada.

LC GV1580
ISSN 0843-218X
CN
DD 793.3/4/0971

CANADIAN DANCERS NEWS (1988). (CANADIAN DANCERS NEWS.). [Can. danc. news]. **Added/Corp** Canadian Square and Round Dance Society. (July 1988)-. Periodical. English. Four times a year. 8.00Can$. Canadian Dancers News, 3608 54th Avenue Southwest, Calgary Alberta T3E 5H4 Canada. **Tel** (403)246-4440, FAX (403)246-9493. **ED** John and Faye Thomson. **Ad Acc. Circ:** 1,200 (ctrl). **Continues** Canadian Dancers News Magazine, 0315-3959.
Desc: General interest reading for square and round-clogging dancing.

ISSN 0739-1994
US

CHARLES FARRELL'S DANCE BUSINESS NEWSLETTER. (CHARLES FARRELL'S DANCE BUSINESS NEWSLETTER : DBN.). **VFOAT** Dance Business Newsletter; DBN; D.B.N. (1978)-. Newsletter. English. Twelve times a year. Charles Farrell, 396 West Mayflower Place, Milford CT 06460. **Tel** (203)874-1656. available on videocassette; available on audiocassette.
Desc: For dance teachers on how to stimulate business.

LC GV1580 .C47
ISSN 0891-6381
DD 792.8/2
SZ
CCC
CODEN CHDAEO

CHOREOGRAPHY AND DANCE. [Choreog. dance]. Vol. 1 (1988)-. Periodical. English. £46.00. Harwood Academic Publishers, PO Box 90, Reading RG1 8JL United Kingdom. **Tel** 011 44 1734 560080, FAX 011 44 1734 568211. **ED** Robert P. Cohan.
Desc: Concerned with ballet and related forms of dance performed on stage, including the techniques whereby choreographers are trained. Also covers historical and social influences on dance.

ISSN 1072-9216
SW

●**CHOREOGRAPHY AND DANCE ARCHIVE.** (CHOREOGRAPHY AND DANCE ARCHIVE [VIDEORECORDING].). (1994)-. English. Harwood Academic Publishers, PO Box 90, Reading RG1 8JL United Kingdom. **Tel** 011 44 1734 560080, FAX 011 44 1734 568211.

ISSN 1053-380X
SZ
DD 792

CHOREOGRAPHY AND DANCE STUDIES. [Choreog. dance stud.]. Vol. 1 (1991)-. Monographic series. English. Price varies per volume. Harwood Academic Publishers, PO Box 90, Reading RG1 8JL United Kingdom. **Tel** 011 44 1734 560080, FAX 011 44 1734 568211. **ED** Robert P. Cohan.
Desc: Book series in which all the authors are themselves dance practitioners, either dancers or choreographers. Focuses on dance composition, its techniques and training and the relationship of choreography to other components of dance performance.

LC GV1580 .C49
KO

CHUM (SEOUL, KOREA). (CHUM.). **VFOAT** The Dance Monthly of Korea; Dance Monthly of Korea. (March 1976)-. Periodical. Korean (Korean). Twelve times a year. 18,000. Kumyonjae, 205 Tonghwa Pilting 188-7, 4-ka Myongyun-dong, Chongno-ku Seoul Korea.

US
COAL COUNTRY CRIER. See Music.

LC GV1580 .C66
ISSN 0198-9634
DD 615.8/2/05
US

CONTACT QUARTERLY. (1980)-. English. Two times a year. $25.00. Contact Quarterly, Box 603, Northampton MA 01061. **Tel** (413)586-1181, FAX (413)586-1181. **ED** Nancy Stark Smith and Lisa Nelson. Index available. **Bk Rev. Ad Acc. Circ:** 1,600. **Continues** Contact Newsletter.
Desc: A contemporary dance/movement journal focusing on current developments in the teaching, practice, and performance of new dance work worldwide.

ISSN 0193-9041
US

CONTRIBUTIONS TO THE STUDY OF MUSIC AND DANCE. See Music.

ISSN 0734-4856
US

CORD NEWSLETTER. (CORD NEWSLETTER / CONGRESS ON RESEARCH IN DANCE.). **Main/Corp** Congress on Research in Dance. **VFOAT** C.O.R.D. Newsletter. **VAT** Congress on Research in Dance Newsletter. Vol. 1, No. 1 (April 1981)-. Newsletter. English. Two times a year. It comes with the Congress on Research in Dance membership. Congress on Research in Dance, State University of New York, College at Brockport, Brockport NY 14420. **Tel** (716)395-2590, FAX (716)395-5413. **ED** Judy Van Zile. ctrl circ.
Desc: Get the calendar on the national and special topics conferences that has been established. Its great for the positions that is open, items for sale, or other information appropriate for a classified ads.

LC GV1580 .C67
ISSN 0070-1262
DD 793.3/1973
US

COUNTRY DANCE AND SONG. (COUNTRY DANCE AND SONG : THE MAGAZINE OF THE COUNTRY DANCE AND SONG SOCIETY OF AMERICA.). [Ctry. dance song]. Vol. 1 (1968)-. English. One time a year. Country Dance and Song Society, 17 New South Street, Northampton MA 01060. **Tel** (413)584-9913. available on microfilm and microfiche from University Microfilms International (UMI). **Continues** Country Dancer.
Ind/Abst Music Index.

ISSN 1070-8251
DD 793
US

COUNTRY DANCE & SONG SOCIETY NEWS. [Ctry. Dance Song Soc. news]. **Added/Corp** Country Dance and Song Society of America. **VFOAT** Country Dance and Song Society News. Issue 1 (19??)-. English. Six times a year. Free to members of the Country Dance and Song Society. Country Dance and Song Society, 17 New South Street, Northampton MA 01060. **Tel** (413)584-9913.
Ind/Abst Music Index.

ISSN 0045-9577
US

DANCE/AMERICA. Periodical. English. Four times a year. Natl Assn for Regional Ballet, 1860 Broadway/Room 410, New York NY 10019. **Tel** (212)645-0042.

LC GV1580 .D232
ISSN 0011-5983
DD 792.8/2/05
UK
CCC
SUSPENDED

DANCE AND DANCERS. VFOAT Dance & Dancers. Vol. 1 (Jan. 1950)-Suspended with Issues 516/517 (1994). Periodical. English. Twelve times a year. Dance & Dancers, 214 Panther House, 38 Mount Pleasant, London WC1X 0AP United Kingdom. **Tel** 011 44 171 8372711, FAX 011 44 171 8372711. **Bk Rev. Ad Acc.** Documents available from The Genuine Article.
Ind/Abst Arts Humanit. Citation Index [Full Cov.]; Curr. Contents Arts Humanit.; Res. Alert [Full Cov.].

LC GV1580 .D36
DD 792
US

DANCE & THE ARTS. VFOAT Dance Pages. (199?)-. Periodical. English. Six times a year. $16.00. Dance & The Arts, 200 West 72nd Street, New York NY 10023. **Tel** (212)362-8160. **Continues** Dance Pages Magazine, 1064-6183.

AT
DANCE AUSTRALIA. Vol. 1, No. 1 (Sept./Nov. 1980)-. Periodical. English (Chinese). Six times a year. 25.90Aus$. Yaffa Publishing Group Pty Ltd., GPO Box 606, Sydney New South Wales 2001 Australia. **Tel** 011 61 2 2812333, FAX 011 61 2 2812750. Index available. cum. index. **Bk Rev. Ad Acc. Circ:** 10,000.
Desc: Covers the work of major ballet and dance companies and dance education.
Ind/Abst Aust. Educ. Index (199?-).

US
DANCE BEAT. (Mar. 1990)-. Periodical. English. Twelve times a year. $30.00. Dance Beat, 12265 South Dixie Highway, Suite 909, Miami FL 33155.

ISSN 0271-9940
US

DANCE BOOK FORUM. [Dance book forum]. **Added/Corp** Dance Institute International. (1981)-. English. Four times a year. Dance Institute International, 22 West 77th Street, Suite 62, New York NY 10024. **Tel** (212)362-9921.

LC GV1580 .D233
ISSN 0147-2526
DD 793.3/05
US
CCC

DANCE CHRONICLE. [Dance chron.]. Vol. 1 (1977)-. Periodical. English. Three times a year. $325.00. Marcel Dekker Inc., 270 Madison Avenue, New York NY 10016. **Tel** (212)696-9000, (800)228-1160, FAX (212)685-4540, telex 421419. (**Subscription address:** Marcel Dekker Inc., PO Box 5017, Monticello NY 12701. **Tel** (800)228-1160). **ED** George Dorris and Jack Anderson. **Bk Rev. Ad Acc.** ctrl circ. available on microfiche. Documents available from The Genuine Article, UMI Article Clearinghouse. **Continues** Dance Perspectives, 0011-6033.
Desc: Covers aesthetics, music, theater, film, literature, painting, and dance. Contains articles from both established dance historians and the new generation of dance scholars.
Ind/Abst Acad. Search; Am. Bibliogr. Slavic East Europ. Stud.; Arts Humanit. Citation Index [Full Cov.]; Curr. Contents Arts Humanit.; EP Collect.; Expand. Acad. Index (1989-); Homework Help.; Humanit. Index; Humanit. Source; INFO-SOUTH Abstr.; Mag. Search; MasterFile FullTEXT 1000; MasterFile FullTEXT 350; MasterFile FullTEXT 650; MasterFile FullTEXT (Jan. 1993-); Music Index (-19??); Newsp. Period. Abstr. (1991-); OCLC; Phys. Educ. Index; Res. Alert [Full Cov.]; Telebase.

US
DANCE COMPANY GRANTS. (1983/84)-. English. One time a year. National Endowment for the Arts, 1100 Pennsylvania Avenue Northwest, Washington DC 20506. **Tel** (202)682-5400, (202)682-5435. **Continues** Dance Touring Program, 0160-0540; Grants to Dance Companies.

LC GV1672.5.A3 D36
ISSN 0838-1313
DD 792.8/097123
CN
SUSPENDED

DANCE CONNECTION. [Dance connect.]. **Added/Corp** Alberta Dance Alliance. (July 1984)-Suspended (Sept.-Oct. 1995). Periodical. English. Five times a year (Feb., Apr., June, Sept., Nov.). $30.00 (institutions). Dance Connection, 815 1st Street southwest #603, Calgary Alta T2P 1N3 Canada. **Tel** (403)237-7327, FAX 403)263-1707. **ED** Heather Elton. Index available. **Bk Rev**, (Qty: 5). **Ad Acc. Circ:** 5,000.
Desc: Provides a forum for written discussion about dance to develop a body of writing from Western Canada which contributes to the advancement of the field, and to document the immediate cultural landscape.

US
DANCE DIMENSIONS. Vol. 1 (Summer 1972)-. Periodical. English. Two times a year. Wisconsin Dance Council, UWEX-UWGB CCC-Studio Arts 115, Green Bay WI 54302. **Tel** (414)465-2735. **Supersedes** Wisconsin Dance Council Newsletter.

ISSN 0306-0128
UK
DANCE GAZETTE. [Dance gaz.]. (1968)-. Periodical. English. Three times a year. $33.00. Royal Academy of Dancing, 48 Vicarage Crescent, London SW11 3LT United Kingdom. **Tel** 011 44 1 223 0091.

LC GV1625 .D36 **ISSN** 0317-9737
DD 793.3/2/0971 CN
SUSPENDED
DANCE IN CANADA. [Dance Can.]. **VFOAT** Danse au Canada. No. 3 (Winter 1975)-(19??). English (French). Four times a year. 10.00Can$ Canada; 16.00Can$ other. Dance in Canada, 322 King Street West/Suite 403, Toronto Ontario M5V 1J2 Canada. **Tel** (416)595-0165, FAX (416)595-0733. **ED** Sandra Evan-Jones. **Bk Rev**. **Ad Acc**. **Circ:** 3,000 (ctrl). available on microfiche from Micromedia Limited. ***Continues*** *Dance Canada, 0318-3076.*
Desc: Glossy magazine presenting commentary on the state of Canadian dance. Contains personality profiles and articles, as well as news and reviews. Strives to cover dance comprehensively from coast to coast. Of interest to students, dancers, teachers and audience members alike.
Ind/Abst Can. Index (?-?); Phys. Educ. Index.

LC GV1580 .D2425 **ISSN** 1047-823X
DD 792.8/05 US
DANCE INK. [Dance ink]. Vol. 1 No. 1 (May/June 1990)- Vol. 4 (Apr. 1993-94)-. Periodical. English. Four times a year (Mar., June, Sept., Dec.). $20.00. Dance Ink Inc., 145 Central Park West, New York NY 10023. **Tel** (212)787-0002. **ED** Lise Friedman (Editor's telephone: 925-5993). **Photos**. **Circ:** 15,000 (ctrl).
Desc: Venue for new ideas on dancing. Photographs, observations and critical essays offer the reader a perspective on this art. A different scope than traditional dance magazines.

LC GV1580 .V34 GV1580 .D3 **ISSN** 1189-9816
DD 792.8/05 CN
•**DANCE INTERNATIONAL (VANCOUVER).** (DANCE INTERNATIONAL.). [Dance int.]. **Added/Corp** Vancouver Ballet Society. Vol. 21, No. 2 (Summer 1993)-. Periodical. English. Four times a year. 35.21Can$. Dance International, Roedde House, 1415 Barclay Street, Vancouver BC V6J 1J6 Canada. **Tel** (604)681-1525. ***Continues*** *Vandance International, 1189-9808.*

LC GV1580 .D244
DD 793.3 US
DANCE LIFE. Vol. 1, No. 2 (Fall 1975)-. English. One time a year. $2.50. D Lindner, 158 East 7th Street, New York NY 10009. ***Continues*** *Dance Life in New York, 0361-5685.*

LC GV1645 .D35
DD 793.3/1941 UK
DANCE (LONDON, ENGLAND : 1986). (DANCE.). No. 1 (1986)-. Periodical. English. £1.20. Imperial Society of Teachers of Dancing, Euston Hall, Birkenhead Street, London WC1H 8BE United Kingdom.

LC GV1580 .A53 **ISSN** 0011-6009
DD 793.3/05 US
DANCE MAGAZINE. [Dance magazine]. **VFOAT** Dancemagazine; Dance. Vol. 22, No. 6 (June 1948)-. Trade Publication. English. Twelve times a year. $34.95. Dance Magazine, 33 West 60th Street, New York NY 10023. **Tel** (212)245-9050, FAX (212)956-6487. **(Subscription address:** Neodata / Colorado, PO Box 2606, Boulder CO 80322. **) ED** Richard Philip. **Ad Acc. Circ:** 51,000. available on microfilm and microfiche from University Microfilms International (UMI). Documents available from The Genuine Article, UMI Article Clearinghouse, Magazine Collection. ***Continues*** *Dance, 0270-2215.*
Desc: Covering ballet, modern, jazz and tap nationally and internationally. For professionals, teachers, and students.
Ind/Abst Acad. Abstr.; Acad. Ind. [Computer File] (1984-); Acad. Search; Am. Bibliogr. Slavic East Europ. Stud.; Arts Humanit. Citation Index [Full Cov.]; Book Rev. Index; Curr. Contents Arts Humanit.; EP Collect.; Expand. Acad. Index (1984-); Film Lit. Index; Gen. Period. Index (1985-); Health Source Plus; Health Source; Homework Help.; Humanit. Index; Humanit. Source; INFO-SOUTH Abstr.; Mag. Artic. Summar. Elite; Mag. Artic. Summar. Select; Mag. Artic. Summar. CD-ROM; Mag. Index Plus (1989-); Mag. Index. Sel. (1986-); Mag. Search; MasterFile FullTEXT 1000; MasterFile FullTEXT 350; MasterFile FullTEXT 650; MasterFile FullTEXT (Jan. 1984-); Med. Rev. Dig.; Newsp. Period. Abstr. (1986-); OCLC; Phys. Educ. Index; Pub. Lib. FullTEXT; Read. Guide Abstr. Select Ed.; Read. Guide Period. Lit.; Res. Alert [Full Cov.]; Soc. Sci. Cit. Index [Select. Cov.]; Telebase; Mag. Index (1977-); Vocat. Search.

UK
DANCE MATTERS. English. Three times a year. £7.50 UK; £12.00 Europe; £15.00 other. National Dance Teachers Association, 29 Larkspur Avenue, Chastown Walsal WS78SR United Kingdom. **Tel** 011 44 1543 685162. **ED** Jeff Meimers (editor's address: University of Central England in Birmingham, Faculty of Education, Westbourne Road, Egbaston Birmingham England). **Bk Rev**. **Ad Acc. Circ:** 1,000.
Desc: A newsheet with articles on dance education.

LC RC489.D3 D35 **ISSN** 1064-7538
DD 615.8/5155/05 US
NLM ZWM 450.5.D2; D173
DANCE / MOVEMENT THERAPY ABSTRACTS. (DANCE/MOVEMENT THERAPY ABSTRACTS : DOCTORAL DISSERTATIONS MASTERS' THESES AND SPECIAL PROJECTS THROUGH ...). [Dance/mov. ther. abstr.]. **Added/Corp** American Dance Therapy Association. Marian Chace Memorial Fund. **VFOAT** Dance Movement Therapy Abstracts. Vol. 1 (1990)-. English. Irregular. $18.00. American Dance Therapy Association, 2000 Century Plaza, Suite 108, Columbia MD 21044. **Tel** (301)997-4040.

ISSN 1038-8931
DD 792.8099423 AT
DANCE NETWORK NEWS (ADELAIDE). (DANCE NETWORK NEWS.). [Dance netw. news (Adel.)]. **Added/Corp** Australian Association for Dance Education. S.A. Branch. (1992)-. Periodical. English. Eleven times a year. Comes with membership to Australian Association for Dance Education - 100.00Aus$ (institutions), 45.00Aus$ (individuals). Ausdance New South Wales, Pier 4 The Wharf, Hickson Road, Walsh Bay New South Wales, 2000 Australia. **Tel** 011 61 2 2414022. ***Continues*** *News - AADE SA Inc., 1031-7481.*

LC GV1587.5 .D34 **ISSN** 0190-7220
DD 793.3/025/73 US
DANCE (NEW YORK, N.Y. 1980). (DANCE.). [Dance]. 1979/80-. English. Association of American Dance Companies, 162 West 56th Street, New York NY 10019-6021.

LC GV1580 .D2317 **ISSN** 0894-4849
DD 792.8 US
DANCE (NEW YORK, N.Y. 1988). (DANCE.). [Dance]. Vol 1 (1989)-. English. One time a year. $37.50. AMS Press Inc., 56 East 13th Street, New York NY 10003. **Tel** (212)777-4700, FAX (212)995-5413, telex 710 581 2302. **ED** Lynnette Y Overby and James H Humphrey. Index available. **Bk Rev**. **Circ:** 350.
Desc: Includes all aspects of dance at research level, theoretical papers, and research reviews.

ISSN 0112-4951
DD 792.82 NZ
CCC
DANCE NEWS WELLINGTON. [Dance news Wellingt.]. (1977). Periodical. English. Three times a year. $17.91. Royal New Zealand Ballet, PO Box 10-786, Wellington 6036 New Zealand. **Tel** 011 64 4 4991107, FAX 011 64 4 4990773. **ED** B. Hyde. **Circ:** 12,000.

LC GV1580 .D1965 **ISSN** 0966-6346
UK
DANCE NOW. Vol. 1, No. 1 (Spring 1992)-. Periodical. English. Four times a year (Mar., June, Sept., Dec.). £12.50 UK; £15.00 other. Dance Books Ltd., 15 Cecil Court, London WC2N 4EZ United Kingdom. **Tel** 011 44 181 8362314, FAX 011 44 181 4970473. **ED** David Leonard and Sanjoy Roy. **Bk Rev**, (Qty: 8-10). **Ad Acc**, **Adv Mgr:** Susan Philo, **Tel** 011 44 1367 820367. **Circ:** 5,000.

LC GV1779 .D36
US
DANCE ON CAMERA NEWS / DANCE FILMS ASSOCIATION, INC. Added/Corp Dance Films Association. (19??)-. Periodical. English. Six times a year. $20.00. Dance Films Association Inc, 1133 Broadway/Suite 507, New York NY 10010.

LC GV1580 .D36 **ISSN** 1064-6183
DD 792 US
TITLE CHANGE
DANCE PAGES MAGAZINE. [Dance pages mag.]. **VFOAT** Dance Pages. Vol. 7, No. 1 (Summer 1989)-(19??). Periodical. English. Dance Pages Incorporated, PO Box 916, Ansonia Station, New York NY 10023. **Tel** (212)227-2090. ***Continues*** *Dance Pages, 0882-5211.* ***Continued by*** *Dance & The Arts.*

US
DANCE PROGRAM, THE. (197?)-. Monographic series. English. Price varies per volume. Marcel Dekker Inc., 270 Madison Avenue, New York NY 10016. **Tel** (212)696-9000, (800)228-1160, FAX (212)685-4540, telex 421419. **(Subscription address:** Marcel Dekker Inc., PO Box 5017, Monticello NY 12701. **Tel** (800)228-1160.**)**

LC GV1580 .D29 **ISSN** 0264-2875
DD 793.3/2 UK
CCC
DANCE RESEARCH. (DANCE RESEARCH : THE JOURNAL OF THE SOCIETY FOR DANCE RESEARCH.). [Dance res.]. **Added/Corp** Society for Dance Research. Vol. 1, No. 1 (Spring 1983)-. Periodical. English. Two times a year. $75.00. Oxford University Press / UK, Walton Street, Oxford OX2 6DP United Kingdom. **Tel** 011 44 1865 56767, FAX 011 44 1865 267773, telex 851/837330 OXPRES G. **(Subscription address:** Oxford University Press / USA, Journals Marketing Department, Oxford University Press, 2001 Evans Road, Cary NC 27513. **Tel** (800)451-7556, (919)677-0977, FAX (919)677-1714.**) ED** Richard Ralph. **Bk Rev**. **Ad Acc**. available on microfilm and microfiche from University Microfilms International (UMI).
Desc: Ranging from the history of European theatrical dance to dance anthropology and renaissance spectacle.

LC GV1580 .C65a **ISSN** 0149-7677
DD 793.3/07/2 US
Pr Rev.
DANCE RESEARCH JOURNAL. [Dance res. j.]. **Added/Corp** Committee on Research in Dance. Vol.7 (Fall/Winter 1974/75)-. Periodical. English. Two times a year (May and Nov.). $48.00 (individuals); $60.00 (institutions), comes with membership. Congress on Research in Dance, State University of New York, College at Brockport, Brockport NY 14420. **Tel** (716)395-2590, FAX (716)395-5413. **ED** Lynn Matluck Brooks. Index available. **Bk Rev**. **Ad Acc**. **Circ:** 1,000. Documents available from The Genuine Article, UMI Article Clearinghouse. ***Continues*** *CORD News, 0588-7356.*
Desc: Research in all aspects of dance, including related fields.
Ind/Abst Arts Humanit. Citation Index [Full Cov.]; Book Rev. Index (1986-); Curr. Contents Arts Humanit.; Expand. Acad. Index (1989-); Humanit. Index; INFO-SOUTH Abstr.; Mag. Search; Newsp. Period. Abstr. (1991-); Phys. Educ. Index; Res. Alert [Full Cov.]; SPORT Discus; SportSearch.

LC GV1580 .D323
DD 793.3/05 UK
DANCE STUDIES. Added/Corp Centre for Dance Studies (St. Peter, Jersey). Vol. 1 (1976)-. English. One time a year. £7.90. Centre for Dance Studies, Les Bois St. Peter, Jersey Channel Islands United Kingdom. **Tel** 011 44 1534 481320. **ED** Roderyk Lange. Index available. **Circ:** 1,000.
Desc: Scholarly magazine devoted to research on dance, dance anthropology, and movement notation.

UK
DANCE TEACHER. Added/Corp International Dance Teachers' Association. (19??)-. Periodical. English. Twelve times a year. $94.11. International Dance Teachers Association Ltd., 76 Bennett Road, Brighton BN2 5JL United Kingdom. **Tel** 011 44 1273 685652, 011 44 1273 685653.

LC GV1580 .D333 **ISSN** 0199-1795
DD 793.3/05 US
DANCE TEACHER NOW. [Dance teach. now]. Vol. 1 (Summer 1979)-. Periodical. English. Ten times a year. $26.00. SMW Communications Inc, 3101 Poplarwood Court, Suite 310, Raleigh NC 27604. **Tel** (919)872-7888, FAX (919)872-6888. **ED** K.C. Patrick. Index available. **Bk Rev**. **Ad Acc**. **Circ:** 7,700.
Desc: Includes dance techniques, business and health articles, plus seminars and competition calendars for teachers of all dance forms: ballet, jazz, modern, aerobic, ballroom, folk, etc.
Ind/Abst Phys. Educ. Index.

LC GV1645 .D36 **ISSN** 0264-9160
DD 793.3/0941 UK
DANCE THEATRE JOURNAL. [Dance theatre j.]. **Added/Corp** Friends of the Laban Centre. Laban Centre for Movement and Dance. Vol. 1, No. 1 (Spring 1983)-. Trade Publication. English. Four times a year. $29.09. Laban Centre for Movement and Dance, Laurie Grove, New Cross London SE14 6NW United Kingdom. **Tel** 011 44 171 6924070. **ED** Chris De Marigny. Index available. cum. index. **Bk Rev**, (Qty: Varies). **Ad Acc**, **Adv Mgr:** D Bromaue. **Circ:** 5000. Documents available from The Genuine Article. ***Continues*** *Labanews.*
Desc: Professional journal covering all aspects of contemporary dance, ballet, dance education, and training.
Ind/Abst Arts Humanit. Citation Index [Full Cov.]; Curr. Contents Arts Humanit.; Res. Alert [Full Cov.].

US
DANCE (WASHINGTON, D.C. : 1986). (DANCE / NATIONAL ENDOWMENT FOR THE ARTS.). **Added/Corp** National Endowment for the Arts. (1986)-. English. One time a year. Free on request. National Endowment for the Arts, 1100 Pennsylvania Avenue Northwest, Washington DC 20506. **Tel** (202)682-5400, (202)682-5435. ***Continues*** *Dance, Mime, 0741-3289.*

LC GV1623 .D26 **ISSN** 0193-1202
DD 793.3/07/1173 US
DANCEMAGAZINE COLLEGE GUIDE. VFOAT Dance College Guide; Dance Magazine College Guide. (1978)-. English. Every 2 years. $18.45 (per copy). DanceMagazine Inc., 33 West 60th Street, New York NY 10023. **Tel** (212)245-9050, FAX (212)956-6487.

US
DANCEVIEW. VFOAT Dance View. Vol. 9, Nos. 1-4 (June 1992)-. Periodical. English. Four times a year. $40.00. DanceView, PO Box 34435, Martin Luther King Station, Washington DC 20043. **Tel** (202)554-5818. **ED** Alexandra Tomalonis. **Bk Rev**, (Qty: 16-20). **Circ:** 600

Dance

(ctrl). *Continues Washington DanceView, 0739-4527.*
Desc: Reviews, interviews, and features about theatrical dancing.

ISSN 0011-605X
UK

DANCING TIMES. No. 1, (1894)-. Periodical. English. Twelve times a year. $62.00. The Dancing Times Ltd, 45-47 Clerkenwell Green, London EC1R 0BE United Kingdom. **Tel** 011 44 171 250 3006, FAX 011 44 171 253 6679. **ED** Mary Clarke. Index available. **Bk Rev. Ad Acc.** available on microfilm from Research Publications. Documents available from The Genuine Article.
Absorbed Ballet Annual and Year Book; Amatuer Dancer and Dancing & the Ballroom.
Desc: Covers reviews, articles, interviews, photographs, news, and student information.
Ind/Abst Arts Humanit. Citation Index [Full Cov.]; Curr. Contents Arts Humanit.; Res. Alert [Full Cov.].

ISSN 1053-5454
DD 793
US

DANCING USA. [Danc. USA]. **VFOAT** Dancing U.S.A. **VAT** Dancing, United States of America. (1989)-. Periodical. English. Six times a year (Jan./Feb., Mar./Apr., May/June, July/Aug., Sept./Oct., Nov./Dec.). $21.97. Dot Publications Inc., 10600 University Avenue Northwest, Minneapolis MN 55433. **Tel** (612)757-4414, FAX (612)757-6605. **ED** Doris Pease. **Bk Rev**, (Qty: 6). **Ad Acc, Adv Mgr:** LeAnn Bamford. *Continues* Ballroom Dancing U.S.A.
Desc: Reflects the romance of ballroom dance. Articles reminisce about big bands, ballrooms, and dance styles; tips and techniques. Source for dance CD's and tapes, apparel, shoes and where to go dancing.

ISSN 0745-3949
DD 793
US

DANCSCENE. [DancScene]. **VFOAT** Dance Scene. Vol. 1, No. 1 (Jan./Feb. 1983)-. Periodical. English. Four times a year. $24.00 US; $40.00 other. Dancscene, PO Box 801371, Dallas TX 75380-1371. **Tel** (214)750-0275. **ED** Suzanna Penn. **Bk Rev. Ad Acc. Circ:** 2,000.
Desc: This magazine carries news and features on ballroom dancers including professional and amateur competitive events with articles of technical and general interest.

ISSN 0755-7639
FR

UDC 793.32
DANSER. [Danser]. (1983)-. Periodical. French. Eleven times a year. $55.56. Sper la Societe Editrice Est, 21 rue du Faubourg St. Antoine, 75550 Paris Cedex 11 France. **Tel** 011 33 1 40026262, FAX 011 33 1 40026260. **ED** Jean Claude Dienis. cum. index. **Bk Rev. Ad Acc.** ctrl circ.

ISSN 0394-722X
IT

UDC 792.8
DANZA & DANZA. [Danza danza]. **VFOAT** Danza e Danza. (1986)-. Periodical. Italian. Ten times a year. L37470. Mediapress, Viale Premuda 42, 20129 Milan Italy. **Tel** 011 39 2 76006387.

US

DCA NEWS. VFOAT D.C.A. News. **VAT** Dance Critics Association News. Periodical. English. Irregular. Dance Critics Association, PO Box 47, Planetarium Station, New York NY 10025.

LC GV1623 .D24   **ISSN** 0363-972X
DD 338.4/7/7933202573   US

DIRECTORY OF DANCE COMPANIES. (DANCE TOURING PROGRAM. DIRECTORY OF DANCE COMPANIES.). **Added/Corp** Charles Reinhart Management, Inc. National Endowment for the Arts. National Endowment for the Arts. Dance Touring Program: Guideline for Sponsors. **VFOAT** Dance Touring Program: National Endowment for the Arts Directory of Dance Companies. (19??)-. Directory. English. Irregular. Charles Reinhart Management, 1697 Broadway, Suite 1201, New York NY 10019.

LC GV1587.5 .D57   **ISSN** 0898-4735
DD 793.3/07/1173   US

DIRECTORY OF DANCE FACULTIES IN COLLEGES AND UNIVERSITIES, U.S. AND CANADA. [Dir. dance fac. coll. univ. U. S. Can.]. **VFOAT** Directory of Dance Faculties in Colleges and Universities, United States and Canada. **VAT** Directory of Dance Faculties in Colleges and Universities, United States and Canada. (1988)-. Directory. English. Irregular. $55.00. College Music Society / CMS Publications, 202 West Spruce Street, Missoula MT 59802. **Tel** (406)728-2002, (800)729-0235, FAX (406)721-9419. **ED** Robby D. Gunstream. **Circ:** 500. available on labels.
Desc: A directory of institutions, listed in alphabetical order within each state or province. A listing by teaching specializations. Contains an international alphabetical index to graduate degrees in dance, and alphabetical listing of institutions.

LC GV1796.D57 D58   **ISSN** 0195-6728
DD 793.3/05   US

DISCOTHEQUE MAGAZINE. (19??)-. Periodical. English. Twelve times a year. Discotheque Magazine, 333 South La Cienega Boulevard, Los Angeles CA 90048.

US

DMA DANCE MUSIC AUTHORITY. See Music.

DD 301.45   US

DRUM MAJOR. See Music.

UK

EARLY DANCE DIRECTORY. Directory. English.

ISSN 0163-528X
US

FOLK DANCE DIRECTORY. Added/Corp Folk Dance Association. (19??)-. Directory. English. One time a year. $3.00 (five-year). Folk Dance Directory, PO Box 500 Midwood Station, Brooklyn NY 11230.

LC GV1587.5 .F65   **ISSN** 1081-2695
DD 793.3/025   US

●**FOLK DANCE PHONE BOOK AND GROUP DIRECTORY.** [Folk dance phone book group dir.]. **Added/Corp** Society of Folk Dance Historians. (1994)-. Directory. English. One time a year. $19.00. Society of Folk Dance Historians, 2100 Rio Grande, Austin TX 78705-5513. **Tel** (512)478-8900, FAX (512)478-9676. **ED** Ron Houston. *Continues* Folk Dance Phone Book and Directory, 1081-2814.

LC GV1623 .F64
DD 793.3/1973   US

FOLK DANCE SCENE. (19??)-. Periodical. English. Twelve times a year. $10.00. Folk Dance Scene, 1841 South Arlington Avenue, Los Angeles CA 90019. **Tel** (310)735-0535. **ED** Marvin Smith. **Ad Acc. Circ:** 1,150 (ctrl).
Desc: Official publication of Folk Dance Federation of California, South, dealing with places to dance and learn, articles of interest about ethnic cultures and related interests.

ISSN 0430-876X
DD 780   UK

FOLK DIRECTORY, THE. See Societies and Clubs.

ISSN 1074-3766
DD 781   US

FOLKALLIANCE (CHAPEL HILL, N.C.). See Music.

US

FOOTNOTES. Vol. 1 (Oct. 1950)-. Periodical. English. Ten times a year. $8.00. Footnotes, PO Box 26, Puyallup WA 98371-0003. **Tel** (206)848-6158. **ED** Kenn and Ginny Trimble. **Ad Acc. Circ:** 1,500.

LC GV1753.5 .N37a   **ISSN** 0735-9608
DD 793.3/06/073   US

HANDBOOK - NATIONAL ASSOCIATION OF SCHOOLS OF DANCE (U.S.). (HANDBOOK / NATIONAL ASSOCIATION OF SCHOOLS OF DANCE.). [Handb. - Natl. Assoc. Schools Dance (U.S.)]. **Main/Corp** National Association of Schools of Dance (U.S.). (1983)-. English. Every 2 years. $7.00. National Association of Schools of Dance, 11250 Roger Bacon Drive, Suite 21, Reston VA 22090. **Tel** (703)437-0700. **ED** David Bading. **Circ:** 500.
Desc: Standards for accreditation for educational programs in dance.

LC WMLC 93/262   **ISSN** 0741-9384
US

HORA (NEW YORK, N.Y.). (HORA.). **Added/Corp** American Zionist Youth Foundation. Vol. 1 (Fall 1968)-. Periodical. English. Two times a year. $3.00. American Zionist Youth Foundation, 110 East 59th Street, New York NY 10022. **Tel** (212)318-6123. **ED** Ruth Goodman Burger and Honey Goldfein-Perry. **Circ:** 5,000. *Continues* Hora (New York : 1962).
Desc: A review of Israeli and Jewish dance news and events.

ISSN 1073-7952
DD 613   US

●**IDEA FITNESS MANAGER FOR OWNERS, PROGRAM DIRECTORS, AND MANAGERS.** See Health-Physical Fitness and Hygiene.

ISSN 1068-087X
DD 796   US

IDEA PERSONAL TRAINER. See Health-Physical Fitness and Hygiene.

LC RA781.15 .D36   **ISSN** 1040-8126
DD 613.7/1/05   US

IDEA TODAY. See Health-Physical Fitness and Hygiene.

ISSN 1063-8520
US
CCC

NLM W1; IM66M
●**IMPULSE (CHAMPAIGN, ILL.).** (IMPULSE.). (1993)-. Periodical. English. Four times a year (Jan., Apr., July, Oct.). $90.00. Human Kinetics Publishers Inc., 1607 North Market Street, PO Box 5076, Champaign IL 61825-5076. **Tel** (217)351-5076, FAX (217)351-2674. **ED** Luke Kahlich. Index available (Included in Oct. issue).
Desc: Publishes the latest in original research articles and scholarly review articles on dance and dance-related issues.

ISSN 0883-9956
CEASED

IN DANCE. Added/Corp San Francisco Bay Area Dance Coalition. (19??)-(19??). Periodical. English. San Francisco Bay Area Dance Coalition, 44 Page Street, Suite 604C, San Francisco CA 94102. **Tel** (415)252-6240. **ED** Daphne Powell. **Bk Rev. Ad Acc. Circ:** 5,000 (ctrl).
Desc: Features articles on dance or dance-related fields and a monthly calendar of dance events in the San Francisco Bay area.

US

INTERNATIONAL DICTIONARY OF BALLET. (1992)-. English. $230.00. St. James Press, An Imprint of Gale Research Inc., PO Box 33477, Detroit MI 48232-5477. **Tel** (800)345-0392. **ED** Martha Bremser.
Desc: Offers a historical perspective on ballet from the Renaissance to the present. Features 550 illustrations, including historical photographs and lithographs; essays by distinguished authorities; and more.

LC GV1705 .I58 GV1705 .I58   **ISSN** 1045-8042
DD 792.8/096   US

INTERNATIONAL JOURNAL OF AFRICAN DANCE. [Int. j. Afri. dance]. **Added/Corp** Institute for African Dance Research and Performance. Vol. 1, No. 1 (Spring 1992)-. Periodical. English. One time a year (Spring & Winter). $36.00. Institute for African Dance Research and Performance, 814 Gladfelter Hall 025-26, Temple University, Philadelphia PA 19122. **Tel** (215)787-8448, (215)787-8626.

LC GV1580 .I56
UK

INTERNATIONAL WORKING PAPERS ON DANCE. Added/Corp Laban Centre for Movement and Dance. **VFOAT** International Working Papers in Dance Studies, Laban Centre. (1991)-. Monographic series. English. One time a year. $27.37. Laban Centre for Movement and Dance, Laurie Grove, New Cross London SE14 6NW United Kingdom. **Tel** 011 44 171 6924070. **Circ:** 200. *Continues* Working Papers in Dance Studies.
Desc: Work in progress on dance scholar's research.

LC ML3712 .J28   **ISSN** 0890-8672
DD 785.4/1/0946   US

JALEO. See Music.

ISSN 0730-3084
US

JOPERD. See Education-Physical Education and Training.

LC GV1588.6 .J68   **ISSN** 0891-7124
DD 793.3/1
Pr Rev.

JOURNAL FOR THE ANTHROPOLOGICAL STUDY OF HUMAN MOVEMENT AT NEW YORK UNIVERSITY. See Anthropology.

LC ML5 .M124
II

JOURNAL OF THE MUSIC ACADEMY, MADRAS, THE. See Music.

IT

JULIET ART MAGAZINE. See The Arts-Art.

LC RC1220.D35 K56   **ISSN** 1058-7438
DD 612   US
NLM W1; KI635I
Pr Rev.   CEASED

KINESIOLOGY AND MEDICINE FOR DANCE. [Kinesiol. med. dance]. Vol. 12, No. 1 (Fall/Winter 1990)-(1994). Periodical. English. Two times a year. A Cappella Books, PO Box 380, Pennington NJ 08534. **Tel** (609)737-6525, FAX (609)737-3787. **ED** Robin Chmelar. **Bk Rev**, (Qty: 7-8). **Ad Acc. Circ:** 600. *Continues* Kinesiology for Dance, 0731-2504.
Ind/Abst Phys. Educ. Index (1991-1994); SPORT Discus.

Dance

LC GV1786.K6 K64A
DD 792.8/09489   DK
KONGELIGE DANSKE BALLET : PROGRAM, DEN. Main/Corp Kongelige Danske Ballet. **VFOAT** Royal Danish Ballet. (19??)-. Danish (English). One time a year.

ISSN 0888-1286
DD 792   US
LANGUAGE OF DANCE SERIES. [Lang. dance ser.]. No. 1 (1987)-. Monographic series. English. Price varies per volume. Gordon & Breach Science Publishers, Inc., PO Box 786, Cooper Station, New York NY 10276. **Tel** (212)206-8900, **FAX** (212)645-2459. **ED** Ann Hutchinson Guest, Ray Cook.
Desc: Offers great works of dance from a range of periods. Each book contains a labanotated score, historical context, and the choreographic significance of the piece, as well as study and performance notes and some sheet music.

LC GV1580 .L4   ISSN 0024-1253
DD 793.305   US
LET'S DANCE. [Let's dance]. **Added/Corp** Folk Dance Federation of California. (1944)-. Periodical. English. Ten times a year (May/June and July/August issues combined). $15.00. Folk Dance Federation of California, PO Box 1282, Alameda CA 94501. **Tel** (510)814-9282. **ED** Genevieve Pereira. Index available. **Bk Rev,** (Qty: occasionally). **Ad Acc. Circ:** 700 (ctrl).
Continues Federation Folkdancer.
Desc: Dance descriptions, costume information, where to dance and folkdancing in general.

LC GV1763 .L38   ISSN 0301-8881
DD 793.3/4/06242   UK
LET'S SQUARE DANCE. [Let's square dance]. (19??)-. Periodical. English. Twelve times a year. British Association of American Square Dance Clubs, 2 Tolmero Cuffley Potters Bar, Hertfordshire 3N6 4JE United Kingdom.

LC PN2000   ISSN 1073-7103
DD 792   US
●**LIMON JOURNAL.** [Limon j.]. **Added/Corp** Limon Institute. Vol. 1, No. 1 (Summer 1993)-. Periodical. English. Four times a year. $5.00. Jose Limon Dance Foundation, 622 Broadway, Suite 5B, New York NY 10012. **Tel** (212)777-3353.

ISSN 1202-5356
DD 787.2/162/009715   CN
MARITIME FIDDLER, THE. See Music.

ISSN 1183-5443
DD 793.9   CN
MECHA-PRESS. [Mecha-press]. Vol. 1, No. 1 (Mar./Apr. [1991])-. Periodical. English. Six times a year. $3.95 (single issue). Mecha-Press, Studio 210, 2360 De Lasalle Avenue, Montreal Quebec H1V 2L1 Canada.

LC RA781.15. .I57a
DD 613.7/1/06073   US
MEMBERSHIP DIRECTORY. See Health-Physical Fitness and Hygiene.

ISSN 0199-1221
    US
MODERN SQUARE, THE. Added/Corp Arkansas State Square Dance Federation. (19??)-. Periodical. English. Twelve times a year. Modern Square, 5508 Crescent Drive, North Little Rock AR 72118.

LC GV1587 .L28
DD 793.3   UK
MOVEMENT AND DANCE : MAGAZINE OF THE LABAN GUILD. Added/Corp Laban Guild. No. 68 (May 1982)-. Periodical. English. Four times a year (Feb., Mat, Aug., Nov.). £12.50 UK; £15.00 other. Movement and Dance, 30 Ringsend Road, Limavady County, Derry BT49 0QJ United Kingdom. **Tel** 011 44 50 4762120. **ED** Lydia Everett. **Bk Rev,** (Qty: 4). **Ad Acc. Circ:** 600 (ctrl). **Continues** Magazine (Laban Art of Movement Guild).
Desc: Current use of Laban in movement and dance. Includes analysis of movement, therapy and recreative dance reviews of practical and philosophical work.

ISSN 1077-0933
DD 792   US
MOVEMENT RESEARCH PERFORMANCE JOURNAL. [Mov. Res. perform. j.]. **Added/Corp** Movement Research (New York, N.Y.). **VFOAT** Movement Research; Performance Journal. (1990)-. Periodical. English. Twenty-four times a year. $25.00. Movement Research Inc., PO Box 794 Village Station, New York NY 10014.

LC ML5 .M6447
DD 780/.5   IS
MUSIC IN TIME. See Music.

LC ML5 .M98917   ISSN 0166-0535
DD 780/.5   NE
MUZIEK & DANS. See Music.

ISSN 0845-4639
DD 792.8/0971   CN
NATIONAL BALLET MAGAZINE. [Natl. ballet mag.]. **Added/Corp** O'Keefe Centre. (1986)-. Periodical. English. Three times a year. 8.00Can$. St. Clair Group, 30 St Clair Avenue West/Suite 805, Toronto Ontario M4V 3A1 Canada. **Tel** (416)926-7595. **Separated from** Performance (Toronto, Ont.), 0229-7965.

LC GV1587.5 .N38
DD 792.8/079   US
NATIONAL DANCE ASSOCIATION'S DANCE SCHOLARSHIP GUIDE. Added/Corp National Dance Association. **VFOAT** Dance Scholarship Guide; NDA Dance Scholarship Guide. (1991)-. English. National Association of Schools of Dance, 11250 Roger Bacon Drive, Suite 21, Reston VA 22090. **Tel** (703)437-0700.

LC GV1623 .N397   ISSN 0196-0040
DD 793.3/4/02573   US
NATIONAL SQUARE DANCE DIRECTORY. (19??)-. Directory. English. One time a year. $12.00. National Square Dance Directory, PO Box 54055, Jackson MS 39288. **Tel** (601)825-6831. **ED** Gordon J. Goss. **Bk Rev. Ad Acc. Circ:** 20,000.
Desc: Listings on over 10,000 square, round, country, and clogging clubs in the United States, Canada, and around the world. Other square dancing information included.

LC GV1580.N48   ISSN 1040-8908
DD 792   CEASED
NEW DANCE REVIEW, THE. [New dance rev.]. (1988)-(Winter 1995). Periodical. English. New Dance Review, 32 West 82nd Street #2F, New York NY 10024. **Tel** (212)799-9057. **ED** Anita Finkel. **Bk Rev,** (Qty: 1-2). **Ad Acc. Circ:** 600.
Desc: Contains critical commentaries on dance and dance-related subjects such as ice skating, interviews, photos and reviews.
Ind/Abst Acad. Search; EP Collect.; Homework Help.; Humanit. Source; MasterFile FullTEXT 1000; MasterFile FullTEXT 350; MasterFile FullTEXT 650; MasterFile FullTEXT (July 1994-) [Full Txt.]; OCLC; Pub. Lib. FullTEXT; Telebase; Vocat. Search.

ISSN 0277-514X
    US
NEW PERFORMANCE. [New perform.]. Vol. 1 (Fall 1977)-. Periodical. English. Three times a year. $10.00 (individuals), $20.00 (institutions) US; $13.00 (individuals), $23.00 (institutions) other. New Performance, c/o San Francisco Dance Management, One 14th Street, San Francisco CA 94103.

ISSN 1060-3972
DD 792   US
ON POINTE. (ON POINTE: THE MAGAZINE FOR YOUNG DANCE ENTHUSIASTS.). [On pointe]. (1992)-. Periodical. English. Six times a year. Solebury Press, PO Box 512, Solebury PA 18963. **Tel** (215)297-0499.

ISSN 0384-5052
    US
ONTARIO FOLKDANCER. Added/Corp Ontario Folk Dance Association. Vol. 4, No. 2 (Apr. 1973)-. Periodical. English. Irregular (every 6 weeks except during the Summer). 16.01Can$. Ontario Folk Dance Association, 22 Latimer Avenue, Toronto Ontario M5N 2L8 Canada. **Tel** (416)489-1621. **ED** Karen Bennett (editor's address: 45 Carlton Street, Apt. 312, Toronto M5B 2H9 Canada; editor's phone: (416)979-3191). Index available. cum. index. **Bk Rev,** (Qty: 1-5). **Ad Acc, Adv Mgr:** Margaret Whelan, **Tel** (416)249-2892. **Circ:** 400 (ctrl). **Continues** Ontario Folk Dance Association. Newsletter, 0384-5044.
Desc: Information on current happenings in the local and international folk dance world. Contains articles on many aspects of folk music and dance.

ISSN 0891-3447
    US
OPEN SQUARES, THE. (THE OPEN SQUARES : PROMENADE OF SOUTHERN CALIFORNIA SQUARE DANCE EVENTS.). (19??)-. Periodical. English. Ten times a year (monthly with combined June/July and Dec./Jan.). $10.00. Open Squares, 9626 Lurline Ave., Unit A, Chatsworth CA 91311. **Tel** (818)993-4648. **ED** Lea and Jim Veronica. **Ad Acc. Circ:** 5,000 (ctrl).

LC ML5 .A22
DD 782.1/05   UK
●**OPERA HOUSE : THE MAGAZINE OF THE ROYAL BALLET, THE ROYAL OPERA AND THE BIRMINGHAM ROYAL BALLET. See** Music.

LC GV1595 .P46   ISSN 0160-5550
DD 793.3/1973   US
PEOPLE'S FOLK DANCE DIRECTORY. (1978)-. Directory. English. Every 3 years. $5.00, $3.25 ten or more copies. People's Folk Dance Directory, PO Box 8575, Austin TX 78713. **Tel** (512)454-0175. **ED** John Steele and Susan Hovorka. **Bk Rev. Ad Acc. Circ:** 4,000.
Desc: Lists international folk dance groups, meeting times and places, contact people, businesses, teachers, camps, publications. Covers North America, references sources of information internationally.

LC GV1580   ISSN 1193-3968
DD 792.8/0971   CN
PERFORMER (TORONTO). (PERFORMER.). [Performer]. **Added/Corp** National Ballet of Canada. Vol. 1, No. 1 (Fall 1991)-. Periodical. English. Three times a year. Free. National Ballet of Canada, 157 King Street East, Toronto Ontario M5C 1G9 Canada. **Tel** (416)362-1041. **Continues** Front Page News., 0838-9268.

LC GV1796.P55 M53   ISSN 0273-6454
DD 793.3/3   US
POLKA NEWS, THE. Vol. 10, No. 21 (Nov. 12, 1980)-. Periodical. English. Six times a year. $17.00. Polka News, PO Box 57, St Charles MI 48655. **Tel** (517)865-6710. **ED** Carl Rohwetter. **Bk Rev. Ad Acc. Circ:** 6,000. **Continues** Michigan Polka News, 0732-3344.
Desc: A newspaper of, for, and about music that originated in Europe; communication of news and events.

LC GV1580 .R43   ISSN 0752-5729
DD 793.3/05   FR
RECHERCHE EN DANSE, LA. Added/Corp Universite de Paris IV: Paris-Sorbonne. No. 1 (June 1982)-. Periodical. French. Association-Danse Sorbonne, 2 rue Francis de Croisset, 75018 Paris France. **Tel** 33 (1)46068290. Index available. **Bk Rev. Ad Acc. Circ:** 500.
Ind/Abst Arts Humanit. Citation Index (19??-19??) [Full Cov.]

ISSN 1061-8120
DD 793   US
RICHMOND DANCE NEWS. [Richmond dance news]. **Added/Corp** United States Amateur Ballroom Dancing Association. Richmond Chapter. (19??)-. Periodical. English. Twelve times a year. $6.00. USABDA, Richmond Chapter, 4020 Berrybrook Drive, Richmond VA 23234. **Tel** (804)276-1262.

LC GV1755 .R69
DD 793.3/3   US
ROUND DANCER MAGAZINE. VFOAT Round Dancer. (Oct. 1979)-. Periodical. English. Ten times a year (monthly except Feb. & Aug.). $22.00. Round Dancer, Rural Route 1 Box 843, Petersburg PA 16669. **Tel** (814)667-2530. **ED** Brian and Sharon Bassett. **Ad Acc, Adv Mgr:** Brian Bassett. **Circ:** 3,000 (ctrl). **Continues** Round Dancer, 0458-5108.

LC GV1763 .R67   ISSN 0485-5140
DD 793.3/4/062776   US
UDC 793.94(776)
ROUNDUP (MINNEAPOLIS, MINN.), THE. (THE ROUNDUP.). (1948)-. Periodical. English. Twelve times a year. $7.00. Square Dance Federation of Minnesota Inc, 3312 Oakland Avenue South, Minneapolis MN 55407. **ED** M Yalley. Index available. **Ad Acc. Circ:** 3,000 (ctrl).
Desc: Specialized magazine for round, folk, clogging, square, dancing for the state of Minnesota.

    FR
SAISONS DE LA DANSE, LES. No. 218 (Nov. 1990)-. Periodical. French. Twelve times a year. 300.00F (surface mail) France; 360.00F (surface mail), 386.00F (airmail) other. Les Saisons de la Danse, 7 Avenue Rachel, 75018 Paris France. **Tel** 011 33 1 48247540, **FAX** 011 33 1 48241202. **Continues** Saisons Nouvelles de la Danse.

ISSN 0749-6435
DD 793   US
SALOME (CHICAGO, ILL.). (SALOME.). [Salome]. Vol. 1, No. 1/2 (Fall/Winter 1976)-. Periodical. English. $12.00. Salome, 5548 N Sawyer, Chicago IL 60625. **Tel** (312)539-5745. **ED** Effie Mihopoulos. **Bk Rev. Ad Acc. Circ:** 1,000.
Desc: An arts magazine with a focus on dance, containing reviews of performances, records, etc. Includes interviews with dancers, choreographers, and writers.

ISSN 1202-3191
DD 787.2/162/0097169   CN
SILVER APPLE NEWS. See Music.

LC GV1580 .D247
DD 791/.025   US
STERN'S PERFORMING ARTS DIRECTORY. VFOAT Performing Arts Directory. (1989)-. Directory. English. One time a year (Sept.). $68.50. Dance Magazine, 33 West 60th Street, New York NY 10023. **Tel** (212)245-9050, **FAX** (212)956-6487. **(Subscription address:** Neodata / Colorado, PO Box 2606, Boulder CO 80322.) **ED** William James Lawson. **Ad Acc. Circ:** 10,000. **Continues** Performing Arts Directory (New York, N.Y.).

Dance

LC GV1601 .S78
DD 792.8/09
Pr Rev.
ISSN 1043-7592
US

STUDIES IN DANCE HISTORY. [Stud. dance hist.]. **Added/Corp** Society of Dance History Scholars (U.S.). **VFOAT** Dance History. Vol. 1, No. 1 (Fall/Winter 1989)-. Academic Scholarly Publication. English. Two times a year (Mar., Oct.). $62.50. Society of Dance History, Dance Program, University of Minnesota, 108 Norris Hall, Minneapolis MN 55455. **ED** Lynn Garafola **Bk Rev. Ad Acc. Adv Mgr** Susan F.. Binding. Full Page $300.00. Documents available from InCover, also available in microform from RPI.
Desc: Covers the history of dance.
Ind/Abst Hist. Abstr. (1993)- ; Amer. Hist. & Life (1993) -.

LC ML3526 .T34
DD 785.4/1
ISSN 0194-1771
US

TALENT & BOOKING'S DISCO. See Music.

DD 613
Pr Rev.
ISSN 0890-1597
US

TENNESSEE JOURNAL OF HEALTH, PHYSICAL EDUCATION, RECREATION, AND DANCE. See Education-Physical Education and Training.

LC GV1580 .A83a
DD 793.3/05
ISSN 0884-3198
US

UCLA JOURNAL OF DANCE ETHNOLOGY. [UCLA j. danc. ethnol.]. **Added/Corp** University of California, Los Angeles. Dept. of Dance. **VFOAT** Journal of Dance Ethnology; Dance Ethnology. **VAT** University of California, Los Angeles Journal of Dance Ethnology. Vol. 8 (1984)-. English. One time a year (Jan.). $18.00. Journal of Dance Ethnology, University of California, Department of Dance, Los Angeles CA 90024. **Tel** (310)825-3951, FAX (310)825-7507. Index available. **Bk Rev. Circ:** 250 (ctrl). **Continues** Journal of the Association of Graduate Dance Ethnologists U.C.L.A., 0273-2068.
Desc: Series of articles addressing dance in a cultural setting. Includes discussion in a dance notation section, notes on resumes, several book reviews, and information on the annual dance ethnology conference.

LC GV1580 .V34
DD 792.8/05
ISSN 1189-9808
CN
TITLE CHANGE

VANDANCE INTERNATIONAL. [Vandance int.]. **Added/Corp** Vancouver Ballet Society. **VFOAT** Vandance. (1992)-(1993). Periodical. English. Dance International, Roedde House, 1415 Barclay Street, Vancouver BC V6J 1J6 Canada. **Tel** (604)681-1525. **Continues** Vandance, 0705-8063. **Continued by** Dance International (Vancouver, B.C.), 1189-9816.
Desc: Provides national and international dance coverage.

LC GV1787 .W67
DD 792.8/05
UK

●**WORLD BALLET AND DANCE.** (1990)-. English. One time a year. Oxford University Press / UK, Walton Street, Oxford OX2 6DP United Kingdom. **Tel** 011 44 1865 56767, FAX 011 44 1865 267773, telex 851/837330 OXPRES G.

ISSN 0144-1205
UK

YEARBOOK (ROYAL BALLET). (YEARBOOK / THE ROYAL BALLET AND SADLER'S WELLS ROYAL BALLET.). [Yearb. R. Ballet, Sadler's Wells R. Ballet]. **Added/Corp** Royal Ballet. Sadler's Wells Royal Ballet. (19??)-. English. One time a year. Friends of Covent Garden Limited, Royal Opera House, Covent Garden, London WC2E 9DD United Kingdom. **Tel** 011 44 71 2401200 Ext. 268. **Continues** Souvenir Book (Royal Ballet).

ABSTRACTING, BIBLIOGRAPHIES AND STATISTICS

LC Z7514.D2 N462a GV1594
DD 016.7933
ISSN 0360-2737
US

BIBLIOGRAPHIC GUIDE TO DANCE.
Main/Corp New York Public Library. Dance Collection. 1st (1975)-. English. One time a year. $490.00. GK Hall & Co., 100 Front Street, Riverside NJ 08075. **Tel** (800)257-5755 ext. 2223. **ED** G K Hall.
Desc: Lists material cataloged by the NYPL Dance Collection, the most comprehensive archive of material relating to dance ever assembled on location.

DENTISTRY

DD 610.69/52/062714
UDC 616.314(714)
ISSN 0384-5915
CN

A C P D Q BULLETIN. **Main/Corp** Association of Councils of Physicians and Dentists of Quebec. Vol. 1, No. 2 (May 1975)-. Bulletin. English. Association of Councils of Physicians and Dentists of Quebec, 306 St. Joseph boulevard East, Montreal Quebec H2T 1J2 Canada. **Continues** A C M D Q Bulletin, 0383-8579.

DD 617
NLM W1; AA101AE
ISSN 1071-9776
US

AACD JOURNAL. (AACD JOURNAL / AMERICAN ACADEMY OF COSMETIC DENTISTRY.). [AACD j.]. **Added/Corp** American Academy of Cosmetic Dentistry. (19??)-. Periodical. English. Four times a year. $100.00. American Academy of Cosmetic Dentistry, 270 Corporate Drive, Madison WI 53714. **Tel** (608)241-5857.

LC RK37 .A24A
DD 617/.522/006073
UDC 616.31-089(060.21)(73)
NLM WU 22; AA1 A512
ISSN 0738-2375
US

AAOMS DIRECTORY / AMERICAN ASSOCIATION OF ORAL AND MAXILLOFACIAL SURGEONS. [AAOMS dir.]. **Main/Corp** American Association of Oral and Maxillofacial Surgeons. **VFOAT** A.A.O.M.S. Directory. **VAT** American Association of Oral and Maxillofacial Surgeons Directory. 1982-. Directory. English. One time a year. American Association of Oral and Maxillofacial Surgeons, 9700 West Bryn Mawr, Rosemont IL 60018. **Continues** American Association of Oral and Maxillofacial Surgeons. Membership Directory, 0162-1483.

DD 617
ISSN 1050-0758
US

ACCESS (CHICAGO, ILL.). (ACCESS : THE NEWSMAGAZINE OF THE AMERICAN DENTAL HYGIENISTS' ASSOCIATION.). [Access]. **Added/Corp** American Dental Hygienists' Association. (19??)-. Trade Publication. English. Ten times a year. $40.00. American Dental Hygienists' Association, 444 North Michigan Avenue, Suite 3400, Chicago IL 60611. **Tel** (312)440-8900. **Continues** ADHA Access, 0894-9042.

NLM W1; AC7836
ISSN 0120-9906
CK

ACTA CLINICA ODONTOLOGICA. (ACTA CLINICA ODONTOLOGICA : ORGANO DE DIFUSION ACADEMICA DE SOCIEDAD ANTIOQUENA DE ENDODONCISTAS ... ET AL.). [Acta clin. odontol.]. **Added/Corp** Sociedad Antioquena de Endodoncistas. Vol. 3, No. 5 (198?)-. Periodical. Spanish. Two times a year. $12.00 US; $6.00 other. Biblioteca University of Antioquia, Apartado Aereo 53232, Medellin Colombia. **Tel** 57 4 263 5411. **Continues** Revista Nacional de Endodoncia.
Ind/Abst Index Dent. Lit. (Vol. 7, No. 13/14, 1984-).

NLM W1 AC789M
ISSN 0252-1032
DR
SUSPENDED

ACTA DE ODONTOLOGIA PEDIATRICA. [Acta odontol. pediatr.]. **Added/Corp** Centro de Odontologia Pediatrica (Santo Domingo, Dominican Republic). Vol. 1, No. 1 (June 1980)-. Periodical. English (Spanish). Two times a year. $25.00. Centro Odontologia Pediatrica, PO Box 2753, Santo Domingo Dominican Republic. **Tel** (809)689-4277. **ED** Federico Garcia-Godoy Jr. Full Page (B&W) $RD780.00. Full Page (Color) $RD1240.00.
Ind/Abst Curr. Titles Dent.; Health Plan. Adminis.; Index Dent. Lit. (1981-).

NLM W1; AC875
ISSN 0326-4815
AG
CODEN AOLAEN

ACTA ODONTOLOGICA LATINOAMERICANA. (ACTA ODONTOLOGICA LATINOAMERICANA : AOL.). [Acta odontol. latinoam.]. **VFOAT** AOL. Vol. 1, No. 1 (1984)-. Periodical. English (Spanish and Portuguese; summaries and/or abstracts in Spanish). Two times a year. $32.00. Acta Odontologica Latinoamericana, La Pampa 2487 University, 1428 Buenos Aires Argentina. **Tel** 011 54 1 7847007. Documents available from BIOSIS Document Express.
Ind/Abst Biol. Abstr. (1984-); Curr. Titles Dent.; Index Dent. Lit. (1984-).

NLM W1 AC876
Pr Rev.
ISSN 0001-6357
NO
CCC
CODEN AOSCAQ

ACTA ODONTOLOGICA SCANDINAVICA. [Acta odontol. Scand.]. Vol. 1 (1939)-. Periodical. Multiple languages (English, German and French). Six times a year. $220.00. Scandinavian University Press, PO Box 2959 Toeyen, N 0608 Oslo 6 Norway. **Tel** 011 47 2 2575400, FAX 011 47 2 2575353, telex 71896 UROR N. (**Subscription address:** Scandinavian University Press, 200 Meacham Ave., Elmont NY 11003. **Tel** (516)352-7300, FAX (516)352-7377.) **ED** Ivar A Mjoer. Index available. **Bk Rev. Ad Acc. Circ:** 1,000. Documents available from The Genuine Article, BIOSIS Document Express, CASDDS.
Desc: Presents dental research in the Scandinavian countries to an international forum. Sponsored by the Dental Associations and Dental School in Scandinavia.
Ind/Abst Biol. Abstr.; Calcium Calcif. Tissue Abstr.; Chem. Abstr.; Curr. Cit.; Curr. Contents Clin. Med.; Curr. Titles Dent.; EMBASE; Energy Res. Abstr.; Health Plan. Adminis.; Index Med.; Index Dent. Lit.; Life Sci. Collect.; Res. Alert [Full Cov.]; Rev. Med. Vet. Mycology; Sci. Cit. Index; SCISEARCH.

NLM W1 AC949L
ISSN 0001-7000
BE
CODEN ASBEBA

ACTA STOMATOLOGICA BELGICA. [Acta stomatol. Belg.]. **Added/Corp** Societe Royale Belge de Stomatologie et de Chirugie Maxillo-Faciale. Societe Belge de Stomatologie. Societe Belge d'Orthopedie Dento-Faciale. Societe Royale Belge de Stomatologie. Vol. 57 (1960)-. Periodical. French (Dutch; summaries and/or abstracts in English and German). Four times a year. 1800F Belgium; 2000F other. Association for the Society of Scientifique Medica Belgique, Avenue Circulaire 138A, B-1180 Brussels Belgium. **Tel** 011 32 2 3745158. **ED** J. Van Reck (editor's address: 20 Rue de la Prison, 1310 Lahulpe Belgium). Index Available, published regularly, free-automatically sent. **Bk Rev. Ad Acc. Circ:** 1,500. Documents available from BIOSIS Document Express. **Continues** Revue Belge de Stomatologie.
Desc: Covers oral medicine and oral pathology. Official publication of the Stomatology Association.
Ind/Abst Biol. Abstr.; Curr. Cit.; Curr. Titles Dent.; EMBASE; Health Plan. Adminis.; Index Med.; Index Dent. Lit.; Life Sci. Collect.

NLM W1 AC949N
ISSN 0001-7019
CI

ACTA STOMATOLOGICA CROATICA. [Acta stomatol. croat.]. Vol. 1 (1966)-. Periodical. Serbo-Croatian (Roman). Four times a year. $42.80. Hrvatski Lijecnicki Zbor, Vinogradska 97, 4100 Zagreb Croatia. (**Subscription address:** Mladost Export Import, Borongajska 69, 41000 Zagreb Croatia. **Tel** 011 385 1 221488, 011 385 1 215853.)
Ind/Abst Health Plan. Adminis.; Index Dent. Lit.

NLM W1 AC996
ISSN 0001-7817
FR
CODEN ACOPAR

ACTUALITES ODONTO-STOMATOLOGIQUES. [Actual. odonto-stomatol.]. (19??)-. Periodical. French. One time a year. $217.63. UD Union Distributor, 106 rue du Petit LeRoy, F 94550 Chevilly LaRue France. **Tel** 011 33 1 41802020. cum. index. **Ad Acc.** ctrl circ. Documents available from BIOSIS Document Express, CASDDS.
Ind/Abst Biol. Abstr.; Chem. Abstr.; Curr. Titles Dent.; Health Plan. Adminis.; Index Dent. Lit.; Life Sci. Collect.

DD 617.6/006/27123
ISSN 0849-5866
CN

ADA NEWSLETTER (EDMONTON). (ADA NEWSLETTER.). [ADA newsl.]. **Added/Corp** Alberta Dental Association. **VFOAT** A.A.D.A. News. **VAT** Alberta Dental Association Newsletter. (1989)-. Newsletter. English. ADA News Information, 611 Medical Centre, 906 8th Avenue SW, Calgary Alberta T2P 1H9 Canada. **Continues** ADA News Information., 0383-6355.

DD 617
ISSN 1053-2668
US

ADEPT REPORT, THE. [ADEPT rep.]. Vol. 1, No. 1 (Winter 1990)-. Periodical. English. Four times a year (Seasonally). $64.00. ADEPT Report Publishing Co., PO Box 5433, Santa Rosa CA 95402. **Tel** (707)544-2586, FAX (707)575-4033. **ED** Harry F. Albers, DDS (editor's address: 2636 Knob Hill Drive, Santa Rosa, CA 95404 phone: (707)544-2586). **Bk Rev.** ctrl circ.
Desc: Newsletter addressing esthetic and adhesive dentistry issues.

LC RK91 .A582a
DD 617.6/007/117
NLM WU 19 A238
Pr Rev.
ISSN 0091-729X
US

ADMISSION REQUIREMENTS OF U.S. AND CANADIAN DENTAL SCHOOLS. [Admiss. requir. U. S. Can. dent. sch.]. **Main/Corp** American Association of Dental Schools. **Added/Corp**

American Dental Association. Council on Dental Education. **VAT** Admission Requirements of United States and Canadian Dental Schools. (1975)-. English. One time a year (Aug.). $25.00. American Association of Dental Schools, 1625 Massachusetts Avenue Northwest, Washington DC 20036. **Tel** (202)667-9433, FAX (202)667-0642. Index Bound in First Issue. **Circ:** 3,500. ***Continues*** *Admission Requirements of American Dental Schools, 0065-1990.*
Desc: A reference book for college and high school students contemplating careers in dentistry. It includes detailed requirements for application and admission to US and Canadian dental schools.

ISSN 0895-9374
DD 617 US
CCC
NLM W1; AD546KJ
Pr Rev.
ADVANCES IN DENTAL RESEARCH. [Adv. dent. res.]. **Added/Corp** International Association for Dental Research. Vol. 1, No. 1 (Oct. 1987)-. English. Irregular. Comes with Journal of Dental Research subscription. American & International Association Dental Research, 1111 14th Street Northwest, Suite 1000, Washington DC 20005. **Tel** (202)898-1050, FAX (202)789-1033. **ED** Arthur Hand. cum. index. **Circ:** 3,000 (ctrl). available on microfiche; available on microfilm.
Desc: Provides a forum for detailed exploration and timely discussion of significant research developments in the sciences relevant to dentistry and to the chemistry, biology and function of the oral cavity in health and disease.
Ind/Abst Curr. Cit.; Dent. Abstr. (-1991); Health Plan. Adminis.; Immunol. Abstr.; Microbiol. Abstr. Sect. B (19??-19??).

ISSN 0794-7348
NR
NLM W1; AF516
AFRICAN DENTAL JOURNAL : OFFICIAL PUBLICATION OF THE FEDERATION OF AFRICAN DENTAL ASSOCIATIONS. **Added/Corp** Federation of African Dental Associations. **VFOAT** Journal Dentaire Africain. Vol. 1, No. 1 (Mar. 1987)-. Periodical. English (French). Two times a year (Mar. & Oct.). $50.00 (institutions); $25.00 (individuals). Federation African Dental Association, University Lagos, College of Medicine, PMB 12003, Lagos Nigeria.
Ind/Abst Health Plan. Adminis.; Index Dent. Lit. (Mar. 1987-).

US
CEASED
AGD DENTAL UPDATE. (19??)-(Jan. 1994). English. Medical Information Systems, 2 Seaview Boulevard, Port Washington NY 11050. **Tel** (516)621-7200.

ISSN 0044-6912
JA
NLM W1 AI52 **CODEN** AGDSAB
AICHI GAKUIN DAIGAKU SHIGAKKAI SHI. [Aichi-Gakuin Daigaku Shigakkai-shi]. **Added/Corp** Aichi Gakuin Daigaku, Nagoya. Shigakkai. **VFOAT** Aichi-Gakuin Journal of Dental Science. (1964)-. Periodical. Japanese (summaries and/or abstracts in English). Aichi Gakuin Daigaku Shigakkai, (Aichi-Gakuin Society of Dental Science), Aichi Gakuin Daigaku, Shigakubu, 1-100 Kusumotocho, Chikusaku Nagoyashi, Aichiken 464 Japan. Documents available from BIOSIS Document Express, CASDDS.
Ind/Abst Biol. Abstr.; Chem. Abstr.

GW
ALAM TUB AL-ASSNAN. **VFOAT** Arab Dental. (19??)-. Arabic (summaries and/or abstracts in English). Four times a year. $20.00. Beta Verlag Marketinggesellsch, Celsiusstrasse 43, D-53125 Bonn 1 Germany. **Tel** 011 49 228 252061, FAX 011 49 228 252067, telex 8869 536 BETA D. **(Subscription address:** Beta Publishing, PO Box 140121, 5300 Bonn 1 Germany. **)** **ED** Rabih Nahas and Taleb Ulama. Index available. cum. index. **Bk Rev. Ad Acc. Circ:** 8,000 (ctrl).
Desc: Contains qualified information such as, reports on dentists and dental technicians, new therapy and materials and articles on science and research.

ISSN 0065-6445
US
ALMA MATER. **See** College and School Publications-Alumni.

ISSN 0002-6417
US
NLM W1 AL984
ALPHA OMEGAN. [Alpha Omegan]. **Added/Corp** Alpha Omega International Dental Fraternity. Vol.1 (Oct. 1916)-. Periodical. English. Three times a year (April, Sept., Dec.). $30.00. Alpha Omega, 347 Fifth Avenue, Room 703, New York NY 10016. **Tel** (212)683-4155, FAX (212)683-0027. **ED** Sidney Tourial. **Bk Rev. Ad Acc. Circ:** 9000 (ctrl).
Desc: Full spectrum of articles on dental medicine and dental science, and news items concerning the fraternity and its individual members.
Ind/Abst Health Plan. Adminis.; Index Dent. Lit.

LC RK **ISSN** 1022-7970
DD 617.6 HK
UDC 616.314
•**AMERICA LATINA NOTICIAS DENTALES.** [Am. Lat. not. dent.]. **VFOAT** Latin American Dental News. (1994)-. Periodical. English (Spanish). Four times a year. MediMedia Asia, Subsidiary of: MediMedia Pacific Ltd., 1501 Tung Sun Commerical Centre, 194-200 Lockhart Road, Wanchai Hong Kong. **Tel** 011 65 8525110765, FAX 011 65 8525073817.

ISSN 0895-2930
DD 617 US
CCC
NLM W1; AM357FH
AMERICAN DENTAL ASSOCIATION NEWS. [Am. Dent. Assoc. news]. **Added/Corp** American Dental Association. **VFOAT** ADA News. Vol. 17, No. 19 (Oct. 6, 1986)-. Periodical. English. Twenty-four times a year. $65.00. American Dental Association, 211 East Chicago Avenue, Chicago IL 60611. **Tel** (312)440-2867, (312)440-2500, FAX (312)440-7494. ***Continues*** *American Dental Association. ADA News, 0001-0855.*
Desc: Provides timely information on social, political and economic developments affecting dentistry and health care in general. It also keeps the reader abreast of association activities affecting the future of dentistry.
Ind/Abst Health Plan. Adminis.; Index Dent. Lit. (1986-).

LC RK37 .A25 **ISSN** 0065-8073
DD 617.6/002573 US
NLM WU 22 AA1 A513
AMERICAN DENTAL DIRECTORY. [Am. dent. dir.]. **Added/Corp** American Dental Association. American Dental Association. Directory and Membership Records Dept. American Dental Association. Membership Records Division. American Dental Association. Bureau of Membership Records. American Dental Association. Bureau of Data Processing Services. American Dental Association. Bureau of Data Processing Services and Membership Records. American Dental Association. Bureau of Data Processing and Membership Records. (1947)-. Directory. English. One time a year. $184.95. American Dental Association, 211 East Chicago Avenue, Chicago IL 60611. **Tel** (312)440-2867, (312)440-2500, FAX (312)440-7494. Index available. **Circ:** 2,500.

ISSN 0894-8275
DD 617 US
NLM W1; AM45MK **CODEN** AJDEES
Pr Rev.
AMERICAN JOURNAL OF DENTISTRY. [Am. j. dent.]. **VFOAT** AJD. Vol. 1, No. 1 (Feb. 1988)-. Periodical. English. Six times a year (Feb., April, June, Aug., Oct., Dec.). $50.00. Mosher & Linder Inc., 9859 IH-10 West, Suite 107/489, San Antonio TX 78230. **Tel** (210)493-9660, FAX (512)493-4660. **ED** Franklin Garcia-Godoy (editor's address: University of Texas 7703 Floyd Curl Drive San Antonio TX 78230). Index available (Bound in Dec. issue). **Bk Rev**, (Qty: 12). **Ad Acc, Adv Mgr:** Katherine J. Godoy. **Circ:** 10,000.
Desc: For the general practitioner. Bridges the gap between dental research and its practical application, including original articles, dental abstracts, and a calendar of meetings.
Ind/Abst Curr. Cit.; Dent. Abstr. (1992-); Health Plan. Adminis.; Index Dent. Lit. (Vol. 1, No. 1, 1988-).

LC RK1 .A615 **ISSN** 0889-5406
DD 617.6/43/005 US
CCC
NLM W1; AM497HD **CODEN** AJOOEB
Pr Rev.
AMERICAN JOURNAL OF ORTHODONTICS AND DENTOFACIAL ORTHOPEDICS. [Am. j. orthod. dentofac. orthop.]. **Added/Corp** American Association of Orthodontists. American Board of Orthodontics. Vol. 90, No. 1 (July 1986)-. Academic Scholarly Publication. English. Twelve times a year. $207.00. Mosby Year Book Inc., 11830 Westline Industrial Drive, St Louis MO 63146. **Tel** (800)325-4177, (314)872-8370, FAX (314)432-1380, telex 44-2402. **ED** T.M. Graber. Index available. **Bk Rev. Ad Acc. Circ:** 15,538. available on microfilm and microfiche from University Microfilms International (UMI). Documents available from The Genuine Article, BIOSIS Document Express. ***Continues*** *American Journal of Orthodontics, 0002-9416.*
Desc: Features diagnostic and clinical coverage.
Ind/Abst Biol. Abstr. (1988-); Curr. Cit.; Curr. Contents Clin. Med.; Curr. Titles Dent.; Dent. Abstr.; EMBASE; Health Plan. Adminis.; Index Med. (1986-); Index Dent. Lit. (1986-); Index Vet.; INIS Atomindex [Micro.]; Res. Alert [Full Cov.]; Sci. Cit. Index; SCISEARCH; Small Anim. Abstr. Bibliogr.; Soc. Sci. Cit. Index [Select. Cov.].

ISSN 1055-7601
DD 617 US
CCC
NLM W1; AN217KG
TITLE CHANGE
ANESTHESIA & PAIN CONTROL IN DENTISTRY. [Anesth. pain control dent.]. **Added/Corp** International Federation of Dental Anesthesiology Societies. European Federation for the Advancement of Anaesthesia in Dentistry. **VFOAT** Anesthesia and Pain Control in Dentistry. Vol. 1, No. 1 (Winter 1992)-Vol. 2, No. 4 (1993). Periodical. English. Quintessence Publishing Company Inc., 551 North Kimberly Drive, Carol Stream IL 60188-1881. **Tel** (708)682-3223, (800)621-0387, FAX (708)682-3288. ***Merged into*** *Quintessence International, 0033-6572.*
Desc: Targeted at anesthesiologists and all dental technicians involved in administering anesthetics. Articles cover techniques/drugs/armamentarium used for local anesthesia, conscious sedation, pain control/emergengy care/treatment of children, elderly, handicapped, and medically-complicated patients.
Ind/Abst Index Dent. Lit. (1992-).

ISSN 0003-3006
DD 617 US
CCC
NLM W1 AN219N
Pr Rev.
ANESTHESIA PROGRESS. [Anesth. prog.]. **Added/Corp** American Dental Society of Anesthesiology. Vol. 13 (Jan. 1966)-. Academic Scholarly Publication. English. Four times a year (1 volume). $185.00. Elsevier Science Publishing Company Inc, Madison Square Station, PO Box 882, New York NY 10159-0882. **Tel** (212)633-3950, FAX (212)633-3990. **ED** Raymond A. Dionne. Index available. **Bk Rev. Ad Acc. Circ:** 3,500 (ctrl). available on microfilm and microfiche from University Microfilms International (UMI); available on an online database from Elsevier Electronic Subscriptions (EES). Documents available from BIOSIS Document Express. ***Continues*** *American Dental Society of Anesthesiology. Journal of the American Dental Society of Anesthesiology.*
Desc: Devoted to the management of pain and anxiety in dental out-patients. Regular features include review articles, original research papers, clinical technique articles, case reports letters and book reports.
Ind/Abst Biol. Abstr.; Curr. Cit.; Curr. Titles Dent.; Dent. Abstr. (-1991); EMBASE; Health Plan. Adminis.; Index Dent. Lit.

ISSN 0003-3219
US
NLM W1 AN227L **CODEN** ANORA
Pr Rev.
ANGLE ORTHODONTIST, THE. [Angle orthod.]. **Added/Corp** Angle Orthodontists Research and Education Foundation. Edward H. Angle Society of Orthodontia. Vol. 1 (Jan. 1931)-. Periodical. English. Six times a year. $60.00. Angle Orthodontist Research Education Foundation, PO Box 2577, Appleton WI 54913. **Tel** (414)738-6938. **ED** David L. Turpin. Index available (bound in Oct. issue). **Circ:** 4,200. available on microfilm and microfiche from University Microfilms International (UMI). Documents available from The Genuine Article.
Desc: Covers all phases of orthodontic treatment as well as the basic sciences relating to orthodontics. Each issue is approximately 80 pages in length. Back issues are available.
Ind/Abst Curr. Cit.; Curr. Contents Clin. Med.; Curr. Titles Dent.; Dent. Abstr.; EMBASE; Health Plan. Adminis.; Index Med.; Index Dent. Lit.; Life Sci. Collect.; Res. Alert [Full Cov.]; Sci. Cit. Index; SCISEARCH.

ISSN 0003-4681
IT
NLM W1 AN523 **CODEN** ASTOAR
ANNALI DI STOMATOLOGIA. [Ann. stomatol.]. (1959)-. Italian. Four times a year. Centro Italiano Congressi Edizioni Internationali, via L Spallanzani 11, 00161 Rome Italy. **Tel** 011 39 6 8412673. Documents available from BIOSIS Document Express, CASDDS. ***Formed by the union of*** *Annali di Stomatologia e dell'Istituto Superiore di Odontoiatria G. Eastman, 0375-8516* ***and*** *Clinica Odontoiatrica, 0366-6794.*
Ind/Abst Biol. Abstr.; Chem. Abstr.

ISSN 0003-4770
DD 617 US
NLM W1 AN573
ANNALS OF DENTISTRY. [Ann. dent.]. **Added/Corp** New York Academy of Dentistry. Vol. 3 (March 1936)-. Periodical. English. Two times a year (June, Dec.). $20.00. New York Academy of Dentistry, PO Box 522, Hackensack NJ 07602. **Tel** (201)440-4498, FAX (201)440-7963. **ED** Murray A Cantor (editor's address: 342 Madison Avenue, #1911, New York, NY 10173). **Bk Rev. Circ:** 1,000. ***Continues*** *Journal of the New York Academy of Dentistry.*
Ind/Abst Curr. Cit.; Curr. Titles Dent.; Dent. Abstr. (-1991); Energy Res. Abstr.; Health Plan. Adminis.; Index Med.; Nutr. Res. Newsl.

ISSN 0158-1570
AT

NLM W1 AN627AS
ANNALS OF THE ROYAL AUSTRALASIAN COLLEGE OF DENTAL SURGEONS. **Added/Corp** Royal Australasian College of Dental Surgeons. Vol. 5 (June 1977)-. English. Irregular. 37.00Aus$. Royal Australia College of Dental Surgeons, 64 Castlereagh Street, Sydney NSW 2000 Australia. **Tel** 011 61 2 2323800, FAX 011 61 2 2218108. **ED** Professor J. K. Harcourt. **Circ:** 1,100. ***Continues*** *Annals of the Royal Australian College of Dental Surgeons, 0312-7923.*

FR

ANNUAIRE DENTAIRE. (1936)-. French. One time a year (June). $117.02. Les Editions de Chabassol S A, 30 rue de Gramont, F 75002 Paris France. **Tel** 011 33 1 42975030, FAX (1)42 86 02 81. **ED** B. Laloup. **Ad Acc. Circ:** 10,000 (ctrl).
Desc: Directory of all French dental professions.

ISSN 0826-2233
DD 617.6/006/0714 CN
UDC 616.314(060.21)(714)
ANNUAIRE DENTAIRE = DENTAL DIRECTORY. [Annu. dent. - Ordre dent. Que]. **Main/Corp** Ordre des Dentistes du Quebec. **VFOAT** Dental Directory. Periodical. English (French). One time a year. Free. Ordre Des Dentistes Du Quebec, Suite 200, 3565 Berri Street, Montreal Quebec H2L 4G3 Canada. ctrl circ.

ISSN 0098-6119
DD 617 US
NLM W1 AN754I CODEN AAOBA7
ANNUAL MEETING - AMERICAN INSTITUTE OF ORAL BIOLOGY. [Annu. meet. - Am. Inst. Oral Biol.]. **Added/Corp** American Institute of Oral Biology. (1944)-. Periodical. English. Seven times a week. $75.00. American Institute of Oral Biology, PO Box 7184, Loma Linda CA 92354-7184. **Tel** (909)824-4671, FAX (909)824-4211. **Circ:** 250 (ctrl). Documents available from CASDDS.
Desc: Proceedings manual of annual seminars.
Ind/Abst Chem. Abstr. (1962-1982).

ISSN 0147-0256
US
UDC 616.314-084
NLM WU 18 A615
ANNUAL REPORT; DENTAL EDUCATION. **VFOAT** Dental Education. Periodical. English. One time a year. Free. Division of Educational Measurements, American Dental Association, 211 East Chicago Avenue, Chicago IL 60611. **Tel** (312)440-2794. available on microfilm from University Microfilms International (UMI). ***Continues*** *Annual Report on Dental Education.*
Desc: Contains information gathered from the annual survey of dental educational institutions.

LC RK80 .N37B ISSN 8756-6885
DD 617.6/0072073 US
UDC 616.314(060.55)(73)
ANNUAL REPORT - NATIONAL INSTITUTE OF DENTAL RESEARCH (U.S.). (ANNUAL REPORT / NATIONAL INSTITUTE OF DENTAL RESEARCH.). [Annu. rep. - Natl. Inst. Dent. Res. (U.S.)]. **Main/Corp** National Institute of Dental Research (U.S.). (1983)-. English. One time a year. National Institute of Dental Research, National Institute of Health, 9000 Rockville Pike, Bethesda MD 20014. available on microfiche (Vols. for (1983-) distributed to depository libraries). ***Formed by the union of*** *National Institute of Dental Research (U.S.). Office of the Director. Annual Report. Part I, Office of the Director; National Institute of Dental Research (U.S.). Annual Report. Part II, National Caries Program, 0735-3219* ***and*** *National Institute of Dental Research (U.S.). Annual Report. Part IV, Intramural Research, 8756-6893.*

US

ANNUAL REPORT ON ALLIED DENTAL EDUCATION. **Added/Corp** American Dental Association. Dept. of Educational Surveys. American Dental Association. Council on Dental Education. **VFOAT** Allied Dental Education; Annual Report, Allied Dental Education. (1991)-. English. One time a year. Free on request. American Dental Association, 211 East Chicago Avenue, Chicago IL 60611. **Tel** (312)440-2867, (312)440-2500, FAX (312)440-7494. ***Continues*** *Annual Report; Dental Auxiliary Education, 0145-5370.*

ISSN 0090-3329
US

NLM W1 AM352
ANNUAL REPORTS AND RESOLUTIONS - AMERICAN DENTAL ASSOCIATION. (ANNUAL REPORTS AND RESOLUTIONS.). **Main/Corp** American Dental Association. (1971)-. Periodical. English. One time a year (published in July). $5.00. American Dental Association, 211 East Chicago Avenue, Chicago IL 60611. **Tel** (312)440-2867, (312)440-2500, FAX (312)440-7494. ***Continues*** *American Dental Association. Reports of Officers and Councils.*

SP

ANUARIO DENTAL ESPANOL Y PORTUGUES. (19??)-. Spanish (Portuguese). One time a year. 4.500ptas Spain; 9.00ptas North America; 6.500 other. Puntex SA, c/ Mare de Deu del Coll 14, 08023 Barcelona Spain. **Tel** (93)237 71 24, FAX (93)217 55 73, telex 97131 GPMM E. **Bk Rev. Ad Acc. Circ:** 10,000.
Desc: Dental businesses and warehouses. Distributors, trademarks, prosthetic products and laboratories, pharmaceutical products, dentists and mouth specialists.

ISSN 0003-6439
UK
NLM W1 AP115
SUSPENDED
APEX. **Added/Corp** University College Hospital, London. Dental Society. (1963)-(19??). Periodical. English. Three times a year. ***Supersedes*** *Journal of the University College Hospital Dental Society.*
Ind/Abst Health Plan. Adminis.

LC RK1 .A6989 ISSN 0003-9969
DD 617.6/005 UK
CCC
NLM W1 AR458 CODEN AOBIAR
Pr Rev.
ARCHIVES OF ORAL BIOLOGY. [Arch. oral biol.]. **Added/Corp** European Organization for Research on Fluorine and Dental Caries Prevention. Proceedings of the Congress. Vol. 1 (Aug. 1959)-. Academic Scholarly Publication. English (French and German). Twelve times a year. $1384.00. Pergamon Press, An Imprint of Elsevier Science Ltd., The Boulevard, Langford Lane, Kidlington, Oxford OX5 1GB United Kingdom. **Tel** 011 44 1865 843000, 011 44 1865 843699, FAX 011 44 1865 843010. **(Subscription address:** Elsevier Science Ltd. / Oxford Fulfillment Centre, PO Box 800, Kidlington OX5 1DX United Kingdom. **Tel** 011 44 865 843355.) **ED** D. B. Ferguson and E. J. Kollar. **Bk Rev. Ad Acc.** available on microfilm and microfiche from University Microfilms International (UMI); and Pergamon International Marketing Company; available on an online database from Elsevier Electronic Subscriptions (EES). Documents available from The Genuine Article, BIOSIS Document Express, CASDDS.
Desc: Publishes papers with new research results on every aspect of oral and dental tissues and bone, over the whole range of vertebrates. The journal covers advances in the anatomy, palaeontology, physiology, chemistry, physics, pathology, immunology, bacteriology, epidemiology and genetics of these tissues.
Ind/Abst Biol. Abstr.; Calcium Calcif. Tissue Abstr.; Chem. Abstr.; CSA Neuro. Abstr. (?-?); Curr. Cit.; Curr. Contents Life Sci.; Curr. Titles Dent.; Dairy Sci. Abstr.; EMBASE; GeoRef; Health Plan. Adminis.; Index Med.; Index Vet.; INIS Atomindex [Micro.]; Microbiol. Abstr. Sect. B (19??-19??); Nutr. Abstr. Rev., Ser. B, Live Feeds and Feed.; Nutr. Abstr. Rev., Ser. A, Hum. Exp.; Nutr. Res. Newsl.; Life Sci. Collect.; Pig News Inf.; Ref. Upd. Deluxe Ed.; Res. Alert [Full Cov.]; Rev. Med. Vet. Mycology; Rev. Plant Pathol.; Sci. Cit. Index; SCISEARCH; Sel. Water Resour. Abstr.; Soc. Sci. Cit. Index [Select. Cov.]; Vet. Bull.

ISSN 0004-0320
IT
NLM W1 AR598
ARCHIVIO STOMATOLOGICO. [Arch. stomatol.]. Vol. 1 (1960)-. Periodical. Italian. Four times a year (Mar., June, Sept., Dec.). L17040. Instituto Clinica Odon Stomatologico, via de Crecchio 6, Sec Univ Stu, 80138 Naples Italy. **Tel** 011 39 81 459655.
Desc: Official journal of the Italian Society of Oral Pathology.
Ind/Abst Curr. Cit.; Index Dent. Lit.

ISSN 0213-4144
SP
NLM W1; AR703F
ARCHIVOS DE ODONTOESTOMATOLOGIA. (ARCHIVOS DE ODONTO ESTOMATOLOGIA.). [Arch. odontoestomatol.]. **VFOAT** Archivos de Odontoestomatologia; Archivos de Odonto-Estomatologia. (198?)-. Periodical. Spanish (summaries and/or abstracts in English). Ten times a year. $75.46. Ediciones Ergon, Antonio Lopez 236 3 Planta, 28029 Madrid Spain. **Tel** 011 34 1 5000114, FAX 011 34 1 7924013. ***Absorbed*** *Archivos de Odonto Estomatolog ia Preventiva y Comunitaria.*
Ind/Abst Index Dent. Lit. (1985-); Indice Med. Esp.

ISSN 1056-4764
DD 617 US
NLM W1; AR805
ARKANSAS DENTISTRY. [Ark. dent.]. **Added/Corp** Arkansas State Dental Association. Vol. 62, No. 1 (Mar. 1991)-. Periodical. English. Four times a year. $15.00. Arkansas State Dental Association, 920 West 2nd Street, Suite 103, Little Rock AR 72201. **Tel** (501)3723368. **ED** Dr. Frank Grammer. **Ad Acc. Circ:** 1200 (ctrl). available on microfilm and microfiche from University Microfilms International (UMI). ***Continues*** *Arkansas Dental Journal, 0004-1769.*
Ind/Abst Energy Res. Abstr.; Health Plan. Adminis.; Index Dent. Lit.

ISSN 0004-2838
BL
UDC 616.314(81)
NLM W1 AR921HM CODEN ACECDB
ARQUIVOS DO CENTRO DE ESTUDOS DO CURSO DE ODONTOLOGIA. UNIVERSIDADE FEDERAL DE MINAS GERAIS. (ARQUIVOS DO CENTRO DE ESTUDOS. CURSO DE ODONTOLOGIA.). [Arq. Cent. Estud. Curso Odontol., Univ. Fed. Minas Gerais]. Vol. 11 (Jan./June 1974)-. Academic Scholarly Publication. Portuguese (Portuguese). Two times a year. Arquivos do Centro de Estudos Faculdade de Odontologia da UFMG, rua Conde de Linhares 141 Cidade Jardim Caixa Postal 359, 30.000 Belo Horizonte Minas Gerais Brazil. Index available in last issue of volume--attached. Documents available from CASDDS. ***Continues*** *Arquivos do Centro de Estudios da Faculdade de Odontologia.*
Ind/Abst Chem. Abstr.; Index Dent. Lit.

ISSN 0272-9067
US
NLM W1 AR954T
ARTICULATOR (COLUMBUS), THE. (THE ARTICULATOR.). [Articulator]. **Added/Corp** Ohio State Dental Laboratory Guild. (1971)-. Periodical. English. Six times a year. North Central Ohio Dental Society, 2355 West State Route 18, Triffin OH 44883. **Tel** (419)447-0253, FAX (419)447-2054. **ED** Robert Dornauer. **Circ:** 100.

US

ASDA GUIDE TO POSTDOCTORAL PROGRAMS. VOLUME 2. (19??)-. English. One time a year. $26.00. American Student Dental Association, 211 East Chicago Avenue, Suite 840, Chicago IL 60611. **Tel** (312)440-2795, FAX (312)440-2820. **ED** Lisa Coghlan (phone: (312)440-2847). ***Absorbed*** *ASDA Guide to Postdoctoral Programs. Endodontics; ASDA Guide to Postdoctoral Programs. Pediatric Dentistry; ASDA Guide to Postdoctoral Programs. Periodontics; ASDA Guide to Postdoctoral Programs. Public Health; ASDA Guide to Postdoctoral Programs. Oral Pathology; ASDA Guide to Postdoctoral Programs. Orthodontics* ***and*** *ASDA Guide to Postdoctoral Programs. Prosthodontics.*

US
NLM WU 22; AA1 A85
ASDA GUIDES TO POSTDOCTORAL PROGRAMS. GENERAL PRACTICE RESIDENCIES AND ADVANCED EDUCATION IN GENERAL DENTISTRY. **Added/Corp** American Student Dental Association. **VFOAT** General Practice Residencies and Advanced Education in General Dentistry; ASDA Guide to General Practice Residencies. (1989/1990)-. English. One time a year (every two years). $26.00. American Student Dental Association, 211 East Chicago Avenue, Suite 840, Chicago IL 60611. **Tel** (312)440-2795, FAX (312)440-2820. ***Continues*** *Guide to General Practice Residences and Advanced Education in General Dentistry.*

US
NLM WU 22; AA1 A81
TITLE CHANGE
ASDA GUIDES TO POSTDOCTORAL PROGRAMS. ORAL PATHOLOGY. **Added/Corp** American Student Dental Association. **VFOAT** Oral Pathology; ASDA Guide to Postdoctoral Programs in Oral Pathology. (1989/1990)-(19??). English. American Student Dental Association, 211 East Chicago Avenue, Suite 840, Chicago IL 60611. **Tel** (312)440-2795, FAX (312)440-2820. ***Continues*** *ASDA Guide to Oral Pathology Postdoctoral Programs.* ***Merged into*** *ASDA Guide to Postdoctoral Programs. Vol. 2.*

LC RK58.5 .A78 ISSN 0277-3619
DD 617.6/0073 US
NLM WU 39; A815
ASDA HANDBOOK. (ASDA HANDBOOK : A PUBLICATION OF THE AMERICAN STUDENT DENTAL ASSOCIATION.). [ASDA handb.]. **Added/Corp** American Student Dental Association. American Student Dental Association. Handbook. **VFOAT** A.S.D. Handbook. **VAT** American Student Dental Association Handbook. (198?)-. English. One time a year (Aug.). $20.00. American Student Dental Association, 211 East Chicago Avenue, Suite 840, Chicago IL 60611. **Tel** (312)440-2795, FAX (312)440-2820.

ISSN 0277-3627
US

ASDA NEWS (1981). (ASDA NEWS : [THE OFFICIAL PUBLICATION OF THE AMERICAN STUDENT DENTAL ASSOCIATION].). [ASDA news]. **Added/Corp** American Student Dental Association. News. American Student Dental Association. **VFOAT** A.S.D.A. News. **VAT** American Student Dental Association News. (1981)-. Periodical. English. Ten times a year (monthly except July & Aug.). $20.00. American Student Dental Association, 211 East Chicago Avenue,

Suite 840, Chicago IL 60611. **Tel** (312)440-2795, FAX (312)440-2820. **Ad Acc. Circ:** 15,000 (ctrl). ***Continues*** *New Dentist, 0161-8431.*
Ind/Abst Dent. Abstr. (-1991); Health Plan. Adminis.; Index Dent. Lit.

IT
NLM W1; AT82M
•ATTUALITA DENTALE : SETTIMANALE DI TECNICA E INFORMAZIONE PROFESSIONALE.
(1994)-. Periodical. Italian. One time a week. L81750. Attualita Dentale, C so Sempione 75, 20149 Milan Italy. **Tel** 011 39 2 4986354. ***Continues*** *Attualita Dentale.*
Ind/Abst Index Dent. Lit. (1994-).

ISSN 1034-6066
AT
NLM W1; AU516L
AUSTRALIAN "BEGG ORTHODONTICS" NEWSLETTER.
(AUSTRALIAN "BEGG ORTHODONTICS" NEWSLETTER : PUBLICATION OF THE AUSTRALIAN BEGG LIGHTWIRE STUDY GROUP.). [Aust. "Begg orthod." newsl.]. **Added/Corp** Australian Begg Lightwire Study Group. **VFOAT** Australian Begg Newsletter. (June 1988)-. Newsletter. English. Australian Begg Lightware Study Group, Ivanhoe Victoria Australia.
Ind/Abst Index Dent. Lit. (1988-).

ISSN 0045-0421
AT
NLM W1 AU522 **CODEN** ADEJA2
Pr Rev.
AUSTRALIAN DENTAL JOURNAL.
[Aust. dent. j.]. **Added/Corp** Australian Dental Association. Vol. 1 (1956)-. Periodical. English. Six times a year (Feb., Apr., June, Aug., Oct., Dec.). 88.80Aus$. Australian Dental Association, PO Box 520, St Leonards NSW 2065 Australia. **Tel** 61 2 9064412, FAX 61 2 9064917. **ED** J. K. Harcourt. Index available. **Bk Rev**. **Ad Acc. Circ:** 7,000 (ctrl). available on microfilm and microfiche from University Microfilms International (UMI). Documents available from The Genuine Article, BIOSIS Document Express, CASDDS. ***Formed by the union of*** *Australian Journal of Dentistry; Dental Journal of Australia* ***and*** *Queensland Dental Journal.*
Desc: Presents original research in all aspects of dentistry, with case reports, surveys, epidemiological studies, assessments of dental materials and equipment, editorial comment, and ADA news.
Ind/Abst Biol. Abstr.; Chem. Abstr.; CIS Abstr.; Curr. Cit.; Curr. Contents Clin. Med.; Curr. Titles Dent.; Dent. Abstr.; EMBASE; Health Plan. Adminis.; Index Med.; Index Dent. Lit.; Nucl. Sci. Abstr.; Nutr. Res. Newsl.; Life Sci. Collect.; Res. Alert [Select. Cov.]; Saf. Health Work; SCISEARCH.

ISSN 1320-2340
AT
NLM W1; AU524C
AUSTRALIAN DENTAL PRACTICE.
[Aust. dent. pract.]. **VFOAT** Dental Practice. Vol. 1, No. 1 (Mar./Apr. 1990)-. Periodical. English. Six times a year. 78.10Aus$. Main Street Publishing, GPO Box 1481, Sydney NSW 2001 Australia. **Tel** 011 61 2 4385333, FAX 011 61 2 4382999. **(Subscription address:** Australian Dental Practice, PO Box 575 Milsons Pt., NSW 2061 Australia. **) ED** Ann Ly. **Bk Rev**, (Qty: 4). **Ad Acc. Circ:** 3,000. ***Continues*** *Dental Reporter.*
Ind/Abst Index Dent. Lit. (1992-).

ISSN 0819-0887
AT
NLM W1; AU644EG
AUSTRALIAN PROSTHODONTIC JOURNAL.
[Aust. prosthodont. j.]. **Added/Corp** Australian Prosthodontic Society. Vol. 1 (1987)-. Periodical. English. One time a year (Sept.). 28.78Aus$. Australian Prosthodontic Journal, Dental Clinical School, Westmead Hospital, Westmead NSW 2145 Australia. **Tel** 011 61 2 6337157, FAX 011 61 2 6334759. **ED** Professor R. W. Bryant. **Bk Rev**, (Qty: 4-6). **Ad Acc. Circ:** 1,000 (ctrl). ***Continues*** *Australian Prosthodontic Society Bulletin, 0816-4460.*
Desc: Covers all aspects of prosthodontics.
Ind/Abst Curr. Cit.; Health Plan. Adminis.; Index Dent. Lit. (1987-).

ISSN 0961-9755
UK
BDA NEWS.
[BDA news]. (1988)-. English. Twenty-four times a year. $66.74. Professional & Scientific Publishers, Tavistock House, East Tavistock Square, London WC1H 9JR United Kingdom. **Tel** 011 44 171 3874499, FAX 011 44 171 3836402, telex 005311. **ED** Norman Whitehouse.
Desc: The newspaper of the British Dental Association and is circulated to all members of the Association. It carries the latest news of the BDA.

ISSN 0775-0285
BE
UDC 616.314
NLM W1 BE462SD
BELGISCH TIJDSCHRIFT VOOR TANDHEELKUNDE.
Vol. 38 (June 1983)-. Periodical. Dutch (French). Six times a year. $89.55. Societe de Medecine Dentaire / ASBL, Avenue de Fre 191, 1180 Brussels Belgium. **Tel** 011 32 2 3758175, FAX 011 32 2 3758612. Index available. **Bk Rev. Ad Acc. Circ:** 3,500 (ctrl). ***Continues in part*** *Revue Belge de Medecine Dentaire.*
Desc: Each issue features four scientific articles, several book reviews and a calendar of scientific activities.
Ind/Abst Index Dent. Lit. (1983-); Life Sci. Collect. (1983-).

LC Z6668-.02
DD 016.6176 BL
BIBLIOGRAFIA BRASILEIRA DE ODONTOLOGIA.
See Dentistry-Abstracting, Bibliographies and Statistics.

LC RK5.M6 B63a **ISSN** 0149-1474
DD 353.9/776/00841976 US
BIENNIAL REPORT - MINNESOTA BOARD OF DENTISTRY.
Main/Corp Minnesota. Board of Dentistry. (19??)-. Periodical. English. Every 2 years. Minnesota Board of Dentistry, 717 SE Delaware, Suite 338, Minneapolis MN 55414.

ISSN 0350-1043
YU
NLM W1; BI617L
BILTEN UDRUZENJA ORTODONATA JUGOSLAVIJE.
Added/Corp Udruzenje Ortodonata Jugoslavije. **VFOAT** Bulletin of Orthodontic Society of Yugoslavia. (196?)-. Bulletin. Serbo-Croatian (Roman) (summaries and/or abstracts in English; table of contents in English). Two times a year.
Ind/Abst Health Plan. Adminis.; Index Dent. Lit. (1968-).

ISSN 0882-1852
DD 617 US
CCC
NLM W1; BI759R
BIOLOGICAL THERAPIES IN DENTISTRY.
[Biol. ther. dent.]. Vol. 1, No. 1, (June 1985)-. Periodical. English. Six times a year (Feb., Apr., Jun., Aug., Oct., Dec.). 68.00Can$. Decker Periodicals Publishing Inc., PO Box 620, Station A, Hamilton Ontario L8N 3K7 Canada. **Tel** (416)522-7017, (800)568-7281, FAX (416)522-7839. **ED** Sebastian G. Cianicio. Index available.
Desc: Contains current developments in dental therapeutics for dental professionals.

ISSN 1054-1713
US
BOOKKEEPER'S JOURNAL FOR DENTAL PRACTICES, THE.
(1991)-. Periodical. English. Twelve times a year. $78.00. Bookkeeper's World, Inc., PO Box 2069, Lebannon NH 03766. ***Continues*** *Bookkeeper's Journal for Dental Offices, 1052-7311.*

ISSN 0007-0610
UK
NLM W1; BR375 **CODEN** BDJOHJ
Pr Rev.
BRITISH DENTAL JOURNAL.
[Br. dent. j.]. **Added/Corp** British Dental Association. Vol. 24, No. 4 (April 1903)-. Periodical. English. Twenty-four times a year. $385.02. Professional & Scientific Publishers, Tavistock House, East Tavistock Square, London WC1H 9JR United Kingdom. **Tel** 011 44 171 3874499, FAX 011 44 171 3836402, telex 005311. **ED** Margaret Seward. available on microfilm and microfiche from University Microfilms International (UMI). Documents available from The Genuine Article, BIOSIS Document Express, CASDDS. ***Continues*** *Journal of the British Dental Association, 0368-1394;* ***Absorbed*** *Dental Gazette; Mouth Mirror; Dental Magazine and Oral Topics, 0308-2245.*
Desc: The official journal of the British Dental Association. Contains general dental interest articles as well as specialist scientific papers from around the world, with many articles illustrated in color.
Ind/Abst Alum. Ind. Abstr.; Biol. Abstr.; Chem. Abstr.; Curr. Cit.; Curr. Contents Clin. Med.; Curr. Titles Dent.; Dent. Abstr. (1992-); Health Plan. Adminis.; Hosp. Health Admin. Index; Index Med.; Index Dent. Lit.; Met. Abstr.; Nutr. Abstr. Rev., Ser. B, Live Feeds and Feed.; Nutr. Abstr. Rev., Ser. A, Hum. Exp.; Nutr. Res. Newsl.; Life Sci. Collect.; Res. Alert [Full Cov.]; Rev. Med. Vet. Mycology; Saf. Health Work; Sci. Cit. Index; SCISEARCH; Soc. Sci. Cit. Index [Select. Cov.]; SportSearch; Trop. Dis. Bull.

LC RK **ISSN** 0007-0629
DD 617.3 UK
NLM W1 BR3736
BRITISH DENTAL SURGERY ASSISTANT.
(THE BRITISH DENTAL SURGERY ASSISTANT.). [Br. dent. surg. assist.]. **Added/Corp** Association of British Dental Surgery Assistants. British Dental Nurses and Assistants Society. Vol. 16 (Aug. 1957)-. Trade Publication. English. Six times a year. $59.89. Association of British Dental Surgery Assistants, DSA House, 29 London Street, Fleetwood Lancashire FY7 6JY United Kingdom. **Tel** 011 44 1253 778631. **ED** The Association of British Dental Surgery Assistants. **Bk Rev. Ad Acc. Circ:** 3,000 (ctrl). available on microfilm. ***Continues*** *British Dental Nurses Journal.*
Desc: Education and training of dental assistants.
Ind/Abst Health Plan. Adminis.; Index Dent. Lit.

ISSN 0301-228X
DD 617.6 UK
CCC
NLM W1 BR595M
BRITISH JOURNAL OF ORTHODONTICS.
[Br. j. orthod.]. **Added/Corp** British Society for the Study of Orthodontics. British Association of Orthodontists. Vol. 1 (Aug. 1973)-. Periodical. English. Four times a year. $140.00. Oxford University Press / UK, Walton Street, Oxford OX2 6DP United Kingdom. **Tel** 011 44 1865 56767, FAX 011 44 1865 267773, telex 851/837330 OXPRES G. **(Subscription address:** Oxford University Press / USA, Journals Marketing Department, Oxford University Press, 2001 Evans Road, Cary NC 27513. **Tel** (800)451-7556, (919)677-0977, FAX (919)677-1714.**) ED** L. A. Usiskin. Index available. **Bk Rev. Ad Acc. Circ:** 1,500 (ctrl). available on microfilm and microfiche from University Microfilms International (UMI). ***Formed by the union of*** *Orthodontist, 0048-2250* ***and*** *Transactions of the British Society for the Study of Orthodontics, 0068-2527.*
Desc: Original articles, reviews, critical commentaries, editorials, book reviews, and correspondence on features of orthodontic practice, teaching and research.
Ind/Abst Curr. Cit.; Curr. Titles Dent.; Dent. Abstr. (-1991); Health Plan. Adminis.; Index Med. (Jan. 1981-); Index Dent. Lit.

GW
UDC 616.314
NLM W1 BR902
BROSCHURE ... DES FORSCHUNGSINSTITUTS FUR DIE ZAHNARZTLICHE VERSORGUNG.
1-. Monographic series. English (French and German). Price varies per volume.

US
BULLETIN, THE.
Added/Corp Dental Society of Western Pennsylvania. Vol. 70, No. 1 (Mar./Apr. 1990)-. Bulletin. English. Six times a year. $36.00. Odontological Society of Western Pennsylvania, 900 Cedar Avenue, Pittsburgh PA 15212. **Tel** (412)321-5810, FAX (412)321-7719. **ED** Dr. Joel A. Casar. **Ad Acc. Circ:** 1,800. ***Continues*** *Odontological Bulletin.*

ISSN 0843-3690
DD 617.6/009711 CN
BULLETIN / COLLEGE OF DENTAL SURGEONS OF BRITISH COLUMBIA, THE.
[Bull. - Coll. Dent. Surg. B.C.]. **Added/Corp** College of Dental Surgeons of British Columbia. (Jan./Feb 1988)-. Bulletin. English. Six times a year. 68.03Can$. College of Dental Surgeons of British Columbia, 1765 West 8th Avenue, #500, Vancouver BC V6J 5CJ Canada. **Tel** (604)736-3621, FAX (604)734-9448. ***Continues*** *B.C. Dental Bulletin., 0831-7941.*

FR
UDC 616.314-089
BULLETIN DE L'ACADEMIE DENTAIRE.
Main/Corp Academie Dentaire. Vol. 1 (1963)-. Bulletin. French. One time a year. Julien Prelat, 17 rue du Petit Pont, 75005 Paris France. ***Continues*** *Academie National de Chirurgie Dentaire. Bulletin.*

ISSN 0339-9710
FR
NLM W1; BU524P
BULLETIN DE L'ACADEMIE NATIONALE DE CHIRURGIE DENTAIRE.
[Bull. Acad. chir. dent.]. **Added/Corp** Academie Nationale de Chirurgie Dentaire (France). (1982/83)-. Bulletin. French. One time a year (November). 200.00F. Academie National Chirurgie Dentaire, 22 rue Emile Menier, 75116 Paris France. **Tel** 011 33 1 47046540, FAX 011 33 1 47043655. **ED** E. Cunin. **Circ:** 300 (ctrl). ***Continues*** *Bulletin de l'Academie de Chirurgie Dentaire, 0339-9710.*
Desc: Report of lectures given at the Academie National de Chirurgie Dentaire and the activities of the ANCD.
Ind/Abst Health Plan. Adminis.; Index Dent. Lit. (1983-).

ISSN 0250-4693
BE
NLM W1 BU6471T
BULLETIN DU GROUPEMENT INTERNATIONAL POUR LA RECHERCHE SCIENTIFIQUE EN STOMATOLOGIE & ODONTOLOGIE.
[Bull. Group. int. rech. sci. stomatol. odontol.]. **VAT** Bulletin du Groupement International pour la Recherche Scientifique en Stomatologie et Odontologie. 19.- Yearly volume; Jan./April 1976-. Bulletin. French (English; summaries and/or abstracts in English, German and Italian). Four times a year. $119.39. Hospital Universite Saint Pierre, rue Haute 322, 1000 Brussels Belgium. ***Continues*** *Bulletin du Groupement Europeen pour la Recherche Scientifique en Stomatologie & Odontologie, 0303-7479.*
Desc: Studies on stomatology.
Ind/Abst Curr. Titles Dent.; EMBASE; Health Plan. Adminis.; Index Med.; Index Dent. Lit.; Life Sci. Collect.

Dentistry

ISSN 0360-2575
US

NLM W1 BU66E
BULLETIN - GREATER ST. LOUIS DENTAL SOCIETY. **Added/Corp** Greater St. Louis Dental Society. Vol. 46 (Jan. 1975)-. Bulletin. English. Six times a year. $25.00. Greater St Louis Dental Society, 13667 Manchester Road, St. Louis MO 63131. **Tel** (314)965-5960. **ED** Gregory N. Newton. **Ad Acc. Circ:** 1,400 (ctrl). *Continues* Greater St. Louis Dental Society Bulletin, 0072-7369.
Desc: Dental information book reviews.

ISSN 0701-1725
CN
DD 617.6/006/27127
UDC 616.314(712)
BULLETIN - MANITOBA DENTAL ASSOCIATION. **Main/Corp** Manitoba Dental Association. Vol. 1 (Apr. 1975)-. Bulletin. English. Illinois State Employment Service, Labor market Unit, 208 South Lasalle Street, Chicago IL 60604.

ISSN 0007-4837
US
Pr Rev.
BULLETIN OF DENTAL EDUCATION.
Added/Corp American Association of Dental Schools. Vol. 1, (1959)-. Bulletin. English. Twelve times a year. $18.00. American Association of Dental Schools, 1625 Massachusetts Avenue Northwest, Washington DC 20036. **Tel** (202)667-9433, FAX (202)667-0642. **ED** Terry Owen. **Ad Acc, Adv Mgr:** A. Siegel. **Circ:** 3,500 (ctrl).
Desc: Reports on innovations in dental education, pertinent federal legislation reports, regulations, individual and institutional members.

ISSN 0190-0277
US

NLM W1 BU846FM
BULLETIN OF THE 8TH DISTRICT DENTAL SOCIETY. **Added/Corp** Eighth District Dental Society of the State of New York. **VFOAT** Bulletin - Eighth District Dental Society of the State of New York. **VAT** Bulletin of the Eighth District Dental Society. (194?)-. Bulletin. English. Four times a year. Eighth District Dental Society, 3514 Delaware Avenue, Kenmore NY 14217. **Tel** (716)876-2115.
Ind/Abst Health Plan. Adminis.

ISSN 0007-5132
US
NLM W1 BU849
Pr Rev. **TITLE CHANGE**
BULLETIN OF THE HISTORY OF DENTISTRY. [Bull. hist. dent.]. **Added/Corp** American Academy of the History of Dentistry. (March 1953)-(March 1996). Bulletin. English. American Academy of the History of Dentistry, 100 South Vail, Arlington Heights IL 60005. **Tel** (708)670-7561. **ED** Malvin E. Ring. cum. index. **Bk Rev. Ad Acc. Circ:** 1,500 (ctrl). available on microfilm and microfiche from University Microfilms International (UMI). *Continued by* Journal of the History of Dentistry.
Desc: Covers all aspects of the history of dentistry.
Ind/Abst Curr. Titles Dent.; Dent. Abstr. (-1991); Index Dent. Lit.

ISSN 0739-1773
US
BULLETIN OF THE INSTITUTE FOR CONTINUING DENTAL EDUCATION OF THE QUEENS COUNTY DENTAL SOCIETY. **Main/Corp** Queens County Dental Society (N.Y.). Institute for Continuing Dental Education. **VFOAT** QCDS Bulletin; Q.C.D.S. Bulletin. Vol. 21, No. 1 (Jan. 1983)-. Bulletin. English. Six times a year (Jan., Mar., May, July, Sept., Nov.). $30.00. Queens County Dental Society, 86 90 188th Street, Jamaica NY 11423. **Tel** (718)454-8344, FAX (718)454-8818. **ED** Alan N. Queens. **Bk Rev. Ad Acc. Circ:** 1,500. *Continues* Bulletin of the Queens County Dental Society.

ISSN 0385-1443
JA
NLM W1; BU854GF **CODEN** BKDCD5
BULLETIN OF THE KANAGAWA DENTAL COLLEGE : BKDC, THE. [Bull. Kanagawa Dent. Coll.]. **Added/Corp** Kanagawa Shika Daigaku. Kanagawa Shika Daigaku. Gakkai. **VFOAT** BKDC. Vol. 1, No. 1 (Mar. 1973)-. Bulletin. English. Two times a year. Kanagawa Shika Daigaku, (Kanagawa Dental College), 82 Inaokacho Yokosukashi, Kanagawaken 238 Japan. Documents available from CASDDS.
Ind/Abst Chem. Abstr.

ISSN 0746-5564
US
NLM W1 BU858H
BULLETIN OF THE MICHIGAN DENTAL HYGIENISTS' ASSOCIATION, THE. [Bull. Mich. Dent. Hyg. Assoc.]. **Main/Corp** Michigan Dental Hygienists' Association. (1968)-. Bulletin. English. Four times a year (Mar., June, Sept., Dec.). $12.00. Michigan Dental Hygienist Association, 1609 East Kalamazoo, Suite 11, Lansing MI 48917. **Tel** (517)484-1352. **ED** Anne Gwozdek. **Ad Acc. Circ:** 1,250. *Continues* Bulletin of the Michigan State Dental Hygieinists Association.
Desc: Stories about dental practice and association activity.
Ind/Abst Health Plan. Adminis.; Index Dent. Lit.

ISSN 0070-3710
US
BULLETIN OF THE NINTH DISTRICT DENTAL SOCIETY. **Main/Corp** Ninth District Dental Society of the State of New York. (1916)-. Bulletin. English. Four times a year.
Ind/Abst Health Plan. Adminis.

ISSN 0040-8891
JA
CCC
NLM W1 BU898H **CODEN** BTDCAV
BULLETIN OF TOKYO DENTAL COLLEGE, THE. [Bull. Tokyo Dent. Coll.]. **Main/Corp** Tokyo Shika Daigaku. Vol. 1 (1960)-. Bulletin. English. Four times a year. $150.50. Tokyo Shika Daigaku, (Tokyo Dental College), 2-2 Masago 1 Chome, Chibashi Chibaken 260, Japan. **(Subscription address:** Japan Publications Trading Company Ltd., PO Box 5030, Tokyo International, Tokyo 100-31 Japan. **Tel** 011 81 3 3292 3753.) Documents available from BIOSIS Document Express, CASDDS. *Supersedes* Ronbun Shu.
Ind/Abst Biol. Abstr.; Chem. Abstr.; Curr. Titles Dent.; Health Plan. Adminis.; Index Dent. Lit.

ISSN 0040-8921
JA
NLM W1 BU898M **CODEN** BTMDAB
BULLETIN OF TOKYO MEDICAL AND DENTAL UNIVERSITY, THE. **See** Medical Sciences.

ISSN 0038-3945
US
NLM W1 BU933T
BULLETIN - SOUTHERN CALIFORNIA DENTAL LABORATORY ASSOCIATION.
[Bull. South. Calif. Dent. Lab. Assoc.]. **Main/Corp** Southern California Dental Laboratory Association. (Oct. 1969)-. Bulletin. English. Six times a year. Southern California Dental Laboratory Association, 3333 Glendale Boulevard, Suite 4, Los Angeles CA 90039. **Tel** (213)661-2188. *Continues* Bulletin - Southern California State Dental Laboratory Society, 0091-3308.

ISSN 0007-6007
US
NLM W1 BU948
BUR (CHICAGO, ILL.), THE. (THE BUR.). **Added/Corp** Loyola University Medical Center. Dept. of Public Relations. Chicago College of Dental Surgery. Loyola University of Chicago. School of Dentistry. (1896)-. Periodical. English. Two times a year (Spring & Fall). Free on request. Loyola Dental Alumni Office, Department of Public Relations, 2160 South First Avenue, Building 131 N, Maywood IL 60153. **Tel** (312)531-3204.
Ind/Abst Health Plan. Adminis.

ISSN 0397-1643
FR
NLM W1 CA1392K
CAHIERS DE PROTHESE, LES. No. 1 (Jan. 1973)-. Periodical. French (summaries and/or abstracts in English). Four times a year. $223.10. Editions CDP, 77 rue de Richelieu, 75002 Paris France. **Tel** 011 33 1 42615065, FAX 011 33 1 42613195, telex 210717 F.
Ind/Abst Curr. Titles Dent.

US
CALIFORNIA DENTAL HYGIENISTS' ASSOCIATION JOURNAL. (19??)-. Periodical. English. Four times a year. $25.00. California Dental Hygienists, 5757 West Century Blvd, Suite 512, Los Angeles CA 90045. **Tel** (310)417-8073. *Absorbed* Southern California Dental Hygienists' Association Journal, 0038-3899.

ISSN 0833-8264
CN
DD 617.6/0233/06071
Pr Rev.
CANADIAN DENTAL ASSISTANTS' ASSOCIATION : JOURNAL. [Can. Dent. Assist. Assoc.]. **Added/Corp** Canadian Dental Assistants' Association. (Fall 1982)-. Trade Publication. English. Four times a year. Free on request. Canadian Dental Assistants' Association, 869 871 Dundas Street, London Ontario N5W 2Z8 Canada. **Tel** (519)679-1582. **ED** Charlotte Peer Miller. **Ad Acc. Circ:** 3,000. *Continues* Canadian Dental Nurses and Assistants Association. Canadian Dental Nurses and Assistants Association., 0317-0438.
Desc: Information of interest to dental assistants, regarding policy, regulations, continuing education, and human interest.

ISSN 0708-2002
CN
DD 617.6/007/1171
UDC 616.314(71)
CANADIAN DENTAL FACULTY AND STAFF REGISTER. (1969)-. English (French). One time a year. Free to members. University of Alberta Faculty of Dentistry, Edmonton Alberta T6G 2E1 Canada.

ISSN 0008-6568
SZ
CCC
NLM W1 CA789 **CODEN** CAREBK
Pr Rev.
CARIES RESEARCH. [Caries res.]. **Added/Corp** European Organization for Caries Research. Vol. 1 (1967)-. Periodical. English (summaries and/or abstracts in French and German). Six times a year. $509.60. S. Karger AG, Allschwilerstrasse 10, PO Box, CH-4009 Basel Switzerland. **Tel** 011 41 61 3061111, FAX 011 41 61 3061234, telex CH 962 652. **ED** J. Tenovuo. **Ad Acc.** available on microfilm and microfiche from University Microfilms International (UMI). Documents available from The Genuine Article, BIOSIS Document Express, CASDDS.
Desc: Advances have been gained in caries prevention, including fluoride applications, development of sugar substitutes, control of intra-oral acid formation. Received international recognition for its contribution to the dissemination of new knowledge in these and related fields. Coverage of human and animal experimental work directs this journal to the investigator, while results of clinical trials with a bearing on treatment and hygiene management are also of value to the practicing dentist.
Ind/Abst Biol. Abstr.; Calcium Calcif. Tissue Abstr.; Chem. Abstr.; Curr. Cit.; Curr. Contents Life Sci.; Curr. Titles Dent.; Dairy Sci. Abstr.; Dent. Abstr.; EMBASE; Health Plan. Adminis.; Index Med.; Index Dent. Lit.; Maize Abstr.; Microbiol. Abstr. Sect. B; NAPRALERT; Nutr. Abstr. Rev., Ser. A, Hum. Exp.; Nutr. Abstr. Rev.; Newsl.; Life Sci. Collect.; Ref. Upd. Deluxe Ed.; Res. Alert [Full Cov.]; Sci. Cit. Index; SCISEARCH.

ISSN 0091-1666
US
NLM W1 C25C
CDS REVIEW. [CDS rev.]. **Added/Corp** Chicago Dental Society. **VFOAT** Chicago Dental Society Review. Vol. 65 (Jan. 1973)-. Periodical. English. Eleven times a year. $30.00. Chicago Dental Society, 401 North Michigan Avenue / #300, Chicago IL 60611-4205. **Tel** (312)836-7300. **ED** Noel T. Maxson. **Bk Rev. Ad Acc. Circ:** 9,000 (ctrl). *Continues* Fortnightly Review of the Chicago Dental Society, 0009-353X.
Desc: Official publication of Chicago Dental Society. Carries national, state and local dental news, editorials and news of the society.
Ind/Abst Index Dent. Lit.

XR
NLM W1; CE76
●**CESKA STOMATOLOGIE.** **Added/Corp** Ceska Lekarska Spolecnost J. Ev. Purkyne. Stomatologicka Spolecnost. (1994)-. Periodical. Czech (summaries and/or abstracts in English; table of contents in English). Six times a year. $86.00. Avicenum Czech Medical Press, Malostranske Nam 28, 118 02 Prague 1 Czech Republic. **(Subscription address:** Artia Pegas Press Ltd., Palac Metro Narodni Trida 25, 11210 Prague 1 Czech Republic. **Tel** 011 42 2 24196265, 011 42 2 24196266.) *Continues* Ceskoslovenska Stomatologie, 0009-0654.
Ind/Abst Index Dent. Lit. (1994-).

ISSN 0009-0654
XR
CCC
NLM W1; CE913
TITLE CHANGE
CESKOSLOVENSKA STOMATOLOGIE.
[Cesk. stomatol.]. **Added/Corp** Ceskoslovenska Lekarska Spolecnost J.E. Purkyne. Stomatologicka Spolecnost. Ceskoslovenska Lekarska Spolecnost J.E. Purkyne. Stomatologicka Sekce. Spolek Ceskych Zubnich Lekaru Pro Zemi Eskou. (1936)-(1993). Periodical. Czech (summaries and/or abstracts in French, English and Russian). Avicenum Czech Medical Press, Malostranske Nam 28, 118 02 Prague 1 Czech Republic. **(Subscription address:** Artia Pegas Press Ltd., Palac Metro Narodni Trida 25, 11210 Prague 1 Czech Republic. **Tel** 011 42 2 24196265, 011 42 2 24196266.) *Continues* Zubni Lekarstvi, 0302-8941. *Continued by* Ceska Stomatologie (Prague, Czech Republic : 1994).
Ind/Abst Index Dent. Lit. (?-?).

KO
UDC 616.314
NLM W1; CH636D
CHIDAE NONMUNJIP. **VFOAT** Journal of Dental College; Journal of Dental College, Seoul National University. Periodical. Korean (English).

ISSN 0009-4838
FR
CCC
NLM W1 CH832H
CHIRURGIEN - DENTISTE DE FRANCE, LE. [Chir. dent. Fr.]. **Added/Corp** Confederation Nationale des Syndicats Dentaires. **VAT** CDF. (1962)-.

Dentistry

Trade Publication. French. Forty times a year (every Thurs. except during Aug.). $223.10. La Confederation Nationale des Syndicats Dentaires, 22 Avenue de Villiers, 75017 Paris France. **Tel** 011 33 1 47660232, FAX 011 33 1 47638072. **ED** Serge Tardy. Index available (free). **Ad Acc. ctrl circ. Continues** Dentiste de France.
Ind/Abst Health Plan. Adminis.; SportSearch.

ISSN 0030-2201
US

NLM W1 CH962K
Pr Rev.
CHRONICLE (OMAHA, NEB.), THE. (THE CHRONICLE.). [Chron.]. **Added/Corp** Omaha District Dental Society. (19??)-. Periodical. English. Ten times a year (monthly except July and Aug.). $10.00. Chronicle / Omaha, 119 North 51st Street, Omaha NE 68132. **Tel** (402)554-1333. **ED** D. O de Shazer. **Bk Rev. Ad Acc. Circ:** 2,000. **Continues** Chronicle of the Omaha District Dental Society.
Desc: Features information on dental and good health, nutrition, cooking, recipes, and book reviews.
Ind/Abst Health Plan. Adminis.; Index Dent. Lit.

ISSN 0894-0975
DD 617 US
NLM W1; CI333E
CINCINNATI DENTAL SOCIETY BULLETIN (1979). (CINCINNATI DENTAL SOCIETY BULLETIN.). [Cincinnati Dent. Soc. bull.]. **Added/Corp** Cincinnati Dental Society (Ohio). Vol. 48, No. 1 (Jan. 1979)-. Bulletin. English. Twelve times a year. Cincinnati Dental Society, 320 Broadway, Cincinnati OH 45202. **Tel** (513)984-3443. **Continues** Bulletin - Cincinnati Dental Society, 0190-0439.
Ind/Abst Energy Res. Abstr. (1979-); Health Plan. Adminis.; Index Dent. Lit. (Jan. 1979-).

ISSN 0393-7593
IT
CLINICA ODONTOIATRICA DEL NORD AMERICA. Italian. Three times a year. L180000. Piccin Editore, Via Altinate 107, 35121 Padua Italy. **Tel** 011 39 49 655566, FAX 011 39 49 8750693.

ISSN 1057-5480
DD 615 US
CEASED
CLINICAL DENTAL BRIEFING. [Clin. dent. brief.]. **Added/Corp** American Health Consultants. Vol. 5, No. 6 (July 1991)-(Nov. 1993). Periodical. English. Spectrum Healthcare Group, 2700 Cumberland Parkway, Suite 525, Atlanta GA 30339. **Tel** (404)432-8558, FAX (404)432-8583. **ED** Fran W. Goldstein. Index available. **Circ:** 500. **Continues** Dental Watch, 0893-665X.
Desc: Summarizes current dental literature and follows with commentary by a panel of well-known clinicians, researchers, and practitioners.

ISSN 0093-8769
US
CLINICAL DENTISTRY. **Added/Corp** Eli Lilly and Company. (Nov. 1972)-. Periodical. English. One time a year. $470.00. J.B. Lippincott Company, 227 East Washington Square, Philadelphia PA 19106-3780. **Tel** (215)238-4200, (212)238-4454, FAX (215)238-4227. **(Subscription address:** J.B. Lippincott, PO Box 350, Hagerstown MD 21740. **Tel** (800)638-3030, FAX (301)824-7390.)

UK
NLM W1; CL69J
CLINICAL DENTISTRY IN HEALTH AND DISEASE. (1988)-. Monographic series. English. Price varies per volume.

ISSN 0905-7161
DK
CCC
NLM W1; CL758
CLINICAL ORAL IMPLANTS RESEARCH. Vol. 1, Issue No. 1 (Dec. 1990)-. Periodical. English. Four times a year. $244.92. Munksgaard International Publishers Ltd, PO Box 2148, DK-1016 Copenhagen K Denmark. **Tel** 011 45 33 127030, FAX 011 45 33 129387, telex 19431 MUNKS DK. Documents available from The Genuine Article.
Ind/Abst Health Plan. Adminis.; Index Dent. Lit. (1990-); Res. Alert [Full Cov.].

LC RK60.7 .C55 ISSN 0163-9633
DD 617.6/01/05 US
CCC
NLM W1 CL767K CODEN CPRDDM
TITLE CHANGE
CLINICAL PREVENTIVE DENTISTRY.
[Clin. prev. dent.]. Vol. 1 (Jan./Feb. 1979)-(199?). Periodical. English. American Health Consultants, 3525 Piedmont Road, Suite 400, Atlanta GA 30305. **Tel** (800)688-2421, (404)262-7436, FAX (800)850-1232, (404)262-7837. **ED** John H. Manhold. **Circ:** 1,900. available on microfilm and microfiche from University Microfilms International (UMI). Documents available from BIOSIS Document Express. **Merged into** GP Monthly Newsletter.
Desc: Information on the application of prevention and control in the management of oral health.

Ind/Abst Biol. Abstr.; Curr. Titles Dent.; Dent. Abstr. (1992-); Health Plan. Adminis.; Nutr. Res. Newsl.; Life Sci. Collect.

US
CLINICAL RESEARCH ASSOCIATES NEWSLETTER. **Added/Corp** Clinical Research Associates. (197?)-. Newsletter. English. Twelve times a year. $49.00. Clinical Research Associates, 3707 North Canyon Road/Suite 6, Provo UT 84604. **Tel** (801)226-2121, FAX (801)226-4726. Index available. **Circ:** 20,000.

SP
CLINICAS ODONTOLOGICAS DE NORTEAMERICA. Spanish. McGraw Hill Interamericana de Espana SA, Manuel Ferrero 13, 28036 Madrid Spain. **Tel** 011 34 1 3154440.

ISSN 0710-5614
DD 617.6/006/071 CN
COMMUNIQUE - CANADIAN DENTAL ASSOCIATION. (COMMUNIQUE / CANADIAN DENTAL ASSOCIATION = COMMUNIQUE DE L'ASSOCIATION DENTAIRE CANADIENNE.). [Commun. - Can. Dent. Assoc.]. **Added/Corp** Canadian Dental Association. **VFOAT** Communique de l'Association Dentaire Canadienne. **VAT** Canadian Dental Association Communique. Vol. 1, No. 1 (March 1977)-. Periodical. English (French). Irregular. Canadian Dental Association, 1815 Alta Vista Drive, Ottawa Ontario K1G 3Y6 Canada. **Tel** (613)523-1770, FAX (613)523-7736.

US
COMMUNIQUE (RICHMOND, VA).
(COMMUNIQUE.). Periodical. English. Four times a year. $10.00 US; $20.00 other. American Association of Public Health Dentistry - AAPHD National Office, 10619 Jousting Lane, Richmond VA 23235. **Tel** (804)272-8344, FAX (804)272-0802. **ED** Marsha Cunningham, University of Iowa, Preventive and Community Dentistry N337-DSB, Iowa City, IA 52242 (319)335-7204. **Ad Acc. Circ:** 800 (ctrl).
Desc: Dental public health newsletter.

ISSN 0265-539X
NLM W1; CO428H UK
CODEN CDHEES
COMMUNITY DENTAL HEALTH.
[Community dent. health]. **Added/Corp** British Association for the Study of Community Dentistry. Vol. 1, No. 1 (March 1984)-. Academic Scholarly Publication. English. Four times a year (Mar., Jun., Sep., Dec.). $148.87. FDI World Dental Press Ltd, 7 Carlisle Street, London W1V 5RG United Kingdom. **Tel** 011 44 171 9357852, FAX 011 44 171 4860183. **ED** P.M.C. James. available on microfilm from University Microfilms International (UMI). Documents available from BIOSIS Document Express.
Desc: Publishes reviews and original communications on a wide range of topics including: oral epidemiology, dental health services research, preventive dentistry, especially in relation to communities, dental health education and promotion, clinical research, with special emphasis on the care of special groups and dental sociology and dental health economics.
Ind/Abst Biol. Abstr. (1986-); Curr. Cit.; Curr. Titles Dent. Vol. 2, no. 2, 1985-; EMBASE Vol. 1, no. 1, 1984-; Health Plan. Adminis.; Index Med. Vol. 2, No. 2, 1985-; Index Dent. Lit. (Vol. 1, No. 1984-).

ISSN 0301-5661
DD 617.6 DK
CCC
NLM W1 CO428I CODEN CDOEAP
Pr Rev.
COMMUNITY DENTISTRY AND ORAL EPIDEMIOLOGY. [Community dent. oral epidemiol.]. Vol. 1, No. 1 (Oct. 1973)-. Academic Scholarly Publication. English. Six times a year. $310.11. Munksgaard International Publishers Ltd, PO Box 2148, DK-1016 Copenhagen K Denmark. **Tel** 011 45 33 127030, FAX 011 45 33 129387, telex 19431 MUNKS DK. **ED** Ole Fejerskov. Index available. **Bk Rev. Ad Acc. Circ:** 800 (ctrl). Documents available from The Genuine Article, BIOSIS Document Express.
Desc: Community dentistry and preventive dentistry, pedodontic aspects, dental care for disabled persons, children with birth defects, old persons, and hospital dentistry.
Ind/Abst Biol. Abstr.; Curr. Cit.; Curr. Contents Clin. Med.; Curr. Titles Dent.; Dent. Abstr.; EMBASE; Energy Res. Abstr. (Sept. 1978-); Index Med.; Index Dent. Lit.; Leis., Rec., Tour. Abstr.; Nutr. Res. Newsl.; Life Sci. Collect.; Res. Alert [Full Cov.]; Rev. Med. Vet. Mycology; Rural Dev. Abstr.; Sci. Cit. Index; SCISEARCH; Soc. Sci. Cit. Index [Select. Cov.]; World Agric. Econ. Rural Sociol. Abstr.

ISSN 0517-127X
US
UDC 616.314
COMPENDIUM. No. 1- 1956-. Periodical. English. South Illinois University, School of Dental Medicine, 2800 College Avenue, Alton IL 62002.

ISSN 0894-1009
DD 617 US
NLM W1; CO437V
Pr Rev.
COMPENDIUM (NEWTOWN, PA.).
(COMPENDIUM.). [Compendium]. **VFOAT** Compendium of Continuing Education in Dentistry; Compend Contin Educ Dent. Vol. 7, No. 8 (Sept. 1986)-. Periodical. English. Twelve times a year (with supplements for each year). $96.00. Dental Learning Systems Company Inc., 9 Pheasant Run Road, Newtown PA 18940. **Tel** (215)860-9595, FAX (215)860-9558. **ED** Allison Walker. Index available (December issue). **Ad Acc. Adv Mgr:** Dan Perkins. **Circ:** 60,000. **Continues** Compendium of Continuing Education in Dentistry, 0734-0338.
Desc: Provides information on clinical dentistry. Written for the general dentist by the specialist.
Ind/Abst Curr. Cit.; Health Plan. Adminis.; Index Dent. Lit. (1986-).

LC RK ISSN 0195-6043
DD 617.6 US
CONTINUUM (L. D. PANKEY INSTITUTE). (CONTINUUM.). **Added/Corp** L. D. Pankey Institute. (1980)-. Periodical. English. One time a year. Science and Medicine, 909 Third Avenue, New York NY 10022.
Ind/Abst Health Plan. Adminis.

ISSN 0162-7279
US
NLM W1 CR118
CRANIOFACIAL GROWTH SERIES. See Medical Sciences-Musculoskeletal System.

ISSN 1045-4411
DD 574 US
CCC
NLM W1; CR216ZEF CODEN CROMEF
CRITICAL REVIEWS IN ORAL BIOLOGY AND MEDICINE. (CRITICAL REVIEWS IN ORAL BIOLOGY AND MEDICINE : OFFICIAL PUBLICATION OF THE AMERICAN ASSOCIATION OF ORAL BIOLOGISTS.). [Crit. rev. oral biol. med.]. **Added/Corp** American Association of Oral Biologists. Vol. 1, Issue 1 (1990)-. Periodical. English. Four times a year. $210.00. International Association for Dental Research, 1619 Duke Street, Alexandria VA 22314. **Tel** (703)548-0066, FAX (703)548-1883. **Bk Rev. Ad Acc. ctrl circ.** Documents available from The Genuine Article, BIOSIS Document Express.
Desc: Devoted to an in-depth analysis of concepts, biological mechanisms, and techniques as well as new developments in the field.
Ind/Abst Biol. Abstr. (1991-); Curr. Cit.; Curr. Contents Clin. Med.; EMBASE; Health Plan. Adminis.; Index Med.; Res. Alert [Select. Cov.].

ISSN 1065-6278
DD 617 US
CCC
●CURRENT OPINION IN COSMETIC DENTISTRY. [Curr. opin. cosmet. dent.]. Vol. 2, No. 4 (1993)-. English. One time a year (May). $163.95. Current Science, 20 North 3rd Street, Philadelphia PA 19106. **Tel** (215)574-2266, (800)552-5866, FAX (215)574-2270. **Continues in part** Current Opinion in Dentistry, 1046-0764.
Desc: Geared toward dentists in clincal and office environments. Features comprehensive review articles, reports new developments in the speciality. Each issue features annotated references and points the reader to current literature available on the subject.

US
CEASED
CURRENT OPINION IN ORTHODONTICS AND PEDODONTICS. (Dec. 1992)-(1993). English. Current Science, 20 North 3rd Street, Philadelphia PA 19106. **Tel** (215)574-2266, (800)552-5866, FAX (215)574-2270. **Continues** Current Opinion in Dentistry.

US
ISSN 1065-626X
DD 617 UK
CCC
NLM W1; CU799GGG
●CURRENT OPINION IN PERIODONTOLOGY. [Curr. opin. periodontol.]. (1993)-.Academic Scholarly Publication. English. One time a year (Mar.). $163.95. Current Science / England, Middlesex House, 34-42 Cleveland Street, London W1P 6LB United Kingdom. **Tel** 011 44 171 5808393, 011 44 171 3230323, FAX 011 44 171 5805646. **(Subscription address:** Current Science, 20 North 3rd Street, Philadelphia PA 19106. **Tel** (800)552-5866.) also available online. Documents available from BLDSC. **Continues in part** Current Opinion in Dentistry, 1046-0764.

LC Z6668.2 ISSN 0903-3483
DD 016.6176 DK
CCC
CURRENT TITLES IN DENTISTRY. See Dentistry-Abstracting, Bibliographies and Statistics.

Dentistry

ISSN 0011-4553
PL
NLM W1 CZ143 **CODEN** CZSTA6
CZASOPISMO STOMATOLOGICZNE.
[Czas. stomatol.]. (1948)-. Academic Scholarly Publication. Polish. Twelve times a year. $123.00. **(Subscription address:** Ars Polona-Ruch, PO Box 1001, Krakowskie Przedmiescie 7, 00-068 Warsaw Poland. **Tel** 011 48 22 261201.) Documents available from CASDDS.
Ind/Abst Chem. Abstr.; Index Dent. Lit.

ISSN 1062-5569
US
DD 617
NLM W1; DA19
TITLE CHANGE
DA UPDATE. (DA UPDATE : NEWSLETTER OF THE AMERICAN DENTAL ASSISTANTS ASSOCIATION.). [DA update]. **Added/Corp** American Dental Assistants Association. **VFOAT** Dental Assistant Update. **VAT** Dental Assistant Update. (1992)-(1993). Newsletter. English. American Dental Assistant Association, 203 North LaSalle Avenue, Suite 1320, Chicago IL 60601. **Tel** (312)541-1550. **Continues** Focus (Chicago, III. : 1982), 0731-101X. **Continued by** Dental Assistant Update.

ISSN 0418-3010
CN
DD 617.6/005
DALHOUSIE DENTAL JOURNAL.
Added/Corp Dalhousie Dental Students' Society. Vol. 1 (1960)-. Periodical. English. One time a year. Free on request. Dalhousie Dental Students Society, Dalhousie University of Dental School, Halifax Nova Scotia B3H 3J5 Canada. **Tel** (902)424-2275. **ED** Heather Carr-Kinnear. Index available. **Ad Acc. Circ:** 2,000 (ctrl).
Desc: Reports concerning current research, issues and trends in dentistry. Written by Dalhousie dental students and faculty. Emphasis is placed on work research, surveys done at the Dalhousie Dental School.

PH
NLM W1; DD201
DDM JOURNAL : A QUARTERLY PUBLICATION OF THE PHILIPPINE DENTAL FOUNDATION, INC, THE.
Added/Corp Philippine Dental Foundation. International College of Dentists. Philippine Section. Philippine Dental Association. (1987)-. Periodical. English. Four times a year. $28.00. **Absorbed** Journal of the Philippine Dental Association.
Ind/Abst Index Dent. Lit. (1990-).

ISSN 0385-0129
JA
CODEN DEDEDP
DE. JOURNAL OF DENTAL ENGINEERING. (THE JOURNAL OF DENTAL ENGINEERING : DE.). [DE, J. dent. eng.]. **Added/Corp** Nihon Shika Riko Gakkai. **VFOAT** DE; D.E. (1967)-. Periodical. Japanese. Four times a year. $81.00. **(Subscription address:** Maruzen Company Ltd., PO Box 5050, Import & Export Department, Tokyo 100 31 Japan. **Tel** 011 81 3 32789224.) Documents available from CASDDS.
Ind/Abst Chem. Abstr.

ISSN 0380-9307
CN
DD 617.6/006/271
UDC 616.314(71)
DELIBERATIONS DE L'ASSOCIATION DENTAIRE CANADIENNE. Main/Corp
Association Dentaire Canadienne. 1969-. French. One time a year. Canadian Dental Association, 1815 Alta Vista Drive, Ottawa Ontario K1G 3Y6 Canada. **Tel** (613)523-1770, FAX (613)523-7736.
Desc: Deliberations of the annual reunion of the Council of Governors.

ISSN 0227-5538
CN
DD 617.6/009714
UDC 616.314-089(714)
DENT POUR DENT. (DENT POUR DENT / ASSOCIATION DES CHIRURGIENS DENTISTES DU QUEBEC.). [Dent dent]. Vol. 1, No. 1 (April 1976)-. Periodical. French. Twelve times a year. Dent Pour Dent, c/o l'Association des Chirurgiens Dentistes du Quebec, 4290 Est rue Beaubien, Montreal Quebec H1T 1S6 Canada.

ISSN 0011-8486
US
LC RK1 .A5416
DD 617.6082
NLM ZWU 100 D412
DENTAL ABSTRACTS (CHICAGO). See Dentistry-Abstracting, Bibliographies and Statistics.

ISSN 0161-7540
US
NLM WU 18 D412
DENTAL ADMISSION TESTING PROGRAM REPORT. Added/Corp American Dental Association. Division of Educational Measurements. (1974/1975)-. English. One time a year. Free on request. American Dental Association, 211 East Chicago Avenue, Chicago IL 60611. **Tel** (312)440-2867, (312)440-2500, FAX (312)440-7494. **ED** Robert E. Sutton. **Circ:** 200 (ctrl). **Continues in part** Annual Report.

Dental Education, 0147-0256.
Desc: Statistical information concerning the dental admission test and applicants to dentistry.

ISSN 0748-4666
US
DD 617
NLM W1; DE166B
DENTAL ADVISOR. (THE DENTAL ADVISOR.). [Dent. advis.]. Vol. 1, No. 1 (Spring 1984)-. Periodical. English. Four times a year. $72.00. Dental Advisor, PO Box 1583, Ann Arbor MI 48106. **Tel** (313)665-2020, FAX (313)665-1648. **ED** John W Farah, John M Powers, William Gregory, and A Jon Goldbug. ctrl circ.
Desc: Ranks dental products according to quality and cost. Provides information essential in maintaining a modern practice.

ISSN 1054-5425
US
DD 617
NLM W1; DE166C
DENTAL ADVISOR PLUS, THE. [Dent. advis. PLUS]. **VFOAT** TDA PLUS. Vol. 1, No. 1 (Jan. 1991)-. Periodical. English. Six times a year. $20.00. Dental Advisor, PO Box 1583, Ann Arbor MI 48106. **Tel** (313)665-2020, FAX (313)665-1648.

ISSN 0311-0699
AT
NLM W1; DE166D
SUSPENDED
DENTAL ANAESTHESIA AND SEDATION. [Dent. anaesth. sedat.]. **Added/Corp** Australian Society for the Advancement of Anaesthesia and Sedation in Dentistry. Vol. 1 (Jan. 1972)-Suspended (1985). Periodical. English. Four times a year. Dental Anaesthesia & Sedation, 116 Pacific Highway, PO Box 564 North, Sydney New South Wales 2060 Australia.
Ind/Abst Index Dent. Lit.

ISSN 0266-6073
UK
LC RK1 .D26
DD 617.6/005
NLM W1; DE166Y
DENTAL ANNUAL (BRISTOL, ENGLAND). (THE DENTAL ANNUAL.). [Dent. annu.]. (1985)-. English. One time a year.

ISSN 0733-9836
US
NLM W1 DE168M
DENTAL ASEPSIS REVIEW. Added/Corp Indiana University. School of Dentistry. Sterilization Monitoring Service. Vol. 1, No. 1 (Mar. 1980)-. Trade Publication. English. Twelve times a year. $10.00. Dental Asepsis Review, Indiana University, School of Dentistry, 1121 West Michigan Street, Indianapolis IN 46202-5186. **Tel** (317)274-5411. **ED** C.J. Palenik and C.H. Miller. Index available. cum. index. **Circ:** 310 (ctrl).
Desc: Methods and materials for reducing the chances of disease transmission in a dental office or clinic.

US
NLM W1; DE169BG
●**DENTAL ASSISTANT : JOURNAL OF THE AMERICAN DENTAL ASSISTANTS ASSOCIATION, THE. Added/Corp** American Dental Assistants Association. Vol. 63, No. 1 (1st Quarter 1994)-. Periodical. English. Four times a year. American Dental Assistant Association, 203 North LaSalle Avenue, Suite 1320, Chicago IL 60601. **Tel** (312)541-1550. **Continues** Dental Assistant Journal, 1072-754X.
Ind/Abst Index Dent. Lit. (1994-).

US
●**DENTAL ASSISTANT UPDATE, THE.**
Added/Corp American Dental Assistants Association. (1993)-. Periodical. English. Four times a year. American Dental Assistant Association, 203 North LaSalle Avenue, Suite 1320, Chicago IL 60601. **Tel** (312)541-1550. **Continues** DA Update, 1062-5569.

ISSN 0011-8524
IT
NLM W1 DE183
DENTAL CADMOS. [Dent. cadmos]. (1933)-. Periodical. English. Twenty times a year. L231000. Masson SPA, via Statuto 2/4, 20121 Milan Italy. **Tel** 011 39 2 63671, FAX 011 39 2 6367211. **Continues** Cadmos.
Ind/Abst Curr. Cit.; Index Dent. Lit.

ISSN 0011-8532
US
LC RK1
DD 617.6/005
UDC 616.314
CCC
NLM W1 DE184
CODEN DCNAAC
DENTAL CLINICS OF NORTH AMERICA.
[Dent. clin. North Am.]. (March 1957)-. Monographic series. English. Four times a year. $110.00. W. B. Saunders Company, A Subsidiary of Harcourt Brace Jovanovich Inc., The Curtis Center, Suite 300, Independence Square West, Philadelphia PA 19106-3399. **Tel** (215)238-7800 or, 5587, FAX (215)238-7883, telex 173146. **(Subscription address:** W. B. Saunders Company / North America Subscriptions, c/o Periodicals, 6277 Sea Harbour Drive, 4th Floor, Orlando FL 32887. **Tel** (800)654-2452, (407)345-3668.) **ED** Brenda Frank. Index available. cum. index. **Circ:** 12,000. available on microfilm and microfiche from University Microfilms International (UMI). Documents available from BIOSIS Document Express, CASDDS.

Desc: Practical updates for the clinician on the latest advances. Each issue addresses a single topic in patient care.
Ind/Abst Biol. Abstr.; Chem. Abstr. (1957-1982); Curr. Cit.; Curr. Titles Dent.; EMBASE; Energy Res. Abstr.; Health Plan. Adminis.; Index Med.; Index Dent. Lit.; INIS Atomindex [Micro.]; Nutr. Abstr. Rev., Ser. B, Live Feeds and Feed.; Nutr. Abstr. Rev., Ser. A, Hum. Exp.; Life Sci. Collect.

GW
DENTAL CORPS INTERNATIONAL.
(19??)-. English. Two times a year. $28.00. Beta Verlag Marketinggesellschaft, Celsiusstrasse 43, D-53125 Bonn Germany. **Tel** 011 49 228 252061.
Ind/Abst Dent. Abstr. (1992-).

ISSN 0191-2542
US
NLM W1 DE1934
Pr Rev.
DENTAL DIMENSIONS. Added/Corp San Fernando Valley Dental Society. Vol. 7, (1972)-. Bulletin. English. Four times a year (Mar., June, Sept., Dec.). $30.00. San Fernando Valley Dental Society, 21201 Victory Boulevard, Suite 260, Canoga Park CA 91303. **Tel** (818)887-7395, FAX (818)884-2341. **ED** Mary Ditto (editor's address: 7525 Topanga Canyon Boulevard, Canoga Park, CA 91303, phone: (818)346-5424). **Ad Acc, Adv Mgr:** Mary Ditto, **Tel** (818)346-5424. **Circ:** 1,200 (ctrl). **Continues** San Fernando Valley Dental Society Bulletin, 0581-4944.
Desc: This bulletin represents the dentists who are members of the San Fernando Valley Dental Society. Each issues contains, letters, opinions, essays and reports on various committees.

ISSN 0011-8575
GW
NLM W1 DE194
DENTAL-ECHO. (DENTAL ECHO; INTERNATIONAL MONATSSCHRIFT FUER DENTAL-INDUSTRIE UND -HANDEL.). [Dent.-Echo]. **Added/Corp** Verband der Deutschen Dental-Fabrikanten. Verband der Deutschen Dental-Industrie. Vol. 1 (1926)-. Periodical. German (English, French, Spanish and Italian). Irregular (eight issues per year). $159.67. Dental Echo Verlag GmbH, Postfach 102663, D-69016 Heidelberg, Germany. **Tel** 011 49 06221 768492. Index available. **Bk Rev. Ad Acc. Circ:** 4,500. **Absorbed** Dental Market.
Desc: Governed by the professional concept of recognizing and appreciating the accomplishments and problems of the working systems, professions and institutions involved in dentistry.
Ind/Abst Health Plan. Adminis.; Index Dent. Lit.

ISSN 0011-8583
US
LC RK1 .O7
DD 338.4/7/6176005
CCC
NLM W1 DE194P
DENTAL ECONOMICS (PITTSBURGH. 1968). (DENTAL ECONOMICS.). [Dent. econ.]. (Jan. 1968)-. Trade Publication. English. Twelve times a year. $72.00. PennWell Publishing Company, 1421 South Sheridan, PO Box 1260, Tulsa OK 74101. **Tel** (918)835-3161, (800)331-4463, FAX (918)831-9497. **(Subscription address:** Dental Economics, Publishing Services, PO Box 3408, Tulsa OK 74101. **Tel** (918)832-9261, FAX (918)832-9295.) **ED** Dick Hale. **Bk Rev. Ad Acc. Circ:** 110,000 (ctrl). available on microfilm and microfiche from University Microfilms International (UMI); available on an online database (file 485/Full-Text) from DIALOG. **Continues** Oral Hygiene/Dental Economics.
Desc: Practice administration, practice-building, personal investment and tax advice for the nation's busiest dentists.
Ind/Abst Account. Tax Datab. (1987-) [Full Txt.]; Curr. Cit.; Dent. Abstr.; Health Plan. Adminis.; Index Dent. Lit.

ISSN 0315-2669
CN
DD 617.6/007/1171
UDC 616.314(71)
DENTAL EDUCATION REGISTER. [Dent. educ. regist.]. 1969/70-. Periodical. English. One time a year. Canadian Dental Association, 1815 Alta Vista Drive, Ottawa Ontario K1G 3Y6 Canada. **Tel** (613)523-1770, FAX (613)523-7736. **Supersedes** Dental Students Register, 0315-2642.

SP
DENTAL EQUIP. GUIA DE EQUIPAMIENTO DENTAL. Spanish. Ediciones Doyma SA, Travesera de Gracia 17 21, 08021 Barcelona Spain. **Tel** 011 34 3 2000711, 011 34 3 4145706, FAX 011 34 3 2091136, telex 51964 INK E.

ISSN 0393-067X
IT
NLM W1; DE194W
DENTAL FLASH. (198?)-. Periodical. Italian (Italian). Eighteen times a year. L6000 Italy. Masson SPA, via Statuto 2/4, 20121 Milan Italy. **Tel** 011 39 2 63671, FAX 011 39 2 6367211.

Dentistry

DD 617.6/0028
ISSN 0070-3656
CN
DENTAL GUIDE. [Dent. guide]. **VAT** Oral Health Dental Guide. (1966)-. Periodical. English. One time a year (Spring). 12.00Can$. Southam Information & Technical Group Inc, 1450 Don Mills Road, Don Mills Ontario M3B 2X7 Canada. **Tel** (416)445-6641, (800)668-2374, FAX (416)442-2261. **Ad Acc.** ctrl circ. *Continues* Oral Health Dental Guide.

JA
DENTAL HAIJIN. (19??)-. Periodical. Japanese. Twelve times a year. $208.00. Ishiyaku Shuppan K.K. / Ishiyaku Publishers Inc., 7-10 Honkomagome 1-chome, Bunkyo-ku Tokyo 113 Japan. **(Subscription address:** Maruzen Company Ltd., PO Box 5050, Import & Export Department, Tokyo 100 31 Japan. **Tel** 011 81 3 32789224.)

ISSN 0011-8605
UK
NLM W1 DE219
DENTAL HEALTH (LONDON, ENGLAND). (DENTAL HEALTH.). [Dent. health]. **Added/Corp** British Dental Hygienists' Association. Vol. 1, No. 1 (Jan./Mar. 1962)-. Periodical. English. Six times a year. $97.54. British Dental Hygienists Association, 13 The Ridge, Yatton Avon BS19 4DQ United Kingdom. **Tel** 011 44 934 833932. available on microfilm and microfiche from University Microfilms International (UMI).
Ind/Abst Curr. Titles Dent.; Health Plan. Adminis.; Index Dent. Lit.; Nutr. Res. Newsl.

ISSN 0958-6687
UK
NLM W1; DE2233
DENTAL HISTORIAN. (DENTAL HISTORIAN: LINDSAY CLUB NEWSLETTER.). [Dent. hist.]. **Added/Corp** Lindsay Club. No. 11 (October 1985)-. Newsletter. English. Two times a year. Lindsay Society, 64 Wimpole Street, British Dental Association, London W1M 8AL United Kingdom. **Tel** 011 44 171 9350875. *Continues* Occasional Newsletter (Lindsay Club). **Ind/Abst** Index Dent. Lit. (Oct. 1985-).

ISSN 0882-9543
US
UDC 616.314-083
DENTAL HYGIENE NEWS (ROCHESTER, N.Y.). (DENTAL HYGIENE NEWS.). [Dent. hyg. news]. (198?)-. Periodical. English. Ten times a year. $25.00. Dental Hygienists' Association of the State of New York Inc, 1070 Sibley Tower, Rochester NY 14604. **Bk Rev. Ad Acc.** *Continues* New York Dental Hygienists' News, 0746-5998.

ISSN 0070-3664
US
DD 617
NLM W1 DE23K
DENTAL IMAGES. [Dent. images]. **Added/Corp** Marquette University. School of Dentistry. Vol. 7 (Fall 1967)-. Periodical. English. Three times a year. Free on request. Marquette University / School of Dentistry, 604 North 16th Street, Milwaukee WI 53233. **Tel** (414) 224-7738. *Continues* Images.
Ind/Abst Health Plan. Adminis.

ISSN 1062-0346
US
DD 617
NLM W1; DE2342
DENTAL IMPLANTOLOGY UPDATE. [Dent. implantol. update]. **Added/Corp** American Health Consultants. (199?)-. Academic Scholarly Publication. English. Twelve times a year. $249.00. American Health Consultants, 3525 Piedmont Road, Suite 400, Atlanta GA 30305. **Tel** (800)688-2421, (404)262-7436, FAX (800)850-1232, (404)262-7837. **(Subscription address:** American Health Consultants, Dept. 5042, Box 71266, Chicago IL 60691.)
Desc: Provides practitioners with information on new materials, new implant systems, and new techniques for dentists skilled in dental implantology.
Ind/Abst Index Dent. Lit. (1991-).

ISSN 0126-8023
MY
UDC 616.314
NLM W1; DE255N
DENTAL JOURNAL OF MALAYSIA. [Dent. j. Malays.]. Vol. 1, No. 1 (June 1974)-. Periodical. English. Malaysian Dental Association, PO Box 237 Jalan Sultan, Jaya Malaysia. *Continues in part* Dental Journal of Malaysia & Singapore, 0011-8648.
Ind/Abst Curr. Titles Dent.; Health Plan. Adminis.

ISSN 0146-9738
US
DD 617
DENTAL LAB PRODUCTS. [Dent. lab prod.]. (197?)-. Periodical. English. Six times a year. $27.00 US; $36.00 (surface mail), $63.00 (airmail) other. Medec Dental Communications, Two Northfield Plaza, Suite 300, Northfield IL 60093-1217. **Tel** (708)441-3700, FAX (708)441-3702. **Bk Rev. Ad Acc.** Circ: 21,000 (ctrl).
Desc: Serving laboratory owners and managers, coverage includes new product introductions, new literature, technical training seminars and videotapes, laboratory conferences, and technique features.

GW
DENTAL-LABOR = LABORATOIRE DENTAIRE = DENTAL LABORATORY, DAS. **Added/Corp** Bundesverband der Rein Gewerblichen Zahntechnischen. Laboratorien. Bundesinnung de Osterreichischen Zahntechniken. Verband Deutscher Zahntechniker-Innung (Bundesinnungsverband). **VFOAT** Laboratoire Dentaire; Dental Laboratory. Vol. 1 (1953)-. Periodical. German. Twelve times a year. $119.75. Verlag Neuer Merkur GmbH, Postfach 460805, D-80916 Munich Germany. **Tel** 011 49 89 3189050. **ED** Edgar Bissinger. **Bk Rev. Ad Acc.** Circ: 17,500.
Desc: Aimed at dental technicians; covers materials, equipment, economy and services.
Ind/Abst Health Plan. Adminis.

ISSN 0957-5138
UK
DD 617.6
DENTAL LABORATORY NOTTINGHAM. (DENTAL LABORATORY.). [Dent. lab.Nottm.]. (1976)-. Trade Publication. English. Twelve times a year. $24.00 UK; £48.00 other. Dental Laboratories Association, Chapel House, Noel Street, Nottingham NG7 6AS United Kingdom. **Tel** 011 44 0602 704321, FAX 011 44 0602 422675. **ED** W. L. Courtney.

ISSN 0109-5641
DK
UDC 616.314-74/-77
NLM W1; DE261F
Pr Rev.
CODEN DEMAEP
DENTAL MATERIALS. [Dent. mater.]. Vol. 1, No. 1 (Feb. 1985)-. Academic Scholarly Publication. English. Six times a year. $175.00. Munksgaard International Publishers Ltd, PO Box 2148, DK-1016 Copenhagen K Denmark. **Tel** 011 45 33 127030, FAX 011 45 33 129387, telex 19431 MUNKS DK. **ED** Franklin A. Young. Index available. **Bk Rev. Ad Acc.** Circ: 800 (ctrl). Documents available from The Genuine Article, BIOSIS Document Express, CASDDS.
Desc: Devoted exclusively to the study of materials used in dentistry. Subject matter includes all aspects of materials science, such as laboratory, clinical, and animal testing of materials and their components, as well as instruments and equipment, interactions of materials, testing methods, and protocols.
Ind/Abst Biol. Abstr. (1985-); Ceram. Abstr. (19??-); Chem. Abstr. (1985-); Curr. Cit.; Curr. Contents Clin. Med. (19??-); Curr. Titles Dent. (19??-); Dent. Abstr. (?-1991); Health Plan. Adminis. (19??-); Index Dent. Lit. (19??-); Ref. Upd. Deluxe Ed. (19??-); Res. Alert (19??-) [Full Cov.]; SCISEARCH (19??-).

ISSN 0287-4547
JA
NLM W1 DE261G **CODEN** DMJOD5
DENTAL MATERIALS JOURNAL. [Dent. mater. j.]. **Added/Corp** Nihon Shika Riko Gakkai. Vol. 1 No. 1 (Dec. 1982)-. Academic Scholarly Publication. English (summaries and/or abstracts in Japanese). Two times a year. $80.00. Nihon Shika Riko Gakkai, (Japanese Society for Dental Materials & Devices), Koku Hoken Kyokai, 44-2 Komagome 1 Chome, Toshimaku Tokyo 170 Japan. **(Subscription address:** Japan Publications Trading Company Ltd., PO Box 5030, Tokyo International, Tokyo 100-31 Japan. **Tel** 011 81 3 3292 3753.) Documents available from CASDDS.
Ind/Abst Chem. Abstr.; Curr. Cit.; Curr. Titles Dent.

ISSN 1049-4871
US
DD 658
NLM W1; DE266K
CCC
CEASED
DENTAL OFFICE. (DENTAL OFFICE : THE MONTHLY PUBLICATION FOR DENTAL OFFICE PROFESSIONALS.). [Dent. off.]. (May 1989)-(Aug. 1995). Periodical. English. Stevens Publishing Corporation, 225 New North Road, Waco TX 76702-2604. **Tel** (800)727-7573, (817)776-9000, FAX (817)776-9018. **(Subscription address:** Stevens Publishing Corp., PO Box 2573, Waco TX 76702.) Index available (bound in last issue). *Continues* Dental Assisting, 0744-012X.
Ind/Abst Index Dent. Lit. (May 1989-).

ISSN 0418-694X
AT
DD 617.601
UDC 616.314
NLM W1 DE27C
SUSPENDED
DENTAL OUTLOOK, THE. [Dent. outlook]. Vol. 1 (1975)-?. Periodical. English. Four times a year. 52.00Aus$. University of Sydney / Dental Health Foundation, Parramatta, Sydney New South Wales 2006 Australia. **Tel** 011 61 2 660 8808. **ED** Graham Craig. Index available. **Bk Rev.** Circ: 7,000 (ctrl). *Supersedes* Dental Outlook, 0418-694X.
Desc: Keeps dentists informed with techniques of value in dental practice.

JA
DENTAL OUTLOOK. SHIKAI TENBO. (19??)-. Periodical. Japanese. Twelve times a year. $298.00. Ishiyaku Shuppan K.K. / Ishiyaku Publishers Inc., 7-10 Honkomagome 1-chome, Bunkyo-ku Tokyo 113 Japan. **(Subscription address:** Maruzen Company Ltd., PO Box 5050, Import & Export Department, Tokyo 100 31 Japan. **Tel** 011 81 3 32789224.)

ISSN 1078-1250
US
DD 338
●**DENTAL PRACTICE & FINANCE.** [Dent. pract. finance]. **VFOAT** Dental Practice and Finance. (1993)-. Periodical. English. Four times a year. $45.00. Medec Dental Communications, Two Northfield Plaza, Suite 300, Northfield IL 60093-1217. **Tel** (708)441-3700, FAX (708)441-3702.

ISSN 0011-8710
UK
NLM W1 DE322C
DENTAL PRACTICE (EWELL). (DENTAL PRACTICE.). [Dent. pract.]. Vol. 8, No. 2 (Feb. 1976)-. Trade Publication. English. Twenty-four times a year. $78.72. A E Morgan Publications Ltd, Stanley House, 9 West Street, Epsom Surrey KT18 7RL United Kingdom. **Tel** 011 44 1372 741411, FAX 011 44 1372 744493, telex 291561 VIA SOS G. **ED** Mary Newing. **Bk Rev. Ad Acc.** Pub. Size: Tabloid. Circ: 23,300 (ctrl). available on microfilm and microfiche from University Microfilms International (UMI); available with illustrations; available with charts. *Continues* DP. Dental Practice.
Desc: Directed at all practicing dentists in the UK, covering all topics of interest to them in their professional life.
Ind/Abst Curr. Titles Dent.; Health Plan. Adminis.

ISSN 0827-1305
CN
DD 617.6/0068
NLM W1; DE322H
DENTAL PRACTICE MANAGEMENT (DON MILLS, ONT.). (DENTAL PRACTICE MANAGEMENT.). [Dent. pract. manage.]. (May 1985)-. Periodical. English. Four times a year. 19.50Can$. Southam Information & Technical Group Inc, 1450 Don Mills Road, Don Mills Ontario M3B 2X7 Canada. **Tel** (416)445-6641, (800)668-2374, FAX (416)442-2261. **Ad Acc.** ctrl circ.
Ind/Abst Dent. Abstr. (?-1991); Health Plan. Adminis.; Index Dent. Lit. (1985-).

UK
DENTAL PRACTITIONERS' FORMULARY. (1954)-. English.

FR
DENTAL PRESS. French. Six times a year. $122.00 US. CCLS Belgique, 5355 rue Cesar Franck, 1050 Brussels Belgium. **Tel** 011 32 2 6464187.

ISSN 0011-8737
US
DD 617
CODEN DPREE3
DENTAL PRODUCTS REPORT. [Dent. prod. rep.]. (19??)-. Trade Publication. English. Twelve times a year. $90.00. Medec Dental Communications, Two Northfield Plaza, Suite 300, Northfield IL 60093-1217. **Tel** (708)441-3700, FAX (708)441-3702. **Bk Rev. Ad Acc.** Circ: 140,000 (ctrl).
Desc: Serving dentists and dental dealers; coverage includes new product introductions, new literature, dental and medical news, and articles on major dental conferences.
Ind/Abst BioBusiness.

ISSN 0149-2853
US
UDC 616.314
NLM W1 DE345
DENTAL REFLECTIONS. Vol. 1 (Nov./Dec. 1976)-. Periodical. English. Six times a year. $50.00. Professional Communications Associates, 625 North Michigan Avenue, Chicago IL 60611.

LC RK80 .D46
ISSN 0147-264X
US
DD 617.6/007/2073
UDC 616.314(73)
NLM WU 22.1 D414
DENTAL RESEARCH IN THE UNITED STATES AND OTHER COUNTRIES. (1975/76)-. English. One time a year. US Department of Health and Human Services National Institutes of Health, 9000 Rockville Pike, Bethesda MD 20892. **Tel** (301)496-9291, FAX (301)496-2443. available on microfiche (Vols. for (1977,1980-) distributed to depository libraries. *Continues* Dental Research in the United States, Canada and Great Britain, 0094-484X.
Desc: A catalog of dental research projects sponsored by federal and non-federal organizations.

Dentistry

ISSN 0255-6928
SZ
NLM W1; DE348E
DENTAL-REVUE. [Dent.-rev.]. **VFOAT** Dental Revue. (198?)-. Periodical. German. Twelve times a year.
Ind/Abst Health Plan. Adminis.; Index Dent. Lit. (1984-).

ISSN 0227-8529
DD 617.6/005 CN
UDC 616.314
DENTAL SPECTRUM (OTTAWA). (DENTAL SPECTRUM.). [Dent. spectr.]. (1979)-. Periodical. English. Six times a year. Jagar Enterprises, Suite 5, 548 Besserer Street, Ottawa K1P 6E7.

ISSN 1183-9996
DD 617.6 CN
DENTAL STUDY CLUB. [Dent. study club]. Vol. 1, No. 1 (Feb. 1992)-. Periodical. English. Six times a year. 105.00Can$. Decker Periodicals Publishing Inc., PO Box 620, Station A, Hamilton Ontario L8N 3K7 Canada. **Tel** (416)522-7017, (800)568-7281, FAX (416)522-7839.

SA
DENTAL SUMMARIES. (1988)-. Periodical. English. Six times a year. MIMS Pty Ltd., PO Box 2059, Pretoria 0001 South Africa. **Tel** 011 27 12 348-5010, FAX 011 27 12 477716. **Ad Acc. Circ:** 1,300 (ctrl).
Desc: Abstracts of important scientific papers published in well known dental journals.

LC RD **ISSN** 0895-318X
DD 617 US
CCC
NLM W1; DE406
DENTAL TEAMWORK. [Dent. teamwork]. **Added/Corp** American Dental Association. Vol. 1, No. 1 (Nov./Dec. 1987)-. Trade Publication. English. Six times a year. $30.00. American Dental Association, 211 East Chicago Avenue, Chicago IL 60611. **Tel** (312)440-2867, (312)440-2500, FAX (312)440-7494.
Desc: Published for all members of the dental team--hygienists, assistants and others with related expertise. It combines clinical care issues with practical information on problems and situations that arise each day in dental practice.
Ind/Abst Dent. Abstr.; Health Plan. Adminis.; Index Dent. Lit. (1987-).

ISSN 0011-8796
UDC 61 UK
NLM W1 DE409
DENTAL TECHNICIAN. [Dent. tech.]. Vol. 1 (1948)-. Directory. English. Twelve times a year. $33.37. A E Morgan Publications Ltd, Stanley House, 9 West Street, Epsom Surrey KT18 7RL United Kingdom. **Tel** 011 44 1372 741411, FAX 011 44 1372 744493, telex 291561 VIA SOS G. **ED** D. Ritchie. **Bk Rev. Ad Acc. Circ:** 3,600. available with illustrations.
Ind/Abst Br. Ceram. Abstr.; Curr. Titles Dent.; Health Plan. Adminis.; Index Dent. Lit.; World Ceram. Abstr.

ISSN 0305-5000
UK
NLM W1 DE414H
DENTAL UPDATE. [Dent. update]. (1974)-. Trade Publication. English. Ten times a year. $106.09. George Warman Publications UK Ltd., 120 126 Lavendar Avenue, Mitcham Surrey CR4 3HP United Kingdom. **Tel** 011 44 1483 304944, FAX 011 44 1483 33191. **ED** Sue Kay. Index available. **Bk Rev. Ad Acc. Circ:** 10,000 (ctrl).
Desc: The publication of clinical review articles and features for practicing dentists. Contains information on products, equipment and services.
Ind/Abst Curr. Cit.; Curr. Titles Dent.; Index Dent. Lit.; Life Sci. Collect.

ISSN 0822-1596
DD 617.6/005 CN
DENTALETTER, THE. [Dentaletter]. Vol. 1, No. 1 (May 1983)-. Periodical. English. Eleven times a year. 119.00Can$. MPL Communications, 133 Richard Street West, Suite 700, Toronto Ontario M5H 3M8 Canada. **Tel** (416)869-1177, FAX (416)869-0456. **ED** Brian N. Feldman. Index available. cum. index. ctrl circ.
Desc: Professional source letter for dentists.

LC RK58 .D49 **ISSN** 0199-736X
DD 617.6/0068 US
UDC 616.314
CEASED
DENTALPRACTICE. [Dentalpractice]. **VAT** Dental Practice (Waco, Tex.). (19??)-(19??). Periodical. English. Stevens Publishing Corporation, 225 North New Road, Waco TX 76702-2604. **Tel** (800)727-7573, (817)776-9000, FAX (817)776-9018. **Continues** Dental Graduate, 0194-4347.

ISSN 0259-563X
SA
DENTEKSA. [Denteksa]. (1980)-. Periodical. English. Four times a year. R15.82 South Africa. MIMS Pty Ltd., PO Box 2059, Pretoria 0001 South Africa. **Tel** 011 27 12 348-5010, FAX 011 27 12 477716. **ED** A. Hacqueboord. **Bk Rev. Ad Acc. Circ:** 750 (ctrl).
Desc: Journal for dental technicians.

IT
NLM W1; DE4292
DENTISTA MODERNO, IL. (198?)-. Periodical. Italian. Twelve times a year. L68130. Utet Periodici Scient, Viale Tunisia 37, 20124 Milan Italy. **Tel** 011 39 2 29003555.

ISSN 1078-7658
DD 627 US
CCC
NLM W1; DE434R
●**DENTISTRY AND MANAGED CARE NEWS.** [Dent. manag. care news]. Vol. 1, No. 1 (Oct. 1994)-. Periodical. English. Six times a year. $65.00. Knolls Publishing Group, 201 Littleton Road, Morris Plains NJ 07950. **Tel** (201)285-0855, FAX (201)285-1472.
Desc: Dedicated to providing current information to dentists and dental industry professionals on managed care, management, administrative, and financial issues.

LC Discard **ISSN** 0277-3635
DD 617 US
NLM W1 DE434 **CODEN** DENTEJ
DENTISTRY (CHICAGO, ILL.). (DENTISTRY.). [Dentistry]. **Added/Corp** American Student Dental Association. Vol. 1, No. 1 (Dec. 1981)-. Trade Publication. English. Four times a year (Feb., Apr., Oct., Dec.). $16.00. American Student Dental Association, 211 East Chicago Avenue, Suite 840, Chicago IL 60611. **Tel** (312)440-2795, FAX (312)440-2820. **ED** Lisa Coghlan. **Bk Rev**, (Qty: 12). **Ad Acc, Adv Mgr:** Debbie Lorimor. **Circ:** 13,500.
Desc: Features information of interest and importance to all dental students and recent graduates. Offers a fresh approach to current topics and features articles of new product announcements, book reviews, case reports, and abstracts.
Ind/Abst Health Plan. Adminis.

ISSN 1057-1418
DD 617 CN
DENTISTRY (HAMILTON, ONT.). (DENTISTRY : AN ILLUSTRATED DESK DIARY.). [Dentistry]. (1992)-. English. $14.45. Decker Periodicals Publishing Inc., PO Box 620, Station A, Hamilton Ontario L8N 3K7 Canada. **Tel** (416)522-7017, (800)568-7281, FAX (416)522-7839.

ISSN 0070-3737
DD 617.6 JA
DENTISTRY IN JAPAN. **Added/Corp** Nippon Shika Ishikai. (1968)-. Periodical. English. Irregular. Japan Dental Association, 4 1 20 Kudan Kita Chiytoda-ku, Tokyo 102 Japan. **Continues** Japanese Dental Journal.
Ind/Abst Health Plan. Adminis.

ISSN 8750-2186
DD 617 US
NLM W1; DE436
DENTISTRY TODAY. [Dent. today]. (198?)-. Periodical. English. Eleven times a year. $40.00. Dentistry Today Inc., 26 Park Street, Montclair NJ 07042. **Tel** (201)783-3935. **ED** Robert Hickox. **Bk Rev. Ad Acc. Circ:** 132,418 (ctrl).
Desc: Latest news in dentistry - new products, computers, clinical articles, practice management, latest in research, personal finance, product profile and seminars.
Ind/Abst Health Plan. Adminis.; Index Dent. Lit. (1990-).

LC RK37 .D5
DD 617.60025 UK
NLM WU 22 FA1 D4
DENTISTS REGISTER, THE. **Added/Corp** General Medical Council (Great Britain) General Dental Council (Great Britain) General Dental. Board. (1879)-. English. One time a year. $31.66. General Dental Council, 37 Wimpole Street, London W1M 8DQ United Kingdom. **Tel** 011 44 171 4862171, FAX 011 44 171 2243294. **Circ:** 2,500.

ISSN 0250-832X
UK
CCC
NLM W1 DE439F
DENTO MAXILLO FACIAL RADIOLOGY. [Dento-maxillo-facial radiol.]. **Added/Corp** International Association of Maxillofacial Radiology. Vol. 1 (1972)-. Monographic series. English (summaries and/or abstracts in German and Spanish). Five times a year. $263.00. Butterworth Heinemann Publishers, Linacre House Jordan Hill, Oxford OX2 8DP United Kingdom. **Tel** 011 44 1865 310366, FAX 011 44 1865 310898. **(Subscription address:** Elsevier Science Ltd. / Oxford Fulfillment Centre, PO Box 800, Kidlington OX5 1DX United Kingdom. **Tel** 011 44 865 843355.) **ED** Stuart C. White. **Bk Rev. Ad Acc. Circ:** 600 (ctrl). available on microfilm and microfiche from University Microfilms International (UMI).
Desc: Publishes scientific articles pertaining to radiology in dentistry.
Ind/Abst Curr. Cit.; Curr. Titles Dent.; Health Plan. Adminis.; Index Dent. Lit.

ISSN 0714-7619
DD 617.6/9/060714 CN
UDC 616.314(714)
DENTURO +. (DENTURO + : JOURNAL DU SYNDICAT PROFESSIONNEL DES DENTUROLOGISTES DU QUEBEC.). [Denturo +]. **VAT** Denturo Plus. Vol. 11, No. 1 (Mar. 1980)-. Periodical. French. Four times a year. Denturo +, c/o Syndicat Professionnel des Denturologistes du Quebec, 4850 Est boulevard Henri-Bourassa, Montreal-Nord Quebec H1G 2R2 Canada. **Continues** Denturo, 0384-8000.

LC LJ105.D38 D4a **ISSN** 0011-9474
DD 378/.198/546176 US
NLM W1 DE516
DESMOS OF DELTA SIGMA DELTA. See Societies and Clubs.

ISSN 0011-9601
US
NLM W1 DE523
DETROIT DENTAL BULLETIN. [Detroit dent. bull.]. **Added/Corp** Detroit District Dental Society. Vol. 1 (Oct. 1933)-. Bulletin. English. Ten times a year. $25.00. Detroit Dental Bulletin, 420 New Center Building, Detroit MI 48202. **Tel** (313)871-3500. **ED** Edward H. Hirsch. Index available. **Ad Acc. Circ:** 1,400 (ctrl).

ISSN 0012-1029
GW
CCC
NLM W1; DE879 **CODEN** DZZEA7
DEUTSCHE ZAHNAERZTLICHE ZEITSCHRIFT. [Dtsch. Zahnarztl. Z.]. **Added/Corp** Bayerische Landeskammer fuer Zahnarzte. Deutsche Gesellschaft fuer Zahn-, Mund- und Kiefer-heilkunde. Deutsche Arbeitsgemeinschaft fuer Paradentose-Forschung. (1946)-. Trade Publication. German. Twelve times a year. $249.18. Carl Hanser Verlag, Postfach 860420, D-81631 Munich Germany. **Tel** 011 49 89 998300, FAX 011 49 89 981264. **ED** Adolf Kroncke and Gerhard Maschinski. Index available. **Bk Rev. Ad Acc. Circ:** 6,000 (ctrl). Documents available from CASDDS. **Absorbed** Deutsche Zahn-, Mund-, und Kieferheilkunde mit Zentralblatt, 0940-855X.
Desc: Original articles from dental specialists world-wide, with interpretations for the reader's practical application. Reports on research as well as new therapy in the field of dentistry and oral health. Case reports included.
Ind/Abst Chem. Abstr.; Curr. Cit.; Curr. Titles Dent.; Health Plan. Adminis.; Life Sci. Collect.

GW
NLM W1; DE895P
DEUTSCHE ZEITSCHRIFT FUER BIOLOGISCHE ZAHNMEDIZIN : BZM. **Added/Corp** Internationale Gesellschaft fuer Ganzheitliche Zahnmedizin. Gesellschaft der Arzte fuer Erfahrungsheilkunde (Germany). Arbeitskreis fuer Ganzheitliche Kieferorthopadie nach Balters. **VFOAT** BZM. (198?)-. Periodical. German. Four times a year. Karl F Haug Verlag, Postfach 102840, D-69018 Heidelberg Germany. **Tel** 011 49 6221 406248. **Continues** Biologisches Zahn-Medizin.

ISSN 0343-3137
GW
CCC
NLM W1; DE903F
DEUTSCHE ZEITSCHRIFT FUER MUND-, KIEFER- UND GESICHTS-CHIRURGIE. [Dtsch. Z. Mund- Kiefer- Gesicht-Chir.]. **Added/Corp** Bundesverband der Fachaerzte fuer Mund- und Kieferchirurgie (Germany) Bundesverband Deutscher Aerzte fuer Mund-Kiefer-Gesichtschirurgie. Deutsche Gesellschaft fuer Mund-, Kiefer- und Gesichtschirurgie. (1977)-. Trade Publication. German (summaries and/or abstracts in English and French; table of contents in English). Six times a year. $310.90. Carl Hanser Verlag, Postfach 860420, D-81631 Munich Germany. **Tel** 011 49 89 998300, FAX 011 49 89 981264. **ED** R. Becker. Index available. **Bk Rev. Ad Acc. Circ:** 7,900 (ctrl).
Desc: Contains articles on oral pathology and new diagnostic and therapeutic methods, to inform the researcher as well as the clinical physician. Reports on conferences and continuing education.
Ind/Abst Curr. Cit.; Curr. Titles Dent.; Health Plan. Adminis.; Index Dent. Lit. (1977-);(1, 1977-).

ISSN 0419-0955
SA
NLM W1 DI278
DIASTEMA. [Diastema]. **Added/Corp** University of the Witwatersrand. Students Dental Council. University of the Witwatersrand. Dental School. Vol. 1 (1963)-. English. One time a year. Free. Faculty of Dentistry / Student Dental Council, University of Witwatsrand, 1 J Smuts Avenue, Johannesburg 2000 South Africa. Index available. cum. index. **Ad Acc. Circ:** 2,000 (ctrl).
Ind/Abst Health Plan. Adminis.; Index Dent. Lit.

Dentistry

DD 617.6/006/07127
UDC 616.314(060.21)(712)
ISSN 0711-2238
CN
DIRECTORY / MANITOBA DENTAL ASSOCIATION. [Dir. - Manit. Dent. Assoc.]. **Main/Corp** Manitoba Dental Association. Directory. English. One time a year. Free. Manitoba Dental Association, 308 Kennedy Street, Winnipeg Manitoba R3B 2M6 Canada. ctrl circ.

LC RK
DD 617.6/006/071
ISSN 1184-6194
CN
DIRECTORY OF CANADIAN DENTAL ASSOCIATION. (DIRECTORY OF CANADIAN DENTAL ASSOCIATION = REPERTOIRE DE L'ASSOCIATION DENTAIRE CANADIENNE.). [Dir. Can. Dent. Assoc.]. **Main/Corp** Association Dentaire Canadienne. **VFOAT** Repertoire de l'Association Dentaire Canadienne. (1991)-. Directory. French (English). Free for members. Association Dentaire Canadienne, 1815 CH Alta Vista, Ottawa Ontario K1G 3Y6 Canada.

NLM WU 22; FA1 D59
●**DIRECTORY OF DENTAL SERVICES.** **VFOAT** Churchill Livingstone Directory of Dental Services. (1993)-. Periodical. English. £75.00 UK. Pearson Professional Ltd., 12-14 Slaidburn Crescent, Southport MSD PR9 9YF United Kingdom. **Tel** 011 44 1704 26881. **(Subscription address:** Pearson Professional Ltd., PO Box 77, Fourth Avenue, Harlow Essex CM19 5BQ United Kingdom. **Tel** 011 44 1279 623924.**)**

NLM WU 22; AA1 A8
US
DIRECTORY OF RESIDENCY TRAINING PROGRAMS IN ORAL AND MAXILLOFACIAL SURGERY. Added/Corp American Association of Oral and Maxillofacial Surgeons. (1992)-. Annual. One time a year. $19.95. American Student Dental Association, 211 East Chicago Avenue, Suite 840, Chicago IL 60611. **Tel** (312)440-2795, FAX (312)440-2820. **Continues** ASDA Guides to Postdoctoral Programs. Oral and Maxillofacial Surgery Residencies.

NLM W1 AN2305
ISSN 0254-5462
TU
DIS HEKIMLIGI YUKSEK OKULU BULTENI. (ANKARA UNIVERSITESI TIB I.E. TIP FAKULTESI : DIS HEKIMLIGIYUKSEK OKULU BULTENI.). [Dis Hekim. Yuksek Okulu bul.]. **VFOAT** Bulletin of the School of Dentistry, Ankara, Turkey. Vol. 1, No. 1 (March 1966)-. Bulletin. Turkish. Irregular.

NLM W1; DI843L
US
DISTRIBUTION OF DENTISTS IN THE UNITED STATES BY REGION AND STATE. Added/Corp American Dental Association. Bureau of Economic and Behavioral Research. (1982)-. English. Irregular. Free. American Dental Association, 211 East Chicago Avenue, Chicago IL 60611. **Tel** (312)440-2867, (312)440-2500, FAX (312)440-7494. **Continues** Distribution of Dentists in the United States by State, Region, District, and County.

NLM W1 ED538F
ISSN 0013-0907
UK
EDINBURGH DENTAL HOSPITAL GAZETTE. Added/Corp Edinburgh Dental Hospital and School. Vol. 13 (Winter 1973)-. Periodical. English. Two times a year. £2.00. Edinburgh Dental Hospital, 1A Buccleuch Place, Edinburgh 8 United Kingdom. **Continues** EDH Gazette, 0013-0907.
Ind/Abst Health Plan. Adminis.

NLM W1; ED587
ISSN 0937-7654
GW
EDS MAGAZINE : OFFICIAL JOURNAL OF THE E.E.C. DENTAL STUDENTS COMMITTEE. Added/Corp European Economic Community. Dental Students Committee. (1990)-. Periodical. English (summaries and/or abstracts in French, German, Italian and Spanish). Four times a year.
Ind/Abst Health Plan. Adminis.; Index Dent. Lit.

LC RK
DD 617.6
ISSN 0731-941X
US
EDUCATION UPDATE (CHICAGO, ILL.). (EDUCATION UPDATE.). **VFOAT** Education Update Newsletter. (19??)-. Periodical. English. Four times a year. American Dental Hygienists Association, 444 North Michigan Avenue/Suite 3400, Chicago IL 60611. **Tel** (312)440-8900, FAX (312)440-8929. **ED** Mary C Munroe and Alexa Sehr. **Circ:** 2,000 (ctrl).
Desc: Newsletter which provides an informal forum for dental hygiene educators and the American Dental Hygienists Association to exchange information.

NLM W1 EG912
UA
CODEN EGDJAS
EGYPTIAN DENTAL JOURNAL. Added/Corp Egyptian Dental Association. Vol. 1 (1955)-. Periodical. English (Arabic). Four times a year. $80.00 one-year. Dar el Hekma 42, Kasr el Eini Street, Cairo Egypt.
Ind/Abst Health Plan. Adminis.

NLM W1; EN362
FR
ENDO : REVUE FRANCAISE D'ENDODONTIE : PUBLICATION OFFICIELLE DE LA SOCIETE FRANCAISE D'ENDODONTIE. Added/Corp Societe Francaise d'Endodontie. Vol. 11, No 2 (June 1992)-. Periodical. French (summaries and/or abstracts in English and Spanish). Four times a year. 519.10F France; 690.00F Europe; 795.00F other. Editions CDP, 77 rue de Richelieu, 75002 Paris France. **Tel** 011 33 1 42615065, FAX 011 33 1 42613195, telex 210717 F. **Continues** Revue Francaise d'Endodontie, 0294-1813.
Ind/Abst Index Dent. Lit. (1992-).

NLM W1; EN396SY
SP
ENDODONCIA : ORGANO DE LA ASOCIACION ESPANOLA DE ENDODONCIA. Added/Corp Asociacion Espanola de Endodoncia. (1990)-. Periodical. Spanish (summaries and/or abstracts in English; table of contents in English). Four times a year. Editorial Garsi SA, Avenida Principe Asturias 20, 08012 Barcelona Spain. **Tel** 011 34 1 4154544. **Continues** Revista Espanola de Endodoncia, 0212-4688.
Ind/Abst Index Dent. Lit. (1990-).

DD 617
NLM W1; EN396UG
ISSN 0899-8973
US
CODEN ENDRE3
CEASED
ENDODONTIC REPORT, THE. [Endod rep.]. (1987)-Vol. 8, No. 2 (1993). Periodical. English. The Endodontic Report Per Inc., 2410 Fletcher Avenue, Suite 203, Santa Barbara CA 93105. **Tel** (805)682-2527. **ED** T. F. Pannkukdds. **Circ:** 8,000 (ctrl).
Desc: Current and original articles by endodontists and their products review section.
Ind/Abst Index Dent. Lit. (Spring/Summer 1987-).

NLM W1; EN396UH
Pr Rev.
ISSN 0109-2502
DK
CCC
CODEN EDTRED
ENDODONTICS & DENTAL TRAUMATOLOGY. [Endod. dent. traumatol.]. **VFOAT** Endodontics and Dental Traumatology. Vol. 1, No. 1 (Feb. 1985)-. Academic Scholarly Publication. English. Six times a year. $266.65. Munksgaard International Publishers Ltd, PO Box 2148, DK-1016 Copenhagen K Denmark. **Tel** 011 45 33 127030, FAX 011 45 33 129387, telex 19431 MUNKS DK. **ED** Leif Tronstad. Index available. **Ad Acc. Circ:** 800 (ctrl). Documents available from The Genuine Article, BIOSIS Document Express, CASDDS.
Desc: Dental biology, endodontics, pediatric endodontics and dental traumatology.
Ind/Abst Biol. Abstr. (1985-); Chem. Abstr. (1985-); Curr. Cit.; Curr. Contents Clin. Med.; Curr. Titles Dent.; Dent. Abstr.; Health Plan. Adminis.; Index Dent. Lit. (Feb. 1985-); Res. Alert [Select. Cov.]; SCISEARCH.

UDC 616
ISSN 0940-9505
GW
ENDODONTIE. [Endodontie]. (1992)-. Trade Publication. Multiple languages. Four times a year. $150.46. Quintessenz Verlag GmbH, Ifenpfad 2 4, D 12107 Berlin Germany. **Tel** 011 49 30 740060, FAX 011 49 30 7415080.

NLM W1 EP462
ISSN 0376-8775
GR
EPISTEMONIKE EPETERIS TES ODONTIATRIKES SCHOLES TOU PANEPISTEMIOU ATHENON. VFOAT Scientific Annual of the Faculty of Dentistry, University of Athens. Vol. 1 (1972)-. Periodical. Greek, Modern (summaries and/or abstracts in French and English). One time a year. University of Athens, Faculty of Dentistry, Athens Greece.

DD 617
NLM W1; ES78
ISSN 1045-9812
US
CCC
ESTHETIC DENTISTRY UPDATE (PHILADELPHIA, PA.). (ESTHETIC DENTISTRY UPDATE.). [Esthet. dent. update]. (1990)-. Periodical. English. Six times a year. $125.00. W. B. Saunders Company, A Subsidiary of Harcourt Brace Jovanovich Inc., The Curtis Center, Suite 300, Independence Square West, Philadelphia PA 19106-3399. **Tel** (215)238-7800 or, 5587, FAX (215)238-7883, telex 173146. **(Subscription address:** W. B. Saunders Company / North America Subscriptions, c/o Periodicals, 6277 Sea Harbour Drive, 4th Floor, Orlando FL 32887. **Tel** (800)654-2452, (407)345-3668.**)**

NLM W1; SC148N
Pr Rev.
DK
CODEN SJDRAN
●**EUROPEAN JOURNAL OF ORAL SCIENCES.** (1995)-. Academic Scholarly Publication. English. Six times a year. $294.30. Munksgaard International Publishers Ltd, PO Box 2148, DK-1016 Copenhagen K Denmark. **Tel** 011 45 33 127030, FAX 011 45 33 129387, telex 19431 MUNKS DK. **ED** Jens Jorgen Pindborg. Index available. **Ad Acc. Circ:** 1,450 (ctrl). Documents available from The Genuine Article, BIOSIS Document Express, CASDDS. **Continues** Scandinavian Journal of Dental Research, 0029-845X.
Desc: Fields within dentistry from basic oral biology to traumatic injuries and diseases of the oral mucosa, to dental materials and endodontics.
Ind/Abst Biol. Abstr.; Calcium Calcif. Tissue Abstr.; Chem. Abstr.; CSA Neuro. Abstr. (?-?); Curr. Cit.; Curr. Contents Clin. Med.; Curr. Contents Life Sci.; Curr. Titles Dent.; Dent. Abstr.; EMBASE [Select. Cov.]; Energy Res. Abstr. (Sept. 1972-); Index Med.; Index Dent. Lit.; Microbiol. Abstr. Sect. B (19??-19??); Nutr. Abstr. Rev., Ser. A, Hum. Exp.; Nutr. Res. Newsl.; Life Sci. Collect.; Res. Alert [Full Cov.]; Sci. Cit. Index; SCISEARCH; Sug. Indus. Abstr.

ISSN 0141-5387
UK
CCC
NLM W1 EU72DN
EUROPEAN JOURNAL OF ORTHODONTICS. [Europ. j. orthodont.]. **Added/Corp** European Orthodontic Society. Vol. 1 (1979)-. Academic Scholarly Publication. English. Six times a year. $195.00. Oxford University Press / UK, Walton Street, Oxford OX2 6DP United Kingdom. **Tel** 011 44 1865 56767, FAX 011 44 1865 267773, telex 851/837330 OXPRES G. **(Subscription address:** Oxford University Press / USA, Journals Marketing Department, Oxford University Press, 2001 Evans Road, Cary NC 27513. **Tel** (800)451-7556, (919)677-0977, FAX (919)677-1714.**) ED** W. J. B. Houston. Index available. **Bk Rev. Ad Acc.** available on microfilm from University Microfilms International (UMI).
Desc: Research or clinical papers of interest to all orthodontists, although the primary intention is to provide a forum for orthodontists in Europe. Welcomes papers from all parts of the world.
Ind/Abst Curr. Cit.; Curr. Titles Dent.; EMBASE; Health Plan. Adminis.; Index Med.; Index Dent. Lit.; SCISEARCH.

ISSN 0965-7452
UK
NLM W1; EU72ECC
EUROPEAN JOURNAL OF PROSTHODONTICS AND RESTORATIVE DENTISTRY, THE. Added/Corp British Society for Restorative Dentistry. Vol. 1, No. 1 (Sept. 1992)-. Periodical. English. Four times a year. $128.34. FDI World Dental Press Ltd, 7 Carlisle Street, London W1V 5RG United Kingdom. **Tel** 011 44 171 9357852, FAX 011 44 171 4860183. **ED** Paul S. Wright. **Continues** Restorative Dentistry, 0266-9315.
Desc: Contains research reports, literature reviews, clinical reports and case studies. Official journal of the British Society for Restorative Dentistry and the Dutch Society for Prosthetic Dentistry.
Ind/Abst Index Dent. Lit. (1992-).

US
EXERCISES IN DENTAL RADIOLOGY (MICROFICHE). (EXERCISES IN DENTAL RADIOLOGY.). Vol. 1 (1978)-. Monographic series. English. Irregular. Price varies per volume. Holt Rinehart and Winston, 6277 Sea Harbor Drive, Orlando FL 32887. **Tel** (407)345-2500, 800 545-2522.

DD 617.6/01/0971405
ISSN 1183-4307
CN
EXPLORATEUR (MONTREAL). (L'EXPLORATEUR.). [Explorateur]. **Added/Corp** Corporation Professionnelle des Hygienistes Dentaires du Quebec. Vol. 1, No 1 (Mar. 1991)-. Periodical. French (summaries and/or abstracts in English). Four times a year. 52.73Can$. Ligue pour la Lecture de la Bible, 1701 Belleville, Lemoyne Quebec J4P 3M2 Canada. **Tel** (514)465-0445, FAX (514)923-8966. **Continues** Info-Corpo (Corporation Professionnelle des Hygienistes Dentaires du Quebec : 1987)., 0845-6534.

DD 617
ISSN 0894-7929
US
EXPLORER (FALLS CHURCH, VA.), THE. (THE EXPLORER : OFFICIAL JOURNAL OF THE NATIONAL ASSOCIATION OF DENTAL ASSISTANTS.). [Explorer]. **Added/Corp** National Association of Dental Assistants (U.S.). (19??)-. Periodical. English. Twelve times a year. $15.00. National Association of Dental Assistants, 900 South Washington Street, Suite G13, Fall Church VA 22046. **Tel** (703)237-8616.

LC RK58.7.A8 A95a ISSN 0157-4094
DD 362.1/9/7600994 AT
NLM W1; FA189D
SUSPENDED

FACTS AND FIGURES. AUSTRALIAN DENTISTRY. (FACTS & FIGURES.). [Facts fig., Aust. dent.]. **Main/Corp** Australian Dental Association. (1971)-Suspended (1988). English. 20.00Aus$. Australian Dental Association, PO Box 520, St Leonards NSW 2065 Australia. **Tel** 61 2 9064412, FAX 61 2 9064917. **ED** P.D. Barnard. **Circ:** 300 (ctrl).
Desc: Summary of Australian population and economic indices, with dental expenditures, workforce services and education.

UK
NLM W1; FO5
●**FDI WORLD. Added/Corp** World Dental Federation. (1994)-. Periodical. English. Six times a year. $59.89. FDI World Dental Press Ltd, 7 Carlisle Street, London W1V 5RG United Kingdom. **Tel** 011 44 171 9357852, FAX 011 44 171 4860183. ***Continues** Dental World/FDI, 0965-9986.*
Ind/Abst Index Dent. Lit. (1994-).

US
FILLING YOU IN --. Added/Corp San Gabriel Valley Dental Society. Vol. 1, Issue 1 (Mar./Apr. 1991)-. Periodical. English. ***Continues** Bulletin (San Gabriel Valley Dental Society).*

ISSN 1042-2528
DD 617 US
NLM W1; FO1005K
FOCUS ON OHIO DENTISTRY. [Focus Ohio dent.]. **Added/Corp** Ohio Dental Association. **VFOAT** Focus. Vol. 63, No. 1 (Jan. 1989)-. Periodical. English. Twelve times a year. $30.00. Ohio Dental Association, 1370 Dublin Road, Columbus OH 43215-1098. **Tel** (614)486-2700, . ***Continues** Newsnotes (Ohio Dental Association), 1040-4945; **Absorbed** Ohio Dental Journal.*
Desc: Coverage of new products, trends in dental care, research, state and federal legislation affecting them, commentary, and member profiles.
Ind/Abst Health Plan. Adminis.; Index Dent. Lit. (1989-).

ISSN 0071-7916
GW
NLM W1 FO855
FORTSCHRITTE DER KIEFER- UND GESICHTS-CHIRURGIE. [Fortschr. Kiefer-Gesichts-Chir.]. Vol. 1 (1955)-. Monographic series. German. Irregular. Price varies per volume. Georg Thieme Verlag Stuttgart, Postfach 301120, D-70451 Stuttgart Germany. **Tel** 011 49 711 89310, FAX 011 49 711 8931298, telex 7 252 275 GTVD. **(Subscription address:** Thieme Medical Publishers Inc., 381 Park Avenue South, New York NY 10016. **Tel** (212)683-5088.**)** cum. index.
Ind/Abst Health Plan. Adminis.; Index Med.; Index Dent. Lit.

ISSN 0015-816X
GW
CCC
NLM W1 FO859
Pr Rev.
FORTSCHRITTE DER KIEFERORTHOPAEDIE. [Fortschr. Kieferorthop.]. **Added/Corp** Deutsche Gesellschaft fuer Kieferorthopadie. (1952)-. German (summaries and/or abstracts in English). Six times a year. $198.05. Urban & Vogel, Postfach 152209, D-80052 Munich Germany. **Tel** 011 49 89 532920, FAX 011 49 89 53292100, telex 521701. **Bk Rev. Ad Acc. Circ:** 2,500. ***Continues in part** Fortschritte der Orthodontik.; Deutsche Zahn- Mund- und Kieferheilkunde.*
Desc: Contains original studies, suggestive methods, surveys, case reports, book reviews, information, and a calendar of meetings.
Ind/Abst Health Plan. Adminis.; Index Med.

ISSN 0820-5949
DD 617.6/007/1171 CN
FORUM / THE ASSOCIATION OF CANADIAN FACULTIES OF DENTISTRY. [Forum - Assoc. Can. Fac. Dent.]. Vol. 19, No. 3 (Feb. 1987)-. Periodical. English. Four times a year. $15.00Can$. Association of Canadian Faculties of Dentistry, Central Office ACFD/AFDC, Suite 10 Alta Vista Drive, Ottawa Ontario K1G 3Y6 Canada. **Tel** (604)228-3413, FAX (604)228-6698. ***Continues** Newsletter - Association of Canadian Faculties of Dentistry, 0044-9555.*

ISSN 0340-1766
GW
NLM W1 FR781K
FREIE ZAHNARZT, DER. [Freie Zahnarzt]. **Added/Corp** Freier Verband Deutscher ZahnEarzte. **VFOAT** Monatsschrift Deutscher Zahnarzte. Vol. 15, No. 7 (July 1971)-. Trade Publication. German. Twelve times a year. DM4.00. Kern & Birner Gmbh & Company, Druckerei und Verlag, Werrastrasse 4, 60486 Frankfurt Main Germany. **Tel** 011 49 69 77 00 01, FAX 011 49 69 70 42 94. **ED** Hubertus Foester. ***Continues** Monatsschrift Deutscher Zahnarzte, 0047-7842.*
Ind/Abst Curr. Titles Dent.; Index Dent. Lit.

ISSN 0301-536X
SZ
CCC
NLM W1 FR946GP **CODEN** FROPBK
FRONTIERS OF ORAL PHYSIOLOGY. [Front. oral physiol.]. Vol. 1 (1974)-. Monographic series. English. One time a year. 160.00F (approx. per volume). S. Karger AG, Allschwilerstrasse 10, PO Box, CH-4009 Basel Switzerland. **Tel** 011 41 61 3061111, FAX 011 41 61 3061234, telex CH 962 652. **ED** D. B. Ferguson. Documents available from BIOSIS Document Express, CASDDS.
Desc: The past two decades have witnessed a rapid advance in the theoretical and technical development of dental and oral medicine, coupled with a substantial increase in the qualitative and quantitative demands made upon the dentist by his patients. This series is designed for the dentist of today who, because of the growing scope of his field, must display more than just a familiarity with all areas of oral physiology, whether fundamental or highly specialized.
Ind/Abst Biol. Abstr.; Chem. Abstr.; Index Med.; Ref. Upd. Deluxe Ed.

ISSN 0385-0064
JA
NLM W1 FU503M **CODEN** FSDZD4
FUKUOKA SHIKA DAIGAKU GAKKAI ZASSHI. [Fukuoka Shika Daigaku Gakkai zasshi]. **Added/Corp** Fukuoka Shika Daigaku. Gakkai. **VFOAT** Fukuoka Dental College Society Journal; Journal of Fukouka Dental College. (1974)-. Periodical. Japanese (English). Three times a year. Fukuoka Dental Gakkai, (Society of Fukuoka Dental College), 700 Ta Sawaraku, Fukuokashi Fukuokaken 811-11 Japan. Documents available from CASDDS.
Ind/Abst Chem. Abstr.; Health Plan. Adminis.

ISSN 8756-3150
DD 617 US
NLM W1; FU518N
FUNCTIONAL ORTHODONTIST, THE. [Funct. orthod.]. **Added/Corp** American Association of Functional Orthodontists. Vol. 1, No. 1 (May/June 1984)-. Periodical. English. Six times a year. $82.00. American Association of Functional Orthodontists, 106 South Kent Street, Winchester VA 22601. **Tel** (703)662-2200. **ED** Craig C. Stoner. cum. index. **Bk Rev. Ad Acc. Circ:** 7,000 (ctrl).
Desc: A continuing source of latest information on functional appliance therapy, treating orthodontic malocclusions and TMJ pain and dysfunction.

US
GDA ACTION : THE JOURNAL OF THE GEORGIA DENTAL ASSOCIATION. **Added/Corp** Georgia Dental Association. **VAT** Georgia Dental Association action. Vol. 7, No. 6 (June 1987)-. Periodical. English. Twelve times a year. $25.00. Georgia Dental Association, 2801 Buford Highway, Suite T60, Atlanta GA 30329. **Tel** (404)636-7553. ***Continues** GDAction.*

ISSN 0363-6771
US
CCC
NLM W1 GE241
Pr Rev.
GENERAL DENTISTRY. [Gen. dent.]. **Added/Corp** Academy of General Dentistry. Vol. 24 (Jan./Feb. 1976)-. Academic Scholarly Publication. English. Six times a year (Jan., Mar., May, July, Sept., Nov.). $40.00. General Dentistry - Academy of General Dentistry, 211 East Chicago Avenue, Suite 1200, Chicago IL 60611-2670. **Tel** (312)440-4300, FAX (312)440-0559. **ED** Janis Forgue. Index available. cum. index. **Bk Rev. Ad Acc. Circ:** 45,500. available on microfilm and microfiche from University Microfilms International (UMI). ***Continues** Journal - Academy of General Dentistry, 0001-4265.*
Desc: Presents clinical data and management information applicable to today's dental practice. Includes case report, literature reviews, techniques, research, clinical reports, oral pathology quizzes, new products and self-instruction program.
Ind/Abst Curr. Cit.; Curr. Titles Dent.; Dent. Abstr. (1992-); Energy Res. Abstr. (April 1982-); Index Med.; Index Dent. Lit.

ISSN 0734-0664
US
UDC 616.314-053.9
NLM W1 GE569 **CODEN** GRDND6
SUSPENDED
GERODONTOLOGY. [Gerodontology]. Vol. 1, No. 1 (Summer 1982)-Suspended Jan 1991. Academic Scholarly Publication. English. Four times a year. $199.00. Beech Hill Publishing Company, PO Box 40, Mt Desert ME 04660. **Tel** (207)667-5048, FAX (207)667-5048. **ED** Edgar A. Tohna. **Bk Rev. Ad Acc. Circ:** 1,000 (ctrl). available on microfilm from University Microfilms International (UMI). Documents available from CASDDS.
Desc: International journal with research articles, clinical studies, reviews of literature, book reviews, recent symposia, and news on the aging patient, dentition, oral tissue and bone.
Ind/Abst Chem. Abstr. (1982-1986); Curr. Titles Dent.; Dent. Abstr. (-1991); EMBASE; Health Plan. Adminis.; Index Dent. Lit. (Vol. 3, No. 2, 1984-); Mod. Med.; Nutr. Res. Newsl.; Life Sci. Collect.; SCISEARCH.

ISSN 0385-0072
JA
NLM W1 GI128
GIFU SHIKA GAKKAI ZASSHI. [Gifu Shika Gakkai zasshi]. **VFOAT** The Journal of Gifu Dental Society. Vol. 1, No. 1 (March 1974)-. Periodical. Japanese (English). Irregular. Do Gakkai, Keto Tsushin 19-ban 30-go Mita, 2-chome Minato-ku, Tokyo 108 Japan.
Ind/Abst Index Dent. Lit.

ISSN 0391-5670
IT
NLM W1; GI478J
GIORNALE DI ANESTESIA STOMATOLOGICA. Added/Corp Associazione Italiana per il Progresso Dell'Anestesia in Odontostomatologia. **VFOAT** Journal of Dental Anaesthesia. (19??)-. Periodical. Italian (English). Four times a year. L55860. Masson SPA, via Statuto 2/4, 20121 Milan Italy. **Tel** 011 39 2 63671, FAX 011 39 2 6367211. **ED** Mario Tiengo. Index available. **Bk Rev. Ad Acc. Circ:** 1,000.
Ind/Abst Index Dent. Lit. (1985-).

ISSN 0884-6898
DD 617 US
GMDA BULLETIN. [GMDA bull.]. **Added/Corp** Greater Milwaukee Dental Association. **VAT** Greater Milwaukee Dental Association Bulletin. Vol. 48, No. 12 (Dec. 1981)-. Bulletin. English. Four times a year (Mar., June, Sept., June). $30.00. Greater Milwaukee Dental Association, 111 East Wisconsin Avenue, Suite 1300, Milwaukee WI 53202. **Tel** (414)276-9911. **ED** Randall F. Johnson. **Ad Acc. Circ:** 1,100 (ctrl). ***Continues** Greater Milwaukee Dental Bulletin.*
Desc: Scientific articles with a dental orientation and news of local dental activities.
Ind/Abst Index Dent. Lit.

ISSN 1063-3324
DD 617 US
NLM W1; GP12
CEASED
GP (ATLANTA, GA.). (GP.). [GP]. **Added/Corp** American Health Consultants. **VAT** General Practitioner. (1992)-(19??). Periodical. English. American Health Consultants, 3525 Piedmont Road, Suite 400, Atlanta GA 30305. **Tel** (800)688-2421, (404)262-7436, FAX (800)850-1232, (404)262-7837. **(Subscription address:** American Health Consultants, Dept. 5042, Box 71266, Chicago IL 60691. **)** ***Formed by the union of** Cosmetic Dentistry for GPs, 1042-1092; Endodontics for GPs, 1050-8767 **and** Periodontics for GPs, 1057-445X.*
Desc: Helps meet more of your patients' needs and increase your income by offering expanded clinical services like endodontics, cosmetic dentistry, implantology, orthodontics and geriatric dentistry.

LC RK78 .A66A **ISSN** 0361-9273
DD 617.6/007/1173 US
NLM WU 22 DC2 G9
GUIDEBOOK OF U.S. & CANADIAN POSTDOCTORAL DENTAL PROGRAMS. Main/Corp American Association of Dental Schools. **VAT** Guidebook of United States and Canadian Postdoctoral Dental Programs. 1976/77-. English. $3.00. American Association of Dental Schools, 1625 Massachusetts Avenue Northwest, Washington DC 20036. **Tel** (202)667-9433, FAX (202)667-0642.

ISSN 1062-029X
DD 378 US
NLM W1; HA63F
HARVARD DENTAL BULLETIN. [Harv. dent. bull.]. **Added/Corp** Harvard School of Dental Medicine. Harvard Dental Alumni Association. Vol. 1, No. 1 (Winter 1990-1991)-. Bulletin. English. Two times a year. Free on request. Harvard School Dental Medicine, 188 Longwood Avenue, Boston MA 02115. **Tel** (617)432-1533. ***Continues** Harvard Dental Alumni Bulletin, 0046-6891.*
Ind/Abst Index Dent. Lit. (1990-1991).

ISSN 0891-9933
DD 617 US
NLM W1; HA966
HAWAII DENTAL JOURNAL. [Hawaii dent. j.]. **Added/Corp** Hawaii Dental Association. Vol. 15, No. 1 (July 1984)-. Periodical. English. Twelve times a year. $20.00. Hawaii Dental Association, 1000 Bishop Street/Suite 805, Honolulu HI 96813. **Tel** (808)536-2135. **ED** Dr. Martin Nweira. **Ad Acc. Circ:** 1,000 (ctrl). ***Formed by the union of** Journal of the Hawaii Dental Association, 0017-8616 **and** Odontoscope.*
Desc: Technical and scientific publication for Hawaii's dental professionals.
Ind/Abst Dent. Abstr. (-1991); Index Dent. Lit. (Vol. 15, No. 1, 1984-).

ISSN 0073-1404
US
HAYES DIRECTORY OF DENTAL SUPPLY HOUSES. [Hayes dir. dent. supply houses]. (1935)-. Directory. English. One time a year.

$80.00. Edward N. Hayes Publisher, 4229 Birch Street, Newport Beach CA 92660. **Tel** (714)756-9063, FAX (714)756-0921.

ISSN 1011-4181
GR

NLM W1 HE784
HELLENIKA STOMATOLOGIKA CHRONIKA. [Ell. stomatol. hron.]. **VFOAT** Hellenic Stomatological Annals. Vol. 14 (1970)-. Periodical. Greek, Modern (English). Four times a year. $15.00. Panhellio Dental Association, Themistocleous 38, Athens 142 Greece. **Tel** (01)36.13.380. ***Continues*** *Stomatologika Chronika.*
Desc: Scientific papers of dental contents written by dentists.
Ind/Abst Index Dent. Lit.

ISSN 1105-1124
GR

NLM W1; HE794H
HELLENIKO PERIODIKO GIA STOMATIKE & GNATHOPROSOPIKE CHEIROURGIKE. **Added/Corp** Hetaireia Stomatognathoprosopikes Cheirourgikes (Greece). **VFOAT** Helleniko Periodiko Gia Stomatike Kai; Gnathoprosopike Cheirourgike; Greek Journal of Oral and Maxillofacial Surgery; Greek Journal of Oral & Maxillofacial Surgery. Vol. 1, No. 1 (March 1986)-. Periodical. Greek, Modern (summaries and/or abstracts in English). Four times a year. $30.00.
Ind/Abst Index Dent. Lit. (March 1986-).

ISSN 0910-9722
JA

NLM W1; HI205H **CODEN** HNSZEX
HIGASHI NIHON SHIGAKU ZASSHI. [Higashi Nippon shigaku zasshi]. **Added/Corp** Higashi Nihon Gakuen Daigaku. Shigakkai. **VFOAT** Higashi Nippon Dental Journal. (1982)-. Periodical. Japanese (summaries and/or abstracts in English; table of contents in English). Two times a year. Higashi Nihon Gakuen Daigaku Shigakkai, Showa 57-Nen, Hokkaido Japan. Documents available from BIOSIS Document Express, CASDDS.
Ind/Abst Biol. Abstr.; Chem. Abstr.

ISSN 0046-7472
JA
CODEN HUDJAN

HIROSHIMA DAIGAKU SHIGAKU ZASSHI. [Hiroshima Daigaku Shigaku zasshi]. **Added/Corp** Hiroshima Daigaku Shigaku Gakkai. **VFOAT** Journal of Hiroshima University Dental Society. (1969)-. Periodical. Japanese. Two times a year. Hiroshima Daigaku Shigaku Gakkai, Hiroshima Japan. available on microfilm from University Microfilms International (UMI). Documents available from CASDDS.
Ind/Abst Chem. Abstr.

ISSN 0360-7224
US

NLM W1 I219F
I.D.A.A. COMMUNIQUE. **Added/Corp** Iowa Dental Assistants Association. **VAT** Iowa Dental Assistants Association Communique. (196?)-. Periodical. English. Four times a year. Iowa Dental Association, 333 Insurance Exchange Building, Des Moines IA 50309. **Tel** (515)282-7250.
Ind/Abst Health Plan. Adminis.

ISSN 0019-1973
US

NLM W1 IL249
TITLE CHANGE
ILLINOIS DENTAL JOURNAL. [Ill. dent. j.]. **Added/Corp** Illinois State Dental Society. (Sept. 1931)-(Sept. 1995). Periodical. English. Illinois State Dental Society, 524 South 5th Street, Springfield IL 62704. **Tel** (217)525-1406, FAX (217)525-8872. **(Subscription address:** Illinois Dental Journal, PO Box 376, Springfield IL 62705. **Tel** (217)525-1406.**)** **ED** D. Milton Salzer. **Ad Acc. Circ:** 6,000. available on microfilm and microfiche from University Microfilms International (UMI). ***Supersedes*** *Illinois State Dental Society. Bulletin.* ***Continued by*** *Illinois Dental News.*
Desc: Contains items of interest to Illinois dentists.
Ind/Abst Dent. Abstr.; Health Plan. Adminis.; Index Dent. Lit.

US

•**ILLINOIS DENTAL NEWS.** (1995)-. English. Six times a year. $30.00. Illinois State Dental Society, 524 South 5th Street, Springfield IL 62704. **Tel** (217)525-1406, FAX (217)525-8872. ***Continues*** *Illinois Dental Journal.*

US

NLM W1; IM5914
IMPACT. **Added/Corp** Academy of General Dentistry. **VFOAT** Academy of General Dentistry Impact; AGD Impact. Vol. 19, No. 1 (Jan. 1991)-. Periodical. English. Eleven times a year (monthly except Aug.). $20.00 (individuals), $32.00 (institutions) US; $25.00 (individuals), $37.00 (institutions) Canada; $35.00Can$ (individuals), $47.00 (institutions) other. General Dentistry - Academy of General Dentistry, 211 East Chicago Avenue, Suite 1200, Chicago IL 60611-2670. **Tel** (312)440-4300, FAX (312)440-0559. **ED** William W. Howard. **Ad Acc, Adv Mgr:** Todd Goldman, **Tel** (813)264-2772. available on microfilm from University Microfilms International (UMI). ***Continues*** *AGD Impact, 0194-729X.*
Desc: Gives general dentists insights into the issues, trends and controversies surrounding techniques, materials, equipment, care management and relationships in the health care community. Also includes business strategies, ethics, legislations, patient question-and-answer fact sheets, national and international news that affect dental practice and continuing education course offerings.

DD 617 **ISSN** 1056-6163
US
CCC

NLM W1; IM661OL
IMPLANT DENTISTRY. [Implant dent.]. **Added/Corp** International Congress of Oral Implantologists. American Academy of Implant Prosthodontics. Academy for Implants & Transplants. (1992)-. Periodical. English. Four times a year. $136.00. Williams & Wilkins Company, 428 East Preston Street, Baltimore MD 21202-3993. **Tel** (410)528-4000, (800)638-6423, FAX (410)528-8596, telex 87669. **(Subscription address:** Williams & Wilkins, PO Box 64380, Baltimore MD 21264. **Tel** 800 638-6423.**)** Documents available from , , Quick Copies. ***Continues*** *International Journal of Oral Implantology, 1048-1842.*
Desc: The official journal of the International Congress of Oral Implantologists and its Component and Affiliated Societies. Directed to general practitioners and specialists offering implant services to edentulous or partially edentulous patients. Covers scientific, educational, and clinical advances in oral implantology.
Ind/Abst Curr. Cit.

ISSN 1059-3489
DD 617 US
NLM W1; IM595G
IMPLANT SOCIETY, THE. (THE IMPLANT SOCIETY : [PERIODICAL].). [Implant Soc.]. **Added/Corp** Implant Society. Vol. 1, No. 1 (Mar./Apr. 1990)-. Periodical. English. Six times a year. $135.00. Implant Society, One Kendall Square, Suite 2200, Cambridge MA 02139. **Tel** (617)621-7170. **ED** M. Thompson. Index available (bound in every issue). cum. index. **Circ:** 15,000.
Ind/Abst Index Dent. Lit. (1990-).

LC Z6668 .I45 RK51 **ISSN** 0019-3992
DD 016.6/001/6 US
NLM ZWU 100 I381
INDEX TO DENTAL LITERATURE. See Dentistry-Abstracting, Bibliographies and Statistics.

ISSN 0325-0679
AG

NLM ZWU 100; I45
INDICE DE LA LITERATURA DENTAL PERIODICA EN CASTELLANO. (INDICE DE LA LITERATURA DENTAL EN CASTELLANO.). [Indice lit. dent. period. castell.]. **Added/Corp** Asociacion Odontologica Argentina. **VFOAT** Indice de la Literatura Dental. (197?)-. Spanish. Every 2 years. $30.00 per volume (1950-1987). Association of Odontologia of Argentina, Junin 959, Buenos Aires Argentina. **Tel** 011 54 1 961 6062 6141. available on CD-ROM. ***Continues*** *Indice de la Literatura Dental Periodica en Castellano, 0325-0679.*

ISSN 1185-7331
DD 617.6 CN
INF-O-RAL (VERDUN). (INF-O-RAL.). [Inf-o-ral]. **Added/Corp** Centre Hospitalier de Verdun. Service de Medecine Dentaire Preventative. **VFOAT** Inforal. Vol. 1, No 1 (Mar. 1991)-. Periodical. French. Twelve times a year. Limited free distribution. Service de Medecine Dentaire Preventative, Centre Hospitalier de Verdun, 4000 boulevard Lasalle, Verdun Quebec H4G 2A3 Canada.

ISSN 0020-0018
FR

NLM W1 IN419
INFORMATION DENTAIRE, L'. [Inf. dent.]. (June 1938)-. Periodical. French. Forty-Four times a year. $426.51. Soc d'Edition l'Info Dentaire, 42 rue Vignon, 75442 Paris Cedex 09 France. **Tel** 011 33 1 42662407. ***Continues*** *Semaine Dentaire.*
Ind/Abst Curr. Titles Dent.; Index Dent. Lit.

ISSN 0020-0336
GW

UDC 616.314-089
INFORMATIONEN AUS ORTHODONTIE UND KIEFERORTHOPADIE. [Inf. Orthod. Kieferorthop.]. **VFOAT** Orthodontie und Kieferorthopadie. (1969)-. Periodical. German. Four times a year. $157.00. Dr. Alfred Huethig Verlag GmbH, Postfach 102869, D-69018 Heidelberg Germany. **Tel** 011 49 6221 489281, FAX 011 49 6221 489279. **(Subscription address:** Huethig Publishing Inc., 29 Macintosh Drive, Oxford CT 06478. **Tel** (203)881-2647.**)**

ISSN 0147-0221
PR

NLM W2 DP8 D7
INFORME ANUAL; SERVICIOS ODONTOLOGICOS. **Main/Corp** Puerto Rico. Division of Oral Health. Periodical. Multiple languages (Spanish and English).

ISSN 0020-6539
UK
CCC

NLM W1 IN742 **CODEN** IDJOAS
INTERNATIONAL DENTAL JOURNAL. [Int. dent. j.]. **Added/Corp** Association Dentaire Mondiale. International Dental Federation. Vol. 1 (Sept. 1950)-. Periodical. English. Six times a year. $171.12. FDI World Dental Press Ltd, 7 Carlisle Street, London W1V 5RG United Kingdom. **Tel** 011 44 171 9357852, FAX 011 44 171 4860183. **ED** R Duckworth (editor's address: London Hostpital Medical College Dental School, London United Kingdom). Index Available in first issue of next volume--loose-unpaged. **Bk Rev. Ad Acc.** available on microfilm and microfiche from University Microfilms International (UMI). Documents available from BIOSIS Document Express, CASDDS.
Desc: Each issue provides new information on scientific and clinical advances in all areas of dentistry, with special emphasis on dental epidemiology and administration of dental health.
Ind/Abst Biol. Abstr. (-1975); Chem. Abstr.; Curr. Cit.; Curr. Titles Dent.; Index Med.; Index Dent. Lit.; Nutr. Abstr. Rev., Ser. B, Live Feeds and Feed.; Nutr. Abstr. Rev., Ser. A, Hum. Exp. (-1988); Nutr. Res. Newsl.; SportSearch.

ISSN 0143-2885
UK
CCC

NLM W1 IN748G **CODEN** IENJEA
Pr Rev.
INTERNATIONAL ENDODONTIC JOURNAL. [Int. endod. j.]. **Added/Corp** British Endodontic Society. Vol. 13 (Jan. 1980)-. Academic Scholarly Publication. English. Six times a year. $244.00. Blackwell Scientific Publications Ltd, Marston Book Services, PO Box 88, Oxford OX2 ONE United Kingdom. **Tel** 011 44 1865 206206, FAX 011 44 1865 206219, telex 837 515 MARDIS G. **ED** T.R. Pitt Ford. Index available. cum. index. **Bk Rev. Ad Acc. Circ:** 1,648. available on microfilm and microfiche from University Microfilms International (UMI). Documents available from The Genuine Article, BIOSIS Document Express. ***Continues*** *Journal of the British Endodontic Society.*
Desc: Covers diseases of dental pulp and periapical tissues, treatment and associated applied microbiology, pharmacology, radiology, toxicology and materials science.
Ind/Abst Biol. Abstr. (1987-); Curr. Cit.; Curr. Contents Clin. Med.; Curr. Titles Dent.; Index Dent. Lit.; Res. Alert [Select. Cov.]; SCISEARCH; Soc. Sci. Cit. Index [Select. Cov.].

ISSN 0742-1931
DD 616 US
CCC

NLM W1; IN7652TC **CODEN** IAOSEE
INTERNATIONAL JOURNAL OF ADULT ORTHODONTICS AND ORTHOGNATHIC SURGERY, THE. Vol. 1, No. 1 (Winter 1986)-. Periodical. English (Italian). Four times a year. $88.00. Quintessence Publishing Company Inc., 551 North Kimberly Drive, Carol Stream IL 60188-1881. **Tel** (708)682-3223, (800)621-0387, FAX (708)682-3288. **ED** Robert Vanarsdall and Raymond White. **Ad Acc. Circ:** 4,000. Documents available from BIOSIS Document Express.
Desc: Targeted at general dentists, orthodontists, oral surgeons and periodontists. Articles depict the latest advancements in treatments of dentofacial deformities. Featured are: current concepts, clinical findings, and research results in orthodontic and orthognathic surgery/new knowledge in anesthesiology, patient monitoring, facial soft tissues, and related areas; also interdisciplinary treatment encompassing orthodontics, oral surgery, periodontics, and restorative dentistry.
Ind/Abst Biol. Abstr. (1987-); Curr. Cit.; Curr. Titles Dent.; Dent. Abstr.

ISSN 0306-9419
UK

NLM W1 IN766K **CODEN** IJFDDK
INTERNATIONAL JOURNAL OF FORENSIC DENTISTRY. (THE INTERNATIONAL JOURNAL OF FORENSIC DENTISTRY.). [Int. j. forensic dent.]. **Added/Corp** American Society of Forensic Odontology. International Society of Forensic Odonto-Stomatology. **VFOAT** Forensic Dentistry. Vol. 1 (July 1973)-. Periodical. English. Four times a year. Forensic Photography, PO Box 18, Bognor Regis PO2 27AA United Kingdom. Documents available from CASDDS.
Ind/Abst Chem. Abstr.

ISSN 0882-2786
DD 617 US
CCC
NLM W1; IN77TJ CODEN IJOIED
INTERNATIONAL JOURNAL OF ORAL AND MAXILLOFACIAL IMPLANTS, THE.
[Int. j. oral maxillofac. implants]. **Added/Corp** Academy of Osseointegration. **VFOAT** JOMI. Vol. 1, No. 1 (Summer 1986)-. Periodical. English (Italian and Japanese). Six times a year. $106.00. Quintessence Publishing Company Inc., 551 North Kimberly Drive, Carol Stream IL 60188-1881. **Tel** (708)682-3223, (800)621-0387, FAX (708)682-3288. **ED** William Laney. Index available. **Ad Acc. Circ:** 5,000. Documents available from BIOSIS Document Express.
Desc: The journal is aimed at oral surgeons, prosthodontists, periodontists, general dentists, and biomaterial specialists to disseminate current information related to dental implants.
Ind/Abst Biol. Abstr. (1986-); Curr. Cit.; Curr. Titles Dent.; Dent. Abstr.; Index Med.; Index Dent. Lit. (Summer 1986-).

ISSN 0901-5027
DK
CCC
NLM W1; IN77TP CODEN IJOSE9
INTERNATIONAL JOURNAL OF ORAL AND MAXILLOFACIAL SURGERY. [Int. j. oral maxillofac. surg.]. **Added/Corp** International Association of Oral and Maxillofacial Surgeons. **VFOAT** Oral and Maxillofacial Surgery. Vol. 15, No. 1 (Feb. 1986)-. Academic Scholarly Publication. English. Six times a year. $353.56. Munksgaard International Publishers Ltd, PO Box 2148, DK-1016 Copenhagen K Denmark. **Tel** 011 45 33 127030, FAX 011 45 33 129387, telex 19431 MUNKS DK. **ED** P.J.W. Stoelinga. Index available. **Bk Rev. Ad Acc. Circ:** 1,200 (ctrl). Documents available from The Genuine Article, BIOSIS Document Express, CASDDS. ***Continues** International Journal of Oral Surgery, 0300-9785.*
Desc: Official publication of the International Association of Oral and Maxillofacial Surgeons.
Ind/Abst Biol. Abstr. (1986-); Chem. Abstr. (1986-); Curr. Cit.; Curr. Contents Clin. Med.; Curr. Titles Dent.; EMBASE; Energy Res. Abstr. (1986-); Helminthol. Abstr. (1991-); Index Med. (1986-); Index Dent. Lit. (1986-); Life Sci. Collect. (1986-); Protozoolog. Abstr.; Res. Alert [Full Cov.]; Rev. Med. Vet. Mycology; Sci. Cit. Index; SCISEARCH.

ISSN 0735-0120
DD 616 US
NLM W1 IN77X
INTERNATIONAL JOURNAL OF OROFACIAL MYOLOGY, THE. (THE INTERNATIONAL JOURNAL OF OROFACIAL MYOLOGY : OFFICIAL PUBLICATION OF THE INTERNATIONAL ASSOCIATION OF OROFACIAL MYOLOGY.). [Int. j. orofac. myol.]. **Added/Corp** International Association of Orofacial Myology. Vol. 6, No. 3 (July 1980)-. Academic Scholarly Publication. English. One time a year. $18.00. International Journal of Orofacial Myology, 2315 187th Avenue Northeast, Redmond WA 98052. **Tel** (206)746-6929. **ED** Jane Van Reenan. Index available. cum. index. **Bk Rev. Circ:** 350 (ctrl). ***Continues** International Journal of Oral Myology, 0360-4004.*
Desc: Research and practical applications of issues of interest to dentists, orthodontists, speech pathologists and physical therapists regarding oral and facial muscle function disorders.
Ind/Abst Curr. Titles Dent.; EMBASE; Energy Res. Abstr. (Aug. 1982-); Index Dent. Lit.

ISSN 0960-7439
UK
CCC
NLM W1; IN771G
INTERNATIONAL JOURNAL OF PAEDIATRIC DENTISTRY. Added/Corp British Paedodontic Society. International Association of Dentistry for Children. Vol. 1, No. 1 Apr. (1991)-. Academic Scholarly Publication. English (summaries and/or abstracts in French, German and Spanish). Three times a year. $275.00. Blackwell Scientific Publications Ltd, Marston Book Services, PO Box 88, Oxford OX2 ONE United Kingdom. **Tel** 011 44 1865 206206, FAX 011 44 1865 206219, telex 837 515 MARDIS G. available on microfilm and microfiche from University Microfilms International (UMI). ***Formed by the union of** Journal of Paediatric Dentistry, 0267-2073 **and** Journal of the International Association of Dentistry for Children, 0309-6858.*
Ind/Abst Index Dent. Lit. (1991-).

ISSN 0198-7569
US
CCC
NLM W1 IN771RM
INTERNATIONAL JOURNAL OF PERIODONTICS & RESTORATIVE DENTISTRY, THE. [Int. j. periodontics restor. dent.]. **VFOAT** International Journal of Periodontics and Restorative Dentistry. Vol. 1, No. 1 (1981)-. Periodical. English (German, French, Italian and Japanese). Six times a year. $168.00. Quintessence Publishing Company Inc., 551 North Kimberly Drive, Carol Stream IL 60188-1881. **Tel** (708)682-3223, (800)621-0387, FAX (708)682-3288. **ED** Gerald M. Kramer and Myron Nevins. Index available. **Ad Acc. Circ:** 6,000.
Desc: Targeted at periodontists and general dentists. Articles deal with the interdependent disciplines of periodontics and restorative dentistry. Each issue contains step-by-step procedures, research developments, and daily practice information.
Ind/Abst Curr. Cit.; Curr. Titles Dent.; Dent. Abstr.; Index Dent. Lit.

ISSN 0893-2174
DD 617 US
CCC
NLM W1; IN775KE CODEN IJLPEJ
INTERNATIONAL JOURNAL OF PROSTHODONTICS, THE. [Int. j. prosthodont.]. **Added/Corp** International College of Prosthodontists. Vol. 1, No. 1 (July/Aug. 1988)-. Periodical. English. Six times a year. $106.00. Quintessence Publishing Company Inc., 551 North Kimberly Drive, Carol Stream IL 60188-1881. **Tel** (708)682-3223, (800)621-0387, FAX (708)682-3288. Documents available from BIOSIS Document Express.
Desc: Provides current articles in all areas of prosthodontics and other interrelated disciplines including periodontics, endodontics, and orthodontics.
Ind/Abst Biol. Abstr. (1989-); Curr. Cit.; Dent. Abstr. (1992-); Health Plan. Adminis.; Index Dent. Lit. (1988-).

ISSN 1059-8081
DD 617 US
CEASED
INTOUCH (KNOXVILLE, TENN.). (INTOUCH : THE MAGAZINE FOR DENTAL HYGIENISTS.). [Intouch]. **VFOAT** Intouch Dental Health Adviser; In Touch. Vol. 1, No. 1 (Spring 1992)-(199?). Periodical. English. Whittle Communications, 333 Main Avenue, Knoxville TN 37902. **Tel** (615)595-5000, FAX (615)595-5877.

ISSN 0021-0498
DD 617 US
NLM W1; IO288
IOWA DENTAL JOURNAL, THE. [Iowa dent. j.]. **Added/Corp** Iowa State Dental Society. Vol. 41, (Feb. 1955)-. Periodical. English. Four times a year (Jan., Apr., July, Oct.). $15.00. Iowa Dental Association, 333 Insurance Exchange Building, Des Moines IA 50309. **Tel** (515)282-7250. **ED** James Heath and Robert Harpster. **Bk Rev. Ad Acc. Circ:** 2,000 (ctrl). ***Continues** Iowa Dental Bulletin, 0021-048X.*
Desc: Scientific and dental news and how it relates to the National Dental affairs and the dentistry in Iowa.
Ind/Abst Curr. Titles Dent.; Dent. Abstr. (1991-); Index Dent. Lit.

ISSN 0886-1064
DD 617 US
NLM W1; JO22CE
Pr Rev.
JOURNAL (AMERICAN ACADEMY OF GNATHOLOGIC ORTHOPEDICS). (THE JOURNAL / AMERICAN ACADEMY OF GNATHOLOGIC ORTHOPEDICS.). **Added/Corp** American Academy of Gnathologic Orthopedics. International Association for Orthodontics. Vol. 1, No. 1 (1984)-. Periodical. English. Four times a year. $80.00. AAGO (American Academy Gnathologic Orthopedics), PO Box 548, Richmond TX 77469. **Tel** (713)341-5250, FAX (312)642-4191. **ED** Joanna Carey. **Bk Rev. Ad Acc. Circ:** 1,800 (ctrl).
Desc: Clinical and scientific articles on orthodontics and related dental topics.
Ind/Abst Index Dent. Lit. (1984-).

ISSN 0709-8936
DD 617.6/005 CN
CCC
NLM W1; CA547
Pr Rev.
JOURNAL - CANADIAN DENTAL ASSOCIATION. [J. - Can. Dent. Assoc.]. **Main/Corp** Canadian Dental Association. **VFOAT** Journal de l'Association Dentaire Canadienne. Vol. 45, No. 5 (May 1979)-. Periodical. English (French). Twelve times a year. 38.42Can$. Canadian Dental Association, 1815 Alta Vista Drive, Ottawa Ontario K1G 3Y6 Canada. **Tel** (613)523-1770, FAX (613)523-7736. **ED** Ralph Crawford. Index available. **Bk Rev**, (Qty: 36/yr). **Ad Acc, Adv Mgr:** Trish Sullivan. **Circ:** 18,000 (ctrl). ***Continues** Dental Journal, 0382-8514.*
Ind/Abst Curr. Cit.; Index Med. (1979-); Index Dent. Lit. (1979-); Nutr. Res. Newsl.; Life Sci. Collect.

ISSN 0010-1559
DD 617 US
NLM W1 JO917D
JOURNAL - COLORADO DENTAL ASSOCIATION. (JOURNAL.). [J. - Colo. Dent. Assoc.]. **Main/Corp** Colorado Dental Association. **VFOAT** Journal of the Colorado Dental Association. Vol. 40, No. 4 (Sept. 1962)-. Periodical. English. Four times a year. $35.00. Colorado Dental Association, 3690 South Yosemite, Suite 100, Denver CO 80237-1808. **Tel** (303)740-6900, FAX (303)740-7989. **ED** Barbara White Melin. **Bk Rev. Ad Acc. Circ:** 2,200 (ctrl). ***Continues** Journal / Colorado State Dental Association.*
Desc: Scientific and association information.
Ind/Abst Index Dent. Lit.

ISSN 0010-6232
DD 617 US
NLM W1 JO236K
Pr Rev.
JOURNAL - CONNECTICUT STATE DENTAL ASSOCIATION, THE. [J. - Conn. St. Dent. Assoc.]. **Main/Corp** Connecticut State Dental Association. Vol. 26 (No. 1)- (Nov. 1952)-. Periodical. English. One time a year. $15.00. Connecticut State Dental Association, 62 Russ Street, Hartford CT 06106. **Tel** (203)278-5550. **ED** Dr. Howard Mark. **Bk Rev. Ad Acc, Adv Mgr:** Sarah Van Dyke, **Tel** (203)278-5550. **Circ:** 2,900 (ctrl). ***Continues** Bulletin of the Connecticut State Dental Association.*
Ind/Abst Index Dent. Lit.

ISSN 0301-3952
FR
NLM W1 JO237F CODEN JBBUA3
CEASED
JOURNAL DE BIOLOGIE BUCCALE. [J. biol. buccale]. **VFOAT** J.B.B. Journal de Biologie Buccale. Vol. 1, Mar. (1973)-March (1993). Academic Scholarly Publication. French (English; summaries and/or abstracts in English, French and German). Soc d'Edition l'Info Dentaire, 42 rue Vignon, 75442 Paris Cedex 09 France. **Tel** 011 33 1 42662407. Documents available from BIOSIS Document Express, CASDDS.
Ind/Abst Biol. Abstr.; Chem. Abstr.; Curr. Titles Dent.; EMBASE; Index Med.; Index Dent. Lit.; Life Sci. Collect.; Protozoolog. Abstr.; Sci. Cit. Index (19??-19??); SCISEARCH.

ISSN 1195-3888
DD 617.6 CN
JOURNAL DE LA SANTE DENTAIRE COMMUNAUTAIRE DU QUEBEC. [J. sante dent. communaut. Que.]. **Added/Corp** Association des Dentistes en Sante Communautaire du Quebec. Vol. 1, No. 1 (Winter 1988)-. Periodical. French. Four times a year. 20.01Can$. Dentist Conseil, 800 boulevard Chomedez Tour A, Laval Quebec H7V 3Y4 Canada. **Tel** (514)694-2055.

FR
NLM W1; JO326RH
•**JOURNAL DE PARODONTOLOGIE & D'IMPLANTOLOGIE ORALE. Added/Corp** Societe Francaise de Parodontologie. **VFOAT** Journal de Parodontologie et d'Implantologie Orale. Vol. 13, No 1 (Febr. 1994)-. Periodical. French (summaries and/or abstracts in English; table of contents in English). Four times a year. $162.95. Societe d'Editions de l'Information Dentaire, 42 rue Vignon, 75442 Paris Cedex 09 France. **Tel** 011 33 1 42662407. ***Continues** Journal de Parodontologie, 0750-1838.*
Ind/Abst Curr. Cit.; Index Dent. Lit. (Feb. 1994-).

CN
NLM W1 JO37CD
JOURNAL DENTAIRE DU QUEBEC. Added/Corp Order of Dentists of Quebec. Dental Association of the Province of Quebec. Quebec Dental Surgeons Association. **VFOAT** Dental Journal; Dentistes du Quebec; Dentists of Canada; Quebec Dental Journal. Vol. 1 (Nov./Dec. 1963)-. Periodical. English (French). Eleven times a year. 42.02Can$. Ordre des Dentistes Quebec, 625 boulevard Rene-Levesque Ouest, 15 Etage, Montreal Quebec H3B 1R2 Canada. **Tel** (514)875-8511. **ED** Denis Forest. Index available. **Bk Rev. Ad Acc. Circ:** 4,200 (ctrl).
Desc: Contains information on continuing education for members, newsletters, information on the corporation and public health.
Ind/Abst Index Dent. Lit.; Repere (1983-).

ISSN 0744-9682
US
JOURNAL : MACOMB COUNTY DENTAL SOCIETY. [J.- Macomb Cty. Dent. Soc. (Mich.)]. **Main/Corp** Macomb County Dental Society (Mich.). **VFOAT** Journal of the Macomb County Dental Society. Periodical. English. Twelve times a year. $5.00. Macomb County Dental Society, 6447 Meldrum, Anchorville MI 48004.
Ind/Abst Index Dent. Lit.

ISSN 0895-8831
DD 617 US
NLM W1; JO587M CODEN JCLDED
Pr Rev.
JOURNAL OF CLINICAL DENTISTRY, THE. [J. clin. dent.]. Vol. 1, No. 1 (Summer 1988)-. Periodical. English. Four times a year. $70.00. Professional Audience Communication, PO Box 243, Yardley PA 19067. **Tel** (215)493-7400, FAX (215)493-9804. **ED** Dr Robert Emling, (215)667-7398. Index available. **Circ:** 1,000 (ctrl). Documents available from BIOSIS Document Express.
Desc: Clinical and applied dental research and review.
Ind/Abst Biol. Abstr. (1988-); Curr. Cit.; Dent. Abstr. (1992-); EMBASE [Select. Cov.]; Health Plan. Adminis.; Index Dent. Lit. (Vol. 1, No. 1, 1988-).

ISSN 0022-3875
DD 617 US
NLM W1 J223W
JOURNAL OF CLINICAL ORTHODONTICS. (JOURNAL OF CLINICAL ORTHODONTICS : JCO.). [J. clin. orthod.]. **VFOAT** JCO. Vol. 4 (1970)-. Periodical. English. Twelve times a year. $155.00. JPO Inc., 1828 Pearl Street, Boulder CO 80302. **Tel** (303)443-1720. **ED** Eugene L Gottlieb. Index available (December issue of each volume). **Bk Rev. Ad Acc. Circ:** 12,000. ***Continues*** *Journal of Practical Orthodontics, 8755-4852.*
Desc: Practical aspects of everyday orthodontic treatment, techniques and practice administration.
Ind/Abst Curr. Titles Dent.; Dent. Abstr. (-199?).

LC RK55.C5 J68 **ISSN** 1053-4628
DD 617.6/45/005 US
NLM W1; JO5896H **CODEN** JCPDEX
JOURNAL OF CLINICAL PEDIATRIC DENTISTRY, THE. [J. clin. pediatr. dent.]. **VFOAT** Clinical Pediatric Dentistry. Vol. 15, No. 1 (Fall 1990)-. Trade Publication. English. Four times a year (Jan., Apr., Jul., Oct.). $129.00. School of Dental Medicine, Tufts University, One Kneeland Street, Boston MA 02111. **Tel** (617)956-6902, telex 78-2661. **(Subscription address:** Journal of Clinical Pediatric Dentistry, Subscription Office, PO Box 830259, Birmingham AL 35283-0259. **Tel** (800)633-4931, (205)991-6920 (outside US and Canada), FAX (205)995-1588.**)** Index available (bound in last issue). available on microfilm and microfiche from University Microfilms International (UMI). ***Continues*** *Journal of Pedodontics, 0145-5508.*
Desc: Covers the study and practice of children's dentistry. Features case reviews and the latest international research.
Ind/Abst Annals Behav. Med.; Curr. Cit.; Dent. Abstr. (1992-); Health Plan. Adminis.; Index Dent. Lit. (Fall 1990-).

ISSN 0303-6979
DK
CCC
NLM W1 JO5896P **CODEN** JCPEDZ
Pr Rev.
JOURNAL OF CLINICAL PERIODONTOLOGY. [J. clin. periodontol.]. **Added/Corp** British Society of Periodontology. **VFOAT** Clinical Periodontology. Vol. 1 (1974)-. Academic Scholarly Publication. English (French and German; summaries and/or abstracts in German and French). Twelve times a year. $310.11. Munksgaard International Publishers Ltd, PO Box 2148, DK-1016 Copenhagen K Denmark. **Tel** 011 45 33 127030, FAX 011 45 33 129387, telex 19431 MUNKS DK. **ED** Jan Lindhe. Index available. **Bk Rev. Ad Acc. Circ:** 8,500 (ctrl). Documents available from The Genuine Article, BIOSIS Document Express, CASDDS.
Desc: Conveys scientific progress in periodontology to those concerned with application of this knowledge for the benefit of dental health.
Ind/Abst Biol. Abstr.; Chem. Abstr.; Curr. Cit.; Curr. Contents Clin. Med.; Curr. Contents Life Sci.; Curr. Titles Dent.; Dent. Abstr. (1992-); EMBASE [Select. Cov.]; Index Med.; Index Dent. Lit.; Life Sci. Collect.; Res. Alert [Full Cov.]; Sci. Cit. Index; SCISEARCH.

LC RK71 .J6 **ISSN** 0022-0337
DD 617.6/007/11 US
NLM W1 JO614
Pr Rev.
JOURNAL OF DENTAL EDUCATION. [J. dent. educ.]. **Added/Corp** American Association of Dental Schools. Vol. 1, (Oct. 1936)-. Periodical. English. Twelve times a year. $75.00. American Association of Dental Schools, 1625 Massachusetts Avenue Northwest, Washington DC 20036. **Tel** (202)667-9433, FAX (202)667-0642. **ED** James Boder (editor's address: University of North Carolina, 725 Airport Road Suite 210, Chapel Hill, N.C. 27599-7590 phone: (919)966-5727). Index available (Bound in Dec. issue). **Bk Rev. Ad Acc, Adv Mgr:** A. Siegel. **Circ:** 4,500 (ctrl). available on microfilm from Princeton Microfilms.
Desc: Contains articles on educational research, teaching methods and materials, curriculum and administration of educational programs.
Ind/Abst Contents Pages Educ.; Curr. Cit.; Curr. Index J. Educ.; Curr. Titles Dent.; Dent. Abstr.; High. Educ. Abstr. (1973-); Index Med.; Index Dent. Lit.; Res. High. Educ. Abstr.

LC RK1 **ISSN** 1043-254X
DD 617.6/01/05 US
NLM W1; JO615
Pr Rev.
JOURNAL OF DENTAL HYGIENE. [J. dent. hyg.]. **VFOAT** JDH. Vol. 62, No. 9 (Oct. 1988)-. Periodical. English. Nine times a year. $40.00. American Dental Hygienists Association, 444 North Michigan Avenue/Suite 3400, Chicago IL 60611. **Tel** (312)440-8900, FAX (312)440-8929. **ED** Rosetta Gervasi and John Thiel. cum. index. **Bk Rev. Ad Acc. Circ:** 30,000 (ctrl). available on microfilm and microfiche from University Microfilms International (UMI). ***Continues*** *Dental Hygiene, 0091-3979.*
Desc: Scholarly and technical articles on dental hygiene practice, education and research.
Ind/Abst Curr. Cit.; Index Dent. Lit. (Oct. 1988-).

LC RK1 .J76 **ISSN** 0022-0345
DD 617.6/005 US
CCC
NLM W1 JO618K **CODEN** JDREAF
Pr Rev.
JOURNAL OF DENTAL RESEARCH. [J. dent. res.]. **Added/Corp** American Association for Dental Research. American Dental Association. International Association for Dental Research. **VFOAT** JDR. Vol. 1, No. 1 (Mar. 1919)-. Academic Scholarly Publication. English. Thirteen times a year (monthly with 1 special issue). $350.00. American & International Association Dental Research, 1111 14th Street Northwest, Suite 1000, Washington DC 20005. **Tel** (202)898-1050, FAX (202)789-1033. **ED** Colin Dawes. Index available (bound in Dec. issue). cum. index. **Ad Acc. Circ:** 6,500. available on microfilm and microfiche from University Microfilms International (UMI). Documents available from The Genuine Article, BIOSIS Document Express, CASDDS, ADONIS. ***Continues*** *Journal of the Allied Dental Societies, 0095-957X.*
Desc: Dedicated to the dissemination of new knowledge and information on all sciences relevant to dentistry and to oral cavity and associated structures in health and disease.
Ind/Abst ADONIS; AgBiotech News Inf.; Alum. Ind. Abstr.; Biol. Abstr.; Ceram. Abstr.; Chem. Abstr.; Curr. Cit.; Curr. Contents Clin. Med.; Curr. Contents Life Sci.; Curr. Titles Dent.; Dairy Sci. Abstr.; Dent. Abstr.; EMBASE [Select. Cov.]; Energy Res. Abstr.; Eng. Mater. Abstr.; Foods Adlibra; Index Med.; Index Dent. Lit.; INIS Atomindex [Micro.]; Met. Abstr.; Microbiol. Abstr. Sect. B; Nutr. Abstr. Rev., Ser. B, Live Feeds and Feed.; Nutr. Abstr. Rev., Ser. A, Hum. Exp.; Nutr. Res. Newsl.; Life Sci. Collect.; Ref. Upd. Deluxe Ed.; Res. Alert [Full Cov.]; Risk Abstr.; Sci. Cit. Index; SCISEARCH; Soc. Sci. Cit. Index [Select. Cov.]; Sug. Indus. Abstr.

ISSN 0300-5712
UK
CCC
NLM W1 JO618R **CODEN** JDENAB
Pr Rev.
JOURNAL OF DENTISTRY. [J. dent.]. Vol. 1 (Oct. 1972)-. Periodical. English. Six times a year. $374.00. Butterworth Heinemann Publishers, Linacre House Jordan Hill, Oxford OX2 8DP United Kingdom. **Tel** 011 44 1865 310366, FAX 011 44 1865 310898. **(Subscription address:** Elsevier Science Ltd. / Oxford Fulfillment Centre, PO Box 800, Kidlington OX5 1DX United Kingdom. **Tel** 011 44 865 843355.**) ED** N. H. F. Wilson (editor's address: University Dental Hospital, Manchester United Kingdom). Index available. **Bk Rev. Ad Acc. Circ:** 700. available on microfilm and microfiche from University Microfilms International (UMI); available on an online database from Elsevier Electronic Subscriptions (EES). Documents available from The Genuine Article, BIOSIS Document Express, CASDDS. ***Continues*** *Dental Practitioner and Dental Record, 0011-8729.*
Desc: Provides an international forum for reporting and discussing all issues relating to research, new developments and the practice of, in particular, restorative dentistry, including dental materials science. The prime purpose of this international journal is to foster the exchange of information among all concerned with the top in dental science and practice.
Ind/Abst Biol. Abstr. (1985-); Chem. Abstr.; Curr. Cit.; Curr. Titles Dent.; Dent. Abstr.; Index Med.; Index Dent. Lit.; Nutr. Abstr. Rev., Ser. B, Live Feeds and Feed.; Nutr. Abstr. Rev., Ser. A, Hum. Exp.; Nutr. Res. Newsl.; Res. Alert [Full Cov.]; Sci. Cit. Index; SCISEARCH.

ISSN 0022-0353
DD 617 US
NLM W1 JO619 **CODEN** JDCHAH
Pr Rev.
JOURNAL OF DENTISTRY FOR CHILDREN. [J. dent. child.]. **Added/Corp** American Society of Dentistry for Children. American Academy of Pedodontics. **VFOAT** ASDC Journal of Dentistry for Children. Vol. 7, No. 4 (Oct. 1940)-. Academic Scholarly Publication. English. Six times a year. $120.00. American Society of Dentistry for Children, 211 East Chicago Avenue, Suite 1430, Chicago IL 60611-2616. **Tel** (312)943-1244, (800)637-2732, FAX (312)943-5341. **ED** George W. Teuscher, Donald W. Kohn and Jimmy R. Pinkham. Index available. cum. index. **Bk Rev. Ad Acc. Circ:** 9,000 (ctrl). available on microfilm and microfiche from University Microfilms International (UMI). Documents available from The Genuine Article, BIOSIS Document Express, CASDDS. ***Continues*** *Review of Dentistry for Children.*
Desc: Papers on pediatric dentistry (research and clinical), child behavior, and related pediatric topics.
Ind/Abst Annals Behav. Med.; Biol. Abstr. (?-1991); Chem. Abstr.; Curr. Cit.; Curr. Contents Clin. Med.; Curr. Titles Dent.; Dent. Abstr. (1992-); Energy Res. Abstr. (Aug. 1982-); Index Dent. Lit.; Nutr. Abstr. Rev., Ser. B, Live Feeds and Feed.; Nutr. Abstr. Rev., Ser. A, Hum. Exp.; Nutr. Res. Newsl.; Life Sci. Collect.; Res. Alert [Full Cov.]; Sci. Cit. Index; SCISEARCH; Soc. Sci. Cit. Index [Select. Cov.].

LC RK351 .J68 **ISSN** 0099-2399
DD 617.6/34 US
CCC
NLM W1 JO643E
Pr Rev.
JOURNAL OF ENDODONTICS. [J. endod.]. **Added/Corp** American Association of Endodontists. American Dental Association. Vol. 1 (Jan. 1975)-. Periodical. English. Twelve times a year. $115.00. Williams & Wilkins Company, 428 East Preston Street, Baltimore MD 21202-3993. **Tel** (410)528-4000, (800)638-6423, FAX (410)528-8596, telex 87669. **(Subscription address:** Williams & Wilkins, PO Box 64380, Baltimore MD 21264. **Tel** 800 638-6423.**) ED** Steve Montgomery. **Ad Acc. Circ:** 5,700. available on microfilm. Documents available from The Genuine Article, Quick Copies.
Desc: Latest methods of pulp conservation, root canal instrumentation, and endodontic treatment for endodontists and general dentists.
Ind/Abst Curr. Cit.; Curr. Contents Clin. Med.; Curr. Titles Dent.; Dent. Abstr.; Energy Res. Abstr. (Aug. 1982-); Index Dent. Lit.; Res. Alert [Full Cov.]; Rev. Med. Vet. Mycology; Sci. Cit. Index; SCISEARCH; Soc. Sci. Cit. Index [Select. Cov.].

ISSN 1040-1466
DD 617 CN
NLM W1; JO644CF
JOURNAL OF ESTHETIC DENTISTRY. [J. esthet. dent.]. Vol. 1, No. 1 (Jan. 1989)-. Periodical. English. Six times a year. 190.00Can$. Decker Periodicals Publishing Inc., PO Box 620, Station A, Hamilton Ontario L8N 3K7 Canada. **Tel** (416)522-7017, (800)568-7281, FAX (416)522-7839. **ED** Ronald E. Jordan.
Desc: Provides color photographs of the latest techniques, procedures, and materials in esthetic dentistry. Contributors present their approach to practice management, marketing considerations, and advancements in orthodontic and oral surgery applications of esthetic dentistry.
Ind/Abst Curr. Cit.; Health Plan. Adminis.; Index Dent. Lit. (1989-).

LC RC **ISSN** 0258-414X
DD 616 AT
NLM W1; JO656
Pr Rev.
JOURNAL OF FORENSIC ODONTO-STOMATOLOGY, THE. [J. forensic odonto-stomatol.]. Vol. 1, No. 1 (Jan./June 1983)-. Academic Scholarly Publication. English. Two times a year (June and Dec.). 28.78Aus$. Journal of Forensic Odonto-Stomatology, University of Adelaide, Adelaide 5005 Australia. **Tel** 011 61 8 3035431, FAX 011 61 8 3034385, telex 89141. **ED** Dr. D Wilson. **Circ:** 300.
Desc: Scientific articles relating to forensic dentistry and case histories.
Ind/Abst EMBASE.

LC RD **ISSN** 1048-1990
DD 617 US
NLM W1; JO668B
Pr Rev.
JOURNAL OF GENERAL ORTHODONTICS. [J. gen. orthod.]. **Added/Corp** International Association for Orthodontics. **VFOAT** JGO. Vol. 1, No. 1 (March 1990)-. Trade Publication. English. Four times a year. $40.00. International Association for Orthodontics, 1100 West Lake Street, Suite 240, Oak Park IL 60301. **Tel** (708)445-0320, FAX (708)445-0321. **ED** Joanna Carey. **Bk Rev**, (Qty: 2). **Ad Acc. Circ:** 3,800 (ctrl).
Desc: Scientific and clinical articles on orthodontics for dentists.
Ind/Abst Health Plan. Adminis.

ISSN 0891-8171
DD 617 US
NLM W1; JO669PC
JOURNAL OF GNATHOLOGY, THE. **Added/Corp** International Academy of Gnathology. **VFOAT** Gnathology. Vol. 1, No. 1 (1982)-. Periodical. English. One time a year. $25.00. International Academy of Gnathology, PO Box 1085, La Mesa CA 91944. **Tel** (619)462-9933.
Ind/Abst Curr. Titles Dent.; Index Dent. Lit. (Vol. 3, No. 1 1984-).

ISSN 0301-5742
II
NLM W1 JO703C
JOURNAL OF INDIAN ORTHODONTIC SOCIETY, THE. **Added/Corp** Indian Orthodontic Society. (196?)-. Periodical. English. Four times a year. $25.00. **(Subscription address:** Prints India, 11 Darya Ganj, New Delhi 110002 India. **Tel** 011 91 11 3268645, FAX 011 91 11 3275542, telex 31-61087 PRIN-IN.**)**

ISSN 0894-8879
US
CCC
NLM W1; JO737
Pr Rev. CEASED

JOURNAL OF LAW AND ETHICS IN DENTISTRY. [J. law ethics dent.]. (1988)-(199?). Periodical. English. Mosby Year Book Inc., 11830 Westline Industrial Drive, St Louis MO 63146. **Tel** (800)325-4177, (314)872-8370, FAX (314)432-1380, telex 44-2402. **ED** Burton R Pollack. Index available. **Bk Rev. Ad Acc. Circ:** 4,500.
Desc: Original articles relating to all aspects of the regulation of dentistry and dental practice by government agencies, voluntary organizations and the courts.
Ind/Abst Index Dent. Lit. (Vol. 1, No. 1, 1988-199?).

ISSN 0029-0432
JA
NLM W1 JO943H CODEN JNUDAT

JOURNAL OF NIHON UNIVERSITY SCHOOL OF DENTISTRY. [J. Nihon Univ. Sch. Dent.]. **Main/Corp** Nihon University School of Dentistry. **VFOAT** Dental Journal of Nihon University. Vol. 1 (June 1958)-. Periodical. English (Japanese and English). Four times a year. $94.00. Nihon Daigaku Shigakubu, (School of Dentistry Nihon University), 8-13 Kanda Surugadai 1 Chome, Chiyodaku Tokyo 101 Japan. **(Subscription address:** Maruzen Company Ltd., PO Box 5050, Import & Export Department, Tokyo 100 31 Japan. **Tel** 011 81 3 32789224.**)** Documents available from BIOSIS Document Express, CASDDS.
Ind/Abst Biol. Abstr.; Chem. Abstr.; Curr. Titles Dent.; Index Med.; Index Dent. Lit.

LC RK1 .J78 ISSN 0278-2391
DD 617 US
CCC
NLM W1 JO803SM CODEN JOMSDA
Pr Rev.

JOURNAL OF ORAL AND MAXILLOFACIAL SURGERY. See Medical Sciences-Surgery.

ISSN 0160-6972
US
NLM W1 JO803TI

JOURNAL OF ORAL IMPLANTOLOGY, THE. [J. oral implantol.]. **Added/Corp** American Academy of Implant Dentistry. AAID Research Foundation. **VFOAT** Oral Implantology. Vol. 7 (1977)-. Periodical. English. Four times a year. $100.00. American & International Association Dental Research, 1111 14th Street Northwest, Suite 1000, Washington DC 20005. **Tel** (202)898-1050, FAX (202)789-1033. **ED** P. J. Mentag. **Ad Acc. Circ:** 2,500 (ctrl). available on microfilm and microfiche from University Microfilms International (UMI). ***Continues*** *Oral Implantology, 0160-6972.*
Desc: Publishes up to date manuscripts of clinical and research findings in the overall related areas of dental implantology.
Ind/Abst Curr. Cit.; Curr. Titles Dent.; Energy Res. Abstr. (Aug. 1982-); Index Dent. Lit.

ISSN 0904-2512
DK
CCC
NLM W1; JO803WG CODEN JPMEEA
Pr Rev.

JOURNAL OF ORAL PATHOLOGY & MEDICINE. (JOURNAL OF ORAL PATHOLOGY & MEDICINE : OFFICIAL PUBLICATION OF THE INTERNATIONAL ASSOCIATION OF ORAL PATHOLOGISTS AND THE AMERICAN ACADEMY OF ORAL PATHOLOGY.). [J. oral pathol. & med.]. **Added/Corp** International Association of Oral Pathologists. American Academy of Oral Pathology. **VFOAT** Journal of Oral Pathology and Medicine. Vol. 18, No. 1 (Jan. 1989)-. Periodical. English. Ten times a year. $602.44. Munksgaard International Publishers Ltd, PO Box 2148, DK-1016 Copenhagen K Denmark. **Tel** 011 45 33 127030, FAX 011 45 33 129387, telex 19431 MUNKS DK. **ED** J J Pindborg. Documents available from The Genuine Article, BIOSIS Document Express. ***Continues*** *Journal of Oral Pathology, 0300-9777.*
Desc: Publishes manuscripts of high scientific quality representing original clinical, diagnostic or experimental work in oral pathology and oral medicine.
Ind/Abst Biol. Abstr.; Curr. Aware. Biol. Sci., CABS; Curr. Cit.; Curr. Contents Life Sci.; EMBASE; Immunol. Abstr.; Index Med. (1989-); Index Dent. Lit. (1989-); Res. Alert [Full Cov.]; Rev. Med. Vet. Mycology; Sci. Cit. Index; SCISEARCH.

ISSN 0305-182X
UK
CCC
NLM W1 JO803Y CODEN JORHBY
Pr Rev.

JOURNAL OF ORAL REHABILITATION. [J. oral rehabil.]. **VFOAT** Clinical Dental Science and Materials. Vol. 1 (Jan. 1974)-. Academic Scholarly Publication. English. Twelve times a year. $647.00. Blackwell Scientific Publications Ltd, Marston Book Services, PO Box 88, Oxford OX2 ONE United Kingdom. **Tel** 011 44 1865 206206, FAX 011 44 1865 206219, telex 837 515 MARDIS G. **ED** A.S.T. Franks. Index available (bound in last issue). **Circ:** 650. available on microfilm and microfiche from University Microfilms International (UMI). Documents available from The Genuine Article, CASDDS.
Desc: Covers oral and facial physiology and dysfunction, prosthetic dentistry, and properties and serviceability of dental materials and instruments.
Ind/Abst Annals Behav. Med.; Chem. Abstr.; Curr. Cit.; Curr. Contents Clin. Med.; Curr. Titles Dent.; Dent. Abstr. (-199?); EMBASE; Index Med.; Index Dent. Lit.; Res. Alert [Full Cov.]; Sci. Cit. Index; SCISEARCH.

ISSN 0475-2058
JA
NLM W1 JO804T CODEN JODUA2

JOURNAL OF OSAKA DENTAL UNIVERSITY. [J. Osaka Dent. Univ.]. **Main/Corp** Osaka Shika Daigaku. **Added/Corp** Osaka Dental University. Vol. 1 (1967)-. Periodical. Japanese. Two times a year. Osaka University Dental School, 3 48 Nakanoshima 4 Chome, Kitaku Osakashi 530 Japan. Documents available from CASDDS.
Ind/Abst Chem. Abstr.

ISSN 0473-4599
JA
NLM W1 JO804U CODEN JOUDA2

JOURNAL OF OSAKA UNIVERSITY DENTAL SCHOOL, THE. [J. Osaka Univ. Dent. Sch.]. **Added/Corp** Osaka Daigaku. Shigakubu. Vol. 1 (July 1961)-. Periodical. English. One time a year. Osaka University Dental School, 3 48 Nakanoshima 4 Chome, Kitaku Osakashi 530 Japan. Documents available from CASDDS. ***Continues*** *Dental Bulletin of Osaka Daigaku.*
Ind/Abst Chem. Abstr.

LC RK361.A1 J68 ISSN 0022-3484
DK
CCC
NLM W1 JO828K CODEN JPDRAY
Pr Rev.

JOURNAL OF PERIODONTAL RESEARCH. [J. periodontal res.]. Vol. 1 (1966)-. Academic Scholarly Publication. English. Eight times a year. $383.19. Munksgaard International Publishers Ltd, PO Box 2148, DK-1016 Copenhagen K Denmark. **Tel** 011 45 33 127030, FAX 011 45 33 129387, telex 19431 MUNKS DK. **ED** Roy C Page. Index available. **Ad Acc. Circ:** 1,400 (ctrl). Documents available from The Genuine Article, BIOSIS Document Express, CASDDS.
Desc: Original investigations concerned with every aspect of periodontology and related sciences.
Ind/Abst Biol. Abstr.; Chem. Abstr.; Curr. Cit.; Curr. Contents Life Sci.; Curr. Titles Dent.; Dent. Abstr.; EMBASE [Select. Cov.]; Energy Res. Abstr. (May 1972-); Index Med.; Index Dent. Lit.; Microbiol. Abstr. Sect. B; Life Sci. Collect.; Res. Alert [Full Cov.]; Sci. Cit. Index; SCISEARCH; Soc. Sci. Cit. Index [Select. Cov.].

ISSN 0022-3492
DD 617 US
CCC
NLM W1 JO828LC CODEN JOPRAJ
Pr Rev.

JOURNAL OF PERIODONTOLOGY (1970). (JOURNAL OF PERIODONTOLOGY.). [J. periodontol.]. **Added/Corp** American Academy of Periodontology. (1970)-. Academic Scholarly Publication. English. Twelve times a year. $190.00. American Academy of Periodontology, 737 North Michigan Avenue, Suite 800, Chicago IL 60611. **Tel** (312)573-3220, FAX (312)787-3670. **ED** Robert J. Genco and Rita Shafer. Index available (bound in last issue). **Ad Acc. Circ:** 8,000. available on microfilm and microfiche from University Microfilms International (UMI). Documents available from The Genuine Article, BIOSIS Document Express, CASDDS. ***Continues*** *Journal of Periodontology-Periodontics, 0095-960X.*
Desc: Keeps dentists in touch with research being carried on in this field and related sciences, and stimulates greater interest in the the supporting tissue of the teeth and their relation to oral and general health.
Ind/Abst Biol. Abstr.; Chem. Abstr.; Curr. Cit.; Curr. Contents Clin. Med.; Curr. Contents Life Sci.; Curr. Titles Dent.; Dent. Abstr.; EMBASE [Select. Cov.]; Energy Res. Abstr.; Index Med.; Index Dent. Lit.; Med. Abstr. Newsl.; Nucl. Sci. Abstr.; Life Sci. Collect.; Res. Alert [Full Cov.]; Sci. Cit. Index; SCISEARCH.

ISSN 0970-2199
II
NLM W1; JO837ABH

JOURNAL OF PIERRE FAUCHARD ACADEMY. INDIA SECTION. (JOURNAL OF PIERRE FAUCHARD ACADEMY.). [J. Pierre Fauchard Acad., India Sect.]. **Added/Corp** Pierre Fauchard Academy. India Section. **VFOAT** Journal of Pierre Fauchard Academy, India Section; JPFA. Vol. 1, No. 1 (Mar. 1987)-. Periodical. English. Four times a year. $30.00. Pierre Fauchard Academy, Indore India. **(Subscription address:** Prints India, 11 Darya Ganj, New Delhi 110002 India. **Tel** 011 91 11 3268645, FAX 011 91 11 3275542, telex 31-61087 PRIN-IN.**)**

ISSN 1072-7965
DD 617 US
NLM W1; JO84N

JOURNAL OF PRACTICAL HYGIENE, THE. [J. pract. hyg.]. **VFOAT** Practical Hygiene. (1992)-. Trade Publication. English. Six times a year (Jan., Mar., May, July, Sept., Nov.). $28.00. Montage Media Corporation, 70 Hilltop Road, Ramsey NJ 07446-1119. **Tel** (201)236-0700, FAX (201)236-1339. **ED** Laura Franklin. **Ad Acc, Adv Mgr:** L. W. Scott Clements, **Tel** (201)236-0700 ext. 117. **Circ:** 60,400 (ctrl).

LC RK1 .A23 ISSN 0022-3913
DD 617.6905 US
CCC
NLM W1 JO851 CODEN JPDEAT
Pr Rev.

JOURNAL OF PROSTHETIC DENTISTRY, THE. [J. prosthet. dent.]. **Added/Corp** Academy of Denture Prosthetics. Vol. 1 (Jan./March 1951)-. Periodical. English. Twelve times a year. $198.00. Mosby Year Book Inc., 11830 Westline Industrial Drive, St Louis MO 63146. **Tel** (800)325-4177, (314)872-8370, FAX (314)432-1380, telex 44-2402. **ED** Judson C. Hickey. Index available. **Bk Rev. Ad Acc. Circ:** 19,360. available on microfilm and microfiche from University Microfilms International (UMI). Documents available from The Genuine Article, CASDDS.
Desc: Coverage of the various phases of restorative dentistry edited for prosthodontists and general dentists who include prosthetics as a major portion of their practice.
Ind/Abst Ceram. Abstr.; Chem. Abstr.; Cumul. Index Nurs. Allied Health Lit.; Curr. Cit.; Curr. Contents Clin. Med.; Curr. Titles Dent.; Dent. Abstr.; Energy Res. Abstr.; Hosp. Health Admin. Index; Index Med.; Index Dent. Lit.; Life Sci. Collect.; Res. Alert [Full Cov.]; Rev. Med. Vet. Mycology; Saf. Health Work; Sci. Cit. Index; SCISEARCH; World Ceram. Abstr.

ISSN 1059-941X
DD 617 US
CCC
NLM W1; JO851EH

JOURNAL OF PROSTHODONTICS. (JOURNAL OF PROSTHODONTICS : OFFICIAL JOURNAL OF THE AMERICAN COLLEGE OF PROSTHODONTISTS.). [J. prosthodont.]. **Added/Corp** American College of Prosthodontists. Vol. 1, No. 1 (Sept. 1992)-. Periodical. English. Four times a year (Mar., June, Sept., Dec.). $118.00. W. B. Saunders Company, A Subsidiary of Harcourt Brace Jovanovich Inc., The Curtis Center, Suite 300, Independence Square West, Philadelphia PA 19106-3399. **Tel** (215)238-7800 or, 5587, FAX (215)238-7883, telex 173146. **(Subscription address:** W. B. Saunders Company / North America Subscriptions, c/o Periodicals, 6277 Sea Harbour Drive, 4th Floor, Orlando FL 32887. **Tel** (800)654-2452, (407)345-3668.**)**

LC RK52 .J68 ISSN 0022-4006
DD 362.1/9/76009 US
NLM W1 JO859Q CODEN JPHDAC
Pr Rev.

JOURNAL OF PUBLIC HEALTH DENTISTRY. [J. public health dent.]. **Added/Corp** American Association of Public Health Dentists. Vol. 25 (Winter 1965)-. Periodical. English. Four times a year (Jan., Apr., July, Oct.). $85.00. American Association of Public Health Dentistry - AAPHD National Office, 10619 Jousting Lane, Richmond VA 23235. **Tel** (804)272-8344, FAX (804)272-0802. **ED** Dr. Gary Rozier, (editor's address: University of North Carolina, McGavran - Greenberg Hall, Chapel Hill, NC 27599-7400, telephone: (919)966-7388). Index available. **Bk Rev**, (Qty: varies). **Ad Acc, Adv Mgr:** Dr. Gary Rozier, **Tel** (919)966-7388. **Circ:** 1,500 (ctrl). available on microfilm from University Microfilms International (UMI). Documents available from The Genuine Article, BIOSIS Document Express. ***Continues*** *Public Health Dentistry, 1069-0476.*
Desc: Contains articles on the science and practice of public health dentistry.
Ind/Abst Biol. Abstr.; Crim. Justice Abstr.; Curr. Cit.; Curr. Contents Clin. Med.; Curr. Titles Dent.; Dent. Abstr.; Energy Res. Abstr. (March 1973-)(Mar. 1973-); Index Med.; Index Dent. Lit.; Nutr. Res. Newsl.; Life Sci. Collect.; Res. Alert [Full Cov.]; Sci. Cit. Index; SCISEARCH; Soc. Sci. Cit. Index [Select. Cov.].

ISSN 0002-4198
DD 617 US
NLM W1 JO222S

JOURNAL OF THE ALABAMA DENTAL ASSOCIATION, THE. [J. Ala. Dent. Assoc.]. **Added/Corp** Alabama Dental Association. Vol. 42, No. 3 (July 1958)-. Periodical. English. Four times a year. $24.00. Alabama Dental Association, 3915 Old Shell Road, Mobile AL 36608. **Tel** (334)342-6410, FAX (334)478-7638. **ED** John H. Mosteller. **Bk Rev**, (Qty: 6-10 per year). **Ad Acc. Circ:** 1,650 (ctrl). available on microfilm and microfiche from University Microfilms International (UMI). ***Continues*** *Bulletin of the Alabama Dental Association, 1056-9456.*
Desc: Publishes articles on dental science and technology; editorials on a variety of social and political issues concerning dentists; dental textbook reviews; and

news items about dentists, dental assistants and dental hygienists.
Ind/Abst Dent. Abstr. (-199?); Index Dent. Lit.

ISSN 0002-7243
DD 615 US
NLM W1 JO222TK **CODEN** JAASBK
TITLE CHANGE

JOURNAL OF THE AMERICAN ANALGESIA SOCIETY. [J. Am. Analg. Soc.]. **Main/Corp** American Analgesia Society. **VFOAT** Journal - American Analgesia Society. (1963)-(199?). Academic Scholarly Publication. English. Arthur A Weiner DMD, 1110 North Main Street, Randolph MA 02368. **Tel** (617)963-0250. **ED** Arthur A. Weiner. cum. index. **Bk Rev**. **Ad Acc**. **Circ:** 750 (ctrl). Documents available from CASDDS. ***Merged into** Anesthesia Progress, 0003-3006.*
Desc: Articles, abstracts and books that deal with Nitrous Oxide-Oxygen Relative analgesia in dentistry and with behavior modification and management of the apprehensive patient.
Ind/Abst Chem. Abstr.

LC RK1 .A515 **ISSN** 0002-7979
DD 617.6/005 US
NLM W1 JO908M
Pr Rev.

JOURNAL OF THE AMERICAN COLLEGE OF DENTISTS, THE. [J. Am. Coll. Dent.]. **Main/Corp** American College of Dentists. Vol. 1 (Jan. 1934)-. Periodical. English. Four times a year (Apr., July, Oct., Dec.). $40.00. American College of Dentists, 839 Quince Orchard Boulevard, Suite J, Gaithersburg MD 20878-1603. **Tel** (301)977-3223, FAX (301)977-3330. **ED** Keith P. Blair. Index available. **Ad Acc**. **Circ:** 5,000 (ctrl). available on microfilm and microfiche from University Microfilms International (UMI).
Desc: Presents ideas and opinions in dentistry.
Ind/Abst Curr. Titles Dent.; Dent. Abstr. (-199?); Energy Res. Abstr. (Aug. 1982-); Index Med.; Index Dent. Lit.

LC RK1. A53 **ISSN** 0002-8177
DD 617 US
CCC
NLM W1 JO908W **CODEN** JADSAY
Pr Rev.

JOURNAL OF THE AMERICAN DENTAL ASSOCIATION (USA ED.), THE. (THE JOURNAL OF THE AMERICAN DENTAL ASSOCIATION.). [J. Am. Dent. Assoc.]. **Main/Corp** American Dental Association. **Added/Corp** American Dental Association. **VFOAT** JADA. Vol. 26, No. 1 (Jan. 1939)-. Periodical. English. Twelve times a year. $105.00. American Dental Association, 211 East Chicago Avenue, Chicago IL 60611. **Tel** (312)440-2867, (312)440-2500, FAX (312)440-7494. available on microfilm and microfiche from University Microfilms International (UMI). Documents available from The Genuine Article, BIOSIS Document Express, CASDDS. ***Continues** Journal of the American Dental Association and the Dental Cosmos, 0375-8451.*
Ind/Abst Acad. Search; Annals Behav. Med.; Biol. Abstr. (1988-); Ceram. Abstr.; Chem. Abstr.; Coal Abstr.; Curr. Cit.; Curr. Contents Clin. Med.; Curr. Titles Dent.; Dent. Abstr.; Energy Res. Abstr.; EP Collect.; Gen. Sci. Index; Gen. Sci. Source; Health Index (1989-); Health Period. Database; Health Ref. Cent. (Jan. 1989-) [Full Cov.]; Health Source Plus; Health Source; Homework Help.; IDIS (1970-); Index Med.; Index Dent. Lit.; INFO-SOUTH Abstr.; INIS Atomindex [Micro.]; Mag. Search; MasterFile FullTEXT 1000; MasterFile FullTEXT 350; MasterFile FullTEXT 650; MasterFile FullTEXT (July 1993-); Med. Abstr. Newsl.; Nutr. Abstr. Rev., Ser. B, Live Feeds and Feed.; Nutr. Abstr. Rev., Ser. A, Hum. Exp.; Nutr. Res. Newsl.; OCLC; Life Sci. Collect.; Protozoolog. Abstr.; Res. Alert [Full Cov.]; Saf. Health Work; Sci. Cit. Index; SCISEARCH; Soc. Sci. Cit. Index [Select. Cov.]; SportSearch; Telebase.

LC RK60.7 .A53A **ISSN** 0093-4518
DD 617.6/01/05 US
NLM W1 JO91X

JOURNAL OF THE AMERICAN SOCIETY FOR PREVENTIVE DENTISTRY. [Am. Soc. Prev. Dent.]. **Main/Corp** American Society for Preventive Dentistry. (1970)-. Periodical. English. Six times a year. $10.00. Michalke Publ Company, 7851 Metro Parkway, Minneapolis MN 55420. available on microfilm and microfiche from University Microfilms International (UMI).
Ind/Abst Energy Res. Abstr. (Aug. 1982-).

ISSN 1043-2256
DD 617 US
NLM W1; JO915B

JOURNAL OF THE CALIFORNIA DENTAL ASSOCIATION. [J. Calif. Dent. Assoc.]. **Added/Corp** California Dental Association. **VFOAT** CDA Journal of the California Dental Association; CDA Journal. **VAT** California Dental Association Journal. Vol. 16, No. 11 (Nov. 1988)-. Periodical. English. Twelve times a year. $24.00. California Dental Association, PO Box 13749, Sacramento CA 95853. **Tel** (800)736-8702, (916)443-0505, FAX (916)443-2943. **ED** Jack F Conley. **Ad Acc**, **Adv Mgr:** Sue Hummel, **Tel** (916)443-3382. **Circ:** 17,000. ***Continues** CDA Journal of the California Dental Association, 0746-424X.*
Ind/Abst Dent. Abstr. (1992-); Index Dent. Lit. (Nov. 1988-).

ISSN 0885-3517
DD 617 US

JOURNAL OF THE CHARLES H. TWEED INTERNATIONAL FOUNDATION. [J. Charles H. Tweed Int. Found.]. **Added/Corp** Charles H. Tweed International Foundation for Orthodontic Research. Vol. 9 (March 1981)-. English. One time a year. Charles H. Tweed International Foundation, 2620 East Broadway, Tuscon AZ 85716. **Tel** (602)326-6002. ***Continues** Journal of the Charles H. Tweed Foundation.*
Ind/Abst Index Dent. Lit.

LC RK **ISSN** 0045-9917
DD 617.6 TH
NLM W1 JO918E

JOURNAL OF THE DENTAL ASSOCIATION OF THAILAND, THE. **Added/Corp** Dental Association of Thailand. (1949)-. Periodical. Multiple languages (English and Thai). Six times a year. $120.00. Dental Association of Thailand, PO Box 355, Samsaen Nai Phyatha, Bangkok 10400 Thailand. **Tel** 011 66 2 5394748. available on an online database from Knowledge Index; STN International; DATA-STAR; and DIALOG.
Ind/Abst Index Dent. Lit.

ISSN 0016-819X
US
NLM W1 JO926I

JOURNAL OF THE GEORGIA DENTAL ASSOCIATION. **Added/Corp** Georgia Dental Association. (1944)-. Periodical. English. Six times a year. Georgia Dental Association, 2801 Buford Highway, Suite T60, Atlanta GA 30329. **Tel** (404)636-7553. ***Continues** Journal of the Georgia State Dental Association.*

ISSN 1062-0265
DD 617 US
NLM W1; JO926P

JOURNAL OF THE GREATER HOUSTON DENTAL SOCIETY, THE. [J. Gt. Houst. Dent. Soc.]. **Added/Corp** Greater Houston Dental Society. (1989)-. Periodical. English. Ten times a year. $45.00. Greater Houston Dental Society, 1 Green Plaza, Suite 110, Houston TX 77146. **Tel** (713)961-4337. **ED** Art Jeske. **Bk Rev**, (Qty: 10). **Ad Acc**, **Adv Mgr:** Becky Ricks. ***Continues** Journal of the Houston District Dental Society.*
Ind/Abst Index Dent. Lit. (1989-).

US
Pr Rev.

•**JOURNAL OF THE HISTORY OF DENTISTRY.** (March 1996)-. English. Three times a year. $45.00. American Academy of the History Dentistry, 100 South Vail, Arlington Heights IL 60005. **Tel** (708)670-7561. ***Continues** Bulletin of the History of Dentistry.*

ISSN 0019-4611
II

JOURNAL OF THE INDIAN DENTAL ASSOCIATION. [J. Indian Dent. Assoc.]. **Main/Corp** Indian Dental Association. Vol. 38, No. 4 (Apr. 1966)-. Periodical. English. Twelve times a year. $70.00. Indian Dental Association, College of Dentistry, Indore 452 India. **(Subscription address:** Prints India, 11 Darya Ganj, New Delhi 110002 India. **Tel** 011 91 11 3268645, FAX 011 91 11 3275542, telex 31-61087 PRIN-IN.) **ED** Ved Prakash Jalili. **Bk Rev**. **Ad Acc**. **Circ:** 6,000. ***Continues** Journal of the All India Dental Association.*
Desc: Covers all aspects of dentistry.
Ind/Abst Curr. Titles Dent.; Index Dent. Lit.

LC RK **ISSN** 0019-6568
DD 617.6 US
NLM W1; JO22M

JOURNAL OF THE INDIANA DENTAL ASSOCIATION. (JOURNAL / INDIANA DENTAL ASSOCIATION.). [J. Indiana Dent. Assoc.]. **Added/Corp** Indiana Dental Association. Vol. 53, No. 1 (Jan./Feb. 1974)-. Trade Publication. English. Six times a year. $10.00 members; $25.00 nonmembers. Indiana Dental Association, PO Box 2467, Indianapolis IN 46206-2467. **Tel** (317)634-2610, FAX (317)634-2612. **ED** Diane M. Buyer. **Ad Acc**, **Adv Mgr:** Jody Eagan. **Circ:** 2,300 (ctrl). ***Continues** Journal of the Indiana Dental Association, 0019-6568.*
Ind/Abst Index Dent. Lit. (Jan./Feb. 1974-).

ISSN 0021-1133
IE
NLM W1 JO932I

JOURNAL OF THE IRISH DENTAL ASSOCIATION, THE. [J. Ir. Dent. Assoc.]. **Added/Corp** Irish Dental Association. Vol. 11 (Feb. 1965)-. Periodical. English. Four times a year. $77.01. Journal of the Irish Dental Association, 10 Richview Office Park, Clonskeagh, Dublin 14 Ireland. **Tel** 011 353 1 283-0499, 283-0496, FAX 011 353 1 283-0515. **ED** Joseph Lemasney. **Bk Rev**. **Ad Acc**. **Circ:** 1,000 (ctrl). available in microform. ***Continues** Irish Dental Review.*
Desc: Covers scientific dentistry.
Ind/Abst Curr. Cit.; Curr. Titles Dent.; Index Dent. Lit.

ISSN 0888-7063
DD 617 US
NLM W1; JO933

JOURNAL OF THE KANSAS DENTAL ASSOCIATION. [J. Kans. Dent. Assoc.]. **Added/Corp** Kansas Dental Association. Vol. 65, No. 3 (July 1981)-. Periodical. English. Four times a year. $10.00. Kansas Dental Association, 5200 Huntoon, Topeka KS 66604. **Tel** (913) 272-7360. ***Continues** Journal of the Kansas State Dental Association, 0022-8796.*
Ind/Abst Dent. Abstr. (-199?).

JA

JOURNAL OF THE KYUSHU DENTAL SOCIETY. ENGLISH ABSTRACTS, THE. **Added/Corp** Kyushu Shika Gakkai. **VFOAT** Journal of the Kyushu Dental Society Supplement: English Abstracts. No. 1 (Mar. 1968)-. Periodical. English (Japanese). Six times a year. Kyushu Shika Gakkai, (Kyushu Dental Soc.), Kyushu Shika Daigaku, Fuzoku Toshokan, 6-1 Manazuru 2 Chome, Kokurakitaku Kitakyushushi, Fukuokaken 803 Japan. **(Subscription address:** Japan Publications Trading Company Ltd., PO Box 5030, Tokyo International, Tokyo 100-31 Japan. **Tel** 011 81 3 3292 3753.)

ISSN 0025-4355
US
NLM W1 JO938K
TITLE CHANGE

JOURNAL OF THE MARYLAND STATE DENTAL ASSOCIATION. [J. Md. State Dent. Assoc.]. **Added/Corp** Maryland State Dental Association. **VFOAT** Journal - Maryland State Dental Association. Vol. 1 (1958)-Vol. 37 (1994). Periodical. English. Four times a year. Maryland State Dental Association, 6450 Dobbin Road, Columbia MD 21045. **Tel** (800)899-3678, (410)964-2880. **Circ:** 2900. ***Continued by** MSDA Journal.*
Ind/Abst Dent. Abstr. (-199?).

ISSN 0025-4800
DD 617 US
NLM W1 JO938M

JOURNAL OF THE MASSACHUSETTS DENTAL SOCIETY. [J. Mass. Dent. Soc.]. **Added/Corp** Massachusetts Dental Society. Vol. 1, (Jan. 1952)-. Periodical. English. Four times a year (March, June, Sept., Dec.). $12.00. Massachusetts Dental Society, 83 Speen Street, Natick MA 01760-4125. **Tel** (508)651-7511, FAX (508)653-7115. **ED** Norman Becker. **Bk Rev**, (Qty: 4). **Ad Acc**, **Adv Mgr:** C. Peterson. **Circ:** 5,000 (ctrl). ***Separated from** New England Dental Journal, 1075-1297.*
Desc: Clinical and practice management articles of particular interest to dentists.
Ind/Abst Index Dent. Lit.

ISSN 0026-2102
DD 617 US
NLM W1 JO94H

JOURNAL OF THE MICHIGAN DENTAL ASSOCIATION, THE. [J. Mich. Dent. Assoc.]. **Added/Corp** Michigan Dental Association. **VFOAT** MDA. The Journal of the Michigan Dental Association. Vol. 50, No. 6 (June 1968)-. Trade Publication. English. Nine times a year (monthly except combined April/May, July/Aug., and Nov./Dec.). $70.00. Michigan Dental Association, 230 North Washington Street/Suite 208, Lansing MI 48933. **Tel** (517)372-9070, FAX (517)372-0008. **ED** Edward D. Barrett. Index available (Bound in last issue). cum. index. **Bk Rev**. **Ad Acc**. **Circ:** 5,800. ***Continues** Journal of the Michigan State Dental Association, 0098-7107.*
Desc: Scientific dental articles and features on members.
Ind/Abst Index Dent. Lit.

ISSN 0093-7347
US
NLM W1 JO942J

JOURNAL OF THE NEW JERSEY DENTAL ASSOCIATION. [J. N. J. Dent. Assoc.]. **Added/Corp** New Jersey Dental Association. **VFOAT** Dental Journal, New Jersey. Vol. 42 (Sept./Oct. 1970)-. Periodical. English. Four times a year. $50.00. New Jersey Dental Association, One Dental Plaza, North Brunswick NJ 08902. **Tel** (908)821-9400, FAX (908)821-1082. **Bk Rev**. **Ad Acc**. **Circ:** 5,000 (ctrl). ***Continues** Journal of the New Jersey State Dental Society.*
Desc: Journal containing scientific articles with features of interest to dentists, with information on continuing education, classifieds, etc.
Ind/Abst Dent. Abstr. (-199?); Index Dent. Lit.

Dentistry

NLM W1 JO942ZC
Pr Rev.
ISSN 0111-1485
NZ
CCC
JOURNAL OF THE NEW ZEALAND SOCIETY OF PERIODONTOLOGY. [J. New Zealand Soc. Periodontol.]. **Added/Corp** New Zealand Society of Periodontology. No. 44 (Aug. 1977)-. Periodical. English. Two times a year. $57.30. New Zealand Society of Periodontology, PO Box 647, Dunedin New Zealand. **Tel** 011 64 34 797108. **ED** A Pack. **Bk Rev. Ad Acc. Circ:** 1,000 (ctrl). **Continues** Bulletin - N. Z. Society of Periodontology.
Ind/Abst Curr. Titles Dent.; Index Dent. Lit.

NLM W1 JO944L
ISSN 0030-4670
US
CEASED
JOURNAL OF THE OREGON DENTAL ASSOCIATION, THE. [J. Or. Dent. Assoc.]. **Added/Corp** Oregon Dental Association. Vol. 37, No. 7 (March 1968)-Vol. 64, No. 3 (1995). Trade Publication. English. Oregon Dental Association, 17898 SW McEwan Road, Portland OR 97223. **Tel** (503)620-3230. **ED** James T. Fratzke. **Ad Acc. Circ:** 2,000 (ctrl). **Continues** Oregon State Dental Journal.
Desc: Presents current news, feature articles and scientific information to the dentists of Oregon.
Ind/Abst Dent. Abstr. (19??-199?); Index Dent. Lit.

US
JOURNAL OF THE PHILADELPHIA COUNTY DENTAL SOCIETY. Vol. 49, No. 1 (July/Aug. 1983)-. Periodical. English. Six times a year. Philadelphia County Dental Society, 225 Washington Square East, Philadelphia PA 19106. **Continues** Bulletin of the Philadelphia County Dental Society (1965).

NLM W1 JO954HP
ISSN 0253-8482
SL
JOURNAL OF THE SIERRA LEONE MEDICAL & DENTAL ASSOCIATION. [J. Sierra Leone Med. Dent. Assoc.]. **Added/Corp** Sierra Leone Medical & Dental Association. **VFOAT** Journal - The Sierra Leone Medical & Dental Association. Vol. 3 (Nov. 1978)-. English. **Continues** Sierra Leone Medical & Dental Association. Bulletin - The Sierra Leone Medical & Dental Association, 0253-8474.
Ind/Abst Trop. Dis. Bull.

NLM W1 JO955V
ISSN 0038-3899
US
TITLE CHANGE
JOURNAL OF THE SOUTHERN CALIFORNIA DENTAL HYGIENISTS' ASSOCIATION. **VFOAT** SCDHA Journal. Vol. 1 (Sept./Oct. 1958)-(19??). Periodical. English. California Dental Hygienists, 5757 West Century Blvd, Suite 512, Los Angeles CA 90045. **Tel** (310)417-8073. **ED** Fred Droz. **Bk Rev. Ad Acc. Circ:** 5,000 (ctrl). available on microfilm and microfiche from University Microfilms International (UMI). **Merged into** Californis Dental Hygienists' Association Journal.
Desc: Academic articles, associations information (events, resolutions by board, etc.), editorials, ads, employment, and information.

NLM W1 JO957G
ISSN 0040-3385
US
CODEN JTDAAB
JOURNAL OF THE TENNESSEE DENTAL ASSOCIATION, THE. [J. Tenn. Dent. Assoc.]. **Added/Corp** Tennessee Dental Association. Tennessee Dental Association. Directory and Membership Roster. Vol. 50, No. 3 (July 1970)-. Periodical. English. Four times a year (Jan., April, July, and Oct.). $9.50. Tennessee Dental Association, 2104 Sunset Place, Nashville TN 37212. **Tel** (615)383-8962. **ED** Stephen Brooks. **Ad Acc, Adv Mgr:** Sharon Melvin, **Tel** same as publisher. **Circ:** 2,100. Documents available from CASDDS. **Continues** Journal - Tennessee State Dental Association, 0091-3987.
Desc: News of the profession of dentistry in Tennessee and scientific articles related to dentistry.
Ind/Abst Chem. Abstr.; Curr. Titles Dent.; Dent. Abstr. (?-199?); Index Dent. Lit.

DD 617
NLM W1 JO972CL
ISSN 0148-4893
US
JOURNAL OF THE WESTERN SOCIETY OF PERIODONTOLOGY / PERIODONTAL ABSTRACTS, THE. [J. West. Soc. Periodontol., Periodontal abstr.]. **Added/Corp** Western Society of Periodontology. Vol. 24 (Spring 1976)-. Periodical. English. Four times a year. $60.00. Western Society of Periodontology, 9010 Reseda Boulevard, Suite 204, Northridge CA 91324. **Tel** (800)367-8386, (818)993-5093. **ED** Thomas N. Sims. Index available in last issue of volume--attached. **Bk Rev. Ad Acc. Circ:** 2,600 (ctrl). **Continues** Periodontal Abstracts, 1069-1502.

Desc: Publication providing literature reviews, original articles, and abstracts of current literature related to periodontology.
Ind/Abst Index Dent. Lit.

US
NLM W1; JO982D
JOURNAL - SEATTLE-KING COUNTY DENTAL SOCIETY. **Added/Corp** Seattle-King County Dental Society. Vol. 8, No. 10 (May 1970)-. Periodical. English. Nine times a year (monthly Sept. - May). $14.00. Journal and Bulletin Agency Inc, PO Box 10249, Bainbridge Island WA 98110. **Tel** (206)623-7325. **Bk Rev. Ad Acc. Circ:** 1,400 (ctrl). **Continues** Journal of the Seattle District Dental Society.
Desc: Newsletter and annual photo roster.

ISSN 0738-7970
US
JOURNAL / SOUTHERN CALIFORNIA DENTAL ASSISTANTS ASSOCIATION. Periodical. English. Six times a year. $12.00. Southern California Dental Assistants Association, PO Box 63, La Mirada CA 90637. **Tel** (213)943-8109.

ISSN 0454-8302
JA
CODEN KSHGDM
KANAGAWA SHIGAKU : KANAGAWA SHIKA DAIGAKU GAKKAI ZASSHI. [Kanagawa shigaku]. **Added/Corp** Kanagawa Shika Daigaku Gakkai. (1967)-. Periodical. Japanese (summaries and/or abstracts in English). Four times a year. Kanagawa Shika Daigaku Gakkai, (Kangawa Odontological Soc.), 82 Ineokacho Yokosukashi, Kanagawaken 238 Japan. Documents available from CASDDS.
Ind/Abst Chem. Abstr.

DD 362
ISSN 0744-396X
US
KENTUCKY DENTAL JOURNAL. [Ky. dent. j.]. **Added/Corp** Kentucky Dental Association. Vol. 34, No. 1 (Jan. 1982)-. Periodical. English. Six times a year. $21.00. Kentucky Dental Association, 1940 Princeton Drive, Louisville KY 40205. **Tel** (502)459-5373. **ED** Joe W Jones. **Ad Acc. Circ:** 1,900 (ctrl). **Continues** Journal of the Kentucky Dental Association, 0023-0162.
Desc: Dental related.

NLM W1 KH53
RU
KHIRURGICHESKAIA I ORTOPEDICHESKAIA STOMATOLOGIIA. Vol. 8 (1978)-. Periodical. Russian. **Continues** Khirurgicheskaia Stomatologiia.

NLM W1; KI589
ISSN 0945-7917
GW
●**KIEFERORTHOPAEDIE : DIE ZEITSCHRIFT FUER DIE PRAXIS.** (March 1994)-. Periodical. German (summaries and/or abstracts in English). Four times a year. DM198.00 Germany; DM209.00 other. Quintessenz Verlag GmbH, Ifenpfad 2 4, D 12107 Berlin Germany. **Tel** 011 49 30 740060, FAX 011 49 30 7415080. **Continues** Praktische Kieferorthopaedie.
Ind/Abst Index Dent. Lit. (1994-).

NLM W1 KO294N
ISSN 0023-2831
JA
CODEN KEGZA7
KOKU EISEI GAKKAI ZASSHI. [Koku Eisei Gakkai zasshi]. **Added/Corp** Koku Eisei Gakkai. **VFOAT** Japanese Journal of Dental Health; Japanese Journal of Oral Hygiene; Journal of Dental Health. Vol. 1 (August 1952)-. Periodical. Japanese (summaries and/or abstracts in English; table of contents in English). Five times a year. $145.50. Nippon Koku Eisei Gakkai, (Japanese Society for Dental Health), Koku hoken kyokai, 44-2 Komagome 1 chome, Tosimaku Tokyo 170 Japan. **(Subscription address:** Japan Publications Trading Company Ltd., PO Box 5030, Tokyo International, Tokyo 100-31 Japan. **Tel** 011 81 3 3292 3753.) Documents available from BIOSIS Document Express, CASDDS.
Ind/Abst Biol. Abstr.; Chem. Abstr.

NLM W1 KO296
ISSN 0300-9149
JA
CODEN KOGZA9
KOKUBYO GAKKAI ZASSHI. [Kokubyo Gakkai Zasshi]. **Main/Corp** Kokubyo Gakkai. **Added/Corp** Kokubyo Gakkai. Journal of the Japan Stomatological Society. **VFOAT** Journal of the Japan Stomatological Society; Vierteljahrschrift - Japanische Gesellschaft fur Stomatologie. Vol. 1 (June 1927)-. Periodical. Japanese (summaries and/or abstracts in English and German). Four times a year. $128.50. Kokubyo Gakkai, (Japan Stomatological Soc.), 44-2 Komagome 1 Chome, Toshimaku Tokyo 170 Japan. **(Subscription address:** Japan Publications Trading Company Ltd., PO Box 5030, Tokyo International, Tokyo 100-31 Japan. **Tel** 011 81 3 3292 3753.) Documents available from CASDDS.
Ind/Abst Chem. Abstr.; Index Med.; Index Dent. Lit.

NLM W1 KO67T
ISSN 0254-0061
CH
KOUQIANG YIXUE. (K'OU CH'IANG I HSUEH.). [Kouqiang yixue]. **VFOAT** Oral Science Review. Vol. 1 (1977)-. Chinese. Six times a year.

LC RK1 .K83
KO
KUGANG SAENGMURHAK YONGU. **VFOAT** Oral Biology Research. Periodical. Korean (summaries and/or abstracts in English). Choson Taehakkyo Kugang, Saengmurhak Yonguso, 17 Pullo-dong Tong-ku, Kwangju-si Korea.

ISSN 0368-6833
JA
CODEN KSGZA3
KYUSHU SHIKA GAKKAI ZASSHI. [Kyushu Shika Gakkai Zasshi]. **Added/Corp** Kyushu Shika Gakkai. **VFOAT** Journal of the Kyushu Dental Society. No. 1 June (1966/Mar. 1933)-. Japanese. Four times a year. $132.50. Kyushu Shika Gakkai, (Kyushu Dental Soc.), Kyushu Shika Daigaku, Fuzoku Toshokan, 6-1 Manazuru 2 Chome, Kokurakitaku Kitakyushushi, Fukuokaken 803 Japan. **(Subscription address:** Japan Publications Trading Company Ltd., PO Box 5030, Tokyo International, Tokyo 100-31 Japan. **Tel** 011 81 3 3292 3753.)

LC R713.67.F5 F55b
ISSN 0780-1785
FI
NLM W 22; GF5 L12
LAAKARIT. **Added/Corp** Finland. Laakintolaitos. **VFOAT** Lakare. (1982)-. Finnish (Swedish). One time a year. Government Printing Centre, PO Box 516, SF-00101 Helsinki 10 Finland. **Continues** Laakarit, Hammaslaakarit.

NLM W1 L101N
ISSN 0092-4458
US
CODEN LDAJE5
LDA JOURNAL. [LDA j.]. **Main/Corp** Louisiana Dental Association. **VFOAT** Journal of the Louisiana Dental Association; DLA Journal. **VAT** Louisiana Dental Association Journal. (1973)-. Periodical. English. Four times a year. $24.00. Louisiana Dental Association, David N. Austin DDS, 230 Carroll Street, Shreveport LA 71105. **Tel** (318)861-4549. **ED** Gary Roberts and David Austin. **Bk Rev. Ad Acc. Circ:** 1,600. **Continues** Journal of the Louisiana Dental Association, 0024-6786.
Desc: Dental, scientific, technical articles and organizational news of local and national dental associations.
Ind/Abst Index Dent. Lit.

LC KF2910.D3 A134
DD 344.73/0413
NLM WU 33 AA1 L4
US
LEGAL CONSIDERATIONS IN DENTISTRY. See Law.

LC RK37 .I47A
DD 617.6/0025/773
US
LICENSEES, DENTAL PRACTICE ACT. **Main/Corp** Illinois. Dept. of Registration and Education. **VFOAT** Dental Roster. English. Illinois Department of Registration and Education, Springfield IL 62701.

ISSN 1064-6698
US
●**LIPPINCOTT'S ORAL AND MAXILLOFACIAL SURGERY.** See Medical Sciences-Surgery.

DD 619
NLM W1; LM102
ISSN 1058-7845
US
LMT (NORWALK, CONN.). (LMT : LAB MANAGEMENT TODAY.). [LMT]. **VFOAT** Lab Management Today. Vol. 8, No. 1 (Sept. 1991)-. Periodical. English. Twelve times a year (with combined June / July and Nov./ Dec.). $17.00. Dental Lab Publications, Inc., 205 Liberty Square, East Norwalk CT 06855. **Tel** (203)866-3302, FAX (203)838-3454. **ED** Kelly Fessel. **Ad Acc, Adv Mgr:** Jim Pouilliard. **Circ:** 18,000 (ctrl). **Continues** Dental Lab Management Today, 8750-9539.
Desc: Offers marketing and management strategies to dental laboratory owners and managers.
Ind/Abst Index Dent. Lit. (1991-).

NLM W1; JO185W
ISSN 0258-4638
JO
MAGALLAT TIBB AL-ASNAN AL-URDUNNIYYAT. (THE JORDAN DENTAL JOURNAL.). [Magallat tibb al-asnan al-urdunniyyat]. **Added/Corp** Niqabat Attiba al-Asnan al-Urduniyah. Jordan. Khadamat al-Tibbiyah al-Malakiyah. Vol. 4, No. 1 (April 1984)-. Periodical. English (summaries and/or abstracts in Arabic). Two times a year. Jordan Dental Association, Shmesani, PO Box 1326, Amman Jordan. **Tel** 665520. **Continues** Majallat Niqabat Attiba Al-Asnan Al-Urduniyah.
Ind/Abst Index Dent. Lit. (Vol. 4, No. 1 1984-).

Dentistry

DD 617.6
NLM W1 MA9309R
ISSN 0277-4445
US
MASSON MONOGRAPHS IN DENTISTRY. [Masson monogr. dent.]. 1-. Monographic series. English. Price varies per volume. Masson Distribution Inc, Box C 762, Brooklyn NY 11205. **ED** L Burket and H M Berry.

DD 617
NLM W1; MA9309VJ
ISSN 1076-7428
US
●**MASTERING CLINICAL PEDIATRIC DENTISTRY.** [Mastering clin. pediatr. dent.]. (1993)-. Periodical. English. Four times a year. $39.00 US; $49.00 Canada. School of Dental Medicine, Tufts University, One Kneeland Street, Boston MA 02111. **Tel** (617)956-6902, telex 78-2661. **Continues** Mastering Pediatric Dentistry, 1065-741X.

DD 617
NLM W1; MA9309WM
ISSN 1065-741X
US
TITLE CHANGE
MASTERING PEDIATRIC DENTISTRY. [Mastering pediatr. dent.]. Vol. 1, No. 1 (Nov./Dec. 1992)-(199?). Periodical. English. School of Dental Medicine, Tufts University, One Kneeland Street, Boston MA 02111. **Tel** (617)956-6902, telex 78-2661. **Continued by** Mastering Clinical Pediatric Dentistry, 1076-7428.

NLM W1; MA94D
ISSN 0175-7326
GW
MATERIALIEN DES FORSCHUNGSINSTITUTS FUR DIE ZAHNARZTLICHE VERSORGUNG. [Mater. Forschungsinst. Zahnarztl. Versorg.]. Vol. 1 (1980)-. Monographic series. German. Price varies per volume.

ISSN 0385-1613
JA
CODEN MATSDE
MATSUMOTO SHIGAKU. [Matsumoto shigaku]. Academic Scholarly Publication. Japanese. Two times a year. Matsumoto Shika Daigaku Gakkai, (Matsumoto Dental College Soc.), 1780 Gohara Hirooka, Shiojirishi Naganoken 399-07, Japan. Documents available from CASDDS.
Ind/Abst Chem. Abstr.

DD 617.6/007/11714281
ISSN 0316-8336
CN
MCGILL UNIVERSITY. FACULTY OF DENTISTRY. (MCGILL UNIVERSITY, FACULTY OF DENTISTRY; CALENDAR.). **Main/Corp** McGill University. Faculty of Dentistry. Periodical. English. McGill University / Faculty of Dentistry, PO Box 6070 Station A, Montreal Quebec H3C 3G1 Canada. **Tel** (514)398-4734.

NLM W 22 AA1 N2745M
ISSN 0730-1448
US
MEDICAL STAFF DIRECTORY. [Med. staff dir.]. **Main/Corp** National Institutes of Health (U.S.). Clinical Center. (1970)-. Directory. English. One time a year. Office of Medical Staff Affairs, The Clinical Center/Room 1N-2005, Bethesda MD 20205.

JA
NLM W1; ME887LH
MEIKAI DAIGAKU SHIGAKU ZASSHI. **Added/Corp** Meikai Daigaku. Shigakubu. **VFOAT** Journal of Meikai University School of Dentistry. Vol. 17, No. 1 (1988)-. Periodical. Japanese (English). Three times a year. Meikai Daigaku Shigakubu, (School of Dentistry Meikai University), 1-1 Keyakidai Sakadoshi, Saitamaken 350-02 Japan. Documents available from CASDDS. **Continues** Josai Shika Daigaku Kiyo, 0301-2662.
Ind/Abst Chem. Abstr.

DD 617
ISSN 1082-4111
US
●**MEMBERSHIP MATTERS (1995).** (MEMBERSHIP MATTERS / ODA.). [Members. matters]. **Added/Corp** Oregon Dental Association. Vol. 1, No. 1 (April 1995)-. Periodical. English. Eleven times a year (monthly except Aug.) $40.00. Oregon Dental Association, 17898 SW McEwan Road, Portland OR 97223. **Tel** (503)620-3230. **Formed by the union of** Membership Matters (Portland, Or. : 1990) and Journal of the Oregon Dental Association, 0030-4670.

NLM W1 ME9381
ISSN 0360-7232
US
MENTALIS. **Added/Corp** University of California, Los Angeles. School of Dentistry. Vol. 1 (Spring 1971)-. Periodical. English. International Tsunami Information Center, PO Box 50027, Honolulu HI 96850-4993. **Tel** (808)541-1658, FAX (808)541-1678.

DD 617
NLM W1 KA541
ISSN 0026-3478
US
MIDWESTERN DENTIST. [Midwest. dent.]. **Added/Corp** Greater Kansas City Dental Society. Kansas City District Dental Society (Mo.). Vol. 35, No. 7 (July 1959)-. Periodical. English. Nine times a year. $20.00. Greater Kansas City Dental Society, 5907 Raytown Trafficway, Kansas City MO 64133. **Tel** (816)737-5353. **ED** Robert Nelson (editor's address: 400 East Red Bridge, Kansas City, MO 64131; phone: (816)942-7696). **Bk Rev. Ad Acc. Circ:** 700 (ctrl). **Formed by the union of** Kansas City District Dental Society (Mo.) Bulletin and Kansas City District Dental Society (Mo.) Journal, 1070-6054.
Desc: Occurrences and innovations pertinent to dentistry of interest to local association members.

NLM W1; MI6489L
ISSN 0394-168X
IT
MINERVA ORTOGNATODONTICA. (198?)-. Periodical. Italian (summaries and/or abstracts in English). Four times a year. L155000. Edizioni Minerva Medica, Corso Bramante 83-85, 10126 Turin Italy. **Tel** 011 39 11 678282, FAX 011 39 11 674502.
Desc: Covers orthognathodontics, gnathology and preventive dentistry.
Ind/Abst Index Dent. Lit. (Vol. 7, No. 2, 1989);(v7n2, 1989).

NLM W1 MI653
ISSN 0026-4970
IT
MINERVA STOMATOLOGICA. [Minerva stomatol.]. (1952)-. Academic Scholarly Publication. Italian. Twelve times a year. L165000. Edizioni Minerva Medica, Corso Bramante 83-85, 10126 Turin Italy. **Tel** 011 39 11 678282, FAX 011 39 11 674502. **ED** B de Michelis. **Bk Rev. Ad Acc.** available on microfilm from University Microfilms International (UMI).
Desc: Journal addressed to practitioners and specialists in dentistry in Italy and abroad. It deals with topics in scientific practice and research.
Ind/Abst Curr. Cit.; EMBASE; Index Med.; Index Dent. Lit.; Nutr. Abstr. Rev., Ser. A, Hum. Exp.

NLM W1 MI811
ISSN 0098-4329
US
MISSISSIPPI DENTAL ASSOCIATION JOURNAL. [Miss. Dent. Assoc. j.]. **Added/Corp** Mississippi Dental Association. Vol. 30, No. 3 (Summer 1974)-. Periodical. English. Four times a year (Feb., May, Aug., Nov.). $20.00. Mississippi Dental Association Journal, 2630 Ridgewood Road, Jackson MS 39216. **Tel** (601)335-6148, FAX (601)378-2836. **ED** William Martin. **Bk Rev. Ad Acc. Circ:** 1,200 (ctrl). **Continues** Journal - Mississippi Dental Association, 0047-7532.
Desc: News about the association and the state dentists.
Ind/Abst Dent. Abstr. (-199?); Index Dent. Lit.

DD 617
NLM W1; MI865G
ISSN 0887-4646
US
MISSOURI DENTAL JOURNAL (JEFFERSON CITY, MO.). (MISSOURI DENTAL JOURNAL : THE JOURNAL OF THE MISSOURI DENTAL ASSOCIATION.). [Mo. dent. j.]. **Added/Corp** Missouri Dental Association. Vol. 65, No. 1 (Jan./Feb. 1985)-. Periodical. English. Six times a year (Jan., Mar., May, July, Sept., Nov.). $12.00. Missouri Dental Association, 230 West McCarty Street, PO Box 1707, Jefferson City MO 65102. **Tel** (314)634-3436, FAX (314)635-0764. **ED** Dr. Elizabeth Ward. **Ad Acc, Adv Mgr:** Tammy Miller. **Circ:** 2,500. **Continues** Journal of the Missouri Dental Association (1980), 0273-3463.
Desc: Covers dentistry; includes scientific articles, association activities and new trends in dentistry.
Ind/Abst Dent. Abstr. (-199?); Index Dent. Lit. (Jan./Feb. 1985-).

ISSN 0739-0963
US
MITTELMAN LETTER, THE. No. 83 (Aug. 1977)-. Periodical. English. Four times a year (Mar., June, Sept., Dec.). $67.00. Once Daily Inc., 263 West End Avenue, Number 2A, New York NY 10023. **Tel** (212)874-4212. **ED** Dr. & Mrs. Jerome S. Mittelman. **Bk Rev. Continues** Once Daily.

NLM W1 MO385G
ISSN 0391-2000
IT
CODEN MOORDG
MONDO ORTODONTICO. [Mondo ortod.]. (1976)-. Periodical. Italian. Six times a year. L203000. Masson SPA, via Statuto 2/4, 20121 Milan Italy. **Tel** 011 39 2 63671, FAX 011 39 2 6367211. Documents available from BIOSIS Document Express.
Ind/Abst Biol. Abstr. (?-1989); Index Dent. Lit.

US
NLM W1; MO559W
MONOGRAPH SERIES ON DENTAL MATERIALS AND THERAPEUTICS / AMERICAN DENTAL ASSOCIATION [AND] COUNCIL ON DENTAL THERAPEUTICS [AND] COUNCIL ON DENTAL MATERIALS, INSTRUMENTS, AND EQUIPMENT. **Added/Corp** American Dental Association. Council on Dental Therapeutics. American Dental Association. Council on Dental Materials, Instruments and Equipment. (1990)-. Monographic series. English. Irregular. Price varies per volume. American Dental Association, 211 East Chicago Avenue, Chicago IL 60611. **Tel** (312)440-2867, (312)440-2500, FAX (312)440-7494. **Formed by the union of** Dentist's Desk Reference, 0732-1325 and Accepted Dental Therapeutics, 0065-079X.

NLM W1 MO568E
ISSN 0077-0892
SZ
CCC
CODEN MGUSCU
MONOGRAPHS IN ORAL SCIENCE. [Monogr. oral sci.]. (1972)-. Monographic series. English. One time a year. 180.00F (approx. per volume). S. Karger AG, Allschwilerstrasse 10, PO Box, CH-4009 Basel Switzerland. **Tel** 011 41 61 3061111, FAX 011 41 61 3061234, telex CH 962 652. **ED** H. M. Myers. Documents available from BIOSIS Document Express.
Desc: Offers a series of books ensuring the publication of new findings in a particular field of study and the frequent revision of established information. Authors are given the opportunity to synthesize the results of their work, and that of others, into a unified view.
Ind/Abst Biol. Abstr.; Index Med.; Index Dent. Lit.; Ref. Upd. Deluxe Ed.

US
●**MSDA JOURNAL.** **Added/Corp** Maryland State Dental Association. **VFOAT** Journal of the Maryland State Dental Association. Vol. 38, No. 1 (Spring 1995)-. Periodical. English. Four times a year. Maryland State Dental Association, 6450 Dobbin Road, Columbia MD 21045. **Tel** (800)899-3678, (410)964-2880. **Continues** Journal of the Maryland State Dental Association.

DD 617
NLM W1; NA398C
ISSN 1050-530X
US
SUSPENDED
NATIONAL DENTAL ASSOCIATION JOURNAL. [Natl. Dent. Assoc. j.]. **Added/Corp** National Dental Association (1932-). **VFOAT** Journal. Vol. 41, No. 1 (June 1984)-Suspended (19??). Periodical. English. Four times a year. $6.00 (single issue) US; $7.50 (single issue) other. National Dental Association, 5506 Connecticut Avenue NW/Suites 24-25, Washington DC 20015. **Tel** (202)244-7555. **Bk Rev. Ad Acc.** available on microfilm from University Microfilms International (UMI). **Continues** National Dental Association (1932-). Quarterly of the National Dental Association, Inc., 0163-5565.
Ind/Abst Index Dent. Lit. (Vol. 41, No. 1, 1984-1986).

LC RK80 .U52a
DD 617.6/007/2073
NLM WU 22 AA1 N2g
ISSN 0360-7763
US
NATIONAL INSTITUTE OF DENTAL RESEARCH PROGRAMS. **Main/Corp** United States. National Institute of Dental Research. **Added/Corp** National Institute of Dental Research (U.S.). Programs. **VFOAT** Programs. (1973)-. Periodical. English. One time a year. Free on request. National Institute of Dental Research, Building 31, 9000 Rockville Pike, Bethesda MD 20892. **ED** Kenneth C. Lynn. **Circ:** 300 (ctrl). **Continues** National Institute of Dental Research Grants and Awards, 0565-7741.
Desc: Contains charts and tables relevant to dental research and training grants, contracts and intramural projects supported by the National Institute of Dental Research.

NE
NEDERLANDS TANDARTSENBLAD. Dutch. Two times a week. Nederlands Tandartsenblad NMT, PO Box 2000, 3430 CA Nieuwegein Netherlands. **Tel** 011 31 3402 76276.

NLM W1 NE14E
ISSN 0028-2200
NE
CODEN NTTAAX
NEDERLANDS TIJDSCHRIFT VOOR TANDHEELKUNDE. [Ned. tijdschr. tandheelkd.]. Vol. 69 (1962)-. Trade Publication. Dutch (English). Eleven times a year. $161.79. Wegener Tijl Tijdschriften Group, Postbus 1860, 1110 CD Diemen Netherlands. **Tel** 011 31 20 6603300. **ED** L J A Van Schijndel. **Bk Rev. Ad Acc. Circ:** 5,500. Documents available from BIOSIS Document Express. **Continues** Tijdschrift voor Tankheelkunde.
Desc: Information on scientific developments within the field of dental surgery.
Ind/Abst Biol. Abstr.; Index Dent. Lit.

DD 617
ISSN 1067-2354
US
CEASED
NEW DENTIST (THOROFARE, N.J.), THE. (THE NEW DENTIST.). [New dent.]. Vol. 1, No. 1 (Mar./Apr. 1993)-(199?). Periodical. English. Slack Inc., 6900 Grove Road, Thorofare NJ 08086. **Tel** (609)848-1000, (800)257-8290, FAX (609)853-5991, telex 517108 SLACK INC VD.

ISSN 0890-3867
DD 617 US
NEW JERSEY DHA QUARTERLY. [N. J. DHA q.]. **Added/Corp** New Jersey Dental Hygienists' Association. **VFOAT** NJDHA Quarterly. **VAT** New Jersey Dental Hygienists' Association Quarterly. (1983)-. Periodical. English. Four times a year. $10.00. NJ Dental Hygienists Association, 27 Tyler Lane, Berlin NJ 08009. **Tel** (609)767-9379. **ED** Dawn Walters. **Ad Acc. Circ:** 1,200 (ctrl). ***Continues*** *The Wisdom Tooth.*

ISSN 0028-6176
US
NLM W1 NE4588J
Pr Rev.
NEW MEXICO DENTAL JOURNAL. [N. M. dent. j.]. **Added/Corp** New Mexico Dental Association. Vol. 8 (1957)-. Periodical. English. Four times a year (Jan., Apr., July, Oct.). $25.00. New Mexico Dental Association, 3736 Eubank Northeast, Suite A-1, Albuquerque NM 87111. **Tel** (505)294-1368. **ED** Dr. JoAnne Allen. **Ad Acc, Adv Mgr:** M.E. Nelson. **Circ:** 750. ***Continues*** *New Mexico State Dental Journal, 0028-6176.*
Desc: Dental education articles, state dental activity and legislative articles.
Ind/Abst Index Dent. Lit.

ISSN 0028-7571
US
NLM W1 NE863
NEW YORK STATE DENTAL JOURNAL. [N. Y. state dent. j.]. **Added/Corp** Dental Society of the State of New York. **VFOAT** Dental Journal; NYS Dental Journal. Vol. 13, (1947)-. Trade Publication. English. Ten times a year (June/July and August/September issues combined). $48.00. Dental Society State of New York, 7 Elk Street, Albany NY 12207. **Tel** (518)465-0044, FAX (518)427-0461. **ED** Mary Grates Stall. Index available. cum. index. **Bk Rev,** (Qty: varies). **Ad Acc, Adv Mgr:** Patricia Zahner. **Circ:** 15,000 (ctrl). available on microfilm and microfiche from University Microfilms International (UMI). ***Continues*** *Journal of the Dental Society of the State of New York, 0093-4100.*
Desc: Features scientific articles including original research reports, case studies, experiences with new techniques and/or products. Also contains articles on practice management, legislative developments, Dental Society activities and news of general interest to practitioners.
Ind/Abst Curr. Cit.; Curr. Titles Dent.; Dent. Abstr.; Energy Res. Abstr.; Index Med.; Index Dent. Lit.

ISSN 0028-8047
NZ
CCC
NLM W1 NE967 **CODEN** NZDJAM
Pr Rev.
NEW ZEALAND DENTAL JOURNAL. [N. Z. dent. j.]. **Added/Corp** New Zealand Dental Association. Vol. 1, (1906)-. Periodical. English. Four times a year (Jan., Apr., July, Oct.). $75.20. New Zealand Dental Association Inc, PO Box 28 084, Auckland 5 New Zealand. **Tel** 011 64 9 5242778, FAX 011 64 9 5205256. **ED** Harvey Brown. Index available. **Bk Rev. Ad Acc, Adv Mgr Tel** 011 64 634 5567. **Circ:** 1,500 (ctrl). Documents available from BIOSIS Document Express.
Desc: Contains clinical papers, association news, reviews and overseas dental news.
Ind/Abst Biol. Abstr.; Curr. Titles Dent.; Index Med.; Index Dent. Lit.; Nutr. Res. Newsl.; Life Sci. Collect.

ISSN 0810-7440
AT
NEWS BULLETIN OF THE AUSTRALIAN DENTAL ASSOCIATION. (AUSTRALIAN DENTAL ASSOCIATION NEWS BULLETIN.). (19??)-. Bulletin. English. Eleven times a year (monthly except Jan.). 69.00Aus$ Australia; 83.00Aus$ other. Australian Dental Association, PO Box 520, St Leonards NSW 2065 Australia. **Tel** 61 2 9064412, FAX 61 2 9064917. **ED** John K. Harcourt, Joyce Campbell, and Julie Green. **Bk Rev,** (Qty: Varies). **Ad Acc. Circ:** 7,050 (ctrl).
Desc: Current information on updates of dental and dentistry care. Other articles are photographs, and product news that helps maintain better care of teeth.

ISSN 1079-4476
US
●**NEWSLETTER/BCDS.** (NEWSLETTER/BCDS.). **VFOAT** Newsletter; Newsletter BCDS. Vol. 1 (Oct. 1994)-. Newsletter. English. Twelve times a year. $14.00. Bergen County Dental Society, 1016 Main Street, River Edge NJ 07661. **Tel** (201)487-1073. **Ad Acc. *Continues*** *Bergen County Dental Society. Journal of the Bergen County Dental Society, 0092-9832.*
Ind/Abst Index Dent. Lit.

LC KF2910.D33 A137 **ISSN** 1044-3142
DD 346.7303/32 US
NEWSLETTER FOR DENTISTS. [Newsl. dent.]. **VFOAT** NMR Newsletter for Dentists. 1989-. Newsletter. English. Three times a year. $24.00. M G Correale, 5114 North Illinois Street, Belleville IL 62221. ***Continues*** *National Malpractice Reporter for Dentists, 0889-499X.*

ISSN 0173-6868
GW
NLM W1 NI376P
NIEDERSACHSISCHES ZAHNARZTEBLATT. [Niedersachs. Zahnarztebl.]. Periodical. German. 3.80. Zahnarztekammer Niedersachsen, Hildescheimer Strasse 35, Postfach 66 43, 3000 Hannover 1 Germany.
Ind/Abst Index Dent. Lit.

ISSN 0385-1605
JA
CODEN NSDKDD
NIHON SHIKA DAIGAKU KIYO. IPPAN KYOIKU KEI. [Nippon Shika Daigaku Kiyo. Ippan Kyoiku-kei]. **Added/Corp** Nihon Shika Daigaku. **VFOAT** Bulletin of Nippon Dental University. General Education. (1972)-. Academic Scholarly Publication. Japanese (English). Nippon Dental University, Fujima 1, Chiyoda-ku, Tokyo Japan. Documents available from CASDDS.
Ind/Abst Chem. Abstr.

ISSN 0385-0110
JA
CODEN NSKADI
NIHON SHISHUBYO GAKKAI KAISHI. [Nihon Shishubyo Gakkai kaishi]. **Added/Corp** Nihon Shishubyo Gakkai. **VFOAT** Journal of the Japanese Association of Periodontology. (1968)-. Academic Scholarly Publication. Japanese (English). Four times a year. Nihon Shishubyo Gakkai, (Japanese Soc. of Gastroenterology), 9-13 Ginza 8 Chome, Chuoku Tokyo 104 Japan. Documents available from CASDDS.
Ind/Abst Chem. Abstr.; Index Dent. Lit.

ISSN 0549-5245
DD 617.6 JA
NIPPON DENTAL UNIVERSITY ANNUAL PUBLICATIONS. [Nippon Dent. Univ. annu. publ.]. **VFOAT** Nippon Dental College Annual Publications. (1964)-. Academic Scholarly Publication. English. One time a year. Society of the Nippon Dental University / Nihon Shika Daigaku Shigakkai, 9-20 Fujimi 1-chome, Chiyodaku Tokyo 102 Japan. **Tel** FAX 011 81 3 2648745.

JA
NIPPON KOKU GEKA GAKKAI ZASSHI. **VFOAT** Japanese Journal of Oral Surgery. (1967)-. Periodical. Japanese. Twelve times a year. $299.50. Nippon Koku Geka Gakkai, (Japanese Soc. of Oral & Maxillofacial Surgeons), 3-1 Doshomachi Higashiku, Osakashi Osakafu 541, Japan. **(Subscription address:** Japan Publications Trading Company Ltd., PO Box 5030, Tokyo International, Tokyo 100-31 Japan. **Tel** 011 81 3 3292 3753.) ***Continues*** *Koku Geka Gakkai Zasshi.*

ISSN 0029-0297
JA
CODEN NKOGAV
NIPPON KOKUKA GAKKAI ZASSHI. (NIHON KOKUKA GAKKAI ZASSHI.). [Nippon Kokuka Gakkai zasshi]. **Added/Corp** Nihon Kokuka Gakkai. **VFOAT** Journal of the Japanese Stomatological Society. Vol. 1 (Jan. 1952)-. Academic Scholarly Publication. Japanese. Five times a year. $209.50. Nihon Kokuka Gakkai, (Japanese Stomatological Soc.), Hitotsubashi Insatsu K.K., Gakkai Jimu Senta, 12-13 Kamiosaki 3 Chome, Shinagawaku Tokyo 141, Japan. **(Subscription address:** Japan Publications Trading Company Ltd., PO Box 5030, Tokyo International, Tokyo 100-31 Japan. **Tel** 011 81 3 3292 3753.) Documents available from CASDDS.
Ind/Abst Chem. Abstr.

JA
NLM W1 NI921N
NIPPON KYOSEI SHIKA GAKKAI ZASSHI. JOURNAL OF JAPAN ORTHODONTIC SOCIETY. **VFOAT** Journal of Japan Orthodontic Society. (1932)-. Periodical. Japanese. Six times a year. $185.00. **(Subscription address:** Maruzen Company Ltd., PO Box 5050, Import & Export Department, Tokyo 100 31 Japan. **Tel** 011 81 3 32789224.) ***Continues*** *Nippon Kyosei Shika Gakkai Kaishi.*
Ind/Abst Index Dent. Lit.

JA
NLM W1 NI933W
NIPPON SHIKA HYORON = THE NIPPON DENTAL REVIEW. **VFOAT** Nippon Dental Review. Vol. 1 (October 1940)-. Trade Publication. Japanese. Twelve times a year. $429.50. **(Subscription address:** Japan Publications Trading Company Ltd., PO Box 5030, Tokyo International, Tokyo 100-31 Japan. **Tel** 011 81 3 3292 3753.) ***Formed by the union of*** *Kuchi, Nippon Koku Eisei Shika Maigetsu Tsushin* ***and*** *Shin Shika Iho.*
Ind/Abst Index Dent. Lit.

ISSN 0387-4346
JA
NLM W1 NI933Y **CODEN** NSIKD4
NIPPON SHIKA IGAKKAI KAIHO. [Nihon Shika Igakkai kaiho]. **VFOAT** Journal of the Japanese Association for Dental Science. Vol. 1 (1975)-. Academic Scholarly Publication. Japanese. Twelve times a year. Documents available from CASDDS.
Ind/Abst Chem. Abstr.

ISSN 0047-1763
JA
NLM W1 NI934 **CODEN** NISIA9
NIPPON SHIKA ISHIKAI ZASSHI. (NIPPON SHIKA ISHIKAI ZASSHI. THE JOURNAL OF THE JAPAN DENTAL ASSOCIATION.). [Nippon Shika Ishikai zasshi]. **Added/Corp** Nippon Shika Ishikai. **VFOAT** Journal of the Japan Dental Association. Vol. 1 (November 1948)-. Academic Scholarly Publication. Japanese. Twelve times a year. $133.00. **(Subscription address:** Japan Publications Trading Company Ltd., PO Box 5030, Tokyo International, Tokyo 100-31 Japan. **Tel** 011 81 3 3292 3753.) available on microfilm from University Microfilms International (UMI). Documents available from CASDDS.
Ind/Abst Chem. Abstr. (1948-1983); Index Dent. Lit.

ISSN 0301-0899
JA
NLM W1 NI934R **CODEN** NSMZDZ
NIPPON SHIKA MASUI GAKKAI ZASSHI. **Main/Corp** Nippon Shika Masui Gakkai. **VFOAT** Journal of Japanese Dental Anaesthesia Society. (1973)-. Academic Scholarly Publication. Japanese. Four times a year. $205.00. **(Subscription address:** Japan Publications Trading Company Ltd., PO Box 5030, Tokyo International, Tokyo 100-31 Japan. **Tel** 011 81 3 3292 3753.) Documents available from CASDDS.
Ind/Abst Chem. Abstr.

ISSN 0091-164X
US
NLM W1 NO382K
NORTH CAROLINA DENTAL GAZETTE. [N.C. dent. j.]. **Added/Corp** North Carolina Dental Society. Vol. 56 (Jan. 1973)-. Newspaper. English. Four times a year. $20.00. North Carolina Dental Society, PO Box 12047, Raleigh NC 27605. **Tel** (919)832-1222, (800)662-8754, FAX (919)832-1222. **ED** Dr. Andy Brown and Thomas V. Bennett (Dr. Brown's phone: (919)467-1966). **Ad Acc. Circ:** 2,800. ***Continues*** *Journal of the North Carolina Dental Society, 0029-2443.*
Ind/Abst Dent. Abstr. (-199?).

LC RK1 .M55 **ISSN** 0029-2915
DD 617.605 US
NLM W1 NO462
NORTHWEST DENTISTRY. [Northwest dent.]. **Added/Corp** Minnesota State Dental Association. North Dakota State Dental Association. South Dakota State Dental Association. (1933)-. Periodical. English. Six times a year (Jan., Mar., May, July, Sept., Nov.). $20.00. Minnesota Dental Association, 2236 Marshall Avenue, St Paul MN 55104. **Tel** (612)646-7454. **ED** Richard A. Johnson. Index available. cum. index. **Ad Acc, Adv Mgr:** Patty Lein. **Circ:** 3400. ***Continues*** *Minnesota State Dental Association. Bulletin.*
Desc: Original articles, editorials, clinical abstracts, research reports, and association reports and news.
Ind/Abst Curr. Cit.; Curr. Titles Dent.; Index Dent. Lit.

ISSN 1062-0311
DD 617 US
NLM W1; NO682
NORTHWESTERN DENTAL RESEARCH. [Northwest. dent. res.]. **Added/Corp** Northwestern University (Evanston, Ill.). Dental School. (1989)-. Periodical. English. Two times a year. $50.00. Northwestern University Dental School, 240 East Huron Street, Chicago IL 60611. **ED** Dr. Evan H. Greener (Editor's address: 311 E. Chicago Ave., Ward 10-186, Chicago IL 60611-3008; Editor's telephone: (312)908-0490). **Ad Acc, Adv Mgr Tel** (312)503-6869. **Circ:** 2,500.
Ind/Abst Index Dent. Lit. (spring 1989-).

ISSN 0394-1388
IT
UDC 616.314
NUOVO LABORATORIO ODONTOTECNICO, IL. [Nuovo lab. odontotec.]. (1985)-. Periodical. Italian. Twelve times a year. L68130. Assoc Naz Titolari Laboratorio Odontotecnico, V Altipiano Asiago 16, 25123 Brescia Italy. **Tel** 011 39 30 300671.

US
NYJD BULLETIN. **Added/Corp** First District Dental Society of New York. **VFOAT** New York Journal of Dentistry Bulletin. Apr./May 1990-. Bulletin. English. Six times a year. New York Journal of Dentistry Inc, 295 Madison Avenue, New York NY 10017. **Tel** (212)889-8940. ***Continues*** *New York Journal of Dentistry.*

ISSN 0826-6905
DD 338.4/36176/009713 CN
ODA SUGGESTED FEE GUIDE FOR GENERAL PRACTITIONERS. (SUGGESTED FEE GUIDE FOR GENERAL PRACTITIONERS.). [ODA suggest. fee guide gen pract.]. **Main/Corp** Ontario Dental Association. **Added/Corp** Ontario Dental Association. Economics of Practice Committee. Ontario Dental Association. **VFOAT** ODA Suggested Fee Guide for General Practitioners; Ontario Dental Association

Dentistry

Suggested Fee Guide for Dental Services Provided by General Practitioners. (1984)-. English. One time a year. 40.01Can$. Ontario Dental Association, 4 New Street, Attn Nina Buttce, Toronto Ontario M5R 1P6 Canada. **Tel** (416)922-3900, FAX (416)922-9005. ctrl circ. *Continues Ontario Dental Association. Suggested Fee Guide for Dental Services Provided by General Practitioners, 0709-6127.*

ISSN 0251-172X
FR

NLM W1 OD72

ODONTO-STOMATOLOGIE TROPICALE. (ODONTO-STOMATOLOGIE TROPICALE / TROPICAL DENTAL JOURNAL.).
[Odonto-stomatol. trop.]. **VFOAT** Tropical Dental Journal. Vol. 1, No. 1 (1978)-. Periodical. English (French). Four times a year. $103.40. Dr. J. L. Miquel / Departement Sante et Developpement, Universite Bordeaux II, 146 rue Leo Saignat, 33076 Bordeaux Cedex France. **Tel** 011 33 56 962893 ext. 539. **ED** Dr. J. L. Miquel. **Bk Rev. Ad Acc. Circ:** 1,500. *Continues Revue du Sesda, 0379-8232.*
Desc: Dental and oral public health in the tropics. Practice and research in tropical environment about oral diseases, continuing education for practitioners in remote areas.
Ind/Abst Curr. Titles Dent.; Index Dent. Lit.

SW

ODONTOLOGISKA FOERENINGEN TIDSKRIFT. Added/Corp Odontologiska Foereningen, Stockholm. VFOAT OFT. (1937)-.
Periodical. Swedish. Six times a year. $24.04. Odontologiska Foereningen Tidskrift, Institutionsvaegen 6, 141 52 Huddinge Sweden.

ISSN 0472-5158
PN

NLM W1 OD569D

ODONTOLOGO (PANAMA), EL. (EL ODONTOLOGO.). Added/Corp Asociacion Odontologica Panamena. (197?)-. Periodical. Spanish. Two times a year. $24.00. Asociacion Odontologica Panamena, Apartado 6777, Panama 5 Panama. **Tel** 69-1603. *Supersedes Odontologo.*

IT

NLM W1; OD699T

ODONTOSTOMATOLOGIA E IMPLANTOPROTESI (MILAN, ITALY : 1989). (ODONTOSTOMATOLOGIA E IMPLANTOPROTESI : O&I.). VFOAT O&I; Odontostomatologia & Implantoprotesi. (198?)-.
Periodical. Italian. Ten times a year. L102190. Stammer Spa, Via della Liberazione 1, 20068 Peschiera Borromeo Italy. **Tel** 011 39 2 55302606, FAX 011 39 2 55302700, telex 321083. *Continues Rivista di Odontostomatologia e Implantoprotesi.*
Ind/Abst Index Dent. Lit. (June 1989-).

ISSN 0029-8506
GR

ODONTOSTOMATOLOGIKE PROODOS.
[Odontostomatol. prood.]. **VFOAT** Odontostomatological Progress. (1947)-. Periodical. Greek, Modern. Six times a year. Soc Odontostomatological Res, 70 Micras Asias Street, Athens 609 Greece.
Ind/Abst Index Dent. Lit.

AU

OESTERREICHISCHE ZAHNARZTE ZEITUNG : OZZ. (19??)-. German. Ten times a year. S350.00 Austria; S430.00 other. Oesterreichische Aerztekammer, Weihburggasse 10-12, A-1011 Vienna Austria. **Tel** 011 43 1 51501233. *Continues Osterreichische Dentistenzeitschrift.*

AU

NLM W1; OS912N

OESTERREICHISCHE ZAHNTECHNIKER HANDWERK : OFFIZIELLES ORGAN DER BUNDESINNUNG DER ZAHNTECHNIKER, DAS. Added/Corp
Bundesinnung der Zahntechniker (Austria). (March 1991)-. Periodical. German. Four times a year.
Ind/Abst Index Dent. Lit. (1991-).

ISSN 0030-087X
US
TITLE CHANGE

DD 617

OHIO DENTAL JOURNAL (COLUMBUS, OHIO. 1959), THE. (THE OHIO DENTAL JOURNAL.). [Ohio dent. j.]. Added/Corp Ohio Dental Association. VFOAT ODJ. (1959)-(1995). Trade Publication. English. Ohio Dental Association, 1370 Dublin Road, Columbus OH 43215-1098. **Tel** (614)486-2700, . **ED** Donald F. Bowers DDS. **Ad Acc. Circ:** 5,400 (ctrl). *Continues ODJ, Ohio Dental Journal, 1076-4178. Merged into Focus on Ohio Dentistry.*
Desc: Membership publication for the Ohio Dental Association dealing with issues and events important to dentists.
Ind/Abst Index Dent. Lit.

ISSN 0916-2313
JA

DD 617.6

OHU DAIGAKU SHIGAKUSHI. VFOAT Ohu University Dental Journal; Ou Daigaku Shigakushi. (1989)-. Periodical. Multiple languages. Four times a year. *Continues Tohoku Shika Daigaku Gakkaishi, 0385-0161.*
Ind/Abst Health Plan. Adminis.

ISSN 0164-9442
US

NLM W1 JO975

OKLAHOMA DENTAL ASSOCIATION JOURNAL. [Okla. Dent. Assoc. J.]. Main/Corp Oklahoma Dental Association. Added/Corp Oklahoma Dental Association. Journal. VFOAT ODA Journal. (1978)-. Periodical. English. Four times a year. $12.00. Oklahoma Dental Association, 629 Northwest Expressway, Oklahoma City OK 73118. **Tel** (405)848-8873. **ED** Earl Mabry, Thomas Murdoch and Frank Miranda. **Bk Rev. Ad Acc. Circ:** 1,600 (ctrl). *Continues Your Oklahoma Dental Association Journal, 0149-2594.*
Desc: Any issues of relevance to dentistry.
Ind/Abst Index Dent. Lit.

ISSN 0300-5275
CN

NLM W1 ON429

ONTARIO DENTIST. [Ont. dent.]. Added/Corp Ontario Dental Association. Vol. 49 (Jan. 1972)-. Periodical. English. Ten times a year (Jan./Feb. and July/August are combined issues). 52.36Can$. Ontario Dental Association, 4 New Street, Attn Nina Buttce, Toronto Ontario M5R 1P6 Canada. **Tel** (416)922-3900, FAX (416)922-9005. **ED** Nadine Hubert. **Ad Acc, Adv Mgr Tel** (416)691-5155. **Circ:** 5,600 (ctrl). *Continues Ontario Dental Association. Journal of the Ontario Dental Association.*
Desc: Communication vehicle for the Ontario Dental Association providing news and clinical articles by and for Ontario dentists.
Ind/Abst Index Dent. Lit.

LC RK501 .O64
DD 617.6
ISSN 0361-7734
US

NLM W1 OP15
Pr Rev.

OPERATIVE DENTISTRY. [Oper. dent.]. Vol. 1 (Winter 1976)-. Periodical. English. Six times a year. $55.00. Institute for Environmental Studies, FM-12, University of Washington, Seattle WA 98195. **Tel** (206)543-1812, FAX (206)543-2025. (Subscription address: Operative Dentistry, School of Dentistry, University of Washington, SM 57, Seattle WA 98195.) **ED** David J. Bales. **Bk Rev. Circ:** 2,000. Documents available from The Genuine Article. *Supersedes Journal of the American Academy of Gold Foil Operators, 0002-7146.*
Desc: Includes conservations and restoration of teeth; the scientific foundation of operative dental therapy; dental materials; dental education; and the social, political, and economic aspects of dentistry.
Ind/Abst Curr. Cit.; Curr. Contents Clin. Med.; Curr. Titles Dent.; Index Dent. Lit.; Res. Alert [Select. Cov.]; SCISEARCH.

ISSN 0163-3473
US

NLM W1 OP15A

OPERATIVE DENTISTRY. SUPPLEMENT. [Oper. dent., Suppl.]. Added/Corp Academy of Operative Dentistry. American Academy of Gold Foil Operators. University of Washington. School of Dentistry. (1977)-. Monographic series. English. Price varies per volume. Operative Dentistry / School of Dentistry, University of Washington, PO Box 357457, Seattle WA 98195. **Tel** (206)543-5913. (Subscription address: Operative Dentistry, School of Dentistry, University of Washington, SM 57, Seattle WA 98195.
Ind/Abst Health Plan. Adminis.

LC RD523 .O7
DD 617/.522/0025
ISSN 0147-1449
US

ORAL AND MAXILLOFACIAL SURGERY DIRECTORY OF THE WORLD. VFOAT Oral Maxillofacial Surgeons Directory of the World. (19??)-. Directory. English. Oral & Maxillofacial Surgery Directory of the World, 761 Osage Road, Pittsburgh PA 15243. *Continues Oral Surgery Directory of the World.*

ISSN 0030-4204
CN
CCC

NLM W1 OR104

ORAL HEALTH. [Oral health]. Vol. 1 (1911)-. Periodical. English. Twelve times a year. 46.00Can$. Southham Information & Technical Group Inc, 1450 Don Mills Road, Don Mills Ontario M3B 2X7 Canada. **Tel** (416)445-6641, (800)668-2374, FAX (416)442-2261. Index available. cum. index. **Bk Rev. Ad Acc.** ctrl circ. available on microfilm and microfiche from University Microfilms International (UMI).
Ind/Abst Dent. Abstr. (-199?); Index Dent. Lit.; Nutr. Res. Newsl.

ISSN 0902-0055
DK
CCC

NLM W1; OR108H
Pr Rev.
CODEN OMIMEE

ORAL MICROBIOLOGY AND IMMUNOLOGY. [Oral microbiol. immunol.]. (1986)-. Periodical. English. Six times a year. $286.41. Munksgaard International Publishers Ltd, PO Box 2148, DK-1016 Copenhagen K Denmark. **Tel** 011 45 33 127030, FAX 011 45 33 129387, telex 19431 MUNKS DK. **ED** Jorgen Slots. Documents available from The Genuine Article, BIOSIS Document Express.
Desc: Pertaining to fundamental and applied aspects of oral infections.
Ind/Abst Biol. Abstr. (1988-); Curr. Aware. Biol. Sci., CABS; Curr. Cit.; Curr. Contents Life Sci.; Curr. Titles Dent.; Immunol. Abstr.; Index Dent. Lit. (1986-); Index Vet.; Microbiol. Abstr. Sect. B; Res. Alert [Select. Cov.]; Rev. Med. Vet. Mycology; Sci. Cit. Index; SCISEARCH; Small Anim. Abstr. Bibliogr.

ISSN 0911-6028
JA

NLM W1; OR109D

ORAL RADIOLOGY. Added/Corp Nihon Shika Hoshasen Gakkai. (198?)-. Periodical. English. Two times a year. $78.87. Japanese Society of Oral & Maxillofacial Radiology, 1-8 Yamadaoka, Osaka University, Osaka 565 Japan. **Tel** 011 81 6 876 5711, FAX 011 44 6 875 5834. **ED** Kanji Kishi. **Ad Acc. Circ:** 1,500.
Desc: Contains original papers concerned with oral and maxillofacial radiology.
Ind/Abst EMBASE.

LC RD1 .O7
DD 617.52
ISSN 0030-4220
US
CCC

NLM W1 OR125
Pr Rev.
CODEN OSOMAE
TITLE CHANGE

ORAL SURGERY, ORAL MEDICINE, ORAL PATHOLOGY. [Oral surg. oral med. oral pathol.]. Added/Corp New England Society of Oral Surgeons. Vol. 1 (Jan. 1948)-(Jan. 1995). Academic Scholarly Publication. English. Mosby Year Book Inc., 11830 Westline Industrial Drive, St Louis MO 63146. **Tel** (800)325-4177, (314)872-8370, FAX (314)432-1380, telex 44-2402. **ED** Robert B. Shira. Index available. **Bk Rev. Ad Acc. Circ:** 10,038. available on microfilm and microfiche from University Microfilms International (UMI). Documents available from The Genuine Article, BIOSIS Document Express, CASDDS. *Absorbed Journal of Endodontics; Supersedes in part American Journal of Orthodontics and Oral Surgery, 0096-6347. Continued by Oral Surgery, Oral Medicine, Oral Pathology, Oral Radiology, and Endodontics.*
Desc: Geared to the medical aspects of dentistry. Concerned with the diagnostic aids, medical treatment and surgical techniques of dental practice and medicine.
Ind/Abst Biol. Abstr.; Chem. Abstr.; Cumul. Index Nurs. Allied Health Lit.; Curr. Cit.; Curr. Contents Clin. Med.; Curr. Titles Dent.; Dent. Abstr.; EMBASE; Energy Res. Abstr.; Index Med.; Index Dent. Lit.; Nutr. Res. Newsl.; Life Sci. Collect.; Physic. Medline Plus; Protozoolog. Abstr.; Res. Alert [Full Cov.]; Rev. Med. Vet. Entomol.; Rev. Med. Vet. Mycology; Sci. Cit. Index; SCISEARCH; Soc. Sci. Cit. Index [Select. Cov.].

US

●ORAL SURGERY, ORAL MEDICINE, ORAL PATHOLOGY, ORAL RADIOLOGY, AND ENDODONTICS.
(1995)-. Periodical. English. Twelve times a year. $186.00 (institutions), $86.00 (individuals) US; $209.00 (institutions), $109.00 (individuals) other. Mosby Year Book Inc., 11830 Westline Industrial Drive, St Louis MO 63146. **Tel** (800)325-4177, (314)872-8370, FAX (314)432-1380, telex 44-2402. *Continues Oral Surgery, Oral Medicine, Oral Pathology.*

US

NLM WU22 O77

ORTHODONTIC DIRECTORY OF THE WORLD. Added/Corp American Association of Orthodontists. (192?)-. English. Every 2 years. $20.00. Orthodontic Directory of the World, 1915 Broadway, Nashville TN 37203. **ED** William H. Oliver. **Ad Acc. Circ:** 5,000.
Desc: Includes names, addresses, and training.

ISSN 0895-5034
US

NLM W1; OR78

ORTHODONTIC REVIEW. [Orthod. rev.]. Vol. 1, No. 1 (Sept./Oct. 1987)-. Periodical. English. Six times a year. $93.00. Orthodontic Review, 2235 SW Westport Dr., Topeka KS 66614. **Tel** (913)272-9493.
Desc: Abstracts of current literature about orthodontics. Features case presentation, book/audio/visual reviews, editorials, and letters to the editor.
Ind/Abst Index Dent. Lit. (1987-).

Dentistry

ISSN 0078-6608
FR
NLM W1 OR79
ORTHODONTIE FRANCAISE, L'. [Orthod. fr.]. Vol.1 (1921/22). Periodical. French. One time a year. $367.45. SID, 9 rue Christine, 75006 Paris. **Tel** 011 33 1 6455311. cum. index.
Ind/Abst Index Med.; Index Dent. Lit.

SP
ORTODONCIA ESPANOLA. Spanish. Sociedad Espanola de Ortodoncia, Avda de Burgos 29/5 D, 28036 Madrid Spain.
Ind/Abst Indice Med. Esp.

ISSN 0937-1532
GW
NLM W1; PA864B
PARODONTOLOGIE : DIE ZEITSCHRIFT FUER DIE PRAXIS. (1990)-. Periodical. German (summaries and/or abstracts in English). Four times a year. $163.51. Quintessenz Verlag GmbH, Ifenpfad 2 4, D 12107 Berlin Germany. **Tel** 011 49 30 740060, FAX 011 49 30 7415080.
Ind/Abst Health Plan. Adminis.; Index Dent. Lit. (1990-).

US
PASSAIC COUNTY DENTAL SOCIETY NEWSLETTER. Newsletter. English. $50.00. Passaic County Dental Society, 642 Broad Street, Clifton NJ 07013. **Tel** (201) 470-0003. **ED** Stuart Katz.

ISSN 0191-7951
US
DD 617
NLM W1 P139
PCSO BULLETIN. (BULLETIN OF PACIFIC COAST SOCIETY OF ORTHODONTISTS.). [PCSO bull.]. **Added/Corp** Pacific Coast Society of Orthodontists. **VAT** Pacific Coast Society of Orthodontists Bulletin. Vol. 50, No. 15 (Fall 1978)-. Bulletin. English. Four times a year (Mar., June, Sept., Dec.). $35.00. Pacific Coast Society of Orthodontists, 1323 Columbus Avenue, Suite 301, San Francisco CA 94133. **Tel** (415)441-2410. **ED** David Crouch. **Ad Acc. Circ:** 3,000. **Continues** Bulletin - Pacific Coast Society of Orthodontists, 0030-8617.
Desc: Content summarizes all material presented during nine regional meetings of the Pacific Coast Society of Orthodontists.

ISSN 0917-2394
JA
NLM W1; PE167DG
PEDIATRIC DENTAL JOURNAL : INTERNATIONAL JOURNAL OF JAPANESE SOCIETY OF PEDIATRIC DENTISTRY. **Added/Corp** Nihon ShÂoni Shika Gakkai. **VFOAT** PDJ. Vol. 1, No. 1 (July 1991)-. Periodical. English. One time a year. $10.00. Japanese Society Pediatric Dentistry Oral Association, 1 44 2 Komagm, Toshima Ku Tokyo Japan.

ISSN 0164-1263
US
NLM W1 PE167E   **CODEN** PEDEDL
PEDIATRIC DENTISTRY. [Pediatr. dent.]. **Added/Corp** American Academy of Pedodontics. American Academy of Pediatric Dentistry. Vol. 1 (Mar. 1979)-. Trade Publication. English. Seven times a year (Feb., Apr., June, Aug., Oct., Dec.). $95.00. American Academy of Pediatric Dentistry, 211 East Chicago Avenue, Suite 1036, Chicago IL 60611. **Tel** (312)337-2169. Index available. Documents available from BIOSIS Document Express.
Desc: Promotes the practice, education, and the research of pediatric dentistry.
Ind/Abst Annals Behav. Med.; Biol. Abstr.; Curr. Cit.; Curr. Titles Dent.; Dent. Abstr.; Index Med.; Index Dent. Lit.

ISSN 1046-2791
US
DD 617
PEDIATRIC DENTISTRY TODAY. (PEDIATRIC DENTISTRY TODAY : NEWSLETTER OF THE AMERICAN ACADEMY OF PEDIATRIC DENTISTRY.). [Pediatr. dent. today]. Vol. 23, No. 7 (Aug. 1988)-. Newsletter. English. Six times a year. $20.00 (Non-Members, Domestic). American Academy of Pediatric Dentistry, AAPD, 211 East Chicago Avenue/Suite 1036, Chicago IL 60611-2616. **Continues** Newsletter of the American Academy of Pediatric Dentistry.

ISSN 0031-4331
US
NLM W1 PE283
PENN DENTAL JOURNAL, THE. **Added/Corp** University of Pennsylvania. School of Dental Medicine. University of Pennsylvania. School of Dentistry. Vol. 1, (May 1897)-. Periodical. English. Two times a year. $40.00. University of Pennsylvania / School of Dental Medicine, A1 4001 Spruce Street, Philadelphia PA 19014. **Tel** (215)898-8951, FAX (215)898-5243. **ED** Tobe Amsterdam. **Ad Acc.**

LC RK1   **ISSN** 0031-4439
DD 617.605   US
UDC 616.314(748)
NLM W1 PE332
PENNSYLVANIA DENTAL JOURNAL. [Pa. dent. j.]. Vol. 16 (Jan. 1949)-. Periodical. English. Six times a year. $12.00. Pennsylvania Dental Association, PO Box 3341, Harrisburg PA 17105. **Tel** (717)234-5941, (800)692-7256, FAX (717)232-7169. **ED** Judith McFadden. **Ad Acc, Adv Mgr:** Stephanie Kalina, **Tel** (717)234-5941. **Circ:** 7,250. available on microfilm and microfiche from University Microfilms International (UMI).
Continues Pennsylvania State Dental Journal, 0887-462X.
Desc: Official publication of the Pennsylvania Dental Association. Includes scientific articles and dental news across Pennsylvania.
Ind/Abst Dent. Abstr. (-199?).

LC RK361.A1 P47   **ISSN** 1055-0712
DD 617   US
PERIO REPORTS. [Perio rep.]. (1989)-. Periodical. English. Six times a year. $32.00. Perio Reports, PO Box 30367, Flagstaff AZ 86003-0367. **Tel** (602)526-2404, FAX (602)526-2523. **ED** Trisha E O'Hehir. cum. index (December). **Circ:** 1,500.
Desc: Contains summaries of current research in the field of periodontics. It is designed for the clinical practitioner.

ISSN 1065-2418
US
DD 617
NLM W1; PE793K
PERIODONTAL CLINICAL INVESTIGATIONS : OFFICIAL PUBLICATION OF THE NORTHEASTERN SOCIETY OF PERIODONTISTS. [Periodontal clin. invest.]. **Added/Corp** Northeastern Society of Periodontists. Vol. 14, No. 1 (1992)-. Periodical. English. Two times a year. $60.00. Medical Science Publishing, 403 Main Street, Port Washington NY 11050. **Tel** (516)944-7340, FAX (516)944-8663. **Continues** Periodontal Case Reports, 0277-4216.

LC RK   **ISSN** 1195-2008
DD 617.6   CN
NLM W1; PE794
●**PERIODONTAL INSIGHTS.** [Periodontal insights]. **Added/Corp** American Academy of Periodontology. Vol. 1, No. 1 (Sept. 1993)-. Periodical. English. Four times a year. $78.00 (institutions), $52.00 (individuals) US and Canada; $105.00 (institutions), $79.00 (individuals) other. Decker Periodicals Publishing Inc., PO Box 620, Station A, Hamilton Ontario L8N 3K7 Canada. **Tel** (416)522-7017, (800)568-7281, FAX (416)522-7839.
Desc: Official publication of the American Academy of Periodontology.

AT
PERIODONTOLOGY. English. Two times a year (May, Oct.). 40.00Aus$. Australian Society of Periodontology, PO Box 80, Maroochudore Queensland, 4558 Australia. **Tel** 011 61 474 438733, FAX 011 61 474 791051. **ED** Dr. Mark Bartold. Index available (Bound in Oct. issue). **Ad Acc. Circ:** 1,500.

ISSN 0906-6713
DK
CCC
NLM W1; PE7955
●**PERIODONTOLOGY 2000.** VFOAT Periodontology Two Thousand. Vol. 1 (1993)-. Monographic series. English. Three times a year. $221.22. Munksgaard International Publishers Ltd, PO Box 2148, DK-1016 Copenhagen K Denmark. **Tel** 011 45 33 127030, FAX 011 45 33 129387, telex 19431 MUNKS DK. **ED** Joergen Slots. **Ad Acc.**

LC R   **ISSN** 1069-269X
DD 610   US
●**PERSONAL REPORT. PRACTICE DEVELOPMENT AND WEALTH ACCUMULATION FOR THE PERIODONTIST, THE.** [Pers. rep., Pract. dev. wealth accumul. periodontist]. **VFOAT** The Personal Report; Practice Development and Wealth Accumulation for the Periodontist. (1993)-. English. Four times a year. $147.00. Personal Report, 17 Arabian Drive, Charleston SC 29407. **Tel** (803)571-1342. **ED** Alvin H Danenberg. Index available in last issue of volume--attached. **Circ:** 4,700. **Continues** Personal Report. Practice Management and Financial Planning for the Periodontist, 1047-434X.
Desc: Provides detailed and updated information on no-load mutual funds, and information on wealth accumulation and financial planning. Features guest expert authors on periodontal practice development.

IT
PICCOLO DI ALESSANDRIA, IL. (19??)-. Italian. Twenty-six times a year. L100000. Editrice de il Piccolo, Via Galilei 62, 15100 Alessandria Italy. **Tel** 011 39 131 444156.

ISSN 0185-5905
MX
NLM W1; PR137F
PRACTICA ODONTOLOGICA. [Pract. odontol.]. Vol. 1, No. 1 (Nov.-Dec. 1979)-. Periodical. Spanish. Twelve times a year. $190.00. Mundo Medico SA, Ejercicto Nacional 381, 11520 Mexico DF Mexico. **Tel** 011 52 5 2038111. **ED** Oscar G Bagnarelli.
Desc: Technical articles on pediatric and adult dentistry, orthodontics and pathology.
Ind/Abst Index Dent. Lit. (Aug. 1986-).

ISSN 1056-7933
DD 617   US
PRACTICAL ENDODONTICS. [Pract. endod.]. **VFOAT** Endodontics. Vol. 1, No. 1 (Oct. 1991)-. Periodical. English. Ten times a year. $195.00. Video Study Club, 14 Hudson S. Road, Griffin GA 30223. **ED** Arthur Weathers (editor's phone: (404)227-3882). Each issue contains an index to its own contents (no volume index)--loose. cum. index. **Bk Rev. Circ:** 1,200 (ctrl).

ISSN 0729-1345
AT
PRACTICAL GUIDES FOR SUCCESSFUL DENTISTRY. Added/Corp Australian Dental Association. Australian Dental Standards Laboratory. 1st ed. (Mar. 1982)-. English. Australian Dental Association, PO Box 520, St Leonards NSW 2065 Australia. **Tel** 61 2 9064412, FAX 61 2 9064917.

ISSN 1042-2722
DD 617   US
NLM W1; PR151
Pr Rev.
PRACTICAL PERIODONTICS AND AESTHETIC DENTISTRY. [Pract. peridontics aesthet. dent.]. **VFOAT** PP&A; PP and A; PP & A. Vol. 1, No. 1 (Jan./Feb. 1989)-. Trade Publication. English. Nine times a year. $80.00. Montage Media Corporation, 70 Hilltop Road, Ramsey NJ 07446-1119. **Tel** (201)236-0700, FAX (201)236-1339. **ED** Laura Franklin. Index available. cum. index. **Ad Acc, Adv Mgr:** L. W. Scott Clements, **Tel** (201)236-0700 ext. 117. **Circ:** 84,000 (ctrl).
Ind/Abst Health Plan. Adminis.

ISSN 1046-7106
DD 617   US
PRACTICAL REVIEWS IN ORTHODONTICS. (PRACTICAL REVIEWS IN ORTHODONTICS [SOUND RECORDING].). [Pract. rev. orthod.]. **Added/Corp** American Association of Orthodontists. Educational Reviews, Inc. (1989)-. Periodical. English. Twelve times a year. $185.00. Educational Reviews Inc., 6801 Cahaba Valley Road, Birmingham AL 35242. **Tel** (205)991-5188, (800)633-4743, FAX (205)995-1926.

LC RK   **ISSN** 1051-0265
DD 617.6   US
PRACTICAL REVIEWS IN PEDIATRIC DENTISTRY [SOUND RECORDING]. [Pract. rev. pediatr. dent.]. **Added/Corp** American Academy of Pediatric Dentistry. **VFOAT** Pediatric Dentistry; PR. Vol. 1, No. 1 (May/June 1990)-. Periodical. English. Six times a year. $160.00. Educational Reviews Inc., 6801 Cahaba Valley Road, Birmingham AL 35242. **Tel** (205)991-5188, (800)633-4743, FAX (205)995-1926.

ISSN 1064-1203
DD 610   US
PRACTICE MANAGEMENT AND MARKETING NEWS IN PEDIATRIC DENTISTRY. (PRACTICE MANAGEMENT AND MARKETING NEWS IN PEDIATRIC DENTISTRY : PMM NEWS.). [Pract. manag. mark. news pediatr. dent.]. **Added/Corp** American Academy of Pediatric Dentistry. **VFOAT** PMM News. Vol. 1, No. 1 (Aug. 1992)-. Periodical. English. Six times a year. American Academy of Pediatric Dentistry, AAPD, 211 East Chicago Avenue/Suite 1036, Chicago IL 60611-2616.

IT
NLM W1; PR507ZD
PREVENZIONE & ASSISTENZA DENTALE. **VFOAT** Prevenzione Ed Assistenza Dentale. (1985)-. Periodical. Italian. Six times a year. $97.00. Masson SPA, via Statuto 2/4, 20121 Milan Italy. **Tel** 011 39 2 63671, FAX 011 39 2 6367211. **Continues** Prevenzione Stomatologica, 0390-1033.
Ind/Abst Index Dent. Lit. (1985-).

LC RK   **ISSN** 1355-7610
DD 617.6   UK
●**PRIMARY DENTAL CARE.** [Prim. dent. care]. (1994)-. Academic Scholarly Publication. English. Twenty-four times a year. £130.00 Europe; £142.00 other. Royal College of Surgeons of England, Faculty of General Dental Practitioners, 35-43 Lincoln's Inn Fields, London WC2A 3PN United Kingdom. **Tel** 011 44 171 4053475, FAX 011 44 171 8317999. **ED** Julian Scott. Documents available from BLDSC.

Dentistry

DD 617.6/01/06071
ISSN 0834-1494
CN
CCC
NLM W1; PR552D
PROBE. (PROBE : THE CANADIAN DENTAL HYGIENISTS' ASSOCIATION REVUE.). [Probe]. **Added/Corp** Canadian Dental Hygienists' Association. **VFOAT** Canadian Dental Hygienists' Association Revue; Revue : Revue de l'Association Canadienne des Hygienistes Dentaires. Vol. 20, No. 3 (Sept. 1986)-. Periodical. English. Six times a year. 52.02Can$. Canadian Dental Hygienist Association, 1018 Merryville Road, Suite 201, Ottawa Ontario K1Z 6A5 Canada. **Tel** (613)728-8730. **Continues** Canadian Dental Hygienist, 0008-3380.
Ind/Abst Index Dent. Lit. (1986-).

ISSN 0032-9185
UK
NLM W1 PR552C
PROBE (LONDON. 1954). (THE PROBE.). [Probe]. **Added/Corp** General Dental Practitioners Association (Great Britain). (1954)-. Periodical. English. Twelve times a year. $102.67. Nexus Business Communications, Warwick House Azalea Drive, Kent BR8 8HY United Kingdom. **Tel** 011 44 1322 660070, FAX 011 44 1322 667633. **ED** Ken Brown. **Bk Rev. Ad Acc. Circ:** 10,481 (ctrl).
Desc: Practice, management, dento/politics, original papers, assessments of new techniques, reviews of new materials, book reviews, forum for dental surgeons at home and abroad.
Ind/Abst Index Dent. Lit.

LC RK1 .A64
DD 617
ISSN 0164-1700
US
NLM W1 PR5822
PROCEEDINGS - AMERICAN SOCIETY FOR THE ADVANCEMENT ANESTHESIA IN DENTISTRY. [Proc. - Am. Soc. Adv. Anesth. Dent.]. **Main/Corp** American Society for the Advancement of Anesthesia in Dentistry. **VFOAT** Pain Control in Dentistry; A.A.S.A.A.D. Pain Control in Dentistry. (1973)-. Proceedings. English. Two times a year. $65.00. American Society for the Advancement of Anesthesia in Dentistry, 475 White Plains, Eastchester NY 10707. **Tel** (914)961-8136. **ED** Louis L. Zall (editor's address: 211 Broadway, Bayonne, NJ 07002). **Bk Rev. Ad Acc. Circ:** 1,100 (ctrl).

UK
Pr Rev.
PROCEEDINGS OF THE BRITISH SOCIETY FOR THE STUDY OF PROSTHETIC DENTISTRY. (1957)-. Proceedings. English. One time a year. £25.00. Quintessence Publishing Co / UK, 2 Blagdon Road New Malden, Surrey KT3 4AD United Kingdom. **Tel** 011 44 181 9496087, FAX 011 44 181 3361484. **(Subscription address:** Sheed and Ward, 14 Cooper's Row, London GC3N 2BM United Kingdom. **Tel** 011 44 181 7029799.) **ED** Dr. Alan R. Ogden (Editor's address: Leeds Dental Institute, Leeds LS2 9LU, United Kingdom). **Ad Acc. Acid Free.**

ISSN 0258-6185
UK
UDC 616.314
PROCEEDINGS OF THE EUROPEAN PROSTHODONTIC ASSOCIATION, THE. Proceedings. English. One time a year. European Prosthodontic Association, Floor 20 Guys Hospital, London SE1 9RT Egland. **Tel** 011 44 171 9554026, FAX 011 44 171 4076736. **ED** P.R. Likeman. **Circ:** 450 (ctrl circ.)
Desc: Papers from annual EPA conference abstract form.

ISSN 0534-669X
US
NLM W1 PR629
PROGRAM AND ABSTRACTS OF PAPERS - INTERNATIONAL ASSOCIATION FOR DENTAL RESEARCH. (PROGRAM AND ABSTRACTS OF PAPERS - INTERNATIONAL ASSOCIATION FOR DENTAL RESEARCH GENERAL MEETING.). **Added/Corp** International Association for Dental Research. **VFOAT** Abstracts of the General Meeting - International Association for Dental Research; IADR Abstracts; Preprinted Abstracts - International Association for Dental Research. (1922)-. Periodical. English. Irregular. $30.00. American & International Association Dental Research, 1111 14th Street Northwest, Suite 1000, Washington DC 20005. **Tel** (202)898-1050, FAX (202)789-1033. **ED** C. Dawes. **Ad Acc. Circ:** 7,000 (ctrl).
Desc: Abstracts of research presented at meeting of the International and American Associations for Dental Research.

LC RK1 .P7
DD 617.6078
ISSN 0033-1236
US
NLM W1 PR722G
PROOFS (TULSA). (PROOFS.). **Added/Corp** Central States Dental Dealers' Club. (1918)-. Trade Publication. English. Ten times a year. $19.95. PennWell Publishing Company, 1421 South Sheridan, PO Box 1260, Tulsa OK 74101. **Tel** (918)835-3161, (800)331-4463, FAX (918)831-9497. **(Subscription address:** Proofs, PO Box 3408, Tulsa OK 74101. **Tel** (918)831-9403, FAX (918)832-9295.) **ED** Mary Elizabeth Good. **Ad Acc. Circ:** 7,796 (ctrl). available on microfilm from University Microfilms International (UMI).
Desc: Serves the dental trade industry by concentrating on news and features about current marketplace trends, government regulations, personnel changes in the field, and annual dental meetings.

ISSN 0750-2524
FR
UDC 616.31
QUESTIONS D'ODONTO-STOMATOLOGIE, LES. [Quest. d'odonto-stomatol.]. **VFOAT** L.Q.O.S. (1976)-. Periodical. French. Four times a year. Chirurgien Dentiste France, 22 Avenue de Villiers, F-75017 Paris France.

IT
QUINTESSENCE INTERNATIONAL. (19??)-. Periodical. Italian. Ten times a year. L195.000. Resch Editrice, Lungadige Matteotti 13/C, 37126 Verona Italy. **Tel** 011 39 45 915499.

GW
QUINTESSENCE INTERNATIONAL (BERLIN : 1985). (QUINTESSENCE INTERNATIONAL.). Vol. 16, No. 1 (Jan. 1985)-. Periodical. English (German, Italian, French and Japanese). Twelve times a year. $98.00. Quintessenz Verlag GmbH, Ifenpfad 2 4, D 12107 Berlin Germany. **Tel** 011 49 30 740060, FAX 011 49 30 7415080. **(Subscription address:** Quintessence Publishing Co. Inc., 551 North Kimberly Drive, Carol Stream IL 60188-1881. **Tel** (708)682-3223, (800)621-0387, FAX (708)682-3288.) **ED** Richard J. Simonsen. Index available in last issue of volume--attached. **Ad Acc. Circ:** 28,000. **Continues in part** Quintessence International Dental Digest; **Absorbed** Anesthesia & Pain Control in Dentistry, 1055-7601.
Desc: Serves as a continuing education source, targeted at general dentists. Provides timely information on clinical and research advances from all fields of dentistry.
Ind/Abst Curr. Cit.; Curr. Titles Dent.; Dent. Abstr.; Index Dent. Lit. (1986-).

US
NLM W1; QU961A
QUINTESSENCE OF DENTAL TECHNOLOGY : QDT. **VFOAT** QDT. Vol. 14 (1990/1991)-. English. One time a year. $56.00. Quintessence Publishing Company Inc., 551 North Kimberly Drive, Carol Stream IL 60188-1881. **Tel** (708)682-3223, (800)621-0387, FAX (708)682-3288. **Continues** QDT Yearbook, 0896-6532.
Desc: Yearbook for Quintessence Publishing.
Ind/Abst Index Dent. Lit. (1990-).

ISSN 0340-4641
GW
NLM W1 QU964L
QUINTESSENZ DER ZAHNTECHNIK, DIE. [Quintessenz Zahntech.]. (1975)-. Periodical. German. Twelve times a year. $159.92. Quintessenz Verlag GmbH, Ifenpfad 2 4, D 12107 Berlin Germany. **Tel** 011 49 30 740060, FAX 011 49 30 7415080.
Ind/Abst Index Dent. Lit.

ISSN 0033-6599
GW
NLM W1 QU964N
QUINTESSENZ JOURNAL. [Quintessenz-J.]. Vol. 1 (1971)-. Periodical. German. Twelve times a year. $199.59. Quintessenz Verlag GmbH, Ifenpfad 2 4, D 12107 Berlin Germany. **Tel** 011 49 30 740060, FAX 011 49 30 7415080.
Ind/Abst Curr. Titles Dent.; Index Dent. Lit.

ISSN 0279-7720
DD 617
US
CCC
NLM W1 RD2
RDH. [RDH.]. **VFOAT** R.D.H. (Jan. 1981)-. Periodical. English. Twelve times a year. $60.00. Stevens Publishing Corporation, 225 North New Road, Waco TX 76702-2604. **Tel** (800)727-7573, (817)776-9000, FAX (817)776-9018. **(Subscription address:** Stevens Publishing Corp., PO Box 2573, Waco TX 76702.) **ED** Sandra Pemberton. Index available (bound in last issue). **Ad Acc. Circ:** 63,210 (ctrl).
Desc: Focuses on establishing and maintaining periodontal and overall health for patients. Also patient education and motivation.
Ind/Abst Curr. Cit.; Int. Nurs. Index.

ISSN 1041-8199
DD 617
US
NLM W1; RE105GF
REALITY (HOUSTON, TEX.). (REALITY.). [Reality]. **Added/Corp** Esthetic Dentistry Research Group. (1986)-. Periodical. English. Twelve times a year (11 newsletters plus 1 reference volume). $197.00. Reality Publishing Company, 11757 Katy Freeway/Suite 200, Houston TX 77079. **Tel** (713)558-9101, FAX (713)493-1558. **(Subscription address:** Reality, Subscription Office, PO Box 11318, Birmingham AL 35202-1318. **Tel** (800)544-4999, (205)995-1567 (outside US and Canada), FAX (205)995-1588.) **ED** Michael B. Miller, Craig A. Mabrito, and Amanda E. Testa. Index available. available on videocassette.
Desc: Covers new techniques and products in cosmetic dentistry.

ISSN 1041-8253
DD 617
US
REALITY NOW (HOUSTON, TEX.). (REALITY NOW.). [Reality now]. **Added/Corp** Esthetic Dentistry Research Group. No. 1 (Jan. 1989)-. Periodical. English. Twelve times a year. Reality Publishing Company, 11757 Katy Freeway/Suite 200, Houston TX 77079. **Tel** (713)558-9101, FAX (713)493-1558.

ISSN 0792-9935
IS
UDC 616.314
●**REPWAT HAPEH WEHASINAYYIM TEL (ABIYB. 1993).** **VFOAT** Journal of the Israel Dental Association. (1993)-. Periodical. Hebrew (English). Four times a year. Israel Dental Association, 22 Shlomzion Hamalca Street, Tel Aviv 62276 Israel. **Tel** 011 972 3 448676. **Continues** Repwat Hasinayyim.

ISSN 0001-0944
MX
NLM W1; RE259
REVISTA ADM. (REVISTA ADM : ORGANO OFICIAL DE LA ASOCIACION DENTAL MEXICANA.). [Rev. ADM]. **Added/Corp** Asociacion Dental Mexicana. **VFOAT** A.ADM. Vol. 37 (1979)-. Periodical. Spanish. Six times a year. $100,000 Mexico; $70.00 other. Revista Oficial Asociacion Dental, Esequiel Montes 92, Mexico 4 DF Mexico. **Tel** 011 52 5 5645702.
Ind/Abst Index Dent. Lit. (1937, 1979-).

ISSN 0034-7507
CU
NLM W1 RE359J
REVISTA CUBANA DE ESTOMATOLOGIA. [Rev. Cuba. estomatol.]. Vol. 1 (June 30, 1964)-. Periodical. Multiple languages (Spanish and Russian; summaries and/or abstracts in English, French and Russian). Three times a year. $21.00 North America; $23.00 South America; $28.00 other. Ediciones Cubanas, Obispo 527 Altos ESQ Bernaza, CP 10100 Havana Cuba.
Desc: Publishes scientific studies on general epidemiology, of dental prosthesis, orthodontics, paradontology and facial (jaw bone) surgery, as well as articles on the development of the stomatology in general.
Ind/Abst Index Dent. Lit.

SP
NLM W1; RE371NH
REVISTA DE ACTUALIDAD ODONTOESTOMATOLOGICA ESPANOLA. **Added/Corp** Ilustre Consejo General de Colegios de Odontologos y Estomatologos de Espana. **VFOAT** Revista de Actualidad Odonto Estomatologica Espanola. (Feb. 1990)-. Periodical. Spanish. Six times a year. Jose M Bueno, Paseo de Miramar 16, Malaga Spain. **Continues** Revista de Actualidad Estomatologica Espanola, 0212-9701.
Ind/Abst Index Dent. Lit. (1990-).

ISSN 0004-4881
AG
NLM W1 RE406T
CODEN RAOABM
Pr Rev.
REVISTA DE LA ASOCIACION ODONTOLOGICA ARGENTINA. [Rev. Asoc. odontol. argent.]. **Main/Corp** Asociacion Odontologica Argentina. Vol. 43 (1955)-. Periodical. Spanish (summaries and/or abstracts in English). Four times a year (Mar., June, Sept., Dec.). $80.00. Asociacion Odontologica de Argentina, Junin 959, 1113 Buenos Aires Argentina. **Tel** 011 54 1 9616062 6141, FAX 011 54 1 9611110. **Bk Rev. Ad Acc. Circ:** 8,000 (ctrl). Documents available from CASDDS. **Continues** Revista Odontologica.
Ind/Abst Chem. Abstr.; Index Dent. Lit.; Life Sci. Collect.

ISSN 0101-1774
BL
NLM W1; RE454CR
CODEN ROUNDL
REVISTA DE ODONTOLOGIA DA UNESP. (REVISTA DE ODONTOLOGIA DA UNESP / UNIVERSIDADE ESTADUAL PAULISTA (UNESP).). [Rev. Odontol. UNESP]. **Added/Corp** Universidade Estadual Paulista. **VFOAT** Revista de Odontologia da U.N.E.S.P. Vol. 8/9 (1979/1980)-. Academic Scholarly Publication. Portuguese (English). Irregular. $30.00 (per copy). Fundacao Desenvolvimento Unesp, Av Rio Branco 1210, 01206 Sao Paulo SP Brazil. **Tel** 011 55 11 2237088. **Circ:** 1,000 (ctrl). Documents available from BIOSIS Document Express, CASDDS. **Formed by the union of** Revista da Faculdade de Odontologia de Aracatuba; Revista da Faculdade de Odontologia de Araraquara **and** Revista da Faculdade de Odontologia de Sao Jose dos Campos.
Desc: Official publication for diffusion of the original investigations in dentistry carried out by researches of the

Dentistry

universidade and from other dental institutes.
Ind/Abst Biol. Abstr.; Calcium Calcif. Tissue Abstr.; Chem. Abstr. (1979/1980-1982); Life Sci. Collect.

ISSN 0103-0663
BL
NLM W1; RE454CV   **CODEN** ROUPES
REVISTA DE ODONTOLOGIA DA UNIVERSIDADE DE SAO PAULO. [Rev. odontol. Univ. Sao Paulo]. **Added/Corp** Universidade de Sao Paulo. Vol. 1, No. 1 (Jan./March 1987)-. Periodical. Portuguese (English; summaries and/or abstracts in English). Four times a year. $50.00. Universidade de Sao Paulo, Cidade Universitaria CP 8191, Sao Paulo Brazil. **Tel** 011 55 11 8150899, FAX 011 55 11 8154272. **ED** Joao Adolfo Caldas Navarro. Index available. ctrl circ. Documents available from BIOSIS Document Express. *Continues* Revista da Faculdade de Odontologia da Universidade de Sao Paulo, 0581-6866.
Ind/Abst Biol. Abstr. (1988-); Index Dent. Lit. (1987-).

SP
REVISTA ESPANOLA DE ORTODONCIA. Spanish. Editorial Garsi SA, Avenida Principe Asturias 20, 08012 Barcelona Spain. **Tel** 011 34 1 4154544.
Ind/Abst Indice Med. Esp.

SP
NLM W1; RE564D
REVISTA EUROPEA DE ODONTO-ESTOMATOLOGIA. **VFOAT** Revista Europea de Odontoestomatologia. Vol. 1, No. 1 (Jan./Feb. 1989)-. Periodical. Spanish. Six times a year. $44.41. Graficas Fomento, C Peligro 8, 08012 Barcelona Spain. **Tel** 011 34 3 2580425. *Continues* Revista Espanola de Estomatologia.
Ind/Abst Index Dent. Lit. (1989-); Indice Med. Esp.

ISSN 0212-193X
SP
NLM W1; RE593T
REVISTA IBERO-AMERICANA DE ORTODONCIA. [Rev. ibero-am. ortod.]. **VFOAT** Revista Iberoamericana de Ortodoncia. (July 1981)-. Periodical. Spanish. Three times a year.
Ind/Abst Index Dent. Lit.; Indice Med. Esp.

ISSN 0484-8020
EC
NLM W1; RE7093R
Pr Rev.
REVISTA ODONTOLOGICA ECUATORIANA. [Rev. odontol. ecuat.]. (1955)-. Periodical. Spanish. Four times a year. $30.00. Revista Odontologica Ecuatoriana, Apartado 6990, Guayaquil Ecuador. **Tel** 011 593 4 342626. **ED** Dr Juan Hidalgo, Telephone: 342-626. **Bk Rev** (Qty: 4). **Ad Acc. Circ:** 1,500 (ctrl).
Ind/Abst Index Dent. Lit.

ISSN 0035-0397
PO
NLM W1 RE7167
Pr Rev.
REVISTA PORTUGUESA DE ESTOMATOLOGIA E CIRURGIA MAXILO-FACIAL. [Rev. port. estomatol. cir. maxilo-fac.]. **Added/Corp** Sociedade Portuguesa de Estomatologia. (1960)-. Periodical. Portuguese (English). Four times a year. $50.00. Sociedade Portuguesa de Estomalogia & Med. Dent., Av. Rainha Amelia 36, 1600 Lisbon Portugal. **Tel** 7593948. **ED** Antonio Mano Azul. Index available. cum. index. **Bk Rev. Ad Acc. Circ:** 2,400 (ctrl).
Desc: Covers maxillofacial surgery and oral aspects of dentistry.
Ind/Abst Index Dent. Lit.; Index Med. Lit.

ISSN 0775-0293
BE
UDC 611
CODEN 615
REVUE BELGE DE MEDECINE DENTAIRE (1984). (1984)-. Periodical. French. Four times a year. $104.47. Societe de Medecine Dentaire / ASBL, Avenue de Fre 191, 1180 Brussels Belgium. **Tel** 011 32 2 3758175, FAX 011 32 2 3758612. **ED** Henri Azonis. **Bk Rev. Ad Acc.** ctrl circ.
Ind/Abst Index Med.

ISSN 0035-1768
FR
NLM W1 RE805L   **CODEN** RSCMAL
REVUE DE STOMATOLOGIE ET DE CHIRURGIE MAXILLO-FACIALE. [Rev. stomatol. chir. maxillo-fac.]. Vol. 70 (1969)-. Academic Scholarly Publication. French. Six times a year. $346.68. Masson Editeur, BP 22, 41354 Vineuil Cedex France. **Tel** 011 33 54 504612, FAX 011 33 54 504611. available on microfilm and microfiche from University Microfilms International (UMI). Documents available from BIOSIS Document Express. *Continues* Revue de Stomatologie.
Ind/Abst Biol. Abstr.; Curr. Cit.; Curr. Titles Dent.; EMBASE; Index Med.; Index Dent. Lit.; Life Sci. Collect.

ISSN 0300-9815
FR
NLM W1 RE833K
REVUE D'ODONTO-STOMATOLOGIE. [Rev. odonto-stomatol.]. **Added/Corp** Societe Odontologique de Paris. Vol. 1 (Jan./Feb. 1972)-. Periodical. French. Six times a year (Feb., Apr., Jun., Sept., Oct., Dec.). $209.98. Secretariat de la Societe Odontologique de Paris, 239 rue du Foubourg, St. Martin, F-75010 Paris France. **Tel** 011 33 1 42092913, FAX 011 33 1 42092908. Index available. **Circ:** 4,000. *Supersedes* Revue Francaise d'Odonto-Stomatologie.
Ind/Abst Curr. Titles Dent.; Index Med.; Index Dent. Lit.

ISSN 0035-2470
FR
NLM W1 RE833L
REVUE D'ODONTO-STOMATOLOGIE DU MIDI DE LA FRANCE. [Rev. odonto-stomatol. midi Fr.]. **Added/Corp** Universite de Bordeaux. Clinique Odonto-Stomatologique. Vol. 23 (1965)-. Periodical. French (summaries and/or abstracts in English). Six times a year. Hopital Pellegrin Tripode, place Amelie Rabadein, 33076 Bordeaux Cedex France. **ED** P. Benoit, P. Ferran and J. Tarrayre. **Bk Rev Ad Acc. Circ:** 1,200. *Supersedes* Revue d'Odonto-Stomatologie.
Desc: Contains original articles, current practice and clinical cases of dentistry or stomatology. Summaries of meetings of 'Societe d'Odonto-Stomatologie de Bordeaux et du sud Ouest' are also included.
Ind/Abst Curr. Titles Dent.; Index Dent. Lit.

ISSN 0337-9736
FR
NLM W1 RE833R
REVUE D'ORTHOPEDIE DENTO-FACIALE. [Rev. orthop. dento-fac.]. **VFOAT** O. D. F. Vol.1 (1967). Periodical. French. Four times a year. $216.53. SID, 9 rue Christine, 75006 Paris. **Tel** 011 33 1 6455311.
Ind/Abst Curr. Titles Dent.; Index Dent. Lit.

ISSN 0721-0078
FR
UDC 616.314
Pr Rev.
REVUE INTERNATIONALE DE PARODONTIE & DENTISTERIE RESTAURATRICE. [Rev. int. parod. dent. restaur.]. **VFOAT** Revue Internationale de Parodontie et Dentisterie Restauratrice. (1981)-. Periodical. English (German, Spanish and Japanese). Six times a year. $279.97. Editions CDP, 77 rue de Richelieu, 75002 Paris France. **Tel** 011 33 1 42615065, FAX 011 33 1 42613195, telex 210717 F. **Ad Acc. Circ:** 2,100.
Desc: International review of dentistry and periodontics.

ISSN 0035-4147
FR
UDC 616.31
REVUE STOMATO ODONTOLOGIQUE DU NORD DE LA FRANCE. [Rev. stomato odontol. Nord Fr.]. (1946)-. Periodical. French. Four times a year. $4.50. Professeur Michel Donazzan, Place de Verdun, 50 Lille France.

ISSN 0103-6440
GW
NLM W1; BR189F
RHEOLOGY GERMANY. **Added/Corp** Fundacao Odontologica de Ribeirao Preto. Vol. 1, (1990)-. Periodical. English (German). Four times a year (Feb., May, Aug., Dec.). $230.29. Curt R. Vincentz Verlag, Postfach 6247, D-30062 Hannover Germany. **Tel** 011 49 511 990980, FAX 011 49 511 9909899, telex 923846.
Ind/Abst Index Dent. Lit. (1990-).

ISSN 0091-8903
US
NLM W1 RH456   **CODEN** RIDJEJ
RHODE ISLAND DENTAL JOURNAL, THE. [R. I. dent. j.]. **Added/Corp** Rhode Island Dental Association. Rhode Island State Dental Association. **VFOAT** R.I. Dental Journal. (1972)-. Periodical. English. Four times a year. $20.00. Rhode Island Dental Association, 200 Centerville Place, Warwick RI 02886. **Tel** (401)732-6833. *Continues* Journal of the Rhode Island State Dental Society, 0035-4643.
Ind/Abst Index Dent. Lit.

ISSN 0035-5488
JA
NLM W1 RI2167K
RINSHO SHIKA. **VFOAT** Folia Odontologica Practica. (1929)-. Periodical. Japanese (summaries and/or abstracts in English). Six times a year. $51.50. Rinsho Shikasha, 29 Ishiicho Nishi 7 Jo, Simogyoku Kyotoshi, Kyotofu 600 Japan. **(Subscription address:**
Japan Publications Trading Company Ltd., PO Box 5030, Tokyo International, Tokyo 100-31 Japan. **Tel** 011 81 3 3292 3753.**)**

IT
RIS : RIVISTA ITALIANA DE STOMATOLOGIA. **Added/Corp** Associazione Medici Dentisti Italiani. **VFOAT** Rivista Italiana di Stomatologia. Vol. 1 No. 1 (1986)-. Periodical. Italian. Irregular. Associazione Medici Dentisti Italiani, Segr Gen V Savoia 78, 00198 Rome Italy. **Tel** 011 39 68549546.
Continues Rivista Italiana di Stomatologia.

IT
RIVISTA INTERNAZIONALE DI PARODONTOLOGIA & ODONTOIATRIA RICOSTRUTTIVA. Italian. Six times a year. Dr Riccardo Ilic Srl, Via Francesco Sforza 19, 20122 Milan Italy. **Tel** 011 39 2 796701 L230000.

ISSN 0391-5611
IT
NLM W1 RI759
RIVISTA ITALIANA DEGLI ODONTOTECNICI. [Riv. ital. odontotec.]. **VFOAT** Dental Press. Vol. 14 (Jan./Feb. 1978)-. Periodical. Italian. Nine times a year. L137000. Masson SPA, via Statuto 2/4, 20121 Milan Italy. **Tel** 011 39 2 63671, FAX 011 39 2 6367211. **ED** Fulvio Tonesi. **Bk Rev. Ad Acc. Circ:** 8,000 (ctrl). *Continues* Dental Press, 0391-5883.
Ind/Abst Index Dent. Lit.

IT
NLM W1; RI776Q
RIVISTA ITALIANA DI ODONTOIATRIA INFANTILE : ORGANO UFFICIALE DELLA SOCIETA ITALIANA DI ODONTOIATRIA INFANTILE. **Added/Corp** Societa Italiana di Odontoiatria Infantile. (1990)-. Periodical. Italian (summaries and/or abstracts in English). Four times a year. L52110. Masson SPA, via Statuto 2/4, 20121 Milan Italy. **Tel** 011 39 2 63671, FAX 011 39 2 6367211.

LC RK5 .M63   ISSN 0360-5582
DD 617.6/0025/776   US
ROSTER OF DENTISTS AND DENTAL HYGIENISTS REGISTERED IN THE STATE OF MINNESOTA. **Added/Corp** Minnesota. State Board of Dentistry. (19??)-. Periodical. English. Minnesota State Board of Dentistry, 209 North Snelling Avenue, St Paul MN 55104. *Continues* Minnesota. State Board of Dental Examiners. Roster of Dentists and Dental Hygienists Registered in the State of Minnesota.

ISSN 0049-1160
UK
NLM W1 S13
S.A.A.D. DIGEST. (SAAD DIGEST.). [SAAD dig.]. **Added/Corp** Society for the Advancement of Anaesthesia in Dentistry (Great Britain). **VAT** Society for the Advancement of Anaesthesia in Dentistry Digest. Vol. 1 (Jan. 1970)-. Periodical. English. Four times a year. $47.92. Society for Advancement Anaesthesia in Dentistry, 59 Summerlands Avenue, London W3 6EW United Kingdom. **Tel** 011 44 181 9936844, FAX 011 44 181 9936844. **ED** P Sykes. Index available. **Bk Rev. Ad Acc. Circ:** 2,500 (ctrl).
Desc: Editorials, original articles, abstracts, correspondence, product information and meeting reports.
Ind/Abst Index Dent. Lit.

ISSN 0325-0741
AG
NLM W1; SA365R
SALUD BUCAL. [Salud bucal]. **Added/Corp** Confederacion Odontologica de la Republica Argentina. (197?)-. Periodical. Spanish. Six times a year.

LC RK1700 .S28
II
SATTARA DASAKA. Periodical. Bengali (Bengali). 6.00. Gita Ganguli, 78/2 Biren Roy Road West, 61 Kalakata India.

ISSN 0029-845X
DK
CCC
NLM W1; SC148N   **CODEN** SJDRAN
Pr Rev.   **TITLE CHANGE**
SCANDINAVIAN JOURNAL OF DENTAL RESEARCH. [Scand. j. dent. res.]. Vol. 78 (1970)-(19??). Academic Scholarly Publication. English. Munksgaard International Publishers Ltd, PO Box 2148, DK-1016 Copenhagen K Denmark. **Tel** 011 45 33 127030, FAX 011 45 33 129387, telex 19431 MUNKS DK. **ED** Jens Jorgen Pindborg. Index available. **Ad Acc. Circ:** 1,450 (ctrl). Documents available from The Genuine Article, BIOSIS Document Express, CASDDS. *Continues* Odontologisk Tidskrift. *Continued by* European Journal of Oral Sciences.
Desc: Fields within dentistry from basic oral biology to traumatic injuries and diseases of the oral mucosa, to dental materials and endodontics.

Ind/Abst Biol. Abstr.; Calcium Calcif. Tissue Abstr.; Chem. Abstr.; CSA Neuro. Abstr. (?-?); Curr. Cit.; Curr. Contents Clin. Med.; Curr. Contents Life Sci.; Curr. Titles Dent.; Dent. Abstr.; EMBASE [Select. Cov.]; Energy Res. Abstr. (Sept. 1972-); Index Med.; Index Dent. Lit.; Microbiol. Abstr. Sect. B (19??-19??); Nutr. Abstr. Rev., Ser. A, Hum. Exp.; Nutr. Res. Newsl.; Life Sci. Collect.; Res. Alert [Full Cov.]; Sci. Cit. Index; SCISEARCH; Sug. Indus. Abstr.

ISSN 1011-4203
SZ
NLM W1; SC396H
SCHWEIZER MONATSSCHRIFT FUER ZAHNMEDIZIN. [Schweiz. Mon.-schr. zahnmed.]. **Added/Corp** SS0 (Society). **VFOAT** Revue Mensuelle Suisse d'Odonto-Stomatologie; Rivista Mensile Svizzera di Odontologia e Stomatologia. Vol. 97 (1987)-. Academic Scholarly Publication. German (French; summaries and/or abstracts in English). Twelve times a year. $278.16. Jean Frey Druck, Edenstrasse 20, CH-8021 Zurich Switzerland. **Tel** 011 41 1 2078257. Index available. cum. index. **Bk Rev. Ad Acc. Circ:** 4,000 (ctrl). Documents available from CASDDS. ***Continues*** *Schweizerische Monatsschrift fur Zahnmedizin, 0256-2855.*
Desc: Covers research science, consulting practice, post graduateeducation, and current dentistry.
Ind/Abst Chem. Abstr. (1987-); Curr. Cit.; Curr. Titles Dent.; Index Med. (1987-); Index Dent. Lit. (1987-).

ISSN 1044-7032
DD 617 US
NLM W1; SE32NU
SELECTED READINGS IN ORAL AND MAXILLOFACIAL SURGERY. [Sel. read. oral maxillofac. surg.]. **Added/Corp** Guild for Scientific Advancement in Oral and Maxillofacial Surgery. Vol. 1, No. 1 (June 1989)-. Monographic series. English. Eight times a year. $185.00 US; $205.00 other. University of Texas Southwestern Medical Center, 5323 Harry Hines Blvd., Dallas TX 75235-9109. **Tel** (214)648-3548, FAX (214)648-2918. **ED** Douglas P. Sinn. **Circ:** 900.
Desc: This a professional publication regarding current topics and areas of new advancement in the field of oral and maxillofacial surgery.

ISSN 1042-718X
DD 617 US
NLM W1; SE487G
SEMINARS IN DENTAL HYGIENE. [Semin. dent. hyg.]. Vol. 1, No. 1 (May 1989)-. Periodical. English. Irregular (2-4 per year). $25.00 (four issues) US; $40.00 (four issues) other. Professional Audience Communications, PO Box 243, Yardley PA 19067. **Tel** (215)493-7400.
Ind/Abst Health Plan. Adminis.

LC RK520 **ISSN** 1073-8746
DD 617 US
•**SEMINARS IN ORTHODONTICS.** [Semin. orthod.]. Vol. 1, No. 1 (March 1995)-. Periodical. English. Four times a year. $99.00. W. B. Saunders Company, A Subsidiary of Harcourt Brace Jovanovich Inc., The Curtis Center, Suite 300, Independence Square West, Philadelphia PA 19106-3399. **Tel** (215)238-7800 or, 5587, FAX (215)238-7883, telex 173146. **(Subscription address:** W. B. Saunders Company / North America Subscriptions, c/o Periodicals, 6277 Sea Harbour Drive, 4th Floor, Orlando FL 32887. **Tel** (800)654-2452, (407)345-3668.**)** **ED** P. Lionel Sadowsky. **Ad Acc.**

ISSN 0037-3710
JA
NLM W1 SH305 **CODEN** SHGKA3
SHIKA GAKUHO. (SHIKA GAKUHO. THE JOURNAL OF THE TOKYO DENTAL COLLEGE SOCIETY.). [Shika gakuho]. **Added/Corp** Tokyo Shika Daigaku. Tokyo Shika Daigaku Gakkai. **VFOAT** Journal of the Tokyo Dental College Society; Shikwa Gakuho; The Journal of the Tokyo Dental College Society. Vol. 5 (March 1900)-. Academic Scholarly Publication. Japanese (summaries and/or abstracts in English; table of contents in English). Twelve times a year. $144.50. Tokyo Shika Diagaku Gakkai, (Tokyo Dental College Soc.), 2-2 Masago 1 Chome, Chibashi Chibaken 260, Japan. **(Subscription address:** Japan Publications Trading Company Ltd., PO Box 5030, Tokyo International, Tokyo 100-31 Japan. **Tel** 011 81 3 3292 3753.**)** Documents available from BIOSIS Document Express, CASDDS. ***Continues*** *Shika Igaku Sodan.*
Ind/Abst Biol. Abstr.; Chem. Abstr.

ISSN 0389-1895
JA
CODEN SHGKD6
SHIKA GIKO. [Shika giko]. **VFOAT** Journal of Dental Technics. (1973)-. Academic Scholarly Publication. Japanese. Twelve times a year. $275.00. Ishiyaku Shuppan K.K. / Ishiyaku Publishers Inc., 7-10 Honkomagome 1-chome, Bunkyo-ku Tokyo 113 Japan. Documents available from CASDDS.
Ind/Abst Chem. Abstr.

JA
SHIKA IGAKU. DENTAL MEDICINE. **Added/Corp** Osaka Shika Gakkai. **VFOAT** Dental Medicine; Zasshi of Osaka Shika Gakkai. Journal of the Osaka Odontological Society; Journal of the Osaka Odontological Society. (1930)-. Academic Scholarly Publication. Japanese (summaries and/or abstracts in English; table of contents in English). Osaka Shika Gakkai, (Osaka Odontological Society), 1-47 Kyobashi Higashiku, Osakashi Osakafu 540, Japan. Documents available from CASDDS.
Ind/Abst Chem. Abstr.

ISSN 0386-4715
DD 617.6 JA
SHIKA JANARU. [Shika janaru]. **VFOAT** Journal of Dental Medicine (Tokyo. 1978). (1978)-. Periodical. Japanese. Twelve times a year. $400.00. **(Subscription address:** Maruzen Company Ltd., PO Box 5050, Import & Export Department, Tokyo 100 31 Japan. **Tel** 011 81 3 32789224.**)** ***Continues*** *Kokusai Shika Janaru, 0386-4707.*

ISSN 0385-0137
JA
CODEN SHKKAN
SHIKA KISO IGAKKAI ZASSHI. [Shika Kiso Igakkai zasshi]. **Added/Corp** Shika Kiso Igakkai (Japan). **VFOAT** Japanese Journal of Oral Biology. (1959)-. Academic Scholarly Publication. Japanese. Four times a year. $114.00. Shika Kiso Igakkai, (Japanese Assoc. for Oral Biology), Koku Hoken Kyokai, 44-2 Komagome 1 Chome, Toshimaku Tokyo 170 Japan. Documents available from CASDDS.
Ind/Abst Chem. Abstr.

ISSN 0286-5858
JA
NLM W1; SH303 **CODEN** SZKIDA
SHIKA ZAIRYO, KIKAI. [Shika zairyo, kikai]. **Added/Corp** Nihon Shika Riko Gakkai. **VFOAT** Journal of the Japanese Society for Dental Materials and Devices. Vol. 1, No. 1 (May 1982)-. Academic Scholarly Publication. Japanese (summaries and/or abstracts in English). Six times a year. $120.00. Nihon Shika Riko Gakkai, (Japanese Society for Dental Materials & Devices), Koku Hoken Kyokai, 44-2 Komagome 1 Chome, Toshimaku Tokyo 170 Japan. Documents available from CASDDS. ***Formed by the union of*** *Shika Rikogaku Zasshi, 0583-0273* ***and*** *Nihon Shika Zairyo Kikai Gakkai Zasshi.*
Ind/Abst Chem. Abstr.; Index Dent. Lit. (Vol. 3, No. 3, 1984-).

ISSN 0285-922X
JA
NLM W1 SH562P **CODEN** SSZADC
SHOWA SHIGAKKAI ZASSHI. [ShÂowa Shigakkai zasshi]. **Added/Corp** Showa Shigakkai. **VFOAT** Journal of Showa University Dental Society. (1981)-. Periodical. Japanese. Two times a year. Showa Daigaku Showa Shigakkai, (Showa University Dental Soc.), 5-8 Hatanodai 1 Chome, Shinagawaku Tokyo 142 Japan.
Ind/Abst Index Dent. Lit. (Vol. 3 No. 2, 1984-).

ISSN 0213-831X
SP
NLM W1; SO8896
SOPRODEN. Vol. 1, No. 1 (May 1985)-. Periodical. Spanish. Four times a year. Editorial Garsi SA, Avenida Principe Asturias 20, 08012 Barcelona Spain. **Tel** 011 34 1 4154544.
Ind/Abst Indice Med. Esp.

LC RK55.H28 S67 **ISSN** 0275-1879
DD 617.6/005 US
NLM W1 SP286H
Pr Rev.
SPECIAL CARE IN DENTISTRY. (SPECIAL CARE IN DENTISTRY : OFFICIAL PUBLICATION OF THE AMERICAN ASSOCIATION OF HOSPITAL DENTISTS, THE ACADEMY OF DENTISTRY FOR THE HANDICAPPED, AND THE AMERICAN SOCIETY FOR GERIATRIC DENTISTRY.). [Spec. care dent.]. **Added/Corp** American Association of Hospital Dentists. Academy of Dentistry for the Handicapped. American Society for Geriatric Dentistry. **VFOAT** SCD. Vol. 1, No. 1 (Jan./Feb. 1981)-. Periodical. English. Six times a year (Jan., Mar., May, Jul., Sept., Nov.). $92.00. Federation Special Care Organization, 211 East Chicago Avenue, Suite 948, Chicago IL 60611. **Tel** (312)440-2661, FAX (312)440-2824. **ED** Dr. Ronald Ettinger. Index available (included in Nov. issue). cum. index. **Bk Rev. Ad Acc. Circ:** 2,500. available on microfilm and microfiche from University Microfilms International (UMI). ***Formed by the union of*** *Journal of Hospital Dental Practice, 0022-1600; Journal of Dentistry for the Handicapped* ***and*** *Journal of the American Society for Geriatric Dentistry, 0003-1054.*
Desc: Dedicated to the management of medically or physically compromised patients. Contains articles by authorities in hospital dentistry, geriatrics, and handicapped care. Subjects include treatment of older adults, homebound, handicapped or medically compromised. Articles describe new treatment settings and techniques, access issues, education, and standards of care.
Ind/Abst Cumul. Index Nurs. Allied Health Lit.; Curr. Cit.; Curr. Titles Dent.; Dent. Abstr.; Energy Res. Abstr. (Aug. 1982-); Health Plan. Adminis.; Hosp. Health Admin. Index; Index Dent. Lit.

IT
NLM W1; ST648R
SUSPENDED
STOMATOLOGIA MEDITERRANEA : SM. **VFOAT** SM. (Jan./Mar. 1981)-Suspended (1994). Periodical. Italian (summaries and/or abstracts in English). Four times a year. L47690. Stomatologia Mediterranea, Via Enrico Amari 32, 90139 Palermo Italy. **Tel** 011 39 91 328269.
Desc: Information on dentistry, mouth diseases and oral surgery.
Ind/Abst Curr. Cit.

LC R **ISSN** 0946-3151
DD 617.6 AU
UDC 61
NLM W1; ZE609F **CODEN** STOMF2
•**STOMATOLOGIE.** **Added/Corp** Oesterreichische Gesellschaft fuer Zahn-, Mund- und Kieferheilkunde. Oesterreichische Aerztekammer. Bundesfachgruppe fuer Zahn-, Mund- und Kieferheilkunde. (Feb. 1995)-. Academic Scholarly Publication. German (summaries and/or abstracts in English; table of contents in English). Ten times a year. $249.00. Springer-Verlag Vienna, Sachsenplatz 4 6, PO Box 89, A-1201 Vienna Austria. **Tel** 011 43 1 33024150, FAX 011 43 1 330242665. **(Subscription address:** Springer-Verlag New York Inc. / North America, PO Box 2485, Journal Fulfillment, Secaucus NJ 07096. **Tel** (201)348-4033, (800)777-4643, FAX (201)348-4505.**)** **ED** G. Watzek, M. Matejka. ***Continues*** *Zeitschrift fuer Stomatologie (1984), 0175-7784.*
Ind/Abst Curr. Aware. Biol. Sci., CABS; Curr. Titles Dent.; EMBASE; Index Dent. Lit. (1995)-.

ISSN 0039-1735
RU
NLM W1 ST6792 **CODEN** STOAAT
STOMATOLOGIJA. (STOMATOLOGIA.). [Stomatologija]. **Added/Corp** Soviet Union. Ministerstvo Zdravookhraneniia. Soviet Union. NarodnyÊi Komissariat Zdravookhraneniia. Vsesoiuznoe Nauchnoe Mediîtsinskoe Obshchestvo Stomatologov (Soviet Union). Vol. 15 (1937)-. Periodical. Russian (English, French and German). Four times a year. $99.95. **(Subscription address:** East View Publications Inc., 3020 Harbor Lane North, Suite 110, Minneapolis MN 55447. **Tel** (800)477-1005, (612)550-0961, FAX (612)559-2931.**)** Index available. **Bk Rev. Ad Acc. Circ:** 3,000. Documents available from CASDDS. ***Continues*** *Sovetskaia Stomatologiia, 0302-5985.*
Ind/Abst Chem. Abstr.; EMBASE [Select. Cov.]; Index Med.

ISSN 0491-0982
BU
NLM W1 ST679 **CODEN** STMYAN
STOMATOLOGIJA (SOFIJA). (STOMATOLOGIIA.). [Stomatologija]. **Added/Corp** Bulgaria. Ministerstvo na Narodnoto Zdrave i Sotsialnite Grizhi. (1952)-. Academic Scholarly Publication. Bulgarian (summaries and/or abstracts in English and Russian; table of contents in English and Russian). Six times a year. 16lv. Izdatelstvo Meditsina i Fizkultura, 11 Pl. Slaveikov, Sofiia Bulgaria. **(Subscription address:** Hemus Foreign Trade Organization, 1B Raiko Daskalov Sq Books, 1000 Sofia Bulgaria. **Tel** 011 359 2 882544, 011 359 2 801575.**)** **ED** E. Atanassova. **Circ:** 2,581. Documents available from CASDDS.
Ind/Abst Chem. Abstr.; EMBASE.

ISSN 0039-1743
YU
CODEN SGLSAB
STOMATOLOSKI GLASNIK SRBIJE. [Stomatol. glas. Srb.]. (195?)-. Academic Scholarly Publication. Serbo-Croatian (Roman) (English, German and French). Six times a year. 150.00 Din Yugoslavia; $25.00 US. Srpsko Lekarsko Drustvo, Stomatoloski Glasnik, Rankeova 4, Stomatoloski Glasnik, Narodnog Fronta 1/II, 11000 Belgrad Yugoslavia. **Tel** 11/686864. cum. index. **Bk Rev. Ad Acc. Circ:** 1,800. Documents available from CASDDS.
Ind/Abst Chem. Abstr. (1954-1983).

ISSN 0039-551X
FI
NLM W1 PR585NN **CODEN** PFDSAX
CEASED
SUOMEN HAMMASLAAKARISEURAN TOIMITUKSIA. (PROCEEDINGS OF THE FINNISH DENTAL SOCIETY.). [Suom. Hammaslaakaris. toim.]. Vol. 68 (1972)-(Dec. 1993). Academic Scholarly Publication. English. Proceedings of the Finnish Dental Society, Rautatielaisendatu 6, SF-00520 Helsinki 52 Finland. **Tel** 358 015021, FAX 358 01496855. **ED** Stina Syrjanen, Matti Narhi. Index available. **Ad Acc. Circ:** 5,800 (ctrl). Documents available from BIOSIS Document Express, CASDDS. ***Continues*** *Suomen Hammaslaadariseuran Toimituksia.*
Desc: Scientific articles and reviews.
Ind/Abst Biol. Abstr.; Chem. Abstr.; Curr. Cit.; Curr. Titles Dent.; Index Med.; Index Dent. Lit.; Life Sci. Collect.

Dentistry

NLM WU 77 A512N
US
SURVEY OF DENTAL PRACTICE.
Main/Corp American Dental Association. Bureau of Economic Research and Statistics. **Added/Corp** American Dental Association. Bureau of Economic Research and Statistics. Survey of the Dental Profession. (1950)-. English. One time a year. $100.00 (members of American Dental Association), $200.00 (nonmembers). American Dental Association, 211 East Chicago Avenue, Chicago IL 60611. **Tel** (312)440-2867, (312)440-2500, FAX (312)440-7494.

ISSN 0347-9994
SW

NLM W1 SW393   **CODEN** SDJOD5
Pr Rev.
SWEDISH DENTAL JOURNAL. [Swed. dent. j.]. **Added/Corp** Swedish Dental Federation. Vol. 1 (1977)-. Academic Scholarly Publication. English (summaries and/or abstracts in Swedish). Six times a year. $96.17. Swedish Dental Journal, Box 5843, S-102 48 Stockholm Sweden. **Tel** 011 46 8 6661500. **ED** Goran Koch. Index available. **Ad Acc. Circ:** 12,000 (ctrl). Documents available from The Genuine Article, CASDDS. **Formed by the union of** Svensk Tandlakare Tidskrift, 0039-6745 **and** Odontologisk Revy.
Desc: Publishes original scientific papers originating from the Scandinavian countries.
Ind/Abst Calcium Calcif. Tissue Abstr.; Chem. Abstr.; Curr. Cit.; Curr. Contents Clin. Med.; Curr. Titles Dent.; Dent. Abstr. (-199?); Index Med.; Nutr. Abstr. Rev., Ser. A, Hum. Exp.; Nutr. Res. Newsl.; Life Sci. Collect.; Res. Alert [Full Cov.]; Sci. Cit. Index; SCISEARCH.

ISSN 0348-6672
SW

NLM W1 SW393A
SWEDISH DENTAL JOURNAL. SUPPLEMENT. [Swed. dent. j., Suppl.]. **Added/Corp** Lunds Universitet. School of Dentistry. (1977)-. Monographic series. English. Irregular. Price varies per volume. Swedish Dental Journal, Box 5843, S-102 48 Stockholm Sweden. **Tel** 011 46 8 6661500. **Formed by the union of** Svensk Tandlakare-Tidskrift. Supplementum **and** Odontologisk Revy. Supplementum, 0472-5131.
Ind/Abst Index Med.; Index Dent. Lit.

ISSN 0251-1657
SZ

SWISS DENT. (1980)-. Periodical. German (and French). Twelve times a year. $188.58. Verlag Dr Felix Wuest AG, Seestrasse 5 Postfach, CH-8700 Kuesnacht Switzerland. **Tel** 011 41 1 9110055, FAX 011 41 1 9106080, telex 825705.
Ind/Abst Curr. Titles Dent.

LC RK1   ISSN 0376-4672
KO

NLM W1 TA392BM   **CODEN** JKDAAG
TAEHAN CHIKWA UISA HYOPHOE CHI. [Daihan cigwa uisa hyebhoiji]. **VFOAT** Journal of the Korean Dental Association. Academic Scholarly Publication. Multiple languages (English and Korean). Twelve times a year. Taehan Chikwa Uisa Hyophoe, 94-114 Yongdungpo-dong Yongdungpo-ku, Seoul Korea. Documents available from CASDDS.
Ind/Abst Chem. Abstr.; Energy Res. Abstr. (Sept. 1980-).

ISSN 0039-9353
DK

TANDLAEGEBLADET. (19??)-. Periodical. Danish. Eighteen times a year. kr.985.00. Tandlaegebladet, Postbus 143, Amaliegade 17, DK 1004 Copenhagen Denmark. **Tel** 011 45 1 157711.

ISSN 0039-6982
SW

NLM W1 TA539C
TANDLAKARTIDNINGEN. [Tandlakartidningen]. **Added/Corp** Sveriges Tandlakarforbund. (196?)-. Periodical. Swedish. Twenty-four times a year. $176.31. Swedish Dental Federation, Nybrogatan 53 Fack, 102 40 Stockholm Sweden. **Bk Rev. Ad Acc. Circ:** 13,000 (ctrl). **Continues** Sveriges Tandlakarforbund.
Desc: Covers odontology union questions, odontological and medical literature.
Ind/Abst Index Dent. Lit.

ISSN 0901-9898
DK

NLM W1; TA539B
TANDLGERNES NYE TIDSSKRIFT. **Added/Corp** Tandlgernes nye Landsforening (Denmark). **VFOAT** TNT. (1986)-. Periodical. Danish. Twelve times a year. **Continues** DB-DBat.
Ind/Abst Health Plan. Adminis.; Index Dent. Lit. (1989-).

ISSN 0303-8866
UN

NLM W1 TE509M   **CODEN** TRPSBI
TERAPEVTICHESKAIA STOMATOLOGIIA. Added/Corp Ukraine. Ministerstvo Okhorony Zdorov'ia. (1973)-. Periodical. Russian. Ministerstvo Okhorony Zdorvia /
Terapevticheskaia Stomatologia, 252001 Kiev 1 Ukraine. Documents available from CASDDS. **Continues** Terapevticheskaia i Ortopedicheskaia Stomatologiia.
Ind/Abst Chem. Abstr. (-1973).

ISSN 0049-3503
US

NLM W1 TE695
TEXAS DENTAL ASSISTANTS ASSOCIATION BULLETIN. [Bull.- Tex. Dent. Assist. Assoc.]. **Added/Corp** Texas Dental Assistants Association. (1940)-. Bulletin. English. Three times a year. $10.00. Texas Dental Assistants Association, 4000 Sixth Avenue, Forth Worth TX 76110. **Tel** (817)924-3388. **ED** Maxine Brown.
Desc: Information on dentistry and personal health in general. Also information on continuing education, seminars and Texas Dental Assistants Association.

ISSN 0040-4284
US

NLM W1 TE71
Pr Rev.
TEXAS DENTAL JOURNAL. [Tex. dent. j.]. **Added/Corp** Texas Dental Association. Vol. 1 (Feb. 1883)-. Periodical. English. Twelve times a year. $49.50. Texas Dental Association, 1946 South Interregional Highway, Austin TX 78704. **Tel** (512)443-3675, (800)460-8700, FAX (512)443-3031. **ED** Douglas B. Willingham. **Ad Acc. Circ:** 7,500 (ctrl).
Desc: Discussion matters of interest to the dental profession.
Ind/Abst Curr. Cit.; Curr. Titles Dent.; Dent. Abstr. (-199?); Index Dent. Lit.

LC RK652 .T47   ISSN 0161-5459
DD 617.6/9/028   US
NLM W1 TH687
THERMOTROL TECHNICIAN, THE.
Added/Corp Jelenko (J. F.) and Company, Inc., New York. Research and Development Dept. Jelenko (J. F.) and Company, Inc., New York. Education Dept. Jelenko (J. F.) and Company, Inc., New York. Technology Division. (1947)-. Periodical. English. Five times a year (bimonthly except July/Aug.). JF Jelenko and Co., 170 Petersville Road, New Rochelle NY 10801.

ISSN 0939-5687
GW

UDC 33
THUERINGER ZAHNAERZTEBLATT.
VFOAT TZB. Theuringer Zahnaerzteblatt. (1991)-. Periodical. German. Twelve times a year. $52.00. Gustav Fischer Verlag Jena, Postfach 100537, D-07705 Jena Germany. **Tel** 011 49 3641 626444, FAX 011 49 3641 626500. **(Subscription address:** VCH Publishers Inc., 303 Northwest 12th Avenue, Journals Department, Deerfield FL 33442. **Tel** (800)367-8249, (305)428-5566.**)**

ISSN 0108-1284
DK

NLM W1; TI249
TIDSSKRIFT FOR TANDLGER (COPENHAGEN, DENMARK : 1981).
(TIDSSKRIFT FOR TANDLGER.). [Tidsskr. tandl.]. **VFOAT** Scandefa. Vol. 1, No. 1 (Aug. 1981)-. Danish. Six times a year. **Continues** Tidsskrift for Praktiserende Tandlger, 0105-0273.
Ind/Abst Index Dent. Lit. (1981-).

ISSN 0885-9191
US

DD 616
NLM ZWU 140; TM91
TMJ UPDATE. [TMJ update]. VAT Temporomandibular Joint Update. (1983)-. Periodical. English. Six times a year (Jan., Mar., May, July, Sept., Nov.). $79.00. Anadem Inc, 3620 North High Street, Columbus OH 43214. **Tel** (614)262-2539, (800)633-0055. **ED** Donald Bowers. Index available.
Desc: Digests medical and dental journal articles about diagnosis and treatment of TMJ and craniomandibular pain.
Ind/Abst Index Dent. Lit. (1987-).

ISSN 1048-5317
US

DD 617
NLM W1; TO167
TODAY'S FDA. (TODAY'S FDA : OFFICIAL MONTHLY JOURNAL OF THE FLORIDA DENTAL ASSOCIATION.). [Today's FDA]. **Added/Corp** Florida Dental Association. (1989)-. Trade Publication. English. Eleven times a year (eleven Today's FDA and 1 sourcebook). $32.10. Florida Dental Association, 1111 East Tennessee Street, Suite 102, Tallahassee FL 32308-6914. **Tel** (904)681-3629, (800)877-9922, FAX (904)561-0504. **ED** Karen Thurston. **Formed by the union of** Dental Times Dispatch, 0886-5094 **and** Florida Dental Journal, 0015-3990.
Ind/Abst Health Plan. Adminis.; Index Dent. Lit. (1989-).

FR

TONUS DENTAIRE. (19??)-. Periodical. French. Six times a year. 97.94F France; 100.00F other. Les Echos, 46 rue de la Boetie, 75381 Paris Cedex 08 France. **Tel** 011 33 1 49536565. **(Subscription address:** Les Echos, 37 Avenue des Champs Elysees, 75008 Paris, France. **Tel** 011 33 1 49536800.**)**

ISSN 0145-9724
US

NLM WU 22 AA1 T7
TRAINEES AND FELLOWS SUPPORTED BY THE NATIONAL INSTITUTE OF DENTAL RESEARCH AND TRAINED DURING FISCAL YEAR ...
. (1968)-. English. One time a year. Dental Research Data Officer, National Institute of Dental Research, Bethesda MD 20014. **Tel** (301)496-7843, FAX (301)496-9241. **Continues** Trainees and Fellows Supported by the National Institute of Dental Research.
Desc: Separate listings of trainees and fellows given grants and awards. Intended to identify young scientists who may be recruited for work in dental research by administrators and investigators.

ISSN 0074-3054
US

NLM W3 IN1742
TRANSACTIONS OF THE INTERNATIONAL CONFERENCE ON ENDODONTICS. Main/Conf International Conference on Endodontics. 2nd 1958-. English. Irregular. University of Pennsylvania / Continuing Education, 4001 Spruce Street A1, Philadelphia PA 19104. **Tel** (215)243-8904. **ED** L I Grossman. **Continues** Transactions of the International Congress on Endodontics.

ISSN 0746-8962
US

NLM W1; TR34R
Pr Rev.
TRENDS & TECHNIQUES IN THE CONTEMPORARY DENTAL LABORATORY. [Trends tech. contemp. dent. lab.]. **Added/Corp** National Association of Dental Laboratories (U.S.). **VFOAT** Trends and Techniques in the Contemporary Dental Laboratory. Vol. 1, No. 1 (Jan. 1984)-. Trade Publication. English. Ten times a year (Jan./Feb. and July/Aug. are combined). $40.00. National Association of Dental Laboratories, 555 East Braddock Road, Alexandria VA 22314. **Tel** (703)683-5263, FAX (703)549-4788. **ED** Jason Warholic. Index available in last issue of volume--attached. cum. index (10-year). **Ad Acc. Circ:** 14,000. **Continues** NADL Journal, 0360-5361.
Desc: Offers information, business management strategies, industry news, ethics, technical tips, new product information, meetings, and literature for dental laboratory technicians, dentists, and related specialists. The official journal of the National Association of Dental Laboratories.
Ind/Abst Dent. Abstr. (-199?).

ISSN 0011-8516
SA

NLM W1 TY119   **CODEN** DASJAG
TYDSKRIF VAN DIE TANDHEELKUNDIGE VERENIGING VAN SUID AFRIKA. [Tydskr. Tandheelkd. Ver. S., Afr.]. **VFOAT** Journal of the D. A. S. A.; Tydskrif van die T. V. S. A.; Journal of the Dental Association of South Africa. Vol. 27 (Jan. 1972)-. Periodical. English (Afrikaans). Twelve times a year. R300.00. Dental Association of South Africa, Private Bag 1 Houghton, 2041 Republic of South Africa. **Tel** 11 27 11 6424687, FAX 642-5718. **ED** Helmut Heydt. Index available. cum. index. **Bk Rev. Ad Acc. Circ:** 3,750 (ctrl). Documents available from CASDDS. **Continues** Tydskrif van die Tandheelkundige Vereniging van Suid-Afrika, 0011-8516.
Desc: Official journal of the Dental Association of South Africa, devoted to publishing original (i.e. not previously published) scientific articles and items of clinical dentistry.
Ind/Abst Chem. Abstr.

US

UNIFORMED SERVICES MEDICAL/DENTAL FACILITIES WORLDWIDE. See Military and Defense.

ISSN 0843-5812
CN

DD 617.6/05
NLM W1; UN96V
UNIVERSITY OF TORONTO DENTAL JOURNAL. [Univ. Tor. dent. j.]. **Added/Corp** University of Toronto. Faculty of Dentistry. **VFOAT** Dental Journal; UTDJ. Vol. 1, No. 1 (Fall 1987)-. Periodical. English. Irregular. 16.01Can$. University of Toronto Dental Journal, 124 Edward Street, Toronto Ontario, M5G 1G6 Canada. **Tel** (416) 979-4302.
Ind/Abst Health Plan. Adminis. (19??-).

ISSN 0897-876X
US

DD 617
NLM W1; UP518D
UPDATE IN PEDIATRIC DENTISTRY.
[Update pediatr. dent.]. **Added/Corp** American Academy of Pediatric Dentistry. Vol. 1, No. 1 (Sept. 1987)-. Periodical. English. Four times a year. Free. Professional Audience Communications, PO Box 243, Yardley PA 19067. **Tel** (215)493-7400.
Ind/Abst Health Plan. Adminis.; Index Dent. Lit. (1987-).

ISSN 0049-6472
DD 617 US
NLM W1 VI776
VIRGINIA DENTAL JOURNAL. [Va. dent. j.]. **Added/Corp** Virginia Dental Association. Virginia State Dental Association. **VFOAT** Bulletin - Virginia State Dental Association. Vol. 41, No. 3 (June 1964)-. Bulletin. English. Four times a year (Feb., May, Aug., Nov.). $12.00. Virginia Dental Association, PO Box 6906, 5006 Monument Avenue, Richmond VA 23230. **Tel** (804)358-4927, FAX (804)353-7342. **ED** Dr. Richard D. Wilson. **Ad Acc. Circ:** 2,900 (ctrl). ***Continues*** *Virginia State Dental Association. Bulletin.*
Desc: News and information about the dental association.
Ind/Abst Index Dent. Lit.

ISSN 1046-9338
DD 617 US
NLM W1; WD13 **CODEN** WDJOEG
WDA JOURNAL. [WDA j.]. **Added/Corp** Wisconsin Dental Association. **VAT** Wisconsin Dental Association Journal. Vol. 64, No. 11 (Nov. 1988)-. Periodical. English. Six times a year. $65.00. Wisconsin Dental Association, 111 East Wisconsin Avenue, Suite 1300, Milwaukee WI 53202. **Tel** (414)276-4520. **ED** Paul R. Mahn. **Bk Rev. Ad Acc. Circ:** 3,100 (ctrl). ***Continues*** *Wisconsin Dental Association Journal, 0887-9699.*
Ind/Abst Health Plan. Adminis. (19??-); Index Dent. Lit. (Nov. 1988-).

ISSN 0043-3225
US
NLM W1 WE454
WEST VIRGINIA DENTAL JOURNAL. [W. V. dent. j.]. **Added/Corp** West Virginia State Dental Society. (193?)-. Periodical. English. Four times a year. $10.00. West Virginia Dental Association, 300 Capitol Street, Suite 1002 Kanawha, Charleston WV 25301. **Tel** (304)344-5246. ***Continues*** *Bulletin of the West Virginia State Dental Society.*
Ind/Abst Dent. Abstr. (-199?); Index Dent. Lit. (19??-).

LC RK37 .W48
DD 617.6/0025/73 US
NLM WU 22; AA1 R476
WHO'S WHO IN BLACK DENTISTRY IN AMERICA. (1987-1988)-. English. $65.00. ***Continues*** *Rhode's Directory of Black Dentists Registered in the United States, 0090-7995.*

US
NLM WU 22; AA1 W65
WHO'S WHO IN DENTAL TECHNOLOGY. **Added/Corp** National Association of Dental Laboratories (U.S.) National Board for Certification in Dental Laboratory Technology (U.S.) National Board for Certification of Dental Laboratories (U.S.). (199?)-. Directory. English. One time a year. National Association of Dental Laboratories, 555 East Braddock Road, Alexandria VA 22314. **Tel** (703)683-5263, FAX (703)549-4788. **ED** Robert W. Stanley and Doug Newcomb. **Ad Acc. Circ:** 43,000. ***Continues*** *Who's Who in the Dental Laboratory Industry, 0195-6221.*
Desc: Membership information, by-laws, committees, officers, state associations, Certified Dental Technicians, Certified Dental Laboratories, manufacturers, distributors, suppliers, product index, staff and other information.

ISSN 0195-6221
US
NLM WU 22; AA1 W65
TITLE CHANGE
WHO'S WHO IN THE DENTAL LABORATORY INDUSTRY. **Added/Corp** National Association of Dental Laboratories (U.S.) National Board for Certification in Dental Laboratory Technology (U.S.) National Board for Certification of Dental Laboratories (U.S.). (1967)-(199?). Directory. English. National Association of Dental Laboratories, 555 East Braddock Road, Alexandria VA 22314. **Tel** (703)683-5263, FAX (703)549-4788. **ED** Robert W. Stanley and Doug Newcomb. **Ad Acc. Circ:** 43,000. ***Continued by*** *Who's Who in Dental Technology.*
Desc: Membership information, by-laws, committees, officers, state associations, Certified Dental Technicians, Certified Dental Laboratories, manufacturers, distributors, suppliers, product index, staff and other information.

ISSN 1062-8746
DD 617 US
WIRELINE (DALLAS, TEX.). (WIRELINE: THE NEWSLETTER OF THE AMERICAN ORTHODONTIC SOCIETY, INC.). [Wireline]. **Added/Corp** American Orthodontic Society. **VFOAT** Wire Line. (Apr. 1992)-. Trade Publication. English. Four times a year. American Orthodontic Society, 9550 Forest Lane, Suite 215, Dallas TX 75243. ***Continues*** *American Orthodontic Society Newsletter.*

US
WSDA MEMBERSHIP DIRECTORY & RESOURCE GUIDE. **Main/Corp** Washington State Dental Association. **VFOAT** WSDA Membership Directory and Resource Guide; Membership Directory and Resource Guide; Membership Directory & Resource Guide. Vol. 60 (Jan. 1992)-. Directory. English. One time a year. $54.10. Washington State Dental Association, 2033 6th Avenue, Suite 333, Seattle WA 98121. **Tel** (206)448-1914. ***Continues*** *Washington State Dental Association. WSDA Membership Roster.*

LC RK16 .Y4 **ISSN** 0084-3717
DD 610.58 S US
NLM W1 YE117
YEAR BOOK OF DENTISTRY, THE. (1936)-. English. One time a year. $59.95. Mosby Year Book Inc., 11830 Westline Industrial Drive, St Louis MO 63146. **Tel** (800)325-4177, (314)872-8370, FAX (314)432-1380, telex 44-2402. **ED** Walter Cohen, Hamilton G.B. Robinson, Robert E. Moyers, Sidney I. Silverman, Ronald Johnson, Barry H. Hendler and Ronald E. Jordan. cum. index. available on an online database from BRS.

ISSN 0733-5784
US
YEARBOOK / INDIANA DENTAL ASSOCIATION. [Yearb. - Indiana Dent. Assoc.]. **Main/Corp** Indiana Dental Association. **VFOAT** IDA Yearbook; Roster Yearbook. (1974)-. English. One time a year. Indiana Dental Association, PO Box 2467, Indianapolis IN 46206-2467. **Tel** (317)634-2610, FAX (317)634-2612. ***Continues in part*** *Journal of the Indiana Dental Association, 0199-6568.*

ISSN 0044-1643
GW
NLM W1 ZA3613
ZAHNAERZTLICHE MITTEILUNGEN. **Added/Corp** Reichsverband der Zahnaertze Deutschland. Deutsche Zahnaertzeschaft. Verband der Deutschen Zahnaertzelichen Berufsvertretungen. Bundesverband der Deutschen Zahnaertze. Kassenzahnaertzliche Bundesvereinigung. No. 1 (1909)-. Periodical. German. Twenty-four times a year. $259.47. Deutscher Aerzte Verlag GmbH, Postfach 404265, D-50832 Cologne Germany. **Tel** 011 49 2234 7011219. **Bk Rev. Ad Acc. Circ:** 52,000 (ctrl).
Ind/Abst Curr. Titles Dent.; Index Dent. Lit.

ISSN 0340-5478
GW
NLM W1 ZA388S
ZAHNARTZLICHER GESUNDHEITSDIENST. (ZAHNARZTLICHER GESUNDHEITSDIENST : OFFIZIELLES ORGAN DES BUNDESVERBANDES DER ZAHNARZTE DES OFFENTLICHEN GESUNDHEITSDIENSTES E.V.). [Zahnartzl. Gesundheitsd.]. (Jan. 15, 1972)-. Periodical. German. Every 2 years.

ISSN 0340-3017
GW
NLM W1 ZA359Z
ZAHNARZTEBLATT BADEN-WURTTEMBERG. [Zahnarztebl. Baden-Wurttemb.]. 1.- Yearly volume; 1973-. Periodical. German. Twelve times a year. DM133.20. AW Gentner Verlag, Postfach 101742, D-70015 Stuttgart Germany. **Tel** 011 49 711 636720, FAX 011 49 711 6367247, telex 841 722244. **Bk Rev. Ad Acc. Circ:** 8,600.
Ind/Abst Index Dent. Lit.

SZ
ZAHNTECHNIK. (19??)-. Periodical. German (French and Italian). Six times a year. 55.00F Switzerland; 62.00F Europe; 75.00F other. Die Zahntechnik, Heidenbuehlstr 2, 8840 Einsiedeln Switzerland. **Tel** 011 41 55 531074. Index available.

LC R **ISSN** 0175-7784
DD 617.6 AU
UDC 61 **CCC**
NLM W1; ZE609F
TITLE CHANGE
ZEITSCHRIFT FUER STOMATOLOGIE (1984). (ZEITSCHRIFT FUER STOMATOLOGIE.). **Added/Corp** Oesterreichische Aerztekammer. Bundesfachgruppe fuer Zahn-, Mund- und Kieferheilkunde. Oesterreichische Gesellschaft fuer Zahn-, Mund- und Kieferheilkunde. (1984)-(1994). Academic Scholarly Publication. German (summaries and/or abstracts in English). Ten times a year. Springer-Verlag Vienna, Sachsenplatz 4 6, PO Box 89, A-1201 Vienna Austria. **Tel** 011 43 1 33024150, FAX 011 43 1 330242665. **(Subscription address:** Springer-Verlag New York Inc. / North America, PO Box 2485, Journal Fulfillment, Secaucus NJ 07096. **Tel** (201)348-4033, (800)777-4643, FAX (201)348-4505.) **ED** G. Watzek, M. Matejka. ***Continues*** *Oesterreichische Zeitschrift fuer Stomatologie.* ***Continued by*** *Stomatologie (Vienna, Austria), 0946-3151.*
Desc: Contains original papers dealing with all topics related to dentistry, stomatology and orthodontics.
Ind/Abst Curr. Aware. Biol. Sci., CABS; Curr. Titles Dent.; EMBASE; Index Dent. Lit.

ISSN 0177-3348
GW
NLM W1; ZE688
ZEITSCHRIFT FUER ZAHNARZTLICHE IMPLANTOLOGIE. **Added/Corp** Deutsche Gesellschaft fuer Zahn-, Mund- und Kieferheilkunde. (198?)-. Periodical. German (English). Four times a year. DM228.80. Carl Hanser Verlag, Postfach 860420, D-81631 Munich Germany. **Tel** 011 49 89 998300, FAX 011 49 89 981264.

ISSN 1002-0098
CC
NLM W1; CH982HQ **CODEN** ZKYZE2
ZHONGHUA KOUQIANG YIXUE ZAZHI. (CHUNG-HUA KOU CHIANG I HSUEH TSA CHIH.). [Zhonghua kouqiang yixue zazhi]. **Added/Corp** Chung-Hua i Hsueh Hui (China : 1949-). **VFOAT** Zhonghua Kouqiang Yixue Zazhi; Chinese Journal of Stomatology. (1987)-. Academic Scholarly Publication. Chinese (summaries and/or abstracts in English; table of contents in English). Six times a year. $34.02. **(Subscription address:** China International Book Trading Corporation, PO Box 399, Library Service Department, Beijing 100044 People's Republic of China. **Tel** 011 86 1 8414284, FAX 011 86 1 8412023, telex 22496 CIBTC CN.) Documents available from CASDDS. ***Continues*** *Chung-Hua Kou Chiang Ko Tsa Chih, 0412-4014.*
Ind/Abst Chem. Abstr.

ISSN 0044-166X
GW
CCC
NLM W1 Z12
ZWR. [ZWR]. Vol. 79 (Jan. 1970)-. Trade Publication. German. Twelve times a year. $152.00. Dr. Alfred Huethig Verlag GmbH, Postfach 102869, D-69018 Heidelberg Germany. **Tel** 011 49 6221 489281, FAX 011 49 6221 489279. **(Subscription address:** Huethig Publishing Inc., 29 Macintosh Drive, Oxford CT 06478. **Tel** (203)881-2647.) **ED** C. Gins, W. Pietsch. **Bk Rev. Ad Acc. Circ:** 17,000 (ctrl). ***Formed by the union of*** *ZWR. Zahnarztliche Welt, Zahnarztliche Rundschau* ***and*** *Deutsche Zahnarzteblatt, 0011-4839;* ***Absorbed*** *Stoma, 0039-1697.*
Desc: Professional journal for the dentist and relating dental technology.
Ind/Abst Curr. Titles Dent.; Index Dent. Lit.

ABSTRACTING, BIBLIOGRAPHIES AND STATISTICS

LC Z6668-.02
DD 016.6176 BL
BIBLIOGRAFIA BRASILEIRA DE ODONTOLOGIA. **Added/Corp** Universidade de Sao Paulo. Seccao de Documentacao Odontologia. **VFOAT** B B O; Brazilian Dental Bibliography. (1967)-. Periodical. Portuguese. Six times a year. Universidade de Sao Paulo / Faculdade de Odontologia 2227, 05508 Sao Paulo SP Brazil. **Tel** 011 55 11 8136944, FAX 011 55 11 8154272. available on CD-ROM.

LC Z6668.2 **ISSN** 0903-3483
DD 016.6176 DK
CCC
CURRENT TITLES IN DENTISTRY. Vol. 1, No. 1 (Jan. 1988)-. Abstracting/Indexing Service. English. Twelve times a year. $88.00. Royal Dental College Library, Vennelyst Boulevard, DK 8000 Aarhus C Denmark. **Tel** 011 45 6 86132533, FAX 011 45 6 86131665. **ED** Preben Junker Jacobsen.
Desc: Lists major international journals in dentistry and related fields. Aids both librarians and clinicians to save costs, and to maintain a range of dental literature. Provides research and survey of new theories, technology, and current achievements in dentistry.

LC RK1 .A5416 **ISSN** 0011-8486
DD 617.6082 US
NLM ZWU 100 D412
DENTAL ABSTRACTS (CHICAGO). (DENTAL ABSTRACTS.). **Added/Corp** American Dental Association. Vol. 1 (Jan. 1956)-. Abstracting/Indexing Service. English. Six times a year. $82.50. Mosby Year Book Inc., 11830 Westline Industrial Drive, St Louis MO 63146. **Tel** (800)325-4177, (314)872-8370, FAX (314)432-1380, telex 44-2402. **ED** Lawrence Meskin. Index available. **Circ:** 9,000. available on microfilm and microfiche from University Microfilms International (UMI).
Desc: Each article presents information in abstract form that includes references for study. The journal reports trends and developments, new technologies, and clinical and research findings in all areas of dental practice.
Ind/Abst Health Plan. Adminis.

LC Z **ISSN** 0730-1308
DD 617.634/2 US
NLM ZWU 230 A512R
ENDODONTIC BIBLIOGRAPHY. [Endod. bibliogr.]. **Added/Corp** American Association of Endodontists. Vol. 4 (June 1979)-. Bibliography. English. Williams & Wilkins Company, 428 East Preston Street,

Baltimore MD 21202-3993. **Tel** (410)528-4000, (800)638-6423, FAX (410)528-8596, telex 87669. ***Continues*** *American Association of Endodontists. Reprint Catalogue.*

ISSN 0367-5920
HK
CODEN HKBJAB

HSIANG-KANG CH'IN HUI HSUEH YUAN HSUEH PAO. [Hsiang-Kang Ch'in Hui Hsueh Yuan Hsueh Pao]. **VFOAT** Hong Kong Baptist College Academic Journal; Hong Kong Ch'in Hui Shu Yuan Hsueh Pao. (1962)-. Multiple languages. Irregular. Kowloon Hong Kong Baptist College. Documents available from CASDDS.
Ind/Abst Chem. Abstr.

LC Z6668 .I45 RK51 **ISSN** 0019-3992
DD 016.6/001/6 US
NLM ZWU 100 I381

INDEX TO DENTAL LITERATURE. [Index dent. lit.]. **Added/Corp** American Dental Association. National Library of Medicine (U.S.). (1962)-. Abstracting/Indexing Service. English. Four times a year. $250.00. American Dental Association, 211 East Chicago Avenue, Chicago IL 60611. **Tel** (312)440-2867, (312)440-2500, FAX (312)440-7494. **ED** Aletha A. Kowitz. **Circ:** 1,400. available on CD-ROM (MEDLINE) from EBSCO Publishing - Peabody; available on microfilm and microfiche from University Microfilms International (UMI). ***Continues*** *Index to Dental Literature in the English Language, 1059-5562.*
Desc: Articles from dental journals from around the world in 41 languages are indexed by authors and subjects. Lists of books and dissertations are also published (world-wide publications).

DRUG ABUSE AND ALCOHOLISM

LC HV5275 .A53
DD 178.6 616.86* US

A.A. GRAPEVINE, THE. Added/Corp Alcoholics Anonymous. Vol. 2, No. 11 (Apr. 1946)-. Periodical. English. Twelve times a year. $12.00. AA Grapevine Inc., PO Box 1980 Grand Central Station, New York NY 10163. **Tel** (212)686-1100 ext. 55. ***Continues*** *Grapevine (Alcoholics Anonymous).*

LC HV697 **ISSN** 0888-5567
DD 362 US
CEASED

ACA JOURNAL, THE. [ACA j.]. **Added/Corp** American Council on Alcoholism. **VFOAT** ACA Quarterly Journal. **VAT** American Council on Alcoholism Journal. (Spring 1987)-(19??). Periodical. English. American Council on Alcoholism, 5024 Campbell Road, Baltimore MD 21236. **Tel** (410)931-9393.

ISSN 0001-7396
US

ACTION (ALBANY). (ACTION.). **Added/Corp** Alcohol Education for Youth. (19??)-. Periodical. English. Twelve times a year. $1.00. Alcohol Education Youth Inc, 1500 Western Avenue, Albany NY 12203. **Tel** (516)456-3800.

LC HV5831.N2 A23A **ISSN** 0097-8973
DD 353.9/782/00765 US

ACTIVITY SUMMARY DRUG AND NARCOTIC CASES. Main/Corp Nebraska. Division of Drug Control. English. Division of Drug Control, PO Box 94637, State House, Lincoln NE 68509.

LC RA11 .B15b
DD 353.0084/2 US
TITLE CHANGE

ADAMHA PUBLIC ADVISORY COMMITTEES. Added/Corp United States. Alcohol, Drug Abuse, and Mental Health Administration. **VFOAT** Public Advisory Committees. **VAT** Alcohol, Drug Abuse, and Mental Health Administration Public Advisory Committees. (19??)-(19??). English. US Department of Health & Human Services / Alcohol Drug Abuse & Mental Health Administration, 5600 Fishers Lane, Rockville MD 20857. **Tel** (301)443-3783, FAX (301)443-1719. ***Continues in part*** *HRA, HSA, CDC, OASH, & ADAMHA Public Advisory Committees.* ***Continued by*** *ADAMHA Advisory Committees.*

LC HV5800 .B7 **ISSN** 0965-2140
DD 362.2/9/05 UK
CCC
NLM W1; AD13L **CODEN** ADICE5

●**ADDICTION. Added/Corp** Society for the Study of Addiction to Alcohol and Other Drugs. Vol. 88, No. 1 (Jan. 1993)-. Periodical. English (summaries and/or abstracts in French and Spanish). Twelve times a year. $896.00. Carfax Publishing Company, PO Box 25, Abingdon, Oxfordshire OX14 3UE United Kingdom. **Tel** 011 44 1235 555335, FAX 011 44 1235 553559, telex 817484. **Bk Rev**. available on microfiche. ***Continues*** *British Journal of Addiction, 0952-0481.*
Desc: Publishes research and reviews in all areas of addiction.
Ind/Abst Curr. Cit.; Curr. Contents Clin. Med.; Curr. Contents Soc. Behav. Sci.; EP Collect.; Health Source Plus; Health Source; Homework Help.; Index Med. (1993-); MasterFile FullTEXT 1000; MasterFile FullTEXT 350; MasterFile FullTEXT 650; MasterFile FullTEXT (July 1994-); Psychol. Abstr.; Sci. Cit. Index; Soc. Sci. Cit. Index; Telebase.

LC HV689 **ISSN** 0968-7610
DD 362.2915 UK
CCC

●**ADDICTION ABSTRACTS.** [Addict. abstr.]. (1994)-. Periodical. English. Four times a year (Mar., Jun., Sept., Dec.). $284.00. Carfax Publishing Company, PO Box 25, Abingdon, Oxfordshire OX14 3UE United Kingdom. **Tel** 011 44 1235 555335, FAX 011 44 1235 553559, telex 817484. **(Subscription address:** Carfax Publishing Co., 875-81 Massachusetts Avenue, Cambridge MA 02139. **) ED** Michael Gossop. **Ad Acc**. available on microfiche. Documents available from UMI Article Clearinghouse.

LC HV5285 .A374a **ISSN** 1052-4614
DD 362.29/05 US
NLM W1; AD133L
TITLE CHANGE

ADDICTION & RECOVERY. [Addict. recovery]. **VFOAT** Addiction and Recovery. Vol. 10, No. 1 (June 1990)-(1993). Periodical. English. Medquest Communications Inc., 629 Euclid Avenue, Suite 500, Cleveland OH 44114. **Tel** (216)522-9700. available on microfilm and microfiche from University Microfilms International (UMI); available on an online database (full text) from DIALOG. ***Continues*** *Alcoholism & Addiction & Recovery Life, 1053-3923.* ***Continued by*** *Behavioral Health Management.*
Ind/Abst Acad. Abstr.; Acad. Search; Consum. Health Nutr. Index; EP Collect.; Health Index (1989-); Health Period. Database [Full Txt.]; Health Ref. Cent. (Jan. 1989-) [Full Txt.] [Full Cov.]; Health Source Plus; Health Source; Homework Help.; INFO-SOUTH Abstr.; Mag. Search; MasterFile FullTEXT 1000; MasterFile FullTEXT 350; MasterFile FullTEXT 650; MasterFile FullTEXT (Jan. 1992-Dec. 1993); OCLC; Pub. Lib. FullTEXT; Telebase.

LC HV5823 **ISSN** 1355-6215
DD 616.86 UK

●**ADDICTION BIOLOGY.** (1996)-. Academic Scholarly Publication. English. Four times a year. £180.00 (institutions), £90.00 (individuals). Carfax Publishing Company, PO Box 25, Abingdon, Oxfordshire OX14 3UE United Kingdom. **Tel** 011 44 1235 555335, FAX 011 44 1235 553559, telex 817484. **(Subscription address:** Carfax Publishing Co., 875-81 Massachusetts Avenue, Cambridge MA 02139.)

LC WMLC 93/1964 **ISSN** 8756-405X
DD 616 US
CCC

ADDICTION LETTER, THE. [Addict. lett.]. Vol. 1, No. 1 (Jan. 1985)-. Newsletter. English. Twelve times a year. $149.00. Manisses Communications Group Inc., 208 Governor Street, PO Box 3357, Providence RI 02906. **Tel** (401)831-6020, (800)333-7771, FAX (401)861-6370. **ED** Marcia J. Lawton and Linda Watts Jackim. Index available. cum. index. **Bk Rev. Circ:** 2,500. available on an online database (full text) from DIALOG.
Desc: Resource exchange on treatment and prevention of alcoholism, drug abuse and all other forms of addiction.
Ind/Abst Acad. Abstr.; Acad. Search; EP Collect.; Health Index (1989-); Health Period. Database [Full Txt.]; Health Ref. Cent. (Jan. 1989-) [Full Txt.] [Full Cov.]; Health Source Plus; Health Source; Homework Help.; INFO-SOUTH Abstr.; Mag. Artic. Summar. Elite; Mag. Artic. Summar. Select; Mag. Artic. Summar. CD-ROM; Mag. Search; MasterFile FullTEXT 1000; MasterFile FullTEXT 350; MasterFile FullTEXT 650; MasterFile FullTEXT (Jan. 1992-) [Full Txt.]; OCLC; Pub. Lib. FullTEXT; Telebase; World Mag. Bank.

ISSN 0899-9112
DD 610 US
NLM W1; AD132
TITLE CHANGE

ADDICTION NURSING NETWORK. See Medical Sciences-Nursing.

ISSN 1058-6989
DD 362 US
CCC
CODEN AREREQ

●**ADDICTION RESEARCH.** [Addict. res.]. Vol. 1, No. 1 (1993)-. Periodical. English. Four times a year. $94.00. Harwood Academic Publishers / New York, PO Box 786, Cooper Station, New York NY 10276. **Tel** (212)206-8900, (201)643-7500.

ISSN 0702-8008
DD 616.8/6/005 CN

ADDICTION THERAPIST, THE. VFOAT Le Toxicotherapeute. Published since 1975. Periodical. French (English). Four times a year. $20.00. Le Toxicotherapeute, 3418 rue Drummond, Montreal Quebec H3G 1Y1 Canada. ***Continues*** *Programme de Portage Relatif a la Dependance de la Drogue Inc. Revue de Portage, 0702-8016.*

LC RC565 .A33 **ISSN** 0306-4603
DD 616.8/6/005 UK
CCC
NLM W1 AD155G **CODEN** ADBEDS
Pr Rev.

ADDICTIVE BEHAVIORS. [Addict. behav.]. Vol. 1 (July 1975)-. Academic Scholarly Publication. English. Six times a year. $554.00. Pergamon Press, An Imprint of Elsevier Science Ltd., The Boulevard, Langford Lane, Kidlington, Oxford OX5 1GB United Kingdom. **Tel** 011 44 1865 843000, 011 44 1865 843699, FAX 011 44 1865 843010. **(Subscription address:** Elsevier Science Ltd. / Oxford Fulfillment Centre, PO Box 800, Kidlington OX5 1DX United Kingdom. **Tel** 011 44 865 843355.**) ED** Peter M. Miller. available on microfilm and microfiche from University Microfilms International (UMI); available on an online database from Elsevier Electronic Subscriptions (EES). Documents available from The Genuine Article, BIOSIS Document Express.
Desc: A professional journal designed to publish original research, theoretical papers and critical reviews in the area of substance abuse. The journal focuses on alcohol and drug abuse, smoking, and problems associated with eating.
Ind/Abst Abstr. Res. Pastor. Care Couns. (19??-); AGRICOLA; Annals Behav. Med.; Biol. Abstr.; Chicano Index; Crim. Penol. Police Sci. Abstr.; Curr. Aware. Biol. Sci., CABS; Curr. Cit.; Curr. Contents Soc. Behav. Sci.; EMBASE; Health Saf. Sci. Abstr.; Health Plan. Adminis.; High. Educ. Abstr. (1980-); Highw. Res. Abstr.; Index Med.; Med. Abstr. Newsl.; Middle East Abstr. Index; Life Sci. Collect.; Physic. Medline Plus; Pollut. Abstr. Indexes; Psychol. Abstr. (1976-); PsycINFO; PsycLit; Res. Alert [Full Cov.]; Risk Abstr.; Soc. Sci. Cit. Index [Full Cov.]; Toxicol. Abstr.

ISSN 0811-9392
DD 026.362290994 AT

ADDLIS NEWS. [ADDLIS news]. **Added/Corp** Alcohol and Drug Depndence Libraries and Information Services Group. **VFOAT** Alcohol and Drug Dependence Libraries and Information Services News. (1982)-. English. Irregular. **ED** B M Allen.
Ind/Abst Aust. Educ. Index.

ISSN 0705-6389
DD 362.2/9 CN

ADE. ALCOHOL AND DRUG EDUCATION. (ADE.). **VAT** Alcohol and Drug Education. Vol. 1 (Feb. 1978)-. Periodical. English. Irregular. $3.00. Alcohol and Drug Education Service, 107-249 1/2 Notre Dame Avenue, Winnipeg Manitoba R3B 1N8 Canada.

ISSN 0214-4840
SP
UDC 364
Pr Rev.

ADICCIONES PALMA DE MALLORCA. [Adicciones Palma de Mallorca]. (1989)-. Periodical. Multiple languages. Four times a year. 4000ptas. Addiciones, Calle Rambla 15 2 3, 07003 Palma Mallorca Spain. **Tel** 011 34 971 714051. **ED** Amador Calafat. **Bk Rev. Ad Acc. Circ:** 4,500.
Desc: Scientific publication of original articles on research, reviews, and other information related to drug addiction, alcoholism and other dependencies.

US
NLM W1; AD37D
TITLE CHANGE

ADOLESCENCE MAGAZINE. VFOAT Adolescence. Vol. 5, No. 3 (Sept. 1992)-(1993). Periodical. English. US Journal Inc., 3201 Southwest 15th Street, Deerfield Beach FL 33442. **Tel** (305)360-0909 ext. 232, (800)851-9100, FAX (305)360-0034. **(Subscription address:** Kable Publishers Aide / Illinois, 308 East Hitt Street, Subscription Department, Mt. Morris IL 61054-1473. **Tel** (815)734-1261.**)** ***Continues*** *Adolescent Counselor, 1042-7589.* ***Merged into*** *Professional Counselor.*
Desc: This publication deals with current issues facing the lives of young people, such as alcohol and drug abuse, teenage sex and AIDS, teenage suicide and eating disorders.

LC HV5280.C2 A24
DD 362.2928 US

ADP PREVENTION HIGHLIGHTS. Added/Corp California. Dept. of Alcohol and Drug Programs. Division of Alcohol Programs. **VFOAT** Prevention Highlights. (19??)-. English.

LC RC563 .A38 **ISSN** 0272-1740
DD 616.86 US
CCC
NLM W1 AD875U

ADVANCES IN SUBSTANCE ABUSE, BEHAVIORAL AND BIOLOGICAL RESEARCH. [Adv. subst. abuse, Behav. biol. res.]. Vol. 1 (1980)-. Monographic series. English. Irregular. Price varies per volume. Jessica Kingsley Publishers, 118 Pentonville Road, London N1 9JN United Kingdom. **Tel** 011 44 171 8332307, FAX 011 44 171 8372917.

(**Subscription address:** Taylor & Francis Inc., 1900 Frost Road, Suite 101, Bristol PA 19007-1598. **Tel** (215)785-5800, (800)821-8312, FAX (215)785-5515.)
Ind/Abst Psychol. Abstr. (1981-).

US

AL ANON Y ALATEEN NEW ACCION CON SELECCIONES DEL FORUM. (19??)-. English (Spanish). Six times a year. $2.00. Al-Anon Family Groups HQ, 1372 Broadway, New York NY 10018. **Tel** (212)302-7240.

LC HV5831.A7 A24a
DD 362.2/9356/09798 US
TITLE CHANGE

ALASKA STATE DRUG ABUSE PLAN. REVISED UPDATE. **Main/Corp** Alaska. State Office of Alcoholism and Drug Abuse. (19??)-(198?). English. Department of Health and Social Services / Office of Alcoholism and Drug Abuse, Pouch H-05F, Juneau AK 99811. **ED** David Pierce. ctrl circ. ***Continued by*** *Alaska. Division of Alcoholism and Drug Abuse. State of Alaska Alcoholism and Drug Abuse Plan.*
Desc: The journal lists priorities, approved programs and indicators in Alaska.

US

ALASKA STATE PLAN FOR THE REDUCTION OF ALCOHOLISM AND ALCOHOL ABUSE, THE. (19??)-. English. Department of Health and Social Services / Office of Alcoholism and Drug Abuse, Pouch H-05F, Juneau AK 99811.

ISSN 1054-1411
DD 362 US

ALATEEN TALK. [Alateen talk]. **Added/Corp** Al-Anon Family Group Headquarters, Inc. (Jan. 1969)-. Periodical. English. Six times a year. $2.50 per year. AFG Inc, Box 862, Midtown Station, New York NY 10018-0862. **Tel** 212-302-7240, FAX 212-869-3757. **ED** Bonnie Cummings. **Circ:** 6,000.
Desc: Personal stories of teenagers affected by the alcoholism of someone close to them.

LC HV5441 .J6 **ISSN** 0735-0414
DD 362.2/92/05 UK
CCC
NLM W1; AL303D **CODEN** ALALDD
Pr Rev.

ALCOHOL AND ALCOHOLISM (OXFORD). (ALCOHOL AND ALCOHOLISM : INTERNATIONAL JOURNAL OF THE MEDICAL COUNCIL ON ALCOHOLISM.). [Alcohol alcohol.]. **Added/Corp** Medical Council on Alcoholism. Vol. 18, No. 1 (1983)-. Academic Scholarly Publication. English. Six times a year. $395.00. Oxford University Press / UK, Walton Street, Oxford OX2 6DP United Kingdom. **Tel** 011 44 1865 56767, FAX 011 44 1865 267773, telex 851/837330 OXPRES G. (**Subscription address:** Oxford University Press / USA, Journals Marketing Department, Oxford University Press, 2001 Evans Road, Cary NC 27513. **Tel** (800)451-7556, (919)677-0977, FAX (919)677-1714.) **ED** A.A-B Badawy. available on microfilm and microfiche from University Microfilms International (UMI). Documents available from The Genuine Article, CASDDS. ***Continues*** *British Journal on Alcohol and Alcoholism, 0309-1635.*
Desc: Publishes original research and review articles on every aspect of alcohol and alcoholism. The areas of interest include all the clinical disciplines of medicines, the basic medical sciences, psychology, sociology and epidemiology.
Ind/Abst Chem. Abstr. (1983-); Crim. Penol. Police Sci. Abstr.; Curr. Aware. Biol. Sci., CABS; Curr. Cit.; Curr. Contents Clin. Med.; Curr. Contents Life Sci.; EMBASE; Health Plan. Adminis.; Index Med. (Vol. 19, No. 1, 1984-); Linguist. Lang. Behav. Abstr.; Psychol. Abstr. (1983-); Res. Alert [Full Cov.]; Sci. Cit. Index; SCISEARCH; Soc. Plann. Policy Dev. Abstr.; Sociol. Abstr.

UK
NLM W1; AL303A
CEASED

ALCOHOL AND ALCOHOLISM. SUPPLEMENT. No. 1 (1987)-(1995). Periodical. English. Oxford University Press / UK, Walton Street, Oxford OX2 6DP United Kingdom. **Tel** 011 44 1865 56767, FAX 011 44 1865 267773, telex 851/837330 OXPRES G. (**Subscription address:** Oxford University Press / UK, PO Box 417, Oxford OX2 6YS United Kingdom. **Tel** 011 44 865 56767.)
Ind/Abst Index Med. (1987-).

LC HV5831.M3 A15a
DD 362.29/186/025752 US

ALCOHOL AND DRUG ABUSE RESOURCE DIRECTORY. **Added/Corp** Maryland. Alcohol and Drug Abuse Administration. **VFOAT** Treatment Resource Directory. Directory. English. Maryland Drug Abuse Administration, O'Conor Building/4th Floor, 201 West Preston Street, Baltimore MD 21201. **Tel** (410)225-6910. ***Formed by the union of*** *Directory of Drug Abuse Treatment Service Units and Organizations Offering Specific Services to Drug Abusers, 0892-0834* ***and*** *Maryland Alcoholism Resource Directory.*

LC HV5297.M2 A58
DD 362.2/9 US

ALCOHOL AND DRUG ABUSE SERVICES IN THE STATE OF MAINE. (19??)-. English. Office of Alcoholism and Drug Abuse Prevention, Bureau of Rehabilitation/Department of Human Services, 32 Winthrop Street, Augusta ME 04330.

LC HV5279 .A68 **ISSN** 0193-3981
DD 362.2/92/02573 US
NLM WM 22 AA1 A2

ALCOHOL AND DRUG ABUSE YEARBOOK/DIRECTORY, THE. (1979/80)-. English. One time a year. Van Nostrand Reinhold Company Inc., 115 5th Avenue, New York NY 10003. **Tel** (212)254-3232, FAX (212)673-1239, telex 272562. **ED** J Norback.

ISSN 0267-3282
UK

ALCOHOL CONCERN. (ALCOHOL CONCERN JOURNAL.). [Alcohol concern]. (1985)-. Newsletter. English. Four times a year. $102.67. Alcohol Concern Magazine, Waterbridge House, 32-26 Loman Street, London SE1 0EE United Kingdom. **Tel** 011 44 71 9287377, FAX 011 44 71 9284644. **ED** Mark Bennett. **Bk Rev**, (Qty: 20 /yr). **Ad Acc**, **Adv Mgr:** Mark Bennett, **Tel** same as publisher. **Circ:** 1,400 (ctrl).
Desc: Contains news of international developments around alcohol abuse, features about alcohol treatment and policies in the UK.

LC RA790.6 .U56a **ISSN** 0096-1485
DD 353.0084/2045 US
NLM WM 22 AA1 A31

ALCOHOL, DRUG ABUSE, MENTAL HEALTH, RESEARCH GRANT AWARDS. **Added/Corp** National Institute of Mental Health (U.S.). Division of Extramural Research Programs. Program Analysis and Evaluation Section. United States. Alcohol, Drug Abuse, and Mental Health Administration. Office of Extramural Programs. United States. Alcohol, Drug Abuse, and Mental Health Administration. Office of Science. United States. Alcohol, Drug Abuse, and Mental Health Administration. Division of Program Analysis. **VFOAT** Alcohol, Drug Abuse, and Mental Health Research Grant Awards. (1973)-. Government Publication. English. One time a year. Free on request. Superintendent of Documents, US Government Printing Office, Washington DC 20402. **Tel** (202)275-3328, FAX (202)786-2377. ***Continues*** *National Institute of Mental Health (U.S.). Mental Health Research Grant Awards, 0565-7768.*

ISSN 0278-5129
US
NLM W1 AL303E

ALCOHOL, DRUGS, AND AGING. USAGE AND PROBLEMS. (ALCOHOL, DRUGS, AND AGING--USAGE AND PROBLEMS.). **Added/Corp** University of Michigan. Institute of Gerontology. **VFOAT** Alcohol, Drugs, and Aging--Usage and Problems Series. No. 1 (1980)-. Monographic series. English. Irregular. Price varies per volume. Institute of Gerontology, Univisersity of Michigan, Ann Arbor MI 48109.

ISSN 0741-8329
US
CCC
NLM W1; AL302 **CODEN** ALCOEX
Pr Rev.

ALCOHOL (FAYETTEVILLE, N.Y.). (ALCOHOL.). [Alcohol]. Vol. 1, No. 1 (Jan./Feb. 1984)-. Academic Scholarly Publication. English. Six times a year. $750.00. Pergamon Press, An Imprint of Elsevier Science Ltd., The Boulevard, Langford Lane, Kidlington, Oxford OX5 1GB United Kingdom. **Tel** 011 44 1865 843000, 011 44 1865 843699, FAX 011 44 1865 843010. (**Subscription address:** Elsevier Science Ltd. / Oxford Fulfillment Centre, PO Box 800, Kidlington OX5 1DX United Kingdom. **Tel** 011 44 865 843355.) **ED** Robert D. Myers. **Bk Rev**. **Ad Acc**. ctrl circ. available on microfilm and microfiche from University Microfilms International (UMI); available on an online database from Elsevier Electronic Subscriptions (EES). Documents available from The Genuine Article, CASDDS. ***Absorbed*** *Alcohol and Drug Research, 0883-1386.*
Desc: Dedicated to in-depth reporting of the burgeoning literature on alcoholism as a disease state. Topics in this regard include: biomedical factors in the etiology of alcoholism, biological and biochemical markers in the identification of alcoholism, new drugs and chemotherapeutic strategies in the treatments of alcoholism, alcohol withdrawal, and fetal alcohol syndrome.
Ind/Abst Anim. Behav. Abstr.; Chem. Abstr. (1984-); CSA Neuro. Abstr.; Curr. Aware. Biol. Sci., CABS; Curr. Cit.; Curr. Contents Life Sci.; EMBASE; Health Saf. Sci. Abstr.; Health Plan. Adminis.; Index Med. (Vol. 1, No. 1, 1984-); INIS Atomindex [Micro.]; Nutr. Abstr. Rev., Ser. A, Hum. Exp.; Nutr. Res. Newsl.; Psychol. Abstr. (1984-); PsycINFO (1990-); Ref. Upd. Deluxe Ed.; Res. Alert [Full Cov.]; Sci. Cit. Index; SCISEARCH; Soc. Sci. Cit. Index [Select. Cov.]; Toxicol. Abstr.

LC HV5285 .A37 **ISSN** 0090-838X
DD 362.2/92/0973 US
NLM W1 AL303H **CODEN** AHRWDZ
Pr Rev.

ALCOHOL HEALTH AND RESEARCH WORLD. [Alcohol health res. world]. **Added/Corp** National Institute on Alcohol Abuse and Alcoholism (U.S.) United States. Alcohol, Drug Abuse, and Mental Health Administration. **VFOAT** Alcohol Health & Research World. Vol. 1, No. 1 (Spring 1973)-. Government Publication. English. Four times a year. $23.00. US Department of Health and Human Services, 200 Independence Avenue Southwest, Washington DC 20201. (**Subscription address:** Superintendent of Documents, US Government Printing Office, Washington DC 20402.) **ED** Dianne Welsh. Index available. cum. index. **Circ:** 8,000 (ctrl). available on microfilm and microfiche from University Microfilms International (UMI); available on an online database (file 149/Full-Text) from DIALOG. Documents available from Magazine Collection, UMI Article Clearinghouse, CASDDS, Documents on Demand.
Desc: Presents current research findings; prevention, treatment, and training program descriptions; and observations with opinions from those working at the base level to provide services to persons affected by alcohol-related problems. Each issue features in-depth coverage of a special topic in the alcohol and allied fields.
Ind/Abst Acad. Abstr.; Acad. Ind. [Computer File] (1992-); Acad. Search; AGRICOLA [Select. Cov.]; Am. Stat. Index; Biol. Dig.; Chem. Abstr.; Curr. Cit.; EP Collect.; Expand. Acad. Index (1992-); Gen. Period. Index (1992-); Gen. Sci. Source; Health Index (1989-); Health Period. Database [Full Txt.]; Health Plan. Adminis.; Health Ref. Cent. (Jan. 1989-) [Full Txt.] [Full Cov.]; Health Source Plus; Health Source; Highw. Res. Abstr.; Homework Help.; Hosp. Health Admin. Index; INFO-SOUTH Abstr.; Mag. Artic. Summar. Elite; Mag. Artic. Summar. Select; Mag. Artic. Summar. CD-ROM; Mag. ASAP Plus [Full Txt.]; Mag. Index Plus (1992-); Mag. Search; MasterFile FullTEXT 1000; MasterFile FullTEXT 350; MasterFile FullTEXT 650; MasterFile FullTEXT (Jan. 1990-) [Full Txt.]; Middle East Abstr. Index; Newsp. Period. Abstr. (1990-); Nutr. Res. Newsl.; OCLC; Psychol. Abstr. (1973-); PsycINFO; PsycLit; Pub. Lib. FullTEXT; Soc. Work Abstr. (Spring 1987-) [Select. Cov.]; Telebase; Vocat. Search; World Mag. Bank.

ISSN 0731-8049
US

ALCOHOL RESEARCH REVIEW SERIES. [Alcohol res. rev. ser.]. (19??)-. Monographic series. English. Irregular. Price varies per volume. Human Sciences Press, PO Box 735, Canal Street Station, New York NY 10013. **Tel** (212)620-8000, FAX (212)807-1047, telex 23421139.

LC HV5001 .O38a **ISSN** 0146-8332
DD 362.2/92/09766 US

ALCOHOL TECHNICAL REPORTS. **Main/Corp** Oklahoma. Dept. of Mental Health. Division On Alcoholism. **Added/Corp** University of Oklahoma. Center for Alcohol and Drug Related Studies. University of Oklahoma. Center for Alcohol-Related Studies. (1973)-. Periodical. English. Four times a year. Okalahoma State Dept. of Mental Health / Divison on Alcoholism, PO Box 53277 Capital Station, Oklahoma City OK 73105.

LC HV5280.S7 A4 **ISSN** 0161-9926
DD 362.2/92/025783 US

ALCOHOLISM AND DRUG ABUSE FACILITIES IN THE STATE OF SOUTH DAKOTA. English. One time a year. $3.50. South Dakota Department of Alcohol and Drug Abuse, 513 East Capitol, Pierre SD 57501. **Tel** (605)773-3123.

ISSN 1042-1394
DD 362 US
CCC
NLM W1; AL312L

ALCOHOLISM & DRUG ABUSE WEEK. [Alcohol. drug abuse week]. **VFOAT** Alcoholism & Drug Abuse Weekly; Alcoholism and Drug Abuse Week. Vol. 1, No. 1 (Jan. 11, 1989)-. Periodical. English. Forty-eight times a year. $499.00. Manisses Communications Group Inc., 208 Governor Street, PO Box 3357, Providence RI 02906. **Tel** (401)831-6020, (800)333-7771, FAX (401)861-6370. **ED** Gary Enos, Eric White and Robert Curley. Index available (free). available on an online database from DATA-STAR; BRS; and DIALOG. ***Continues*** *Drug Abuse Report, 0889-7050.*
Desc: Drug testing, AIDS and drugs prevention, treatment and education issues as well as Washington legislative and administrative developments affecting the field of alcoholism and drug abuse.
Ind/Abst Acad. Search; EP Collect.; Health Index (1989-1991); Health Period. Database [Full Txt.]; Health Ref. Cent. (Jan. 1989-) [Full Txt.] [Full Cov.]; Health Source Plus; Health Source; Homework Help.; MasterFile FullTEXT 1000; MasterFile FullTEXT 350; MasterFile FullTEXT 650; MasterFile FullTEXT (July 1994-) [Full Txt.]; OCLC; Soc. Sci. Source; Telebase.

LC HV **ISSN** 1076-2507
DD 362 US
UDC 36
ALCOHOLISM BRIEFS. [Alcohol. briefs]. **VFOAT** Alcoholism. (1986)-. Periodical. English. Four times a year (Jan., Apr., July, Oct.). $8.95. Del Mar Publications Inc., 1165 Elmwood Place, Deerfield IL 60015. **Tel** (312)945-1790.
Desc: Provides a clearing house and exchange for concise news and information on alcoholism and related subjects.

LC RC565 .A4456 **ISSN** 0145-6008
DD 616.8/61/005 US
CCC
NLM W1 AL309R **CODEN** ACRSDM
Pr Rev.
ALCOHOLISM : CLINICAL AND EXPERIMENTAL RESEARCH. [Alcohol., clin. exp. res.]. **Added/Corp** American Medical Society on Alcoholism. Research Society on Alcoholism (U.S.) National Council on Alcoholism. American Medical Society on Alcoholism and Other Drug Dependencies. International Society for Biomedical Research on Alcoholism. **VFOAT** Alcoholism. Vol. 1 (Jan. 1977)-. Academic Scholarly Publication. English. Six times a year. $345.00. Williams & Wilkins Company, 428 East Preston Street, Baltimore MD 21202-3993. **Tel** (410)528-4000, (800)638-6423, FAX (410)528-8596, telex 87669. **(Subscription address:** Williams & Wilkins, PO Box 64380, Baltimore MD 21264. **Tel** 800 638-6423.) **ED** Marcus A. Rothschild. **Ad Acc. Circ:** 1,500. available on microfilm. Documents available from The Genuine Article, BIOSIS Document Express, CASDDS, Quick Copies.
Desc: Presents the current articles on alcoholism, including clinical studies and research findings on alcoholism and alcohol-induced syndromes and organ damage.
Ind/Abst Annals Behav. Med.; Biol. Abstr.; Chem. Abstr.; Cumul. Index Nurs. Allied Health Lit.; Curr. Cit.; Curr. Contents Life Sci.; Dairy Sci. Abstr.; EMBASE; Entomol. Abstr.; Health Plan. Adminis.; Index Med.; Med. Abstr. Newsl.; Nutr. Abstr. Rev., Ser. B, Live Feeds and Feed.; Nutr. Abstr. Rev., Ser. A, Hum. Exp.; Psychol. Abstr. (1981-); PsycINFO; PsycLit; Ref. Upd. Deluxe Ed.; Res. Alert [Full Cov.]; Sci. Cit. Index; SCISEARCH; Soc. Sci. Cit. Index [Select. Cov.]; Trop. Dis. Bull.

LC HV5001 .A34 **ISSN** 0093-3279
DD 362.2/92 US
NLM ZWM 274 A354
ALCOHOLISM DIGEST ANNUAL, THE. [Alcohol. dig. annu.]. Vol. 1 (1972/73)-. English. Information Planning Associates / Maryland, 310 Maple Drive, Rockville MD 20850.

ISSN 0276-3613
DD 362 US
ALCOHOLISM REPORT, THE. [Alcohol. rep.]. **Added/Corp** Johnson Institute (Minneapolis, Minn.). Vol. 1 (1972)-. Newsletter. English. Twelve times a year (monthly). $97.00. National Council on Alcoholism and Drug Dependence, 1511 K Street Northwest, Suite 938, Washington DC 20005. **Tel** (202)737-7342, FAX (202)628-4731. **(Subscription address:** Alcoholism Report, Subscription Office, PO Box 11318, Birmingham AL 35202-1318. **Tel** (800)633-4931, FAX (205)995-1588.) **ED** Neil Scott. Index available (free). **Circ:** 2,500.
Desc: Covering national developments in the field of alcoholism and drug dependence, with a special emphasis on events at the federal level.
Ind/Abst Acad. Abstr.; Acad. Search; EP Collect.; Gen. Sci. Source; Health Index (1989-); Health Period. Database [Full Txt.]; Health Ref. Cent. (Jan. 1989-) [Full Txt.] [Full Cov.]; Health Source Plus; Health Source; Homework Help.; INFO-SOUTH Abstr.; Mag. Artic. Summar. Elite; Mag. Artic. Summar. Select; Mag. Artic. Summar. CD-ROM; Mag. Search; MasterFile FullTEXT 1000; MasterFile FullTEXT 350; MasterFile FullTEXT 650; MasterFile FullTEXT (Jan. 1992-) [Full Txt.]; OCLC; Pub. Lib. FullTEXT; Telebase; Vocat. Search.

LC WMLC 93/1994 **ISSN** 0734-7324
DD 616 US
NLM W1; AL3147
Pr Rev.
ALCOHOLISM TREATMENT QUARTERLY. [Alcohol. treat. q.]. Vol. 1, No. 1 (Spring 1984)-. Periodical. English. Four times a year. $235.00. The Haworth Press Inc., 10 Alice Street, Binghamton NY 13904-1580. **Tel** (607)722-5857, (800)3-HAWORTH, FAX (607)722-1424. **ED** Thomas F. McGovern (editor's address: Southwest Institute for Addictive Diseases, Department of Psychiatry, Texas Tech University, Health Sciences Center, PO Box 5864, Lubbock, TX 79417). **Bk Rev. Ad Acc. Acid Free. Circ:** 628. available on microfilm and microfiche from University Microfilms International (UMI). Documents available from Haworth Document Delivery Service.
Desc: Dedicated to the needs of clinicians who work with alcoholic clients and their families. A wide variety of helping professionals consult the journal in their everyday practice.
Ind/Abst Abstr. Res. Pastor. Care Couns. (19??-); Crim. Justice Abstr.; Crim. Penol. Police Sci. Abstr.; Curr. Cit.; EMBASE; EP Collect.; Health Source Plus; Health Source; Homework Help.; Index Period. Artic. Relat. Law; Linguist. Lang. Behav. Abstr.; MasterFile FullTEXT 1000; MasterFile FullTEXT 350; MasterFile FullTEXT 650; MasterFile FullTEXT; OCLC; Psychol. Abstr. (1984-); PsycINFO; Refer. Z.; Soc. Plann. Policy Dev. Abstr.; Soc. Work Abstr. [Select. Cov.]; Sociol. Abstr.; Stud. Women Abstr.; Telebase.

ISSN 0002-502X
CI
NLM W1 AL309P **CODEN** ALCMAN
ALCOHOLISM (ZAGREB). (ALCOHOLISM.). [Alcoholism]. **Added/Corp** International Council on Alcohol and Addictions, Centar za Proucavanje i Suzbijanje Alkoholizma i Drugih Ovisnosti (Zagreb, Croatia). Vol. 1 (1965)-. Academic Scholarly Publication. English. Two times a year. $30.00. Center of Study Control Alcoholism, Vinogradska 29, 41000 Zagreb Croatia. available on microfilm and microfiche from University Microfilms International (UMI). Documents available from BIOSIS Document Express.
Ind/Abst Biol. Abstr.; EMBASE; Nutr. Res. Newsl.

ISSN 0394-9826
IT
UDC 178
Pr Rev.
ALCOLOGIA. [Alcologia]. (1989)-. Periodical. Multiple languages (Italian). Three times a year. L54500. Editrice Compositori SRL, Viale Stalingrado 97 2, 40128 Bologna Italy. **Tel** 011 39 51 327811. **ED** G. Gasbarrini, R. Naccarato and C. Surrenti. Index available. **Bk Rev. Ad Acc. Circ:** 3,000.
Desc: Publishes original and unpublished articles that strive to widen and improve knowledge of the topics connected with alcohology. Alcohology includes all subjects studying the relationships between alcohol and man as concerns production, preservation, distribution, and consumption with special reference to the physical, psychological, economic and legal implications at a social and individual level.

ISSN 0002-5054
FR
UDC 362.1:613.81
ALCOOL OU SANTE PARIS. [Alcool sante Paris]. **Added/Corp** Association Nationale de Prevention de l'Alcoolisme (France). (1951)-. Periodical. French. Four times a year. $22.97. ANPA, 20 rue Saint Fiacre, 75002 Paris France. **Tel** 011 33 1 42335104, FAX 45 08 17 02. **Bk Rev. Circ:** 10,000 (ctrl). ***Continues*** *L'Etoile Bleue (Saint-Hippolyte-du-Fort), 0999-2650.*
Desc: Medico-social aspects of alcoholism in France and in the world. Alcohol control policies (schools, firms, road, etc.).

ISSN 0345-0732
SW
UDC 364
ALKOHOL OCH NARKOTIKA. [Alkohol nark.]. (1973)-. Periodical. Multiple languages. Six times a year. Kr275.00. CAN, Box 27302, S-102 54 Stockholm Sweden. **Tel** 011 46 8 667-9720. ***Continues*** *Alkoholfragan, 0002-5518.*

LC Z7721 .A43 HY5515.5
DD 016.36229/2/094897 FI
CEASED
ALKOHOLIKIRJALLISUUS SUOMESSA. **Added/Corp** Alkon Kirjasto- Ja Tietopalvelu. **VFOAT** Alcohol Literature in Finland in ... . (1972)-(1993). English (Finnish). Alko Ltd, Box 350, 00101 Helsinki Finland. **Tel** 011 358 01332982, FAX 011 358 01332386.

ISSN 0355-9750
FI
UDC 364
ALKOHOLIPOLITIIKKA. [Alkoholipolitiikka]. **VFOAT** Alcohol Policy. (1953)-. Periodical. Finnish. Six times a year. Alko Ltd, Box 350, 00101 Helsinki Finland. **Tel** 011 358 01332982, FAX 011 358 01332386.
Ind/Abst Soc. Plann. Policy Dev. Abstr.

LC HD9365.F5 V86 **ISSN** 0783-1374
FI
ALKOHOLITILASTOLLINEN VUOSIKIRJA = ALKOHOLSTATISTISK AARSBOK = ALCOHOL STATISTICAL YEARBOOK. **Added/Corp** Alko Oy. **VFOAT** Alkoholstatistisk Aarsbok; Alcohol Statistical Yearbook. (198?)-. Statistical Publication. Finnish (English, Finnish and Swedish). Tiedotuspalvelu, PO Box 350, SF-00101 Helsinki 10, Finland. ***Continues*** *Vuosikirja (Alko Oy), 0356-6730.*

LC HV5537 .A3
DD 362.29209 SW
ALKOHOLSTATISTIK. **See** Drug Abuse and Alcoholism-Abstracting, Bibliographies and Statistics.

LC HV5285 .A5 **ISSN** 0195-1556
DD 178.505 US
AMERICAN ISSUE (DES MOINES), THE. (THE AMERICAN ISSUE.). **Added/Corp** Anti-saloon League of America. National Temperance League (U.S.) American Council on Alcohol Problems. (1906)-. English. Twelve times a year (with monthly donor letter). Comes with membership to American Council of Alcohol Problems - $25.00. American Council of Alcohol Problems, 3426 Bridgeland Drive, Bridgeton MO 63044. **Tel** (314)739-5944, FAX (314)739-0848. **Circ:** 1,000 (ctrl). ***Absorbed*** *American Patriot; New Republic* ***and*** *National Daily.*

LC HV5800 .A43 **ISSN** 0095-2990
DD 362.2/9/05 US
CCC
NLM W1 AM45S **CODEN** AJDABD
Pr Rev.
AMERICAN JOURNAL OF DRUG AND ALCOHOL ABUSE, THE. [Am. j. drug alcohol abuse]. Vol. 1 (1974)-. Academic Scholarly Publication. English. Four times a year. $495.00. Marcel Dekker Inc., 270 Madison Avenue, New York NY 10016. **Tel** (212)696-9000, (800)228-1160, FAX (212)685-4540, telex 421419. **(Subscription address:** Marcel Dekker Inc., PO Box 5017, Monticello NY 12701. **Tel** (800)228-1160.) **ED** Edward Kaufman, Richard J. Frances and E. Mansell Pattison. **Bk Rev. Ad Acc.** available on microfiche. Documents available from The Genuine Article, BIOSIS Document Express, CASDDS.
Desc: Dedicated to the presentation of essential aspects of drug and alcohol abuse by established workers in their respective fields. Epidemiology, causes, effects, and treatment are all critically covered, as is the exciting work in endogenous opiates and opiate and benzodiazepine receptors. Interdisciplinary in scope, it provides the essential forum for exchanging ideas among the full range of disciplines - including sociology, medicine, and public health - that contribute to the understanding and treatment of drug and alcohol abuse.
Ind/Abst Acad. Search; Annals Behav. Med.; Biol. Abstr.; Chem. Abstr.; Curr. Cit.; Curr. Contents Soc. Behav. Sci.; EMBASE; EP Collect.; Gen. Sci. Index; Gen. Sci. Source; Health Index (1989-); Health Period. Database [Full Txt.]; Health Ref. Cent. (Jan. 1989-) [Full Cov.]; Health Source Plus; Health Source; Highw. Res. Abstr.; Homework Help.; Index Med.; INFO-SOUTH Abstr.; Int. Pharm. Abstr.; Linguist. Lang. Behav. Abstr.; Mag. Search; MasterFile FullTEXT 1000; MasterFile FullTEXT 350; MasterFile FullTEXT 650; MasterFile FullTEXT (Jan. 1993-); Middle East Abstr. Index; Nutr. Res. Newsl.; OCLC; Life Sci. Collect.; Psychol. Abstr. (1976-); PsycINFO; PsycLit; Ref. Upd. Deluxe Ed.; Res. Alert [Full Cov.]; Risk Abstr.; Soc. Plann. Policy Dev. Abstr.; Soc. Sci. Cit. Index [Full Cov.]; Soc. Work Abstr. (Spring, Summer 1987-) [Select. Cov.]; Sociol. Abstr.; Telebase.

ISSN 1055-0496
DD 616 US
NLM W1; AM532
Pr Rev.
AMERICAN JOURNAL ON ADDICTIONS, THE. (THE AMERICAN JOURNAL ON ADDICTIONS/ AMERICAN ACADEMY OF PSYCHIATRISTS IN ALCOHOLISM AND ADDICTIONS.). [Am. j. addict.]. **Added/Corp** American Academy of Psychiatrists in Alcoholism and Addictions. Vol. 1, No. 1 (Winter 1992)-. Periodical. English. Four times a year. $135.00. American Psychiatric Press Inc., 1400 K Street Northwest, Suite 1101, Washington DC 20005. **Tel** (202)682-6222, FAX (202)789-2648. **Ad Acc.**
Desc: Covers everything from co-dependence to genetics, epidemiology to dual diagnosis, and more. Editorial features include overview articles, original reports and clinical studies, and case reports.

LC HV5825 .A7215
DD 362.2/9/05 US
ANNUAL EDITIONS. DRUGS, SOCIETY, AND BEHAVIOR. **VFOAT** Drugs, Society, and Behavior. 1st Ed. (1986/87)-. Periodical. English. One time a year. $10.95. Dushkin Publishing Group Inc., Sluice Dock, Guilford CT 06437. **Tel** (203)453-4351, (800)243-6532, FAX (203)453-6000. **ED** Erich Goode.
Desc: A broad collection of carefully selected current articles addressing the widespread use and abuse of drugs in society and their physical, social, and psychological effects.

LC HV5825 .U5634a **ISSN** 0739-246X
DD 362.2/93/0973 US
ANNUAL REPORT FROM THE SECRETARY OF THE DEPARTMENT OF HEALTH AND HUMAN SERVICES TO THE PRESIDENT AND CONGRESS OF THE UNITED STATES : DRUG ABUSE PREVENTION, TREATMENT, AND REHABILITATION. [Annu. rep. Secr. Dep. Health Hum. Serv. Pres. Congr. U. S., Drug abuse prev., treat., rehabil.]. **Main/Corp** United States. Dept. of Health and Human Services. **Added/Corp** National Institute on Drug Abuse. **VFOAT** Drug Abuse Prevention, Treatment, and Rehabilitation. (Fiscal Year 1980)-. English. One time a year. US Department of Health and Human Services, 200 Independence Avenue Southwest, Washington DC 20201. ***Continues*** *United States. Dept. of Health, Education, and Welfare. Annual Report from the Secretary of the Department of Health, Education, and Welfare to the President and the Congress of the United States, 0270-1502.*

Drug Abuse and Alcoholism

LC HV5831.P4 A2A **ISSN** 0149-7596
DD 353.9/748/008429 US
ANNUAL REPORT - GOVERNOR'S COUNCIL ON DRUG AND ALCOHOL ABUSE. (ANNUAL REPORT - GOVERNOR'S COUNCIL ON DRUG AND ALCOHOL ABUSE (PENNSYLVANIA).). **Main/Corp** Pennsylvania. Governor's Council on Drug and Alcohol Abuse. English. One time a year. Governor's Council on Drug and Alcohol Abuse, 2101 North Front Street, Building No. 1, Harrisburg PA 17110.

LC HV5297.M3 M36A **ISSN** 0883-3249
DD 362.2/9286/09752 US
ANNUAL REPORT - MARYLAND. ADVISORY COUNCIL ON ALCOHOLISM CONTROL. (ANNUAL REPORT / ADVISORY COUNCIL ON ALCOHOLISM CONTROL.). **Main/Corp** Maryland. Advisory Council on Alcoholism Control. English. One time a year. Advisory Council on Alcoholism Control, 201 West Preston Street, Baltimore MD 21201.

LC HV5086.O5 O38a **ISSN** 0093-6243
DD 353.9/766/00761 US
ANNUAL REPORT OF THE OKLAHOMA ALCOHOLIC BEVERAGE CONTROL BOARD. (ANNUAL REPORT.). **Main/Corp** Oklahoma. Alcoholic Beverage Control Board. (19??)-. Periodical. English. One time a year. Alcoholic Beverage Control Board, 210 NE 4th, Room 100, Oklahoma City OK 73104.

LC HV5280.I4 I34A **ISSN** 0160-161X
DD 353.9/773/008429205 US
ANNUAL REPORT, STATE OF ILLINOIS ALCOHOLISM PLANS AND PROGRAMS. **Main/Corp** Illinois. Alcoholism Division. English. One time a year. Illinois Alcoholism Plans and Programs, Department of Mental Health and Developmental Disabilities, Suite 1900 188 West Randolph Street, Chicago IL 60601.

LC HV5840.C32 B72a **ISSN** 0704-2493
DD 354/.711/00842905 CN
ANNUAL REPORT TO THE LEGISLATURE OF THE ALCOHOL AND DRUG COMMISSION (VICTORIA). (ANNUAL REPORT TO THE LEGISLATURE OF THE ALCOHOL AND DRUG COMMISSION.). **Main/Corp** British Columbia. Alcohol and Drug Commission. **VAT** Annual Report - B.C. Alcohol & Drug Commission; Annual Report - British Columbia Alcohol and Drug Commission; Annual Report - Alcohol and Drug Commission (Victoria). (1974)-. English. One time a year. Alcohol and Drug Commission, #705 805 W. Broadway, Box 50, Vancouver BC V5Z 1K1. **Continues** British Columbia. Alcohol and Drug Commission. Special Report to the Legislature of the Alcohol and Drug Commission.

LC RC563 .A56 **ISSN** 0955-663X
US
CCC
NLM W1; AN769IE **CODEN** AARTEC
TITLE CHANGE
ANNUAL REVIEW OF ADDICTIONS RESEARCH AND TREATMENT. **VFOAT** Addictions Research and Treatment. Vol. 1 (1991/-199?). English. Pergamon Press, An Imprint of Elsevier Science Ltd., The Boulevard, Langford Lane, Kidlington, Oxford OX5 1GB United Kingdom. **Tel** 011 44 1865 843000, 011 44 1865 843699, FAX 011 44 1865 843010. **ED** Peter Nathan. **Continued by** Addictive Behaviors, 0306-4603.

LC JX1977 .A2
DD 614.3 178.8 US
ANNUAL SUMMARY OF LAWS AND REGULATIONS RELATING TO THE CONTROL OF NARCOTIC DRUGS. See Law-International Law.

LC HV5297.A4 A46B **ISSN** 0146-9053
DD 362.2/92/09798 US
ANNUAL UPDATE TO THE ALASKA STATE PLAN FOR THE REDUCTION OF ALCOHOLISM AND ALCOHOL ABUSE. **Main/Corp** Alaska. Office of Alcoholism. English. One time a year. Department of Health and Social Services / Office of Alcoholism and Drug Abuse, Pouch H-05F, Juneau AK 99811.

ISSN 0389-4118
JA
NLM W1 AR962C **CODEN** AKYIDF
ARUKORU KENKYU TO YAKUBUTSU IZON. [Arukoru kenkyu to yakubutsu izon]. **Added/Corp** Nihon Arukoru Igakkai. **VFOAT** Japanese Journal of Alcohol Studies and Drug Dependence; Japanese Journal of Alcohol Studies & Drug Dependence. Vol. 16, No. 1 (March 1981)-. Academic Scholarly Publication. Japanese (English; summaries and/or abstracts in English). Four times a year. $45.00. Japanese Medical Society of Alcohol Studies, Kawaramachi Hirokoji Kamikyoku, Kyoto 602 Japan. **Tel** 011 81 75-251-5343, FAX (075)241-0824. Index available. cum. index. **Ad Acc.** ctrl circ. Documents available from BIOSIS Document Express, CASDDS. **Continues** Arukoru Kenkyu, 0021-5244.
Desc: Covers topics on alcohol, alcoholism and drug dependence.
Ind/Abst Biol. Abstr.; Chem. Abstr.; EMBASE; Health Plan. Adminis.; Index Med.

US
AUDIOVISUAL CATALOG - NIDA RESOURCE CENTER. **Main/Corp** National Institute on Drug Abuse. Resource Center. Catalog. English. National Institute on Drug Abuse, 5600 Fishers Lane, Room 199 - 55, Rockville MD 20852. **Tel** (301)443-6637.

LC HV5297.T4 **ISSN** 0737-6383
DD 353.97640084/29 US
AUDIT REPORT. TEXAS COMMISSION ON ALCOHOLISM. **Main/Corp** Texas Commission on Alcoholism. **VFOAT** Texas Commission on Alcoholism. (1955)-. English. One time a year. State Auditor, John H Reagan, State Office Building, PO Box 12067, Austin TX 78711.

ISSN 0812-3837
AT
NLM W1; AU46U
AUSTRALIAN ADVERSE DRUG REACTIONS BULLETIN. [Aust. adverse drug react. bull.]. **Added/Corp** Australian Drug Evaluation Committee. Adverse Drug Reactions Advisory Committee. (1982)-. Bulletin. English. Four times a year. Free on request. Australian Adverse Drug Reactions Bulletin, PO Box 100, Woden Australian Capital Territory 2606 Australia. **Tel** 011 61 62 898538.

ISSN 1075-6701
DD 362 US
NLM W1; BE13GM
●**BEHAVIORAL HEALTH MANAGEMENT.** [Behav. health man.]. Vol. 14, No. 1 (Jan./Feb. 1994)-. Periodical. English. Six times a year. $60.00. Medquest Communications Inc., 629 Euclid Avenue, Suite 500, Cleveland OH 44114. **Tel** (216)522-9700. **ED** Richard Peck. **Continues** Addiction & Recovery, 1052-4614.
Desc: Looks at the field of behavioral health with a continued emphasis on addictions treatment. Subjects include networking trends, risk management, and legal liabilities.
Ind/Abst Acad. Abstr.; Acad. Search; EP Collect.; Health Source Plus; Health Source; Homework Help.; MasterFile FullTEXT 1000; MasterFile FullTEXT 350; MasterFile FullTEXT 650; MasterFile FullTEXT (Jan. 1994-) [Full Txt.]; OCLC; Telebase.

ISSN 0227-1567
DD 362.2/9286/09714 CN
BENEVOLE, LE. [Benevole]. Vol. 1 (Jan. 1974)-. Periodical. French. Six times a year. Free. Federation Des Organismes Benevoles Pour Le Traitement, Et La Prevention Des Alcooliques Et Des Toxicomanes Du Quebec, Chamber 10, 945 rue Turnbull Sous-Sol, Quebec Quebec G1R 2X6. ctrl circ.

ISSN 0273-0162
US
BLUE BOOK (TULSA), THE. (THE BLUE BOOK.). [Blue Book]. **Main/Conf** National Clergy Conference on Alcoholism, Vol. 1 (1949)-. Proceedings. English. One time a year. $10.00. National Catholic Council on Alcoholism, 1550 Hendrickson Street, Brooklyn NY 11234. **Tel** (718)951-7177, FAX (718)951-7233. **ED** James J. Ruddick. **Circ:** 1,000.

ISSN 0392-3126
IT
UDC 178
BOLLETTINO PER LE FARMACODIPENDENZE E L'ALCOOLISMO. [Boll. Farmacodipend. alcool.]. (1978)-. Periodical. Italian (English). Six times a year. Free on request. Ministero Della Sanita, Viale Dell Industria #20, 00100 Rome Italy. **Tel** 011 39 6 5944 Ext 513. Index available. cum. index. **Bk Rev**. **Ad Acc**. **Circ:** 7,000.
Desc: Contains the recent legislative acts, and drug abuse and AIDS prevention policies at a national and international level.

ISSN 0891-6950
DD 362 US
NLM W1; BO917IL
BOTTOM LINE ON ALCOHOL IN SOCIETY, THE. **Added/Corp** American Business Men's Research Foundation. Alcohol Research Information Service (Lansing, Mich.). **VFOAT** Bottom Line. Vol. 2, No. 1 (Spring 1978)-. Periodical. English. Four times a year. $20.00. Alcohol Research Information Service, 1106 East Oakland Avenue, Box 10212, Lansing MI 48906. **Tel** (517)485-9900. **Continues** Bottom Line, 0161-1267.
Desc: Deals with research, issues, events and opinions relating to public policy in the field of alcohol problems, with special emphasis on prevention.

LC HV5275 .A53 **ISSN** 0362-2584
DD 362.2/92/05 US
BOX 1980. **VFOAT** AA Grapevine. **VAT** Box Nineteen Eighty. Vol. 30, No. 12 (May 1974)-. Periodical. English. Twelve times a year. $12.00 (one-year), $23.00 (two-year). AA Grapevine Inc., PO Box 1980 Grand Central Station, New York NY 10163. **Tel** (212)686-1100 ext. 55. **Continues** A.A. Grapevine.
Desc: The international monthly journal of Alcoholics Anonymous. The magazine is written almost entirely by AA members, who share their recovery with other AAs and air opinions and insights on what's happening in the Fellowship. There are occasional articles by nonalcoholics, and a section on AA's history several times a year. Many AAs use the magazine, not only as a tool for their own sobriety but for twelfth-stepping beginners, group discussion ideas, carrying the message to prisons and treatment centers, or for introducing interested nonalcoholics to the Fellowship.

LC RC563 .D54 **ISSN** 1040-6328
DD 616.86 US
CCC
NLM W1; BR91H
BROWN UNIVERSITY DIGEST OF ADDICTION THEORY AND APPLICATION. (BROWN UNIVERSITY DIGEST OF ADDICTION THEORY AND APPLICATION : DATA.). [Brown Univ. dig. addict. theory appl.]. **Added/Corp** Brown University. Center for Alcohol and Addiction Studies. **VFOAT** Digest of Addiction Theory and Application; DATA. Vol. 6, No. 2 (Feb. 1987)-. Academic Scholarly Publication. Twelve times a year (monthly). $179.00. Manisses Communications Group Inc., 208 Governor Street, PO Box 3357, Providence RI 02906. **Tel** (401)831-6020, (800)333-7771, FAX (401)861-6370. **ED** Dr. David Lewis and Dr. Anne Marshall Christner. Index available. cum. index. **Ad Acc**. **Circ:** 3,500. available on an online database (file 149/Full-Text) from DIALOG. **Continues** Digest of Addiction Theory and Application, 0887-8145.
Desc: Digest of articles that have appeared in medical and professional journals concerning addiction.
Ind/Abst EP Collect.; Health Index (1989-); Health Period. Database [Full Txt.]; Health Source Plus; Health Source; Homework Help.; MasterFile FullTEXT 1000; MasterFile FullTEXT 350; MasterFile FullTEXT 650; MasterFile FullTEXT; OCLC; Telebase.

ISSN 0995-3671
FR
UDC 362.1:613.81
Pr Rev.
BULLETIN DE LIAISON DU CNDT. **VFOAT** Bulletin de Liaison - Centre National de Documentation sur les toxicomanies; Bulletin de Liaison du Centre National de Documentation sur les Toxicomanies. (1982)-. Bulletin. French. Two times a year. 250.00F France; 500.00F other. Centre National de Documentation sur la Toxicomanie, Centre Berthelot, 14 Avenue Berthelot, 69007 Lyon France. **Tel** 011 33 1 72792307. Acid Free.
Desc: Focus is based on the issues of illegal drugs with a multidisciplinary approach.

CN
NLM W2; DC2 A5c
CANADIAN PROFILE. ALCOHOL & OTHER DRUGS. **Added/Corp** Addiction Research Foundation (Ont.). **VFOAT** Alcohol & other Drugs; Canadian Profile: Alcohol and other Drugs; Alcohol and other Drugs. (1992)-. Periodical. English. One time a year. 30.77Can$. Addiction Research Foundation, 33 Russell Street, Toronto Ontario M5S 2S1 Canada. **Tel** (416)595-6000, FAX (416)595-5017. **Continues in part** Statistics on Alcohol and Drug Use in Canada and other Countries.

LC HV5297.I3 I43a
DD 362.2/9 US
COMPREHENSIVE STATE PLAN AND HUMAN SERVICES PLAN FOR THE PREVENTION/INTERVENTION/ TREATMENT OF ALCOHOLISM AND OTHER DRUG DEPENDENCY FOR FISCAL YEARS, A. **Main/Corp** Illinois. Dept. of Alcoholism & Substance Abuse. **VFOAT** Comprehensive State Plan for Drug/Alcohol Services. (1992)-. English. Every 3 years. Illinois Department of Alcoholism and, Substance Abuse, 100 West Randolph Street, Suite 5-600, Chicago IL 60601. **Continues** Comprehensive State Plan for Alcoholism and Substance Abuse Services.

LC HV5831.V8 A27 **ISSN** 0361-9176
DD 362.2/93/09755 US
COMPREHENSIVE STATE PLAN FOR DRUG ABUSE CONTROL (VIRGINIA). **Main/Corp** Virginia. Dept. of Mental Health and Mental Retardation. Fiscal year 1978-. English. One time a year. Virginia Department of Mental Health and Mental Retardation, PO Box 1797, Richmond VA 23214. **Continues** Virginia. Division of Drug Abuse Control. Comprehensive State Plan for Drug Abuse Control, 0361-9176.

ISSN 0045-799X CN

CONCERNS (DON MILLS). (CONCERNS.). **Added/Corp** Alcohol and Drug Concerns, inc. Vol. 1 (Nov. 1970)-. Periodical. English. Four times a year. 12.00Can$. Alcohol and Drug Concerns Inc., 11 Progress Avenue/Suite 200, Scarborough Ontario M1P 4S7 Canada. **Tel** (905)293-3400. **ED** Karl N. Burgen. **Circ:** 16,000. ***Supersedes** Advocate, 0319-8065.*
Desc: Information about the work and programs of the organization, and articles about current issues.

LC HV5800 .C66 **ISSN** 0091-4509
DD 362.2/93/05 US
NLM W1 CO769MK
CONTEMPORARY DRUG PROBLEMS. [Contemp. drug probl.]. Vol. 1 (Winter 1972)-. Periodical. English. Four times a year. $45.00. Federal Legal Publications Inc., 157 Chambers Street, New York NY 10007. **Tel** (212)619-4949, FAX (212)608-3141. **ED** Robin Room. Index available. **Bk Rev**. **Ad Acc. Circ:** 3,000. available on microfilm and microfiche from University Microfilms International (UMI). Documents available from UMI Article Clearinghouse.
Desc: A journal designed to provide guidance to attorneys, educators, social workers, administrators, sociologists and doctors.
Ind/Abst Acad. Abstr.; Acad. Search; Crim. Justice Abstr.; Crim. Penol. Police Sci. Abstr.; Curr. Cit.; Curr. Law Index (1980-); EMBASE; EP Collect.; Expand. Acad. Index (1984-); Health Source Plus; Health Source; Homework Help.; Hum. Resour. Abstr. (?-?); INFO-SOUTH Abstr.; Int. Pharm. Abstr.; Leg. Resour. Index (1980-); LegalTrac (1980-); Linguist. Lang. Behav. Abstr.; Mag. Search; MasterFile FullTEXT 1000; MasterFile FullTEXT 350; MasterFile FullTEXT 650; MasterFile FullTEXT (Jan. 1992-); Middle East Abstr. Index; Newsp. Period. Abstr. (1991-); OCLC; Pub. Lib. FullTEXT; Soc. Plann. Policy Dev. Abstr.; Soc. Sci. Source; Soc. Sci. Index; Soc. Sci. Index Fulltext (Summer 1988-) [Full Txt.]; Sociol. Abstr.; Telebase.

US

CORNELL/SMITHERS REPORT ON WORKPLACE SUBSTANCE ABUSE POLICY. **Added/Corp** R. Brinkley Smithers Institute for Alcohol-Related Workplace Studies. **VFOAT** Report on Workplace Substance Abuse Policy. Vol. 1, Issue 1 (Jan. 1992)-. Periodical. English. Four times a year. New York State School of Industrial and Labor Relations, Cornell University, Ithaca NY 14853.

LC HV5279 .C68 **ISSN** 1047-7314
DD 362.29/15323/097305 US
Pr Rev.
COUNSELOR (ARLINGTON, VA.), THE. (THE COUNSELOR.). [Counselor]. **Added/Corp** National Association of Alcoholism and Drug Abuse Counselors (U.S.). (19??)-. Periodical. English. Six times a year. $36.00. NAADAC / National Association of Alcoholism and Drug Abuse Counselors, 3717 Columbia Pike, Suite 300, Arlington VA 22204. **Tel** (703)920-4644, FAX (703)920-4672. **ED** Laura Schmidt. **Ad Acc. Circ:** 17,000.
Desc: Covers developments, issues, research and treatment practices relating to the alcohol and drug abuse counseling profession.

US

NLM W1; CS199
CSAP TECHNICAL REPORT. **Added/Corp** Center for Substance Abuse Prevention (U.S.). (199?)-. Monographic series. English. US Department of Health and Human Services National Institutes of Health, 9000 Rockville Pike, Bethesda MD 20892. **Tel** (301)496-9291, FAX (301)496-2443. ***Continues** OSAP Technical Report.*

LC RC565 .C87 **ISSN** 0161-8504
US
NLM W3 CU615 **CODEN** CUALDU
CURRENTS IN ALCOHOLISM. [Curr. alcohol.]. Vol. 1 (1977)-. Academic Scholarly Publication. English. Price varies per volume. Grune & Stratton Inc., 6277 Sea Harbor Drive, Orlando FL 32887. **Tel** (800)782-4479, (407)345-2567. Documents available from CASDDS.
Ind/Abst Chem. Abstr.

LC Z7164.N17 D2 **ISSN** 0091-424X
DD 016.3622/93/0973 US
NLM ZWM 270 D111
DACAS: DRUG ABUSE CURRENT AWARENESS SYSTEM. [DACAS Drug abuse curr. awareness syst.]. **Added/Corp** National Clearinghouse for Drug Abuse Information. National Institute on Drug Abuse. **VFOAT** Drug Abuse Current Awareness System. Vol. 1 (July 3, 1972)-. Periodical. English. Twenty-six times a year. National Clearinghouse for Drug Abuse Information, 5600 Fishers Lane, Room 10 A 43, Rockville MD 20857. **Tel** (301)443-6500.

LC HV5825 .A72 **ISSN** 0196-4879
DD 362.2/9 US
DATA FROM THE CLIENT ORIENTED DATA ACQUISITION PROCESS. ANNUAL DATA. (ANNUAL DATA, DATA FROM THE CLIENT ORIENTED DATA ACQUISITION PROCESS.). [Data client oriented data acquis. process, Annu. data]. **VFOAT** Data from the Client Oriented Data Acquisition Process. (197?)-. English. One time a year. National Institute on Drug Abuse, 5600 Fishers Lane, Room 199 - 55, Rockville MD 20852. **Tel** (301)443-6637.

LC HV5825 .T75 **ISSN** 0197-0259
DD 362.2/9 US
DATA FROM THE CLIENT ORIENTED DATA ACQUISITION PROCESS. TREND REPORT. (TREND REPORT, DATA FROM THE CLIENT ORIENTED DATA ACQUISITION PROCESS / NATIONAL INSTITUTE ON DRUG ABUSE.). [Data client oriented data acquis. process, Trend rep.]. **Added/Corp** National Institute on Drug Abuse. Division of Scientific and Program Information. National Institute on Drug Abuse. Division of Data and Information Development. **VFOAT** Data from the Client Oriented Data Acquisition Process. (197?)-. English. One time a year. National Institute on Drug Abuse, 5600 Fishers Lane, Room 199 - 55, Rockville MD 20852. **Tel** (301)443-6637.

LC RC563 .N37 **ISSN** 0884-2132
US

DATA FROM THE DRUG ABUSE WARNING NETWORK. SEMIANNUAL REPORT. (SEMIANNUAL REPORT : DATA FROM THE DRUG ABUSE WARNING NETWORK.). [Data Drug Abuse Warn. Netw., Semiannu. rep.]. **VFOAT** DAWN Semiannual Reports; Data From the Drug Abuse Warning Network (DAWN). Semiannual Reports, Provisional Data. July-Dec. 1983-. English. Six times a year. Free. National Institute on Drug Abuse, 5600 Fishers Lane, Room 199 - 55, Rockville MD 20852. **Tel** (301)443-6637. **Circ:** 800 (ctrl). available on microfiche (Vols. for (1985-) distributed to depository libraries). ***Continues** Quarterly Report, Provisional Data.*
Desc: Trends in the semi-annual numbers of mentions of selected drugs in emergency room episodes and medical examiner cases.

ISSN 1121-0311
IT
UDC 613.83
DELFINO ROMA, IL. (IL DELFINO.). [Delfino Roma]. (1976)-. Periodical. Italian. Six times a year. L27250. Centro Italiano Di Solidarieta, Via Ambrosini 129, 00147 Rome Italy. **Tel** 011 39 6 5405945. **Bk Rev**, (Qty: 70/yr).

ISSN 0714-1017
DD 362.2/9/097123 CN
DEVELOPMENTS (EDMONTON). (DEVELOPMENTS / ALBERTA ALCOHOLISM AND DRUG ABUSE COMMISSION.). [Developments]. **Added/Corp** Alberta Alcoholism and Drug Abuse Commission. Vol. 1, Issue No. 1 (July 1981)-. Periodical. English. Ten times a year. Free on request. AAdac Production adn Distribution, 2nd Floor 10909 Jasper Avenue, Edmonton Alta T5J 3M9 Canada. **Tel** (403)427-7319. **Bk Rev**. **Circ:** 10,000 (ctrl).
Desc: Maintains a current awareness of addictions issues to professionals in the field and to interested others whose work may relate to addictions issues.

ISSN 1044-4149
DD 810 US
Pr Rev.
DIONYSOS (SUPERIOR, WISC.). (DIONYSOS.). [Dionysos]. **Added/Corp** University of Wisconsin--Superior. Vol. 1, No. 1 (Spring 1989)-. Periodical. English. Three times a year (Feb., June, Oct.). $12.00 (institutions); $8.00 (individuals). Dionysos, 1800 Grand Avenue, University of Wisconsin, Superior WI 54880. **Tel** (715)394-8480, FAX (715)394-8454. **ED** Roger Forseth (phone: (715)394-4577). Index available (Bound in Jan. iss.). **Bk Rev**, (Qty: 12-15). **Ad Acc. Circ:** 200.
Desc: This literature is devoted to critical and scholarly work concerning both the destructive and creative dimensions of intoxication in literary texts and biography.
Ind/Abst MLA Int. Bibl. Books Artic. Mod. Lang. Lit.

LC HV5275 .A88a **ISSN** 0145-2401
DD 362.2/92/0257 US
DIRECTORY - ASSOCIATION OF HALFWAY HOUSE ALCOHOLISM PROGRAMS OF NORTH AMERICA. **Main/Corp** Association of Halfway House Alcoholism Programs of North America. **VAT** Directory - Association of Halfway House Alcoholism Programs of North America, Incorporated. (19??)-. Directory. English. Association of Halfway House Programs of North America, 786 East 7th Street, St Paul MN 55106.

ISSN 0705-5587
DD 362.2/93/02571 CN
DIRECTORY. OCCUPATIONAL PROGRAMS - CANADIAN ADDICTIONS FOUNDATION. (DIRECTORY, OCCUPATIONAL PROGRAMS.). **VFOAT** Repertoire, Programmes Industriels. 1977-. Directory. English. Canadian Addictions Foundation, 303 Kendal Road, Vanier Ontario K1L 7S7 Canada.

LC HV5279 .D54 **ISSN** 0148-9771
DD 362.2/92/02573 US
DIRECTORY OF ALCOHOLISM COUNCILS IN AMERICA. Directory. English. American Council on Alcoholism, 5024 Campbell Road, Baltimore MD 21236. **Tel** (410)931-9393.

LC HV5831.M6 D57 **ISSN** 0734-0192
DD 362.2/9 US
DIRECTORY OF CHEMICAL DEPENDENCY PROGRAMS IN MINNESOTA. **Added/Corp** Minnesota. Dept. of Public Welfare. **VFOAT** Chemical Dependency Programs in Minnesota. (19??)-. English. Every 2 years. Minnesota Department of Human Services, Chemical Dependency Program Division, Human Services Building, 444 Lafayette Road, St Paul MN 55155-3823. **Tel** (612)296-3991. **ED** Carl C. Haerle. **Circ:** 1,500.
Desc: Comprehensive listing of chemical dependency treatment programs found in the state of Minnesota.

LC HV5825 .D56 **ISSN** 0361-1493
DD 362.2/9/02573 US
NLM WM 22 AA1 D3
DIRECTORY OF DRUG INFORMATION AND TREATMENT ORGANIZATIONS. (1972)-. Directory. English. Twelve times a year. Stash Library, 118 South Bedford Street, Madison WI 53703. ***Continues** Directory of Drug Information Groups, 0098-4701.*

LC HV5285 .R87A **ISSN** 0273-1657
DD 362.2/922/0973 US
DRINKERS, DRINKING AND ALCOHOL-RELATED MORTALITY AND HOSPITALIZATIONS. [Drink. drink. alcohol-relat. mortal. hosp.]. **Main/Corp** Rutgers University, New Brunswick, N.J. Center of Alcohol Studies. Publications Division. **VAT** Drinkers, Drinking and Alcohol Related Mortality and Hospitalizations. English. Publications Division of Rutgers Center of Alcohol Studies, PO Box 969, Piscataway NJ 08854. **Tel** (201)932-2190.
Desc: A publication related to statistics on alcohol problems and alcoholism.

ISSN 0363-0811
US
SUSPENDED
DRINKING AND DRUG PRACTICES SURVEYOR, THE. [Drink. drug pract. surv.]. **Added/Corp** University of California, Berkeley. School of Public Health. Social Research Group. No. 1 (Spring 1970)-No. 24 (June 1992). Periodical. English. Irregular. Alcohol Research Group, PO Box 9513, 1816 Scenic Avenue, Berkeley CA 94709. **Tel** (510)642-5208, FAX (510)642-7175, telex 6501015906 MCI UW. **ED** Robin Room. Index available. cum. index. **Bk Rev**. **Circ:** 600.
Desc: Multidisciplinary perspectives on general-population studies of alcohol and other drug practices and problems.
Ind/Abst EMBASE.

LC KF2231.A15 D74 **ISSN** 0730-2568
DD 345.73/0247 347.305247 US
DRINKING/DRIVING LAW LETTER. **See** Law.

ISSN 1062-3337
US

DRINKING, DRUGS & DRIVING. (DRINKING, DRUGS & DRIVING: RESEARCH INSTITUTE ON ALCOHOLISM.). **Added/Corp** New York (State). Division of Alcoholism and Alcohol Abuse. New York (State). Research Institute on Alcoholism. **VFOAT** Drinking, Drugs, and Driving. (1992)-. Monographic series. English. Price varies per volume. Research Institute on Alcoholism, Attn: Special Projects Coordinator, 1021 Main Street, Buffalo NY 14203-1016. ***Continues** Research Note (Problem-Drinker Driver Project (New York)), 1049-1813.*

ISSN 0160-0028
US
NLM W1 DR393 **CODEN** DAAND4
DRUG ABUSE & ALCOHOLISM NEWSLETTER. [Drug abuse alcohol. newsl.]. **VFOAT** Drug Abuse and Alcoholism Newsletter. Vol. 1 (Sept. 1971)-. Newsletter. English. Irregular. Free. Vista Hill Foundation, 3420 Camino Del Rio North/Suite 100, San Diego CA 92108. **Tel** (619)563-1770. **ED** Sid Cohen. **Circ:** 12,000 (ctrl). available on microfilm and microfiche from University Microfilms International (UMI).
Desc: Essays on state-of-art of abuse research and treatment.

UK

DRUG ABUSE CURRENT AWARENESS BULLETIN. (19??)-. Bulletin. English. Twelve times a year. £30.00 UK and Europe; £50.00 other. Institute for the Study of Drug Dependence, 32-36 Loman Street, Waterbridge House, London SE1 0EE United Kingdom. **Tel** 011 44 171 9281211, FAX 011 44 171 9281771.

LC HV5831.W2 A26B
DD 362.2/9386 US
DRUG ABUSE PREVENTION PLAN.
Main/Corp Washington (State). Dept. of Social and Health Services. English. One time a year. Department of Social and Health Services / Washington, Mail Stop OB-41K, Olympia WA 98504.

LC HV5825 .D774 **ISSN** 0091-5025
DD 362.2/93/0973 US
DRUG ABUSE PREVENTION REPORT.
Added/Corp National Clearinghouse for Drug Abuse Information. United States. Special Action Office for Drug Abuse Prevention. (19??)-. English. Twelve times a year. National Clearinghouse for Alcohol and Drug Information, PO Box 2345, Rockville MD 20852. **Tel** (800)729-6686, (301)468-2600.

US
NLM W1; DR397
DRUG ABUSE SERVICES RESEARCH SERIES. **Added/Corp** National Institute on Drug Abuse. United States. Alcohol, Drug Abuse, and Mental Health Administration. **VFOAT** NIDA Drug Abuse Services Research Series. No. 1 (1991)-. English. US Department of Health and Human Services, 200 Independence Avenue Southwest, Washington DC 20201.

ISSN 0283-8117
SW
DRUG ABUSE. **Added/Corp** Centralforbundet for Alkohol- Och Narkotikaupplysning (Sweden) Norway. Statens Edruskapsdirektorat. Centralforbundet for Alkohol- och Narkotikaupplysning (Sweden). Information and Documentation Center. (1986)-. Periodical. English. Four times a year. Free on request. Swedish Council for Information, PO Box 27302, S-10254 Stockholm Sweden. **Tel** 011 46 8 6616484. ***Continues** Drogmissbruk, 0349-1773.*

LC HV5825 .D776184 **ISSN** 0739-6562
DD 362.29/0973/05 US
DRUG ABUSE UPDATE. (DRUG ABUSE UPDATE : FROM THE FAMILIES IN ACTION DRUG INFORMATION CENTER.). [Drug abuse update]. **Added/Corp** Families in Action. Drug Information Center. Families in Action. National Drug Information Center. Scott Newman Center. No. 1 (June 1982)-. Newsletter. English. Four times a year (Mar., June, Spet.,Dec.). $30.00. National Families in Action, 2296 Henderson Mill Road, Suite 204, Atlanta GA 30345. **Tel** (404)934-6364, FAX (404)934-7137. **ED** Paula Kemp. Index available (additional $5.00). **Bk Rev**. **Ad Acc**. **Circ:** 16,000 (ctrl). ***Continues** Families in Action Newsletter.*
Desc: Abstracts current medical and scientific journals and common press for articles related to drug abuse.

LC RC564.73 .D775 **ISSN** 1067-814X
DD 362.29/025/73 US
DRUG, ALCOHOL, AND OTHER ADDICTIONS. (DRUG, ALCOHOL, AND OTHER ADDICTIONS : A DIRECTORY OF TREATMENT CENTERS AND PREVENTION PROGRAMS NATIONWIDE.). [Drug alcohol addict.]. **Added/Corp** Oryx Press. 1st Edition (1989)-. Directory. English. Irregular. $195.00 US; $234.00 other. Oryx Press, 4041 North Central Avenue #700, Phoenix AZ 85012-3397. **Tel** (800)279-6799, (602)265-2651, FAX (602)265-6250, (800)279-4663, (800)279-6799. **(Subscription address:** Eurospan Ltd., 3 Henrietta Street Covent Garden, London WC2E 8LU United Kingdom. **Tel** 011 44 181 2400856, FAX 011 44 181 3790609.)

LC RC566.A1 D66 **ISSN** 0376-8716
DD 616.8/6/005 SZ
CCC
NLM W1 DR46 **CODEN** DADEDV
Pr Rev.
DRUG AND ALCOHOL DEPENDENCE.
[Drug alcohol depend.]. **Added/Corp** International Council on Alcohol and Addictions. Vol. 1 (Sept. 1975)-. Academic Scholarly Publication. English. Twelve times a year (4 vols.). $986.00. Elsevier Science Ireland Ltd., Bay 15, Shannon Industrial Estate, Co Clare Ireland. **Tel** 011 353 61 471944. **ED** C.E. Johanson. Index available. available on microfilm and microfiche from University Microfilms International (UMI); available on an online database from Elsevier Electronic Subscriptions (EES). Documents available from The Genuine Article, BIOSIS Document Express, CASDDS.
Desc: Endeavours to be multidisciplinary and to promote rational approaches in research and intervention activities. Journal open to workers in the fields of biomedical as well as clinical, epidemiological, socio-cultural, education and medico-legal research.
Ind/Abst Abstr. Res. Pastor. Care Couns. (19??-); Appl. Soc. Sci. Index Abstr.; Biol. Abstr.; Chem. Abstr.; Crim. Penol. Police Sci. Abstr.; CSA Neuro. Abstr. (?-?); Cumul. Index Nurs. Allied Health Lit.; Curr. Cit.; Curr. Contents Life Sci.; EMBASE; Health Saf. Sci. Abstr.; Highw. Res. Abstr.; Index Med.; Int. Pharm. Abstr.; Middle East Abstr. Index; Life Sci. Collect.; Physic. Medline Plus; Psychol. Abstr. (1975-); PsycINFO; PsycLit; Ref. Upd. Deluxe Ed.; Res. Alert [Full Cov.]; Sci. Cit. Index; SCISEARCH; Soc. Plann. Policy Dev. Abstr.; Soc. Sci. Cit. Index [Select. Cov.]; Sociol. Abstr.; Toxicol. Abstr.

ISSN 0959-5236
UK
CCC
NLM W1; DR46D
DRUG AND ALCOHOL REVIEW.
Added/Corp Australian Medical and Professional Society on Alcohol and Other Drugs. (1990)-. Periodical. English. Four times a year. $382.00. Carfax Publishing Company, PO Box 25, Abingdon, Oxfordshire OX14 3UE United Kingdom. **Tel** 011 44 1235 555335, FAX 011 44 1235 553559, telex 817484. available on microfiche. ***Continues** Australian Drug and Alcohol Review, 0819-5331.*
Ind/Abst Curr. Cit.

ISSN 1076-1519
US
•**DRUG & CRIME PREVENTION FUNDING NEWS.** (June 1994)-. English. One time a week. $239.00. Government Information Services / Virginia, 4301 North Fairfax Drive, Suite 875, Arlington VA 22203. **Tel** (703)528-1082, FAX (703)528-6060, telex RCA 263591 GIS UR. **ED** Stephanie Neuben. ***Continues** Anti-Drug Funding Alert, 1060-4707.*
Desc: Covers developments affecting federal aid for anti-drug programs and law enforcement.

LC HV5825 .D7765 **ISSN** 0894-1300
DD 363.4/5/0973 US
DRUG ENFORCEMENT REPORT (NEW YORK, N.Y.). (DRUG ENFORCEMENT REPORT.). [Drug enforc. rep.]. Vol. 1, No. 1 (Oct. 8, 1984)-. Periodical. English. Twenty-four times a year. $197.00. Pace Publications / New York, PO Box 2972, Grand Central Station, New York NY 10163. **Tel** (212)685-5450, FAX (212)679-4701.

CN
DRUG FILE UPDATE. English. Two times a year. 49.00Can$. Sport Information Resource Centre, 1600 Promenade James Naismith Drive, Gloucester Ontario K1B 5N4 Canada. **Tel** (613)748-5658, FAX (613)748-5701, telex 053-3660 Sportrec Ott.
Desc: A current awareness index to publications on drugs and doping in sports.

US
DRUG FREE WORKPLACE REPORT.
(19??)-. English. Four times a year. $45.00. Institute for Drug Free Workplace, 1301 K Street Northwest, East Tower 1010, Washington DC 20005. **Tel** (202)842-7400.

ISSN 1073-8649
DD 364 US
CCC
•**DRUG POLICY REPORT.** [Drug policy rep.]. **Added/Corp** Drug Policy Research Institute (Arlington, Va.). (1994)-. Periodical. English. Twelve times a year. $189.00. Drug Policy Report, PO Box 3423, Arlington VA 22203. **Tel** (800)608-4618.

US
DRUG USE AMONG AMERICAN HIGH SCHOOL STUDENTS. (1977)-. Periodical. English. One time a year. US Department of Health and Human Services, 200 Independence Avenue Southwest, Washington DC 20201.

ISSN 0305-4349
UK
DRUGLINK INFORMATION LETTER.
VFOAT Druglink. Vol. 1, Issue 1 (Sept. 1974)-. Periodical. English. Six times a year. £12.00 UK; £15.00 US. Institute for the Study of Drug Dependence, 32-36 Loman Street, Waterbridge House, London SE1 0EE United Kingdom. **Tel** 011 44 171 9281211, FAX 011 44 171 9281771. **ED** Michael Ashton. **Bk Rev**. **Ad Acc**. **Circ:** 1,300 (ctrl).
Desc: A magazine for readers with a professional occupational interest in the response to drug misuse in Britain.

ISSN 0957-3100
UK
DRUGLINK LONDON. (DRUGLINK.). [Druglink Lond.]. (1986)-. Periodical. English. Six times a year (Jan., March, May, July, Sept., Nov.). $59.89. Institute for the Study of Drug Dependence, 32-36 Loman Street, Waterbridge House, London SE1 0EE United Kingdom. **Tel** 011 44 171 9281211, FAX 011 44 171 9281771. ***Continues** Druglink Information Letter, 0305-4349.*
Ind/Abst Appl. Soc. Sci. Index Abstr.; Curr. Cit.; SPORT Discus.

LC HV5825 .W3813 **ISSN** 0744-2823
DD 362.2/93/0973 US
NLM W1 DR892F
DRUGS AND DRUG ABUSE EDUCATION NEWSLETTER, (1982).
(DRUGS AND DRUG ABUSE EDUCATION NEWSLETTER.). [Drug and drug abus. educ. newsl.]. **Added/Corp** Editorial Resources, Inc. **VFOAT** Drugs & Drug Abuse Education. Vol. 13, No. 1 (Jan. 1982)-. Newsletter. English. Twelve times a year. $92.00. Editorial Resources Inc, PO Box 20754, Seattle WA 98102. **Tel** (206)322-8387. **ED** David L. Howell. **Bk Rev**. ***Continues** Washington Drug Review, 0146-728X;* ***Absorbed** Alcoholism & Alcohol Education.*

Desc: Independent focus on drug prevention, treatment and issues. Thorough coverage of federal policy, legislation, research, and successful local programs. Includes a calendar and a book list.

LC HV5800 .D784 **ISSN** 8756-8233
DD 362.2/9 US
NLM W1; DR514E **CODEN** DRSOEI
Pr Rev.
DRUGS & SOCIETY (NEW YORK, N.Y.).
(DRUGS & SOCIETY.). [Drugs soc.]. **VFOAT** Drugs and Society. Vol. 1, No. 1 (Fall 1986)-. Periodical. English. Four times a year (Published on the academic year). $150.00. The Haworth Press Inc., 10 Alice Street, Binghamton NY 13904-1580. **Tel** (607)722-5857, (800)3-HAWORTH, FAX (607)722-1424. **ED** Bernard Segal (editor's address: Center for Alcohol and Addiction Studies, University of Alaska, 3211 Providence Drive, Anchorage, AK 99508). **Bk Rev**. **Ad Acc**. **Acid Free**. **Circ:** 105. available on microfilm and microfiche from University Microfilms International (UMI). Documents available from BIOSIS Document Express, Haworth Document Delivery Service.
Desc: Addresses current controversies in the alcoholism and substance abuse field. Presents articles by experts that critically review issues; also provides reports of innovative contemporary research that have direct implications for practitioners and researchers.
Ind/Abst Abstr. Anthropol. (19??-); Appl. Soc. Sci. Index Abstr.; Biol. Abstr. (1986-); Child Dev. Abstr. Bibliogr.; Crim. Justice Abstr.; Crim. Justice Period. Index; Crim. Penol. Police Sci. Abstr.; Curr. Cit.; EMBASE; EP Collect.; Health Saf. Sci. Abstr.; Health Source Plus; Health Source; Homework Help.; Hum. Resour. Abstr. (?-?); Index Period. Artic. Relat. Law; Int. Pharm. Abstr.; Int. Polit. Sci. Abstr.; MasterFile FullTEXT 1000; MasterFile FullTEXT 350; MasterFile FullTEXT 650; MasterFile FullTEXT; OCLC; PAIS Int. Print (1991-?); Person. Manage. Abstr.; Psychol. Abstr. (1986-); PsycINFO; PsycLit; Refer. Z.; Sage Fam. Stud. Abstr. (?-?); Soc. Plann. Policy Dev. Abstr.; Soc. Work Abstr. [Select. Cov.]; Telebase; Urban Aff. Abstr.

LC HV5825 .D779 **ISSN** 0273-2505
DD 362.2/93/0973 US
DRUGS (BOCA RATON). (DRUGS.). (1970)-. English. One time a year. Social Issues Resources Series Inc, PO Box 2348, Boca Raton FL 33427. **Tel** (800)327-0513, (407)994-0079. **ED** Eleanor C. Goldstein.
Desc: Interdisciplinary resource material consisting of reprinted articles from popular and professional journals, newspapers, magazines and government documents.
Ind/Abst Curr. Aware. Biol. Sci., CABS; IDIS.

LC HV5800 **ISSN** 0968-7637
DD 362.29160941 UK
CCC
Pr Rev.
•**DRUGS: EDUCATION, PREVENTION POLICY.** [Drugs educ. prev. policy]. Vol. 1 (1994)-. Academic Scholarly Publication. English. Three times a year. $248.00. Carfax Publishing Company, PO Box 25, Abingdon, Oxfordshire OX14 3UE United Kingdom. **Tel** 011 44 1235 555335, FAX 011 44 1235 553559, telex 817484. **(Subscription address:** Carfax Publishing Co., 875-81 Massachusetts Avenue, Cambridge MA 02139.) **ED** Stuart Ware. Index available. **Bk Rev**. **Ad Acc**. available on microfiche. Documents available from BLDSC, UMI Article Clearinghouse.
Desc: Publishes multi-disciplinary papers on the prevention of substance misuse and related problems.

ISSN 1188-0260
DD 362.29/08/8796 CN
NLM W1; DR893TF
DRUGS IN SPORTS. [Drugs sports]. Vol. 1, No. 1 (Feb. 1992)-. Periodical. English. Four times a year. 65.00Can$. MGD Press, 23 Main Street, Workworth Ontario K0K 3K0 Canada. **Tel** (705)924-2341.
Ind/Abst Int. Pharm. Abstr.; SPORT Discus.

ISSN 1040-4228
DD 362 US
DRUGS IN THE WORKPLACE. [Drugs workplace]. (198?)-. Periodical. English. Twelve times a year. $275.00. Business Research Publications, 1333 H Street Northwest, 2nd Floor West, Washington DC 20005. **Tel** (202)842-3022, (800)822-6338, FAX (202)842-3023.
Desc: Reports on scientific, legal and government issues regarding alcohol and drug abuse in the workplace. News and features focus on drug-testing methods, insurance and benefits requirements and limitations, etc.

LC HV6251 **ISSN** 1190-9048
DD 364.177097105 CN
DRUGS, RCMP NATIONAL DRUG INTELLIGENCE ESTIMATE ... WITH TREND INDICATORS. (DRUGS, RCMP NATIONAL DRUG INTELLIGENCE ESTIMATE ... WITH TREND INDICATORS THROUGH. . .). [Drugs RCMP natl. drug intell. estim. trend indic.]. **VFOAT** RCMP National Drug Intelligence Estimate; Drogues, Rapport Annuel National sur les Drogues ... et Indicateurs de Tendance d'Ici .. (199?)-. Multiple languages. One time a year. Royal Canadian Mounted Police, Ottawa Ontario K1A 0R2 Canada. **Tel** (613)998-6317. ***Continues** National Drug Intelligence Estimate, 0848-4740.*

ISSN 8755-8181
DD 362 US
EMPLOYER-EMPLOYEE ALCOHOLISM ADVISOR. [Empl.-empl. alcohol. advis.]. **VFOAT** Employer Employee Alcoholism Advisor; Alcoholism Advisor; E.E.A.A. (Aug. 1984)-. Periodical. English. Twelve times a year. $35.00. Quinlan Publishing Company Inc., 23 Drydock Avenue, Boston MA 02210. **Tel** (617)542-0048, (800)229-2084, FAX (617)345-9646.

ISSN 0566-764X
US
ESTIMATED WORLD REQUIREMENTS OF NARCOTIC DRUGS AND ESTIMATES OF WORLD PRODUCTION OF OPIUM. **Main/Corp** International Narcotics Control Board. **VFOAT** Evaluations des Besoins du Monde en Stupefiants et de la Production Mondiale d'Opium; Previsiones de las Necesidades Mundiales de Estupefacientes y de la Produccion Mundial de Opio. (19??)-. Government Publication. Multiple languages (English, French and Spanish). Irregular. $2.00. United Nations Publications, 2 United Nations Plaza, Room DC2 0853, Department 007C, New York NY 10017. **Tel** (212)963-8303, (800)253-9646.
Desc: Provides estimates of requirements of narcotic drugs, opium production, the cultivation of the opium poppy for purposes other than the harvesting of opium, and drugs.

ISSN 1022-6877
SZ
NLM W1; EU612D
•**EUROPEAN ADDICTION RESEARCH.** Vol. 1 (1995)-. Periodical. English. Four times a year. $245.40. S. Karger AG, Allschwilerstrasse 10, PO Box, CH-4009 Basel Switzerland. **Tel** 011 41 61 3061111, FAX 011 41 61 3061234, telex CH 962 652. **ED** M. Krausz, A. Uchtenhagen.
Desc: International forum for the exchange of interdisciplinary information and expert opinions on all aspects of addiction research.

LC HV4999.2 .N37a ISSN 0161-5068
DD 362.2/9 US
EXECUTIVE REPORT, DATA FROM THE NATIONAL DRUG ABUSE TREATMENT UTILIZATION SURVEY (NDATUS). **Main/Corp** National Institute on Drug Abuse. Division of Scientific and Program Information. (19??)-. English. National Institute on Drug Abuse, 5600 Fishers Lane, Room 199 - 55, Rockville MD 20852. **Tel** (301)443-6637.

US
FEDERAL SUPERVISORS GUIDE TO DRUG TESTING. (19??)-. English. Irregular. $8.95 (US); $12.45 (Canada). FPMI Communications Inc., 707 Fiber Street, Huntsville AL 35801. **Tel** (205)539-1850, FAX (205)539-0911, .

ISSN 0733-9658
US
FLORIDA, IN REVIEW. Vol. 1, No. 1 (Apr. 1981)-. Periodical. English. Twelve times a year. Florida Alcohol and Drug Abuse Association, 1300 Executive Center Frive, Suite 300-302, Tallahassee FL. ***Formed by the union of*** *Dateline* ***and*** *FAC Sheet.*

ISSN 1048-8731
DD 362 US
FORENSIC DRUG ABUSE ADVISOR, THE. [Forensic drug abuse advis.]. **Added/Corp** Forensic Drug Abuse Advisory Service. (1989)-. Periodical. English. Ten times a year (monthly with June/July and Nov./Dec. issues combined). $187.00 US, Canada and Mexico; $207.00 other. Forensic Drug Abuse Advisor Inc., PO Box 5139, Berkeley CA 94705. **Tel** (510)849-0923, FAX (510)849-0958. **ED** Steven B. Karch. Index available (bound in Feb. issue). **Bk Rev**, (Qty: Varies). **Circ:** 1,200. available on an online database from NEWSNET.
Desc: Provides concise information about recent scientific discoveries related to drug abuse. Emphasis is placed on the forensic significance of these discoveries, and how they apply in the courts.

ISSN 0194-8121
US
Pr Rev.
FORUM (AL-ANON), THE. (THE FORUM.). Periodical. English. Twelve times a year. $9.00. Al-Anon Family Groups HQ, 1372 Broadway, New York NY 10018. **Tel** (212)302-7240. **Circ:** 57500.

ISSN 0801-2547
DD 178 UK
GLOBE OSLO. [Globe Oslo]. (1975)-. Periodical. English. Four times a year. £7.00. Globe, 1 the Quay Saint Ives, Cambridgeshire PE17 4AR United Kingdom. **Tel** 011 44 1480 466766, FAX 011 44 1480 466766. **ED** Derek Rutherford. **Bk Rev. Circ:** 5,000 (ctrl).
Desc: An international magazine on alcohol and drug problems.

US
GRANT$ FOR ALCOHOL AND DRUG ABUSE. **See** Philanthropy.

LC HV5825. G85 ISSN 1056-9340
DD 353.0084/29 US
GUIDE TO FEDERAL FUNDING FOR ANTI-DRUG PROGRAMS. [Guide fed. funding anti drug programs]. **Added/Corp** Government Information Services. (19??)-. English. Irregular. $199.50. Government Information Services / Virginia, 4301 North Fairfax Drive, Suite 875, Arlington VA 22203. **Tel** (703)528-1082, FAX (703)528-6060, telex RCA 263591 GIS UR. **ED** Charles Edwards, Heather Bodell, Natascha Ovando, Amy McAuliffe.
Desc: Lists federal grant programs for drug abuse and alcoholism prevention, education, treatment, rehabilitation, and research, as well as domestic law enforcement.

ISSN 1051-4236
US
HAWORTH SERIES IN DRUG THERAPY FOR ADDICTION PROBLEMS. (1991)-. Monographic series. English. Irregular. Price varies per volume. The Haworth Press Inc., 10 Alice Street, Binghamton NY 13904-1580. **Tel** (607)722-5857, (800)3-HAWORTH, FAX (607)722-1424. **Acid Free.** Documents available from Haworth Document Delivery Service.

LC HV5800 .H53a ISSN 0362-630X
DD 301.2/2 US
HIGH TIMES. (19??)-. Periodical. English. Twelve times a year. $29.95. Trans High Corporation, 211 East 43rd Street, New York NY 10023. **Tel** (212)972-8484. **(Subscription address:** Kable Publishers Aide / Illinois, 308 East Hitt Street, Subscription Department, Mt. Morris IL 61054-1473. **Tel** (815)734-1261.)

US
TITLE CHANGE
HIGHLIGHTS FROM STUDENT DRUG USE IN AMERICA. **Added/Corp** National Institute on Drug Abuse. Division of Research. University of Michigan. Institute for Social Research. **VFOAT** Student Drug Use in America. (1975/1980)-(198?). English. National Institute on Drug Abuse, 5600 Fishers Lane, Room 199 - 55, Rockville MD 20852. **Tel** (301)443-6637. ***Continues*** *Highlights, Drugs and the Nation's High School Students, Five Year National Trends.* ***Continued by*** *Highlights from Drugs and American High School Students.*

ISSN 1012-8360
SZ
ICAA NEWS. [ICAA news]. **VFOAT** International Council on Alcohol and Addictions News. (19??)-. Periodical. English. Four times a year. $37.72. International Council Alcohol Addiction, Case Postale 189, CH-1001 Lausanne Switzerland. **Tel** 011 41 21 3209865, FAX 011 41 21 3209817.

ISSN 0932-4240
GW
NLM ZWM 270; I19
IDIS-LITERATURLISTE. SUCHTINFORMATION / IDIS. **Added/Corp** Institut fuer Dokumentation und Information Uber Sozialmedizin und Offentliches Gesundheitswesen. **VFOAT** IDIS Literaturliste. Suchtinformation; Suchtinformation. (1987)-. Monographic series. German (English). Irregular. Price varies per volume. Institut fuer Dokumentation und Information, Sozialmedizin und Oeffentliches Gesundheitswesen, Westerfeldstr 35-37, Postfach 20 10 12, D-4800 Bielefeld 1 Germany. **Tel** 0521/86033-35, FAX 0521/870050. **ED** Dr Med Rudolf Welteke-Bethge. Index available. **Bk Rev. Circ:** 300.
Desc: Bibliographic documentation that provides actual information in the field of drug abuse, alcoholism and smoking.

LC HV5275 .I57 ISSN 0361-7459
DD 362.2/92 US
INTERNATIONAL A. A. DIRECTORY. **VAT** International Alcoholics Anonymous Directory. (1975)-. Directory. English. Alcoholics Anonymous World Services Inc, Box 459 Grand Central Station, New York NY 10017.

LC RC566.A1 I5 ISSN 0020-773X
DD 362.2/9/05 US
CCC
NLM W1 IN791N CODEN INJABN
Pr Rev. **TITLE CHANGE**
INTERNATIONAL JOURNAL OF THE ADDICTIONS, THE. [Int. j. addict.]. **Added/Corp** Institute for the Study of Drug Addiction. Vol. 1 (Jan. 1966)-(1995). Academic Scholarly Publication. English. Marcel Dekker Inc., 270 Madison Avenue, New York NY 10016. **Tel** (212)696-9000, (800)228-1160, FAX (212)685-4540, telex 421419. **(Subscription address:** Marcel Dekker Inc., PO Box 5017, Monticello NY 12701. **Tel** (800)228-1160.) **ED** Stanley Einstein. **Bk Rev. Ad Acc.** ctrl circ. available on microfiche. Documents available from The Genuine Article, BIOSIS Document Express. ***Continued by*** *Substance Use and Misuse.*
Desc: Presents reports on the serious problems facing individuals and communities in the areas of drug, alcohol, and tobacco use, abuse, and dependency. Offers an forum for the exchange of theory and empirical information - in a format designed for non-professionals as well as medical practitioners.
Ind/Abst Abstr. Res. Pastor. Care Couns. (19??-); Appl. Soc. Sci. Index Abstr.; Biol. Abstr.; Chicano Index; Crim. Justice Abstr.; Cumul. Index Nurs. Allied Health Lit.; Curr. Cit.; Curr. Contents Clin. Med.; Curr. Contents Soc. Behav. Sci.; EMBASE; Energy Res. Abstr. (Aug. 1982-); Health Saf. Sci. Abstr.; High. Educ. Abstr. (19??-19??); IDIS (1971-); Index Med.; Int. Pharm. Abstr.; Med. Abstr. Newsl.; Middle East Abstr. Index; Nutr. Res. Newsl.; Life Sci. Collect.; Psychol. Abstr. (1971-); PsycINFO; PsycLit; Ref. Upd. Deluxe Ed.; Res. Alert [Full Cov.]; Sci. Cit. Index; SCISEARCH; Soc. Plann. Policy Dev. Abstr.; Soc. Sci. Cit. Index [Full Cov.]; Soc. Work Abstr. [Select. Cov.].

LC HV5800 .I5228 ISSN 0955-3959
DD 362.29/05 UK
NLM W1; IN7966 CODEN IJDPED
Pr Rev.
INTERNATIONAL JOURNAL ON DRUG POLICY, THE. [Int. j. drug policy]. (198?)-. Periodical. English. Four times a year. $79.00. Whurr Publishers Ltd., 19B Compton Terrace, London N1 2UN United Kingdom. **Tel** 011 44 171 3595979, FAX 011 44 171 2265290. **(Subscription address:** Turpin Distribution Services Limited, Blackhorse Road, Letchworth, Hertfordshire SH6 1HN United Kingdom. **Tel** 011 44 1462 672555, FAX 011 44 1462 480947.) **ED** Pat O'Hare. Index available. **Bk Rev. Ad Acc.** Full Page (B&W) £250.00. Half Page (B&W) £150.00. **Circ:** 500. Documents available from ADONIS. ***Continues*** *Mersey Drugs Journal, 0955-5412.*
Desc: Features research, information and policy analysis current happenings in the field of drug treatment and control. Addresses the legal, social, medical and educational issues surrounding the use of psychoactive substances.
Ind/Abst ADONIS; Curr. Cit.; Trop. Dis. Bull.

ISSN 0823-213X
DD 362.2/9/09714 CN
INTERVENANT. (L'INTERVENANT / AITQ.). [Intervenant]. **Added/Corp** Association des Intervenants en Toxicomanie du Quebec. **VFOAT** Revue l'Intervenant. Vol. 1, No. 1 (1983)-. Periodical. French. Four times a year (Mar., June, Sept., Dec.). 12.01Can$. Association des Intervenants en Toxicomanie de Quebec, 2033 Est St. Joseph, Montreal Quebec H2H 1E5 Canada. **Tel** (514)523-1196. **Bk Rev**, (Qty: 10). **Circ:** 1,500 (ctrl).
Ind/Abst Repere.

LC HV5831.I8 A17a
DD 362.2/9/09777 US
IOWA COMPREHENSIVE STATE PLAN FOR SUBSTANCE ABUSE. **Main/Corp** Iowa. Division of Substance Abuse. (1986/87)-. English. Iowa Department of Public Health, Division of Substance Abuse, Lucas Building, Des Moines IA 50319. ***Continues*** *Iowa Comprehensive State Plan for Substance Abuse.*

LC RC563 .I86 ISSN 0235-6007
RU
ITOGI NAUKI I TEKHNIKI. SERIIA NARKOLOGIIA. **Added/Corp** Vsesoiuznyi Institut Nauchnoi i Tekhnicheskoi Informatsii (Soviet Union). **VFOAT** Seriia Narkologiia; Narkologiia; Itogi Nauki i Tekhniki. (1988)-. Monographic series. Russian. Price varies per volume. VINITI - Vsesoyuznyi Institut Nauchno-Tekhnicheskoi Informatsii, All-Union Scientific and Technical Information Institute, Baltiiskaia ulitsa 14, 125219 Moscow Russia. **Tel** 011 7 95 2384600, FAX 011 7 95 9430060, telex 411160.

GW
NLM W1; JA449
JAHRESSTATISTIK ... DER AMBULANTEN BERATUNGS- UND BEHANDLUNGSSTELLEN FUR SUCHTKRANKE IN DER BUNDESREPUBLIK DEUTSCHLAND. **See** Drug Abuse and Alcoholism-Abstracting, Bibliographies and Statistics.

ISSN 0044-6203
CN
NLM W1 JO222P
JOURNAL - ADDICTION RESEARCH FOUNDATION, THE. [J. - Addict. Res. Found.]. **Main/Corp** Addiction Research Foundation of Ontario. **Added/Corp** Addiction Research Foundation of Ontario. Ontario. Addiction Research Foundation. Vol. 1 (June 1972)-. Periodical. English. Six times a year. 15.00Can$ Canada; 19.00Can$ other. Addiction Research Foundation, 33 Russell Street, Toronto Ontario M5S 2S1 Canada. **Tel** (416)595-6000, FAX (416)595-5017. **ED** Anne MacLennan. Index available. **Bk Rev. Ad Acc. Circ:** 24,000. available on microfiche.
Desc: News publication for professionals in addictions

and related health, enforcement, research, and education fields.
Ind/Abst Can. Index (?-?); Can. Period. Index (19??-).

US
•JOURNAL OF ADDICTIONS NURSING.
See Medical Sciences-Nursing.

LC HV5800 .A356 **ISSN** 1055-0887
DD 362.29/05 US
NLM W1; JO533PU **CODEN** JADDER
Pr Rev.
JOURNAL OF ADDICTIVE DISEASES.
(JOURNAL OF ADDICTIVE DISEASES : THE OFFICIAL JOURNAL OF ASAM, AMERICAN SOCIETY OF ADDICTION MEDICINE.). [J. addict. dis.]. **Added/Corp** American Society of Addiction Medicine. Vol. 10, No. 1/2 (1991)-. Academic Scholarly Publication. English. Four times a year. $275.00. The Haworth Press Inc., 10 Alice Street, Binghamton NY 13904-1580. **Tel** (607)722-5857, (800)3-HAWORTH, FAX (607)722-1424. **ED** Barry Stimmel, MD (society's address: 5225 Wisconsin Avenue, NW, Suite 409, Washington, DC 20015). **Acid Free.** available on microfiche. Documents available from BIOSIS Document Express, Haworth Document Delivery Service, CASDDS. ***Continues** Advances in Alcohol & Substance Abuse, 0270-3106.*
Desc: Provides an integrated, multi-specialty perspective on clinically relevant research, treatment and public policy for specialists in addiction medicine. Will review important findings in etiology, epidemiology and clinical care. Represents the scholarly commitment of the field and reflects the highest standards of investigation, clinical practice, medical education and evaluation of patient care.
Ind/Abst Abstr. Anthropol. (19??-); Abstr. Res. Pastor. Care Couns. (19??-); Biol. Abstr. (1991-); Chem. Abstr.; Child Dev. Abstr. Bibliogr.; Crim. Justice Abstr.; Crim. Justice Period. Index; Crim. Penol. Police Sci. Abstr.; Curr. Aware. Biol. Sci., CABS; Curr. Cit.; EMBASE; EP Collect.; Health Saf. Sci. Abstr.; Health Plan. Adminis.; Health Source Plus; Health Source; Homework Help.; Index Med. (1991-); Index Period. Artic. Relat. Law; Int. Pharm. Abstr.; MasterFile FullTEXT 1000; MasterFile FullTEXT 350; MasterFile FullTEXT 650; MasterFile FullTEXT; OCLC; Physic. Medline Plus; Pollut. Abstr. Indexes; Psychol. Abstr. (1981-); PsycINFO; Risk Abstr.; Soc. Plann. Policy Dev. Abstr.; Soc. Work Abstr. [Select. Cov.]; Sociol. Abstr.; Stud. Women Abstr.; Telebase.

LC RJ506.D78 J68 **ISSN** 0896-7768
DD 616.86/0083 US
NLM W1; JO533RL **CODEN** JACDEM
Pr Rev. **TITLE CHANGE**
JOURNAL OF ADOLESCENT CHEMICAL DEPENDENCY. [J. adolesc. chem. depend.]. (1990)-Vol. 3, No. 1 (Fall 1993). Academic Scholarly Publication. English. The Haworth Press Inc., 10 Alice Street, Binghamton NY 13904-1580. **Tel** (607)722-5857, (800)3-HAWORTH, FAX (607)722-1424. **ED** Paul B. Henry (editor's address: UHS/Keystone Center, 2001 Providence Avenue, Chester, PA 19013). **Bk Rev. Ad Acc. Circ:** 317. available on microfilm and microfiche from University Microfilms International (UMI). Documents available from Haworth Document Delivery Service, CASDDS. ***Continued by** Journal of Child & Adolescent Substance Abuse, 1067-828X.*
Desc: Devoted entirely to meeting the needs of all professionals who work with adolescents on a daily basis, and specifically for chemical dependency clinicians and prevention/treatment specialists who deal with the unique needs of adolescents with alcohol and drug problems. Emphasis on an entire range of new prevention and intervention strategies covering both school and community based programs.
Ind/Abst Chem. Abstr.; Except. Child Educ. Resour.; Index Med.; Soc. Plann. Policy Dev. Abstr.; Soc. Work Abstr. [Select. Cov.]; Spec. Educ. Needs Abstr.

LC HV5128.U5 J68 **ISSN** 0090-1482
DD 362.2/92/07073 US
NLM W1 JO534M **CODEN** JADEDT
Pr Rev.
JOURNAL OF ALCOHOL AND DRUG EDUCATION. [J. alcohol drug educ.]. **Added/Corp** Alcohol and Drug Problems Association of North America. Alcohol and Drug Problems Association of North America. Education Section. (Winter 1972)-. Periodical. English. Three times a year. $45.00. Journal of Alcohol and Drug Education, PO Box 10212, 1120 East Oakland, Lansing MI 48901. **Tel** (517)484-2636. **ED** Gerald Globetti. **Acid Free. Circ:** 800. available on microfilm from University Microfilms International (UMI). Documents available from The Genuine Article. ***Continues** Journal of Alcohol Education, 0021-8677.*
Desc: Various educational philosophies, differing points of view in regard to alcohol and drugs. Reports teacher experience and experiments. Provides reference resource for actual teaching materials, techniques and procedures.
Ind/Abst Acad. Search; Commun. Abstr.; Contents Pages Educ.; Crim. Justice Abstr.; Curr. Cit.; Curr. Contents Soc. Behav. Sci.; Curr. Index J. Educ.; Educ. Index; EP Collect.; Health Source Plus; Health Source; High. Educ. Abstr. (1975-19??); Highw. Res. Abstr.; Homework Help.; Mag. Search; MasterFile FullTEXT 1000; MasterFile FullTEXT 350; MasterFile FullTEXT 650; MasterFile FullTEXT (July 1993-); OCLC; Psychol. Abstr. (1972-); PsycINFO; PsycLit; Res. Alert [Full Cov.]; Soc. Sci. Cit. Index [Full Cov.]; Spec. Educ. Needs Abstr.; SPORT Discus; Telebase.

LC RC563 .J66 **ISSN** 0885-4734
DD 616.86 US
NLM W1; JO58L
Pr Rev.
JOURNAL OF CHEMICAL DEPENDENCY TREATMENT. [J. chem. depend. treat.]. Vol. 1, No. 1 (1987)-. Periodical. English. Two times a year. $125.00. The Haworth Press Inc., 10 Alice Street, Binghamton NY 13904-1580. **Tel** (607)722-5857, (800)3-HAWORTH, FAX (607)722-1424. **ED** Bruce Carruth (editor's address: Little Rock Psychotherapy Center, PO Box 5011 Hillcrest Station, Little Rock, AR 72205). **Bk Rev. Ad Acc. Acid Free. Circ:** 449. available on microfilm and microfiche from University Microfilms International (UMI). Documents available from Haworth Document Delivery Service.
Desc: Provides focused, thematic issues dealing with current, practical clinical topics for drug abuse/substance abuse counselors and treatment professionals, covering both maintenance and drug-free philosophies.
Ind/Abst Curr. Cit.; EP Collect.; Health Source Plus; Health Source; Homework Help.; MasterFile FullTEXT 1000; MasterFile FullTEXT 350; MasterFile FullTEXT 650; MasterFile FullTEXT; OCLC; Psychol. Abstr. (1987-); PsycINFO (1990-); PsycLit; Soc. Work Abstr. [Select. Cov.]; Telebase.

ISSN 1067-828X
US
NLM W1; JO583KD
•JOURNAL OF CHILD & ADOLESCENT SUBSTANCE ABUSE. (1994)-. Academic Scholarly Publication. English. Four times a year (published during the academic year). $105.00. The Haworth Press Inc., 10 Alice Street, Binghamton NY 13904-1580. **Tel** (607)722-5857, (800)3-HAWORTH, FAX (607)722-1424. **ED** Frank DePiano, PhD and Vincent B. Van Hasselt, PhD. **Acid Free.** Documents available from Haworth Document Delivery Service. ***Continues** Journal of Adolescent Chemical Dependency, 0896-7768.*
Desc: Includes the treatment of substance abuse in all ages of children. Serves as a vehicle for communication and dissemination of information to the many practitioners and researchers working with these young people.
Ind/Abst Biol. Dig. (1994-); Child Dev. Abstr. Bibliogr. (1994-); Crim. Justice Abstr. (1994-); Cumul. Index Nurs. Allied Health Lit. (1994-); EP Collect.; Except. Child Educ. Resour. (1994-); Health Source Plus; Health Source; Homework Help.; Index Period. Artic. Relat. Law (1994-); MasterFile FullTEXT 1000; MasterFile FullTEXT 350; MasterFile FullTEXT 650; MasterFile FullTEXT; OCLC; PsycINFO (1994-); Refer. Z. (1994-); Soc. Plann. Policy Dev. Abstr. (1994-); Soc. Work Abstr. (1994-); Sociol. Abstr. (1994-); Spec. Educ. Needs Abstr. (1994-); Telebase.

LC HV5808 .J68 **ISSN** 0047-2379
DD 613.8/05 US
NLM W1 JO623 **CODEN** JDGEBT
Pr Rev.
JOURNAL OF DRUG EDUCATION. [J. drug educ.]. **VFOAT** Drug Education. Vol. 1 (March 1971)-. Periodical. English. Four times a year. $132.50. Baywood Publishing Company Inc., 26 Austin Avenue, PO Box 337, Amityville NY 11701. **Tel** (516)691-1270, (800)638-7819, FAX (516)691-1770. **ED** Seymour Eiseman. cum. index. Documents available from The Genuine Article, BIOSIS Document Express.
Desc: Peer-refereed, wide-ranging coverage of important trends and developments in the drug education field.
Ind/Abst Abstr. Anthropol. (19??-); Acad. Search; AGRICOLA [Select. Cov.]; Biol. Abstr.; Contents Pages Educ.; Crim. Penol. Police Sci. Abstr. (?-?); Cumul. Index Nurs. Allied Health Lit.; Curr. Cit.; Curr. Contents Soc. Behav. Sci.; Curr. Index J. Educ.; Educ. Index; EMBASE; EP Collect.; Health Source Plus; Health Source; Homework Help.; Index Med. (1984-); INFO-SOUTH Abstr.; Int. Pharm. Abstr.; Mag. Search; MasterFile FullTEXT 1000; MasterFile FullTEXT 350; MasterFile FullTEXT 650; MasterFile FullTEXT (July 1993-); Middle East Abstr. Index; OCLC; Psychol. Abstr. (1971-); PsycINFO; PsycLit; Res. Alert [Full Cov.]; Soc. Plann. Policy Dev. Abstr.; Soc. Sci. Cit. Index [Full Cov.]; Soc. Work Abstr. [Select. Cov.]; Sociol. Abstr.; Spec. Educ. Needs Abstr.; SPORT Discus; Stud. Women Abstr.; Telebase.

LC HV5800 .J68 **ISSN** 0022-0426
DD 362.2/93/05 US
CCC
NLM W1 JO624 **CODEN** JDGIA6
Pr Rev.
JOURNAL OF DRUG ISSUES. [J. drug issues]. **VFOAT** Drug Issues. (Jan. 1971)-. Academic Scholarly Publication. English. Four times a year (Jan., April, July, Oct.). $80.00. Journal of Drug Issues, PO Box 4021, Tallahassee FL 32315. **Tel** (904)386-6551. **ED** Richard L. Rachin, Eugene H. Czajkoski, Alexander Bassin, James D. Orcutt, Nils Retterstol. Index available. cum. index. **Bk Rev. Ad Acc. Circ:** 910. available on microfilm and microfiche from University Microfilms International (UMI). Documents available from The Genuine Article, BIOSIS Document Express, UMI Article Clearinghouse.
Desc: An interdisciplinary focus on alcohol and drug use and their social, legal, political, economic and medically related ramifications on society, its institutions and people.
Ind/Abst Acad. Abstr. Full Text Elite; Acad. Abstr.; Acad. Search; Appl. Soc. Sci. Index Abstr.; Biol. Abstr.; Chicano Index; Crim. Justice Abstr.; Curr. Cit.; Curr. Contents Soc. Behav. Sci.; EMBASE; EP Collect.; Expand. Acad. Index (1989-); Health Source Plus; Health Source; Homework Help.; Index Period. Artic. Relat. Law; INFO-SOUTH Abstr.; Int. Pharm. Abstr.; Mag. Search; MasterFile FullTEXT 1000; MasterFile FullTEXT 350; MasterFile FullTEXT 650; MasterFile FullTEXT (July 1990-); Med. Abstr. Newsl.; Middle East Abstr. Index; Newsp. Period. Abstr. (1988-); OCLC; Psychol. Abstr. (1972-); PsycINFO; PsycLit; Pub. Lib. FullTEXT; Res. Alert [Full Cov.]; Soc. Plann. Policy Dev. Abstr.; Soc. Sci. Source; Soc. Sci. Cit. Index [Full Cov.]; Soc. Sci. Index; Soc. Sci. Index Fulltext (Fall 1988-) [Full Txt.]; Soc. Work Abstr. [Select. Cov.]; Sociol. Abstr.; Telebase.

LC RC
DD 616.86 US
Pr Rev.
•JOURNAL OF MAINTENANCE IN THE ADDICTIONS. Vol. 1, No. 1 (1996)-. Academic Scholarly Publication. English. Four times a year. $60.00 US; $84.00 other. The Haworth Press Inc., 10 Alice Street, Binghamton NY 13904-1580. **Tel** (607)722-5857, (800)3-HAWORTH, FAX (607)722-1424. **ED** J. Thomas Payte. **Acid Free.** Documents available from Haworth Document Delivery Service.
Desc: Provides articles that assist in the understanding of clinical management at a practical level. This includes the development of innovative models for delivery of services in methadone treatment programs leading to a multi-level care system.

ISSN 1053-8755
US
NLM W1; JO77MI
Pr Rev.
•JOURNAL OF MINISTRY IN ADDICTION & RECOVERY. Vol. 1 (Spring 1994)-. Periodical. English. Two times a year. $75.00. The Haworth Press Inc., 10 Alice Street, Binghamton NY 13904-1580. **Tel** (607)722-5857, (800)3-HAWORTH, FAX (607)722-1424. **ED** Robert H. Albers, PhD (editor's address: Luther Northwestern Theological Seminary, 2481 Como Avenue, St Paul, MN 55108). **Bk Rev. Ad Acc. Acid Free.** available on microfiche. Documents available from Haworth Document Delivery Service.
Desc: Provides pastoral caregivers with the latest and most innovative ways of ministry as it relates to a variety of addictive behaviors. Provides an opportunity to think theologically about issues of addiction as it relates to the ministry.
Ind/Abst Abstr. Res. Pastor. Care Couns.; EP Collect.; Guide Soc. Sci. Relig.; Health Source Plus; Health Source; Homework Help.; Hum. Resour. Abstr.; MasterFile FullTEXT 1000; MasterFile FullTEXT 350; MasterFile FullTEXT 650; MasterFile FullTEXT; OCLC; Refer. Z.; Telebase.

LC BF207 .J68 **ISSN** 0279-1072
DD 362.2/93 US
NLM W1 JO856L **CODEN** JPDRD3
Pr Rev.
JOURNAL OF PSYCHOACTIVE DRUGS. [J. psychoact. drugs]. **Added/Corp** Haight-Ashbury Free Medical Clinic. Vol. 13, No. 1 (Jan.-March 1981)-. Academic Scholarly Publication. English. Four times a year. $140.00. Haight-Ashbury Publications, 409 Clayton street, 2nd Floor, San Francisco CA 94117. **Tel** (415)565-1904, FAX (415)621-7354. **ED** Jeffrey H. Novey. **Bk Rev. Ad Acc. Circ:** 1,200. available on microfilm and microfiche from University Microfilms International (UMI); available with illustrations; available with charts. Documents available from The Genuine Article, BIOSIS Document Express, CASDDS, BLDSC, FAXON Xpress, The UnCover Company, SWETS, UMI Article Clearinghouse. ***Continues** Journal of Psychedelic Drugs, 0022-393X.*
Desc: A multidisciplinary forum offering information on the social, psychological, and medical aspects of drug use and abuse.
Ind/Abst Arts Humanit. Citation Index [Select. Cov.]; Biol. Abstr.; Chem. Abstr.; Chicano Index; Crim. Justice Abstr.; Curr. Cit.; Curr. Contents Soc. Behav. Sci.; EMBASE; Highw. Res. Abstr.; IDIS (1967-); Index Med.; NAPRALERT; Psychol. Abstr. (1981-); PsycINFO; PsycLit; Res. Alert [Full Cov.]; Sage Urban Stud. Abstr; Soc. Sci. Cit. Index [Full Cov.].

LC RC565 .Q28 **ISSN** 0096-882X
DD 616.86/005 US
CCC
NLM W1 JO904X **CODEN** JSALDP
Pr Rev.
JOURNAL OF STUDIES ON ALCOHOL. [J. stud. alcohol]. **Added/Corp** Rutgers Center of Alcohol Studies. **VFOAT** Studies on Alcohol. Vol. 36 (Jan. 1975)-. Academic Scholarly Publication. English. Six times a year. $175.00 (one-year), $340.00 (two-year), $495.00 (three-year) institutions; $140.00 (one-year), $270.00 (two-year), $390.00 (three-year) individuals. Alcohol Research Documentation, Inc., Publications Division, PO Box 969, Piscataway NJ 08855-0969. **Tel** (908)932-2190, FAX (908)445-3500. **ED** Jack H. Mendelson and Nancy

K. Mello. (Bound in Nov. issue). cum. index. **Bk Rev. Ad Acc. Circ:** 3,000. available on microfilm and microfiche from University Microfilms International (UMI). Documents available from The Genuine Article, BIOSIS Document Express, UMI Article Clearinghouse, CASDDS. ***Continues** Quarterly Journal of Studies on Alcohol, 0033-5649.*
Desc: Contains original research reports that contribute fundamental knowledge about alcohol, its use and misuse, and its biomedical, behavioral and sociocultural effects.
Ind/Abst Acad. Abstr.; Acad. Search; Am. Hist. Life (1968-1973); Annals Behav. Med.; Appl. Soc. Sci. Index Abstr.; Biol. Abstr.; Chem. Abstr.; Commun. Abstr. (?-?); Crim. Justice Abstr.; Crim. Penol. Police Sci. Abstr.; Cumul. Index Nurs. Allied Health Lit.; Curr. Aware. Biol. Sci., CABS; Curr. Cit.; Curr. Contents Clin. Med.; Curr. Contents Life Sci.; Curr. Contents Soc. Behav. Sci.; EMBASE; EP Collect.; Expand. Acad. Index (1992-); Health Saf. Sci. Abstr.; Health Source Plus; Health Source; High. Educ. Abstr. (1981-); Highw. Res. Abstr.; Homework Help.; Index Med.; INFO-SOUTH Abstr.; Mag. Search; MasterFile FullTEXT 1000; MasterFile FullTEXT 350; MasterFile FullTEXT 650; MasterFile FullTEXT (July 1990-); Middle East Abstr. Index; Newsp. Period. Abstr. (1989-); Nutr. Abstr. Rev., Ser. A, Hum. Exp.; OCLC; PAIS Int. Print (1991-); Life Sci. Collect.; Psychol. Abstr. (1975-); PsycINFO; PsycLit; Public Aff. Inf. Serv. Bull.; Pub. Lib. FullTEXT; Res. Alert [Full Cov.]; Risk Abstr.; Sci. Cit. Index; SCISEARCH; Soc. Plann. Policy Dev. Abstr.; Soc. Sci. Source; Soc. Sci. Cit. Index [Full Cov.]; Soc. Sci. Index; Soc. Sci. Index Fulltext (Nov. 1988-) [Full Txt.]; Soc. Work Abstr. [Select. Cov.]; Sociol. Abstr.; SportSearch; Telebase; Vitis Vitic. Enol. Abstr.; Women Stud. Abstr.

ISSN 0363-468X
US
NLM W1 JO904X
JOURNAL OF STUDIES ON ALCOHOL. SUPPLEMENT.
[J. stud. alcohol, Suppl.]. **Added/Corp** Rutgers Center of Alcohol Studies. (Nov. 1975)-. Monographic series. English. Irregular. $175.00. Alcohol Research Documentation, Inc., Publications Division, PO Box 969, Piscataway NJ 08855-0969. **Tel** (908)932-2190, FAX (908)445-3500. ***ED*** Alex Fundock ***Ad Acc Circ:*** 3,000 available on microfilm from UMI. ***Continues** Quarterly Journal of Studies on Alcohol. Supplement, 0079-8312.*
Ind/Abst Biol. Abstr.; Bull Signal.; Chem.Abstr.; Curr.Cont.; Excerp.Med.; Hist.Abstr.; Index Med.; P.A.I.S.; Psychol.Abstr.

LC RC563 .J67 **ISSN** 0899-3289
DD 616.86/005 US
CCC
NLM W1; JO905CJ **CODEN** JSABEU
JOURNAL OF SUBSTANCE ABUSE.
[J. subst. abuse]. Vol. 1, No. 1 (1988)-. Periodical. English. Four times a year. $140.00. Ablex Publishing Corporation, 355 Chestnut Street, Norwood NJ 07648. **Tel** (201)767-8450, (201)767-8455 (Customer Service), FAX (201)767-6717. **ED** Ted D. Nirenberg. Index available. cum. index. **Bk Rev. Ad Acc. Circ:** 400.
Desc: This journal publishes articles pertaining to alcohol abuse, drug abuse, smoking, and eating disorders. Each issue includes research reports, review articles, and brief communications. The journal is committed to publishing articles on the most timely and significant trends, issues, problems, and applications in substance abuse.
Ind/Abst Curr. Cit.; Health Saf. Sci. Abstr.; Index Med. (1988-); Neuropsych. Abstr.; Psychoanal. Abstr.; Psychol. Abstr. (1989-); PsycLit; PsycScan: Appl. Exp. Eng. Psych.; PsycScan: LD/MR.

LC RC563 .J68 **ISSN** 0740-5472
DD 616.86/06/05 US
CCC
NLM W1; JO905DF **CODEN** JSATEG
Pr Rev.
JOURNAL OF SUBSTANCE ABUSE TREATMENT.
[J. subst. abuse treat.]. **Added/Corp** North Shore University Hospital. Vol. 1, No. 1 (1984)-. Periodical. English. Six times a year. $315.00. Pergamon Press, An Imprint of Elsevier Science Ltd., The Boulevard, Langford Lane, Kidlington, Oxford OX5 1GB United Kingdom. **Tel** 011 44 1865 843000, 011 44 1865 843699, FAX 011 44 1865 843010. **(Subscription address:** Elsevier Science Ltd. / Oxford Fulfillment Centre, PO Box 800, Kidlington OX5 1DX United Kingdom. **Tel** 011 44 865 843355.**)** **ED** John Imhoff and Robert Hirsch. available on microfilm and microfiche from University Microfilms International (UMI); available on an online database from Elsevier Electronic Subscriptions (EES). Documents available from The Genuine Article, BIOSIS Document Express, UMI Article Clearinghouse.
Desc: Features original contributions and articles on the clinical treatment of substance abuse and alcoholism. The journal is directed toward treatment practitioners in both the private and public sectors including those involved in health centers, clinics, hospitals, and community agencies.
Ind/Abst Abstr. Anthropol. (19??-); Biol. Abstr. (1984-); Curr. Aware. Biol. Sci., CABS; Curr. Cit.; Curr. Contents Soc. Behav. Sci.; EMBASE; Expand. Acad. Index (1992-); Index Med. (1984-); Newsp. Period. Abstr. (1992-); Psychol. Abstr. (1984-); PsycINFO; PsycLit; Res. Alert [Full Cov.]; Soc. Plann. Policy Dev. Abstr.; Soc. Sci. Cit. Index [Full Cov.]; Sociol. Abstr.

ISSN 0882-3375
DD 616 US
JOURNAL OF TECHNOLOGY IN ADDICTION & RECOVERY.
[J. technol. addict. recovery]. **VFOAT** Journal of Technology in Addiction and Recovery. Vol. 1, No. 1 (Fall 1984)-. Periodical. English. Four times a year. $17.95. Person Centered Consulting, 511-11th Avenue South, Minneapolis MI 55415.

LC HV5297.K2 K24A **ISSN** 0098-003X
DD 362.2/92/09781 US
NLM W2 AK3 A3K
KANSAS STATE PLAN FOR COMPREHENSIVE ALCOHOL ABUSE AND ALCOHOLISM PREVENTION, TREATMENT AND REHABILITATION.
Main/Corp Kansas. Commission on Alcoholism. English. One time a year. Commission on Alcoholism, 535 Kansas Avenue, Topeka KS 66603.

ISSN 0895-4127
US
LIFELINE (SEATTLE, WASH.).
(LIFELINE.). (19??)-. Periodical. English. $15.00. National Foundation for Alcoholism Communications, 352 Halladay, Seattle WA 98109.
Desc: Teaches recovering addicts, their family, employers and medical professionals about addiction.

LC HV5285 .L65 **ISSN** 0024-435X
DD 178.05 US
LISTEN (MOUNTAIN VIEW, CALIF.).
(LISTEN.). [Listen]. **Added/Corp** American Temperance Society. Narcotics Education, Inc. Vol. 1 (July/Sept. 1948)-. Periodical. English. Twelve times a year. $18.97. Review and Herald Publishing Association, 55 West Oak Ridge Drive, Hagerstown MD 21740. **Tel** (301)791-7000 ext. 2534, FAX (301)790-9734. **ED** Gary Swanson. Index available in last issue of volume--attached. **Bk Rev. Circ:** 100,000 (ctrl). available on microfilm and microfiche from University Microfilms International (UMI).
Desc: Designed to provide a positive, educational approach to problems arising from tobacco, alcohol and other drugs.
Ind/Abst Seventh-Day Adventist Period. Index (19??-).

PY
NLM W1; MA641G
MARANDU.
Added/Corp Proyecto de Apoyo al Programa Nacional de Prevencion al Abuso de Drogas (Paraguay). No. 1, Bulletin No. 1 (Feb. 1991)-. Periodical. Spanish. Proyecto de Apoyo al Programa Nacional de Prevencion al Abuso de Drogras, Asuncion Paraquay.

ISSN 0889-3926
DD 362 US
Pr Rev.
MICAP RECAP.
[MICAP recap]. **Added/Corp** Michigan Interfaith Council on Alcohol Problems. **VAT** Michigan Interfaith Council on Alcohol Problems Recap. (198?)-. Periodical. English. Twenty-four times a year. $35.00. Michigan Council Alcohol Problems, 1120 East Oakland, Box 10212, Lansing MI 48901-0212. **Tel** (517)484-0016. **ED** Allen B. Rice II, (phone: 484-0016).

LC HV5831.M8 A2 **ISSN** 0362-8388
DD 362.2/93/09778 US
MISSOURI COMPREHENSIVE STATE PLAN FOR DRUG ABUSE PREVENTION AND TREATMENT.
Main/Corp Missouri. Division of Mental Health. 1973/74-. English. One time a year. Missouri Division of Mental Health, 722 Jefferson Street, Jefferson City MO 65101.

LC HV5297.M8 M57A **ISSN** 0148-7752
DD 362.2/92/09779 US
MISSOURI STATE PLAN FOR THE IMPLEMENTATION OF THE COMPREHENSIVE ALCOHOL ABUSE AND ALCOHOLISM PREVENTION, TREATMENT AND REHABILITATION ACT OF 1970.
Main/Corp Missouri. Division of Alcoholism and Drug Abuse. **VFOAT** State Plan on Alcohol Abuse. **VAT** Missouri State Plan for the Implementation of the Comprehensive Alcohol Abuse and Alcoholism Prevention, Treatment and Rehabilitation Act of Nineteen Seventy. English. Missouri Department of Mental Health, 2002 Missouri Boulevard, Jefferson City MO 65101. ***Continues** State Plan for the Implementation of the Comprehensive Alcohol Abuse and Alcoholism Prevention, Treatment and Rehabilitation Act of 1970.*

ISSN 0080-4983
US
NLM W1 MO569R **CODEN** RUAMAP
MONOGRAPHS OF THE RUTGERS CENTER OF ALCOHOL STUDIES.
[Monogr. Rutgers Cent. Alcohol Stud.]. No. 4 (1964)-. Monographic series. English. Six times a year. $29.95 (cloth bound), $19.95 (paper bound). Rutgers State University of New Jersey, Smithers Hall, Allison Road, Piscataway NJ 08854. **Tel** (908)445-2190. Documents available from BIOSIS Document Express. ***Continues** Monographs of the Yale Center of Alcohol Studies.*
Desc: Works published in this series report the results of original research on alcohol, its use and misuse in any of the scientific disciplines.
Ind/Abst Biol. Abstr.

LC RC565 .M63 **ISSN** 0090-3809
DD 362.2/92/09786 US
NLM W2 AM9 A3M
MONTANA STATE PLAN FOR ALCOHOL ABUSE AND ALCOHOLISM PREVENTION, TREATMENT, AND REHABILITATION, THE.
Main/Corp Montana. Dept. of Health and Environmental Sciences. English. One time a year. Montana Department of Health & Environmental Sciences, 1400 Broadway, Cogswell Building, Room C108, Helena MT 59620. **Tel** (406)444-2544, FAX (406)444-2606.

LC WMLC 93/1088 **ISSN** 1046-5421
DD 362 US
N.A. WAY MAGAZINE, THE.
[N. A. way mag.]. **Added/Corp** Narcotics Anonymous. Narcotics Anonymous. World Service Office. **VFOAT** NA Way Magazine. **VAT** Narcotics Anonymous Way Magazine. (1988)-. Periodical. English. Twelve times a year. $15.00. World Service Office, PO Box 9999, 16155 Wyandotte Street, Van Nuys CA 91409. **Tel** (818)780-3951. **(Subscription address:** Subscriber Services, PO Box 15665, North Hollywood CA 91615. **Tel** (818)760-8983.**)** Index available in last issue of volume--attached. **Circ:** 6,000. ***Continues** NA Way, 0896-9116.*

LC HV5800 .N33 **ISSN** 0094-3991
DD 362.2/93/05 US
NLM WM 22 AA1 N15
NARCOTICS AND DRUG ABUSE.
(19??)-. Periodical. English. Four times a year. $79.90. Croner Publications Inc., 34 Jericho Turnpike, Jericho NY 11753. **Tel** (516)333-9085.
Desc: Directory includes dictionary section explaining drugs, terms and slang expressions. Also includes most abused substances, symptom descriptions, historical highlights, treatment facilities, services, admission requirements and bibliography.

US
•NARCOTICS ENFORCEMENT & PREVENTION DIGEST.
(Jan. 1995)-. English. One time a week. $345.00. Washington Crime News Services, 3918 Prosperity Avenue, Suite 318, Fairfax VA 22031-3334. **Tel** (703)573-1600, (800)422-9267, FAX (703)573-1604. ***Absorbed** Narcotics Control Digest, 0889-5708 **and** Narcotics Demand Reduction, 1043-8572.*

LC KF3890.A59 N37 **ISSN** 8755-8289
DD 344.73/0545 347.304545 US
CCC
NARCOTICS LAW BULLETIN.
See Law.

LC HV5840.H6 A36A
DD 362.2/93/095125 HK
NARCOTICS PROGRESS REPORT.
Main/Corp Action Committee Against Narcotics. **VFOAT** Hong Kong Narcotics Progress Report. English. Departmental Report by the Commissioner of Transport, Government Printer, Java Road, Hong Kong Hong Kong.

LC HV5840.D4 N37
DK
NARKOSTATISTIK.
Danish. Kbenhavns Politiadvokatur Afdeling N Politigarden, 1567 Copenhagen V Denmark.

LC HV5840.S8 N35 **ISSN** 0346-5632
SW
NARKOTIKAUTVECKLINGEN.
Added/Corp Brottsforebyggande Radet (Sweden). Utvecklingsenheten. (19??)-. Periodical. Swedish. Irregular. Liber Distribution, Prenumberationsorder, Forlagsorder 162 89, Stockholm Sweden.

ISSN 0270-2770
US
NASADAD ALCOHOL AND DRUG ABUSE REPORT. MONTHLY REPORT.
Main/Corp National Association of State Alcohol and Drug Abuse Directors. **VFOAT** Alcohol and Drug abuse Report. Monthly Report. **VAT** National Association of State Alcohol and Drug Abuse Directors Alcohol and Drug Abuse Report. Monthly Report. (19??)-. Periodical. English. Twelve times a year. $80.00. National Association of State Alcohol and Drug Abuse Directors, 444 North Capital Street Northwest, Suite 642, Washington DC 20001. **Tel** (202)783-6868, FAX (202)783-2704.

ISSN 0270-2789
US
NASADAD ALCOHOL AND DRUG ABUSE REPORT. SPECIAL REPORT.
Main/Corp National Association of State Alcohol and Drug Abuse Directors. **VAT** National Association of State Alcohol and Drug Abuse Directors Alcohol and Drug Abuse Report. Special Report. Periodical. English. Twenty-four times a year. $55.00. National Association of

State Alcohol and Drug Abuse Directors, 444 North Capital Street Northwest, Suite 642, Washington DC 20001. **Tel** (202)783-6868, FAX (202)783-2704.

LC HV5825 .N323
DD 362.29/18/02573
NLM WM 22; AA1 N224
US

NATIONAL DIRECTORY OF DRUG ABUSE AND ALCOHOLISM TREATMENT AND PREVENTION PROGRAMS. **Added/Corp** National Institute on Drug Abuse. National Institute on Alcohol Abuse and Alcoholism (U.S.). (Sept. 1982)-. English. Every 2 years. Free on request. National Clearinghouse for Alcohol and Drug Information, PO Box 2345, Rockville MD 20852. **Tel** (800)729-6686, (301)468-2600. **Formed by the union of** National Directory, Drug Abuse Treatment Programs **and** National Directory of Alcoholism Treatment Programs.

LC HV6251
DD 364.1/77/0971
ISSN 0848-4740
CN
TITLE CHANGE

NATIONAL DRUG INTELLIGENCE ESTIMATE (1988). (NATIONAL DRUG INTELLIGENCE ESTIMATE.). [Natl. drug intell. estim.]. **Added/Corp** Royal Canadian Mounted Police. Drug Enforcement Directorate. **VFOAT** Rapport Annuel National sur les Drogues. (1987/88)-(199?). English (French). Royal Canadian Mounted Police, Ottawa Ontario K1A 0R2 Canada. **Tel** (613)998-6317. **Continues** RCMP National Drug Intelligence Estimate, 0820-6228. **Continued by** Drugs, RCMP National Drug Intelligence Estimate ... With Trend Indicators Through ..., 1190-9048.

DD 362.2/9
NLM W2 A N223S
ISSN 0731-2458
US

NATIONAL INSTITUTE ON DRUG ABUSE STATISTICAL SERIES. SERIES C. **See** Drug Abuse and Alcoholism-Abstracting, Bibliographies and Statistics.

LC HV4997
DD 362.29
NLM W2; A N223
ISSN 0896-1190
US

NATIONAL INSTITUTE ON DRUG ABUSE STATISTICAL SERIES. SERIES H. **See** Drug Abuse and Alcoholism-Abstracting, Bibliographies and Statistics.

LC HV4997 .N37
DD 362.2/9
ISSN 0891-5709
US
CCC

NATIONAL REPORT ON SUBSTANCE ABUSE, THE. [Natl. rep. subst. abuse]. Vol. 1, No. 1 (Dec. 10, 1986)-. Periodical. English. Twenty-four times a year. $387.00. Buraff Publications Inc., 714 Church Street, Alexandria VA 22314. **Tel** (800)333-1291, (703)739-8500. **ED** Richard Hagan.
Desc: A newsletter covering substance abuse in the workplace: testing, employee privacy rights, pre-employment screening, legislation, regulation, employer liability, court decisions, and more.

LC HV5280.N2 N45A
DD 362.2/92/09782
ISSN 0364-5673
US

NEBRASKA NUMBERS. **Main/Corp** Nebraska. Division on Alcoholism. English. One time a year. Division of Alcoholism, PO Box 94728, Lincoln NE 68509.

LC HV5280.N2 N43A
DD 362.2/92/09782
ISSN 0149-2101
US

NEBRASKA STATE PLAN FOR ALCOHOLISM, THE. **Main/Corp** Nebraska. Division on Alcoholism. English. **VFOAT** State Plan for Alcoholism. 1977-. English. Division of Alcoholism, PO Box 94728, Lincoln NE 68509. **Continues** Nebraska Comprehensive State Plan for Alcoholism, 0363-9940.

DD 615/.1
ISSN 0849-0902
CN

NEW DRUG INFORMATION DIGEST. [New drug inf. dig.]. No. 1 (Feb. 1989)-. Periodical. English. Irregular. STA Communications Inc., 955 St. John Boulevard, Suite 306, Pointe-Claire Quebec H9R 5K3 Canada. **Tel** (514)695-7623. **Continues** Drugs in Family Medicine., 0826-3094.

DD 362
ISSN 1068-302X
US

NEWSLETTER FROM DICK B. ON THE SPIRITUAL ROOTS OF ALCOHOLICS ANONYMOUS, A. **See** Religions and Theology.

ISSN 0147-0515
US

NLM W1 N127

NIAAA-RUCAS ALCOHOLISM TREATMENT SERIES. [NIAAA-RUCAS alcohol. treat. ser.]. **Added/Corp** National Institute on Alcohol Abuse and Alcoholism (U.S.) Rutgers Center of Alcohol Studies. Rutgers Center of Alcohol Studies. Publications Division. **VFOAT** NIAAA RUCAS Alcoholism Treatment Series. **VAT** National Institute on Alcohol Abuse and Alcoholism and the Rutgers University Center of Alcohol Studies Alcoholism Treatment Series. No. 1 (1978)-. Monographic series. English. Irregular. Price varies per volume. Center of Alcohol Studies, Rutgers University, National Institute of Alcohol Abuse, Publishing Division, New Brunswick NJ 08903. **Tel** (201)932-2011. **ED** E.P. Noble.
Desc: Makes available to the therapeutic and allied professions systematic current knowledge on helping, treating and rehabilitating those affected by alcoholism.
Ind/Abst Psychol. Abstr. (1982-).

DD 362
NLM W1; NA486Q
ISSN 1046-9516
US

NIDA RESEARCH MONOGRAPH. [NIDA res. monogr.]. **Added/Corp** National Institute on Drug Abuse. National Institute on Drug Abuse. Division of Research. National Institute on Drug Abuse. Office of Science. United States. Alcohol, Drug Abuse, and Mental Health Administration. **VFOAT** National Institute on Drug Abuse Research Monograph Series. **VAT** National Institute on Drug Abuse Research Monograph. Vol. 5 (Feb. 1976)-. Academic Scholarly Publication. English. Irregular. Free on request. National Clearinghouse for Alcohol and Drug Information, PO Box 2345, Rockville MD 20852. **Tel** (800)729-6686, (301)468-2600. Documents available from BIOSIS Document Express, CASDDS. **Continues** National Institute on Drug Abuse Research monograph Series, 0361-8595.
Ind/Abst Biol. Abstr.; Chem. Abstr.; Curr. Cit.; EMBASE; Energy Res. Abstr. (March 1982-); Index Med. Feb. 1976-; Psychol. Abstr. (1975-).

ISSN 0782-9671
FI

NORDISK ALKOHOL TIDSKRIFT. **Added/Corp** Alko Oy. Nordiska Namden for Alkohol- och Drogforskning. Systembolaget (Sweden) Vinmonopolet (Norway). **VFOAT** Nordic Alcohol Studies; Nordisk Alkoholtidskrift. No. 1 (1991)-. Academic Scholarly Publication. Danish (Norwegian and Swedish; summaries and/or abstracts in English). Six times a year. Fmk100.00. Alko-Bolagen Ab, PO Box 350, SF-00101, Helsinki Finland. **Tel** 358 0 133 2949, FAX 358 0 1332386. **ED** Jorma Hentila, Kerstin Stenius. **Bk Rev**, (Qty: 15). **Ad Acc. Circ:** 2,000 (ctrl). Documents available from BLDSC. **Continues** Alkoholpolitik, 0355-9769.
Desc: Presents Nordic alcohol and drug research, policy debate, book reviews, and Nordic alcohol statistics.
Ind/Abst Soc. Plann. Policy Dev. Abstr.

ISSN 0789-6069
FI

UDC 364

●**NORDISK ALKOHOLTIDSKRIFT.** [Nordisk alkoholtidskr.]. **VFOAT** Nordic Alcohol Studies. (1991)-. Periodical. Multiple languages. Six times a year. Alko Ltd, Box 350, 00101 Helsinki Finland. **Tel** 011 358 01332982, FAX 011 358 01332386. **ED** Kerstin Stenius. **Continues** Alkoholpolitik (Helsingfors. 1984), 0782-9671.

LC HV5280.N8
DD 362.2/9256/09756
NLM W2 AN8 D5N
ISSN 0193-9424
US

NORTH CAROLINA STATE PLAN FOR ALCOHOL AND DRUG ABUSE. **Main/Corp** North Carolina. Dept. of Human Resources. 1978/79-. English. One time a year. State Department of Human Resources / North Carolina, 701 Barbour Street, Raleigh NC 27603. **Tel** (919)733-4283. **Formed by the union of** North Carolina State Plan for the Prevention, Treatment, and Control of Alcohol Abuse and Alcoholism **and** North Carolina State Plan for Drug Abuse Prevention Functions.

LC HV5831.N8 A32a
DD 353.97560084/29
ISSN 0197-1050
US

NORTH CAROLINA STATE PLAN FOR DRUG ABUSE PREVENTION FUNCTIONS, THE. **Main/Corp** North Carolina. Drug Commission. (19??)-. English. Irregular. North Carolina Drug Commission, 375 North Salisbury Street, Sixth Floor, Raleigh NC 27611. **Continues** North Carolina State Plan for Drug Abuse Prevention Functions, 0197-1050.

LC HV5831.N9 A17b
DD 362.2/9/09784
NLM W2 AN9 D5N
US

NORTH DAKOTA STATE PLAN FOR ALCOHOL, DRUG ABUSE PREVENTION, TREATMENT, AND REHABILITATION PROGRAMS. **Main/Corp** North Dakota. Division of Alcoholism and Drug Abuse. **Added/Corp** North Dakota. Division of Alcoholism and Drug Abuse. Plan for Prevention, Treatment & Rehabilitation. **VFOAT** Plan for Prevention, Treatment & Rehabilitation. (1980)-. English. One time a year. Division of Alcoholism and Drug Abuse / North Dakota, 909 Basin Avenue, Bismarck ND 58505. **Formed by the union of** North Dakota. Division of Alcoholism and Drug Abuse. North Dakota State Plan for Alcohol Abuse and Alcoholism Prevention, Treatment, and Rehabilitation Programs (DLC) 80640562 **and** North Dakota. Division of Alcoholism and Drug Abuse. North Dakota State Plan for Drug Abuse Prevention, Treatment, and Rehabilitation Programs.

Drug Abuse and Alcoholism

LC RF52.5
DD 610.73
NLM W1; PE872C
ISSN 1057-1639
US

PERSPECTIVES ON ADDICTIONS NURSING : A PUBLICATION OF THE NATIONAL NURSES SOCIETY ON ADDICTIONS. **See** Medical Sciences-Nursing.

ISSN 0032-0412
US
CEASED

PLAIN RAPPER. **Added/Corp** Project Eden (Hayward, Calif.). (1970)-(19??). Periodical. English. Project Eden, 680 West Tennyson Road, Hayward CA 94544. **Tel** (510)887-0566. **ED** Linda Cherry. **Bk Rev**. **Ad Acc. Circ:** 2,400 (ctrl).
Desc: Newsletter of substance abuse, education, prevention, and counseling program for youth and families in Hayward, Castro Valley, and San Lorenzo (Alameda County), California.

UDC 61
SP

PONS INFORMATIU. Spanish. Associa Prevencio Alcoholisme, Toxicomanies Pza Catalunya 9-4, 08002 Barcelona Spain. **Tel** 011 34 3 9172691.

DD 616
NLM W1; PR1387
ISSN 0891-8910
US

PRACTICAL COMMUNICATIONS. (PRACTICAL COMMUNICATIONS : ACCREDITATION & CERTIFICATION.). [Pract. commun.]. **VFOAT** Accreditation & Certification; Accreditation and Certification; A.PC. (1986)-. Periodical. English. Six times a year (Feb., Apr., June, Aug., Oct., Dec.). $102.00. Practical Communications, Dr. A. Goldman, PO Box 742, Bala Cynwyd PA 19004. **Tel** (610)667-8019, FAX (610)667-9858. **ED** Arnold Goldman. cum. index. **Circ:** 650.
Desc: A newsletter about accreditation and certification for psychiatric, alcoholism, and drug abuse services.

LC HV5035 .A45
DD 362.29209
US

PREVENTION PIPELINE, THE. **Added/Corp** Center for Substance Abuse Prevention (U.S.) National Clearinghouse for Alcohol and Drug Information (U.S.). Vol. 5, No. 6 (Nov./Dec. 1992)-. Periodical. English. Six times a year. National Clearinghouse for Alcohol and Drug Information, PO Box 2345, Rockville MD 20852. **Tel** (800)729-6686, (301)468-2600. **Continues** CSAP Prevention Pipeline.

ISSN 0032-9495
PL

PROBLEMY ALKOHOLIZMU (1976). (PROBLEMY ALKOHOLIZMU.). [Probl. Alkohol. 1976]. (1976)-. Periodical. Multiple languages. Twelve times a year. Price on request. **(Subscription address:** Ars Polona-Ruch, PO Box 1001, Krakowskie Przedmiescie 7, 00-068 Warsaw Poland. **Tel** 011 48 22 261201.)
Continues in part Problemy Alkoholizmu, Zdrowie i Trzezwosc, 0137-3889.

DD 362
ISSN 1046-7785
US

PROFESSIONALS AND THEIR ADDICTIONS. [Prof. their addict.]. (1989)-. English. One time a year. Charter Peachford Hospital, Publications Department, 2151 Peachford Road, Atlanta GA 30338.

PE

PSICOACTIVA : REVISTA CIENTIFICA DEL CENTRO DE INFORMACION Y EDUCACION PARA LA PREVENCION DEL ABUSO DE DROGAS. **Added/Corp** Centro de Informacion y Educacion para la Prevencion del Abuso de Drogas (Lima, Peru). (1987)-. Periodical. Spanish (summaries and/or abstracts in English). Two times a year. $30.00. CEDRO / Centro de Informacion y Educacion para la Prevencion del Abuso de Drogas, Roca y Bolona 271, Miraflores, Lima 18 Peru. **Tel** 011 51 14 466682, 467046, FAX 011 51 14 460751. **ED** Jorge Zavaleta Alegre.
Desc: Publishes original articles relating to addictive substances and their impact at different levels, based on empirical, theoretical or applied investigational work.

DD 362.2/93/05
ISSN 0715-9684
CN
CEASED

PSYCHOTROPES (MONTREAL). (PSYCHOTROPES : UN JOURNAL D'INFORMATION SUR LES DROGUES ET LEURS USAGES.). [Psychotropes]. Vol. 1, No. 1 (Spring/Summer 1983)-Vol. 8, No. 3 (19??). Periodical. French (English; summaries and/or abstracts in English). Psychotropes, C P 592 Succursale Outremont, Montreal Quebec H2V 4N2 Canada. **Tel** (418)274-6956. Index available. cum. index. **Bk Rev**. **Ad Acc. Circ:** 2,000 (ctrl).
Desc: An international journal publishing articles in French on psychoactive drug uses and abuses,

cross-cultural data and current developments aimed at the medical, social and educational professions.
Ind/Abst EMBASE.

LC HV5823
DD 616.86 FR
●**PSYCHOTROPES (PARIS).** (1996)-. French. Four times a year. 400.00F (institutions), 350.00F (individuals) France; 500.00F (institutions), 450.00F (individuals) other. Masson - Periodiques, Villa Laromiguiere, 75005 Paris France. **Tel** 011 1 40466200, FAX 011 1 40466201.

US
PULSE BEATS ALCOHOL & DRUG ABUSE. (19??)-. English. Twelve times a year. $47.00 US; $54.00 other. Insurance Field Company, PO Box 948, Northbrook IL 60065. **Tel** (708)498-0100. **Bk Rev. Circ:** 500.
Desc: Provides clear concise details on the rapidly changing and complex field of drug and alcohol abuse for timely action by citizens, businesses, civic/religious groups, and public officials.

LC RC563 .Q37 **ISSN** 0737-5956
DD 362.2/93/09748 US
QUARTERLY EXECUTIVE TREND REPORT. English. Four times a year. Governor's Council on Drug and Alcohol Abuse, 2101 North Front Street, Building No. 1, Harrisburg PA 17110.

LC HV5001 .R4 **ISSN** 0738-422X
DD 616.86/1/05 US
CCC
NLM W1 RE106AH (P) **CODEN** RDALE9
RECENT DEVELOPMENTS IN ALCOHOLISM. (RECENT DEVELOPMENTS IN ALCOHOLISM : AN OFFICIAL PUBLICATION OF THE AMERICAN MEDICAL SOCIETY ON ALCOHOLISM, AND THE RESEARCH SOCIETY ON ALCOHOLISM, AND THE NATIONAL COUNCIL ON ALCOHOLISM.). [Recent dev. alcohol.]. **Added/Corp** American Medical Society on Alcoholism. Research Society on Alcoholism (U.S.) National Council on Alcoholism. American Medical Society on Alcoholism and Other Related Dependencies. (1983)-. Academic Scholarly Publication. English. Irregular. Price varies per volume. Plenum Press, 233 Spring Street, New York NY 10013-1578. **Tel** (212)620-8000, (800)221-9369, FAX (212)463-0742, (212)807-1047, telex 23/421139. **ED** Marc Galanter. Documents available from CASDDS.
Ind/Abst Chem. Abstr. (1983-); Curr. Cit.; Index Med.; Psychol. Abstr. (1983-); PsycINFO (?-?).

ISSN 0896-2391
DD 362 US
RECOVERING (SAN FRANCISCO, CALIF.). (RECOVERING.). [Recovering]. **Added/Corp** Recovery Information Services (San Francisco, Calif.). (Summer 1987)-. Periodical. English. Twelve times a year. $20.00. Recovery Informations Services, 490 6th Avenue #202, San Francisco CA 94118. **Tel** (415)752-2246. **ED** Michelle Garcia. **Bk Rev**, (Qty: 12). **Ad Acc, Adv Mgr:** Corin Hylton. **Circ:** 25,000.
Desc: News magazine for people recovering from addictive diseases (alcoholism, co-dependency, gambling, etc.).

LC HV5831.W2 A26A
DD 362.2/9386 US
REPORT : DRUG ABUSE PREVENTION PLAN. Main/Corp Washington (State). Dept. of Social and Health Services. **VFOAT** State of Washington Annual Drug Abuse Plan. (19??)-. English. One time a year. Director Office of Drug Abuse Prevention, Department of Social and Health Services, OB-43E, Olympia WA 98505.

LC RC565 .U53A **ISSN** 0193-0494
DD 353.008/42 US
NLM W2 A A38R
REPORT OF THE ADMINISTRATOR / ALCOHOL, DRUG ABUSE, AND MENTAL HEALTH ADMINISTRATION. Main/Corp United States. Alcohol, Drug Abuse, and Mental Health Administration. (1978)-. English. One time a year. US Department of Health and Human Services, 200 Independence Avenue Southwest, Washington DC 20201.

LC HV5800 .I525
DD 363.4/5/05 US
NLM W2 MI5 I6R
REPORT OF THE INTERNATIONAL NARCOTICS CONTROL BOARD. (REPORT OF THE INTERNATIONAL NARCOTICS CONTROL BOARD FOR ...). **Main/Corp** International Narcotics Control Board. **VFOAT** Report of the International Narcotics Control Board on its Work in .... (1968)-. Government Publication. English. One time a year. $15.00. United Nations Publications, 2 United Nations Plaza, Room DC2 0853, Department 007C, New York NY 10017. **Tel** (212)963-8303, (800)253-9646. ***Continues*** *Report to the Economic and Social Council on the Work of the Board in ... .*
Desc: Report of the Board's yearly activities that is submitted to the Economic and Social Council.

LC HV5297.A4 A46a **ISSN** 0095-3318
DD 353.9/798/0084292 US
REPORT - OFFICE OF ALCOHOLISM, DEPARTMENT OF HEALTH AND SOCIAL SERVICES, STATE OF ALASKA. (REPORT - OFFICE OF ALCOHOLISM.). **Main/Corp** Alaska. Office of Alcoholism. **Added/Corp** Alaska. Office of Alcoholism. Annual Status Report. **VFOAT** Annual Status Report. (19??)-. English. One time a year. Office of Alcoholism, Juneau AK 99801.

LC HE5620.D7 R46
DD 364.1/47 US
REPORT ON DRIVING UNDER THE INFLUENCE OF ALCOHOL, OPERATING AFTER LICENSE SUSPENSION, AND HABITUAL OFFENDER REVOCATION VIOLATIONS. **See** Law-Law Enforcement and Criminology.

LC RC565 .R37 **ISSN** 0093-9714
DD 616.8/6/005 US
CCC
NLM W1 RE215AD
RESEARCH ADVANCES IN ALCOHOL AND DRUG PROBLEMS. [Res. adv. alcohol drug probl.]. **VAT** Research Advances in Alcohol and Drug Problems. Vol. 1 (1974)-. Monographic series. English. Irregular. Price varies per volume. Plenum Press, 233 Spring Street, New York NY 10013-1578. **Tel** (212)620-8000, (800)221-9369, FAX (212)463-0742, (212)807-1047, telex 23/421139. Documents available from The Genuine Article.
Ind/Abst Res. Alert [Full Cov.].

ISSN 1080-8388
US
CCC
NLM W1; RE216HS
●**RESEARCH COMMUNICATIONS IN ALCOHOL AND SUBSTANCES OF ABUSE.** (1994)-. Periodical. English. Four times a year. $90.00. PJD Publications Ltd., PO Box 966, Westbury NY 11590. **Tel** (516)626-0650, FAX (516)626-5546. ***Continues*** *Research Communications in Alcohol and Substances of Abuse, 0193-0818.*

ISSN 0193-0818
DD 615 US
CCC
NLM W1; RE216HS
Pr Rev. **TITLE CHANGE**
RESEARCH COMMUNICATIONS IN SUBSTANCES OF ABUSE. [Res. commun. subst. abuse]. Vol. 2, No. 4 (1981)-(1994). Academic Scholarly Publication. English. PJD Publications Ltd., PO Box 966, Westbury NY 11590. **Tel** (516)626-0650, FAX (516)626-5546. Documents available from The Genuine Article, BIOSIS Document Express, CASDDS. ***Continues*** *Research Communications in Substance Abuse, 0193-0818.* ***Continued by*** *Research Communications in Alcohol and Substances of Abuse.*
Ind/Abst Biol. Abstr. (1981-); Chem. Abstr. (1981-); Curr. Aware. Biol. Sci., CABS; Curr. Cit.; Curr. Contents Life Sci.; EMBASE; Res. Alert [Full Cov.]; Sci. Cit. Index; SCISEARCH.

ISSN 0360-7631
US
NLM W1 RE231G **CODEN** RIUPDJ
RESEARCH ISSUES. [Res. issues]. (1975)-. Monographic series. English. Price varies per volume. National Institute on Drug Abuse, 5600 Fishers Lane, Room 199 - 55, Rockville MD 20852. **Tel** (301)443-6637. Documents available from BIOSIS Document Express.
Ind/Abst Biol. Abstr.

ISSN 0270-7772
US
NLM W1 RE232FN **CODEN** RMNAE2
RESEARCH MONOGRAPH - NATIONAL INSTITUTE ON ALCOHOL ABUSE AND ALCOHOLISM. [Res. monogr., Natl. Inst. Alcohol Abuse Alcohol.]. **Added/Corp** National Institute on Alcohol Abuse and Alcoholism (U.S.). **VFOAT** NIAAA Research Monograph. (1979)-. Academic Scholarly Publication. English. Irregular. Price varies per volume. Superintendent of Documents, US Government Printing Office, Washington DC 20402. **Tel** (202)275-3328, FAX (202)786-2377. Documents available from CASDDS.
Ind/Abst Chem. Abstr.

ISSN 0361-8595
US
NLM W1 NA486Q
RESEARCH MONOGRAPH SERIES - NATIONAL INSTITUTE ON DRUG ABUSE. (NATIONAL INSTITUTE ON DRUG ABUSE RESEARCH MONOGRAPH SERIES.). **VFOAT** NIDA Research Monograph. 1- 1975-. Monographic series. English. Price varies per volume. National Institute on Drug Abuse, 5600 Fishers Lane, Room 199 - 55, Rockville MD 20852. **Tel** (301)443-6637.
Ind/Abst Psychol. Abstr. (1975-); PsycINFO (1990-); PsycLit.

ISSN 0213-7615
SP
NLM W1; RE532R
Pr Rev.
REVISTA ESPANOLA DE DROGODEPENCENCIAS. Vol. 12, No. 1 (1987)-. Periodical. Spanish (summaries and/or abstracts in English and French). Four times a year (Mar., June, Sept., Dec.). $71.06. Revista Espanola Drogodependencias, Apartado de Correos 477, 46080 Valencia Spain. **Tel** 011 34 96 3601506. **Bk Rev**, (Qty: 12-13). **Ad Acc, Adv Mgr:** Joaqvin Cuevas. ***Continues*** *Drogalcohol.*
Ind/Abst Indice Med. Esp.

ISSN 1072-4567
DD 026 US
SALIS NEWS. (SALIS NEWS : SUBSTANCE ABUSE LIBRARIANS & INFORMATION SPECIALISTS NEWSLETTER.). [SALIS news]. **Added/Corp** Substance Abuse Librarians & Information Specialists. **VAT** Substance Abuse Librarians & Information Specialists News. (1981)-. Periodical. English. Four times a year. $20.00. Alcohol Research Group, PO Box 9513, 1816 Scenic Avenue, Berkeley CA 94709. **Tel** (510)642-5208, FAX (510)642-7175, telex 6501015906 MCI UW.

ISSN 0814-2025
AT
SAM. SUBSTANCE ABUSE MONTHLY. (1980)-. Periodical. English. Twelve times a year. 49.34Aus$. Substance Abuse Monthly, Alcohol and Drug Foundation, PO Box 529, South Melbourne 3205 Australia. **Tel** 011 61 3 6906000, FAX 011 61 3 6903271.

US
NLM W1; SA488UM
●**SAMHSA NEWS. Added/Corp** United States. Substance Abuse and Mental Health Services Administration. Vol. 1, No. 1 (Winter 1993)-. Government Publication. English. Six times a year. $11.00 US; $13.75 other. Superintendent of Documents, US Government Printing Office, Washington DC 20402. **Tel** (202)275-3328, FAX (202)786-2377. ***Continues*** *ADAMHA News (Rockville, Md. : 1990), 1057-6215.*
Desc: Contains articles on agency-related issues, such as AIDS, alcoholism, drug abuse, and mental health, and events of the Substance Abuse and Mental Health Services Administration.

UK
SCODA NEWSLETTER : STANDING CONFERENCE ON DRUG ABUSE. (19??)-. Newsletter. English. Six times a year. £10.00. Institute for the Study of Drug Dependence, 32-36 Loman Street, Waterbridge House, London SE1 0EE United Kingdom. **Tel** 011 44 171 9281211, FAX 011 44 171 9281771.
Desc: News on services for people with drug problems. The law, funding, prevention, training and articles and personal views from people working with drug users. Includes book reviews and parliamentary reports.

US
SELECTED PUBLICATIONS - NATIONAL CLEARINGHOUSE FOR ALCOHOL INFORMATION. Main/Corp National Clearinghouse for Alcohol Information. (19??)-. Periodical. English. US Department of Health & Human Services / Alcohol Drug Abuse & Mental Health Administration, 5600 Fishers Lane, Rockville MD 20857. **Tel** (301)443-3783, FAX (301)443-1719.
Desc: The aim of the bibliographies is to provide the reader with a regularly published series of bibliographic references for recent, topical literature in designated areas.

ISSN 1059-6259
DD 362 US
SOBER TIMES. (SOBER TIMES : THE RECOVERY MAGAZINE.). [Sober times]. (1987)-. Periodical. English. Twelve times a year. $12.50. Sober Times, PO Box 31967, Seattle WA 98013. **Tel** (206)523-8005.

ISSN 1071-4111
DD 362 US
SOBERING THOUGHTS. (SOBERING THOUGHTS : A PUBLICATION OF WOMEN FOR SOBRIETY, INC.). [Sobering thoughts]. **Added/Corp** Women for Sobriety, Inc. (19??)-. Periodical. English. Twelve times a year. $18.00 (one-year), $28.00 (two-year), $38.00 (three-year). Women for Sobriety Inc., PO Box 618, Quakertown PA 18951. **Tel** (215)536-8026, FAX (215)536-8026. **ED** Jean Kirkpatrick. **Circ:** 2,000.
Desc: Newsletter written by recovering alcoholic women using the New Life Program.

ISSN 0887-2783
DD 394 US
Pr Rev.
SOCIAL HISTORY OF ALCOHOL REVIEW, THE. [Soc. hist. alcohol rev.]. **Added/Corp** Alcohol and Temperance History Group. No. 12 (Fall 1985)-. Periodical. English. Two times a year (June, & Oct.). $20.00. Alcohol Temperance History Society, Department of History, Albany NY 12222. **Tel** (417)836-5065. **ED** Scott Haine, (editor's address: 6 Park

Drug Abuse and Alcoholism

Ridge Court, Belmont, CA 94002, (phone: (415)591-2254). **Bk Rev. Continues** Alcohol in History, 0749-7989.
 Desc: The journal of the alcohol and temperance history society.

DD 362   **ISSN** 1071-1422 US
SOS INTERNATIONAL NEWSLETTER.
[SOS int. newsl.]. **Main/Corp** Secular Organizations for Sobriety. **VFOAT** International Newsletter. **VAT** Secular Organizations for Sobriety International Newsletter. (19??)-. Newsletter. English. Four times a year. $15.00. SOS National Clearinghouse, PO Box 5, Central Park Station, Buffalo NY 14215. **Tel** (716)834-2921, FAX (716)834-0841. **ED** Jim Christopher.
 Desc: Newsletter of the Secular Organizations for Sobriety.

LC Z7164.N17 S67
DD 016.3622/93   **ISSN** 0092-4229 US
NLM ZWM 270 S742
SPEED (BELOIT). (SPEED : THE CURRENT INDEX TO THE DRUG ABUSE LITERATURE.). [Speed].
Vol. 1 (Jan. 1, 1973)-. Periodical. English. Twenty-four times a year. $20.00. Stash Library, 118 South Bedford Street, Madison WI 53703.

DD 016.812/54   **ISSN** 1189-3397 CN
SPOTLIGHTING PLAYS ON ALCOHOL AND OTHER DRUGS. See Theater.

NLM W1; ST31D
    US
CEASED
STATE ADM REPORTS : ALCOHOLISM, DRUG ABUSE & MENTAL HEALTH.
Added/Corp George Washington University. Intergovernmental Health Policy Project. **VFOAT** Alcoholism, Drug Abuse & Mental Health. (Jan. 1991)-(June 1995). Periodical. English. Intergovernmental Health Policy Project, 2021 K Street NW, Suite 800, Washington DC 20006. **Tel** (202)872-1445, FAX (202)785-0114. **Circ:** 1,900.
Continues State Health Reports.
 Desc: Covers important research and policy developments affecting mental health, alcoholism, and drug abuse programs within the fifty states.

LC HV5280.I4 I34B
DD 362.2/9286/09773   **ISSN** 0736-766X US
STATE OF ILLINOIS PLAN FOR THE TREATMENT AND PREVENTION OF ALCOHOL ABUSE AND ALCOHOLISM.
(STATE OF ILLINOIS PLAN FOR THE TREATMENT AND PREVENTION OF ALCOHOL ABUSE AND ALCOHOLISM FOR ILLINOIS FISCAL YEAR ...). **Main/Corp** Illinois. Division of Alcoholism. **VFOAT** Plan for the Treatment and Prevention of Alcohol Abuse and Alcoholism. English. Illinois Department of Mental Health, 401 State Office Building, Springfield IL 62706.
Continues State of Illinois Plan for the Treatment and Prevention of Alcoholism and Alcohol Abuse, 0191-0744.

LC HV5297.O7 S84
DD 362.2/9286   US
STATE PLAN FOR ALCOHOL PROBLEMS.
English. Oregon Mental Health Division, 2575 Bittern Street NE, Salem OR 97310.

    US
STATE PLAN PROFILES. English. US
Department of Health and Human Services, 200 Independence Avenue Southwest, Washington DC 20201.

LC HV5831.N8 A33A
DD 364.1/7   **ISSN** 0145-8531 US
STATISTICAL DATA. See Drug Abuse and Alcoholism-Abstracting, Bibliographies and Statistics.

LC HV5840.G7
DD 364.1/77/0941   **ISSN** 0143-1463 UK
NLM W2; FA1 H6s
STATISTICS OF THE MISUSE OF DRUGS UNITED KINGDOM, SUPPLEMENTARY TABLES. See Drug Abuse and Alcoholism-Abstracting, Bibliographies and Statistics.

LC Discard
    NO
STOFF MISBRUK : INFORMASJON FRA SENTRALRADET FOR NARKOTIKAPROBLEMER. Vol. 1, (1971)-.
Norwegian. Six times a year. Kr415.00, $75.00. Scandinavian University Press, PO Box 2959 Toeyen, N 0608 Oslo 6 Norway. **Tel** 011 47 2 2575400, FAX 011 47 2 2575353, telex 71896 UROR N. **(Subscription address:** Scandinavian University Press, 200 Meacham Ave., Elmont NY 11003. **Tel** (516)352-7300, FAX (516)352-7377.**)** **ED** Martin Blindheim. **Bk Rev. Ad Acc. Circ:** 5,000.
 Desc: A journal for information and debate on drug problems in Norway and internationally.

DD 371   **ISSN** 1042-6388 US
STUDENT ASSISTANCE JOURNAL. [Stud. assist. j.]. (1988)-. Trade Publication. English. Five times a year (bimonthly except July/Aug.). $34.00. Performance Resource Press, Inc., 1863 Technology Drive, Suite 200, Troy MI 48083. **Tel** (810)588-7733, (800)453-7733, FAX (810)588-6633. **ED** Geraldine Andrews. **Ad Acc.**
 Desc: Devoted to disseminating information about alcohol and other drug problems to educators, treatment personnel, and others who work with youths.

    US
STUDENT DRUG USE IN AMERICA.
(1975-1979)-. English. One time a year. National Institute on Drug Abuse, 5600 Fishers Lane, Room 199 - 55, Rockville MD 20852. **Tel** (301)443-6637.

LC RC563 .S83
DD 362.29/05   **ISSN** 0889-7077 US
NLM W1; SU147G
SUBSTANCE ABUSE. (SUBSTANCE ABUSE : OFFICIAL PUBLICATION OF THE ASSOCIATION FOR MEDICAL EDUCATION AND RESEARCH IN SUBSTANCE ABUSE.). [Subst. abuse]. **Added/Corp** Association for Medical Education and Research in Substance Abuse (U.S.) Brown University. Center for Alcohol and Addiction Studies. (19??)-. Periodical. English. Four times a year. $165.00. Plenum Press, 233 Spring Street, New York NY 10013-1578. **Tel** (212)620-8000, (800)221-9369, FAX (212)463-0742, (212)807-1047, telex 23/421139. **ED** Marc Galanter.

DD 362   **ISSN** 1067-0165 US
SUBSTANCE ABUSE FUNDING NEWS.
[Subst. abuse funding news]. (19??)-. Periodical. English. Twenty-four times a year. $259.00. CD Publications, 8204 Fenton Street, Silver Spring MD 20910. **Tel** (800)666-6380, (301)588-6380, FAX (301)588-6385.

DD 371   **ISSN** 0895-8874 US
TITLE CHANGE
SUBSTANCE ABUSE IN SCHOOLS.
[Subst. abuse sch.]. Vol. 1, No. 1 (Sept. 1987)-(19??). Periodical. English. National Professional Resources, PO Box 1479, 25 South Regent Street, Port Chester NY 10573. **Tel** (914)937-8879, FAX (914)937-9327. **ED** Robert Hanson. **Bk Rev.** ctrl circ. **Continues** Aids Education. **Merged with** Challenging Times.
 Desc: A publication to keep schools informed by presenting the current issues, identifying national resources, and disseminating information about programs that work to stop substance abuse in the schools.

DD 362   **ISSN** 1076-979X US
NLM W1; SU147D
●SUBSTANCE ABUSE LETTER. [Subst. abuse lett.]. Vol. 1, No. 1 (July 5, 1994)-. Periodical. English. Twenty-four times a year. $195.00. Pace Publications / New York, PO Box 2972, Grand Central Station, New York NY 10163. **Tel** (212)685-5450, FAX (212)679-4701.

DD 362   **ISSN** 1040-4163 US
SUBSTANCE ABUSE REPORT (NEW YORK, N.Y.). (SUBSTANCE ABUSE REPORT.).
[Subst. abuse rep.]. Vol. 15, No. 9 (Sept. 1984)-. Periodical. English. Twelve times a year. $275.00. Business Research Publications, 1333 H Street Northwest, 2nd Floor West, Washington DC 20005. **Tel** (202)842-3022, (800)822-6338, FAX (202)842-3023. **ED** Alison Knopf. **Continues** Addiction and Substance Abuse Report, 0160-967X.
 Desc: Concentrates on regulatory news, trends, and developments in the field of drug and alcohol abuse. Discusses treatment methods and community facilities for handling substance abuse.

    ISSN 1082-6084 US
●SUBSTANCE USE & MISUSE. VFOAT
Substance Use and Misuse. (1996)-. Periodical. English. Fourteen times a year. $1395.00. Marcel Dekker Inc., 270 Madison Avenue, New York NY 10016. **Tel** (212)696-9000, (800)228-1160, FAX (212)685-4540, telex 421419. **(Subscription address:** Marcel Dekker Inc., PO Box 5017, Monticello NY 12701. **Tel** (800)228-1160.**) Continues** International Journal of the Addictions, 0020-773X.

LC HE5614.3.W2 W38B
DD 614.8/62   **ISSN** 0146-1192 US
SUMMARY OF ACCIDENTS INVOLVING THE DRINKING DRIVER. See Transportation-Roads and Traffic.

LC HV5825 .N35f
DD 362.2/938/0973   **ISSN** 0161-5041 US
SUMMARY REPORT, DATA FROM THE NATIONAL DRUG ABUSE TREATMENT UTILIZATION SURVEY (NDATUS).
Main/Corp National Institute on Drug Abuse. Division of Scientific and Program Information. (19??)-. English. National Institute on Drug Abuse, 5600 Fishers Lane, Room 199 - 55, Rockville MD 20852. **Tel** (301)443-6637.

LC HV5280.T47 T48A
DD 362.2/92/09764   **ISSN** 0364-8850 US
TEXAS STATE PLAN FOR THE PREVENTION, TREATMENT, AND CONTROL OF ALCOHOL ABUSE AND ALCOHOLISM. Main/Corp Texas. Commission on Alcoholism. English. One time a year. Texas Commission on Alcoholism, 809 Sam Houston Office Building, Austin TX 78701. **Tel** (512)475-5452.

LC RC566.A1 T54   **ISSN** 0378-2778 NE
NLM W1 TI64
TIJDSCHRIFT VOOR ALCOHOL, DRUGS EN ANDERE PSYCHOTROPE STOFFEN.
[Tijdschr. alkohol, drugs andere psychotr. stoffen]. **Added/Corp** Volksbond tegen Drankmisbruik. **VFOAT** Journal of Alcohol, Drugs and Other Psychotropic Substances. Vol. 1 (1975)-. Periodical. Dutch (summaries and/or abstracts in English). Four times a year. $82.73. Swets & Zeitlinger BV, Heereweg 347B PO Box 825, 2160 SZ Lisse Netherlands. **Tel** 011 31 2521 35111, FAX 011 31 2521 15888, telex 41325. **ED** Prof C H Gips, Dr A F W Kok, Dr H J van der Wal. **Bk Rev. Ad Acc. Circ:** 6 (ctrl).
 Desc: Alcohol and drug policy, scientific articles and discussions on the treatment of alcohol and drug dependence and other psychotopics.
 Ind/Abst EMBASE; Psychol. Abstr. (1984-); PsycINFO (1984-); PsycLit.

LC HV5800 .T7
DD 362.29   US
TRANSLATIONS ON NARCOTICS AND DANGEROUS DRUGS. Main/Corp U.S. Joint Publications Research Service. **Added/Corp** United States. Joint Publications Research Service. No. 1 (Aug. 2, 1971)-. Periodical. English. National Technical Information Service - NTIS, Room 2027S, 5285 Port Royal Road, Springfield VA 22161. **Tel** (703)487-4630, (703)487-4660, (703)487-4650, FAX (703)321-8547, telex 89-9405.

LC HV5001
DD 362.291802571   **ISSN** 1201-3374 CN
●TREATMENT OTTAWA. (TREATMENT.).
[Treatment Ott.]. **VFOAT** Canadian Directory of Substance Abuse Services; Repertoire Canadien des Services en Toxicomanie; Readaptation, Repertoire Canadien des Services en Toxicomanie. (1994)-. Mult,ple languages. Every 2 years. Canadian Centre on Substance Abuse, 112 Kent Street, Suite 480, Ottawa Ontario K1P 5P2 Canada. **Continues** Directory of Substance Abuse Organizations in Canada, 1188-4886.

LC HV4999.3.S6 U54
DD 364.1/77/0973021   US
UNIFORM CRIME REPORT ARREST INFORMATION RELATING TO SUBSTANCE ABUSE IN SOUTH CAROLINA. **Added/Corp** South Carolina Commission on Alcohol and Drug Abuse. Division of Research and Evaluation. South Carolina Commission on Alcohol and Drug Abuse. Division of Planning, Evaluation, and Grants Management. South Carolina Commission on Alcohol and Drug Abuse. Division of Program Support. (19??)-. English. Commission on Alcohol and Drug Abuse / South Carolina / Division of Planning Evaluation and Grant Management, 3700 Forest Drive, Suite 300, Columbia SC 29204.

DD 362.2/9/09711   **ISSN** 0824-4839 CN
UPDATE - ALCOHOL-DRUG EDUCATION SERVICE. (UPDATE : NEWSLETTER OF THE ALCOHOL-DRUG EDUCATION SERVICE.). [Update - Alcohol-Drug Educ. Serv.]. **Added/Corp** Alcohol-Drug Education Service (Vancouver, B.C.). (July 1982)-. Newsletter. English. Four times a year. 4.01Can$. Alcohol-Drug Education Service, 212 96 East Broadway, Vancouver British Columbia, V5T 1V6 Canada. **Tel** (604)874-3466, FAX (604)874-0903. **ED** Art Steinmann. **Circ:** 20,000. **Continues** Alcohol-Drug Education Service (Vancouver, B.C.). Newsletter, 0700-396X.
 Desc: Emphasizes prevention and education as well as lobbying decision makers regarding sound alcohol/drug policy.

LC HV5831.V47 A15A
DD 362.2/93/09743   US
NLM W2 AV5 A25V
VERMONT STATE PLAN FOR DRUG ABUSE PREVENTION AND TREATMENT, THE. Main/Corp Vermont. Alcohol and Drug Abuse Division. English. Department of Social and Rehabilitation Services / Vermont, Alcohol & Drug Abuse Division, State Office Building, Montpelier VT 05602. **Continues** Vermont State Drug Plan, 0164-2626.

Drug Abuse and Alcoholism — Abstracting, Bibliographies and Statistics

DD 362.2/92/05   **ISSN** 0708-6377   CN
VIGNE A A, LA. Main/Corp Alcooliques Anonymes. Vol. 1 (April/May 1965)-. Periodical. French. Six times a year. 0.50Can$ per no. Comite Provincial des Alcooliques Anonymes du Quebec, 7210 rue St. Denis, Montreal Quebec H2R 2E2 Canada.

DD 360   **ISSN** 1043-8572   US
NLM W1; NA1753
TITLE CHANGE
WASHINGTON CRIME NEWS SERVICES' NARCOTICS DEMAND REDUCTION DIGEST. [Wash. Crime News Serv. narc. demand reduct. dig.]. **Added/Corp** Washington Crime News Services (U.S.). **VFOAT** Narcotics Demand Reduction Digest. Vol. 1, No. 1 (June 1989)-(1995). Periodical. English. Washington Crime News Services, 3918 Prosperity Avenue, Suite 318, Fairfax VA 22031-3334. **Tel** (703)573-1600, (800)422-9267, FAX (703)573-1604. **Absorbed by** Narcotics Enforcement and Prevention Digest.

ISSN 0250-4936   AU
CODEN WZSUDS
WIENER ZEITSCHRIFT FUER SUCHTFORSCHUNG. [Wien. Z. Suchtforsch.]. **Added/Corp** Ludwig Boltzmann Institut fuer Suchtforschung. Anton Proksch-Institut. (1977)-. Academic Scholarly Publication. German (summaries and/or abstracts in English). Four times a year. $53.44. Ludwig Boltzmann Institut fuer Suchtforschung, Mackgasse 7 9, A 1237 Vienna Austria. Documents available from CASDDS.
Ind/Abst Chem. Abstr. (-1987); EMBASE.

ISSN 0966-9094   UK
WINDOW ON DRUG MONITORING. (1993)-. Academic Scholarly Publication. English. Twelve times a year. $90.00. Royal Society of Chemistry, Thomas Graham House, Science Park, Cambridge CB4 4WF United Kingdom. **Tel** 011 44 1223 420066, FAX 011 44 1223 423623, telex 818293 ROYAL. (**Subscription address:** Royal Society of Chemistry, Turpin Distribution Services Ltd., Blackhorse Road, Letchworth, Hertfordshire SG6 1HN United Kingdom. **Tel** 011 44 1462 672555, FAX 011 44 1462 480947.) **ED** Judith Barnsby
Desc: includes developments in the analysis of therapeutic drugs and drugs of abuse in biological tissues and fluids.

ISSN 0043-5937   US
WINNER (WASHINGTON, D.C.), THE. See Children and Youth Interests.

LC HV5001 .A29a   **ISSN** 0512-2716   US
DD 362.2/92/025
WORLD DIRECTORY OF AL-ANON FAMILY GROUPS AND ALATEENS. **Main/Corp** Al-Anon Family Group Headquarters, Inc. **Added/Corp** Al-Anon Family Group Headquarters, Inc. Al-Anon World Directory. **VFOAT** Al-Anon World Directory. (19??)-. English. Every 2 years. $3.00. Al-Anon Family Groups HQ, 1372 Broadway, New York NY 10018. **Tel** (212)302-7240. **Circ:** 22,000 (ctrl).
Desc: A directory of members and meetings held for members who have been affected by someone else's drinking problems.

ABSTRACTING, BIBLIOGRAPHIES AND STATISTICS

LC HE5620.D7 A588   **ISSN** 0891-7086   US
DD 363.1/251
CODEN ADRDEJ
Pr Rev.
ALCOHOL, DRUGS AND DRIVING. (ALCOHOL, DRUGS, AND DRIVING : ABSTRACTS AND REVIEWS.). [Alcohol drugs driv.]. **Added/Corp** University of California, Los Angeles. Alcohol Information Service. Vol. 1, No. 1-2 (Jan./June 1985)-. Abstracting/Indexing Service. English. Four times a year (Jan., Apr., July, Oct.). Free on request. Brain Information Service, 43 367 CHS, UCLA School of Medicine, Los Angeles CA 90024. **Tel** (310)825-3417, FAX (310)206-3499. **ED** Michael H. Chase, Ph.D and Thomas Roth, Ph.D. **Circ:** 8,000 (ctrl). **Continues** Abstracts & Reviews in Alcohol & Driving, 0882-9578 (DLC)sc 84004231.
Ind/Abst Curr. Cit.; Linguist. Lang. Behav. Abstr.; Psychol. Abstr. (1981-); PsycINFO; Soc. Plann. Policy Dev. Abstr.; Sociol. Abstr.

LC HE5620.D7 A59   **ISSN** 0280-7645   SW
DD 363.1/251
ALCOHOL, DRUGS, AND TRAFFIC SAFETY : CURRENT RESEARCH LITERATURE. Vol. 1, No. 1 (1983)-. Abstracting/Indexing Service. English. Four times a year (March, June, Sept., Dec.). $105.00. Valverius Medinres Inc., Gimlevagen 32A, S 182 33 Danderyd Sweden. **Tel** 011 46 8 7555379, FAX 011 46 8 7536516.
(**Subscription address:** BTJ Tryck AB, Traktorvagen 13, S 226 60 Lund Sweden. **Tel** 011 46 46 180380, FAX 011 46 46 304400.) **ED** Peter Valverius. Index available. cum. index (as a database). **Circ:** 500.
Desc: Covers literature references with abstracts to the world's literature in the biomedical and social sciences related to the incidence and effects of alcohol, drugs, narcotics, and transportation.

US
ALCOHOL STUDIES, RETROSPECTIVE BIBLIOGRAPHIES. 1980-. Periodical. English.

LC HV5537 .A3   SW
DD 362.29209
ALKOHOLSTATISTIK. Main/Corp Sweden. Socialstyrelsen. **VFOAT** Alcohol Statistics. 1977-. Swedish (summaries and/or abstracts in English). One time a year. Liber Distribution, Prenumberationsorder, Forlagsorder 162 89, Stockholm Sweden. **Continues** Alkoholstatistik.

LC Z7254   US
DD 362.29
ANNOTATED BIBLIOGRAPHY OF DRUG ABUSE RESEARCH REPORTS AND EVALUATIONS. Added/Corp New York (State). Office of Drug Abuse Services. Vol. 4 (1977)-. Bibliography. English. One time a year. New York Office of Drug Abuse Services, Executive Park South, Albany NY 12203. **Continues** Annotated Bibliography of Research Reports & Program Studies.

LC HV5825 .S58   **ISSN** 0161-5033   US
DD 362.2/9
DATA FROM THE CLIENT ORIENTED DATA ACQUISITION PROCESS. SMSA STATISTICS. (SMSA STATISTICS, DATA FROM THE CLIENT ORIENTED DATA ACQUISITION PROCESS.). [Data client oriented data acquis. process, SMSA stat.]. **Added/Corp** National Institute on Drug Abuse. Division of Scientific and Program Information. National Institute on Drug Abuse. Division of Data and Information Development. **VFOAT** Data from the Client Oriented Acquisition Process. **VAT** Data from the Client Oriented Data Acquisition Process. Standard Metropolitan Statistical Area Statistics. (197?)-. English. One time a year. National Institute on Drug Abuse, 5600 Fishers Lane, Room 199 - 55, Rockville MD 20852. **Tel** (301)443-6637.

LC HV5825 .S67   **ISSN** 0161-4967   US
DD 362.2/9
DATA FROM THE CLIENT ORIENTED DATA ACQUISITION PROCESS. STATE OFFICIALS. (STATE STATISTICS, DATA FROM THE CLIENT ORIENTED DATA ACQUISITION PROCESS.). [Data client oriented data acquis. process, State stat.]. **Added/Corp** Data from the Client Oriented Data Acquisition Process. English. One time a year. National Institute on Drug Abuse, 5600 Fishers Lane, Room 199 - 55, Rockville MD 20852. **Tel** (301)443-6637.

US
INTERNATIONAL BIBLIOGRAPHY OF STUDIES ON ALCOHOL. (1966)-. English. One time a year. $100.00. Rutgers University Center, National Institute of Alcohol Abuse, Publishing Division, New Brunswick NJ 08903. **Tel** (201)932-2011. **ED** Jack H. Mendelson and Nancy K. Mello. **Bk Rev. Ad Acc. Circ:** 3,000.
Desc: Publishes original research reports that contribute significantly to fundamental knowledge about alcohol, its use and mis-use, and its biomedical, behavioral and sociocultural effects.

GW
NLM W1; JA449
JAHRESSTATISTIK ... DER AMBULANTEN BERATUNGS- UND BEHANDLUNGSSTELLEN FUR SUCHTKRANKE IN DER BUNDESREPUBLIK DEUTSCHLAND. **VFOAT** Annual Statistical Report ... of the Out-Patient Advisory and Treatment Facilities for Addicts in the Federal Republic of Germany. (1980)-. German. One time a year.

DD 362.2/9   **ISSN** 0731-2458   US
NLM W2 A N223S
NATIONAL INSTITUTE ON DRUG ABUSE STATISTICAL SERIES. SERIES C. [Natl. Inst. Drug Abuse stat. ser., Ser. C]. **Added/Corp** National Institute on Drug Abuse. **VFOAT** Statistical Series. Series C; Client Oriented Data Acquisition Process Topical Reports; CODAP Topical Reports. No. 1 (1980)-. Statistical Publication. English. Price varies per volume. National Institute on Drug Abuse, 5600 Fishers Lane, Room 199 - 55, Rockville MD 20852. **Tel** (301)443-6637.

LC HV4997   **ISSN** 0896-1190   US
DD 362.29
NLM W2; A N223
NATIONAL INSTITUTE ON DRUG ABUSE STATISTICAL SERIES. SERIES H. [Natl. Int. Drug Abuse stat. ser., H]. **VFOAT** Statistical Series. Series H. No. 1 (1981)-. Statistical Publication. English. Price varies per volume. US Department of Health and Human Services, 200 Independence Avenue Southwest, Washington DC 20201.

DD 016.36229   **ISSN** 1181-8646   CN
PRODUCT CATALOGUE - ONTARIO. ADDICTION RESEARCH FOUNDATION. (PRODUCT CATALOGUE.). [Prod. cat. - Ont., Addict. Res. Found.]. **Main/Corp** Ontario. Addiction Research Foundation. (1991)-. English (summaries and/or abstracts in French). Addiction Research Foundation, 33 Russell Street, Toronto Ontario M5S 2S1 Canada. **Tel** (416)595-6000, FAX (416)595-5017. **Continues** Education Materials Catalogue., 0848-3701.

LC Z   **ISSN** 0095-0572   US
DD 011
NLM ZWM 270 S741
SPECIAL BIBLIOGRAPHIES (ROCKVILLE). (SPECIAL BIBLIOGRAPHIES.). **Added/Corp** National Clearinghouse for Drug Abuse Information. National Institute on Drug Abuse. No. 1 (Sept. 1974)-. Government Publication. English. Irregular. Superintendent of Documents, US Government Printing Office, Washington DC 20402. **Tel** (202)275-3328, FAX (202)786-2377.

LC HV5831.N8 A33A   **ISSN** 0145-8531   US
DD 364.1/7
STATISTICAL DATA. (STATISTICAL DATA / NORTH CAROLINA. DRUG COMMISSION.). **Main/Corp** North Carolina. Drug Commission. Statistical Publication. English. One time a year. North Carolina Drug Commission, 375 North Salisbury Street, Sixth Floor, Raleigh NC 27611.

DD 362.29/09713/05   **ISSN** 1189-038X   CN
●**STATISTICAL UPDATE.** [Stat. update].
Added/Corp Ontario. Addiction Research Foundation. Statistical Information Service. Vol. 1, No. 1 (1991)-. Statistical Publication. English.

LC HV5840.G7   **ISSN** 0143-1463   UK
DD 364.1/77/0941
NLM W2; FA1 H6s
STATISTICS OF THE MISUSE OF DRUGS UNITED KINGDOM, SUPPLEMENTARY TABLES. English. £2.00. Home Office Statistical Department, Room 1706 Tolworth Tower, Surbiton Surrey KT6 7DS United Kingdom.